SEMICONDUCTOR CROSS REFERENCE BOOK

From the Engineers of Howard W. Sams

©1994 by Howard W. Sams & Company
2647 Waterfront Parkway East Drive
Suite 300
Indianapolis, IN 46214-2041

SECOND EDITION—1994

PROMPT® Publications is an imprint of Howard W. Sams & Company.

International Standard Book Number: 0-7906-1050-7

Editor: Candace M. Drake
Assistant Editors: Rebecca A. Hartford, Natalie F. Houck
Compilation: Barry Buchanan, Karen Montgomery
Typesetting: Leah Marckel
Cover Design: Sara Wright

Printed in the United States of America

10 9 8 7 6 5 4 3 2 1

TABLE OF CONTENTS

How to Use This Book

To find a suitable replacement for a semiconductor, follow these simple steps:

1 **Locate the part number stamped on the part** you wish to replace, or find the part number in a parts list.

2 **Look up the old part number in Section 1** of this cross-reference. To the right of the number will be a replacement code/block number.

3 **Look up the replacement code in Section 2** (pages identified with black bars). To find right, find part numbers of suitable replacements from NTE, ECG, Radio Shack, and Thomson Consumer Electronics.

Other Important Information

The engineering staff of Howard W. Sams & Company has assembled this cross-reference guide to help you find replacements or substitutions for more than 490,000 semiconductors. It has been compiled from manufacturers' data and from the analysis of consumer electronics devices for PHOTOFACT® service data, which has been relied upon since 1946 by service technicians worldwide. Here are some important notes to help you use the two sections of this book effectively.

Section 1—Original Device Types

This section lists device types in alphanumeric order by manufacturer's part number, type number, or other identification, including numbers from the U.S., Europe, and the Far East. At the right of the part number is a replacement code that you will use to look up replacements in section 2.

We have included part numbers for which alternates have not yet been identified from NTE, ECG, Radio Shack, or TCE. For these items, the abbreviation "OEM" appears at the right of the part number. Contact the original equipment manufacturer for appropriate replacements for these parts. For your convenience, a list of manufacturers' addresses is provided.

Occasionally you will find the same part number listed twice. This is because different manufacturers have used the same part number for different devices. In these cases, we provide identifying notes (device type, manufacturer, or color) in parentheses following the part number. For example, AR-31 (DIO) is the part number for a diode, and AR-31 (XSTR) is the part number for a transistor.

Section 2—Replacements

This section provides substitutions and replacements for the semiconductors listed in section 1. The data for this cross-reference was developed from the application parameters found during our PHOTOFACT® analysis. Using manufacturer's specifications and their suggested replacements, we have compiled the most complete replacement guide available.

Some of the replacement numbers are followed by the letter N and another number. These notations provide additional information about the use of the recommended replacement. The key to these notes is as follows:

N1   Two required, connect in series—anode to anode.

N2   Two required, connect in series—cathode to cathode.

N3   Two required, connect in series—anode to cathode.

N4   Caution: Replacement device threads may differ from the original.

N5   Four required, connect as in original circuit.

N6   Five required, connect as in original circuit.

N7   Six required, connect as in original circuit.

N8   Seven required, connect as in original circuit.

N9   Eight required, connect as in original circuit.

*   Lead configuration may vary from original.

%   Use insulating hardware supplied with replacement.

Some manufacturers make modules of discrete components (transistors, resistors, and capacitors) dipped into potting compound. The modules may be completely encapsulated or may have one or more discrete components exposed. The ICs listed as substitutes for these modules are electrically suitable replacements but may not have the same pin-basing arrangement.

Manufacturers and Importers

A

A.C.T. ELECTRONICS ★ †
2345 E ANAHEIM ST.
LONG BEACH, CA 90804
310-433-0475

AC-DELCO GENERAL MOTORS CORP. ★
SERVICE PARTS OPERATIONS
NEW CENTER ONE BUILDING
3031 WEST GRAND BOULEVARD,PO BOX 33115
DETROIT, MI 48202
313 974-0190

ADCOM
11 ELKINS RD
EAST BRUNSWICK, NJ 08816
908-390-1130
908-390-5657 FAX

AIWA AMERICA INC. ★ †
800 CORPORATE DR
MAHWAH, NJ 07430
201-512-3600

AKAI AMERICA LTD.
5757 PLAZA DRIVE
CYPRESS, CA 90630-0007
800-553-7278

ALARON, INC. ★ †
ATTN:SERVICE DEPT.
P.O. BOX 550 185 PARK ST.
TROY, MI 48099
313-585-8400

ALPINE ELECTRONICS OF AMERICA INC. ★ †
19145 GRAMERCY PLACE
ATTN: PARTS DEPARTMENT
TORRANCE, CA 90501
310-326-8000
310-533-0369 FAX

ALTEC LANSING INT'L
CUSTOMER SERVICE/REPAIR
10500 W. RENO AVE.
OKLAHOMA CITY, OK 73126
405-324-5311

AM-COMM SYSTEMS, INC.
1801 OCEAN AVE.
SAN FRANCISCO, CA 94112
415-239-4188

AMERICAN ELECTRONICS INC. ★ †
PO BOX 301
GREENWOOD, IN 46142
317-888-7265

AMERICAN MOTORS CORP.
1200 CHRYSLER DR
DETROIT, MI 48288-1118
313-959-5741

AMPEX CORP. ★ †
401 BROADWAY
REDWOOD CITY, CA 94063-3199
415-367-2011

AMPRO CORPORATION
5 WHEELING AVE
WOBURN, MA 01801
617-932-4800

ANDREA RADIO CORP. ★ †
11-40 45TH ROAD
LONG ISLAND CITY, NY 11101
718-729-8500

AOC INTERNATIONAL (USA) LTD. ★ †
311 SINCLAIR FRONTAGE ROAD
MILPITAS, CA 95035
800-343-5777

APELCO CO.
446 RIVER RD
HUDSON, NH 03051
603-881-4750

APPLE COMPUTER
20525 MARIANI AVE
CUPERTINO, CA 95014
408-996-1010

ARTHUR FULMER,INC.
122 GAYOSO
MEMPHIS, TN 38103
901-525-5711

ARVIN INDUSTRIES INC.
1531 13TH ST
COLUMBUS, IN 47201
812-379-3000

ASSOCIATED MERCHANDISING CORP
1440 BROADWAY
NEW YORK, NY 10018
212-536-4000

ASTATIC/CTI ★ †
PO BOX 120
HARBOR & JACKSON STREETS
CONNEAUT, OH 44030-0120
216-593-1111

AT&T
CUSTOMER INFORMATION
DOCUMENTS ONLY
PO BOX 19901
INDIANAPOLIS, IN 46219
800-432-6600

ATARI CORP
1196 BORREGAS AVE
SUNNYVALE, CA 94089
408-745-2000

AUDIO INDUSTRIES,INC.
532 W. FOURTH ST.
PO BOX N
MICHIGAN CITY, IN 46360
219-874-7251

AUDIO-TECHNICA US INC
ATTN: SERVICE DEPARTMENT
1221 COMMERCE DRIVE
STOW, OH 44224
216-686-2600

AUDIOVOX CORP.
PARTS DEPT
150 MARCUS BLVD
HAUPPAUGE, NY 11788
516-231-6057

AUTORADIO U.S.A. ★ †
613-19 S. 24TH ST.
PHILADELPHIA, PA 19146
215-545-2434

B

BARCUS-BERRY ELECT INC
5381 PRODUCTION DR
HUNTINGTON BCH, CA 92649
708-865-5388

BELL & HOWELL
A DIVISION OF E.I.K.I INTL INC
27882 CAMINO CAPISTRANO
LAGUNA NIGUEL, CA 92677
714-457-0220

BLONDER-TONGUE LABS,INC. ★ †
ONE JAKE BROWN RD.
OLD BRIDGE, NJ 08857
908-679-4000

BOGEN COMMUNICATIONS, INC. ★ †
50 SPRING ST. P.O. BOX 575
RAMSEY, NJ 07446
201-934-8500

BOMAN INDUSTRIES
7906 CRUSADER AVE
CERRITOS, CA 90701
213-403-7045

BORG-WARNER AUTOMOTIVE CORP.
700 S. 25TH AVE.
BELLWOOD, IL 60104
708-547-2600

BRUNSWICK CORPORATION
525 W. LAKETON AVE
MUSKEGON, MI 49443
616-725-3300

C

C.ITOH DIGITAL ELECTRONICS,INC ★ †
2505 MCCABE WAY
IRVIN, CA 92714
800-347-2484

CAB SERVICE & PARTS CORP
1157 W MONROE
CHICAGO, IL 60607
312-421-1122

CANON U.S.A. INC (EAST)
100 JAMESBURG RD
JAMESBURG, NJ 08831-1000
908-521-7230
800-258-0900 FAX

CANON U.S.A. INC (WEST)
CANON PARTS CENTER
15955 ALTON PKWY
IRVINE, CA 92718-3616
714-753-4120
800-443-3766 FAX

CANTON ELECTRONICS CORP INC
915 WASHINGTON AVE SO
MINNEAPOLIS, MN 55415-1245
612-333-1150

CASIO INC
570 MT PLEASANT AVE
P O BOX 7000
DOVER, NJ 07801
201-361-5400

CHANNEL MASTER ★ †
DIVISION OF AVNET,INC
INDUSTRIAL PARK DR
PO BOX 1416
SMITHFIELD, NC 27577
919-934-1484
919-989-2200 FAX

CLARION CORP. OF AMERICA ★ †
661 W REDONDO BEACH BLVD
GARDENA, CA 90247-4201
310-327-9100

COBRA ELECTRONICS CORP
6500 W CORTLAND ST
CHICAGO, IL 60635
312-889-8870

COMMAND ELECTRONICS,INC.
11811 SHAVER RD.
SCHOOLCRAFT, MI 49087

COMMODORE BUSINESS MACHINES
1200 WILSON DRIVE
C-2655
WEST CHESTER, PA 19380
215-431-9100

★ SERVICE DATA AVAILABLE ON REQUEST   † PARTS AVAILABLE ON REQUEST

COMPAQ COMPUTER CORP
PO BOX 692000
HOUSTON, TX 77269-2000
713-370-0670

CORNELL-DUBILIER/SANGAMO COMPONENTS
DIV.
INSIDE SALES
1605 RODNEY FRENCH BLVD
NEW BEDFORD, MA 02744
508-996-8561

CRAIG CONSUMER ELECT. CORP. ★
13845 ARTESIA BLVD
CERRITOS, CA 90701-5067
310-926-9944
310-926-9269 FAX

CROWN INTERNATIONAL INC. ★ †
1718 W. MISHAWAKA RD.
ELKHART, IN 46517
219-294-8000

CUBIC COMMUNICATIONS INC.
PO BOX 85587
SAN DIEGO, CA 92186-5587
619-277-6780

D

DAEWOO ELECTRONICS OF AMERICA ★ †
100 DAEWOO PLACE
CARLSTADT, NJ 07072
201-935-8700
201-935-5284 FAX

DENON AMERICA INC
222 NEW RD
PO BOX 5370
PARSIPPANY, NJ 07054-5370
201-882-7490
201-575-1213 FAX

DYNASCAN CORP. ★ †
COBRA ELECTRONICS CORP
6500 W CORTLAND ST
CHICAGO, IL 60635
312-889-8870

E

EASTMAN KODAK COMPANY
800 LEE RD
ROCHESTER, NY 14650
716-724-7278

EICO ELECTRONIC INSTRUMENT CO. INC. ★ †
363 MERRICK ROAD
LYNBROOK, NY 11563
516-599-5744

ELECTRO BRAND INC. ★ †
5410 W. ROOSEVELT ROAD
CHICAGO, IL 60650
312-261-5000

ELECTRO-VOICE, INC. ★ †
600 CECIL ST.
BUCHANAN, MI 49107
616-695-6831

ELECTRONIC ENGINEERS,INC. ★ †
2522 W ARMITAGE AVE
CHICAGO, IL 60647
312-227-2600

ELECTRONIC SYSTEMS PRODUCTS
1301 ARMSTRONG DR
TITUSVILLE, FL 32780-7999
800-327-3644

EMERSON RADIO CORP. ★ †
NATIONAL PARTS DISTRIBUTION
6 ENGINE ROAD
PARSIPPANY, NJ 07054-0432
800-695-0095
812-386-6502 FAX

ESQUIRE RADIO & ELECTRONICS,INC
4100 FIRST AVENUE
BROOKLYN, NY 11232-3321
718-449-0020

F

FANON COURIER INC. ★ †
14811 MYFORD RD.
TUSTIN, CA 92680-7253
714-669-9890
714-669-1081 FAX
85-2263 TELEX

FARADAY INC
805 S. MAUMEE ST.
TECUMSEH, MI 49286
517-423-2111

FIRESTIK ANTENNA CO
A DIV. OF PAL INTERNATIONAL CORP.
2614 E ADAMS
PHOENIX, AZ 85034
602-273-7151
800-528-8113

FISHER
See SFS Corp.
800-421-5013

FUJITSU TEN CORP. OF AMERICA
NATIONAL SERVICE HEADQUARTERS
1210 E 223RD ST
SUITE 301
CARSON, CA 90745
800-423-8161
213-513-0411

FUNAI USA CORPORATION
PARTS DEPARTMENT
100 N STREET
TETERBORO, NJ 07608
201-288-2666

G

GENERAL TIME CORP. ★ †
WESTCLOX/SETH THOMAS
520 GUTHRIDGE COURT
NORCROSS, GA 30092
404-447-5300

GENERAL TIME CORP
WESTCLOX/SETH THOMAS
520 GUTHRIDGE COURT
NORCROSS, GA 30092
404-447-5300

GOLD STAR ELECTRONICS INT'L ★ †
SERVICE DIVISION
201 JAMES RECORD ROAD
HUNTSVILLE, AL 35824-0166
800-562-0244
800-442-2561 FAX

GRAN PRIX ELECTRONICS ★ †
108 MADISON ST.
ST. LOUIS, MO 63102
314-621-3314

H

HARMAN KARDON INC. ★ †
JBL,EPI,CONCORD
240 CROSSWAYS PARK WEST
WOODBURY, NY 11797
516-496-3400

HITACHI SALES CORP. OF AMERICA ★ †
401 W ARTESIA BLVD
COMPTON, CA 90220
800-448-2244

I

IBM CORP
1000 NW 51ST ST
BOCA RATON, FL 33432
800-443-2000

INTERNATIONAL CRYSTAL MFG. CO.,INC.
10 N. LEE
PO BOX 26330
OKLAHOMA CITY, OK 73126
405-236-3741

ITT CORPORATION ★ †
1330 AVENUE OF THE AMERICAS
NEW YORK, NY 10019
212-258-1000 212-752-6000

J

JCPENNEY CO. INC. ★ †
NATIONAL PARTS CENTER
6840 BARTON RD
MORROW, GA 30260
800-933-7115

JENSEN
A DIVISION OF INTL JENSEN INC
SUITE 400
25 TRI-STATE INTL OFFICE CENTER
LINCOLNSHIRE, IL 60069
800-323-4815
708-317-3826 FAX

E.F. JOHNSON CO. ★ †
PO BOX 1249
299 JOHNSON AVE.
WASECA, MN 56093
507-835-6222

JVC (MIDWEST REGION)
705 ENTERPRISE STREET
AURORA, IL 60504-8149
708-851-7855
708-851-0036 FAX

JVC (SOUTHWEST REGION)
407 GARDEN OAKS BLVD
HOUSTON, TX 77018
713-694-3331

JVC (WEST COAST REGION)
5665 CORPORATE AVE
CYPRESS, CA 90630
213-637-0305

JVC ★ †
DIV. OF US JVC CORP
107 LITTLE FALLS RD.
FAIRFIELD, NJ 07006
201-808-2100

K

KENWOOD
PO BOX 22745
LONG BEACH, CA 90801-5745
800-367-7514
310-609-2127 FAX

KRACO ENTERPRISES,INC.
505 E. EUCLID AVE.
COMPTON, CA 90224
800-421-1910

S.S. KRESGE CO.
3100 W. BIG BEAVER
TROY, MI 48084
313-643-2971

KTV INC. ★ †
SERVICE DEPARTMENT
205 MOONACHIE RD
MOONACHIE, NJ 07074
201-440-9090

KYOCERA ELECTRONICS INC
ATTN: PARTS DEPARTMENT
100 RANDOLPH RD
SOMERSET, NJ 08875-6727
908-560-3400

L

LLOYD'S ELECTRONICS INC.
SEE COBRA
312-889-8870

M

MAGNADYNE CORP.
1111 W. VICTORIA ST.
COMPTON, CA 90220
213-639-2200

★ SERVICE DATA AVAILABLE ON REQUEST

MARANTZ COMPANY,INC ★ †
A DIVISION OF BANG & OLUFEN OF AMERICAN INC
1150 FEEHANVILLE DR
MOUNT PROSPECT, IL 60056
708-299-4000
708-299-4004 FAX

MATSUSHITA SERVICES CO. †
PARTS DIVISION
50 MEADOWLAND PARKWAY
SECAUCUS, NJ 07094
800-447-4700

McINTOSH LABORATORY,INC ★ †
2 CHAMBERS ST
BINGHAMTON, NY 13903
607-723-3512

MIDLAND INTERNATIONAL CORP. ★ †
CUSTOMER SERVICE (PARTS DEPT.)
1690 NORTH TOPPING AVE.
KANSAS CITY, MO 64120
800-643-5263 1-800-MIDLAND

MITSUBISHI ELECTRIC SALES AMERICA,INC. ★ †
PRODUCT SUPPORT GROUP
5757 PLAZA DRIVE
PO BOX 6007
CYPRESS, CA 90630-0007
800-553-7278
800-888-6773
800-825-6655 FAX

MONTGOMERY WARD
MONTGOMERY WARD PLAZA
CHICAGO, IL 60671
800-323-1965

N

NAD (USA) INC
1600 PROVIEDENCE HWY #286
WALPOLE, MA 02081-2544
508-660-1667

NATM BUYING CORP. ★ †
45 W. 34TH ST.
SUITES 1204-5
NEW YORK, NY 10001
212-239-7222

NEC TECHNOLOGIES INC ★ †
ATTN: PARTS ORDER DEPT
1255 MICHAEL DR
WOOD DALE, IL 60191-1094
708-860-0335
800-366-3632 PARTS
800-356-2415 FAX

NICHOLS ELECTRONICS INC. ★ †
HCR69 BOX 254 SCHOOL ST.
TILTON, NH 03276-7701
603-286-4421

NORTRONICS CO. INC. †
1000 SUPERIOR SUITE 302
WAYZATA, MN 55391
612-476-7356
612-476-7316 FAX

O

OKIDATA
800-654-3282

ONKYO U.S.A. CORP. ★ †
ATTN: PARTS DEPARTMENT
200 WILLIAMS DR
RAMSEY, NJ 07446
201-825-7950

ORTOFON INC
DUAL PARTS AND SERVICES
122 DUPONT STREET
PLAINVILLE, NY 11803
516-349-7757

P

PANASONIC
50 MEADOWLANDS PARKWAY
SECAUCUS, NJ 07094
800-545-2672

PC'S LIMITED
1611 HEADWAY CIRCLE, BLDG 3
AUSTIN, TX 78754
800-624-9896 (TECH SUPPORT)

PERMA POWER ELECTRONICS,INC. ★ †
5601 W. HOWARD
NILES, IL 60714
800-323-4255
800-523-0130 FAX

PHILIPS CONSUMER ELECTRONICS CO. ★ †
PRODUCT SERVICES PARTS ORGANIZATION
112 POLK ST
PO BOX 967
GREENVILLE, TN 37744
800-851-8885
800-535-3715 FAX

PHILIPS ECG
1025 WESTMINSTER DR
WILLIAMSPORT, PA 17701
800-526-9354
800-346-6621 FAX

PILOT AUDIO/VIDEO SYSTEMS ★ †
1450 FLATCREEK RD.
ATHENS, TX 75751
903-675-6886

PIONEER ELECTRONICS SERVICE, INC. ★ †
1925 EAST DOMINGUEZ ST
LONG BEACH, CA 90810
800-457-2881
310-952-2247 FAX

PROSCAN
SEE THOMPSON CONSUMER ELECTRONICS
800-336-1900

PROTON
PROTON PARTS DEPARTMENT
5630 CERRITOS AVE
CYPRESS, CA 90630
800-829-3444

Q

QUASAR
50 MEADOWLANDS PARKWAY
SECAUCUS, NJ 07094
800-545-2672

R

RADIO SHACK
NATIONAL PARTS DEPARTMENT
900 E NORTHSIDE DR
FT. WORTH, TX 76102
800-442-2425
817-870-5737 FAX

RANGAIRE CORP. ★
PO BOX 177
CLEBURNE, TX 76031
817-645-9111

RAY JEFFERSON ★ †
4200 MITCHELL STREET
PHILADELPHIA, PA 19128
215-487-2800

READERS DIGEST
READERS DIGEST RD
PLEASANTVILLE, NY 10570
914-238-8585

REGENCY ELECTRONICS,INC. ★ †
7707 RECORDS ST.
INDIANAPOLIS, IN 46226
317-545-4281

RELM COMMUNICATIONS INC
7707 RECORDS ST
INDIANAPOLIS , IN 46226
317-545-4281

RF PARTS CO. ★
435 S PACIFIC ST
SAN MARCOS, CA 92069
619-744-0700
619-744-1943 FAX

ROBERT BOSCH CORP. ★ †
2800 S. 25TH AVE.
BROADVIEW, IL 60153
708-865-5200

ROTEL OF AMERICA
A DIVISION OF EQUITY INTNL INC
54 CONCORD ST
PO BOX 8
NORTH READING, MA 01864-0008
800-543-0471

ROYAL CONSUMER BUSINESS PRODUCTS ★ †
C/O OLIVETTI USA
765 US HWY 202
BRIDGEWATER, NJ 08807
800-243-3234
800-222-2310

RTL ELECTRONICS
1213 W. 135TH ST.
GARDENA, CA 90247
310-327-8792

S

SAAB-SCANIA OF AMERICA,INC.
ATTN: PARTS
4405A SAAB DRIVE
PO BOX 9000
NORCROSS, GA 30091
404-279-0100

SAMPO CORP. OF AMERICA ★ †
PARTS & SERVICE
5550 PEACHTREE INDUSTRIAL BLVD
NORCROSS, GA 30071
404-449-6220
404-447-1109 FAX

SAMSUNG ELECTRONICS AMERICA, INC. ★
PARTS DEPARTMENT
ONE SAMSUNG PLACE
LEDGEWOOD, NJ 07852
800-634-9276
201-691-6200
800-248-0498 FAX

SANSUI ELECTRONICS CORP.
17150 S MARGAY AVE
PO BOX 4687
CARSON, CA 90746
310-604-7300
310-604-1664 FAX

SANYO
SEE SFS CORP. LISTING
800-421-5013

H.H. SCOTT,INC.
STATE ROUTE 41 & COUNTY RD 100 W
PRINCETON, IN 47670
800-695-0095

SFS CORP (WESTERN REGION) ★ †
PARTS ORDERING DEPT
1200 ARTESIA BLVD
COMPTON, CA 90224-9038
310-605-6741
310-605-6744 FAX

SFS CORP (EASTERN REGION)
PARTS ORDERING DEPT
210 RISER RD
LITTLE FERRY, NJ 07643
201-641-3000

SFS CORP (MIDWEST REGION)
PARTS ORDERING DEPT
BENSENVILLE, IL 60106
708-350-1505
708-350-1621 FAX

SFS CORP (SOUTHERN REGION)
PARTS ORDERING DEPT
1790 CORPORATE DRIVE #340
NORCROSS, GA 30090
404-925-8900
404-925-9308 FAX

† PARTS AVAILABLE ON REQUEST

MANUFACTURERS AND IMPORTERS

SHAKESPEARE ELECTRONICS & FIBERGLASS
DIV.
PO BOX 733
NEWBERRY, SC 29108
803-276-5504

SHARP ELECTRONICS CORP.
PO BOX 650
SHARP PLAZA
MAHWAH, NJ 07430-2135
800-526-0264
201-512-0055
201-529-9284 FAX

SHERWOOD/INKEL CORP. ★ †
14830 ALONDRA BLVD
LA MIRANDA, CA 90638
714-521-6100

SHINTOM WEST CORP OF AMERICA
20435 S WESTERN AVE
TORRANCE , CA 90501
213-328-7200

SHURE BROTHERS INC ★ †
ATTN: SERVICE DEPARTMENT
222 HARTREY AVE
EVANSTON, IL 60202-3696
708-866-2553
708-866-2279 FAX

SIGNET
SERVICE MANAGER
4701 HUDSON DR
STOW, OH 44224
216-688-9400

SMITH CORONA NATL SERVICE STORES
ROUTE 13
PO BOX 2020
CORTLAND, NY 13045
607-753-6011
800-523-2881 FAX

SONAR RADIO CORP. ★ †
3000 STIRLING RD.
HOLLYWOOD, FL 33021
305-981-8800

SONY SERVICE CO. ★ †
PARTS DIVISION
8281 N.W. 107TH TERRACE
KANSAS CITY, MO 64153
816-891-7550
861-821-5662 FAX

SOUNDCRAFTSMEN
ATTN: PARTS DEPT
2200 S RITCHEY
SANTA ANA, CA 92705
714-556-6191

SOUNDESIGN CORP (SDI) ★ †
800 FEDERAL BLVD
CARTERET, NJ 07008
800-888-4491

SPARKOMATIC CORPORATION
ATTN: PARTS DEPT
PO BOX 277
MILFORD, PA 18337
800-338-5085

SPIEGEL CUSTOMER SERVICE
PO BOX 6105
RAPID CITY, SD 57709-6105
605-348-8100

STANDARD COMMUNICATIONS CORP. ★ †
PO BOX 92151
LOS ANGELES, CA 90009-2151
213-532-5300

STUDER REVOX AMERICA INC
1425 ELM HILL PIKE
NASHVILLE, TN 37210
615-254-5651
615-256-7619 FAX

STUDER REVOX CANADA LTD
TORONTO,
416-510-1294

SYMPHONIC
100 NORTH STREET
FUNAI USA CORP
TETERBORO, NJ 07608
800-242-7158
201-288-2666

T

TANDY NATIONAL PARTS ★ †
A DIVISION OF TANDY ELECTRONICS
900 E NORTHSIDE DRIVE
FORT WORTH, TX 76102
800-442-2425
817-870-5737 FAX

TATUNG CO. OF AMERICA INC. ★ †
2850 EL PRESIDIO ST.
LONG BEACH, CA 90810
310-637-2105
213-979-7055

TCE PUBLICATIONS ★
10003 BUNSEN WAY
LOUISVILLE, KY 40299
502-491-8110

TEAC CORP. OF AMERICA
7733 TELEGRAPH ROAD
MONTEBELLO, CA 90640
213-726-0303

TECHNICS
50 MEADOWLANDS PARKWAY
SECAUCUS, NJ 07094
800-545-2672

TEKNIKA ELECTRONICS CORP. ★ †
DIVISION OF FUJITSU LTD
ATTN: PARTS DEPT
353 ROUTE 46 WEST
FAIRFIELD, NJ 07004
201-575-0380
800-835-6452

TELEDYNE ACOUSTIC RES
ATTN: PARTS DEPTS
330 TURNPIKE ST
CANTON, MA 02021
617-821-2300

TELEX COMMUNICATIONS,INC. ★ †
9600 ALDRICH AVE. S.
MINNEAPOLIS, MN 55420
612-884-4051 TECH.CUST.SERV.

TERRYVILLE ELECTRONICS ★ †
693 OLD TOWN ROAD
TERRYVILLE, NY 11776
516-473-0192

TESI
100 RISER ROAD
LITTLE FERRY, NJ 07643
201-641-3680

THOMSON CONSUMER ELECTRONICS
PO BOX 1976
INDIANAPOLIS, IN 46206
800-336-1900

TMK
SEE TESI
201-641-3680

TOMEN
SEE TESI
201-641-3680

TORO WHEEL HORSE CO
8111 LYNDALE AVE SOUTH
BLOOMINGTON, MN 55420
612-887-8255 612-887-8402
612-887-8260

TOSHIBA AMERICA CONSUMER PRODUCTS
INC ★ †
NATIONAL PARTS CENTER
1420 TOSHIBA DRIVE
LEBANON, TN 37087
800-345-9785
615-444-7481 FAX

TOYOMENKA (AMERICA),INC.
SEE TESI
201-641-3680

U

UNIDEN CORP. OF AMERICA ★ †
9319 CASTLEGATE DR.
INDIANAPOLIS, IN 46256
317-842-1036

UNISONIC PRODUCTS CORP.
FACTORY PARTS CTR
16 WEST 25TH ST
NEW YORK, NY 10010
212-255-5400

UNIVERSITY SOUND,INC ★ †
13278 RALSTON AVE.
SYLMAR, CA 91342
818-362-9516

UTAH-AMERICAN CORP.
DIVISION OXFORD SPEAKER CO.
4237 W. 42ND PLACE
CHICAGO, IL 60632
312-927-3715

V

VOLKSWAGEN OF AMERICA,INC.
3800 HAMLIN ROAD
AUBURN HILLS, MI 48326
313-340-5000

W

WELLS-GARDNER ELECTRONICS CORP. ★ †
SERVICE PARTS DEPT
2701 N KILDARE AVE
CHICAGO, IL 60639
312-252-8220

WESTERN AUTO SUPPLY CO.
2107 GRAND AVE.
KANSAS CITY, MO 64108

WINEGARD CO. ★ †
3000 KIRKWOOD
BURLINGTON, IA 52601-1007
319-753-0121
800-843-4741

Y

YAMAHA ELECTRONICS CORP USA
ATTN: PARTS OFFICE
660 ORANGETHORPE AVE
BUENA PARK, CA 90620
714-994-3312
800-634-0355 FAX

YORX ELECTRONICS CORP. ★ †
ATTN: PARTS DEPT
405 MINNISINK RD
TOTOWA, NJ 07512-1899
201-256-0500

Z

ZENITH ELECTRONICS CORP.
1900 AUSTIN AVE.
CHICAGO, IL 60639
312-745-2000

ZENITH DATA SYSTEMS ★
2150 EAST LAKE COOK RD
BUFFALO GROVE, IL 60089
708-808-5000

★ SERVICE DATA AVAILABLE ON REQUEST

SECTION 1

Original Device Types
and Replacement Codes

DEVICE TYPE	REPL CODE
0000000FR1	0015
0000000FR2	0023
0000000FRI	0015
0000000MV4	0133
0000000S15	0102
0000001N60	0019
0000001S85	0715
00000010D1	0023
000000DG13	0918
000000DS17	0015
000000DS18	0015
000000DS-38	0015
000000DS38	0015
000000SD1A	0102
000000SD1AB	0015
000000SD1AB(BOOST)	0102
000000SD1AB/(BOOST)	0102
000000SD1Y	0023
000000SD46	0143
000000SV31	0164
000000SZT8	0644
000001S188	0143
000001S334	0012
000001S553	0755
000001S990	0133
000002SB22	0164
0000010DC1	0015
0000015330A	0041
00000DS18	0023
00000DS-38	0071
00000DS131	0015
00000DS410	0133
00000FR202	2068
00000MZ206	0157
00000SIB01	0015
00000WZ090	0057
0000-00011-053	0843
0000-0071	0676
0000-04	0079
0000-0141	0006
0000-0150	0006
0000-0300	0006
00001S155	0133
00001S188	0143
00001S330A	0041
00001S1210	0139
00001S1555	0133
00001S1849	0015
00001S2076	0133
00001S4460	0143
00002SA10	0050
00002SA101	0136
00002SA202	0628
00002SA550	0037
00002SB22	0004
00002SB185	0004
00002SB185-0	0004
00002SB186	0004
00002SB186-0	0004
00002SB187	0004
00002SB303	0004
00002SB303-0	0004
00002SB405	0164
00002SB405R	0164
00002SB435	0919
00002SB460	0127
00002SB474	1004
00002SB481	0816
00002SB492	0841
00002SB968	0079
00002SC373	0076
00002SC460	0151
00002SC460A	0144
00002SC460B	0144
00002SC460C	0144
00002SC461	0151
00002SC492	0841
00002SC535	0127
00002SC536	0532
00002SC537	0191
00002SC606	0144
00002SC609	1401
00002SC644	0111
00002SC668	0127
00002SC735	0191
00002SC772	1136
00002SC828	1211
00002SC829	0127
00002SC838	0191
00002SC858	0111
00002SC870	0016
00002SC870A	0016
00002SC870B	0016
00002SC870C	0016
00002SC929	1060
00002SC930	2195
00002SC945	0076
00002SC968	0198
00002SC1023	0079
00002SC1026	0007
00002SC1032	0007
00002SC1061	0419
00002SD235	0042
00002SD261	0590
0000101	0136
0000102	0136
0000103	0004
0000104	0004
00001201	0574

DEVICE TYPE	REPL CODE
000071090	0222
000071120	1257
000071130	1045
000071131	1045
000071150	0037
000071151	0037
000072020	0015
000072050	0015
000072090	0143
000072150	0012
000072160	0143
000072180	0244
000072190	0012
000073070	0111
000073080	0111
000073090	0016
000073100	0016
000073110	0086
000073120	0016
000073130	0016
000073140	0224
000073230	0016
000073231	0016
000073280	0555
000073290	0016
000073300	0590
000073301	0590
000073302	0590
000073303	0590
000073310	0016
000073320	0555
000073332	0016
000073333	0016
000073351	0111
000073361	0111
000073370	0079
000073380	0555
000073381	0219
000073390	0016
000073391	0016
000074010	1206
000074020	6968
000074030	1469
0000DS410R	0133
0000FR202	0015
0000LA3301	1206
0000LD3000	2388
0000RS1542	0015
0000SD-1AUF	0133
000-04	0016
0001S188	0143
0001S188AM	0143
0001S188FM	0143
0002SB187	0004
0002SB303-0	0004
0002SB405R	0164
0002SB1860	0211
0002SB3030	0004
0002SC373	0016
0002SC373W	0076
0002SC458B	0076
0002SC458C	0076
0002SC537F	0155
0002SC644Q	0111
0002SC644S,R,Q	0111
0002SC710B	0284
0002SC710C	0284
0002SC772C	0127
0002SC828	1211
0002SC828H	1211
0002SC828Q	1211
0002SC930D	0111
0002SC930E	0111
0002SC968P	2901
0002SC1023	0127
0002SC1026	0127
0002SC1026A	0127
0002SC1026B	0127
0002SC1026C	0127
0002SC1032	0127
0002SC1032A	0127
0002SC1032B	0127
0002SC1032C	0127
0002SC1061	0042
0002SC1061A	0042
0002SC1061B	0042
0002SC1061C	0042
0002SC1162	0558
0003-009700	0137
000157GN	0143
000188-4	0178
000188GN	0143
000192-3	0178
000192GN	4432
000546-1	0016
000704	0079
0001849	0015
0001849R	0015
0004203	0222
00023645	0079
000583954	0315
0002500040	3333
00031011049	0079
00031013045	0079
00031014007	0023
00031014021	0143
00031014022	0015
000HA1306U	2247
000LA1201B	0574

DEVICE TYPE	REPL CODE
000LA1306U	2247
000LD1020A	0021
000WG1010	0124
00	0111
00-06-006	OEM
001	1659
001-0000-00	0143
001-00	0016
001-002	5270
001-003	5270
001-004	5270
001-007-00	0015
001-0010-00	0143
001-0020-00	0123
001-0020-0	0143
001-0020-02	1012
001-0022-00	0143
001-0036	0438
001-0072-00	0015
001-0072-00(MUNTZ)	0196
001-0077-00	0023
001-0081	0143
001-0081-00	0229
001-0082-00	0631
001-0085-00	0030
001-0091	2845
001-0095-00	0133
001-0095-02	0124
001-0099-00	0644
001-0099-01	0062
001-0099-02	0077
001-007100	OEM
001-02	0037
001-03	0037
001-04	0037
001-0101-01	1075
001-0112-00	0124
001-0125-00	0133
001-0127-00	0064
001-0130-00	0623
001-0130-01	0623
001-0140-00	OEM
001-0151-00	0133
001-0151-01	0133
001-0152-00	0244
001-0153-00	0015
001-0156-00	OEM
001-0160-00	0030
001-0161-00	0244
001-0163-02	0041
001-0163-04	0253
001-0163-10	0077
001-0163-13	0165
001-0163-15	0012
001-0176-00	0030
001-01101-0	0595
001-01202-1	0279
001-01203-1	0279
001-01204	0435
001-01204-0	0085
001-01205-0	0085
001-01205-1	0085
001-01206-0	0211
001-01250	0160
001-01251	0160
001-01252	0160
001-01253	0160
001-01254	0160
001-01255	0160
001-01256	0160
001-01257	0160
001-01258	0160
001-01259	0160
001-01501-0	0143
001-02101-0	0016
001-02101-1	0016
001-02102-0	0016
001-02103-0	0016
001-02104-0	0016
001-02105-0	0016
001-02106-0	0016
001-02107-0	0016
001-02108-0	0016
001-02109-0	0016
001-02110-0	0016
001-02111-0	0079
001-02111-1	0016
001-02113-2	0016
001-02113-3	0016
001-02113-4	0016
001-02113-5	0016
001-02114-0	0168
001-02115-0	0142
001-02116-0	0142
001-02117-2	0786
001-02119-0	0086
001-02121-0	0016
001-02201-0	0037
001-02303-0	0162
001-02303-3	0631
001-02303-4	0002
001-02405-0	0015
001-02405-1	0015
001-02405-2	0015
001-02406-0	0087
001-02406-1	0087
001-02601-0	0015
001-02603-0	0015
001-02701-1	0321

DEVICE TYPE	REPL CODE
001-02702-0	0321
001-02703-0	0321
001-011010	0595
001-012010	0211
001-012011	0211
001-012020	0279
001-012021	0279
001-012030	0279
001-012031	0279
001-012040	0085
001-012050	0599
001-012051	0085
001-012052	0085
001-012053	0085
001-012060	0211
001-015010	0143
001-015011	0143
001-021010	0155
001-021011	0155
001-021020	0155
001-021030	0155
001-021040	0155
001-021050	0155
001-021060	0155
001-021070	0111
001-021080	0155
001-021090	0155
001-021100	0855
001-021110	0086
001-021111	0086
001-021130	0155
001-021131	0155
001-021132	0155
001-021133	0155
001-021134	0155
001-021135	0155
001-021136	0111
001-021140	0187
001-021150	0142
001-021160	0142
001-021161	0142
001-021163	0142
001-021172	0037
001-021180	0103
001-021190	0086
001-021200	0103
001-021210	0016
001-021218	0016
001-021230	0218
001-021231	0218
001-021232	0218
001-021270-1	0103
001-021280	0130
001-021290	0086
001-022010	0037
001-022020	0006
001-022030	0218
001-022032	1233
001-022050	0312
001-023020	0221
001-023021	1725
001-023027	0436
001-023030	0162
001-023031	0560
001-023033	0631
001-023034	0002
001-023035	0170
001-023036	0451
001-023037	0446
001-023038	0416
001-023041	0247
001-023042	0475
001-024010	0015
001-024020	0015
001-024030	0015
001-024040	1116
001-024050	0015
001-024051	0015
001-024052	0015
001-024060	0947
001-024061	0947
001-024070	3160
001-024080	0155
001-026010	0133
001-026030	0133
001-026050	0312
001-026060	0124
001-027010	2959
001-027020	2959
001-027030	0321
001-044272-002	0155
001-044273-002	0086
001-044275-002	0178
001-044277-002	0015
001-044672-001	0004
001-044673-001	0004
001-044674-001	0155
001-044676-001	0133
001-044677-001	0111
001-1	0396
001-157-00	OEM
001-163-10	OEM
001-21011	0016
001-223027	0436
001-223034	0002
001-226030	0015
002	0823
002-00840	0211
002-00900	0050

DEVICE TYPE	REPL CODE
002-005100	0004
002-006300	0211
002-006500	0198
002-006600	0211
002-006800	0004
002-006900	0211
002-007000	0085
002-007100	0136
002-007200	0050
002-007300	0004
002-007400	0050
002-008100	0085
002-008200	OEM
002-008300	0111
002-008400	0164
002-008800	0160
002-009000	0050
002-009100	0142
002-009500	0016
002-009500H	OEM
002-009501	0004
002-009502	0016
002-009502-12	0198
002-009600	0144
002-009601	0144
002-009601-12	0007
002-009700	0085
002-009701	0085
002-009800	0037
002-009800-12	0126
002-009800A	0006
002-009900	0016
002-03	0016
002-010100	0160
002-010300	0160
002-010300-6	0126
002-010300A	0037
002-010400	0016
002-010500	0037
002-010500A	0037
002-010600	0086
002-010700	0126
002-010800	0016
002-010900	0037
002-010900A	0037
002-011000	0004
002-011100	OEM
002-011400	0007
002-011500	0007
002-011600	0136
002-011700	0208
002-011800	0841
002-011900	0004
002-012000	0198
002-012100	0455
002-012200	0161
002-012300	0919
002-012400	0042
002-012500	0086
002-012600	0126
002-012700	0160
002-012700-12	0969
002-012800	0037
002-012800A	0037
002-9501	0111
002-9502	0111
002-9502-12	0111
002-9601	0144
002-9601-12	0144
002-9700	0160
002-9800-12	0126
002-9800-A	0037
002-11700	0208
002-11800	0004
002-11900	0004
002-12000	0016
002-SANYO	OEM
002D235RY	0042
002SA203AA	0136
002SB185AA	0004
002SB435RY	0919
002SC203	0590
002SC203A	0590
002SC203AA	0590
002SC668D	0127
002SC735-0Y	0079
002SC7350Y	0191
002SC1061	0555
002SC1209C	0076
002SC7350Y	0155
002SD235RY	0228
003	0123
003-00	0224
003-00200	0123
003-002200	0196
003-004200	0123
003-005400	0143
003-006700	0143
003-007500	0123
003-009000	0143
003-009100	0002
003-009200	0143
003-009400	0015
003-009600	0143
003-009700	0137
003-009900	0015
003-0	0895
003-01	0224
003-02000	0123

DEVICE TYPE	REPL CODE
003-010000	0137
003PV-T018	OEM
004	3901
004(TOYOTA)	3901
004-00	0016
004-001	0599
004-0027-00	0015
004-00900	0133
004-002000	0015
004-002700	0015
004-002800	0015
004-002900	0196
004-003000	0015
004-003100	1293
004-003200	0769
004-003300	0015
004-003400	0015
004-003500	0102
004-003600	0015
004-003700	0469
004-003900	0015
004-004000	0071
004-004100	0015
004-009200	0143
004-03100	1293
004-03200	0769
004-03300	0015
004-03500	0015
004-03600	0015
004-03700	0015
004-1	0378
004-1A	0126
004-2	0042
004-175-9-001	0139
004-8000	0160
005-02	0016
005-010300	0190
005-010400	1493
005-010800	1493
005-010900	1493
005-011000	1493
005-011200	1493
005-012200	2954
005-013500	0405
005-013600	2777
005-1	0042
006-0000137A	0103
006-0000146	0232
006-0000147	0507
006-0000151	1417
006-0000155A	0004
006-0000162	0936
006-000138B	0130
006-0001003	0233
006-0001011	0233
006-0002034	3579
006-0002088	0233
006-0004443	0321
006-0004779	1340
006-0005545	1918
006-0006903	0434
006-02	0037
006B2M	0696
007-00	0283
007-009-00	2593
007-0051-00	0086
007-0051-01	0086
007-0072-00	0130
007-0074	0178
007-0112-00	0419
007-0112-04	0419
007-0150-00	2480
007-0189-00	0212
007-0197-00	2006
007-0214-00	0321
007-0214-01	0321
007-023200	0334
007-117-02	0212
007-214-00	0321
007-25853-01RB	4159
007-25853-02	4159
007-73203-01	0004
007-73401-02	0050
007-1671101	1686
007-1681301	1918
007-1695001	0232
007-1695101	0692
007-1695301	0357
007-1695701	1018
007-1695901	0507
007-1696001	0370
007-1696101	2228
007-1696201	0310
007-1696301	3478
007-1696701	0522
007-1696801	0614
007-1696901	1197
007-1697701	1818
007-1697801	1032
007-1698301	1910
007-1698401	1915
007-1698901	0738
007-1699201	0522
007-1699301	0462
007-1699401	0331
007-1699801	1303
007-7450301C	0103
009-00	0065
0010-0150	0713

DEVICE TYPE	REPL CODE
0010-0180	1638
0010-0190	0455
0018	0079
0018-162-60002	OEM
0018-162-60203	OEM
0018-162-70005	OEM
0018-165-60005	OEM
0018-165-60304	OEM
0019-003485	0178
0019-003485A	0006
0019-1313	2599
0020-0191	0076
0020-0221	0386
0020-0250	0191
0020-0321	1060
0020-0322	1060
0020-0330	0076
0020-0332	0076
0020-0351	1505
0020-0381	1505
0020-0442	0076
0020-0521	0224
0020-0531	0127
0020-0540	1317
0020-0541	1317
0020-0630	0836
0020-0643	0275
0020-0650	0723
0020-0710	0261
0020-0711	0261
0020-0720	0219
0020-0761	0168
0020-0800	0949
0020-0801	0949
0030-007-0	OEM
0030-0041	1779
0030-0091	1274
0030-0150	0723
0030-0161	1274
0030-0370	0055
0036-001	0037
0036-181-32215	OEM
0050-0011	0019
0050-0014	0143
0050-0021	0123
0050-0023	0123
0050-0032	0123
0050-0033	0123
0050-0050	1914
0050-0070	0124
0050-0130	0133
0050-0250	0124
0050-0300	0124
0050-0301	0124
0050-0302	0124
0051-0010	0023
0051-0070	0023
0051-0100	0023
0051-0110	0023
0051-0130	0023
0051-0160	0015
0051-0170	0102
0051-0290	1089
0051-0291	1791
0051-0340	0023
0051-0400	0095
0052-0060	0715
0053-015-71100	0064
0053-015-71330	0166
0053-015-71629	0466
0053-015-71829	0165
0053-015-71919	0057
0053-017-11002	0604
0053-018-11001	0133
0053-018-11002	0124
0053-024-71001	0911
0053-024-91439	OEM
0053-024-91519	0582
0053-024-91629	0292
0053-026-01002	0031
0053-026-11001	0023
0053-026-21001	0071
0053-026-91002	OEM
0053-027-40002	OEM
0053-029-70001	OEM
0053-029-91002	1082
0053-030-51003	0031
0053-030-61001	0947
0053-031-01001	0031
0053-032-11100	OEM
0053-032-91439	0274
0053-032-91629	0292
0053-033-71120	0052
0053-033-71330	0166
0053-033-71479	0140
0053-033-71629	2500
0053-033-71919	0057
0053-901-30479	0140
0053-901-50479	0140
0053-901-50519	0041
0053-912-00520	0015
0053-915-00270	0124
0053-915-00330	OEM
0053-915-00610	0031
0053-915-00800	OEM
0053-919-00100	0057
0054-0010	0372
0054-0020	0140
0054-0050	0253

If replacement code is OEM, contact original manufacturer for replacement.

DEVICE TYPE	REPL CODE
0054-0060	0077
0054-0091	0057
0054-0110	0181
0054-0115	0181
0054-0152	0195
0054-0191	0041
0054-0240	0999
0054-0250	0124
0054-0611	0450
0061-015-80003	0037
0061-022-39001	OEM
0061-022-40001	0079
0061-022-49001	0111
0061-043-49001	0079
0061-043-49002	0037
0061-043-49003	0037
0061-043-59001	0079
0061-043-59002	0079
0061-044-00019	OEM
0061-044-00119	OEM
0061-044-00120	0076
0061-044-00123	0148
0061-044-30001	3749
0061-044-39001	OEM
0061-049-99001	0079
0061-055-49001	0261
0061-055-50002	1533
0061-056-30001	OEM
0061-058-50001	0168
0061-058-70001	0551
0061-232-70001	4521
0061-238-00001	0101
0061-247-90001	0619
0061-247-90004	OEM
0061-253-54078	OEM
0061-257-40001	2929
0061-258-60003	3897
0061-258-60004	2348
0061-261-90001	OEM
0061-262-50001	0727
0061-266-30004	OEM
0061-900-01002	0261
0061-900-04412	2666
0061-900-05200	3950
0061-900-05600	0860
0061-901-00660	0148
0061-901-01401	OEM
0061-901-02160	4062
0061-920-01330	4349
0061-920-20620	OEM
0061-920-60090	0970
0061-969-90120	OEM
0061-969-90130	1288
0061-969-90140	OEM
0062-0061	OEM
0070-0120	4571
0070-0210	2868
0070-0500	2180
0071-0030	2609
0073-0020	1319
0073-0030	2898
0073-0180	0069
0079-0060	4554
0079-0150	5101
0079-0160	3564
0079-0170	2008
0079-0220	5136
0079-0500	0906
0079-0510	0328
0079-0780	0485
0079-1313	2599
0081-0050	0120
0086-0173	OEM
0098-0520	OEM
0098-0530	OEM
0098-0550	OEM
0098-0570	OEM
0098-0580	OEM
0098-0620	OEM
0098-0640	OEM
0098-0660	OEM
0098-0670	OEM
0098-0680	OEM
0098-0690	OEM
0098-0710	2037
0099-1030	0023
0099-1040	0124
00192-6	0178
00192GN	4432
00508	OEM
00509	OEM
00764-16	0178
00764GN	4432
00765A	0178
00765GN	4432
00766-18	0178
00766GN	4432
00963	OEM
001422	0079
002112A010	OEM
002112P010	OEM
002132Q010	OEM
002132Q030	OEM
003002	0143
003007	0015
003008	0133
003015	0015
003016	0019
003017	0133
003023	0023
003102	0012
003111	0057
003113	0162
003114	0999
003307	0124
003449	0224
003460	0111
003461	0111
003501	0574
003515	0514
003516	0412
003519	2008
003522	0428
003526	2512
003536	1805
003542	0331
004567	0015
004746	0037
004747	3495
004763	0133
004781	0848
004792	0127
004795	2593
004887	0137
0022481	0222
0023645	0127
0023828	0016
0023829	0127
0030058	OEM
0044028-014	0016
0044028-14	0016
0048000	0004
0099201-325	0057
0099202-128	0039
0099203-005	0015
0099203-007	0015
00148907	OEM
00200118	0080
002007300	OEM
008010028	0124
0021120030	OEM
0021120150	OEM
0021121050	OEM
0021121090	OEM
0021150030	OEM
0021151050	1767
0021320010	OEM
0021321070	OEM
0021321080	OEM
0021321110	OEM
0021520130	OEM
0021521100	OEM
0021721010	OEM
0031013026	0079
0031013029	0144
0031013045	0079
0031013049	0079
0031013050	0037
0031013052	0037
0031013056	0224
0031013064	1045
0031013065	0786
0031014003	0023
0031014007	0023
0031014008	0023
0031014009	0077
0031014021	0143
0031014022	0015
0031014024	0023
0031014029	0124
0031014030	0023
0031015012	0167
0042122001	4262
0063050118	0015
0072585411A	4159
00HA1306PU	2247
00S08	1042
00S09	OEM
0-00(AMPEX)	0126
01-031-018	OEM
01-03945	0111
01-010473	0919
01-010495	0006
01-010562	0006
01-010564	0203
01-010628	0006
01-010673	0148
01-010719	0006
01-010733	0006
01-010844	0688
01-020562	0527
01-020566	0676
01-030372	0076
01-030373	0111
01-030380	0224
01-030388	0326
01-030394	0155
01-030454	0076
01-030458	0076
01-030460	0151
01-030495	1581
01-030509	0155
01-030536	0532
01-030643	0309
01-030668	0127
01-030682	0047
01-030710	0364
01-030711	0376
01-030719	0006
01-030732	0111
01-030733	0006
01-030734	0076
01-030735	0191
01-030763	0127
01-030784	1136
01-030785	1136
01-030828	1211
01-030829	0151
01-030900	1212
01-030930	2195
01-030945	0076
01-030983	0066
01-031018	2039
01-031047	0113
01-031096	0386
01-031166	0728
01-031173	0042
01-031175	0191
01-031213	0191
01-031239	1897
01-031293	1060
01-031306	0833
01-031317	0155
01-031318	0155
01-031327	1212
01-031359	0151
01-031360	1653
01-031364	0076
01-031446	0638
01-031507	0949
01-031514	1077
01-031520	0168
01-031550	0275
01-031664	0625
01-031674	1060
01-031675	0076
01-031678	0930
01-031685	0284
01-031686	0224
01-031687	0224
01-031688	0016
01-031756	0638
01-031760	1935
01-031815	0076
01-031846	0781
01-031855	0224
01-031906	0127
01-031909	0930
01-031921	0261
01-031923	0224
01-031957	2684
01-031964	2475
01-031974	0830
01-032028	1581
01-032029	0930
01-032057	0224
01-032076	0079
01-032078	0930
01-032092	0930
01-032314	1581
01-040201	0861
01-040234	0042
01-040243	0228
01-040299	0223
01-040313	0419
01-040389	0042
01-040471	0018
01-040476	0419
01-040724	0388
01-070019	3043
01-070030	0321
01-080019	3043
01-080045	0410
01-080059	0212
01-0318145	0111
01-201-0	0079
01-9011-5/2221-3	0079
01-9013-7/2221-3	0079
01-9014-2/2221-3	0079
01-9016-4/2221-3	0079
01-9018-6/2221-3	0079
01-30828	0224
01-30829	0079
01-57291	0042
01-117005	0144
01-117006	0144
01-119185-01	0375
01-119185-02	0375
01-119185-03	0375
01-121365	0167
01-349418	0086
01-349423	0016
01-349426	0224
01-349634	0079
01-349681	0037
01-472814	0155
01-571591	0037
01-571751	0037
01-571794	0007
01-571804	0326
01-571811	0079
01-571821	0079
01-571831	0233
01-571921	0142
01-571941	0016
01-572088	0283
01-572588	0037
01-572631	0309
01-572774	0919
01-572784	0042
01-572791	0042
01-572811	0006
01-572814	0155
01-572831	0233
01-572861	0042
01-680415	0710
01-680815	0079
01-690261	0590
01-690471	0018
01-690564	0527
01-690643	1233
01-690733	0037
01-690945	0076
01-691187	0224
01-691674	0144
01-700542	0037
01K-3.6E	0188
01K-3.8E	0451
01K-4.6E	0446
01K-5.0E	0162
01K-5.2E	0162
01K-5.4E	0157
01K5.4E	0162
01K-5.8E	0157
01K-6.5E	0631
01K6.5E	0631
01M1371008B	OEM
01S60	OEM
01S67	OEM
01ST-2SC945P	0076
01ST-MPS9700D	0079
02-004558	0356
02-07150-01	OEM
02-010103	1532
02-010241	3977
02-010245	3238
02-010331	2579
02-010612	3980
02-091128	0167
02-091366	1120
02-2SC458LGC	0076
02-1001-1/2221-3	0143
02-1006-2/2221-3	0133
02-1006-22221-3	0133
02-3002-2/2221-3	0015
02-3002-22221-3	0015
02-5004	2007
02-5004-6	2006
02-5184-11	0147
02-33379-6	0086
02-33379-7	0396
02-103898	2702
02-121201	0574
02-121365	0167
02-124400	3286
02-124422	1044
02-151204	0866
02-161204	0866
02-161521	5243
02-165143	0167
02-173710	1805
02-173756	4567
02-217660	0780
02-235104	2592
02-252222	4571
02-257130	2008
02-257205	1044
02-257222	4571
02-257310	1532
02-263001	1532
02-269106	2801
02-280007	4564
02-300023	0523
02-300574	1319
02-300577	2246
02-301181	0749
02-301182	0751
02-301380	1049
02-310023	0523
02-311380	1049
02-341125	0167
02-341128	0167
02-341358	0167
02-343065	0167
02-360002	1704
02-360003	3515
02-373001	1532
02-392816	2312
02-403065	0167
02-435624	4558
02-437205	1044
02-437310	1532
02-455804	0356
02-507120	4766
02-507130	OEM
02-537666	0167
02-540800	4084
02-561171	1327
02-561201	0797
02-561251	0842
02-561410	0348
02-561492	OEM
02-561551	OEM
02-561651	OEM
02-781050	1288
02-781060	2285
02-ST-2SD1178C	0558
02A20A	OEM
02BZ2R7	0755
02BZ2.2	1266
02BZ2.7	0755
02BZ3.3	0289
02BZ3.9	0451
02BZ4.7	0446
02CZ2.0	OEM
02CZ2.2	OEM
02CZ2.4	OEM
02CZ2.7	OEM
02CZ3.0	OEM
02CZ3.3	OEM
02CZ3.6	OEM
02CZ3.9	OEM
02CZ4.3	OEM
02CZ4.7	OEM
02CZ5.1	OEM
02CZ5.6	OEM
02CZ6.2	OEM
02CZ6.8	OEM
02CZ7.5	OEM
02CZ8.2	OEM
02CZ9.1	OEM
02CZ10	OEM
02CZ11	OEM
02CZ12	OEM
02CZ13	OEM
02CZ15	OEM
02CZ16	OEM
02CZ18	OEM
02CZ20	OEM
02CZ22	OEM
02CZ24	OEM
02CZ27	OEM
02CZ30	OEM
02CZ33	OEM
02CZ36	OEM
02CZ39	OEM
02DZ3.3	OEM
02P1B	0037
02RECT-UG-1004	0106
02SI-TDB2033	OEM
02ST-2SC1815	0076
02ST-2SC1815Y	0076
02ST-2SC1875	2636
02ST-2SD1178C	0558
02Z5.6	0157
02Z5.6A	0253
02Z5.6Y	0253
02Z-6.2A	0631
02Z6.2A	0466
02Z6.2W	0466
02Z6.2W(FA-1)	0466
02Z6.2WFA-1	0466
02Z6.8A	0025
02Z7.5	0644
02Z-7.5A	0644
02Z7.5A	0077
02Z8.2	0244
02Z8.2A	0165
02Z9.1	0012
02Z-9.1A	0057
02Z9.1A	0057
02Z-10A	0170
02Z10A	0064
02Z10A-U	0170
02Z11A	0313
02Z12A	0052
02Z12GR	0052
02Z13A	0053
02Z15	0002
02Z15A	0440
02Z16A	0416
02Z18	0526
02Z18A	0490
02Z20A	0695
02Z22A	0700
02Z24	0398
02Z24A	0489
02Z62A	0631
02Z82A	0623
03-0018-0	0015
03-0020-0	0211
03-0023-0	0211
03-0247	OEM
03-0248	OEM
03-156B	0004
03-160	0143
03-460C	0144
03-461B	0144
03-535A	0144
03-1585/G	0016
03-3016	0015
03-931051	0143
03-931601	0015
03-931609	0015
03-931641	0599
03-931642	0133
03-931645	0133
03-931771	0143
03-931971	0015
03-933935	0346
03-933943	0137
03-936011	0102
03A02	0018
03A03	0016
03A04	0006
03A05	0016
03A06	0527
03A09	0321
03A10	0212
03A10	0212
03A11	0079
03A12	0079
03K-3.5E	0188
03K-4.2E	0451
03P05M	0340
03P1M	0895
03P2M	0058
03P3M	0403
03P4M	0403
03P4MG	OEM
03P4MGC	OEM
03P5MG	OEM
03P5MGC	OEM
03P6MGC	OEM
03SI-MC1352P	0391
03SZ-RD12EB	0999
03SZ-RD12EB(AO)	0999
03SZ-RD12EB(AU)	0052
04-00072-01	0208
04-000655-1	0124
04-00156-03	0164
04-00460-03	0016
04-00461-02	0127
04-00535-02	0127
04-00535-06	0144
04-01585-06	0016
04-01585-07	0016
04-01585-08	0127
04-02090-02	0079
04-07150-01	0520
04-2	0549
04-4600-02	0224
04-11620-01	0558
04-15850-06	0016
04-38190-01	0321
04-46000-02	0224
04-67000-01	0037
04AZ2.0	OEM
04AZ2.0-Z	OEM
04AZ2.0Z	OEM
04AZ2.2	OEM
04AZ2.2-Z	OEM
04AZ2.2Z	OEM
04AZ2.4	1266
04AZ2.7	0755
04AZ2.7X	OEM
04AZ2.7Y	OEM
04AZ2.7Z	0755
04AZ3.0	0118
04AZ3.3	0296
04AZ3.6	0372
04AZ3.9	0036
04AZ4.3	0274
04AZ4.3-Y	0274
04AZ4.3X	0274
04AZ4.3Y	0274
04AZ4.3Z	0274
04AZ4.7	0140
04AZ4.7-X	0582
04AZ4.7-Y	0140
04AZ4.7X	0582
04AZ4.7Y	0140
04AZ4.7Z	OEM
04AZ5.1	0041
04AZ5.1-X	0582
04AZ5.1X	0041
04AZ5.1Y	0582
04AZ5.1ZTPA7	OEM
04AZ5.6	0253
04AZ5.6-X	0877
04AZ5.6X	0041
04AZ5.6Y	0253
04AZ5.6Z	0877
04AZ6.2	0466
04AZ6.2-Y	0292
04AZ6.2X	0292
04AZ6.2Y	0466
04AZ6.2Z	0292
04AZ6.8	0062
04AZ6.8-Y	0062
04AZ6.8-Z	0062
04AZ6.8X	0062
04AZ6.8Y	0062
04AZ6.8Z	0062
04AZ7.5	0077
04AZ7.5-X	0077
04AZ7.5X	0062
04AZ7.5Y	OEM
04AZ7.5Z	0077
04AZ8.2	0165
04AZ8.2X	0077
04AZ8.2Z	0165
04AZ9.1	0057
04AZ9.1X	0057
04AZ9.1Y	0057
04AZ9.1Z	0057
04AZ9.1ZTPA7	OEM
04AZ10	0064
04AZ10-X	0248
04AZ10X	0057
04AZ10Y	OEM
04AZ10Z	OEM
04AZ11	0181
04AZ12	0052
04AZ12-X	0999
04AZ12-Y	0999
04AZ12X	0999
04AZ12Y	0999
04AZ12Z	0999
04AZ13	0053
04AZ13X	OEM
04AZ15	0681
04AZ15-Z	0681
04AZ15X	4446
04AZ15Y	4446
04AZ15Z	0681
04AZ16	0440
04AZ16ZTPA7	OEM
04AZ18	0371
04AZ20	0695
04AZ20-Y	0666
04AZ20X	0666
04AZ20Y	0666
04AZ20Z	0666
04AZ22	0700
04AZ24	0489
04AZ27	0450
04AZ30	0195
04AZ30Y	OEM
04AZ33	0166
04AZ33-Y	OEM
04AZ33Y	OEM
04AZ36	0010
04AZ36X	OEM
04AZ39	0032
04AZ39Z	OEM
04BZ4.7	0140
04BZ5.1	0041
04BZ5.6	0253
04BZ6.2	0466
04BZ6.8	0062
04BZ7.5	0077
04BZ8.2	0165
04BZ9.1	0057
04BZ10	0064
04BZ11	0181
04BZ12	0052
04BZ13	0053
04BZ15	0681
04BZ16	0440
04BZ18	0371
04BZ20	0695
04BZ22	0700
04BZ24	0489
04DZ2.0	OEM
04DZ2.2	OEM
04DZ2.4	1266
04DZ2.7	0755
04DZ3.0	0118
04DZ3.3	0296
04DZ3.6	0372
04DZ3.9	0036
04DZ4.3	0274
04DZ4.7	0140
04DZ5.1	0041
04HFL40S05	OEM
04HFL80S05	OEM
04S05	2039
04S06	0930
04S4	6611
04S30	0037
04S48	0079
04S51	0710
04ST-2SC945Q(AU)E	0076
04SZ-UZ-6.2B	0466
04Z2.0	OEM
04Z2.2	OEM
04Z2.4	OEM
04Z2.7	OEM
04Z3.0	OEM
04Z3.3	OEM
04Z3.6	OEM
04Z3.9	OEM
04Z4.3	OEM
04Z4.7	OEM
04Z5.1	OEM
04Z5.6	OEM
04Z6.2	OEM
04Z6.8	OEM
04Z7.5	OEM
04Z8.2	OEM
04Z9.1	OEM
04Z10	OEM
04Z11	OEM
04Z12	OEM
04Z13	OEM
04Z15	OEM
04Z16	OEM
04Z18	OEM
04Z20	OEM
04Z22	OEM
04Z24	OEM
05-00000-00	0143
05-00060-00	0143
05-00060-01	0019
05-00085-00	0030
05-000104	0023
05-0085-00	OEM
05-00160-01	0143
05-00608-01	OEM
05-001100	0015
05-002139	0005
05-02160-01	0133

If replacement code is OEM, contact original manufacturer for replacement.

DEVICE TYPE	REPL CODE
05-02638-01	0030
05-03016-01	0015
05-04001-02	0023
05-04800-02	0244
05-040004	0102
05-040006	0102
05-060110	0313
05-18155	0133
05-69669-01	0025
05-95017	0490
05-110046	0102
05-110106	0091
05-110107	0062
05-110108	0062
05-110442	0133
05-111011	0313
05-112404	0023
05-112406	0102
05-123103	0023
05-141025	0015
05-150018	0023
05-150046	0120
05-170034	0123
05-170060	0019
05-174002	0015
05-174004	0790
05-180034	0143
05-180053	0133
05-180188	0143
05-180553	0755
05-180953	0124
05-181555	0133
05-181658	0030
05-181885	0023
05-182076	0124
05-182236	0005
05-182688	0030
05-190060	0143
05-190061	0023
05-200310	0623
05-200410	0030
05-320301	0133
05-328518	1914
05-330150	0133
05-330161	0133
05-331091	0057
05-370151	0286
05-429602	0015
05-472209	0030
05-480086	0318
05-480204	0451
05-480205	0162
05-480209	0623
05-480306	0298
05-490090	0019
05-490091	0019
05-490095	0143
05-540001	0023
05-540082	0165
05-540091	0012
05-540094	0012
05-540112	0023
05-610046	0143
05-740012	0102
05-750010	0015
05-780251	0030
05-800015	0182
05-860002	0023
05-860091	0012
05-900006	0023
05-931601	0015
05-931609	0023
05-931642	0133
05-931645	0133
05-931771	0143
05-931971	0015
05-932510	0143
05-933935	0346
05-933943	0137
05-933945	0398
05-933948	1639
05-933949	0296
05-933950	0416
05-935201	0023
05-936010	0623
05-936470	0133
05-950177	1639
05-990094	0012
05-2000310	0623
05A	0140
05A01	0133
05A03	0143
05A05	0133
05A06	0124
05A07	0015
05A08	0030
05AZ2.0	OEM
05AZ2.2	OEM
05AZ2.4	1266
05AZ2.7	0755
05AZ3.0	0118
05AZ3.3	0296
05AZ3.6	0372
05AZ3.9	0036
05AZ4.3	0274
05AZ4.7	0140
05AZ5.1	0041
05AZ5.6	0253
05AZ5.6Y	0877

DEVICE TYPE	REPL CODE
05AZ6.2	0466
05AZ6.8	0062
05AZ7.5	0077
05AZ8.2	0165
05AZ9.1	0057
05AZ10	0064
05AZ11	0181
05AZ12	0052
05AZ13	0053
05AZ15	0681
05AZ16	0440
05AZ18	0371
05AZ20	0695
05AZ22	0700
05AZ24	0489
05AZ27	0450
05AZ30	0195
05AZ33	0166
05AZ36	0010
05AZ39	0032
05AZ43	0054
05AZ47	0068
05AZ51	0092
05AZ56	0125
05AZ62	0152
05AZ68	0173
05AZ75	0094
05AZ75-R	0094
05AZ82	0049
05AZ91	0156
05AZ100	0189
05B	0140
05B2B	0167
05B2D	0167
05B2M	0167
05B486	0007
05C	0041
05D	0041
05M1	0041
05RECT-SI-56	OEM
05RECT-SI-156	0790
05RM80	OEM
05RM100	OEM
05RM120	OEM
05RM150	OEM
05RM200	OEM
05RM250	OEM
05SM05	OEM
05SM1	1325
05ST-2SA844C	0688
05ST-2SC2482	0261
05V-50	0080
05V50	0015
05WM05	1325
05Z2.0	OEM
05Z2.0-X	OEM
05Z2.0X	OEM
05Z2.2	OEM
05Z2.4	1266
05Z2.4X	1268
05Z2.4Z	5833
05Z2.7	0755
05Z3.0	0118
05Z3.0-Y	0118
05Z3.0X	4256
05Z3.0Y	0296
05Z3.0Z	5899
05Z3.3	0296
05Z3.3XLC-5	0296
05Z3.6	0372
05Z3.6X	5904
05Z3.6Y	5904
05Z3.6Z	OEM
05Z3.9	0036
05Z3.9X	0036
05Z3.9Y	0036
05Z3.9Z	5142
05Z4-3Y	0274
05Z4.3	0274
05Z4.3-X	0274
05Z4.3-Y	0274
05Z4.3X	0274
05Z4.3Y	0274
05Z4.3Z	5986
05Z4.7	0140
05Z4.7-X	0140
05Z4.7-Z	0140
05Z4.7X	0140
05Z4.7Y	5986
05Z4.7Z	5986
05Z5-1X	0041
05Z5-1Y	0041
05Z5.1	0041
05Z5.1-X	0041
05Z5.1L	0041
05Z5.1U	0041
05Z5.1X	0041
05Z5.1Y	0041
05Z5.1Z	0041
05Z5.4Z	OEM
05Z5.6	0253
05Z5.6-X	0253
05Z5.6U	6065
05Z5.6X	0041
05Z5.6Y	0253
05Z5.6Z	0253
05Z6.2	0466
05Z6.2-Z	0466
05Z-6.2L	0466

DEVICE TYPE	REPL CODE
05Z6.2L	0091
05Z6.2U	6108
05Z6.2W	0466
05Z6.2WFA-1	0466
05Z6.2X	6109
05Z6.2Y	0466
05Z6.2Z	0466
05Z6.8	0062
05Z6.8-X	0062
05Z6.8-Y	0062
05Z6.8U	OEM
05Z6.8X	0062
05Z-6.8Y	0062
05Z6.8Y	0062
05Z6.8Z	0062
05Z7.5	0077
05Z7.5-UNI	0644
05Z7.5-Y	0077
05Z7.5X	6220
05Z7.5Y	0077
05Z7.5Z	6220
05Z8.2	0165
05Z8.2-U	0244
05Z8.2X	0244
05Z8.2Y	4245
05Z8.2Z	0057
05Z9.1	0057
05Z9.1-Z	0057
05Z9.1L	0012
05Z9.1U	0012
05Z9.1X	6405
05Z9.1Z	0057
05Z-10	6652
05Z10	0006
05Z10L	0170
05Z10X	6094
05Z10Y	6094
05Z10Z	6094
05Z11	0181
05Z11-Z	0181
05Z11Y	0181
05Z11Z	0181
05Z12	0052
05Z12-X	0052
05Z12-Y	0052
05Z12-Z	0361
05Z12X	0999
05Z12Y	0137
05Z12Z	0361
05Z13	0053
05Z13X	0053
05Z13Y	0053
05Z13Z	0361
05Z15	0681
05Z15-Y	0681
05Z15X	0873
05Z15Y	0681
05Z15Z	0681
05Z16	0440
05Z16X	0440
05Z16Y	1220
05Z18	0371
05Z18L	0490
05Z18X	4764
05Z18Y	4764
05Z18Z	4764
05Z20	0695
05Z20-X	0695
05Z20-Y	0695
05Z20X	0666
05Z20Y	0695
05Z22	0700
05Z22L	0700
05Z-22X	0700
05Z22X	0700
05Z22Z	4855
05Z24	0489
05Z24I	0489
05Z24K	OEM
05Z24L	0489
05Z24X	2448
05Z24Y	0489
05Z24Z	2448
05Z27	0450
05Z30	0195
05Z30Y	2419
05Z33	0166
05Z33-Y	0166
05Z33Y	0166
05Z36	0010
05Z36X	0010
05Z36Y	0010
05Z36Z	0010
05Z39	0032
05Z43	0054
05Z47	0068
05Z51	0092
05Z56	0125
05Z62	0152
05Z68	0173
05Z72	1181
05Z72(TP)	1181
05Z75	0094
05Z82	0049
05Z91	0156
05Z100	0189
06A	0253
06B1AH	0696
06B1B	0696

DEVICE TYPE	REPL CODE
06B1D	0696
06B1M	0696
06C	0091
06D	0091
06M	0091
06M6	0091
06SI-SAB3034	OEM
06SP-LT-3233G	OEM
06ST-2SC1906	0127
06X90514A75	0058
07-07159	3017
07-07459	0007
07-72	0111
07-1077-02	0004
07-1777-03	0359
07-5085-36	0030
07-5134-14	0143
07-5160-15	0123
07-5331-86	0631
07-22816-90	0124
07-28777-40	3973
07-28777-41	0167
07-28777-42	2932
07-28777-45	4004
07-28777-49	4017
07-28777-56	4665
07-28777-70	0203
07-28777-71	0006
07-28777-72	0520
07-28777-76	2208
07-28777-83	0781
07-28777-84	0577
07-28777-87	0558
07-28777-92	0133
07-28777-95	0120
07-28777-96	0911
07-28777-100	0466
07-28778-70	4663
07-28778-72	4677
07-28778-73	4671
07-28778-74	4666
07-28778-75	4670
07-28778-76	4981
07-28778-77	4678
07-28778-78	4099
07-28778-79	0558
07-28778-80	0155
07-28778-82	4076
07-28778-84	0527
07-28778-85	0321
07-28778-86	0133
07-28815-75	0355
07-28815-76	0819
07-28815-77	0819
07-28815-82	2208
07-28815-83	2208
07-28815-84	0577
07-28815-85	0577
07-28815-86	0155
07-28815-89	0577
07-28815-92	0023
07-28815-97	0253
07-28815-100	3809
07-28815-101	2244
07-28815-103	0919
07-28815-108	0819
07-28815-116	0124
07-28815-118	0199
07-28815-119	1009
07-28816-70	1570
07-28816-71	1572
07-28816-72	1575
07-28816-73	1516
07-28816-74	0676
07-28816-75	0284
07-28816-76	0019
07-28816-77	0023
07-28816-78	0036
07-28816-81	1319
07-28816-82	OEM
07-28816-83	1589
07-28816-84	1135
07-28816-85	0394
07-28816-86	0119
07-28816-87	1593
07-28816-88	1211
07-28816-89	0124
07-28816-90	0124
07-28816-91	0143
07-28816-92	0100
07-28816-93	0039
07-28816-94	1603
07B	0062
07B2B	0659
07B2Z	2728
07B3B	0659
07B3M	0659
07B3Z	0659
07B27	0659
07D	0077
07M	0062
07M6	0062
07SD-1S1555	0133
07SD-1S1887	0023
07SD-1S1887(AU)	0023
07ST-2SC383W	0076
07SZ-UZP-11B	0313
08-0040	0015
08-0821	0015

DEVICE TYPE	REPL CODE
08-08112	0019
08-302152	0224
08A	0077
08A159-001	0139
08A159-006	OEM
08A159-007	0133
08A159-009	0139
08A165-001	0133
08D	0087
08P-2-12	0004
08SD-1K34A	2217
08SI-UPD4556BC	3397
08ST-2SC945Q(AU)E	0076
08ST-2SC945R(AU)E	0076
08ST-JE9015C	0037
08V-50	0080
08V-100	0604
08V-200	0790
09-004	0649
09-011	0438
09-05032	1202
09-030214	0198
09-033006	0208
09-309-070	0111
09-309-071	0042
09-30012	0050
09-30036	0126
09-30126	0004
09-30205	0626
09-30313	0004
09-30514	0321
09-30636	0123
09-30924	OEM
09-30970	0111
09-36154	0124
09-207039	0139
09-300002	0136
09-300005	0164
09-300006	0628
09-300007	0136
09-300011	0136
09-300012	0136
09-300015	0136
09-300016	0136
09-300017	0004
09-300021	0050
09-300024	0004
09-300026	0203
09-300027	0136
09-300028	0050
09-300029	0136
09-300036	0203
09-300037	0006
09-300037A	0160
09-300043	0126
09-300059	0006
09-300061	0037
09-300062	0037
09-300063	0006
09-300064	0006
09-300067	1421
09-300068	0676
09-300070	0006
09-300071	0527
09-300072	1233
09-300073	0676
09-300074	0037
09-300076	0527
09-300077	0037
09-300078	0136
09-300079	0136
09-300080	0006
09-300081	0006
09-300084	0050
09-300090	0919
09-300307	0037
09-301001	0164
09-301002	0004
09-301002-6	0004
09-301003	0004
09-301004	0004
09-301005	0004
09-301006	0004
09-301007	0004
09-301008	0164
09-301008-18	0004
09-301009	0004
09-301010	0085
09-301012	0164
09-301014	0164
09-301015	0841
09-301016	0004
09-301019	0164
09-301020	0004
09-301022	1056
09-301023	0004
09-301024	0222
09-301025	0004
09-301025-6	0004
09-301026	0004
09-301027	0164
09-301030	1004
09-301031	0841
09-301032	0004
09-301034	0222
09-301036	0004
09-301039	0007
09-301048	0004
09-301050	0527

DEVICE TYPE	REPL CODE
09-301052	0160
09-301054	0004
09-301056	0004
09-301066	0164
09-301071	0969
09-301072	0004
09-301073	0969
09-301074	0004
09-301075	0222
09-301077	0919
09-301079	0969
09-301081	1900
09-302002	0284
09-302003	0155
09-302004	0151
09-302005	0144
09-302006	0127
09-302007	0191
09-302009	0127
09-302010	1136
09-302012	0364
09-302014	0127
09-302015	1390
09-302016	0836
09-302017	0144
09-302019	0711
09-302020	0076
09-302026	OEM
09-302028	0007
09-302030	0208
09-302032	0127
09-302033	0151
09-302034	0076
09-302036	1060
09-302037	2195
09-302038	1211
09-302039	0155
09-302040	0191
09-302041	0079
09-302042	OEM
09-302044	0127
09-302045	0016
09-302045-12	0016
09-302046	2035
09-302050	1401
09-302051	1897
09-302053	0532
09-302054	0191
09-302055	1583
09-302056	1401
09-302058	0284
09-302060	0470
09-302061	0544
09-302062	0155
09-302063	0470
09-302068	1390
09-302072	0470
09-302073	0127
09-302074	0783
09-302074(SHARP)	0111
09-302075	0079
09-302078	0783
09-302079	0127
09-302080	2035
09-302081	1390
09-302082	0626
09-302083	0042
09-302085	0111
09-302086	0532
09-302090	0076
09-302090(DIODE)	0133
09-302092	0191
09-302093	1212
09-302095	1136
09-302097	0547
09-302099	0233
09-302101	0284
09-302102	2039
09-302103	0127
09-302106	0151
09-302107	0111
09-302113	0555
09-302117	4144
09-302118	0076
09-302119	0086
09-302121	0219
09-302122	0615
09-302123	0219
09-302124	0076
09-302125	0076
09-302126	0386
09-302127	0111
09-302128	0047
09-302129	0127
09-302130	0855
09-302131	0016
09-302132	0042
09-302135	2039
09-302136	0781
09-302138	1136
09-302139	0111
09-302140	0155
09-302141	0144
09-302142	0127
09-302143	0127
09-302144	0127
09-302145	0076
09-302146	0142
09-302148	0216

DEVICE TYPE	REPL CODE
09-302149	1146
09-302150	0693
09-302151	0127
09-302152	0127
09-302153	0016
09-302155	0018
09-302156	0142
09-302157	0003
09-302158	0637
09-302159	0074
09-302160	0142
09-302161	0786
09-302162	0127
09-302164	0042
09-302165	0076
09-302166	0617
09-302169	1897
09-302170	0042
09-302171	0086
09-302172	0016
09-302173	0155
09-302174	0007
09-302175	0191
09-302176	2420
09-302177	0637
09-302185	0142
09-302186	0168
09-302187	0065
09-302188	1021
09-302189	0016
09-302190	0470
09-302191	0470
09-302192	0930
09-302193	0830
09-302194	0111
09-302199	0007
09-302201	0007
09-302202	1967
09-302204	0016
09-302206	0284
09-302207	0155
09-302212	0076
09-302215	0224
09-302216	0224
09-302218	0178
09-302219	1165
09-302220	0127
09-302222	0155
09-302224	1060
09-302225	0076
09-302226	0218
09-302227	0155
09-302236	0042
09-302237	0949
09-302238	1142
09-302240	0007
09-302241	0224
09-302242	0224
09-302243	0066
09-302244	0191
09-302245	1142
09-302246	2636
09-302325	0631
09-303005	0178
09-303006	0208
09-303012	0208
09-303013	0208
09-303018	0228
09-303019	0218
09-303020	0419
09-303021	0042
09-303022	0555
09-303023	0208
09-303025	1409
09-303028	0142
09-303029	0168
09-303030	0004
09-303031	0419
09-303032	1597
09-303033	0042
09-303034	0388
09-303036	0018
09-303042	0224
09-303058	0198
09-304011	0050
09-304012	0037
09-304017	1382
09-304019	0127
09-304042	0224
09-304043	0224
09-304044	0016
09-304045	0016
09-304046	0283
09-304047	0037
09-304048	0079
09-304049	0037
09-304050	0037
09-304051	0037
09-304052	0334
09-304055	0556
09-304056	0065
09-304057	0003
09-304058	0016
09-304264	OEM
09-305006	0007
09-305007	0127
09-305011	0007
09-305014	0683
09-305021	3017

If replacement code is OEM, contact original manufacturer for replacement.

DEVICE TYPE	REPL CODE
09-305023	0321
09-305024	0037
09-305031	0321
09-305032	0321
09-305033	0127
09-305034	0016
09-305035	OEM
09-305036	0127
09-305040	0349
09-305041	0127
09-305048	0111
09-305049	2035
09-305050	0224
09-305051	2195
09-305052	0111
09-305058	0688
09-305062	0016
09-305063	0076
09-305068	0016
09-305069	0144
09-305072	0144
09-305074	0144
09-305077	0016
09-305091	1897
09-305092	0728
09-305093	0155
09-305094	1136
09-305095	0042
09-305124	1967
09-305126	0111
09-305131	0004
09-305132	1146
09-305133	0321
09-305134	0006
09-305135	0321
09-305136	0833
09-305137	0830
09-305138	0103
09-305139	0076
09-305140	0042
09-305148	0079
09-305149	0037
09-305150	0710
09-305151	0338
09-305152	0079
09-306002	0143
09-306008	0030
09-306009	0143
09-306010	0143
09-306012	0143
09-306014	0030
09-306015	0030
09-306018	0030
09-306019	0123
09-306020	0123
09-306021	0030
09-306023	0005
09-306024	0002
09-306024(ZENER)	0002
09-306028	6169
09-306030	0102
09-306031	0914
09-306033	0015
09-306034	0015
09-306036	0019
09-306037	0143
09-306039	0030
09-306040	0143
09-306042	0015
09-306042(DIO)	2613
09-306042(ZENER)	0244
09-306047	0143
09-306049	0143
09-306050	0023
09-306051	0143
09-306052	0062
09-306053	0087
09-306054	0015
09-306055	0631
09-306057	0123
09-306058	0143
09-306059	0015
09-306060	0139
09-306061	0143
09-306062	0133
09-306063	0015
09-306073	0298
09-306077	0911
09-306083	0087
09-306084	OEM
09-306088	0015
09-306089	0911
09-306093	0143
09-306100	0023
09-306101	0196
09-306102	0071
09-306103	0015
09-306104	0133
09-306106	0012
09-306107	0143
09-306108	0143
09-306109	0298
09-306110	0139
09-306110(ZENER)	0002
09-306111	0133
09-306112	1141
09-306113	0120
09-306114	0139
09-306115	0015

DEVICE TYPE	REPL CODE
09-306119	0015
09-306124	0012
09-306125	0015
09-306126	0030
09-306127	0361
09-306129	0139
09-306134	0133
09-306135	0133
09-306138	0015
09-306141	0102
09-306144	0102
09-306145	0133
09-306148	0143
09-306149	0023
09-306151	0124
09-306154	0133
09-306157	0015
09-306158	0012
09-306159	0133
09-306160	0015
09-306161	0133
09-306162	0015
09-306163	0133
09-306165	0012
09-306167	0030
09-306168	1141
09-306169	0015
09-306170	0133
09-306171	0133
09-306172	0015
09-306173	0053
09-306176	0015
09-306177	0015
09-306178	0023
09-306179	0137
09-306180	0012
09-306181	0644
09-306183	0091
09-306191	0041
09-306192	0015
09-306193	0196
09-306194	0012
09-306195	0133
09-306196	0244
09-306197	0644
09-306198	0133
09-306199	0139
09-306200	0139
09-306201	0030
09-306202	0133
09-306204	0133
09-306205	0015
09-306206	0133
09-306208	0298
09-306209	0911
09-306210	0911
09-306211	0133
09-306211(RECT)	0133
09-306212	0077
09-306212(RECT)	0015
09-306213	0015
09-306214	0015
09-306215	0025
09-306216	0911
09-306219	0143
09-306220	0002
09-306221	0133
09-306222	0133
09-306223	0139
09-306224	0139
09-306225	0071
09-306226	0071
09-306227	0015
09-306228	0064
09-306229	0019
09-306230	0030
09-306231	0133
09-306233	0139
09-306235	0170
09-306236	0133
09-306237	0102
09-306238	0165
09-306239	0012
09-306240	0715
09-306241	0012
09-306242	0077
09-306244	0133
09-306245	0023
09-306247	0012
09-306248	0133
09-306249	0015
09-306250	0015
09-306251	0030
09-306253	0030
09-306254	0015
09-306255	0015
09-306256	0139
09-306257	0071
09-306258	0182
09-306259	0102
09-306260	0102
09-306261	0911
09-306262	0911
09-306263	0015
09-306264	0015
09-306265	0030
09-306266	0133
09-306270	0143
09-306274	0015

DEVICE TYPE	REPL CODE
09-306276	0133
09-306277	0244
09-306278	0100
09-306283	0133
09-306285	0015
09-306286	0062
09-306287	0012
09-306288	0163
09-306289	0528
09-306290	0143
09-306300	0015
09-306301	0918
09-306302	0015
09-306303	0133
09-306304	0087
09-306305	0644
09-306306	0120
09-306309	0133
09-306310	0752
09-306311	0071
09-306312	0015
09-306313	0133
09-306314	0244
09-306315	0080
09-306323	0015
09-306324	0416
09-306325	0025
09-306326	0124
09-306327	0012
09-306329	0030
09-306330	0143
09-306332	0057
09-306333	0015
09-306334	0143
09-306335	0123
09-306336	0019
09-306349	0143
09-306350	0015
09-306351	0012
09-306352	0030
09-306353	0139
09-306354	0244
09-306355	1639
09-306356	0165
09-306359	0005
09-306365	0015
09-306366	0023
09-306367	0002
09-306368	0133
09-306369	0005
09-306370	0143
09-306371	5024
09-306372	0120
09-306373	0133
09-306374	0030
09-306375	0012
09-306376	0015
09-306377	0091
09-306378	0244
09-306379	0087
09-306380	0451
09-306381	0244
09-306382	0012
09-306384	0015
09-306389	0015
09-306390	0133
09-306391	0137
09-306392	0102
09-306394	0015
09-306400	OEM
09-306401	0012
09-306417	0023
09-306418	0071
09-306419	0025
09-306420	0374
09-306421	0071
09-306422	0015
09-306423	0023
09-306424	0344
09-306425	0344
09-306426	0133
09-306427	0015
09-306428	0313
09-306429	0313
09-306430	0286
09-306431	0023
09-306432	0015
09-306433	0023
09-307037	0139
09-307039	0133
09-307043	0139
09-307045	0139
09-307055	0133
09-307056	0120
09-307080	0133
09-307081	0120
09-307082	0644
09-307083	0133
09-307084	0139
09-307085	0139
09-307088	0025
09-307089	0133
09-307093	0005
09-307094	OEM
09-308002	0817
09-308003	0817
09-308004	0627
09-308005	OEM
09-308007	0817

DEVICE TYPE	REPL CODE
09-308008	0574
09-308009	0523
09-308010	2593
09-308011	2554
09-308012	OEM
09-308013	0627
09-308015	OEM
09-308017	2600
09-308019	0627
09-308021	0141
09-308022	0232
09-308024	2142
09-308025	0940
09-308026	0958
09-308027	2855
09-308028	0924
09-308029	2860
09-308030	0633
09-308031	0668
09-308033	1739
09-308034	1206
09-308041	0905
09-308043	1983
09-308044	2020
09-308045	0350
09-308046	0350
09-308047	0661
09-308048	0661
09-308049	2487
09-308050	2582
09-308051	2145
09-308052	2246
09-308053	0465
09-308054	2377
09-308055	OEM
09-308056	OEM
09-308059	0905
09-308061	3232
09-308062	0574
09-308063	0574
09-308064	1206
09-308065	2390
09-308066	2606
09-308067	3625
09-308069	2855
09-308070	1383
09-308071	1469
09-308072	0127
09-308074	2100
09-308076	0428
09-308077	0021
09-308079	0348
09-308080	1044
09-308083	0648
09-308084	4348
09-308086	3332
09-308089	0872
09-308090	0391
09-308094	4553
09-308095	1012
09-308096	2300
09-308098	0167
09-308099	1327
09-308100	0167
09-308102	0648
09-308103	5640
09-308208	0631
09-309006	0224
09-309007	0144
09-309012	0016
09-309013	0144
09-309015	0144
09-309023	0016
09-309024	0144
09-309027	0144
09-309028	0144
09-309029	0396
09-309030	0786
09-309031	0590
09-309032	0144
09-309038	0037
09-309040	OEM
09-309042	0037
09-309049	0016
09-309050	0016
09-309059	0111
09-309060	0016
09-309061	0155
09-309062	0693
09-309069	0127
09-309070	0111
09-309071	0219
09-309072	0931
09-309073	0144
09-309075	0208
09-309076	0016
09-309171	0133
09-310171	0969
09-395148	OEM
09-3060111	0133
09-ST-BF459	0275
09A001-00	1024
09A02	0780
09A04	1682
09A05	1651
09A07	2242
09A08	3231
09A10	4331
09C5	0057

DEVICE TYPE	REPL CODE
09D	0057
09ST-2SA755C	0919
09ST-BF459	0275
010-694	0283
010PIN-T05	OEM
010PV-T05	OEM
010UV-PV-T05	OEM
011-00	0334
011H01	0279
012-00	0556
012-1020	OEM
012-1020-005	0133
012-1021-001	0133
012-1022-002	0479
012-1023-007	0157
012-1024-001	0133
012-1025-002	0087
012E	0016
012H01	0279
013-005002-06	0718
013-005005	1865
013-005005-6	1865
013-005007	1865
013-005007-6	1865
013-005009-6	0618
013-0144-6438	0015
013-1	4272
013-3	6104
013-339	0015
014-611	0037
014-652	0037
014-698	0016
014-784	0016
014-862	0111
015-002	0015
015-006	0015
015-1	1129
016	0589
016B12	0016
016B810	0016
016B812	0016
017E824	0016
018-00001	0037
018-00002	0037
018-00003	0016
018-00004	1257
018-00005	0555
018-00006	0015
018-00007	0015
018-00008	0015
018-00009	0015
018-0008	0015
018-0009	0015
019-00009	0016
019-00010	0016
019-001918	0143
019-001980	0143
019-002935	0015
019-002964	0133
019-003315	0050
019-003317	0038
019-003318	0038
019-003319	0038
019-003324	0279
019-003342	0279
019-003343	0279
019-003349	0086
019-003411	0170
019-003415	0164
019-003416	0164
019-003420	0015
019-003485	0178
019-003691	0693
019-003692	1390
019-003777	0136
019-003778	0050
019-003870-013	0015
019-003870-020	0015
019-003929	0144
019-003932	0016
019-003934	0016
019-005006	0016
019-005010	0037
019-005043	0143
019-005045	0959
019-102311	2217
019-301980	0143
020-00011	0123
020-00012	0123
020-00023	0136
020-00024	0127
020-00025	0127
020-00026	0144
020-00027	0144
020-00028	0127
020-00030	0143
020-00031	0819
020-1110-004	0150
020-1110-004(SCOTT)	0037
020-1110-004C	0037
020-1110-005	0688
020-1110-005(SCOTT)	0037
020-1110-005C	0006
020-1110-006	0050
020-1110-006(SCOTT)	0050
020-1110-007(SCOTT)	0126
020-1110-008	0086
020-1110-008(SCOTT)	0086
020-1110-009	0126

DEVICE TYPE	REPL CODE
020-1110-009(SCOTT)	0126
020-1110-010	0111
020-1110-010(SCOTT)	0016
020-1110-011	0079
020-1110-011(SCOTT)	0016
020-1110-012	0111
020-1110-012(SCOTT)	0016
020-1110-013	0111
020-1110-013(SCOTT)	0016
020-1110-014	0126
020-1110-014(SCOTT)	0233
020-1110-015(SCOTT)	0126
020-1110-016	0321
020-1110-016(SCOTT)	0321
020-1110-017	0079
020-1110-017(SCOTT)	0016
020-1110-018	0321
020-1110-018(SCOTT)	0321
020-1110-021	0321
020-1110-022	0321
020-1110-025	0164
020-1110-025(SCOTT)	0004
020-1110-027	0688
020-1110-038	0855
020-1111-002	0103
020-1111-002(SCOTT)	0103
020-1111-003	0074
020-1111-003(SCOTT)	0103
020-1111-004	0919
020-1111-005	0042
020-1111-006(SCOTT)	0599
020-1111-007	0103
020-1111-007(SCOTT)	0103
020-1111-008	0103
020-1111-008(SCOTT)	0103
020-1111-017	0126
020-1111-018	0086
020-1112-001	0016
020-1112-002	0321
020-1112-004	0127
020-1112-004(SCOTT)	0016
020-1112-005	0321
020-1112-006	0321
020-1112-007	0321
020-1112-008	0321
020-1112-009	0321
020-1114-004	OEM
020-1114-006	0649
020-1114-007	0627
020-1114-008	0627
020-1114-009	0438
020-1114-010	OEM
020-1114-016	1686
022-006500	0198
022-009600	0079
022-2823-001	0559
022-2823-002	0012
022-2823-003	0019
022-2823-004	0133
022-2823-005	0133
022-2823-006	0123
022-2823-007	0123
022-2823-008	0143
022-2823-009	0015
022-2823-010	0133
022-2823-011	0015
022-2823-501	0715
022-2823-503	0030
022-2844-001	4331
022-2844-002	6889
022-2844-501	2285
022-2844-502	OEM
022-2844-701	2285
022-2844-702	1888
022-2844-703	4331
022-2876-001	0321
022-2876-002	0208
022-2876-003	0076
022-2876-004	0037
022-2876-005	0321
022-2876-006	0321
022-2876-007	0364
022-2876-008	1025
022-2876-009	0683
022-2876-010	0161
022-2876-011	0833
022-2876-012	0830
022-2876-704	0930
022-3504-060	0211
022-3505-910	0211
022-3511-770	0050
022-3511-780	0050
022-3511-790	0050
022-3516-380	0136
022-3640-050	0160
022-3640-080	0144
022-3640-081	0693
022-3640-082	0693
022-3640-253	0164
022-3901-001	0143
022-3905-001	0015
022-5311-770	0136
022-5311-780	0136
022-5511-790	0136
022-3511780	0050
022-3511790	0050
022D	0015
022.3504-040	0211
024	0899

DEVICE TYPE	REPL CODE
025-009600	0127
025-1	2716
025-100003	0144
025-100004	0144
025-100005	OEM
025-100006	OEM
025-100008	0911
025-100009	0144
025-100010	OEM
025-100011	0030
025-100012	0007
025-100013	0144
025-100014	0144
025-100015	0086
025-100016	0015
025-100017	0111
025-100018	0079
025-100019	OEM
025-100024	0015
025-100026	0127
025-100027	0143
025-100028	0015
025-100029	0015
025-100030	0016
025-100031	0164
025-100035	0015
025-100036	0007
025-100036-12	0007
025-100037	0007
025-100037-12	0007
025-100038	0007
025-100038-12	0007
025-100039	0030
025-100040	0016
025B	0016
025B1C	2716
025B-YEL	0016
026-1000-20	0085
026-100003	0160
026-100004	0265
026-100005	0211
026-100012	0211
026-100013	0086
026-100017	0198
026-100018	0211
026-100020	0265
026-100026	0016
026-100028	0160
027-000296	0015
027-000306	0015
027-000312	0015
027-300226	0196
028	0142
028-300-226	0123
030	0087
030-007-0	0688
030-034-0	0208
031	0087
031-002-0	2035
031-025-0	0364
031-098-0	0930
031A	0016
032	0087
033-00234	1021
033-005400	OEM
033-014-0	0410
033-3	0086
033-4	OEM
033A	0111
034-001-0	0123
034-018-0	0139
034-032-0	0124
035	0087
035-013-0	0005
037	0016
037-250	0398
038	0086
039	0126
040-014-0	OEM
041	0016
041A	0212
042	0016
044-0603-210	0259
045	0349
045-1	0127
045-1(SYLVANIA)	0144
045-2	0127
045-2(SYLVANIA)	0144
046-0134	0133
046-0909	0133
046-07037	0743
046-1	0555
046-1(SYLVANIA)	0555
046-40209	0090
047	0349
047-1	1257
047-1(SYLVANIA)	1257
048	0843
050-0011-00	0015
050A1GOF	1694
050A1OOF	1694
050A2GOF	OEM
050A2OOF	OEM
050A3GOF	OEM
050A3OOF	OEM
050A4GOF	OEM
050A4OOF	OEM
050AAGOF	1694
050AAOOF	1694

If replacement code is OEM, contact original manufacturer for replacement.

5

Original Device Types

DEVICE TYPE	REPL CODE
050BBGOF	1694
050BBOOF	1694
050PIN-RM	OEM
050PIN-T08	OEM
050PV-RM	OEM
051-0003	0133
051-0006	0015
051-003	0133
051-0010-00	4477
051-0011-00	1983
051-0011-00-04	1983
051-0011-00-05	3625
051-0011-04	2898
051-0012-00	0438
051-0012-11	0438
051-0016-00	0015
051-0017-00	0696
051-0020	0133
051-0020-00	1012
051-0020-02	1012
051-0021-00	0780
051-0022-00	0673
051-0035-01	1012
051-0035-02	1012
051-0035-03	1012
051-0035-04	1012
051-0035-4	OEM
051-0036-00	4031
051-0036-01	4031
051-0036-02	4031
051-0036-03	4031
051-0036-0102	4031
051-0038-00	2546
051-0039-00	1469
051-0046	0016
051-0047	0016
051-0049	0127
051-0050-00	0514
051-0050-01	0514
051-0055-02	1044
051-0055-03	1044
051-0055-0203	1044
051-0062	0050
051-0063	0050
051-0066-00	4027
051-0068-02	0574
051-0079	0136
051-0086-00	0701
051-0087-00	3763
051-0088-00	0412
051-0088-00101	0412
051-0099-00	OEM
051-0100-00	1704
051-0107	0037
051-0107B	0006
051-0151	0178
051-0155	0016
051-0156	0693
051-0157	0693
052	0396
052A	0396
052ALRLF	OEM
053-602	OEM
054-50	OEM
055	0016
055C	0320
056	0037
057	0016
057B474H	0007
058	0015
058-001138	1135
059	0142
062	0016
063N	OEM
065	0178
065-001	0321
065-002	0321
065-004	0016
065-006	0111
065-007	0219
065-008	0590
065-011	OEM
065-012	0133
065-013	0143
065-014	0123
065-015	0015
065-016	0087
065-1	0050
065-1-12	0050
065-1-12-7	0050
065-2	0208
065-2-12	0208
065-4	0595
065-4-12	0595
065-4-12-7	0595
065-14	0143
065-210	0830
065A	0050
065A-12	0050
065A-12-7	0050
065B	0136
065B-12	0136
065B-12-7	0136
065C	0160
065C-12	0160
065C-12-7	0160
066	0086
066-1	0004
066-1-12	0004
066-1-12-7	0004
066-2	0004
066-2-12	0004
066-2-12-7	0004
066-3	0004
066-3-12	0004
066-3-12-7	0004
066C	0431
069	0016
070	0103
070-001	0050
070-003	0123
070-004	0071
070-005	0071
070-006	0071
070-007	0071
070-008	0071
070-009	0071
070-010	0071
070-011	0170
070-013	0071
070-014	0071
070-015	0071
070-016	0071
070-017	0071
070-019	0015
070-020	0279
070-021	0002
070-022	0133
070-024	0170
070-027	0916
070-028	0071
070-030	0071
070-031	0087
070-032	0071
070-033	0071
070-035	0087
070-036	0916
070-041	0087
070-043	0916
070-047	0133
072-1	0133
074-1	0219
074-3	0279
074-3-12-7	0279
075-045037	1303
075-046270	1417
075B	OEM
077A	0435
077A-12	0435
077A-12-7	0435
077C	0160
077C-12	0160
077C-12-7	0160
078-0016	0015
078-1696	0015
078-2400	0015
078-5001	0015
083	OEM
083-1	0037
083-2	OEM
083-6	0037
084A	0160
084A-12	0160
084A-12-7	0160
085	0103
088C	0279
088C-12	0279
088C-12-7	0279
089-4	0187
089-4(SYL)	1698
089-4(SYLVANIA)	0275
089-214	0144
089-215	0144
089-216	0144
089-220	0136
089-222	0004
089-223	0016
089-226	0016
089-231	0164
089-233	0038
089-235	0030
089-236	0143
089-241	0133
089-248	0143
089-252	0229
089-293	0143
090A64-1	0143
092-1	0435
092-1-12	0435
092-1-12-7	0435
093	OEM
094-007	0133
094-010	0023
094-011	0023
094-012	0023
094-013	0160
094-014	0019
094K	OEM
095C	3891
098-1	0015
098GI219	0071
099-1	0042
099-1(SYL)	0042
0100	0015
0100(IC)	OEM
0101-0034	0136
0101-0222	0136
0101-0439	0786
0101-0448	1257
0101-0448A	1257
0101-0465	0919
0101-0466	1257
0101-0491	0016
0101-0531	0144
0101-0540	0016
0101-439	0126
0102	0015
0103	0321
0103-0014	0016
0103-0014(R,S)	0086
0103-0014R	0086
0103-0014S	0086
0103-0014T	0086
0103-0014U	0086
0103-0051	0086
0103-0060	0144
0103-0060(B)	0079
0103-0060-6438	0144
0103-0060A	0079
0103-0060B	0144
0103-0088	0111
0103-0088/4460	0111
0103-0088H	0016
0103-0088R	0016
0103-0088S	0016
0103-00608	0079
0103-052	0007
0103-0191	0144
0103-0389	0144
0103-0419	0555
0103-0419A	0555
0103-0473	0016
0103-0491	0076
0103-0491-6438	0198
0103-0503	0155
0103-0503S	0086
0103-0504	0016
0103-0521	0144
0103-0521(B)	0079
0103-0521B	0144
0103-0531	0076
0103-0531-4460	0016
0103-0531-6438	0016
0103-0540	0016
0103-0568	2365
0103-0607	0086
0103-0616	0086
0103-389	0144
0103-512M	0555
0104-0013	0086
0104-0013-6438	0086
0105-0012	0321
0110	0015
0110-0011	0015
0110-0141	0015
0110-0141-6438	0015
0110-0209	0015
0110-0209-6438	0015
0111	0133
0112	0015
0112-0019	0143
0112-0028	0143
0112-0028/5462	0143
0112-0028-6438	0019
0112-0037	0143
0112-0037-6438	0143
0112-0046	0143
0112-0073	0143
0112-0082	0143
0113-0027	0030
0113-0036	0030
0113-0036/4460	0143
0113-0036-6438	1208
0114	0133
0114-0017	0012
0114-0026	OEM
0114-0090	0012
0114-0090-6438	0012
0114-0260	0062
0117-02	0349
0121	0016
0122-0028-6438	0143
0124	0161
0124(KNIGHT)	0037
0124A	0037
0125	0016
0126	0016
0126(WARDS)	0378
0127	0016
0128	0016
0130	0086
0131	0016
0131-000101	0004
0131-000102	0004
0131-000192	0160
0131-000335	0037
0131-000336	0160
0131-000337	0160
0131-000418	0050
0131-000419	0050
0131-000473	0016
0131-000498	0050
0131-000561	0086
0131-000562	0160
0131-000563	0004
0131-000704	0016
0131-000802	0050
0131-000859	0050
0131-000862	0050
0131-000863	0050
0131-0026	0015
0131-0044	0015
0131-0053	0015
0131-001050	0164
0131-001056	0164
0131-001182	0050
0131-001314	0050
0131-001328	0037
0131-001329	0037
0131-001332	0050
0131-001417	0016
0131-001418	0016
0131-001419	0004
0131-001420	0037
0131-001421	0016
0131-001422	0016
0131-001423	0016
0131-001424	0016
0131-001425	0160
0131-001426	0004
0131-001427	0126
0131-001428	0126
0131-001429	0086
0131-001430	0086
0131-001433	0050
0131-001434	0050
0131-001435	0050
0131-001436	0050
0131-001438	0150
0131-001439	0037
0131-001464	0016
0131-001597	0103
0131-001697	0050
0131-001864	0016
0131-002049	0919
0131-002068	0103
0131-002656	0004
0131-003029	0050
0131-004560	0178
0131-005807	0086
0131-026	0015
0131-053	0015
0131-0144	OEM
0131-0144-6438	0139
0131-5352	0419
0132	0103
0133	0037
0133-0024	OEM
0134	0016
0135-1	0947
0142	0144
0148	4333
0154	1403
0200	1241
0201	1241
0210	1241
0211	1241
0212A	OEM
0220	1241
0221	1241
0234	0015
0243	0994
0244	0015
0245	2070
0248	0087
0276.8A	0025
0300	0015
0301	0015
0302	0015
0304	0015
0307	0071
0310	0015
0311	0015
0312	0015
0314	0015
0317	0071
0320	0015
0321	0015
0322	0015
0324	0015
0327	0071
0361S	OEM
0366L	OEM
0400	0015
0401	0015
0402	0015
0404	OEM
0404-1	OEM
0404-2	OEM
0410	0015
0411	0015
0412	0015
0413	OEM
0414	OEM
0415	0419
0450	0015
0460	0015
0461	OEM
0462	OEM
0463	OEM
0491	OEM
0492	OEM
0493	OEM
0500	0133
0516-3101-250	0470
0516-3101-406	0470
0557-010	0015
0575-005	0143
0602	0109
0604	0122
0606	0145
0615	0676
0648R	0025
0684R	0025
0700	0015
0701	0015
0702	0015
0703	0144
0704	0015
0707	0071
0710	0015
0727-50	0015
0737R	0025
0770	0455
0772	0161
0773	0455
0783Z	0673
0801	OEM
0802	OEM
0803	OEM
0831	0688
0847T0R402	3858
0847TR2501	1796
0912	0338
0912-7	OEM
0912-25	OEM
0912-45	OEM
0912-125A	OEM
0912-125B	OEM
0912P200	OEM
0912P250	OEM
0912P250A	OEM
0912P250B	OEM
0912P400A	OEM
0912P400B	OEM
0912P600A	OEM
0912P600B	OEM
01103-0036	0623
01122-0073	0143
01339	0015
02164	OEM
0220100F	0707
0220100L	1640
0220100N	1837
0220200F	0464
0220200L	1640
0220200N	1837
0220300F	0717
0220300L	2623
0220300N	1844
0220400F	0717
0220400L	2623
0220400N	1844
0220500F	0720
0220500L	2625
0220500N	3185
0230100F	0707
0230100N	3883
0230200F	0464
0230200N	1837
0230300F	0717
0230300N	1844
0230400F	0717
0230400N	1844
0230500F	0720
0230500N	3185
0230600F	0720
0230600N	3185
02375-A	0178
02724A	0398
03002	0130
03008-1	0016
03500	0143
03507FWF	OEM
03507FXF	OEM
03507GUF	OEM
03507GWF	OEM
03507GXF	OEM
03507HWF	OEM
03507HXF	OEM
03507IWF	OEM
03507IXF	OEM
03508FWF	OEM
03508FXF	OEM
03508GUF	OEM
03508GWF	OEM
03508GXF	OEM
03508HWF	OEM
03508HXF	OEM
03508IWF	OEM
03508IXF	OEM
03509FWF	OEM
03509FXF	OEM
03509GUF	OEM
03509GWF	OEM
03509GXF	OEM
03509HWF	OEM
03509HXF	OEM
03509IWS	OEM
03509IXF	OEM
03510FWF	OEM
03510FXF	OEM
03510GUF	OEM
03510GWF	OEM
03510GXF	OEM
03510HWF	OEM
03510HXF	OEM
03510IWF	OEM
03510IXF	OEM
03511FWF	OEM
03511FXF	OEM
03511GUF	OEM
03511GWF	OEM
03511GXF	OEM
03511HWF	OEM
03511HXF	OEM
03511IWF	OEM
03511IXF	OEM
03512FWF	OEM
03512FXF	OEM
03512GUF	OEM
03512GWF	OEM
03512GXF	OEM
03512HWF	OEM
03512HXF	OEM
03512IWF	OEM
03512IXF	OEM
03571	0143
03901FPF	OEM
03901FRF	OEM
03901FUF	OEM
03901GPF	OEM
03901GRF	OEM
03901GUF	OEM
03901HPF	OEM
03901HRF	OEM
03901HUF	OEM
03902FPF	OEM
03902FRF	OEM
03902FUF	OEM
03902GPF	OEM
03902GRF	OEM
03902GUF	OEM
03902HPF	OEM
03902HRF	OEM
03902HUF	OEM
03903FPF	OEM
03903FRF	OEM
03903FUF	OEM
03903GPF	OEM
03903GRF	OEM
03903GUF	OEM
03903HPF	OEM
03903HRF	OEM
03903HUF	OEM
03904FPF	OEM
03904FRF	OEM
03904FUF	OEM
03904GPF	OEM
03904GRF	OEM
03904GUF	OEM
03904HPF	OEM
03904HRF	OEM
03904HUF	OEM
03905FPF	OEM
03905FRF	OEM
03905FUF	OEM
03905GPF	OEM
03905GRF	OEM
03905GUF	OEM
03905HPF	OEM
03905HRF	OEM
03905HUF	OEM
03906FPF	OEM
03906FRF	OEM
03906FUF	OEM
03906GPF	OEM
03906GRF	OEM
03906GUF	OEM
03906HPF	OEM
03906HRF	OEM
03906HUF	OEM
04049B	0015
04170	0276
04306A	OEM
04770	0143
04970	0071
05001GOF	OEM
0500100F	1694
05002GOF	1694
0500200F	1694
05003GOF	3970
0500300F	3970
05004GOF	3970
0500400F	3970
05005GOF	3970
0500500F	3970
05007GOF	0674
0500700F	0674
05008GOF	0674
0500800F	0674
05009GOF	0674
0500900F	0674
05010GOF	0674
0501000F	0674
0501100F	0674
05012GOF	0674
0501200F	0674
05070	0918
05201G0A	0603
05201GOD	0636
0520100A	0603
0520100D	OEM
05202G0A	0603
05202GOD	0636
0520200A	0603
0520200D	OEM
05203GOA	0605
05203GOD	0217
0520300A	0605
0520300D	OEM
05204GOA	0605
05204GOD	0217
0520400A	0605
0520400D	OEM
05205GOA	0605
05205GOD	0217
0520500A	0605
0520500D	OEM
05206-0	0111
05206GOA	0605
05206GOD	0217
0520600A	0605
0520600D	0605
05253	0160
05470	0644
07101GOA	0603
07101GOD	0636
0710100A	OEM
0710100D	OEM
07102GOA	0603
07102GOD	0636
0710200D	OEM
0710200Z	OEM
07103GOA	0605
07103GOD	0217
0710300A	OEM
0710300D	OEM
07104GOA	0605
07104GOD	0217
0710400A	OEM
0710400D	OEM
07105GOA	0605
07105GOD	0217
0710500	OEM
07106GOA	0605
07106GOD	0217
0710600A	OEM
0710600D	OEM
07607GUA	OEM
07607GUD	OEM
07607GWA	OEM
07607GWD	OEM
07607GXA	OEM
07607GXD	OEM
07607HUA	OEM
07607HUD	OEM
07607HWA	OEM
07607HWD	OEM
07607HXA	OEM
07607HXD	OEM
07607IUA	OEM
07607IUD	OEM
07607IWA	OEM
07607IWD	OEM
07607IXA	OEM
07607IXD	OEM
07608GUA	OEM
07608GUD	OEM
07608GWA	OEM
07608GWD	OEM
07608GXA	OEM
07608GXD	OEM
07608HUA	OEM
07608HUD	OEM
07608HWA	OEM
07608HWD	OEM
07608HXA	OEM
07608HXD	OEM
07608IUA	OEM
07608IUD	OEM
07608IWA	OEM
07608IWD	OEM
07608IXA	OEM
07608IXD	OEM
07609GUA	OEM
07609GUD	OEM
07609GWA	OEM
07609GWD	OEM
07609GXA	OEM
07609GXD	OEM
07609HUA	OEM
07609HUD	OEM
07609HWA	OEM
07609HWD	OEM
07609HXD	OEM
07609IUA	OEM
07609IUD	OEM
07609IWA	OEM
07609IWD	OEM
07609IXA	OEM
07609IXD	OEM
07609NXA	OEM
07610GUA	OEM
07610GUD	OEM
07610GWA	OEM
07610GWD	OEM
07610GXA	OEM
07610GXD	OEM
07610HUA	OEM
07610HUD	OEM
07610HWA	OEM
07610HWD	OEM

If replacement code is OEM, contact original manufacturer for replacement.

DEVICE TYPE	REPL CODE
07610HXA	OEM
07610HXD	OEM
07610IUA	OEM
07610IUD	OEM
07610IWA	OEM
07610IWD	OEM
07610IXA	OEM
07610IXD	OEM
07611GUA	OEM
07611GUD	OEM
07611GWA	OEM
07611GWD	OEM
07611GXA	OEM
07611GXD	OEM
07611HUA	OEM
07611HUD	OEM
07611HWA	OEM
07611HWD	OEM
07611HXA	OEM
07611HXD	OEM
07611IUA	OEM
07611IUD	OEM
07611IWA	OEM
07611IWD	OEM
07611IXA	OEM
07611IXD	OEM
07612GUA	OEM
07612GUD	OEM
07612GWA	OEM
07612GWD	OEM
07612GXA	OEM
07612GXD	OEM
07612HUD	OEM
07612HWA	OEM
07612HWD	OEM
07612HXA	OEM
07612HXD	OEM
07612IUA	OEM
07612IUD	OEM
07612IWA	OEM
07612IWD	OEM
07612IXA	OEM
07612IXD	OEM
07621HUA	OEM
07901GRA	OEM
07901GRD	OEM
07901GUA	OEM
07901GUD	OEM
07901GWA	OEM
07901HRA	OEM
07901HUA	OEM
07901HUD	OEM
07901HWA	OEM
07901HWD	OEM
07901IRA	OEM
07901IRD	OEM
07901IUA	OEM
07901IUD	OEM
07902GRA	OEM
07902GRD	OEM
07902GUA	OEM
07902GUD	OEM
07902GWA	OEM
07902GWD	OEM
07902HRA	OEM
07902HRD	OEM
07902HUA	OEM
07902HUD	OEM
07902HWA	OEM
07902HWD	OEM
07902IRA	OEM
07902IRD	OEM
07902IUA	OEM
07902IUD	OEM
07903GRA	OEM
07903GRD	OEM
07903GUA	OEM
07903GUD	OEM
07903GWA	OEM
07903GWD	OEM
07903HRA	OEM
07903HRD	OEM
07903HUA	OEM
07903HUD	OEM
07903HWA	OEM
07903HWD	OEM
07903IRA	OEM
07903IRD	OEM
07903IUA	OEM
07903IUD	OEM
07904GRA	OEM
07904GRD	OEM
07904GUA	OEM
07904GUD	OEM
07904GWA	OEM
07904GWD	OEM
07904HRA	OEM
07904HRD	OEM
07904HUA	OEM
07904HUD	OEM
07904HWA	OEM
07904HWD	OEM
07904IRA	OEM
07904IRD	OEM
07904IUA	OEM
07904IUD	OEM
07905GRA	OEM
07905GRD	OEM
07905GUA	OEM

DEVICE TYPE	REPL CODE
07905GUD	OEM
07905GWA	OEM
07905GWD	OEM
07905HRA	OEM
07905HRD	OEM
07905HUA	OEM
07905HUD	OEM
07905HWA	OEM
07905HWD	OEM
07905IRA	OEM
07905IRD	OEM
07905IUA	OEM
07905IUD	OEM
07906GRA	OEM
07906GRD	OEM
07906GUA	OEM
07906GUD	OEM
07906GWA	OEM
07906GWD	OEM
07906HRA	OEM
07906HRD	OEM
07906HUA	OEM
07906HUD	OEM
07906HWA	OEM
07906HWD	OEM
07906IRA	OEM
07906IRD	OEM
07906IUA	OEM
07906IUD	OEM
08001G0A	0603
08001G0D	0636
0800100A	OEM
0800100D	OEM
08002G0A	0603
08002G0D	0636
0800200A	OEM
0800200D	OEM
08003G0A	0605
08003G0D	0636
0800300A	OEM
0800300D	OEM
08004G0A	0605
08004G0D	0217
0800400A	OEM
0800400D	OEM
08005G0A	0605
08005G0D	0217
0800500A	OEM
0800500D	OEM
08006G0A	0605
08006G0D	0217
0800600A	OEM
0800600D	OEM
08050	0015
09501	0111
09502	0111
09502-8	0016
09800	0037
09800-12	0126
09800C	0006
010562	0006
010694	1698
011103	0196
011119	0123
011406	OEM
013339	0229
013339(RECTIFIER)	0071
013684	0122
014382	0160
014558	0233
015040/7	0357
018069	0126
018077	0086
020156	0279
021154	0015
022939	0187
023606	0321
023754	0178
023762	0103
025026	0015
025056	0015
025072	0071
026237	0079
030010	0079
030010-1	0079
030011	0086
030011-1	0086
030011-2	0086
030387	0934
030512-1	0079
030512-2	0079
030515	0079
030515-4	0079
030527	0079
030531-1	0435
030536	0079
030536-1	0079
030537	0079
030537-1	0079
030537-2	0079
030538	0079
030539-1	0103
030542	0079
030542-1	0079
030543	0079
030543-1	0079
030543-2	0079
030548	0079
030828	0111

DEVICE TYPE	REPL CODE
030930	0224
031033	0143
031034	0015
031040	0143
031450	0242
033370	0914
033421	0914
033549	0914
033563	0007
033571	0126
033589	0037
036001	0627
037077	0178
037085	0103
037085BL	0130
037085BR	0130
037085GR	0130
037085OR	0130
037085R	0130
037085Y	0130
040001	0127
040048	1004
041001	0006
041200-30110	0133
041616	0133
043001	0144
053328	0050
053480	0007
055210	0229
055210H	0015
055228	0071
055228H	0071
057001	0143
057001H	0143
057005	0123
057005H	0143
057019H	0143
057174	0739
057500	0143
057524	0030
059395	0143
061366	0079
062971	1403
071964-001	0103
075005	0143
075085-36	0030
080001	0136
080003	0004
080004	0004
080006	0144
080021	0144
080022	0144
080023	0144
080026	0050
080027	0050
080028	0050
080040	0015
080041	0144
080042	0144
080043	0004
080047	0004
080048	0160
080050	0015
080052	0004
080059	0144
080060	0144
080061	0050
080071	0050
080072	0136
080073	0004
080114	0050
080206	0136
080224	0136
080225	0136
080228	0136
080236	0136
080244	0050
080245	0050
080253	0136
080258	0050
080266	0050
080267	0050
080269	0050
080274	0136
080275	0136
080276	0136
080277	0136
081001	0004
081018	0004
081019	0004
081026	0164
081027	0164
081029	0164
081038	0004
081042	0816
081046	0004
081047	0004
081048	0004
081049	0004
081050	0004
081056	0004
081059	0164
082006	0079
082019	0079
082020	0326
082022	0693
082025	1401
082028	0155
082029	1401

DEVICE TYPE	REPL CODE
082033	0693
084001	0037
084001C	0160
085002	0143
085003	0133
085004	0143
085005	0123
085006	0143
085016	0143
085026	0123
087003	0004
094013	0599
0112945	0276
0112945(ELGIN)	0276
0170301	0133
0201201	0574
0207046	1383
0207120	1012
0207205	1044
0220600L	2625
0230100N	1837
0260540	0012
0300005	0004
0300006	0208
0300008B	0004
0303303	OEM
0310002	0841
0320031	0079
0320051	0233
0320064	0155
0330302	0137
0404011-001	1824
0404012-001	1833
0444028-010	0016
0444028-014	0016
0510006	0015
0510079	0050
0510079H	0050
0517022	0143
0517132	0133
0517133	0133
0517261B	0030
0517550	0015
0517550-3	0015
0517750	0015
0517750H	0015
0517826	0143
0517828	0143
0517829	0143
0518926	0133
0525001	0030
0525002	0143
0525002H	0143
0526224	0143
0526232	0133
0531014	0004
0531015	0004
0531016	0004
0535001	0143
0535005	0143
0537125	0004
0537640	0004
0537640(DIO)	0015
0537820	0143
0539860	0030
0551029	0276
0551029H	0276
0552005	0102
0552005H	0229
0552006	0015
0552006H	0015
0552007	0102
0552007H	0229
0552010	0015
0552010H	0015
0563012H	0004
0570519	0143
0572480	0076
0573001	0004
0573001-14	0004
0573001H	0004
0573002	0136
0573003	0004
0573003H	0004
0573004	0004
0573005	0004
0573005-14	0004
0573005H	0004
0573011	0004
0573012	0004
0573012H	0004
0573018	0004
0573018H	0004
0573022	0004
0573022H	0004
0573023	0004
0573023A	0004
0573023H	0004
0573024	0004
0573024-14	0004
0573025	0004
0573030	0222
0573030-14	0222
0573031	0816
0573034	0004
0573036	0004
0573036H	0004
0573037	0208
0573037H	0208

DEVICE TYPE	REPL CODE
0573040	0160
0573055	0164
0573056	0004
0573066	0016
0573103	0211
0573114	0004
0573114H	0004
0573117	0004
0573117-14	0004
0573119	0004
0573124H	0136
0573125	0004
0573131	0004
0573139	0208
0573142	0004
0573142H	0004
0573152	0004
0573153	0004
0573153H	0004
0573166	0085
0573184	0164
0573185	0841
0573187	0004
0573199	0969
0573199H	0969
0573200	0004
0573202	0016
0573204	0164
0573205	0160
0573212	0222
0573212H	0969
0573328	0004
0573330	0136
0573335	0050
0573366	0050
0573398	0136
0573415	0142
0573418	0016
0573422	0004
0573422H	0004
0573427	0136
0573428	0050
0573429	0004
0573430	0016
0573468	0016
0573468(HITACHI)	0127
0573469	0016
0573469H	0016
0573471	0136
0573474	0047
0573474H	0007
0573475	0007
0573479	0155
0573479H	0016
0573480	0076
0573480H	0086
0573481	0076
0573481H	0016
0573485	0127
0573486	0127
0573486H	0326
0573487	0151
0573487H	0326
0573490	0016
0573491	0076
0573491H	0155
0573492	0076
0573494	0144
0573495	0144
0573497	OEM
0573501	0233
0573506	0144
0573506H	0144
0573507	0127
0573507H	0144
0573508	0127
0573509	0224
0573509H	0127
0573510	0127
0573510H	0127
0573511	0144
0573511H	0127
0573515	0142
0573515H	0142
0573517	0949
0573518	0136
0573519	0233
0573523	0016
0573525	0178
0573526	2420
0573527	0086
0573529	0016
0573532	0016
0573541	1401
0573542	0126
0573556	0016
0573557	0086
0573559	0126
0573560	0126
0573562	0103
0573570	0144
0573607	0127
0573742	0004
0573981	0016
0575001	0123
0575001H	0143
0575002	0143
0575002AH	0143
0575002H	0143

DEVICE TYPE	REPL CODE
0575004	0143
0575005	0123
0575005H	0143
0575007	0143
0575010	0030
0575010H	0030
0575019	0123
0575019H	0123
0575024	0030
0575024(8)	0030
0575024H	0030
0575027	0030
0575047	0102
0575047H	0102
0575048	0102
0575048H	0918
0575049	0102
0575049H	0102
0575050	0071
0575051	0015
0575054	0102
0575066	0102
0575067	0143
0575099	0143
0576001	0004
0576054	0015
0576054(BIAS)	0015
0576054(SW)	0133
0577001	0143
0610007	OEM
0610008	OEM
0610083	0006
0610084	0148
0612016/1	0261
0613761A02	1982
0613785A03	OEM
0620001	OEM
0620017	0143
0621063	0178
0622070	0023
0630049	0906
0690403A47	1982
0690524A04	OEM
0800040	OEM
0899024	0319
0900296	0817
01310131-0035	0015
02600043	0143
04440028-002	0016
04440028-007	0016
04450023-007	0130
04450300-1	0147
04450303-001	0739
04450303-002	0739
04450304	0739
05320023	0016
05320074	0016
05734815	0076
05750011	0123
06100007	1298
06100008	1298
06100015	0148
06100016	0148
06100030	0006
06100033	0919
06100034	0006
06100035	0006
06100047	0006
06100053	0688
06100058	0643
06100061	0688
06100062	0006
06100063	1900
06100076	1900
06100081	0006
06100082	0006
06100083	0006
06100084	0148
06100085	0006
06100086	0527
06100089	1638
06100090	0148
06100094	0006
06100095	0006
06100096	0006
06100131	2116
06100132	OEM
06100137	0527
06110032	1638
06120001	0711
06120003	0042
06120005	0076
06120006	0076
06120008	0151
06120009	0127
06120012	2420
06120015	0127
06120018	0042
06120021	0042
06120025	0836
06120026	0284
06120028	0155
06120029	0079
06120030	0042
06120041	0638
06120044	2420
06120053	0275
06120063	0191
06120073	0224

DEVICE TYPE	REPL CODE
06120083	1077
06120085	0224
06120087	0284
06120088	0168
06120091	0168
06120096	0111
06120097	0168
06120098	0168
06120100	1488
06120109	0168
06120110	0168
06120126	0261
06120128	0261
06120129	0261
06120130	0130
06120134	4092
06120141	0949
06120144	0275
06120145	0388
06120148	1274
06120149	0638
06120150	0638
06120151	0945
06120152	0261
06120153	0309
06120155	0275
06120156	0275
06120161	0066
06120162	0261
06120168	0284
06120169	0284
06120170	0284
06120171	0284
06120172	0284
06120173	0155
06120174	0155
06120175	0155
06120181	0219
06120182	0219
06120186	0168
06120187	0168
06120200	0275
06120201	1274
06120202	1274
06120204	0076
06120207	1274
06120208	2636
06120212	1376
06120217	0261
06120218	0066
06120220	0638
06120221	0638
06120224	0079
06120225	0261
06120227	0079
06120228	0079
06120229	0079
06120230	0079
06120231	0037
06120232	0037
06120233	0079
06120235	0836
06120236	0261
06120238	0261
06120239	0284
06120240	0284
06120253	0148
06120255	0261
06120365	0860
06120619	0284
06130014	1274
06130017	1274
06130018	1274
06130019	0309
06130033	0456
06130034	0042
06130036	1157
06130037	0065
06130040	1967
06130042	0055
06130046	0388
06130047	0388
06130052	0388
06130053	0388
06130063	0713
06130086	3454
06130118	1533
06130134	0551
06150012	0261
06150031	0079
06160006	0055
06160008	0127
06170014	0079
06170028	1533
06170030	1533
06179462	OEM
06179495	0261
06179501	0338
06179502	0261
06200001	0123
06200002	0019
06200003	0123
06200005	0071
06200009	0015
06200010	0023
06200012	0025
06200013	0133
06200014	0023
06200017	0143

If replacement code is OEM, contact original manufacturer for replacement.

DEVICE TYPE	REPL CODE
06200027	0023
06200030	0023
06200032	0313
06200037	0959
06200038	0182
06200039	0023
06200041	0143
06200044	0133
06200045	0143
06200046	0120
06200047	0139
06200048	0133
06200050	0102
06200051	0023
06200052	0015
06200055	0631
06200056	0100
06200057	0025
06200058	0137
06200059	0137
06200060	0293
06200061	6398
06200062	0023
06200063	0790
06200064	0124
06200065	0071
06200067	0071
06200069	0031
06200071	0790
06200072	3048
06200073	0133
06200076	0286
06200083	0091
06200084	0181
06200085	0057
06200088	0023
06200089	0120
06200090	0559
06200091	1258
06200095	2217
06200096	0143
06200100	0023
06200102	0023
06200103	0023
06200104	0023
06200105	0023
06200106	0102
06200107	0071
06200108	0466
06200109	0071
06200112	0466
06200113	0057
06200114	0181
06200115	0133
06200116	0133
06200117	0133
06200118	0080
06200119	0790
06200120	0344
06200121	6687
06200122	0023
06200123	0023
06200124	0015
06200127	0137
06200129	0466
06200130	0133
06200149	0248
06200150	0124
06200159	0023
06200164	0253
06200167	0124
06200168	0137
06200170	0071
06200177	0181
06200179	0133
06200180	0999
06200181	0023
06200182	0023
06200183	0023
06200186	0143
06200189	0023
06200194	0313
06200202	0023
06200203	0023
06200206	0181
06200207	0023
06200211	0023
06200212	0023
06200223	0181
06200226	0124
06200228	0181
06200229	0023
06200230	0023
06200231	0023
06200232	0023
06200233	0181
06200255	0023
06200263	0031
06200272	0041
06200283	0023
06200284	0023
06200285	0023
06200286	0023
06200287	0102
06200288	0023
06200295	0248
06200323	0023
06210010	OEM
06210011	2604

DEVICE TYPE	REPL CODE
06210017	OEM
06210018	OEM
06210018(DS2(LED))	OEM
06210020	OEM
06220017	0023
06220021	0023
06220022	0947
06220069	0080
06220070	0604
06220071	0790
06220120	0057
06220127	0137
06220132	0041
06220137	OEM
06220167	0124
06220168	0372
06220227	0041
06220228	0253
06220233	0057
06220235	0181
06220241	OEM
06220242	0195
06300001	3242
06300003	3238
06300004	1049
06300005	0523
06300009	0167
06300028	OEM
06300029	OEM
06300030	3250
06300031	1420
06300034	0485
06300039	0619
06300049	0906
06300050	2043
06300051	2043
06300052	4071
06300056	2079
06300058	3461
06300066	2511
06300069	0167
06300071	0678
06300072	2079
06300080	1192
06300089	0619
06300090	1192
06300095	2015
06300104	OEM
06300105	0624
06300106	OEM
06300107	4075
06300108	OEM
06300111	2092
06300113	2104
06300115	2109
06300116	2092
06300117	OEM
06300120	0167
06300121	2641
06300144	0619
06300154	4083
06300160	3726
06300163	OEM
06300191	0034
06300192	0034
06300219	0330
06300248	1585
06300253	OEM
06300311	1888
06300315	1008
06300316	0409
06300317	1542
06300318	OEM
06300320	OEM
06300323	4126
06300330	OEM
06300331	OEM
06300332	OEM
06300334	4009
06300335	0536
06300336	4131
06300337	0311
06300342	0619
06300357	0534
06300359	0552
06300360	0727
06300365	2109
06300373	OEM
06300394	0624
06300395	OEM
06300403	3896
06300411	OEM
06300440	0311
06300441	OEM
06300450	OEM
06300456	3054
06300457	2843
06300488	3590
06300491	2929
06300508	1934
06300514	0517
06300516	OEM
06300517	OEM
06300519	0457
06300536	OEM
06300537	OEM
06300546	1192
06300554	0024
06300564	OEM

DEVICE TYPE	REPL CODE
06300565	0765
06300574	0534
06300575	OEM
06300615	OEM
06300616	0552
06300621	3590
06300629	2348
06300634	OEM
06300656	1230
06300661	OEM
06300662	OEM
06300688	1631
06300714	OEM
06300724	OEM
06300733	OEM
06300736	OEM
06300737	OEM
06300738	0101
06300739	OEM
06300740	OEM
06300741	OEM
06300742	OEM
06300743	OEM
06300744	OEM
06300745	OEM
06300746	OEM
06300761	3357
06300763	3473
06300764	OEM
06300765	OEM
06300766	3223
06300767	1022
06300769	OEM
06300778	OEM
06300779	OEM
06363040	OEM
06363045	OEM
06400001	0058
06400002	0239
06400537	OEM
06500004	0120
07009502	1338
07011751	3580
07011752	0148
07011757	0148
07012611	1190
07107071	0848
07107951	2869
07108251	0848
07108841	0597
07108861	2222
07108951	2869
07109741	0597
07110121	OEM
07110991	0597
07111351	4062
07111681	0455
07113591	OEM
07220031	0284
07227851	0249
07227853	0151
07233301	2926
07233312	0018
07307741	2019
07308631	1376
07308821	0161
07309861	2942
07311951	1203
07311961	2220
07312371	1157
07312731	0922
07312771	1203
07313081	3107
07313761	3658
07313951	2350
07315931	OEM
07316371	1055
07317251	0161
07320101	OEM
07506562	0571
07602002	0826
07650003	OEM
07650004	OEM
07650013	OEM
07650016	3910
07650017	OEM
07650020	OEM
07650021	OEM
07650023	OEM
07650024	OEM
07650027	OEM
07650029	OEM
07650031	OEM
08000001	0133
08000015	0124
08000016	0087
08000017	0916
08000018	0133
08000022	0071
08000028	0124
08000039	0133
08000040	1082
08000044	0080
08000045	1082
08000048	1082
08020007	0631
08020020	0526
08020022	1596
08020025	0023

DEVICE TYPE	REPL CODE
08020028	0053
08020029	0466
08020030	0140
08020033	0062
08020036	0755
08020037	0273
08020040	0372
08020052	0039
08020054	0436
08020056	0064
08020059	OEM
08020066	OEM
08020067	0274
08020073	0253
08020075	0140
08020077	0165
08030001	2520
08030002	0023
08030003	2219
08030005	2520
08200040	0866
08200043	0619
08200045	1817
08200050	1825
08200064	1825
08200068	OEM
08200069	1288
08200070	2893
08200071	OEM
08200073	OEM
08200074	OEM
08200077	2893
08200086	OEM
08200091	0624
08200093	2517
08200095	OEM
08200096	OEM
08200101	OEM
08200103	OEM
08200105	OEM
08200109	OEM
08200111	OEM
08200112	OEM
08200114	OEM
08200115	OEM
08202003	OEM
08210001	1519
08210002	1585
08210004	1830
08210006	1197
08210008	0967
08210017	1598
08210022	1877
08210023	1688
08210029	0422
08210030	0209
08210032	1623
08210033	0243
08210038	0704
08210039	1153
08210040	1733
08210043	4956
08210046	0153
08210047	0503
08210048	0506
08210050	0770
08210052	0708
08210053	0088
08210058	1657
08210059	0973
08210063	1764
08210064	0813
08210068	0937
08210069	0453
08210070	0288
08210071	1636
08210072	1550
08210103	OEM
08220014	2672
08220027	1887
08220028	OEM
08220029	OEM
08220030	0806
08220031	1887
08220032	OEM
08220033	0806
08220036	OEM
08220037	OEM
08220038	OEM
08220039	OEM
08220041	OEM
08220042	OEM
08220043	OEM
08220047	1628
08220048	OEM
08220070	OEM
08220072	1550
08220073	OEM
08220082	OEM
08220086	OEM
08220090	0806
08220092	0176
08220096	OEM
08220099	OEM
08220101	OEM
08220102	OEM
08220102(HD63A03YF)	OEM
08220103	OEM
08220106	OEM

DEVICE TYPE	REPL CODE
08220108	OEM
08220116	OEM
08221002	OEM
08221007	OEM
08230028	OEM
08230040	OEM
08240001	OEM
08240002	OEM
08240013	OEM
08250001	OEM
08300027	OEM
08300028	OEM
08300032	OEM
08300055	OEM
08300058	OEM
08990202	2994
08990207	0319
08990208	0276
08990210	0319
08990211	0468
08990214	0319
09301027	0164
09302090	0076
09306244	0133
09391000A	2863
061300053	0388
0847000202	OEM
0A10	0959
0A70	0143
0A90	0019
0A90A-G	0019
0A90A-M	0019
0A90AM	0019
0A90FM	0123
0A90G	0019
0A90LF	0143
0A90M	0143
0A90MLF	0143
0A90Z	0143
0A90ZA	0143
0A91	0019
0A95	0123
0A99	0143
0A126/10	0181
0A126/12	0137
0AZ209	0162
0AZ243	0631
0AZ244	0062
0AZ246	0165
0AZ269	0162
0C3K	0211
0C-16	0160
0C16	0085
0C19	0160
0C20	0160
0C-22	0160
0C22	0085
0C-23	0160
0C23	0085
0C-24	0160
0C24	0085
0C-25	0160
0C25	0085
0C-26	0160
0C26	0085
0C-30A	0160
0C32	0211
0C-35	0160
0C35	0085
0C-36	0160
0C36	0085
0C41	0211
0C-44	0279
0C-45	0023
0C-46	0279
0C-47	0279
0C56	0211
0C74N	0164
0C83	0164
0C84	0164
0C-130	0279
0C169	0050
0C-304	0841
0C308	0164
0C463K	0855
0DD2000AF	0023
0DD20000AE	0559
0DD20000AF	0023
0DD100009AC	0023
0DD100009AE	0023
0DD100009BA	0023
0DD120000BB	1119
0DD200009AC	0031
0DD200009AE	0559
0DD200009AF	0023
0DD247109AA	0124
0DD300000EJ	0023
0DD300009AB	0282
0DD400000AE	0031
0DD400000AF	0102
0DD400000AG	0031
0DD400209AA	0080
0DD400409AA	4147
0DD400509BA	5886
0DD414809ED	0133
0DD606000AA	1039
0DL206000AA	OEM
0DL206000AC	OEM
0DZ10009BA	0057

DEVICE TYPE	REPL CODE
0DZ110009AA	0181
0DZ120009AA	0052
0DZ240009BB	5878
0DZ300009BA	0195
0DZ360000BA	0372
0DZ360009AB	0372
0DZ510009AB	0041
0DZ512000AA	4049
0DZ560009AA	0253
0DZ620000BA	0631
0DZ620009AA	6649
0DZ680009AA	0062
0DZ750009AA	0077
0DZ910009BA	0012
0DZ911000AC	0057
0F66	0102
0F160	0015
0F162	0133
0F173	0143
0F612	OEM
0F643	OEM
0G02	0105
0IGL301300A	2348
0IGS348000A	OEM
0IGS381200A	OEM
0IGS382000A	OEM
0IGS406600A	0101
0IGS455800A	OEM
0IGS781200A	4342
0IGS781500A	1311
0IHI115660A	OEM
0IHY934600A	OEM
0IKE703300A	OEM
0IKE780120A	0330
0IM0800809A	OEM
0IM1371008B	OEM
0IMA300800A	OEM
0IMA310100A	OEM
0IMA530200A	OEM
0IMI371008B	OEM
0IMI514940A	OEM
0IMI1514940A	OEM
0IM0800809A	OEM
0INE187000A	OEM
0INE187100A	OEM
0INNS745950A	OEM
0INS199200A	OEM
0INS745950A	OEM
0INS934600B	OEM
0INS1999200A	OEM
0IO111000CA	OEM
0IPH842500A	OEM
0IS0111000A	OEM
0IS0112400A	OEM
0ISA426100A	3223
0ISA701600A	1022
0ISA722200A	OEM
0ISA755500A	OEM
0ISA783000A	0727
0ISA783100A	2929
0ISG382000A	OEM
0ISK120000A	OEM
0ISK500410A	3310
0ISM460500A	OEM
0ISM4605500A	OEM
0ISO111000A	OEM
0ISO112400A	OEM
0ISS330000A	1319
0IT063100A	0311
0IT0631000A	OEM
0IT0762900A	OEM
0IT0820000A	OEM
0IT0868000A	3473
0IT0890802D	OEM
0IT0631000A	0311
0IT0820000A	OEM
0LD206000AC	OEM
0N008341C-2	0004
0N008351	0279
0N049874	3843
0N064071-1	0004
0N088598	2664
0N097164	0142
0N271	0079
0N1105	OEM
0N1112	OEM
0N2170-R	OEM
0N2170-RLF	OEM
0N2170-RS	OEM
0N3161-QR	OEM
0N101880	2662
0N101881	2515
0N161646C	0004
0N188320-2	0473
0N198382-2	1135
0PP28	OEM
0S40	OEM
0SD-0033	0644
0SD0033	0644
0T3	OEM
0TF325000AA	OEM
0TR100100AA	OEM
0TR101509AA	0006
0TR105009AB	OEM
0TR126609AA	4440
0TR127009AA	0006
0TR127109AA	0472
0TR135100AB	0402
0TR155400AA	1533

DEVICE TYPE	REPL CODE
0TR162700AC	1376
0TR162709AB	1376
0TR165100AA	0551
0TR181509AB	0284
0TR187900AA	2116
0TR188600AA	3454
0TR195909AA	0284
0TR206800BA	0638
0TR206800BB	0638
0TR222909AB	0261
0TR223009AB	0261
0TR223500AA	OEM
0TR223800AA	0388
0TR248200AA	0066
0TR248209AA	0261
0TR319709AB	OEM
0TR319809AA	5817
0TR320209AA	0379
0TR320309AA	OEM
0TR320609AB	0261
0TR322700AC	0320
0TR322709AA	OEM
0TR387500AA	0719
0TR388000AC	0836
0TR388009AA	0379
0TR388100AA	OEM
0TR508000EA	3326
0TR562009AA	0006
0TR595000AB	0713
0TR880000AB	4439
0TR949000AB	1514
0TR966000AA	OEM
0TR968000AA	1638
0V02	0102
0Z27T5	0436
0Z27T10	0436
0.4M9.1SZ5	OEM
0.5Z5.1U	0041
.2KT12.8A	0361
.4M3.3AZ5	0289
.4M3.3AZ10	0289
.4M3.6AZ5	0188
.4M3.6AZ10	0188
.4M3.9AZ5	0451
.4M3.9AZ10	0451
.4M4.3AZ5	0528
.4M4.3AZ10	0528
.4M4.7AZ5	0446
.4M4.7AZ10	0446
.4M10AZ5	0064
.4M10AZ10	0064
.4M13Z5	0361
.4M16Z5	0416
.4M18Z5	0490
.4M30Z5	0721
.4T5.6	0157
.4T5.6A	0157
.4T5.6B	0157
.4T6.8	0025
.4T6.8B	0025
.4T7.5	0644
.4T7.5A	0644
.4T7.5B	0644
.4T8.2	0244
.4T9.1	0012
.4T9.1A	0012
.4T9.1B	0012
.4T10	0170
.4T10A	0170
.4T10B	0170
.4T12A	0137
.4T12B	0137
.4T15	0002
.4T15A	0002
.4T15B	0002
.4T18	0490
.4T18A	0490
.4T18B	0490
.4T22	0560
.4T22A	0560
.4T22B	0560
.4T22V	0560
.4T27	0436
.4T27A	0436
.4T27B	0436
.4T33	0039
.4T33A	0039
.4T33B	0039
.4T39	0346
.4T39A	0346
.4T39B	0346
.4T47	0993
.4T47A	0993
.4T47B	0993
.4T56	0863
.4T56A	0863
.4T56B	0863
.4T68	3174
.4T68A	3174
.4T68B	3174
.4T82	0327
.4T82A	0327
.4T82B	0327
.4T100	0098
.4T100A	0098
.4T100B	0098
.4T110B	0098
.4T120	0186
.4T120A	0186

If replacement code is OEM, contact original manufacturer for replacement.

DEVICE TYPE	REPL CODE
.4T120B	0186
.4T150	0028
.4T150A	0028
.4T150B	0028
.4T180	0363
.4T180A	0363
.4T180B	0363
.4T688	1258
.4Z14D	0873
.4Z14D5	0873
.4Z14D10	0873
.4Z17D	0210
.4Z17D5	0210
.4Z17D10	0210
.4Z19D	0666
.4Z19D5	0666
.4Z19D10	0666
.4Z25D	0709
.4Z25D5	0709
.4Z25D10	0709
.4Z45D	0054
.4Z45D5	0054
.4Z45D10	0054
.4Z50D	0092
.4Z50D5	0092
.4Z50D10	0092
.4Z52D	0092
.4Z52D5	0092
.4Z52D10	0092
.4Z105D	0189
.4Z105D5	0189
.4Z105D10	0189
.4Z140D	0252
.4Z140D5	0252
.4Z140D10	0252
.4Z175D	0390
.4Z175D5	0390
.4Z175D10	0390
.5E05	0015
.5E1	0015
.5E2	0015
.5E3	0015
.5E4	0015
.5E5	0015
.5E6	0015
.5E7	0071
.5E8	0071
.5E10	0071
.5E12	0102
.5J05	0015
.5J1	0015
.5J2	0015
.5J3	0015
.5J4	0015
.5J5	0015
.5J6	0015
.5J7	0071
.5J8	0071
.5J10	0071
.5J12	0102
.5L1-2	OEM
.5LS1-3	OEM
.5LS1-3S	OEM
.5LS1.2-3.6	OEM
.5LS1.2-3.6S	OEM
.5LS1.5-3	OEM
.5M3.3ZS5	0289
.5M3.3ZS10	0289
.5M3.6ZS5	0188
.5M3.6ZS10	0188
.5M3.9ZS5	0451
.5M3.9ZS10	0451
.5M4.3ZS5	0528
.5M4.3ZS10	0528
.5M4.7ZS5	0446
.5M4.7ZS10	0446
.5M5.1ZS3	0041
.5M8.7ZS5	1075
.5M13ZS5	0361
.5M16ZS5	0416
.5M18ZS5	0490
.5M25Z55	1596
.5M28Z55	1664
.5M30ZS5	0721
.5PL.5-1.5	OEM
.5PL.5-1.5S	OEM
.5PL.8-2.4	OEM
.5PL.8-2.4S	OEM
.5P.2-.4	OEM
.5P.2-.4S	OEM
.5P.5-1	OEM
.5P.5-1.5	OEM
.5P.25-.5	OEM
.5P.25-.5S	OEM
.7E05	0015
.7E1	0015
.7E2	0015
.7E3	0015
.7E4	0015
.7E5	0015
.7E6	0015
.7E7	0071
.7E8	0071
.7E10	0071
.7E12	0102
.7J05	0015
.7J1	0015
.7J2	0015
.7J3	0015

DEVICE TYPE	REPL CODE
.7J5	0015
.7J6	0015
.7J7	0071
.7J8	0071
.7J10	0071
.7J12	0102
.7J2100	0098
.7J2120	0186
.7JM13A	0361
.7JM13B	0361
.7JM13C	0361
.7JM13D	0361
.7JZ6.8	0025
.7JZ7.5	0644
.7JZ9.1	0012
.7JZ10	0170
.7JZ12	0137
.7JZ15	0002
.7JZ18	0490
.7JZ22	0560
.7JZ27	0436
.7JZ33	0039
.7JZ39	0346
.7JZ45	0993
.7JZ47	0993
.7JZ68	1258
.7JZ82	0327
.7JZ100	0098
.7JZ105	0098
.7JZ110	0401
.7JZ120	0186
.7JZ130	0213
.7JZ140	0245
.7JZ150	0028
.7JZ160	0255
.7JZ175	0871
.7JZ180	0363
.7JZ200	2831
.7JZ220	2335
.7Z6.8	0025
.7Z6.8A	0025
.7Z6.8B	0025
.7Z6.8C	0025
.7Z6.8D	0025
.7Z7.5	0644
.7Z7.5A	0644
.7Z7.5B	0644
.7Z7.5C	0644
.7Z7.5D	0644
.7Z8.2	0244
.7Z8.2A	0244
.7Z8.2B	0244
.7Z8.2C	0244
.7Z8.2D	0244
.7Z9.1	0012
.7Z9.1A	0012
.7Z9.1B	0012
.7Z9.1C	0012
.7Z9.1D	0012
.7Z10	0170
.7Z10A	0170
.7Z10B	0170
.7Z10C	0170
.7Z10D	0170
.7Z11	0313
.7Z11A	0313
.7Z11B	0313
.7Z11C	0313
.7Z11D	0313
.7Z12	0137
.7Z12A	0137
.7Z12B	0137
.7Z12C	0137
.7Z12D	0137
.7Z13	0361
.7Z13A	0361
.7Z13B	0361
.7Z13C	0361
.7Z13D	0361
.7Z14	0100
.7Z14A	0002
.7Z14B	0100
.7Z14C	0002
.7Z14D	0100
.7Z15	0002
.7Z15A	0002
.7Z15B	0137
.7Z15C	0002
.7Z15D	0002
.7Z16	0416
.7Z16A	0416
.7Z16B	0416
.7Z16C	0416
.7Z16D	0416
.7Z17	1639
.7Z17A	1639
.7Z17B	1639
.7Z17C	1639
.7Z17D	1639
.7Z18	0490
.7Z18A	0490
.7Z18B	0490
.7Z18C	0490
.7Z18D	0490
.7Z19	0943
.7Z19A	0943
.7Z19B	0943
.7Z19C	0943
.7Z19D	0943

DEVICE TYPE	REPL CODE
.7Z20	0526
.7Z20A	0526
.7Z20B	0526
.7Z20C	0526
.7Z20D	0526
.7Z22	0560
.7Z22A	0560
.7Z22B	0560
.7Z22C	0560
.7Z22D	0560
.7Z24	0398
.7Z24A	0398
.7Z24B	0398
.7Z24C	0398
.7Z24D	0398
.7Z25	1596
.7Z25A	1596
.7Z25B	1596
.7Z25C	1596
.7Z25D	1596
.7Z27	0436
.7Z27A	0436
.7Z27B	0436
.7Z27C	0436
.7Z27D	0436
.7Z30	0721
.7Z30A	0721
.7Z30B	0721
.7Z30C	0721
.7Z30D	0721
.7Z33	0039
.7Z33A	0039
.7Z33B	0039
.7Z33C	0039
.7Z33D	0039
.7Z36	0814
.7Z36A	0814
.7Z36B	0814
.7Z36C	0814
.7Z36D	0814
.7Z39	0346
.7Z39A	0346
.7Z39B	0346
.7Z39C	0346
.7Z39D	0346
.7Z43	0925
.7Z43A	0925
.7Z43B	0925
.7Z43C	0925
.7Z43D	0925
.7Z45	0925
.7Z45A	0993
.7Z45B	0993
.7Z45C	0993
.7Z45D	0993
.7Z47	0993
.7Z47A	0993
.7Z47B	0993
.7Z47C	0993
.7Z47D	0993
.7Z50	0497
.7Z50A	0497
.7Z50B	0497
.7Z50C	0497
.7Z50D	0497
.7Z51	0497
.7Z51A	0497
.7Z51B	0497
.7Z51C	0497
.7Z51D	0497
.7Z52	0497
.7Z52A	0497
.7Z52B	0497
.7Z52C	0497
.7Z52D	0497
.7Z56	0863
.7Z56A	1823
.7Z56B	0863
.7Z56C	1823
.7Z56D	1823
.7Z62	0778
.7Z62A	0778
.7Z62B	0778
.7Z62C	0778
.7Z62D	0778
.7Z68	2144
.7Z68A	1258
.7Z68B	1258
.7Z68C	1258
.7Z68D	1258
.7Z75	1181
.7Z75A	1181
.7Z75B	1181
.7Z75C	1181
.7Z75D	1181
.7Z82	0327
.7Z82A	0327
.7Z82B	0327
.7Z82C	0327
.7Z82D	0327
.7Z91	1301
.7Z91A	1301
.7Z91B	1301
.7Z91C	1301
.7Z91D	1301
.7Z100	0098
.7Z100A	0098
.7Z100B	0098
.7Z100C	0098

DEVICE TYPE	REPL CODE
.7Z100D	0098
.7Z105	0098
.7Z105A	0098
.7Z105B	0098
.7Z105C	0098
.7Z105D	OEM
.7Z110	0149
.7Z110A	0149
.7Z110B	0149
.7Z110C	0149
.7Z110D	0149
.7Z120	0186
.7Z120A	0186
.7Z120B	0186
.7Z120C	0186
.7Z120D	0186
.7Z130	0213
.7Z130A	0213
.7Z130B	0213
.7Z130C	0213
.7Z130D	0213
.7Z140	0245
.7Z140A	0245
.7Z140B	0245
.7Z140C	0245
.7Z140D	0245
.7Z150	0028
.7Z150A	0028
.7Z150B	0028
.7Z150C	0028
.7Z150D	0028
.7Z160	0255
.7Z160A	0255
.7Z160B	0255
.7Z160C	0255
.7Z160D	0255
.7Z175	0871
.7Z175A	0871
.7Z175B	0871
.7Z175C	0871
.7Z175D	OEM
.7Z180	0363
.7Z180A	0363
.7Z180B	0363
.7Z180C	0363
.7Z180D	0363
.7Z200	0417
.7Z200A	0417
.7Z200B	0417
.7Z200C	0417
.7Z200D	0417
.7Z220	OEM
.7Z220A	2335
.7Z220B	2335
.7Z220C	2335
.7Z220D	2335
.7ZM6.8	0025
.7ZM6.8A	0025
.7ZM6.8B	0025
.7ZM6.8C	0025
.7ZM6.8D	0025
.7ZM7.5	0644
.7ZM7.5A	0644
.7ZM7.5B	0644
.7ZM7.5C	0644
.7ZM7.5D	0644
.7ZM8.2	0244
.7ZM8.2A	0244
.7ZM8.2B	0244
.7ZM8.2C	0244
.7ZM8.2D	0244
.7ZM9.1	0012
.7ZM9.1A	0012
.7ZM9.1B	0012
.7ZM9.1C	0012
.7ZM9.1D	0012
.7ZM10	0170
.7ZM10A	0170
.7ZM10B	0170
.7ZM10C	0170
.7ZM10D	0170
.7ZM11	0313
.7ZM11A	0313
.7ZM11B	0313
.7ZM11C	0313
.7ZM11D	0313
.7ZM12	0137
.7ZM12A	0137
.7ZM12B	0137
.7ZM12C	0137
.7ZM12D	0137
.7ZM13	0361
.7ZM13A	0361
.7ZM13B	0361
.7ZM13C	0361
.7ZM13D	0361
.7ZM14	0100
.7ZM14A	0100
.7ZM14B	0100
.7ZM14C	0100
.7ZM14D	0100
.7ZM15	0002
.7ZM15A	0002
.7ZM15B	0002
.7ZM15C	0002
.7ZM15D	0002
.7ZM16	0416
.7ZM16A	0416
.7ZM16B	0416

DEVICE TYPE	REPL CODE
.7ZM16C	0416
.7ZM16D	0416
.7ZM17	1639
.7ZM17A	1639
.7ZM17B	1639
.7ZM17C	1639
.7ZM17D	1639
.7ZM18	0490
.7ZM18A	0490
.7ZM18B	0490
.7ZM18C	0490
.7ZM18D	0490
.7ZM19	0943
.7ZM19A	0943
.7ZM19B	0943
.7ZM19C	0943
.7ZM19D	0943
.7ZM20	0526
.7ZM20A	0526
.7ZM20B	0526
.7ZM20C	0526
.7ZM20D	0526
.7ZM22	0560
.7ZM22A	0560
.7ZM22B	0560
.7ZM22C	0560
.7ZM22D	0560
.7ZM24	0398
.7ZM24A	0398
.7ZM24B	0398
.7ZM24C	0398
.7ZM24D	0398
.7ZM25	1596
.7ZM25A	1596
.7ZM25B	1596
.7ZM25C	1596
.7ZM25D	1596
.7ZM27	0436
.7ZM27A	0436
.7ZM27B	0436
.7ZM27C	0436
.7ZM27D	0436
.7ZM30	0721
.7ZM30A	0721
.7ZM30B	0721
.7ZM30C	0721
.7ZM30D	0721
.7ZM33	0039
.7ZM33A	0039
.7ZM33B	0039
.7ZM33C	0039
.7ZM33D	0039
.7ZM36	0814
.7ZM36A	0814
.7ZM36B	0814
.7ZM36C	0814
.7ZM36D	0814
.7ZM39	0346
.7ZM39A	0346
.7ZM39B	0346
.7ZM39C	0346
.7ZM39D	0346
.7ZM43	0925
.7ZM43A	0925
.7ZM43B	0925
.7ZM43C	0925
.7ZM43D	0925
.7ZM45	0925
.7ZM45A	0925
.7ZM45B	0925
.7ZM45C	0925
.7ZM45D	OEM
.7ZM47	0993
.7ZM47A	0993
.7ZM47B	0993
.7ZM47C	0993
.7ZM47D	0993
.7ZM50	0497
.7ZM50A	0497
.7ZM50B	0497
.7ZM50C	0497
.7ZM50D	0497
.7ZM51	0497
.7ZM51A	0497
.7ZM51B	0497
.7ZM51C	0497
.7ZM51D	0497
.7ZM52	0497
.7ZM52A	0497
.7ZM52B	0497
.7ZM52C	0497
.7ZM52D	0497
.7ZM56	0863
.7ZM56A	0863
.7ZM56B	0863
.7ZM56C	0863
.7ZM56D	0863
.7ZM62	0778
.7ZM62A	0778
.7ZM62B	0778
.7ZM62C	0778
.7ZM62D	0778
.7ZM68	2144
.7ZM68A	1258
.7ZM68B	1258
.7ZM68C	1258
.7ZM68D	1258
.7ZM75	1181
.7ZM75A	1181

DEVICE TYPE	REPL CODE
.7ZM75B	1181
.7ZM75C	1181
.7ZM75D	1181
.7ZM82	0327
.7ZM82A	0327
.7ZM82B	0327
.7ZM82C	0327
.7ZM82D	0327
.7ZM91	1301
.7ZM91A	1301
.7ZM91B	1301
.7ZM91C	1301
.7ZM91D	1301
.7ZM100	0098
.7ZM100A	0098
.7ZM100B	0098
.7ZM100C	0098
.7ZM100D	0098
.7ZM105	0098
.7ZM105A	0098
.7ZM105B	0098
.7ZM105C	0098
.7ZM105D	OEM
.7ZM110	0149
.7ZM110A	0149
.7ZM110B	0149
.7ZM110C	0149
.7ZM110D	0149
.7ZM120	0186
.7ZM120A	0186
.7ZM120B	0186
.7ZM120C	0186
.7ZM120D	0186
.7ZM130	0213
.7ZM130A	0213
.7ZM130B	0213
.7ZM130C	0213
.7ZM130D	0213
.7ZM140	0245
.7ZM140A	0245
.7ZM140B	0245
.7ZM140C	0245
.7ZM140D	0245
.7ZM150	0028
.7ZM150A	0028
.7ZM150B	0028
.7ZM150C	0028
.7ZM150D	0028
.7ZM160	0255
.7ZM160A	0255
.7ZM160B	0255
.7ZM160C	0255
.7ZM160D	0255
.7ZM175	0871
.7ZM175A	0871
.7ZM175B	0871
.7ZM175C	0871
.7ZM175D	OEM
.7ZM180	0363
.7ZM180A	0363
.7ZM180B	0363
.7ZM180C	0363
.7ZM180D	0363
.7ZM200	0417
.7ZM200A	0417
.7ZM200B	0417
.7ZM200C	0417
.7ZM200D	0417
.7ZM220	OEM
.7ZM220A	2335
.7ZM220B	2335
.7ZM220C	2335
.7ZM220D	OEM
.25N6.8	0062
.25N7.5	0077
.25N8.2	0165
.25N9.1	0057
.25N10	0064
.25N11	0181
.25N12	0052
.25N13	0053
.25N14	0873
.25N15	0681
.25N16	0440
.25N17	0210
.25N18	0371
.25N19	0666
.25N20	0695
.25N22	0700
.25N24	0489
.25N25	0709
.25N27	0450
.25N30	0195
.25N33	0166
.25N36	0010
.25N39	0032
.25N43	0054
.25N45	0068
.25N47	0068
.25N50	0068
.25N52	0068
.25N56	0125
.25N62	0152
.25N68	0173
.25N75	0094
.25N82	0049
.25N91	0156
.25N100	0189
.25N105	0099

DEVICE TYPE	REPL CODE
.25N110	0099
.25N120	0089
.25N130	0285
.25N140	0252
.25N150	0336
.25N175	0420
.25N200	1464
.25NN15	0681
.25P25-.75S	OEM
.25P25A-.75	OEM
.25PL4-1.2	OEM
.25PL4-1.2S	OEM
.25P.35-1	OEM
.25P.35-1S	OEM
.25T5.6	0157
.25T5.6A	0157
.25T5.6B	0157
.25T6.8	0025
.25T6.8A	0025
.25T7.1	0025
.25T7.1A	0025
.25T7.5	0644
.25T7.5A	0644
.25T7.5B	0644
.25T8.2	0244
.25T8.8A	1075
.25T9.1	0012
.25T9.1A	0012
.25T9.1B	0012
.25T10	0170
.25T10A	0170
.25T10B	0170
.25T10.5	0170
.25T10.5A	0170
.25T12	0137
.25T12A	0137
.25T12B	0137
.25T15	0002
.25T15A	0002
.25T15B	0002
.25T18	0490
.25T18A	0490
.25T22	0560
.25T22A	0560
.25T24.	0398
.25T27	0436
.25T27A	0436
.25T27B	0436
.25T33	0039
.25T33A	0039
.25T33B	0039
.25T39	0346
.25T39A	0346
.25T47	0993
.25T47A	0993
.25T56	0863
.25T56A	0863
.25T68	3174
.25T68A	3174
.25T82	0327
.25T82A	0327
.25T82B	0327
.25T87A	2997
.25T100	0098
.25T100A	0098
.25T110A	0401
.25T120	0186
.25T120A	0186
.25T140	0245
.25T150	0028
.25T150A	0028
.25T180	0363
.25T180A	0363
.72M6.8A	0025
.72M6.8B	0025
.72M6.8C	0025
.72M6.8D	0025
.72M16A	0416
.72M20B	0526
.72M20C	0526
.72M20D	0526
.72M36C	0814
.72M36D	0814
.75N5	0002
.75N5.1	0162
.75N5.6	0157
.75N6.2	0631
.75N7.5	0644
.75N12	0137
.75N27	0436
.75N33	0039
.75N82	0327
.75N110	0149
.728.2A	0244
.728.2B	0244
.728.2C	0244
.MZ18D	0490
.MZ24C	0398
.MZ110B	0149
.MZM14A	0100
1/47M.1AZ5	0162
1/4A6.8	0062
1/4A6.8A	0062
1/4A6.8B	0062
1/4A7.5	0077
1/4A7.5A	0077
1/4A7.5B	0077
1/4A8.2	0165
1/4A8.2A	0165

If replacement code is OEM, contact original manufacturer for replacement.

DEVICE TYPE	REPL CODE
1/4A8.2B	0165
1/4A9.1	0057
1/4A9.1A	0057
1/4A9.1B	0057
1/4A10	0170
1/4A10A	0170
1/4A10B	0170
1/4A11	0181
1/4A11A	0181
1/4A11B	0181
1/4A12	0052
1/4A12A	0052
1/4A12B	0052
1/4A13	0053
1/4A13A	0053
1/4A13B	0053
1/4A14	0100
1/4A14A	0100
1/4A14B	0100
1/4A15	0681
1/4A15A	0681
1/4A15B	0681
1/4A16	0440
1/4A16A	0440
1/4A16B	0440
1/4A17	0210
1/4A17A	0210
1/4A17B	0210
1/4A18	0371
1/4A18A	0371
1/4A18B	0371
1/4A19	0666
1/4A19A	0666
1/4A19B	0666
1/4A20	0695
1/4A20A	0695
1/4A20B	0695
1/4A22	0700
1/4A22A	0700
1/4A22B	0700
1/4A24	0489
1/4A24A	0489
1/4A24B	0489
1/4A25	0709
1/4A25A	0709
1/4A25B	0709
1/4A27	0436
1/4A27A	0436
1/4A27B	0436
1/4A30	0195
1/4A30A	0195
1/4A30B	0195
1/4A33	0039
1/4A33A	0039
1/4A33B	0039
1/4A36	0010
1/4A36A	0010
1/4A36B	0010
1/4A39	0032
1/4A39A	0032
1/4A39B	0032
1/4A43	0054
1/4A43A	0054
1/4A43B	0054
1/4A45	0054
1/4A45A	0054
1/4A45B	0054
1/4A47	0068
1/4A47A	0068
1/4A47B	0068
1/4A50	0092
1/4A50A	0092
1/4A50B	0092
1/4A52	0092
1/4A52A	0092
1/4A52B	0092
1/4A56	0125
1/4A56A	0125
1/4A56B	0125
1/4A62	0778
1/4A62A	0778
1/4A62B	0778
1/4A68	0173
1/4A68A	0173
1/4A68B	0173
1/4A75	0094
1/4A75A	0094
1/4A75B	0094
1/4A82	0327
1/4A82A	0327
1/4A82B	0327
1/4A91	0156
1/4A91A	0156
1/4A91B	0156
1/4A100	0189
1/4A100A	0189
1/4A100B	0189
1/4A105	0189
1/4A105A	0189
1/4A105B	0390
1/4A110	0149
1/4A110A	0149
1/4A110B	0149
1/4A120	0089
1/4A120A	0089
1/4A120B	0089
1/4A130	0285
1/4A130A	0285
1/4A130B	0285

DEVICE TYPE	REPL CODE
1/4A140	0252
1/4A140A	0252
1/4A140B	0252
1/4A150	0336
1/4A150A	0336
1/4A150B	0336
1/4A175	0390
1/4A175A	0390
1/4A175B	0390
1/4A200	1464
1/4A200A	1464
1/4A200B	1464
1/4AZ2.2D	OEM
1/4AZ2.2D5	OEM
1/4AZ2.2D10	OEM
1/4AZ2.4D5	1266
1/4AZ2.4D10	1266
1/4AZ2.7D	0755
1/4AZ2.7D5	0755
1/4AZ2.7D10	0755
1/4AZ3.0D	0118
1/4AZ3.0D5	0118
1/4AZ3.0D10	0118
1/4AZ3.3D	0296
1/4AZ3.3D5	0296
1/4AZ3.3D10	0296
1/4AZ3.6D	0372
1/4AZ3.6D5	0188
1/4AZ3.6D10	0188
1/4AZ3.9D	0036
1/4AZ3.9D5	0036
1/4AZ3.9D10	0036
1/4AZ4.3D	0274
1/4AZ4.3D5	0274
1/4AZ4.3D10	0274
1/4AZ4.7D	0140
1/4AZ4.7D5	0140
1/4AZ4.7D10	0140
1/4AZ5.1D	0162
1/4AZ5.1D5	0162
1/4AZ5.1D10	0162
1/4AZ5.6D	0157
1/4AZ5.6D5	0157
1/4AZ5.6D10	0157
1/4AZ6.2D	0466
1/4AZ6.2D5	0466
1/4AZ6.2D10	0466
1/4AZ6.8D	0062
1/4AZ6.8D5	0062
1/4AZ6.8D10	0062
1/4LZ2.2D	OEM
1/4LZ2.2D5	OEM
1/4LZ2.2D10	OEM
1/4LZ2.4D	1266
1/4LZ2.4D5	1266
1/4LZ2.4D10	1266
1/4LZ2.7D	0755
1/4LZ2.7D5	0755
1/4LZ2.7D10	0755
1/4LZ3.0D	0118
1/4LZ3.0D5	0118
1/4LZ3.0D10	0118
1/4LZ3.3D	0296
1/4LZ3.3D5	0296
1/4LZ3.3D10	0296
1/4LZ3.6D	0211
1/4LZ3.6D5	0211
1/4LZ3.6D10	0372
1/4LZ3.9D	0036
1/4LZ3.9D5	0036
1/4LZ3.9D10	0036
1/4LZ4.3D	0274
1/4LZ4.3D5	0274
1/4LZ4.3D10	0274
1/4LZ4.7D	0140
1/4LZ4.7D5	0140
1/4LZ4.7D10	0140
1/4LZ5.1D	0041
1/4LZ5.1D5	0041
1/4LZ5.1D10	0041
1/4LZ5.6D	0157
1/4LZ5.6D5	0157
1/4LZ5.6D10	0157
1/4LZ6.2D	0466
1/4LZ6.2D5	0466
1/4LZ6.2D10	0466
1/4LZ6.8D	0062
1/4LZ6.8D5	0062
1/4LZ6.8D10	0062
1/4M2.4AZ	1266
1/4M2.4AZ5	1266
1/4M2.4AZ10	1266
1/4M2.4AZ10.5	OEM
1/4M2.7AZ	0755
1/4M2.7AZ5	0755
1/4M2.7AZ10	0755
1/4M2.7AZ10.5	OEM
1/4M3.0AZ	0118
1/4M3.0AZ5	0118
1/4M3.0AZ10	0118
1/4M3.3AZ	0296
1/4M3.3AZ5	0296
1/4M3.3AZ10	0296
1/4M3.3AZ10.5	OEM
1/4M3.6AZ	0372
1/4M3.6AZ5	0188
1/4M3.6AZ10	0188
1/4M3.6AZ10.5	OEM
1/4M3.9AZ	0036

DEVICE TYPE	REPL CODE
1/4M3.9AZ5	0036
1/4M3.9AZ10	0036
1/4M4.3AZ	0274
1/4M4.3AZ5	0274
1/4M4.3AZ10	0274
1/4M4.3AZ10.5	OEM
1/4M4.7AZ	0140
1/4M4.7AZ5	0140
1/4M4.7AZ10	0140
1/4M5.1	0041
1/4M5.1AZ	0041
1/4M5.1AZ5	0162
1/4M5.1AZ10	0041
1/4M5.1AZ25	0162
1/4M5.6AZ	0157
1/4M5.6AZ5	0157
1/4M5.6AZ10	0253
1/4M5.6AZ10.5	OEM
1/4M5.6AZ25	0157
1/4M6.2AZ	0466
1/4M6.2AZ5	0466
1/4M6.2AZ10	0466
1/4M6.2AZ10.5	OEM
1/4M6.8AZ	0062
1/4M6.8AZ5	0062
1/4M6.8AZ10	0062
1/4M6.8Z	0062
1/4M6.8Z5	0062
1/4M6.8Z10	0062
1/4M6.8Z10.5	OEM
1/4M7.5Z	0077
1/4M7.5Z5	0077
1/4M7.5Z10	0077
1/4M8/27	0165
1/4M8.2Z	0165
1/4M8.2Z5	0165
1/4M8.2Z10	0165
1/4M9.1Z	0057
1/4M9.1Z5	0057
1/4M9.1Z10	0057
1/4M9.1Z10.5	OEM
1/4M10Z	0170
1/4M10Z5	0064
1/4M10Z10	0170
1/4M10Z10.5	OEM
1/4M11Z5	0181
1/4M11Z10	0181
1/4M12Z	0052
1/4M12Z5	0052
1/4M12Z10	0052
1/4M12Z10.5	OEM
1/4M13Z	OEM
1/4M13Z5	0361
1/4M13Z10	0053
1/4M14	0100
1/4M14Z	0100
1/4M14Z5	0100
1/4M14Z10	0064
1/4M15Z	0002
1/4M15Z5	0681
1/4M15Z10	0681
1/4M16Z5	0416
1/4M16Z10	0440
1/4M17Z10	0210
1/4M18Z5	0490
1/4M18Z10	0371
1/4M19Z10	0666
1/4M20Z10	0695
1/4M22Z	0700
1/4M22Z10	0700
1/4M24Z	0489
1/4M24Z5	0489
1/4M24Z10	0489
1/4M24Z10.5	OEM
1/4M25Z5	0709
1/4M25Z10	0709
1/4M27Z	0436
1/4M27Z5	0436
1/4M27Z10	0450
1/4M30Z10	0195
1/4M33Z	0039
1/4M33Z5	0039
1/4M33Z10	0166
1/4M36Z10	0010
1/4M39Z10	0032
1/4M43Z10	0054
1/4M45Z10	0068
1/4M47Z10	0068
1/4M50Z10	0092
1/4M51Z	0092
1/4M51Z5	0092
1/4M51Z10	0092
1/4M52Z10	0092
1/4M56Z10	0125
1/4M62Z	0778
1/4M62Z5	0778
1/4M62Z10	0152
1/4M68Z10	0173
1/4M68.Z10	0025
1/4M75Z10	0094
1/4M82Z	0327
1/4M82Z5	0327
1/4M82Z10	0049
1/4M91Z10	0156
1/4M100Z10	0189
1/4M105Z10	0099
1/4M110Z	0149
1/4M110Z5	0149
1/4M110Z10	0149

DEVICE TYPE	REPL CODE
1/4M120Z10	0089
1/4M150Z	0336
1/4M150Z5	0336
1/4M150Z10	0336
1/4M160Z	0366
1/4M160Z5	0366
1/4M160Z10	0366
1/4M175Z	0390
1/4M175Z5	0390
1/4M175Z10	0390
1/4M180	0420
1/4M180Z	0420
1/4M180Z5	0420
1/4M180Z10	0420
1/4M200Z	1464
1/4M200Z5	1464
1/4M200Z10	1464
1/4M227	0560
1/4M3025	0721
1/4Z5.6T5	0253
1/4Z6.8D	0062
1/4Z6.8D5	0062
1/4Z6.8D10	0062
1/4Z7.5D	0077
1/4Z7.5D5	0077
1/4Z7.5D10	0077
1/4Z8.2D	0165
1/4Z8.2D5	0165
1/4Z8.2D10	0165
1/4Z9.1D	0057
1/4Z9.1D5	0140
1/4Z9.1D10	0057
1/4Z10D	0064
1/4Z10D5	0064
1/4Z10D10	0064
1/4Z11D	0181
1/4Z11D5	0181
1/4Z11D10	0181
1/4Z12D	0052
1/4Z12D5	0052
1/4Z12D10	0052
1/4Z12T5	0137
1/4Z13D	0053
1/4Z13D5	0053
1/4Z13D10	0053
1/4Z14D	0100
1/4Z14D5	0100
1/4Z14D10	0100
1/4Z15D	0681
1/4Z15D5	0681
1/4Z15D10	0681
1/4Z15T5	0681
1/4Z16D	0440
1/4Z16D5	0440
1/4Z16D10	0440
1/4Z17D	0210
1/4Z17D5	0210
1/4Z17D10	0210
1/4Z18D	0371
1/4Z18D5	0371
1/4Z18D10	0371
1/4Z19D	0666
1/4Z19D5	0666
1/4Z19D10	0666
1/4Z20D	0695
1/4Z20D5	0695
1/4Z20D10	0695
1/4Z22D	0700
1/4Z22D5	0700
1/4Z22D10	0700
1/4Z24D	0489
1/4Z24D5	0489
1/4Z24D10	0489
1/4Z25D	0709
1/4Z25D5	0709
1/4Z25D10	0709
1/4Z27D	0436
1/4Z27D5	0436
1/4Z27D10	0436
1/4Z27T5	0450
1/4Z30D	0195
1/4Z30D5	0195
1/4Z30D10	0195
1/4Z33D	0039
1/4Z33D5	0039
1/4Z33D10	0039
1/4Z33T5	0166
1/4Z36D	0010
1/4Z36D5	0010
1/4Z36D10	0010
1/4Z39D	0032
1/4Z39D5	0032
1/4Z39D10	0032
1/4Z43D	0054
1/4Z43D5	0054
1/4Z43D10	0054
1/4Z45D	0054
1/4Z45D5	0054
1/4Z45D10	0054
1/4Z47D	0068
1/4Z47D5	0068
1/4Z47D10	0068
1/4Z50D	0092
1/4Z50D5	0092
1/4Z50D10	0092
1/4Z51D	0092
1/4Z51D5	0092
1/4Z51D10	0092
1/4Z52D	0092

DEVICE TYPE	REPL CODE
1/4Z52D5	0092
1/4Z52D10	0092
1/4Z56D	0125
1/4Z56D5	0125
1/4Z56D10	0125
1/4Z62D	0778
1/4Z62D5	0778
1/4Z62D10	0778
1/4Z68D	0173
1/4Z68D5	0173
1/4Z68D10	0173
1/4Z75D	0094
1/4Z75D5	0094
1/4Z75D10	0094
1/4Z82D	0327
1/4Z82D5	0049
1/4Z82D10	0327
1/4Z91D	0156
1/4Z91D5	0156
1/4Z91D10	0156
1/4Z100D	0189
1/4Z100D5	0189
1/4Z100D10	0189
1/4Z105D	0189
1/4Z105D5	0189
1/4Z105D10	0189
1/4Z110D	0149
1/4Z110D5	0149
1/4Z110D10	0149
1/4Z120D	0089
1/4Z120D5	0089
1/4Z120D10	0089
1/4Z130D	0285
1/4Z130D5	0285
1/4Z130D10	0285
1/4Z140D	0252
1/4Z140D5	0252
1/4Z140D10	0252
1/4Z150D	0336
1/4Z150D5	0336
1/4Z150D10	0336
1/4Z160D	0366
1/4Z160D5	0366
1/4Z160D10	0366
1/4Z175D	0390
1/4Z175D5	0390
1/4Z175D10	0390
1/4Z180D	0420
1/4Z180D5	0420
1/4Z180D10	0420
1/4Z200D	1464
1/4Z200D5	1464
1/4Z200D10	1464
1/276.5T5	0644
1/2Z2TT5	0436
1/2Z3.3T5	0296
1/2Z3.5T5	OEM
1/2Z3.6T5	0372
1/2Z3.9T5	0036
1/2Z4.3T5	0274
1/2Z4.7T5	0140
1/2Z5.1T5	0041
1/2Z5.6T5	0253
1/2Z6.2T5	0466
1/2Z6.5T5	0157
1/2Z6.8T5	0062
1/2Z7.5T5	0077
1/2Z8.2T5	0165
1/2Z9.1T5	0057
1/2Z10T5	0064
1/2Z11T5	0181
1/2Z12T5	0052
1/2Z13T5	0053
1/2Z15T5	0681
1/2Z16T5	0440
1/2Z18T5	0371
1/2Z20T5	0695
1/2Z22T5	0700
1/2Z24T5	0489
1/2Z27T5	0450
1/2Z30T5	0195
1/2Z33T5	0170
1/2Z36T5	0010
1/2Z39T5	0032
1/2Z43T5	0054
1/2Z47T5	0068
1/2Z51T5	0068
1/2Z56T5	0125
1/2Z62T5	0152
1/2Z68T5	0173
1/2Z75T5	0094
1/2Z82T5	0049
1/2Z91T5	0156
1/2Z100T5	0189
1/2Z105T5	0170
1/2Z276.5T5	0012
3/4D25D5	OEM
3/4M14Z	0100
3/4M14Z5	0100
3/4M14Z10	0100
3/4M17Z	1639
3/4M17Z5	1639
3/4M17Z10	1639
3/4M19Z	0943
3/4M19Z5	0943
3/4M19Z10	0943
3/4M25Z	1596
3/4M25Z5	1596
3/4M25Z10	1596

DEVICE TYPE	REPL CODE
3/4M140Z	0245
3/4M150Z5	0245
3/4M140Z10	0245
3/4T12D5	0137
3/4Z12D5	0137
3/4Z12D10	0137
3/4Z14D	0100
3/4Z14D5	0100
3/4Z14D10	0100
3/4Z17D	1639
3/4Z17D5	1639
3/4Z17D10	1639
3/4Z19D	0943
3/4Z19D5	0943
3/4Z19D10	0943
3/4Z25D	1596
3/4Z25D10	1596
3/4Z45D	OEM
3/4Z45D5	OEM
3/4Z45D10	OEM
3/4Z50D	OEM
3/4Z50D5	OEM
3/4Z50D10	OEM
3/4Z52D	OEM
3/4Z52D5	OEM
3/4Z52D10	OEM
3/4Z105D	OEM
3/4Z105D5	OEM
3/4Z105D10	OEM
3/4Z140D	0245
3/4Z140D5	0245
3/4Z140D10	0245
3/4Z175D	OEM
3/4Z175D5	OEM
3/4Z175D10	OEM
1	OEM
1/042/2207	0079
1-00004-064	0124
1-00006-003	0079
1-00006-007	0143
1-00006-281	0124
1-000-099-00	1199
1-0002-001	0124
1-00011-043	0012
1-00030-010	0229
1-00032-027	0208
1-00038-008	0124
1-001	OEM
1-001/2207	0133
1-001-003-15	0016
1-014/2207	0133
1-034/2207	0037
1-035/2207	0086
1-037/2207	0143
1-041/2207	0144
1-042/2207	0016
1-043/2207	0037
1-044/2207	0016
1-20-001-890	0015
1-20-001890	0015
1-21-73	0279
1-21-74	0279
1-21-75	0279
1-21-76	0279
1-21-78	0279
1-21-83	0279
1-21-91	0279
1-21-92	0279
1-21-93	0279
1-21-95	0004
1-21-96	0004
1-21-100	0279
1-21-102	0279
1-21-103	0279
1-21-104	0279
1-21-105	0279
1-21-106	0004
1-21-107	0004
1-21-120	0004
1-21-128	0279
1-21-135	0050
1-21-137	0050
1-21-138	0136
1-21-139	0050
1-21-148	0004
1-21-150	0050
1-21-157	0050
1-21-161	0279
1-21-162	0279
1-21-164	0004
1-21-179	0279
1-21-180	0279
1-21-184	0004
1-21-186	0279
1-21-189	0136
1-21-190	0050
1-21-191	0004
1-21-192	0004
1-21-225	0004
1-21-226	0004
1-21-227	0004
1-21-228	0050
1-21-229	0050
1-21-230	0050
1-21-231	0050
1-21-232	0004
1-21-233	0050
1-21-234	0279
1-21-235	0279

DEVICE TYPE	REPL CODE
1-21-236	0279
1-21-240	0279
1-21-241	0279
1-21-242	0136
1-21-243	0136
1-21-244	0136
1-21-246	0004
1-21-254	0279
1-21-256	0050
1-21-257	0136
1-21-258	0050
1-21-259	0050
1-21-260	0050
1-21-266	0004
1-21-267	0004
1-21-270	0160
1-21-271	0160
1-21-272	0004
1-21-273	0279
1-21-274	0004
1-21-275	0279
1-21-276	0016
1-21-277	0016
1-21-278	0016
1-21-279	0016
1-21-289	0279
1-63-5209	OEM
1-101	0015
1-231-416-00	OEM
1-231-443	OEM
1-231-443-00	OEM
1-231-462-00	OEM
1-231-462-11	OEM
1-231-705-00	OEM
1-232-680-11	0466
1-235-031-00	OEM
1-235-034-00	OEM
1-235-058-00	OEM
1-235-120-00	OEM
1-235-217-00	OEM
1-235-217-11	OEM
1-235-223-11	OEM
1-235-444-11	1411
1-235-783-11	OEM
1-235-783-21	OEM
1-235-784-11	OEM
1-235-784-12	OEM
1-235-963-11	OEM
1-235-971-12	0514
1-424-115-11	3530
1-425-636	0143
1-453-032-13	OEM
1-453-032-16	OEM
1-453-041-12	OEM
1-453-043-00	OEM
1-453-050-00	OEM
1-453-050-31	OEM
1-453-063-00	OEM
1-453-067-13	OEM
1-453-071-00	OEM
1-453-082-00	OEM
1-464-756-21	OEM
1-506-319	0087
1-530-012-11	0015
1-531-016	0015
1-531-024	0287
1-531-027	0015
1-531-028	0286
1-531-028-21	0286
1-531-036-11	0769
1-531-052	0201
1-531-055	0201
1-531-105	0015
1-531-105-11	0015
1-531-105-13	0015
1-531-106	0015
1-531-106-13	0015
1-531-106-17	0015
1-534-105-13	0015
1-534-106-13	0015
1-590-1261	1018
1-800-662-11	1470
1-800-945-00	OEM
1-801-003	0016
1-801-003-12	0144
1-801-003-13	0144
1-801-003-14	0144
1-801-003-15	0144
1-801-004	0016
1-801-004-17	0016
1-801-005	0164
1-801-005-23	0004
1-801-006	0164
1-801-006-12	0004
1-801-006-14	0004
1-801-009-11	2337
1-801-010	OEM
1-801-099-11	4169
1-801-301-13	0142
1-801-301-14	0142
1-801-301-15	0142
1-801-304-15	0127
1-801-305-13	0144
1-801-306	0144
1-801-306-13	0144
1-801-306-14	0144
1-801-306-15	0144
1-801-308	0004
1-801-308-24	0004

If replacement code is OEM, contact original manufacturer for replacement.

DEVICE TYPE	REPL CODE
1-801-309	0208
1-801-310	0164
1-801-314	0016
1-801-314-15	0016
1-801-314-16	0016
1-801-951	OEM
1-805-104	OEM
1-805-104-11	OEM
1-805-105-11	1624
1-806-214-11	OEM
1-806-476-00	1404
1-806-549-41	0017
1-807-643-11	OEM
1-807-745-11	OEM
1-808-592-11	0031
1-808-919-11	OEM
1-808-948-11	OEM
1-809-120-21	OEM
1-809-365-11	OEM
1-809-366-11	OEM
1-809-401-11	OEM
1-809-401-31	OEM
1-810-039-11	OEM
1-810-050-11	OEM
1-810-052-21	OEM
1-6732	0419
1-8259	0015
1-12689	0123
1-16549	0133
1-18341	0030
1-20363	0057
1-20398	0064
1-40159E01	OEM
1-79990A	0086
1-464607-3	0405
1-464607-5	0405
1-464860-1	0405
1-464865-1	0405
1-464984-1	0405
1-466860-1	0405
1-52221011	0004
1-522210111	0004
1-522210131	0050
1-522210300	0050
1-522210921	0050
1-522211021	0050
1-522211200	0004
1-522211328	0004
1-522211921	0050
1-522214400	0050
1-522214411	0050
1-522214435	0050
1-522214821	0050
1-522214831	0050
1-522216500	0004
1-522216600	0050
1-522217400	0050
1-522223720	0016
1-6147191229	0016
1-6171191368	0079
1-6207190405	0004
1-6501190016	0015
1-B527-062	0196
1-TD-2684	0004
1-TR-016	2279
1+12/1	0015
1A0013	0617
1A0020	0470
1A0021	0155
1A0022	0155
1A0024	0111
1A0025	0079
1A0027	0178
1A0029	0079
1A0032	0079
1A0033	0155
1A0034	0016
1A0035	0016
1A0037	0155
1A0038	0142
1A0043	0016
1A0044	0127
1A0045	0155
1A0046	0236
1A0048	0178
1A0051	0155
1A0055	0004
1A0056	0004
1A0058	0042
1A0059	0236
1A0063	0016
1A0066	0086
1A0067	0155
1A0070	0079
1A0076	0079
1A0077	0079
1A0078	0079
1A0079	0016
1A0080	0016
1A0081	0016
1A0083	0155
1A0084	0155
1A01	0086
1A02	0126
1A03	0086
1A04	4507
1A05	0126
1A06	0086
1A07	0086
1A08	0126
1A09	0187
1A1/18	OEM
1A1/52	OEM
1A2/18	OEM
1A2/52	OEM
1A3	OEM
1A3-F	OEM
1A3F	OEM
1A5/18	OEM
1A5/52	OEM
1A6.8M	0025
1A6.8MA	0025
1A6.8MB	0025
1A7.5M	0644
1A7.5MA	0644
1A7.5MB	0644
1A8-1A82	0050
1A8.2M	0244
1A8.2MA	0244
1A8.2MB	0244
1A9.1M	0012
1A9.1MA	0012
1A9.1MB	0012
1A10M	0170
1A10MA	0170
1A10MB	0170
1A11	0187
1A11M	0313
1A11MA	0313
1A11MB	0313
1A12	OEM
1A12/18	OEM
1A12M	0137
1A12MA	0137
1A12MB	0137
1A13	0187
1A13/18	OEM
1A13M	0361
1A13MA	0361
1A13MB	0361
1A14	OEM
1A14/18	OEM
1A15	0187
1A15/18	OEM
1A15M	0002
1A15MA	0002
1A15MB	0002
1A16	0334
1A16/18	OEM
1A16M	0416
1A16MA	0416
1A16MB	0416
1A17	0086
1A18	0086
1A18M	0490
1A18MA	0490
1A18MB	0490
1A19	0126
1A20M	0526
1A20MA	0526
1A20MB	0526
1A22	OEM
1A22/18	OEM
1A22M	0560
1A22MA	0560
1A22MB	0560
1A23	OEM
1A23/18	OEM
1A24	OEM
1A24/18	OEM
1A24M	0398
1A24MA	0398
1A24MB	0398
1A25	OEM
1A25/18	OEM
1A26	OEM
1A26/18	OEM
1A27M	0436
1A27MA	0436
1A27MB	0436
1A30M	0721
1A30MA	0721
1A30MB	0721
1A33M	0039
1A33MA	0039
1A33MB	0039
1A34(R)	0590
1A36M	0814
1A36MA	0814
1A36MB	0814
1A37	OEM
1A38	0590
1A38(R)	0590
1A38R	0590
1A39M	0346
1A39MA	0346
1A39MB	0346
1A40	OEM
1A43M	0925
1A43MA	0925
1A43MB	0925
1A47M	0993
1A47MA	0993
1A47MB	0993
1A48B	OEM
1A48C	OEM
1A48FB	OEM
1A48FC	OEM
1A51M	0497
1A51MA	0497
1A51MB	0497
1A52	1266
1A52/18	OEM
1A53	0755
1A53/18	OEM
1A54	0118
1A54/18	OEM
1A55	0296
1A55/18	OEM
1A56	0372
1A56/18	OEM
1A56M	1823
1A56MA	1823
1A56MB	0863
1A57	0036
1A58	0274
1A59	0140
1A60	0041
1A61	0777
1A62	0466
1A62M	0778
1A62MA	0778
1A62MB	0778
1A68M	2144
1A68MA	2144
1A68MB	2144
1A75M	1181
1A75MA	1181
1A75MB	1181
1A82M	0327
1A82MA	0327
1A82MB	0327
1A83	OEM
1A91M	1301
1A91MA	1301
1A91MB	1301
1A100M	0098
1A100MA	0098
1A100MB	0098
1A104	OEM
1A110M	0149
1A110MA	0149
1A110MB	0149
1A120M	0186
1A120MA	0186
1A120MB	0186
1A124	OEM
1A129	OEM
1A130	OEM
1A130M	0213
1A130MA	0213
1A130MB	0213
1A150M	0028
1A150MA	0028
1A150MB	0028
1A160M	0255
1A160MA	0255
1A160MB	0255
1A180M	0363
1A180MA	0363
1A180MB	0363
1A200M	0417
1A200MA	0417
1A200MB	0417
1A348(R)	0590
1A4102	3161
1A10425	0015
1A10952	0102
1A11184	0015
1A11306	0143
1A11671	0015
1A12214	0015
1A12407	0015
1A12687	0030
1A12688	0012
1A12689	0143
1A12690	0015
1A13219	0015
1A13719	0015
1A13720	0015
1A14384	0143
1A15790	0015
1A16549	0133
1A16550	0015
1A16551	0133
1A17273	OEM
1A66102-02C	OEM
1A66102-03C	OEM
1A66400-05B	OEM
1AC12	0137
1AC12A	0137
1AC12B	0137
1AC15	0002
1AC15A	0002
1AC15B	0002
1AC27	0436
1AC27A	0436
1AC27B	0436
1AC33	0039
1AC33A	0039
1AC33B	0039
1AC62	0778
1AC62A	0778
1AC62B	0778
1AC82	0327
1AC82A	0327
1AC82B	0327
1AC110	0149
1AC110A	0149
1AC110B	0149
1AMH2	0344
1AR	OEM
1AS027	0087
1AS029	0087
1AU3	1296
1AU601	OEM
1AU601A	OEM
1AU601B	OEM
1AV20	OEM
1AV30	OEM
1AV35	OEM
1AV40	OEM
1AV48	OEM
1AV50	OEM
1AV51	OEM
1AV56	OEM
1AV57	OEM
1AV58	OEM
1AV59	OEM
1AV60	OEM
1AV61	OEM
1AV62	OEM
1AV65	OEM
1AV67	OEM
1AV68	OEM
1AV69	OEM
1AV80	OEM
1AV81	OEM
1AV82	OEM
1AV83	OEM
1AV84	OEM
1AV85	OEM
1AV86	OEM
1AV87	OEM
1AV88	OEM
1AV89	OEM
1AV95	OEM
1AV96	OEM
1AV97	OEM
1AV97A	OEM
1AV98	OEM
1AV98A	OEM
1AV99	OEM
1AV99A	OEM
1AV100	OEM
1AV120	OEM
1AV130	OEM
1AZ6.8	0025
1AZ7.5	0644
1AZ8.2	0244
1AZ9.1	0012
1AZ10	0170
1AZ11	0313
1AZ12	0137
1AZ13	0361
1AZ15	0002
1AZ16	0416
1AZ18	0490
1AZ20	0526
1AZ22	0560
1AZ24	0273
1AZ27	0436
1AZ30	0721
1AZ33	0039
1AZ36	0814
1AZ47	0993
1AZ51	0497
1AZ200	0417
1AZ270	OEM
1AZ300	OEM
1AZ330	OEM
1B01	0615
1B04	0074
1B05	0276
1B05J05	0276
1B05J20	0015
1B05J40	0015
1B06	0177
1B07	2411
1B08	2411
1B08T05	0276
1B08T10	0276
1B08T20	0287
1B09	0359
1B1	0276
1B1/18	OEM
1B1/52	OEM
1B1.1	0106
1B2	0287
1B2/18	OEM
1B2/52	OEM
1B2C1	0196
1B2C1-LC2	OEM
1B2Z1	0015
1B2Z1-LC2	OEM
1B2Z1AY	0015
1B3	1296
1B4	0293
1B4B1	0106
1B4B41	0276
1B4B42	0241
1B4.1	0106
1B5/18	OEM
1B5/52	OEM
1B6	0299
1B8	0250
1B10	0250
1B10J20	0015
1B12	OEM
1B12/18	OEM
1B13	OEM
1B13/18	OEM
1B14	OEM
1B14/18	OEM
1B15	OEM
1B15/18	OEM
1B15CL05	OEM
1B15CL10	OEM
1B15CL20	OEM
1B15CL30	OEM
1B15CL40	OEM
1B16	OEM
1B16/18	OEM
1B22	OEM
1B22/18	OEM
1B23	OEM
1B23/18	OEM
1B24	OEM
1B24/18	OEM
1B24A	OEM
1B24A/MXT14	OEM
1B25	OEM
1B25/18	OEM
1B26	OEM
1B26/18	OEM
1B27	OEM
1B35A	OEM
1B35A/MXA14	OEM
1B37A	OEM
1B37A/MXA19	OEM
1B38	OEM
1B38/MST26	OEM
1B40CL05	OEM
1B40CL10	OEM
1B40CL20	OEM
1B40CL30	OEM
1B40CL40	OEM
1B42IG1	0895
1B44	OEM
1B44/MSA12	OEM
1B52	OEM
1B52/18	OEM
1B52/MSA21	OEM
1B53	OEM
1B53/18	OEM
1B53/MSA15	OEM
1B54	OEM
1B54/18	OEM
1B54/MST27	OEM
1B55	OEM
1B55/18	OEM
1B55/MST18	OEM
1B56	OEM
1B56/18	OEM
1B56/MSA11	OEM
1B58A	OEM
1B58A/MST12	OEM
1B63A	OEM
1B63A/MXT15	OEM
1B63B	OEM
1B759	0137
1B1055	OEM
1B12421	0122
1BH62	0080
1BZ61	0015
1BZ61-A	0015
1BZ61-B	0015
1BZ61-C	0015
1BZ61-D	0015
1BZ61-K	0015
1BZ61-L	0015
1BZ61-OR	0015
1BZ61-Y	0015
1C0009	0015
1C0017	0133
1C0020	0644
1C0025	0015
1C0026	0015
1C0029	0143
1C0031	0015
1C0038	0631
1C03	0236
1C04	0848
1C05	0015
1C06	0848
1C07	0556
1C08	1190
1C09	0042
1C2	0015
1C4	0015
1C6	4149
1C8	0784
1C9.1Z	0012
1C9.1ZA	0012
1C10	0071
1C10Z	0170
1C10ZA	0170
1C11	0848
1C11Z	0313
1C11ZA	0313
1C12	2803
1C12Z	0137
1C12ZA	0137
1C13	0350
1C13Z	0361
1C13ZA	0361
1C14	0419
1C15	0167
1C15A	0002
1C15Z	0002
1C15ZA	0002
1C16	2222
1C16Z	0416
1C16ZA	0416
1C17	0780
1C18	1797
1C18Z	0490
1C18ZA	0490
1C-19	0368
1C20	1070
1C20Z	0526
1C20ZA	0526
1C21	6967
1C22Z	0560
1C22ZA	0560
1C-24	0574
1C24Z	0398
1C24ZA	0398
1C26	0167
1C27Z	0436
1C27ZA	0436
1C-30	1601
1C30Z	0721
1C30ZA	0721
1C33Z	0039
1C33ZA	0039
1C36Z	0814
1C36ZA	0814
1C39Z	0346
1C39ZA	0346
1C43Z	0925
1C43ZA	0925
1C47Z	0993
1C47ZA	0993
1C51Z	0497
1C51ZA	0497
1C56Z	0863
1C56ZA	0863
1C62Z	0778
1C62ZA	0778
1C68Z	2144
1C68ZA	2144
1C75Z	1181
1C75ZA	1181
1C82Z	0327
1C82ZA	0327
1C91	0627
1C91Z	1301
1C91ZA	1301
1C100Z	0098
1C100ZA	0098
1C-101	0396
1C110Z	0149
1C110ZA	0149
1C-112	0849
1C120Z	0186
1C120ZA	0186
1C-126	4502
1C129M	OEM
1C130Z	0213
1C130ZA	0213
1C-142	0167
1C150Z	0028
1C150ZA	0028
1C160Z	0255
1C160ZA	0255
1C180Z	0363
1C180ZA	0363
1C200Z	0417
1C200ZA	0417
1C202	1797
1C204	3189
1C288	0368
1C-289	1742
1C311	2716
1C319	2688
1C-502	0748
1C504	0659
1C505	0673
1C-507	0574
1C507	2377
1C508	0661
1C509	0348
1C510	0350
1C511	0649
1C513	0696
1C-602	2535
1C821	OEM
1C821A	OEM
1C823	OEM
1C823A	OEM
1C825	OEM
1C825A	OEM
1C2992	OEM
1C2993	OEM
1C2995	OEM
1C3003	OEM
1C3004	OEM
1C3005	OEM
1C3006	OEM
1C3007	OEM
1C3008	OEM
1C3009	OEM
1C3010	OEM
1C3011	OEM
1C3012	OEM
1C3014	OEM
1C3015	OEM
1C3041	OEM
1C3993	OEM
1C4728	OEM
1C4729	OEM
1C4730	OEM
1C4731	OEM
1C4732	OEM
1C4733	OEM
1C4734	OEM
1C4735	OEM
1C4736	OEM
1C4737	OEM
1C4738	OEM
1C4739	OEM
1C4740	OEM
1C4741	OEM
1C4742	OEM
1C4743	OEM
1C4744	OEM
1C4745	OEM
1C4746	OEM
1C4747	OEM
1C4748	OEM
1C4749	OEM
1C4750	OEM
1C4751	OEM
1C4752	OEM
1C4753	OEM
1C4754	OEM
1C4755	OEM
1C4756	OEM
1C4757	OEM
1C4758	OEM
1C4759	OEM
1C4760	OEM
1C4761	OEM
1C4762	OEM
1C4763	OEM
1C4764	OEM
1C5247	OEM
1C5283	OEM
1C5284	OEM
1C5285	OEM
1C5286	OEM
1C5287	OEM
1C5288	OEM
1C5289	OEM
1C5290	OEM
1C5291	OEM
1C5292	OEM
1C5293	OEM
1C5294	OEM
1C5295	OEM
1C5296	OEM
1C5297	OEM
1C5298	OEM
1C5299	OEM
1C5300	OEM
1C5301	OEM
1C5302	OEM
1C5303	OEM
1C5304	OEM
1C5305	OEM
1C5306	OEM
1C5307	OEM
1C5308	OEM
1C5309	OEM
1C5310	OEM
1C5311	OEM
1C5312	OEM
1C5313	OEM
1C5314	OEM
1C5333	OEM
1C5334	OEM
1C5335	OEM
1C5336	OEM
1C5337	OEM
1C5338	OEM
1C5339	OEM
1C5340	OEM
1C5341	OEM
1C5342	OEM
1C5343	OEM
1C5344	OEM
1C5345	OEM
1C5346	OEM
1C5347	OEM
1C5348	OEM
1C5349	OEM
1C5350	OEM
1C5351	OEM
1C5352	OEM
1C5353	OEM
1C5354	OEM
1C5355	OEM
1C5356	OEM
1C5357	OEM
1C5358	OEM
1C5359	OEM
1C5360	OEM
1C5361	OEM
1C5362	OEM
1C5363	OEM
1C5364	OEM
1C5365	OEM

If replacement code is OEM, contact original manufacturer for replacement.

DEVICE TYPE	REPL CODE
1C5367	OEM
1C5368	OEM
1C5369	OEM
1C5370	OEM
1C5371	OEM
1C5372	OEM
1C5373	OEM
1C5374	OEM
1C5375	OEM
1C5376	OEM
1C5377	OEM
1C5378	OEM
1C5379	OEM
1C5380	OEM
1C5381	OEM
1C5382	OEM
1C5383	OEM
1C5384	OEM
1C5385	OEM
1C5386	OEM
1C5387	OEM
1C5388	OEM
1C6267	OEM
1C6267A	OEM
1C6268	OEM
1C6268A	OEM
1C6269	OEM
1C6269A	OEM
1C6270	OEM
1C6270A	OEM
1C6271	OEM
1C6271A	OEM
1C6272	OEM
1C6272A	OEM
1C6273	OEM
1C6273A	OEM
1C6274	OEM
1C6274A	OEM
1C6275	OEM
1C6275A	OEM
1C6276	OEM
1C6276A	OEM
1C6277	OEM
1C6277A	OEM
1C6278	OEM
1C6278A	OEM
1C6279	OEM
1C6279A	OEM
1C6280	OEM
1C6280A	OEM
1C6281	OEM
1C6281A	OEM
1C6282	OEM
1C6282A	OEM
1C6283	OEM
1C6283A	OEM
1C6284	OEM
1C6284A	OEM
1C6285	OEM
1C6285A	OEM
1C6286	OEM
1C6286A	OEM
1C6287	OEM
1C6287A	OEM
1C6288	OEM
1C6288A	OEM
1C6289	OEM
1C6289A	OEM
1C6290	OEM
1C6290A	OEM
1C6291	OEM
1C6291A	OEM
1C6292	OEM
1C6292A	OEM
1C6293	OEM
1C6293A	OEM
1C6294	OEM
1C6294A	OEM
1C6295	OEM
1C6295A	OEM
1C6296	OEM
1C6296A	OEM
1C6297	OEM
1C6297A	OEM
1C6298	OEM
1C6298A	OEM
1C6299	OEM
1C6299A	OEM
1C6300	OEM
1C6300A	OEM
1C6301	OEM
1C6301A	OEM
1C6302	OEM
1C6302A	OEM
1C6303	OEM
1C6303A	OEM
1C25681	2524
1C73045	0042
1C744005	0007
1C744006	0018
1C744009	0830
1CL-101-TY	0093
1CL-101A-TY	0093
1CL-201-TY	0093
1CL-201A-TY	0093
1CL-301A-PA	0093
1CL-301A-TY	0093
1CL-748-TY	0093
1CP-N5	1796

DEVICE TYPE	REPL CODE
1D08	0002
1D059	1257
1D2	0015
1D2C1	0199
1D2C1LC2	0199
1D2Z1	0015
1D3.9	0451
1D3.9A	0451
1D3.9B	0451
1D4B1	0106
1D4B41	0287
1D4B42	1864
1D4.7	0446
1D4.7A	0446
1D4.7B	0446
1D5.1A	0162
1D5.1B	0437
1D5.6	0157
1D5.6A	0157
1D5.6B	0157
1D6.2A	0631
1D6.2B	0631
1D6.2SA	0631
1D6.2SB	0631
1D8	0071
1D10	0071
1D12	OEM
1D20M	OEM
1D27Z5	0436
1D40M	OEM
1D60M	OEM
1D80M	OEM
1D80MS	OEM
1D100	1129
1D100M	OEM
1D100MS	OEM
1D101	0340
1D102	0895
1D103	2326
1D104	0058
1D150M	OEM
1D150MS	OEM
1D200M	OEM
1D200MA	OEM
1D261	0015
1D300MA	OEM
1D600M	OEM
1DA1Z8.2A	0244
1DA1Z8.2B	0244
1DA1Z8.2C	0244
1DA1Z8.20	0244
1DA1Z18B	0490
1DAZ3401	0244
1DAZ3401A	0244
1DAZ3401B	0244
1DAZ3401C	0244
1DAZ34010	0244
1DAZ3405B	0490
1DB050	1864
1DB100	1864
1DB200	1864
1DB400	1864
1DB600	1864
1DC1	0015
1DF251	OEM
1DG2	0143
1DH62	0604
1DMB10	0241
1DMB20	0241
1DMB40	4501
1DMB60	1864
1D-S	OEM
1DZ12	0137
1DZ61	0015
1DZ61-A	0015
1DZ61-B	0015
1DZ61-C	0015
1DZ61-D	0015
1DZ61-K	0015
1DZ61-L	0015
1DZ61-OR	0015
1DZ61-Y	0015
1DZ120	0186
1E02	0015
1E05	0015
1E-1	0086
1E1	0015
1E2	0015
1E3	0015
1E4	0015
1E5	0015
1E6	0015
1E6.8Z5	0025
1E6.8Z10	0025
1E7	0071
1E7.5Z	0644
1E7.5Z5	0644
1E7.5Z10	0644
1E8	0071
1E8.2Z	0244
1E8.2Z5	0244
1E8.2Z10	0244
1E-9A	0050
1E9.1D	0012
1E9.1D5	0012
1E9.1D10	0012
1E9.1Z	0012
1E9.1Z5	0012
1E9.1Z10	0012

DEVICE TYPE	REPL CODE
1E10	0071
1E10Z	0170
1E10Z5	0170
1E10Z10	0170
1E11Z	0789
1E11Z5	0313
1E11Z10	0789
1E12	OEM
1E12Z	0137
1E12Z5	0137
1E12Z10	0137
1E13Z	0361
1E13Z5	0361
1E13Z10	0361
1E14	OEM
1E14Z	0100
1E14Z5	0100
1E14Z10	0100
1E15Z	0002
1E15Z5	0002
1E15Z10	0002
1E16	OEM
1E16Z	0416
1E16Z5	0416
1E16Z10	0416
1E17Z	1639
1E17Z5	1639
1E17Z10	1639
1E18	OEM
1E18Z	0490
1E18Z5	0490
1E18Z10	0490
1E19Z	0943
1E19Z5	0943
1E19Z10	0943
1E20	OEM
1E20Z	0526
1E20Z5	0526
1E20Z10	0526
1E22Z	0560
1E22Z5	0560
1E22Z10	0560
1E24Z	0398
1E24Z5	0398
1E24Z10	0398
1E25	OEM
1E25Z	1596
1E25Z5	1596
1E25Z10	1596
1E27Z	0436
1E27Z5	0436
1E27Z10	0436
1E30Z	0721
1E30Z5	0721
1E30Z10	0721
1E33Z	0039
1E33Z5	0039
1E33Z10	0039
1E36Z	0814
1E36Z5	0814
1E36Z10	0814
1E39Z	0346
1E39Z5	0346
1E39Z10	0346
1E43Z	0925
1E43Z5	0925
1E43Z10	0925
1E45Z	0993
1E45Z5	0993
1E45Z10	0993
1E47Z	0993
1E47Z5	0993
1E47Z10	0993
1E50A	OEM
1E50Z	0497
1E50Z5	0497
1E50Z10	0497
1E51Z	0497
1E51Z5	0497
1E51Z10	0497
1E52Z	0497
1E52Z5	0497
1E52Z10	0497
1E56Z	0863
1E56Z5	0863
1E56Z10	0863
1E62Z	0778
1E62Z5	0778
1E62Z10	0778
1E68Z	2144
1E68Z5	2144
1E68Z10	2144
1E75Z	1181
1E75Z5	1181
1E75Z10	1181
1E82Z	0327
1E82Z5	0327
1E82Z10	0327
1E91Z	1301
1E91Z5	1301
1E91Z10	1301
1E100Z	0098
1E100Z5	0098
1E100Z10	0098
1E110Z	0149
1E110Z5	0149
1E110Z10	0149
1E120Z	0186
1E120Z5	0186

DEVICE TYPE	REPL CODE
1E120Z10	0186
1E130Z	0213
1E130Z5	0213
1E130Z10	0213
1E150Z	0028
1E150Z5	0028
1E150Z10	0028
1E160Z	0255
1E160Z5	0255
1E160Z10	0255
1E180Z	0363
1E180Z5	0363
1E180Z10	0363
1E200Z	0417
1E200Z5	0417
1E200Z10	0417
1E535A	0224
1E535B	0127
1E703E	0627
1EA10A	0229
1EA20A	0229
1EA30A	0229
1EA40A	0229
1EA50A	0229
1EA60A	0229
1EA70A	4193
1EA80A	4193
1EA100A	0071
1EA120A	OEM
1EB10A	0090
1EB20A	0097
1EB30A	0105
1EB40A	0109
1EB50A	0204
1EB60A	0122
1EB70A	0131
1EB80A	0131
1EB100A	0145
1EK200	OEM
1EK220	OEM
1EK250	OEM
1EK300	OEM
1ER100A	0145
1ET02	0015
1ET05	0015
1ET1	0015
1ET2	0015
1ET3	0015
1ET4	0015
1ET5	0015
1ET6	0015
1ET7	0071
1ET8	0071
1ET10	0071
1EZ3.3D	0289
1EZ3.3D5	0289
1EZ3.3D10	0289
1EZ3.3T10	0289
1EZ3.6	0188
1EZ3.6D	0188
1EZ3.6D5	0188
1EZ3.6D10	0188
1EZ3.6T10	0188
1EZ3.9D	0451
1EZ3.9D5	0451
1EZ3.9D10	0451
1EZ3.9T10	0451
1EZ4.3D	0528
1EZ4.3D5	0528
1EZ4.3D10	0528
1EZ4.3T10	0528
1EZ4.7D	0446
1EZ4.7D5	0446
1EZ4.7D10	0446
1EZ4.7T10	0446
1EZ-5Z10	0644
1EZ5.1	0162
1EZ5.1D	0162
1EZ5.1D5	0162
1EZ5.1D10	0162
1EZ5.1T10	0162
1EZ5.6	0157
1EZ5.6D	0157
1EZ5.6D5	0157
1EZ5.6D10	0157
1EZ5.6T10	0157
1EZ6.2D	0631
1EZ6.2D5	0631
1EZ6.2D10	0631
1EZ6.2T10	0631
1EZ6.8D	0025
1EZ6.8D5	0025
1EZ6.8D10	0025
1EZ6.8T10	0025
1EZ7.5D	0644
1EZ7.5D5	0644
1EZ7.5D10	0644
1EZ7.5T10	0644
1EZ7.5Z	0644
1EZ8.2D	0244
1EZ8.2D5	0244
1EZ8.2D10	0244
1EZ8.2T10	0244
1EZ9.1	0012
1EZ9.1D	0012
1EZ9.1D5	0012
1EZ9.1D10	0012
1EZ9.1T10	0012
1EZ10D	0170

DEVICE TYPE	REPL CODE
1EZ10D5	0170
1EZ10D10	0170
1EZ10T10	0170
1EZ11D	0313
1EZ11D5	0313
1EZ11D10	0313
1EZ11T10	0313
1EZ12	0137
1EZ12D	0137
1EZ12D5	0137
1EZ12D10	0137
1EZ12T10	0137
1EZ13D	0361
1EZ13D5	0361
1EZ13D10	0361
1EZ13T10	0361
1EZ14D	0100
1EZ14D5	0100
1EZ14D10	0100
1EZ15	0002
1EZ15D	0002
1EZ15D5	0002
1EZ15D10	0002
1EZ15T10	0002
1EZ16D	0416
1EZ16D5	0416
1EZ16D10	0416
1EZ16T10	0416
1EZ17D	1639
1EZ17D5	1639
1EZ17D10	1639
1EZ18D	0490
1EZ18D5	0490
1EZ18D10	0490
1EZ18T10	0490
1EZ19D	0943
1EZ19D5	0943
1EZ19D10	0943
1EZ20D	0526
1EZ20D5	0526
1EZ20D10	0526
1EZ20T10	0526
1EZ22D	0560
1EZ22D5	0560
1EZ22D10	0560
1EZ22T10	0560
1EZ24D	0398
1EZ24D5	0398
1EZ24D10	0398
1EZ24T10	0398
1EZ27	0436
1EZ27D	0436
1EZ27D5	0436
1EZ27D10	0436
1EZ27T10	0436
1EZ30D	0721
1EZ30D5	0721
1EZ30D10	0721
1EZ30T10	0721
1EZ33D	0039
1EZ33D5	0039
1EZ33D10	0039
1EZ36D	0814
1EZ36D5	0814
1EZ36D10	0814
1EZ39D	0346
1EZ39D5	0346
1EZ39D10	0346
1EZ43D	0925
1EZ43D5	0925
1EZ43D10	0925
1EZ47D	0993
1EZ47D5	0993
1EZ47D10	0993
1EZ50D	OEM
1EZ50D5	OEM
1EZ50D10	OEM
1EZ51D	0497
1EZ51D5	0497
1EZ51D10	0497
1EZ52D	OEM
1EZ52D5	OEM
1EZ52D10	OEM
1EZ56D	0863
1EZ56D5	0863
1EZ56D10	0863
1EZ62D	0778
1EZ62D5	0778
1EZ62D10	0778
1EZ68D	2144
1EZ68D5	2144
1EZ68D10	2144
1EZ75D	1181
1EZ75D5	1181
1EZ75D10	1181
1EZ82D	0327
1EZ82D5	0327
1EZ82D10	0327
1EZ91D	1301
1EZ91D5	1301
1EZ91D10	1301
1EZ100D	0098
1EZ100D5	0098
1EZ100D10	0098
1EZ110D	0149
1EZ110D5	0149
1EZ110D10	0149
1EZ120D	0186
1EZ120D5	0186

DEVICE TYPE	REPL CODE
1EZ120D10	0186
1EZ130D	0213
1EZ130D5	0213
1EZ130D10	0213
1EZ140D	0245
1EZ140D5	0245
1EZ140D10	0245
1EZ150D	0028
1EZ150D5	0028
1EZ150D10	0028
1EZ160D	0255
1EZ160D5	0255
1EZ160D10	0255
1EZ170D	0871
1EZ170D5	0871
1EZ170D10	0871
1EZ180D	0363
1EZ180D5	0363
1EZ180D10	0363
1EZ190D	2831
1EZ190D5	2831
1EZ190D10	2831
1EZ200D	0417
1EZ200D5	0417
1EZ200D10	0417
1EZ1905	2831
1E.5	OEM
1F05	0015
1F1	1082
1F2	0015
1F3	1082
1F4	OEM
1F6	OEM
1F8	0071
1F10	0071
1F12	OEM
1F14	OEM
1F14A	0015
1F16	OEM
1F18	OEM
1F20	OEM
1F101	OEM
1F104	OEM
1F105	2496
1F106	2496
1F112	OEM
1F911	OEM
1F911N	OEM
1F916	OEM
1F918H	OEM
1F935	OEM
1F941M	OEM
1F941N	OEM
1F942N	OEM
1F943M	OEM
1FB100R	OEM
1FJ0	OEM
1FJ0(F)	OEM
1FJ1	OEM
1FJ1(F)	OEM
1FJ2	OEM
1FJ2(F)	OEM
1FJ3	OEM
1FJ3(F)	OEM
1FM2	0015
1FP70020H	2549
1G	OEM
1G01	0143
1G1	OEM
1G2	0071
1G2C1	0196
1G2Z	0015
1G2Z1	1089
1G3	1296
1G3(RECT)	0071
1G3.3	0289
1G3.3A	0289
1G3.6	0188
1G3.6A	0188
1G3.9	0451
1G3.9A	0451
1G4	0071
1G4B1	0106
1G4B41	0293
1G4B42	1864
1G4.3	0528
1G4.3A	0528
1G4.7	0446
1G4.7A	0446
1G5	OEM
1G5.1	0162
1G5.1A	0162
1G5.6	0157
1G5.6A	0157
1G6	0071
1G6.2	0631
1G6.2A	0631
1G6.8	0025
1G6.8A	0025
1G7.5	0644
1G7.5A	0644
1G8	0071
1G8.2	0244
1G8.2A	0244
1G9.1	0012
1G9.1A	0012
1G10	0170
1G10A	0170
1G11	0313

DEVICE TYPE	REPL CODE
1G11A	0313
1G12	0137
1G12A	0137
1G13	0361
1G13A	0361
1G15	0100
1G15A	0002
1G16	0416
1G16A	0416
1G18	0490
1G18A	0490
1G20	0526
1G20A	0526
1G22	0560
1G22A	0560
1G24	0398
1G24A	0398
1G25	0143
1G27	0436
1G27A	0436
1G30	0721
1G30A	0721
1G33	0039
1G33A	0039
1G36	0814
1G36A	0814
1G39	0346
1G39A	0346
1G43	0925
1G43A	0925
1G47	0993
1G47A	0993
1G51	0497
1G51A	0497
1G56	0863
1G56A	0863
1G62	0778
1G62A	0778
1G68	2144
1G68A	2144
1G75	1181
1G75A	1181
1G82	0327
1G82A	0327
1G86	0143
1G91	0156
1G91A	1301
1G100	0435
1G100(ZENER)	0098
1G100A	0098
1G110	0149
1G110A	0149
1G120	0186
1G120A	0186
1G130	0213
1G130A	0213
1G150	0028
1G150A	0028
1G160	0255
1G160A	0255
1G180	0363
1G180A	0363
1G200	0417
1G200A	0417
1GD2	0143
1GD4	0143
1GD5	0030
1GD5X	0143
1GD6	0143
1GD10	0143
1GH11	0182
1GH11F-FA	0102
1GH62	0023
1GWJ43	0730
1GZ61	0015
1GZ61-A	0015
1GZ61-B	0015
1GZ61-C	0015
1GZ61-D	0015
1GZ61-K	0015
1GZ61-L	0015
1GZ61-OR	0015
1GZ61-Y	0015
1GZZ1	0015
1H3	0182
1H20M	OEM
1H40M	OEM
1H40MS	OEM
1H60H	OEM
1H60M	OEM
1H60S	OEM
1H80M	OEM
1H80MS	OEM
1H100M	OEM
1H120M	OEM
1H120MS	OEM
1H140M	OEM
1H160M	OEM
1H160MS	OEM
1H180M	OEM
1H200M	OEM
1H200MS	OEM
1H250M	OEM
1H300M	OEM
1H400M	OEM
1HC-10F	0015
1HC-10R	0015
1HC-15F	0015
1HC-15R	0015

If replacement code is OEM, contact original manufacturer for replacement.

DEVICE TYPE	REPL CODE
1HC-20F	0015
1HC-20R	0015
1HC-25F	0015
1HC-25R	0015
1HC-30F	0015
1HC-30R	0015
1HC-40F	0015
1HC-40R	0015
1HC-50F	0015
1HC-50R	0015
1HC-60F	0015
1HC-60R	0015
1HC-80F	0071
1HC-80R	0071
1HC-100F	0071
1HC-100R	0071
1HC-120F	0102
1HC-120R	0102
1HY40	0015
1HY50	0015
1HY80	0071
1HY100	0071
1J1	0016
1J2C1	0199
1J2Z1	1009
1J3	1296
1J4B1	1999
1J4B41	0299
1J4B42	1864
1JA16	0160
1JH11	OEM
1JH11F	0015
1JH62	0023
1JK30	OEM
1JK60	OEM
1JK90	OEM
1JK100	OEM
1JK120	OEM
1JK150	OEM
1JK160	OEM
1JK180	OEM
1JL50	0015
1JL51	0015
1JL52	0015
1JL53	0015
1JL56	0015
1JL57	0015
1JL58	0071
1JL59	0071
1JL63	0071
1JL64	0071
1JLA10	OEM
1JM11F	OEM
1JUS.540A	OEM
1JZ61	0023
1JZ61-A	0015
1JZ61-B	0015
1JZ61-C	0015
1JZ61-D	0015
1JZ61-K	0015
1JZ61-L	0015
1JZ61-OR	0015
1JZ61-Y	0015
1K	OEM
1K01	OEM
1K2	0242
1K3	1296
1K-3.5E	0188
1K34A	2217
1K60	0143
1K60A	0143
1K60P	0143
1K60R	0143
1K75CH	OEM
1K75CK	OEM
1K75CK8199	OEM
1K75CLA	OEM
1K75CS	OEM
1K90	0143
1K110	0143
1K125CA	OEM
1K125CB	OEM
1K125CB-B	OEM
1K125CD	OEM
1K188	0143
1K188F1	OEM
1K188FM	0143
1K188FM-1	0143
1K188FM1	OEM
1K261	0143
1KAB100E	OEM
1KF20-04	0143
1KK-HA1196	4716
1KK-HA11225	2237
1L1-2R	OEM
1LE11	0087
1LE11-A	0071
1LE11-B	0071
1LE11-C	0071
1LE11-D	0071
1LE11-K	0071
1LE11-L	0071
1LE11-OR	0071
1LE11-Y	0071
1LE11A	0071
1LE11B	0071
1LE11C	0071
1LE11D	0071
1LE11K	0071
1LE11L	0071
1LE11R	0071
1LE11Y	0071
1LF11	0087
1LH62	0072
1LM340T12	0330
1LZ61	0071
1LZ61-A	0071
1LZ61-B	0071
1LZ61-C	0071
1LZ61-D	0071
1LZ61-K	0071
1LZ61-L	0071
1LZ61-OR	0071
1LZ61-Y	0071
1M3.3AZ3	0296
1M3.3AZ10	0289
1M3.6AZ3	0188
1M3.6AZ5	0188
1M3.6AZ10	0188
1M3.6ZS10	0188
1M3.9AZ3	OEM
1M3.9AZ10	0451
1M3.9ZS5	0451
1M3.9ZS10	0451
1M4.3AZ3	OEM
1M4.3AZ10	0528
1M4.7AZ3	OEM
1M4.7AZ10	0446
1M4.7ZS5	0446
1M4.7ZS10	0446
1M5.1AZ3	0162
1M5.1AZ10	0162
1M5.1ZS5	0437
1M5.1ZS10	0162
1M5.6AZ3	OEM
1M5.6AZ10	0157
1M5.6ZS5	0157
1M5.6ZS10	0157
1M6.2AZ3	0631
1M6.2AZ10	0631
1M6.2ZS10	0631
1M6.8AZ3	OEM
1M6.8AZ10	0025
1M6.8Z	0025
1M6.8Z3	OEM
1M6.8Z5	0025
1M6.8Z10	0025
1M6.8ZS5	0025
1M6.8ZS10	0025
1M7.5AZ3	OEM
1M7.5AZ10	0644
1M7.5Z	0644
1M7.5Z3	OEM
1M7.5Z5	0644
1M7.5Z10	0644
1M7.5ZS5	0644
1M7.5ZS10	0644
1M8.2Z	0244
1M8.2Z3	3071
1M8.2Z5	0244
1M8.2Z10	0244
1M8.2ZS5	0244
1M8.2ZS10	0244
1M9.1Z	0012
1M9.1Z3	OEM
1M9.1Z5	0012
1M9.1Z10	0012
1M9.1ZS5	0012
1M9.1ZS10	0012
1M10Z	0170
1M10Z3	OEM
1M10Z5	0170
1M10Z10	0170
1M10ZS5	0170
1M10ZS10	0170
1M11Z	0313
1M11Z3	OEM
1M11Z5	0313
1M11Z10	0313
1M11ZS5	0313
1M11ZS10	0313
1M12Z	0137
1M12Z3	0137
1M12Z5	0137
1M12Z10	0137
1M12ZS5	0137
1M12ZS10	0137
1M13Z3	OEM
1M13Z5	0361
1M13Z10	0361
1M13ZS10	0361
1M140Z	0245
1M14Z	0100
1M14Z5	0100
1M14Z10	0100
1M15/1B	OEM
1M15Z	0002
1M15Z3	0002
1M15Z5	0002
1M15Z10	0002
1M15ZS5	0002
1M15ZS10	0002
1M16Z	0416
1M16Z3	OEM
1M16Z5	0416
1M16Z10	0416
1M16ZS5	0416
1M16ZS10	0416
1M17Z	1639
1M17Z5	1639
1M17Z10	1639
1M18Z	0490
1M18Z3	OEM
1M18Z5	0490
1M18Z10	0490
1M18ZS5	0490
1M18ZS10	0490
1M19Z	0943
1M19Z5	0943
1M19Z10	0943
1M20Z	0526
1M20Z3	0526
1M20Z5	0526
1M20Z10	0526
1M20ZS5	0186
1M20ZS10	0526
1M22Z	0560
1M22Z3	OEM
1M22Z5	0560
1M22Z10	0560
1M22ZS5	0560
1M22ZS10	0560
1M24Z	0398
1M24Z3	OEM
1M24Z5	0398
1M24Z10	0398
1M24ZS5	0398
1M24ZS10	0398
1M25Z	1596
1M25Z5	1596
1M25Z10	1596
1M27Z	0436
1M27Z3	OEM
1M27Z5	0436
1M27Z10	0436
1M27ZS5	0436
1M27ZS10	0436
1M30Z	0721
1M30Z3	OEM
1M30Z5	0721
1M30Z10	0721
1M33Z	0039
1M33Z3	OEM
1M33Z5	0039
1M33Z10	0039
1M33ZS5	0039
1M33ZS10	0039
1M36Z	0814
1M36Z3	OEM
1M36Z5	0814
1M36Z10	0814
1M39Z	0346
1M39Z3	OEM
1M39Z5	0346
1M39Z10	0346
1M39ZS5	0346
1M39ZS10	0346
1M43Z	0925
1M43Z3	OEM
1M43Z5	0925
1M43Z10	0925
1M47Z	0993
1M47Z3	OEM
1M47Z5	0993
1M47Z10	0993
1M47ZS5	0993
1M47ZS10	0993
1M51Z	0497
1M51Z3	OEM
1M51Z5	0497
1M51Z10	0497
1M56Z	0863
1M56Z3	OEM
1M56Z5	0863
1M56Z10	0863
1M56ZS5	0863
1M56ZS10	0863
1M62Z	0778
1M62Z5	0778
1M62Z10	0778
1M62ZS5	0778
1M62ZS10	0778
1M68Z	1258
1M68Z3	1258
1M68Z5	1258
1M68Z10	1258
1M68ZS5	1258
1M68ZS10	1258
1M70A	OEM
1M75Z	1181
1M75Z3	1181
1M75Z5	1181
1M75Z10	1181
1M82Z	0327
1M82Z3	OEM
1M82Z5	0327
1M82Z10	0327
1M82ZS5	0327
1M82ZS10	0327
1M87ZS5	2997
1M91Z	1301
1M91Z3	1301
1M91Z5	1301
1M91Z10	1301
1M99	OEM
1M100Z	0098
1M100Z3	OEM
1M100Z5	0098
1M100Z10	0098
1M100ZS5	0098
1M100ZS10	0098
1M110Z	0149
1M110Z3	0149
1M110Z5	0149
1M110Z10	0149
1M110ZS5	0149
1M110ZS5RL	OEM
1M110ZS10	0149
1M110ZS10RL	OEM
1M110ZS10.5	OEM
1M120Z	0186
1M120Z3	0186
1M120Z5	0186
1M120Z10	0186
1M120ZS5	0186
1M120ZS5RL	OEM
1M120ZS10	0186
1M120ZS10RL	OEM
1M120ZS10.5	OEM
1M130Z	0213
1M130Z3	0213
1M130Z5	0213
1M130Z10	0213
1M130ZS5	0213
1M130ZS5RL	OEM
1M130ZS10	0213
1M130ZS10RL	OEM
1M130ZS10.5	OEM
1M130Z.5	OEM
1M140Z	0245
1M140Z5	0245
1M140Z10	0245
1M140ZS5	0245
1M140ZS5RL	OEM
1M140ZS10	0245
1M140ZS10RL	OEM
1M150Z	0028
1M150Z3	0028
1M150Z5	0028
1M150Z10	0028
1M150ZS5	0028
1M150ZS5RL	OEM
1M150ZS10	0028
1M150ZS10RL	OEM
1M150Z.5	OEM
1M151	OEM
1M160Z	0255
1M160Z3	0255
1M160Z5	0255
1M160Z10	0255
1M160ZS5	0255
1M160ZS5RL	OEM
1M160ZS10	0255
1M160ZS10RL	OEM
1M160Z.5	OEM
1M170ZS5	0871
1M175ZS5	0363
1M175ZS5RL	OEM
1M175ZS10	0363
1M175ZS10RL	OEM
1M180Z	0363
1M180Z3	0363
1M180Z5	0363
1M180Z10	0363
1M180ZS5	0363
1M180ZS5RL	OEM
1M180ZS10	0363
1M180ZS10RL	OEM
1M180Z.5	OEM
1M200Z	0417
1M200Z3	0417
1M200Z5	0417
1M200Z10	0417
1M200ZS5	0417
1M200ZS5RL	OEM
1M200ZS10	0417
1M200ZS10RL	OEM
1M200Z.5	OEM
1M383T	1042
1M392S10	0346
1M430B	OEM
1M1140Z5	0245
1M2086	0015
1M4796D	OEM
1M8513A	0015
1M39000A30	OEM
1MA4	0015
1MC110Z10	OEM
1MC120Z10	OEM
1MC130Z10	OEM
1MC150Z10	OEM
1MC160Z10	OEM
1MC180Z10	OEM
1MC200Z10	OEM
1MC1358P	0167
1MJJ3.6	0188
1MJJ3.6A	0188
1MJJ6.2	0631
1MJJ6.2A	0631
1MJJ9.1	0769
1MJJ9.1A	0769
1MJJ12	0137
1MJJ12A	0137
1MZ9.1T5	0012
1MZ9.1T10	0012
1MZ9.1T20	0012
1MZS22ZS10	0560
1N0188A	OEM
1N1055	OEM
1N2	1296
1N4020A	OEM
1N4084A	OEM
1N6E11	OEM
1N9	OEM
1N21	1105
1N21A	0601
1N21B	0601
1N21BM	0601
1N21BMR	0601
1N21BR	0601
1N21C	0601
1N21CM	0601
1N21CMR	0601
1N21CR	0601
1N21D	0601
1N21DM	0601
1N21DMR	0601
1N21DR	0601
1N21E	0601
1N21EM	0601
1N21EMR	0601
1N21ER	0601
1N21F	0601
1N21FM	0601
1N21FMR	0601
1N21FR	0601
1N21G	0601
1N21GM	0601
1N21GMR	0601
1N21GR	0601
1N21WD	0601
1N21WDM	0601
1N21WE	0601
1N21WEM	0601
1N21WF	0601
1N21WFM	0601
1N21WG	0601
1N21WGM	0601
1N-22	0143
1N22	1106
1N22WA	OEM
1N22WB	OEM
1N23	1107
1N23A	0046
1N23B	0601
1N23BM	0601
1N23BMR	0601
1N23BR	0601
1N23C	1107
1N23CM	1107
1N23CMR	1107
1N23CR	1107
1N23D	0046
1N23DM	0046
1N23DMR	0046
1N23DR	0046
1N23E	0046
1N23EM	0046
1N23EMR	0046
1N23ER	0046
1N23F	0601
1N23FM	0601
1N23FMR	0601
1N23FR	0601
1N23G	0601
1N23GM	0601
1N23GMR	0601
1N23GR	0601
1N23H	0911
1N23WD	0601
1N23WDM	0601
1N23WE	0046
1N23WEM	0046
1N23WF	0601
1N23WFM	0601
1N23WG	0601
1N23WGM	0601
1N25	0162
1N25A	0133
1N25B	OEM
1N25WA	OEM
1N26	OEM
1N26A	OEM
1N26B	OEM
1N26C	OEM
1N27C	OEM
1N28G	0911
1N28J	OEM
1N31	OEM
1N31A	0143
1N32	OEM
1N32A	OEM
1N34	0143
1N34A	0123
1N34A(AU)	0143
1N34A(H)	0143
1N34A(K)	0143
1N34AM	0143
1N34AS	0143
1N34A-T	0143
1N34ATF1	0143
1N34A-Z	0143
1N34G	0143
1N34GA	0143
1N34M	0123
1N34N	0143
1N34Z	0143
1N35	0143
1N35(H)	OEM
1N36	0143
1N38	0143
1N38A	0143
1N38A(H)	0143
1N38B	0143
1N39	OEM
1N39A	0604
1N39B	OEM
1N40	0143
1N41	0143
1N42	0143
1N43	0143
1N44	0143
1N44A1	OEM
1N45	0143
1N46	0143
1N46A	0143
1N47	0143
1N48	0143
1N48A	0143
1N48N	0143
1N49	0143
1N50	0143
1N51	0143
1N52	0143
1N52A	0143
1N52A1	OEM
1N53	OEM
1N53A	OEM
1N53B	OEM
1N53C	OEM
1N53D	OEM
1N54	0143
1N54A	0143
1N54G	0143
1N54GA	0143
1N55	OEM
1N55A	0143
1N55B	OEM
1N56	0143
1N56A	0143
1N57	0143
1N57A	0143
1N58	0143
1N58A	0143
1N59	OEM
1N60	0019
1N60(GA)	0019
1N60(GB)	0019
1N60(H)	0019
1N60/7825B	0019
1N60-1	0019
1N60-5	0123
1N60-FA1	0019
1N60-FD1	0019
1N60-FM	0019
1N60-M3	0019
1N60-S	0019
1N60-T	0019
1N60-TF1	0019
1N60-Z	0019
1N60A	0019
1N60AM	0019
1N60AM2000-302	OEM
1N60B	0019
1N60C	0019
1N60D	0019
1N60F	0019
1N60FA1	0019
1N60FD1	0019
1N60FM	0019
1N60FM-1	0019
1N60FM1	0019
1N60FMX	0019
1N60G	0019
1N60GA	0019
1N60GB	0019
1N60M	0019
1N60M3	0019
1N60MP	0123
1N60N	0019
1N60P	0123
1N60R	0019
1N60S	0019
1N60SD60	0019
1N60T	0019
1N60TF1	0019
1N60TPGL	0019
1N60TV	0019
1N60TVG1	1106
1N60TVGL	0019
1N60TV-TDGL	1106
1N60TV-TOGL	0019
1N60TVTP	0019
1N60TV-TPGL	0019
1N60TVTPGL	0019
1N60Z	0019
1N61	OEM
1N61A	0143
1N61A1	OEM
1N62	0143
1N63	0143
1N63A	0143
1N64	0143
1N64A	0143
1N64B	0143
1N64G	0143
1N64GA	0143
1N64N	OEM
1N64P	0143
1N64S	0124
1N65	0143
1N65A	0143
1N66	0143
1N66A	0143
1N67	0143
1N67A	0143
1N67D	0143
1N68	0143
1N68A	0143
1N69	0143
1N69A	0143
1N70	0143
1N70A	0143
1N71	0143
1N72	0143
1N72G	0143
1N73	0143
1N74	0143
1N75	0143
1N75A	0143
1N76	0143
1N76A	0143
1N76C	0143
1N76G	0143
1N78	OEM
1N78A	OEM
1N78B	OEM
1N78C	OEM
1N78D	OEM
1N78E	OEM
1N78F	OEM
1N78G	OEM
1N81	0143
1N81A	0143
1N82	0911
1N82A	0911
1N82AD	0911
1N82AG	0911
1N82G	0911
1N83	OEM
1N84	0143
1N86	0143
1N86AG	0143
1N87	0143
1N87A	0143
1N87AN	OEM
1N87G	0143
1N87GA	0143
1N87S	0143
1N87T	0143
1N88	0123
1N89	0143
1N90	0143
1N90G	0143
1N90GA	0143
1N91	0143
1N92	0015
1N93	0015
1N93A	0015
1N95	0143
1N96	0143
1N96A	0143
1N96B	OEM
1N97	0143
1N97A	0143
1N98	0143
1N98A	0143
1N99	0143
1N99A	0143
1N100	0143
1N100A	0143
1N102	OEM
1N103	0143
1N104	0143
1N105	0143
1N107	0143
1N108	0143
1N109	0143
1N110	0911
1N111	0143
1N112	0143
1N113	0143
1N114	0143
1N115	0143
1N116	0143
1N116A	0143
1N117	0143
1N117A	0143
1N118	0143
1N118A	0143
1N119	0143
1N119A	0143
1N120	0143
1N120A	0143
1N122B	0229
1N124	0911
1N124A	0911
1N125	0143
1N126	0143
1N126A	0143
1N127	0143
1N127A	0143
1N128	0143

If replacement code is OEM, contact original manufacturer for replacement.

13

DEVICE TYPE	REPL CODE
1N128A	0143
1N132	0143
1N133	0143
1N134	0143
1N135	0133
1N136	0143
1N137	0143
1N137A	0133
1N137B	0133
1N138	0133
1N138A	0133
1N138B	0133
1N139	0143
1N140	0143
1N141	0143
1N142	0143
1N143	0143
1N144	0143
1N145	0143
1N147	0911
1N147A	0911
1N148	0143
1N149	OEM
1N150	OEM
1N151	0015
1N152	0015
1N153	0015
1N156	OEM
1N158	0015
1N160	OEM
1N169	0015
1N172	0911
1N173	0911
1N175	OEM
1N191	0143
1N192	0143
1N194	0133
1N194A	0133
1N194B	0133
1N195	0133
1N196	0133
1N197B	OEM
1N198	0143
1N198A	0143
1N198B	0143
1N198N	0143
1N200	0133
1N200AR	0133
1N201	0133
1N202	0133
1N203	0133
1N204	0133
1N205	0133
1N206	0133
1N207	0133
1N208	0133
1N209	0133
1N210	0133
1N211	0133
1N212	0133
1N213	0133
1N214	0133
1N215	0133
1N216	0133
1N217	0133
1N218	0133
1N219	0790
1N220	0790
1N221	0790
1N222	0790
1N225	0318
1N225A	0318
1N226	0064
1N226A	0064
1N227	0053
1N227A	0053
1N228	0440
1N228A	0440
1N229	0666
1N229A	0666
1N230	0489
1N230A	0489
1N231	0257
1N231A	0257
1N232	0010
1N232A	0010
1N233	0054
1N233A	0054
1N234	0068
1N234A	0068
1N235	2301
1N235A	2301
1N236	OEM
1N237	0104
1N237A	0104
1N238	OEM
1N239	0285
1N248	3160
1N248A	3160
1N248AR	1620
1N248B	3160
1N248BR	1620
1N248C	1116
1N248CR	1620
1N248R	1620
1N248RA	1620
1N248RB	1620
1N248RC	1620
1N249	1116

DEVICE TYPE	REPL CODE
1N249A	2873
1N249AR	0254
1N249B	2873
1N249BR	0254
1N249C	2873
1N249CR	0254
1N249R	1099
1N249RA	0254
1N249RB	0254
1N249RC	0254
1N250	1241
1N250A	1116
1N250AR	1099
1N250B	1116
1N250BR	1099
1N250C	0800
1N250CR	1099
1N250R	1567
1N250RA	1099
1N250RB	1099
1N250RC	0258
1N251	0133
1N251A	0133
1N252	0133
1N252A	0133
1N253	0575
1N253R	2275
1N254	0575
1N254R	OEM
1N255	0994
1N255R	0471
1N256	2070
1N256R	0471
1N258	OEM
1N263	0911
1N265	0143
1N266	0143
1N267	0143
1N268	0143
1N270	0143
1N273	0143
1N276	0023
1N277	0143
1N278	0143
1N279	0143
1N281	0143
1N282	0143
1N283	0143
1N285	0143
1N286	OEM
1N286A	OEM
1N287	0143
1N288	0143
1N289	0143
1N290	0143
1N291	0143
1N292	0143
1N294	0143
1N294A	0143
1N295	0143
1N295A	0143
1N295S	0143
1N295X	0143
1N296	0143
1N297	0143
1N297A	0143
1N298	0143
1N298A	0143
1N299	0911
1N300	0133
1N300A	0133
1N300B	0133
1N301	0133
1N301A	0133
1N301B	0133
1N302	0133
1N302A	0133
1N302B	0133
1N303	0133
1N303A	0133
1N303B	0133
1N304	0143
1N305	0143
1N306	0143
1N307	0143
1N308	0143
1N309	0143
1N310	0143
1N312	0143
1N313	0143
1N314	0143
1N315	0015
1N315A	0015
1N316	0015
1N316A	0015
1N317	0015
1N317A	0015
1N318	0015
1N318A	0015
1N319	0015
1N319A	0015
1N320	0015
1N320A	0015
1N321	0071
1N321A	0071
1N322	0071
1N322A	0071
1N323	0015
1N323A	0015

DEVICE TYPE	REPL CODE
1N324	0015
1N324A	0015
1N325	0015
1N325A	0015
1N326	0015
1N326A	0015
1N326B	OEM
1N327	0015
1N327A	0015
1N328	0071
1N328A	0071
1N329	0071
1N329A	0071
1N330	0133
1N331	0133
1N332	0994
1N332R	1006
1N333	0994
1N333R	1006
1N334	2049
1N334R	4443
1N335	0994
1N335R	4443
1N336	0575
1N336R	0941
1N337	0575
1N337R	0941
1N338	0575
1N338R	5420
1N339	0575
1N339R	5420
1N340	0575
1N340R	5420
1N341	0994
1N341R	1006
1N342	0994
1N342R	1006
1N343	0994
1N343R	4443
1N344	0994
1N344R	4443
1N345	0575
1N345R	0941
1N346	0575
1N346R	0941
1N347	0575
1N347R	5420
1N348	0575
1N348R	5420
1N349	0575
1N349R	5420
1N350	0133
1N351	0133
1N352	0133
1N353	0133
1N354	0790
1N355	0143
1N358	OEM
1N358A	OEM
1N359	0015
1N359A	0015
1N360	0015
1N360A	0015
1N361	0015
1N361A	0015
1N362	0015
1N362A	0015
1N363	0015
1N363A	0015
1N364	0071
1N364A	0071
1N365	0071
1N365A	0071
1N367	0143
1N367B	0143
1N368	0015
1N369	OEM
1N369A	OEM
1N370	OEM
1N371	1266
1N372	1703
1N373	0188
1N374	0274
1N375	0274
1N376	0162
1N377	0298
1N378	0062
1N379	0133
1N380	0133
1N381	0133
1N382	0133
1N383	0133
1N384	0133
1N385	0133
1N386	0133
1N387	0133
1N388	0133
1N389	0133
1N390	0133
1N391	0133
1N392	0133
1N393	0133
1N394	0133
1N400	0071
1N400B	0015
1N411B	0594
1N411RB	1337
1N412B	0594
1N412RB	1337

DEVICE TYPE	REPL CODE
1N413B	0594
1N413RB	1337
1N415B	1107
1N415C	1107
1N415D	0046
1N415E	0046
1N415F	OEM
1N415G	OEM
1N415H	OEM
1N416B	0911
1N416C	1105
1N416D	0601
1N416E	0601
1N416F	OEM
1N416G	OEM
1N417	0143
1N417SA	0814
1N418	0143
1N419	0143
1N422A	OEM
1N429	0466
1N430	0165
1N430A	0165
1N430B	0165
1N431	0133
1N432	0133
1N432A	0133
1N432B	0133
1N433	0133
1N433A	0133
1N433B	0133
1N434	0133
1N434A	0133
1N434B	0133
1N435	0143
1N440	0015
1N440B	0015
1N441	0015
1N441A	0526
1N441B	0015
1N442	0015
1N442B	0015
1N443	0015
1N443B	0015
1N444	0015
1N444B	0015
1N445	0015
1N445B	0015
1N446	0143
1N447	0143
1N447A	OEM
1N448	0143
1N449	0143
1N450	0143
1N451	0143
1N452	0143
1N453	0143
1N454	0143
1N455	0143
1N456	0133
1N456A	0133
1N456AM	OEM
1N457	0133
1N457A	0133
1N457AM	0080
1N457M	0133
1N458	0133
1N458A	0133
1N458AM	0133
1N458M	0133
1N459	0133
1N459A	0133
1N459M	0133
1N460	0133
1N460A	0133
1N460B	0133
1N461	0133
1N461A	0133
1N461AM	OEM
1N461M	OEM
1N462	0133
1N462A	0080
1N462AM	0080
1N462M	0133
1N463	0133
1N463A	0133
1N464	0133
1N464A	0133
1N465	0755
1N465A	0755
1N465B	OEM
1N466	0372
1N466A	0372
1N466B	OEM
1N467	0036
1N467A	0036
1N467B	OEM
1N468	0140
1N468A	0140
1N468B	0582
1N469	0253
1N469A	0062
1N469B	0877
1N470	0077
1N470A	0062
1N470B	0292
1N471	0372
1N471A	0372
1N471B	OEM

DEVICE TYPE	REPL CODE
1N472	0274
1N472A	0274
1N472B	0274
1N473	0041
1N473A	0041
1N473B	0162
1N474	0091
1N474A	0091
1N474B	0091
1N475	0062
1N475A	0062
1N475B	0062
1N476	0143
1N477	0143
1N478	0143
1N479	0143
1N480	0143
1N480B	0015
1N481A	OEM
1N482	0133
1N482A	0133
1N482AM	0133
1N482B	0133
1N482BM	0133
1N482C	0133
1N482M	0133
1N482TH	0015
1N483	0133
1N483A	0133
1N483AM	0133
1N483B	0133
1N483BM	0133
1N483C	0133
1N483M	0080
1N483TH	0015
1N484	0133
1N484A	0133
1N484B	0133
1N484C	0133
1N484TH	0015
1N485	0133
1N485A	0133
1N485B	0133
1N485C	0133
1N485TH	0015
1N486	0133
1N486A	0133
1N486B	0133
1N486TH	0015
1N487	0102
1N487A	0102
1N487B	0102
1N487TH	0015
1N488	0102
1N488A	0102
1N488B	0102
1N488TH	0015
1N490	0143
1N492	0789
1N493	0789
1N497	0143
1N498	0143
1N499	0143
1N500	0143
1N501	0143
1N502	OEM
1N503	0015
1N504	0015
1N505	0015
1N506	0015
1N507	0015
1N508	0015
1N509	0071
1N510	0071
1N511	0015
1N512	0015
1N513	0015
1N514	0015
1N515	0015
1N516	0015
1N517	0071
1N518	0071
1N519	0015
1N520	0015
1N521	0015
1N522	0015
1N523	0015
1N524	0015
1N525	0071
1N526	0071
1N527	0143
1N530	0015
1N531	0015
1N532	0015
1N533	0015
1N534	0015
1N535	0015
1N536	0015
1N536ARL	OEM
1N537	0015
1N538	0015
1N539	0015
1N540	0015
1N541	0123
1N542	0143
1N542A	0143
1N542MP	0143
1N543	0102
1N543A	0102

DEVICE TYPE	REPL CODE
1N547	0015
1N547A	OEM
1N548	0071
1N549	0102
1N550	4077
1N550R	5420
1N551	0575
1N551R	0941
1N552	2049
1N552R	4443
1N553	0994
1N553R	1006
1N554	2065
1N554R	5467
1N555	2070
1N555R	1067
1N560	0071
1N561	0071
1N562	2077
1N562R	1130
1N563	0607
1N563R	1180
1N564	0143
1N566	OEM
1N567	OEM
1N568	0143
1N569	0143
1N570	2077
1N571	0143
1N580A	OEM
1N588	0017
1N589	0017
1N590	OEM
1N591	OEM
1N596	0015
1N597	0071
1N598	0071
1N599	0015
1N599A	0015
1N600	0015
1N600A	0015
1N600KB	0133
1N601	0015
1N601A	0015
1N601S34	0143
1N602	0015
1N602A	0015
1N603	0015
1N603A	0015
1N604	0015
1N604A	0015
1N605	0015
1N605A	0015
1N606	0015
1N606A	0015
1N607	0703
1N607A	0703
1N607R	2275
1N608	0575
1N608A	0575
1N608R	2275
1N609	0575
1N609A	0575
1N609R	2275
1N610	0575
1N610A	0575
1N610R	2275
1N611	0941
1N611A	0941
1N611R	0471
1N612	0994
1N612A	0994
1N612R	0471
1N613	2065
1N613A	2065
1N613R	0471
1N614	2070
1N614A	2070
1N614R	0471
1N616	0143
1N617	0143
1N618	0143
1N619	0133
1N619M	OEM
1N622	0133
1N625	0133
1N625A	0133
1N625M	0133
1N626	0133
1N626A	0133
1N626M	0133
1N627	0133
1N627A	0133
1N628	0133
1N628A	0133
1N629	0133
1N629A	0133
1N630	OEM
1N630A	OEM
1N631	0143
1N632	0143
1N633	0133
1N634	OEM
1N635	OEM
1N636	0143
1N636A	0143
1N643	0133
1N643A	0133
1N645	0015

DEVICE TYPE	REPL CODE
1N645-1	0015
1N645A	0790
1N645B	0790
1N645J	0790
1N645TH	0015
1N646	0015
1N646TH	0015
1N647	0015
1N647-1	0015
1N647TH	0015
1N648	0015
1N648TH	0015
1N649	0015
1N649-1	0015
1N649TH	0015
1N658	0133
1N658A	0133
1N658M	0133
1N659	0133
1N659/A	0133
1N659A	0133
1N659AM	OEM
1N659M	OEM
1N660	0133
1N660A	0133
1N661	0133
1N661A	0133
1N662	0133
1N662A	0133
1N663	0133
1N663A	0133
1N663M	0133
1N664	0165
1N665	0052
1N666	0681
1N667	0371
1N668	0700
1N669	0436
1N670	0173
1N671	0189
1N672	0336
1N673	0015
1N674	0140
1N675	0466
1N676	0015
1N677	0015
1N678	0015
1N679	0015
1N681	0015
1N682	0015
1N683	0015
1N684	0015
1N685	0015
1N686	0015
1N687	0015
1N689	0015
1N690	0133
1N691	0133
1N692	0133
1N693	0133
1N695	0143
1N695A	0143
1N696	0133
1N697	0133
1N698	0143
1N699	0143
1N701	0064
1N702	0755
1N702A	0755
1N702A0	OEM
1N702A1	OEM
1N702A3	OEM
1N702A4	OEM
1N702A5	OEM
1N702A7	OEM
1N702A8	OEM
1N702A9	OEM
1N703	0372
1N703A	0372
1N703A0	OEM
1N703A1	OEM
1N703A3	OEM
1N703A4	OEM
1N703A5	OEM
1N703A6	OEM
1N704	0036
1N704A	0036
1N704A1	OEM
1N704A2	OEM
1N704A3	OEM
1N704A4	OEM
1N704A5	OEM
1N705	0140
1N705A	0140
1N705A0	OEM
1N705A1	OEM
1N705A2	OEM
1N705A4	OEM
1N705A5	OEM
1N705A6	OEM
1N705A7	OEM
1N705A8	OEM
1N706	0091
1N706A	0091
1N706A1	OEM
1N706A4	OEM
1N706A6	OEM
1N706A8	OEM
1N706A9	OEM

If replacement code is OEM, contact original manufacturer for replacement.

DEVICE TYPE	REPL CODE
1N707	0062
1N707A	0062
1N707A0	OEM
1N707A2	OEM
1N707A3	OEM
1N707A6	OEM
1N708	0253
1N708A	0253
1N708B	0253
1N709	0466
1N709A	0466
1N709B	0466
1N710	0062
1N710A	0062
1N710B	0062
1N711	0077
1N711A	0077
1N711B	0099
1N712	0165
1N712A	0165
1N712B	0165
1N713	0057
1N713A	0057
1N713B	0057
1N714	0064
1N714A	0064
1N714B	0064
1N715	0181
1N715A	0181
1N715B	0181
1N716	0052
1N716A	0052
1N716B	0137
1N717	0053
1N717A	0053
1N717B	0053
1N718	0681
1N718A	0681
1N718B	0002
1N719	0440
1N719A	0440
1N719B	0440
1N720	0371
1N720A	0371
1N720B	0371
1N721	0695
1N721A	0695
1N721B	0695
1N722	0700
1N722A	0700
1N722B	0700
1N723	0489
1N723A	0489
1N723B	0489
1N724	0450
1N724A	0450
1N724B	0436
1N725	0195
1N725A	0195
1N725B	0195
1N726	0166
1N726A	0166
1N726B	0166
1N727	0010
1N727A	0010
1N727B	0814
1N728	0032
1N728A	0032
1N728B	0032
1N729	0054
1N729A	0054
1N729B	0054
1N729RL	OEM
1N730	0068
1N730A	0068
1N730B	0068
1N731	0092
1N731A	0092
1N731B	0092
1N732	0125
1N732A	0125
1N732B	0125
1N733	0778
1N733A	0152
1N733B	0152
1N734	0173
1N734A	0173
1N734B	0173
1N735	0094
1N735A	0094
1N735B	0094
1N736	0327
1N736A	0049
1N736B	0049
1N737	0156
1N737A	0156
1N737B	0156
1N738	0189
1N738A	0189
1N738B	0189
1N739	0149
1N739A	0099
1N739B	0099
1N740	0089
1N740A	0089
1N740B	0089
1N741	0285
1N741A	0285
1N741B	0336

DEVICE TYPE	REPL CODE
1N742	0336
1N742A	0336
1N742B	0336
1N743	0366
1N743A	0366
1N743B	0366
1N744	0420
1N744A	0420
1N744B	0420
1N745	1464
1N745A	1464
1N745B	1464
1N745N	OEM
1N746	0296
1N746A	0296
1N746RL	OEM
1N747	0372
1N747A	0372
1N747B	0188
1N747RL	OEM
1N748	0036
1N748A	0036
1N748RL	OEM
1N749	0274
1N749A	0274
1N749ARL	OEM
1N749RL	OEM
1N750	0140
1N750A	0140
1N750ARL	OEM
1N750RL	OEM
1N751	0041
1N751A	0041
1N751ARL	OEM
1N751RL	OEM
1N752	0253
1N752A	0253
1N752ARL	OEM
1N752RL	OEM
1N753	0466
1N753A	0466
1N753ARL	OEM
1N753D	OEM
1N753RL	OEM
1N754	0062
1N754A	0062
1N754ARL	OEM
1N754RL	OEM
1N755	0077
1N755A	0077
1N755ARL	OEM
1N755RL	OEM
1N756	0165
1N756A	0165
1N756ARL	OEM
1N756RL	OEM
1N757	0057
1N757A	0057
1N757ARL	OEM
1N757RL	OEM
1N758	0064
1N758A	0064
1N758ARL	OEM
1N758RL	OEM
1N759	0052
1N759A	0052
1N759ARL	OEM
1N759RL	OEM
1N760	0133
1N761	0140
1N761-1	0140
1N761-2	0041
1N761A	0162
1N762	0091
1N762-1	0253
1N762-2	0091
1N762A	0157
1N763	0077
1N763-1	0062
1N763-2	0062
1N763-3	0077
1N763A	0077
1N764	0318
1N764-1	0165
1N764-2	0318
1N764-3	0057
1N764-4	0057
1N764A	0318
1N765	0181
1N765-1	0064
1N765-2	0181
1N765A	0064
1N766	0053
1N766-1	0052
1N766-2	0053
1N766-3	0100
1N766A	0361
1N767	0440
1N767-1	0681
1N767-2	0440
1N767-3	0210
1N767-22	0440
1N767A	0440
1N768	0666
1N768-1	0371
1N768-2	0666
1N768-3	0695
1N768A	0666
1N769	0489

DEVICE TYPE	REPL CODE
1N769-1	0700
1N769-2	0489
1N769-3	0450
1N769-4	0257
1N769A	0489
1N770	0143
1N771	0143
1N771A	0143
1N771B	0143
1N772	0133
1N772A	0143
1N773	0143
1N773A	0143
1N774	0143
1N774A	0143
1N775	0143
1N776	0143
1N777	0143
1N778	0133
1N779	0133
1N781	0143
1N781A	0143
1N788	0133
1N789	0133
1N789M	0133
1N790	0133
1N790M	0133
1N791	0133
1N791M	0133
1N792	0133
1N792M	0133
1N793	0133
1N793M	0133
1N794	0133
1N794M	OEM
1N795	0133
1N795M	OEM
1N796	0133
1N796M	OEM
1N797	0133
1N798	0133
1N799	0133
1N800	0133
1N801	0133
1N802	0133
1N803	0133
1N804	0133
1N805	0143
1N806	0133
1N807	0133
1N808	0133
1N809	0133
1N810	0133
1N811	0133
1N811M	0133
1N812	0133
1N812M	0133
1N813	0133
1N813M	0133
1N814	0133
1N814M	0133
1N815	0133
1N815M	0133
1N816	0133
1N817	0133
1N818	0133
1N818M	0133
1N819	0015
1N821	0466
1N821-1	OEM
1N821A	0466
1N821A1	OEM
1N821ARL	OEM
1N821RL	OEM
1N822	0466
1N822A	0466
1N822AG	0466
1N823	0466
1N823-1	OEM
1N823A	0466
1N823A1	OEM
1N823ARL	OEM
1N823RL	OEM
1N824	0466
1N824A	0466
1N825	0466
1N825-1	OEM
1N825A	0466
1N825A1	OEM
1N825ARL	OEM
1N825RL	OEM
1N826	0062
1N826A	0062
1N827	0466
1N827-1	OEM
1N827A	0466
1N827A1	OEM
1N827ARL	OEM
1N827RL	OEM
1N828	0062
1N828A	0062
1N829	0466
1N829-1	OEM
1N829A	0466
1N829A1	OEM
1N829ARL	OEM
1N829RL	OEM
1N830	OEM
1N830A	OEM

DEVICE TYPE	REPL CODE
1N831	OEM
1N831A	OEM
1N831B	OEM
1N831C	OEM
1N832	OEM
1N832A	OEM
1N832B	OEM
1N832C	OEM
1N832D	OEM
1N833	OEM
1N833A	OEM
1N835	0143
1N837	0133
1N837A	0133
1N838	0133
1N839	0133
1N840	0133
1N840M	0133
1N841	0133
1N842	0133
1N843	0133
1N844	0133
1N845	0133
1N846	0015
1N847	0015
1N848	0015
1N849	0015
1N850	0015
1N851	0015
1N852	0015
1N853	0071
1N854	0071
1N855	0071
1N856	0071
1N857	0015
1N858	0015
1N859	0015
1N860	0015
1N861	0015
1N862	0015
1N863	0015
1N864	0071
1N865	0071
1N866	0071
1N867	0071
1N868	0015
1N869	0015
1N870	0015
1N871	0015
1N872	0015
1N873	0015
1N874	0015
1N875	0071
1N876	0071
1N877	0071
1N878	0071
1N879	0015
1N880	0015
1N881	0015
1N881B	0015
1N882	0015
1N883	0015
1N884	0015
1N885	0015
1N886	0071
1N887	0071
1N888	0071
1N889	0071
1N890	0133
1N890M	0133
1N891	0133
1N891M	OEM
1N892	0133
1N893	0102
1N894	OEM
1N897	0133
1N898	0133
1N899	0133
1N900	0133
1N901	0133
1N902	0133
1N903	0133
1N903/A	0133
1N903A	0133
1N903AM	0133
1N903M	0133
1N904	0133
1N904/A	0133
1N904A	0133
1N904AM	0133
1N904M	0133
1N905	0133
1N905/A	0133
1N905A	0133
1N905AM	0133
1N905M	0133
1N906	0133
1N906/A	0133
1N906A	0133
1N906AM	0133
1N906M	0133
1N907	0133
1N907/A	0133
1N907A	0133
1N907AM	0133
1N907M	0133
1N908	0133
1N908/A	0133
1N908A	0133

DEVICE TYPE	REPL CODE
1N908AM	0133
1N908M	0133
1N909	0143
1N910	0143
1N911	0143
1N912	OEM
1N912A	OEM
1N913	OEM
1N913A	OEM
1N914	0124
1N914/A/B	0124
1N914A	0124
1N914B	0124
1N914F	0133
1N914M	0124
1N915	0133
1N916	0124
1N916A	0133
1N916B	0133
1N917	0133
1N918	OEM
1N919	0133
1N920	0133
1N921	0133
1N922	0133
1N923	0133
1N924	0133
1N925	0133
1N926	0133
1N927	0133
1N928	0133
1N929	0133
1N930	0133
1N931	0133
1N932	0133
1N933	0133
1N934	0133
1N935	0057
1N935-1	OEM
1N935A1	OEM
1N935ARL	OEM
1N935B1	OEM
1N935BRL	OEM
1N935RL	OEM
1N936	0057
1N936A	0057
1N936ARL	OEM
1N936B	0057
1N936BRL	OEM
1N936RL	OEM
1N937	0057
1N937-1	OEM
1N937A	0057
1N937A1	OEM
1N937ARL	OEM
1N937B	0057
1N937B1	OEM
1N937BRL	OEM
1N937RL	OEM
1N938	0057
1N938-1	OEM
1N938A	0057
1N938A1	OEM
1N938B	0057
1N938B1	OEM
1N939	0057
1N939A	0057
1N939ARL	OEM
1N939B	0057
1N939BRL	OEM
1N939RL	OEM
1N940	0057
1N940A	0057
1N940B	0057
1N941	0789
1N941-1	OEM
1N941A	0789
1N941A1	OEM
1N941ARL	OEM
1N941B	0789
1N941B1	OEM
1N941RL	OEM
1N942	0789
1N942A	0137
1N942B	0137
1N942BRL	OEM
1N942RL	OEM
1N943	0137
1N943-1	OEM
1N943A	0137
1N943A1	OEM
1N943ARL	OEM
1N943B	0137
1N943B1	OEM
1N943BRL	OEM
1N943RL	OEM
1N944	0137
1N944-1	OEM
1N944A	0137
1N944A1	OEM
1N944ARL	OEM
1N944B	0137
1N944B1	OEM
1N944BRL	OEM
1N944RL	OEM
1N945	0789
1N945-1	OEM
1N945A	0789
1N945A1	OEM

DEVICE TYPE	REPL CODE
1N945B	0789
1N945B1	OEM
1N946	0789
1N946A	0789
1N946B	0789
1N947	0015
1N948	0133
1N949	0143
1N950	OEM
1N950A	OEM
1N950B	OEM
1N951	0064
1N951A	0064
1N951B	OEM
1N952	OEM
1N952A	OEM
1N952B	OEM
1N953	OEM
1N953A	OEM
1N953B	OEM
1N954	0030
1N954A	OEM
1N954B	OEM
1N955	OEM
1N955A	OEM
1N955B	OEM
1N956	OEM
1N956A	OEM
1N956B	OEM
1N957	0062
1N957A	0062
1N957ARL	OEM
1N957B	0062
1N957BRL	OEM
1N958	0077
1N958A	0077
1N958ARL	OEM
1N958B	0077
1N958BRL	OEM
1N959	0165
1N959A	0165
1N959ARL	OEM
1N959B	0165
1N959BRL	OEM
1N960	0057
1N960A	0057
1N960ARL	OEM
1N960B	0057
1N960BRL	OEM
1N961	0170
1N961A	0064
1N961ARL	OEM
1N961B	0064
1N961BRL	OEM
1N962	0181
1N962A	0181
1N962ARL	OEM
1N962B	0181
1N962BRL	OEM
1N963	0052
1N963A	0052
1N963ARL	OEM
1N963B	0052
1N963BRL	OEM
1N964	0053
1N964A	0053
1N964ARL	OEM
1N964B	0053
1N964B-F	0361
1N964BRL	OEM
1N965	0681
1N965A	0681
1N965ARL	OEM
1N965B	0681
1N965BRL	OEM
1N966	0440
1N966A	0440
1N966ARL	OEM
1N966B	0440
1N966B-F	0440
1N966BRL	OEM
1N967	0371
1N967A	0371
1N967ARL	OEM
1N967B	0371
1N967B-F	0490
1N967BRL	OEM
1N968	0695
1N968A	0695
1N968ARL	OEM
1N968B	0695
1N968B-F	0695
1N968BRL	OEM
1N969	0700
1N969A	0700
1N969ARL	OEM
1N969B	0560
1N969BRL	OEM
1N970	0489
1N970A	0489
1N970ARL	OEM
1N970B	0489
1N970BRL	OEM
1N971	0450
1N971A	0450
1N971ARL	OEM
1N971B	0450
1N971BRL	OEM
1N972	0195

DEVICE TYPE	REPL CODE
1N972A	0195
1N972ARL	OEM
1N972B	0195
1N972B-F	0721
1N972BRL	OEM
1N973	0166
1N973A	0166
1N973ARL	OEM
1N973B	0166
1N973BRL	OEM
1N974	0010
1N974A	0010
1N974ARL	OEM
1N974B	0010
1N974BRL	OEM
1N975	0032
1N975A	0032
1N975ARL	OEM
1N975B	0032
1N975BRL	OEM
1N976	0054
1N976A	0054
1N976ARL	OEM
1N976B	0054
1N976BRL	OEM
1N977	0068
1N977A	0068
1N977ARL	OEM
1N977B	0068
1N977BRL	OEM
1N978	0092
1N978A	0092
1N978ARL	OEM
1N978B	0092
1N978BRL	OEM
1N979	0125
1N979A	0125
1N979ARL	OEM
1N979B	0125
1N979BRL	OEM
1N980	0152
1N980A	0152
1N980ARL	OEM
1N980B	0152
1N980BRL	OEM
1N981	0173
1N981A	0173
1N981ARL	OEM
1N981B	0173
1N981BRL	OEM
1N982	0094
1N982A	0094
1N982ARL	OEM
1N982B	0094
1N982BRL	OEM
1N983	0049
1N983A	0049
1N983ARL	OEM
1N983B	0049
1N983BRL	OEM
1N984	0156
1N984A	0156
1N984ARL	OEM
1N984B	0156
1N984BRL	OEM
1N985	0189
1N985A	0189
1N985ARL	OEM
1N985B	0189
1N985BRL	OEM
1N986	0099
1N986A	0099
1N986ARL	OEM
1N986B	0099
1N987	0089
1N987A	0089
1N987ARL	OEM
1N987B	0089
1N987BRL	OEM
1N988	0285
1N988A	0285
1N988ARL	OEM
1N988B	0285
1N988BRL	OEM
1N989	0336
1N989A	0336
1N989ARL	OEM
1N989B	0336
1N989BRL	OEM
1N990	0366
1N990A	0366
1N990ARL	OEM
1N990B	0366
1N990BRL	OEM
1N991	0420
1N991A	0420
1N991ARL	OEM
1N991B	0420
1N991BRL	OEM
1N992	1464
1N992A	1464
1N992ARL	OEM
1N992B	1464
1N992BRL	OEM
1N993	0133
1N994	0143
1N995	0143
1N995M	0143
1N996	0143

If replacement code is OEM, contact original manufacturer for replacement.

15

DEVICE TYPE	REPL CODE
1N997	0133
1N998	0015
1N999	0133
1N1008	0015
1N1028	0015
1N1029	0015
1N1030	0015
1N1031	0015
1N1032	0015
1N1033	0015
1N1034	0703
1N1035	5420
1N1036	0941
1N1037	0941
1N1038	4443
1N1039	1006
1N1040	0927
1N1041	5420
1N1042	0941
1N1043	0941
1N1044	4443
1N1045	1006
1N1046	0927
1N1047	5420
1N1048	0941
1N1049	0941
1N1050	4443
1N1051	1006
1N1052	0015
1N1053	0015
1N1054	0071
1N1055	0071
1N1056	0087
1N1057	0087
1N1058	0979
1N1059	0904
1N1060	0984
1N1061	0984
1N1062	0987
1N1063	0991
1N1064	0979
1N1064R	2275
1N1065	0904
1N1065R	2275
1N1066	0983
1N1066R	2275
1N1067	0983
1N1067R	2275
1N1068	3697
1N1068R	0471
1N1069	0991
1N1069R	0471
1N1070	0979
1N1071	0904
1N1072	0984
1N1073	0984
1N1074	0987
1N1075	0991
1N1076	4917
1N1077	1231
1N1078	1241
1N1079	1232
1N1080	3244
1N1081	0015
1N1081A	0015
1N1082	0015
1N1082A	0015
1N1083	0015
1N1083A	0015
1N1083C	OEM
1N1084	0015
1N1084A	0015
1N1085	OEM
1N1085A	OEM
1N1086	OEM
1N1086A	OEM
1N1087	OEM
1N1087A	OEM
1N1088	OEM
1N1088A	OEM
1N1089	OEM
1N1089A	OEM
1N1090	OEM
1N1090A	OEM
1N1091	OEM
1N1091A	OEM
1N1092	OEM
1N1092A	OEM
1N1093	0143
1N1095	0015
1N1096	0015
1N1100	0015
1N1101	0015
1N1102	0015
1N1103	0015
1N1104	0015
1N1104R	0015
1N1105	0015
1N1108	0071
1N1109	OEM
1N1110	OEM
1N1111	OEM
1N1112	OEM
1N1113	OEM
1N1115	0575
1N1115R	2275
1N1116	0575
1N1116R	2275
1N1117	2049

DEVICE TYPE	REPL CODE
1N1117R	0471
1N1118	0994
1N1118R	0471
1N1119	2065
1N1119R	0471
1N1120	2070
1N1120R	0471
1N1122A	0015
1N1124	0575
1N1124A	0983
1N1124AR	0984
1N1124R	0941
1N1124RA	0471
1N1125	2049
1N1125A	3697
1N1125AR	0987
1N1125R	4443
1N1125RA	0471
1N1126	0994
1N1126A	0197
1N1126AR	0991
1N1126R	1006
1N1126RA	0471
1N1127	2065
1N1127A	0200
1N1127AR	0995
1N1127R	5467
1N1127RA	0471
1N1128	2070
1N1128A	0204
1N1128AR	0510
1N1128R	1067
1N1128RA	0444
1N1130	OEM
1N1131	OEM
1N1132	OEM
1N1133	OEM
1N1134	OEM
1N1135	OEM
1N1136	OEM
1N1137	OEM
1N1138	OEM
1N1139	OEM
1N1140	OEM
1N1141	OEM
1N1142	OEM
1N1143	OEM
1N1143A	OEM
1N1144	OEM
1N1145	OEM
1N1146	OEM
1N1147	OEM
1N1148	OEM
1N1149	OEM
1N1150	OEM
1N1150A	OEM
1N1157	OEM
1N1158	OEM
1N1159	OEM
1N1160	OEM
1N1161	OEM
1N1162	OEM
1N1163	OEM
1N1164	OEM
1N1165	OEM
1N1166	OEM
1N1167	OEM
1N1168	OEM
1N1169	0015
1N1169A	0015
1N1182	0315
1N1183	3160
1N1183A	3160
1N1183AR	1620
1N1183R	1620
1N1183RA	1620
1N1184	2873
1N1184A	2873
1N1184AR	0254
1N1184R	0254
1N1184RA	1099
1N1185	1116
1N1185A	1116
1N1185AR	1099
1N1185R	1099
1N1185RA	1099
1N1186	1116
1N1186A	1116
1N1186AR	1099
1N1186R	1099
1N1186RA	1099
1N1187	0800
1N1187A	1118
1N1187AR	1103
1N1187R	1103
1N1187RA	1103
1N1188	0800
1N1188A	0800
1N1188AR	0258
1N1188R	0258
1N1188RA	0258
1N1189	1186
1N1189A	1186
1N1189AR	1634
1N1189R	1634
1N1189RA	1634
1N1190	0315
1N1190A	0315
1N1190AR	0267

DEVICE TYPE	REPL CODE
1N1190R	0267
1N1190RA	0267
1N1191	3160
1N1191A	3160
1N1191AR	1620
1N1191R	1620
1N1191RA	1620
1N1192	2873
1N1192A	2873
1N1192AR	0254
1N1192R	0254
1N1192RA	0254
1N1193	1116
1N1193A	1116
1N1193AR	1099
1N1193R	1099
1N1193RA	1099
1N1194	1116
1N1194A	1116
1N1194AR	1099
1N1194R	1099
1N1194RA	1099
1N1195	1118
1N1195A	1118
1N1195AR	1103
1N1195R	1103
1N1195RA	0258
1N1196	0800
1N1196A	0800
1N1196AR	0258
1N1196R	0258
1N1196RA	0258
1N1197	1186
1N1197A	1186
1N1197AR	1634
1N1197R	1634
1N1197RA	0267
1N1198	0315
1N1198A	0315
1N1198AR	0267
1N1198R	0267
1N1198RA	0267
1N1199	0084
1N1199A	0084
1N1199AR	0529
1N1199B	0084
1N1199BR	0529
1N1199C	0084
1N1199R	0529
1N1199RA	0529
1N1199RB	2275
1N1199RC	0084
1N1200	0090
1N1200A	0090
1N1200AR	0743
1N1200B	0090
1N1200BR	0743
1N1200C	0575
1N1200R	0743
1N1200RA	0760
1N1200RB	2275
1N1200RC	5420
1N1201	0097
1N1201A	0097
1N1201AR	0760
1N1201B	0097
1N1201BR	0760
1N1201C	OEM
1N1201R	0760
1N1201RA	0760
1N1201RB	2275
1N1201RC	OEM
1N1202	0097
1N1202A	0097
1N1202AR	0760
1N1202B	0097
1N1202BR	0760
1N1202C	0575
1N1202R	0760
1N1202RA	0760
1N1202RB	2275
1N1202RC	0941
1N1203	0105
1N1203A	0105
1N1203AR	0772
1N1203B	0105
1N1203BR	0772
1N1203C	OEM
1N1203R	0772
1N1203RA	0772
1N1203RB	0471
1N1203RC	OEM
1N1204	0109
1N1204A	0109
1N1204AR	0533
1N1204B	0109
1N1204BR	0533
1N1204C	0994
1N1204R	0533
1N1204RA	0533
1N1204RB	0471
1N1204RC	1006
1N1205	0116
1N1205A	0116
1N1205AR	0796
1N1205B	0116
1N1205BR	0796
1N1205C	1627
1N1205R	0796

DEVICE TYPE	REPL CODE
1N1205RA	0796
1N1205RB	0471
1N1205RC	5478
1N1206	0122
1N1206A	0122
1N1206AR	0810
1N1206B	0122
1N1206BR	0810
1N1206C	2065
1N1206R	0810
1N1206RA	0810
1N1206RB	0471
1N1206RC	5467
1N1216R	OEM
1N1217	0023
1N1217A	0071
1N1217B	0071
1N1218	0071
1N1218A	0071
1N1218B	0071
1N1219	0071
1N1219A	0071
1N1219B	0071
1N1220	0242
1N1220A	0242
1N1220B	0242
1N1221	1736
1N1221A	1736
1N1221B	1736
1N1222	0535
1N1222A	0535
1N1222B	0535
1N1223	1760
1N1223A	1760
1N1223B	1760
1N1224	0959
1N1224A	0959
1N1224B	0959
1N1225	0071
1N1225A	0071
1N1225B	0087
1N1226	0071
1N1226A	0071
1N1226B	0087
1N1227	0703
1N1227A	0703
1N1227B	0703
1N1228	0575
1N1228A	0575
1N1228B	0575
1N1229	0575
1N1229A	0575
1N1229B	0575
1N1230	0575
1N1230A	0575
1N1230B	0575
1N1231	2049
1N1231A	2049
1N1231B	2049
1N1232	0994
1N1232A	0994
1N1232B	0994
1N1233	2065
1N1233A	2065
1N1233B	2065
1N1234	2070
1N1234A	2070
1N1234B	2070
1N1235	2077
1N1235A	2077
1N1235B	2077
1N1236	2077
1N1236A	2077
1N1236B	2077
1N1237	OEM
1N1238	OEM
1N1239	OEM
1N1251	0015
1N1252	0015
1N1253	0015
1N1254	0015
1N1254(WEST)	3160
1N1255	0015
1N1255(WEST)	2873
1N1255A	0015
1N1256	0015
1N1256(WEST)	1116
1N1257	0015
1N1257(WEST)	1118
1N1258	0071
1N1259	0071
1N1259(WEST)	1186
1N1260	0071
1N1260(WEST)	0315
1N1261	0071
1N1262	OEM
1N1281	OEM
1N1282	OEM
1N1283	OEM
1N1284	OEM
1N1285	OEM
1N1286	OEM
1N1287	OEM
1N1291	OEM
1N1292	OEM
1N1293	OEM
1N1294	OEM
1N1295	OEM
1N1296	OEM

DEVICE TYPE	REPL CODE
1N1297	OEM
1N1301	3160
1N1301R	2786
1N1302	2873
1N1302R	2786
1N1303	2786
1N1303R	2786
1N1304	1116
1N1304R	2786
1N1305	2786
1N1305R	2786
1N1306	1118
1N1306R	2786
1N1313	0318
1N1313A	0318
1N1314	0181
1N1314A	0181
1N1315	0053
1N1315A	0053
1N1316	0440
1N1316A	0440
1N1317	0666
1N1317A	0666
1N1318	0489
1N1318A	0489
1N1319	0257
1N1319A	0257
1N1320	0166
1N1320A	0166
1N1321	0032
1N1321A	0032
1N1322	0068
1N1322A	0068
1N1323	2301
1N1323A	2301
1N1324	0173
1N1324A	2144
1N1325	0104
1N1325A	0104
1N1326	0099
1N1326A	0149
1N1327	0285
1N1327A	0213
1N1329	OEM
1N1330	OEM
1N1331	OEM
1N1332	OEM
1N1333	OEM
1N1334	OEM
1N1335	OEM
1N1336	OEM
1N1337-5	0015
1N1341	0964
1N1341A	0964
1N1341AR	0979
1N1341B	0964
1N1341BR	0979
1N1341C	OEM
1N1341R	0979
1N1341RA	0979
1N1341RB	0979
1N1342	3688
1N1342A	3688
1N1342AR	0904
1N1342B	3688
1N1342BR	0904
1N1342C	OEM
1N1342R	0904
1N1342RA	0904
1N1342RB	0904
1N1343	0983
1N1343A	0983
1N1343AR	0984
1N1343B	0983
1N1343BR	0984
1N1343C	OEM
1N1343R	0984
1N1343RA	0984
1N1343RB	2275
1N1344	0983
1N1344A	0983
1N1344AR	0984
1N1344B	0983
1N1344BR	0984
1N1344C	OEM
1N1344R	0984
1N1344RA	0984
1N1344RB	0984
1N1345	3697
1N1345A	3697
1N1345AR	0987
1N1345B	0987
1N1345BR	0987
1N1345C	OEM
1N1345R	0987
1N1345RA	0987
1N1346	0197
1N1346A	0197
1N1346AR	0991
1N1346B	0197
1N1346BR	0991
1N1346C	OEM
1N1346R	0991
1N1346RA	0991
1N1346RB	0991
1N1347	0200
1N1347A	0200
1N1347AR	0995
1N1347B	0995

DEVICE TYPE	REPL CODE
1N1347BR	0995
1N1347C	OEM
1N1347R	0995
1N1347RA	0995
1N1347RB	0995
1N1348	0204
1N1348A	0204
1N1348AR	0510
1N1348B	0204
1N1348BR	0510
1N1348C	OEM
1N1348R	0510
1N1348RA	0510
1N1348RB	0510
1N1351	0505
1N1351A	0505
1N1351B	0505
1N1351C	0505
1N1351CA	OEM
1N1351R	0986
1N1351RA	0986
1N1351RB	0986
1N1352	0686
1N1352A	0686
1N1352B	0686
1N1352C	0686
1N1352CA	OEM
1N1352R	0989
1N1352RA	0989
1N1352RB	0989
1N1353	0864
1N1353A	0864
1N1353B	0864
1N1353C	0864
1N1353CA	OEM
1N1353R	1254
1N1353RA	1254
1N1353RB	1254
1N1354	1014
1N1354A	1014
1N1354B	1014
1N1354C	1014
1N1354CA	OEM
1N1354R	1240
1N1354RA	1240
1N1354RB	1240
1N1355	1264
1N1355A	1264
1N1355B	1264
1N1355C	1264
1N1355CA	OEM
1N1355R	1629
1N1355RA	1629
1N1355RB	1629
1N1356	1392
1N1356A	1392
1N1356B	1392
1N1356C	1392
1N1356CA	OEM
1N1356R	1693
1N1356RA	1693
1N1356RB	1693
1N1357	1071
1N1357A	1071
1N1357B	1071
1N1357C	OEM
1N1357CA	OEM
1N1357R	1706
1N1357RA	1706
1N1357RB	1706
1N1358	1707
1N1358A	1707
1N1358B	1707
1N1358C	OEM
1N1358CA	OEM
1N1358R	1720
1N1358RA	1720
1N1358RB	1720
1N1359	1712
1N1359A	1712
1N1359B	1712
1N1359C	OEM
1N1359CA	OEM
1N1359R	0722
1N1359RA	0722
1N1359RB	0722
1N1360	1725
1N1360A	1725
1N1360B	1725
1N1360C	OEM
1N1360CA	OEM
1N1360R	1745
1N1360RA	1745
1N1360RB	1745
1N1361	1750
1N1361A	1750
1N1361B	1750
1N1361C	1771
1N1361CA	OEM
1N1361R	1771
1N1361RA	1771
1N1361RB	1771
1N1361RC	1771
1N1362	1761
1N1362A	1761
1N1362B	1761
1N1362C	OEM
1N1362CA	OEM
1N1362R	1783

DEVICE TYPE	REPL CODE
1N1362RA	1783
1N1362RB	1783
1N1363	1777
1N1363A	1777
1N1363B	1777
1N1363C	OEM
1N1363CA	OEM
1N1363R	1788
1N1363RA	1788
1N1363RB	1788
1N1364	1785
1N1364A	1785
1N1364B	1785
1N1364C	OEM
1N1364CA	OEM
1N1364R	1798
1N1364RA	1798
1N1364RB	1798
1N1365	1793
1N1365A	1793
1N1365B	1793
1N1365C	OEM
1N1365CA	OEM
1N1365R	1806
1N1365RA	1806
1N1365RB	1806
1N1366	1185
1N1366A	1185
1N1366B	1185
1N1366C	OEM
1N1366CA	OEM
1N1366R	1815
1N1366RA	1815
1N1366RB	1815
1N1367	0022
1N1367A	0022
1N1367B	0022
1N1367C	OEM
1N1367CA	OEM
1N1367R	1842
1N1367RA	1842
1N1367RB	1842
1N1368	0132
1N1368A	0132
1N1368B	0132
1N1368C	OEM
1N1368CA	OEM
1N1368R	1855
1N1368RA	1855
1N1368RB	1855
1N1369	0207
1N1369A	0207
1N1369B	0207
1N1369C	OEM
1N1369CA	OEM
1N1369R	1873
1N1369RA	1873
1N1369RB	1873
1N1370	0263
1N1370A	0263
1N1370B	0263
1N1370C	OEM
1N1370CA	OEM
1N1370R	1884
1N1370RA	1884
1N1370RB	1884
1N1371	0306
1N1371A	0306
1N1371B	0306
1N1371C	OEM
1N1371CA	OEM
1N1371R	1891
1N1371RA	1891
1N1371RB	1891
1N1372	0325
1N1372A	0325
1N1372B	0325
1N1372C	OEM
1N1372CA	OEM
1N1372R	0731
1N1372RA	0731
1N1372RB	0731
1N1373	0352
1N1373A	0352
1N1373B	0352
1N1373C	OEM
1N1373CA	OEM
1N1373R	1898
1N1373RA	1898
1N1373RB	1898
1N1374	0408
1N1374A	0408
1N1374B	0408
1N1374C	OEM
1N1374CA	OEM
1N1374R	1903
1N1374RA	1903
1N1374RB	1903
1N1375	0433
1N1375A	0433
1N1375B	0433
1N1375C	OEM
1N1375CA	OEM
1N1375R	1155
1N1375RA	1155
1N1375RB	1155
1N1376	OEM
1N1377	OEM
1N1378	OEM

If replacement code is OEM, contact original manufacturer for replacement.

DEVICE TYPE	REPL CODE
1N1379	OEM
1N1380	OEM
1N1381	OEM
1N1382	OEM
1N1391	0143
1N1396	1551
1N1396R	1337
1N1397	0594
1N1397R	1337
1N1398	0594
1N1398R	1337
1N1399	2633
1N1399R	1337
1N1400	0594
1N1400R	1337
1N1401	2823
1N1401R	1894
1N1402	1975
1N1402R	1894
1N1403	1975
1N1403R	1894
1N1406	0015
1N1407	0071
1N1408	0071
1N1409	0102
1N1410	0182
1N1411	0344
1N1412	0344
1N1413	OEM
1N1415	0015
1N1416	1481
1N1416R	1612
1N1417	0864
1N1417R	1254
1N1418	1264
1N1418R	1629
1N1419	1071
1N1419R	1706
1N1420	1712
1N1420R	0722
1N1421	1750
1N1421R	1771
1N1422	0306
1N1422R	1891
1N1423	0433
1N1423R	1155
1N1424	0063
1N1424R	1950
1N1425	0244
1N1426	0137
1N1427	0002
1N1428	0490
1N1429	0560
1N1430	0436
1N1431	1258
1N1432	0098
1N1433	0028
1N1434	3160
1N1434R	0315
1N1435	2873
1N1435R	0315
1N1436	1116
1N1436R	0315
1N1437	0800
1N1437R	0315
1N1438	0315
1N1438R	0315
1N1439	0015
1N1440	0015
1N1441	0015
1N1442	0015
1N1443	0071
1N1443A	0071
1N1443B	0071
1N1444	0607
1N1444A	0607
1N1444B	0607
1N1446	0575
1N1447	0575
1N1448	2049
1N1449	0994
1N1450	0575
1N1451	0575
1N1452	2049
1N1453	0994
1N1454	OEM
1N1455	OEM
1N1456	OEM
1N1457	OEM
1N1458	OEM
1N1459	OEM
1N1460	OEM
1N1461	OEM
1N1462	OEM
1N1463	OEM
1N1464	OEM
1N1465	OEM
1N1466	OEM
1N1467	OEM
1N1468	OEM
1N1469	OEM
1N1470	OEM
1N1471	OEM
1N1472	OEM
1N1473	OEM
1N1474	OEM
1N1475	OEM
1N1476	OEM
1N1477	OEM

DEVICE TYPE	REPL CODE
1N1478	OEM
1N1479	OEM
1N1480	OEM
1N1481	OEM
1N1482	1429
1N1482R	2101
1N1483	2206
1N1483R	0691
1N1484	0446
1N1485	0631
1N1486	0015
1N1487	0015
1N1488	0015
1N1489	0015
1N1490	0015
1N1491	0015
1N1492	0015
1N1507	0451
1N1507A	0451
1N1508	0446
1N1508A	0446
1N1509	0157
1N1509A	0157
1N1510	0025
1N1510A	0025
1N1511	0244
1N1511A	0244
1N1512	0170
1N1512A	0170
1N1513	0137
1N1513A	0137
1N1514	0002
1N1514A	0002
1N1515	0490
1N1515A	0490
1N1516	0560
1N1516A	0560
1N1517	0436
1N1517A	0436
1N1518	0451
1N1518A	0451
1N1519	0446
1N1519A	0446
1N1520	0157
1N1520A	0157
1N1521	0025
1N1521A	0025
1N1522	0244
1N1522A	0244
1N1523	0170
1N1523A	0170
1N1524	0137
1N1524A	0137
1N1524R	0810
1N1525	0002
1N1525A	0002
1N1526	0490
1N1526A	0490
1N1527	0560
1N1527A	0560
1N1528	0436
1N1528A	0436
1N1530	1075
1N1530A	1075
1N1531A	0436
1N1537	0703
1N1537R	0927
1N1538	0575
1N1538R	0941
1N1539	0575
1N1539R	0941
1N1540	0575
1N1540R	0941
1N1541	0941
1N1541R	4443
1N1542	0994
1N1542R	1006
1N1543	2065
1N1543R	5467
1N1544	2070
1N1544A	0873
1N1544R	1067
1N1551	0575
1N1551R	2275
1N1552	0575
1N1552R	2275
1N1553	2049
1N1553R	0471
1N1554	0994
1N1554R	0471
1N1555	2065
1N1555A	0257
1N1555R	0471
1N1556	0947
1N1557	0242
1N1558	1736
1N1559	0535
1N1560	1760
1N1561	0143
1N1562	0143
1N1563	0947
1N1563A	0015
1N1564	0242
1N1564A	0015
1N1565	1736
1N1565A	0015
1N1566	0535
1N1566A	0015
1N1567	1760

DEVICE TYPE	REPL CODE
1N1567A	0015
1N1568	0959
1N1568A	0015
1N1575	0094
1N1576	OEM
1N1577	OEM
1N1578	OEM
1N1581	0703
1N1581R	0927
1N1582	0575
1N1582R	5420
1N1583	0575
1N1583R	0941
1N1584	2049
1N1584R	4443
1N1585	0994
1N1585R	1006
1N1586	2065
1N1586R	5467
1N1587	2070
1N1587R	1067
1N1588	0542
1N1588A	0542
1N1588AR	2024
1N1588B	0542
1N1588R	2024
1N1588RA	2024
1N1588RB	2024
1N1589	2101
1N1589A	2101
1N1589AR	1429
1N1589B	2101
1N1589R	1429
1N1589RA	2385
1N1589RB	2385
1N1590	1890
1N1590A	1890
1N1590AR	1436
1N1590B	1890
1N1590R	1436
1N1590RA	1436
1N1590RB	1436
1N1591	1591
1N1591A	1591
1N1591AR	1449
1N1591B	1591
1N1591R	1449
1N1591RA	1449
1N1591RB	1449
1N1592	1612
1N1592A	1612
1N1592AR	1481
1N1592B	1612
1N1592R	1481
1N1592RA	1481
1N1592RB	1481
1N1593	0986
1N1593A	0986
1N1593AR	0505
1N1593B	0986
1N1593R	0505
1N1593RA	0505
1N1593RB	0505
1N1594	1254
1N1594A	1254
1N1594AR	0864
1N1594B	1254
1N1594R	0864
1N1594RA	0864
1N1594RB	0864
1N1595	1629
1N1595A	1629
1N1595AR	1264
1N1595B	1629
1N1595R	1264
1N1595RA	1264
1N1595RB	1264
1N1596	1706
1N1596A	1706
1N1596AR	1071
1N1596B	1706
1N1596R	1071
1N1596RA	1071
1N1596RB	1071
1N1597	0722
1N1597A	0722
1N1597AR	1712
1N1597B	0722
1N1597R	1712
1N1597RA	1712
1N1597RB	1712
1N1598	1771
1N1598A	1771
1N1598AR	1750
1N1598B	1771
1N1598R	1750
1N1598RA	1750
1N1598RB	1750
1N1599	0542
1N1599A	0542
1N1599AR	2024
1N1599R	2024
1N1599RA	2024
1N1600	2101
1N1600A	0542
1N1600AR	1429
1N1600R	1429
1N1600RA	1429
1N1601	1890

DEVICE TYPE	REPL CODE
1N1601A	1890
1N1601AR	1436
1N1601R	1436
1N1601RA	1436
1N1602	1591
1N1602A	1591
1N1602AR	1449
1N1602R	1449
1N1602RA	1449
1N1603	1612
1N1603A	1612
1N1603AR	1481
1N1603R	1481
1N1603RA	1481
1N1604	0986
1N1604A	0986
1N1604AR	0505
1N1604R	0505
1N1604RA	0505
1N1605	1254
1N1605A	1254
1N1605AR	0864
1N1605R	0864
1N1605RA	0864
1N1606	1629
1N1606A	1629
1N1606AR	1264
1N1606R	1264
1N1606RA	1264
1N1607	1706
1N1607A	1706
1N1607AR	1071
1N1607R	1071
1N1607RA	1071
1N1608	0722
1N1608A	0722
1N1608AR	1712
1N1608R	1712
1N1608RA	1712
1N1609	1771
1N1609A	1771
1N1609AR	1750
1N1609R	1750
1N1609RA	1750
1N1610	OEM
1N1611	OEM
1N1611A	OEM
1N1611B	OEM
1N1612	0964
1N1612(REV.POL.)	0979
1N1612A	0964
1N1612AR	0979
1N1612R	0979
1N1612RA	2275
1N1613	3688
1N1613(REV.POL.)	0904
1N1613A	3688
1N1613AR	0904
1N1613R	0904
1N1613RA	2275
1N1614	0983
1N1614(REV.POL.)	0984
1N1614A	0983
1N1614AR	0984
1N1614B	0984
1N1614R	0984
1N1614RA	2275
1N1615	0197
1N1615A	0197
1N1615AR	0991
1N1615R	0991
1N1615RA	0471
1N1616	0204
1N1616(REV.POL.)	0510
1N1616A	0204
1N1616AR	0510
1N1616R	0510
1N1616RA	0471
1N1617	0947
1N1617AR	0947
1N1618	0015
1N1619	0015
1N1620	0015
1N1621	0090
1N1622	0097
1N1623	0105
1N1624	0109
1N1625	OEM
1N1625A	OEM
1N1626	OEM
1N1626A	OEM
1N1627	OEM
1N1628	OEM
1N1629	OEM
1N1630	0133
1N1631	OEM
1N1632	OEM
1N1633	OEM
1N1634	OEM
1N1635	OEM
1N1636	OEM
1N1637	OEM
1N1638	0133
1N1639	OEM
1N1640	OEM
1N1641	OEM
1N1642	OEM
1N1644	0110
1N1645	0947

DEVICE TYPE	REPL CODE
1N1646	0242
1N1647	0242
1N1648	1736
1N1649	1736
1N1650	0535
1N1651	0535
1N1652	1760
1N1653	0959
1N1660	1017
1N1661	1017
1N1662	1017
1N1663	1017
1N1664	1017
1N1665	1030
1N1666	1030
1N1670	1017
1N1671	1017
1N1672	1017
1N1673	1017
1N1674	1017
1N1675	1030
1N1676	1030
1N1680	0594
1N1680R	1337
1N1681	0594
1N1681R	1337
1N1682	0594
1N1682R	1337
1N1683	0594
1N1683R	1894
1N1684	1975
1N1684R	1894
1N1685	1975
1N1685R	1894
1N1686	1975
1N1686R	1894
1N1687	1975
1N1687R	1894
1N1688	0652
1N1688R	0193
1N1689	0652
1N1689R	0193
1N1690	0652
1N1690R	0193
1N1691	0652
1N1691R	0193
1N1692	0015
1N1693	0015
1N1694	0015
1N1695	0015
1N1696	0015
1N1697	0015
1N1698	OEM
1N1699	OEM
1N1700	OEM
1N1701	0015
1N1702	0015
1N1703	0015
1N1704	0015
1N1705	0015
1N1706	0015
1N1707	0015
1N1708	0015
1N1709	0015
1N1710	0015
1N1711	0015
1N1712	0015
1N1713	0137
1N1730	0071
1N1730A	0071
1N1731	0344
1N1731A	0344
1N1732	0344
1N1732A	0344
1N1733	3835
1N1733A	3835
1N1734	3835
1N1734A	3835
1N1735	0466
1N1736	0052
1N1736A	0052
1N1737	0943
1N1737A	0943
1N1738	1596
1N1738A	1596
1N1739	0721
1N1739A	0721
1N1740	0316
1N1740A	0316
1N1741	0333
1N1741A	0333
1N1742	0027
1N1742A	0027
1N1743	0505
1N1743R	0986
1N1744	0170
1N1745	OEM
1N1746	OEM
1N1747	OEM
1N1748	OEM
1N1749	OEM
1N1750	OEM
1N1751	OEM
1N1752	OEM
1N1753	OEM
1N1754	OEM
1N1755	OEM
1N1756	OEM
1N1757	OEM

DEVICE TYPE	REPL CODE
1N1758	OEM
1N1759	OEM
1N1760	OEM
1N1761	OEM
1N1762	OEM
1N1763	0023
1N1763A	0535
1N1764	0015
1N1764A	1760
1N1765	0157
1N1765A	0157
1N1766	0631
1N1766A	0631
1N1767	0025
1N1767A	0025
1N1768	0644
1N1768A	0644
1N1769	0244
1N1769A	0244
1N1770	0012
1N1770A	0012
1N1771	0170
1N1771A	0170
1N1772	0313
1N1772A	0313
1N1773	0137
1N1773A	0137
1N1774	0361
1N1774A	0361
1N1775	0002
1N1775A	0002
1N1776	0416
1N1776A	0416
1N1777	0490
1N1777A	0490
1N1778	0526
1N1778A	0526
1N1779	0298
1N1779A	0560
1N1780	0398
1N1780A	0526
1N1781	0436
1N1781A	0436
1N1782	0721
1N1782A	0721
1N1783	0361
1N1783A	0039
1N1784	0814
1N1784A	0814
1N1785	0346
1N1785A	0346
1N1786	0925
1N1786A	0925
1N1787	0993
1N1787A	0993
1N1788	0497
1N1788A	0497
1N1789	0863
1N1789A	0863
1N1790	0778
1N1790A	0778
1N1791	1258
1N1791A	1258
1N1792	1181
1N1792A	1181
1N1793	0327
1N1793A	0327
1N1794	1301
1N1794A	1301
1N1795	0098
1N1795A	0098
1N1796	0149
1N1796A	0149
1N1797	0186
1N1797A	0186
1N1798	0213
1N1798A	0213
1N1799	0028
1N1799A	0028
1N1800	0255
1N1800A	0255
1N1801	0363
1N1801A	0363
1N1802	0417
1N1802A	0417
1N1803	1436
1N1803A	1436
1N1803AR	1890
1N1803B	1436
1N1803BR	1890
1N1803C	1436
1N1803CA	OEM
1N1803R	1890
1N1803RA	1890
1N1804	2206
1N1804A	2206
1N1804B	2206
1N1804C	2206
1N1804R	0691
1N1804RA	0691
1N1805	1449
1N1805A	1449
1N1805AR	1591
1N1805B	1449
1N1805BR	1449
1N1805C	1449
1N1805CA	OEM
1N1805R	1591
1N1805RA	1591

DEVICE TYPE	REPL CODE
1N1805RB	1591
1N1806	0221
1N1806A	0221
1N1806B	0213
1N1806C	0221
1N1806CA	OEM
1N1806R	1606
1N1806RA	1606
1N1807	1481
1N1807A	1481
1N1807AR	1612
1N1807B	1481
1N1807BR	1612
1N1807C	1481
1N1807CA	OEM
1N1807R	1612
1N1807RA	1612
1N1808	1608
1N1808A	1608
1N1808B	1608
1N1808C	1608
1N1808CA	OEM
1N1808R	0622
1N1808RA	0622
1N1809	0483
1N1809A	0483
1N1809B	0483
1N1809C	0483
1N1809CA	OEM
1N1809R	1922
1N1809RA	1922
1N1810	0504
1N1810A	0504
1N1810AR	1930
1N1810B	0504
1N1810BR	1930
1N1810C	0504
1N1810CA	OEM
1N1810R	1930
1N1810RA	1930
1N1811	0519
1N1811A	0519
1N1811B	0519
1N1811C	0519
1N1811CA	OEM
1N1811R	1936
1N1811RA	1936
1N1812	0063
1N1812A	0063
1N1812AR	1950
1N1812B	0063
1N1812BR	1950
1N1812C	0063
1N1812CA	OEM
1N1812R	1950
1N1812RA	1950
1N1813	0397
1N1813A	0397
1N1813B	0397
1N1813C	0397
1N1813CA	OEM
1N1813R	0353
1N1813RA	0353
1N1814	0629
1N1814A	0629
1N1814AR	0771
1N1814B	0629
1N1814BR	0771
1N1814C	0629
1N1814CA	OEM
1N1814R	0771
1N1814RA	0771
1N1815	0663
1N1815A	0663
1N1815B	0663
1N1815C	0663
1N1815CA	OEM
1N1815R	1065
1N1815RA	1065
1N1816	1014
1N1816A	1014
1N1816C	1014
1N1816R	1240
1N1816RA	1240
1N1817	1264
1N1817A	1264
1N1817AR	1629
1N1817B	1264
1N1817BR	1629
1N1817C	1264
1N1817R	1629
1N1817RA	1629
1N1818	1392
1N1818A	1392
1N1818C	1392
1N1818R	1693
1N1818RA	1693
1N1819	1071
1N1819A	1071
1N1819AR	1706
1N1819B	1071
1N1819BR	1706
1N1819C	1071
1N1819R	1706
1N1819RA	1706
1N1820	1707
1N1820A	1707
1N1820C	1707
1N1820R	1720

If replacement code is OEM, contact original manufacturer for replacement.

DEVICE TYPE	REPL CODE
1N1820RA	1720
1N1821	1712
1N1821A	1712
1N1821AR	0722
1N1821B	1712
1N1821BR	0722
1N1821C	1712
1N1821R	0722
1N1821RA	0722
1N1822	1725
1N1822A	1725
1N1822C	1725
1N1822R	1745
1N1822RA	1745
1N1823	1750
1N1823A	1750
1N1823AR	1771
1N1823B	1750
1N1823BR	1771
1N1823C	1750
1N1823R	1771
1N1823RA	1771
1N1824	1761
1N1824A	1761
1N1824C	1761
1N1824CA	OEM
1N1824R	1783
1N1824RA	1783
1N1825	1777
1N1825A	1777
1N1825AR	1788
1N1825B	1777
1N1825BR	1788
1N1825C	1777
1N1825R	1788
1N1825RA	1788
1N1826	1785
1N1826A	1785
1N1826C	1785
1N1826R	1798
1N1826RA	1798
1N1827	1793
1N1827A	1793
1N1827AR	1806
1N1827B	1793
1N1827BR	1806
1N1827C	1793
1N1827R	1806
1N1827RA	1806
1N1828	1185
1N1828A	1185
1N1828C	1185
1N1828R	1815
1N1828RA	1815
1N1829	0022
1N1829A	0022
1N1829AR	1842
1N1829B	0022
1N1829BR	1842
1N1829C	0022
1N1829R	1842
1N1829RA	1842
1N1830	0132
1N1830A	0132
1N1830C	0132
1N1830R	1855
1N1830RA	1855
1N1831	0207
1N1831A	0207
1N1831AR	1873
1N1831B	0207
1N1831BR	1873
1N1831C	0207
1N1831R	1873
1N1831RA	1873
1N1832	0263
1N1832A	0263
1N1832C	0263
1N1832R	1884
1N1832RA	1884
1N1833	0306
1N1833A	0306
1N1833AR	1891
1N1833B	0306
1N1833BR	1891
1N1833C	0306
1N1833R	1891
1N1833RA	1891
1N1834	0325
1N1834A	0325
1N1834C	0325
1N1834R	0731
1N1834RA	0731
1N1835	0352
1N1835A	0352
1N1835AR	1898
1N1835B	0352
1N1835BR	1898
1N1835C	0352
1N1835R	1898
1N1835RA	1898
1N1836	0408
1N1836A	0408
1N1836C	0408
1N1836R	1903
1N1836RA	1903
1N1838	OEM
1N1839	0133
1N1840	0133
1N1841	0133
1N1842	0133
1N1843	0133
1N1844	0133
1N1845	0133
1N1846	0133
1N1847	0133
1N1848	0133
1N1849	0790
1N1850	0790
1N1875	0244
1N1875A	0244
1N1875B	0244
1N1876	0170
1N1876A	0170
1N1876B	OEM
1N1877	0137
1N1877A	0137
1N1877B	OEM
1N1878	0002
1N1878A	0002
1N1878B	OEM
1N1879	0490
1N1879A	0490
1N1879B	OEM
1N1880	0560
1N1880A	0560
1N1880B	OEM
1N1881	0436
1N1881A	0436
1N1881B	OEM
1N1882	0039
1N1882A	0039
1N1882B	OEM
1N1883	0346
1N1883A	0346
1N1883B	OEM
1N1884	0993
1N1884A	0993
1N1884B	OEM
1N1885	0863
1N1885A	0863
1N1885B	OEM
1N1886	1258
1N1886A	1258
1N1886B	OEM
1N1887	0327
1N1887A	0327
1N1887B	OEM
1N1888	0098
1N1888A	0098
1N1888B	OEM
1N1889	0186
1N1889A	0504
1N1889B	OEM
1N1890	0028
1N1890A	0028
1N1890B	OEM
1N1891	1612
1N1891A	1612
1N1891R	1481
1N1891RA	1481
1N1892	0986
1N1892A	0986
1N1892R	0505
1N1892RA	0505
1N1893	1254
1N1893A	1254
1N1893R	0864
1N1893RA	0864
1N1894	1629
1N1894A	1629
1N1894R	1264
1N1894RA	1264
1N1895	1706
1N1895A	1706
1N1895R	1071
1N1895RA	1071
1N1896	0722
1N1896A	0722
1N1896R	1712
1N1896RA	1712
1N1897	1771
1N1897A	1771
1N1897R	1750
1N1897RA	1750
1N1898	1788
1N1898A	1788
1N1898R	1777
1N1898RA	1777
1N1899	1806
1N1899A	1806
1N1899R	1793
1N1899RA	1793
1N1900	1842
1N1900A	1842
1N1900R	0022
1N1900RA	0022
1N1901	1873
1N1901A	1873
1N1901R	0207
1N1901RA	0207
1N1902	1891
1N1902A	1891
1N1902R	0306
1N1902RA	0306
1N1903	1898
1N1903A	1898
1N1903R	0352
1N1903RA	0352
1N1904	1155
1N1904A	1155
1N1904R	0433
1N1904RA	0433
1N1905	0504
1N1906	0063
1N1907	0015
1N1908	0015
1N1909	0015
1N1910	1736
1N1911	0015
1N1912	0015
1N1913	0015
1N1914	0071
1N1915	0071
1N1916	0071
1N1917	0964
1N1918	OEM
1N1919	OEM
1N1920	OEM
1N1921	OEM
1N1922	OEM
1N1923	OEM
1N1924	OEM
1N1925	OEM
1N1926	OEM
1N1927	0036
1N1927A	0036
1N1927B	OEM
1N1928	0140
1N1928A	0140
1N1928B	OEM
1N1929	0253
1N1929A	0253
1N1929B	0253
1N1930	0062
1N1930A	0062
1N1930B	OEM
1N1931	0165
1N1931A	0165
1N1931B	0244
1N1932	0064
1N1932A	0170
1N1932B	0064
1N1933	0052
1N1933A	0052
1N1933B	0999
1N1934	0681
1N1934A	0002
1N1934B	0681
1N1935	0371
1N1935A	0371
1N1935B	OEM
1N1936	0700
1N1936A	0700
1N1936B	OEM
1N1937	0450
1N1937A	0436
1N1937B	0450
1N1938	0166
1N1938A	0039
1N1938B	0166
1N1939	0032
1N1939A	0032
1N1939B	OEM
1N1940	0068
1N1940A	0068
1N1940B	OEM
1N1941	0125
1N1941A	0125
1N1941B	OEM
1N1942	0125
1N1942A	0173
1N1942B	OEM
1N1943	0049
1N1943A	0327
1N1943B	0049
1N1944	0189
1N1944A	0189
1N1944B	OEM
1N1945	0089
1N1945A	0186
1N1945B	OEM
1N1946	0336
1N1946A	0336
1N1946B	OEM
1N1947	0420
1N1947A	0420
1N1947B	OEM
1N1948	OEM
1N1948A	OEM
1N1948B	OEM
1N1949	OEM
1N1949A	OEM
1N1949B	OEM
1N1950	OEM
1N1950A	OEM
1N1950B	OEM
1N1951	OEM
1N1951A	OEM
1N1951B	OEM
1N1952	OEM
1N1952A	OEM
1N1952B	OEM
1N1953	OEM
1N1953A	OEM
1N1953B	OEM
1N1954	0036
1N1954A	0036
1N1954B	0036
1N1955	0140
1N1955A	0140
1N1955B	OEM
1N1956	0253
1N1956A	0253
1N1956B	OEM
1N1957	0062
1N1957A	0062
1N1957B	OEM
1N1958	0165
1N1958A	0165
1N1958B	OEM
1N1959	0064
1N1959A	0064
1N1959B	OEM
1N1960	0052
1N1960A	0052
1N1960B	0052
1N1961	0873
1N1961A	0873
1N1961B	OEM
1N1962	0371
1N1962A	0371
1N1962B	OEM
1N1963	0700
1N1963A	0700
1N1963B	OEM
1N1964	0450
1N1964A	0436
1N1964B	0450
1N1965	0166
1N1965A	0039
1N1965B	0166
1N1966	0032
1N1967	0068
1N1968	0125
1N1969	0173
1N1970	0049
1N1971	0189
1N1972	0089
1N1973	0336
1N1973/T59277	OEM
1N1974	0420
1N1975	2335
1N1981	0036
1N1981A	0036
1N1981B	0036
1N1982	0140
1N1982A	0140
1N1982B	OEM
1N1983	0253
1N1983A	0253
1N1983B	0253
1N1984	0062
1N1984A	0062
1N1984B	OEM
1N1985	0165
1N1985A	0165
1N1985B	0165
1N1986	0064
1N1986A	0170
1N1986B	0064
1N1987	0052
1N1987A	0052
1N1987B	0052
1N1988	0681
1N1988A	0002
1N1988B	0681
1N1989	0371
1N1989A	0371
1N1989B	0371
1N1990	0700
1N1990A	0700
1N1990B	OEM
1N1991	0450
1N1991A	0436
1N1991B	0436
1N1992	0166
1N1992A	0039
1N1992B	0039
1N1993	0032
1N1993A	0032
1N1993B	OEM
1N1994	0068
1N1994A	0068
1N1994B	OEM
1N1995	0125
1N1995A	0125
1N1995B	OEM
1N1996	0173
1N1996A	0173
1N1996B	OEM
1N1997	0049
1N1997A	0327
1N1997B	4431
1N1998	0189
1N1998A	0189
1N1998B	OEM
1N1999	0089
1N1999A	0089
1N1999B	OEM
1N2000	0336
1N2000A	0336
1N2000B	OEM
1N2001	0420
1N2001A	0420
1N2001B	0420
1N2002	OEM
1N2002A	OEM
1N2002B	OEM
1N2003	6488
1N2003A	OEM
1N2003B	OEM
1N2004	OEM
1N2004A	OEM
1N2004B	OEM
1N2005	OEM
1N2005A	OEM
1N2005B	OEM
1N2006	OEM
1N2006A	OEM
1N2006B	OEM
1N2007	OEM
1N2007A	OEM
1N2007B	OEM
1N2008	0433
1N2008A	0433
1N2008AR	1155
1N2008C	0433
1N2008R	1155
1N2008RA	1155
1N2009	0483
1N2009A	0483
1N2009C	0483
1N2009R	1922
1N2009RA	1922
1N2010	0504
1N2010A	0504
1N2010AR	1930
1N2010C	0504
1N2010R	1930
1N2010RA	1930
1N2011	0519
1N2011A	0519
1N2011C	0519
1N2011R	1936
1N2011RA	1936
1N2012	0063
1N2012A	0063
1N2012AR	1950
1N2012C	0063
1N2012R	1950
1N2012RA	1950
1N2013	0110
1N2014	0947
1N2015	0242
1N2016	0242
1N2017	1736
1N2018	1736
1N2019	0535
1N2020	0535
1N2021	1241
1N2021R	0267
1N2022	5487
1N2022R	0267
1N2023	5487
1N2023R	0267
1N2024	1571
1N2024R	0267
1N2025	1571
1N2025R	0267
1N2026	0110
1N2026R	2275
1N2027	0575
1N2027R	2275
1N2028	2049
1N2028R	0471
1N2029	0994
1N2029R	0471
1N2030	2065
1N2031	2070
1N2032	0446
1N2032-1	0446
1N2032-2	0162
1N2032A	0446
1N2033	0298
1N2033-1	0157
1N2033-2	0298
1N2033A	0157
1N2034	0025
1N2034-1	0025
1N2034-2	0025
1N2034-3	0644
1N2034A	0025
1N2035	1075
1N2035-1	0244
1N2035-2	1075
1N2035-3	0012
1N2035-4	0012
1N2035A	0244
1N2036	0170
1N2036-1	0170
1N2036-2	0313
1N2036A	0170
1N2037	0361
1N2037-1	0137
1N2037-2	0361
1N2037-3	0100
1N2037A	0137
1N2038	0416
1N2038-1	0002
1N2038-2	0416
1N2038-3	1639
1N2038A	0416
1N2039	0943
1N2039-1	0490
1N2039-2	0943
1N2039-3	0526
1N2039A	0943
1N2040	0398
1N2040-1	0560
1N2040-2	0398
1N2040-3	1596
1N2040A	0398
1N2041	2101
1N2041-1	2101
1N2041-2	2101
1N2041A	2101
1N2041B	2394
1N2041C	2394
1N2041RA	1429
1N2041RB	2391
1N2042	1890
1N2042-1	1890
1N2042-2	2400
1N2042A	1890
1N2042B	0691
1N2042C	2400
1N2042RA	1436
1N2042RB	2206
1N2043	1591
1N2043-1	1591
1N2043-2	1591
1N2043-3	1606
1N2043A	1591
1N2043B	1591
1N2043C	1606
1N2043RA	1449
1N2043RB	1449
1N2043RC	0221
1N2044	2408
1N2044-1	1612
1N2044-2	2408
1N2044-3	0622
1N2044-4	0622
1N2044A	1612
1N2044B	1612
1N2044C	0622
1N2044D	0622
1N2044RA	1481
1N2044RB	1481
1N2044RC	1608
1N2044RD	1608
1N2045	0986
1N2045-1	0989
1N2045-2	0989
1N2045A	0986
1N2045B	0989
1N2045C	0989
1N2045RA	0505
1N2045RB	0686
1N2046	1240
1N2046-1	1240
1N2046-2	1240
1N2046-3	1626
1N2046A	1254
1N2046B	1240
1N2046C	1626
1N2046R	1014
1N2046RA	0864
1N2046RB	1014
1N2046RC	1145
1N2047	1693
1N2047-1	1693
1N2047-2	1693
1N2047-3	1630
1N2047A	1629
1N2047B	1693
1N2047C	1630
1N2047RA	1264
1N2047RB	1392
1N2047RC	1524
1N2048	1709
1N2048-1	1709
1N2048-2	1709
1N2048-3	1720
1N2048A	1706
1N2048B	1709
1N2048C	1720
1N2048RA	1071
1N2048RB	1701
1N2048RC	1707
1N2049	1745
1N2049-1	1745
1N2049-2	1745
1N2049-3	1771
1N2049-4	2434
1N2049A	0722
1N2049B	1745
1N2049C	1757
1N2049D	1771
1N2049RA	1712
1N2049RB	1725
1N2049RC	1737
1N2049RD	1750
1N2050AR	1099
1N2050BR	1099
1N2054	1017
1N2054-68	1017
1N2054R	0496
1N2055	1017
1N2055R	0496
1N2056	1017
1N2056R	0496
1N2057	1017
1N2057R	0496
1N2058	1017
1N2058R	0496
1N2059	1017
1N2059R	0496
1N2060	1017
1N2060R	1766
1N2061	1017
1N2061R	1766
1N2062	1030
1N2062R	1766
1N2063	1030
1N2063R	1766
1N2064	1030
1N2064R	1766
1N2065	1040
1N2065R	1778
1N2066	1040
1N2066R	1778
1N2067	1040
1N2067R	1778
1N2068	1040
1N2068R	1778
1N2069	0015
1N2069A	0015
1N2070	0023
1N2070A	0015
1N2071	0015
1N2071A	0015
1N2072	0015
1N2073	0015
1N2074	0015
1N2075	0015
1N2076	0015
1N2077	0015
1N2078	0015
1N2079	0015
1N2080	0015
1N2081	0015
1N2082	0015
1N2083	0015
1N2084	0015
1N2085	0015
1N2086	0015
1N2088	0015
1N2089	0015
1N2090	0015
1N2091	0015
1N2092	0015
1N2093	0015
1N2094	0015
1N2095	0015
1N2096	0015
1N2102	OEM
1N2103	0015
1N2104	0015
1N2105	0015
1N2106	0015
1N2107	0015
1N2108	0015
1N2109	0703
1N2110	OEM
1N2115	0015
1N2116	0015
1N2117	0015
1N2127	OEM
1N2127A	OEM
1N2128	3716
1N2128A	3716
1N2128AR	2640
1N2128R	2640
1N2128RA	1772
1N2129	2629
1N2129A	2629
1N2129AR	2670
1N2129R	2670
1N2129RA	1772
1N2130	2633
1N2130A	2633
1N2130AR	2741
1N2130R	2741
1N2130RA	1772
1N2131	2633
1N2131A	2633
1N2131AR	2741
1N2131R	2741
1N2131RA	1772
1N2132	2639
1N2132A	2639
1N2132AR	2828
1N2132R	2828
1N2132RA	1772
1N2133	2639
1N2133A	2639
1N2133AR	2828
1N2133R	2828
1N2133RA	1772
1N2134	1995
1N2134A	1995
1N2134AR	2879
1N2134R	2879
1N2134RA	1772
1N2135	1995
1N2135A	1995
1N2135AR	2879
1N2135R	2879
1N2135RA	1772
1N2136	2652
1N2136A	2652

If replacement code is OEM, contact original manufacturer for replacement.

DEVICE TYPE	REPL CODE
1N2136AR	2946
1N2136R	2946
1N2136RA	1772
1N2137	2652
1N2137A	2652
1N2137AR	2946
1N2137R	2946
1N2137RA	1772
1N2138	2657
1N2138A	2657
1N2138AR	3022
1N2138R	3022
1N2138RA	1772
1N2139	2657
1N2139A	2657
1N2139AR	3022
1N2139R	3022
1N2147	0964
1N2147A	0964
1N2148	3688
1N2148A	3688
1N2149	0983
1N2149A	0983
1N2150	3697
1N2150A	3697
1N2151	0200
1N2151A	0197
1N2152	5417
1N2152A	0200
1N2153	0204
1N2153A	0204
1N2154	3160
1N2154R	1620
1N2155	2873
1N2155R	0254
1N2156	1116
1N2156R	1099
1N2157	1118
1N2157R	1103
1N2158	0800
1N2158R	0258
1N2159	1186
1N2159R	1634
1N2160	0315
1N2160R	0267
1N2163	0012
1N2163A	0012
1N2164	0012
1N2164A	0012
1N2165	0012
1N2165A	0012
1N2166	0012
1N2166A	0012
1N2167	0012
1N2167A	0012
1N2168	0012
1N2168A	0012
1N2169	0012
1N2169A	0012
1N2170	0012
1N2170A	0012
1N2171	0012
1N2171A	0012
1N2172	0594
1N2172R	1337
1N2173	0594
1N2173R	1337
1N2174	0594
1N2174R	1337
1N2181	0015
1N2214	0157
1N2216	0703
1N2216R	2275
1N2217	0703
1N2218	2065
1N2218R	2275
1N2219	2065
1N2220	2070
1N2220R	2275
1N2221	2070
1N2222	2077
1N2222A	2077
1N2222R	0444
1N2223	2077
1N2223A	2077
1N2224	0607
1N2224A	0607
1N2224R	0444
1N2225	0607
1N2225A	0607
1N2226	0811
1N2226A	0811
1N2227	OEM
1N2227A	OEM
1N2228	0964
1N2228A	0964
1N2228R	2872
1N2228RA	2872
1N2229	0964
1N2229A	0964
1N2230	0983
1N2230A	0983
1N2231	0983
1N2231A	0983
1N2232	3697
1N2232A	3697
1N2233	3697
1N2233A	3697
1N2234	0197

DEVICE TYPE	REPL CODE
1N2234A	0197
1N2235	0197
1N2235A	0197
1N2236	0200
1N2236A	0200
1N2237	0200
1N2237A	0200
1N2238	0204
1N2238A	0204
1N2239	0204
1N2239A	0204
1N2240	0206
1N2240A	0206
1N2241	0206
1N2241A	0206
1N2242	0583
1N2242A	0583
1N2243	0583
1N2243A	0583
1N2244	OEM
1N2244A	OEM
1N2245	OEM
1N2245A	OEM
1N2246	0084
1N2246A	0084
1N2246R	2275
1N2246RA	2275
1N2247	0084
1N2247A	0084
1N2248	0090
1N2248A	0090
1N2248R	2275
1N2248RA	2275
1N2249	0090
1N2249A	0090
1N2250	0097
1N2250A	0097
1N2250R	2275
1N2250RA	2275
1N2251	0097
1N2251A	0097
1N2252	0105
1N2252A	0105
1N2252R	0471
1N2252RA	0471
1N2253	0105
1N2253A	0105
1N2254	0109
1N2254A	0109
1N2254R	0471
1N2254RA	0471
1N2255	0109
1N2255A	0109
1N2256	0116
1N2256A	0116
1N2256R	0471
1N2256RA	0471
1N2257	0116
1N2257A	0116
1N2258	0122
1N2258A	0122
1N2258R	0471
1N2258RA	0471
1N2259	0122
1N2259A	0122
1N2260	0131
1N2260A	0131
1N2260R	0444
1N2260RA	0444
1N2261	0131
1N2261A	0131
1N2262	0145
1N2262A	0145
1N2262R	0444
1N2262RA	0444
1N2263	0145
1N2263A	0145
1N2264	OEM
1N2264A	OEM
1N2265	OEM
1N2265A	OEM
1N2266	0703
1N2266R	2275
1N2267	0703
1N2268	2065
1N2268R	0471
1N2269	2065
1N2270	2070
1N2270R	0471
1N2271	2070
1N2272	1590
1N2272R	0267
1N2273	0585
1N2273R	0267
1N2274	1241
1N2274R	0267
1N2275	5487
1N2275R	0267
1N2276	1571
1N2276R	0267
1N2277	5489
1N2277R	0267
1N2278	1576
1N2278R	0267
1N2279	1124
1N2279R	0280
1N2280	0045
1N2281	OEM
1N2282	1118

DEVICE TYPE	REPL CODE
1N2282R	0267
1N2283	0800
1N2283R	0267
1N2284	1186
1N2284R	0267
1N2285	0315
1N2285R	0267
1N2286	1124
1N2286R	0280
1N2287	0045
1N2287R	0280
1N2288	OEM
1N2289	0703
1N2289A	0703
1N2290	0703
1N2290A	0703
1N2291	0575
1N2291A	2049
1N2292	2049
1N2292A	2049
1N2293	0994
1N2293A	0994
1N2323	0015
1N2326	3638
1N2327	0102
1N2328	OEM
1N2348	0703
1N2348R	4949
1N2349	0575
1N2349R	2275
1N2350	0575
1N2350R	2275
1N2357	0102
1N2358	0344
1N2359	0344
1N2360	0344
1N2361	0344
1N2362	OEM
1N2362A	OEM
1N2362B	OEM
1N2363	OEM
1N2363A	OEM
1N2363B	OEM
1N2364	OEM
1N2364A	OEM
1N2364B	OEM
1N2365	OEM
1N2365A	OEM
1N2365B	OEM
1N2366	OEM
1N2366A	OEM
1N2366B	OEM
1N2367	OEM
1N2367A	OEM
1N2367B	OEM
1N2368	OEM
1N2368A	OEM
1N2368B	OEM
1N2369	OEM
1N2369A	OEM
1N2369B	OEM
1N2370	OEM
1N2370A	OEM
1N2370B	OEM
1N2371	OEM
1N2371A	OEM
1N2371B	OEM
1N2372	0607
1N2373	0959
1N2374	0811
1N2375	0182
1N2376	0344
1N2377	OEM
1N2378	OEM
1N2379	OEM
1N2380	OEM
1N2381	1780
1N2382	3835
1N2382A	3835
1N2383	3835
1N2383A	3835
1N2384	OEM
1N2384A	OEM
1N2385	OEM
1N2385A	OEM
1N2387	0721
1N2389	OEM
1N2390	0110
1N2391	0947
1N2392	0242
1N2393	1736
1N2394	0535
1N2395	1760
1N2396	0959
1N2397	0811
1N2398	0811
1N2399	0110
1N2400	0947
1N2401	0242
1N2402	1736
1N2403	0535
1N2404	1760
1N2405	0959
1N2406	0811
1N2407	0811
1N2408	0110
1N2409	0947
1N2410	0242
1N2411	1736

DEVICE TYPE	REPL CODE
1N2412	0535
1N2413	1760
1N2414	0959
1N2415	0811
1N2416	0811
1N2417	0071
1N2418	0071
1N2419	0071
1N2420	0071
1N2421	0071
1N2422	0071
1N2423	0071
1N2424	0071
1N2425	0071
1N2426	0594
1N2426R	1337
1N2427	0594
1N2427R	1337
1N2428	0594
1N2428R	1337
1N2429	0594
1N2429R	1337
1N2430	0594
1N2430R	1337
1N2431	0594
1N2431R	1337
1N2432	0594
1N2432R	1766
1N2433	0594
1N2433R	1766
1N2434	1975
1N2434R	1766
1N2435	1975
1N2435R	1766
1N2436	0594
1N2436R	1337
1N2437	0594
1N2437R	1337
1N2438	0594
1N2438R	1337
1N2439	0594
1N2439R	1337
1N2440	0594
1N2440R	1337
1N2441	0594
1N2441R	1337
1N2442	1975
1N2442R	1894
1N2443	0594
1N2443R	1894
1N2444	1975
1N2444R	1894
1N2445	1975
1N2445R	1894
1N2446	3160
1N2446R	1620
1N2447	2873
1N2447R	0254
1N2448	1116
1N2448R	1099
1N2449	1116
1N2449R	1099
1N2450	1118
1N2450R	1103
1N2451	1118
1N2451R	1103
1N2452	0800
1N2452R	0258
1N2453	0800
1N2453R	0258
1N2454	1186
1N2454R	1634
1N2455	0315
1N2455R	0267
1N2456	1124
1N2456R	1111
1N2457	1124
1N2457R	1111
1N2458	3160
1N2458R	1620
1N2459	2873
1N2459R	0254
1N2460	1116
1N2460R	1099
1N2461	1116
1N2461R	1099
1N2462	1118
1N2462R	1103
1N2463	1118
1N2463R	1103
1N2464	0800
1N2464R	0258
1N2465	0800
1N2465R	0258
1N2466	1186
1N2466R	1634
1N2467	0315
1N2467R	0267
1N2468	1124
1N2468R	1111
1N2469	1124
1N2469R	1111
1N2482	0015
1N2483	0015
1N2484	0015
1N2485	0015
1N2486	0015
1N2487	0015
1N2488	0015

DEVICE TYPE	REPL CODE
1N2489	0015
1N2490	OEM
1N2491	0964
1N2491R	2275
1N2492	3688
1N2492R	2275
1N2493	0983
1N2493R	2275
1N2494	3697
1N2494R	0471
1N2495	0197
1N2495R	0471
1N2496	0200
1N2496R	0471
1N2497	0204
1N2497R	0471
1N2498	0505
1N2498A	0505
1N2498AR	0986
1N2498C	0505
1N2498R	0986
1N2498RA	0986
1N2498RC	0986
1N2499	0686
1N2499A	0686
1N2499C	0686
1N2499R	0989
1N2499RA	0989
1N2499RC	0989
1N2500	0864
1N2500A	0864
1N2500AR	1254
1N2500B	0864
1N2500C	0864
1N2500CA	0864
1N2500R	1254
1N2500RA	1254
1N2500RB	1254
1N2500RC	1254
1N2500RCA	1254
1N2501	0811
1N2502	0916
1N2503	0102
1N2504	0344
1N2505	0811
1N2506	0916
1N2507	0102
1N2508	0344
1N2509	OEM
1N2510	OEM
1N2512	0983
1N2512R	2275
1N2513	0983
1N2513R	2275
1N2514	1104
1N2514R	0471
1N2515	0197
1N2515R	0471
1N2516	0200
1N2516R	0471
1N2517	0204
1N2517R	0471
1N2518	3688
1N2519	0983
1N2520	2049
1N2521	0994
1N2522	0200
1N2523	2070
1N2524	0703
1N2525	0575
1N2526	0575
1N2527	2049
1N2528	0994
1N2529	2065
1N2530	2070
1N2531	2077
1N2532	2077
1N2533	0607
1N2534	0607
1N2535	0703
1N2536	0575
1N2537	0575
1N2538	2049
1N2539	0994
1N2540	2065
1N2541	2070
1N2542	2077
1N2543	2077
1N2544	0607
1N2545	0607
1N2546	0703
1N2547	0575
1N2548	0575
1N2549	2049
1N2550	0994
1N2551	2065
1N2552	2070
1N2553	2077
1N2554	2077
1N2555	0607
1N2556	0607
1N2557	0206
1N2558	0206
1N2559	0583
1N2560	0583
1N2561	0206
1N2562	0206
1N2563	0583
1N2564	0583

DEVICE TYPE	REPL CODE
1N2565	0964
1N2566	3688
1N2567	0983
1N2568	3697
1N2569	0197
1N2570	0200
1N2571	0204
1N2572	0206
1N2573	0206
1N2574	0583
1N2575	0583
1N2576	0084
1N2577	0090
1N2578	0097
1N2579	0105
1N2580	0109
1N2581	0116
1N2582	0122
1N2583	0131
1N2584	0131
1N2585	0145
1N2586	0145
1N2587	0084
1N2588	0090
1N2589	0097
1N2590	0105
1N2591	0109
1N2592	0116
1N2593	0122
1N2594	0131
1N2595	0131
1N2596	0145
1N2597	0145
1N2598	0084
1N2598R	1104
1N2599	0090
1N2600	0097
1N2601	0105
1N2602	0109
1N2603	0116
1N2604	0122
1N2605	0131
1N2606	0131
1N2607	0145
1N2608	0145
1N2609	0015
1N2610	0015
1N2611	0015
1N2612	0015
1N2613	0535
1N2614	0015
1N2615	0015
1N2616	0071
1N2617	0071
1N2618	0102
1N2619	0344
1N2620	0012
1N2620A	0012
1N2620B	0012
1N2621	0012
1N2621A	0012
1N2621B	0012
1N2622	0012
1N2622A	0012
1N2622B	0012
1N2623	0012
1N2623A	0012
1N2623B	0012
1N2624	0012
1N2624A	0012
1N2624B	0012
1N2625	OEM
1N2626	OEM
1N2630	OEM
1N2631	3298
1N2632	OEM
1N2633	OEM
1N2634	4335
1N2635	OEM
1N2636	OEM
1N2637	OEM
1N2638	0015
1N2641	OEM
1N2644	OEM
1N2647	OEM
1N2650	0015
1N2653	0071
1N2656	OEM
1N2659	OEM
1N2662	OEM
1N2664	OEM
1N2666	OEM
1N2667	OEM
1N2668	OEM
1N2669	OEM
1N2673	OEM
1N2677	OEM
1N2681	OEM
1N2685	OEM
1N2685A	OEM
1N2687	OEM
1N2689	OEM
1N2689A	OEM
1N2690	OEM
1N2691	OEM
1N2692	OEM
1N2694	OEM
1N2696	OEM
1N2698	OEM

DEVICE TYPE	REPL CODE
1N2700	OEM
1N2701	OEM
1N2702	0575
1N2705	OEM
1N2708	OEM
1N2711	OEM
1N2714	OEM
1N2717	OEM
1N2720	OEM
1N2722	OEM
1N2723	OEM
1N2724	OEM
1N2725	OEM
1N2728	OEM
1N2731	OEM
1N2734	OEM
1N2737	OEM
1N2738	OEM
1N2739	OEM
1N2740	OEM
1N2742	OEM
1N2744	OEM
1N2746	OEM
1N2748	OEM
1N2749	OEM
1N2750	0575
1N2753	OEM
1N2756	OEM
1N2759	OEM
1N2762	OEM
1N2763	OEM
1N2764	OEM
1N2765	0062
1N2765A	0062
1N2766	0873
1N2766A	0873
1N2767	0526
1N2767A	0526
1N2768	0436
1N2768A	0436
1N2769	OEM
1N2769A	OEM
1N2770	OEM
1N2770A	OEM
1N2771	OEM
1N2772	0811
1N2773	0811
1N2774	0916
1N2775	0916
1N2776	0102
1N2777	0102
1N2778	0102
1N2779	0102
1N2780	OEM
1N2781	OEM
1N2783	0382
1N2784	0865
1N2785	0847
1N2786	1241
1N2786R	1567
1N2787	1571
1N2787R	3251
1N2788	2633
1N2788R	2741
1N2789	1995
1N2789R	2879
1N2790	1075
1N2791	OEM
1N2792	OEM
1N2792A	OEM
1N2792B	OEM
1N2793	1991
1N2793R	0267
1N2794	0585
1N2794R	0267
1N2795	1241
1N2795R	0267
1N2796	1241
1N2796R	0267
1N2797	5487
1N2797R	0267
1N2798	5487
1N2798R	0267
1N2799	1571
1N2799R	0267
1N2800	1571
1N2800A	0267
1N2801	0143
1N2802	OEM
1N2804	OEM
1N2804A	OEM
1N2804B	OEM
1N2804R	OEM
1N2804RA	OEM
1N2804RB	OEM
1N2805	OEM
1N2805A	OEM
1N2805B	OEM
1N2805R	OEM
1N2805RA	OEM
1N2805RB	OEM
1N2806	OEM
1N2806A	OEM
1N2806B	OEM
1N2806R	OEM
1N2806RA	OEM
1N2806RB	OEM
1N2807	OEM
1N2807A	OEM

If replacement code is OEM, contact original manufacturer for replacement.

19

DEVICE TYPE	REPL CODE
1N2807B	OEM
1N2807R	OEM
1N2807RA	OEM
1N2807RB	OEM
1N2808	OEM
1N2808A	OEM
1N2808B	OEM
1N2808R	OEM
1N2808RA	OEM
1N2808RB	OEM
1N2809	OEM
1N2809A	OEM
1N2809B	OEM
1N2809R	OEM
1N2809RA	OEM
1N2809RB	OEM
1N2810	OEM
1N2810A	OEM
1N2810B	OEM
1N2810R	OEM
1N2810RA	OEM
1N2810RB	OEM
1N2811	OEM
1N2811A	OEM
1N2811B	OEM
1N2811R	OEM
1N2811RA	OEM
1N2811RB	OEM
1N2812	OEM
1N2812A	OEM
1N2812B	OEM
1N2812R	OEM
1N2812RA	OEM
1N2812RB	OEM
1N2813	OEM
1N2813A	OEM
1N2813B	OEM
1N2813R	OEM
1N2813RA	OEM
1N2813RB	OEM
1N2814	OEM
1N2814A	OEM
1N2814B	OEM
1N2814R	OEM
1N2814RA	OEM
1N2814RB	OEM
1N2815	OEM
1N2815A	OEM
1N2815B	OEM
1N2815R	OEM
1N2815RA	OEM
1N2815RB	OEM
1N2816	OEM
1N2816A	OEM
1N2816B	OEM
1N2816R	OEM
1N2816RA	OEM
1N2816RB	OEM
1N2817	OEM
1N2817A	OEM
1N2817B	OEM
1N2817R	OEM
1N2817RA	OEM
1N2817RB	OEM
1N2818	OEM
1N2818A	OEM
1N2818B	OEM
1N2818R	OEM
1N2818RA	OEM
1N2818RB	OEM
1N2819	OEM
1N2819A	OEM
1N2819B	OEM
1N2819R	OEM
1N2819RA	OEM
1N2819RB	OEM
1N2820	OEM
1N2820A	OEM
1N2820B	OEM
1N2820R	OEM
1N2820RA	OEM
1N2820RB	OEM
1N2821	OEM
1N2821A	OEM
1N2821B	OEM
1N2821R	OEM
1N2821RA	OEM
1N2821RB	OEM
1N2822	OEM
1N2822A	OEM
1N2822B	OEM
1N2822R	OEM
1N2822RA	OEM
1N2822RB	OEM
1N2823	OEM
1N2823A	OEM
1N2823B	OEM
1N2823R	OEM
1N2823RA	OEM
1N2823RB	OEM
1N2824	OEM
1N2824A	OEM
1N2824B	OEM
1N2824R	OEM
1N2824RA	OEM
1N2824RB	OEM
1N2825	OEM
1N2825A	OEM
1N2825B	OEM
1N2825R	OEM
1N2825RA	OEM
1N2825RB	OEM
1N2826	OEM
1N2826A	OEM
1N2826B	OEM
1N2826R	OEM
1N2826RA	OEM
1N2826RB	OEM
1N2827	OEM
1N2827A	OEM
1N2827B	OEM
1N2827R	OEM
1N2827RA	OEM
1N2827RB	OEM
1N2828	OEM
1N2828A	OEM
1N2828B	OEM
1N2828R	OEM
1N2828RA	OEM
1N2828RB	OEM
1N2829	OEM
1N2829A	OEM
1N2829B	OEM
1N2829R	OEM
1N2829RA	OEM
1N2829RB	OEM
1N2830	OEM
1N2830A	OEM
1N2830B	OEM
1N2830R	OEM
1N2830RA	OEM
1N2830RB	OEM
1N2831	OEM
1N2831A	OEM
1N2831B	OEM
1N2831R	OEM
1N2831RA	OEM
1N2831RB	OEM
1N2832	OEM
1N2832A	OEM
1N2832B	OEM
1N2832R	OEM
1N2832RA	OEM
1N2832RB	OEM
1N2833	OEM
1N2833A	OEM
1N2833B	OEM
1N2833R	OEM
1N2833RA	OEM
1N2833RB	OEM
1N2834	OEM
1N2834A	OEM
1N2834B	OEM
1N2834R	OEM
1N2834RA	OEM
1N2834RB	OEM
1N2835	OEM
1N2835A	OEM
1N2835B	OEM
1N2835R	OEM
1N2835RA	OEM
1N2835RB	OEM
1N2836	OEM
1N2836A	OEM
1N2836B	OEM
1N2836R	OEM
1N2836RA	OEM
1N2836RB	OEM
1N2837	OEM
1N2837A	OEM
1N2837B	OEM
1N2837R	OEM
1N2837RA	OEM
1N2837RB	OEM
1N2838	OEM
1N2838A	OEM
1N2838B	OEM
1N2838R	OEM
1N2838RA	OEM
1N2838RB	OEM
1N2839	OEM
1N2839A	OEM
1N2839B	OEM
1N2839R	OEM
1N2839RA	OEM
1N2839RB	OEM
1N2840	OEM
1N2840A	OEM
1N2840B	OEM
1N2840R	OEM
1N2840RA	OEM
1N2840RB	OEM
1N2841	OEM
1N2841A	OEM
1N2841B	OEM
1N2841R	OEM
1N2841RA	OEM
1N2841RB	OEM
1N2842	OEM
1N2842A	OEM
1N2842B	OEM
1N2842R	OEM
1N2842RA	OEM
1N2842RB	OEM
1N2843	OEM
1N2843A	OEM
1N2843B	OEM
1N2843R	OEM
1N2843RA	OEM
1N2843RB	OEM
1N2844	OEM
1N2844A	OEM
1N2844B	OEM
1N2844R	OEM
1N2844RA	OEM
1N2844RB	OEM
1N2845	OEM
1N2845A	OEM
1N2845B	OEM
1N2845R	OEM
1N2845RA	OEM
1N2845RB	OEM
1N2846	OEM
1N2846A	OEM
1N2846B	OEM
1N2846R	OEM
1N2846RA	OEM
1N2846RB	OEM
1N2847	0575
1N2848	0575
1N2849	2049
1N2850	0994
1N2851	2065
1N2852	2070
1N2858	0015
1N2858A	0110
1N2859	0947
1N2859A	0947
1N2860	0023
1N2860A	0242
1N2861	0015
1N2861A	1736
1N2862	0015
1N2862A	0535
1N2863	0015
1N2863A	1760
1N2864	0015
1N2864A	0959
1N2865	0811
1N2866	0916
1N2867	0811
1N2868	0916
1N2878	0071
1N2879	0071
1N2880	0071
1N2881	0071
1N2882	0071
1N2883	0071
1N2884	0102
1N2885	0102
1N2886	0182
1N2887	0182
1N2887R	0267
1N2888	0344
1N2889	0344
1N2890	0344
1N2891	0344
1N2892	OEM
1N2893	OEM
1N2894	OEM
1N2895	OEM
1N2896	OEM
1N2897	OEM
1N2898	OEM
1N2899	OEM
1N2900	OEM
1N2901	OEM
1N2902	OEM
1N2903	OEM
1N2904	OEM
1N2905	OEM
1N2906	OEM
1N2907	OEM
1N2908	OEM
1N2909	OEM
1N2910	OEM
1N2911	OEM
1N2912	OEM
1N2913	OEM
1N2914	OEM
1N2915	OEM
1N2916	OEM
1N2917	OEM
1N2918	OEM
1N2919	OEM
1N2920	OEM
1N2921	OEM
1N2922	OEM
1N2923	OEM
1N2924	OEM
1N2925	OEM
1N2926	OEM
1N2926A	OEM
1N2929A	OEM
1N2930A	OEM
1N2937	OEM
1N2938	OEM
1N2939	OEM
1N2939A	OEM
1N2940	OEM
1N2940A	OEM
1N2941	OEM
1N2941A	OEM
1N2942	0952
1N2942R	1216
1N2943	0988
1N2943R	1228
1N2944	1003
1N2944R	1243
1N2945	1013
1N2945R	1259
1N2946	0883
1N2946R	1267
1N2947	1043
1N2947R	1283
1N2948	0926
1N2948R	1292
1N2949	1072
1N2949R	1300
1N2950	1098
1N2950R	1314
1N2951	1127
1N2951R	1323
1N2952	1144
1N2952R	1334
1N2953	1156
1N2953R	1346
1N2954	1176
1N2954R	1361
1N2955	1201
1N2955R	1377
1N2956	1214
1N2956R	1396
1N2957	1223
1N2957R	1405
1N2958	1237
1N2958R	1419
1N2959	1256
1N2959R	1431
1N2960	1280
1N2960R	1438
1N2961	1297
1N2961R	1452
1N2962	1321
1N2962R	1465
1N2963	1343
1N2963R	0608
1N2964	1355
1N2964R	1502
1N2965	1374
1N2965R	1515
1N2966	1391
1N2966R	1529
1N2967	1402
1N2967R	1541
1N2968	1413
1N2968R	1565
1N2969	1402
1N2969A	OEM
1N2970	1449
1N2970A	1449
1N2970AR	1591
1N2970B	1449
1N2970BR	1591
1N2970R	1591
1N2970RA	1591
1N2970RB	1591
1N2971	0221
1N2971A	0221
1N2971B	0221
1N2971R	1606
1N2971RA	1606
1N2971RB	1606
1N2972	1481
1N2972A	1481
1N2972AR	1612
1N2972B	1481
1N2972BR	1612
1N2972R	1612
1N2972RA	1612
1N2972RB	1612
1N2973	1608
1N2973A	1608
1N2973B	1608
1N2973R	0622
1N2973RA	0622
1N2973RB	0622
1N2974	0505
1N2974A	0505
1N2974AR	0986
1N2974B	0505
1N2974BR	0986
1N2974R	0986
1N2974RA	0986
1N2974RB	0986
1N2975	0686
1N2975A	0686
1N2975B	0686
1N2975R	0989
1N2975RA	0989
1N2975RB	0989
1N2976	0864
1N2976A	0864
1N2976AR	1254
1N2976B	0864
1N2976BR	1254
1N2976R	1254
1N2976RA	1254
1N2976RB	1254
1N2976RC	1254
1N2977	1014
1N2977A	1014
1N2977B	1014
1N2977R	1240
1N2977RA	1240
1N2977RB	1240
1N2978	1145
1N2978A	1145
1N2978B	1145
1N2978R	1626
1N2978RA	1626
1N2978RB	1626
1N2979	1264
1N2979A	1264
1N2979AR	1629
1N2979B	1264
1N2979BR	1629
1N2979R	1629
1N2979RA	1629
1N2979RB	1629
1N2980	1392
1N2980A	1392
1N2980B	1392
1N2980R	1693
1N2980RA	1693
1N2980RB	1693
1N2981	1524
1N2981A	1524
1N2981B	1524
1N2981R	1630
1N2981RA	1630
1N2981RB	1630
1N2982	1071
1N2982A	1071
1N2982AR	1706
1N2982B	1071
1N2982BR	1706
1N2982R	1706
1N2982RA	1706
1N2982RB	1706
1N2983	1701
1N2983A	1701
1N2983B	1701
1N2983R	1709
1N2983RA	1709
1N2983RB	1709
1N2984	1707
1N2984A	1707
1N2984B	1707
1N2984R	1720
1N2984RA	1720
1N2984RB	1720
1N2985	1712
1N2985A	1712
1N2985AR	0722
1N2985B	1712
1N2985BR	0722
1N2985R	0722
1N2985RA	0722
1N2985RB	0722
1N2986	1725
1N2986A	1725
1N2986AN	1745
1N2986B	1725
1N2986R	1745
1N2986RA	1745
1N2986RB	1745
1N2987	1737
1N2987A	1737
1N2987B	1737
1N2987R	1757
1N2987RA	1757
1N2987RB	1757
1N2988	1750
1N2988A	1750
1N2988AR	1771
1N2988B	1750
1N2988BR	1771
1N2988R	1771
1N2988RA	1771
1N2988RB	1771
1N2989	1761
1N2989A	1761
1N2989B	1761
1N2989R	1783
1N2989RA	1783
1N2989RB	1783
1N2990	1777
1N2990A	1777
1N2990AR	1788
1N2990B	1777
1N2990BR	1788
1N2990R	1788
1N2990RA	1788
1N2990RB	1788
1N2991	1785
1N2991A	1785
1N2991B	1785
1N2991R	1798
1N2991RA	1798
1N2991RB	1798
1N2992	1793
1N2992A	1793
1N2992AR	1806
1N2992B	1793
1N2992BR	1806
1N2992R	1806
1N2992RA	1806
1N2992RB	1806
1N2993	1185
1N2993A	1185
1N2993B	1185
1N2993R	1815
1N2993RA	1815
1N2993RB	1815
1N2994	1810
1N2994A	1810
1N2994B	1810
1N2994R	1829
1N2994RA	1829
1N2994RB	1829
1N2995	0022
1N2995A	0022
1N2995AR	1842
1N2995B	0022
1N2995BR	1842
1N2995R	1842
1N2995RA	1842
1N2995RB	1842
1N2996	0070
1N2996A	0070
1N2996B	0070
1N2996R	1850
1N2996RA	1850
1N2996RB	1850
1N2997	0132
1N2997A	0132
1N2997B	0132
1N2997R	1855
1N2997RA	1855
1N2997RB	1855
1N2998	0172
1N2998A	0172
1N2998B	0172
1N2998R	1863
1N2998RA	1863
1N2998RB	1863
1N2999	0207
1N2999A	0207
1N2999AR	1873
1N2999B	0207
1N2999BR	1873
1N2999R	1873
1N2999RA	1873
1N2999RB	1873
1N3000	0263
1N3000A	0263
1N3000B	0263
1N3000R	1884
1N3000RA	1884
1N3000RB	1884
1N3001	0306
1N3001A	0306
1N3001AR	1891
1N3001B	0306
1N3001BR	1891
1N3001R	1891
1N3001RA	1891
1N3001RB	1891
1N3002	0325
1N3002A	0325
1N3002B	0325
1N3002R	0731
1N3002RA	0731
1N3002RB	0731
1N3003	0352
1N3003A	0352
1N3003AR	1898
1N3003B	0352
1N3003BR	1898
1N3003R	1898
1N3003RA	1898
1N3003RB	1898
1N3004	0408
1N3004A	0408
1N3004B	0408
1N3004R	1903
1N3004RA	1903
1N3004RB	1903
1N3005	0433
1N3005A	0433
1N3005AR	1155
1N3005B	0433
1N3005BR	1155
1N3005R	1155
1N3005RA	1155
1N3005RB	1155
1N3006	0459
1N3006A	0459
1N3006B	0459
1N3006R	1913
1N3006RA	1913
1N3006RB	1913
1N3007	0483
1N3007A	0483
1N3007B	0483
1N3007R	1922
1N3007RA	1922
1N3007RB	1922
1N3008	0504
1N3008A	0504
1N3008AR	1930
1N3008B	0504
1N3008BR	1930
1N3008R	1930
1N3008RA	1930
1N3008RB	1930
1N3009	0519
1N3009A	0519
1N3009B	0519
1N3009R	1936
1N3009RA	1936
1N3009RB	1936
1N3010	0537
1N3010A	0537
1N3010B	0537
1N3010R	1942
1N3010RA	1942
1N3010RB	1942
1N3011	0063
1N3011A	0063
1N3011AR	1950
1N3011B	0063
1N3011BR	1950
1N3011R	1950
1N3011RA	1950
1N3011RB	1950
1N3012	0397
1N3012A	0397
1N3012B	0397
1N3012R	0353
1N3012RA	0353
1N3012RB	0353
1N3013	0611
1N3013A	0611
1N3013B	0611
1N3013R	0665
1N3013RA	0665
1N3013RB	0665
1N3014	0629
1N3014A	0629
1N3014AR	0771
1N3014B	0629
1N3014BR	0771
1N3014R	0771
1N3014RA	0771
1N3014RB	0771
1N3015	0663
1N3015A	0663
1N3015B	0663
1N3015R	1065
1N3015RA	1065
1N3015RB	1065
1N3016	0025
1N3016A	0025
1N3016B	0025
1N3017	0644
1N3017A	0644
1N3017B	0644
1N3018	0244
1N3018A	0244
1N3018B	0244
1N3018BA	0244
1N3019	0012
1N3019A	0012
1N3019B	0012
1N3020	0170
1N3020A	0170
1N3020B	0170
1N3021	0313
1N3021A	0313
1N3021B	0313
1N3022	0137
1N3022A	0137
1N3022B	0137
1N3023	0361
1N3023A	0361
1N3023B	0361
1N3024	0002
1N3024A	0002
1N3024B	0002
1N3025	0416
1N3025A	0416
1N3025B	0416
1N3026	0490
1N3026A	0490
1N3026B	0490
1N3027	0526
1N3027A	0526
1N3027B	0526
1N3028	0560
1N3028A	0560
1N3028B	0560
1N3029	0398
1N3029A	0398
1N3029B	0398
1N3030	0436
1N3030A	0436
1N3030B	0436
1N3031	0721
1N3031A	0721
1N3031B	0721
1N3032	0039
1N3032A	0039
1N3032B	0039
1N3033	0814
1N3033A	0814
1N3033B	0814
1N3034	0346
1N3034A	0346
1N3034B	0346
1N3035	0925
1N3035A	0925
1N3035B	0925
1N3036	0993
1N3036A	0993
1N3036B	0993
1N3037	0497
1N3037A	0497
1N3037B	0497
1N3038	0863
1N3038A	0863
1N3038B	0863

If replacement code is OEM, contact original manufacturer for replacement.

DEVICE TYPE	REPL CODE
1N3039	0778
1N3039A	0778
1N3039B	0778
1N3040	1258
1N3040A	1258
1N3040B	1258
1N3041	1181
1N3041A	1181
1N3041B	1181
1N3042	0327
1N3042A	0327
1N3042B	0327
1N3043	1301
1N3043A	1301
1N3043B	1301
1N3044	0098
1N3044A	0098
1N3044B	0098
1N3045	0149
1N3045A	0149
1N3045B	0149
1N3046	0186
1N3046A	0186
1N3046B	0186
1N3047	0213
1N3047A	0213
1N3047B	0213
1N3048	0028
1N3048A	0028
1N3048B	0028
1N3049	0255
1N3049A	0255
1N3049B	0255
1N3050	0363
1N3050A	0363
1N3050B	0363
1N3051	0417
1N3051A	0417
1N3051B	0417
1N3052	5625
1N3053	5625
1N3054	5625
1N3055	5625
1N3056	5625
1N3057	5625
1N3058	5625
1N3059	5625
1N3060	5625
1N3061	5625
1N3062	0124
1N3063	0133
1N3064	0133
1N3065	0133
1N3066	0133
1N3066M	OEM
1N3067	0133
1N3068	0133
1N3069	0133
1N3069M	0133
1N3070	0133
1N3071	0133
1N3072	0110
1N3073	0947
1N3074	0242
1N3075	0242
1N3076	1736
1N3077	1736
1N3078	0535
1N3079	0535
1N3080	0811
1N3081	0031
1N3082	0242
1N3083	0535
1N3084	0959
1N3085	0594
1N3085R	1337
1N3086	0594
1N3086R	1337
1N3087	0594
1N3087R	1337
1N3088	1975
1N3088R	1894
1N3089	1975
1N3089R	1894
1N3090	1975
1N3090R	1894
1N3091	0652
1N3091R	0193
1N3092	0652
1N3092R	0193
1N3094	0015
1N3097	OEM
1N3098	0186
1N3098A	0186
1N3099	0028
1N3099A	0028
1N3100	0363
1N3100A	0363
1N3102	1930
1N3102A	1930
1N3102R	0504
1N3102RA	0504
1N3103	1950
1N3103A	1950
1N3103R	0063
1N3103RA	0063
1N3104	0771
1N3104A	0771
1N3104R	0629
1N3104RA	0629
1N3105	OEM
1N3105A	OEM
1N3105R	OEM
1N3105RA	OEM
1N3106	0959
1N3107	0916
1N3108	0012
1N3109	0607
1N3110	0143
1N3111	0594
1N3111R	1337
1N3112	0086
1N3118	OEM
1N3121	0143
1N3122	0143
1N3123	0133
1N3124	0133
1N3125	0143
1N3128	OEM
1N3129	OEM
1N3130	6599
1N3138	OEM
1N3139	1551
1N3140	1551
1N3141	OEM
1N3142	2633
1N3143	OEM
1N3146	0143
1N3147	0133
1N3148	0318
1N3149	OEM
1N3149A	OEM
1N3150	OEM
1N3151	OEM
1N3154	0244
1N3154-1	OEM
1N3154A	0244
1N3154A1	OEM
1N3155	0244
1N3155A	0244
1N3155A-1	OEM
1N3155A1	OEM
1N3156	0244
1N3156-1	OEM
1N3156A	0244
1N3156A1	OEM
1N3157	0244
1N3157-1	OEM
1N3157A	0244
1N3157A1	OEM
1N3159	OEM
1N3160	0015
1N3161	1017
1N3161R	0496
1N3161RC	1771
1N3162	1017
1N3162R	0496
1N3163	1017
1N3163R	0496
1N3164	1017
1N3164R	0496
1N3165	1017
1N3165R	0496
1N3166	1017
1N3166R	0496
1N3167	1017
1N3167R	1766
1N3168	1017
1N3168R	1766
1N3169	1030
1N3169R	1766
1N3170	1030
1N3170R	1766
1N3171	1040
1N3171A	1040
1N3171R	1778
1N3171RA	1778
1N3172	1040
1N3172A	1040
1N3172R	1778
1N3172RA	1778
1N3173	1040
1N3173A	1040
1N3173R	1778
1N3173RA	1778
1N3174	1040
1N3174A	1040
1N3174R	1778
1N3174RA	1778
1N3175	3872
1N3176	OEM
1N3177	OEM
1N3179	0604
1N3180	0604
1N3181	0644
1N3182	0030
1N3183	0015
1N3184	0015
1N3185	0071
1N3186	0071
1N3187	OEM
1N3188	OEM
1N3189	0015
1N3190	0015
1N3191	0015
1N3193	0015
1N3194	0023
1N3195	0023
1N3196	0023
1N3197	0133
1N3198	OEM
1N3199	0165
1N3200	OEM
1N3201	OEM
1N3202	OEM
1N3203	0015
1N3204	0143
1N3205	OEM
1N3206	0133
1N3207	0133
1N3208	1991
1N3208R	1992
1N3209	0585
1N3209R	3234
1N3210	1241
1N3210R	1567
1N3211	5487
1N3211R	3244
1N3212	1571
1N3212R	3251
1N3213	5489
1N3213R	3256
1N3214	1576
1N3214R	3263
1N3215	OEM
1N3217	OEM
1N3218	OEM
1N3219	OEM
1N3220	OEM
1N3221	0071
1N3222	OEM
1N3223	0133
1N3224	OEM
1N3225	OEM
1N3227	0947
1N3228	0242
1N3229	1760
1N3230	0959
1N3231	0811
1N3232	0916
1N3233	0102
1N3234	6445
1N3235	0344
1N3236	0344
1N3237	0110
1N3238	0947
1N3239	0242
1N3240	0535
1N3241	0959
1N3242	0811
1N3243	0916
1N3244	0102
1N3245	6445
1N3246	0110
1N3247	0947
1N3248	0242
1N3249	0535
1N3250	0959
1N3251	0811
1N3252	0916
1N3253	0015
1N3254	0015
1N3255	0015
1N3256	0071
1N3257	0133
1N3258	0133
1N3260	1017
1N3260R	0496
1N3261	1017
1N3261R	0496
1N3262	1017
1N3262R	0496
1N3263	1017
1N3263R	0496
1N3264	1017
1N3264R	0496
1N3265	1017
1N3265R	0496
1N3266	1017
1N3266R	0496
1N3267	1017
1N3267R	0496
1N3268	1030
1N3268R	1766
1N3269	1030
1N3269R	0800
1N3270	1040
1N3270R	1778
1N3271	1040
1N3271R	1778
1N3272	1040
1N3272R	1778
1N3273	1040
1N3273R	1778
1N3274	3872
1N3274R	3489
1N3275	2805
1N3275R	3138
1N3276	OEM
1N3276R	OEM
1N3277	0015
1N3278	0015
1N3279	0015
1N3280	0071
1N3281	0071
1N3282	0071
1N3283	0344
1N3284	OEM
1N3285	OEM
1N3286	OEM
1N3287	0143
1N3287N	0143
1N3287W	0143
1N3288	0594
1N3288A	0594
1N3288AR	1337
1N3288R	1337
1N3288RA	1337
1N3289	0594
1N3289A	0594
1N3289AR	1337
1N3289R	1337
1N3289RA	1337
1N3290	0594
1N3290A	0594
1N3290AR	1337
1N3290R	1337
1N3290RA	1337
1N3291	0594
1N3291A	0594
1N3291AR	1337
1N3291R	1337
1N3291RA	1337
1N3292	1975
1N3292A	1975
1N3292AR	1894
1N3292B	1975
1N3292BR	1894
1N3292R	1894
1N3292RA	1894
1N3292RB	1894
1N3293	1975
1N3293A	1975
1N3293AR	1894
1N3293R	1894
1N3293RA	1894
1N3294	0652
1N3294A	0652
1N3294AR	0193
1N3294R	0193
1N3294RA	0193
1N3295	0652
1N3295A	0652
1N3295AR	0193
1N3295R	0193
1N3295RA	0193
1N3296	3277
1N3296A	3277
1N3296AR	0202
1N3296R	0202
1N3296RA	0202
1N3297	OEM
1N3297A	3277
1N3297AR	0202
1N3297RA	3277
1N3298	0023
1N3298A	OEM
1N3299	OEM
1N3300	3603
1N3300A	3603
1N3301	3298
1N3301A	3298
1N3302	2704
1N3302A	2704
1N3303	OEM
1N3303A	2704
1N3304	OEM
1N3304A	OEM
1N3305	0920
1N3305A	0920
1N3305AR	2713
1N3305B	0920
1N3305BR	2713
1N3305R	2713
1N3305RA	2713
1N3305RB	2713
1N3306	0938
1N3306A	0938
1N3306B	0938
1N3306R	2717
1N3306RA	2717
1N3306RB	2717
1N3307	0952
1N3307A	0952
1N3307AR	1216
1N3307B	0952
1N3307BR	1216
1N3307R	1216
1N3307RA	1216
1N3307RB	1216
1N3308	0988
1N3308A	0988
1N3308B	0988
1N3308R	1228
1N3308RA	1228
1N3308RB	1228
1N3309	1003
1N3309A	1003
1N3309AR	1243
1N3309B	1003
1N3309BR	1243
1N3309R	1243
1N3309RA	1243
1N3309RB	1243
1N3310	1013
1N3310A	1013
1N3310B	1013
1N3310R	1259
1N3310RA	1259
1N3310RB	1259
1N3311	0883
1N3311A	0883
1N3311AR	1267
1N3311B	0883
1N3311BR	1267
1N3311R	1267
1N3311RA	1267
1N3311RB	1267
1N3312	1043
1N3312A	1043
1N3312B	1043
1N3312R	1283
1N3312RA	1283
1N3312RB	1283
1N3313	1052
1N3313A	1052
1N3313B	1052
1N3313R	2725
1N3313RA	2725
1N3313RB	2725
1N3314	0926
1N3314A	0926
1N3314AR	1292
1N3314B	0926
1N3314BR	1292
1N3314R	1292
1N3314RA	1292
1N3314RB	1292
1N3315	1072
1N3315A	1072
1N3315B	1072
1N3315R	1300
1N3315RA	1300
1N3315RB	1300
1N3316	1088
1N3316A	1088
1N3316B	1088
1N3316R	2729
1N3316RA	2729
1N3316RB	2729
1N3317	1098
1N3317A	1098
1N3317AR	1314
1N3317B	1098
1N3317BR	1314
1N3317R	1314
1N3317RA	1314
1N3317RB	1314
1N3318	1115
1N3318A	1115
1N3318B	1115
1N3318R	2731
1N3318RA	2731
1N3318RB	2731
1N3319	1127
1N3319A	1127
1N3319B	1127
1N3319R	1323
1N3319RA	1323
1N3319RB	1323
1N3320	1144
1N3320A	1144
1N3320AR	1334
1N3320B	1144
1N3320BR	1334
1N3320R	1334
1N3320RA	1334
1N3320RB	1334
1N3321	1156
1N3321A	1156
1N3321B	1156
1N3321R	1346
1N3321RA	1346
1N3321RB	1346
1N3322	1166
1N3322A	1166
1N3322B	1166
1N3322R	2733
1N3322RA	2733
1N3322RB	2733
1N3323	1176
1N3323A	1176
1N3323AR	1361
1N3323B	1176
1N3323BR	1361
1N3323R	1361
1N3323RA	1361
1N3323RB	1361
1N3324	1201
1N3324A	1201
1N3324B	1201
1N3324R	1377
1N3324RA	1377
1N3324RB	1377
1N3325	1214
1N3325A	1214
1N3325AR	1396
1N3325B	1214
1N3325BR	1396
1N3325R	1396
1N3325RA	1396
1N3325RB	1396
1N3326	1223
1N3326A	1223
1N3326B	1223
1N3326R	1405
1N3326RA	1405
1N3326RB	1405
1N3327	1237
1N3327A	1237
1N3327AR	1419
1N3327B	1237
1N3327BR	1419
1N3327R	1419
1N3327RA	1419
1N3327RB	1419
1N3328	1256
1N3328A	1256
1N3328B	1256
1N3328R	1431
1N3328RA	1431
1N3328RB	1431
1N3329	1263
1N3329A	1263
1N3329B	1263
1N3329R	2745
1N3329RA	2745
1N3329RB	2745
1N3330	1280
1N3330A	1280
1N3330B	1280
1N3330R	1438
1N3330RA	1438
1N3330RB	1438
1N3331	1289
1N3331A	1289
1N3331B	1289
1N3331R	2749
1N3331RA	2749
1N3331RB	2749
1N3332	1297
1N3332A	1297
1N3332B	1297
1N3332R	1452
1N3332RA	1452
1N3332RB	1452
1N3333	1312
1N3333A	1312
1N3333B	1312
1N3333R	2752
1N3333RA	2752
1N3333RB	2752
1N3334	1321
1N3334A	1321
1N3334AR	1465
1N3334B	1321
1N3334BR	1465
1N3334R	1465
1N3334RA	1465
1N3334RB	1465
1N3335	1343
1N3335A	1343
1N3335B	1343
1N3335R	0608
1N3335RA	0608
1N3335RB	0608
1N3336	1355
1N3336A	1355
1N3336B	1355
1N3336R	1502
1N3336RA	1502
1N3336RB	1502
1N3337	1374
1N3337A	1374
1N3337B	1374
1N3337R	1515
1N3337RA	1515
1N3337RB	1515
1N3338	1391
1N3338A	1391
1N3338B	1391
1N3338R	1529
1N3338RA	1529
1N3338RB	1529
1N3339	1402
1N3339A	1402
1N3339B	1402
1N3339R	1541
1N3339RA	1541
1N3339RB	1541
1N3340	1413
1N3340A	1413
1N3340AR	1565
1N3340B	1413
1N3340BR	1565
1N3340R	1565
1N3340RA	1565
1N3340RB	1565
1N3341	1427
1N3341A	1427
1N3341B	1427
1N3341R	2775
1N3341RA	2775
1N3341RB	2775
1N3342	1435
1N3342A	1435
1N3342B	1435
1N3342R	2776
1N3342RA	2776
1N3342RB	2776
1N3343	1448
1N3343A	1448
1N3343B	1448
1N3343R	1499
1N3343RA	1499
1N3343RB	1499
1N3344	1461
1N3344A	1461
1N3344B	1461
1N3344R	2778
1N3344RA	2778
1N3344RB	2778
1N3345	1475
1N3345A	1475
1N3345B	1475
1N3345R	2780
1N3345RA	2780
1N3345RB	2780
1N3346	1497
1N3346A	1497
1N3346B	1497
1N3346R	2783
1N3346RA	2783
1N3346RB	2783
1N3347	1513
1N3347A	1513
1N3347B	1513
1N3347R	2788
1N3347RA	2788
1N3347RB	2788
1N3348	1523
1N3348A	1523
1N3348B	1523
1N3348R	2791
1N3348RA	2791
1N3348RB	2791
1N3349	1539
1N3349A	1539
1N3349B	1539
1N3349R	2793
1N3349RA	2793
1N3349RB	2793
1N3350	1577
1N3350A	1577
1N3350B	1577
1N3350R	2797
1N3350RA	2797
1N3350RB	2797
1N3353	OEM
1N3354	OEM
1N3355	OEM
1N3356	OEM
1N3357	OEM
1N3358	OEM
1N3359	OEM
1N3360	OEM
1N3361	OEM
1N3362	OEM
1N3363	OEM
1N3364	OEM
1N3365	OEM
1N3366	OEM
1N3367	OEM
1N3368	OEM
1N3369	OEM
1N3370	OEM
1N3371	OEM
1N3372	OEM
1N3373	OEM
1N3374	OEM
1N3375	OEM
1N3376	OEM
1N3377	OEM
1N3378	OEM
1N3379	OEM
1N3380	OEM
1N3381	1325
1N3382	0133
1N3383	1325
1N3384	0080
1N3385	0080
1N3386	0604
1N3387	0604
1N3388	0790
1N3389	0790
1N3390	0790
1N3391	OEM
1N3392	OEM
1N3393	OEM
1N3394	OEM
1N3395	OEM
1N3396	0296
1N3397	OEM
1N3398	OEM
1N3399	0157
1N3400	0062
1N3401	0165
1N3401-0	0244
1N34010	0244
1N3402	0064
1N3403	0052
1N3404	0681
1N3405	0371
1N3406	0700
1N3407	0450
1N3408	0166
1N3409	0032
1N3410	0068
1N3411	0466
1N3412	0062
1N3413	0077
1N3414	0165
1N3415	0064

If replacement code is OEM, contact original manufacturer for replacement.

DEVICE TYPE	REPL CODE
1N3416	0052
1N3417	0681
1N3418	0371
1N3419	0700
1N3420	0450
1N3421	0195
1N3422	0166
1N3423	0032
1N3424	0068
1N3425	0125
1N3426	0173
1N3427	0049
1N3428	0189
1N3429	0089
1N3430	0336
1N3431	0420
1N3432	OEM
1N3433	1481
1N3433A	1481
1N3433C	OEM
1N3433R	1612
1N3433RA	1612
1N3434	0505
1N3434A	0505
1N3434C	OEM
1N3434R	0986
1N3434RA	0986
1N3435	0864
1N3435A	0864
1N3435C	OEM
1N3435R	1254
1N3435RA	1254
1N3436	1264
1N3436A	1264
1N3436C	OEM
1N3436R	1629
1N3436RA	1629
1N3437	1071
1N3437A	1071
1N3437C	OEM
1N3437R	1706
1N3437RA	1706
1N3438	1712
1N3438A	1712
1N3438C	OEM
1N3438R	0722
1N3438RA	0722
1N3439	1750
1N3439A	1750
1N3439C	OEM
1N3439R	1771
1N3439RA	1771
1N3440	1777
1N3440A	1777
1N3440C	OEM
1N3440R	1788
1N3440RA	1788
1N3441	1793
1N3441A	1793
1N3441C	OEM
1N3441R	1806
1N3441RA	1806
1N3442	0022
1N3442A	0022
1N3442C	OEM
1N3442R	1842
1N3442RA	1842
1N3443	0691
1N3443A	0691
1N3443R	2206
1N3443RA	2206
1N3444	1591
1N3444A	1591
1N3444R	1449
1N3444RA	1449
1N3445	1606
1N3445A	1606
1N3445R	0221
1N3445RA	0221
1N3446	0986
1N3446A	0986
1N3446R	0505
1N3446RA	0505
1N3447	1254
1N3447A	1254
1N3447R	0864
1N3447RA	0864
1N3448	1629
1N3448A	1629
1N3448R	1264
1N3448RA	1264
1N3449	1706
1N3449A	1706
1N3449R	1071
1N3449RA	1071
1N3450	0722
1N3450A	0722
1N3450R	1712
1N3450RA	1712
1N3451	1771
1N3451A	1771
1N3451R	1750
1N3451RA	1750
1N3452	1783
1N3452A	1783
1N3452R	1761
1N3452RA	1761
1N3453	1788
1N3453A	1788
1N3453R	1777
1N3453RA	1777
1N3454	1806
1N3454A	1806
1N3454R	1793
1N3454RA	1793
1N3455	1842
1N3455A	1842
1N3455R	0022
1N3455RA	0022
1N3456	1873
1N3456A	1873
1N3456R	0207
1N3456RA	0207
1N3457	1891
1N3457A	1891
1N3457R	0306
1N3457RA	0306
1N3458	1898
1N3458A	1898
1N3458R	0352
1N3458RA	0352
1N3459	1155
1N3459A	1155
1N3459R	0433
1N3459RA	0433
1N3460	1930
1N3460A	1930
1N3460R	0504
1N3460RA	0504
1N3461	1950
1N3461A	1950
1N3461R	0063
1N3461RA	0063
1N3462	0771
1N3462A	0771
1N3462R	0629
1N3462RA	0629
1N3463	OEM
1N3463A	OEM
1N3463R	OEM
1N3463RA	OEM
1N3464	OEM
1N3465	0143
1N3466	0143
1N3467	0143
1N3468	0143
1N3469	0143
1N3470	0143
1N3471	0133
1N3473	0015
1N3474	0015
1N3475	0015
1N3476	0071
1N3477	OEM
1N3477A	OEM
1N3481	OEM
1N3482	0143
1N3483	0143
1N3484	0143
1N3485	OEM
1N3486	0947
1N3487	0102
1N3488	OEM
1N3489	OEM
1N3489A	OEM
1N3490	OEM
1N3491	4938
1N3491R	2537
1N3492	2591
1N3492R	2544
1N3493	2591
1N3493R	2544
1N3494	4938
1N3494R	2537
1N3495	4938
1N3495R	2537
1N3496	0466
1N3497	0466
1N3498	0466
1N3499	0466
1N3500	0466
1N3501	OEM
1N3502	OEM
1N3503	OEM
1N3503A	OEM
1N3504	OEM
1N3504A	OEM
1N3506	0296
1N3507	0372
1N3508	0036
1N3509	0274
1N3510	0140
1N3511	0162
1N3512	0253
1N3513	0466
1N3514	0062
1N3514R	0267
1N3515	0077
1N3516	0165
1N3517	0057
1N3518	0064
1N3519	0181
1N3520	0052
1N3521	0053
1N3522	0681
1N3523	0440
1N3524	0371
1N3525	0695
1N3526	0700
1N3527	0489
1N3528	0450
1N3529	0195
1N3530	0166
1N3531	0814
1N3532	0032
1N3533	0054
1N3534	0068
1N3537	0137
1N3539	OEM
1N3539A	OEM
1N3540	OEM
1N3540A	OEM
1N3541	OEM
1N3541A	OEM
1N3541B	0122
1N3542	OEM
1N3542A	OEM
1N3542B	0122
1N3543	OEM
1N3543A	OEM
1N3544	0015
1N3544B	0122
1N3545	0015
1N3545B	0959
1N3546	0015
1N3546B	0122
1N3547	0015
1N3547B	0122
1N3548	0015
1N3548B	0122
1N3549	0015
1N3550	0133
1N3551	OEM
1N3552	OEM
1N3553	0466
1N3554	0715
1N3555	OEM
1N3556	OEM
1N3557	OEM
1N3558	OEM
1N3559	0143
1N3560	OEM
1N3561	OEM
1N3562	OEM
1N3563	0916
1N3564	0143
1N3565	0703
1N3566	OEM
1N3567	OEM
1N3568	OEM
1N3569	3688
1N3569R	2275
1N3570	0983
1N3570R	2275
1N3571	3697
1N3571R	0471
1N3572	0197
1N3572R	0471
1N3573	0200
1N3573R	0471
1N3574	0204
1N3574R	0471
1N3575	0133
1N3576	0133
1N3577	0133
1N3578	0790
1N3579	0790
1N3580	0789
1N3580A	0789
1N3580B	0789
1N3581	0789
1N3581A	0789
1N3581B	0789
1N3582	0789
1N3582A	0789
1N3582B	0789
1N3583	0137
1N3583A	0137
1N3583B	0137
1N3584	0789
1N3584A	0789
1N3584B	0789
1N3585	OEM
1N3586	OEM
1N3587	OEM
1N3588	OEM
1N3589	OEM
1N3590	OEM
1N3591	OEM
1N3592	0143
1N3593	0133
1N3594	0133
1N3595	0133
1N3596	0133
1N3597	OEM
1N3598	0133
1N3599	0133
1N3600	0124
1N3601	0133
1N3602	0133
1N3603	0133
1N3604	0133
1N3605	0133
1N3606	0133
1N3607	0133
1N3608	0133
1N3609	0133
1N3610	2872
1N3611	0604
1N3611GP	0604
1N3612	0790
1N3612GP	0790
1N3613	0015
1N3613GP	0015
1N3614	0072
1N3614GP	0072
1N3615	5417
1N3615R	1229
1N3616	5482
1N3616R	1231
1N3617	2872
1N3617R	1232
1N3618	2872
1N3618R	1232
1N3619	3705
1N3619R	2349
1N3620	3705
1N3620R	2349
1N3621	3711
1N3621R	1244
1N3622	1599
1N3622R	2360
1N3623	3722
1N3623R	1255
1N3624	2982
1N3624R	0444
1N3625	0133
1N3626	0133
1N3627	OEM
1N3628	OEM
1N3629	0015
1N3630	0015
1N3631	0015
1N3632	0015
1N3633	0015
1N3634	0015
1N3635	0071
1N3636	0071
1N3637	0071
1N3638	0071
1N3639	0015
1N3640	0015
1N3641	0015
1N3642	0071
1N3643	0369
1N3644	0344
1N3645	0344
1N3646	OEM
1N3647	OEM
1N3648	OEM
1N3649	0206
1N3649(REV.POL.)	1002
1N3649R	1002
1N3650	0583
1N3650R	0444
1N3653	0133
1N3654	0133
1N3655	OEM
1N3655A	0601
1N3655B	OEM
1N3656	0242
1N3657	0535
1N3658	0959
1N3659	4938
1N3659R	2537
1N3660	4938
1N3660R	2537
1N3661	4938
1N3661R	2537
1N3662	4938
1N3662R	2537
1N3663	4938
1N3663R	2537
1N3664	2591
1N3665	2591
1N3665R	OEM
1N3666	0133
1N3667	OEM
1N3668	0133
1N3669	0015
1N3670	0131
1N3670A	0131
1N3670AR	0540
1N3670R	0540
1N3670RA	0540
1N3671	0131
1N3671A	0131
1N3671AR	0540
1N3671R	0540
1N3671RA	0540
1N3672	0145
1N3672A	0145
1N3672AR	0545
1N3672R	0545
1N3672RA	0545
1N3673	0145
1N3673A	0145
1N3673AR	0545
1N3673R	0545
1N3673RA	0545
1N3675	0025
1N3675A	0025
1N3675B	0025
1N3676	0644
1N3676A	0644
1N3676B	0644
1N3677	0244
1N3677A	0244
1N3677B	0244
1N3678	0012
1N3678A	0012
1N3678B	0012
1N3679	0170
1N3679A	0170
1N3679B	0170
1N3680	0313
1N3680A	0313
1N3680B	0313
1N3681	0137
1N3681A	0137
1N3681B	0137
1N3682	0361
1N3682A	0361
1N3682B	0361
1N3683	0002
1N3683A	0002
1N3683B	0002
1N3684	0416
1N3684A	0416
1N3684B	0416
1N3685	0490
1N3685A	0490
1N3685B	0490
1N3686	0526
1N3686A	0526
1N3686B	0526
1N3687	0560
1N3687A	0560
1N3687B	0560
1N3688	0398
1N3688A	0398
1N3688B	0398
1N3689	0436
1N3689A	0436
1N3689B	0436
1N3690	0721
1N3690A	0721
1N3690B	0721
1N3691	0039
1N3691A	0039
1N3691B	0039
1N3692	0814
1N3692A	0814
1N3692B	0814
1N3693	0346
1N3693A	0346
1N3693B	0346
1N3694	0925
1N3694A	0925
1N3694B	0925
1N3695	0993
1N3695A	0993
1N3695B	0993
1N3696	0497
1N3696A	0497
1N3696B	0497
1N3697	0863
1N3697A	0863
1N3697B	0863
1N3698	0778
1N3698A	0778
1N3698B	0778
1N3699	1258
1N3699A	1258
1N3699B	1258
1N3700	1181
1N3700A	1181
1N3700B	1181
1N3701	0327
1N3701A	0327
1N3701B	0327
1N3702	1301
1N3702A	1301
1N3702B	1301
1N3703	0098
1N3703A	0098
1N3703B	0098
1N3704	0149
1N3704A	0149
1N3704B	0149
1N3705	0186
1N3705A	0186
1N3705B	0186
1N3706	0213
1N3706A	0213
1N3706B	0213
1N3707	0028
1N3707A	0028
1N3707B	0028
1N3708	0255
1N3708A	0255
1N3708B	0255
1N3709	0363
1N3709A	0363
1N3709B	0363
1N3710	0417
1N3710A	0417
1N3710B	0417
1N3711	OEM
1N3712	OEM
1N3713	OEM
1N3714	OEM
1N3715	OEM
1N3716	OEM
1N3717	OEM
1N3718	OEM
1N3719	OEM
1N3720	OEM
1N3721	OEM
1N3722	0133
1N3723	0916
1N3724	0102
1N3725	0102
1N3726	0344
1N3727	0344
1N3728	0790
1N3729	0102
1N3730	OEM
1N3731	0023
1N3732	0162
1N3733	OEM
1N3734	OEM
1N3735	1017
1N3735R	0496
1N3736	1017
1N3736A	0298
1N3736R	0496
1N3737	1017
1N3737R	0496
1N3738	1017
1N3738R	0496
1N3739	1030
1N3739R	1766
1N3740	1030
1N3740R	1766
1N3741	1040
1N3741R	1778
1N3742	1040
1N3742R	1778
1N3743	3872
1N3743R	2765
1N3744	2805
1N3744R	3138
1N3745	1107
1N3746	OEM
1N3747	OEM
1N3747W	OEM
1N3748	0242
1N3749	0535
1N3750	0959
1N3751	0811
1N3752	0916
1N3753	0143
1N3754	0015
1N3755	0242
1N3756	0023
1N3757	0242
1N3758	0535
1N3759	0959
1N3760	0811
1N3761	0916
1N3762	OEM
1N3763	0262
1N3764	OEM
1N3765	1124
1N3765R	1111
1N3766	1124
1N3766R	1111
1N3767	0045
1N3767R	0280
1N3768	0045
1N3768R	0280
1N3769	0143
1N3770	OEM
1N3771	OEM
1N3772	OEM
1N3773	0143
1N3774	OEM
1N3775	OEM
1N3776	0170
1N3777	1124
1N3778	OEM
1N3779	0062
1N3780	0062
1N3781	0062
1N3782	0789
1N3782A	0789
1N3782B	0789
1N3783	0062
1N3784	0789
1N3784A	0789
1N3784B	0789
1N3785	0205
1N3785A	0205
1N3785B	0205
1N3786	0475
1N3786A	0475
1N3786B	0475
1N3787	0499
1N3787A	0499
1N3787B	0499
1N3788	0679
1N3788A	0679
1N3788B	0679
1N3789	0225
1N3789A	0225
1N3789B	0225
1N3790	0230
1N3790A	0230
1N3790B	0230
1N3791	0234
1N3791A	0234
1N3791B	0234
1N3792	0237
1N3792A	0237
1N3792B	0237
1N3793	0247
1N3793A	0247
1N3793B	0247
1N3794	0251
1N3794A	0251
1N3794B	0251
1N3795	0256
1N3795A	0256
1N3795B	0256
1N3796	0262
1N3796A	0262
1N3796B	0262
1N3797	0269
1N3797A	0269
1N3797B	0269
1N3798	0273
1N3798A	0273
1N3798B	0273
1N3799	0291
1N3799A	0291
1N3799B	0291
1N3800	0305
1N3800A	0305
1N3800B	0305
1N3801	0314
1N3801A	0314
1N3801B	0314
1N3802	0316
1N3802A	0316
1N3802B	0316
1N3803	0322
1N3803A	0322
1N3803B	0322
1N3804	0333
1N3804A	0333
1N3804B	0333
1N3805	0343
1N3805A	0343
1N3805B	0343
1N3806	0027
1N3806A	0027
1N3806B	0027
1N3807	0266
1N3807A	0266
1N3807B	0266
1N3808	0382
1N3808A	0382
1N3808B	0382
1N3809	0401
1N3809A	0401
1N3809B	0401
1N3810	0421
1N3810A	0421
1N3810B	0421
1N3811	0439
1N3811A	0439
1N3811B	0439
1N3812	0238
1N3812A	0238
1N3812B	0238
1N3813	1172
1N3813A	1172
1N3813B	1172
1N3814	1182
1N3814A	1182
1N3814B	1182
1N3815	1198
1N3815A	1198
1N3815B	1198
1N3816	1209
1N3816A	1209
1N3816B	1209
1N3817	0642
1N3817A	0642
1N3817B	0642
1N3818	1246
1N3818A	1246
1N3818B	1246
1N3819	1269
1N3819A	1269
1N3819B	1269
1N3820	0600
1N3820A	0600
1N3820B	0600
1N3821	0289
1N3821A	0289
1N3822	0188
1N3822A	0188
1N3823	0451
1N3823A	0451
1N3824	0528
1N3824A	0528
1N3825	0446
1N3825A	0446
1N3826	0162
1N3826A	0162
1N3827	0157
1N3827A	0157
1N3828	0631
1N3828A	0631
1N3829	0025
1N3829A	0025
1N3829B	OEM
1N3830	0644
1N3830A	0644
1N3831	OEM
1N3832	OEM

If replacement code is OEM, contact original manufacturer for replacement.

DEVICE TYPE	REPL CODE
1N3833	OEM
1N3834	OEM
1N3835	OEM
1N3836	OEM
1N3837	OEM
1N3838	OEM
1N3839	OEM
1N3840	OEM
1N3841	OEM
1N3842	OEM
1N3843	OEM
1N3844	OEM
1N3845	OEM
1N3846	OEM
1N3847	OEM
1N3848	OEM
1N3849	OEM
1N3850	OEM
1N3851	OEM
1N3852	OEM
1N3853	OEM
1N3854	OEM
1N3855A	0012
1N3856	OEM
1N3857	OEM
1N3858	OEM
1N3859	OEM
1N3860	OEM
1N3862	OEM
1N3864	0133
1N3865	1325
1N3866	0242
1N3867	0535
1N3868	0959
1N3869	0916
1N3870	0182
1N3871	OEM
1N3872	0133
1N3873	0133
1N3874	0914
1N3875	0015
1N3876	OEM
1N3877	OEM
1N3878	OEM
1N3879	1557
1N3879A	1557
1N3879R	1538
1N3879RA	1538
1N3880	1557
1N3880A	1557
1N3880R	1538
1N3880RA	1538
1N3881	1557
1N3881A	1557
1N3881R	1538
1N3881RA	1538
1N3882	2140
1N3882A	2140
1N3882R	3110
1N3882RA	3110
1N3883	2140
1N3883A	2140
1N3883R	3110
1N3883RA	3110
1N3884	OEM
1N3885	OEM
1N3886	OEM
1N3887	OEM
1N3888	OEM
1N3889	1557
1N3889A	1266
1N3889R	1538
1N3889RA	1538
1N3890	1557
1N3890A	1557
1N3890R	1538
1N3890RA	1538
1N3891	1557
1N3891A	1557
1N3891R	1538
1N3891RA	1538
1N3892	2140
1N3892A	2140
1N3892R	3110
1N3892RA	3110
1N3893	2140
1N3893A	2140
1N3893R	3110
1N3893RA	3110
1N3894	0790
1N3895	0790
1N3896	OEM
1N3897	OEM
1N3898	OEM
1N3899	1522
1N3899R	1512
1N3900	1522
1N3900R	1512
1N3901	1522
1N3901R	1512
1N3902	0029
1N3902R	1836
1N3903	0029
1N3903R	1836
1N3904	OEM
1N3905	OEM
1N3906	OEM
1N3907	OEM
1N3908	OEM
1N3909	1522
1N3909R	1512
1N3910	1522
1N3910R	1512
1N3911	1522
1N3911R	1512
1N3912	0029
1N3912R	1836
1N3913	0029
1N3913R	1836
1N3914	0914
1N3915	0102
1N3916	OEM
1N3917	OEM
1N3918	OEM
1N3919	0583
1N3920	OEM
1N3921	OEM
1N3922	OEM
1N3923	OEM
1N3924	0145
1N3925	OEM
1N3926	OEM
1N3927	OEM
1N3928	OEM
1N3929	0071
1N3930	OEM
1N3931	OEM
1N3932	OEM
1N3933	OEM
1N3934	OEM
1N3935	OEM
1N3936	OEM
1N3938	0242
1N3939	0535
1N3940	0959
1N3941	0811
1N3942	0916
1N3943	OEM
1N3944	OEM
1N3945	OEM
1N3946	OEM
1N3947	0631
1N3949	1707
1N3949A	1707
1N3950	0262
1N3951	2383
1N3952	0242
1N3953	0133
1N3954	0133
1N3955	OEM
1N3956	0133
1N3957	0071
1N3957GP	0071
1N3958	0097
1N3958C	OEM
1N3959	0097
1N3959C	OEM
1N3960	0097
1N3960C	OEM
1N3961	0097
1N3961C	OEM
1N3962	0097
1N3962C	OEM
1N3963	OEM
1N3963C	OEM
1N3964	0865
1N3965	0847
1N3966	1599
1N3966R	1196
1N3967	1600
1N3968	2633
1N3968R	2741
1N3969	1995
1N3969R	2879
1N3970	2657
1N3970R	3022
1N3971	3846
1N3971R	3088
1N3972	0594
1N3973	0594
1N3974	1975
1N3975	0652
1N3976	1017
1N3977	1017
1N3978	1241
1N3979	OEM
1N3980	OEM
1N3981	0242
1N3982	0535
1N3983	0959
1N3984	1890
1N3984A	1890
1N3985	2400
1N3985A	2400
1N3986	0691
1N3986A	0691
1N3987	0206
1N3987R	1002
1N3988	0206
1N3988R	1002
1N3989	0583
1N3989R	0942
1N3990	0583
1N3990R	0545
1N3991	0143
1N3992	OEM
1N3993	0542
1N3993A	0542
1N3993B	0542
1N3993R	2024
1N3993RA	2024
1N3993RB	2024
1N3994	2387
1N3994A	2387
1N3994B	2387
1N3994R	2385
1N3994RA	2385
1N3994RB	2385
1N3995	2101
1N3995A	2101
1N3995B	2101
1N3995R	1429
1N3995RA	1429
1N3995RB	1429
1N3996	2394
1N3996A	2394
1N399C?	2394
1N3996R	2391
1N3996RA	2391
1N3996RB	2391
1N3997	1890
1N3997A	1890
1N3997B	1890
1N3997R	1436
1N3997RA	1436
1N3997RB	1436
1N3998	0691
1N3998A	0691
1N3998R	2206
1N3998RA	2206
1N3998RB	2206
1N3999	1591
1N3999A	1591
1N3999R	1449
1N3999RA	1449
1N4000	1606
1N4000A	1606
1N4000R	0221
1N4000RA	0221
1N4001	5551
1N4001A	1325
1N4001F	OEM
1N4001G	1325
1N4001GP	1325
1N4001RL	OEM
1N4002	0080
1N4002A	0080
1N4002F	OEM
1N4002G	0080
1N4002GP	6398
1N4002ID	0080
1N4002IO	0080
1N4002L	0080
1N4002RL	OEM
1N4002TA	6398
1N4003	5627
1N4003-T3	0023
1N4003-Z	0604
1N4003A	0604
1N4003F	OEM
1N4003G	0604
1N4003GP	0023
1N4003K	OEM
1N4003PX	0604
1N4003RL	0604
1N4003TA	0604
1N4004	0790
1N4004A	0790
1N4004F	OEM
1N4004G	0790
1N4004GP	0790
1N4004RL	OEM
1N4004TA	0790
1N4004TP	OEM
1N4005	0015
1N4005BP	0015
1N4005F	OEM
1N4005G	0015
1N4005GP	0015
1N4005RL	OEM
1N4006	0072
1N4006F	OEM
1N4006G	0071
1N4006GP	0072
1N4006RL	OEM
1N4007	0023
1N4007F	OEM
1N4007G	0071
1N4007GP	0071
1N4007RL	OEM
1N4008	OEM
1N4009	0133
1N4010	0466
1N4011	0071
1N4012	0131
1N4012R	0540
1N4013	0131
1N4013R	0540
1N4014	0145
1N4014R	0545
1N4015	0145
1N4015R	0545
1N4016	1481
1N4016A	1481
1N4016B	1481
1N4017	1608
1N4017A	1608
1N4017B	1608
1N4018	0505
1N4018A	0505
1N4018B	0505
1N4019	0686
1N4019A	0686
1N4019B	0686
1N4020	0864
1N4020A	0864
1N4020B	0864
1N4021	1014
1N4021A	1014
1N4021B	1014
1N4022	1264
1N4022A	1264
1N4022B	1264
1N4023	1392
1N4023A	1392
1N4023B	1392
1N4024	1071
1N4024A	1071
1N4024B	1071
1N4025	1707
1N4025A	1707
1N4025B	1707
1N4026	1712
1N4026A	1712
1N4026B	1712
1N4027	1725
1N4027A	1725
1N4027B	1725
1N4028	1750
1N4028A	1750
1N4028B	1750
1N4029	1761
1N4029A	1761
1N4029B	0883
1N4030	1777
1N4030A	1777
1N4030B	1777
1N4031	1785
1N4031A	1785
1N4031B	1785
1N4032	1793
1N4032A	1793
1N4032B	1793
1N4033	1185
1N4033A	1185
1N4033B	1185
1N4034	0022
1N4034A	0022
1N4034B	0022
1N4035	0132
1N4035A	0132
1N4035B	0132
1N4036	0207
1N4036A	0207
1N4036B	0207
1N4037	0263
1N4037A	0263
1N4037B	0263
1N4038	0306
1N4038A	0306
1N4038B	0306
1N4039	0325
1N4039A	0325
1N4039B	0325
1N4040	0352
1N4040A	0352
1N4040B	0352
1N4041	0408
1N4041A	0408
1N4041B	0408
1N4042	0433
1N4042A	0433
1N4042B	0433
1N4043	0133
1N4044	1017
1N4044R	0496
1N4045	1017
1N4045R	0496
1N4046	1017
1N4046R	0496
1N4047	1017
1N4047R	0496
1N4048	1017
1N4048R	0496
1N4049	1017
1N4049R	0496
1N4050	1017
1N4050R	0496
1N4051	1030
1N4051R	1766
1N4052	1030
1N4052R	1766
1N4053	1040
1N4053R	1778
1N4054	1040
1N4054R	1778
1N4055	1040
1N4055R	1778
1N4056	1040
1N4056R	1778
1N4057	0234
1N4057A	0234
1N4058	0247
1N4058A	0247
1N4059	1170
1N4059A	1170
1N4060	2379
1N4060A	2379
1N4061	0262
1N4061A	0262
1N4062	0269
1N4062A	0269
1N4063	0291
1N4063A	0291
1N4064	0305
1N4064A	0305
1N4065	0314
1N4065A	0314
1N4066	0316
1N4066A	0316
1N4067	0333
1N4067A	0333
1N4068	0343
1N4068A	0343
1N4069	0027
1N4069A	0027
1N4070	0266
1N4070A	0266
1N4071	0382
1N4071A	0382
1N4072	0401
1N4072A	0401
1N4073	0421
1N4073A	0421
1N4074	0439
1N4074A	0439
1N4075	2999
1N4075A	2999
1N4076	0238
1N4076A	0238
1N4077	1172
1N4077A	1172
1N4078	1182
1N4078A	1182
1N4079	1182
1N4079A	1182
1N4080	1198
1N4080A	1198
1N4081	1209
1N4081A	1209
1N4082	1870
1N4082A	1870
1N4083	0642
1N4083A	0642
1N4084	1269
1N4084A	1269
1N4085	0600
1N4085A	0600
1N4086	2491
1N4087	0133
1N4088	0143
1N4089	0535
1N4090	OEM
1N4091	OEM
1N4092	0133
1N4093	0907
1N4094	OEM
1N4095	0041
1N4096	0238
1N4097	1172
1N4098	0642
1N4099	0062
1N4099-1	OEM
1N4099RL	OEM
1N4100	0077
1N4100-1	OEM
1N4100RL	OEM
1N4101	0165
1N4101-1	OEM
1N4101RL	OEM
1N4102	0318
1N4102-1	OEM
1N4102RL	OEM
1N4103	0057
1N4103-1	OEM
1N4103A	0012
1N4103RL	OEM
1N4104	0064
1N4104-1	OEM
1N4104RL	OEM
1N4105	0181
1N4105-1	OEM
1N4106	0052
1N4106-1	OEM
1N4106A	0137
1N4106RL	OEM
1N4107	0053
1N4107-1	OEM
1N4107RL	OEM
1N4108	0873
1N4108-1	OEM
1N4108A	0100
1N4108B	0100
1N4108RL	OEM
1N4109	0681
1N4109-1	OEM
1N4109RL	OEM
1N4110	0440
1N4110-1	OEM
1N4110RL	OEM
1N4111	0210
1N4111RL	OEM
1N4112	0371
1N4112-1	OEM
1N4112RL	OEM
1N4113	0666
1N4113-1	OEM
1N4113RL	OEM
1N4114	0695
1N4114-1	OEM
1N4114RL	OEM
1N4115	0700
1N4115JAN	OEM
1N4115JTX	OEM
1N4115JTXV	OEM
1N4115RL	OEM
1N4116	0489
1N4116-1	OEM
1N4116RL	OEM
1N4117	0709
1N4117-1	OEM
1N4117RL	OEM
1N4118	0450
1N4118-1	OEM
1N4118RL	OEM
1N4119	0257
1N4119-1	OEM
1N4119RL	OEM
1N4120	0195
1N4120-1	OEM
1N4120RL	OEM
1N4121	0166
1N4121A	0039
1N4121B	0039
1N4121RL	OEM
1N4122	0010
1N4122RL	OEM
1N4123	0032
1N4123RL	OEM
1N4124	0054
1N4124RL	OEM
1N4125	0068
1N4125RL	OEM
1N4126	0068
1N4126RL	OEM
1N4127	0125
1N4127A	0863
1N4127B	0863
1N4127RL	OEM
1N4128	2301
1N4128RL	OEM
1N4129	0152
1N4129A	0778
1N4129B	0778
1N4129RL	OEM
1N4130	0173
1N4130RL	OEM
1N4131	0094
1N4131RL	OEM
1N4132	0049
1N4132A	0327
1N4132B	0327
1N4132RL	OEM
1N4133	0104
1N4133RL	OEM
1N4134	0156
1N4134RL	OEM
1N4135	0189
1N4135RL	OEM
1N4136	2813
1N4136R	1772
1N4137	2823
1N4137R	1772
1N4138	2844
1N4138R	1772
1N4139	0110
1N4140	0947
1N4141	0242
1N4142	0535
1N4143	0959
1N4144	0811
1N4145	0916
1N4146	0102
1N4147	0133
1N4148	0124
1N4148(AU)	0124
1N4148B	OEM
1N4148F	0124
1N4148RE	OEM
1N4148T	0124
1N4148TA	0124
1N4148TD	0124
1N4148TE	0124
1N4148V	0124
1N4149	0124
1N4150	0124
1N4150V	0133
1N4151	0133
1N4152	0133
1N4153	0124
1N4154	0124
1N4155	0102
1N4156	0133
1N4157	0133
1N4158	0025
1N4158A	0025
1N4158B	0025
1N4159	0644
1N4159A	0644
1N4159B	0644
1N4160	0244
1N4160A	0244
1N4160B	0244
1N4161	0012
1N4161A	0012
1N4161B	0012
1N4162	0170
1N4162A	0170
1N4162B	0170
1N4163	0313
1N4163A	0313
1N4163B	0313
1N4164	0137
1N4164A	0137
1N4164B	0137
1N4165	0361
1N4165A	0361
1N4165B	0361
1N4166	0002
1N4166A	0002
1N4166B	0002
1N4167	0416
1N4167A	0416
1N4167B	0416
1N4168	0490
1N4168A	0490
1N4168B	0490
1N4169	0526
1N4169A	0526
1N4169B	0526
1N4170	0560
1N4170A	0560
1N4170B	0560
1N4171	0398
1N4171A	0398
1N4171B	0398
1N4172	0436
1N4172A	0436
1N4172B	0436
1N4173	0721
1N4173A	0721
1N4173B	0721
1N4174	0039
1N4174A	0039
1N4174B	0039
1N4175	0814
1N4175A	0814
1N4175B	0814
1N4176	0346
1N4176A	0346
1N4176B	0346
1N4177	0925
1N4177A	0925
1N4177B	0925
1N4178	0993
1N4178A	0993
1N4178B	0993
1N4179	0497
1N4179A	0497
1N4179B	0497
1N4180	0863
1N4180A	0863
1N4180B	0863
1N4181	0778
1N4181A	0778
1N4181B	0778
1N4182	1258
1N4182A	1258
1N4182B	1258
1N4183	1181
1N4183A	1181
1N4183B	1181
1N4184	0327
1N4184A	0327
1N4184B	0327
1N4185	1301
1N4185A	1301
1N4185B	1301
1N4186	0098
1N4186A	0098
1N4186B	0098
1N4187	0149
1N4187A	0149
1N4187B	0149
1N4188	0186
1N4188A	0186
1N4188B	0186
1N4189	0213
1N4189A	0213
1N4189B	0213
1N4190	0028
1N4190A	0028
1N4190B	0028
1N4191	0255
1N4191A	0255
1N4191B	0255
1N4192	0363
1N4192A	0363
1N4192B	0363
1N4193	0417
1N4193A	0417
1N4193B	0417
1N4194	1449
1N4194A	1449
1N4194B	OEM
1N4195	0221
1N4195A	0221
1N4195B	OEM
1N4196	1481
1N4196A	1481
1N4196B	OEM
1N4197	1608
1N4197A	1608

If replacement code is OEM, contact original manufacturer for replacement.

23

DEVICE TYPE	REPL CODE
1N4197B	OEM
1N4198	0505
1N4198A	0505
1N4198B	OEM
1N4199	0686
1N4199A	0686
1N4199B	OEM
1N4200	0864
1N4200A	0864
1N4200B	OEM
1N4201	1014
1N4201A	1014
1N4201B	OEM
1N4202	1145
1N4202A	1145
1N4202B	OEM
1N4203	1264
1N4203A	1264
1N4203B	OEM
1N4204	1392
1N4204A	1392
1N4204B	OEM
1N4205	1524
1N4205A	1524
1N4205B	OEM
1N4206	1071
1N4206A	1071
1N4206B	OEM
1N4207	1701
1N4207A	1701
1N4207B	OEM
1N4208	1707
1N4208A	1707
1N4208B	OEM
1N4209	1712
1N4209A	1712
1N4209B	OEM
1N4210	1725
1N4210A	1725
1N4210B	OEM
1N4211	1737
1N4211A	1737
1N4211B	OEM
1N4212	1750
1N4212A	1750
1N4212B	OEM
1N4213	1761
1N4213A	1761
1N4213B	OEM
1N4214	1777
1N4214A	1777
1N4214B	OEM
1N4215	1785
1N4215A	1785
1N4215B	OEM
1N4216	1793
1N4216A	1793
1N4216B	OEM
1N4217	1185
1N4217A	1185
1N4217B	OEM
1N4218	1810
1N4218A	1810
1N4218B	OEM
1N4219	0022
1N4219A	0022
1N4219B	OEM
1N4220	0070
1N4220A	0070
1N4220B	OEM
1N4221	0132
1N4221A	0132
1N4221B	OEM
1N4222	0172
1N4222A	0172
1N4222B	OEM
1N4223	0207
1N4223A	0207
1N4223B	OEM
1N4224	0263
1N4224A	0263
1N4224B	OEM
1N4225	0306
1N4225A	0306
1N4225B	OEM
1N4226	0325
1N4226A	0325
1N4226B	OEM
1N4227	0352
1N4227A	0352
1N4227B	OEM
1N4228	0408
1N4228A	0408
1N4228B	OEM
1N4229	0433
1N4229A	0433
1N4229B	OEM
1N4230	0459
1N4230A	0459
1N4230B	OEM
1N4231	0483
1N4231A	0483
1N4231B	OEM
1N4232	0504
1N4232A	0504
1N4232B	OEM
1N4233	0519
1N4233A	0519
1N4233B	OEM

DEVICE TYPE	REPL CODE
1N4234	0537
1N4234A	0537
1N4234B	OEM
1N4235	0063
1N4235A	0063
1N4235B	OEM
1N4236	0397
1N4236A	0397
1N4236B	OEM
1N4237	0611
1N4237A	0611
1N4237B	OEM
1N4238	0629
1N4238A	0629
1N4238B	OEM
1N4239	0663
1N4239A	0663
1N4239B	OEM
1N4240	2391
1N4241	2399
1N4242	0133
1N4243	0133
1N4244	0124
1N4245	0604
1N4245GP	0604
1N4246	0015
1N4246GP	0790
1N4247	0015
1N4247GP	0015
1N4248	0071
1N4248GP	0072
1N4249	0071
1N4249GP	0071
1N4250	0071
1N4251	0071
1N4252	0102
1N4253	6445
1N4254	0017
1N4255	0344
1N4256	OEM
1N4257	OEM
1N4258	1449
1N4258A	1449
1N4258B	OEM
1N4259	0221
1N4259A	0221
1N4259B	OEM
1N4260	1481
1N4260A	1481
1N4260B	OEM
1N4261	1608
1N4261A	1608
1N4261B	OEM
1N4262	0505
1N4262A	0505
1N4262B	OEM
1N4263	0686
1N4263A	0686
1N4263B	0686
1N4264	0864
1N4264A	0864
1N4264B	OEM
1N4265	1014
1N4265A	1014
1N4265B	OEM
1N4266	1264
1N4266A	1264
1N4266B	OEM
1N4267	1392
1N4267A	1392
1N4267B	OEM
1N4268	1071
1N4268A	1071
1N4268B	OEM
1N4269	1707
1N4269A	1707
1N4269B	OEM
1N4270	1712
1N4270A	1712
1N4270B	OEM
1N4271	1725
1N4271A	1725
1N4271B	OEM
1N4272	1750
1N4272A	1750
1N4272B	OEM
1N4273	1761
1N4273A	1761
1N4273B	OEM
1N4274	1777
1N4274A	1777
1N4274B	OEM
1N4275	1785
1N4275A	1785
1N4275B	OEM
1N4276	1793
1N4276A	1793
1N4276B	OEM
1N4277	1185
1N4277A	1185
1N4277B	OEM
1N4278	0022
1N4278A	0022
1N4278B	OEM
1N4279	0132
1N4279A	0132
1N4279B	OEM
1N4280	0207
1N4280A	0207

DEVICE TYPE	REPL CODE
1N4280B	OEM
1N4281	0263
1N4281A	0263
1N4281B	OEM
1N4282	0306
1N4282A	0306
1N4282B	OEM
1N4283	0325
1N4283A	0325
1N4283B	OEM
1N4284	0352
1N4284A	0352
1N4284B	OEM
1N4285	0408
1N4285A	0408
1N4285B	OEM
1N4286	0433
1N4286A	0433
1N4286B	OEM
1N4287	0483
1N4287A	0483
1N4287B	OEM
1N4288	0504
1N4288A	0504
1N4288B	OEM
1N4289	0519
1N4289A	0519
1N4289B	OEM
1N4290	0063
1N4290A	0063
1N4290B	OEM
1N4291	0397
1N4291A	0397
1N4291B	OEM
1N4292	0629
1N4292A	0629
1N4292B	OEM
1N4293	0663
1N4293A	0663
1N4293B	0663
1N4294	OEM
1N4295	0170
1N4295A	0170
1N4296	0170
1N4296A	0170
1N4297	1075
1N4297A	1075
1N4297B	OEM
1N4298	1075
1N4298A	1075
1N4298B	OEM
1N4299	0313
1N4299A	0313
1N4299B	0789
1N4300	0313
1N4300A	0313
1N4300B	0789
1N4301	0313
1N4301A	0313
1N4301B	OEM
1N4302	1075
1N4302A	1075
1N4302B	OEM
1N4303	0313
1N4303A	0313
1N4303B	0789
1N4304	0313
1N4304A	0313
1N4304B	0789
1N4305	0124
1N4305F	0124
1N4306	0133
1N4307	0133
1N4308	0133
1N4309	0133
1N4310	OEM
1N4311	0133
1N4312	OEM
1N4313	OEM
1N4314	OEM
1N4315	0133
1N4316	OEM
1N4317	OEM
1N4318	0133
1N4319	OEM
1N4320	OEM
1N4321	0497
1N4322	0133
1N4323	0025
1N4323A	0025
1N4323B	0025
1N4324	0644
1N4324A	0644
1N4324B	0644
1N4325	0244
1N4325A	0244
1N4325B	0244
1N4326	0012
1N4326A	0012
1N4326B	0012
1N4327	0170
1N4327A	0170
1N4327B	0170
1N4328	0313
1N4328A	0313
1N4328B	0313
1N4329	0137
1N4329A	0137
1N4329B	0137

DEVICE TYPE	REPL CODE
1N4330	0361
1N4330A	0361
1N4330B	0361
1N4331	0002
1N4331A	0002
1N4331B	0002
1N4332	0416
1N4332A	0416
1N4332B	0416
1N4333	0490
1N4333A	0490
1N4333B	0490
1N4334	0526
1N4334A	0526
1N4334B	0526
1N4335	0560
1N4335A	0560
1N4335B	0560
1N4336	0398
1N4336A	0398
1N4336B	0398
1N4337	0436
1N4337A	0436
1N4337B	0039
1N4338	0721
1N4338A	0721
1N4338B	0721
1N4339	0039
1N4339A	0039
1N4339B	0039
1N4340	0814
1N4340A	0814
1N4340B	0814
1N4341	0346
1N4341A	0346
1N4341B	0346
1N4342	0925
1N4342A	0925
1N4342B	0925
1N4343	0993
1N4343A	0993
1N4343B	0993
1N4344	0497
1N4344A	0497
1N4344B	0497
1N4345	0863
1N4345A	0863
1N4345B	0863
1N4346	0778
1N4346A	0778
1N4346B	0778
1N4347	1258
1N4347A	1258
1N4347B	1258
1N4348	1181
1N4348A	1181
1N4348B	1181
1N4349	0327
1N4349A	0327
1N4349B	0327
1N4350	1301
1N4350A	1301
1N4350B	1301
1N4351	0098
1N4351A	0098
1N4351B	0098
1N4352	0149
1N4352A	0149
1N4352B	0149
1N4353	0186
1N4353A	0186
1N4353B	0186
1N4354	0213
1N4354A	0213
1N4354B	0213
1N4355	0028
1N4355A	0028
1N4355B	0028
1N4356	0255
1N4356A	0255
1N4356B	0255
1N4357	0363
1N4357A	0363
1N4357B	0363
1N4358	0417
1N4358A	0417
1N4358B	0417
1N4359	OEM
1N4360	1266
1N4361	0071
1N4362	OEM
1N4363	0133
1N4364	0015
1N4365	0276
1N4366	0276
1N4367	0015
1N4368	0015
1N4369	0015
1N4370	1266
1N4370A	1266
1N4370ARL	OEM
1N4370RL	OEM
1N4371	0755
1N4371A	0755
1N4371ARL	OEM
1N4371RL	OEM
1N4372	0118
1N4372A	0118
1N4372ARL	OEM

DEVICE TYPE	REPL CODE
1N4372RL	OEM
1N4374	OEM
1N4375	0133
1N4376	0133
1N4377	OEM
1N4378	OEM
1N4379	OEM
1N4380	OEM
1N4381	OEM
1N4382	0133
1N4383	0015
1N4383GP	0604
1N4384	0015
1N4384GP	0790
1N4385	0015
1N4385GP	0015
1N4386	OEM
1N4387	OEM
1N4388	OEM
1N4389	0133
1N4390	OEM
1N4391	OEM
1N4392	0133
1N4393	OEM
1N4393A	OEM
1N4393B	OEM
1N4394	OEM
1N4394A	OEM
1N4394B	OEM
1N4395	0133
1N4395A	0133
1N4395B	OEM
1N4396	OEM
1N4396A	OEM
1N4396B	OEM
1N4397	OEM
1N4397A	OEM
1N4397B	OEM
1N4398	OEM
1N4398A	OEM
1N4398B	OEM
1N4399	OEM
1N4399A	OEM
1N4399B	OEM
1N4400	0025
1N4400A	0025
1N4400B	0025
1N4401	0644
1N4401A	0644
1N4401B	0644
1N4402	0244
1N4402A	0244
1N4402B	0244
1N4403	0012
1N4403A	0012
1N4403B	0012
1N4404	0170
1N4404A	0170
1N4404B	0170
1N4405	0313
1N4405A	0313
1N4405B	0313
1N4406	0137
1N4406A	0137
1N4406B	0137
1N4407	0361
1N4407A	0361
1N4407B	0361
1N4408	0002
1N4408A	0002
1N4408B	0002
1N4409	0416
1N4409A	0416
1N4409B	0416
1N4410	0490
1N4410A	0490
1N4410B	0490
1N4411	0526
1N4411A	0526
1N4411B	0526
1N4412	0560
1N4412A	0560
1N4412B	0560
1N4413	0398
1N4413A	0398
1N4413B	0398
1N4414	0436
1N4414A	0436
1N4414B	0436
1N4415	0721
1N4415A	0721
1N4415B	0721
1N4416	0039
1N4416A	0039
1N4416B	0039
1N4417	0814
1N4417A	0814
1N4417B	0814
1N4418	0346
1N4418A	0346
1N4418B	0346
1N4419	0925
1N4419A	0925
1N4419B	0925
1N4420	0993
1N4420A	0993
1N4420B	0993
1N4421	0497
1N4421A	0497

DEVICE TYPE	REPL CODE
1N4421B	0497
1N4422	0863
1N4422A	0863
1N4422B	0863
1N4423	0778
1N4423A	0778
1N4423B	0778
1N4424	1258
1N4424A	1258
1N4424B	1258
1N4425	1181
1N4425A	1181
1N4425B	1181
1N4426	0327
1N4426A	0327
1N4426B	0327
1N4427	1301
1N4427A	1301
1N4427B	1301
1N4428	0098
1N4428A	0098
1N4428B	0098
1N4429	0149
1N4429A	0149
1N4429B	0149
1N4430	0186
1N4430A	0186
1N4430B	0186
1N4431	0213
1N4431A	0213
1N4431B	0213
1N4432	0028
1N4432A	0028
1N4432B	0028
1N4433	0255
1N4433A	0255
1N4434	0363
1N4434A	0363
1N4434B	0363
1N4435	0417
1N4435A	0417
1N4435B	0417
1N4436	OEM
1N4436F	OEM
1N4436S	OEM
1N4436T	OEM
1N4437	OEM
1N4437F	OEM
1N4437S	OEM
1N4437T	OEM
1N4438	OEM
1N4438F	OEM
1N4438S	OEM
1N4438T	OEM
1N4440	OEM
1N4441	OEM
1N4444	0133
1N4445	OEM
1N4445A	OEM
1N4446	0124
1N4447	0124
1N4448	0124
1N4449	0124
1N4450	0133
1N4451	0133
1N4452	OEM
1N4453	0133
1N4453A	OEM
1N4454	0124
1N4455	0133
1N4456	OEM
1N4457	OEM
1N4458	0206
1N4458R	1002
1N4459	0583
1N4459R	0942
1N4460	0185
1N4461	0205
1N4462	0475
1N4463	0499
1N4464	0679
1N4465	0225
1N4466	0230
1N4467	0234
1N4468	0237
1N4469	0247
1N4470	0251
1N4471	0256
1N4472	0262
1N4472B	OEM
1N4473	0269
1N4474	0273
1N4475	0291
1N4476	0305
1N4477	0314
1N4478	0316
1N4479	0322
1N4480	0333
1N4481	0343
1N4482	0027
1N4483	0266
1N4484	0382
1N4485	0401
1N4486	0421
1N4487	0439
1N4488	0238
1N4489	1172
1N4490	1182
1N4491	1198

DEVICE TYPE	REPL CODE
1N4492	1209
1N4493	0642
1N4494	1246
1N4495	1269
1N4496	0600
1N4497	OEM
1N4498	OEM
1N4499	0631
1N4500	0959
1N4501	0062
1N4502	0143
1N4503	0314
1N4504	0600
1N4505	OEM
1N4506	0097
1N4507	0109
1N4508	0122
1N4509	0131
1N4510	0145
1N4510R	OEM
1N4511	OEM
1N4511R	OEM
1N4512	1325
1N4513	OEM
1N4514	0811
1N4517	0242
1N4523	0143
1N4524	OEM
1N4525	1116
1N4526	0800
1N4527	0315
1N4528	1124
1N4528B	OEM
1N4529	0045
1N4529R	OEM
1N4530	OEM
1N4530R	OEM
1N4531	0133
1N4532	0133
1N4533	0133
1N4534	0133
1N4535	0289
1N4536	0133
1N4537	OEM
1N4538	OEM
1N4539	OEM
1N4540	OEM
1N4541	0790
1N4542	0790
1N4543	OEM
1N4544	OEM
1N4545	0369
1N4546	OEM
1N4547	0133
1N4548	0133
1N4549	0809
1N4549A	0809
1N4549B	0809
1N4549R	2695
1N4549RA	2695
1N4549RB	2695
1N4550	0821
1N4550A	0821
1N4550B	0821
1N4550R	2698
1N4550RA	2698
1N4550RB	2698
1N4551	0840
1N4551A	0840
1N4551B	0840
1N4551R	2700
1N4551RA	2700
1N4551RB	2700
1N4552	0862
1N4552A	0862
1N4552B	0862
1N4552R	2703
1N4552RA	2703
1N4552RB	2703
1N4553	0879
1N4553A	0879
1N4553B	0879
1N4553R	2706
1N4553RA	2706
1N4553RB	2706
1N4554	0908
1N4554A	0908
1N4554B	0908
1N4554R	2711
1N4554RA	2711
1N4554RB	2711
1N4555	0920
1N4555A	0920
1N4555AR	2713
1N4555B	0920
1N4555BR	2713
1N4555R	2713
1N4555RA	2713
1N4555RB	2713
1N4556	0938
1N4556A	0938
1N4556B	0938
1N4556R	2717
1N4556RA	2717
1N4556RB	2717
1N4557	OEM
1N4557A	OEM
1N4557B	OEM
1N4557R	OEM

If replacement code is OEM, contact original manufacturer for replacement.

DEVICE TYPE	REPL CODE	DEVICE TYPE	REPL CODE	DEVICE TYPE	REPL CODE	DEVICE TYPE	REPL CODE	DEVICE TYPE	REPL CODE	DEVICE TYPE	REPL CODE	DEVICE TYPE	REPL CODE
1N4557RA	OEM	1N4578	0631	1N4625	0041	1N4699	0052	1N4738ARL	OEM	1N4762RL	OEM	1N4793B	OEM
1N4557RB	OEM	1N4578-1	OEM	1N4625-1	OEM	1N4699RL	OEM	1N4738RL	OEM	1N4763	1301	1N4793C	OEM
1N4558	OEM	1N4578A	0631	1N4625RL	OEM	1N4700	0053	1N4739	0012	1N4763A	1301	1N4793D	OEM
1N4558A	OEM	1N4578A1	OEM	1N4626	0253	1N4700RL	OEM	1N4739A	0012	1N4763AE	1301	1N4794	0030
1N4558B	OEM	1N4578B	OEM	1N4626-1	OEM	1N4701	0873	1N4739ARL	OEM	1N4763AG	1301	1N4794A	0030
1N4558R	OEM	1N4579	0631	1N4626RL	OEM	1N4701RL	OEM	1N4739RL	OEM	1N4763ARL	OEM	1N4794B	OEM
1N4558RA	OEM	1N4579-1	OEM	1N4627	0466	1N4702	0681	1N4740	0170	1N4763RL	OEM	1N4794C	OEM
1N4558RB	OEM	1N4579A	0631	1N4627-1	OEM	1N4702RL	OEM	1N4740A	0170	1N4764	0098	1N4794D	OEM
1N4559	OEM	1N4579A1	OEM	1N4627RL	OEM	1N4703	0440	1N4740ARL	OEM	1N4764A	0098	1N4795	OEM
1N4559A	OEM	1N4579B	OEM	1N4628	0025	1N4703A	OEM	1N4740RL	OEM	1N4764ARL	OEM	1N4795A	OEM
1N4559B	OEM	1N4580	0631	1N4629	0644	1N4703B	OEM	1N4741	0313	1N4764RL	OEM	1N4795B	OEM
1N4559R	OEM	1N4580-1	OEM	1N4630	0244	1N4703C	OEM	1N4741A	0313	1N4765	0057	1N4795C	OEM
1N4559RA	OEM	1N4580A	0631	1N4631	0012	1N4703D	OEM	1N4741ARL	OEM	1N4765A	0057	1N4795D	OEM
1N4559RB	OEM	1N4580A1	OEM	1N4632	0170	1N4703RL	OEM	1N4741RL	OEM	1N4765B	0057	1N4796	OEM
1N4560	OEM	1N4580B	OEM	1N4632A	OEM	1N4704	0210	1N4742	0137	1N4766	0012	1N4796A	OEM
1N4560A	OEM	1N4581	0631	1N4633	0313	1N4704RL	OEM	1N4742A	0137	1N4766A	0012	1N4796B	OEM
1N4560B	OEM	1N4581-1	OEM	1N4633A	OEM	1N4705	0371	1N4742ARL	OEM	1N4766B	0057	1N4796C	OEM
1N4560R	OEM	1N4581A	0631	1N4634	0137	1N4705RL	OEM	1N4742RL	OEM	1N4767	0012	1N4796D	OEM
1N4560RA	OEM	1N4581A1	OEM	1N4634A	OEM	1N4706	0666	1N4743	0361	1N4767A	0012	1N4797	OEM
1N4560RB	OEM	1N4581B	OEM	1N4635	0361	1N4706RL	OEM	1N4743A	0361	1N4767B	0057	1N4797A	OEM
1N4561	OEM	1N4582	0631	1N4635A	OEM	1N4707	0695	1N4743ARL	OEM	1N4768	0012	1N4797B	OEM
1N4561A	OEM	1N4582-1	OEM	1N4636	0002	1N4707RL	OEM	1N4743RL	OEM	1N4768A	0012	1N4797C	OEM
1N4561B	OEM	1N4582A	0631	1N4636A	OEM	1N4708	0700	1N4744	0002	1N4768B	0057	1N4797D	OEM
1N4561R	OEM	1N4582A1	OEM	1N4637	0416	1N4708RL	OEM	1N4744A	0002	1N4769	0012	1N4798	OEM
1N4561RA	OEM	1N4582B	OEM	1N4637A	OEM	1N4709	0489	1N4744ARL	OEM	1N4769A	0012	1N4798A	OEM
1N4561RB	OEM	1N4583	0789	1N4638	0490	1N4709RL	OEM	1N4744RL	OEM	1N4769B	0057	1N4798B	OEM
1N4562	OEM	1N4583-1	OEM	1N4638A	OEM	1N4710	0709	1N4745	0416	1N4770	0057	1N4798C	OEM
1N4562A	OEM	1N4583A	0789	1N4639	0526	1N4710RL	OEM	1N4745(A)	0416	1N4770A	0057	1N4798D	OEM
1N4562B	OEM	1N4583A1	OEM	1N4639A	OEM	1N4711	0450	1N4745A	0416	1N4770B	0057	1N4799	OEM
1N4562R	OEM	1N4583B	0631	1N4640	0560	1N4711RL	OEM	1N4745ARL	OEM	1N4771	0057	1N4799A	OEM
1N4562RA	OEM	1N4584	0631	1N4641	0398	1N4712	0257	1N4745RL	OEM	1N4771A	0057	1N4799B	OEM
1N4562RB	OEM	1N4584-1	OEM	1N4642	0436	1N4712RL	OEM	1N4746	0490	1N4771B	0057	1N4799C	OEM
1N4563	OEM	1N4584A	0631	1N4643	0721	1N4713	0195	1N4746A	0490	1N4772	0057	1N4799D	OEM
1N4563A	OEM	1N4584A1	OEM	1N4644	0039	1N4713RL	OEM	1N4746ARL	OEM	1N4772A	0057	1N4800	OEM
1N4563B	OEM	1N4584B	OEM	1N4645	0814	1N4714	0166	1N4746RL	OEM	1N4772B	0057	1N4800A	OEM
1N4563R	OEM	1N4585	0811	1N4646	0346	1N4714RL	OEM	1N4747	0526	1N4773	0057	1N4800B	OEM
1N4563RA	OEM	1N4585GP	0072	1N4647	0925	1N4715	0010	1N4747A	0526	1N4773A	0057	1N4800C	OEM
1N4563RB	OEM	1N4586	0811	1N4648	0993	1N4715RL	OEM	1N4747ARL	OEM	1N4773B	0057	1N4800D	OEM
1N4564	OEM	1N4586GP	0071	1N4649	0289	1N4716	0032	1N4747RL	OEM	1N4774	0057	1N4801	0549
1N4564A	OEM	1N4587	0594	1N4650	0188	1N4716RL	OEM	1N4748	0560	1N4774A	0057	1N4801A	0549
1N4564B	OEM	1N4587R	1337	1N4651	0451	1N4717	0054	1N4748A	0560	1N4774B	0057	1N4801B	OEM
1N4564R	OEM	1N4588	0594	1N4652	0528	1N4717RL	OEM	1N4748ARL	OEM	1N4775	1075	1N4801C	OEM
1N4564RA	OEM	1N4588R	1337	1N4653	0446	1N4718	0914	1N4748RL	OEM	1N4775A	1075	1N4801D	OEM
1N4564RB	OEM	1N4589	0594	1N4654	0162	1N4719	0110	1N4749	0398	1N4775B	OEM	1N4802	OEM
1N4565	0631	1N4589R	1337	1N4655	0157	1N4719E	OEM	1N4749(A)	0398	1N4776	1075	1N4802A	OEM
1N4565-1	OEM	1N4590	0594	1N4656	0631	1N4719R	0087	1N4749A	0398	1N4776A	1075	1N4802B	OEM
1N4565A	0631	1N4590R	1894	1N4657	0025	1N4720	0947	1N4749ARL	OEM	1N4776B	OEM	1N4802C	OEM
1N4565A1	OEM	1N4591	1975	1N4658	0644	1N4720E	OEM	1N4749RL	OEM	1N4777	1075	1N4802D	OEM
1N4565B	OEM	1N4591R	1894	1N4659	0244	1N4720R	0087	1N4750	0436	1N4777A	1075	1N4803	OEM
1N4566	0631	1N4592	1975	1N4660	0012	1N4721	0242	1N4750A	0436	1N4777B	OEM	1N4803A	OEM
1N4566-1	OEM	1N4592R	1894	1N4661	0170	1N4721E	OEM	1N4750ARL	OEM	1N4778	1075	1N4803B	OEM
1N4566A	0631	1N4593	0652	1N4662	0313	1N4721R	0242	1N4750RL	OEM	1N4778A	1075	1N4803C	OEM
1N4566A1	OEM	1N4593R	0193	1N4663	0137	1N4722	0535	1N4751	0721	1N4778B	OEM	1N4803D	OEM
1N4566B	OEM	1N4594	0652	1N4664	0361	1N4722E	OEM	1N4751A	0721	1N4779	1075	1N4804	OEM
1N4567	0631	1N4594R	0193	1N4665	0002	1N4722R	0087	1N4751ARL	OEM	1N4779A	1075	1N4804A	OEM
1N4567-1	OEM	1N4595	3277	1N4666	0416	1N4723	0959	1N4751RL	OEM	1N4779B	OEM	1N4804B	OEM
1N4567A	0631	1N4595R	0202	1N4667	0490	1N4723E	OEM	1N4752	0039	1N4780	1075	1N4804C	OEM
1N4567A1	OEM	1N4596	3277	1N4668	0526	1N4723R	0087	1N4752A	0039	1N4780A	1075	1N4804D	OEM
1N4567B	OEM	1N4596R	0202	1N4669	0560	1N4724	0811	1N4752ARL	OEM	1N4780B	OEM	1N4805	OEM
1N4568	0631	1N4597	OEM	1N4670	0398	1N4724E	OEM	1N4752RL	OEM	1N4781	1075	1N4805A	OEM
1N4568-1	OEM	1N4598	OEM	1N4671	0436	1N4724R	0087	1N4753	0814	1N4781A	1075	1N4805B	OEM
1N4568A	0631	1N4599	OEM	1N4672	0721	1N4725	0916	1N4753A	0814	1N4781B	OEM	1N4805C	OEM
1N4568A1	OEM	1N4600	OEM	1N4673	0039	1N4725E	OEM	1N4753ARL	OEM	1N4782	1075	1N4805D	OEM
1N4568B	OEM	1N4601	OEM	1N4674	0814	1N4725R	0087	1N4753RL	OEM	1N4782A	1075	1N4806	OEM
1N4569	0631	1N4602	OEM	1N4675	0346	1N4726	0133	1N4754	0346	1N4782B	OEM	1N4806A	OEM
1N4569-1	OEM	1N4603	OEM	1N4676	0925	1N4727	0133	1N4754A	0346	1N4783	1075	1N4806B	OEM
1N4569A	0631	1N4604	OEM	1N4677	0993	1N4728	0289	1N4754ARL	OEM	1N4783A	1075	1N4806C	OEM
1N4569A1	OEM	1N4605	OEM	1N4678	OEM	1N4728A	0289	1N4754RL	OEM	1N4783B	OEM	1N4806D	OEM
1N4569B	OEM	1N4606	0133	1N4678RL	OEM	1N4728AG	0289	1N4755	0925	1N4784	1075	1N4807	OEM
1N4570	0631	1N4606R	0124	1N4679	OEM	1N4728ARL	OEM	1N4755A	0925	1N4784A	1075	1N4807A	OEM
1N4570-1	OEM	1N4607	0133	1N4679RL	OEM	1N4728RL	OEM	1N4755AE	0925	1N4784B	OEM	1N4807B	OEM
1N4570A	0631	1N4608	0133	1N4680	0289	1N4729	0188	1N4755AG	0925	1N4785	OEM	1N4807C	OEM
1N4570A1	OEM	1N4609	0623	1N4680RL	OEM	1N4729A	0188	1N4755ARL	OEM	1N4786	0549	1N4807D	OEM
1N4570B	OEM	1N4609A	0623	1N4681	1266	1N4729ARL	OEM	1N4755RL	OEM	1N4786A	0549	1N4808	OEM
1N4571	0631	1N4610	0133	1N4681RL	OEM	1N4730	0451	1N4756	0993	1N4786B	OEM	1N4808A	OEM
1N4571-1	OEM	1N4611	0025	1N4682	0755	1N4730A	0451	1N4756A	0993	1N4786C	OEM	1N4808B	OEM
1N4571A	0631	1N4611A	OEM	1N4682RL	OEM	1N4730AG	0451	1N4756AE	0993	1N4786D	OEM	1N4808C	OEM
1N4571A1	OEM	1N4611B	OEM	1N4683	0118	1N4730ARL	OEM	1N4756AG	0993	1N4787	OEM	1N4808D	OEM
1N4571B	OEM	1N4611C	OEM	1N4683RL	OEM	1N4730RL	OEM	1N4756ARL	OEM	1N4787A	OEM	1N4809	OEM
1N4572	0631	1N4612	0025	1N4684	0296	1N4731	0755	1N4756RL	OEM	1N4787B	OEM	1N4809A	OEM
1N4572-1	OEM	1N4612A	0025	1N4684RL	OEM	1N4731A	0528	1N4757	0497	1N4787C	OEM	1N4809B	OEM
1N4572A	0631	1N4612B	0025	1N4685	0372	1N4731ARL	OEM	1N4757A	0497	1N4787D	OEM	1N4809C	OEM
1N4572A1	OEM	1N4612C	0025	1N4685RL	OEM	1N4731RL	OEM	1N4757AE	0497	1N4788	0005	1N4809D	OEM
1N4572B	OEM	1N4613	0025	1N4686	0036	1N4732	0446	1N4757AG	0497	1N4788A	0005	1N4810	OEM
1N4573	0631	1N4613A	OEM	1N4686RL	OEM	1N4732A	0446	1N4757ARL	OEM	1N4788B	OEM	1N4810A	OEM
1N4573-1	OEM	1N4613B	OEM	1N4687	0274	1N4732ARL	OEM	1N4757RL	OEM	1N4788C	OEM	1N4810B	OEM
1N4573A	0631	1N4613C	OEM	1N4687RL	OEM	1N4732RL	OEM	1N4758	0863	1N4788D	OEM	1N4810C	OEM
1N4573A1	OEM	1N4614	OEM	1N4688	0140	1N4733	0162	1N4758A	0863	1N4789	0715	1N4810D	OEM
1N4573B	OEM	1N4614RL	OEM	1N4688RL	OEM	1N4733A	0437	1N4758AG	0863	1N4789A	0715	1N4811	OEM
1N4574	0631	1N4615	OEM	1N4689	0041	1N4733ARL	OEM	1N4758ARL	OEM	1N4789B	OEM	1N4811A	OEM
1N4574-1	OEM	1N4615RL	OEM	1N4689RL	OEM	1N4733RL	OEM	1N4758E	0863	1N4789C	OEM	1N4811B	OEM
1N4574A	0631	1N4616	OEM	1N4690	0253	1N4734	0157	1N4758RL	OEM	1N4789D	OEM	1N4811C	OEM
1N4574A1	OEM	1N4616RL	OEM	1N4690RL	OEM	1N4734A	0157	1N4759	0778	1N4790	OEM	1N4811D	OEM
1N4574B	OEM	1N4617	1266	1N4691	0466	1N4734ARL	OEM	1N4759A	0778	1N4790A	OEM	1N4812	OEM
1N4575	0631	1N4617RL	OEM	1N4691RL	OEM	1N4734RL	OEM	1N4759ARL	OEM	1N4790B	OEM	1N4812A	OEM
1N4575-1	OEM	1N4618	0755	1N4692	0062	1N4735	0631	1N4759RL	OEM	1N4790C	OEM	1N4812B	OEM
1N4575A	0631	1N4618RL	OEM	1N4692RL	OEM	1N4735A	0631	1N4760	1258	1N4790D	OEM	1N4812C	OEM
1N4575A1	OEM	1N4619	0118	1N4693	0077	1N4735ARL	OEM	1N4760A	1258	1N4791	OEM	1N4812D	OEM
1N4575B	OEM	1N4619RL	OEM	1N4693RL	OEM	1N4735RL	OEM	1N4760AE	1258	1N4791A	OEM	1N4813	OEM
1N4576	0631	1N4620	0296	1N4694	0165	1N4736	0025	1N4760AG	1258	1N4791B	OEM	1N4813A	OEM
1N4576-1	OEM	1N4620RL	OEM	1N4694RL	OEM	1N4736A	0025	1N4760ARL	OEM	1N4791C	OEM	1N4813B	0679
1N4576A	0631	1N4621	0372	1N4695	0318	1N4736ARL	OEM	1N4760RL	OEM	1N4791D	OEM	1N4813C	OEM
1N4576A1	OEM	1N4621RL	OEM	1N4695RL	OEM	1N4736RL	OEM	1N4761	1181	1N4792	0623	1N4813D	OEM
1N4576B	OEM	1N4622	0036	1N4696	0057	1N4737	0644	1N4761A	1181	1N4792A	0623	1N4814	OEM
1N4577	0631	1N4622RL	OEM	1N4696RL	OEM	1N4737A	0644	1N4761ARL	OEM	1N4792B	OEM	1N4814A	OEM
1N4577-1	OEM	1N4623	0274	1N4697	0064	1N4737ARL	OEM	1N4761RL	OEM	1N4792C	OEM	1N4814B	OEM
1N4577A	0631	1N4623RL	OEM	1N4697RL	OEM	1N4737RL	OEM	1N4762	0327	1N4792D	OEM	1N4814C	OEM
1N4577A1	OEM	1N4624	0140	1N4698	0181	1N4738	0244	1N4762A	0327	1N4793	OEM	1N4814D	OEM
1N4577B	OEM	1N4624RL	OEM	1N4698RL	OEM	1N4738A	0244	1N4762ARL	OEM	1N4793A	OEM	1N4815	OEM

If replacement code is OEM, contact original manufacturer for replacement.

DEVICE TYPE	REPL CODE
1N4815A	OEM
1N4815B	OEM
1N4815C	OEM
1N4815D	OEM
1N4816	0110
1N4817	0071
1N4818	0071
1N4819	1736
1N4820	0535
1N4821	1760
1N4822	0959
1N4823	0015
1N4824	0015
1N4825	0015
1N4826	0102
1N4827	0133
1N4828	0133
1N4829	0133
1N4830	0133
1N4831	0679
1N4831A	0679
1N4831B	0679
1N4832	0225
1N4832A	0225
1N4832B	0225
1N4833	0230
1N4833A	0230
1N4833B	0230
1N4834	0234
1N4834A	0234
1N4834B	0234
1N4835	0237
1N4835A	0237
1N4835B	0237
1N4836	0247
1N4836A	0247
1N4836B	0247
1N4837	0251
1N4837A	0251
1N4837B	0251
1N4838	0256
1N4838A	0256
1N4838B	0256
1N4839	0262
1N4839A	0262
1N4839B	0262
1N4840	0269
1N4840A	0269
1N4840B	0269
1N4841	0273
1N4841A	0273
1N4841B	0273
1N4842	0291
1N4842A	0291
1N4842B	0291
1N4843	0305
1N4843A	0305
1N4843B	0305
1N4844	0314
1N4844A	0314
1N4844B	0314
1N4845	0316
1N4845A	0316
1N4845B	0316
1N4846	0322
1N4846A	0322
1N4846B	0322
1N4847	0333
1N4847A	0333
1N4847B	0333
1N4848	0343
1N4848A	0343
1N4848B	0343
1N4849	0027
1N4849A	0027
1N4849B	0027
1N4850	0266
1N4850A	0266
1N4850B	0266
1N4851	0382
1N4851A	0382
1N4851B	0382
1N4852	0401
1N4852A	0401
1N4852B	0401
1N4853	0421
1N4853A	0421
1N4853B	0421
1N4854	0439
1N4854A	0439
1N4854B	0439
1N4855	0238
1N4855A	0238
1N4855B	0238
1N4856	1172
1N4856A	1172
1N4856B	1172
1N4857	1182
1N4857A	1182
1N4857B	1182
1N4858	1198
1N4858A	0186
1N4858B	1198
1N4859	0213
1N4859A	0213
1N4859B	1209
1N4860	0028
1N4860A	0028
1N4860B	0642

DEVICE TYPE	REPL CODE
1N4861	0133
1N4862	0133
1N4863	0133
1N4864	0133
1N4865	OEM
1N4866	OEM
1N4867	OEM
1N4868	OEM
1N4869	OEM
1N4870	OEM
1N4871	OEM
1N4872	OEM
1N4873	OEM
1N4874	OEM
1N4875	OEM
1N4876	OEM
1N4877	OEM
1N4878	0594
1N4879	1017
1N4880	1017
1N4881	0262
1N4882	0316
1N4883	0234
1N4884	0262
1N4885	OEM
1N4886	OEM
1N4887	OEM
1N4888	OEM
1N4889	0382
1N4890	OEM
1N4890A	OEM
1N4891	OEM
1N4891A	OEM
1N4892	OEM
1N4892A	OEM
1N4893	OEM
1N4893A	OEM
1N4894	OEM
1N4894A	OEM
1N4895	OEM
1N4895A	OEM
1N4896	0053
1N4896A	0053
1N4897	0053
1N4897A	0053
1N4898	0053
1N4898A	0053
1N4899	0053
1N4899A	0053
1N4900	0053
1N4900A	0053
1N4901	0053
1N4901A	0053
1N4902	0053
1N4902A	0053
1N4903	0053
1N4903A	0053
1N4904	0053
1N4904A	0053
1N4905	0053
1N4905A	0053
1N4906	0053
1N4906A	0053
1N4907	0053
1N4907A	0053
1N4908	0053
1N4908A	0053
1N4909	0053
1N4909A	0053
1N4910	0053
1N4910A	0053
1N4911	0053
1N4911A	0053
1N4912	0053
1N4912A	0053
1N4913	0053
1N4913A	0053
1N4914	0053
1N4914A	0053
1N4915	0053
1N4915A	0053
1N4916	0943
1N4916A	0943
1N4917	0943
1N4917A	0943
1N4918	0943
1N4918A	0943
1N4919	0943
1N4919A	0943
1N4920	0943
1N4920A	0943
1N4921	0943
1N4921A	0943
1N4922	0943
1N4922A	0943
1N4923	0943
1N4923A	0943
1N4924	0943
1N4924A	0943
1N4925	0943
1N4925A	0943
1N4926	0943
1N4926A	0943
1N4927	0943
1N4927A	0943
1N4928	0943
1N4928A	0943
1N4929	0943
1N4929A	0943

DEVICE TYPE	REPL CODE
1N4930	0943
1N4930A	0943
1N4931	0943
1N4931A	0943
1N4932	0943
1N4932A	0943
1N4933	0023
1N4933G	OEM
1N4933GP	0023
1N4933RL	OEM
1N4934	0023
1N4934G	OEM
1N4934GP	0023
1N4934RL	OEM
1N4935	0023
1N4935G	OEM
1N4935GP	0023
1N4935RL	OEM
1N4936	0023
1N4936G	OEM
1N4936GP	0023
1N4936RL	OEM
1N4937	0023
1N4937G	OEM
1N4937GP	0023
1N4937RL	OEM
1N4938	0133
1N4939	OEM
1N4940	OEM
1N4941	OEM
1N4942	0023
1N4942G	OEM
1N4942GP	0023
1N4943	0087
1N4944	0023
1N4944G	OEM
1N4944GP	0023
1N4945	0102
1N4946	0023
1N4946G	OEM
1N4946GP	0023
1N4947	0017
1N4947G	OEM
1N4947GP	0017
1N4948	0017
1N4948G	OEM
1N4948GP	0017
1N4949	0133
1N4950	0133
1N4951	0133
1N4952	0133
1N4953	OEM
1N4954	0205
1N4954A	OEM
1N4954B	OEM
1N4955	0475
1N4955A	OEM
1N4955B	OEM
1N4956	0499
1N4956A	OEM
1N4956B	OEM
1N4957	0679
1N4957A	OEM
1N4957B	OEM
1N4958	0225
1N4958A	OEM
1N4958B	OEM
1N4959	0230
1N4959A	1976
1N4959B	OEM
1N4960	0234
1N4960A	OEM
1N4960B	OEM
1N4960D	0234
1N4961	0237
1N4961A	OEM
1N4961B	OEM
1N4962	0247
1N4962A	OEM
1N4962B	OEM
1N4963	0251
1N4963A	OEM
1N4963B	OEM
1N4964	0256
1N4964A	OEM
1N4964B	OEM
1N4965	0262
1N4965A	OEM
1N4965B	OEM
1N4966	0269
1N4966A	OEM
1N4966B	OEM
1N4967	0273
1N4967A	OEM
1N4967B	OEM
1N4968	0291
1N4968A	OEM
1N4968B	OEM
1N4969	0305
1N4969A	OEM
1N4969B	OEM
1N4970	0314
1N4970A	OEM
1N4970B	OEM
1N4971	0316
1N4971A	OEM
1N4971B	OEM
1N4972	0322
1N4972A	OEM

DEVICE TYPE	REPL CODE
1N4972B	OEM
1N4973	0333
1N4973A	OEM
1N4973B	OEM
1N4974	0343
1N4974A	OEM
1N4974B	OEM
1N4975	0027
1N4975A	OEM
1N4975B	OEM
1N4976	0266
1N4976A	OEM
1N4976B	OEM
1N4977	0382
1N4977A	OEM
1N4977B	OEM
1N4978	0401
1N4978A	OEM
1N4978B	OEM
1N4979	0421
1N4979A	OEM
1N4979B	OEM
1N4980	0439
1N4980A	OEM
1N4980B	OEM
1N4981	0238
1N4981A	OEM
1N4981B	OEM
1N4982	1172
1N4982A	OEM
1N4982B	OEM
1N4983	1182
1N4983A	OEM
1N4983B	OEM
1N4984	1198
1N4984A	OEM
1N4984B	OEM
1N4985	1209
1N4985A	OEM
1N4985B	OEM
1N4986	0642
1N4986A	OEM
1N4986B	OEM
1N4987	1246
1N4987A	OEM
1N4987B	OEM
1N4988	1269
1N4988A	OEM
1N4988B	OEM
1N4989	0600
1N4989A	OEM
1N4989B	OEM
1N4990	OEM
1N4990A	OEM
1N4990B	OEM
1N4991	OEM
1N4991A	OEM
1N4991B	OEM
1N4991D	OEM
1N4992	OEM
1N4992A	OEM
1N4992B	OEM
1N4993	OEM
1N4993A	OEM
1N4993B	OEM
1N4994	OEM
1N4994A	OEM
1N4994B	OEM
1N4995	OEM
1N4995A	OEM
1N4995B	OEM
1N4996	OEM
1N4996A	OEM
1N4996B	OEM
1N4997	0110
1N4997R	0087
1N4998	0947
1N4998R	0087
1N4999	0242
1N4999R	0087
1N5000	0535
1N5000R	0087
1N5001	0959
1N5001R	0087
1N5002	0811
1N5002R	0087
1N5003	0916
1N5003R	0087
1N5004	0947
1N5005	0242
1N5006	0535
1N5007	0959
1N5008	0777
1N5008A	0777
1N5009	0791
1N5009A	0791
1N5010	0801
1N5010A	0801
1N5011	0815
1N5011A	0815
1N5012	0827
1N5012A	0827
1N5013	0437
1N5013A	0437
1N5014	0870
1N5014A	0870
1N5015	0185
1N5015A	0185
1N5016	0205

DEVICE TYPE	REPL CODE
1N5016A	0205
1N5017	0475
1N5017A	0475
1N5018	0499
1N5018A	0499
1N5019	0679
1N5019A	0679
1N5020	0225
1N5020A	0225
1N5021	0230
1N5021A	0230
1N5022	0234
1N5022A	0234
1N5023	0237
1N5023A	0237
1N5024	1387
1N5024A	1387
1N5025	0247
1N5025A	0247
1N5026	0251
1N5026A	0251
1N5027	1170
1N5027A	1170
1N5028	0256
1N5028A	0256
1N5029	2379
1N5029A	2379
1N5030	0262
1N5030A	0262
1N5031	0269
1N5031A	0269
1N5032	0273
1N5032A	0273
1N5033	2383
1N5033A	2383
1N5034	0291
1N5034A	0291
1N5035	0305
1N5035A	0305
1N5036	0314
1N5036A	0314
1N5037	0316
1N5037A	0316
1N5038	0322
1N5038A	0322
1N5039	0333
1N5039A	0333
1N5040	0343
1N5040A	0343
1N5041	0343
1N5041A	0343
1N5042	0027
1N5042A	0027
1N5043	0027
1N5043A	0027
1N5044	0027
1N5044A	0027
1N5045	0266
1N5045A	0266
1N5046	0382
1N5046A	0382
1N5047	0401
1N5047A	0401
1N5048	0421
1N5048A	0421
1N5049	0439
1N5049A	0439
1N5050	0238
1N5050A	0238
1N5051	1172
1N5051A	1172
1N5052	0811
1N5053	0811
1N5054	0071
1N5055	0947
1N5056	0242
1N5057	1736
1N5058	0535
1N5059	0102
1N5059GP	0604
1N5060	0102
1N5060GP	0790
1N5061	0023
1N5061GP	0015
1N5062	0071
1N5062GP	0072
1N5063	0205
1N5064	0475
1N5065	0499
1N5066	0679
1N5067	0225
1N5068	0230
1N5069	0237
1N5070	1387
1N5071	0247
1N5072	0251
1N5073	0256
1N5074	0269
1N5075	0273
1N5076	0291
1N5077	0305
1N5078	0314
1N5079	0316
1N5080	0322
1N5081	0322
1N5082	0333
1N5083	0343
1N5084	0343
1N5085	0027

DEVICE TYPE	REPL CODE
1N5086	0027
1N5087	0266
1N5088	2829
1N5089	0382
1N5090	0401
1N5091	OEM
1N5092	0421
1N5093	0439
1N5094	0439
1N5095	0238
1N5096	1182
1N5097	1198
1N5098	1209
1N5099	1870
1N5100	1246
1N5101	2091
1N5102	1269
1N5103	2210
1N5104	0600
1N5105	OEM
1N5106	OEM
1N5107	OEM
1N5108	OEM
1N5109	OEM
1N5110	OEM
1N5111	OEM
1N5112	OEM
1N5113	OEM
1N5114	OEM
1N5115	OEM
1N5116	OEM
1N5117	OEM
1N5118	1387
1N5119	0322
1N5120	0343
1N5121	0027
1N5122	2829
1N5123	0401
1N5124	0439
1N5125	0238
1N5126	1870
1N5127	2091
1N5128	2210
1N5129	6719
1N5130	OEM
1N5131	6720
1N5132	6721
1N5133	6722
1N5134	6723
1N5135	OEM
1N5136	OEM
1N5136A	OEM
1N5137	OEM
1N5137A	OEM
1N5138	OEM
1N5138A	OEM
1N5139	0549
1N5139A	0549
1N5140	0005
1N5140A	0005
1N5141	0715
1N5141A	0715
1N5142	0715
1N5142A	0715
1N5143	0623
1N5143A	0623
1N5144	0623
1N5144A	0623
1N5145	0623
1N5145A	0623
1N5146	0030
1N5146A	0030
1N5147	0030
1N5147A	0030
1N5148	0030
1N5148A	0030
1N5149	OEM
1N5150	OEM
1N5150A	OEM
1N5151	OEM
1N5152	OEM
1N5152A	OEM
1N5153	OEM
1N5153A	OEM
1N5154	OEM
1N5154B	0436
1N5155	OEM
1N5155A	OEM
1N5156	OEM
1N5157	OEM
1N5158	OEM
1N5159	OEM
1N5160	OEM
1N5161	OEM
1N5162	OEM
1N5163	OEM
1N5164	OEM
1N5165	OEM
1N5166	OEM
1N5167	OEM
1N5168	OEM
1N5169	OEM
1N5170	0087
1N5171	0110
1N5172	0087
1N5173	1736
1N5174	0535
1N5175	1760
1N5176	0959

DEVICE TYPE	REPL CODE
1N5177	0087
1N5178	0087
1N5179	0133
1N5180	1272
1N5181	OEM
1N5182	OEM
1N5183	OEM
1N5184	OEM
1N5185	0959
1N5185GP	0959
1N5186	0959
1N5186GP	0959
1N5187	0959
1N5187GP	0959
1N5188	0102
1N5188A	0959
1N5188GP	0959
1N5189	0102
1N5189GP	0959
1N5190	0102
1N5190GP	0087
1N5194	0133
1N5195	0133
1N5196	0133
1N5197	0110
1N5198	0229
1N5199	0242
1N5200	0535
1N5201	0959
1N5206	0959
1N5207	1282
1N5208	0133
1N5209	0133
1N5210	0133
1N5211	0015
1N5212	0015
1N5213	0015
1N5214	0071
1N5215	0015
1N5216	0015
1N5217	0015
1N5218	0071
1N5219	0133
1N5220	0133
1N5221	1266
1N5221A	1266
1N5221ARL	OEM
1N5221B	1266
1N5221BRL	OEM
1N5222	2847
1N5222A	2847
1N5222ARL	OEM
1N5222B	1266
1N5222BRL	OEM
1N5222RL	OEM
1N5223	0755
1N5223A	0755
1N5223ARL	OEM
1N5223B	0755
1N5223BRL	OEM
1N5223RL	OEM
1N5224	0672
1N5224A	0672
1N5224ARL	OEM
1N5224B	0672
1N5224BRL	OEM
1N5224RL	OEM
1N5225	0118
1N5225A	0118
1N5225ARL	OEM
1N5225B	0118
1N5225BRL	OEM
1N5225RL	OEM
1N5226	0296
1N5226A	0296
1N5226ARL	OEM
1N5226B	0296
1N5226BRL	OEM
1N5226C	0296
1N5226D	OEM
1N5226RL	OEM
1N5227	0372
1N5227A	0372
1N5227ARL	OEM
1N5227B	0188
1N5227BRL	OEM
1N5227C	OEM
1N5227D	OEM
1N5227RL	OEM
1N5228	0036
1N5228A	0036
1N5228ARL	OEM
1N5228B	0036
1N5228BRL	OEM
1N5228C	OEM
1N5228D	OEM
1N5228RL	OEM
1N5229	0274
1N5229A	0274
1N5229ARL	OEM
1N5229B	0528
1N5229BRL	OEM
1N5229C	OEM
1N5229D	OEM
1N5229RL	OEM
1N5230	0140
1N5230A	0140
1N5230ARL	OEM
1N5230B	0140

If replacement code is OEM, contact original manufacturer for replacement.

DEVICE TYPE	REPL CODE
1N5230BRL	OEM
1N5230C	OEM
1N5230D	OEM
1N5230RL	OEM
1N5231	0041
1N5231A	0041
1N5231ARL	OEM
1N5231B	0041
1N5231BRL	OEM
1N5231C	OEM
1N5231D	OEM
1N5232	0253
1N5232A	0253
1N5232ARL	OEM
1N5232B	0253
1N5232BRL	OEM
1N5232C	OEM
1N5232D	OEM
1N5232RL	OEM
1N5233	0091
1N5233A	0091
1N5233ARL	OEM
1N5233B	0091
1N5233BRL	OEM
1N5233C	OEM
1N5233D	OEM
1N5233RL	OEM
1N5234	0466
1N5234A	0466
1N5234ARL	OEM
1N5234B	0466
1N5234BRL	OEM
1N5234C	OEM
1N5234D	OEM
1N5234RL	OEM
1N5235	0062
1N5235A	0062
1N5235ARL	OEM
1N5235B	0062
1N5235BRL	OEM
1N5235C	OEM
1N5235D	OEM
1N5235RL	OEM
1N5236	0077
1N5236A	0077
1N5236ARL	OEM
1N5236B	0077
1N5236BRL	OEM
1N5236C	OEM
1N5236D	OEM
1N5236RL	OEM
1N5237	0165
1N5237A	0165
1N5237ARL	OEM
1N5237B	0165
1N5237BRL	OEM
1N5237C	OEM
1N5237D	OEM
1N5237RL	OEM
1N5238	0318
1N5238-BRL	1075
1N5238A	0318
1N5238ARL	OEM
1N5238B	0318
1N5238BRL	OEM
1N5238C	OEM
1N5238D	OEM
1N5238RL	OEM
1N5239	0057
1N5239A	0057
1N5239ARL	OEM
1N5239B	0057
1N5239BRL	OEM
1N5239C	OEM
1N5239D	OEM
1N5239RL	OEM
1N5240	0064
1N5240A	0064
1N5240ARL	OEM
1N5240B	0064
1N5240BRL	OEM
1N5240C	OEM
1N5240D	OEM
1N5240RL	OEM
1N5241	0181
1N5241A	0181
1N5241ARL	OEM
1N5241B	0181
1N5241BRL	OEM
1N5241C	OEM
1N5241D	OEM
1N5241RL	OEM
1N5242	0052
1N5242A	0052
1N5242ARL	OEM
1N5242B	0052
1N5242BRL	OEM
1N5242C	OEM
1N5242D	OEM
1N5242RL	OEM
1N5243	0053
1N5243-BRL	0053
1N5243A	0053
1N5243ARL	OEM
1N5243B	0053
1N5243BRL	OEM
1N5243C	OEM
1N5243D	OEM
1N5243RL	OEM

DEVICE TYPE	REPL CODE
1N5244	0873
1N5244A	0873
1N5244ARL	OEM
1N5244B	0873
1N5244BRL	OEM
1N5244C	OEM
1N5244D	OEM
1N5244RL	OEM
1N5245	0681
1N5245A	0681
1N5245ARL	OEM
1N5245B	0681
1N5245BRL	OEM
1N5245C	OEM
1N5245D	OEM
1N5245RL	OEM
1N5246	0440
1N5246A	0440
1N5246ARL	OEM
1N5246B	0440
1N5246BRL	OEM
1N5246C	OEM
1N5246D	OEM
1N5246RL	OEM
1N5247	0210
1N5247A	0210
1N5247ARL	OEM
1N5247B	0210
1N5247BRL	OEM
1N5247C	OEM
1N5247D	OEM
1N5247RL	OEM
1N5248	0371
1N5248A	0371
1N5248ARL	OEM
1N5248B	0371
1N5248BRL	OEM
1N5248C	OEM
1N5248D	OEM
1N5248RL	OEM
1N5249	0666
1N5249A	0666
1N5249ARL	OEM
1N5249B	0666
1N5249BRL	OEM
1N5249C	OEM
1N5249D	OEM
1N5249RL	OEM
1N5250	0695
1N5250A	0695
1N5250ARL	OEM
1N5250B	0695
1N5250BRL	OEM
1N5250C	OEM
1N5250D	OEM
1N5250RL	OEM
1N5251	0700
1N5251A	0700
1N5251ARL	OEM
1N5251B	0700
1N5251BRL	OEM
1N5251C	OEM
1N5251D	OEM
1N5251RL	OEM
1N5252	0489
1N5252A	0489
1N5252ARL	OEM
1N5252B	0489
1N5252BRL	OEM
1N5252C	OEM
1N5252D	OEM
1N5252RL	OEM
1N5253	0709
1N5253A	0709
1N5253ARL	OEM
1N5253B	0709
1N5253BRL	OEM
1N5253C	OEM
1N5253D	OEM
1N5253RL	OEM
1N5254	0450
1N5254A	0450
1N5254ARL	OEM
1N5254B	0450
1N5254BRL	OEM
1N5254C	OEM
1N5254D	OEM
1N5254RL	OEM
1N5255	0257
1N5255A	0257
1N5255ARL	OEM
1N5255B	0257
1N5255BRL	OEM
1N5255C	OEM
1N5255D	OEM
1N5255RL	OEM
1N5256	0195
1N5256A	0195
1N5256ARL	OEM
1N5256B	0195
1N5256BRL	OEM
1N5256C	OEM
1N5256D	OEM
1N5256RL	OEM
1N5257	0166
1N5257A	0166
1N5257ARL	OEM
1N5257B	0166
1N5257BRL	OEM

DEVICE TYPE	REPL CODE
1N5257C	OEM
1N5257D	OEM
1N5257RL	OEM
1N5258	0010
1N5258A	0010
1N5258ARL	OEM
1N5258B	0010
1N5258BRL	OEM
1N5258C	OEM
1N5258D	OEM
1N5258RL	OEM
1N5259	0032
1N5259A	0032
1N5259ARL	OEM
1N5259B	0032
1N5259BRL	OEM
1N5259C	OEM
1N5259D	OEM
1N5259RL	OEM
1N5260	0054
1N5260A	0054
1N5260ARL	OEM
1N5260B	0054
1N5260BRL	OEM
1N5260C	OEM
1N5260D	OEM
1N5260RL	OEM
1N5261	0068
1N5261A	0068
1N5261ARL	OEM
1N5261B	0068
1N5261BRL	OEM
1N5261C	OEM
1N5261D	OEM
1N5261RL	OEM
1N5262	0092
1N5262A	0092
1N5262ARL	OEM
1N5262B	0092
1N5262BRL	OEM
1N5262C	OEM
1N5262D	OEM
1N5262RL	OEM
1N5263	0125
1N5263A	0125
1N5263ARL	OEM
1N5263B	0125
1N5263BRL	OEM
1N5263C	OEM
1N5263D	OEM
1N5263RL	OEM
1N5264	2301
1N5264A	2301
1N5264ARL	OEM
1N5264B	2301
1N5264BRL	OEM
1N5264C	OEM
1N5264D	OEM
1N5264RL	OEM
1N5265	0152
1N5265A	0152
1N5265ARL	OEM
1N5265B	0152
1N5265BRL	OEM
1N5265C	OEM
1N5265D	OEM
1N5265RL	OEM
1N5266	0173
1N5266A	0173
1N5266ARL	OEM
1N5266B	0173
1N5266BRL	OEM
1N5266C	OEM
1N5266D	OEM
1N5266RL	OEM
1N5267	0094
1N5267A	0094
1N5267ARL	OEM
1N5267B	0094
1N5267BRL	OEM
1N5267RL	OEM
1N5268	0049
1N5268A	0049
1N5268ARL	OEM
1N5268B	0049
1N5268BRL	OEM
1N5268RL	OEM
1N5269	0104
1N5269A	0104
1N5269ARL	OEM
1N5269B	0104
1N5269BRL	OEM
1N5269RL	OEM
1N5270	0156
1N5270A	0156
1N5270ARL	OEM
1N5270B	0156
1N5270BRL	OEM
1N5270RL	OEM
1N5271	0189
1N5271A	0189
1N5271ARL	OEM
1N5271B	0189
1N5271BRL	OEM
1N5271RL	OEM
1N5272	0099
1N5272A	0099
1N5272ARL	OEM
1N5272B	0099

DEVICE TYPE	REPL CODE
1N5272BRL	OEM
1N5272RL	OEM
1N5273	0089
1N5273A	0089
1N5273ARL	OEM
1N5273B	0089
1N5273BE	0089
1N5273BRL	OEM
1N5273RL	OEM
1N5274	0285
1N5274A	0285
1N5274ARL	OEM
1N5274B	0285
1N5274BRL	OEM
1N5274RL	OEM
1N5275	0252
1N5275A	0252
1N5275ARL	OEM
1N5275B	0252
1N5275BRL	OEM
1N5275RL	OEM
1N5276	0336
1N5276A	0336
1N5276ARL	OEM
1N5276B	0028
1N5276BRL	OEM
1N5276RL	OEM
1N5277	0366
1N5277A	0366
1N5277ARL	OEM
1N5277B	0255
1N5277BRL	OEM
1N5277RL	OEM
1N5278	0390
1N5278A	0390
1N5278ARL	OEM
1N5278B	0871
1N5278BRL	OEM
1N5278RL	OEM
1N5279	0420
1N5279A	0420
1N5279ARL	OEM
1N5279B	0363
1N5279BRL	OEM
1N5279RL	OEM
1N5280	0448
1N5280A	0448
1N5280ARL	OEM
1N5280B	2831
1N5280BRL	OEM
1N5280RL	OEM
1N5281	1464
1N5281A	1464
1N5281ARL	OEM
1N5281B	0417
1N5281BRL	OEM
1N5281RL	OEM
1N5282	0124
1N5283	OEM
1N5284	OEM
1N5285	OEM
1N5286	OEM
1N5287	OEM
1N5288	OEM
1N5289	OEM
1N5290	OEM
1N5291	OEM
1N5292	OEM
1N5293	OEM
1N5294	OEM
1N5295	OEM
1N5296	OEM
1N5297	OEM
1N5298	OEM
1N5299	OEM
1N5300	OEM
1N5301	OEM
1N5302	OEM
1N5303	OEM
1N5304	OEM
1N5305	OEM
1N5306	OEM
1N5307	OEM
1N5308	OEM
1N5309	OEM
1N5310	OEM
1N5311	OEM
1N5312	OEM
1N5313	OEM
1N5314	OEM
1N5315	0133
1N5316	0133
1N5317	0133
1N5318	0133
1N5319	0133
1N5320	0133
1N5321	OEM
1N5322	OEM
1N5323	OEM
1N5324	0466
1N5324A	0466
1N5324B	0253
1N5326	1272
1N5329	OEM
1N5330	0437
1N5331	OEM
1N5331R	OEM
1N5332	OEM
1N5332R	OEM

DEVICE TYPE	REPL CODE
1N5333	0777
1N5333A	0777
1N5333ARL	OEM
1N5333B	0777
1N5333BE	0777
1N5333BRL	OEM
1N5334	0791
1N5334A	0791
1N5334ARL	OEM
1N5334B	0791
1N5334BE	0791
1N5334BRL	OEM
1N5335	0801
1N5335A	0801
1N5335ARL	OEM
1N5335B	0801
1N5335BE	0801
1N5335BRL	OEM
1N5336	0815
1N5336A	0815
1N5336ARL	OEM
1N5336B	0815
1N5336BE	0815
1N5336BRL	OEM
1N5337	0827
1N5337A	0827
1N5337ARL	OEM
1N5337B	0827
1N5337BE	0827
1N5337BRL	OEM
1N5338	0437
1N5338A	0437
1N5338ARL	OEM
1N5338B	0437
1N5338BE	0437
1N5338BRL	OEM
1N5339	0870
1N5339A	0870
1N5339ARL	OEM
1N5339B	0870
1N5339BE	0870
1N5339BRL	OEM
1N5340	3099
1N5340A	3099
1N5340ARL	OEM
1N5340B	3099
1N5340BE	3099
1N5340BRL	OEM
1N5341	0185
1N5341A	0185
1N5341ARL	OEM
1N5341B	0185
1N5341BE	0185
1N5341BRL	OEM
1N5342	0205
1N5342A	0205
1N5342ARL	OEM
1N5342B	0205
1N5342BE	0205
1N5342BRL	OEM
1N5343	0475
1N5343A	0475
1N5343ARL	OEM
1N5343B	0475
1N5343BE	0475
1N5343BRL	OEM
1N5344	0499
1N5344A	0499
1N5344ARL	OEM
1N5344B	0499
1N5344BE	0499
1N5344BRL	OEM
1N5345	3285
1N5345A	3285
1N5345ARL	OEM
1N5345B	3285
1N5345BE	3285
1N5345BRL	OEM
1N5346	0679
1N5346A	0679
1N5346ARL	OEM
1N5346B	0679
1N5346BE	0679
1N5346BRL	OEM
1N5347	0225
1N5347A	0225
1N5347ARL	OEM
1N5347B	0225
1N5347BE	0225
1N5347BRL	OEM
1N5348	0230
1N5348A	0230
1N5348ARL	OEM
1N5348B	0170
1N5348BE	0230
1N5348BRL	OEM
1N5349	0234
1N5349A	0234
1N5349ARL	OEM
1N5349B	0234
1N5349BE	0234
1N5349BRL	OEM
1N5350	0237
1N5350A	0237
1N5350ARL	OEM
1N5350B	0237
1N5350BE	0237
1N5350BRL	OEM
1N5351	1387

DEVICE TYPE	REPL CODE
1N5351A	1387
1N5351ARL	OEM
1N5351B	1387
1N5351BE	1387
1N5351BRL	OEM
1N5352	0247
1N5352A	0247
1N5352ARL	OEM
1N5352B	0251
1N5352BE	0247
1N5352BRL	OEM
1N5353	0251
1N5353A	0251
1N5353ARL	OEM
1N5353B	0251
1N5353BE	0251
1N5353BRL	OEM
1N5354	1170
1N5354A	1170
1N5354ARL	OEM
1N5354B	1170
1N5354BE	1170
1N5354BRL	OEM
1N5355	0256
1N5355A	0256
1N5355ARL	OEM
1N5355B	0256
1N5355BE	0256
1N5355BRL	OEM
1N5356	2379
1N5356A	2379
1N5356ARL	OEM
1N5356B	2999
1N5356BE	2379
1N5356BRL	OEM
1N5357	0262
1N5357A	0262
1N5357ARL	OEM
1N5357B	0262
1N5357BE	0262
1N5357BRL	OEM
1N5358	0269
1N5358A	0269
1N5358ARL	OEM
1N5358B	0269
1N5358BE	0269
1N5358BRL	OEM
1N5359	0273
1N5359A	0273
1N5359ARL	OEM
1N5359B	0273
1N5359BE	0273
1N5359BRL	OEM
1N5360	2383
1N5360A	2383
1N5360ARL	OEM
1N5360B	2383
1N5360BE	2383
1N5360BRL	OEM
1N5361	0291
1N5361A	0291
1N5361B	0291
1N5361BE	0291
1N5361BRL	OEM
1N5362	1169
1N5362A	1169
1N5362ARL	OEM
1N5362B	1169
1N5362BE	1169
1N5362BRL	OEM
1N5363	0305
1N5363A	0305
1N5363ARL	OEM
1N5363B	0305
1N5363BE	0305
1N5363BRL	OEM
1N5364	0314
1N5364A	0314
1N5364ARL	OEM
1N5364B	0314
1N5364BE	0314
1N5364BRL	OEM
1N5365	0316
1N5365A	0316
1N5365ARL	OEM
1N5365B	0316
1N5365BE	0316
1N5365BRL	OEM
1N5366	0322
1N5366A	0322
1N5366ARL	OEM
1N5366B	0322
1N5366BE	0322
1N5366BRL	OEM
1N5367	0333
1N5367A	0333
1N5367ARL	OEM
1N5367B	0333
1N5367BE	0333
1N5367BRL	OEM
1N5368	0343
1N5368A	0343
1N5368ARL	OEM
1N5368B	0343
1N5368BE	0343
1N5368BRL	OEM
1N5369	0027
1N5369A	0027
1N5369ARL	OEM

DEVICE TYPE	REPL CODE
1N5369B	0027
1N5369BE	0027
1N5369BRL	OEM
1N5370	0266
1N5370A	0266
1N5370ARL	OEM
1N5370B	0266
1N5370BE	0266
1N5370BRL	OEM
1N5371	2829
1N5371A	2829
1N5371ARL	OEM
1N5371B	2829
1N5371BE	2829
1N5371BRL	OEM
1N5372	0382
1N5372A	0382
1N5372ARL	OEM
1N5372B	0382
1N5372BRL	OEM
1N5373	0401
1N5373A	0401
1N5373ARL	OEM
1N5373B	0401
1N5373BE	0401
1N5373BRL	OEM
1N5374	0421
1N5374A	0421
1N5374ARL	OEM
1N5374B	0421
1N5374BE	0401
1N5374BRL	OEM
1N5375	0439
1N5375A	0439
1N5375ARL	OEM
1N5375B	0439
1N5375BE	0439
1N5375BRL	OEM
1N5376	2999
1N5376A	2999
1N5376ARL	OEM
1N5376B	2999
1N5376BE	2999
1N5376BRL	OEM
1N5377	0238
1N5377A	0238
1N5377ARL	OEM
1N5377B	0238
1N5377BE	0238
1N5377BRL	OEM
1N5378	1172
1N5378A	1172
1N5378ARL	OEM
1N5378B	1172
1N5378BE	1172
1N5378BRL	OEM
1N5379	1182
1N5379A	1182
1N5379ARL	OEM
1N5379B	1182
1N5379BE	1182
1N5379BRL	OEM
1N5380	1198
1N5380A	1198
1N5380ARL	OEM
1N5380B	1198
1N5380BE	1198
1N5380BRL	OEM
1N5381	1209
1N5381A	1209
1N5381ARL	OEM
1N5381B	1209
1N5381BE	1209
1N5381BRL	OEM
1N5382	1870
1N5382A	1870
1N5382ARL	OEM
1N5382B	1870
1N5382BE	1870
1N5382BRL	OEM
1N5383	0642
1N5383A	0642
1N5383ARL	OEM
1N5383B	0642
1N5383BE	0642
1N5383BRL	OEM
1N5384	1246
1N5384A	1246
1N5384ARL	OEM
1N5384B	1246
1N5384BE	1246
1N5384BRL	OEM
1N5385	2091
1N5385A	2091
1N5385ARL	OEM
1N5385B	2091
1N5385BRL	OEM
1N5386	1269
1N5386A	1269
1N5386ARL	OEM
1N5386B	1269
1N5386BE	1269
1N5386BRL	OEM
1N5387	2210
1N5387A	2210
1N5387ARL	OEM
1N5387B	2210
1N5387BRL	OEM
1N5388	0600

If replacement code is OEM, contact original manufacturer for replacement.

DEVICE TYPE	REPL CODE
1N5388A	0600
1N5388ARL	OEM
1N5388B	0600
1N5388BE	0600
1N5388BRL	OEM
1N5389	OEM
1N5390	0911
1N5391	0110
1N5391G	0071
1N5391GP	0071
1N5391RL	OEM
1N5392	0071
1N5392(GP)	0087
1N5392G	0071
1N5392G2	0947
1N5392GP	0071
1N5392RL	OEM
1N5393	0242
1N5393G	0071
1N5393GP	0071
1N5393L	OEM
1N5394	1736
1N5394G	0071
1N5394GP	0071
1N5395	0535
1N5395G	0071
1N5395GP	0071
1N5395RL	OEM
1N5396	1760
1N5396G	0071
1N5396GP	0071
1N5396RB	2391
1N5397	0959
1N5397G	0071
1N5397GP	0071
1N5397RL	OEM
1N5398	0811
1N5398G	0071
1N5398GP	0071
1N5398RL	OEM
1N5399	0087
1N5399G	0071
1N5399GP	0071
1N5399RL	OEM
1N5400	0110
1N5400G	0110
1N5400RL	OEM
1N5401	0947
1N5401G	0947
1N5401RL	OEM
1N5402	0242
1N5402-M21	OEM
1N5402G	0242
1N5402RL	OEM
1N5403	1736
1N5403G	OEM
1N5404	0535
1N5404G	0535
1N5404RL	OEM
1N5405	1760
1N5405G	OEM
1N5406	0959
1N5406G	0959
1N5406RL	OEM
1N5407	0811
1N5407G	0811
1N5408	0916
1N5408G	0916
1N5409	1118
1N5409R	1103
1N5410	0105
1N5410R	0772
1N5411	2704
1N5412	0229
1N5413	0133
1N5414	0133
1N5415	0914
1N5416	0031
1N5417	0031
1N5418	0102
1N5419	0102
1N5420	0087
1N5421	OEM
1N5422	OEM
1N5423	OEM
1N5424	OEM
1N5425	OEM
1N5426	0133
1N5427	OEM
1N5428	OEM
1N5429	OEM
1N5430	OEM
1N5431	OEM
1N5432	OEM
1N5433	0102
1N5434	0102
1N5435	0131
1N5436	OEM
1N5437	OEM
1N5438	OEM
1N5439	OEM
1N5439A	OEM
1N5439B	OEM
1N5439C	OEM
1N5439D	OEM
1N5440	OEM
1N5440A	OEM
1N5440B	OEM
1N5440C	OEM
1N5440D	OEM
1N5441	0549
1N5441A	0549
1N5441B	0549
1N5441C	0549
1N5441D	OEM
1N5442	OEM
1N5442A	0549
1N5442B	0549
1N5442C	0549
1N5442D	OEM
1N5443	0005
1N5443A	0005
1N5443B	0005
1N5443C	0005
1N5443D	OEM
1N5444	0715
1N5444A	0715
1N5444B	0715
1N5444C	0715
1N5444D	OEM
1N5445	OEM
1N5445A	0715
1N5445B	0715
1N5445C	0715
1N5445D	OEM
1N5446	OEM
1N5446A	0623
1N5446B	0623
1N5446C	0623
1N5446D	OEM
1N5447	0623
1N5447A	0623
1N5447B	0623
1N5447C	0623
1N5447D	OEM
1N5448	0623
1N5448A	0623
1N5448B	0623
1N5448C	0623
1N5448D	OEM
1N5449	OEM
1N5449A	0623
1N5449B	0623
1N5449C	0623
1N5449D	OEM
1N5450	0030
1N5450A	0030
1N5450B	0030
1N5450C	0030
1N5450D	OEM
1N5451	OEM
1N5451A	OEM
1N5451B	OEM
1N5451C	OEM
1N5451D	OEM
1N5452	OEM
1N5452A	OEM
1N5452B	OEM
1N5452C	OEM
1N5452D	OEM
1N5453	OEM
1N5453A	OEM
1N5453B	OEM
1N5453C	OEM
1N5453D	OEM
1N5454	OEM
1N5454A	OEM
1N5454B	OEM
1N5454C	OEM
1N5454D	OEM
1N5455	OEM
1N5455A	OEM
1N5455B	OEM
1N5455C	OEM
1N5455D	OEM
1N5456	OEM
1N5456A	OEM
1N5456B	OEM
1N5456C	OEM
1N5456D	OEM
1N5457	OEM
1N5457A	OEM
1N5457B	OEM
1N5457C	OEM
1N5457D	OEM
1N5458	OEM
1N5458A	OEM
1N5458B	OEM
1N5458C	OEM
1N5458D	OEM
1N5459	OEM
1N5459A	OEM
1N5459B	OEM
1N5459C	OEM
1N5459D	OEM
1N5460	OEM
1N5460A	OEM
1N5460B	OEM
1N5460C	OEM
1N5460D	OEM
1N5461	0549
1N5461A	0549
1N5461B	0549
1N5461C	0549
1N5461D	OEM
1N5462	OEM
1N5462A	OEM
1N5462B	OEM
1N5462C	OEM
1N5462D	OEM
1N5463	0005
1N5463A	0005
1N5463B	0005
1N5463C	0005
1N5463D	OEM
1N5464	0715
1N5464A	0715
1N5464B	0715
1N5464C	0715
1N5464D	OEM
1N5465	OEM
1N5465A	OEM
1N5465B	OEM
1N5465C	OEM
1N5465D	OEM
1N5466	OEM
1N5466A	OEM
1N5466B	OEM
1N5466C	OEM
1N5466D	OEM
1N5467	OEM
1N5467A	OEM
1N5467B	OEM
1N5467C	OEM
1N5467D	OEM
1N5468	0623
1N5468A	0623
1N5468B	0623
1N5468C	0623
1N5468D	OEM
1N5469	OEM
1N5469A	OEM
1N5469B	OEM
1N5469C	OEM
1N5469D	OEM
1N5470	0030
1N5470A	0030
1N5470B	0030
1N5470C	0030
1N5470D	OEM
1N5471	OEM
1N5471A	OEM
1N5471B	OEM
1N5471C	OEM
1N5471D	OEM
1N5472	OEM
1N5472A	OEM
1N5472B	OEM
1N5472C	OEM
1N5472D	OEM
1N5473	OEM
1N5473A	OEM
1N5473B	OEM
1N5473C	OEM
1N5473D	OEM
1N5474	OEM
1N5474A	OEM
1N5474B	OEM
1N5474C	OEM
1N5474D	OEM
1N5475	OEM
1N5475A	OEM
1N5475B	OEM
1N5475C	OEM
1N5475D	OEM
1N5476	OEM
1N5476A	OEM
1N5476B	OEM
1N5476C	OEM
1N5476D	OEM
1N5477	OEM
1N5478	OEM
1N5479	OEM
1N5480	OEM
1N5481	OEM
1N5482	OEM
1N5483	OEM
1N5484	OEM
1N5485	OEM
1N5518	0296
1N5518A	0296
1N5518B	0296
1N5518C	OEM
1N5518D	OEM
1N5519	0372
1N5519A	0372
1N5519B	0372
1N5519C	OEM
1N5519D	OEM
1N5520	0036
1N5520A	0036
1N5520B	0036
1N5520C	0036
1N5520D	0036
1N5521	0274
1N5521A	0274
1N5521B	0274
1N5521C	OEM
1N5521D	OEM
1N5522	0140
1N5522A	0140
1N5522B	0140
1N5522C	OEM
1N5522D	OEM
1N5523	0041
1N5523A	0041
1N5523B	0041
1N5523C	0466
1N5523D	0582
1N5524	0253
1N5524A	0253
1N5524B	0253
1N5524C	0877
1N5524D	0877
1N5525	0466
1N5525A	0466
1N5525B	0466
1N5525C	OEM
1N5525D	OEM
1N5526	0062
1N5526A	0062
1N5526B	0062
1N5526B1	0062
1N5526C	OEM
1N5526D	OEM
1N5527	0077
1N5527A	0077
1N5527B	0077
1N5527B1	0077
1N5527C	OEM
1N5527D	OEM
1N5528	0165
1N5528A	0165
1N5528B	0165
1N5528B1	0165
1N5528C	4245
1N5528D	4245
1N5529	0057
1N5529A	0057
1N5529B	0057
1N5529B1	0057
1N5529C	OEM
1N5529D	OEM
1N5530	0064
1N5530A	0064
1N5530B	0064
1N5530B1	0064
1N5530C	0248
1N5530D	0248
1N5531	0181
1N5531A	0181
1N5531B	0181
1N5531B1	0181
1N5531C	OEM
1N5531D	OEM
1N5532	0052
1N5532A	0052
1N5532B	0052
1N5532B1	0052
1N5532C	0999
1N5532D	0999
1N5533	0053
1N5533A	0053
1N5533B	0053
1N5533B1	0053
1N5533C	OEM
1N5533D	OEM
1N5534	0873
1N5534A	0873
1N5534B	0873
1N5534B1	0873
1N5534C	OEM
1N5534D	OEM
1N5535	0681
1N5535A	0681
1N5535B	0681
1N5535B1	0681
1N5535C	OEM
1N5535D	OEM
1N5536	0440
1N5536A	0440
1N5536B	0440
1N5536B1	0440
1N5536C	OEM
1N5536D	OEM
1N5537	0210
1N5537A	0210
1N5537B	0210
1N5537B1	0210
1N5537C	OEM
1N5537D	OEM
1N5538	0371
1N5538A	0371
1N5538B	0371
1N5538B1	0371
1N5538C	OEM
1N5538D	OEM
1N5539	0666
1N5539A	0666
1N5539B	0666
1N5539B1	0666
1N5539C	OEM
1N5539D	OEM
1N5540	0695
1N5540A	0695
1N5540B	0695
1N5540B1	0695
1N5540C	OEM
1N5540D	OEM
1N5541	0700
1N5541A	0700
1N5541B	0700
1N5541B1	0700
1N5541C	OEM
1N5541D	OEM
1N5542	0489
1N5542A	0489
1N5542B	0489
1N5542B1	0489
1N5542C	OEM
1N5542D	OEM
1N5543	0709
1N5543A	0709
1N5543B	0709
1N5543B1	0709
1N5543C	OEM
1N5543D	OEM
1N5544	0257
1N5544A	0257
1N5544B	0257
1N5544B1	0257
1N5544C	OEM
1N5544D	OEM
1N5545	0195
1N5545A	0195
1N5545B	0195
1N5545B1	0195
1N5545C	OEM
1N5545D	OEM
1N5546	0166
1N5546A	0166
1N5546B	0166
1N5546B1	0166
1N5546C	OEM
1N5546D	OEM
1N5550	0087
1N5551	0087
1N5552	0087
1N5553	0102
1N5554	0102
1N5555	OEM
1N5556	OEM
1N5557	OEM
1N5558	OEM
1N5559	0025
1N5559A	0025
1N5559B	0025
1N5560	0644
1N5560A	0644
1N5560B	0644
1N5561	0244
1N5561A	0244
1N5561B	0244
1N5562	0012
1N5562A	0012
1N5562B	0644
1N5563	0170
1N5563A	0170
1N5563B	0012
1N5564	0313
1N5564A	0313
1N5564B	0313
1N5565	0137
1N5565A	0137
1N5565B	0137
1N5566	0361
1N5566A	0361
1N5566B	0361
1N5567	0002
1N5567A	0002
1N5567B	0002
1N5568	0416
1N5568A	0416
1N5568B	0416
1N5569	0490
1N5569A	0490
1N5569B	0490
1N5570	0526
1N5570A	0526
1N5570B	0526
1N5571	0560
1N5571A	0560
1N5571B	0560
1N5572	0398
1N5572A	0398
1N5572B	0398
1N5573	0436
1N5573A	0436
1N5573B	0436
1N5574	0721
1N5574A	0721
1N5574B	0721
1N5575	0039
1N5575A	0039
1N5575B	0039
1N5576	0814
1N5576A	0814
1N5576B	0814
1N5577	0346
1N5577A	0346
1N5577B	0814
1N5578	0925
1N5578A	0925
1N5578B	0925
1N5579	0993
1N5579A	0993
1N5579B	0993
1N5580	0497
1N5580A	0497
1N5580B	0497
1N5581	0863
1N5581A	0863
1N5581B	0863
1N5582	0778
1N5582A	0778
1N5582B	0778
1N5583	1258
1N5583A	1258
1N5583B	1258
1N5584	1181
1N5584A	1181
1N5584B	1181
1N5585	0327
1N5585A	0327
1N5585B	0327
1N5586	1301
1N5586A	1301
1N5586B	1301
1N5587	0098
1N5587A	0098
1N5587B	0098
1N5588	0149
1N5588A	0149
1N5588B	0149
1N5589	0186
1N5589A	0186
1N5589B	0186
1N5590	0213
1N5590A	0213
1N5590B	0213
1N5591	0028
1N5591A	0028
1N5591B	0028
1N5592	0255
1N5592A	0255
1N5592B	0255
1N5593	0363
1N5593A	0363
1N5593B	0363
1N5594	0417
1N5594A	0417
1N5594B	0417
1N5595	OEM
1N5596	OEM
1N5597	OEM
1N5598	OEM
1N5599	OEM
1N5600	OEM
1N5601	OEM
1N5602	OEM
1N5603	OEM
1N5604	OEM
1N5605	0133
1N5606	0133
1N5607	0133
1N5608	0133
1N5609	0133
1N5610	0133
1N5611	OEM
1N5614	0023
1N5614GP	0023
1N5615	0023
1N5615GP	0023
1N5616	0023
1N5616GP	0023
1N5617	0023
1N5617GP	0023
1N5618	0017
1N5618GP	0017
1N5619	0017
1N5619GP	0017
1N5620	0017
1N5620GP	0017
1N5621	0017
1N5621GP	0017
1N5622	0017
1N5622GP	0017
1N5623	0017
1N5623GP	0017
1N5624	0242
1N5624GP	0242
1N5625	0535
1N5625GP	0535
1N5626	0959
1N5626G	OEM
1N5626GP	0959
1N5627	0811
1N5627GP	0811
1N5628	OEM
1N5629	3085
1N5629A	3085
1N5629AP1	OEM
1N5629P1	OEM
1N5630	OEM
1N5630A	OEM
1N5630AP1	OEM
1N5630P1	OEM
1N5631	OEM
1N5631A	OEM
1N5631AP1	OEM
1N5631P1	OEM
1N5632	OEM
1N5632A	OEM
1N5632AP1	OEM
1N5632P1	OEM
1N5633	OEM
1N5633A	OEM
1N5633AP1	OEM
1N5633P1	OEM
1N5634	OEM
1N5634A	OEM
1N5634AP1	OEM
1N5634P1	OEM
1N5635	OEM
1N5635A	OEM
1N5635AP1	OEM
1N5635P1	OEM
1N5636	3143
1N5636A	3143
1N5636AP1	OEM
1N5636P1	OEM
1N5637	OEM
1N5637A	OEM
1N5637AP1	OEM
1N5637P1	OEM
1N5638	OEM
1N5638A	OEM
1N5638AP1	OEM
1N5638P1	OEM
1N5639	3162
1N5639A	3162
1N5639AP1	OEM
1N5639P1	OEM
1N5640	3171
1N5640A	3171
1N5640AP1	OEM
1N5640P1	OEM
1N5641	OEM
1N5641A	OEM
1N5641AP1	OEM
1N5641P1	OEM
1N5642	OEM
1N5642A	OEM
1N5642AP1	OEM
1N5642P1	OEM
1N5643	1904
1N5643A	1904
1N5643AP1	OEM
1N5643P1	OEM
1N5644	OEM
1N5644A	OEM
1N5644AP1	OEM
1N5644P1	OEM
1N5645	OEM
1N5645A	OEM
1N5645AP1	OEM
1N5645P1	OEM
1N5646	OEM
1N5646A	OEM
1N5646AP1	OEM
1N5646P1	OEM
1N5647	OEM
1N5647A	OEM
1N5647AP1	OEM
1N5647P1	OEM
1N5648	OEM
1N5648A	OEM
1N5648AP1	OEM
1N5648P1	OEM
1N5649	OEM
1N5649A	OEM
1N5649AP1	OEM
1N5649P1	OEM
1N5650	0563
1N5650A	0563
1N5650AP1	OEM
1N5650P1	OEM
1N5651	OEM
1N5651A	OEM
1N5651AP1	OEM
1N5651P1	OEM
1N5652	OEM
1N5652A	OEM
1N5652AP1	OEM
1N5652P1	OEM
1N5653	0825
1N5653A	0825
1N5653AP1	OEM
1N5653P1	OEM
1N5654	OEM
1N5654A	OEM
1N5654AP1	OEM
1N5654P1	OEM
1N5655	OEM
1N5655A	OEM
1N5655AP1	OEM
1N5655P1	OEM
1N5656	OEM
1N5656A	OEM
1N5656AP1	OEM
1N5656P1	OEM
1N5657	OEM
1N5657A	OEM
1N5657AP1	OEM
1N5657P1	OEM
1N5658	OEM
1N5658A	OEM
1N5658AP1	OEM
1N5658P1	OEM
1N5659	OEM
1N5659A	OEM
1N5659AP1	OEM
1N5659P1	OEM
1N5660	OEM
1N5660A	OEM
1N5660AP1	OEM
1N5660P1	OEM
1N5661	OEM
1N5661A	OEM
1N5661AP1	OEM
1N5661P1	OEM
1N5662	OEM
1N5662A	OEM

If replacement code is OEM, contact original manufacturer for replacement.

DEVICE TYPE	REPL CODE
1N5662AP1	OEM
1N5662P1	OEM
1N5663	OEM
1N5663A	OEM
1N5663AP1	OEM
1N5663P1	OEM
1N5664	OEM
1N5664A	OEM
1N5664AP1	OEM
1N5664P1	OEM
1N5665	1395
1N5665A	1395
1N5665AP1	OEM
1N5665P1	OEM
1N5670A	2847
1N5671A	0672
1N5676A	OEM
1N5678A	OEM
1N5679	0015
1N5680	0015
1N5681	0549
1N5681A	0549
1N5681B	OEM
1N5682	OEM
1N5682A	OEM
1N5682B	OEM
1N5683	0005
1N5683A	0005
1N5683B	OEM
1N5684	0715
1N5684A	0715
1N5684B	OEM
1N5685	OEM
1N5685A	OEM
1N5685B	OEM
1N5686	OEM
1N5686A	OEM
1N5686B	OEM
1N5687	0623
1N5687A	0623
1N5687B	OEM
1N5688	OEM
1N5688A	OEM
1N5688B	OEM
1N5689	0030
1N5689A	0030
1N5689B	OEM
1N5690	OEM
1N5690A	OEM
1N5690B	OEM
1N5691	OEM
1N5691A	OEM
1N5691B	OEM
1N5692	OEM
1N5692A	OEM
1N5692B	OEM
1N5693	OEM
1N5693A	OEM
1N5693B	OEM
1N5694	OEM
1N5694A	OEM
1N5694B	OEM
1N5695	OEM
1N5695A	OEM
1N5695B	OEM
1N5696	0549
1N5696A	0549
1N5696B	OEM
1N5697	OEM
1N5697A	OEM
1N5697B	OEM
1N5698	OEM
1N5698A	OEM
1N5698B	OEM
1N5699	0715
1N5699A	0715
1N5699B	OEM
1N5700	OEM
1N5700A	OEM
1N5700B	OEM
1N5701	OEM
1N5701A	OEM
1N5701B	OEM
1N5702	0623
1N5702A	0623
1N5702B	OEM
1N5703	OEM
1N5703A	OEM
1N5703B	OEM
1N5704	OEM
1N5704A	OEM
1N5704B	OEM
1N5705	OEM
1N5705A	OEM
1N5705B	OEM
1N5706	OEM
1N5706A	OEM
1N5706B	OEM
1N5707	OEM
1N5707A	OEM
1N5707B	OEM
1N5708	OEM
1N5708A	OEM
1N5708B	OEM
1N5709	OEM
1N5709A	OEM
1N5709B	OEM
1N5710	OEM
1N5710A	OEM
1N5710B	OEM
1N5711	0133
1N5712	6776
1N5713	0133
1N5714	OEM
1N5715	OEM
1N5716	OEM
1N5717	OEM
1N5718	OEM
1N5719	0133
1N5720	0124
1N5721	0124
1N5722	OEM
1N5723	OEM
1N5724	OEM
1N5725	OEM
1N5726	0124
1N5726A	OEM
1N5727	0124
1N5728	0140
1N5728B	0140
1N5728C	OEM
1N5728D	OEM
1N5729	0041
1N5729B	0041
1N5729C	0582
1N5729D	0582
1N5730	0253
1N5730B	0253
1N5730C	OEM
1N5730D	OEM
1N5731	0466
1N5731B	0466
1N5731C	OEM
1N5731D	OEM
1N5732B	0062
1N5732C	OEM
1N5732D	OEM
1N5733	0077
1N5733B	0077
1N5733C	OEM
1N5733D	OEM
1N5734	0165
1N5734A	0165
1N5734B	0244
1N5734C	0165
1N5734D	0165
1N5735B	0057
1N5735C	OEM
1N5735D	OEM
1N5736	0064
1N5736B	0052
1N5736C	OEM
1N5736D	OEM
1N5737B	0181
1N5737C	OEM
1N5737D	OEM
1N5738	0052
1N5738B	0052
1N5738C	OEM
1N5738D	OEM
1N5739A	0053
1N5739B	0053
1N5739C	OEM
1N5739D	OEM
1N5740	0681
1N5740B	0681
1N5740C	OEM
1N5740D	OEM
1N5741	0440
1N5741B	0416
1N5741C	OEM
1N5741D	OEM
1N5742	0371
1N5742B	0490
1N5742C	OEM
1N5742D	OEM
1N5743B	0695
1N5743C	OEM
1N5743D	OEM
1N5744	0700
1N5744B	0700
1N5744C	OEM
1N5744D	OEM
1N5745B	0489
1N5745C	OEM
1N5745D	OEM
1N5746	0450
1N5746B	0450
1N5746C	0450
1N5746D	0450
1N5747B	0721
1N5747C	OEM
1N5747D	OEM
1N5748B	0166
1N5748C	OEM
1N5748D	OEM
1N5749	0010
1N5749B	0010
1N5749C	OEM
1N5749D	OEM
1N5750	0032
1N5750B	0032
1N5750C	OEM
1N5750D	OEM
1N5751	0054
1N5751B	0054
1N5751C	OEM
1N5751D	OEM
1N5752	0068
1N5752B	0068
1N5752C	OEM
1N5752D	OEM
1N5753	0092
1N5753B	0092
1N5753C	OEM
1N5753D	OEM
1N5754B	0125
1N5754C	OEM
1N5754D	OEM
1N5755B	0152
1N5755C	OEM
1N5755D	OEM
1N5756B	0173
1N5756C	OEM
1N5756D	OEM
1N5757B	0094
1N5757C	OEM
1N5757D	OEM
1N5758	3603
1N5758A	3603
1N5759	3298
1N5759A	3298
1N5760	3298
1N5760A	2704
1N5761	2704
1N5761A	3298
1N5762	OEM
1N5762A	OEM
1N5763	OEM
1N5764	OEM
1N5765	OEM
1N5767	0133
1N5768	OEM
1N5769	OEM
1N5770	OEM
1N5771	OEM
1N5772	OEM
1N5773	OEM
1N5774	OEM
1N5775	OEM
1N5779	OEM
1N5780	OEM
1N5781	OEM
1N5782	OEM
1N5783	OEM
1N5784	OEM
1N5785	OEM
1N5786	OEM
1N5787	OEM
1N5788	OEM
1N5789	OEM
1N5790	OEM
1N5791	OEM
1N5792	OEM
1N5793	OEM
1N5794	OEM
1N5795	OEM
1N5796	OEM
1N5797	OEM
1N5798	OEM
1N5799	OEM
1N5800	OEM
1N5802	0124
1N5803	0124
1N5804	0133
1N5805	0133
1N5806	0133
1N5807	0124
1N5808	0124
1N5809	0133
1N5810	0133
1N5811	0133
1N5812	OEM
1N5813	OEM
1N5814	OEM
1N5815	OEM
1N5816	OEM
1N5817	1325
1N5817RL	OEM
1N5818	1325
1N5818RL	OEM
1N5819	0730
1N5819RL	OEM
1N5820	0087
1N5820RL	OEM
1N5821	2520
1N5821RL	OEM
1N5822	2520
1N5822RL	OEM
1N5823	OEM
1N5824	OEM
1N5825	OEM
1N5826	0610
1N5827	0610
1N5828	0610
1N5829	0610
1N5830	6786
1N5831	6786
1N5832	1536
1N5833	1536
1N5834	1536
1N5835	0068
1N5836	0068
1N5837	1266
1N5837A	1266
1N5837B	1266
1N5837C	OEM
1N5837D	OEM
1N5838	2847
1N5838A	2847
1N5838B	2847
1N5838C	OEM
1N5838D	OEM
1N5839	0755
1N5839A	0755
1N5839B	0755
1N5839C	OEM
1N5839D	OEM
1N5840	0672
1N5840A	0672
1N5840B	0672
1N5840C	OEM
1N5840D	OEM
1N5841	0118
1N5841A	0118
1N5841B	0118
1N5841C	OEM
1N5841D	OEM
1N5842	0296
1N5842A	0296
1N5842B	0296
1N5842C	OEM
1N5842D	OEM
1N5843	0372
1N5843A	0372
1N5843B	0372
1N5843C	OEM
1N5843D	OEM
1N5844	0036
1N5844A	0036
1N5844B	0036
1N5844C	OEM
1N5844D	OEM
1N5845	0274
1N5845A	0274
1N5845B	0528
1N5845C	OEM
1N5845D	OEM
1N5846	0140
1N5846A	0140
1N5846B	0140
1N5846C	OEM
1N5846D	OEM
1N5847	0041
1N5847A	0041
1N5847B	0041
1N5847C	OEM
1N5847D	OEM
1N5848	0253
1N5848A	0253
1N5848B	0253
1N5848C	OEM
1N5848D	OEM
1N5849	0091
1N5849A	0091
1N5849B	0091
1N5849C	OEM
1N5849D	OEM
1N5850	0466
1N5850A	0466
1N5850B	0466
1N5850C	OEM
1N5850D	OEM
1N5851	0062
1N5851A	0062
1N5851B	0025
1N5851C	OEM
1N5851D	OEM
1N5852	0644
1N5852A	0644
1N5852B	0077
1N5852C	OEM
1N5852D	OEM
1N5853	0165
1N5853A	0165
1N5853B	0165
1N5853C	OEM
1N5853D	OEM
1N5854	0318
1N5854A	0318
1N5854B	0318
1N5854C	OEM
1N5854D	OEM
1N5855	0057
1N5855A	0057
1N5855B	0057
1N5855C	OEM
1N5855D	OEM
1N5856	0064
1N5856A	0064
1N5856B	0064
1N5856C	OEM
1N5856D	OEM
1N5857	0181
1N5857A	0181
1N5857B	0181
1N5857C	OEM
1N5857D	OEM
1N5858	0052
1N5858A	0052
1N5858B	0052
1N5858C	OEM
1N5858D	OEM
1N5859	0053
1N5859A	0053
1N5859B	0053
1N5859C	OEM
1N5859D	OEM
1N5860	0873
1N5860A	0873
1N5860B	0873
1N5860C	OEM
1N5860D	OEM
1N5861	0681
1N5861A	0681
1N5861B	0681
1N5861C	OEM
1N5861D	OEM
1N5862	0440
1N5862A	0440
1N5862B	0440
1N5862C	OEM
1N5862D	OEM
1N5863	0210
1N5863A	0210
1N5863B	0210
1N5863C	OEM
1N5863D	OEM
1N5864	0371
1N5864A	0371
1N5864B	0371
1N5864C	OEM
1N5864D	OEM
1N5865	0666
1N5865A	0666
1N5865B	0666
1N5865C	OEM
1N5865D	OEM
1N5866	0695
1N5866A	0695
1N5866B	0695
1N5866C	OEM
1N5866D	OEM
1N5867	0700
1N5867A	0700
1N5867B	0700
1N5867C	OEM
1N5867D	OEM
1N5868	0489
1N5868A	0489
1N5868B	0489
1N5868C	OEM
1N5868D	OEM
1N5869	0709
1N5869A	0709
1N5869B	0709
1N5869C	OEM
1N5869D	OEM
1N5870	0450
1N5870A	0450
1N5870B	0450
1N5870C	OEM
1N5870D	OEM
1N5871	0257
1N5871A	0257
1N5871B	0257
1N5871C	OEM
1N5871D	OEM
1N5872	0195
1N5872A	0195
1N5872B	0195
1N5872C	OEM
1N5872D	OEM
1N5873	0166
1N5873A	0166
1N5873B	0166
1N5873C	OEM
1N5873D	OEM
1N5874	0010
1N5874A	0010
1N5874B	0010
1N5874C	OEM
1N5874D	OEM
1N5875	0032
1N5875A	0032
1N5875B	0032
1N5875C	OEM
1N5875D	OEM
1N5876	0054
1N5876A	0054
1N5876B	0054
1N5876C	OEM
1N5876D	OEM
1N5877	0068
1N5877A	0068
1N5877B	0068
1N5877C	OEM
1N5877D	OEM
1N5878	0092
1N5878A	0092
1N5878B	0092
1N5878C	OEM
1N5878D	OEM
1N5879	0125
1N5879A	0125
1N5879B	0125
1N5879C	OEM
1N5879D	OEM
1N5880	2301
1N5880A	2301
1N5880B	6985
1N5880C	OEM
1N5880D	OEM
1N5881	0152
1N5881A	0152
1N5881B	0152
1N5881C	OEM
1N5881D	OEM
1N5882	0173
1N5882A	0173
1N5882B	0173
1N5882C	OEM
1N5882D	OEM
1N5883	0094
1N5883A	0094
1N5883B	0094
1N5883C	OEM
1N5883D	OEM
1N5884	0049
1N5884A	0049
1N5884B	0049
1N5884C	OEM
1N5884D	OEM
1N5885	0104
1N5885A	0104
1N5885B	0104
1N5885C	OEM
1N5885D	OEM
1N5886	0156
1N5886A	0156
1N5886B	0156
1N5886C	OEM
1N5886D	OEM
1N5887	0189
1N5887A	0189
1N5887B	0189
1N5887C	OEM
1N5887D	OEM
1N5888	0099
1N5888A	0099
1N5888B	0099
1N5888C	OEM
1N5888D	OEM
1N5889	0089
1N5889A	0244
1N5889B	0089
1N5889C	OEM
1N5889D	OEM
1N5890	0213
1N5890A	0213
1N5890B	0285
1N5890C	OEM
1N5890D	OEM
1N5891	0245
1N5891A	0245
1N5891B	0252
1N5891C	OEM
1N5891D	OEM
1N5892	0336
1N5892A	0336
1N5892B	0336
1N5892C	OEM
1N5892D	OEM
1N5893	0366
1N5893A	0366
1N5893B	0366
1N5893C	OEM
1N5893D	OEM
1N5894	0390
1N5894A	0390
1N5894B	0390
1N5894C	OEM
1N5894D	OEM
1N5895	0420
1N5895A	0420
1N5895B	0420
1N5895C	OEM
1N5895D	OEM
1N5896	0448
1N5896A	0448
1N5896B	0448
1N5896C	OEM
1N5896D	OEM
1N5897	0448
1N5897A	0448
1N5897B	0448
1N5897C	OEM
1N5897D	OEM
1N5898	0110
1N5899	0947
1N5900	0242
1N5901	0535
1N5902	0959
1N5903	0811
1N5904	0916
1N5905	OEM
1N5906	OEM
1N5907	2380
1N5908	2380
1N5908C	OEM
1N5913	0777
1N5913A	0777
1N5913ARL	OEM
1N5913B	0777
1N5913BRL	OEM
1N5913C	OEM
1N5913D	OEM
1N5914	0791
1N5914A	0791
1N5914ARL	OEM
1N5914B	0791
1N5914BRL	OEM
1N5914C	OEM
1N5914D	0582
1N5915	0801
1N5915A	0801
1N5915ARL	OEM
1N5915B	0801
1N5915BRL	OEM
1N5915C	OEM
1N5915D	OEM
1N5916	0815
1N5916A	0815
1N5916ARL	OEM
1N5916B	0815
1N5916BRL	OEM
1N5916C	OEM
1N5916D	OEM
1N5917	0827
1N5917A	0827
1N5917ARL	OEM
1N5917B	0827
1N5917BRL	OEM
1N5917C	OEM
1N5917D	OEM
1N5918	0437
1N5918A	0437
1N5918ARL	OEM
1N5918B	0437
1N5918BRL	OEM
1N5918C	OEM
1N5918D	0582
1N5919	0870
1N5919A	0870
1N5919ARL	OEM
1N5919B	0870
1N5919BRL	OEM
1N5919C	OEM
1N5919D	0877
1N5920	0185
1N5920A	0185
1N5920ARL	OEM
1N5920B	0185
1N5920BRL	OEM
1N5920C	OEM
1N5920D	0292
1N5920E	OEM
1N5921	0205
1N5921A	0205
1N5921ARL	OEM
1N5921B	0205
1N5921BRL	OEM
1N5921C	OEM
1N5921D	OEM
1N5922	0475
1N5922A	0475
1N5922ARL	OEM
1N5922B	0475
1N5922BRL	OEM
1N5922C	OEM
1N5922D	OEM
1N5923	0499
1N5923A	0499
1N5923ARL	OEM
1N5923B	0499
1N5923BRL	OEM
1N5923C	OEM
1N5923D	OEM
1N5924	0679
1N5924A	0679
1N5924ARL	OEM
1N5924B	0679
1N5924BRL	OEM
1N5924C	OEM
1N5924D	OEM
1N5925	0225
1N5925A	0225
1N5925ARL	OEM
1N5925B	0225
1N5925BRL	OEM
1N5925C	OEM
1N5925D	0248
1N5926	0230
1N5926A	0230
1N5926ARL	OEM
1N5926B	0230
1N5926BRL	OEM
1N5926C	OEM
1N5926D	OEM
1N5927	0234
1N5927A	0234
1N5927ARL	OEM
1N5927B	0234
1N5927BRL	OEM
1N5927C	OEM
1N5927D	0999
1N5928	0237
1N5928A	0237
1N5928ARL	OEM
1N5928B	0237
1N5928BRL	OEM
1N5928C	OEM
1N5928D	OEM
1N5929	0247
1N5929A	0247
1N5929ARL	OEM
1N5929B	0247
1N5929BRL	OEM
1N5929C	OEM
1N5929D	OEM
1N5930	0251
1N5930A	0251
1N5930ARL	OEM

If replacement code is OEM, contact original manufacturer for replacement.
29

DEVICE TYPE	REPL CODE
1N5930B	0251
1N5930BRL	OEM
1N5930C	OEM
1N5930D	OEM
1N5931	0256
1N5931A	0256
1N5931ARL	OEM
1N5931B	0256
1N5931BRL	OEM
1N5931C	OEM
1N5931D	OEM
1N5932	0262
1N5932A	0262
1N5932ARL	OEM
1N5932B	0262
1N5932BRL	OEM
1N5932C	OEM
1N5932D	OEM
1N5933	0269
1N5933A	0269
1N5933ARL	OEM
1N5933B	0269
1N5933BRL	OEM
1N5933C	OEM
1N5933D	OEM
1N5934	0273
1N5934A	0273
1N5934ARL	OEM
1N5934B	0273
1N5934BRL	OEM
1N5934C	OEM
1N5934D	OEM
1N5935	0291
1N5935A	0291
1N5935ARL	OEM
1N5935B	0291
1N5935BRL	OEM
1N5935C	OEM
1N5935D	OEM
1N5936	0305
1N5936A	0305
1N5936ARL	OEM
1N5936B	0305
1N5936BRL	OEM
1N5936C	OEM
1N5936D	OEM
1N5937	0314
1N5937A	0314
1N5937ARL	OEM
1N5937B	0314
1N5937BRL	OEM
1N5937C	OEM
1N5937D	OEM
1N5938	0316
1N5938A	0316
1N5938ARL	OEM
1N5938B	0316
1N5938BRL	OEM
1N5938C	OEM
1N5938D	OEM
1N5939	0322
1N5939A	0322
1N5939ARL	OEM
1N5939B	0322
1N5939BRL	OEM
1N5939C	OEM
1N5939D	OEM
1N5940	0333
1N5940A	0333
1N5940ARL	OEM
1N5940B	0333
1N5940BRL	OEM
1N5940C	OEM
1N5940D	OEM
1N5941	0343
1N5941A	0343
1N5941ARL	OEM
1N5941B	0343
1N5941BRL	OEM
1N5941C	OEM
1N5941D	OEM
1N5942	0027
1N5942A	0027
1N5942ARL	OEM
1N5942B	0027
1N5942BRL	OEM
1N5942C	OEM
1N5942D	OEM
1N5943	0266
1N5943A	0266
1N5943ARL	OEM
1N5943B	0266
1N5943BRL	OEM
1N5943C	OEM
1N5943D	OEM
1N5944	0382
1N5944A	0382
1N5944ARL	OEM
1N5944B	0382
1N5944BRL	OEM
1N5944C	OEM
1N5944D	OEM
1N5945	0401
1N5945A	0401
1N5945ARL	OEM
1N5945B	0401
1N5945BRL	OEM
1N5945C	OEM
1N5945D	OEM
1N5946	0421
1N5946A	0421
1N5946ARL	OEM
1N5946B	0421
1N5946BRL	OEM
1N5946C	OEM
1N5946D	OEM
1N5947	0439
1N5947A	0439
1N5947ARL	OEM
1N5947B	0439
1N5947BRL	OEM
1N5947C	OEM
1N5947D	OEM
1N5948	0238
1N5948A	0238
1N5948ARL	OEM
1N5948B	0238
1N5948BRL	OEM
1N5948C	OEM
1N5948D	OEM
1N5949	1172
1N5949A	1172
1N5949ARL	OEM
1N5949B	1172
1N5949BRL	OEM
1N5949C	OEM
1N5949D	OEM
1N5949GP	1172
1N5950	1182
1N5950A	1182
1N5950ARL	OEM
1N5950B	1182
1N5950BRL	OEM
1N5950C	OEM
1N5950D	OEM
1N5950GP	1182
1N5951	1198
1N5951A	1198
1N5951ARL	OEM
1N5951B	1198
1N5951BRL	OEM
1N5951C	OEM
1N5951D	OEM
1N5951GP	1198
1N5952	1209
1N5952A	1209
1N5952ARL	OEM
1N5952B	1209
1N5952BRL	OEM
1N5952C	OEM
1N5952D	OEM
1N5952GP	1209
1N5953	0642
1N5953A	0642
1N5953ARL	OEM
1N5953B	0642
1N5953BRL	OEM
1N5953C	OEM
1N5953D	OEM
1N5953GP	0642
1N5954	1246
1N5954A	1246
1N5954ARL	OEM
1N5954B	1246
1N5954BRL	OEM
1N5954C	OEM
1N5954D	OEM
1N5954GP	1246
1N5955	1269
1N5955A	1269
1N5955ARL	OEM
1N5955B	1269
1N5955BRL	OEM
1N5955C	OEM
1N5955D	OEM
1N5955GP	1269
1N5956	0600
1N5956A	0600
1N5956ARL	OEM
1N5956B	0600
1N5956BRL	OEM
1N5956C	OEM
1N5956D	OEM
1N5956GP	0600
1N5957	OEM
1N5968	0005
1N5968A	0005
1N5969	0185
1N5985	1266
1N5985A	1266
1N5985ARL	OEM
1N5985B	1266
1N5985BRL	OEM
1N5985C	OEM
1N5985D	OEM
1N5986	0755
1N5986A	0755
1N5986ARL	OEM
1N5986B	1302
1N5986BRL	OEM
1N5986C	OEM
1N5986D	OEM
1N5987	0118
1N5987A	0118
1N5987ARL	OEM
1N5987B	1703
1N5987BRL	OEM
1N5987C	OEM
1N5987D	OEM
1N5988	0296
1N5988A	0296
1N5988ARL	OEM
1N5988B	0289
1N5988BRL	OEM
1N5988C	OEM
1N5988D	OEM
1N5989	0372
1N5989A	0372
1N5989ARL	OEM
1N5989B	0372
1N5989BRL	OEM
1N5989C	OEM
1N5989D	OEM
1N5990	0036
1N5990A	0036
1N5990ARL	OEM
1N5990B	0036
1N5990BRL	OEM
1N5990C	OEM
1N5990D	OEM
1N5991	0274
1N5991A	0274
1N5991ARL	OEM
1N5991B	0274
1N5991BRL	OEM
1N5991C	OEM
1N5991D	OEM
1N5992	0140
1N5992A	0140
1N5992ARL	OEM
1N5992B	0140
1N5992BRL	OEM
1N5992C	OEM
1N5992D	OEM
1N5993	0041
1N5993A	0041
1N5993ARL	OEM
1N5993B	0041
1N5993BRL	OEM
1N5993C	0582
1N5993D	0582
1N5994	0253
1N5994A	0253
1N5994ARL	OEM
1N5994B	0253
1N5994BRL	OEM
1N5994C	0877
1N5994D	0877
1N5995	0466
1N5995A	0466
1N5995ARL	OEM
1N5995B	0466
1N5995BRL	OEM
1N5995C	0292
1N5995D	0292
1N5996	0062
1N5996A	0062
1N5996ARL	OEM
1N5996B	0062
1N5996BRL	OEM
1N5996C	OEM
1N5996D	OEM
1N5997	0077
1N5997A	0077
1N5997ARL	OEM
1N5997B	0077
1N5997BRL	OEM
1N5997C	OEM
1N5997D	OEM
1N5998	0165
1N5998A	0165
1N5998ARL	OEM
1N5998B	0165
1N5998BRL	OEM
1N5998C	OEM
1N5998D	OEM
1N5999	0057
1N5999A	0057
1N5999ARL	OEM
1N5999B	0057
1N5999BRL	OEM
1N5999C	OEM
1N5999D	OEM
1N6000	0064
1N6000A	0064
1N6000ARL	OEM
1N6000B	0064
1N6000BRL	OEM
1N6000C	0248
1N6000D	0248
1N6001	0181
1N6001A	0181
1N6001ARL	OEM
1N6001B	0181
1N6001BRL	OEM
1N6001C	OEM
1N6001D	OEM
1N6002	0052
1N6002A	0052
1N6002ARL	OEM
1N6002B	0052
1N6002BRL	OEM
1N6002C	0999
1N6002D	0999
1N6003	0053
1N6003A	0053
1N6003ARL	OEM
1N6003B	0361
1N6003BRL	OEM
1N6003C	0053
1N6003D	OEM
1N6004	0681
1N6004A	0681
1N6004ARL	OEM
1N6004B	0681
1N6004BRL	OEM
1N6004C	OEM
1N6004D	OEM
1N6005	0440
1N6005A	0440
1N6005ARL	OEM
1N6005B	0440
1N6005BRL	OEM
1N6005C	OEM
1N6005D	OEM
1N6006	0371
1N6006A	0371
1N6006ARL	OEM
1N6006B	0490
1N6006BRL	OEM
1N6006C	OEM
1N6006D	OEM
1N6007	0695
1N6007A	0695
1N6007ARL	OEM
1N6007B	0695
1N6007BRL	OEM
1N6007C	OEM
1N6007D	OEM
1N6008	0700
1N6008A	0700
1N6008ARL	OEM
1N6008B	0700
1N6008BRL	OEM
1N6008C	OEM
1N6008D	OEM
1N6009	0489
1N6009A	0489
1N6009ARL	OEM
1N6009B	0489
1N6009BRL	OEM
1N6009C	OEM
1N6009D	OEM
1N6010	0450
1N6010A	0450
1N6010ARL	OEM
1N6010B	0450
1N6010BRL	OEM
1N6010C	OEM
1N6010D	OEM
1N6011	0257
1N6011A	0257
1N6011ARL	OEM
1N6011B	0257
1N6011C	OEM
1N6011D	OEM
1N6012	0166
1N6012A	0166
1N6012ARL	OEM
1N6012B	0166
1N6012BRL	OEM
1N6012C	OEM
1N6012D	OEM
1N6013	0010
1N6013A	0010
1N6013ARL	OEM
1N6013B	0010
1N6013BRL	OEM
1N6013C	OEM
1N6013D	OEM
1N6014	0032
1N6014A	0032
1N6014ARL	OEM
1N6014B	0032
1N6014BRL	OEM
1N6014C	OEM
1N6014D	OEM
1N6015	0054
1N6015A	0054
1N6015ARL	OEM
1N6015B	0054
1N6015BRL	OEM
1N6015C	OEM
1N6015D	OEM
1N6016	0068
1N6016A	0068
1N6016ARL	OEM
1N6016B	0068
1N6016BRL	OEM
1N6016C	OEM
1N6016D	OEM
1N6017	0092
1N6017A	0092
1N6017ARL	OEM
1N6017B	0092
1N6017BRL	OEM
1N6017C	OEM
1N6017D	OEM
1N6018	0125
1N6018A	0125
1N6018B	0125
1N6018BRL	OEM
1N6018C	OEM
1N6018D	OEM
1N6019	0152
1N6019A	0152
1N6019ARL	OEM
1N6019B	0152
1N6019BRL	OEM
1N6019C	OEM
1N6019D	OEM
1N6020	0173
1N6020A	0173
1N6020ARL	OEM
1N6020B	0173
1N6020BRL	OEM
1N6020C	OEM
1N6020D	OEM
1N6021	0094
1N6021A	0094
1N6021B	0094
1N6021BRL	OEM
1N6021C	OEM
1N6021D	OEM
1N6022	0049
1N6022A	0049
1N6022ARL	OEM
1N6022B	0049
1N6022BRL	OEM
1N6022C	OEM
1N6022D	OEM
1N6023	0156
1N6023A	0156
1N6023B	0156
1N6023BRL	OEM
1N6023C	OEM
1N6023D	OEM
1N6024	0189
1N6024A	0189
1N6024B	0099
1N6024C	OEM
1N6024D	OEM
1N6025	0099
1N6025A	0099
1N6025B	0099
1N6025C	OEM
1N6025D	OEM
1N6026	0089
1N6026A	0089
1N6026B	0089
1N6026C	OEM
1N6026D	OEM
1N6027	0285
1N6027A	0285
1N6027B	0285
1N6027C	OEM
1N6027D	OEM
1N6028	0336
1N6028A	0336
1N6028B	0336
1N6028C	OEM
1N6028D	OEM
1N6029	0366
1N6029A	0366
1N6029B	0366
1N6029C	OEM
1N6029D	OEM
1N6030	0420
1N6030A	0420
1N6030B	0420
1N6030C	OEM
1N6030D	OEM
1N6031	1464
1N6031A	1464
1N6031B	0417
1N6031C	OEM
1N6031D	OEM
1N6036	OEM
1N6036A	2120
1N6037	OEM
1N6037A	OEM
1N6038	OEM
1N6038A	OEM
1N6039	OEM
1N6039A	OEM
1N6040	OEM
1N6040A	OEM
1N6041	OEM
1N6041A	OEM
1N6042	1161
1N6042A	1161
1N6043	OEM
1N6043A	OEM
1N6044	OEM
1N6044A	OEM
1N6045	1756
1N6045A	1756
1N6046	1921
1N6046A	1921
1N6047	OEM
1N6047A	OEM
1N6048	OEM
1N6048A	OEM
1N6049	1941
1N6049A	1941
1N6050	OEM
1N6050A	OEM
1N6051	OEM
1N6051A	OEM
1N6052	OEM
1N6052A	OEM
1N6053	OEM
1N6053A	OEM
1N6054	OEM
1N6054A	OEM
1N6055	OEM
1N6055A	OEM
1N6056	1961
1N6056A	1961
1N6057	OEM
1N6057A	OEM
1N6058	OEM
1N6058A	OEM
1N6059	1976
1N6059A	1976
1N6060	OEM
1N6060A	OEM
1N6061	OEM
1N6061A	OEM
1N6062	OEM
1N6062A	OEM
1N6063	OEM
1N6063A	OEM
1N6064	OEM
1N6064A	OEM
1N6065	OEM
1N6065A	OEM
1N6066	OEM
1N6066A	OEM
1N6067	OEM
1N6067A	OEM
1N6068	OEM
1N6068A	OEM
1N6069	OEM
1N6069A	OEM
1N6070	OEM
1N6070A	OEM
1N6071	1398
1N6071A	1398
1N6072	OEM
1N6072A	OEM
1N6073	0541
1N6074	2501
1N6075	3048
1N6076	OEM
1N6077	OEM
1N6078	OEM
1N6079	OEM
1N6080	OEM
1N6081	OEM
1N6082	0274
1N6082A	0274
1N6082B	0274
1N6082C	OEM
1N6082D	OEM
1N6083	0140
1N6083A	0140
1N6083B	0140
1N6083C	0582
1N6083D	0582
1N6084	0041
1N6084A	0041
1N6084B	0041
1N6084C	0877
1N6084D	0877
1N6085	0253
1N6085A	0253
1N6085B	0253
1N6085C	OEM
1N6085D	OEM
1N6086	0466
1N6086A	0466
1N6086B	0466
1N6086C	OEM
1N6086D	OEM
1N6087	0062
1N6087A	0062
1N6087B	0062
1N6087C	OEM
1N6087D	OEM
1N6088	0077
1N6088A	0077
1N6088B	0077
1N6088C	OEM
1N6088D	OEM
1N6089	0165
1N6089A	0165
1N6089B	0165
1N6089C	OEM
1N6089D	OEM
1N6090	0057
1N6090A	0057
1N6090B	0057
1N6090C	OEM
1N6090D	OEM
1N6091	0064
1N6091A	0064
1N6091B	0064
1N6091C	OEM
1N6091D	OEM
1N6092	OEM
1N6093	OEM
1N6094	OEM
1N6095	0610
1N6096	0610
1N6097	1536
1N6098	1536
1N6099	0133
1N6099A	OEM
1N6102	OEM
1N6102A	OEM
1N6103	OEM
1N6103A	OEM
1N6104	OEM
1N6104A	OEM
1N6105	OEM
1N6105A	OEM
1N6106	OEM
1N6106A	OEM
1N6107	OEM
1N6107A	OEM
1N6108	OEM
1N6108A	OEM
1N6109	OEM
1N6109A	OEM
1N6110	OEM
1N6110A	OEM
1N6111	OEM
1N6111A	OEM
1N6112	OEM
1N6112A	OEM
1N6113	OEM
1N6113A	OEM
1N6114	OEM
1N6114A	OEM
1N6115	OEM
1N6115A	OEM
1N6116	OEM
1N6116A	OEM
1N6117	OEM
1N6117A	OEM
1N6118	OEM
1N6118A	OEM
1N6119	OEM
1N6119A	OEM
1N6120	OEM
1N6120A	OEM
1N6121	OEM
1N6121A	OEM
1N6122	OEM
1N6122A	OEM
1N6123	OEM
1N6123A	OEM
1N6124	OEM
1N6124A	OEM
1N6125	OEM
1N6125A	OEM
1N6126	OEM
1N6126A	OEM
1N6127	OEM
1N6127A	OEM
1N6128	OEM
1N6128A	OEM
1N6129	OEM
1N6129A	OEM
1N6130	OEM
1N6130A	OEM
1N6131	OEM
1N6131A	OEM
1N6132	OEM
1N6132A	OEM
1N6133	OEM
1N6133A	OEM
1N6134	OEM
1N6134A	OEM
1N6135	OEM
1N6135A	OEM
1N6136	OEM
1N6136A	OEM
1N6137	OEM
1N6137A	OEM
1N6138	OEM
1N6138A	OEM
1N6139	OEM
1N6139A	OEM
1N6140	OEM
1N6140A	OEM
1N6141	OEM
1N6141A	OEM
1N6142	OEM
1N6142A	OEM
1N6143	OEM
1N6143A	OEM
1N6144	OEM
1N6144A	OEM
1N6145	OEM
1N6145A	OEM
1N6146	OEM
1N6146A	OEM
1N6147	OEM
1N6147A	OEM
1N6148	OEM
1N6148A	OEM
1N6149	OEM
1N6149A	OEM
1N6150	OEM
1N6150A	OEM
1N6151	OEM
1N6151A	OEM
1N6152	OEM
1N6152A	OEM
1N6153	OEM
1N6153A	OEM
1N6154	OEM
1N6154A	OEM
1N6155	OEM
1N6155A	OEM
1N6156	OEM
1N6156A	OEM
1N6157	OEM
1N6157A	OEM
1N6158	OEM
1N6158A	OEM

If replacement code is OEM, contact original manufacturer for replacement.

DEVICE TYPE	REPL CODE
1N6159	OEM
1N6159A	OEM
1N6160	OEM
1N6160A	OEM
1N6161	OEM
1N6161A	OEM
1N6162	OEM
1N6162A	OEM
1N6163	OEM
1N6163A	OEM
1N6164	OEM
1N6164A	OEM
1N6165	OEM
1N6165A	OEM
1N6166	OEM
1N6166A	OEM
1N6167	OEM
1N6167A	OEM
1N6168	OEM
1N6168A	OEM
1N6169	OEM
1N6169A	OEM
1N6170	OEM
1N6170A	OEM
1N6171	OEM
1N6171A	OEM
1N6172	OEM
1N6172A	OEM
1N6173	OEM
1N6173A	OEM
1N6176A	OEM
1N6262	OEM
1N6263	3837
1N6264	OEM
1N6265	OEM
1N6266	OEM
1N6267	3085
1N6267A	3085
1N6267C	2120
1N6267CA	2120
1N6268	OEM
1N6268A	OEM
1N6268C	OEM
1N6268CA	OEM
1N6269	OEM
1N6269A	OEM
1N6269C	OEM
1N6269CA	OEM
1N6270	OEM
1N6270A	OEM
1N6270C	OEM
1N6270CA	OEM
1N6271	OEM
1N6271A	OEM
1N6271CA	OEM
1N6272	OEM
1N6272A	OEM
1N6272C	OEM
1N6272CA	OEM
1N6273	OEM
1N6273A	OEM
1N6273C	OEM
1N6273CA	OEM
1N6274	3143
1N6274A	3143
1N6274C	1161
1N6274CA	1161
1N6275	OEM
1N6275A	OEM
1N6275C	OEM
1N6275CA	OEM
1N6276	OEM
1N6276A	OEM
1N6276C	OEM
1N6276CA	OEM
1N6277	3162
1N6277A	3162
1N6277C	1756
1N6277CA	1756
1N6278	3171
1N6278A	3171
1N6278C	1921
1N6278CA	1921
1N6279	OEM
1N6279A	OEM
1N6279C	OEM
1N6279CA	OEM
1N6280	OEM
1N6280A	OEM
1N6280C	OEM
1N6280CA	OEM
1N6281	1904
1N6281A	1904
1N6281C	1941
1N6281CA	1941
1N6282	OEM
1N6282A	OEM
1N6282C	OEM
1N6282CA	OEM
1N6283	OEM
1N6283A	OEM
1N6283C	OEM
1N6283CA	OEM
1N6284	OEM
1N6284A	OEM
1N6284C	OEM
1N6284CA	OEM
1N6285	OEM
1N6285A	OEM
1N6285C	OEM
1N6285CA	OEM
1N6286	OEM
1N6286A	OEM
1N6286C	OEM
1N6286CA	OEM
1N6287	OEM
1N6287A	OEM
1N6287C	OEM
1N6287CA	OEM
1N6288	0563
1N6288A	0563
1N6288C	1961
1N6288CA	1961
1N6289	OEM
1N6289A	OEM
1N6289C	OEM
1N6289CA	OEM
1N6290	OEM
1N6290A	OEM
1N6290C	OEM
1N6290CA	OEM
1N6291	0825
1N6291A	0825
1N6291C	1976
1N6291CA	1976
1N6292	OEM
1N6292A	OEM
1N6292C	OEM
1N6292CA	OEM
1N6293	OEM
1N6293A	OEM
1N6293C	OEM
1N6293CA	OEM
1N6294	OEM
1N6294A	OEM
1N6294C	OEM
1N6294CA	OEM
1N6295	OEM
1N6295A	OEM
1N6295C	OEM
1N6295CA	OEM
1N6296	OEM
1N6296A	OEM
1N6296C	OEM
1N6296CA	OEM
1N6297	OEM
1N6297A	OEM
1N6297C	OEM
1N6297CA	OEM
1N6298	OEM
1N6298A	OEM
1N6298C	OEM
1N6298CA	OEM
1N6299	OEM
1N6299A	OEM
1N6299C	OEM
1N6299CA	OEM
1N6300	OEM
1N6300A	OEM
1N6300C	OEM
1N6300CA	OEM
1N6301	OEM
1N6301A	OEM
1N6301C	OEM
1N6301CA	OEM
1N6302	OEM
1N6302A	OEM
1N6302C	OEM
1N6302CA	OEM
1N6303	1395
1N6303A	1395
1N6303C	1398
1N6303CA	1398
1N6304	OEM
1N6305	OEM
1N6306	OEM
1N6309	1266
1N6310	0755
1N6311	0118
1N6312	0296
1N6313	0372
1N6314	0036
1N6315	0274
1N6316	0140
1N6317	0041
1N6318	0253
1N6319	0466
1N6320	0062
1N6321	0077
1N6322	0165
1N6323	0057
1N6324	0064
1N6325	0181
1N6326	0052
1N6327	0053
1N6328	0873
1N6329	0440
1N6330	0371
1N6331	0695
1N6332	0700
1N6333	0489
1N6334	0450
1N6335	0195
1N6336	0166
1N6337	0010
1N6338	0032
1N6339	0054
1N6340	0068
1N6341	0092
1N6342	0125
1N6343	2301
1N6344	0173
1N6345	0094
1N6346	0049
1N6347	0156
1N6348	0189
1N6349	0099
1N6350	0089
1N6351	0285
1N6352	0336
1N6353	0366
1N6354	0420
1N6355	1464
1N6356	OEM
1N6357	OEM
1N6358	OEM
1N6359	OEM
1N6360	OEM
1N6361	OEM
1N6362	OEM
1N6363	OEM
1N6364	OEM
1N6365	OEM
1N6366	OEM
1N6367	OEM
1N6368	OEM
1N6369	OEM
1N6370	OEM
1N6371	OEM
1N6371C	OEM
1N6372	OEM
1N6373	OEM
1N6373C	OEM
1N6374	OEM
1N6374C	OEM
1N6375	OEM
1N6375C	OEM
1N6376	OEM
1N6376C	OEM
1N6377	OEM
1N6377C	OEM
1N6378	OEM
1N6378C	OEM
1N6379	OEM
1N6379C	OEM
1N6380	OEM
1N6380C	OEM
1N6381	OEM
1N6381C	OEM
1N6382	OEM
1N6382C	OEM
1N6383	OEM
1N6383C	OEM
1N6384	OEM
1N6384C	OEM
1N6385	OEM
1N6385C	OEM
1N6386	OEM
1N6386C	OEM
1N6387	OEM
1N6387C	OEM
1N6388	OEM
1N6388C	OEM
1N6389	OEM
1N6389C	OEM
1N6391	OEM
1N6392	OEM
1N6402	OEM
1N6402A	OEM
1N6403	OEM
1N6403A	OEM
1N6404	OEM
1N6404A	OEM
1N6405	OEM
1N6405A	OEM
1N6406	OEM
1N6406A	OEM
1N6407	OEM
1N6407A	OEM
1N6408	OEM
1N6408A	OEM
1N6409	OEM
1N6409A	OEM
1N6410	OEM
1N6410A	OEM
1N6411	OEM
1N6411A	OEM
1N6412	OEM
1N6412A	OEM
1N6413	OEM
1N6413A	OEM
1N6414	OEM
1N6414A	OEM
1N6415	OEM
1N6415A	OEM
1N6416	OEM
1N6416A	OEM
1N6417	OEM
1N6417A	OEM
1N6418	OEM
1N6418A	OEM
1N6419	OEM
1N6419A	OEM
1N6420	OEM
1N6420A	OEM
1N6421	OEM
1N6421A	OEM
1N6422	OEM
1N6422A	OEM
1N6423	OEM
1N6423A	OEM
1N6424	OEM
1N6424A	OEM
1N6425	OEM
1N6425A	OEM
1N6426	OEM
1N6426A	OEM
1N6427	OEM
1N6427A	OEM
1N6428	OEM
1N6428A	OEM
1N6429	OEM
1N6429A	OEM
1N6430	OEM
1N6430A	OEM
1N6431	OEM
1N6431A	OEM
1N6432	OEM
1N6432A	OEM
1N6433	OEM
1N6433A	OEM
1N6434	OEM
1N6434A	OEM
1N6435	OEM
1N6435A	OEM
1N6436	OEM
1N6436A	OEM
1N6437	OEM
1N6437A	OEM
1N6438	OEM
1N6438A	OEM
1N6439	OEM
1N6439A	OEM
1N6440	OEM
1N6440A	OEM
1N6441	OEM
1N6441A	OEM
1N6442	OEM
1N6442A	OEM
1N6443	OEM
1N6443A	OEM
1N6444	OEM
1N6444A	OEM
1N6445	OEM
1N6445A	OEM
1N6446	OEM
1N6446A	OEM
1N6447	OEM
1N6447A	OEM
1N6448	OEM
1N6448A	OEM
1N6449	OEM
1N6449A	OEM
1N6450	OEM
1N6450A	OEM
1N6451	OEM
1N6451A	OEM
1N6452	OEM
1N6452A	OEM
1N6453	OEM
1N6453A	OEM
1N6454	OEM
1N6454A	OEM
1N6455	OEM
1N6455A	OEM
1N6456	OEM
1N6456A	OEM
1N6478	OEM
1N6479	OEM
1N6480	OEM
1N6481	OEM
1N6482	OEM
1N6483	OEM
1N6484	OEM
1N9221RA	OEM
1N19161	OEM
1N29864A	OEM
1N33974	0012
1N36001	0124
1N40021D	0023
1N43182	0030
1N47551	OEM
1N63402	OEM
1N70980	0133
1N601000-17	0143
1NA4	0143
1NA4G	0143
1NAG1	0143
1NC61684	0015
1NE11	0087
1NE11-0R	0071
1NE11-A	0071
1NE11-B	0071
1NE11-C	0071
1NE11-D	0071
1NE11-K	0071
1NE11-L	0071
1NE11-Y	0071
1NE11A	0071
1NE11B	0071
1NE11C	0071
1NE11D	0071
1NE11K	0071
1NE11L	0071
1NE11R	0071
1NE11Y	0071
1NF11	0087
1NH61	0071
1NH62	0017
1NJ27	0071
1NJ33233	0143
1NJ60284	0143
1NJ61224	0143
1NJ61225	0157
1NJ61433	0133
1NJ61675	0143
1NJ61676	0015
1NJ61677	0133
1NJ61725	0133
1NJ70972	0196
1NJ70973	0143
1NJ70976	0102
1NJ70980	0133
1NJ70989	0143
1NJ71126	0914
1NJ71185	0143
1NJ71186	0914
1NJ71223	0196
1NJ71224	0133
1NK862B	0416
1NL749A	OEM
1NL750A	OEM
1NL751A	OEM
1NL752A	OEM
1NL753A	OEM
1NL754A	OEM
1NL755A	OEM
1NL756A	OEM
1NL757A	OEM
1NL914	OEM
1NL914A	OEM
1NL914B	OEM
1NL915	OEM
1NL4148	OEM
1NL4153	OEM
1NLD914	OEM
1NLD914A	OEM
1NLD914B	OEM
1NLD915	OEM
1NLD4148	OEM
1NLD4153	OEM
1NT175	OEM
1NZ61	0071
1NZ61-A	0071
1NZ61-B	0071
1NZ61-C	0071
1NZ61-D	0071
1NZ61-K	0071
1NZ61-L	0071
1NZ61-OR	0071
1NZ61-Y	0071
1OM30	0800
1P	OEM
1P5-1	OEM
1P20-0006	0086
1P20-0023	0102
1P20-0029	0144
1P20-0032	0155
1P20-0034	0144
1P20-0036	0419
1P20-0037	0144
1P20-0041	0079
1P20-0046	0006
1P20-0060	0143
1P20-0061	0124
1P20-0083	0042
1P20-0086	0162
1P20-0103	1581
1P20-0110	0144
1P20-0120	0015
1P20-0122	0079
1P20-0155	0830
1P20-0157	0212
1P20-0159	0037
1P20-0167	0178
1P20-0172	1973
1P20-0213	0006
1P20-0214	0198
1P35-1	OEM
1P60F	0019
1P100	1129
1P101	0340
1P102	0895
1P103	2326
1P541	0143
1P542	0143
1P643	0023
1P644	0023
1P645	0023
1P646	0023
1P647	0023
1P648	0271
1P649	0023
1PT	OEM
1PX	OEM
1P.5-1	OEM
1P.5-1R	OEM
1P.5-1S	OEM
1P.25-5	OEM
1P.25-5S	OEM
1P.375-75	OEM
1P.375-75S	OEM
1QE11	0102
1QZ61	0102
1R0	0133
1R01	0015
1R0E	0071
1R0F	0071
1R0H	0015
1R1D	0015
1R1K	0015
1R2	0133
1R2A	0015
1R2D	0015
1R2E	0015
1R2E01	OEM
1R2E02	OEM
1R2E16	OEM
1R3A	0133
1R3D	0015
1R3G	0015
1R3J	0015
1R3.6	0188
1R4JA	OEM
1R5B	0015
1R5BZ61	0087
1R5BZ61-A	0071
1R5BZ61-B	0071
1R5BZ61-C	0071
1R5BZ61-D	0071
1R5BZ61-K	0071
1R5BZ61-L	0071
1R5BZ61-OR	0071
1R5BZ61-Y	0071
1R5DZ61	0242
1R5DZ61-A	0071
1R5DZ61-B	0071
1R5DZ61-C	0071
1R5DZ61-D	0071
1R5DZ61-K	0361
1R5DZ61-L	0071
1R5DZ61-OR	0071
1R5DZ61-Y	0071
1R5G	0559
1R5GU41	3058
1R5GZ41	0031
1R5GZ61	0071
1R5GZ61(FA-1)	0071
1R5GZ61-A	0071
1R5GZ61-B	0071
1R5GZ61-C	0071
1R5GZ61-D	0071
1R5GZ61-K	0071
1R5GZ61-L	0071
1R5GZ61-OR	0071
1R5GZ61-Y	0071
1R5GZ61FA-1	0071
1R5GZ61FA1	0071
1R5H	0015
1R5JZ61	0959
1R5JZ61-A	0071
1R5JZ61-B	0071
1R5JZ61-C	0071
1R5JZ61-D	0071
1R5JZ61-K	0071
1R5JZ61-L	0071
1R5JZ61-OR	0071
1R5JZ61-V	0071
1R5TH61	0017
1R5.1	0162
1R6.8	OEM
1R6.8A	OEM
1R6.8B	OEM
1R7.5	0644
1R7.5A	0644
1R7.5B	OEM
1R9	0015
1R9D	0015
1R9H	0015
1R9I	0015
1R9J	0015
1R9L	0015
1R9P	0015
1R9U	0015
1R9.1	0222
1R9.1A	0012
1R9.1B	0012
1R10D3K	0133
1R10D3L	0102
1R11	0313
1R11A	0313
1R11B	0313
1R12	0137
1R12A	0137
1R12B	0137
1R13	0361
1R13A	0361
1R13B	0361
1R15	0002
1R15A	0002
1R15B	0002
1R18	0490
1R18A	0490
1R18B	0490
1R20	0526
1R22	0560
1R22A	0560
1R22B	0560
1R27	0436
1R27A	0436
1R27B	0436
1R31	0102
1R33	0039
1R33A	0039
1R33B	0039
1R39A	0346
1R39B	0346
1R47	0993
1R47A	0993
1R47B	0993
1R56	0863
1R56A	0863
1R56B	0863
1R61	OEM
1R62	0778
1R62A	0778
1R62B	0778
1R68	1258
1R68A	1258
1R68B	1258
1R81	0015
1R82	0327
1R82A	0327
1R82B	0327
1R90	0015
1R91	1301
1R96	0071
1R100	0098
1R100A	0098
1R100B	0098
1R106B1	0934
1R106B1-C	0934
1R106B2	0934
1R106B3	0934
1R106B4	0934
1R106B41	0934
1R106D1	0095
1R106D2	0095
1R106D3	0095
1R106D4	0095
1R106D41	0095
1R110	0149
1R110A	0149
1R110B	0149
1R120	0186
1R120A	0186
1R120B	0186
1R140	0245
1R140A	0245
1R140B	0245
1R150	0028
1R150A	0028
1R150B	0028
1R161R16B	0416
1R180	0363
1R180A	0363
1R180B	0363
1R914	0124
1R1600	0240
1R1601	0240
1R1602	0240
1R1771	0240
1R1772	0240
1R1774	0240
1RBB2T	OEM
1RC5	1250
1RC10	0442
1RC20	0934
1RC30	1213
1RC40	0095
1RC60	OEM
1RE02	OEM
1RE10	0015
1RE20	OEM
1RE40	OEM
1RE60	OEM
1RE80	OEM
1RE100	OEM
1RE120	OEM
1RM40	OEM
1RM60	OEM
1RM80	OEM
1RM100	OEM
1RM120	OEM
1RM150	OEM
1RM200	OEM
1RM250	OEM
1ROE	0133
1ROF	0015
1ROH	0015
1RRGZ61	OEM
1RS	OEM
1RS35-200AT	OEM
1R-TR24	0144
1R-TR25	0144
1RTR51	0111
1R-TR57	2085
1RTR75	0334
1R-TR77	0848
1R-TR87	0218
1S005	0015
1S016	0015
1S020	0947
1S021	0242
1S023	0535
1S025	0959
1S027	0811
1S030	0110
1S031	0947
1S032	0242
1S034	0535
1S036	0959
1S038	0811

If replacement code is OEM, contact original manufacturer for replacement.

DEVICE TYPE	REPL CODE
1S054	0015
1S058	0071
1S-0142	1434
1S0S2-2.65	OEM
1S1Z09	0015
1S11	0143
1S11A	0157
1S12	0143
1S13	0143
1S14	0143
1S15	0143
1S16	0143
1S17	0143
1S17D1	0143
1S18	0143
1S19	0143
1S20	0143
1S21	OEM
1S22	OEM
1S23	OEM
1S24	OEM
1S25	OEM
1S28	0500
1S32	0143
1S33	0143
1S34	0143
1S34(TP)	0143
1S34(TV)	0143
1S34A	0143
1S34S	0143
1S35	0143
1S36	0015
1S37	0298
1S38	0133
1S39	0071
1S40	0947
1S41	0755
1S42	1736
1S43	0535
1S44	0023
1S45	0959
1S46	0811
1S47	0015
1S48	0715
1S48A	0623
1S49	0030
1S50	0123
1S51	0446
1S52	0157
1S53	0025
1S54	0644
1S55	0012
1S56	0012
1S57	OEM
1S58	0143
1S60	0123
1S60(RECT)	0015
1S60P	0143
1S61	0015
1S62	0015
1S63	0015
1S64	0015
1S65	0015
1S66	0015
1S71	0015
1S72	0143
1S73	0143
1S73A	0143
1S74	0143
1S75	0143
1S77	0143
1S77(H)	0143
1S77H	0143
1S78	0143
1S78(H)	0143
1S78H	0143
1S79	0143
1S79(H)	0143
1S79H	0143
1S80	0143
1S81	0015
1S82	0123
1S83	0015
1S83(H)	0015
1S84	0133
1S84H	0015
1S85	0715
1S85(Y)	0030
1S85(YL)	OEM
1S85/0575024	0030
1S85B0	0030
1S85H	0715
1S85L	0030
1S85M	0030
1S85SW	0030
1S85V	0015
1S85W	0030
1S85W7	0030
1S85WR	0030
1S85WT	0030
1S85Y	0030
1S85YL	0030
1S86	0755
1S87	0143
1S88	0143
1S89	0133
1S90	0015
1S90R	0133
1S91	0015

DEVICE TYPE	REPL CODE
1S91R	0015
1S92	0015
1S92R	0015
1S93	0015
1S93/SGJ	0015
1S93R	0015
1S94	0015
1S94R	0015
1S95	0015
1S95R	0015
1S96	0071
1S96R	0071
1S97	0071
1S97R	0071
1S98	0071
1S98R	0071
1S99	0071
1S99A	0015
1S99R	0015
1S100	0015
1S100R	0015
1S101	0015
1S101R	0015
1S102	0015
1S102R	0015
1S103	0015
1S103R	0015
1S104	0015
1S104R	0015
1S105	0015
1S105R	0015
1S106	0015
1S106A	5428
1S106R	0015
1S107	0071
1S107R	0071
1S108	0071
1S108R	0071
1S109	0071
1S109R	0071
1S110	0015
1S110A	5428
1S111	0015
1S112	0015
1S113	0015
1S113A	0015
1S114	0015
1S115	0015
1S116	0015
1S117	0071
1S118	0015
1S119	0015
1S120	0015
1S121	0015
1S121(RECT)	0015
1S122	0015
1S123	0015
1S124	0015
1S125	0015
1S126	0015
1S127	0143
1S128	0143
1S128FM	0123
1S129	0143
1S130	0133
1S131	0133
1S132	0133
1S133	1075
1S134	0140
1S135	0023
1S135E	OEM
1S136	0062
1S136(RECT)	0015
1S136Q	0790
1S137	0077
1S138	0318
1S138(RECT)	0071
1S138(ZENER)	0318
1S139	0057
1S140	0181
1S141	0052
1S142	0681
1S143	0440
1S144	0133
1S145	0005
1S146	4077
1S147	0015
1S148	0015
1S149	0015
1S150	0015
1S151	0097
1S152	0097
1S153	0800
1S154	0800
1S155	0133
1S155-1	0133
1S156	2077
1S157	4077
1S158	0575
1S159	2049
1S160	0084
1S161	0090
1S162	0097
1S163	0105
1S164	0109
1S165	0116
1S166	0122
1S167	0865
1S168	0865

DEVICE TYPE	REPL CODE
1S169	0847
1S170	1590
1S171	5189
1S172	0865
1S173	5190
1S174	0847
1S175	5192
1S176	1599
1S177	0865
1S178	0865
1S179	0847
1S180	0133
1S180/5GB	0015
1S180-M	0015
1S180B	0133
1S181	0023
1S181-M	0015
1S181FA	0133
1S182	0133
1S182-M	0015
1S183	0015
1S183-M	0015
1S184	0907
1S185	0143
1S186	0143
1S186(FM)	0143
1S186FM	0123
1S186G	0015
1S187	0143
1S187(S)	0143
1S187S	3284
1S-188	0019
1S188	0143
1S188(AM)	0143
1S188(FM)	1106
1S188-FM	2217
1S188-TV-M	0143
1S188A	0143
1S188AM	0143
1S188AM-T	OEM
1S188AR	0143
1S188F	0143
1S188F1	OEM
1S188FM	0143
1S188FM-1	0143
1S188FM1	0143
1S188FM1A	0143
1S188FM-2	0143
1S188FM2	0143
1S188FMA	0143
1S188FMI	0123
1S188G	0143
1S188MPX	0123
1S188P	0123
1S188S	0143
1S188TV	0143
1S188TV(MP)	0123
1S189	0143
1S189FM	0123
1S189FM(MP)	0123
1S190	0041
1S191	0091
1S192	0062
1S193	0244
1S194	0057
1S195	0064
1S196	0181
1S197	0052
1S198	0100
1S199	0490
1S200	0143
1S204	0015
1S205	0015
1S206	0015
1S207	0015
1S208	0015
1S208/2SJ2A	0229
1S209	0015
1S209/2SJ4A	0229
1S210	0071
1S210/2SJ6A	0071
1S211	0071
1S211/2SJ8A	0071
1S211A	0071
1S212	0318
1S213	0318
1S213C	0030
1S214	0318
1S215	0170
1S216	0170
1S217	0012
1S218	0133
1S219	OEM
1S220	0528
1S221	0157
1S222	0025
1S223	0644
1S224	1075
1S225	0170
1S226	0313
1S227	0137
1S228	0361
1S229	0100
1S230	0002
1S231	0416
1S232	1639
1S233	0490
1S234	0943
1S235	0526

DEVICE TYPE	REPL CODE
1S236	0560
1S237	0398
1S238	1596
1S239	0436
1S240	0721
1S241	0039
1S242	0814
1S243	0346
1S244	0925
1S245	0993
1S246	0993
1S247	0133
1S248	0497
1S249	0863
1S250	0778
1S251	1258
1S251B	0030
1S252	1181
1S253	0327
1S254	1301
1S255	0098
1S256	0149
1S257	0149
1S258	0186
1S259	0213
1S260	0245
1S261	0028
1S262	2101
1S263	1890
1S264	1591
1S265	1606
1S266	2408
1S267	0986
1S268	0686
1S268A	0989
1S268AA	0989
1S268AA,T	0015
1S268T	0015
1S269	1254
1S270	1240
1S271	1626
1S272	1629
1S273	1693
1S274	1630
1S275	1706
1S276	1709
1S277	1720
1S278	0722
1S279	1745
1S279WT	OEM
1S280	1757
1S281	1771
1S282	1783
1S283	1788
1S284	1798
1S285	1806
1S286	1815
1S287	1842
1S288	1842
1S289	1850
1S290	1863
1S291	1873
1S292	1884
1S293	1891
1S294	0731
1S295	1898
1S296	1903
1S297	1155
1S298	1913
1S299	1922
1S300	1930
1S301	0519
1S301GR	1936
1S301.5	0002
1S302	1942
1S303	1950
1S304	0318
1S305	0318
1S306	0124
1S306M	0124
1S307	0133
1S308	OEM
1S309	0015
1S310	0015
1S310H	0015
1S311	0229
1S311H	0015
1S311N	0015
1S312	0015
1S312A	0015
1S312H	0015
1S313	0015
1S313H	0015
1S314	0023
1S314H	0015
1S314N	0015
1S315	0023
1S315FR1MD	0071
1S315H	0015
1S316	0071
1S317	0071
1S318	0143
1S319	0143
1S320	0162
1S322	0133
1S323	0143
1S324	0124
1S325	0124
1S326	0124

DEVICE TYPE	REPL CODE
1S327	0015
1S328	0015
1S329	0071
1S330	0041
1S330A	0041
1S-331	0631
1S331	0091
1S331A	0091
1S331AZ	0091
1S332	0644
1S332M	0025
1S333	0244
1S333Y	0244
1S334	0012
1S334M	0012
1S334N	0012
1S335	0064
1S336	0181
1S337	0052
1S337-Y	0137
1S337A	0137
1S337E	0137
1S337Y	0137
1S338	0100
1S338Q	0361
1S338U	0100
1S339	0371
1S340	0437
1S341	3099
1S341W1	0030
1S341W2	0030
1S341W3	0030
1S342	0205
1S343	0499
1S344	0679
1S345	0225
1S346	0230
1S347	0298
1S348	1387
1S349	0256
1S351	0005
1S351-S	0005
1S351B	0005
1S351M	0005
1S351R	0005
1S351S	0005
1S351W	0005
1S351W1	0005
1S351W2	0005
1S351W3	0005
1S352	0030
1S352A	0030
1S352M	0030
1S352N	0715
1S352R	0030
1S353	0623
1S353M	0030
1S354	0143
1S355	0143
1S356	0143
1S357	0143
1S358	0015
1S358A	0015
1S358S	0015
1S359	0015
1S360	OEM
1S361	OEM
1S362	OEM
1S362.3	OEM
1S363	OEM
1S367	0015
1S368	0015
1S369	0015
1S370	0015
1S371	0015
1S372	0015
1S373	0015
1S374	0015
1S375	0015
1S376	0015
1S377	0015
1S378	0015
1S379	0015
1S380	0015
1S381	0015
1S382	0015
1S383	0865
1S384	0865
1S385	0847
1S388	0865
1S389	0865
1S390	0015
1S393	0015
1S394	0015
1S395	0015
1S396	0015
1S397	0071
1S398	0071
1S399	0015
1S400	0015
1S401	0071
1S402	0071
1S403	0102
1S404	0015
1S405	0071
1S406	0071
1S407	0102
1S408	OEM
1S409	OEM

DEVICE TYPE	REPL CODE
1S410	0575
1S411	0575
1S412	OEM
1S413	0994
1S414	OEM
1S415	2070
1S416	OEM
1S417	2077
1S418	0865
1S419	0607
1S420	0090
1S421	0097
1S422	0847
1S423	0109
1S425	0122
1S426	0123
1S426G	0143
1S426GFM	0143
1S427	0873
1S428	0143
1S430	0110
1S431	0947
1S431R	OEM
1S432	0242
1S432R	OEM
1S433	OEM
1S433R	OEM
1S434	0535
1S434R	OEM
1S435	OEM
1S435R	OEM
1S436	0959
1S436R	OEM
1S437	OEM
1S438	0811
1S438R	OEM
1S439	OEM
1S440	OEM
1S440R	OEM
1S441	0143
1S441(RECT)	0703
1S442	0143
1S442(RECT)	0703
1S443	0703
1S443(RECT)	0703
1S444	0133
1S444(RECT)	0575
1S445	OEM
1S445(RECT)	0575
1S446	0143
1S446(RECT)	0575
1S446D	0143
1S447	0143
1S448	0143
1S449	0143
1S450	OEM
1S451	0143
1S452	0143
1S453	0143
1S454	0143
1S455	0143
1S456	0124
1S457	0124
1S458	0023
1S459	0023
1S460	0124
1S461	0124
1S462	0124
1S463	0242
1S464	0133
1S465	0124
1S466	0163
1S467	OEM
1S467R	0143
1S468	0124
1S470	0091
1S471	0062
1S472	0057
1S473	0181
1S474	0873
1S475	0371
1S476	0700
1S477	0257
1S478	0010
1S479	0068
1S480	0298
1S481	0025
1S482	0012
1S483	0313
1S484	0100
1S485	0490
1S486	0560
1S487	1664
1S488	0814
1S489	0993
1S490	2400
1S491	0205
1S492	0622
1S493	0230
1S494	1145
1S495	1706
1S496	1712
1S497	2434
1S498	1798
1S499	0343
1S500	0124
1S501	0124
1S501M	0124
1S502	OEM

DEVICE TYPE	REPL CODE
1S503	OEM
1S504	OEM
1S505	OEM
1S506	OEM
1S507	OEM
1S508	OEM
1S509	OEM
1S510	0946
1S511	OEM
1S512	OEM
1S513	OEM
1S514	OEM
1S515	OEM
1S516	OEM
1S517	OEM
1S518	OEM
1S519	OEM
1S520	0946
1S521	OEM
1S522	OEM
1S523	OEM
1S524	OEM
1S525	OEM
1S526	OEM
1S527	OEM
1S528	OEM
1S529	OEM
1S530	OEM
1S531	OEM
1S532	OEM
1S533	OEM
1S534	OEM
1S535	0549
1S535-1	0030
1S536	OEM
1S537	OEM
1S538	OEM
1S539	OEM
1S540	OEM
1S541	OEM
1S542	0143
1S543	0911
1S544	0131
1S545	0145
1S546	1600
1S547	1604
1S548	0124
1S550	0165
1S551	0165
1S552	0165
1S553	0755
1S553T	0755
1S554	0623
1S554T	0623
1S555	0623
1S556	0030
1S557	0023
1S557H	0071
1S558	0023
1S559	0015
1S560	0133
1S560(H)	OEM
1S560H	0133
1S561	OEM
1S561A	OEM
1S562	OEM
1S562A	OEM
1S563	OEM
1S563A	OEM
1S564	OEM
1S564A	OEM
1S565	OEM
1S565A	OEM
1S566	OEM
1S566A	OEM
1S567	OEM
1S567A	OEM
1S568	0133
1S568A	OEM
1S569	OEM
1S569A	OEM
1S582	OEM
1S588	0015
1S589	0143
1S593	0015
1S597	0002
1S600	OEM
1S601	OEM
1S602	OEM
1S603	OEM
1S604	OEM
1S610	0946
1S611	0755
1S612	0372
1S613	0528
1S614	0528
1S615	0253
1S616	0644
1S617	0644
1S618	0170
1S619	0361
1S620	0416
1S621	0666
1S622	0398
1S623	1664
1S624	0010
1S630	OEM
1S631	OEM
1S632	0372

If replacement code is OEM, contact original manufacturer for replacement.

DEVICE TYPE	REPL CODE
1S633	0446
1S634	0162
1S635	0298
1S636	0025
1S661	0015
1S662	0071
1S663	0071
1S664	0102
1S665	OEM
1S666	OEM
1S667	OEM
1S668	OEM
1S669	0847
1S673	0847
1S685	0015
1S686	0071
1S687	0071
1S688	0102
1S689	0918
1S689A	0918
1S689BK	0918
1S690	0451
1S691	0446
1S692	0157
1S693	0133
1S694	0244
1S695	0170
1S696	0137
1S697	0002
1S698	0490
1S699	0560
1S700	0436
1S701	2024
1S702	1429
1S703	1436
1S704	1449
1S704A	0274
1S704B	0274
1S705	1481
1S706	0505
1S707	0864
1S708	1264
1S709	1071
1S710	1712
1S711	1750
1S712	2024
1S713	1429
1S714	1436
1S715	1449
1S716	1481
1S717	0505
1S718	0864
1S719	1264
1S720	1071
1S721	1712
1S722	1750
1S731	0124
1S732	OEM
1S733	OEM
1S734	OEM
1S735	OEM
1S735R	OEM
1S736	OEM
1S736R	OEM
1S737	OEM
1S738	OEM
1S738R	OEM
1S739	OEM
1S740R	OEM
1S741	OEM
1S742	OEM
1S742R	OEM
1S743	OEM
1S744	0143
1S745	0143
1S746	0143
1S747	0143
1S748	0143
1S749	OEM
1S750	0911
1S750(2)	0911
1S750S	0911
1S751	0918
1S752	0755
1S752(H)	0755
1S753	0372
1S753(H)	0296
1S753H	0289
1S754	0274
1S754(H)	0274
1S754H	0451
1S755	0140
1S755(H)	0041
1S755H	0446
1S756	0091
1S756(H)	0253
1S757	0062
1S757(H)	0077
1S757A	0012
1S758	0318
1S758(H)	0318
1S758GS	0012
1S758H	1075
1S759	0064
1S759(H)	0181
1S759H	0170
1S760	0053
1S760(H)	0053
1S760H	0361
1S761	0440
1S761(H)	0440
1S762	0666
1S762(H)	0666
1S763	0489
1S763(H)	0489
1S764	0450
1S764(H)	0257
1S765	0039
1S765(H)	0010
1S765H	0039
1S766	0005
1S767	0005
1S767A	0005
1S768	OEM
1S769	0005
1S770	OEM
1S770R	OEM
1S773	0124
1S773A	0124
1S774	0124
1S774A	0124
1S775	0124
1S775FA-1	0023
1S776	0124
1S776A	0124
1S777	0015
1S778	0865
1S779	OEM
1S780	OEM
1S781	0847
1S782	OEM
1S783	OEM
1S784	OEM
1S785	OEM
1S786	OEM
1S787	OEM
1S788	0143
1S789	OEM
1S790	0847
1S791	OEM
1S792	OEM
1S793	OEM
1S794	OEM
1S796	OEM
1S797	OEM
1S798	OEM
1S799	OEM
1S800	OEM
1S801	0124
1S802	0124
1S803	0124
1S804	0124
1S805	0124
1S806	0124
1S807	0124
1S808	0124
1S811	0015
1S812	0015
1S813	0071
1S814	0071
1S815	0102
1S816	0015
1S817	0015
1S818	0071
1S819	0071
1S820	0102
1S821	0847
1S822	0847
1S823	OEM
1S824	OEM
1S825	OEM
1S826	0847
1S827	0847
1S831	0847
1S832	0847
1S836	0847
1S837	0847
1S841	0015
1S842	0015
1S843	0015
1S844	0015
1S844N	0015
1S845	0015
1S846	0015
1S846N	0015
1S847	0071
1S848	0071
1S848N	0071
1S849	0015
1S849,R	0015
1S849R	0015
1S850	0071
1S850N	0071
1S851	0143
1S852	0102
1S853	0030
1S854	0535
1S854L	0030
1S855	0959
1S856	0959
1S857	0811
1S858	0811
1S859	0916
1S860	0916
1S871	0015
1S871A	0015
1S871B	0071
1S871C	0071
1S871D	0102
1S871E	0102
1S872	0015
1S872A	0015
1S872B	0071
1S872C	0071
1S872D	0102
1S873	0847
1S874	0847
1S881	OEM
1S881A	0015
1S881B	0071
1S881C	0071
1S881D	0102
1S881E	0102
1S882	0015
1S882A	0015
1S882B	0071
1S882C	0071
1S882D	0102
1S882E	0102
1S885	0015
1S887	0015
1S891	0005
1S892	0715
1S893	0623
1S894	0201
1S895	0201
1S896	0201
1S897	0201
1S920	0133
1S921	0133
1S921(RECT)	0242
1S922	0535
1S922(DIODE)	0133
1S922(RECT)	0535
1S923	0133
1S923(RECT)	0959
1S923A	OEM
1S924	0811
1S925	0916
1S926	0097
1S927	0109
1S928	0122
1S929	0131
1S930	0145
1S931	0594
1S932	1975
1S933	0652
1S934	0652
1S935	0652
1S936	1116
1S937	OEM
1S938	OEM
1S939	0652
1S940	0652
1S941	0133
1S942	0133
1S943	0015
1S946	0015
1S947	0015
1S948	0015
1S949	0071
1S950	0071
1S951	0124
1S952	0124
1S953	0133
1S954	0133
1S954(2)	0124
1S955	0124
1S956	0242
1S957	0535
1S958	0959
1S959	0811
1S960	0916
1S961	0124
1S962	0847
1S963	0229
1S967	0847
1S977	0124
1S978	0124
1S981	0124
1S982	0124
1S983	0133
1S984	0124
1S985	0124
1S986	0124
1S987	0124
1S988	0124
1S989	1709
1S990	0133
1S990-A	OEM
1S990-AM	0133
1S990A	0133
1S990AM	0143
1S990S	0002
1S991	OEM
1S993	0118
1S994	0451
1S994A	0133
1S994S	0446
1S994Y	0644
1S995	0005
1S1000	0911
1S1000A	0911
1S1001	0133
1S1004	0015
1S1005	OEM
1S1006	0143
1S1007	0143
1S1007S	0143
1S1008	0143
1S1009	0143
1S1010	0143
1S1011	OEM
1S1012	0015
1S1013	0015
1S1014	0071
1S1015	0071
1S1016	0102
1S1017	0102
1S1021	0015
1S1022	0015
1S1023	0071
1S1024	0071
1S1025	0102
1S1026	0102
1S1027	0015
1S1028	0015
1S1029	0071
1S1030	0071
1S1031	0102
1S1032	0102
1S1033	1017
1S1034	1017
1S1035	1017
1S1036	1030
1S1037	1040
1S1038	1040
1S1039	0535
1S1040	0959
1S1041	0811
1S1042	0916
1S1043	0015
1S1044	0015
1S1045	0071
1S1046	0071
1S1047	0102
1S1048	0102
1S1052	0133
1S-1053	0124
1S1053	0133
1S1061	0015
1S1062	0015
1S1063	0015
1S1064	0015
1S1065	0071
1S1066	0071
1S1067	0102
1S1068	0102
1S1071	0087
1S1072	0242
1S1073	0535
1S1074	0959
1S1075	0811
1S1076	0087
1S1076TF1	0124
1S1081	0865
1S1094	0077
1S1095	0057
1S1096	0015
1S1097	0361
1S1098	0440
1S1099	0666
1S1100	0489
1S1101	0257
1S1102	0814
1S1103	OEM
1S1104	OEM
1S1105	OEM
1S1106	OEM
1S1107	OEM
1S1108	OEM
1S1109	OEM
1S1110	OEM
1S1111	OEM
1S1112	OEM
1S1113	OEM
1S1114	0644
1S1114A	0644
1S1115	OEM
1S1116	OEM
1S1117	OEM
1S1118	OEM
1S1119	OEM
1S1120	OEM
1S1121	0276
1S1122	0287
1S1123	0293
1S1124	0293
1S1125	0299
1S1126	0250
1S1127	0250
1S1128	0319
1S1129	1404
1S1130	0468
1S1131	0468
1S1132	0441
1S1135	0319
1S1136	1404
1S1137	0468
1S1138	0468
1S1139	0441
1S1144	OEM
1S1145	OEM
1S1146	0015
1S1147	0124
1S1148	0124
1S1149	0124
1S1154	0077
1S1155	0165
1S1156	0064
1S1160	0372
1S1161	0140
1S1162	0091
1S1163	0077
1S1164	0165
1S1165	0064
1S1166	0053
1S1167	0440
1S1168	0666
1S1169	0489
1S1170	0257
1S1171	0010
1S1172	0446
1S1173	0298
1S1174	0025
1S1175	1075
1S1176	0313
1S1177	0002
1S1178	0416
1S1179	0943
1S1180	0398
1S1181	1664
1S1182	0814
1S1183	0925
1S1184	0497
1S1185	1429
1S1186	1436
1S1187	1449
1S1188	1481
1S1189	0505
1S1190	0864
1S1191	1524
1S1192	1071
1S1193	1712
1S1194	1750
1S1195	1793
1S1196	0022
1S1197	0207
1S1198	OEM
1S1198A	OEM
1S1199	OEM
1S1199A	OEM
1S1200	OEM
1S1200A	OEM
1S1201	0466
1S1201(H)	0466
1S1202	0062
1S1202(H)	0062
1S1203	0165
1S1204	0139
1S1207	0133
1S1208	0124
1S1209	0139
1S1210	0139
1S1211	0139
1S1212	0139
1S1212A	0139
1S1213	0133
1S1214	0133
1S1215	0133
1S1216	0133
1S1217	0133
1S1218	0133
1S1219	0133
1S1219H	0124
1S1220	0133
1S1221	0015
1S1222	0015
1S1223	0071
1S1224	0015
1S1225	0071
1S1225A	0071
1S1226	0102
1S1230	0015
1S1230H	0015
1S1231	0015
1S1231H	0015
1S1232	0015
1S1232H	0015
1S1232N	0015
1S1233	0071
1S1233H	0071
1S1233N	0071
1S1234	0071
1S1234H	0071
1S1234N	0071
1S1235	0327
1S1236	0959
1S1237	0023
1S1238	0102
1S1239	0143
1S1244	0143
1S1245	0143
1S1246	0143
1S1255A	0071
1S1260	0865
1S1260R	1625
1S1261	0865
1S1261R	1625
1S1262	0847
1S1262R	1242
1S1263	0847
1S1263R	1242
1S1264	1599
1S1264R	1196
1S1265	1599
1S1265R	1196
1S1266	1600
1S1266R	2124
1S1267	1600
1S1267R	2124
1S1268	1604
1S1268R	2236
1S1269	1604
1S1269R	2236
1S1270	0865
1S1270R	1625
1S1271	0865
1S1271R	1625
1S1272	0847
1S1272R	1242
1S1273	0847
1S1280	0865
1S1281	0847
1S1282	0847
1S1288	5189
1S1288R	OEM
1S1289	0865
1S1290	0847
1S1295	0124
1S1296	0124
1S1297	0276
1S1298	0015
1S1299	0015
1S1300	OEM
1S1301	0124
1S1302	0124
1S1303	0124
1S1304	0133
1S1305	0133
1S1308	0361
1S1314	1325
1S1315	0005
1S1316	0124
1S1317	0124
1S1318	0023
1S1319	0023
1S1320	0023
1S1321	1272
1S1322	1272
1S1323	1277
1S1324	1277
1S1325	1282
1S1326	1282
1S1327	1285
1S1328	1285
1S1329	1285
1S1329B	0030
1S1330	1285
1S1331	OEM
1S1332	OEM
1S1333	0023
1S1333(RECT)	OEM
1S1333R	OEM
1S1334	OEM
1S1334R	OEM
1S1335	OEM
1S1335R	OEM
1S1336	OEM
1S1336R	OEM
1S1337	OEM
1S1337R	OEM
1S1338	OEM
1S1338R	OEM
1S1339	OEM
1S1339R	OEM
1S1340	OEM
1S1341	0015
1S1342	0015
1S1343	0015
1S1344	0015
1S1345	0071
1S1346	0015
1S1347	0071
1S1348	0071
1S1349	0102
1S1350	1590
1S1351	4077
1S1352	0575
1S1353	2049
1S1354	0994
1S1355	2070
1S1356	2077
1S1357	0607
1S1358	OEM
1S1359	0015
1S1359A	0015
1S1360	0015
1S1360A	0015
1S1361	0015
1S1361A	0015
1S1362	0071
1S1362A	0071
1S1363	0071
1S1363A	0071
1S1364	0102
1S1364A	0102
1S1365	0015
1S1365A	0015
1S1366	0015
1S1366A	0015
1S1367	0015
1S1367A	0015
1S1368	0071
1S1368A	0071
1S1369	0071
1S1369A	0071
1S1370	0102
1S1370A	0102
1S1371	2847
1S1371A	2847
1S1372	0372
1S1372A	0372
1S1373	0528
1S1373A	0528
1S1374	0157
1S1374A	0157
1S1375	0631
1S1375A	0631
1S1376	0025
1S1376A	0025
1S1377	1075
1S1377A	1075
1S1378	0170
1S1378A	0064
1S1379	0361
1S1379A	0361
1S1380	0416
1S1380A	0416
1S1381	0695
1S1381A	0695
1S1382	1596
1S1382A	1596
1S1383	0721
1S1383A	0721
1S1384	0814
1S1384A	0814
1S1385	0054
1S1385A	0054
1S1386	0755
1S1386A	0755
1S1387	0372
1S1387A	0372
1S1388	0528
1S1388A	0528
1S1389	0157
1S1389A	0157
1S1390	0631
1S1390A	0631
1S1391	0644
1S1391A	0644
1S1392	1075
1S1392A	1075
1S1393	0170
1S1393A	0170
1S1394	0361
1S1394A	0361
1S1395	0416
1S1395A	0416
1S1396	0695
1S1396A	0695
1S1397	1596
1S1397A	1596
1S1398	0721
1S1398A	0721
1S1399	0814
1S1399A	0814
1S1400	0054
1S1400A	0054
1S1401	0497
1S1401A	0497
1S1402	1302
1S1402R	1302
1S1403	0188
1S1403R	0188
1S1404	0446
1S1404R	0446
1S1405	0157
1S1405R	0157
1S1406	0631
1S1406R	0631
1S1407	0644
1S1407R	0644
1S1408	1075
1S1408R	1075
1S1409	0170
1S1409R	0170
1S1410	0100
1S1410R	0100
1S1411	0416
1S1411R	0416
1S1412	0526
1S1412R	0526
1S1413	1596
1S1413R	1596
1S1414	0721
1S1414R	0721
1S1415	0814
1S1415R	0814
1S1417	1111
1S1418	0280
1S1419	OEM
1S1420	OEM
1S1420(H)	0133
1S1420H	0133
1S1421	0925
1S1421R	0925
1S1422	1823
1S1422R	1823
1S1424	2024
1S1424R	0542
1S1425	1429
1S1425R	2101

If replacement code is OEM, contact original manufacturer for replacement.

33

DEVICE TYPE	REPL CODE
1S1426	1436
1S1426R	1890
1S1427	1449
1S1427R	1591
1S1429	1481
1S1429R	1612
1S1430	0505
1S1430R	0986
1S1439	1429
1S1439R	2101
1S1440	1436
1S1440R	1890
1S1441	1449
1S1441R	1591
1S1443	1481
1S1443R	1612
1S1444	0505
1S1444R	0986
1S1445	0864
1S1445R	1254
1S1454	0847
1S1461	OEM
1S1462	OEM
1S1463	OEM
1S1464	0911
1S1465	0918
1S1471	0071
1S1472	0229
1S1473	0124
1S1474	0242
1S1475	0535
1S1476	0959
1S1477	0811
1S1478	0916
1S1480	0865
1S1481	0847
1S1486	0015
1S1487	0015
1S1488	0242
1S1489	0535
1S1490	0959
1S1491	0811
1S1492	0916
1S1500	0549
1S1501	0549
1S1502	0005
1S1502C	0005
1S1503	0755
1S1514	0133
1S1515	0133
1S1516	0133
1S1517	0182
1S1517A	0102
1S1532	0133
1S1533	0030
1S1540	OEM
1S1544	0163
1S1544A	0163
1S1545	0163
1S1546	0015
1S1547	0015
1S1548	0015
1S1549	0911
1S1551	OEM
1S1552	0124
1S1553	0133
1S1553(TV)	0133
1S1553V	0133
1S1553V(TV)	0133
1S1554	0133
1S1554(TV)	0133
1S1554V	0133
1S1554V(TV)	0133
1S1555	0133
1S1555(TV)	0133
1S1555-1	0133
1S1555-5	0102
1S1555-K	0133
1S1555-S	0133
1S-1555-Z	0133
1S1555FA-1	0133
1S1555FA1	0133
1S1555TP	0133
1S1555TP3	0133
1S1555TV	4116
1S-1555V	0133
1S1555V	0133
1S1555V(TV)	0133
1S1555Z	0133
1S1556	OEM
1S1557	OEM
1S1558	0030
1S1560	OEM
1S1560R	OEM
1S1561	OEM
1S1562	OEM
1S1563	OEM
1S1564	OEM
1S1571	OEM
1S1572	OEM
1S1573	OEM
1S1574	OEM
1S1575	0109
1S1576	0122
1S1577	0131
1S1578	0145
1S1579	0133
1S1580	0133
1S1581	OEM
1S1582	0549
1S1583	OEM
1S1585	0124
1S1585(TPE3)	0124
1S1586	0124
1S1587	0124
1S1588	0133
1S1588-FM	0143
1S1588-T	OEM
1S1588T	OEM
1S1588V	0124
1S1589	0133
1S1591	0102
1S1592	0102
1S1593	0102
1S1594	0102
1S1595	0102
1S1596	0102
1S1597	0015
1S1598	0015
1S1599	0015
1S1600	0023
1S1601	0023
1S1602	0023
1S1604	0015
1S1605	0071
1S1606	0865
1S1607	0847
1S1608	0071
1S1609	0102
1S1610	0102
1S1611	0201
1S1612	0201
1S1613	0374
1S1614	2806
1S1615	2454
1S1616	OEM
1S1617	OEM
1S1618	OEM
1S1619	OEM
1S1621	0133
1S1621-O	0133
1S1621-R	0133
1S1621-Y	0133
1S1622	0015
1S1623	0015
1S1624	0015
1S1625	0015
1S1626	0206
1S1627	0583
1S1628	OEM
1S1629	2077
1S1630	0607
1S1631	OEM
1S1632	OEM
1S1640	0865
1S1641	0865
1S1642	OEM
1S1642R	OEM
1S1643	0594
1S1643R	1337
1S1644	0594
1S1644R	1337
1S1645	OEM
1S1646	OEM
1S1647	OEM
1S1648	0030
1S1650	0133
1S1651	0133
1S1652	1241
1S1652R	0760
1S1653	5487
1S1653R	0772
1S1654	1116
1S1654R	1099
1S1655	1118
1S1655R	1103
1S1656	OEM
1S1657	0918
1S1658	0030
1S1658(FA-3)	OEM
1S1658FA-2	0030
1S1658FA2	0030
1S1658FA-3	0030
1S1659	OEM
1S1660	0575
1S1660R	0941
1S1661	2049
1S1661R	4443
1S1662	0983
1S1662R	0984
1S1663	3697
1S1663R	0987
1S1664	0015
1S1665	0229
1S1666	0015
1S1667	0015
1S1668	0015
1S1668F	0015
1S1669	0071
1S1670	0276
017031	0287
1S1671	0287
1S1672	0293
1S1673	0299
1S1674	0250
1S1675	0250
1S1676	OEM
1S1677	OEM
1S1678	0015
1S1679	0015
1S1680	0015
1S1681	0015
1S1682	0071
1S1683	0071
1S1684	0015
1S1685	0015
1S1686	0015
1S1687	0015
1S1688	0071
1S1689	0071
1S1690	0143
1S1690A	0015
1S1691	0015
1S1691A	0015
1S1692	0229
1S1692A	0015
1S1693	0015
1S1693A	0015
1S1694	0229
1S1694A	0015
1S1695	0071
1S1695A	0015
1S1696	0015
1S1696A	0015
1S1697	0015
1S1698	0015
1S1699	0167
1S1700	0167
1S1701	5493
1S1702	0102
1S1703	0102
1S1704	0102
1S1704A	0102
1S1705	0102
1S1705A	0102
1S1706	0102
1S1707	0102
1S1707A	0102
1S1708	0102
1S1709	0102
1S1710	0124
1S1711	0124
1S1712	0124
1S1712A	0124
1S1713	0124
1S1714	0124
1S1715	0631
1S1716	0077
1S1717	1075
1S1717L	0012
1S1718	0012
1S1719	OEM
1S1720	0087
1S1720R	0087
1S1721	0911
1S1722	0911
1S1723	0015
1S1724	0015
1S1724R	0015
1S1725	0015
1S1725R	0015
1S1726	0015
1S1726R	0015
1S1727	0015
1S1727R	0015
1S1728	0012
1S1728R	0015
1S1729	0015
1S1729R	0015
1S1730	0015
1S1730R	0015
1S1731	0071
1S1731R	0071
1S1732	0071
1S1732R	0071
1S1733	0102
1S1733R	0102
1S1734	0162
1S1735	0631
1S1736	0644
1S1737	1075
1S1738	0313
1S1739	0137
1S1740	0002
1S1741	1639
1S1742	0526
1S1743	1596
1S1744	0721
1S1745	0814
1S1746	0925
1S1747	1823
1S1748	0778
1S1749	1181
1S1750	0327
1S1751	1301
1S1752	0098
1S1753	0149
1S1754	0186
1S1755	0213
1S1756	0245
1S1757	0623
1S1758	0623
1S1759	0623
1S1760	OEM
1S1761	OEM
1S1762	OEM
1S1763	OEM
1S1764	OEM
1S1765	OEM
1S1766	0162
1S1767	0298
1S1768	0644
1S1769	1075
1S1770	0313
1S1771	0361
1S1772	0002
1S1773	1639
1S1774	0695
1S1775	0398
1S1776	0721
1S1777	0039
1S1781	1075
1S1782	1075
1S1783	1075
1S1784	0778
1S1785	2144
1S1786	0327
1S1787	0098
1S1788	0186
1S1789	0213
1S1790	0028
1S1791	0363
1S1792	0417
1S1796	0124
1S1798	0097
1S1798R	0760
1S1799	0097
1S1799R	0760
1S1800	OEM
1S1800R	OEM
1S1801	0109
1S1801-02	0124
1S1801R	2938
1S1802	0122
1S1802R	0122
1S1803	0131
1S1803R	0540
1S1804	0145
1S1804R	0545
1S1805	0005
1S1805A	0005
1S1806	0005
1S1806A	0005
1S1807	0911
1S1820	0911
1S1821	0072
1S1821R	0072
1S1822	OEM
1S1822R	OEM
1S1823	OEM
1S1823R	OEM
1S1824	OEM
1S1824R	OEM
1S1825	0133
1S1825R	OEM
1S1829	0071
1S1829A	0071
1S1829B	0071
1S1829C	0071
1S1829D	0071
1S1829K	0071
1S1829L	0071
1S1829Y	0071
1S1830	0071
1S1830A	0071
1S1830B	0071
1S1830C	0071
1S1830D	0071
1S1830K	0071
1S1830L	0071
1S1830Y	0071
1S1832	0182
1S1833	0023
1S1834	0023
1S1835	0023
1S1836	0286
1S1837	0374
1S1838	OEM
1S1841	0800
1S1842	0315
1S1843	1124
1S1844	0045
1S1845	0015
1S1845A	0015
1S1845B	0015
1S1845C	0071
1S1845D	0071
1S1845E	0102
1S1846	0015
1S1846A	0015
1S1846B	0015
1S1846C	0071
1S1846D	0071
1S1846E	0102
1S1847A	0847
1S1848	0015
1S1848A	0847
1S1849	0015
1S1849R	0023
1S1850	0023
1S1850R	0023
1S1851	0015
1S1851R	0015
1S1855	0124
1S1856	OEM
1S1857	OEM
1S1858	OEM
1S1860	0911
1S1876	OEM
1S1881AM	0015
1S1882	0102
1S1885	0023
1S1885(FA)	0023
1S1885-3	0015
1S1885A	0604
1S1885FA	0604
1S1886	0023
1S1886A	0604
1S1887	0023
1S1887(AU)	0790
1S1887(FA)	0790
1S1887A	0023
1S1887A(FA)	OEM
1S1887A(FA-1)	0015
1S1887AFA	0015
1S1887AFA-1	0790
1S1887ALC	0790
1S1887A-LC7	0023
1S1887ALC-7	0790
1S1887A-T3	0023
1S1887A-Z	0790
1S1887FA	0015
1S1887FA-1	0015
1S1888	0023
1S1888H	OEM
1S1888J	OEM
1S1888V	0015
1S1890	0959
1S1891	0023
1S1892	0087
1S1893	0549
1S1894A	OEM
1S1894B	OEM
1S1894C	OEM
1S1895	0715
1S1895A	OEM
1S1895B	OEM
1S1895C	OEM
1S1895D	OEM
1S1897	0959
1S1898	0811
1S1899	0916
1S1906	0015
1S1910	0102
1S1911	0102
1S1912	0201
1S1914	0947
1S1915	0242
1S1916	0535
1S1917	0959
1S1918	0811
1S1919	0916
1S1920	0182
1S1921A	0023
1S1921B	0023
1S1921C	0023
1S1921D	0023
1S1921E	0023
1S1921F	0023
1S1922	0549
1S1922DS	OEM
1S1922G	0911
1S1923	0005
1S1923A	0549
1S1924	0715
1S1925	0911
1S1926	0911
1S1926K	0911
1S1926P	0911
1S1928	0911
1S1934	0865
1S1934R	1625
1S1935	0865
1S1935R	1625
1S1936	0847
1S1936R	1242
1S1937	1599
1S1937R	1196
1S1938	1600
1S1938R	2124
1S1939	1604
1S1939R	2236
1S1941	0023
1S1941B	0133
1S1941L	1325
1S1942	0023
1S1943	0015
1S1944	0023
1S1944H	OEM
1S1944J	OEM
1S1945	OEM
1S1946	OEM
1S1947	OEM
1S1948	0015
1S1949	0015
1S1950	0015
1S1951	0039
1S1953	1703
1S1954	OEM
1S1955	OEM
1S1956	0298
1S1957	0025
1S1958	0244
1S1959	0012
1S1960	0170
1S1961	0313
1S1962	0137
1S1963	0100
1S1964	0002
1S1965	0416
1S1966	0490
1S1967	0526
1S1968	0560
1S1969	0398
1S1970	0436
1S1971	0721
1S1972	0124
1S1972-M	0124
1S1973	0124
1S1973-M	0124
1S1991	0242
1S1992	2496
1S1993	2496
1S1994	2496
1S1995	2496
1S1996	0865
1S1997	0847
1S2000	0847
1S2003	OEM
1S2003R	OEM
1S2004	OEM
1S2004R	OEM
1S2005	0847
1S2019	0071
1S2030A	0118
1S2031	0036
1S2033	0296
1S2033A	0296
1S2034	OEM
1S2034R	OEM
1S2035	OEM
1S2035R	OEM
1S2036	0372
1S2036A	0372
1S2036R	OEM
1S2037	OEM
1S2037R	OEM
1S2039	0451
1S2039A	0036
1S2043	0274
1S2043A	0274
1S2045(STUD)	0542
1S2046(STUD)	2101
1S2047	0140
1S2047(STUD)	1890
1S2047A	0140
1S2049(STUD)	1612
1S2051	0041
1S2051(STUD)	0986
1S2051A	0041
1S2051B	0162
1S2053(STUD)	1254
1S2055(STUD)	1264
1S2056	0253
1S2056A	0253
1S2056B	0253
1S2057(STUD)	1706
1S2059(STUD)	0722
1S2061(STUD)	1771
1S2062	0466
1S2062A	0466
1S2063	0071
1S2064	0916
1S2067	0318
1S2068	0318
1S2068A	0062
1S2069	0318
1S2070	0124
1S2071	0124
1S2071A	0124
1S2072	0124
1S2073-A	OEM
1S2074	0124
1S2074H	0133
1S2075	0133
1S2075A	0077
1S2075K	0133
1S2076	0133
1S2076-27	0124
1S2076-TF1	0124
1S2076-TFI	0124
1S2076A	0124
1S2076A/-07-27	0124
1S2076A-07	0124
1S2076A-07-27	0124
1S2076MC	0124
1S2076P	0124
1S2076S4	OEM
1S2076T	0124
1S2076TF1	0124
1S2076TFI	0392
1S2080	0023
1S2081	0015
1S2082	0165
1S2082A	0165
1S2083	OEM
1S2083R	OEM
1S2085	0715
1S2085A	0715
1S2086	0715
1S2086A	0715
1S2087	0715
1S2087A	0715
1S2088	0715
1S2088A	0715
1S2089	0005
1S2090	0549
1S2091	0133
1S2091-BK	0133
1S2091-BL	0133
1S2091-W	0133
1S2091A	0057
1S2091BK	0133
1S2091BL	0133
1S2091W	0133
1S2092	0133
1S2093	2704
1S2094	0005
1S2095	0124
1S2095A	0124
1S2097	0133
1S2098	0133
1S2099	0124
1S2100	0064
1S2100A	0064
1S2107	0451
1S2107A	0451
1S2108	0528
1S2108A	0528
1S2109	0140
1S2109A	0446
1S2110	0181
1S2110A	0181
1S2111	0157
1S2111A	0157
1S2112	0091
1S2112A	0466
1S2112A(FA-1)	OEM
1S2112AFA-1	0631
1S2112FA-1	OEM
1S2113	0025
1S2113A	0025
1S2114	0644
1S2114A	0644
1S2115	0244
1S2115A	0244
1S2116	0012
1S2116A	0012
1S2117	5546
1S2117A	0170
1S2118	0313
1S2118A	0313
1S2119	0052
1S2119A	0052
1S2120	0052
1S2120A	0052
1S2121	0002
1S2121A	0002
1S2122	1639
1S2122A	0416
1S2123	0490
1S2123A	0490
1S2124	0015
1S2125	0091
1S2126	0318
1S2127	0052
1S2128	0298
1S2129	1075
1S2130	0137
1S2130A	0053
1S2131	0943
1S2131C	0030
1S2132	0098
1S2133	0213
1S2134	0124
1S2135	0124
1S2136	0091
1S2137	1075
1S2138	0137
1S2139	0005
1S2139-A	0549
1S2139-B	0005
1S2139-C	0715
1S2139A	0549
1S2139B	0005
1S2139C	0715
1S2139D	0030
1S2139P	0005
1S2140	0015
1S2142	0005
1S2143	0005
1S2144	0133
1S2144A	0133
1S-2144Z	0133
1S2144Z	0133
1S2145	0124
1S2147	0549
1S2147A	0715
1S2147B	0715
1S2147C	0715
1S2147D	OEM
1S2148	OEM
1S2149	OEM
1S2150	0681
1S2150A	0681
1S2160	4851
1S2160A	0440
1S2175	OEM
1S2176	OEM
1S2180	0371
1S2180A	0371
1S2181	OEM
1S2186	0133

If replacement code is OEM, contact original manufacturer for replacement.

DEVICE TYPE	REPL CODE	DEVICE TYPE	REPL CODE	DEVICE TYPE	REPL CODE	DEVICE TYPE	REPL CODE	DEVICE TYPE	REPL CODE	DEVICE TYPE	REPL CODE	DEVICE TYPE	REPL CODE
1S2186GR	4116	1S2293(STUD)	1629	1S2400	0071	1S2473-2	0124	1S2564	0814	1S2757	0015	1S4010A	0225
1S2187	0911	1S2293A	1264	1S2401	0015	1S2473-K	0124	1S2565	0528	1S2758	0916	1S4011	0230
1S2188	0005	1S2295	1071	1S2402	0015	1S2473-T72	0124	1S2566	0054	1S2759	0916	1S4011A	0230
1S2189	0030	1S2295(STUD)	1706	1S2403	0071	1S2473C	OEM	1S2567	0068	1S2760	0110	1S4012	0234
1S2190	0165	1S2295A	1071	1S2404	0015	1S2473H	0133	1S2568	0092	1S2761	0947	1S4012A	0234
1S2191	0165	1S2297	1712	1S2405	0071	1S2473HC	0133	1S2569	1823	1S2762	0242	1S4013	0237
1S2192	0165	1S2297(STUD)	0722	1S2406	0071	1S2473H-R	0133	1S2570	0778	1S2763	0535	1S4013A	0237
1S2193	0165	1S2297A	1712	1S2407	0102	1S2473H-Y	0124	1S2571	2144	1S2764	0535	1S4015	0247
1S2194	0091	1S2299	1712	1S2408	0110	1S2473I	0124	1S2572	0094	1S2765	0959	1S4015A	0247
1S2195	0318	1S2299(STUD)	1771	1S2409	0087	1S2473K	0124	1S2573	0327	1S2766	0959	1S4016	0251
1S2196	0052	1S2299A	1750	1S2410	0242	1S2473T	0133	1S2574	0156	1S2766A	1208	1S4016A	0251
1S2197	0030	1S2300	1761	1S2411	1736	1S2473T72	0124	1S2575	0189	1S2767	0811	1S4018	0256
1S2197A	0030	1S2300A	1761	1S2412	0535	1S2473T-83	OEM	1S2588	0124	1S2768	0811	1S4018A	0256
1S2198	0911	1S2302	0289	1S2413	1760	1S2473TA	0133	1S2589	0015	1S2768A	0087	1S4020	0262
1S2198HC	0911	1S2303	0451	1S2414	0959	1S2473TV	OEM	1S2590	0015	1S2769	0062	1S4020A	0262
1S2199	OEM	1S2304	0162	1S2415	0110	1S2473UJ	0133	1S2591	0023	1S2770	0062	1S4022	0269
1S2200	0695	1S2305	OEM	1S2416	0947	1S2473V	0124	1S2592	0017	1S2771	0062	1S4022A	0269
1S2200A	0695	1S2306	0102	1S2417	0242	1S2473VE	0133	1S2593	0017	1S2772	0062	1S4024	0273
1S2201	OEM	1S2307	0102	1S2418	1736	1S2473VH	OEM	1S2594	0017	1S2773	0062	1S4024A	0273
1S2203	OEM	1S2308	0102	1S2419	0535	1S2479	0143	1S2595	0017	1S2774	0062	1S4027	0291
1S2204	0124	1S2309	0102	1S2420	1760	1S2480	1302	1S2596	0023	1S2775	0023	1S4027A	0291
1S2206	0030	1S2310	0102	1S2421	0959	1S2480R	1302	1S2597	0133	1S2775(FA-1)	0023	1S4030	0305
1S-2207	0549	1S2311	0071	1S2422	4938	1S2481	1703	1S2598	0959	1S2775FA-1	0494	1S4030A	0305
1S2207	0030	1S2312	0071	1S2422R	2537	1S2481R	1703	1S2602	0015	1S2775FA1	0015	1S4033	0314
1S2207-9	0005	1S2313	0015	1S2423	4938	1S2482	0289	1S2603	0015	1S2775TPA2	0494	1S4033A	0314
1S2208	1023	1S2314	0071	1S2423R	2537	1S2482R	0289	1S2604	0015	1S2776	0087	1S4036	0316
1S2208B	5529	1S2315	0071	1S2424	4938	1S2483	0188	1S2605	0015	1S2777	0015	1S4036A	0316
1S2209	1023	1S2316	0023	1S2424R	2537	1S2483R	0188	1S2606	0015	1S2778	0959	1S4039	0322
1S2209B	OEM	1S2317	0023	1S2425	4938	1S2484	0451	1S2607	0071	1S2779	0535	1S4039A	0322
1S2210	2496	1S2318	0017	1S2425R	2537	1S2484R	0451	1S2608	0071	1S2780	0959	1S4043	0333
1S2211	2496	1S2319	0017	1S2426	4938	1S2485	0528	1S2609	0071	1S2781	0811	1S4043A	0333
1S2212	0124	1S2323	0017	1S2426R	2537	1S2485R	0528	1S2610	0071	1S2782	0916	1S4047	0343
1S2220	0700	1S2324	0017	1S2427	2591	1S2486	0446	1S2611	0017	1S2787	0124	1S4047A	0343
1S2220A	0700	1S2325	0017	1S2427R	2544	1S2486R	0446	1S2612	0017	1S2788	0124	1S4050	OEM
1S2222	2496	1S2326	0017	1S2428	OEM	1S2487	0162	1S2613	0017	1S2788B	0133	1S4051	0027
1S2226	0015	1S2329	OEM	1S2428R	OEM	1S2488	0157	1S2614	0017	1S2789	0715	1S4051A	0027
1S2227	0015	1S2330	0166	1S2429	OEM	1S2489	0631	1S2615	OEM	1S2789W	0005	1S4056	0266
1S2228	0015	1S2330A	0166	1S2429R	OEM	1S2490	0025	1S2616	OEM	1S2790	0623	1S4056A	0266
1S2229	0015	1S2331	OEM	1S2430	OEM	1S2491	0644	1S2617	OEM	1S2790W	0623	1S4062	0382
1S2230	0015	1S2332	OEM	1S2430R	OEM	1S2492	0244	1S2618	0071	1S2790WT	0623	1S4062A	0382
1S2231	0071	1S2333	OEM	1S2431	OEM	1S2493	0012	1S2619	0201	1S2790Y	OEM	1S4068	0401
1S2233	0959	1S2334	OEM	1S2431R	OEM	1S2494	0170	1S2620	0374	1S2790YL	0030	1S4068A	0401
1S2234	0811	1S2335	OEM	1S2432	OEM	1S2495	0313	1S2628	0865	1S2791	0911	1S4075	0421
1S2235	0916	1S2336	0005	1S2432R	OEM	1S2496	0137	1S2629	0865	1S2792	0865	1S4075A	0421
1S2236	0005	1S2337	OEM	1S2433	OEM	1S2497	0361	1S2630	0865	1S2793	0847	1S4082	0439
1S2237	OEM	1S2339	0549	1S2433R	OEM	1S2498	0100	1S2631	0865	1S2794	0847	1S4082A	0439
1S2238	0071	1S2339-C	0549	1S2434	1991	1S2499	0416	1S2632	0865	1S2795	0847	1S4091	0238
1S2239	0071	1S2339C	0005	1S2434R	1992	1S2500	0490	1S2633	0865	1S2827A	0242	1S4091A	0238
1S2239C	0715	1S2339K	0030	1S2435	1241	1S2501	0526	1S2638	0005	1S2828A	0535	1S4100	1172
1S2240	0071	1S2340	0005	1S2435R	1567	1S2502	0560	1S2638VVC	0030	1S2830A	0811	1S4100A	1172
1S2240A	0489	1S2342	OEM	1S2436	1241	1S2503	0398	1S2666	OEM	1S2831A	0916	1S4110	1182
1S2241	0071	1S2343	OEM	1S2436R	1567	1S2504	0436	1S2667	OEM	1S2832	0015	1S4110A	1182
1S2242	0071	1S2344	OEM	1S2437	1571	1S2505	0721	1S2668	OEM	1S2833	0037	1S4120	1198
1S2243	0071	1S2345	OEM	1S2437R	3251	1S2506	0039	1S2669	OEM	1S2834	0102	1S4120A	1198
1S2244	0023	1S2346	OEM	1S2438	1576	1S2507	0814	1S2670	OEM	1S2835	0133	1S4130	1209
1S2245	0023	1S2347	OEM	1S2438R	3263	1S2508	0346	1S2671	OEM	1S2835CHIP	OEM	1S4130A	1209
1S2246	0023	1S2348	0124	1S2439	1576	1S2509	0925	1S2672	0102	1S2836	0133	1S4148	OEM
1S2247	OEM	1S2348H	OEM	1S2439R	3263	1S2510	0993	1S2673	0102	1S2837	0901	1S4150	0642
1S2248	OEM	1S2349	OEM	1S2440	OEM	1S2511	0497	1S2674	0102	1S2837CHIP	OEM	1S4150A	0642
1S2249	OEM	1S2350	0535	1S2440R	OEM	1S2512	1823	1S2675	0023	1S2838	0901	1S4160	1246
1S2250	OEM	1S2351	0015	1S2441	OEM	1S2513	0778	1S2676	0023	1S2867T	0715	1S4160A	1246
1S2251	OEM	1S2352	0015	1S2441R	OEM	1S2514	5613	1S2677	0017	1S2880	OEM	1S4180	1269
1S2252	OEM	1S2353	0071	1S2442	OEM	1S2515	1181	1S2678	0017	1S2885	0494	1S4180A	1269
1S2253	OEM	1S2354	0071	1S2442R	OEM	1S2516	0327	1S2679	0017	1S2888	OEM	1S4200	0600
1S2254	OEM	1S2355	0102	1S2443	OEM	1S2517	1301	1S2682D	OEM	1S2939	OEM	1S4200A	0600
1S2255	OEM	1S2356	0015	1S2443R	OEM	1S2518	0098	1S2685	OEM	1S2970WT	OEM	1S4266	0143
1S2256	OEM	1S2357	0015	1S2444	OEM	1S2519	0149	1S2686	0005	1S2976	OEM	1S4266FM	0143
1S2257	OEM	1S2358	0015	1S2444R	OEM	1S2520	0186	1S2686D	0005	1S3006	0025	1S4735	0041
1S2258	OEM	1S2359	0015	1S2445	OEM	1S2521	0213	1S2687	0715	1S3007	0644	1S5006	1449
1S2259	OEM	1S2361	0015	1S2445R	OEM	1S2522	0028	1S2687-1	0715	1S3008	0244	1S5006A	1449
1S2260	OEM	1S2362	0015	1S2446	3160	1S2523	0255	1S2687A	0715	1S3009	0012	1S5007	0221
1S2261	OEM	1S2363	0015	1S2446R	1620	1S2524	0363	1S2687AA	0715	1S3010	0170	1S5007A	0221
1S2262	OEM	1S2364	0071	1S2447	2873	1S2525	0417	1S2687D	0715	1S3011	0313	1S5008	1481
1S2263	OEM	1S2365	0071	1S2447R	0254	1S2536	1266	1S2688	0030	1S3012	0137	1S5008A	1481
1S2264	OEM	1S2366	0102	1S2448	1116	1S2536R	1266	1S2688A	OEM	1S3013	0361	1S5009	1608
1S2265	OEM	1S2367	0023	1S2448R	1099	1S2537	0755	1S2688B	0030	1S3016	0002	1S5009A	1608
1S2266	OEM	1S2368	0102	1S2449	1118	1S2537R	0755	1S2688C	0030	1S3016(RECT)	0015	1S5010	0505
1S2267	0715	1S2369	0102	1S2449R	1103	1S2538	0118	1S2688E	0030	1S3016(ZENER)	0416	1S5010A	0505
1S2268	0715	1S2370	0017	1S2450	0800	1S2538R	0118	1S2688EA	0015	1S3016R	0015	1S5011	0686
1S2269	0015	1S2371	0276	1S2450R	0258	1S2539	0289	1S2688EB	0030	1S3018	0490	1S5011A	0686
1S2270	0450	1S2371A	0276	1S2451	1186	1S2539R	0372	1S2688T	OEM	1S3022	0560	1S5012	0864
1S2270A	0450	1S2372	0015	1S2451R	1634	1S2540	0188	1S2689	0030	1S3027	0436	1S5012A	0864
1S2271	0015	1S2372A	0287	1S2452	0631	1S2540R	0188	1S2689B	0030	1S3033	0039	1S5013	1014
1S2272	0015	1S2373	0015	1S2453	0631	1S2541	0451	1S2689K	0030	1S3039	0346	1S5013A	1014
1S2273	0071	1S2373A	0293	1S2454	0631	1S2541R	0451	1S2692	2496	1S3047	0993	1S5015	1264
1S2274	0071	1S2374	0015	1S2455	0559	1S2542	0528	1S2692A	2496	1S3056	0863	1S5015A	1264
1S2275FA-1	0015	1S2374A	0299	1S2456	0242	1S2542R	0528	1S2692AB	0124	1S3068	1258	1S5015C	OEM
1S2276	0133	1S2375	0015	1S2457	0535	1S2543	0446	1S2692B	6050	1S3082	0327	1S5016	1392
1S2277	0023	1S2375A	0287	1S2458	1208	1S2543R	0446	1S2701	OEM	1S3091A	OEM	1S5016A	1392
1S2278	0023	1S2376	0015	1S2459	1760	1S2544	0157	1S2701R	OEM	1S3100	0098	1S5016C	OEM
1S2279	0023	1S2376A	0293	1S2460	0133	1S2545	0157	1S2702	OEM	1S3100A	OEM	1S5018	1071
1S2280	0017	1S2377	0087	1S2461	0133	1S2546	0298	1S2702R	OEM	1S3110	0149	1S5018A	1071
1S2281	0017	1S2378	0575	1S2461V-Y	0124	1S2547	0631	1S2703	OEM	1S3120	0186	1S5018C	OEM
1S2283(STUD)	0542	1S2378R	0941	1S2462	0023	1S2548	0644	1S2703R	OEM	1S3150	0028	1S5020	1707
1S2284(STUD)	2101	1S2379	0535	1S2463	0023	1S2549	0165	1S2711	0182	1S3180	0363	1S5020A	1707
1S2285(STUD)	1890	1S2380	0959	1S2464	OEM	1S2550	0012	1S2712	OEM	1S3195	0015	1S5020C	OEM
1S2286	1449	1S2387	OEM	1S2469	0374	1S2551	0170	1S2712F-FA	0102	1S3302	OEM	1S5022	1712
1S2286(STUD)	1591	1S2388	OEM	1S2470	0374	1S2552	0313	1S2713	OEM	1S3305	0041	1S5022A	1712
1S2286A	1449	1S2389	OEM	1S2471	0124	1S2553	0137	1S2714	0865	1S3332	0025	1S5022C	OEM
1S2287	1481	1S2390	0015	1S2471A	0124	1S2554	0361	1S2715	0865	1S3585	0143	1S5024	1725
1S2287(STUD)	1612	1S2391	0015	1S2471B	0124	1S2555	0100	1S2716	0847	1S4006	0205	1S5024A	1725
1S2287A	1481	1S2392	0015	1S2471C	OEM	1S2556	0416	1S2717	0847	1S4006A	0205	1S5024C	OEM
1S2289	0505	1S2393	0015	1S2471TA	0133	1S2557	0490	1S2724	OEM	1S4007	0475	1S5027	1750
1S2289(STUD)	0986	1S2394	0015	1S-2472	0133	1S2558	0695	1S2725	OEM	1S4007A	0475	1S5027A	1750
1S2289A	0505	1S2395	0015	1S2472	0133	1S2559	0560	1S2726	OEM	1S4008	0499	1S5027C	OEM
1S2291	0864	1S2396	0015	1S2472T-77	0133	1S2560	0398	1S2745	1208	1S4008A	0499	1S5030	1761
1S2291(STUD)	1254	1S2397	0071	1S2473	0133	1S2561	0436	1S2746	1208	1S4009	0679	1S5030A	1761
1S2291A	0864	1S2398	0071	1S2473*7A	3844	1S2562	1664	1S2747	0916	1S4009A	0679	1S5030C	OEM
1S2293	1264	1S2399	0071	1S2473*7K	3844	1S2563	0039	1S2756	0023	1S4010	0225	1S5033	1777

If replacement code is OEM, contact original manufacturer for replacement.

35

DEVICE TYPE	REPL CODE
1S5033A	1777
1S5033C	OEM
1S5036	1785
1S5036A	1785
1S5036C	OEM
1S5039	1793
1S5039A	1793
1S5039C	OEM
1S5043	1185
1S5043A	1185
1S5043C	OEM
1S5047	0022
1S5047A	0022
1S5047C	OEM
1S5051	0132
1S5051A	0132
1S5051C	OEM
1S5056	0207
1S5056A	0207
1S5056C	OEM
1S5062	0263
1S5062A	0263
1S5062C	OEM
1S5068	0306
1S5068A	0306
1S5068C	OEM
1S5075	0325
1S5075A	0325
1S5075C	OEM
1S5082	0352
1S5082A	0352
1S5082C	OEM
1S5091	0408
1S5091A	0408
1S5091C	OEM
1S5100	0433
1S5100A	0433
1S5100C	OEM
1S5110	0483
1S5110A	0483
1S5110C	OEM
1S5120	0504
1S5120A	0504
1S5120C	OEM
1S5130	0519
1S5130A	0519
1S5130C	OEM
1S5150	0063
1S5150A	0063
1S5150C	OEM
1S5277B	0080
1S5295G	0023
1S5295J	0023
1S5351	0030
1S5454	0143
1S5566B	OEM
1S6006	1449
1S6006A	1449
1S6007	0221
1S6007A	0221
1S6008	1481
1S6008A	1481
1S6009	1608
1S6009A	1608
1S6010	0505
1S6010A	0505
1S6011	0686
1S6011A	0686
1S6012	0864
1S6012A	0864
1S6013	1014
1S6013A	1014
1S6015	1264
1S6015A	1264
1S6016	1392
1S6016A	1392
1S6018	1071
1S6018A	1071
1S6020	1707
1S6020A	1707
1S6022	1712
1S6022A	1712
1S6024	1725
1S6024A	1725
1S6027	1750
1S6027A	1750
1S6030	1761
1S6030A	1761
1S6033	1777
1S6033A	1777
1S6036	1785
1S6036A	1785
1S6039	1793
1S6039A	1793
1S6043	1185
1S6043A	1185
1S6047	0022
1S6047A	0022
1S6051	0132
1S6051A	0132
1S6056	0207
1S6056A	0207
1S6062	0263
1S6062A	0263
1S6068	0306
1S6068A	0306
1S6075	0325
1S6075A	0325
1S6082	0352

DEVICE TYPE	REPL CODE
1S6082A	0352
1S6091	0408
1S6091A	0408
1S6100	0433
1S6100A	0433
1S6110	0483
1S6110A	0483
1S6120	0504
1S6120A	0504
1S6130	0519
1S6130A	0519
1S6150	0063
1S6150A	0063
1S6160	0397
1S6160A	0397
1S6180	0629
1S6180A	0629
1S6200	0663
1S6200A	0663
1S6288B	0715
1S6289	0715
1S7026A	OEM
1S7026B	OEM
1S7030A	0118
1S7033	0296
1S7033A	0296
1S7033B	0296
1S7036	0372
1S7036A	0372
1S7036B	0372
1S7039	0036
1S7039A	0036
1S7039B	0036
1S7043	0274
1S7043A	0274
1S7043B	0274
1S7047	0140
1S7047A	0140
1S7047B	0140
1S7051	0041
1S7051A	0041
1S7051B	0041
1S7056	0253
1S7056A	0253
1S7056B	0253
1S7062	0466
1S7062A	0466
1S7062B	0466
1S7068	0062
1S7068A	0062
1S7068B	0062
1S7075	0077
1S7075A	0077
1S7075B	0077
1S7082	0165
1S7082A	0165
1S7082B	0165
1S7091	0057
1S7091A	0057
1S7091B	0057
1S7100	0064
1S7100A	0064
1S7100B	0064
1S7110	0181
1S7110A	0181
1S7110B	0181
1S7120	0052
1S7120A	0052
1S7120B	0052
1S7130	0053
1S7130A	0053
1S7130B	0053
1S7150	0681
1S7150A	0681
1S7150B	0681
1S7160A	0440
1S7209	0139
1S7230A	OEM
1S7581S759	OEM
1S9413	0015
1S9908	0143
1S15188	0124
1S16009	1608
1S16009A	1608
1S18813	OEM
1S18853	OEM
1S19413	0015
1S19413T	0015
1S21447	0124
1S22079	0715
1S23396	OEM
1S26870	0715
1SB01-02	0015
1SB34	OEM
1SB50S	0030
1SB69-06	0715
1SC301A	OEM
1SC301B	OEM
1SC301C	OEM
1SC301D	OEM
1SC301E	OEM
1SC683	0007
1SC929	0007
1SC1566	0275
1SC2367	0133
1SD-2	0015
1SD2	0015
1SD1212	0015
1SF1	1557

DEVICE TYPE	REPL CODE
1SF2	1557
1SF4	2140
1SG11	OEM
1SG12	OEM
1SG13	OEM
1SG14	OEM
1SG15	OEM
1SG16	OEM
1SG17	OEM
1SG18	OEM
1SG19	OEM
1SG20	OEM
1SG21	OEM
1SG22	OEM
1SG23	OEM
1SG24	OEM
1SG25	OEM
1SG26	OEM
1SG27	OEM
1SG28	OEM
1SG29	OEM
1SG30	OEM
1SIZ09	0015
1SM1	0080
1SM3	0031
1SM6	OEM
1SM15	OEM
1SM25	OEM
1SM40	OEM
1SM55	OEM
1SM70	OEM
1SM100	OEM
1SM150	OEM
1SM-150A	0102
1SM200	OEM
1S-M2511-8010S035B	0124
1SN1835	0102
1S030	0015
1S031	0015
1S032	0015
1S034	0015
1S036	0015
1S038	0071
1S058	0071
1SR1FM4	0015
1SR1K	0015
1SR11-100	0087
1SR11-200	0015
1SR11-400	0087
1SR11-600	0015
1SR11-800	0072
1SR11-1000	0071
1SR11-1200	0102
1SR11-1500	0102
1SR12-50	0087
1SR12-100	0087
1SR12-200	0015
1SR12-400	0087
1SR12-600	0015
1SR12-800	0037
1SR12-1000	0071
1SR13-50	0087
1SR13-100	0087
1SR13-200	0015
1SR13-400	0087
1SR13-600	0015
1SR13-800	0037
1SR13-1000	0071
1SR14-50	0087
1SR14-100	0087
1SR14-200	0015
1SR14-400	0087
1SR15-50	0110
1SR15-100	0947
1SR15-200	0242
1SR15-400	0535
1SR15-600	0959
1SR15-800	0811
1SR15-1000	0916
1SR16-50	0110
1SR16-100	0947
1SR16-200	0242
1SR16-400	0535
1SR16-600	0959
1SR16-800	0811
1SR16-1000	0916
1SR17-50	0110
1SR17-100	0947
1SR17-200	0242
1SR17-400	0535
1SR17-600	0959
1SR17-800	0811
1SR17-1000	0916
1SR19-100	OEM
1SR19-250	OEM
1SR19-400	OEM
1SR20-100	OEM
1SR20-250	OEM
1SR20-400	OEM
1SR29-200	OEM
1SR29-400	OEM
1SR29-600	OEM
1SR29-800	OEM
1SR29-1000	OEM
1SR30-200	0015
1SR30-400	0087
1SR30-600	0015
1SR31-800	0037
1SR31-1000	0071

DEVICE TYPE	REPL CODE
1SR32-1200	0102
1SR32-1400	0102
1SR32-1500	0102
1SR34	0023
1SR34-200	4176
1SR35	0023
1SR35-50	1325
1SR35-50A	1325
1SR-35-100	0015
1SR35-100	0080
1SR35-100-F	0015
1SR35-100-HT	0080
1SR35-100-T3	0080
1SR35-100-Z	0080
1SR35-100A	0023
1SR35-100A-Y	0080
1SR35-200	0023
1SR35-200A	0604
1SR-35-400	0790
1SR35-400	0790
1SR35-400A	0790
1SR36	0102
1SR37	0865
1SR55-50	0087
1SR55-100	0087
1SR55-200	0015
1SR56-50	0102
1SR56-100	0102
1SR56-200	0102
1SR57-200	OEM
1SR57-300	OEM
1SR58-200	OEM
1SR58-300	OEM
1SR62-2000	OEM
1SR62-2500	OEM
1SR62-2800	OEM
1SR62-3000	OEM
1SR63-2000	OEM
1SR63-2500	OEM
1SR64-200	OEM
1SR64-400	OEM
1SR64-600	OEM
1SR67-200	1404
1SR68	0071
1SR69	0015
1SR70-100	0276
1SR70-200	0287
1SR70-400	0293
1SR70-800	0250
1SR70-1000	0250
1SR71-30	1590
1SR71-40	1590
1SR74-200	0865
1SR74-300	0847
1SR74-400	0847
1SR74-600	OEM
1SR74-800	OEM
1SR74-1000	OEM
1SR74R-200	OEM
1SR74R-300	OEM
1SR74R-400	OEM
1SR74R-600	OEM
1SR74R-800	OEM
1SR74R-1000	OEM
1SR75-200	0865
1SR75-300	0847
1SR75-400	0847
1SR75-600	OEM
1SR75-800	OEM
1SR75-1000	OEM
1SR75R-200	OEM
1SR75R-300	OEM
1SR75R-400	OEM
1SR75R-600	OEM
1SR75R-800	OEM
1SR75R-1000	OEM
1SR77-200	0015
1SR77-400	0087
1SR77-600	0015
1SR77-800	0072
1SR77-1000	0071
1SR78-200	0015
1SR78-400	0087
1SR79-800	0037
1SR79-1000	0071
1SR80-100	0865
1SR80-200	0865
1SR80-400	0847
1SR80-600	OEM
1SR80R-100	OEM
1SR80R-200	OEM
1SR80R-400	OEM
1SR80R-600	OEM
1SR81-800	OEM
1SR81R-800	OEM
1SR82-100	0865
1SR82-200	0865
1SR82-400	0847
1SR82-600	OEM
1SR82-800	OEM
1SR82-1000	OEM
1SR82R-100	OEM
1SR82R-200	OEM
1SR82R-600	OEM
1SR83-800	OEM
1SR83R-800	OEM
1SR84-100	OEM
1SR84-200	OEM
1SR84-400	OEM

DEVICE TYPE	REPL CODE
1SR90-200	OEM
1SR90-400	OEM
1SR90-600	OEM
1SR90-800	OEM
1SR90R-200	OEM
1SR90R-400	OEM
1SR90R-600	OEM
1SR90R-800	OEM
1SR91-100	0087
1SR91-200	0087
1SR91-400	0087
1SR95-1600	0344
1SR95A-1600	0344
1SR96-200	0604
1SR96-400	0790
1SR96-600	0015
1SR97-800	0072
1SR97-1000	0071
1SR98-100	0031
1SR98-200	0031
1SR99-100	0080
1SR99-200	0604
1SR99-400	0790
1SR99A-100	0080
1SR99A-200	0604
1SR99A-400	0790
1SR100-200	0604
1SR100-400	0790
1SR100-600	0015
1SR100-800	0072
1SR100-1200	0344
1SR100-1500	0344
1SR101-800	0072
1SR101-1200	0344
1SR101-1500	0344
1SR102-2000	0344
1SR106-200	OEM
1SR106-400	OEM
1SR106-600	OEM
1SR106-800	OEM
1SR106R-200	OEM
1SR106R-400	OEM
1SR106R-600	OEM
1SR106R-800	OEM
1SR107-50	OEM
1SR107-100	OEM
1SR107-200	OEM
1SR107R-50	OEM
1SR107R-100	OEM
1SR107R-200	OEM
1SR108-50	OEM
1SR108-100	OEM
1SR108-200	OEM
1SR108R-50	OEM
1SR108R-100	OEM
1SR108R-200	OEM
1SR109-50	OEM
1SR109-100	OEM
1SR109-200	OEM
1SR109R-50	OEM
1SR109R-100	OEM
1SR109R-200	OEM
1SR112-800	0072
1SR112-1000	0071
1SR112-1300	0344
1SR112-1500	0344
1SR117-100	0087
1SR117-200	0087
1SR117-400	0087
1SR117-600	0087
1SR117-800	0087
1SR119-100	0080
1SR119-200	0604
1SR119-400	0790
1SR124-50	1325
1SR124-50A	1325
1SR124-100	0023
1SR124-100A	0023
1SR124-200	0023
1SR124-200A	0023
1SR124-400	0023
1SR124-400-Z	0023
1SR124-400A	0023
1SR124-400V-Z	0023
1SR133-200	OEM
1SR133-200R	OEM
1SR133-400	OEM
1SR133-400R	OEM
1SR133-600	OEM
1SR133-600R	OEM
1SR135	0182
1SR135-100	OEM
1SR135-100-Z	OEM
1SR136	OEM
1SR137	OEM
1SR138	0124
1SR139	0031
1SR139-100	0581
1SR139-100AT	OEM
1SR139-200	0581
1SR139-400	0581
1SR140	0031
1SR141	0031
1SR142	0031
1SR143	OEM
1SR35200TB	OEM
1SRBA20Z	0287
1SS11	OEM
1SS12	OEM

DEVICE TYPE	REPL CODE
1SS13	OEM
1SS14	OEM
1SS15	OEM
1SS-16	0911
1SS16	0911
1SS19	0124
1SS23	0143
1SS24	0907
1SS25	0907
1SS26	0907
1SS27	0143
1SS28	0907
1SS29	0907
1SS30	0124
1SS31	0124
1SS40	OEM
1SS41	0124
1SS43	0911
1SS48	OEM
1SS49	0124
1SS50	0124
1SS51	0124
1SS52	2496
1SS-53	0133
1SS53	0133
1SS54	0133
1SS54-T4	0124
1SS55	0023
1SS68	0124
1SS69	OEM
1SS70	OEM
1SS78	0911
1SS81	0133
1SS81-F1	OEM
1SS81-R	0133
1SS81-T2	0133
1SS81-Y	0133
1SS-82	0023
1SS82	0023
1SS82-Y	0023
1SS83	0133
1SS84	0133
1SS85	0163
1SS86	0911
1SS87	0911
1SS88	0335
1SS90	0911
1SS91	OEM
1SS91-G	0163
1SS91-S	0163
1SS92	0124
1SS93	0124
1SS94	0124
1SS95	0133
1SS96	OEM
1SS97	0335
1SS98	0911
1SS99	0911
1SS101	3837
1SS102	0133
1SS103	2496
1SS104	0133
1SS104(FA)	0133
1SS104FA	0133
1SS105	OEM
1SS105A	OEM
1SS106	3144
1SS107	0335
1SS108	3837
1SS109	0124
1SS110	0015
1SS110FQ	0124
1SS110T	0124
1SS110Y	0124
1SS111	0163
1SS112	0163
1SS113	0392
1SS114	OEM
1SS115	OEM
1SS116	0911
1SS117	0124
1SS118	0124
1SS118-S3	OEM
1SS119	0124
1SS119/VHD1SS119//-1	OEM
1SS119-041T	0124
1SS119-14	0124
1SS119-14FQ	0124
1SS119-T	0124
1SS119TD	0124
1SS119TG	0124
1SS120	0124
1SS121	0124
1SS122	0023
1SS122H	OEM
1SS123	0124
1SS124	0124
1SS125	OEM
1SS130	0133
1SS131	0124
1SS131T-77	0124
1SS131T-177	OEM
1SS132	0124
1SS132T	0124
1SS132T-77	0124
1SS133	0133
1SS133-T2	0133
1SS133-Y	0124
1SS133HV	0133

DEVICE TYPE	REPL CODE
1SS133T	0133
1SS133T-72	OEM
1SS133VT	OEM
1SS134	0124
1SS135	0124
1SS136	0124
1SS137	0124
1SS138	0124
1SS139	0133
1SS140	0133
1SS141	0133
1SS142	0023
1SS143	0023
1SS144	0023
1SS145	0023
1SS146	0023
1SS146-T2	0023
1SS146-Y	0023
1SS147	0023
1SS148	0133
1SS149	0023
1SS149H	OEM
1SS150	0124
1SS150(A)	0133
1SS151	0911
1SS151(A)	OEM
1SS152	0124
1SS152(A)	0133
1SS153	3842
1SS154	OEM
1SS155	0392
1SS156	OEM
1SS157	OEM
1SS158	OEM
1SS162	OEM
1SS163	0124
1SS164	0124
1SS165	0163
1SS165(A)	OEM
1SS166	0163
1SS166(A)	OEM
1SS166-03TE	OEM
1SS168	0163
1SS168(A)	0133
1SS169	0124
1SS170	0124
1SS171	0124
1SS172	0023
1SS173	0163
1SS173A	0124
1SS174	0911
1SS175	0133
1SS175A	0133
1SS176	0133
1SS176(FA)	0124
1SS176-TPA7	OEM
1SS176FA	0124
1SS176TPA7	OEM
1SS177	0124
1SS178	0124
1SS178(FA)	0124
1SS178-Y	0124
1SS178FA	0124
1SS179	OEM
1SS181	0897
1SS182	OEM
1SS184	0901
1SS184-TE85L	0901
1SS184TE85L	0901
1SS184TE85R	OEM
1SS187	0124
1SS188-03TD	OEM
1SS190	0124
1SS193	0124
1SS196	0124
1SS197	0163
1SS198	0335
1SS199	OEM
1SS200	6070
1SS201	0124
1SS202	0124
1SS202-1	OEM
1SS203	0124
1SS204	0124
1SS205	0133
1SS206	0124
1SS207	0133
1SS208	0124
1SS209	0124
1SS210	0124
1SS211	0124
1SS212	0124
1SS213	0124
1SS214	0124
1SS215	0124
1SS216	0163
1SS217	0133
1SS218	0124
1SS219	0133
1SS220	0124
1SS221	0124
1SS222	0124
1SS223	0124
1SS226	0124
1SS227	1083
1SS228	OEM
1SS229	0689
1SS230	0689
1SS231	2189

36 If replacement code is OEM, contact original manufacturer for replacement.

DEVICE TYPE	REPL CODE	DEVICE TYPE	REPL CODE	DEVICE TYPE	REPL CODE	DEVICE TYPE	REPL CODE	DEVICE TYPE	REPL CODE	DEVICE TYPE	REPL CODE	DEVICE TYPE	REPL CODE
1SS232	2189	1SV53A	OEM	1SV177	OEM	1SZ56-08	0475	1T33	0039	1T1102	OEM	1VA100	OEM
1SS233	0689	1SV54	OEM	1SV178	OEM	1SZ56-09	3285	1T33A	0039	1T1103	OEM	1VA120	OEM
1SS233F	3163	1SV54-G	OEM	1SV179	OEM	1SZ56-10	0679	1T33B	0039	1T1104	OEM	1VR10A	OEM
1SS234	0689	1SV55	0030	1SV180	OEM	1SZ56-11	0225	1T33C	OEM	1T1110	OEM	1VR10B	OEM
1SS235	2189	1SV56	OEM	1SV181	OEM	1SZ56-12	0230	1T33CT	OEM	1T1331	0123	1W01-08J	0313
1SS236	2189	1SV57	OEM	1SV182	OEM	1SZ56-13	0234	1T36	0550	1T1401	OEM	1W20	OEM
1SS237	0335	1SV58	1023	1SV186	OEM	1SZ56-15	1387	1T36A	0814	1T1402	OEM	1W20A	OEM
1SS238	OEM	1SV59	1023	1SV187	OEM	1SZ56-16	0247	1T36B	0814	1T2011	0015	1W50	OEM
1SS239	0335	1SV65	OEM	1SV188	OEM	1SZ56-18	1170	1T38	0739	1T2012	0015	1W80	OEM
1SS240	0124	1SV66	OEM	1SV189	OEM	1SZ56-20	2379	1T39	0346	1T2013	0015	1W1706	0321
1SS241	0163	1SV68	0030	1SV190	OEM	1SZ56-22	0262	1T39A	0346	1T2014	0015	1W9640	0037
1SS242	0911	1SV68-01	OEM	1SV191	OEM	1SZ56-24	0269	1T39B	0346	1T2015	0015	1W9640A	0037
1SS243	0133	1SV69	1023	1SV192	OEM	1SZ56-27	2383	1T40	0133	1T2016	0015	1W9728	0037
1SS244	1082	1SV69-06	0715	1SV193	OEM	1SZ56-30	1169	1T43	0925	1T20105	0015	1W9728A	0037
1SS244-T2	1082	1SV70	1023	1SV194	OEM	1SZ56-33	0305	1T43A	0925	1TA5.6	0157	1W9782	0037
1SS244-T77	OEM	1SV70-06	0715	1SV195	OEM	1SZ57	0292	1T43B	0925	1TA5.6A	0157	1W9782A	0037
1SS245	1082	1SV71	OEM	1SV196	OEM	1SZ58	0292	1T46	0550	1TA5.6B	0157	1W9787	0016
1SS246	OEM	1SV72	OEM	1SV197	OEM	1SZ59	0292	1T47	0993	1TA6.2	0631	1W9810	0037
1SS247	OEM	1SV73	OEM	1SV198	OEM	1SZ60	0292	1T47A	0993	1TA6.2A	0631	1W9810A	0037
1SS248	0392	1SV74	OEM	1SV201	OEM	1SZ61	0466	1T47B	0993	1TA6.2B	0631	1W9810S	0037
1SS248TP3	5261	1SV75	OEM	1SV203	OEM	1SZ62	0165	1T48	0550	1TA6.8	0025	1W9810SA	0037
1SS249	OEM	1SV77	0005	1SV206	OEM	1SZ63	0052	1T51	0497	1TA7.5	0644	1W11700	0037
1SS250	0133	1SV80	OEM	1SV207	OEM	1SZ64	0451	1T51A	0497	1TA7.5A	0644	1W11700A	0037
1SS251	0023	1SV84	1023	1SV209	OEM	1SZ65	OEM	1T51B	0497	1TA8.2	0244	1W11702	0037
1SS252	0133	1SV87	OEM	1SV1615	OEM	1SZ66	0166	1T56	0863	1TA9.1	0012	1W11702A	0037
1SS253	0124	1SV88	OEM	1SX170	0023	1SZ67	0062	1T56A	0863	1TA9.1A	0012	1W11706	0321
1SS254	0124	1SV89	0715	1SX171	0023	1SZ68	OEM	1T56B	0863	1TA9.1B	0012	1W11708-1	0016
1SS267	0023	1SV89A	0715	1SX172	0023	1SZ69	OEM	1T58	0550	1TA10	0170	1W11708-2	0016
1SS268	0901	1SV89B01	0715	1SX173	0023	1SZ70	OEM	1T62	0778	1TA10A	0170	1W11711	0037
1SS269	0897	1SV89BFG	0715	1SX174	0023	1SZ71	OEM	1T62A	0778	1TA11	0313	1W11711A	0006
1SS270	0133	1SV90	OEM	1SX175	0023	1SZ72	OEM	1T62B	0778	1TA12	0137	1WB-5A	0162
1SS270A	0124	1SV90A	3643	1SZ11	0210	1T06	0550	1T66	0550	1TA12A	0137	1WB-6A	0157
1SS270TA	0133	1SV91	3643	1SZ12	0666	1T08	0550	1T68	0550	1TA13	0361	1WB-7A	0025
1SS270TD	OEM	1SV92	OEM	1SZ13	0010	1T010	0767	1T68A	2144	1TA13A	0361	1WB-9D	1075
1SS271	OEM	1SV93	OEM	1SZ14	OEM	1T015	0767	1T68B	2144	1TA13B	0361	1WB-11D	0313
1SS272	0124	1SV94	OEM	1SZ21	1639	1T1	OEM	1T75	1181	1TA14	0100	1WB-13D	0361
1SS273	0124	1SV95	OEM	1SZ22	0371	1T1TA14	0100	1T75A	1181	1TA14A	0100	1WB-15D	0002
1SS274	0911	1SV96	OEM	1SZ23	0010	1T2C1	0015	1T75B	1181	1TA14B	0100	1WB-17D	1639
1SS275	0911	1SV97	0623	1SZ24	OEM	1T2Z1	0015	1T82	0327	1TA15	0002	1WB-20D	0526
1SS276	0911	1SV98	OEM	1SZ25	0165	1T3	OEM	1T82A	0327	1TA15A	0002	1WB-25D	0398
1SS277	0163	1SV100	OEM	1SZ26	0466	1T5.6	0157	1T82B	0327	1TA16	0416	1WB-30D	0721
1SS278	0163	1SV101	OEM	1SZ27	0165	1T5.6B	0157	1T91	1301	1TA18	0490	1WB-35D	0814
1SS279	2496	1SV102	OEM	1SZ28	0440	1T6	OEM	1T91A	1301	1TA20	0526	1WB-45D	0925
1SS280	2496	1SV103	OEM	1SZ29	0709	1T6.2	0631	1T91B	1301	1TA22	0560	1WB-55D	1823
1SS281	0335	1SV108	OEM	1SZ30	0064	1T6.2A	0631	1T100	0098	1TA24	0398	1WB-65D	0778
1SS282	0335	1SV109	3642	1SZ39	0631	1T6.2B	0631	1T100A	0098	1TA25A	0398	1WB-75D	1181
1SS283	0335	1SV110	OEM	1SZ40-11	0313	1T7.5	0644	1T100B	0098	1TA27	0436	1WB-85D	0327
1SS284	0335	1SV110-07	OEM	1SZ40-12	0137	1T7.5A	0644	1T110	0550	1TA27A	0436	1WB-95D	1301
1SS285	3837	1SV111	1023	1SZ40-13	0361	1T7.5B	0644	1T110A	0149	1TA30	0721	1WB-100D	0098
1SS290	0133	1SV111-06	1023	1SZ40-15	0002	1T9.1	0012	1T110B	0149	1TA33	0039	1WB-110D	0149
1SS291	0133	1SV111-14	OEM	1SZ40-16	0416	1T9.1A	0012	1T120	0186	1TA33A	0039	1WB-120D	0186
1SS292	0133	1SV112	OEM	1SZ40-18	0490	1T9.1B	0012	1T120A	0186	1TA36	0814	1WB-130D	0213
1SS292T-72	OEM	1SV113	0623	1SZ40-20	0526	1T10	0170	1T120B	0186	1TA39	0346	1WB-140D	0245
1SS312	OEM	1SV114	OEM	1SZ40-22	0560	1T10B	0170	1T130	0213	1TA43	0925	1WM6	0015
1SS355	0124	1SV114(A)	OEM	1SZ40-24	0398	1T11	0313	1T130A	0213	1TA47	0993	1WS1	0087
1SS585	OEM	1SV115	OEM	1SZ40-27	0436	1T11A	0313	1T130B	0213	1TA51	0497	1WS2	0087
1SS916	OEM	1SV116	OEM	1SZ40-30	0721	1T11B	0313	1T150	0028	1TA56	0863	1WS4	0535
1SS1555	0392	1SV117	OEM	1SZ40-33	0039	1T11.5A	0789	1T150A	0028	1TA62	0778	1WS6	0959
1SS53125	OEM	1SV118	OEM	1SZ41	OEM	1T12	0137	1T150B	0028	1TA68	1258	1WS8	0087
1ST11	OEM	1SV121	OEM	1SZ42	OEM	1T12A	0137	1T160	0255	1TA75	1181	1WS10	0087
1ST11-UR	OEM	1SV122	OEM	1SZ43	0157	1T12B	0137	1T160A	0255	1TA82	0327	1X8055	0133
1ST12	OEM	1SV123	0715	1SZ45	0292	1T13	0911	1T160B	0255	1TA82A	0327	1X9179	0133
1ST12-UR	OEM	1SV124	0623	1SZ45A	0292	1T13A	0911	1T180	0363	1TA91	1301	1X9805	0133
1ST13	OEM	1SV125	OEM	1SZ46	0292	1T13B	0911	1T180A	0363	1TA100	0098	1X9809	0133
1ST13-UR	OEM	1SV125(A)	OEM	1SZ46A	0292	1T14	0100	1T180B	0363	1TA110	0149	1XG1	OEM
1ST14	OEM	1SV126	OEM	1SZ47	0292	1T14A	0100	1T188	0143	1TA120	0186	1XG2	OEM
1ST14-UR	OEM	1SV128	OEM	1SZ47A	0292	1T14B	0100	1T200	0417	1TA130	0213	1XV1	OEM
1ST15	OEM	1SV132	OEM	1SZ48	0292	1T15	0002	1T200A	0417	1TA150	0028	1XV2	OEM
1ST15-UR	OEM	1SV132(A)	OEM	1SZ48A	0292	1T15B	0002	1T200B	0417	1TA160	0255	1XV3	OEM
1ST16	OEM	1SV133	0623	1SZ49	0292	1T16	0550	1T205A	0050	1TA180	0363	1Z3.3	0289
1ST16-UR	OEM	1SV134	OEM	1SZ49A	0292	1T16A	0416	1T210	0550	1TA200	0417	1Z3.3A	0289
1ST17	OEM	1SV135	OEM	1SZ50	0466	1T16B	0416	1T213	0143	1TA7607AP	0906	1Z3.3B	0289
1ST17-UR	OEM	1SV136	OEM	1SZ51	0466	1T18	0550	1T215	0767	1TA7608CP5	2043	1Z3.3T10.5	0289
1ST18	OEM	1SV136(A)	OEM	1SZ52	0466	1T19-15B	0002	1T220	0321	1TA7609P-2	4071	1Z3.6	0188
1ST18-UR	OEM	1SV141	OEM	1SZ53	0466	1T20	0526	1T229-2	0015	1TB06	0015	1Z3.6A	0188
1ST20	OEM	1SV141(A)	OEM	1SZ54	0466	1T20A	0526	1T231	0143	1TH60	OEM	1Z3.6B	0188
1ST21	OEM	1SV142	OEM	1SZ55-C2V2	OEM	1T20B	0526	1T236	0143	1TH61	0071	1Z3.6T5	0188
1ST22	OEM	1SV143	OEM	1SZ55-C2V4	1266	1T22	0143	1T240	0143	1TH62	0017	1Z3.6T10	0188
1ST37	OEM	1SV144	OEM	1SZ55-C2V7	0755	1T22(A)	0143	1T240A	0143	1TS05	0015	1Z3.6TS	0188
1SV11	OEM	1SV145	OEM	1SZ55-C2V0	OEM	1T22A	0143	1T243	0133	1TT210	OEM	1Z3.9	0451
1SV25	OEM	1SV146	OEM	1SZ55-C3V0	0118	1T22AJ	0143	1T243M	0012	1TT-410	0030	1Z3.9A	0451
1SV25/S3015A	OEM	1SV147	OEM	1SZ55-C3V3	0296	1T22AM	0143	1T261	0019	1TT410	0030	1Z3.9B	0451
1SV26	OEM	1SV148	OEM	1SZ55-C3V6	0372	1T22B	0143	1T261T	0143	1TT921	0102	1Z4.3	0528
1SV27	OEM	1SV149	OEM	1SZ55-C3V9	0036	1T22G	0143	1T262	0143	1TT1168	0030	1Z4.3A	0528
1SV28	OEM	1SV151S	OEM	1SZ55-C4V3	0274	1T22M	0143	1T263	0497	1TT7215	0102	1Z4.3B	0528
1SV29	OEM	1SV153	OEM	1SZ55-C4V7	0140	1T23	0143	1T264	0497	1TV24237	0469	1Z4.7	0446
1SV30	OEM	1SV154	OEM	1SZ55-C5V1	0041	1T23A	0143	1T310	0550	1TW85B	0030	1Z4.7A	0446
1SV31	OEM	1SV154FQ	OEM	1SZ55-C5V6	0253	1T23B	0143	1T315	0739	1TWC8H	1075	1Z4.7B	0446
1SV32	OEM	1SV156	OEM	1SZ55-C6V2	0466	1T23G	0143	1T377	OEM	1TWC8L	1075	1Z5	OEM
1SV33	OEM	1SV157	OEM	1SZ55-C6V8	0062	1T23J	0143	1T378	0015	1TWC8M	1075	1Z5.1	0162
1SV34	0124	1SV158	OEM	1SZ55-C7V5	0077	1T23M	0143	1T410	0550	1TZ61	0017	1Z5.1A	0162
1SV35	0124	1SV160	OEM	1SZ55-C8V2	0165	1T23S	0123	1T415	0739	1U585F	0016	1Z5.1B	0162
1SV36	OEM	1SV161	OEM	1SZ55-C9V1	0057	1T24	0398	1T495	0164	1UPC1363C	0678	1Z5.1T5	0162
1SV37	OEM	1SV161S	OEM	1SZ55-C10	0064	1T24A	0398	1T501	0015	1UPD1937C	2079	1Z5.6	0157
1SV45	OEM	1SV162	OEM	1SZ55-C11	0181	1T24B	0398	1T502	0015	1UPD1986C	4706	1Z5.6A	0157
1SV46	OEM	1SV164	OEM	1SZ55-C12	0052	1T25	0715	1T503	0015	1V2	1440	1Z5.6B	0157
1SV47	OEM	1SV165	OEM	1SZ55-C13	0053	1T25-4	OEM	1T504	0015	1V3074A20	0015	1Z6.2	0631
1SV48	OEM	1SV166	OEM	1SZ55-C15	0681	1T26	0143	1T505	0015	1V3074A21	0015	1Z6.2A	0631
1SV48-1	OEM	1SV166(1)	OEM	1SZ55-C16	0440	1T26-2	0143	1T506	0015	1V9002	0143	1Z6.2B	0631
1SV48-2	OEM	1SV166S	OEM	1SZ55-C18	0371	1T26TRIAC	0767	1T507	0071	1V68611A47	0037	1Z6.2T5	0631
1SV49	OEM	1SV167	OEM	1SZ55-C20	0695	1T27	0436	1T508	0071	1V68611A47A	0037	1Z6.2T20	0631
1SV50	0030	1SV168	OEM	1SZ55-C22	0700	1T27B	0436	1T509	0071	1VA10	0015	1Z6.8	0025
1SV50(1)	OEM	1SV169	OEM	1SZ55-C24	0489	1T28	0550	1T510	0071	1VA20	OEM	1Z6.8A	0025
1SV50-1	OEM	1SV170	OEM	1SZ55-C27	0450	1T30	0721	1T515	0612	1VA30	OEM	1Z6.8B	0025
1SV50S	0030	1SV172	OEM	1SZ55-C30	0195	1T30A	0721	1T610	0550	1VA40	OEM	1Z6.8C	OEM
1SV52	OEM	1SV173	OEM	1SZ55-C33	0166	1T30B	0721	1T615	0612	1VA50	OEM	1Z6.8D	0025
1SV53	0030	1SV174	OEM	1SZ55-C36	0010	1T31	OEM	1T929	0079	1VA60	OEM	1Z6.8D5	0025
1SV53-A	OEM	1SV175	OEM	1SZ55-C39	0032	1T32	OEM	1T930	0079	1VA70	OEM	1Z6.8D10	0025
1SV53-B	OEM	1SV176	OEM	1SZ56-07	0185	1T32-2	OEM	1T1101	OEM	1VA80	OEM	1Z7.5	0644

If replacement code is OEM, contact original manufacturer for replacement. 37

DEVICE TYPE	REPL CODE
1Z7.5A	0644
1Z7.5B	0644
1Z7.5C	OEM
1Z7.5D	0644
1Z7.5D5	0644
1Z7.5D10	0644
1Z8.2	0244
1Z8.2A	0244
1Z8.2B	0244
1Z8.2C	OEM
1Z8.2D	0244
1Z8.2D5	0244
1Z8.2D10	0244
1Z8.3	0244
1Z9.1	0012
1Z9.1A	0012
1Z9.1B	0012
1Z9.1C	0012
1Z9.1D	0012
1Z9.1D5	0012
1Z9.1D10	0012
1Z9.1D15	0012
1Z9.1T5	0012
1Z9.1T10	0012
1Z9.1T20	0012
1Z10	0170
1Z10A	0170
1Z10B	0170
1Z10C	OEM
1Z10D	0170
1Z10D5	0170
1Z10D10	0170
1Z10T10	0170
1Z10T20	0170
1Z11	0313
1Z11A	0313
1Z11B	0313
1Z11C	OEM
1Z11D	0313
1Z11D5	0313
1Z11D10	0313
1Z11T5	0313
1Z11T10	0313
1Z11T20	0313
1Z-12	0137
1Z12	0137
1Z12A	0137
1Z12B	0137
1Z12C	0137
1Z12D	0137
1Z12D5	0137
1Z12D10	0137
1Z12T5	0137
1Z12T10	0137
1Z12T20	0137
1Z13	0361
1Z13A	0361
1Z13B	0361
1Z13C	0361
1Z13D	0361
1Z13D5	0361
1Z13D10	0361
1Z13T5	0361
1Z13T10	0361
1Z13T20	0361
1Z14	0100
1Z14A	0100
1Z14B	0100
1Z14C	0100
1Z14D	0100
1Z14D5	0100
1Z14D10	0100
1Z15	0002
1Z15A	0002
1Z15B	0002
1Z15C	0002
1Z15D	0002
1Z15D5	0002
1Z15D10	0002
1Z15D20	0002
1Z15T5	0002
1Z15T10	0002
1Z15T20	0002
1Z16	0416
1Z16A	0416
1Z16B	0416
1Z16C	OEM
1Z16D	0416
1Z16D5	0416
1Z16D10	0416
1Z17	1639
1Z17A	1639
1Z17B	1639
1Z17C	OEM
1Z17D	1639
1Z17D5	1639
1Z17D10	1639
1Z18	0490
1Z18A	0490
1Z18B	0490
1Z18C	OEM
1Z18D	0490
1Z18D5	0490
1Z18D10	0490
1Z18T5	0490
1Z18T10	0490
1Z18T20	0490
1Z19	0943
1Z19A	0943

DEVICE TYPE	REPL CODE
1Z19B	0943
1Z19C	OEM
1Z19D	0943
1Z19D5	0943
1Z19D10	0943
1Z20	0526
1Z20A	0526
1Z20B	0526
1Z20C	OEM
1Z20D	0526
1Z20D5	0526
1Z20D10	0526
1Z22	0560
1Z22A	0560
1Z22B	0560
1Z22C	OEM
1Z22D	0560
1Z22D5	0560
1Z22D10	0560
1Z22T5	0560
1Z22T10	0560
1Z22T20	0560
1Z24	0273
1Z24A	0398
1Z24B	0398
1Z24C	OEM
1Z24D	0398
1Z24D5	0398
1Z24D10	0398
1Z25	1596
1Z25A	1596
1Z25B	1596
1Z25C	OEM
1Z25D	1596
1Z25D5	1596
1Z25D10	1596
1Z26A	2553
1Z27	0436
1Z27A	0436
1Z27B	0436
1Z27C	0436
1Z27D	0436
1Z27D5	0436
1Z27D10	0436
1Z27T5	0436
1Z27T10	0436
1Z27T20	0436
1Z30	0721
1Z30A	0721
1Z30B	0721
1Z30C	OEM
1Z30D	0721
1Z30D5	0721
1Z30D10	0721
1Z33	0039
1Z33-A	0039
1Z33A	0039
1Z33B	0039
1Z33C	0039
1Z33D	0039
1Z33D5	0039
1Z33D10	0039
1Z33T5	0039
1Z33T10	0039
1Z33T20	0039
1Z36	0814
1Z36B	0814
1Z36C	OEM
1Z36D	0814
1Z36D5	0814
1Z36D10	0814
1Z39	0346
1Z39A	0346
1Z39B	0346
1Z39C	OEM
1Z39D	0346
1Z39D5	0346
1Z39D10	0346
1Z43	0925
1Z43A	0925
1Z43B	0925
1Z43C	OEM
1Z43D	0925
1Z43D5	0925
1Z43D10	0925
1Z45	0993
1Z45A	0993
1Z45B	0993
1Z45C	OEM
1Z45D	0993
1Z45D5	0993
1Z45D10	0993
1Z47	0993
1Z47A	0993
1Z47B	0993
1Z47C	OEM
1Z47D	0993
1Z47D5	0993
1Z47D10	0993
1Z50	0497
1Z50A	0497
1Z50B	0497
1Z50C	OEM
1Z50D	0497
1Z50D5	0497
1Z50D10	0497
1Z51	0497
1Z51A	0497
1Z51B	0497

DEVICE TYPE	REPL CODE
1Z51C	OEM
1Z51D	0497
1Z51D5	0497
1Z51D10	0497
1Z52	0497
1Z52A	0497
1Z52B	0497
1Z52C	OEM
1Z52D	0497
1Z52D5	0497
1Z52D10	0497
1Z56	0863
1Z56A	0863
1Z56B	0863
1Z56C	1823
1Z56D	0863
1Z56D5	0863
1Z56D10	0863
1Z62	0778
1Z62A	0778
1Z62B	0778
1Z62C	0778
1Z62D	0778
1Z62D5	0778
1Z62D10	0778
1Z68	1258
1Z68A	1258
1Z68B	2144
1Z68C	OEM
1Z68D	2144
1Z68D5	2144
1Z68D10	2144
1Z72	1181
1Z75	1181
1Z75A	1181
1Z75B	1181
1Z75C	OEM
1Z75D	1181
1Z75D5	1181
1Z75D10	1181
1Z75FA	1181
1Z82	0012
1Z82A	0327
1Z82B	0327
1Z82C	0327
1Z82D	0327
1Z82D5	0327
1Z82D10	0327
1Z91	1301
1Z91A	1301
1Z91B	1301
1Z91C	OEM
1Z91D	1301
1Z91D5	1301
1Z91D10	1301
1Z91.1D10	0012
1Z91.D10	0012
1Z100	0098
1Z100A	0098
1Z100B	0098
1Z100C	OEM
1Z100D	0098
1Z100D5	0098
1Z100D10	0098
1Z105	0149
1Z105A	0149
1Z105B	0149
1Z105C	OEM
1Z105D	0149
1Z105D5	0149
1Z105D10	0149
1Z110	0149
1Z110A	0149
1Z110B	0149
1Z110C	0149
1Z110D	0149
1Z110D5	0149
1Z110D10	0149
1Z120	0186
1Z120A	0186
1Z120B	0186
1Z120C	OEM
1Z120D	0186
1Z120D5	0186
1Z120D10	0186
1Z130	0213
1Z130A	0213
1Z130B	0213
1Z130C	OEM
1Z130D	0213
1Z130D5	0213
1Z130D10	0213
1Z140	0245
1Z140A	0245
1Z140B	0245
1Z140C	OEM
1Z140D	0245
1Z140D5	0245
1Z140D10	0245
1Z150	0028
1Z150A	0028
1Z150B	0028
1Z150C	OEM
1Z150D	0028
1Z150D5	0028
1Z150D10	0028
1Z160	0255
1Z160A	0255
1Z160B	0255

DEVICE TYPE	REPL CODE
1Z160C	OEM
1Z160D	0255
1Z160D5	0255
1Z160D10	0255
1Z175	0363
1Z175A	0363
1Z175B	0363
1Z175C	OEM
1Z175D	0363
1Z175D5	0363
1Z175D10	0363
1Z180	0363
1Z180A	0363
1Z180B	0363
1Z180C	OEM
1Z180D	0363
1Z180D5	0363
1Z180D10	0363
1Z200	0417
1Z200A	0417
1Z200B	0417
1Z200C	OEM
1Z200D	0417
1Z200D5	0417
1Z200D10	0417
1Z261-02	OEM
1Z330	OEM
1Z390	OEM
1ZB10	0170
1ZB10B	0170
1ZB12	0137
1ZB12B	0137
1ZB15	0002
1ZB15B	0002
1ZB22	0560
1ZB22B	0560
1ZB27	0436
1ZB27B	0436
1ZB33	0039
1ZB33B	0039
1ZB39	0346
1ZB39B	0346
1ZB47	0993
1ZB47B	0993
1ZB56	0863
1ZB56B	0863
1ZB68	2144
1ZB68B	2144
1ZB82	0327
1ZB82B	0327
1ZB100	0098
1ZB100B	0098
1ZC1LT10	0416
1ZC3.6	0188
1ZC3.6T5	0372
1ZC3.6T10	0372
1ZC5.1	0162
1ZC5.6	0157
1ZC5.6T10.5	0157
1ZC6.2	0631
1ZC9.1	0012
1ZC9.1T5	0012
1ZC9.1T10	0012
1ZC10T5	0170
1ZC12	0137
1ZC12T5	0137
1ZC12T10	0137
1ZC12T20	0137
1ZC15	0002
1ZC15T5	0002
1ZC15T10	0002
1ZC18T5	0490
1ZC18T10	0490
1ZC22T5	0560
1ZC22T10	0560
1ZC27	0436
1ZC27T5	0436
1ZC27T10	0436
1ZCT10	0170
1ZD6	0644
1ZD8-2	0244
1ZD8-5	0244
1ZD8.2	0244
1ZD8.2V	0244
1ZD12	0137
1ZD82S	0244
1ZD120	0186
1ZD825	0244
1ZD892	0244
1ZF5.1T5	0162
1ZF5.1T10	0162
1ZF5.1T20	0162
1ZF5.6T5	0157
1ZF5.6T10	0157
1ZF5.6T20	0157
1ZF9.1T5	0012
1ZF9.1T10	0012
1ZF9.1T20	0012
1ZF12T5	0137
1ZF12T10	0137
1ZF12T20	0137
1ZF15T5	0002
1ZF15T10	0002
1ZF15T20	0002
1ZF27T5	0436
1ZF27T10	0436
1ZF27T20	0436
1ZF33T5	0039
1ZF33T10	0039

DEVICE TYPE	REPL CODE
1ZF33T20	0039
1ZG10	OEM
1ZG10B	OEM
1ZG15	OEM
1ZG15B	OEM
1ZG18	OEM
1ZG18B	OEM
1ZG22	OEM
1ZG22B	OEM
1ZG27	OEM
1ZG27B	OEM
1ZG33	OEM
1ZG33B	OEM
1ZG39	OEM
1ZG39B	OEM
1ZG47	OEM
1ZG47B	OEM
1ZG56	OEM
1ZG56B	OEM
1ZG68	OEM
1ZG68B	OEM
1ZG82	OEM
1ZG82B	OEM
1ZG100	OEM
1ZG100B	OEM
1ZK10	OEM
1ZK10B	OEM
1ZK12	OEM
1ZK12B	OEM
1ZK15	OEM
1ZK15B	OEM
1ZK18	OEM
1ZK18B	OEM
1ZK22	OEM
1ZK22B	OEM
1ZK27	OEM
1ZK27B	OEM
1ZK33	OEM
1ZK33B	OEM
1ZK39	OEM
1ZK39B	OEM
1ZK47	OEM
1ZK47B	OEM
1ZK56	OEM
1ZK56B	OEM
1ZK68	OEM
1ZK68B	OEM
1ZK82	OEM
1ZK82B	OEM
1ZK100	OEM
1ZK100B	OEM
1ZM3.3T5	0289
1ZM3.3T10	0289
1ZM3.3T20	0289
1ZM3.6T5	0188
1ZM3.6T10	0188
1ZM3.6T20	0188
1ZM3.9T5	0451
1ZM3.9T10	0451
1ZM3.9T20	0451
1ZM4.3T5	0528
1ZM4.3T10	0528
1ZM4.3T20	0528
1ZM4.7T5	0446
1ZM4.7T10	0446
1ZM4.7T20	0446
1ZM5.1T5	0162
1ZM5.1T10	0162
1ZM5.1T20	0162
1ZM5.6T5	0157
1ZM5.6T10	0157
1ZM5.6T20	0157
1ZM6.2T5	0631
1ZM6.2T10	0631
1ZM6.2T20	0631
1ZM6.8T5	0025
1ZM6.8T10	0025
1ZM6.8T20	0025
1ZM7.5T5	0644
1ZM7.5T10	0644
1ZM7.5T20	0644
1ZM8.2T5	0244
1ZM8.2T10	0244
1ZM8.2T20	0244
1ZM9.1T5	0012
1ZM9.1T10	0012
1ZM9.1T20	0012
1ZM10T5	0170
1ZM10T10	0170
1ZM10T20	0170
1ZM11T5	0313
1ZM11T10	0313
1ZM11T20	0313
1ZM12T5	0137
1ZM12T10	0137
1ZM12T20	0137
1ZM13T5	0361
1ZM13T10	0361
1ZM13T20	0361
1ZM15T5	0002
1ZM15T10	0002
1ZM15T20	0002
1ZM16T5	0416
1ZM16T10	0416
1ZM16T20	0416
1ZM18T5	0490
1ZM18T10	0490
1ZM18T20	0490
1ZM20T5	0526

DEVICE TYPE	REPL CODE
1ZM20T10	0526
1ZM20T20	0526
1ZM22T5	0560
1ZM22T10	0560
1ZM24T5	0398
1ZM24T10	0398
1ZM27	0436
1ZM27T5	0436
1ZM27T10	0436
1ZM30	0721
1ZM30T5	0721
1ZM30T10	0721
1ZM33T5	0039
1ZM33T10	0039
1ZM36T5	0814
1ZM36T10	0814
1ZM39T5	0346
1ZM39T10	0346
1ZM43T5	0925
1ZM43T10	0925
1ZM47	0993
1ZM47T5	0993
1ZM47T10	0993
1ZM50	0497
1ZM51T5	0497
1ZM51T10	0497
1ZM56T5	0863
1ZM56T10	0863
1ZM62T5	0778
1ZM62T10	0778
1ZM68T5	1258
1ZM68T10	2144
1ZM75T5	1181
1ZM75T10	1181
1ZM82T5	0327
1ZM82T10	0327
1ZM91T5	1301
1ZM91T10	1301
1ZM100	0098
1ZM100T5	0098
1ZM100T10	0098
1ZM110T5	0149
1ZM110T10	0149
1ZM120T5	0186
1ZM120T10	0186
1ZM130T5	0213
1ZM130T10	0213
1ZM150T5	0028
1ZM150T10	0028
1ZM160T5	0255
1ZM160T10	0255
1ZM180	0363
1ZM180T5	0363
1ZM180T10	0363
1ZM200T5	0417
1ZM200T10	0417
1ZM330	OEM
1ZM390	OEM
1ZS13A	0361
1ZS16A	0416
1ZS18A	0490
1ZT10	0170
1ZT10B	0170
1ZT12	0137
1ZT12B	0137
1ZT15	0002
1ZT15B	0002
1ZT18	0490
1ZT18B	0490
1ZT22	0560
1ZT22B	0560
1ZT27	0436
1ZT27B	0436
1ZT33	0039
1ZT33B	0039
1ZT39	0346
1ZT39B	0346
1ZT47	0993
1ZT47B	0993
1ZT56	0863
1ZT56B	0863
1ZT68	2144
1ZT68B	2144
1ZT82	0327
1ZT82B	0327
1ZT100	0098
1ZT100B	0098
1ZT110A	0149
1ZT120A	0186
1ZT130A	0213
1ZT150A	0028
1ZT160A	0255
1ZT180A	0363
1ZT200A	0417
1.000.111-00	0037
1.4Z45D10	OEM
1.5B05	0087
1.5B1	2501
1.5B2	2501
1.5B4	2505
1.5B6	2505
1.5B8	2506
1.5B10	6296
1.5B12	0182
1.5B14	0182
1.5B16	0344
1.5B18	0344
1.5B20	0344
1.5BZ100D	1172

DEVICE TYPE	REPL CODE
1.5BZ110B	1182
1.5BZ120	1198
1.5BZ120C	1198
1.5BZ130D	1209
1.5BZ140B	1870
1.5BZ150	0642
1.5BZ150C	0642
1.5C05	0087
1.5C1	2501
1.5C2	2501
1.5C4	2505
1.5C6	2505
1.5C8	2506
1.5C10	6296
1.5C12	0182
1.5C14	0182
1.5C16	0344
1.5C18	0344
1.5C20	0344
1.5DKZ6.8	0205
1.5DKZ6.8A	0205
1.5DKZ6.8B	0205
1.5DKZ7.5	0475
1.5DKZ7.5A	0475
1.5DKZ7.5B	0475
1.5DKZ8.2	0499
1.5DKZ8.2A	0499
1.5DKZ8.2B	0499
1.5DKZ9.1	0679
1.5DKZ9.1A	0679
1.5DKZ9.1B	0679
1.5DKZ10	0225
1.5DKZ10A	0225
1.5DKZ10B	0225
1.5DKZ11	0230
1.5DKZ11A	0230
1.5DKZ11B	0230
1.5DKZ12	0234
1.5DKZ12A	0234
1.5DKZ12B	0234
1.5DKZ13	0237
1.5DKZ13A	0237
1.5DKZ13B	0237
1.5DKZ15	0247
1.5DKZ15A	0247
1.5DKZ15B	0247
1.5DKZ16	0251
1.5DKZ16A	0251
1.5DKZ16B	0251
1.5DKZ18	0256
1.5DKZ18A	0256
1.5DKZ18B	0256
1.5DKZ20	0262
1.5DKZ20A	0262
1.5DKZ20B	0262
1.5DKZ22	0269
1.5DKZ22A	0269
1.5DKZ22B	0269
1.5DKZ24	0273
1.5DKZ24A	0273
1.5DKZ24B	0273
1.5DKZ27	0291
1.5DKZ27A	0291
1.5DKZ27B	0291
1.5DKZ30	0305
1.5DKZ30A	0305
1.5DKZ30B	0305
1.5DKZ33	0314
1.5DKZ33A	0314
1.5DKZ33B	0314
1.5DKZ36	0316
1.5DKZ36A	0316
1.5DKZ36B	0316
1.5DKZ39	0322
1.5DKZ39A	0322
1.5DKZ39B	0322
1.5DKZ43	0333
1.5DKZ43A	0333
1.5DKZ43B	0333
1.5DKZ47	0343
1.5DKZ47A	0343
1.5DKZ47B	0343
1.5DKZ51	0027
1.5DKZ51A	0027
1.5DKZ51B	0027
1.5DKZ56	0266
1.5DKZ56A	0266
1.5DKZ56B	0266
1.5DKZ62	0382
1.5DKZ62A	0382
1.5DKZ62B	0382
1.5DKZ68	0401
1.5DKZ68A	0401
1.5DKZ68B	0401
1.5DKZ75	0421
1.5DKZ75A	0421
1.5DKZ75B	0421
1.5E05	0110
1.5E1	0947
1.5E2	0242
1.5E3	0087
1.5E4	0535
1.5E5	1760
1.5E6	0959
1.5E7	0087
1.5E8	0087
1.5E10	0087
1.5E12	0102
1.5E14	0182

If replacement code is OEM, contact original manufacturer for replacement.

DEVICE TYPE	REPL CODE
1.5E16	0344
1.5E18	0344
1.5E20	0344
1.5E25	OEM
1.5E50A	OEM
1.5E100	OEM
1.5E140	1870
1.5F05	OEM
1.5F1	2501
1.5F2	2501
1.5F4	2505
1.5F6	2505
1.5F8	2506
1.5F10	6296
1.5F12	0182
1.5F14	0182
1.5F16	0344
1.5F18	0344
1.5F20	0344
1.5J05	0110
1.5J1	0947
1.5J2	0242
1.5J3	1736
1.5J4	0535
1.5J5	1760
1.5J6	0959
1.5J7	0087
1.5J8	0087
1.5J10	0087
1.5J12	0102
1.5JA19B	2379
1.5JZ6.8	0205
1.5JZ6.8A	0205
1.5JZ6.8B	0205
1.5JZ6.8C	0205
1.5JZ6.8D	0205
1.5JZ7.5	0475
1.5JZ7.5A	0475
1.5JZ7.5B	0475
1.5JZ7.5C	0475
1.5JZ7.5D	0475
1.5JZ8.2	0499
1.5JZ8.2A	0499
1.5JZ8.2B	0499
1.5JZ8.2C	0499
1.5JZ8.2D	0499
1.5JZ9.1	0679
1.5JZ9.1A	0679
1.5JZ9.1B	0679
1.5JZ9.1C	0679
1.5JZ9.1D	0679
1.5JZ10	0225
1.5JZ10A	0225
1.5JZ10B	0225
1.5JZ10C	0225
1.5JZ10D	0225
1.5JZ11	0230
1.5JZ11A	0230
1.5JZ11B	0230
1.5JZ11C	0230
1.5JZ11D	0230
1.5JZ12	0234
1.5JZ12A	0234
1.5JZ12B	0234
1.5JZ12C	0234
1.5JZ12D	0234
1.5JZ13	0237
1.5JZ13A	0237
1.5JZ13B	0237
1.5JZ13C	0237
1.5JZ13D	0237
1.5JZ14	1387
1.5JZ14A	1387
1.5JZ14B	1387
1.5JZ14C	1387
1.5JZ14D	1387
1.5JZ15	0247
1.5JZ15A	0247
1.5JZ15B	0247
1.5JZ15C	0247
1.5JZ15D	0247
1.5JZ16	0251
1.5JZ16A	0251
1.5JZ16B	0251
1.5JZ16C	0251
1.5JZ16D	0251
1.5JZ17	1170
1.5JZ17A	1170
1.5JZ17B	1170
1.5JZ17C	1170
1.5JZ17D	1170
1.5JZ18	0256
1.5JZ18A	0256
1.5JZ18B	0256
1.5JZ18C	0256
1.5JZ18D	0256
1.5JZ19	2379
1.5JZ19A	2379
1.5JZ19B	2379
1.5JZ19C	2379
1.5JZ19D	2379
1.5JZ20	0262
1.5JZ20A	0262
1.5JZ20B	0262
1.5JZ20C	0262
1.5JZ20D	0262
1.5JZ22	0269
1.5JZ22A	0269
1.5JZ22B	0269

DEVICE TYPE	REPL CODE
1.5JZ22C	0269
1.5JZ22D	0269
1.5JZ24	0273
1.5JZ24A	0273
1.5JZ24B	0273
1.5JZ24C	0273
1.5JZ24D	0273
1.5JZ25	2383
1.5JZ25A	2383
1.5JZ25B	2383
1.5JZ25C	1170
1.5JZ25D	2383
1.5JZ27	0291
1.5JZ27A	0291
1.5JZ27B	0291
1.5JZ27C	0291
1.5JZ27D	0291
1.5JZ30	0305
1.5JZ30A	0305
1.5JZ30B	0305
1.5JZ30C	0305
1.5JZ30D	0305
1.5JZ33	0314
1.5JZ33A	0314
1.5JZ33B	0314
1.5JZ33C	0314
1.5JZ33D	0314
1.5JZ36	0316
1.5JZ36A	0316
1.5JZ36B	0316
1.5JZ36C	0316
1.5JZ36D	0316
1.5JZ39	0322
1.5JZ39A	0322
1.5JZ39B	0322
1.5JZ39C	0322
1.5JZ39D	0322
1.5JZ43	0333
1.5JZ43A	0333
1.5JZ43B	0333
1.5JZ43C	0333
1.5JZ43D	0333
1.5JZ45	0333
1.5JZ45A	0333
1.5JZ45B	0333
1.5JZ45C	0333
1.5JZ45D	OEM
1.5JZ47	0343
1.5JZ47A	0343
1.5JZ47B	0343
1.5JZ47C	0343
1.5JZ47D	0343
1.5JZ50	0027
1.5JZ50A	0027
1.5JZ50B	0027
1.5JZ50C	0027
1.5JZ50D	OEM
1.5JZ51	0027
1.5JZ51A	0027
1.5JZ51B	0027
1.5JZ51C	0027
1.5JZ51D	0027
1.5JZ52	0027
1.5JZ52A	0027
1.5JZ52B	0027
1.5JZ52C	0027
1.5JZ52D	OEM
1.5JZ56	0266
1.5JZ56A	0266
1.5JZ56B	0266
1.5JZ56C	0266
1.5JZ56D	0266
1.5JZ62	0382
1.5JZ62A	0382
1.5JZ62B	0382
1.5JZ62C	0382
1.5JZ62D	0382
1.5JZ68	0401
1.5JZ68A	0401
1.5JZ68B	0401
1.5JZ68C	0401
1.5JZ68D	OEM
1.5JZ75	0421
1.5JZ75A	0421
1.5JZ75B	0421
1.5JZ75C	0421
1.5JZ75D	0421
1.5JZ82	0439
1.5JZ82A	0439
1.5JZ82B	0439
1.5JZ82C	0439
1.5JZ82D	0439
1.5JZ91	0238
1.5JZ91A	0238
1.5JZ91B	0238
1.5JZ91C	0238
1.5JZ91D	0238
1.5JZ100	1172
1.5JZ100A	1172
1.5JZ100B	1172
1.5JZ100C	1172
1.5JZ100D	OEM
1.5JZ105	1172
1.5JZ105A	1172
1.5JZ105B	1172
1.5JZ105C	1172
1.5JZ105D	OEM
1.5JZ110	1182
1.5JZ110A	1182

DEVICE TYPE	REPL CODE
1.5JZ110B	1182
1.5JZ110C	1182
1.5JZ110D	1182
1.5JZ120	1198
1.5JZ120A	1198
1.5JZ120B	1198
1.5JZ120C	1198
1.5JZ120D	1198
1.5JZ130	1209
1.5JZ130A	1209
1.5JZ130B	1209
1.5JZ130C	1209
1.5JZ130D	1209
1.5JZ140	1870
1.5JZ140A	1870
1.5JZ140B	1870
1.5JZ140C	1870
1.5JZ140D	1870
1.5JZ150	0642
1.5JZ150A	0642
1.5JZ150B	0642
1.5JZ150C	0642
1.5JZ150D	0642
1.5JZ160	1246
1.5JZ160A	1246
1.5JZ160B	1246
1.5JZ160C	1246
1.5JZ160D	1246
1.5JZ175	2091
1.5JZ175A	2091
1.5JZ175B	2091
1.5JZ175C	2091
1.5JZ175D	OEM
1.5JZ180	1269
1.5JZ180A	1269
1.5JZ180B	1269
1.5JZ180C	1269
1.5JZ180D	OEM
1.5JZ200	0600
1.5JZ200A	0600
1.5JZ200B	0600
1.5JZ200C	0600
1.5JZ200D	0600
1.5JZ220	OEM
1.5JZ220A	OEM
1.5JZ220B	OEM
1.5JZ220C	OEM
1.5JZ220D	OEM
1.5K6.8	3085
1.5K6.8A	3085
1.5K6.8R	3085
1.5K6.8RA	3085
1.5K7.5	OEM
1.5K7.5A	OEM
1.5K7.5R	OEM
1.5K7.5RA	OEM
1.5K8.2	OEM
1.5K8.2A	OEM
1.5K8.2R	OEM
1.5K8.2RA	OEM
1.5K9.1	OEM
1.5K9.1A	OEM
1.5K9.1R	OEM
1.5K9.1RA	OEM
1.5K10	OEM
1.5K10A	OEM
1.5K10R	OEM
1.5K10RA	OEM
1.5K11	OEM
1.5K11A	OEM
1.5K11R	OEM
1.5K11RA	OEM
1.5K12	OEM
1.5K12A	OEM
1.5K12R	OEM
1.5K12RA	OEM
1.5K13	3143
1.5K13A	3143
1.5K13R	3143
1.5K13RA	3143
1.5K15	OEM
1.5K15A	OEM
1.5K15R	OEM
1.5K15RA	OEM
1.5K16	OEM
1.5K16A	OEM
1.5K16R	OEM
1.5K16RA	OEM
1.5K18	3162
1.5K18A	3162
1.5K18R	3162
1.5K18RA	3162
1.5K20	3171
1.5K20A	3171
1.5K20R	3171
1.5K20RA	3171
1.5K22	OEM
1.5K22A	OEM
1.5K22R	OEM
1.5K22RA	OEM
1.5K24	OEM
1.5K24A	OEM
1.5K24R	OEM
1.5K24RA	OEM
1.5K27	1904
1.5K27A	1904
1.5K27R	1904
1.5K27RA	1904
1.5K30	OEM

DEVICE TYPE	REPL CODE
1.5K30A	OEM
1.5K30R	OEM
1.5K30RA	OEM
1.5K33	OEM
1.5K33A	OEM
1.5K33R	OEM
1.5K33RA	OEM
1.5K36	OEM
1.5K36A	OEM
1.5K36R	OEM
1.5K36RA	OEM
1.5K39	OEM
1.5K39A	OEM
1.5K39R	OEM
1.5K39RA	OEM
1.5K43	OEM
1.5K43A	OEM
1.5K43R	OEM
1.5K43RA	OEM
1.5K47	OEM
1.5K47A	OEM
1.5K47R	OEM
1.5K47RA	OEM
1.5K51	0563
1.5K51A	0563
1.5K51R	0563
1.5K51RA	0563
1.5K56	OEM
1.5K56A	OEM
1.5K56R	OEM
1.5K56RA	OEM
1.5K62	OEM
1.5K62A	OEM
1.5K62R	OEM
1.5K62RA	OEM
1.5K68	0825
1.5K68A	0825
1.5K68R	0825
1.5K68RA	0825
1.5K75	OEM
1.5K75(1N5654)	OEM
1.5K75A	OEM
1.5K75R	OEM
1.5K75RA	OEM
1.5K82	OEM
1.5K82A	OEM
1.5K82R	OEM
1.5K82RA	OEM
1.5K91	OEM
1.5K91A	OEM
1.5K91R	OEM
1.5K91RA	OEM
1.5K100	OEM
1.5K100A	OEM
1.5K100R	OEM
1.5K100RA	OEM
1.5K110	OEM
1.5K110A	OEM
1.5K110R	OEM
1.5K110RA	OEM
1.5K120	OEM
1.5K120A	OEM
1.5K120R	OEM
1.5K120RA	OEM
1.5K130	OEM
1.5K130A	OEM
1.5K130R	OEM
1.5K130RA	OEM
1.5K150	OEM
1.5K150A	OEM
1.5K150R	OEM
1.5K150RA	OEM
1.5K160	OEM
1.5K160A	OEM
1.5K160R	OEM
1.5K160RA	OEM
1.5K170	OEM
1.5K170A	OEM
1.5K170R	OEM
1.5K170RA	OEM
1.5K180	OEM
1.5K180A	OEM
1.5K180R	OEM
1.5K180RA	OEM
1.5K200	1395
1.5K200A	1395
1.5K200R	1395
1.5K200RA	1395
1.5KC6.8	OEM
1.5KC6.8A	3085
1.5KC7.5	OEM
1.5KC7.5A	OEM
1.5KC7.5C	OEM
1.5KC7.5CA	OEM
1.5KC8.2	OEM
1.5KC8.2A	OEM
1.5KC8.2C	OEM
1.5KC8.2CA	OEM
1.5KC9.1	OEM
1.5KC9.1A	OEM
1.5KC9.1C	OEM
1.5KC9.1CA	OEM
1.5KC10	OEM
1.5KC10A	OEM
1.5KC10C	OEM
1.5KC10CA	OEM
1.5KC11	OEM
1.5KC11A	OEM
1.5KC11C	OEM

DEVICE TYPE	REPL CODE
1.5KC11CA	OEM
1.5KC12	OEM
1.5KC12A	OEM
1.5KC13	OEM
1.5KC13A	3143
1.5KC15	OEM
1.5KC15A	OEM
1.5KC16	OEM
1.5KC16A	OEM
1.5KC18	OEM
1.5KC18A	3162
1.5KC20	OEM
1.5KC20A	3171
1.5KC22	OEM
1.5KC22A	OEM
1.5KC24	OEM
1.5KC24A	OEM
1.5KC27	OEM
1.5KC27A	1904
1.5KC30	OEM
1.5KC30A	OEM
1.5KC33	OEM
1.5KC33A	OEM
1.5KC36	OEM
1.5KC36A	OEM
1.5KC39	OEM
1.5KC39A	OEM
1.5KC43	OEM
1.5KC43A	OEM
1.5KC47	OEM
1.5KC47A	OEM
1.5KC51	OEM
1.5KC51A	0563
1.5KC56	OEM
1.5KC56A	OEM
1.5KC62	OEM
1.5KC62A	OEM
1.5KC68	OEM
1.5KC68A	0825
1.5KC75	OEM
1.5KC75A	OEM
1.5KC82	OEM
1.5KC82A	OEM
1.5KC91	OEM
1.5KC91A	OEM
1.5KC100	OEM
1.5KC100A	OEM
1.5KC110	OEM
1.5KC110A	OEM
1.5KE6V8A	OEM
1.5KE6V8CA	OEM
1.5KE6V8CP	OEM
1.5KE6V8P	OEM
1.5KE6.8	3085
1.5KE6.8A	3085
1.5KE6.8C	2120
1.5KE6.8CA	2120
1.5KE7V5A	OEM
1.5KE7V5CA	OEM
1.5KE7V5CP	OEM
1.5KE7V5P	OEM
1.5KE7.5	OEM
1.5KE7.5A	OEM
1.5KE7.5C	OEM
1.5KE7.5CA	OEM
1.5KE8V2A	OEM
1.5KE8V2CA	OEM
1.5KE8V2CP	OEM
1.5KE8V2P	OEM
1.5KE8.2	OEM
1.5KE8.2A	OEM
1.5KE8.2C	OEM
1.5KE8.2CA	OEM
1.5KE9V1A	OEM
1.5KE9V1CA	OEM
1.5KE9V1CP	OEM
1.5KE9V1P	OEM
1.5KE9.1	OEM
1.5KE9.1A	OEM
1.5KE9.1C	OEM
1.5KE9.1CA	OEM
1.5KE10	OEM
1.5KE10A	OEM
1.5KE10C	OEM
1.5KE10CA	OEM
1.5KE10CP	OEM
1.5KE10P	OEM
1.5KE11	OEM
1.5KE11A	OEM
1.5KE11C	OEM
1.5KE11CA	OEM
1.5KE11CP	OEM
1.5KE11P	OEM
1.5KE12	OEM
1.5KE12A	OEM
1.5KE12C	OEM
1.5KE12CA	OEM
1.5KE12CP	OEM
1.5KE12P	OEM
1.5KE13	3143
1.5KE13A	3143
1.5KE13C	1161
1.5KE13CA	1161
1.5KE13CP	OEM
1.5KE13P	OEM
1.5KE15	OEM
1.5KE15A	OEM
1.5KE15C	OEM
1.5KE15CA	OEM

DEVICE TYPE	REPL CODE
1.5KE15CP	OEM
1.5KE15P	OEM
1.5KE16	OEM
1.5KE16A	OEM
1.5KE16C	OEM
1.5KE16CA	OEM
1.5KE16CP	OEM
1.5KE16P	OEM
1.5KE18	3162
1.5KE18A	3162
1.5KE18C	1756
1.5KE18CA	1756
1.5KE18CP	OEM
1.5KE18P	OEM
1.5KE20	3171
1.5KE20A	3171
1.5KE20C	1921
1.5KE20CA	1921
1.5KE20CP	OEM
1.5KE20P	OEM
1.5KE22	OEM
1.5KE22A	OEM
1.5KE22C	OEM
1.5KE22CA	OEM
1.5KE22CP	OEM
1.5KE22P	OEM
1.5KE24	OEM
1.5KE24A	OEM
1.5KE24C	OEM
1.5KE24CA	OEM
1.5KE24CP	OEM
1.5KE24P	OEM
1.5KE27	1904
1.5KE27A	1904
1.5KE27C	1941
1.5KE27CA	1941
1.5KE27CP	OEM
1.5KE27P	OEM
1.5KE30	OEM
1.5KE30A	OEM
1.5KE30C	OEM
1.5KE30CA	OEM
1.5KE30CP	OEM
1.5KE30P	OEM
1.5KE33	OEM
1.5KE33A	OEM
1.5KE33C	OEM
1.5KE33CA	OEM
1.5KE33CP	OEM
1.5KE33P	OEM
1.5KE36	OEM
1.5KE36A	OEM
1.5KE36C	OEM
1.5KE36CA	OEM
1.5KE36CP	OEM
1.5KE36P	OEM
1.5KE39	OEM
1.5KE39A	OEM
1.5KE39C	OEM
1.5KE39CA	OEM
1.5KE39CP	OEM
1.5KE39P	OEM
1.5KE43	OEM
1.5KE43A	OEM
1.5KE43C	OEM
1.5KE43CA	OEM
1.5KE43CP	OEM
1.5KE43P	OEM
1.5KE47	OEM
1.5KE47A	OEM
1.5KE47C	OEM
1.5KE47CA	OEM
1.5KE47CP	OEM
1.5KE47P	OEM
1.5KE51	0563
1.5KE51A	0563
1.5KE51C	1961
1.5KE51CA	1961
1.5KE51CP	OEM
1.5KE51P	OEM
1.5KE56	OEM
1.5KE56A	OEM
1.5KE56C	OEM
1.5KE56CA	OEM
1.5KE56CP	OEM
1.5KE56P	OEM
1.5KE62	OEM
1.5KE62A	OEM
1.5KE62C	OEM
1.5KE62CA	OEM
1.5KE62CP	OEM
1.5KE62P	OEM
1.5KE68	0825
1.5KE68A	0825
1.5KE68C	1976
1.5KE68CA	1976
1.5KE68CP	OEM
1.5KE68P	OEM
1.5KE75	OEM
1.5KE75A	OEM
1.5KE75C	OEM
1.5KE75CA	OEM
1.5KE75CP	OEM
1.5KE75P	OEM
1.5KE82	OEM
1.5KE82A	OEM
1.5KE82C	OEM
1.5KE82CA	OEM
1.5KE82CP	OEM

DEVICE TYPE	REPL CODE
1.5KE82P	OEM
1.5KE91	OEM
1.5KE91A	OEM
1.5KE91C	OEM
1.5KE91CA	OEM
1.5KE91CP	OEM
1.5KE91P	OEM
1.5KE100	OEM
1.5KE100A	OEM
1.5KE100C	OEM
1.5KE100CA	OEM
1.5KE100CP	OEM
1.5KE100P	OEM
1.5KE110	OEM
1.5KE110A	OEM
1.5KE110C	OEM
1.5KE110CA	OEM
1.5KE110CP	OEM
1.5KE110P	OEM
1.5KE120	OEM
1.5KE120A	OEM
1.5KE120C	OEM
1.5KE120CA	OEM
1.5KE120CP	OEM
1.5KE120P	OEM
1.5KE130	OEM
1.5KE130A	OEM
1.5KE130C	OEM
1.5KE130CA	OEM
1.5KE130CP	OEM
1.5KE130P	OEM
1.5KE150	OEM
1.5KE150A	OEM
1.5KE150C	OEM
1.5KE150CA	OEM
1.5KE160	OEM
1.5KE160A	OEM
1.5KE160C	OEM
1.5KE160CA	OEM
1.5KE170	OEM
1.5KE170A	OEM
1.5KE170C	OEM
1.5KE170CA	OEM
1.5KE180	OEM
1.5KE180A	OEM
1.5KE180C	OEM
1.5KE180CA	OEM
1.5KE180CP	OEM
1.5KE200	1395
1.5KE200A	1395
1.5KE200C	1398
1.5KE200CA	1398
1.5KE200CP	OEM
1.5KE200P	OEM
1.5KE220	OEM
1.5KE220A	OEM
1.5KE220C	OEM
1.5KE220CA	OEM
1.5KE220CP	OEM
1.5KE220P	OEM
1.5KE250	OEM
1.5KE250A	OEM
1.5KE250C	OEM
1.5KE250CA	OEM
1.5KE250CP	OEM
1.5KE250P	OEM
1.5KE280	OEM
1.5KE280A	OEM
1.5KE280CA	OEM
1.5KE280CP	OEM
1.5KE280P	OEM
1.5KE300	OEM
1.5KE300A	OEM
1.5KE300CA	OEM
1.5KE300CP	OEM
1.5KE300P	OEM
1.5KE320	OEM
1.5KE320A	OEM
1.5KE320CA	OEM
1.5KE320CP	OEM
1.5KE320P	OEM
1.5KE350	OEM
1.5KE350A	OEM
1.5KE350CA	OEM
1.5KE350CP	OEM
1.5KE350P	OEM
1.5KE400	OEM
1.5KE400A	OEM
1.5KE400CA	OEM
1.5KE400CP	OEM
1.5KE400P	OEM
1.5KE440	OEM
1.5KE440A	OEM
1.5KE440CA	OEM
1.5KE440CP	OEM
1.5KE440P	OEM
1.5L56A	OEM
1.5M14Z	1387
1.5M14Z5	1387
1.5M14Z10	1387
1.5M17Z	1170
1.5M17Z5	1170
1.5M17Z10	1170
1.5M19Z	2379
1.5M19Z5	2379
1.5M19Z10	2379
1.5M25Z	2383
1.5M25Z5	2383
1.5M25Z10	2383

If replacement code is OEM, contact original manufacturer for replacement.

DEVICE TYPE	REPL CODE
1.5M140Z	1870
1.5M140Z5	1870
1.5M140Z10	1870
1.5R7.5	0475
1.5R7.5A	0475
1.5R7.5B	0475
1.5R8.2	0499
1.5R8.2A	0499
1.5R8.2B	0499
1.5R9.1	0679
1.5R9.1A	0679
1.5R9.1B	0679
1.5R10	0225
1.5R10A	0225
1.5R10B	0225
1.5R11	0230
1.5R11A	0230
1.5R11B	0230
1.5R12	0234
1.5R12A	0234
1.5R12B	0234
1.5R13	0237
1.5R13A	0237
1.5R13B	0237
1.5R15	0247
1.5R15A	0247
1.5R15B	0247
1.5R16	0251
1.5R16A	0251
1.5R16B	0251
1.5R18	0256
1.5R18A	0256
1.5R18B	0256
1.5R20	0262
1.5R20A	0262
1.5R20B	0262
1.5R22	0269
1.5R22A	0269
1.5R22B	0269
1.5R24	0273
1.5R24A	0273
1.5R24B	0273
1.5R27	0291
1.5R27A	0291
1.5R27B	0291
1.5R30	0305
1.5R30A	0305
1.5R30B	0305
1.5R31	0322
1.5R33	0314
1.5R33A	0314
1.5R33B	0314
1.5R36	0316
1.5R36A	0316
1.5R36B	0316
1.5R39A	0322
1.5R39B	0322
1.5R43	0333
1.5R43A	0333
1.5R43B	0333
1.5R47	0343
1.5R47A	0343
1.5R47B	0343
1.5R51	0027
1.5R51A	0027
1.5R51B	0027
1.5R56	0266
1.5R56A	0266
1.5R56B	0266
1.5R62	0382
1.5R62A	0382
1.5R62B	0382
1.5R68	0401
1.5R68A	0401
1.5R68B	0401
1.5R91	0238
1.5R91A	0238
1.5R91B	0238
1.5R100	1172
1.5R100A	1172
1.5R100B	1172
1.5R110	1182
1.5R110A	1182
1.5R110B	1182
1.5R120	1198
1.5R120A	1198
1.5R120B	1198
1.5R130	1209
1.5R130A	1209
1.5R130B	1209
1.5R140	1870
1.5R140A	1870
1.5R140B	1870
1.5R150	0642
1.5R150A	0642
1.5R150B	0642
1.5R160	1246
1.5R160A	1246
1.5R160B	1246
1.5R180	1269
1.5R180A	1269
1.5R180B	1269
1.5R200	0600
1.5R200A	0600
1.5R200B	0600
1.5S220	OEM
1.5S220A	OEM
1.5S250	OEM
1.5S250A	OEM

DEVICE TYPE	REPL CODE
1.5S300	OEM
1.5S300A	OEM
1.5S350	OEM
1.5S350A	OEM
1.5S400	OEM
1.5S400A	OEM
1.5SE6.8	3085
1.5SE6.8A	3085
1.5SE7.5	OEM
1.5SE7.5A	OEM
1.5SE8.2	OEM
1.5SE8.2A	OEM
1.5SE9.1	OEM
1.5SE9.1A	OEM
1.5SE10	OEM
1.5SE10A	OEM
1.5SE11	OEM
1.5SE11A	OEM
1.5SE12	OEM
1.5SE12A	OEM
1.5SE13	3143
1.5SE13A	3143
1.5SE15	OEM
1.5SE15A	OEM
1.5SE16	OEM
1.5SE16A	OEM
1.5SE18	3162
1.5SE18A	3162
1.5SE20	3171
1.5SE20A	3171
1.5SE22	OEM
1.5SE22A	OEM
1.5SE24	OEM
1.5SE24A	OEM
1.5SE27	1904
1.5SE27A	1904
1.5SE30	OEM
1.5SE30A	OEM
1.5SE33	OEM
1.5SE33A	OEM
1.5SE36	OEM
1.5SE36A	OEM
1.5SE39	OEM
1.5SE39A	OEM
1.5SE43	OEM
1.5SE43A	OEM
1.5SE47	OEM
1.5SE47A	OEM
1.5SE51	0563
1.5SE51A	0563
1.5SE56	OEM
1.5SE56A	OEM
1.5SE62	OEM
1.5SE62A	OEM
1.5SE68	0825
1.5SE68A	0825
1.5SE75	OEM
1.5SE75A	OEM
1.5SE82	OEM
1.5SE82A	OEM
1.5SE91	OEM
1.5SE91A	OEM
1.5SE100	OEM
1.5SE100A	OEM
1.5SE110	OEM
1.5SE110A	OEM
1.5SE120	OEM
1.5SE120A	OEM
1.5SE130	OEM
1.5SE130A	OEM
1.5SE150	OEM
1.5SE150A	OEM
1.5SE160	OEM
1.5SE160A	OEM
1.5SE170	OEM
1.5SE170A	OEM
1.5SE180	OEM
1.5SE180A	OEM
1.5SE200	1395
1.5SE200A	1395
1.5SE220	OEM
1.5SE220A	OEM
1.5SE250	OEM
1.5SE250A	OEM
1.5SE300	OEM
1.5SE300A	OEM
1.5SE350	OEM
1.5SE350A	OEM
1.5SE400	OEM
1.5SE400A	OEM
1.5X52D5	OEM
1.5X180A	OEM
1.5Z6.8	0205
1.5Z6.8A	0205
1.5Z6.8B	0205
1.5Z6.8C	0205
1.5Z6.8D	0205
1.5Z7.5	0475
1.5Z7.5A	0475
1.5Z7.5B	0475
1.5Z7.5C	0475
1.5Z7.5D	0475
1.5Z8.2	0499
1.5Z8.2A	0499
1.5Z8.2B	0499
1.5Z8.2C	0499
1.5Z8.2D	0499
1.5Z9.1	0679
1.5Z9.1A	0679

DEVICE TYPE	REPL CODE
1.5Z9.1B	0679
1.5Z9.1C	0679
1.5Z9.1D	0679
1.5Z10	0225
1.5Z10A	0225
1.5Z10B	0225
1.5Z10C	0225
1.5Z10D	0225
1.5Z11	0230
1.5Z11A	0230
1.5Z11B	0230
1.5Z11C	0230
1.5Z11D	0230
1.5Z12	0234
1.5Z12A	0234
1.5Z12B	0234
1.5Z12C	0234
1.5Z12D	0234
1.5Z13	0237
1.5Z13A	0237
1.5Z13B	0237
1.5Z13C	0237
1.5Z13D	0237
1.5Z14	1387
1.5Z14A	1387
1.5Z14B	1387
1.5Z14C	1387
1.5Z14D	1387
1.5Z15	0247
1.5Z15A	0247
1.5Z15B	0247
1.5Z15C	0247
1.5Z15D	0247
1.5Z16	0251
1.5Z16A	0251
1.5Z16B	0251
1.5Z16C	0251
1.5Z16D	0251
1.5Z17	1170
1.5Z17A	1170
1.5Z17B	1170
1.5Z17C	1170
1.5Z17D	1170
1.5Z17D5	1170
1.5Z17D10	1170
1.5Z18	0256
1.5Z18A	0256
1.5Z18B	0256
1.5Z18C	0256
1.5Z18D	0256
1.5Z19	2379
1.5Z19A	2379
1.5Z19B	2379
1.5Z19C	2379
1.5Z19D	2379
1.5Z19D5	2379
1.5Z19D10	2379
1.5Z20	0262
1.5Z20A	0262
1.5Z20B	0262
1.5Z20C	0262
1.5Z20D	0262
1.5Z22	0269
1.5Z22A	0269
1.5Z22B	0269
1.5Z22C	0269
1.5Z22D	0269
1.5Z24	0273
1.5Z24A	0273
1.5Z24B	0273
1.5Z24C	0273
1.5Z24D	0273
1.5Z25	2383
1.5Z25A	2383
1.5Z25B	2383
1.5Z25C	2383
1.5Z25D	2383
1.5Z25D5	2383
1.5Z25D10	2383
1.5Z27	0291
1.5Z27A	0291
1.5Z27B	0291
1.5Z27C	0291
1.5Z27D	0291
1.5Z30	0305
1.5Z30A	0305
1.5Z30B	0305
1.5Z30C	0305
1.5Z30D	0305
1.5Z31C	0322
1.5Z33	0314
1.5Z33A	0314
1.5Z33B	0314
1.5Z33C	0314
1.5Z33D	0314
1.5Z36	0316
1.5Z36A	0316
1.5Z36B	0316
1.5Z36C	0316
1.5Z36D	0316
1.5Z39	0322
1.5Z39A	0322
1.5Z39B	0322
1.5Z39C	0322
1.5Z39D	0322
1.5Z43	0333
1.5Z43A	0333
1.5Z43B	0333
1.5Z43C	0333

DEVICE TYPE	REPL CODE
1.5Z43D	0333
1.5Z45	0333
1.5Z45A	0333
1.5Z45B	0333
1.5Z45C	0333
1.5Z45D	0333
1.5Z45D5	0333
1.5Z47	0343
1.5Z47A	0343
1.5Z47B	0343
1.5Z47C	0343
1.5Z47D	0343
1.5Z50	0027
1.5Z50A	0027
1.5Z50B	0027
1.5Z50C	0027
1.5Z50D	0027
1.5Z50D5	0027
1.5Z50D10	0027
1.5Z51	0027
1.5Z51A	0027
1.5Z51B	0027
1.5Z51C	0027
1.5Z51D	0027
1.5Z52	0027
1.5Z52A	0027
1.5Z52B	0027
1.5Z52C	0027
1.5Z52D	0027
1.5Z52D10	0027
1.5Z56	0266
1.5Z56A	0266
1.5Z56B	0266
1.5Z56C	0266
1.5Z56D	0266
1.5Z62	0382
1.5Z62A	0382
1.5Z62B	0382
1.5Z62C	0382
1.5Z62D	0382
1.5Z68	0401
1.5Z68A	0401
1.5Z68B	0401
1.5Z68C	0401
1.5Z68D	0401
1.5Z75	0421
1.5Z75A	0421
1.5Z75B	0421
1.5Z75C	0421
1.5Z75D	0421
1.5Z82	0439
1.5Z82A	0439
1.5Z82B	0439
1.5Z82C	0439
1.5Z82D	0439
1.5Z91	0238
1.5Z91A	0238
1.5Z91B	0238
1.5Z91C	0238
1.5Z91D	0238
1.5Z100	1172
1.5Z100A	1172
1.5Z100B	1172
1.5Z100C	1172
1.5Z100D	1172
1.5Z105	1172
1.5Z105A	1172
1.5Z105B	1172
1.5Z105C	1172
1.5Z105D	1172
1.5Z105D5	0247
1.5Z105D10	1172
1.5Z110	1182
1.5Z110A	1182
1.5Z110B	1182
1.5Z110C	1182
1.5Z110D	1182
1.5Z120	1198
1.5Z120A	1198
1.5Z120B	1198
1.5Z120C	1198
1.5Z120D	1198
1.5Z130	1209
1.5Z130A	1209
1.5Z130B	1209
1.5Z130C	1209
1.5Z130D	1209
1.5Z140	1870
1.5Z140A	1870
1.5Z140B	1870
1.5Z140C	1870
1.5Z140D	1870
1.5Z140D5	1870
1.5Z140D10	1870
1.5Z150	0642
1.5Z150A	0642
1.5Z150B	0642
1.5Z150C	0642
1.5Z150D	0642
1.5Z160	1246
1.5Z160A	1246
1.5Z160B	1246
1.5Z160C	1246
1.5Z160D	1246
1.5Z175	2091
1.5Z175A	2091
1.5Z175B	2091
1.5Z175C	2091
1.5Z175D	2091

DEVICE TYPE	REPL CODE
1.5Z175D5	2091
1.5Z175D10	2091
1.5Z180	1269
1.5Z180A	1269
1.5Z180B	1269
1.5Z180C	1269
1.5Z180D	1269
1.5Z200	0600
1.5Z200A	0600
1.5Z200B	0600
1.5Z200C	0600
1.5Z200D	0600
1.5Z220	OEM
1.5Z220A	OEM
1.5Z220B	OEM
1.5Z220C	OEM
1.5Z220D	OEM
1.25AGD	OEM
1.ZZ9.1	OEM
2(3395	0079
2-00020-327F	0315
2-00037-955	0160
2-00045-345	0079
2-00045-424	0079
2-0A70	OEM
2-0A90	0123
2-0A90-H	0143
2-1K60	0143
2-1K261	0143
2-5SR3	0079
2-80	0911
2-131	2955
2-136	2955
2-140	2955
2-140-01	2955
2-312	OEM
2-412	OEM
2-5004-6	2006
2-5004-14	2007
2-5184-11	0147
2-D2K	0015
2-D2L	0015
2-D2R	0015
2-0A90	0143
2-0A90-M	0143
2-0A90A	0143
2-0A90A-H	0143
2-0A90A-M	0143
2-0A99	0143
2-0A99A	0143
2A	0136
2A1/18	OEM
2A1/52	OEM
2A2/18	OEM
2A2/52	OEM
2A5/18	OEM
2A5/52	OEM
2A12	0126
2A12/18	OEM
2A12/52	OEM
2A13	OEM
2A13/18	OEM
2A13/52	OEM
2A14	OEM
2A14/18	OEM
2A14/52	OEM
2A15	OEM
2A15/18	OEM
2A15/52	OEM
2A16	OEM
2A16/18	OEM
2A16/52	OEM
2A21	0041
2A21(ZENER)	0041
2A22	0041
2A22(ZENER)	0041
2A22/18	OEM
2A23	OEM
2A23/18	OEM
2A24	OEM
2A24/18	OEM
2A25	0188
2A25/18	OEM
2A26	OEM
2A26/18	OEM
2A28(ZENER)	0118
2A30	0087
2A43	0672
2A46	0451
2A50	0124
2A52	OEM
2A52/18	OEM
2A53	OEM
2A53/18	OEM
2A54	OEM
2A54/18	OEM
2A55	OEM
2A55/18	OEM
2A56	OEM
2A56/18	OEM
2A64	0166
2A100	0087
2A112	OEM
2A113	OEM
2A119	0143
2A200	0087
2A300	0071
2A400	0071
2A500	0071

DEVICE TYPE	REPL CODE
2A600	0071
2A800	0071
2A1000	0071
2A1200	0102
2AA112	0019
2AA113	0143
2AA116	0143
2AA117	OEM
2AA118	OEM
2AA119	0123
2AA119(MP)	0123
2AC127	OEM
2AC128	0136
2AC128-01	OEM
2AC132	0004
2AC187	0841
2AC188	0164
2AC188-01	OEM
2AD140	0160
2AD149	0265
2AD161	OEM
2AF1	0071
2AF1LH	OEM
2AF1LV	OEM
2AF2	0071
2AF2LH	OEM
2AF2LV	OEM
2AF4	0071
2AF4LH	OEM
2AF4LV	OEM
2AG	0007
2AH	0007
2AM-1	0934
2AS160	OEM
2AS429	OEM
2ASCP30	OEM
2ASCP40	OEM
2ASCP45	OEM
2ASCP120	OEM
2ASLD1	OEM
2ASLD2	OEM
2ASLD3	OEM
2ASLD4	OEM
2ASLD5	OEM
2ASLD6	OEM
2ASLD7	OEM
2ASLD8	OEM
2ASLD9	OEM
2ASLD10	OEM
2ASLD10TRA	OEM
2ASLD10TRB	OEM
2ASLD15	OEM
2ASLD15TR	OEM
2ASLD20	OEM
2ASLD25	OEM
2ASLD30	OEM
2ASLD35	OEM
2ASLD40	OEM
2ASLD40TR	OEM
2ASLD45	OEM
2ASLD50	OEM
2ASLD75	OEM
2ASLD100	OEM
2ASLD120	OEM
2ASPC1	OEM
2ASPC2	OEM
2ASPC3	OEM
2ASPC4	OEM
2ASPC5	OEM
2ASPC6	OEM
2ASPC7	OEM
2ASPC8	OEM
2ASPC9	OEM
2ASPC10	OEM
2ASPC15	OEM
2ASPC20	OEM
2ASPC25	OEM
2ASPC30	OEM
2ASPC35	OEM
2ASPC40	OEM
2ASPC45	OEM
2ASPC50	OEM
2ASPC75	OEM
2ASPC100	OEM
2ASPC120	OEM
2ASPF16	OEM
2ASPF20	OEM
2ASPF30	OEM
2ASPF40	OEM
2ASPF50	OEM
2ASPF60	OEM
2ASPF70	OEM
2ASPF80	OEM
2ASPF90	OEM
2ASPF100	OEM
2ASPF150	OEM
2ASPF200	OEM
2ASPF250	OEM
2ASPF300	OEM
2ASPF350	OEM
2ASPF400	OEM
2ASPF450	OEM
2ASPF500	OEM
2ASPF750	OEM
2ASPF1000	OEM
2ASPF1200	OEM
2ASPS16	OEM
2ASPS20	OEM
2ASPS30	OEM

DEVICE TYPE	REPL CODE
2ASPS40	OEM
2ASPS50	OEM
2ASPS60	OEM
2ASPS70	OEM
2ASPS80	OEM
2ASPS90	OEM
2ASPS100	OEM
2ASPS150	OEM
2ASPS200	OEM
2ASPS250	OEM
2ASPS300	OEM
2ASPS350	OEM
2ASPS400	OEM
2ASPS450	OEM
2ASPS500	OEM
2ASPS750	OEM
2ASPS1000	OEM
2ASPS1200	OEM
2ASZ15	OEM
2AT128	OEM
2AT329	OEM
2AT331	OEM
2ATPF16	OEM
2ATPF20	OEM
2ATPF30	OEM
2ATPF40	OEM
2ATPF50	OEM
2ATPF60	OEM
2ATPF70	OEM
2ATPF80	OEM
2ATPF90	OEM
2ATPF100	OEM
2ATPF150	OEM
2ATPF200	OEM
2ATPF250	OEM
2ATPF300	OEM
2ATPF350	OEM
2ATPF400	OEM
2ATPF450	OEM
2ATPF500	OEM
2ATPF750	OEM
2ATPF1000	OEM
2ATPF1200	OEM
2ATPH16	OEM
2ATPH20	OEM
2ATPH30	OEM
2ATPH40	OEM
2ATPH50	OEM
2ATPH60	OEM
2ATPH70	OEM
2ATPH80	OEM
2ATPH90	OEM
2ATPH100	OEM
2ATPH150	OEM
2ATPH200	OEM
2ATPH250	OEM
2ATPH300	OEM
2ATPH350	OEM
2ATPH400	OEM
2ATPH450	OEM
2ATPH500	OEM
2ATPH750	OEM
2ATPH1000	OEM
2ATPH1200	OEM
2AV2	1440
2AV30	OEM
2AV41	OEM
2B	0279
2B1/18	OEM
2B1/52	OEM
2B-2	0102
2B2/18	OEM
2B2/52	OEM
2B-2D10DE	0102
2B-2DIODE	0102
2B2DM	0276
2B2M	0276
2B2MS	0276
2B3.L	0319
2B4B41	0319
2B4DM	0287
2B4M	0287
2B4MS	0287
2B4.E	1404
2B5/18	OEM
2B5/52	OEM
2B6DM	0293
2B6M	0293
2B6MS	0293
2B8	OEM
2B8DM	0293
2B8M	0293
2B8MS	0293
2B10DM	0299
2B10M	0299
2B10MS	0299
2B12	OEM
2B12/18	OEM
2B12DM	0299
2B12DS	0299
2B12M	0250
2B12MS	0250
2B13	OEM
2B13/18	OEM
2B14	OEM
2B14/18	OEM
2B15	OEM
2B15/18	OEM
2B16	OEM

If replacement code is OEM, contact original manufacturer for replacement.

DEVICE TYPE	REPL CODE
2B16/18	OEM
2B16DM	0250
2B16M	0250
2B20A	OEM
2B20B	OEM
2B20DM	0250
2B20M	0250
2B22	OEM
2B22/18	OEM
2B22J	OEM
2B22K	OEM
2B22L	OEM
2B23	OEM
2B23/18	OEM
2B24	OEM
2B24/18	OEM
2B25	OEM
2B25/18	OEM
2B26	OEM
2B26/18	OEM
2B35J	OEM
2B35K	OEM
2B50B	OEM
2B50C	OEM
2B50FB	OEM
2B50FC	OEM
2B52	OEM
2B52/18	OEM
2B52A-1J01	OEM
2B52A-1J05	OEM
2B52A-1K01	OEM
2B52A-1K04	OEM
2B52A-1K06	OEM
2B52A-1T01	OEM
2B53	OEM
2B53/18	OEM
2B53A-1J01	OEM
2B53A-1J03	OEM
2B53A-1J05	OEM
2B53A-1K01	OEM
2B53A-1K04	OEM
2B53A-1K06	OEM
2B53A-1T01	OEM
2B53A-1T02	OEM
2B54	OEM
2B54/18	OEM
2B55	OEM
2B55/18	OEM
2B56	OEM
2B56/18	OEM
2B56A	OEM
2B57A	OEM
2B58A-1-1-01	OEM
2B58A-1-1-02	OEM
2B58A-1-1-03	OEM
2B58A-1-1-04	OEM
2B59A-0-1-01	OEM
2B59A-0-1-02	OEM
2B59A-0-1-03	OEM
2B59A-0-1-04	OEM
2B59A-02-01	OEM
2B59A-02-02	OEM
2B59A-02-03	OEM
2B59A-02-04	OEM
2B1202	0435
2BA2	1440
2BC119	OEM
2BC138	OEM
2BC139	OEM
2BC142	OEM
2BC143	OEM
2BC144	OEM
2BC221	OEM
2BC222	OEM
2BC286	OEM
2BC288	OEM
2BD117	OEM
2BD181	1506
2BD182	OEM
2BD183	1506
2BDY20	OEM
2BDY38	OEM
2B-E	OEM
2BG2C41	0199
2BG2Z41	1009
2BZ61	OEM
2C	0279
2C05	0087
2C05/18	OEM
2C05/52	OEM
2C054	OEM
2C054/18	OEM
2C055	OEM
2C055/18	OEM
2C056	OEM
2C056/18	OEM
2C057	OEM
2C057/18	OEM
2C1	OEM
2C1/18	OEM
2C1/52	OEM
2C2	OEM
2C2/18	OEM
2C2/52	OEM
2C2DM	0199
2C2M	0199
2C4-6S	OEM
2C4DM	0199
2C4M	0199

DEVICE TYPE	REPL CODE
2C6	0087
2C6-7S	OEM
2C6DM	0199
2C6M	0199
2C8	0087
2C8DM	0199
2C8M	0199
2C10	0087
2C10DM	0199
2C10M	0199
2C12	OEM
2C12DM	0199
2C12M	0199
2C13B	0237
2C14	OEM
2C14/18	OEM
2C15	OEM
2C15/18	OEM
2C16	OEM
2C16/18	OEM
2C16DM	0199
2C16M	0199
2C17	OEM
2C17/18	OEM
2C18	OEM
2C20	OEM
2C20DM	0199
2C20M	0199
2C24	OEM
2C24/18	OEM
2C25	OEM
2C25/18	OEM
2C26	OEM
2C26/18	OEM
2C27	OEM
2C27/18	OEM
2C34	OEM
2C91G	0595
2C111	OEM
2C415	OEM
2C425	OEM
2C444	OEM
2C918	OEM
2C2102	OEM
2C2222A	OEM
2C2369A	OEM
2C2484	OEM
2C2546	OEM
2C2857	OEM
2C2894	OEM
2C2907A	OEM
2C2946	OEM
2C3303	OEM
2C3308	OEM
2C3439	OEM
2C3468	OEM
2C3501	OEM
2C3506	OEM
2C3511	OEM
2C3553	OEM
2C3635	OEM
2C3724	OEM
2C3762	OEM
2C3767	OEM
2C3796	OEM
2C3799	OEM
2C3866	OEM
2C3868	OEM
2C3904	OEM
2C3906	OEM
2C3960	OEM
2C4091	OEM
2C4117	OEM
2C4220	OEM
2C4261	OEM
2C4352	OEM
2C4405	OEM
2C4416	OEM
2C4427	OEM
2C4900	OEM
2C4920	OEM
2C4923	OEM
2C4957	OEM
2C5031	OEM
2C5038	OEM
2C5108	OEM
2C5109	OEM
2C5160	OEM
2C5179	OEM
2C5192	OEM
2C5195	OEM
2C5208	OEM
2C5339	OEM
2C5345	OEM
2C5401	OEM
2C5416	OEM
2C5462	OEM
2C5551	OEM
2C5583	OEM
2C5631	OEM
2C5641	OEM
2C5642	OEM
2C5680	OEM
2C5682	OEM
2C5760	OEM
2C5836	OEM
2C5841	OEM
2CN3	1296
2CS537FC	0111

DEVICE TYPE	REPL CODE
2CY30	0855
2CY31	0855
2CY32	0855
2CY33	0855
2CY34	0855
2CY38	0037
2CY39	0037
2CZ6.8	OEM
2CZ6.8A	OEM
2CZ6.8B	OEM
2CZ7.5	OEM
2CZ7.5A	OEM
2CZ7.5B	OEM
2CZ8.2	OEM
2CZ8.2A	OEM
2CZ8.2B	OEM
2CZ9.1	OEM
2CZ9.1A	OEM
2CZ9.1B	OEM
2CZ10	OEM
2CZ10A	OEM
2CZ10B	OEM
2CZ11	OEM
2CZ11A	OEM
2CZ11B	OEM
2CZ12	OEM
2CZ12A	OEM
2CZ12B	OEM
2CZ13	OEM
2CZ13A	OEM
2CZ13B	OEM
2CZ15	OEM
2CZ15A	OEM
2CZ15B	OEM
2CZ16	OEM
2CZ16A	OEM
2CZ16B	OEM
2CZ18	OEM
2CZ18A	OEM
2CZ18B	OEM
2CZ20	OEM
2CZ20A	OEM
2CZ20B	OEM
2CZ22	OEM
2CZ22A	OEM
2CZ22B	OEM
2CZ24	OEM
2CZ24A	OEM
2CZ24B	OEM
2CZ27	OEM
2CZ27A	OEM
2CZ27B	OEM
2CZ30	OEM
2CZ30A	OEM
2CZ30B	OEM
2CZ33	OEM
2CZ33A	OEM
2CZ33B	OEM
2CZ36	OEM
2CZ36A	OEM
2CZ36B	OEM
2CZ39	OEM
2CZ39A	OEM
2CZ39B	OEM
2CZ43	OEM
2CZ43A	OEM
2CZ43B	OEM
2CZ47	OEM
2CZ47A	OEM
2CZ47B	OEM
2CZ51	OEM
2CZ51A	OEM
2CZ51B	OEM
2CZ56	OEM
2CZ56A	OEM
2CZ56B	OEM
2CZ62	OEM
2CZ62A	OEM
2CZ62B	OEM
2CZ68	OEM
2CZ68A	OEM
2CZ68B	OEM
2CZ75	OEM
2CZ75A	OEM
2CZ75B	OEM
2CZ82	OEM
2CZ82A	OEM
2CZ82B	OEM
2CZ91	OEM
2CZ91A	OEM
2CZ91B	OEM
2CZ100	OEM
2CZ100A	OEM
2CZ100B	OEM
2CZ110	OEM
2CZ110A	OEM
2CZ110B	OEM
2CZ120	OEM
2CZ120A	OEM
2CZ120B	OEM
2CZ130	OEM
2CZ130A	OEM
2CZ130B	OEM
2CZ150	OEM
2CZ150A	OEM
2CZ150B	OEM
2CZ160	OEM
2CZ160A	OEM
2CZ160B	OEM

DEVICE TYPE	REPL CODE
2CZ170	OEM
2CZ170A	OEM
2CZ170B	OEM
2CZ180	OEM
2CZ180A	OEM
2CZ180B	OEM
2CZ200	OEM
2CZ200A	OEM
2CZ200B	OEM
2D	0279
2D001	0160
2D002	0079
2D002-41	0079
2D002-168	0016
2D002-169	0016
2D002-170	0079
2D002-171	0283
2D002-175	0079
2D004	0160
2D004-9	0160
2D010	0103
2D013-13	0211
2D013-54	0211
2D013-109	0211
2D013-160	0211
2D016	0211
2D016-45	0211
2D016-54	0211
2D017-165	0037
2D017-166	0037
2D017-167	0037
2D017-169	0037
2D020-173	0855
2D020-174	0855
2D021	0279
2D021-8	0279
2D021-11	0279
2D021-56	0279
2D022	1659
2D022-211	1659
2D023	0211
2D026	0079
2D026-274	0079
2D027	0037
2D030	1882
2D031	2922
2D033	0155
2D036	0004
2D038	0470
2D039	0004
2D040	0187
2D1	OEM
2D1PDA	OEM
2D4B41	OEM
2D7A	0098
2D7AM	0098
2D41	1129
2D600M	OEM
2DB2A	0287
2DB4A	0293
2DB6A	0299
2DF12	OEM
2DG2	0143
2DG2C41	0199
2DG2Z41	1009
2DL8	OEM
2DL10	OEM
2DL-15	0102
2DL15	0017
2DL15A	0017
2DL18A	0344
2DL20	OEM
2D021-56	0164
2D023	0164
2D033	0079
2DS24YD	0142
2DS500	OEM
2DS503	OEM
2DS506	OEM
2E	0136
2E05	0015
2E1	0015
2E2	0087
2E2DM	1009
2E4	0015
2E4DM	1009
2E6	0087
2E6DM	1009
2E8	0087
2E8DM	1009
2E10	0087
2E10DM	1009
2E12	OEM
2E12DM	1009
2E14	OEM
2E16	OEM
2E16DM	1009
2E18	OEM
2E20	OEM
2E20DM	1009
2E40A	OEM
2EM03	0071
2EM05	0071
2EM015	0087
2EM1	OEM
2EM2	OEM
2EM3	OEM
2EM4	OEM
2EM5	OEM

DEVICE TYPE	REPL CODE
2EM6	0087
2EM8	0087
2EM10	0087
2EM12	OEM
2EZ3.6D	0791
2EZ3.6D5	0791
2EZ3.6D10	0791
2EZ3.9D	0801
2EZ3.9D5	0801
2EZ3.9D10	0801
2EZ4.3D	0815
2EZ4.3D5	0815
2EZ4.3D10	0815
2EZ4.7D	0827
2EZ4.7D5	0827
2EZ4.7D10	0827
2EZ5.1D	0437
2EZ5.1D5	0437
2EZ5.1D10	0437
2EZ5.6D	0870
2EZ5.6D5	0870
2EZ5.6D10	0870
2EZ6.2D	0185
2EZ6.2D5	0185
2EZ6.2D10	0185
2EZ6.3D10	OEM
2EZ6.8D	0205
2EZ6.8D5	0205
2EZ6.8D10	0205
2EZ7.5D	0475
2EZ7.5D5	0475
2EZ7.5D10	0475
2EZ8.2D	0499
2EZ8.2D5	0499
2EZ8.2D10	0499
2EZ9.1D	0679
2EZ9.1D5	0679
2EZ9.1D10	0679
2EZ10D	0225
2EZ10D5	0225
2EZ10D10	0225
2EZ11D	0230
2EZ11D5	0230
2EZ11D10	0230
2EZ12D	0234
2EZ12D5	0234
2EZ12D10	0234
2EZ13D	0237
2EZ13D5	0237
2EZ13D10	0237
2EZ14D	1387
2EZ14D5	1387
2EZ14D10	1387
2EZ15D	0247
2EZ15D5	0247
2EZ15D10	0247
2EZ16D	0251
2EZ16D5	0251
2EZ16D10	0251
2EZ17D	1170
2EZ17D5	1170
2EZ17D10	1170
2EZ18D	0256
2EZ18D5	0256
2EZ18D10	0256
2EZ19D	2379
2EZ19D5	2379
2EZ19D10	2379
2EZ20D	0262
2EZ20D5	0262
2EZ20D10	0262
2EZ22D	0269
2EZ22D5	0269
2EZ22D10	0269
2EZ24C	0273
2EZ24D	0273
2EZ24D5	0273
2EZ24D10	0273
2EZ27D	0291
2EZ27D5	0291
2EZ27D10	0291
2EZ30D	0305
2EZ30D5	0305
2EZ30D10	0305
2EZ33D	0314
2EZ33D5	0314
2EZ33D10	0314
2EZ36D	0316
2EZ36D5	0316
2EZ36D10	0316
2EZ39D	0322
2EZ39D5	0322
2EZ39D10	0322
2EZ43D	0333
2EZ43D5	0333
2EZ43D10	0333
2EZ47D	0343
2EZ47D5	0343
2EZ47D10	0343
2EZ51D	0027
2EZ51D5	0027
2EZ51D10	0027
2EZ56D	0266
2EZ56D5	0266
2EZ56D10	0266
2EZ62D	0382
2EZ62D5	0382
2EZ62D10	0382
2EZ68D	0401

DEVICE TYPE	REPL CODE
2EZ68D5	0401
2EZ68D10	0401
2EZ75D	0421
2EZ75D5	0499
2EZ75D10	0421
2EZ82D	0439
2EZ82D5	0439
2EZ82D10	0439
2EZ91D	0238
2EZ91D5	0238
2EZ91D10	0238
2EZ100D	1172
2EZ100D5	1172
2EZ100D10	1172
2EZ110D	1182
2EZ110D5	1182
2EZ110D10	1182
2EZ120D	1198
2EZ120D5	1198
2EZ120D10	1198
2EZ130D	1209
2EZ130D5	1209
2EZ130D10	1209
2EZ140D	1870
2EZ140D5	1870
2EZ140D10	1870
2EZ150D	0642
2EZ150D5	0642
2EZ150D10	0642
2EZ160D	1246
2EZ160D5	1246
2EZ160D10	1246
2EZ170D	2091
2EZ170D5	2091
2EZ170D10	2091
2EZ180D	1269
2EZ180D5	1269
2EZ180D10	1269
2EZ190D	2210
2EZ190D5	2210
2EZ190D10	2210
2EZ200D	0600
2EZ200D5	0600
2EZ200D10	0600
2E.5	OEM
2F	0050
2F05	0110
2F1	OEM
2F2	OEM
2F2CN1	0087
2F2CN5	0087
2F3	OEM
2F4	0015
2F5CN1	0071
2F6	0087
2F8	0087
2F10	0087
2F12	OEM
2F14	OEM
2F16	OEM
2F18	OEM
2F20	OEM
2FB050	0276
2FB050R	0276
2FB100	0276
2FB100R	0276
2FB200	0287
2FB200R	0287
2FB400	0293
2FB400R	0293
2FB600	0299
2FB600R	0299
2FB800	0250
2FB800R	0250
2FB1000	0250
2FB1000R	0250
2G	0136
2G022	0211
2G1	0071
2G2	0071
2G4	0071
2G4B41	0468
2G6	0071
2G8	0071
2G10	0071
2G13	0015
2G101	0136
2G102	0050
2G103	0050
2G104	0050
2G106	0050
2G108	0211
2G109	0050
2G110	0050
2G138	0279
2G139	0279
2G140	0279
2G141	OEM
2G201	0050
2G202	0050
2G210	0160
2G220	0160
2G221	2691
2G222	0160
2G223	0085
2G224	0160
2G225	0160
2G226	0599
2G227	0599

DEVICE TYPE	REPL CODE
2G228	0599
2G229	OEM
2G230	OEM
2G231	OEM
2G240	0160
2G270	0211
2G271	0211
2G301	0050
2G302	0211
2G303	0004
2G304	0004
2G306	0211
2G308	0004
2G309	0004
2G319	0211
2G320	0211
2G321	0211
2G322	0211
2G323	0211
2G324	0211
2G339	0038
2G339A	0595
2G344	0004
2G345	0004
2G371	0004
2G371A	0004
2G374	0004
2G374A	0004
2G376	0004
2G377	0004
2G381	0004
2G381A	0004
2G382	0004
2G383	0279
2G384	0211
2G385	0211
2G386	0211
2G387	0211
2G394	0279
2G395	0211
2G396	0279
2G397	0279
2G398	OEM
2G401	0136
2G402	0136
2G403	0050
2G404	0050
2G413	0050
2G414	0136
2G415	0136
2G416	0136
2G417	0136
2G508	0211
2G509	0211
2G524	0279
2G525	0279
2G526	0279
2G527	0279
2G577	0279
2G601	0279
2G602	0279
2G603	0279
2G604	0279
2G605	0279
2G805	0015
2G1024	0279
2G1025	0279
2G1026	0279
2G1027	0211
2GA	0015
2GG2C41	0199
2GG2Z41	1009
2GL05	0279
2GU026	0279
2H1254	0037
2H1255	0037
2H1256	0150
2H1257	0150
2H1258	0037
2H1259	0037
2HR3J	0071
2HR3M	0071
2HR3N	OEM
2HR3P	OEM
2HT-2L	0769
2HT-6	0752
2HT-9	OEM
2HT-11C	0286
2HT-11L	0286
2HT-13C	0286
2HT-13L	0286
2HT-16	0201
2HT-18C	0752
2HT-20C	0752
2ISD235-R	0042
2J4B41	0441
2J30	OEM
2J31	OEM
2J32	OEM
2J33	OEM
2J34	OEM
2J42	OEM
2J42A	OEM
2J42A-6027	OEM
2J42H	OEM
2J50	OEM
2J51	OEM
2J51A	OEM
2J53	OEM

DEVICE TYPE	REPL CODE
2J55	OEM
2J70A	OEM
2J70B	OEM
2J72	0050
2J73	0050
2J8138	0015
2JG2C41	0199
2JG2Z41	1009
2JUS1.08A	OEM
2JUS1.08B	OEM
2JUS1.23A	OEM
2JUS1.23B	OEM
2JUS1.30A	OEM
2JUS1.30B	OEM
2JUS1.46A	OEM
2JUS1.46B	OEM
2JUS1.52A	OEM
2JUS1.52B	OEM
2K02	0071
2K19H	0321
2K22	OEM
2K25	OEM
2K25A	OEM
2K26	OEM
2K28	OEM
2K28A	OEM
2K29	OEM
2K45	OEM
2K48	0050
2K56	OEM
2KBP005	0276
2KBP01	0276
2KBP02	0287
2KBP04	0293
2KBP06	0299
2KBP08	0250
2KBP10	0250
2KBP20	OEM
2KZ6.8	OEM
2KZ6.8A	OEM
2KZ6.8B	OEM
2KZ7.5	OEM
2KZ7.5A	OEM
2KZ7.5B	OEM
2KZ8.2	OEM
2KZ8.2A	OEM
2KZ8.2B	OEM
2KZ9	OEM
2KZ9A	OEM
2KZ9B	OEM
2KZ9.1	OEM
2KZ9.1A	OEM
2KZ9.1B	OEM
2KZ10	OEM
2KZ10A	OEM
2KZ10B	OEM
2KZ11	OEM
2KZ11A	OEM
2KZ11B	OEM
2KZ12	OEM
2KZ12A	OEM
2KZ12B	OEM
2KZ13	OEM
2KZ13A	OEM
2KZ13B	OEM
2KZ15	OEM
2KZ15A	OEM
2KZ15B	OEM
2KZ16	OEM
2KZ16A	OEM
2KZ16B	OEM
2KZ18	OEM
2KZ18A	OEM
2KZ18B	OEM
2KZ20	OEM
2KZ20A	OEM
2KZ20B	OEM
2KZ22	OEM
2KZ22A	OEM
2KZ22B	OEM
2KZ24	OEM
2KZ24A	OEM
2KZ24B	OEM
2KZ27	OEM
2KZ27A	OEM
2KZ27B	OEM
2KZ30	OEM
2KZ30A	OEM
2KZ30B	OEM
2KZ33	OEM
2KZ33A	OEM
2KZ33B	OEM
2KZ36	OEM
2KZ36A	OEM
2KZ36B	OEM
2KZ39	OEM
2KZ39A	OEM
2KZ39B	OEM
2KZ43	OEM
2KZ43A	OEM
2KZ43B	OEM
2KZ47	OEM
2KZ47A	OEM
2KZ47B	OEM
2KZ51	OEM
2KZ51A	OEM
2KZ51B	OEM
2KZ56	OEM
2KZ56A	OEM
2KZ56B	OEM
2KZ62	OEM
2KZ62A	OEM
2KZ62B	OEM
2KZ68	OEM
2KZ68A	OEM
2KZ68B	OEM
2KZ75	OEM
2KZ75A	OEM
2KZ75B	OEM
2KZ82	OEM
2KZ82A	OEM
2KZ82B	OEM
2KZ90	OEM
2KZ90A	OEM
2KZ90B	OEM
2KZ91	OEM
2KZ91A	OEM
2KZ91B	OEM
2KZ100	OEM
2KZ100A	OEM
2KZ100B	OEM
2KZ110	OEM
2KZ110A	OEM
2KZ110B	OEM
2KZ120	OEM
2KZ120A	OEM
2KZ120B	OEM
2KZ130	OEM
2KZ130A	OEM
2KZ130B	OEM
2KZ150	OEM
2KZ150A	OEM
2KZ150B	OEM
2KZ160	OEM
2KZ160A	OEM
2KZ160B	OEM
2KZ170	OEM
2KZ170A	OEM
2KZ170B	OEM
2KZ180	OEM
2KZ180A	OEM
2KZ180B	OEM
2KZ200	OEM
2KZ200A	OEM
2KZ200B	OEM
2L02	OEM
2L08	OEM
2L1-2	OEM
2L1-2S	OEM
2L15	0344
2L15A	OEM
2L15B	OEM
2L15C	OEM
2L20	OEM
2L25	OEM
2L30	OEM
2L35	OEM
2L40	OEM
2L45	OEM
2L50	OEM
2L55	OEM
2L60	OEM
2L65	OEM
2L70	OEM
2L75	OEM
2L80	OEM
2L85	OEM
2L90	OEM
2L95	OEM
2L100	OEM
2L110	OEM
2L120	OEM
2L130	OEM
2L140	OEM
2L150	OEM
2L160	OEM
2L170	OEM
2L180	OEM
2L190	OEM
2L200	OEM
2L210	OEM
2L220	OEM
2L230	OEM
2L240	OEM
2L250	OEM
2L260	OEM
2L270	OEM
2L280	OEM
2L290	OEM
2L300	OEM
2LS1.5-3	OEM
2M13	OEM
2M53	OEM
2M53G	OEM
2M54	OEM
2M57A	OEM
2M60A	OEM
2M66	OEM
2M68	OEM
2M76	0142
2M78	0595
2M105	OEM
2M107A	OEM
2M109	OEM
2M110	OEM
2M115	OEM
2M115G	OEM
2M120	OEM
2M121	OEM
2M125	OEM
2M125H	OEM
2M125J	OEM
2M130	OEM
2M131	OEM
2M132	OEM
2M132A	OEM
2M140	OEM
2M140A	OEM
2M142	OEM
2M142G	OEM
2M142H	OEM
2M142J	OEM
2M151A	OEM
2M152	OEM
2M152G	OEM
2M152H	OEM
2M152J	OEM
2M158	OEM
2M158H	OEM
2M158J	OEM
2M162	OEM
2M162G	OEM
2M162H	OEM
2M162J	OEM
2M164	OEM
2M172	OEM
2M172G	OEM
2M172H	OEM
2M172J	OEM
2M182	OEM
2M214	1075
2M1127	0211
2M1303	0164
2M1305	0050
2M1849	0720
2M6219	0144
2M6504	OEM
2MA	1293
2MA509	0431
2MC	0136
2MC509	0018
2MN6374	0144
2MW665	0143
2N0681	OEM
2N0682	OEM
2N0682J	OEM
2N0682TX	OEM
2N0683	OEM
2N0683J	OEM
2N0683TX	OEM
2N0684	OEM
2N0685	OEM
2N0685J	OEM
2N0685TX	OEM
2N0686	OEM
2N0686J	OEM
2N0686TX	OEM
2N0687	OEM
2N0687J	OEM
2N0687TX	OEM
2N0688	OEM
2N0688J	OEM
2N0688TX	OEM
2N0689	OEM
2N0690	OEM
2N0690J	OEM
2N0690TX	OEM
2N0697	OEM
2N0699	OEM
2N2G374	0211
2N2J324	0086
2N2J374	0590
2N404A	OEM
2N15	0211
2N21	0164
2N21A	OEM
2N22	0164
2N23	0211
2N24	0211
2N25	0211
2N26	0211
2N27	0279
2N28	0595
2N29	0595
2N30	0279
2N31	0279
2N32	0211
2N32A	0211
2N33	0136
2N34	0004
2N34/5	OEM
2N34A	0004
2N35	0208
2N36	0004
2N37	0136
2N38	0136
2N38A	0004
2N39	0211
2N40	0211
2N41	0211
2N42	0211
2N43	0211
2N43A	0211
2N44	0211
2N44A	0004
2N45	0004
2N45A	0004
2N46	0211
2N47	0211
2N48	0211
2N48A	0211
2N49	0211
2N50	0211
2N51	0211
2N52	0211
2N53	0211
2N54	0211
2N55	0211
2N56	0211
2N57	0085
2N58	0211
2N59	0279
2N59A	0211
2N59B	0211
2N59C	0211
2N59D	0211
2N60	0279
2N60A	0211
2N60B	0211
2N60C	0211
2N60R	0211
2N61	0279
2N61A	0211
2N61B	0211
2N61C	0211
2N62	0004
2N63	0004
2N64	0004
2N65	0211
2N66	0085
2N67	0085
2N68	0085
2N70	OEM
2N71	0211
2N72	0136
2N73	0211
2N74	0211
2N75	0136
2N76	0211
2N77	0004
2N78	0595
2N78A	0595
2N79	0211
2N80	0211
2N81	0211
2N82	0211
2N82AG	0911
2N83	0279
2N84	0050
2N85	0136
2N86	0136
2N87	0136
2N88	0136
2N89	0136
2N90	0136
2N94	0038
2N94A	0038
2N95	2167
2N96	0211
2N97	0038
2N97A	0595
2N98	0595
2N98A	0595
2N99	0595
2N100	0595
2N102	0595
2N103	0595
2N104	0004
2N105	0004
2N106	0004
2N107	0279
2N108	0004
2N109	0086
2N109/5	0211
2N109BLU	0004
2N109GRN	0004
2N109M1	0004
2N109M2	0004
2N109WHT	0004
2N109YEL	0004
2N110	OEM
2N111	0211
2N111A	0211
2N111B	0136
2N111M1	0136
2N111M2	0136
2N112	0136
2N112A	0211
2N112M1	0136
2N113	0279
2N114	0279
2N115	0160
2N117	0079
2N117(T1)	0855
2N118	0079
2N118(T1)	0855
2N118A	0079
2N118A(T1)	0855
2N119	0079
2N119(T1)	0855
2N120	0079
2N120(T1)	0855
2N122	0168
2N123	0279
2N123(GE)	0211
2N123/5	0050
2N123A	0136
2N123A5	0050
2N124	0595
2N124(T1)	0595
2N125	0595
2N125(T1)	0595
2N126	0595
2N126(T1)	0595
2N127	0595
2N128	0136
2N129	0136
2N130	0211
2N130A	0211
2N130B	0038
2N131	0211
2N131A	0211
2N132	0211
2N132A	0004
2N133	0211
2N133A	0004
2N135	0279
2N136	0279
2N137	0279
2N138	0136
2N138A	0004
2N138B	0004
2N139	0136
2N140	0136
2N140M1	0136
2N140M2	0136
2N141	0160
2N143	0160
2N145	0595
2N146	0595
2N147	0595
2N148	0208
2N148A	0208
2N148B	0208
2N148C	0208
2N148C/D	0208
2N148D	0208
2N149	0208
2N149A	0208
2N149B	0164
2N150	0595
2N150A	0595
2N151	0211
2N155	0160
2N156	0160
2N157	0160
2N157A	0160
2N158	0160
2N158A	0160
2N159	0211
2N160	0079
2N160A	0079
2N161	0079
2N161A	0079
2N162	0079
2N162A	0127
2N163	0079
2N163A	0079
2N164	0595
2N164A	0595
2N165	0595
2N166	0595
2N167	0595
2N167A	0595
2N168	0595
2N168A	0595
2N169	0595
2N169A	0595
2N170	0595
2N171	0038
2N172	0595
2N173	0040
2N174	0040
2N174A	0040
2N174RED	0040
2N175	0004
2N176	0160
2N176(WHT/BRN)	0160
2N176(WHT/GRN	0160
2N176(WHT/GRN)G	0160
2N176(WHT/RED)	0160
2N176-1	0085
2N176-1BLU	0160
2N176-1WHT	0160
2N176-1YEL	0160
2N176-3PUR	0160
2N176-4PUR	0160
2N176-5WHT	0160
2N176-6WHT	0160
2N176A	0085
2N176BLK	0160
2N176BLU	0160
2N176G	0085
2N176GRN	0160
2N176PUR	0160
2N176RED	0160
2N176W	0085
2N176WHT	0160
2N176YEL	0160
2N178	0085
2N178A	OEM
2N179	0085
2N180	0004
2N181	0004
2N182	0208
2N183	0595
2N184	0595
2N185	0004
2N185BLU	0004
2N186	0004
2N186A	0004
2N187	0004
2N187A	0211
2N188	0211
2N188A	0211
2N189	0211
2N190	0211
2N191	0211
2N192	0211
2N193	0038
2N194	0038
2N194A	0038
2N195	0211
2N196	0211
2N197	0211
2N198	0211
2N199	0211
2N200	0211
2N204	0211
2N205	0211
2N206	0211
2N207	0211
2N207A	0211
2N207B	0211
2N207BLU	0211
2N211	0038
2N211M2	0050
2N212	0038
2N213	0208
2N213A	0208
2N214	0208
2N214A	0038
2N214MP	OEM
2N215	0004
2N216	0038
2N217	0164
2N217A	0004
2N217EQ	OEM
2N217RED	0004
2N217WHT	0004
2N217YEL	0004
2N218	0136
2N219	0050
2N220	0004
2N222	0004
2N222A	0004
2N223	0004
2N224	0004
2N225	0004
2N226	0004
2N227	0004
2N228	0208
2N228A	0164
2N229	0038
2N230	0085
2N231	0136
2N231-YEL-RED	0136
2N231BLU	0136
2N231RED	0136
2N231YEL	0136
2N232	0136
2N233	0038
2N233A	0038
2N234	0160
2N234A	0160
2N235	0160
2N235A	0160
2N235B	0160
2N236	0160
2N236A	0160
2N236B	0160
2N237	0211
2N238	0004
2N238-ORN	0004
2N238D	0004
2N238E	0004
2N238F	0004
2N240	0136
2N241	0004
2N241A	0004
2N242	0160
2N243	0018
2N244	0018
2N245	0590
2N246	0590
2N247	0136
2N247/33	0136
2N248	0136
2N249	0004
2N250	0085
2N250A	0085
2N251	0160
2N251A	0160
2N252	0136
2N253	0595
2N254	0595
2N255	0085
2N255A	0085
2N256	0085
2N256A	0085
2N257	0160
2N257-B	0085
2N257-BLK	0969
2N257-GRN	0969
2N257-W	0085
2N257-WHT	0599
2N257A	0085
2N257B	0085
2N257G	0085
2N257GRN	0085
2N257W	0085
2N260	OEM
2N260A	OEM
2N261	OEM
2N262	0279
2N262A	OEM
2N263	0079
2N264	0079
2N265	0211
2N266	0211
2N267	0050
2N268	0599
2N268A	0599
2N269	0004
2N270	0004
2N270A	0211
2N270SM	0279
2N271	0279
2N271A	0279
2N272	0211
2N273	0279
2N274	0050
2N274BLU	0050
2N274WHT	0050
2N275	0136
2N275W	0085
2N276	0050
2N277	0040
2N278	0040
2N279	0004
2N280	0004
2N281	0004
2N282	0211
2N283	0004
2N284	0004
2N284A	0004
2N285	0085
2N285A	0085
2N285B	0085
2N286	0050
2N289	0050
2N290	0435
2N291	0211
2N292	0595
2N292A	0595
2N293	0595
2N296	0085
2N297	0160
2N297A	0160
2N299	0136
2N300	0050
2N301	0160
2N301A	0160
2N301B	0160
2N301G	0136
2N301W	0160
2N302	0211
2N303	0211
2N306	0208
2N306A	0208
2N307	0599
2N307A	0599
2N307B	0599
2N308	0279
2N309	0279
2N310	0211
2N311	0279
2N312	0595
2N313	0595
2N314	0595
2N315	0279
2N315A	0279
2N315B	0279
2N316	0279
2N316A	0211
2N317	0279
2N317A	0279
2N318	0136
2N319	0211
2N320	0004
2N321	0211
2N322	0211
2N323	0211
2N324	0211
2N325	0085
2N327	0279
2N327A	0279
2N327B	0126
2N328	0126
2N328A	0126
2N328B	0126
2N329	0126
2N329A	0126
2N329B	0126
2N330	0126
2N330A	0126
2N331	0050
2N331M	0211
2N332	0198
2N332A	0198
2N333	0198
2N333A	0198
2N334	0198

If replacement code is OEM, contact original manufacturer for replacement.

DEVICE TYPE	REPL CODE
2N334A	0198
2N334B	0198
2N335	0198
2N335A	0198
2N335B	0198
2N336	0198
2N336A	0198
2N337	0198
2N337A	0198
2N338	0198
2N338A	0198
2N339	0086
2N339A	0086
2N3390-U29	0079
2N340	0086
2N340A	0086
2N341	0233
2N341A	0233
2N342	0086
2N342A	0086
2N342B	0086
2N343	0086
2N343A	0086
2N343B	0590
2N344	0136
2N345	0136
2N346	0136
2N347	OEM
2N348	OEM
2N349	OEM
2N350	0085
2N350A	0085
2N351	0085
2N351A	0085
2N352	0160
2N353	0160
2N355	0855
2N356	0595
2N356A	0038
2N357	0595
2N357A	0038
2N358	0595
2N358A	0038
2N359	0211
2N360	0211
2N361	0211
2N362	0211
2N363	0211
2N364	0038
2N365	0038
2N366	0038
2N367	0211
2N368	0211
2N369	0211
2N370	0136
2N370/33	0136
2N370A	0136
2N371	0136
2N371/33	0136
2N372	0136
2N372/33	0136
2N373	0136
2N374	0136
2N375	0085
2N376	0085
2N376A	0085
2N377	0595
2N377A	0595
2N378	0085
2N379	0599
2N380	0085
2N381	0211
2N382	0211
2N383	0211
2N384	0050
2N384/33	0050
2N385	0595
2N385/46	0079
2N385A	0595
2N386	0085
2N387	0085
2N388	0595
2N388A	0595
2N389/I	OEM
2N389A/I	OEM
2N391	OEM
2N392	0085
2N393	0136
2N394	0279
2N394A	0279
2N395	0279
2N396	0279
2N396A	0279
2N397	0279
2N399	0085
2N400	0085
2N401	0085
2N401A	0085
2N402	0211
2N403	0279
2N404	0004
2N404A	0211
2N405	0004
2N406	0004
2N406BLU	0004
2N406BRN	0004
2N406GRN	0004
2N406GRN-YEL	0004
2N406ORN	0004
2N406RED	0004
2N407	0136
2N407BLK	0004
2N407GRN	0004
2N407J	0004
2N407RED	0004
2N407WHT	0004
2N407YEL	0004
2N408	0004
2N408J	0004
2N408WHT	0004
2N409	0136
2N410	0136
2N411	0136
2N412	0136
2N413	0279
2N413A	0279
2N414	0279
2N414A	0279
2N414B	0211
2N414C	0211
2N415	0279
2N415A	0279
2N416	0279
2N417	0279
2N418	0599
2N419	0085
2N420	0160
2N420A	0160
2N421	OEM
2N422	0211
2N422/A	0321
2N422A	0211
2N424/I	OEM
2N424A/I	OEM
2N425	0211
2N425A	0150
2N426	0279
2N427	0279
2N427A	0004
2N428	0279
2N428A	0279
2N431	0198
2N432	0198
2N433	0198
2N435	0164
2N438	0038
2N438A	0038
2N439	0038
2N439A	0279
2N440	0595
2N440A	0038
2N441	0040
2N441BLU	0432
2N442	0040
2N443	0040
2N444	0595
2N444A	0038
2N445	0595
2N445A	0038
2N446	0595
2N446A	0038
2N447	0595
2N447A	0038
2N447B	0038
2N448	0595
2N449	0595
2N450	0004
2N451	OEM
2N452	OEM
2N453	OEM
2N454	OEM
2N456	0085
2N456A	0085
2N456B	0085
2N457	0085
2N457A	0085
2N457B	0085
2N458	0085
2N458A	0085
2N458B	0160
2N459	0599
2N459A	0599
2N460	0211
2N461	0211
2N462	0211
2N464	0211
2N465	0211
2N466	0211
2N467	0211
2N468	0211
2N469	0164
2N470	0198
2N471	0198
2N471A	0198
2N472	0016
2N472A	0016
2N473	0198
2N474	0198
2N474A	0198
2N475	0016
2N475A	0016
2N476	0198
2N476A	0127
2N477	0198
2N477A	0855
2N478	0198
2N478A	0855
2N479	0198
2N479A	0198
2N480	0016
2N480A	0016
2N480B	0086
2N481	0279
2N482	0279
2N483	0279
2N483-6M	0211
2N483-B	0279
2N483B	0211
2N484	0279
2N485	0279
2N486	0279
2N486B	0279
2N487	0279
2N489	OEM
2N489A	OEM
2N489B	OEM
2N490	OEM
2N490A	OEM
2N490B	OEM
2N490C	OEM
2N491	1659
2N491A	1659
2N491B	1659
2N492	OEM
2N492A	OEM
2N492B	OEM
2N492C	OEM
2N493	OEM
2N493A	OEM
2N493B	OEM
2N494	OEM
2N494A	OEM
2N494B	OEM
2N494C	OEM
2N495	0150
2N495/18	0150
2N496	0150
2N496/18	OEM
2N497	0086
2N497A	0086
2N498	0086
2N498A	0168
2N499	0136
2N499A	0136
2N500	0136
2N500BLU	0136
2N500RED	0136
2N500WHT	0136
2N501	0136
2N501/18	0136
2N501A	0136
2N502	0136
2N502A	0136
2N502B	0136
2N502BRN	0050
2N502GRN	0050
2N502RED	0050
2N503	0136
2N504	0136
2N505	0279
2N506	0136
2N507	0208
2N508	0211
2N508A	0211
2N509	0050
2N511	0085
2N511A	0085
2N511B	0085
2N512	0085
2N512A	0085
2N512B	0085
2N513	0085
2N513A	0085
2N513B	0085
2N514	0599
2N514A	0599
2N514B	0160
2N515	0038
2N516	0038
2N517	0038
2N518	0279
2N519	0279
2N519A	0279
2N520	0279
2N520A	0279
2N521	0279
2N521A	0279
2N522	0279
2N522A	0279
2N523	0279
2N523A	0279
2N524	0211
2N524A	0211
2N525	0211
2N525A	0211
2N526	0211
2N526A	0211
2N527	0211
2N527A	0211
2N529	0279
2N529/N	0595
2N529/P	0050
2N530	0279
2N530/N	0595
2N530/P	0050
2N531	0279
2N531/N	0595
2N531/P	0841
2N532	0279
2N532/N	0595
2N532/P	0050
2N533	0279
2N533/N	0595
2N533/P	0050
2N534	0004
2N535	0004
2N535A	0004
2N535B	0004
2N536	0004
2N537	0050
2N538	0160
2N538A	0160
2N539	0085
2N539A	0085
2N540	0085
2N540A	0085
2N541	0198
2N541/A	OEM
2N541A	0007
2N542	0086
2N542A	0198
2N543	0016
2N543A	0016
2N544	0136
2N544/33	0136
2N545	0086
2N546	0016
2N547	0086
2N548	0016
2N549	0086
2N550	0016
2N551	0016
2N552	0198
2N553	0160
2N554	0160
2N555	0160
2N556	0595
2N557	0595
2N558	0595
2N559	0050
2N560	0086
2N561	0599
2N563	0004
2N564	0211
2N565	0004
2N566	0211
2N567	0004
2N568	0211
2N569	0004
2N570	0211
2N571	0004
2N572	0279
2N573	0211
2N573BLU	0211
2N573BRN	0211
2N573ORN	0211
2N573RED	0211
2N574	0435
2N574A	0435
2N575	0040
2N575A	0040
2N576	0595
2N576A	0595
2N577	OEM
2N578	0279
2N579	0279
2N580	0279
2N581	0279
2N582	0279
2N583	0279
2N584	0004
2N585	0595
2N586	0279
2N587	0595
2N588	0136
2N588A	0136
2N589	0160
2N591	0164
2N591/5	0004
2N591A	0004
2N592	0279
2N593	0279
2N594	0595
2N595	0595
2N596	0595
2N597	0279
2N598	0279
2N599	0279
2N600	0279
2N601	0050
2N602	0136
2N602A	0136
2N603	0136
2N603A	0136
2N604	0136
2N604A	0136
2N605	0136
2N606	0136
2N607	0136
2N608	0136
2N609	0211
2N610	0211
2N611	0211
2N612	0211
2N613	0211
2N614	0279
2N615	0279
2N616	0279
2N617	0279
2N618	0085
2N619	0016
2N620	0016
2N621	0016
2N622	0016
2N623	0136
2N624	0136
2N625	0038
2N626	0150
2N627	0599
2N628	0599
2N628A	OEM
2N629	0599
2N630	0599
2N631	0211
2N632	0211
2N633	0211
2N633B	0211
2N634	0595
2N634A	0595
2N635	0595
2N635A	0595
2N636	0595
2N636A	0595
2N637	0085
2N637A	0085
2N637B	0085
2N638	0085
2N638A	0085
2N638B	0085
2N639	0085
2N639A	0085
2N639B	0085
2N640	0136
2N641	0136
2N641REDM/F	0136
2N642	0136
2N643	0136
2N644	0136
2N645	0136
2N646	0208
2N647	0208
2N647/22	0208
2N648	0038
2N649	0208
2N649/5	0208
2N649/22	0038
2N650	0211
2N650A	0211
2N651	0211
2N651A	0211
2N651BLA	0211
2N652	0211
2N652A	0211
2N653	0211
2N654	0211
2N654(TAD)	0164
2N655	0211
2N655(TAD)	0211
2N655A	0086
2N655GRN	0211
2N655RED	0211
2N656	0086
2N656A	0086
2N656S	0086
2N657	0086
2N657A	0168
2N657S	0086
2N658	0126
2N659	0126
2N660	0841
2N661	0841
2N662	0085
2N663	0160
2N665	0160
2N669	0085
2N669TX	OEM
2N670	0164
2N671	0164
2N672	0841
2N673	0164
2N674	0279
2N675	0164
2N676	OEM
2N677	0599
2N677A	0599
2N677B	0599
2N677C	0599
2N678	0599
2N678A	0599
2N678B	0599
2N678C	0599
2N679	0595
2N680	0164
2N681	3275
2N681A	2174
2N682	2174
2N682A	2174
2N683	0562
2N683A	0562
2N683AS	OEM
2N683S	OEM
2N684	3227
2N684A	3227
2N685	0757
2N685A	0757
2N685AS	OEM
2N685S	OEM
2N686	3237
2N686A	3237
2N687	3240
2N687-300R	OEM
2N687A	3240
2N687AS	OEM
2N687S	OEM
2N688	0735
2N688A	0735
2N688AS	OEM
2N688S	OEM
2N689	3260
2N689A	3260
2N689AS	OEM
2N689S	OEM
2N690	0759
2N690A	0759
2N690AS	OEM
2N690S	OEM
2N691	0761
2N691A	0761
2N691AS	OEM
2N691S	OEM
2N692	0761
2N692A	0761
2N692AS	OEM
2N692S	OEM
2N694	0136
2N695	0136
2N696	0198
2N696A	0086
2N696S	0086
2N697	0086
2N697A	0086
2N698	0187
2N699	0086
2N699A	0086
2N699A,B	0086
2N699B	0086
2N700	0050
2N700/18	0050
2N700A	0050
2N700A/18	0050
2N701	0198
2N702	0016
2N703	0016
2N705	0136
2N705A	0136
2N706	0016
2N706/46	0016
2N706/51	0016
2N706/KVT	OEM
2N706/TNT	0016
2N706/TPT	OEM
2N706A	0016
2N706A/46	0016
2N706A/51	0016
2N706A/TNT	0016
2N706A/TPT	OEM
2N706B	0016
2N706B/46	0016
2N706B/51	0016
2N706C	0016
2N706C/46	OEM
2N706C/51	OEM
2N706M-JAN	0016
2N707	0488
2N707A	0016
2N708	0016
2N708/46	0016
2N708/51	0016
2N708/KVT	OEM
2N708/TNT	0016
2N708/TPT	OEM
2N708A	0016
2N709	0144
2N709/46	0414
2N709/51	0414
2N709/52	0144
2N709/KVT	OEM
2N709/TNT	0414
2N709/TPT	OEM
2N709A	0144
2N709A/46	OEM
2N709A/51	0414
2N709A46	0414
2N710	0136
2N710A	0136
2N711	0136
2N711/46	0144
2N711A	0136
2N711B	0136
2N715	0016
2N716	0079
2N717	0016
2N717A	0144
2N718	0016
2N718A	0016
2N719	0855
2N719A	0855
2N720	0855
2N720A	0855
2N721	0037
2N721A	0037
2N721AB	0006
2N722	0037
2N722A	0037
2N722AB	0037
2N723	0150
2N725	0136
2N726	0150
2N727	0150
2N728	0198
2N729	0016
2N730	0086
2N731	0086
2N734	0086
2N734A	0086
2N735	0086
2N735A	0086
2N736	0086
2N736A	0086
2N736B	0086
2N738	0233
2N738A	0710
2N738B	OEM
2N739	0086
2N739A	0086
2N740	0086
2N740A	0086
2N741	0136
2N741A	0050
2N742	0016
2N742A	0016
2N743	0016
2N743/46	0590
2N743/51	0590
2N743A	0488
2N744	0016
2N744/46	0590
2N744/51	0590
2N744A	0488
2N745	0016
2N746	0016
2N747	0016
2N748	0016
2N749	0016
2N750	0855
2N751	0855
2N752	0086
2N753	0016
2N753/46	0079
2N753/51	0590
2N754	0016
2N755	0086
2N756	0016
2N756A	0016
2N757	0016
2N757A	0016
2N757B	0155
2N758	0016
2N758A	0016
2N758B	0016
2N759	0016
2N759A	0016
2N759B	0016
2N760	0016
2N760A	0016
2N760B	0016
2N761	0016
2N762	0016
2N764	OEM
2N765	OEM
2N766	OEM
2N767	OEM
2N768	0136
2N769	0136
2N770	0198
2N771	0198
2N772	0198
2N773	0198
2N774	0198
2N775	0198
2N776	0198
2N777	0198
2N778	0198
2N779	0136
2N779A	0136
2N779B	0050
2N780	0016
2N781	0136
2N782	0136
2N783	0016
2N784	0016
2N784/51	0198
2N784A	0016
2N784A/46	0016
2N784A/51	0016
2N784A46	0079
2N789	0198
2N790	0198
2N791	0198
2N792	0198
2N793	0198
2N794	0136
2N795	0136
2N796	0136
2N797	0038
2N799	0211
2N800	0004
2N801	0279
2N802	0279
2N803	0164
2N804	0164
2N805	0164
2N806	0164

If replacement code is OEM, contact original manufacturer for replacement.

DEVICE TYPE	REPL CODE	DEVICE TYPE	REPL CODE	DEVICE TYPE	REPL CODE	DEVICE TYPE	REPL CODE	DEVICE TYPE	REPL CODE	DEVICE TYPE	REPL CODE	DEVICE TYPE	REPL CODE
2N807	0004	2N903	0007	2N969	0136	2N1055	0086	2N1138A	0599	2N1212/I	OEM	2N1299	0595
2N808	0004	2N904	0007	2N970	0136	2N1056	0211	2N1138B	0599	2N1213	0136	2N1300	0136
2N809	0279	2N904AS	0855	2N971	0136	2N1057	0211	2N1139	0198	2N1214	0136	2N1301	0050
2N810	0279	2N905	0007	2N972	0136	2N1058	0595	2N1140	0016	2N1215	0136	2N1302	0208
2N811	0279	2N906	0079	2N973	0136	2N1059	0208	2N1141	0050	2N1216	0136	2N1303	0211
2N812	0279	2N907	0590	2N974	0136	2N1059-1	0038	2N1141A	0050	2N1217	0595	2N1304	0595
2N813	0004	2N908	0086	2N975	0136	2N1060	0144	2N1142	0050	2N1218	0599	2N1305	0211
2N814	0004	2N909	0016	2N976	0050	2N1065	0050	2N1142A	0050	2N1219	0037	2N1306	0595
2N815	0004	2N910	0086	2N977	0136	2N1066	0050	2N1143	0050	2N1220	0037	2N1307	0279
2N816	0004	2N911	0086	2N978	0150	2N1067	0555	2N1143A	0050	2N1221	0037	2N1308	0595
2N817	0164	2N912	0086	2N979	0136	2N1068	0555	2N1144	0211	2N1222	0037	2N1309	0279
2N818	0164	2N913	0016	2N980	0136	2N1069	0103	2N1145	0211	2N1223	0037	2N1309A	0279
2N819	0004	2N914	0016	2N981	0086	2N1070	0103	2N1146	0599	2N1224	0136	2N1310	0595
2N820	0004	2N914/46	0016	2N982	0136	2N1072	0103	2N1146A	0599	2N1225	0136	2N1311	0595
2N821	0595	2N914/51	0144	2N983	0136	2N1073	0599	2N1146B	0599	2N1226	0136	2N1312	0038
2N822	0595	2N914A	0016	2N984	0136	2N1073A	0599	2N1146C	0599	2N1227	0085	2N1313	0136
2N823	0595	2N915	0016	2N985	0136	2N1073B	0969	2N1147	0599	2N1227-3	0085	2N1314	0085
2N824	0595	2N915A	0016	2N986	0136	2N1077	0016	2N1147A	0599	2N1227-4	0085	2N1314R	0085
2N825	0211	2N916	0016	2N987	0050	2N1078	0208	2N1147B	0599	2N1227-4A	0085	2N1315	0841
2N826	0211	2N916A	0016	2N988	0016	2N1081	0086	2N1147C	0599	2N1227-4R	0085	2N1316	0279
2N827	0136	2N916B	0016	2N989	0016	2N1082	0198	2N1149	0079	2N1227A	0085	2N1317	0279
2N828	0136	2N917	0007	2N990	0136	2N1084	0855	2N1150	0079	2N1228	0126	2N1318	0279
2N828A	0136	2N917/46	0224	2N991	0136	2N1085	0144	2N1150/904	0079	2N1229	0126	2N1319	0279
2N829	0136	2N917/51	0127	2N992	0136	2N1086	0595	2N1151	0079	2N1230	0126	2N1330	0155
2N834	0016	2N917A	0007	2N993	0136	2N1086A	0595	2N1151/904A	0079	2N1231	0126	2N1335	0233
2N834/46	0016	2N918	0144	2N994	0136	2N1087	0595	2N1152	0079	2N1232	0126	2N1336	0233
2N834/51	0016	2N918/46	0144	2N995	0150	2N1090	0595	2N1153	0079	2N1232A	OEM	2N1337	0233
2N834A	0016	2N918/51	0144	2N995A	0150	2N1091	0595	2N1153/910	0079	2N1233	0126	2N1338	0086
2N835	0016	2N919	0016	2N996	0150	2N1092	0086	2N1154	0018	2N1234	0126	2N1339	0233
2N835/46	0016	2N920	0016	2N997	0396	2N1093	0211	2N1154/951	0018	2N1238	0150	2N1340	0233
2N835/51	0016	2N921	0016	2N998	0396	2N1094	0050	2N1155	0018	2N1239	0150	2N1341	0233
2N837	0136	2N922	0016	2N999	0396	2N1095	0038	2N1155/952	0018	2N1240	0150	2N1342	0233
2N838	0136	2N923	0037	2N1000	0595	2N1096	0038	2N1156	0086	2N1241	0150	2N1342A#	0233
2N839	0016	2N923A	0037	2N1003	0136	2N1097	0211	2N1156/953	0086	2N1242	0786	2N1343	0279
2N840	0016	2N924	0037	2N1004	0136	2N1098	0211	2N1157	0040	2N1242A	OEM	2N1344	0279
2N841	0016	2N924A	0037	2N1005	0144	2N1099	0435	2N1157A	0040	2N1243	0786	2N1345	0279
2N841/46	0016	2N925	0037	2N1006	0198	2N1100	0435	2N1158	0136	2N1245	0085	2N1346	0279
2N841/51	OEM	2N925A	0037	2N1007	0085	2N1101	0208	2N1158A	0136	2N1246	0085	2N1347	0279
2N841/KVT	0016	2N926	0037	2N1008	0211	2N1102	0208	2N1159	0599	2N1247	0198	2N1348	0211
2N841/TNT	OEM	2N926A	0037	2N1008A	0211	2N1102/5	0595	2N1160	0599	2N1248	0198	2N1349	0279
2N841/TPT	OEM	2N927	0037	2N1008B	0211	2N1103	0016	2N1162	0599	2N1249	0198	2N1350	0279
2N842	0016	2N927A	0037	2N1009	0211	2N1104	0198	2N1162A	0599	2N1250/I	OEM	2N1351	0279
2N843	0016	2N928	0037	2N1010	0208	2N1105	0855	2N1163	0599	2N1251	0208	2N1352	0211
2N844	0016	2N928A	0037	2N1011	0599	2N1106	0626	2N1163A	0599	2N1252	0198	2N1353	0211
2N845	0086	2N929	0016	2N1012	0595	2N1107	0136	2N1164	0599	2N1252A	0198	2N1354	0279
2N846	0050	2N929/46	0016	2N1013	OEM	2N1108	0136	2N1164A	0599	2N1253	0198	2N1355	0279
2N846A	0136	2N929/51	OEM	2N1014	0599	2N1108RED	0136	2N1165	0085	2N1253A	0198	2N1356	0279
2N846B	0050	2N929A	0016	2N1016B/M	OEM	2N1109	0136	2N1165A	0599	2N1254	0126	2N1357	0279
2N847	OEM	2N930	0016	2N1016C/M	OEM	2N1110	0136	2N1166	0599	2N1255	0126	2N1358	0040
2N848	OEM	2N930/5P5	OEM	2N1017	0050	2N1111	0136	2N1166A	0599	2N1256	0037	2N1358A	0040
2N849	0144	2N930/46	0016	2N1018	0050	2N1111A	0136	2N1167	0969	2N1257	0037	2N1358M	0040
2N850	0144	2N930/51	OEM	2N1019	OEM	2N1111B	0136	2N1167A	0969	2N1258	0126	2N1359	0160
2N851	0144	2N930/KVT	0016	2N1020	0160	2N1111RED	0136	2N1168	0160	2N1259	0126	2N1360	0599
2N852	0144	2N930/TNT	0016	2N1021	0599	2N1112	0595	2N1169	0038	2N1261	0435	2N1361	0279
2N858	0037	2N930A	0016	2N1021A	0599	2N1114	0595	2N1170	0038	2N1261A	OEM	2N1361A	0279
2N858C	0037	2N930A/46	0016	2N1022	0599	2N1115	0004	2N1171	0279	2N1262	0435	2N1362	0599
2N859	0037	2N930A/51	OEM	2N1022A	0599	2N1115A	0050	2N1172	0085	2N1262A	OEM	2N1363	0599
2N859D	0037	2N930B	0016	2N1023	0050	2N1116	0086	2N1173	0208	2N1263	0435	2N1364	0160
2N860	0037	2N933	0136	2N1024	0150	2N1117	0086	2N1173W	0208	2N1263A	OEM	2N1365	0160
2N860A	0037	2N934	0136	2N1025	0037	2N1118	0037	2N1174	0211	2N1264	0279	2N1366	0595
2N861	0037	2N935	0037	2N1025A	0037	2N1118A	0037	2N1174W	0841	2N1264/13	OEM	2N1367	0595
2N861A	0037	2N935A	0037	2N1025M	0037	2N1118AB	0037	2N1175	0211	2N1265	0211	2N1370	0211
2N862	0037	2N936	0037	2N1026	0037	2N1119	0037	2N1175A	0211	2N1265/5	0279	2N1371	0211
2N862A	0037	2N936A	0037	2N1026A	0037	2N1119A	0037	2N1176	0279	2N1265A	0211	2N1372	0211
2N863	0037	2N937	0037	2N1026AC	0037	2N1120	0599	2N1176A	0279	2N1266	0136	2N1373	0211
2N863A	0037	2N937A	0037	2N1027	0037	2N1121	0595	2N1176B	0279	2N1267	0198	2N1374	0211
2N864	0037	2N938	0037	2N1027A	0037	2N1122	0050	2N1177	0050	2N1268	0198	2N1375	0211
2N864A	0150	2N938A	0037	2N1028	0037	2N1122A	0050	2N1178	0050	2N1269	0198	2N1376	0211
2N865	0150	2N939	0037	2N1028A	0037	2N1123	0164	2N1179	0050	2N1270	0198	2N1377	0211
2N865A	0150	2N939A	0037	2N1029	0599	2N1124	0211	2N1180	0136	2N1271	0198	2N1378	0211
2N866	0016	2N940	0037	2N1029A	0599	2N1125	0211	2N1182	0599	2N1272	0198	2N1379	0211
2N867	0016	2N940A	0037	2N1029B	0599	2N1126	0211	2N1183	0841	2N1273	0004	2N1380	0211
2N869	0150	2N941	0037	2N1029C	0599	2N1127	0164	2N1183A	0841	2N1273BLU	0211	2N1381	0211
2N869A	0150	2N941A	0037	2N1030	0599	2N1128	0841	2N1183B	0841	2N1273GRN	0211	2N1382	0211
2N870	0086	2N942	0037	2N1030A	0599	2N1129	0164	2N1184	0841	2N1273ORN	0211	2N1383	0211
2N871	0086	2N942A	0338	2N1030B	0599	2N1130	0004	2N1184A	0841	2N1273RED	0211	2N1384	0136
2N876	1129	2N943	0037	2N1030C	0599	2N1131	0037	2N1184B	0841	2N1273YEL	0211	2N1385	0050
2N877	1129	2N943A	0037	2N1031	0599	2N1131/46	0037	2N1185	0279	2N1274	0004	2N1386	0198
2N878	0340	2N944	0037	2N1031A	0599	2N1131/51	0037	2N1186	0279	2N1274BLU	0211	2N1387	0198
2N879	0895	2N944A	0037	2N1031B	0599	2N1131A	0037	2N1187	0279	2N1274BRN	0211	2N1388	0016
2N880	2326	2N945	0037	2N1031C	0599	2N1131A/51	0037	2N1188	0279	2N1274GRN	0211	2N1389	0016
2N881	0058	2N945A	0037	2N1032	0599	2N1131AD	0037	2N1189	0211	2N1274ORN	0211	2N1390	0198
2N882	OEM	2N946	0037	2N1032A	0599	2N1131AS	0037	2N1190	0211	2N1274PUR	0211	2N1391	0038
2N883	OEM	2N946A	0037	2N1032B	0599	2N1131S	0037	2N1191	0211	2N1274RED	0211	2N1392	0211
2N884	OEM	2N947	0016	2N1032C	0599	2N1132	0037	2N1192	0211	2N1274V10	0841	2N1393	0279
2N884A	OEM	2N948	OEM	2N1033	0160	2N1132/46	0037	2N1193	0211	2N1274VIO	0841	2N1394	0050
2N885	1129	2N949	OEM	2N1034	0126	2N1132/51	0037	2N1194	0211	2N1275	0126	2N1395	0279
2N885A	1129	2N950	OEM	2N1035	0126	2N1132/KVT	OEM	2N1195	0050	2N1276	0016	2N1396	0136
2N886	0340	2N951	0079	2N1036	0126	2N1132/TNT	0037	2N1196	0037	2N1277	0016	2N1397	0136
2N886A	OEM	2N955	0595	2N1037	0126	2N1132/TPT	OEM	2N1197	0126	2N1278	0198	2N1398	0136
2N887	OEM	2N955A	0595	2N1038	0841	2N1132A	0037	2N1198	0595	2N1279	0016	2N1399	0136
2N887A	OEM	2N956	0016	2N1039	0160	2N1132A/46	0037	2N1199	0198	2N1280	0279	2N1400	0136
2N888	OEM	2N957	0016	2N1040	0085	2N1132A/51	0037	2N1199A	0198	2N1281	0279	2N1401	0136
2N888A	2326	2N958	0079	2N1041	0160	2N1132A46	0037	2N1200	0198	2N1282	0279	2N1401A	0136
2N889	OEM	2N959	0079	2N1042	0136	2N1132AC	0037	2N1201	0198	2N1284	0279	2N1402	0136
2N889A	OEM	2N960	0136	2N1043	0136	2N1132B	0037	2N1202	0435	2N1285	0050	2N1403	0050
2N890	OEM	2N960/46	0050	2N1044	0211	2N1132B/46	0037	2N1203	0435	2N1287	0211	2N1404	0211
2N891	OEM	2N961	0136	2N1045	0211	2N1132B/51	0037	2N1204	0136	2N1287A	0211	2N1404A	0279
2N892	OEM	2N961/46	0136	2N1046	0599	2N1132B46	0037	2N1204A	0136	2N1288	0595	2N1405	0050
2N893	OEM	2N962	0136	2N1046A	0969	2N1135	0037	2N1205	0198	2N1289	0595	2N1406	0050
2N894	OEM	2N962/46	0136	2N1046B	0160	2N1135A	0037	2N1206	0590	2N1290	0279	2N1407	0050
2N895	OEM	2N963	0136	2N1047	0042	2N1136	0085	2N1207	0233	2N1291	0085	2N1408	0050
2N896	OEM	2N964	0136	2N1048	0042	2N1136A	0085	2N1208	2637	2N1292	2687	2N1409	0016
2N897	OEM	2N964/46	0050	2N1049	0042	2N1136B	0085	2N1208/I	OEM	2N1293	0160	2N1409A	0198
2N898	OEM	2N964A	0136	2N1050	0168	2N1136C	0085	2N1209	2637	2N1294	0599	2N1410	0086
2N899	OEM	2N965	0136	2N1051	0086	2N1137	0599	2N1209/I	OEM	2N1295	0599	2N1410A	0086
2N900	OEM	2N966	0136	2N1052	0233	2N1137A	0599	2N1210/I	OEM	2N1296	2691	2N1411	0050
2N901	OEM	2N967	0136	2N1053	0233	2N1137B	0599	2N1211/I	OEM	2N1297	0599	2N1412	0432
2N902	0007	2N968	0050	2N1054	0233	2N1138	0599	2N1212	2637	2N1298	0208	2N1412A	0432

44

If replacement code is OEM, contact original manufacturer for replacement.

DEVICE TYPE	REPL CODE	DEVICE TYPE	REPL CODE	DEVICE TYPE	REPL CODE	DEVICE TYPE	REPL CODE	DEVICE TYPE	REPL CODE	DEVICE TYPE	REPL CODE	DEVICE TYPE	REPL CODE
2N1413	0211	2N1524/33	0050	2N1602	0957	2N1700	0086	2N1796	0217	2N1911	0603	2N2011	OEM
2N1414	0211	2N1524-1	0050	2N1603	2905	2N1701	0042	2N1797	0217	2N1912	0603	2N2012	OEM
2N1415	0211	2N1524-2	0050	2N1604	2908	2N1702	0359	2N1798	0217	2N1913	0603	2N2013	OEM
2N1416	0004	2N1525	0050	2N1605	0595	2N1703	0103	2N1799	0217	2N1914	0605	2N2014	OEM
2N1417	0198	2N1526	0050	2N1605-A	0038	2N1704	0016	2N1800	0217	2N1914A	OEM	2N2017	0086
2N1418	0198	2N1526/33	0050	2N1605A	0595	2N1705	0211	2N1801	0653	2N1914B	OEM	2N2018	2985
2N1419	0599	2N1527	0136	2N1606	0126	2N1706	0211	2N1802	0653	2N1915	0605	2N2019	2985
2N1420	0086	2N1528	0198	2N1607	0037	2N1707	0211	2N1803	0653	2N1916	0605	2N2020	2985
2N1420A	0086	2N1529	0599	2N1608	0037	2N1708	0016	2N1804	0653	2N1916A	OEM	2N2021	2985
2N1422	0103	2N1529A	0599	2N1609	0085	2N1708A	0016	2N1805	0605	2N1917	0338	2N2022	0050
2N1423	0103	2N1530	0599	2N1610	0085	2N1709	0042	2N1806	0605	2N1918	0338	2N2023	0603
2N1425	0136	2N1530A	0160	2N1611	0160	2N1710	0555	2N1807	0463	2N1919	0037	2N2024	0603
2N1426	0136	2N1531	0599	2N1612	0160	2N1711	0086	2N1808	0595	2N1920	0037	2N2025	0603
2N1427	0136	2N1531A	0599	2N1613	0076	2N1711/46	0016	2N1837	0086	2N1921	0037	2N2026	0603
2N1428	0037	2N1532	0599	2N1613/46	0016	2N1711/51	OEM	2N1837A	0086	2N1922	0126	2N2027	0603
2N1429	0126	2N1532A	0599	2N1613/51	OEM	2N1711/KVT	OEM	2N1837B	0086	2N1923	0086	2N2028	0605
2N1430	0160	2N1533	0160	2N1613/KVT	OEM	2N1711/TNT	0855	2N1838	0086	2N1924	0004	2N2029	0605
2N1431	0038	2N1534	0599	2N1613/TNT	OEM	2N1711/TPT	OEM	2N1839	0086	2N1925	0004	2N2030	0605
2N1432	0211	2N1534A	0599	2N1613/TPT	OEM	2N1711A	0086	2N1839A	0086	2N1926	0004	2N2031	OEM
2N1433	0435	2N1535	0599	2N1613A	0016	2N1711B	0086	2N1840	0016	2N1929	1129	2N2032	0144
2N1434	0435	2N1535A	0160	2N1613B	0016	2N1711S	0086	2N1841	OEM	2N1930	OEM	2N2032/I	OEM
2N1435	0435	2N1536	0599	2N1613S	0086	2N1713	0136	2N1842	3073	2N1931	0240	2N2033	0617
2N1436	0050	2N1536A	0160	2N1614	0164	2N1714	0086	2N1842A	3073	2N1932	0240	2N2033/S	OEM
2N1437	0160	2N1537	0599	2N1615	0086	2N1715	0187	2N1842B	0717	2N1933	0240	2N2034	0617
2N1438	0160	2N1537A	0599	2N1616	2637	2N1716	0086	2N1843	2497	2N1934	OEM	2N2034/S	OEM
2N1439	0037	2N1538	0160	2N1616/I	OEM	2N1717	0187	2N1843A	2497	2N1935	OEM	2N2035	0042
2N1440	0037	2N1538A	0160	2N1616A	2637	2N1718	0042	2N1843B	2497	2N1940	0279	2N2036	2298
2N1441	0037	2N1539	0599	2N1616A/I	OEM	2N1719	OEM	2N1844	0736	2N1941	0086	2N2038	0086
2N1442	0037	2N1539A	0599	2N1617	2637	2N1720	0042	2N1844A	0736	2N1942	0279	2N2039	0086
2N1443	0037	2N1540	0599	2N1617/I	OEM	2N1721	OEM	2N1844B	0736	2N1943	0086	2N2040	0086
2N1444	0086	2N1540A	0599	2N1617A	2637	2N1722	0556	2N1845	3076	2N1944	0016	2N2041	0086
2N1445	0187	2N1541	0599	2N1617A/I	OEM	2N1722/I	OEM	2N1845A	3076	2N1945	0016	2N2044	OEM
2N1446	0211	2N1541A	0599	2N1618	2637	2N1722A/I	OEM	2N1845B	0740	2N1946	0016	2N2045	OEM
2N1447	0211	2N1542	0599	2N1618/I	OEM	2N1723	0060	2N1846	0740	2N1947	0016	2N2046	OEM
2N1448	0211	2N1542A	0599	2N1618A	2637	2N1724	2637	2N1846A	0740	2N1948	0016	2N2047	OEM
2N1449	0211	2N1543	0599	2N1618A/I	OEM	2N1724/I	OEM	2N1846B	0740	2N1949	0016	2N2048	0136
2N1450	0136	2N1543A	0599	2N1619	OEM	2N1724A	2637	2N1847	3080	2N1950	0016	2N2048A	0136
2N1451	0211	2N1544	0599	2N1620/I	OEM	2N1724A/I	OEM	2N1847A	3080	2N1951	0016	2N2049	0086
2N1452	0211	2N1544A	0599	2N1622	0595	2N1725	2637	2N1847B	3080	2N1952	0016	2N2059	0136
2N1468	OEM	2N1545	0599	2N1623	0126	2N1726	0136	2N1848	2889	2N1953	0086	2N2060	2034
2N1469	0279	2N1545A	0599	2N1624	0595	2N1727	0136	2N1848A	2889	2N1954	0004	2N2060A	2034
2N1470	0279	2N1546	0599	2N1625	0050	2N1728	0136	2N1848B	2889	2N1955	0004	2N2060B	OEM
2N1471	0279	2N1546A	0599	2N1631	0136	2N1729	0279	2N1849	0742	2N1956	0004	2N2061	0085
2N1472	0086	2N1547	0599	2N1632	0136	2N1730	0595	2N1849A	0742	2N1957	0004	2N2061A	0085
2N1473	0595	2N1547A	0599	2N1633	0136	2N1731	0279	2N1849B	0742	2N1958	0086	2N2062	0085
2N1474	0037	2N1548	0599	2N1634	0136	2N1732	0595	2N1850	0747	2N1958/18	0086	2N2062A	0085
2N1474A	0037	2N1548A	0599	2N1635	0136	2N1741	OEM	2N1850A	3213	2N1958A	0086	2N2063	0085
2N1475	0037	2N1549	0599	2N1636	0136	2N1742	0136	2N1850B	3213	2N1958A/51	0086	2N2063A	0085
2N1476	0037	2N1549A	0599	2N1637	0050	2N1743	0136	2N1853	0136	2N1959	0086	2N2064	0085
2N1477	0037	2N1550	0599	2N1637/33	0050	2N1744	0136	2N1853/18	0050	2N1959/18	0086	2N2064A	0085
2N1478	0211	2N1550A	0599	2N1638	0136	2N1745	0136	2N1854	0136	2N1959A	0086	2N2065	0085
2N1479	1471	2N1551	0599	2N1638/33	0136	2N1746	0136	2N1858	0038	2N1959A/51	0086	2N2065A	0085
2N1479J	OEM	2N1551A	0599	2N1639	0136	2N1747	0136	2N1864	0136	2N1960	0050	2N2066	0085
2N1480	1471	2N1552	0599	2N1639/33	0050	2N1748	0136	2N1865	0136	2N1960/46	0050	2N2066A	0085
2N1480J	OEM	2N1552A	0599	2N1640	0150	2N1748A	0136	2N1866	0050	2N1961	0050	2N2067	0085
2N1481	1471	2N1553	0599	2N1641	0150	2N1749	0050	2N1867	0050	2N1961/46	0211	2N2067-O	OEM
2N1481J	OEM	2N1553A	0599	2N1642	0150	2N1750	0050	2N1868	0136	2N1962	0016	2N2067B	0085
2N1482	1471	2N1554	0599	2N1643	0037	2N1751	0599	2N1869	OEM	2N1962/46	0016	2N2067G	0085
2N1482J	OEM	2N1554A	0599	2N1644	0086	2N1752	0136	2N1869A	OEM	2N1963	0016	2N2067W	0085
2N1483	0042	2N1555	0599	2N1644A	0086	2N1753	0004	2N1870	OEM	2N1963/46	0016	2N2068-O	OEM
2N1483J	OEM	2N1555A	0599	2N1645	OEM	2N1754	0136	2N1870A	OEM	2N1964	0016	2N2069	0599
2N1483TX	OEM	2N1556	0599	2N1646	0050	2N1755	0085	2N1871	OEM	2N1964/46	0016	2N2070	0599
2N1484	0042	2N1556A	0599	2N1647	2936	2N1756	0085	2N1871A	OEM	2N1965	0016	2N2071	0160
2N1484TX	OEM	2N1557	0599	2N1648	2936	2N1757	0085	2N1872	0050	2N1965/46	0016	2N2072	0160
2N1485	0042	2N1557A	0599	2N1649	2936	2N1758	0085	2N1872A	OEM	2N1969	0279	2N2075	0040
2N1485J	OEM	2N1558	0599	2N1650	2936	2N1759	0085	2N1873	0050	2N1970	0040	2N2075A	0040
2N1485TX	OEM	2N1558A	0599	2N1651	0599	2N1760	0085	2N1873A	OEM	2N1971	0160	2N2076	0040
2N1486	0042	2N1559	0599	2N1652	0599	2N1761	0085	2N1874	0050	2N1972	0086	2N2076A	0040
2N1486J	OEM	2N1559A	0599	2N1653	0160	2N1762	0085	2N1874A	OEM	2N1973	0086	2N2077	0040
2N1486TX	OEM	2N1560	0599	2N1654	0126	2N1763	0198	2N1875	0050	2N1974	0086	2N2077A	0040
2N1487	0177	2N1560A	0599	2N1655	0338	2N1764	0086	2N1875A	OEM	2N1975	0016	2N2078	0040
2N1487J	OEM	2N1561	0211	2N1656	0338	2N1765	OEM	2N1876	OEM	2N1978	OEM	2N2078A	0040
2N1488	0177	2N1562	0211	2N1657	OEM	2N1768	0042	2N1876A	OEM	2N1980	0040	2N2079	0040
2N1488J	OEM	2N1564	0086	2N1662	0136	2N1769	0042	2N1877	OEM	2N1981	0040	2N2079A	0040
2N1489	0177	2N1565	0086	2N1663	0198	2N1770	1095	2N1877A	OEM	2N1982	0040	2N2080	0040
2N1489J	OEM	2N1566	0086	2N1664	0279	2N1770A	3385	2N1878	OEM	2N1983	0086	2N2080A	0040
2N1490	0359	2N1566A	0086	2N1665	0050	2N1771	1102	2N1878A	OEM	2N1983/T59276	OEM	2N2081	0040
2N1490J	OEM	2N1567	0435	2N1666	0599	2N1771A	1095	2N1879	OEM	2N1984	0086	2N2081A	0040
2N1491	0086	2N1568	0435	2N1667	0160	2N1772	2904	2N1879A	OEM	2N1985	0086	2N2082	0040
2N1492	0086	2N1569	0435	2N1668	0085	2N1772A	2471	2N1880	OEM	2N1986	0086	2N2082A	0435
2N1493	0233	2N1570	0279	2N1669	0085	2N1773	0240	2N1880A	OEM	2N1987	0086	2N2083	3186
2N1494	0050	2N1572	0233	2N1670	0050	2N1773A	0240	2N1881	OEM	2N1988	0086	2N2084	0050
2N1495	0050	2N1573	0233	2N1671	1659	2N1774	0957	2N1882	OEM	2N1989	0086	2N2085	0595
2N1499	0136	2N1574	0233	2N1671A	1659	2N1774A	0240	2N1883	OEM	2N1990	0086	2N2086	0086
2N1499A	0136	2N1581	0279	2N1671B	1659	2N1775	0671	2N1884	OEM	2N1990/46	0710	2N2087	0079
2N1499B	0136	2N1583	0279	2N1671BP	OEM	2N1775A	2635	2N1885	OEM	2N1990R	0710	2N2089	0136
2N1500	0136	2N1584	0279	2N1671C	1659	2N1776	3024	2N1886	0042	2N1990S	0710	2N2090	0136
2N1500/18	0050	2N1585	0595	2N1671CX	OEM	2N1776A	2635	2N1889	0086	2N1990W	0710	2N2091	0136
2N1501	0085	2N1586	0127	2N1672	0208	2N1776B	2635	2N1890	0086	2N1991	0037	2N2092	0136
2N1502	0085	2N1587	0079	2N1672A	0208	2N1777	2908	2N1890S	0086	2N1991S	0150	2N2093	0136
2N1504/10	OEM	2N1588	0079	2N1673	0050	2N1777A	0671	2N1891	0595	2N1992	0016	2N2094	0086
2N1505	0016	2N1589	0127	2N1674	0016	2N1778	3026	2N1892	0211	2N1993	0038	2N2094A	0086
2N1506	0016	2N1590	0079	2N1676	0037	2N1778A	2782	2N1893	0233	2N1994	0595	2N2095	0164
2N1506A	0016	2N1591	0079	2N1677	0037	2N1779	0595	2N1893/46	0233	2N1995	0595	2N2095A	0164
2N1507	0086	2N1592	0127	2N1678	0050	2N1780	0595	2N1893/51	OEM	2N1996	0595	2N2096	0164
2N1508	0086	2N1593	0079	2N1679	0626	2N1781	0595	2N1893/KVT	OEM	2N1997	0279	2N2096A	0016
2N1509	0086	2N1594	0079	2N1680	0590	2N1782	0050	2N1893/T59235A	OEM	2N1998	0279	2N2097	0050
2N1510	0595	2N1595	0179	2N1681	0211	2N1783	0595	2N1893/TNT	OEM	2N1999	0050	2N2097A	0016
2N1515	0136	2N1595A	0179	2N1682	0198	2N1784	0050	2N1893/TPT	OEM	2N2000	0004	2N2098	0050
2N1516	0136	2N1596	0934	2N1683	0136	2N1785	0136	2N1893A	0233	2N2001	0211	2N2099	0136
2N1517	0136	2N1596A	0179	2N1684	0279	2N1786	0136	2N1893S	0086	2N2002	0037	2N2100	0050
2N1517A	0050	2N1597	0934	2N1685	0595	2N1787	0136	2N1905	0969	2N2003	0037	2N2100A	0164
2N1518	0040	2N1597A	0179	2N1686	OEM	2N1788	0050	2N1906	0599	2N2004	0037	2N2102	0086
2N1519	0040	2N1598	0342	2N1687	OEM	2N1789	0050	2N1907	0599	2N2005	0037	2N2102A	0086
2N1520	0040	2N1598A	0342	2N1688	OEM	2N1790	0050	2N1907A	0599	2N2006	0037	2N2102S	0086
2N1521	0040	2N1599	0342	2N1689	OEM	2N1792	0636	2N1908	0599	2N2007	0037	2N2104	0037
2N1522	0432	2N1599A	0342	2N1691	0168	2N1793	0636	2N1908A	0599	2N2008	0233	2N2105	0037
2N1523	0435	2N1600	1102	2N1694	0595	2N1794	0636	2N1909	0603	2N2009	0050	2N2106	0086
2N1524	0050	2N1601	2904	2N1699	0136	2N1795	0636	2N1910	0603	2N2010	OEM	2N2107	0086

If replacement code is OEM, contact original manufacturer for replacement.

45

DEVICE TYPE	REPL CODE
2N2108	0086
2N2121	0037
2N2137	0085
2N2137A	0085
2N2138	0085
2N2138A	0085
2N2139	0085
2N2139A	0085
2N2140	0085
2N2140A	0085
2N2141	0085
2N2141A	0085
2N2142	0085
2N2142A	0085
2N2143	0085
2N2143A	0085
2N2144	0085
2N2144A	0085
2N2145	0085
2N2145A	0085
2N2146	0085
2N2146A	0085
2N2147	0160
2N2148	0160
2N2149	OEM
2N2150	2936
2N2151	2936
2N2152	0040
2N2152A	0040
2N2153	0040
2N2153A	0040
2N2154	0040
2N2154A	0040
2N2155	0040
2N2155A	0040
2N2156	0040
2N2156A	0040
2N2157	0040
2N2157A	0040
2N2158	0040
2N2158A	0040
2N2159	0040
2N2159A	0040
2N2160	1659
2N2161	0086
2N2162	0037
2N2163	0037
2N2164	0037
2N2165	0037
2N2166	0037
2N2167	0037
2N2168	0136
2N2169	0136
2N2170	0136
2N2171	0279
2N2172	0279
2N2173	0841
2N2174	OEM
2N2175	0150
2N2176	0150
2N2177	0150
2N2178	0037
2N2180	0136
2N2181	0037
2N2182	0037
2N2183	0037
2N2184	0037
2N2185	0037
2N2186	0037
2N2187	0037
2N2188	0136
2N2189	0136
2N2190	0050
2N2191	0050
2N2192	0086
2N2192A	0086
2N2192B	0086
2N2193	0086
2N2193A	0086
2N2193AS	0086
2N2193B	0086
2N2194	0086
2N2194A	0086
2N2194B	0086
2N2195	0086
2N2195A	0086
2N2195B	0086
2N2196	0626
2N2197	0144
2N2198	0086
2N2199	0136
2N2200	0136
2N2204	0142
2N2205	0016
2N2206	0016
2N2207	0136
2N2208	0136
2N2209	0211
2N2210	0435
2N2212	0160
2N2213	OEM
2N2214	0198
2N2216	0283
2N2217	0086
2N2217/51	0079
2N2217A	OEM
2N2218	0086
2N2218/51	0079
2N2218/TNT	0079
2N2218/TPT	OEM
2N2218A	0086
2N2218AS	0016
2N2218S	0016
2N2219	0086
2N2219/51	0079
2N2219/TNT	0079
2N2219/TPT	OEM
2N2219A	0086
2N2219AS	0016
2N2219S	0016
2N2220	0016
2N2220A	0016
2N2221	0016
2N2221A	0016
2N2222	0016
2N2222A	0016
2N2223	2034
2N2223A	0710
2N2224	0016
2N2225	0136
2N2226	OEM
2N2230S	0198
2N2233A	2034
2N2234	0198
2N2235	0198
2N2236	0016
2N2237	0016
2N2238	0050
2N2239	3247
2N2240	0198
2N2241	0198
2N2242	0016
2N2243	0086
2N2243A	0086
2N2244	0016
2N2245	0016
2N2246	0016
2N2247	0016
2N2248	0016
2N2249	0016
2N2250	0016
2N2251	0016
2N2252	0016
2N2253	0016
2N2254	0016
2N2255	0016
2N2256	0016
2N2257	0016
2N2258	0136
2N2259	0136
2N2266	0435
2N2267	0435
2N2268	0435
2N2269	0435
2N2270	0086
2N2270S	0086
2N2271	0211
2N2272	0016
2N2273	0136
2N2274	0037
2N2275	0037
2N2276	0037
2N2277	0037
2N2278	0037
2N2279	0037
2N2279/51	0590
2N2280	0037
2N2281	0037
2N2282	0085
2N2285	0599
2N2286	0599
2N2287	0160
2N2288	0599
2N2289	0599
2N2290	0599
2N2291	0599
2N2292	0599
2N2293	0160
2N2294	0160
2N2295	0160
2N2296	0160
2N2297	0086
2N2297/51	0079
2N2297S	0086
2N2303	0037
2N2303/46	0037
2N2303/51	OEM
2N2303/KVT	OEM
2N2303/TNT	0037
2N2303/TPT	OEM
2N2304	0086
2N2305	0103
2N2307	OEM
2N2309	0198
2N2310	0710
2N2311	0710
2N2312	0710
2N2313	0710
2N2314	0016
2N2315	0016
2N2316	0710
2N2317	0086
2N2318	0016
2N2319	0016
2N2320	0016
2N2322	0934
2N2322A	OEM
2N2323	0934
2N2323A	OEM
2N2324	0934
2N2324A	OEM
2N2325	0934
2N2325A	OEM
2N2326	0934
2N2326A	OEM
2N2327	1213
2N2327A	OEM
2N2328	0342
2N2328A	OEM
2N2329	3291
2N2329A	OEM
2N2330	0198
2N2330S	0018
2N2331	0016
2N2331S	0198
2N2332	0037
2N2333	0037
2N2334	0037
2N2335	0037
2N2336	0037
2N2337	0037
2N2339	0042
2N2340	1401
2N2341	1401
2N2342	0321
2N2343	0321
2N2344	OEM
2N2345	OEM
2N2346	OEM
2N2347	OEM
2N2348	OEM
2N2349	0016
2N2350	0086
2N2350A	0086
2N2351	0086
2N2351A	0086
2N2352	0086
2N2352A	0086
2N2353	0086
2N2353A	0086
2N2354	0038
2N2356	OEM
2N2356A	0710
2N2357	0160
2N2358	0160
2N2360	0050
2N2361	0050
2N2362	0050
2N2363	0136
2N2364	0187
2N2364A	0187
2N2368	0016
2N2368/51	0590
2N2369	0016
2N2369/46	0016
2N2369/51	0590
2N2369/KVT	OEM
2N2369/TNT	OEM
2N2369/TPT	OEM
2N2369A	0488
2N2370	0037
2N2371	0037
2N2372	0037
2N2373	0037
2N2374	0211
2N2375	0211
2N2376	0211
2N2377	0037
2N2378	0037
2N2379	0435
2N2380	0086
2N2380A	0086
2N2381	0086
2N2382	0050
2N2383	0103
2N2384	0103
2N2385	0222
2N2386	1133
2N2386A	1133
2N2387	0079
2N2388	0079
2N2389	0198
2N2390	0198
2N2391	0855
2N2392	0855
2N2393	0037
2N2394	0037
2N2395	0150
2N2396	0198
2N2397	0198
2N2398	0050
2N2399	0050
2N2400	0136
2N2401	0136
2N2402	0136
2N2403	0590
2N2404	0590
2N2405	0639
2N2405L	0639
2N2405S	0086
2N2406	0841
2N2410	0086
2N2410/51	0018
2N2410A	OEM
2N2411	0037
2N2412	0037
2N2413	0016
2N2414	0320
2N2415	0050
2N2416	0050
2N2417	0016
2N2417A	OEM
2N2417B	OEM
2N2418	OEM
2N2418A	OEM
2N2418B	OEM
2N2419	OEM
2N2419A	OEM
2N2419B	OEM
2N2420	OEM
2N2420B	OEM
2N2421	0164
2N2421A	OEM
2N2421B	OEM
2N2422	OEM
2N2422A	OEM
2N2422B	OEM
2N2423	0599
2N2424	0037
2N2425	0037
2N2426	0595
2N2427	0016
2N2428	0004
2N2429	0004
2N2429/353	0211
2N2430	0208
2N2431	0164
2N2431B	0211
2N2432	0016
2N2432A	0111
2N2433	0086
2N2434	0086
2N2435	0710
2N2436	0710
2N2437	0710
2N2438	0710
2N2439	0710
2N2440	0233
2N2443	0233
2N2446	0599
2N2447	0004
2N2448	0004
2N2449	0004
2N2450	0004
2N2451	0136
2N2453	2034
2N2454	2908
2N2455	0050
2N2456	0050
2N2457	OEM
2N2458	OEM
2N2459	0710
2N2460	0710
2N2461	0710
2N2462	0710
2N2463	0086
2N2464	0086
2N2465	0086
2N2466	0086
2N2468	0211
2N2469	0211
2N2472	0079
2N2473	0079
2N2474	0037
2N2475	0144
2N2475/46	0224
2N2475/51	0224
2N2476	0016
2N2477	0016
2N2478	0086
2N2479	0086
2N2480	2034
2N2480A	2034
2N2481	0016
2N2482	0038
2N2483	0016
2N2484	0127
2N2484A	0590
2N2485	OEM
2N2486	OEM
2N2487	0136
2N2488	0136
2N2489	0136
2N2489A	0086
2N2490	0040
2N2491	0040
2N2492	0040
2N2493	0040
2N2494	0136
2N2495	0050
2N2496	0050
2N2497	2959
2N2498	1133
2N2499	OEM
2N2500	OEM
2N2501	0016
2N2503	OEM
2N2504	OEM
2N2505	OEM
2N2506	OEM
2N2507	OEM
2N2508	OEM
2N2509	0233
2N2510	0086
2N2511	0086
2N2512	0050
2N2514	0016
2N2515	0016
2N2516	0086
2N2517	0710
2N2518	0710
2N2519	0710
2N2520	0710
2N2521	0710
2N2522	0710
2N2523	0016
2N2524	0016
2N2526	0599
2N2527	0969
2N2528	0969
2N2529	0016
2N2530	0016
2N2531	0016
2N2532	0016
2N2533	0016
2N2534	0016
2N2537	0086
2N2538	0086
2N2539	0016
2N2540	0016
2N2541	0841
2N2542	0733
2N2543	0733
2N2544	0733
2N2545	0733
2N2546	0733
2N2547	0733
2N2548	0733
2N2549	0733
2N2550	OEM
2N2551	0338
2N2564	0211
2N2564/5	0841
2N2565	0211
2N2568	OEM
2N2569	0016
2N2570	0016
2N2571	0016
2N2572	0016
2N2573	1814
2N2574	1814
2N2575	1814
2N2576	1814
2N2577	1814
2N2578	1814
2N2579	1814
2N2586	0016
2N2587	0050
2N2588	0136
2N2590	0126
2N2591	0126
2N2592	0126
2N2593	0126
2N2594	0086
2N2594/TNT	OEM
2N2594/TPT	OEM
2N2595	0037
2N2596	0037
2N2597	0037
2N2598	0338
2N2599	0338
2N2599A	0338
2N2600	0338
2N2600A	0037
2N2601	0037
2N2602	0037
2N2603	0037
2N2604	0037
2N2605	0037
2N2605A	0037
2N2606	OEM
2N2607	OEM
2N2608	OEM
2N2609	1133
2N2610	0127
2N2611	0264
2N2612	0599
2N2613	0004
2N2614	0004
2N2615	0144
2N2616	0144
2N2617	0079
2N2618	0233
2N2618/46	0079
2N2619	3405
2N2620	OEM
2N2621	0136
2N2622	0136
2N2623	0136
2N2624	0136
2N2625	0136
2N2626	0136
2N2627	0136
2N2628	0136
2N2629	0136
2N2630	0136
2N2631	2846
2N2632	2846
2N2633	2846
2N2635	0136
2N2636	0599
2N2637	0599
2N2638	0599
2N2639	2034
2N2640	2034
2N2641	2034
2N2642	2034
2N2643	2034
2N2644	2034
2N2645	0016
2N2646	2123
2N2646P	OEM
2N2647	1167
2N2648	0279
2N2649	OEM
2N2650	OEM
2N2650A	OEM
2N2651	0016
2N2652	0855
2N2652A	0855
2N2653	2908
2N2654	0050
2N2655	0144
2N2656	0016
2N2657	0042
2N2671	0050
2N2672	0841
2N2672A	0050
2N2672BLK	0050
2N2672GRN	0050
2N2673	0016
2N2674	0016
2N2675	0016
2N2676	0016
2N2677	0016
2N2678	0016
2N2679	1129
2N2679A	OEM
2N2680	0340
2N2680A	0340
2N2681	OEM
2N2681A	OEM
2N2682	OEM
2N2682A	OEM
2N2683	OEM
2N2683A	OEM
2N2684	OEM
2N2684A	OEM
2N2685	OEM
2N2685A	OEM
2N2686	OEM
2N2686A	OEM
2N2687	1129
2N2688	0340
2N2689	0895
2N2690	0058
2N2691	0599
2N2691A	0599
2N2692	0016
2N2693	0016
2N2694	0111
2N2695	0037
2N2696	0037
2N2699	0595
2N2706	0164
2N2706MP	OEM
2N2707	0164
2N2708	0259
2N2709	0037
2N2710	0488
2N2711	0155
2N2712	0076
2N2712BLUE	0144
2N2712ORANGE	0144
2N2713	0155
2N2714	0155
2N2715	0127
2N2716	0127
2N2717	0136
2N2718	0136
2N2719	0016
2N2720	2034
2N2721	2034
2N2722	2034
2N2723	2243
2N2724	2243
2N2725	0396
2N2726	0233
2N2727	0283
2N2728	0435
2N2729	0488
2N2730	0435
2N2731	0435
2N2732	0435
2N2757	3449
2N2758	3449
2N2759	3449
2N2763	3449
2N2764	3449
2N2765	3449
2N2769	3449
2N2770	3449
2N2771	3449
2N2775	3449
2N2776	3449
2N2777	3449
2N2783	0136
2N2784	0144
2N2784/46	0414
2N2784/52	0144
2N2784/KVT	OEM
2N2784/TNT	0079
2N2784/TPT	OEM
2N2786	0050
2N2786A	0050
2N2787	0086
2N2788	0086
2N2789	0086
2N2789S	0086
2N2790	0016
2N2791	0016
2N2792	0016
2N2793	0435
2N2794	OEM
2N2795	0136
2N2796	0136
2N2797	0050
2N2798	0050
2N2799	0050
2N2800	0126
2N2800/46	0037
2N2800/51	0150
2N2800S	0126
2N2801	0037
2N2801/46	0126
2N2801/51	0150
2N2802	2449
2N2803	2449
2N2804	2449
2N2805	2449
2N2806	2449
2N2807	2449
2N2808	0079
2N2808A	0079
2N2809	0007
2N2809A	0079
2N2810	0007
2N2810A	0079
2N2811	2637
2N2812	2637
2N2813	2637
2N2814	2637
2N2815	3470
2N2816	3470
2N2819	3449
2N2820	3449
2N2821	3449
2N2822	3449
2N2823	3449
2N2824	3449
2N2825	3449
2N2828	0042
2N2829	0042
2N2831	0016
2N2832	0599
2N2835	0222
2N2836	0160
2N2837	0037
2N2838	0037
2N2840	OEM
2N2841	OEM
2N2842	OEM
2N2843	OEM
2N2844	OEM
2N2845	0016
2N2846	0016
2N2847	0016
2N2848	0016
2N2849	0617
2N2849-1	0617
2N2849-2	2846
2N2850	0617
2N2850-1	0617
2N2850-2	2846
2N2851	0617
2N2851-1	0617
2N2851-2	2846
2N2852	0617
2N2852-1	0617
2N2852-2	2846
2N2853	0617
2N2853-1	0617
2N2853-2	0617
2N2854	0617
2N2854-1	0617
2N2854-2	0617
2N2855	0617
2N2855-1	0617
2N2855-2	0617
2N2855-3	0617
2N2856	0617
2N2856-1	0617
2N2856-2	0617
2N2857	0259
2N2857J	OEM
2N2860	0050
2N2861	0037
2N2862	0037
2N2863	0086
2N2864	0086
2N2865	0007
2N2868	0086
2N2869	0599
2N2869/2N301	0599
2N2870	0160
2N2870/2N301A	0969
2N2873	0050
2N2874	0626
2N2875	0919
2N2876	0830
2N2877	2936
2N2878	2936
2N2879	2936

If replacement code is OEM, contact original manufacturer for replacement.

DEVICE TYPE	REPL CODE
2N2880	2936
2N2882	0886
2N2883	0016
2N2884	0016
2N2885	0111
2N2886	0018
2N2888	0757
2N2889	3237
2N2890	0086
2N2891	0086
2N2892	2846
2N2893	2846
2N2894	0037
2N2894A	0037
2N2895	0086
2N2896	0639
2N2897	0086
2N2898	0187
2N2899	0187
2N2900	0086
2N2901	0127
2N2903	2034
2N2903A	2034
2N2904	0148
2N2904/TNT	0037
2N2904/TPT	OEM
2N2904A	0126
2N2904AS	0037
2N2904S	0037
2N2905	0126
2N2905A	0126
2N2905AS	0037
2N2905S	0037
2N2906	0037
2N2906A	0037
2N2907	0037
2N2907A	5052
2N2909	0086
2N2910	0079
2N2913	2034
2N2914	0079
2N2915	2034
2N2915A	2034
2N2916	0016
2N2916A	0079
2N2917	2034
2N2918	0079
2N2919	2034
2N2919A	2034
2N2920	0016
2N2920A	0079
2N2921	0155
2N2922	0155
2N2923	0155
2N2924	0155
2N2924-8	OEM
2N2924B	OEM
2N2925	0155
2N2926	0076
2N2926-6	0016
2N2926-B	0007
2N2926-BRN	0111
2N2926-G	0079
2N2926-GRN	0111
2N2926-O	0007
2N2926-ORG	0111
2N2926-R	0007
2N2926-RED	0111
2N2926-Y	0079
2N2926-YEL	0111
2N2926G	0016
2N2926GRN	0016
2N2926O	0590
2N2926ORN	0016
2N2926R	0590
2N2926Y	0079
2N2927	0037
2N2927/46	0037
2N2927/51	0150
2N2928	0050
2N2929	0050
2N2930	0211
2N2931	0111
2N2932	0111
2N2933	0111
2N2934	0111
2N2935	0111
2N2936	0079
2N2937	0079
2N2938	0016
2N2939	0086
2N2940	0187
2N2941	0187
2N2942	0050
2N2943	0050
2N2944	0037
2N2944A	0037
2N2945	0037
2N2945A	0037
2N2946	0037
2N2946A	0037
2N2947	0042
2N2948	0103
2N2949	0693
2N2950	1581
2N2951	0016
2N2951S	0086
2N2952	0016
2N2953	0004

DEVICE TYPE	REPL CODE
2N2954	0079
2N2955	0136
2N2956	0136
2N2957	0136
2N2958	0016
2N2959	0016
2N2959S	0016
2N2960	0016
2N2961	0016
2N2966	0279
2N2967	0007
2N2968	0150
2N2968A	0321
2N2969	0150
2N2970	0150
2N2971	0150
2N2972	2034
2N2973	0079
2N2974	2034
2N2975	0079
2N2976	2034
2N2977	0079
2N2978	2034
2N2979	0079
2N2980	0086
2N2987	0168
2N2988	0168
2N2989	0168
2N2990	0168
2N2991	0136
2N2992	0136
2N2993	0136
2N2994	0136
2N2995	0626
2N2996	0050
2N2997	0050
2N2998	0050
2N2999	0050
2N3001	OEM
2N3002	OEM
2N3003	OEM
2N3004	OEM
2N3005	1129
2N3006	0340
2N3007	0895
2N3008	0058
2N3009	0016
2N3010	0144
2N3011	0016
2N3012	0037
2N3013	0016
2N3014	0016
2N3015	0016
2N3016	0561
2N3017	0561
2N3019	0086
2N3019S	0187
2N3020	0086
2N3020S	0086
2N3021	0919
2N3022	0919
2N3023	0919
2N3024	0919
2N3025	0919
2N3026	0919
2N3027	1129
2N3028	0340
2N3029	0895
2N3030	1129
2N3031	0340
2N3032	0895
2N3033	0855
2N3034	0855
2N3035	0144
2N3036	0086
2N3037	0710
2N3038	0086
2N3039	0126
2N3040	0126
2N3043	0079
2N3044	0079
2N3045	0079
2N3046	0079
2N3047	0079
2N3048	0079
2N3049	0150
2N3050	0150
2N3051	0150
2N3052	0590
2N3053	0076
2N3053/4053	0626
2N3053/40053	0590
2N3053A	0086
2N3053S	0626
2N3054	0424
2N3054A	0178
2N3055	0103
2N3055-1	0103
2N3055-2	0103
2N3055-3	0130
2N3055-4	0103
2N3055-5	0103
2N3055-6	0130
2N3055-7	0130
2N3055-8	0130
2N3055-9	0103
2N3055-10	0103
2N3055A	0103
2N3055AH	0103

DEVICE TYPE	REPL CODE
2N3055C	OEM
2N3055H	0103
2N3055HOM	1822
2N3055J	OEM
2N3055MP	0103
2N3055S	0103
2N3055SD	0103
2N3055TX	OEM
2N3055UB	0103
2N3056	0086
2N3056A	0187
2N3057	0710
2N3057A	0187
2N3058	0037
2N3059	0037
2N3059AS	0086
2N3060	0037
2N3061	0037
2N3062	0037
2N3063	0338
2N3064	0338
2N3065	0338
2N3066	0321
2N3066A	OEM
2N3067	0321
2N3067A	OEM
2N3068	0321
2N3068A	OEM
2N3069	0321
2N3069A	OEM
2N3070	0321
2N3070A	OEM
2N3071	0321
2N3072	0037
2N3073	0037
2N3074	0050
2N3075	0279
2N3077	0086
2N3078	0086
2N3081	0037
2N3081/46	0786
2N3081/51	OEM
2N3082	0127
2N3083	0127
2N3084	0321
2N3085	0321
2N3086	0321
2N3087	0321
2N3088	0321
2N3088A	0321
2N3089	0321
2N3089A	0321
2N3091	0605
2N3091-96	OEM
2N3092	0463
2N3093	0463
2N3094	0463
2N3095	0463
2N3096	0463
2N3097	0463
2N3098	OEM
2N3099	OEM
2N3100	OEM
2N3101	OEM
2N3102	OEM
2N3103	OEM
2N3104	OEM
2N3105	OEM
2N3106	OEM
2N3107	0086
2N3108	0086
2N3109	0086
2N3110	0086
2N3110S	0086
2N3112	OEM
2N3113	OEM
2N3114	0233
2N3114S	0334
2N3115	0016
2N3116	0016
2N3117	0111
2N3118	0086
2N3119	0283
2N3120	0126
2N3121	0037
2N3122	0086
2N3123	0016
2N3124	0599
2N3125	0599
2N3126	0160
2N3127	0050
2N3128	0079
2N3129	0079
2N3130	0079
2N3131	0007
2N3132	0599
2N3133	0126
2N3133S	0233
2N3134	0126
2N3135	0037
2N3136	0037
2N3137	0488
2N3138	0042
2N3140	0042
2N3142	0042
2N3144	0042
2N3146	0160
2N3147	0160
2N3148	0050

DEVICE TYPE	REPL CODE
2N3153	0050
2N3162	OEM
2N3171	1671
2N3172	1671
2N3173	1671
2N3174	1671
2N3183	1671
2N3184	1671
2N3185	1671
2N3186	1671
2N3195	1671
2N3196	1671
2N3197	1671
2N3198	1671
2N3199	0919
2N3200	0919
2N3202	0126
2N3203	0126
2N3205	0919
2N3206	0919
2N3208	0126
2N3209	0150
2N3210	0016
2N3211	0016
2N3212	2687
2N3213	0160
2N3214	2687
2N3215	2687
2N3216	0279
2N3217	0037
2N3218	0037
2N3219	0037
2N3224	0434
2N3225	0434
2N3226	0103
2N3227	0488
2N3228	3651
2N3229	0042
2N3230	OEM
2N3231	OEM
2N3232	0103
2N3233	0103
2N3234	0103
2N3235	0103
2N3236	3656
2N3237	0130
2N3238	0130
2N3239	0130
2N3241	0016
2N3241A	0016
2N3242	0016
2N3242A	0016
2N3244	0126
2N3244S	0126
2N3245	0126
2N3245S	0126
2N3246	0016
2N3247	0016
2N3248	0037
2N3249	0037
2N3250	0037
2N3250A	0037
2N3251	0037
2N3251A	0037
2N3252	0590
2N3252S	0626
2N3253	0830
2N3253S	0626
2N3254	0626
2N3255	OEM
2N3256	OEM
2N3257	OEM
2N3258	OEM
2N3259	0340
2N3261	0016
2N3262	0617
2N3265	3470
2N3266	3470
2N3267	0050
2N3268	0016
2N3269	OEM
2N3270	OEM
2N3271	OEM
2N3272	OEM
2N3273	OEM
2N3274	OEM
2N3275	OEM
2N3276	OEM
2N3277	OEM
2N3278	OEM
2N3279	0050
2N3280	0050
2N3281	0050
2N3282	0050
2N3283	0050
2N3284	0050
2N3285	0050
2N3286	0050
2N3287	0007
2N3288	0007
2N3289	0007
2N3290	0007
2N3291	0007
2N3292	0007
2N3293	0007
2N3294	0007
2N3295	0590
2N3296	0555
2N3297	0103

DEVICE TYPE	REPL CODE
2N3298	0079
2N3299	0016
2N3299S	0488
2N3300	0016
2N3300S	0488
2N3301	0016
2N3302	0016
2N3303	2675
2N3304	0150
2N3305	0037
2N3306	0037
2N3307	0037
2N3308	0037
2N3309	0930
2N3309A	OEM
2N3310	0016
2N3311	0040
2N3312	0040
2N3313	0040
2N3314	0040
2N3315	0040
2N3316	0435
2N3317	0037
2N3318	0037
2N3319	0037
2N3320	0136
2N3321	0136
2N3322	0136
2N3323	0136
2N3324	0136
2N3325	0136
2N3326	0086
2N3328	0050
2N3329	1133
2N3330	1133
2N3331	1133
2N3332	1133
2N3333	OEM
2N3334	OEM
2N3335	OEM
2N3336	OEM
2N3337	0007
2N3338	0007
2N3339	0007
2N3340	0016
2N3341	0037
2N3342	0150
2N3343	0126
2N3344	0126
2N3345	0126
2N3346	0037
2N3347	2449
2N3348	2449
2N3349	2449
2N3350	2449
2N3351	2449
2N3352	2449
2N3353	OEM
2N3354	OEM
2N3355	OEM
2N3356	OEM
2N3357	OEM
2N3358	OEM
2N3359	OEM
2N3360	OEM
2N3361	OEM
2N3362	OEM
2N3363	OEM
2N3364	OEM
2N3365	0321
2N3366	0321
2N3367	0321
2N3368	0321
2N3369	0321
2N3370	0321
2N3371	0050
2N3374	0590
2N3375	0555
2N3375J	OEM
2N3375TX	OEM
2N3376	1133
2N3377	1133
2N3378	1133
2N3379	1133
2N3380	OEM
2N3381	OEM
2N3382	OEM
2N3383	OEM
2N3384	OEM
2N3385	OEM
2N3386	OEM
2N3387	OEM
2N3388	0233
2N3389	0233
2N3390	0111
2N3390-U29	0111
2N3391	0111
2N3391-U29	0111
2N3391A	0111
2N3392	0155
2N3392-U29	0111
2N3393	0155
2N3393-U29	0111
2N3394	0155
2N3394-U29	0111
2N3395	0155
2N3395-W	0079
2N3395-WHT	0111
2N3395-Y	0079

DEVICE TYPE	REPL CODE
2N3395-YEL	0111
2N3396	0155
2N3396-O	0086
2N3396-ORG	0111
2N3396-W	0079
2N3396-WHT	0111
2N3396-Y	0079
2N3396-YEL	0111
2N3397	0155
2N3397-O	0086
2N3397-ORG	0111
2N3397-R	0086
2N3397-RED	0111
2N3397-W	0079
2N3397-WHT	0111
2N3397-Y	0079
2N3397-YEL	0111
2N3398	0111
2N3398-B	0079
2N3398-BLU	0111
2N3398-O	0086
2N3398-ORG	0111
2N3398-R	0086
2N3398-RED	0111
2N3398-W	0079
2N3398-WHT	0111
2N3398-YEL	0224
2N3399	0050
2N3400	0136
2N3401	0037
2N3402	0284
2N3403	0284
2N3404	0284
2N3405	0284
2N3406	OEM
2N3407	0007
2N3408	OEM
2N3409	0079
2N3410	0079
2N3411	0079
2N3412	0136
2N3413	0338
2N3414	0155
2N3415	0016
2N3416	0155
2N3417	0218
2N3418	0555
2N3420	0555
2N3423	0079
2N3424	0079
2N3425	0224
2N3426	0693
2N3427	0211
2N3428	0211
2N3435	0590
2N3436	0321
2N3437	0321
2N3438	0321
2N3439	0187
2N3439J	OEM
2N3439TX	OEM
2N3440	0187
2N3440J	OEM
2N3440S	0187
2N3440TX	OEM
2N3441	1021
2N3441J	OEM
2N3441TX	OEM
2N3442	0538
2N3442J	OEM
2N3442TX	OEM
2N3443	0136
2N3444	0626
2N3444S	0626
2N3445	0103
2N3446	1955
2N3447	2002
2N3448	0103
2N3449	0136
2N3450	0187
2N3451	0037
2N3452	0321
2N3453	0321
2N3454	0321
2N3455	0321
2N3456	0321
2N3457	0321
2N3458	0321
2N3459	0321
2N3460	0321
2N3461	0164
2N3462	0016
2N3463	0016
2N3464	0037
2N3465	0321
2N3466	0321
2N3467	0126
2N3467S	0126
2N3468	0126
2N3468S	0126
2N3469	0086
2N3478	0259
2N3479	OEM
2N3480	OEM
2N3481	OEM
2N3482	OEM
2N3483	0178
2N3484	OEM
2N3485	0037

DEVICE TYPE	REPL CODE
2N3485A	0037
2N3486	0037
2N3486A	0037
2N3487	0556
2N3488	0556
2N3490	0556
2N3491	0556
2N3493	0007
2N3494	0126
2N3494S	0037
2N3495	0338
2N3495S	0338
2N3496	0037
2N3497	0338
2N3498	0086
2N3498S	0334
2N3499	0086
2N3499S	0334
2N3500	0168
2N3500S	0334
2N3501	0086
2N3501S	0334
2N3502	0126
2N3503	0126
2N3504	0037
2N3505	0037
2N3506	0617
2N3506S	0626
2N3507	0617
2N3507S	0626
2N3508	0016
2N3509	0016
2N3510	0016
2N3511	0016
2N3512	0016
2N3513	OEM
2N3514	OEM
2N3515	OEM
2N3516	OEM
2N3517	OEM
2N3518	OEM
2N3519	OEM
2N3520	OEM
2N3521	OEM
2N3522	OEM
2N3523	OEM
2N3524	OEM
2N3525	3349
2N3525A	0555
2N3526	0233
2N3527	0037
2N3528	2378
2N3529	0705
2N3530	OEM
2N3531	OEM
2N3532	OEM
2N3533	OEM
2N3533J	OEM
2N3533TX	OEM
2N3534	OEM
2N3535	OEM
2N3536	OEM
2N3537	OEM
2N3538	OEM
2N3539	OEM
2N3540	OEM
2N3541	OEM
2N3542	0079
2N3544	0144
2N3545	0037
2N3546	0037
2N3547	0037
2N3548	0037
2N3549	0037
2N3550	0037
2N3553	1588
2N3554	0693
2N3555	OEM
2N3556	OEM
2N3557	OEM
2N3558	OEM
2N3559	OEM
2N3560	OEM
2N3561	OEM
2N3562	0144
2N3563	0144
2N3563-1	0144
2N3564	0016
2N3565	0016
2N3566	0076
2N3567	0076
2N3568	0086
2N3569	0076
2N3570	0144
2N3571	0259
2N3572	0259
2N3573	OEM
2N3574	OEM
2N3575	OEM
2N3576	0150
2N3577	OEM
2N3578	OEM
2N3579	0037
2N3580	0037
2N3581	0037
2N3582	0037
2N3583	1021
2N3584	0424
2N3584J	OEM

If replacement code is OEM, contact original manufacturer for replacement.

47

DEVICE TYPE	REPL CODE
2N3584TX	OEM
2N3585	1021
2N3585J	OEM
2N3585TX	OEM
2N3586	OEM
2N3587	2034
2N3588	0050
2N3589	0168
2N3590	0168
2N3591	0168
2N3592	0168
2N3593	0168
2N3594	0168
2N3597	3470
2N3598	3470
2N3599	3470
2N3600	0007
2N3601	OEM
2N3602	OEM
2N3603	OEM
2N3604	OEM
2N3605	0155
2N3605A	0155
2N3606	0155
2N3606A	0155
2N3607	0155
2N3608	0321
2N3609	OEM
2N3610	OEM
2N3611	0599
2N3612	0599
2N3613	0599
2N3614	0599
2N3615	0599
2N3616	0599
2N3617	0599
2N3618	0599
2N3619	0555
2N3620	0555
2N3621	0933
2N3622	2637
2N3623	0555
2N3624	0555
2N3625	0933
2N3626	0042
2N3627	0042
2N3628	0555
2N3629	0933
2N3630	0042
2N3631	3583
2N3632	0042
2N3633	0414
2N3633/46	0127
2N3633/51	OEM
2N3633/52	0590
2N3633/KVT	0855
2N3633/TNT	0127
2N3633/TPT	OEM
2N3637S	1814
2N3638	0006
2N3638A	0037
2N3639	0037
2N3640	0037
2N3641	0016
2N3642	0016
2N3643	0016
2N3644	0006
2N3645	0006
2N3646	0016
2N3647	0016
2N3648	0016
2N3649	0799
2N3650	0799
2N3651	0799
2N3652	0799
2N3653	0799
2N3654	0799
2N3655	0799
2N3656	0799
2N3657	0799
2N3658	0799
2N3659	0168
2N3660	0886
2N3661	0886
2N3662	0127
2N3663	0127
2N3665	0086
2N3666	0086
2N3667	0103
2N3668	1814
2N3669	3804
2N3670	1814
2N3671	0126
2N3672	0037
2N3673	0037
2N3675	0042
2N3677	0126
2N3678	0086
2N3679	OEM
2N3681	0007
2N3682	0144
2N3683	0007
2N3684	3104
2N3684A	0321
2N3685	0321
2N3685A	0321
2N3686	0321
2N3686A	0321
2N3687	0321

DEVICE TYPE	REPL CODE
2N3687A	0488
2N3688	0224
2N3689	0016
2N3690	0016
2N3691	0016
2N3692	0016
2N3693	0016
2N3694	0076
2N3695	0144
2N3696	OEM
2N3697	3577
2N3698	OEM
2N3700	0233
2N3701	0233
2N3702	0006
2N3703	0037
2N3704	0076
2N3705	0076
2N3706	0079
2N3707	0155
2N3708	1212
2N3708-BLU	0111
2N3708-BRN	0111
2N3708-G	0079
2N3708-GRN	0111
2N3708-O	0086
2N3708-ORG	0111
2N3708-R	0086
2N3708-RED	0111
2N3708-V	0079
2N3708-VIO	0111
2N3708-Y	0086
2N3708-YEL	0111
2N3709	0127
2N3710	1212
2N3711	0155
2N3712	0233
2N3712S	0233
2N3713	3820
2N3713HS	0538
2N3714	3820
2N3714HS	0538
2N3715	3820
2N3716	3820
2N3716HS	1955
2N3717	OEM
2N3719	0126
2N3720	0126
2N3721	0155
2N3722	0086
2N3723	0086
2N3724	0488
2N3724A	0930
2N3725	0016
2N3725A	0419
2N3726	2449
2N3727	2449
2N3728	OEM
2N3729	OEM
2N3730	0969
2N3731	0969
2N3732	0969
2N3733	0830
2N3734	0930
2N3734S	0626
2N3735	0626
2N3735S	0626
2N3736	0079
2N3737	0626
2N3738	1021
2N3739	1021
2N3740	0899
2N3740A	0919
2N3740Q	OEM
2N3741	0676
2N3741A	0676
2N3742	0233
2N3742S	0233
2N3743	0233
2N3743S	0434
2N3744	0042
2N3745	0042
2N3747	0042
2N3748	0042
2N3753	2430
2N3754	0799
2N3755	OEM
2N3756	OEM
2N3757	OEM
2N3758	OEM
2N3759	OEM
2N3760	OEM
2N3761	OEM
2N3762	0126
2N3762A	0626
2N3762S	0626
2N3763	0126
2N3763S	0626
2N3764	0126
2N3764A	0626
2N3765	0527
2N3766	0424
2N3767	0424
2N3770	0050
2N3771	0130
2N3771J	OEM
2N3771TX	OEM
2N3772	0130
2N3772C	5535

DEVICE TYPE	REPL CODE
2N3772J	OEM
2N3772TX	OEM
2N3773	0538
2N3774	0126
2N3775	0126
2N3776	0126
2N3777	0886
2N3778	0126
2N3779	0126
2N3780	0126
2N3781	1973
2N3782	0126
2N3783	0050
2N3784	0050
2N3785	0050
2N3788	0637
2N3789	0486
2N3790	0486
2N3791	0486
2N3792	3853
2N3793	0079
2N3794	0079
2N3795	0886
2N3796	3583
2N3797	3583
2N3798	0037
2N3798A	0037
2N3799	0037
2N3799A	0037
2N3800	2449
2N3801	OEM
2N3802	OEM
2N3803	OEM
2N3804	OEM
2N3804A	OEM
2N3805	OEM
2N3805A	OEM
2N3806	2449
2N3807	0016
2N3808	2449
2N3809	0016
2N3810	2449
2N3810A	2449
2N3811	0016
2N3811A	0016
2N3812	0037
2N3813	0016
2N3814	0037
2N3815	0016
2N3816	0037
2N3816A	0037
2N3817	0016
2N3817A	0016
2N3818	0042
2N3819	0321
2N3820	2959
2N3821	0321
2N3822	3104
2N3823	0843
2N3824	3104
2N3825	0155
2N3826	0155
2N3827	0155
2N3828	0079
2N3829	0037
2N3830	0086
2N3831	0617
2N3832	0007
2N3833	0414
2N3834	0414
2N3835	0414
2N3836	OEM
2N3837	OEM
2N3838	3863
2N3839	0259
2N3840	0037
2N3841	0338
2N3842	0037
2N3843	0155
2N3843A	0155
2N3844	0155
2N3844A	0155
2N3845	0155
2N3845A	0155
2N3846	0127
2N3850	2846
2N3851	2846
2N3852	2846
2N3853	2846
2N3854	0155
2N3854A	0155
2N3855	0155
2N3855A	0127
2N3856	0155
2N3856A	0155
2N3857	0037
2N3858	0155
2N3858A	0155
2N3859	0155
2N3859A	0155
2N3860	0155
2N3861	3249
2N3862	0488
2N3863	0103
2N3864	0103
2N3865	0074
2N3866	0488
2N3866A	0488
2N3866AJ	OEM

DEVICE TYPE	REPL CODE
2N3866ATX	OEM
2N3866J	OEM
2N3866TX	OEM
2N3867	0126
2N3868	0126
2N3869	0488
2N3870	1640
2N3871	1640
2N3872	2623
2N3873	2625
2N3877	0086
2N3877A	0155
2N3878	0424
2N3879	0178
2N3879J	3328
2N3879TX	OEM
2N3880	0259
2N3881	0086
2N3882	OEM
2N3883	0136
2N3884	1076
2N3885	1076
2N3886	1076
2N3887	1078
2N3888	1078
2N3889	1078
2N3890	1078
2N3891	1094
2N3892	1094
2N3893	1094
2N3894	1094
2N3895	1094
2N3896	0562
2N3897	0464
2N3898	0717
2N3899	0720
2N3900	0155
2N3900A	0155
2N3901	0111
2N3902	0359
2N3903	0076
2N3904	0076
2N3905	0037
2N3906	0006
2N3907	2034
2N3908	2034
2N3909	OEM
2N3909A	OEM
2N3910	0037
2N3911	0037
2N3912	0037
2N3913	0037
2N3914	0037
2N3915	0150
2N3916	0168
2N3917	0103
2N3918	0103
2N3919	0615
2N3920	0615
2N3921	OEM
2N3922	OEM
2N3923	0233
2N3924	0198
2N3925	0555
2N3926	3289
2N3927	3290
2N3930	0037
2N3931	0037
2N3932	0007
2N3933	0007
2N3934	OEM
2N3935	OEM
2N3936	0240
2N3937	0240
2N3938	0671
2N3939	0671
2N3940	0332
2N3941	OEM
2N3942	OEM
2N3943	OEM
2N3944	OEM
2N3945	0930
2N3946	0016
2N3947	0016
2N3948	0488
2N3950	0830
2N3953	0259
2N3954	OEM
2N3954A	OEM
2N3955	OEM
2N3955A	OEM
2N3956	OEM
2N3957	2917
2N3958	OEM
2N3959	0414
2N3960	0414
2N3961	0555
2N3962	0037
2N3963	0037
2N3964	0037
2N3965	0037
2N3966	0321
2N3967	0321
2N3967A	0321
2N3968	0321
2N3968A	0321
2N3969	0321
2N3969A	0321
2N3970	1147

DEVICE TYPE	REPL CODE
2N3971	1147
2N3972	OEM
2N3973	0018
2N3974	0018
2N3975	0018
2N3976	0018
2N3977	0037
2N3978	0037
2N3979	0037
2N3980	1882
2N3981	0590
2N3982	0590
2N3983	0127
2N3984	0127
2N3985	0127
2N3986	0463
2N3987	0463
2N3988	0463
2N3989	0463
2N3990	0463
2N3991	0463
2N3992	0463
2N3993	OEM
2N3993A	OEM
2N3994	0155
2N3994A	OEM
2N3995	0050
2N3996	2936
2N3997	2936
2N3998	2846
2N3999	2846
2N4000	0168
2N4001	0617
2N4002	3449
2N4003	3449
2N4006	0037
2N4007	0037
2N4008	0037
2N4009	OEM
2N4010	OEM
2N4011	OEM
2N4012	0555
2N4013	0016
2N4014	0016
2N4015	2449
2N4016	0037
2N4018	2449
2N4020	OEM
2N4021	2449
2N4022	OEM
2N4023	OEM
2N4024	2449
2N4025	OEM
2N4026	0126
2N4027	0126
2N4028	0126
2N4029	0126
2N4030	0126
2N4031	0126
2N4032	0126
2N4033	0126
2N4034	0150
2N4035	0150
2N4036	0126
2N4037	0126
2N4038	0977
2N4039	0977
2N4040	0555
2N4041	0555
2N4042	OEM
2N4043	OEM
2N4044	0079
2N4045	0079
2N4046	0016
2N4047	0086
2N4048	3955
2N4049	3955
2N4050	3955
2N4051	0432
2N4052	3955
2N4053	0432
2N4054	0275
2N4055	0275
2N4056	0275
2N4057	0275
2N4058	0150
2N4059	0150
2N4060	0150
2N4061	0150
2N4062	0150
2N4063	3964
2N4064	3964
2N4065	0838
2N4066	OEM
2N4067	OEM
2N4068	0233
2N4069	0168
2N4070	3510
2N4071	1955
2N4071MP	0177
2N4072	0016
2N4073	0488
2N4074	0016
2N4075	3969
2N4076	3969
2N4077	2736
2N4078	0222
2N4079	3502
2N4080	3971

DEVICE TYPE	REPL CODE
2N4081	0007
2N4082	OEM
2N4083	OEM
2N4084	OEM
2N4085	OEM
2N4086	0111
2N4087	0111
2N4087A	0111
2N4088	OEM
2N4089	OEM
2N4090	OEM
2N4091	1147
2N4091A	OEM
2N4092	1147
2N4092A	OEM
2N4093	3519
2N4093A	OEM
2N4094	OEM
2N4095	OEM
2N4096	OEM
2N4097	OEM
2N4098	OEM
2N4099	OEM
2N4100	0079
2N4101	3579
2N4102	OEM
2N4103	3979
2N4104	0079
2N4105	0038
2N4106	0164
2N4107	0164
2N4108	OEM
2N4109	OEM
2N4110	OEM
2N4111	0615
2N4112	0103
2N4113	0615
2N4114	0103
2N4117	0321
2N4117A	0321
2N4118	0321
2N4118A	3350
2N4119	0321
2N4119A	0321
2N4120	0838
2N4121	0037
2N4122	0150
2N4123	0079
2N4124	0076
2N4125	0037
2N4126	0037
2N4127	1224
2N4128	1966
2N4130	0103
2N4134	0007
2N4135	0007
2N4136	0208
2N4137	0488
2N4138	0016
2N4139	OEM
2N4140	0016
2N4141	0016
2N4142	0037
2N4143	0037
2N4144	1129
2N4145	1129
2N4146	0340
2N4147	0895
2N4148	0058
2N4149	0058
2N4150	0617
2N4151	1478
2N4152	1478
2N4153	1478
2N4154	1478
2N4155	1478
2N4156	1478
2N4157	OEM
2N4158	OEM
2N4159	1478
2N4160	1478
2N4161	1478
2N4162	1478
2N4163	1478
2N4164	1478
2N4165	OEM
2N4166	OEM
2N4167	3385
2N4168	1095
2N4169	2471
2N4170	0240
2N4171	2635
2N4172	0671
2N4173	2782
2N4174	0332
2N4175	1095
2N4176	3385
2N4177	2471
2N4178	0240
2N4179	2635
2N4180	0671
2N4181	0332
2N4182	0332
2N4183	1478
2N4184	1478
2N4185	1478
2N4186	1478
2N4187	1478
2N4188	1478

DEVICE TYPE	REPL CODE
2N4189	OEM
2N4190	OEM
2N4191	1478
2N4192	1478
2N4193	1478
2N4194	1478
2N4195	1478
2N4196	1478
2N4197	OEM
2N4198	OEM
2N4199	OEM
2N4200	OEM
2N4201	OEM
2N4202	OEM
2N4203	OEM
2N4204	OEM
2N4205	OEM
2N4207	0037
2N4208	0037
2N4209	0037
2N4210	3470
2N4211	3470
2N4212	OEM
2N4213	OEM
2N4214	OEM
2N4215	OEM
2N4216	OEM
2N4217	OEM
2N4218	0403
2N4219	OEM
2N4220	3577
2N4220A	0321
2N4221	3577
2N4221A	3577
2N4222	0321
2N4222A	0321
2N4223	0321
2N4224	0321
2N4225	0555
2N4226	0555
2N4227	0016
2N4228	0037
2N4231	0178
2N4231A	0161
2N4232	0178
2N4232A	0419
2N4233	0178
2N4233A	0419
2N4234	0126
2N4235	0126
2N4236	0126
2N4237	0086
2N4238	0086
2N4239	0086
2N4240	1021
2N4241	0160
2N4241MP	OEM
2N4242	0599
2N4243	0599
2N4244	0085
2N4245	0599
2N4246	0599
2N4247	0085
2N4248	0006
2N4249	0037
2N4250	0037
2N4250A	0037
2N4251	0414
2N4252	0007
2N4253	0007
2N4254	0127
2N4255	0127
2N4256	0155
2N4257	0037
2N4257A	0037
2N4258	0037
2N4258A	0037
2N4259	0007
2N4260	1581
2N4261	3562
2N4261JAN	OEM
2N4261JTX	OEM
2N4262	OEM
2N4263	OEM
2N4264	0079
2N4265	0079
2N4267	0838
2N4269	0233
2N4270	0233
2N4271	0168
2N4273	0424
2N4274	0016
2N4275	0016
2N4276	0085
2N4277	0085
2N4278	0085
2N4279	0085
2N4280	4037
2N4281	0085
2N4282	0085
2N4283	0085
2N4284	0037
2N4285	0037
2N4286	0155
2N4287	0155
2N4288	0037
2N4289	0037
2N4290	0037
2N4291	0037

48 If replacement code is OEM, contact original manufacturer for replacement.

DEVICE TYPE	REPL CODE
2N4292	0144
2N4293	0144
2N4294	0079
2N4295	0007
2N4296	1021
2N4297	1021
2N4298	0142
2N4299	0142
2N4301	2637
2N4302	2922
2N4303	2922
2N4304	2922
2N4307	0042
2N4308	0042
2N4311	0042
2N4312	0042
2N4313	0037
2N4314	0126
2N4315	OEM
2N4316	0500
2N4317	0500
2N4318	0500
2N4319	OEM
2N4320	OEM
2N4321	OEM
2N4322	OEM
2N4323	OEM
2N4324	OEM
2N4325	OEM
2N4326	OEM
2N4327	OEM
2N4328	OEM
2N4329	OEM
2N4330	OEM
2N4331	OEM
2N4332	OEM
2N4333	OEM
2N4334	OEM
2N4335	OEM
2N4336	OEM
2N4337	OEM
2N4338	0321
2N4339	0321
2N4340	3104
2N4341	0321
2N4342	OEM
2N4343	OEM
2N4346	0969
2N4347	0177
2N4348	0177
2N4349	0930
2N4350	0555
2N4351	0977
2N4352	0838
2N4353	0838
2N4354	0037
2N4355	0037
2N4356	0037
2N4357	0338
2N4359	0037
2N4360	2959
2N4361	0463
2N4362	0463
2N4363	0463
2N4364	0463
2N4365	0463
2N4366	0463
2N4367	0463
2N4368	OEM
2N4369	OEM
2N4370	OEM
2N4371	0653
2N4372	0653
2N4373	0653
2N4374	0653
2N4375	0653
2N4376	0653
2N4377	0653
2N4378	OEM
2N4379	OEM
2N4380	OEM
2N4381	1133
2N4382	OEM
2N4383	0086
2N4384	0018
2N4385	0086
2N4386	0018
2N4387	0919
2N4388	0919
2N4389	0037
2N4390	0855
2N4391	1147
2N4392	1147
2N4393	OEM
2N4395	0103
2N4396	0103
2N4397	0007
2N4398	1671
2N4399	1671
2N4400	0076
2N4401	0076
2N4402	0037
2N4403	0037
2N4404	0126
2N4405	0126
2N4406	0126
2N4407	0126
2N4409	0855
2N4410	0076
2N4411	0037
2N4412	0126
2N4412A	0126
2N4413	0037
2N4413A	0037
2N4414	0126
2N4414A	0126
2N4415	0037
2N4415A	0037
2N4416	2861
2N4416A	2861
2N4417	2861
2N4418	0016
2N4419	0016
2N4420	0079
2N4421	0079
2N4422	0079
2N4423	0150
2N4424	0155
2N4425	0218
2N4427	2030
2N4427M	2030
2N4428	0555
2N4429	0555
2N4430	0555
2N4432	0016
2N4432A	0016
2N4433	0007
2N4434	0007
2N4435	0007
2N4436	0016
2N4437	0016
2N4440	0555
2N4440J	OEM
2N4440TX	OEM
2N4441	0424
2N4442	2255
2N4443	3368
2N4444	3370
2N4445	OEM
2N4446	OEM
2N4447	OEM
2N4448	OEM
2N4449	0488
2N4450	0016
2N4451	0150
2N4452	0037
2N4453	0150
2N4625	0079
2N4836M	0841
2N4848A	OEM
2N4851	2123
2N4852	1167
2N4853	1167
2N4854	0855
2N4855	0855
2N4856	1147
2N4856A	1147
2N4857	1147
2N4857A	1147
2N4858	1147
2N4858A	1147
2N4859	1147
2N4859A	1147
2N4860	1147
2N4860A	1147
2N4861	1147
2N4861A	1147
2N4864	0178
2N4867	0321
2N4867A	0321
2N4868	0321
2N4868A	0321
2N4869	3104
2N4869A	3104
2N4870	1882
2N4871	1882
2N4872	0150
2N4873	0488
2N4874	0488
2N4875	0488
2N4876	0488
2N4877	0617
2N4878	0079
2N4879	0079
2N4880	0079
2N4881	OEM
2N4882	OEM
2N4884	OEM
2N4885	OEM
2N4886	OEM
2N4888	0338
2N4889	0037
2N4890	0126
2N4890S	0126
2N4891	1659
2N4892	OEM
2N4893	2123
2N4894	OEM
2N4895	0617
2N4896	0617
2N4897	0617
2N4898	0899
2N4899	0899
2N4900	0899
2N4901	0486
2N4902	0486
2N4903	0486
2N4904	2002
2N4905	2002
2N4906	2002
2N4907	0486
2N4908	0486
2N4909	0486
2N4910	0424
2N4911	0424
2N4912	0424
2N4913	0177
2N4914	0177
2N4915	0177
2N4916	0006
2N4917	0037
2N4918	0455
2N4919	0455
2N4920	0455
2N4921	0161
2N4922	0161
2N4923	0161
2N4924	4161
2N4924S	0264
2N4925	0233
2N4926	0233
2N4927	0233
2N4928	0126
2N4928S	0378
2N4929	0434
2N4930	0434
2N4930S	0434
2N4931	0434
2N4931S	0434
2N4932	0617
2N4934	0259
2N4935	0488
2N4936	0488
2N4937	0150
2N4938	0150
2N4939	0150
2N4940	0150
2N4941	0150
2N4942	0150
2N4943	0086
2N4944	0086
2N4945	0855
2N4946	0086
2N4947	OEM
2N4948	1167
2N4949	1659
2N4950	0079
2N4951	0079
2N4952	0079
2N4953	0079
2N4954	0155
2N4955	OEM
2N4956	OEM
2N4957	3562
2N4958	3562
2N4959	3562
2N4960	0086
2N4961	0086
2N4962	0086
2N4963	0086
2N4964	0086
2N4965	0037
2N4966	0016
2N4967	0111
2N4968	0016
2N4969	0016
2N4970	0079
2N4971	0037
2N4971A	0786
2N4972	0037
2N4972A	0786
2N4973	OEM
2N4976	0555
2N4977	OEM
2N4978	OEM
2N4979	OEM
2N4980	0037
2N4981	0037
2N4982	0037
2N4982A	0786
2N4983	3373
2N4984	OEM
2N4985	OEM
2N4986	OEM
2N4987	3373
2N4988	OEM
2N4989	OEM
2N4990	3373
2N4991	4169
2N4992	4169
2N4993	4169
2N4994	0079
2N4995	0079
2N4996	0144
2N4997	0076
2N4998	3969
2N5000	3969
2N5006	0933
2N5008	0933
2N5010	0168
2N5018	OEM
2N5019	OEM
2N5020	OEM
2N5021	OEM
2N5022	0126
2N5023	0126
2N5024	0259
2N5027	0079
2N5028	0079
2N5029	0079
2N5030	0079
2N5031	0007
2N5032	0127
2N5033	2959
2N5034	0103
2N5035	0103
2N5036	0103
2N5037	0103
2N5038	2465
2N5038-1	2465
2N5038J	OEM
2N5038TX	OEM
2N5039	2465
2N5039-1	2465
2N5039J	OEM
2N5039TX	OEM
2N5040	0126
2N5041	0126
2N5042	0126
2N5045	0321
2N5046	0321
2N5047	0321
2N5048	2637
2N5049	2637
2N5050	0424
2N5051	0424
2N5052	0007
2N5053	0259
2N5054	0259
2N5055	0786
2N5058	0233
2N5058S	0144
2N5059	0233
2N5059S	0144
2N5060	1129
2N5061	0340
2N5062	0895
2N5063	2326
2N5064	0058
2N5066	0079
2N5067	0177
2N5068	0177
2N5069	0177
2N5070	0930
2N5071J	OEM
2N5071TX	OEM
2N5073	0233
2N5074	4187
2N5075	4187
2N5076	4187
2N5077	4187
2N5078	2861
2N5078A	0321
2N5079	0555
2N5080	0555
2N5081	0016
2N5082	0016
2N5086	0037
2N5086A	0786
2N5087	0037
2N5087A	0786
2N5088	1212
2N5089	1212
2N5090	0617
2N5092	0168
2N5095	0168
2N5097	0103
2N5101	3249
2N5102	0130
2N5103	0079
2N5103A	0321
2N5104	OEM
2N5104A	0321
2N5105	OEM
2N5105A	0321
2N5106	0018
2N5107	0016
2N5108	0414
2N5108A	0414
2N5109	0414
2N5109J	OEM
2N5109TX	OEM
2N5110	0126
2N5111	0126
2N5112	0919
2N5114	1147
2N5115	OEM
2N5116	OEM
2N5117	OEM
2N5118	OEM
2N5119	OEM
2N5120	0086
2N5121	OEM
2N5122	OEM
2N5123	OEM
2N5124	OEM
2N5125	OEM
2N5126	0007
2N5127	0016
2N5128	0016
2N5129	0016
2N5130	0007
2N5131	0079
2N5132	0007
2N5133	0007
2N5134	0016
2N5135	0198
2N5136	0198
2N5137	0016
2N5138	0037
2N5138A	0786
2N5139	0037
2N5139A	0786
2N5140	0150
2N5141	0150
2N5142	0037
2N5142A	0786
2N5143	0037
2N5143A	0786
2N5144	0079
2N5145	0016
2N5146	OEM
2N5148	0617
2N5150	0617
2N5155	0969
2N5156	0599
2N5157	0359
2N5158	OEM
2N5159	OEM
2N5160	0126
2N5161	0919
2N5163	0321
2N5163A	0321
2N5164	1641
2N5165	1641
2N5166	1574
2N5167	1655
2N5168	2174
2N5169	0757
2N5170	0717
2N5171	0759
2N5172	0155
2N5174	0155
2N5175	0855
2N5176	0233
2N5179	0259
2N5180	0007
2N5181	0007
2N5182	0007
2N5183	0198
2N5184	0233
2N5185	0233
2N5186	0016
2N5187	0016
2N5188	0086
2N5189	4207
2N5190	0236
2N5191	0161
2N5192	0161
2N5193	0676
2N5194	0455
2N5195	0455
2N5196	2917
2N5197	2917
2N5198	2917
2N5199	2917
2N5200	0414
2N5201	0710
2N5202	0424
2N5204	0720
2N5205	0761
2N5206	0674
2N5207	0674
2N5208	0150
2N5209	0079
2N5210	0079
2N5211	0086
2N5213	0419
2N5218	2637
2N5219	0079
2N5220	0079
2N5221	0006
2N5222	0224
2N5223	0079
2N5224	0079
2N5225	0076
2N5226	0037
2N5226A	0786
2N5227	0037
2N5227A	0786
2N5228	0150
2N5229	0037
2N5230	0007
2N5231	0037
2N5232	0111
2N5232A	0111
2N5233	0320
2N5234	0320
2N5235	0320
2N5236	0488
2N5238	OEM
2N5239	0270
2N5240	0270
2N5241	0359
2N5242	0126
2N5243	0126
2N5245	0321
2N5245A	0321
2N5246	0321
2N5246A	0321
2N5247	0321
2N5247A	0321
2N5248	0321
2N5248A	0321
2N5249	0111
2N5249A	0111
2N5252	0168
2N5253	0168
2N5254	OEM
2N5255	OEM
2N5256	OEM
2N5257	OEM
2N5258	0321
2N5259	OEM
2N5260	OEM
2N5261	OEM
2N5262	4207
2N5264	1955
2N5265	OEM
2N5266	OEM
2N5267	0321
2N5268	0321
2N5269	0321
2N5270	0321
2N5271	OEM
2N5272	0488
2N5273	3121
2N5274	3123
2N5275	2007
2N5276	OEM
2N5277	0321
2N5278	4218
2N5278A	0321
2N5279	0168
2N5281	0434
2N5282	0434
2N5288	0933
2N5289	0933
2N5291	0434
2N5292	0488
2N5293	0042
2N5294	0419
2N5295	0042
2N5296	0236
2N5297	0419
2N5298	0042
2N5300	0086
2N5301	0130
2N5302	0130
2N5302J	OEM
2N5302TX	OEM
2N5303	0130
2N5303J	OEM
2N5303TX	OEM
2N5304	0144
2N5305	0396
2N5306	0396
2N5306A	0396
2N5307	0396
2N5308	0396
2N5308A	0396
2N5309	0155
2N5310	0155
2N5311	0155
2N5313	2637
2N5315	2637
2N5317	0933
2N5319	0933
2N5320	3296
2N5320HS	0590
2N5321	0617
2N5322	0126
2N5323	0126
2N5324	0969
2N5325	0969
2N5328	0934
2N5331	3449
2N5334	0042
2N5335	0617
2N5336	0617
2N5337	0617
2N5338	0617
2N5339	0617
2N5344	0168
2N5345	0168
2N5346	3969
2N5347	3969
2N5348	3969
2N5349	2846
2N5352	0150
2N5354	0006
2N5354A	0786
2N5355	0006
2N5355A	0786
2N5356	0037
2N5356A	0786
2N5358	0321
2N5359	0321
2N5360	0321
2N5360A	0321
2N5361	0321
2N5362	0321
2N5363	0321
2N5364	0321
2N5365	0037
2N5365A	0786
2N5366	0037
2N5366A	0786
2N5367	0037
2N5367A	0786
2N5368	0079
2N5369	0079
2N5370	0079
2N5371	0079
2N5372	0037
2N5372A	0786
2N5373	0037
2N5373A	0786
2N5374	0037
2N5374A	0786
2N5375	0037
2N5375A	0786
2N5376	1212
2N5377	0079
2N5378	0037
2N5378A	0786
2N5379	0037
2N5379A	0786
2N5380	0079
2N5381	0079
2N5382	0037
2N5382A	0786
2N5383	0037
2N5383A	0786
2N5385	2936
2N5390	OEM
2N5391	0321
2N5392	0321
2N5393	0321
2N5394	0321
2N5395	0321
2N5396	0321
2N5397	2861
2N5398	2861
2N5399	0488
2N5400	0338
2N5401	0338
2N5402	OEM
2N5410(TRW)	0105
2N5415	0434
2N5415J	OEM
2N5415TX	OEM
2N5416	0434
2N5416J	OEM
2N5416TX	OEM
2N5417	0016
2N5418	0155
2N5419	0155
2N5420	0155
2N5421	2030
2N5422	0555
2N5423	0555
2N5424	0042
2N5425	OEM
2N5427	0419
2N5428	0419
2N5429	0419
2N5430	0419
2N5431	1659
2N5432	0321
2N5433	0321
2N5434	0321
2N5435	0085
2N5438	0085
2N5441	1058
2N5442	1307
2N5443	1880
2N5444	2004
2N5445	2006
2N5446	2007
2N5447	0037
2N5447A	0786
2N5448	0133
2N5448A	0786
2N5449	0016
2N5450	0086
2N5451	0086
2N5452	2917
2N5453	2917
2N5454	2917
2N5455	0126
2N5456	0079
2N5457	2922
2N5458	2922
2N5459	3104
2N5460	2959
2N5461	2959
2N5462	2959
2N5463	2959
2N5464	2959
2N5465	OEM
2N5466	0797
2N5467	0359
2N5470	0419
2N5471	OEM
2N5472	OEM
2N5473	OEM
2N5474	OEM
2N5475	OEM
2N5476	OEM
2N5477	2846
2N5478	2846
2N5479	2846
2N5480	2846
2N5481	0555
2N5482	0555
2N5483	0042
2N5484	0321
2N5485	1382
2N5485-1	1382
2N5486	0321
2N5487-1	0144
2N5487-3	0144

If replacement code is OEM, contact original manufacturer for replacement. 49

DEVICE TYPE	REPL CODE
2N5489	0555
2N5490	0419
2N5491	0419
2N5492	0419
2N5493	0419
2N5494	0419
2N5495	0419
2N5496	0042
2N5497	0419
2N5505	OEM
2N5506	OEM
2N5507	OEM
2N5508	OEM
2N5509	OEM
2N5510	OEM
2N5511	OEM
2N5512	OEM
2N5513	OEM
2N5514	OEM
2N5515	2917
2N5516	2917
2N5517	2917
2N5518	2917
2N5519	2917
2N5520	2917
2N5521	2917
2N5522	2917
2N5523	2917
2N5524	2917
2N5525	0396
2N5526	0396
2N5539	3449
2N5541	0168
2N5542	2637
2N5543	3104
2N5544	3104
2N5545	2917
2N5546	2917
2N5547	2917
2N5548	OEM
2N5549	0321
2N5550	0076
2N5551	0076
2N5555	0321
2N5556	0321
2N5557	0321
2N5558	0321
2N5559	0074
2N5561	0321
2N5562	0321
2N5563	0321
2N5564	2917
2N5565	2917
2N5566	2917
2N5567	1058
2N5568	1307
2N5569	0154
2N5570	0147
2N5571	1058
2N5572	1307
2N5573	0154
2N5574	0147
2N5581	0079
2N5582	0079
2N5589	3532
2N5590	1224
2N5591	1966
2N5592	3104
2N5593	3104
2N5594	3104
2N5597	0919
2N5598	0178
2N5600	0178
2N5601	0178
2N5602	0178
2N5603	3328
2N5604	0178
2N5606	0042
2N5608	0555
2N5610	0555
2N5612	0555
2N5614	0615
2N5616	0615
2N5618	0615
2N5620	0615
2N5621	1671
2N5622	0615
2N5623	1671
2N5624	0615
2N5625	1671
2N5626	0615
2N5628	0615
2N5629	0538
2N5630	0538
2N5631	0538
2N5632	1955
2N5633	1955
2N5634	1955
2N5637	0042
2N5638	3102
2N5639	3102
2N5640	0321
2N5641	3542
2N5642	3543
2N5643	2485
2N5644	3516
2N5645	2080
2N5646	1224
2N5647	OEM

DEVICE TYPE	REPL CODE
2N5648	0321
2N5649	0321
2N5650	0259
2N5651	0259
2N5652	0259
2N5653	3102
2N5654	1967
2N5655	0275
2N5656	0275
2N5657	0168
2N5658	2637
2N5659	0933
2N5660	2085
2N5661	2085
2N5662	0168
2N5663	0168
2N5664	0424
2N5665	0424
2N5668	2922
2N5669	0321
2N5670	0321
2N5671	2465
2N5671J	OEM
2N5671TX	OEM
2N5672	2465
2N5672J	OEM
2N5672TX	OEM
2N5679	0886
2N5680	0886
2N5681	0086
2N5682	0639
2N5683	4279
2N5684	4279
2N5685	4280
2N5686	4280
2N5687	2030
2N5688	0555
2N5689	3524
2N5690	3525
2N5692	0085
2N5693	0085
2N5697	0684
2N5698	3516
2N5699	0555
2N5700	0042
2N5701	0042
2N5702	0488
2N5703	0555
2N5704	0042
2N5705	0042
2N5710	0693
2N5711	3542
2N5712	3543
2N5713	3543
2N5715	0617
2N5716	0321
2N5717	0321
2N5718	2922
2N5719	OEM
2N5720	OEM
2N5721	OEM
2N5722	OEM
2N5723	OEM
2N5724	OEM
2N5725	OEM
2N5726	OEM
2N5727	OEM
2N5728	OEM
2N5730	0103
2N5731	0933
2N5733	3449
2N5735	0079
2N5736	0079
2N5737	0486
2N5738	2002
2N5741	1671
2N5742	1671
2N5745	1671
2N5754	2367
2N5755	2378
2N5756	1403
2N5757	2371
2N5758	0074
2N5759	1955
2N5760	1955
2N5763	0150
2N5764	0555
2N5765	0042
2N5766	0555
2N5767	0555
2N5768	0042
2N5769	0103
2N5770	0144
2N5771	0338
2N5772	0079
2N5777	3156
2N5778	3156
2N5779	3156
2N5780	3156
2N5781	4296
2N5782	1257
2N5783	1257
2N5784	0639
2N5785	0639
2N5786	0626
2N5787	1129
2N5788	0340
2N5789	0895
2N5790	0058

DEVICE TYPE	REPL CODE
2N5791	OEM
2N5792	OEM
2N5793	0855
2N5794	2034
2N5795	0037
2N5795JTX	OEM
2N5796	2449
2N5797	OEM
2N5798	OEM
2N5799	OEM
2N5800	OEM
2N5801	OEM
2N5802	OEM
2N5803	OEM
2N5804	0359
2N5805	0359
2N5806	0464
2N5806J	OEM
2N5807	0717
2N5807J	OEM
2N5808	0773
2N5808J	OEM
2N5809	0720
2N5809J	OEM
2N5810	0079
2N5811	0037
2N5812	0079
2N5813	0527
2N5814	0086
2N5815	0527
2N5816	0086
2N5817	0527
2N5818	0086
2N5819	0527
2N5820	0076
2N5820HS	0590
2N5821	0126
2N5821HS	0786
2N5822	0086
2N5823	0786
2N5824	0076
2N5825	0076
2N5826	0079
2N5827	0079
2N5827A	0079
2N5828	0079
2N5828A	0079
2N5829	3562
2N5830	0076
2N5830A	0224
2N5831	0710
2N5832	0710
2N5833	0710
2N5834	0126
2N5835	0007
2N5836	0626
2N5837	0414
2N5838	0270
2N5839	0270
2N5840	0220
2N5841	0855
2N5842	0855
2N5843	OEM
2N5844	OEM
2N5845	0079
2N5845A	0079
2N5846	0617
2N5847	3524
2N5848	3525
2N5849	3526
2N5851	0007
2N5852	0007
2N5855	0786
2N5856	0086
2N5857	0037
2N5857TX	OEM
2N5858	0076
2N5859	0086
2N5861	0617
2N5864	0886
2N5865	0126
2N5867	0486
2N5868	2002
2N5869	0359
2N5870	0359
2N5871	2002
2N5872	2002
2N5873	0103
2N5874	0177
2N5875	0486
2N5876	1588
2N5877	0103
2N5878	0538
2N5879	1588
2N5880	1588
2N5881	0615
2N5882	0615
2N5883	1671
2N5884	1671
2N5885	0130
2N5886	0130
2N5887	0222
2N5888	0222
2N5889	0222
2N5890	0222
2N5891	0222
2N5892	0222
2N5893	0222
2N5894	0222

DEVICE TYPE	REPL CODE
2N5895	0222
2N5896	0222
2N5897	0222
2N5898	0222
2N5899	0222
2N5900	0222
2N5901	0222
2N5902	OEM
2N5903	OEM
2N5904	OEM
2N5905	OEM
2N5906	OEM
2N5907	OEM
2N5908	OEM
2N5909	OEM
2N5910	0037
2N5911	OEM
2N5912	OEM
2N5913	3387
2N5914	3516
2N5915	1410
2N5916	OEM
2N5917	1963
2N5920	2675
2N5922	2156
2N5923	2156
2N5924	1189
2N5925	1189
2N5930	3510
2N5933	3510
2N5941	2523
2N5942	2523
2N5943	2194
2N5944	3516
2N5945	2080
2N5946	1410
2N5947	2059
2N5949	0321
2N5950	0321
2N5951	0321
2N5952	0321
2N5953	0321
2N5954	1190
2N5955	1190
2N5956	1190
2N5961	0079
2N5962	0079
2N5963	0079
2N5964	0086
2N5965	0233
2N5970	0538
2N5971	0538
2N5972	0538
2N5973	0538
2N5974	1190
2N5975	1190
2N5976	1190
2N5977	0556
2N5978	0556
2N5979	0556
2N5980	1190
2N5981	1190
2N5982	1190
2N5983	0556
2N5984	0556
2N5985	0556
2N5986	1190
2N5987	1190
2N5988	1190
2N5989	0556
2N5991	0556
2N5992	1189
2N5993	1963
2N5994	2485
2N5995	1963
2N5996	1224
2N5998	0155
2N5999	0006
2N6000	0079
2N6001	0527
2N6002	0079
2N6003	0037
2N6004	0016
2N6005	0037
2N6006	0079
2N6007	0527
2N6008	0155
2N6009	0527
2N6010	0086
2N6011	0527
2N6012	0018
2N6013	0037
2N6014	0086
2N6015	0786
2N6016	0018
2N6017	0037
2N6021	0919
2N6022	0676
2N6023	0676
2N6024	0676
2N6025	0676
2N6026	0676
2N6027	0312
2N6028	0312
2N6029	1588
2N6030	1588
2N6031	1588
2N6032	2416
2N6032J	OEM

DEVICE TYPE	REPL CODE
2N6032TX	OEM
2N6033	2416
2N6033J	OEM
2N6033TX	OEM
2N6034	2869
2N6035	2869
2N6036	2869
2N6037	0553
2N6038	0553
2N6039	0553
2N6040	3488
2N6041	0597
2N6042	0597
2N6043	3487
2N6044	1203
2N6045	1203
2N6049	0899
2N6050	2415
2N6051	2415
2N6052	2415
2N6053	2262
2N6054	2262
2N6055	2411
2N6056	2411
2N6057	2422
2N6058	2422
2N6059	2422
2N6067	0037
2N6068	4341
2N6068A	0588
2N6068B	0588
2N6069	1744
2N6069A	0588
2N6069B	0588
2N6070	4343
2N6070A	0588
2N6070B	0588
2N6071	3458
2N6071A	0588
2N6071B	0588
2N6072	4058
2N6072A	OEM
2N6072B	OEM
2N6073	0480
2N6073A	0480
2N6073B	OEM
2N6074	4345
2N6074A	OEM
2N6074B	OEM
2N6075	4346
2N6075A	OEM
2N6075B	OEM
2N6076	0037
2N6077	0424
2N6078	0424
2N6079	0424
2N6080	3534
2N6081	1224
2N6082	1966
2N6083	1966
2N6084	1963
2N6085	OEM
2N6086	OEM
2N6087	OEM
2N6088	OEM
2N6089	OEM
2N6090	OEM
2N6091	OEM
2N6092	OEM
2N6093	2523
2N6094	3536
2N6095	3538
2N6096	3539
2N6097	3540
2N6098	0060
2N6099	0477
2N6100	0477
2N6101	0477
2N6102	0477
2N6103	0477
2N6105	1963
2N6106	0848
2N6107	0848
2N6108	0848
2N6109	0919
2N6110	0848
2N6111	0848
2N6112	0111
2N6114	OEM
2N6115	OEM
2N6116	0312
2N6117	OEM
2N6118	OEM
2N6119	OEM
2N6120	OEM
2N6121	0236
2N6122	0060
2N6123	0060
2N6124	0676
2N6125	4357
2N6126	0676
2N6128	0933
2N6129	0144
2N6130	0144
2N6131	0144
2N6132	0848
2N6133	0848
2N6134	0848
2N6135	2059

DEVICE TYPE	REPL CODE
2N6137	OEM
2N6138	OEM
2N6139	0418
2N6140	0418
2N6141	0418
2N6142	OEM
2N6143	OEM
2N6144	OEM
2N6145	3169
2N6146	0147
2N6147	3192
2N6148	OEM
2N6149	OEM
2N6150	OEM
2N6151	4366
2N6152	0954
2N6153	0960
2N6154	0407
2N6155	0411
2N6156	1092
2N6157	2004
2N6158	2006
2N6159	1880
2N6160	2004
2N6161	2006
2N6162	2007
2N6163	3169
2N6164	3177
2N6165	3192
2N6167	1837
2N6168	1837
2N6169	1844
2N6170	3185
2N6171	1837
2N6172	1837
2N6173	1844
2N6174	3185
2N6175	1698
2N6176	1698
2N6177	1698
2N6178	0060
2N6179	0161
2N6180	1298
2N6181	0455
2N6186	1190
2N6187	1190
2N6188	0477
2N6189	0477
2N6190	0886
2N6191	0886
2N6198	3542
2N6199	3543
2N6200	2485
2N6207	1963
2N6208	1963
2N6211	0074
2N6211JK	OEM
2N6212	0074
2N6212J	OEM
2N6213	0074
2N6213J	OEM
2N6214	2714
2N6215	3449
2N6216	0074
2N6218	0144
2N6219	0710
2N6220	0144
2N6221	0144
2N6222	0144
2N6223	0037
2N6224	0037
2N6225	0855
2N6226	1588
2N6227	1588
2N6228	1588
2N6229	1588
2N6230	1588
2N6231	1588
2N6232	0144
2N6232-4	0144
2N6233	0178
2N6234	0424
2N6235	0424
2N6236	4384
2N6237	0174
2N6238	3801
2N6239	3575
2N6240	3291
2N6241	1494
2N6246	0486
2N6247	0486
2N6248	1671
2N6249	1980
2N6250	1980
2N6251	1980
2N6253	0103
2N6254	0103
2N6255	4390
2N6256	1203
2N6257	0130
2N6258	2416
2N6259	2416
2N6260	0178
2N6261	0424
2N6262	0538
2N6263	0178
2N6264	0178
2N6271	3510
2N6274	2416

DEVICE TYPE	REPL CODE
2N6275	2416
2N6276	2416
2N6277	2416
2N6278	3449
2N6279	3449
2N6280	3449
2N6281	3449
2N6282	3483
2N6283	3483
2N6283J	OEM
2N6283TX	OEM
2N6284	3483
2N6284J	OEM
2N6284TX	OEM
2N6285	2429
2N6286	3484
2N6287	3484
2N6288	0042
2N6289	0042
2N6290	0042
2N6291	0419
2N6292	0419
2N6293	0419
2N6294	3336
2N6295	3336
2N6296	3497
2N6297	3497
2N6298	0597
2N6299	0597
2N6300	1203
2N6301	1203
2N6302	0538
2N6303	0126
2N6304	0259
2N6305	0259
2N6306	0359
2N6306J	OEM
2N6306TX	OEM
2N6307	0359
2N6307M	0074
2N6308	0359
2N6308J	OEM
2N6308M	0074
2N6308TX	OEM
2N6312	0676
2N6313	0676
2N6314	0676
2N6315	0419
2N6316	0419
2N6317	0848
2N6318	0848
2N6322	0538
2N6322MP	0538
2N6326	0130
2N6327	0130
2N6328	0130
2N6329	1671
2N6330	1671
2N6331	1671
2N6332	OEM
2N6333	OEM
2N6334	OEM
2N6335	OEM
2N6336	OEM
2N6337	OEM
2N6338	2465
2N6339	2465
2N6340	2465
2N6341	2465
2N6342	0767
2N6342A	0767
2N6343	0739
2N6343A	0739
2N6344	0612
2N6344A	0612
2N6345	0869
2N6345A	0869
2N6346	0767
2N6346A	0767
2N6347	0739
2N6347A	0739
2N6348	0612
2N6348A	0612
2N6349	0869
2N6349A	0869
2N6354	0615
2N6355	3483
2N6356	3483
2N6357	2422
2N6358	3483
2N6359	0538
2N6360	0538
2N6365	0050
2N6365A	0050
2N6366	1581
2N6367	0144
2N6368	2918
2N6370	0144
2N6371	0103
2N6372	0144
2N6373	0424
2N6374	0424
2N6375	0693
2N6383	3339
2N6383J	OEM
2N6383TX	OEM
2N6384	3339
2N6384J	OEM
2N6384TX	OEM

If replacement code is OEM, contact original manufacturer for replacement.

DEVICE TYPE	REPL CODE
2N6385	3339
2N6385J	OEM
2N6385TX	OEM
2N6386	2220
2N6387	2220
2N6388	2220
2N6389	0259
2N6394	2499
2N6395	4411
2N6396	4412
2N6397	4413
2N6398	4414
2N6399	1504
2N6400	4415
2N6401	4412
2N6402	4412
2N6403	4413
2N6404	4414
2N6405	1504
2N6413	0161
2N6420	0787
2N6421	0787
2N6422	0787
2N6423	0787
2N6424	0142
2N6425	0142
2N6426	3749
2N6427	3749
2N6428	0079
2N6428A	0079
2N6429	0079
2N6429A	0079
2N6430	0187
2N6431	0187
2N6432	0338
2N6433	0338
2N6436	1671
2N6437	1671
2N6438	2465
2N6441	OEM
2N6442	OEM
2N6443	OEM
2N6444	OEM
2N6445	OEM
2N6446	OEM
2N6447	OEM
2N6448	OEM
2N6449	OEM
2N6450	OEM
2N6451	OEM
2N6452	OEM
2N6453	OEM
2N6454	OEM
2N6455	2296
2N6456	2296
2N6457	2296
2N6458	0615
2N6459	3521
2N6465	0178
2N6466	0928
2N6467	0676
2N6468	0676
2N6469	0486
2N6470	0103
2N6471	0103
2N6472	0130
2N6473	0236
2N6474	0236
2N6475	0676
2N6476	0676
2N6477	0723
2N6478	0723
2N6483	OEM
2N6484	OEM
2N6485	OEM
2N6486	0477
2N6487	0477
2N6488	1359
2N6489	1359
2N6490	1359
2N6491	1359
2N6492	2411
2N6493	2411
2N6494	2411
2N6496	0615
2N6497	0723
2N6498	0723
2N6499	2985
2N6500	0178
2N6504	2499
2N6505	0393
2N6506	0393
2N6507	0606
2N6508	0946
2N6509	1504
2N6510	0359
2N6511	0359
2N6512	0359
2N6513	0359
2N6514	0359
2N6515	0710
2N6516	0710
2N6518	0338
2N6519	0338
2N6526	OEM
2N6530	2220
2N6531	1203
2N6532	1203
2N6534	1203

DEVICE TYPE	REPL CODE
2N6535	1203
2N6536	1203
2N6538	0079
2N6539	0079
2N6540	0855
2N6541	0855
2N6542	0359
2N6543	0359
2N6544	0359
2N6545	3236
2N6546	1331
2N6546J	OEM
2N6546TX	OEM
2N6547	3009
2N6548	3492
2N6549	3492
2N6550	OEM
2N6551	0555
2N6552	0818
2N6553	0818
2N6554	3294
2N6555	3294
2N6556	3294
2N6557	0283
2N6558	0638
2N6558L	0283
2N6560	1841
2N6561	1955
2N6564	OEM
2N6565	OEM
2N6569	0103
2N6573	0270
2N6574	1841
2N6575	1841
2N6576	1384
2N6577	1384
2N6578	2412
2N6579	OEM
2N6580	OEM
2N6581	OEM
2N6582	1955
2N6583	1955
2N6584	OEM
2N6585	OEM
2N6586	OEM
2N6587	OEM
2N6588	OEM
2N6589	OEM
2N6590	OEM
2N6591	0283
2N6592	0283
2N6593	0283
2N6594	0486
2N6601	0007
2N6605	OEM
2N6606	OEM
2N6607	OEM
2N6608	OEM
2N6609	4454
2N6617	OEM
2N6618	OEM
2N6619	OEM
2N6620	OEM
2N6621	OEM
2N6623	OEM
2N6624	OEM
2N6625	OEM
2N6626	OEM
2N6627	OEM
2N6628	OEM
2N6629	OEM
2N6630	OEM
2N6631	OEM
2N6632	OEM
2N6633	OEM
2N6634	OEM
2N6635	OEM
2N6636	OEM
2N6637	OEM
2N6638	OEM
2N6639	OEM
2N6640	OEM
2N6641	OEM
2N6642	OEM
2N6643	OEM
2N6644	OEM
2N6645	OEM
2N6646	OEM
2N6648	3340
2N6648J	OEM
2N6648TX	OEM
2N6649	3340
2N6649J	OEM
2N6650	3340
2N6650J	OEM
2N6650TX	OEM
2N6653	1841
2N6654	1841
2N6655	1841
2N6656	OEM
2N6657	OEM
2N6658	OEM
2N6659	OEM
2N6660	OEM
2N6661	OEM
2N6665	OEM
2N6666	2222
2N6667	2222
2N6668	2222

DEVICE TYPE	REPL CODE
2N6669	4459
2N6671	1955
2N6672	1955
2N6673	3354
2N6674	1331
2N6675	1331
2N6676	4460
2N6677	4460
2N6678	4460
2N6679	OEM
2N6680	OEM
2N6681	OEM
2N6682	OEM
2N6683	OEM
2N6684	OEM
2N6685	OEM
2N6686	OEM
2N6687	OEM
2N6688	OEM
2N6689	OEM
2N6690	OEM
2N6691	0477
2N6692	OEM
2N6693	OEM
2N6701	OEM
2N6702	1157
2N6703	1157
2N6704	OEM
2N6705	3882
2N6706	3882
2N6707	3882
2N6708	4468
2N6709	4468
2N6710	4468
2N6711	0261
2N6712	0261
2N6713	0261
2N6714	1518
2N6715	1518
2N6716	1518
2N6717	0086
2N6718	0086
2N6719	0261
2N6720	3718
2N6721	3718
2N6722	3718
2N6723	3718
2N6724	3749
2N6725	3749
2N6726	1587
2N6727	1587
2N6728	1587
2N6729	1587
2N6730	1587
2N6731	1587
2N6732	1587
2N6733	3708
2N6734	3708
2N6735	3708
2N6736	OEM
2N6737	1518
2N6738	0723
2N6740H	0723
2N6751	4487
2N6752	4487
2N6753	3031
2N6754	2965
2N6755	OEM
2N6756	OEM
2N6757	OEM
2N6758	OEM
2N6759	OEM
2N6760	OEM
2N6761	OEM
2N6762	OEM
2N6763	4492
2N6764	OEM
2N6764H	5266
2N6765	OEM
2N6766	OEM
2N6767	OEM
2N6768	OEM
2N6769	OEM
2N6770	OEM
2N6781	OEM
2N6782	OEM
2N6783	OEM
2N6784	OEM
2N6785	OEM
2N6786	OEM
2N6787	OEM
2N6788	OEM
2N6789	OEM
2N6790	OEM
2N6791	OEM
2N6792	OEM
2N6793	OEM
2N6794	OEM
2N6795	OEM
2N6796	OEM
2N6797	OEM
2N6798	OEM
2N6799	OEM
2N6800	OEM
2N6801	OEM
2N6802	OEM
2N6826	OEM
2N6832	OEM
2N6833	4510

DEVICE TYPE	REPL CODE
2N6834	4511
2N6835	OEM
2N6836	3354
2N6837	OEM
2N6838	OEM
2N6839	OEM
2N7000	OEM
2N7002	OEM
2N7008	OEM
2N19616	0050
2N29260RN	0079
2N54433	0050
2N67425	OEM
2N91446	0079
2NFP4339	OEM
2NFP4340	OEM
2NJ5A	0279
2NJ5D	0211
2NJ6	0279
2NJ8A	0279
2NJ9A	0211
2NJ9D	0211
2NJ50	0136
2NJ51	0136
2NJ52	0136
2NJ53	0136
2NJ59D	0136
2NJ224	OEM
2NJ233B	0321
2NJ584	1021
2NJ770A	OEM
2NJ771A	OEM
2NL48	0590
2NS31	0211
2NS32	0211
2NS121	0211
2NSM-1	0071
2NU/9	0841
2NU/9WHT	0841
2NU/9YEL	0841
20A72	OEM
20A79	OEM
20A90	0123
20A90A-M	0123
20A90M	0123
20A99	0143
20A99A	0143
20C6	OEM
20C26	OEM
20C28	OEM
20C29	OEM
20C30	OEM
20C35	OEM
20C36	OEM
20C72	0164
20C74	OEM
20C83	OEM
20C84	OEM
2P05M	1250
2P1M	2255
2P2M	0934
2P4M	0095
2P5M	1234
2P6M	1234
2P389	OEM
2P389A	OEM
2P424	OEM
2P424A	OEM
2PB187	0004
2PD56	OEM
2PD57	OEM
2PD58	OEM
2PD-358	0143
2PL.75-1.5	OEM
2PL.75-1.5S	OEM
2PS428	0079
2PT6	OEM
2P.5-1	OEM
2P.5-1S	OEM
2QT2222	2877
2QT2905	0281
2R0/18	OEM
2R1/18	OEM
2R1/52	OEM
2R2/18	OEM
2R2B	OEM
2R2JA	OEM
2R2S	OEM
2R3B	OEM
2R3S	OEM
2R4C	OEM
2R4S	OEM
2R5C	OEM
2R5S	OEM
2R6C	OEM
2R6S	OEM
2R7CD	OEM
2R7S	OEM
2R8CD	OEM
2R8S	OEM
2R9.1	0679
2R9.1A	0679
2R9.1B	0679
2R10	0225
2R10A	0225
2R10B	0225
2R11	0230
2R11A	0230
2R11B	0230

DEVICE TYPE	REPL CODE
2R12	0234
2R12A	0234
2R12B	0234
2R13	0237
2R13A	0237
2R13B	0237
2R15	0247
2R15A	0247
2R15B	0247
2R16	0251
2R16A	0251
2R16B	0251
2R18	0256
2R18A	0256
2R18B	0256
2R20	0262
2R20A	0262
2R20B	0262
2R22	0269
2R22A	0269
2R22B	0269
2R24	0273
2R24A	0273
2R24B	0273
2R27	0291
2R27A	0291
2R27B	0291
2R30	0305
2R30A	0305
2R30B	0305
2R33	0314
2R33A	0314
2R33B	0314
2R36	0316
2R36A	0316
2R36B	0316
2R39	0322
2R39A	0322
2R39B	0322
2R43	0333
2R43A	0333
2R43B	0333
2R47	0343
2R47A	0343
2R47B	0343
2R51	0027
2R51A	0027
2R51B	0027
2R52	OEM
2R56	0266
2R56A	0266
2R56B	0266
2R68	0401
2R68A	0401
2R68B	0401
2R75	0421
2R75A	0421
2R75B	0421
2R91	0238
2R91A	0238
2R91B	0238
2R100	1172
2R100A	1172
2R100B	1172
2R110	1182
2R110A	1182
2R110B	1182
2R120	1198
2R120A	1198
2R120B	1198
2R130	1209
2R130A	1209
2R130B	1209
2R140	1870
2R140A	1870
2R140B	1870
2R150	0642
2R150A	0642
2R150B	0642
2R160	1246
2R160A	1246
2R160B	1246
2R180	1269
2R180A	1269
2R180B	1269
2R200	0600
2R200A	0600
2R200B	0600
2R430M	OEM
2RD402B1X16	OEM
2RD402B1X32	OEM
2RD402B1X36	OEM
2RD402B1X72	OEM
2RE52	OEM
2S001	0016
2S002	0016
2S003	0016
2S004	0016
2S005	0016
2S006	0144
2S012	0042
2S013	OEM
2S014	0086
2S017	0086
2S018	0086
2S019	0086
2S020	0086
2S021	0126
2S022	0126

DEVICE TYPE	REPL CODE
2S023	0126
2S033	0103
2S034	0103
2S035	0074
2S036	0074
2S043	OEM
2S044	OEM
2S045	OEM
2S046	OEM
2S095A	0079
2S0781	0558
2S2-4	OEM
2S2-4S	OEM
2S2M	OEM
2S3M	OEM
2S4M	OEM
2S12	0279
2S13	0279
2S14	0211
2S15	0211
2S15A	0211
2S15X90	0037
2S22	0211
2S24	0211
2S25	0279
2S26	0160
2S26A	0160
2S30	0279
2S31	0279
2S32	0211
2S33	0211
2S34	0211
2S35	0136
2S36	0136
2S37	0211
2S38	0211
2S39	0211
2S40	0211
2S41	0085
2S41A	0085
2S42	0085
2S43	0211
2S44	0211
2S45	0279
2S46	0211
2S47	0211
2S49	0279
2S51	0279
2S52	0279
2S53	0279
2S54	0211
2S56	0211
2S57	0050
2S58	0136
2S60	0279
2S82	0127
2S91	0279
2S92	0279
2S92A	0279
2S93	0279
2S93A	0279
2S95A	0016
2S96	0136
2S97	0136
2S98	0136
2S101	0016
2S102	0016
2S103	0016
2S104	0016
2S109	0136
2S110	0136
2S111	0279
2S112	0136
2S128Y	0208
2S131	0016
2S134	0841
2S141	0136
2S142	0136
2S143	0136
2S144	0050
2S145	0136
2S146	0136
2S148	0050
2S155	0279
2S159	0279
2S160	0208
2S163	0211
2S167	0279
2S174	0279
2S174R	OEM
2S175	0050
2S176	0136
2S178	0279
2S179	0211
2S189	0004
2S201	0050
2S257	1257
2S273	0004
2S277C	0208
2S301	0126
2S302	0126
2S302A	0126
2S303	0126
2S304	0126
2S305	0037
2S306	0037
2S307	0037
2S307A	0786
2S321	0037

DEVICE TYPE	REPL CODE
2S321A	0786
2S322	0037
2S322A	0037
2S322AB	0786
2S323	0037
2S323A	0786
2S324	0037
2S324A	0786
2S325	0855
2S326	0037
2S326A	0786
2S327	0037
2S327A	0786
2S351B	0050
2S363	0079
2S375B	0211
2S471-1	0050
2S494-YE	0786
2S501	0016
2S502	0016
2S503	0016
2S512	0016
2S564R	0150
2S644(S)	0086
2S645	0079
2S701	0198
2S702	0198
2S703	0198
2S711	0016
2S712	0016
2S720	OEM
2S731	0016
2S732	0016
2S733	0016
2S741	0198
2S741A	0016
2S742	0086
2S742A	0086
2S743	0233
2S743A	0233
2S744	0198
2S744A	0016
2S745	0086
2S745A	0086
2S746	0233
2S746A	0233
2S858	0338
2S1182D	0079
2S1505	OEM
2S1685QR	OEM
2S1760	0211
2S3010	0126
2S3020	0037
2S3020A	0786
2S3021	0037
2S3021A	0786
2S3030	0037
2S3030A	0786
2S3040	0037
2S3040A	0786
2S3187	0279
2S3210	0037
2S3210A	0786
2S3220	0037
2S3220A	0786
2S3221	0037
2S3221A	0786
2S3230	0037
2S3230A	0786
2S3240	0037
2S3240A	0786
2S3324	0279
2S3370	0136
2S6856	0283
2S20141	0079
2SA007H	0164
2SA076F	0050
2SA081C	0164
2SA098R	0050
2SA12	0004
2SA12(V)	0004
2SA12A	0004
2SA12B	0004
2SA12C	0004
2SA12D	0004
2SA12H	0004
2SA12V	0004
2SA13	0050
2SA13A	0050
2SA13B	0050
2SA13C	0050
2SA13D	0050
2SA13G	0050
2SA13L	0050
2SA13M	0050
2SA13OR	0050
2SA13R	0050
2SA13X	0050
2SA13Y	0050
2SA14	0050
2SA14A	0050
2SA14B	0050
2SA14C	0050
2SA14D	0050
2SA14E	0050
2SA14G	0050
2SA14L	0050
2SA14M	0050
2SA14OR	0050

If replacement code is OEM, contact original manufacturer for replacement.

DEVICE TYPE	REPL CODE
2SA14R	0050
2SA14X	0050
2SA14Y	0050
2SA15	0004
2SA15-6	0004
2SA15A	0004
2SA15B	0004
2SA15BK	0004
2SA15C	0004
2SA15D	0004
2SA15E	0004
2SA15F	0004
2SA15G	0004
2SA15H	0004
2SA15K	0004
2SA15L	0004
2SA15M	0004
2SA15OR	0004
2SA15R	0004
2SA15RD	0004
2SA15U	0004
2SA15V	0004
2SA15V/R	0004
2SA15VR	0004
2SA15X	0004
2SA15Y	0004
2SA16	0004
2SA16A	0004
2SA16B	0004
2SA16C	0004
2SA16D	0004
2SA16E	0004
2SA16F	0004
2SA16L	0004
2SA16M	0004
2SA16OR	0004
2SA16R	0004
2SA16X	0004
2SA16Y	0004
2SA17	0050
2SA17A	0050
2SA17B	0050
2SA17C	0050
2SA17D	0050
2SA17E	0050
2SA17F	0050
2SA17G	0050
2SA17H	0050
2SA17L	0050
2SA17OR	0050
2SA17R	0050
2SA17X	0050
2SA17Y	0050
2SA18	0050
2SA18A	0050
2SA18B	0050
2SA18C	0050
2SA18D	0050
2SA18E	0050
2SA18F	0050
2SA18G	0050
2SA18H	0050
2SA18L	0050
2SA18M	0050
2SA18OR	0050
2SA18R	0050
2SA18X	0050
2SA18Y	0050
2SA19	0164
2SA19A	0164
2SA19B	0164
2SA19C	0164
2SA19D	0164
2SA19E	0164
2SA19F	0164
2SA19G	0164
2SA19L	0164
2SA19M	0164
2SA19OR	0164
2SA19R	0164
2SA19X	0164
2SA19Y	0164
2SA20	0164
2SA20A	0164
2SA20B	0164
2SA20C	0164
2SA20D	0164
2SA20E	0164
2SA20F	0164
2SA20G	0164
2SA20L	0164
2SA20M	0164
2SA20OR	0164
2SA20R	0164
2SA20X	0164
2SA20Y	0164
2SA21	0164
2SA21A	0164
2SA21B	0164
2SA21C	0164
2SA21D	0164
2SA21E	0164
2SA21F	0164
2SA21G	0164
2SA21L	0164
2SA21M	0164
2SA21OR	0164
2SA21R	0164
2SA21X	0164

DEVICE TYPE	REPL CODE
2SA21Y	0164
2SA22	0050
2SA23	0050
2SA24	0050
2SA25	0050
2SA26	0050
2SA26A	0050
2SA26B	0050
2SA26C	0050
2SA26D	0050
2SA26E	0050
2SA26F	0050
2SA26G	0050
2SA26L	0050
2SA26M	0050
2SA26OR	0050
2SA26R	0050
2SA26X	0050
2SA26Y	0050
2SA27	0050
2SA28	0050
2SA28A	0050
2SA28B	0050
2SA28C	0050
2SA28D	0050
2SA28E	0050
2SA28F	0050
2SA28G	0050
2SA28L	0050
2SA28M	0050
2SA28OR	0050
2SA28X	0050
2SA28Y	0050
2SA29	0164
2SA29A	0164
2SA29B	0164
2SA29C	0164
2SA29D	0164
2SA29E	0164
2SA29F	0164
2SA29G	0164
2SA29L	0164
2SA29M	0164
2SA29R	0164
2SA29X	0164
2SA29Y	0164
2SA30	0136
2SA30A	0136
2SA30B	0136
2SA30C	0136
2SA30D	0136
2SA30E	0136
2SA30F	0136
2SA30G	0136
2SA30L	0136
2SA30M	0136
2SA30OR	0136
2SA30X	0136
2SA30Y	0136
2SA31	0279
2SA31A	0279
2SA31B	0279
2SA31C	0279
2SA31D	0279
2SA31E	0279
2SA31F	0279
2SA31G	0279
2SA31L	0279
2SA31M	0279
2SA31OR	0279
2SA31X	0279
2SA31Y	0279
2SA32	0050
2SA32A	0050
2SA32B	0050
2SA32C	0050
2SA32D	0050
2SA32E	0050
2SA32F	0050
2SA32G	0050
2SA32L	0050
2SA32M	0050
2SA32OR	0050
2SA32X	0050
2SA32Y	0050
2SA33	0004
2SA35	0004
2SA35A	0004
2SA35B	0004
2SA35C	0004
2SA35D	0004
2SA35E	0004
2SA35F	0004
2SA35G	0004
2SA35L	0004
2SA35M	0004
2SA35OR	0004
2SA35X	0004
2SA35Y	0004
2SA36	0050
2SA36A	0050
2SA36B	0050
2SA36C	0050
2SA36D	0050
2SA36E	0050
2SA36F	0050
2SA36G	0050
2SA36L	0050
2SA36M	0050

DEVICE TYPE	REPL CODE
2SA36OR	0050
2SA36R	0050
2SA36X	0050
2SA36Y	0050
2SA37	0050
2SA37A	0050
2SA37B	0050
2SA37C	0050
2SA37D	0050
2SA37E	0050
2SA37F	0050
2SA37G	0050
2SA37L	0050
2SA37M	0050
2SA37OR	0050
2SA37R	0050
2SA37X	0050
2SA37Y	0050
2SA38	0050
2SA38A	0050
2SA38B	0050
2SA38C	0050
2SA38D	0050
2SA38E	0050
2SA38F	0050
2SA38G	0050
2SA38L	0050
2SA38M	0050
2SA38OR	0050
2SA38R	0050
2SA38X	0050
2SA38Y	0050
2SA39	0050
2SA39A	0050
2SA39B	0050
2SA39C	0050
2SA39D	0050
2SA39E	0050
2SA39F	0050
2SA39G	0050
2SA39L	0050
2SA39M	0050
2SA39OR	0050
2SA39R	0050
2SA39X	0050
2SA39Y	0050
2SA40	0279
2SA40A	0279
2SA40B	0279
2SA40C	0279
2SA40D	0279
2SA40E	0279
2SA40F	0279
2SA40G	0279
2SA40L	0279
2SA40M	0279
2SA40OR	0279
2SA40R	0279
2SA40X	0279
2SA40Y	0279
2SA41	0050
2SA41A	0050
2SA41B	0050
2SA41C	0050
2SA41D	0050
2SA41E	0050
2SA41F	0050
2SA41G	0050
2SA41L	0050
2SA41M	0050
2SA41OR	0050
2SA41R	0050
2SA41X	0050
2SA41Y	0050
2SA42	0050
2SA43	0136
2SA44	0136
2SA44A	0136
2SA44B	0136
2SA44C	0136
2SA44D	0136
2SA44E	0136
2SA44F	0136
2SA44G	0136
2SA44L	0136
2SA44M	0136
2SA44OR	0136
2SA44R	0136
2SA44X	0136
2SA44Y	0136
2SA45	0136
2SA45-1	0136
2SA45-2	0136
2SA45-3	0136
2SA46	0279
2SA47	0050
2SA48	0050
2SA49	0628
2SA49A	0628
2SA49B	0628
2SA49C	0628
2SA49D	0628
2SA49E	0628
2SA49F	0628
2SA49G	0628
2SA49L	0628
2SA49M	0628
2SA49OR	0628
2SA49R	0628

DEVICE TYPE	REPL CODE
2SA49X	0628
2SA49Y	0628
2SA50	0050
2SA50A	0050
2SA50B	0050
2SA50C	0050
2SA50D	0050
2SA50E	0050
2SA50F	0050
2SA50G	0050
2SA50L	0050
2SA50M	0050
2SA50OR	0050
2SA50R	0050
2SA50X	0050
2SA50Y	0050
2SA51	0136
2SA51A	0136
2SA51B	0136
2SA51C	0136
2SA51D	0136
2SA51E	0136
2SA51F	0136
2SA51G	0136
2SA51L	0136
2SA51M	0136
2SA51OR	0136
2SA51R	0136
2SA51X	0136
2SA51Y	0136
2SA52	0136
2SA52A	0136
2SA52B	0136
2SA52C	0136
2SA52D	0136
2SA52E	0136
2SA52F	0136
2SA52G	0136
2SA52L	0136
2SA52M	0136
2SA52OR	0136
2SA52R	0136
2SA52X	0136
2SA52Y	0136
2SA53	0628
2SA53A	0628
2SA53B	0628
2SA53C	0628
2SA53D	0628
2SA53E	0628
2SA53F	0628
2SA53G	0628
2SA53L	0628
2SA53M	0628
2SA53OR	0628
2SA53R	0628
2SA53X	0628
2SA53Y	0628
2SA54	0050
2SA54A	0050
2SA54B	0050
2SA54C	0050
2SA54D	0050
2SA54E	0050
2SA54F	0050
2SA54G	0050
2SA54L	0050
2SA54M	0050
2SA54OR	0050
2SA54R	0050
2SA54X	0050
2SA54Y	0050
2SA55	0136
2SA55A	0136
2SA55B	0136
2SA55C	0136
2SA55D	0136
2SA55E	0136
2SA55F	0136
2SA55G	0136
2SA55L	0136
2SA55M	0136
2SA55OR	0136
2SA55R	0136
2SA55X	0136
2SA55Y	0136
2SA56	0136
2SA56A	0136
2SA57	0136
2SA57A	0136
2SA57B	0136
2SA57C	0136
2SA57D	0136
2SA57E	0136
2SA57F	0136
2SA57G	0136
2SA57L	0136
2SA57M	0136
2SA57OR	0136
2SA57R	0136
2SA57X	0136
2SA57Y	0136
2SA58	0050
2SA58A	0050
2SA58B	0050
2SA58C	0050
2SA58D	0050
2SA58E	0050
2SA58F	0050

DEVICE TYPE	REPL CODE
2SA58G	0050
2SA58H	0050
2SA58J	0050
2SA58K	0050
2SA58L	0050
2SA58M	0050
2SA58OR	0050
2SA58R	0050
2SA58X	0050
2SA58Y	0050
2SA59	0050
2SA59A	0050
2SA59B	0050
2SA59C	0050
2SA59D	0050
2SA59E	0050
2SA59F	0050
2SA59G	0050
2SA59L	0050
2SA59M	0050
2SA59OR	0050
2SA59R	0050
2SA59X	0050
2SA59Y	0050
2SA60	0050
2SA60A	0050
2SA60B	0050
2SA60C	0050
2SA60D	0050
2SA60E	0050
2SA60F	0050
2SA60G	0050
2SA60H	0050
2SA60K	0050
2SA60L	0050
2SA60M	0050
2SA60OR	0050
2SA60R	0050
2SA60X	0050
2SA60Y	0050
2SA61	0050
2SA61A	0050
2SA61C	0050
2SA61D	0050
2SA61E	0050
2SA61G	0050
2SA61K	0050
2SA61L	0050
2SA61OR	0050
2SA61R	0050
2SA61X	0050
2SA61Y	0050
2SA64	0164
2SA64A	0164
2SA64B	0164
2SA64C	0164
2SA64D	0164
2SA64E	0164
2SA64F	0164
2SA64G	0164
2SA64GN	0164
2SA64H	0164
2SA64J	0164
2SA64K	0164
2SA64L	0164
2SA64M	0164
2SA64OR	0164
2SA64R	0164
2SA64X	0164
2SA64Y	0164
2SA65	0050
2SA65A	0050
2SA65B	0050
2SA65C	0050
2SA65D	0050
2SA65E	0050
2SA65F	0050
2SA65G	0050
2SA65K	0050
2SA65L	0050
2SA65M	0050
2SA65OR	0050
2SA65R	0050
2SA65X	0050
2SA65Y	0050
2SA66	0050
2SA66A	0050
2SA66B	0050
2SA66C	0050
2SA66D	0050
2SA66E	0050
2SA66F	0050
2SA66G	0050
2SA66K	0050
2SA66L	0050
2SA66M	0050
2SA66OR	0050
2SA66R	0050
2SA66X	0050
2SA66Y	0050
2SA67	0004
2SA67A	0004
2SA67B	0004
2SA67C	0004
2SA67D	0004
2SA67E	0004
2SA67F	0004
2SA67G	0004
2SA67H	0004

DEVICE TYPE	REPL CODE
2SA67K	0004
2SA67L	0004
2SA67OR	0004
2SA67R	0004
2SA67X	0004
2SA67Y	0004
2SA68	0050
2SA69	0136
2SA69A	0136
2SA69B	0136
2SA69C	0136
2SA69D	0136
2SA69E	0136
2SA69F	0136
2SA69G	0136
2SA69H	0136
2SA69K	0136
2SA69L	0136
2SA69M	0136
2SA69OR	0136
2SA69R	0136
2SA69X	0136
2SA69Y	0136
2SA70	0050
2SA70-08	0050
2SA70-0B	0050
2SA70-OB	0050
2SA70A	0050
2SA70B	0050
2SA70C	0050
2SA70D	0050
2SA70E	0050
2SA70F	0050
2SA70G	0050
2SA70H	0050
2SA70K	0050
2SA70L	0050
2SA70MA	0050
2SA70OA	0050
2SA70OR	0050
2SA70R	0050
2SA70X	0050
2SA70Y	0050
2SA71	0050
2SA71A	0050
2SA71AB	0050
2SA71AC	0050
2SA71B	0050
2SA71BS	0050
2SA71C	0050
2SA71D	0050
2SA71E	0050
2SA71F	0050
2SA71G	0050
2SA71H	0050
2SA71K	0050
2SA71L	0050
2SA71M	0050
2SA71OR	0050
2SA71R	0050
2SA71X	0050
2SA71Y	0050
2SA71YA	0050
2SA72	0136
2SA72BLU	0136
2SA72BLU-BLU	0136
2SA72BRN	0136
2SA72ORN	0136
2SA72WHT	0136
2SA73	0050
2SA73A	0050
2SA73B	0050
2SA73C	0050
2SA73D	0050
2SA73E	0050
2SA73F	0050
2SA73G	0050
2SA73H	0050
2SA73K	0050
2SA73L	0050
2SA73M	0050
2SA73OR	0050
2SA73R	0050
2SA73X	0050
2SA73Y	0050
2SA74	0136
2SA74A	0136
2SA74B	0136
2SA74C	0136
2SA74D	0136
2SA74E	0136
2SA74F	0136
2SA74G	0136
2SA74H	0136
2SA74K	0136
2SA74L	0136
2SA74M	0136
2SA74OR	0136
2SA74R	0136
2SA74X	0136
2SA74Y	0136
2SA75	0136
2SA75A	0136
2SA75B	0136
2SA75C	0136
2SA75D	0136
2SA75E	0136
2SA75F	0136
2SA75G	0136

DEVICE TYPE	REPL CODE
2SA75H	0136
2SA75K	0136
2SA75L	0136
2SA75M	0136
2SA75OR	0136
2SA75R	0136
2SA75X	0136
2SA75Y	0136
2SA76	0050
2SA76A	0050
2SA76B	0050
2SA76C	0050
2SA76D	0050
2SA76E	0050
2SA76F	0050
2SA76G	0050
2SA76H	0050
2SA76K	0050
2SA76L	0050
2SA76OR	0050
2SA76R	0050
2SA76X	0050
2SA76Y	0050
2SA77	0628
2SA77A	0628
2SA77B	0628
2SA77C	0628
2SA77D	0628
2SA77E	0628
2SA77F	0628
2SA77G	0628
2SA77H	0628
2SA77K	0628
2SA77L	0628
2SA77M	0628
2SA77OR	0628
2SA77R	0628
2SA77X	0628
2SA77Y	0628
2SA78	0004
2SA79	0004
2SA80	0164
2SA80A	0164
2SA80B	0164
2SA80D	0164
2SA80E	0164
2SA80F	0164
2SA80G	0164
2SA80H	0164
2SA80K	0164
2SA80L	0164
2SA80M	0164
2SA80OR	0164
2SA80R	0164
2SA80X	0164
2SA80Y	0164
2SA81	0050
2SA82	0164
2SA82A	0164
2SA82B	0164
2SA82C	0164
2SA82D	0164
2SA82E	0164
2SA82F	0164
2SA82G	0164
2SA82H	0164
2SA82K	0164
2SA82M	0164
2SA82OR	0164
2SA82R	0164
2SA82X	0164
2SA82Y	0164
2SA83	0050
2SA83A	0050
2SA83B	0050
2SA83C	0050
2SA83D	0050
2SA83E	0050
2SA83F	0050
2SA83G	0050
2SA83H	0050
2SA83K	0050
2SA83L	0050
2SA83M	0050
2SA83OR	0050
2SA83R	0050
2SA83X	0050
2SA83Y	0050
2SA84	0050
2SA84A	0050
2SA84B	0050
2SA84C	0050
2SA84D	0050
2SA84E	0050
2SA84F	0050
2SA84G	0050
2SA84H	0050
2SA84K	0050
2SA84L	0050
2SA84M	0050
2SA84OR	0050
2SA84R	0050
2SA84X	0050
2SA84Y	0050
2SA85	0136
2SA85L	0136
2SA86	0050
2SA87	0050
2SA87A	0050

If replacement code is OEM, contact original manufacturer for replacement.

DEVICE TYPE	REPL CODE
2SA87B	0050
2SA87C	0050
2SA87D	0050
2SA87E	0050
2SA87F	0050
2SA87G	0050
2SA87H	0050
2SA87K	0050
2SA87L	0050
2SA87M	0050
2SA87OR	0050
2SA87R	0050
2SA87X	0050
2SA87Y	0050
2SA88	0050
2SA89	0050
2SA90	0136
2SA92	0050
2SA92A	0050
2SA92B	0050
2SA92C	0050
2SA92D	0050
2SA92E	0050
2SA92F	0050
2SA92G	0050
2SA92H	0050
2SA92K	0050
2SA92L	0050
2SA92M	0050
2SA92OR	0050
2SA92R	0050
2SA92X	0050
2SA92Y	0050
2SA93	0050
2SA93A	0050
2SA93B	0050
2SA93C	0050
2SA93E	0050
2SA93F	0050
2SA93G	0050
2SA93H	0050
2SA93K	0050
2SA93L	0050
2SA93M	0050
2SA93OR	0050
2SA93R	0050
2SA93X	0050
2SA93Y	0050
2SA94	0164
2SA94A	0164
2SA94C	0164
2SA94D	0164
2SA94E	0164
2SA94F	0164
2SA94G	0164
2SA94H	0164
2SA94K	0164
2SA94L	0164
2SA94M	0164
2SA94OR	0164
2SA94R	0164
2SA94X	0164
2SA94Y	0164
2SA95	0050
2SA96	0050
2SA97	0050
2SA98	0050
2SA99	0050
2SA100	0136
2SA100A	0136
2SA100B	0136
2SA100C	0136
2SA100D	0136
2SA100E	0136
2SA100F	0136
2SA100G	0136
2SA100H	0136
2SA100J	0136
2SA100K	0136
2SA100M	0136
2SA100OR	0136
2SA100R	0136
2SA100X	0136
2SA100Y	0136
2SA101	0136
2SA101(C)	0136
2SA101(V)	0136
2SA101-OR	0136
2SA101A	0136
2SA101AA	0136
2SA101AY	0136
2SA101B	0136
2SA101BA	0136
2SA101BB	0136
2SA101BC	0136
2SA101BX	0136
2SA101C	0136
2SA101CA	0136
2SA101CV	0136
2SA101CX	0136
2SA101D	0136
2SA101E	0136
2SA101F	0136
2SA101G	0136
2SA101H	0136
2SA101K	0136
2SA101L	0136
2SA101M	0136
2SA101OR	0136

DEVICE TYPE	REPL CODE
2SA101QA	0136
2SA101R	0136
2SA101X	0136
2SA101XBX	0136
2SA101Y	0136
2SA101YA	0136
2SA101Z	0136
2SA102	0136
2SA102(BA)	0136
2SA102-OR	0136
2SA102A	0136
2SA102AA	0136
2SA102AB	0136
2SA102B	0136
2SA102BA	0136
2SA102BA-2	0136
2SA102BN	0136
2SA102C	0136
2SA102CA	0136
2SA102CA-1	0136
2SA102D	0136
2SA102E	0136
2SA102F	0136
2SA102G	0136
2SA102H	0136
2SA102K	0136
2SA102L	0136
2SA102M	0136
2SA102OR	0136
2SA102TV	0136
2SA102TV-2	0136
2SA102X	0136
2SA102Y	0136
2SA103	0136
2SA103(CA)	0136
2SA103A	0136
2SA103B	0136
2SA103C	0136
2SA103CA	0136
2SA103CAK	0136
2SA103CB	0136
2SA103CG	0136
2SA103D	0136
2SA103DA	0136
2SA103E	0136
2SA103F	0136
2SA103G	0136
2SA103GA	0136
2SA103K	0136
2SA103L	0136
2SA103M	0136
2SA103OR	0136
2SA103R	0136
2SA103X	0136
2SA103Y	0136
2SA104	0050
2SA104A	0050
2SA104B	0050
2SA104C	0050
2SA104D	0050
2SA104E	0050
2SA104F	0050
2SA104G	0050
2SA104H	0050
2SA104K	0050
2SA104L	0050
2SA104M	0050
2SA104OR	0050
2SA104P	0050
2SA104R	0050
2SA104X	0050
2SA104Y	0050
2SA105	0136
2SA105A	0136
2SA105B	0136
2SA105C	0136
2SA105D	0136
2SA105E	0136
2SA105G	0136
2SA105H	0136
2SA105K	0136
2SA105L	0136
2SA105M	0136
2SA105OR	0136
2SA105R	0136
2SA105X	0136
2SA105Y	0136
2SA106	0136
2SA106A	0136
2SA106B	0136
2SA106C	0136
2SA106D	0136
2SA106E	0136
2SA106F	0136
2SA106G	0136
2SA106H	0136
2SA106K	0136
2SA106L	0136
2SA106M	0136
2SA106OR	0136
2SA106R	0136
2SA106X	0136
2SA106Y	0136
2SA107	0136
2SA107A	0136
2SA107B	0136
2SA107C	0136
2SA107D	0136
2SA107E	0136

DEVICE TYPE	REPL CODE
2SA107F	0136
2SA107G	0136
2SA107H	0136
2SA107K	0136
2SA107L	0136
2SA107M	0136
2SA107OR	0136
2SA107R	0136
2SA107X	0136
2SA107Y	0136
2SA108	0136
2SA108A	0136
2SA108B	0136
2SA108C	0136
2SA108D	0136
2SA108E	0136
2SA108F	0136
2SA108G	0136
2SA108H	0136
2SA108K	0136
2SA108L	0136
2SA108M	0136
2SA108OR	0136
2SA108R	0136
2SA108X	0136
2SA108Y	0136
2SA109	0136
2SA109A	0136
2SA109B	0136
2SA109C	0136
2SA109D	0136
2SA109E	0136
2SA109F	0136
2SA109G	0136
2SA109K	0136
2SA109L	0136
2SA109M	0136
2SA109OR	0136
2SA109R	0136
2SA109X	0136
2SA109Y	0136
2SA110	0136
2SA110A	0136
2SA110B	0136
2SA110C	0136
2SA110D	0136
2SA110E	0136
2SA110F	0136
2SA110G	0136
2SA110K	0136
2SA110L	0136
2SA110M	0136
2SA110OR	0136
2SA110R	0136
2SA110X	0136
2SA110Y	0136
2SA111	0136
2SA111A	0136
2SA111B	0136
2SA111C	0136
2SA111D	0136
2SA111E	0136
2SA111F	0136
2SA111G	0136
2SA111K	0136
2SA111L	0136
2SA111M	0136
2SA111OR	0136
2SA111R	0136
2SA111X	0136
2SA111Y	0136
2SA112	0136
2SA112A	0136
2SA112B	0136
2SA112C	0136
2SA112D	0136
2SA112E	0136
2SA112F	0136
2SA112G	0136
2SA112GN	0136
2SA112H	0136
2SA112K	0136
2SA112L	0136
2SA112M	0136
2SA112OR	0136
2SA112R	0136
2SA112X	0136
2SA112Y	0136
2SA113	0136
2SA113A	0136
2SA113B	0136
2SA113C	0136
2SA113D	0136
2SA113E	0136
2SA113F	0136
2SA113G	0136
2SA113GN	0136
2SA113H	0136
2SA113J	0136
2SA113L	0136
2SA113M	0136
2SA113R	0136
2SA113X	0136
2SA113Y	0136
2SA114	0136
2SA114A	0136
2SA114B	0136
2SA114C	0136
2SA114D	0136

DEVICE TYPE	REPL CODE
2SA114E	0136
2SA114F	0136
2SA114G	0136
2SA114H	0136
2SA114K	0136
2SA114L	0136
2SA114M	0136
2SA114OR	0136
2SA114R	0136
2SA114X	0136
2SA114Y	0136
2SA115	0136
2SA115A	0136
2SA115B	0136
2SA115C	0136
2SA115D	0136
2SA115E	0136
2SA115F	0136
2SA115G	0136
2SA115GN	0136
2SA115H	0136
2SA115J	0136
2SA115K	0136
2SA115L	0136
2SA115M	0136
2SA115OR	0136
2SA115R	0136
2SA115X	0136
2SA115Y	0136
2SA116	0136
2SA116A	0136
2SA116B	0136
2SA116C	0136
2SA116D	0136
2SA116E	0136
2SA116F	0136
2SA116G	0136
2SA116GN	0136
2SA116H	0136
2SA116J	0136
2SA116K	0136
2SA116L	0136
2SA116M	0136
2SA116OR	0136
2SA116R	0136
2SA116X	0136
2SA116Y	0136
2SA117	0136
2SA117A	0136
2SA117B	0136
2SA117C	0136
2SA117D	0136
2SA117E	0136
2SA117F	0136
2SA117G	0136
2SA117GN	0136
2SA117H	0136
2SA117J	0136
2SA117K	0136
2SA117L	0136
2SA117M	0136
2SA117OR	0136
2SA117R	0136
2SA117X	0136
2SA117Y	0136
2SA118	0136
2SA118A	0136
2SA118B	0136
2SA118C	0136
2SA118D	0136
2SA118E	0136
2SA118F	0136
2SA118G	0136
2SA118GN	0136
2SA118H	0136
2SA118J	0136
2SA118K	0136
2SA118L	0136
2SA118M	0136
2SA118OR	0136
2SA118R	0136
2SA118X	0136
2SA118Y	0136
2SA119	0126
2SA120	0126
2SA120A	0126
2SA121	0136
2SA121A	0136
2SA121B	0136
2SA121C	0136
2SA121D	0136
2SA121E	0136
2SA121F	0136
2SA121G	0136
2SA121GN	0136
2SA121H	0136
2SA121J	0136
2SA121K	0136
2SA121L	0136
2SA121M	0136
2SA121OR	0136
2SA121R	0136
2SA121X	0136
2SA121Y	0136
2SA122	0136
2SA122A	0136
2SA122B	0136
2SA122C	0136
2SA122D	0136

DEVICE TYPE	REPL CODE
2SA122E	0136
2SA122F	0136
2SA122G	0136
2SA122GN	0136
2SA122H	0136
2SA122K	0136
2SA122L	0136
2SA122M	0136
2SA122OR	0136
2SA122R	0136
2SA122X	0136
2SA122Y	0136
2SA123	0136
2SA123A	0136
2SA123B	0136
2SA123C	0136
2SA123D	0136
2SA123E	0136
2SA123F	0136
2SA123G	0136
2SA123GN	0136
2SA123H	0136
2SA123J	0136
2SA123K	0136
2SA123L	0136
2SA123M	0136
2SA123OR	0136
2SA123R	0136
2SA123X	0136
2SA123Y	0136
2SA124	0136
2SA124A	0136
2SA124B	0136
2SA124C	0136
2SA124D	0136
2SA124E	0136
2SA124F	0136
2SA124G	0136
2SA124GN	0136
2SA124H	0136
2SA124J	0136
2SA124K	0136
2SA124L	0136
2SA124M	0136
2SA124OR	0136
2SA124R	0136
2SA124X	0136
2SA124Y	0136
2SA125	0136
2SA125A	0136
2SA125B	0136
2SA125C	0136
2SA125D	0136
2SA125E	0136
2SA125F	0136
2SA125G	0136
2SA125GN	0136
2SA125H	0136
2SA125J	0136
2SA125K	0136
2SA125L	0136
2SA125M	0136
2SA125OR	0136
2SA125R	0136
2SA125X	0136
2SA125Y	0136
2SA126	0136
2SA127	0136
2SA128	0164
2SA128A	0164
2SA128B	0164
2SA128C	0164
2SA128D	0164
2SA128E	0164
2SA128F	0164
2SA128G	0164
2SA128GN	0164
2SA128H	0164
2SA128J	0164
2SA128K	0164
2SA128L	0164
2SA128M	0164
2SA128OR	0164
2SA128R	0164
2SA128X	0164
2SA128Y	0164
2SA129	0164
2SA129A	0164
2SA129B	0164
2SA129C	0164
2SA129D	0164
2SA129E	0164
2SA129F	0164
2SA129G	0164
2SA129GN	0164
2SA129H	0164
2SA129J	0164
2SA129K	0164
2SA129L	0164
2SA129M	0164
2SA129OR	0164
2SA129R	0164
2SA129X	0164
2SA129Y	0164
2SA130	0050
2SA130A	0050
2SA130B	0050
2SA130C	0050
2SA130D	0050

DEVICE TYPE	REPL CODE
2SA130E	0050
2SA130F	0050
2SA130G	0050
2SA130GN	0050
2SA130H	0050
2SA130J	0050
2SA130K	0050
2SA130L	0050
2SA130M	0050
2SA130OR	0050
2SA130R	0050
2SA130X	0050
2SA130Y	0050
2SA131	0136
2SA131A	0136
2SA131B	0136
2SA131C	0136
2SA131D	0136
2SA131E	0136
2SA131F	0136
2SA131G	0136
2SA131GN	0136
2SA131H	0136
2SA131J	0136
2SA131K	0136
2SA131L	0136
2SA131M	0136
2SA131OR	0136
2SA131R	0136
2SA131X	0136
2SA131Y	0136
2SA132	0136
2SA132A	0136
2SA132B	0136
2SA132C	0136
2SA132D	0136
2SA132E	0136
2SA132F	0136
2SA132G	0136
2SA132H	0136
2SA132J	0136
2SA132K	0136
2SA132L	0136
2SA132M	0136
2SA132OR	0136
2SA132X	0136
2SA132Y	0136
2SA133	0136
2SA133A	0136
2SA133B	0136
2SA133C	0136
2SA133D	0136
2SA133E	0136
2SA133F	0136
2SA133G	0136
2SA133GN	0136
2SA133H	0136
2SA133J	0136
2SA133K	0136
2SA133L	0136
2SA133M	0136
2SA133OR	0136
2SA133R	0136
2SA133X	0136
2SA133Y	0136
2SA134	0136
2SA134A	0136
2SA134B	0136
2SA134C	0136
2SA134D	0136
2SA134E	0136
2SA134F	0136
2SA134G	0136
2SA134H	0136
2SA134J	0136
2SA134K	0136
2SA134L	0136
2SA134OR	0136
2SA134R	0136
2SA134X	0136
2SA134Y	0136
2SA135	0050
2SA135A	0050
2SA135B	0050
2SA135C	0050
2SA135D	0050
2SA135E	0050
2SA135F	0050
2SA135G	0050
2SA135GN	0050
2SA135H	0050
2SA135J	0050
2SA135K	0050
2SA135L	0050
2SA135M	0050
2SA135OR	0050
2SA135R	0050
2SA135X	0050
2SA135Y	0050
2SA136	0050
2SA136A	0050
2SA136B	0050
2SA136C	0050
2SA136D	0050
2SA136E	0050
2SA136F	0050
2SA136G	0050
2SA136GN	0050
2SA136H	0050

DEVICE TYPE	REPL CODE
2SA136J	0050
2SA136K	0050
2SA136L	0050
2SA136M	0050
2SA136OR	0050
2SA136R	0050
2SA136X	0050
2SA136Y	0050
2SA137	0136
2SA137A	0136
2SA137B	0136
2SA137C	0136
2SA137D	0136
2SA137E	0136
2SA137F	0136
2SA137G	0136
2SA137GN	0136
2SA137H	0136
2SA137J	0136
2SA137K	0136
2SA137L	0136
2SA137M	0136
2SA137OR	0136
2SA137R	0136
2SA137X	0136
2SA137Y	0136
2SA138	0004
2SA139	0136
2SA139A	0136
2SA139B	0136
2SA139C	0136
2SA139D	0136
2SA139E	0136
2SA139F	0136
2SA139G	0136
2SA139GN	0136
2SA139J	0136
2SA139K	0136
2SA139L	0136
2SA139M	0136
2SA139OR	0136
2SA139R	0136
2SA139X	0136
2SA139Y	0136
2SA141	0136
2SA141A	0136
2SA141B	0136
2SA141C	0136
2SA141D	0136
2SA141E	0136
2SA141F	0136
2SA141G	0136
2SA141GN	0136
2SA141H	0136
2SA141K	0136
2SA141L	0136
2SA141M	0136
2SA141OR	0136
2SA141R	0136
2SA141X	0136
2SA141Y	0136
2SA142	0136
2SA142A	0136
2SA142B	0136
2SA142C	0136
2SA142D	0136
2SA142E	0136
2SA142F	0136
2SA142G	0136
2SA142GN	0136
2SA142H	0136
2SA142J	0136
2SA142K	0136
2SA142L	0136
2SA142M	0136
2SA142OR	0136
2SA142R	0136
2SA142X	0136
2SA142Y	0136
2SA143	0136
2SA143A	0136
2SA143B	0136
2SA143C	0136
2SA143D	0136
2SA143E	0136
2SA143F	0136
2SA143G	0136
2SA143GN	0136
2SA143H	0136
2SA143J	0136
2SA143K	0136
2SA143L	0136
2SA143M	0136
2SA143OR	0136
2SA143R	0136
2SA143X	0136
2SA143Y	0136
2SA144	0136
2SA144A	0136
2SA144B	0136
2SA144C	0136
2SA144D	0136
2SA144E	0136
2SA144F	0136
2SA144G	0136
2SA144GN	0136
2SA144H	0136
2SA144J	0136
2SA144K	0136

If replacement code is OEM, contact original manufacturer for replacement.

DEVICE TYPE	REPL CODE
2SA144L	0136
2SA144M	0136
2SA144OR	0136
2SA144R	0136
2SA144X	0136
2SA144Y	0136
2SA145	0136
2SA145A	0136
2SA145B	0136
2SA145C	0136
2SA145D	0136
2SA145E	0136
2SA145G	0136
2SA145GN	0136
2SA145K	0136
2SA145M	0136
2SA145OR	0136
2SA145R	0136
2SA145X	0136
2SA145Y	0136
2SA146	0136
2SA146A	0136
2SA146B	0136
2SA146C	0136
2SA146D	0136
2SA146E	0136
2SA146F	0136
2SA146G	0136
2SA146GN	0136
2SA146H	0136
2SA146J	0136
2SA146K	0136
2SA146L	0136
2SA146M	0136
2SA146OR	0136
2SA146X	0136
2SA146Y	0136
2SA147	0136
2SA147A	0136
2SA147B	0136
2SA147C	0136
2SA147D	0136
2SA147E	0136
2SA147F	0136
2SA147G	0136
2SA147H	0136
2SA147J	0136
2SA147K	0136
2SA147L	0136
2SA147M	0136
2SA147OR	0136
2SA147R	0136
2SA147X	0136
2SA147Y	0136
2SA148	0136
2SA148A	0136
2SA148B	0136
2SA148C	0136
2SA148D	0136
2SA148E	0136
2SA148F	0136
2SA148G	0136
2SA148GN	0136
2SA148H	0136
2SA148J	0136
2SA148K	0136
2SA148L	0136
2SA148M	0136
2SA148OR	0136
2SA148R	0136
2SA148X	0136
2SA148Y	0136
2SA149	0136
2SA149A	0136
2SA149B	0136
2SA149C	0136
2SA149D	0136
2SA149E	0136
2SA149F	0136
2SA149G	0136
2SA149GN	0136
2SA149H	0136
2SA149J	0136
2SA149K	0136
2SA149L	0136
2SA149M	0136
2SA149OR	0136
2SA149R	0136
2SA149X	0136
2SA149Y	0136
2SA150	0136
2SA150A	0136
2SA150B	0136
2SA150C	0136
2SA150D	0136
2SA150E	0136
2SA150F	0136
2SA150G	0136
2SA150GN	0136
2SA150H	0136
2SA150J	0136
2SA150K	0136
2SA150L	0136
2SA150M	0136
2SA150OR	0136
2SA150R	0136
2SA150X	0136
2SA150Y	0136
2SA151	0136
2SA151A	0136
2SA151B	0136
2SA151C	0136
2SA151D	0136
2SA151E	0136
2SA151F	0136
2SA151G	0136
2SA151GN	0136
2SA151H	0136
2SA151J	0136
2SA151K	0136
2SA151L	0136
2SA151M	0136
2SA151OR	0136
2SA151R	0136
2SA151X	0136
2SA151Y	0136
2SA152	0136
2SA152A	0136
2SA152B	0136
2SA152C	0136
2SA152D	0136
2SA152E	0136
2SA152F	0136
2SA152G	0136
2SA152GN	0136
2SA152H	0136
2SA152J	0136
2SA152K	0136
2SA152L	0136
2SA152M	0136
2SA152OR	0136
2SA152R	0136
2SA152X	0136
2SA152Y	0136
2SA153	0136
2SA153A	0136
2SA153B	0136
2SA153C	0136
2SA153D	0136
2SA153E	0136
2SA153F	0136
2SA153G	0136
2SA153GN	0136
2SA153H	0136
2SA153J	0136
2SA153K	0136
2SA153L	0136
2SA153M	0136
2SA153OR	0136
2SA153R	0136
2SA153X	0136
2SA153Y	0136
2SA154	0136
2SA154A	0136
2SA154B	0136
2SA154C	0136
2SA154D	0136
2SA154E	0136
2SA154F	0136
2SA154G	0136
2SA154GN	0136
2SA154H	0136
2SA154J	0136
2SA154K	0136
2SA154L	0136
2SA154M	0136
2SA154OR	0136
2SA154R	0136
2SA154X	0136
2SA154Y	0136
2SA155	0136
2SA155A	0136
2SA155B	0136
2SA155C	0136
2SA155D	0136
2SA155E	0136
2SA155F	0136
2SA155G	0136
2SA155GN	0136
2SA155H	0136
2SA155J	0136
2SA155K	0136
2SA155L	0136
2SA155M	0136
2SA155OR	0136
2SA155R	0136
2SA155X	0136
2SA155Y	0136
2SA156	0136
2SA156A	0136
2SA156B	0136
2SA156C	0136
2SA156D	0136
2SA156E	0136
2SA156F	0136
2SA156G	0136
2SA156GN	0136
2SA156H	0136
2SA156J	0136
2SA156K	0136
2SA156L	0136
2SA156M	0136
2SA156OR	0136
2SA156R	0136
2SA156X	0136
2SA156Y	0136
2SA157	0136
2SA157A	0136
2SA157B	0136
2SA157C	0136
2SA157D	0136
2SA157E	0136
2SA157F	0136
2SA157G	0136
2SA157GN	0136
2SA157H	0136
2SA157J	0136
2SA157K	0136
2SA157L	0136
2SA157M	0136
2SA157OR	0136
2SA157R	0136
2SA157X	0136
2SA157Y	0136
2SA159	0136
2SA159A	0136
2SA159B	0136
2SA159C	0136
2SA159D	0136
2SA159E	0136
2SA159F	0136
2SA159G	0136
2SA159GN	0136
2SA159H	0136
2SA159J	0136
2SA159K	0136
2SA159L	0136
2SA159M	0136
2SA159OR	0136
2SA159R	0136
2SA159X	0136
2SA159Y	0136
2SA160	0136
2SA160A	0136
2SA160B	0136
2SA160C	0136
2SA160D	0136
2SA160E	0136
2SA160F	0136
2SA160GN	0136
2SA160H	0136
2SA160J	0136
2SA160K	0136
2SA160L	0136
2SA160M	0136
2SA160OR	0136
2SA160R	0136
2SA160X	0136
2SA160Y	0136
2SA161	0136
2SA161A	0136
2SA161B	0136
2SA161C	0136
2SA161D	0136
2SA161E	0136
2SA161F	0136
2SA161G	0136
2SA161GN	0136
2SA161H	0136
2SA161J	0136
2SA161K	0136
2SA161L	0136
2SA161M	0136
2SA161OR	0136
2SA161R	0136
2SA161X	0136
2SA161Y	0136
2SA162	0136
2SA162A	0136
2SA162B	0136
2SA162C	0136
2SA162D	0136
2SA162E	0136
2SA162F	0136
2SA162G	0136
2SA162GN	0136
2SA162H	0136
2SA162J	0136
2SA162K	0136
2SA162L	0136
2SA162M	0136
2SA162OR	0136
2SA162R	0136
2SA162X	0136
2SA162Y	0136
2SA163	0136
2SA163A	0136
2SA163B	0136
2SA163C	0136
2SA163D	0136
2SA163E	0136
2SA163F	0136
2SA163G	0136
2SA163GN	0136
2SA163H	0136
2SA163J	0136
2SA163K	0136
2SA163L	0136
2SA163M	0136
2SA163OR	0136
2SA163R	0136
2SA163X	0136
2SA163Y	0136
2SA164	0136
2SA164A	0136
2SA164B	0136
2SA164C	0136
2SA164D	0136
2SA164E	0136
2SA164F	0136
2SA164G	0136
2SA164GN	0136
2SA164H	0136
2SA164J	0136
2SA164K	0136
2SA164L	0136
2SA164M	0136
2SA164OR	0136
2SA164R	0136
2SA164X	0136
2SA164Y	0136
2SA165	0136
2SA165A	0136
2SA165B	0136
2SA165C	0136
2SA165D	0136
2SA165E	0136
2SA165F	0136
2SA165G	0136
2SA165GN	0136
2SA165H	0136
2SA165J	0136
2SA165K	0136
2SA165L	0136
2SA165M	0136
2SA165OR	0136
2SA165R	0136
2SA165X	0136
2SA165Y	0136
2SA166	0136
2SA166A	0136
2SA166B	0136
2SA166C	0136
2SA166D	0136
2SA166E	0136
2SA166F	0136
2SA166G	0136
2SA166GN	0136
2SA166H	0136
2SA166J	0136
2SA166K	0136
2SA166L	0136
2SA166M	0136
2SA166OR	0136
2SA166R	0136
2SA166X	0136
2SA166Y	0136
2SA167	0279
2SA167A	0279
2SA167B	0279
2SA167C	0279
2SA167D	0279
2SA167E	0279
2SA167F	0279
2SA167G	0279
2SA167GN	0279
2SA167H	0279
2SA167J	0279
2SA167K	0279
2SA167L	0279
2SA167M	0279
2SA167OR	0279
2SA167R	0279
2SA167X	0279
2SA167Y	0279
2SA168	0279
2SA168A	0279
2SA168B	0279
2SA168C	0279
2SA168D	0279
2SA168E	0279
2SA168F	0279
2SA168G	0279
2SA168GN	0279
2SA168H	0279
2SA168J	0279
2SA168K	0279
2SA168L	0279
2SA168M	0279
2SA168OR	0279
2SA168R	0279
2SA168X	0279
2SA168Y	0279
2SA169	0279
2SA169A	0279
2SA169B	0279
2SA169C	0279
2SA169D	0279
2SA169E	0279
2SA169F	0279
2SA169G	0279
2SA169GN	0279
2SA169H	0279
2SA169J	0279
2SA169K	0279
2SA169L	0279
2SA169M	0279
2SA169OR	0279
2SA169R	0279
2SA169X	0279
2SA169Y	0279
2SA170	0279
2SA170A	0279
2SA170B	0279
2SA170C	0279
2SA170D	0279
2SA170E	0279
2SA170F	0279
2SA170G	0279
2SA170GN	0279
2SA170H	0279
2SA170J	0279
2SA170K	0279
2SA170L	0279
2SA170M	0279
2SA170OR	0279
2SA170R	0279
2SA170X	0279
2SA170Y	0279
2SA171	0279
2SA171A	0279
2SA171B	0279
2SA171C	0279
2SA171D	0279
2SA171E	0279
2SA171F	0279
2SA171G	0279
2SA171GN	0279
2SA171H	0279
2SA171J	0279
2SA171K	0279
2SA171L	0279
2SA171M	0279
2SA171OR	0279
2SA171R	0279
2SA171X	0279
2SA171Y	0279
2SA172	0279
2SA172A	0279
2SA172B	0279
2SA172C	0279
2SA172D	0279
2SA172E	0279
2SA172F	0279
2SA172G	0279
2SA172GN	0279
2SA172H	0279
2SA172J	0279
2SA172K	0279
2SA172L	0279
2SA172M	0279
2SA172OR	0279
2SA172R	0279
2SA172X	0279
2SA172Y	0279
2SA173	0004
2SA173A	0004
2SA173B	0004
2SA173C	0004
2SA173D	0004
2SA173E	0004
2SA173F	0004
2SA173G	0004
2SA173GN	0004
2SA173H	0004
2SA173J	0004
2SA173K	0004
2SA173L	0004
2SA173M	0004
2SA173OR	0004
2SA173R	0004
2SA173X	0004
2SA173Y	0004
2SA174	0211
2SA174A	0211
2SA174B	0211
2SA174C	0211
2SA174D	0211
2SA174E	0211
2SA174F	0211
2SA174G	0211
2SA174GN	0211
2SA174H	0211
2SA174J	0211
2SA174K	0211
2SA174L	0211
2SA174M	0211
2SA174OR	0211
2SA174R	0211
2SA174X	0211
2SA174Y	0211
2SA175	0136
2SA175A	0136
2SA175B	0136
2SA175C	0136
2SA175D	0136
2SA175E	0136
2SA175F	0136
2SA175G	0136
2SA175GN	0136
2SA175H	0136
2SA175J	0136
2SA175K	0136
2SA175L	0136
2SA175M	0136
2SA175OR	0136
2SA175R	0136
2SA175X	0136
2SA175Y	0136
2SA176	0136
2SA176A	0136
2SA176B	0136
2SA176C	0136
2SA176D	0136
2SA176E	0136
2SA176F	0136
2SA176G	0136
2SA176GN	0136
2SA176H	0136
2SA176J	0136
2SA176K	0136
2SA176L	0136
2SA176M	0136
2SA176OR	0136
2SA176R	0136
2SA176X	0136
2SA176Y	0136
2SA178	0050
2SA180	0136
2SA180A	0136
2SA180B	0136
2SA180C	0136
2SA180D	0136
2SA180E	0136
2SA180F	0136
2SA180G	0136
2SA180GN	0136
2SA180H	0136
2SA180J	0136
2SA180K	0136
2SA180L	0136
2SA180M	0136
2SA180OR	0136
2SA180R	0136
2SA180X	0136
2SA180Y	0136
2SA181	0136
2SA181A	0136
2SA181B	0136
2SA181C	0136
2SA181D	0136
2SA181E	0136
2SA181F	0136
2SA181G	0136
2SA181GN	0136
2SA181H	0136
2SA181J	0136
2SA181K	0136
2SA181L	0136
2SA181M	0136
2SA181OR	0136
2SA181R	0136
2SA181X	0136
2SA181Y	0136
2SA182	0050
2SA182A	0050
2SA182B	0050
2SA182C	0050
2SA182D	0050
2SA182E	0050
2SA182F	0050
2SA182G	0050
2SA182GN	0050
2SA182H	0050
2SA182J	0050
2SA182K	0050
2SA182L	0050
2SA182M	0050
2SA182OR	0050
2SA182R	0050
2SA182X	0050
2SA182Y	0050
2SA183	0136
2SA183A	0136
2SA183B	0136
2SA183C	0136
2SA183D	0136
2SA183E	0136
2SA183F	0136
2SA183G	0136
2SA183GN	0136
2SA183H	0136
2SA183J	0136
2SA183K	0136
2SA183L	0136
2SA183M	0136
2SA183OR	0136
2SA183R	0136
2SA183X	0136
2SA183Y	0136
2SA184	0050
2SA186	0164
2SA187TV	0004
2SA188	0136
2SA188A	0136
2SA188B	0136
2SA188C	0136
2SA188D	0136
2SA188E	0136
2SA188F	0136
2SA188G	0136
2SA188GN	0136
2SA188H	0136
2SA188J	0136
2SA188K	0136
2SA188L	0136
2SA188M	0136
2SA188OR	0136
2SA188R	0136
2SA188X	0136
2SA188Y	0136
2SA189	0136
2SA189A	0136
2SA189B	0136
2SA189C	0136
2SA189D	0136
2SA189E	0136
2SA189F	0136
2SA189G	0136
2SA189GN	0136
2SA189H	0136
2SA189J	0136
2SA189K	0136
2SA189L	0136
2SA189M	0136
2SA189OR	0136
2SA189R	0136
2SA189X	0136
2SA189Y	0136
2SA190	0050
2SA191	0050
2SA192	0050
2SA193	0050
2SA194	0050
2SA195	0050
2SA196	0050
2SA197	0136
2SA197A	0136
2SA197B	0136
2SA197C	0136
2SA197D	0136
2SA197E	0136
2SA197F	0136
2SA197G	0136
2SA197GN	0136
2SA197H	0136
2SA197J	0136
2SA197K	0136
2SA197L	0136
2SA197M	0136
2SA197OR	0136
2SA197R	0136
2SA197X	0136
2SA197Y	0136
2SA198	0050
2SA198A	0050
2SA198B	0050
2SA198C	0050
2SA198D	0050
2SA198E	0050
2SA198F	0050
2SA198G	0050
2SA198GN	0050
2SA198H	0050
2SA198J	0050
2SA198K	0050
2SA198L	0050
2SA198M	0050
2SA198OR	0050
2SA198R	0050
2SA198X	0050
2SA198Y	0050
2SA199	0050
2SA200	0136
2SA201	0136
2SA201(0)	0136
2SA201-0	0136
2SA201-N	0136
2SA201-O	0136
2SA201-OR	0136
2SA201A	0136
2SA201B	0136
2SA201CL	0136
2SA201D	0136
2SA201E	0136
2SA201F	0136
2SA201G	0136
2SA201GN	0136
2SA201H	0136
2SA201J	0136
2SA201K	0136
2SA201L	0136
2SA201M	0136
2SA201N	0136
2SA201O	0136
2SA201OR	0136
2SA201R	0136
2SA201TV	0136
2SA201TVO	0136
2SA201X	0136
2SA201Y	0136
2SA202	0628
2SA202-OR	0628
2SA202A	0628
2SA202AP	0628
2SA202B	0628
2SA202C	0628
2SA202D	0628
2SA202D-4	0628
2SA202E	0628
2SA202F	0628
2SA202G	0628
2SA202GN	0628
2SA202H	0628
2SA202J	0628
2SA202K	0628
2SA202L	0628
2SA202M	0628
2SA202OR	0628
2SA202R	0628
2SA202X	0628
2SA202Y	0628
2SA203	0628

If replacement code is OEM, contact original manufacturer for replacement.

DEVICE TYPE	REPL CODE
2SA203A	0628
2SA203AA	0628
2SA203B	0628
2SA203C	0628
2SA203D	0628
2SA203P	0628
2SA204	0279
2SA204A	0279
2SA204B	0279
2SA204C	0279
2SA204D	0279
2SA204E	0279
2SA204F	0279
2SA204G	0279
2SA204GN	0279
2SA204H	0279
2SA204J	0279
2SA204K	0279
2SA204L	0279
2SA204M	0279
2SA204OR	0279
2SA204R	0279
2SA204X	0279
2SA204Y	0279
2SA205	0279
2SA205A	0279
2SA205B	0279
2SA205C	0279
2SA205D	0279
2SA205E	0279
2SA205F	0279
2SA205G	0279
2SA205GN	0279
2SA205H	0279
2SA205J	0279
2SA205K	0279
2SA205L	0279
2SA205M	0279
2SA205OR	0279
2SA205R	0279
2SA205X	0279
2SA205Y	0279
2SA206	0279
2SA206A	0279
2SA206B	0279
2SA206C	0279
2SA206D	0279
2SA206E	0279
2SA206F	0279
2SA206G	0279
2SA206GN	0279
2SA206H	0279
2SA206J	0279
2SA206K	0279
2SA206L	0279
2SA206M	0279
2SA206OR	0279
2SA206R	0279
2SA206X	0279
2SA206Y	0279
2SA207	0279
2SA207A	0279
2SA207B	0279
2SA207C	0279
2SA207D	0279
2SA207E	0279
2SA207F	0279
2SA207G	0279
2SA207GN	0279
2SA207H	0279
2SA207J	0279
2SA207K	0279
2SA207L	0279
2SA207M	0279
2SA207OR	0279
2SA207R	0279
2SA207X	0279
2SA207Y	0279
2SA208	0841
2SA208A	0841
2SA208B	0841
2SA208C	0841
2SA208D	0841
2SA208E	0841
2SA208F	0841
2SA208G	0841
2SA208GN	0841
2SA208H	0841
2SA208J	0841
2SA208K	0841
2SA208L	0841
2SA208M	0841
2SA208OR	0841
2SA208R	0841
2SA208X	0841
2SA208Y	0841
2SA209	0841
2SA209A	0841
2SA209B	0841
2SA209C	0841
2SA209D	0841
2SA209E	0841
2SA209F	0841
2SA209G	0841
2SA209GN	0841
2SA209H	0841
2SA209J	0841
2SA209K	0841
2SA209L	0841
2SA209M	0841
2SA209OR	0841
2SA209R	0841
2SA209X	0841
2SA209Y	0841
2SA210	0841
2SA210A	0841
2SA210B	0841
2SA210C	0841
2SA210D	0841
2SA210E	0841
2SA210F	0841
2SA210G	0841
2SA210GN	0841
2SA210H	0841
2SA210J	0841
2SA210K	0841
2SA210L	0841
2SA210M	0841
2SA210OR	0841
2SA210R	0841
2SA210X	0841
2SA210Y	0841
2SA211	0279
2SA211A	0279
2SA211B	0279
2SA211C	0279
2SA211D	0279
2SA211E	0279
2SA211F	0279
2SA211G	0279
2SA211GN	0279
2SA211H	0279
2SA211J	0279
2SA211K	0279
2SA211L	0279
2SA211M	0279
2SA211OR	0279
2SA211R	0279
2SA211X	0279
2SA211Y	0279
2SA212	0050
2SA212A	0050
2SA212B	0050
2SA212C	0050
2SA212D	0050
2SA212E	0050
2SA212F	0050
2SA212G	0050
2SA212GN	0050
2SA212H	0050
2SA212J	0050
2SA212K	0050
2SA212L	0050
2SA212M	0050
2SA212OR	0050
2SA212R	0050
2SA212X	0050
2SA212Y	0050
2SA213	0136
2SA213A	0136
2SA213B	0136
2SA213C	0136
2SA213D	0136
2SA213E	0136
2SA213F	0136
2SA213G	0136
2SA213GN	0136
2SA213H	0136
2SA213J	0136
2SA213K	0136
2SA213L	0136
2SA213M	0136
2SA213OR	0136
2SA213R	0136
2SA213X	0136
2SA213Y	0136
2SA214	0136
2SA214A	0136
2SA214B	0136
2SA214C	0136
2SA214D	0136
2SA214E	0136
2SA214F	0136
2SA214G	0136
2SA214GN	0136
2SA214H	0136
2SA214J	0136
2SA214K	0136
2SA214L	0136
2SA214M	0136
2SA214OR	0136
2SA214R	0136
2SA214X	0136
2SA214Y	0136
2SA215	0136
2SA215A	0136
2SA215B	0136
2SA215C	0136
2SA215D	0136
2SA215E	0136
2SA215F	0136
2SA215G	0136
2SA215GN	0136
2SA215H	0136
2SA215J	0136
2SA215K	0136
2SA215L	0136
2SA215M	0136
2SA215OR	0136
2SA215R	0136
2SA215X	0136
2SA215Y	0136
2SA216	0136
2SA216A	0136
2SA216B	0136
2SA216C	0136
2SA216D	0136
2SA216E	0136
2SA216F	0136
2SA216G	0136
2SA216GN	0136
2SA216H	0136
2SA216J	0136
2SA216K	0136
2SA216L	0136
2SA216M	0136
2SA216OR	0136
2SA216R	0136
2SA216X	0136
2SA216Y	0136
2SA217	0279
2SA217A	0279
2SA217B	0279
2SA217C	0279
2SA217D	0279
2SA217E	0279
2SA217F	0279
2SA217G	0279
2SA217GN	0279
2SA217H	0279
2SA217J	0279
2SA217K	0279
2SA217L	0279
2SA217M	0279
2SA217OR	0279
2SA217R	0279
2SA217X	0279
2SA217Y	0279
2SA218	0050
2SA218A	0050
2SA218B	0050
2SA218C	0050
2SA218D	0050
2SA218E	0050
2SA218F	0050
2SA218G	0050
2SA218GN	0050
2SA218H	0050
2SA218J	0050
2SA218K	0050
2SA218L	0050
2SA218M	0050
2SA218OR	0050
2SA218R	0050
2SA218X	0050
2SA218Y	0050
2SA219	0136
2SA219A	0136
2SA219B	0136
2SA219C	0136
2SA219D	0136
2SA219E	0136
2SA219F	0136
2SA219G	0136
2SA219GN	0136
2SA219H	0136
2SA219J	0136
2SA219K	0136
2SA219L	0136
2SA219M	0136
2SA219OR	0136
2SA219R	0136
2SA219X	0136
2SA219Y	0136
2SA220	0136
2SA220A	0136
2SA220B	0136
2SA220C	0136
2SA220D	0136
2SA220E	0136
2SA220F	0136
2SA220G	0136
2SA220GN	0136
2SA220H	0136
2SA220J	0136
2SA220K	0136
2SA220L	0136
2SA220M	0136
2SA220OR	0136
2SA220R	0136
2SA220X	0136
2SA220Y	0136
2SA221	0136
2SA221-OR	0136
2SA221A	0136
2SA221B	0136
2SA221C	0136
2SA221D	0136
2SA221E	0136
2SA221F	0136
2SA221G	0136
2SA221GN	0136
2SA221H	0136
2SA221J	0136
2SA221K	0136
2SA221L	0136
2SA221M	0136
2SA221OR	0136
2SA221R	0136
2SA221X	0136
2SA221Y	0136
2SA222	0136
2SA222A	0136
2SA222B	0136
2SA222C	0136
2SA222D	0136
2SA222E	0136
2SA222F	0136
2SA222G	0136
2SA222GN	0136
2SA222H	0136
2SA222J	0136
2SA222K	0136
2SA222L	0136
2SA222M	0136
2SA222OR	0136
2SA222R	0136
2SA222X	0136
2SA222Y	0136
2SA223	0136
2SA223A	0136
2SA223B	0136
2SA223C	0136
2SA223D	0136
2SA223E	0136
2SA223F	0136
2SA223G	0136
2SA223GN	0136
2SA223H	0136
2SA223J	0136
2SA223K	0136
2SA223L	0136
2SA223M	0136
2SA223OR	0136
2SA223R	0136
2SA223X	0136
2SA223Y	0136
2SA224	0050
2SA224A	0050
2SA224B	0050
2SA224C	0050
2SA224D	0050
2SA224E	0050
2SA224F	0050
2SA224G	0050
2SA224GN	0050
2SA224H	0050
2SA224J	0050
2SA224K	0050
2SA224L	0050
2SA224M	0050
2SA224OR	0050
2SA224R	0050
2SA224X	0050
2SA224Y	0050
2SA225	0628
2SA225A	0628
2SA225B	0628
2SA225C	0628
2SA225D	0628
2SA225E	0628
2SA225F	0628
2SA225G	0628
2SA225GN	0628
2SA225H	0628
2SA225J	0628
2SA225K	0628
2SA225L	0628
2SA225M	0628
2SA225OR	0628
2SA225R	0628
2SA225X	0628
2SA225Y	0628
2SA226	0050
2SA227	0050
2SA227A	0050
2SA227B	0050
2SA227C	0050
2SA227D	0050
2SA227E	0050
2SA227F	0050
2SA227G	0050
2SA227GN	0050
2SA227H	0050
2SA227J	0050
2SA227K	0050
2SA227L	0050
2SA227M	0050
2SA227OR	0050
2SA227R	0050
2SA227X	0050
2SA227Y	0050
2SA228	0050
2SA229	0050
2SA229A	0050
2SA229B	0050
2SA229C	0050
2SA229D	0050
2SA229E	0050
2SA229F	0050
2SA229G	0050
2SA229GN	0050
2SA229H	0050
2SA229J	0050
2SA229K	0050
2SA229L	0050
2SA229OR	0050
2SA229R	0050
2SA229X	0050
2SA229Y	0050
2SA230	0050
2SA230A	0050
2SA230B	0050
2SA230C	0050
2SA230D	0050
2SA230E	0050
2SA230F	0050
2SA230G	0050
2SA230GN	0050
2SA230H	0050
2SA230J	0050
2SA230K	0050
2SA230L	0050
2SA230M	0050
2SA230OR	0050
2SA230R	0050
2SA230X	0050
2SA230Y	0050
2SA231	0841
2SA232	0841
2SA233	0050
2SA233A	0050
2SA233B	0050
2SA233C	0050
2SA233D	0050
2SA233E	0050
2SA233F	0050
2SA233G	0050
2SA233GN	0050
2SA233H	0050
2SA233J	0050
2SA233K	0050
2SA233L	0050
2SA233M	0050
2SA233OR	0050
2SA233R	0050
2SA233X	0050
2SA233Y	0050
2SA234	0050
2SA234A	0050
2SA234B	0050
2SA234C	0050
2SA234D	0050
2SA234E	0050
2SA234F	0050
2SA234G	0050
2SA234GN	0050
2SA234H	0050
2SA234J	0050
2SA234K	0050
2SA234L	0050
2SA234M	0050
2SA234OR	0050
2SA234R	0050
2SA234X	0050
2SA234Y	0050
2SA235	0050
2SA235A	0050
2SA235A57B2-14	0050
2SA235B	0050
2SA235C	0050
2SA235C57B2-13	0050
2SA235D	0050
2SA235E	0050
2SA235F	0050
2SA235G	0050
2SA235GN	0050
2SA235H	0050
2SA235K	0050
2SA235M	0050
2SA235OR	0050
2SA235R	0050
2SA235X	0050
2SA235Y	0050
2SA236	0136
2SA236A	0136
2SA236B	0136
2SA236C	0136
2SA236D	0136
2SA236E	0136
2SA236F	0136
2SA236G	0136
2SA236GN	0136
2SA236H	0136
2SA236J	0136
2SA236K	0136
2SA236L	0136
2SA236M	0136
2SA236OR	0136
2SA236R	0136
2SA236X	0136
2SA236Y	0136
2SA237	0136
2SA237A	0136
2SA237B	0136
2SA237C	0136
2SA237D	0136
2SA237E	0136
2SA237F	0136
2SA237G	0136
2SA237GN	0136
2SA237H	0136
2SA237J	0136
2SA237K	0136
2SA237L	0136
2SA237M	0136
2SA237OR	0136
2SA237R	0136
2SA237X	0136
2SA237Y	0136
2SA238	0136
2SA238A	0136
2SA238B	0136
2SA238C	0136
2SA238D	0136
2SA238E	0136
2SA238F	0136
2SA238G	0136
2SA238GN	0136
2SA238H	0136
2SA238J	0136
2SA238K	0136
2SA238L	0136
2SA239	0050
2SA239A	0050
2SA239B	0050
2SA239C	0050
2SA239D	0050
2SA239E	0050
2SA239F	0050
2SA239G	0050
2SA239GN	0050
2SA239GREEN	0050
2SA239H	0050
2SA239J	0050
2SA239K	0050
2SA239L	0050
2SA239M	0050
2SA239OR	0050
2SA239R	0050
2SA239RED	0050
2SA239X	0050
2SA239Y	0050
2SA240	0050
2SA240-BL	OEM
2SA240-OR	OEM
2SA240A	0050
2SA240B	0050
2SA240B2	0050
2SA240BL	0050
2SA240C	0050
2SA240D	0050
2SA240E	0050
2SA240F	0050
2SA240G	0050
2SA240GN	0050
2SA240GREEN	0050
2SA240H	0050
2SA240J	0050
2SA240K	0050
2SA240L	0050
2SA240M	0050
2SA240OR	0050
2SA240R	0050
2SA240RED	0050
2SA240X	0050
2SA240Y	0050
2SA241	0050
2SA241A	0050
2SA241B	0050
2SA241C	0050
2SA241D	0050
2SA241E	0050
2SA241F	0050
2SA241G	0050
2SA241GN	0050
2SA241H	0050
2SA241J	0050
2SA241K	0050
2SA241L	0050
2SA241M	0050
2SA241OR	0050
2SA241R	0050
2SA241X	0050
2SA241Y	0050
2SA242	0050
2SA243	0050
2SA243A	0050
2SA244	0050
2SA244A	0050
2SA245	0050
2SA246	0136
2SA246A	0136
2SA246B	0136
2SA246C	0136
2SA246D	0136
2SA246E	0136
2SA246F	0136
2SA246G	0136
2SA246GN	0136
2SA246H	0136
2SA246J	0136
2SA246K	0136
2SA246L	0136
2SA246M	0136
2SA246OR	0136
2SA246R	0136
2SA246V	0136
2SA246X	0136
2SA246Y	0136
2SA247	0136
2SA247A	0136
2SA247B	0136
2SA247C	0136
2SA247D	0136
2SA247E	0136
2SA247F	0136
2SA247G	0136
2SA247GN	0136
2SA247H	0136
2SA247J	0136
2SA247K	0136
2SA247L	0136
2SA247M	0136
2SA247OR	0136
2SA247R	0136
2SA247X	0136
2SA247Y	0136
2SA248	0004
2SA248A	0004
2SA248B	0004
2SA248C	0004
2SA248D	0004
2SA248E	0004
2SA248F	0004
2SA248G	0004
2SA248GN	0004
2SA248H	0004
2SA248J	0004
2SA248K	0004
2SA248L	0004
2SA248M	0004
2SA248OR	0004
2SA248R	0004
2SA248X	0004
2SA248Y	0004
2SA249	0164
2SA250	0136
2SA250A	0136
2SA250B	0136
2SA250C	0136
2SA250D	0136
2SA250E	0136
2SA250F	0136
2SA250G	0136
2SA250GN	0136
2SA250H	0136
2SA250J	0136
2SA250L	0136
2SA250M	0136
2SA250OR	0136
2SA250X	0136
2SA250Y	0136
2SA251	0136
2SA251A	0136
2SA251B	0136
2SA251C	0136
2SA251D	0136
2SA251E	0136
2SA251F	0136
2SA251G	0136
2SA251H	0136
2SA251J	0136
2SA251K	0136
2SA251L	0136
2SA251M	0136
2SA251OR	0136
2SA251R	0136
2SA251X	0136
2SA251Y	0136
2SA252	0136
2SA252A	0136
2SA252B	0136
2SA252C	0136
2SA252D	0136
2SA252E	0136
2SA252F	0136
2SA252G	0136
2SA252H	0136
2SA252J	0136
2SA252K	0136
2SA252L	0136
2SA252M	0136
2SA252OR	0136
2SA252R	0136
2SA252X	0136
2SA252Y	0136
2SA253	0136
2SA253A	0136
2SA253B	0136
2SA253C	0136
2SA253D	0136
2SA253E	0136
2SA253F	0136
2SA253G	0136
2SA253GN	0136
2SA253H	0136
2SA253J	0136
2SA253K	0136
2SA253L	0136
2SA253M	0136
2SA253OR	0136
2SA253R	0136
2SA253X	0136
2SA253Y	0136
2SA254	0136
2SA254A	0136
2SA254B	0136
2SA254C	0136
2SA254D	0136
2SA254E	0136
2SA254F	0136
2SA254G	0136

If replacement code is OEM, contact original manufacturer for replacement.

DEVICE TYPE	REPL CODE
2SA254H	0136
2SA254J	0136
2SA254K	0136
2SA254L	0136
2SA254M	0136
2SA254OR	0136
2SA254R	0136
2SA254X	0136
2SA254Y	0136
2SA255	0136
2SA255A	0136
2SA255B	0136
2SA255C	0136
2SA255D	0136
2SA255E	0136
2SA255F	0136
2SA255G	0136
2SA255GN	0136
2SA255H	0136
2SA255J	0136
2SA255K	0136
2SA255L	0136
2SA255M	0136
2SA255OR	0136
2SA255R	0136
2SA255X	0136
2SA255Y	0136
2SA256	0136
2SA256A	0136
2SA256B	0136
2SA256C	0136
2SA256D	0136
2SA256E	0136
2SA256F	0136
2SA256G	0136
2SA256GN	0136
2SA256H	0136
2SA256J	0136
2SA256K	0136
2SA256L	0136
2SA256M	0136
2SA256OR	0136
2SA256R	0136
2SA256X	0136
2SA256Y	0136
2SA257	0136
2SA257A	0136
2SA257B	0136
2SA257C	0136
2SA257D	0136
2SA257E	0136
2SA257F	0136
2SA257G	0136
2SA257GN	0136
2SA257H	0136
2SA257J	0136
2SA257K	0136
2SA257L	0136
2SA257OR	0136
2SA257R	0136
2SA257X	0136
2SA257Y	0136
2SA258	0136
2SA258A	0136
2SA258B	0136
2SA258C	0136
2SA258D	0136
2SA258E	0136
2SA258F	0136
2SA258G	0136
2SA258GN	0136
2SA258H	0136
2SA258J	0136
2SA258K	0136
2SA258L	0136
2SA258M	0136
2SA258OR	0136
2SA258R	0136
2SA258X	0136
2SA258Y	0136
2SA259	0136
2SA259B	0136
2SA259C	0136
2SA259D	0136
2SA259E	0136
2SA259F	0136
2SA259G	0136
2SA259GN	0136
2SA259H	0136
2SA259J	0136
2SA259L	0136
2SA259M	0136
2SA259OR	0136
2SA259R	0136
2SA259X	0136
2SA259Y	0136
2SA260	0050
2SA260A	0050
2SA260B	0050
2SA260C	0050
2SA260D	0050
2SA260E	0050
2SA260F	0050
2SA260G	0050
2SA260GN	0050
2SA260H	0050
2SA260J	0050
2SA260K	0050
2SA260L	0050
2SA260M	0050
2SA260OR	0050
2SA260R	0050
2SA260X	0050
2SA260Y	0050
2SA261	0050
2SA261A	0050
2SA261B	0050
2SA261C	0050
2SA261D	0050
2SA261E	0050
2SA261F	0050
2SA261G	0050
2SA261GN	0050
2SA261H	0050
2SA261K	0050
2SA261L	0050
2SA261M	0050
2SA261OR	0050
2SA261R	0050
2SA261X	0050
2SA261Y	0050
2SA262	0050
2SA262A	0050
2SA262B	0050
2SA262C	0050
2SA262D	0050
2SA262E	0050
2SA262F	0050
2SA262G	0050
2SA262GN	0050
2SA262H	0050
2SA262J	0050
2SA262K	0050
2SA262L	0050
2SA262M	0050
2SA262OR	0050
2SA262R	0050
2SA262X	0050
2SA262Y	0050
2SA263	0050
2SA263A	0050
2SA263B	0050
2SA263C	0050
2SA263D	0050
2SA263E	0050
2SA263F	0050
2SA263G	0050
2SA263GN	0050
2SA263H	0050
2SA263J	0050
2SA263K	0050
2SA263L	0050
2SA263M	0050
2SA263OR	0050
2SA263R	0050
2SA263X	0050
2SA263Y	0050
2SA264	0050
2SA264(1)	0050
2SA264A	0050
2SA264B	0050
2SA264C	0050
2SA264D	0050
2SA264E	0050
2SA264F	0050
2SA264G	0050
2SA264GN	0050
2SA264H	0050
2SA264K	0050
2SA264L	0050
2SA264M	0050
2SA264OR	0050
2SA264R	0050
2SA264X	0050
2SA264Y	0050
2SA265	0050
2SA265A	0050
2SA265B	0050
2SA265C	0050
2SA265D	0050
2SA265E	0050
2SA265F	0050
2SA265G	0050
2SA265GN	0050
2SA265H	0050
2SA265J	0050
2SA265K	0050
2SA265L	0050
2SA265M	0050
2SA265OR	0050
2SA265R	0050
2SA265X	0050
2SA265Y	0050
2SA266	0136
2SA266A	0136
2SA266B	0136
2SA266C	0136
2SA266D	0136
2SA266E	0136
2SA266F	0136
2SA266G	0136
2SA266GN	0136
2SA266GREEN	0136
2SA266H	0136
2SA266J	0136
2SA266K	0136
2SA266L	0136
2SA266M	0136
2SA266OR	0136
2SA266R	0136
2SA266X	0136
2SA266Y	0136
2SA267	0136
2SA267A	0136
2SA267B	0136
2SA267C	0136
2SA267D	0136
2SA267E	0136
2SA267F	0136
2SA267G	0136
2SA267GN	0136
2SA267H	0136
2SA267J	0136
2SA267K	0136
2SA267L	0136
2SA267M	0136
2SA267OR	0136
2SA267R	0136
2SA267X	0136
2SA267Y	0136
2SA268	0136
2SA268A	0136
2SA268B	0136
2SA268C	0136
2SA268D	0136
2SA268E	0136
2SA268F	0136
2SA268G	0136
2SA268GN	0136
2SA268H	0136
2SA268J	0136
2SA268K	0136
2SA268L	0136
2SA268M	0136
2SA268OR	0136
2SA268R	0136
2SA268X	0136
2SA268Y	0136
2SA269	0136
2SA269A	0136
2SA269B	0136
2SA269C	0136
2SA269D	0136
2SA269E	0136
2SA269F	0136
2SA269GN	0136
2SA269H	0136
2SA269J	0136
2SA269K	0136
2SA269L	0136
2SA269M	0136
2SA269OR	0136
2SA269X	0136
2SA269Y	0136
2SA270	0136
2SA270A	0136
2SA270B	0136
2SA270C	0136
2SA270D	0136
2SA270E	0136
2SA270F	0136
2SA270G	0136
2SA270GN	0136
2SA270H	0136
2SA270J	0136
2SA270K	0136
2SA270L	0136
2SA270M	0136
2SA270OR	0136
2SA270R	0136
2SA270X	0136
2SA270Y	0136
2SA271	0136
2SA271(2)	0136
2SA271(3)	0136
2SA271A	0136
2SA271B	0136
2SA271C	0136
2SA271D	0136
2SA271E	0136
2SA271F	0136
2SA271G	0136
2SA271GN	0136
2SA271H	0136
2SA271J	0136
2SA271K	0136
2SA271L	0136
2SA271M	0136
2SA271OR	0136
2SA271R	0136
2SA271X	0136
2SA271Y	0136
2SA272	0136
2SA272A	0136
2SA272B	0136
2SA272C	0136
2SA272D	0136
2SA272E	0136
2SA272F	0136
2SA272G	0136
2SA272GN	0136
2SA272H	0136
2SA272J	0136
2SA272K	0136
2SA272L	0136
2SA272M	0136
2SA272OR	0136
2SA272R	0136
2SA272X	0136
2SA272Y	0136
2SA273	0136
2SA273A	0136
2SA273B	0136
2SA273C	0136
2SA273D	0136
2SA273E	0136
2SA273F	0136
2SA273G	0136
2SA273GN	0136
2SA273H	0136
2SA273J	0136
2SA273K	0136
2SA273L	0136
2SA273M	0136
2SA273OR	0136
2SA273X	0136
2SA273Y	0136
2SA274	0136
2SA274A	0136
2SA274B	0136
2SA274C	0136
2SA274D	0136
2SA274E	0136
2SA274F	0136
2SA274G	0136
2SA274GN	0136
2SA274H	0136
2SA274J	0136
2SA274K	0136
2SA274L	0136
2SA274M	0136
2SA274OR	0136
2SA274R	0136
2SA274X	0136
2SA274Y	0136
2SA275	0136
2SA275A	0136
2SA275B	0136
2SA275C	0136
2SA275D	0136
2SA275E	0136
2SA275F	0136
2SA275G	0136
2SA275GN	0136
2SA275H	0136
2SA275J	0136
2SA275L	0136
2SA275M	0136
2SA275OR	0136
2SA275R	0136
2SA275X	0136
2SA275Y	0136
2SA276	0050
2SA277	0279
2SA277A	0279
2SA277B	0279
2SA277C	0279
2SA277D	0279
2SA277E	0279
2SA277F	0279
2SA277G	0279
2SA277GN	0279
2SA277H	0279
2SA277J	0279
2SA277K	0279
2SA277L	0279
2SA277M	0279
2SA277OR	0279
2SA277X	0279
2SA277Y	0279
2SA278	0279
2SA278A	0279
2SA278B	0279
2SA278C	0279
2SA278D	0279
2SA278E	0279
2SA278F	0279
2SA278G	0279
2SA278GN	0279
2SA278J	0279
2SA278K	0279
2SA278L	0279
2SA278M	0279
2SA278OR	0279
2SA278R	0279
2SA278X	0279
2SA278Y	0279
2SA279	0279
2SA279A	0279
2SA279B	0279
2SA279C	0279
2SA279D	0279
2SA279E	0279
2SA279F	0279
2SA279G	0279
2SA279GN	0279
2SA279H	0279
2SA279J	0279
2SA279K	0279
2SA279L	0279
2SA279OR	0279
2SA279R	0279
2SA279X	0279
2SA279Y	0279
2SA280	0279
2SA280A	0279
2SA280B	0279
2SA280C	0279
2SA280D	0279
2SA280E	0279
2SA280F	0279
2SA280G	0279
2SA280GN	0279
2SA280H	0279
2SA280J	0279
2SA280K	0279
2SA280L	0279
2SA280M	0279
2SA280OR	0279
2SA280R	0279
2SA280X	0279
2SA280Y	0279
2SA281	0279
2SA281A	0279
2SA281B	0279
2SA281C	0279
2SA281D	0279
2SA281E	0279
2SA281F	0279
2SA281G	0279
2SA281GN	0279
2SA281H	0279
2SA281J	0279
2SA281K	0279
2SA281L	0279
2SA281M	0279
2SA281OR	0279
2SA281R	0279
2SA281X	0279
2SA281Y	0279
2SA282	0004
2SA282A	0004
2SA282B	0004
2SA282C	0004
2SA282D	0004
2SA282E	0004
2SA282F	0004
2SA282G	0004
2SA282GN	0004
2SA282H	0004
2SA282J	0004
2SA282K	0004
2SA282L	0004
2SA282M	0004
2SA282OR	0004
2SA282R	0004
2SA282X	0004
2SA282Y	0004
2SA283	0279
2SA283A	0279
2SA283B	0279
2SA283C	0279
2SA283D	0279
2SA283E	0279
2SA283F	0279
2SA283G	0279
2SA283GN	0279
2SA283H	0279
2SA283J	0279
2SA283K	0279
2SA283L	0279
2SA283M	0279
2SA283OR	0279
2SA283R	0279
2SA283X	0279
2SA283Y	0279
2SA284	0279
2SA284A	0279
2SA284B	0279
2SA284C	0279
2SA284D	0279
2SA284E	0279
2SA284F	0279
2SA284G	0279
2SA284GN	0279
2SA284J	0279
2SA284K	0279
2SA284L	0279
2SA284M	0279
2SA284OR	0279
2SA284R	0279
2SA284X	0279
2SA284Y	0279
2SA285	0050
2SA285B	0050
2SA285C	0050
2SA285E	0050
2SA285F	0050
2SA285G	0050
2SA285GN	0050
2SA285H	0050
2SA285J	0050
2SA285L	0050
2SA285M	0050
2SA285OR	0050
2SA285R	0050
2SA285X	0050
2SA285Y	0050
2SA286	0050
2SA286A	0050
2SA286B	0050
2SA286C	0050
2SA286D	0050
2SA286E	0050
2SA286F	0050
2SA286G	0050
2SA286GN	0050
2SA286H	0050
2SA286K	0050
2SA286M	0050
2SA286OR	0050
2SA286R	0050
2SA286X	0050
2SA286Y	0050
2SA287	0050
2SA287A	0050
2SA287B	0050
2SA287C	0050
2SA287D	0050
2SA287E	0050
2SA287F	0050
2SA287G	0050
2SA287GN	0050
2SA287H	0050
2SA287J	0050
2SA287K	0050
2SA287L	0050
2SA287M	0050
2SA287OR	0050
2SA287X	0050
2SA287Y	0050
2SA288	0136
2SA288A	0136
2SA288B	0136
2SA288C	0136
2SA288D	0136
2SA288E	0136
2SA288F	0136
2SA288G	0136
2SA288GN	0136
2SA288J	0136
2SA288K	0136
2SA288L	0136
2SA288M	0136
2SA288OR	0136
2SA288X	0136
2SA288Y	0136
2SA289	0136
2SA289A	0136
2SA289B	0136
2SA289C	0136
2SA289D	0136
2SA289E	0136
2SA289F	0136
2SA289G	0136
2SA289GN	0136
2SA289H	0136
2SA289J	0136
2SA289K	0136
2SA289L	0136
2SA289M	0136
2SA289OR	0136
2SA289R	0136
2SA289X	0136
2SA289Y	0136
2SA290	0136
2SA290A	0136
2SA290B	0136
2SA290C	0136
2SA290D	0136
2SA290E	0136
2SA290F	0136
2SA290G	0136
2SA290GN	0136
2SA290H	0136
2SA290J	0136
2SA290K	0136
2SA290L	0136
2SA290M	0136
2SA290OR	0136
2SA290R	0136
2SA290X	0136
2SA290Y	0136
2SA291	0136
2SA291A	0136
2SA291B	0136
2SA291C	0136
2SA291D	0136
2SA291E	0136
2SA291F	0136
2SA291G	0136
2SA291GN	0136
2SA291H	0136
2SA291J	0136
2SA291K	0136
2SA291L	0136
2SA291M	0136
2SA291OR	0136
2SA291R	0136
2SA291X	0136
2SA291Y	0136
2SA292	0136
2SA292A	0136
2SA292B	0136
2SA292C	0136
2SA292D	0136
2SA292E	0136
2SA292F	0136
2SA292G	0136
2SA292GN	0136
2SA292H	0136
2SA292J	0136
2SA292K	0136
2SA292L	0136
2SA292M	0136
2SA292OR	0136
2SA292R	0136
2SA292X	0136
2SA292Y	0136
2SA293	0136
2SA293A	0136
2SA293B	0136
2SA293C	0136
2SA293D	0136
2SA293E	0136
2SA293G	0136
2SA293GN	0136
2SA293H	0136
2SA293J	0136
2SA293K	0136
2SA293L	0136
2SA293M	0136
2SA293OR	0136
2SA293R	0136
2SA293X	0136
2SA293Y	0136
2SA294	0136
2SA294A	0136
2SA294B	0136
2SA294C	0136
2SA294D	0136
2SA294E	0136
2SA294F	0136
2SA294GN	0136
2SA294H	0136
2SA294J	0136
2SA294K	0136
2SA294L	0136
2SA294M	0136
2SA294OR	0136
2SA294R	0136
2SA294X	0136
2SA294Y	0136
2SA295	0136
2SA295A	0136
2SA295B	0136
2SA295C	0136
2SA295D	0136
2SA295E	0136
2SA295F	0136
2SA295G	0136
2SA295GN	0136
2SA295H	0136
2SA295J	0136
2SA295K	0136
2SA295L	0136
2SA295OR	0136
2SA295R	0136
2SA295Y	0136
2SA296	0136
2SA296A	0136
2SA296B	0136
2SA296C	0136
2SA296D	0136
2SA296E	0136
2SA296F	0136
2SA296G	0136
2SA296GN	0136
2SA296H	0136
2SA296J	0136
2SA296K	0136
2SA296L	0136
2SA296M	0136
2SA296OR	0136
2SA296R	0136
2SA296X	0136
2SA296Y	0136
2SA297	0136
2SA297A	0136
2SA297B	0136
2SA297C	0136
2SA297D	0136
2SA297E	0136
2SA297F	0136
2SA297G	0136
2SA297H	0136
2SA297J	0136
2SA297K	0136
2SA297L	0136
2SA297M	0136
2SA297OR	0136
2SA297R	0136
2SA297X	0136
2SA297Y	0136
2SA298	0050
2SA298A	0050
2SA298B	0050
2SA298C	0050
2SA298D	0050
2SA298E	0050
2SA298F	0050
2SA298G	0050
2SA298GN	0050
2SA298H	0050
2SA298J	0050
2SA298K	0050
2SA298L	0050
2SA298M	0050
2SA298OR	0050
2SA298R	0050
2SA298X	0050
2SA298Y	0050
2SA299	0279

If replacement code is OEM, contact original manufacturer for replacement.

DEVICE TYPE	REPL CODE
2SA300	0050
2SA301	0164
2SA301A	0164
2SA301B	0164
2SA301C	0164
2SA301D	0164
2SA301E	0164
2SA301F	0164
2SA301G	0164
2SA301GN	0164
2SA301H	0164
2SA301J	0164
2SA301K	0164
2SA301L	0164
2SA301M	0164
2SA301OR	0164
2SA301R	0164
2SA301X	0164
2SA301Y	0164
2SA302	0004
2SA303	0004
2SA304	0279
2SA304-GREEN	0279
2SA304-RED	0279
2SA304-YELLOW	0279
2SA304A	0279
2SA304B	0279
2SA304C	0279
2SA304D	0279
2SA304F	0279
2SA304G	0279
2SA304GN	0279
2SA304J	0279
2SA304K	0279
2SA304L	0279
2SA304M	0279
2SA304OR	0279
2SA304R	0279
2SA304X	0279
2SA304Y	0279
2SA305	0279
2SA305-GREEN	0279
2SA305-RED	0279
2SA305-YELLOW	0279
2SA305A	0279
2SA305B	0279
2SA305C	0279
2SA305D	0279
2SA305E	0279
2SA305F	0279
2SA305G	0279
2SA305GN	0279
2SA305H	0279
2SA305J	0279
2SA305K	0279
2SA305L	0279
2SA305M	0279
2SA305OR	0279
2SA305R	0279
2SA305X	0279
2SA305Y	0279
2SA306	0050
2SA307	0050
2SA307A	0050
2SA307B	0050
2SA307C	0050
2SA307D	0050
2SA307E	0050
2SA307F	0050
2SA307G	0050
2SA307GN	0050
2SA307J	0050
2SA307K	0050
2SA307L	0050
2SA307M	0050
2SA307OR	0050
2SA307R	0050
2SA307X	0050
2SA307Y	0050
2SA308	0136
2SA308A	0136
2SA308B	0136
2SA308C	0136
2SA308D	0136
2SA308E	0136
2SA308F	0136
2SA308G	0136
2SA308GN	0136
2SA308H	0136
2SA308J	0136
2SA308K	0136
2SA308L	0136
2SA308M	0136
2SA308OR	0136
2SA308R	0136
2SA308X	0136
2SA308Y	0136
2SA309	1774
2SA309A	1774
2SA309B	1774
2SA309C	1774
2SA309D	1774
2SA309E	1774
2SA309F	1774
2SA309G	1774
2SA309GN	1774
2SA309H	1774
2SA309J	1774
2SA309K	1774
2SA309L	1774
2SA309M	1774
2SA309OR	1774
2SA309R	1774
2SA309X	1774
2SA309Y	1774
2SA310	0136
2SA310A	0136
2SA310B	0136
2SA310C	0136
2SA310D	0136
2SA310E	0136
2SA310F	0136
2SA310G	0136
2SA310GN	0136
2SA310H	0136
2SA310J	0136
2SA310K	0136
2SA310L	0136
2SA310M	0136
2SA310OR	0136
2SA310R	0136
2SA310X	0136
2SA310Y	0136
2SA311	0004
2SA311A	0004
2SA311B	0004
2SA311C	0004
2SA311D	0004
2SA311E	0004
2SA311F	0004
2SA311G	0004
2SA311GN	0004
2SA311H	0004
2SA311J	0004
2SA311K	0004
2SA311L	0004
2SA311M	0004
2SA311OR	0004
2SA311R	0004
2SA311X	0004
2SA311Y	0004
2SA312	0004
2SA312A	0004
2SA312B	0004
2SA312C	0004
2SA312D	0004
2SA312E	0004
2SA312F	0004
2SA312G	0004
2SA312GN	0004
2SA312H	0004
2SA312J	0004
2SA312K	0004
2SA312L	0004
2SA312M	0004
2SA312OR	0004
2SA312R	0004
2SA312X	0004
2SA312Y	0004
2SA313	0136
2SA313-BLUE	0136
2SA313-GREEN	0136
2SA313-RED	0136
2SA313-YELLOW	0136
2SA313A	0136
2SA313B	0136
2SA313C	0136
2SA313D	0136
2SA313E	0136
2SA313F	0136
2SA313G	0136
2SA313GN	0136
2SA313H	0136
2SA313J	0136
2SA313K	0136
2SA313L	0136
2SA313M	0136
2SA313OR	0136
2SA313R	0136
2SA313X	0136
2SA313Y	0136
2SA314	0136
2SA314-GREEN	0136
2SA314-RED	0136
2SA314-YELLOW	0136
2SA314A	0136
2SA314B	0136
2SA314C	0136
2SA314D	0136
2SA314E	0136
2SA314F	0136
2SA314G	0136
2SA314GN	0136
2SA314H	0136
2SA314J	0136
2SA314K	0136
2SA314L	0136
2SA314M	0136
2SA314OR	0136
2SA314R	0136
2SA314X	0136
2SA314Y	0136
2SA315	0136
2SA315-GREEN	0136
2SA315-RED	0136
2SA315-YELLOW	0136
2SA315A	0136
2SA315B	0136
2SA315C	0136
2SA315D	0136
2SA315E	0136
2SA315F	0136
2SA315G	0136
2SA315GN	0136
2SA315H	0136
2SA315J	0136
2SA315K	0136
2SA315L	0136
2SA315M	0136
2SA315OR	0136
2SA315R	0136
2SA315X	0136
2SA315Y	0136
2SA316	0136
2SA316-GREEN	0136
2SA316-RED	0136
2SA316-YELLOW	0136
2SA316A	0136
2SA316B	0136
2SA316C	0136
2SA316D	0136
2SA316E	0136
2SA316F	0136
2SA316G	0136
2SA316GN	0136
2SA316H	0136
2SA316J	0136
2SA316K	0136
2SA316L	0136
2SA316M	0136
2SA316OR	0136
2SA316R	0136
2SA316X	0136
2SA316Y	0136
2SA321	0004
2SA321-1	0004
2SA321A	0004
2SA321B	0004
2SA321C	0004
2SA321D	0004
2SA321E	0004
2SA321F	0004
2SA321G	0004
2SA321GN	0004
2SA321H	0004
2SA321J	0004
2SA321K	0004
2SA321L	0004
2SA321M	0004
2SA321OR	0004
2SA321R	0004
2SA321X	0004
2SA321Y	0004
2SA322	0004
2SA322A	0004
2SA322B	0004
2SA322C	0004
2SA322D	0004
2SA322E	0004
2SA322F	0004
2SA322G	0004
2SA322GN	0004
2SA322H	0004
2SA322K	0004
2SA322L	0004
2SA322M	0004
2SA322OR	0004
2SA322R	0004
2SA322X	0004
2SA322Y	0004
2SA323	0050
2SA323A	0050
2SA323B	0050
2SA323C	0050
2SA323D	0050
2SA323E	0050
2SA323F	0050
2SA323G	0050
2SA323GN	0050
2SA323J	0050
2SA323K	0050
2SA323L	0050
2SA323M	0050
2SA323R	0050
2SA323X	0050
2SA323Y	0050
2SA324	0136
2SA324A	0136
2SA324B	0136
2SA324C	0136
2SA324D	0136
2SA324E	0136
2SA324F	0136
2SA324G	0136
2SA324GN	0136
2SA324H	0136
2SA324K	0136
2SA324L	0136
2SA324M	0136
2SA324OR	0136
2SA324R	0136
2SA324X	0136
2SA324Y	0136
2SA325	0136
2SA325A	0136
2SA325B	0136
2SA325D	0136
2SA325E	0136
2SA325G	0136
2SA325GN	0136
2SA325H	0136
2SA325J	0136
2SA325K	0136
2SA325L	0136
2SA325M	0136
2SA325OR	0136
2SA325R	0136
2SA325X	0136
2SA325Y	0136
2SA326	0136
2SA326A	0136
2SA326B	0136
2SA326C	0136
2SA326D	0136
2SA326E	0136
2SA326F	0136
2SA326G	0136
2SA326GN	0136
2SA326H	0136
2SA326J	0136
2SA326K	0136
2SA326L	0136
2SA326M	0136
2SA326OR	0136
2SA326R	0136
2SA326X	0136
2SA326Y	0136
2SA327	0050
2SA328	0279
2SA329	0136
2SA329A	0136
2SA329B	0136
2SA329C	0136
2SA329D	0136
2SA329E	0136
2SA329F	0136
2SA329G	0136
2SA329GN	0136
2SA329H	0136
2SA329J	0136
2SA329K	0136
2SA329L	0136
2SA329M	0136
2SA329OR	0136
2SA329R	0136
2SA329X	0136
2SA329Y	0136
2SA330	0136
2SA330A	0136
2SA330B	0136
2SA330C	0136
2SA330D	0136
2SA330E	0136
2SA330F	0136
2SA330G	0136
2SA330GN	0136
2SA330H	0136
2SA330K	0136
2SA330L	0136
2SA330M	0136
2SA330OR	0136
2SA330X	0136
2SA330Y	0136
2SA331	0136
2SA331A	0136
2SA331B	0136
2SA331C	0136
2SA331D	0136
2SA331E	0136
2SA331F	0136
2SA331G	0136
2SA331GN	0136
2SA331H	0136
2SA331J	0136
2SA331K	0136
2SA331L	0136
2SA331M	0136
2SA331OR	0136
2SA331R	0136
2SA331X	0136
2SA331Y	0136
2SA332	0050
2SA332A	0050
2SA332B	0050
2SA332C	0050
2SA332D	0050
2SA332E	0050
2SA332F	0050
2SA332G	0050
2SA332GN	0050
2SA332H	0050
2SA332J	0050
2SA332K	0050
2SA332L	0050
2SA332M	0050
2SA332OR	0050
2SA332R	0050
2SA332X	0050
2SA332Y	0050
2SA333	5121
2SA334	5121
2SA335	0136
2SA335A	0136
2SA335B	0136
2SA335C	0136
2SA335D	0136
2SA335E	0136
2SA335F	0136
2SA335G	0136
2SA335GN	0136
2SA335H	0136
2SA335J	0136
2SA335K	0136
2SA335L	0136
2SA335M	0136
2SA335OR	0136
2SA335R	0136
2SA335X	0136
2SA335Y	0136
2SA336	0050
2SA337	0136
2SA337A	0136
2SA337B	0136
2SA337C	0136
2SA337D	0136
2SA337E	0136
2SA337F	0136
2SA337G	0136
2SA337GN	0136
2SA337H	0136
2SA337J	0136
2SA337K	0136
2SA337L	0136
2SA337M	0136
2SA337OR	0136
2SA337R	0136
2SA337X	0136
2SA337Y	0136
2SA338	0136
2SA338A	0136
2SA338B	0136
2SA338C	0136
2SA338D	0136
2SA338E	0136
2SA338F	0136
2SA338G	0136
2SA338GN	0136
2SA338H	0136
2SA338J	0136
2SA338K	0136
2SA338L	0136
2SA338M	0136
2SA338OR	0136
2SA338R	0136
2SA338X	0136
2SA338Y	0136
2SA339	0136
2SA339A	0136
2SA339B	0136
2SA339C	0136
2SA339D	0136
2SA339E	0136
2SA339F	0136
2SA339G	0136
2SA339GN	0136
2SA339H	0136
2SA339J	0136
2SA339K	0136
2SA339L	0136
2SA339M	0136
2SA339OR	0136
2SA339R	0136
2SA339X	0136
2SA339Y	0136
2SA340	0050
2SA341	0050
2SA341-NB	OEM
2SA341-OA	0050
2SA341-OB	0050
2SA341A	0050
2SA341B	0050
2SA341C	0050
2SA341D	0050
2SA341E	0050
2SA341F	0050
2SA341G	0050
2SA341GN	0050
2SA341H	0050
2SA341J	0050
2SA341K	0050
2SA341L	0050
2SA341M	0050
2SA341OR	0050
2SA341R	0050
2SA341X	0050
2SA341Y	0050
2SA342	0050
2SA342A	0050
2SA342B	0050
2SA342C	0050
2SA342D	0050
2SA342E	0050
2SA342F	0050
2SA342G	0050
2SA342GN	0050
2SA342H	0050
2SA342J	0050
2SA342K	0050
2SA342L	0050
2SA342M	0050
2SA342OR	0050
2SA342R	0050
2SA342X	0050
2SA342Y	0050
2SA343	0050
2SA343A	0050
2SA343B	0050
2SA343C	0050
2SA343D	0050
2SA343E	0050
2SA343F	0050
2SA343G	0050
2SA343H	0050
2SA343J	0050
2SA343K	0050
2SA343L	0050
2SA343M	0050
2SA343OR	0050
2SA343R	0050
2SA343X	0050
2SA343Y	0050
2SA344	0136
2SA344A	0136
2SA344B	0136
2SA344C	0136
2SA344D	0136
2SA344E	0136
2SA344F	0136
2SA344G	0136
2SA344GN	0136
2SA344H	0136
2SA344J	0136
2SA344K	0136
2SA344L	0136
2SA344M	0136
2SA344OR	0136
2SA344R	0136
2SA344X	0136
2SA344Y	0136
2SA345	0050
2SA346	0050
2SA347	0050
2SA348	0050
2SA348A	0050
2SA348B	0050
2SA348C	0050
2SA348D	0050
2SA348E	0050
2SA348F	0050
2SA348G	0050
2SA348GN	0050
2SA348H	0050
2SA348J	0050
2SA348K	0050
2SA348L	0050
2SA348M	0050
2SA348OR	0050
2SA348R	0050
2SA348X	0050
2SA348Y	0050
2SA349	0050
2SA350	0136
2SA350A	0136
2SA350AV	0136
2SA350B	0136
2SA350BK	0136
2SA350C	0136
2SA350D	0136
2SA350E	0136
2SA350F	0136
2SA350G	0136
2SA350GN	0136
2SA350H	0136
2SA350J	0136
2SA350K	0136
2SA350L	0136
2SA350M	0136
2SA350OR	0136
2SA350R	0136
2SA350T	0136
2SA350TY	0136
2SA350X	0136
2SA350Y	0136
2SA351	0136
2SA351(B)	0136
2SA351(GR)	0136
2SA351A	0136
2SA351A-2	0136
2SA351B	0136
2SA351C	0136
2SA351D	0136
2SA351E	0136
2SA351F	0136
2SA351G	0136
2SA351GN	0136
2SA351GR	0136
2SA351K	0136
2SA351L	0136
2SA351M	0136
2SA351OR	0136
2SA351R	0136
2SA351X	0136
2SA351Y	0136
2SA352	0136
2SA352A	0136
2SA352B	0136
2SA352C	0136
2SA352D	0136
2SA352E	0136
2SA352F	0136
2SA352G	0136
2SA352GN	0136
2SA352H	0136
2SA352J	0136
2SA352K	0136
2SA352L	0136
2SA352M	0136
2SA352OR	0136
2SA352R	0136
2SA352X	0136
2SA352Y	0136
2SA353	0136
2SA353(A)	0136
2SA353(C)	0136
2SA353-AC	0136
2SA353A	0136
2SA353AL	0136
2SA353B	0136
2SA353C	0136
2SA353CL	0136
2SA353D	0136
2SA353E	0136
2SA353F	0136
2SA353G	0136
2SA353GN	0136
2SA353H	0136
2SA353J	0136
2SA353K	0136
2SA353L	0136
2SA353M	0136
2SA353OR	0136
2SA353R	0136
2SA353X	0136
2SA353Y	0136
2SA354	0136
2SA354-B	0136
2SA354A	0136
2SA354B	0136
2SA354BK	0136
2SA354C	0136
2SA354D	0136
2SA354E	0136
2SA354F	0136
2SA354G	0136
2SA354GN	0136
2SA354H	0136
2SA354J	0136
2SA354K	0136
2SA354L	0136
2SA354M	0136
2SA354OR	0136
2SA354R	0136
2SA354X	0136
2SA354Y	0136
2SA355	0136
2SA355A	0136
2SA355B	0136
2SA355C	0136
2SA355D	0136
2SA355E	0136
2SA355F	0136
2SA355G	0136
2SA355H	0136
2SA355J	0136
2SA355K	0136
2SA355L	0136
2SA355M	0136
2SA355OR	0136
2SA355R	0136
2SA355X	0136
2SA355Y	0136
2SA356	0136
2SA356A	0136
2SA356B	0136
2SA356C	0136
2SA356D	0136
2SA356E	0136
2SA356F	0136
2SA356G	0136
2SA356GN	0136
2SA356H	0136
2SA356J	0136
2SA356K	0136
2SA356L	0136
2SA356M	0136
2SA356OR	0136
2SA356R	0136
2SA357	0136
2SA357A	0136
2SA357B	0136
2SA357C	0136
2SA357D	0136
2SA357E	0136
2SA357F	0136
2SA357G	0136
2SA357GN	0136
2SA357H	0136
2SA357J	0136
2SA357K	0136
2SA357L	0136
2SA357M	0136
2SA357OR	0136
2SA357R	0136
2SA357X	0136
2SA357Y	0136
2SA358	0136
2SA358-3	0136
2SA358A	0136
2SA358B	0136
2SA358C	0136
2SA358D	0136
2SA358E	0136

If replacement code is OEM, contact original manufacturer for replacement.

DEVICE TYPE	REPL CODE	DEVICE TYPE	REPL CODE	DEVICE TYPE	REPL CODE	DEVICE TYPE	REPL CODE	DEVICE TYPE	REPL CODE	DEVICE TYPE	REPL CODE	DEVICE TYPE	REPL CODE
2SA358F	0136	2SA366F	0136	2SA377C	0050	2SA385D	0136	2SA398X	0211	2SA407X	0004	2SA417	0211
2SA358G	0136	2SA366G	0136	2SA377D	0050	2SA385E	0136	2SA398Y	0211	2SA407Y	0004	2SA419	0050
2SA358GN	0136	2SA366GN	0136	2SA377E	0050	2SA385F	0136	2SA399	0211	2SA408	0136	2SA420	0050
2SA358H	0136	2SA366H	0136	2SA377F	0050	2SA385G	0136	2SA399A	0211	2SA408A	0136	2SA420A	0050
2SA358J	0136	2SA366J	0136	2SA377G	0050	2SA385GN	0136	2SA399B	0211	2SA408B	0136	2SA420B	0050
2SA358K	0136	2SA366K	0136	2SA377GN	0050	2SA385H	0136	2SA399C	0211	2SA408D	0136	2SA420C	0050
2SA358L	0136	2SA366L	0136	2SA377H	0050	2SA385J	0136	2SA399D	0211	2SA408E	0136	2SA420D	0050
2SA358M	0136	2SA366M	0136	2SA377J	0050	2SA385K	0136	2SA399E	0211	2SA408F	0136	2SA420E	0050
2SA358OR	0136	2SA366OR	0136	2SA377K	0050	2SA385L	0136	2SA399F	0211	2SA408GN	0136	2SA420F	0050
2SA358R	0136	2SA366R	0136	2SA377L	0050	2SA385M	0136	2SA399G	0211	2SA408H	0136	2SA420G	0050
2SA358X	0136	2SA366X	0136	2SA377M	0050	2SA385OR	0136	2SA399GN	0211	2SA408J	0136	2SA420H	0050
2SA358Y	0136	2SA366Y	0136	2SA377OR	0050	2SA385R	0136	2SA399H	0211	2SA408K	0136	2SA420J	0050
2SA359	0136	2SA367	0136	2SA377R	0050	2SA385X	0136	2SA399J	0211	2SA408L	0136	2SA420K	0050
2SA359A	0136	2SA367A	0136	2SA377X	0050	2SA385Y	0136	2SA399K	0211	2SA408M	0136	2SA420L	0050
2SA359B	0136	2SA367B	0136	2SA377Y	0050	2SA386	0050	2SA399L	0211	2SA408OR	0136	2SA420M	0050
2SA359C	0136	2SA367C	0136	2SA378	0050	2SA387	0050	2SA399M	0211	2SA408R	0136	2SA420OR	0050
2SA359D	0136	2SA367D	0136	2SA379	0050	2SA389	0050	2SA399OR	0211	2SA408X	0136	2SA420R	0050
2SA359E	0136	2SA367E	0136	2SA380	0136	2SA390	0050	2SA399X	0211	2SA408Y	0136	2SA420X	0050
2SA359F	0136	2SA367F	0136	2SA380A	0136	2SA391	0279	2SA399Y	0211	2SA409	0136	2SA420Y	0050
2SA359G	0136	2SA367G	0136	2SA380B	0136	2SA391A	0279	2SA400	0136	2SA409A	0136	2SA421	0050
2SA359GN	0136	2SA367GN	0136	2SA380C	0136	2SA391B	0279	2SA400A	0136	2SA409B	0136	2SA422	0050
2SA359H	0136	2SA367H	0136	2SA380D	0136	2SA391C	0279	2SA400B	0136	2SA409C	0136	2SA423	0279
2SA359J	0136	2SA367J	0136	2SA380E	0136	2SA391D	0279	2SA400C	0136	2SA409D	0136	2SA424	0279
2SA359K	0136	2SA367K	0136	2SA380F	0136	2SA391E	0279	2SA400D	0136	2SA409E	0136	2SA425	0050
2SA359L	0136	2SA367L	0136	2SA380G	0136	2SA391F	0279	2SA400E	0136	2SA409F	0136	2SA426	0050
2SA359M	0136	2SA367M	0136	2SA380GN	0136	2SA391G	0279	2SA400F	0136	2SA409G	0136	2SA426GN	0050
2SA359OR	0136	2SA367OR	0136	2SA380H	0136	2SA391GN	0279	2SA400G	0136	2SA409GN	0136	2SA427	0136
2SA359R	0136	2SA367R	0136	2SA380J	0136	2SA391H	0279	2SA400GN	0136	2SA409H	0136	2SA427A	0136
2SA359X	0136	2SA367X	0136	2SA380K	0136	2SA391J	0279	2SA400H	0136	2SA409J	0136	2SA427B	0136
2SA359Y	0136	2SA367Y	0136	2SA380L	0136	2SA391K	0279	2SA400J	0136	2SA409K	0136	2SA427C	0136
2SA360	0050	2SA368	0136	2SA380M	0136	2SA391L	0279	2SA400K	0136	2SA409L	0136	2SA427D	0136
2SA360A	0050	2SA368A	0136	2SA380OR	0136	2SA391M	0279	2SA400L	0136	2SA409M	0136	2SA427E	0136
2SA360B	0050	2SA368B	0136	2SA380R	0136	2SA391OR	0279	2SA400M	0136	2SA409OR	0136	2SA427F	0136
2SA360C	0050	2SA368C	0136	2SA380X	0136	2SA391R	0279	2SA400OR	0136	2SA409R	0136	2SA427G	0136
2SA360E	0050	2SA368D	0136	2SA380Y	0136	2SA391X	0279	2SA400R	0136	2SA409X	0136	2SA427GN	0136
2SA360F	0050	2SA368E	0136	2SA381	0136	2SA391Y	0279	2SA400X	0136	2SA409Y	0136	2SA427H	0136
2SA360G	0050	2SA368F	0136	2SA381A	0136	2SA392	0279	2SA400Y	0136	2SA410	0050	2SA427J	0136
2SA360GN	0050	2SA368G	0136	2SA381B	0136	2SA392A	0279	2SA401	0136	2SA411	0050	2SA427K	0136
2SA360H	0050	2SA368GN	0136	2SA381D	0136	2SA392B	0279	2SA402	0037	2SA412	0136	2SA427L	0136
2SA360J	0050	2SA368H	0136	2SA381E	0136	2SA392C	0279	2SA403	0050	2SA412A	0136	2SA427M	0136
2SA360K	0050	2SA368J	0136	2SA381F	0136	2SA392D	0279	2SA403A	0050	2SA412B	0136	2SA427OR	0136
2SA360L	0050	2SA368K	0136	2SA381G	0136	2SA392E	0279	2SA403B	0050	2SA412C	0136	2SA427R	0136
2SA360M	0050	2SA368L	0136	2SA381GN	0136	2SA392F	0279	2SA403C	0050	2SA412D	0136	2SA427X	0136
2SA360OR	0050	2SA368M	0136	2SA381H	0136	2SA392G	0279	2SA403D	0050	2SA412E	0136	2SA427Y	0136
2SA360R	0050	2SA368OR	0136	2SA381K	0136	2SA392GN	0279	2SA403E	0050	2SA412F	0136	2SA428	0136
2SA360X	0050	2SA368R	0136	2SA381L	0136	2SA392H	0279	2SA403F	0050	2SA412G	0136	2SA428A	0136
2SA360Y	0050	2SA368X	0136	2SA381M	0136	2SA392J	0279	2SA403G	0050	2SA412GN	0136	2SA428B	0136
2SA361	0050	2SA368Y	0136	2SA381OR	0136	2SA392K	0279	2SA403GN	0050	2SA412H	0136	2SA428C	0136
2SA361A	0050	2SA369	0136	2SA381R	0136	2SA392L	0279	2SA403H	0050	2SA412J	0136	2SA428D	0136
2SA361B	0050	2SA369A	0136	2SA381X	0136	2SA392M	0279	2SA403J	0050	2SA412K	0136	2SA428E	0136
2SA361C	0050	2SA369B	0136	2SA381Y	0136	2SA392OR	0279	2SA403K	0050	2SA412L	0136	2SA428F	0136
2SA361D	0050	2SA369C	0136	2SA382	0136	2SA392R	0279	2SA403L	0050	2SA412M	0136	2SA428G	0136
2SA361E	0050	2SA369D	0136	2SA382A	0136	2SA392X	0279	2SA403M	0050	2SA412OR	0136	2SA428GN	0136
2SA361F	0050	2SA369E	0136	2SA382B	0136	2SA392Y	0279	2SA403OR	0050	2SA412R	0136	2SA428H	0136
2SA361G	0050	2SA369F	0136	2SA382C	0136	2SA393	0279	2SA403R	0050	2SA412X	0136	2SA428J	0136
2SA361GN	0050	2SA369G	0136	2SA382D	0136	2SA393A	0279	2SA403X	0050	2SA412Y	0136	2SA428K	0136
2SA361H	0050	2SA369GN	0136	2SA382E	0136	2SA394	0279	2SA403Y	0050	2SA413	0050	2SA428L	0136
2SA361J	0050	2SA369H	0136	2SA382F	0136	2SA394A	0279	2SA404	0050	2SA414	0279	2SA428M	0136
2SA361K	0050	2SA369J	0136	2SA382G	0136	2SA394B	0279	2SA404A	0050	2SA414A	0279	2SA428OR	0136
2SA361L	0050	2SA369K	0136	2SA382GN	0136	2SA394C	0279	2SA404B	0050	2SA414B	0279	2SA428R	0136
2SA361M	0050	2SA369L	0136	2SA382H	0136	2SA394D	0279	2SA404C	0050	2SA414C	0279	2SA428X	0136
2SA361OR	0050	2SA369M	0136	2SA382J	0136	2SA394E	0279	2SA404D	0050	2SA414D	0279	2SA428Y	0136
2SA361R	0050	2SA369OR	0136	2SA382K	0136	2SA394F	0279	2SA404E	0050	2SA414E	0279	2SA429	2714
2SA361X	0050	2SA369R	0136	2SA382L	0136	2SA394G	0279	2SA404F	0050	2SA414F	0279	2SA429-0	2714
2SA361Y	0050	2SA369X	0136	2SA382M	0136	2SA394GN	0279	2SA404G	0050	2SA414G	0279	2SA429A	2714
2SA362	0050	2SA369Y	0136	2SA382OR	0136	2SA394H	0279	2SA404GN	0050	2SA414GN	0279	2SA429B	2714
2SA363	0050	2SA370	0164	2SA382R	0136	2SA394J	0279	2SA404H	0050	2SA414H	0279	2SA429C	2714
2SA364	0136	2SA371	0164	2SA382X	0136	2SA394K	0279	2SA404K	0050	2SA414J	0279	2SA429D	2714
2SA364A	0136	2SA372	0050	2SA382Y	0136	2SA394L	0279	2SA404L	0050	2SA414K	0279	2SA429E	2714
2SA364B	0136	2SA373	0004	2SA383	0136	2SA394M	0279	2SA404M	0050	2SA414L	0279	2SA429F	2714
2SA364C	0136	2SA373A	0004	2SA383A	0136	2SA394OR	0279	2SA404OR	0050	2SA414M	0279	2SA429G	2714
2SA364D	0136	2SA374	0004	2SA383B	0136	2SA394R	0279	2SA404R	0050	2SA414OR	0279	2SA429GN	2714
2SA364E	0136	2SA375	0004	2SA383C	0136	2SA394X	0279	2SA404X	0050	2SA414R	0279	2SA429G-0	2714
2SA364F	0136	2SA375A	0004	2SA383D	0136	2SA394Y	0279	2SA404Y	0050	2SA414X	0279	2SA429G-R	2714
2SA364G	0136	2SA375B	0004	2SA383E	0136	2SA395	0279	2SA405	0050	2SA415	0279	2SA429G-Y	2714
2SA364GN	0136	2SA375C	0004	2SA383F	0136	2SA395A	0279	2SA405-0	0050	2SA415A	0279	2SA429H	2714
2SA364H	0136	2SA375D	0004	2SA383G	0136	2SA395B	0279	2SA406	0004	2SA415B	0279	2SA429J	2714
2SA364J	0136	2SA375E	0004	2SA383GN	0136	2SA395C	0279	2SA406A	0004	2SA415C	0279	2SA429K	2714
2SA364K	0136	2SA375F	0004	2SA383H	0136	2SA395D	0279	2SA406B	0004	2SA415D	0279	2SA429L	2714
2SA364L	0136	2SA375G	0004	2SA383J	0136	2SA395E	0279	2SA406C	0004	2SA415E	0279	2SA429M	2714
2SA364M	0136	2SA375GN	0004	2SA383K	0136	2SA395F	0279	2SA406D	0004	2SA415F	0279	2SA429OR	2714
2SA364OR	0136	2SA375H	0004	2SA383L	0136	2SA395G	0279	2SA406E	0004	2SA415G	0279	2SA429R	2714
2SA364R	0136	2SA375J	0004	2SA383M	0136	2SA395GN	0279	2SA406G	0004	2SA415H	0279	2SA429X	2714
2SA364X	0136	2SA375K	0004	2SA383OR	0136	2SA395H	0279	2SA406GN	0004	2SA415J	0279	2SA430	0050
2SA364Y	0136	2SA375L	0004	2SA383R	0136	2SA395J	0279	2SA406H	0004	2SA415K	0279	2SA431	0050
2SA365	0136	2SA375M	0004	2SA383X	0136	2SA395K	0279	2SA406J	0004	2SA415L	0279	2SA431A	0050
2SA365A	0136	2SA375OR	0004	2SA383Y	0136	2SA395L	0279	2SA406K	0004	2SA415M	0279	2SA432	0050
2SA365B	0136	2SA375R	0004	2SA384	0136	2SA395M	0279	2SA406L	0004	2SA415OR	0279	2SA432A	0050
2SA365C	0136	2SA375X	0004	2SA384A	0136	2SA395OR	0279	2SA406M	0004	2SA415R	0279	2SA432B	0050
2SA365D	0136	2SA375Y	0004	2SA384B	0136	2SA395R	0279	2SA406OR	0004	2SA415X	0279	2SA432C	0050
2SA365E	0136	2SA376	0136	2SA384C	0136	2SA395X	0279	2SA406R	0004	2SA415Y	0279	2SA432D	0050
2SA365F	0136	2SA376A	0136	2SA384D	0136	2SA395Y	0279	2SA406X	0004	2SA416	0160	2SA432E	0050
2SA365G	0136	2SA376B	0136	2SA384E	0136	2SA396	0211	2SA406Y	0004	2SA416A	0160	2SA432F	0050
2SA365GN	0136	2SA376C	0136	2SA384F	0136	2SA397	0211	2SA407	0004	2SA416B	0160	2SA432G	0050
2SA365H	0136	2SA376D	0136	2SA384G	0136	2SA398	0211	2SA407A	0004	2SA416C	0160	2SA432GN	0050
2SA365J	0136	2SA376E	0136	2SA384GN	0136	2SA398A	0211	2SA407B	0004	2SA416D	0160	2SA432H	0050
2SA365K	0136	2SA376F	0136	2SA384H	0136	2SA398B	0211	2SA407C	0004	2SA416E	0160	2SA432K	0050
2SA365L	0136	2SA376GN	0136	2SA384J	0136	2SA398C	0211	2SA407D	0004	2SA416F	0160	2SA432L	0050
2SA365M	0136	2SA376H	0136	2SA384K	0136	2SA398D	0211	2SA407E	0004	2SA416G	0160	2SA432M	0050
2SA365OR	0136	2SA376J	0136	2SA384L	0136	2SA398E	0211	2SA407F	0004	2SA416GN	0160	2SA432OR	0050
2SA365R	0136	2SA376K	0136	2SA384M	0136	2SA398F	0211	2SA407G	0004	2SA416H	0160	2SA432R	0050
2SA365X	0136	2SA376L	0136	2SA384OR	0136	2SA398G	0211	2SA407GN	0004	2SA416J	0160	2SA432X	0050
2SA365Y	0136	2SA376OR	0136	2SA384R	0136	2SA398GN	0211	2SA407H	0004	2SA416K	0160	2SA432Y	0050
2SA366	0136	2SA376R	0136	2SA384X	0136	2SA398H	0211	2SA407J	0004	2SA416L	0160	2SA433	0050
2SA366A	0136	2SA376X	0136	2SA384Y	0136	2SA398J	0211	2SA407K	0004	2SA416M	0160	2SA433A	0050
2SA366B	0136	2SA376Y	0136	2SA385	0136	2SA398K	0211	2SA407L	0004	2SA416OR	0160	2SA433B	0050
2SA366C	0136	2SA377	0050	2SA385A	0136	2SA398L	0211	2SA407M	0004	2SA416R	0160	2SA433C	0050
2SA366D	0136	2SA377A	0050	2SA385B	0136	2SA398M	0211	2SA407OR	0004	2SA416X	0160	2SA433D	0050
2SA366E	0136	2SA377B	0050	2SA385C	0136	2SA398OR	0211	2SA407R	0004	2SA416Y	0160	2SA433E	0050

If replacement code is OEM, contact original manufacturer for replacement.

DEVICE TYPE	REPL CODE
2SA433F	0050
2SA433G	0050
2SA433GN	0050
2SA433H	0050
2SA433K	0050
2SA433L	0050
2SA433M	0050
2SA433OR	0050
2SA433R	0050
2SA433X	0050
2SA433Y	0050
2SA434	0050
2SA434A	0050
2SA434B	0050
2SA434C	0050
2SA434D	0050
2SA434E	0050
2SA434F	0050
2SA434G	0050
2SA434GN	0050
2SA434H	0050
2SA434J	0050
2SA434K	0050
2SA434L	0050
2SA434M	0050
2SA434OR	0050
2SA434R	0050
2SA434X	0050
2SA434Y	0050
2SA435	0050
2SA435A	0050
2SA435B	0050
2SA435C	0050
2SA435D	0050
2SA435E	0050
2SA435F	0050
2SA435G	0050
2SA435GN	0050
2SA435H	0050
2SA435J	0050
2SA435L	0050
2SA435M	0050
2SA435OR	0050
2SA435R	0050
2SA435X	0050
2SA435Y	0050
2SA436	0136
2SA436A	0136
2SA436B	0136
2SA436C	0136
2SA436D	0136
2SA436E	0136
2SA436F	0136
2SA436G	0136
2SA436GN	0136
2SA436H	0136
2SA436J	0136
2SA436K	0136
2SA437	0136
2SA437A	0136
2SA437B	0136
2SA437C	0136
2SA437D	0136
2SA437E	0136
2SA437F	0136
2SA437G	0136
2SA437GN	0136
2SA437H	0136
2SA437J	0136
2SA437K	0136
2SA437L	0136
2SA437M	0136
2SA437OR	0136
2SA437R	0136
2SA437X	0136
2SA437Y	0136
2SA438	0136
2SA438A	0136
2SA438B	0136
2SA438C	0136
2SA438D	0136
2SA438E	0136
2SA438F	0136
2SA438G	0136
2SA438GN	0136
2SA438H	0136
2SA438J	0136
2SA438K	0136
2SA438L	0136
2SA438M	0136
2SA438OR	0136
2SA438R	0136
2SA438X	0136
2SA438Y	0136
2SA440	0050
2SA440A	0050
2SA440AL	0050
2SA440B	0050
2SA440C	0050
2SA440D	0050
2SA440E	0050
2SA440F	0050
2SA440G	0050
2SA440GN	0050
2SA440H	0050
2SA440J	0050
2SA440K	0050
2SA440L	0050
2SA440M	0050

DEVICE TYPE	REPL CODE
2SA440OR	0050
2SA440R	0050
2SA440X	0050
2SA440Y	0050
2SA441	0050
2SA443	0004
2SA444	0004
2SA445	0004
2SA446	0211
2SA446A	0211
2SA446B	0211
2SA446C	0211
2SA446D	0211
2SA446E	0211
2SA446F	0211
2SA446G	0211
2SA446GN	0211
2SA446H	0211
2SA446J	0211
2SA446K	0211
2SA446L	0211
2SA446M	0211
2SA446OR	0211
2SA446R	0211
2SA446X	0211
2SA446Y	0211
2SA447	0136
2SA447A	0136
2SA447B	0136
2SA447C	0136
2SA447D	0136
2SA447E	0136
2SA447F	0136
2SA447G	0136
2SA447GN	0136
2SA447H	0136
2SA447J	0136
2SA447K	0136
2SA447L	0136
2SA447M	0136
2SA447OR	0136
2SA447R	0136
2SA447X	0136
2SA447Y	0136
2SA448	0050
2SA449	0136
2SA450	0050
2SA450H	0050
2SA451	0050
2SA451H	0050
2SA452	0050
2SA452H	0050
2SA453	0136
2SA453A	0136
2SA453B	0136
2SA453C	0136
2SA453D	0136
2SA453E	0136
2SA453F	0136
2SA453G	0136
2SA453GN	0136
2SA453H	0136
2SA453J	0136
2SA453K	0136
2SA453L	0136
2SA453M	0136
2SA453OR	0136
2SA453R	0136
2SA453X	0136
2SA453Y	0136
2SA454	0136
2SA454A	0136
2SA454B	0136
2SA454C	0136
2SA454D	0136
2SA454E	0136
2SA454F	0136
2SA454G	0136
2SA454GN	0136
2SA454H	0136
2SA454J	0136
2SA454K	0136
2SA454L	0136
2SA454OR	0136
2SA454R	0136
2SA454X	0136
2SA454Y	0136
2SA455	0136
2SA455A	0136
2SA455B	0136
2SA455C	0136
2SA455D	0136
2SA455E	0136
2SA455F	0136
2SA455G	0136
2SA455GN	0136
2SA455H	0136
2SA455J	0136
2SA455K	0136
2SA455L	0136
2SA455M	0136
2SA455OR	0136
2SA455R	0136
2SA455X	0136
2SA455Y	0136
2SA456	0136
2SA456A	0136
2SA456B	0136
2SA456C	0136

DEVICE TYPE	REPL CODE
2SA456D	0136
2SA456E	0136
2SA456F	0136
2SA456G	0136
2SA456GN	0136
2SA456H	0136
2SA456J	0136
2SA456K	0136
2SA456L	0136
2SA456M	0136
2SA456OR	0136
2SA456R	0136
2SA456X	0136
2SA456Y	0136
2SA457	0136
2SA457A	0136
2SA457B	0136
2SA457C	0136
2SA457D	0136
2SA457E	0136
2SA457F	0136
2SA457G	0136
2SA457GN	0136
2SA457H	0136
2SA457J	0136
2SA457K	0136
2SA457L	0136
2SA457M	0136
2SA457OR	0136
2SA457R	0136
2SA457X	0136
2SA457Y	0136
2SA458	1056
2SA458C	1056
2SA459	0004
2SA459Y	0004
2SA460	0050
2SA461	0050
2SA462	0050
2SA463	0050
2SA463C	0050
2SA464	0050
2SA465	0150
2SA466	0136
2SA466-2	0136
2SA466-3	0136
2SA466A	0136
2SA466B	0136
2SA466BLK	0136
2SA466BLU	0136
2SA466C	0136
2SA466D	0136
2SA466E	0136
2SA466F	0136
2SA466G	0136
2SA466GN	0136
2SA466H	0136
2SA466J	0136
2SA466K	0136
2SA466L	0136
2SA466M	0136
2SA466OR	0136
2SA466R	0136
2SA466X	0136
2SA466Y	0136
2SA466YEL	0136
2SA467	0006
2SA467A	0006
2SA467B	0006
2SA467C	0006
2SA467D	0006
2SA467E	0006
2SA467F	0006
2SA467G	0006
2SA467GN	0006
2SA467G-O	0006
2SA467G-R	0006
2SA467G-Y	0006
2SA467H	0006
2SA467J	0006
2SA467K	0006
2SA467L	0006
2SA467M	0006
2SA467OR	0006
2SA467R	0006
2SA467X	0006
2SA467Y	0006
2SA468	0136
2SA468A	0136
2SA468B	0136
2SA468C	0136
2SA468D	0136
2SA468E	0136
2SA468F	0136
2SA468G	0136
2SA468GN	0136
2SA468H	0136
2SA468J	0136
2SA468K	0136
2SA468L	0136
2SA468M	0136
2SA468OR	0136
2SA468R	0136
2SA468X	0136
2SA468Y	0136
2SA469	0136
2SA469A	0136
2SA469B	0136
2SA469C	0136

DEVICE TYPE	REPL CODE
2SA469D	0136
2SA469E	0136
2SA469F	0136
2SA469G	0136
2SA469GN	0136
2SA469H	0136
2SA469J	0136
2SA469K	0136
2SA469L	0136
2SA469M	0136
2SA469OR	0136
2SA469R	0136
2SA469X	0136
2SA469Y	0136
2SA470	0136
2SA470A	0136
2SA470B	0136
2SA470C	0136
2SA470D	0136
2SA470E	0136
2SA470F	0136
2SA470G	0136
2SA470GN	0136
2SA470H	0136
2SA470J	0136
2SA470K	0136
2SA470L	0136
2SA470M	0136
2SA470OR	0136
2SA470R	0136
2SA470X	0136
2SA470Y	0136
2SA471	0136
2SA471-1	0136
2SA471-2	0136
2SA471-3	0136
2SA471A	0136
2SA471B	0136
2SA471C	0136
2SA471D	0136
2SA471E	0136
2SA471F	0136
2SA471G	0136
2SA471GN	0136
2SA471H	0136
2SA471J	0136
2SA471K	0136
2SA471L	0136
2SA471M	0136
2SA471OR	0136
2SA471R	0136
2SA471X	0136
2SA471Y	0136
2SA472	0136
2SA472-1	0136
2SA472-2	0136
2SA472-3	0136
2SA472-4	0136
2SA472-5	0136
2SA472-6	0136
2SA472A	0136
2SA472B	0136
2SA472C	0136
2SA472D	0136
2SA472E	0136
2SA472F	0136
2SA472G	0136
2SA472GN	0136
2SA472H	0136
2SA472J	0136
2SA472K	0136
2SA472L	0136
2SA472M	0136
2SA472OR	0136
2SA472R	0136
2SA472X	0136
2SA472Y	0136
2SA473	0919
2SA473(0)	0919
2SA473(O)	0919
2SA473-GR	0919
2SA473-O	0919
2SA473-R	0919
2SA473-Y	0919
2SA473B	0919
2SA473D	0919
2SA473GR	0919
2SA473R	0919
2SA473Y	0919
2SA474	0136
2SA474-G	0136
2SA474A	0136
2SA474B	0136
2SA474C	0136
2SA474D	0136
2SA474E	0136
2SA474F	0136
2SA474G	0136
2SA474GN	0136
2SA474H	0136
2SA474OR	0136
2SA474R	0136
2SA474X	0136
2SA474Y	0136
2SA475	0050
2SA476	0136
2SA476A	0136
2SA476B	0136
2SA476C	0136

DEVICE TYPE	REPL CODE
2SA476D	0136
2SA476E	0136
2SA476F	0136
2SA476G	0136
2SA476GN	0136
2SA476H	0136
2SA476J	0136
2SA476K	0136
2SA476L	0136
2SA476M	0136
2SA476OR	0136
2SA476R	0136
2SA476X	0136
2SA476Y	0136
2SA477	0136
2SA477A	0136
2SA477B	0136
2SA477C	0136
2SA477D	0136
2SA477E	0136
2SA477F	0136
2SA477G	0136
2SA477GN	0136
2SA477H	0136
2SA477J	0136
2SA477K	0136
2SA477L	0136
2SA477M	0136
2SA477OR	0136
2SA477R	0136
2SA477X	0136
2SA477Y	0136
2SA478	0004
2SA478-G	0004
2SA478A	0004
2SA478B	0004
2SA478C	0004
2SA478D	0004
2SA478E	0004
2SA478F	0004
2SA478G	0004
2SA478GN	0004
2SA478H	0004
2SA478J	0004
2SA478K	0004
2SA478L	0004
2SA478M	0004
2SA478OR	0004
2SA478R	0004
2SA478X	0004
2SA478Y	0004
2SA479	0004
2SA479A	0004
2SA479B	0004
2SA479C	0004
2SA479D	0004
2SA479E	0004
2SA479F	0004
2SA479G	0004
2SA479GN	0004
2SA479H	0004
2SA479J	0004
2SA479K	0004
2SA479L	0004
2SA479M	0004
2SA479OR	0004
2SA479R	0004
2SA479X	0004
2SA479Y	0004
2SA480	0037
2SA480-OR	0037
2SA480A	0037
2SA480B	0037
2SA480C	0037
2SA480D	0037
2SA480E	0037
2SA480F	0037
2SA480G	0037
2SA480GN	0037
2SA480H	0037
2SA480J	0037
2SA480K	0037
2SA480L	0037
2SA480M	0037
2SA480OR	0037
2SA480R	0037
2SA480X	0037
2SA480Y	0037
2SA482	0037
2SA482A	0037
2SA482B	0037
2SA482C	0037
2SA482D	0037
2SA482E	0037
2SA482F	0037
2SA482G	0037
2SA482GN	0037
2SA482H	0037
2SA482J	0037
2SA482K	0037
2SA482L	0037
2SA482M	0037
2SA482OR	0037
2SA482R	0037
2SA482X	0037
2SA482Y	0037
2SA483	0899
2SA483-O	0899
2SA483-R	0899

DEVICE TYPE	REPL CODE
2SA483-Y	0899
2SA484	0886
2SA484-BL	0886
2SA484-R	0886
2SA484-Y	0886
2SA485	0886
2SA485-BL	0886
2SA485-BLU	0886
2SA485-R	0886
2SA485-RED	0886
2SA485-Y	0886
2SA485-YEL	0886
2SA485Y	0886
2SA486	0886
2SA486-BL	0886
2SA486-BLU	0886
2SA486-R	0886
2SA486-RED	0886
2SA486-Y	0886
2SA486-YEL	0886
2SA489	0919
2SA489-0	0919
2SA489-O	0919
2SA489-R	0919
2SA489-Y	0919
2SA490	1490
2SA490(POWER)	1490
2SA490-0	1490
2SA490-O	1490
2SA490-R	1490
2SA490-Y	1490
2SA490A	1490
2SA490B	1490
2SA490C	1490
2SA490D	1490
2SA490E	1490
2SA490F	1490
2SA490G	1490
2SA490GN	1490
2SA490H	1490
2SA490J	1490
2SA490K	1490
2SA490L	1490
2SA490LBG1	1490
2SA490M	1490
2SA490OR	1490
2SA490R	1490
2SA490X	1490
2SA490Y	1490
2SA490YA	1490
2SA490YLBG11	1490
2SA490YLBGL1	1490
2SA493	0006
2SA493-GR	0006
2SA493-O	0006
2SA493-Y	0006
2SA493A	0006
2SA493B	0006
2SA493C	0006
2SA493D	0006
2SA493E	0006
2SA493F	0006
2SA493G	0006
2SA493G-GR	0006
2SA493GN	0006
2SA493GR	3552
2SA493G-Y	0006
2SA493H	0006
2SA493J	0006
2SA493K	0006
2SA493L	0006
2SA493M	0006
2SA493OR	0006
2SA493R	0006
2SA493X	0006
2SA493Y	0006
2SA494	0688
2SA494(Y)	0688
2SA494-GR	0688
2SA494-GR-1	0688
2SA494-O	0688
2SA494-OR	0688
2SA494-Y	0688
2SA494A	0688
2SA494B	0688
2SA494C	0688
2SA494D	0688
2SA494E	0688
2SA494F	0688
2SA494G	0688
2SA494GN	0688
2SA494GR	0688
2SA494H	0688
2SA494J	0688
2SA494K	0688
2SA494L	0688
2SA494M	0688
2SA494O	0688
2SA494OR	0688
2SA494R	0688
2SA494X	0688
2SA494Y	0688
2SA495	0006
2SA495(O)	0006
2SA495(R)	0006
2SA495(Y)	0006
2SA495-0	0006
2SA495-1	0006
2SA495-GN	0006

DEVICE TYPE	REPL CODE
2SA495-O	0006
2SA495-OF	0006
2SA495-OR	0006
2SA495-ORG	0006
2SA495-ORG-G	0006
2SA495-Q	0006
2SA495-R	0006
2SA495-RD	0006
2SA495-RED	0006
2SA495-RED-G	0006
2SA495-Y	0006
2SA495-YEL	0006
2SA495-YEL-G	0006
2SA495-YL	0006
2SA495A	0006
2SA495B	0006
2SA495C	0006
2SA495D	0006
2SA495E	0006
2SA495F	0006
2SA495G	0006
2SA495G-GR	0006
2SA495GN	0006
2SA495G-O	0006
2SA495G-R	0006
2SA495G-Y	0006
2SA495H	0006
2SA495J	0006
2SA495K	0006
2SA495L	0006
2SA495M	0006
2SA495O	0006
2SA495OF	0006
2SA495OR	0006
2SA495Q	0006
2SA495R	0006
2SA495RD	0006
2SA495RED	0006
2SA495RED-G	0006
2SA495RO	0006
2SA495W	0006
2SA495W1	0006
2SA495WI	0006
2SA495X	0006
2SA495Y	0006
2SA495Y(FA-1)	OEM
2SA495YEL	0006
2SA495YEL-G	0006
2SA495YL	0006
2SA496	0520
2SA496(O)	0520
2SA496(Y)	0520
2SA496-0	0520
2SA496-O	0520
2SA496-ORG	0520
2SA496-R	0520
2SA496-RED	0520
2SA496-Y	0520
2SA496-YEL	0520
2SA496O	0520
2SA496ORG	0520
2SA496R	0520
2SA496RED	0520
2SA496Y	0520
2SA496YEL	0520
2SA497	0126
2SA497-O	0126
2SA497-ORG	0126
2SA497-R	0126
2SA497-RED	0126
2SA497-Y	0126
2SA497-YEL	0126
2SA497R	0126
2SA497RED	0126
2SA497Y	0126
2SA498	0126
2SA498(Y)	0126
2SA498-O	0126
2SA498-ORG	0126
2SA498-R	0126
2SA498-RED	0126
2SA498-Y	0126
2SA498-YEL	0126
2SA498R	0126
2SA498RED	0126
2SA498Y	0126
2SA499	0150
2SA499-O	0150
2SA499-ORG	0150
2SA499-R	0150
2SA499-RED	0150
2SA499-Y	0150
2SA499-YEL	0150
2SA499A	0150
2SA499B	0150
2SA499C	0150
2SA499D	0150
2SA499E	0150
2SA499F	0150
2SA499G	0150
2SA499GN	0150
2SA499H	0150
2SA499J	0150
2SA499K	0150
2SA499L	0150
2SA499M	0150
2SA499O	0150
2SA499OR	0150
2SA499R	0150

If replacement code is OEM, contact original manufacturer for replacement.

DEVICE TYPE	REPL CODE
2SA499X	0150
2SA499Y	0150
2SA500	0150
2SA500-0	0150
2SA500-OR	0150
2SA500-ORG	0150
2SA500-R	0150
2SA500-RED	0150
2SA500-Y	0150
2SA500-YEL	0150
2SA500A	0150
2SA500B	0150
2SA500C	0150
2SA500D	0150
2SA500E	0150
2SA500F	0150
2SA500G	0150
2SA500GN	0150
2SA500H	0150
2SA500J	0150
2SA500K	0150
2SA500L	0150
2SA500M	0150
2SA5000	0150
2SA5000R	0150
2SA500R	0150
2SA500X	0150
2SA500Y	0150
2SA501	0126
2SA502	0006
2SA502-0	0006
2SA502-OR	0006
2SA502-R	0006
2SA502-Y	0006
2SA502A	0006
2SA502B	0006
2SA502C	0006
2SA502D	0006
2SA502E	0006
2SA502F	0006
2SA502G	0006
2SA502GN	0006
2SA502H	0006
2SA502J	0006
2SA502K	0006
2SA502L	0006
2SA502M	0006
2SA5020R	0006
2SA502R	0006
2SA502X	0006
2SA502Y	0006
2SA503	0126
2SA503-GR	0126
2SA503-GRN	0126
2SA503-0	0126
2SA503-ORG	0126
2SA503-R	0126
2SA503-Y	0126
2SA503-YEL	0126
2SA503G	0126
2SA5030	0126
2SA503Y	0126
2SA504	0126
2SA504-GR	0126
2SA504-GRN	0126
2SA504-0	0126
2SA504-ORG	0126
2SA504-R	0126
2SA504-Y	0126
2SA504-YEL	0126
2SA504G	0126
2SA5040	0126
2SA504Y	0126
2SA505	0520
2SA505-0	0520
2SA505-ORG	0520
2SA505-R	0520
2SA505-RED	0520
2SA505-Y	0520
2SA505-YEL	0520
2SA5050	0520
2SA5050RG	0520
2SA505R	0520
2SA505RED	0520
2SA505Y	0520
2SA505YEL	0520
2SA506	0050
2SA506R	OEM
2SA506Y	OEM
2SA507	0050
2SA507A	0050
2SA507B	0050
2SA507C	0050
2SA507D	0050
2SA507E	0050
2SA507F	0050
2SA507G	0050
2SA507GN	0050
2SA507H	0050
2SA507J	0050
2SA507K	0050
2SA507L	0050
2SA5070R	0050
2SA507R	0050
2SA507X	0050
2SA507Y	0050
2SA508	0050
2SA508D	0050
2SA508F	0050

DEVICE TYPE	REPL CODE
2SA509	0006
2SA509(A)	0006
2SA509(0)	0006
2SA509-0	0006
2SA509-O	0006
2SA509-OR	0006
2SA509-R	0006
2SA509-RD	0006
2SA509-Y	0006
2SA509-YE	0006
2SA509A	0006
2SA509B	0006
2SA509BL	0006
2SA509C	0006
2SA509D	0006
2SA509E	0006
2SA509F	0006
2SA509G	0006
2SA509GN	0006
2SA509G-0	0006
2SA509GR	0006
2SA509GR-1	0006
2SA509G-Y	0006
2SA509H	0006
2SA509J	0006
2SA509K	0006
2SA509L	0006
2SA509M	0006
2SA5090R	0006
2SA509Q	0006
2SA509R	0006
2SA509RD	0006
2SA509T	0006
2SA509V	0006
2SA509X	0006
2SA509Y	0006
2SA509YE	0006
2SA510	0886
2SA510-0	0886
2SA510-OR	0886
2SA510-ORG	0886
2SA510-R	0886
2SA510-RD	0886
2SA510-RED	0886
2SA510A	0886
2SA510B	0886
2SA510C	0886
2SA510D	0886
2SA510E	0886
2SA510F	0886
2SA510G	0886
2SA510GN	0886
2SA510H	0886
2SA510J	0886
2SA510K	0886
2SA510L	0886
2SA510M	0886
2SA5100R	0886
2SA510R	0886
2SA510X	0886
2SA510Y	0886
2SA511	0886
2SA511-G	0886
2SA511-0	0886
2SA511-OR	0886
2SA511-ORG	0886
2SA511-R	0886
2SA511-RD	0886
2SA511-RED	0886
2SA511A	0886
2SA511B	0886
2SA511C	0886
2SA511D	0886
2SA511E	0886
2SA511F	0886
2SA511G	0886
2SA511GN	0886
2SA511H	0886
2SA511J	0886
2SA511K	0886
2SA511L	0886
2SA511M	0886
2SA5110R	0886
2SA511R	0886
2SA511X	0886
2SA511Y	0886
2SA512	0886
2SA512-0	0886
2SA512-OR	0886
2SA512-OR1	0886
2SA512-ORG	0886
2SA512-R	0886
2SA512-RD	0886
2SA512-RED	0886
2SA512A	0886
2SA512B	0886
2SA512C	0886
2SA512D	0886
2SA512E	0886
2SA512F	0886
2SA512G	0886
2SA512GN	0886
2SA512H	0886
2SA512J	0886
2SA512K	0886
2SA512L	0886
2SA512M	0886
2SA5120R	0886
2SA512R	0886

DEVICE TYPE	REPL CODE
2SA512X	0886
2SA512Y	0886
2SA513	0886
2SA513-0	0886
2SA513-OR	0886
2SA513-ORG	0886
2SA513-R	0886
2SA513-RD	0886
2SA513-RED	0886
2SA513A	0886
2SA513B	0886
2SA513C	0886
2SA513D	0886
2SA513E	0886
2SA513F	0886
2SA513G	0886
2SA513GN	0886
2SA513H	0886
2SA513J	0886
2SA513K	0886
2SA513L	0886
2SA513M	0886
2SA5130R	0886
2SA513R	0886
2SA513X	0886
2SA513Y	0886
2SA514A-Q	OEM
2SA514A-QR	OEM
2SA514A-R	OEM
2SA516	0886
2SA516A	0886
2SA517	0136
2SA518	0136
2SA518-G	0136
2SA518A	0136
2SA518B	0136
2SA518C	0136
2SA518D	0136
2SA518E	0136
2SA518F	0136
2SA518G	0136
2SA518GN	0136
2SA518H	0136
2SA518J	0136
2SA518K	0136
2SA518L	0136
2SA518M	0136
2SA5180R	0136
2SA518R	0136
2SA518X	0136
2SA518Y	0136
2SA522	0037
2SA522A	0037
2SA522AL	0037
2SA522B	0037
2SA522C	0037
2SA522D	0037
2SA522E	0037
2SA522F	0037
2SA522G	0037
2SA522GN	0037
2SA522H	0037
2SA522J	0037
2SA522K	0037
2SA522L	0037
2SA522M	0037
2SA5220R	0037
2SA522R	0037
2SA522X	0037
2SA522Y	0037
2SA523	0126
2SA523A	0126
2SA524	0037
2SA525	0050
2SA525A	0050
2SA525B	0050
2SA525C	0050
2SA525D	0050
2SA525E	0050
2SA525F	0050
2SA525GN	0050
2SA525H	0050
2SA525J	0050
2SA525K	0050
2SA525L	0050
2SA525M	0050
2SA5250R	0050
2SA525R	0050
2SA525X	0050
2SA525Y	0050
2SA526	0037
2SA527	0126
2SA528	0126
2SA529	0126
2SA530	0037
2SA530A	0037
2SA530B	0037
2SA530C	0037
2SA530D	0037
2SA530E	0037
2SA530F	0037
2SA530G	0037
2SA530GN	0037
2SA530GR	0037
2SA530H	0037
2SA530H1	0037
2SA530HA	0037
2SA530HB	0037
2SA530HC	0037

DEVICE TYPE	REPL CODE
2SA530J	0037
2SA530K	0037
2SA530L	0037
2SA530M	0037
2SA5300R	0037
2SA530R	0037
2SA530X	0037
2SA530Y	0037
2SA532	0126
2SA532A	0126
2SA532B	0126
2SA532C	0126
2SA532D	0126
2SA532E	0126
2SA532F	0126
2SA535	0037
2SA536	0050
2SA537	0126
2SA537A	0126
2SA537AA	0126
2SA537AB	0126
2SA537AC	0126
2SA537AH	0126
2SA537AHA	0126
2SA537AHB	0126
2SA537AHC	0126
2SA537H	0126
2SA537HA	0126
2SA537HB	0126
2SA537HC	0126
2SA537K	0126
2SA537L	0126
2SA538	0004
2SA538-G	0004
2SA538G	0004
2SA539	0006
2SA539(K)	0006
2SA539(L)	0006
2SA539(M)	0006
2SA539-Y	0006
2SA539A	0006
2SA539B	0006
2SA539C	0006
2SA539D	0006
2SA539E	0006
2SA539F	0006
2SA539G	0006
2SA539GN	0006
2SA539H	0006
2SA539J	0006
2SA539K	0006
2SA539L	0006
2SA539M	0006
2SA5390R	0006
2SA539R	0006
2SA539X	0006
2SA539Y	0006
2SA542	0037
2SA542A	0037
2SA542B	0037
2SA542C	0037
2SA542D	0037
2SA542E	0037
2SA542F	0037
2SA542G	0037
2SA542GN	0037
2SA542H	0037
2SA542J	0037
2SA542K	0037
2SA542L	0037
2SA542M	0037
2SA5420R	0037
2SA542R	0037
2SA542X	0037
2SA542Y	0037
2SA543	0688
2SA544	0126
2SA544A	0126
2SA544B	0126
2SA544C	0126
2SA544D	0126
2SA544E	0126
2SA544F	0126
2SA544G	0126
2SA544GN	0126
2SA544H	0126
2SA544J	0126
2SA544K	0126
2SA544L	0126
2SA544M	0126
2SA5440R	0126
2SA544R	0126
2SA544X	0126
2SA544Y	0126
2SA545	0786
2SA545(K)	0786
2SA545(L)	0786
2SA545A	0786
2SA545B	0786
2SA545C	0786
2SA545D	0786
2SA545E	0786
2SA545F	0786
2SA545G	0786
2SA545GN	0786
2SA545H	0786
2SA545J	0786
2SA545K	0786
2SA545KLM	0786

DEVICE TYPE	REPL CODE
2SA545L	0786
2SA545LM	0786
2SA545M	0786
2SA5450R	0786
2SA545R	0786
2SA545X	0786
2SA545Y	0786
2SA546	0126
2SA546A	0126
2SA546B	0126
2SA546E	0126
2SA546H	0126
2SA547	0786
2SA547A	0786
2SA548	0150
2SA548G	0150
2SA548GN	0150
2SA548H	0150
2SA548HA	0150
2SA548HB	0150
2SA548HC	0150
2SA5480R	0150
2SA548R	0150
2SA548Y	0150
2SA549	0338
2SA549A	0338
2SA549AH	0338
2SA550	0037
2SA550(Q)	0037
2SA550(R)	0037
2SA550(S)	0037
2SA550A	0037
2SA550A(Q)	0037
2SA550A(R)	0037
2SA550A(R,Q,S	0037
2SA550A(S)	0037
2SA550AB	0037
2SA550AQ	0037
2SA550AR	0037
2SA550AS	0037
2SA550B	0037
2SA550BC	0037
2SA550BL	0037
2SA550C	0037
2SA550D	0037
2SA550P	0037
2SA550Q	0037
2SA550R	0037
2SA550S	0037
2SA550Y	0037
2SA551	0126
2SA551C	0126
2SA551D	0126
2SA551E	0126
2SA552	0126
2SA553	0037
2SA554	0037
2SA554A	0037
2SA555	0006
2SA556	0006
2SA557	0150
2SA558	0037
2SA559	0037
2SA559A	0037
2SA560	0126
2SA560A	0126
2SA561	0006
2SA561(0)	0006
2SA561-0	0006
2SA561-GR	0006
2SA561-GRN	0006
2SA561-O	0006
2SA561-OR	0006
2SA561-ORG	0006
2SA561-R	0006
2SA561-RD	0006
2SA561-RED	0006
2SA561-Y	0006
2SA561-YEL	0006
2SA561-YL	0006
2SA561GRN	0006
2SA561R	0006
2SA561RD	0006
2SA561RED	0006
2SA561Y	0006
2SA561YEL	0006
2SA561YL	0006
2SA562	0006
2SA562(0)	0006
2SA562(T)	0006
2SA562(Y)	0006
2SA562-0	0006
2SA562-GR	0006
2SA562-GRN	0006
2SA562-O	0006
2SA562-OR	0006
2SA562-ORG	0006
2SA562-OTM	0006
2SA562-R	0006
2SA562-RD	0006
2SA562-RED	0006
2SA562-TMO	0006
2SA562-Y	0006
2SA562-YE	0006
2SA562-YEL	0006
2SA562-Y-TM	0006
2SA562D	0006
2SA562E	0006
2SA562G	0006

DEVICE TYPE	REPL CODE
2SA562GR	0006
2SA562GRN	0006
2SA562O	0006
2SA562Q	0006
2SA562R	0006
2SA562RD	0006
2SA562RED	0006
2SA562T	0006
2SA562T(O)	0006
2SA562T(Q)	0006
2SA562TM	0006
2SA562TM(Y)	0006
2SA562TM-0	0006
2SA562TML	0006
2SA562TMM-O	0006
2SA562TM-O	0006
2SA562TMO	0006
2SA562TM-O(FA)	0006
2SA562TM-OFA	0006
2SA562TM-Y	0006
2SA562TMY	0006
2SA562TM-Y(FA)	0006
2SA562TM-Y(T)	5817
2SA562TM-YFA	0006
2SA562TO	0006
2SA562TQ	0006
2SA562V	0006
2SA562VO	0006
2SA562Y	0006
2SA562YE	0006
2SA562YEL	0006
2SA562Y-TM	0006
2SA562YTM	0006
2SA564	0203
2SA564(0)	0203
2SA564(L)	0203
2SA564(O)	0203
2SA564(P)	0203
2SA564(Q)	0203
2SA564(R)	0203
2SA564(S)	0203
2SA564(S,T)	0203
2SA564(T)	0203
2SA564(Y)	0203
2SA564-0	0203
2SA564-1	0203
2SA564-O	0203
2SA564-OGD	0203
2SA564-OR	0203
2SA564-P	0203
2SA564-PQR	0203
2SA564-Q	0203
2SA564-QR	0203
2SA564-Q.R	0203
2SA564-R	0203
2SA564-S	0203
2SA564A	0203
2SA564A(P)	0203
2SA564A(Q)	0203
2SA564A(R)	0203
2SA564A(S)	0203
2SA564A2	0203
2SA564ABQ-1	0203
2SA564AG	0203
2SA564AK	0203
2SA564AL	0203
2SA564A-P	0203
2SA564AP	0203
2SA564A-P(CU)	0203
2SA564A-PQR	0203
2SA564APQR	0203
2SA564A-Q	0203
2SA564AQ	0203
2SA564A-Q(CU)	0203
2SA564AQ-(HD)	0203
2SA564A-QCU	0203
2SA564AQR	0203
2SA564AQRS	0203
2SA564A-Q.R	0203
2SA564A-R	0203
2SA564AR	0203
2SA564A-R(CU)	0203
2SA564ARS	0203
2SA564A-S	0203
2SA564AS	0203
2SA564AT	0203
2SA564ATAQR	0203
2SA564ATAQRS	0203
2SA564B	0203
2SA564BL	0203
2SA564C	0203
2SA564D	0203
2SA564E	0203
2SA564F	0203
2SA564FQ	0203
2SA564FQ-1	0203
2SA564FR	5306
2SA564FR-1	0203
2SA564G	0203
2SA564GN	0203
2SA564H	0203
2SA564J	0203
2SA564K	0203
2SA564L	0203
2SA564M	0203
2SA5640R	0203
2SA564P	0203
2SA564PQR	0203
2SA564P.A	0203

DEVICE TYPE	REPL CODE
2SA564Q	0203
2SA564QP	0203
2SA564QR	0203
2SA564QRS	0203
2SA564R	0203
2SA564RQS	0203
2SA564RS	0203
2SA564S	0203
2SA564T	0203
2SA564X	0203
2SA564XL	0203
2SA564Y	0203
2SA565	0037
2SA565(C)	0037
2SA565(D)	0037
2SA565(D,C)	0037
2SA565A	0037
2SA565AB	0037
2SA565B	0037
2SA565BA	0037
2SA565C	0037
2SA565D	0037
2SA565E	0037
2SA565F	0037
2SA565G	0037
2SA565GN	0037
2SA565H	0037
2SA565J	0037
2SA565K	0037
2SA565L	0037
2SA565M	0037
2SA5650R	0037
2SA565R	0037
2SA565X	0037
2SA565Y	0037
2SA566	0899
2SA566A	0899
2SA566B	0899
2SA566C	0899
2SA566H	0899
2SA567	0037
2SA567A	0037
2SA567B	0037
2SA567C	0037
2SA567D	0037
2SA567E	0037
2SA567F	0037
2SA567G	0037
2SA567GN	0037
2SA567GR	0037
2SA567H	0037
2SA567J	0037
2SA567K	0037
2SA567L	0037
2SA567M	0037
2SA5670R	0037
2SA567R	0037
2SA567X	0037
2SA567Y	0037
2SA568	0006
2SA568-OR	0006
2SA568A	0006
2SA568B	0006
2SA568C	0006
2SA568D	0006
2SA568E	0006
2SA568F	0006
2SA568G	0006
2SA568GN	0006
2SA568H	0006
2SA568J	0006
2SA568K	0006
2SA568L	0006
2SA568M	0006
2SA5680R	0006
2SA568R	0006
2SA568X	0006
2SA568Y	0006
2SA569	0006
2SA569A	0006
2SA569B	0006
2SA569C	0006
2SA569D	0006
2SA569E	0006
2SA569F	0006
2SA569G	0006
2SA569GN	0006
2SA569H	0006
2SA569J	0006
2SA569K	0006
2SA569L	0006
2SA569M	0006
2SA5690R	0006
2SA569R	0006
2SA569X	0006
2SA569Y	0006
2SA570	0006
2SA570A	0006
2SA570B	0006
2SA570C	0006
2SA570D	0006
2SA570E	0006
2SA570F	0006
2SA570G	0006
2SA570GN	0006
2SA570H	0006
2SA570J	0006
2SA570K	0006
2SA570L	0006

60

If replacement code is OEM, contact original manufacturer for replacement.

DEVICE TYPE	REPL CODE
2SA570M	0006
2SA570OR	0006
2SA570R	0006
2SA570X	0006
2SA570Y	0006
2SA571	0126
2SA572	0688
2SA572Y	0688
2SA573	0006
2SA574	0431
2SA575	0006
2SA576	0150
2SA577	0431
2SA578	0688
2SA579	0688
2SA580	0126
2SA581	0126
2SA594	0126
2SA594-O	0126
2SA594-R	0126
2SA594-Y	0126
2SA594N	0126
2SA597	0126
2SA598	OEM
2SA599	0786
2SA599(Y)	0786
2SA599Y	0786
2SA603	0037
2SA603A	0037
2SA603B	0037
2SA603C	0037
2SA603D	0037
2SA603E	0037
2SA603F	0037
2SA603G	0037
2SA603GN	0037
2SA603H	0037
2SA603J	0037
2SA603K	0037
2SA603L	0037
2SA603M	0037
2SA603OR	0037
2SA603R	0037
2SA603X	0037
2SA603Y	0037
2SA604	0126
2SA605	0126
2SA606	0126
2SA607	4920
2SA607A	4920
2SA607B	4920
2SA607C	4920
2SA607D	4920
2SA607E	4920
2SA607F	4920
2SA607G	4920
2SA607GN	4920
2SA607H	4920
2SA607J	4920
2SA607K	4920
2SA607L	4920
2SA607M	4920
2SA607OR	4920
2SA607R	4920
2SA607S	4920
2SA607SA	4920
2SA607SB	4920
2SA607SC	4920
2SA607SD	4920
2SA607X	4920
2SA607Y	4920
2SA608	0006
2SA608(C)	0006
2SA608(D)	0006
2SA608(E)	0006
2SA608(F)	0006
2SA608-0	0006
2SA608-C	0006
2SA608-E	0006
2SA608-E-CTV-NP	0006
2SA608-F	0006
2SA608-F-CTV-NP	0006
2SA608-F-NP-AA	0006
2SA608-F-SPA-AC	0006
2SA608-G-NP-AA	0006
2SA608-G-SPA-AC	0006
2SA608-O	0006
2SA608-OR	0006
2SA608A	0006
2SA608A(E)	0006
2SA608A(F)	0006
2SA608AE	0006
2SA608AF	0006
2SA608B	0006
2SA608BL	0006
2SA608C	0006
2SA608D	0006
2SA608D(F)	0006
2SA608E	0006
2SA608E-SP	OEM
2SA608EZ	0006
2SA608F	0006
2SA608F-NP	OEM
2SA608F-SP	OEM
2SA608FZ	0006
2SA608G	0006
2SA608GN	0006
2SA608G-SP	OEM
2SA608H	0006

DEVICE TYPE	REPL CODE
2SA608J	0006
2SA608K	0006
2SA608K(E)	0006
2SA608K(F)	0006
2SA608K-A-NP	OEM
2SA608KE	0006
2SA608KF	0006
2SA608KG	0006
2SA608KNP	3079
2SA608KNPET	0006
2SA608KNPFT	0006
2SA608KNP-T	0006
2SA608L	0006
2SA608M	0006
2SA608NP	0006
2SA608NP(F)	0006
2SA608NP(G)	0006
2SA608NP-F	OEM
2SA608NP-G	OEM
2SA608NP-T	0006
2SA608OR	0006
2SA608P	0006
2SA608R	0006
2SA608SE	0006
2SA608SEZ	0006
2SA608SF	0006
2SA608SFZ	0006
2SA608SP	0006
2SA608SP(F)	0006
2SA608SP(G)	0006
2SA608SP-E	OEM
2SA608SPE	0006
2SA608SP-F	OEM
2SA608SPF	0006
2SA608SP-G	OEM
2SA608X	0006
2SA608Y	0006
2SA609	0037
2SA609A	0037
2SA609B	0037
2SA609C	0037
2SA609D	0037
2SA609E	0037
2SA609F	0037
2SA609G	0037
2SA609GN	0037
2SA609J	0037
2SA609K	0037
2SA609L	0037
2SA609M	0037
2SA609OR	0037
2SA609R	0037
2SA609Y	0037
2SA610	0006
2SA611	0006
2SA612	0126
2SA613	0899
2SA614	0899
2SA615	0899
2SA616	0899
2SA616(1)	0899
2SA616(1,2)	0899
2SA616(2)	0899
2SA617	0338
2SA617K	0338
2SA618	0338
2SA618K	0338
2SA620	0006
2SA621	0037
2SA622	3477
2SA623	1421
2SA623-0	1421
2SA624	1421
2SA625	0126
2SA626	3459
2SA626L	3459
2SA627	3459
2SA628	0006
2SA628(EF)	0006
2SA628(F)	0006
2SA628-E	0006
2SA628-O	0006
2SA628-OR	0006
2SA628A	0006
2SA628A(E)	0006
2SA628AA	0006
2SA628AD	0006
2SA628A-E	0006
2SA628AE	0006
2SA628A-F	0006
2SA628AF	0006
2SA628B	0006
2SA628C	0006
2SA628D	0006
2SA628E	0006
2SA628E,F	0006
2SA628EF	0006
2SA628F	0006
2SA628G	0006
2SA628GN	0006
2SA628H	0006
2SA628J	0006
2SA628K	0006
2SA628L	0006
2SA628M	0006
2SA628OR	0006
2SA628R	0006
2SA628X	0006
2SA628Y	0006

DEVICE TYPE	REPL CODE
2SA629	0688
2SA629A	0688
2SA629B	0688
2SA629C	0688
2SA629D	0688
2SA629E	0688
2SA629F	0688
2SA629G	0688
2SA629GN	0688
2SA629H	0688
2SA629J	0688
2SA629K	0688
2SA629L	0688
2SA629M	0688
2SA629OR	0688
2SA629R	0688
2SA629X	0688
2SA629Y	0688
2SA633	1045
2SA633A	1045
2SA634	0676
2SA634(4)K	0676
2SA634(4)L	0676
2SA634(L)	0676
2SA634(L,K)	0676
2SA634(M)	0676
2SA634A	0676
2SA634K	0676
2SA634L	0676
2SA634M	0676
2SA635	0378
2SA636	2010
2SA636(4)K	2010
2SA636(4)L	2010
2SA636(L)	2010
2SA636(M)	2010
2SA636-4K	2010
2SA636-4L	2010
2SA636A	2010
2SA636B	2010
2SA636C	2010
2SA636D	2010
2SA636K	2010
2SA636L	2010
2SA636M	2010
2SA637	0338
2SA637C	0338
2SA637D	0338
2SA637M(Q)	0338
2SA637M(R)	0338
2SA637M(S)	0338
2SA638	0338
2SA638E	0338
2SA638E,F	0338
2SA638F	0338
2SA638S	0338
2SA639	0338
2SA639L	0338
2SA639S	0338
2SA640	0688
2SA640(M)	0688
2SA640A	0688
2SA640B	0688
2SA640C	0688
2SA640D	0688
2SA640M	0688
2SA641	0688
2SA641A	0688
2SA641B	0688
2SA641BL	0688
2SA641C	0688
2SA641D	0688
2SA641G	0688
2SA641GR	0688
2SA641K	0688
2SA641L	0688
2SA641M	0688
2SA641O	0688
2SA641OR	0688
2SA641R	0688
2SA641Y	0688
2SA642	0006
2SA642-O	5817
2SA642A	0006
2SA642B	0006
2SA642C	0006
2SA642D	0006
2SA642E	0006
2SA642F	0006
2SA642G	0006
2SA642GN	0006
2SA642H	0006
2SA642J	0006
2SA642K	0006
2SA642L	0006
2SA642M	0006
2SA642OR	0006
2SA642R	0006
2SA642S	0006
2SA642V	0006
2SA642W	0006
2SA642X	0006
2SA642Y	0006
2SA643	1233
2SA643(R)	1233
2SA643(V)	1233
2SA643(V,R)	1233
2SA643(W)	1233
2SA643R	1233

DEVICE TYPE	REPL CODE
2SA643S	1233
2SA643V	1233
2SA643W	1233
2SA645	1357
2SA646	1357
2SA647	0126
2SA648	2002
2SA649	2002
2SA649A	2002
2SA650	2002
2SA651	2002
2SA652	0787
2SA653	0787
2SA653A	0787
2SA653L	0787
2SA654ARS	OEM
2SA656	3459
2SA656A	3459
2SA656L	3459
2SA656M	3459
2SA657	3459
2SA657A	3459
2SA658	3459
2SA658A	3459
2SA659	0006
2SA659(D)	0006
2SA659(E)	0006
2SA659A	0006
2SA659B	0006
2SA659D	0006
2SA659E	0006
2SA659F	0006
2SA659G	0006
2SA659L	0006
2SA659P	0006
2SA659R	0006
2SA659Y	0006
2SA661	0006
2SA661-GR	0006
2SA661-O	0006
2SA661-R	0006
2SA661-Y	0006
2SA661Y	0006
2SA663	0486
2SA663-BL	0486
2SA663-R	0486
2SA663-Y	0486
2SA664	0527
2SA666	0006
2SA666A	0006
2SA666B	0006
2SA666BL	0006
2SA666C	0006
2SA666D	0006
2SA666E	0006
2SA666H	0006
2SA666HR	0006
2SA666I	0006
2SA666IQRS	0006
2SA666QRS	0006
2SA666R	0006
2SA666S	0006
2SA666Y	0006
2SA668	0126
2SA669	0338
2SA670	0919
2SA670A	0919
2SA670B	0919
2SA670C	0919
2SA671	1298
2SA671A	1298
2SA671B	1298
2SA671C	1298
2SA671K	1298
2SA671KA	1298
2SA671KB	1298
2SA671KC	1298
2SA671TD	1298
2SA672	0037
2SA672(B)	0037
2SA672A	0037
2SA672B	0037
2SA672C	0037
2SA673	0148
2SA673(B)	0148
2SA673(C)	0148
2SA673(C)-Y	0148
2SA673(D)	0148
2SA673-C	0148
2SA673-D	0148
2SA673-O	0148
2SA673-OR	0148
2SA673-Y	0148
2SA673A	0148
2SA673A(C)	0148
2SA673AB	0148
2SA673A-C	0148
2SA673AC	0148
2SA673AD	0148
2SA673AK	0148
2SA673AKA	0148
2SA673AKB	0148
2SA673AKC	0148
2SA673AKD	0148
2SA673AS	0148
2SA673AS(C)	0148
2SA673B	0148
2SA673C	0148
2SA673C2	0148

DEVICE TYPE	REPL CODE
2SA673CD	5055
2SA673C-TB	0148
2SA673D	0148
2SA673E	0148
2SA673F	0148
2SA673G	0148
2SA673GN	0148
2SA673H	0148
2SA673J	0148
2SA673K	0148
2SA673L	0148
2SA673M	0148
2SA673OR	0148
2SA673R	0148
2SA673X	0148
2SA673Y	0148
2SA675	0006
2SA677	0006
2SA677-0	0006
2SA677-O	0006
2SA677-OR	0006
2SA677A	0006
2SA677B	0006
2SA677C	0006
2SA677D	0006
2SA677E	0006
2SA677F	0006
2SA677G	0006
2SA677GN	0006
2SA677H	0006
2SA677HL	0006
2SA677J	0006
2SA677K	0006
2SA677L	0006
2SA677M	0006
2SA677OR	0006
2SA677R	0006
2SA677X	0006
2SA677Y	0006
2SA678	0006
2SA678(C)	0006
2SA678(SONY)	0006
2SA678-O	0006
2SA678-OR	0006
2SA678A	0006
2SA678B	0006
2SA678C	0006
2SA678D	0006
2SA678E	0006
2SA678F	0006
2SA678G	0006
2SA678GN	0006
2SA678H	0006
2SA678J	0006
2SA678K	0006
2SA678L	0006
2SA678M	0006
2SA678OR	0006
2SA678R	0006
2SA678X	0006
2SA678Y	0006
2SA679	2002
2SA679-R	2002
2SA679-Y	2002
2SA680	2002
2SA680-R	2002
2SA680-Y	2002
2SA681	0126
2SA682	0520
2SA682-O	0520
2SA682-Y	0520
2SA682O	0520
2SA683	0527
2SA683(Q)	0527
2SA683(R)	0527
2SA683NC	0527
2SA683O	0527
2SA683P	0527
2SA683Q	0527
2SA683R	0527
2SA683S	0527
2SA683.4	0527
2SA684	0527
2SA684(Q)	0527
2SA684(R)	0527
2SA684(S)	0527
2SA684NC	0527
2SA684Q	0527
2SA684R	0527
2SA684RS	0527
2SA684S	0527
2SA685	0006
2SA693	0006
2SA693C	0006
2SA695	0431
2SA695-F	0431
2SA695C	0431
2SA695D	0431
2SA696	0006
2SA696D	0006
2SA697	0006
2SA697C	0006
2SA698	0676
2SA699	0676
2SA699(AP)	0676
2SA699(H)	0676
2SA699(Q)	0676
2SA699(R)	0676
2SA699A	0676

DEVICE TYPE	REPL CODE
2SA699A(P)	0676
2SA699A(R)	0676
2SA699A(RPQ)	0676
2SA699AP	0676
2SA699AQ	0676
2SA699AR	0676
2SA699CF	0676
2SA699P	0676
2SA699Q	0676
2SA699R	0676
2SA700	0919
2SA700(B)	0919
2SA700B	0919
2SA700Y	0919
2SA701	0037
2SA701F	0037
2SA701F0	0037
2SA701FJ	0037
2SA701FO	0037
2SA702	0688
2SA702F	3078
2SA703	1421
2SA704	0006
2SA704A	0006
2SA704B	0006
2SA704C	0006
2SA704D	0006
2SA704E	0006
2SA704F	0006
2SA704G	0006
2SA704GN	0006
2SA704H	0006
2SA704J	0006
2SA704K	0006
2SA704L	0006
2SA704M	0006
2SA704OR	0006
2SA704R	0006
2SA704X	0006
2SA704Y	0006
2SA705	0006
2SA705A	0006
2SA705B	0006
2SA705C	0006
2SA705D	0006
2SA705E	0006
2SA705F	0006
2SA705G	0006
2SA705GN	0006
2SA705H	0006
2SA705J	0006
2SA705K	0006
2SA705L	0006
2SA705M	0006
2SA705OR	0006
2SA705R	0006
2SA705X	0006
2SA705Y	0006
2SA706	0378
2SA706(3)	0378
2SA706-2	0378
2SA706-3	0378
2SA706-4	0378
2SA706H	0378
2SA706J	0378
2SA707	0431
2SA707(V)	0431
2SA708	0126
2SA708A	0126
2SA709	0037
2SA710	0150
2SA711	0150
2SA712	0434
2SA713	3477
2SA713A	3477
2SA714	2002
2SA714-L	2002
2SA714L	2002
2SA715	0520
2SA715B	0520
2SA715C	0520
2SA715D	0520
2SA715WBP	0520
2SA715WT	0520
2SA715WT(C,B)	0520
2SA715WT-B	0520
2SA715WTB	0520
2SA715WTBC	0520
2SA715WT-C	0520
2SA715WTC	0520
2SA717	0126
2SA718	0037
2SA719	0006
2SA719(Q)	0006
2SA719(R)	0006
2SA719(RS)	0006
2SA719(S)	0006
2SA719-P	0006
2SA719-PQR	0006
2SA719-Q	0006
2SA719-R	0006
2SA719-S	0006
2SA719,R	0006
2SA719A	0006
2SA719K	0006
2SA719NC	0006
2SA719O	0006
2SA719P	0006
2SA719PQR	0006

DEVICE TYPE	REPL CODE
2SA719Q	0006
2SA719QR	0006
2SA719R	0006
2SA719RS	0006
2SA719S	0006
2SA719TAQR	0006
2SA720	0006
2SA720-G	0006
2SA720-O	0006
2SA720-Q	0006
2SA720-R	0006
2SA720A	0006
2SA720A(R)	0006
2SA720A(S)	0006
2SA720B	0006
2SA720C	0006
2SA720D	0006
2SA720L	0006
2SA720NC	0006
2SA720Q	0006
2SA720QR	0006
2SA720QS	0006
2SA720R	0006
2SA720RST	0006
2SA720S	0006
2SA720Y	0006
2SA721	0688
2SA721Q	0688
2SA721R	0688
2SA721S	0688
2SA721T	0688
2SA721U	0688
2SA722	0688
2SA722-S	OEM
2SA722S	0688
2SA723	0006
2SA723R	0006
2SA724	0148
2SA725	0688
2SA725Y	0688
2SA726	0688
2SA726Y	0688
2SA728	0006
2SA728A	0006
2SA730	1233
2SA731	1233
2SA732	0126
2SA733	0006
2SA733(C)Q	0006
2SA733(C)-T	0006
2SA733(E)	0006
2SA733(K)	0006
2SA733(P)	0006
2SA733(Q)	0006
2SA733-P	0006
2SA733-Q	0006
2SA733-T	0006
2SA733A	0006
2SA733A-K	OEM
2SA733AK	0006
2SA733A-KY	OEM
2SA733AP	0006
2SA733APT	0006
2SA733A-Q	OEM
2SA733AQ	0006
2SA733AR	0006
2SA733H	0006
2SA733IO	0006
2SA733IQ	0006
2SA733K	0006
2SA733P	0006
2SA733PQ	0006
2SA733Q	0006
2SA733Q1P	0006
2SA733QP	0006
2SA733QT	0006
2SA733R	0006
2SA733TP	0006
2SA734	0126
2SA735	0037
2SA736	0126
2SA738	0455
2SA738(B)	0455
2SA738A	0455
2SA738C	0455
2SA738D	0455
2SA739	3561
2SA740	1638
2SA740A	1638
2SA740AB	1638
2SA741	0150
2SA741H	0150
2SA742	0126
2SA742H	0126
2SA743	0520
2SA743A	0520
2SA743AB	0520
2SA743AC	0520
2SA743C	0520
2SA744	0486
2SA745	2002
2SA745A	2002
2SA746	2002
2SA747	2002
2SA747A	2002
2SA748	0676
2SA748Q	0676
2SA749	0338
2SA749A	0338

If replacement code is OEM, contact original manufacturer for replacement.

61

DEVICE TYPE	REPL CODE
2SA750	0688
2SA751	0472
2SA751(P)	0472
2SA751(Q)	0472
2SA751(R)	0472
2SA751Q	0472
2SA751R	0472
2SA752	0472
2SA753	2002
2SA754	0919
2SA755	0919
2SA755B	0919
2SA755C	0919
2SA756	3459
2SA757	3459
2SA758	2002
2SA759	0037
2SA760	0688
2SA761	0126
2SA761-1	0126
2SA761-2	0126
2SA762	0787
2SA762-1	0787
2SA762-2	0787
2SA763	0688
2SA764	0899
2SA765	0899
2SA766	1638
2SA766S	1638
2SA767	0037
2SA768	0919
2SA768G	0919
2SA768O	0919
2SA768Q	0919
2SA768Y	0919
2SA768Y-G	OEM
2SA769	0848
2SA770	0848
2SA771	1359
2SA772	0527
2SA772-1	0527
2SA772-2	0527
2SA772-23	0527
2SA772J	0527
2SA773	2027
2SA773-1	2027
2SA773-2	2027
2SA773H	2027
2SA774	0688
2SA774A	0688
2SA775	0676
2SA775A	0676
2SA775AA	0676
2SA775AB	0676
2SA775AC	0676
2SA775B	0676
2SA775C	0676
2SA776	0150
2SA776A	0150
2SA777	0431
2SA777NC	0431
2SA777Q	0431
2SA777R	5504
2SA778	0338
2SA778(A-K)	0338
2SA778A	0338
2SA778AF-02	0338
2SA778AK	0338
2SA778AK-02	0338
2SA778K	0338
2SA778K-02	0338
2SA779	1045
2SA779K	1045
2SA779KB	1045
2SA780	1357
2SA780A	1357
2SA780AK	1357
2SA780AKB	1357
2SA781	0150
2SA781K	0150
2SA782	0037
2SA783	0148
2SA784	3477
2SA785	4971
2SA786	0037
2SA786-Q	0037
2SA786Q	0037
2SA786QL	0037
2SA786R	0037
2SA787	0688
2SA788	0037
2SA789	0148
2SA790	0630
2SA790M	0630
2SA791	3477
2SA793	0126
2SA794	0520
2SA794A	0520
2SA795	0520
2SA795A	0520
2SA796	3477
2SA797	OEM
2SA798	0688
2SA798-G-DU	0688
2SA798G	6081
2SA799	0126
2SA800	3562
2SA802	0338
2SA803	1514
2SA804	1514
2SA805	0338
2SA806	0338
2SA807	3459
2SA808	3459
2SA808A	3459
2SA809	0338
2SA810	0338
2SA811	0037
2SA811A	0037
2SA811C5	0037
2SA811C6	0037
2SA811C7	0037
2SA811C8	0037
2SA812	1731
2SA812-M51E	1731
2SA812M3	1731
2SA812M4	1731
2SA812M5	1731
2SA812M6	1731
2SA812M7	1731
2SA813	0150
2SA813S2	0150
2SA813S3	0150
2SA813S4	0150
2SA814	0676
2SA814-O	0676
2SA814-Y	0676
2SA815	0676
2SA815-O	0676
2SA815-Y	0676
2SA816	1638
2SA816-0	1638
2SA816-O	1638
2SA816-Y	1638
2SA817	0431
2SA817(Y)	0431
2SA817-Y	0431
2SA817A	0431
2SA817A-Y	OEM
2SA817AY	0431
2SA817Y	0431
2SA818	0676
2SA818-O	0676
2SA818-Y	0676
2SA819	0006
2SA820	0338
2SA821	0338
2SA822	0431
2SA823	0527
2SA824	0527
2SA825	0006
2SA825Q	0006
2SA825R	0006
2SA825S	0006
2SA826	0037
2SA826P	0037
2SA826Q	0037
2SA826R	0037
2SA826S	0037
2SA827	0148
2SA828	0527
2SA828A	0527
2SA829	0527
2SA830	3477
2SA831	0630
2SA832	0338
2SA833	OEM
2SA834	1514
2SA835	0338
2SA835H	0338
2SA836	0688
2SA836(D)	0688
2SA836(E)	0688
2SA836C	0688
2SA836D	0688
2SA836E	0688
2SA836F	0688
2SA837	3459
2SA838	5280
2SA838A	6091
2SA838B	5280
2SA838C	5280
2SA839	1638
2SA839-O	1638
2SA839-R	1638
2SA839-Y	1638
2SA840	1638
2SA840H	1638
2SA840JC	1638
2SA840JM	1638
2SA840K	1638
2SA841	0688
2SA841-BL	0688
2SA841-GR	0688
2SA842	0688
2SA842-BL	0688
2SA842-GR	0688
2SA843	1638
2SA844	0006
2SA844(D)	0688
2SA844(E)	0688
2SA844C	0688
2SA844CD	0006
2SA844CD-TB	0006
2SA844D	0688
2SA844E	0688
2SA844F	0688
2SA844O	0688
2SA845	0338
2SA845A	0338
2SA845AH	0338
2SA845H	0338
2SA847	0643
2SA847A	0643
2SA848	0434
2SA849	0434
2SA850	0006
2SA851	3572
2SA852	3572
2SA853	OEM
2SA-854	1338
2SA854	1338
2SA854(Q)	1338
2SA854-Q	1338
2SA854G	1338
2SA854PQ	1338
2SA-854Q	1338
2SA854Q	1338
2SA854QE	1338
2SA854QR	1338
2SA854QV	1338
2SA854QY	1338
2SA854QZ	1338
2SA854R	1338
2SA854RA	OEM
2SA854S	1338
2SA854SQ	1338
2SA854SQR	OEM
2SA854SR	1338
2SA855	0688
2SA856	0688
2SA856A	0688
2SA857	0338
2SA858	0338
2SA859	0037
2SA860	0338
2SA861	1045
2SA861(3)	1045
2SA861JK	1045
2SA866	0037
2SA866V	0037
2SA866VG	0037
2SA867	0150
2SA868	0037
2SA869	0037
2SA870	0037
2SA871	5270
2SA872	0643
2SA872A	0643
2SA872AD	0643
2SA872AE	0643
2SA872AF	0643
2SA872C	0643
2SA872D	0643
2SA872E	0643
2SA872F	0643
2SA873	0150
2SA874	0355
2SA874M	0355
2SA874P	0355
2SA874PQ	0355
2SA874Q	0355
2SA876	0037
2SA876HA	0037
2SA876HB	0037
2SA876HC	0037
2SA877	3459
2SA878	3459
2SA879	0338
2SA879NC	0338
2SA879P	0338
2SA879Q	0338
2SA880	0688
2SA881	0006
2SA881Q	0006
2SA881R	0006
2SA882	2002
2SA883	0527
2SA884	0527
2SA885	0520
2SA886	0520
2SA886Q	0520
2SA886V	0520
2SA886VQ	0520
2SA886VR	0520
2SA886VS	0520
2SA887	1257
2SA887P	1257
2SA887Q	1257
2SA887R	1257
2SA888	0037
2SA889	0037
2SA890	0037
2SA891	0037
2SA892	0597
2SA893	0643
2SA893A	0643
2SA893AC	0643
2SA893AD	0643
2SA893AE	0643
2SA893AF	0643
2SA893D	0643
2SA893E	0643
2SA894	0431
2SA895	0150
2SA896	0338
2SA896-1	0338
2SA896-2	0338
2SA897	0643
2SA898	0520
2SA899	5283
2SA900	0520
2SA900-R	0520
2SA900-S	0520
2SA900-T	0520
2SA901	0688
2SA902	0688
2SA903	0688
2SA904	0643
2SA904A	0643
2SA905	0643
2SA906	0688
2SA907	1671
2SA908	1588
2SA909	1588
2SA911	OEM
2SA912	0338
2SA912Q	0338
2SA912R	0338
2SA912S	0338
2SA913	1638
2SA913A	1638
2SA913A(Q)	1638
2SA913A(R)	1638
2SA913AQ	1638
2SA913ARQ	OEM
2SA914	0520
2SA915	0338
2SA916	0338
2SA916K	0338
2SA916L	0338
2SA916M	0338
2SA917	0472
2SA918	0150
2SA919	OEM
2SA920	3712
2SA921	0643
2SA921A	0643
2SA921AS	0643
2SA922	0126
2SA923	0338
2SA923-1	0338
2SA923-2	0338
2SA924	3572
2SA925	0150
2SA925-1	0150
2SA925-2	0150
2SA927	0006
2SA928	1593
2SA928A	OEM
2SA929	0688
2SA929G	0688
2SA929H	0688
2SA930	0688
2SA931	5270
2SA932	5270
2SA933	0148
2SA933(Q)	0148
2SA933(Q)-Y	0148
2SA933(Q,R)	0148
2SA933(R)	0148
2SA933(R)-Y	0148
2SA933(S)	0148
2SA933-Q	0148
2SA933-R	0148
2SA933-S	0148
2SA933-T	0148
2SA933-T-93-R	0148
2SA933-T-93-S	0148
2SA933-Y	0148
2SA933A(Q)	0148
2SA933A(Q)-Y	0148
2SA933A(R)	0148
2SA933A(R)-Y	0148
2SA933AQ	0148
2SA933AR	0148
2SA933LN	0148
2SA933P	0148
2SA933Q	0148
2SA933QL	0148
2SA933QR	0148
2SA933QV	0148
2SA933QY	0148
2SA933QZ	0148
2SA933R	0148
2SA933RA	0148
2SA933RC	0148
2SA933RK	0148
2SA933RZ	0148
2SA933S	0148
2SA933S(Q)	0148
2SA933S(Q)-Y	0148
2SA933S(QR)	0148
2SA933S(QR)-T	0148
2SA933S(R)	0148
2SA933S(R)-Y	0148
2SA933S(S)	0148
2SA933SP	0148
2SA933S-Q	0148
2SA933SQ	0148
2SA933SQR	0148
2SA933SQRSTA	OEM
2SA933SQT	0148
2SA933SQZ	0148
2SA933S-R	0148
2SA933SR	0148
2SA933SRC	0148
2SA933SRD	0148
2SA933SRF	0148
2SA933SRN	0148
2SA933SRQ	0148
2SA933SRR	0148
2SA933SRU	0148
2SA933SRX	0148
2SA933SRY	0148
2SA933S-S	0148
2SA933SS	0148
2SA933SSA	0148
2SA933SSD	0148
2SA933SSJ	0148
2SA933SSK	0148
2SA933SSU	0148
2SA933XTPR	0148
2SA933XTPS	0148
2SA933Z	OEM
2SA934	0527
2SA934Q	0527
2SA934R	0527
2SA935	0431
2SA935R	0431
2SA935T103	0431
2SA936	3477
2SA-937	2464
2SA937	2464
2SA937(R)	2464
2SA937-Q	2464
2SA937-R	2464
2SA937F	OEM
2SA937LN	2464
2SA937M	2464
2SA937M(Q)	2464
2SA937M(R)	2464
2SA937M(S)	2464
2SA937MQRS	2464
2SA937M-R	OEM
2SA937MR	2464
2SA937MRS	2464
2SA937M-S	OEM
2SA937MS	2464
2SA937P	2464
2SA937Q	2464
2SA937R	2464
2SA937RQ	2464
2SA937RZ	2464
2SA937S	2464
2SA938	3154
2SA939	4402
2SA940	1900
2SA940-AR(D)	1900
2SA940-AR(E)	1900
2SA940-O	1900
2SA940-R-D(LB-SAN-5)	1900
2SA940-R-E(LB-SAN-5)	1900
2SA940-Z	1900
2SA940AD	1900
2SA940AR-D	OEM
2SA940AR-E	OEM
2SA940D	1900
2SA940E	1900
2SA940GL2	1900
2SA940LB	1900
2SA940LBGL2	1900
2SA940LBGLR	1900
2SA940R	1900
2SA940R(D)	1900
2SA940R(E)	1900
2SA940RD	1900
2SA940RE	1900
2SA940T-D	OEM
2SA940T-E	OEM
2SA940Z	3500
2SA941	0006
2SA942	0006
2SA945	0164
2SA945-0	0164
2SA945-O	0164
2SA945-Q	0164
2SA948	0126
2SA948E	0126
2SA949	0472
2SA949-Y(C)	0472
2SA949Y	0472
2SA949Y(FA-1)	OEM
2SA950	1338
2SA950(GR)	1338
2SA950(O)	1338
2SA950(Y)	1338
2SA950-0	1338
2SA950-O	1338
2SA950-Y	1338
2SA950FA	1338
2SA950GR	3079
2SA950Y	1338
2SA950Y(FA)	OEM
2SA951	0676
2SA951-10	0676
2SA951KA	0676
2SA951KD	0676
2SA951LC	0676
2SA951M	0676
2SA951MU	0676
2SA952	0006
2SA952(C)-T	0006
2SA952(C)-TL	0006
2SA952(L)	0006
2SA952(M)	0006
2SA952C	0006
2SA952K	0006
2SA952L	0006
2SA952LK	0006
2SA952LT	0006
2SA952M	0006
2SA952ML	0006
2SA952ML2	0006
2SA952NL2	OEM
2SA953	1338
2SA953(K)	1338
2SA953(L)	1338
2SA953K	1338
2SA953L	1338
2SA954	0006
2SA956	0150
2SA956H3	0150
2SA956H4	0150
2SA956H5	0150
2SA956H6	0150
2SA957	1638
2SA957Y	1638
2SA958	1900
2SA958-O	OEM
2SA958-O-N03	1900
2SA958-Y-N03	1900
2SA958Y	1900
2SA959	OEM
2SA962	0378
2SA963	0520
2SA964	3712
2SA964A	3712
2SA965	5233
2SA965(Y)	5233
2SA965-O	0472
2SA965Y	0472
2SA966	0527
2SA966(Y)	0527
2SA966-O	0527
2SA966O	0527
2SA966Y	0527
2SA967	OEM
2SA968	1638
2SA968(Y)	1638
2SA968A	1638
2SA968B	1638
2SA968Y	1638
2SA969	0787
2SA970	0006
2SA970BL	0006
2SA970GR	0006
2SA970NEW-BL	0006
2SA971	1588
2SA972	0527
2SA973	0688
2SA977	0520
2SA977A	0520
2SA978	0688
2SA979	4967
2SA979G	6221
2SA980	2002
2SA981	2002
2SA982	2002
2SA983	OEM
2SA984	0006
2SA984(E)	0006
2SA984(F)	0006
2SA984-E-AA	0006
2SA984-F-AA	0006
2SA984E	0006
2SA984F	3079
2SA984K	0006
2SA984K(E)	0006
2SA984K(F)	0006
2SA984K-E	OEM
2SA984KE	0006
2SA984K-F	OEM
2SA984K-T	0006
2SA985	5288
2SA985A	5288
2SA985P	3500
2SA986	3527
2SA987	0006
2SA988	0643
2SA988E	0643
2SA988F	0643
2SA988FE	0643
2SA989	0527
2SA990	0688
2SA991	0688
2SA992	0643
2SA992E	0643
2SA992EF	OEM
2SA992F	0643
2SA993	0037
2SA994	0006
2SA995	4969
2SA997	0527
2SA998	0527
2SA999	0006
2SA999-O	0006
2SA999F	OEM
2SA999L	0006
2SA1001	2002
2SA1002	2002
2SA1003	1588
2SA1004	0037
2SA1005	0037
2SA1005L	0037
2SA1006	3500
2SA1006A	3500
2SA1006B	OEM
2SA1007	1588
2SA1007A	1588
2SA1008	3501
2SA1009	OEM
2SA1009A	OEM
2SA1010	1359
2SA1010V	1359
2SA1010Y	1359
2SA1011	1638
2SA1011(D)	1638
2SA1011(E)	1638
2SA1011D	1638
2SA1011E	1638
2SA1011RA	OEM
2SA1012	3505
2SA1012-O	3505
2SA1012-Y	3505
2SA1012Y	3505
2SA-1013	1514
2SA1013	1514
2SA1013-0	1514
2SA1013-O	1514
2SA1013-O(C)	1514
2SA1013-R	1514
2SA1013R	1514
2SA1013Y	1514
2SA1014	OEM
2SA-1015	0148
2SA1015	0148
2SA1015(G)	0148
2SA1015(GR)	0148
2SA1015(GR)L	0148
2SA1015(GR)Y	0148
2SA1015(H)-Y	0148
2SA1015(J)-Y	0148
2SA1015(O)	0148
2SA1015(Y)	0148
2SA1015(Y)L	0148
2SA1015(Y)Y	0148
2SA1015(Y,GR)Y	0148
2SA1015(YG)	0148
2SA1015(YG)-LB	0148
2SA1015(YG)-T	0148
2SA1015-0	0148
2SA1015-GR	0148
2SA1015-GR-(SAN)	0148
2SA1015-GR(SAN)	0148
2SA1015-O	0148
2SA1015-O(FA)	0148
2SA1015-O(SAN)	0148
2SA1015-O(TE)	5055
2SA1015-OFA	0148
2SA1015-TPE2	0148
2SA1015-Y	0148
2SA1015-Y(FA)	0148
2SA1015-Y(SAN)	0148
2SA1015-Y(TE)	0148
2SA1015-YFA	0148
2SA1015ABL	0148
2SA1015FA	0148
2SA1015G	0148
2SA1015GR	0148
2SA1015L	0148
2SA1015O	0148
2SA1015TPE2	0148
2SA-1015Y	0148
2SA1015Y	0148
2SA1015Y(FA)	0148
2SA1015Y-TYPE1	0148
2SA1016	0688
2SA1016(F)	0688
2SA1016(G)	0688
2SA1016E	OEM
2SA1016F	0688
2SA1016G	0688
2SA1016K	0688
2SA1016K-F	0688
2SA1016KF	0688
2SA1016KFG	0688
2SA1017	0338
2SA1017G	6610
2SA1018	0338
2SA1018-V	0338
2SA1018Q	6613
2SA1018R	6613
2SA1018V	0338
2SA1019	0643
2SA1020	0429
2SA1020(Y)	0429
2SA1020-O	0429
2SA1020-Y	0429
2SA1020O	0429
2SA1020Y	0429
2SA1020YTPE6	0429
2SA1021	0520
2SA1021-O	0520
2SA1021-R	0520
2SA1021R	2533
2SA1021Y	0520
2SA1022	1741
2SA1022(B)	1741
2SA1022(C)	1741
2SA1022C	6620
2SA1023	1593
2SA1023P	1593

If replacement code is OEM, contact original manufacturer for replacement.

DEVICE TYPE	REPL CODE
2SA1023Q	1593
2SA1024	OEM
2SA1024H	OEM
2SA1025	0037
2SA1025D	0037
2SA1025E	0037
2SA1026	0006
2SA1027	0037
2SA1027(R)	0037
2SA1027R	0037
2SA1028	2002
2SA1029	0006
2SA1029B	0006
2SA1029C	0006
2SA1029D	0006
2SA1030	0006
2SA1030B	0006
2SA1030C	0006
2SA1031	0037
2SA1031B	0037
2SA1031C	0037
2SA1031D	0037
2SA1032	0037
2SA1032B	0037
2SA1032C	0037
2SA1033	0037
2SA1034	1731
2SA1035	1731
2SA1036	1741
2SA1036K	1741
2SA1036KQ	OEM
2SA1037	1731
2SA1037(R)	1731
2SA1037K	1731
2SA1037K(FR)	1731
2SA1037KA	1731
2SA1037KERS	OEM
2SA1037K-Q	1731
2SA1037KQ	1731
2SA1037K-QR	1731
2SA1037K-R	1731
2SA1037KR	1731
2SA1037K-S	1731
2SA1037KS	1731
2SA1037KT97	1731
2SA1037KT147	1731
2SA1038	0643
2SA1039	0643
2SA1039(Q)	0643
2SA1039(R)	0643
2SA1039(S)	0643
2SA1040	0006
2SA1041	1588
2SA1042	0486
2SA1043	1671
2SA1044	1671
2SA1045	0486
2SA1046	0486
2SA1047	0520
2SA1047F	2533
2SA1048	0013
2SA1048-0	0013
2SA1048-GR	0013
2SA1048-O	0013
2SA1048G	0013
2SA1048GR	0013
2SA1048O	0013
2SA1048Y	0013
2SA1049	0006
2SA1050	0148
2SA1050A	0148
2SA1051	1588
2SA1051A	1588
2SA1052	1731
2SA1052B	1731
2SA1052C	1731
2SA1052D	1731
2SA1053	0037
2SA1054	0037
2SA1055	0037
2SA1056	0037
2SA1057	OEM
2SA1058	OEM
2SA1059	OEM
2SA1060	0853
2SA1060P	0853
2SA1060Q	0853
2SA1061	0853
2SA1061P	0853
2SA1061Q	0853
2SA1061R	0853
2SA1062	3527
2SA1063	1588
2SA1064	1588
2SA1065	1588
2SA1066	0472
2SA1067	1588
2SA1068	1588
2SA1069	3533
2SA1069A	3533
2SA1069C	3533
2SA1069L	3533
2SA1071-O	OEM
2SA1072	1588
2SA1072A	1588
2SA1073	1588
2SA1075	3537
2SA1076	3537
2SA1077	0713

DEVICE TYPE	REPL CODE
2SA1078	3541
2SA1079	0713
2SA1080	0676
2SA1081	0037
2SA1081D	0037
2SA1081E	0037
2SA1082	0037
2SA1082D	0037
2SA1082E	0037
2SA1083	0037
2SA1083D	0037
2SA1083E	0037
2SA1084	1587
2SA1084D	1587
2SA1084E	1587
2SA1085	1587
2SA1085D	1587
2SA1085E	1587
2SA1090	0037
2SA1091	0338
2SA1091-O	0338
2SA1091R	0338
2SA1092	0688
2SA1093	3527
2SA1094	3537
2SA1095	3537
2SA1096	0520
2SA1096A	0520
2SA1097-1	OEM
2SA1097-2	OEM
2SA1100	0006
2SA1100D	0006
2SA1100F	0006
2SA1100L	0006
2SA1102	0853
2SA1103	0853
2SA1104	3082
2SA1104A	OEM
2SA1105	3082
2SA1106	3082
2SA1107	3585
2SA1107A	3585
2SA1108	3585
2SA1108A	3585
2SA1109	3601
2SA1110	0520
2SA1111	1638
2SA1112	1638
2SA1113	OEM
2SA1114	OEM
2SA1115	3282
2SA1115(E)	3282
2SA1115(F)	3282
2SA1115(G)	3282
2SA1115-E	3282
2SA1115-EF	3282
2SA1115-F	3282
2SA1115E	3282
2SA1115F	3282
2SA1115G	3282
2SA1116	3561
2SA1117	3561
2SA1120	0520
2SA1121	1741
2SA1121(SC)	OEM
2SA1121C(SC)	OEM
2SA1121SB	1741
2SA1121SC	1741
2SA1121SD	1741
2SA1122	1731
2SA1122(CD)	1731
2SA1122CC	1731
2SA1122CD	1731
2SA1122CE	1731
2SA1123	1514
2SA1124	1514
2SA1125	1638
2SA1126	OEM
2SA1126H	OEM
2SA1127	0688
2SA1127NC	0688
2SA1128	0006
2SA1129	1298
2SA1133	1900
2SA1133A	1900
2SA1135	0853
2SA1136	0472
2SA1137	0643
2SA1138	0643
2SA1141	3082
2SA1142	0520
2SA1143	0688
2SA1144	0136
2SA1145	1514
2SA1146	3527
2SA1147	3561
2SA1150	0006
2SA1150Y	0006
2SA1151	0527
2SA1152	0037
2SA1153	3572
2SA1154	0527
2SA1155	OEM
2SA1156	4402
2SA1158	0431
2SA1160	0527
2SA1161	OEM
2SA1162	1731
2SA1162-G	1731

DEVICE TYPE	REPL CODE
2SA1162G	1731
2SA1162Y	1731
2SA1163	5357
2SA1164	0037
2SA1166	3585
2SA1166A	3585
2SA1169	3537
2SA1170	3601
2SA1171	5357
2SA1171PD	5357
2SA1171PE	5357
2SA1173	1514
2SA1174	0688
2SA1175	3580
2SA1175(E)	3580
2SA1175(F)	3580
2SA1175(H)	3580
2SA1175(H)-Y	3580
2SA1175(J)	3580
2SA1175(J)-Y	3580
2SA1175(J,H)-Y	3580
2SA1175-E	3580
2SA1175-F	3580
2SA1175-FEK	5775
2SA1175-HFE	3580
2SA1175-Y	3580
2SA1175E	3580
2SA1175F	3580
2SA1175F(H)	3580
2SA1175FH	3580
2SA1175H	3580
2SA1175HO	3580
2SA1175J	3580
2SA1175JHFE	3580
2SA1175TP	3580
2SA1177	OEM
2SA1177E	OEM
2SA1178	3082
2SA1179	1741
2SA1179-M5	OEM
2SA1179-M5TA	OEM
2SA1179-M6TA	OEM
2SA1179-TA	1741
2SA1180	1588
2SA1180A	1588
2SA1182	1741
2SA1183	0853
2SA1184	0520
2SA1185	0853
2SA1186	3527
2SA1187	3585
2SA1188	0472
2SA1188D	0472
2SA1188E	0472
2SA1189	0472
2SA1189D	0472
2SA1189E	0472
2SA1190	0472
2SA1190D	0472
2SA1190E	0472
2SA1191	0472
2SA1191D	0472
2SA1191E	0472
2SA1193	3836
2SA1193K	3836
2SA1194	2869
2SA1194K	2869
2SA1195	1045
2SA1195-O	1045
2SA1195O	1045
2SA1195R	1045
2SA1196	OEM
2SA1197	OEM
2SA1198	0688
2SA1198(E)	0688
2SA1198(S)	0688
2SA1198R	OEM
2SA1198RS	0688
2SA1198S	0688
2SA1199	0037
2SA1200	OEM
2SA1201	OEM
2SA1202	3600
2SA1203	OEM
2SA1204	3600
2SA1205	3082
2SA1206	5365
2SA1206K	5365
2SA1207	1514
2SA1207S	6610
2SA1207T	OEM
2SA1208	1514
2SA1208S	6610
2SA1208T	6610
2SA1209	0520
2SA1209-T	OEM
2SA1209S	2533
2SA1210	0520
2SA1211	3572
2SA1213	OEM
2SA1214	0520
2SA1215	3537
2SA1216	3601
2SA1217	0520
2SA1218	0037
2SA1219	0688
2SA1220	0520
2SA1220A	0520
2SA1220A-P	0520

DEVICE TYPE	REPL CODE
2SA1220AP	0520
2SA1220A-Q	0520
2SA1220AQ	0520
2SA1221	0520
2SA1221-L	0520
2SA1221L	0520
2SA1222	5270
2SA1223	OEM
2SA1224	OEM
2SA1225	5367
2SA1226	1741
2SA1227	3082
2SA1227A	3082
2SA1228	OEM
2SA1229	OEM
2SA1230	OEM
2SA1231	OEM
2SA1232	3082
2SA1233	OEM
2SA1233L	OEM
2SA1235	1741
2SA1235-E	1741
2SA1236	OEM
2SA1237	OEM
2SA1238	OEM
2SA1239	OEM
2SA1240	OEM
2SA1241	5367
2SA1242	5367
2SA1243	5367
2SA1244	5367
2SA1245	4419
2SA1246	3609
2SA1246(R)	3609
2SA1246(S)	3609
2SA1246(T)	3609
2SA1246(U)	3609
2SA1246R	3609
2SA1246S	3609
2SA1246T	3609
2SA1246U	3609
2SA1247	5357
2SA1248	0520
2SA1249	0520
2SA1249-R	OEM
2SA1249-S	OEM
2SA1249-T	OEM
2SA1249R	0520
2SA1249S	0520
2SA1250	OEM
2SA1251	OEM
2SA1252	1731
2SA1252-D6-TB	OEM
2SA1252-D7-TB	OEM
2SA1252D4	1731
2SA1252D5	1731
2SA1253	0472
2SA1254	0148
2SA1255	5271
2SA1256	1731
2SA1257	5357
2SA1258	0597
2SA1259	0597
2SA1260	0597
2SA1261	1190
2SA1262	1298
2SA1262-O	OEM
2SA1262R	OEM
2SA1262Y	OEM
2SA1263	3082
2SA1264	3082
2SA1264N	OEM
2SA1264O	OEM
2SA1264T	3082
2SA1265	3082
2SA1265-O	OEM
2SA1265N	3082
2SA1265NFA-1	3082
2SA1266	0148
2SA1266GR	0148
2SA1266Y	0148
2SA1267	0148
2SA1268	1514
2SA1269	0472
2SA1270	0006
2SA1271	5376
2SA1272	5376
2SA1273	3154
2SA1274	0431
2SA1275	1514
2SA1276	0848
2SA1277	1298
2SA1278	3500
2SA1279	1298
2SA1280	3500
2SA1281	5270
2SA1282	3154
2SA1282A	3154
2SA1283	0472
2SA1283(DE)-T	0472
2SA1284	0472
2SA1285	0472
2SA1285A	0472
2SA1286	OEM
2SA1287	OEM
2SA1288	1298
2SA1289	1298
2SA1290	1298
2SA1291	1298

DEVICE TYPE	REPL CODE
2SA1292	3082
2SA1293	1190
2SA1294	OEM
2SA1295	OEM
2SA1296	3954
2SA1297	3154
2SA1298	1741
2SA1299	OEM
2SA1300	3954
2SA1301	3628
2SA1301-0	OEM
2SA1302	5252
2SA1302-0	OEM
2SA1302-O	OEM
2SA1302O	5252
2SA1302R	5252
2SA1303	3628
2SA1304	1638
2SA1304(OEC.1)	1638
2SA1305	0919
2SA1305Y	0919
2SA1306	OEM
2SA1306(Y)	OEM
2SA1306-Y	OEM
2SA1306A	OEM
2SA1306A-O	OEM
2SA1306A-O(LB-SAN)	OEM
2SA1306A-Y	OEM
2SA1306AY	OEM
2SA1306A-Y(LB-SAN)	OEM
2SA1306Y	OEM
2SA1307	1298
2SA1307Y	OEM
2SA1308	5378
2SA1309	0013
2SA1309(Q)	0013
2SA1309(R)	0013
2SA1309(S)	0013
2SA1309A	0013
2SA1309A(Q)	0013
2SA1309A(Q)Y	0013
2SA1309A(R)	0013
2SA1309A(R)Y	0013
2SA1309AQ	0013
2SA1309A-QRS	0013
2SA1309AQSTA	OEM
2SA1309AR	0013
2SA1309AS	0013
2SA1309Q	5322
2SA1309QRS	OEM
2SA1309R	0013
2SA1309S	0013
2SA1310	OEM
2SA1311	OEM
2SA1312	5357
2SA1313	1741
2SA1314	OEM
2SA1315	OEM
2SA1316	0643
2SA1317	0013
2SA1317(S)	0013
2SA1317S	0013
2SA1317SZ	0013
2SA1317T	0013
2SA1317T-AC	OEM
2SA1318	0037
2SA1318S	0037
2SA1318T	0037
2SA1319	OEM
2SA1319R	OEM
2SA1319S	OEM
2SA1319T	OEM
2SA1320	0338
2SA1321	0338
2SA1321(TPE6)	0338
2SA1322	OEM
2SA1323	OEM
2SA1324	OEM
2SA1325	OEM
2SA1326	OEM
2SA1327	1298
2SA1328	OEM
2SA1329	OEM
2SA1330	OEM
2SA1331	1741
2SA1332	OEM
2SA1333	OEM
2SA1334	OEM
2SA1335	OEM
2SA1336	OEM
2SA1337	0013
2SA1338	1741
2SA1339	0013
2SA1339ST	0013
2SA1340	OEM
2SA1341	3241
2SA1342	0698
2SA1343	OEM
2SA1344	1881
2SA1344-TA	1881
2SA1345	4067
2SA1346	3114
2SA1346-AC	3114
2SA1346Z	3114
2SA1347	OEM
2SA1348	4109
2SA1349	OEM
2SA1350	0013
2SA1351	OEM

DEVICE TYPE	REPL CODE
2SA1352	OEM
2SA1353	OEM
2SA1354	OEM
2SA1355	OEM
2SA1355-O	OEM
2SA1355G	OEM
2SA1355Y	OEM
2SA1356	0520
2SA1357	OEM
2SA1358	0520
2SA1359	OEM
2SA1360	0520
2SA1361	OEM
2SA1362	1741
2SA1363	OEM
2SA1364	3600
2SA1365	1741
2SA1366	1741
2SA1367	OEM
2SA1368	OEM
2SA1369	OEM
2SA1370	OEM
2SA1371	OEM
2SA1371(D)-AE	OEM
2SA1371(E)-AE	OEM
2SA1371-AE	OEM
2SA1371D	OEM
2SA1371E	OEM
2SA1372	OEM
2SA1373	OEM
2SA1374	0013
2SA1375	OEM
2SA1376	OEM
2SA1376A	OEM
2SA1376A-K	OEM
2SA1376A-L	OEM
2SA1376A-L/K	OEM
2SA1377	OEM
2SA1378	0013
2SA1379	OEM
2SA1380	OEM
2SA1381	4402
2SA1382	OEM
2SA1383	OEM
2SA1384	OEM
2SA1385	OEM
2SA1385L	OEM
2SA1386	5383
2SA1386A	OEM
2SA1387	OEM
2SA1388	OEM
2SA1389	3585
2SA1390	0013
2SA1390B	0013
2SA1390C	0013
2SA1390D-TZ	0013
2SA1391	OEM
2SA1392	OEM
2SA1393	OEM
2SA1394	OEM
2SA1395	0676
2SA1396	1359
2SA1397	OEM
2SA1398	OEM
2SA1399	OEM
2SA1400	OEM
2SA1401	OEM
2SA1402	OEM
2SA1403	OEM
2SA1404	OEM
2SA1405	OEM
2SA1406	OEM
2SA1407	OEM
2SA1408	0520
2SA1408(O)	0520
2SA1408(R)	0520
2SA1408-O	0520
2SA1408-O(LB-SAN-2)	0520
2SA1408-O(SAN-1)	0520
2SA1408-OY	OEM
2SA1408-R(LB-SAN-2)	0520
2SA1408-R(SAN-1)	0520
2SA1408R	0520
2SA1408RY	OEM
2SA1408Y(O)	0520
2SA1408Y(R)	0520
2SA1409	OEM
2SA1410	OEM
2SA1411	OEM
2SA1412	OEM
2SA1413	OEM
2SA1414	OEM
2SA1415	5274
2SA1416	OEM
2SA1417	OEM
2SA1418	5274
2SA1420	4067
2SA1421	1026
2SA1422	OEM
2SA1423	4109
2SA1424	OEM
2SA1425	OEM
2SA1426	4043
2SA1426Y	OEM
2SA1427	4043
2SA1428	OEM
2SA1429	OEM
2SA1430	4043
2SA1431	3954

DEVICE TYPE	REPL CODE
2SA1432	OEM
2SA1433	OEM
2SA1441	5388
2SA1441L	5388
2SA1442	0713
2SA1443	OEM
2SA1444	OEM
2SA1450	0472
2SA1450R	0472
2SA1450S	0472
2SA1450T	0472
2SA1451	OEM
2SA1452	OEM
2SA1453	OEM
2SA1458	0013
2SA1459	OEM
2SA1460	OEM
2SA1461	OEM
2SA1462	OEM
2SA1463	OEM
2SA1464	OEM
2SA1465	0472
2SA1466	OEM
2SA1467	OEM
2SA1468	OEM
2SA1469	1298
2SA1469R	1298
2SA1470	OEM
2SA1470S	OEM
2SA1471	OEM
2SA1474	OEM
2SA1475	OEM
2SA1476	OEM
2SA1477	OEM
2SA1478	OEM
2SA1479	OEM
2SA1480	OEM
2SA1481	0013
2SA1482	1514
2SA1483	OEM
2SA1484	OEM
2SA1485	OEM
2SA1488	0676
2SA1489	0853
2SA1490	3082
2SA1491	3082
2SA1492	5397
2SA1493	3537
2SA1494	3601
2SA1495	OEM
2SA1498	OEM
2SA1499	OEM
2SA1500	OEM
2SA1501	OEM
2SA1503	OEM
2SA1504	1731
2SA1505	OEM
2SA1506	OEM
2SA1507-R-RA	5767
2SA1507-S-CTV-YA	0520
2SA1507-S-RA	OEM
2SA1507-T-CTV-YA	0520
2SA1507S	5767
2SA1507S-CTV-YA	2098
2SA1507T-CTV-YA	2098
2SA1515	0037
2SA1516	OEM
2SA1517	OEM
2SA1524	OEM
2SA1532	OEM
2SA1532BC	OEM
2SA1546L	OEM
2SA1546M	OEM
2SA1547QSTV2	OEM
2SA1561	2464
2SA1561Q	OEM
2SA1561R	OEM
2SA1567	OEM
2SA1606	0713
2SA1606A	0713
2SA1606D	0713
2SA1606E	0713
2SA1624	0338
2SA1624(D)-AA	0338
2SA1624(E)-AA	0338
2SA1624D	0338
2SA1624E	0338
2SA1706	OEM
2SA1706-AN	OEM
2SA1706F	OEM
2SA1738QR	OEM
2SA2109	OEM
2SA2408	OEM
2SA3410A	0050
2SA3410B	0050
2SA-4551	0050
2SA-4561	0050
2SA4728B	0050
2SA4930	0786
2SA4940	0786
2SA4940LBGL2	0786
2SA4950	0006
2SA4950R	0006
2SA4964	0455
2SA5610	0037
2SA5620	0786
2SA5670	0786
2SA5670R	0786
2SA5680	0786

If replacement code is OEM, contact original manufacturer for replacement.

DEVICE TYPE	REPL CODE
2SA5680R	0786
2SA5690	0786
2SA5690R	0786
2SA6111	0150
2SA6361	1257
2SA6361,K	1257
2SA6361K	1257
2SA24082	0050
2SA492057B2-60	0211
2SA4712057B2-65	0050
2SA4712057B2-66	0050
2SAD7160	OEM
2SAJ15GN	0050
2SA-NJ-101	0037
2SANJ101	0037
2SAU/3H	0050
2SAU03	0050
2SAU03H	0050
2SAUUJ	0841
2SB12	0150
2SB13	0004
2SB14	0050
2SB15	0164
2SB15D	0164
2SB15E	0164
2SB16	0435
2SB16A	0435
2SB16B	0435
2SB16C	0435
2SB16D	0435
2SB16E	0435
2SB16F	0435
2SB16G	0435
2SB16GN	0435
2SB16H	0435
2SB16J	0435
2SB16K	0435
2SB16L	0435
2SB16M	0435
2SB16OR	0435
2SB16R	0435
2SB16X	0435
2SB16Y	0435
2SB17	0435
2SB17A	0435
2SB17B	0435
2SB17C	0435
2SB17D	0435
2SB17E	0435
2SB17F	0435
2SB17G	0435
2SB17GN	0435
2SB17H	0435
2SB17J	0435
2SB17K	0435
2SB17L	0435
2SB17M	0435
2SB17OR	0435
2SB17R	0435
2SB17X	0435
2SB17Y	0435
2SB18	0435
2SB18A	0435
2SB18B	0435
2SB18C	0435
2SB18D	0435
2SB18E	0435
2SB18F	0435
2SB18G	0435
2SB18GN	0435
2SB18H	0435
2SB18J	0435
2SB18K	0435
2SB18L	0435
2SB18LA	0435
2SB18M	0435
2SB18OR	0435
2SB18R	0435
2SB18X	0435
2SB18Y	0435
2SB19	0969
2SB19A	0969
2SB19B	0969
2SB19C	0969
2SB19D	0969
2SB19E	0969
2SB19F	0969
2SB19G	0969
2SB19GN	0969
2SB19H	0969
2SB19J	0969
2SB19K	0969
2SB19L	0969
2SB19M	0969
2SB19OR	0969
2SB19R	0969
2SB19X	0969
2SB19Y	0969
2SB20	0969
2SB20A	0969
2SB20B	0969
2SB20C	0969
2SB20D	0969
2SB20E	0969
2SB20F	0969
2SB20G	0969
2SB20GN	0969
2SB20H	0969
2SB20J	0969
2SB20K	0969
2SB20L	0969
2SB20M	0969
2SB20OR	0969
2SB20R	0969
2SB20X	0969
2SB20Y	0969
2SB21	0969
2SB21A	0969
2SB21B	0969
2SB21C	0969
2SB21D	0969
2SB21E	0969
2SB21F	0969
2SB21G	0969
2SB21GN	0969
2SB21H	0969
2SB21J	0969
2SB21K	0969
2SB21L	0969
2SB21M	0969
2SB21OR	0969
2SB21R	0969
2SB21X	0969
2SB21Y	0969
2SB22	0164
2SB22/09-30100	0164
2SB22A	0164
2SB22B	0164
2SB22C	0164
2SB22D	0164
2SB22E	0164
2SB22F	0164
2SB22G	0164
2SB22GN	0164
2SB22H	0164
2SB22I	0164
2SB22J	0164
2SB22K	0164
2SB22L	0164
2SB22M	0164
2SB22OR	0164
2SB22P	0164
2SB22R	0164
2SB22X	0164
2SB22Y	0164
2SB23	0004
2SB23A	0004
2SB23B	0004
2SB23C	0004
2SB23D	0004
2SB23E	0004
2SB23F	0004
2SB23G	0004
2SB23GN	0004
2SB23H	0004
2SB23J	0004
2SB23K	0004
2SB23L	0004
2SB23M	0004
2SB23OR	0004
2SB23R	0004
2SB23X	0004
2SB23Y	0004
2SB24	0164
2SB24A	0164
2SB24B	0164
2SB24C	0164
2SB24D	0164
2SB24E	0164
2SB24F	0164
2SB24G	0164
2SB24GN	0164
2SB24H	0164
2SB24J	0164
2SB24K	0164
2SB24L	0164
2SB24M	0164
2SB24OR	0164
2SB24R	0164
2SB24X	0164
2SB24Y	0164
2SB25	0160
2SB25-N	0160
2SB25A	0160
2SB25B	0160
2SB25C	0160
2SB25D	0160
2SB25E	0160
2SB25F	0160
2SB25G	0160
2SB25GN	0160
2SB25H	0160
2SB25J	0160
2SB25K	0160
2SB25L	0160
2SB25M	0160
2SB25N	0160
2SB25OR	0160
2SB25R	0160
2SB25X	0160
2SB25Y	0160
2SB26	0085
2SB26A	0085
2SB26B	0085
2SB26C	0085
2SB26D	0085
2SB26E	0085
2SB26F	0085
2SB26G	0085
2SB26GN	0085
2SB26H	0085
2SB26J	0085
2SB26K	0085
2SB26L	0085
2SB26M	0085
2SB26OR	0085
2SB26R	0085
2SB26X	0085
2SB26Y	0085
2SB27	0085
2SB27A	0085
2SB27B	0085
2SB27C	0085
2SB27D	0085
2SB27E	0085
2SB27F	0085
2SB27G	0085
2SB27GN	0085
2SB27H	0085
2SB27J	0085
2SB27K	0085
2SB27L	0085
2SB27M	0085
2SB27OR	0085
2SB27R	0085
2SB27X	0085
2SB27Y	0085
2SB28	0085
2SB28A	0085
2SB28B	0085
2SB28C	0085
2SB28D	0085
2SB28E	0085
2SB28F	0085
2SB28G	0085
2SB28GN	0085
2SB28H	0085
2SB28J	0085
2SB28K	0085
2SB28L	0085
2SB28M	0085
2SB28OR	0085
2SB28R	0085
2SB28X	0085
2SB28Y	0085
2SB29	0085
2SB29A	0085
2SB29B	0085
2SB29C	0085
2SB29D	0085
2SB29E	0085
2SB29F	0085
2SB29G	0085
2SB29GN	0085
2SB29H	0085
2SB29J	0085
2SB29K	0085
2SB29L	0085
2SB29M	0085
2SB29OR	0085
2SB29R	0085
2SB29X	0085
2SB29Y	0085
2SB30	0085
2SB30A	0085
2SB30B	0085
2SB30C	0085
2SB30D	0085
2SB30E	0085
2SB30F	0085
2SB30G	0085
2SB30GN	0085
2SB30H	0085
2SB30J	0085
2SB30K	0085
2SB30L	0085
2SB30M	0085
2SB30OR	0085
2SB30R	0085
2SB30X	0085
2SB30Y	0085
2SB31	0085
2SB31A	0085
2SB31B	0085
2SB31C	0085
2SB31D	0085
2SB31E	0085
2SB31F	0085
2SB31G	0085
2SB31GN	0085
2SB31H	0085
2SB31J	0085
2SB31K	0085
2SB31L	0085
2SB31M	0085
2SB31OR	0085
2SB31R	0085
2SB31X	0085
2SB31Y	0085
2SB32	0004
2SB32(3)	0004
2SB32(N)	0004
2SB32-0	0004
2SB32-1	0004
2SB32-2	0004
2SB32-4	0004
2SB32A	0004
2SB32B	0004
2SB32C	0004
2SB32D	0004
2SB32E	0004
2SB32F	0004
2SB32G	0004
2SB32GN	0004
2SB32H	0004
2SB32J	0004
2SB32K	0004
2SB32M	0004
2SB32OR	0004
2SB32R	0004
2SB32X	0004
2SB32Y	0004
2SB33	0004
2SB33(3)	0004
2SB33(4)	0004
2SB33(5)	0004
2SB33-4	0004
2SB33-5	0004
2SB33A	0004
2SB33B	0004
2SB33BK	0004
2SB33C	0004
2SB33D	0004
2SB33E	0004
2SB33F	0004
2SB33G	0004
2SB33GN	0004
2SB33H	0004
2SB33J	0004
2SB33K	0004
2SB33L	0004
2SB33M	0004
2SB33OR	0004
2SB33R	0004
2SB33X	0004
2SB33Y	0004
2SB34	0211
2SB34A	0211
2SB34B	0211
2SB34C	0211
2SB34D	0211
2SB34E	0211
2SB34F	0211
2SB34G	0211
2SB34GN	0211
2SB34H	0211
2SB34J	0211
2SB34K	0211
2SB34L	0211
2SB34M	0211
2SB34N	0211
2SB34OR	0211
2SB34R	0211
2SB34X	0211
2SB34Y	0211
2SB35	0164
2SB35A	0164
2SB35B	0164
2SB35C	0164
2SB35D	0164
2SB35E	0164
2SB35F	0164
2SB35G	0164
2SB35GN	0164
2SB35H	0164
2SB35J	0164
2SB35K	0164
2SB35L	0164
2SB35M	0164
2SB35OR	0164
2SB35R	0164
2SB35X	0164
2SB35Y	0164
2SB37	0004
2SB37A	0004
2SB37B	0004
2SB37C	0004
2SB37D	0004
2SB37E	0004
2SB37F	0004
2SB37G	0004
2SB37GN	0004
2SB37H	0004
2SB37J	0004
2SB37K	0004
2SB37L	0004
2SB37M	0004
2SB37OR	0004
2SB37R	0004
2SB37X	0004
2SB37Y	0004
2SB38	0211
2SB38A	0211
2SB38B	0211
2SB38C	0211
2SB38D	0211
2SB38E	0211
2SB38F	0211
2SB38G	0211
2SB38GN	0211
2SB38H	0211
2SB38J	0211
2SB38K	0211
2SB38L	0211
2SB38M	0211
2SB38OR	0211
2SB38R	0211
2SB38X	0211
2SB38Y	0211
2SB39	0004
2SB39A	0004
2SB39B	0004
2SB39C	0004
2SB39D	0004
2SB39E	0004
2SB39F	0004
2SB39G	0004
2SB39GN	0004
2SB39H	0004
2SB39J	0004
2SB39K	0004
2SB39L	0004
2SB39M	0004
2SB39OR	0004
2SB39R	0004
2SB39X	0004
2SB39Y	0004
2SB40	0004
2SB40A	0004
2SB40B	0004
2SB40C	0004
2SB40D	0004
2SB40E	0004
2SB40F	0004
2SB40G	0004
2SB40GN	0004
2SB40H	0004
2SB40J	0004
2SB40K	0004
2SB40L	0004
2SB40M	0004
2SB40OR	0004
2SB40R	0004
2SB40X	0004
2SB40Y	0004
2SB41	0085
2SB41A	0085
2SB41B	0085
2SB41C	0085
2SB41D	0085
2SB41E	0085
2SB41F	0085
2SB41G	0085
2SB41GN	0085
2SB41H	0085
2SB41J	0085
2SB41K	0085
2SB41L	0085
2SB41M	0085
2SB41OR	0085
2SB41R	0085
2SB41X	0085
2SB41Y	0085
2SB42	0085
2SB42A	0085
2SB42B	0085
2SB42C	0085
2SB42D	0085
2SB42E	0085
2SB42F	0085
2SB42G	0085
2SB42GN	0085
2SB42H	0085
2SB42J	0085
2SB42K	0085
2SB42L	0085
2SB42M	0085
2SB42OR	0085
2SB42R	0085
2SB42X	0085
2SB42Y	0085
2SB43	0004
2SB43A	0004
2SB43B	0004
2SB43C	0004
2SB43D	0004
2SB43E	0004
2SB43F	0004
2SB43G	0004
2SB43GN	0004
2SB43H	0004
2SB43J	0004
2SB43K	0004
2SB43L	0004
2SB43M	0004
2SB43OR	0004
2SB43R	0004
2SB43X	0004
2SB43Y	0004
2SB44	0004
2SB44A	0004
2SB44B	0004
2SB44C	0004
2SB44D	0004
2SB44E	0004
2SB44F	0004
2SB44G	0004
2SB44GN	0004
2SB44H	0004
2SB44J	0004
2SB44K	0004
2SB44L	0004
2SB44M	0004
2SB44OR	0004
2SB44R	0004
2SB44X	0004
2SB44Y	0004
2SB46	0004
2SB46A	0004
2SB46B	0004
2SB46C	0004
2SB46D	0004
2SB46E	0004
2SB46F	0004
2SB46G	0004
2SB46GN	0004
2SB46H	0004
2SB46J	0004
2SB46K	0004
2SB46L	0004
2SB46M	0004
2SB46OR	0004
2SB46R	0004
2SB46X	0004
2SB46Y	0004
2SB47	0004
2SB47A	0004
2SB47B	0004
2SB47C	0004
2SB47D	0004
2SB47E	0004
2SB47F	0004
2SB47G	0004
2SB47GN	0004
2SB47H	0004
2SB47J	0004
2SB47K	0004
2SB47L	0004
2SB47M	0004
2SB47OR	0004
2SB47R	0004
2SB47X	0004
2SB47Y	0004
2SB48	0211
2SB48A	0211
2SB48B	0211
2SB48C	0211
2SB48D	0211
2SB48E	0211
2SB48F	0211
2SB48G	0211
2SB48GN	0211
2SB48H	0211
2SB48J	0211
2SB48K	0211
2SB48L	0211
2SB48M	0211
2SB48OR	0211
2SB48R	0211
2SB48X	0211
2SB48Y	0211
2SB49	0211
2SB49A	0211
2SB49B	0211
2SB49C	0211
2SB49D	0211
2SB49E	0211
2SB49F	0211
2SB49G	0211
2SB49GN	0211
2SB49H	0211
2SB49J	0211
2SB49K	0211
2SB49L	0211
2SB49M	0211
2SB49OR	0211
2SB49R	0211
2SB49X	0211
2SB49Y	0211
2SB50	0211
2SB50(RECT)	0319
2SB50A	0211
2SB50B	0211
2SB50C	0211
2SB50D	0211
2SB50E	0211
2SB50F	0211
2SB50G	0211
2SB50GN	0211
2SB50H	0211
2SB50J	0211
2SB50K	0211
2SB50L	0211
2SB50M	0211
2SB50OR	0211
2SB50R	0211
2SB50X	0211
2SB50Y	0211
2SB51	0211
2SB51A	0211
2SB51B	0211
2SB51C	0211
2SB51D	0211
2SB51E	0211
2SB51F	0211
2SB51G	0211
2SB51GN	0211
2SB51H	0211
2SB51J	0211
2SB51K	0211
2SB51L	0211
2SB51M	0211
2SB51OR	0211
2SB51R	0211
2SB51X	0211
2SB51Y	0211
2SB52	0211
2SB52A	0211
2SB52B	0211
2SB52C	0211
2SB52D	0211
2SB52E	0211
2SB52F	0211
2SB52G	0211
2SB52GN	0211
2SB52H	0211
2SB52J	0211
2SB52K	0211
2SB52L	0211
2SB52M	0211
2SB52OR	0211
2SB52R	0211
2SB52X	0211
2SB52Y	0211
2SB53	0211
2SB53A	0211
2SB53B	0211
2SB53C	0211
2SB53D	0211
2SB53E	0211
2SB53F	0211
2SB53G	0211
2SB53GN	0211
2SB53H	0211
2SB53J	0211
2SB53K	0211
2SB53L	0211
2SB53M	0211
2SB53OR	0211
2SB53R	0211
2SB53X	0211
2SB53Y	0211
2SB54	0004
2SB54A	0004
2SB54B	0004
2SB54BA	0004
2SB54C	0004
2SB54D	0004
2SB54E	0004
2SB54F	0004
2SB54G	0004
2SB54GN	0004
2SB54H	0004
2SB54J	0004
2SB54K	0004
2SB54L	0004
2SB54L1	0004
2SB54M	0004
2SB54OR	0004
2SB54R	0004
2SB54X	0004
2SB54Y	0004
2SB55	0004
2SB55A	0004
2SB55B	0004
2SB55C	0004
2SB55D	0004
2SB55E	0004
2SB55F	0004
2SB55G	0004
2SB55GN	0004
2SB55H	0004
2SB55J	0004
2SB55K	0004
2SB55L	0004
2SB55M	0004
2SB55OR	0004
2SB55R	0004
2SB55X	0004
2SB55Y	0004
2SB56	0004
2SB56(C)	0004
2SB56(F1)	OEM
2SB56/8020	0004
2SB56/117728	0004
2SB56/80205600	0004
2SB56A	0004
2SB56B	0004
2SB56C	0004
2SB56CK	0004
2SB56D	0004
2SB56E	0004
2SB56F	0004
2SB56G	0004
2SB56GN	0004
2SB56H	0004
2SB56J	0004
2SB56K	0004
2SB56L	0004
2SB56OR	0004
2SB56R	0004
2SB56X	0004
2SB56Y	0004
2SB57	0004
2SB57A	0004
2SB57B	0004
2SB57C	0004
2SB57D	0004
2SB57E	0004
2SB57F	0004
2SB57G	0004
2SB57GN	0004
2SB57H	0004

64

If replacement code is OEM, contact original manufacturer for replacement.

DEVICE TYPE	REPL CODE
2SB57J	0004
2SB57K	0004
2SB57L	0004
2SB57M	0004
2SB57OR	0004
2SB57R	0004
2SB57X	0004
2SB57Y	0004
2SB58	0164
2SB59	0004
2SB59A	0004
2SB59B	0004
2SB59C	0004
2SB59D	0004
2SB59E	0004
2SB59F	0004
2SB59G	0004
2SB59GN	0004
2SB59J	0004
2SB59K	0004
2SB59L	0004
2SB59M	0004
2SB59OR	0004
2SB59R	0004
2SB59X	0004
2SB59Y	0004
2SB60	0004
2SB60A	0004
2SB60B	0004
2SB60C	0004
2SB60D	0004
2SB60E	0004
2SB60F	0004
2SB60G	0004
2SB60GN	0004
2SB60H	0004
2SB60J	0004
2SB60K	0004
2SB60L	0004
2SB60M	0004
2SB60OR	0004
2SB60R	0004
2SB60X	0004
2SB60Y	0004
2SB61	0004
2SB61A	0004
2SB61B	0004
2SB61C	0004
2SB61D	0004
2SB61E	0004
2SB61F	0004
2SB61G	0004
2SB61GN	0004
2SB61H	0004
2SB61J	0004
2SB61K	0004
2SB61L	0004
2SB61M	0004
2SB61OR	0004
2SB61R	0004
2SB61X	0004
2SB61Y	0004
2SB62	1004
2SB62A	1004
2SB62B	1004
2SB62C	1004
2SB62D	1004
2SB62E	1004
2SB62F	1004
2SB62G	1004
2SB62GN	1004
2SB62H	1004
2SB62J	1004
2SB62K	1004
2SB62L	1004
2SB62M	1004
2SB62OR	1004
2SB62R	1004
2SB62X	1004
2SB62Y	1004
2SB63	0222
2SB63A	0222
2SB63B	0222
2SB63C	0222
2SB63D	0222
2SB63E	0222
2SB63F	0222
2SB63G	0222
2SB63GN	0222
2SB63H	0222
2SB63K	0222
2SB63L	0222
2SB63M	0222
2SB63OR	0222
2SB63R	0222
2SB63X	0222
2SB63Y	0222
2SB64	0969
2SB64A	0969
2SB64B	0969
2SB64C	0969
2SB64D	0969
2SB64E	0969
2SB64F	0969
2SB64G	0969
2SB64H	0969
2SB64J	0969
2SB64K	0969
2SB64L	0969

DEVICE TYPE	REPL CODE
2SB64M	0969
2SB64OR	0969
2SB64R	0969
2SB64X	0969
2SB64Y	0969
2SB65	0004
2SB65A	0004
2SB65B	0004
2SB65C	0004
2SB65D	0004
2SB65F	0004
2SB65G	0004
2SB65GN	0004
2SB65H	0004
2SB65J	0004
2SB65K	0004
2SB65L	0004
2SB65M	0004
2SB65OR	0004
2SB65R	0004
2SB65X	0004
2SB65Y	0004
2SB66	0004
2SB66A	0004
2SB66B	0004
2SB66C	0004
2SB66D	0004
2SB66E	0004
2SB66F	0004
2SB66G	0004
2SB66GN	0004
2SB66H	0004
2SB66J	0004
2SB66K	0004
2SB66L	0004
2SB66M	0004
2SB66OR	0004
2SB66R	0004
2SB66X	0004
2SB66Y	0004
2SB67	0004
2SB67A	0004
2SB67AH	0004
2SB67B	0004
2SB67C	0004
2SB67D	0004
2SB67E	0004
2SB67F	0004
2SB67G	0004
2SB67GN	0004
2SB67H	0004
2SB67J	0004
2SB67K	0004
2SB67L	0004
2SB67M	0004
2SB67OR	0004
2SB67R	0004
2SB67X	0004
2SB67Y	0004
2SB68	0004
2SB68A	0004
2SB68B	0004
2SB68C	0004
2SB68D	0004
2SB68E	0004
2SB68F	0004
2SB68G	0004
2SB68GN	0004
2SB68H	0004
2SB68J	0004
2SB68K	0004
2SB68L	0004
2SB68M	0004
2SB68OR	0004
2SB68R	0004
2SB68X	0004
2SB68Y	0004
2SB69	0160
2SB69A	0160
2SB69B	0160
2SB69C	0160
2SB69D	0160
2SB69E	0160
2SB69F	0160
2SB69G	0160
2SB69GN	0160
2SB69H	0160
2SB69J	0160
2SB69K	0160
2SB69L	0160
2SB69M	0160
2SB69OR	0160
2SB69R	0160
2SB69X	0160
2SB69Y	0160
2SB70	0164
2SB71	0004
2SB71A	0004
2SB71B	0004
2SB71C	0004
2SB71D	0004
2SB71E	0004
2SB71F	0004
2SB71G	0004
2SB71GN	0004
2SB71H	0004
2SB71J	0004
2SB71K	0004
2SB71L	0004

DEVICE TYPE	REPL CODE
2SB71M	0004
2SB71OR	0004
2SB71R	0004
2SB71X	0004
2SB71Y	0004
2SB72	0211
2SB72A	0211
2SB72B	0211
2SB72C	0211
2SB72D	0211
2SB72E	0211
2SB72F	0211
2SB72G	0211
2SB72GN	0211
2SB72H	0211
2SB72J	0211
2SB72K	0211
2SB72L	0211
2SB72M	0211
2SB72OR	0211
2SB72R	0211
2SB72X	0211
2SB72Y	0211
2SB73	0004
2SB73/123	0004
2SB73/123806	0004
2SB73A	0004
2SB73A-1	0004
2SB73B	0004
2SB73B/0573018	0004
2SB73C	0004
2SB73D	0004
2SB73E	0004
2SB73F	0004
2SB73G	0004
2SB73GN	0004
2SB73GR	0004
2SB73H	0004
2SB73J	0004
2SB73K	0004
2SB73L	0004
2SB73M	0004
2SB73OR	0004
2SB73R	0004
2SB73S	0004
2SB73X	0004
2SB73Y	0004
2SB74	0164
2SB74A	0164
2SB74B	0164
2SB74C	0164
2SB74D	0164
2SB74E	0164
2SB74F	0164
2SB74G	0164
2SB74GN	0164
2SB74H	0164
2SB74J	0164
2SB74K	0164
2SB74L	0164
2SB74M	0164
2SB74OR	0164
2SB74R	0164
2SB74X	0164
2SB74Y	0164
2SB75	0004
2SB75(C)	0004
2SB75A	0004
2SB75AH	0004
2SB75B	0004
2SB75C	0004
2SB75C/0573153	0004
2SB75C1	0004
2SB75C-4	0004
2SB75D	0004
2SB75E	0004
2SB75F	0004
2SB75F/0573125	0004
2SB75G	0004
2SB75GN	0004
2SB75H	0004
2SB75J	0004
2SB75L	0004
2SB75LB	0004
2SB75M	0004
2SB75OR	0004
2SB75R	0004
2SB75X	0004
2SB75Y	0004
2SB76	0004
2SB76A	0004
2SB76B	0004
2SB76C	0004
2SB76D	0004
2SB76E	0004
2SB76F	0004
2SB76G	0004
2SB76GN	0004
2SB76H	0004
2SB76J	0004
2SB76K	0004
2SB76L	0004
2SB76M	0004
2SB76OR	0004
2SB76R	0004
2SB76X	0004
2SB76Y	0004
2SB77	0004
2SB77(B)	0004

DEVICE TYPE	REPL CODE
2SB77(C)	0004
2SB77(C)SHARP	0004
2SB77(D)	0004
2SB77(V)	0004
2SB77/1222	0004
2SB77/122244	0004
2SB77-A	0004
2SB77-C	0004
2SB77-OR	0004
2SB77A	0004
2SB77A/P	0004
2SB77AA	0004
2SB77AB	0004
2SB77AC	0004
2SB77AD	0004
2SB77AH	0004
2SB77AP	0004
2SB77B	0004
2SB77B/0573114	0004
2SB77B2	0004
2SB77B-11	0004
2SB77B57B2-24	0004
2SB77C	0004
2SB77D	0004
2SB77E	0004
2SB77F	0004
2SB77G	0004
2SB77GN	0004
2SB77H	0004
2SB77K	0004
2SB77L	0004
2SB77M	0004
2SB77OR	0004
2SB77P	0004
2SB77PD	0004
2SB77R	0004
2SB77RED	0004
2SB77V	0004
2SB77VRED	0004
2SB77X	0004
2SB77Y	0004
2SB78	0004
2SB78A	0004
2SB78B	0004
2SB78C	0004
2SB78D	0004
2SB78E	0004
2SB78F	0004
2SB78G	0004
2SB78GN	0004
2SB78H	0004
2SB78J	0004
2SB78K	0004
2SB78L	0004
2SB78M	0004
2SB78OR	0004
2SB78R	0004
2SB78X	0004
2SB78Y	0004
2SB79	0004
2SB79A	0004
2SB79B	0004
2SB79C	0004
2SB79D	0004
2SB79E	0004
2SB79F	0004
2SB79G	0004
2SB79GN	0004
2SB79H	0004
2SB79J	0004
2SB79K	0004
2SB79L	0004
2SB79M	0004
2SB79OR	0004
2SB79R	0004
2SB79X	0004
2SB79Y	0004
2SB80	0222
2SB80A	0222
2SB80B	0222
2SB80C	0222
2SB80D	0222
2SB80E	0222
2SB80F	0222
2SB80G	0222
2SB80GN	0222
2SB80H	0222
2SB80J	0222
2SB80K	0222
2SB80L	0222
2SB80M	0222
2SB80OR	0222
2SB80R	0222
2SB80X	0222
2SB80Y	0222
2SB81	0969
2SB81A	0969
2SB81B	0969
2SB81C	0969
2SB81D	0969
2SB81E	0969
2SB81F	0969
2SB81GN	0969
2SB81H	0969
2SB81J	0969
2SB81K	0969
2SB81L	0969
2SB81M	0969
2SB81OR	0969

DEVICE TYPE	REPL CODE
2SB81R	0969
2SB81X	0969
2SB81Y	0969
2SB82	0969
2SB82A	0969
2SB82B	0969
2SB82C	0969
2SB82D	0969
2SB82E	0969
2SB82F	0969
2SB82G	0969
2SB82GN	0969
2SB82H	0969
2SB82J	0969
2SB82K	0969
2SB82L	0969
2SB82M	0969
2SB82OR	0969
2SB82R	0969
2SB82X	0969
2SB82Y	0969
2SB83	0969
2SB83A	0969
2SB83B	0969
2SB83C	0969
2SB83D	0969
2SB83E	0969
2SB83F	0969
2SB83G	0969
2SB83GN	0969
2SB83H	0969
2SB83J	0969
2SB83K	0969
2SB83L	0969
2SB83M	0969
2SB83OR	0969
2SB83R	0969
2SB83X	0969
2SB83Y	0969
2SB84	0085
2SB84A	0085
2SB84B	0085
2SB84C	0085
2SB84D	0085
2SB84E	0085
2SB84F	0085
2SB84G	0085
2SB84GN	0085
2SB84H	0085
2SB84J	0085
2SB84K	0085
2SB84L	0085
2SB84M	0085
2SB84OR	0085
2SB84R	0085
2SB84X	0085
2SB84Y	0085
2SB85	0164
2SB85A	0164
2SB85B	0164
2SB85C	0164
2SB85D	0164
2SB85E	0164
2SB85F	0164
2SB85G	0164
2SB85GN	0164
2SB85H	0164
2SB85J	0164
2SB85K	0164
2SB85L	0164
2SB85M	0164
2SB85OR	0164
2SB85R	0164
2SB85X	0164
2SB85Y	0164
2SB86	0160
2SB87	0164
2SB87A	0164
2SB87B	0164
2SB87C	0164
2SB87D	0164
2SB87E	0164
2SB87F	0164
2SB87G	0164
2SB87GN	0164
2SB87H	0164
2SB87J	0164
2SB87K	0164
2SB87L	0164
2SB87M	0164
2SB87OR	0164
2SB87R	0164
2SB87X	0164
2SB87Y	0164
2SB88	0969
2SB89	0004
2SB89A	0004
2SB89AH	0004
2SB89C	0004
2SB89D	0004
2SB89E	0004
2SB89F	0004
2SB89G	0004
2SB89GN	0004
2SB89H	0004
2SB89J	0004
2SB89K	0004
2SB89L	0004
2SB89M	0004

DEVICE TYPE	REPL CODE
2SB89OR	0004
2SB89R	0004
2SB89X	0004
2SB89Y	0004
2SB90	0004
2SB90A	0004
2SB90B	0004
2SB90C	0004
2SB90D	0004
2SB90E	0004
2SB90F	0004
2SB90G	0004
2SB90GN	0004
2SB90H	0004
2SB90J	0004
2SB90K	0004
2SB90L	0004
2SB90M	0004
2SB90OR	0004
2SB90R	0004
2SB90X	0004
2SB90Y	0004
2SB91	0004
2SB91A	0004
2SB91B	0004
2SB91C	0004
2SB91D	0004
2SB91E	0004
2SB91F	0004
2SB91G	0004
2SB91GN	0004
2SB91H	0004
2SB91J	0004
2SB91K	0004
2SB91L	0004
2SB91M	0004
2SB91OR	0004
2SB91R	0004
2SB91X	0004
2SB91Y	0004
2SB92	0004
2SB92A	0004
2SB92B	0004
2SB92C	0004
2SB92D	0004
2SB92E	0004
2SB92F	0004
2SB92G	0004
2SB92GN	0004
2SB92H	0004
2SB92J	0004
2SB92K	0004
2SB92L	0004
2SB92M	0004
2SB92X	0004
2SB92Y	0004
2SB93	0004
2SB94	0004
2SB94A	0004
2SB94B	0004
2SB94C	0004
2SB94D	0004
2SB94E	0004
2SB94F	0004
2SB94G	0004
2SB94GN	0004
2SB94H	0004
2SB94J	0004
2SB94K	0004
2SB94M	0004
2SB94OR	0004
2SB94R	0004
2SB94X	0004
2SB94Y	0004
2SB95	0004
2SB95A	0004
2SB95B	0004
2SB95C	0004
2SB95D	0004
2SB95E	0004
2SB95F	0004
2SB95G	0004
2SB95GN	0004
2SB95H	0004
2SB95J	0004
2SB95L	0004
2SB95M	0004
2SB95OR	0004
2SB95R	0004
2SB95X	0004
2SB95Y	0004
2SB96	0211
2SB97	0004
2SB97A	0004
2SB97B	0004
2SB97C	0004
2SB97D	0004
2SB97F	0004
2SB97G	0004
2SB97GN	0004
2SB97H	0004
2SB97K	0004
2SB97L	0004
2SB97M	0004
2SB97OR	0004
2SB97R	0004
2SB97X	0004
2SB97Y	0004
2SB98	0211

DEVICE TYPE	REPL CODE
2SB98A	0211
2SB98B	0211
2SB98C	0211
2SB98D	0211
2SB98E	0211
2SB98F	0211
2SB98G	0211
2SB98GN	0211
2SB98H	0211
2SB98J	0211
2SB98K	0211
2SB98L	0211
2SB98M	0211
2SB98OR	0211
2SB98R	0211
2SB98X	0211
2SB98Y	0211
2SB99	0164
2SB99A	0164
2SB99B	0164
2SB99C	0164
2SB99D	0164
2SB99E	0164
2SB99F	0164
2SB99G	0164
2SB99GN	0164
2SB99H	0164
2SB99J	0164
2SB99K	0164
2SB99L	0164
2SB99M	0164
2SB99OR	0164
2SB99R	0164
2SB99X	0164
2SB99Y	0164
2SB100	0211
2SB100(RECT)	0319
2SB100A	0211
2SB100B	0211
2SB100C	0211
2SB100D	0211
2SB100E	0211
2SB100F	0211
2SB100G	0211
2SB100GN	0211
2SB100H	0211
2SB100J	0211
2SB100K	0211
2SB100L	0211
2SB100M	0211
2SB100OR	0211
2SB100R	0211
2SB100X	0211
2SB100Y	0211
2SB101	0211
2SB101A	0211
2SB101B	0211
2SB101C	0211
2SB101D	0211
2SB101E	0211
2SB101F	0211
2SB101G	0211
2SB101GN	0211
2SB101H	0211
2SB101J	0211
2SB101K	0211
2SB101L	0211
2SB101M	0211
2SB101OR	0211
2SB101R	0211
2SB101X	0211
2SB101Y	0211
2SB102	0211
2SB102A	0211
2SB102B	0211
2SB102C	0211
2SB102D	0211
2SB102E	0211
2SB102F	0211
2SB102G	0211
2SB102GN	0211
2SB102H	0211
2SB102J	0211
2SB102K	0211
2SB102L	0211
2SB102M	0211
2SB102OR	0211
2SB102R	0211
2SB102X	0211
2SB102Y	0211
2SB103	0211
2SB103A	0211
2SB103B	0211
2SB103C	0211
2SB103D	0211
2SB103E	0211
2SB103F	0211
2SB103G	0211
2SB103GN	0211
2SB103H	0211
2SB103J	0211
2SB103K	0211
2SB103L	0211
2SB103M	0211
2SB103OR	0211
2SB103R	0211
2SB103X	0211
2SB103Y	0211
2SB104	0164

If replacement code is OEM, contact original manufacturer for replacement.

65

DEVICE TYPE	REPL CODE
2SB104A	0164
2SB104B	0164
2SB104C	0164
2SB104D	0164
2SB104E	0164
2SB104F	0164
2SB104G	0164
2SB104GN	0164
2SB104H	0164
2SB104J	0164
2SB104K	0164
2SB104L	0164
2SB104M	0164
2SB104OR	0164
2SB104R	0164
2SB104X	0164
2SB104Y	0164
2SB105	0164
2SB105A	0164
2SB105B	0164
2SB105C	0164
2SB105D	0164
2SB105E	0164
2SB105F	0164
2SB105G	0164
2SB105GN	0164
2SB105H	0164
2SB105K	0164
2SB105L	0164
2SB105M	0164
2SB105OR	0164
2SB105R	0164
2SB105X	0164
2SB105Y	0164
2SB106	0164
2SB107	0160
2SB107A	0160
2SB107B	0160
2SB107C	0160
2SB107D	0160
2SB107E	0160
2SB107F	0160
2SB107G	0160
2SB107GN	0160
2SB107H	0160
2SB107J	0160
2SB107K	0160
2SB107L	0160
2SB107M	0160
2SB107OR	0160
2SB107R	0160
2SB107X	0160
2SB107Y	0160
2SB108	0164
2SB108A	0164
2SB108B	0164
2SB108C	0164
2SB108D	0164
2SB108E	0164
2SB108F	0164
2SB108G	0164
2SB108GN	0164
2SB108H	0164
2SB108J	0164
2SB108K	0164
2SB108L	0164
2SB108M	0164
2SB108OR	0164
2SB108X	0164
2SB108Y	0164
2SB109	0164
2SB109A	0164
2SB109B	0164
2SB110	0004
2SB110A	0004
2SB110B	0004
2SB110C	0004
2SB110D	0004
2SB110E	0004
2SB110F	0004
2SB110G	0004
2SB110GN	0004
2SB110H	0004
2SB110J	0004
2SB110K	0004
2SB110L	0004
2SB110M	0004
2SB110OR	0004
2SB110R	0004
2SB110X	0004
2SB110Y	0004
2SB111	0004
2SB111A	0004
2SB111B	0004
2SB111C	0004
2SB111D	0004
2SB111E	0004
2SB111F	0004
2SB111G	0004
2SB111GN	0004
2SB111H	0004
2SB111J	0004
2SB111K	0004
2SB111L	0004
2SB111M	0004
2SB111OR	0004
2SB111R	0004
2SB111X	0004
2SB111Y	0004
2SB112	0004
2SB112A	0004
2SB112B	0004
2SB112C	0004
2SB112D	0004
2SB112E	0004
2SB112F	0004
2SB112G	0004
2SB112H	0004
2SB112J	0004
2SB112K	0004
2SB112L	0004
2SB112M	0004
2SB112OR	0004
2SB112R	0004
2SB112X	0004
2SB112Y	0004
2SB113	0004
2SB113A	0004
2SB113B	0004
2SB113C	0004
2SB113D	0004
2SB113E	0004
2SB113F	0004
2SB113G	0004
2SB113GN	0004
2SB113H	0004
2SB113J	0004
2SB113K	0004
2SB113L	0004
2SB113M	0004
2SB113OR	0004
2SB113R	0004
2SB113X	0004
2SB113Y	0004
2SB114	0004
2SB114A	0004
2SB114B	0004
2SB114C	0004
2SB114D	0004
2SB114E	0004
2SB114F	0004
2SB114G	0004
2SB114GN	0004
2SB114H	0004
2SB114J	0004
2SB114K	0004
2SB114L	0004
2SB114M	0004
2SB114OR	0004
2SB114R	0004
2SB114X	0004
2SB114Y	0004
2SB115	0004
2SB115A	0004
2SB115B	0004
2SB115C	0004
2SB115D	0004
2SB115E	0004
2SB115F	0004
2SB115G	0004
2SB115GN	0004
2SB115H	0004
2SB115J	0004
2SB115K	0004
2SB115L	0004
2SB115M	0004
2SB115OR	0004
2SB115R	0004
2SB115X	0004
2SB115Y	0004
2SB116	0004
2SB116A	0004
2SB116B	0004
2SB116C	0004
2SB116D	0004
2SB116E	0004
2SB116F	0004
2SB116G	0004
2SB116GN	0004
2SB116H	0004
2SB116J	0004
2SB116K	0004
2SB116L	0004
2SB116M	0004
2SB116OR	0004
2SB116R	0004
2SB116X	0004
2SB116Y	0004
2SB117	0004
2SB117A	0004
2SB117B	0004
2SB117C	0004
2SB117D	0004
2SB117E	0004
2SB117F	0004
2SB117G	0004
2SB117GN	0004
2SB117H	0004
2SB117J	0004
2SB117K	0004
2SB117L	0004
2SB117M	0004
2SB117OR	0004
2SB117R	0004
2SB117X	0004
2SB117Y	0004
2SB118	0164
2SB119	0160
2SB119A	0160
2SB119B	0160
2SB119C	0160
2SB119D	0160
2SB119E	0160
2SB119F	0160
2SB119G	0160
2SB119GN	0160
2SB119H	0160
2SB119J	0160
2SB119K	0160
2SB119L	0160
2SB119M	0160
2SB119OR	0160
2SB119R	0160
2SB119X	0160
2SB119Y	0160
2SB120	0004
2SB120A	0004
2SB120B	0004
2SB120C	0004
2SB120D	0004
2SB120E	0004
2SB120F	0004
2SB120G	0004
2SB120GN	0004
2SB120H	0004
2SB120J	0004
2SB120K	0004
2SB120L	0004
2SB120M	0004
2SB120OR	0004
2SB120R	0004
2SB120X	0004
2SB120Y	0004
2SB122	0160
2SB122A	0160
2SB122B	0160
2SB122C	0160
2SB122D	0160
2SB122E	0160
2SB122F	0160
2SB122G	0160
2SB122GN	0160
2SB122H	0160
2SB122J	0160
2SB122K	0160
2SB122L	0160
2SB122M	0160
2SB122OR	0160
2SB122R	0160
2SB122X	0160
2SB122Y	0160
2SB123	0085
2SB123A	0085
2SB123B	0085
2SB123C	0085
2SB123D	0085
2SB123E	0085
2SB123F	0085
2SB123G	0085
2SB123GN	0085
2SB123H	0085
2SB123J	0085
2SB123K	0085
2SB123L	0085
2SB123M	0085
2SB123OR	0085
2SB123R	0085
2SB123X	0085
2SB123Y	0085
2SB124	0160
2SB124A	0160
2SB124B	0160
2SB124C	0160
2SB124D	0160
2SB124E	0160
2SB124F	0160
2SB124G	0160
2SB124H	0160
2SB124J	0160
2SB124K	0160
2SB124L	0160
2SB124M	0160
2SB124OR	0160
2SB124R	0160
2SB124X	0160
2SB124Y	0160
2SB125	0599
2SB126	0160
2SB126(F)	0160
2SB126(V)	0160
2SB126A	0160
2SB126AA	0160
2SB126AB	0160
2SB126AC	0160
2SB126AD	0160
2SB126AE	0160
2SB126AF	0160
2SB126AG	0160
2SB126AH	0160
2SB126B	0160
2SB126C	0160
2SB126D	0160
2SB126E	0160
2SB126F	0160
2SB126FV	0160
2SB126G	0160
2SB126GN	0160
2SB126H	0160
2SB126J	0160
2SB126K	0160
2SB126L	0160
2SB126M	0160
2SB126OR	0160
2SB126P	0160
2SB126R	0160
2SB126V	0160
2SB126X	0160
2SB126Y	0160
2SB127	0160
2SB127A	0160
2SB127B	0160
2SB127C	0160
2SB127D	0160
2SB127E	0160
2SB127F	0160
2SB127G	0160
2SB127GN	0160
2SB127H	0160
2SB127J	0160
2SB127K	0160
2SB127L	0160
2SB127M	0160
2SB127OR	0160
2SB127R	0160
2SB127X	0160
2SB127Y	0160
2SB128	0969
2SB128(V)	0969
2SB128A	0969
2SB128B	0969
2SB128C	0969
2SB128D	0969
2SB128E	0969
2SB128F	0969
2SB128G	0969
2SB128GN	0969
2SB128H	0969
2SB128J	0969
2SB128K	0969
2SB128L	0969
2SB128M	0969
2SB128OR	0969
2SB128R	0969
2SB128V	0969
2SB128X	0969
2SB128Y	0969
2SB129	0969
2SB129A	0969
2SB129B	0969
2SB129C	0969
2SB129D	0969
2SB129E	0969
2SB129F	0969
2SB129G	0969
2SB129GN	0969
2SB129H	0969
2SB129J	0969
2SB129K	0969
2SB129L	0969
2SB129M	0969
2SB129OR	0969
2SB129R	0969
2SB129X	0969
2SB129Y	0969
2SB130	0222
2SB130A	0222
2SB130B	0222
2SB130C	0222
2SB130D	0222
2SB130E	0222
2SB130F	0222
2SB130G	0222
2SB130GN	0222
2SB130H	0222
2SB130J	0222
2SB130K	0222
2SB130L	0222
2SB130M	0222
2SB130OR	0222
2SB130R	0222
2SB130X	0222
2SB130Y	0222
2SB131	0160
2SB131A	0160
2SB131B	0160
2SB131C	0160
2SB131D	0160
2SB131E	0160
2SB131F	0160
2SB131G	0160
2SB131GN	0160
2SB131H	0160
2SB131J	0160
2SB131K	0160
2SB131L	0160
2SB131M	0160
2SB131OR	0160
2SB131R	0160
2SB131X	0160
2SB131Y	0160
2SB132	0160
2SB132A	0160
2SB132B	0160
2SB132C	0160
2SB132D	0160
2SB132E	0160
2SB132F	0160
2SB132G	0160
2SB132GN	0160
2SB132H	0160
2SB132J	0160
2SB132L	0160
2SB132M	0160
2SB132OR	0160
2SB132R	0160
2SB132X	0160
2SB132Y	0160
2SB134	0004
2SB134A	0004
2SB134B	0004
2SB134C	0004
2SB134D	0004
2SB134E	0004
2SB134F	0004
2SB134G	0004
2SB134GN	0004
2SB134H	0004
2SB134J	0004
2SB134K	0004
2SB134L	0004
2SB134M	0004
2SB134OR	0004
2SB134R	0004
2SB134X	0004
2SB134Y	0004
2SB135	0004
2SB135(C)	0004
2SB135A	0004
2SB135B	0004
2SB135C	0004
2SB135D	0004
2SB135E	0004
2SB135F	0004
2SB135G	0004
2SB135GN	0004
2SB135H	0004
2SB135J	0004
2SB135K	0004
2SB135L	0004
2SB135M	0004
2SB135OR	0004
2SB135R	0004
2SB135X	0004
2SB135Y	0004
2SB136	0004
2SB136(C)	0004
2SB136A	0004
2SB136B	0004
2SB136C	0004
2SB136D	0004
2SB136E	0004
2SB136F	0004
2SB136G	0004
2SB136GN	0004
2SB136H	0004
2SB136J	0004
2SB136K	0004
2SB136L	0004
2SB136M	0004
2SB136OR	0004
2SB136R	0004
2SB136U	0004
2SB136X	0004
2SB137	0160
2SB137A	0160
2SB137B	0160
2SB137C	0160
2SB137D	0160
2SB137E	0160
2SB137F	0160
2SB137G	0160
2SB137GN	0160
2SB137H	0160
2SB137K	0160
2SB137L	0160
2SB137OR	0160
2SB137R	0160
2SB137X	0160
2SB137Y	0160
2SB138	0160
2SB138A	0160
2SB138B	0160
2SB138C	0160
2SB138D	0160
2SB138E	0160
2SB138G	0160
2SB138GN	0160
2SB138H	0160
2SB138J	0160
2SB138K	0160
2SB138L	0160
2SB138M	0160
2SB138OR	0160
2SB138R	0160
2SB138X	0160
2SB138Y	0160
2SB140	0085
2SB140A	0085
2SB140B	0085
2SB140C	0085
2SB140D	0085
2SB140E	0085
2SB140F	0085
2SB140G	0085
2SB140GN	0085
2SB140H	0085
2SB140J	0085
2SB140K	0085
2SB140L	0085
2SB140M	0085
2SB140OR	0085
2SB140X	0085
2SB140Y	0085
2SB141	0085
2SB142	0085
2SB142A	0085
2SB142B	0085
2SB142C	0085
2SB142D	0085
2SB142E	0085
2SB142F	0085
2SB142G	0085
2SB142GN	0085
2SB142H	0085
2SB142J	0085
2SB142K	0085
2SB142L	0085
2SB142M	0085
2SB142OR	0085
2SB142R	0085
2SB142X	0085
2SB142Y	0085
2SB143	0085
2SB143A	0085
2SB143B	0085
2SB143C	0085
2SB143D	0085
2SB143E	0085
2SB143F	0085
2SB143G	0085
2SB143GN	0085
2SB143H	0085
2SB143J	0085
2SB143K	0085
2SB143L	0085
2SB143M	0085
2SB143OR	0085
2SB143P	0085
2SB143X	0085
2SB143Y	0085
2SB144	0085
2SB144A	0085
2SB144B	0085
2SB144C	0085
2SB144D	0085
2SB144E	0085
2SB144F	0085
2SB144G	0085
2SB144GN	0085
2SB144H	0085
2SB144J	0085
2SB144K	0085
2SB144L	0085
2SB144M	0085
2SB144OR	0085
2SB144P	0085
2SB144R	0085
2SB144X	0085
2SB144Y	0085
2SB145	0085
2SB145A	0085
2SB145B	0085
2SB145C	0085
2SB145D	0085
2SB145E	0085
2SB145F	0085
2SB145G	0085
2SB145GN	0085
2SB145H	0085
2SB145J	0085
2SB145K	0085
2SB145L	0085
2SB145M	0085
2SB145OR	0085
2SB145R	0085
2SB145X	0085
2SB145Y	0085
2SB146	0085
2SB146A	0085
2SB146B	0085
2SB146C	0085
2SB146D	0085
2SB146E	0085
2SB146F	0085
2SB146G	0085
2SB146GN	0085
2SB146H	0085
2SB146J	0085
2SB146K	0085
2SB146L	0085
2SB146M	0085
2SB146OR	0085
2SB146R	0085
2SB146X	0085
2SB146Y	0085
2SB147	0085
2SB147A	0085
2SB147B	0085
2SB147C	0085
2SB147D	0085
2SB147E	0085
2SB147F	0085
2SB147G	0085
2SB147H	0085
2SB147J	0085
2SB147K	0085
2SB147L	0085
2SB147M	0085
2SB147OR	0085
2SB147X	0085
2SB147Y	0085
2SB148	0599
2SB149	0085
2SB149-N	0085
2SB149A	0085
2SB149B	0085
2SB149C	0085
2SB149D	0085
2SB149E	0085
2SB149F	0085
2SB149G	0085
2SB149GN	0085
2SB149H	0085
2SB149J	0085
2SB149K	0085
2SB149L	0085
2SB149M	0085
2SB149OR	0085
2SB149R	0085
2SB149X	0085
2SB149Y	0085
2SB150	0164
2SB150A	0164
2SB150B	0164
2SB150C	0164
2SB150D	0164
2SB150E	0164
2SB150F	0164
2SB150G	0164
2SB150GN	0164
2SB150H	0164
2SB150J	0164
2SB150K	0164
2SB150L	0164
2SB150M	0164
2SB150OR	0164
2SB150R	0164
2SB150X	0164
2SB150Y	0164
2SB151	0969
2SB151A	0969
2SB151B	0969
2SB151C	0969
2SB151D	0969
2SB151E	0969
2SB151F	0969
2SB151G	0969
2SB151GN	0969
2SB151H	0969
2SB151J	0969
2SB151K	0969
2SB151L	0969
2SB151M	0969
2SB151OR	0969
2SB151R	0969
2SB151X	0969
2SB151Y	0969
2SB152	0969
2SB152A	0969
2SB152B	0969
2SB152C	0969
2SB152D	0969
2SB152E	0969
2SB152F	0969
2SB152G	0969
2SB152GN	0969
2SB152H	0969
2SB152J	0969
2SB152K	0969
2SB152L	0969
2SB152M	0969
2SB152OR	0969
2SB152R	0969
2SB152X	0969
2SB152Y	0969
2SB153	0004
2SB153A	0004
2SB153B	0004
2SB153C	0004
2SB153D	0004
2SB153E	0004
2SB153F	0004
2SB153G	0004
2SB153GN	0004
2SB153H	0004
2SB153J	0004
2SB153K	0004
2SB153L	0004
2SB153M	0004
2SB153OR	0004
2SB153R	0004
2SB153X	0004
2SB153Y	0004
2SB154	0004
2SB154A	0004
2SB154B	0004
2SB154C	0004
2SB154D	0004
2SB154E	0004
2SB154F	0004
2SB154G	0004
2SB154GN	0004
2SB154H	0004

If replacement code is OEM, contact original manufacturer for replacement.

DEVICE TYPE	REPL CODE
2SB154J	0004
2SB154K	0004
2SB154L	0004
2SB154M	0004
2SB154OR	0004
2SB154R	0004
2SB154X	0004
2SB154Y	0004
2SB155	0004
2SB155A	0004
2SB155B	0004
2SB155C	0004
2SB155D	0004
2SB155E	0004
2SB155F	0004
2SB155G	0004
2SB155GN	0004
2SB155H	0004
2SB155J	0004
2SB155K	0004
2SB155L	0004
2SB155M	0004
2SB155OR	0004
2SB155R	0004
2SB155X	0004
2SB155Y	0004
2SB156	0004
2SB156-A	0004
2SB156A	0004
2SB156AA	0004
2SB156AB	0004
2SB156AC	0004
2SB156AD	0004
2SB156B	0004
2SB156B3	0004
2SB156BK	0004
2SB156C	0004
2SB156D	0004
2SB156E	0004
2SB156F	0004
2SB156G	0004
2SB156GN	0004
2SB156H	0004
2SB156J	0004
2SB156K	0004
2SB156L	0004
2SB156M	0004
2SB156OR	0004
2SB156P	0004
2SB156R	0004
2SB156X	0004
2SB156Y	0004
2SB157	0136
2SB157A	0136
2SB157B	0136
2SB157C	0136
2SB157D	0136
2SB157E	0136
2SB157F	0136
2SB157G	0136
2SB157GN	0136
2SB157H	0136
2SB157J	0136
2SB157K	0136
2SB157L	0136
2SB157M	0136
2SB157OR	0136
2SB157R	0136
2SB157X	0136
2SB157Y	0136
2SB158	0136
2SB158A	0136
2SB158B	0136
2SB158C	0136
2SB158D	0136
2SB158E	0136
2SB158F	0136
2SB158G	0136
2SB158GN	0136
2SB158H	0136
2SB158J	0136
2SB158K	0136
2SB158L	0136
2SB158M	0136
2SB158OR	0136
2SB158R	0136
2SB158X	0136
2SB158Y	0136
2SB159	0136
2SB159A	0136
2SB159B	0136
2SB159C	0136
2SB159D	0136
2SB159E	0136
2SB159F	0136
2SB159G	0136
2SB159GN	0136
2SB159H	0136
2SB159J	0136
2SB159K	0136
2SB159L	0136
2SB159M	0136
2SB159OR	0136
2SB159R	0136
2SB159X	0136
2SB159Y	0136
2SB160	0136
2SB160A	0136
2SB160B	0136

DEVICE TYPE	REPL CODE
2SB160C	0136
2SB160D	0136
2SB160E	0136
2SB160F	0136
2SB160G	0136
2SB160GN	0136
2SB160H	0136
2SB160J	0136
2SB160K	0136
2SB160L	0136
2SB160M	0136
2SB160OR	0136
2SB160R	0136
2SB160X	0136
2SB160Y	0136
2SB161	0211
2SB161A	0211
2SB161B	0211
2SB161C	0211
2SB161D	0211
2SB161E	0211
2SB161F	0211
2SB161G	0211
2SB161GN	0211
2SB161H	0211
2SB161J	0211
2SB161K	0211
2SB161L	0211
2SB161M	0211
2SB161OR	0211
2SB161R	0211
2SB161X	0211
2SB161Y	0211
2SB162	0004
2SB162A	0004
2SB162B	0004
2SB162C	0004
2SB162D	0004
2SB162E	0004
2SB162F	0004
2SB162G	0004
2SB162GN	0004
2SB162H	0004
2SB162J	0004
2SB162K	0004
2SB162L	0004
2SB162M	0004
2SB162OR	0004
2SB162R	0004
2SB162X	0004
2SB162Y	0004
2SB163	0211
2SB163A	0211
2SB163B	0211
2SB163C	0211
2SB163D	0211
2SB163E	0211
2SB163F	0211
2SB163G	0211
2SB163GN	0211
2SB163H	0211
2SB163J	0211
2SB163K	0211
2SB163L	0211
2SB163M	0211
2SB163OR	0211
2SB163R	0211
2SB163X	0211
2SB163Y	0211
2SB164	0211
2SB164A	0211
2SB164B	0211
2SB164C	0211
2SB164D	0211
2SB164E	0211
2SB164F	0211
2SB164G	0211
2SB164GN	0211
2SB164H	0211
2SB164J	0211
2SB164L	0211
2SB164M	0211
2SB164OR	0211
2SB164R	0211
2SB164X	0211
2SB164Y	0211
2SB165	0211
2SB165A	0211
2SB165B	0211
2SB165C	0211
2SB165D	0211
2SB165E	0211
2SB165F	0211
2SB165G	0211
2SB165GN	0211
2SB165H	0211
2SB165J	0211
2SB165K	0211
2SB165M	0211
2SB165OR	0211
2SB165R	0211
2SB165X	0211
2SB165Y	0211
2SB166	0004
2SB166A	0004
2SB166B	0004
2SB166C	0004
2SB166D	0004
2SB166E	0004

DEVICE TYPE	REPL CODE
2SB166F	0004
2SB166G	0004
2SB166GN	0004
2SB166H	0004
2SB166J	0004
2SB166K	0004
2SB166L	0004
2SB166M	0004
2SB166OR	0004
2SB166R	0004
2SB166X	0004
2SB166Y	0004
2SB167	0164
2SB167A	0164
2SB167B	0164
2SB167BK	0164
2SB167C	0164
2SB167D	0164
2SB167E	0164
2SB167F	0164
2SB167G	0164
2SB167GN	0164
2SB167H	0164
2SB167J	0164
2SB167K	0164
2SB167L	0164
2SB167M	0164
2SB167OR	0164
2SB167R	0164
2SB167X	0164
2SB167Y	0164
2SB168	0004
2SB168A	0004
2SB168B	0004
2SB168C	0004
2SB168D	0004
2SB168E	0004
2SB168F	0004
2SB168G	0004
2SB168GN	0004
2SB168H	0004
2SB168J	0004
2SB168K	0004
2SB168L	0004
2SB168M	0004
2SB168OR	0004
2SB168R	0004
2SB168X	0004
2SB168Y	0004
2SB169	0004
2SB169A	0004
2SB169B	0004
2SB169C	0004
2SB169D	0004
2SB169E	0004
2SB169F	0004
2SB169G	0004
2SB169GN	0004
2SB169H	0004
2SB169J	0004
2SB169K	0004
2SB169L	0004
2SB169M	0004
2SB169OR	0004
2SB169R	0004
2SB169X	0004
2SB169Y	0004
2SB170	0004
2SB170A	0004
2SB170B	0004
2SB170C	0004
2SB170D	0004
2SB170E	0004
2SB170F	0004
2SB170G	0004
2SB170GN	0004
2SB170H	0004
2SB170J	0004
2SB170K	0004
2SB170L	0004
2SB170M	0004
2SB170OR	0004
2SB170R	0004
2SB170X	0004
2SB170Y	0004
2SB171	0004
2SB171A	0004
2SB171B	0004
2SB171C	0004
2SB171D	0004
2SB171E	0004
2SB171F	0004
2SB171G	0004
2SB171GN	0004
2SB171H	0004
2SB171J	0004
2SB171K	0004
2SB171L	0004
2SB171M	0004
2SB171OR	0004
2SB171X	0004
2SB171Y	0004
2SB172	0004
2SB172(F)	0004
2SB172A	0004
2SB172A-1	0004
2SB172A-F	0004
2SB172AF	0004
2SB172AL	0004

DEVICE TYPE	REPL CODE
2SB172B	0004
2SB172C	0004
2SB172D	0004
2SB172E	0004
2SB172F	0004
2SB172FN	0004
2SB172G	0004
2SB172GN	0004
2SB172H	0004
2SB172J	0004
2SB172K	0004
2SB172L	0004
2SB172M	0004
2SB172OR	0004
2SB172P	0004
2SB172R	0004
2SB172X	0004
2SB172Y	0004
2SB173	0004
2SB173(C)	0004
2SB173A	0004
2SB173B	0004
2SB173BL	0004
2SB173C	0004
2SB173CL	0004
2SB173D	0004
2SB173E	0004
2SB173F	0004
2SB173G	0004
2SB173GN	0004
2SB173H	0004
2SB173J	0004
2SB173K	0004
2SB173L	0004
2SB173M	0004
2SB173OR	0004
2SB173R	0004
2SB173X	0004
2SB173Y	0004
2SB174	0004
2SB174A	0004
2SB174B	0004
2SB174C	0004
2SB174D	0004
2SB174E	0004
2SB174F	0004
2SB174G	0004
2SB174GN	0004
2SB174H	0004
2SB174K	0004
2SB174L	0004
2SB174M	0004
2SB174OR	0004
2SB174R	0004
2SB174X	0004
2SB174Y	0004
2SB175	0004
2SB175(A)	0004
2SB175(B)	0004
2SB175(C)	0004
2SB175A	0004
2SB175B	0004
2SB175B-1	0004
2SB175BL	0004
2SB175C	0004
2SB175CL	0004
2SB175D	0004
2SB175E	0004
2SB175F	0004
2SB175G	0004
2SB175GN	0004
2SB175H	0004
2SB175L	0004
2SB175M	0004
2SB175OR	0004
2SB175R	0004
2SB175X	0004
2SB175Y	0004
2SB176	0004
2SB176(O)	0004
2SB176(P)	0004
2SB176-O	0004
2SB176-P	0004
2SB176-PR	0004
2SB176A	0004
2SB176B	0004
2SB176C	0004
2SB176D	0004
2SB176E	0004
2SB176F	0004
2SB176G	0004
2SB176GN	0004
2SB176H	0004
2SB176J	0004
2SB176K	0004
2SB176L	0004
2SB176M	0004
2SB176O	0004
2SB176OR	0004
2SB176P	0004
2SB176PL	0004
2SB176PR	0004
2SB176PRC	0004
2SB176R	0004
2SB176R(1)	0004
2SB176RG	0004
2SB176X	0004
2SB176Y	0004
2SB177	0004

DEVICE TYPE	REPL CODE
2SB177A	0004
2SB177B	0004
2SB177C	0004
2SB177D	0004
2SB177E	0004
2SB177F	0004
2SB177G	0004
2SB177GN	0004
2SB177H	0004
2SB177K	0004
2SB177L	0004
2SB177M	0004
2SB177OR	0004
2SB177R	0004
2SB177X	0004
2SB177Y	0004
2SB178	0004
2SB178(M)	0004
2SB178-O	0004
2SB178-OR	0004
2SB178-S	0004
2SB178A	0004
2SB178B	0004
2SB178C	0004
2SB178D	0004
2SB178E	0004
2SB178F	0004
2SB178G	0004
2SB178GN	0004
2SB178H	0004
2SB178J	0004
2SB178K	0004
2SB178L	0004
2SB178M	0004
2SB178N	0004
2SB178OR	0004
2SB178R	0004
2SB178S	0004
2SB178T	0004
2SB178TC	0004
2SB178TS	0004
2SB178U	0004
2SB178V	0004
2SB178X	0004
2SB178Y	0004
2SB179	0050
2SB180	0164
2SB180A	0164
2SB181	0164
2SB181A	0164
2SB182	0050
2SB183	0004
2SB183A	0004
2SB183B	0004
2SB183C	0004
2SB183D	0004
2SB183E	0004
2SB183F	0004
2SB183G	0004
2SB183GN	0004
2SB183H	0004
2SB183J	0004
2SB183K	0004
2SB183L	0004
2SB183M	0004
2SB183OR	0004
2SB183R	0004
2SB183X	0004
2SB183Y	0004
2SB184	0004
2SB184A	0004
2SB184B	0004
2SB184C	0004
2SB184D	0004
2SB184E	0004
2SB184F	0004
2SB184G	0004
2SB184GN	0004
2SB184H	0004
2SB184J	0004
2SB184K	0004
2SB184L	0004
2SB184M	0004
2SB184OR	0004
2SB184R	0004
2SB184X	0004
2SB184Y	0004
2SB185	0004
2SB185(O)	0004
2SB185(P)	0004
2SB185-O	0004
2SB185A	0004
2SB185AA	0004
2SB185B	0004
2SB185C	0004
2SB185D	0004
2SB185E	0004
2SB185F	0004
2SB185G	0004
2SB185GN	0004
2SB185H	0004
2SB185I	0004
2SB185J	0004
2SB185L	0004
2SB185M	0004
2SB185OR	0004
2SB185P	0004
2SB185R	0004
2SB185X	0004

DEVICE TYPE	REPL CODE
2SB185Y	0004
2SB186	0004
2SB186(A)	0004
2SB186(O)	0004
2SB186-1	0004
2SB186-7	0004
2SB186-K	0004
2SB186-O	0004
2SB186-OR	0004
2SB186A	0004
2SB186AG	0004
2SB186B	0004
2SB186BY	0004
2SB186C	0004
2SB186D	0004
2SB186E	0004
2SB186F	0004
2SB186G	0004
2SB186GN	0004
2SB186H	0004
2SB186J	0004
2SB186K	0004
2SB186L	0004
2SB186M	0004
2SB186OR	0004
2SB186R	0004
2SB186X	0004
2SB186Y	0004
2SB187	0004
2SB187(1)	0004
2SB187(K)	0004
2SB187-1	0004
2SB187-OR	0004
2SB187A	0004
2SB187AA	3511
2SB187B	3511
2SB187BK	0004
2SB187C	0004
2SB187D	0004
2SB187E	0004
2SB187F	0004
2SB187G	0004
2SB187GN	0004
2SB187H	0004
2SB187K	0004
2SB187L	0004
2SB187M	0004
2SB187OR	0004
2SB187R	0004
2SB187S	0004
2SB187TV	0004
2SB187X	0004
2SB187Y	0004
2SB188	0004
2SB188A	0004
2SB188B	0004
2SB188C	0004
2SB188D	0004
2SB188E	0004
2SB188F	0004
2SB188G	0004
2SB188GN	0004
2SB188H	0004
2SB188J	0004
2SB188K	0004
2SB188L	0004
2SB188M	0004
2SB188OR	0004
2SB188R	0004
2SB188X	0004
2SB188Y	0004
2SB189	0004
2SB189A	0004
2SB189B	0004
2SB189C	0004
2SB189D	0004
2SB189E	0004
2SB189F	0004
2SB189G	0004
2SB189GN	0004
2SB189H	0004
2SB189J	0004
2SB189K	0004
2SB189L	0004
2SB189M	0004
2SB189OR	0004
2SB189R	0004
2SB189X	0004
2SB189Y	0004
2SB190	0164
2SB191	0279
2SB192	0164
2SB193	0164
2SB194	0164
2SB195	0164
2SB196	0164
2SB197	0164
2SB198	0164
2SB199	0211
2SB199A	0211
2SB199B	0211
2SB199C	0211
2SB199D	0211
2SB199E	0211
2SB199F	0211
2SB199G	0211
2SB199GN	0211
2SB199H	0211
2SB199J	0211

DEVICE TYPE	REPL CODE
2SB199L	0211
2SB199M	0211
2SB199OR	0211
2SB199R	0211
2SB199X	0211
2SB199Y	0211
2SB200	0004
2SB200(RECT)	1404
2SB200A	0004
2SB200B	0004
2SB200C	0004
2SB200D	0004
2SB200E	0004
2SB200F	0004
2SB200G	0004
2SB200GN	0004
2SB200H	0004
2SB200J	0004
2SB200K	0004
2SB200L	0004
2SB200M	0004
2SB200OR	0004
2SB200R	0004
2SB200X	0004
2SB200Y	0004
2SB201	0004
2SB202	0004
2SB202A	0004
2SB202B	0004
2SB202C	0004
2SB202D	0004
2SB202E	0004
2SB202F	0004
2SB202G	0004
2SB202GN	0004
2SB202H	0004
2SB202J	0004
2SB202L	0004
2SB202M	0004
2SB202OR	0004
2SB202R	0004
2SB202X	0004
2SB202Y	0004
2SB203	0599
2SB203A	0599
2SB203AA	0599
2SB203B	0599
2SB203C	0599
2SB203D	0599
2SB203E	0599
2SB203F	0599
2SB203G	0599
2SB203GN	0599
2SB203H	0599
2SB203J	0599
2SB203K	0599
2SB203L	0599
2SB203M	0599
2SB203OR	0599
2SB203R	0599
2SB203X	0599
2SB203Y	0599
2SB204	0599
2SB205	0599
2SB206	0599
2SB207	0599
2SB207A	0599
2SB208	0599
2SB208A	0599
2SB209	0599
2SB210	0599
2SB211	0599
2SB212	0599
2SB213	0599
2SB213A	0599
2SB214	0599
2SB214A	0599
2SB215	0969
2SB215A	0969
2SB215B	0969
2SB215C	0969
2SB215D	0969
2SB215E	0969
2SB215F	0969
2SB215G	0969
2SB215GN	0969
2SB215H	0969
2SB215J	0969
2SB215K	0969
2SB215L	0969
2SB215M	0969
2SB215OR	0969
2SB215R	0969
2SB215X	0969
2SB215Y	0969
2SB216	0160
2SB216A	0160
2SB216B	0160
2SB216C	0160
2SB216D	0160
2SB216E	0160
2SB216F	0160
2SB216G	0160
2SB216GN	0160
2SB216H	0160
2SB216J	0160
2SB216K	0160
2SB216L	0160
2SB216M	0160

If replacement code is OEM, contact original manufacturer for replacement.

67

DEVICE TYPE	REPL CODE
2SB216OR	0160
2SB216R	0160
2SB216X	0160
2SB216Y	0160
2SB217	0160
2SB217A	0160
2SB217B	0160
2SB217C	0160
2SB217D	0160
2SB217E	0160
2SB217F	0160
2SB217G	0160
2SB217GN	0160
2SB217H	0160
2SB217K	0160
2SB217L	0160
2SB217M	0160
2SB217OR	0160
2SB217R	0160
2SB217U	0160
2SB217X	0160
2SB217Y	0160
2SB218	0211
2SB218A	0211
2SB218B	0211
2SB218C	0211
2SB218D	0211
2SB218E	0211
2SB218F	0211
2SB218G	0211
2SB218GN	0211
2SB218H	0211
2SB218J	0211
2SB218K	0211
2SB218L	0211
2SB218M	0211
2SB218OR	0211
2SB218R	0211
2SB218X	0211
2SB218Y	0211
2SB219	0211
2SB219A	0211
2SB219B	0211
2SB219E	0211
2SB219F	0211
2SB219G	0211
2SB219H	0211
2SB219J	0211
2SB219K	0211
2SB219L	0211
2SB219R	0211
2SB219X	0211
2SB219Y	0211
2SB220	0211
2SB220A	0211
2SB220B	0211
2SB220C	0211
2SB220D	0211
2SB220E	0211
2SB220F	0211
2SB220GN	0211
2SB220H	0211
2SB220J	0211
2SB220K	0211
2SB220L	0211
2SB220M	0211
2SB220OR	0211
2SB220R	0211
2SB220X	0211
2SB220Y	0211
2SB221	0211
2SB221A	0211
2SB221B	0211
2SB221C	0211
2SB221D	0211
2SB221E	0211
2SB221F	0211
2SB221G	0211
2SB221GN	0211
2SB221H	0211
2SB221J	0211
2SB221K	0211
2SB221L	0211
2SB221M	0211
2SB221OR	0211
2SB221R	0211
2SB221X	0211
2SB221Y	0211
2SB222	0211
2SB222A	0211
2SB222B	0211
2SB222C	0211
2SB222D	0211
2SB222E	0211
2SB222F	0211
2SB222G	0211
2SB222GN	0211
2SB222H	0211
2SB222J	0211
2SB222K	0211
2SB222L	0211
2SB222M	0211
2SB222OR	0211
2SB222R	0211
2SB222X	0211
2SB222Y	0211
2SB223	0211
2SB223A	0211
2SB223B	0211
2SB223C	0211
2SB223D	0211
2SB223E	0211
2SB223F	0211
2SB223G	0211
2SB223Y	0211
2SB224	0004
2SB224A	0004
2SB224B	0004
2SB224C	0004
2SB224D	0004
2SB224E	0004
2SB224F	0004
2SB224G	0004
2SB224GN	0004
2SB224H	0004
2SB224K	0004
2SB224L	0004
2SB224M	0004
2SB224OR	0004
2SB224R	0004
2SB224X	0004
2SB224Y	0004
2SB225	0211
2SB225A	0211
2SB225B	0211
2SB225C	0211
2SB225D	0211
2SB225E	0211
2SB225F	0211
2SB225G	0211
2SB225GN	0211
2SB225H	0211
2SB225K	0211
2SB225L	0211
2SB225M	0211
2SB225OR	0211
2SB225R	0211
2SB225X	0211
2SB225Y	0211
2SB226	0211
2SB226A	0211
2SB226B	0211
2SB226C	0211
2SB226D	0211
2SB226E	0211
2SB226F	0211
2SB226G	0211
2SB226GN	0211
2SB226J	0211
2SB226K	0211
2SB226L	0211
2SB226M	0211
2SB226OR	0211
2SB226R	0211
2SB226X	0211
2SB226Y	0211
2SB227	0004
2SB227A	0004
2SB227B	0004
2SB227C	0004
2SB227D	0004
2SB227E	0004
2SB227F	0004
2SB227G	0004
2SB227GN	0004
2SB227H	0004
2SB227J	0004
2SB227K	0004
2SB227L	0004
2SB227M	0004
2SB227OR	0004
2SB227R	0004
2SB227X	0004
2SB227Y	0004
2SB228	0969
2SB228A	0969
2SB228B	0969
2SB228C	0969
2SB228D	0969
2SB228E	0969
2SB228F	0969
2SB228G	0969
2SB228GN	0969
2SB228H	0969
2SB228J	0969
2SB228K	0969
2SB228L	0969
2SB228M	0969
2SB228OR	0969
2SB228R	0969
2SB228X	0969
2SB228Y	0969
2SB229	0969
2SB229A	0969
2SB229B	0969
2SB229C	0969
2SB229D	0969
2SB229E	0969
2SB229F	0969
2SB229G	0969
2SB229GN	0969
2SB229J	0969
2SB229K	0969
2SB229L	0969
2SB229M	0969
2SB229OR	0969
2SB229R	0969
2SB229X	0969
2SB229Y	0969
2SB230	0969
2SB230A	0969
2SB230B	0969
2SB230C	0969
2SB230D	0969
2SB230E	0969
2SB230F	0969
2SB230G	0969
2SB230GN	0969
2SB230H	0969
2SB230J	0969
2SB230K	0969
2SB230L	0969
2SB230M	0969
2SB230OR	0969
2SB230R	0969
2SB230X	0969
2SB230Y	0969
2SB231	0969
2SB231A	0969
2SB231B	0969
2SB231C	0969
2SB231D	0969
2SB231E	0969
2SB231F	0969
2SB231G	0969
2SB231GN	0969
2SB231H	0969
2SB231J	0969
2SB231K	0969
2SB231L	0969
2SB231M	0969
2SB231OR	0969
2SB231R	0969
2SB231X	0969
2SB231Y	0969
2SB232	0969
2SB232A	0969
2SB232B	0969
2SB232C	0969
2SB232D	0969
2SB232E	0969
2SB232F	0969
2SB232G	0969
2SB232GN	0969
2SB232H	0969
2SB232K	0969
2SB232L	0969
2SB232M	0969
2SB232OR	0969
2SB232R	0969
2SB232X	0969
2SB232Y	0969
2SB233	0969
2SB233A	0969
2SB233B	0969
2SB233C	0969
2SB233D	0969
2SB233E	0969
2SB233F	0969
2SB233G	0969
2SB233GN	0969
2SB233H	0969
2SB233J	0969
2SB233K	0969
2SB233L	0969
2SB233M	0969
2SB233OR	0969
2SB233R	0969
2SB233X	0969
2SB233Y	0969
2SB234	0969
2SB234A	0969
2SB234B	0969
2SB234C	0969
2SB234D	0969
2SB234E	0969
2SB234F	0969
2SB234G	0969
2SB234GN	0969
2SB234H	0969
2SB234J	0969
2SB234K	0969
2SB234L	0969
2SB234M	0969
2SB234N	0969
2SB234OR	0969
2SB234R	0969
2SB234X	0969
2SB234Y	0969
2SB235	0040
2SB235A	0040
2SB235B	0040
2SB235C	0040
2SB235D	0040
2SB235E	0040
2SB235F	0040
2SB235G	0040
2SB235GN	0040
2SB235H	0040
2SB235L	0040
2SB235M	0040
2SB235OR	0040
2SB235R	0040
2SB235X	0040
2SB235Y	0040
2SB236	0435
2SB236A	0435
2SB236B	0435
2SB236C	0435
2SB236D	0435
2SB236E	0435
2SB236F	0435
2SB236G	0435
2SB236GN	0435
2SB236H	0435
2SB236J	0435
2SB236K	0435
2SB236L	0435
2SB236M	0435
2SB236OR	0435
2SB236R	0435
2SB236X	0435
2SB236Y	0435
2SB237	0435
2SB237-12A	0435
2SB237-12B	0435
2SB237A	0435
2SB237B	0435
2SB237C	0435
2SB237D	0435
2SB237E	0435
2SB237F	0435
2SB237G	0435
2SB237GN	0435
2SB237H	0435
2SB237J	0435
2SB237K	0435
2SB237L	0435
2SB237M	0435
2SB237OR	0435
2SB237R	0435
2SB237X	0435
2SB237Y	0435
2SB238	0164
2SB238-12A	0164
2SB238-12B	0164
2SB238-12C	0164
2SB238A	0164
2SB238B	0164
2SB238C	0164
2SB238D	0164
2SB238E	0164
2SB238F	0164
2SB238G	0164
2SB238GN	0164
2SB238H	0164
2SB238J	0164
2SB238K	0164
2SB238L	0164
2SB238M	0164
2SB238OR	0164
2SB238R	0164
2SB238X	0164
2SB238Y	0164
2SB239	0160
2SB239A	0160
2SB239B	0160
2SB239C	0160
2SB239D	0160
2SB239E	0160
2SB239F	0160
2SB239G	0160
2SB239GN	0160
2SB239H	0160
2SB239J	0160
2SB239K	0160
2SB239L	0160
2SB239M	0160
2SB239OR	0160
2SB239R	0160
2SB239X	0160
2SB239Y	0160
2SB240	0050
2SB240A	0050
2SB240B	0050
2SB240C	0050
2SB240D	0050
2SB240E	0050
2SB240F	0050
2SB240GN	0050
2SB240H	0050
2SB240J	0050
2SB240K	0050
2SB240L	0050
2SB240M	0050
2SB240OR	0050
2SB240R	0050
2SB240X	0050
2SB240Y	0050
2SB241	0164
2SB241A	0164
2SB241B	0164
2SB241C	0164
2SB241D	0164
2SB241E	0164
2SB241F	0164
2SB241G	0164
2SB241GN	0164
2SB241H	0164
2SB241J	0164
2SB241K	0164
2SB241L	0164
2SB241M	0164
2SB241OR	0164
2SB241R	0164
2SB241V	0164
2SB241X	0164
2SB241Y	0164
2SB242	0164
2SB242A	0164
2SB242B	0164
2SB242C	0164
2SB242D	0164
2SB242E	0164
2SB242F	0164
2SB242G	0164
2SB242GN	0164
2SB242H	0164
2SB242J	0164
2SB242K	0164
2SB242L	0164
2SB242M	0164
2SB242OR	0164
2SB242R	0164
2SB242X	0164
2SB242Y	0164
2SB243	0969
2SB243A	0969
2SB243B	0969
2SB243C	0969
2SB243D	0969
2SB243E	0969
2SB243F	0969
2SB243G	0969
2SB243GN	0969
2SB243H	0969
2SB243J	0969
2SB243K	0969
2SB243L	0969
2SB243M	0969
2SB243OR	0969
2SB243R	0969
2SB243X	0969
2SB243Y	0969
2SB244	0969
2SB244A	0969
2SB244B	0969
2SB244C	0969
2SB244D	0969
2SB244E	0969
2SB244F	0969
2SB244G	0969
2SB244GN	0969
2SB244H	0969
2SB244J	0969
2SB244K	0969
2SB244L	0969
2SB244M	0969
2SB244OR	0969
2SB244R	0969
2SB244X	0969
2SB244Y	0969
2SB245	0969
2SB245A	0969
2SB245B	0969
2SB245C	0969
2SB245D	0969
2SB245E	0969
2SB245F	0969
2SB245G	0969
2SB245H	0969
2SB245J	0969
2SB245L	0969
2SB245M	0969
2SB245OR	0969
2SB245R	0969
2SB245X	0969
2SB245Y	0969
2SB246	0085
2SB246A	0085
2SB246B	0085
2SB246C	0085
2SB246D	0085
2SB246E	0085
2SB246F	0085
2SB246G	0085
2SB246GN	0085
2SB246H	0085
2SB246J	0085
2SB246K	0085
2SB246L	0085
2SB246M	0085
2SB246OR	0085
2SB246R	0085
2SB246X	0085
2SB246Y	0085
2SB247	0160
2SB247A	0160
2SB247B	0160
2SB247C	0160
2SB247D	0160
2SB247E	0160
2SB247F	0160
2SB247G	0160
2SB247GN	0160
2SB247H	0160
2SB247J	0160
2SB247K	0160
2SB247L	0160
2SB247M	0160
2SB247OR	0160
2SB247R	0160
2SB247X	0160
2SB247Y	0160
2SB248	0085
2SB248A	0085
2SB248B	0085
2SB248C	0085
2SB248D	0085
2SB248E	0085
2SB248F	0085
2SB248G	0085
2SB248GN	0085
2SB248H	0085
2SB248J	0085
2SB248K	0085
2SB248L	0085
2SB248M	0085
2SB248OR	0085
2SB248R	0085
2SB248X	0085
2SB248Y	0085
2SB249	0599
2SB249A	0599
2SB249B	0599
2SB249C	0599
2SB249D	0599
2SB249E	0599
2SB249F	0599
2SB249G	0599
2SB249GN	0599
2SB249H	0599
2SB249J	0599
2SB249K	0599
2SB249L	0599
2SB249M	0599
2SB249OR	0599
2SB249X	0599
2SB249Y	0599
2SB250	0085
2SB250A	0085
2SB250B	0085
2SB250D	0085
2SB250E	0085
2SB250F	0085
2SB250G	0085
2SB250GN	0085
2SB250H	0085
2SB250K	0085
2SB250L	0085
2SB250M	0085
2SB250OR	0085
2SB250X	0085
2SB250Y	0085
2SB251	0969
2SB251A	0969
2SB251B	0969
2SB251C	0969
2SB251D	0969
2SB251E	0969
2SB251F	0969
2SB251G	0969
2SB251GN	0969
2SB251H	0969
2SB251J	0969
2SB251K	0969
2SB251L	0969
2SB251M	0969
2SB251OR	0969
2SB251R	0969
2SB251X	0969
2SB252	0969
2SB252A	0969
2SB252B	0969
2SB252C	0969
2SB252D	0969
2SB252E	0969
2SB252F	0969
2SB252G	0969
2SB252GN	0969
2SB252H	0969
2SB252J	0969
2SB252L	0969
2SB252M	0969
2SB252OR	0969
2SB252R	0969
2SB252X	0969
2SB252Y	0969
2SB253	0969
2SB253A	0969
2SB253B	0969
2SB253C	0969
2SB253D	0969
2SB253E	0969
2SB253F	0969
2SB253G	0969
2SB253GN	0969
2SB253H	0969
2SB253K	0969
2SB253L	0969
2SB253M	0969
2SB253OR	0969
2SB253X	0969
2SB253Y	0969
2SB254	1004
2SB254(D)	1004
2SB254A	1004
2SB254B	1004
2SB254C	1004
2SB254D	1004
2SB254E	1004
2SB254F	1004
2SB254G	1004
2SB254GN	1004
2SB254H	1004
2SB254J	1004
2SB254K	1004
2SB254L	1004
2SB254M	1004
2SB254OR	1004
2SB254R	1004
2SB254X	1004
2SB254Y	1004
2SB255	1004
2SB255A	1004
2SB255B	1004
2SB255C	1004
2SB255D	1004
2SB255E	1004
2SB255F	1004
2SB255G	1004
2SB255GN	1004
2SB255H	1004
2SB255J	1004
2SB255K	1004
2SB255L	1004
2SB255M	1004
2SB255OR	1004
2SB255R	1004
2SB255X	1004
2SB255Y	1004
2SB256	1004
2SB256A	1004
2SB256B	1004
2SB256C	1004
2SB256D	1004
2SB256E	1004
2SB256F	1004
2SB256G	1004
2SB256GN	1004
2SB256H	1004
2SB256J	1004
2SB256L	1004
2SB256M	1004
2SB256OR	1004
2SB256R	1004
2SB256X	1004
2SB256Y	1004
2SB257	0004
2SB257A	0004
2SB257B	0004
2SB257C	0004
2SB257D	0004
2SB257E	0004
2SB257F	0004
2SB257G	0004
2SB257GN	0004
2SB257H	0004
2SB257K	0004
2SB257L	0004
2SB257M	0004
2SB257OR	0004
2SB257R	0004
2SB257X	0004
2SB257Y	0004
2SB258	0432
2SB258A	0432
2SB258B	0432
2SB258C	0432
2SB258D	0432
2SB258E	0432
2SB258F	0432
2SB258G	0432
2SB258GN	0432
2SB258H	0432
2SB258J	0432
2SB258K	0432
2SB258L	0432
2SB258M	0432
2SB258OR	0432
2SB258R	0432
2SB258X	0432
2SB258Y	0432
2SB259	0432
2SB259A	0432
2SB259B	0432
2SB259C	0432
2SB259D	0432
2SB259E	0432
2SB259F	0432
2SB259GN	0432
2SB259H	0432
2SB259J	0432
2SB259K	0432
2SB259L	0432
2SB259OR	0432
2SB259R	0432
2SB259X	0432
2SB259Y	0432
2SB260	0040
2SB260A	0040
2SB260B	0040
2SB260C	0040
2SB260D	0040
2SB260E	0040
2SB260F	0040
2SB260G	0040
2SB260GN	0040
2SB260H	0040
2SB260J	0040
2SB260K	0040
2SB260L	0040
2SB260M	0040

If replacement code is OEM, contact original manufacturer for replacement.

DEVICE TYPE	REPL CODE	DEVICE TYPE	REPL CODE	DEVICE TYPE	REPL CODE	DEVICE TYPE	REPL CODE	DEVICE TYPE	REPL CODE	DEVICE TYPE	REPL CODE	DEVICE TYPE	REPL CODE
2SB260OR	0040	2SB266P	0004	2SB273X	0004	2SB284M	0160	2SB293L	0004	2SB301R	0969	2SB311X	0969
2SB260R	0040	2SB266Q	0004	2SB273Y	0004	2SB284OR	0160	2SB293M	0004	2SB301X	0969	2SB311Y	0969
2SB260X	0040	2SB266R	0004	2SB274	0969	2SB284R	0160	2SB293OR	0004	2SB301Y	0969	2SB312	0969
2SB260Y	0040	2SB266X	0004	2SB274A	0969	2SB284X	0160	2SB293R	0004	2SB302	0004	2SB312A	0969
2SB261	0004	2SB266Y	0004	2SB274B	0969	2SB284Y	0160	2SB293X	0004	2SB302A	0004	2SB312B	0969
2SB261A	0004	2SB267	0004	2SB274C	0969	2SB285	0969	2SB293Y	0004	2SB302B	0004	2SB312C	0969
2SB261B	0004	2SB267A	0004	2SB274D	0969	2SB285A	0969	2SB294	0004	2SB302C	0004	2SB312D	0969
2SB261C	0004	2SB267B	0004	2SB274E	0969	2SB285B	0969	2SB294A	0004	2SB302D	0004	2SB312E	0969
2SB261D	0004	2SB267C	0004	2SB274F	0969	2SB285C	0969	2SB294B	0004	2SB302E	0004	2SB312F	0969
2SB261E	0004	2SB267D	0004	2SB274G	0969	2SB285D	0969	2SB294C	0004	2SB302F	0004	2SB312G	0969
2SB261F	0004	2SB267E	0004	2SB274H	0969	2SB285E	0969	2SB294D	0004	2SB302G	0004	2SB312GN	0969
2SB261G	0004	2SB267F	0004	2SB274J	0969	2SB285F	0969	2SB294E	0004	2SB302J	0004	2SB312H	0969
2SB261GN	0004	2SB267G	0004	2SB274K	0969	2SB285G	0969	2SB294F	0004	2SB302K	0004	2SB312J	0969
2SB261H	0004	2SB267GN	0004	2SB274L	0969	2SB285GN	0969	2SB294G	0004	2SB302L	0004	2SB312K	0969
2SB261J	0004	2SB267H	0004	2SB274M	0969	2SB285H	0969	2SB294GN	0004	2SB302M	0004	2SB312L	0969
2SB261K	0004	2SB267J	0004	2SB274OR	0969	2SB285J	0969	2SB294H	0004	2SB302OR	0004	2SB312M	0969
2SB261L	0004	2SB267K	0004	2SB274R	0969	2SB285K	0969	2SB294J	0004	2SB302R	0004	2SB312X	0969
2SB261M	0004	2SB267L	0004	2SB274V	0969	2SB285L	0969	2SB294K	0004	2SB302X	0004	2SB312Y	0969
2SB261N	0004	2SB267M	0004	2SB274X	0969	2SB285M	0969	2SB294L	0004	2SB302Y	0004	2SB313	0969
2SB261OR	0004	2SB267OR	0004	2SB274Y	0969	2SB285OR	0969	2SB294M	0004	2SB303	0004	2SB313A	0969
2SB261R	0004	2SB267R	0004	2SB275	0969	2SB285R	0969	2SB294OR	0004	2SB303(0)	0004	2SB313B	0969
2SB261X	0004	2SB267X	0004	2SB275A	0969	2SB285X	0969	2SB294R	0004	2SB303-0	0004	2SB313C	0969
2SB261Y	0004	2SB267Y	0004	2SB275B	0969	2SB285Y	0969	2SB294X	0004	2SB303A	0004	2SB313D	0969
2SB262	0004	2SB268	0004	2SB275C	0969	2SB286	0969	2SB294Y	0004	2SB303B	0004	2SB313E	0969
2SB262A	0004	2SB268A	0004	2SB275D	0969	2SB287	0969	2SB295	0969	2SB303BK	0004	2SB313F	0969
2SB262B	0004	2SB268B	0004	2SB275E	0969	2SB288	0050	2SB295A	0969	2SB303C	0004	2SB313G	0969
2SB262C	0004	2SB268C	0004	2SB275F	0969	2SB289	0050	2SB295B	0969	2SB303D	0004	2SB313GN	0969
2SB262D	0004	2SB268D	0004	2SB275G	0969	2SB290	0279	2SB295C	0969	2SB303E	0004	2SB313H	0969
2SB262E	0004	2SB268E	0004	2SB275GN	0969	2SB290-GREEN	0279	2SB295D	0969	2SB303F	0004	2SB313J	0969
2SB262F	0004	2SB268F	0004	2SB275H	0969	2SB290-YELLOW	0279	2SB295E	0969	2SB303G	0004	2SB313K	0969
2SB262G	0004	2SB268G	0004	2SB275J	0969	2SB290A	0279	2SB295F	0969	2SB303GN	0004	2SB313L	0969
2SB262GN	0004	2SB268GN	0004	2SB275K	0969	2SB290A-BLUE	0279	2SB295G	0969	2SB303H	0004	2SB313M	0969
2SB262H	0004	2SB268H	0004	2SB275L	0969	2SB290B	0279	2SB295GN	0969	2SB303J	0004	2SB313OR	0969
2SB262J	0004	2SB268J	0004	2SB275M	0969	2SB290C	0279	2SB295H	0969	2SB303K	0004	2SB313R	0969
2SB262K	0004	2SB268K	0004	2SB275OR	0969	2SB290D	0279	2SB295J	0969	2SB303L	0004	2SB313X	0969
2SB262L	0004	2SB268L	0004	2SB275R	0969	2SB290E	0279	2SB295K	0969	2SB303M	0004	2SB313Y	0969
2SB262M	0004	2SB268M	0004	2SB275X	0969	2SB290F	0279	2SB295L	0969	2SB303OR	0004	2SB314	0279
2SB262OR	0004	2SB268OR	0004	2SB275Y	0969	2SB290G	0279	2SB295M	0969	2SB303R	0004	2SB314A	0279
2SB262R	0004	2SB268R	0004	2SB276	0969	2SB290GN	0279	2SB295OR	0969	2SB303X	0004	2SB314B	0279
2SB262X	0004	2SB268X	0004	2SB276A	0969	2SB290H	0279	2SB295R	0969	2SB303Y	0004	2SB314C	0279
2SB262Y	0004	2SB268Y	0004	2SB276B	0969	2SB290J	0279	2SB295X	0969	2SB304	0164	2SB314D	0279
2SB263	0004	2SB269	0004	2SB276C	0969	2SB290K	0279	2SB295Y	0969	2SB304A	0164	2SB314E	0279
2SB263A	0004	2SB269A	0004	2SB276D	0969	2SB290L	0279	2SB296	0969	2SB304B	0164	2SB314F	0279
2SB263B	0004	2SB269C	0004	2SB276E	0969	2SB290M	0279	2SB296A	0969	2SB304C	0164	2SB314GN	0279
2SB263C	0004	2SB269D	0004	2SB276F	0969	2SB290OR	0279	2SB296B	0969	2SB304D	0164	2SB314H	0279
2SB263D	0004	2SB269E	0004	2SB276G	0969	2SB290R	0279	2SB296C	0969	2SB304E	0164	2SB314J	0279
2SB263E	0004	2SB269F	0004	2SB276GN	0969	2SB290X	0279	2SB296D	0969	2SB304F	0164	2SB314K	0279
2SB263F	0004	2SB269G	0004	2SB276H	0969	2SB290Y	0279	2SB296E	0969	2SB304G	0164	2SB314L	0279
2SB263G	0004	2SB269GN	0004	2SB276J	0969	2SB291	0279	2SB296F	0969	2SB304GN	0164	2SB314M	0279
2SB263GN	0004	2SB269J	0004	2SB276K	0969	2SB291-GREEN	0279	2SB296G	0969	2SB304H	0164	2SB314OR	0279
2SB263H	0004	2SB269K	0004	2SB276L	0969	2SB291-RED	0279	2SB296GN	0969	2SB304J	0164	2SB314R	0279
2SB263J	0004	2SB269L	0004	2SB276M	0969	2SB291-YELLOW	0279	2SB296H	0969	2SB304K	0164	2SB314X	0279
2SB263K	0004	2SB269M	0004	2SB276OR	0969	2SB291A	0279	2SB296J	0969	2SB304L	0164	2SB314Y	0279
2SB263L	0004	2SB269OR	0004	2SB276R	0969	2SB291B	0279	2SB296K	0969	2SB304M	0164	2SB315	0004
2SB263M	0004	2SB269R	0004	2SB276X	0969	2SB291C	0279	2SB296L	0969	2SB304OR	0164	2SB315A	0004
2SB263OR	0004	2SB269X	0004	2SB276Y	0969	2SB291D	0279	2SB296M	0969	2SB304R	0164	2SB315B	0004
2SB263R	0004	2SB269Y	0004	2SB277	0050	2SB291E	0279	2SB296OR	0969	2SB304X	0164	2SB315C	0004
2SB263X	0004	2SB270	0004	2SB278	0164	2SB291F	0279	2SB296R	0969	2SB304Y	0164	2SB315D	0004
2SB263Y	0004	2SB270A	0004	2SB279	0164	2SB291G	0279	2SB296X	0969	2SB309	0969	2SB315E	0004
2SB264	0004	2SB270B	0004	2SB280	0004	2SB291GN	0279	2SB296Y	0969	2SB309A	0969	2SB315F	0004
2SB264A	0004	2SB270C	0004	2SB281	0527	2SB291H	0279	2SB299	0004	2SB309B	0969	2SB315G	0004
2SB264B	0004	2SB270D	0004	2SB281C	0527	2SB291J	0279	2SB299A	0004	2SB309C	0969	2SB315GN	0004
2SB264C	0004	2SB270E	0004	2SB282	0599	2SB291K	0279	2SB299B	0004	2SB309D	0969	2SB315H	0004
2SB264D	0004	2SB270F	0004	2SB282A	0599	2SB291L	0279	2SB299C	0004	2SB309E	0969	2SB315J	0004
2SB264E	0004	2SB270G	0004	2SB282B	0599	2SB291M	0279	2SB299D	0004	2SB309F	0969	2SB315L	0004
2SB264F	0004	2SB270GN	0004	2SB282C	0599	2SB291OR	0279	2SB299E	0004	2SB309G	0969	2SB315M	0004
2SB264G	0004	2SB270H	0004	2SB282D	0599	2SB291R	0279	2SB299F	0004	2SB309GN	0969	2SB315OR	0004
2SB264GN	0004	2SB270J	0004	2SB282E	0599	2SB291X	0279	2SB299G	0004	2SB309H	0969	2SB315R	0004
2SB264H	0004	2SB270K	0004	2SB282G	0599	2SB291Y	0279	2SB299GN	0004	2SB309K	0969	2SB315X	0004
2SB264J	0004	2SB270L	0004	2SB282GN	0599	2SB292	0279	2SB299H	0004	2SB309L	0969	2SB315Y	0004
2SB264K	0004	2SB270M	0004	2SB282H	0599	2SB292-BLUE	0279	2SB299J	0004	2SB309M	0969	2SB316	0004
2SB264L	0004	2SB270OR	0004	2SB282J	0599	2SB292-GREEN	0279	2SB299K	0004	2SB309OR	0969	2SB316A	0004
2SB264M	0004	2SB270R	0004	2SB282K	0599	2SB292-ORANGE	0279	2SB299L	0004	2SB309R	0969	2SB316B	0004
2SB264OR	0004	2SB270X	0004	2SB282L	0599	2SB292-RED	0279	2SB299M	0004	2SB309X	0969	2SB316C	0004
2SB264R	0004	2SB270Y	0004	2SB282M	0599	2SB292-YELLOW	0279	2SB299OR	0004	2SB309Y	0969	2SB316D	0004
2SB264X	0004	2SB271	0004	2SB282OR	0599	2SB292A	0279	2SB299R	0004	2SB310	0969	2SB316E	0004
2SB264Y	0004	2SB272	0004	2SB282R	0599	2SB292A-BLUE	0279	2SB299X	0004	2SB310A	0969	2SB316F	0004
2SB265	0004	2SB272A	0004	2SB282X	0599	2SB292A-GREEN	0279	2SB299Y	0004	2SB310B	0969	2SB316G	0004
2SB265A	0004	2SB272B	0004	2SB282Y	0599	2SB292A-ORANG	0279	2SB300	0969	2SB310C	0969	2SB316GN	0004
2SB265B	0004	2SB272C	0004	2SB283	0160	2SB292A-RED	0279	2SB300A	0969	2SB310D	0969	2SB316H	0004
2SB265C	0004	2SB272D	0004	2SB283A	0160	2SB292A-YELLO	0279	2SB300B	0969	2SB310E	0969	2SB316OR	0004
2SB265D	0004	2SB272E	0004	2SB283B	0160	2SB292B	0279	2SB300C	0969	2SB310F	0969	2SB316R	0004
2SB265E	0004	2SB272F	0004	2SB283C	0160	2SB292C	0279	2SB300D	0969	2SB310G	0969	2SB316X	0004
2SB265F	0004	2SB272G	0004	2SB283D	0160	2SB292D	0279	2SB300E	0969	2SB310GN	0969	2SB316Y	0004
2SB265G	0004	2SB272GN	0004	2SB283E	0160	2SB292E	0279	2SB300F	0969	2SB310H	0969	2SB317	0004
2SB265GN	0004	2SB272J	0004	2SB283F	0160	2SB292F	0279	2SB300G	0969	2SB310J	0969	2SB318	0969
2SB265H	0004	2SB272K	0004	2SB283G	0160	2SB292G	0279	2SB300GN	0969	2SB310K	0969	2SB318A	0969
2SB265J	0004	2SB272L	0004	2SB283GN	0160	2SB292GN	0279	2SB300H	0969	2SB310L	0969	2SB318B	0969
2SB265K	0004	2SB272M	0004	2SB283H	0160	2SB292H	0279	2SB300J	0969	2SB310M	0969	2SB318C	0969
2SB265L	0004	2SB272OR	0004	2SB283J	0160	2SB292J	0279	2SB300K	0969	2SB310OR	0969	2SB318D	0969
2SB265M	0004	2SB272R	0004	2SB283K	0160	2SB292K	0279	2SB300L	0969	2SB310R	0969	2SB318E	0969
2SB265OR	0004	2SB272X	0004	2SB283L	0160	2SB292L	0279	2SB300M	0969	2SB310X	0969	2SB318F	0969
2SB265X	0004	2SB272Y	0004	2SB283M	0160	2SB292M	0279	2SB300R	0969	2SB310Y	0969	2SB318G	0969
2SB265Y	0004	2SB273	0004	2SB283OR	0160	2SB292OR	0279	2SB300X	0969	2SB311	0969	2SB318GN	0969
2SB266	0004	2SB273A	0004	2SB283R	0160	2SB292R	0279	2SB300Y	0969	2SB311A	0969	2SB318H	0969
2SB266A	0004	2SB273B	0004	2SB283X	0160	2SB292X	0279	2SB301	0969	2SB311B	0969	2SB318J	0969
2SB266B	0004	2SB273C	0004	2SB283Y	0160	2SB292Y	0279	2SB301A	0969	2SB311C	0969	2SB318K	0969
2SB266C	0004	2SB273D	0004	2SB284	0160	2SB293	0004	2SB301B	0969	2SB311D	0969	2SB318L	0969
2SB266D	0004	2SB273E	0004	2SB284A	0160	2SB293A	0004	2SB301C	0969	2SB311E	0969	2SB318M	0969
2SB266E	0004	2SB273F	0004	2SB284B	0160	2SB293B	0004	2SB301D	0969	2SB311F	0969	2SB318OR	0969
2SB266F	0004	2SB273G	0004	2SB284C	0160	2SB293C	0004	2SB301E	0969	2SB311G	0969	2SB318R	0969
2SB266G	0004	2SB273GN	0004	2SB284D	0160	2SB293D	0004	2SB301F	0969	2SB311GN	0969	2SB318X	0969
2SB266GN	0004	2SB273H	0004	2SB284E	0160	2SB293E	0004	2SB301G	0969	2SB311H	0969	2SB318Y	0969
2SB266H	0004	2SB273J	0004	2SB284F	0160	2SB293F	0004	2SB301GN	0969	2SB311J	0969	2SB319	0969
2SB266J	0004	2SB273K	0004	2SB284G	0160	2SB293G	0004	2SB301H	0969	2SB311K	0969	2SB319A	0969
2SB266K	0004	2SB273L	0004	2SB284H	0160	2SB293GN	0004	2SB301J	0969	2SB311L	0969	2SB319B	0969
2SB266L	0004	2SB273M	0004	2SB284J	0160	2SB293H	0004	2SB301L	0969	2SB311M	0969	2SB319C	0969
2SB266M	0004	2SB273OR	0004	2SB284K	0160	2SB293J	0004	2SB301M	0969	2SB311OR	0969	2SB319D	0969
2SB266OR	0004	2SB273R	0004	2SB284L	0160	2SB293K	0004	2SB301OR	0969	2SB311R	0969	2SB319E	0969

If replacement code is OEM, contact original manufacturer for replacement.

DEVICE TYPE	REPL CODE
2SB319F	0969
2SB319G	0969
2SB319GN	0969
2SB319H	0969
2SB319J	0969
2SB319K	0969
2SB319L	0969
2SB319M	0969
2SB319OR	0969
2SB319R	0969
2SB319X	0969
2SB319Y	0969
2SB320	0969
2SB320A	0969
2SB320B	0969
2SB320C	0969
2SB320D	0969
2SB320E	0969
2SB320F	0969
2SB320G	0969
2SB320GN	0969
2SB320H	0969
2SB320J	0969
2SB320K	0969
2SB320L	0969
2SB320M	0969
2SB320OR	0969
2SB320R	0969
2SB320X	0969
2SB320Y	0969
2SB321	0004
2SB322	0004
2SB323	0004
2SB324	1056
2SB324(E)	1056
2SB324(F)	1056
2SB324(I)	1056
2SB324(K)	1056
2SB324(L)	1056
2SB324(N)	1056
2SB324(V)	1056
2SB324-OR	1056
2SB324,K	1056
2SB324A	1056
2SB324B	1056
2SB324C	1056
2SB324D	1056
2SB324E	1056
2SB324E-1	1056
2SB324E-L	1056
2SB324F	1056
2SB324G	1056
2SB324GN	1056
2SB324H	1056
2SB324I	1056
2SB324J	1056
2SB324K	1056
2SB324L	1056
2SB324M	1056
2SB324N	1056
2SB324OR	1056
2SB324P	1056
2SB324R	1056
2SB324S	1056
2SB324V	1056
2SB324X	1056
2SB324Y	1056
2SB326	0004
2SB326A	0004
2SB326B	0004
2SB326C	0004
2SB326D	0004
2SB326E	0004
2SB326F	0004
2SB326G	0004
2SB326GN	0004
2SB326H	0004
2SB326J	0004
2SB326K	0004
2SB326L	0004
2SB326M	0004
2SB326OR	0004
2SB326R	0004
2SB326X	0004
2SB326Y	0004
2SB327	0004
2SB327A	0004
2SB327B	0004
2SB327C	0004
2SB327D	0004
2SB327E	0004
2SB327F	0004
2SB327G	0004
2SB327GN	0004
2SB327H	0004
2SB327J	0004
2SB327K	0004
2SB327L	0004
2SB327M	0004
2SB327OR	0004
2SB327R	0004
2SB327X	0004
2SB327Y	0004
2SB328	0211
2SB328A	0211
2SB328B	0211
2SB328C	0211
2SB328D	0211
2SB328E	0211

DEVICE TYPE	REPL CODE
2SB328F	0211
2SB328G	0211
2SB328GN	0211
2SB328H	0211
2SB328J	0211
2SB328K	0211
2SB328L	0211
2SB328M	0211
2SB328OR	0211
2SB328R	0211
2SB328X	0211
2SB328Y	0211
2SB329	0004
2SB329A	0004
2SB329B	0004
2SB329C	0004
2SB329D	0004
2SB329E	0004
2SB329F	0004
2SB329G	0004
2SB329GN	0004
2SB329H	0004
2SB329J	0004
2SB329K	0004
2SB329L	0004
2SB329M	0004
2SB329OR	0004
2SB329R	0004
2SB329X	0004
2SB329Y	0004
2SB331	0040
2SB331A	0040
2SB331B	0040
2SB331C	0040
2SB331D	0040
2SB331E	0040
2SB331F	0040
2SB331G	0040
2SB331GN	0040
2SB331H	0040
2SB331J	0040
2SB331K	0040
2SB331L	0040
2SB331M	0040
2SB331OR	0040
2SB331R	0040
2SB331X	0040
2SB331Y	0040
2SB332	0040
2SB332A	0040
2SB332B	0040
2SB332C	0040
2SB332D	0040
2SB332E	0040
2SB332F	0040
2SB332G	0040
2SB332GN	0040
2SB332H	0040
2SB332J	0040
2SB332K	0040
2SB332L	0040
2SB332M	0040
2SB332OR	0040
2SB332R	0040
2SB332X	0040
2SB332Y	0040
2SB333	0040
2SB333A	0040
2SB333B	0040
2SB333D	0040
2SB333E	0040
2SB333F	0040
2SB333G	0040
2SB333GN	0040
2SB333H	0040
2SB333HA	0040
2SB333HB	0040
2SB333J	0040
2SB333K	0040
2SB333L	0040
2SB333M	0040
2SB333OR	0040
2SB333R	0040
2SB333X	0040
2SB333Y	0040
2SB334	0435
2SB334-OR	0435
2SB334A	0435
2SB334B	0435
2SB334C	0435
2SB334D	0435
2SB334E	0435
2SB334F	0435
2SB334G	0435
2SB334GN	0435
2SB334H	0435
2SB334J	0435
2SB334K	0435
2SB334L	0435
2SB334M	0435
2SB334OR	0435
2SB334R	0435
2SB334X	0435
2SB334Y	0435
2SB335	0211
2SB336	0004
2SB337	0160
2SB337(A)	0160
2SB337(B)	0160

DEVICE TYPE	REPL CODE
2SB337(C)	0160
2SB337-B	0160
2SB337-OR	0160
2SB337A	0160
2SB337B	0160
2SB337BK	0160
2SB337C	0160
2SB337D	0160
2SB337E	0160
2SB337F	0160
2SB337G	0160
2SB337GN	0160
2SB337H	0160
2SB337J	0160
2SB337K	0160
2SB337L	0160
2SB337LB	0160
2SB337M	0160
2SB337OR	0160
2SB337R	0160
2SB337X	0160
2SB337Y	0160
2SB338	0160
2SB338A	0160
2SB338B	0160
2SB338C	0160
2SB338D	0160
2SB338E	0160
2SB338F	0160
2SB338G	0160
2SB338GN	0160
2SB338H	0160
2SB338HA	0160
2SB338HB	0160
2SB338J	0160
2SB338K	0160
2SB338L	0160
2SB338M	0160
2SB338OR	0160
2SB338R	0160
2SB338X	0160
2SB338Y	0160
2SB339	0599
2SB339H	0599
2SB340	0599
2SB340H	0599
2SB341	0969
2SB341(V)	0969
2SB341A	0969
2SB341B	0969
2SB341C	0969
2SB341D	0969
2SB341E	0969
2SB341F	0969
2SB341G	0969
2SB341GN	0969
2SB341H	0969
2SB341J	0969
2SB341K	0969
2SB341L	0969
2SB341M	0969
2SB341OR	0969
2SB341R	0969
2SB341S	0969
2SB341V	0969
2SB341V(S)	0969
2SB341X	0969
2SB341Y	0969
2SB342	0969
2SB342A	0969
2SB342B	0969
2SB342C	0969
2SB342D	0969
2SB342E	0969
2SB342F	0969
2SB342G	0969
2SB342GN	0969
2SB342H	0969
2SB342J	0969
2SB342K	0969
2SB342L	0969
2SB342M	0969
2SB342OR	0969
2SB342R	0969
2SB342X	0969
2SB342Y	0969
2SB343	0969
2SB343A	0969
2SB343B	0969
2SB343C	0969
2SB343D	0969
2SB343E	0969
2SB343F	0969
2SB343G	0969
2SB343GN	0969
2SB343H	0969
2SB343J	0969
2SB343K	0969
2SB343L	0969
2SB343M	0969
2SB343OR	0969
2SB343R	0969
2SB343X	0969
2SB343Y	0969
2SB345	0004
2SB345A	0004
2SB345B	0004
2SB345C	0004
2SB345D	0004

DEVICE TYPE	REPL CODE
2SB345E	0004
2SB345F	0004
2SB345G	0004
2SB345GN	0004
2SB345H	0004
2SB345J	0004
2SB345K	0004
2SB345L	0004
2SB345M	0004
2SB345OR	0004
2SB345R	0004
2SB345X	0004
2SB345Y	0004
2SB346	0004
2SB346(Q)	0004
2SB346A	0004
2SB346B	0004
2SB346C	0004
2SB346D	0004
2SB346E	0004
2SB346F	0004
2SB346G	0004
2SB346GN	0004
2SB346H	0004
2SB346J	0004
2SB346K	0004
2SB346L	0004
2SB346M	0004
2SB346OR	0004
2SB346Q	0004
2SB346R	0004
2SB346X	0004
2SB346Y	0004
2SB347	0004
2SB347A	0004
2SB347B	0004
2SB347C	0004
2SB347D	0004
2SB347E	0004
2SB347F	0004
2SB347G	0004
2SB347GN	0004
2SB347H	0004
2SB347J	0004
2SB347K	0004
2SB347L	0004
2SB347M	0004
2SB347OR	0004
2SB347R	0004
2SB347X	0004
2SB347Y	0004
2SB348	0004
2SB348(Q)	0004
2SB348A	0004
2SB348B	0004
2SB348C	0004
2SB348D	0004
2SB348E	0004
2SB348F	0004
2SB348G	0004
2SB348GN	0004
2SB348H	0004
2SB348J	0004
2SB348K	0004
2SB348L	0004
2SB348M	0004
2SB348OR	0004
2SB348Q	0004
2SB348R	0004
2SB348X	0004
2SB348Y	0004
2SB349	0004
2SB350	0211
2SB350A	0211
2SB350B	0211
2SB350C	0211
2SB350D	0211
2SB350E	0211
2SB350F	0211
2SB350G	0211
2SB350GN	0211
2SB350H	0211
2SB350J	0211
2SB350K	0211
2SB350L	0211
2SB350M	0211
2SB350OR	0211
2SB350R	0211
2SB350X	0211
2SB350Y	0211
2SB351	0435
2SB351A	0435
2SB351B	0435
2SB351C	0435
2SB351D	0435
2SB351E	0435
2SB351F	0435
2SB351G	0435
2SB351GN	0435
2SB351H	0435
2SB351J	0435
2SB351K	0435
2SB351L	0435
2SB351M	0435
2SB351OR	0435
2SB351R	0435
2SB351X	0435
2SB351Y	0435
2SB352	0040

DEVICE TYPE	REPL CODE
2SB352A	0040
2SB352B	0040
2SB352C	0040
2SB352D	0040
2SB352E	0040
2SB352F	0040
2SB352G	0040
2SB352GN	0040
2SB352H	0040
2SB352J	0040
2SB352K	0040
2SB352L	0040
2SB352M	0040
2SB352OR	0040
2SB352R	0040
2SB352X	0040
2SB352Y	0040
2SB353	0040
2SB353A	0040
2SB353B	0040
2SB353C	0040
2SB353D	0040
2SB353E	0040
2SB353F	0040
2SB353G	0040
2SB353GN	0040
2SB353H	0040
2SB353J	0040
2SB353K	0040
2SB353L	0040
2SB353M	0040
2SB353OR	0040
2SB353R	0040
2SB353X	0040
2SB353Y	0040
2SB354	0432
2SB354A	0432
2SB354B	0432
2SB354C	0432
2SB354D	0432
2SB354E	0432
2SB354F	0432
2SB354G	0432
2SB354GN	0432
2SB354H	0432
2SB354J	0432
2SB354K	0432
2SB354L	0432
2SB354M	0432
2SB354OR	0432
2SB354R	0432
2SB354X	0432
2SB354Y	0432
2SB355	0085
2SB355A	0085
2SB355B	0085
2SB355C	0085
2SB355D	0085
2SB355E	0085
2SB355F	0085
2SB355G	0085
2SB355GN	0085
2SB355H	0085
2SB355J	0085
2SB355K	0085
2SB355L	0085
2SB355M	0085
2SB355OR	0085
2SB355R	0085
2SB355X	0085
2SB355Y	0085
2SB356	0085
2SB356A	0085
2SB356B	0085
2SB356C	0085
2SB356D	0085
2SB356E	0085
2SB356F	0085
2SB356G	0085
2SB356GN	0085
2SB356H	0085
2SB356J	0085
2SB356K	0085
2SB356L	0085
2SB356M	0085
2SB356OR	0085
2SB356R	0085
2SB356X	0085
2SB356Y	0085
2SB357	0969
2SB357A	0969
2SB357B	0969
2SB357C	0969
2SB357D	0969
2SB357E	0969
2SB357F	0969
2SB357G	0969
2SB357GN	0969
2SB357H	0969
2SB357J	0969
2SB357K	0969
2SB357L	0969
2SB357M	0969
2SB357OR	0969
2SB357R	0969
2SB357X	0969
2SB357Y	0969
2SB358	0969
2SB358A	0969

DEVICE TYPE	REPL CODE
2SB358B	0969
2SB358C	0969
2SB358D	0969
2SB358E	0969
2SB358F	0969
2SB358G	0969
2SB358GN	0969
2SB358H	0969
2SB358J	0969
2SB358K	0969
2SB358L	0969
2SB358M	0969
2SB358OR	0969
2SB358R	0969
2SB358X	0969
2SB358Y	0969
2SB359	0969
2SB359A	0969
2SB359B	0969
2SB359C	0969
2SB359D	0969
2SB359E	0969
2SB359F	0969
2SB359G	0969
2SB359GN	0969
2SB359H	0969
2SB359J	0969
2SB359K	0969
2SB359L	0969
2SB359M	0969
2SB359OR	0969
2SB359R	0969
2SB359X	0969
2SB359Y	0969
2SB360	0969
2SB360A	0969
2SB360B	0969
2SB360C	0969
2SB360D	0969
2SB360E	0969
2SB360F	0969
2SB360G	0969
2SB360GN	0969
2SB360H	0969
2SB360J	0969
2SB360K	0969
2SB360L	0969
2SB360M	0969
2SB360OR	0969
2SB360R	0969
2SB360X	0969
2SB360Y	0969
2SB361	0969
2SB361A	0969
2SB361B	0969
2SB361C	0969
2SB361D	0969
2SB361E	0969
2SB361F	0969
2SB361G	0969
2SB361GN	0969
2SB361H	0969
2SB361J	0969
2SB361K	0969
2SB361L	0969
2SB361M	0969
2SB361OR	0969
2SB361R	0969
2SB361X	0969
2SB361Y	0969
2SB362	0969
2SB362A	0969
2SB362B	0969
2SB362C	0969
2SB362D	0969
2SB362E	0969
2SB362F	0969
2SB362G	0969
2SB362GN	0969
2SB362H	0969
2SB362J	0969
2SB362K	0969
2SB362L	0969
2SB362M	0969
2SB362OR	0969
2SB362R	0969
2SB362X	0969
2SB362Y	0969
2SB363	0848
2SB364	0164
2SB364/8023	0164
2SB364/80236400	0164
2SB364-OR	0164
2SB364A	0164
2SB364B	0164
2SB364C	0164
2SB364D	0164
2SB364E	0164
2SB364F	0164
2SB364G	0164
2SB364GN	0164
2SB364H	0164
2SB364J	0164
2SB364K	0164
2SB364L	0164
2SB364M	0164
2SB364OR	0164
2SB364R	0164
2SB364X	0164

DEVICE TYPE	REPL CODE
2SB364Y	0164
2SB365	0164
2SB365A	0164
2SB365B	0164
2SB365C	0164
2SB365D	0164
2SB365E	0164
2SB365F	0164
2SB365G	0164
2SB365GN	0164
2SB365H	0164
2SB365J	0164
2SB365K	0164
2SB365L	0164
2SB365M	0164
2SB365OR	0164
2SB365R	0164
2SB365X	0164
2SB365Y	0164
2SB366	0969
2SB366A	0969
2SB366B	0969
2SB366C	0969
2SB366D	0969
2SB366E	0969
2SB366F	0969
2SB366G	0969
2SB366GN	0969
2SB366H	0969
2SB366J	0969
2SB366K	0969
2SB366L	0969
2SB366M	0969
2SB366OR	0969
2SB366R	0969
2SB366X	0969
2SB366Y	0969
2SB367	0222
2SB367(B)	0222
2SB367(B)P	0222
2SB367-4	0222
2SB367-5	0222
2SB367-OR	0222
2SB367A	0222
2SB367AL	0222
2SB367B	0222
2SB367B-2	0222
2SB367BL	0222
2SB367BP	0222
2SB367C	0222
2SB367D	0222
2SB367E	0222
2SB367F	0222
2SB367G	0222
2SB367H	0222
2SB367J	0222
2SB367K	0222
2SB367L	0222
2SB367M	0222
2SB367OR	0222
2SB367P	0222
2SB367R	0222
2SB367X	0222
2SB367Y	0222
2SB368	0222
2SB368(B)	0222
2SB368-OR	0222
2SB368A	0222
2SB368B	0222
2SB368C	0222
2SB368D	0222
2SB368E	0222
2SB368F	0222
2SB368G	0222
2SB368GN	0222
2SB368H	0222
2SB368J	0222
2SB368K	0222
2SB368L	0222
2SB368M	0222
2SB368OR	0222
2SB368X	0222
2SB368Y	0222
2SB370	0004
2SB370(A)	0004
2SB370(B)	0004
2SB370/123	0004
2SB370/123877	0004
2SB370-O	0004
2SB370A	0004
2SB370AA	0004
2SB370AB	0004
2SB370AC	0004
2SB370AH	0004
2SB370AHA	0004
2SB370AHB	0004
2SB370B	0004
2SB370C	0004
2SB370D	0004
2SB370E	0004
2SB370F	0004
2SB370G	0004
2SB370GN	0004
2SB370H	0004
2SB370J	0004
2SB370K	0004
2SB370L	0004
2SB370M	0004
2SB370OR	0004

If replacement code is OEM, contact original manufacturer for replacement.

DEVICE TYPE	REPL CODE
2SB370P	0004
2SB370R	0004
2SB370V	0004
2SB370X	0004
2SB370Y	0004
2SB371	0004
2SB371A	0004
2SB371B	0004
2SB371C	0004
2SB371D	0004
2SB371E	0004
2SB371F	0004
2SB371G	0004
2SB371GN	0004
2SB371H	0004
2SB371J	0004
2SB371K	0004
2SB371L	0004
2SB371M	0004
2SB371OR	0004
2SB371R	0004
2SB371X	0004
2SB371Y	0004
2SB372	0841
2SB373	0841
2SB373A	0841
2SB373B	0841
2SB373C	0841
2SB373D	0841
2SB373E	0841
2SB373F	0841
2SB373G	0841
2SB373GN	0841
2SB373H	0841
2SB373K	0841
2SB373L	0841
2SB373M	0841
2SB373OR	0841
2SB373R	0841
2SB373X	0841
2SB373Y	0841
2SB374	0164
2SB375	1665
2SB375-2B	1665
2SB375-5B	1665
2SB375-OR	1665
2SB375A	1665
2SB375A-2B	1665
2SB375A-5B	1665
2SB375AL	1665
2SB375A-NB	1665
2SB375ATV	1665
2SB375B	1665
2SB375C	1665
2SB375D	1665
2SB375E	1665
2SB375F	1665
2SB375G	1665
2SB375GN	1665
2SB375H	1665
2SB375J	1665
2SB375K	1665
2SB375L	1665
2SB375M	1665
2SB375OR	1665
2SB375R	1665
2SB375X	1665
2SB375Y	1665
2SB376	0004
2SB376A	0004
2SB376B	0004
2SB376C	0004
2SB376D	0004
2SB376E	0004
2SB376F	0004
2SB376G	0004
2SB376GN	0004
2SB376J	0004
2SB376K	0004
2SB376L	0004
2SB376M	0004
2SB376OR	0004
2SB376R	0004
2SB376X	0004
2SB376Y	0004
2SB377	0211
2SB377B	0211
2SB378	0004
2SB378A	0004
2SB378B	0004
2SB378C	0004
2SB378D	0004
2SB378E	0004
2SB378F	0004
2SB378GN	0004
2SB378J	0004
2SB378K	0004
2SB378L	0004
2SB378M	0004
2SB378OR	0004
2SB378R	0004
2SB378X	0004
2SB378Y	0004
2SB379	0211
2SB379-2	0211
2SB379A	0211
2SB379B	0211
2SB379C	0211
2SB379D	0211
2SB379E	0211
2SB379F	0211
2SB379G	0211
2SB379GN	0211
2SB379H	0211
2SB379J	0211
2SB379K	0211
2SB379L	0211
2SB379M	0211
2SB379OR	0211
2SB379R	0211
2SB379Y	0211
2SB380	0211
2SB380A	0211
2SB380B	0211
2SB380C	0211
2SB380D	0211
2SB380E	0211
2SB380F	0211
2SB380GN	0211
2SB380J	0211
2SB380K	0211
2SB380L	0211
2SB380OR	0211
2SB380R	0211
2SB380X	0211
2SB380Y	0211
2SB381	0004
2SB381A	0004
2SB381B	0004
2SB381C	0004
2SB381D	0004
2SB381E	0004
2SB381F	0004
2SB381G	0004
2SB381GN	0004
2SB381H	0004
2SB381J	0004
2SB381K	0004
2SB381L	0004
2SB381M	0004
2SB381OR	0004
2SB381R	0004
2SB381X	0004
2SB381Y	0004
2SB382	0004
2SB382A	0004
2SB382B	0004
2SB382BK	0004
2SB382BN	0004
2SB382C	0004
2SB382D	0004
2SB382E	0004
2SB382F	0004
2SB382G	0004
2SB382GN	0004
2SB382H	0004
2SB382J	0004
2SB382K	0004
2SB382L	0004
2SB382OR	0004
2SB382R	0004
2SB382X	0004
2SB382Y	0004
2SB383	0004
2SB383(2SB382)	0004
2SB383(2SB495)	0004
2SB383-1	0004
2SB383-2	0004
2SB383A	0004
2SB383B	0004
2SB383C	0004
2SB383D	0004
2SB383E	0004
2SB383F	0004
2SB383G	0004
2SB383GN	0004
2SB383H	0004
2SB383J	0004
2SB383K	0004
2SB383L	0004
2SB383M	0004
2SB383OR	0004
2SB383R	0004
2SB383X	0004
2SB383Y	0004
2SB384	0004
2SB384A	0004
2SB384B	0004
2SB384C	0004
2SB384D	0004
2SB384E	0004
2SB384F	0004
2SB384G	0004
2SB384GN	0004
2SB384H	0004
2SB384J	0004
2SB384K	0004
2SB384L	0004
2SB384M	0004
2SB384OR	0004
2SB384R	0004
2SB384X	0004
2SB384Y	0004
2SB385	0004
2SB385A	0004
2SB385B	0004
2SB385C	0004
2SB385D	0004
2SB385E	0004
2SB385F	0004
2SB385G	0004
2SB385GN	0004
2SB385H	0004
2SB385J	0004
2SB385K	0004
2SB385L	0004
2SB385M	0004
2SB385OR	0004
2SB385R	0004
2SB385X	0004
2SB385Y	0004
2SB386	0004
2SB386A	0004
2SB386B	0004
2SB386C	0004
2SB386D	0004
2SB386E	0004
2SB386F	0004
2SB386G	0004
2SB386GN	0004
2SB386H	0004
2SB386K	0004
2SB386L	0004
2SB386M	0004
2SB386OR	0004
2SB386R	0004
2SB386X	0004
2SB386Y	0004
2SB387	0004
2SB387A	0004
2SB387B	0004
2SB387D	0004
2SB387E	0004
2SB387F	0004
2SB387G	0004
2SB387GN	0004
2SB387H	0004
2SB387J	0004
2SB387K	0004
2SB387L	0004
2SB387M	0004
2SB387OR	0004
2SB387R	0004
2SB387X	0004
2SB387Y	0004
2SB389	0004
2SB389-O	0004
2SB389A	0004
2SB389B	0004
2SB389BK	0004
2SB389C	0004
2SB389D	0004
2SB389E	0004
2SB389F	0004
2SB389G	0004
2SB389GN	0004
2SB389H	0004
2SB389J	0004
2SB389K	0004
2SB389L	0004
2SB389M	0004
2SB389OR	0004
2SB389R	0004
2SB389X	0004
2SB389Y	0004
2SB390	0969
2SB390A	0969
2SB390B	0969
2SB390C	0969
2SB390D	0969
2SB390E	0969
2SB390F	0969
2SB390G	0969
2SB390GN	0969
2SB390H	0969
2SB390J	0969
2SB390K	0969
2SB390L	0969
2SB390M	0969
2SB390OR	0969
2SB390R	0969
2SB390X	0969
2SB390Y	0969
2SB391	0160
2SB391A	0160
2SB391B	0160
2SB391C	0160
2SB391D	0160
2SB391E	0160
2SB391F	0160
2SB391G	0160
2SB391GN	0160
2SB391H	0160
2SB391J	0160
2SB391K	0160
2SB391L	0160
2SB391M	0160
2SB391OR	0160
2SB391R	0160
2SB391X	0160
2SB391Y	0160
2SB392	0279
2SB392A	0279
2SB392B	0279
2SB392C	0279
2SB392D	0279
2SB392E	0279
2SB392F	0279
2SB392G	0279
2SB392GN	0279
2SB392H	0279
2SB392J	0279
2SB392K	0279
2SB392L	0279
2SB392M	0279
2SB392OR	0279
2SB392R	0279
2SB392X	0279
2SB392Y	0279
2SB393	0279
2SB393A	0279
2SB393B	0279
2SB393C	0279
2SB393D	0279
2SB393E	0279
2SB393F	0279
2SB393G	0279
2SB393GN	0279
2SB393H	0279
2SB393J	0279
2SB393K	0279
2SB393L	0279
2SB393M	0279
2SB393OR	0279
2SB393R	0279
2SB393X	0279
2SB393Y	0279
2SB394	0279
2SB394A	0279
2SB394B	0279
2SB394C	0279
2SB394D	0279
2SB394E	0279
2SB394F	0279
2SB394G	0279
2SB394GN	0279
2SB394H	0279
2SB394J	0279
2SB394K	0279
2SB394L	0279
2SB394M	0279
2SB394OR	0279
2SB394R	0279
2SB394X	0279
2SB394Y	0279
2SB395	0279
2SB395A	0279
2SB395B	0279
2SB395C	0279
2SB395D	0279
2SB395E	0279
2SB395F	0279
2SB395G	0279
2SB395GN	0279
2SB395H	0279
2SB395J	0279
2SB395K	0279
2SB395M	0279
2SB395OR	0279
2SB395R	0279
2SB395X	0279
2SB395Y	0279
2SB396	0211
2SB396A	0211
2SB396B	0211
2SB396C	0211
2SB396D	0211
2SB396E	0211
2SB396F	0211
2SB396G	0211
2SB396GN	0211
2SB396H	0211
2SB396J	0211
2SB396K	0211
2SB396L	0211
2SB396M	0211
2SB396OR	0211
2SB396R	0211
2SB396X	0211
2SB396Y	0211
2SB397	0050
2SB398	0164
2SB400	0004
2SB400(RECT)	0468
2SB400A	0004
2SB400B	0004
2SB400BK	0004
2SB400C	0004
2SB400D	0004
2SB400E	0004
2SB400F	0004
2SB400G	0004
2SB400GN	0004
2SB400H	0004
2SB400J	0004
2SB400K	0004
2SB400L	0004
2SB400M	0004
2SB400OR	0004
2SB400R	0004
2SB400X	0004
2SB400Y	0004
2SB401	0279
2SB401A	0279
2SB401B	0279
2SB401C	0279
2SB401D	0279
2SB401E	0279
2SB401F	0279
2SB401G	0279
2SB401GN	0279
2SB401H	0279
2SB401K	0279
2SB401L	0279
2SB401M	0279
2SB401OR	0279
2SB401R	0279
2SB401X	0279
2SB401Y	0279
2SB402	0279
2SB402A	0279
2SB402B	0279
2SB402C	0279
2SB402D	0279
2SB402E	0279
2SB402F	0279
2SB402G	0279
2SB402GN	0279
2SB402H	0279
2SB402J	0279
2SB402K	0279
2SB402L	0279
2SB402M	0279
2SB402OR	0279
2SB402R	0279
2SB402X	0279
2SB402Y	0279
2SB403	0279
2SB403A	0279
2SB403B	0279
2SB403C	0279
2SB403D	0279
2SB403E	0279
2SB403F	0279
2SB403G	0279
2SB403GN	0279
2SB403H	0279
2SB403J	0279
2SB403K	0279
2SB403L	0279
2SB403M	0279
2SB403OR	0279
2SB403R	0279
2SB403X	0279
2SB403Y	0279
2SB405	0164
2SB405(K)	0164
2SB405-0	0164
2SB405-1	0164
2SB405-2C	0164
2SB405-3C	0164
2SB405-4C	0164
2SB405-O	0164
2SB405-OR	0164
2SB405-R	0164
2SB405A	0164
2SB405AG	0164
2SB405B	0164
2SB405C	0164
2SB405D	0164
2SB405DK	0164
2SB405E	0164
2SB405EK	0164
2SB405F	0164
2SB405G	0164
2SB405GN	0164
2SB405H	0164
2SB405J	0164
2SB405K	0164
2SB405L	0164
2SB405M	0164
2SB405OR	0164
2SB405R	0164
2SB405RE	0164
2SB405X	0164
2SB405Y	0164
2SB406	0969
2SB407	0160
2SB407-0	0160
2SB407-O	0160
2SB407-OR	0160
2SB407A	0160
2SB407B	0160
2SB407BK	0160
2SB407C	0160
2SB407D	0160
2SB407E	0160
2SB407F	0160
2SB407G	0160
2SB407GN	0160
2SB407H	0160
2SB407J	0160
2SB407K	0160
2SB407M	0160
2SB407OR	0160
2SB407R	0160
2SB407TV	0160
2SB407TV-2	0160
2SB407X	0160
2SB407Y	0160
2SB408	0004
2SB408A	0004
2SB408B	0004
2SB408C	0004
2SB408D	0004
2SB408E	0004
2SB408F	0004
2SB408G	0004
2SB408GN	0004
2SB408H	0004
2SB408J	0004
2SB408K	0004
2SB408L	0004
2SB408M	0004
2SB408OR	0004
2SB408R	0004
2SB408X	0004
2SB408Y	0004
2SB409	0279
2SB410	0969
2SB411	0969
2SB411TV	0969
2SB412	0969
2SB413	0222
2SB413A	0222
2SB413B	0222
2SB413C	0222
2SB413D	0222
2SB413E	0222
2SB413F	0222
2SB413G	0222
2SB413GN	0222
2SB413H	0222
2SB413J	0222
2SB413K	0222
2SB413L	0222
2SB413M	0222
2SB413OR	0222
2SB413R	0222
2SB413X	0222
2SB413Y	0222
2SB414	1004
2SB414B	1004
2SB414C	1004
2SB414D	1004
2SB414E	1004
2SB414F	1004
2SB414G	1004
2SB414GN	1004
2SB414H	1004
2SB414J	1004
2SB414K	1004
2SB414L	1004
2SB414M	1004
2SB414OR	1004
2SB414R	1004
2SB414X	1004
2SB414Y	1004
2SB415	0164
2SB415(1)	0164
2SB415-OR	0164
2SB415A	0164
2SB415B	0164
2SB415C	0164
2SB415D	0164
2SB415E	0164
2SB415F	0164
2SB415G	0164
2SB415GN	0164
2SB415H	0164
2SB415J	0164
2SB415K	0164
2SB415L	0164
2SB415M	0164
2SB415OR	0164
2SB415R	0164
2SB415X	0164
2SB415Y	0164
2SB416	0279
2SB416A	0279
2SB416B	0279
2SB416C	0279
2SB416D	0279
2SB416E	0279
2SB416F	0279
2SB416G	0279
2SB416GN	0279
2SB416H	0279
2SB416J	0279
2SB416K	0279
2SB416L	0279
2SB416M	0279
2SB416OR	0279
2SB416R	0279
2SB416X	0279
2SB416Y	0279
2SB417	0279
2SB417A	0279
2SB417B	0279
2SB417C	0279
2SB417D	0279
2SB417E	0279
2SB417F	0279
2SB417G	0279
2SB417GN	0279
2SB417H	0279
2SB417J	0279
2SB417K	0279
2SB417L	0279
2SB417M	0279
2SB417OR	0279
2SB417R	0279
2SB417X	0279
2SB417Y	0279
2SB419	0222
2SB421	0004
2SB422	0211
2SB422A	0211
2SB422B	0211
2SB422C	0211
2SB422D	0211
2SB422E	0211
2SB422F	0211
2SB422G	0211
2SB422GN	0211
2SB422H	0211
2SB422J	0211
2SB422K	0211
2SB422L	0211
2SB422M	0211
2SB422OR	0211
2SB422R	0211
2SB422X	0211
2SB422Y	0211
2SB423	0004
2SB423A	0004
2SB423B	0004
2SB423C	0004
2SB423D	0004
2SB423E	0004
2SB423F	0004
2SB423G	0004
2SB423GN	0004
2SB423H	0004
2SB423J	0004
2SB423K	0004
2SB423L	0004
2SB423M	0004
2SB423OR	0004
2SB423R	0004
2SB423X	0004
2SB423Y	0004
2SB424	0599
2SB424A	0599
2SB424B	0599
2SB424C	0599
2SB424D	0599
2SB424E	0599
2SB424F	0599
2SB424G	0599
2SB424GN	0599
2SB424H	0599
2SB424J	0599
2SB424K	0599
2SB424L	0599
2SB424M	0599
2SB424OR	0599
2SB424R	0599
2SB424X	0599
2SB424Y	0599
2SB425	0160
2SB425-BL	0160
2SB425-R	0160
2SB425-Y	0160
2SB425A	0160
2SB425B	0160
2SB425C	0160
2SB425D	0160
2SB425E	0160
2SB425F	0160
2SB425G	0160
2SB425G-BL	0160
2SB425G-R	0160
2SB425G-Y	0160
2SB425H	0160
2SB425J	0160
2SB425K	0160
2SB425L	0160
2SB425M	0160
2SB425R	0160
2SB425X	0160
2SB425Y	0160
2SB426	0160
2SB426-BL	0160
2SB426-R	0160
2SB426-Y	0160
2SB426A	0160
2SB426B	0160
2SB426BL	0160
2SB426C	0160
2SB426D	0160
2SB426E	0160
2SB426F	0160
2SB426G	0160
2SB426G-BL	0160
2SB426GN	0160
2SB426G-R	0160
2SB426G-Y	0160
2SB426J	0160
2SB426K	0160
2SB426L	0160
2SB426M	0160
2SB426OR	0160
2SB426R	0160
2SB426X	0160
2SB426Y	0160
2SB427	0004
2SB427A	0004
2SB427B	0004
2SB427C	0004
2SB427D	0004
2SB427E	0004
2SB427F	0004
2SB427G	0004

DEVICE TYPE	REPL CODE
2SB427GN	0004
2SB427H	0004
2SB427J	0004
2SB427K	0004
2SB427L	0004
2SB427M	0004
2SB427OR	0004
2SB427R	0004
2SB427X	0004
2SB427Y	0004
2SB428	0004
2SB428A	0004
2SB428B	0004
2SB428C	0004
2SB428D	0004
2SB428E	0004
2SB428F	0004
2SB428G	0004
2SB428GN	0004
2SB428H	0004
2SB428J	0004
2SB428K	0004
2SB428L	0004
2SB428M	0004
2SB428OR	0004
2SB428R	0004
2SB428X	0004
2SB428Y	0004
2SB429	0279
2SB430	0040
2SB431	0164
2SB432	0969
2SB432A	0969
2SB432B	0969
2SB432C	0969
2SB432D	0969
2SB432E	0969
2SB432F	0969
2SB432G	0969
2SB432GN	0969
2SB432H	0969
2SB432J	0969
2SB432K	0969
2SB432L	0969
2SB432M	0969
2SB432OR	0969
2SB432R	0969
2SB432X	0969
2SB432Y	0969
2SB433	5334
2SB434	0919
2SB434(O)	0919
2SB434-O	0919
2SB434-ORG	0919
2SB434-R	0919
2SB434-RED	0919
2SB434-Y	0919
2SB434-YEL	0919
2SB434G	0919
2SB434G-O	0919
2SB434G-R	0919
2SB434G-Y	0919
2SB434R	0919
2SB435	0919
2SB435-0	0919
2SB435-O	0919
2SB435-ORG	0919
2SB435-R	0919
2SB435-RED	0919
2SB435-Y	0919
2SB435-YEL	0919
2SB435G-O	0919
2SB435G-R	0919
2SB435G-Y	0919
2SB435O	0919
2SB435R	0919
2SB435RY	0919
2SB435Y	0919
2SB436	0050
2SB437	0050
2SB438	1056
2SB439	0004
2SB439/802	0004
2SB439/120144	0004
2SB439/80243900	0004
2SB439A	0004
2SB439B	0004
2SB439C	0004
2SB439D	0004
2SB439E	0004
2SB439F	0004
2SB439G	0004
2SB439GN	0004
2SB439H	0004
2SB439J	0004
2SB439L	0004
2SB439M	0004
2SB439OR	0004
2SB439R	0004
2SB439X	0004
2SB439Y	0004
2SB440	0004
2SB440A	0004
2SB440B	0004
2SB440C	0004
2SB440E	0004
2SB440F	0004
2SB440G	0004
2SB440GN	0004
2SB440H	0004
2SB440K	0004
2SB440L	0004
2SB440M	0004
2SB440OR	0004
2SB440R	0004
2SB440X	0004
2SB440Y	0004
2SB441	0969
2SB442	0969
2SB443	0004
2SB443A	0004
2SB443B	0004
2SB443C	0004
2SB443D	0004
2SB443E	0004
2SB443F	0004
2SB443G	0004
2SB443GN	0004
2SB443H	0004
2SB443J	0004
2SB443K	0004
2SB443L	0004
2SB443M	0004
2SB443OR	0004
2SB443R	0004
2SB443X	0004
2SB443Y	0004
2SB444	0136
2SB444A	0136
2SB444B	0136
2SB444C	0136
2SB444D	0136
2SB444E	0136
2SB444F	0136
2SB444G	0136
2SB444GN	0136
2SB444H	0136
2SB444K	0136
2SB444L	0136
2SB444M	0136
2SB444OR	0136
2SB444R	0136
2SB444X	0136
2SB444Y	0136
2SB445	1004
2SB445A	1004
2SB445B	1004
2SB445C	1004
2SB445D	1004
2SB445E	1004
2SB445F	1004
2SB445G	1004
2SB445GN	1004
2SB445H	1004
2SB445J	1004
2SB445K	1004
2SB445L	1004
2SB445M	1004
2SB445OR	1004
2SB445R	1004
2SB445X	1004
2SB445Y	1004
2SB446	1004
2SB446A	1004
2SB446B	1004
2SB446C	1004
2SB446D	1004
2SB446E	1004
2SB446F	1004
2SB446G	1004
2SB446GN	1004
2SB446H	1004
2SB446J	1004
2SB446K	1004
2SB446L	1004
2SB446M	1004
2SB446OR	1004
2SB446R	1004
2SB446X	1004
2SB446Y	1004
2SB447	0969
2SB447A	0969
2SB447B	0969
2SB447C	0969
2SB447D	0969
2SB447E	0969
2SB447F	0969
2SB447G	0969
2SB447GN	0969
2SB447H	0969
2SB447J	0969
2SB447K	0969
2SB447L	0969
2SB447OR	0969
2SB447R	0969
2SB447X	0969
2SB447Y	0969
2SB448	0222
2SB448A	0222
2SB448B	0222
2SB448C	0222
2SB448D	0222
2SB448E	0222
2SB448F	0222
2SB448G	0222
2SB448GN	0222
2SB448H	0222
2SB448K	0222
2SB448L	0222
2SB448M	0222
2SB448OR	0222
2SB448R	0222
2SB448X	0222
2SB448Y	0222
2SB449	0160
2SB449(F)	0160
2SB449A	0160
2SB449B	0160
2SB449C	0160
2SB449D	0160
2SB449E	0160
2SB449F	0160
2SB449G	0160
2SB449GN	0160
2SB449H	0160
2SB449J	0160
2SB449K	0160
2SB449L	0160
2SB449M	0160
2SB449OR	0160
2SB449P	0160
2SB449PG	0160
2SB449X	0160
2SB449Y	0160
2SB450	0164
2SB450A	0164
2SB451	0164
2SB452	0164
2SB452A	0164
2SB453	0164
2SB454	0164
2SB455	0164
2SB456	0164
2SB457	0164
2SB457A	0164
2SB457A(C)	0164
2SB457AC	0164
2SB457B	0164
2SB457C	0164
2SB457D	0164
2SB457E	0164
2SB457F	0164
2SB457G	0164
2SB457GN	0164
2SB457H	0164
2SB457J	0164
2SB457K	0164
2SB457L	0164
2SB457M	0164
2SB457OR	0164
2SB457R	0164
2SB457X	0164
2SB457Y	0164
2SB458	0222
2SB458A	0222
2SB458B	0222
2SB458BC	0222
2SB458BL	0222
2SB458C	0222
2SB458D	0222
2SB458E	0222
2SB458F	0222
2SB458G	0222
2SB458GN	0222
2SB458H	0222
2SB458J	0222
2SB458K	0222
2SB458L	0222
2SB458M	0222
2SB458OR	0222
2SB458R	0222
2SB458X	0222
2SB458Y	0222
2SB459	0004
2SB459(C)	0004
2SB459-O	0004
2SB459A	0004
2SB459B	0004
2SB459C	0004
2SB459C-2	0004
2SB459D	0004
2SB459E	0004
2SB459F	0004
2SB459G	0004
2SB459GN	0004
2SB459H	0004
2SB459J	0004
2SB459K	0004
2SB459L	0004
2SB459M	0004
2SB459OR	0004
2SB459R	0004
2SB459X	0004
2SB459Y	0004
2SB460	0004
2SB460A	0004
2SB460B	0004
2SB460C	0004
2SB460D	0004
2SB460E	0004
2SB460F	0004
2SB460G	0004
2SB460GN	0004
2SB460H	0004
2SB460J	0004
2SB460K	0004
2SB460L	0004
2SB460M	0004
2SB460OR	0004
2SB460R	0004
2SB460X	0004
2SB460Y	0004
2SB461	0841
2SB461A	0841
2SB461B	0841
2SB461BL	0841
2SB461C	0841
2SB461D	0841
2SB461E	0841
2SB461F	0841
2SB461G	0841
2SB461H	0841
2SB461J	0841
2SB461K	0841
2SB461L	0841
2SB461M	0841
2SB461OR	0841
2SB461R	0841
2SB461X	0841
2SB461Y	0841
2SB462	0222
2SB462-BL	0222
2SB462-BLU	0222
2SB462-BLU-G	0222
2SB462-R	0222
2SB462-RED	0222
2SB462-RED-G	0222
2SB462-Y	0222
2SB462-YEL	0222
2SB462-YEL-G	0222
2SB462A	0222
2SB462B	0222
2SB462C	0222
2SB462D	0222
2SB462E	0222
2SB462F	0222
2SB462G	0222
2SB462G-BL	0222
2SB462GN	0222
2SB462G-R	0222
2SB462G-Y	0222
2SB462H	0222
2SB462K	0222
2SB462L	0222
2SB462M	0222
2SB462OR	0222
2SB462R	0222
2SB462X	0222
2SB462Y	0222
2SB463	0222
2SB463(1)	0222
2SB463(Y)	0222
2SB463-BL	0222
2SB463-BLU	0222
2SB463-BLU-G	0222
2SB463-O	0222
2SB463-R	0222
2SB463-RED	0222
2SB463-RED-G	0222
2SB463-Y	0222
2SB463-YEL	0222
2SB463-YEL-G	0222
2SB463A	0222
2SB463B	0222
2SB463BL	0222
2SB463BLU	0222
2SB463BLU-G	0222
2SB463C	0222
2SB463D	0222
2SB463E	0222
2SB463F	0222
2SB463G	0222
2SB463G-BL	0222
2SB463GN	0222
2SB463G-R	0222
2SB463G-Y	0222
2SB463H	0222
2SB463J	0222
2SB463K	0222
2SB463L	0222
2SB463M	0222
2SB463OR	0222
2SB463R	5845
2SB463RED	0222
2SB463RED-G	0222
2SB463X	0222
2SB463XL	0222
2SB463Y	0222
2SB463YEL	0222
2SB463YEL-G	0222
2SB464	0969
2SB464A	0969
2SB464B	0969
2SB464C	0969
2SB464D	0969
2SB464E	0969
2SB464F	0969
2SB464G	0969
2SB464GN	0969
2SB464H	0969
2SB464J	0969
2SB464K	0969
2SB464M	0969
2SB464OR	0969
2SB464X	0969
2SB464Y	0969
2SB465	0969
2SB465A	0969
2SB465B	0969
2SB465C	0969
2SB465D	0969
2SB465E	0969
2SB465F	0969
2SB465G	0969
2SB465GN	0969
2SB465H	0969
2SB465J	0969
2SB465K	0969
2SB465L	0969
2SB465M	0969
2SB465R	0969
2SB465X	0969
2SB465Y	0969
2SB466	1004
2SB466A	1004
2SB466B	1004
2SB466C	1004
2SB466D	1004
2SB466E	1004
2SB466F	1004
2SB466G	1004
2SB466GN	1004
2SB466H	1004
2SB466J	1004
2SB466K	1004
2SB466L	1004
2SB466M	1004
2SB466OR	1004
2SB466R	1004
2SB466X	1004
2SB466Y	1004
2SB467	1004
2SB467A	1004
2SB467C	1004
2SB467D	1004
2SB467E	1004
2SB467F	1004
2SB467G	1004
2SB467GN	1004
2SB467H	1004
2SB467J	1004
2SB467K	1004
2SB467L	1004
2SB467M	1004
2SB467OR	1004
2SB467X	1004
2SB467Y	1004
2SB468	0969
2SB468-OR	0969
2SB468A	0969
2SB468B	0969
2SB468B-5	0969
2SB468C	0969
2SB468D	0969
2SB468E	0969
2SB468F	0969
2SB468G	0969
2SB468GN	0969
2SB468H	0969
2SB468J	0969
2SB468K	0969
2SB468L	0969
2SB468OR	0969
2SB468X	0969
2SB468Y	0969
2SB470	0004
2SB470A	0004
2SB470B	0004
2SB470C	0004
2SB470D	0004
2SB470E	0004
2SB470F	0004
2SB470G	0004
2SB470GN	0004
2SB470H	0004
2SB470J	0004
2SB470K	0004
2SB470L	0004
2SB470M	0004
2SB470OR	0004
2SB470R	0004
2SB470X	0004
2SB470Y	0004
2SB471	0160
2SB471-2	0160
2SB471-O	0160
2SB471A	0160
2SB471B	0160
2SB471C	0160
2SB471D	0160
2SB471E	0160
2SB471F	0160
2SB471G	0160
2SB471GN	0160
2SB471H	0160
2SB471J	0160
2SB471K	0160
2SB471L	0160
2SB471M	0160
2SB471OR	0160
2SB471R	0160
2SB471X	0160
2SB471Y	0160
2SB472	0599
2SB472(B)	0599
2SB472A	0599
2SB472B	0599
2SB472C	0599
2SB472D	0599
2SB472E	0599
2SB472F	0599
2SB472G	0599
2SB472GN	0599
2SB472H	0599
2SB472J	0599
2SB472K	0599
2SB472M	0599
2SB472OR	0599
2SB472X	0599
2SB472Y	0599
2SB473	0222
2SB473(H)	0222
2SB473A	0222
2SB473B	0222
2SB473C	0222
2SB473D	0222
2SB473E	0222
2SB473F	0222
2SB473G	0222
2SB473GN	0222
2SB473H	0222
2SB473K	0222
2SB473L	0222
2SB473M	0222
2SB473X	0222
2SB473Y	0222
2SB474	1004
2SB474(C)	1004
2SB474(MP)	1851
2SB474-2	1004
2SB474-3	1004
2SB474-4	1004
2SB474-6D	1004
2SB474-OR	1004
2SB474A	1004
2SB474B	1004
2SB474C	1004
2SB474D	1004
2SB474E	1004
2SB474F	1004
2SB474G	1004
2SB474GN	1004
2SB474H	1004
2SB474J	1004
2SB474K	1004
2SB474L	1004
2SB474M	1004
2SB474MP	1004
2SB474OR	1004
2SB474R	1004
2SB474S	1004
2SB474V4	1004
2SB474V10	1004
2SB474X	1004
2SB474Y	1004
2SB474YE1	1004
2SB474YEL	1004
2SB475	0004
2SB475A	0004
2SB475B	0004
2SB475C	0004
2SB475D	0004
2SB475E	0004
2SB475F	0004
2SB475G	0004
2SB475GN	0004
2SB475H	0004
2SB475J	0004
2SB475K	0004
2SB475L	0004
2SB475M	0004
2SB475OR	0004
2SB475P	0004
2SB475PL	0004
2SB475Q	0004
2SB475R	0004
2SB475X	0004
2SB475Y	0004
2SB476	0841
2SB476S	0841
2SB476W	0841
2SB477	0435
2SB477(C)	0435
2SB477A	0435
2SB477C	0435
2SB477D	0435
2SB477E	0435
2SB477F	0435
2SB477G	0435
2SB477GN	0435
2SB477H	0435
2SB477J	0435
2SB477K	0435
2SB477L	0435
2SB477M	0435
2SB477OR	0435
2SB477R	0435
2SB477X	0435
2SB477Y	0435
2SB478	0432
2SB478BS	0432
2SB479	0432
2SB480	0432
2SB481	0222
2SB481-OR	0222
2SB481A	0222
2SB481B	0222
2SB481C	0222
2SB481D	0222
2SB481E	0222
2SB481F	0222
2SB481G	0222
2SB481GN	0222
2SB481H	0222
2SB481J	0222
2SB481K	0222
2SB481L	0222
2SB481M	0222
2SB481OR	0222
2SB481R	0222
2SB481X	0222
2SB482	0004
2SB482A	0004
2SB482B	0004
2SB482C	0004
2SB482D	0004
2SB482E	0004
2SB482F	0004
2SB482G	0004
2SB482GN	0004
2SB482H	0004
2SB482J	0004
2SB482K	0004
2SB482L	0004
2SB482M	0004
2SB482V	0004
2SB482X	0004
2SB482Y	0004
2SB483	0599
2SB484	0599
2SB485	0599
2SB486	0004
2SB486A	0004
2SB486B	0004
2SB486C	0004
2SB486D	0004
2SB486E	0004
2SB486F	0004
2SB486G	0004
2SB486GN	0004
2SB486H	0004
2SB486J	0004
2SB486K	0004
2SB486L	0004
2SB486M	0004
2SB486OR	0004
2SB486R	0004
2SB486X	0004
2SB486Y	0004
2SB491	OEM
2SB492	0841
2SB492A	0841
2SB492B	0841
2SB492C	0841
2SB492D	0841
2SB492E	0841
2SB492F	0841
2SB492G	0841
2SB492GN	0841
2SB492H	0841
2SB492J	0841
2SB492K	0841
2SB492L	0841
2SB492M	0841
2SB492OR	0841
2SB492R	0841
2SB492X	0841
2SB492Y	0841
2SB493	0164
2SB493W	0164
2SB494	0164
2SB495	0164
2SB495A	0164
2SB495B	0164
2SB495C	0164
2SB495D	0164
2SB495E	0164
2SB495F	0164
2SB495G	0164
2SB495GN	0164
2SB495H	0164
2SB495J	0164
2SB495K	0164
2SB495L	0164
2SB495M	0164
2SB495OR	0164
2SB495R	0164
2SB495T	0164
2SB495X	0164
2SB495Y	0164
2SB496	0004
2SB496A	0004
2SB496B	0004
2SB496C	0004
2SB496D	0004
2SB496E	0004
2SB496F	0004
2SB496G	0004
2SB496GN	0004
2SB496H	0004
2SB496J	0004
2SB496K	0004
2SB496L	0004

If replacement code is OEM, contact original manufacturer for replacement.

DEVICE TYPE	REPL CODE
2SB496M	0004
2SB4960R	0004
2SB496R	0004
2SB496X	0004
2SB496Y	0004
2SB497	0004
2SB497A	0004
2SB497B	0004
2SB497C	0004
2SB497D	0004
2SB497E	0004
2SB497F	0004
2SB497G	0004
2SB497GN	0004
2SB497H	0004
2SB497J	0004
2SB497K	0004
2SB497L	0004
2SB497M	0004
2SB4970R	0004
2SB497R	0004
2SB497X	0004
2SB497Y	0004
2SB498	0004
2SB498A	0004
2SB498B	0004
2SB498C	0004
2SB498D	0004
2SB498E	0004
2SB498F	0004
2SB498G	0004
2SB498GN	0004
2SB498H	0004
2SB498J	0004
2SB498K	0004
2SB498L	0004
2SB498M	0004
2SB4980R	0004
2SB498R	0004
2SB498X	0004
2SB498Y	0004
2SB502	0899
2SB502-0	0899
2SB502-R	0899
2SB502-Y	0899
2SB502A	0899
2SB502A-0	0899
2SB502A-R	0899
2SB502A-Y	0899
2SB503	0848
2SB503-0	0848
2SB503-R	0848
2SB503-Y	0848
2SB503A	0848
2SB503A-0	0848
2SB503A-R	0848
2SB503A-Y	0848
2SB504	0126
2SB504A	0126
2SB505	0676
2SB506	3459
2SB506A	3459
2SB507	0676
2SB507D	3706
2SB507E	0676
2SB508	0919
2SB509	0919
2SB510	0126
2SB510S	0126
2SB511	0919
2SB511-1	0919
2SB511C	0919
2SB511D	0919
2SB511E	0919
2SB512	0919
2SB512-0	0919
2SB512-0	0919
2SB512A	0919
2SB512P	0919
2SB513	0919
2SB513A	0919
2SB513P	0919
2SB513Q	0919
2SB513R	0919
2SB514	0919
2SB514D	3706
2SB514E	3706
2SB515	0919
2SB516	0004
2SB516(C)	0004
2SB516(D)	0004
2SB516C	0004
2SB516CD	0004
2SB516CD(P)	0004
2SB516D	0004
2SB516P	0004
2SB518	1671
2SB519	1671
2SB520	2002
2SB520-1	2002
2SB520-2	2002
2SB521	0848
2SB522	0848
2SB523	0919
2SB524	0919
2SB525	0527
2SB525C	0527
2SB525D	0527
2SB525E	0527

DEVICE TYPE	REPL CODE
2SB526	0676
2SB526C	0676
2SB527	0676
2SB528	0676
2SB528D	2407
2SB529	0919
2SB530	2002
2SB531	2002
2SB531-0	2002
2SB531-R	2002
2SB531-Y	2002
2SB532	2002
2SB533	0848
2SB533-0	0848
2SB5330	0848
2SB533Y	0848
2SB534	0004
2SB534(A)	0004
2SB535	0164
2SB535G	0164
2SB536	0676
2SB536K	0676
2SB536L	0676
2SB536M	0676
2SB537	0676
2SB537K	0676
2SB537L	0676
2SB538	0599
2SB539	1588
2SB539A	1588
2SB539B	1588
2SB539C	1588
2SB540	0164
2SB541	3459
2SB542	0006
2SB542D	0006
2SB544	0527
2SB544(E)	0527
2SB544(F)	0527
2SB544D	0527
2SB544E	0527
2SB544E-MP	0527
2SB544F	0527
2SB544P1	0527
2SB544P2	0527
2SB546	1638
2SB546A	1638
2SB546AK	1638
2SB546AL	1638
2SB546AM	1638
2SB546C	1638
2SB546E	1638
2SB546I	1638
2SB546K	1638
2SB546L	1638
2SB546M	1638
2SB547	1638
2SB547A	1638
2SB548	0520
2SB549	0520
2SB549P	0520
2SB549Q	0520
2SB549R	0520
2SB550	3459
2SB551	0899
2SB551H	0899
2SB552	1588
2SB553	0713
2SB553Y	0713
2SB554	1588
2SB554-0	1588
2SB554R	1588
2SB555	2002
2SB555-0	2002
2SB555-R	2002
2SB555R	2002
2SB556	2002
2SB556-0	2002
2SB556-R	2002
2SB557	2002
2SB557-0	2002
2SB557-R	2002
2SB558	2002
2SB558-0	2002
2SB558-R	2002
2SB559	0455
2SB560	0472
2SB560(E)	0472
2SB560(F)	0472
2SB560-0-MP	OEM
2SB560-F-MP-AE	0472
2SB560E	6712
2SB560F	6712
2SB561	0431
2SB561B	0431
2SB561C	0431
2SB562	0527
2SB562(C)	0527
2SB562-C	0527
2SB562A	3552
2SB562B	0527
2SB562BC	OEM
2SB562C	0527
2SB562D	0527
2SB563	0899
2SB564	0527
2SB564(1)K	0527
2SB564(1)L	0527
2SB564(L)	0527

DEVICE TYPE	REPL CODE
2SB564(M)	0527
2SB564A	3552
2SB564K	0527
2SB564L	0527
2SB564M	0527
2SB564Q	0527
2SB564QRS	0527
2SB564R	0527
2SB564S	0527
2SB565	0164
2SB565A	0164
2SB565B	0164
2SB565C	0164
2SB565D	0164
2SB565E	0164
2SB565F	0164
2SB565G	0164
2SB565GN	0164
2SB565H	0164
2SB565J	0164
2SB565K	0164
2SB565L	0164
2SB565M	0164
2SB5650R	0164
2SB565R	0164
2SB565X	0164
2SB565Y	0164
2SB566	0676
2SB566A	0676
2SB566AKB	0676
2SB566AKC	0676
2SB566B	0676
2SB566C	0676
2SB566D	0676
2SB566K	0676
2SB566KB	0676
2SB566KC	0676
2SB567	3500
2SB568	1900
2SB568-C	1900
2SB568B	1900
2SB568C	1900
2SB568D	1900
2SB569	0455
2SB570	0455
2SB571	0455
2SB572	1045
2SB573	1045
2SB574	1045
2SB575	0455
2SB576	0455
2SB577	0455
2SB578	1190
2SB579	1190
2SB580	1190
2SB581	1190
2SB582	1190
2SB583	1190
2SB584	3488
2SB585	2262
2SB586	2262
2SB587	2415
2SB588	2415
2SB589	2415
2SB595	1359
2SB595-0	1359
2SB595-Y	1359
2SB595Y	1359
2SB596	0848
2SB596-0	0848
2SB596-0	0848
2SB596R	0848
2SB596Y	0848
2SB598	3760
2SB598(E)	3760
2SB598(F)	3760
2SB598-F-NP-AA	3760
2SB598E	3760
2SB598F	3760
2SB598F-NP	OEM
2SB598NP	OEM
2SB599	0676
2SB600	3459
2SB600(RECT)	0441
2SB601	0597
2SB601K	0597
2SB602	OEM
2SB603	OEM
2SB604	0848
2SB605	0527
2SB605K	0527
2SB606	0338
2SB607	0164
2SB608	0431
2SB609	0676
2SB611	2002
2SB611A	2002
2SB612	1588
2SB612A	1588
2SB613	3561
2SB616	3527
2SB616A	3527
2SB617	3527
2SB617A	3527
2SB618	3527
2SB618A	3527
2SB619	0164
2SB620	0150
2SB621	0527

DEVICE TYPE	REPL CODE
2SB621A	0527
2SB621ARSTA	OEM
2SB621C	0527
2SB621N	0527
2SB621NC	0527
2SB621Q	0527
2SB621R	0527
2SB622	0434
2SB624	1741
2SB624-BV4	1741
2SB624BV1	1741
2SB624BV2	1741
2SB624BV3	1741
2SB624BV4	1741
2SB624BV5	1741
2SB625	OEM
2SB626	1671
2SB627	3267
2SB628	1638
2SB628A	1638
2SB630	5370
2SB631	0520
2SB631D	2533
2SB631E	2533
2SB631F	2533
2SB631K	0520
2SB631KE	0520
2SB631KF	2533
2SB632	0455
2SB632D	2533
2SB632E	0455
2SB632F	2533
2SB632K	0455
2SB632K(E)	0455
2SB632KE	0455
2SB632KF	2533
2SB632K-SA-E	0455
2SB633	5372
2SB633E	5372
2SB633P	5372
2SB634	3459
2SB634-Y	3459
2SB634Y	3459
2SB635	0004
2SB636	0004
2SB637	0643
2SB637KC	0643
2SB637KD	0643
2SB637KE	0643
2SB638	2415
2SB638H	2415
2SB639	2415
2SB639H	2415
2SB640	0037
2SB641	0355
2SB641(P)	0355
2SB641(Q)	0355
2SB641(R)	0355
2SB641(S)	0355
2SB641(T)	0355
2SB641-P	0355
2SB641-Q	0355
2SB641-QR	0355
2SB641-R	0355
2SB641-S	0355
2SB641B	0355
2SB641P	0355
2SB641Q	0355
2SB641QR	0355
2SB641QRS	0355
2SB641R	0355
2SB641RS	0355
2SB641S	0355
2SB641T	0355
2SB642	0819
2SB642(Q)	0819
2SB642(R)	0819
2SB642(S)	0819
2SB642(T)	0819
2SB642-0	0819
2SB642-P	0819
2SB642-PQR	0819
2SB642-Q	0819
2SB642-QR	0819
2SB642-R	0819
2SB642-S	0819
2SB642A	0819
2SB642P	0819
2SB642PQR	0819
2SB642Q	0819
2SB642QR	0819
2SB642QRS	0819
2SB642R	0819
2SB642RS	0819
2SB642RST	0819
2SB642S	0819
2SB643	0819
2SB643(Q)	0819
2SB643(R)	0819
2SB643(S)	0819
2SB643-0	0819
2SB643-P	0819
2SB643-PQR	0819
2SB643-Q	0819
2SB643-QRS	OEM
2SB643-R	0819
2SB643-S	0819
2SB643P	0819
2SB643PQR	0819

DEVICE TYPE	REPL CODE
2SB643Q	0819
2SB643QR	0819
2SB643QRS	0819
2SB643R	0819
2SB643RS	0819
2SB643S	0819
2SB644	0819
2SB644(C)	0819
2SB644(Q)	0819
2SB644(R)	0819
2SB644(S)	0819
2SB644-Q	0819
2SB644-R	0819
2SB644Q	0819
2SB644QR	0819
2SB644R	0819
2SB644S	0819
2SB645	1588
2SB645E	1588
2SB646	0472
2SB646A	0472
2SB646AB	0472
2SB646B	0472
2SB646C	0472
2SB646D	0472
2SB647	0472
2SB647A	0472
2SB647AB	0472
2SB647AC	0472
2SB647B	0472
2SB647C	0472
2SB647D	0472
2SB648	0520
2SB648A	0520
2SB648B	0520
2SB648C	0520
2SB649	0520
2SB649A	0520
2SB649AB	0520
2SB649AC	0520
2SB649AD	0520
2SB649B	0520
2SB649C	0520
2SB649D	0520
2SB650	2415
2SB650H	2415
2SB653	3459
2SB653A	3459
2SB654	3459
2SB654A	3459
2SB655	1588
2SB655A	1588
2SB656	1588
2SB656A	1588
2SB668	0597
2SB668A	0597
2SB669	0597
2SB669A	0597
2SB669Q	0597
2SB669R	0597
2SB673	0597
2SB674	0597
2SB675	0597
2SB676	0676
2SB677	0919
2SB678	OEM
2SB679	0597
2SB681	1588
2SB682	0676
2SB683	0848
2SB683C	0848
2SB683D	0848
2SB684	0527
2SB685	0073
2SB686	0853
2SB686R	OEM
2SB688	3082
2SB688-0	3082
2SB688-0(BS)	3082
2SB688R	3082
2SB689	0676
2SB690	0676
2SB691	3082
2SB692	3082
2SB693	3484
2SB693H	3484
2SB694	OEM
2SB694H	OEM
2SB695	5380
2SB696	3459
2SB696K	3459
2SB697	1588
2SB697K	1588
2SB698	0006
2SB698(F)	0006
2SB698(G)	0006
2SB698-AA	0006
2SB698-T	0006
2SB698D	3079
2SB698E	3079
2SB698F	0006
2SB698G	3079
2SB699	0919
2SB699A-B-B/C	0919
2SB699Q	0919
2SB700	3537
2SB700A	3537
2SB701	3537
2SB702	3537

DEVICE TYPE	REPL CODE
2SB702A	3537
2SB703	0676
2SB703A	0676
2SB703QRS	0676
2SB703Q	0676
2SB705	3537
2SB705A	3537
2SB705B	3537
2SB706	OEM
2SB706A	OEM
2SB707	0848
2SB708	0848
2SB709	1731
2SB709(Q)	1731
2SB709(R)	1731
2SB709(S)	1731
2SB709A	1731
2SB709AORB	1731
2SB709A-Q	1731
2SB709AQ	OEM
2SB709AQRB	1731
2SB709AQRS	1731
2SB709AQRW	1731
2SB709A-QW	1731
2SB709AQW	1731
2SB709A-RST	OEM
2SB709ATW	1731
2SB709AW	1731
2SB709QRSTW	OEM
2SB709QR-TX	1731
2SB709R(AR)	OEM
2SB709S	1731
2SB710	1741
2SB710(Q)	1741
2SB710(R)	1741
2SB710(S)	1741
2SB710A	1741
2SB710AQRS	1741
2SB710AW	1741
2SB711	0597
2SB712	0597
2SB713	5381
2SB714	0841
2SB715	0643
2SB716	0643
2SB716A	0643
2SB716AD	0643
2SB716D	0643
2SB716E	0643
2SB717	5382
2SB717B	5382
2SB717C	5382
2SB717D	5382
2SB718	5382
2SB719	1638
2SB720	0431
2SB721	0037
2SB722	1588
2SB723	1588
2SB724	0919
2SB725	0006
2SB726	1593
2SB726(R)	1593
2SB726(S)	1593
2SB726(T)	1593
2SB726Q	1593
2SB726R	1593
2SB726S	1593
2SB726T	1593
2SB727	1957
2SB727K	1957
2SB731	0520
2SB731K	OEM
2SB733	0527
2SB733K	0527
2SB7330	0527
2SB733U	0527
2SB734	0527
2SB734-34	0527
2SB734A	0527
2SB734K	0527
2SB734U	0527
2SB736	5357
2SB736A	5357
2SB737	0643
2SB738	0472
2SB738B	0472
2SB738C	0472
2SB739	0527
2SB739B	0527
2SB739C	0527
2SB740	0472
2SB740-3	0472
2SB740B	0472
2SB740C	0472
2SB741	0472
2SB741B	0472
2SB741C	0472
2SB742	0688
2SB743	0520
2SB743Q	0520
2SB744	1603
2SB744A	1603
2SB744Q	1603
2SB744R	1603
2SB744S	1603
2SB745	4076
2SB745(S)	4076
2SB745(T)	4076
2SB745A	4076

DEVICE TYPE	REPL CODE
2SB745AS	4076
2SB745S	4076
2SB745T	4076
2SB746	0148
2SB747	0848
2SB748	3537
2SB748A	3537
2SB749	3537
2SB749A	3537
2SB750	0597
2SB750A	0597
2SB750B	0597
2SB751	0597
2SB751A	0597
2SB751B	0597
2SB753	1359
2SB754	5381
2SB755	3537
2SB756K	1957
2SB757	5244
2SB758	3527
2SB758A	3527
2SB759	0643
2SB759A	0643
2SB760	0713
2SB760A	0713
2SB760B	0713
2SB761	3136
2SB761(P)	3136
2SB761(Q)	3136
2SB761A	3136
2SB761B	3136
2SB761L	3136
2SB761LB	3136
2SB761LBP	3136
2SB761LBQ	3136
2SB761P	3136
2SB761Q	3136
2SB761QLB	3136
2SB761QP	3136
2SB761R	3136
2SB762	0713
2SB762A	0713
2SB762B	0713
2SB762P	0713
2SB762Q	0713
2SB763	5381
2SB763A	5381
2SB763B	5381
2SB764	0472
2SB764(F)	0472
2SB764E	OEM
2SB764F	6712
2SB765	1957
2SB765K	1957
2SB765SK	1957
2SB766	3600
2SB766-QR	OEM
2SB766A	3600
2SB766QR	OEM
2SB767	3600
2SB768	OEM
2SB772	0455
2SB772(P)	0455
2SB772(Q)	0455
2SB772(R)	0455
2SB772-P	0455
2SB772-Q	0455
2SB772P	0455
2SB772Q	0455
2SB772QR	0455
2SB772R	0455
2SB773	3527
2SB773A	3527
2SB774	1603
2SB774(Q)	1603
2SB774(R)	1603
2SB774(RS)-T	1603
2SB774(S)	1603
2SB774Q	1603
2SB774R	1603
2SB774S	1603
2SB774T	1603
2SB775	5381
2SB775E	5380
2SB776	5381
2SB776E	5380
2SB777	3082
2SB778	5380
2SB779	1741
2SB780	0006
2SB781	0676
2SB782	0676
2SB783	0676
2SB786	2869
2SB787	0338
2SB788	0643
2SB788(S)	0643
2SB788(T)	0643
2SB788Q	0643
2SB788S	0643
2SB788T	0643
2SB788U	0643
2SB789	5274
2SB789A	5274
2SB790	0148
2SB791	1957
2SB791K	1957
2SB792	5357

If replacement code is OEM, contact original manufacturer for replacement.

DEVICE TYPE	REPL CODE
2SB792S	OEM
2SB792T	OEM
2SB793	0472
2SB793(Q)	0472
2SB793(R)	0472
2SB793(S)	0472
2SB793-QRS	0472
2SB793A	0472
2SB793Q	0472
2SB793QRS	0472
2SB793R	0472
2SB793S	0472
2SB794	2869
2SB794A	2869
2SB794K	2869
2SB794L	2869
2SB794M	2869
2SB795	2869
2SB795L	2869
2SB796	3561
2SB798	3600
2SB799	3600
2SB800	3600
2SB800(RECT)	1412
2SB801	OEM
2SB802	OEM
2SB803	OEM
2SB804	OEM
2SB804AW	OEM
2SB805	OEM
2SB806	OEM
2SB807	OEM
2SB808	0006
2SB808F	0006
2SB808F-SP	OEM
2SB808F-SPA	OEM
2SB808FT	OEM
2SB808G	6712
2SB808G1	0006
2SB810	0527
2SB810(E)	0527
2SB810(F)	0527
2SB810(H)	0527
2SB810F	0527
2SB810H	0527
2SB810HJ	0527
2SB810HJ-T	0527
2SB810HT-T	0527
2SB810J	0527
2SB811	0472
2SB812	0853
2SB812A	0853
2SB813	0676
2SB814	5357
2SB815	1741
2SB816	3082
2SB817	3082
2SB818	OEM
2SB818K	OEM
2SB819	4282
2SB819(Q)	4282
2SB819(R)	4282
2SB819AU(Q)	4282
2SB819AU(R)	4282
2SB819AUR	4282
2SB819Q	4282
2SB819QR	4282
2SB819R	4282
2SB820	OEM
2SB821	0472
2SB822	4043
2SB822(Q)	4043
2SB822(R)	4043
2SB822Q	4043
2SB823	0848
2SB824	1298
2SB824Q	1298
2SB824R	1298
2SB825	0848
2SB825R	0848
2SB825S	2558
2SB826	1298
2SB827	5381
2SB827R	6926
2SB827S	6926
2SB828	5381
2SB828Q	6926
2SB828R	6926
2SB828S	5381
2SB829	5244
2SB829R	6926
2SB829S	OEM
2SB830	0472
2SB831	1741
2SB831BB	1741
2SB831BC	1741
2SB832	OEM
2SB833	4043
2SB833(Q)	4043
2SB834	0848
2SB834(O)	0848
2SB834(Y)	0848
2SB834-O	0848
2SB834O	0848
2SB834Y	0848
2SB835	0527
2SB835(Q)	0527
2SB835(R)	0527
2SB835(S)	0527

DEVICE TYPE	REPL CODE
2SB835(T)	0527
2SB835R	3552
2SB835T	0527
2SB836	3457
2SB836L	3457
2SB837	3457
2SB837B	3457
2SB837C	3457
2SB837D	3457
2SB837LB	3457
2SB837LC	3457
2SB837LD	3457
2SB838	3457
2SB838B	3457
2SB839	3457
2SB839B	3457
2SB840	3457
2SB840B	3457
2SB840C	3457
2SB840LB	3457
2SB841	3457
2SB841C	3457
2SB841LB	3457
2SB841LC	3457
2SB842	OEM
2SB843	OEM
2SB844	3457
2SB845	3457
2SB846	3457
2SB848	0853
2SB849	5381
2SB849A	5381
2SB850	1298
2SB850A	1298
2SB851	4971
2SB851P	4971
2SB851Q	4971
2SB851R	4971
2SB852	OEM
2SB853	OEM
2SB853K	OEM
2SB854	OEM
2SB854K	OEM
2SB855	5395
2SB855A	5395
2SB855B	5395
2SB856	0713
2SB856B	0713
2SB856C	0713
2SB857	2895
2SB857-F1	OEM
2SB857B	2895
2SB857C	2895
2SB857D	2895
2SB858	2895
2SB858B	2895
2SB858C	2895
2SB858D	2895
2SB859	0676
2SB859B	0676
2SB859C	0676
2SB860	1359
2SB861	1638
2SB861-02	1638
2SB861-02-C	1638
2SB861-02C	1638
2SB861B	1638
2SB861C	1638
2SB861D	1638
2SB862	OEM
2SB863	5381
2SB864	0688
2SB865	0630
2SB867	0713
2SB868	0676
2SB869	0713
2SB870	0713
2SB871	1298
2SB871A	1298
2SB872	0597
2SB872A	0597
2SB873	OEM
2SB874	0520
2SB875	0713
2SB876	2533
2SB877	0520
2SB878	OEM
2SB879	OEM
2SB880	2222
2SB881	2222
2SB882	2222
2SB883	0073
2SB884	0597
2SB885	0597
2SB886	2222
2SB887	0073
2SB888	OEM
2SB889	0455
2SB889Q	OEM
2SB890	0006
2SB891	0455
2SB892	0472
2SB892S	0472
2SB892SZ	0472
2SB892T	0472
2SB892TZ	0472
2SB893	OEM
2SB894	2464
2SB894(Q)	2464

DEVICE TYPE	REPL CODE
2SB894(R)	2464
2SB894(S)	2464
2SB894S	2464
2SB895	2869
2SB895A	2869
2SB896	1298
2SB896A	1298
2SB897	3459
2SB898	0676
2SB899	0676
2SB900	1298
2SB901	0676
2SB902	1731
2SB902P	OEM
2SB902Q	OEM
2SB903	1190
2SB904	0558
2SB905	OEM
2SB906	OEM
2SB907	5256
2SB908	5256
2SB-909	4043
2SB909	4043
2SB909M	4043
2SB909MQ	OEM
2SB909MR	OEM
2SB910	0355
2SB910M	0355
2SB910MP	0355
2SB910MQ	0355
2SB910MR	0355
2SB911	4043
2SB911-M	OEM
2SB911M	4043
2SB911MP	4043
2SB911MQ	4043
2SB911MR	4043
2SB912	0073
2SB913	0073
2SB914	2429
2SB915	2429
2SB916	2429
2SB917	OEM
2SB918	0338
2SB919	0713
2SB920	0713
2SB921	0713
2SB922	5380
2SB923	4081
2SB924	4081
2SB925	1298
2SB925A	1298
2SB926	3954
2SB926-T	3954
2SB927	OEM
2SB928	OEM
2SB928A	OEM
2SB929	5367
2SB929A	5367
2SB930	5367
2SB930A	5367
2SB931	5367
2SB932	5367
2SB933	5367
2SB934	5367
2SB935	5367
2SB935A	5367
2SB936	5367
2SB936A	5367
2SB937	5256
2SB937A	5256
2SB938	5256
2SB938A	5256
2SB939	OEM
2SB939A	OEM
2SB940	1638
2SB940-P	1638
2SB940A	1638
2SB940ALBP	1638
2SB940A-P	1638
2SB940AP	1638
2SB940APLB	1638
2SB940LBP	1638
2SB940P	1638
2SB940PLB	1638
2SB941	2895
2SB941(P)	2895
2SB941(Q)	2895
2SB941A	2895
2SB941A-PLT	OEM
2SB941A-PVJ	OEM
2SB941B	2895
2SB941D	2895
2SB941P	2895
2SB941PB	2895
2SB941PD	2895
2SB941PQ	2895
2SB941Q	2895
2SB942	0713
2SB942A	0713
2SB942A-PVJ	OEM
2SB943	0713
2SB943Q	5403
2SB944	0713
2SB945	5403
2SB945P	5403
2SB946	0713
2SB947	1298
2SB947A	1298

DEVICE TYPE	REPL CODE
2SB948	1298
2SB948A	1298
2SB949	0597
2SB949(P)	0597
2SB949(Q)	0597
2SB949A	0597
2SB949P	0597
2SB950	0597
2SB950A	0597
2SB951	0597
2SB951A	0597
2SB952	5367
2SB952(P)	5367
2SB952(Q)	5367
2SB952A	5367
2SB952PQ	5367
2SB952Q	5367
2SB953	1298
2SB953A	1298
2SB954	3136
2SB954A	3136
2SB955	1957
2SB955(K)	1957
2SB956	3600
2SB956S	OEM
2SB957	3457
2SB958	3457
2SB959	3457
2SB960	3457
2SB962	OEM
2SB962P	OEM
2SB962Q	OEM
2SB963	OEM
2SB964	OEM
2SB965	5380
2SB966	3082
2SB967	OEM
2SB968	3457
2SB969	OEM
2SB970	1741
2SB970-QR	OEM
2SB970QR	OEM
2SB970QRSTW	OEM
2SB971	3154
2SB972	OEM
2SB973	1741
2SB974	0597
2SB974L	0597
2SB974M	0597
2SB975	0597
2SB976	0643
2SB976(Q)	0643
2SB976(R)	0643
2SB976QR	0643
2SB976R	0643
2SB977	0630
2SB977A	0630
2SB978	3154
2SB979	3082
2SB980	3082
2SB981	3082
2SB982	3082
2SB983	1190
2SB984	1514
2SB985	0805
2SB985G	OEM
2SB985S	0805
2SB986	0455
2SB987	1514
2SB988	0919
2SB989	0676
2SB990	OEM
2SB991	1638
2SB992	1298
2SB993	1298
2SB994	1298
2SB995	0713
2SB996	3136
2SB997	0597
2SB998	2222
2SB999	2222
2SB1000	3600
2SB1000(RECT)	2425
2SB1000A	3600
2SB1001	OEM
2SB1002	3600
2SB1003	OEM
2SB1004	OEM
2SB1005	0597
2SB1007	0520
2SB1008	2869
2SB1009	0455
2SB1009P	0455
2SB1010	3154
2SB1010(Q)	3154
2SB1010Q	3154
2SB1010QZ	3154
2SB1010R	3154
2SB1010RZ	3154
2SB1011	OEM
2SB1011RL	OEM
2SB1012	OEM
2SB1012(K)	OEM
2SB1012K	OEM
2SB1013	OEM
2SB1014	OEM
2SB1015	1298
2SB1015Y	OEM
2SB1016	1359

DEVICE TYPE	REPL CODE
2SB1017	0676
2SB1018	0713
2SB1019	1298
2SB1020	2222
2SB1021	0597
2SB1022	0597
2SB1023	OEM
2SB1024	OEM
2SB1025	OEM
2SB1026	OEM
2SB1027	OEM
2SB1028	OEM
2SB1029	OEM
2SB1030	0013
2SB1030AR	0013
2SB1030ARS	0013
2SB1030AS	0013
2SB1030R	0013
2SB1030RSTTA	OEM
2SB1030S	0013
2SB1031	OEM
2SB1032	OEM
2SB1033	OEM
2SB1034	2869
2SB1035	OEM
2SB1036	OEM
2SB1037	1638
2SB1038	0676
2SB1039	0676
2SB1040	OEM
2SB1040A	OEM
2SB1041	6300
2SB1042	OEM
2SB1042M	0355
2SB1043	6300
2SB1044	OEM
2SB1044M	0355
2SB1045	OEM
2SB1046	OEM
2SB1047	OEM
2SB1048	OEM
2SB1049	OEM
2SB1050	3954
2SB1050(Q)	3954
2SB1050(R)	3954
2SB1050-Q	OEM
2SB1050R	3786
2SB1051	OEM
2SB1052	OEM
2SB1052B	OEM
2SB1052D	OEM
2SB1053	OEM
2SB1054	3082
2SB1055	3082
2SB1056	OEM
2SB1057	3082
2SB1058	3954
2SB1059	0037
2SB1060	0456
2SB1061	OEM
2SB1062	OEM
2SB1062S	OEM
2SB1063	0713
2SB1064	1298
2SB1065	0455
2SB1066	OEM
2SB1067	2869
2SB1068	3954
2SB1068-K	OEM
2SB1069	OEM
2SB1070	OEM
2SB1071	OEM
2SB1072	OEM
2SB1073	OEM
2SB1074	OEM
2SB1075	OEM
2SB1076	OEM
2SB1077	0597
2SB1078	1957
2SB1079	OEM
2SB1080	3294
2SB1085	1638
2SB1086	0520
2SB1087	OEM
2SB1088	OEM
2SB1089	OEM
2SB1090	OEM
2SB1091	0597
2SB1092	OEM
2SB1093	OEM
2SB1093-T	OEM
2SB1093L	OEM
2SB1093Q	OEM
2SB1094	3954
2SB1094L	3954
2SB1095	0676
2SB1096	1638
2SB1097	OEM
2SB1098	1957
2SB1099	0597
2SB1099K	0597
2SB1099L	0597
2SB1100	OEM
2SB1101	0597
2SB1102	0597
2SB1103	0597
2SB1104	0597
2SB1105	1957
2SB1106	1957

DEVICE TYPE	REPL CODE
2SB1107	OEM
2SB1108	1957
2SB1109	0520
2SB1110	OEM
2SB1111	OEM
2SB1112	OEM
2SB1113	OEM
2SB1114	OEM
2SB1115	3600
2SB1115A	3600
2SB1116	0472
2SB1116A	4028
2SB1117	OEM
2SB1118	3600
2SB1119	3600
2SB1120	OEM
2SB1121	OEM
2SB1122	3600
2SB1123	OEM
2SB1124	OEM
2SB1125	OEM
2SB1126	OEM
2SB1127	OEM
2SB1128	OEM
2SB1129	OEM
2SB1130	OEM
2SB1131	OEM
2SB1132	OEM
2SB1133	1298
2SB1133R	OEM
2SB1134	0919
2SB1134Q	OEM
2SB1134R	0919
2SB1134R-SA	0919
2SB1135	4062
2SB1135(R)	4062
2SB1135R	4061
2SB1135S	4062
2SB1136	OEM
2SB1137	OEM
2SB1140	OEM
2SB1141	0520
2SB1142	OEM
2SB1143	OEM
2SB1144	0520
2SB1145	1957
2SB1146	1957
2SB1147	1957
2SB1148	OEM
2SB1149	OEM
2SB1150	OEM
2SB1151	0455
2SB1152	OEM
2SB1153	OEM
2SB1154	OEM
2SB1155	OEM
2SB1156	OEM
2SB1157	OEM
2SB1158	OEM
2SB1159	OEM
2SB1160	OEM
2SB1161	OEM
2SB1162	5252
2SB1163	5252
2SB1164	OEM
2SB1165	OEM
2SB1165S	OEM
2SB1166	OEM
2SB1167	OEM
2SB1168	0455
2SB1168S	0455
2SB1169	OEM
2SB1170	OEM
2SB1171	OEM
2SB1172	OEM
2SB1173	OEM
2SB1174	OEM
2SB1175	OEM
2SB1176	OEM
2SB1177	OEM
2SB1178	OEM
2SB1179	OEM
2SB1180	OEM
2SB1181	OEM
2SB1182R	OEM
2SB1184	OEM
2SB1185	1298
2SB1185E	OEM
2SB1186	1638
2SB1186A	OEM
2SB1187	5378
2SB1187E	OEM
2SB1188	OEM
2SB1189	OEM
2SB1190	1638
2SB1191	OEM
2SB1192	1638
2SB1193	1957
2SB1194	OEM
2SB1195	OEM
2SB1203S	OEM
2SB1212	OEM
2SB1212-P	OEM
2SB1212P	OEM
2SB1218-QRS	OEM
2SB1218QRS	OEM
2SB1223	OEM
2SB1238	OEM
2SB1238QS	OEM

DEVICE TYPE	REPL CODE
2SB1238QSTV6	OEM
2SB1240	4043
2SB1240-P	OEM
2SB1240QRTV6	OEM
2SB1240R	OEM
2SB1243	OEM
2SB1262	OEM
2SB1272	OEM
2SB1272M	OEM
2SB1274(Q)	0919
2SB1274(R)	0919
2SB1274-Q-RA	0919
2SB1274-R-RA	0919
2SB1274Q	0919
2SB1274Q-RA	0919
2SB1274R	0919
2SB1274S	0919
2SB1277	4318
2SB1277P	4318
2SB1318	OEM
2SB1318L	OEM
2SB1357	5378
2SB1357DEFTA	OEM
2SB1359	6183
2SB1364	0211
2SB1366Y	OEM
2SB1367O	OEM
2SB1367Y	OEM
2SB1370-EF	OEM
2SB1370E	OEM
2SB1370EF	OEM
2SB1375	OEM
2SB1382	OEM
2SB1420	OEM
2SB1760	0211
2SB1780	0164
2SB1780A	0164
2SB1780B	0164
2SB1780C	0164
2SB1780D	0164
2SB1780E	0164
2SB1780F	0164
2SB1780G	0164
2SB1780GN	0164
2SB1780H	0164
2SB1780J	0164
2SB1780K	0164
2SB1780L	0164
2SB1780M	0164
2SB1780OR	0164
2SB1780R	0164
2SB1780X	0164
2SB1780Y	0164
2SB1785	0211
2SB1851	0004
2SB1860	0211
2SB2821	2464
2SB3030	0004
2SB3224E	0211
2SB3240	0164
2SB3240A	0164
2SB3240B	0164
2SB3240C	0164
2SB3240D	0164
2SB3240E	0164
2SB3240F	0164
2SB3240G	0164
2SB3240GN	0164
2SB3240H	0164
2SB3240J	0164
2SB3240K	0164
2SB3240L	0164
2SB3240M	0164
2SB3240OR	0164
2SB3240R	0164
2SB3240X	0164
2SB3240Y	0164
2SB3244	0279
2SB-3783	0164
2SB3783A	0164
2SB3783B	0164
2SB3783C	0164
2SB3783D	0164
2SB3783E	0164
2SB3783F	0164
2SB3783G	0164
2SB3783GN	0164
2SB3783H	0164
2SB3783J	0164
2SB3783K	0164
2SB3783L	0164
2SB3783M	0164
2SB3783OR	0164
2SB3783R	0164
2SB3783X	0164
2SB3783Y	0164
2SB-3812	0164
2SB3812A	0164
2SB3812B	0164
2SB3812C	0164
2SB3812D	0164
2SB3812F	0164
2SB3812G	0164
2SB3812GN	0164
2SB3812H	0164
2SB3812J	0164
2SB3812K	0164
2SB3812L	0164
2SB3812M	0164

If replacement code is OEM, contact original manufacturer for replacement.

DEVICE TYPE	REPL CODE
2SB3812OR	0164
2SB3812R	0164
2SB3812X	0164
2SB3812Y	0164
2SB-3813	0164
2SB3813A	0164
2SB3813B	0164
2SB3813C	0164
2SB3813D	0164
2SB3813E	0164
2SB3813F	0164
2SB3813G	0164
2SB3813GN	0164
2SB3813H	0164
2SB3813J	0164
2SB3813K	0164
2SB3813L	0164
2SB3813M	0164
2SB3813OR	0164
2SB3813R	0164
2SB3813X	0164
2SB3813Y	0164
2SB4151	0211
2SB4340	0848
2SB4440D	0164
2SB4631	0222
2SB4718	OEM
2SB7513	0279
2SB17313	0211
2SB-C731	0015
2SBF1	0004
2SB-F1A	0004
2SBF1A	0004
2SBF2	0004
2SBF2A	0164
2SBF5	0160
2SBF20	1404
2SBF40	0468
2SBF60	0441
2SBF80	1412
2SBF100	2425
2SBM77	0164
2SB-S131	0087
2SB-S851	0276
2SBU86	0211
2SBZ	0969
2SC11	0208
2SC11A	0208
2SC11B	0208
2SC11C	0208
2SC11D	0208
2SC11E	0208
2SC11F	0208
2SC11G	0208
2SC11GN	0208
2SC11H	0208
2SC11J	0208
2SC11K	0208
2SC11L	0208
2SC11M	0208
2SC11OR	0208
2SC11R	0208
2SC11X	0208
2SC11Y	0208
2SC12	0086
2SC12A	0086
2SC12B	0086
2SC12C	0086
2SC12D	0086
2SC12E	0086
2SC12F	0086
2SC12G	0086
2SC12GN	0086
2SC12H	0086
2SC12J	0086
2SC12K	0086
2SC12L	0086
2SC12M	0086
2SC12OR	0086
2SC12R	0086
2SC12X	0086
2SC12Y	0086
2SC13	0595
2SC13A	0595
2SC13B	0595
2SC13C	0595
2SC13D	0595
2SC13E	0595
2SC13F	0595
2SC13G	0595
2SC13GN	0595
2SC13H	0595
2SC13J	0595
2SC13K	0595
2SC13L	0595
2SC13M	0595
2SC13OR	0595
2SC13R	0595
2SC13X	0595
2SC13Y	0595
2SC14	0595
2SC14A	0595
2SC14B	0595
2SC14C	0595
2SC14D	0595
2SC14E	0595
2SC14F	0595
2SC14G	0595
2SC14GN	0595

DEVICE TYPE	REPL CODE
2SC14H	0595
2SC14J	0595
2SC14K	0595
2SC14L	0595
2SC14M	0595
2SC14OR	0595
2SC14R	0595
2SC14X	0595
2SC14Y	0595
2SC15	0016
2SC15-0	0016
2SC15-1	0016
2SC15-2	0016
2SC15-3	0016
2SC15A	0016
2SC15B	0016
2SC15C	0016
2SC15D	0016
2SC15E	0016
2SC15F	0016
2SC15G	0016
2SC15GN	0016
2SC15H	0016
2SC15J	0016
2SC15K	0016
2SC15L	0016
2SC15M	0016
2SC15OR	0016
2SC15R	0016
2SC15X	0016
2SC15Y	0016
2SC16	0016
2SC16A	0016
2SC16B	0016
2SC16C	0016
2SC16D	0016
2SC16E	0016
2SC16F	0016
2SC16G	0016
2SC16GN	0016
2SC16H	0016
2SC16J	0016
2SC16K	0016
2SC16L	0016
2SC16M	0016
2SC16OR	0016
2SC16R	0016
2SC16X	0016
2SC16Y	0016
2SC17	0016
2SC17A	0016
2SC17B	0016
2SC17C	0016
2SC17D	0016
2SC17E	0016
2SC17F	0016
2SC17G	0016
2SC17GN	0016
2SC17H	0016
2SC17J	0016
2SC17K	0016
2SC17L	0016
2SC17M	0016
2SC17OR	0016
2SC17R	0016
2SC17X	0016
2SC17Y	0016
2SC18	0079
2SC18A	0079
2SC18B	0079
2SC18C	0079
2SC18D	0079
2SC18E	0079
2SC18F	0079
2SC18G	0079
2SC18GN	0079
2SC18H	0079
2SC18J	0079
2SC18K	0079
2SC18L	0079
2SC18M	0079
2SC18OR	0079
2SC18R	0079
2SC18X	0079
2SC19	0086
2SC19A	0086
2SC19B	0086
2SC19C	0086
2SC19D	0086
2SC19E	0086
2SC19F	0086
2SC19G	0086
2SC19GN	0086
2SC19H	0086
2SC19J	0086
2SC19K	0086
2SC19L	0086
2SC19M	0086
2SC19OR	0086
2SC19R	0086
2SC19X	0086
2SC19Y	0086
2SC20	0086
2SC20A	0086
2SC20B	0086
2SC20C	0086
2SC20D	0086
2SC20E	0086
2SC20F	0086

DEVICE TYPE	REPL CODE
2SC20G	0086
2SC20GN	0086
2SC20H	0086
2SC20J	0086
2SC20K	0086
2SC20L	0086
2SC20M	0086
2SC20OR	0086
2SC20R	0086
2SC20X	0086
2SC20Y	0086
2SC21	0103
2SC21A	0103
2SC21B	0103
2SC21C	0103
2SC21D	0103
2SC21E	0103
2SC21F	0103
2SC21G	0103
2SC21GN	0103
2SC21H	0103
2SC21J	0103
2SC21K	0103
2SC21L	0103
2SC21M	0103
2SC21OR	0103
2SC21R	0103
2SC21X	0103
2SC21Y	0103
2SC22	0086
2SC22A	0086
2SC22B	0086
2SC22D	0086
2SC22E	0086
2SC22F	0086
2SC22G	0086
2SC22GN	0086
2SC22H	0086
2SC22J	0086
2SC22K	0086
2SC22L	0086
2SC22M	0086
2SC22OR	0086
2SC22R	0086
2SC22X	0086
2SC22Y	0086
2SC23	0086
2SC23A	0086
2SC23B	0086
2SC23D	0086
2SC23E	0086
2SC23F	0086
2SC23G	0086
2SC23GN	0086
2SC23H	0086
2SC23J	0086
2SC23K	0086
2SC23L	0086
2SC23M	0086
2SC23OR	0086
2SC23R	0086
2SC23X	0086
2SC23Y	0086
2SC24	0086
2SC24A	0086
2SC24B	0086
2SC24C	0086
2SC24D	0086
2SC24E	0086
2SC24F	0086
2SC24G	0086
2SC24GN	0086
2SC24H	0086
2SC24J	0086
2SC24K	0086
2SC24L	0086
2SC24M	0086
2SC24OR	0086
2SC24R	0086
2SC24X	0086
2SC24Y	0086
2SC25	1077
2SC26	0016
2SC26A	0016
2SC26B	0016
2SC26C	0016
2SC26D	0016
2SC26E	0016
2SC26F	0016
2SC26G	0016
2SC26GN	0016
2SC26H	0016
2SC26J	0016
2SC26K	0016
2SC26L	0016
2SC26M	0016
2SC26OR	0016
2SC26R	0016
2SC26X	0016
2SC26Y	0016
2SC27	0016
2SC27A	0016
2SC27B	0016
2SC27D	0016
2SC27E	0016
2SC27F	0016
2SC27G	0016
2SC27GN	0016
2SC27H	0016

DEVICE TYPE	REPL CODE
2SC27J	0016
2SC27K	0016
2SC27L	0016
2SC27M	0016
2SC27OR	0016
2SC27R	0016
2SC27X	0016
2SC27Y	0016
2SC28	0198
2SC28A	0198
2SC28B	0198
2SC28C	0198
2SC28D	0198
2SC28E	0198
2SC28F	0198
2SC28G	0198
2SC28GN	0198
2SC28H	0198
2SC28J	0198
2SC28K	0198
2SC28L	0198
2SC28M	0198
2SC28OR	0198
2SC28R	0198
2SC28X	0198
2SC28Y	0198
2SC29	0198
2SC29A	0198
2SC29B	0198
2SC29C	0198
2SC29D	0198
2SC29E	0198
2SC29F	0198
2SC29G	0198
2SC29GN	0198
2SC29H	0198
2SC29J	0198
2SC29K	0198
2SC29L	0198
2SC29M	0198
2SC29OR	0198
2SC29R	0198
2SC29X	0198
2SC29Y	0198
2SC30	0086
2SC30-OR	0086
2SC30A	0086
2SC30B	0086
2SC30C	0086
2SC30D	0086
2SC30E	0086
2SC30F	0086
2SC30G	0086
2SC30GN	0086
2SC30H	0086
2SC30J	0086
2SC30K	0086
2SC30L	0086
2SC30M	0086
2SC30OR	0086
2SC30R	0086
2SC30X	0086
2SC30Y	0086
2SC31	0086
2SC31A	0086
2SC31B	0086
2SC31C	0086
2SC31D	0086
2SC31E	0086
2SC31F	0086
2SC31G	0086
2SC31GN	0086
2SC31H	0086
2SC31J	0086
2SC31K	0086
2SC31L	0086
2SC31M	0086
2SC31OR	0086
2SC31R	0086
2SC31X	0086
2SC31Y	0086
2SC32	0086
2SC32A	0086
2SC32B	0086
2SC32C	0086
2SC32D	0086
2SC32E	0086
2SC32F	0086
2SC32G	0086
2SC32GN	0086
2SC32H	0086
2SC32J	0086
2SC32K	0086
2SC32L	0086
2SC32M	0086
2SC32OR	0086
2SC32R	0086
2SC32X	0086
2SC32Y	0086
2SC33	0079
2SC33A	0079
2SC33B	0079
2SC33C	0079
2SC33D	0079
2SC33E	0079
2SC33F	0079
2SC33G	0079
2SC33GN	0079
2SC33H	0079
2SC33J	0079

DEVICE TYPE	REPL CODE
2SC33K	0079
2SC33L	0079
2SC33M	0079
2SC33OR	0079
2SC33R	0079
2SC33X	0079
2SC33Y	0079
2SC34	0208
2SC34A	0208
2SC34C	0208
2SC34D	0208
2SC34E	0208
2SC34F	0208
2SC34G	0208
2SC34GN	0208
2SC34H	0208
2SC34J	0208
2SC34K	0208
2SC34L	0208
2SC34M	0208
2SC34OR	0208
2SC34R	0208
2SC34X	0208
2SC34Y	0208
2SC35	0208
2SC35A	0208
2SC35B	0208
2SC35C	0208
2SC35E	0208
2SC35F	0208
2SC35G	0208
2SC35GN	0208
2SC35H	0208
2SC35J	0208
2SC35K	0208
2SC35L	0208
2SC35M	0208
2SC35OR	0208
2SC35R	0208
2SC35X	0208
2SC35Y	0208
2SC36	0208
2SC36B	0208
2SC36C	0208
2SC36D	0208
2SC36E	0208
2SC36F	0208
2SC36G	0208
2SC36GN	0208
2SC36H	0208
2SC36J	0208
2SC36K	0208
2SC36L	0208
2SC36M	0208
2SC36OR	0208
2SC36R	0208
2SC36X	0208
2SC36Y	0208
2SC37	0016
2SC37A	0016
2SC37B	0016
2SC37C	0016
2SC37D	0016
2SC37E	0016
2SC37F	0016
2SC37G	0016
2SC37GN	0016
2SC37H	0016
2SC37J	0016
2SC37K	0016
2SC37L	0016
2SC37M	0016
2SC37OR	0016
2SC37R	0016
2SC37X	0016
2SC37Y	0016
2SC38	0016
2SC38A	0016
2SC38B	0016
2SC38C	0016
2SC38D	0016
2SC38E	0016
2SC38F	0016
2SC38G	0016
2SC38H	0016
2SC38J	0016
2SC38K	0016
2SC38L	0016
2SC38M	0016
2SC38OR	0016
2SC38R	0016
2SC38X	0016
2SC38Y	0016
2SC39	0144
2SC39A	0144
2SC39B	0144
2SC39C	0144
2SC39D	0144
2SC39E	0144
2SC39F	0144
2SC39G	0144
2SC39GN	0144
2SC39H	0144
2SC39J	0144
2SC39K	0144
2SC39L	0144
2SC39M	0144
2SC39OR	0144
2SC39R	0144

DEVICE TYPE	REPL CODE
2SC39X	0144
2SC39Y	0144
2SC40	0144
2SC40A	0144
2SC40B	0144
2SC40C	0144
2SC40D	0144
2SC40E	0144
2SC40F	0144
2SC40G	0144
2SC40GN	0144
2SC40H	0144
2SC40J	0144
2SC40K	0144
2SC40L	0144
2SC40OR	0144
2SC40R	0144
2SC40X	0144
2SC40Y	0144
2SC41	0615
2SC41B	0615
2SC41C	0615
2SC41F	0615
2SC41GN	0615
2SC41H	0615
2SC41J	0615
2SC41M	0615
2SC41OR	0615
2SC41R	0615
2SC41TV	0615
2SC41X	0615
2SC41Y	0615
2SC42	0074
2SC42A	0074
2SC42B	0074
2SC42C	0074
2SC42E	0074
2SC42F	0074
2SC42G	0074
2SC42GN	0074
2SC42H	0074
2SC42J	0074
2SC42K	0074
2SC42L	0074
2SC42M	0074
2SC42OR	0074
2SC42R	0074
2SC42X	0074
2SC42Y	0074
2SC43	0074
2SC44	0074
2SC45	0016
2SC45B-GR	0016
2SC45B-O	0016
2SC45B-Y	0016
2SC46	0086
2SC46A	0086
2SC46B	0086
2SC46C	0086
2SC46DB	0086
2SC46E	0086
2SC46F	0086
2SC46G	0086
2SC46GN	0086
2SC46H	0086
2SC46J	0086
2SC46K	0086
2SC46L	0086
2SC46M	0086
2SC46OR	0086
2SC46X	0086
2SC46Y	0086
2SC47	0086
2SC47A	0086
2SC47B	0086
2SC47C	0086
2SC47D	0086
2SC47E	0086
2SC47G	0086
2SC47GN	0086
2SC47H	0086
2SC47J	0086
2SC47K	0086
2SC47L	0086
2SC47M	0086
2SC47OR	0086
2SC47R	0086
2SC47X	0086
2SC47Y	0086
2SC48	0086
2SC48A	0086
2SC48B	0086
2SC48C	0086
2SC48D	0086
2SC48E	0086
2SC48F	0086
2SC48G	0086
2SC48GN	0086
2SC48H	0086
2SC48J	0086
2SC48K	0086
2SC48L	0086
2SC48M	0086
2SC48OR	0086
2SC48R	0086
2SC48X	0086
2SC48Y	0086
2SC49	0086
2SC49A	0086

DEVICE TYPE	REPL CODE
2SC49B	0086
2SC49C	0086
2SC49D	0086
2SC49E	0086
2SC49F	0086
2SC49G	0086
2SC49GN	0086
2SC49H	0086
2SC49J	0086
2SC49K	0086
2SC49L	0086
2SC49M	0086
2SC49OR	0086
2SC49X	0086
2SC49Y	0086
2SC50	0595
2SC50A	0595
2SC50B	0595
2SC50C	0595
2SC50E	0595
2SC50F	0595
2SC50G	0595
2SC50GN	0595
2SC50H	0595
2SC50J	0595
2SC50K	0595
2SC50L	0595
2SC50M	0595
2SC50OR	0595
2SC50R	0595
2SC50X	0595
2SC50Y	0595
2SC51	0086
2SC51A	0086
2SC51B	0086
2SC51C	0086
2SC51D	0086
2SC51E	0086
2SC51F	0086
2SC51G	0086
2SC51GN	0086
2SC51H	0086
2SC51J	0086
2SC51K	0086
2SC51L	0086
2SC51M	0086
2SC51OR	0086
2SC51R	0086
2SC51X	0086
2SC51Y	0086
2SC52	0016
2SC52A	0016
2SC52B	0016
2SC52C	0016
2SC52D	0016
2SC52E	0016
2SC52F	0016
2SC52G	0016
2SC52GN	0016
2SC52H	0016
2SC52J	0016
2SC52K	0016
2SC52L	0016
2SC52M	0016
2SC52OR	0016
2SC52X	0016
2SC52Y	0016
2SC53	0016
2SC53A	0016
2SC53B	0016
2SC53C	0016
2SC53D	0016
2SC53E	0016
2SC53F	0016
2SC53G	0016
2SC53GN	0016
2SC53H	0016
2SC53J	0016
2SC53L	0016
2SC53OR	0016
2SC53R	0016
2SC53X	0016
2SC53Y	0016
2SC54	0016
2SC54A	0016
2SC54B	0016
2SC54C	0016
2SC54D	0016
2SC54E	0016
2SC54F	0016
2SC54G	0016
2SC54H	0016
2SC54J	0016
2SC54K	0016
2SC54L	0016
2SC54M	0016
2SC54OR	0016
2SC54X	0016
2SC54Y	0016
2SC55	0016
2SC55A	0016
2SC55B	0016
2SC55C	0016
2SC55D	0016
2SC55E	0016
2SC55F	0016
2SC55G	0016
2SC55GN	0016
2SC55H	0016

If replacement code is OEM, contact original manufacturer for replacement.

75

DEVICE TYPE	REPL CODE
2SC55J	0016
2SC55K	0016
2SC55L	0016
2SC55M	0016
2SC55OR	0016
2SC55R	0016
2SC55X	0016
2SC55Y	0016
2SC56	0127
2SC56A	0127
2SC56B	0127
2SC56C	0127
2SC56D	0127
2SC56E	0127
2SC56F	0127
2SC56G	0127
2SC56GN	0127
2SC56H	0127
2SC56J	0127
2SC56K	0127
2SC56L	0127
2SC56M	0127
2SC56OR	0127
2SC56R	0127
2SC56X	0127
2SC56Y	0127
2SC57	0590
2SC58	0233
2SC58A	0233
2SC58AC	0233
2SC58B	0233
2SC58D	0233
2SC58E	0233
2SC58F	0233
2SC58G	0233
2SC58GN	0233
2SC58H	0233
2SC58J	0233
2SC58K	0233
2SC58L	0233
2SC58M	0233
2SC58OR	0233
2SC58R	0233
2SC58X	0233
2SC58Y	0233
2SC59	0086
2SC59A	0086
2SC59B	0086
2SC59C	0086
2SC59D	0086
2SC59E	0086
2SC59F	0086
2SC59G	0086
2SC59GN	0086
2SC59H	0086
2SC59J	0086
2SC59K	0086
2SC59L	0086
2SC59M	0086
2SC59OR	0086
2SC59R	0086
2SC59X	0086
2SC59Y	0086
2SC60	0208
2SC60A	0208
2SC60B	0208
2SC60C	0208
2SC60D	0208
2SC60E	0208
2SC60F	0208
2SC60G	0208
2SC60GN	0208
2SC60H	0208
2SC60J	0208
2SC60K	0208
2SC60L	0208
2SC60M	0208
2SC60OR	0208
2SC60R	0208
2SC60X	0208
2SC60Y	0208
2SC61	0086
2SC61A	0086
2SC61B	0086
2SC61C	0086
2SC61D	0086
2SC61E	0086
2SC61F	0086
2SC61G	0086
2SC61GN	0086
2SC61H	0086
2SC61J	0086
2SC61K	0086
2SC61L	0086
2SC61M	0086
2SC61OR	0086
2SC61R	0086
2SC61Y	0086
2SC62	0016
2SC62A	0016
2SC62B	0016
2SC62C	0016
2SC62D	0016
2SC62E	0016
2SC62F	0016
2SC62G	0016
2SC62GN	0016
2SC62H	0016
2SC62J	0016

DEVICE TYPE	REPL CODE
2SC62L	0016
2SC62M	0016
2SC62OR	0016
2SC62R	0016
2SC62X	0016
2SC62Y	0016
2SC63	0144
2SC63A	0144
2SC63B	0144
2SC63D	0144
2SC63E	0144
2SC63F	0144
2SC63G	0144
2SC63GN	0144
2SC63H	0144
2SC63J	0144
2SC63K	0144
2SC63L	0144
2SC63M	0144
2SC63OR	0144
2SC63R	0144
2SC63X	0144
2SC63Y	0144
2SC64	0086
2SC64A	0086
2SC64B	0086
2SC64C	0086
2SC64D	0086
2SC64E	0086
2SC64F	0086
2SC64G	0086
2SC64GN	0086
2SC64H	0086
2SC64K	0086
2SC64L	0086
2SC64M	0086
2SC64OR	0086
2SC64R	0086
2SC64X	0086
2SC64Y	0086
2SC64Y-RST	0086
2SC65	0233
2SC65(Y)	0233
2SC65-O	0233
2SC65-OR	0233
2SC65A	0233
2SC65B	0233
2SC65C	0233
2SC65D	0233
2SC65E	0233
2SC65F	0233
2SC65G	0233
2SC65GN	0233
2SC65H	0233
2SC65K	0233
2SC65L	0233
2SC65M	0233
2SC65N	0233
2SC65OR	0233
2SC65R	0233
2SC65X	0233
2SC65Y	0233
2SC65Y(B)	0233
2SC65YA	0233
2SC65YB	0233
2SC65YTV	0233
2SC65YTV1	0233
2SC66	0233
2SC66A	0233
2SC66B	0233
2SC66C	0233
2SC66D	0233
2SC66E	0233
2SC66EV	0233
2SC66F	0233
2SC66G	0233
2SC66GN	0233
2SC66H	0233
2SC66J	0233
2SC66K	0233
2SC66L	0233
2SC66M	0233
2SC66OR	0233
2SC66R	0233
2SC66X	0233
2SC66Y	0233
2SC67	0016
2SC67A	0016
2SC67B	0016
2SC67C	0016
2SC67D	0016
2SC67E	0016
2SC67F	0016
2SC67G	0016
2SC67GN	0016
2SC67H	0016
2SC67J	0016
2SC67K	0016
2SC67L	0016
2SC67M	0016
2SC67R	0016
2SC67X	0016
2SC67Y	0016
2SC68	0016
2SC68A	0016
2SC68B	0016
2SC68C	0016
2SC68D	0016
2SC68E	0016

DEVICE TYPE	REPL CODE
2SC68F	0016
2SC68G	0016
2SC68GN	0016
2SC68H	0016
2SC68J	0016
2SC68K	0016
2SC68L	0016
2SC68M	0016
2SC68OR	0016
2SC68R	0016
2SC68X	0016
2SC68Y	0016
2SC69	0086
2SC69A	0086
2SC69B	0086
2SC69C	0086
2SC69D	0086
2SC69E	0086
2SC69F	0086
2SC69G	0086
2SC69GN	0086
2SC69H	0086
2SC69J	0086
2SC69K	0086
2SC69L	0086
2SC69M	0086
2SC69OR	0086
2SC69R	0086
2SC69X	0086
2SC69Y	0086
2SC70	0233
2SC70A	0233
2SC70B	0233
2SC70C	0233
2SC70D	0233
2SC70E	0233
2SC70F	0233
2SC70G	0233
2SC70GN	0233
2SC70H	0233
2SC70J	0233
2SC70K	0233
2SC70L	0233
2SC70M	0233
2SC70OR	0233
2SC70R	0233
2SC70X	0233
2SC70Y	0233
2SC71	0595
2SC71A	0595
2SC71B	0595
2SC71C	0595
2SC71D	0595
2SC71E	0595
2SC71F	0595
2SC71G	0595
2SC71GN	0595
2SC71H	0595
2SC71J	0595
2SC71M	0595
2SC71OR	0595
2SC71R	0595
2SC71X	0595
2SC72	0595
2SC72A	0595
2SC72B	0595
2SC72C	0595
2SC72D	0595
2SC72E	0595
2SC72F	0595
2SC72G	0595
2SC72GN	0595
2SC72H	0595
2SC72J	0595
2SC72K	0595
2SC72L	0595
2SC72M	0595
2SC72OR	0595
2SC72R	0595
2SC72X	0595
2SC72Y	0595
2SC73	0595
2SC73A	0595
2SC73B	0595
2SC73C	0595
2SC73D	0595
2SC73E	0595
2SC73F	0595
2SC73G	0595
2SC73GN	0595
2SC73H	0595
2SC73J	0595
2SC73K	0595
2SC73L	0595
2SC73LBGL	0595
2SC73M	0595
2SC73OR	0595
2SC73R	0595
2SC73X	0595
2SC73Y	0595
2SC74	0198
2SC74-GR	0198
2SC74-O	0198
2SC74-R	0198
2SC74-Y	0198
2SC74A	0198
2SC74B	0198
2SC74C	0198
2SC74D	0198

DEVICE TYPE	REPL CODE
2SC74E	0198
2SC74F	0198
2SC74G	0198
2SC74GN	0198
2SC74H	0198
2SC74J	0198
2SC74K	0198
2SC74L	0198
2SC74M	0198
2SC74R	0198
2SC74X	0198
2SC74Y	0198
2SC75	0595
2SC75A	0595
2SC75B	0595
2SC75B-1	0595
2SC75C	0595
2SC75E	0595
2SC75F	0595
2SC75G	0595
2SC75GN	0595
2SC75H	0595
2SC75J	0595
2SC75K	0595
2SC75L	0595
2SC75M	0595
2SC75OR	0595
2SC75R	0595
2SC75X	0595
2SC75Y	0595
2SC76	0595
2SC76A	0595
2SC76B	0595
2SC76C	0595
2SC76D	0595
2SC76E	0595
2SC76F	0595
2SC76G	0595
2SC76GN	0595
2SC76H	0595
2SC76J	0595
2SC76K	0595
2SC76L	0595
2SC76M	0595
2SC76OR	0595
2SC76R	0595
2SC76X	0595
2SC76Y	0595
2SC77	0595
2SC77A	0595
2SC77B	0595
2SC77C	0595
2SC77D	0595
2SC77F	0595
2SC77G	0595
2SC77GN	0595
2SC77H	0595
2SC77J	0595
2SC77K	0595
2SC77L	0595
2SC77M	0595
2SC77OR	0595
2SC77R	0595
2SC77X	0595
2SC77Y	0595
2SC77Z	0595
2SC78	0595
2SC78A	0595
2SC78B	0595
2SC78C	0595
2SC78D	0595
2SC78E	0595
2SC78F	0595
2SC78G	0595
2SC78GN	0595
2SC78H	0595
2SC78J	0595
2SC78K	0595
2SC78L	0595
2SC78M	0595
2SC78OR	0595
2SC78R	0595
2SC78X	0595
2SC78Y	0595
2SC79	0224
2SC79A	0224
2SC79B	0224
2SC79C	0224
2SC79D	0224
2SC79E	0224
2SC79F	0224
2SC79G	0224
2SC79GN	0224
2SC79H	0224
2SC79J	0224
2SC79K	0224
2SC79L	0224
2SC79M	0224
2SC79OR	0224
2SC79R	0224
2SC79X	0224
2SC79Y	0224
2SC80	0007
2SC80A	0007
2SC80B	0007
2SC80C	0007
2SC80D	0007
2SC80E	0007
2SC80F	0007

DEVICE TYPE	REPL CODE
2SC80G	0007
2SC80GN	0007
2SC80H	0007
2SC80J	0007
2SC80K	0007
2SC80L	0007
2SC80M	0007
2SC80OR	0007
2SC80R	0007
2SC80X	0007
2SC80Y	0007
2SC81	0018
2SC81A	0018
2SC81B	0018
2SC81C	0018
2SC81D	0018
2SC81E	0018
2SC81F	0018
2SC81G	0018
2SC81GN	0018
2SC81H	0018
2SC81J	0018
2SC81K	0018
2SC81L	0018
2SC81M	0018
2SC81OR	0018
2SC81R	0018
2SC82	0127
2SC82BN	0127
2SC82R	0127
2SC83	0127
2SC84	0595
2SC85	0208
2SC85O	0208
2SC86	0208
2SC87	0016
2SC87A	0016
2SC87B	0016
2SC87C	0016
2SC87D	0016
2SC87E	0016
2SC87F	0016
2SC87G	0016
2SC87GN	0016
2SC87H	0016
2SC87J	0016
2SC87K	0016
2SC87L	0016
2SC87M	0016
2SC87OR	0016
2SC87R	0016
2SC87X	0016
2SC87Y	0016
2SC88	0086
2SC88A	0086
2SC88B	0086
2SC88C	0086
2SC88D	0086
2SC88E	0086
2SC88F	0086
2SC88G	0086
2SC88GN	0086
2SC88H	0086
2SC88J	0086
2SC88K	0086
2SC88L	0086
2SC88M	0086
2SC88OR	0086
2SC88R	0086
2SC88X	0086
2SC88Y	0086
2SC89	0595
2SC89A	0595
2SC89B	0595
2SC89C	0595
2SC89D	0595
2SC89E	0595
2SC89F	0595
2SC89G	0595
2SC89GN	0595
2SC89H	0595
2SC89J	0595
2SC89K	0595
2SC89L	0595
2SC89M	0595
2SC89OR	0595
2SC89R	0595
2SC89X	0595
2SC89Y	0595
2SC90	0595
2SC90A	0595
2SC90B	0595
2SC90C	0595
2SC90D	0595
2SC90E	0595
2SC90F	0595
2SC90G	0595
2SC90GN	0595
2SC90H	0595
2SC90J	0595
2SC90K	0595
2SC90L	0595
2SC90M	0595
2SC90OR	0595
2SC90R	0595
2SC90X	0595
2SC90Y	0595
2SC91	0595
2SC91A	0595

DEVICE TYPE	REPL CODE
2SC91B	0595
2SC91C	0595
2SC91D	0595
2SC91E	0595
2SC91F	0595
2SC91G	0595
2SC91GN	0595
2SC91H	0595
2SC91J	0595
2SC91K	0595
2SC91L	0595
2SC91M	0595
2SC91OR	0595
2SC91R	0595
2SC91X	0595
2SC91Y	0595
2SC92	0042
2SC93	0042
2SC94	0042
2SC94AP	0042
2SC95	0086
2SC95A	0086
2SC95B	0086
2SC95C	0086
2SC95D	0086
2SC95E	0086
2SC95F	0086
2SC95G	0086
2SC95GN	0086
2SC95H	0086
2SC95J	0086
2SC95K	0086
2SC95L	0086
2SC95M	0086
2SC95OR	0086
2SC95R	0086
2SC95X	0086
2SC95Y	0086
2SC96	0079
2SC97	0086
2SC97A	0086
2SC97B	0086
2SC97C	0086
2SC97D	0086
2SC97E	0086
2SC97F	0086
2SC97G	0086
2SC97GN	0086
2SC97H	0086
2SC97J	0086
2SC97K	0086
2SC97L	0086
2SC97M	0086
2SC97OR	0086
2SC97R	0086
2SC97X	0086
2SC97Y	0086
2SC98	0016
2SC98A	0016
2SC98B	0016
2SC98C	0016
2SC98D	0016
2SC98E	0016
2SC98F	0016
2SC98G	0016
2SC98GN	0016
2SC98H	0016
2SC98J	0016
2SC98K	0016
2SC98L	0016
2SC98M	0016
2SC98OR	0016
2SC98R	0016
2SC98X	0016
2SC98Y	0016
2SC99	0016
2SC99A	0016
2SC99B	0016
2SC99C	0016
2SC99D	0016
2SC99E	0016
2SC99F	0016
2SC99G	0016
2SC99GN	0016
2SC99H	0016
2SC99J	0016
2SC99K	0016
2SC99L	0016
2SC99M	0016
2SC99OR	0016
2SC99R	0016
2SC99X	0016
2SC99Y	0016
2SC100	0016
2SC100-OY	0016
2SC100A	0016
2SC100B	0016
2SC100C	0016
2SC100D	0016
2SC100E	0016
2SC100F	0016
2SC100G	0016
2SC100GN	0016
2SC100J	0016
2SC100L	0016
2SC100M	0016
2SC100OR	0016
2SC100R	0016
2SC100X	0016

DEVICE TYPE	REPL CODE
2SC100Y	0016
2SC101	0074
2SC101A	0074
2SC101B	0074
2SC101C	0074
2SC101D	0074
2SC101E	0074
2SC101F	0074
2SC101G	0074
2SC101GN	0074
2SC101H	0074
2SC101J	0074
2SC101K	0074
2SC101L	0074
2SC101M	0074
2SC101OR	0074
2SC101R	0074
2SC101X	0074
2SC101XL	0074
2SC101Y	0074
2SC102	OEM
2SC103	0016
2SC103A	0016
2SC103B	0016
2SC103C	0016
2SC103D	0016
2SC103E	0016
2SC103F	0016
2SC103G	0016
2SC103GN	0016
2SC103H	0016
2SC103J	0016
2SC103K	0016
2SC103L	0016
2SC103M	0016
2SC103X	0016
2SC103Y	0016
2SC104	0016
2SC104A	0016
2SC104B	0016
2SC104C	0016
2SC104D	0016
2SC104E	0016
2SC104F	0016
2SC104G	0016
2SC104GN	0016
2SC104H	0016
2SC104J	0016
2SC104K	0016
2SC104L	0016
2SC104M	0016
2SC104OR	0016
2SC104R	0016
2SC104X	0016
2SC104Y	0016
2SC105	0016
2SC105B	0016
2SC106	0617
2SC106A	0617
2SC106B	0617
2SC106C	0617
2SC106G	0617
2SC106GN	0617
2SC106H	0617
2SC106J	0617
2SC106K	0617
2SC106L	0617
2SC106M	0617
2SC106OR	0617
2SC106R	0617
2SC106X	0617
2SC106Y	0617
2SC107	0042
2SC107G4	0042
2SC107G5	0042
2SC107G6	0042
2SC108	0086
2SC108A	0086
2SC108A-O	0086
2SC108A-R	0086
2SC108B	0086
2SC108C	0086
2SC108D	0086
2SC108E	0086
2SC108F	0086
2SC108G	0086
2SC108GN	0086
2SC108H	0086
2SC108J	0086
2SC108K	0086
2SC108L	0086
2SC108M	0086
2SC108OR	0086
2SC108R	0086
2SC108X	0086
2SC108Y	0086
2SC109	0086
2SC109A	0086
2SC109A-O	0086
2SC109A-R	0086
2SC109A-Y	0086
2SC109B	0086
2SC109C	0086
2SC109D	0086
2SC109E	0086
2SC109F	0086
2SC109G	0086
2SC109G1	0086
2SC109GN	0086

If replacement code is OEM, contact original manufacturer for replacement.

DEVICE TYPE	REPL CODE
2SC109J	0086
2SC109K	0086
2SC109L	0086
2SC109OR	0086
2SC109R	0086
2SC109X	0086
2SC109Y	0086
2SC110	0016
2SC110A	0016
2SC110B	0016
2SC110C	0016
2SC110D	0016
2SC110E	0016
2SC110F	0016
2SC110G	0016
2SC110GN	0016
2SC110H	0016
2SC110J	0016
2SC110K	0016
2SC110L	0016
2SC110M	0016
2SC110OR	0016
2SC110R	0016
2SC110X	0016
2SC110Y	0016
2SC111	0016
2SC111A	0016
2SC111B	0016
2SC111C	0016
2SC111D	0016
2SC111E	0016
2SC111F	0016
2SC111G	0016
2SC111GN	0016
2SC111H	0016
2SC111J	0016
2SC111K	0016
2SC111L	0016
2SC111M	0016
2SC111OR	0016
2SC111R	0016
2SC111X	0016
2SC111Y	0016
2SC112	0086
2SC112A	0086
2SC112B	0086
2SC112C	0086
2SC112D	0086
2SC112E	0086
2SC112F	0086
2SC112G	0086
2SC112GN	0086
2SC112H	0086
2SC112J	0086
2SC112K	0086
2SC112L	0086
2SC112M	0086
2SC112OR	0086
2SC112R	0086
2SC112X	0086
2SC112Y	0086
2SC113	0086
2SC113A	0086
2SC113B	0086
2SC113C	0086
2SC113D	0086
2SC113E	0086
2SC113F	0086
2SC113G	0086
2SC113GN	0086
2SC113H	0086
2SC113J	0086
2SC113K	0086
2SC113L	0086
2SC113M	0086
2SC113OR	0086
2SC113R	0086
2SC113X	0086
2SC113Y	0086
2SC114	0086
2SC114A	0086
2SC114B	0086
2SC114C	0086
2SC114D	0086
2SC114E	0086
2SC114EF	0086
2SC114F	0086
2SC114G	0086
2SC114GN	0086
2SC114H	0086
2SC114J	0086
2SC114K	0086
2SC114L	0086
2SC114M	0086
2SC114OR	0086
2SC114R	0086
2SC114X	0086
2SC114Y	0086
2SC115	0086
2SC115-1	0086
2SC115-2	0086
2SC115-3	0086
2SC115-43	0086
2SC115A	0086
2SC115B	0086
2SC115C	0086
2SC115D	0086
2SC115E	0086
2SC115F	0086

DEVICE TYPE	REPL CODE
2SC115G	0086
2SC115GN	0086
2SC115H	0086
2SC115J	0086
2SC115K	0086
2SC115L	0086
2SC115M	0086
2SC115OR	0086
2SC115R	0086
2SC115X	0086
2SC115Y	0086
2SC116	2050
2SC116-OR	2050
2SC116A	2050
2SC116B	2050
2SC116C	2050
2SC116D	2050
2SC116E	2050
2SC116F	2050
2SC116G	2050
2SC116GN	2050
2SC116H	2050
2SC116J	2050
2SC116K	2050
2SC116L	2050
2SC116M	2050
2SC116OR	2050
2SC116R	2050
2SC116T	2050
2SC116X	2050
2SC116Y	2050
2SC117	0086
2SC117A	0086
2SC117B	0086
2SC117C	0086
2SC117D	0086
2SC117F	0086
2SC117G	0086
2SC117GN	0086
2SC117H	0086
2SC117J	0086
2SC117K	0086
2SC117L	0086
2SC117M	0086
2SC117OR	0086
2SC117R	0086
2SC117X	0086
2SC117Y	0086
2SC118	0086
2SC118A	0086
2SC118B	0086
2SC118C	0086
2SC118D	0086
2SC118E	0086
2SC118F	0086
2SC118G	0086
2SC118GN	0086
2SC118H	0086
2SC118J	0086
2SC118L	0086
2SC118M	0086
2SC118OR	0086
2SC118R	0086
2SC118X	0086
2SC118Y	0086
2SC119	0086
2SC119A	0086
2SC119B	0086
2SC119C	0086
2SC119D	0086
2SC119E	0086
2SC119F	0086
2SC119G	0086
2SC119GN	0086
2SC119H	0086
2SC119J	0086
2SC119K	0086
2SC119L	0086
2SC119M	0086
2SC119OR	0086
2SC119R	0086
2SC119X	0086
2SC119Y	0086
2SC120	0016
2SC120A	0016
2SC120B	0016
2SC120C	0016
2SC120D	0016
2SC120E	0016
2SC120F	0016
2SC120G	0016
2SC120GN	0016
2SC120H	0016
2SC120J	0016
2SC120K	0016
2SC120M	0016
2SC120R	0016
2SC120Y	0016
2SC121	0086
2SC121A	0086
2SC121B	0086
2SC121C	0086
2SC121D	0086
2SC121E	0086
2SC121F	0086
2SC121G	0086
2SC121GN	0086
2SC121H	0086
2SC121J	0086

DEVICE TYPE	REPL CODE
2SC121L	0086
2SC121M	0086
2SC121OR	0086
2SC121R	0086
2SC121X	0086
2SC121Y	0086
2SC122	0086
2SC122A	0086
2SC122B	0086
2SC122C	0086
2SC122D	0086
2SC122E	0086
2SC122F	0086
2SC122G	0086
2SC122GN	0086
2SC122H	0086
2SC122J	0086
2SC122K	0086
2SC122L	0086
2SC122M	0086
2SC122OR	0086
2SC122R	0086
2SC122X	0086
2SC122Y	0086
2SC123	0086
2SC123A	0086
2SC123B	0086
2SC123C	0086
2SC123D	0086
2SC123E	0086
2SC123F	0086
2SC123G	0086
2SC123GN	0086
2SC123H	0086
2SC123J	0086
2SC123K	0086
2SC123L	0086
2SC123M	0086
2SC123OR	0086
2SC123R	0086
2SC123X	0086
2SC123Y	0086
2SC124	0086
2SC124A	0086
2SC124B	0086
2SC124C	0086
2SC124D	0086
2SC124E	0086
2SC124F	0086
2SC124G	0086
2SC124GN	0086
2SC124H	0086
2SC124J	0086
2SC124K	0086
2SC124L	0086
2SC124M	0086
2SC124OR	0086
2SC124R	0086
2SC124X	0086
2SC124Y	0086
2SC125	0086
2SC126	0283
2SC127	0016
2SC127A	0016
2SC127B	0016
2SC127C	0016
2SC127D	0016
2SC127E	0016
2SC127F	0016
2SC127G	0016
2SC127GN	0016
2SC127H	0016
2SC127J	0016
2SC127K	0016
2SC127L	0016
2SC127M	0016
2SC127OR	0016
2SC127R	0016
2SC127X	0016
2SC127Y	0016
2SC128	0595
2SC128A	0595
2SC128B	0595
2SC128C	0595
2SC128D	0595
2SC128E	0595
2SC128F	0595
2SC128G	0595
2SC128GN	0595
2SC128H	0595
2SC128J	0595
2SC128K	0595
2SC128L	0595
2SC128M	0595
2SC128OR	0595
2SC128R	0595
2SC128X	0595
2SC128Y	0595
2SC129	0595
2SC129A	0595
2SC129B	0595
2SC129C	0595
2SC129D	0595
2SC129E	0595
2SC129F	0595
2SC129GN	0595
2SC129H	0595
2SC129J	0595
2SC129K	0595

DEVICE TYPE	REPL CODE
2SC129L	0595
2SC129M	0595
2SC129OR	0595
2SC129R	0595
2SC129X	0595
2SC129Y	0595
2SC130	0086
2SC130A	0086
2SC130B	0086
2SC130C	0086
2SC130D	0086
2SC130E	0086
2SC130F	0086
2SC130GN	0086
2SC130H	0086
2SC130J	0086
2SC130K	0086
2SC130L	0086
2SC130M	0086
2SC130OR	0086
2SC130R	0086
2SC130X	0086
2SC130Y	0086
2SC131	0016
2SC131A	0016
2SC131B	0016
2SC131C	0016
2SC131D	0016
2SC131E	0016
2SC131F	0016
2SC131G	0016
2SC131GN	0016
2SC131H	0016
2SC131J	0016
2SC131L	0016
2SC131M	0016
2SC131OR	0016
2SC131R	0016
2SC131T	0016
2SC131Y	0016
2SC132	0016
2SC132A	0016
2SC132B	0016
2SC132C	0016
2SC132D	0016
2SC132E	0016
2SC132F	0016
2SC132G	0016
2SC132GN	0016
2SC132H	0016
2SC132J	0016
2SC132K	0016
2SC132L	0016
2SC132M	0016
2SC132OR	0016
2SC132R	0016
2SC132X	0016
2SC132Y	0016
2SC133	0016
2SC133A	0016
2SC133C	0016
2SC133D	0016
2SC133E	0016
2SC133F	0016
2SC133G	0016
2SC133GN	0016
2SC133H	0016
2SC133J	0016
2SC133K	0016
2SC133L	0016
2SC133M	0016
2SC133OR	0016
2SC133X	0016
2SC133Y	0016
2SC134	0016
2SC134A	0016
2SC134B	0016
2SC134C	0016
2SC134D	0016
2SC134E	0016
2SC134F	0016
2SC134G	0016
2SC134GN	0016
2SC134H	0016
2SC134J	0016
2SC134K	0016
2SC134L	0016
2SC134M	0016
2SC134OR	0016
2SC134R	0016
2SC134X	0016
2SC134Y	0016
2SC135	0016
2SC135A	0016
2SC135B	0016
2SC135C	0016
2SC135D	0016
2SC135E	0016
2SC135F	0016
2SC135G	0016
2SC135GN	0016
2SC135H	0016
2SC135J	0016
2SC135L	0016
2SC135M	0016
2SC135OR	0016
2SC135R	0016
2SC135X	0016
2SC135Y	0016

DEVICE TYPE	REPL CODE
2SC136	0016
2SC136D	0016
2SC137	0016
2SC137A	0016
2SC137B	0016
2SC137C	0016
2SC137D	0016
2SC137E	0016
2SC137F	0016
2SC137G	0016
2SC137GN	0016
2SC137H	0016
2SC137J	0016
2SC137K	0016
2SC137L	0016
2SC137M	0016
2SC137OR	0016
2SC137R	0016
2SC137X	0016
2SC137Y	0016
2SC138	0016
2SC138A	0016
2SC138B	0016
2SC138C	0016
2SC138D	0016
2SC138E	0016
2SC138F	0016
2SC138G	0016
2SC138GN	0016
2SC138H	0016
2SC138J	0016
2SC138L	0016
2SC138M	0016
2SC138OR	0016
2SC138R	0016
2SC138S	0016
2SC138X	0016
2SC139	0016
2SC139A	0016
2SC139B	0016
2SC139C	0016
2SC139D	0016
2SC139E	0016
2SC139F	0016
2SC139G	0016
2SC139GN	0016
2SC139H	0016
2SC139J	0016
2SC139K	0016
2SC139M	0016
2SC139OR	0016
2SC139R	0016
2SC139X	0016
2SC139Y	0016
2SC140	0086
2SC140A	0086
2SC140C	0086
2SC140D	0086
2SC140E	0086
2SC140F	0086
2SC140G	0086
2SC140GN	0086
2SC140H	0086
2SC140J	0086
2SC140K	0086
2SC140L	0086
2SC140M	0086
2SC140OR	0086
2SC140R	0086
2SC140X	0086
2SC140Y	0086
2SC141	0079
2SC142	0079
2SC143	0079
2SC144	0079
2SC144A	0079
2SC145	0079
2SC146	0079
2SC146A	0079
2SC147	2338
2SC147A	2338
2SC147B	2338
2SC147C	2338
2SC147D	2338
2SC147F	2338
2SC147G	2338
2SC147GN	2338
2SC147H	2338
2SC147J	2338
2SC147K	2338
2SC147L	2338
2SC147M	2338
2SC147R	2338
2SC147X	2338
2SC147Y	2338
2SC148	0144
2SC148A	0144
2SC148B	0144
2SC148D	0144
2SC148E	0144
2SC148F	0144
2SC148G	0144
2SC148GN	0144
2SC148H	0144
2SC148J	0144
2SC148K	0144
2SC148L	0144
2SC148M	0144
2SC148OR	0144

DEVICE TYPE	REPL CODE
2SC148R	0144
2SC148X	0144
2SC148Y	0144
2SC149	0086
2SC150	2361
2SC150-OR	2361
2SC150A	2361
2SC150B	2361
2SC150C	2361
2SC150D	2361
2SC150E	2361
2SC150F	2361
2SC150G	2361
2SC150GN	2361
2SC150H	2361
2SC150J	2361
2SC150K	2361
2SC150L	2361
2SC150M	2361
2SC150OR	2361
2SC150R	2361
2SC150T	2361
2SC150X	2361
2SC150Y	2361
2SC151	0198
2SC151A	0198
2SC151B	0198
2SC151C	0198
2SC151D	0198
2SC151E	0198
2SC151G	0198
2SC151GN	0198
2SC151H	0198
2SC151HA	0198
2SC151HB	0198
2SC151HC	0198
2SC151J	0198
2SC151K	0198
2SC151L	0198
2SC151M	0198
2SC151OR	0198
2SC151R	0198
2SC151X	0198
2SC151Y	0198
2SC152	0198
2SC152A	0198
2SC152B	0198
2SC152C	0198
2SC152D	0198
2SC152E	0198
2SC152F	0198
2SC152G	0198
2SC152GN	0198
2SC152H	0198
2SC152HA	0198
2SC152HB	0198
2SC152HC	0198
2SC152J	0198
2SC152K	0198
2SC152L	0198
2SC152M	0198
2SC152OR	0198
2SC152R	0198
2SC152X	0198
2SC152Y	0198
2SC153	0079
2SC154	0711
2SC154(C)	0711
2SC154-OR	0711
2SC154A	0711
2SC154B	0711
2SC154C	0711
2SC154D	0711
2SC154E	0711
2SC154F	0711
2SC154G	0711
2SC154GN	0711
2SC154H	0711
2SC154HA	0711
2SC154HB	0711
2SC154HC	0711
2SC154J	0711
2SC154K	0711
2SC154L	0711
2SC154M	0711
2SC154OR	0711
2SC154R	0711
2SC154X	0711
2SC154Y	0711
2SC155	0127
2SC155A	0127
2SC155B	0127
2SC155C	0127
2SC155D	0127
2SC155E	0127
2SC155F	0127
2SC155GN	0127
2SC155H	0127
2SC155J	0127
2SC155K	0127
2SC155L	0127
2SC155M	0127
2SC155OR	0127
2SC155R	0127
2SC155X	0127
2SC155Y	0127
2SC156	0127
2SC156A	0127
2SC156B	0127

DEVICE TYPE	REPL CODE
2SC156C	0127
2SC156D	0127
2SC156E	0127
2SC156F	0127
2SC156G	0127
2SC156GN	0127
2SC156H	0127
2SC156J	0127
2SC156K	0127
2SC156L	0127
2SC156M	0127
2SC156OR	0127
2SC156R	0127
2SC156X	0127
2SC156Y	0127
2SC157	0198
2SC157A	0198
2SC157B	0198
2SC157C	0198
2SC157D	0198
2SC157E	0198
2SC157F	0198
2SC157G	0198
2SC157GN	0198
2SC157J	0198
2SC157K	0198
2SC157L	0198
2SC157M	0198
2SC157OR	0198
2SC157R	0198
2SC157Y	0198
2SC158	0198
2SC158A	0198
2SC158B	0198
2SC158C	0198
2SC158D	0198
2SC158E	0198
2SC158F	0198
2SC158G	0198
2SC158GN	0198
2SC158H	0198
2SC158J	0198
2SC158K	0198
2SC158L	0198
2SC158M	0198
2SC158OR	0198
2SC158R	0198
2SC158X	0198
2SC158Y	0198
2SC159	0016
2SC159A	0016
2SC159B	0016
2SC159C	0016
2SC159D	0016
2SC159E	0016
2SC159F	0016
2SC159GN	0016
2SC159H	0016
2SC159J	0016
2SC159K	0016
2SC159L	0016
2SC159M	0016
2SC159OR	0016
2SC159R	0016
2SC159X	0016
2SC159Y	0016
2SC160	0016
2SC160A	0016
2SC160B	0016
2SC160C	0016
2SC160D	0016
2SC160E	0016
2SC160F	0016
2SC160G	0016
2SC160GN	0016
2SC160H	0016
2SC160J	0016
2SC160K	0016
2SC160L	0016
2SC160M	0016
2SC160OR	0016
2SC160R	0016
2SC160X	0016
2SC160Y	0016
2SC161	0538
2SC162	0079
2SC163	0488
2SC163A	0488
2SC163B	0488
2SC163C	0488
2SC163D	0488
2SC163E	0488
2SC163F	0488
2SC163G	0488
2SC163GN	0488
2SC163H	0488
2SC163J	0488
2SC163K	0488
2SC163L	0488
2SC163M	0488
2SC163OR	0488
2SC163R	0488
2SC163X	0488
2SC163Y	0488
2SC164	0018
2SC164(E)	0018
2SC164A	0018
2SC164B	0018
2SC164C	0018

If replacement code is OEM, contact original manufacturer for replacement. 77

DEVICE TYPE	REPL CODE
2SC164D	0018
2SC164E	0018
2SC164F	0018
2SC164G	0018
2SC164GN	0018
2SC164H	0018
2SC164J	0018
2SC164K	0018
2SC164L	0018
2SC164OR	0018
2SC164R	0018
2SC164X	0018
2SC164Y	0018
2SC165	0590
2SC166	0016
2SC166A	0016
2SC166B	0016
2SC166C	0016
2SC166D	0016
2SC166E	0016
2SC166F	0016
2SC166G	0016
2SC166GN	0016
2SC166H	0016
2SC166J	0016
2SC166K	0016
2SC166L	0016
2SC166M	0016
2SC166OR	0016
2SC166R	0016
2SC166X	0016
2SC166Y	0016
2SC167	0016
2SC167A	0016
2SC167B	0016
2SC167C	0016
2SC167D	0016
2SC167E	0016
2SC167F	0016
2SC167G	0016
2SC167GN	0016
2SC167H	0016
2SC167K	0016
2SC167L	0016
2SC167M	0016
2SC167OR	0016
2SC167X	0016
2SC167Y	0016
2SC168	0079
2SC169	0016
2SC170	0016
2SC170A	0016
2SC170B	0016
2SC170C	0016
2SC170D	0016
2SC170E	0016
2SC170F	0016
2SC170G	0016
2SC170GN	0016
2SC170H	0016
2SC170J	0016
2SC170K	0016
2SC170L	0016
2SC170M	0016
2SC170OR	0016
2SC170R	0016
2SC170X	0016
2SC170Y	0016
2SC171	0016
2SC171A	0016
2SC171B	0016
2SC171C	0016
2SC171D	0016
2SC171E	0016
2SC171F	0016
2SC171G	0016
2SC171GN	0016
2SC171H	0016
2SC171J	0016
2SC171K	0016
2SC171L	0016
2SC171M	0016
2SC171OR	0016
2SC171R	0016
2SC171X	0016
2SC171Y	0016
2SC172	0016
2SC172A	0016
2SC172B	0016
2SC172C	0016
2SC172D	0016
2SC172E	0016
2SC172F	0016
2SC172G	0016
2SC172GN	0016
2SC172H	0016
2SC172J	0016
2SC172K	0016
2SC172L	0016
2SC172M	0016
2SC172OR	0016
2SC172R	0016
2SC172Y	0016
2SC173	0595
2SC173A	0595
2SC173B	0595
2SC173C	0595
2SC173D	0595
2SC173E	0595
2SC173F	0595
2SC173G	0595
2SC173GN	0595
2SC173H	0595
2SC173J	0595
2SC173K	0595
2SC173L	0595
2SC173M	0595
2SC173OR	0595
2SC173R	0595
2SC173X	0595
2SC173Y	0595
2SC174	0016
2SC174A	0016
2SC174B	0016
2SC174C	0016
2SC174D	0016
2SC174E	0016
2SC174F	0016
2SC174G	0016
2SC174GN	0016
2SC174H	0016
2SC174J	0016
2SC174K	0016
2SC174L	0016
2SC174M	0016
2SC174OR	0016
2SC174Q	0016
2SC174R	0016
2SC174S	0016
2SC174X	0016
2SC174Y	0016
2SC175	0595
2SC175A	0595
2SC175B	0595
2SC175BL	0595
2SC175C	0595
2SC175D	0595
2SC175E	0595
2SC175F	0595
2SC175G	0595
2SC175GN	0595
2SC175H	0595
2SC175J	0595
2SC175K	0595
2SC175L	0595
2SC175M	0595
2SC175OR	0595
2SC175R	0595
2SC175X	0595
2SC175Y	0595
2SC176	0595
2SC176A	0595
2SC176B	0595
2SC176C	0595
2SC176D	0595
2SC176E	0595
2SC176F	0595
2SC176G	0595
2SC176GN	0595
2SC176H	0595
2SC176J	0595
2SC176K	0595
2SC176L	0595
2SC176OR	0595
2SC176R	0595
2SC176X	0595
2SC176Y	0595
2SC177	0595
2SC177A	0595
2SC177B	0595
2SC177C	0595
2SC177D	0595
2SC177E	0595
2SC177F	0595
2SC177G	0595
2SC177GN	0595
2SC177H	0595
2SC177J	0595
2SC177K	0595
2SC177L	0595
2SC177M	0595
2SC177OR	0595
2SC177R	0595
2SC177X	0595
2SC177Y	0595
2SC178	0595
2SC178A	0595
2SC178B	0595
2SC178C	0595
2SC178D	0595
2SC178E	0595
2SC178F	0595
2SC178G	0595
2SC178H	0595
2SC178J	0595
2SC178K	0595
2SC178L	0595
2SC178M	0595
2SC178OR	0595
2SC178R	0595
2SC178X	0595
2SC178Y	0595
2SC179	0208
2SC179A	0208
2SC179B	0208
2SC179C	0208
2SC179D	0208
2SC179E	0208
2SC179F	0208
2SC179G	0208
2SC179GN	0208
2SC179H	0208
2SC179J	0208
2SC179K	0208
2SC179L	0208
2SC179M	0208
2SC179OR	0208
2SC179R	0208
2SC179X	0208
2SC179Y	0208
2SC180	0208
2SC180A	0208
2SC180B	0208
2SC180C	0208
2SC180D	0208
2SC180E	0208
2SC180F	0208
2SC180G	0208
2SC180GN	0208
2SC180H	0208
2SC180J	0208
2SC180K	0208
2SC180L	0208
2SC180M	0208
2SC180OR	0208
2SC180R	0208
2SC180X	0208
2SC180Y	0208
2SC181	0208
2SC181A	0208
2SC181B	0208
2SC181C	0208
2SC181D	0208
2SC181E	0208
2SC181F	0208
2SC181G	0208
2SC181GN	0208
2SC181H	0208
2SC181J	0208
2SC181L	0208
2SC181M	0208
2SC181OR	0208
2SC181R	0208
2SC181X	0208
2SC181Y	0208
2SC182	0470
2SC182(Q)	0470
2SC182(V)	0470
2SC182A	0470
2SC182B	0470
2SC182C	0470
2SC182D	0470
2SC182E	0470
2SC182F	0470
2SC182G	0470
2SC182GN	0470
2SC182H	0470
2SC182J	0470
2SC182K	0470
2SC182L	0470
2SC182M	0470
2SC182Q	0470
2SC182R	0470
2SC182V	0470
2SC182X	0470
2SC182Y	0470
2SC183	0470
2SC183(P)	0470
2SC183(Q)(R)	0470
2SC183(R)	0470
2SC183-1	0470
2SC183-OR	0470
2SC183A	0470
2SC183AP	0470
2SC183B	0470
2SC183BK	0470
2SC183C	0470
2SC183D	0470
2SC183E	0470
2SC183F	0470
2SC183G	0470
2SC183GN	0470
2SC183H	0470
2SC183J	0470
2SC183K	0470
2SC183L	0470
2SC183M	0470
2SC183OR	0470
2SC183P	0470
2SC183Q	0470
2SC183R	0470
2SC183S	0470
2SC183W	0470
2SC183X	0470
2SC183Y	0470
2SC184	0470
2SC184(R)	0470
2SC184-OR	0470
2SC184A	0470
2SC184AP	0470
2SC184B	0470
2SC184BK	0470
2SC184C	0470
2SC184D	0470
2SC184E	0470
2SC184F	0470
2SC184G	0470
2SC184GN	0470
2SC184H	0470
2SC184J	0470
2SC184K	0470
2SC184L	0470
2SC184M	0470
2SC184OR	0470
2SC184P	0470
2SC184Q	0470
2SC184R	0470
2SC184X	0470
2SC184Y	0470
2SC185	0470
2SC185A	0470
2SC185B	0470
2SC185C	0470
2SC185E	0470
2SC185F	0470
2SC185G	0470
2SC185GN	0470
2SC185H	0470
2SC185J	0470
2SC185K	0470
2SC185L	0470
2SC185M	0470
2SC185OR	0470
2SC185Q	0470
2SC185R	0470
2SC185V	0470
2SC185X	0470
2SC185Y	0470
2SC186	0127
2SC186A	0127
2SC186B	0127
2SC186C	0127
2SC186D	0127
2SC186E	0127
2SC186F	0127
2SC186G	0127
2SC186GN	0127
2SC186H	0127
2SC186J	0127
2SC186K	0127
2SC186L	0127
2SC186M	0127
2SC186OR	0127
2SC186R	0127
2SC186X	0127
2SC186Y	0127
2SC187	0669
2SC187(I)	0669
2SC187-OR	0669
2SC187A	0669
2SC187B	0669
2SC187C	0669
2SC187D	0669
2SC187E	0669
2SC187F	0669
2SC187G	0669
2SC187H	0669
2SC187I	0669
2SC187J	0669
2SC187K	0669
2SC187L	0669
2SC187M	0669
2SC187OR	0669
2SC187R	0669
2SC187X	0669
2SC187Y	0669
2SC188	0086
2SC188A	0086
2SC188AB	0086
2SC188B	0086
2SC188C	0086
2SC188D	0086
2SC188E	0086
2SC188F	0086
2SC188G	0086
2SC188GN	0086
2SC188J	0086
2SC188K	0086
2SC188L	0086
2SC188M	0086
2SC188OR	0086
2SC188R	0086
2SC188X	0086
2SC188Y	0086
2SC189	0086
2SC189A	0086
2SC189B	0086
2SC189C	0086
2SC189D	0086
2SC189E	0086
2SC189F	0086
2SC189G	0086
2SC189GN	0086
2SC189H	0086
2SC189J	0086
2SC189K	0086
2SC189L	0086
2SC189M	0086
2SC189OR	0086
2SC189R	0086
2SC189X	0086
2SC189Y	0086
2SC190	0086
2SC190A	0086
2SC190B	0086
2SC190C	0086
2SC190D	0086
2SC190E	0086
2SC190F	0086
2SC190GN	0086
2SC190H	0086
2SC190J	0086
2SC190K	0086
2SC190L	0086
2SC190M	0086
2SC190OR	0086
2SC190R	0086
2SC190X	0086
2SC190Y	0086
2SC191	0016
2SC191A	0016
2SC191B	0016
2SC191C	0016
2SC191D	0016
2SC191E	0016
2SC191F	0016
2SC191G	0016
2SC191GN	0016
2SC191H	0016
2SC191J	0016
2SC191K	0016
2SC191L	0016
2SC191M	0016
2SC191OR	0016
2SC191R	0016
2SC191X	0016
2SC191Y	0016
2SC192	0016
2SC192A	0016
2SC192B	0016
2SC192C	0016
2SC192D	0016
2SC192E	0016
2SC192F	0016
2SC192G	0016
2SC192GN	0016
2SC192H	0016
2SC192J	0016
2SC192K	0016
2SC192L	0016
2SC192M	0016
2SC192OR	0016
2SC192R	0016
2SC192X	0016
2SC192Y	0016
2SC193	0016
2SC193A	0016
2SC193B	0016
2SC193C	0016
2SC193D	0016
2SC193E	0016
2SC193F	0016
2SC193G	0016
2SC193GN	0016
2SC193H	0016
2SC193J	0016
2SC193K	0016
2SC193L	0016
2SC193M	0016
2SC193OR	0016
2SC193R	0016
2SC193X	0016
2SC194	0016
2SC194A	0016
2SC194B	0016
2SC194C	0016
2SC194D	0016
2SC194E	0016
2SC194F	0016
2SC194G	0016
2SC194GN	0016
2SC194H	0016
2SC194J	0016
2SC194K	0016
2SC194L	0016
2SC194M	0016
2SC194OR	0016
2SC194X	0016
2SC194Y	0016
2SC195	0016
2SC195A	0016
2SC195B	0016
2SC195C	0016
2SC195D	0016
2SC195E	0016
2SC195F	0016
2SC195G	0016
2SC195GN	0016
2SC195H	0016
2SC195J	0016
2SC195K	0016
2SC195L	0016
2SC195M	0016
2SC195OR	0016
2SC195R	0016
2SC195X	0016
2SC195Y	0016
2SC196	0016
2SC196A	0016
2SC196B	0016
2SC196C	0016
2SC196D	0016
2SC196E	0016
2SC196F	0016
2SC196G	0016
2SC196GN	0016
2SC196H	0016
2SC196J	0016
2SC196K	0016
2SC196L	0016
2SC196M	0016
2SC196OR	0016
2SC196R	0016
2SC196X	0016
2SC196Y	0016
2SC197	0016
2SC197A	0016
2SC197B	0016
2SC197C	0016
2SC197D	0016
2SC197E	0016
2SC197F	0016
2SC197G	0016
2SC197GN	0016
2SC197H	0016
2SC197J	0016
2SC197K	0016
2SC197L	0016
2SC197M	0016
2SC197OR	0016
2SC197R	0016
2SC197X	0016
2SC197Y	0016
2SC198	0525
2SC198A	0525
2SC198H	0525
2SC198S	0525
2SC198T	0525
2SC199	0016
2SC199A	0016
2SC199B	0016
2SC199C	0016
2SC199D	0016
2SC199E	0016
2SC199F	0016
2SC199G	0016
2SC199GN	0016
2SC199H	0016
2SC199J	0016
2SC199K	0016
2SC199L	0016
2SC199M	0016
2SC199OR	0016
2SC199R	0016
2SC199X	0016
2SC199Y	0016
2SC200	0016
2SC200A	0016
2SC200B	0016
2SC200C	0016
2SC200D	0016
2SC200E	0016
2SC200F	0016
2SC200G	0016
2SC200GN	0016
2SC200H	0016
2SC200J	0016
2SC200K	0016
2SC200L	0016
2SC200M	0016
2SC200OR	0016
2SC200R	0016
2SC200X	0016
2SC200Y	0016
2SC201	0016
2SC201A	0016
2SC201B	0016
2SC201C	0016
2SC201D	0016
2SC201E	0016
2SC201F	0016
2SC201G	0016
2SC201GN	0016
2SC201H	0016
2SC201J	0016
2SC201K	0016
2SC201L	0016
2SC201M	0016
2SC201R	0016
2SC201X	0016
2SC201Y	0016
2SC202	0016
2SC202A	0016
2SC202B	0016
2SC202C	0016
2SC202D	0016
2SC202E	0016
2SC202F	0016
2SC202G	0016
2SC202GN	0016
2SC202H	0016
2SC202J	0016
2SC202K	0016
2SC202L	0016
2SC202M	0016
2SC202OR	0016
2SC202R	0016
2SC202X	0016
2SC202Y	0016
2SC203	0590
2SC203A	0590
2SC203AA	0590
2SC203B	0590
2SC203C	0590
2SC203D	0590
2SC203E	0590
2SC203F	0590
2SC203G	0590
2SC203GN	0590
2SC203H	0590
2SC203J	0590
2SC203K	0590
2SC203L	0590
2SC203M	0590
2SC203OR	0590
2SC203R	0590
2SC203X	0590
2SC203Y	0590
2SC204	0016
2SC204A	0016
2SC204B	0016
2SC204C	0016
2SC204D	0016
2SC204E	0016
2SC204F	0016
2SC204G	0016
2SC204GN	0016
2SC204H	0016
2SC204J	0016
2SC204K	0016
2SC204L	0016
2SC204M	0016
2SC204OR	0016
2SC204R	0016
2SC204X	0016
2SC204Y	0016
2SC205	0016
2SC205A	0016
2SC205B	0016
2SC205C	0016
2SC205D	0016
2SC205F	0016
2SC205G	0016
2SC205GN	0016
2SC205H	0016
2SC205J	0016
2SC205K	0016
2SC205L	0016
2SC205M	0016
2SC205OR	0016
2SC205R	0016
2SC205X	0016
2SC205Y	0016
2SC206	0216
2SC206-OR	0216
2SC206A	0216
2SC206B	0216
2SC206C	0216
2SC206D	0216
2SC206E	0216
2SC206G	0216
2SC206GN	0216
2SC206H	0216
2SC206J	0216
2SC206K	0216
2SC206L	0216
2SC206M	0216
2SC206OR	0216
2SC206R	0216
2SC206RED	0216
2SC206WHITE	0216
2SC206X	0216
2SC206Y	0216
2SC207	0259
2SC208	0007
2SC208A	0007
2SC208B	0007
2SC208C	0007
2SC208D	0007
2SC208E	0007
2SC208F	0007
2SC208G	0007
2SC208GN	0007
2SC208H	0007
2SC208J	0007
2SC208K	0007
2SC208L	0007
2SC208M	0007
2SC208OR	0007
2SC208R	0007
2SC208X	0007
2SC208Y	0007
2SC209	0259
2SC210	0086
2SC210A	0086
2SC210B	0086
2SC210C	0086
2SC210D	0086
2SC210E	0086
2SC210F	0086
2SC210G	0086
2SC210GN	0086
2SC210H	0086
2SC210J	0086
2SC210K	0086
2SC210L	0086
2SC210M	0086
2SC210OR	0086
2SC210R	0086
2SC210X	0086
2SC210Y	0086
2SC211	0086
2SC211A	0086

If replacement code is OEM, contact original manufacturer for replacement.

DEVICE TYPE	REPL CODE
2SC211B	0086
2SC211C	0086
2SC211D	0086
2SC211F	0086
2SC211G	0086
2SC211GN	0086
2SC211H	0086
2SC211J	0086
2SC211K	0086
2SC211L	0086
2SC211M	0086
2SC211OR	0086
2SC211R	0086
2SC211X	0086
2SC211Y	0086
2SC212	0086
2SC212A	0086
2SC212B	0086
2SC212C	0086
2SC212D	0086
2SC212E	0086
2SC212F	0086
2SC212G	0086
2SC212GN	0086
2SC212H	0086
2SC212J	0086
2SC212K	0086
2SC212L	0086
2SC212M	0086
2SC212OR	0086
2SC212R	0086
2SC212X	0086
2SC212Y	0086
2SC213	0617
2SC213A	0617
2SC213B	0617
2SC213C	0617
2SC213D	0617
2SC213E	0617
2SC213F	0617
2SC213G	0617
2SC213GN	0617
2SC213H	0617
2SC213J	0617
2SC213K	0617
2SC213L	0617
2SC213M	0617
2SC213OR	0617
2SC213R	0617
2SC213X	0617
2SC213Y	0617
2SC214	0617
2SC214A	0617
2SC214B	0617
2SC214C	0617
2SC214D	0617
2SC214E	0617
2SC214F	0617
2SC214G	0617
2SC214GN	0617
2SC214H	0617
2SC214J	0617
2SC214K	0617
2SC214L	0617
2SC214M	0617
2SC214OR	0617
2SC214X	0617
2SC214Y	0617
2SC215	0617
2SC215A	0617
2SC215B	0617
2SC215C	0617
2SC215E	0617
2SC215F	0617
2SC215G	0617
2SC215GN	0617
2SC215H	0617
2SC215J	0617
2SC215K	0617
2SC215L	0617
2SC215M	0617
2SC215OR	0617
2SC215R	0617
2SC215X	0617
2SC215Y	0617
2SC216	0086
2SC216A	0086
2SC216B	0086
2SC216C	0086
2SC216D	0086
2SC216E	0086
2SC216F	0086
2SC216G	0086
2SC216GN	0086
2SC216H	0086
2SC216J	0086
2SC216K	0086
2SC216L	0086
2SC216M	0086
2SC216OR	0086
2SC216R	0086
2SC216X	0086
2SC216Y	0086
2SC217	0086
2SC217A	0086
2SC217B	0086
2SC217C	0086
2SC217D	0086
2SC217E	0086
2SC217F	0086
2SC217G	0086
2SC217GN	0086
2SC217H	0086
2SC217J	0086
2SC217K	0086
2SC217L	0086
2SC217M	0086
2SC217OR	0086
2SC217R	0086
2SC217X	0086
2SC217Y	0086
2SC218	0086
2SC218A	0086
2SC218B	0086
2SC218C	0086
2SC218D	0086
2SC218E	0086
2SC218F	0086
2SC218G	0086
2SC218GN	0086
2SC218H	0086
2SC218J	0086
2SC218L	0086
2SC218M	0086
2SC218OR	0086
2SC218R	0086
2SC218X	0086
2SC218Y	0086
2SC219	0007
2SC220	0086
2SC220A	0086
2SC220B	0086
2SC220C	0086
2SC220D	0086
2SC220E	0086
2SC220F	0086
2SC220G	0086
2SC220GN	0086
2SC220H	0086
2SC220K	0086
2SC220L	0086
2SC220M	0086
2SC220OR	0086
2SC220R	0086
2SC220X	0086
2SC220Y	0086
2SC221	0086
2SC221A	0086
2SC221B	0086
2SC221C	0086
2SC221D	0086
2SC221E	0086
2SC221F	0086
2SC221G	0086
2SC221GN	0086
2SC221H	0086
2SC221J	0086
2SC221K	0086
2SC221L	0086
2SC221M	0086
2SC221OR	0086
2SC221R	0086
2SC221X	0086
2SC221Y	0086
2SC222	0086
2SC222A	0086
2SC222B	0086
2SC222C	0086
2SC222D	0086
2SC222E	0086
2SC222F	0086
2SC222G	0086
2SC222GN	0086
2SC222H	0086
2SC222J	0086
2SC222L	0086
2SC222M	0086
2SC222OR	0086
2SC222R	0086
2SC222X	0086
2SC222Y	0086
2SC223	0617
2SC223A	0617
2SC223B	0617
2SC223C	0617
2SC223D	0617
2SC223E	0617
2SC223F	0617
2SC223G	0617
2SC223GN	0617
2SC223H	0617
2SC223J	0617
2SC223L	0617
2SC223M	0617
2SC223OR	0617
2SC223R	0617
2SC223X	0617
2SC223Y	0617
2SC224	0617
2SC224A	0617
2SC224B	0617
2SC224C	0617
2SC224D	0617
2SC224E	0617
2SC224F	0617
2SC224G	0617
2SC224GN	0617
2SC224GR-GL	0617
2SC224H	0617
2SC224J	0617
2SC224K	0617
2SC224L	0617
2SC224M	0617
2SC224OR	0617
2SC224R	0617
2SC224X	0617
2SC224Y	0617
2SC225	0086
2SC225A	0086
2SC225B	0086
2SC225C	0086
2SC225D	0086
2SC225E	0086
2SC225F	0086
2SC225G	0086
2SC225GN	0086
2SC225H	0086
2SC225J	0086
2SC225L	0086
2SC225M	0086
2SC225OR	0086
2SC225R	0086
2SC225X	0086
2SC225Y	0086
2SC226	0086
2SC226A	0086
2SC226B	0086
2SC226C	0086
2SC226D	0086
2SC226E	0086
2SC226F	0086
2SC226G	0086
2SC226GN	0086
2SC226H	0086
2SC226J	0086
2SC226K	0086
2SC226L	0086
2SC226M	0086
2SC226OR	0086
2SC226R	0086
2SC226X	0086
2SC226Y	0086
2SC227	0086
2SC227A	0086
2SC227B	0086
2SC227C	0086
2SC227D	0086
2SC227E	0086
2SC227F	0086
2SC227G	0086
2SC227GN	0086
2SC227H	0086
2SC227J	0086
2SC227K	0086
2SC227L	0086
2SC227M	0086
2SC227OR	0086
2SC227R	0086
2SC227X	0086
2SC227Y	0086
2SC228	0086
2SC228A	0086
2SC228B	0086
2SC228C	0086
2SC228D	0086
2SC228E	0086
2SC228F	0086
2SC228G	0086
2SC228GN	0086
2SC228H	0086
2SC228J	0086
2SC228K	0086
2SC228L	0086
2SC228M	0086
2SC228OR	0086
2SC228R	0086
2SC228X	0086
2SC228Y	0086
2SC229	0617
2SC229A	0617
2SC229B	0617
2SC229C	0617
2SC229D	0617
2SC229E	0617
2SC229F	0617
2SC229G	0617
2SC229GN	0617
2SC229H	0617
2SC229J	0617
2SC229K	0617
2SC229L	0617
2SC229M	0617
2SC229OR	0617
2SC229R	0617
2SC229X	0617
2SC229Y	0617
2SC230	2960
2SC230A	2960
2SC230B	2960
2SC230C	2960
2SC230D	2960
2SC230E	2960
2SC230F	2960
2SC230G	2960
2SC230GN	2960
2SC230H	2960
2SC230J	2960
2SC230K	2960
2SC230L	2960
2SC230M	2960
2SC230OR	2960
2SC230R	2960
2SC230X	2960
2SC230Y	2960
2SC231	2968
2SC231A	2968
2SC231B	2968
2SC231C	2968
2SC231D	2968
2SC231E	2968
2SC231F	2968
2SC231G	2968
2SC231GN	2968
2SC231H	2968
2SC231J	2968
2SC231K	2968
2SC231L	2968
2SC231M	2968
2SC231OR	2968
2SC231R	2968
2SC231X	2968
2SC231Y	2968
2SC232	2980
2SC232A	2980
2SC232B	2980
2SC232C	2980
2SC232D	2980
2SC232E	2980
2SC232F	2980
2SC232G	2980
2SC232GN	2980
2SC232H	2980
2SC232J	2980
2SC232K	2980
2SC232L	2980
2SC232M	2980
2SC232OR	2980
2SC232R	2980
2SC232X	2980
2SC232Y	2980
2SC233	0617
2SC233A	0617
2SC233B	0617
2SC233C	0617
2SC233D	0617
2SC233F	0617
2SC233G	0617
2SC233GN	0617
2SC233H	0617
2SC233J	0617
2SC233L	0617
2SC233M	0617
2SC233OR	0617
2SC233R	0617
2SC233X	0617
2SC233Y	0617
2SC234	0086
2SC234A	0086
2SC234B	0086
2SC234C	0086
2SC234D	0086
2SC234E	0086
2SC234F	0086
2SC234G	0086
2SC234GN	0086
2SC234H	0086
2SC234J	0086
2SC234K	0086
2SC234L	0086
2SC234M	0086
2SC234OR	0086
2SC234R	0086
2SC234X	0086
2SC234Y	0086
2SC235	0018
2SC235(0)	0018
2SC235-0	0018
2SC235-O	0018
2SC235A	0018
2SC235B	0018
2SC235C	0018
2SC235D	0018
2SC235E	0018
2SC235F	0018
2SC235G	0018
2SC235GN	0018
2SC235H	0018
2SC235J	0018
2SC235K	0018
2SC235L	0018
2SC235M	0018
2SC235OR	0018
2SC235R	0018
2SC235X	0018
2SC235Y	0018
2SC236	0086
2SC236A	0086
2SC236B	0086
2SC236C	0086
2SC236D	0086
2SC236E	0086
2SC236F	0086
2SC236G	0086
2SC236GN	0086
2SC236H	0086
2SC236J	0086
2SC236K	0086
2SC236L	0086
2SC236M	0086
2SC236OR	0086
2SC236R	0086
2SC236X	0086
2SC236Y	0086
2SC237	0016
2SC237A	0016
2SC237B	0016
2SC237C	0016
2SC237D	0016
2SC237E	0016
2SC237F	0016
2SC237G	0016
2SC237GN	0016
2SC237H	0016
2SC237J	0016
2SC237K	0016
2SC237L	0016
2SC237M	0016
2SC237OR	0016
2SC237R	0016
2SC237X	0016
2SC237Y	0016
2SC238	0016
2SC238A	0016
2SC238B	0016
2SC238C	0016
2SC238D	0016
2SC238E	0016
2SC238F	0016
2SC238G	0016
2SC238GN	0016
2SC238H	0016
2SC238J	0016
2SC238K	0016
2SC238L	0016
2SC238M	0016
2SC238OR	0016
2SC238R	0016
2SC238X	0016
2SC238Y	0016
2SC239	0016
2SC239A	0016
2SC239B	0016
2SC239C	0016
2SC239D	0016
2SC239E	0016
2SC239F	0016
2SC239G	0016
2SC239GN	0016
2SC239H	0016
2SC239J	0016
2SC239K	0016
2SC239L	0016
2SC239M	0016
2SC239OR	0016
2SC239R	0016
2SC239X	0016
2SC239Y	0016
2SC240	0103
2SC240A	0103
2SC240B	0103
2SC240C	0103
2SC240D	0103
2SC240E	0103
2SC240F	0103
2SC240G	0103
2SC240GN	0103
2SC240H	0103
2SC240J	0103
2SC240K	0103
2SC240L	0103
2SC240M	0103
2SC240OR	0103
2SC240R	0103
2SC240X	0103
2SC240Y	0103
2SC241	0103
2SC241A	0103
2SC241B	0103
2SC241C	0103
2SC241D	0103
2SC241E	0103
2SC241F	0103
2SC241G	0103
2SC241GN	0103
2SC241H	0103
2SC241K	0103
2SC241L	0103
2SC241M	0103
2SC241OR	0103
2SC241R	0103
2SC241X	0103
2SC241Y	0103
2SC242	0103
2SC242A	0103
2SC242B	0103
2SC242C	0103
2SC242D	0103
2SC242E	0103
2SC242F	0103
2SC242G	0103
2SC242GN	0103
2SC242H	0103
2SC242J	0103
2SC242K	0103
2SC242L	0103
2SC242M	0103
2SC242OR	0103
2SC242R	0103
2SC242X	0103
2SC242Y	0103
2SC243	0177
2SC244	1955
2SC244A	1955
2SC244B	1955
2SC244C	1955
2SC244D	1955
2SC244E	1955
2SC244F	1955
2SC244G	1955
2SC244GN	1955
2SC244J	1955
2SC244K	1955
2SC244L	1955
2SC244M	1955
2SC244OR	1955
2SC244R	1955
2SC244X	1955
2SC244Y	1955
2SC245	1955
2SC246	1955
2SC247	0086
2SC247A	0086
2SC247B	0086
2SC247C	0086
2SC247D	0086
2SC247E	0086
2SC247F	0086
2SC247G	0086
2SC247GN	0086
2SC247H	0086
2SC247J	0086
2SC247L	0086
2SC247M	0086
2SC247OR	0086
2SC247R	0086
2SC247X	0086
2SC247Y	0086
2SC248	0016
2SC248(0)	0016
2SC248A	0016
2SC248B	0016
2SC248C	0016
2SC248D	0016
2SC248E	0016
2SC248F	0016
2SC248G	0016
2SC248J	0016
2SC248K	0016
2SC248L	0016
2SC248M	0016
2SC248OR	0016
2SC248R	0016
2SC248X	0016
2SC248Y	0016
2SC249	0086
2SC249A	0086
2SC249B	0086
2SC249C	0086
2SC249D	0086
2SC249E	0086
2SC249F	0086
2SC249G	0086
2SC249GN	0086
2SC249H	0086
2SC249J	0086
2SC249K	0086
2SC249L	0086
2SC249M	0086
2SC249OR	0086
2SC249R	0086
2SC249X	0086
2SC249Y	0086
2SC250	0016
2SC250A	0016
2SC250B	0016
2SC250C	0016
2SC250D	0016
2SC250E	0016
2SC250F	0016
2SC250G	0016
2SC250GN	0016
2SC250H	0016
2SC250J	0016
2SC250K	0016
2SC250L	0016
2SC250M	0016
2SC250OR	0016
2SC250R	0016
2SC250X	0016
2SC250Y	0016
2SC251	0259
2SC251A	0259
2SC251B	0259
2SC251C	0259
2SC251D	0259
2SC251E	0259
2SC251F	0259
2SC251G	0259
2SC251GN	0259
2SC251H	0259
2SC251J	0259
2SC251K	0259
2SC251L	0259
2SC251M	0259
2SC251OR	0259
2SC251R	0259
2SC251X	0259
2SC251Y	0259
2SC252	0259
2SC252A	0259
2SC252B	0259
2SC252C	0259
2SC252D	0259
2SC252E	0259
2SC252F	0259
2SC252G	0259
2SC252GN	0259
2SC252H	0259
2SC252J	0259
2SC252K	0259
2SC252L	0259
2SC252M	0259
2SC252OR	0259
2SC252R	0259
2SC252X	0259
2SC252Y	0259
2SC253	0259
2SC253A	0259
2SC253B	0259
2SC253C	0259
2SC253D	0259
2SC253E	0259
2SC253F	0259
2SC253G	0259
2SC253GN	0259
2SC253H	0259
2SC253J	0259
2SC253K	0259
2SC253L	0259
2SC253M	0259
2SC253OR	0259
2SC253R	0259
2SC253RS	0259
2SC253X	0259
2SC253Y	0259
2SC254	0086
2SC255	0086
2SC256	0086
2SC257	1973
2SC258	0264
2SC259	0264
2SC260	0590
2SC260D	0590
2SC260E	0590
2SC261	0693
2SC262	0590
2SC263	0144
2SC263A	0144
2SC263B	0144
2SC263C	0144
2SC263D	0144
2SC263E	0144
2SC263F	0144
2SC263G	0144
2SC263GN	0144
2SC263H	0144
2SC263J	0144
2SC263K	0144
2SC263L	0144
2SC263M	0144
2SC263OR	0144
2SC263R	0144
2SC263X	0144
2SC263Y	0144
2SC264	0079
2SC265	0079
2SC266	0470
2SC266A	0470
2SC266B	0470
2SC266C	0470
2SC266D	0470
2SC266E	0470
2SC266F	0470
2SC266G	0470
2SC266GN	0470
2SC266H	0470
2SC266J	0470
2SC266K	0470
2SC266L	0470
2SC266M	0470
2SC266OR	0470
2SC266R	0470
2SC266X	0470
2SC266Y	0470
2SC267	0016
2SC267A	0016
2SC267B	0016
2SC267C	0016
2SC267D	0016
2SC267E	0016
2SC267F	0016
2SC267G	0016
2SC267GN	0016
2SC267H	0016
2SC267J	0016
2SC267K	0016
2SC267L	0016
2SC267M	0016
2SC267OR	0016
2SC267R	0016
2SC267X	0016
2SC267Y	0016
2SC268	0086

If replacement code is OEM, contact original manufacturer for replacement.

DEVICE TYPE	REPL CODE
2SC268-OR	0086
2SC268A	0086
2SC268B	0086
2SC268C	0086
2SC268D	0086
2SC268E	0086
2SC268F	0086
2SC268G	0086
2SC268GN	0086
2SC268H	0086
2SC268J	0086
2SC268K	0086
2SC268L	0086
2SC268M	0086
2SC268OR	0086
2SC268R	0086
2SC268X	0086
2SC268Y	0086
2SC269	0144
2SC269A	0144
2SC269B	0144
2SC269C	0144
2SC269D	0144
2SC269E	0144
2SC269F	0144
2SC269G	0144
2SC269GN	0144
2SC269H	0144
2SC269J	0144
2SC269K	0144
2SC269L	0144
2SC269M	0144
2SC269OR	0144
2SC269R	0144
2SC269X	0144
2SC269Y	0144
2SC270	0074
2SC271	0144
2SC271A	0144
2SC271B	0144
2SC271C	0144
2SC271D	0144
2SC271E	0144
2SC271F	0144
2SC271G	0144
2SC271GN	0144
2SC271H	0144
2SC271J	0144
2SC271K	0144
2SC271L	0144
2SC271M	0144
2SC271OR	0144
2SC271R	0144
2SC271X	0144
2SC271Y	0144
2SC272	0144
2SC272A	0144
2SC272B	0144
2SC272C	0144
2SC272D	0144
2SC272E	0144
2SC272F	0144
2SC272G	0144
2SC272GN	0144
2SC272H	0144
2SC272J	0144
2SC272K	0144
2SC272L	0144
2SC272M	0144
2SC272OR	0144
2SC272R	0144
2SC272X	0144
2SC272Y	0144
2SC273	0233
2SC277C	0208
2SC278-OR	0470
2SC280	0111
2SC280A0	0111
2SC281	0531
2SC281(B)	0531
2SC281-OR	0531
2SC281A	0531
2SC281B	0531
2SC281BL	0531
2SC281C	0531
2SC281C-EP	0531
2SC281D	0531
2SC281E	0531
2SC281EP	0531
2SC281F	0531
2SC281G	0531
2SC281GN	0531
2SC281H	0531
2SC281J	0531
2SC281K	0531
2SC281L	0531
2SC281M	0531
2SC281OR	0531
2SC281R	0531
2SC281X	0531
2SC281Y	0531
2SC282	0016
2SC282A	0016
2SC282B	0016
2SC282C	0016
2SC282D	0016
2SC282E	0016
2SC282F	0016
2SC282G	0016

DEVICE TYPE	REPL CODE
2SC282GN	0016
2SC282H	0016
2SC282J	0016
2SC282K	0016
2SC282L	0016
2SC282M	0016
2SC282OR	0016
2SC282R	0016
2SC282X	0016
2SC282Y	0016
2SC283	1553
2SC283A	1553
2SC283B	1553
2SC283C	1553
2SC283D	1553
2SC283E	1553
2SC283F	1553
2SC283G	1553
2SC283GN	1553
2SC283H	1553
2SC283J	1553
2SC283K	1553
2SC283L	1553
2SC283M	1553
2SC283OR	1553
2SC283R	1553
2SC283X	1553
2SC283Y	1553
2SC284	0016
2SC284A	0016
2SC284B	0016
2SC284C	0016
2SC284D	0016
2SC284E	0016
2SC284F	0016
2SC284G	0016
2SC284GN	0016
2SC284H	0016
2SC284J	0016
2SC284K	0016
2SC284L	0016
2SC284M	0016
2SC284OR	0016
2SC284R	0016
2SC284X	0016
2SC284Y	0016
2SC285	0488
2SC285A	0488
2SC285B	0488
2SC285C	0488
2SC285D	0488
2SC285E	0488
2SC285F	0488
2SC285G	0488
2SC285GN	0488
2SC285H	0488
2SC285J	0488
2SC285K	0488
2SC285L	0488
2SC285M	0488
2SC285OR	0488
2SC285R	0488
2SC285X	0488
2SC285Y	0488
2SC286	0144
2SC286A	0144
2SC286B	0144
2SC286C	0144
2SC286D	0144
2SC286E	0144
2SC286F	0144
2SC286G	0144
2SC286GN	0144
2SC286H	0144
2SC286J	0144
2SC286K	0144
2SC286L	0144
2SC286M	0144
2SC286OR	0144
2SC286R	0144
2SC286X	0144
2SC286Y	0144
2SC287	0470
2SC287-OR	0470
2SC287A	0470
2SC287A-B	OEM
2SC287B	0470
2SC287C	0470
2SC287D	0470
2SC287E	0470
2SC287F	0470
2SC287G	0470
2SC287GN	0470
2SC287H	0470
2SC287J	0470
2SC287K	0470
2SC287L	0470
2SC287M	0470
2SC287OR	0470
2SC287R	0470
2SC287X	0470
2SC287Y	0470
2SC288	1332
2SC288A	1332
2SC288A(5B)	1332
2SC288A1	1332
2SC288A1B	1332
2SC288A5-B	1332
2SC288AB	1332

DEVICE TYPE	REPL CODE
2SC288B	1332
2SC288C	1332
2SC288D	1332
2SC288E	1332
2SC288F	1332
2SC288G	1332
2SC288GN	1332
2SC288H	1332
2SC288J	1332
2SC288K	1332
2SC288L	1332
2SC288M	1332
2SC288OR	1332
2SC288R	1332
2SC288X	1332
2SC288Y	1332
2SC289	0144
2SC289A	0144
2SC289B	0144
2SC289C	0144
2SC289D	0144
2SC289E	0144
2SC289F	0144
2SC289G	0144
2SC289GN	0144
2SC289H	0144
2SC289J	0144
2SC289K	0144
2SC289L	0144
2SC289M	0144
2SC289OR	0144
2SC289R	0144
2SC289X	0144
2SC289Y	0144
2SC290	0693
2SC291	0086
2SC291A	0086
2SC291B	0086
2SC291C	0086
2SC291D	0086
2SC291E	0086
2SC291F	0086
2SC291G	0086
2SC291GN	0086
2SC291H	0086
2SC291J	0086
2SC291K	0086
2SC291M	0086
2SC291OR	0086
2SC291R	0086
2SC291X	0086
2SC291Y	0086
2SC292	0617
2SC292A	0617
2SC292B	0617
2SC292C	0617
2SC292D	0617
2SC292E	0617
2SC292F	0617
2SC292G	0617
2SC292GN	0617
2SC292H	0617
2SC292J	0617
2SC292K	0617
2SC292L	0617
2SC292M	0617
2SC292OR	0617
2SC292R	0617
2SC292X	0617
2SC292Y	0617
2SC293	0617
2SC293A	0617
2SC293B	0617
2SC293C	0617
2SC293D	0617
2SC293E	0617
2SC293F	0617
2SC293G	0617
2SC293GN	0617
2SC293H	0617
2SC293J	0617
2SC293K	0617
2SC293L	0617
2SC293M	0617
2SC293OR	0617
2SC293R	0617
2SC293X	0617
2SC293Y	0617
2SC294	0283
2SC294X	0283
2SC295	0079
2SC296	0419
2SC297	0555
2SC298	0617
2SC298-4	0617
2SC299	3302
2SC299A	3302
2SC299B	3302
2SC299C	3302
2SC299D	3302
2SC299E	3302
2SC299F	3302
2SC299G	3302
2SC299GN	3302
2SC299H	3302
2SC299J	3302
2SC299K	3302
2SC299L	3302
2SC299M	3302

DEVICE TYPE	REPL CODE
2SC299OR	3302
2SC299R	3302
2SC299X	3302
2SC299Y	3302
2SC300	0016
2SC300A	0016
2SC300B	0016
2SC300C	0016
2SC300D	0016
2SC300E	0016
2SC300F	0016
2SC300G	0016
2SC300GN	0016
2SC300H	0016
2SC300J	0016
2SC300K	0016
2SC300L	0016
2SC300M	0016
2SC300OR	0016
2SC300R	0016
2SC300X	0016
2SC300Y	0016
2SC301	0016
2SC301A	0016
2SC301B	0016
2SC301C	0016
2SC301D	0016
2SC301E	0016
2SC301F	0016
2SC301G	0016
2SC301GN	0016
2SC301H	0016
2SC301J	0016
2SC301K	0016
2SC301L	0016
2SC301M	0016
2SC301OR	0016
2SC301R	0016
2SC301X	0016
2SC301Y	0016
2SC302	0016
2SC302A	0016
2SC302B	0016
2SC302C	0016
2SC302D	0016
2SC302E	0016
2SC302F	0016
2SC302G	0016
2SC302GN	0016
2SC302H	0016
2SC302J	0016
2SC302K	0016
2SC302L	0016
2SC302M	0016
2SC302OR	0016
2SC302R	0016
2SC302X	0016
2SC302Y	0016
2SC303	0590
2SC304	0590
2SC305	0590
2SC305A	0590
2SC305B	0590
2SC305C	0590
2SC305D	0590
2SC305E	0590
2SC305F	0590
2SC305G	0590
2SC305GN	0590
2SC305H	0590
2SC305J	0590
2SC305K	0590
2SC305L	0590
2SC305M	0590
2SC305OR	0590
2SC305R	0590
2SC305X	0590
2SC305Y	0590
2SC306	0086
2SC306A	0086
2SC306B	0086
2SC306C	0086
2SC306D	0086
2SC306E	0086
2SC306F	0086
2SC306G	0086
2SC306GN	0086
2SC306H	0086
2SC306J	0086
2SC306K	0086
2SC306L	0086
2SC306M	0086
2SC306OR	0086
2SC306R	0086
2SC306X	0086
2SC306Y	0086
2SC307	0086
2SC307-OR	0086
2SC307A	0086
2SC307B	0086
2SC307C	0086
2SC307D	0086
2SC307E	0086
2SC307F	0086
2SC307G	0086
2SC307GN	0086
2SC307H	0086
2SC307J	0086
2SC307K	0086

DEVICE TYPE	REPL CODE
2SC307L	0086
2SC307M	0086
2SC307OR	0086
2SC307R	0086
2SC307X	0086
2SC307Y	0086
2SC308	0086
2SC308A	0086
2SC308B	0086
2SC308C	0086
2SC308D	0086
2SC308E	0086
2SC308F	0086
2SC308G	0086
2SC308GN	0086
2SC308H	0086
2SC308J	0086
2SC308K	0086
2SC308L	0086
2SC308M	0086
2SC308OR	0086
2SC308R	0086
2SC308X	0086
2SC308Y	0086
2SC309	0086
2SC309A	0086
2SC309B	0086
2SC309C	0086
2SC309D	0086
2SC309E	0086
2SC309F	0086
2SC309G	0086
2SC309GN	0086
2SC309H	0086
2SC309J	0086
2SC309K	0086
2SC309L	0086
2SC309M	0086
2SC309OR	0086
2SC309R	0086
2SC309X	0086
2SC309Y	0086
2SC310	0086
2SC310A	0086
2SC310B	0086
2SC310C	0086
2SC310D	0086
2SC310E	0086
2SC310F	0086
2SC310G	0086
2SC310GN	0086
2SC310H	0086
2SC310J	0086
2SC310K	0086
2SC310L	0086
2SC310M	0086
2SC310OR	0086
2SC310R	0086
2SC310X	0086
2SC310Y	0086
2SC311	0693
2SC311A	OEM
2SC311B	0693
2SC311C	0693
2SC311D	0693
2SC311E	0693
2SC311F	0693
2SC311G	0693
2SC311GN	0693
2SC311H	0693
2SC311J	0693
2SC311K	0693
2SC311L	0693
2SC311M	0693
2SC311OR	0693
2SC311R	0693
2SC311X	0693
2SC311Y	0693
2SC312	0626
2SC312A	0626
2SC312B	0626
2SC312C	0626
2SC312D	0626
2SC312E	0626
2SC312F	0626
2SC312G	0626
2SC312GN	0626
2SC312H	0626
2SC312J	0626
2SC312K	0626
2SC312L	0626
2SC312M	0626
2SC312OR	0626
2SC312R	0626
2SC312X	0626
2SC312Y	0626
2SC-313	3356
2SC313	3356
2SC313-OR	3356
2SC313A	3356
2SC313B	3356
2SC313C	3356
2SC313D	3356
2SC313E	3356
2SC313F	3356
2SC313G	3356
2SC313GN	3356
2SC313H	3356
2SC313J	3356

DEVICE TYPE	REPL CODE
2SC313K	3356
2SC313L	3356
2SC313M	3356
2SC313OR	3356
2SC313R	3356
2SC313X	3356
2SC313Y	3356
2SC314	0626
2SC314TA	OEM
2SC315	0016
2SC315A	0016
2SC315B	0016
2SC315C	0016
2SC315D	0016
2SC315E	0016
2SC315F	0016
2SC315G	0016
2SC315GN	0016
2SC315H	0016
2SC315J	0016
2SC315K	0016
2SC315L	0016
2SC315M	0016
2SC315OR	0016
2SC315R	0016
2SC315X	0016
2SC315Y	0016
2SC316	0016
2SC316A	0016
2SC316B	0016
2SC316C	0016
2SC316D	0016
2SC316E	0016
2SC316F	0016
2SC316G	0016
2SC316GN	0016
2SC316H	0016
2SC316J	0016
2SC316K	0016
2SC316L	0016
2SC316M	0016
2SC316OR	0016
2SC316R	0016
2SC316X	0016
2SC316Y	0016
2SC317	0016
2SC317A	0016
2SC317B	0016
2SC317C	0016
2SC317D	0016
2SC317E	0016
2SC317F	0016
2SC317G	0016
2SC317GN	0016
2SC317H	0016
2SC317J	0016
2SC317K	0016
2SC317L	0016
2SC317M	0016
2SC317OR	0016
2SC317R	0016
2SC317X	0016
2SC317Y	0016
2SC318	0016
2SC318A	0016
2SC318AB	0016
2SC318B	0016
2SC318C	0016
2SC318D	0016
2SC318E	0016
2SC318F	0016
2SC318G	0016
2SC318GN	0016
2SC318H	0016
2SC318J	0016
2SC318K	0016
2SC318L	0016
2SC318M	0016
2SC318OR	0016
2SC318R	0016
2SC318X	0016
2SC318Y	0016
2SC319	0488
2SC319A	0488
2SC319B	0488
2SC319C	0488
2SC319D	0488
2SC319E	0488
2SC319F	0488
2SC319G	0488
2SC319GN	0488
2SC319H	0488
2SC319J	0488
2SC319K	0488
2SC319L	0488
2SC319M	0488
2SC319OR	0488
2SC319R	0488
2SC319X	0488
2SC319Y	0488
2SC320	3387
2SC320A	3387
2SC320B	3387
2SC320C	3387
2SC320D	3387
2SC320E	3387
2SC320F	3387
2SC320G	3387
2SC320GN	3387

DEVICE TYPE	REPL CODE
2SC320H	3387
2SC320J	3387
2SC320K	3387
2SC320L	3387
2SC320M	3387
2SC320OR	3387
2SC320R	3387
2SC320X	3387
2SC320Y	3387
2SC321	0016
2SC321A	0016
2SC321B	0016
2SC321C	0016
2SC321D	0016
2SC321E	0016
2SC321F	0016
2SC321G	0016
2SC321GN	0016
2SC321H	0016
2SC321HA	0016
2SC321HB	0016
2SC321HC	0016
2SC321J	0016
2SC321K	0016
2SC321L	0016
2SC321M	0016
2SC321OR	0016
2SC321R	0016
2SC321X	0016
2SC321Y	0016
2SC322	0079
2SC323	0016
2SC323A	0016
2SC323B	0016
2SC323C	0016
2SC323D	0016
2SC323E	0016
2SC323F	0016
2SC323G	0016
2SC323GN	0016
2SC323H	0016
2SC323J	0016
2SC323K	0016
2SC323L	0016
2SC323M	0016
2SC323OR	0016
2SC323R	0016
2SC323X	0016
2SC323Y	0016
2SC324	0016
2SC324(H)	0016
2SC324A	0016
2SC324B	0016
2SC324C	0016
2SC324D	0016
2SC324E	0016
2SC324F	0016
2SC324G	0016
2SC324GN	0016
2SC324H	0016
2SC324HA	0016
2SC324J	0016
2SC324K	0016
2SC324L	0016
2SC324M	0016
2SC324OR	0016
2SC324R	0016
2SC324X	0016
2SC324Y	0016
2SC325	0259
2SC325C	0259
2SC326	0414
2SC327	0127
2SC328	0259
2SC329	0259
2SC330	2817
2SC331	2817
2SC332	0079
2SC333	0016
2SC334	0016
2SC335	0531
2SC336	0016
2SC337	0016
2SC338	0076
2SC339	0079
2SC340	0470
2SC340H	OEM
2SC341	0320
2SC342	0079
2SC343	0016
2SC344	0127
2SC344(Y)	0127
2SC344Y	0127
2SC345	0320
2SC346	0016
2SC347	0016
2SC348	0016
2SC348A	0016
2SC348B	0016
2SC348C	0016
2SC348D	0016
2SC348E	0016
2SC348F	0016
2SC348G	0016
2SC348GN	0016
2SC348H	0016
2SC348J	0016
2SC348K	0016
2SC348L	0016

If replacement code is OEM, contact original manufacturer for replacement.

DEVICE TYPE	REPL CODE
2SC348M	0016
2SC348OR	0016
2SC348X	0016
2SC348Y	0016
2SC349	0127
2SC349R	0127
2SC350	0016
2SC350A	0016
2SC350B	0016
2SC350C	0016
2SC350D	0016
2SC350E	0016
2SC350F	0016
2SC350G	0016
2SC350GN	0016
2SC350H	0016
2SC350J	0016
2SC350K	0016
2SC350L	0016
2SC350M	0016
2SC350OR	0016
2SC350R	0016
2SC350X	0016
2SC350Y	0016
2SC351	0127
2SC351(FA)	0127
2SC351(FA-1)	OEM
2SC351A	0127
2SC351B	0127
2SC351C	0127
2SC351D	0127
2SC351E	0127
2SC351F	0127
2SC351FA1	0127
2SC351G	0127
2SC351GN	0127
2SC351H	0127
2SC351J	0127
2SC351K	0127
2SC351L	0127
2SC351M	0127
2SC351OR	0127
2SC351R	0127
2SC351X	0127
2SC351Y	0127
2SC352	0449
2SC352-OR	0449
2SC352A	0449
2SC352AC	0449
2SC352B	0449
2SC352C	0449
2SC352D	0449
2SC352E	0449
2SC352F	0449
2SC352G	0449
2SC352GN	0449
2SC352H	0449
2SC352J	0449
2SC352K	0449
2SC352L	0449
2SC352M	0449
2SC352OR	0449
2SC352R	0449
2SC352X	0449
2SC352Y	0449
2SC353	0086
2SC353A	0086
2SC353AC	0086
2SC353B	0086
2SC353C	0086
2SC353D	0086
2SC353E	0086
2SC353F	0086
2SC353G	0086
2SC353GN	0086
2SC353H	0086
2SC353J	0086
2SC353K	0086
2SC353L	0086
2SC353M	0086
2SC353OR	0086
2SC353R	0086
2SC353X	0086
2SC353Y	0086
2SC354	0930
2SC355	0930
2SC356	0079
2SC356A	0079
2SC356B	0079
2SC356C	0079
2SC356D	0079
2SC356E	0079
2SC356F	0079
2SC356G	0079
2SC356GN	0079
2SC356H	0079
2SC356J	0079
2SC356K	0079
2SC356L	0079
2SC356M	0079
2SC356OR	0079
2SC356R	0079
2SC356X	0079
2SC356Y	0079
2SC360	0016
2SC360-OR	0016
2SC360A	0016
2SC360B	0016
2SC360C	0016
2SC360D	0016
2SC360E	0016
2SC360F	0016
2SC360G	0016
2SC360GN	0016
2SC360H	0016
2SC360J	0016
2SC360K	0016
2SC360L	0016
2SC360M	0016
2SC360OR	0016
2SC360R	0016
2SC360X	0016
2SC360Y	0016
2SC361	0155
2SC361A	0155
2SC361B	0155
2SC361C	0155
2SC361D	0155
2SC361E	0155
2SC361F	0155
2SC361G	0155
2SC361GN	0155
2SC361H	0155
2SC361J	0155
2SC361K	0155
2SC361L	0155
2SC361M	0155
2SC361OR	0155
2SC361R	0155
2SC361X	0155
2SC361Y	0155
2SC362	0155
2SC362A	0155
2SC362B	0155
2SC362C	0155
2SC362D	0155
2SC362E	0155
2SC362F	0155
2SC362G	0155
2SC362GN	0155
2SC362H	0155
2SC362J	0155
2SC362K	0155
2SC362L	0155
2SC362M	0155
2SC362OR	0155
2SC362R	0155
2SC362X	0155
2SC362Y	0155
2SC363	0016
2SC363-OR	0016
2SC363A	0016
2SC363B	0016
2SC363C	0016
2SC363D	0016
2SC363E	0016
2SC363F	0016
2SC363G	0016
2SC363GN	0016
2SC363H	0016
2SC363J	0016
2SC363K	0016
2SC363L	0016
2SC363M	0016
2SC363OR	0016
2SC363R	0016
2SC363X	0016
2SC363Y	0016
2SC364	0525
2SC366	0284
2SC366-O	0284
2SC366-ORG-G	0284
2SC366-RED-G	0284
2SC366A	0284
2SC366B	0284
2SC366C	0284
2SC366D	0284
2SC366E	0284
2SC366F	0284
2SC366G	0284
2SC366GN	0284
2SC366G-O	0284
2SC366G-R	0284
2SC366G-Y	0284
2SC366H	0284
2SC366J	0284
2SC366K	0284
2SC366L	0284
2SC366M	0284
2SC366OR	0284
2SC366X	0284
2SC367	0284
2SC367-O	0284
2SC367-ORG-G	0284
2SC367-R	0284
2SC367-RED-G	0284
2SC367-Y	0284
2SC367-YEL-G	0284
2SC367A	0284
2SC367B	0284
2SC367C	0284
2SC367D	0284
2SC367E	0284
2SC367F	0284
2SC367G	0284
2SC367GN	0284
2SC367G-O	0284
2SC367G-R	0284
2SC367G-Y	0284
2SC367H	0284
2SC367J	0284
2SC367K	0284
2SC367L	0284
2SC367M	0284
2SC367OR	0284
2SC367R	0284
2SC367X	0284
2SC367Y	0284
2SC368	0111
2SC368-BL	0111
2SC368-GR	0111
2SC368A	0111
2SC368B	0111
2SC368C	0111
2SC368D	0111
2SC368E	0111
2SC368F	0111
2SC368G	0111
2SC368GN	0111
2SC368H	0111
2SC368J	0111
2SC368K	0111
2SC368L	0111
2SC368M	0111
2SC368OR	0111
2SC368R	0111
2SC368V	0111
2SC368X	0111
2SC368Y	0111
2SC369	0111
2SC369-BL	0111
2SC369-BLU-G	0111
2SC369-GR	0111
2SC369-GRN-G	0111
2SC369-V	0111
2SC369A	0111
2SC369B	0111
2SC369BL	0111
2SC369C	0111
2SC369D	0111
2SC369E	0111
2SC369F	0111
2SC369G	0111
2SC369G/BL	0111
2SC369G/GR	0111
2SC369G-BL	0111
2SC369GBL	0111
2SC369G-GR	0111
2SC369GGR	0111
2SC369GN	0111
2SC369GR	0111
2SC369G-V	0111
2SC369H	0111
2SC369J	0111
2SC369K	0111
2SC369L	0111
2SC369M	0111
2SC369OR	0111
2SC369R	0111
2SC369V	0111
2SC369X	0111
2SC369Y	0111
2SC370	0155
2SC370-O	0155
2SC370-G	0155
2SC370-O	0155
2SC370-T	0155
2SC370A	0155
2SC370B	0155
2SC370C	0155
2SC370D	0155
2SC370E	0155
2SC370F	0155
2SC370G	0155
2SC370GN	0155
2SC370H	0155
2SC370I	0155
2SC370J	0155
2SC370K	0155
2SC370L	0155
2SC370M	0155
2SC370OR	0155
2SC370R	0155
2SC370X	0155
2SC370Y	0155
2SC371	0191
2SC371(O)	0191
2SC371(O)	0191
2SC371-O	0191
2SC371-O	0191
2SC371-OR	0191
2SC371-ORG-G	0191
2SC371-R	0191
2SC371-RED-G	0191
2SC371-T	0191
2SC371A	0191
2SC371B	0191
2SC371C	0191
2SC371D	0191
2SC371E	0191
2SC371F	0191
2SC371G	0191
2SC371GN	0191
2SC371G-O	0191
2SC371G-R	0191
2SC371H	0191
2SC371J	0191
2SC371K	0191
2SC371L	0191
2SC371M	0191
2SC371O	0191
2SC371OR	0191
2SC371R	0191
2SC371R-1	0191
2SC371RED-G	0191
2SC371T	0191
2SC371X	0191
2SC371Y	0191
2SC372	0076
2SC372(H)	0076
2SC372(O)	0076
2SC372(Y)	0076
2SC372-0	0076
2SC372-1	0076
2SC372-2	0076
2SC372-O	0076
2SC372-OR	0076
2SC372-ORG	0076
2SC372-ORG-G	0076
2SC372-Y	0076
2SC372-YEL-G	0076
2SC372A	0076
2SC372AR	0076
2SC372B	0076
2SC372C	0076
2SC372D	0076
2SC372E	0076
2SC372F	0076
2SC372G	0076
2SC372GN	0076
2SC372G-O	0076
2SC372G-Y	0076
2SC372J	0076
2SC372K	0076
2SC372L	0076
2SC372M	0076
2SC372O	0076
2SC372OR	0076
2SC372R	0076
2SC372X	0076
2SC372Y	0076
2SC372Y1	0076
2SC372YEL	0076
2SC372YEL-G	0076
2SC372Z	0076
2SC373	0076
2SC373(GR)	0076
2SC373-0	0076
2SC373-14	0076
2SC373-G	0076
2SC373-O	0076
2SC373-OR	0076
2SC373A	0076
2SC373AL	0076
2SC373B	0076
2SC373C	0076
2SC373D	0076
2SC373E	0076
2SC373F	0076
2SC373G	0076
2SC373GN	0076
2SC373GR	0076
2SC373H	0076
2SC373J	0076
2SC373K	0076
2SC373L	0076
2SC373M	0076
2SC373OR	0076
2SC373R	0076
2SC373W	0076
2SC373X	0076
2SC373Y	0076
2SC374	0547
2SC374(BL)	0547
2SC374(V)	0547
2SC374-BL	0547
2SC374-OR	0547
2SC374-V	0547
2SC374A	0547
2SC374B	0547
2SC374BL	0547
2SC374BLK	0547
2SC374C	0547
2SC374D	0547
2SC374E	0547
2SC374F	0547
2SC374G	0547
2SC374GN	0547
2SC374H	0547
2SC374J	0547
2SC374K	0547
2SC374L	0547
2SC374M	0547
2SC374OR	0547
2SC374R	0547
2SC374V	0547
2SC374X	0547
2SC374Y	0547
2SC375	0127
2SC375-O	0127
2SC375-O	0127
2SC375-Y	0127
2SC375A	0127
2SC375B	0127
2SC375C	0127
2SC375D	0127
2SC375E	0127
2SC375F	0127
2SC375G	0127
2SC375GN	0127
2SC375H	0127
2SC375J	0127
2SC375K	0127
2SC375L	0127
2SC375M	0127
2SC375OR	0127
2SC375R	0127
2SC375X	0127
2SC376	0284
2SC376A	0284
2SC376B	0284
2SC376C	0284
2SC376D	0284
2SC376E	0284
2SC376F	0284
2SC376G	0284
2SC376GN	0284
2SC376H	0284
2SC376J	0284
2SC376K	0284
2SC376L	0284
2SC376M	0284
2SC376OR	0284
2SC376R	0284
2SC376X	0284
2SC376Y	0284
2SC377	0076
2SC377-0	0076
2SC377-BN	0076
2SC377-BRN	0076
2SC377-O	0076
2SC377-OR	0076
2SC377-ORG	0076
2SC377-R	0076
2SC377-RED	0076
2SC377A	0076
2SC377B	0076
2SC377BN	0076
2SC377BRN	0076
2SC377C	0076
2SC377D	0076
2SC377E	0076
2SC377F	0076
2SC377G	0076
2SC377GN	0076
2SC377H	0076
2SC377J	0076
2SC377K	0076
2SC377L	0076
2SC377M	0076
2SC377O	0076
2SC377OR	0076
2SC377R	0076
2SC377RED	0076
2SC377X	0076
2SC377Y	0076
2SC378	0155
2SC378-O	0155
2SC378-ORG	0155
2SC378-R	0155
2SC378-RED	0155
2SC378-Y	0155
2SC378-YEL	0155
2SC378A	0155
2SC378B	0155
2SC378C	0155
2SC378D	0155
2SC378E	0155
2SC378F	0155
2SC378G	0155
2SC378GN	0155
2SC378H	0155
2SC378J	0155
2SC378K	0155
2SC378L	0155
2SC378M	0155
2SC378O	0155
2SC378OR	0155
2SC378R	0155
2SC378X	0155
2SC378Y	0155
2SC379	0284
2SC379A	0284
2SC379B	0284
2SC379C	0284
2SC379D	0284
2SC379E	0284
2SC379F	0284
2SC379G	0284
2SC379GN	0284
2SC379H	0284
2SC379J	0284
2SC379K	0284
2SC379L	0284
2SC379M	0284
2SC379OR	0284
2SC379R	0284
2SC379X	0284
2SC379Y	0284
2SC380	0284
2SC380(O)	0284
2SC380(R)	0284
2SC380(Y)	0284
2SC380-0	0284
2SC380-0/4454C	0284
2SC380-BRN	0284
2SC380-O	0284
2SC380-O/4454C	0284
2SC380-OR	0284
2SC380-ORG	0284
2SC380-R	0284
2SC380-RED	0284
2SC380-Y	0284
2SC380-YEL	0284
2SC380A	0284
2SC380A(D)	0284
2SC380A(O)	0284
2SC380A(R)	0284
2SC380A(Y)	0284
2SC380A-O	0284
2SC380AO	0284
2SC380A-JA-8	OEM
2SC380A-JA-Y	OEM
2SC380A-O	0284
2SC380AO	0284
2SC380A-O(TV)	0284
2SC380A-R	0284
2SC380AR	0284
2SC380ATV	0284
2SC380A-Y	0284
2SC380AY	0284
2SC380B	0284
2SC380B-Y	0284
2SC380BY	0284
2SC380C	0284
2SC380C-Y	0284
2SC380CY	0284
2SC380D	0284
2SC380D-Y	0284
2SC380DY	0284
2SC380E	0284
2SC380E-Y	0284
2SC380EY	0284
2SC380F	0284
2SC380F-Y	0284
2SC380FY	0284
2SC380G	0284
2SC380GN	0284
2SC380H	0284
2SC380J	0284
2SC380K	0284
2SC380L	0284
2SC380M	0284
2SC380O	0284
2SC380OR	0284
2SC380R	0284
2SC380RED	0284
2SC380T	0284
2SC380TM-O	0284
2SC380TM-Y	0284
2SC380V	0284
2SC380X	0284
2SC380Y	0284
2SC380YEL	0284
2SC381	0113
2SC381(BN)	0113
2SC381-0	0113
2SC381-BN	0113
2SC381-BRN	0113
2SC381-O	0113
2SC381-OR	0113
2SC381-ORG	0113
2SC381-R	0113
2SC381-RED	0113
2SC381A	0113
2SC381B	0113
2SC381BN	0113
2SC381BN-1	0113
2SC381C	0113
2SC381D	0113
2SC381E	0113
2SC381F	0113
2SC381G	0113
2SC381GN	0113
2SC381H	0113
2SC381J	0113
2SC381K	0113
2SC381L	0113
2SC381M	0113
2SC381O	0113
2SC381OR	0113
2SC381R	0113
2SC381RED	0113
2SC381RL	0113
2SC381X	0113
2SC381Y	0113
2SC382	0184
2SC382(BL)	0184
2SC382(BN)	0184
2SC382(R)	0184
2SC382-BK	OEM
2SC382-BK(1)	0184
2SC382-BK(2)	0184
2SC382-BL	OEM
2SC382-BR	OEM
2SC382-G	0184
2SC382-GR	0184
2SC382-GY	0184
2SC382-OR	0184
2SC382-R	0184
2SC382-V	0184
2SC382A	0184
2SC382B	0184
2SC382BK	0184
2SC382BK1	0184
2SC382BK2	0184
2SC382BL	0184
2SC382BN	0184
2SC382BR	0184
2SC382C	0184
2SC382D	0184
2SC382E	0184
2SC382F	0184
2SC382G	0184
2SC382GN	0184
2SC382GR	0184
2SC382GY	0184
2SC382H	0184
2SC382J	0184
2SC382K	0184
2SC382L	0184
2SC382M	0184
2SC382OR	0184
2SC382R	0184
2SC382TM	0184
2SC382V	0184
2SC382W	0184
2SC382W,R	0184
2SC382X	0184
2SC382Y	0184
2SC383	0076
2SC383(T)	0076
2SC383-OR	0076
2SC383A	0076
2SC383B	0076
2SC383C	0076
2SC383D	0076
2SC383E	0076
2SC383F	0076
2SC383G	0076
2SC383GN	0076
2SC383H	0076
2SC383J	0076
2SC383K	0076
2SC383L	0076
2SC383M	0076
2SC383OR	0076
2SC383R	0076
2SC383T	0076
2SC383TM	0076
2SC383W	0076
2SC383WT	0076
2SC383X	0076
2SC383Y	0076
2SC384	0127
2SC384(O)	0127
2SC384(Y)	0127
2SC384-O	0127
2SC384A	0127
2SC384B	0127
2SC384C	0127
2SC384D	0127
2SC384E	0127
2SC384F	0127
2SC384G	0127
2SC384GN	0127
2SC384H	0127
2SC384J	0127
2SC384K	0127
2SC384L	0127
2SC384M	0127
2SC384OR	0127
2SC384R	0127
2SC384X	0127
2SC384Y	0127
2SC385	0544
2SC385A	0544
2SC385B	0544
2SC385C	0544
2SC385D	0544
2SC385E	0544
2SC385F	0544
2SC385G	0544
2SC385GN	0544
2SC385H	0544
2SC385J	0544
2SC385K	0544
2SC385L	0544
2SC385M	0544
2SC385OR	0544
2SC385R	0544
2SC385X	0544
2SC385Y	0544
2SC386	0127
2SC386-O	0127
2SC386A	0127
2SC386A-O(TV)	0127
2SC386AO	0127
2SC386B	0127
2SC386C	0127
2SC386D	0127
2SC386E	0127
2SC386F	0127
2SC386G	0127
2SC386GN	0127
2SC386H	0127
2SC386J	0127
2SC386K	0127
2SC386L	0127
2SC386M	0127
2SC386OR	0127
2SC386R	0127
2SC386X	0127

If replacement code is OEM, contact original manufacturer for replacement. 81

DEVICE TYPE	REPL CODE
2SC386Y	0127
2SC387	0544
2SC387(FA-3)	0544
2SC387-G	0544
2SC387-OR	0544
2SC387A	0544
2SC387A(FA-3)	0544
2SC387AG	0544
2SC387B	0544
2SC387C	0544
2SC387D	0544
2SC387E	0544
2SC387F	0544
2SC387FA3	0544
2SC387G	0544
2SC387GN	0544
2SC387H	0544
2SC387J	0544
2SC387K	0544
2SC387L	0544
2SC387M	0544
2SC387OR	0544
2SC387R	0544
2SC387X	0544
2SC387Y	0544
2SC388	0836
2SC388(FA-1)	OEM
2SC388-A	0836
2SC388-O	0836
2SC388-OR	0836
2SC388A	0127
2SC388ABC	0836
2SC388ACC	0836
2SC388A-TM	0836
2SC388ATM	0836
2SC388ATM(FA)	0836
2SC388ATM(FA-1)	OEM
2SC388ATMFA	0836
2SC388B	0836
2SC388C	0836
2SC388D	0836
2SC388E	0836
2SC388F	0836
2SC388FA	0836
2SC388G	0836
2SC388GN	0836
2SC388H	0836
2SC388J	0836
2SC388K	0836
2SC388L	0836
2SC388M	0836
2SC388OR	0836
2SC388R	0836
2SC388TM	0836
2SC388X	0836
2SC388Y	0836
2SC389	0007
2SC389-O	0007
2SC389-OR	0007
2SC389A	0007
2SC389AFP	0007
2SC389B	0007
2SC389BLB-O	0007
2SC389C	0007
2SC389D	0007
2SC389E	0007
2SC389F	0007
2SC389G	0007
2SC389GN	0007
2SC389H	0007
2SC389J	0007
2SC389K	0007
2SC389L	0007
2SC389LP	0007
2SC389M	0007
2SC389O	0007
2SC389OR	0007
2SC389P	0007
2SC389R	0007
2SC389X	0007
2SC389Y	0007
2SC390	0259
2SC390A	0259
2SC390B	0259
2SC390C	0259
2SC390D	0259
2SC390E	0259
2SC390F	0259
2SC390G	0259
2SC390GN	0259
2SC390H	0259
2SC390J	0259
2SC390K	0259
2SC390L	0259
2SC390M	0259
2SC390OR	0259
2SC390R	0259
2SC390X	0259
2SC390Y	0259
2SC391	0008
2SC391A	0008
2SC391B	0008
2SC391C	0008
2SC391D	0008
2SC391E	0008
2SC391F	0008
2SC391G	0008
2SC391GN	0008
2SC391H	0008

DEVICE TYPE	REPL CODE
2SC391J	0008
2SC391K	0008
2SC391L	0008
2SC391M	0008
2SC391OR	0008
2SC391R	0008
2SC391X	0008
2SC391Y	0008
2SC392	0259
2SC392A	0259
2SC392B	0259
2SC392C	0259
2SC392D	0259
2SC392E	0259
2SC392F	0259
2SC392G	0259
2SC392GN	0259
2SC392H	0259
2SC392J	0259
2SC392K	0259
2SC392L	0259
2SC392M	0259
2SC392OR	0259
2SC392R	0259
2SC392X	0259
2SC392Y	0259
2SC393	0079
2SC394	0155
2SC394(0)	0155
2SC394(O)	0155
2SC394-0	0155
2SC394-GR	0155
2SC394-GRN	0155
2SC394-O	0155
2SC394-OR	0155
2SC394-ORG	0155
2SC394-R	0155
2SC394-RED	0155
2SC394-Y	0155
2SC394-YEL	0155
2SC394A	0155
2SC394AP	0155
2SC394B	0155
2SC394C	0155
2SC394D	0155
2SC394E	0155
2SC394F	0155
2SC394G	0155
2SC394GN	0155
2SC394GR	0155
2SC394GRN	0155
2SC394H	0155
2SC394J	0155
2SC394K	0155
2SC394L	0155
2SC394M	0155
2SC394O	0155
2SC394OR	0155
2SC394R	0155
2SC394RED	0155
2SC394W	0155
2SC394X	0155
2SC394Y	0155
2SC394YEL	0155
2SC395	0016
2SC395A	0016
2SC395A-O	0016
2SC395A-ORG	0016
2SC395A-R	0016
2SC395A-RED	0016
2SC395A-Y	0016
2SC395A-YEL	0016
2SC395B	0016
2SC395C	0016
2SC395D	0016
2SC395E	0016
2SC395F	0016
2SC395G	0016
2SC395GN	0016
2SC395H	0016
2SC395J	0016
2SC395K	0016
2SC395L	0016
2SC395M	0016
2SC395OR	0016
2SC395R	0016
2SC395X	0016
2SC395Y	0016
2SC396	0488
2SC396A	0488
2SC396B	0488
2SC396C	0488
2SC396D	0488
2SC396E	0488
2SC396F	0488
2SC396G	0488
2SC396GN	0488
2SC396GR	0488
2SC396H	0488
2SC396J	0488
2SC396K	0488
2SC396L	0488
2SC396M	0488
2SC396OR	0488
2SC396R	0488
2SC396X	0488
2SC396Y	0488
2SC397	0007
2SC397A	0007

DEVICE TYPE	REPL CODE
2SC397B	0007
2SC397C	0007
2SC397D	0007
2SC397E	0007
2SC397F	0007
2SC397G	0007
2SC397GN	0007
2SC397H	0007
2SC397J	0007
2SC397K	0007
2SC397L	0007
2SC397M	0007
2SC397OR	0007
2SC397R	0007
2SC397X	0007
2SC397Y	0007
2SC398	0008
2SC398(FA-1)	0008
2SC398A	0008
2SC398B	0008
2SC398C	0008
2SC398D	0008
2SC398E	0008
2SC398F	0008
2SC398FA1	0008
2SC398G	0008
2SC398GN	0008
2SC398H	0008
2SC398J	0008
2SC398K	0008
2SC398L	0008
2SC398M	0008
2SC398OR	0008
2SC398R	0008
2SC398X	0008
2SC398Y	0008
2SC399	0008
2SC399A	0008
2SC399B	0008
2SC399C	0008
2SC399D	0008
2SC399E	0008
2SC399F	0008
2SC399FA1	0008
2SC399G	0008
2SC399GN	0008
2SC399H	0008
2SC399J	0008
2SC399K	0008
2SC399L	0008
2SC399M	0008
2SC399OR	0008
2SC399R	0008
2SC399X	0008
2SC399Y	0008
2SC400	0016
2SC400-0	0016
2SC400-GR	0016
2SC400-O	0016
2SC400-R	0016
2SC400-Y	0016
2SC400A	0016
2SC400B	0016
2SC400C	0016
2SC400D	0016
2SC400E	0016
2SC400F	0016
2SC400G	0016
2SC400GN	0016
2SC400H	0016
2SC400J	0016
2SC400K	0016
2SC400L	0016
2SC400M	0016
2SC400OR	0016
2SC400R	0016
2SC400X	0016
2SC400Y	0016
2SC401	0155
2SC401A	0155
2SC401B	0155
2SC401C	0155
2SC401D	0155
2SC401E	0155
2SC401F	0155
2SC401G	0155
2SC401GN	0155
2SC401H	0155
2SC401J	0155
2SC401K	0155
2SC401L	0155
2SC401M	0155
2SC401OR	0155
2SC401R	0155
2SC401X	0155
2SC401Y	0155
2SC402	0155
2SC402A	0155
2SC402B	0155
2SC402C	0155
2SC402D	0155
2SC402E	0155
2SC402F	0155
2SC402G	0155
2SC402GN	0155
2SC402H	0155
2SC402J	0155
2SC402K	0155
2SC402L	0155

DEVICE TYPE	REPL CODE
2SC402M	0155
2SC402OR	0155
2SC402R	0155
2SC402X	0155
2SC402Y	0155
2SC403	0155
2SC403(C)	0155
2SC403(SONY)	0155
2SC403-OR	0155
2SC403A	0155
2SC403AL	0155
2SC403B	0155
2SC403C	0155
2SC403C4	OEM
2SC403CG	0155
2SC403D	0155
2SC403E	0155
2SC403F	0155
2SC403G	0155
2SC403GN	0155
2SC403H	0155
2SC403J	0155
2SC403K	0155
2SC403L	0155
2SC403M	0155
2SC403OR	0155
2SC403R	0155
2SC403SP3	OEM
2SC403X	0155
2SC403Y	0155
2SC404	0155
2SC404A	0155
2SC404B	0155
2SC404C	0155
2SC404D	0155
2SC404E	0155
2SC404F	0155
2SC404G	0155
2SC404GN	0155
2SC404H	0155
2SC404J	0155
2SC404K	0155
2SC404L	0155
2SC404M	0155
2SC404OR	0155
2SC404R	0155
2SC404X	0155
2SC404Y	0155
2SC405	0016
2SC405A	0016
2SC405B	0016
2SC405C	0016
2SC405D	0016
2SC405E	0016
2SC405F	0016
2SC405G	0016
2SC405GN	0016
2SC405H	0016
2SC405J	0016
2SC405K	0016
2SC405L	0016
2SC405M	0016
2SC405OR	0016
2SC405R	0016
2SC405X	0016
2SC405Y	0016
2SC406	0016
2SC406A	0016
2SC406B	0016
2SC406C	0016
2SC406D	0016
2SC406E	0016
2SC406F	0016
2SC406G	0016
2SC406GN	0016
2SC406H	0016
2SC406J	0016
2SC406K	0016
2SC406L	0016
2SC406M	0016
2SC406OR	0016
2SC406R	0016
2SC406X	0016
2SC406Y	0016
2SC407	1955
2SC408	1955
2SC409	1955
2SC410	1955
2SC410A	1955
2SC411	1955
2SC412	0637
2SC413	0626
2SC414	0626
2SC415	0626
2SC416	0626
2SC420	0626
2SC423	0016
2SC423-0	0016
2SC423A	0016
2SC423B	0016
2SC423C	0016
2SC423D	0016
2SC423E	0016
2SC423F	0016
2SC423G	0016
2SC423GN	0016
2SC423H	0016
2SC423J	0016
2SC423K	0016

DEVICE TYPE	REPL CODE
2SC423L	0016
2SC423M	0016
2SC423OR	0016
2SC423R	0016
2SC423X	0016
2SC423Y	0016
2SC424	0016
2SC424D	0016
2SC425	0016
2SC425A	0016
2SC425B	0016
2SC425C	0016
2SC425D	0016
2SC425E	0016
2SC425F	0016
2SC425G	0016
2SC425GN	0016
2SC425H	0016
2SC425K	0016
2SC425L	0016
2SC425M	0016
2SC425OR	0016
2SC425R	0016
2SC425X	0016
2SC425Y	0016
2SC426	0079
2SC427	0079
2SC428	0079
2SC429	0470
2SC429A	0470
2SC429B	0470
2SC429C	0470
2SC429D	0470
2SC429E	0470
2SC429F	0470
2SC429G	0470
2SC429GN	0470
2SC429H	0470
2SC429J	0470
2SC429K	0470
2SC429L	0470
2SC429M	0470
2SC429OR	0470
2SC429R	0470
2SC429X	0470
2SC429Y	0470
2SC430	0470
2SC430A	0470
2SC430B	0470
2SC430C	0470
2SC430D	0470
2SC430E	0470
2SC430F	0470
2SC430G	0470
2SC430GN	0470
2SC430H	0470
2SC430J	0470
2SC430K	0470
2SC430L	0470
2SC430M	0470
2SC430OR	0470
2SC430R	0470
2SC430W	0470
2SC430X	0470
2SC430Y	0470
2SC433	0079
2SC437	0626
2SC438	0693
2SC439	0018
2SC440	0488
2SC441	0488
2SC441A	0488
2SC441B	0488
2SC441C	0488
2SC441D	0488
2SC441E	0488
2SC441F	0488
2SC441G	0488
2SC441GN	0488
2SC441H	0488
2SC441J	0488
2SC441K	0488
2SC441L	0488
2SC441M	0488
2SC441OR	0488
2SC441R	0488
2SC441X	0488
2SC441Y	0488
2SC442	0488
2SC442A	0488
2SC442B	0488
2SC442C	0488
2SC442D	0488
2SC442E	0488
2SC442F	0488
2SC442G	0488
2SC442GN	0488
2SC442H	0488
2SC442J	0488
2SC442K	0488
2SC442L	0488
2SC442M	0488
2SC442OR	0488
2SC442R	0488
2SC442X	0488
2SC442Y	0488
2SC443	0086
2SC443A	0086
2SC443B	0086

DEVICE TYPE	REPL CODE
2SC443C	0086
2SC443D	0086
2SC443E	0086
2SC443F	0086
2SC443G	0086
2SC443GN	0086
2SC443H	0086
2SC443J	0086
2SC443K	0086
2SC443L	0086
2SC443M	0086
2SC443OR	0086
2SC443R	0086
2SC443X	0086
2SC443Y	0086
2SC444	0590
2SC445	0168
2SC445A	0168
2SC445B	0168
2SC445C	0168
2SC445D	0168
2SC445E	0168
2SC445F	0168
2SC445G	0168
2SC445GN	0168
2SC445H	0168
2SC445J	0168
2SC445K	0168
2SC445L	0168
2SC445M	0168
2SC445OR	0168
2SC445R	0168
2SC445X	0168
2SC445Y	0168
2SC446	5468
2SC454	0076
2SC454(B)	0076
2SC454(C)	0076
2SC454-3	0076
2SC454-5	0076
2SC454-C	0076
2SC454-OR	0076
2SC454A	0076
2SC454B	0076
2SC454B-6	0076
2SC454BL	0076
2SC454C	0076
2SC454D	0076
2SC454E	0076
2SC454F	0076
2SC454G	0076
2SC454GN	0076
2SC454H	0076
2SC454J	0076
2SC454K	0076
2SC454L	0076
2SC454LA	0076
2SC454M	0076
2SC454OR	0076
2SC454R	0076
2SC454X	0076
2SC454Y	0076
2SC455	0155
2SC455-OR	0155
2SC455A	0155
2SC455B	0155
2SC455C	0155
2SC455D	0155
2SC455E	0155
2SC455F	0155
2SC455G	0155
2SC455GN	0155
2SC455H	0155
2SC455J	0155
2SC455K	0155
2SC455L	0155
2SC455M	0155
2SC455OR	0155
2SC455R	0155
2SC455X	0155
2SC455Y	0155
2SC456	0693
2SC456A	0693
2SC456B	0693
2SC456C	0693
2SC456D	0693
2SC456E	0693
2SC456F	0693
2SC456G	0693
2SC456GN	0693
2SC456H	0693
2SC456J	0693
2SC456K	0693
2SC456L	0693
2SC456M	0693
2SC456OR	0693
2SC456R	0693
2SC456X	0693
2SC456Y	0693
2SC457	0079
2SC458	0076
2SC458(A)	0076
2SC458(B)	0076
2SC458(C)	0076
2SC458(C,D)	0076
2SC458(D)	0076
2SC458(LG)	0076
2SC458-4	0076
2SC458-5	0076

DEVICE TYPE	REPL CODE
2SC458-B	0076
2SC458-C	0076
2SC458-D	0076
2SC458-GR	0076
2SC458-O	0076
2SC458-OR	0076
2SC458-Y	0076
2SC458A	0076
2SC458AD	0076
2SC458AK	0076
2SC458B	0076
2SC458BC	0076
2SC458BD	0076
2SC458B-GR	0076
2SC458BL	0076
2SC458BM	0076
2SC458B-O	0076
2SC458B-Y	0076
2SC458C	0076
2SC458C/L6	0076
2SC458CD	0076
2SC458CD-TB	0076
2SC458CL	0076
2SC458CLG	0076
2SC458CM	0076
2SC458D	0076
2SC458E	0076
2SC458F	0076
2SC458G	0076
2SC458GN	0076
2SC458H	0076
2SC458J	0076
2SC458K	0076
2SC458KB	0076
2SC458L	0076
2SC458L(C)	0076
2SC458L6	0076
2SC458LB	0076
2SC458LC	0076
2SC458LD	0076
2SC458LG	0076
2SC458LG(B)	0076
2SC458LG(C)	0076
2SC458LG(D)	0076
2SC458LGA	0076
2SC458LGB	0076
2SC458LGBM	0076
2SC458LGC	0076
2SC458LGC-6	0076
2SC458LGD	0076
2SC458LGO	0076
2SC458LGR	0076
2SC458LGS	0076
2SC458M	0076
2SC458OR	0076
2SC458R	0076
2SC458RGS	0076
2SC458X	0076
2SC458Y	0076
2SC459	0284
2SC459A	0284
2SC459B	0284
2SC459C	0284
2SC459D	0284
2SC459E	0284
2SC459F	0284
2SC459G	0284
2SC459GN	0284
2SC459H	0284
2SC459J	0284
2SC459K	0284
2SC459L	0284
2SC459M	0284
2SC459OR	0284
2SC459R	0284
2SC459X	0284
2SC459Y	0284
2SC460	0151
2SC460(A)	0151
2SC460(B)	0151
2SC460(C)	0151
2SC460-5	0151
2SC460-B	0151
2SC460-C	0151
2SC460-OR	0151
2SC460A	0151
2SC460A2302-17	0151
2SC460B	0151
2SC460BL	0151
2SC460C	0151
2SC460D	0151
2SC460E	0151
2SC460F	0151
2SC460G	0151
2SC460GB	0151
2SC460GN	0151
2SC460H	0151
2SC460J	0151
2SC460K	0151
2SC460L	0151
2SC460M	0151
2SC460OR	0151
2SC460R	0151
2SC460X	0151
2SC460Y	0151
2SC461	0151
2SC461(8F)	0151
2SC461-8F	0151
2SC461-A	0151

If replacement code is OEM, contact original manufacturer for replacement.

DEVICE TYPE	REPL CODE
2SC461-B	0151
2SC461A	0151
2SC461AL	0151
2SC461B	0151
2SC461BF	0151
2SC461BK	0151
2SC461BL	0151
2SC461C	0151
2SC461E	0151
2SC461EP	0151
2SC461F	0151
2SC461L	0151
2SC462	0079
2SC463	0007
2SC463A	0007
2SC463B	0007
2SC463C	0007
2SC463D	0007
2SC463E	0007
2SC463F	0007
2SC463G	0007
2SC463GN	0007
2SC463H	0007
2SC463J	0007
2SC463K	0007
2SC463L	0007
2SC463M	0007
2SC463OR	0007
2SC463R	0007
2SC463X	0007
2SC463Y	0007
2SC464	0259
2SC464A	0259
2SC464B	0259
2SC464C	0259
2SC464D	0259
2SC464E	0259
2SC464F	0259
2SC464G	0259
2SC464GN	0259
2SC464H	0259
2SC464J	0259
2SC464K	0259
2SC464L	0259
2SC464M	0259
2SC464OR	0259
2SC464R	0259
2SC464X	0259
2SC464Y	0259
2SC465	0259
2SC465A	0259
2SC465B	0259
2SC465C	0259
2SC465D	0259
2SC465E	0259
2SC465F	0259
2SC465G	0259
2SC465GN	0259
2SC465H	0259
2SC465J	0259
2SC465K	0259
2SC465L	0259
2SC465M	0259
2SC465OR	0259
2SC465R	0259
2SC465X	0259
2SC465Y	0259
2SC466	0259
2SC466A	0259
2SC466B	0259
2SC466C	0259
2SC466D	0259
2SC466E	0259
2SC466F	0259
2SC466G	0259
2SC466GN	0259
2SC466H	0259
2SC466J	0259
2SC466K	0259
2SC466L	0259
2SC466M	0259
2SC466OR	0259
2SC466R	0259
2SC466X	0259
2SC466Y	0259
2SC467	0144
2SC468	0016
2SC468A	0016
2SC468B	0016
2SC468H	0016
2SC468LGR	0016
2SC469	0470
2SC469-OR	0470
2SC469A	0470
2SC469B	0470
2SC469C	0470
2SC469D	0470
2SC469E	0470
2SC469F	0470
2SC469G	0470
2SC469GN	0470
2SC469H	0470
2SC469J	0470
2SC469K	0470
2SC469L	0470
2SC469M	0470
2SC469OR	0470
2SC469Q	0470
2SC469R	0470

DEVICE TYPE	REPL CODE
2SC469X	0470
2SC469Y	0470
2SC470	0233
2SC470-3	0233
2SC470-4	0233
2SC470-5	0233
2SC470-6	0233
2SC470A	0233
2SC470B	0233
2SC470C	0233
2SC470D	0233
2SC470E	0233
2SC470F	0233
2SC470G	0233
2SC470GN	0233
2SC470H	0233
2SC470J	0233
2SC470K	0233
2SC470L	0233
2SC470M	0233
2SC470OR	0233
2SC470R	0233
2SC470X	0233
2SC470Y	0233
2SC471	0018
2SC472	0224
2SC472A	0224
2SC472B	0224
2SC472C	0224
2SC472D	0224
2SC472E	0224
2SC472F	0224
2SC472G	0224
2SC472GN	0224
2SC472H	0224
2SC472J	0224
2SC472K	0224
2SC472L	0224
2SC472M	0224
2SC472OR	0224
2SC472R	0224
2SC472X	0224
2SC472Y	0224
2SC473	0016
2SC473AC	0016
2SC474	0079
2SC475	0470
2SC475A	0470
2SC475B	0470
2SC475C	0470
2SC475D	0470
2SC475E	0470
2SC475F	0470
2SC475G	0470
2SC475GN	0470
2SC475H.TEMP	0470
2SC475M	0470
2SC475OR	0470
2SC475R	0470
2SC475X	0470
2SC475Y	0470
2SC476	0470
2SC476C	0470
2SC476D	0470
2SC476E	0470
2SC476F	0470
2SC476G	0470
2SC476GN	0470
2SC476H	0470
2SC476J	0470
2SC476K	0470
2SC476L	0470
2SC476M	0470
2SC476OR	0470
2SC476R	0470
2SC476X	0470
2SC476Y	0470
2SC477	0007
2SC477A	0007
2SC477B	0007
2SC477C	0007
2SC477D	0007
2SC477E	0007
2SC477F	0007
2SC477G	0007
2SC477GN	0007
2SC477H	0007
2SC477J	0007
2SC477K	0007
2SC477L	0007
2SC477M	0007
2SC477OR	0007
2SC477R	0007
2SC477X	0007
2SC477Y	0007
2SC478	0016
2SC478(D)	0016
2SC478-4	0016
2SC478-O	0016
2SC478A	0016
2SC478B	0016
2SC478C	0016
2SC478D	0016
2SC478E	0016
2SC478F	0016
2SC478G	0016
2SC478GN	0016
2SC478H	0016
2SC478J	0016

DEVICE TYPE	REPL CODE
2SC478K	0016
2SC478L	0016
2SC478M	0016
2SC478OR	0016
2SC478R	0016
2SC478X	0016
2SC478Y	0016
2SC479	0086
2SC479A	0086
2SC479B	0086
2SC479C	0086
2SC479D	0086
2SC479E	0086
2SC479F	0086
2SC479G	0086
2SC479GN	0086
2SC479H	0086
2SC479J	0086
2SC479K	0086
2SC479L	0086
2SC479M	0086
2SC479OR	0086
2SC479R	0086
2SC479X	0086
2SC479Y	0086
2SC480	0320
2SC481	0693
2SC481-OR	0693
2SC481A	0693
2SC481B	0693
2SC481C	0693
2SC481D	0693
2SC481E	0693
2SC481F	0693
2SC481G	0693
2SC481GN	0693
2SC481H	0693
2SC481J	0693
2SC481K	0693
2SC481L	0693
2SC481M	0693
2SC481OR	0693
2SC481R	0693
2SC481X	0693
2SC481Y	0693
2SC482	1583
2SC482(Y)	1583
2SC482-0	1583
2SC482-GR	1583
2SC482-GRN	1583
2SC482-O	1583
2SC482-OR	1583
2SC482-ORG	1583
2SC482-Y	1583
2SC482-YEL	1583
2SC482A	1583
2SC482B	1583
2SC482C	1583
2SC482D	1583
2SC482E	1583
2SC482F	1583
2SC482G	1583
2SC482GN	1583
2SC482GR	1583
2SC482GRN	1583
2SC482GRY	1583
2SC482H	1583
2SC482J	1583
2SC482K	1583
2SC482L	1583
2SC482M	1583
2SC482OR	1583
2SC482R	1583
2SC482X	1583
2SC482Y	1583
2SC482YEL	1583
2SC483	1021
2SC484	1471
2SC484-BL	1471
2SC484-BLU	1471
2SC484-R	1471
2SC484-RED	1471
2SC484-Y	1471
2SC484-YEL	1471
2SC484A	1471
2SC484B	1471
2SC484BL	1471
2SC484C	1471
2SC484D	1471
2SC484E	1471
2SC484F	1471
2SC484G	1471
2SC484GN	1471
2SC484H	1471
2SC484J	1471
2SC484K	1471
2SC484L	1471
2SC484M	1471
2SC484OR	1471
2SC484R	1471
2SC484X	1471
2SC484Y	1471
2SC485	1471
2SC485(Y)	1471
2SC485-BL	1471
2SC485-BLU	1471
2SC485-OR	1471
2SC485-R	1471
2SC485-RED	1471

DEVICE TYPE	REPL CODE
2SC485-Y	1471
2SC485-YEL	1471
2SC485A	1471
2SC485B	1471
2SC485BL	1471
2SC485C	1471
2SC485D	1471
2SC485E	1471
2SC485F	1471
2SC485G	1471
2SC485GN	1471
2SC485H	1471
2SC485J	1471
2SC485K	1471
2SC485L	1471
2SC485M	1471
2SC485OR	1471
2SC485R	1471
2SC485X	1471
2SC485Y	1471
2SC486	1471
2SC486(Y)	1471
2SC486-BL	1471
2SC486-BLU	1471
2SC486-R	1471
2SC486-RED	1471
2SC486-Y	1471
2SC486-YEL	1471
2SC486A	1471
2SC486B	1471
2SC486BL	1471
2SC486C	1471
2SC486D	1471
2SC486E	1471
2SC486F	1471
2SC486G	1471
2SC486GN	1471
2SC486H	1471
2SC486J	1471
2SC486K	1471
2SC486L	1471
2SC486M	1471
2SC486OR	1471
2SC486R	1471
2SC486X	1471
2SC486Y	1471
2SC487	0178
2SC487A	0178
2SC488	0178
2SC488H	0178
2SC489	0178
2SC489-BL	0178
2SC489-BLU	0178
2SC489-R	0178
2SC489-RED	0178
2SC489-Y	0178
2SC489-YEL	0178
2SC489A	0178
2SC489B	0178
2SC489C	0178
2SC489D	0178
2SC489E	0178
2SC489F	0178
2SC489G	0178
2SC489GN	0178
2SC489H	0178
2SC489J	0178
2SC489K	0178
2SC489L	0178
2SC489M	0178
2SC489OR	0178
2SC489R	0178
2SC489X	0178
2SC489Y	0178
2SC490	0178
2SC490-BL	0178
2SC490-BLU	0178
2SC490-R	0178
2SC490-RED	0178
2SC490-Y	0178
2SC490-YEL	0178
2SC491	0178
2SC491-BL	0178
2SC491-BLU	0178
2SC491-R	0178
2SC491-RED	0178
2SC491-Y	0178
2SC491-YEL	0178
2SC491A	0178
2SC491B	0178
2SC491BL	0178
2SC491C	0178
2SC491D	0178
2SC491E	0178
2SC491F	0178
2SC491G	0178
2SC491GN	0178
2SC491H	0178
2SC491J	0178
2SC491K	0178
2SC491L	0178
2SC491M	0178
2SC491OR	0178
2SC491R	0178
2SC491X	0178
2SC491Y	0178
2SC492	0177
2SC493	0861
2SC493-BL	0861

DEVICE TYPE	REPL CODE
2SC493-R	0861
2SC493-Y	0861
2SC493A	0861
2SC493B	0861
2SC493C	0861
2SC493D	0861
2SC493E	0861
2SC493F	0861
2SC493G	0861
2SC493GN	0861
2SC493H	0861
2SC493J	0861
2SC493K	0861
2SC493L	0861
2SC493M	0861
2SC493OR	0861
2SC493R	0861
2SC493X	0861
2SC493Y	0861
2SC494	0615
2SC494-BL	0615
2SC494-R	0615
2SC494-Y	0615
2SC494A	0615
2SC494B	0615
2SC494BL	0615
2SC494C	0615
2SC494D	0615
2SC494E	0615
2SC494F	0615
2SC494G	0615
2SC494GN	0615
2SC494H	0615
2SC494J	0615
2SC494K	0615
2SC494L	0615
2SC494M	0615
2SC494OR	0615
2SC494R	0615
2SC494X	0615
2SC494Y	0615
2SC495	0781
2SC495-0	0781
2SC495-O	0781
2SC495-OR	0781
2SC495-ORG	0781
2SC495-R	0781
2SC495-RED	0781
2SC495-Y	0781
2SC495-YEL	0781
2SC495A	0781
2SC495B	0781
2SC495C	0781
2SC495D	0781
2SC495E	0781
2SC495F	0781
2SC495G	0781
2SC495GN	0781
2SC495H	0781
2SC495J	0781
2SC495K	0781
2SC495L	0781
2SC495M	0781
2SC495O	0781
2SC495OR	0781
2SC495P	0781
2SC495R	0781
2SC495RED	0781
2SC495T	0781
2SC495X	0781
2SC495Y	0781
2SC495YEL	0781
2SC495Y-X	OEM
2SC496	0781
2SC496(O)	0781
2SC496(Y)	0781
2SC496-0	0781
2SC496-O	0781
2SC496-OR	0781
2SC496-ORG	0781
2SC496-R	0781
2SC496-RED	0781
2SC496-Y	0781
2SC496-YEL	0781
2SC496A	0781
2SC496B	0781
2SC496C	0781
2SC496D	0781
2SC496E	0781
2SC496F	0781
2SC496G	0781
2SC496GN	0781
2SC496H	0781
2SC496J	0781
2SC496K	0781
2SC496L	0781
2SC496M	0781
2SC496OR	0781
2SC496R	0781
2SC496RED	0781
2SC496X	0781
2SC496Y	0781
2SC496YEL	0781
2SC497	0086
2SC497-0	0086
2SC497-O	0086
2SC497-OR	0086
2SC497-ORG	0086
2SC497-R	0086

DEVICE TYPE	REPL CODE
2SC497-RED	0086
2SC497-Y	0086
2SC497-YEL	0086
2SC497A	0086
2SC497B	0086
2SC497C	0086
2SC497D	0086
2SC497E	0086
2SC497F	0086
2SC497G	0086
2SC497GN	0086
2SC497H	0086
2SC497J	0086
2SC497K	0086
2SC497L	0086
2SC497M	0086
2SC497OR	0086
2SC497R	0086
2SC497RED	0086
2SC497X	0086
2SC497Y	0086
2SC498	0086
2SC498-0	0086
2SC498-O	0086
2SC498-OR	0086
2SC498-ORG	0086
2SC498-R	0086
2SC498-RED	0086
2SC498-Y	0086
2SC498-YEL	0086
2SC498A	0086
2SC498B	0086
2SC498C	0086
2SC498D	0086
2SC498E	0086
2SC498F	0086
2SC498G	0086
2SC498GN	0086
2SC498H	0086
2SC498J	0086
2SC498K	0086
2SC498L	0086
2SC498M	0086
2SC498OR	0086
2SC498R	0086
2SC498RED	0086
2SC498X	0086
2SC498Y	0086
2SC498YEL	0086
2SC499	2359
2SC499(A)	2359
2SC499(R)	2359
2SC499(Y)	2359
2SC499-OR	2359
2SC499-R	2359
2SC499-R(FA-1)	2359
2SC499-RED	2359
2SC499-RY	2359
2SC499-Y	2359
2SC499-Y(FA-1)	2359
2SC499-YEL	2359
2SC499A	2359
2SC499B	2359
2SC499C	2359
2SC499D	2359
2SC499E	2359
2SC499F	2359
2SC499FA1	2359
2SC499G	2359
2SC499GN	2359
2SC499H	2359
2SC499J	2359
2SC499K	2359
2SC499L	2359
2SC499M	2359
2SC499OR	2359
2SC499R	2359
2SC499RED	2359
2SC499RY	2359
2SC499X	2359
2SC499Y	2359
2SC499YEL	2359
2SC500	0233
2SC500(N)	0233
2SC500(Y)	0233
2SC500A	0233
2SC500B	0233
2SC500C	0233
2SC500D	0233
2SC500E	0233
2SC500F	0233
2SC500G	0233
2SC500GN	0233
2SC500H	0233
2SC500J	0233
2SC500K	0233
2SC500L	0233
2SC500M	0233
2SC500OR	0233
2SC500R	0233
2SC500X	0233
2SC500Y	0233
2SC501	0086
2SC501-O	0086
2SC501-ORG	0086
2SC501-R	0086
2SC501-RED	0086
2SC501-Y	0086
2SC501-YEL	0086

DEVICE TYPE	REPL CODE
2SC501A	0086
2SC501B	0086
2SC501C	0086
2SC501D	0086
2SC501E	0086
2SC501F	0086
2SC501G	0086
2SC501GN	0086
2SC501H	0086
2SC501J	0086
2SC501K	0086
2SC501L	0086
2SC501M	0086
2SC501O	0086
2SC501OR	0086
2SC501R	0086
2SC501X	0086
2SC501Y	0086
2SC502	0693
2SC502A	0693
2SC502B	0693
2SC502C	0693
2SC502D	0693
2SC502E	0693
2SC502F	0693
2SC502G	0693
2SC502GN	0693
2SC502H	0693
2SC502J	0693
2SC502K	0693
2SC502L	0693
2SC502M	0693
2SC502OR	0593
2SC502R	0693
2SC502X	0693
2SC502Y	0693
2SC503	0086
2SC503-GR	0086
2SC503-O	0086
2SC503-Y	0086
2SC503A	0086
2SC503B	0086
2SC503C	0086
2SC503D	0086
2SC503E	0086
2SC503F	0086
2SC503G	0086
2SC503GN	0086
2SC503GR	0086
2SC503H	0086
2SC503J	0086
2SC503K	0086
2SC503L	0086
2SC503M	0086
2SC503OR	0086
2SC503R	0086
2SC503X	0086
2SC504	0086
2SC504-GR	0086
2SC504-O	0086
2SC504-Y	0086
2SC504A	0086
2SC504B	0086
2SC504C	0086
2SC504D	0086
2SC504E	0086
2SC504F	0086
2SC504G	0086
2SC504GN	0086
2SC504GR	0086
2SC504H	0086
2SC504J	0086
2SC504K	0086
2SC504L	0086
2SC504M	0086
2SC504OR	0086
2SC504R	0086
2SC504X	0086
2SC505	0233
2SC505-O	0233
2SC505-ORG	0233
2SC505-R	0233
2SC505-RED	0233
2SC505A	0233
2SC505B	0233
2SC505C	0233
2SC505D	0233
2SC505E	0233
2SC505F	0233
2SC505G	0233
2SC505GN	0233
2SC505H	0233
2SC505J	0233
2SC505K	0233
2SC505L	0233
2SC505M	0233
2SC505O	0233
2SC505OR	0233
2SC505R	0233
2SC505X	0233
2SC505Y	0233
2SC506	0233
2SC506-O	0233
2SC506-ORG	0233
2SC506-R	0233
2SC506-RED	0233
2SC506A	0233
2SC506B	0233
2SC506C	0233

If replacement code is OEM, contact original manufacturer for replacement.

DEVICE TYPE	REPL CODE
2SC506D	0233
2SC506E	0233
2SC506F	0233
2SC506G	0233
2SC506GN	0233
2SC506H	0233
2SC506J	0233
2SC506K	0233
2SC506L	0233
2SC506M	0233
2SC5060	0233
2SC5060R	0233
2SC506R	0233
2SC506X	0233
2SC506Y	0233
2SC507	0233
2SC507-0	0233
2SC507-O	0233
2SC507-R	0233
2SC507-Y	0233
2SC507A	0233
2SC507B	0233
2SC507C	0233
2SC507D	0233
2SC507E	0233
2SC507F	0233
2SC507G	0233
2SC507GN	0233
2SC507H	0233
2SC507J	0233
2SC507K	0233
2SC507L	0233
2SC507M	0233
2SC5070R	0233
2SC507R	0233
2SC507X	0233
2SC507Y	0233
2SC508	0178
2SC508A	0178
2SC508B	0178
2SC508C	0178
2SC508D	0178
2SC508E	0178
2SC508F	0178
2SC508G	0178
2SC508GN	0178
2SC5080R	0178
2SC508X	0178
2SC508Y	0178
2SC509	0155
2SC509(0)	0155
2SC509(O)	0155
2SC509(Y)	0155
2SC509-0	0155
2SC509-O	0155
2SC509-Y	0155
2SC509G	0155
2SC509G-O	0155
2SC509G-Y	0155
2SC5090	0155
2SC509Y	0155
2SC510	1471
2SC510-0	1471
2SC510-ORG	1471
2SC510-R	1471
2SC510-RED	1471
2SC510A	1471
2SC510B	1471
2SC510C	1471
2SC510D	1471
2SC510E	1471
2SC510F	1471
2SC510G	1471
2SC510GN	1471
2SC510H	1471
2SC510J	1471
2SC510K	1471
2SC510L	1471
2SC510M	1471
2SC5100	1471
2SC5100R	1471
2SC510R	1471
2SC510X	1471
2SC510Y	1471
2SC511	1471
2SC511-0	1471
2SC511-ORG	1471
2SC511-R	1471
2SC511-RED	1471
2SC511A	1471
2SC511B	1471
2SC511C	1471
2SC511D	1471
2SC511E	1471
2SC511F	1471
2SC511G	1471
2SC511GN	1471
2SC511H	1471
2SC511J	1471
2SC511K	1471
2SC511L	1471
2SC511M	1471
2SC5110	1471
2SC5110R	1471
2SC511R	1471
2SC511X	1471
2SC511Y	1471
2SC512	1471
2SC512-0	1471
2SC512-O	1471
2SC512-ORG	1471
2SC512-R	1471
2SC512-RED	1471
2SC512A	1471
2SC512B	1471
2SC512C	1471
2SC512D	1471
2SC512E	1471
2SC512F	1471
2SC512G	1471
2SC512GN	1471
2SC512H	1471
2SC512J	1471
2SC512K	1471
2SC512L	1471
2SC512M	1471
2SC5120	1471
2SC5120R	1471
2SC512R	1471
2SC512X	1471
2SC512Y	1471
2SC513	1471
2SC513-0	1471
2SC513-O	1471
2SC513-ORG	1471
2SC513-R	1471
2SC513-RED	1471
2SC513A	1471
2SC513B	1471
2SC513C	1471
2SC513D	1471
2SC513E	1471
2SC513F	1471
2SC513G	1471
2SC513GN	1471
2SC513H	1471
2SC513J	1471
2SC513K	1471
2SC513L	1471
2SC513M	1471
2SC5130	1471
2SC5130R	1471
2SC513R	1471
2SC513X	1471
2SC513Y	1471
2SC514	0142
2SC514A	0142
2SC514B	0142
2SC514C	0142
2SC514D	0142
2SC514E	0142
2SC514F	0142
2SC514G	0142
2SC514GN	0142
2SC514H	0142
2SC514J	0142
2SC514K	0142
2SC514L	0142
2SC514M	0142
2SC5140R	0142
2SC514R	0142
2SC514X	0142
2SC514Y	0142
2SC515	0142
2SC515-OR	0142
2SC515A	0142
2SC515A(BK)	0142
2SC515AM	0142
2SC515AX	0142
2SC515AY	0142
2SC515B	0142
2SC515BK	0142
2SC515C	0142
2SC515D	0142
2SC515E	0142
2SC515F	0142
2SC515G	0142
2SC515GN	0142
2SC515H	0142
2SC515J	0142
2SC515K	0142
2SC515L	0142
2SC515M	0142
2SC5150R	0142
2SC515R	0142
2SC515X	0142
2SC515Y	0142
2SC516	0086
2SC516A	0086
2SC516B	0086
2SC516C	0086
2SC516D	0086
2SC516E	0086
2SC516F	0086
2SC516G	0086
2SC516GN	0086
2SC516H	0086
2SC516J	0086
2SC516K	0086
2SC516L	0086
2SC516M	0086
2SC5160R	0086
2SC516R	0086
2SC516X	0086
2SC516Y	0086
2SC517	1401
2SC517-OR	1401
2SC517A	1401
2SC517B	1401
2SC517C	1401
2SC517D	1401
2SC517E	1401
2SC517F	1401
2SC517G	1401
2SC517GN	1401
2SC517H	1401
2SC517J	1401
2SC517K	1401
2SC517L	1401
2SC517M	1401
2SC5170R	1401
2SC517R	1401
2SC517S	1401
2SC517X	1401
2SC517Y	1401
2SC518	0168
2SC518A	0168
2SC519	0861
2SC519A	0861
2SC520	0861
2SC520A	0861
2SC521	0861
2SC521A	0861
2SC522	2298
2SC522-0	2298
2SC522-O	2298
2SC522-ORG	2298
2SC522-R	2298
2SC522-RED	2298
2SC5220	2298
2SC522R	2298
2SC523	2298
2SC523-0	2298
2SC523-ORG	2298
2SC523-R	2298
2SC523-RED	2298
2SC5230	2298
2SC523R	2298
2SC524	3302
2SC524-0	3302
2SC524-O	3302
2SC524-ORG	3302
2SC524-R	3302
2SC524-RED	3302
2SC5240	3302
2SC524R	3302
2SC525	1401
2SC525-0	1401
2SC525-O	1401
2SC525-ORG	1401
2SC525-R	1401
2SC525-RED	1401
2SC5250	1401
2SC525R	1401
2SC526	0233
2SC526-0	0233
2SC526A	0233
2SC526B	0233
2SC526C	0233
2SC526D	0233
2SC526E	0233
2SC526F	0233
2SC526G	0233
2SC526GN	0233
2SC526H	0233
2SC526J	0233
2SC526K	0233
2SC526L	0233
2SC526M	0233
2SC5260R	0233
2SC526R	0233
2SC526X	0233
2SC526Y	0233
2SC527	0007
2SC528	0111
2SC529	0284
2SC529A	0284
2SC529B	0284
2SC529C	0284
2SC529D	0284
2SC529E	0284
2SC529F	0284
2SC529G	0284
2SC529GN	0284
2SC529H	0284
2SC529J	0284
2SC529K	0284
2SC529L	0284
2SC529M	0284
2SC5290R	0284
2SC529R	0284
2SC529X	0284
2SC529Y	0284
2SC530	0079
2SC531	0155
2SC532	0079
2SC5320	0079
2SC533	0079
2SC534	0079
2SC535	0127
2SC535(B)	0127
2SC535(C)	0127
2SC535-OR	0127
2SC535A	0127
2SC535ABC	0127
2SC535AL	0127
2SC535B	0127
2SC535C	0127
2SC535D	0127
2SC535E	0127
2SC535F	0127
2SC535G	0127
2SC535GN	0127
2SC535H	0127
2SC535J	0127
2SC535K	0127
2SC535L	0127
2SC535M	0127
2SC535NB	OEM
2SC5350R	0127
2SC535R	0127
2SC535X	0127
2SC535Y	0127
2SC536	0532
2SC536(C)	0532
2SC536(D)	0532
2SC536(E)	0532
2SC536(F)	0532
2SC536(G)	0532
2SC536(RED)	OEM
2SC536-AUD-SPA	OEM
2SC536-D	0532
2SC536-E	0532
2SC536-E-NP	0532
2SC536-F	0532
2SC536-F-NP	0532
2SC536-F-NP-AA	0532
2SC536-F-SPA-AC	0532
2SC536-G	0532
2SC536-G-NP	0532
2SC536-G-NP-AA	0532
2SC536-G-SP	OEM
2SC536-G-SPT-AC	0532
2SC536-OR	0532
2SC536A	0502
2SC536AE-NP	OEM
2SC536AE-SP	OEM
2SC536AF	0532
2SC536AF-SP	OEM
2SC536AG	0532
2SC536AG-SP	OEM
2SC536AUD	OEM
2SC536AUD-G	OEM
2SC536AUD-H	OEM
2SC536AUD-KG	OEM
2SC536B	0532
2SC536C	0532
2SC536D	0532
2SC536DK	0532
2SC536E	0532
2SC536ED	0532
2SC536EH	0532
2SC536EJ	0532
2SC536EN	0532
2SC536EP	0532
2SC536ER	0532
2SC536ESP	OEM
2SC536ET	0532
2SC536EW	OEM
2SC536EZ	0532
2SC536F	0532
2SC536F1	0532
2SC536F2	0532
2SC536FC	0532
2SC536F-NP	0532
2SC536FP	0532
2SC536FS	0532
2SC536FS6	0532
2SC536FSP	OEM
2SC536FZ	0532
2SC536G	0532
2SC536G-1	0532
2SC536G1	0532
2SC536G2	0532
2SC536GF	0532
2SC536GJ	0532
2SC536GK	0532
2SC536GL	0532
2SC536GM	0532
2SC536GN	0532
2SC536G-NP	0532
2SC536GP	0532
2SC536GT	0532
2SC536GV	0532
2SC536GY	0532
2SC536GZ	0532
2SC536H	0532
2SC536J	0532
2SC536K	0532
2SC536K(F)	0532
2SC536K(G)	0532
2SC536KE	0532
2SC536KF	0532
2SC536K-F-NP-AA	0532
2SC536KG	0532
2SC536K-G-NP-AA	0532
2SC536KN(PG)	0532
2SC536KNP	0532
2SC536KNP-AA	0532
2SC536K-NP-E	OEM
2SC536K-NP-F	OEM
2SC536KNPFT	0532
2SC536KNP-T	0532
2SC536L	0532
2SC536M	0532
2SC536NP	0532
2SC536NP(E)	0532
2SC536NP(F)	0532
2SC536NP(G)	0532
2SC536NP-E	0532
2SC536NPE	0532
2SC536NP-F	OEM
2SC536NPF	0532
2SC536NP-G	OEM
2SC536NPG	0532
2SC536NP-T	0532
2SC5360R	0532
2SC536R	0532
2SC536SE	0532
2SC536SEZ	0532
2SC536SF	0532
2SC536SFZ	0532
2SC536SP	0532
2SC536SP(F)	0532
2SC536SP(G)	0532
2SC536SP-AC	0532
2SC536SP-E	OEM
2SC536SPE	0532
2SC536SP-F	OEM
2SC536SPF	0532
2SC536SP-G	OEM
2SC536W	0532
2SC536X	0532
2SC536XL	0532
2SC536Y	0502
2SC536YF	0532
2SC537	0191
2SC537(F)	0191
2SC537(G)	0191
2SC537-C7	0191
2SC537-EV	0191
2SC537ALC	0191
2SC537B	0191
2SC537BK	0191
2SC537C	0191
2SC537C7	0191
2SC537D	0191
2SC537D1	0191
2SC537D2	0191
2SC537E	0191
2SC537EF	0191
2SC537EH	0191
2SC537EJ	0191
2SC537EV	0191
2SC537F	0191
2SC537F1	0191
2SC537F2	0191
2SC537FC	0191
2SC537F-C7	0191
2SC537FC7	0191
2SC537FJ	0191
2SC537FK	0191
2SC537FV	0191
2SC537G	0191
2SC537G1	0191
2SC537G2	0191
2SC537GFL	0191
2SC537GI	0191
2SC537H	0191
2SC537HT	0191
2SC537WF	0191
2SC538	0079
2SC538(A)	0079
2SC538(P)	0079
2SC538(R)	0079
2SC538-Q	0079
2SC538A	0079
2SC538A(Q)	0079
2SC538A-P	0079
2SC538AQ	0079
2SC538A-R	0079
2SC538AR	0079
2SC538AS	0079
2SC538K	0079
2SC538P	0079
2SC538Q	0079
2SC538R	0079
2SC538S	0079
2SC538T	0079
2SC539	0016
2SC539(L)(K)	0016
2SC539(R)	0016
2SC539R	0016
2SC539S	0016
2SC539T	0016
2SC540	0470
2SC540A	0470
2SC540B	0470
2SC540C	0470
2SC540D	0470
2SC540E	0470
2SC540F	0470
2SC540G	0470
2SC540GN	0470
2SC540H	0470
2SC540J	0470
2SC540K	0470
2SC540L	0470
2SC540M	0470
2SC5400R	0470
2SC540R	0470
2SC540X	0470
2SC540Y	0470
2SC541	0555
2SC542	0555
2SC543	0042
2SC543A	0042
2SC543B	0042
2SC543C	0042
2SC543D	0042
2SC543E	0042
2SC543F	0042
2SC543G	0042
2SC543GN	0042
2SC543H	0042
2SC543J	0042
2SC543K	0042
2SC543L	0042
2SC543M	0042
2SC5430R	0042
2SC543R	0042
2SC543X	0042
2SC543Y	0042
2SC544	2195
2SC544A	2195
2SC544AG	2195
2SC544B	2195
2SC544C	2195
2SC544D	0127
2SC544D(VHF)	0127
2SC544E	2195
2SC544F	2195
2SC544G	2195
2SC544GN	2195
2SC544H	2195
2SC544J	2195
2SC544K	2195
2SC544L	2195
2SC544M	2195
2SC5440R	2195
2SC544R	2195
2SC544X	2195
2SC544Y	2195
2SC545	0127
2SC545A	0127
2SC545B	0127
2SC545C	0127
2SC545D	0127
2SC545E	0127
2SC546	0007
2SC546K	0007
2SC547	0111
2SC547B	OEM
2SC547C	OEM
2SC548	0555
2SC548C	OEM
2SC549	OEM
2SC550	0555
2SC550A	0555
2SC551	0042
2SC552	0042
2SC553	0042
2SC554	0042
2SC555	0488
2SC556	0224
2SC556B	OEM
2SC557	OEM
2SC557C	OEM
2SC558	4841
2SC558A	OEM
2SC558B	OEM
2SC559	0018
2SC559B	OEM
2SC560	0086
2SC560A	0086
2SC560B	0086
2SC560C	0086
2SC560D	0086
2SC560E	0086
2SC560F	0086
2SC560G	0086
2SC560GN	0086
2SC560H	0086
2SC560J	0086
2SC560K	0086
2SC560L	0086
2SC560M	0086
2SC5600R	0086
2SC560R	0086
2SC560X	0086
2SC560Y	0086
2SC561	1422
2SC561-OR	1422
2SC561A	1422
2SC561B	1422
2SC561C	1422
2SC561D	1422
2SC561E	1422
2SC561F	1422
2SC561G	1422
2SC561GN	1422
2SC561H	1422
2SC561J	1422
2SC561K	1422
2SC561L	1422
2SC561M	1422
2SC5610R	1422
2SC561R	1422
2SC561X	1422
2SC561Y	1422
2SC562	0216
2SC562(O)	0216
2SC562-OR	0216
2SC562A	0216
2SC562B	0216
2SC562C	0216
2SC562D	0216
2SC562E	0216
2SC562F	0216
2SC562G	0216
2SC562GN	0216
2SC562H	0216
2SC562J	0216
2SC562K	0216
2SC562L	0216
2SC562M	0216
2SC5620R	0216
2SC562R	0216
2SC562X	0216
2SC562Y	0216
2SC563	0829
2SC563(A)	0829
2SC563-F	0829
2SC563-G	0829
2SC563-OR	0829
2SC563A	0829
2SC563B	0829
2SC563C	0829
2SC563D	0829
2SC563E	0829
2SC563F	0829
2SC563G	0829
2SC563GN	0829
2SC563H	0829
2SC563J	0829
2SC563K	0829
2SC563L	0829
2SC563M	0829
2SC5630R	0829
2SC563R	0829
2SC563X	0829
2SC563Y	0829
2SC564	0016
2SC564(Q)	0016
2SC564(Q)(R)	0016
2SC564(S)	0016
2SC564A	0016
2SC564AP	0016
2SC564B	0016
2SC564C	0016
2SC564D	0016
2SC564E	0016
2SC564F	0016
2SC564G	0016
2SC564GN	0016
2SC564H	0016
2SC564J	0016
2SC564K	0016
2SC564L	0016
2SC564M	0016
2SC5640R	0016
2SC564P	0016
2SC564PL	0016
2SC564Q	0016
2SC564QC	0016
2SC564R	0016
2SC564S	0016
2SC564T	0016
2SC564X	0016
2SC564Y	0016
2SC565	0016
2SC566	0259
2SC566A	0259
2SC566B	0259
2SC566C	0259
2SC566D	0259
2SC566E	0259
2SC566F	0259
2SC566G	0259
2SC566GN	0259
2SC566H	0259
2SC566J	0259
2SC566K	0259
2SC566L	0259
2SC566M	0259
2SC5660R	0259
2SC566R	0259
2SC566X	0259
2SC566Y	0259
2SC567	0259
2SC567A	0259
2SC567B	0259
2SC567C	0259
2SC567D	0259
2SC567E	0259
2SC567F	0259
2SC567G	0259
2SC567GN	0259
2SC567H	0259
2SC567J	0259
2SC567K	0259
2SC567L	0259
2SC567M	0259
2SC5670R	0259
2SC567R	0259
2SC567X	0259
2SC567Y	0259
2SC568	0259
2SC568A	0259
2SC568B	0259
2SC568C	0259
2SC568D	0259

84
If replacement code is OEM, contact original manufacturer for replacement.

DEVICE TYPE	REPL CODE
2SC568E	0259
2SC568F	0259
2SC568G	0259
2SC568GN	0259
2SC568H	0259
2SC568J	0259
2SC568K	0259
2SC568L	0259
2SC568M	0259
2SC568OR	0259
2SC568R	0259
2SC568X	0259
2SC568Y	0259
2SC569	0016
2SC570	0016
2SC571	2030
2SC572	3289
2SC573	3290
2SC575	0086
2SC576	0016
2SC576E	0016
2SC576F	0016
2SC576G	0016
2SC577	0016
2SC578	0855
2SC579	0396
2SC580	0086
2SC580A	0086
2SC580B	0086
2SC580C	0086
2SC580D	0086
2SC580E	0086
2SC580F	0086
2SC580G	0086
2SC580GN	0086
2SC580H	0086
2SC580J	0086
2SC580K	0086
2SC580L	0086
2SC580M	0086
2SC580OR	0086
2SC580R	0086
2SC580T	0086
2SC580X	0086
2SC580Y	0086
2SC581	0007
2SC582	2634
2SC582(BX)	2634
2SC582(BX)(BY)	2634
2SC582(BY)	2634
2SC582-OR	2634
2SC582,B	2634
2SC582A	2634
2SC582B	2634
2SC582BC	2634
2SC582BX	2634
2SC582BY	2634
2SC582C	2634
2SC582D	2634
2SC582E	2634
2SC582EA	2634
2SC582EH	2634
2SC582F	2634
2SC582G	2634
2SC582GN	2634
2SC582H	2634
2SC582J	2634
2SC582K	2634
2SC582L	2634
2SC582M	2634
2SC582OR	2634
2SC582R	2634
2SC582X	2634
2SC582Y	2634
2SC583	0259
2SC584	0219
2SC585	0042
2SC586	0177
2SC587	0016
2SC587A	0016
2SC587B	0016
2SC587C	0016
2SC587D	0016
2SC587E	0016
2SC587F	0016
2SC587G	0016
2SC587GN	0016
2SC587H	0016
2SC587J	0016
2SC587K	0016
2SC587L	0016
2SC587M	0016
2SC587OR	0016
2SC587R	0016
2SC587X	0016
2SC587Y	0016
2SC588	0016
2SC588A	0016
2SC588B	0016
2SC588C	0016
2SC588D	0016
2SC588E	0016
2SC588F	0016
2SC588G	0016
2SC588GN	0016
2SC588H	0016
2SC588J	0016
2SC588K	0016
2SC588L	0016

DEVICE TYPE	REPL CODE
2SC588M	0016
2SC588OR	0016
2SC588R	0016
2SC588X	0016
2SC588Y	0016
2SC589	0233
2SC589A	0233
2SC589B	0233
2SC589C	0233
2SC589D	0233
2SC589E	0233
2SC589F	0233
2SC589G	0233
2SC589GN	0233
2SC589H	0233
2SC589J	0233
2SC589K	0233
2SC589L	0233
2SC589M	0233
2SC589OR	0233
2SC589R	0233
2SC589X	0233
2SC589Y	0233
2SC590	0233
2SC590A	0233
2SC590B	0233
2SC590C	0233
2SC590D	0233
2SC590E	0233
2SC590F	0233
2SC590G	0233
2SC590GN	0233
2SC590H	0233
2SC590J	0233
2SC590K	0233
2SC590L	0233
2SC590M	0233
2SC590OR	0233
2SC590X	0233
2SC590Y	0233
2SC591	0168
2SC591A	0168
2SC591B	0168
2SC591C	0168
2SC591D	0168
2SC591E	0168
2SC591F	0168
2SC591G	0168
2SC591GN	0168
2SC591H	0168
2SC591J	0168
2SC591K	0168
2SC591L	0168
2SC591M	0168
2SC591OR	0168
2SC591R	0168
2SC591X	0168
2SC591Y	0168
2SC592	0555
2SC593	0016
2SC594	0016
2SC594-O	0016
2SC594-R	0016
2SC594-Y	0016
2SC594A	0016
2SC594B	0016
2SC594C	0016
2SC594D	0016
2SC594E	0016
2SC594F	0016
2SC594G	0016
2SC594GN	0016
2SC594H	0016
2SC594J	0016
2SC594K	0016
2SC594L	0016
2SC594M	0016
2SC594OR	0016
2SC594R	0016
2SC594Y	0016
2SC595	0016
2SC595A	0016
2SC595B	0016
2SC595C	0016
2SC595D	0016
2SC595E	0016
2SC595F	0016
2SC595G	0016
2SC595GN	0016
2SC595H	0016
2SC595J	0016
2SC595K	0016
2SC595L	0016
2SC595M	0016
2SC595OR	0016
2SC595X	0016
2SC595Y	0016
2SC596	0016
2SC596A	0016
2SC596B	0016
2SC596C	0016
2SC596E	0016
2SC596F	0016
2SC596G	0016
2SC596GN	0016
2SC596H	0016
2SC596J	0016
2SC596K	0016
2SC596L	0016

DEVICE TYPE	REPL CODE
2SC596M	0016
2SC596OR	0016
2SC596R	0016
2SC596X	0016
2SC596Y	0016
2SC597	0930
2SC598	0555
2SC599	0042
2SC600	0042
2SC601	0488
2SC601N	0488
2SC602	0007
2SC603	0396
2SC604	0127
2SC605	0470
2SC605(B)	0470
2SC605(L)	0470
2SC605-B	0470
2SC605-OR	0470
2SC605A	0470
2SC605B	0470
2SC605C	0470
2SC605D	0470
2SC605E	0470
2SC605F	0470
2SC605G	0470
2SC605GN	0470
2SC605H	0470
2SC605J	0470
2SC605K	0470
2SC605L	0470
2SC605M	0470
2SC605OR	0470
2SC605Q	0470
2SC605R	0470
2SC605TW	0470
2SC605X	0470
2SC605Y	0470
2SC606	0470
2SC606(B)	0470
2SC606(VHF)	0470
2SC606-B	0470
2SC606A	0470
2SC606B	0470
2SC606C	0470
2SC606D	0470
2SC606E	0470
2SC606F	0470
2SC606G	0470
2SC606GN	0470
2SC606H	0470
2SC606J	0470
2SC606K	0470
2SC606L	0470
2SC606M	0470
2SC606N	0470
2SC606OR	0470
2SC606R	0470
2SC606X	0470
2SC606Y	0470
2SC607	0086
2SC608	1401
2SC608A	1401
2SC608AA	1401
2SC608B	1401
2SC608C	1401
2SC608D	1401
2SC608E	1401
2SC608F	1401
2SC608G	1401
2SC608GN	1401
2SC608H	1401
2SC608J	1401
2SC608K	1401
2SC608L	1401
2SC608M	1401
2SC608OR	1401
2SC608R	1401
2SC608T	1401
2SC608X	1401
2SC608Y	1401
2SC609	1401
2SC609-OR	1401
2SC609A	1401
2SC609B	1401
2SC609C	1401
2SC609D	1401
2SC609E	1401
2SC609F	1401
2SC609G	1401
2SC609GN	1401
2SC609H	1401
2SC609J	1401
2SC609K	1401
2SC609L	1401
2SC609M	1401
2SC609OR	1401
2SC609R	1401
2SC609T	1401
2SC609X	1401
2SC609Y	1401
2SC610	0086
2SC610A	0086
2SC610B	0086
2SC610C	0086
2SC610D	0086
2SC610E	0086
2SC610F	0086
2SC610G	0086

DEVICE TYPE	REPL CODE
2SC610GN	0086
2SC610H	0086
2SC610J	0086
2SC610K	0086
2SC610L	0086
2SC610M	0086
2SC610OR	0086
2SC610R	0086
2SC610X	0086
2SC610Y	0086
2SC611	0259
2SC611A	0259
2SC611B	0259
2SC611C	0259
2SC611D	0259
2SC611E	0259
2SC611F	0259
2SC611G	0259
2SC611GN	0259
2SC611H	0259
2SC611J	0259
2SC611K	0259
2SC611L	0259
2SC611M	0259
2SC611OR	0259
2SC611R	0259
2SC611X	0259
2SC611Y	0259
2SC612	0259
2SC612A	0259
2SC612B	0259
2SC612C	0259
2SC612D	0259
2SC612E	0259
2SC612F	0259
2SC612G	0259
2SC612GN	0259
2SC612H	0259
2SC612J	0259
2SC612K	0259
2SC612L	0259
2SC612M	0259
2SC612OR	0259
2SC612R	0259
2SC612X	0259
2SC612Y	0259
2SC613	0144
2SC613A	0144
2SC613B	0144
2SC613C	0144
2SC613D	0144
2SC613E	0144
2SC613F	0144
2SC613G	0144
2SC613GN	0144
2SC613H	0144
2SC613J	0144
2SC613K	0144
2SC613L	0144
2SC613M	0144
2SC613OR	0144
2SC613R	0144
2SC613X	0144
2SC613Y	0144
2SC614	0693
2SC614A	0693
2SC614B	0693
2SC614C	0693
2SC614D	0693
2SC614E	0693
2SC614F	0693
2SC614G	0693
2SC614GN	0693
2SC614H	0693
2SC614J	0693
2SC614K	0693
2SC614L	0693
2SC614M	0693
2SC614OR	0693
2SC614R	0693
2SC614X	0693
2SC614Y	0693
2SC615	0693
2SC615-OR	0693
2SC615A	0693
2SC615B	0693
2SC615C	0693
2SC615D	0693
2SC615E	0693
2SC615F	0693
2SC615G	0693
2SC615GN	0693
2SC615H	0693
2SC615J	0693
2SC615K	0693
2SC615L	0693
2SC615M	0693
2SC615OR	0693
2SC615R	0693
2SC615X	0693
2SC615Y	0693
2SC616	0626
2SC617	0626
2SC618	0007
2SC618A	0007
2SC619	0284
2SC619(B)	0284
2SC619(C)	0284
2SC619A	0284

DEVICE TYPE	REPL CODE
2SC619B	0284
2SC619C	0284
2SC619D	0284
2SC619E	0284
2SC619F	0284
2SC619G	0284
2SC619GN	0284
2SC619H	0284
2SC619J	0284
2SC619K	0284
2SC619L	0284
2SC619M	0284
2SC619OR	0284
2SC619R	0284
2SC619X	0284
2SC619Y	0284
2SC620	0076
2SC620(C)	0076
2SC620(D)	0076
2SC620(E)	0076
2SC620-D	0076
2SC620-E	0076
2SC620-OR	0076
2SC620A	0076
2SC620B	0076
2SC620C	0076
2SC620CD	0076
2SC620D	0076
2SC620DE	0076
2SC620E	0076
2SC620F	0076
2SC620G	0076
2SC620GN	0076
2SC620H	0076
2SC620J	0076
2SC620K	0076
2SC620L	0076
2SC620M	0076
2SC620OR	0076
2SC620R	0076
2SC620X	0076
2SC620Y	0076
2SC621	0284
2SC621A	0284
2SC621B	0284
2SC621C	0284
2SC621D	0284
2SC621E	0284
2SC621F	0284
2SC621G	0284
2SC621GN	0284
2SC621H	0284
2SC621J	0284
2SC621K	0284
2SC621L	0284
2SC621M	0284
2SC621OR	0284
2SC621R	0284
2SC621X	0284
2SC621Y	0284
2SC622	0016
2SC622A	0016
2SC622B	0016
2SC622C	0016
2SC622D	0016
2SC622E	0016
2SC622F	0016
2SC622G	0016
2SC622GN	0016
2SC622H	0016
2SC622J	0016
2SC622K	0016
2SC622L	0016
2SC622M	0016
2SC622OR	0016
2SC622R	0016
2SC622X	0016
2SC622Y	0016
2SC623	0016
2SC624	0016
2SC626	0016
2SC627	0233
2SC628	0488
2SC628E	0488
2SC628F	0488
2SC629	0224
2SC629-31	0224
2SC629-41	0224
2SC629A	0224
2SC629B	0224
2SC629C	0224
2SC629D	0224
2SC629E	0224
2SC629F	0224
2SC629G	0224
2SC629GN	0224
2SC629H	0224
2SC629J	0224
2SC629K	0224
2SC629L	0224
2SC629M	0224
2SC629OR	0224
2SC629R	0224
2SC629X	0224
2SC629Y	0224
2SC631	0284
2SC631A	0284
2SC631B	0284
2SC631C	0284

DEVICE TYPE	REPL CODE
2SC631D	0284
2SC631E	0284
2SC631F	0284
2SC631G	0284
2SC631GN	0284
2SC631H	0284
2SC631J	0284
2SC631K	0284
2SC631L	0284
2SC631M	0284
2SC631OR	0284
2SC631R	0284
2SC631X	0284
2SC631Y	0284
2SC632	2064
2SC632(1)	2064
2SC632-OR	2064
2SC632A	2064
2SC632B	2064
2SC632C	2064
2SC632D	2064
2SC632E	2064
2SC632F	2064
2SC632G	2064
2SC632GN	2064
2SC632H	2064
2SC632J	2064
2SC632K	2064
2SC632L	2064
2SC632M	2064
2SC632OR	2064
2SC632R	2064
2SC632X	2064
2SC632Y	2064
2SC633	2064
2SC633-7	2064
2SC633-OR	2064
2SC633A	2064
2SC633B	2064
2SC633C	2064
2SC633D	2064
2SC633E	2064
2SC633F	2064
2SC633G	2064
2SC633GN	2064
2SC633H	2064
2SC633J	2064
2SC633K	2064
2SC633L	2064
2SC633M	2064
2SC633OR	2064
2SC633R	2064
2SC633X	2064
2SC633Y	2064
2SC634	2064
2SC634(2)	2064
2SC634-O	2064
2SC634-OR	2064
2SC634-SP	2064
2SC634-SP8	2064
2SC634A	2064
2SC634AK	2064
2SC634AL	2064
2SC634AXL	2064
2SC634B	2064
2SC634C	2064
2SC634D	2064
2SC634E	2064
2SC634F	2064
2SC634G	2064
2SC634GN	2064
2SC634H	2064
2SC634J	2064
2SC634K	2064
2SC634L	2064
2SC634M	2064
2SC634OR	2064
2SC634R	2064
2SC634SP	2064
2SC634SP-8	2064
2SC634SP8	2064
2SC634X	2064
2SC634Y	2064
2SC635	0079
2SC635A	0079
2SC636	0042
2SC637	3289
2SC638	3290
2SC638C	3290
2SC639	0016
2SC640	0470
2SC640A	0470
2SC640B	0470
2SC640C	0470
2SC640D	0470
2SC640E	0470
2SC640F	0470
2SC640G	0470
2SC640GN	0470
2SC640J	0470
2SC640K	0470
2SC640L	0470
2SC640M	0470
2SC640R	0470
2SC640X	0470
2SC641	0284
2SC641A	0284
2SC641B	0284
2SC641C	0284

DEVICE TYPE	REPL CODE
2SC641D	0284
2SC641E	0284
2SC641F	0284
2SC641G	0284
2SC641GN	0284
2SC641H	0284
2SC641J	0284
2SC641K	0284
2SC641K-B	OEM
2SC641L	0284
2SC641M	0284
2SC641OR	0284
2SC641R	0284
2SC641X	0284
2SC641Y	0284
2SC642	0003
2SC642A	0003
2SC643	1142
2SC643-OR	1142
2SC643A	1142
2SC643B	1142
2SC643C	1142
2SC643D	1142
2SC643E	1142
2SC643F	1142
2SC643G	1142
2SC643GN	1142
2SC643H	1142
2SC643J	1142
2SC643K	1142
2SC643L	1142
2SC643M	1142
2SC643OR	1142
2SC643R	1142
2SC643X	1142
2SC643Y	1142
2SC644	0111
2SC644(F)	0111
2SC644(H)	0111
2SC644(R)	0111
2SC644(R,S)	0111
2SC644(S)	0111
2SC644(T)	0111
2SC644-OR	0111
2SC644A	0111
2SC644B	0111
2SC644C	0111
2SC644D	0111
2SC644E	0111
2SC644F	0111
2SC644F(H)(S)	0111
2SC644FH	0111
2SC644FHS	0111
2SC644FR	0111
2SC644FS	0111
2SC644G	0111
2SC644GN	0111
2SC644H	0111
2SC644H(S)	0111
2SC644J	0111
2SC644K	0111
2SC644L	0111
2SC644M	0111
2SC644OR	0111
2SC644P	0111
2SC644PJ	0111
2SC644Q	0111
2SC644R	0111
2SC644S	0111
2SC644T	0111
2SC644X	0111
2SC644Y	0111
2SC645	0669
2SC645(B)	0669
2SC645-OR	0669
2SC645A	0669
2SC645B	0669
2SC645B-1	0669
2SC645C	0669
2SC645D	0669
2SC645E	0669
2SC645F	0669
2SC645G	0669
2SC645GN	0669
2SC645GR	0669
2SC645H	0669
2SC645J	0669
2SC645K	0669
2SC645L	0669
2SC645M	0669
2SC645N	0669
2SC645OR	0669
2SC645R	0669
2SC645V	0669
2SC645X	0669
2SC645Y	0669
2SC646	0615
2SC647	4316
2SC647Q	4316
2SC647R	4316
2SC648	0016
2SC648A	0016
2SC648B	0016
2SC648C	0016
2SC648D	0016
2SC648E	0016
2SC648F	0016
2SC648G	0016
2SC648H	0016

If replacement code is OEM, contact original manufacturer for replacement.

85

DEVICE TYPE	REPL CODE
2SC648J	0016
2SC648K	0016
2SC648L	0016
2SC648M	0016
2SC648OR	0016
2SC648R	0016
2SC648X	0016
2SC648Y	0016
2SC649	0016
2SC649A	0016
2SC649B	0016
2SC649C	0016
2SC649D	0016
2SC649E	0016
2SC649F	0016
2SC649G	0016
2SC649GN	0016
2SC649H	0016
2SC649J	0016
2SC649K	0016
2SC649L	0016
2SC649M	0016
2SC649OR	0016
2SC649R	0016
2SC649X	0016
2SC649Y	0016
2SC650	0531
2SC650-OR	0531
2SC650-Y	0531
2SC650A	0531
2SC650B	0531
2SC650C	0531
2SC650D	0531
2SC650E	0531
2SC650F	0531
2SC650G	0531
2SC650GN	0531
2SC650H	0531
2SC650J	0531
2SC650K	0531
2SC650L	0531
2SC650M	0531
2SC650OR	0531
2SC650R	0531
2SC650X	0531
2SC650Y	0531
2SC651	0488
2SC652	0488
2SC653	0259
2SC654	0488
2SC654A	0488
2SC654B	0488
2SC654C	0488
2SC654D	0488
2SC654E	0488
2SC654F	0488
2SC654G	0488
2SC654GN	0488
2SC654H	0488
2SC654J	0488
2SC654K	0488
2SC654L	0488
2SC654M	0488
2SC654OR	0488
2SC654R	0488
2SC654X	0488
2SC654Y	0488
2SC655	0016
2SC655A	0016
2SC655B	0016
2SC655C	0016
2SC655D	0016
2SC655E	0016
2SC655F	0016
2SC655G	0016
2SC655GN	0016
2SC655H	0016
2SC655J	0016
2SC655K	0016
2SC655L	0016
2SC655M	0016
2SC655OR	0016
2SC655R	0016
2SC655X	0016
2SC655Y	0016
2SC656	0259
2SC656A	0259
2SC656B	0259
2SC656C	0259
2SC656D	0259
2SC656E	0259
2SC656F	0259
2SC656G	0259
2SC656GN	0259
2SC656H	0259
2SC656J	0259
2SC656K	0259
2SC656L	0259
2SC656M	0259
2SC656OR	0259
2SC656R	0259
2SC656X	0259
2SC656Y	0259
2SC657	0127
2SC657A	0127
2SC657B	0127
2SC657C	0127
2SC657D	0127
2SC657E	0127
2SC657F	0127
2SC657G	0127
2SC657GN	0127
2SC657H	0127
2SC657J	0127
2SC657K	0127
2SC657L	0127
2SC657M	0127
2SC657OR	0127
2SC657R	0127
2SC657X	0127
2SC657Y	0127
2SC658	0127
2SC658A	0127
2SC658B	0127
2SC658C	0127
2SC658D	0127
2SC658E	0127
2SC658F	0127
2SC658G	0127
2SC658GN	0127
2SC658H	0127
2SC658J	0127
2SC658K	0127
2SC658L	0127
2SC658M	0127
2SC658OR	0127
2SC658R	0127
2SC658X	0127
2SC658Y	0127
2SC659	0127
2SC659A	0127
2SC659B	0127
2SC659C	0127
2SC659D	0127
2SC659E	0127
2SC659F	0127
2SC659G	0127
2SC659GN	0127
2SC659H	0127
2SC659J	0127
2SC659K	0127
2SC659L	0127
2SC659M	0127
2SC659OR	0127
2SC659R	0127
2SC659X	0127
2SC659Y	0127
2SC660	0007
2SC661	0007
2SC662	0144
2SC662A	0144
2SC662B	0144
2SC662C	0144
2SC662D	0144
2SC662E	0144
2SC662F	0144
2SC662G	0144
2SC662GN	0144
2SC662H	0144
2SC662J	0144
2SC662K	0144
2SC662L	0144
2SC662M	0144
2SC662OR	0144
2SC662R	0144
2SC662X	0144
2SC662Y	0144
2SC663	0007
2SC663A	0007
2SC663B	0007
2SC663C	0007
2SC663D	0007
2SC663E	0007
2SC663F	0007
2SC663G	0007
2SC663GN	0007
2SC663H	0007
2SC663J	0007
2SC663K	0007
2SC663L	0007
2SC663M	0007
2SC663OR	0007
2SC663R	0007
2SC663X	0007
2SC663Y	0007
2SC664	0103
2SC664(B)	0103
2SC664(C)	0103
2SC664-OR	0103
2SC664A	0103
2SC664B	0103
2SC664C	0103
2SC664D	0103
2SC664E	0103
2SC664F	0103
2SC664L	0103
2SC664MNP-F	OEM
2SC664OR	0103
2SC664R	0103
2SC664Y	0103
2SC665	0861
2SC665H	0861
2SC665HA	0861
2SC665HB	0861
2SC666	0177
2SC666C	0177
2SC667	0007
2SC668	0127
2SC668(AUDIO)	0127
2SC668(C)	0127
2SC668(D)	0127
2SC668-OR	0127
2SC668-SP	0127
2SC668A	0127
2SC668B	0127
2SC668B1	0127
2SC668BC2	0127
2SC668C	0127
2SC668C1	0127
2SC668C2	0127
2SC668CD	0127
2SC668D	0127
2SC668D0	0127
2SC668D1	0127
2SC668DE	0127
2SC668DO	0127
2SC668DV	0127
2SC668DX	0127
2SC668DZ	0127
2SC668E	0127
2SC668E1	0127
2SC668E2	0127
2SC668EP	0127
2SC668EV	0127
2SC668EX	0127
2SC668F	0127
2SC668G	0127
2SC668GN	0127
2SC668H	0127
2SC668K	0127
2SC668L	0127
2SC668M	0127
2SC668OR	0127
2SC668R	0127
2SC668SP	0127
2SC668X	0127
2SC668Y	0127
2SC669	0617
2SC669A	0617
2SC669AB	0617
2SC669C	0617
2SC669D	0617
2SC673	0007
2SC673(B)	0007
2SC673B	0007
2SC673C	0007
2SC673C2	0007
2SC673D	0007
2SC674	0127
2SC674(C)	0127
2SC674(D)	0127
2SC674(F)	0127
2SC674(G)	0127
2SC674-B	0127
2SC674-F	0127
2SC674B	0127
2SC674C	0127
2SC674CK	0127
2SC674CL	0127
2SC674D	0127
2SC674E	0127
2SC674F	0127
2SC674G	0127
2SC675	0359
2SC676	0168
2SC677	0861
2SC678	0103
2SC679	1021
2SC679H	1021
2SC680	1496
2SC680(A)	1496
2SC680A	1496
2SC680B	1496
2SC680C	1496
2SC680G	1496
2SC680GN	1496
2SC680H	1496
2SC680J	1496
2SC680K	1496
2SC680L	1496
2SC680M	1496
2SC680R	1496
2SC680X	1496
2SC681	2420
2SC681(A)	2420
2SC681(B)	2420
2SC681A	2420
2SC681AYL	2420
2SC681AYL-12	OEM
2SC681L	2420
2SC681Y	2420
2SC681YL	2420
2SC682	0047
2SC682(B)	0047
2SC682-OR	0047
2SC682A	0047
2SC682B	0047
2SC682C	0047
2SC682D	0047
2SC682E	0047
2SC682F	0047
2SC682G	0047
2SC682GN	0047
2SC682H	0047
2SC682J	0047
2SC682K	0047
2SC682L	0047
2SC682M	0047
2SC682OR	0047
2SC682R	0047
2SC682X	0047
2SC682Y	0047
2SC683	0047
2SC683(B)	0047
2SC683-0	0047
2SC683-OR	0047
2SC683A	0047
2SC683B	0047
2SC683C	0047
2SC683D	0047
2SC683E	0047
2SC683F	0047
2SC683G	0047
2SC683GN	0047
2SC683H	0047
2SC683J	0047
2SC683K	0047
2SC683L	0047
2SC683M	0047
2SC683OR	0047
2SC683P	0047
2SC683Q	0047
2SC683R	0047
2SC683S	0047
2SC683V	0047
2SC683X	0047
2SC683Y	0047
2SC684	0127
2SC684-OR	0127
2SC684A	0127
2SC684B	0127
2SC684BK	0127
2SC684C	0127
2SC684D	0127
2SC684E	0127
2SC684F	0127
2SC684G	0127
2SC684GN	0127
2SC684H	0127
2SC684J	0127
2SC684K	0127
2SC684L	0127
2SC684M	0127
2SC684OR	0127
2SC684R	0127
2SC684TM	0127
2SC684X	0127
2SC684Y	0127
2SC685	0142
2SC685(0)	0142
2SC685-0	0142
2SC685-O	0142
2SC685A	0142
2SC685ABK	0142
2SC685AL	0142
2SC685B	0142
2SC685BK	0142
2SC685C	0142
2SC685D	0142
2SC685E	0142
2SC685F	0142
2SC685G	0142
2SC685GN	0142
2SC685H	0142
2SC685J	0142
2SC685K	0142
2SC685L	0142
2SC685M	0142
2SC685OR	0142
2SC685P	0142
2SC685R	0142
2SC685SY	0142
2SC685X	0142
2SC685Y	0142
2SC686	0233
2SC686A	0233
2SC686B	0233
2SC686C	0233
2SC686D	0233
2SC686E	0233
2SC686F	0233
2SC686G	0233
2SC686GN	0233
2SC686H	0233
2SC686J	0233
2SC686K	0233
2SC686L	0233
2SC686M	0233
2SC686OR	0233
2SC686R	0233
2SC686X	0233
2SC686Y	0233
2SC687	0177
2SC687A	0177
2SC687B	0177
2SC687C	0177
2SC687D	0177
2SC687E	0177
2SC687F	0177
2SC687G	0177
2SC687GN	0177
2SC687H	0177
2SC687J	0177
2SC687K	0177
2SC687L	0177
2SC687M	0177
2SC687OR	0177
2SC687R	0177
2SC687X	0177
2SC687Y	0177
2SC688	0224
2SC688-SP	0224
2SC688A	0224
2SC688B	0224
2SC688C	0224
2SC688D	0224
2SC688E	0224
2SC688F	0224
2SC688G	0224
2SC688GN	0224
2SC688H	0224
2SC688J	0224
2SC688K	0224
2SC688L	0224
2SC688M	0224
2SC688OR	0224
2SC688R	0224
2SC688X	0224
2SC688Y	0224
2SC689	0016
2SC689A	0016
2SC689B	0016
2SC689C	0016
2SC689D	0016
2SC689E	0016
2SC689G	0016
2SC689GN	0016
2SC689H	0016
2SC689J	0016
2SC689K	0016
2SC689L	0016
2SC689M	0016
2SC689OR	0016
2SC689R	0016
2SC689X	0016
2SC689Y	0016
2SC690	3543
2SC690A	3543
2SC691	0555
2SC692	0555
2SC693	0547
2SC693-OR	0547
2SC693A	0547
2SC693B	0547
2SC693C	0547
2SC693D	0547
2SC693E	0547
2SC693EB	0547
2SC693ET	0547
2SC693F	0547
2SC693FC	0547
2SC693FL	0547
2SC693FP	0547
2SC693FU	0547
2SC693G	0547
2SC693GL	0547
2SC693GN	0547
2SC693GS	0547
2SC693GU	0547
2SC693GZ	0547
2SC693H	0547
2SC693J	0547
2SC693K	0547
2SC693L	0547
2SC693M	0547
2SC693NP	0547
2SC693OR	0547
2SC693R	0547
2SC693U	0547
2SC693X	0547
2SC693Y	0547
2SC694	0111
2SC694A	0111
2SC694B	0111
2SC694C	0111
2SC694D	0111
2SC694E	0111
2SC694F	0111
2SC694G	0111
2SC694GN	0111
2SC694H	0111
2SC694J	0111
2SC694K	0111
2SC694L	0111
2SC694M	0111
2SC694OR	0111
2SC694R	0111
2SC694X	0111
2SC694Y	0111
2SC694Z	0111
2SC695	0470
2SC696	0639
2SC696(B)	0639
2SC696(D)	0639
2SC696(E)	0639
2SC696(H)	0639
2SC696-4	0639
2SC696-OR	0639
2SC696A	0639
2SC696AA	0639
2SC696AB	0639
2SC696AD	0639
2SC696AE	0639
2SC696AF	0639
2SC696AG	0639
2SC696AH	0639
2SC696AI	0639
2SC696B	0639
2SC696BL	0639
2SC696C	0639
2SC696D	0639
2SC696E	0639
2SC696F	0639
2SC696G	0639
2SC696GN	0639
2SC696GU	0639
2SC696H	0639
2SC696I	0639
2SC696J	0639
2SC696K	0639
2SC696L	0639
2SC696M	0639
2SC696OR	0639
2SC696R	0639
2SC696U	0639
2SC696X	0639
2SC696Y	0639
2SC697	1897
2SC697-OR	1897
2SC697A	1897
2SC697B	1897
2SC697C	1897
2SC697D	1897
2SC697E	1897
2SC697F	1897
2SC697G	1897
2SC697GN	1897
2SC697H	1897
2SC697J	1897
2SC697K	1897
2SC697L	1897
2SC697M	1897
2SC697OR	1897
2SC697R	1897
2SC697X	1897
2SC697Y	1897
2SC698	0626
2SC699	0590
2SC700	0590
2SC701	0018
2SC701A	0018
2SC701B	0018
2SC701C	0018
2SC701D	0018
2SC701E	0018
2SC701F	0018
2SC701G	0018
2SC701GN	0018
2SC701H	0018
2SC701J	0018
2SC701K	0018
2SC701L	0018
2SC701M	0018
2SC701OR	0018
2SC701R	0018
2SC701X	0018
2SC701Y	0018
2SC702	0018
2SC702A	0018
2SC702B	0018
2SC702C	0018
2SC702D	0018
2SC702E	0018
2SC702F	0018
2SC702G	0018
2SC702GN	0018
2SC702H	0018
2SC702J	0018
2SC702K	0018
2SC702L	0018
2SC702M	0018
2SC702OR	0018
2SC702R	0018
2SC702X	0018
2SC702Y	0018
2SC703	0042
2SC704	0042
2SC705	0127
2SC705A	0127
2SC705B	0127
2SC705C	0127
2SC705D	0127
2SC705E	0127
2SC705F	0127
2SC705G	0127
2SC705GN	0127
2SC705J	0127
2SC705K	0127
2SC705L	0127
2SC705M	0127
2SC705OR	0127
2SC705R	0127
2SC705TV	0127
2SC705TVV	0127
2SC705TW	0127
2SC705X	0127
2SC705Y	0127
2SC706	0007
2SC707	0259
2SC707A	0259
2SC707B	0259
2SC707C	0259
2SC707D	0259
2SC707E	0259
2SC707F	0259
2SC707G	0259
2SC707GN	0259
2SC707H	0259
2SC707K	0259
2SC707L	0259
2SC707M	0259
2SC707OR	0259
2SC707R	0259
2SC707X	0259
2SC707Y	0259
2SC708	0086
2SC708(A)	0086
2SC708(B)	0086
2SC708(C)	0086
2SC708-OR	0086
2SC708A	0086
2SC708AA	0086
2SC708AB	0086
2SC708AC	0086
2SC708AH	0086
2SC708B	0086
2SC708C	0086
2SC708D	0086
2SC708E	0086
2SC708F	0086
2SC708G	0086
2SC708GN	0086
2SC708H	0086
2SC708HA	0086
2SC708HB	0086
2SC708L	0086
2SC708M	0086
2SC708OR	0086
2SC708R	0086
2SC708X	0086
2SC708Y	0086
2SC709	0284
2SC709(B)(C)	0284
2SC709(C)	0284
2SC709A	0284
2SC709B	0284
2SC709C	0284
2SC709CD	0284
2SC709D	0284
2SC709E	0284
2SC709F	0284
2SC709G	0284
2SC709GN	0284
2SC709H	0284
2SC709J	0284
2SC709L	0284
2SC709M	0284
2SC709OR	0284
2SC709X	0284
2SC709Y	0284
2SC710	0364
2SC710(B)	0364
2SC710(C)	0364
2SC710(D)	0364
2SC710(E)	0364
2SC710-0	0364
2SC710-3	0364
2SC710-5	0364
2SC710-13	0364
2SC710-14	0364
2SC710-D	0364
2SC710-E	0364
2SC710-OR	0364
2SC710AL	0364
2SC710B	0364
2SC710B2	0364
2SC710BC	0364
2SC710C	0364
2SC710D	0364
2SC710DB	0364
2SC710DE	0364
2SC710E	0364
2SC710F	0364
2SC710G	0364
2SC710GN	0364
2SC710H	0364
2SC710K	0364
2SC710L	0364
2SC710M	0364
2SC710OR	0364
2SC710R	0364
2SC710S	0364
2SC710X	0364
2SC710XL	0364
2SC710Y	0364
2SC711	0376
2SC711(D)	0376
2SC711(E)	0376
2SC711(F)	0376
2SC711-OR	0376
2SC711A	0376
2SC711A(E)	0376
2SC711A(F)	0376
2SC711A-E	0376
2SC711AE	0376
2SC711A-F	0376
2SC711AF	0376
2SC711AG	0376
2SC711AN	0376
2SC711B	0376
2SC711C	0376
2SC711D	0376
2SC711E	0376

If replacement code is OEM, contact original manufacturer for replacement.

DEVICE TYPE	REPL CODE
2SC711EF	0376
2SC711F	0376
2SC711G	2446
2SC711GN	0376
2SC711H	0376
2SC711J	0376
2SC711L	0376
2SC711M	0376
2SC711OR	0376
2SC711R	0376
2SC711X	0376
2SC711Y	0376
2SC712	0076
2SC712(D)	0076
2SC712A	0076
2SC712B	0076
2SC712BC	0076
2SC712C	0076
2SC712CD	0076
2SC712D	0076
2SC712DC	0076
2SC712E	0076
2SC712F	0076
2SC712G	0076
2SC712GN	0076
2SC712H	0076
2SC712J	0076
2SC712K	0076
2SC712L	0076
2SC712M	0076
2SC712OR	0076
2SC712R	0076
2SC712W	0076
2SC712X	0076
2SC712Y	0076
2SC713	0284
2SC713A	0284
2SC713B	0284
2SC713C	0284
2SC713D	0284
2SC713E	0284
2SC713F	0284
2SC713G	0284
2SC713GN	0284
2SC713H	0284
2SC713J	0284
2SC713K	0284
2SC713L	0284
2SC713M	0284
2SC713MC	0284
2SC713MD	0284
2SC713ME	0284
2SC713OR	0284
2SC713R	0284
2SC713W	0284
2SC713X	0284
2SC713Y	0284
2SC714	0155
2SC714A	0155
2SC714B	0155
2SC714C	0155
2SC714D	0155
2SC714E	0155
2SC714F	0155
2SC714G	0155
2SC714GN	0155
2SC714H	0155
2SC714J	0155
2SC714K	0155
2SC714L	0155
2SC714M	0155
2SC714OR	0155
2SC714R	0155
2SC714X	0155
2SC714Y	0155
2SC715	0284
2SC715(D)	0284
2SC715(E)	0284
2SC715-OR	0284
2SC715A	0284
2SC715B	0284
2SC715C	0284
2SC715D	0284
2SC715E	0284
2SC715EJ	0284
2SC715EV	0284
2SC715F	0284
2SC715G	0284
2SC715GN	0284
2SC715H	0284
2SC715J	0284
2SC715K	0284
2SC715L	0284
2SC715M	0284
2SC715OR	0284
2SC715R	0284
2SC715X	0284
2SC715XL	0284
2SC715Y	0284
2SC716	0155
2SC716A	0155
2SC716B	0155
2SC716C	0155
2SC716D	0155
2SC716E	0155
2SC716F	0155
2SC716G	0155
2SC716GN	0155
2SC716H	0155
2SC716J	0155
2SC716K	0155
2SC716L	0155
2SC716M	0155
2SC716OR	0155
2SC716R	0155
2SC716X	0155
2SC716Y	0155
2SC717	0127
2SC717-TM	0127
2SC717B	0127
2SC717BK	0127
2SC717BLK	0127
2SC717F	0127
2SC717G	0127
2SC717GN	0127
2SC717H	0127
2SC717K	0127
2SC717L	0127
2SC717M	0127
2SC717TM	0127
2SC717X	0127
2SC718	0079
2SC719	0155
2SC719Q	0155
2SC720	0007
2SC721	0079
2SC722	0127
2SC723	0127
2SC723BL	0127
2SC724	0155
2SC725	0155
2SC725-06	0155
2SC726	0079
2SC727	0710
2SC727A	0710
2SC727B	0710
2SC727C	0710
2SC727D	0710
2SC727E	0710
2SC727F	0710
2SC727G	0710
2SC727GN	0710
2SC727H	0710
2SC727J	0710
2SC727K	0710
2SC727L	0710
2SC727M	0710
2SC727R	0710
2SC727X	0710
2SC727Y	0710
2SC728	0710
2SC728A	0710
2SC728B	0710
2SC728D	0710
2SC728E	0710
2SC728F	0710
2SC728G	0710
2SC728GN	0710
2SC728H	0710
2SC728J	0710
2SC728K	0710
2SC728L	0710
2SC728M	0710
2SC728OR	0710
2SC728R	0710
2SC728X	0710
2SC728Y	0710
2SC729	0414
2SC730	2030
2SC731	0488
2SC731R	0488
2SC732	0111
2SC732(BL)	0111
2SC732-B	0111
2SC732-BL	0111
2SC732-BLU	0111
2SC732-G	0111
2SC732-GR	0111
2SC732-GRN	0111
2SC732-OR	0111
2SC732-V	0111
2SC732-V10	0111
2SC732-VIO	0111
2SC732A	0111
2SC732B	0111
2SC732BL	0111
2SC732BL-1	0111
2SC732BLU	0111
2SC732C	0111
2SC732D	0111
2SC732E	0111
2SC732F	0111
2SC732G	0111
2SC732GN	0111
2SC732GR	0111
2SC732GR/4454C	0111
2SC732GRB	0111
2SC732GRGRN	0111
2SC732H	0111
2SC732J	0111
2SC732L	0111
2SC732M	0111
2SC732NEW-BL	OEM
2SC732OR	0111
2SC732R	0111
2SC732S	0111
2SC732TM	OEM
2SC732V	0111
2SC732V10	0111
2SC732VIO	0111
2SC732X	0111
2SC732Y	0111
2SC733	0111
2SC733(BL)	0111
2SC733(GR)	0111
2SC733(Y)	0111
2SC733-0	0111
2SC733-B	0111
2SC733-BL	0111
2SC733-BLU	0111
2SC733-G	0111
2SC733-GR	0111
2SC733-GRN	0111
2SC733-O	0111
2SC733-OR	0111
2SC733-ORG	0111
2SC733-Y	0111
2SC733-YEL	0111
2SC733A	OEM
2SC733B	0111
2SC733BL	0111
2SC733BLK	0111
2SC733BLU	0111
2SC733C	0111
2SC733D	0111
2SC733E	0111
2SC733ER	0111
2SC733F	0111
2SC733G	0111
2SC733GN	0111
2SC733GR	0111
2SC733GRN	0111
2SC733H	0111
2SC733J	0111
2SC733K	0111
2SC733L	0111
2SC733M	0111
2SC733O	0111
2SC733OR	0111
2SC733Q	0111
2SC733R	0111
2SC733S	0111
2SC733S-BL	0111
2SC733V	0111
2SC733X	0111
2SC733Y	0111
2SC733YEL	0111
2SC734	0076
2SC734(O)	0076
2SC734(R)	0076
2SC734(Y)	0076
2SC734-0	0076
2SC734-G	0076
2SC734-GR	0076
2SC734-GRN	0076
2SC734-O	0076
2SC734-OR	0076
2SC734-ORG	0076
2SC734-OY	0076
2SC734-R	0076
2SC734-RED	0076
2SC734-Y	0076
2SC734-YEL	0076
2SC734A	0076
2SC734B	0076
2SC734C	0076
2SC734D	0076
2SC734E	0076
2SC734F	0076
2SC734G	0076
2SC734GN	0076
2SC734GR	0076
2SC734GRN	0076
2SC734H	0076
2SC734J	0076
2SC734K	0076
2SC734K/GR	0076
2SC734L	0076
2SC734M	0076
2SC734OR	0076
2SC734R	0076
2SC734RED	0076
2SC734X	0076
2SC734Y	0076
2SC734YEL	0076
2SC735	0191
2SC735(0)	0191
2SC735(FA-4)	OEM
2SC735(O)	0191
2SC735(Y)	0191
2SC735-0	0191
2SC735-GR	0191
2SC735-GRN	0191
2SC735-O	0191
2SC735-OR	0191
2SC735-ORG	0191
2SC735-ORN	0191
2SC735-OY	0191
2SC735-R	0191
2SC735-RED	0191
2SC735-Y	0191
2SC735-YEL	0191
2SC735A	0191
2SC735B	0191
2SC735C	0191
2SC735D	0191
2SC735E	0191
2SC735F	0191
2SC735FA3	0191
2SC735G	0191
2SC735GN	0191
2SC735GR	0191
2SC735GRN	0191
2SC735H	0191
2SC735J	0191
2SC735K	0191
2SC735L	0191
2SC735M	0191
2SC735O	0191
2SC735OR	0191
2SC735RED	0191
2SC735X	0191
2SC735Y	0191
2SC735YEL	0191
2SC735YFA-5	0191
2SC736	0861
2SC736A	0861
2SC736B	0861
2SC736C	0861
2SC736D	0861
2SC736E	0861
2SC736F	0861
2SC736G	0861
2SC736GN	0861
2SC736H	0861
2SC736J	0861
2SC736K	0861
2SC736L	0861
2SC736M	0861
2SC736OR	0861
2SC736R	0861
2SC736X	0861
2SC736Y	0861
2SC737	0079
2SC737Y	0079
2SC738	0889
2SC738A	0889
2SC738B	0889
2SC738C	0889
2SC738D	0889
2SC738E	0889
2SC738F	0889
2SC738G	0889
2SC738GN	0889
2SC738H	0889
2SC738J	0889
2SC738K	0889
2SC738L	0889
2SC738M	0889
2SC738OR	0889
2SC738R	0889
2SC738X	0889
2SC738Y	0889
2SC739	0127
2SC739A	0127
2SC739B	0127
2SC739C	0127
2SC739D	0127
2SC739E	0127
2SC739F	0127
2SC739G	0127
2SC739GN	0127
2SC739H	0127
2SC739K	0127
2SC739L	0127
2SC739M	0127
2SC739OR	0127
2SC739R	0127
2SC739Y	0127
2SC740	0144
2SC740A	0144
2SC740B	0144
2SC740C	0144
2SC740D	0144
2SC740E	0144
2SC740F	0144
2SC740G	0144
2SC740GN	0144
2SC740H	0144
2SC740J	0144
2SC740K	0144
2SC740L	0144
2SC740M	0144
2SC740OR	0144
2SC740R	0144
2SC740X	0144
2SC740Y	0144
2SC741	0684
2SC741B	0684
2SC741C	0684
2SC741D	0684
2SC741E	0684
2SC741F	0684
2SC741GN	0684
2SC741H	0684
2SC741J	0684
2SC741K	0684
2SC741L	0684
2SC741M	0684
2SC741OR	0684
2SC741R	0684
2SC741X	0684
2SC741Y	0684
2SC742	0930
2SC743	0930
2SC743A	0930
2SC744	0086
2SC744A	0086
2SC745	0930
2SC746	0168
2SC746A	0168
2SC746B	0168
2SC746C	0168
2SC746D	0168
2SC746E	0168
2SC746F	0168
2SC746GN	0168
2SC746H	0168
2SC746J	0168
2SC746K	0168
2SC746L	0168
2SC746M	0168
2SC746OR	0168
2SC746R	0168
2SC746X	0168
2SC746Y	0168
2SC748	0144
2SC748A	0144
2SC748C	0144
2SC748D	0144
2SC748E	0144
2SC748F	0144
2SC748G	0144
2SC748GN	0144
2SC748H	0144
2SC748J	0144
2SC748K	0144
2SC748L	0144
2SC748M	0144
2SC748OR	0144
2SC748R	0144
2SC748X	0144
2SC748Y	0144
2SC749	0930
2SC751	0111
2SC752	0546
2SC752(G)TM-Y	0546
2SC752-ORG-G	0546
2SC752-RED-G	0546
2SC752-YEL-G	0546
2SC752A	0546
2SC752B	0546
2SC752C	0546
2SC752D	0546
2SC752E	0546
2SC752F	0546
2SC752G	0546
2SC752GA	0546
2SC752GN	0546
2SC752G-O	0546
2SC752G-R	0546
2SC752GTM-O	0546
2SC752G-TM-Y	0546
2SC752GTM-Y	0546
2SC752GTMY	0546
2SC752G-Y	0546
2SC752H	0546
2SC752J	0546
2SC752K	0546
2SC752L	0546
2SC752M	0546
2SC752OR	0546
2SC752R	0546
2SC752TM-YFA	0546
2SC752X	0546
2SC752Y	0546
2SC753	0470
2SC753GTM-Y	0470
2SC754	0079
2SC755	0016
2SC756	0617
2SC756(4-4)	0617
2SC756(44)	0617
2SC756-1	0617
2SC756-2	0617
2SC756-2-4	0617
2SC756-2-5	0617
2SC756-3	0617
2SC756-4	0617
2SC756-OR	0617
2SC756A	0617
2SC756B	0617
2SC756C	0617
2SC756D	0617
2SC756E	0617
2SC756F	0617
2SC756G	0617
2SC756GN	0617
2SC756H	0617
2SC756J	0617
2SC756K	0617
2SC756L	0617
2SC756M	0617
2SC756OR	0617
2SC756R	0617
2SC756X	0617
2SC756Y	0617
2SC757	0470
2SC758	0074
2SC758OR	0074
2SC759	0538
2SC760	0103
2SC761	1146
2SC761(Y)	1146
2SC761A	1146
2SC761B	1146
2SC761C	1146
2SC761D	1146
2SC761E	1146
2SC761F	1146
2SC761G	1146
2SC761GN	1146
2SC761H	1146
2SC761J	1146
2SC761K	1146
2SC761L	1146
2SC761M	1146
2SC761OR	1146
2SC761P	1146
2SC761R	1146
2SC761X	1146
2SC761Y	1146
2SC761Z	1146
2SC762	1146
2SC762B	1146
2SC762C	1146
2SC762D	1146
2SC762E	1146
2SC762F	1146
2SC762G	1146
2SC762GN	1146
2SC762H	1146
2SC762J	1146
2SC762K	1146
2SC762L	1146
2SC762M	1146
2SC762R	1146
2SC762X	1146
2SC762Y	1146
2SC763	0127
2SC763(C)	0127
2SC763-C	0127
2SC763-OR	0127
2SC763A	0127
2SC763B	0127
2SC763C	0127
2SC763D	0127
2SC763E	0127
2SC763F	0127
2SC763G	0127
2SC763GN	0127
2SC763H	0127
2SC763J	0127
2SC763K	0127
2SC763L	0127
2SC763M	0127
2SC763OR	0127
2SC763R	0127
2SC763S	0127
2SC763T	0127
2SC763X	0127
2SC763Y	0127
2SC764	0079
2SC765	0130
2SC765A	0130
2SC765B	0130
2SC765C	0130
2SC765D	0130
2SC765E	0130
2SC765F	0130
2SC765G	0130
2SC765GN	0130
2SC765H	0130
2SC765J	0130
2SC765K	0130
2SC765L	0130
2SC765M	0130
2SC765OR	0130
2SC765R	0130
2SC765X	0130
2SC765Y	0130
2SC766	0103
2SC767	0103
2SC768	0615
2SC768A	0615
2SC768B	0615
2SC768C	0615
2SC768D	0615
2SC768E	0615
2SC768F	0615
2SC768G	0615
2SC768GN	0615
2SC768H	0615
2SC768J	0615
2SC768K	0615
2SC768L	0615
2SC768M	0615
2SC768OR	0615
2SC768R	0615
2SC768X	0615
2SC768Y	0615
2SC769	0615
2SC770	0074
2SC771	0224
2SC771A	0224
2SC771B	0224
2SC771BX	0224
2SC771C	0224
2SC771D	0224
2SC771E	0224
2SC771F	0224
2SC771G	0224
2SC771GN	0224
2SC771H	0224
2SC771J	0224
2SC771K	0224
2SC771L	0224
2SC771M	0224
2SC771OR	0224
2SC771R	0224
2SC771X	0224
2SC771Y	0224
2SC772	1136
2SC772-OR	1136
2SC772A	1136
2SC772B	1136
2SC772BG	1136
2SC772BH	1136
2SC772BV	1136
2SC772BX	1136
2SC772BY	1136
2SC772C	1136
2SC772C1	1136
2SC772C2	1136
2SC772CA	1136
2SC772CK	1136
2SC772CL	1136
2SC772CS	1136
2SC772CU	1136
2SC772CV	1136
2SC772CX	1136
2SC772D	1136
2SC772DJ	1136
2SC772DU	1136
2SC772DV	1136
2SC772DX	1136
2SC772DY	1136
2SC772E	1136
2SC772F	1136
2SC772G	1136
2SC772GN	1136
2SC772H	1136
2SC772J	1136
2SC772K	1136
2SC772KB	1136
2SC772KC	1136
2SC772KD	1136
2SC772KD1	1136
2SC772KD2	1136
2SC772L	1136
2SC772M	1136
2SC772OR	1136
2SC772R	1136
2SC772RB-D	1136
2SC772RD	1136
2SC772RS-D	1136
2SC772X	1136
2SC772Y	1136
2SC773	0783
2SC773(E)	0783
2SC773A	0783
2SC773B	0783
2SC773C	0783
2SC773D	0783
2SC773E	0783
2SC773F	0783
2SC773G	0783
2SC773GN	0783
2SC773H	0783
2SC773J	0783
2SC773K	0783
2SC773L	0783
2SC773M	0783
2SC773OR	0783
2SC773R	0783
2SC773X	0783
2SC773Y	0783
2SC774	0693
2SC774B	0693
2SC774C	0693
2SC774D	0693
2SC774E	0693
2SC774F	0693
2SC774G	0693
2SC774GN	0693
2SC774H	0693
2SC774J	0693
2SC774K	0693
2SC774L	0693
2SC774M	0693
2SC774R	0693
2SC774X	0693
2SC774Y	0693
2SC775	0693
2SC775A	0693
2SC775B	0693
2SC775C	0693
2SC775D	0693
2SC775E	0693
2SC775F	0693
2SC775G	0693
2SC775GN	0693
2SC775H	0693
2SC775J	0693
2SC775K	0693
2SC775L	0693
2SC775M	0693
2SC775OR	0693
2SC775R	0693
2SC775X	0693
2SC775Y	0693
2SC776	1390
2SC776(Y)	1390

If replacement code is OEM, contact original manufacturer for replacement.

DEVICE TYPE	REPL CODE	DEVICE TYPE	REPL CODE	DEVICE TYPE	REPL CODE	DEVICE TYPE	REPL CODE	DEVICE TYPE	REPL CODE	DEVICE TYPE	REPL CODE	DEVICE TYPE	REPL CODE
2SC776A	1390	2SC781X	0693	2SC786F	0216	2SC793GN	0103	2SC799GN	1401	2SC814A	0079	2SC826E	0086
2SC776B	1390	2SC781Y	0693	2SC786G	0216	2SC793H	0103	2SC799H	1401	2SC814B	0079	2SC826F	0086
2SC776C	1390	2SC782	1460	2SC786GN	0216	2SC793J	0103	2SC799J	1401	2SC814C	0079	2SC826G	0086
2SC776D	1390	2SC782(FA6)	OEM	2SC786H	0216	2SC793K	0103	2SC799K	1401	2SC814D	0079	2SC826H	0086
2SC776E	1390	2SC782(FAZ-1)	OEM	2SC786J	0216	2SC793L	0103	2SC799L	1401	2SC814E	0079	2SC826J	0086
2SC776F	1390	2SC782-OR	1460	2SC786K	0216	2SC793M	0103	2SC799M	1401	2SC814F	0079	2SC826K	0086
2SC776G	1390	2SC782A	1460	2SC786L	0216	2SC793OR	0103	2SC799OR	1401	2SC814G	0079	2SC826L	0086
2SC776GN	1390	2SC782B	1460	2SC786M	0216	2SC793R	0103	2SC799R	1401	2SC814GN	0079	2SC826M	0086
2SC776H	1390	2SC782C	1460	2SC786OR	0216	2SC793X	0103	2SC799X	1401	2SC814H	0079	2SC826OR	0086
2SC776J	1390	2SC782D	1460	2SC786R	0216	2SC793Y	0103	2SC799Y	1401	2SC814J	0079	2SC826R	0086
2SC776K	1390	2SC782E	1460	2SC786X	0216	2SC794	0103	2SC800	0626	2SC814K	0079	2SC826X	0086
2SC776L	1390	2SC782F	1460	2SC786Y	0216	2SC794A	0103	2SC800A	0626	2SC814M	0079	2SC826Y	0086
2SC776M	1390	2SC782G	1460	2SC787	1146	2SC794B	0103	2SC800B	0626	2SC814OR	0079	2SC827	0086
2SC776OR	1390	2SC782GN	1460	2SC787A	1146	2SC794C	0103	2SC800C	0626	2SC814R	0079	2SC827A	0086
2SC776R	1390	2SC782H	1460	2SC787B	1146	2SC794D	0103	2SC800D	0626	2SC814X	0079	2SC827B	0086
2SC776X	1390	2SC782J	1460	2SC787C	1146	2SC794E	0103	2SC800E	0626	2SC814Y	0079	2SC827C	0086
2SC776Y	1390	2SC782K	1460	2SC787D	1146	2SC794F	0103	2SC800F	0626	2SC815	0155	2SC827D	0086
2SC777	1401	2SC782L	1460	2SC787E	1146	2SC794G	0103	2SC800G	0626	2SC815(K)	0155	2SC827E	0086
2SC777-OR	1401	2SC782OR	1460	2SC787F	1146	2SC794GN	0103	2SC800GN	0626	2SC815(L)	0155	2SC827F	0086
2SC777A	1401	2SC782R	1460	2SC787G	1146	2SC794H	0103	2SC800H	0626	2SC815-1	0155	2SC827G	0086
2SC777AP	1401	2SC782X	1460	2SC787GN	1146	2SC794J	0103	2SC800J	0626	2SC815-Y	6683	2SC827GN	0086
2SC777B	1401	2SC782Y	1460	2SC787H	1146	2SC794K	0103	2SC800K	0626	2SC815A	0155	2SC827H	0086
2SC777C	1401	2SC783	1021	2SC787K	1146	2SC794L	0103	2SC800L	0626	2SC815B	0155	2SC827J	0086
2SC777D	1401	2SC783-O	1021	2SC787L	1146	2SC794OR	0103	2SC800M	0626	2SC815BK	0155	2SC827K	0086
2SC777E	1401	2SC783-R	1021	2SC787M	1146	2SC794R	0103	2SC800OR	0626	2SC815C	0155	2SC827M	0086
2SC777F	1401	2SC783-Y	1021	2SC787OR	1146	2SC794RA	0103	2SC800R	0626	2SC815D	0155	2SC827OR	0086
2SC777G	1401	2SC784	1136	2SC787R	1146	2SC794X	0103	2SC800X	0626	2SC815E	0155	2SC827R	0086
2SC777GN	1401	2SC784(BN)	1136	2SC787X	1146	2SC794Y	0103	2SC800Y	0626	2SC815F	0155	2SC827X	0086
2SC777H	1401	2SC784(R)	1136	2SC787Y	1146	2SC795	0142	2SC801	0086	2SC815G	0155	2SC827Y	0086
2SC777J	1401	2SC784-0	1136	2SC788	0233	2SC795(BN)	0142	2SC802	0086	2SC815GN	0155	2SC828	1211
2SC777K	1401	2SC784-6	1136	2SC788B	0233	2SC795A	0142	2SC803	0693	2SC815H	0155	2SC828(A)	1211
2SC777L	1401	2SC784-B	1136	2SC788C	0233	2SC795B	0142	2SC803A	0693	2SC815J	0155	2SC828(H)	1211
2SC777M	1401	2SC784-BN	1136	2SC788D	0233	2SC795BN	0142	2SC803B	0693	2SC815K	0155	2SC828(K)	1211
2SC777OR	1401	2SC784-BRN	1136	2SC788E	0233	2SC795C	0142	2SC803C	0693	2SC815K,L	0155	2SC828(N)	1211
2SC777R	1401	2SC784-O	1136	2SC788F	0233	2SC795D	0142	2SC803D	0693	2SC815L	0155	2SC828(O)	1211
2SC777X	1401	2SC784-OR	1136	2SC788G	0233	2SC795F	0142	2SC803E	0693	2SC815LJ	0155	2SC828(P)	1211
2SC777Y	1401	2SC784-ORG	1136	2SC788GN	0233	2SC795G	0142	2SC803F	0693	2SC815M	0155	2SC828(P)(Q)	1211
2SC778	1401	2SC784-R	1136	2SC788J	0233	2SC795GN	0142	2SC803G	0693	2SC815OR	0155	2SC828(Q)	1211
2SC778A	1401	2SC784-RED	1136	2SC788K	0233	2SC795H	0142	2SC803H	0693	2SC815R	0155	2SC828(R)	1211
2SC778B	1401	2SC784-Y	1136	2SC788L	0233	2SC795J	0142	2SC803J	0693	2SC815S	0155	2SC828(R)(Q)	1211
2SC778C	1401	2SC784A	1136	2SC788M	0233	2SC795L	0142	2SC803K	0693	2SC815SA	0155	2SC828(R)(S)	1211
2SC778D	1401	2SC784B	1136	2SC788OR	0233	2SC795M	0142	2SC803L	0693	2SC815SC	0155	2SC828(R,Q,P)	1211
2SC778E	1401	2SC784BN	1136	2SC788R	0233	2SC795OR	0142	2SC803M	0693	2SC815X	0155	2SC828(R,S,T)	1211
2SC778F	1401	2SC784BN-1	1136	2SC788X	0233	2SC795R	0142	2SC803OR	0693	2SC815Y	0155	2SC828(S)	1211
2SC778G	1401	2SC784BRN	1136	2SC788Y	0233	2SC795X	0142	2SC803R	0693	2SC816	0086	2SC828(S)(T)	1211
2SC778GN	1401	2SC784C	1136	2SC789	0228	2SC795Y	0142	2SC803X	0693	2SC816A	0086	2SC828(T)	1211
2SC778H	1401	2SC784D	1136	2SC789-0	0228	2SC796	0016	2SC803Y	0693	2SC816B	0086	2SC828-0	1211
2SC778J	1401	2SC784E	1136	2SC789-O	0228	2SC796A	0016	2SC804	0470	2SC816C	0086	2SC828-O	1211
2SC778K	1401	2SC784F	1136	2SC789-R	0228	2SC796B	0016	2SC804H	0470	2SC816D	0086	2SC828-OR	1211
2SC778L	1401	2SC784G	1136	2SC789-Y	0228	2SC796C	0016	2SC805	0711	2SC816E	0086	2SC828A	1211
2SC778M	1401	2SC784GN	1136	2SC789A	0228	2SC796D	0016	2SC805A	0711	2SC816F	0086	2SC828A(P)	1211
2SC778OR	1401	2SC784H	1136	2SC789B	0228	2SC796E	0016	2SC805A1	0711	2SC816G	0086	2SC828A(Q)	1211
2SC778R	1401	2SC784J	1136	2SC789C	0228	2SC796F	0016	2SC805A2	0711	2SC816GN	0086	2SC828A(R)	1211
2SC778X	1401	2SC784K	1136	2SC789D	0228	2SC796G	0016	2SC805B	0711	2SC816H	0086	2SC828A(R.S.)	1211
2SC778Y	1401	2SC784L	1136	2SC789E	0228	2SC796GN	0016	2SC805C	0711	2SC816HL	0086	2SC828A(S)	1211
2SC779	1021	2SC784M	1136	2SC789F	0228	2SC796H	0016	2SC805D	0711	2SC816K	0086	2SC828A(T)	1211
2SC779-O	1021	2SC784OR	1136	2SC789G	0228	2SC796J	0016	2SC805E	0711	2SC816L	0086	2SC828AO	1211
2SC779-R	1021	2SC784P	1136	2SC789GN	0228	2SC796K	0016	2SC805F	0711	2SC816M	0086	2SC828AP	1211
2SC779-Y	1021	2SC784Q	1136	2SC789H	0228	2SC796L	0016	2SC805G	0711	2SC816OR	0086	2SC828AQ	1211
2SC779O	1021	2SC784R	1136	2SC789J	0228	2SC796M	0016	2SC805GN	0711	2SC816R	0086	2SC828AR	1211
2SC780	0855	2SC784RA	1136	2SC789K	0228	2SC796OR	0016	2SC805H	0711	2SC816X	0086	2SC828AS	1211
2SC780-O	0855	2SC784RED	1136	2SC789L	0228	2SC796R	0016	2SC805J	0711	2SC816Y	0086	2SC828AT	1211
2SC780-ORG-G	0855	2SC784X	1136	2SC789M	0228	2SC796X	0016	2SC805L	0711	2SC817	0259	2SC828B	1211
2SC780-R	0855	2SC785	1136	2SC789OR	0228	2SC796Y	0016	2SC805OR	0711	2SC818	0168	2SC828C	1211
2SC780-RED-G	0855	2SC785(E)(D)	1136	2SC789R	0228	2SC797	0079	2SC805R	0711	2SC818A	0168	2SC828D	1211
2SC780-Y	0855	2SC785(R)	1136	2SC789X	0228	2SC797A	0079	2SC805X	0711	2SC818B	0168	2SC828E	1211
2SC780-YEL-G	0855	2SC785-0	1136	2SC789Y	0228	2SC797B	0079	2SC805Y	0711	2SC818C	0168	2SC828F	1211
2SC780A	0855	2SC785-B	1136	2SC790	1488	2SC797C	0079	2SC806	0359	2SC818D	0168	2SC828G	1211
2SC780A/G	0855	2SC785-BN	1136	2SC790(O)	1488	2SC797D	0079	2SC806(A)	0359	2SC818E	0168	2SC828GN	1211
2SC780AG	0855	2SC785-BRN	1136	2SC790-O	1488	2SC797E	0079	2SC806A	0359	2SC818F	0168	2SC828H	1211
2SC780AG-O	0855	2SC785-O	1136	2SC790-R	1488	2SC797F	0079	2SC806B	0359	2SC818G	0168	2SC828HR	1211
2SC780AG-R	0855	2SC785-ORG	1136	2SC790-Y	1488	2SC797G	0079	2SC806C	0359	2SC818GN	0168	2SC828K	1211
2SC780AG-Y	0855	2SC785-O.JA	1136	2SC790Y	1488	2SC797GN	0079	2SC806D	0359	2SC818H	0168	2SC828L	1211
2SC780B	0855	2SC785-R	1136	2SC791	1139	2SC797H	0079	2SC806E	0359	2SC818J	0168	2SC828LS	1211
2SC780C	0855	2SC785-RED	1136	2SC791-OR	1139	2SC797J	0079	2SC806F	0359	2SC818K	0168	2SC828M	1211
2SC780D	0855	2SC785-Y	1136	2SC791A	1139	2SC797K	0079	2SC806G	0359	2SC818L	0168	2SC828OR	1211
2SC780E	0855	2SC785-YEL	1136	2SC791B	1139	2SC797L	0079	2SC806J	0359	2SC818M	0168	2SC828P	1211
2SC780F	0855	2SC785A	1136	2SC791C	1139	2SC797M	0079	2SC806L	0359	2SC818OR	0168	2SC828PQ	1211
2SC780G	0855	2SC785B	1136	2SC791D	1139	2SC797OR	0079	2SC806M	0359	2SC818R	0168	2SC828Q	1211
2SC780GA	0855	2SC785BL	1136	2SC791E	1139	2SC797R	0079	2SC806OR	0359	2SC818X	0168	2SC828Q-6	1211
2SC780GN	0855	2SC785BN	1136	2SC791F	1139	2SC797X	0079	2SC806R	0359	2SC818Y	0168	2SC828QR	1211
2SC780G-O	0855	2SC785BR	1136	2SC791FA1	1139	2SC797Y	0079	2SC806X	0359	2SC819	2675	2SC828QRS	1211
2SC780G-R	0855	2SC785BRN	1136	2SC791G	1139	2SC798	0693	2SC806Y	0359	2SC821	2030	2SC828R	1211
2SC780G-Y	0855	2SC785C	1136	2SC791GN	1139	2SC798A	0693	2SC807	1955	2SC822	2030	2SC828R-1	1211
2SC780H	0855	2SC785D	1136	2SC791H	1139	2SC798B	0693	2SC807(A)	1955	2SC823	0414	2SC828RA	1211
2SC780J	0855	2SC785E	1136	2SC791J	1139	2SC798C	0693	2SC807A	1955	2SC824	0414	2SC828RH	1211
2SC780K	0855	2SC785F	1136	2SC791K	1139	2SC798D	0693	2SC807AK	1955	2SC825	1021	2SC828RS	1211
2SC780L	0855	2SC785G	1136	2SC791M	1139	2SC798E	0693	2SC808	2398	2SC825A	1021	2SC828RST	1211
2SC780M	0855	2SC785GN	1136	2SC791OR	1139	2SC798G	0693	2SC809	0259	2SC825B	1021	2SC828RT	1211
2SC780O	0855	2SC785GR	1136	2SC791R	1139	2SC798GN	0693	2SC810	0488	2SC825C	1021	2SC828S	1211
2SC780OR	0855	2SC785H	1136	2SC791X	1139	2SC798H	0693	2SC811	0007	2SC825D	1021	2SC828T	1211
2SC780R	0855	2SC785JA	1136	2SC791Y	1139	2SC798J	0693	2SC812	0626	2SC825E	1021	2SC828X	1211
2SC780X	0855	2SC785K	1136	2SC792	0220	2SC798K	0693	2SC812A	0626	2SC825F	1021	2SC828Y	1211
2SC780Y	0855	2SC785L	1136	2SC792(FA-3)	OEM	2SC798L	0693	2SC812B	0626	2SC825G	1021	2SC828YL	1211
2SC781	0693	2SC785M	1136	2SC792FA-3	0220	2SC798M	0693	2SC812C	0626	2SC825GN	1021	2SC829	0151
2SC781A	0693	2SC785O	1136	2SC793	0103	2SC798OR	0693	2SC812D	0626	2SC825H	1021	2SC829(B)	0151
2SC781AK	0693	2SC785R	1136	2SC793-BL	0103	2SC798R	0693	2SC812E	0626	2SC825J	1021	2SC829(C)	0151
2SC781B	0693	2SC785RA	1136	2SC793-BLU	0103	2SC798X	0693	2SC812F	0626	2SC825K	1021	2SC829(Y)	0151
2SC781C	0693	2SC785RED	1136	2SC793-R	0103	2SC798Y	0693	2SC812G	0626	2SC825L	1021	2SC829/4454C	0151
2SC781D	0693	2SC785V	1136	2SC793-RED	0103	2SC799	1401	2SC812GN	0626	2SC825M	1021	2SC829-OR	0151
2SC781E	0693	2SC785X	1136	2SC793-Y	0103	2SC799-4	1401	2SC812H	0626	2SC825OR	1021	2SC829A	0151
2SC781F	0693	2SC785Y	1136	2SC793-YEL	0103	2SC799A	1401	2SC812J	0626	2SC825R	1021	2SC829AK	0151
2SC781G	0693	2SC785YEL	1136	2SC793A	0103	2SC799AP	1401	2SC812K	0626	2SC825X	1021	2SC829B	0151
2SC781H	0693	2SC786	0216	2SC793B	0103	2SC799B	1401	2SC812L	0626	2SC825Y	1021	2SC829BC	0151
2SC781J	0693	2SC786A	0216	2SC793BL	0103	2SC799C	1401	2SC812M	0626	2SC826	0086	2SC829BJ	0151
2SC781K	0693	2SC786B	0216	2SC793C	0103	2SC799D	1401	2SC812OR	0626	2SC826A	0086	2SC829BK	0151
2SC781M	0693	2SC786C	0216	2SC793E	0103	2SC799E	1401	2SC812R	0626	2SC826B	0086	2SC829C	0151
2SC781OR	0693	2SC786D	0216	2SC793F	0103	2SC799F	1401	2SC812Y	0626	2SC826C	0086	2SC829CL	0151
2SC781R	0693	2SC786E	0216	2SC793G	0103	2SC799G	1401	2SC814	0079	2SC826D	0086	2SC829D	0151

If replacement code is OEM, contact original manufacturer for replacement.

DEVICE TYPE	REPL CODE
2SC829E	0151
2SC829G	0151
2SC829GN	0151
2SC829H	0151
2SC829K	0151
2SC829L	0151
2SC829M	0151
2SC829OR	0151
2SC829R	0151
2SC829X	0151
2SC829Y	0151
2SC830	1139
2SC830A	1139
2SC830B	1139
2SC830C	1139
2SC830D	1139
2SC830E	1139
2SC830F	1139
2SC830G	1139
2SC830GN	1139
2SC830H	1139
2SC830J	1139
2SC830K	1139
2SC830L	1139
2SC830M	1139
2SC830OR	1139
2SC830R	1139
2SC830X	1139
2SC830Y	1139
2SC831	0042
2SC833	0424
2SC833BL	0424
2SC834L	0424
2SC835	0127
2SC836	0127
2SC836M	0127
2SC837	0224
2SC837(K)	0224
2SC837(KL)	0224
2SC837(L)	0224
2SC837A	0224
2SC837B	0224
2SC837C	0224
2SC837D	0224
2SC837E	0224
2SC837F	0224
2SC837G	0224
2SC837GN	0224
2SC837H	0224
2SC837J	0224
2SC837K	0224
2SC837KL	0224
2SC837L	0224
2SC837M	0224
2SC837OR	0224
2SC837R	0224
2SC837WF	0224
2SC837X	0224
2SC837Y	0224
2SC838	0191
2SC838(A)	0191
2SC838(E)	0191
2SC838(F)	0191
2SC838(H)	0191
2SC838(J)	0191
2SC838(K)	0191
2SC838(L)	0191
2SC838(M)	0191
2SC838(O)	0191
2SC838(S)	0191
2SC838-2	0191
2SC838-O	0191
2SC838A	0191
2SC838BL	0191
2SC838C	0191
2SC838E	0191
2SC838F	0191
2SC838H	0191
2SC838HF	0191
2SC838I	0191
2SC838J	0191
2SC838K	0191
2SC838L	0191
2SC838M	0191
2SC839	0076
2SC839(F)	0076
2SC839(H)	0076
2SC839(J)	0076
2SC839(JI)	0076
2SC839(L)	0076
2SC839(M)	0076
2SC839-E	0076
2SC839-F	0076
2SC839A	0076
2SC839B	0076
2SC839C	0076
2SC839D	0076
2SC839E	0076
2SC839F	0076
2SC839G	0076
2SC839GN	0076
2SC839H	0076
2SC839J	0076
2SC839J1	0076
2SC839JH	0076
2SC839K	0076
2SC839L	0076
2SC839M	0076
2SC839OR	0076

DEVICE TYPE	REPL CODE
2SC839R	0076
2SC839X	0076
2SC839Y	0076
2SC840	2017
2SC840(P)	2017
2SC840/A	2017
2SC840A	2017
2SC840AC	2017
2SC840B	2017
2SC840C	2017
2SC840D	2017
2SC840E	2017
2SC840F	2017
2SC840G	2017
2SC840GN	2017
2SC840H	2017
2SC840HP	2017
2SC840J	2017
2SC840K	2017
2SC840L	2017
2SC840M	2017
2SC840OR	2017
2SC840P	2017
2SC840Q	2017
2SC840R	2017
2SC840X	2017
2SC840Y	2017
2SC841	2030
2SC841H	2030
2SC844	0488
2SC844D	0488
2SC845	0488
2SC847	0016
2SC847A	0016
2SC847B	0016
2SC847C	0016
2SC847D	0016
2SC847E	0016
2SC847F	0016
2SC847G	0016
2SC847GN	0016
2SC847H	0016
2SC847J	0016
2SC847K	0016
2SC847L	0016
2SC847M	0016
2SC847OR	0016
2SC847R	0016
2SC847X	0016
2SC848	0016
2SC848A	0016
2SC848B	0016
2SC848C	0016
2SC848D	0016
2SC848E	0016
2SC848F	0016
2SC848G	0016
2SC848GN	0016
2SC848H	0016
2SC848J	0016
2SC848K	0016
2SC848L	0016
2SC848M	0016
2SC848OR	0016
2SC848R	0016
2SC848X	0016
2SC848Y	0016
2SC849	0016
2SC849A	0016
2SC849B	0016
2SC849C	0016
2SC849D	0016
2SC849E	0016
2SC849F	0016
2SC849G	0016
2SC849GN	0016
2SC849H	0016
2SC849J	0016
2SC849K	0016
2SC849L	0016
2SC849M	0016
2SC849OR	0016
2SC849R	0016
2SC849X	0016
2SC849Y	0016
2SC850	0016
2SC850A	0016
2SC850B	0016
2SC850C	0016
2SC850D	0016
2SC850E	0016
2SC850F	0016
2SC850G	0016
2SC850GN	0016
2SC850H	0016
2SC850J	0016
2SC850K	0016
2SC850L	0016
2SC850M	0016
2SC850OR	0016
2SC850R	0016
2SC850X	0016
2SC850Y	0016
2SC851	0130
2SC851A	0130
2SC851B	0130
2SC851C	0130
2SC851D	0130
2SC851E	0130

DEVICE TYPE	REPL CODE
2SC851F	0130
2SC851G	0130
2SC851GN	0130
2SC851H	0130
2SC851K	0130
2SC851L	0130
2SC851M	0130
2SC851OR	0130
2SC851R	0130
2SC851X	0130
2SC851Y	0130
2SC852	0488
2SC852A	0488
2SC853	0218
2SC853-OR	0218
2SC853A	0218
2SC853B	0218
2SC853C	0218
2SC853D	0218
2SC853E	0218
2SC853F	0218
2SC853G	0218
2SC853GN	0218
2SC853H	0218
2SC853J	0218
2SC853K	0218
2SC853KLM	0218
2SC853L	0218
2SC853M	0218
2SC853OR	0218
2SC853R	0218
2SC853X	0218
2SC853Y	0218
2SC854	0414
2SC855	0414
2SC856	0725
2SC856-02	0725
2SC856-OR	0725
2SC856A	0725
2SC856B	0725
2SC856C	0725
2SC856D	0725
2SC856E	0725
2SC856F	0725
2SC856G	0725
2SC856GN	0725
2SC856J	0725
2SC856K	0725
2SC856L	0725
2SC856M	0725
2SC856OR	0725
2SC856R	0725
2SC856X	0725
2SC856Y	0725
2SC857	0233
2SC857H	0233
2SC857K	0233
2SC858	0111
2SC858A	0111
2SC858B	0111
2SC858C	0111
2SC858D	0111
2SC858E	0111
2SC858F	0111
2SC858FG	0111
2SC858G	0111
2SC858GA	0111
2SC858GN	0111
2SC858H	0111
2SC858J	0111
2SC858K	0111
2SC858L	0111
2SC858M	0111
2SC858OR	0111
2SC858R	0111
2SC858X	0111
2SC858Y	0111
2SC859	0111
2SC859A	0111
2SC859B	0111
2SC859D	0111
2SC859E	0111
2SC859F	0111
2SC859FG	0111
2SC859G	0111
2SC859GK	0111
2SC859GL	0111
2SC859GM	0111
2SC859GN	0111
2SC859H	0111
2SC859J	0111
2SC859K	0111
2SC859L	0111
2SC859M	0111
2SC859OR	0111
2SC859R	0111
2SC859X	0111
2SC859Y	0111
2SC860	0007
2SC860A	0007
2SC860B	0007
2SC860C	0007
2SC860D	0007
2SC860E	0007
2SC860F	0007
2SC860G	0007
2SC860GN	0007
2SC860H	0007
2SC860J	0007

DEVICE TYPE	REPL CODE
2SC860K	0007
2SC860L	0007
2SC860M	0007
2SC860OR	0007
2SC860R	0007
2SC860X	0007
2SC860Y	0007
2SC861	0637
2SC862	0359
2SC863	0007
2SC863A	0007
2SC863B	0007
2SC863C	0007
2SC863D	0007
2SC863E	0007
2SC863F	0007
2SC863G	0007
2SC863GN	0007
2SC863H	0007
2SC863J	0007
2SC863K	0007
2SC863L	0007
2SC863M	0007
2SC863OR	0007
2SC863R	0007
2SC863X	0007
2SC863Y	0007
2SC864	0007
2SC865	0693
2SC866	0626
2SC866A	0626
2SC866B	0626
2SC866C	0626
2SC866D	0626
2SC866E	0626
2SC866F	0626
2SC866G	0626
2SC866GN	0626
2SC866H	0626
2SC866J	0626
2SC866K	0626
2SC866L	0626
2SC866M	0626
2SC866OR	0626
2SC866R	0626
2SC866X	0626
2SC866Y	0626
2SC867	1350
2SC867-0R	1350
2SC867-2	1350
2SC867-3	1350
2SC867-4	1350
2SC867-5	1350
2SC867-OR	1350
2SC867A	1350
2SC867B	1350
2SC867C	1350
2SC867D	1350
2SC867E	1350
2SC867F	1350
2SC867G	1350
2SC867GN	1350
2SC867H	1350
2SC867J	1350
2SC867K	1350
2SC867L	1350
2SC867M	1350
2SC867OR	1350
2SC867R	1350
2SC867X	1350
2SC867Y	1350
2SC868	0855
2SC868A	0855
2SC868B	0855
2SC868C	0855
2SC868D	0855
2SC868E	0855
2SC868F	0855
2SC868G	0855
2SC868GN	0855
2SC868H	0855
2SC868J	0855
2SC868K	0855
2SC868L	0855
2SC868M	0855
2SC868OR	0855
2SC868R	0855
2SC868X	0855
2SC868Y	0855
2SC869	0855
2SC869A	0855
2SC869B	0855
2SC869C	0855
2SC869D	0855
2SC869E	0855
2SC869F	0855
2SC869G	0855
2SC869GN	0855
2SC869J	0855
2SC869K	0855
2SC869L	0855
2SC869M	0855
2SC869OR	0855
2SC869R	0855
2SC869X	0855
2SC869Y	0855
2SC870	0076
2SC870A	0076
2SC870B	0076

DEVICE TYPE	REPL CODE
2SC870C	0076
2SC870D	0076
2SC870E	0076
2SC870F	0076
2SC870FL	0076
2SC870G	0076
2SC870GN	0076
2SC870H	0076
2SC870J	0076
2SC870K	0076
2SC870L	0076
2SC870M	0076
2SC870OR	0076
2SC870R	0076
2SC870X	0076
2SC870Y	0076
2SC871	0151
2SC871(F)	0151
2SC871-G	0151
2SC871A	0151
2SC871AM	0151
2SC871B	0151
2SC871C	0151
2SC871D	0151
2SC871E	0151
2SC871F	0151
2SC871G	0151
2SC871GN	0151
2SC871H	0151
2SC871J	0151
2SC871K	0151
2SC871L	0151
2SC871M	0151
2SC871OR	0151
2SC871R	0151
2SC871X	0151
2SC871Y	0151
2SC872	0414
2SC873	4389
2SC874	0018
2SC875	0086
2SC875(D)	0086
2SC875(E)	0086
2SC875(F)	0086
2SC875-1	0086
2SC875-1C	0086
2SC875-1D	0086
2SC875-1E	0086
2SC875-1F	0086
2SC875-2	0086
2SC875-2C	0086
2SC875-2D	0086
2SC875-2E	0086
2SC875-2F	0086
2SC875-3	0086
2SC875-3C	0086
2SC875-3D	0086
2SC875-3E	0086
2SC875-3F	0086
2SC875B	0086
2SC875C	0086
2SC875D	3392
2SC875DL	0086
2SC875E	3392
2SC875EL	0086
2SC875F	0086
2SC875G	0086
2SC875GN	0086
2SC875J	0086
2SC875K	0086
2SC875L	0086
2SC875M	0086
2SC875OR	0086
2SC875X	0086
2SC875Y	0086
2SC876	0086
2SC876(F)	0086
2SC876-E	0086
2SC876-F	0086
2SC876A	0086
2SC876B	0086
2SC876C	0086
2SC876D	0086
2SC876E	0086
2SC876F	0086
2SC876G	0086
2SC876GN	0086
2SC876H	0086
2SC876J	0086
2SC876K	0086
2SC876L	0086
2SC876M	0086
2SC876OR	0086
2SC876R	0086
2SC876TV	0086
2SC876TV(D)	0086
2SC876TV(E)	0086
2SC876TVD	0086
2SC876TV-E	0086
2SC876TVE	0086
2SC876TVEF	0086
2SC876TV-F	0086
2SC876TVF	0086
2SC876X	0086
2SC876Y	0086
2SC877	0016
2SC878	0016
2SC879	0127
2SC880	0320

DEVICE TYPE	REPL CODE
2SC880R	0320
2SC881	0218
2SC881A	0218
2SC881B	0218
2SC881C	0218
2SC881D	0218
2SC881E	0218
2SC881F	0218
2SC881G	0218
2SC881GN	0218
2SC881H	0218
2SC881K	0218
2SC881L	0218
2SC881M	0218
2SC881OR	0218
2SC881R	0218
2SC881X	0218
2SC881Y	0218
2SC882	0615
2SC883	0419
2SC884	0178
2SC885	0074
2SC886	0074
2SC887	0074
2SC888	0074
2SC889	0103
2SC890	3794
2SC891	2080
2SC892	0042
2SC893	2298
2SC894	0155
2SC894A	0155
2SC894B	0155
2SC894C	0155
2SC894D	0155
2SC894E	0155
2SC894F	0155
2SC894G	0155
2SC894GN	0155
2SC894H	0155
2SC894J	0155
2SC894K	0155
2SC894L	0155
2SC894M	0155
2SC894OR	0155
2SC894R	0155
2SC894X	0155
2SC894Y	0155
2SC895	0074
2SC895-2	0074
2SC895-3	0074
2SC895-4	0074
2SC895-5	0074
2SC896	0016
2SC896A	0016
2SC896B	0016
2SC896C	0016
2SC896D	0016
2SC896E	0016
2SC896F	0016
2SC896G	0016
2SC896GN	0016
2SC896J	0016
2SC896K	0016
2SC896L	0016
2SC896M	0016
2SC896OR	0016
2SC896R	0016
2SC896X	0016
2SC896Y	0016
2SC897	0177
2SC897A	0177
2SC897B	0177
2SC898	0177
2SC898A	0177
2SC898B	0177
2SC898D	0177
2SC898E	0177
2SC898F	0177
2SC898G	0177
2SC898GN	0177
2SC898H	0177
2SC898J	0177
2SC898K	0177
2SC898L	0177
2SC898M	0177
2SC898OR	0177
2SC898X	0177
2SC898Y	0177
2SC899	2386
2SC899A	2386
2SC899B	2386
2SC899C	2386
2SC899D	2386
2SC899E	2386
2SC899F	2386
2SC899G	2386
2SC899GN	2386
2SC899H	2386
2SC899J	2386
2SC899K	2386
2SC899L	2386
2SC899M	2386
2SC899OR	2386
2SC899R	2386
2SC899X	2386
2SC899Y	2386
2SC900	1212
2SC900(E)	1212

DEVICE TYPE	REPL CODE
2SC900(E)(L)	1212
2SC900(F)	1212
2SC900(U)	1212
2SC900-OR	1212
2SC900A	1212
2SC900AF	1212
2SC900B	1212
2SC900C	1212
2SC900D	1212
2SC900E	1212
2SC900F	1212
2SC900G	1212
2SC900J	1212
2SC900K	1212
2SC900L	1212
2SC900M	1212
2SC900OR	1212
2SC900R	1212
2SC900S	1212
2SC900SA	1212
2SC900SB	1212
2SC900SC	1212
2SC900SD	1212
2SC900U	1212
2SC900UE	1212
2SC900V	1212
2SC900VE	1212
2SC900X	1212
2SC900Y	1212
2SC901	0637
2SC901A	0637
2SC901B	0637
2SC901C	0637
2SC901D	0637
2SC901E	0637
2SC901F	0637
2SC901G	0637
2SC901GN	0637
2SC901H	0637
2SC901J	0637
2SC901K	0637
2SC901L	0637
2SC901M	0637
2SC901OR	0637
2SC901R	0637
2SC901X	0637
2SC901Y	0637
2SC902	0615
2SC903	0155
2SC904	0155
2SC905	0855
2SC906	0016
2SC906(F)	0016
2SC906F	0016
2SC907	0016
2SC907A	0016
2SC907AC	0016
2SC907AD	0016
2SC907AH	0016
2SC907B	0016
2SC907C	0016
2SC907D	0016
2SC907E	0016
2SC907F	0016
2SC907G	0016
2SC907GN	0016
2SC907H	0016
2SC907HA	0016
2SC907J	0016
2SC907K	0016
2SC907L	0016
2SC907M	0016
2SC907OR	0016
2SC907R	0016
2SC907X	0016
2SC907Y	0016
2SC908	1344
2SC909	0555
2SC910	OEM
2SC911	0555
2SC911A	0555
2SC912	0144
2SC912M	0144
2SC913	0855
2SC913A	0855
2SC913B	0855
2SC913C	0855
2SC913D	0855
2SC913E	0855
2SC913F	0855
2SC913G	0855
2SC913GN	0855
2SC913H	0855
2SC913J	0855
2SC913K	0855
2SC913L	0855
2SC913M	0855
2SC913OR	0855
2SC913R	0855
2SC913X	0855
2SC913Y	0855
2SC914	0016
2SC914A	0016
2SC915	0016
2SC915A	0016
2SC916	0042
2SC917	0007
2SC917(K)	0007
2SC917A	0007

If replacement code is OEM, contact original manufacturer for replacement.

89

DEVICE TYPE	REPL CODE
2SC917B	0007
2SC917C	0007
2SC917D	0007
2SC917E	0007
2SC917F	0007
2SC917G	0007
2SC917GN	0007
2SC917H	0007
2SC917J	0007
2SC917K	0007
2SC917L	0007
2SC917M	0007
2SC917OR	0007
2SC917R	0007
2SC917X	0007
2SC917Y	0007
2SC918	0224
2SC918A	0224
2SC918AL	0224
2SC918B	0224
2SC918C	0224
2SC918D	0224
2SC918E	0224
2SC918F	0224
2SC918G	0224
2SC918GN	0224
2SC918H	0224
2SC918J	0224
2SC918K	0224
2SC918L	0224
2SC918LF	0224
2SC918M	0224
2SC918OR	0224
2SC918R	0224
2SC918X	0224
2SC918XL	0224
2SC918Y	0224
2SC920	1204
2SC920-OQ	1204
2SC920-OR	1204
2SC920A	1204
2SC920B	1204
2SC920C	1204
2SC920CL	1204
2SC920D	1204
2SC920E	1204
2SC920F	1204
2SC920G	1204
2SC920GN	1204
2SC920H	1204
2SC920L	1204
2SC920M	1204
2SC920OR	1204
2SC920Q	1204
2SC920R	1204
2SC920X	1204
2SC920Y	1204
2SC921	2365
2SC921(L)	2365
2SC921(VHF)	2365
2SC921A	2365
2SC921B	2365
2SC921C	2365
2SC921C1	2365
2SC921CL	2365
2SC921D	2365
2SC921E	2365
2SC921F	2365
2SC921G	2365
2SC921GN	2365
2SC921H	2365
2SC921J	2365
2SC921K	2365
2SC921L	2365
2SC921M	2365
2SC921OR	2365
2SC921R	2365
2SC921W	2365
2SC921X	2365
2SC921Y	2365
2SC922	0931
2SC922A	0931
2SC922B	0931
2SC922C	0931
2SC922K	0931
2SC922L	0931
2SC922M	0931
2SC-923	0547
2SC923	0547
2SC923(E)	0547
2SC923(E)(F)	0547
2SC923(F)	0547
2SC923A	0547
2SC923B	0547
2SC923C	0547
2SC923D	0547
2SC923E	0547
2SC923F	0547
2SC923G	0547
2SC923GN	0547
2SC923H	0547
2SC923K	0547
2SC923L	0547
2SC923M	0547
2SC923OR	0547
2SC923R	0547
2SC923X	0547
2SC923Y	0547
2SC924	0544
2SC924A	0544
2SC924B	0544
2SC924C	0544
2SC924D	0544
2SC924E	0544
2SC924F	0544
2SC924G	0544
2SC924GN	0544
2SC924H	0544
2SC924J	0544
2SC924K	0544
2SC924L	0544
2SC924M	0544
2SC924OR	0544
2SC924R	0544
2SC924X	0544
2SC924Y	0544
2SC925	0284
2SC925(M)	0284
2SC925A	0284
2SC925B	0284
2SC925C	0284
2SC925D	0284
2SC925E	0284
2SC925F	0284
2SC925G	0284
2SC925GN	0284
2SC925H	0284
2SC925J	0284
2SC925K	0284
2SC925L	0284
2SC925M	0284
2SC925OR	0284
2SC925R	0284
2SC925X	0284
2SC925Y	0284
2SC926	0261
2SC926(A)	0261
2SC926-OR	0261
2SC926A	0261
2SC926B	0261
2SC926C	0261
2SC926D	0261
2SC926E	0261
2SC926F	0261
2SC926G	0261
2SC926GN	0261
2SC926H	0261
2SC926J	0261
2SC926K	0261
2SC926L	0261
2SC926M	0261
2SC926OR	0261
2SC926R	0261
2SC926X	0261
2SC926Y	0261
2SC927	0007
2SC927(C)	0007
2SC927(D)	0007
2SC927(E)	0007
2SC927A	0007
2SC927B	0007
2SC927C	0007
2SC927C(E)	0007
2SC927C(K)	0007
2SC927CJ	0007
2SC927CK	0007
2SC927CT	0007
2SC927CU	0007
2SC927CW	0007
2SC927D	0007
2SC927E	0007
2SC927E,Z	0007
2SC927F	0007
2SC927G	0007
2SC927GN	0007
2SC927H	0007
2SC927J	0007
2SC927K	0007
2SC927L	0007
2SC927M	0007
2SC927OR	0007
2SC927R	0007
2SC927X	0007
2SC927XL	0007
2SC927Y	0007
2SC927Z	0007
2SC928	0007
2SC928A	0007
2SC928B	0007
2SC928C	0007
2SC928D	0007
2SC928E	0007
2SC928F	0007
2SC928G	0007
2SC928GN	0007
2SC928H	0007
2SC928J	0007
2SC928K	0007
2SC928L	0007
2SC928M	0007
2SC928OR	0007
2SC928R	0007
2SC928X	0007
2SC928Y	0007
2SC929	1060
2SC929(0)	1060
2SC929(E)	1060
2SC929-0	1060
2SC929-O	1060
2SC929A	1060
2SC929B	1060
2SC929C	1060
2SC929C1	1060
2SC929D	1060
2SC929D1	1060
2SC929DE	1060
2SC929DP	1060
2SC929DU	1060
2SC929DV	1060
2SC929E	1489
2SC929ED	1060
2SC929EZ	1060
2SC929F	1060
2SC929FK	1060
2SC929G	1060
2SC929GN	1060
2SC929H	1060
2SC929J	1060
2SC929K	1060
2SC929L	1060
2SC929M	1060
2SC929NP	1060
2SC929OR	1060
2SC929R	1060
2SC929SP	1060
2SC929X	1060
2SC929Y	1060
2SC930	2195
2SC930(C)	2195
2SC930(D)	2195
2SC930(E)	2195
2SC930(F)	2195
2SC930-E-SP	OEM
2SC930-E-SPA-AC	OEM
2SC930-F-SPA-AC	OEM
2SC930-OR	2195
2SC930A	2195
2SC930B	2195
2SC930BK	2195
2SC930C	2195
2SC930C-IF	2195
2SC930CK	2195
2SC930CL	2195
2SC930CS	2195
2SC930D	2195
2SC930DB	2195
2SC930DC	2195
2SC930DE	2195
2SC930DK	2195
2SC930DS	2195
2SC930DT	2195
2SC930DT-2	2195
2SC930DX	2195
2SC930DZ	2195
2SC930E	2195
2SC930E1	4438
2SC930E2	OEM
2SC930EP	2195
2SC930E-SP	OEM
2SC930ET	2195
2SC930EV	2195
2SC930EX	2195
2SC930F	2195
2SC930F-SP	OEM
2SC930G	2195
2SC930GN	2195
2SC930H	2195
2SC930J	2195
2SC930K	2195
2SC930L	2195
2SC930M	2195
2SC930NP	2195
2SC930OR	2195
2SC930R	2195
2SC930SP	2195
2SC930SPE	4438
2SC930X	2195
2SC930Y	2195
2SC931	0219
2SC931C	0219
2SC931D	0219
2SC931E	0219
2SC932	0555
2SC932(E)	0555
2SC932A	0555
2SC932B	0555
2SC932BK	0555
2SC932C	0555
2SC932D	0555
2SC932E	0555
2SC932F	0555
2SC932G	0555
2SC932GN	0555
2SC932H	0555
2SC932J	0555
2SC932K	0555
2SC932L	0555
2SC932M	0555
2SC932OR	0555
2SC932R	0555
2SC932X	0555
2SC932Y	0555
2SC933	0191
2SC933(D)	0191
2SC933(F)	0191
2SC933(G)	0191
2SC933A	0191
2SC933B	0191
2SC933BB	0191
2SC933C	0191
2SC933D	0191
2SC933D(F)	0191
2SC933E	0191
2SC933E(F)	0191
2SC933F	0191
2SC933FB	0191
2SC933FP	0191
2SC933G	0191
2SC933GN	0191
2SC933H	0191
2SC933J	0191
2SC933K	0191
2SC933L	0191
2SC933M	0191
2SC933OR	0191
2SC933R	0191
2SC933X	0191
2SC933Y	0191
2SC934	0016
2SC934-O	0016
2SC934A	0016
2SC934B	0016
2SC934C	0016
2SC934D	0016
2SC934E	0016
2SC934F	0016
2SC934G	0016
2SC934GN	0016
2SC934H	0016
2SC934J	0016
2SC934K	0016
2SC934L	0016
2SC934M	0016
2SC934OR	0016
2SC934Q	0016
2SC934R	0016
2SC934X	0016
2SC934Y	0016
2SC935	0074
2SC935-OR	0074
2SC935A	0074
2SC935B	0074
2SC935C	0074
2SC935D	0074
2SC935E	0074
2SC935F	0074
2SC935G	0074
2SC935GN	0074
2SC935H	0074
2SC935J	0074
2SC935K	0074
2SC935M	0074
2SC935OR	0074
2SC935R	0074
2SC935X	0074
2SC935Y	0074
2SC936	0003
2SC936(BK)	0003
2SC936A	0003
2SC936B	0003
2SC936BK	0003
2SC936C	0003
2SC936D	0003
2SC936E	0003
2SC936F	0003
2SC936G	0003
2SC936GN	0003
2SC936H	0003
2SC936J	0003
2SC936K	0003
2SC936L	0003
2SC936M	0003
2SC936OR	0003
2SC936R	0003
2SC936X	0003
2SC936Y	0003
2SC937	0103
2SC937(BK)	0103
2SC937(XL)	0103
2SC937(YL,BK)	0103
2SC937-01	0103
2SC937A	0103
2SC937B	0103
2SC937BK	0103
2SC937C	0103
2SC937D	0103
2SC937E	0103
2SC937F	0103
2SC937G	0103
2SC937GN	0103
2SC937H	0103
2SC937J	0103
2SC937K	0103
2SC937L	0103
2SC937M	0103
2SC937OR	0103
2SC937R	OEM
2SC937X	0103
2SC937Y	0103
2SC938	0155
2SC938-O	0155
2SC938A	0155
2SC938B	0155
2SC938C	0155
2SC938D	0155
2SC938E	0155
2SC938F	0155
2SC938G	0155
2SC938GN	0155
2SC938H	0155
2SC938J	0155
2SC938K	0155
2SC938L	0155
2SC938M	0155
2SC938OR	0155
2SC938R	0155
2SC938X	0155
2SC938Y	0155
2SC939	0637
2SC939(L)	0637
2SC939I	0637
2SC939L	0637
2SC940	0820
2SC940(L)(M)	0820
2SC940(M)	0820
2SC940(P)	0820
2SC940(Q)	0820
2SC940(R)	0820
2SC940L	0820
2SC940M	0820
2SC940Q	0820
2SC941	0155
2SC941(O)	0155
2SC941(O),(R)	0155
2SC941(R)	0155
2SC941-04	0155
2SC941-OY	0155
2SC941-O	0155
2SC941-R	0155
2SC941-TM.O.JA	0155
2SC941-Y	0155
2SC941K	0155
2SC941O	0155
2SC941R	0155
2SC941TM	0155
2SC941TM-0	OEM
2SC941TM-O	0155
2SC941Y	0155
2SC942	0016
2SC943	0016
2SC943A	0016
2SC943B	0016
2SC943C	0016
2SC943D	0016
2SC943E	0016
2SC943F	0016
2SC943G	0016
2SC943GN	0016
2SC943H	0016
2SC943J	0016
2SC943K	0016
2SC943L	0016
2SC943M	0016
2SC943OR	0016
2SC943R	0016
2SC943X	0016
2SC943Y	0016
2SC944	0076
2SC944S	0076
2SC-945	0076
2SC945	0076
2SC945(C)-T	0076
2SC945(C)T	0076
2SC945(K)	0076
2SC945(L)	0076
2SC945(L)Q	0076
2SC945(P)	0076
2SC945(Q)	0076
2SC945(R)	0076
2SC945(TK)	0076
2SC945(TK,P)	0076
2SC945(TP)	0076
2SC945(TQ)	0076
2SC945(TQ,Q)	0076
2SC945-0	0076
2SC945-K	0076
2SC945-O	0076
2SC945-OR	0076
2SC945-P	0076
2SC945-Q	0076
2SC945-T	0076
2SC945-TQ	0076
2SC945-YX	0076
2SC-945A	0076
2SC945A	0076
2SC945A(C)	0076
2SC945A(C)P	0076
2SC945A(C)Q	0076
2SC945A(C)-T	0076
2SC945A(C)T	0076
2SC945A(K)	0076
2SC945A(P)	0076
2SC945A(Q)	0076
2SC945A(Q.R)	0076
2SC945A(R)	0076
2SC945A/D	0076
2SC945A-AQ	0076
2SC945A-D	OEM
2SC945A-K	OEM
2SC945AK	0076
2SC945AKT	0076
2SC945A-P	OEM
2SC945AP	0076
2SC945A-PA	0076
2SC945APT	0076
2SC945A-Q	0076
2SC945AQ	0076
2SC945A-QA	0076
2SC945A-R	OEM
2SC945AR	0076
2SC945A-RA	0076
2SC945B	0076
2SC945C	0076
2SC945D	0076
2SC945E	0076
2SC945F	0076
2SC945G	0076
2SC945GN	0076
2SC945H	0076
2SC945J	0076
2SC945K	0076
2SC945L	0076
2SC945LP	0076
2SC945LQ	0076
2SC945M	0076
2SC945OR	0076
2SC945P	0076
2SC945P1	0076
2SC945PA	0076
2SC945PJ	0076
2SC945PQ	0076
2SC945Q	0076
2SC945QL	0076
2SC945QP	0076
2SC945QZ	0076
2SC945R	0076
2SC945RA	0076
2SC945S	0076
2SC945T	0076
2SC945TK	0076
2SC945TP	0076
2SC945TQ	0076
2SC945X	0076
2SC945Y	0076
2SC945Z	OEM
2SC945ZA	0076
2SC947	0007
2SC947A	0007
2SC947B	0007
2SC947C	0007
2SC947D	0007
2SC947E	0007
2SC947F	0007
2SC947G	0007
2SC947GN	0007
2SC947H	0007
2SC947J	0007
2SC947K	0007
2SC947L	0007
2SC947M	0007
2SC947OR	0007
2SC947R	0007
2SC947X	0007
2SC947Y	0007
2SC948	0216
2SC948A	0216
2SC948B	0216
2SC948D	0216
2SC948E	0216
2SC948F	0216
2SC948G	0216
2SC948GN	0216
2SC948H	0216
2SC948J	0216
2SC948K	0216
2SC948L	0216
2SC948M	0216
2SC948OR	0216
2SC948R	0216
2SC948X	0216
2SC948Y	0216
2SC949	0216
2SC950	0016
2SC951	0079
2SC952	0079
2SC953	0016
2SC954	0016
2SC955	0016
2SC956	0016
2SC957	0144
2SC957A	0144
2SC957AL	0144
2SC957B	0144
2SC957C	0144
2SC957D	0144
2SC957E	0144
2SC957F	0144
2SC957G	0144
2SC957GN	0144
2SC957H	0144
2SC957J	0144
2SC957K	0144
2SC957L	0144
2SC957M	0144
2SC957OR	0144
2SC957R	0144
2SC957X	0144
2SC957XL	0144
2SC957Y	0144
2SC959	0086
2SC959A	0086
2SC959B	0086
2SC959C	0086
2SC959D	0086
2SC959E	0086
2SC959F	0086
2SC959G	0086
2SC959GN	0086
2SC959H	0086
2SC959J	0086
2SC959K	0086
2SC959L	0086
2SC959M	0086
2SC959OR	0086
2SC959R	0086
2SC959S	0086
2SC959SA	0086
2SC959SB	0086
2SC959SC	0086
2SC959SD	0086
2SC959X	0086
2SC959Y	0086
2SC960	5522
2SC961	0615
2SC962	0615
2SC963	0016
2SC964	0016
2SC965	0016
2SC966	0016
2SC966A	0016
2SC966B	0016
2SC966C	0016
2SC966D	0016
2SC966E	0016
2SC966F	0016
2SC966G	0016
2SC966GN	0016
2SC966H	0016
2SC966J	0016
2SC966K	0016
2SC966L	0016
2SC966M	0016
2SC966OR	0016
2SC966R	0016
2SC966X	0016
2SC966Y	0016
2SC967	0016
2SC967A	0016
2SC967B	0016
2SC967C	0016
2SC967D	0016
2SC967E	0016
2SC967F	0016
2SC967G	0016
2SC967GN	0016
2SC967H	0016
2SC967J	0016
2SC967K	0016
2SC967L	0016
2SC967M	0016
2SC967OR	0016
2SC967R	0016
2SC967X	0016
2SC967Y	0016
2SC968	2901
2SC968A	2901
2SC968B	2901
2SC968C	2901
2SC968D	2901
2SC968E	2901
2SC968F	2901
2SC968G	2901
2SC968GN	2901
2SC968H	2901
2SC968J	2901
2SC968K	2901
2SC968L	2901
2SC968M	2901
2SC968OR	2901
2SC968P	2901
2SC968R	2901
2SC968X	2901
2SC968Y	2901
2SC969	0016
2SC970	0016
2SC971	2924
2SC971A	2924
2SC971B	2924
2SC971BK	2924
2SC971C	2924
2SC971D	2924
2SC971E	2924
2SC971F	2924
2SC971G	2924
2SC971GN	2924
2SC971H	2924
2SC971J	2924
2SC971K	2924
2SC971L	2924
2SC971M	2924
2SC971OR	2924
2SC971R	2924
2SC971X	2924
2SC971Y	2924
2SC972	0086
2SC972A	0086
2SC972B	0086
2SC972C	0086
2SC972D	0086
2SC972E	0086
2SC972F	0086
2SC972G	0086
2SC972GN	0086

If replacement code is OEM, contact original manufacturer for replacement.

DEVICE TYPE	REPL CODE
2SC972H	0086
2SC972J	0086
2SC972K	0086
2SC972L	0086
2SC972M	0086
2SC972OR	0086
2SC972R	0086
2SC972X	0086
2SC972Y	0086
2SC973	2080
2SC973A	2080
2SC975	1410
2SC975A	1410
2SC976	0086
2SC976TV	0086
2SC979	0016
2SC979-O	0016
2SC979-R	0016
2SC979-Y	0016
2SC979A	0016
2SC979A-O	0016
2SC979A-R	0016
2SC980	0284
2SC980A	0284
2SC980A/G	0284
2SC980AG	0284
2SC980AG-O	0284
2SC980AG-R	0284
2SC980G	0284
2SC980G-O	0284
2SC980G-R	0284
2SC980G-Y	0284
2SC981	0178
2SC982	0396
2SC983	0066
2SC983(FA-1)	OEM
2SC983(O)	0066
2SC983-0	0066
2SC983-O	0066
2SC983-R	0066
2SC983-Y	0066
2SC983D	0066
2SC983FA-1	0066
2SC983FH-1	0066
2SC983O	0066
2SC983R	0066
2SC983S	0066
2SC983Y	0066
2SC983YFA-1	0066
2SC984	0531
2SC984A	0531
2SC984B	0531
2SC984C	0531
2SC984D	0531
2SC984E	0531
2SC984F	0531
2SC984G	0531
2SC984GN	0531
2SC984H	0531
2SC984J	0531
2SC984L	0531
2SC984M	0531
2SC984OR	0531
2SC984R	0531
2SC984X	0531
2SC984Y	0531
2SC985	0111
2SC985A	0111
2SC987	0007
2SC987A	0007
2SC988	0007
2SC988A	0007
2SC988B	0007
2SC990	0042
2SC991	0488
2SC991A	0488
2SC991B	0488
2SC991C	0488
2SC991D	0488
2SC991E	0488
2SC991F	0488
2SC991G	0488
2SC991GN	0488
2SC991H	0488
2SC991J	0488
2SC991K	0488
2SC991L	0488
2SC991M	0488
2SC991OR	0488
2SC991R	0488
2SC991X	0488
2SC991Y	0488
2SC992	0488
2SC992A	0488
2SC992B	0488
2SC992C	0488
2SC992D	0488
2SC992E	0488
2SC992F	0488
2SC992G	0488
2SC992GN	0488
2SC992H	0488
2SC992J	0488
2SC992K	0488
2SC992L	0488
2SC992M	0488
2SC992OR	0488
2SC992R	0488
2SC992X	0488

DEVICE TYPE	REPL CODE
2SC992Y	0488
2SC993	0016
2SC993D	0016
2SC993E	0016
2SC994	0079
2SC995	0168
2SC995A	0168
2SC995B	0168
2SC995C	0168
2SC995E	0168
2SC995F	0168
2SC995G	0168
2SC995GN	0168
2SC995H	0168
2SC995J	0168
2SC995K	0168
2SC995L	0168
2SC995M	0168
2SC995OR	0168
2SC995R	0168
2SC995X	0168
2SC995Y	0168
2SC996	3249
2SC997	0224
2SC997A	0224
2SC997B	0224
2SC997C	0224
2SC997D	0224
2SC997E	0224
2SC997F	0224
2SC997G	0224
2SC997GN	0224
2SC997H	0224
2SC997J	0224
2SC997K	0224
2SC997L	0224
2SC997M	0224
2SC997OR	0224
2SC997R	0224
2SC997X	0224
2SC997Y	0224
2SC998	3794
2SC999	0065
2SC999A	0065
2SC999B	0065
2SC999C	0065
2SC999D	0065
2SC999E	0065
2SC999F	0065
2SC999G	0065
2SC999GN	0065
2SC999H	0065
2SC999J	0065
2SC999K	0065
2SC999L	0065
2SC999M	0065
2SC999OR	0065
2SC999R	0065
2SC999X	0065
2SC999Y	0065
2SC1000	0111
2SC1000(BL)	0111
2SC1000(GR)	0111
2SC1000-BL	0111
2SC1000-GR	0111
2SC1000-Y	0111
2SC1000A	0111
2SC1000B	0111
2SC1000BL	0111
2SC1000C	0111
2SC1000D	0111
2SC1000E	0111
2SC1000F	0111
2SC1000G	0111
2SC1000G-BL	0111
2SC1000GBL	0111
2SC1000G-GR	0111
2SC1000GN	0111
2SC1000GR	0111
2SC1000GR(FA-1)	OEM
2SC1000H	0111
2SC1000J	0111
2SC1000K	0111
2SC1000L	0111
2SC1000M	0111
2SC1000OR	0111
2SC1000R	0111
2SC1000X	0111
2SC1000Y	0111
2SC1001	2028
2SC1004	0003
2SC1004A	0003
2SC1004B	0003
2SC1004C	0003
2SC1004D	0003
2SC1004E	0003
2SC1004F	0003
2SC1004G	0003
2SC1004GN	0003
2SC1004H	0003
2SC1004J	0003
2SC1004K	0003
2SC1004L	0003
2SC1004M	0003
2SC1004OR	0003
2SC1004R	0003
2SC1004X	0003
2SC1004Y	0003
2SC1005	0065

DEVICE TYPE	REPL CODE
2SC1005A	0065
2SC1005B	0065
2SC1005C	0065
2SC1005D	0065
2SC1005E	0065
2SC1005F	0065
2SC1005G	0065
2SC1005GN	0065
2SC1005H	0065
2SC1005J	0065
2SC1005K	0065
2SC1005L	0065
2SC1005M	0065
2SC1005OR	0065
2SC1005R	0065
2SC1005X	0065
2SC1005Y	0065
2SC1006	0111
2SC1006A	0111
2SC1006B	0111
2SC1006C	0111
2SC1007	0016
2SC1008	0086
2SC1008A	0086
2SC1009	0224
2SC1009A	0224
2SC1009F1	0224
2SC1009F2	0224
2SC1009F3	0224
2SC1009F4	0224
2SC1009F5	0224
2SC1010	0111
2SC1010A	0111
2SC1010B	0111
2SC1010C	0111
2SC1010D	0111
2SC1010E	0111
2SC1010F	0111
2SC1010G	0111
2SC1010GN	0111
2SC1010H	0111
2SC1010J	0111
2SC1010K	0111
2SC1010L	0111
2SC1010M	0111
2SC1010OR	0111
2SC1010R	0111
2SC1010X	0111
2SC1010Y	0111
2SC1011	0693
2SC1012	0233
2SC1012A	0233
2SC1012B	0233
2SC1012C	0233
2SC1012D	0233
2SC1012E	0233
2SC1012F	0233
2SC1012G	0233
2SC1012GN	0233
2SC1012H	0233
2SC1012J	0233
2SC1012K	0233
2SC1012L	0233
2SC1012M	0233
2SC1012OR	0233
2SC1012R	0233
2SC1012X	0233
2SC1012Y	0233
2SC1013	2035
2SC1013-OR	2035
2SC1013A	2035
2SC1013B	2035
2SC1013C	2035
2SC1013D	2035
2SC1013E	2035
2SC1013F	2035
2SC1013G	2035
2SC1013GN	2035
2SC1013H	2035
2SC1013J	2035
2SC1013K	2035
2SC1013L	2035
2SC1013LJ	2035
2SC1013M	2035
2SC1013OR	2035
2SC1013PJ	2035
2SC1013R	2035
2SC1013X	2035
2SC1013Y	2035
2SC1014	2035
2SC1014-1	2035
2SC1014-2	2035
2SC1014A	2035
2SC1014B	2035
2SC1014BY	2035
2SC1014C	2035
2SC1014CD	2035
2SC1014D	2035
2SC1014D1	2035
2SC1014E	2035
2SC1014F	2035
2SC1014G	2035
2SC1014GA	2035
2SC1014GN	2035
2SC1014H	2035
2SC1014J	2035
2SC1014K	2035
2SC1014L	2035
2SC1014LG	2035

DEVICE TYPE	REPL CODE
2SC1014LR	2035
2SC1014M	2035
2SC1014OR	2035
2SC1014R	2035
2SC1014W	2035
2SC1014X	2035
2SC1014Y	2035
2SC1015	OEM
2SC1015-O	OEM
2SC1015Y	OEM
2SC1016	OEM
2SC1017	2039
2SC1018	2039
2SC1018A	2039
2SC1018B	2039
2SC1018C	2039
2SC1018D	2039
2SC1018E	2039
2SC1018F	2039
2SC1018G	2039
2SC1018GN	2039
2SC1018H	2039
2SC1018J	2039
2SC1018K	2039
2SC1018L	2039
2SC1018M	2039
2SC1018R	2039
2SC1018X	2039
2SC1018Y	2039
2SC1019	OEM
2SC1019C	0042
2SC1020	OEM
2SC1021Q	OEM
2SC1023	0127
2SC1023(0)	0127
2SC1023(O)	0127
2SC1023-O	0127
2SC1023-Y	0127
2SC1023A	0127
2SC1023B	0127
2SC1023C	0127
2SC1023D	0127
2SC1023E	0127
2SC1023F	0127
2SC1023G	0127
2SC1023GN	0127
2SC1023H	0127
2SC1023J	0127
2SC1023K	0127
2SC1023L	0127
2SC1023M	0127
2SC1023OR	0127
2SC1023R	0127
2SC1023X	0127
2SC1023Y	0127
2SC1024	0178
2SC1024(D)	0178
2SC1024(F)	0178
2SC1024-E	0178
2SC1024A	0178
2SC1024B	0178
2SC1024C	0178
2SC1024D	0178
2SC1024E	0178
2SC1024F	0178
2SC1024G	0178
2SC1024L	0178
2SC1024Y	0178
2SC1025	0928
2SC1025(D)	0928
2SC1025C	OEM
2SC1025CTV	0928
2SC1025D	0928
2SC1025E	0928
2SC1025J	0928
2SC1025MT	0928
2SC1026	0127
2SC1026(G)	0127
2SC1026-O	0127
2SC1026-R	0127
2SC1026A	0127
2SC1026B	0127
2SC1026BL	0127
2SC1026C	0127
2SC1026D	0127
2SC1026E	0127
2SC1026F	0127
2SC1026G	0127
2SC1026GN	0127
2SC1026GR	0127
2SC1026H	0127
2SC1026J	0127
2SC1026K	0127
2SC1026L	0127
2SC1026M	0127
2SC1026OR	0127
2SC1026R	0127
2SC1026X	0127
2SC1026Y	0127
2SC1027	0637
2SC1030	2048
2SC1030-OR	2048
2SC1030A	2048
2SC1030B	2048
2SC1030B2C	2048
2SC1030C	2048
2SC1030D	2048
2SC1030E	2048
2SC1030F	2048

DEVICE TYPE	REPL CODE
2SC1030G	2048
2SC1030H	2048
2SC1030J	2048
2SC1030K	2048
2SC1030L	2048
2SC1030M	2048
2SC1030OR	2048
2SC1030R	2048
2SC1030X	2048
2SC1030Y	2048
2SC1031	1021
2SC1032	0127
2SC1032(Y)	0127
2SC1032A	0127
2SC1032B	0127
2SC1032BL	0127
2SC1032C	0127
2SC1032D	0127
2SC1032E	0127
2SC1032F	0127
2SC1032G	0127
2SC1032GN	0127
2SC1032H	0127
2SC1032J	0127
2SC1032K	0127
2SC1032L	0127
2SC1032M	0127
2SC1032OR	0127
2SC1032R	0127
2SC1032X	0127
2SC1032Y	0127
2SC1033	0710
2SC1033A	0710
2SC1033B	0710
2SC1033C	0710
2SC1033D	0710
2SC1033E	0710
2SC1033F	0710
2SC1033G	0710
2SC1033GN	0710
2SC1033H	0710
2SC1033J	0710
2SC1033K	0710
2SC1033L	0710
2SC1033OR	0710
2SC1033R	0710
2SC1033X	0710
2SC1033Y	0710
2SC1034	2053
2SC1034-3	2053
2SC1034-4	2053
2SC1034-5	2053
2SC1035	0007
2SC1035A	0007
2SC1035B	0007
2SC1035C	0007
2SC1035D	0007
2SC1035E	0007
2SC1035F	0007
2SC1035GN	0007
2SC1035H	0007
2SC1035J	0007
2SC1035L	0007
2SC1035M	0007
2SC1035OR	0007
2SC1035R	0007
2SC1035X	0007
2SC1035Y	0007
2SC1036	0007
2SC1036A	0007
2SC1036B	0007
2SC1036C	0007
2SC1036D	0007
2SC1036E	0007
2SC1036F	0007
2SC1036G	0007
2SC1036GN	0007
2SC1036H	0007
2SC1036J	0007
2SC1036K	0007
2SC1036L	0007
2SC1036M	0007
2SC1036OR	0007
2SC1036R	0007
2SC1036X	0007
2SC1036Y	0007
2SC1037	OEM
2SC1042	1581
2SC1043	2059
2SC1044	0007
2SC1045	0003
2SC1045(B)	0003
2SC1045B	0003
2SC1045C	0003
2SC1045D	0003
2SC1045E	0003
2SC1045F	0003
2SC1045G	0003
2SC1045GN	0003
2SC1045H	0003
2SC1045J	0003
2SC1045K	0003
2SC1045L	0003
2SC1045M	0003
2SC1045OR	0003
2SC1045R	0003
2SC1045X	0003
2SC1045Y	0003
2SC1046	0065

DEVICE TYPE	REPL CODE
2SC1046-OR	0065
2SC1046A	0065
2SC1046B	0065
2SC1046C	0065
2SC1046D	0065
2SC1046E	0065
2SC1046F	0065
2SC1046G	0065
2SC1046GN	0065
2SC1046H	0065
2SC1046J	0065
2SC1046K	0065
2SC1046L	0065
2SC1046M	0065
2SC1046N	0065
2SC1046OR	0065
2SC1046R	0065
2SC1046X	0065
2SC1046Y	0065
2SC1047	0113
2SC1047(B)	0113
2SC1047(C)	0113
2SC1047(CD)	0113
2SC1047-C	0113
2SC1047-D	0113
2SC1047A	0113
2SC1047B	0113
2SC1047BC	0113
2SC1047BCD	0113
2SC1047C	0113
2SC1047D	0113
2SC1047E	0113
2SC1047F	0113
2SC1047G	0113
2SC1047GN	0113
2SC1047GR	0113
2SC1047H	0113
2SC1047J	0113
2SC1047K	0113
2SC1047L	0113
2SC1047M	0113
2SC1047R	0113
2SC1047X	0113
2SC1047Y	0113
2SC1048	0233
2SC1048(C)	0233
2SC1048(D)	0233
2SC1048B	0233
2SC1048C	0233
2SC1048D	0233
2SC1048D,C	0233
2SC1048DC	0233
2SC1048E	0233
2SC1048F	0233
2SC1050	0220
2SC1050C	0220
2SC1050D	0220
2SC1050E	0220
2SC1050F	0220
2SC1051	0177
2SC1051L	0177
2SC1052	0086
2SC1053	0086
2SC1054	0007
2SC1055	0424
2SC1055H	0424
2SC1055U	0424
2SC1056	0233
2SC1056A	0233
2SC1056B	0233
2SC1056C	0233
2SC1056D	0233
2SC1056E	0233
2SC1056F	0233
2SC1056G	0233
2SC1056GN	0233
2SC1056H	0233
2SC1056J	0233
2SC1056K	0233
2SC1056L	0233
2SC1056M	0233
2SC1056OR	0233
2SC1056R	0233
2SC1056X	0233
2SC1056Y	0233
2SC1057	OEM
2SC1058	OEM
2SC1059	0142
2SC1059A	0142
2SC1059B	0142
2SC1059C	0142
2SC1059D	0142
2SC1059E	0142
2SC1059F	0142
2SC1059G	0142
2SC1059GN	0142
2SC1059H	0142
2SC1059J	0142
2SC1059K	0142
2SC1059L	0142
2SC1059M	0142
2SC1059OR	0142
2SC1059R	0142
2SC1059X	0142
2SC1059Y	0142
2SC1060	0042
2SC1060(C,D)	0042
2SC1060A	0042
2SC1060B	0042

DEVICE TYPE	REPL CODE
2SC1060BL	0042
2SC1060BM	0042
2SC1060BY	0042
2SC1060C	0042
2SC1060D	0042
2SC1060E	0042
2SC1060F	0042
2SC1060G	0042
2SC1060GN	0042
2SC1060H	0042
2SC1060J	0042
2SC1060K	0042
2SC1060L	0042
2SC1060M	0042
2SC1060OR	0042
2SC1060R	0042
2SC1060X	0042
2SC1060Y	0042
2SC1061	0042
2SC1061(B)	0042
2SC1061(C)	0042
2SC1061-C	0042
2SC1061A	0042
2SC1061B	0042
2SC1061BM	0042
2SC1061C	0042
2SC1061D	0042
2SC1061K	0042
2SC1061KA	0042
2SC1061KB	0042
2SC1061KC	0042
2SC1061SC	0042
2SC1061T	0042
2SC1061TB	0042
2SC1062	0233
2SC1063	0018
2SC1064	0320
2SC1066	0259
2SC1067	0007
2SC1068	0414
2SC1069	0626
2SC1070	0007
2SC1070-1	0007
2SC1070-2	0007
2SC1070-B	0007
2SC1071	0016
2SC1072	0086
2SC1072A	0086
2SC1072B	0086
2SC1072C	0086
2SC1072D	0086
2SC1072E	0086
2SC1072F	0086
2SC1072G	0086
2SC1072GN	0086
2SC1072H	0086
2SC1072J	0086
2SC1072K	0086
2SC1072L	0086
2SC1072M	0086
2SC1072OR	0086
2SC1072R	0086
2SC1072X	0086
2SC1072Y	0086
2SC1073BGS2	OEM
2SC1074	2080
2SC1075	1410
2SC1076	2082
2SC1078	2085
2SC1079	0177
2SC1079-R	0177
2SC1079-Y	0177
2SC1080	0177
2SC1080-R	0177
2SC1080-Y	0177
2SC1080B	0177
2SC1080LB	0177
2SC1082	OEM
2SC1083	2030
2SC1084	0224
2SC1085	0178
2SC1086	0223
2SC1086A	0223
2SC1086B	0223
2SC1086C	0223
2SC1086D	0223
2SC1086E	0223
2SC1086F	0223
2SC1086G	0223
2SC1086GN	0223
2SC1086H	0223
2SC1086J	0223
2SC1086K	0223
2SC1086L	0223
2SC1086M	0223
2SC1086OR	0223
2SC1086R	0223
2SC1086X	0223
2SC1086Y	0223
2SC1087	OEM
2SC1088	0283
2SC1089	0283
2SC1089(B)	0283
2SC1089(B,D)	0283
2SC1089(D)	0283
2SC1089B	0283
2SC1089C	0283
2SC1089D	0283
2SC1090	0233

If replacement code is OEM, contact original manufacturer for replacement.

DEVICE TYPE	REPL CODE
2SC1091A	0555
2SC1092	OEM
2SC1092FA	OEM
2SC1093	OEM
2SC1095	0219
2SC1095-K	0219
2SC1096	0386
2SC1096(M)	0386
2SC1096-4Z-L	0386
2SC1096-4ZL	0386
2SC1096-OR	0386
2SC1096A	0386
2SC1096B	0386
2SC1096C	0386
2SC1096D	0386
2SC1096E	0386
2SC1096F	0386
2SC1096G	0386
2SC1096GN	0386
2SC1096H	0386
2SC1096J	0386
2SC1096K	0386
2SC1096L	0386
2SC1096LM	0386
2SC1096M	0386
2SC1096N	0386
2SC1096OR	0386
2SC1096Q	0386
2SC1096R	0386
2SC1096X	0386
2SC1096Y	0386
2SC1097	OEM
2SC1098	0555
2SC1098(4)K	0555
2SC1098(4)L	0555
2SC1098(L)	0555
2SC1098(M)	0555
2SC1098-4K	0555
2SC1098-4L	0555
2SC1098-42M	0555
2SC1098A	0555
2SC1098B	0555
2SC1098C	0555
2SC1098D	0555
2SC1098L	0555
2SC1098M	0555
2SC1099	1138
2SC1099(K)	1138
2SC1099K	1138
2SC1100	1142
2SC1100A	1142
2SC1100B	1142
2SC1100C	1142
2SC1100D	1142
2SC1100E	1142
2SC1100F	1142
2SC1100G	1142
2SC1100GN	1142
2SC1100H	1142
2SC1100J	1142
2SC1100K	1142
2SC1100L	1142
2SC1100M	1142
2SC1100OR	1142
2SC1100R	1142
2SC1100X	1142
2SC1100Y	1142
2SC1101	0003
2SC1101A	0003
2SC1101B	0003
2SC1101C	0003
2SC1101D	0003
2SC1101E	0003
2SC1101F	0003
2SC1101G	0003
2SC1101GN	0003
2SC1101H	0003
2SC1101J	0003
2SC1101K	0003
2SC1101L	0003
2SC1101M	0003
2SC1101OR	0003
2SC1101R	0003
2SC1101X	0003
2SC1101Y	0003
2SC1102	0142
2SC1102(L)	0142
2SC1102(M)	0142
2SC1102A	0142
2SC1102B	0142
2SC1102C	0142
2SC1102K	0142
2SC1102L	0142
2SC1102M	0142
2SC1103	0233
2SC1103(A)	0233
2SC1103(L)	0233
2SC1103A	0233
2SC1103B	0233
2SC1103C	0233
2SC1103L	0233
2SC1104	1200
2SC1104A	1200
2SC1104B	1200
2SC1104C	1200
2SC1104L	1200
2SC1105	0142
2SC1105(K)	0142
2SC1105(L)	0142
2SC1105(M)	0142
2SC1105A	0142
2SC1105B	0142
2SC1105C	0142
2SC1105D	0142
2SC1105E	0142
2SC1105F	0142
2SC1105G	0142
2SC1105GN	0142
2SC1105H	0142
2SC1105J	0142
2SC1105K	0142
2SC1105L	0142
2SC1105M	0142
2SC1105OR	0142
2SC1105R	0142
2SC1105X	0142
2SC1105Y	0142
2SC1106	0220
2SC1106(K)	0220
2SC1106(L)	0220
2SC1106(M)	0220
2SC1106A	0220
2SC1106B	0220
2SC1106C	0220
2SC1106K	0220
2SC1106L	0220
2SC1106M	0220
2SC1106P	0220
2SC1106PQ	0220
2SC1106Q	0220
2SC1107	0236
2SC1107Q	0236
2SC1107YG	0236
2SC1108	0236
2SC1109	0236
2SC1110	0236
2SC1111	0861
2SC1112	0861
2SC1113	0424
2SC1114	2112
2SC1114-O	OEM
2SC1115	0177
2SC1116	0538
2SC1116-0	0538
2SC1116-O	0538
2SC1116A	0538
2SC1117	0007
2SC1117A	0007
2SC1117B	0007
2SC1117C	0007
2SC1117D	0007
2SC1117E	0007
2SC1117F	0007
2SC1117G	0007
2SC1117GN	0007
2SC1117H	0007
2SC1117J	0007
2SC1117K	0007
2SC1117L	0007
2SC1117M	0007
2SC1117OR	0007
2SC1117R	0007
2SC1117X	0007
2SC1117Y	0007
2SC1122	1410
2SC1122A	1410
2SC1123	0079
2SC1123A	0079
2SC1123B	0079
2SC1123C	0079
2SC1123D	0079
2SC1123E	0079
2SC1123F	0079
2SC1123GN	0079
2SC1123H	0079
2SC1123J	0079
2SC1123K	0079
2SC1123L	0079
2SC1123M	0079
2SC1123OR	0079
2SC1123R	0079
2SC1123X	0079
2SC1123Y	0079
2SC1124	0264
2SC1124(13)	0264
2SC1124-2	0570
2SC1124-OR	0264
2SC1124A	0264
2SC1124B	0264
2SC1124C	0264
2SC1124D	0264
2SC1124E	0264
2SC1124F	0264
2SC1124G	0264
2SC1124GN	0264
2SC1124H	0264
2SC1124J	0264
2SC1124K	0264
2SC1124L	0264
2SC1124M	0264
2SC1124OR	0264
2SC1124R	0264
2SC1124X	0264
2SC1124Y	0264
2SC1126	0224
2SC1126A	0224
2SC1126E	0224
2SC1126F	0224
2SC1126GN	0224
2SC1126J	0224
2SC1126K	0224
2SC1126L	0224
2SC1126M	0224
2SC1126OR	0224
2SC1126R	0224
2SC1126X	0224
2SC1126Y	0224
2SC1127	1062
2SC1127-1	1062
2SC1127-2	1062
2SC1127-0	1062
2SC1127-OR	1062
2SC1127A	1062
2SC1127B	1062
2SC1127C	1062
2SC1127D	1062
2SC1127E	1062
2SC1127F	1062
2SC1127G	1062
2SC1127GA	1062
2SC1127GN	1062
2SC1127H	1062
2SC1127J	1062
2SC1127JR	1062
2SC1127K	1062
2SC1127L	1062
2SC1127M	1062
2SC1127OR	1062
2SC1127R	1062
2SC1127X	1062
2SC1127Y	1062
2SC1128	0224
2SC1128(M)	0224
2SC1128(S)	0224
2SC1128-O	0224
2SC1128A	0224
2SC1128B	0224
2SC1128BL	0224
2SC1128C	0224
2SC1128D	0224
2SC1128G	0224
2SC1128H	0224
2SC1128M	0224
2SC1128R	0224
2SC1128S	0224
2SC1128Y	0224
2SC1129	0224
2SC1129(M)	0224
2SC1129(R)	0224
2SC1129-0	0224
2SC1129A	0224
2SC1129B	0224
2SC1129BL	0224
2SC1129C	0224
2SC1129G	0224
2SC1129M	0224
2SC1129R	0224
2SC1129Y	0224
2SC1130	0003
2SC1131	0637
2SC1132	0065
2SC1133	0065
2SC1133D	0065
2SC1138	2133
2SC1140	1841
2SC1141	1841
2SC1142	0359
2SC1143	0359
2SC1150	0086
2SC1151	0003
2SC1151A	0003
2SC1152	0074
2SC1152(F)	0074
2SC1152F	0074
2SC1152G	0074
2SC1153	1142
2SC1153A	1142
2SC1154	0223
2SC1155	0264
2SC1156	0264
2SC1156A	0264
2SC1156B	0264
2SC1156C	0264
2SC1156D	0264
2SC1156E	0264
2SC1156F	0264
2SC1156G	0264
2SC1156GN	0264
2SC1156H	0264
2SC1156K	0264
2SC1156L	0264
2SC1156M	0264
2SC1156OR	0264
2SC1156R	0264
2SC1156X	0264
2SC1156Y	0264
2SC1157	0264
2SC1157A	0264
2SC1157B	0264
2SC1157C	0264
2SC1157E	0264
2SC1157F	0264
2SC1157G	0264
2SC1157GN	0264
2SC1157H	0264
2SC1157J	0264
2SC1157K	0264
2SC1157L	0264
2SC1157M	0264
2SC1157OR	0264
2SC1157R	0264
2SC1157X	0264
2SC1157Y	0264
2SC1158	0470
2SC1159	0007
2SC1160	0178
2SC1160(L)	0178
2SC1160-O	0178
2SC1160K	0178
2SC1160L	0178
2SC1161	0178
2SC1162	0558
2SC1162(C)	0558
2SC1162A	0558
2SC1162B	0558
2SC1162C	0558
2SC1162CP	0558
2SC1162D	0558
2SC1162W	0558
2SC1162W(C)	0558
2SC1162W(D)	0558
2SC1162WBP	0558
2SC1162WT	0558
2SC1162WTB	0558
2SC1162WTC	0558
2SC1163	0275
2SC1164	0414
2SC1164-O	0414
2SC1164-R	0414
2SC1165	0684
2SC1166	0728
2SC1166(O)	0728
2SC1166-GR	0728
2SC1166-O	0728
2SC1166-R	0728
2SC1166-Y	0728
2SC1166A	0728
2SC1166B	0728
2SC1166C	0728
2SC1166E	0728
2SC1166F	0728
2SC1166G	0728
2SC1166GN	0728
2SC1166H	0728
2SC1166K	0728
2SC1166L	0728
2SC1166M	0728
2SC1166O	0728
2SC1166OR	0728
2SC1166U	0728
2SC1166Y	0728
2SC1167	0309
2SC1168	0142
2SC1168X	0142
2SC1169	0626
2SC1170	1142
2SC1170(B)	1142
2SC1170-OR	1142
2SC1170A	1142
2SC1170B	1142
2SC1170B(FA-2)	OEM
2SC1170BFA-2	1142
2SC1170C	1142
2SC1170D	1142
2SC1170E	1142
2SC1170F	1142
2SC1170FA-2	1142
2SC1170G	1142
2SC1170GN	1142
2SC1170H	1142
2SC1170J	1142
2SC1170K	1142
2SC1170L	1142
2SC1170M	1142
2SC1170OR	1142
2SC1170R	1142
2SC1170X	1142
2SC1170Y	1142
2SC1171	0065
2SC1172	0309
2SC1172A	0309
2SC1172B	0309
2SC1172C	0309
2SC1172D	0309
2SC1172E	0309
2SC1172F	0309
2SC1172G	0309
2SC1172GN	0309
2SC1172H	0309
2SC1172J	0309
2SC1172K	0309
2SC1172L	0309
2SC1172M	0309
2SC1172R	0309
2SC1172X	0309
2SC1172Y	0309
2SC1173	0042
2SC1173(O)	0042
2SC1173(X)	0042
2SC1173-0	0042
2SC1173-B	0042
2SC1173-C	0042
2SC1173-GR	0042
2SC1173-O	0042
2SC1173-R	0042
2SC1173-Y	0042
2SC1173A	0042
2SC1173B	0042
2SC1173GR	0042
2SC1173R	0042
2SC1173X	0042
2SC1173X(Y)	0042
2SC1173XO	0042
2SC1173XY	0042
2SC1173Y	0042
2SC1173YX	OEM
2SC1174	0309
2SC1174-OR	0309
2SC1174A	0309
2SC1174B	0309
2SC1174C	0309
2SC1174D	0309
2SC1174E	0309
2SC1174F	0309
2SC1174G	0309
2SC1174GN	0309
2SC1174H	0309
2SC1174J	0309
2SC1174K	0309
2SC1174L	0309
2SC1174M	0309
2SC1174OR	0309
2SC1174R	0309
2SC1174X	0309
2SC1174Y	0309
2SC1175	0191
2SC1175(C)	0191
2SC1175(D,E,F)	0191
2SC1175C	0191
2SC1175CTV	0191
2SC1175CTV-D	OEM
2SC1175CTV-E	OEM
2SC1175CTV-F	OEM
2SC1175D	0191
2SC1175E	0191
2SC1175E,D,F	0191
2SC1175F	0191
2SC1175F(H)	0191
2SC1176	2156
2SC1177	1189
2SC1178	OEM
2SC1178A	1966
2SC1180	0007
2SC1181	0047
2SC1182	0007
2SC1182B	0007
2SC1182C	0007
2SC1182D	0007
2SC1184	0003
2SC1184A	0003
2SC1184B	0003
2SC1184C	0003
2SC1184D	0003
2SC1184E	0003
2SC1185	0074
2SC1185A	0074
2SC1185B	0074
2SC1185C	0074
2SC1185K	0074
2SC1185L	0074
2SC1185M	0074
2SC1187	0224
2SC1188	0224
2SC1188-O	0224
2SC1189	0224
2SC1189L	0224
2SC1190	1224
2SC1195	0103
2SC1195(FA-1)	0103
2SC1195A	0103
2SC1195B	0103
2SC1195C	0103
2SC1195D	0103
2SC1195E	0103
2SC1195F	0103
2SC1195FA-1	0103
2SC1195FA-5	0103
2SC1195G	0103
2SC1195GN	0103
2SC1195GR	0103
2SC1195H	0103
2SC1195J	0103
2SC1195K	0103
2SC1195L	0103
2SC1195M	0103
2SC1195O	0103
2SC1195OR	0103
2SC1195R	0103
2SC1195X	0103
2SC1195Y	0103
2SC1196A	OEM
2SC1197A	OEM
2SC1199	0414
2SC1204	0155
2SC1204B	5897
2SC1204C	0155
2SC1204D	0155
2SC1205	2169
2SC1205A	2169
2SC1205B	2169
2SC1205C	2169
2SC1206	0086
2SC1206A	0086
2SC1206B	0086
2SC1207	OEM
2SC1207A	OEM
2SC1207B	OEM
2SC1208	OEM
2SC1209	0076
2SC1209(C)	0076
2SC1209(D)	0076
2SC1209C	0076
2SC1209D	0076
2SC1209E	0076
2SC1210	0945
2SC1210Y	0945
2SC1211	0155
2SC1212	0558
2SC1212A	0558
2SC1212AB	0558
2SC1212ABWT	0558
2SC1212AC	0558
2SC1212ACWT	0558
2SC1212B	0558
2SC1212C	0558
2SC1213	0191
2SC1213(A)	0191
2SC1213(B)	0191
2SC1213(C)	0191
2SC1213(D)	0191
2SC1213-OR	0191
2SC1213A	0191
2SC1213A(C)	0191
2SC1213AA	0191
2SC1213AB	0191
2SC1213A-C	0191
2SC1213AC	0191
2SC1213AD	0191
2SC1213AK	0191
2SC1213AKB	0191
2SC1213AKC	0191
2SC1213AKD	0191
2SC1213B	0191
2SC1213BC	0191
2SC1213C	0191
2SC1213CD	0191
2SC1213D	0191
2SC1213D-24	0191
2SC1213E	0191
2SC1213F	0191
2SC1213G	0191
2SC1213GN	0191
2SC1213H	0191
2SC1213J	0191
2SC1213K	0191
2SC1213L	0191
2SC1213M	0191
2SC1213OR	0191
2SC1213Q	0191
2SC1213X	0191
2SC1213Y	0191
2SC1214	0155
2SC1214(B)	0155
2SC1214A	0155
2SC1214B	0155
2SC1214C	0155
2SC1214D	0155
2SC1215	0127
2SC1215(R)	0127
2SC1215C	0127
2SC1215D	0127
2SC1215E	0127
2SC1215F	0127
2SC1215G	0127
2SC1215GN	0127
2SC1215H	0127
2SC1215J	0127
2SC1215K	0127
2SC1215L	0127
2SC1215M	0127
2SC1215OR	0127
2SC1215R	0127
2SC1215X	0127
2SC1215Y	0127
2SC1216	0224
2SC1217	0283
2SC1218	0086
2SC1219	0155
2SC1220	0155
2SC1220(E)	0155
2SC1220-003	0155
2SC1220A	0155
2SC1220A(QPR)	0155
2SC1220AP	0155
2SC1220AQ	0155
2SC1220AR	0155
2SC1220E	0155
2SC1220P	0155
2SC1220Q	0155
2SC1220R	0155
2SC1222	2176
2SC1222(E)	2176
2SC1222A	2176
2SC1222B	2176
2SC1222C	2176
2SC1222D	2176
2SC1222E	2176
2SC1222H	2176
2SC1222U	2176
2SC1223	0414
2SC1224	0334
2SC1226	0219
2SC1226(A)	0219
2SC1226(AP)	0219
2SC1226(P)	0219
2SC1226(Q)	0219
2SC1226(R)	0219
2SC1226-0	0219
2SC1226A	0219
2SC1226A(P)	0219
2SC1226A(Q)	0219
2SC1226A(QPR)	0219
2SC1226A(R)	0219
2SC1226AC	0219
2SC1226ACF	0219
2SC1226AF	0219
2SC1226AP	0219
2SC1226AQ	0219
2SC1226AR	0219
2SC1226ARL	0219
2SC1226ARL(P)	0219
2SC1226ARL(Q)	0219
2SC1226ARL(R)	0219
2SC1226B	0219
2SC1226BL	0219
2SC1226C	0219
2SC1226CF	0219
2SC1226D	0219
2SC1226E	0219
2SC1226F	0219
2SC1226G	0219
2SC1226H	0219
2SC1226L	0219
2SC1226OR	0219
2SC1226P	0219
2SC1226Q	0219
2SC1226R	0219
2SC1226RL	0219
2SC1226RL(P)	0219
2SC1226RL(Q)	0219
2SC1226RL(QR)	0219
2SC1226RL(R)	0219
2SC1226RL/P	0219
2SC1226RLP	0219
2SC1226RLQ	0219
2SC1226RLR	0219
2SC1226Y	0219
2SC1227	0074
2SC1228	1955
2SC1229	0168
2SC1229Q	0168
2SC1229R	0168
2SC1230	1955
2SC1231	0855
2SC1232	OEM
2SC1233	OEM
2SC1235	0142
2SC1235A	0142
2SC1235AL	0142
2SC1235AM	0142
2SC1235G	0142
2SC1236	0224
2SC1237	0930
2SC1237E	0930
2SC1239	1897
2SC1240	0224
2SC1241	1189
2SC1241A	1189
2SC1243	2005
2SC1243-24	2005
2SC1243C1	2005
2SC1243C2	2005
2SC1243D1	2005
2SC1243D2	2005
2SC1244	0079
2SC1246	0155
2SC1246A	0155
2SC1246R	0155
2SC1246S	0155
2SC1246T	0155
2SC1247	0155
2SC1247A	0155
2SC1247AF	0155
2SC1252	2194
2SC1253	0414
2SC1254	0007
2SC1256	2198
2SC1257	2156
2SC1258	1224
2SC1259	1963
2SC1260	0259
2SC1266	0086
2SC1267	2156
2SC1268	1157
2SC1271A	OEM
2SC1273	OEM
2SC1274	0016
2SC1275	0259
2SC1276	0111
2SC1277	0320
2SC1278	0855
2SC1278S	0855
2SC1279	0855
2SC1279S	0855
2SC1280	0396
2SC1280A	0396
2SC1280AS	0396
2SC1280S	0396
2SC1281	0079
2SC1282	0320
2SC1283	0079
2SC1284	0127

If replacement code is OEM, contact original manufacturer for replacement.

DEVICE TYPE	REPL CODE
2SC1285	0155
2SC1290	2214
2SC1292	0637
2SC1293	1060
2SC1293(A)	1060
2SC1293A	1060
2SC1293B	1060
2SC1293C	1060
2SC1293D	1060
2SC1295	1142
2SC1295(O)	1142
2SC1295-0	1142
2SC1295-O	1142
2SC1296	0065
2SC1298	1963
2SC1300	0065
2SC1302	OEM
2SC1303	1854
2SC1304	1496
2SC1306	0833
2SC1306A	0833
2SC1306I	0833
2SC1306K	0833
2SC-1307	0830
2SC1307	0830
2SC1307-1	0830
2SC1308	0309
2SC1308(K)	0309
2SC1308K	0309
2SC1308L	0309
2SC1308N	0309
2SC1309	0065
2SC1310	0284
2SC1311	0284
2SC1312	1212
2SC1312A	1212
2SC1312BC	1212
2SC1312C	1212
2SC1312D	1212
2SC1312E	1212
2SC1312F	1212
2SC1312G	1212
2SC1312GN	1212
2SC1312H	1212
2SC1312J	1212
2SC1312K	1212
2SC1312L	1212
2SC1312M	1212
2SC1312OR	1212
2SC1312R	1212
2SC1312X	1212
2SC1312Y	1212
2SC1313	0111
2SC1313(G)	0111
2SC1313B	0111
2SC1313Y	0111
2SC1314	1963
2SC1315	0233
2SC1316	2230
2SC1316-3	2230
2SC1316T	OEM
2SC1317	0155
2SC1317(P)	0155
2SC1317(Q)	0155
2SC1317(R)	0155
2SC1317(S)	0155
2SC1317-OR	0155
2SC1317-Q	0155
2SC1317-R	0155
2SC1317-S	0155
2SC1317-T	0155
2SC1317A	0155
2SC1317BC	0155
2SC1317C	0155
2SC1317E	0155
2SC1317G	0155
2SC1317GR	0155
2SC1317L	0155
2SC1317NC	0155
2SC1317NC(Q)	0155
2SC1317OR	0155
2SC1317Q	0155
2SC1317R	0155
2SC1317S	0155
2SC1317T	0155
2SC1317V	0155
2SC1317Y	0155
2SC1318	0155
2SC1318(P)	0155
2SC1318(P,R)	0155
2SC1318(Q)	0155
2SC1318(R)	0155
2SC1318(S)	0155
2SC1318-R	0155
2SC1318-S	0155
2SC1318A	0155
2SC1318B	0155
2SC1318C	0155
2SC1318E	0155
2SC1318F	0155
2SC1318G	0155
2SC1318GN	0155
2SC1318H	0155
2SC1318J	0155
2SC1318K	0155
2SC1318L	0155
2SC1318M	0155
2SC1318P	0155
2SC1318PR	0155

DEVICE TYPE	REPL CODE
2SC1318Q	0155
2SC1318QP	0155
2SC1318QR	0155
2SC1318R	0155
2SC1318S	0155
2SC1318S,R	0155
2SC1318Y	0155
2SC1319	0007
2SC1319C	0007
2SC1320	0224
2SC1320(K)	0224
2SC1320A	0224
2SC1320B	0224
2SC1320C	0224
2SC1320D	0224
2SC1320E	0224
2SC1320F	0224
2SC1320G	0224
2SC1320GN	0224
2SC1320H	0224
2SC1320J	0224
2SC1320K	0224
2SC1320L	0224
2SC1320M	0224
2SC1320OR	0224
2SC1320R	0224
2SC1320X	0224
2SC1320Y	0224
2SC1321	0007
2SC1321Q2	0007
2SC1321Q3	0007
2SC1321Q4	0007
2SC1321Q5	0007
2SC1322	0177
2SC1324	0414
2SC1324(C)	0414
2SC1324C	0414
2SC1325	0885
2SC1325A	0885
2SC1325AK	0885
2SC1325AL	0885
2SC1326	0488
2SC1327	1212
2SC1327FS	1212
2SC1327R	1212
2SC1327S	1212
2SC1327T	1212
2SC1327TU	1212
2SC1327TV	1212
2SC1327U	1212
2SC1328	0111
2SC1328(U)	0111
2SC1328(U)(T)	0111
2SC1328T	0111
2SC1328U	0111
2SC1330	0218
2SC1331	0007
2SC1335	1212
2SC1335(B)	1212
2SC1335(C)	1212
2SC1335(D)	1212
2SC1335(E)	1212
2SC1335-OR	1212
2SC1335A	1212
2SC1335B	1212
2SC1335C	1212
2SC1335D	1212
2SC1335E	1212
2SC1335F	1212
2SC1335G	1212
2SC1335GN	1212
2SC1335H	1212
2SC1335J	1212
2SC1335K	1212
2SC1335L	1212
2SC1335M	1212
2SC1335OR	1212
2SC1335R	1212
2SC1335X	1212
2SC1335Y	1212
2SC1336	0144
2SC1336JK	0144
2SC1337	1410
2SC1337A	1410
2SC1338A	OEM
2SC1339	OEM
2SC1340	2156
2SC1342	0127
2SC1342(A)	0127
2SC1342(B)	0127
2SC1342(C)	0127
2SC1342-OR	0127
2SC1342A	0127
2SC1342B	0127
2SC1342C	0127
2SC1342D	0127
2SC1342E	0127
2SC1342F	0127
2SC1342G	0127
2SC1342GN	0127
2SC1342J	0127
2SC1342K	0127
2SC1342L	0127
2SC1342M	0127
2SC1342OR	0127
2SC1342R	0127
2SC1342X	0127
2SC1342Y	0127
2SC1343	0171

DEVICE TYPE	REPL CODE
2SC1343-05	0171
2SC1343B	0171
2SC1343BL	0171
2SC1343D	0171
2SC1343E	0171
2SC1343F	0171
2SC1343G	0171
2SC1343GN	0171
2SC1343G-R	0171
2SC1343GR	0171
2SC1343H	0171
2SC1343J	0171
2SC1343K	0171
2SC1343L	0171
2SC1343M	0171
2SC1343O	0171
2SC1343OR	0171
2SC1343R	0171
2SC1343X	0171
2SC1343Y	0171
2SC1344	0547
2SC1344(E)	0547
2SC1344C	0547
2SC1344D	0547
2SC1344E	0547
2SC1344F	0547
2SC1345	0547
2SC1345(E)	0547
2SC1345C	0547
2SC1345D	0547
2SC1345E	0547
2SC1345F	0547
2SC1345KD	0547
2SC1345KE	0547
2SC1345KF	0547
2SC1346	0218
2SC1346(Q)	0218
2SC1346(R)	0218
2SC1346R	0218
2SC1346S	0218
2SC1347	0218
2SC1347(Q)	0218
2SC1347(R)	0218
2SC1347(S)	0218
2SC1347A	0218
2SC1347B	0218
2SC1347C	0218
2SC1347D	0218
2SC1347F	0218
2SC1347G	0218
2SC1347L	0218
2SC1347Q	0218
2SC1347R	0218
2SC1347RQ	0218
2SC1347X	0218
2SC1347Y	0218
2SC1348	0223
2SC1348-1	0223
2SC1348-2	0223
2SC1348-3	0223
2SC1349	0855
2SC1350	OEM
2SC1351	0626
2SC1352	0079
2SC1353	0626
2SC1355	OEM
2SC1356	OEM
2SC1358	2040
2SC1358A	2040
2SC1358K	2040
2SC1358K1	2040
2SC1358K2	2040
2SC1358K3	2040
2SC1358L	2040
2SC1358M	2040
2SC1359	0151
2SC1359(A)	0151
2SC1359(B)	0151
2SC1359(C)	0151
2SC1359(C,B)	0151
2SC1359-C	0151
2SC1359A	0151
2SC1359B	0151
2SC1359BC	0151
2SC1359C	0151
2SC1359Q	0151
2SC1360	1653
2SC1360-C	6563
2SC1360A	1653
2SC1360ANC	1653
2SC1361	0155
2SC1362	0155
2SC1362(47)	0155
2SC1363	0076
2SC1364	0076
2SC1364-6	0076
2SC1364-7	0076
2SC1364-8	0076
2SC1364-OR	0076
2SC1364A	0076
2SC1364B	0076
2SC1364C	0076
2SC1364D	0076
2SC1364E	0076
2SC1364H	0076
2SC1364K	0076
2SC1364L	0076
2SC1364M	0076
2SC1364OR	0076

DEVICE TYPE	REPL CODE
2SC1364R	0076
2SC1364X	0076
2SC1364Y	0076
2SC1365	0414
2SC1366	0414
2SC1367	0003
2SC1367A	0003
2SC1368	1779
2SC1368(B)	1779
2SC1368B	1779
2SC1368C	1779
2SC1368D	1779
2SC1372	0155
2SC1372Y	0155
2SC1373	0111
2SC1374	2257
2SC1374H	2257
2SC1375	0111
2SC1375H	0111
2SC1376	0079
2SC1376H	0079
2SC1377	0830
2SC1380	0016
2SC1380-BL	0016
2SC1380-GR	0016
2SC1380A	0016
2SC1380A-BL	0016
2SC1380A-GR	0016
2SC1381	1581
2SC1382	0558
2SC1382-0	0558
2SC1382-O	0558
2SC1382-Y	0558
2SC1383	0018
2SC1383(P,Q,R)	0018
2SC1383(R)	0018
2SC1383(S)	0018
2SC1383-P	0018
2SC1383-Q	0018
2SC1383-QR	0018
2SC1383-R	0018
2SC1383,RS	0018
2SC1383NC	0018
2SC1383NC(R)	0018
2SC1383NC-P	0018
2SC1383NCP	0018
2SC1383NCPQR	0018
2SC1383NC-Q	0018
2SC1383NCQ	0018
2SC1383NC-R	0018
2SC1383NCR	0018
2SC1383NOPQR	0018
2SC1383P	0018
2SC1383PQR	0018
2SC1383Q	0018
2SC1383QR	0018
2SC1383R	0018
2SC1383RS	0018
2SC1383S	0018
2SC1383X	0018
2SC1384	0018
2SC1384(Q)	0018
2SC1384-OR	0018
2SC1384A	0018
2SC1384B	0018
2SC1384C	0018
2SC1384D	0018
2SC1384E	0018
2SC1384F	0018
2SC1384G	0018
2SC1384GN	0018
2SC1384H	0018
2SC1384J	0018
2SC1384K	0018
2SC1384L	0018
2SC1384M	0018
2SC1384NC	0018
2SC1384NC-R	OEM
2SC1384OR	0018
2SC1384Q	0018
2SC1384Q,R	0018
2SC1384R	0018
2SC1384RS	0018
2SC1384S	0018
2SC1384X	0018
2SC1384Y	0018
2SC1385	0016
2SC1385H	0016
2SC1386	0086
2SC1386H	0086
2SC1387	0414
2SC1388	0086
2SC1390	0592
2SC1390(L)	0592
2SC1390(L,Y)	0592
2SC1390(V)	0592
2SC1390(W)	0592
2SC1390(X)	0592
2SC1390(Y)	0592
2SC1390I(W)	0592
2SC1390IW	0592
2SC1390J(X)	0592
2SC1390JX	0592
2SC1390W	0592
2SC1390WH	0592
2SC1390WX	0592
2SC1390X	0592
2SC1390XK	0592
2SC1390YM	0592

DEVICE TYPE	REPL CODE
2SC1391	0142
2SC1391VL	0142
2SC1393	0224
2SC1393K	0224
2SC1393L	0224
2SC1393M	0224
2SC1394	0224
2SC1395	0007
2SC1396	0007
2SC1398	0042
2SC1398(Q)	0042
2SC1398A	0042
2SC1398P	0042
2SC1398Q	0042
2SC1399	0558
2SC1399E	0558
2SC1400	0525
2SC1402	0177
2SC1403	0538
2SC1403A	0538
2SC1404	OEM
2SC1406	2271
2SC1406(P)	2271
2SC1406Q	2271
2SC1407	2271
2SC1407(Q)	2271
2SC1407B	2271
2SC1407Q	2271
2SC1407X	2271
2SC1409	0388
2SC1409(B)	0388
2SC1409(C)	0388
2SC1409A	0388
2SC1409A(B)	0388
2SC1409AA	0388
2SC1409AB	0388
2SC1409AC	0388
2SC1409B	0388
2SC1409C	0388
2SC1410	0388
2SC1410A	0388
2SC1410AA	0388
2SC1410AB	0388
2SC1410AC	0388
2SC1410B	0388
2SC1410C	0388
2SC1411	0016
2SC1412	0855
2SC1413	0065
2SC1413A	0065
2SC1413AH	0065
2SC1413B	0065
2SC1413C	0065
2SC1413D	0065
2SC1413E	0065
2SC1413F	0065
2SC1413G	0065
2SC1413GN	0065
2SC1413K	0065
2SC1413L	0065
2SC1413R	0065
2SC1413X	0065
2SC1413Y	0065
2SC1414	OEM
2SC1415	1077
2SC1415-05	1077
2SC1416	0016
2SC1416A	0016
2SC1417	0127
2SC1417(G)	0127
2SC1417(V)	0127
2SC1417(V,G)	0127
2SC1417(W)	0127
2SC1417D(V)	0127
2SC1417F	0127
2SC1417V	0127
2SC1417VF	0127
2SC1417VW	0127
2SC1417W	0127
2SC1418	0042
2SC1419	2276
2SC1419-C	2276
2SC1419B	2276
2SC1419C	2276
2SC1424	0259
2SC1426	0626
2SC1427	0224
2SC1428	0111
2SC1429	0546
2SC1429-1	0546
2SC1429-2	0546
2SC1430	0617
2SC1431	1021
2SC1431-1	1021
2SC1431-2	1021
2SC1432	OEM
2SC1433	0637
2SC1434	1841
2SC1436	1841
2SC1437-NC	0261
2SC1438	0079
2SC1439	0079
2SC1440	1841
2SC1441	1841
2SC1444	0419
2SC1445	0419
2SC1446	0638
2SC1446(LA)(P)	0638
2SC1446(LA)(Q)	0638

DEVICE TYPE	REPL CODE
2SC1446(LB)(P)	0638
2SC1446(LB)(Q)	0638
2SC1446(P)	0638
2SC1446(Q)	0638
2SC1446-O	0638
2SC1446LB	0638
2SC1446LB(Q)	0638
2SC1446LB(R)	0638
2SC1446LBQ	0638
2SC1446LBR	0638
2SC1446P	0638
2SC1446Q	0638
2SC1447	0638
2SC1447(R)	0638
2SC1447-0	0638
2SC1447-O	0638
2SC1447FA-2	0638
2SC1447GL	0638
2SC1447GL3	0638
2SC1448	1274
2SC1448A	1274
2SC1448A(FA-1)	OEM
2SC1448C	1274
2SC1448LB	1274
2SC1449	0161
2SC1449(K)	0161
2SC1449(L)	0161
2SC1449CB	0161
2SC1449M	0161
2SC1450	1021
2SC1450S	1021
2SC1451	0710
2SC1452	0710
2SC1453	0111
2SC1454	0220
2SC1454-0	0220
2SC1454-O	0220
2SC1456	0142
2SC1456(L)	0142
2SC1456(M)	0142
2SC1457	0855
2SC1463	0637
2SC1464	0626
2SC1465	OEM
2SC1466	0065
2SC1467	0065
2SC1468	1955
2SC1469	0359
2SC1469A	0359
2SC1471	0284
2SC1472	0396
2SC1472K	0396
2SC1472KA	0396
2SC1472KB	0396
2SC1473	0261
2SC1473(NC)	0261
2SC1473(Q)	0261
2SC1473(R)	0261
2SC1473-Q	0261
2SC1473-QNC	0261
2SC1473-QRNC	0261
2SC1473-R	0261
2SC1473-RNC	0261
2SC1473A	0261
2SC1473A(Q)	0261
2SC1473A(R)	0261
2SC1473AE	0261
2SC1473AH	0261
2SC1473AQ	0261
2SC1473AQH	0261
2SC1473AR	0261
2SC1473C	0261
2SC1473CN	0261
2SC1473N	0261
2SC1473NC	0261
2SC1473NC(P)	0261
2SC1473NC(Q)	0261
2SC1473NC(R)	0261
2SC1473NC-P	0261
2SC1473NC-Q	0261
2SC1473NCQ	0261
2SC1473NCQR	0261
2SC1473NC-R	0261
2SC1473NCR	0261
2SC1473NE	0261
2SC1473P	0261
2SC1473Q	0261
2SC1473QNC	0261
2SC1473QR	0261
2SC1473QRNC	0261
2SC1473R	0261
2SC1473RNC	0261
2SC1474	0018
2SC1474-3	0018
2SC1474-4	0018
2SC1474J	0018
2SC1474S	0018
2SC1475	1967
2SC1475(13)	1967
2SC1475-13	1967
2SC1475A	1967
2SC1475D	1967
2SC1475H	1967
2SC1475K	1967
2SC1477	0359
2SC1478	0224
2SC1478A	0224
2SC1479	0414
2SC1480	OEM

DEVICE TYPE	REPL CODE
2SC1481	OEM
2SC1482	2319
2SC1485	0710
2SC1486	OEM
2SC1487	OEM
2SC1488	OEM
2SC1489	OEM
2SC1490	2156
2SC1491	1189
2SC1492	1966
2SC1493	0710
2SC1493NC	0710
2SC1493P4	0710
2SC1494	1963
2SC1495	OEM
2SC1498	OEM
2SC1499	OEM
2SC1500	OEM
2SC1501	0275
2SC1501(Q)	0275
2SC1501(R)	0275
2SC1501P	0275
2SC1501Q	0275
2SC1501R	0275
2SC1502L	0168
2SC1504	2085
2SC1504E	OEM
2SC1505	0949
2SC1505(1)	0949
2SC1505(1)K	0949
2SC1505(1)L	0949
2SC1505(I)	0949
2SC1505(K)	0949
2SC1505-1	0949
2SC1505A	0949
2SC1505H(LB)	0949
2SC1505I	0949
2SC1505K	0949
2SC1505L	0949
2SC1505LA	0949
2SC1505M	6105
2SC1506	0168
2SC1506K	0168
2SC1506L	0168
2SC1506M	0168
2SC1507	0949
2SC1507(1)K	OEM
2SC1507(1)L	OEM
2SC1507(1)M	OEM
2SC1507(2)	OEM
2SC1507(K)	0949
2SC1507(L)	0949
2SC1507-1	OEM
2SC1507-K	0949
2SC1507-L	0949
2SC1507-O	0949
2SC1507-Y	0949
2SC1507H	0949
2SC1507J	0949
2SC1507K	0949
2SC1507K,L,M	0949
2SC1507L	0949
2SC1507LK	0949
2SC1507M	0949
2SC1507Y	0949
2SC1509	0320
2SC1509-O	0320
2SC1509NC	0320
2SC1509O	0320
2SC1509Q	0320
2SC1509R	0320
2SC1509Y	0320
2SC1511	OEM
2SC1512	OEM
2SC1513	0414
2SC1514	1077
2SC1514-05	1077
2SC1514-14	1077
2SC1514-15	1077
2SC1514BK	1077
2SC1514BVC	1077
2SC1514CS	1077
2SC1514CS-CVC	1077
2SC1514CVC	1077
2SC1514VC	1077
2SC1515	0710
2SC1515AX	0710
2SC1515C	0710
2SC1515K	0710
2SC1516	1935
2SC1516K	1935
2SC1516K-B	1935
2SC1516KC	1935
2SC1517	1698
2SC1517A	1698
2SC1517AK	1698
2SC1517AKB	1698
2SC1517AKC	1698
2SC1518	0018
2SC1518NC	0018
2SC1519	0168
2SC1520	0168
2SC1520-1	0168
2SC1520C	0168
2SC1520I	0168
2SC1520K	0168
2SC1520K-1	0168
2SC1520L	0168
2SC1520L-1	0168

If replacement code is OEM, contact original manufacturer for replacement.

DEVICE TYPE	REPL CODE
2SC1520M	0168
2SC1520M-1	0168
2SC1521	2343
2SC1521K	2343
2SC1521L	2343
2SC1522	1077
2SC1523	OEM
2SC1524	OEM
2SC1525	OEM
2SC1526	OEM
2SC1529	0259
2SC1533	OEM
2SC1534	OEM
2SC1535	OEM
2SC1536	OEM
2SC1537	0111
2SC1537(S)	0111
2SC1537-0	0111
2SC1537-O	0111
2SC1537B	0111
2SC1538	0111
2SC1538S	0111
2SC1538S(A)	0111
2SC1538SA	0111
2SC1539	0079
2SC1540	0079
2SC1541	0155
2SC1542	0111
2SC1543	0224
2SC1544	0079
2SC1545	0396
2SC1545M	0396
2SC1546	0396
2SC1547	0007
2SC1549	0855
2SC1550	0275
2SC1550(K)	0275
2SC1550(L)	0275
2SC1550(M)	0275
2SC1550-1	0275
2SC1552	2366
2SC1553	0007
2SC1553A	0007
2SC1556	0693
2SC1561	OEM
2SC1562	OEM
2SC1563	OEM
2SC1564	OEM
2SC1565	0558
2SC1565A	OEM
2SC1566	0275
2SC1566F	0275
2SC1567	0558
2SC1567A	0558
2SC1567A-Q	OEM
2SC1567R	0558
2SC1568	1779
2SC1568(R)	1779
2SC1568-R	1779
2SC1568-S	1779
2SC1568R	1779
2SC1568S	1779
2SC1569	0638
2SC1569(FA-2)	OEM
2SC1569(FA-5)	0638
2SC1569(K)	0638
2SC1569-0	0638
2SC1569-O	0638
2SC1569BK	0638
2SC1569FA-1	0638
2SC1569FA-3	0638
2SC1569FA-5	0638
2SC1569FA5	0638
2SC1569K	0638
2SC1569L	0638
2SC1569LB	0638
2SC1569LB-O	OEM
2SC1569LBO	0638
2SC1569LB-R	OEM
2SC1569LBR	0638
2SC1569LB-Y	OEM
2SC1569LBY	0638
2SC15690	0638
2SC1569R	0638
2SC1569Y	0638
2SC1570	0111
2SC1570F	0502
2SC1570FL	0111
2SC1570G	0502
2SC1570GL	0111
2SC1570HL	0111
2SC1570LH	0111
2SC1571	0111
2SC1571F	0502
2SC1571G	0111
2SC1571H	0111
2SC1571L	0111
2SC1571L-F	OEM
2SC1571L-G	OEM
2SC1571L-H	OEM
2SC1572	OEM
2SC1573	0261
2SC1573(P)	0261
2SC1573(Q)	0261
2SC1573(TO126)	0261
2SC1573-0	0261
2SC1573A	0261
2SC1573A(Q)	0261
2SC1573A(R)	0261
2SC1573AH	0261
2SC1573AQ	0261
2SC1573AQH	0261
2SC1573AQR	0261
2SC1573AR	0261
2SC1573B	0261
2SC1573B(R)	0261
2SC1573BR	0261
2SC1573NC	0261
2SC1573NC(Q)	0261
2SC1573NC-Q	0261
2SC1573NC-R	0261
2SC1573P	0261
2SC1573P(TO126)	0261
2SC1573PQ	0261
2SC1573PQ(TO126)	0261
2SC1573Q	0261
2SC1573Q(TO126)	0261
2SC1573QNC	0261
2SC1573QR	0261
2SC1573R	0261
2SC1574	0103
2SC1576	0359
2SC1577	0359
2SC1577A	0359
2SC1578	0359
2SC1579	0359
2SC1580	0359
2SC1581	2296
2SC1582	2296
2SC1583	2395
2SC1583F	2395
2SC1583G	2395
2SC1583H	2395
2SC1584	0538
2SC1585	2398
2SC1585F	2398
2SC1585F,H	2398
2SC1585H	2398
2SC1586	2398
2SC1587	OEM
2SC1588	0414
2SC1589	2039
2SC1592	OEM
2SC1593	OEM
2SC1594	OEM
2SC1595	OEM
2SC1596	0079
2SC1597	0855
2SC1600	OEM
2SC1601	0224
2SC1602	0079
2SC1603	OEM
2SC1604	OEM
2SC1605	1966
2SC1605A	1966
2SC1606	0555
2SC1607	0326
2SC1608	0626
2SC1609	2416
2SC1610	0615
2SC1613	0710
2SC1613A	0710
2SC1614	0710
2SC1615	0710
2SC1617	2420
2SC1618	2421
2SC1618B	2421
2SC1619	0861
2SC1619A	0861
2SC1620-0	OEM
2SC1620-Y	OEM
2SC1621	0144
2SC1621-0	0144
2SC1621B2	0144
2SC1621B3	0144
2SC1621B4	0144
2SC1622	0007
2SC1622A	0007
2SC1622D6	0007
2SC1622D7	0007
2SC1622D8	0007
2SC16220	0007
2SC1622Y	0007
2SC1623	0719
2SC1623(L6)	0719
2SC1623-L5L6	OEM
2SC1623-L6	0719
2SC1623L	OEM
2SC1623L3	0719
2SC1623L4	0719
2SC1623L5	0719
2SC1623L5L6	0719
2SC1623L6	0719
2SC1623L7	0719
2SC1623L51E	0719
2SC1624	0236
2SC1624-0	0236
2SC1624-Y	0236
2SC1625	0236
2SC1625-0	0236
2SC1625-O	0236
2SC1625-Y	0236
2SC1625Y	0236
2SC1625YLBGH	0236
2SC1625YLBGL	0236
2SC1625YLBGL1	0236
2SC1626	0236
2SC1626-0	0236
2SC1626-Y	0236
2SC16260	0236
2SC1626Y	0236
2SC1627	0728
2SC1627(Y)	0728
2SC1627-0	0728
2SC1627-Y	0728
2SC1627-Y(FA)	0728
2SC1627-YFA	0728
2SC1627A	0728
2SC1627AO	0728
2SC1627A-Y	0728
2SC1627AY	0728
2SC1627Y	0728
2SC1627Y(FA)	0728
2SC1628	0264
2SC1628-0	0264
2SC1628-Y	0264
2SC1628-Y.JA	0264
2SC1629	0130
2SC1629A	0130
2SC1629A(O)	0130
2SC1629A(R)	0130
2SC1629AO	0130
2SC1629AR	0130
2SC1629M	0130
2SC1629R	0130
2SC1630	0233
2SC1631	0018
2SC1632	0284
2SC1633	2437
2SC1634	2440
2SC1634-7	0076
2SC1635	0086
2SC1636	2441
2SC1636(22)	2441
2SC1637	0111
2SC1638	0414
2SC1639	0016
2SC1640	2446
2SC1641	0016
2SC1641Q	0016
2SC1641R	0016
2SC1642	0111
2SC1643	0155
2SC1644	0155
2SC1645	0396
2SC1645B	0396
2SC1646	0396
2SC1646A	0396
2SC1646B	0396
2SC1647	0111
2SC1647Q	0111
2SC1647RY	0111
2SC1648	0111
2SC1648E	0111
2SC1648EF	0111
2SC1648SH	0111
2SC1649	0710
2SC1650	0710
2SC1651	0710
2SC-1652	2452
2SC1652	2452
2SC1652(Q)	2452
2SC1652(R)	2452
2SC1652-0	2452
2SC1652-Q	2452
2SC1652M	2452
2SC1652Q	5784
2SC1652QY	2452
2SC1652R	2452
2SC1652RE	2452
2SC1652RQ	2452
2SC1652S	2452
2SC1653	0855
2SC1653N2	0855
2SC1653N3	0855
2SC1653N4	0855
2SC1654	0855
2SC1654N5	0855
2SC1654N6	0855
2SC1654N7	0855
2SC1655	OEM
2SC1655A	OEM
2SC1657	OEM
2SC1658	OEM
2SC1658(C)	0577
2SC1658(R)	0577
2SC1659	OEM
2SC1661	OEM
2SC1662	OEM
2SC1663	0264
2SC1663H	0264
2SC1664	0625
2SC1664A	0625
2SC16640	0625
2SC1664OR	0625
2SC1664Q	0625
2SC1664R	0625
2SC1665	0259
2SC1666	0359
2SC1667	0103
2SC1668	1966
2SC1669	0388
2SC1669-0	0388
2SC1669-R	0388
2SC1669-Y	0388
2SC1670	2463
2SC1670H	2463
2SC1670J	2463
2SC1670JA	2463
2SC1670JD	2463
2SC1670JW	2463
2SC1672	2465
2SC1673	OEM
2SC1674	1060
2SC1674(L)	1060
2SC1674(M)	1060
2SC1674-M	1060
2SC1674AL	1060
2SC1674K	1060
2SC1674L	1060
2SC1674M	1060
2SC1675	0076
2SC1675B	0076
2SC1675K	0076
2SC1675L	0076
2SC1675L1	OEM
2SC1675L1TA	OEM
2SC1675L-FM	OEM
2SC1675M	0076
2SC1676	1963
2SC1678	2475
2SC1678E	2475
2SC1679	0830
2SC1680	OEM
2SC1681	1746
2SC1681-BL	1746
2SC1681-GR	1746
2SC1681A	1746
2SC1681B	1746
2SC1681B6	1746
2SC1681BL	1746
2SC1681C	1746
2SC1681F	1746
2SC1681G	1746
2SC1681GN	1746
2SC1681GR	1746
2SC1681H	1746
2SC1681J	1746
2SC1681K	1746
2SC1681L	1746
2SC1681M	1746
2SC1681O	1746
2SC1681OR	1746
2SC1681R	1746
2SC1681V	1746
2SC1682	0111
2SC1682-BL	0111
2SC1682-GR	0111
2SC1682V	0111
2SC1683	0388
2SC1683(LB)	0388
2SC1683(LB)P	0388
2SC1683(LB)Q	0388
2SC1683-0	0388
2SC1683-O	0388
2SC1683-Q	0388
2SC1683A	0388
2SC1683LA	0388
2SC1683LB	0388
2SC1683LD	0388
2SC1683LDP	0388
2SC1683LDQ	0388
2SC1683P	0388
2SC1683Q	0388
2SC1683Q(LB)	0388
2SC1683R	0388
2SC1684	0155
2SC1684(Q)	0155
2SC1684(QR)	0155
2SC1684(Q.R)	0155
2SC1684(R)	0155
2SC1684(S)	0155
2SC1684(T)	0155
2SC1684-P	0155
2SC1684-Q	0155
2SC1684-Q.R	0155
2SC1684-R	0155
2SC1684-S	0155
2SC1684A(Q)	0155
2SC1684A(R)	0155
2SC1684A(S)	0155
2SC1684BL	0155
2SC1684H(R)	0155
2SC1684HE	0155
2SC1684K	0155
2SC1684P	0155
2SC1684Q	0155
2SC1684QR	0155
2SC1684QRS	0155
2SC1684R	0155
2SC1684RSTTA	OEM
2SC1684S	0155
2SC1684T	0155
2SC1685	0284
2SC1685(C)	0284
2SC1685(Q)	0284
2SC1685(R)	0284
2SC1685(S)	0284
2SC1685-0	0284
2SC1685-P	0284
2SC1685-PQR	0284
2SC1685-Q	0284
2SC1685-QR	0284
2SC1685-QRS	0284
2SC1685-R	0284
2SC1685-RS	0284
2SC1685-S	0284
2SC1685A(Q)	0284
2SC1685A(R)	0284
2SC1685A(S)	0284
2SC1685AQR	OEM
2SC1685AQRS	0379
2SC1685C	0284
2SC1685CR	0284
2SC1685CR-Q	0284
2SC1685NCQRS	OEM
2SC1685P	0284
2SC1685PQ	0284
2SC1685PQR	0284
2SC1685PQR(M)	0284
2SC1685PR	0284
2SC1685Q	0284
2SC1685QL	0284
2SC1685QR	0284
2SC1685QRS	0284
2SC1685R	0284
2SC1685RS	0284
2SC1685RST	0284
2SC1685S	0284
2SC1685ST	0284
2SC1685T	0284
2SC1685TAQR	0284
2SC1685TAQRS	0284
2SC1686	0224
2SC1686B	0224
2SC1686V	0224
2SC1687	0224
2SC1688	0016
2SC1688D	OEM
2SC1689	2485
2SC1698	OEM
2SC1703	OEM
2SC1706	0710
2SC1706H	0710
2SC1707	0016
2SC1707A	0016
2SC1707AH	0016
2SC1707AHB	0016
2SC1707H	0016
2SC1707HB	0016
2SC1707HC	0016
2SC1707HD	0016
2SC1708	0525
2SC1708A	0525
2SC1709	0079
2SC1711	OEM
2SC1711A	OEM
2SC1717	0626
2SC1718	OEM
2SC1719	0855
2SC1720	0855
2SC1721	0018
2SC1722	1077
2SC1722BK	1077
2SC1722BKS	1077
2SC1722S	1077
2SC1723	1077
2SC1723-02	1077
2SC1723A	1077
2SC1724	0626
2SC1725	OEM
2SC1726	OEM
2SC1727	2503
2SC1728	1165
2SC1728-3	1165
2SC1728D	1165
2SC1728F	1165
2SC1728H	1165
2SC1729	2504
2SC1730	0127
2SC1730K	0127
2SC1730L	0127
2SC1731	OEM
2SC1732	OEM
2SC1733	OEM
2SC1734	0016
2SC1734H	0016
2SC1735	0284
2SC1736	0111
2SC1737	0111
2SC1738	0111
2SC1739	0016
2SC1740	0151
2SC1740(Q)	0151
2SC1740(Q)-L	0151
2SC1740(Q)-Y	0151
2SC1740(Q)Y	0151
2SC1740(QR)-T	0151
2SC1740(R)	0151
2SC1740(R)-L	0151
2SC1740(R)-Y	0151
2SC1740(R)Y	0151
2SC1740(S)	0151
2SC1740-E	OEM
2SC1740-Q	0151
2SC1740-R	0151
2SC1740-S	0151
2SC1740-T-93-R	0151
2SC1740-T-93-S	0151
2SC1740-Y	0151
2SC1740C	0151
2SC1740D	0151
2SC1740EF	0151
2SC1740FF	0151
2SC1740HF	0151
2SC1740JF	0151
2SC1740L	0151
2SC1740LN	0151
2SC1740LNCS	0151
2SC1740LN-E	OEM
2SC1740LNE	0151
2SC1740LN-R	OEM
2SC1740LN-S	OEM
2SC1740LNS	0151
2SC1740LNT	OEM
2SC1740LN-Z	OEM
2SC1740P	0151
2SC1740Q	0151
2SC1740QH	0151
2SC1740QJ	0151
2SC1740QN	0151
2SC1740QP	0151
2SC1740QQ	0151
2SC1740QR	0151
2SC1740QU	0151
2SC1740QV	0151
2SC1740QW	0151
2SC1740QZ	0151
2SC1740R	0151
2SC1740RE	0151
2SC1740RH	0151
2SC1740RL	0151
2SC1740RM	0151
2SC1740RQ	0151
2SC1740RR	0151
2SC1740RS	0151
2SC1740RS(RS)	0151
2SC1740RS(S)	0151
2SC1740RS-TB	0151
2SC1740RU	0151
2SC1740RV	0151
2SC1740RZ	0151
2SC1740S	0151
2SC1740S(Q)	0151
2SC1740S(Q)Y	0151
2SC1740S(QR)	0151
2SC1740S(QR)-T	0151
2SC1740S(QR)-Y	0151
2SC1740S(QRS)	0151
2SC1740S(R)	0151
2SC1740S(R)Y	0151
2SC1740S(RS)	0151
2SC1740S(S)	0151
2SC1740S(S35)	0151
2SC1740S,B40	0151
2SC1740S-E	0151
2SC1740SE	0151
2SC1740SED	0151
2SC1740SEE	0151
2SC1740SEH	0151
2SC1740SER	0151
2SC1740SES	0151
2SC1740SEY	0151
2SC1740SLNST	OEM
2SC1740S-Q	0151
2SC1740SQ	0151
2SC1740SQA	0151
2SC1740S-QF	0151
2SC1740SQR	0151
2SC1740SQT	0151
2SC1740SQY	0151
2SC1740S-R	0151
2SC1740SR	0151
2SC1740SRC	0151
2SC1740SRF	0151
2SC1740SRJ	0151
2SC1740SRK	0151
2SC1740SRM	0151
2SC1740SRP	0151
2SC1740SRQ	0151
2SC1740SRR	0151
2SC1740S-RS	0151
2SC1740SRS	0151
2SC1740S-RSF	OEM
2SC1740SRT	0151
2SC1740SRY	0151
2SC1740S-S	0151
2SC1740S-SF	OEM
2SC1740SSJ	0151
2SC1740SSK	0151
2SC1740SSN	0151
2SC1740SSS	0151
2SC1740SST	0151
2SC1740SSU	0151
2SC1740SSX	0151
2SC1740SSZ	0151
2SC1740ST-93	0151
2SC1740TPQ	0151
2SC1740TPR	0151
2SC1740TPS	0151
2SC1740XTPQ	0151
2SC1740XTPQR	0151
2SC1740XTPQS	0151
2SC1740XTPR	0151
2SC1740XTPS	0151
2SC1740Z	OEM
2SC1741	1505
2SC1741A	1505
2SC1741AP	1505
2SC1741AQ	1505
2SC1741P	1505
2SC1741Q	1505
2SC1741QR	1505
2SC1741R	1505
2SC1741S	1505
2SC1741SQ	1505
2SC1741SR	1505
2SC1742	OEM
2SC1743	0261
2SC1743NCR	0261
2SC1744	OEM
2SC1745	OEM
2SC1746	OEM
2SC1746A	0079
2SC1747	2503
2SC1748	0187
2SC1748Q	0187
2SC1748R	0187
2SC1749	1077
2SC1749XD	1077
2SC1752	0710
2SC1753	0710
2SC1755	1077
2SC1755C	1077
2SC1755D	1077
2SC1755E	1077
2SC1756	0638
2SC1756(C)	0638
2SC1756(D)	0638
2SC1756(E)	0638
2SC1756-0	0638
2SC1756-F	0638
2SC1756C	0638
2SC1756C,D,E	0638
2SC1756D	0638
2SC1756E	0638
2SC1756HP	0638
2SC1756K	0638
2SC1756M	0638
2SC1756M-C	OEM
2SC1756M-D	OEM
2SC1756M-E	OEM
2SC1757	1077
2SC1758	0283
2SC1760	1935
2SC1760-2	1935
2SC1760-3	1935
2SC1760H	1935
2SC1760K	1935
2SC1761	1935
2SC1761KJ	1935
2SC1761LE	1935
2SC1761MC	1935
2SC1762-1	OEM
2SC1762-2	OEM
2SC1763	2522
2SC1764	2523
2SC1765	0626
2SC1766	0376
2SC1766B	0376
2SC1768	2526
2SC1769	2528
2SC1770	0079
2SC1771	0016
2SC1772	0111
2SC1773	2534
2SC1774	0079
2SC1775	0525
2SC1775A	0525
2SC1775AE	0525
2SC1775E	0525
2SC1775F	0525
2SC1776	0079
2SC1777	2534
2SC1778	0224
2SC1779	0224
2SC1780	0086
2SC1781	0016
2SC1781H	0016
2SC1781HA	0016
2SC1781HB	0016
2SC1781HC	0016
2SC1782	0861
2SC1783	0861
2SC1784	0538
2SC1785	2398
2SC1786	2398
2SC1787	1260
2SC1788	0155
2SC1788A	0155
2SC1788R	0155
2SC1789	0007
2SC1790	0259
2SC1790JD	0259
2SC1791	0142
2SC1792	OEM
2SC1797	OEM
2SC1798	OEM
2SC1799	OEM
2SC1800	OEM
2SC1801	0259
2SC1802	0224
2SC1803	OEM
2SC1804	OEM
2SC1805	OEM
2SC1806	OEM
2SC1807	0488
2SC1808	OEM
2SC1809	0127
2SC1810	2575
2SC1810HU	2575
2SC1810J	2575
2SC1810JL	2575

If replacement code is OEM, contact original manufacturer for replacement.

DEVICE TYPE	REPL CODE
2SC1811	0261
2SC1811-1	0261
2SC1811-2	0261
2SC1811KC	0261
2SC1812	OEM
2SC1812-P	OEM
2SC1813	0016
2SC-1815	0076
2SC1815	0076
2SC1815(FA)	OEM
2SC1815(G)	0076
2SC1815(G)-T	0076
2SC1815(GR)	0076
2SC1815(GR)L	0076
2SC1815(GR)-Y	0076
2SC1815(GR)Y	0076
2SC1815(O)	0076
2SC1815(Y)	0076
2SC1815(Y)L	0076
2SC1815(Y)Y	0076
2SC1815(Y,GR)Y	0076
2SC1815(YG)	0076
2SC1815(YG)-T	0076
2SC1815-0	0076
2SC1815-BL	0076
2SC1815-GR	0076
2SC1815-GR(FA)	0076
2SC1815-GRFA	0076
2SC1815-O	0076
2SC1815-OFA	0076
2SC1815-Y	0076
2SC1815-Y(FA)	0076
2SC1815-YFA	0076
2SC1815BL	0076
2SC1815FA	0076
2SC1815G	0076
2SC1815GR	0076
2SC1815GR(FA-2)	OEM
2SC1815N(GR)	0076
2SC1815N-BL	0076
2SC1815NEW-BL	0076
2SC1815NEW-GR	0076
2SC1815NEW-O	0076
2SC1815NEW-Y	0076
2SC1815N-GR	0076
2SC1815N-Y	0076
2SC1815O	0076
2SC1815TPE2	0076
2SC-1815Y	0076
2SC1815Y	0076
2SC1815Y(FA)	0076
2SC1815Y(GR)	0076
2SC1816	2475
2SC1816H	2475
2SC1816HL	2475
2SC1817	0830
2SC1818	0177
2SC1819	0638
2SC1819M	0638
2SC1819MIS	0638
2SC1819ML	0638
2SC1819MR	0638
2SC1819RL	0638
2SC1820	0233
2SC1821	OEM
2SC1822	OEM
2SC1823	OEM
2SC1824	OEM
2SC1825	OEM
2SC1826	0419
2SC1826(P)	0419
2SC1826(Q)	0419
2SC1826(R)	0419
2SC1826(Y)	0419
2SC1826-0	0419
2SC1826-G	0419
2SC1826-O	0419
2SC1826-Y	0419
2SC1826D	0419
2SC1826G	0419
2SC1826O	0419
2SC1826P	0419
2SC1826Q	0419
2SC1826R	0419
2SC1826Y	0419
2SC1827	0236
2SC1827(Y)	0236
2SC1828	2085
2SC1828B	2085
2SC1828R	2085
2SC1829	2596
2SC1829(FA-2)	OEM
2SC1829C	2596
2SC1829FA-1	2596
2SC1830	0538
2SC1831	0556
2SC1832	2602
2SC1833	0284
2SC1834	0284
2SC1835	OEM
2SC1836	0930
2SC1837	OEM
2SC1838	OEM
2SC1840	0111
2SC1840E	0111
2SC1840F	0111
2SC1840P	0111
2SC1841	0525
2SC1841(E)	0525

DEVICE TYPE	REPL CODE
2SC1841E	0525
2SC1841F	0525
2SC1841FE	0525
2SC1841FP	0525
2SC1841P	0525
2SC1841Q	0525
2SC1841R	0525
2SC1841U	0525
2SC1842	0111
2SC1842E	0111
2SC1843	0111
2SC1844	0111
2SC1844E	0111
2SC1844F	0111
2SC1845	0525
2SC1845(E)	0525
2SC1845(U)	0525
2SC1845E	0525
2SC1845EF	0525
2SC1845F	0525
2SC1845Q	0525
2SC1845R	0525
2SC1845S	0525
2SC1845U	0525
2SC1846	0781
2SC1846(Q)	0781
2SC1846(R)	0781
2SC1846-Q	OEM
2SC1846-R	0781
2SC1846-S	0781
2SC1846B	0781
2SC1846P	0781
2SC1846Q	0781
2SC1846Q/R/S	0781
2SC1846QRS	0781
2SC1846R	0781
2SC1846RS	0781
2SC1846RSLB	0781
2SC1846RSRL	0781
2SC1846S	0781
2SC1847	0558
2SC1847(Q)	0558
2SC1847(R)	0558
2SC1847-O	0558
2SC1847A	0558
2SC1847B	0558
2SC1847C	0558
2SC1847D	0558
2SC1847E	0558
2SC1847F	0558
2SC1847G	0558
2SC1847GN	0558
2SC1847LG	0558
2SC1847NV	0558
2SC1847P	0558
2SC1847Q	0558
2SC1847R	0558
2SC1847V	0558
2SC1847V(Q)	0558
2SC1847V(R)	0558
2SC1847VG	0558
2SC1847VQ	0558
2SC1847VR	0558
2SC1847X	0558
2SC1847Y	0558
2SC1848	0219
2SC1848(Q)	0219
2SC1848(R)	0219
2SC1848P	0219
2SC1848Q	0219
2SC1848R	0219
2SC1848V	0219
2SC1849	0079
2SC1850	0079
2SC1851	0079
2SC1852	0079
2SC1853	1211
2SC1853B	1211
2SC1853C	1211
2SC1854	0284
2SC1854C	0284
2SC1854R	0284
2SC1854S	0284
2SC1855	0224
2SC1856	0224
2SC1856-02	0224
2SC1856M	0224
2SC1857	0079
2SC1859	0626
2SC1860	2626
2SC1861	2626
2SC1862	0187
2SC1863	0424
2SC1864	0424
2SC1864A	0424
2SC1865	0723
2SC1866	0615
2SC1867	1955
2SC1867A	1955
2SC1868	1955
2SC1869	0615
2SC1870	2398
2SC1871	1955
2SC1871A	1955
2SC1872	OEM
2SC1873	OEM
2SC1874	OEM
2SC1875	2636
2SC1875(K)	2636

DEVICE TYPE	REPL CODE
2SC1875K	2636
2SC1875L	2636
2SC1875R	2636
2SC1876	OEM
2SC1879	OEM
2SC1880	OEM
2SC1880K	OEM
2SC1881	1203
2SC1881K	1203
2SC1882	OEM
2SC1883	OEM
2SC1883K	OEM
2SC1884	OEM
2SC1885	0261
2SC1886	0259
2SC1887	0259
2SC1888	0626
2SC-1890	0525
2SC1890	0525
2SC1890(E)	0525
2SC1890A	0525
2SC1890A(D)	0525
2SC1890A(E)	0525
2SC1890A(E)L.P.F.	0525
2SC1890A-D	0525
2SC1890AD	0525
2SC1890A-E	0525
2SC1890AE	0525
2SC1890A-EV	0525
2SC1890A-F	OEM
2SC1890AF	0525
2SC1890AL	0525
2SC1890D	0525
2SC-1890E	0525
2SC1890E	0525
2SC1890F	0525
2SC1890F(E)	0525
2SC1890P	0525
2SC1891	0223
2SC1892	2636
2SC1893	2643
2SC1893-O	2643
2SC1893FA-1	2643
2SC1894	0309
2SC1894(ARV)	0309
2SC1894K	0309
2SC1894N	0309
2SC1895	0309
2SC1896	0309
2SC1897	0086
2SC1898	0008
2SC1899	0008
2SC1900	0525
2SC1901	0414
2SC1902	2030
2SC1903	0558
2SC1904	0558
2SC1905	0949
2SC1905(1)	0949
2SC1905(H)B	0949
2SC1905(H)L	0949
2SC1905(LB)	0949
2SC1905(M)	0949
2SC1905H	0949
2SC1905H(LB)	0949
2SC1905HLB	0949
2SC1905LB	0949
2SC1905M	0949
2SC-1906	0127
2SC1906	0127
2SC1906-T	0127
2SC1906-Y	0127
2SC1906F	0127
2SC1907	0127
2SC1908	2654
2SC1908E	2654
2SC1908H	2654
2SC1909	0930
2SC1909K	0930
2SC1909R	0930
2SC1913	0388
2SC1913A	0388
2SC1913A(Q)	0388
2SC1913A(R)	0388
2SC1913AQ	3084
2SC1913AR	0388
2SC1914	0525
2SC1914A	0525
2SC1915	0525
2SC1915-T	OEM
2SC1916	1967
2SC1917	1967
2SC1918	1967
2SC1919	0127
2SC1919C	0127
2SC1921	0261
2SC1921-03	0261
2SC1922	2643
2SC1923	2666
2SC1923(O)	2666
2SC1923(Y)	2666
2SC1923-0	2666
2SC1923-02	OEM
2SC1923-O	2666
2SC1923A	2666
2SC1923BN	2666
2SC1923R	1489
2SC1923Y	2666
2SC1924	OEM

DEVICE TYPE	REPL CODE
2SC1925	OEM
2SC1926	OEM
2SC1927	OEM
2SC1928	1967
2SC1929	0168
2SC1929(Q)	0168
2SC1929(R)	0168
2SC1929LB	0168
2SC1929Q	0168
2SC1929R	0168
2SC1940	0079
2SC1941	1317
2SC1941-OY	1317
2SC1941K	1317
2SC1941L	1317
2SC1941M	1317
2SC1942	2636
2SC1942-03	2636
2SC1942-10	2636
2SC1942-10/03	0048
2SC1943	OEM
2SC1944	0830
2SC1945	0830
2SC1946	2504
2SC1946A	2504
2SC1947	2677
2SC1948	OEM
2SC1948-1	OEM
2SC1948-2	OEM
2SC1948-5	OEM
2SC1949	OEM
2SC1950	OEM
2SC1951	1376
2SC1952	OEM
2SC1953	0558
2SC1954	0127
2SC1955	2677
2SC1956	0626
2SC1957	2684
2SC1957K	2684
2SC1958Y	OEM
2SC1959	0284
2SC1959(Y)	0284
2SC1959(Y)-T	0284
2SC1959(Y)-Y	0284
2SC1959-O	0284
2SC1959-Y	0284
2SC1959-Y(FA)	0284
2SC1959-YFA	0284
2SC1959GR	0284
2SC1959NEW-Y	0284
2SC1959Y	0284
2SC1959Y(FA)	0284
2SC1960	0284
2SC1961	0224
2SC1962	0334
2SC1962-O	0334
2SC1963	1935
2SC1963-1	1935
2SC1963Y	1935
2SC1964	2475
2SC1964D	2475
2SC1965	2677
2SC1965A	2677
2SC1966	OEM
2SC1967	OEM
2SC1968	OEM
2SC1968A	OEM
2SC1969	0830
2SC1969B	0830
2SC1969BH	0830
2SC1969H	0830
2SC1970	2693
2SC1971	2693
2SC1972	2694
2SC1973	0018
2SC1974	0830
2SC1974C	0830
2SC1975	0930
2SC1976	2699
2SC1977	OEM
2SC1978	2693
2SC1980	1260
2SC1980(S)	1260
2SC1980(T)	1260
2SC1980R	1260
2SC1980S	1260
2SC1980T	1260
2SC1981	OEM
2SC1982	0264
2SC-1983	2047
2SC1983	2047
2SC1983(O)	2047
2SC1983(R)	2047
2SC1983(Y)	2047
2SC1983-O	2047
2SC1983D	2047
2SC1983K	2047
2SC1983O	2047
2SC1983P	2303
2SC1983Q	2047
2SC1983R	2047
2SC1983Y	2047
2SC1984	1203
2SC1985	0419
2SC1986	0477
2SC1987	0424
2SC1989	0007
2SC1990	0127

DEVICE TYPE	REPL CODE
2SC1990B	0127
2SC1991	0079
2SC1992	0016
2SC1993	0016
2SC1994	0016
2SC1995	0016
2SC1996	0016
2SC1997	0016
2SC1998	0079
2SC1999	0111
2SC2000	0284
2SC2000L	0284
2SC2001	1505
2SC2001(L)	1505
2SC2001-L	1505
2SC2001F	1505
2SC2001G	1505
2SC2001I	1505
2SC2001K	1505
2SC2001KTA	OEM
2SC2001L	1505
2SC2001L1	1505
2SC2001LK	1505
2SC2001M	1505
2SC2001R	1505
2SC-2002	0945
2SC2002	0945
2SC2002(K)	0945
2SC2002(L)	0945
2SC2002(M)	0945
2SC2002-L	0945
2SC2002-M	0945
2SC2002B	0945
2SC2002K	0945
2SC2002L	0945
2SC2002M	0945
2SC2002Y	OEM
2SC2003	0284
2SC2003K	0284
2SC2008	OEM
2SC2009	0224
2SC2010	0224
2SC2011	0224
2SC2011L	0224
2SC2012	2730
2SC2013	0224
2SC2014	1376
2SC2017	1841
2SC2018	1841
2SC2019	1841
2SC2020	0930
2SC-2021	1132
2SC2021	1132
2SC2021-Q	1132
2SC2021-R	1132
2SC2021E	1132
2SC2021F	OEM
2SC2021L	1132
2SC2021LN	1132
2SC2021LR	OEM
2SC2021LS	OEM
2SC2021M	1132
2SC2021M(Q)	1132
2SC2021M(R)	1132
2SC2021M(S)	1132
2SC2021MLN	1132
2SC2021MQR	1132
2SC2021M-QRS	1132
2SC2021MQRS	1132
2SC2021M-R	OEM
2SC2021MR	1132
2SC2021MRS	1132
2SC2021M-S	OEM
2SC2021MS	1132
2SC2021P	1132
2SC2021Q	1132
2SC2021R	1132
2SC2021RJ	1132
2SC2021RS	1132
2SC2021S	1132
2SC2021SE	OEM
2SC2021Y	1132
2SC2022	0949
2SC2023	2589
2SC2024	1581
2SC2025	0259
2SC2026	1795
2SC2026K	1795
2SC2027	0309
2SC2028	0884
2SC2028-B/20	0884
2SC2028B	0884
2SC2028B/20	0884
2SC2028B20	0884
2SC2028D	0884
2SC2028L	0884
2SC2029	0930
2SC2029/1	0930
2SC2029/3	0930
2SC2029-1	0930
2SC2029-3	0930
2SC2029-B/10	0930
2SC2029B	0930
2SC2029B/10	0930
2SC2029B10	0930
2SC2029C	0930
2SC2031	OEM
2SC2032	OEM
2SC2033	OEM

DEVICE TYPE	REPL CODE
2SC2034	2742
2SC2035	0079
2SC2036	0558
2SC2037	2743
2SC2038	OEM
2SC2039	OEM
2SC2040	2747
2SC2043	0830
2SC2044	OEM
2SC2050	0930
2SC2051	0284
2SC2053	0079
2SC2055	0079
2SC2056	2677
2SC2057	0224
2SC2057-C	0224
2SC2057C	0224
2SC2057D	0224
2SC2057E	0224
2SC2057E1	0224
2SC2057F	0224
2SC2058	0284
2SC2058(P)	0284
2SC2058P-SP	OEM
2SC2058PZ	0284
2SC2058Q	6055
2SC2058Q-SP	OEM
2SC2058QZ	0284
2SC2058S	0284
2SC2058S-P	0284
2SC2058Z	OEM
2SC2059	0719
2SC2059K	0719
2SC2059KN	0719
2SC2060	0018
2SC2060(Q)	0018
2SC2060(R)	0018
2SC2060-O	OEM
2SC2060K	0018
2SC2060Q	0018
2SC2060QC	0018
2SC2060QZ	0018
2SC2060R	0018
2SC2060RD	0018
2SC2060RQ	0018
2SC2060RZ	0018
2SC2060Y	OEM
2SC2061	0320
2SC2061QU	OEM
2SC2062	2770
2SC2063	0577
2SC2063M	0577
2SC2063P	0577
2SC2065	OEM
2SC2066	OEM
2SC2067	1967
2SC-2068	0638
2SC2068	0638
2SC2068(FA-1)	0638
2SC2068(LB)	0638
2SC2068-GS-1	0638
2SC2068-LB	0638
2SC2068-O	OEM
2SC2068BK	0638
2SC2068BKLB	0638
2SC2068BXLB	0638
2SC2068FA-1	0638
2SC2068GS-1	0638
2SC-2068LB	0638
2SC2068LB	0638
2SC2068LBBK	0638
2SC2068R	6105
2SC2068S	6105
2SC2068Y	OEM
2SC2069	0016
2SC2070	0016
2SC2071	0275
2SC2072	OEM
2SC2072-1	OEM
2SC2072-2	OEM
2SC2073	1274
2SC2073(B)	1274
2SC2073(C)	1274
2SC2073(FA-1)	1274
2SC2073(FA-3)	1274
2SC2073-AR(D)	1274
2SC2073-AR(E)	1274
2SC2073-B	1274
2SC2073-C	1274
2SC2073-LBGL2	1274
2SC2073-Z	1274
2SC2073A	1274
2SC2073A-D	OEM
2SC2073AD	1274
2SC2073A-E	OEM
2SC2073AE	1274
2SC2073AR	OEM
2SC2073AR-D	OEM
2SC2073AR-E	OEM
2SC2073B	1274
2SC2073BGS2	1274
2SC2073BGSC	1274
2SC2073BLGL2	1274
2SC2073C	1274
2SC2073D	1274
2SC2073E	1274
2SC2073FA-1	1274
2SC2073FA-4	1274
2SC2073GL2	1274

DEVICE TYPE	REPL CODE
2SC2073J	1274
2SC2073L	1274
2SC2073LB	1274
2SC2073LBGL	1274
2SC2073LBGL2	1274
2SC2073LBGS2	1274
2SC2073LBL2	1274
2SC2073R	1274
2SC2073R(D)	1274
2SC2073R(E)	1274
2SC2073R-D	OEM
2SC2073RD	1274
2SC2073R-E	OEM
2SC2073RE	1274
2SC2073SO	1274
2SC2073T	1274
2SC2073Y	1274
2SC2073Z	3084
2SC2074	1973
2SC2074C	1973
2SC2074Y	1973
2SC2075	2475
2SC2076	2787
2SC2076B	2787
2SC2076C	2787
2SC2076CB	2787
2SC2076CD	2787
2SC2076D	2787
2SC2078	2475
2SC2079	1581
2SC2079E	1581
2SC2080	0161
2SC2081	2794
2SC2082	OEM
2SC2083	OEM
2SC2085	0638
2SC2085P	0638
2SC2085Q	0638
2SC2086	2798
2SC2087	0079
2SC2088	1553
2SC2089	0525
2SC2091	1581
2SC2092	0930
2SC2093	0830
2SC2094	2504
2SC2097	OEM
2SC2098	0830
2SC2099	2808
2SC2100	2296
2SC2101	1189
2SC2102	1224
2SC2103	1963
2SC2103A	1963
2SC2104	OEM
2SC2105	1410
2SC2106	OEM
2SC2107	0079
2SC2107G3	0079
2SC2108	OEM
2SC2109	0079
2SC2110	0086
2SC2111	0016
2SC2113	0558
2SC2114	OEM
2SC2115	2817
2SC2116	OEM
2SC2117	2677
2SC2118	2677
2SC2119	OEM
2SC2120	0860
2SC2120(Y)	0860
2SC2120-0	0860
2SC2120-O	0860
2SC2120-Y	0860
2SC2120FA	0860
2SC-2120Y	0860
2SC2120Y	0860
2SC2120Y-FA	OEM
2SC2120YFA	0860
2SC2121	0359
2SC2122	0359
2SC2122A	0359
2SC2123	0065
2SC2124	2820
2SC2125	2820
2SC2126	0178
2SC2126A	0178
2SC2127	0538
2SC2127A	0538
2SC2128	OEM
2SC2128A	OEM
2SC2129	1967
2SC2130	1967
2SC2131	0187
2SC2132	2825
2SC2133	OEM
2SC2134	OEM
2SC2135	2833
2SC2137	1955
2SC2138	0168
2SC2139	1841
2SC2139A	1841
2SC2140	0074
2SC2141	0264
2SC2141-10	0264
2SC2141KC	0264
2SC2141KD	0264
2SC2141LC	0264

If replacement code is OEM, contact original manufacturer for replacement.

DEVICE TYPE	REPL CODE	DEVICE TYPE	REPL CODE	DEVICE TYPE	REPL CODE	DEVICE TYPE	REPL CODE	DEVICE TYPE	REPL CODE	DEVICE TYPE	REPL CODE	DEVICE TYPE	REPL CODE
2SC2141M	0264	2SC2228A-C	OEM	2SC2253	OEM	2SC2309(E)	0111	2SC2371(K)	0275	2SC2428	0538	2SC2483(Y)	0219
2SC2141NE	0264	2SC2228A-D	OEM	2SC2254	OEM	2SC2309(F)	0111	2SC2371(L)	0275	2SC2429	1841	2SC2483-O	0219
2SC2142	OEM	2SC2228A-E	OEM	2SC2255	OEM	2SC2309D	0111	2SC2371(N)-L	0275	2SC2429A	1841	2SC2483-R	0219
2SC2143	2817	2SC2228C	1317	2SC2256	2398	2SC2309E	0111	2SC2371(P)-L	0275	2SC2430	0615	2SC2483-Y	0219
2SC2144	OEM	2SC2228D	1317	2SC2257	0275	2SC2309F	0111	2SC2371K	0275	2SC2431	0615	2SC24830	0219
2SC2145	0693	2SC2228E	1317	2SC2257A	0275	2SC2309L	0111	2SC2371L	0275	2SC2432	0615	2SC2483R	0219
2SC2146	0930	2SC2228F	1317	2SC2258	0275	2SC2310	0284	2SC2371M	0275	2SC2433	2416	2SC2483Y	0219
2SC2147	OEM	2SC2228K	1317	2SC2258A	0275	2SC2311	0161	2SC2372(L)	0723	2SC2434	2416	2SC2484	3052
2SC2148	OEM	2SC2228K(D)	1317	2SC2258B	0275	2SC2312	0830	2SC2373	0723	2SC2435	1980	2SC2484P	3052
2SC2149	OEM	2SC2228K(E)	1317	2SC2259	2896	2SC2313	OEM	2SC2373(1)K	0723	2SC2436	2602	2SC2485	3052
2SC2150	OEM	2SC2228K-D	OEM	2SC2259C	2896	2SC2314	1581	2SC2373(1)L	0723	2SC2437	3009	2SC2486	3053
2SC2151	1841	2SC2228K-E	OEM	2SC2259G	2896	2SC2314D	1581	2SC2373(1)M	0723	2SC2438	OEM	2SC2487	0538
2SC2152	OEM	2SC2228M	1317	2SC2260	0177	2SC2315	0419	2SC2373(1)Y	0723	2SC2439	OEM	2SC2488	0538
2SC2153	0079	2SC2228Y	1317	2SC2261	0177	2SC2316	OEM	2SC2373K	0723	2SC2440	0723	2SC2489	0538
2SC2159	OEM	2SC2228Y(E)	1317	2SC2262	0177	2SC2317	0388	2SC2373L	0723	2SC2441	0558	2SC2490	OEM
2SC2160	OEM	2SC-2229	0066	2SC2263	0111	2SC2318	OEM	2SC2373M	0723	2SC2441E	2529	2SC2491	1157
2SC2161	OEM	2SC2229	0066	2SC2264	1967	2SC2319	OEM	2SC2375	0261	2SC2442	OEM	2SC2492	0538
2SC2162	OEM	2SC2229(FA-2)	OEM	2SC2265	0007	2SC2320	0151	2SC2376	0275	2SC2443	OEM	2SC2493	0538
2SC2163	OEM	2SC2229(O)	0066	2SC2266	2900	2SC2320GR	OEM	2SC2377	2208	2SC2443-24	0546	2SC2494	OEM
2SC2164	OEM	2SC2229(Y)	0066	2SC2267	0187	2SC2320L	0151	2SC2377(B)	2208	2SC2444	OEM	2SC2494K	OEM
2SC2165	OEM	2SC2229-0	0066	2SC2267H	0187	2SC2321	0615	2SC2377(C)	2208	2SC2445	OEM	2SC2494M	OEM
2SC2166	2475	2SC2229-C	0066	2SC2270	OEM	2SC2322	0615	2SC2377(CD)	2208	2SC2447	0259	2SC2495	OEM
2SC2167	1274	2SC2229-M	0066	2SC2270B	OEM	2SC2323	0615	2SC2377(D)	2208	2SC2448	3029	2SC2495K	OEM
2SC2167-Y	1274	2SC2229-M(SAN-1)	0066	2SC2271	0261	2SC2324	2942	2SC2377-C	2208	2SC2449	3029	2SC2495M	OEM
2SC2167Y	1274	2SC2229-O	0066	2SC2271(D)	0261	2SC2324K	2942	2SC2377C	2208	2SC2450	1841	2SC2496	OEM
2SC2168	1274	2SC2229-O(FA)	0066	2SC2271(D)-AE	0261	2SC2325	OEM	2SC2377D	2208	2SC2451	1841	2SC2496A	OEM
2SC2168(O)	1274	2SC2229-OY	0066	2SC2271(E)	0261	2SC2326	OEM	2SC2378	1376	2SC2452	3031	2SC2497	0558
2SC2168(Y)	1274	2SC2229-Y	0066	2SC2271(E)-AE	0261	2SC2327	OEM	2SC2379	OEM	2SC2453	3031	2SC2497A	0558
2SC2168-O	1274	2SC2229E	0066	2SC2271(M)	0261	2SC2328	OEM	2SC2380	OEM	2SC2454	OEM	2SC2497Q	0558
2SC2168-O-N03	1274	2SC2229M	0066	2SC2271(N)	0261	2SC2329	2675	2SC2381	OEM	2SC2455	OEM	2SC2497R	0558
2SC2168-OY	1274	2SC2229O	0066	2SC2271-AE	0261	2SC2330	0261	2SC2382	1963	2SC2456	0275	2SC2498	1795
2SC2168-B-Y	1274	2SC2229Y	0066	2SC2271-B-CTV	0261	2SC2330-0	0261	2SC2383	1553	2SC2456(LB-SAN-1)	0275	2SC2499	2824
2SC2168-Y-N03	1274	2SC2229Y-TYPE6	0066	2SC2271-D-CTV	0261	2SC2330-Y	OEM	2SC-2383	1553	2SC2456LB	0275	2SC2500	3064
2SC2168Y	1274	2SC2230	0261	2SC2271-E-CTV	0261	2SC2330A	0261	2SC2383(O)	1553	2SC2456LB(Z)	0275	2SC2501	0723
2SC2169	OEM	2SC2230(G)	0261	2SC2271-WB	0261	2SC2330A-GR	0261	2SC2383(Q)	1553	2SC2456Z	0275	2SC2502	0723
2SC2172	OEM	2SC2230(GR)	0261	2SC2271C	0261	2SC2330A-Y	0261	2SC2383(R)	1553	2SC2458	0076	2SC2503	OEM
2SC2173	OEM	2SC2230(GR)Y	0261	2SC2271CTV	OEM	2SC2330GR	OEM	2SC2383-0	1553	2SC2458(G)	0076	2SC2504	OEM
2SC2174	OEM	2SC2230(Y)	0261	2SC2271D	0261	2SC2330Y	0261	2SC2383-O(SAN)	1553	2SC2458(GR)	0076	2SC2505	0723
2SC2175	1955	2SC2230-A	0261	2SC2271E	0261	2SC2331	0388	2SC2383-R(SAN)	1553	2SC2458(LB-SAN-1)	0076	2SC2506	0723
2SC2176	OEM	2SC2230-GR	0261	2SC2271M	0261	2SC2331-Y	1614	2SC2383-Y	1553	2SC2458(Y)	0076	2SC2507	1841
2SC2177	OEM	2SC2230-Y	0261	2SC2271N	0261	2SC2331Y	0388	2SC2383-Y(C)	1553	2SC2458-GR	0076	2SC2508	2857
2SC2178	0388	2SC2230A	0261	2SC2271O	0261	2SC2333	0261	2SC23830	1553	2SC2458-0	0076	2SC2509	3072
2SC2178Y	0388	2SC2230A(G)	0261	2SC2271Z	0261	2SC2334	2253	2SC2383R	1553	2SC2458BL	0076	2SC2510	OEM
2SC2179	OEM	2SC2230A(GR)	0261	2SC2272	OEM	2SC2334K	2253	2SC2383Y	1553	2SC2458GR	0076	2SC2511	0155
2SC2180	1963	2SC2230A(Y)	0261	2SC2273	OEM	2SC2334L	2253	2SC2384	0334	2SC2458GR-T	OEM	2SC2512	0224
2SC2181	2857	2SC2230AG	0261	2SC2274	0155	2SC2335	0723	2SC2385	0111	2SC2458Y	0076	2SC2512-03	0224
2SC2182	2485	2SC2230A-GR	0261	2SC2274(D)	0155	2SC2336	0388	2SC2386	1967	2SC2459	1260	2SC2512-04	0224
2SC2183	OEM	2SC2230A-Y	0261	2SC2274(E)	0155	2SC2336A	0388	2SC2387	2900	2SC2459BL	1260	2SC2516	1157
2SC2184	0830	2SC2230AP	0261	2SC2274(F)	0155	2SC2336B	0388	2SC2388	1841	2SC2459GR	1260	2SC2516A	1157
2SC2185	OEM	2SC2230A-Y	0261	2SC2274-D	0155	2SC2337	0861	2SC2388A	1841	2SC2460	0177	2SC2516AK	1157
2SC2186	OEM	2SC2230AY	0261	2SC2274-DE	0155	2SC2337A	0861	2SC2389	0525	2SC2460A	0177	2SC2516AL	1157
2SC2188	2041	2SC2230AYG	0261	2SC2274-E	0155	2SC2338	OEM	2SC2389Z	OEM	2SC2461	0538	2SC2516K	1157
2SC2189	0615	2SC2230G	0261	2SC2274-E-AA	0155	2SC2339	OEM	2SC2390	0525	2SC2461B	0538	2SC2516L	1157
2SC2190	0065	2SC2230GR	0261	2SC2274-F	0155	2SC2340	0261	2SC2391	OEM	2SC2462	0719	2SC2516M	1157
2SC2191	0359	2SC2230Y	0261	2SC2274-F-AA	0155	2SC2341	OEM	2SC2392	OEM	2SC2462(LD)	0719	2SC2517	1157
2SC2192	OEM	2SC2230YGR	0261	2SC2274D	2514	2SC2342	OEM	2SC2393	0261	2SC2462B	0719	2SC2518	0723
2SC2193	0710	2SC2231	0168	2SC2274E	0155	2SC2344	1274	2SC2393D	0261	2SC2462C	0719	2SC2519	0127
2SC2194	0546	2SC2231A	0168	2SC2274F	0155	2SC2344(D)	1274	2SC2394	0830	2SC2462CD	OEM	2SC2522	0538
2SC2195	0830	2SC2231Y	0168	2SC2274K	0155	2SC2344(E)	1274	2SC2394D	0830	2SC2462D	0719	2SC2522A	0538
2SC2196	0626	2SC2233	1530	2SC2274K-D	OEM	2SC2344D	1274	2SC2395	OEM	2SC2462L	OEM	2SC2523	0538
2SC2197	1963	2SC2233LBGL2	1530	2SC2274KE	0155	2SC2344E	1274	2SC2396	0111	2SC2462LD	OEM	2SC2525	2261
2SC2198	0625	2SC2234	1963	2SC2274K-T	0155	2SC2344RA	OEM	2SC2397	OEM	2SC2463	0719	2SC2526	2261
2SC2199	0615	2SC2235	1376	2SC2275	1274	2SC2345	OEM	2SC2398	0177	2SC2463D	0719	2SC2527	1157
2SC2199(FA-1)	OEM	2SC2235-0	1376	2SC2275A	1274	2SC2347	1581	2SC2399	0144	2SC2463E	OEM	2SC2528	3083
2SC2200	0723	2SC-2236	2882	2SC2276	2911	2SC2348	0224	2SC2400	OEM	2SC2463E(DE)	OEM	2SC2529	3084
2SC2204	OEM	2SC2236	2882	2SC2277	0079	2SC2349	0127	2SC2401	2996	2SC2463F	0719	2SC2530	3086
2SC2205	OEM	2SC2236(D)	2882	2SC2278	0283	2SC2350	0042	2SC2402	0538	2SC2464	OEM	2SC2532	OEM
2SC2206	2208	2SC2236(O)	2882	2SC2279	0334	2SC2351	OEM	2SC2403	OEM	2SC2465	2978	2SC2534	0723
2SC2206(B)	2208	2SC2236(Y)	2882	2SC2281	1189	2SC2352	0224	2SC2404	OEM	2SC2466	2978	2SC2535	0177
2SC2206(C)	2208	2SC2236-CY	2882	2SC2282	OEM	2SC2353	2963	2SC2404(C)	OEM	2SC2467	2978	2SC2536	1498
2SC2206(D)	2208	2SC2236-0	2882	2SC2283	OEM	2SC2354	0424	2SC2404(D)	OEM	2SC2468	OEM	2SC2537	2171
2SC2206(R)	2208	2SC2236-OY	2882	2SC2284	OEM	2SC2356	1841	2SC2404C	OEM	2SC2469	OEM	2SC2538	OEM
2SC2206(S)	2208	2SC2236-Y	2882	2SC2284A	OEM	2SC2357	2965	2SC2405	1722	2SC2470	2978	2SC2539	OEM
2SC2206-C	2208	2SC2236A	OEM	2SC2285	OEM	2SC2358	2965	2SC2406	OEM	2SC2471	0224	2SC2540	3090
2SC2206B	2208	2SC2236GR	2882	2SC2285A	OEM	2SC2359	0723	2SC2407	OEM	2SC2472	1795	2SC2541	2171
2SC2206BC	2208	2SC2236Q	2882	2SC2286	OEM	2SC2360	OEM	2SC2407-1	OEM	2SC2473	2824	2SC2542	0723
2SC2206C	2208	2SC2236Y	2882	2SC2287	OEM	2SC2361	2969	2SC2408	OEM	2SC2474	2257	2SC2543	3091
2SC2206CD	2208	2SC2237	2504	2SC2287K	OEM	2SC2361A	2969	2SC2409	0111	2SC2475	0855	2SC2544	3091
2SC2206Q	2208	2SC2238	2883	2SC2287M	OEM	2SC2362	1218	2SC2410	0008	2SC2476	2257	2SC2544E	OEM
2SC2206R	2208	2SC2238(Y)	3084	2SC2288	OEM	2SC2362-T	1218	2SC2411	1722	2SC2477	2257	2SC2545	0111
2SC2206S	2208	2SC2238A	2883	2SC2288K	OEM	2SC2362G	1218	2SC2412	0719	2SC2480	OEM	2SC2545D	0111
2SC2207	0830	2SC2238B	3084	2SC2288M	OEM	2SC2362H	1218	2SC2412K	0719	2SC2481	0558	2SC2545E	0111
2SC2208	OEM	2SC2238Y	3084	2SC2289	OEM	2SC2362K	1218	2SC2412K(BR)	0719	2SC2481-0	0558	2SC2545F	0111
2SC2209	0161	2SC2239	1021	2SC2289K	OEM	2SC2362K(F)-AA	1218	2SC2412KBRST	OEM	2SC2481-OLBGL1	0558	2SC2545T44	OEM
2SC2209R	0161	2SC2240	2900	2SC2289M	OEM	2SC2362K(G)-AA	1218	2SC2412K-Q	0719	2SC2481-Y	0558	2SC2546	3091
2SC2210	0224	2SC2240BL	2118	2SC2290	2918	2SC2362K-AA	1218	2SC2412K-QR	0719	2SC2481R	0558	2SC2546D	OEM
2SC2210E	2514	2SC2240GL	2118	2SC2291	2919	2SC2362KD	1218	2SC2412KQ	0719	2SC2481RLBGL1	0558	2SC2546E	OEM
2SC2210F	2514	2SC2240GR	2118	2SC2292	2900	2SC2362KE	1218	2SC2412K-R	0719	2SC2481Y	0558	2SC2546F	OEM
2SC2212	0144	2SC2240NEW-BL	2118	2SC2293	2900	2SC2362KF	1218	2SC2412KR	0719	2SC-2482	0261	2SC2547	3091
2SC2212A	0144	2SC2241	1077	2SC2294	0127	2SC2362K-T	1218	2SC2412KR(BS)	0719	2SC2482	0261	2SC2547D	OEM
2SC2213	0144	2SC2242	1077	2SC2295	1722	2SC2363	0079	2SC2412KS	0719	2SC2482(C)	0261	2SC2547E	OEM
2SC2214	OEM	2SC2242BK	1077	2SC2296	0525	2SC2363G	6831	2SC2412KT147	0719	2SC2482(C1)	0261	2SC2548	1498
2SC2215	0224	2SC2242GL2	1077	2SC2297	0419	2SC2364	2973	2SC2412Q	0719	2SC2482(C1)-T	0261	2SC2548(FA)	OEM
2SC2216	2874	2SC2242LB	1077	2SC2298	0161	2SC2365	0637	2SC2412R	0719	2SC2482(FA-1)	0261	2SC2549	0224
2SC2217	0224	2SC2242LBGL2	1077	2SC2298A	0161	2SC2366	OEM	2SC2413	0719	2SC2482-1	0261	2SC2550	0016
2SC2218	OEM	2SC2243	2885	2SC2298B	0161	2SC2367	OEM	2SC2414	3008	2SC2482A	0261	2SC2551	0261
2SC2219	OEM	2SC2244	0074	2SC2299	1967	2SC2368	2978	2SC2415	3009	2SC2482BK	0261	2SC2551(O)	0261
2SC2220	OEM	2SC2245	0074	2SC2300	0930	2SC2369	2978	2SC2416	3009	2SC2482C	OEM	2SC2551-0	0261
2SC2221	1973	2SC2246	0359	2SC2301	OEM	2SC2370	OEM	2SC2417	OEM	2SC2482FA-1	0261	2SC2551O	0261
2SC2222	1973	2SC2247	0723	2SC2302	OEM	2SC2371	0275	2SC2419	OEM	2SC2482FA1	0261	2SC2551R	0261
2SC2223	OEM	2SC2248	0723	2SC2303	1841	2SC2371(1)	0275	2SC2420	3012	2SC2482K	0261	2SC2551R0	0261
2SC2223F14	OEM	2SC2249	OEM	2SC2304	1841	2SC2371(1)K	0275	2SC2421	2526	2SC2482V	0261	2SC2552	0723
2SC2224	0334	2SC2250	OEM	2SC2305	2171	2SC2371(1)L	0275	2SC2422	2526	2SC2482Z	0261	2SC2553	0723
2SC2224A	0334	2SC2251	OEM	2SC2307	1498	2SC2371(1)LD	0275	2SC2422A	2526	2SC2483	0219	2SC-2555	2171
2SC2227	OEM	2SC2251-0	0261	2SC2308	0155	2SC2371(1)M	0275	2SC2423	OEM	2SC2483(O)	0219	2SC2555	2171
2SC2228	1317	2SC2252	OEM	2SC2308B	0155	2SC2371(1)MK	0275	2SC2424	OEM	2SC2483(R)	0219	2SC2555Z	2171
2SC2228(D)	1317			2SC2308C	0155	2SC2371(8)K	0275	2SC2425	0949			2SC2556	0558
2SC2228(E)	1317			2SC2309	0111	2SC2371(8)L	0275	2SC2427	0723				
2SC2228A	1317					2SC2371(8)M	0275						

If replacement code is OEM, contact original manufacturer for replacement.

DEVICE TYPE	REPL CODE
2SC2556A	0558
2SC2557	0111
2SC2558	OEM
2SC2559	OEM
2SC2561	0127
2SC2562	3096
2SC2563	3053
2SC2564	2261
2SC2565	2261
2SC2566	OEM
2SC2567	OEM
2SC2567A	OEM
2SC2568	0275
2SC2568*1*	0275
2SC2568*1*(K)	0275
2SC2568*1*(L)	0275
2SC2568*1*(M)	0275
2SC2568(1)	0275
2SC2568(1)(K)	0275
2SC2568(1)(L)	0275
2SC2568(1)(M)	0275
2SC2568(1)-K	0275
2SC2568(1)K	0275
2SC2568(1)KD	0275
2SC2568(1)-L	0275
2SC2568(1)L	0275
2SC2568(1)LD	0275
2SC2568(1)-M	0275
2SC2568(1)M	0275
2SC2568(K)	0275
2SC2568(L)	0275
2SC2568(M)	0275
2SC2568-1	0275
2SC2568-1-(K)	0275
2SC2568-1-(L)	0275
2SC2568-1-(M)	0275
2SC2568K	0275
2SC2568KD	0275
2SC2568L	0275
2SC2568LD	0275
2SC2568LM	0275
2SC2568M	0275
2SC2569	0723
2SC2570	2824
2SC2570A	2824
2SC2570AE	2824
2SC2571	OEM
2SC2571-1	OEM
2SC2571-2	OEM
2SC2572	0016
2SC2575	0284
2SC2575L	0284
2SC2577	0194
2SC2578	0194
2SC2579	3053
2SC2580	3053
2SC2581	3053
2SC2582	0558
2SC2584	OEM
2SC2585	OEM
2SC2586	OEM
2SC2587	0044
2SC2587A	0044
2SC2588	0044
2SC2588A	0044
2SC2589	0861
2SC2590	0558
2SC2591	0388
2SC2592	0388
2SC2593	OEM
2SC2594	0161
2SC2594V	0161
2SC2595	OEM
2SC2596	OEM
2SC2597	OEM
2SC2598	OEM
2SC2599	OEM
2SC2600	OEM
2SC2601	OEM
2SC2602	0111
2SC2602G	0502
2SC2603	0513
2SC2603(D)	0513
2SC2603(E)	0513
2SC2603(F)	0513
2SC2603(G)	0513
2SC2603-D	0513
2SC2603-E	0513
2SC2603-F	0513
2SC2603-G	0513
2SC2603E	0513
2SC2603F	0513
2SC2603G	0513
2SC2603R	0513
2SC2603S	0513
2SC2604	0191
2SC2605	0191
2SC2606	0283
2SC2607	2398
2SC2608	2398
2SC2609	OEM
2SC-2610	0261
2SC2610	0261
2SC2610(BK)	0261
2SC2610(BR)	0261
2SC2610(Y)	0261
2SC2610-05	0261
2SC2610-5	0261
2SC2610B	0261
2SC2610BK	0261
2SC2610K	0261
2SC2610KK	0261
2SC2611	0275
2SC2611-06	0275
2SC2611-5	0275
2SC2611BK	OEM
2SC2612	0168
2SC2613	0723
2SC2613K	0723
2SC2614	OEM
2SC2615	OEM
2SC2615K	OEM
2SC2616	2900
2SC2617	2900
2SC2618	1722
2SC2619	0719
2SC2619A	0719
2SC2619B	0719
2SC2619C	0719
2SC2620	OEM
2SC2620A	OEM
2SC2620B	OEM
2SC2620C	OEM
2SC2621	0275
2SC2621(C)	0275
2SC2621(D)	0275
2SC2621(D)-RAC	0275
2SC2621(E)	0275
2SC2621(E)-RAC	0275
2SC2621-C	0275
2SC2621-C-RA	0275
2SC2621-D	0275
2SC2621-D-RA	0275
2SC2621-E	0275
2SC2621-E-RA	0275
2SC2621-RA	0275
2SC2621-RA(C)	0275
2SC2621-RA(D)	0275
2SC2621-RA(E)	0275
2SC2621-RAC	0275
2SC2621-RAD	0275
2SC2621-RAE	0275
2SC2621C	0275
2SC2621D	0275
2SC2621E	0275
2SC2621RA	0275
2SC2621RA(C)	0275
2SC2621RA(D)	0275
2SC2621RA(E)	0275
2SC2621RA-C	OEM
2SC2621RA-D	OEM
2SC2621RA-E	OEM
2SC2621S	OEM
2SC2623	1841
2SC2624	2171
2SC2625	2171
2SC2626	1498
2SC2627	3131
2SC2628	OEM
2SC2629	3135
2SC2630	3090
2SC2631	0261
2SC2631QRS	OEM
2SC2632	0261
2SC2633	1077
2SC2634	0111
2SC2634-R	0111
2SC2634-RS	0111
2SC2634-S	0111
2SC2634NC	0111
2SC2634NC-T	OEM
2SC2634R	0111
2SC2634RS	0111
2SC2634S	0111
2SC2635	OEM
2SC2635H	OEM
2SC2636	0127
2SC2636(R)	0127
2SC2636S	0127
2SC2636T	0127
2SC2637	1077
2SC2637K	1077
2SC2637L	1077
2SC2637Q	1077
2SC2637R	1077
2SC2637RL	1077
2SC2638	OEM
2SC2639	OEM
2SC2640	3141
2SC2641	OEM
2SC2642	OEM
2SC2643	OEM
2SC2644	OEM
2SC2644S	OEM
2SC2645	OEM
2SC2646	0127
2SC2647	0224
2SC2647C	0224
2SC2648	OEM
2SC2649	OEM
2SC2650	OEM
2SC2651	OEM
2SC2652	OEM
2SC2653	0168
2SC2653(H)	0168
2SC2653(H)CL	0168
2SC2653(H)CL(LB)	0168
2SC2653(H)LB	0168
2SC2653(LB)	0168
2SC2653B	0168
2SC2653C	0168
2SC2653CL	0168
2SC2653H	0168
2SC2653H(C)	0168
2SC2653H(L)	0168
2SC2653H(LB)	0168
2SC2653H-CL	0168
2SC2653HCL	0168
2SC2653HCL(LB)	0168
2SC2653HLB	0168
2SC2653H.C	0168
2SC2653H.L	0168
2SC2653L	0168
2SC2653LB	0168
2SC2653LBA	0168
2SC2653Q	0168
2SC2654	3149
2SC2655	0018
2SC2655(Y)	0018
2SC2655(Y)-T	0018
2SC2655(Y)-Y	0018
2SC2655-O	0018
2SC2655-Y	0018
2SC2655-Y(C)	0018
2SC26550	0018
2SC26550YTPE6	0018
2SC2655Y	0018
2SC2655YTPE6	0018
2SC2656	2171
2SC2657	1315
2SC2657A	1315
2SC2658	0275
2SC2658A	0275
2SC2659	0309
2SC2659A	0309
2SC2660	0388
2SC2660A	0388
2SC2662	0617
2SC2664	0617
2SC2665	3052
2SC2666	OEM
2SC2667	OEM
2SC2668	1136
2SC2668-O	1489
2SC2668Y	1489
2SC2669	0155
2SC2669-O	0155
2SC2669-Y	0155
2SC2669Y	1510
2SC2670	0155
2SC2671	2824
2SC2672	OEM
2SC2673	0009
2SC2673-Q	0009
2SC2673-R	0009
2SC2673Q	1556
2SC2673R	1559
2SC2674	1376
2SC2675	0155
2SC2676	0525
2SC2677	0326
2SC2678	0326
2SC2679	0144
2SC2680	OEM
2SC2681	0194
2SC2682	0558
2SC2684	OEM
2SC2685	OEM
2SC2686	OEM
2SC2687	0261
2SC2688	0275
2SC2688(2)	0275
2SC2688(K)	0275
2SC2688(L)	0275
2SC2688(M)	0275
2SC2688(N)	0275
2SC2688-K	0275
2SC2688-L	0275
2SC2688-LK	0275
2SC2688-M	0275
2SC2688-N	0275
2SC2688A	0275
2SC2688K	0275
2SC2688KA	0275
2SC2688L	0275
2SC2688LA	0275
2SC2688LK	0275
2SC2688LM	0275
2SC2688M	0275
2SC2688MA	0275
2SC2688N	0275
2SC2689	OEM
2SC2690	0558
2SC2690A	0558
2SC2690A-Q	0558
2SC2691	0155
2SC2692	OEM
2SC2693	OEM
2SC2694	3165
2SC2695	OEM
2SC2700	OEM
2SC2701	OEM
2SC2702	OEM
2SC-2703	1553
2SC2703	1553
2SC2703Y	1553
2SC2704	0558
2SC2705	1553
2SC2705P	OEM
2SC2706	3053
2SC2707	3170
2SC2710	0155
2SC2710(Y)	0155
2SC2710-O	0155
2SC2710-Y	0155
2SC2710Y	0155
2SC2711	OEM
2SC2712	0719
2SC2712(Y)	0719
2SC2712-YG	0719
2SC2712G	0719
2SC2712GR	0719
2SC2712Y	0719
2SC2713	2316
2SC2713-L	4922
2SC2714	OEM
2SC2715	0719
2SC2716	0719
2SC2717	0309
2SC2717(FA)	OEM
2SC2717FA	0309
2SC2718	0018
2SC2719	0155
2SC2719K	0155
2SC2719L	0155
2SC2720	3173
2SC2721	0018
2SC2722	0044
2SC2723	1498
2SC2724	0191
2SC2724(D)	0191
2SC2724(E)	0191
2SC2724-C	0191
2SC2724-CD	0191
2SC2724-D	0191
2SC2724-E	0191
2SC2724C	0191
2SC2724D	0191
2SC2724E	0191
2SC2724T	0191
2SC2725	OEM
2SC2726	OEM
2SC2727	2817
2SC2728	OEM
2SC2729	2817
2SC2730	OEM
2SC2731	OEM
2SC2732	OEM
2SC2733	OEM
2SC2734	2891
2SC2735	2891
2SC2735J-L	2891
2SC2736	2891
2SC2737	2824
2SC2738	3179
2SC2739	0723
2SC2740	3181
2SC2741	OEM
2SC2743	OEM
2SC2744	OEM
2SC2745	OEM
2SC2746	OEM
2SC2748	OEM
2SC2749	2171
2SC2749A	2171
2SC2750	0194
2SC2751	1498
2SC2751A	1498
2SC2752	3187
2SC2753	1498
2SC2754	0261
2SC2755	OEM
2SC2756	OEM
2SC2757	OEM
2SC2757R	OEM
2SC2758	OEM
2SC2759	OEM
2SC2760	OEM
2SC2761	OEM
2SC2762	0488
2SC2763	OEM
2SC2766	2261
2SC2766A	2261
2SC2767	0723
2SC2768	0723
2SC2768A	0723
2SC2769	2171
2SC2770	OEM
2SC2771	OEM
2SC2773	3196
2SC2774	3196
2SC2775	2316
2SC2776	1722
2SC2776VA	1722
2SC2776VB	1722
2SC2776VC	1722
2SC2778	OEM
2SC2780	1553
2SC2781	OEM
2SC2782	OEM
2SC2783	OEM
2SC2784	1260
2SC2784E	1260
2SC2784EU	OEM
2SC2784F	1260
2SC2785	0249
2SC2785(E)	0249
2SC2785(F)	0249
2SC2785(H)	0249
2SC2785(H)-Y	0249
2SC2785(J)	0249
2SC2785(J)-Y	0249
2SC2785(J,H)-Y	0249
2SC2785(JH)-T	0249
2SC2785-E	0249
2SC2785-F	0249
2SC2785-FEK	OEM
2SC2785-HFE	0249
2SC2785-K	0249
2SC2785-Y	0249
2SC2785E	0249
2SC2785EE	0249
2SC2785EF	0249
2SC2785F	0249
2SC2785F(H)	0249
2SC2785FF	0249
2SC2785H	0249
2SC2785J	0249
2SC2785JHFE	0249
2SC2785K	0249
2SC2785TP	0249
2SC2785Y	0249
2SC2786	0284
2SC2786L	0284
2SC2786MTA	OEM
2SC2786SP	OEM
2SC2787	0127
2SC2787L	0127
2SC2788	2171
2SC2789	2171
2SC2789C	0275
2SC2789CD	0275
2SC2790	2424
2SC2790A	2424
2SC2791	3199
2SC2792	3201
2SC2793	OEM
2SC2794	0558
2SC2796	OEM
2SC2797	OEM
2SC2798	OEM
2SC2799	OEM
2SC2800	OEM
2SC2802	OEM
2SC2803	2757
2SC2804	OEM
2SC2805	OEM
2SC2806	OEM
2SC2808	0525
2SC2809	2589
2SC2809-O	2589
2SC28090	2589
2SC2809Q	2589
2SC2809R	OEM
2SC2809V	2589
2SC2810	0723
2SC2811	OEM
2SC2812	0719
2SC2812-L5	0719
2SC2812-L5TA	0719
2SC2812-L5TA(E)	0719
2SC2812-L6	0719
2SC2812-L6TA	0719
2SC2812-L6TA(F)	0719
2SC2812-L7	0719
2SC2812-L7-TA	0719
2SC2812-L7TA	0719
2SC2812-L7TA(G)	0719
2SC2812-TA	0719
2SC2812L6	0719
2SC2813	OEM
2SC2814	0719
2SC2814-F5TA	OEM
2SC2814-TA	0719
2SC2814F5-TA	OEM
2SC2815	0723
2SC2816	0723
2SC2817	OEM
2SC2818	0079
2SC2818H	0079
2SC2819	1841
2SC2819H	1841
2SC2820	1841
2SC2821	2316
2SC2821UD	2316
2SC2821UE	2316
2SC2821UF	2316
2SC2822	0016
2SC2823	OEM
2SC2824	0558
2SC2825	3212
2SC2826	2985
2SC2827	0723
2SC2828	2171
2SC2829	1955
2SC2830	1841
2SC2831	2739
2SC2831A	2739
2SC2832	0168
2SC2832A	0168
2SC2832K	0168
2SC2832L	0168
2SC2833	2757
2SC2833A	2757
2SC2834	3218
2SC2834-AM	2768
2SC2834A	2768
2SC2834AM	2768
2SC2837	0194
2SC2838	0044
2SC2839	0151
2SC2839-D	0151
2SC2839-F-SPA-AC	0151
2SC2839D	0151
2SC2839E	0151
2SC2839EZ	0151
2SC2839F	0151
2SC2839FZ	0151
2SC2840	0127
2SC2840D	0127
2SC2840E	2821
2SC2841	2171
2SC2844	OEM
2SC2845	OEM
2SC2847	OEM
2SC2850	OEM
2SC2851	OEM
2SC2852	0414
2SC2853	1376
2SC2853D	1376
2SC2853E	1376
2SC2854	1376
2SC2854D	1376
2SC2854E	1376
2SC2855	1376
2SC2855D	1376
2SC2855E	1376
2SC2856	1376
2SC2856E	1376
2SC2857	0261
2SC2857D	0261
2SC2857E	0261
2SC2858	OEM
2SC2858K	OEM
2SC2859	1722
2SC2860	1489
2SC2865	1841
2SC2865A	1841
2SC2867	0723
2SC2868	0155
2SC2869	OEM
2SC2870	OEM
2SC2870L	OEM
2SC2871	OEM
2SC2872	0320
2SC2873	OEM
2SC2875	OEM
2SC2876	2817
2SC2877	0161
2SC2878	3065
2SC2878(A)	3065
2SC2878(B)	3065
2SC2878(B)-T	3065
2SC2878(B)-Y	3065
2SC2878-A	3065
2SC2878A	3065
2SC-2878B	3065
2SC2878B	3065
2SC2879	OEM
2SC2880	OEM
2SC2881	OEM
2SC2882	0662
2SC2883	OEM
2SC2884	0127
2SC2885	OEM
2SC2885K	OEM
2SC2885L	OEM
2SC2885M	OEM
2SC2886	OEM
2SC2887	OEM
2SC2888	OEM
2SC2889	OEM
2SC2890	OEM
2SC2891	OEM
2SC2892	OEM
2SC2893	OEM
2SC2894	OEM
2SC2895	OEM
2SC2896	OEM
2SC2897	OEM
2SC2898	0723
2SC2899	3187
2SC2900	2589
2SC2901	3243
2SC2902	1841
2SC2903	1841
2SC2904	OEM
2SC2905	OEM
2SC2906	OEM
2SC2906A	OEM
2SC2907	OEM
2SC2908	3248
2SC2909	0261
2SC2909R	0261
2SC2909S	0261
2SC2909T	OEM
2SC2910	1553
2SC2910S	OEM
2SC2910T	OEM
2SC2911	0558
2SC2911-T	OEM
2SC2911S	0558
2SC2912	0558
2SC2913	0723
2SC2914	3236
2SC2914(Z)	3236
2SC2914Z	3236
2SC2915	OEM
2SC2917	OEM
2SC2918	OEM
2SC2920	1331
2SC2921	3255
2SC2922	3196
2SC2923	0275
2SC2923-RL	0275
2SC2923RL	0275
2SC2924	OEM
2SC2925	0396
2SC2926	0127
2SC2927	2575
2SC2928	3261
2SC2928-01	3261
2SC2929	2985
2SC2930	1841
2SC2931	OEM
2SC2932	OEM
2SC2933	OEM
2SC2934	0275
2SC2935	0275
2SC2936	OEM
2SC2937	2171
2SC2938	2171
2SC2939	1498
2SC2940	OEM
2SC2941	OEM
2SC2942	OEM
2SC2943	1498
2SC2944	1498
2SC2946	OEM
2SC2946-1K	OEM
2SC2946-1L	OEM
2SC2946-1M	OEM
2SC2946-1N	OEM
2SC2946K	OEM
2SC2946L	OEM
2SC2946M	OEM
2SC2946N	OEM
2SC2947	0155
2SC2948	OEM
2SC2949	OEM
2SC2950	OEM
2SC2951	OEM
2SC2952	OEM
2SC2953	OEM
2SC2954	OEM
2SC2955	OEM
2SC2956	OEM
2SC2957	OEM
2SC2958	1376
2SC2959	1553
2SC2960	3270
2SC2960E	3270
2SC2960F	3270
2SC2960G	3270
2SC2961	2171
2SC2962	2757
2SC2963	0060
2SC2964	2900
2SC2965	2900
2SC2966	OEM
2SC2967	0127
2SC2968	0525
2SC2969	OEM
2SC2970	OEM
2SC2971	1331
2SC2972	1331
2SC2973	OEM
2SC2974	OEM
2SC2975	OEM
2SC2976	3031
2SC2977	OEM
2SC2978	OEM
2SC2979	2085
2SC2980	OEM
2SC2981	3031
2SC2982	OEM
2SC2983	OEM
2SC2984	OEM
2SC2985	OEM
2SC2986	0127
2SC2987	0194
2SC2987A	0194
2SC2988	OEM
2SC2989	OEM
2SC2991	OEM
2SC2992	OEM
2SC2995	0525
2SC2996	1722
2SC2997	OEM
2SC2998	0284
2SC2999	0127
2SC2999(E)	0127
2SC2999D	0127
2SC2999E	0127
2SC3000	0284
2SC3000(D)-AA	0284
2SC3000(E)-AA	0284
2SC3000-AA	0284
2SC3000-D	0284
2SC3000-E	0284
2SC3000-F-AA	0284
2SC3000D	0284
2SC3000E	0284

If replacement code is OEM, contact original manufacturer for replacement.

97

DEVICE TYPE	REPL CODE
2SC3000F	0284
2SC3001	OEM
2SC3004	OEM
2SC3005	OEM
2SC3006	OEM
2SC3007	3296
2SC3008	OEM
2SC3009	OEM
2SC3010	OEM
2SC3011	OEM
2SC3011MA	OEM
2SC3012	0194
2SC3013	OEM
2SC3014	OEM
2SC3015	2891
2SC3016	2891
2SC3017	0693
2SC3018	OEM
2SC3019	OEM
2SC3020	OEM
2SC3021	OEM
2SC3022	OEM
2SC3023	0223
2SC3024	2820
2SC3025	0065
2SC3026	2820
2SC3027	0065
2SC3028	OEM
2SC3029	2817
2SC3030	1498
2SC3031	3031
2SC3032	1498
2SC3033	3031
2SC3034	3029
2SC3035	0424
2SC3036	2085
2SC3037	2824
2SC3038	2985
2SC3038N	2985
2SC3039	0723
2SC3040	3181
2SC3041	3009
2SC3042	2171
2SC3043	3009
2SC3044	1331
2SC3044A	1331
2SC3045	1331
2SC3046	3304
2SC3047	3305
2SC3048	3031
2SC3049	3031
2SC3050	0223
2SC3051	3187
2SC3052	1722
2SC3052E	1722
2SC3053	1722
2SC3054	3311
2SC3055	0723
2SC3056	0723
2SC3056A	0723
2SC3057	0723
2SC3058	OEM
2SC3058A	OEM
2SC3059	0223
2SC3060	0223
2SC3061	OEM
2SC3062	OEM
2SC3063	0275
2SC3063-RL	0275
2SC3063RL	0275
2SC3064	OEM
2SC3064-E	OEM
2SC3064E	OEM
2SC3065	OEM
2SC3066	OEM
2SC3066-F	OEM
2SC3067	OEM
2SC3068	OEM
2SC3068-AA	OEM
2SC3069	OEM
2SC3070	OEM
2SC3071	OEM
2SC3072	OEM
2SC3073	3316
2SC3073Y	3316
2SC3074	OEM
2SC3075	OEM
2SC3076	3316
2SC3077	OEM
2SC3078	0577
2SC3078M	0577
2SC3079	1489
2SC3079M	1489
2SC3080	2208
2SC3080M	2208
2SC3080MM	2208
2SC3080MN	2208
2SC3080MP	2208
2SC3080MQ	2208
2SC3081	0127
2SC3082	OEM
2SC3082I	OEM
2SC3083	2757
2SC3084	3009
2SC3085	0259
2SC3086	3323
2SC3087	OEM
2SC3088	2757
2SC3089	3326
2SC3090	1498
2SC3091	1841
2SC3092	1841
2SC3093	1841
2SC3094	0259
2SC3095	OEM
2SC3096	OEM
2SC3098	OEM
2SC3099	2891
2SC3101	0693
2SC3102	OEM
2SC3103	OEM
2SC3104	OEM
2SC3105	OEM
2SC3106	OEM
2SC3107	OEM
2SC3108	OEM
2SC3109	OEM
2SC3110	2891
2SC3111	OEM
2SC3112	0111
2SC3112(A)	0111
2SC3112(B)	0111
2SC3112A	0111
2SC3112AB	0111
2SC3113	OEM
2SC3114	0155
2SC3114(S)	0155
2SC3114(T)	0155
2SC3114-R	0155
2SC3114-S	0155
2SC3114-T	0155
2SC3114R	0155
2SC3114S	OEM
2SC3114T	0155
2SC3114U	OEM
2SC3115	2316
2SC3116	0558
2SC3116(T)	0558
2SC3116S	0558
2SC3116ST	OEM
2SC3116T	0558
2SC3117	0558
2SC3117-R	OEM
2SC3117-S	OEM
2SC3117R	0558
2SC3117S	0558
2SC3118	OEM
2SC3119	2891
2SC3120	3338
2SC3121	OEM
2SC3122	OEM
2SC3123	OEM
2SC3124	3338
2SC3125	3338
2SC3125HH	OEM
2SC3126	2817
2SC3127	2891
2SC3128	2824
2SC3129	OEM
2SC3130	2891
2SC3131	3341
2SC3132	OEM
2SC3133	OEM
2SC3134	0719
2SC3135	1376
2SC3136	1795
2SC3137	OEM
2SC3138	3345
2SC3139	OEM
2SC3140	OEM
2SC3141	OEM
2SC3142	OEM
2SC3143	2316
2SC3144	1203
2SC3145	1203
2SC3146	2220
2SC3147	OEM
2SC3148	2739
2SC3149	3323
2SC3149L	3323
2SC3150	3323
2SC3151	2757
2SC3152	2757
2SC3153	2757
2SC3153K	2757
2SC3153L	2757
2SC3153M	2757
2SC3154	0223
2SC3155	0223
2SC3156	3351
2SC3157	3031
2SC3157K	3031
2SC3157L	3031
2SC3158	0723
2SC3159	0723
2SC3159L	0723
2SC3160	0723
2SC3161	OEM
2SC3162	2985
2SC3163	0723
2SC3164	3353
2SC3165	2985
2SC3166	0723
2SC3167	3354
2SC3168	0259
2SC3169	2985
2SC3169KT	2985
2SC3170	0723
2SC3170-P	0723
2SC3171	2171
2SC3172	OEM
2SC3173	1157
2SC3174	0723
2SC3174R	0723
2SC3174S	0723
2SC3175	0723
2SC3176	0723
2SC3177	0127
2SC3178	OEM
2SC3179	0060
2SC3179(G)	0060
2SC3179(Y)	0060
2SC3179-O	OEM
2SC3179G	0060
2SC3179R	OEM
2SC3179Y	0060
2SC3180	3053
2SC3180N	OEM
2SC3181	0194
2SC3181-O	OEM
2SC3181N	OEM
2SC3182	0194
2SC3182N	0194
2SC3182NFA-1	0194
2SC3183	3323
2SC3184	3323
2SC3185	2936
2SC3186	OEM
2SC3187	3358
2SC3187V	3358
2SC3189	0723
2SC3190	0191
2SC3191	0191
2SC3192	0127
2SC3193	0127
2SC3194	3362
2SC3195	1489
2SC3196	1489
2SC3197	1060
2SC3198	0284
2SC3198GR	0284
2SC3198Y	0284
2SC3199	0284
2SC3200	OEM
2SC3201	OEM
2SC3202	0155
2SC3203	3364
2SC3204	0284
2SC3205	3064
2SC3206	0086
2SC3207	0086
2SC3208	1077
2SC3209	0261
2SC3209K	0261
2SC3209L	0261
2SC3209LK	0261
2SC3209M	0261
2SC3210	2171
2SC3211	2757
2SC3211A	2757
2SC3212	3326
2SC3212A	3326
2SC3213	OEM
2SC3214	0065
2SC3215	OEM
2SC3216	OEM
2SC3217	OEM
2SC3218	OEM
2SC3219	0723
2SC3220	3353
2SC3221	OEM
2SC3222	3354
2SC3223	OEM
2SC3224	OEM
2SC3225	OEM
2SC3226	3372
2SC3227	0320
2SC3228	1553
2SC3229	2575
2SC3230	3086
2SC3231	2985
2SC3232	1498
2SC3233	OEM
2SC3234	3084
2SC3235	2985
2SC3236	0723
2SC3237	3377
2SC3238	1077
2SC3239	0060
2SC3240	OEM
2SC3241	OEM
2SC3242	3064
2SC3242A	3064
2SC3242G	3064
2SC3243	1376
2SC3243(DE)-T	1376
2SC3243D	1376
2SC3243DE	1376
2SC3243E	1376
2SC3244	1376
2SC3245	1376
2SC3245A	1376
2SC3246	OEM
2SC3247	0396
2SC3248	0261
2SC3249	0261
2SC3250	OEM
2SC3251	OEM
2SC3252	1498
2SC3253	0060
2SC3254	0060
2SC3255	0060
2SC3256	1351
2SC3257	0723
2SC3258	0060
2SC3259	3323
2SC3260	2757
2SC3261	2757
2SC3262	OEM
2SC3263	1498
2SC3264	OEM
2SC3265	1722
2SC3265Y	OEM
2SC3266	1492
2SC3267	3064
2SC3268	OEM
2SC3269	0261
2SC3270	0261
2SC3271	0275
2SC3271(N)	0275
2SC3271(N)-L	0275
2SC3271(NP)	0275
2SC3271(NP)-C1	0275
2SC3271(NP)-L	0275
2SC3271(P)	0275
2SC3271(P)-L	0275
2SC3271-N	0275
2SC3271F	0275
2SC3271F-N	0275
2SC3271N	0275
2SC3271P	0275
2SC3272	0275
2SC3273	2824
2SC3274	OEM
2SC3275	OEM
2SC3276	OEM
2SC3277	2171
2SC3278	1955
2SC3279	1492
2SC3280	3401
2SC3280-0	3657
2SC3280R	OEM
2SC3281	3402
2SC3281-0	3657
2SC3281-O	3402
2SC3281-R	3402
2SC3281G	OEM
2SC3282	OEM
2SC3282A	OEM
2SC3283	OEM
2SC3283A	OEM
2SC3283R	1553
2SC3284	3401
2SC3284-O	OEM
2SC3285	3404
2SC3286	OEM
2SC3287	OEM
2SC3288	OEM
2SC3289	OEM
2SC3290	OEM
2SC3291	OEM
2SC3292	0277
2SC3293	0277
2SC3294	2350
2SC3295	OEM
2SC3296	0388
2SC3296D	OEM
2SC3296E	OEM
2SC3297	0042
2SC3298	OEM
2SC3298(Y)	OEM
2SC3298A	OEM
2SC3298A-O	OEM
2SC3298A-O(LB-SAN)	OEM
2SC3298A-T(LB-SAN)	OEM
2SC3298A-Y	OEM
2SC3298AY	OEM
2SC3298A-Y(LB-SAN)	OEM
2SC3298B	OEM
2SC3298B-Y	OEM
2SC3298Y	OEM
2SC3299	0060
2SC3299(Y)	0060
2SC3299Y	0060
2SC3300	2351
2SC3300A	2351
2SC3300ALF	2351
2SC3301	OEM
2SC3301G	OEM
2SC3302	2817
2SC3303	OEM
2SC3303Y	OEM
2SC3304	OEM
2SC3305	OEM
2SC3306	2171
2SC3306S	OEM
2SC3307	OEM
2SC3308	3411
2SC3309	2985
2SC3310	0723
2SC3311	2926
2SC3311(Q)	2926
2SC3311(R)	2926
2SC3311(S)	2926
2SC3311-Q	OEM
2SC3311-QRS	OEM
2SC3311A	2926
2SC3311A(Q)	2926
2SC3311A(Q)Y	2926
2SC3311A(Q,R)-Y	2926
2SC3311A(R)	2926
2SC3311A(R)Y	2926
2SC3311A-Q	OEM
2SC3311AQ	2926
2SC3311A-QRS	2926
2SC3311AQRS	2926
2SC3311AQSTA	OEM
2SC3311A-R	2926
2SC3311AR	2926
2SC3311ARS	2926
2SC3311A-RTA	2926
2SC3311AS	2926
2SC3311Q	2926
2SC3311QR	2926
2SC3311QRS	OEM
2SC3311QRSTA	OEM
2SC3311QS	2926
2SC3311R	2926
2SC3311S	2926
2SC3312	3412
2SC3313	OEM
2SC3314	OEM
2SC3315	OEM
2SC3315C	4378
2SC3316	3414
2SC3317	2985
2SC3317-S	2985
2SC3317S	2985
2SC3318	3353
2SC3319	3354
2SC3320	OEM
2SC3321	3354
2SC3322	2757
2SC3323	OEM
2SC3324	2316
2SC3325	1722
2SC3326	OEM
2SC3327	OEM
2SC3328	OEM
2SC3329	0525
2SC3330	2926
2SC3330-S-AC	2926
2SC3330T	2926
2SC3331	0018
2SC3331-V	OEM
2SC3331S	0018
2SC3331ST	0018
2SC3331T	0018
2SC3331U	0018
2SC3332	OEM
2SC3333	0261
2SC3334	0261
2SC3335	3187
2SC3336	1498
2SC3337	3419
2SC3338	OEM
2SC3339	OEM
2SC3340	OEM
2SC3341	OEM
2SC3342	OEM
2SC3343	OEM
2SC3344	0723
2SC3345	OEM
2SC3346	OEM
2SC3347	OEM
2SC3348	OEM
2SC3349	OEM
2SC3350	OEM
2SC3351	OEM
2SC3352	3424
2SC3353	3426
2SC3354	OEM
2SC3354S	OEM
2SC3354T	OEM
2SC3355	OEM
2SC3356	OEM
2SC3357	OEM
2SC3358	OEM
2SC3359	0155
2SC3360	OEM
2SC3361	1722
2SC3362	OEM
2SC3363	OEM
2SC3364	OEM
2SC3365	2171
2SC3366	OEM
2SC3367	OEM
2SC3368	OEM
2SC3369	OEM
2SC3370	OEM
2SC3371	OEM
2SC3372	OEM
2SC3372-5	OEM
2SC3373	OEM
2SC3374	3431
2SC3374-O	OEM
2SC3375	OEM
2SC3376	2757
2SC3377	OEM
2SC3377P	OEM
2SC3377Q	OEM
2SC3377R	OEM
2SC3378	OEM
2SC3379	OEM
2SC3380	3433
2SC3381	OEM
2SC3382	OEM
2SC3383	OEM
2SC3384	3354
2SC3385	3354
2SC3386	OEM
2SC3387	3437
2SC3387-01AB	3437
2SC3387-SY	3437
2SC3388	OEM
2SC3389	OEM
2SC3390	2926
2SC3391	OEM
2SC3391C	OEM
2SC3392	1722
2SC3393	2926
2SC3393ST	2926
2SC3394	OEM
2SC3395	3439
2SC3396	0975
2SC3396(CY)-TA	0975
2SC3396TA	OEM
2SC3397	OEM
2SC3398	3442
2SC3398-TA	3442
2SC3399	0892
2SC3399-AC	0892
2SC3400	2307
2SC3400-AC	2307
2SC3400-T	2307
2SC3400Z	2307
2SC3401	OEM
2SC3402	0826
2SC3402-T	0826
2SC3403	OEM
2SC3404	OEM
2SC3405	OEM
2SC3406	OEM
2SC3407	OEM
2SC3408	OEM
2SC3409	2757
2SC3410	OEM
2SC3411	3354
2SC3412	3446
2SC3413	2926
2SC3413(C)	2926
2SC3413(D)	2926
2SC3413B	2926
2SC3413BC	OEM
2SC3413C	2926
2SC3413CD	OEM
2SC3413D-TZ	2926
2SC3414	OEM
2SC3415	3447
2SC3416	OEM
2SC3417	0275
2SC3418	OEM
2SC3419	0558
2SC3420	OEM
2SC3421	0558
2SC3422	OEM
2SC3422Y	OEM
2SC3423	0558
2SC3424	OEM
2SC3425	OEM
2SC3426	1722
2SC3427	OEM
2SC3428	OEM
2SC3429	OEM
2SC3430	OEM
2SC3431	OEM
2SC3432	OEM
2SC3433	OEM
2SC3434	1498
2SC3435	1498
2SC3436	OEM
2SC3437	OEM
2SC3438	OEM
2SC3439	OEM
2SC3440	1722
2SC3441	1722
2SC3442	OEM
2SC3443	OEM
2SC3444	0662
2SC3445	OEM
2SC3446	3424
2SC3447	OEM
2SC3448	3452
2SC3449	3454
2SC3450	OEM
2SC3450M	OEM
2SC3451	OEM
2SC3452	OEM
2SC3453	OEM
2SC3454	OEM
2SC3455	OEM
2SC3456	3456
2SC3457	OEM
2SC3458	3404
2SC3459	3404
2SC3460	3326
2SC3461	3326
2SC3462	OEM
2SC3463	OEM
2SC3464	OEM
2SC3465	OEM
2SC3466	3326
2SC3467	0261
2SC3467D	0261
2SC3467E	0261
2SC3468	0261
2SC3468(D)-AE	0261
2SC3468(E)-AE	0261
2SC3468-AE	0261
2SC3468-D	0261
2SC3468D	0261
2SC3468E	0261
2SC3468F	0261
2SC3469	OEM
2SC3470	2926
2SC3471	OEM
2SC3472	OEM
2SC3473	OEM
2SC3474	OEM
2SC3475	OEM
2SC3476	OEM
2SC3477	OEM
2SC3478	OEM
2SC3478A	OEM
2SC3479	3465
2SC3480	3465
2SC3481	3465
2SC3482	3465
2SC3483	3469
2SC3484	3469
2SC3485	3471
2SC3486	3472
2SC3487	OEM
2SC3488	2926
2SC3489	OEM
2SC3490	3323
2SC3491	OEM
2SC3492	OEM
2SC3493	2891
2SC3494	2926
2SC3495	0525
2SC3496	OEM
2SC3497	OEM
2SC3498	OEM
2SC3499	OEM
2SC3500	OEM
2SC3501	OEM
2SC3502	0275
2SC3503	0275
2SC3503-RA	0275
2SC3503CDEF	OEM
2SC3503D	0275
2SC3503E	0275
2SC3503F	0275
2SC3504	OEM
2SC3505	2757
2SC3506	3404
2SC3507	3404
2SC3508	OEM
2SC3509	OEM
2SC3510	2824
2SC3511	OEM
2SC3512	3419
2SC3513	OEM
2SC3514	OEM
2SC3515	3433
2SC3516	OEM
2SC3517	OEM
2SC3518	OEM
2SC3518L	OEM
2SC3519	3482
2SC3519A	OEM
2SC3520	OEM
2SC3521	1722
2SC3522	OEM
2SC3523	OEM
2SC3524	OEM
2SC3525	OEM
2SC3526	OEM
2SC3527	1498
2SC3528	OEM
2SC3529	OEM
2SC3531	OEM
2SC3532	OEM
2SC3533	3454
2SC3534	3454
2SC3535	3454
2SC3536	3454
2SC3537	OEM
2SC3538	OEM
2SC3539	OEM
2SC3540	OEM
2SC3541	OEM
2SC3542	OEM
2SC3544	OEM
2SC3545	OEM
2SC3545T44	OEM
2SC3546	0044
2SC3547	2891
2SC3548	OEM
2SC3549	3323
2SC3550	2757
2SC3551	2757
2SC3552	3499
2SC3552L	3499
2SC3553	2116
2SC3553BC	2116
2SC3553CD	OEM
2SC3554	OEM
2SC3555	OEM
2SC3556	OEM
2SC3557	OEM
2SC3558	OEM

If replacement code is OEM, contact original manufacturer for replacement.

DEVICE TYPE	REPL CODE
2SC3559	3424
2SC3560	3504
2SC3561	3504
2SC3562	OEM
2SC3563	OEM
2SC3564	OEM
2SC3565	OEM
2SC3566	1157
2SC3567	1157
2SC3568	0723
2SC3568K	0723
2SC3568L	0723
2SC3569	2985
2SC3570	3426
2SC3571	3426
2SC3572	0723
2SC3573	OEM
2SC3574	OEM
2SC3575	OEM
2SC3576	OEM
2SC3577	3326
2SC3578	OEM
2SC3579	OEM
2SC3580	OEM
2SC3581	OEM
2SC3582	OEM
2SC3583	OEM
2SC3584	OEM
2SC3585	OEM
2SC3586	OEM
2SC3587	OEM
2SC3588	OEM
2SC3589	OEM
2SC3590	OEM
2SC3591	OEM
2SC3592	OEM
2SC3593	OEM
2SC3594	OEM
2SC3595	OEM
2SC3596	OEM
2SC3597	OEM
2SC3598	OEM
2SC3599	OEM
2SC3600	OEM
2SC3601	OEM
2SC3602	OEM
2SC3603	3518
2SC3604	OEM
2SC3605	3419
2SC3606	OEM
2SC3607	OEM
2SC3608	OEM
2SC3609	OEM
2SC3610	OEM
2SC3611	OEM
2SC3612	OEM
2SC3613	OEM
2SC3614	OEM
2SC3615	OEM
2SC3616	OEM
2SC3617	OEM
2SC3618	OEM
2SC3619	0275
2SC3620	0275
2SC3620(LB)	0275
2SC3620(LB-SAN-1)	0275
2SC3620EQ	0275
2SC3620LB	0275
2SC3621	0558
2SC3621(O)	0558
2SC3621(R)	0558
2SC3621-O	0558
2SC3621-O(LB-SAN-2)	0558
2SC3621-O(SAN-1)	0558
2SC3621-OY	OEM
2SC3621-R	0558
2SC3621-R(LB-SAN-2)	0558
2SC3621-R(SAN-1)	0558
2SC3621R	0558
2SC3621RY	OEM
2SC3621Y	0558
2SC3621Y(O)	0558
2SC3621Y(R)	0558
2SC3622	OEM
2SC3622A	OEM
2SC3622AK	OEM
2SC3622AL	OEM
2SC3623	OEM
2SC3623-K	OEM
2SC3623A	OEM
2SC3623A-L	OEM
2SC3623K	OEM
2SC3623L	OEM
2SC3624	OEM
2SC3624A	OEM
2SC3625	0723
2SC3626	2880
2SC3627	0723
2SC3628	OEM
2SC3629	OEM
2SC3630	OEM
2SC3631	OEM
2SC3632	OEM
2SC3633	OEM
2SC3634	OEM
2SC3635	OEM
2SC3636	3454
2SC3637	OEM
2SC3638	OEM

DEVICE TYPE	REPL CODE
2SC3639	OEM
2SC3640	OEM
2SC3641	OEM
2SC3642	3454
2SC3643	3454
2SC3644	OEM
2SC3645	3433
2SC3646	OEM
2SC3647	OEM
2SC3648	3433
2SC3649	OEM
2SC3650	OEM
2SC3651	OEM
2SC3652	OEM
2SC3653	0892
2SC3657	2757
2SC3658	0055
2SC3659	0055
2SC3660	OEM
2SC3661	OEM
2SC3662	OEM
2SC3663	OEM
2SC3664	OEM
2SC3665	OEM
2SC3666	3563
2SC3667	0009
2SC3668	OEM
2SC3669	OEM
2SC3670	0009
2SC3671	3433
2SC3672	OEM
2SC3673	OEM
2SC3674	OEM
2SC3675	OEM
2SC3676	OEM
2SC3677	OEM
2SC3678	2757
2SC3679	2757
2SC3680	3446
2SC3681	OEM
2SC3682	OEM
2SC3683	OEM
2SC3684	OEM
2SC3685	3454
2SC3686	3454
2SC3687	3454
2SC3688	3454
2SC3689	OEM
2SC3690	OEM
2SC3691	0060
2SC3691K	0060
2SC3691L	0060
2SC3692	OEM
2SC3693	OEM
2SC3694	OEM
2SC3695	OEM
2SC3696	OEM
2SC3697	OEM
2SC3698	OEM
2SC3699	OEM
2SC3700	OEM
2SC3701	OEM
2SC3702	OEM
2SC3703	OEM
2SC3704	OEM
2SC3705	1055
2SC3706	OEM
2SC3707	2891
2SC3708	1376
2SC3708-R	1376
2SC3708-S	1376
2SC3708R	1376
2SC3708S	1376
2SC3708T	OEM
2SC3709	OEM
2SC3710	OEM
2SC3711	OEM
2SC3712	OEM
2SC3713	OEM
2SC3714	OEM
2SC3715	OEM
2SC3716	OEM
2SC3717	0127
2SC3718	OEM
2SC3719	OEM
2SC3720	0224
2SC3720A	0224
2SC3720B	0224
2SC3720C	0224
2SC3720D	0224
2SC3720F	0224
2SC3720G	0224
2SC3720GN	0224
2SC3720H	0224
2SC3720J	0224
2SC3720K	0224
2SC3720L	0224
2SC3720OR	0224
2SC3720R	0224
2SC3720X	0224
2SC3720Y	0224
2SC3721	0079
2SC3722	OEM
2SC3723	OEM
2SC3724	1498
2SC3725	1498
2SC3726	OEM
2SC3727	OEM
2SC3728	OEM

DEVICE TYPE	REPL CODE
2SC3729	3446
2SC3730	OEM
2SC3731	2926
2SC3732	OEM
2SC3733	OEM
2SC3734	OEM
2SC3735	OEM
2SC3736	OEM
2SC3737	3454
2SC3738	OEM
2SC3739	OEM
2SC3740	1492
2SC3741	OEM
2SC3742	OEM
2SC3743	3323
2SC3744	OEM
2SC3745	OEM
2SC3746	0060
2SC3746R	0060
2SC3747	0060
2SC3748	0060
2SC3748R	0060
2SC3749	3424
2SC3750	3426
2SC3751	3594
2SC3752	3456
2SC3753	OEM
2SC3754	OEM
2SC3755	OEM
2SC3756	OEM
2SC3757	OEM
2SC3757QR	OEM
2SC3758	OEM
2SC3759	OEM
2SC3760	OEM
2SC3761	OEM
2SC3762	OEM
2SC3763	OEM
2SC3764	OEM
2SC3765	OEM
2SC3766	OEM
2SC3769	OEM
2SC3770	OEM
2SC3771	OEM
2SC3772	OEM
2SC3773	OEM
2SC3774	OEM
2SC3775	OEM
2SC3776	2824
2SC3777	2824
2SC3778	2824
2SC3779	3419
2SC3780	OEM
2SC3781	OEM
2SC3782	OEM
2SC3783	2757
2SC3784	1055
2SC3785	1055
2SC3786	OEM
2SC3787	OEM
2SC3788	OEM
2SC3789	0275
2SC3789-C	0275
2SC3789-CD	0275
2SC3789-D	0275
2SC3789-DE	0275
2SC3789-E	0275
2SC3789D	0275
2SC3789E	0275
2SC3790	0275
2SC3790D	0275
2SC3791	OEM
2SC3792	OEM
2SC3793	OEM
2SC3794	3323
2SC3795	3608
2SC3795B	3608
2SC3796	2757
2SC3797	3454
2SC3798	2757
2SC3799	3454
2SC3800	0224
2SC3800A	0224
2SC3800B	0224
2SC3800C	0224
2SC3800D	0224
2SC3800E	0224
2SC3800F	0224
2SC3800G	0224
2SC3800GN	0224
2SC3800H	0224
2SC3800J	0224
2SC3800K	0224
2SC3800L	0224
2SC3800M	0224
2SC3800OR	0224
2SC3800R	0224
2SC3800X	0224
2SC3800Y	0224
2SC3801	OEM
2SC3802	OEM
2SC3803	OEM
2SC3804	OEM
2SC3805	OEM
2SC3806	OEM
2SC3807	OEM
2SC3807-R-CTV-YA	OEM
2SC3807K	OEM
2SC3807R	OEM

DEVICE TYPE	REPL CODE
2SC3808	OEM
2SC3809	OEM
2SC3810	OEM
2SC3811	0734
2SC3811-QRS	OEM
2SC3812	OEM
2SC3813	2171
2SC3814	OEM
2SC3815	OEM
2SC3816	OEM
2SC3817	OEM
2SC3818	OEM
2SC3819	OEM
2SC3820	OEM
2SC3821	2880
2SC3822	OEM
2SC3823	OEM
2SC3824	OEM
2SC3825	OEM
2SC3826	OEM
2SC3827	OEM
2SC3828	OEM
2SC3829	OEM
2SC3830	3623
2SC3831	3353
2SC3832	2880
2SC3833	1498
2SC3833LF-128	1498
2SC3834	OEM
2SC3835	OEM
2SC3836	OEM
2SC3841	OEM
2SC3842	OEM
2SC3843	OEM
2SC3844	OEM
2SC3845	OEM
2SC3846	OEM
2SC3847	OEM
2SC3850	OEM
2SC3851	0236
2SC3852	3629
2SC3853	3630
2SC3854	0127
2SC3855	0194
2SC3856	3633
2SC3857	2261
2SC3858	3196
2SC3868	3424
2SC3869	3426
2SC3870	3426
2SC3871	3637
2SC3871LP	3637
2SC3872	2171
2SC3873	2171
2SC3874	OEM
2SC3875	0719
2SC3875S(LO)	0719
2SC3876	1426
2SC3877	OEM
2SC3878	OEM
2SC3879	0719
2SC3880	OEM
2SC3881	OEM
2SC3886A	5520
2SC3890	0723
2SC3892A	OEM
2SC3898	OEM
2SC3902	0558
2SC3902-R-RA	0558
2SC3902-S-CTV-YA	0558
2SC3902-S-RA	OEM
2SC3902-T-CTV-YA	0558
2SC3902S	0558
2SC3902S-CTV-YA	4179
2SC3902T-CTV-YA	0558
2SC3907	3657
2SC3931	OEM
2SC3938	OEM
2SC3939R	OEM
2SC3940	0224
2SC3940A	0224
2SC3940AQSTA	OEM
2SC3940B	0224
2SC3940C	0224
2SC3940D	0224
2SC3940E	0224
2SC3940F	0224
2SC3940G	0224
2SC3940GN	0224
2SC3940H	0224
2SC3940J	0224
2SC3940K	0224
2SC3940L	0224
2SC3940M	0224
2SC3940OR	0224
2SC3940R	0224
2SC3940X	0224
2SC3940Y	0224
2SC3942	3664
2SC3942RL	5479
2SC3987	3678
2SC4006	3678
2SC-4012	0018
2SC4012A	0018
2SC4012B	0018
2SC4012C	0018
2SC4012D	0018
2SC4012E	0018
2SC4012F	0018

DEVICE TYPE	REPL CODE
2SC4012G	0018
2SC4012GN	0018
2SC4012H	0018
2SC4012J	0018
2SC4012L	0018
2SC4012M	0018
2SC4012X	0018
2SC4012Y	0018
2SC4026	OEM
2SC-4033	0224
2SC4033A	0224
2SC4033B	0224
2SC4033C	0224
2SC4033D	0224
2SC4033E	0224
2SC4033F	0224
2SC4033G	0224
2SC4033GN	0224
2SC4033H	0224
2SC4033J	0224
2SC4033K	0224
2SC4033L	0224
2SC4033M	0224
2SC4033OR	0224
2SC4033R	0224
2SC4033X	0224
2SC4033Y	0224
2SC4038LN	OEM
2SC4038Q-TL2	OEM
2SC4038R-TL2	OEM
2SC4048	OEM
2SC4052	OEM
2SC4054	OEM
2SC4059	1498
2SC4073	OEM
2SC4075	1077
2SC4075(D)-YAC	1077
2SC4075(E)-YAC	1077
2SC4075-YAC	1077
2SC4075D	1077
2SC4075E	1077
2SC4108	1498
2SC4108-CTV-YB	1498
2SC4108N	1498
2SC4108Z	1498
2SC4109	OEM
2SC4115S	1492
2SC4115SQR	1492
2SC4116	0042
2SC4116A	0042
2SC4116B	0042
2SC4116C	0042
2SC4116D	0042
2SC4116E	0042
2SC4116F	0042
2SC4116G	0042
2SC4116GN	0042
2SC4116H	0042
2SC4116J	0042
2SC4116K	0042
2SC4116L	0042
2SC4116M	0042
2SC4116OR	0042
2SC4116R	0042
2SC4116X	0042
2SC4116Y	0042
2SC4130	3745
2SC4159	1157
2SC4159-E	1157
2SC4159D	1157
2SC4159E	1157
2SC4161L	OEM
2SC4161M	OEM
2SC4169	1055
2SC4170	OEM
2SC4212(H)	OEM
2SC4212H	OEM
2SC4212HL	OEM
2SC4212HLB	OEM
2SC4212HLBS	OEM
2SC4217	0275
2SC4217(D)-RAC	0275
2SC4217(E)-RAC	0275
2SC4217-RAC	0275
2SC4217D	0275
2SC4217E	0275
2SC4226	OEM
2SC4237	OEM
2SC4274	0723
2SC4274-02	0723
2SC4274-02F9	0723
2SC4304	3323
2SC4417	OEM
2SC4418	2880
2SC4418LF608	2880
2SC4418Y	2880
2SC4418Y-F	2880
2SC4421LP	OEM
2SC4423	2171
2SC4423-CTV	2171
2SC4423-CTV-YB	2171
2SC4424	3069
2SC4424-L-YB	3069
2SC4424-M-YB	3069
2SC4424L	3069
2SC4424M	3069
2SC4440	OEM
2SC4475	OEM
2SC4502	OEM

DEVICE TYPE	REPL CODE
2SC4502-Y	OEM
2SC4533	OEM
2SC4533LP	OEM
2SC4544	3870
2SC4547	OEM
2SC4589	OEM
2SC4601B	OEM
2SC4634	OEM
2SC4636	OEM
2SC4664	OEM
2SC4664MNP-F	OEM
2SC4833MNP	OEM
2SC4833N	OEM
2SC4834MNP	OEM
2SC4927-01	OEM
2SC5100	0168
2SC5100A	0168
2SC5100B	0168
2SC5100C	0168
2SC5100D	0168
2SC5100E	0168
2SC5100F	0168
2SC5100G	0168
2SC5100GN	0168
2SC5100H	0168
2SC5100J	0168
2SC5100K	0168
2SC5100L	0168
2SC5100M	0168
2SC5100OR	0168
2SC5100R	0168
2SC5100Y	0168
2SC5110	0168
2SC5110A	0168
2SC5110B	0168
2SC5110C	0168
2SC5110D	0168
2SC5110E	0168
2SC5110F	0168
2SC5110G	0168
2SC5110GN	0168
2SC5110H	0168
2SC5110J	0168
2SC5110K	0168
2SC5110L	0168
2SC5110M	0168
2SC5110OR	0168
2SC5110R	0168
2SC5110X	0168
2SC5110Y	0168
2SC5120	0555
2SC5130	0555
2SC5370	0018
2SC5370A	0018
2SC5370B	0018
2SC5370C	0018
2SC5370D	0018
2SC5370E	0018
2SC5370F	0018
2SC5370G	0018
2SC5370GN	0018
2SC5370H	0018
2SC5370J	0018
2SC5370K	0018
2SC5370L	0018
2SC5370M	0018
2SC5370OR	0018
2SC5370R	0018
2SC5370X	0018
2SC5370Y	0018
2SC54300R	0224
2SC5488	OEM
2SC5598	OEM
2SC5884	OEM
2SC5886	OEM
2SC5944	OEM
2SC5945	OEM
2SC5946	OEM
2SC5947	OEM
2SC5988	OEM
2SC5991	OEM
2SC6031	OEM
2SC6036	OEM
2SC6039	OEM
2SC6042	OEM
2SC6045	OEM
2SC6052	OEM
2SC6056	OEM
2SC6059	OEM
2SC6080	OEM
2SC6081	OEM
2SC6082	OEM
2SC6094	OEM
2SC6095	OEM
2SC6096	OEM
2SC6193	OEM
2SC6228	OEM
2SC6235	OEM
2SC6251	OEM
2SC6277	OEM
2SC6284	OEM
2SC6287	OEM
2SC6292	OEM
2SC6295	OEM
2SC6297	OEM
2SC6299	OEM
2SC6301	OEM
2SC6304	OEM
2SC6316	OEM

DEVICE TYPE	REPL CODE
2SC6318	OEM
2SC6341	OEM
2SC6379	OEM
2SC6423	OEM
2SC6438	OEM
2SC6488	OEM
2SC6491	OEM
2SC6543	OEM
2SC6545	OEM
2SC6547	OEM
2SC6556	OEM
2SC6603	OEM
2SC6604	OEM
2SC8146	0018
2SC8290	0079
2SC9011E	0079
2SC9011F	0079
2SC9011H	0079
2SC9012A	OEM
2SC9013	OEM
2SC9633	OEM
2SC10148	0555
2SC11070	0555
2SC14505	0042
2SC15211	0168
2SC17401	0198
2SC17405	0198
2SC32816	OEM
2SC32840	OEM
2SC82915	OEM
2SCD78	0042
2SCF1	0144
2SCF1A	0224
2SCF1B	0224
2SCF1C	0224
2SCF1D	0224
2SCF1E	0224
2SCF1F	0224
2SCF1G	0224
2SCF1GN	0224
2SCF1H	0224
2SCF1J	0224
2SCF1K	0224
2SCF1L	0224
2SCF1M	0224
2SCF1OR	0224
2SCF1R	0224
2SCF1X	0224
2SCF1Y	0224
2SCF-2	0016
2SCF2A	0224
2SCF2B	0224
2SCF2C	0224
2SCF2D	0224
2SCF2E	0224
2SCF2G	0224
2SCF2GN	0224
2SCF2H	0224
2SCF2J	0224
2SCF2K	0224
2SCF2L	0224
2SCF2M	0224
2SCF2R	0224
2SCF2X	0224
2SCF2Y	0224
2SCF3	0626
2SCF3A	0626
2SCF3B	0626
2SCF3C	0626
2SCF3D	0626
2SCF3E	0626
2SCF3F	0626
2SCF3G	0626
2SCF3GN	0626
2SCF3H	0626
2SCF3J	0626
2SCF3K	0626
2SCF3L	0626
2SCF3M	0626
2SCF3OR	0626
2SCF3R	0626
2SCF3X	0626
2SCF3Y	0626
2SCF5	0016
2SCF5A	0079
2SCF5B	0079
2SCF5C	0079
2SCF5D	0079
2SCF5E	0079
2SCF5F	0079
2SCF5G	0079
2SCF5GN	0079
2SCF5H	0079
2SCF5J	0079
2SCF5K	0079
2SCF5L	0079
2SCF5M	0079
2SCF5OR	0079
2SCF5R	0079
2SCF5X	0079
2SCF5Y	0079
2SC-F6	0079
2SCF6	1390
2SCF6A	0086
2SCF6B	0086
2SCF6C	0086
2SCF6D	0086
2SCF6E	0086
2SCF6F	0086

If replacement code is OEM, contact original manufacturer for replacement.

DEVICE TYPE	REPL CODE
2SCF6G	0086
2SCF6GN	0086
2SCF6H	0086
2SCF6J	0086
2SCF6K	0086
2SCF6L	0086
2SCF6M	0086
2SCF6OR	0086
2SCF6R	0086
2SCF6X	0086
2SCF6Y	0086
2SCF-8	4144
2SCF8	4144
2SCF8A	4144
2SCF8B	4144
2SCF8C	4144
2SCF8D	4144
2SCF8E	4144
2SCF8F	4144
2SCF8G	4144
2SCF8GN	4144
2SCF8H	4144
2SCF8J	4144
2SCF8K	4144
2SCF8L	4144
2SCF8OR	4144
2SCF8R	4144
2SCF8X	4144
2SCF8Y	4144
2SC-F11	0224
2SCF11	0470
2SC-F11A	0224
2SC-F11B	0224
2SC-F11C	0224
2SC-F11D	0224
2SC-F11E	0224
2SC-F11F	0224
2SC-F11G	0224
2SC-F11GN	0224
2SC-F11H	0224
2SC-F11J	0224
2SC-F11K	0224
2SC-F11L	0224
2SC-F11M	0224
2SC-F11OR	0224
2SC-F11R	0224
2SC-F11X	0224
2SC-F11Y	0224
2SCF12A	0626
2SCF12B	0626
2SCF12C	0626
2SCF12D	0626
2SCF12E	0626
2SCF12F	0626
2SCF12G	0626
2SCF12GN	0626
2SCF12H	0626
2SCF12J	0626
2SCF12K	0626
2SCF12L	0626
2SCF12M	0626
2SCF12OR	0626
2SCF12R	0626
2SCF12X	0626
2SCF12Y	0626
2SC-F14	0224
2SC-F14A	0224
2SC-F14B	0224
2SC-F14C	0224
2SC-F14D	0224
2SC-F14E	0224
2SC-F14F	0224
2SC-F14G	0224
2SC-F14GN	0224
2SC-F14H	0224
2SC-F14J	0224
2SC-F14K	0224
2SC-F14L	0224
2SC-F14M	0224
2SC-F14OR	0224
2SC-F14R	0224
2SC-F14X	0224
2SC-F14Y	0224
2SCF812	0626
2SCI090B	0233
2SCI520K	0168
2SCM39J	0224
2SCM39X	0224
2SCM93D	0103
2SCM95K	0142
2SCM98F	0086
2SC-NJ-100	0111
2SC-NJ100	0111
2SCNJ100	0111
2SC-NJ-107	0086
2SCNJ107	0086
2SCS183A	0018
2SCS183B	0018
2SCS183C	0018
2SCS183D	0018
2SCS183E	0198
2SCS183F	0018
2SCS183G	0018
2SCS183GN	0018
2SCS183H	0018
2SCS183J	0018
2SCS183K	0018
2SCS183L	0018
2SCS183M	0018

DEVICE TYPE	REPL CODE
2SCS183OR	0018
2SCS183R	0018
2SCS183Y	0018
2SCS184	0018
2SCS184A	0018
2SCS184B	0018
2SCS184C	0018
2SCS184D	0018
2SCS184E	0198
2SCS184F	0018
2SCS184G	0018
2SCS184GN	0018
2SCS184H	0018
2SCS184J	0144
2SCS184K	0018
2SCS184L	0018
2SCS184M	0018
2SCS184OR	0018
2SCS184R	0018
2SCS184X	0018
2SCS184Y	0018
2SCS429	0224
2SCS429A	0224
2SCS429B	0224
2SCS429C	0224
2SCS429D	0224
2SCS429E	0224
2SCS429F	0224
2SCS429G	0224
2SCS429GN	0224
2SCS429H	0224
2SCS429J	0144
2SCS429K	0224
2SCS429L	0224
2SCS429M	0224
2SCS429OR	0224
2SCS429R	0224
2SCS429X	0224
2SCS429Y	0224
2SCS430	0224
2SCS430A	0224
2SCS430B	0224
2SCS430C	0224
2SCS430D	0224
2SCS430E	0224
2SCS430F	0224
2SCS430GN	0224
2SCS430H	0144
2SCS430J	0224
2SCS430K	0224
2SCS430L	0224
2SCS430M	0224
2SCS430R	0224
2SCS430X	0224
2SCS430Y	0224
2SCS461	0224
2SCS461A	0224
2SCS461B	0224
2SCS461C	0224
2SCS461D	0224
2SCS461E	0224
2SCS461F	0144
2SCS461G	0224
2SCS461GN	0224
2SCS461H	0224
2SCS461J	0224
2SCS461K	0224
2SCS461L	0224
2SCS461M	0224
2SCS461OR	0224
2SCS461R	0224
2SCS461X	0224
2SCS461Y	0224
2SCS469	0224
2SCS469A	0224
2SCS469B	0224
2SCS469C	0224
2SCS469D	0224
2SCS469E	0224
2SCS469F	0144
2SCS469G	0224
2SCS469GN	0224
2SCS469H	0224
2SCS469J	0224
2SCS469K	0224
2SCS469L	0224
2SCS469M	0224
2SCS469R	0224
2SCS469X	0224
2SCS469Y	0224
2SCU64M	1390
2SD2A	OEM
2SD11	0208
2SD11A	0208
2SD11B	0208
2SD11C	0208
2SD11D	0208
2SD11E	0208
2SD11F	0208
2SD11G	0208
2SD11GN	0208
2SD11H	0208
2SD11J	0208
2SD11K	0208
2SD11L	0208
2SD11M	0208
2SD11OR	0208
2SD11R	0208
2SD11X	0208

DEVICE TYPE	REPL CODE
2SD11Y	0208
2SD12	0074
2SD12A	0074
2SD12B	0074
2SD12C	0074
2SD12E	0074
2SD12F	0074
2SD12G	0074
2SD12GN	0074
2SD12H	0074
2SD12J	0074
2SD12K	0074
2SD12L	0074
2SD12M	0074
2SD12OR	0074
2SD12R	0074
2SD12X	0074
2SD12Y	0074
2SD13	OEM
2SD14	OEM
2SD15	0130
2SD15A	0130
2SD15B	0130
2SD15C	0130
2SD15D	0130
2SD15E	0130
2SD15F	0130
2SD15G	0130
2SD15GN	0130
2SD15H	0130
2SD15J	0130
2SD15K	0130
2SD15L	0130
2SD15M	0130
2SD15OR	0130
2SD15R	0130
2SD15X	0130
2SD15Y	0130
2SD16	0130
2SD16A	0130
2SD16B	0130
2SD16C	0130
2SD16D	0130
2SD16E	0130
2SD16F	0130
2SD16G	0130
2SD16GN	0130
2SD16H	0130
2SD16J	0130
2SD16K	0130
2SD16L	0130
2SD16M	0130
2SD16OR	0130
2SD16R	0130
2SD16X	0130
2SD16Y	0130
2SD17	0130
2SD17A	0130
2SD17C	0130
2SD17D	0130
2SD17E	0130
2SD17F	0130
2SD17GN	0130
2SD17H	0130
2SD17J	0130
2SD17K	0130
2SD17L	0130
2SD17M	0130
2SD17R	0130
2SD17X	0130
2SD17Y	0130
2SD18	0861
2SD19	0208
2SD19A	0208
2SD19B	0208
2SD19C	0208
2SD19E	0208
2SD19F	0208
2SD19G	0208
2SD19GN	0208
2SD19H	0208
2SD19J	0208
2SD19K	0208
2SD19M	0208
2SD19Y	0208
2SD20	0208
2SD20A	0208
2SD20B	0208
2SD20C	0208
2SD20D	0208
2SD20E	0208
2SD20F	0208
2SD20G	0208
2SD20GN	0208
2SD20H	0208
2SD20J	0208
2SD20K	0208
2SD20L	0208
2SD20M	0208
2SD20OR	0208
2SD20R	0208
2SD20X	0208
2SD20Y	0208
2SD21	0208
2SD21A	0208
2SD21B	0208
2SD21C	0208
2SD21D	0208
2SD21E	0208

DEVICE TYPE	REPL CODE
2SD21F	0208
2SD21G	0208
2SD21GN	0208
2SD21H	0208
2SD21J	0208
2SD21K	0208
2SD21L	0208
2SD21M	0208
2SD21OR	0208
2SD21R	0208
2SD21X	0208
2SD21Y	0208
2SD22	0208
2SD22A	0208
2SD22B	0208
2SD22C	0208
2SD22D	0208
2SD22E	0208
2SD22F	0208
2SD22G	0208
2SD22GN	0208
2SD22H	0208
2SD22J	0208
2SD22K	0208
2SD22L	0208
2SD22M	0208
2SD22OR	0208
2SD22R	0208
2SD22X	0208
2SD22Y	0208
2SD23	0208
2SD23A	0208
2SD23B	0208
2SD23C	0208
2SD23D	0208
2SD23E	0208
2SD23F	0208
2SD23G	0208
2SD23GN	0208
2SD23H	0208
2SD23J	0208
2SD23K	0208
2SD23L	0208
2SD23M	0208
2SD23OR	0208
2SD23R	0208
2SD23X	0208
2SD23Y	0208
2SD24	0142
2SD24(D)	0142
2SD24(F)	0142
2SD24A	0142
2SD24B	0142
2SD24C	0142
2SD24CK	0142
2SD24D	0142
2SD24DR	0142
2SD24E	0142
2SD24F	0142
2SD24G	0142
2SD24GN	0142
2SD24H	0142
2SD24J	0142
2SD24K	OEM
2SD24K(C)	0142
2SD24K(E)	0142
2SD24KC	0142
2SD24KD	0142
2SD24KE	0142
2SD24L	0142
2SD24M	0142
2SD24OR	0142
2SD24R	0142
2SD24X	0142
2SD24Y	0142
2SD24Y(C)	0142
2SD24Y(D,E)	0142
2SD24Y(E,F)	0142
2SD24Y(KC)	0142
2SD24YC	0142
2SD24YD	0142
2SD24YE	0142
2SD24YF	0142
2SD24YK	0142
2SD24YKC	0142
2SD24YL	0142
2SD24YLC	0142
2SD24YLD	0142
2SD24YLE	0142
2SD24YLF	0142
2SD24YM	0142
2SD24YM(C-E)	0142
2SD24YMC	0142
2SD24YME	0142
2SD25	0208
2SD25A	0208
2SD25B	0208
2SD25C	0208
2SD25D	0208
2SD25E	0208
2SD25G	0208
2SD25GN	0208
2SD25H	0208
2SD25J	0208
2SD25K	0208
2SD25L	0208
2SD25M	0208
2SD25OR	0208
2SD25R	0208

DEVICE TYPE	REPL CODE
2SD25X	0208
2SD25Y	0208
2SD26	0861
2SD26A	0861
2SD26B	0861
2SD26C	0861
2SD26D	0861
2SD26E	0861
2SD26F	0861
2SD26G	0861
2SD26GN	0861
2SD26H	0861
2SD26J	0861
2SD26K	0861
2SD26L	0861
2SD26M	0861
2SD26OR	0861
2SD26R	0861
2SD26X	0861
2SD26Y	0861
2SD27	0208
2SD28	0042
2SD28A	0042
2SD28B	0042
2SD28C	0042
2SD28D	0042
2SD28E	0042
2SD28F	0042
2SD28G	0042
2SD28GN	0042
2SD28H	0042
2SD28J	0042
2SD28K	0042
2SD28L	0042
2SD28M	0042
2SD28OR	0042
2SD28R	0042
2SD28X	0042
2SD28Y	0042
2SD29	0042
2SD29A	0042
2SD29B	0042
2SD29E	0042
2SD29F	0042
2SD29GN	0042
2SD29J	0042
2SD29K	0042
2SD29L	0042
2SD29M	0042
2SD29OR	0042
2SD29R	0042
2SD29X	0042
2SD29Y	0042
2SD30	0208
2SD30-0	0208
2SD30-0R	0208
2SD30-N	0208
2SD30-O	0208
2SD30-OR	0208
2SD30A	0208
2SD30B	0208
2SD30C	0208
2SD30D	0208
2SD30E	0208
2SD30F	0208
2SD30G	0208
2SD30GN	0208
2SD30H	0208
2SD30J	0208
2SD30K	0208
2SD30L	0208
2SD30M	0208
2SD30N	0208
2SD30OR	0208
2SD30P	0208
2SD30R	0208
2SD30X	0208
2SD30Y	0208
2SD31	0208
2SD31B	0208
2SD31C	0208
2SD31D	0208
2SD31E	0208
2SD31F	0208
2SD31G	0208
2SD31GN	0208
2SD31H	0208
2SD31J	0208
2SD31K	0208
2SD31L	0208
2SD31M	0208
2SD31OR	0208
2SD31R	0208
2SD31X	0208
2SD31Y	0208
2SD32	0208
2SD32A	0208
2SD32B	0208
2SD32C	0208
2SD32D	0208
2SD32E	0208
2SD32F	0208
2SD32G	0208
2SD32GN	0208
2SD32H	0208
2SD32J	0208
2SD32K	0208
2SD32L	0208
2SD32M	0208

DEVICE TYPE	REPL CODE
2SD32OR	0208
2SD32R	0208
2SD32X	0208
2SD32Y	0208
2SD33	0007
2SD33A	0007
2SD33B	0007
2SD33C	0007
2SD33D	0007
2SD33E	0007
2SD33F	0007
2SD33G	0007
2SD33GN	0007
2SD33H	0007
2SD33J	0007
2SD33K	0007
2SD33L	0007
2SD33OR	0007
2SD33X	0007
2SD33Y	0007
2SD34	0208
2SD34A	0208
2SD34B	0208
2SD34C	0208
2SD34D	0208
2SD34E	0208
2SD34F	0208
2SD34G	0208
2SD34GN	0208
2SD34H	0208
2SD34J	0208
2SD34K	0208
2SD34L	0208
2SD34M	0208
2SD34OR	0208
2SD34R	0208
2SD34X	0208
2SD34Y	0208
2SD35	0208
2SD36	0208
2SD36A	0208
2SD36B	0208
2SD36C	0208
2SD36D	0208
2SD36E	0208
2SD36F	0208
2SD36G	0208
2SD36GN	0208
2SD36H	0208
2SD36J	0208
2SD36K	0208
2SD36L	0208
2SD36M	0208
2SD36OR	0208
2SD36R	0208
2SD36X	0208
2SD36Y	0208
2SD37	0208
2SD37A	0208
2SD37B	0208
2SD37C	0208
2SD37D	0208
2SD37E	0208
2SD37F	0208
2SD37G	0208
2SD37GN	0208
2SD37H	0208
2SD37K	0208
2SD37L	0208
2SD37M	0208
2SD37OR	0208
2SD37R	0208
2SD37X	0208
2SD37Y	0208
2SD38	0208
2SD38A	0208
2SD38B	0208
2SD38C	0208
2SD38D	0208
2SD38E	0208
2SD38F	0208
2SD38G	0208
2SD38GN	0208
2SD38H	0208
2SD38J	0208
2SD38K	0208
2SD38L	0208
2SD38M	0208
2SD38OR	0208
2SD38R	0208
2SD38X	0208
2SD38Y	0208
2SD40V5	OEM
2SD41	0130
2SD41A	0130
2SD41B	0130
2SD41C	0130
2SD41D	0130
2SD41E	0130
2SD41F	0130
2SD41G	0130
2SD41GN	0130
2SD41H	0130
2SD41J	0130
2SD41K	0130
2SD41L	0130
2SD41M	0130
2SD41OR	0130
2SD41R	0130

DEVICE TYPE	REPL CODE
2SD41X	0130
2SD41Y	0130
2SD43	0208
2SD43A	0208
2SD43B	0208
2SD43C	0208
2SD43D	0208
2SD43E	0208
2SD43F	0208
2SD43G	0208
2SD43GN	0208
2SD43H	0208
2SD43J	0208
2SD43K	0208
2SD43L	0208
2SD43M	0208
2SD43OR	0208
2SD43R	0208
2SD43X	0208
2SD43Y	0208
2SD44	0208
2SD44A	0208
2SD44B	0208
2SD44C	0208
2SD44D	0208
2SD44E	0208
2SD44F	0208
2SD44G	0208
2SD44GN	0208
2SD44H	0208
2SD44J	0208
2SD44K	0208
2SD44L	0208
2SD44M	0208
2SD44R	0208
2SD44X	0208
2SD44Y	0208
2SD45	0074
2SD46	0074
2SD47	0615
2SD48	0042
2SD49	0042
2SD49A	0042
2SD49B	0042
2SD49C	0042
2SD49D	0042
2SD49E	0042
2SD49F	0042
2SD49G	0042
2SD49GN	0042
2SD49J	0042
2SD49K	0042
2SD49L	0042
2SD49M	0042
2SD49OR	0042
2SD49R	0042
2SD49X	0042
2SD49Y	0042
2SD50	0861
2SD50A	0861
2SD50B	0861
2SD50C	0861
2SD50D	0861
2SD50E	0861
2SD50F	0861
2SD50G	0861
2SD50GN	0861
2SD50H	0861
2SD50J	0861
2SD50K	0861
2SD50L	0861
2SD50M	0861
2SD50OR	0861
2SD50R	0861
2SD50X	0861
2SD50Y	0861
2SD51	0861
2SD51A	0861
2SD51B	0861
2SD51C	0861
2SD51D	0861
2SD51E	0861
2SD51F	0861
2SD51G	0861
2SD51GN	0861
2SD51H	0861
2SD51J	0861
2SD51K	0861
2SD51L	0861
2SD51M	0861
2SD51OR	0861
2SD51R	0861
2SD51X	0861
2SD51Y	0861
2SD52	0103
2SD53	0130
2SD53A	0130
2SD53B	0130
2SD53C	0130
2SD53E	0130
2SD53F	0130
2SD53G	0130
2SD53GN	0130
2SD53H	0130
2SD53J	0130
2SD53K	0130
2SD53L	0130
2SD53M	0130
2SD53OR	0130

If replacement code is OEM, contact original manufacturer for replacement.

DEVICE TYPE	REPL CODE
2SD53R	0130
2SD53X	0130
2SD53Y	0130
2SD54	0130
2SD55	0130
2SD55A	0130
2SD56	4397
2SD56A	4397
2SD56B	4397
2SD56C	4397
2SD56D	4397
2SD56E	4397
2SD56F	4397
2SD56G	4397
2SD56GN	4397
2SD56H	4397
2SD56J	4397
2SD56K	4397
2SD56L	4397
2SD56M	4397
2SD56OR	4397
2SD56R	4397
2SD56X	4397
2SD56Y	4397
2SD57	0178
2SD58	0178
2SD59	0074
2SD60	0074
2SD61	0208
2SD61A	0208
2SD61B	0208
2SD61C	0208
2SD61D	0208
2SD61E	0208
2SD61F	0208
2SD61G	0208
2SD61GN	0208
2SD61H	0208
2SD61J	0208
2SD61K	0208
2SD61L	0208
2SD61M	0208
2SD61OR	0208
2SD61R	0208
2SD61X	0208
2SD61Y	0208
2SD62	0208
2SD62A	0208
2SD62B	0208
2SD62C	0208
2SD62D	0208
2SD62E	0208
2SD62G	0208
2SD62GN	0208
2SD62H	0208
2SD62J	0208
2SD62K	0208
2SD62L	0208
2SD62M	0208
2SD62R	0208
2SD62X	0208
2SD62Y	0208
2SD63	0208
2SD63A	0208
2SD63B	0208
2SD63C	0208
2SD63E	0208
2SD63F	0208
2SD63G	0208
2SD63GN	0208
2SD63H	0208
2SD63J	0208
2SD63K	0208
2SD63L	0208
2SD63M	0208
2SD63OR	0208
2SD63R	0208
2SD63X	0208
2SD63Y	0208
2SD64	0208
2SD64A	0208
2SD64B	0208
2SD64C	0208
2SD64D	0208
2SD64E	0208
2SD64F	0208
2SD64G	0208
2SD64GN	0208
2SD64H	0208
2SD64J	0208
2SD64K	0208
2SD64M	0208
2SD64OR	0208
2SD64R	0208
2SD64X	0208
2SD64Y	0208
2SD65	0208
2SD65-1	0208
2SD65A	0208
2SD65B	0208
2SD65C	0208
2SD65D	0208
2SD65E	0208
2SD65F	0208
2SD65G	0208
2SD65GN	0208
2SD65H	0208
2SD65J	0208
2SD65K	0208

DEVICE TYPE	REPL CODE
2SD65L	0208
2SD65M	0208
2SD65OR	0208
2SD65R	0208
2SD65X	0208
2SD65Y	0208
2SD66	0208
2SD66A	0208
2SD66B	0208
2SD66C	0208
2SD66D	0208
2SD66E	0208
2SD66F	0208
2SD66G	0208
2SD66GN	0208
2SD66H	0208
2SD66J	0208
2SD66K	0208
2SD66L	0208
2SD66M	0208
2SD66OR	0208
2SD66R	0208
2SD66X	0208
2SD66Y	0208
2SD67	0177
2SD67B	0177
2SD67C	0177
2SD67D	0177
2SD67E	0177
2SD68	0130
2SD68A	0130
2SD68B	0130
2SD68C	0130
2SD68D	0130
2SD68E	0130
2SD68F	0130
2SD68G	0130
2SD68GN	0130
2SD68H	0130
2SD68J	0130
2SD68L	0130
2SD68M	0130
2SD68OR	0130
2SD68R	0130
2SD68X	0130
2SD68Y	0130
2SD69	6001
2SD70	0130
2SD70A	0130
2SD70B	0130
2SD70C	0130
2SD70D	0130
2SD70E	0130
2SD70F	0130
2SD70G	0130
2SD70GN	0130
2SD70H	0130
2SD70J	0130
2SD70K	0130
2SD70L	0130
2SD70M	0130
2SD70OR	0130
2SD70R	0130
2SD70X	0130
2SD70Y	0130
2SD71	0178
2SD72	0208
2SD72(K)	0208
2SD72-2C	0208
2SD72-3C	0208
2SD72-4C	0208
2SD72-6	0208
2SD72-OR	0208
2SD72A	0208
2SD72B	0208
2SD72C	0208
2SD72D	0208
2SD72E	0208
2SD72EJ	0208
2SD72F	0208
2SD72G	0208
2SD72GA	0208
2SD72H	0208
2SD72J	0208
2SD72K	0208
2SD72L	0208
2SD72M	0208
2SD72OR	0208
2SD72P	0208
2SD72R	0208
2SD72RE	0208
2SD72X	0208
2SD72Y	0208
2SD73	0861
2SD74	0284
2SD75	0208
2SD75(A)	0208
2SD75(B)	0208
2SD75A	0208
2SD75AH	0208
2SD75B	0208
2SD75C	0208
2SD75D	0208
2SD75E	0208
2SD75F	0208
2SD75G	0208
2SD75GN	0208
2SD75H	0208
2SD75J	0208

DEVICE TYPE	REPL CODE
2SD75K	0208
2SD75L	0208
2SD75M	0208
2SD75OR	0208
2SD77	0208
2SD77(C)	0208
2SD77-A	0208
2SD77A	0208
2SD77AH	0208
2SD77B	0208
2SD77C	0208
2SD77D	0208
2SD77E	0208
2SD77F	0208
2SD77G	0208
2SD77GN	0208
2SD77H	0208
2SD77J	0208
2SD77L	0208
2SD77M	0208
2SD77OR	0208
2SD77P	0208
2SD77R	0208
2SD77X	0208
2SD77Y	0208
2SD78	2980
2SD78A	2980
2SD79	6667
2SD80	0130
2SD80A	0130
2SD80B	0130
2SD80C	0130
2SD80D	0130
2SD80E	0130
2SD80F	0130
2SD80G	0130
2SD80GN	0130
2SD80H	0130
2SD80J	0130
2SD80K	0130
2SD80L	0130
2SD80OR	0130
2SD80R	0130
2SD80X	0130
2SD80Y	0130
2SD81	0861
2SD81A	0861
2SD81B	0861
2SD81C	0861
2SD81E	0861
2SD81F	0861
2SD81G	0861
2SD81GN	0861
2SD81H	0861
2SD81J	0861
2SD81K	0861
2SD81L	0861
2SD81M	0861
2SD81OR	0861
2SD81R	0861
2SD81X	0861
2SD81Y	0861
2SD82	0861
2SD82-OR	0861
2SD82A	0861
2SD82B	0861
2SD82C	0861
2SD82D	0861
2SD82E	0861
2SD82F	0861
2SD82G	0861
2SD82GN	0861
2SD82H	0861
2SD82J	0861
2SD82K	0861
2SD82L	0861
2SD82M	0861
2SD82OR	0861
2SD82R	0861
2SD82X	0861
2SD82Y	0861
2SD83	0861
2SD84	0861
2SD85GR	0723
2SD88	0861
2SD88A	0861
2SD88OY	0861
2SD90	0042
2SD90A	0042
2SD90B	0042
2SD90C	0042
2SD90D	0042
2SD90E	0042
2SD90F	0042
2SD90G	0042
2SD90GN	0042
2SD90H	0042
2SD90J	0042
2SD90K	0042
2SD90L	0042
2SD90M	0042
2SD90OR	0042
2SD90X	0042
2SD90Y	0042
2SD91	0042
2SD91A	0042
2SD91B	0042
2SD91F	0042

DEVICE TYPE	REPL CODE
2SD91G	0042
2SD91GN	0042
2SD91H	0042
2SD91J	0042
2SD91L	0042
2SD91M	0042
2SD91OR	0042
2SD91R	0042
2SD91X	0042
2SD91Y	0042
2SD92	0178
2SD92D	0178
2SD93	0074
2SD94	0388
2SD96	0208
2SD96A	0208
2SD96B	0208
2SD96C	0208
2SD96D	0208
2SD96E	0208
2SD96F	0208
2SD96G	0208
2SD96GN	0208
2SD96H	0208
2SD96J	0208
2SD96K	0208
2SD96L	0208
2SD96OR	0208
2SD96R	0208
2SD96X	0208
2SD96Y	0208
2SD100	0208
2SD100A	0208
2SD100B	0208
2SD100C	0208
2SD100D	0208
2SD100E	0208
2SD100F	0208
2SD100G	0208
2SD100GN	0208
2SD100H	0208
2SD100J	0208
2SD100K	0208
2SD100L	0208
2SD100M	0208
2SD100OR	0208
2SD100R	0208
2SD100X	0208
2SD100Y	0208
2SD101	0595
2SD101AK	0595
2SD102	0178
2SD102-O	0178
2SD102-R	0178
2SD102-Y	0178
2SD102A	0178
2SD102B	0178
2SD102C	0178
2SD102D	0178
2SD102E	0178
2SD102F	0178
2SD102G	0178
2SD102GN	0178
2SD102H	0178
2SD102J	0178
2SD102K	0178
2SD102L	0178
2SD102M	0178
2SD102OR	0178
2SD102R	0178
2SD102X	0178
2SD102Y	0178
2SD103	0178
2SD103-O	0178
2SD103-R	0178
2SD103-Y	0178
2SD104	0208
2SD104A	0208
2SD104B	0208
2SD104C	0208
2SD104D	0208
2SD104E	0208
2SD104F	0208
2SD104G	0208
2SD104GN	0208
2SD104H	0208
2SD104K	0208
2SD104L	0208
2SD104M	0208
2SD104OR	0208
2SD104R	0208
2SD104X	0208
2SD104Y	0208
2SD105	0208
2SD105A	0208
2SD105B	0208
2SD105C	0208
2SD105D	0208
2SD105E	0208
2SD105F	0208
2SD105G	0208
2SD105GN	0208
2SD105H	0208
2SD105J	0208
2SD105K	0208
2SD105L	0208
2SD105M	0208
2SD105OR	0208
2SD105R	0208

DEVICE TYPE	REPL CODE
2SD105X	0208
2SD105Y	0208
2SD107	0103
2SD108	0103
2SD110	0177
2SD110-0	0177
2SD110-O	0177
2SD110-ORG	0177
2SD110-R	0177
2SD110-RED	0177
2SD110-Y	0177
2SD110-YEL	0177
2SD111	0177
2SD111-O	0177
2SD111-ORG	0177
2SD111-R	0177
2SD111-RED	0177
2SD111-Y	0177
2SD111-YEL	0177
2SD111R	0177
2SD113	0130
2SD113-O	0130
2SD113-ORG	0130
2SD113-R	0130
2SD113-RED	0130
2SD113-Y	0130
2SD113-YEL	0130
2SD113R	0130
2SD114	0130
2SD114-O	0130
2SD114-ORG	0130
2SD114-R	0130
2SD114-RED	0130
2SD114-Y	0130
2SD114-YEL	0130
2SD114R	0130
2SD116	0103
2SD117	0615
2SD117C	0615
2SD118	0177
2SD118-B	0177
2SD118-BL	0177
2SD118-BLU	0177
2SD118-R	0177
2SD118-RED	0177
2SD118-Y	0177
2SD118-YEL	0177
2SD118A	0177
2SD118BL	0177
2SD118C	0177
2SD118D	0177
2SD118R	0177
2SD118Y	0177
2SD119	0177
2SD119-BL	0177
2SD119-BLU	0177
2SD119-R	0177
2SD119-RED	0177
2SD119-Y	0177
2SD119-YEL	0177
2SD119A	0177
2SD119B	0177
2SD119BL	0177
2SD119C	0177
2SD119D	0177
2SD119R	0177
2SD119Y	0177
2SD120	1471
2SD120D	1471
2SD120E	1471
2SD120F	1471
2SD120G	1471
2SD120GN	1471
2SD120H	1471
2SD120J	1471
2SD120K	1471
2SD120L	1471
2SD120M	1471
2SD120OR	1471
2SD120R	1471
2SD120X	1471
2SD120Y	1471
2SD121	1471
2SD121C	1471
2SD121D	1471
2SD121E	1471
2SD121F	1471
2SD121G	1471
2SD121GN	1471
2SD121H	1471
2SD121J	1471
2SD121K	1471
2SD121L	1471
2SD121M	1471
2SD121OR	1471
2SD121R	1471
2SD121X	1471
2SD121Y	1471
2SD122	0042
2SD123	0236
2SD123(P)	OEM
2SD124	0861
2SD124A	0861
2SD124AH	0861
2SD124B	0861
2SD124C	0861
2SD124E	0861
2SD124F	0861
2SD124G	0861

DEVICE TYPE	REPL CODE
2SD124GN	0861
2SD124H	0861
2SD124J	0861
2SD124K	0861
2SD124L	0861
2SD124M	0861
2SD124OR	0861
2SD124R	0861
2SD124X	0861
2SD124Y	0861
2SD125	0861
2SD125A	0861
2SD125AH	0861
2SD125B	0861
2SD125C	0861
2SD125E	0861
2SD125F	0861
2SD125G	0861
2SD125GN	0861
2SD125H	0861
2SD125J	0861
2SD125K	0861
2SD125L	0861
2SD125M	0861
2SD125OR	0861
2SD125R	0861
2SD125X	0861
2SD125Y	0861
2SD126	0861
2SD126H	0861
2SD126HA	0861
2SD126HB	0861
2SD126S	0861
2SD127	0208
2SD127A	0208
2SD127B	0208
2SD127C	0208
2SD127D	0208
2SD127E	0208
2SD127F	0208
2SD127G	0208
2SD127GN	0208
2SD127H	0208
2SD127J	0208
2SD127K	0208
2SD127L	0208
2SD127M	0208
2SD127OR	0208
2SD127R	0208
2SD127X	0208
2SD127Y	0208
2SD128	0208
2SD128A	0208
2SD128B	0208
2SD128C	0208
2SD128D	0208
2SD128E	0208
2SD128F	0208
2SD128G	0208
2SD128GN	0208
2SD128H	0208
2SD128J	0208
2SD128K	0208
2SD128L	0208
2SD128M	0208
2SD128OR	0208
2SD128R	0208
2SD128X	0208
2SD128Y	0208
2SD129	0178
2SD129-BL	0178
2SD129-BLU	0178
2SD129-R	0178
2SD129-RED	0178
2SD129-Y	0178
2SD129-YEL	0178
2SD130	1139
2SD130(BL)	1139
2SD130(FA-1)	OEM
2SD130(Y)	1139
2SD130-BL	1139
2SD130-BLU	1139
2SD130-R	1139
2SD130-RED	1139
2SD130-Y	1139
2SD130-YEL	1139
2SD130A	1139
2SD130B	1139
2SD130BL	1139
2SD130C	1139
2SD130D	1139
2SD130E	1139
2SD130F	1139
2SD130G	1139
2SD130GN	1139
2SD130H	1139
2SD130J	1139
2SD130K	1139
2SD130OR	1139
2SD130R	1139
2SD130X	1139
2SD130Y	1139
2SD131	0615
2SD132	0130
2SD134	0018
2SD134A	0018
2SD134C	0018
2SD134D	0018
2SD134F	0018

DEVICE TYPE	REPL CODE
2SD134G	0018
2SD134GN	0018
2SD134H	0018
2SD134J	0018
2SD134K	0018
2SD134L	0018
2SD134M	0018
2SD134OR	0018
2SD134R	0018
2SD134X	0018
2SD134Y	0018
2SD136	0142
2SD136D	0142
2SD136E	0142
2SD136F	0142
2SD136G	0142
2SD136GN	0142
2SD136J	0142
2SD136K	0142
2SD136L	0142
2SD136M	0142
2SD136OR	0142
2SD136R	0142
2SD136X	0142
2SD136Y	0142
2SD137	0142
2SD137A	0142
2SD137B	0142
2SD137C	0142
2SD137D	0142
2SD137F	0142
2SD137G	0142
2SD137H	0142
2SD137J	0142
2SD137K	0142
2SD137L	0142
2SD137M	0142
2SD137OR	0142
2SD137R	0142
2SD137X	0142
2SD137Y	0142
2SD138	0168
2SD139	0168
2SD141	0042
2SD141A	0042
2SD141B	0042
2SD141C	0042
2SD141E	0042
2SD141F	0042
2SD141G	0042
2SD141GN	0042
2SD141H	0042
2SD141H01	0042
2SD141J	0042
2SD141K	0042
2SD141L	0042
2SD141M	0042
2SD141OR	0042
2SD141R	0042
2SD141X	0042
2SD141Y	0042
2SD142	0178
2SD142A	0178
2SD142B	0178
2SD142C	0178
2SD142D	0178
2SD142E	0178
2SD142F	0178
2SD142G	0178
2SD142GN	0178
2SD142H	0178
2SD142J	0178
2SD142K	0178
2SD142L	0178
2SD142M	0178
2SD142OR	0178
2SD142R	0178
2SD142X	0178
2SD142Y	0178
2SD143	0178
2SD144	0178
2SD145	0178
2SD146	0042
2SD146A	0042
2SD146B	0042
2SD146C	0042
2SD146D	0042
2SD146E	0042
2SD146F	0042
2SD146G	0042
2SD146GN	0042
2SD146H	0042
2SD146J	0042
2SD146K	0042
2SD146L	0042
2SD146OR	0042
2SD146R	0042
2SD146UK	0042
2SD146VK	0042
2SD146X	0042
2SD146Y	0042
2SD147	0042
2SD147A	0042
2SD147B	0042
2SD147C	0042
2SD147D	0042
2SD147E	0042
2SD147F	0042
2SD147GN	0042

If replacement code is OEM, contact original manufacturer for replacement.

101

DEVICE TYPE	REPL CODE
2SD147H	0042
2SD147J	0042
2SD147K	0042
2SD147L	0042
2SD147M	0042
2SD147OR	0042
2SD147R	0042
2SD147X	0042
2SD147Y	0042
2SD148	0042
2SD149	0086
2SD150	0178
2SD150A	0178
2SD150B	0178
2SD150C	0178
2SD150E	0178
2SD150F	0178
2SD150G	0178
2SD150GN	0178
2SD150H	0178
2SD150J	0178
2SD150K	0178
2SD150L	0178
2SD150M	0178
2SD150OR	0178
2SD150R	0178
2SD150X	0178
2SD150Y	0178
2SD151	0615
2SD151A	0615
2SD151B	0615
2SD151C	0615
2SD151E	0615
2SD151F	0615
2SD151G	0615
2SD151GN	0615
2SD151H	0615
2SD151J	0615
2SD151K	0615
2SD151L	0615
2SD151M	0615
2SD151OR	0615
2SD151R	0615
2SD151Y	0615
2SD152	0388
2SD152(L)	0388
2SD152(M)	0388
2SD152A	0388
2SD152B	0388
2SD152C	0388
2SD152D	0388
2SD152E	0388
2SD152F	0388
2SD152G	0388
2SD152GN	0388
2SD152H	0388
2SD152J	0388
2SD152K	0388
2SD152L	0388
2SD152M	0388
2SD152OR	0388
2SD152R	0388
2SD152X	0388
2SD152Y	0388
2SD154	0236
2SD154(L)	0236
2SD154A	0236
2SD154B	0236
2SD154C	0236
2SD154E	0236
2SD154F	0236
2SD154G	0236
2SD154GN	0236
2SD154H	0236
2SD154J	0236
2SD154K	0236
2SD154L	0236
2SD154M	0236
2SD154R	0236
2SD154X	0236
2SD154Y	0236
2SD155	0178
2SD155(K)	0178
2SD155(L)	0178
2SD155-H	0178
2SD155-K	0178
2SD155H	0178
2SD155K	0178
2SD155L	0178
2SD156	0142
2SD156B	0142
2SD156C	0142
2SD156D	0142
2SD156E	0142
2SD156F	0142
2SD156G	0142
2SD156GN	0142
2SD156H	0142
2SD156K	0142
2SD156L	0142
2SD156M	0142
2SD156OR	0142
2SD156R	0142
2SD156X	0142
2SD156Y	0142
2SD157	0142
2SD157A	0142
2SD157B	0142
2SD157C	0142

DEVICE TYPE	REPL CODE
2SD157D	0142
2SD157G	0142
2SD157GN	0142
2SD157H	0142
2SD157J	0142
2SD157K	0142
2SD157L	0142
2SD157OR	0142
2SD157R	0142
2SD157X	0142
2SD157Y	0142
2SD158	1021
2SD158A	1021
2SD158B	1021
2SD158C	1021
2SD158D	1021
2SD158E	1021
2SD158F	1021
2SD158GN	1021
2SD158H	1021
2SD158J	1021
2SD158K	1021
2SD158L	1021
2SD158M	1021
2SD158OR	1021
2SD158R	1021
2SD158X	1021
2SD158Y	1021
2SD159	1021
2SD159A	1021
2SD159B	1021
2SD159C	1021
2SD159D	1021
2SD159E	1021
2SD159F	1021
2SD159G	1021
2SD159GN	1021
2SD159H	1021
2SD159J	1021
2SD159K	1021
2SD159L	1021
2SD159M	1021
2SD159OR	1021
2SD159R	1021
2SD159X	1021
2SD159Y	1021
2SD160	0626
2SD161	0615
2SD161A	0615
2SD161B	0615
2SD161C	0615
2SD161D	0615
2SD161E	0615
2SD161F	0615
2SD161G	0615
2SD161GN	0615
2SD161H	0615
2SD161J	0615
2SD161K	0615
2SD161L	0615
2SD161M	0615
2SD161OR	0615
2SD161R	0615
2SD161X	0615
2SD161Y	0615
2SD162	0208
2SD162A	0208
2SD162B	0208
2SD162C	0208
2SD162D	0208
2SD162E	0208
2SD162F	0208
2SD162G	0208
2SD162GN	0208
2SD162H	0208
2SD162J	0208
2SD162K	0208
2SD162L	0208
2SD162M	0208
2SD162OR	0208
2SD162R	0208
2SD162X	0208
2SD162Y	0208
2SD163	0103
2SD163A	0103
2SD163B	0103
2SD163C	0103
2SD163D	0103
2SD163E	0103
2SD163F	0103
2SD163G	0103
2SD163GN	0103
2SD163H	0103
2SD163J	0103
2SD163K	0103
2SD163L	0103
2SD163M	0103
2SD163OR	0103
2SD163R	0103
2SD163X	0103
2SD163Y	0103
2SD164	0103
2SD164A	0103
2SD164B	0103
2SD164C	0103
2SD164D	0103
2SD164E	0103
2SD164F	0103
2SD164G	0103

DEVICE TYPE	REPL CODE
2SD164GN	0103
2SD164H	0103
2SD164J	0103
2SD164K	0103
2SD164L	0103
2SD164M	0103
2SD164OR	0103
2SD164R	0103
2SD164X	0103
2SD164Y	0103
2SD165	1955
2SD166	1955
2SD167	0208
2SD167A	0208
2SD167B	0208
2SD167C	0208
2SD167E	0208
2SD167F	0208
2SD167G	0208
2SD167GN	0208
2SD167H	0208
2SD167J	0208
2SD167K	0208
2SD167L	0208
2SD167M	0208
2SD167OR	0208
2SD167R	0208
2SD167X	0208
2SD167Y	0208
2SD168	3339
2SD170	0208
2SD170(A)	0208
2SD170(B)	0208
2SD170A	0208
2SD170A/PB	0208
2SD170AA	0208
2SD170AB	0208
2SD170AC	0208
2SD170B	0208
2SD170BC	0208
2SD170C	0208
2SD171	0637
2SD172	0103
2SD172A	0103
2SD172B	0103
2SD172C	0103
2SD172D	0103
2SD172E	0103
2SD172F	0103
2SD172G	0103
2SD172GN	0103
2SD172H	0103
2SD172J	0103
2SD172K	0103
2SD172L	0103
2SD172M	0103
2SD172OR	0103
2SD172R	0103
2SD172X	0103
2SD172Y	0103
2SD173	0130
2SD173A	0130
2SD173B	0130
2SD173C	0130
2SD173D	0130
2SD173E	0130
2SD173F	0130
2SD173G	0130
2SD173GN	0130
2SD173H	0130
2SD173J	0130
2SD173K	0130
2SD173M	0130
2SD173OR	0130
2SD173X	0130
2SD173Y	0130
2SD174	0103
2SD174A	0103
2SD174B	0103
2SD174C	0103
2SD174D	0103
2SD174E	0103
2SD174F	0103
2SD174G	0103
2SD174GN	0103
2SD174H	0103
2SD174J	0103
2SD174K	0103
2SD174L	0103
2SD174M	0103
2SD174R	0103
2SD174X	0103
2SD174Y	0103
2SD175	0103
2SD175A	0103
2SD175B	0103
2SD175C	0103
2SD175D	0103
2SD175E	0103
2SD175F	0103
2SD175G	0103
2SD175GN	0103
2SD175H	0103
2SD175J	0103
2SD175K	0103
2SD175L	0103
2SD175M	0103
2SD175OR	0103
2SD175R	0103

DEVICE TYPE	REPL CODE
2SD175X	0103
2SD175Y	0103
2SD176	0130
2SD176A	0130
2SD176B	0130
2SD176C	0130
2SD176D	0130
2SD176E	0130
2SD176F	0130
2SD176G	0130
2SD176GN	0130
2SD176H	0130
2SD176J	0130
2SD176K	0130
2SD176L	0130
2SD176M	0130
2SD176OR	0130
2SD176X	0130
2SD176Y	0130
2SD177	0615
2SD178	0208
2SD178A	0208
2SD178B	0208
2SD178C	0208
2SD178D	0208
2SD178E	0208
2SD178F	0208
2SD178G	0208
2SD178GN	0208
2SD178H	0208
2SD178J	0208
2SD178K	0208
2SD178L	0208
2SD178M	0208
2SD178Q	0208
2SD178T	0208
2SD178X	0208
2SD178Y	0208
2SD180	2766
2SD180A	2766
2SD180B	2766
2SD180C	2766
2SD180D	2766
2SD180F	2766
2SD180G	2766
2SD180GN	2766
2SD180H	2766
2SD180J	2766
2SD180K	2766
2SD180L	2766
2SD180M	2766
2SD180OR	2766
2SD180R	2766
2SD180X	2766
2SD180Y	2766
2SD181	1955
2SD181A	1955
2SD182	0086
2SD182A	0086
2SD182B	0086
2SD182C	0086
2SD182D	0086
2SD182E	0086
2SD182F	0086
2SD182G	0086
2SD182GN	0086
2SD182H	0086
2SD182J	0086
2SD182K	0086
2SD182L	0086
2SD182OR	0086
2SD182R	0086
2SD182X	0086
2SD182Y	0086
2SD183	0086
2SD183B	0086
2SD183E	0086
2SD183GN	0086
2SD183K	0086
2SD183L	0086
2SD183OR	0086
2SD183R	0086
2SD184	0042
2SD184A	0042
2SD184B	0042
2SD184C	0042
2SD184D	0042
2SD184E	0042
2SD184F	0042
2SD184H	0042
2SD184J	0042
2SD184K	0042
2SD184L	0042
2SD184M	0042
2SD184OR	0042
2SD184Y	0042
2SD185	0042
2SD186	0208
2SD186A	0208
2SD186B	0208
2SD186C	0208
2SD186D	0208
2SD186E	0208
2SD186F	0208
2SD186G	0208
2SD186GN	0208
2SD186H	0208
2SD186J	0208
2SD186K	0208

DEVICE TYPE	REPL CODE
2SD186L	0208
2SD186M	0208
2SD186OR	0208
2SD186R	0208
2SD186X	0208
2SD186Y	0208
2SD187	0208
2SD187-OR	0208
2SD187A	0208
2SD187B	0208
2SD187C	0208
2SD187D	0208
2SD187E	0208
2SD187F	0208
2SD187G	0208
2SD187GN	0208
2SD187H	0208
2SD187J	0208
2SD187K	0208
2SD187L	0208
2SD187M	0208
2SD187OR	0208
2SD187R	0208
2SD187X	0208
2SD187Y	0208
2SD188	2534
2SD188A	2534
2SD188B	2534
2SD188C	2534
2SD188D	2534
2SD188E	2534
2SD188F	2534
2SD188G	2534
2SD188GN	2534
2SD188H	2534
2SD188J	2534
2SD188L	2534
2SD188M	2534
2SD188OR	2534
2SD188R	2534
2SD188X	2534
2SD188Y	2534
2SD189	0177
2SD189A	0177
2SD189B	0177
2SD189C	0177
2SD189D	0177
2SD189E	0177
2SD189F	0177
2SD189G	0177
2SD189GN	0177
2SD189H	0177
2SD189J	0177
2SD189K	0177
2SD189L	0177
2SD189M	0177
2SD189OR	0177
2SD189R	0177
2SD189X	0177
2SD189Y	0177
2SD190	0142
2SD190B	0142
2SD190C	0142
2SD190D	0142
2SD190E	0142
2SD190F	0142
2SD190GN	0142
2SD190H	0142
2SD190J	0142
2SD190K	0142
2SD190L	0142
2SD190M	0142
2SD190OR	0142
2SD190R	0142
2SD190X	0142
2SD190Y	0142
2SD191	0208
2SD192	0208
2SD193	0208
2SD194	0208
2SD195	0208
2SD195A	0208
2SD195B	0208
2SD195C	0208
2SD195D	0208
2SD195E	0208
2SD195F	0208
2SD195G	0208
2SD195GN	0208
2SD195H	0208
2SD195J	0208
2SD195K	0208
2SD195L	0208
2SD195M	0208
2SD195OR	0208
2SD195R	0208
2SD195X	0208
2SD195Y	0208
2SD198	0042
2SD198(H)	0042
2SD198(R)	0042
2SD198A	0042
2SD198AP	0042
2SD198A-Q	OEM
2SD198AQ	0042
2SD198A-R	OEM
2SD198AR	0042
2SD198B	0042
2SD198C	0042

DEVICE TYPE	REPL CODE
2SD198D	0042
2SD198F	0042
2SD198G	0042
2SD198H	0042
2SD198HQ	0042
2SD198HR	0042
2SD198J	0042
2SD198K	0042
2SD198OR	0042
2SD198P	0042
2SD198Q	0042
2SD198R	0042
2SD198S	0042
2SD198V	0042
2SD198X	0042
2SD198Y	0042
2SD199	0003
2SD200	0223
2SD200-OR	0223
2SD200A	0223
2SD200B	0223
2SD200C	0223
2SD200D	0223
2SD200E	0223
2SD200F	0223
2SD200G	0223
2SD200GN	0223
2SD200H	0223
2SD200J	0223
2SD200K	0223
2SD200L	0223
2SD200M	0223
2SD200OR	0223
2SD200X	0223
2SD200Y	0223
2SD201	0861
2SD201-O	0861
2SD201A	0861
2SD201B	0861
2SD201C	0861
2SD201F	0861
2SD201G	0861
2SD201GN	0861
2SD201H	0861
2SD201J	0861
2SD201K	0861
2SD201L	0861
2SD201M	0861
2SD201M(O)	0861
2SD201M(O,Y)	0861
2SD201M(Y)	0861
2SD201MO	0861
2SD201MY	0861
2SD201Q	0861
2SD201X	0861
2SD201Y	0861
2SD202	0861
2SD203	0861
2SD204	0086
2SD204(L)	0086
2SD204A	0086
2SD204B	0086
2SD204BL	0086
2SD204C	0086
2SD204D	0086
2SD204E	0086
2SD204F	0086
2SD204G	0086
2SD204GA	0086
2SD204GN	0086
2SD204H	0086
2SD204K	0086
2SD204L	0086
2SD204M	0086
2SD204R	0086
2SD204Y	0086
2SD205	0086
2SD205(L)	0086
2SD205(M)	0086
2SD205A	0086
2SD205B	0086
2SD205C	0086
2SD205D	0086
2SD205E	0086
2SD205F	0086
2SD205G	0086
2SD205GN	0086
2SD205H	0086
2SD205J	0086
2SD205L	0086
2SD205M	0086
2SD205OR	0086
2SD205R	0086
2SD205X	0086
2SD205Y	0086
2SD206	0538
2SD206A	0538
2SD207	0103
2SD207A	0103
2SD208	0615
2SD208A	0615
2SD211	0103
2SD211-O	0103
2SD211-OR	0103
2SD211A	0103
2SD211B	0103
2SD211C	0103
2SD211D	0103
2SD211E	0103

DEVICE TYPE	REPL CODE
2SD211F	0103
2SD211G	0103
2SD211GN	0103
2SD211H	0103
2SD211J	0103
2SD211K	0103
2SD211L	0103
2SD211M	0103
2SD211M(O)	0103
2SD211M(Y)	0103
2SD211OR	0103
2SD211R	0103
2SD211X	0103
2SD211Y	0103
2SD212	0103
2SD212A	0103
2SD212B	0103
2SD212C	0103
2SD212D	0103
2SD212E	0103
2SD212F	0103
2SD212G	0103
2SD212GN	0103
2SD212H	0103
2SD212J	0103
2SD212K	0103
2SD212L	0103
2SD212M	0103
2SD212OR	0103
2SD212R	0103
2SD212X	0103
2SD212Y	0103
2SD213	0177
2SD214	0177
2SD215	0086
2SD216	0086
2SD217	0861
2SD218	0861
2SD219	0086
2SD219A	0086
2SD219B	0086
2SD219C	0086
2SD219D	0086
2SD219E	0086
2SD219F	0086
2SD219G	0086
2SD219GN	0086
2SD219H	0086
2SD219J	0086
2SD219K	0086
2SD219L	0086
2SD219M	0086
2SD219OR	0086
2SD219R	0086
2SD219X	0086
2SD219Y	0086
2SD220	0086
2SD220A	0086
2SD220B	0086
2SD220C	0086
2SD220D	0086
2SD220E	0086
2SD220F	0086
2SD220G	0086
2SD220GN	0086
2SD220H	0086
2SD220J	0086
2SD220K	0086
2SD220L	0086
2SD220M	0086
2SD220OR	0086
2SD220R	0086
2SD220X	0086
2SD220Y	0086
2SD221	0086
2SD221F	0086
2SD222	1471
2SD222A	1471
2SD222B	1471
2SD222C	1471
2SD222D	1471
2SD222E	1471
2SD222F	1471
2SD222G	1471
2SD222GN	1471
2SD222H	1471
2SD222J	1471
2SD222K	1471
2SD222L	1471
2SD222M	1471
2SD222OR	1471
2SD222R	1471
2SD222X	1471
2SD222Y	1471
2SD223	1471
2SD223A	1471
2SD223B	1471
2SD223C	1471
2SD223D	1471
2SD223E	1471
2SD223F	1471
2SD223G	1471
2SD223GN	1471
2SD223H	1471
2SD223J	1471
2SD223K	1471
2SD223L	1471
2SD223M	1471
2SD223OR	1471

If replacement code is OEM, contact original manufacturer for replacement.

DEVICE TYPE	REPL CODE
2SD223R	1471
2SD223X	1471
2SD223Y	1471
2SD224	1471
2SD226	0178
2SD226-0	0178
2SD226-O	0178
2SD226A	0178
2SD226A(0)	0178
2SD226AO	0178
2SD226AP	0178
2SD226B	0178
2SD226BP	0178
2SD226C	0178
2SD226E	0178
2SD226F	0178
2SD226G	0178
2SD226GN	0178
2SD226H	0178
2SD226J	0178
2SD226K	0178
2SD226L	0178
2SD226M	0178
2SD226OR	0178
2SD226P	0178
2SD226Q	0178
2SD226R	0178
2SD226X	0178
2SD226Y	0178
2SD227	1409
2SD227(PANASONIC)	1409
2SD227(R)	1409
2SD227-175	1409
2SD227-OR	1409
2SD227A	1409
2SD227B	1409
2SD227C	1409
2SD227D	1409
2SD227E	1409
2SD227G	1409
2SD227GN	1409
2SD227H	1409
2SD227J	1409
2SD227K	1409
2SD227L	1409
2SD227LF	1409
2SD227M	1409
2SD227OR	1409
2SD227R	1409
2SD227V	1409
2SD227X	1409
2SD227Y	1409
2SD228	0155
2SD228F	0155
2SD228G	0155
2SD228GN	0155
2SD228H	0155
2SD228J	0155
2SD228K	0155
2SD228L	0155
2SD228M	0155
2SD228OR	0155
2SD228R	0155
2SD228X	0155
2SD228Y	0155
2SD231	0130
2SD232	0130
2SD232A	0130
2SD234	0228
2SD234(0)	0228
2SD234-0	0228
2SD234-O	0228
2SD234-ORG	0228
2SD234-R	0228
2SD234-RED	0228
2SD234-Y	0228
2SD234-YEL	0228
2SD234A	0228
2SD234B	0228
2SD234C	0228
2SD234D	0228
2SD234E	0228
2SD234F	0228
2SD234G	0228
2SD234GA	0228
2SD234GN	0228
2SD234G-O	0228
2SD234G-R	0228
2SD234GR	0228
2SD234G-Y	0228
2SD234H	0228
2SD234J	0228
2SD234K	0228
2SD234L	0228
2SD234M	0228
2SD234N	0228
2SD234O	0228
2SD234OR	0228
2SD234R	0228
2SD234X	0228
2SD234Y	0228
2SD235	0228
2SD235(O)	0228
2SD235(R)	0228
2SD235(Y)	0228
2SD235-0	0228
2SD235-O	0228
2SD235-OR	0228
2SD235-ORG	0228
2SD235-R	0228
2SD235-RED	0228
2SD235-Y	0228
2SD235-YEL	0228
2SD235-Y.JA	0228
2SD235A	0228
2SD235B	0228
2SD235C	0228
2SD235D	0228
2SD235E	0228
2SD235F	0228
2SD235G	0228
2SD235GN	0228
2SD235G-O	0228
2SD235G-R	0228
2SD235G-Y	0228
2SD235H	0228
2SD235J	0228
2SD235L	0228
2SD235LBY	0228
2SD235M	0228
2SD235O	0228
2SD235OR	0228
2SD235R	0228
2SD235RED	0228
2SD235RY	0228
2SD235X	0228
2SD235Y	0228
2SD236	4036
2SD236(02Y)	4036
2SD236A	4036
2SD236B	4036
2SD236C	4036
2SD236D	4036
2SD236E	4036
2SD236F	4036
2SD236G	4036
2SD236GN	4036
2SD236H	4036
2SD236J	4036
2SD236K	4036
2SD236L	4036
2SD236M	4036
2SD236R	4036
2SD236X	4036
2SD236Y	4036
2SD237	0178
2SD238	0178
2SD238(F)	0178
2SD238F	0178
2SD241	0042
2SD242	0419
2SD242YLC	0419
2SD243	0236
2SD244	0236
2SD245K(C)	OEM
2SD246	0223
2SD246A	0223
2SD246B	0223
2SD246C	0223
2SD246D	0223
2SD246E	0223
2SD246F	0223
2SD246G	0223
2SD246GN	0223
2SD246H	0223
2SD246J	0223
2SD246K	0223
2SD246L	0223
2SD246M	0223
2SD246OR	0223
2SD246R	0223
2SD246X	0223
2SD246Y	0223
2SD247	0615
2SD247K	0615
2SD249	0130
2SD250	0130
2SD251	1021
2SD254	0178
2SD255	0178
2SD256	0042
2SD257	0419
2SD258	0236
2SD259	0236
2SD260	0615
2SD261	0218
2SD261(L)	0218
2SD261(O)	0218
2SD261(O,Q)	0218
2SD261(Q)	0218
2SD261(R)	0218
2SD261(V)	0218
2SD261-0	0218
2SD261-O	0218
2SD261A	0218
2SD261B	0218
2SD261C	0218
2SD261D	0218
2SD261E	0218
2SD261F	0218
2SD261G	0218
2SD261GN	0218
2SD261H	0218
2SD261J	0218
2SD261K	0218
2SD261L	0218
2SD261M	0218
2SD261OR	0218
2SD261P	0218
2SD261Q	0218
2SD261R	0218
2SD261S	0218
2SD261U	0218
2SD261V	0218
2SD261W	0218
2SD261X	0218
2SD261Y	0218
2SD262	0359
2SD265	0359
2SD266	0359
2SD271R	OEM
2SD272	0359
2SD273	0359
2SD274	0359
2SD280	OEM
2SD283	0074
2SD284	0424
2SD285	0074
2SD286	0538
2SD287	0538
2SD287A	0538
2SD287B	0538
2SD287C	0538
2SD288	0419
2SD288(O)	0419
2SD288A	0419
2SD288B	0419
2SD288C	0419
2SD288K	0419
2SD288L	0419
2SD289	0419
2SD289A	0419
2SD289B	0419
2SD289C	0419
2SD290	0178
2SD291	4036
2SD291(R)	4036
2SD291-0	4036
2SD291B	4036
2SD291BL	4036
2SD291C	4036
2SD291D	4036
2SD291E	4036
2SD291F	4036
2SD291G	4036
2SD291GA	4036
2SD291GN	4036
2SD291H	4036
2SD291J	4036
2SD291K	4036
2SD291L	4036
2SD291M	4036
2SD291OR	4036
2SD291R	4036
2SD291X	4036
2SD291Y	4036
2SD292	0042
2SD292-0	0042
2SD292A	0042
2SD292B	0042
2SD292BL	0042
2SD292C	0042
2SD292D	0042
2SD292E	0042
2SD292F	0042
2SD292G	0042
2SD292GA	0042
2SD292GN	0042
2SD292H	0042
2SD292J	0042
2SD292K	0042
2SD292L	0042
2SD292M	0042
2SD292OR	0042
2SD292R	0042
2SD292X	0042
2SD292Y	0042
2SD293	0359
2SD294	0359
2SD297	0178
2SD299	0223
2SD299(V)	0223
2SD299A	0223
2SD299B	0223
2SD299C	0223
2SD299E	0223
2SD299F	0223
2SD299G	0223
2SD299GN	0223
2SD299H	0223
2SD299J	0223
2SD299K	0223
2SD299M	0223
2SD299OR	0223
2SD299R	0223
2SD299SL	0223
2SD299X	0223
2SD299Y	0223
2SD300	0223
2SD300A	0223
2SD300B	0223
2SD300C	0223
2SD300D	0223
2SD300G	0223
2SD300H	0223
2SD300J	0223
2SD301	3956
2SD310	1841
2SD311	1841
2SD312	0003
2SD312A	0003
2SD312B	0003
2SD312C	0003
2SD312D	0003
2SD312E	0003
2SD312F	0003
2SD312G	0003
2SD312GN	0003
2SD312H	0003
2SD312J	0003
2SD312K	0003
2SD312L	0003
2SD312M	0003
2SD312X	0003
2SD312Y	0003
2SD313	0042
2SD313(D)	0042
2SD313(D,E)	0042
2SD313(DE)	0042
2SD313(E)	0042
2SD313(EF)	0042
2SD313(F)	0042
2SD313A	0042
2SD313B	0042
2SD313C	0042
2SD313D	0042
2SD313DE	0042
2SD313D-RA	OEM
2SD313E	0042
2SD313E-RA	OEM
2SD313F	0042
2SD313G	0042
2SD313GN	0042
2SD313H	0042
2SD313HP	0042
2SD313HP-D	0042
2SD313HP-E	0042
2SD313L	0042
2SD313M	0042
2SD313N	0042
2SD313R	0042
2SD313RA	0042
2SD313RA(D)	0042
2SD313RA(E)	0042
2SD313RA(F)	0042
2SD313Y	0042
2SD314	0042
2SD314A	0042
2SD314B	0042
2SD314C	0042
2SD314D	0042
2SD314E	0042
2SD314F	0042
2SD314GN	0042
2SD314H	0042
2SD314L	0042
2SD314M	0042
2SD314N	0042
2SD314R	0042
2SD314Y	0042
2SD315	4186
2SD315C	4186
2SD315D	4186
2SD315E	4186
2SD316	0177
2SD316-1	0177
2SD316-2	0177
2SD317	0419
2SD317A	0419
2SD317A(F)	0419
2SD317A(F)(P)	0419
2SD317A(P)	0419
2SD317AF	0419
2SD317AP	0419
2SD317F	0419
2SD317P	0419
2SD318	0419
2SD318-O	0419
2SD318A	0419
2SD318B	0419
2SD318P	0419
2SD318Q	0419
2SD319	0538
2SD320	0074
2SD321	0359
2SD322	0177
2SD322A	0177
2SD322B	0177
2SD322C	0177
2SD323	0177
2SD323A	0177
2SD323B	0177
2SD323C	0177
2SD324	0142
2SD324E	0142
2SD325	0555
2SD325-1	0555
2SD325-OR	0555
2SD325A	0555
2SD325B	0555
2SD325C	0555
2SD325D	0555
2SD325DS	OEM
2SD325E	0555
2SD325ES	OEM
2SD325F	0555
2SD325G	0555
2SD325GN	0555
2SD325H	0555
2SD325J	0555
2SD325K	0555
2SD325L	0555
2SD325M	0555
2SD325OR	0555
2SD325R	OEM
2SD325X	0555
2SD325Y	0555
2SD326	0142
2SD326A	0142
2SD326B	0142
2SD326C	0142
2SD326D	0142
2SD326E	0142
2SD326L	0142
2SD326M	0142
2SD326OR	0142
2SD326X	0142
2SD326Y	0142
2SD327	0284
2SD327-V	0284
2SD327A	0284
2SD327B	0284
2SD327C	0284
2SD327D	0284
2SD327E	0284
2SD327F	0284
2SD327L	0284
2SD327OR	0284
2SD327R	0284
2SD328	0086
2SD328S	0086
2SD329	0187
2SD330	1597
2SD330(E)	1597
2SD330D	1597
2SD330E	1597
2SD330F	OEM
2SD331	0042
2SD332	0861
2SD334	0177
2SD334A	0177
2SD334R	0177
2SD335	0130
2SD336	0320
2SD336(R)	0320
2SD336(Y)	0320
2SD338	0130
2SD339	0177
2SD339-1	0177
2SD339-2	0177
2SD340	0177
2SD340-1	0177
2SD340-2	0177
2SD341	0103
2SD341H	0103
2SD342	0419
2SD343	0228
2SD343A	0228
2SD343B	0228
2SD343C	0228
2SD343D	0228
2SD343H	0228
2SD343J	0228
2SD343K	0228
2SD344	0419
2SD345	0419
2SD346	0419
2SD347	0419
2SD348	0309
2SD349	0396
2SD350	2040
2SD350(Q)	2040
2SD350A	2040
2SD350Q	2040
2SD350T	2040
2SD351	0359
2SD352	0208
2SD352D	0208
2SD352H	0208
2SD353	0220
2SD355	0018
2SD355C	0018
2SD355D	0018
2SD356	0236
2SD356E	0236
2SD357	0236
2SD357E	0236
2SD358	0236
2SD358E	0236
2SD359	1597
2SD359C	1597
2SD359C2	1597
2SD359D	1597
2SD359D1	1597
2SD359D2	1597
2SD360	0042
2SD360D	0042
2SD360E	0042
2SD361	0042
2SD361C	0042
2SD361D	0042
2SD362	1157
2SD365	0042
2SD365A	0042
2SD365B	0042
2SD365H	0042
2SD365HP	0042
2SD365P	0042
2SD366	0042
2SD366A	0042
2SD367	0208
2SD367A	0208
2SD367B	0208
2SD367C	0208
2SD367E	0208
2SD367F	0208
2SD367H	0208
2SD367J	0208
2SD367K	0208
2SD367L	0208
2SD367M	0208
2SD367OR	0208
2SD367R	0208
2SD367X	0208
2SD367Y	0208
2SD368	0309
2SD368A-D	0309
2SD368A-E	0309
2SD369	0538
2SD369-0	0538
2SD369-O	0538
2SD369C	0538
2SD369Y	0538
2SD369Y(FA)	OEM
2SD370	0177
2SD371	0861
2SD371-0	0861
2SD371-R	0861
2SD371-Y	0861
2SD375	0615
2SD376	1955
2SD376A	1955
2SD377	1955
2SD378	0626
2SD379	0177
2SD380	0309
2SD380A	0309
2SD381	0236
2SD381CDTA	OEM
2SD381K	0236
2SD381L	0236
2SD382	0236
2SD383	0359
2SD384	3336
2SD385	1203
2SD386	0388
2SD386A	0388
2SD386A(D)	0388
2SD386A(E)	0388
2SD386A-D	0388
2SD386AD	0388
2SD386A-E	0388
2SD386AE	0388
2SD386A-Y	OEM
2SD386AY	2133
2SD386A-YD	OEM
2SD386A-YE	OEM
2SD386E	0388
2SD386Y	0388
2SD387	0388
2SD387A	0388
2SD387AC	0388
2SD387AD	0388
2SD387A-E	OEM
2SD387AE	0388
2SD387A-F	OEM
2SD387AF	0388
2SD387AS	0388
2SD387D	0388
2SD387E	0388
2SD387S	0388
2SD388	0861
2SD389	0042
2SD389(LP)	0042
2SD389(O)	0042
2SD389(O,LP,P)	0042
2SD389(P)	0042
2SD389-0	0042
2SD389-O	0042
2SD389A	0042
2SD389A(F)	0042
2SD389A(O)	0042
2SD389A(P)	0042
2SD389AF	0042
2SD389AFO	0042
2SD389AFO	0042
2SD389AFP	0042
2SD389AFPQ	0042
2SD389AO	0042
2SD389AP	0042
2SD389AQ	0042
2SD389B	0042
2SD389B(O)	0042
2SD389B(P)	0042
2SD389BLB	0042
2SD389BLB-O	0042
2SD389BLB-P	0042
2SD389BP	0042
2SD389BQ	0042
2SD389L	0042
2SD389LB	0042
2SD389LBP	0042
2SD389LP	0042
2SD389P	0042
2SD389Q	0042
2SD389R	0042
2SD390	0042
2SD390A	0042
2SD390P	0042
2SD390Q	0042
2SD392	0284
2SD393	0359
2SD394	0309
2SD395	0359
2SD396	0359
2SD400	2882
2SD400(E)	2882
2SD400(F)	2882
2SD400-D-MP	2882
2SD400-E-MP	2882
2SD400-F-MP	2882
2SD400D	1559
2SD400E	2882
2SD400F	2882
2SD400FZ	2882
2SD400G	OEM
2SD400P1	2882
2SD400P2	2882
2SD401	1274
2SD401(A)	1274
2SD401(K)	1274
2SD401(L)	1274
2SD401-O	1274
2SD401-Y	1274
2SD401A	1274
2SD401A(K)	1274
2SD401A(L)	1274
2SD401A-K	1274
2SD401AK	1274
2SD401A-L	1274
2SD401AL	1274
2SD401A-M	OEM
2SD401AM	1274
2SD401E	1274
2SD401EK	1274
2SD401H	1274
2SD401I	1274
2SD401IJ	1274
2SD401K	1274
2SD401KL	1274
2SD401L	1274
2SD401LA	1274
2SD401LM	1274
2SD401M	1274
2SD401R	1274
2SD401Y	1274
2SD402	0388
2SD402A	0388
2SD402A-K	OEM
2SD402AK	0388
2SD402A-L	OEM
2SD402AL	0388
2SD402A-M	OEM
2SD402AM	0388
2SD402K	0388
2SD402L	0388
2SD402M	0388
2SD404	0419
2SD404G	0419
2SD405	1203
2SD407	OEM
2SD408	OEM
2SD409	1203
2SD410	OEM
2SD411	2422
2SD412	OEM
2SD413	0233
2SD414	0558
2SD414Q	0558
2SD415	0558
2SD415P	0558
2SD415Q	0558
2SD415R	0558
2SD415Y	0558
2SD416	0309
2SD417	0861
2SD418	0065
2SD419	1203
2SD422	0424
2SD423	0424
2SD424	0538
2SD424-O	0538
2SD424R	0538
2SD425	0177
2SD425-O	0177
2SD425-R	0177
2SD426	0177
2SD426-O	0177
2SD426-R	0177
2SD427	0177
2SD427-O	0177
2SD427-R	0177
2SD428	0861
2SD428-O	0861
2SD428-R	0861
2SD429	0359
2SD430	0615
2SD431	0615
2SD432	0615
2SD433	2398
2SD434	2398
2SD435	2398
2SD436	2398

If replacement code is OEM, contact original manufacturer for replacement.

DEVICE TYPE	REPL CODE
2SD437	0359
2SD437W	0359
2SD438	0191
2SD438(E)	0191
2SD438(F)	0191
2SD438D	5784
2SD438E	0191
2SD438F	0191
2SD438TV	OEM
2SD439	0558
2SD439E	0558
2SD439F	2529
2SD445	OEM
2SD457	OEM
2SD458	0359
2SD458C	0359
2SD459	2220
2SD460	1203
2SD461	0637
2SD463	2411
2SD464	2422
2SD467	0945
2SD467(B)	0945
2SD467(C)	0945
2SD467-C	0945
2SD467B	0945
2SD467BC	0945
2SD467C	0945
2SD468	0018
2SD468(C)	0018
2SD468A	0018
2SD468AC	0018
2SD468B	0018
2SD468BC	0018
2SD468C	0018
2SD468D	0018
2SD468E	0018
2SD468F	0018
2SD468G	0018
2SD468GN	0018
2SD468H	0018
2SD468L	0018
2SD468LN	0018
2SD468Y	0018
2SD469	0177
2SD470	1740
2SD470-A	1740
2SD470-B	1740
2SD470A	1740
2SD470B	1740
2SD471	0018
2SD471(1)L	0018
2SD471(A)	0018
2SD471(K)	0018
2SD471(L)	0018
2SD471-L	0018
2SD471A	0018
2SD471B	0018
2SD471C	0018
2SD471D	0018
2SD471E	0018
2SD471G	0018
2SD471GN	0018
2SD471K	0018
2SD471KA	0018
2SD471L	0018
2SD471LA	0018
2SD471M	0018
2SD471N	0018
2SD471OR	0018
2SD471P	0018
2SD471Q	0018
2SD471R	0018
2SD471X	0018
2SD471Y	0018
2SD472	OEM
2SD472H	OEM
2SD473	0018
2SD473H	0018
2SD474K	0007
2SD475	0042
2SD475A	0042
2SD476	0419
2SD476A	0419
2SD476AKB	0419
2SD476AKC	0419
2SD476B	0419
2SD476C	0419
2SD476D	0419
2SD476G	0419
2SD476KB	0419
2SD476KC	0419
2SD476O	0419
2SD476YL	0419
2SD477	0042
2SD478	0388
2SD478-08	0388
2SD478-C	0388
2SD478A-01	0388
2SD478B	0388
2SD478BS	0388
2SD478C	0388
2SD478CS	0388
2SD478D	0388
2SD478Y	0388
2SD478YL	0388
2SD479	0161
2SD480	0161
2SD481	0161
2SD482	0275
2SD483	0275
2SD484	0168
2SD485	0161
2SD486	0161
2SD487	0161
2SD488	0161
2SD489	0161
2SD490	0161
2SD491	0556
2SD492	0103
2SD493	0556
2SD494	0556
2SD495	0556
2SD496	3487
2SD497	3487
2SD498	3487
2SD499	0556
2SD500	0556
2SD501	0556
2SD502	2411
2SD503	2411
2SD504	2422
2SD505	2422
2SD506	2422
2SD511A	OEM
2SD517	0309
2SD518	0178
2SD519	0424
2SD520	0130
2SD522	0103
2SD523	2411
2SD524	1384
2SD525	4183
2SD525-O	4183
2SD525-Y	4183
2SD525R	4183
2SD525Y	4183
2SD526	2969
2SD526(O)	2969
2SD526-O	2969
2SD528	OEM
2SD529	1841
2SD530	OEM
2SD531	0419
2SD532	5604
2SD533	0359
2SD534	0538
2SD535	2398
2SD536	1955
2SD537	1955
2SD538	1841
2SD538A	1841
2SD539	0359
2SD539A	0359
2SD540	OEM
2SD541	OEM
2SD542	OEM
2SD543	OEM
2SD544	0419
2SD545	0018
2SD545(E)	0018
2SD545(F)	0018
2SD545(G)	0018
2SD545E	0018
2SD545F	0018
2SD545G	0018
2SD545NP	OEM
2SD546	2085
2SD546K	2085
2SD547	OEM
2SD548	OEM
2SD549	0553
2SD550	3328
2SD551	0538
2SD552	2398
2SD553	4800
2SD553-Y	4800
2SD553Y	4800
2SD554	1021
2SD555	0861
2SD556	0538
2SD557	0538
2SD558	OEM
2SD560	1203
2SD560L	OEM
2SD560M	OEM
2SD562	0830
2SD562A	0830
2SD562B	0830
2SD562C	0830
2SD562D	0830
2SD562E	0830
2SD562K	0830
2SD562L	0830
2SD562OR	0830
2SD562R	0830
2SD562X	0830
2SD562Y	0830
2SD564	4182
2SD565	1980
2SD568	0419
2SD568(K)	0419
2SD569	0419
2SD570	0419
2SD571	1967
2SD571(L)	1967
2SD571-L	OEM
2SD571K	1967
2SD571L	1967
2SD572	0359
2SD573	0359
2SD575	4841
2SD575L	4841
2SD576	0233
2SD577	0065
2SD578	OEM
2SD579	0178
2SD580	0742
2SD581	0177
2SD581A	0177
2SD582	4857
2SD582A	4857
2SD583	2398
2SD586	2911
2SD586A	2911
2SD586R	2911
2SD587	2911
2SD587A	2911
2SD588	2911
2SD588A	2911
2SD589	0065
2SD590	0086
2SD591	0111
2SD591R	0111
2SD592	0284
2SD592A	0284
2SD592ANC	0284
2SD592AQ	1559
2SD592AR	1559
2SD592NC	0284
2SD592R	0284
2SD593	0168
2SD594	OEM
2SD596	1722
2SD596DV1	1722
2SD596DV2	1722
2SD596DV3	1722
2SD596DV4	1722
2SD596DV5	1722
2SD597	0861
2SD598	0861
2SD599	0111
2SD600	0558
2SD600D	2529
2SD600E	2529
2SD600F	2529
2SD600K	0558
2SD600KE	2529
2SD600KF	2529
2SD601	0719
2SD601(Q)	0719
2SD601(R)	0719
2SD601(S)	0719
2SD601-QRS	OEM
2SD601A	0719
2SD601A-Q	0719
2SD601AQRS	0719
2SD601AQRW	0719
2SD601A-QW	0719
2SD601AQW	0719
2SD601AR	0719
2SD601ATW	0719
2SD601AW	0719
2SD601Q	0719
2SD601QR	OEM
2SD601QRSTW	OEM
2SD601R	0719
2SD601R(TR)	OEM
2SD601S	0719
2SD602	1722
2SD602(R)	1722
2SD602(S)	1722
2SD602A	1722
2SD602R	OEM
2SD602R(W-R)	OEM
2SD602S	1722
2SD603	0155
2SD604	0074
2SD605	0359
2SD606	0359
2SD608	0388
2SD608A	0388
2SD610	1021
2SD611	0424
2SD612	1779
2SD612(E)	1779
2SD612(F)	1779
2SD612E	1779
2SD612F	2529
2SD612K	1779
2SD612K(E)	1779
2SD612KE	1779
2SD612KF	2529
2SD612K-SA-E	1779
2SD613	0060
2SD613(D)	0060
2SD613(E)	0060
2SD613E	0060
2SD613P	0060
2SD614	OEM
2SD615	OEM
2SD616	0861
2SD617	2422
2SD619	1935
2SD620	0161
2SD621	2820
2SD622	0424
2SD624	0233
2SD625	5622
2SD626	OEM
2SD627	2636
2SD628	2422
2SD628H	2422
2SD629	2422
2SD629H	2422
2SD630	0130
2SD631	2416
2SD632	0270
2SD632P	0270
2SD632Q	0270
2SD632R	0270
2SD633	1203
2SD634	1203
2SD635	1203
2SD636	0577
2SD636(O)	0577
2SD636(P)	0577
2SD636(Q)	0577
2SD636(R)	0577
2SD636(R.S.T)	0577
2SD636(S)	0577
2SD636(T)	0577
2SD636-0	0577
2SD636-O	0577
2SD636-P	0577
2SD636-Q	0577
2SD636-QRS	0577
2SD636-Q.R	0577
2SD636-R	0577
2SD636-R.S.T	0577
2SD636-S	0577
2SD636P	0577
2SD636Q	0577
2SD636QR	0577
2SD636QRS	0577
2SD636R	0577
2SD636RS	0577
2SD636S	0577
2SD636T	0577
2SD637	0577
2SD637(C)	0577
2SD637(CR)	0577
2SD637(Q)	0577
2SD637(R)	0577
2SD637(S)	0577
2SD637(T)	0577
2SD637-O	0577
2SD637-P	0577
2SD637-PQR	0577
2SD637-Q	0577
2SD637-QR	0577
2SD637-QRS	0577
2SD637-R	0577
2SD637-RS	0577
2SD637-S	0577
2SD637C	0577
2SD637CR	0577
2SD637O	0577
2SD637P	0577
2SD637PQ	0577
2SD637PQR	0577
2SD637PR	0577
2SD637Q	0577
2SD637QR	0577
2SD637QRS	0577
2SD637R	0577
2SD637RS	0577
2SD637RST	0577
2SD637S	0577
2SD637ST	0577
2SD637T	0577
2SD638	0667
2SD638(Q)	0667
2SD638(R)	0667
2SD638(S)	0667
2SD638-Q	0667
2SD638-R	0667
2SD638-RS	0667
2SD638-S	0667
2SD638P	0667
2SD638PQR	0667
2SD638Q	0667
2SD638QR	0667
2SD638QRS	0667
2SD638R	0667
2SD638RS	0667
2SD638S	0667
2SD638T	0667
2SD639	0667
2SD639(Q)	0667
2SD639(R)	0667
2SD639(S)	0667
2SD639-R	0667
2SD639-S	0667
2SD639P	0667
2SD639Q	0667
2SD639QR	0667
2SD639QRST	0667
2SD639R	0667
2SD639S	0667
2SD639T	0667
2SD640	0359
2SD641	1841
2SD642	OEM
2SD643	OEM
2SD644	OEM
2SD645	OEM
2SD646	OEM
2SD646A	OEM
2SD647	OEM
2SD647A	1376
2SD648	OEM
2SD648A	OEM
2SD649	0065
2SD649(Q)	0065
2SD649Q	0065
2SD650	OEM
2SD650H	OEM
2SD651	OEM
2SD652	OEM
2SD654	0086
2SD655	1967
2SD655(D)	1967
2SD655(E)	1967
2SD655(F)	1967
2SD655D	1967
2SD655E	1967
2SD655EF	1967
2SD655F	1967
2SD656	0178
2SD657	0074
2SD658	0065
2SD660	0626
2SD661	0577
2SD661(R)	0577
2SD661(S)	0577
2SD661(T)	0577
2SD661-R	0577
2SD661-S	0577
2SD661RS	0577
2SD661S	0577
2SD661ST	0577
2SD661T	0577
2SD662	0710
2SD662(Q)	0710
2SD662(R)	0710
2SD663	0359
2SD664	1203
2SD665	0538
2SD666	1376
2SD666A	1376
2SD666AB	1376
2SD666AC	1376
2SD666B	1376
2SD666C	1376
2SD666D	1376
2SD667	1376
2SD667(A)	1376
2SD667(B)	1376
2SD667A	1376
2SD667AB	1376
2SD667AC	1376
2SD667B	1376
2SD667C	1376
2SD667D	1376
2SD668	0558
2SD668A	0558
2SD668AB	0558
2SD668AC	0558
2SD668B	0558
2SD668D	0558
2SD669	0558
2SD669A	0558
2SD669AB	0558
2SD669AC	0558
2SD669B	0558
2SD669C	0558
2SD669D	0558
2SD670	1384
2SD670H	1384
2SD671	0155
2SD671(L)	0155
2SD672	0074
2SD673	0861
2SD673A	0861
2SD674	0861
2SD674A	0861
2SD675	0538
2SD675A	0538
2SD676	0538
2SD676A	0538
2SD677	0074
2SD678	1203
2SD678A	1203
2SD679	1203
2SD679A	1203
2SD683	1841
2SD683A	1841
2SD683S	1841
2SD684	OEM
2SD684A	OEM
2SD685	1841
2SD686	1203
2SD687	1203
2SD688	1471
2SD689	0055
2SD690	0424
2SD691	1203
2SD692	2411
2SD692(Q)	2411
2SD692M	2411
2SD692P	2411
2SD692Q	2411
2SD693	0074
2SD694	OEM
2SD695	OEM
2SD696	0014
2SD696A	0014
2SD696AB	OEM
2SD696AC	OEM
2SD697	OEM
2SD698	OEM
2SD698B	OEM
2SD699	OEM
2SD700	OEM
2SD701QR-TW	OEM
2SD702	OEM
2SD703	OEM
2SD704	0060
2SD704D	0060
2SD704E	0060
2SD705	0359
2SD706	0074
2SD707	0359
2SD708	OEM
2SD709	OEM
2SD710	1722
2SD711	2602
2SD711A	2602
2SD712	0477
2SD712A	0477
2SD713	0477
2SD715	0134
2SD716	3052
2SD716R	OEM
2SD717	3052
2SD718	0194
2SD720	OEM
2SD720D	0208
2SD720E	0208
2SD720PJ	0208
2SD721	1203
2SD722	5641
2SD723	0236
2SD724	0388
2SD725	0065
2SD725-06	0065
2SD726	0236
2SD726B	6031
2SD726C	6031
2SD727	3557
2SD728	3052
2SD729	3483
2SD729H	3483
2SD730	1384
2SD730H	1384
2SD731	3248
2SD732	0861
2SD732K	0861
2SD733	0538
2SD733K	0538
2SD733U	0538
2SD734	1505
2SD734(E)-AA	1505
2SD734(F)	1505
2SD734(F)-AA	1505
2SD734(G)	1505
2SD734(G)-AA	1505
2SD734-AA	1505
2SD734-F-AA	1505
2SD734-G-AA	1505
2SD734-NP	1505
2SD734-T	1505
2SD734E	1505
2SD734F	1505
2SD734G	1505
2SD735	2261
2SD735-O	2261
2SD735A-B-B/C	2261
2SD736	2261
2SD736A	2261
2SD737	2261
2SD738	2261
2SD738A	2261
2SD741	OEM
2SD743	1274
2SD743A	1274
2SD743R	1274
2SD745	2261
2SD745A	2261
2SD745B	2261
2SD746	OEM
2SD746A	OEM
2SD746A-01	OEM
2SD747	0079
2SD748	3197
2SD748A	3197
2SD748A-01	3197
2SD748A-01A	3197
2SD748B	3197
2SD749	0359
2SD749P	0359
2SD750	0538
2SD751	0194
2SD752	0538
2SD753	0538
2SD754	0320
2SD755	0525
2SD755D	0525
2SD755E	0525
2SD755F	0525
2SD756	0525
2SD756A	0525
2SD756AF	0525
2SD756D	0525
2SD756E	0525
2SD757	0168
2SD757C	0168
2SD757D	0168
2SD758	1077
2SD758C	1077
2SD758D	1077
2SD759	0388
2SD760	0388
2SD761	0388
2SD761D	0388
2SD761E	0388
2SD761V	0388
2SD761VL	0388
2SD761VL-D	OEM
2SD761VL-E	OEM
2SD761VR	0388
2SD761VR-D	OEM
2SD761VRD	0388
2SD761VR-E	OEM
2SD761VRE	0388
2SD762	0690
2SD762-O	0690
2SD762-OP	0690
2SD762-P	0690
2SD762A	0690
2SD762LB	0690
2SD762OP	0690
2SD762OPLB	0690
2SD762P	0690
2SD762PLB	0690
2SD762Q	0690
2SD763	1376
2SD764	0223
2SD765	0223
2SD766	2085
2SD766D	2085
2SD766P	2085
2SD766Q	2085
2SD766R	2085
2SD767	0155
2SD767(R)	0155
2SD767(S)	0155
2SD767R	0155
2SD767S	0155
2SD768	1948
2SD768K	1948
2SD769	0284
2SD770	0155
2SD771	0111
2SD772	0388
2SD772A	0388
2SD772B	0388
2SD772BLB	0388
2SD773	0018
2SD773-4	0018
2SD773-34	0018
2SD773K	0018
2SD773L	0018
2SD773U	0018
2SD774	2019
2SD774(U2)	2019
2SD774-3	2019
2SD774-4	2019
2SD774-34	2019
2SD774-K	2019
2SD774K	2019
2SD774R	2019
2SD774U	2019
2SD774U2	2019
2SD776	2526
2SD777	0270
2SD777(FA-4)	OEM
2SD777(FA-5)	0270
2SD777-1	0270
2SD777FA-1	0270
2SD777FA-5	0270
2SD777FA5	0270
2SD778	0284
2SD778(Q)	0284
2SD778(R)	0284
2SD778Q	0284
2SD778QR	0284
2SD778R	0284
2SD779	0284
2SD780	2316
2SD780A	2316
2SD780DW1	2316
2SD780DW2	2316
2SD780DW3	2316
2SD780DW4	2316
2SD780DW5	2316
2SD781	0558
2SD782	0723
2SD783	0309
2SD784	2820
2SD785	2820
2SD786	0525
2SD787	0710
2SD787B	0710
2SD787C	0710
2SD787D	0710
2SD787E	0710
2SD788	1492
2SD788-3	0018
2SD788-4	0018
2SD788-5	0018
2SD788-34TZ	1492

104

If replacement code is OEM, contact original manufacturer for replacement.

DEVICE TYPE	REPL CODE
2SD788-C	0018
2SD788B	0018
2SD788C	1492
2SD788D	0018
2SD788E	0018
2SD789	2539
2SD789(B)	2539
2SD789(C)	2539
2SD789(D)	2539
2SD789(E)	2539
2SD789-03C	2539
2SD789-3	2539
2SD789-4	2539
2SD789B	2539
2SD789C	2539
2SD789D	2539
2SD789DE	2539
2SD789E	2539
2SD789M	2539
2SD789P	2539
2SD790	1376
2SD790B	1376
2SD790C	1376
2SD792	0309
2SD792S	0309
2SD792T	0309
2SD793	0558
2SD793Q	0558
2SD794	0161
2SD794(2)	0161
2SD794A	0161
2SD794AD	0161
2SD794AQ	0161
2SD794D	0161
2SD794P	0161
2SD794Q	0161
2SD794R	0161
2SD795	0830
2SD795A	0830
2SD795AQ	0830
2SD795P	0830
2SD795Q	0830
2SD796	OEM
2SD797	2416
2SD798	OEM
2SD799	OEM
2SD800	1841
2SD801	1841
2SD802	3031
2SD803	2422
2SD803Q	2422
2SD804	0042
2SD804B	0042
2SD804H	0042
2SD804HLB	0042
2SD804HP	0042
2SD804L	0042
2SD804P	0042
2SD805	OEM
2SD806	OEM
2SD807	1485
2SD807M	1485
2SD808	0191
2SD809	0558
2SD809D	OEM
2SD809E	OEM
2SD810	4376
2SD811	5650
2SD812	1157
2SD812-Q	1157
2SD812Q	1157
2SD813	1722
2SD814	2316
2SD814A	2316
2SD814S	OEM
2SD815	OEM
2SD816	5212
2SD817	OEM
2SD818	2636
2SD819	2643
2SD820	2040
2SD820(FA-1)	2040
2SD820FA-1	2040
2SD821	0309
2SD822	5309
2SD822P	5309
2SD822Q	5309
2SD823	1157
2SD824	2261
2SD824A	2261
2SD825	2261
2SD825A	2261
2SD826	OEM
2SD827	OEM
2SD827K	OEM
2SD828	OEM
2SD829	OEM
2SD829K	OEM
2SD830	OEM
2SD832	OEM
2SD833	1203
2SD834	5212
2SD835	5212
2SD836	1203
2SD836A	1203
2SD836B	1203
2SD836Q	1203
2SD836R	1203
2SD837	1203

DEVICE TYPE	REPL CODE
2SD837A	1203
2SD837AB	1203
2SD837AD	1203
2SD837AQ	1203
2SD837AR	1203
2SD837B	1203
2SD837LB	1203
2SD837LBPQ	1203
2SD837O	1203
2SD837P	1203
2SD837PQ	1203
2SD837Q	1203
2SD837R	1203
2SD838	2820
2SD838B	2820
2SD839	1203
2SD840	1203
2SD841	2985
2SD842	2412
2SD843	0060
2SD843(Y)	0060
2SD844	0194
2SD844E	0194
2SD845	2261
2SD845O	2261
2SD847	2351
2SD848	2911
2SD848A	2911
2SD849	0065
2SD850	2643
2SD851	OEM
2SD852	OEM
2SD854	0617
2SD855	1157
2SD855A	1157
2SD855B	1157
2SD856	0060
2SD856(P)	0060
2SD856(Q)	0060
2SD856(R)	0060
2SD856A	0060
2SD856B	0060
2SD856L	0060
2SD856LB	0060
2SD856M	0060
2SD856M(LB)	0060
2SD856MLB	0060
2SD856MLD	0060
2SD856O	0060
2SD856P	0060
2SD856PLB	0060
2SD856PQ	0060
2SD856PQ(LB)	0060
2SD856PQR	0060
2SD856Q	0060
2SD856Q(LB)	0060
2SD856R	0060
2SD856S	0060
2SD857	0060
2SD857A	0060
2SD857B	0060
2SD858	5354
2SD858A	5354
2SD858B	5354
2SD859	0168
2SD859A	0168
2SD859B	0168
2SD860	0168
2SD860A	0168
2SD860B	0168
2SD861	0168
2SD861A	0168
2SD861B	0168
2SD862	OEM
2SD863	1376
2SD863E	1376
2SD863E-AE	1376
2SD863F	1376
2SD864	1948
2SD864K	1948
2SD865	OEM
2SD866	3096
2SD866(P)	3096
2SD866(Q)	3096
2SD866A	3096
2SD866B	3096
2SD866D	3096
2SD866P	3096
2SD866Q	3096
2SD866R	3096
2SD866S	3096
2SD867	0177
2SD868	0055
2SD868(FA)	OEM
2SD869	0055
2SD869(L)	0055
2SD869-14	0055
2SD869-L	0055
2SD869B	0055
2SD869FA	0055
2SD869L	0055
2SD870	0055
2SD870(FA)	0055
2SD870A	0055
2SD870FA	0055
2SD870Z	0055
2SD871	0055
2SD871(Z)	0055
2SD871Z	0055

DEVICE TYPE	REPL CODE
2SD872	0723
2SD873	4704
2SD874	0662
2SD874(R)	0662
2SD874-QR	OEM
2SD874A	0662
2SD874QR	OEM
2SD874QRS	OEM
2SD874R	0662
2SD875	0662
2SD876	0388
2SD877	0178
2SD877Y	2345
2SD878	0103
2SD878(FA-1)	OEM
2SD879	1492
2SD880	0456
2SD880-0	0456
2SD880-O	0456
2SD880-OLBGL2	0456
2SD880-Y	0456
2SD880GR	0456
2SD880OLBGL2	0456
2SD880Y	0456
2SD880YLBGL2	0456
2SD882	0161
2SD882(P)	0161
2SD882-P	0161
2SD882P	0161
2SD882PM	0161
2SD882Q	0161
2SD882R	0161
2SD883	2911
2SD883A	2911
2SD884	0723
2SD885	0723
2SD886	0060
2SD886A	0060
2SD886F	0060
2SD886P	0060
2SD886Q	0060
2SD887	1203
2SD888	1203
2SD889	0111
2SD889Q	0111
2SD889R	0111
2SD889S	0502
2SD889T	0111
2SD890	0525
2SD891	0396
2SD891A	0396
2SD892	2770
2SD892A	2770
2SD892A-Q	2770
2SD892AQ	2770
2SD892AR	2770
2SD893	0396
2SD893A	0396
2SD893Q	0396
2SD893R	0396
2SD894	0553
2SD894E	OEM
2SD894K	OEM
2SD895	3053
2SD896	3053
2SD897	0055
2SD897A	0055
2SD898	0055
2SD898-B13	0055
2SD898A	0055
2SD898B	0055
2SD899	0055
2SD899A	0055
2SD900	0055
2SD900A	0055
2SD900B	0055
2SD900B-06	0055
2SD900D	0055
2SD901	0388
2SD901D	OEM
2SD901E	OEM
2SD902	0074
2SD903	0055
2SD904	0055
2SD904K	0055
2SD904P	0055
2SD905	0309
2SD906	0055
2SD907	3052
2SD908	0194
2SD909	3401
2SD910	0194
2SD911	0538
2SD912	0538
2SD913	2416
2SD914	2416
2SD915	OEM
2SD916	1203
2SD917	0723
2SD918	0477
2SD919	0155
2SD920	0074
2SD920B	0074
2SD921	2973
2SD921-03	OEM
2SD922	OEM
2SD923	OEM
2SD926	0236
2SD927	0236

DEVICE TYPE	REPL CODE
2SD928	0236
2SD929	2526
2SD929A	OEM
2SD929B	6186
2SD930	OEM
2SD931	2973
2SD932	OEM
2SD933	5321
2SD933A	5321
2SD933H	5321
2SD934	OEM
2SD934K	OEM
2SD935	2589
2SD936	OEM
2SD937	OEM
2SD938	OEM
2SD939	OEM
2SD940	OEM
2SD941	OEM
2SD942	OEM
2SD943	OEM
2SD944	1055
2SD946	0553
2SD946-Q	0553
2SD946-Q.R	0553
2SD946-R	0553
2SD946A	0553
2SD946B	0553
2SD946S	OEM
2SD947	0553
2SD948	0016
2SD949	0309
2SD950	2643
2SD950Q	2643
2SD951	0055
2SD952	0223
2SD953	0223
2SD954	0223
2SD955	0710
2SD956	0055
2SD957	0055
2SD957A	0055
2SD957A-03	0055
2SD958	0525
2SD958(R)	0525
2SD958(S)	0525
2SD958(T)	0525
2SD958R	0525
2SD958S	0525
2SD958T	0525
2SD958U	0525
2SD959	1157
2SD959LB	1157
2SD959Q	1157
2SD960	0236
2SD961	1157
2SD962	OEM
2SD963	OEM
2SD965	1492
2SD966	OEM
2SD966(R)	OEM
2SD967	0396
2SD968	3433
2SD968A	3433
2SD968A-RS	OEM
2SD969	0667
2SD970	1948
2SD970K	1948
2SD971	OEM
2SD972	2350
2SD973	0009
2SD973(Q)	0009
2SD973(R)	0009
2SD973(S)	0009
2SD973A	0009
2SD973A-QRS	OEM
2SD973AR	1376
2SD973ARS	OEM
2SD973Q	0009
2SD973QRS	0009
2SD973R	0009
2SD973RS	0009
2SD973S	0009
2SD974	1376
2SD975	0558
2SD975C	0558
2SD976	0723
2SD976A	0723
2SD977	5212
2SD978	5212
2SD979	5245
2SD980	OEM
2SD981	OEM
2SD981-03	OEM
2SD982	OEM
2SD983	OEM
2SD985	3658
2SD985-L	3658
2SD985K	3658
2SD985L	3658
2SD985M	3658
2SD985T	3658
2SD986	2942
2SD986K	2942
2SD987	0723
2SD990	OEM
2SD990K	OEM
2SD991	5212
2SD991K	5212

DEVICE TYPE	REPL CODE
2SD992	3316
2SD992M	3316
2SD993	0055
2SD993A	0055
2SD994	0055
2SD995	2820
2SD997	2398
2SD998	3658
2SD999	0662
2SD1000	0662
2SD1001	0662
2SD1002	OEM
2SD1003	OEM
2SD1004	OEM
2SD1005	OEM
2SD1006	OEM
2SD1007	OEM
2SD1009	OEM
2SD1010	0111
2SD1010R	6596
2SD1010S	0111
2SD1011	0525
2SD1011R	0525
2SD1011S	0525
2SD1011T	0525
2SD1012	0284
2SD1012F	0284
2SD1012G	5784
2SD1012G1	0284
2SD1012G-SPA	OEM
2SD1012H	5784
2SD1014	OEM
2SD1015	OEM
2SD1015C	OEM
2SD1016	0055
2SD1017	2589
2SD1018	2589
2SD1020	0018
2SD1020H	0018
2SD1021	0018
2SD1022	1203
2SD1023	5319
2SD1024	1203
2SD1025	2085
2SD1026	OEM
2SD1027	OEM
2SD1029	0042
2SD1030	OEM
2SD1031	1948
2SD1032	3052
2SD1032A	3052
2SD1032B	3052
2SD1033	3316
2SD1034	OEM
2SD1034A	OEM
2SD1035	1157
2SD1036	2261
2SD1037	OEM
2SD1038	OEM
2SD1039	3509
2SD1040	0538
2SD1040A	0538
2SD1041	3510
2SD1042	OEM
2SD1043	5321
2SD1044	0134
2SD1044A	0134
2SD1045	OEM
2SD1046	0194
2SD1046D-L	OEM
2SD1046E-L	OEM
2SD1047	0194
2SD1048	1722
2SD1048-X6	1722
2SD1048-X6-TA	1722
2SD1048-X6TA	1722
2SD1048-X6TA(F)	1722
2SD1048-X7	1722
2SD1048-X7-TA	1722
2SD1048-X7-TA(G)	1722
2SD1048-X7TA	1722
2SD1048-X7TA(G)	1722
2SD1048-X8	1722
2SD1048-X8-TA	1722
2SD1048-X8-TA(H)	1722
2SD1048-X8TA	1722
2SD1048-X8TA(H)	1722
2SD1049	3557
2SD1050	OEM
2SD1051	0018
2SD1051(Q)	0018
2SD1051(R)	0018
2SD1051Q	0018
2SD1051QR	0018
2SD1051R	0018
2SD1052	2058
2SD1052-A	2058
2SD1052A	2058
2SD1052A(FA)	2058
2SD1052A-FA	2058
2SD1052AFA	2058
2SD1052FA	2058
2SD1053	3316
2SD1054	5324
2SD1055	0009
2SD1055Q	0009
2SD1055R	0009
2SD1056	OEM
2SD1059	2187

DEVICE TYPE	REPL CODE
2SD1060	0060
2SD1060K	0060
2SD1061	0060
2SD1062	1955
2SD1063	3052
2SD1064	3052
2SD1065	2351
2SD1065Q	2351
2SD1065R	2351
2SD1065S	2351
2SD1066	OEM
2SD1067	OEM
2SD1068	2965
2SD1069	0723
2SD1070	3052
2SD1071	OEM
2SD1072	OEM
2SD1073	OEM
2SD1074	3316
2SD1075	3316
2SD1076	3316
2SD1076L	3316
2SD1077	3316
2SD1078	3316
2SD1078B	3316
2SD1079	3316
2SD1079C	3316
2SD1079LB	3316
2SD1079LC	3316
2SD1080	3316
2SD1080C	3316
2SD1080LC	3316
2SD1081	3316
2SD1081B	3316
2SD1081C	3316
2SD1081LB	3316
2SD1081LC	3316
2SD1082	OEM
2SD1083	3316
2SD1083L	3316
2SD1084	OEM
2SD1085	5212
2SD1085K	5212
2SD1087	OEM
2SD1088	OEM
2SD1089	OEM
2SD1090	2973
2SD1091	OEM
2SD1092	3474
2SD1092(FA)	OEM
2SD1092(FA-1)	OEM
2SD1092FA	3474
2SD1093	2965
2SD1094	3544
2SD1095	0065
2SD1096	3316
2SD1097	0065
2SD1098	0065
2SD1098-42M	0065
2SD1099	0065
2SD1100	OEM
2SD1101	1722
2SD1101AB	1722
2SD1101AC	1722
2SD1102	0065
2SD1103	0065
2SD1104	0065
2SD1105	2398
2SD1106	OEM
2SD1107	OEM
2SD1109	3052
2SD1109A	3052
2SD1110	0130
2SD1110A	0130
2SD1111	OEM
2SD1111-T	OEM
2SD1112	OEM
2SD1113	OEM
2SD1113K	OEM
2SD1114	OEM
2SD1114K	OEM
2SD1115	5212
2SD1115K	5212
2SD1116	OEM
2SD1116K	OEM
2SD1117	0060
2SD1117A	0060
2SD1118	OEM
2SD1119	OEM
2SD1120	5212
2SD1121	5212
2SD1122	OEM
2SD1123	OEM
2SD1124	5212
2SD1125	OEM
2SD1126	1948
2SD1126K	1948
2SD1127	1948
2SD1127K	1948
2SD1128	OEM
2SD1129	OEM
2SD1129K	OEM
2SD1130	0130
2SD1130K	0130
2SD1131	0236
2SD1131B	0236
2SD1131C	0236
2SD1131D	0236
2SD1132	0236

DEVICE TYPE	REPL CODE
2SD1132B	0236
2SD1132C	0236
2SD1132D	0236
2SD1133	0236
2SD1133(D)	0236
2SD1133B	0236
2SD1133C	0236
2SD1133D	0236
2SD1134	0236
2SD1134-C	0236
2SD1134C	0236
2SD1135	0236
2SD1136	0388
2SD1137	0236
2SD1138	0388
2SD1138(C)	0388
2SD1138(D)	0388
2SD1138(G)	0388
2SD1138-02-C	0388
2SD1138-02C	0388
2SD1138-C	0388
2SD1138-D	0388
2SD1138-O	0388
2SD1138-Y	0388
2SD1138B	0388
2SD1138C	0388
2SD1138D	0388
2SD1138Y	0388
2SD1139	0388
2SD1139B	0388
2SD1140	0130
2SD1141	OEM
2SD1141K	OEM
2SD1142	1533
2SD1143	0065
2SD1145	OEM
2SD1146	3064
2SD1147	OEM
2SD1148	3053
2SD1149	OEM
2SD1150	0723
2SD1151	0223
2SD1152	OEM
2SD1153	0396
2SD1154	0359
2SD1155	OEM
2SD1156	OEM
2SD1157	2058
2SD1158	OEM
2SD1159	2985
2SD1160	5353
2SD1160-O	OEM
2SD1160Y	5353
2SD1161	OEM
2SD1162	5212
2SD1162K	5212
2SD1162L	5212
2SD1162M	5212
2SD1163	2792
2SD1163A	2792
2SD1164	3195
2SD1164K	3195
2SD1164L	3195
2SD1164M	3195
2SD1165	OEM
2SD1165A	OEM
2SD1166	OEM
2SD1168	0065
2SD1169	5355
2SD1170	5356
2SD1171	0055
2SD1172	0055
2SD1173	0055
2SD1174	0055
2SD1175	3574
2SD1176	1203
2SD1176A	1203
2SD1177	0558
2SD1177C	0558
2SD1178	0558
2SD1178C	0558
2SD1179	0558
2SD1180	0558
2SD1181	OEM
2SD1182	OEM
2SD1183	0309
2SD1184	0309
2SD1185	0309
2SD1186	0309
2SD1187	5359
2SD1189	0161
2SD1190	5360
2SD1191	2220
2SD1192	2220
2SD1193	3582
2SD1194	1203
2SD1195	1203
2SD1196	2220
2SD1197	1563
2SD1198	0396
2SD1198A	0396
2SD1199	0577
2SD1199-R	0577
2SD1200	0161
2SD1201	1841
2SD1202	3009
2SD1203	3009
2SD1204	3009
2SD1205	0396

If replacement code is OEM, contact original manufacturer for replacement.

105

DEVICE TYPE	REPL CODE
2SD1205(P)	0396
2SD1205(Q)	0396
2SD1205(R)	0396
2SD1205A	0396
2SD1205PQR	0396
2SD1205R	0396
2SD1206	0667
2SD1206(Q)	0667
2SD1206(R)	0667
2SD1206(S)	0667
2SD1206Q	0667
2SD1206R	0667
2SD1206S	0667
2SD1207	3882
2SD1207-F	3882
2SD1207-T	3882
2SD1207S	3882
2SD1207SZ	3882
2SD1207T	3882
2SD1207TZ	3882
2SD1208	2411
2SD1208(FA)	2411
2SD1208FA	2411
2SD1209	3838
2SD1210	3582
2SD1211	1553
2SD1212	3086
2SD1213	3557
2SD1213C	OEM
2SD1214	1203
2SD1215	1203
2SD1216	1203
2SD1217	0277
2SD1218	2350
2SD1219	1203
2SD1220	OEM
2SD1220-0Y	OEM
2SD1221	5353
2SD1222	5255
2SD1223	5255
2SD1224	5366
2SD1225	0009
2SD1225M	0009
2SD1225M(Q)	0009
2SD1225M(R)	0009
2SD1225MQ	1556
2SD1225MR	1556
2SD1226	2452
2SD1226M	2452
2SD1226MP	2452
2SD1226MQ	2452
2SD1226MR	2452
2SD1226Q	2452
2SD1227	0009
2SD1227M	0009
2SD1227MF	OEM
2SD1227MP	0009
2SD1227MQ	0009
2SD1227MR	0009
2SD1228	2452
2SD1228M	2452
2SD1229	3700
2SD1230	3702
2SD1231	1384
2SD1232	1384
2SD1233	1384
2SD1234	1384
2SD1235	1157
2SD1236	1157
2SD1237	1157
2SD1237R	1157
2SD1238	3248
2SD1239	2465
2SD1240	2465
2SD1241	3052
2SD1241A	3052
2SD1242	3052
2SD1242A	3052
2SD1243	0194
2SD1243A	0194
2SD1244	1492
2SD1244R	OEM
2SD1245	5212
2SD1246	1492
2SD1246-T	1492
2SD1246-U	1492
2SD1246T	1492
2SD1246U	6750
2SD1247	OEM
2SD1247S	OEM
2SD1247T	OEM
2SD1248	1948
2SD1249	OEM
2SD1249A	OEM
2SD1250	OEM
2SD1250A	OEM
2SD1251	5353
2SD1251A	5353
2SD1252	5353
2SD1252A	5353
2SD1253	5353
2SD1253A	5353
2SD1254	5353
2SD1255	5353
2SD1256	5353
2SD1257	5353
2SD1257A	5353
2SD1258	OEM
2SD1259	0553

DEVICE TYPE	REPL CODE
2SD1259A	0553
2SD1260	5255
2SD1260A	5255
2SD1261	5255
2SD1261A	5255
2SD1262	OEM
2SD1262A	OEM
2SD1263	0168
2SD1263A	0168
2SD1264	0388
2SD1264-D	0388
2SD1264-P	0388
2SD1264-PLB	0388
2SD1264A	0388
2SD1264ALBP	0388
2SD1264A-P	0388
2SD1264AP	0388
2SD1264APLB	0388
2SD1264LBP	0388
2SD1264P	0388
2SD1264PLB	0388
2SD1265	1154
2SD1265(LB)	1154
2SD1265(LB)O	1154
2SD1265(P)	1154
2SD1265(Q)	1154
2SD1265(QP)	1154
2SD1265-0	1154
2SD1265-0P	1154
2SD1265-LB	1154
2SD1265-O	1154
2SD1265-OP	1154
2SD1265-OP(LB)	1154
2SD1265-P	1154
2SD1265-Q	1154
2SD1265-R	1154
2SD1265A	1154
2SD1265B	1154
2SD1265L	1154
2SD1265LB	1154
2SD1265LB-O	1154
2SD1265LB-P	1154
2SD1265O	1154
2SD1265OLB	1154
2SD1265OP	1154
2SD1265OPQ	1154
2SD1265P	1154
2SD1266	0060
2SD1266(P)	0060
2SD1266(Q)	0060
2SD1266(R)	0060
2SD1266-P	0060
2SD1266-PQ	0060
2SD1266-Q	0060
2SD1266A	0060
2SD1266A(P)	0060
2SD1266A(P,Q)	0060
2SD1266A(Q)	0060
2SD1266A-P	OEM
2SD1266AP	0060
2SD1266A-PLT	OEM
2SD1266A-PVJ	OEM
2SD1266A-Q	0060
2SD1266AQ	0060
2SD1266LB	0060
2SD1266LB(P)	0060
2SD1266LB(Q)	0060
2SD1266LBPQ	0060
2SD1266LVPQ	0060
2SD1266P	0060
2SD1266PQ	0060
2SD1266PQR	0060
2SD1266Q	0060
2SD1267	0060
2SD1267(P)	0060
2SD1267A	0060
2SD1267ALBPQ	0060
2SD1267AP	OEM
2SD1267APQ	OEM
2SD1267A-PVJ	OEM
2SD1267P	0060
2SD1267Q	6031
2SD1268	1157
2SD1269	1157
2SD1270	1157
2SD1271	1157
2SD1271A	1157
2SD1271B	OEM
2SD1271BP	OEM
2SD1272	OEM
2SD1273	0922
2SD1273(P)	0922
2SD1273(Q)	0922
2SD1273A	0922
2SD1273LB-O	0922
2SD1273LB-P	0922
2SD1273P	0922
2SD1273Q	0922
2SD1273QP	0922
2SD1274	3950
2SD1274A	3950
2SD1274B	3950
2SD1275	1203
2SD1275A	1203
2SD1276	1203
2SD1276(LB)	1203
2SD1276-AP	1203
2SD1276-LB	1203
2SD1276A	1203

DEVICE TYPE	REPL CODE
2SD1276A(LB)P	1203
2SD1276A(LP)	1203
2SD1276AP	1203
2SD1276B	1203
2SD1276LB	1203
2SD1276P	1203
2SD1276PLB	1203
2SD1276Q	6778
2SD1276QLB	1203
2SD1277	1203
2SD1277A	1203
2SD1277B	1203
2SD1277BP	1203
2SD1277R	1203
2SD1278	5375
2SD1279	0309
2SD1279FA	0309
2SD1280	0662
2SD1280R	0662
2SD1281	3316
2SD1282	3316
2SD-1283	0208
2SD1283	0208
2SD1284	3316
2SD1286	3195
2SD1287	3956
2SD1288	OEM
2SD1289	0194
2SD1290	1533
2SD1291	1533
2SD1292	1553
2SD1292T103Q	1553
2SD1292T103R	1553
2SD1293	3563
2SD1293M	3563
2SD1293MP	3563
2SD1293MQ	3563
2SD1293MR	3563
2SD1294	2961
2SD1294(FA)	2961
2SD1294FA	2961
2SD1295	3316
2SD1296	OEM
2SD1297	OEM
2SD1298	OEM
2SD1299	OEM
2SD1300	0309
2SD1301	0055
2SD1302	1492
2SD1302STTA	OEM
2SD1302T	OEM
2SD1303	1376
2SD1304	OEM
2SD1305	OEM
2SD1306	1722
2SD1306E	1722
2SD1307	OEM
2SD1308	3107
2SD1308L	3107
2SD1309	3107
2SD1310	0236
2SD1311	0236
2SD1312	3882
2SD1313	OEM
2SD1314	1498
2SD1315	5355
2SD1316	0553
2SD1317	0553
2SD1318	0086
2SD1319	5253
2SD1320	5253
2SD1321	5253
2SD1322	2220
2SD1323	2220
2SD1324	2220
2SD1325	3678
2SD1326	3678
2SD1327	3678
2SD1328	1722
2SD1328(DS)	1722
2SD1328STTW	OEM
2SD1329	5253
2SD1330	0014
2SD1330(R)	0014
2SD1330(S)	0014
2SD1330(T)	0014
2SD1330-RS	0014
2SD1330R	0014
2SD1330RST	0014
2SD1330S	0014
2SD1330ST	0014
2SD1330T	0014
2SD1331	OEM
2SD1332	0194
2SD1333	0194
2SD1334	0194
2SD1335	0194
2SD1336	3107
2SD1336A	3107
2SD1337	OEM
2SD1338	OEM
2SD1339	OEM
2SD1340	OEM
2SD1341	0065
2SD1341P	OEM
2SD1342	0055
2SD1343	OEM
2SD1344	0055
2SD1344E	0055

DEVICE TYPE	REPL CODE
2SD1345	0060
2SD1346	OEM
2SD1347	0018
2SD1348	0161
2SD1348S	OEM
2SD1348T	OEM
2SD1349	OEM
2SD1350	OEM
2SD1351	0042
2SD1352	0236
2SD1353	3646
2SD1354	3647
2SD1355	3648
2SD1356	3649
2SD1357	1203
2SD1358	2220
2SD1359	2220
2SD1360	OEM
2SD1361	OEM
2SD1362	3149
2SD1363	0060
2SD1363-Y	0060
2SD1364	0723
2SD1365	OEM
2SD1366	1722
2SD1366A	1722
2SD1367	OEM
2SD1368	0662
2SD1369	2220
2SD1370	1203
2SD1371	OEM
2SD1372	2985
2SD1373	2589
2SD1374	0270
2SD1375	0270
2SD1376	3658
2SD1376K	3658
2SD1377	1948
2SD1378	0558
2SD1379	0161
2SD1380	0558
2SD1381	0558
2SD1382	2942
2SD1383	5267
2SD1384	3064
2SD1384(R)	3064
2SD1384Q	3064
2SD1384QZ	3064
2SD1384R	3064
2SD1384RZ	3064
2SD1385	OEM
2SD1386	OEM
2SD1387	OEM
2SD1387-2	OEM
2SD1387-3	OEM
2SD1387-4	OEM
2SD1388	OEM
2SD1388-4	OEM
2SD1389	5375
2SD1390	2739
2SD1391	1533
2SD1392	2350
2SD1392L	2350
2SD1393	0277
2SD1394	2350
2SD1395	2350
2SD1396	1533
2SD1397	1533
2SD1397-OR1-YB	1533
2SD1397B	1533
2SD1398	1533
2SD1398-CTV-YB	1533
2SD1398-OR1-YB	1533
2SD1398-ORI-YB	1533
2SD1398S	1533
2SD1398S-CA	1533
2SD1399	1533
2SD1400	3404
2SD1401	3404
2SD1402	5384
2SD1403	3326
2SD1404	0723
2SD1405	2058
2SD1405BL	OEM
2SD1406	3096
2SD1406-O	3096
2SD1406-Y	3096
2SD1406-YGR	3096
2SD1406GR	3096
2SD1406OR	OEM
2SD1406Y	3096
2SD1406YR	OEM
2SD1407	0477
2SD1408	0236
2SD1408-Y	0236
2SD1409	OEM
2SD1410	OEM
2SD1411	1157
2SD1412	3096
2SD1413	OEM
2SD1414	OEM
2SD1415	3107
2SD1416	3107
2SD1417	3107
2SD1418	OEM
2SD1419	OEM
2SD1420	OEM
2SD1421	OEM
2SD1422	OEM

DEVICE TYPE	REPL CODE
2SD1423	2926
2SD1423AS	2926
2SD1423Q	OEM
2SD1424	OEM
2SD1425	1533
2SD-1426	1533
2SD1426	1533
2SD1426(E)	1533
2SD1426(F)	1533
2SD1426FA	1533
2SD1426Y	OEM
2SD1427	1533
2SD1427(FA-1)	1533
2SD1427-LB	1533
2SD1427FA-1	1533
2SD1428	5385
2SD1428E	5385
2SD1428FA	1533
2SD1428FA-3	1533
2SD1428Y	OEM
2SD1429	3404
2SD1430	3404
2SD1431	3437
2SD1432	3326
2SD1433	3326
2SD1434	OEM
2SD1435	OEM
2SD1436	OEM
2SD1437	OEM
2SD1438	3658
2SD1439	1533
2SD1439-Q	1533
2SD1439-Q(LB)	1533
2SD1439-QLB	1533
2SD1439LB	1533
2SD1439P	1533
2SD1439PLB	1533
2SD1439Q	1533
2SD1439R	1533
2SD1439RL	1533
2SD1440	1533
2SD1441	1533
2SD1441(B)	1533
2SD1441(L)	1533
2SD1441-LB	1533
2SD1441LB	1533
2SD1441R	1533
2SD1441RL	1533
2SD1442	0060
2SD1443	0060
2SD1444	0060
2SD1445	0060
2SD1446	OEM
2SD1447	OEM
2SD1448	OEM
2SD1449	OEM
2SD1449S	OEM
2SD1449T	OEM
2SD1450	3412
2SD1450QRSTA	OEM
2SD1450R	OEM
2SD1450RS	OEM
2SD1450S	OEM
2SD1450T	OEM
2SD1451	3404
2SD1452	3404
2SD1453	1533
2SD1453-04	1533
2SD1453-06	1533
2SD1454	3404
2SD1455	1533
2SD1455-04	1533
2SD1455-05	1533
2SD1456	3326
2SD1457	OEM
2SD1457A	OEM
2SD1457AKU	OEM
2SD1457A-P	OEM
2SD1457AP	OEM
2SD1458	0640
2SD1458(Q)	0640
2SD1458(R)	0640
2SD1458(S)	OEM
2SD1459	3683
2SD1459D	3683
2SD1459Q	3683
2SD1459R	3683
2SD1460	OEM
2SD1461	OEM
2SD1462	OEM
2SD1463	OEM
2SD1464	OEM
2SD1465	OEM
2SD1466	OEM
2SD1468	1492
2SD1468S	1492
2SD1468SQ	OEM
2SD1468SR	OEM
2SD1468SS	OEM
2SD1469	0009
2SD1469F	OEM
2SD1469Q	OEM
2SD1469R	OEM
2SD1469S	OEM
2SD1470	OEM
2SD1471	5272
2SD1472	OEM
2SD1473	OEM
2SD1474	OEM

DEVICE TYPE	REPL CODE
2SD1475	1157
2SD1475(Q)	1157
2SD1475(R)	1157
2SD1475Q	1157
2SD1476	1157
2SD1476(Q)	1157
2SD1476(R)	1157
2SD1477	OEM
2SD1478	5267
2SD1479	3404
2SD1480	0236
2SD1481	0277
2SD1482	OEM
2SD1483	OEM
2SD1484	OEM
2SD1485	0194
2SD1486	0194
2SD1487	0194
2SD1488	0194
2SD1489	1492
2SD1490	1376
2SD1491	1055
2SD1492	3404
2SD1493	3404
2SD1494	3404
2SD1495	3404
2SD1496	3404
2SD1497	3326
2SD1497-06	3326
2SD1498	3326
2SD1499	1157
2SD1500	OEM
2SD1501	OEM
2SD1501Q	OEM
2SD1502	OEM
2SD1503	2757
2SD1504	OEM
2SD1504E	OEM
2SD1505	0060
2SD1506	0161
2SD1507	OEM
2SD1508	OEM
2SD1509	5255
2SD1510	1203
2SD1511	OEM
2SD1512	OEM
2SD1513	1492
2SD1513(Q)	1492
2SD1513(R)	1492
2SD1513R	1492
2SD1514	OEM
2SD1515	OEM
2SD1516	OEM
2SD1517	OEM
2SD1518	4376
2SD1519	OEM
2SD1520	OEM
2SD1521	1055
2SD1522	5245
2SD1523	4269
2SD1524	5245
2SD1525	OEM
2SD1526	OEM
2SD1527	OEM
2SD1528	OEM
2SD1529	OEM
2SD1530	OEM
2SD1531	5400
2SD1531(Q)	OEM
2SD1531(R)	OEM
2SD1531R	5400
2SD1532	OEM
2SD1533	OEM
2SD1534	OEM
2SD1535	OEM
2SD1536	OEM
2SD1537	OEM
2SD1538	OEM
2SD1539	0060
2SD1540	OEM
2SD1541	1533
2SD1542	3404
2SD1543	3404
2SD1544	3404
2SD1545	3404
2SD1546	3326
2SD1547	3326
2SD1548	OEM
2SD1549	4376
2SD1550	1498
2SD1551	3404
2SD1552	3404
2SD1553	1533
2SD1554	1533
2SD1554-C1	1533
2SD1554-LB	1533
2SD1554FA	1533
2SD1555	0551
2SD1555(E)	0551
2SD1555(LBOEC)	0551
2SD1555-1	0551
2SD1555-LB	0551
2SD1555-LB-S1	0551
2SD1555LBS1	0551
2SD1556	2116
2SD1556(E)	1533
2SD1556-LB	2116
2SD1556LBMA	2116
2SD1556MA	2116

DEVICE TYPE	REPL CODE
2SD1557	OEM
2SD1558	1203
2SD1559	OEM
2SD1562	0388
2SD1563	0558
2SD1564	OEM
2SD1565	5319
2SD1566	OEM
2SD1567	OEM
2SD1568	OEM
2SD1569	OEM
2SD1569FA-5	OEM
2SD1571	3323
2SD1572	1203
2SD1573	OEM
2SD1574	OEM
2SD1575	2739
2SD1576	3404
2SD1577	3326
2SD1578	OEM
2SD1579	OEM
2SD1579K	OEM
2SD1580	0060
2SD1581	OEM
2SD1581L	OEM
2SD1582	OEM
2SD1583	OEM
2SD1584	OEM
2SD1585	0236
2SD1585-K	0236
2SD1585K	0236
2SD1585L	OEM
2SD1585LK	0236
2SD1586	0236
2SD1587	0388
2SD1588	OEM
2SD1589	3107
2SD1590	3107
2SD1591	OEM
2SD1592	OEM
2SD1593	OEM
2SD1593KL	OEM
2SD1593L	OEM
2SD1593M	OEM
2SD1594	OEM
2SD1595	3678
2SD1597	OEM
2SD1598	OEM
2SD1599	5407
2SD1600	5407
2SD1601	2220
2SD1602	2220
2SD1603	2220
2SD1604	2220
2SD1605	1948
2SD1606	1948
2SD1607	OEM
2SD1608	1948
2SD1609	0558
2SD1610	OEM
2SD1611	OEM
2SD1612	OEM
2SD1613	OEM
2SD1614	OEM
2SD1615	0662
2SD1615A	0662
2SD1615A-GP	OEM
2SD1615Y-GP	OEM
2SD1616	0558
2SD1616A	0558
2SD1617	5411
2SD1618	0662
2SD1619	0662
2SD1620	OEM
2SD1621	OEM
2SD1622	5413
2SD1623	OEM
2SD1624	OEM
2SD1625	OEM
2SD1626	OEM
2SD1627	OEM
2SD1628	OEM
2SD1629	1055
2SD1630	1055
2SD1631	OEM
2SD1632	1533
2SD1633	3107
2SD1634	3107
2SD1635	OEM
2SD1636	OEM
2SD1637	1055
2SD1637Y	1055
2SD1638	OEM
2SD1639	OEM
2SD1640	OEM
2SD1641	3474
2SD1642	OEM
2SD1643	OEM
2SD1644	OEM
2SD1645	1055
2SD1646	5319
2SD1647	0277
2SD1647C3	0277
2SD1648	OEM
2SD1649	1533
2SD1649-CA	1533
2SD1649-CTV-YB	1533
2SD-1650	1533
2SD1650	1533

If replacement code is OEM, contact original manufacturer for replacement.

DEVICE TYPE	REPL CODE
2SD1650-CTV-YB	1533
2SD1650YD	1533
2SD1651	0551
2SD1651-CTV-TB	0551
2SD1651-CTV-YB	0551
2SD1651-KR	0551
2SD1651YB	0551
2SD1651YD	0551
2SD1652	1533
2SD1652-CTV-YB	1533
2SD1653	3454
2SD1654	3454
2SD1655	3454
2SD1656	3454
2SD1657	OEM
2SD1658	1055
2SD1659	OEM
2SD1660	OEM
2SD1661	OEM
2SD1662	OEM
2SD1663	3454
2SD1664	OEM
2SD1664R	OEM
2SD1665	OEM
2SD1666	0060
2SD1666Q	0060
2SD1666R	0060
2SD1666S	0060
2SD1667	0060
2SD1668	0060
2SD1669	OEM
2SD1670	OEM
2SD1671	OEM
2SD1672	OEM
2SD1673	OEM
2SD1676	OEM
2SD1677	OEM
2SD1678	OEM
2SD1679	OEM
2SD1680	4376
2SD1681	0558
2SD1682	OEM
2SD1682S	OEM
2SD1683	OEM
2SD1684	0558
2SD1685	0284
2SD1685RS	0284
2SD1686	OEM
2SD1687	OEM
2SD1688	OEM
2SD1689	OEM
2SD1690	OEM
2SD1691	OEM
2SD1692	OEM
2SD1693	OEM
2SD1694	OEM
2SD1695	OEM
2SD1696	OEM
2SD1697	OEM
2SD1698	OEM
2SD1699	OEM
2SD1700	OEM
2SD1701	OEM
2SD1702	OEM
2SD1703	OEM
2SD1704	OEM
2SD1705	0194
2SD1706	OEM
2SD1706Q	OEM
2SD1707	OEM
2SD1708	OEM
2SD1709	1533
2SD1710	OEM
2SD1711	1533
2SD1712	OEM
2SD1713	OEM
2SD1714	OEM
2SD1715	OEM
2SD1716	OEM
2SD1717	3402
2SD1718	3402
2SD1719	OEM
2SD1720	0042
2SD1721	OEM
2SD1722	OEM
2SD1723	OEM
2SD1724	OEM
2SD1725	0161
2SD1725S	0161
2SD1726	OEM
2SD1727	1533
2SD1728	1533
2SD1729	1533
2SD1730	1533
2SD1731	1533
2SD1732	5248
2SD1733	OEM
2SD1734	2739
2SD1735	3454
2SD1736	3454
2SD1737	3454
2SD1738	3454
2SD1739	3454
2SD1740	OEM
2SD1741	OEM
2SD1742	OEM
2SD1743	OEM
2SD1744	OEM
2SD1745	OEM
2SD1746	OEM
2SD1747	OEM
2SD1748	5255
2SD1749	5255
2SD1750	OEM
2SD1751	OEM
2SD1752	OEM
2SD1753	OEM
2SD1754	OEM
2SD1755	OEM
2SD1756	OEM
2SD1757	OEM
2SD1757KQSTW	OEM
2SD1757KR	OEM
2SD1757KS	OEM
2SD1758F5	OEM
2SD1758R	OEM
2SD1760	OEM
2SD1761	OEM
2SD1761-E	OEM
2SD1761-F	OEM
2SD1761DEF	OEM
2SD1761F	OEM
2SD1762	0060
2SD1763	0388
2SD1764	0277
2SD1765	1203
2SD1765S	OEM
2SD1766	OEM
2SD1767	OEM
2SD1768	OEM
2SD1768S	OEM
2SD1769	1948
2SD1770	0388
2SD1771	OEM
2SD1772	0388
2SD1773	1948
2SD1774	2058
2SD1775	OEM
2SD1776	2058
2SD1776(P)	2058
2SD1776(Q)	2058
2SD1776-PQ0	OEM
2SD1776P	2303
2SD1776Q	2303
2SD1777	OEM
2SD1779	OEM
2SD1781K	2333
2SD1781KAFR	OEM
2SD1783L	2350
2SD1785	OEM
2SD1788	3107
2SD1796	OEM
2SD1812P	OEM
2SD1812Q	OEM
2SD1819	OEM
2SD1819A	OEM
2SD1823	OEM
2SD1825	3107
2SD1825-LU	3107
2SD1832	0042
2SD1832C4	0042
2SD1833	0042
2SD1833C4	0042
2SD1833F	0042
2SD1843	2822
2SD1843-T	OEM
2SD1843L	2822
2SD1843T	2822
2SD1846	2116
2SD1847	3465
2SD1855	0060
2SD1855E	0060
2SD1856	3678
2SD1858Q	OEM
2SD1858R2	OEM
2SD1859	2452
2SD1862	0009
2SD1862-P	OEM
2SD1876	2116
2SD1876-CA	2116
2SD1877	2116
2SD1878	2116
2SD1878-CA	2116
2SD1878CA	2116
2SD1879	2116
2SD1879-CTV-YB	2116
2SD1880	5437
2SD1881	OEM
2SD1885	5333
2SD1886	3454
2SD1886CA	3454
2SD1887	2470
2SD1888	OEM
2SD1894	0065
2SD1900	OEM
2SD1910	1533
2SD1911	1533
2SD1913	0042
2SD1913-O	0042
2SD1913-Q-RA	0042
2SD1913-R-RA	0042
2SD1913Q	0042
2SD1913QRA	0042
2SD1913R	0042
2SD1913RRA	6690
2SD1913S	OEM
2SD1915T	OEM
2SD1919	0009
2SD1920	0009
2SD1929	1055
2SD1929Q	1055
2SD1929TP	1055
2SD1941	3326
2SD1941-06	3326
2SD1941-07	3326
2SD1944	2058
2SD1959	3454
2SD1959-02	3454
2SD1978	OEM
2SD1981	OEM
2SD1991	OEM
2SD2005Q	OEM
2SD2005R	OEM
2SD2006	1376
2SD2010	5455
2SD2010P	OEM
2SD2012	1157
2SD2021	OEM
2SD2021M	OEM
2SD2023E	0456
2SD2023F18E	0456
2SD2037	3411
2SD2037EFTA	OEM
2SD2046	OEM
2SD2057	1533
2SD2057LB	1533
2SD2059Y	OEM
2SD2061	OEM
2SD2061DE	0042
2SD2089	2116
2SD2089-LBSONY	2116
2SD2095	2116
2SD2096	OEM
2SD2096-EF	OEM
2SD2096EL	OEM
2SD2096F	OEM
2SD2125	2116
2SD2144S	OEM
2SD2148	OEM
2SD2148-C1	OEM
2SD2157P	OEM
2SD2271D	OEM
2SD2340	0042
2SD2350	0042
2SD2394-EF	OEM
2SD2394E	OEM
2SD2394EF	OEM
2SD2724D	OEM
2SD3243DE	OEM
2SD3311(R)	OEM
2SD5254	OEM
2SD7180	OEM
2SD7620P	0763
2SD9008	OEM
2SD-F1	0595
2SDF1	0595
2SD-F1A	0595
2SDF1A	0595
2SD-F1B	0208
2SD-F1C	0208
2SD-F1D	0208
2SD-F1E	0208
2SD-F1F	0208
2SD-F1G	0208
2SD-F1GN	0208
2SD-F1H	0208
2SD-F1J	0208
2SD-F1K	0208
2SD-F1L	0208
2SD-F1M	0208
2SD-F1OR	0208
2SD-F1R	0208
2SD-F1X	0208
2SD-F1Y	0208
2SDF2A	0130
2SDF2B	0130
2SDF2C	0130
2SDF2D	0130
2SDF2E	0130
2SDF2F	0130
2SDF2G	0130
2SDF2GN	0130
2SDF2H	0130
2SDF2J	0130
2SDF2K	0130
2SDF2L	0130
2SDF2M	0130
2SDF2OR	0130
2SDF2R	0130
2SDF2X	0130
2SDF2Y	0130
2SDF946A	OEM
2SDL2F	0208
2SD026	0142
2SDQ22Q	0161
2SDU36C	0142
2SDU37E	0142
2SDU47X	0130
2SDU57M	0142
2SDU780R	0018
2SDU84GN	0086
2SDU90R	0208
2SE629	0144
2SE4002	0111
2SE4002-1	0208
2SF1	OEM
2SF2	OEM
2SF4	OEM
2SF11	1095
2SF11Q	2320
2SF12	2471
2SF13	0430
2SF14	0240
2SF15	1478
2SF16	2635
2SF18	0671
2SF21	2497
2SF22	0736
2SF23	3076
2SF24	0740
2SF25	3080
2SF26	2889
2SF28	0742
2SF31A	0726
2SF32	0707
2SF32A	0707
2SF33	0464
2SF33A	0464
2SF34	0464
2SF34A	0464
2SF35	0716
2SF35A	0716
2SF36	0716
2SF36A	0716
2SF38	0717
2SF38A	0717
2SF41	OEM
2SF41F	0321
2SF42	OEM
2SF43	OEM
2SF44	OEM
2SF45	OEM
2SF46	OEM
2SF47	OEM
2SF48	OEM
2SF49	OEM
2SF50	OEM
2SF51	OEM
2SF52	OEM
2SF53	OEM
2SF54	OEM
2SF55	2174
2SF56	2174
2SF57	0562
2SF58	0757
2SF59	0757
2SF60	0735
2SF61	0735
2SF62	0735
2SF63	0736
2SF64	0736
2SF65	0736
2SF66	0740
2SF67	0740
2SF68	0742
2SF69	0742
2SF70	0742
2SF71	3275
2SF72	2174
2SF73	0562
2SF74	3227
2SF75	0757
2SF76	3240
2SF77	0735
2SF101	0340
2SF101B	0340
2SF102	0895
2SF102A	0895
2SF102B	0895
2SF103	2326
2SF104	0058
2SF104A	0058
2SF104B	0058
2SF105	0403
2SF106	0403
2SF106A	0403
2SF106B	0403
2SF108	0403
2SF108A	0403
2SF108B	0403
2SF110B	1673
2SF111	OEM
2SF112	OEM
2SF113	OEM
2SF114	OEM
2SF115	OEM
2SF116	0705
2SF116A	0705
2SF118	OEM
2SF120	OEM
2SF121	OEM
2SF123	OEM
2SF125	OEM
2SF131	3246
2SF132	0726
2SF133	0707
2SF134	0464
2SF135	0464
2SF136	0716
2SF137	0717
2SF138	0773
2SF139	3260
2SF200	2782
2SF201	0332
2SF205	3213
2SF206	0759
2SF207	2848
2SF210	0773
2SF210A	0773
2SF211	0720
2SF211A	0759
2SF212	2848
2SF212A	2848
2SF215	0759
2SF216	0759
2SF217	0720
2SF218	0720
2SF219	OEM
2SF220	OEM
2SF221	3385
2SF222	1095
2SF223	2471
2SF224	0240
2SF225	0240
2SF226	2635
2SF227	0671
2SF228	2782
2SF229	2326
2SF230	2174
2SF231	2174
2SF232	2174
2SF233	0757
2SF234	0757
2SF235	0735
2SF236	0735
2SF237	0735
2SF239	0726
2SF240	0707
2SF241	0464
2SF242	0464
2SF243	0716
2SF244	0716
2SF245	0717
2SF248	1814
2SF248A	1814
2SF248T	0042
2SF261	1095
2SF261A	1095
2SF262	2471
2SF262A	2471
2SF263	0240
2SF263A	0240
2SF264	0240
2SF264A	0240
2SF265	2635
2SF265A	2635
2SF266	2635
2SF266A	2635
2SF267	0671
2SF267A	0671
2SF268	0671
2SF268A	0671
2SF269	2782
2SF269A	2782
2SF271	2430
2SF271A	2430
2SF272	2471
2SF272A	2471
2SF273	0240
2SF273A	0240
2SF274	0430
2SF274A	0430
2SF275	0430
2SF275A	0430
2SF276	2635
2SF276A	2635
2SF277	1478
2SF277A	1478
2SF278	0742
2SF278A	0742
2SF279	3213
2SF279A	3213
2SF281	2174
2SF281A	2174
2SF282	0562
2SF282A	0562
2SF283	3227
2SF283A	3227
2SF284	0757
2SF284A	0757
2SF285	3237
2SF285A	3237
2SF286	3240
2SF286A	3240
2SF287	0735
2SF287A	0735
2SF288	0735
2SF288A	0735
2SF289	3260
2SF289A	3260
2SF291	0726
2SF291A	0726
2SF292	0707
2SF292A	0707
2SF293	0464
2SF293A	0464
2SF294	0464
2SF294A	0464
2SF295	0716
2SF295A	0716
2SF296	0716
2SF296A	0716
2SF297	0717
2SF297A	0717
2SF298	0717
2SF298A	0717
2SF299	0773
2SF299A	0773
2SF301	OEM
2SF302	OEM
2SF303	OEM
2SF304	OEM
2SF305	OEM
2SF306	OEM
2SF307	OEM
2SF308	OEM
2SF309	OEM
2SF316	OEM
2SF321	3385
2SF321A	3385
2SF322	1095
2SF322A	1095
2SF323	2471
2SF323A	2471
2SF324	0240
2SF324A	0240
2SF325	0240
2SF325A	0240
2SF326	2635
2SF326A	2635
2SF327	2635
2SF327A	2635
2SF328	0671
2SF328A	0671
2SF329	2782
2SF329A	2782
2SF330	0332
2SF330A	0332
2SF331	OEM
2SF332	OEM
2SF333	OEM
2SF334	OEM
2SF335	OEM
2SF336	OEM
2SF337	OEM
2SF338	OEM
2SF339	OEM
2SF340	OEM
2SF341	OEM
2SF342	OEM
2SF343	OEM
2SF344	OEM
2SF345	OEM
2SF346	OEM
2SF347	OEM
2SF348	OEM
2SF352	OEM
2SF353	OEM
2SF354	OEM
2SF355	OEM
2SF356	OEM
2SF357	0442
2SF358	OEM
2SF359	OEM
2SF360	OEM
2SF361	OEM
2SF362	OEM
2SF363	OEM
2SF364	OEM
2SF365	OEM
2SF366	OEM
2SF367	OEM
2SF371	OEM
2SF373	OEM
2SF374	OEM
2SF375	OEM
2SF376	OEM
2SF377	OEM
2SF378	OEM
2SF379	OEM
2SF401	OEM
2SF402	OEM
2SF403	OEM
2SF404	OEM
2SF405	OEM
2SF406	OEM
2SF407	OEM
2SF408	OEM
2SF416	OEM
2SF421	OEM
2SF422	OEM
2SF426	OEM
2SF427	OEM
2SF431	0759
2SF432	0759
2SF433	2848
2SF434	0761
2SF435	OEM
2SF436	OEM
2SF437	OEM
2SF438	2848
2SF439	0761
2SF440	OEM
2SF441	0500
2SF442	0500
2SF443	OEM
2SF448	0332
2SF448A	0332
2SF449	2848
2SF450	OEM
2SF451	0682
2SF452	0761
2SF453	OEM
2SF454	0759
2SF454A	0759
2SF455	0761
2SF456	OEM
2SF457	0759
2SF458	0761
2SF459	0745
2SF460	0707
2SF461	0464
2SF462	0716
2SF463	0735
2SF464	3260
2SF478	OEM
2SF479	OEM
2SF480	OEM
2SF481	OEM
2SF482	OEM
2SF483	OEM
2SF484	OEM
2SF485	OEM
2SF486	OEM
2SF487	OEM
2SF490	OEM
2SF491	OEM
2SF492	OEM
2SF493	OEM
2SF494	OEM
2SF495	OEM
2SF496	OEM
2SF497	OEM
2SF511	OEM
2SF512	OEM
2SF513	OEM
2SF514	OEM
2SF515	OEM
2SF516	OEM
2SF517	OEM
2SF518	OEM
2SF521	0340
2SF522	0442
2SF523	0058
2SF524	0403
2SF525	0403
2SF526	1673
2SF527	1673
2SF528	2084
2SF529	OEM
2SF530	0500
2SF531	0857
2SF532	0705
2SF533	OEM
2SF534	OEM
2SF535	OEM
2SF536	OEM
2SF537	OEM
2SF538	OEM
2SF539	OEM
2SF540	OEM
2SF541	OEM
2SF542	OEM
2SF543	OEM
2SF544	OEM
2SF562	OEM
2SF563	OEM
2SF564	OEM
2SF565	OEM
2SF566	OEM
2SF605	OEM
2SF644S	OEM
2SF656	0895
2SF656ZS	0895
2SF657	0895
2SF658	0058
2SF660	1102
2SF661	2904
2SF662	0957
2SF664	0895
2SF664S	0895
2SF665	1095
2SF666	2471
2SF667	0240
2SF668	0671
2SF674S	0895
2SF676S	0895
2SF694	OEM
2SF695	OEM
2SF696	OEM
2SF711	0562
2SF713	3240
2SF714	0742
2SF716	OEM
2SF717	0761
2SF721	0707
2SF722	0464
2SF724	0717
2SF725	0773
2SF726	0720
2SF727	0761
2SF732	0464
2SF733	0716
2SF734	0717
2SF743	OEM
2SF744	OEM
2SF745	OEM
2SF746	OEM
2SF747	OEM
2SF748	OEM
2SF752	0757
2SF752A	0740
2SF755	3260

If replacement code is OEM, contact original manufacturer for replacement.

107

DEVICE TYPE	REPL CODE
2SF762	0757
2SF762A	0757
2SF775	0693
2SF812	OEM
2SF813	OEM
2SF814	OEM
2SF815	OEM
2SF816	OEM
2SF817	OEM
2SF832	OEM
2SF833	OEM
2SF834	OEM
2SF835	OEM
2SF836	OEM
2SF837	OEM
2SF861	OEM
2SF862	OEM
2SF863	OEM
2SF875	OEM
2SF876	OEM
2SF877	OEM
2SF894	OEM
2SF932	OEM
2SF933	OEM
2SF934	OEM
2SF935	OEM
2SF936	OEM
2SF937	OEM
2SF938	OEM
2SF939	OEM
2SF940	0500
2SF941	0442
2SF942	0934
2SF1060	0500
2SF1110	0340
2SF1111	0340
2SF1112	0058
2SF1113	0403
2SF1114	0403
2SF1115	2084
2SF1116	2078
2SF1117	0500
2SF1118	0705
2SF1119	OEM
2SF1125	OEM
2SF1126	OEM
2SF1127	OEM
2SF1128	OEM
2SF1129	OEM
2SF1130	OEM
2SF1141	OEM
2SF1145	1889
2SF1146	1889
2SF1147	0733
2SF1148	0733
2SF1149	2134
2SF1150	OEM
2SF1151	OEM
2SF1152	OEM
2SF1168	0239
2SF1168A	0239
2SF1188	0239
2SF1188A	0239
2SF1188B	0239
2SF1188C	0239
2SF1188D	0239
2SF1188E	0239
2SF1188F	0239
2SF1188G	0239
2SF1188H	0239
2SF1188K	0239
2SF1188L	0239
2SF1188M	0239
2SF1188N	0239
2SF1188R	0239
2SF1188Y	0239
2SF1189	0061
2SF1189A	0061
2SF1189C	0061
2SF1189D	0061
2SF1189E	0061
2SF1189F	0061
2SF1189G	0061
2SF1189H	0061
2SF1189K	0061
2SF1189L	0061
2SF1189M	0061
2SF1189N	0061
2SF1189R	0061
2SF1189Y	0061
2SF1365	OEM
2SF1366	OEM
2SF1367	OEM
2SF1368	OEM
2SF1369	OEM
2SF1370	OEM
2SF1418C	0500
2SF1418D	0857
2SF1418E	0705
2SF1419	0705
2SF1420	0705
2SF1420D	0239
2SF1420E	0705
2SF1420F	0705
2SF1421	0705
2SF1422	0239
2SF1422A	0239
2SF1422B	0239
2SF1422C	0239

DEVICE TYPE	REPL CODE
2SF1422D	0239
2SFD111	0143
2SFF05	OEM
2SFF10	OEM
2SFF15	OEM
2SFT212	0160
2SF.T212	0085
2SG536GN	0016
2SH11	2123
2SH12	1659
2SH13	OEM
2SH14	OEM
2SH18	2123
2SH18K	2123
2SH18L	2123
2SH18M	2123
2SH18N	2123
2SH19	2123
2SH19K	2123
2SH19L	2123
2SH19M	2123
2SH19N	2123
2SH20	2123
2SH21	1659
2SH22	1167
2SH203	0279
2SH460	0435
2SH643	0786
2SH678	0150
2SJ2A	0015
2SJ4A	0015
2SJ8A	0071
2SJ11	0321
2SJ12	0321
2SJ13	OEM
2SJ15	OEM
2SJ16	OEM
2SJ17	OEM
2SJ18	OEM
2SJ19	OEM
2SJ20	OEM
2SJ22	OEM
2SJ29	OEM
2SJ32	OEM
2SJ33	OEM
2SJ39	OEM
2SJ40	OEM
2SJ40CD	OEM
2SJ40CTA	OEM
2SJ43	OEM
2SJ44	OEM
2SJ45	OEM
2SJ47	OEM
2SJ48	OEM
2SJ49	OEM
2SJ49(H)	OEM
2SJ49H	OEM
2SJ50	OEM
2SJ50H	OEM
2SJ51	OEM
2SJ55	OEM
2SJ56	OEM
2SJ56(H)	OEM
2SJ56H	OEM
2SJ59(H)	OEM
2SJ60A	0015
2SJ68	OEM
2SJ69	OEM
2SJ70	OEM
2SJ72	OEM
2SJ73	OEM
2SJ74	OEM
2SJ75	OEM
2SJ76	OEM
2SJ77	OEM
2SJ77(K)	OEM
2SJ77K	OEM
2SJ78	OEM
2SJ79	OEM
2SJ79(K)	OEM
2SJ79K	OEM
2SJ81	OEM
2SJ82	OEM
2SJ83	OEM
2SJ84	OEM
2SJ90	OEM
2SJ91	OEM
2SJ92	OEM
2SJ96	OEM
2SJ99	OEM
2SJ100	OEM
2SJ101	OEM
2SJ102	2256
2SJ103	2959
2SJ103GR	OEM
2SJ104	OEM
2SJ104V	OEM
2SJ105	2959
2SJ105-Y	2959
2SJ105Y	2959
2SJ106	OEM
2SJ106G-TE85L	OEM
2SJ107	OEM
2SJ108	OEM
2SJ109	OEM
2SJ110	OEM
2SJ111	OEM
2SJ112	OEM
2SJ113	OEM

DEVICE TYPE	REPL CODE
2SJ114	OEM
2SJ115	OEM
2SJ116	OEM
2SJ117	5263
2SJ118	OEM
2SJ119	OEM
2SJ120(L)	OEM
2SJ120(S)	OEM
2SJ120L	OEM
2SJ120S	OEM
2SJ122	OEM
2SJ123	OEM
2SJ125	OEM
2SJ126	OEM
2SJ164PQRTA	OEM
2SK2SET	0321
2SK11	0321
2SK12	0321
2SK13	0321
2SK15	3350
2SK16(H)	0321
2SK16HA	0321
2SK17	0321
2SK17(O)	0321
2SK17-O	0321
2SK17-OR	0321
2SK17A	0321
2SK17B	0321
2SK17BL	0321
2SK17GR	0321
2SK17O	0321
2SK17R	0321
2SK17Y	0321
2SK18	OEM
2SK18A	OEM
2SK18L	OEM
2SK19	0683
2SK19(BL)	0683
2SK19(GN)	0683
2SK19(GR)	0683
2SK19-14	0683
2SK19-BL	0683
2SK19-GR	0683
2SK19-Y	0683
2SK19A	0683
2SK19B	0683
2SK19BB	0683
2SK19BL	0683
2SK19FET	0683
2SK19GB	0683
2SK19GE	0683
2SK19GR	0683
2SK19H	0683
2SK19K	0683
2SK19TM	0683
2SK19V	0683
2SK19Y	0683
2SK22Y	0321
2SK23	3672
2SK23A	3672
2SK23A(812)	3672
2SK23A-8	3672
2SK23A8	3672
2SK23A-9	3672
2SK23A9	3672
2SK23A-540	3672
2SK23A540	3672
2SK23AL	3672
2SK23G	3672
2SK24	0321
2SK24C	0321
2SK24D	0321
2SK24DR	0321
2SK24E	0321
2SK24F	0321
2SK24G	0321
2SK25	0321
2SK25C	0321
2SK25D	0321
2SK25E	0321
2SK25ET	0321
2SK25F	0321
2SK25G	0321
2SK30	3017
2SK30(O)	3017
2SK30-O	3017
2SK30-Y	3017
2SK30A	3017
2SK30A(D)	3017
2SK30A(FA-1)	3017
2SK30A(G)	3017
2SK30A(G)F	3017
2SK30A(G)L	3017
2SK30A(G)P	3017
2SK30A(GR)	3017
2SK30A-1	3017
2SK30A-GR	3017
2SK30AGR	3017
2SK30A-O	3017
2SK30AO	3017
2SK30A-R	3017
2SK30ATM	3017
2SK30A-TM(FA-1)	3017
2SK30ATM(FA-1)	OEM
2SK30ATM(O)	3017
2SK30ATM(Y)	3017
2SK30ATMFA-1	3017
2SK30ATMFA1	3017
2SK30ATMFA-I	3017

DEVICE TYPE	REPL CODE
2SK30ATM-G	OEM
2SK30ATM-GR	3017
2SK30ATMGR	3017
2SK30ATM-O	3017
2SK30ATM-R	3017
2SK30ATM-Y	3017
2SK30A-Y	3017
2SK30AY	3017
2SK30D	3017
2SK30GR	3017
2SK30O	3017
2SK30R	3017
2SK30Y	3017
2SK31(C)	0321
2SK31C	0321
2SK32	0321
2SK32B	0321
2SK33	1270
2SK33D	1270
2SK33E	1270
2SK33F	1270
2SK33H	1270
2SK34	3126
2SK34(C)	3126
2SK34(D)	3126
2SK34(D)(E)	3126
2SK34(E)	3126
2SK34-D	3126
2SK34A	3126
2SK34B	3126
2SK34C	3126
2SK34D	3126
2SK34E	3126
2SK35	0321
2SK35-0	0321
2SK35-1	0321
2SK35-2	0321
2SK35A	0321
2SK35BL	0321
2SK35C	0321
2SK35GN	0321
2SK35R	0321
2SK35Y	0321
2SK37	0321
2SK37(K)	0321
2SK37H	0321
2SK38	OEM
2SK38A	OEM
2SK39	0212
2SK39(P)	0212
2SK39A	0212
2SK39B	0212
2SK39P	0212
2SK39Q	0212
2SK40	3320
2SK40(C)	3320
2SK40(D)	3320
2SK40-3	3320
2SK40A	3320
2SK40B	3320
2SK40C	3320
2SK40D	3320
2SK41	1202
2SK41C	1202
2SK41D	1202
2SK41E	1202
2SK41E1	1202
2SK41F	1202
2SK42	0321
2SK42-CM1	0321
2SK42-CMI	0321
2SK43	1747
2SK43(03)	1747
2SK43(2)	1747
2SK43(3A)	1747
2SK43(S)	1747
2SK43(S)-D	1747
2SK43-3	1747
2SK43-4	1747
2SK43-OR	1747
2SK43A	1747
2SK43B	1747
2SK43C	1747
2SK43D	1747
2SK43E	1747
2SK43F	1747
2SK43GN	1747
2SK43H	1747
2SK43J	1747
2SK43OR	1747
2SK43R	1747
2SK43S	1747
2SK43X	1747
2SK43Y	1747
2SK44	0321
2SK44(D)	0321
2SK45	0843
2SK45B	0843
2SK46	OEM
2SK47	2922
2SK48	3219
2SK49	1270
2SK49E2	1270
2SK49F	1270
2SK49H	1270
2SK49H1	1270
2SK49H2	1270
2SK49I	1270
2SK49M	1270

DEVICE TYPE	REPL CODE
2SK50	OEM
2SK54	1270
2SK54B	1270
2SK54C	1270
2SK55	0321
2SK55(CD)	0321
2SK55C	0321
2SK55CD	0321
2SK55D	0321
2SK55DE	0321
2SK55R	0321
2SK56	OEM
2SK57	OEM
2SK58	OEM
2SK59	1747
2SK60	OEM
2SK61	1202
2SK61(Y)	1202
2SK61-LV	OEM
2SK61-O	1202
2SK61GR	1202
2SK61Y	1202
2SK63	OEM
2SK65	OEM
2SK66	3104
2SK67	OEM
2SK67A	OEM
2SK67J2	OEM
2SK67J3	OEM
2SK67J4	OEM
2SK67J5	OEM
2SK67J6	OEM
2SK67J7	OEM
2SK67J8	OEM
2SK68	3308
2SK68-L	3308
2SK68-M	3308
2SK68A	3308
2SK68A(L)	3308
2SK68A(M)	3308
2SK68AK	3308
2SK68AL	3308
2SK68A-M	3308
2SK68AM	3308
2SK68L	3308
2SK68M	3308
2SK68Q	3308
2SK69	OEM
2SK70	OEM
2SK72	2917
2SK73	OEM
2SK74	OEM
2SK79	OEM
2SK80	OEM
2SK81	OEM
2SK83	0321
2SK83R	0321
2SK84	3104
2SK84R	OEM
2SK85	OEM
2SK87(H)	3104
2SK87HB	3104
2SK87HD	3104
2SK88	OEM
2SK92	OEM
2SK93	OEM
2SK94	OEM
2SK94X1	OEM
2SK95	OEM
2SK96	OEM
2SK97	OEM
2SK101	OEM
2SK102	OEM
2SK103	OEM
2SK104	0321
2SK104E	0321
2SK104F	0321
2SK104H	0321
2SK105	1747
2SK105(E)	1747
2SK105(F)	1747
2SK105A	1747
2SK105A-10	1747
2SK105A-30	1747
2SK105E	1747
2SK105F	1747
2SK106	0321
2SK106(D)	0321
2SK106D	0321
2SK107	0321
2SK107(3)	0321
2SK107-1	0321
2SK107-2	0321
2SK107-4	0321
2SK108	OEM
2SK108-C	OEM
2SK108C	OEM
2SK109	OEM
2SK109A	OEM
2SK110	OEM
2SK111	OEM
2SK112	OEM
2SK113	1147
2SK117	3104
2SK117(BL)	3104
2SK117-BL	3104
2SK117-GR	3104
2SK117-GR(TPE2)	3104
2SK117-GR-FA-2	3104

DEVICE TYPE	REPL CODE
2SK117-GRFA-2	3104
2SK117-Y	3104
2SK117A	3104
2SK117B(C)	3104
2SK117BL	3104
2SK117GR	3104
2SK117Y	3104
2SK118	1747
2SK118(O)	1747
2SK118-O	1747
2SK118-R	1747
2SK118NEW-R	OEM
2SK118Q	1747
2SK118R	1747
2SK119	0321
2SK120	1382
2SK121	1747
2SK121-2	1747
2SK121-3	OEM
2SK121-4	OEM
2SK121-5	OEM
2SK121-6	OEM
2SK123	OEM
2SK124	OEM
2SK125	OEM
2SK127	1747
2SK127A	OEM
2SK128	OEM
2SK130	OEM
2SK130A	OEM
2SK131	OEM
2SK132	OEM
2SK133	OEM
2SK134	OEM
2SK134(H)	OEM
2SK134H	OEM
2SK135	OEM
2SK135(H)	OEM
2SK135H	OEM
2SK136	3672
2SK137	OEM
2SK137A	OEM
2SK138	OEM
2SK140	OEM
2SK141	1147
2SK141A	1147
2SK146	OEM
2SK147	OEM
2SK148	0321
2SK149	OEM
2SK150	OEM
2SK151	OEM
2SK152	0321
2SK152(2)	0321
2SK152(4)	0321
2SK152-1	0321
2SK152-2	0321
2SK152-3	0321
2SK152-4	OEM
2SK152L	0321
2SK152LA	0321
2SK154	OEM
2SK155	OEM
2SK156	OEM
2SK157	OEM
2SK158	OEM
2SK159	OEM
2SK160	OEM
2SK160A	OEM
2SK160K4	OEM
2SK160K5	OEM
2SK160K6	OEM
2SK160K7	OEM
2SK161	3577
2SK161-O	OEM
2SK161Y	OEM
2SK162	OEM
2SK163	OEM
2SK163L	OEM
2SK163M	OEM
2SK165	OEM
2SK168	0321
2SK168D	0321
2SK168F	0321
2SK169	OEM
2SK170	0321
2SK170V	0321
2SK171	OEM
2SK173	OEM
2SK175	OEM
2SK176	OEM
2SK176(H)	OEM
2SK176H	OEM
2SK184	OEM
2SK185	OEM
2SK186	3104
2SK186B	3104
2SK186C	3104
2SK186D	3104
2SK186E	3104
2SK187	OEM
2SK187C	OEM
2SK187D	OEM
2SK187E	OEM
2SK187F	OEM
2SK190	OEM
2SK190E	OEM
2SK190F	OEM
2SK190G	OEM

DEVICE TYPE	REPL CODE
2SK190H	OEM
2SK191	3219
2SK192	0321
2SK192A	0321
2SK193	OEM
2SK194	0321
2SK195	1382
2SK195H	1382
2SK196	3219
2SK196(H)	OEM
2SK196R	3219
2SK197	0321
2SK197YC	0321
2SK197YD	0321
2SK197YE	0321
2SK198	OEM
2SK198L	OEM
2SK199	OEM
2SK201	OEM
2SK203	OEM
2SK208	OEM
2SK209	OEM
2SK209-GR	OEM
2SK209G	OEM
2SK210	OEM
2SK211	OEM
2SK212	1382
2SK212A	1382
2SK212A-E	OEM
2SK212AE	1382
2SK212E	1382
2SK212F	OEM
2SK213	OEM
2SK214	OEM
2SK214(K)	OEM
2SK214K	OEM
2SK215	OEM
2SK216	OEM
2SK216(K)	OEM
2SK216K	OEM
2SK217	OEM
2SK217ZD	OEM
2SK217ZE	OEM
2SK218	OEM
2SK218(Q)	OEM
2SK218Q	OEM
2SK218R	OEM
2SK220(H)	OEM
2SK220H	OEM
2SK221(H)	OEM
2SK221H	OEM
2SK222	OEM
2SK222E	OEM
2SK223	OEM
2SK225	OEM
2SK226	OEM
2SK227	OEM
2SK238	OEM
2SK240	OEM
2SK241	OEM
2SK242	OEM
2SK246	OEM
2SK246-Y	OEM
2SK246BL	OEM
2SK246GR	OEM
2SK246GR3	OEM
2SK246Y	OEM
2SK247	OEM
2SK258(H)	OEM
2SK258H	OEM
2SK259(H)	OEM
2SK259H	OEM
2SK260(H)	OEM
2SK260H	OEM
2SK266	OEM
2SK270	OEM
2SK271	OEM
2SK272	OEM
2SK273	OEM
2SK274	OEM
2SK275	OEM
2SK276	OEM
2SK277	OEM
2SK278	OEM
2SK279	OEM
2SK280	OEM
2SK281	OEM
2SK283	OEM
2SK286	OEM
2SK287(K)	OEM
2SK287K	OEM
2SK288(K)	OEM
2SK288K	OEM
2SK289(H)	OEM
2SK290(H)	OEM
2SK291	OEM
2SK291E	OEM
2SK291F	OEM
2SK291G	OEM
2SK291H	OEM
2SK292	OEM
2SK293	OEM
2SK293A	OEM
2SK294	6228
2SK295	4970
2SK296	1457
2SK298	OEM
2SK299	OEM
2SK300	OEM

108

If replacement code is OEM, contact original manufacturer for replacement.

DEVICE TYPE	REPL CODE
2SK301	3104
2SK301(O)	3104
2SK301(P)	3104
2SK301(Q)	3104
2SK301(R)	3104
2SK301Q	3104
2SK301QR	3104
2SK301QTA	OEM
2SK301R	3104
2SK302	OEM
2SK303	OEM
2SK304	0321
2SK304D	OEM
2SK304E	OEM
2SK308	OEM
2SK310	1456
2SK311	OEM
2SK312	OEM
2SK313	OEM
2SK314	OEM
2SK315	OEM
2SK315E	OEM
2SK316	OEM
2SK317	OEM
2SK318	OEM
2SK319	1456
2SK320	OEM
2SK321	OEM
2SK322	OEM
2SK322WE	OEM
2SK322WF	OEM
2SK322WG	OEM
2SK322WH	OEM
2SK323	OEM
2SK323KB	OEM
2SK323KC	OEM
2SK323KD	OEM
2SK323KE	OEM
2SK324	OEM
2SK325	OEM
2SK330	OEM
2SK331	OEM
2SK332	OEM
2SK333	OEM
2SK334	OEM
2SK336	OEM
2SK337	OEM
2SK343	OEM
2SK344	OEM
2SK345	5264
2SK346	5264
2SK347	OEM
2SK349	OEM
2SK350	OEM
2SK351	5764
2SK352	OEM
2SK353	OEM
2SK354	OEM
2SK354A	OEM
2SK355	OEM
2SK356	OEM
2SK357	OEM
2SK358	OEM
2SK359	OEM
2SK360	OEM
2SK362	1747
2SK363	OEM
2SK364	OEM
2SK365	OEM
2SK366	OEM
2SK367	OEM
2SK368	OEM
2SK369	OEM
2SK370	OEM
2SK371	OEM
2SK372	OEM
2SK373	OEM
2SK374	OEM
2SK375(L)	OEM
2SK375(S)	OEM
2SK376	OEM
2SK377	OEM
2SK378	OEM
2SK379	OEM
2SK380	OEM
2SK381	1747
2SK381-B	1747
2SK381-E	1747
2SK381B	1747
2SK381C	4218
2SK381D	4218
2SK381TP-C	1747
2SK382	1457
2SK383	4970
2SK384(L)	OEM
2SK384(S)	OEM
2SK385	OEM
2SK386	OEM
2SK387	OEM
2SK388	OEM
2SK389	OEM
2SK398	5266
2SK399	OEM
2SK400	OEM
2SK401	OEM
2SK402	OEM
2SK403	OEM
2SK404	OEM
2SK405	OEM

DEVICE TYPE	REPL CODE
2SK406	OEM
2SK407	OEM
2SK408	OEM
2SK409	OEM
2SK410	OEM
2SK411	1658
2SK412	OEM
2SK413	OEM
2SK414	OEM
2SK415	OEM
2SK416	OEM
2SK416(L)	OEM
2SK416(S)	OEM
2SK417	OEM
2SK418	OEM
2SK419	OEM
2SK420	OEM
2SK421	OEM
2SK422	OEM
2SK423	OEM
2SK424	1658
2SK425	OEM
2SK426	OEM
2SK427	OEM
2SK428	4970
2SK429	OEM
2SK429(L)	OEM
2SK429(S)	OEM
2SK430	OEM
2SK430(L)	OEM
2SK430(S)	OEM
2SK431	OEM
2SK433	OEM
2SK435	OEM
2SK436	OEM
2SK437	OEM
2SK437(H)	OEM
2SK438	OEM
2SK439	OEM
2SK440	2162
2SK441	OEM
2SK442	OEM
2SK443	OEM
2SK444	OEM
2SK445	OEM
2SK446	OEM
2SK447	OEM
2SK448	OEM
2SK449	OEM
2SK453	OEM
2SK454	OEM
2SK455	OEM
2SK456	OEM
2SK457	OEM
2SK458	OEM
2SK459	OEM
2SK462	OEM
2SK463	OEM
2SK464	OEM
2SK468	OEM
2SK470	OEM
2SK477	OEM
2SK479	OEM
2SK482	OEM
2SK484	OEM
2SK493G	OEM
2SK494	OEM
2SK503A	OEM
2SK505	OEM
2SK507	OEM
2SK508	OEM
2SK511	OEM
2SK512	OEM
2SK513	3673
2SK518	OEM
2SK519	OEM
2SK520	OEM
2SK521	OEM
2SK522	OEM
2SK525	OEM
2SK526	OEM
2SK527	OEM
2SK528	OEM
2SK529	OEM
2SK530	OEM
2SK531	OEM
2SK532	OEM
2SK534	OEM
2SK535	OEM
2SK535(L)	OEM
2SK535(S)	OEM
2SK537	OEM
2SK538	OEM
2SK539	OEM
2SK541	OEM
2SK543	OEM
2SK544	OEM
2SK544F	OEM
2SK545	OEM
2SK546	OEM
2SK549	OEM
2SK551	OEM
2SK552	OEM
2SK553	OEM
2SK554	5661
2SK555	5661
2SK556	OEM
2SK557	OEM
2SK559	OEM

DEVICE TYPE	REPL CODE
2SK560	OEM
2SK562	OEM
2SK564	OEM
2SK565	OEM
2SK566	OEM
2SK568	OEM
2SK570	OEM
2SK570S	OEM
2SK572	OEM
2SK573	OEM
2SK575	OEM
2SK578	OEM
2SK579(L)	OEM
2SK579(S)	OEM
2SK580(L)	OEM
2SK580(S)	OEM
2SK581	OEM
2SK582	OEM
2SK583	OEM
2SK585	OEM
2SK586	OEM
2SK587	OEM
2SK590	OEM
2SK593	OEM
2SK600	OEM
2SK601	OEM
2SK602	OEM
2SK603	OEM
2SK604	OEM
2SK606	0321
2SK607	OEM
2SK608	OEM
2SK609	OEM
2SK610	OEM
2SK614	OEM
2SK615	OEM
2SK616	OEM
2SK617	OEM
2SK618	OEM
2SK619	OEM
2SK621	OEM
2SK624	OEM
2SK625	OEM
2SK626	OEM
2SK627	OEM
2SK628	OEM
2SK629	OEM
2SK630	OEM
2SK631	OEM
2SK632	OEM
2SK633	OEM
2SK634	OEM
2SK635	OEM
2SK636	OEM
2SK637	OEM
2SK638	OEM
2SK646	OEM
2SK652Q	OEM
2SK652R	OEM
2SK656	OEM
2SK739	OEM
2SK774	OEM
2SK786	OEM
2SK796	OEM
2SK817	OEM
2SK824	OEM
2SK824(1)	OEM
2SK1033B	0321
2SK1059	OEM
2SK1105	OEM
2SK1199	OEM
2SK1206-01	OEM
2SK1429	OEM
2SK1521A	0321
2SL17	OEM
2SL24F	OEM
2SM1	0015
2SM3	0087
2SM6	OEM
2SM11	OEM
2SM12	OEM
2SM13	OEM
2SM15	0418
2SM20	OEM
2SM21	OEM
2SM22	OEM
2SM25	0418
2SM40	OEM
2SM41	OEM
2SM42	OEM
2SM43	OEM
2SM55	OEM
2SM58	OEM
2SM63	OEM
2SM64	OEM
2SM65	OEM
2SM66	OEM
2SM67	OEM
2SM68	OEM
2SM69	OEM
2SM70	OEM
2SM71	0404
2SM72	0418
2SM73	0147
2SM74	0147
2SM75	OEM
2SM79	OEM
2SM100	3123
2SM125	OEM

DEVICE TYPE	REPL CODE
2SM125A	OEM
2SM136	OEM
2SM137	OEM
2SM138	OEM
2SM139	OEM
2SM140	OEM
2SM141	OEM
2SM142	OEM
2SM143	OEM
2SM144	0154
2SM145	0147
2SM146	0147
2SM147	0278
2SM150	OEM
2SM151	OEM
2SM200	OEM
2SM610B	0037
2SM1020A4	OEM
2SM1020A4PL	OEM
2SM1020A4T	OEM
2SM1020A5	OEM
2SM1020A5PL	OEM
2SM1020A5T	OEM
2SM1020A6	OEM
2SM1020A6PL	OEM
2SM1020A6T	OEM
2SM1020A7	OEM
2SM1020A7PL	OEM
2SM1020A7T	OEM
2SM1020A8PL	OEM
2SM1020A8T	OEM
2SM1020AB	OEM
2SM1020E4	OEM
2SM1020E4PL	OEM
2SM1020E4T	OEM
2SM1020E5	OEM
2SM1020E5PL	OEM
2SM1020E5T	OEM
2SM1020E6	OEM
2SM1020E6PL	OEM
2SM1020E6T	OEM
2SM1020E7	OEM
2SM1020E7T	OEM
2SM1020GE8	OEM
2SM1020GE8PL	OEM
2SM1020GE8T	OEM
2SM1020GE9	OEM
2SM1020GE9PL	OEM
2SM1020GE9T	OEM
2SM1020GE10	OEM
2SM1020GE10PL	OEM
2SM1020GE10T	OEM
2SN733	0079
2SN784	0488
2SN3841	0037
2SO12	0042
2SO14	0007
2SO17	0626
2SO18	0626
2SO20	0626
2SO33	0103
2SO34	0103
2SO35	0103
2SO36	0103
2SO95A	0079
2SOO2	0855
2SP405	0086
2SQ371	0144
2SR05K	0015
2SR1K	0015
2SR1K-2	OEM
2SR1K-4	OEM
2SR24	0321
2SR54	0086
2SR68AM	0321
2SR173	0086
2SR677	0786
2SV341V	0969
2SVB	0319
2SVB10	1404
2T1	OEM
2T2P	0211
2T3	0004
2T11	0164
2T12	0164
2T13	0164
2T14	0164
2T14A	0136
2T15	0164
2T15X3	0127
2T16	0164
2T17	0164
2T20	0050
2T21	0164
2T22	0164
2T23	0164
2T24	0164
2T25	0164
2T26	0164
2T40	0079
2T41	0079
2T42	0079
2T43	0079
2T44	0079
2T51	0038
2T52	0595
2T53	0595
2T54	0595
2T55	0595

DEVICE TYPE	REPL CODE
2T56	0595
2T57	0595
2T58	0595
2T61	0038
2T62	0038
2T63	0038
2T64	0038
2T64R	0038
2T65	0038
2T65R	0038
2T66	0038
2T66R	0038
2T67	0595
2T69	0038
2T71	0595
2T72	0595
2T73	0595
2T73R	0595
2T74	0595
2T75	0595
2T75R	0595
2T76	0595
2T76R	0595
2T77	0595
2T77R	0595
2T78	0595
2T78R	0595
2T82	0595
2T83	0595
2T84	0038
2T85	0038
2T85A	0038
2T86	0038
2T89	0038
2T172	0079
2T201	0050
2T202	0079
2T203	0050
2T204	0050
2T204A	0050
2T205	0050
2T205A	0050
2T230	0211
2T231	0211
2T311	0164
2T312	0164
2T313	0164
2T314	0164
2T315	0164
2T321	0164
2T322	0164
2T323	0164
2T324	0164
2T383	0164
2T402	0198
2T403	0079
2T404	0079
2T501	0015
2T502	0015
2T503	0015
2T504	0015
2T505	0015
2T506	0015
2T507	0071
2T508	0071
2T509	0071
2T510	0071
2T513	0595
2T520	0595
2T521	0595
2T522	0038
2T523	0038
2T524	0595
2T551	0595
2T552	0038
2T650	0595
2T681	0038
2T682	0038
2T918	0079
2T919	0127
2T2001	0211
2T2102	0590
2T2708	0079
2T2785	0079
2T2857	0079
2T3011	0160
2T3021	0160
2T3022	0160
2T3030	0160
2T3031	0160
2T3032	0160
2T3033	0160
2T3041	0160
2T3042	0160
2T3043	0160
2TDA1054M	OEM
2TN15	0279
2TN32	0279
2TN45A	0211
2TN48	0279
2TN49	0279
2TN52	0279
2TN53	0279
2TN56	0211
2TN95	0211
2TN95A	0211
2U4	0023
2U8	0023
2U12	0023

DEVICE TYPE	REPL CODE
2U16	0017
2U20	0017
2V58.5B	OEM
2V110A	OEM
2V110B	OEM
2V205	OEM
2V362	0211
2V363	0211
2V435	OEM
2V464	0279
2V465	0279
2V466	0279
2V467	0279
2V482	0279
2V483	0279
2V484	0279
2V485	0050
2V486	0279
2V559	0050
2V560	0050
2V561	0050
2V562	0050
2V563	0050
2V631	0279
2V632	0279
2V633	0279
2VR5.6	0870
2VR5.6A	0870
2VR5.6B	0870
2VR6	3099
2VR6A	3099
2VR6B	3099
2VR6.2	3099
2VR6.2A	3099
2VR6.2B	3099
2VR6.8	0205
2VR6.8A	0205
2VR6.8B	0205
2VR7	0205
2VR7A	0205
2VR7B	0205
2VR7.5	0475
2VR7.5A	0475
2VR7.5B	0475
2VR8.2	0499
2VR8.2A	0499
2VR8.2B	0499
2VR8.5	3285
2VR8.5A	3285
2VR8.5B	3285
2VR9.1	0679
2VR9.1A	0679
2VR9.1B	0679
2VR10	0225
2VR10A	0225
2VR10B	0225
2VR11	0230
2VR11A	0230
2VR11B	0230
2VR12	0234
2VR12A	0234
2VR12B	0234
2VR13	0237
2VR13A	0237
2VR13B	0237
2VR13R	0237
2VR14	1387
2VR14A	1387
2VR14B	1387
2VR15	0247
2VR15A	0247
2VR15B	0247
2VR16	0251
2VR16A	0251
2VR16B	0251
2VR18	0256
2VR18A	0256
2VR18B	0256
2VR20	0262
2VR20A	0262
2VR20B	0262
2VR22	0269
2VR22A	0269
2VR22B	0269
2VR24	0273
2VR24A	0273
2VR24B	0273
2VR27	0291
2VR27A	0291
2VR27B	0291
2VR28	1169
2VR28A	1169
2VR28B	1169
2VR30	0305
2VR30A	0305
2VR30B	0305
2VR33	0314
2VR33A	0314
2VR33B	0314
2VR36	0316
2VR36A	0316
2VR36B	0316
2VR39	0322
2VR39A	0322
2VR39B	0322
2VR43	0333
2VR43A	0333
2VR43B	0333
2VR47	0343

DEVICE TYPE	REPL CODE
2VR47A	0343
2VR47B	0343
2VR51	0027
2VR51A	0027
2VR51B	0027
2VR56	0266
2VR56A	0266
2VR56B	0266
2VR62	0382
2VR62A	0382
2VR62B	0382
2VR67	0401
2VR67A	0401
2VR67B	0401
2VR68	0401
2VR68A	0401
2VR68B	0401
2VR75	0421
2VR75A	0421
2VR75B	0421
2VR80	0439
2VR80A	0439
2VR80B	0439
2VR82	0439
2VR82A	0439
2VR82B	0439
2VR90	0238
2VR90A	0238
2VR90B	0238
2VR91	0238
2VR91A	0238
2VR91B	0238
2VR100	1172
2VR100A	1172
2VR100B	1172
2VR105	1172
2VR105A	1172
2VR105B	1172
2VR110	1182
2VR110A	1182
2VR110B	1182
2VR120	1198
2VR120A	1198
2VR120B	1198
2VR130	1209
2VR130A	1209
2VR130B	1209
2VR150	0642
2VR150A	0642
2VR150B	0642
2VR160	1246
2VR160A	1246
2VR160B	1246
2VR180	1269
2VR180A	1269
2VR180B	1269
2VR200	0600
2VR200A	0600
2VR200B	0600
2W005	0106
2W005G	OEM
2W005M	1847
2W01	0106
2W01G	OEM
2W01M	2758
2W02	0106
2W02-5008-L	OEM
2W02-5008L	OEM
2W02G	OEM
2W02M	2758
2W04	0106
2W04G	OEM
2W04M	2758
2W06	0672
2W06G	OEM
2W06M	2175
2W08	0118
2W08G	OEM
2W08M	6600
2W010	0782
2W3A	0015
2W4A	0015
2W5A	0015
2W6A	0071
2W7A	0071
2W9A	0071
2W10	0782
2W10G	5620
2W10M	5620
2W12A	OEM
2W15A	OEM
2W20A	OEM
2WCDR152-1203B	OEM
2WDCR7K603B35	OEM
2WDCR7K703B35	OEM
2WDCR7K803B35	OEM
2WDCR7K903B35	OEM
2WDCR7K1003B35	OEM
2WDCR7K1103B4	OEM
2WDCR7K1103B35	OEM
2WDCR7K1203B35	OEM
2WDCR7K1203BR	OEM
2WDCR7K1303B4	OEM
2WDCR7K1303B35	OEM
2WDCR7K1403B4	OEM
2WDCR7K1503B4	OEM
2WDCR152-603B	OEM
2WDCR152-703B	OEM
2WDCR152-803B	OEM

If replacement code is OEM, contact original manufacturer for replacement.

DEVICE TYPE	REPL CODE	DEVICE TYPE	REPL CODE	DEVICE TYPE	REPL CODE	DEVICE TYPE	REPL CODE	DEVICE TYPE	REPL CODE	DEVICE TYPE	REPL CODE	DEVICE TYPE	REPL CODE
2WDCR152-903B	OEM	2.5Z47D5	0343	3A3150	OEM	3BZ62	0382	3BZD51A	OEM	3C1200A	OEM	3CZ100B	OEM
2WDCR152-1003B	OEM	2.5Z47D10	0343	3A3150A	OEM	3BZ62A	0382	3BZD51B	OEM	3C2030	OEM	3CZ110	OEM
2WDCR152-1103B	OEM	2.5Z50D	0027	3A3200	OEM	3BZ62B	0382	3BZD56	OEM	3C2030A	OEM	3CZ110A	OEM
2WDCR152-1303B	OEM	2.5Z50D5	0027	3A3200A	OEM	3BZ68	0401	3BZD56A	OEM	3C2060	OEM	3CZ110B	OEM
2WMT1	1241	2.5Z50D10	0027	3AF2	0087	3BZ68A	0401	3BZD56B	OEM	3C2060A	OEM	3CZ120	OEM
2WMT2	1567	2.5Z51D	0027	3AF4	1736	3BZ68B	0401	3BZD62	OEM	3C2100	OEM	3CZ120A	OEM
2WMT4	1571	2.5Z51D5	0027	3AF6	0959	3BZ75	0421	3BZD62A	OEM	3C2100A	OEM	3CZ120B	OEM
2WMT6	1576	2.5Z51D10	0027	3AF8	0811	3BZ75A	0421	3BZD62B	OEM	3C2200	OEM	3CZ130	OEM
2WMT8	1124	2.5Z52D	0027	3ALB	OEM	3BZ75B	0421	3BZD68	OEM	3C2200A	OEM	3CZ130A	OEM
2WMT10	0045	2.5Z52D5	0027	3AS1	0015	3BZ82	0439	3BZD68A	OEM	3C6030	1129	3CZ130B	OEM
2WMT12	OEM	2.5Z52D10	0027	3AS2	0015	3BZ82A	0439	3BZD68B	OEM	3C6060	OEM	3CZ150	OEM
2X2N3055	OEM	2.5Z56D	0266	3B4B41	0319	3BZ82B	0439	3BZD75	OEM	3C6100	0442	3CZ150A	OEM
2X9A116	0015	2.5Z56D5	0266	3B4.1	0319	3BZ91	0238	3BZD75A	OEM	3C6150	OEM	3CZ150B	OEM
2XAA111	0143	2.5Z56D10	0266	3B15	0211	3BZ91A	0238	3BZD75B	OEM	3C6200	OEM	3CZ160	OEM
2XAA112	0143	2.5Z62D	0382	3B15-1	0211	3BZ91B	0238	3BZD82	OEM	3CC11	OEM	3CZ160A	OEM
2XAA113	0143	2.5Z62D5	0382	3B30S	OEM	3BZ100	1172	3BZD82A	OEM	3CC12	0865	3CZ160B	OEM
2XAA119	0143	2.5Z62D10	0382	3B60S	OEM	3BZ100A	1172	3BZD82B	OEM	3CC13	0865	3CZ180	OEM
2XBD181	OEM	2.5Z68D	0401	3B100S	OEM	3BZ100B	1172	3BZD91	OEM	3CD12	0865	3CZ180A	OEM
2XBD182	OEM	2.5Z68D5	0401	3B150S	OEM	3BZ110	1182	3BZD91A	OEM	3CD13	0865	3CZ180B	OEM
2XBD183	OEM	2.5Z68D10	0401	3B200S	OEM	3BZ110A	1182	3BZD91B	OEM	3CG0R	1067	3CZ200	OEM
2XBD184	OEM	2.5Z75D	0421	3B1034	OEM	3BZ110B	1182	3BZD100	OEM	3CG0R	1067	3CZ200A	OEM
2XBDY20	OEM	2.5Z75D5	0421	3B3015	OEM	3BZ120	1198	3BZD100A	OEM	3CS1	0015	3CZ200B	OEM
2XR440M	OEM	2.5Z75D10	0421	3B3030	OEM	3BZ120A	1198	3BZD100B	OEM	3CS2	0015	3D1.E	0319
2XT95423C	OEM	2.5Z82D	0439	3B3060	OEM	3BZ120B	1198	3BZD110	OEM	3CZ6.8	OEM	3D4B41	1404
2YQ	OEM	2.5Z82D5	0439	3B3100	OEM	3BZ130	1209	3BZD110A	OEM	3CZ6.8A	OEM	3D5R5	OEM
2Z	OEM	2.5Z82D10	0439	3B3150	OEM	3BZ130A	1209	3BZD110B	OEM	3CZ6.8B	OEM	3D5R12-12	OEM
2Z16A	0251	2.5Z91D	0238	3B3200	OEM	3BZ130B	1209	3BZD120	OEM	3CZ7.5	OEM	3D5R15-15	OEM
2Z18A	0256	2.5Z91D5	0238	3BB-20B01	0276	3BZ150	0642	3BZD120A	OEM	3CZ7.5A	OEM	3D24R5	OEM
2Z27A	0291	2.5Z91D10	0238	3BB-20801	0015	3BZ150A	0642	3BZD120B	OEM	3CZ7.5B	OEM	3D24R12-12	OEM
2.2B	OEM	2.5Z100D	1172	3BH61	0087	3BZ150B	0642	3BZD130	OEM	3CZ8.2	OEM	3D24R15-15	OEM
2.2Z22D10	OEM	2.5Z100D5	1172	3BS1	0015	3BZ160	1246	3BZD130A	OEM	3CZ8.2A	OEM	3D-702	0398
2.3L15	OEM	2.5Z100D10	1172	3BS2	0015	3BZ160A	1246	3BZD130B	OEM	3CZ8.2B	OEM	3DC11	OEM
2.3L30	OEM	2.7B	0755	3BZ5.6	0870	3BZ160B	1246	3BZD150	OEM	3CZ9.1	OEM	3DC12	0865
2.3L60	OEM	2.7B2	0755	3BZ5.6A	0870	3BZ180	1269	3BZD150A	OEM	3CZ9.1A	OEM	3DC13	0865
2.5Z6.8D	0205	2.7B3	0755	3BZ5.6B	0870	3BZ180A	1269	3BZD150B	OEM	3CZ9.1B	OEM	3DD10	0369
2.5Z6.8D5	0205	2.7L1	0755	3BZ6.2	0185	3BZ180B	1269	3BZD160	OEM	3CZ10	OEM	3DD12	0865
2.5Z6.8D10	0205	2.4341.0018	0160	3BZ6.2A	0185	3BZ200	0600	3BZD160A	OEM	3CZ10A	OEM	3DD15	OEM
2.5Z7.5D	0475	2.V008M01	0279	3BZ6.2B	0185	3BZ200A	0600	3BZD160B	OEM	3CZ10B	OEM	3DD20	OEM
2.5Z7.5D5	0475	2.V0038H03	0211	3BZ6.8	0205	3BZ200B	0600	3BZD180	OEM	3CZ11	OEM	3DD25	OEM
2.5Z7.5D10	0475	2x0C318	OEM	3BZ6.8A	0205	3BZD5.6	OEM	3BZD180A	OEM	3CZ11A	OEM	3DD30	OEM
2.5Z8.2D	0499	2x0C308	OEM	3BZ6.8B	0205	3BZD5.6A	OEM	3BZD180B	OEM	3CZ11B	OEM	3DE15	OEM
2.5Z8.2D5	0499	3-1477	0535	3BZ7.5	0475	3BZD5.6B	OEM	3BZD200	OEM	3CZ12	OEM	3DF10	OEM
2.5Z8.2D10	0499	3-DL2	0023	3BZ7.5A	0475	3BZD6.2	OEM	3BZD200A	OEM	3CZ12A	OEM	3DF20	OEM
2.5Z9.1D	0679	3A03	OEM	3BZ7.5B	0475	3BZD6.2A	OEM	3BZD200B	OEM	3CZ12B	OEM	3DF25	OEM
2.5Z9.1D5	0679	3A05	OEM	3BZ8.2	0499	3BZD6.2B	OEM	3C05	0703	3CZ13	OEM	3DF30	OEM
2.5Z9.1D10	0679	3A1	0087	3BZ8.2A	0499	3BZD6.8	OEM	3C05R	0927	3CZ13A	OEM	3DH61	0087
2.5Z10	0225	3A2	OEM	3BZ8.2B	0499	3BZD6.8A	OEM	3C1	2873	3CZ13B	OEM	3DL2	0023
2.5Z10D5	0225	3A4	OEM	3BZ9.1	0679	3BZD6.8B	OEM	3C2	1116	3CZ15	OEM	3DL4C	0023
2.5Z10D10	0225	3A5R5	OEM	3BZ9.1A	0679	3BZD7.5	OEM	3C4	0800	3CZ15A	OEM	3DS1	0015
2.5Z11D	0230	3A5R12-12	OEM	3BZ9.1B	0679	3BZD7.5A	OEM	3C6	0315	3CZ15B	OEM	3DS2	0015
2.5Z11D5	0230	3A5R15-15	OEM	3BZ10	0225	3BZD7.5B	OEM	3C6RH	0991	3CZ16	OEM	3DS3	0087
2.5Z11D10	0230	3A6	OEM	3BZ10A	0225	3BZD8.2	OEM	3C8	1124	3CZ16A	OEM	3DZ61	0087
2.5Z12D	0234	3A8	OEM	3BZ10B	0225	3BZD8.2A	OEM	3C10	0045	3CZ16B	OEM	3E05	0110
2.5Z12D5	0234	3A12R5	OEM	3BZ11	0230	3BZD8.2B	OEM	3C10R	0941	3CZ18	OEM	3E-1	0016
2.5Z12D10	0234	3A12R12-12	OEM	3BZ11A	0230	3BZD9.1	OEM	3C12	OEM	3CZ18A	OEM	3E1	0947
2.5Z13D	0237	3A12R15-15	OEM	3BZ11B	0230	3BZD9.1A	OEM	3C14	OEM	3CZ18B	OEM	3E-2	0016
2.5Z13D5	0237	3A15	0110	3BZ12	0234	3BZD9.1B	OEM	3C15	0575	3CZ20	OEM	3E2	0242
2.5Z13D10	0237	3A24R5	OEM	3BZ12A	0234	3BZD10	OEM	3C15A	OEM	3CZ20A	OEM	3E-3	0016
2.5Z14D	1387	3A24R12-12	OEM	3BZ12B	0234	3BZD10A	OEM	3C15R	0941	3CZ20B	OEM	3E-4	0143
2.5Z14D5	1387	3A24R15-15	OEM	3BZ13	0237	3BZD10B	OEM	3C16	OEM	3CZ22	OEM	3E4	0535
2.5Z14D10	1387	3A30	0110	3BZ13A	0237	3BZD11	OEM	3C20	0575	3CZ22A	OEM	3E6	0959
2.5Z15D	0247	3A50	0087	3BZ13B	0237	3BZD11A	OEM	3C20R	0941	3CZ22B	OEM	3E8	0811
2.5Z15D5	0247	3A50FS	0087	3BZ15	0247	3BZD11B	OEM	3C30	2049	3CZ24	OEM	3E10	0916
2.5Z15D10	0247	3A69-34000-001	OEM	3BZ15A	0247	3BZD12	OEM	3C30A	OEM	3CZ24A	OEM	3E25	OEM
2.5Z16D	0251	3A100	0087	3BZ15B	0247	3BZD12A	OEM	3C30R	4443	3CZ24B	OEM	3E-27	0004
2.5Z16D5	0251	3A100FS	0087	3BZ16	0251	3BZD12B	OEM	3C40	0994	3CZ27	OEM	3E-28	0164
2.5Z16D10	0251	3A120	OEM	3BZ16A	0251	3BZD13	OEM	3C40R	1006	3CZ27A	OEM	3E-29	0164
2.5Z17D	1170	3A133	OEM	3BZ16B	0251	3BZD13A	OEM	3C50	2065	3CZ27B	OEM	3E50A	OEM
2.5Z17D5	1170	3A152	0015	3BZ18	0256	3BZD13B	OEM	3C50R	5467	3CZ30	OEM	3E-64	0015
2.5Z17D10	1170	3A154	0015	3BZ18A	0256	3BZD15	OEM	3C51	OEM	3CZ30A	OEM	3E-65	0015
2.5Z18D	0256	3A156	0015	3BZ18B	0256	3BZD15A	OEM	3C60	2070	3CZ30B	OEM	3ES1	0015
2.5Z18D5	0256	3A158	0071	3BZ20	0262	3BZD15B	OEM	3C60A	OEM	3CZ33	OEM	3ES2	0015
2.5Z18D10	0256	3A-200	0071	3BZ20A	0262	3BZD16	OEM	3C60R	1067	3CZ33A	OEM	3EZ3.9D	0801
2.5Z19D	2379	3A200	0015	3BZ20B	0262	3BZD16A	OEM	3C63B	OEM	3CZ33B	OEM	3EZ3.9D1	OEM
2.5Z19D5	2379	3A200FS	0087	3BZ22	0269	3BZD16B	OEM	3C63C	OEM	3CZ36	OEM	3EZ3.9D2	OEM
2.5Z19D10	2379	3A252	0015	3BZ22A	0269	3BZD18	OEM	3C70	2077	3CZ36A	OEM	3EZ3.9D3	OEM
2.5Z20D	0262	3A254	0015	3BZ22B	0269	3BZD18A	OEM	3C70R	1130	3CZ36B	OEM	3EZ3.9D4	OEM
2.5Z20D5	0262	3A256	0015	3BZ24	0273	3BZD18B	OEM	3C80	2077	3CZ39	OEM	3EZ3.9D5	0801
2.5Z20D10	0262	3A258	0071	3BZ24A	0273	3BZD20	OEM	3C80R	1130	3CZ39A	OEM	3EZ3.9D10	0801
2.5Z22D	0269	3A300	1736	3BZ24B	0273	3BZD20A	OEM	3C90	0607	3CZ39B	OEM	3EZ4.3D	0815
2.5Z22D5	0269	3A300FS	OEM	3BZ27	0291	3BZD20B	OEM	3C90R	1180	3CZ43	OEM	3EZ4.3D1	OEM
2.5Z24D	0269	3A400	0087	3BZ27A	0291	3BZD22	OEM	3C91B	OEM	3CZ43A	OEM	3EZ4.3D2	OEM
2.5Z24D5	0273	3A400FS	0087	3BZ27B	0291	3BZD22A	OEM	3C91C	OEM	3CZ43B	OEM	3EZ4.3D3	OEM
2.5Z24D10	0273	3A500	1760	3BZ30	0305	3BZD22B	OEM	3C92B	OEM	3CZ47	OEM	3EZ4.3D4	OEM
2.5Z25D	2383	3A500FS	0087	3BZ30A	0305	3BZD24	OEM	3C92C	OEM	3CZ47A	OEM	3EZ4.3D5	0815
2.5Z25D5	2383	3A600	0087	3BZ30B	0305	3BZD24A	OEM	3C100	0607	3CZ47B	OEM	3EZ4.3D10	0815
2.5Z25D10	2383	3A600FS	0087	3BZ33	0314	3BZD24B	OEM	3C100A	OEM	3CZ51	OEM	3EZ4.7D	0827
2.5Z27D	0291	3A700	0087	3BZ33A	0314	3BZD27	OEM	3C100R	1180	3CZ51A	OEM	3EZ4.7D1	OEM
2.5Z27D5	0291	3A700FS	0087	3BZ33B	0314	3BZD27A	OEM	3C128	OEM	3CZ51B	OEM	3EZ4.7D2	OEM
2.5Z27D10	0291	3A800	0087	3BZ36	0316	3BZD27B	OEM	3C169	OEM	3CZ56	OEM	3EZ4.7D3	OEM
2.5Z30D	0305	3A800FS	0087	3BZ36A	0316	3BZD30	OEM	3C200	OEM	3CZ56A	OEM	3EZ4.7D4	OEM
2.5Z30D5	0305	3A900	0087	3BZ36B	0316	3BZD30A	OEM	3C200A	OEM	3CZ56B	OEM	3EZ4.7D5	0827
2.5Z30D10	0305	3A900FS	0087	3BZ39	0322	3BZD30B	OEM	3C201	OEM	3CZ62	OEM	3EZ4.7D10	0827
2.5Z33D	0314	3A1000	0087	3BZ39A	0322	3BZD33	OEM	3C211	OEM	3CZ62A	OEM	3EZ5.1D	0437
2.5Z33D5	0314	3A1000FS	0087	3BZ39B	0322	3BZD33A	OEM	3C300	OEM	3CZ62B	OEM	3EZ5.1D1	OEM
2.5Z33D10	0314	3A1100	OEM	3BZ43	0333	3BZD33B	OEM	3C400	OEM	3CZ66	OEM	3EZ5.1D2	OEM
2.5Z36D	0316	3A1100FS	OEM	3BZ43A	0333	3BZD36	OEM	3C500	OEM	3CZ66A	OEM	3EZ5.1D3	OEM
2.5Z36D5	0316	3A1200	OEM	3BZ43B	0333	3BZD36A	OEM	3C600	OEM	3CZ66B	OEM	3EZ5.1D4	OEM
2.5Z36D10	0316	3A1200FS	OEM	3BZ47	0343	3BZD36B	OEM	3C800	OEM	3CZ75	OEM	3EZ5.1D5	0437
2.5Z39D	0322	3A1300	OEM	3BZ47A	0343	3BZD39	OEM	3C1000	OEM	3CZ75A	OEM	3EZ5.1D10	0437
2.5Z39D5	0322	3A1300FS	OEM	3BZ47B	0343	3BZD39A	OEM	3C1030	OEM	3CZ75B	OEM	3EZ5.6D	0870
2.5Z39D10	0322	3A1510	0071	3BZ51	0027	3BZD39B	OEM	3C1030A	OEM	3CZ82	OEM	3EZ5.6D1	OEM
2.5Z43D	0333	3A2510	0071	3BZ51A	0027	3BZD43	OEM	3C1060	OEM	3CZ82A	OEM	3EZ5.6D2	OEM
2.5Z43D5	0333	3A3030	OEM	3BZ51B	0027	3BZD43A	OEM	3C1060A	OEM	3CZ82B	OEM	3EZ5.6D3	OEM
2.5Z43D10	0333	3A3030A	OEM	3BZ56	0266	3BZD43B	OEM	3C1100	OEM	3CZ91	OEM	3EZ5.6D4	OEM
2.5Z45	0343	3A3060	OEM	3BZ56A	0266	3BZD47	OEM	3C1100A	OEM	3CZ91A	OEM	3EZ5.6D5	0870
2.5Z45D5	0343	3A3060A	OEM	3BZ56B	0266	3BZD47A	OEM	3C1150	OEM	3CZ91B	OEM	3EZ5.6D10	0870
2.5Z45D10	0343	3A3100	OEM	3BZ-61	0087	3BZD47B	OEM	3C1150A	OEM	3CZ100	OEM	3EZ6.2D	0185
2.5Z47D	0343	3A3100A	OEM	3BZ61	0559	3BZD51	OEM	3C1200	OEM	3CZ100A	OEM	3EZ6.2D1	OEM

If replacement code is OEM, contact original manufacturer for replacement.

DEVICE TYPE	REPL CODE
3EZ6.2D2	OEM
3EZ6.2D3	OEM
3EZ6.2D4	OEM
3EZ6.2D5	0185
3EZ6.2D10	0185
3EZ6.8D	0205
3EZ6.8D1	OEM
3EZ6.8D2	OEM
3EZ6.8D3	OEM
3EZ6.8D4	OEM
3EZ6.8D5	0205
3EZ6.8D10	0205
3EZ7.5D	0475
3EZ7.5D1	OEM
3EZ7.5D2	OEM
3EZ7.5D3	OEM
3EZ7.5D4	OEM
3EZ7.5D5	0475
3EZ7.5D10	0475
3EZ8.2D	0499
3EZ8.2D1	OEM
3EZ8.2D2	OEM
3EZ8.2D3	OEM
3EZ8.2D4	OEM
3EZ8.2D5	0499
3EZ8.2D10	0499
3EZ9.1D	0679
3EZ9.1D1	OEM
3EZ9.1D2	OEM
3EZ9.1D3	OEM
3EZ9.1D4	OEM
3EZ9.1D5	0679
3EZ9.1D10	0679
3EZ10D	0225
3EZ10D1	OEM
3EZ10D2	OEM
3EZ10D3	OEM
3EZ10D4	OEM
3EZ10D5	0225
3EZ10D10	0225
3EZ11D	0230
3EZ11D1	OEM
3EZ11D2	OEM
3EZ11D3	OEM
3EZ11D4	OEM
3EZ11D5	0230
3EZ11D10	0230
3EZ12D	0234
3EZ12D1	OEM
3EZ12D2	OEM
3EZ12D3	OEM
3EZ12D4	OEM
3EZ12D5	0234
3EZ12D10	0234
3EZ13D	0237
3EZ13D1	OEM
3EZ13D2	OEM
3EZ13D3	OEM
3EZ13D4	OEM
3EZ13D5	0237
3EZ13D10	0237
3EZ14D	1387
3EZ14D1	OEM
3EZ14D2	OEM
3EZ14D3	OEM
3EZ14D4	OEM
3EZ14D5	1387
3EZ14D10	1387
3EZ15D	0247
3EZ15D1	OEM
3EZ15D2	OEM
3EZ15D3	OEM
3EZ15D4	OEM
3EZ15D5	0247
3EZ15D10	0247
3EZ16D	0251
3EZ16D1	OEM
3EZ16D2	OEM
3EZ16D3	OEM
3EZ16D4	OEM
3EZ16D5	0251
3EZ16D10	0251
3EZ17	1170
3EZ17D	1170
3EZ17D1	OEM
3EZ17D2	OEM
3EZ17D3	OEM
3EZ17D4	OEM
3EZ17D5	1170
3EZ17D10	1170
3EZ18D	0256
3EZ18D1	OEM
3EZ18D2	OEM
3EZ18D3	OEM
3EZ18D4	OEM
3EZ18D5	0256
3EZ18D10	0256
3EZ19	2379
3EZ19D	OEM
3EZ19D1	OEM
3EZ19D2	OEM
3EZ19D3	OEM
3EZ19D4	OEM
3EZ19D5	2379
3EZ19D10	2379
3EZ20D	0262
3EZ20D1	OEM
3EZ20D2	OEM
3EZ20D3	OEM

DEVICE TYPE	REPL CODE
3EZ20D4	OEM
3EZ20D5	0262
3EZ20D10	0262
3EZ22D	0269
3EZ22D1	OEM
3EZ22D2	OEM
3EZ22D3	OEM
3EZ22D4	OEM
3EZ22D5	0269
3EZ22D10	0269
3EZ24D	0273
3EZ24D1	OEM
3EZ24D2	OEM
3EZ24D3	OEM
3EZ24D4	OEM
3EZ24D5	0273
3EZ24D10	0273
3EZ27D	0291
3EZ27D1	OEM
3EZ27D2	OEM
3EZ27D3	OEM
3EZ27D4	OEM
3EZ27D5	0291
3EZ27D10	0291
3EZ28D	1169
3EZ28D1	OEM
3EZ28D2	OEM
3EZ28D3	OEM
3EZ28D4	OEM
3EZ28D5	1169
3EZ28D10	1169
3EZ30D	0305
3EZ30D1	OEM
3EZ30D2	OEM
3EZ30D3	OEM
3EZ30D4	OEM
3EZ30D5	0305
3EZ30D10	0305
3EZ33D	0314
3EZ33D1	OEM
3EZ33D2	OEM
3EZ33D3	OEM
3EZ33D4	OEM
3EZ33D5	0314
3EZ33D10	0314
3EZ36D	0316
3EZ36D1	OEM
3EZ36D2	OEM
3EZ36D3	OEM
3EZ36D4	OEM
3EZ36D5	0316
3EZ36D10	0316
3EZ39D	0322
3EZ39D1	OEM
3EZ39D2	OEM
3EZ39D3	OEM
3EZ39D4	OEM
3EZ39D5	0322
3EZ39D10	0322
3EZ43D	0333
3EZ43D1	OEM
3EZ43D2	OEM
3EZ43D3	OEM
3EZ43D4	OEM
3EZ43D5	0333
3EZ43D10	0333
3EZ47D	0343
3EZ47D1	OEM
3EZ47D2	OEM
3EZ47D3	OEM
3EZ47D4	OEM
3EZ47D5	0343
3EZ47D10	0343
3EZ51D	0027
3EZ51D1	OEM
3EZ51D2	OEM
3EZ51D3	OEM
3EZ51D4	OEM
3EZ51D5	0027
3EZ51D10	0027
3EZ56D	0266
3EZ56D1	OEM
3EZ56D2	OEM
3EZ56D3	OEM
3EZ56D4	OEM
3EZ56D5	0266
3EZ56D10	0266
3EZ62D	0382
3EZ62D1	OEM
3EZ62D2	OEM
3EZ62D3	OEM
3EZ62D4	OEM
3EZ62D5	0382
3EZ62D10	0382
3EZ68D	0401
3EZ68D1	OEM
3EZ68D2	OEM
3EZ68D3	OEM
3EZ68D4	OEM
3EZ68D5	0401
3EZ68D10	0401
3EZ75D	0421
3EZ75D1	OEM
3EZ75D2	OEM
3EZ75D3	OEM
3EZ75D4	OEM
3EZ75D5	0421
3EZ75D10	0421
3EZ82D	0439

DEVICE TYPE	REPL CODE
3EZ82D1	OEM
3EZ82D2	OEM
3EZ82D3	OEM
3EZ82D4	OEM
3EZ82D5	0439
3EZ82D10	0439
3EZ91D	0238
3EZ91D1	OEM
3EZ91D2	OEM
3EZ91D3	OEM
3EZ91D4	OEM
3EZ91D5	0238
3EZ91D10	0238
3EZ100D	1172
3EZ100D1	OEM
3EZ100D2	OEM
3EZ100D3	OEM
3EZ100D4	OEM
3EZ100D5	1172
3EZ100D10	1172
3EZ110D	1182
3EZ110D1	OEM
3EZ110D2	OEM
3EZ110D3	OEM
3EZ110D4	OEM
3EZ110D5	1182
3EZ110D10	1182
3EZ120D	1198
3EZ120D1	OEM
3EZ120D2	OEM
3EZ120D3	OEM
3EZ120D4	OEM
3EZ120D5	1198
3EZ120D10	1198
3EZ130D	1209
3EZ130D1	OEM
3EZ130D2	OEM
3EZ130D3	OEM
3EZ130D4	OEM
3EZ130D5	1209
3EZ130D10	1209
3EZ140D	1870
3EZ140D1	OEM
3EZ140D2	OEM
3EZ140D3	OEM
3EZ140D4	OEM
3EZ140D5	1870
3EZ140D10	1870
3EZ150D	0642
3EZ150D1	OEM
3EZ150D2	OEM
3EZ150D3	OEM
3EZ150D4	OEM
3EZ150D5	0642
3EZ150D10	0642
3EZ160D	1246
3EZ160D1	OEM
3EZ160D2	OEM
3EZ160D3	OEM
3EZ160D4	OEM
3EZ160D5	1246
3EZ160D10	1246
3EZ170D	2091
3EZ170D1	OEM
3EZ170D2	OEM
3EZ170D3	OEM
3EZ170D4	OEM
3EZ170D5	2091
3EZ170D10	2091
3EZ180D	1269
3EZ180D1	OEM
3EZ180D2	OEM
3EZ180D3	OEM
3EZ180D4	OEM
3EZ180D5	1269
3EZ180D10	1269
3EZ190D	2210
3EZ190D1	OEM
3EZ190D2	OEM
3EZ190D3	OEM
3EZ190D4	OEM
3EZ190D5	2210
3EZ190D10	2210
3EZ200D	0600
3EZ200D1	OEM
3EZ200D2	OEM
3EZ200D3	OEM
3EZ200D4	OEM
3EZ200D5	0600
3EZ200D10	0600
3E.5	OEM
3F5	0703
3F5-D	0703
3F5D	0097
3F5R	2275
3F10	0575
3F10D	0575
3F10D-C	0575
3F10R	2275
3F15	0575
3F20	0575
3F20D	0575
3F20D-C	0575
3F20R	2275
3F30	2049
3F30(SCR)	1129
3F30D	2049
3F30R	0471
3F40	0575

DEVICE TYPE	REPL CODE
3F40D	0994
3F40D-C	0994
3F40R	0471
3F50	2065
3F50D	2065
3F50R	0471
3F60	2070
3F60(SCR)	0340
3F60D	2070
3F60R	0471
3F80	2077
3F80D	2077
3F80R	0444
3F100	0607
3F100(SCR)	0895
3F100D	0607
3F100R	0444
3F120	OEM
3F150	0058
3F150(SCR)	2326
3F200	0058
3F200(SCR)	0058
3FB050R	0724
3FB100R	0724
3FB200R	0724
3FB400R	0732
3FB600R	0732
3FB800R	0737
3FB1000R	0737
3FC11	OEM
3FC12	0847
3FC13	0994
3FD	OEM
3FD12	0847
3FD13	1006
3FF05	OEM
3FF10	OEM
3FF15	OEM
3FF30	OEM
3FF40	OEM
3FF50	OEM
3FR5	0927
3FR10	0941
3FR15	0941
3FR20	0941
3FR30	4443
3FR40	1006
3FR50	5467
3FR60	1067
3FR80	1130
3FR100	1180
3FS1	0015
3FS2	0015
3G1	0087
3G2	2922
3G2(RECT)	0087
3G4	0087
3G4B41	0468
3G6	0087
3G8	0087
3G10	0087
3G15	OEM
3G30	OEM
3G42IG5	OEM
3G60	OEM
3G100	OEM
3G150	OEM
3G152	0015
3G154	0015
3G156	0015
3G158	0071
3G200	OEM
3G252	0015
3G254	0015
3G256	0015
3G258	0071
3G421G5	0403
3G1510	0071
3G2510	0071
3GA	0015
3GC11	OEM
3GC12	0994
3GCRCX	OEM
3GCRCY	OEM
3GCRCZ	OEM
3GCRDX	OEM
3GCRDY	OEM
3GCRDZ	OEM
3GCREX	OEM
3GCREY	OEM
3GCREZ	OEM
3GCRFX	OEM
3GCRFY	OEM
3GCRFZ	OEM
3GCRGX	OEM
3GCRGY	OEM
3GCRGZ	OEM
3GCRHX	OEM
3GCRHY	OEM
3GCRHZ	OEM
3GCRIX	OEM
3GCRIY	OEM
3GCRIZ	OEM
3GCRJX	OEM
3GCRJY	OEM
3GCRJZ	OEM
3GD12	0847
3GH61	0087
3GS1	0015

DEVICE TYPE	REPL CODE
3GS2	0015
3GZ61	0535
3H81-00050-001	OEM
3H82-00020-000	0330
3H82-00030-003	1157
3H83-00050-000	2164
3H83-00050-002	OEM
3H83-00160-000	2273
3H84-00040-004	0638
3H750M	OEM
3H7500H	OEM
3HC11	OEM
3HS1	0015
3HS2	0015
3J	OEM
3J4B41	0441
3J15	1129
3J30	1129
3J60	0340
3J100	0895
3J301	OEM
3JC11	OEM
3JC12	2070
3JH41	OEM
3JH-61	0023
3JH61	0023
3JH61(FA-2)	0023
3JH61(FA2)	0023
3JH61-FA-2	0023
3JH61FA-2	0023
3JH441	OEM
3JM61	OEM
3JU21.95B	OEM
3JUS1.62A	OEM
3JUS1.62B	OEM
3JUS1.85A	OEM
3JUS1.85B	OEM
3JUS1.95A	OEM
3JUS2.19A	OEM
3JUS2.19B	OEM
3JUS2.29A	OEM
3JUS2.29B	OEM
3JZ61	0959
3K	OEM
3K15	1129
3K101	OEM
3K121	OEM
3K301	OEM
3K3000LO	OEM
3K5797	0037
3K210000LO	OEM
3KC11	OEM
3KCB10	0724
3KCB20	0724
3KCB40	0732
3KCB60	0732
3KD8	OEM
3KM3LB	OEM
3KM300LA	OEM
3KM3000LA	OEM
3KM50000PA2	OEM
3KS110	OEM
3KZ6.8	0205
3KZ6.8A	OEM
3KZ6.8B	OEM
3KZ7.5	0475
3KZ7.5A	OEM
3KZ7.5B	OEM
3KZ8.2	0499
3KZ8.2A	OEM
3KZ8.2B	OEM
3KZ9.1	0679
3KZ9.1A	OEM
3KZ9.1B	OEM
3KZ10	0225
3KZ10A	OEM
3KZ10B	OEM
3KZ11	0230
3KZ11A	OEM
3KZ11B	OEM
3KZ12	0234
3KZ12A	OEM
3KZ12B	OEM
3KZ13	0237
3KZ13A	OEM
3KZ13B	OEM
3KZ14	OEM
3KZ14A	OEM
3KZ14B	OEM
3KZ15	0247
3KZ15A	OEM
3KZ15B	OEM
3KZ16	OEM
3KZ16A	OEM
3KZ16B	OEM
3KZ17	OEM
3KZ17A	OEM
3KZ17B	OEM
3KZ18	OEM
3KZ18A	OEM
3KZ18B	OEM
3KZ19	OEM
3KZ19A	OEM
3KZ19B	OEM
3KZ20	0262
3KZ20A	OEM
3KZ20B	OEM
3KZ22	0269
3KZ22A	OEM

DEVICE TYPE	REPL CODE
3KZ22B	OEM
3KZ24	0273
3KZ24A	OEM
3KZ24B	OEM
3KZ27	0291
3KZ27A	OEM
3KZ27B	OEM
3KZ28	OEM
3KZ28A	OEM
3KZ28B	OEM
3KZ30	0305
3KZ30A	OEM
3KZ30B	OEM
3KZ33	0314
3KZ33A	OEM
3KZ33B	OEM
3KZ36	0316
3KZ36A	OEM
3KZ36B	OEM
3KZ39	0322
3KZ39A	OEM
3KZ39B	OEM
3KZ43	0314
3KZ43A	OEM
3KZ43B	OEM
3KZ47	0343
3KZ47A	OEM
3KZ47B	OEM
3KZ51	0027
3KZ51A	OEM
3KZ51B	OEM
3KZ56	0266
3KZ56A	OEM
3KZ56B	OEM
3KZ62	0382
3KZ62A	OEM
3KZ62B	OEM
3KZ66	0401
3KZ68	OEM
3KZ68A	OEM
3KZ68B	OEM
3KZ75	0421
3KZ75A	OEM
3KZ75B	OEM
3KZ82	0439
3KZ82A	OEM
3KZ82B	OEM
3KZ91	0238
3KZ91A	OEM
3KZ91B	OEM
3KZ100	1172
3KZ100A	OEM
3KZ100B	OEM
3KZ110	OEM
3KZ110A	OEM
3KZ110B	OEM
3KZ120	1198
3KZ120A	OEM
3KZ120B	OEM
3KZ130	1209
3KZ130A	OEM
3KZ130B	OEM
3KZ140	OEM
3KZ140A	OEM
3KZ140B	OEM
3KZ150	0642
3KZ150A	OEM
3KZ150B	OEM
3KZ160	1246
3KZ160A	OEM
3KZ160B	OEM
3KZ170	OEM
3KZ170A	OEM
3KZ170B	OEM
3KZ180	1269
3KZ180A	OEM
3KZ180B	OEM
3KZ190	OEM
3KZ190A	OEM
3KZ190B	OEM
3KZ200	0600
3KZ200A	OEM
3KZ200B	OEM
3L1.4-1.6	OEM
3L1.8-2.1	OEM
3L4-2001	0143
3L4-2001-1	0019
3L4-2001-1A	0143
3L4-2001-3	0133
3L4-2001-4	0133
3L4-2003-1	0019
3L4-2003-3	0143
3L4-2003-4	0143
3L4-2003-7	0019
3L4-3001-1	0133
3L4-3001-5	0023
3L4-3001-7	0133
3L4-3001-8	0023
3L4-3002-7	0133
3L4-3002-10	0133
3L4-3002-13	0790
3L4-3002-20	0133
3L4-3002-25	0133
3L4-3002-30	0015
3L4-3002-31	0133
3L4-3002-32	0133
3L4-3002-33	0133
3L4-3501-1	OEM
3L4-3503-1	1023

DEVICE TYPE	REPL CODE
3L4-3503-5	0030
3L4-3503-6	0030
3L4-3504-1	3642
3L4-3504-1(G)	OEM
3L4-3504-1G	OEM
3L4-3504-1GREEN	OEM
3L4-3504-2	3642
3L4-3504-2(B)	3642
3L4-3504-2B	3642
3L4-3504-2BLUE	3642
3L4-3504-3	3642
3L4-3504-3(W)	3642
3L4-3504-3W	3642
3L4-3504-3WHITE	3642
3L4-3504-4	3642
3L4-3504-4(R)	3642
3L4-3504-4R	3642
3L4-3504-9	OEM
3L4-3504-11	OEM
3L4-3504-12	OEM
3L4-3504-RED	OEM
3L4-3505-1	0244
3L4-3505-2	0025
3L4-3505-3	0644
3L4-3505-4	0313
3L4-3506-1	OEM
3L4-3506-2	0025
3L4-3506-3	0644
3L4-3506-4	OEM
3L4-3506-7	0244
3L4-3506-12	0025
3L4-3506-21	0157
3L4-3506-29	0002
3L4-3506-31	0162
3L4-3506-40	0416
3L4-3506-43	0025
3L4-3506-45	0490
3L4-3506-49	0436
3L4-3508-1	3642
3L4-3508-2	3642
3L4-5007-3	0144
3L4-6001-01	0103
3L4-6004	0178
3L4-6005-1	0178
3L4-6005-3	0161
3L4-6005-5	0178
3L4-6006-1	0142
3L4-6007-1	0178
3L4-6007-2	0016
3L4-6007-3	0144
3L4-6007-4	0590
3L4-6007-9	OEM
3L4-6007-10	0007
3L4-6007-11	0007
3L4-6007-12	0007
3L4-6007-13	0144
3L4-6007-14	0007
3L4-6007-15	0111
3L4-6007-19	0590
3L4-6007-20	0007
3L4-6007-21	0007
3L4-6007-22	0007
3L4-6007-23	0007
3L4-6007-34	0037
3L4-6007-35	0007
3L4-6007-41	0224
3L4-6007-51	0144
3L4-6010-1	0419
3L4-6010-3	0079
3L4-6010-4	0786
3L4-6010-6	0086
3L4-6010-8	0126
3L4-6011-1	0419
3L4-6011-2	1357
3L4-6011-3	1357
3L4-6011-9	0919
3L4-6011-11	0919
3L4-6011-12	0919
3L4-6011-14	0919
3L4-6011-52	1357
3L4-6011-53	1357
3L4-6012-2	0419
3L4-6012-3	0419
3L4-6012-4	0161
3L4-6012-5	0419
3L4-6012-6	0419
3L4-6012-8	0419
3L4-6012-55	0555
3L4-6012-56	0419
3L4-6012-58	0419
3L4-6013-2	0848
3L4-6013-4	0455
3L4-6013-5	0848
3L4-6013-6	0919
3L4-6013-8	0848
3L4-6013-15	0919
3L4-6013-55	0848
3L4-6013-56	0848
3L4-6013-58	0848
3L4-6021-01	2422
3L4-6024-1	3493
3L4-6503-1	0212
3L4-6503-2	0212
3L4-6504-2	OEM
3L4-7004-1	0312
3L4-9002-1	2688
3L4-9004-1	1385
3L4-9004-3	1385
3L4-9004-4	1385

If replacement code is OEM, contact original manufacturer for replacement.

111

DEVICE TYPE	REPL CODE
3L4-9004-6	1385
3L4-9004-51	1385
3L4-9006-1	2593
3L4-9006-51	2593
3L4-9007-0	1335
3L4-9007-1	1434
3L4-9007-51	1434
3L4-9008-01	1832
3L4-9008-51	1832
3L4-9009-1	OEM
3L4-9013-01	0141
3L4-9014-1	OEM
3L4-9015-1	3050
3L4-9020-1	1042
3L4-9021-1	OEM
3L4-9022-1	OEM
3L4-9024-1	OEM
3L4-9025-1	OEM
3L5-0011-4	OEM
3L5-0016-01	OEM
3L5-0016-02	OEM
3L5-0016-1	OEM
3L5-0016-2	OEM
3L5-1002-02	OEM
3L5-1002-04	OEM
3L5-1002-05	OEM
3L5-1002-2	OEM
3L5-1002-4	OEM
3L5-1002-5	OEM
3L1015	OEM
3L1030	1129
3L1060	OEM
3L2015	1129
3L2100	OEM
3L46007-1	0079
3L46007-2	0079
3LA-6007-4	0590
3LC11	OEM
3LC12	2077
3LF11	0810
3LH61	0087
3LK-2001-1	OEM
3LR	OEM
3LZ61	0811
3M5U12-5	OEM
3M90	OEM
3M95	OEM
3MA	0769
3MC	0050
3MC11	OEM
3MCCV102	OEM
3MS5	0015
3MS10	0015
3MS20	0015
3MS30	0015
3MS40	0015
3MS50	0015
3N	OEM
3N0128	OEM
3N0138	OEM
3N0139	OEM
3N0140	OEM
3N0141	OEM
3N0142	OEM
3N0143	OEM
3N0152	OEM
3N0153	OEM
3N0154	OEM
3N0159	OEM
3N0187	OEM
3N0200	OEM
3N0204	OEM
3N0205	OEM
3N0206	OEM
3N0211	OEM
3N0212	OEM
3N0213	OEM
3N21	0136
3N22	0595
3N23	0595
3N23A	0595
3N23B	0595
3N23C	0595
3N25	OEM
3N25/501	0050
3N26	OEM
3N27	OEM
3N29	0595
3N30	0595
3N31	0595
3N32	OEM
3N33	OEM
3N34	0050
3N35	0016
3N35A	0050
3N36	0595
3N37	0595
3N39	OEM
3N40	OEM
3N41	OEM
3N42	OEM
3N43	OEM
3N44	OEM
3N44A	OEM
3N49	0435
3N50	0435
3N51	0435
3N52	0435
3N56	OEM
3N57	OEM
3N58	OEM
3N59	OEM
3N60	OEM
3N62	OEM
3N63	OEM
3N64	OEM
3N65	OEM
3N66	OEM
3N67	OEM
3N68	OEM
3N68A	OEM
3N69	OEM
3N70	OEM
3N71	0127
3N72	0127
3N73	0127
3N74	0111
3N75	0111
3N76	0111
3N77	0111
3N78	0111
3N79	0111
3N80	OEM
3N81	OEM
3N82	OEM
3N83	2320
3N84	OEM
3N85	OEM
3N86	OEM
3N87	0127
3N88	0127
3N90	0037
3N91	0037
3N92	0037
3N93	0037
3N94	0037
3N95	0037
3N96	OEM
3N97	OEM
3N98	OEM
3N99	OEM
3N100	OEM
3N101	OEM
3N102	OEM
3N103	OEM
3N104	OEM
3N105	OEM
3N106	OEM
3N107	OEM
3N112	0150
3N113	0150
3N114	0037
3N115	0037
3N116	0037
3N117	0037
3N118	0037
3N119	0037
3N120	0127
3N121	0127
3N123	0688
3N124	OEM
3N125	OEM
3N126	OEM
3N127	0007
3N128	0843
3N129	0037
3N130	0037
3N131	0037
3N132	0037
3N133	0037
3N134	0037
3N135	0037
3N136	0037
3N138	OEM
3N139	OEM
3N140	0349
3N141	0212
3N142	0843
3N143	0843
3N152	0843
3N153	0843
3N154	0843
3N155	OEM
3N155A	OEM
3N156	OEM
3N156A	OEM
3N157	OEM
3N157A	OEM
3N158	OEM
3N158A	OEM
3N159	0212
3N161	2439
3N163	OEM
3N164	OEM
3N165	OEM
3N166	OEM
3N169	OEM
3N170	OEM
3N171	OEM
3N172	OEM
3N173	OEM
3N175	0977
3N176	0977
3N182	OEM
3N187	0212
3N188	OEM
3N189	OEM
3N190	OEM
3N191	OEM
3N200	2439
3N201	0212
3N201A	0212
3N202	2439
3N203	2439
3N203A	OEM
3N204	2439
3N205	2439
3N206	2439
3N208	3787
3N209	2439
3N211	2439
3N212	4432
3N213	0212
3N219	OEM
3N220	OEM
3N221	OEM
3N222	OEM
3N225	OEM
3N225A	OEM
3N243	OEM
3N244	OEM
3N245	OEM
3N246	0276
3N247	0276
3N248	0287
3N249	0293
3N250	0299
3N251	0250
3N252	0250
3N253	0276
3N254	0287
3N255	0287
3N256	0293
3N257	0299
3N258	0250
3N259	0250
3N261	OEM
3N262	OEM
3N263	OEM
3N2603	OEM
3N3536	OEM
3N6285	3483
3NC11	OEM
3NC12	0607
3NF11	OEM
3NV10	0017
3NV10F	0017
3NV15	0017
3NV15F	0017
3NV20	OEM
3NV20F	OEM
3NV30	OEM
3NV30F	OEM
3NVF10	0017
3NVF12	0017
3NVF15	0017
3NZ61	0087
3P1M	OEM
3P1MH	0442
3P2M	OEM
3P2MH	0342
3P2MM	OEM
3P4M	OEM
3P4MH	0095
3P5M	OEM
3P6M	OEM
3PT40	OEM
3PT60	OEM
3PT80	OEM
3PT100	OEM
3QF11	OEM
3R0/18	OEM
3R1/18	OEM
3R2/18	OEM
3R2B	OEM
3R2S	OEM
3R3B	OEM
3R3S	OEM
3R4C	OEM
3R4S	OEM
3R5C	OEM
3R5S	OEM
3R6C	OEM
3R6S	OEM
3R7CD	OEM
3R7.5	0475
3R7.5A	0475
3R7.5B	0475
3R8CD	OEM
3R8S	OEM
3R8.2	0499
3R8.2A	0499
3R8.2B	0499
3R9.1	0679
3R9.1A	0679
3R9.1B	0679
3R10	0225
3R10A	0225
3R10B	0225
3R11	0230
3R11A	0230
3R11B	0230
3R12	0234
3R12A	0234
3R12B	0234
3R13	0237
3R13B	0237
3R15	0247
3R15A	0247
3R15B	0247
3R16	0251
3R16B	0251
3R18	0256
3R18A	0256
3R18B	0256
3R20	0262
3R20A	0262
3R20B	0262
3R22	0269
3R22A	0269
3R22B	0269
3R24	0273
3R24A	0273
3R24B	0273
3R27	0291
3R27A	0291
3R27B	0291
3R30	0305
3R30A	0305
3R30B	0305
3R33	0314
3R33A	0314
3R33B	0314
3R35	0316
3R35A	0316
3R35B	0316
3R36	0316
3R36A	0316
3R36B	0316
3R39	0322
3R39A	0322
3R39B	0322
3R43	0333
3R43A	0333
3R43B	0333
3R47	0343
3R47A	0343
3R47B	0343
3R51	0027
3R51A	0027
3R51B	0027
3R52	OEM
3R56	0266
3R56A	0266
3R56B	0266
3R62	0382
3R62A	0382
3R62B	0382
3R68	0401
3R68A	0401
3R68B	0401
3R75	0421
3R75A	0421
3R75B	0421
3R82	0439
3R82A	0439
3R82B	0439
3R91	0238
3R91A	0238
3R91B	0238
3R100	1172
3R100A	1172
3R100B	1172
3R110	1182
3R110A	1182
3R110B	1182
3R120	1198
3R120A	1198
3R120B	1198
3R130	1209
3R130A	1209
3R130B	1209
3R140	1870
3R140A	1870
3R140B	1870
3R150	0642
3R150A	0642
3R150B	0642
3R160	1246
3R160A	1246
3R180	1269
3R180A	1269
3R180B	1269
3R200	0600
3R200A	0600
3R200B	0600
3RB20/6	OEM
3RB20/10	OEM
3RB80/6	OEM
3RB80/10	OEM
3RC2	1102
3RC5	1102
3RC5A	1102
3RC10	2904
3RC10A	2904
3RC15	0957
3RC15A	0957
3RC20	0957
3RC20A	0957
3RC25	2905
3RC30	2905
3RC30A	2905
3RC40	2908
3RC40A	2908
3RC50	3626
3RC50A	3626
3RC60	3405
3RC60A	3405
3RCF	1102
3RL5A	1102
3RL10A	2904
3RL20A	0957
3RL30A	2905
3RL40A	2908
3RL50A	3626
3RL60A	3405
3RO/18	OEM
3RUS2120	OEM
3RUS2150	OEM
3RUS2180	OEM
3S001	OEM
3S002	OEM
3S003	OEM
3S004	0016
3S05E	0110
3S1E	0947
3S2E	0242
3S2.8-3.1	OEM
3S3E	1736
3S4E	0535
3S4M	0095
3S4M//LB	0095
3S4M//LB1E	0095
3S4M/LB1E	0095
3S5E	1760
3S5R15-15	OEM
3S6E	0959
3S11	OEM
3S12	OEM
3S12R15-15	OEM
3S14	OEM
3S16	OEM
3S24R15-15	OEM
3S28R15-15	OEM
3S30B	0321
3S105	0087
3S271	OEM
3S331	OEM
3SA324	0050
3SB05	OEM
3SB10	OEM
3SB20	OEM
3SB40	OEM
3SB60	OEM
3SB80	OEM
3SB100	6284
3SB629	0015
3SBMA1F	OEM
3SBMA2	0724
3SBMA2F	0724
3SBMA4	0724
3SBMA4F	0724
3SBMA6	0732
3SBMA8	0737
3SBMA05F	OEM
3SBMB1F	OEM
3SBMB2	0724
3SBMB2F	0724
3SBMB4	0724
3SBMB4F	0724
3SBMB6	0732
3SBMB8	0732
3SBMB05F	OEM
3SBMC05F	OEM
3SBMC1F	OEM
3SBMC2	0724
3SBMC2F	0724
3SBMC4	0724
3SBMC4F	0724
3SBMC6	0732
3SBMC8	0732
3SC1358K1	0359
3SC1415	1077
3SF1	OEM
3SF2	3348
3SF4	OEM
3SF11	2320
3SF11(Q)	2320
3SF11P	2320
3SF11Q	2320
3SFR0	OEM
3SJ11	0838
3SJ11A	0838
3SK072	OEM
3SK3E	0212
3SK14	0843
3SK15	OEM
3SK15A	OEM
3SK16	OEM
3SK17	OEM
3SK18	OEM
3SK19	OEM
3SK20	0349
3SK20(H)	OEM
3SK20H	0349
3SK20HW	0349
3SK20HY	0349
3SK21	0212
3SK21(H)	OEM
3SK21H	0212
3SK22	0212
3SK22-Y	0212
3SK22GR	0843
3SK22Y	0212
3SK23	0321
3SK28	0212
3SK29	0843
3SK30	0321
3SK30(B)	0212
3SK30A	0321
3SK-30B	0843
3SK30B	0321
3SK30C	0321
3SK32	0349
3SK32(B)	0212
3SK32A	0349
3SK32B	0349
3SK32B-6	0349
3SK32C	0349
3SK32D	0349
3SK32E	0349
3SK32E-4	0349
3SK33	0843
3SK34	0212
3SK34C	0321
3SK-35	0212
3SK35	0212
3SK35-BL	0212
3SK35-GR	0212
3SK35-Y	0212
3SK35BL	0212
3SK35G	0212
3SK37	0212
3SK38	0977
3SK38A	0977
3SK-39	0212
3SK39	0349
3SK39(E)	0212
3SK39(P)	0212
3SK39(Z)	OEM
3SK39E	0349
3SK39P	0349
3SK39Q	0349
3SK39R	0349
3SK40	0349
3SK40I	0212
3SK40M	0212
3SK-41	OEM
3SK41	1025
3SK41(L)	1025
3SK41C	1025
3SK41L	1025
3SK41M	1025
3SK44	0212
3SK45	0410
3SK45-B04	0410
3SK45-B09	0410
3SK45B	0410
3SK45B-09	0410
3SK45B09	0410
3SK47	2439
3SK48	0349
3SK49	0349
3SK49(Z)	OEM
3SK49E2	0212
3SK49NC	0212
3SK49Q	0212
3SK51	0349
3SK53	0212
3SK55	OEM
3SK59	0212
3SK59(GR)	0212
3SK59BL	0212
3SK59GR	0212
3SK60	2439
3SK61	2439
3SK63	2439
3SK66	OEM
3SK70	2439
3SK71	OEM
3SK72	0367
3SK73	0212
3SK73(Y)	0212
3SK73-GR	0212
3SK73Y	1441
3SK74	0367
3SK74L	OEM
3SK76	OEM
3SK77	OEM
3SK78	2439
3SK79	OEM
3SK80	0367
3SK81	4173
3SK82	OEM
3SK83	0367
3SK85	0367
3SK87	0367
3SK87(K)	0367
3SK88	0367
3SK88(K)	0367
3SK90	OEM
3SK95	0367
3SK96	OEM
3SK97	OEM
3SK100	OEM
3SK101	0365
3SK102	0367
3SK103	OEM
3SK104	OEM
3SK104V	OEM
3SK107	OEM
3SK108	0380
3SK112	OEM
3SK113	0367
3SK114	0367
3SK115	0367
3SK116	OEM
3SK118	OEM
3SK119	OEM
3SK120	OEM
3SK121	OEM
3SK122	OEM
3SK122L	OEM
3SK122M	OEM
3SK123	OEM
3SK125	OEM
3SK126	OEM
3SK127	OEM
3SK128	OEM
3SK129	OEM
3SK131	OEM
3SK132	OEM
3SK133	OEM
3SK134	OEM
3SK135	OEM
3SK136	OEM
3SK137	OEM
3SK138	OEM
3SK139	OEM
3SK140	OEM
3SK140-0	OEM
3SK140-0	OEM
3SK141	OEM
3SK142	OEM
3SK143	OEM
3SK144	OEM
3SK145	OEM
3SK146	OEM
3SK150	OEM
3SK151	OEM
3SK152	OEM
3SK153	OEM
3SK156	OEM
3SK159	OEM
3SK160	OEM
3SK162	OEM
3SK164	OEM
3SK165	OEM
3SK166	OEM
3SK169	OEM
3SK179	OEM
3SK183	OEM
3SK184	OEM
3SK186	OEM
3SK411	0212
3SK458	OEM
3SM0	OEM
3SM2	3348
3SM4	0095
3SM6	0031
3SM8	OEM
3SM1020A4	OEM
3SM1020A4PL	OEM
3SM1020A4T	OEM
3SM1020A5	OEM
3SM1020A5PL	OEM
3SM1020A5T	OEM
3SM1020A6	OEM
3SM1020A6PL	OEM
3SM1020A6T	OEM
3SM1020A7	OEM
3SM1020A7PL	OEM
3SM1020A7T	OEM
3SM1020A8	OEM
3SM1020A8PL	OEM
3SM1020A8T	OEM
3SM1020E4	OEM
3SM1020E4PL	OEM
3SM1020E4T	OEM
3SM1020E5	OEM
3SM1020E5PL	OEM
3SM1020E5T	OEM
3SM1020E6	OEM
3SM1020E6PL	OEM
3SM1020E6T	OEM
3SM1020E7	OEM
3SM1020E7PL	OEM
3SM1020E7T	OEM
3SM1020GE8	OEM
3SM1020GE8PL	OEM
3SM1020GE8T	OEM
3SM1020GE9	OEM
3SM1020GE9PL	OEM
3SM1020GE9T	OEM
3SM1020GE10	OEM
3SM1020GE10PL	OEM
3SM1020GE10T	OEM
3SS4M	0095
3T6.2	2206
3T6.2A	2206
3T6.2B	2206
3T7.5	0221
3T7.5A	0221
3T7.5B	0221
3T9.1	1608
3T9.1A	1608
3T9.1B	1608
3T11	0686
3T11A	0686
3T11B	0686
3T12	0864
3T12A	0864
3T12B	0864

If replacement code is OEM, contact original manufacturer for replacement.

DEVICE TYPE	REPL CODE
3T13	1014
3T13A	1014
3T13B	1014
3T16	1392
3T16A	1392
3T16B	1392
3T20	1707
3T20A	1707
3T20B	1707
3T24	1725
3T24A	1725
3T24B	1725
3T30	1761
3T30A	1761
3T30B	1761
3T33	1777
3T33A	1777
3T33B	1777
3T36	1785
3T36A	1785
3T36B	1785
3T39	1793
3T39A	1793
3T39B	1793
3T43	1185
3T43A	1185
3T43B	1185
3T47	0022
3T47A	0022
3T47B	0022
3T51	0132
3T51A	0132
3T51B	0132
3T56	0207
3T56A	0207
3T56B	0207
3T62	0263
3T62A	0263
3T62B	0263
3T68	0306
3T68A	0306
3T68B	0306
3T75	0325
3T75A	0325
3T75B	0325
3T82	0352
3T82A	0352
3T82B	0352
3T91	0408
3T91A	0408
3T91B	0408
3T100	0433
3T100A	0433
3T100B	0433
3T110	0483
3T110A	0483
3T110B	0483
3T120	0504
3T120A	0504
3T120B	0504
3T130	0519
3T130A	0519
3T130B	0519
3T150	0063
3T150A	0063
3T150B	0063
3T160	0397
3T160A	0397
3T160B	0397
3T180	0629
3T180A	0629
3T180B	0629
3T200	0663
3T200A	0663
3T200B	0663
3T201	0595
3T202	0595
3T203	0595
3T501	0015
3T502	0015
3T503	0015
3T504	0015
3T505	0015
3T506	0015
3T507	0071
3T508	0071
3T509	0071
3T510	0071
3TCRA	1102
3TCRB	1102
3TCRC	2904
3TCRD	0957
3TCRE	0957
3TCRF	2905
3TCRG	2905
3TCRH	2908
3TCRI	3626
3TCRJ	3405
3TCRK	OEM
3TCRL	OEM
3TE120	0103
3TE130	OEM
3TE140	0103
3TE150	0590
3TE160	0590
3TE220	0065
3TE225	OEM
3TE230	0103
3TE240	0103

DEVICE TYPE	REPL CODE
3TE250	0590
3TE260	0590
3TE467	OEM
3TE477	OEM
3TH62	0087
3TRC10A	0636
3TX002	0065
3TX003	0103
3TX004	0103
3TX621	3516
3TX622	2080
3TX820	3516
3TX822	2080
3TZ3.6	0791
3TZ3.6A	0791
3TZ3.6B	0791
3TZ3.6C	0791
3TZ3.6D	0791
3TZ3.9	0801
3TZ3.9A	0801
3TZ3.9B	0801
3TZ3.9C	0801
3TZ3.9D	0801
3TZ4.3	0815
3TZ4.3A	0815
3TZ4.3B	0815
3TZ4.3C	0815
3TZ4.3D	0815
3TZ4.7	0827
3TZ4.7A	0827
3TZ4.7B	0827
3TZ4.7C	0827
3TZ4.7D	0827
3TZ5.1	0437
3TZ5.1A	0437
3TZ5.1B	0437
3TZ5.1C	0437
3TZ5.1D	0437
3TZ5.6	0870
3TZ5.6A	0870
3TZ5.6B	0870
3TZ5.6C	0870
3TZ5.6D	0870
3TZ6.2	0185
3TZ6.2A	0185
3TZ6.2B	0185
3TZ6.2C	0185
3TZ6.2D	0185
3TZ6.8	0205
3TZ6.8A	0205
3TZ6.8B	0205
3TZ6.8C	0205
3TZ6.8D	0205
3TZ7.5	0475
3TZ7.5A	0475
3TZ7.5B	0475
3TZ7.5C	0475
3TZ7.5D	0475
3TZ8.2	0499
3TZ8.2A	0499
3TZ8.2B	0499
3TZ8.2C	0499
3TZ8.2D	0499
3TZ9.1	0679
3TZ9.1A	0679
3TZ9.1B	0679
3TZ9.1C	0679
3TZ9.1D	0679
3TZ10	0225
3TZ10A	0225
3TZ10B	0225
3TZ10C	0225
3TZ10D	0225
3TZ11	0230
3TZ11A	0230
3TZ11B	0230
3TZ11C	0230
3TZ11D	0230
3TZ12	0234
3TZ12A	0234
3TZ12B	0234
3TZ12C	0234
3TZ12D	0234
3TZ13	0237
3TZ13A	0237
3TZ13B	0237
3TZ13C	0237
3TZ13D	0237
3TZ14	1387
3TZ14A	1387
3TZ14B	1387
3TZ14C	1387
3TZ14D	1387
3TZ15	0247
3TZ15A	0247
3TZ15B	0247
3TZ15C	0247
3TZ15D	0247
3TZ16	0251
3TZ16A	0251
3TZ16B	0251
3TZ16C	0251
3TZ16D	0251
3TZ17	1170
3TZ17A	1170
3TZ17B	1170
3TZ17C	1170
3TZ17D	1170
3TZ18	0256

DEVICE TYPE	REPL CODE
3TZ18A	0256
3TZ18B	0256
3TZ18C	0256
3TZ18D	0256
3TZ19	2379
3TZ19A	2379
3TZ19B	2379
3TZ19C	2379
3TZ19D	2379
3TZ20	0262
3TZ20A	0262
3TZ20B	0262
3TZ20C	0262
3TZ20D	0262
3TZ22	0269
3TZ22A	0269
3TZ22B	0269
3TZ22C	0269
3TZ22D	0269
3TZ24	0273
3TZ24A	0273
3TZ24B	0273
3TZ24C	0273
3TZ24D	0273
3TZ27	0291
3TZ27A	0291
3TZ27B	0291
3TZ27C	0291
3TZ27D	0291
3TZ30	0305
3TZ30A	0305
3TZ30B	0305
3TZ30C	0305
3TZ30D	0305
3TZ33	0314
3TZ33A	0314
3TZ33B	0314
3TZ33C	0314
3TZ33D	0314
3TZ34C	0314
3TZ34D	OEM
3TZ36	0316
3TZ36A	0316
3TZ36B	0316
3TZ36C	0316
3TZ36D	0316
3TZ39	0322
3TZ39A	0322
3TZ39B	0322
3TZ39C	0322
3TZ39D	0322
3TZ43	0333
3TZ43A	0333
3TZ43B	0333
3TZ43C	0333
3TZ43D	0333
3TZ45A	0343
3TZ45B	0343
3TZ45C	0343
3TZ45D	OEM
3TZ47	0343
3TZ47A	0343
3TZ47B	0343
3TZ47C	0343
3TZ47D	0343
3TZ50	0027
3TZ50A	0027
3TZ50B	0027
3TZ50C	0027
3TZ50D	0027
3TZ51	0027
3TZ51A	0027
3TZ51B	0027
3TZ51C	0027
3TZ51D	0027
3TZ52	0027
3TZ52A	0027
3TZ52B	0027
3TZ52C	0027
3TZ52D	OEM
3TZ56	0266
3TZ56A	0266
3TZ56B	0266
3TZ56C	0266
3TZ56D	0266
3TZ62	0382
3TZ62A	0382
3TZ62B	0382
3TZ62C	0382
3TZ62D	0382
3TZ68	0401
3TZ68A	0401
3TZ68B	0401
3TZ68C	0401
3TZ68D	0401
3TZ75	0421
3TZ75A	0421
3TZ75B	0421
3TZ75C	0421
3TZ75D	0421
3TZ82	0439
3TZ82A	0439
3TZ82B	0439
3TZ82C	0439
3TZ82D	0439
3TZ91	0238
3TZ91A	0238
3TZ91B	0238
3TZ91C	0238

DEVICE TYPE	REPL CODE
3TZ91D	0238
3TZ100	1172
3TZ100A	1172
3TZ100B	1172
3TZ100C	1172
3TZ100D	1172
3TZ105	1182
3TZ105A	1182
3TZ105B	1182
3TZ105C	1182
3TZ105D	OEM
3TZ110	1182
3TZ110A	1182
3TZ110B	1182
3TZ110C	1182
3TZ110D	1182
3TZ120	1198
3TZ120A	1198
3TZ120B	1198
3TZ120C	1198
3TZ120D	1198
3TZ130	1209
3TZ130A	1209
3TZ130B	1209
3TZ130C	1209
3TZ130D	1209
3TZ140	1870
3TZ140A	1870
3TZ140B	1870
3TZ140C	1870
3TZ140D	1870
3TZ150	0642
3TZ150A	0642
3TZ150B	0642
3TZ150C	0642
3TZ150D	0642
3TZ160	1246
3TZ160A	1246
3TZ160A0A	OEM
3TZ160B	1246
3TZ160C	1246
3TZ160D	1246
3TZ175	1269
3TZ175A	1269
3TZ175B	1269
3TZ175C	1269
3TZ175D	OEM
3TZ180	1269
3TZ180A	1269
3TZ180B	1269
3TZ180C	1269
3TZ180D	1269
3TZ200	0600
3TZ200A	0600
3TZ200B	0600
3TZ200C	0600
3TZ200D	0600
3TZ220	OEM
3TZ220A	OEM
3TZ220B	OEM
3TZ220C	OEM
3TZ220D	OEM
3TZ455	OEM
3UT40	OEM
3VR5.6	0870
3VR5.6A	0870
3VR5.6B	0870
3VR6	3099
3VR6A	3099
3VR6B	3099
3VR6.2	0185
3VR6.2A	0185
3VR6.2B	0185
3VR6.8	0205
3VR6.8A	0205
3VR6.8B	0205
3VR7.5	0475
3VR7.5A	0475
3VR7.5B	0475
3VR8.2	0499
3VR8.2A	0499
3VR8.2B	0499
3VR8.5	3285
3VR8.5A	3285
3VR8.5B	3285
3VR9.1	0679
3VR9.1A	0679
3VR9.1B	0679
3VR10	0225
3VR10A	0225
3VR10B	0225
3VR11	0230
3VR11A	0230
3VR11B	0230
3VR12	0234
3VR12A	0234
3VR12B	0234
3VR13	0237
3VR13A	0237
3VR13B	0237
3VR15	0247
3VR15A	0247
3VR15B	0247
3VR16	0251
3VR16A	0251
3VR16B	0251
3VR18	0256
3VR18A	0256
3VR18B	0256

DEVICE TYPE	REPL CODE
3VR20	0262
3VR20A	0262
3VR20B	0262
3VR22	0269
3VR22A	0269
3VR22B	0269
3VR24	0273
3VR24A	0273
3VR24B	0273
3VR27	0291
3VR27A	0291
3VR27B	0291
3VR30	0305
3VR30A	0305
3VR30B	0305
3VR33	0314
3VR33A	0314
3VR33B	0314
3VR36	0316
3VR36A	0316
3VR36B	0316
3VR39	0322
3VR39A	0322
3VR39B	0322
3VR43	0333
3VR43A	0333
3VR43B	0333
3VR47	0343
3VR47A	0343
3VR47B	0343
3VR51	0027
3VR51A	0027
3VR51B	0027
3VR56	0266
3VR56A	0266
3VR56B	0266
3VR62	0382
3VR62A	0382
3VR62B	0382
3VR67	0401
3VR67A	0401
3VR67B	0401
3VR68	0401
3VR68A	0401
3VR68B	0401
3VR75	0421
3VR75A	0421
3VR75B	0421
3VR82	0439
3VR82A	0439
3VR82B	0439
3VR90	0238
3VR90A	0238
3VR90B	0238
3VR91	0238
3VR91A	0238
3VR91B	0238
3VR100	1172
3VR100A	1172
3VR100B	1172
3VR110	1182
3VR110A	1182
3VR110B	1182
3VR120	1198
3VR120A	1198
3VR120B	1198
3VR130	1209
3VR130A	1209
3VR130B	1209
3VR150	0642
3VR150A	0642
3VR150B	0642
3VR160	1246
3VR160A	1246
3VR160B	1246
3VR180	1269
3VR180A	1269
3VR180B	1269
3VR200	0600
3VR200A	0600
3VR200B	0600
3W5R5	OEM
3W5R12-12	OEM
3W5R15-15	OEM
3W12R5	OEM
3W12R15-15	OEM
3W24R5	OEM
3W24R12-12	OEM
3W24R15-15	OEM
3W28R5	OEM
3W28R12-12	OEM
3W28R15-15	OEM
3W5412-5	OEM
3W12412-12	OEM
3WB-5A	1429
3WB-6A	1436
3WB-7A	1449
3WB-9D	1481
3WB-11D	0505
3WB-13	0237
3WB-13D	0864
3WB-15D	0247
3WB-17D	1071
3WB-25D	2383
3WB-30D	1777
3WB-55D	0207
3WB-85D	0352
3WB-100D	0433
3WB-120D	0504

DEVICE TYPE	REPL CODE
3WC-13D	0237
3WC-15D	0247
3WC-25D	2383
3WM1	OEM
3WM2	OEM
3WM4	OEM
3WM6	OEM
3WM8	OEM
3WM10	OEM
3WM12	OEM
3X11/1	0015
3Z3.9M	2024
3Z3.9T5	6174
3Z3.9T10	0542
3Z3.9T20	0542
3Z4.3T5	2387
3Z4.3T10	2387
3Z4.3T20	2387
3Z4.7M	1429
3Z4.7T5	6959
3Z4.7T10	2101
3Z4.7T20	2101
3Z5.1T5	2394
3Z5.1T10	2394
3Z5.1T20	2394
3Z5.6M	1890
3Z5.6T5	1890
3Z5.6T10	1890
3Z5.6T20	1890
3Z6.2T5	0691
3Z6.2T10	0691
3Z6.2T20	0691
3Z6.8	0205
3Z6.8A	0205
3Z6.8B	0205
3Z6.8M	1591
3Z6.8T5	1591
3Z6.8T10	1591
3Z6.8T20	1591
3Z7.5T5	1606
3Z7.5T10	1606
3Z7.5T20	1606
3Z8.2M	1612
3Z8.2T5	1612
3Z8.2T10	1612
3Z8.2T20	1612
3Z9.0	0679
3Z9.0A	0679
3Z9.0B	0679
3Z9.1T5	0622
3Z9.1T10	0622
3Z9.1T20	0622
3Z10M	0505
3Z10T5	0986
3Z10T10	0986
3Z10T20	0986
3Z11T5	0989
3Z11T10	0989
3Z11T20	0989
3Z12	0234
3Z12A	0234
3Z12B	0234
3Z12M	0864
3Z12T5	1254
3Z12T10	1254
3Z12T20	1254
3Z13T5	1240
3Z13T10	1240
3Z13T20	1240
3Z15	0247
3Z15A	0247
3Z15B	0247
3Z15M	1264
3Z15T5	1629
3Z15T10	1629
3Z15T20	1629
3Z16T5	1693
3Z16T10	1693
3Z16T20	1693
3Z18	0256
3Z18A	0256
3Z18B	0256
3Z18M	1071
3Z18T5	1706
3Z18T10	1706
3Z18T20	1706
3Z20T5	5624
3Z20T10	1720
3Z20T20	1720
3Z21	0262
3Z21A	0262
3Z21B	0262
3Z22M	1712
3Z22T5	0722
3Z22T10	0722
3Z22T20	0722
3Z24	0273
3Z24A	0273
3Z24B	0273
3Z24T5	1745
3Z24T10	1745
3Z24T20	1745
3Z27	0291
3Z27A	0291
3Z27B	0291
3Z27M	1750
3Z27T5	1771
3Z27T10	1771
3Z27T20	1771

DEVICE TYPE	REPL CODE
3Z30	0305
3Z30A	0305
3Z30B	0305
3Z30T5	1783
3Z30T10	1783
3Z30T20	1783
3Z33	0314
3Z33A	0314
3Z33B	0314
3Z33T5	1777
3Z33T10	1777
3Z36	0316
3Z36A	0316
3Z36B	0316
3Z524A	OEM
3.0B2	0118
3.3B1	1073
3.3B1(ZENER)	0296
3.3B2	OEM
3.3Y	0296
3.6B	0372
3.6B1	0188
3.6C	0188
3.6CP	0372
3.6E25	OEM
3.6E50A	OEM
3.6E100	OEM
3.6E250	OEM
3.6EB1	0372
3.6L1	0372
3.6N1	0372
3.9B2	0036
3.9N2	0036
3.9Y	0036
3.58MC	4391
4-009	0438
4-08018-667	1248
4-4A-1A7-1	0160
4-6B-3A7-1	0265
4-8P-2A7-1	0004
4-9L-4A7-1	0004
4-12-1A7-1	0016
4-14A17-1	0160
4-46	0111
4-47	0191
4-47(SEARS)	0016
4-48	1851
4-48(SEARS)	1851
4-50	0015
4-65-1A7-1	0050
4-65-2A7-1	0208
4-65-4A7-1	0595
4-65A17-1	0050
4-65B17-1	0050
4-65C17-1	0160
4-66-1A7-1	0004
4-66-2A7-1	0004
4-66-3A7-1	0004
4-74-3A7-1	0279
4-77A17-1	0435
4-77C17-1	0160
4-88A17-1	0160
4-88B17-1	0050
4-88C17-1	0279
4-92-1A7-1	0435
4-142	0222
4-142-1(SEARS)	0841
4-202A16	0143
4-202R101	0015
4-203-5100-69372	0547
4-221R806	OEM
4-221R807	OEM
4-227R801	OEM
4-279	0136
4-280	0136
4-282	0143
4-324	0321
4-397	0086
4-398	0086
4-399	0144
4-400	0144
4-432	0050
4-433	0144
4-434	0144
4-435	0085
4-436	0157
4-436(SEARS)	0157
4-437	0030
4-443	0127
4-850	0127
4-851	0016
4-852	0143
4-853	0143
4-854	0143
4-855	0143
4-856	0244
4-857	0143
4-882	0143
4-1544	0111
4-1545	0016
4-1546	0841
4-1723	0451
4-1724	0133
4-1726	0133
4-1790	0016
4-1791	0111
4-1792	0590
4-1807	0015
4-1848	0816

If replacement code is OEM, contact original manufacturer for replacement.

113

DEVICE TYPE	REPL CODE
4-2020	0143
4-2020-03173	0015
4-2020-03200	0015
4-2020-03500	0143
4-2020-03571	0143
4-2020-03700	0102
4-2020-03800	0102
4-2020-03900	0071
4-2020-05000	0196
4-2020-05200	0015
4-2020-05400	0196
4-2020-05600	0123
4-2020-05800	0133
4-2020-06100	0133
4-2020-06200	0133
4-2020-06300	1293
4-2020-06400	0133
4-2020-06500	0102
4-2020-06600	0053
4-2020-06700	0102
4-2020-06800	0015
4-2020-07300	0015
4-2020-07500	0631
4-2020-07600	0015
4-2020-07601	0015
4-2020-07700	0015
4-2020-07800	0102
4-2020-07801	0102
4-2020-07802	0102
4-2020-07900	0196
4-2020-08000	0102
4-2020-08001	0133
4-2020-08200	0133
4-2020-08500	0015
4-2020-08600	0123
4-2020-08700	0196
4-2020-08900	0015
4-2020-09200	0490
4-2020-09400	1293
4-2020-09600	OEM
4-2020-10100	0133
4-2020-10500	0015
4-2020-11300	0025
4-2020-11600	OEM
4-2020-12000	0490
4-2020-12300	0313
4-2020-12400	0137
4-2020-13300	0814
4-2020-14400	0102
4-2020-14500	0015
4-2020-14600	0102
4-2020-15100	0102
4-2020-15600	0133
4-2021	0918
4-2021-04170	0276
4-2021-04470	0071
4-2021-04570	0102
4-2021-04770	0071
4-2021-04870	0102
4-2021-04970	0015
4-2021-05000	1141
4-2021-05070	0969
4-2021-05170	0911
4-2021-05470	0644
4-2021-05870	0143
4-2021-06970	0102
4-2021-07470	0133
4-2021-07570	0752
4-2021-07670	0124
4-2021-08070	0752
4-2021-08270	0015
4-2021-08570	0560
4-2021-09070	0313
4-2021-09370	0023
4-2021-10270	0023
4-2021-10470	0023
4-2021-10870	0313
4-2021-14970	0017
4-2029-70791	0030
4-2029-70860	0124
4-2029-71590	0133
4-2039-70380	1060
4-2039-70431	0076
4-2040-08000	0133
4-2060-02300	0872
4-2060-02400	0872
4-2060-02600	0849
4-2060-02900	0849
4-2060-03900	0849
4-2060-04000	0167
4-2060-04200	0043
4-2060-04300	0385
4-2060-04600	0167
4-2060-04800	0602
4-2060-04900	0602
4-2060-05200	0878
4-2060-07200	0043
4-2060-07300	0385
4-2060-07500	0875
4-2060-09100	3660
4-2060-09200	0850
4-2061-05170	0391
4-2061-05370	2615
4-2069-70232	2898
4-2069-70430	OEM
4-2069-71660	4339
4-2069-71710	4750
4-2069-71730	3680
4-2069-71842	OEM

DEVICE TYPE	REPL CODE
4-2073	0050
4-3033	0015
4-3034	0133
4-3036	2247
4-5145	0016
4-18341	0030
4-68681-2	0004
4-68681-3	0004
4-68682-3	0016
4-68687-3	0229
4-68689-3	0071
4-68695-3	0144
4-68697-3	0071
4-684120-3	0144
4-685285-3	0144
4-686105-3	0071
4-686106-3	0071
4-686107-3	0144
4-686108-3	0144
4-686112-3	0144
4-686114-3	0144
4-686116-3	0229
4-686118-3	0144
4-686119-3	0144
4-686120-3	0144
4-686126-3	0144
4-686127-3	0144
4-686130-3	0178
4-686131-3	0144
4-686132-3	0016
4-686139-3	0071
4-686140-3	0144
4-686143-3	0016
4-686144-3	0016
4-686145-3	0233
4-686147-3	0229
4-686148-3	0229
4-686149-3	0015
4-686150-3	0229
4-686151-3	0229
4-686163-3	0004
4-686169-3	0144
4-686170-3	0126
4-686171-3	0144
4-686172-3	0144
4-686173-3	0016
4-686177-3	0229
4-686179-3	0071
4-686182-3	0086
4-686183-3	0016
4-686184-3	0071
4-686186-3	0071
4-686189-3	0071
4-686195-3	0004
4-686196-3	0004
4-686199-3	0071
4-686201-3	0071
4-686207-3	0144
4-686208-3	0144
4-686209-3	0144
4-686212-3	0071
4-686213-3	0160
4-686224-3	0144
4-686226-3	0178
4-686227-3	0201
4-686228-3	0144
4-686229-3	0126
4-686230-3	0126
4-686231-3	0016
4-686232-3	0233
4-686234-3	0419
4-686235-3	0126
4-686238-3	0126
4-686244-3	0144
4-686251-3	0144
4-686252-3	0334
4-686256-1	0136
4-686256-2	0136
4-686256-3	0136
4-686257-3	0016
4-3022861	0144
4-3023190	0130
4-3023212	0016
4-3023221	0016
4-3023222	0126
4-3023223	0086
4-3023843	0103
4-3023844	0086
4-3025763	0144
4-3025764	0144
4-3025765	0144
4-3025766	0016
4-3025767	0144
4-3540012	0015
4-8134842	0334
4-30203845	0126
4-202003571	0143
4-202104170	0015
4-202104570	0102
4-202104770	0164
4-202104970	0133
4-202105070	0918
4-202105470	0644
4-202115770	0102
4-2020035000	0143
4-AAZ10	0143
4A-1	0160
4A-1-70	0160
4A-1-70-12	0160

DEVICE TYPE	REPL CODE
4A-1-70-12-7	0160
4A-1-A-7B	0160
4A-1A	0160
4A-1A0	0160
4A-1A0R	0160
4A-1A1	0160
4A-1A2	0160
4A-1A3	0160
4A-1A3P	0160
4A-1A4	0160
4A-1A4-7	0160
4A-1A5	0160
4A-1A5L	0160
4A-1A6	0160
4A-1A6-4	0160
4A-1A7	0160
4A-1A7-1	0160
4A-1A8	0160
4A-1A9	0160
4A-1A9G	0160
4A-1A19	0160
4A-1A21	0160
4A-1A82	0160
4A2	0372
4A-10	0160
4A-11	0160
4A-12	0160
4A-13	0160
4A-14	0160
4A-15	0160
4A-16	0160
4A-17	0160
4A-18	0160
4A-19	0160
4A132	1241
4A162	0315
4A232	0315
4A262	0315
4A600	0315
4A1122	0315
4A2122	0315
4AF05NLH	OEM
4AF05NLV	OEM
4AF05NPP	OEM
4AF1	OEM
4AF1LH	OEM
4AF1LV	OEM
4AF1NLH	OEM
4AF1NLV	OEM
4AF1NPP	OEM
4AF2	OEM
4AF2LH	OEM
4AF2LV	OEM
4AF2NLH	OEM
4AF2NLV	OEM
4AF2NPP	OEM
4AF4	OEM
4AF4LH	OEM
4AF4LV	OEM
4AF4NLH	OEM
4AF4NLV	OEM
4AF4NPP	OEM
4AF6NLH	OEM
4AF6NLV	OEM
4AF6NPP	OEM
4AJ4DX52D	0015
4AJ4DX520	0015
4B1	0036
4B4B41	0319
4B10Y	OEM
4B20Y	OEM
4B30Y	OEM
4B40Y	OEM
4BA4B41	OEM
4BV60	OEM
4BV80	OEM
4BV100	OEM
4BV120	OEM
4BV130	OEM
4C1	2873
4C2	1116
4C4	0800
4C6	0315
4C8	1124
4C10	0045
4C12	OEM
4C14	OEM
4C16	OEM
4C28	0086
4C29	0086
4C30	0086
4C31	0086
4C43	0079
4D4	0015
4D4B41	1404
4D4B42	OEM
4D4B44	OEM
4D6	0015
4D8	0015
4D20	0016
4D21	0016
4D22	0016
4D24	0016
4D25	0016
4D26	0016
4D48B41	OEM
4E20	OEM
4E20-8	OEM
4E20-28	OEM

DEVICE TYPE	REPL CODE
4E20A	OEM
4E20M-8	OEM
4E20M8	OEM
4E20M-28	OEM
4E20M28	OEM
4E30-8	OEM
4E30-28	OEM
4E30A	OEM
4E30M-8	OEM
4E30M8	OEM
4E30M-28	OEM
4E40-8	OEM
4E40-28	OEM
4E40A	OEM
4E40M-8	OEM
4E40M8	OEM
4E40M-28	OEM
4E40M28	OEM
4E50-8	OEM
4E50-28	OEM
4E50A	OEM
4E50M-8	OEM
4E50M8	OEM
4E50M-28	OEM
4E50M28	OEM
4E80-8	OEM
4E80-28	OEM
4E100-8	OEM
4E100-28	OEM
4E100A	OEM
4E100M-8	OEM
4E100M8	OEM
4E100M-28	OEM
4E100M28	OEM
4E200-8	OEM
4E200-28	OEM
4E200A	OEM
4E200M-8	OEM
4E200M-28	OEM
4EP30-3	OEM
4EP30-8	OEM
4EP30-28	OEM
4EP30A	OEM
4EP30M3	OEM
4EP30M8	OEM
4EP30M28	OEM
4EX580	OEM
4EX581	OEM
4EX582	OEM
4EX583	OEM
4E.5	OEM
4F05	OEM
4F1	OEM
4F2	OEM
4F3	OEM
4F4	OEM
4F5	OEM
4F6	OEM
4F8	OEM
4F10	OEM
4F12	OEM
4FB5	0015
4FB10	0015
4FB20	0015
4FB30	0015
4FB40	0015
4FC5	OEM
4FC10	OEM
4FC20	OEM
4FC30	OEM
4FC40	OEM
4FDC	OEM
4G2	3219
4G4	OEM
4G4B41	0468
4G5	OEM
4G8	0071
4G50	OEM
4G100	OEM
4G132	0315
4G162	0315
4G200	OEM
4G232	0315
4G262	0315
4G1122	0315
4G2122	0315
4GA	0015
4GZ10A	0505
4GZ10B	0505
4GZ12A	0864
4GZ12B	0504
4GZ15A	1264
4GZ15B	0063
4GZ18A	1071
4GZ18B	0629
4GZ22A	1712
4GZ27A	1750
4GZ33A	1777
4GZ39A	1793
4GZ47A	0022
4GZ56A	0207
4GZ68A	0306
4GZ82A	0352
4H1HA	OEM
4H-130-30302	0015
4H-130-30312	0123
4H-130-30702	0015
4H-130-30845	0549
4H-130-30862	0057

DEVICE TYPE	REPL CODE
4H-130-30869	0123
4H-130-30993	1404
4H-130-31012	0019
4H-130-31438	0023
4H-130-31907	0549
4H-130-34173	0253
4H-130-40936	0079
4H-130-40937	0079
4H-130-41356	3756
4H-130-41395	3572
4H-130-41448	0802
4H-130-41461	3756
4H-130-44121	0079
4H-130-44196	0079
4H-209-80751	0491
4H-209-80786	5515
4H-209-80821	1251
4H-209-80967	2898
4H-209-81252	5080
4H-209-81473	4493
4H1034-4196	0079
4H1034-4283	0472
4H1303-0219	0143
4H1303-0613	0124
4H1303-1201	0023
4H1303-1356	0015
4H1303-1393	0023
4H1304	OEM
4H1304-0938	0079
4H1304-0941	0037
4H1304-1025	0224
4H1304-1084	0261
4H1304-1558	2739
4H1304-4104	0006
4H1304-4121	0079
4H1304-4154	0224
4H1304-4196	0079
4H1304-4283	0472
4H1304-4349	1376
4H1304-4358	0037
4H2098-0357	3416
4H13030621	0133
4H13030847	0124
4H13030862	0057
4H13030983	0124
4H13030984	0124
4H13031168	0071
4H13031173	0087
4H13031174	0023
4H13031201	0102
4H13032214	OEM
4H13034167	0466
4H13034197	0999
4H13034278	0062
4H13034328	OEM
4H13040938	0079
4H13040941	0037
4H13040995	0919
4H13041025	OEM
4H13041041	0320
4H13041085	0723
4H13041275	0071
4H13041436	2833
4H13041487	0031
4H13041773	0275
4H13041782	0261
4H13041803	0261
4H13041817	OEM
4H13044196	0079
4H13044197	0037
4H13044283	0472
4H13044349	1376
4H13044358	0037
4H13044503	0079
4H20980587	4191
4H20981194	1051
4H20981472	OEM
4H20981787	1769
4HEADIC	OEM
4I29200602	0123
4IC-402	4406
4IC-407	0574
4IC-409	2289
4J4B41	0441
4J24X539	0137
4J31	OEM
4J32	OEM
4J33	OEM
4J34	OEM
4J35	OEM
4J36	OEM
4J37	OEM
4J43	OEM
4J44	OEM
4J50	OEM
4J50-5	OEM
4J50A	OEM
4J50M5	OEM
4J50M25	OEM
4J50TO	OEM
4J50TR	OEM
4J52A	OEM
4J53	OEM
4J57	OEM
4J58	OEM
4J59	OEM
4J100-5	OEM
4J100M5	OEM
4J100M25	OEM

DEVICE TYPE	REPL CODE
4J200-5	OEM
4J200-25	OEM
4J200M5	OEM
4J200M25	OEM
4JA2FX355	0015
4JA2X355	0015
4JA4DR700	0015
4JA4DX520	0015
4JA6MR700	0015
4JA10DX3	0015
4JA10DX32	0015
4JA10EX3	0015
4JA11BX4	0097
4JA12C101	OEM
4JA16MR700M	0071
4JA27DR700	0109
4JA38DR700	1124
4JA70MR700	1975
4JA211A	0015
4JB2C6	0911
4JBC12	0911
4JC12X070	OEM
4JD1A17	0279
4JD1A73	0211
4JD1B2	OEM
4JD1B3	OEM
4JD1B4	OEM
4JD3B1	0595
4JD4A2	OEM
4JD4A3	OEM
4JD4A4	OEM
4JD4A5	OEM
4JD5E29	1659
4JD7A35	OEM
4JD12C102	OEM
4JD12X009	OEM
4JD12X010	OEM
4JD12X011	OEM
4JD12X012	OEM
4JD12X013	OEM
4JD12X014	OEM
4JD12X043	OEM
4JD12X047	OEM
4JD12X132	OEM
4JD20AB	OEM
4JFBD1	OEM
4JFBD2	OEM
4JFBD3	OEM
4JFBD4	OEM
4JFBD5	OEM
4JFBD6	OEM
4JFBD7	OEM
4JUS2.16A	OEM
4JUS2.16B	OEM
4JUS2.46A	OEM
4JUS2.46B	OEM
4JUS2.60A	OEM
4JUS2.60B	OEM
4JUS2.92A	OEM
4JUS2.92B	OEM
4JUS3.05A	OEM
4JUS3.05B	OEM
4JX1A520	0211
4JX1A520B	0211
4JX1A520C	0211
4JX1A520D	0279
4JX1A520E	0279
4JX1A813	0050
4JX1C707	0050
4JX1C850	0211
4JX1C850A	0279
4JX1C1224	0211
4JX1D925	0004
4JX1E596	0016
4JX1E821	0279
4JX1E850	0038
4JX2A60	0279
4JX2A601	0038
4JX2A616	0208
4JX2A801	0595
4JX2A816	0038
4JX2A822	0038
4JX5E670	1659
4JX7A972	0016
4JX8D404	0160
4JX8P404	0160
4JX8P409	0160
4JX11C2848	0086
4JX16A567	0016
4JX16A569	0038
4JX16A667	0016
4JX16A667/G	0079
4JX16A667/O	0079
4JX16A667/R	0079
4JX16A667/Y	0079
4JX16A667G	0016
4JX16A6670	0016
4JX16A667R	0016
4JX16A667Y	0016
4JX16A668	0016
4JX16A668/G	0079
4JX16A668/O	0079
4JX16A668/Y	0079
4JX16A668G	0016
4JX16A6680	0079
4JX16A668Y	0016
4JX16A669	0016
4JX16A669/G	1510
4JX16A669/Y	1510

DEVICE TYPE	REPL CODE
4JX16A669G	0016
4JX16A669Y	0016
4JX16A670	0016
4JX16A670G	0016
4JX16A6670	0079
4JX16A6680	0016
4JX16B670/B	0079
4JX16B670/G	1510
4JX16B670/R	0079
4JX16B670/Y	0079
4JX16B670B	0016
4JX16B670G	0016
4JX16B670R	0016
4JX16B670Y	0016
4JX16E3860	0016
4JX16E3890	0016
4JX16E3960	0016
4JX17A567	OEM
4JX24X539	0137
4JX29A826	0037
4JX29A829	0037
4JX2816	0038
4JX2825	0038
4JZ4X539	0137
4JZ4XL12	0137
4K3CB	OEM
4K3CC	OEM
4K3SJ	OEM
4K3SK	OEM
4K3SL	OEM
4K3SN	OEM
4K5SL1	OEM
4K5SL3	OEM
4K30	1129
4K60	0340
4K100	0895
4K200LW	OEM
4K200LX	OEM
4KD20A7	OEM
4KM50LB	OEM
4KM50LC	OEM
4KM50SI	OEM
4KM50SJ	OEM
4KM50SK	OEM
4KM70LH	OEM
4KM70LH2	OEM
4KM70SJ	OEM
4KM70SK	OEM
4KM100LA	OEM
4KM100LF	OEM
4KM100LH	OEM
4KM150LA	OEM
4KM150LB	OEM
4KM150LF	OEM
4KM150LH	OEM
4KM150LH1	OEM
4KM3000LR	OEM
4KM50000LA3	OEM
4KM50000LA5	OEM
4KM50000LQ	OEM
4KM50000LR	OEM
4KMP300LU	OEM
4KMP10000LF	OEM
4KMV150LH1	OEM
4KP3SN	OEM
4KZ	OEM
4L30	1129
4L60	OEM
4L100	0895
4N22	OEM
4N22A	OEM
4N23	OEM
4N23A	OEM
4N24	OEM
4N24A	OEM
4N25	0536
4N25A	0536
4N26	0536
4N27	0536
4N28	0536
4N29	1047
4N29A	1047
4N30	1047
4N31	1047
4N32	1101
4N32A	1101
4N33	1101
4N35	0311
4N36	0311
4N37	0311
4N38	OEM
4N38A	0536
4N39	OEM
4N40	OEM
4N41	OEM
4N45	OEM
4N46	OEM
4N47	OEM
4N48	OEM
4N49	OEM
4N51	OEM
4N52	OEM
4N53	OEM
4N54	OEM
4N55	OEM
4N55TXV	OEM
4N55TXVB	OEM
4NT100	OEM
4NT175	OEM

If replacement code is OEM, contact original manufacturer for replacement.

DEVICE TYPE	REPL CODE
4O9C	0030
4R0/18	OEM
4R1/18	OEM
4R2/18	OEM
4R2B	OEM
4R2S	OEM
4R3B	OEM
4R3S	OEM
4R4C	OEM
4R4S	OEM
4R5C	OEM
4R5S	OEM
4R6C	OEM
4R6S	OEM
4R7CD	OEM
4R8CD	OEM
4R8S	OEM
4R52	OEM
4RCM5	1095
4RCM10	OEM
4RCM20	OEM
4RCM30	2635
4RCM40	OEM
4RCM50	OEM
4RCM60	OEM
4RO/18	OEM
4SD46-2	0143
4SM1	0015
4SM3	0087
4SM6	OEM
4SM15	OEM
4SM25	OEM
4SM40	OEM
4SM55	OEM
4SM70	OEM
4SM100	OEM
4SM150	OEM
4SM200	OEM
4ST41	OEM
4T6.2	0631
4T6.2A	0631
4T10T	OEM
4T20T	OEM
4T40T	OEM
4T60T	OEM
4T80T	OEM
4T100T	OEM
4T501	0015
4T502	0015
4T503	0015
4T504	0015
4T505	0015
4T506	0015
4T507	0071
4T508	0071
4T509	0071
4T510	0071
4TP001	OEM
4V27	OEM
4W01-13	0137
4W70	OEM
4W80	OEM
4W81	OEM
4W82	OEM
4X11	OEM
4Z9-4Z12	OEM
4.3Y	0274
4.7B	OEM
4.7B1	0140
4.7B2	0140
4.7B3	0140
4.7EB1	0140
4.7EB3	0140
4.7X	0140
4.7Z	0041
5	OEM
5-8	0016
5-30082.3	0071
5-30082.4	0071
5-30086.1	0015
5-30088.1	0015
5-30088.2	0229
5-30088.3	0071
5-30094.1	0015
5-30095.1	0015
5-30098.1	0015
5-30099.1	0015
5-30099.3	0015
5-30099.4	0015
5-30106.1	0015
5-30109.1	0015
5-30111.1	0229
5-30113.1	0015
5-30119.1	0286
5-30120.1	0015
5-30122.1	0229
5-30132.1	0769
5-113641	0141
5-70004503	0016
5-70005452	0016
5-70005503	0016
5-7000901504	0016
5A1	0015
5A1/18	OEM
5A1/52	OEM
5A2	0015
5A2/18	OEM
5A2/52	OEM
5A3	0015

DEVICE TYPE	REPL CODE
5A4	0015
5A4D	0015
5A4D-C	0015
5A5	0015
5A5/18	OEM
5A5/52	OEM
5A5D	0015
5A5R5	OEM
5A5R12-12	OEM
5A5R15-15	OEM
5A6	0015
5A6D	0015
5A6D-C	0015
5A8	0071
5A8D	2613
5A8DC	0071
5A10	0071
5A10C	0071
5A10D	2613
5A10D-C	0071
5A12	OEM
5A12/18	OEM
5A12R5	OEM
5A12R12-12	OEM
5A12R15-15	OEM
5A13	OEM
5A13/18	OEM
5A14	OEM
5A14/18	OEM
5A15	1129
5A15/18	OEM
5A16	OEM
5A16/18	OEM
5A22	OEM
5A22/18	OEM
5A23	OEM
5A23/18	OEM
5A24	OEM
5A24/18	OEM
5A24R5	OEM
5A24R12-12	OEM
5A24R15-15	OEM
5A25	OEM
5A25/18	OEM
5A26	OEM
5A26/18	OEM
5A30	OEM
5A50	OEM
5A52	OEM
5A52/18	OEM
5A53	OEM
5A53/18	OEM
5A54	OEM
5A54/18	OEM
5A55	OEM
5A55/18	OEM
5A56	OEM
5A56/18	OEM
5A60	OEM
5A100	OEM
5A200	OEM
5A400	OEM
5A600	OEM
5A800	OEM
5A1000	OEM
5AA5-1	0435
5A-D	0015
5AD8	0087
5AD8DC	0087
5AD10	0087
5AD10C	0087
5AD10D	0087
5AGD	OEM
5AV20	OEM
5AV30	OEM
5AV50	OEM
5AV60	OEM
5AV65	OEM
5AV80	OEM
5AV100	OEM
5AV120	OEM
5AV130	OEM
5AX90518A72	OEM
5B05	OEM
5B-1	0015
5B1	0015
5B1/18	OEM
5B1/52	OEM
5B-2	0015
5B2	0087
5B2/18	OEM
5B2/52	OEM
5B-2-H5W	0015
5B2C11	OEM
5B2Z11	OEM
5B3	0015
5B4	0299
5B5/18	OEM
5B5/52	OEM
5B7	0253
5B12	OEM
5B12/18	OEM
5B13	OEM
5B13/18	OEM
5B14	OEM
5B14/18	OEM
5B15	OEM
5B15/18	OEM
5B-15H	0015

DEVICE TYPE	REPL CODE
5B16	OEM
5B16/18	OEM
5B22	OEM
5B22/18	OEM
5B23	OEM
5B23/18	OEM
5B24	OEM
5B24/18	OEM
5B25	OEM
5B25/18	OEM
5B26	OEM
5B26/18	OEM
5B52	OEM
5B52/18	OEM
5B53	OEM
5B53/18	OEM
5B54	OEM
5B54/18	OEM
5B55	OEM
5B55/18	OEM
5B56	OEM
5B56/18	OEM
5B2012	OEM
5BG2C11	OEM
5BG2C41	1227
5BG2Z11	OEM
5BG2Z41	1716
5BL2C41	1227
5BL41	1119
5C	OEM
5C(C)1	0582
5C05/18	OEM
5C05/52	OEM
5C054	OEM
5C054/18	OEM
5C055	OEM
5C055/18	OEM
5C056	OEM
5C056/18	OEM
5C057	OEM
5C057/18	OEM
5C1/52	OEM
5C1R10	OEM
5C1R20	OEM
5C1R30	OEM
5C1S10	OEM
5C1S20	OEM
5C1S30	OEM
5C2/18	OEM
5C2/52	OEM
5C3	0582
5C4-5S	OEM
5C4.5-5.5S	OEM
5C5.4-5.9S	OEM
5C5.5-6.5S	OEM
5C5.6S	OEM
5C6.7S	OEM
5C14	OEM
5C14/18	OEM
5C15	OEM
5C15/18	OEM
5C16	OEM
5C16/18	OEM
5C17	OEM
5C17/18	OEM
5C24	OEM
5C24/18	OEM
5C25	OEM
5C25/18	OEM
5C26	OEM
5C26/18	OEM
5C27	OEM
5C27/18	OEM
5C28	OEM
5C29	OEM
5C30	OEM
5C50	OEM
5C100	OEM
5C200	OEM
5C400	OEM
5C600	OEM
5C800	OEM
5C1000	OEM
5CA/18	OEM
5CH1M	1227
5CH1MU	1227
5CH2M	1227
5CH2MU	1227
5CH2SM	1227
5CH3M	OEM
5CH4M	OEM
5CL2C41	1227
5CL41	1119
5CS04SM	1227
5D1	0015
5D2	0015
5D2C11	OEM
5D2Z11	OEM
5D4	OEM
5D5R5	OEM
5D5R12-12	OEM
5D5R15-15	OEM
5D6	OEM
5D8	0071
5D10	0071
5D12R5	OEM
5D12R12-12	OEM
5D12R15-15	OEM
5D15	OEM

DEVICE TYPE	REPL CODE
5D20	OEM
5D20-1	0797
5D24R5	OEM
5D24R12-12	OEM
5D24R15-15	OEM
5D25	OEM
5D30	OEM
5D40	OEM
5D50	OEM
5D50FS	OEM
5D100	OEM
5D100FS	OEM
5D200	OEM
5D200FS	OEM
5D400	OEM
5D400FS	OEM
5D600	OEM
5D600FS	OEM
5D800	OEM
5D800FS	OEM
5D1000	OEM
5DG2C11	OEM
5DG2C41	1227
5DG2Z11	OEM
5DG2Z41	1716
5DH1M	OEM
5DH2M	OEM
5DH3M	OEM
5DH4M	OEM
5DL2C41	1227
5DL2CZ41A-LB	OEM
5DL41	1119
5E1	0015
5E1R20	OEM
5E1R40	OEM
5E1R60	OEM
5E1S20	OEM
5E1S40	OEM
5E1S60	OEM
5E2	0015
5E3	0015
5E4	0015
5E5	0015
5E6	0015
5E8	0071
5E25	OEM
5E29	OEM
5E50A	OEM
5E100	OEM
5E150	OEM
5E200	OEM
5E250	OEM
5EH1M	1716
5EH2M	1716
5EH3M	1716
5EH4M	1716
5EZ3.3D	0777
5EZ3.6D	0791
5EZ3.6D5	0791
5EZ3.6D10	0791
5EZ3.9D	0801
5EZ3.9D5	0801
5EZ3.9D10	0801
5EZ4.3D5	0815
5EZ4.3D10	0815
5EZ4.7D	0827
5EZ4.7D5	0827
5EZ4.7D10	0827
5EZ5.1D	0437
5EZ5.1D5	0437
5EZ5.1D10	0437
5EZ5.6D	0870
5EZ5.6D5	0870
5EZ5.6D10	0870
5EZ6.2D	0185
5EZ6.2D5	0185
5EZ6.2D10	0185
5EZ6.8D	0205
5EZ6.8D5	0205
5EZ6.8D10	0205
5EZ7.5D	0475
5EZ7.5D5	0475
5EZ7.5D10	0475
5EZ8.2D	0499
5EZ8.2D5	0499
5EZ8.2D10	0499
5EZ8.7D	0499
5EZ8.7D5	3285
5EZ8.7D10	3285
5EZ9.1D	0679
5EZ9.1D5	0679
5EZ9.1D10	0679
5EZ10D	0225
5EZ10D5	0225
5EZ10D10	0225
5EZ11D	0230
5EZ11D5	0230
5EZ11D10	0230
5EZ12D	0234
5EZ12D5	0234
5EZ12D10	0234
5EZ13D	0237
5EZ13D5	0237
5EZ13D10	0237
5EZ14D	1387
5EZ14D5	1387
5EZ14D10	1387
5EZ15D	0247
5EZ15D5	OEM

DEVICE TYPE	REPL CODE
5EZ15D10	0247
5EZ16D	0251
5EZ16D5	0251
5EZ16D10	0251
5EZ17D	1170
5EZ17D5	1170
5EZ17D10	1170
5EZ18D	0256
5EZ18D5	0256
5EZ18D10	0256
5EZ19D	2379
5EZ19D5	2379
5EZ19D10	2379
5EZ20D5	0262
5EZ20D10	0262
5EZ22D	0269
5EZ22D5	0269
5EZ22D10	0269
5EZ24D	0273
5EZ24D5	0273
5EZ24D10	0273
5EZ25D	2383
5EZ25D5	2383
5EZ25D10	2383
5EZ27D	0291
5EZ27D5	0291
5EZ27D10	0291
5EZ28D	1169
5EZ28D5	1169
5EZ28D10	1169
5EZ30D	0305
5EZ30D5	0305
5EZ30D10	0305
5EZ33D	0314
5EZ33D5	0314
5EZ33D10	0314
5EZ36D	0316
5EZ36D5	0316
5EZ36D10	0314
5EZ39D	0322
5EZ39D5	0322
5EZ39D10	0322
5EZ43D	0343
5EZ43D5	0333
5EZ43D10	0333
5EZ47D	0343
5EZ47D10	0343
5EZ51D	0027
5EZ51D5	0027
5EZ51D10	0027
5EZ56D	0266
5EZ56D5	0266
5EZ56D10	0266
5EZ60D	2829
5EZ60D5	2829
5EZ60D10	2829
5EZ62D5	0382
5EZ75D	0421
5EZ75D10	0421
5EZ82D	0439
5EZ82D5	0439
5EZ82D10	0439
5EZ87D	2999
5EZ87D5	2999
5EZ87D10	2999
5EZ91D	0238
5EZ91D5	0238
5EZ91D10	0238
5EZ100D	1172
5EZ100D5	1172
5EZ100D10	1172
5EZ110D5	1182
5EZ110D10	1182
5EZ120D	1198
5EZ120D5	1198
5EZ130D	1209
5EZ130D10	OEM
5EZ140D	1870
5EZ140D5	1870
5EZ140D10	1870
5EZ150D	0642
5EZ150D5	0642
5EZ150D10	0642
5EZ160D	1246
5EZ160D5	1246
5EZ160D10	1246
5EZ170D	2091
5EZ170D5	2091
5EZ170D10	2091
5EZ180D	1269
5EZ180D5	1269
5EZ180D10	1269
5EZ190D	2210
5EZ190D5	2210
5EZ190D10	2210
5EZ200D	0600
5EZ200D5	0600
5EZ200D10	0600
5EZ1200D10	OEM
5E.5	OEM
5F1	0703
5F1R07	OEM
5F1R15	OEM
5F1S07	OEM
5F1S15	OEM
5F1S07	OEM
5F5	0964
5F10	0865
5F15	0315

DEVICE TYPE	REPL CODE
5F15E2	OEM
5F15E3	OEM
5F20	1241
5F25	OEM
5F30	0847
5F40	0759
5F50	OEM
5F60	OEM
5F80	OEM
5FF05	OEM
5FF10	OEM
5FF15	OEM
5FF30	OEM
5FF40	OEM
5FF50	OEM
5FWJ2C41	1227
5G1	OEM
5G2	4224
5G2C11	OEM
5G2Z11	OEM
5G3	OEM
5G4	OEM
5G5	OEM
5G8	0071
5G514	OEM
5G515	OEM
5G516	OEM
5GA	0015
5G-D	0015
5GD	0015
5GF	0071
5GFH	0015
5GG2C11	OEM
5GG2C41	OEM
5GG2Z11	OEM
5GG2Z41	OEM
5GJ	0071
5GJ/FR1N	0015
5GWJ2C41	1227
5H	0015
5H3P	0964
5H3PN	0979
5H4D1	0015
5H300RT	OEM
5H500RT	OEM
5H750M	0015
5H20984841	OEM
5J2C11	OEM
5J2Z11	OEM
5J3P	0084
5J26	OEM
5J-F1	0015
5JG2C11	OEM
5JG2Z11	OEM
5JG2Z41	OEM
5JH3	OEM
5JUS2.70A	OEM
5JUS2.70B	OEM
5JUS3.08A	OEM
5JUS3.08B	OEM
5JUS3.25A	OEM
5JUS3.25B	OEM
5JUS3.65A	OEM
5JUS3.65B	OEM
5JUS3.81A	OEM
5JUS3.81B	OEM
5K090B	OEM
5K10	0071
5K20	OEM
5K40	OEM
5K50	OEM
5K50SE	OEM
5K50SG	OEM
5K60	OEM
5K70SG	OEM
5K70SG-WB	OEM
5K70SH1	OEM
5K100	OEM
5K300SK	OEM
5K4164ANP-15	2341
5KF10(B)	OEM
5KF20(B)	OEM
5KF20B	1227
5KF30	1654
5KF30B	5684
5KF40	1654
5KF40B	5684
5KFU10	OEM
5KFU10B	OEM
5KFU20	OEM
5KFU20B	OEM
5KM50SJ	OEM
5KM70SI	OEM
5KM70SJ	OEM
5KM300SI	OEM
5KM1000SG	OEM
5KP5.0	2380
5KP5.0A	2380
5KP6.0	3085
5KP6.0A	3085
5KP6.5	OEM
5KP6.5A	OEM
5KP7.0	OEM
5KP7.0A	OEM
5KP7.5	OEM
5KP7.5A	OEM
5KP8.0	OEM
5KP8.0A	OEM
5KP8.5	OEM

DEVICE TYPE	REPL CODE
5KP8.5A	OEM
5KP9.0	OEM
5KP9.0A	OEM
5KP10	OEM
5KP10A	OEM
5KP11	3143
5KP11A	3143
5KP12	OEM
5KP12A	OEM
5KP13	OEM
5KP13A	OEM
5KP14	OEM
5KP14A	OEM
5KP15	3162
5KP15A	3162
5KP16	OEM
5KP16A	OEM
5KP17	OEM
5KP17A	3171
5KP18	OEM
5KP18A	OEM
5KP20	OEM
5KP20A	OEM
5KP22	1904
5KP22A	1904
5KP24	OEM
5KP24A	OEM
5KP26	OEM
5KP26A	OEM
5KP28	OEM
5KP28A	OEM
5KP30	OEM
5KP30A	OEM
5KP33	OEM
5KP33A	OEM
5KP36	OEM
5KP36A	OEM
5KP40	OEM
5KP40A	OEM
5KP43	0563
5KP43A	0563
5KP45	OEM
5KP45A	OEM
5KP48	OEM
5KP48A	OEM
5KP51	OEM
5KP51A	OEM
5KP54	OEM
5KP54A	OEM
5KP58	0825
5KP58A	0825
5KP60	OEM
5KP60A	OEM
5KP64	OEM
5KP64A	OEM
5KP64P	OEM
5KP70	OEM
5KP70A	OEM
5KP75	OEM
5KP75A	OEM
5KP78	OEM
5KP78A	OEM
5KP85	OEM
5KP85A	OEM
5KP90	OEM
5KP90A	OEM
5KP100	OEM
5KP100A	OEM
5KP110	OEM
5KP110A	OEM
5KQ30	OEM
5KQ30(B)	OEM
5KQ30B	OEM
5KQ40	OEM
5KQ40(B)	OEM
5KQ40B	OEM
5KQ50	OEM
5KQ50(B)	OEM
5KQ50B	OEM
5KQ60	OEM
5KQ60(B)	OEM
5KQ60B	OEM
5KQ90	OEM
5KQ90B	OEM
5KQ100	OEM
5KQ100B	OEM
5L1-2	OEM
5L1-2S	OEM
5L15	0344
5L20	OEM
5L20(1)	OEM
5L25	OEM
5L30	OEM
5L30(1)	OEM
5L35	OEM
5L40	OEM
5L40(1)	OEM
5L45	OEM
5L50	OEM
5L55	OEM
5L60	OEM
5L60(1)	OEM
5L65	OEM
5L70	OEM
5L75	OEM
5L75(1)	OEM
5L80	OEM
5L85	OEM
5L90	OEM

If replacement code is OEM, contact original manufacturer for replacement.

115

DEVICE TYPE	REPL CODE
5L95	OEM
5L100	OEM
5L100(1)	OEM
5L110	OEM
5L120	OEM
5L130	OEM
5L140	OEM
5L150	OEM
5L150(1)	OEM
5L160	OEM
5L170	OEM
5L180	OEM
5L190	OEM
5L200	OEM
5L200(1)	OEM
5L209	OEM
5L210	OEM
5L220	OEM
5L230	OEM
5L240	OEM
5L250	OEM
5L260	OEM
5L270	OEM
5L280	OEM
5L290	OEM
5L300	OEM
5LT32	OEM
5LT36ZY1	OEM
5LT61ZK	OEM
5M10	OEM
5M15	OEM
5M20	OEM
5M30	OEM
5M40	3705
5M47ZS5	6639
5M47ZS10	OEM
5M47ZS10.5	OEM
5M50	3711
5M60	1104
5M80	3722
5M80/E3517	OEM
5M81	OEM
5M100	2982
5MA1	OEM
5MA2	0015
5MA3	OEM
5MA4	0015
5MA4D	0015
5MA5	0015
5MA6	0015
5MA8	0071
5MA10	0071
5MF1	0015
5MS5	0015
5MS10	0015
5MS20	0015
5MS30	0015
5MS40	0015
5MS50	0015
5N02F1-A	OEM
5N05M1	OEM
5N1	0015
5N2	0097
5N3	0097
5N10K1	OEM
5N15A	OEM
5N15A9	OEM
5N20A	OEM
5N20A9	OEM
5N25A	OEM
5N25A9	OEM
5N30A	OEM
5N30A9	OEM
5N35A	OEM
5N35A9	OEM
5N40A	OEM
5N40A9	OEM
5N45A	OEM
5N45A9	OEM
5N50A	OEM
5N50A9	OEM
5N55A	OEM
5N55A9	OEM
5N60A	OEM
5N60A9	OEM
5N65A	OEM
5N65A9	OEM
5N70A	OEM
5N70A9	OEM
5N75A	OEM
5N75A9	OEM
5N80A	OEM
5N80A9	OEM
5N85A	OEM
5N85A9	OEM
5N90A	OEM
5N90A9	OEM
5N95A	OEM
5N95A9	OEM
5N100A	OEM
5N100A9	OEM
5N110A	OEM
5N120A	OEM
5N130A	OEM
5N140A	OEM
5N150A	OEM
5N160A	OEM
5N170A	OEM
5N190A	OEM

DEVICE TYPE	REPL CODE
5N200A	OEM
5N210A	OEM
5N220A	OEM
5N230A	OEM
5N240A	OEM
5N250A	OEM
5N260A	OEM
50	0143
5P-01	0015
5P05M	2084
5P1M	3816
5P2	0097
5P2M	3823
5P3	0097
5P4M	0705
5P5M	0857
5P6M	0857
5P15	OEM
5P30	OEM
5P60	OEM
5P100	OEM
5PL.6-1.2	OEM
5PL.6-1.2S	OEM
5P.4-.8	OEM
5P.4-.8S	OEM
5P.35-.5	OEM
5P.35-.5S	OEM
5Q3	1620
5R	OEM
5R0/18	OEM
5R1/18	OEM
5R1/52	OEM
5R2/4	OEM
5R2/18	OEM
5R2/66	OEM
5R2B	OEM
5R2S	OEM
5R3/4	OEM
5R3/66	OEM
5R3B	OEM
5R3P	OEM
5R3S	OEM
5R4/3	OEM
5R4/3C	OEM
5R4/4	OEM
5R4/59	OEM
5R4C	OEM
5R4S	OEM
5R5/3	OEM
5R5/3D	OEM
5R5/5	OEM
5R5/61	OEM
5R5C	OEM
5R5S	OEM
5R6/3	OEM
5R6/3D	OEM
5R6/5	OEM
5R6/61	OEM
5R6C	OEM
5R6S	OEM
5R7/3	OEM
5R7/3D	OEM
5R7/5	OEM
5R7/61	OEM
5R7CD	OEM
5R7S	OEM
5R8/3	OEM
5R8/3D	OEM
5R8/5	OEM
5R8/63	OEM
5R8CD	OEM
5R8S	OEM
5R52	OEM
5RC2	3385
5RC5	1095
5RC5A	1095
5RC10	2471
5RC10A	2471
5RC10G	0240
5RC15	0240
5RC15A	0240
5RC20	0240
5RC20A	0240
5RC25	2635
5RC30	2635
5RC30A	2635
5RC40	0671
5RC40A	0671
5RC50	2782
5RC50A	2782
5RC50B	2782
5RC60	0332
5RC60A	0332
5RCF5A	OEM
5RCF10A	OEM
5RCF20A	OEM
5RCF25A	OEM
5RCF30A	OEM
5RCF40A	OEM
5RCF50A	OEM
5RCF60A	OEM
5RCL2	3385
5RCL5	1095
5RCL10	2471
5RCL15	0240
5RCL20	0240
5RE52	OEM
5RKB1	OEM
5RKB2	OEM

DEVICE TYPE	REPL CODE
5RKB3	OEM
5RKB4	OEM
5RKB5	OEM
5RKB6	OEM
5RKB7	OEM
5RKB8	OEM
5RO/18	OEM
5S1S03	OEM
5S1S04	OEM
5S2.8-2.85	OEM
5S3P	OEM
5S3.4-3.7	OEM
5S4M	OEM
5SB05	OEM
5SB10	OEM
5SB20	OEM
5SB40	OEM
5SB60	OEM
5SB80	OEM
5SB100	OEM
5SKB1	OEM
5SKB2	OEM
5SKB3	OEM
5SKB4	OEM
5SKB5	OEM
5SKB6	OEM
5SKB7	OEM
5SKB8	OEM
5SM1020A4	OEM
5SM1020A4PL	OEM
5SM1020A4T	OEM
5SM1020A5	OEM
5SM1020A5PL	OEM
5SM1020A5T	OEM
5SM1020A6	OEM
5SM1020A6PL	OEM
5SM1020A6T	OEM
5SM1020A7	OEM
5SM1020A7PL	OEM
5SM1020A7T	OEM
5SM1020A8	OEM
5SM1020A8PL	OEM
5SM1020A8T	OEM
5SM1020E4	OEM
5SM1020E4PL	OEM
5SM1020E4T	OEM
5SM1020E5	OEM
5SM1020E5PL	OEM
5SM1020E5T	OEM
5SM1020E6	OEM
5SM1020E6PL	OEM
5SM1020E6T	OEM
5SM1020E7	OEM
5SM1020E7PL	OEM
5SM1020E7T	OEM
5SM1020GE8PL	OEM
5SM1020GE8T	OEM
5SM1020GE9	OEM
5SM1020GE9PL	OEM
5SM1020GE9T	OEM
5SM1020GE10	OEM
5SM1020GE10PL	OEM
5SM1020GE10T	OEM
5SP510-6	OEM
5SPT10-4	OEM
5SPT10-5	OEM
5SPT12-4	OEM
5SPT12-5	OEM
5T3P	OEM
5TB1	2471
5TB1-CE00	OEM
5TB1-CH00	OEM
5TB1-EE00	OEM
5TB1-EH00	OEM
5TB1-GE00	OEM
5TB1-GH00	OEM
5TB1-JE00	OEM
5TB2	0240
5TB2-CE00	OEM
5TB2-CH00	OEM
5TB2-EE00	OEM
5TB2-EH00	OEM
5TB2-GE00	OEM
5TB2-GH00	OEM
5TB2-JE00	OEM
5TB3	2635
5TB3-CE00	OEM
5TB3-CH00	OEM
5TB3-EE00	OEM
5TB3-EH00	OEM
5TB3-GE00	OEM
5TB3-GH00	OEM
5TB3-JE00	OEM
5TB4	0671
5TB4-CE00	OEM
5TB4-CH00	OEM
5TB4-EE00	OEM
5TB4-EH00	OEM
5TB4-GE00	OEM
5TB4-GH00	OEM
5TB4-JE00	OEM
5TB5	2782
5TB5-CE00	OEM
5TB5-CH00	OEM
5TB5-EE00	OEM
5TB5-EH00	OEM
5TB5-GE00	OEM
5TB5-GH00	OEM
5TB5-JE00	OEM

DEVICE TYPE	REPL CODE
5TB6	0332
5TB6-CE00	OEM
5TB6-CH00	OEM
5TB6-EE00	OEM
5TB6-EH00	OEM
5TB6-GE00	OEM
5TB6-GH00	OEM
5TB6-JE00	OEM
5TB7	OEM
5TB7-CE00	OEM
5TB7-CH00	OEM
5TB7-EE00	OEM
5TB7-EH00	OEM
5TB7-GE00	OEM
5TB7-GH00	OEM
5TB7-JE00	OEM
5TB8	OEM
5TC05	OEM
5TC025	OEM
5TC10	OEM
5TC15	OEM
5TC20	OEM
5TC25	OEM
5TC30	OEM
5TC35	OEM
5TC40	OEM
5TC50	OEM
5TC60	OEM
5TC70	OEM
5TC80	OEM
5TC90	OEM
5TC100	OEM
5TC110	OEM
5TC120	OEM
5TCA10	OEM
5TCA20	OEM
5TCA30	OEM
5TCA40	OEM
5TCA50	OEM
5TCA60	OEM
5TCA70	OEM
5TCA80	OEM
5TCA90	OEM
5TCA100	OEM
5TCA110	OEM
5TCA120	OEM
5TCRA	3385
5TCRB	1095
5TCRC	2471
5TCRD	OEM
5TCRE	0240
5TCRF	OEM
5TCRG	6780
5TCRH	0671
5TCRI	0332
5TCRJ	0332
5TCRK	OEM
5TCRL	OEM
5V	OEM
5V3P	OEM
5W3P	OEM
5W5R5	OEM
5W5R12-12	OEM
5W5R15-15	OEM
5W12R5	OEM
5W12R12-12	OEM
5W12R15-15	OEM
5W24R5	OEM
5W24R12-12	OEM
5W24R15-15	OEM
5W28R5	OEM
5W28R12-12	OEM
5W28R15-15	OEM
5W70	OEM
5W71	OEM
5WM1020GE8	OEM
5X3P	OEM
5X10	OEM
5Y3P	OEM
5Z27	0291
5Z30	0305
5Z82B	0439
5ZB	OEM
5ZS3.3	0777
5ZS3.3A	0777
5ZS3.3B	0777
5ZS3.6	0791
5ZS3.6A	0791
5ZS3.6B	0791
5ZS3.9	0801
5ZS3.9A	0801
5ZS3.9B	0801
5ZS4.3	0815
5ZS4.3A	0815
5ZS4.3B	0815
5ZS5.1	0437
5ZS5.1A	0437
5ZS5.1B	0437
5ZS5.6	0870
5ZS5.6A	0870
5ZS5.6B	0870
5ZS6.0A	3099
5ZS6.0B	3099
5ZS6.2	0185
5ZS6.2A	0185
5ZS6.2B	0185
5ZS7.5	0475
5ZS7.5A	0475
5ZS7.5B	0475

DEVICE TYPE	REPL CODE
5ZS8.2	0499
5ZS8.2A	0499
5ZS8.2B	0499
5ZS8.7	3285
5ZS8.7B	1481
5ZS9.1	0679
5ZS9.1A	0679
5ZS9.1B	0679
5ZS10	0225
5ZS10A	0225
5ZS10B	0225
5ZS11	0230
5ZS11A	0230
5ZS12	0234
5ZS12A	0234
5ZS12B	0234
5ZS13	0237
5ZS13B	0237
5ZS14	1387
5ZS14B	1387
5ZS15	0247
5ZS15A	0247
5ZS15B	0247
5ZS18	0256
5ZS18A	0256
5ZS18B	0256
5ZS20	0262
5ZS20A	0262
5ZS20B	0262
5ZS22	0269
5ZS22A	0269
5ZS22B	0269
5ZS24	0273
5ZS24A	0273
5ZS24B	0273
5ZS27	0291
5ZS27A	0291
5ZS27B	0291
5ZS30	0305
5ZS30A	0305
5ZS30B	0305
5ZS33	0314
5ZS33A	0314
5ZS33B	0314
5ZS36	0316
5ZS36A	0316
5ZS36B	0316
5ZS39	0322
5ZS39A	0322
5ZS39B	0322
5ZS43	0333
5ZS43A	0333
5ZS43B	0333
5ZS47	0343
5ZS47A	0343
5ZS47B	0343
5ZS51	0027
5ZS51A	0027
5ZS51B	0027
5ZS68	0401
5ZS68A	0401
5ZS68B	0401
5ZS75	0421
5ZS75A	0421
5ZS75B	0421
5ZS82	0439
5ZS82A	0439
5ZS87	0439
5ZS87A	0439
5ZS87B	0439
5ZS91	0238
5ZS91A	0238
5ZS91B	0238
5ZS100	1172
5ZS100A	1172
5ZS100B	1172
5.1	0041
5.1B	0041
5.1B1	0041
5.1B2	0041
5.1B2	0041
5.1EB(3)	0041
5.1EB2	0041
5.1EB3	0041
5.1N1	0041
5.1N2	0041
5.1N3	0041
5.1X	0041
5.6B	0253
5.6B1	0253
5.6B2	0253
5.6B3	0253
5.6EB	0253
5.6EB1	0877
5.6L2	0253
5.6M	OEM
5.6N1	0253
5.6N2	0253
5.6V	0157
5.6X	0041
5.6Y	0253
5.6Z	0253
6	0079
6-0004799	0571
6-02	0079
6-04	0016
6-04GRN	0016
6-04ORN	0016
6-04S1	0016

DEVICE TYPE	REPL CODE
6-04S2	0016
6-05	0016
6-05F	0016
6-05YEL	0016
6-0451	0016
6-0452	0016
6-11	0016
6-13	0004
6-19	0016
6-24	0178
6-30	0016
6-31	0037
6-31A	0037
6-38	0037
6-38A	0037
6-49	0688
6-50	0136
6-53	0164
6-53/63	0211
6-53A	0004
6-53F	0004
6-60	0050
6-60-P	0211
6-60A	0050
6-60B	0136
6-60C	0050
6-60D	0136
6-60E	0050
6-60F	0050
6-60P	0004
6-60T	0050
6-60X	0050
6-61	0136
6-61-P	0211
6-61A	0050
6-61B	0004
6-61D	0136
6-61E	0050
6-61F	0050
6-61P	0004
6-61T	0050
6-61X	0050
6-62	0136
6-62-P	0211
6-62A	0004
6-62B	0004
6-62C	0050
6-62D	0004
6-62E	0050
6-62F	0136
6-62P	0136
6-62X	0136
6-63	0004
6-63A	0004
6-63T	0004
6-65	0004
6-65T	0004
6-66	0004
6-66T	0004
6-67	0004
6-67T	0004
6-69	0050
6-69X	0050
6-70	0136
6-71	0136
6-72	0136
6-84F	0050
6-85F	0050
6-87	0004
6-88	0004
6-88(AUTOMATIC)	0222
6-89	0136
6-89X	0136
6-90	0007
6-93	1212
6-223-636	1954
6-2708	0144
6-4799	0571
6-5363	0004
6-13759A02	OEM
6-13780A01	OEM
6-59010	0015
6-1260039	0050
6-1260039A	0050
6-6490004	0103
6A05	3612
6A05G	3612
6A1	0582
6A1(RECT)	1272
6A1G	1272
6A2	1272
6A2G	1277
6A4	1277
6A4G	1277
6A6	1282
6A6F	0706
6A6F1	OEM
6A6G	1282
6A8	1285
6A8-1A5L	0050
6A8F	OEM
6A8F1	OEM
6A8G	1285
6A10	1285
6A10F	OEM
6A10F1	OEM
6A10G	1285
6A15	0964
6A30	0964

DEVICE TYPE	REPL CODE
6A50	0964
6A100	3688
6A150	OEM
6A200	0983
6A300	3697
6A400	0197
6A500	0200
6A600	0204
6A700	0206
6A753	OEM
6A800	0206
6A900	0583
6A1000	0583
6A1200	OEM
6A10227	0016
6A10228	0086
6A10229	0222
6A10422	0016
6A10423	0016
6A10520	0016
6A10622	0164
6A10624	0004
6A10851	0016
6A10855	0016
6A11180	0016
6A11223	0007
6A11301	0628
6A11665	0004
6A11668	0004
6A12515	0164
6A12516	0004
6A12517	0164
6A12677	0144
6A12678	0279
6A12679	0144
6A12680	0136
6A12681	0016
6A12682	0079
6A12683	0016
6A12684	0004
6A12685	0004
6A12725	0016
6A12788	0016
6A12789	0016
6A12889	0050
6A12988	0233
6A12989	0004
6A12990	0004
6A12992	0208
6A12993	0038
6A16399	0076
6AKB7	OEM
6ALZ1	OEM
6ALZ6.8	OEM
6ALZ6.8A	OEM
6ALZ6.8B	OEM
6ALZ7.5	OEM
6ALZ7.5A	OEM
6ALZ7.5B	OEM
6ALZ8.2	OEM
6ALZ8.2A	OEM
6ALZ8.2B	OEM
6ALZ8.7	OEM
6ALZ8.7A	OEM
6ALZ8.7B	OEM
6ALZ9.1	OEM
6ALZ9.1A	OEM
6ALZ9.1B	OEM
6ALZ10	OEM
6ALZ10A	OEM
6ALZ10B	OEM
6ALZ11	OEM
6ALZ11A	OEM
6ALZ11B	OEM
6ALZ12	OEM
6ALZ12A	OEM
6ALZ12B	OEM
6ALZ13	OEM
6ALZ13A	OEM
6ALZ13B	OEM
6ALZ14	OEM
6ALZ14A	OEM
6ALZ14B	OEM
6ALZ15	OEM
6ALZ15A	OEM
6ALZ15B	OEM
6ALZ16	OEM
6ALZ16A	OEM
6ALZ16B	OEM
6ALZ17	OEM
6ALZ17A	OEM
6ALZ17B	OEM
6ALZ18	OEM
6ALZ18A	OEM
6ALZ18B	OEM
6ALZ19	OEM
6ALZ19A	OEM
6ALZ19B	OEM
6ALZ20	OEM
6ALZ20A	OEM
6ALZ20B	OEM
6ALZ22	OEM
6ALZ22A	OEM
6ALZ22B	OEM
6ALZ23	OEM
6ALZ23A	OEM
6ALZ23B	OEM
6ALZ24	OEM
6ALZ24A	OEM

If replacement code is OEM, contact original manufacturer for replacement.

DEVICE TYPE	REPL CODE
6ALZ24B	OEM
6ALZ25	OEM
6ALZ25A	OEM
6ALZ25B	OEM
6ALZ27	OEM
6ALZ27A	OEM
6ALZ27B	OEM
6ALZ28	OEM
6ALZ28A	OEM
6ALZ28B	OEM
6ALZ30	OEM
6ALZ30A	OEM
6ALZ30B	OEM
6ALZ33	OEM
6ALZ33A	OEM
6ALZ33B	OEM
6ALZ36	OEM
6ALZ36A	OEM
6ALZ36B	OEM
6ALZ39	OEM
6ALZ39A	OEM
6ALZ39B	OEM
6ALZ43	OEM
6ALZ43A	OEM
6ALZ43B	OEM
6ALZ47	OEM
6ALZ47A	OEM
6ALZ47B	OEM
6ALZ51	OEM
6ALZ51A	OEM
6ALZ51B	OEM
6ALZ56	OEM
6ALZ56A	OEM
6ALZ56B	OEM
6ALZ60	OEM
6ALZ60A	OEM
6ALZ60B	OEM
6ALZ62	OEM
6ALZ62A	OEM
6ALZ62B	OEM
6ALZ68	OEM
6ALZ68A	OEM
6ALZ68B	OEM
6ALZ75	OEM
6ALZ75A	OEM
6ALZ75B	OEM
6ALZ82	OEM
6ALZ82A	OEM
6ALZ82B	OEM
6ALZ87	OEM
6ALZ87A	OEM
6ALZ87B	OEM
6ALZ91	OEM
6ALZ91A	OEM
6ALZ91B	OEM
6ALZ100	OEM
6ALZ100A	OEM
6ALZ100B	OEM
6ALZ110	OEM
6ALZ110A	OEM
6ALZ110B	OEM
6ALZ120	OEM
6ALZ120A	OEM
6ALZ120B	OEM
6ALZ130	OEM
6ALZ130A	OEM
6ALZ130B	OEM
6ALZ140	OEM
6ALZ140A	OEM
6ALZ140B	OEM
6ALZ150	OEM
6ALZ150A	OEM
6ALZ150B	OEM
6ALZ160	OEM
6ALZ160A	OEM
6ALZ160B	OEM
6ALZ170	OEM
6ALZ170A	OEM
6ALZ170B	OEM
6ALZ180	OEM
6ALZ180A	OEM
6ALZ180B	OEM
6ALZ190	OEM
6ALZ190A	OEM
6ALZ190B	OEM
6ALZ200	OEM
6ALZ200A	OEM
6ALZ200B	OEM
6ALZ561	OEM
6B	OEM
6B1	0253
6B2	0631
6B2(3%)	0157
6B2CTA	OEM
6B3	0253
6B4B41	4011
6B4CTA	OEM
6B4DM	OEM
6B4HA	OEM
6B8CTA	OEM
6B8DM	OEM
6B8HA	OEM
6B10	OEM
6B12DM	OEM
6B12MA	OEM
6B16DM	OEM
6B16MA	OEM
6B20	OEM
6B40	OEM

DEVICE TYPE	REPL CODE
6B60	0441
6B82	OEM
6BCTA	OEM
6BG11	1557
6BL6	OEM
6BM6	OEM
6BM61	OEM
6C	OEM
6C05	0964
6C05R	0979
6C1	0091
6C2	0466
6C3	0292
6C7	OEM
6C8	OEM
6C9	OEM
6C10	3688
6C10R	0904
6C15	0983
6C15R	0984
6C20	3694
6C20R	0984
6C30	3697
6C30R	0987
6C40	0197
6C40R	0991
6C50	0200
6C50R	0995
6C60	0204
6C60R	0510
6C70	0206
6C70R	1002
6C80	0206
6C80R	1002
6C90	0583
6C90R	0942
6C100	0583
6C100R	0942
6C153S	OEM
6CC11	1241
6CC12	0865
6CC13	0983
6CD12	0865
6CD13	0983
6CG12	0197
6CM7	OEM
6CZ5.0	OEM
6CZ5.0A	OEM
6CZ5.0B	OEM
6CZ6.0	OEM
6CZ6.0A	OEM
6CZ6.0B	OEM
6CZ6.5	OEM
6CZ6.5A	OEM
6CZ6.5B	OEM
6CZ7.0	OEM
6CZ7.0A	OEM
6CZ7.0B	OEM
6CZ7.5	OEM
6CZ7.5A	OEM
6CZ7.5B	OEM
6CZ8.0	OEM
6CZ8.0A	OEM
6CZ8.0B	OEM
6CZ8.5	OEM
6CZ8.5A	OEM
6CZ8.5B	OEM
6CZ9.0	OEM
6CZ9.0A	OEM
6CZ9.0B	OEM
6CZ10	OEM
6CZ10A	OEM
6CZ10B	OEM
6CZ11	OEM
6CZ11A	OEM
6CZ11B	OEM
6CZ12	OEM
6CZ12A	OEM
6CZ12B	OEM
6CZ13	OEM
6CZ13A	OEM
6CZ13B	OEM
6CZ14	OEM
6CZ14A	OEM
6CZ14B	OEM
6CZ15	OEM
6CZ15A	OEM
6CZ15B	OEM
6CZ16	OEM
6CZ16A	OEM
6CZ16B	OEM
6CZ17	OEM
6CZ17A	OEM
6CZ17B	OEM
6CZ18	OEM
6CZ18A	OEM
6CZ18B	OEM
6CZ20	OEM
6CZ20A	OEM
6CZ20B	OEM
6CZ22	OEM
6CZ22A	OEM
6CZ22B	OEM
6CZ24	OEM
6CZ24A	OEM
6CZ24B	OEM
6CZ26	OEM
6CZ26A	OEM
6CZ26B	OEM

DEVICE TYPE	REPL CODE
6CZ28	OEM
6CZ28A	OEM
6CZ28B	OEM
6CZ30	OEM
6CZ30A	OEM
6CZ30B	OEM
6CZ33	OEM
6CZ33A	OEM
6CZ33B	OEM
6CZ36	OEM
6CZ36A	OEM
6CZ36B	OEM
6CZ40	OEM
6CZ40A	OEM
6CZ40B	OEM
6CZ43	OEM
6CZ43A	OEM
6CZ43B	OEM
6CZ45	OEM
6CZ45A	OEM
6CZ45B	OEM
6CZ48	OEM
6CZ48A	OEM
6CZ48B	OEM
6CZ51	OEM
6CZ51A	OEM
6CZ51B	OEM
6CZ54	OEM
6CZ54A	OEM
6CZ54B	OEM
6CZ58	OEM
6CZ58A	OEM
6CZ58B	OEM
6CZ60	OEM
6CZ60A	OEM
6CZ60B	OEM
6CZ64	OEM
6CZ64A	OEM
6CZ64B	OEM
6CZ70	OEM
6CZ70A	OEM
6CZ70B	OEM
6CZ75	OEM
6CZ75A	OEM
6CZ75B	OEM
6CZ78	OEM
6CZ78A	OEM
6CZ78B	OEM
6CZ85	OEM
6CZ85A	OEM
6CZ85B	OEM
6CZ90	OEM
6CZ90A	OEM
6CZ90B	OEM
6CZ100	OEM
6CZ100A	OEM
6CZ100B	OEM
6CZ110	OEM
6CZ110A	OEM
6CZ110B	OEM
6D02M1-A	OEM
6D05M1	OEM
6D4B41	1404
6D10K1	OEM
6D20	OEM
6D50	OEM
6D50FS	OEM
6D72	OEM
6D73	OEM
6D100	OEM
6D100FS	OEM
6D122	0004
6D122R	0004
6D122T	0004
6D122TC	0004
6D122TH	0004
6D122U	0004
6D122V	0004
6D122W	0004
6D122Y	0004
6D200	OEM
6D200FS	OEM
6D300A	0023
6D400	OEM
6D400FS	OEM
6D450A	OEM
6D600	OEM
6D600FS	OEM
6D800	OEM
6D800FS	OEM
6D1000	OEM
6D67800A03	0769
6DC11	0315
6DC12	0865
6DD12	0865
6DG11	1557
6DM	0244
6E	OEM
6E20	OEM
6E40A	OEM
6E55	OEM
6E100	OEM
6E175	OEM
6F	OEM
6F4	OEM
6F5	0964
6F5-D	0964
6F5A	0964
6F5B	0964

DEVICE TYPE	REPL CODE
6F5D	0097
6F5R	2275
6F5RA	2275
6F5RB	2275
6F8	OEM
6F10	3688
6F10-D	3688
6F10A	3688
6F10B	3688
6F10D	0097
6F10R	2275
6F10RA	2275
6F10RB	2275
6F12	OEM
6F15	0983
6F15-D	0983
6F15A	0983
6F15B	0983
6F15D	0983
6F15R	2275
6F15RA	2275
6F15RB	2275
6F16	OEM
6F20	0983
6F20-D	0983
6F20A	0983
6F20B	0983
6F20D	0097
6F20R	2275
6F20RA	2275
6F20RB	2275
6F30	3697
6F30-D	3697
6F30A	3697
6F30B	3697
6F30R	0471
6F30RA	0471
6F30RB	0471
6F40	0197
6F40-D	0197
6F40A	0197
6F40B	0197
6F40D	0800
6F40R	0471
6F40RA	0471
6F40RB	0471
6F50	0200
6F50-D	0200
6F50A	0200
6F50B	0200
6F50R	0471
6F50RA	0471
6F50RB	0471
6F60	0204
6F60-D	0204
6F60A	0204
6F60B	0204
6F60D	0204
6F60R	0471
6F60RA	0471
6F60RB	0471
6F70	0206
6F70A	0206
6F70B	0206
6F70R	0444
6F70RA	0444
6F70RB	0444
6F80	0206
6F80-D	0206
6F80A	0206
6F80B	0206
6F80D	0206
6F80R	0444
6F80RA	0444
6F80RB	0444
6F90	0583
6F90A	0583
6F90B	0583
6F90R	0444
6F90RA	0444
6F90RB	0444
6F100	0583
6F100-D	0583
6F100A	0583
6F100B	0583
6F100D	0583
6F100R	0444
6F100RA	0444
6F100RB	0444
6F120	OEM
6FA10-D	0904
6FB050	1036
6FB1L	0319
6FB2L	1404
6FB4L	0468
6FB6L	0441
6FB100	1036
6FB200	1036
6FB400	1039
6FB600	1039
6FB800	OEM
6FB1000	OEM
6FC11	OEM
6FC12	0847
6FC13	0197
6FD12	0847
6FD13	0991
6FG11	2140
6FH05S	1557

DEVICE TYPE	REPL CODE
6FH1S	1557
6FH2S	1557
6FH3S	2140
6FH4S	2140
6FL10S02	OEM
6FL20S02	OEM
6FL40S02	5231
6FL50	OEM
6FL60	OEM
6FL60S02	OEM
6FR5	0979
6FR5-D	0979
6FR5A	0979
6FR10	0904
6FR10-D	0904
6FR10A	0904
6FR10B	0904
6FR15	0984
6FR15A	0984
6FR15B	0984
6FR20	0984
6FR20-D	0984
6FR20A	0984
6FR20B	0984
6FR30	0987
6FR30A	0987
6FR30B	0987
6FR40	0991
6FR40-D	0991
6FR40A	0991
6FR40B	0991
6FR50	0995
6FR50A	0995
6FR50B	0995
6FR58	0979
6FR60	0510
6FR60-D	0510
6FR60A	0510
6FR60B	0510
6FR70	1002
6FR70A	1002
6FR70B	1002
6FR80	1002
6FR80-D	1002
6FR80A	1002
6FR80B	1002
6FR90	0942
6FR90A	0942
6FR90B	0942
6FR100	0942
6FR100A	0942
6FR100B	0942
6FXF11	OEM
6FXF12	OEM
6G2	OEM
6G4	0196
6G4B41	0468
6G8	0015
6GA175D	0015
6GA1750	0015
6GC1	0196
6GC1BY1	3553
6GC11	OEM
6GC12	0197
6GD1	0479
6GD12	0847
6GG11	2140
6GX1	1073
6H65F	OEM
6H65FW	OEM
6H65H	OEM
6H65HW	OEM
6H75AE	OEM
6H100AE	OEM
6H150AE	OEM
6H200A	OEM
6H250AR	OEM
6H300AE	OEM
6H350A	OEM
6H400AE	OEM
6H450A	OEM
6H500A	OEM
6H600A	OEM
6H740AC	1908
6H750A	OEM
6HC11	OEM
6J4B41	0441
6J7L	OEM
6JB41	OEM
6JC11	OEM
6JC12	0204
6JG11	0706
6JUS3.24	OEM
6JUS3.24B	OEM
6JUS3.70A	OEM
6JUS3.70B	OEM
6JUS3.90A	OEM
6JUS3.90B	OEM
6JUS4.38A	OEM
6JUS4.38B	OEM
6JUS4.57A	OEM
6JUS4.57B	OEM
6KB7	OEM
6KC11	OEM
6KZ5.0	OEM
6KZ5.0A	OEM
6KZ5.0B	OEM
6KZ6.0	OEM
6KZ6.0A	OEM

DEVICE TYPE	REPL CODE
6KZ6.0B	OEM
6KZ6.5	OEM
6KZ6.5A	OEM
6KZ6.5B	OEM
6KZ7.0	OEM
6KZ7.0A	OEM
6KZ7.0B	OEM
6KZ7.5	OEM
6KZ7.5A	OEM
6KZ7.5B	OEM
6KZ8.0	OEM
6KZ8.0A	OEM
6KZ8.0B	OEM
6KZ8.5	OEM
6KZ8.5A	OEM
6KZ8.5B	OEM
6KZ9.0	OEM
6KZ9.0A	OEM
6KZ9.0B	OEM
6KZ10	OEM
6KZ10A	OEM
6KZ10B	OEM
6KZ11	OEM
6KZ11A	OEM
6KZ11B	OEM
6KZ12	OEM
6KZ12A	OEM
6KZ12B	OEM
6KZ13	OEM
6KZ13A	OEM
6KZ13B	OEM
6KZ14	OEM
6KZ14A	OEM
6KZ14B	OEM
6KZ15	OEM
6KZ15A	OEM
6KZ15B	OEM
6KZ16	OEM
6KZ16A	OEM
6KZ16B	OEM
6KZ17	OEM
6KZ17A	OEM
6KZ17B	OEM
6KZ18	OEM
6KZ18A	OEM
6KZ18B	OEM
6KZ20	OEM
6KZ20A	OEM
6KZ20B	OEM
6KZ22	OEM
6KZ22A	OEM
6KZ22B	OEM
6KZ24	OEM
6KZ24A	OEM
6KZ24B	OEM
6KZ26	OEM
6KZ26A	OEM
6KZ26B	OEM
6KZ28	OEM
6KZ28A	OEM
6KZ28B	OEM
6KZ30	OEM
6KZ30A	OEM
6KZ30B	OEM
6KZ33	OEM
6KZ33A	OEM
6KZ33B	OEM
6KZ36	OEM
6KZ36A	OEM
6KZ36B	OEM
6KZ40	OEM
6KZ40A	OEM
6KZ40B	OEM
6KZ43	OEM
6KZ43A	OEM
6KZ43B	OEM
6KZ45	OEM
6KZ45A	OEM
6KZ45B	OEM
6KZ48	OEM
6KZ48A	OEM
6KZ48B	OEM
6KZ51	OEM
6KZ51A	OEM
6KZ51B	OEM
6KZ54	OEM
6KZ54A	OEM
6KZ54B	OEM
6KZ58	OEM
6KZ58A	OEM
6KZ58B	OEM
6KZ60	OEM
6KZ60A	OEM
6KZ60B	OEM
6KZ64	OEM
6KZ64A	OEM
6KZ65B	OEM
6KZ70	OEM
6KZ70A	OEM
6KZ70B	OEM
6KZ75	OEM
6KZ75A	OEM
6KZ75B	OEM
6KZ78	OEM
6KZ78A	OEM
6KZ78B	OEM
6KZ85	OEM
6KZ85A	OEM
6KZ85B	OEM

DEVICE TYPE	REPL CODE
6KZ90	OEM
6KZ90A	OEM
6KZ90B	OEM
6KZ100	OEM
6KZ100A	OEM
6KZ100B	OEM
6KZ110	OEM
6KZ110A	OEM
6KZ110B	OEM
6L122	0004
6LC11	OEM
6LC12	0206
6LF11	1002
6M4	0015
6M10	0865
6M20	0865
6M30	1118
6M40	0847
6M60	0315
6M70	OEM
6M72	OEM
6M80	1124
6M100	0045
6M404-1	0015
6M404-2	0015
6M404-3	0015
6M404-4	0015
6M404-5	0015
6M404-6	0015
6M404-7	0015
6MA10	0865
6MA20	0865
6MA40	0847
6MA60	0267
6MA80	1111
6MA100	0280
6MC	0050
6MC11	OEM
6N02F1	OEM
6N05M1	OEM
6N10K1	OEM
6N126	OEM
6N127	OEM
6N128	OEM
6N129	OEM
6N130	OEM
6N131	OEM
6N132	OEM
6N133	OEM
6N134	OEM
6N135	5328
6N136	1281
6N136-020	1281
6N136-HP	1281
6N137	5325
6N138	5329
6N139	5329
6N140	OEM
6N-1039E-32	OEM
6NC11	OEM
6NC12	0583
6NF11	0942
6P05M1A	OEM
6P10K1	OEM
6P02F1-A	OEM
6QF11	OEM
6RH05S	1538
6RH1S	1557
6RH2S	1557
6RH3S	2140
6RH4S	3110
6RKB1	OEM
6RKB2	OEM
6RKB3	OEM
6RKB4	OEM
6RKB5	OEM
6RKB6	OEM
6RKB7	OEM
6RKB8	OEM
6RM36	OEM
6RM40	OEM
6RM42	OEM
6RM48	OEM
6RM56	OEM
6RM60	OEM
6RM64	OEM
6RM72	OEM
6RM80	OEM
6RM100	OEM
6RM120	OEM
6RM150	OEM
6RM200	OEM
6RM250	OEM
6RS1DH4	OEM
6RS1DH6	OEM
6RS5AJ1B1	OEM
6RS5SJ5B5	OEM
6RS5SP1B1	OEM
6RS5SP2B2	OEM
6RS5SP3B3	OEM
6RS5SP4B4	OEM
6RS5SP5B5	4337
6RS5SP6B6	OEM
6RS5SP7B7	OEM
6RS5SP8B8	OEM
6RS5SP9B9	OEM
6RS5SP10B10	4394
6RS5SP11B11	3226
6RS5SP12B12	3226

If replacement code is OEM, contact original manufacturer for replacement. 117

DEVICE TYPE	REPL CODE
6RS5SP13B13	3226
6RS5SP14B14	3226
6RS5SP15B15	OEM
6RS5SP16B16	1093
6RS5SP17B17	OEM
6RS5SP18B18	OEM
6RS5SP19B19	OEM
6RS5SP20B20	OEM
6RS5VP1B	OEM
6RS5VP2B	OEM
6RS5VP3B	OEM
6RS5VP4B	OEM
6RS5VP5B	OEM
6RS5VP6B	OEM
6RS5VP7B	OEM
6RS5VP8B	OEM
6RS5VP9B	OEM
6RS5VP10B	OEM
6RS5VP11B	OEM
6RS5VP12B	OEM
6RS5VP13B	OEM
6RS5VP14B	OEM
6RS5VP15B	OEM
6RS5VP16B	OEM
6RS5VP17B	OEM
6RS5VP18B	OEM
6RS5VP19B	OEM
6RS5VP20B	OEM
6RS5VP21B	OEM
6RS5VP22B	OEM
6RS5VP23B	OEM
6RS5VP24B	OEM
6RS6PH13BCJ1	1293
6RS6PH13BJJ1	1293
6RS6PH13BKJ1	1293
6RS6PH13BMJ1	1293
6RS7PH13BKJ1	1293
6RS7PH30BCB1	0769
6RS7PH130BCB1	0769
6RS17DH4	OEM
6RS17DH6	OEM
6RS18PH110BEB1	0769
6RS18PH110BHB1	0769
6RS18PH110BMB1	0769
6RS18PH110BNB1	0769
6RS20AP62B2	0246
6RS20AP181	OEM
6RS20PH6RGD1	OEM
6RS20SJ3BB	1364
6RS20SJ5B5	OEM
6RS20SP1B1	OEM
6RS20SP2B2	OEM
6RS20SP3B3	OEM
6RS20SP4B4	OEM
6RS20SP5B5	3381
6RS20SP6B6	OEM
6RS20SP7B7	OEM
6RS20SP8B8	OEM
6RS20SP10B10	OEM
6RS20SP11B11	OEM
6RS20SP12B12	OEM
6RS20SP13B13	OEM
6RS20SP14B14	OEM
6RS20SP15B15	OEM
6RS20SP16B16	OEM
6RS20SP17B17	OEM
6RS20SP18B18	OEM
6RS20SP19B19	OEM
6RS20SP20B20	OEM
6RS20VJ10B	0246
6RS20VP1B	OEM
6RS20VP2B	OEM
6RS20VP3B	OEM
6RS20VP4B	OEM
6RS20VP5B	OEM
6RS20VP6B	OEM
6RS20VP7B	OEM
6RS20VP8B	OEM
6RS20VP9B	OEM
6RS20VP10B	OEM
6RS20VP11B	OEM
6RS20VP12B	OEM
6RS20VP13B	OEM
6RS20VP14B	OEM
6RS20VP15B	OEM
6RS20VP16B	OEM
6RS20VP17B	OEM
6RS20VP18B	OEM
6RS20VP19B	OEM
6RS20VP20B	OEM
6RS20VP21B	OEM
6RS20VP22B	OEM
6RS20VP23B	OEM
6RS20VP24B	OEM
6RS36PH13BJJ1	1293
6RS36PH13BJK1	1293
6RS36PH13BKJ1	1293
6RS36PH13BLJ1	1293
6RS51GX12	0469
6RS56PHL3BKJ1	1293
6RW32DEB3	1337
6RW32FEB3	1337
6RW32HEB3	1894
6RW32KEB3	1894
6RW32MEB3	1894
6RW32PEB3	0193
6RW32REB3	0193
6RW56AC	OEM
6RW56BC	OEM

DEVICE TYPE	REPL CODE
6RW56CC	OEM
6RW56DC	OEM
6RW56EC	OEM
6RW56FC	OEM
6RW56GC	OEM
6RW56HC	OEM
6RW56KC	OEM
6RW59PY	OEM
6RW59RY	OEM
6RW59SY	OEM
6RW59UY	OEM
6RW59VY	OEM
6RW59WY	OEM
6RW62HY	0015
6RW71AY	OEM
6RW71B	OEM
6RW71BY	OEM
6RW71C	OEM
6RW71CY	OEM
6RW71D	OEM
6RW71DY	OEM
6RW71E	OEM
6RW71EY	OEM
6RW71F	OEM
6RW71FY	OEM
6RW71G	OEM
6RW71GY	OEM
6RW71H	OEM
6RW71HY	OEM
6RW71KY	OEM
6RW71MY	OEM
6RW71PY	OEM
6RW71RY	OEM
6Rs20SP9B9	OEM
6S	OEM
6S08	OEM
6S010	OEM
6S015	OEM
6S020	OEM
6S2	1659
6S4	1277
6S6	1282
6S8	1285
6S10	1285
6S18	OEM
6S28	OEM
6S38	OEM
6S48	OEM
6S58	OEM
6S68	OEM
6S110	OEM
6S115	OEM
6S120	OEM
6S210	OEM
6S215	OEM
6S220	OEM
6S310	OEM
6S315	OEM
6S320	OEM
6S410	OEM
6S415	OEM
6S420	OEM
6S510	OEM
6S515	OEM
6S520	OEM
6S610	OEM
6S615	OEM
6S620	OEM
6S10729A01	OEM
6S13759A01	OEM
6S13759A02	OEM
6S13761-A01	OEM
6S13761A01	OEM
6SB050	0319
6SB50	0319
6SB100	0319
6SB200	1404
6SB400	0468
6SB600	0441
6SB800	1412
6SB1000	2425
6SBF20	OEM
6SBF40	OEM
6SBF60	OEM
6SBF80	OEM
6SBF100	OEM
6SKB1	OEM
6SKB2	OEM
6SKB3	OEM
6SKB4	OEM
6SKB5	OEM
6SKB6	OEM
6SKB7	OEM
6SKB8	OEM
6SM1	OEM
6SM3	OEM
6SM6	OEM
6SM15	OEM
6SM25	OEM
6SM40	OEM
6SM55	OEM
6SM70	OEM
6SM100	OEM
6SM150	OEM
6SM200	OEM
6T06	4180
6T06A	OEM
6T06B	OEM
6T06C	OEM

DEVICE TYPE	REPL CODE
6T06HA	OEM
6T06HX	OEM
6T010	OEM
6T010A	OEM
6T010B	OEM
6T010C	OEM
6T010HA	OEM
6T010HX	OEM
6T015	OEM
6T015A	OEM
6T015B	OEM
6T015C	OEM
6T015HA	OEM
6T015HX	OEM
6T10T	OEM
6T16	4180
6T16A	OEM
6T16B	OEM
6T16C	OEM
6T16HA	OEM
6T16HX	OEM
6T20T	OEM
6T26	4180
6T26A	OEM
6T26B	OEM
6T26C	OEM
6T26HA	OEM
6T26HX	OEM
6T36	OEM
6T36A	OEM
6T36B	OEM
6T36C	OEM
6T36HA	OEM
6T36HX	OEM
6T40T	OEM
6T46	OEM
6T46A	OEM
6T46B	OEM
6T46C	OEM
6T46HA	OEM
6T46HX	OEM
6T56	OEM
6T56A	OEM
6T56B	OEM
6T56C	OEM
6T56HA	OEM
6T56HX	OEM
6T60T	OEM
6T66	OEM
6T66A	OEM
6T66B	OEM
6T66C	OEM
6T66HA	OEM
6T66HX	OEM
6T80T	OEM
6T100T	OEM
6T110	OEM
6T110A	OEM
6T110B	OEM
6T110C	OEM
6T110HA	OEM
6T110HX	OEM
6T115	OEM
6T115A	OEM
6T115B	OEM
6T115C	OEM
6T115HA	OEM
6T115HX	OEM
6T210	OEM
6T210A	OEM
6T210B	OEM
6T210C	OEM
6T210HA	OEM
6T210HX	OEM
6T215	OEM
6T215A	OEM
6T215B	OEM
6T215C	OEM
6T215HA	OEM
6T215HX	OEM
6T310	OEM
6T310A	OEM
6T310B	OEM
6T310C	OEM
6T310HA	OEM
6T310HX	OEM
6T315	OEM
6T315A	OEM
6T315B	OEM
6T315C	OEM
6T315HA	OEM
6T315HX	OEM
6T410	OEM
6T410A	OEM
6T410B	OEM
6T410C	OEM
6T410HA	OEM
6T410HX	OEM
6T415	OEM
6T415A	OEM
6T415B	OEM
6T415C	OEM
6T415HA	OEM
6T415HX	OEM
6T510	OEM
6T510A	OEM
6T510B	OEM
6T510C	OEM
6T510HA	OEM

DEVICE TYPE	REPL CODE
6T510HX	OEM
6T515	OEM
6T515A	OEM
6T515B	OEM
6T515C	OEM
6T515HA	OEM
6T515HX	OEM
6T610	OEM
6T610A	OEM
6T610B	OEM
6T610C	OEM
6T610HA	OEM
6T610HX	OEM
6T615	OEM
6T615A	OEM
6T615B	OEM
6T615C	OEM
6T615HA	OEM
6T615HX	OEM
6TC10	OEM
6TC20	OEM
6TC30	OEM
6TC40	OEM
6TC50	OEM
6TC60	OEM
6TC70	OEM
6TC80	OEM
6TC90	OEM
6TC100	OEM
6TC110	OEM
6TC120	OEM
6TCA10	OEM
6TCA20	OEM
6TCA30	OEM
6TCA40	OEM
6TCA50	OEM
6TCA60	OEM
6TCA70	OEM
6TCA80	OEM
6TCA90	OEM
6TCA100	OEM
6TCA110	OEM
6TCA120	OEM
6TW1	OEM
6TW2	OEM
6TW3	OEM
6TW4	OEM
6TW5	OEM
6TW6	OEM
6U4	OEM
6U8	OEM
6U12	OEM
6V23	OEM
6V-200	0157
6V200	0157
6V203	OEM
6V211	OEM
6V221	OEM
6W52	OEM
6W70	OEM
6W73	OEM
6W411	OEM
6W411V	OEM
6WM1	OEM
6WM2	OEM
6WM4	OEM
6WM6	OEM
6WM10	OEM
6WM12	OEM
6X2C	OEM
6X97047A01	0016
6X97047A02	0004
6X97174A01	0133
6X97174XA08	0133
6Z0345	OEM
6.2B	0466
6.2B1	0091
6.2B1(1WATT)	0631
6.2B2	0466
6.2B3	0466
6.2EB3	0466
6.2N1	0466
6.2N2	0466
6.2Y	0466
6.2Z	0466
6.8	0062
6.8B	0062
6.8B1	0062
6.8B2	0062
6.8B2(ZENER)	3335
6.8B2(ZENER)	0062
6.8B3	0062
6.8EB1	0062
6.8EB3	0062
6.8EN2	0062
6.8L	OEM
6.8M	OEM
6.8N2	0062
6.8SC20	OEM
6.8V	0062
6.8X	0062
6.8Y	0062
6.8Z	0062
7	OEM
7-0002	0015
7-0003	0276
7-0004	0015
7-0005	0143
7-0006	0143

DEVICE TYPE	REPL CODE
7-0007	0063
7-0008	0015
7-0009	0433
7-0013	0133
7-0014	0037
7-0015	0016
7-1(SARKES)	0016
7-1(STANDEL)	0160
7-2	0160
7-2(SARKES)	0016
7-2(STANDEL)	3004
7-3(SARKES)	0016
7-3(STANDEL)	0126
7-4	0144
7-4(SARKES)	0016
7-4(STANDEL)	0126
7-6	0144
7-6(SARKES)	0079
7-7	0144
7-7(SARKES)	0016
7-8	0144
7-8(SARKES)	0016
7-8(STANDEL)	0293
7-9	0007
7-9(SARKES)	0007
7-10	0007
7-10(SARKES)	0007
7-11(SARKES)	0007
7-12	0103
7-12(STANDEL)	0103
7-13	0103
7-13(STANDEL)	0103
7-14A	0126
7-15(SARKES)	0016
7-15(STANDEL)	0071
7-16	0127
7-16(SARKES)	0016
7-17	0016
7-17(SARKES)	0016
7-18(SARKES)	0016
7-19	0142
7-19(SARKES)	0016
7-19(STANDEL)	0142
7-20	0127
7-20(SARKES)	0016
7-21(SARKES)	0007
7-22	0127
7-22(SARKES)	0007
7-23	0127
7-23(SARKES)	0007
7-24(SARKES)	0007
7-25(SARKES)	0007
7-26	0127
7-27	OEM
7-28	0007
7-28(STANDEL)	0899
7-29	0030
7-29(STANDEL)	0178
7-36	0127
7-40	0212
7-43	0127
7-44	0144
7-45	0127
7-59-001/3477	0143
7-59-005/3477	0276
7-59-0013477	0143
7-59-0053477	0276
7-59-010/3477	0211
7-59-019/3477	0079
7-59-020/3477	0079
7-59-021/3477	0079
7-59-022/3477	0079
7-59-023/3477	0079
7-59-024/3477	0079
7-59-029/3477	0279
7-59-060/3477	0211
7-59-068	0016
7-59-0103477	0164
7-59-0193477	0144
7-59-0203477	0144
7-59-0213477	0144
7-59-0223477	0144
7-59-0233477	0144
7-59-0243477	0016
7-59-0293477	0004
7-59-0603477	0004
7-117-02	0349
7-759-651-35	0872
7-5806	0720
7-5851	0147
7-5851-02	0147
7-5851V	0147
7-5853	2337
7-5853A	1403
7-5853B	1403
7-6006-00	0947
7-25806-01	0720
7-73004-02	0841
7-73004-03	0841
7-73004-04	0841
7-73004-1	0841
7-466201	0130
7-1585122	0147
7-2580504	1478
7-2585301-01	2337
7-2585301-02	1403
7-2585303	1403
7A1/18	OEM
7A1/52	OEM

DEVICE TYPE	REPL CODE
7A2	0062
7A2/18	OEM
7A2/52	OEM
7A5/18	OEM
7A5/52	OEM
7A12	OEM
7A12/18	OEM
7A13	OEM
7A13/18	OEM
7A14	OEM
7A14/18	OEM
7A15	OEM
7A15/18	OEM
7A16	OEM
7A16/18	OEM
7A22	OEM
7A22/18	OEM
7A23	OEM
7A23/18	OEM
7A24	OEM
7A24/18	OEM
7A25	OEM
7A25/18	OEM
7A26	OEM
7A26/18	OEM
7A30	0127
7A30(GE)	0086
7A30(SHERWOOD)	0016
7A31	0127
7A31(GE)	0086
7A31(SHERWOOD)	0016
7A32	0127
7A32(GE)	0086
7A32(SHERWOOD)	0086
7A35	0590
7A35(GE)	0086
7A52	OEM
7A52/18	OEM
7A53	OEM
7A53/18	OEM
7A54	OEM
7A54/18	OEM
7A55	OEM
7A55/18	OEM
7A56	OEM
7A56/18	OEM
7A995	0086
7A995(GE)	0086
7A995(SHERWOOD)	0086
7A1011	0086
7A1011(GE)	0086
7A1011(SHERWOOD)	0086
7AAC299M	OEM
7B1	0142
7B1(2%)	OEM
7B1(ZENER)	OEM
7B1/18	OEM
7B1/52	OEM
7B2	0142
7B2(ZENER)	0062
7B2/18	OEM
7B2/52	OEM
7B3	OEM
7B-3B1	0299
7B4	OEM
7B5/18	OEM
7B5/52	OEM
7B12	OEM
7B12/18	OEM
7B13	0142
7B13/18	OEM
7B14	OEM
7B14/18	OEM
7B15	OEM
7B15/18	OEM
7B16	OEM
7B16/18	OEM
7B20T	OEM
7B22	OEM
7B22/18	OEM
7B23	OEM
7B23/18	OEM
7B24	OEM
7B24/18	OEM
7B25	OEM
7B25/18	OEM
7B26	OEM
7B26/18	OEM
7B33	0142
7B34	0142
7B40T	OEM
7B52	OEM
7B52/18	OEM
7B53	OEM
7B53/18	OEM
7B54	OEM
7B54/18	OEM
7B55	OEM
7B55/18	OEM
7B56	OEM
7B56/18	OEM
7B60T	OEM
7B80T	OEM
7BM10	OEM
7BM10A	OEM
7BT13ZRK	OEM
7BT25ZYK	OEM
7C05/18	OEM
7C05/52	OEM

DEVICE TYPE	REPL CODE
7C054	OEM
7C054/18	OEM
7C055	OEM
7C055/18	OEM
7C056	OEM
7C056/18	OEM
7C057	OEM
7C057/18	OEM
7C1	0142
7C1(ZENER)	0077
7C1/18	OEM
7C1/52	OEM
7C2	0142
7C2/18	OEM
7C2/52	OEM
7C3	0142
7C4	OEM
7C13	0590
7C14	OEM
7C14/18	OEM
7C15	OEM
7C15/18	OEM
7C16	OEM
7C16/18	OEM
7C17	OEM
7C17/18	OEM
7C24	OEM
7C24/18	OEM
7C25	OEM
7C25/18	OEM
7C26	OEM
7C26/18	OEM
7C27	OEM
7C27/18	OEM
7CM8	OEM
7D	0015
7D1	0142
7D2	0142
7D3	0142
7D4	OEM
7D8	OEM
7D10	OEM
7D12	OEM
7D13	0590
7D15	OEM
7D33	0142
7D34	0142
7D75A	OEM
7D150A	OEM
7D210	0071
7D210A	0071
7D300A	OEM
7E1	0142
7E2	0142
7E3	0142
7E4	OEM
7E13	0590
7E17	OEM
7E34A	OEM
7E45	OEM
7E90	OEM
7E115	OEM
7EM11	OEM
7E.5	OEM
7F13	0590
7G1	0142
7G2	0142
7G3	0142
7G4	0142
7G13	0590
7G33	OEM
7G34	OEM
7GM7	OEM
7GM10	OEM
7H75AE	OEM
7H150AE	OEM
7H300AE	OEM
7H450A	OEM
7JUS3.78A	OEM
7JUS3.78B	OEM
7JUS4.31A	OEM
7JUS4.31B	OEM
7JUS4.55A	OEM
7JUS4.55B	OEM
7JUS5.11A	OEM
7JUS5.11B	OEM
7JUS5.33A	OEM
7JUS5.33B	OEM
7K705M	0196
7L	OEM
7L6-0105	0178
7L6-0444-1	4229
7L6-0495-14	0015
7L6-0531-1	4229
7L6-0531-2	4229
7L6-0531-19	4033
7L6-0592-1	4229
7L6-0592-1(NPN)	OEM
7L6-0592-1(PNP)	OEM
7MA60	0015
7OR2S	0145
7R0/18	OEM
7R1/18	OEM
7R1/52	OEM
7R2/4	OEM
7R2/18	OEM
7R2/66	OEM
7R2B	OEM
7R2S	OEM

If replacement code is OEM, contact original manufacturer for replacement.

DEVICE TYPE	REPL CODE
7R3/4	OEM
7R3/66	OEM
7R3B	OEM
7R3S	OEM
7R4/3	OEM
7R4/3C	OEM
7R4/4	OEM
7R4/59	OEM
7R4C	OEM
7R4S	OEM
7R5/3	OEM
7R5/3D	OEM
7R5/5	OEM
7R5/61	OEM
7R5C	OEM
7R5S	OEM
7R6/3	OEM
7R6/3D	OEM
7R6/5	OEM
7R6/61	OEM
7R6C	OEM
7R6S	OEM
7R7/3	OEM
7R7/3D	OEM
7R7/5	OEM
7R7/61	OEM
7R7CD	OEM
7R7S	OEM
7R8/3	OEM
7R8/3D	OEM
7R8/5	OEM
7R8/63	OEM
7R8CD	OEM
7R8S	OEM
7R52	OEM
7RE52	OEM
7RO/18	OEM
7S133DC	OEM
7SA15	0050
7SB33E	0211
7TB1	2430
7TB1-CE00	OEM
7TB1-CH00	OEM
7TB1-EE00	OEM
7TB1-EH00	OEM
7TB1-GE00	OEM
7TB1-JE00	OEM
7TB2	0240
7TB2-CE00	OEM
7TB2-CH00	OEM
7TB2-EE00	OEM
7TB2-EH00	OEM
7TB2-GE00	OEM
7TB2-GH00	OEM
7TB2-JE00	OEM
7TB3	2635
7TB3-CE00	OEM
7TB3-CH00	OEM
7TB3-EE00	OEM
7TB3-EH00	OEM
7TB3-GE00	OEM
7TB3-JE00	OEM
7TB4	0742
7TB4-CE00	OEM
7TB4-CH00	OEM
7TB4-EE00	OEM
7TB4-EH00	OEM
7TB4-GE00	OEM
7TB4-GH00	OEM
7TB4-JE00	OEM
7TB5	3260
7TB5-CE00	OEM
7TB5-CH00	OEM
7TB5-EE00	OEM
7TB5-EH00	OEM
7TB5-GE00	OEM
7TB5-GH00	OEM
7TB5-JE00	OEM
7TB6	0682
7TB6-CE00	OEM
7TB6-CH00	OEM
7TB6-EE00	OEM
7TB6-EH00	OEM
7TB6-GE00	OEM
7TB6-GH00	OEM
7TB6-JE00	OEM
7TB7	OEM
7TB7-CE00	OEM
7TB7-CH00	OEM
7TB7-EE00	OEM
7TB7-EH00	OEM
7TB7-GE00	OEM
7TB7-GH00	OEM
7TB8	0761
7TB8-CE00	OEM
7TB8-CH00	OEM
7TB8-EE00	OEM
7TB8-EH00	OEM
7TB8-GE00	OEM
7TB8-GH00	OEM
7TB8-JE00	OEM
7TCRA	OEM
7TCRB	OEM
7TCRC	OEM
7TCRD	OEM
7TCRE	OEM
7TCRF	OEM
7TCRG	OEM
7TCRH	OEM

DEVICE TYPE	REPL CODE
7TCRI	OEM
7TCRJ	OEM
7TCRK	OEM
7TCRL	OEM
7UV10	OEM
7V10T	OEM
7V204	OEM
7V205	OEM
7V224	OEM
7V242	OEM
7V254	OEM
7V272	OEM
7V273	OEM
7V312	OEM
7VM705M	0196
7W412	OEM
7W412V	OEM
7XF	OEM
7Z3	OEM
7.5B	0077
7.5B1	0062
7.5B2	0077
7.5JB2	0077
8-0001300	0071
8-0001400	0071
8-0024-1	0144
8-0024-2	0144
8-0024-3	0198
8-0060	0279
8-0062	0211
8-00243	0016
8-005202	0016
8-0050100	0016
8-0050300	0208
8-0050400	0050
8-0050500	0050
8-0050600	0208
8-0050700	0160
8-0051500	0016
8-0051600	0126
8-0052102	0016
8-0052302	0079
8-0052402	0103
8-0052600	0016
8-0052700	0126
8-0052800	0208
8-0053001	0016
8-0053300	0086
8-0053400	0016
8-0053600	0144
8-0053702	1506
8-0104900	0050
8-0105200	0050
8-0105300	0050
8-0205400	0004
8-0205600	0004
8-0222631U	0004
8-0236400	0004
8-0236430	0004
8-0243900	0004
8-0318250	0016
8-0337390	0016
8-0338030	0144
8-0338040	0144
8-0339430	0144
8-0339440	0144
8-0383840	0144
8-0383930	0144
8-0383940	0016
8-0389910	0016
8-0389930	0016
8-0414120	0103
8-0414130	0103
8-0421980	0016
8-1	0178
8-1(BENDIX)	0178
8-4(BENDIX)	0016
8-9V	0244
8-22	0015
8-25	0015
8-38	0015
8-179-918-77	0017
8-543-640-00	OEM
8-619-030-007	0004
8-619-030-008	0004
8-619-030-009	0004
8-619-030-011	0143
8-619-030-012	0015
8-619-030-014	0004
8-619-030-015	0222
8-619-030-016	0004
8-619-030-017	0004
8-639-001-095	0015
8-697-020-567	0004
8-697-020-568	0004
8-697-020-569	0004
8-697-020-570	0016
8-697-020-571	0143
8-709-801-71	0102
8-710-222-21	0015
8-710-815-55	0133
8-712-540-00	OEM
8-712-600-00	0143
8-713-300-57	0039
8-719-000-04	2189
8-719-000-05	0319
8-719-000-08	OEM
8-719-000-24	0058
8-719-000-28	0403

DEVICE TYPE	REPL CODE
8-719-022-97	OEM
8-719-026-11	0143
8-719-027-43	OEM
8-719-028-72	OEM
8-719-031-68	OEM
8-719-031-80	OEM
8-719-032-13	OEM
8-719-100-06	1970
8-719-100-23	0274
8-719-100-30	0041
8-719-100-35	0253
8-719-100-37	0466
8-719-100-38	0466
8-719-100-43	0077
8-719-100-44	0077
8-719-100-55	0057
8-719-100-64	0052
8-719-100-65	0052
8-719-100-68	0053
8-719-100-72	0681
8-719-100-76	0371
8-719-100-80	0666
8-719-101-03	0166
8-719-101-04	0166
8-719-101-08	OEM
8-719-101-14	0010
8-719-101-38	0372
8-719-101-39	0372
8-719-101-40	0036
8-719-101-58	0253
8-719-101-67	0077
8-719-102-47	0755
8-719-102-57	0372
8-719-102-58	0372
8-719-102-60	0036
8-719-102-61	0036
8-719-102-64	0140
8-719-102-67	0041
8-719-102-68	0041
8-719-102-69	0041
8-719-102-70	0253
8-719-102-71	0253
8-719-102-72	0253
8-719-102-73	0466
8-719-102-74	0466
8-719-102-76	0062
8-719-102-88	0057
8-719-102-89	0064
8-719-102-90	0064
8-719-102-91	0064
8-719-102-99	0053
8-719-103-06	0053
8-719-103-09	0681
8-719-103-11	0681
8-719-103-16	0416
8-719-105-51	OEM
8-719-105-82	OEM
8-719-105-91	OEM
8-719-106-07	0010
8-719-106-16	OEM
8-719-106-34	OEM
8-719-106-43	OEM
8-719-106-63	OEM
8-719-106-70	OEM
8-719-107-16	OEM
8-719-107-82	OEM
8-719-108-32	0253
8-719-109-68	0372
8-719-109-69	0372
8-719-109-71	OEM
8-719-109-72	0036
8-719-109-74	0274
8-719-109-81	0140
8-719-109-84	0041
8-719-109-85	0041
8-719-109-86	0582
8-719-109-88	0253
8-719-109-89	0253
8-719-109-90	0253
8-719-109-92	0466
8-719-109-93	0466
8-719-109-96	0292
8-719-109-97	0062
8-719-109-98	0062
8-719-110-06	OEM
8-719-110-09	0165
8-719-110-12	OEM
8-719-110-13	0057
8-719-110-14	OEM
8-719-110-16	0064
8-719-110-17	0064
8-719-110-18	0064
8-719-110-26	0064
8-719-110-31	0052
8-719-110-32	OEM
8-719-110-33	0052
8-719-110-34	0053
8-719-110-35	OEM
8-719-110-36	0053
8-719-110-48	0210
8-719-110-49	0371
8-719-110-52	0666
8-719-110-53	0666
8-719-110-61	0489
8-719-110-66	0709
8-719-110-72	0195
8-719-110-76	OEM
8-719-110-78	0166
8-719-110-90	OEM

DEVICE TYPE	REPL CODE
8-719-111-07	0181
8-719-112-01	0052
8-719-112-07	0052
8-719-112-24	0052
8-719-112-25	0052
8-719-113-07	0053
8-719-113-21	0053
8-719-113-25	0053
8-719-113-63	0678
8-719-114-34	OEM
8-719-119-97	OEM
8-719-120-53	OEM
8-719-121-98	0911
8-719-122-00	0120
8-719-122-03	0120
8-719-122-07	0700
8-719-123-25	OEM
8-719-124-07	0489
8-719-124-08	0398
8-719-127-07	0755
8-719-127-25	0450
8-719-130-07	0289
8-719-130-25	0195
8-719-133-07	0296
8-719-136-07	0188
8-719-139-07	0036
8-719-143-07	0274
8-719-151-07	0041
8-719-151-77	0041
8-719-156-07	0253
8-719-156-23	0253
8-719-156-25	0253
8-719-156-27	0253
8-719-156-73	OEM
8-719-158-39	OEM
8-719-160-24	0162
8-719-160-44	0057
8-719-162-07	0466
8-719-168-07	0062
8-719-168-08	OEM
8-719-168-77	0062
8-719-175-07	0077
8-719-175-26	0077
8-719-182-07	0165
8-719-182-25	0165
8-719-190-00	0489
8-719-191-81	2911
8-719-193-03	OEM
8-719-200-01	0015
8-719-200-02	0015
8-719-200-2	0015
8-719-200-10	0015
8-719-205-10	0015
8-719-210-10	0071
8-719-300-07	0441
8-719-300-09	1227
8-719-300-33	0282
8-719-300-38	0023
8-719-300-45	0023
8-719-300-59	1227
8-719-300-65	0017
8-719-300-70	0102
8-719-300-76	0023
8-719-300-91	0604
8-719-301-14	0344
8-719-301-18	0071
8-719-301-45	2520
8-719-301-64	0102
8-719-302-00	0023
8-719-302-06	0023
8-719-302-43	0017
8-719-302-44	0023
8-719-303-21	0023
8-719-304-63	0071
8-719-305-07	1039
8-719-305-15	0158
8-719-311-23	OEM
8-719-311-31	0023
8-719-311-72	1039
8-719-311-87	OEM
8-719-311-89	OEM
8-719-312-10	0031
8-719-312-61	0023
8-719-312-62	0023
8-719-312-71	OEM
8-719-312-72	OEM
8-719-320-11	0102
8-719-320-31	0102
8-719-331-10	0023
8-719-400-18	0901
8-719-404-46	OEM
8-719-422-21	0143
8-719-500-01	0241
8-719-500-04	4501
8-719-500-26	OEM
8-719-500-34	0199
8-719-500-41	1227
8-719-500-67	1227
8-719-500-69	OEM
8-719-501-34	1009
8-719-502-20	1404
8-719-503-06	0732
8-719-503-40	0087
8-719-504-10	0319
8-719-510-02	OEM
8-719-510-09	OEM
8-719-510-26	1082
8-719-510-48	OEM
8-719-510-53	OEM

DEVICE TYPE	REPL CODE
8-719-510-63	OEM
8-719-510-64	OEM
8-719-511-10	0276
8-719-511-20	0287
8-719-511-40	0293
8-719-512-20	2219
8-719-521-10	0276
8-719-549-41	0017
8-719-713-93	0715
8-719-768-71	0715
8-719-800-34	0199
8-719-800-43	1281
8-719-800-69	OEM
8-719-800-83	0311
8-719-801-02	OEM
8-719-801-35	OEM
8-719-801-70	0102
8-719-801-71	0102
8-719-802-30	0133
8-719-803-06	OEM
8-719-810-20	OEM
8-719-812-41	2990
8-719-812-43	0835
8-719-815-55	0133
8-719-815-80	0124
8-719-815-85	0124
8-719-820-13	OEM
8-719-900-02	0015
8-719-900-26	1208
8-719-900-63	0023
8-719-900-93	0023
8-719-900-95	0023
8-719-901-02	0080
8-719-901-03	0023
8-719-901-09	0023
8-719-901-13	0015
8-719-901-19	0023
8-719-901-21	0120
8-719-901-24	0095
8-719-901-31	OEM
8-719-901-39	0102
8-719-901-58	0031
8-719-901-83	0133
8-719-901-92	0023
8-719-901-93	0023
8-719-901-94	0023
8-719-901-95	0023
8-719-901-96	OEM
8-719-901-98	0311
8-719-902-85	0031
8-719-903-06	3559
8-719-903-09	0023
8-719-903-29	0023
8-719-906-15	0102
8-719-906-24	0398
8-719-907-30	0031
8-719-907-40	0023
8-719-907-50	OEM
8-719-908-03	0087
8-719-908-06	OEM
8-719-911-06	3144
8-719-911-19	0124
8-719-911-53	0959
8-719-911-54	0535
8-719-911-55	0535
8-719-912-54	0087
8-719-918-77	0017
8-719-920-04	0023
8-719-920-62	OEM
8-719-921-53	0031
8-719-923-64	3643
8-719-923-76	0124
8-719-924-06	0023
8-719-924-73	0133
8-719-925-06	0023
8-719-926-06	0023
8-719-927-74	1158
8-719-928-04	0031
8-719-928-08	0102
8-719-930-11	0313
8-719-930-12	0137
8-719-931-05	0162
8-719-931-06	0298
8-719-931-07	0644
8-719-931-08	0244
8-719-931-10	0170
8-719-931-13	0361
8-719-933-13	0031
8-719-935-08	0077
8-719-936-12	0999
8-719-936-82	OEM
8-719-936-83	0087
8-719-936-84	OEM
8-719-936-85	0023
8-719-936-96	1158
8-719-937-08	0165
8-719-937-10	0064
8-719-938-36	0023
8-719-938-40	0604
8-719-938-68	OEM
8-719-941-13	0087
8-719-941-17	OEM
8-719-941-74	1082
8-719-945-80	0344
8-719-945-84	OEM
8-719-945-91	0039
8-719-948-59	0541
8-719-950-10	OEM
8-719-951-28	OEM

DEVICE TYPE	REPL CODE
8-719-961-03	0023
8-719-971-20	3833
8-719-974-81	0623
8-719-976-64	OEM
8-719-979-85	0031
8-719-980-78	OEM
8-719-981-00	0031
8-719-981-01	0023
8-719-982-04	2520
8-719-987-06	OEM
8-719-988-55	OEM
8-719-988-57	2077
8-719-991-18	OEM
8-720-177-54	2019
8-721-323-00	0004
8-722-381-20	3672
8-722-383	3672
8-722-923-00	0617
8-723-302-00	1747
8-723-303	3308
8-723-303-03	1747
8-723-303-20	1747
8-723-304-00	1747
8-723-650	0038
8-724-034-00	0155
8-724-375-01	0155
8-724-733-30	0233
8-725-412-00	0264
8-725-413-00	0309
8-725-800-00	0224
8-725-923-00	0224
8-726-357-10	0284
8-726-368-10	0155
8-726-388-00	0076
8-727-225-00	OEM
8-727-632-00	0378
8-727-786-00	0006
8-727-786-01	0037
8-729-016-15	OEM
8-729-016-32	OEM
8-729-019-01	OEM
8-729-019-51	OEM
8-729-100-09	2888
8-729-100-66	0719
8-729-101-13	0312
8-729-101-31	0312
8-729-103-41	0527
8-729-103-42	0527
8-729-103-43	0527
8-729-104-33	1274
8-729-107-26	0236
8-729-107-78	OEM
8-729-107-84	OEM
8-729-108-53	0249
8-729-109-53	0830
8-729-113-32	0527
8-729-115-10	1747
8-729-115-30	1747
8-729-116-42	3195
8-729-117-43	2019
8-729-117-54	3580
8-729-117-63	0191
8-729-118-76	2636
8-729-119-76	3580
8-729-119-78	0249
8-729-119-79	4200
8-729-119-80	0275
8-729-120-28	0719
8-729-122-01	0520
8-729-122-03	0520
8-729-122-12	0520
8-729-133-40	2253
8-729-133-53	0723
8-729-137-32	0723
8-729-138-72	0367
8-729-138-82	0367
8-729-140-50	0261
8-729-140-96	2019
8-729-140-97	0527
8-729-140-98	0018
8-729-141-89	0236
8-729-157-11	1967
8-729-167-42	1060
8-729-168-82	0275
8-729-169-01	0558
8-729-169-02	OEM
8-729-173-37	0006
8-729-177-22	0455
8-729-177-32	0018
8-729-177-33	0018
8-729-177-41	2019
8-729-177-42	2019
8-729-177-43	2019
8-729-178-54	0249
8-729-178-56	0249
8-729-188-23	0161
8-729-191-81	0477
8-729-194-58	0076
8-729-198-52	3658
8-729-200-02	0015
8-729-200-17	0338
8-729-200-33	0042
8-729-201-32	1514
8-729-201-62	2171
8-729-201-78	3096
8-729-201-96	0284
8-729-201-98	1533
8-729-202-03	0236
8-729-202-53	1533

DEVICE TYPE	REPL CODE
8-729-202-58	0551
8-729-203-80	0551
8-729-204-82	0013
8-729-204-83	0013
8-729-207-35	2959
8-729-208-39	OEM
8-729-208-72	OEM
8-729-209-03	0261
8-729-212-02	0860
8-729-212-12	0261
8-729-213-01	0261
8-729-213-02	0261
8-729-213-11	0261
8-729-213-12	0261
8-729-216-22	1731
8-729-230-49	0719
8-729-231-60	3096
8-729-231-95	2116
8-729-238-32	1553
8-729-245-83	0076
8-729-245-84	0076
8-729-255-12	0261
8-729-265-52	0018
8-729-266-93	0155
8-729-271-02	0155
8-729-271-32	2316
8-729-286-90	0055
8-729-287-00	0055
8-729-287-10	0055
8-729-288-02	0456
8-729-300-90	3326
8-729-301-11	3437
8-729-301-46	0261
8-729-301-56	3437
8-729-304-00	1747
8-729-304-50	3326
8-729-304-92	0520
8-729-305-01	3326
8-729-305-42	1270
8-729-306-92	0558
8-729-307-62	0419
8-729-307-82	0388
8-729-308-92	2539
8-729-309-06	0525
8-729-309-08	0525
8-729-309-36	0643
8-729-311-42	0270
8-729-313-42	0236
8-729-313-82	0388
8-729-316-12	0042
8-729-316-16	0042
8-729-317-12	1298
8-729-320-61	1492
8-729-322-78	0283
8-729-323-82	0388
8-729-326-11	0275
8-729-326-82	1900
8-729-331-53	0419
8-729-336-11	1638
8-729-341-34	0065
8-729-341-93	2276
8-729-345-42	0220
8-729-348-47	0688
8-729-364-12	0284
8-729-372-31	1077
8-729-372-52	0155
8-729-374-02	0472
8-729-375-01	0155
8-729-377-12	1359
8-729-378-82	0018
8-729-378-84	0018
8-729-378-91	2539
8-729-378-92	2539
8-729-378-93	2539
8-729-382-64	0419
8-729-383-03	0194
8-729-386-12	1638
8-729-390-06	0055
8-729-395-70	0055
8-729-395-73	0055
8-729-398-09	0055
8-729-400-81	0060
8-729-400-82	0060
8-729-420-00	1642
8-729-422-27	0719
8-729-422-36	OEM
8-729-423-35	2926
8-729-423-37	2926
8-729-423-44	0013
8-729-424-00	1056
8-729-432-44	OEM
8-729-447-53	0004
8-729-468-43	0527
8-729-600-08	1747
8-729-600-12	OEM
8-729-600-21	1741
8-729-600-27	2064
8-729-600-28	2064
8-729-609-06	0076
8-729-612-77	0037
8-729-617-77	0037
8-729-660-37	0003
8-729-663-47	0076
8-729-665-47	0155
8-729-671-13	0364
8-729-671-14	0364
8-729-671-15	0364
8-729-800-03	1533
8-729-800-87	1533

If replacement code is OEM, contact original manufacturer for replacement.

119

DEVICE TYPE	REPL CODE
8-729-801-22	0284
8-729-801-45	OEM
8-729-801-71	1533
8-729-801-76	1533
8-729-802-50	1533
8-729-803-04	2195
8-729-803-81	0261
8-729-806-84	0127
8-729-809-29	1157
8-729-809-41	2116
8-729-820-50	0688
8-729-821-87	2116
8-729-822-65	3454
8-729-831-33	0042
8-729-880-82	0006
8-729-883-91	0076
8-729-883-92	0151
8-729-900-36	0881
8-729-900-61	4109
8-729-900-65	4067
8-729-900-89	0892
8-729-901-01	3439
8-729-901-04	1881
8-729-902-07	OEM
8-729-902-10	2985
8-729-902-11	1132
8-729-903-30	OEM
8-729-903-80	4970
8-729-905-52	0009
8-729-906-24	5212
8-729-906-38	0275
8-729-906-39	0275
8-729-920-71	1731
8-729-920-74	0719
8-729-920-90	0723
8-729-920-92	OEM
8-729-922-68	0013
8-729-922-69	2926
8-729-924-82	OEM
8-729-924-83	1157
8-729-924-86	OEM
8-729-924-90	OEM
8-729-926-73	OEM
8-729-927-12	1492
8-729-927-22	OEM
8-729-931-43	0723
8-729-965-22	2452
8-729-967-32	0009
8-729-978-62	0037
8-729-982-22	4043
8-729-993-72	2464
8-729-37501	0155
8-739-100-00	0367
8-739-178-54	OEM
8-741-013-00	OEM
8-741-013-10	OEM
8-741-100-62	OEM
8-741-101-60	OEM
8-741-103-00	OEM
8-741-103-80	OEM
8-741-103-90	OEM
8-741-104-10	OEM
8-741-104-30	OEM
8-741-104-40	OEM
8-741-104-41	OEM
8-741-104-50	OEM
8-741-104-60	OEM
8-741-104-70	OEM
8-741-108-30	OEM
8-741-108-40	OEM
8-741-108-60	OEM
8-741-108-70	OEM
8-741-108-80	OEM
8-741-109-00	OEM
8-741-109-10	OEM
8-741-109-20	OEM
8-741-109-30	OEM
8-741-109-40	OEM
8-741-109-50	OEM
8-741-115-30	OEM
8-741-131-70	OEM
8-741-132-30	OEM
8-741-135-70	OEM
8-741-138-70	OEM
8-741-139-80	OEM
8-741-148-33	OEM
8-741-156-80	OEM
8-741-618-11	OEM
8-741-637-11	OEM
8-742-230	OEM
8-743-350-00	OEM
8-743-420-00	OEM
8-743-580-00	OEM
8-743-600-00	OEM
8-743-610-00	OEM
8-743-640-00	OEM
8-743-690-00	OEM
8-743-760-00	OEM
8-743-780-00	OEM
8-743-790-00	OEM
8-743-800-00	OEM
8-743-830-00	OEM
8-743-840-00	OEM
8-743-901-00	OEM
8-743-903-00	OEM
8-743-904-00	OEM
8-743-912-00	OEM
8-743-921-00	OEM
8-743-945-10	OEM

DEVICE TYPE	REPL CODE
8-743-946-10	OEM
8-743-947-20	OEM
8-743-948-10	OEM
8-743-949-00	OEM
8-743-950-10	OEM
8-743-951-20	OEM
8-743-952-00	OEM
8-743-953-00	OEM
8-743-954-00	OEM
8-743-955-00	OEM
8-743-956-10	OEM
8-743-958-10	OEM
8-743-959-10	OEM
8-743-960-00	OEM
8-743-969-10	OEM
8-743-970-10	OEM
8-743-971-00	OEM
8-743-972-00	OEM
8-743-973-00	OEM
8-743-976-00	OEM
8-743-977-00	OEM
8-743-978-00	OEM
8-743-980-00	OEM
8-743-981-00	OEM
8-743-982-10	OEM
8-743-982-20	OEM
8-743-983-00	OEM
8-743-984-00	OEM
8-743-988-00	OEM
8-743-999-00	OEM
8-743-999-10	OEM
8-749-20-81	OEM
8-749-900-15	5183
8-749-900-36	OEM
8-749-900-80	OEM
8-749-901-35	3857
8-749-901-43	OEM
8-749-920-57	OEM
8-749-920-61	OEM
8-749-920-62	OEM
8-749-920-65	OEM
8-749-920-81	OEM
8-749-921-10	OEM
8-749-922-13	OEM
8-749-930-35	3410
8-749-933-35	OEM
8-749-938-30	OEM
8-749-939-69	OEM
8-749-939-70	OEM
8-749-939-71	OEM
8-749-953-14	OEM
8-749-956-10	1525
8-749-956-11	OEM
8-749-956-30	1562
8-749-958-30	1562
8-749-960-11	OEM
8-749-960-21	OEM
8-750-105-11	1624
8-750-253-20	OEM
8-750-930-00	OEM
8-750-990-00	OEM
8-751-001-00	4360
8-751-300-00	3904
8-751-310-00	4197
8-751-340-00	3662
8-751-350-00	3907
8-751-360-00	3909
8-751-370-00	4230
8-751-380-00	3911
8-751-390-00	4178
8-751-410-00	3913
8-751-430-00	3916
8-751-450-00	3918
8-751-500-00	OEM
8-751-700-10	3935
8-751-771-00	3943
8-751-771-10	3943
8-751-830-02	OEM
8-751-860-00	OEM
8-751-870-00	OEM
8-751-880-00	OEM
8-751-940-02	OEM
8-751-941-01	OEM
8-751-960-00	OEM
8-751-3300-00	3652
8-752-000-80	OEM
8-752-001-30	OEM
8-752-001-31	OEM
8-752-001-40	OEM
8-752-001-41	OEM
8-752-006-10	OEM
8-752-006-12	OEM
8-752-007-30	OEM
8-752-008-20	OEM
8-752-010-00	OEM
8-752-010-60	OEM
8-752-011-20	2843
8-752-012-52	OEM
8-752-012-91	OEM
8-752-013-90	OEM
8-752-019-20	OEM
8-752-019-30	OEM
8-752-030-26	3054
8-752-030-69	OEM
8-752-031-72	OEM
8-752-032-27	OEM
8-752-033-32	OEM
8-752-034-95	OEM
8-752-035-29	OEM

DEVICE TYPE	REPL CODE
8-752-035-32	OEM
8-752-035-39	OEM
8-752-035-52	OEM
8-752-035-53	OEM
8-752-035-54	OEM
8-752-036-60	OEM
8-752-037-15	OEM
8-752-037-24	OEM
8-752-052-88	OEM
8-752-053-17	OEM
8-752-053-30	OEM
8-752-053-38	OEM
8-752-059-67	OEM
8-752-062-86	OEM
8-752-321-18	OEM
8-752-332-83	OEM
8-752-602-54	OEM
8-752-813-89	OEM
8-752-817-58	OEM
8-752-830-22	OEM
8-752-841-16	OEM
8-757-280-00	OEM
8-757-604-00	OEM
8-757-605-00	OEM
8-757-611-00	OEM
8-757-660-00	OEM
8-757-959-00	OEM
8-758-040-00	OEM
8-758-100-00	OEM
8-758-140-00	OEM
8-758-150-00	OEM
8-758-160-00	OEM
8-758-220-00	OEM
8-758-320-00	OEM
8-758-480-00	4103
8-758-660-00	OEM
8-758-690-00	OEM
8-758-740-00	OEM
8-758-850-00	OEM
8-758-851-00	OEM
8-758-852-00	OEM
8-759-000-49	0101
8-759-001-20	6062
8-759-006-10	OEM
8-759-011-65	OEM
8-759-013-06	0619
8-759-013-09	0330
8-759-014-40	OEM
8-759-030-99	1336
8-759-038-39	OEM
8-759-040-00	OEM
8-759-040-46	3394
8-759-040-53	0034
8-759-043-86	OEM
8-759-045-38	1057
8-759-069-14	OEM
8-759-084-09	OEM
8-759-088-00	OEM
8-759-089-13	OEM
8-759-090-21	OEM
8-759-093-26	OEM
8-759-093-28	OEM
8-759-093-29	OEM
8-759-10-31	0898
8-759-32-89	OEM
8-759-100-06	OEM
8-759-100-07	2888
8-759-100-09	2888
8-759-100-38	OEM
8-759-100-54	OEM
8-759-100-56	OEM
8-759-100-60	5117
8-759-100-75	4959
8-759-101-60	1739
8-759-101-72	OEM
8-759-101-77	OEM
8-759-101-80	4584
8-759-102-12	OEM
8-759-102-28	OEM
8-759-103-00	0548
8-759-103-68	0670
8-759-103-93	0624
8-759-104-05	1869
8-759-105-56	2599
8-759-105-57	2601
8-759-105-59	OEM
8-759-105-82	2031
8-759-106-61	3220
8-759-108-05	1288
8-759-110-17	2898
8-759-110-31	0898
8-759-111-44	OEM
8-759-111-85	4584
8-759-111-88	4713
8-759-112-06	OEM
8-759-112-22	4935
8-759-112-38	1042
8-759-112-77	4756
8-759-112-93	OEM
8-759-113-53	4554
8-759-113-58	0548
8-759-113-63	0678
8-759-113-65	OEM
8-759-113-68	0670
8-759-113-73	2015
8-759-113-78	2031
8-759-115-17	OEM
8-759-115-18	OEM
8-759-115-56	2599

DEVICE TYPE	REPL CODE
8-759-116-18	OEM
8-759-125-56	0485
8-759-131-11	2093
8-759-131-49	OEM
8-759-132-40	0620
8-759-133-90	0176
8-759-135-80	0765
8-759-140-01	0473
8-759-140-11	0215
8-759-140-29	2218
8-759-140-53	0034
8-759-140-66	0101
8-759-142-04	OEM
8-759-145-27	4009
8-759-145-58	0356
8-759-146-17	OEM
8-759-146-37	OEM
8-759-147-49	OEM
8-759-147-60	OEM
8-759-148-68	OEM
8-759-148-69	OEM
8-759-149-90	OEM
8-759-150-61	1288
8-759-153-20	OEM
8-759-153-42	OEM
8-759-154-62	OEM
8-759-155-21	OEM
8-759-157-40	1319
8-759-157-41	1319
8-759-157-52	2845
8-759-157-60	1470
8-759-164-18	OEM
8-759-170-08	1187
8-759-170-12	OEM
8-759-171-05	0619
8-759-171-12	OEM
8-759-178-05	1288
8-759-178-12	1817
8-759-200-93	OEM
8-759-204-96	OEM
8-759-206-12	OEM
8-759-208-67	OEM
8-759-208-92	OEM
8-759-208-94	OEM
8-759-220-00	OEM
8-759-220-04	OEM
8-759-231-56	OEM
8-759-234-63	OEM
8-759-240-01	0473
8-759-240-11	0215
8-759-240-12	0493
8-759-240-13	0409
8-759-240-16	0101
8-759-240-27	1938
8-759-240-29	2218
8-759-240-30	0495
8-759-240-49	0001
8-759-240-51	0362
8-759-240-52	0024
8-759-240-53	0034
8-759-240-66	0101
8-759-240-69	0119
8-759-240-71	0129
8-759-240-81	0328
8-759-243-19	OEM
8-759-245-20	2650
8-759-245-28	3168
8-759-250-26	OEM
8-759-271-20	1012
8-759-271-33	OEM
8-759-272-15	0087
8-759-273-20	3753
8-759-276-07	0906
8-759-276-14	5113
8-759-276-30	3726
8-759-276-58	5080
8-759-312-21	4724
8-759-312-44	4770
8-759-400-01	4662
8-759-400-88	3403
8-759-402-35	4066
8-759-403-42	OEM
8-759-403-44	OEM
8-759-420-37	OEM
8-759-420-48	OEM
8-759-424	3977
8-759-424-00	0167
8-759-425	3977
8-759-425-00	0167
8-759-500-31	OEM
8-759-510-89	OEM
8-759-510-90	OEM
8-759-512-50	OEM
8-759-512-85	OEM
8-759-512-86	OEM
8-759-517-74	OEM
8-759-518-39	OEM
8-759-600-05	0762
8-759-600-08	OEM
8-759-600-43	4102
8-759-600-50	OEM
8-759-600-95	3891
8-759-601-12	OEM
8-759-601-77	OEM
8-759-601-86	OEM
8-759-601-87	OEM
8-759-601-95	3891
8-759-602-54	OEM
8-759-603-94	OEM

DEVICE TYPE	REPL CODE
8-759-604-29	0619
8-759-604-37	OEM
8-759-604-83	OEM
8-759-605-14	OEM
8-759-605-15	OEM
8-759-605-39	OEM
8-759-605-55	0762
8-759-608-07	OEM
8-759-608-11	OEM
8-759-608-43	4102
8-759-608-64	OEM
8-759-608-65	OEM
8-759-608-82	OEM
8-759-608-83	OEM
8-759-610-95	3891
8-759-618-30	OEM
8-759-618-48	3899
8-759-619-03	0804
8-759-630-78	OEM
8-759-631-22	OEM
8-759-632-89	OEM
8-759-633-67	OEM
8-759-634-45	OEM
8-759-634-46	OEM
8-759-634-50	OEM
8-759-634-54	OEM
8-759-634-69	OEM
8-759-635-34	OEM
8-759-636-30	OEM
8-759-636-31	OEM
8-759-636-45	OEM
8-759-645-19	0963
8-759-651-34	1624
8-759-651-35	0872
8-759-651-42	1624
8-759-660-00	OEM
8-759-679-32	OEM
8-759-684-78	4050
8-759-701-79	0330
8-759-701-92	OEM
8-759-710-04	OEM
8-759-710-40	OEM
8-759-710-68	OEM
8-759-710-69	OEM
8-759-711-23	OEM
8-759-720-74	OEM
8-759-748-69	OEM
8-759-800-12	4313
8-759-800-15	3299
8-759-800-18	OEM
8-759-800-65	2641
8-759-800-81	1022
8-759-801-25	1940
8-759-801-98	0727
8-759-802-10	2052
8-759-803-24	OEM
8-759-803-25	OEM
8-759-803-29	3068
8-759-805-37	OEM
8-759-812-01	0574
8-759-814-05	4746
8-759-820-63	OEM
8-759-820-92	2330
8-759-820-93	4032
8-759-822-02	2330
8-759-822-03	OEM
8-759-826-01	3074
8-759-832-10	2052
8-759-833-01	1206
8-759-833-61	1251
8-759-841-25	1940
8-759-841-40	0358
8-759-878-02	1580
8-759-878-03	1580
8-759-879-03	1580
8-759-900-04	1585
8-759-900-09	1632
8-759-900-10	1652
8-759-900-45	OEM
8-759-900-46	OEM
8-759-900-70	OEM
8-759-900-74	0243
8-759-900-86	0288
8-759-900-93	1877
8-759-901-03	OEM
8-759-901-23	0973
8-759-901-38	0422
8-759-902-22	OEM
8-759-903-86	3034
8-759-904-69	0119
8-759-904-94	4349
8-759-905-15	OEM
8-759-905-16	OEM
8-759-905-17	OEM
8-759-905-19	OEM
8-759-905-35	OEM
8-759-905-45	OEM
8-759-905-86	OEM
8-759-905-94	OEM
8-759-906-09	OEM
8-759-907-16	OEM
8-759-907-22	OEM
8-759-907-76	OEM
8-759-907-79	OEM
8-759-907-86	OEM
8-759-908-13	OEM
8-759-908-24	OEM
8-759-908-25	OEM
8-759-908-41	OEM

DEVICE TYPE	REPL CODE
8-759-908-68	OEM
8-759-908-75	OEM
8-759-909-15	OEM
8-759-909-49	OEM
8-759-909-50	OEM
8-759-910-21	OEM
8-759-910-39	OEM
8-759-911-66	OEM
8-759-913-11	OEM
8-759-914-09	OEM
8-759-914-66	OEM
8-759-915-31	OEM
8-759-918-29	OEM
8-759-918-75	OEM
8-759-919-05	OEM
8-759-920-81	OEM
8-759-922-85	OEM
8-759-923-41	OEM
8-759-924-12	1801
8-759-925-74	OEM
8-759-927-51	OEM
8-759-928-10	OEM
8-759-929-62	5885
8-759-932-33	0101
8-759-932-80	2323
8-759-933-00	OEM
8-759-934-19	OEM
8-759-937-59	1813
8-759-940-88	OEM
8-759-945-58	0356
8-759-947-18	OEM
8-759-951-02	2094
8-759-953-87	2279
8-759-955-50	OEM
8-759-965-60	OEM
8-759-966-81	OEM
8-759-971-56	OEM
8-759-972-43	OEM
8-759-978-66	OEM
8-759-980-10	OEM
8-759-980-43	OEM
8-759-980-58	4314
8-759-980-59	OEM
8-759-981-40	OEM
8-759-981-41	OEM
8-759-981-80	OEM
8-759-982-10	OEM
8-759-982-13	0330
8-759-982-21	1288
8-759-982-25	OEM
8-759-982-26	1817
8-759-982-31	0619
8-759-982-34	OEM
8-759-982-37	OEM
8-759-983-38	OEM
8-759-983-44	OEM
8-759-983-69	OEM
8-759-984-06	OEM
8-759-985-20	2650
8-759-985-27	OEM
8-759-985-28	OEM
8-759-986-39	OEM
8-759-987-16	0624
8-759-987-47	OEM
8-759-987-58	OEM
8-759-987-89	OEM
8-759-989-67	OEM
8-759-994-51	0970
8-759-996-43	OEM
8-759-997-64	OEM
8-760-335-10	0018
8-760-343-10	0018
8-760-413	1967
8-760-413-10	1967
8-760-514-10	0527
8-760-523-10	0527
8-761-622-00	2441
8-762-020-00	0338
8-763-113-00	1935
8-763-213-00	1045
8-764-803-00	2475
8-765-170-01	0334
8-765-212-20	0150
8-765-222-20	1935
8-765-401-00	0144
8-765-422-00	0321
8-765-423-00	0321
8-765-424-00	0321
8-765-440-00	OEM
8-765-500-00	0264
8-765-510-00	0676
8-765-620-00	OEM
8-769-132-00	1747
8-769-194-00	1747
8-769-200-00	0321
8-769-200-10	0321
8-769-200-30	0321
8-769-200-40	0321
8-795-145-58	0356
8-795-270-70	0872
8-795-600-95	3891
8-851-340-00	3662
8-902-0706-071	0016
8-905-013-752	0015
8-905-013-759	0015
8-905-013-760	0015
8-905-014-017	0016
8-905-198-001	0015
8-905-198-004	0015

DEVICE TYPE	REPL CODE
8-905-198-005	0015
8-905-198-007	0015
8-905-198-008	0015
8-905-198-010	0015
8-905-198-034	0015
8-905-305-004	0123
8-905-305-007	0143
8-905-305-020	0143
8-905-305-023	0123
8-905-305-055	0143
8-905-305-318	0143
8-905-305-327	0143
8-905-305-330	0143
8-905-305-336	0143
8-905-305-338	0143
8-905-305-339	0143
8-905-305-342	0143
8-905-305-348	0143
8-905-305-400	0015
8-905-305-405	0143
8-905-305-555	0143
8-905-305-561	0143
8-905-305-580	0143
8-905-305-635	0143
8-905-313-007	0123
8-905-313-008	0123
8-905-313-010	0143
8-905-313-011	0143
8-905-313-018	0123
8-905-313-100	0143
8-905-313-101	0143
8-905-313-120	0143
8-905-405-002	0015
8-905-405-026	0015
8-905-405-069	0015
8-905-405-077	0143
8-905-405-098	0133
8-905-405-105	0071
8-905-405-134	0015
8-905-405-146	0015
8-905-405-160	0071
8-905-405-170	0071
8-905-405-206	0015
8-905-405-838	0143
8-905-406-020	0133
8-905-413-092	0015
8-905-421-109	0157
8-905-421-118	0012
8-905-421-128	0002
8-905-421-215	0446
8-905-421-228	0012
8-905-421-234	0137
8-905-421-239	0002
8-905-421-300	0133
8-905-421-315	0327
8-905-421-319	0137
8-905-421-715	0002
8-905-605-016	0004
8-905-605-030	0004
8-905-605-032	0004
8-905-605-050	0004
8-905-605-051	0004
8-905-605-075	0004
8-905-605-090	0004
8-905-605-091	0004
8-905-605-105	0208
8-905-605-108	0208
8-905-605-109	0208
8-905-605-110	0208
8-905-605-111	0208
8-905-605-112	0208
8-905-605-113	0208
8-905-605-120	0164
8-905-605-123	0164
8-905-605-124	0164
8-905-605-125	0164
8-905-605-126	0164
8-905-605-127	0164
8-905-605-128	0164
8-905-605-129	0164
8-905-605-230	0004
8-905-605-232	0004
8-905-605-234	0004
8-905-605-250	0164
8-905-605-255	0164
8-905-605-260	0164
8-905-605-264	0164
8-905-605-266	0164
8-905-605-268	0164
8-905-605-269	0164
8-905-605-292	0004
8-905-605-305	0004
8-905-605-320	0050
8-905-605-365	0208
8-905-605-384	0208
8-905-605-390	0208
8-905-605-607	0222
8-905-605-624	0160
8-905-605-635	0160
8-905-605-636	0160
8-905-605-637	0160
8-905-605-644	0007
8-905-605-650	0222
8-905-605-775	0969
8-905-605-908	0969
8-905-606-001	0050
8-905-606-003	0050
8-905-606-007	0050
8-905-606-008	0050

If replacement code is OEM, contact original manufacturer for replacement.

DEVICE TYPE	REPL CODE
8-905-606-010	0050
8-905-606-016	0050
8-905-606-051	0050
8-905-606-075	0050
8-905-606-077	0050
8-905-606-090	0050
8-905-606-105	0050
8-905-606-106	0050
8-905-606-120	0050
8-905-606-142	0050
8-905-606-152	0050
8-905-606-153	0050
8-905-606-154	0050
8-905-606-155	0050
8-905-606-158	0050
8-905-606-165	0050
8-905-606-168	0050
8-905-606-180	0050
8-905-606-211	0050
8-905-606-225	0050
8-905-606-241	0050
8-905-606-255	0050
8-905-606-256	0050
8-905-606-349	0050
8-905-606-350	0050
8-905-606-351	0050
8-905-606-352	0050
8-905-606-360	0050
8-905-606-375	0050
8-905-606-390	0050
8-905-606-391	0050
8-905-606-392	0050
8-905-606-405	0050
8-905-606-419	0050
8-905-606-420	0050
8-905-606-423	0050
8-905-606-720	0160
8-905-606-750	0004
8-905-606-800	0004
8-905-606-815	0004
8-905-606-817	0004
8-905-606-885	0004
8-905-613-010	0004
8-905-613-015	0208
8-905-613-062	0208
8-905-613-070	0164
8-905-613-071	0164
8-905-613-131	0164
8-905-613-132	0164
8-905-613-133	0164
8-905-613-150	2839
8-905-613-160	0164
8-905-613-210	0160
8-905-613-215	0160
8-905-613-232	0969
8-905-613-240	0222
8-905-613-241	0222
8-905-613-242	0222
8-905-613-245	0222
8-905-613-250	0160
8-905-613-265	0222
8-905-613-266	0222
8-905-613-277	0222
8-905-613-282	0222
8-905-613-283	0222
8-905-613-284	0222
8-905-613-295	0969
8-905-613-555	0222
8-905-613-640	0004
8-905-613-710	0004
8-905-613-955	0004
8-905-615-156	0004
8-905-705-112	0016
8-905-705-403	0016
8-905-705-405	0016
8-905-705-410	0086
8-905-706-010	0283
8-905-706-044	0007
8-905-706-055	0007
8-905-706-060	0007
8-905-706-067	0283
8-905-706-068	0283
8-905-706-070	0007
8-905-706-071	0007
8-905-706-075	0007
8-905-706-080	0007
8-905-706-101	0007
8-905-706-104	0016
8-905-706-110	0007
8-905-706-112	0007
8-905-706-201	0016
8-905-706-202	0016
8-905-706-203	0016
8-905-706-206	0016
8-905-706-208	0016
8-905-706-211	0016
8-905-706-215	0016
8-905-706-235	0016
8-905-706-236	0016
8-905-706-238	0016
8-905-706-239	0016
8-905-706-240	0016
8-905-706-242	0016
8-905-706-244	0016
8-905-706-245	0016
8-905-706-246	0016
8-905-706-247	0037
8-905-706-250	0016
8-905-706-251	0037

DEVICE TYPE	REPL CODE
8-905-706-253	0037
8-905-706-254	0037
8-905-706-255	0037
8-905-706-256	0037
8-905-706-257	0016
8-905-706-260	0016
8-905-706-263	0016
8-905-706-280	0037
8-905-706-286	0037
8-905-706-287	0037
8-905-706-288	0037
8-905-706-289	0037
8-905-706-290	0037
8-905-706-336	0016
8-905-706-545	0126
8-905-706-555	0103
8-905-706-556	0103
8-905-706-557	0103
8-905-706-606	0016
8-905-706-730	0007
8-905-706-790	0050
8-905-706-801	0161
8-905-706-901	0321
8-905-707-254	0016
8-905-707-265	0016
8-905-707-313	0016
8-905-713-058	0037
8-905-713-101	0103
8-905-713-110	0161
8-905-713-556	0103
8-905-713-810	0126
8-917-300-70	0023
8-2409501	0016
8-2410300	0126
8-81250108	0111
8-81250109	0016
8-B	OEM
8-C	OEM
8A	OEM
8A01	0143
8A1ABG0	OEM
8A1ABG1	OEM
8A1HA1	OEM
8A1HS0	OEM
8A1HS1	OEM
8A1PA1	OEM
8A1PG0	OEM
8A1PG1	OEM
8A1PS0	OEM
8A1PS1	OEM
8A1QBG0	OEM
8A1QBG1	OEM
8A2ABG0	OEM
8A2ABG2	OEM
8A2HA2	OEM
8A2HS0	OEM
8A2HS1	OEM
8A2PA2	OEM
8A2PG0	OEM
8A2PG2	OEM
8A2PS0	OEM
8A2PS1	OEM
8A2QBG0	OEM
8A2QBG2	OEM
8A3ABG0	OEM
8A3ABG3	OEM
8A3HA3	OEM
8A3HS0	OEM
8A3HS1	OEM
8A3PA3	OEM
8A3PG0	OEM
8A3PG3	OEM
8A3PS0	OEM
8A3PS1	OEM
8A3QBG0	OEM
8A3QBG3	OEM
8A4ABG0	OEM
8A4ABG4	OEM
8A4HA4	OEM
8A4HS0	OEM
8A4HS1	OEM
8A4PA4	OEM
8A4PG0	OEM
8A4PG4	OEM
8A4PS0	OEM
8A4PS1	OEM
8A4QBG0	OEM
8A4QBG4	OEM
8A5ABG0	OEM
8A5ABG5	OEM
8A5HA5	OEM
8A5HS0	OEM
8A5HS1	OEM
8A5PA5	OEM
8A5PG0	OEM
8A5PG5	OEM
8A5PS0	OEM
8A5PS1	OEM
8A5QBG0	OEM
8A5QBG5	OEM
8A6ABG0	OEM
8A6ABG6	OEM
8A6HS0	OEM
8A6HS1	OEM
8A6PG0	OEM
8A6PG6	OEM
8A6PS0	OEM
8A6PS1	OEM
8A6QBG0	OEM

DEVICE TYPE	REPL CODE
8A6QBG6	OEM
8A7ABG0	OEM
8A7ABG7	OEM
8A7HS0	OEM
8A7HS1	OEM
8A7PG0	OEM
8A7PG7	OEM
8A7PS0	OEM
8A7PS1	OEM
8A7QBG0	OEM
8A7QBG7	OEM
8A8ABG0	OEM
8A8ABG8	OEM
8A8HS0	OEM
8A8HS1	OEM
8A8PG0	OEM
8A8PG8	OEM
8A8PS0	OEM
8A8PS1	OEM
8A8QBG0	OEM
8A8QBG8	OEM
8A9ABG0	OEM
8A9ABG9	OEM
8A9HS0	OEM
8A9HS1	OEM
8A9PG0	OEM
8A9PG9	OEM
8A9PS0	OEM
8A9PS1	OEM
8A9QBG0	OEM
8A9QBG9	OEM
8A10ABG0	OEM
8A10ABG10	OEM
8A10HS0	OEM
8A10HS1	OEM
8A10PG0	OEM
8A10PG10	OEM
8A10PS0	OEM
8A10PS1	OEM
8A10QBG0	OEM
8A10QBG10	OEM
8A11ABG0	OEM
8A11ABG11	OEM
8A11HS0	OEM
8A11HS1	OEM
8A11PG0	OEM
8A11PG11	OEM
8A11PS0	OEM
8A11PS1	OEM
8A11QBG0	OEM
8A11QBG11	OEM
8A12ABG0	OEM
8A12ABG12	OEM
8A12HS0	OEM
8A12HS1	OEM
8A12PG0	OEM
8A12PG12	OEM
8A12PS0	OEM
8A12PS1	OEM
8A12QBG0	OEM
8A12QBG12	OEM
8A13ABG0	OEM
8A13ABG13	OEM
8A13PG0	OEM
8A13PG13	OEM
8A13QBG0	OEM
8A13QBG13	OEM
8A14ABG0	OEM
8A14ABG14	OEM
8A14PG0	OEM
8A14PG14	OEM
8A14QBG0	OEM
8A14QBG14	OEM
8A15ABG0	OEM
8A15ABG15	OEM
8A15PG0	OEM
8A15PG15	OEM
8A15QBG0	OEM
8A15QBG15	OEM
8A16ABG0	OEM
8A16ABG16	OEM
8A16PG0	OEM
8A16PG16	OEM
8A16QBG0	OEM
8A16QBG16	OEM
8A17ABG0	OEM
8A17ABG17	OEM
8A17PG0	OEM
8A17PG17	OEM
8A17QBG0	OEM
8A17QBG17	OEM
8A18ABG0	OEM
8A18ABG18	OEM
8A18PG0	OEM
8A18PG18	OEM
8A18QBG0	OEM
8A18QBG18	OEM
8A19ABG0	OEM
8A19ABG19	OEM
8A19PG0	OEM
8A19PG19	OEM
8A19QBG0	OEM
8A19QBG19	OEM
8A20ABG0	OEM
8A20ABG20	OEM
8A20PG0	OEM
8A20PG20	OEM
8A20QBG0	OEM
8A20QBG20	OEM

DEVICE TYPE	REPL CODE
8A1002	0396
8A1003	0396
8A10521	0222
8A10625	0222
8A11083	0222
8A11667	0015
8A11721	0222
8A12359	0222
8A12789	0016
8A12991	0085
8A13164	0222
8A13718	0164
8AF05NLH	OEM
8AF05NLV	OEM
8AF05NPP	OEM
8AF1NLH	OEM
8AF1NLV	OEM
8AF1NPP	OEM
8AF2NLH	OEM
8AF2NLV	OEM
8AF2NPP	OEM
8AF4NLH	OEM
8AF4NLV	OEM
8AF4NPP	OEM
8AN10	1567
8AN20	1567
8AN30	0109
8AN40	3705
8AN50	OEM
8AN60	OEM
8AN80	OEM
8AN100	2982
8AN120	OEM
8AN140	OEM
8AN160	OEM
8B	OEM
8BT30ZK	OEM
8C1	OEM
8C2	OEM
8C4	OEM
8C6	OEM
8C8	OEM
8C12	OEM
8C14	OEM
8C16	OEM
8C91	0012
8C200	0037
8C201	0037
8C202	0037
8C203	0037
8C204	0037
8C205	0037
8C206	0037
8C207	0037
8C327-25	OEM
8C430	0037
8C430K	0037
8C440	0037
8C440K	0037
8C443	0037
8C443K	0037
8C445	0037
8C445K	0037
8C449	0037
8C449K	0037
8C450	0037
8C460	0037
8C460K	0037
8C463	0037
8C463K	0037
8C465	0037
8C465K	0037
8C466	0037
8C466K	0037
8C467	0037
8C467K	0037
8C468	0037
8C468K	0037
8C469	0037
8C469K	0037
8C470	0037
8C470K	0037
8C700	0037
8C700A	0037
8C700B	0037
8C702	0037
8C702A	0037
8C702B	0037
8C704	0037
8C740	0037
8C740G	0037
8C740M	0037
8C742	0037
8C742G	0037
8C742M	0037
8C7400	0037
8C7420	0037
8CG15	0015
8CG15RE	0015
8D	1273
8D4	0015
8D6	0015
8D8	0071
8D10	0071
8E	0050
8E(AUTOMATIC)	0136
8E0	OEM
8E1	OEM
8E7H	OEM

DEVICE TYPE	REPL CODE
8E15	OEM
8E30A	OEM
8E70	OEM
8E110	OEM
8F	0050
8F(AUTOMATIC)	0136
8F5H	OEM
8F5H1	OEM
8F6H	OEM
8F6H1	OEM
8FR	OEM
8G6H	OEM
8G6H1	OEM
8G7	0071
8GA	0071
8H303	0160
8J5091	OEM
8JUS4.32A	OEM
8JUS4.32B	OEM
8JUS5.20A	OEM
8JUS5.20B	OEM
8JUS5.84A	OEM
8JUS5.84B	OEM
8JUS6.10A	OEM
8JUS6.10B	OEM
8JV30	OEM
8JV60	OEM
8JV100	OEM
8JV120	OEM
8JV150	OEM
8JV160	OEM
8JV180	OEM
8KBS	OEM
8L	0050
8L201	0160
8L201B	0160
8L201C	0160
8L201R	0160
8L201V	0160
8L301V	0085
8L404	0160
8M-26102	1024
8MT05ZYK	OEM
8N	OEM
8NA	0196
8P	0050
8P1M	2078
8P-2	0004
8P-2-70	0004
8P-2-70-12	0004
8P-2-70-12-7	0004
8P-2A	0004
8P-2A0	0004
8P-2A0R	0004
8P-2A1	0004
8P-2A2	0004
8P-2A3	0004
8P-2A3P	0004
8P-2A4	0004
8P-2A4-7	0004
8P-2A4-7B	0004
8P-2A5	0004
8P-2A5L	0004
8P-2A6	0004
8P-2A6-2	0004
8P-2A7	0004
8P-2A7-1	0004
8P-2A8	0004
8P-2A9	0004
8P-2A9G	0004
8P-2A19	0211
8P-2A21	0004
8P-2A82	0004
8P-2AO	0164
8P-2AOR	0164
8P2M	0500
8P7OBLU	0042
8P10	OEM
8P-20	0004
8P-21	0004
8P-22	0004
8P-23	0004
8P-24	0004
8P-25	0004
8P-26	0004
8P-27	0004
8P-28	0004
8P-29	0004
8P40	0085
8P50S	0222
8P73BLU	0042
8P111	0321
8P202	0222
8P345	0042
8P-404	0160
8P404	0160
8P404B	0160
8P404F	0085
8P404M	0160
8P404M-1	0160
8P404N	0160
8P404ORN	0085
8P-404R	0160
8P404R	0160
8P404T	0222
8P404V	0160
8P415C	0160
8P416C	0160
8P-505	0222

DEVICE TYPE	REPL CODE
8P505	0222
8P880	0435
8P880B	0435
8P9253	0149
8PC60	0160
8PS60	0160
8Q-3-01	0111
8Q-3-02	0150
8Q-3-04	0208
8Q-3-10	0111
8Q-3-11	0037
8Q-3-12	0079
8Q-3-13	0086
8Q-3-14	0037
8Q-3-23	2736
8Q-7-01	0015
8Q-7-02	0015
8Q-7-03	0015
8RCM5	2497
8RCM10	OEM
8RCM20	0740
8RCM30	OEM
8RCM40	OEM
8RCM50	OEM
8RCM60	OEM
8RCU5	OEM
8RCU10	OEM
8RCU20	OEM
8RCU30	OEM
8RCU40	OEM
8RCU50	OEM
8RCU60	OEM
8RCV5	2497
8RCV20	0740
8S	OEM
8S191A04	0015
8SB050	OEM
8SB100	0319
8SB200	1404
8SB400	0468
8SB600	0441
8SM1	OEM
8SM3	OEM
8SM6	OEM
8SM15	OEM
8SM25	OEM
8SM40	OEM
8SM55	OEM
8SM70	OEM
8SM100	OEM
8SM150	OEM
8SM200	OEM
8T04A	2284
8T04HA	2284
8T14A	2284
8T14HA	2284
8T24A	2284
8T24HA	2284
8T28	0576
8T32F	OEM
8T33	OEM
8T34A	2284
8T34HA	2284
8T35F	OEM
8T36F	OEM
8T44A	2284
8T44HA	2284
8T54A	OEM
8T54HA	OEM
8T64A	OEM
8T64HA	OEM
8T95	4566
8T3404F	OEM
8T3404N	OEM
8TW1	OEM
8TW2	OEM
8TW3	OEM
8TW4	OEM
8TW5	OEM
8TW6	OEM
8U4	0790
8U8	0015
8U12	0072
8V228	OEM
8V257	OEM
8V274	OEM
8V301	OEM
8VT01	OEM
8VT02	OEM
8W413	OEM
8W413V	OEM
8.2B1	0077
8.2M	OEM
8.2Z	0165
8.75VZENER	0012
9-719-000-04	2189
9-900-285-01	OEM
9-900-615-01	1376
9-900-616-01	0472
9-900-617-01	1404
9-900-618-01	0023
9-900-619-01	0681
9-900-910-01	OEM
9-900-930-01	OEM
9-900-931-01	0023
9-901-371-01	1319
9-901-372-01	OEM
9-901-373-01	OEM
9-901-374-01	OEM

DEVICE TYPE	REPL CODE
9-901-375-01	OEM
9-901-376-01	OEM
9-901-385-01	OEM
9-901-386-01	2891
9-901-387-01	OEM
9-901-403-01	OEM
9-901-496-01	OEM
9-901-499-01	0541
9-901-500-01	OEM
9-901-504-01	0457
9-901-505-01	1022
9-901-506-01	OEM
9-901-507-01	2330
9-901-518-01	OEM
9-901-519-01	OEM
9-901-548-01	0541
9-901-549-01	OEM
9-901-550-01	3559
9-901-551-01	2384
9-901-557-01	OEM
9-905-606-001	0050
9-982-051-00	OEM
9-982-071-00	OEM
9-982-071-02	OEM
9-5108	0050
9-5110	0050
9-5111	0050
9-5112	0595
9-5113	0595
9-5114	0595
9-5116	0050
9-5117	0050
9-5118	0050
9-5119	0050
9-5120	0050
9-5120A	0279
9-5121	0050
9-5122	0050
9-5123	0050
9-5124	0050
9-5125	0144
9-5126	0144
9-5127	0144
9-5128	0144
9-5129	0144
9-5130	0144
9-5131	0144
9-5201	0004
9-5202	0208
9-5203	0004
9-5204	0004
9-5208	0004
9-5209	0004
9-5212	0004
9-5213	0004
9-5214	0004
9-5216	0016
9-5217	0004
9-5218	0004
9-5220	0086
9-5221	0079
9-5222-1	0004
9-5222-2	0208
9-5223	0144
9-5224-1	0004
9-5224-2	0208
9-5225	0016
9-5226-003	0126
9-5226-004	0086
9-5226-1	0126
9-5226-2	0016
9-5226-3	0126
9-5226-4	0086
9-5227	0016
9-5250	0160
9-5251	0160
9-5252	0142
9-5252-1	0142
9-5252-2	0142
9-5252-3	0142
9-5252-4	0142
9-5257	0265
9-5296	0016
9-9101	0136
9-9102	0136
9-9103	0136
9-9104	0004
9-9105	0050
9-9106	0050
9-9107	0050
9-9108	0050
9-9109-1	0016
9-9109-2	0016
9-9120	0050
9-9121	0050
9-9201	0004
9-9202	0004
9-9203	0004
9-51141400	0160
9-511410100	0004
9-511410200	0004
9-511410900	0004
9-511413500	0004
9-511511500	0071
9A1	1024
9A1(3%)	OEM
9A2	0165
9A8-1A64	0050
9A1000	OEM

If replacement code is OEM, contact original manufacturer for replacement.

121

DEVICE TYPE	REPL CODE
9ACW	OEM
9AM10	OEM
9B7	OEM
9BM10	OEM
9C3	0057
9CR12U02G	OEM
9CR12U04G	OEM
9CR12U06G	OEM
9CR12U08G	OEM
9CR12U10G	OEM
9CR12U12G	OEM
9CR20U08G	OEM
9CR20U10G	OEM
9CR20U11G	OEM
9CR30U02G	OEM
9CR30U04G	OEM
9CR30U06G	OEM
9CR30U08G	OEM
9D02M1	OEM
9D05M1	OEM
9D10K1	OEM
9D11	0133
9D12	0143
9D13	0015
9D14	0139
9D15	0012
9D16	0143
9D141003-12	0012
9DI	0133
9DI1	0133
9DI2	0143
9DI3	0015
9DI4	0139
9DI5	0012
9DT1100310	0143
9E13	OEM
9E26A	OEM
9E45	OEM
9E85	OEM
9E150	OEM
9GR2	0016
9H00DC	0677
9H00PC	0677
9H01DC	5241
9H01PC	5241
9H04DC	1896
9H04PC	1896
9H05DC	3221
9H05PC	3221
9H08DC	5258
9H08PC	5258
9H10DC	0680
9H10PC	0680
9H11DC	2382
9H11PC	2382
9H20DC	3670
9H20PC	3670
9H21DC	4772
9H21PC	4772
9H22	4516
9H22DC	4516
9H22PC	4516
9H30DC	5284
9H30PC	5284
9H40DC	0554
9H40PC	0554
9H50DC	1781
9H50PC	1781
9H51DC	1933
9H51PC	1933
9H52DC	2009
9H52PC	2009
9H53DC	2090
9H53PC	2090
9H54DC	2158
9H54PC	2158
9H55DC	3129
9H55PC	3129
9H60DC	5312
9H60PC	5312
9H61DC	2638
9H61PC	2638
9H62DC	2705
9H62PC	2705
9H71DC	3233
9H71PC	3233
9H72DC	3281
9H72PC	3281
9H73DC	2444
9H73PC	2444
9H74DC	2472
9H74PC	2472
9H76DC	5208
9H76PC	5208
9H78DC	5320
9H78PC	5320
9H101DC	5424
9H101PC	5424
9H102DC	5426
9H102PC	5426
9H103DC	2941
9H103PC	2941
9H106DC	5159
9H106PC	5159
9H108DC	0180
9H108PC	0180
9H450A	OEM
9H600A	OEM
9HM7	OEM

DEVICE TYPE	REPL CODE
9JUS4.86A	OEM
9JUS4.86B	OEM
9JUS5.54A	OEM
9JUS5.54B	OEM
9JUS5.85A	OEM
9JUS5.85B	OEM
9JUS6.57A	OEM
9JUS6.57B	OEM
9JUS6.86A	OEM
9JUS6.86B	OEM
9K	OEM
9L	OEM
9L-4	0004
9L-4-70	0004
9L-4-70-12	0004
9L-4-70-12-7	0004
9L-4A	0004
9L-4A0	0004
9L-4A0R	0004
9L-4A1	0004
9L-4A2	0004
9L-4A3	0004
9L-4A3P	0004
9L-4A4	0004
9L-4A4-7	0004
9L-4A4-7B	0004
9L-4A5	0004
9L-4A5L	0004
9L-4A6	0004
9L-4A6-1	0004
9L-4A7	0004
9L-4A7-1	0004
9L-4A8	0004
9L-4A9	0004
9L-4A9G	0004
9L-4A19	0004
9L-4A21	0004
9L-4A82	0004
9L-40	0004
9L-41	0004
9L-42	0004
9L-43	0004
9L-44	0004
9L-45	0004
9L-46	0004
9L-47	0004
9L-48	0004
9L-49	0004
9LR2	0196
9LR2-1	0196
9LR2-1S	OEM
9LR2-2	0479
9LR2-3	0196
9LR2-4	1073
9LR2-24	0196
9LR2-385	OEM
9LR2-S	0196
9LR2-S1	0196
9LR21	0196
9LS17TDM	OEM
9LS95DC	OEM
9LS95DM	OEM
9LS95FC	OEM
9LS95FM	OEM
9LS95PC	OEM
9LS164DC	OEM
9LS164DM	OEM
9LS164FC	OEM
9LS164FM	OEM
9LS164PC	4418
9LS170DC	OEM
9LS170DM	OEM
9LS170FC	OEM
9LS170FM	OEM
9LS170PC	OEM
9LS174DC	0260
9LS174DM	0260
9LS174FM	OEM
9LS174PC	0260
9LS175DC	1662
9LS175FC	OEM
9LS175FM	OEM
9LS175PC	1662
9LS194DC	1294
9LS194DM	1294
9LS194FC	OEM
9LS194FM	OEM
9LS194PC	1294
9LS195DC	OEM
9LS195DM	OEM
9LS195FC	OEM
9LS195FM	OEM
9LS195PC	1305
9LS295DC	OEM
9LS295DM	OEM
9LS295FC	OEM
9LS295FM	OEM
9LS295PC	OEM
9LS670DC	OEM
9LS670DM	OEM
9LS670FC	OEM
9LS670FM	OEM
9LS670PC	OEM
9M	OEM
9M12	OEM
9M13	OEM
9M31	OEM
9M40	OEM
9M61	OEM

DEVICE TYPE	REPL CODE
9M62A	OEM
9M64A	OEM
9M65	OEM
9M65A	OEM
9M66	OEM
9M72	OEM
9M73	OEM
9M80	OEM
9M80A	OEM
9M90	OEM
9M301	OEM
9M302	OEM
9M303	OEM
9M501	OEM
9M502	OEM
9M503	OEM
9M601	OEM
9M602	OEM
9M603	OEM
9M611	OEM
9M612	OEM
9M613	OEM
9M751	OEM
9M752	OEM
9M753	OEM
9MF2A100	OEM
9MF2A200	OEM
9MF2A400	OEM
9MF2B100	OEM
9MF2B200	OEM
9MF2B400	OEM
9MF2B600	OEM
9MF2B800	OEM
9MF10B100	OEM
9MF10B100R	OEM
9MF10B200	OEM
9MF10B200R	OEM
9MF10B400	OEM
9MF10B400R	OEM
9MF10B600	OEM
9MF10B600R	OEM
9MF10B800	OEM
9MF10B800R	OEM
9MT19ZK	OEM
9N00	0232
9N00DC	0232
9N00PC	0232
9N01DC	0268
9N01PC	0268
9N02	0310
9N02DC	0310
9N02F1	OEM
9N02PC	0310
9N03DC	0331
9N03PC	0331
9N04	0357
9N04DC	0357
9N04PC	0357
9N05DC	0381
9N05M1	OEM
9N05PC	0381
9N06	1197
9N06DC	1197
9N06PC	1197
9N07DC	1329
9N07PC	1329
9N08	0462
9N08DC	0462
9N08PC	0462
9N09DC	0487
9N09PC	0487
9N10	0507
9N10DC	0507
9N10K1	OEM
9N10PC	0507
9N11DC	0522
9N11PC	0522
9N12DC	2227
9N12PC	2227
9N13	1432
9N13DC	1432
9N13PC	1432
9N14DC	2228
9N14PC	2228
9N16DC	1339
9N16PC	1339
9N17DC	1342
9N17PC	1342
9N20	0692
9N20DC	0692
9N20PC	0692
9N21DC	1347
9N21PC	1347
9N23DC	3429
9N23PC	3429
9N25DC	3438
9N25PC	3438
9N26DC	0798
9N26PC	0798
9N27	0812
9N27DC	0812
9N27PC	0812
9N30DC	0867
9N30PC	0867
9N32	0893
9N32DC	0893
9N32PC	0893
9N37DC	3478
9N37PC	3478

DEVICE TYPE	REPL CODE
9N38DC	0990
9N39DC	5722
9N39PC	5722
9N40DC	1018
9N40PC	1018
9N50DC	0738
9N50PC	0738
9N51	1160
9N51DC	1160
9N51PC	1160
9N53DC	1177
9N53PC	1177
9N54DC	1193
9N54PC	1193
9N60DC	1265
9N60PC	1265
9N70DC	1394
9N70PC	1394
9N72DC	1417
9N72PC	1417
9N73	1164
9N73DC	1164
9N73PC	1164
9N74	1303
9N74DC	1303
9N74PC	1303
9N76	1150
9N76DC	1150
9N76PC	1150
9N86	1358
9N86DC	1358
9N86PC	1358
9N107DC	0936
9N107PC	0936
9N122DC	1131
9N122PC	1131
9N123	1149
9N123DC	1149
9N123PC	1149
9N132DC	1261
9N132PC	1261
9OC69-1	0015
9P10K1	OEM
9PO2F1-A	OEM
9RE1	0015
9S00DC	0699
9S00PC	0699
9S03DC	2203
9S03PC	2203
9S04DC	2248
9S04PC	2248
9S05DC	2305
9S05PC	2305
9S011	0004
9S037	0016
9S10DC	2426
9S10PC	2426
9S11DC	2428
9S11PC	2428
9S15DC	2432
9S15PC	2432
9S20DC	1011
9S20PC	1011
9S22DC	2442
9S22PC	2442
9S40DC	2456
9S40PC	2456
9S64DC	2476
9S64PC	2476
9S65DC	2477
9S65PC	2477
9S74DC	2483
9S74PC	2483
9S112DC	1607
9S112PC	1607
9S113DC	1613
9S113PC	1613
9S114DC	1619
9S114PC	1619
9S133DC	1808
9S133PC	1808
9S134DC	1816
9S134PC	1816
9S140DC	1875
9S140PC	1875
9T10T	OEM
9T20T	OEM
9T40T	OEM
9T60T	OEM
9T80T	OEM
9T100T	OEM
9TR1	0127
9TR2	0364
9TR3	0364
9TR4	1390
9TR5	1897
9TR6	1390
9TR7	0155
9TR8	0236
9TR9	2261
9TR10	0016
9TR11	1390
9TR11001-01	0127
9TR21001-02	0016
9TR31001-03	0016
9TR61001-07	0086
9TR91001-09	0103
9TRZ1001-02	0016
9V54	OEM

DEVICE TYPE	REPL CODE
9V58	OEM
9VT01	OEM
9VT02	OEM
9X64	OEM
9XT2107-501	OEM
9.0B2	OEM
9.1B	0057
9.1B2	6242
9.1B3	0057
9.1BL	OEM
9.1M	OEM
9.1N3	0057
9.1Z	0057
9.S037	0079
10	0016
10-0007	0930
10-0009	0386
10-001	3763
10-002	0076
10-003	0076
10-004	1202
10-004#	1532
10-004(IC)	1532
10-004IC	1532
10-005	3980
10-005(IC)	3980
10-006	0884
10-007	0930
10-008	0155
10-009	0930
10-010	0133
10-010#	1187
10-010(IC)	1187
10-010IC	1187
10-012	0023
10-013	0012
10-015	0030
10-016	0253
10-024	2911
10-080009	0144
10-080010	0016
10-085001	0143
10-085004	0123
10-085005	0133
10-085006	0015
10-085009	0015
10-085010	0015
10-085013	0030
10-085014	0143
10-085018	0143
10-085025	0133
10-085026	0015
10-085027	0162
10-085030	0015
10-0800010	0016
10-1	0007
10-2	0007
10-2SA49	0136
10-2SB54	0004
10-2SB56	0004
10-2SC80	0144
10-2SC94	0144
10-2SC380	0127
10-7	0015
10-12	0015
10-42	0015
10-102005	0071
10-I3002-004	0103
10A	0050
10A1/18	OEM
10A1/52	OEM
10A2/18	OEM
10A2/52	OEM
10A5/18	OEM
10A5/52	OEM
10A12	OEM
10A12/18	OEM
10A13	OEM
10A13/18	OEM
10A14	OEM
10A14/18	OEM
10A15	OEM
10A15/18	OEM
10A16	OEM
10A16/18	OEM
10A22	OEM
10A22/18	OEM
10A23	OEM
10A23/18	OEM
10A24	OEM
10A24/18	OEM
10A25	OEM
10A25/18	OEM
10A26	OEM
10A26/18	OEM
10A50	OEM
10A52	OEM
10A52/18	OEM
10A53	OEM
10A53/18	OEM
10A54	OEM
10A54/18	OEM
10A55	OEM
10A55/18	OEM
10A56	OEM
10A56/18	OEM
10A100	OEM
10A200	OEM
10A400	OEM

DEVICE TYPE	REPL CODE
10A590B	0015
10A600	OEM
10A800	OEM
10AG2	0015
10AG4	0015
10AG6	0015
10AG8	0071
10AG10	0071
10AL2	0015
10AL6	0015
10AM10	OEM
10AS	0015
10AT2	0015
10AT4	0015
10AT6	0015
10AT8	0071
10AT10	0071
10B	0050
10B05T	OEM
10B1	0015
10B1(ZENER)	0057
10B1(ZENER)	0064
10B1/18	OEM
10B1/52	OEM
10B-2	0015
10B2	0064
10B2(ZENER)	OEM
10B2/18	OEM
10B2/52	OEM
10B-2-B1W	0015
10B2-B1W	0276
10B-2-N1W	0015
10B2FR	OEM
10B3	0015
10B3(1W-ZENER)	0170
10B3(ZENER)	0064
10B-4	0469
10B4	0015
10B-4-C4	0469
10B4B41	OEM
10B4FR	OEM
10B5	0015
10B5/18	OEM
10B5/52	OEM
10B6	0015
10B6FR	OEM
10B8	0071
10B10	0087
10B10T	OEM
10B12	OEM
10B12/18	OEM
10B13	OEM
10B13/18	OEM
10B14	OEM
10B14/18	OEM
10B15	OEM
10B15/18	OEM
10B16	OEM
10B16/18	OEM
10B20T	OEM
10B22	OEM
10B22/18	OEM
10B23	OEM
10B23/18	OEM
10B24	OEM
10B24/18	OEM
10B25	OEM
10B25/18	OEM
10B26	OEM
10B26/18	OEM
10B40T	OEM
10B52	OEM
10B52/18	OEM
10B53	OEM
10B53/18	OEM
10B54	OEM
10B54/18	OEM
10B55	OEM
10B55/18	OEM
10B56	OEM
10B56/18	OEM
10B62	0170
10B80T	OEM
10B551	0144
10B551-2	0007
10B551-3	0007
10B553	0144
10B553-2	0007
10B553-2,3	OEM
10B553-3	0007
10B555	0144
10B555-2	0144
10B555-2,3	OEM
10B555-3	0144
10B556	0144
10B556-2	0144
10B556-2,3	OEM
10B556-3	0144
10B701	OEM
10B705	OEM
10B1051	0144
10B1055	0144
10BG2C11	OEM
10BG2Z11	OEM
10BL2C41	0903
10BT16ZK	OEM
10B-Y	0015
10BYZ1400	OEM
10BYZ1600	OEM

DEVICE TYPE	REPL CODE
10BZX79C	0064
10C	0015
10C05	0015
10C05/18	OEM
10C05/52	OEM
10C054	OEM
10C054/18	OEM
10C055	OEM
10C055/18	OEM
10C056	OEM
10C056/18	OEM
10C057	OEM
10C057/18	OEM
10C1	0015
10C1R10	OEM
10C1R20	OEM
10C1R30	OEM
10C1S10	OEM
10C1S20	OEM
10C1S30	OEM
10C2	0015
10C2/18	OEM
10C2/52	OEM
10C2R10	OEM
10C2R11	OEM
10C2R20	OEM
10C2R21	OEM
10C2R30	OEM
10C2R31	OEM
10C2S10	OEM
10C2S11	OEM
10C2S20	OEM
10C2S21	OEM
10C2S30	OEM
10C2S31	OEM
10C2SR11	OEM
10C2SR20	OEM
10C2SR21	OEM
10C2SR30	OEM
10C2SR31	OEM
10C2SS11	OEM
10C2SS21	OEM
10C2SS30	OEM
10C2SS31	OEM
10C3	0015
10C4	0015
10C4D	0015
10C4.5	OEM
10C4.5-5.5	OEM
10C5	0015
10C5.5-6.5	OEM
10C5.6	OEM
10C6	0015
10C6.5-7.5	OEM
10C6.7	OEM
10C8	0071
10C10	0071
10C11/18	OEM
10C11/52	OEM
10C12	OEM
10C14/18	OEM
10C15	OEM
10C15/18	OEM
10C16/18	OEM
10C17	OEM
10C17/18	OEM
10C24	OEM
10C24/18	OEM
10C25	OEM
10C25/18	OEM
10C26	OEM
10C26/18	OEM
10C27	OEM
10C27/18	OEM
10C573	0144
10C573-2	0007
10C573-2,3	OEM
10C573-3	0007
10C574	0144
10C574-2	0007
10C574-2,3	OEM
10C574-3	0007
10CC11	OEM
10CH2SM	1227
10CL2C41	0903
10CS04SM	OEM
10CZ6.8	OEM
10CZ6.8A	OEM
10CZ6.8B	OEM
10CZ7.5	OEM
10CZ7.5A	OEM
10CZ7.5B	OEM
10CZ8.2	OEM
10CZ8.2A	OEM
10CZ8.2B	OEM
10CZ9.1	OEM
10CZ9.1A	OEM
10CZ9.1B	OEM
10CZ10	OEM
10CZ10A	OEM
10CZ10B	OEM
10CZ11	OEM
10CZ11A	OEM
10CZ11B	OEM
10CZ12	OEM
10CZ12A	OEM
10CZ12B	OEM
10CZ13	OEM
10CZ13A	OEM

122

If replacement code is OEM, contact original manufacturer for replacement.

DEVICE TYPE	REPL CODE
10CZ13B	OEM
10CZ15	OEM
10CZ15A	OEM
10CZ15B	OEM
10CZ16	OEM
10CZ16A	OEM
10CZ16B	OEM
10CZ18	OEM
10CZ18A	OEM
10CZ18B	OEM
10CZ20	OEM
10CZ20A	OEM
10CZ20B	OEM
10CZ22	OEM
10CZ22A	OEM
10CZ22B	OEM
10CZ24	OEM
10CZ24A	OEM
10CZ24B	OEM
10CZ27	OEM
10CZ27A	OEM
10CZ27B	OEM
10CZ30	OEM
10CZ30A	OEM
10CZ30B	OEM
10CZ33	OEM
10CZ33A	OEM
10CZ33B	OEM
10CZ36	OEM
10CZ36A	OEM
10CZ36B	OEM
10CZ39	OEM
10CZ39A	OEM
10CZ39B	OEM
10CZ43	OEM
10CZ43A	OEM
10CZ43B	OEM
10CZ47	OEM
10CZ47A	OEM
10CZ47B	OEM
10CZ51	OEM
10CZ51A	OEM
10CZ51B	OEM
10CZ56	OEM
10CZ56A	OEM
10CZ56B	OEM
10CZ62	OEM
10CZ62A	OEM
10CZ62B	OEM
10CZ66	OEM
10CZ66A	OEM
10CZ66B	OEM
10CZ75	OEM
10CZ75A	OEM
10CZ75B	OEM
10CZ82	OEM
10CZ82A	OEM
10CZ82B	OEM
10CZ91	OEM
10CZ91A	OEM
10CZ91B	OEM
10CZ100	OEM
10CZ100A	OEM
10CZ100B	OEM
10CZ103	OEM
10CZ110	OEM
10CZ110A	OEM
10CZ110B	OEM
10CZ120	OEM
10CZ120A	OEM
10CZ120B	OEM
10CZ130A	OEM
10CZ130B	OEM
10CZ150	OEM
10CZ150A	OEM
10CZ150B	OEM
10CZ160	OEM
10CZ160A	OEM
10CZ160B	OEM
10CZ180	OEM
10CZ180A	OEM
10CZ180B	OEM
10CZ200	OEM
10CZ200A	OEM
10CZ200B	OEM
10D	0015
10D(ZENER)	0248
10D-02	0015
10D-05	0015
10D05	0015
10D-06	0015
10D06	0535
10D0.5	0015
10D-1	0015
10D1	0023
10D-2	0023
10D2	0023
10D-2B	0015
10D-2B(-4)	0015
10D-2B(4)	0015
10D-2B-4	0102
10D3	0015
10D3G	0015
10D-4	0071
10D4	0023
10D4A	0023
10D4B	0023
10D4B41	OEM
10D4E	0015
10D4L	0102
10D-5	0102
10D5	0015
10D5A	0102
10D5B	0015
10D5D	0102
10D5E	0015
10D-6	0015
10D6	0023
10D6D	0015
10D6E	0015
10D6FD	OEM
10D7	0071
10D7E	0071
10D7F	0071
10D-7K	0071
10D8	0023
10D-10	0071
10D10	0071
10D556-2,3	OEM
10D701	OEM
10D702	OEM
10DB	0015
10DB1	0276
10DB2	0287
10DB2A	0287
10DB2P	0293
10DB4	0293
10DB4A	0293
10DB4P	0299
10DB6	0299
10DB6A	0293
10DB6A-C	0293
10DB6P	1999
10DB8	0250
10DB10	0250
10DC	0015
10DC05	0581
10DC0B	0015
10DC0H	0015
10DC0.5	0015
10DC-1	OEM
10DC1	0015
10DC1BLACK	0015
10DC-1N	0196
10DC-1R	0015
10DC1R	0071
10DC-2	0023
10DC2	0015
10DC-2B	0015
10DC-2C	0015
10DC-2F	0015
10DC2F	0015
10DC-2J	0015
10DC-4	0015
10DC4	0015
10DC-4R	0015
10DC4R	0015
10DC-4R-202	0015
10DC5	0015
10DC8	0071
10DC8R	0071
10DC11	OEM
10DCIN	0015
10DCIR	0015
10DCOB	0015
10DCOH	0015
10DCO.5	0015
10DCR	4890
10DF1	0604
10DF2	0790
10DF4	0015
10DF6	0072
10DF8	0071
10DG2C11	OEM
10DG2Z11	OEM
10DI	0071
10DK241U	OEM
10DL1	0015
10DL2	0015
10DL2C41	0903
10D-V	0015
10DX2	0015
10DZ	0015
10E-1	0015
10E1	0015
10E1LF	0015
10E1R20	OEM
10E1R40	OEM
10E1R60	OEM
10E1S20	OEM
10E1S40	OEM
10E1S60	OEM
10E-2	0015
10E2	0015
10E2-TA2B	0015
10E2N	OEM
10E2R20	OEM
10E2R21	OEM
10E2R40	OEM
10E2R41	OEM
10E2R60	OEM
10E2R61	OEM
10E2S20	OEM
10E2S21	OEM
10E2S40	OEM
10E2S41	OEM
10E2S60	OEM
10E2S61	OEM
10E4	0015
10E4A	0015
10E4B	0015
10E6	0015
10E-7L	0015
10E8	0071
10E10	0071
10E10(FA-8)	0071
10E10-TA2B5	0071
10E-10P	0015
10E10P	0015
10E11F	0015
10E12	OEM
10E24A	OEM
10E40	OEM
10E75	OEM
10E120	OEM
10E1051	OEM
10EB1	0170
10ELS4	0023
10ELS4-TA-1	0023
10ELS6	0023
10ELS6TA1	0023
10EN2	OEM
10EZ3.3D	OEM
10EZ3.3D5	OEM
10EZ3.3D10	OEM
10EZ3.6D	OEM
10EZ3.6D5	OEM
10EZ3.6D10	OEM
10EZ3.9D	OEM
10EZ3.9D5	OEM
10EZ3.9D10	OEM
10EZ4.3D	OEM
10EZ4.3D5	OEM
10EZ4.3D10	OEM
10EZ4.7D	OEM
10EZ4.7D5	OEM
10EZ4.7D10	OEM
10EZ5.1D	OEM
10EZ5.1D5	OEM
10EZ5.1D10	OEM
10EZ5.6D	OEM
10EZ5.6D5	OEM
10EZ5.6D10	OEM
10EZ6.2D	OEM
10EZ6.2D5	OEM
10EZ6.2D10	OEM
10EZ6.8D	OEM
10EZ6.8D5	OEM
10EZ6.8D10	OEM
10EZ7.5D	OEM
10EZ7.5D5	OEM
10EZ7.5D10	OEM
10EZ8.2D	OEM
10EZ8.2D5	OEM
10EZ8.2D10	OEM
10EZ9.1D	OEM
10EZ9.1D5	OEM
10EZ9.1D10	OEM
10EZ10D	OEM
10EZ10D5	OEM
10EZ10D10	OEM
10EZ11D	OEM
10EZ11D5	OEM
10EZ11D10	OEM
10EZ12D	OEM
10EZ12D5	OEM
10EZ12D10	OEM
10EZ13D	OEM
10EZ13D5	OEM
10EZ13D10	OEM
10EZ14D	OEM
10EZ14D5	OEM
10EZ14D10	OEM
10EZ15D	OEM
10EZ15D5	OEM
10EZ15D10	OEM
10EZ16D	OEM
10EZ16D5	OEM
10EZ16D10	OEM
10EZ17D	OEM
10EZ17D5	OEM
10EZ17D10	OEM
10EZ18D	OEM
10EZ18D5	OEM
10EZ18D10	OEM
10EZ19D	OEM
10EZ19D5	OEM
10EZ19D10	OEM
10EZ20D	OEM
10EZ20D5	OEM
10EZ20D10	OEM
10EZ22D	OEM
10EZ22D5	OEM
10EZ22D10	OEM
10EZ24D	OEM
10EZ24D5	OEM
10EZ24D10	OEM
10EZ25D	OEM
10EZ25D5	OEM
10EZ25D10	OEM
10EZ27D	OEM
10EZ27D5	OEM
10EZ27D10	OEM
10EZ30D	OEM
10EZ30D5	OEM
10EZ30D10	OEM
10EZ33D	OEM
10EZ33D5	OEM
10EZ33D10	OEM
10EZ36D	OEM
10EZ36D5	OEM
10EZ36D10	OEM
10EZ39D	OEM
10EZ39D5	OEM
10EZ39D10	OEM
10EZ43D	OEM
10EZ43D5	OEM
10EZ43D10	OEM
10EZ45D	OEM
10EZ45D5	OEM
10EZ45D10	OEM
10EZ47D	OEM
10EZ47D5	OEM
10EZ47D10	OEM
10EZ50D	OEM
10EZ50D5	OEM
10EZ50D10	OEM
10EZ51D	OEM
10EZ51D5	OEM
10EZ51D10	OEM
10EZ52D	OEM
10EZ52D5	OEM
10EZ52D10	OEM
10EZ56D	OEM
10EZ56D5	OEM
10EZ56D10	OEM
10EZ62D	OEM
10EZ62D5	OEM
10EZ62D10	OEM
10EZ68D	OEM
10EZ68D5	OEM
10EZ68D10	OEM
10EZ82D	OEM
10EZ82D5	OEM
10EZ82D10	OEM
10EZ91D	OEM
10EZ91D5	OEM
10EZ91D10	OEM
10EZ100D	OEM
10EZ100D5	OEM
10EZ100D10	OEM
10EZ105D	OEM
10EZ105D5	OEM
10EZ105D10	OEM
10EZ110D	OEM
10EZ110D5	OEM
10EZ110D10	OEM
10EZ120D	OEM
10EZ120D5	OEM
10EZ120D10	OEM
10EZ130D	OEM
10EZ130D5	OEM
10EZ130D10	OEM
10EZ140D	OEM
10EZ140D5	OEM
10EZ140D10	OEM
10EZ150D	OEM
10EZ150D5	OEM
10EZ150D10	OEM
10EZ160D	OEM
10EZ160D5	OEM
10EZ160D10	OEM
10EZ175D	OEM
10EZ175D5	OEM
10EZ175D10	OEM
10EZ180D	OEM
10EZ180D5	OEM
10EZ180D10	OEM
10EZ200D	OEM
10EZ200D5	OEM
10EZ200D10	OEM
10E.5	OEM
10F1	0015
10F1R07	OEM
10F1R15	OEM
10F1S07	OEM
10F1S15	OEM
10F2R07	OEM
10F2R15	OEM
10F2S07	OEM
10F2S15	OEM
10F2S07	OEM
10F5	3688
10F10	0865
10F15	0865
10F20	0865
10F30	0847
10F40	0847
10F50	1599
10FC11	OEM
10FCRA	1814
10FCRB	1814
10FCRC	1814
10FCRD	1814
10FCRE	1814
10FCRF	1814
10FCRG	1814
10FCRH	1814
10FCRI	OEM
10FCRJ	OEM
10FCRK	OEM
10FCRL	OEM
10FIR15	OEM
10FWJ2C11	3235
10FWJ2C41	3235
10G4	0071
10G4B41	OEM
10G1051	0144
10G1052	0144
10GA	0071
10GC11	0847
10GD11	0847
10GG2C11	OEM
10GG2Z11	OEM
10GW2C11	OEM
10GW2C41	OEM
10GWJ2C11	3235
10GWJ2C41	3235
10H	0015
10H3	0097
10H3N	2275
10H3P	3688
10H3PN	0904
10H380RT	OEM
10H551	0144
10H551-2,3	OEM
10H553	0144
10H553-2,3	OEM
10H1051	0144
10H1053	0144
10HB05	2347
10HB10	2347
10HB20	2347
10HB40	2353
10HB60	2354
10HB80	2356
10HC11	OEM
10I10	0071
10IP005	OEM
10IP005D	OEM
10IP005N	OEM
10IP01	OEM
10IP01D	OEM
10IP01N	OEM
10IP02	OEM
10IP02D	OEM
10IP02N	OEM
10IP04	OEM
10IP04D	OEM
10IP04N	OEM
10IP06	OEM
10IP06D	OEM
10IP06N	OEM
10IP08	OEM
10IP08D	OEM
10IP08N	OEM
10IP10	OEM
10IP10D	OEM
10IP10N	OEM
10J1	1219
10J2	0015
10J2F	0015
10J3P	0090
10J4	OEM
10J4B41	OEM
10JC11	OEM
10JF1	OEM
10JF2	OEM
10JG2C11	OEM
10JG2Z11	OEM
10JH3	1551
10JUS5.04A	OEM
10JUS5.04B	OEM
10JUS6.16A	OEM
10JUS6.16B	OEM
10JUS6.50A	OEM
10JUS6.50AB	OEM
10JUS7.30A	OEM
10JUS7.30B	OEM
10JUS7.62A	OEM
10JUS7.62B	OEM
10K	0015
10K241U	1982
10KB7	OEM
10KC11	OEM
10KM7	OEM
10KZ6.8	OEM
10KZ6.8A	OEM
10KZ6.8B	OEM
10KZ7.5	OEM
10KZ7.5A	OEM
10KZ7.5B	OEM
10KZ8.2	OEM
10KZ8.2A	OEM
10KZ8.2B	OEM
10KZ9.1	OEM
10KZ9.1A	OEM
10KZ9.1B	OEM
10KZ10	OEM
10KZ10A	OEM
10KZ10B	OEM
10KZ11	OEM
10KZ11A	OEM
10KZ11B	OEM
10KZ12	OEM
10KZ12A	OEM
10KZ12B	OEM
10KZ13	OEM
10KZ13A	OEM
10KZ13B	OEM
10KZ15	OEM
10KZ15A	OEM
10KZ15B	OEM
10KZ16	OEM
10KZ16A	OEM
10KZ16B	OEM
10KZ18	OEM
10KZ18A	OEM
10KZ18B	OEM
10KZ20	OEM
10KZ20A	OEM
10KZ20B	OEM
10KZ22	OEM
10KZ22A	OEM
10KZ22B	OEM
10KZ24	OEM
10KZ24A	OEM
10KZ24B	OEM
10KZ27	OEM
10KZ27A	OEM
10KZ27B	OEM
10KZ30	OEM
10KZ30A	OEM
10KZ30B	OEM
10KZ33	OEM
10KZ33A	OEM
10KZ33B	OEM
10KZ36	OEM
10KZ36A	OEM
10KZ36B	OEM
10KZ39	OEM
10KZ39A	OEM
10KZ39B	OEM
10KZ43	OEM
10KZ43A	OEM
10KZ43B	OEM
10KZ47	OEM
10KZ47A	OEM
10KZ47B	OEM
10KZ51	OEM
10KZ51A	OEM
10KZ51B	OEM
10KZ56	OEM
10KZ56A	OEM
10KZ56B	OEM
10KZ62	OEM
10KZ62A	OEM
10KZ62B	OEM
10KZ66	OEM
10KZ66A	OEM
10KZ66B	OEM
10KZ75	OEM
10KZ75A	OEM
10KZ75B	OEM
10KZ82	OEM
10KZ82A	OEM
10KZ82B	OEM
10KZ91	OEM
10KZ91A	OEM
10KZ91B	OEM
10KZ100	OEM
10KZ100A	OEM
10KZ100B	OEM
10KZ110	OEM
10KZ110A	OEM
10KZ110B	OEM
10KZ120	OEM
10KZ120A	OEM
10KZ120B	OEM
10KZ130	OEM
10KZ130A	OEM
10KZ130B	OEM
10KZ150	OEM
10KZ150A	OEM
10KZ150B	OEM
10KZ160	OEM
10KZ160A	OEM
10KZ160B	OEM
10KZ180	OEM
10KZ180A	OEM
10KZ180B	OEM
10KZ200	OEM
10KZ200A	OEM
10KZ200B	OEM
10L1-1.5	OEM
10L1-1.5S	OEM
10L1.5-2	OEM
10L1.5-2S	OEM
10L15	0344
10L20	OEM
10L25	OEM
10L30	OEM
10L35	OEM
10L40	OEM
10L45	OEM
10L50	OEM
10L55	OEM
10L60	OEM
10L65	OEM
10L70	OEM
10L75	OEM
10L80	OEM
10L85	OEM
10L90	OEM
10L95	OEM
10L100	OEM
10L110	OEM
10L120	OEM
10L130	OEM
10L140	OEM
10L150	OEM
10L160	OEM
10L170	OEM
10L180	OEM
10L190	OEM
10L200	OEM
10L210	OEM
10L220	OEM
10L230	OEM
10L240	OEM
10L250	OEM
10L260	OEM
10L270	OEM
10L280	OEM
10L290	OEM
10L300	OEM
10LC11	OEM
10LZ3.3D5	OEM
10LZ3.3D10	OEM
10LZ3.6D5	OEM
10LZ3.6D10	OEM
10M	0015
10M10	2873
10M15	1116
10M17Z	1524
10M17Z5	1524
10M17Z10	1524
10M20	1116
10M25Z	1737
10M25Z5	1737
10M25Z10	1737
10M30	1118
10M40	0800
10M50	1186
10M60	0315
10M80	1124
10M100	0045
10MA10	0254
10MA20	1099
10MA30	1103
10MA40	0258
10MA60	0267
10MA80	1111
10MA100	0280
10MA120	OEM
10MA140	OEM
10MA160	OEM
10MC11	OEM
10N1	0015
10N2	0097
10N2(ZENER)	0064
10N3	0064
10N15A	OEM
10N15A9	OEM
10N20A	OEM
10N20A9	OEM
10N25A	OEM
10N25A9	OEM
10N30A	OEM
10N30A9	OEM
10N35A	OEM
10N35A9	OEM
10N40A	OEM
10N40A9	OEM
10N45A	OEM
10N45A9	OEM
10N50A	OEM
10N50A9	OEM
10N55A	OEM
10N55A9	OEM
10N60A	OEM
10N60A9	OEM
10N65A	OEM
10N65A9	OEM
10N70A	OEM
10N70A9	OEM
10N75A	OEM
10N75A9	OEM
10N80A	OEM
10N80A9	OEM
10N85A	OEM
10N85A9	OEM
10N90A	OEM
10N90A9	OEM
10N95A	OEM
10N95A9	OEM
10N100A	OEM
10N100A9	OEM
10N110A	OEM
10N130A	OEM
10N140A	OEM
10N150A	OEM
10N160A	OEM
10N170A	OEM
10N180A	OEM
10N190A	OEM
10N200A	OEM
10N210A	OEM
10N220A	OEM
10N230A	OEM
10N240A	OEM
10N250A	OEM
10N260A	OEM
10NC11	OEM
100-202	0143
10P1	0037
10P1A	0037
10P1S	0562
10P1SG	0562
10P2	0097
10P2S	0757
10P2SG	0757
10P3	0097

If replacement code is OEM, contact original manufacturer for replacement. 123

DEVICE TYPE	REPL CODE
10P3S	3240
10P3SG	0735
10P4	OEM
10P4S	0735
10P4SG	0735
10P5S	3260
10P5SG	0759
10P6S	0759
10P6SG	0759
10P8S	0761
10P8SG	0761
10P10SG	OEM
10P12SG	OEM
10PCRA	1641
10PCRB	1641
10PCRC	1641
10PCRD	1641
10PCRE	1641
10PCRF	1574
10PCRG	1574
10PCRH	1574
10PCRI	1655
10PCRJ	1655
10PCRK	OEM
10PCRL	OEM
10PCRNA	OEM
10PCRNB	OEM
10PCRNC	OEM
10PCRND	OEM
10PCRNE	OEM
10PCRNF	OEM
10PCRNG	OEM
10PCRNH	OEM
10PCRNI	OEM
10PCRNJ	OEM
10PCRNK	OEM
10PCRNL	OEM
10PCRSA	2497
10PCRSB	2497
10PCRSC	0736
10PCRSD	0740
10PCRSE	0740
10PCRSF	0742
10PCRSG	0742
10PCRSH	0742
10PCRSI	0747
10PCRSJ	0747
10PCRSK	OEM
10PCRSL	OEM
10PF	0030
10PM8	OEM
10PZ6.8	1449
10PZ6.8A	1449
10PZ6.8B	1449
10PZ6.8C	1449
10PZ6.8D	1449
10PZ7.5	0221
10PZ7.5A	0221
10PZ7.5B	0221
10PZ7.5C	0221
10PZ7.5D	0221
10PZ8.2	1481
10PZ8.2A	1481
10PZ8.2B	1481
10PZ8.2C	1481
10PZ8.2D	1481
10PZ9.1	1608
10PZ9.1A	1608
10PZ9.1B	1608
10PZ9.1C	1608
10PZ9.1D	1608
10PZ10	0505
10PZ10A	0505
10PZ10B	0505
10PZ10C	0505
10PZ10D	0505
10PZ11	0686
10PZ11A	0686
10PZ11B	0686
10PZ11C	0686
10PZ11D	0686
10PZ12	0864
10PZ12A	0864
10PZ12B	0864
10PZ12C	0864
10PZ12D	0864
10PZ13	1014
10PZ13A	1014
10PZ13B	1014
10PZ13C	1014
10PZ13D	1014
10PZ14	1145
10PZ14A	1145
10PZ14B	1145
10PZ14C	1145
10PZ14D	1145
10PZ15	1264
10PZ15A	1264
10PZ15B	1264
10PZ15C	1264
10PZ15D	1264
10PZ16	1392
10PZ16A	1392
10PZ16B	1392
10PZ16C	1392
10PZ16D	1392
10PZ18	1071
10PZ18A	1071
10PZ18B	1071

DEVICE TYPE	REPL CODE
10PZ18C	1071
10PZ18D	1071
10PZ20	1707
10PZ20A	1707
10PZ20B	1707
10PZ20C	1707
10PZ20D	1707
10PZ22	1712
10PZ22A	1712
10PZ22B	1712
10PZ22C	1712
10PZ22D	1712
10PZ24	1725
10PZ24A	1725
10PZ24B	1725
10PZ24C	1725
10PZ24D	1725
10PZ27	1750
10PZ27A	1750
10PZ27B	1750
10PZ27C	1750
10PZ27D	1750
10PZ30	1761
10PZ30A	1761
10PZ30B	1761
10PZ30C	1761
10PZ30D	1761
10PZ33	1777
10PZ33A	1777
10PZ33B	1777
10PZ33C	1777
10PZ33D	1777
10PZ36	1785
10PZ36A	1785
10PZ36B	1785
10PZ36C	1785
10PZ36D	1785
10PZ39	1793
10PZ39A	1793
10PZ39B	1793
10PZ39C	1793
10PZ39D	1793
10PZ43	1185
10PZ43A	1185
10PZ43B	1185
10PZ43C	1185
10PZ43D	1185
10PZ47	0022
10PZ47A	0022
10PZ47B	0022
10PZ47C	0022
10PZ47D	0022
10PZ51	0132
10PZ51A	0132
10PZ51B	0132
10PZ51C	0132
10PZ51D	0132
10PZ56	0207
10PZ56A	0207
10PZ56B	0207
10PZ56C	0207
10PZ56D	0207
10PZ62	0263
10PZ62A	0263
10PZ62B	0263
10PZ62C	0263
10PZ62D	0263
10PZ68	0306
10PZ68A	0306
10PZ68B	0306
10PZ68C	0306
10PZ68D	0306
10PZ75	0325
10PZ75A	0325
10PZ75B	0325
10PZ75C	0325
10PZ75D	0352
10PZ82	0352
10PZ82A	0352
10PZ82B	0352
10PZ82C	0352
10PZ82D	0352
10PZ91	0408
10PZ91A	0408
10PZ91B	0408
10PZ91C	0408
10PZ91D	0408
10PZ100	0433
10PZ100A	0433
10PZ100B	0433
10PZ100C	0433
10PZ100D	0433
10PZ110	0483
10PZ110A	0483
10PZ110B	0483
10PZ110C	0483
10PZ110D	0483
10PZ120	0504
10PZ120A	0504
10PZ120B	0504
10PZ120C	0504
10PZ120D	0504
10PZ130	0519
10PZ130A	0519
10PZ130B	0519
10PZ130C	0519
10PZ130D	0519
10PZ150	0063
10PZ150A	0063

DEVICE TYPE	REPL CODE
10PZ150B	0063
10PZ150C	0063
10PZ150D	0063
10PZ160	0397
10PZ160A	0397
10PZ160B	0397
10PZ160C	0397
10PZ160D	0397
10PZ180	0629
10PZ180A	0629
10PZ180B	0629
10PZ180C	0629
10PZ180D	0629
10PZ200	0663
10PZ200A	0663
10PZ200B	0663
10PZ200C	0663
10PZ200D	0663
10PZ220	OEM
10PZ220A	OEM
10PZ220B	OEM
10PZ220C	OEM
10PZ220D	OEM
10P.5-.75	OEM
10P.5-.75S	OEM
10P.75-1	OEM
10P.75-1S	OEM
10Q3	1241
10R0/18	OEM
10R1/18	OEM
10R1/52	OEM
10R1A10	OEM
10R1A10M	OEM
10R1A20	OEM
10R1A20M	OEM
10R1A40	OEM
10R1A40M	OEM
10R1A60	OEM
10R1A60M	OEM
10R1A80	OEM
10R1A80M	OEM
10R1A100	OEM
10R1A100M	OEM
10R1A110	OEM
10R1A110M	OEM
10R1A120	OEM
10R1A120M	OEM
10R1B	0015
10R2	4917
10R2/4	OEM
10R2/18	OEM
10R2/66	OEM
10R2B	0015
10R2S	OEM
10R3/4	OEM
10R3/66	OEM
10R3B	0015
10R3P	OEM
10R3S	OEM
10R4/3	OEM
10R4/3C	OEM
10R4/4	OEM
10R4/59	OEM
10R4B	0015
10R4C	OEM
10R4S	OEM
10R5/3	OEM
10R5/3D	OEM
10R5/5	OEM
10R5/61	OEM
10R5B	0015
10R5C	OEM
10R5S	OEM
10R6/3	OEM
10R6/3D	OEM
10R6/5	OEM
10R6/61	OEM
10R6B	0015
10R6C	OEM
10R6S	OEM
10R7/3	OEM
10R7/3D	OEM
10R7/5	OEM
10R7/61	OEM
10R7B	0071
10R7CD	OEM
10R7S	OEM
10R8/3	OEM
10R8/3D	OEM
10R8/5	OEM
10R8/63	OEM
10R8B	0071
10R8CD	OEM
10R8S	OEM
10R9B	0071
10R10B	0071
10R11B	0102
10R12B	0102
10R13B	0102
10R14B	0102
10R15B	0344
10R16B	OEM
10R18B	OEM
10R20B	OEM
10R22B	OEM
10R24B	OEM
10R26B	OEM
10R27.5	OEM
10R27.5A	OEM

DEVICE TYPE	REPL CODE
10R27.5B	OEM
10R27.5C	OEM
10R27.5D	OEM
10R28B	OEM
10R30B	OEM
10R32B	OEM
10R34B	OEM
10R36B	OEM
10R38B	OEM
10R40B	OEM
10R42B	OEM
10R44B	OEM
10R46B	OEM
10R48B	OEM
10R50B	OEM
10RC2	3275
10RC2A	3275
10RC5	2174
10RC5A	2174
10RC10	0562
10RC10A	0562
10RC15	3227
10RC15A	3227
10RC20	0757
10RC20A	0757
10RC25	3237
10RC25A	0716
10RC30	3240
10RC30A	3240
10RC40	0735
10RC40A	0735
10RC50	3260
10RC50A	3260
10RC60	0759
10RC60A	0759
10RC70	2848
10RC70A	2848
10RC80	0761
10RC80A	0761
10RC90	OEM
10RC100	0674
10RC110	0674
10RC110A	0674
10RC120	0674
10RCF2A	OEM
10RCF5A	OEM
10RCF10A	OEM
10RCF15A	OEM
10RCF20A	OEM
10RCF25A	OEM
10RCF30A	OEM
10RCF40A	OEM
10RCF50A	OEM
10RCF60A	OEM
10RCF70A	OEM
10RCF80A	OEM
10RCU5	OEM
10RCU10	OEM
10RCU20	OEM
10RCU30	OEM
10RCU40	OEM
10RCU50	OEM
10RCU60	OEM
10RE52	OEM
10RIA10	0464
10RIA20	0464
10RIA40	0717
10RIA60	0720
10RIA80	0674
10RIA100	0674
10RIA110	0674
10RIA120	0674
10RM60	OEM
10RM80	OEM
10RM100	OEM
10RM120	OEM
10RM150	OEM
10RM200	OEM
10RM220	OEM
10RM250	OEM
10R0/18	OEM
10RZ6.8	1591
10RZ6.8A	1591
10RZ6.8B	1591
10RZ6.8C	1449
10RZ6.8D	1449
10RZ7.1C	OEM
10RZ7.1D	OEM
10RZ7.5	1606
10RZ7.5A	1606
10RZ7.5B	1606
10RZ7.5C	0221
10RZ7.5D	0221
10RZ8.2	1612
10RZ8.2A	1481
10RZ8.2B	1612
10RZ8.2C	1481
10RZ8.2D	1481
10RZ9.1	0622
10RZ9.1A	0622
10RZ9.1B	0622
10RZ9.1C	1608
10RZ9.1D	1608
10RZ10	0505
10RZ10A	0986
10RZ10B	0986
10RZ10C	0505
10RZ10D	0505
10RZ11	0989

DEVICE TYPE	REPL CODE
10RZ11A	0989
10RZ11B	0686
10RZ11C	0686
10RZ11D	0686
10RZ12	1254
10RZ12A	1254
10RZ12B	1254
10RZ12C	0864
10RZ12D	0864
10RZ13	1240
10RZ13A	1240
10RZ13B	1240
10RZ13C	1014
10RZ13D	1014
10RZ15	1629
10RZ15A	1629
10RZ15B	1629
10RZ15C	1264
10RZ15D	1264
10RZ16	1693
10RZ16A	1693
10RZ16B	1693
10RZ16C	1392
10RZ16D	1392
10RZ18	1706
10RZ18A	1706
10RZ18B	1706
10RZ18C	1071
10RZ18D	1071
10RZ20	1720
10RZ20A	1720
10RZ20B	1720
10RZ20C	1707
10RZ20D	1707
10RZ22	0722
10RZ22A	0722
10RZ22B	0722
10RZ22C	1712
10RZ22D	1712
10RZ24	1745
10RZ24A	1745
10RZ24B	1745
10RZ24C	1725
10RZ24D	1725
10RZ27	1771
10RZ27A	1771
10RZ27B	1771
10RZ27C	1750
10RZ27D	1750
10RZ30	1783
10RZ30A	1783
10RZ30B	1783
10RZ30C	1761
10RZ30D	1761
10RZ33	1788
10RZ33A	1788
10RZ33B	1788
10RZ33C	1777
10RZ33D	1777
10RZ36	1785
10RZ36A	1798
10RZ36B	1798
10RZ36C	1785
10RZ36D	1785
10RZ39	1806
10RZ39A	1806
10RZ39B	1806
10RZ39C	1793
10RZ39D	1793
10RZ43	1815
10RZ43A	1815
10RZ43B	1815
10RZ43C	6820
10RZ43D	6820
10RZ47	1842
10RZ47A	1842
10RZ47B	1842
10RZ47C	0022
10RZ47D	0022
10RZ51	1855
10RZ51A	1855
10RZ51B	1855
10RZ51C	0132
10RZ51D	0132
10RZ56	1873
10RZ56A	1873
10RZ56B	1873
10RZ56C	0207
10RZ56D	0207
10RZ62	0263
10RZ62A	0263
10RZ62B	0263
10RZ62C	0263
10RZ62D	0263
10RZ68	1891
10RZ68A	1891
10RZ68B	1891
10RZ68C	0306
10RZ68D	0306
10RZ75	0731
10RZ75A	0731
10RZ75B	0731
10RZ75C	0325
10RZ75D	0325
10RZ82	1898
10RZ82A	1898
10RZ82B	1898
10RZ82C	0352
10RZ82D	0352

DEVICE TYPE	REPL CODE
10RZ91	1903
10RZ91A	1903
10RZ91B	1903
10RZ91C	0408
10RZ91D	0408
10RZ100	1155
10RZ100A	1155
10RZ100B	1155
10RZ100C	0433
10RZ100D	0433
10RZ110	1922
10RZ110A	1922
10RZ110B	1922
10RZ110C	0483
10RZ110D	0483
10RZ120	1930
10RZ120A	1930
10RZ120B	0504
10RZ120C	0504
10RZ120D	0504
10RZ130	1936
10RZ130A	1936
10RZ130B	1936
10RZ130C	0519
10RZ130D	0519
10RZ150	1950
10RZ150A	1950
10RZ150B	1950
10RZ150C	0063
10RZ150D	0063
10RZ160	0353
10RZ160A	0353
10RZ160B	0353
10RZ160C	0397
10RZ160D	0397
10RZ180	0771
10RZ180A	0771
10RZ180B	0771
10RZ180C	0629
10RZ180D	0629
10RZ200	1065
10RZ200A	1065
10RZ200B	1065
10RZ200C	0663
10RZ200D	0663
10RZ220	OEM
10RZ220A	OEM
10RZ220B	OEM
10RZ220C	OEM
10RZ220D	OEM
10S1S03	OEM
10S1S04	OEM
10S2-3	OEM
10S2-3S	OEM
10S2S03	OEM
10S2S04	OEM
10S2SC	OEM
10S2.5-3R	OEM
10S2.5-3.5	OEM
10S2.5-3.5S	OEM
10S3-4	OEM
10S3-4S	OEM
10S3P	OEM
10S3SC	OEM
10S3.5R	OEM
10S4SC	OEM
10S5SC	OEM
10S6SC	OEM
10S20	OEM
10S30	OEM
10S40	OEM
10S50	OEM
10SB050	OEM
10SB100	OEM
10SB200	OEM
10SB400	OEM
10SB600	OEM
10SC05	OEM
10SC1	OEM
10SC2	OEM
10SC3	OEM
10SC3.5-3.5S	OEM
10SC3.5-4.5	OEM
10SC4	OEM
10SC6	OEM
10SL101	OEM
10SM1	OEM
10SM3	OEM
10SM6	OEM
10SM15	OEM
10SM25	OEM
10SM40	OEM
10SM55	OEM
10SM70	OEM
10SM100	OEM
10SM150	OEM
10SM200	OEM
10SP005	OEM
10SP005D	OEM
10SP005N	OEM
10SP01	OEM
10SP01D	OEM
10SP01N	OEM
10SP02	OEM
10SP02D	OEM
10SP02N	OEM
10SP04	OEM
10SP04D	OEM
10SP04N	OEM

DEVICE TYPE	REPL CODE
10SP06	OEM
10SP06D	OEM
10SP06N	OEM
10SP08	OEM
10SP08D	OEM
10SP08N	OEM
10SP10	OEM
10SP10D	OEM
10SP10N	OEM
10SS2SC	OEM
10SS3SC	OEM
10SS4SC	OEM
10SS5SC	OEM
10SS6SC	OEM
10T2	OEM
10T2FR	OEM
10T3P	OEM
10T4	OEM
10T4FR	OEM
10T4S	OEM
10T5.6	1436
10T6FR	OEM
10T6.2	2206
10T6.8	1449
10T7.5	0221
10T8.2	1481
10T9.1	1608
10T10	0505
10T11	0686
10T12	0864
10T13	1014
10T15	1264
10T16	1392
10T18	1071
10T20	1707
10T22	1712
10T24	1725
10T27	1750
10T30	1761
10T33	1777
10T36	1785
10T39	1793
10T43	1185
10T47	0022
10T51	0132
10T56	0207
10T62	0263
10T68	0306
10T75	0325
10T82	0352
10T91	0408
10T100	0433
10T110	0483
10T120	0504
10T130	0519
10T150	0063
10T160	0397
10T180	0629
10T200	0663
10TB050	OEM
10TB1	0736
10TB1-CE00	OEM
10TB1-CH00	OEM
10TB1-EE00	OEM
10TB1-EH00	OEM
10TB1-GE00	OEM
10TB1-GH00	OEM
10TB1-JE00	OEM
10TB2	0740
10TB2-CE00	OEM
10TB2-CH00	OEM
10TB2-EE00	OEM
10TB2-EH00	OEM
10TB2-GE00	OEM
10TB2-GH00	OEM
10TB2-JE00	OEM
10TB3	2889
10TB3-CE00	OEM
10TB3-CH00	OEM
10TB3-EE00	OEM
10TB3-EH00	OEM
10TB3-GE00	OEM
10TB3-GH00	OEM
10TB3-JE00	OEM
10TB4	0742
10TB4-CE00	OEM
10TB4-CH00	OEM
10TB4-EE00	OEM
10TB4-EH00	OEM
10TB4-GE00	OEM
10TB4-GH00	OEM
10TB4-J300	OEM
10TB5	3260
10TB5-CE00	OEM
10TB5-CH00	OEM
10TB5-EE00	OEM
10TB5-EH00	OEM
10TB5-GE00	OEM
10TB5-GH00	OEM
10TB5-JE00	OEM
10TB6	0759
10TB6-CE00	OEM
10TB6-CH00	OEM
10TB6-EE00	OEM
10TB6-EH00	OEM
10TB6-GE00	OEM
10TB6-GH00	OEM
10TB6-JE00	OEM
10TB7	2848

124 If replacement code is OEM, contact original manufacturer for replacement.

DEVICE TYPE	REPL CODE
10TB7-CE00	OEM
10TB7-CH00	OEM
10TB7-EE00	OEM
10TB7-EH00	OEM
10TB7-GE00	OEM
10TB7-GH00	OEM
10TB7-JE00	OEM
10TB8	0761
10TB8-CE00	OEM
10TB8-CH00	OEM
10TB8-EE00	OEM
10TB8-EH00	OEM
10TB8-GE00	OEM
10TB8-GH00	OEM
10TB8-JE00	OEM
10TB100	OEM
10TB200	OEM
10TB400	OEM
10TB600	OEM
10TC05	OEM
10TC05B	OEM
10TC10	OEM
10TC10B	OEM
10TC15	OEM
10TC15B	OEM
10TC20	OEM
10TC20B	OEM
10TC25	OEM
10TC30	OEM
10TC30B	OEM
10TC35	OEM
10TC40	OEM
10TC40B	OEM
10TC50	OEM
10TC50B	OEM
10TC60	OEM
10TC60B	OEM
10TC70	OEM
10TC80	OEM
10TC90	OEM
10TC100	OEM
10TC110	OEM
10TC120	OEM
10TCA10	OEM
10TCA20	OEM
10TCA30	OEM
10TCA40	OEM
10TCA50	OEM
10TCA60	OEM
10TCA70	OEM
10TCA80	OEM
10TCA90	OEM
10TCA100	OEM
10TCA110	OEM
10TCA120	OEM
10TQ030	OEM
10TQ035	OEM
10TQ040	OEM
10TQ045	OEM
10V3P	OEM
10V13	OEM
10V-50	0080
10V-100	0604
10V-200	0790
10VJ	0170
10VT01	OEM
10VZENER	0170
10W3P	OEM
10W5R12-12	OEM
10W5R15-15	OEM
10W12R5	OEM
10W12R12-12	OEM
10W12R15-15	OEM
10W24R12-12	OEM
10W24R15-15	OEM
10WM1	OEM
10WM2	OEM
10WM4	OEM
10WM5	OEM
10WM8	OEM
10WM10	OEM
10X3P	OEM
10X7-8	OEM
10X7.5-8.5	OEM
10X8-9	OEM
10X8.5-9.6	OEM
10X9-10	OEM
10XT26	0211
10Y	0064
10Y3P	OEM
10YHB10	OEM
10Z3.3T	4167
10Z3.3T5	1000
10Z3.3T10	1000
10Z3.6T	2381
10Z3.6T5	1370
10Z3.6T10	1370
10Z3.9M	2024
10Z3.9T5	0542
10Z3.9T10	0542
10Z3.9T20	0542
10Z4.3T5	2387
10Z4.3T10	2387
10Z4.3T20	2387
10Z4.7M	1429
10Z4.7T5	2101
10Z4.7T10	2101
10Z4.7T20	2101
10Z5.1T5	2394
10Z5.1T10	2394
10Z5.1T20	2394
10Z5.6M	1436
10Z5.6T5	1890
10Z5.6T10	1890
10Z5.6T20	1890
10Z6	0015
10Z6.2T5	0691
10Z6.2T10	0691
10Z6.2T20	0691
10Z6.8M	1449
10Z6.8T5	1591
10Z6.8T10	1591
10Z6.8T20	1591
10Z7.5T5	1606
10Z7.5T10	1606
10Z7.5T20	1606
10Z8.2M	1481
10Z8.2T5	1612
10Z8.2T10	1612
10Z8.2T20	1612
10Z9.1T5	0622
10Z9.1T10	0622
10Z9.1T20	0622
10Z10	0505
10Z10M	0505
10Z10T5	0986
10Z10T10	0986
10Z10T20	0986
10Z11T5	0989
10Z11T10	0989
10Z11T20	0989
10Z12	0864
10Z12M	0864
10Z12T5	1254
10Z12T10	1254
10Z12T20	1254
10Z13T5	1240
10Z13T10	1240
10Z13T20	1240
10Z15M	1264
10Z15T5	1629
10Z15T10	1629
10Z15T20	1629
10Z16T5	1693
10Z16T10	1693
10Z16T20	1693
10Z18M	1071
10Z18T10	1706
10Z18T20	1706
10Z20T5	1720
10Z20T10	1720
10Z20T20	1720
10Z22M	1712
10Z22T5	0722
10Z22T10	0722
10Z22T20	0722
10Z24T5	1745
10Z24T10	1745
10Z24T20	1745
10Z27M	1750
10Z27T5	1771
10Z27T10	1771
10Z27T20	1771
10Z30T5	1761
10Z30T20	1783
10Z33T5	1788
10Z33T10	1788
10ZB	OEM
11/1	0133
11/1+12/1	0015
11/1&12/1	0015
11/10	0102
11/15	0015
11/20	1293
11/1592	0015
11-0399	0160
11-0400	0160
11-0422	0155
11-0423	0396
11-0429	0015
11-0430	0133
11-0769	0015
11-0770	0455
11-0771	0015
11-0772	0161
11-0773	0455
11-0774	0155
11-0775	0396
11-0778	0155
11-0781	0133
11-085001	0143
11-085003	0015
11-085004	0143
11-085005	0143
11-085007	0143
11-085008	0143
11-085010	0016
11-085012	0133
11-085013	0015
11-085014	0143
11-085015	0143
11-085022	0143
11-085024	0015
11-60	2285
11-102	4559
11-102-001	0276
11-103	0621
11-104	OEM
11-113	1532
11-115	4227
11-116	OEM
11-117	1775
11-1592	0015
11-11911-1	0130
11-102001	0015
11-102003	0276
11-108002	0276
11-120007	0015
11A1	0181
11B	0181
11B1	0248
11B2	0181
11B3	0181
11B551	0144
11B551-2	0111
11B551-2,3	OEM
11B551-3	0111
11B552	0144
11B552-2	0111
11B552-2,3	OEM
11B552-3	0111
11B554	0144
11B554-2	0111
11B554-2,3	OEM
11B554-3	0111
11B555	0144
11B555-2	0111
11B555-2,3	OEM
11B555-3	0111
11B556	0590
11B556-2	0855
11B556-2,3	OEM
11B556-3	0855
11B560	0590
11B560-2	0855
11B560-2,3	OEM
11B560-3	0855
11B1052	0144
11B1055	0144
11B1257	0855
11B1258	0855
11B1259	0855
11B1260	0855
11BT23GK	OEM
11BT33ZK	OEM
11C1B1	0142
11C2	0181
11C3B1	0142
11C3B3	0142
11C5B1	0142
11C7B1	0142
11C10B1	0142
11C11B1	0142
11C11B20	0626
11C44DC	0011
11C211B20	0590
11C551	0144
11C551-2	0111
11C551-2,3	OEM
11C551-3	0111
11C553	0144
11C553-2	0111
11C553-2,3	OEM
11C553-3	0111
11C557	0144
11C557-2	0007
11C557-2,3	OEM
11C557-3	0007
11C702	0018
11C1051	0144
11C1053	0144
11C1057	0144
11C1536	0086
11CB1	OEM
11CB2	OEM
11CB3	OEM
11CB4	OEM
11CB5	OEM
11CB6	OEM
11CB7	OEM
11CB8	OEM
11CF1	OEM
11CF2	OEM
11CF3	OEM
11CF4	OEM
11CF5	OEM
11CF6	OEM
11CF7	OEM
11CF8	OEM
11CM6	OEM
11DF1	0080
11DF2	0080
11DF3	0790
11DF4	0790
11DM6	OEM
11DQ03	0730
11DQ04	1325
11DQ05	1325
11DQ06	3834
11DQ09	3834
11DQ10	OEM
11E1	0015
11E1TA1	0015
11E1TA1-T	0015
11E2	0015
11E2TA-1	0015
11E2TA1	0015
11E4	0015
11E11	OEM
11E22A	OEM
11E35	OEM
11E60	OEM
11E100	OEM
11EB2	OEM
11EQS04	6646
11ES1	0015
11ES1TA1	0015
11ES1TB3	OEM
11ES2	0015
11F1SC	0865
11F2SC	0865
11F3SC	0847
11FA30S	OEM
11G702	OEM
11G703	OEM
11G1052	0007
11G1053	0007
11HM6	OEM
11J2	0015
11J2F	0015
11JUS5.94A	OEM
11JUS5.94B	OEM
11JUS6.78A	OEM
11JUS6.78B	OEM
11JUS7.15A	OEM
11JUS7.15B	OEM
11JUS8.03A	OEM
11JUS8.03B	OEM
11JUS8.38A	OEM
11JUS8.38B	OEM
11K60	0201
11N1	0181
11N267	0143
11PD18M	OEM
11PD18P	OEM
11PH18M	OEM
11PS18M	OEM
11R05S	0084
11R055	0097
11R1S	0090
11R1SC	0097
11R2	OEM
11R2S	0097
11R2SC	0097
11R3S	0105
11R3SC	0109
11R4S	0109
11R5S	0116
11R6S	0122
11R8S	0131
11R10S	0145
11R12S	OEM
11R45	0109
11R105	0145
11R106	0142
11RA10S	OEM
11RC10	0562
11RC20	0757
11RC30	0735
11RC40	0735
11RC50	0759
11RC60	0759
11RC80	0761
11RC100	OEM
11RT1	0150
11T1	OEM
11T2	OEM
11T4	0179
11T4S	1250
11V53A	OEM
11V54	OEM
11V64	OEM
11V651	OEM
11V652	OEM
11W71	OEM
11W72	OEM
11Y	0181
11YM6	OEM
11Z4	OEM
11Z6	OEM
11Z6A	OEM
11Z6AF	0289
11Z6F	0289
11Z6FAF	OEM
12/1	0196
12/1N	1073
12/1N10	1141
12/3	0196
12/100	0196
12-085005	0143
12-085006	0143
12-085009	0143
12-085029	0143
12-085031	0015
12-085034	0143
12-085035	0143
12-085038	0143
12-085040	0015
12-085041	0123
12-087003	0143
12-087004	0133
12-1	0233
12-1-70	0016
12-1-70-12	0016
12-1-70-12-7	0016
12-1-73	0279
12-1-74	0279
12-1-75	0279
12-1-76	0279
12-1-78	0279
12-1-83	0279
12-1-91	0279
12-1-92	0279
12-1-93	0279
12-1-95	0004
12-1-96	0004
12-1-100	0279
12-1-102	0279
12-1-103	0279
12-1-104	0279
12-1-105	0279
12-1-106	0004
12-1-107	0004
12-1-120	0004
12-1-128	0279
12-1-135	0050
12-1-137	0050
12-1-138	0050
12-1-139	0050
12-1-148	0004
12-1-150	0050
12-1-157	0050
12-1-161	0279
12-1-162	0279
12-1-164	0004
12-1-179	0279
12-1-180	0279
12-1-184	0004
12-1-186	0279
12-1-189	0136
12-1-190	0050
12-1-191	0004
12-1-226	0004
12-1-227	0004
12-1-228	0050
12-1-229	0050
12-1-230	0050
12-1-231	0050
12-1-232	0004
12-1-233	0050
12-1-234	0279
12-1-235	0279
12-1-236	0279
12-1-240	0279
12-1-241	0279
12-1-242	0136
12-1-243	0136
12-1-244	0136
12-1-246	0004
12-1-254	0279
12-1-256	0050
12-1-257	0136
12-1-258	0050
12-1-259	0050
12-1-260	0050
12-1-266	0004
12-1-267	0004
12-1-270	0160
12-1-271	0160
12-1-272	0004
12-1-273	0279
12-1-274	0004
12-1-275	0279
12-1-276	0016
12-1-277	0016
12-1-278	0016
12-1-279	0016
12-1-289	0279
12-1A	0016
12-1A0	0016
12-1A0R	0016
12-1A1	0016
12-1A2	0016
12-1A3	0016
12-1A3P	0016
12-1A4	0016
12-1A4-7	0016
12-1A4-7B	0016
12-1A5	0016
12-1A5L	0016
12-1A6	0016
12-1A6A	0016
12-1A7	0016
12-1A7-1	0016
12-1A8	0016
12-1A9	0016
12-1A9G	0016
12-1A19	0016
12-1A21	0016
12-1A82	0016
12-4	0016
12-10	0016
12-11	0016
12-12	0016
12-13	0016
12-14	0016
12-15	0016
12-16	0016
12-17	0016
12-18	0016
12-19	0016
12-1032-41	2503
12-23163-3	0113
12-100001	0015
12-100003	0015
12-102001	0015
12-679115-01	0720
12-680701-05	0720
12A	0053
12A1	0052
12A2	0999
12A3	0999
12A6F	0706
12A6F1	OEM
12A8	OEM
12A8F	OEM
12A8F1	OEM
12A10F	OEM
12A10F1	OEM
12A50	OEM
12A100	OEM
12A104	OEM
12A105	OEM
12A107	OEM
12A108	OEM
12A200	OEM
12A300	OEM
12A304	OEM
12A308	OEM
12A400	OEM
12A500	OEM
12A600	OEM
12A700	0131
12A800	0131
12A900	0145
12A904	OEM
12A1000	0145
12A9275	0211
12A9275-1	0211
12AL240	0279
12B	0052
12B(1WATT)	0137
12B	0052
12B1	0999
12B1(1-WATT)	0137
12B1(1WATT)	0137
12B-2	0015
12B2	0137
12B2(.5W)	0999
12B-2-BIP-M	0071
12B-2B1P-M	0015
12B3	0052
12B20	OEM
12B40	OEM
12B490100	OEM
12BG11	1522
12BH11	1512
12BL2C41	2259
12BM	1207
12C05	0084
12C05R	0529
12C1	0999
12C2	0015
12C2(ZENER)	0052
12C2P-114	0276
12C3	0052
12C5Y	0137
12C7OR	0545
12C10	0090
12C10R	0743
12C15	0097
12C15R	0760
12C20	0097
12C20R	0760
12C30	0105
12C30R	0772
12C40	0105
12C40R	0533
12C50	0116
12C50R	0796
12C60	0122
12C60R	0810
12C70	0131
12C70R	0540
12C80	0131
12C80R	0540
12C90	0145
12C90R	0545
12C100	0145
12C100R	0545
12C101	OEM
12C102	OEM
12CC12	1241
12CD12	1567
12CF11	0540
12CG11	0847
12CH1FM	OEM
12CH1M	2219
12CH2FM	OEM
12CH2M	2219
12CH3FM	OEM
12CH3M	OEM
12CH4FM	OEM
12CH4M	OEM
12CLN	0016
12CTQ030	3235
12CTQ035	3235
12CTQ040	3235
12CTQ045	6730
12D02M1	OEM
12D05M1	OEM
12D2C41	OEM
12D10K1-A	OEM
12DF15E1	OEM
12DF15E2	OEM
12DF15E3	OEM
12DG11	1522
12DH11	1512
12E10	OEM
12E20A	OEM
12E40	OEM
12E70	OEM
12E109	OEM
12E120	OEM
12F5	0084
12F5A	0084
12F5B	0084
12F5R	2275
12F5RA	2275
12F5RB	2275
12F10	0090
12F10A	0090
12F10B	0090
12F10R	2275
12F10RA	2275
12F10RB	2275
12F15	0097
12F15A	0097
12F15B	0097
12F15E1	OEM
12F15E3	OEM
12F15R	2275
12F15RA	2275
12F15RB	2275
12F20	0097
12F20A	0097
12F20B	0097
12F20R	2275
12F20RA	2275
12F20RB	2275
12F30	0105
12F30A	0105
12F30B	0105
12F30R	0471
12F30RA	0471
12F30RB	0471
12F40	0109
12F40A	0109
12F40B	0109
12F40R	0471
12F40RA	0471
12F40RB	0471
12F50	0116
12F50A	0116
12F50B	0116
12F50R	0471
12F50RA	0471
12F50RB	0471
12F60	0122
12F60A	0122
12F60B	0122
12F60R	0471
12F60RA	0471
12F60RB	0471
12F70	2982
12F70A	2982
12F70B	0131
12F70R	2982
12F70RA	0444
12F70RB	0444
12F80	0131
12F80A	0131
12F80B	0131
12F80R	0444
12F80RA	0444
12F80RB	0444
12F90	0145
12F90A	0145
12F90B	0145
12F90R	0444
12F90RA	0444
12F90RB	0444
12F100	0145
12F100A	0145
12F100B	0145
12F100R	0444
12F100RA	0444
12F100RB	0444
12F120	OEM
12FC12	1571
12FD12	3251
12FG11	0029
12FH05S	1557
12FH1S	1557
12FH2S	1557
12FH3S	2140
12FH4S	2140
12FH11	1836
12FL5S02	1557
12FL5S05	1557
12FL5S10	1557
12FL10S02	1557
12FL10S05	1557
12FL10S10	1557
12FL20S02	1557
12FL20S05	1557
12FL20S10	1557
12FL40S02	2140
12FL40S05	2140
12FL40S10	2140
12FL60S02	0706
12FL60S05	0706
12FL60S10	OEM

If replacement code is OEM, contact original manufacturer for replacement.

125

DEVICE TYPE	REPL CODE
12FL80S05	OEM
12FL80S10	OEM
12FL100S05	OEM
12FL100S10	OEM
12FR5	0529
12FR5A	0529
12FR5B	0529
12FR10	0743
12FR10A	0743
12FR10B	4949
12FR15	0760
12FR15A	0760
12FR15B	0760
12FR20	0760
12FR20A	0760
12FR20B	0760
12FR30	0772
12FR30A	0772
12FR30B	0772
12FR40	0533
12FR40A	0533
12FR40B	0533
12FR50	0796
12FR50A	0796
12FR50B	0796
12FR60	0810
12FR60A	0810
12FR60B	0810
12FR70B	0540
12FR80	0540
12FR80A	0540
12FR80B	0540
12FR90	0545
12FR90A	0545
12FR90B	0545
12FR100	0545
12FR100A	0545
12FR100B	0545
12FX11	OEM
12FX12	OEM
12FXF11	OEM
12G1	OEM
12G2	OEM
12G4	0102
12G101	OEM
12G301	OEM
12G302	OEM
12GC11	1571
12GG11	0029
12GH11	1836
12H301	OEM
12H302	OEM
12H303	OEM
12H901	OEM
12H902	OEM
12J2	0015
12J2F	0015
12J301	OEM
12J302	OEM
12J303	OEM
12J901	OEM
12J902	OEM
12J905	OEM
12JC11	1576
12JG11	0596
12JH11	1840
12JUS6.48A	OEM
12JUS6.48B	OEM
12JUS7.39A	OEM
12JUS7.39B	OEM
12JUS7.80A	OEM
12JUS7.80B	OEM
12JUS8.76A	OEM
12JUS8.76B	OEM
12JUS9.14A	OEM
12JUS9.14B	OEM
12K60	0286
12KM7	OEM
12L2C41	OEM
12LC11	1124
12LF11	0540
12M2	0160
12MC	0050
12MF5	1557
12MF10	1557
12MF15	1557
12MF20	1557
12MF30	OEM
12MF40	OEM
12MZ	0050
12N02F1	OEM
12N05M1	OEM
12N10K1	OEM
12NC11	0045
12NF11	0545
12P02F1-A	OEM
12P05M1-A	OEM
12P2	0133
12P10K1	OEM
12PR40B	0533
12PR60B	0810
12QF11	OEM
12R0/18	OEM
12R1/18	OEM
12R1/52	OEM
12R2	OEM
12R2/4	OEM
12R2/66	OEM
12R2B	OEM

DEVICE TYPE	REPL CODE
12R2S	OEM
12R3/4	OEM
12R3/66	OEM
12R3B	OEM
12R3S	OEM
12R4/3	OEM
12R4/3C	OEM
12R4/4	OEM
12R4/59	OEM
12R4C	OEM
12R4S	OEM
12R5/3	OEM
12R5/3D	OEM
12R5/5	OEM
12R5/61	OEM
12R5C	OEM
12R5S	OEM
12R6/3	OEM
12R6/3D	OEM
12R6/5	OEM
12R6/61	OEM
12R6C	OEM
12R6S	OEM
12R7/3	OEM
12R7/3D	OEM
12R7/5	OEM
12R7/61	OEM
12R7CD	OEM
12R7S	OEM
12R8/3	OEM
12R8/3D	OEM
12R8/5	OEM
12R8/63	OEM
12R8CD	OEM
12R8S	OEM
12R52	OEM
12RCM5	2174
12RCM10	0562
12RCM20	OEM
12RCM30	OEM
12RCM40	OEM
12RCM50	OEM
12RCM60	OEM
12RH05S	1557
12RH1S	1557
12RH2S	1538
12RH3S	3110
12RH4S	2140
12RO/18	OEM
12S1573	OEM
12S1831	OEM
12SM1	OEM
12SM3	OEM
12SM6	OEM
12SM15	OEM
12SM25	OEM
12SM40	OEM
12SM55	OEM
12SM70	OEM
12SM100	OEM
12SM150	OEM
12SM200	OEM
12SZ-EQB01-12A	0137
12T05T	OEM
12T1	OEM
12T2	OEM
12T4	OEM
12T4S	OEM
12T10T	OEM
12T20T	OEM
12T40T	OEM
12T60T	OEM
12T80T	OEM
12TB050	OEM
12TB100	OEM
12TB200	OEM
12TB400	OEM
12TB600	OEM
12TC10	OEM
12TC20	OEM
12TC30	OEM
12TC40	OEM
12TC50	OEM
12TC60	OEM
12TC70	OEM
12TC80	OEM
12TC90	OEM
12TC100	OEM
12TC110	OEM
12TC120	OEM
12TCA10	OEM
12TCA20	OEM
12TCA30	OEM
12TCA40	OEM
12TCA50	OEM
12TCA60	OEM
12TCA70	OEM
12TCA80	OEM
12TCA90	OEM
12TCA100	OEM
12TCA110	OEM
12TCA120	OEM
12V	0137
12V1W	0137
12V66	OEM
12X	0052
12X006	OEM
12X008	OEM
12X010	OEM

DEVICE TYPE	REPL CODE
12X011	OEM
12X012	OEM
12X013	OEM
12X014	OEM
12X015	OEM
12X040	OEM
12X043	OEM
12X047	0016
12X058	OEM
12X059	OEM
12X070	OEM
12X084A	OEM
12X084B	OEM
12X165	OEM
12Y	0137
12Z	0361
12Z4	OEM
12Z6	OEM
12Z6A	OEM
12Z6F	0188
12Z6FAF	3890
13-0002	0170
13-0003	0133
13-0003(PACE)	0124
13-0004	0143
13-0006	0006
13-0006A	0037
13-0009	0155
13-0010	0155
13-0014	0424
13-0015	0015
13-0017	0316
13-0020	0144
13-0021	0016
13-0022	0076
13-0024	0016
13-0028	0693
13-0029	0156
13-0032	0103
13-0035	0079
13-0040	0016
13-0041	0037
13-0043	0037
13-0043A	0037
13-0044	0006
13-0044A	0037
13-0048	0037
13-0049	0161
13-0050	0023
13-0058	0155
13-0061	0037
13-0061A	0037
13-0062	0144
13-0062-1	0224
13-0063	0076
13-0064	0079
13-0065	0144
13-0065(1)	0007
13-0078	0247
13-0079	5468
13-0079A	5468
13-0097	0556
13-001200-00X	0123
13-0022345-00X	OEM
13-0023511-04X	0527
13-0023534-03X	OEM
13-0023535-03X	OEM
13-0023713-08X	OEM
13-0106	1258
13-0117	0030
13-0118	0212
13-0129	4972
13-0130	3747
13-0158	OEM
13-0161	0083
13-0164	0446
13-0165	0212
13-0167	OEM
13-0178	0018
13-0321-5	0016
13-0321-6	0016
13-0321-7	0016
13-0321-8	0016
13-0321-9	0016
13-0321-10	0016
13-0321-11	0016
13-0321-12	0016
13-0321-14	0144
13-0321-15	0144
13-0321-16	0144
13-0321-17	0144
13-0321-21	0144
13-0321-81	0016
13-076003	OEM
13-085002	0133
13-085012	0123
13-085015	0133
13-085022	0133
13-085023	0133
13-085024	0071
13-085026	0133
13-085027	0071
13-085028	0012
13-085029	0123
13-085039	0015
13-085042	0012
13-086028	1914
13-087005	0133
13-087005(DIODE)	0133

DEVICE TYPE	REPL CODE
13-087005(TRANS)	0004
13-087027	0015
13-1-6	0627
13-3-6	6920
13-4P63-I	0042
13-9-6	0627
13-10-6	0627
13-11-6	0627
13-12-03-0	0143
13-17-6	0016
13-17-6(SEARS)*	0079
13-26-6	0649
13-27-6	2689
13-28-6	2549
13-29-5	0167
13-29-6	0167
13-30-6	0360
13-36-6	0649
13-40-6	0350
13-41-6	0345
13-42-6	0348
13-43-6	OEM
13-46-6	OEM
13-50-6	0618
13-52-6	0696
13-53-6	4175
13-54-6	OEM
13-56-6	0850
13-57-6	0746
13-59-6	2535
13-60-6	0696
13-61-6	2535
13-62-6	OEM
13-64-6	0167
13-66-9	OEM
13-67-6	0746
13-72-6	OEM
13-73-6	0797
13-74-6	6258
13-100-6	6496
13-101-6	OEM
13-103-6	OEM
13-105-6	5206
13-106-6	OEM
13-107-6	OEM
13-108-6	OEM
13-109-6	OEM
13-110-6	OEM
13-111-6	OEM
13-112-6	OEM
13-113-6	OEM
13-114-6	OEM
13-115-6	OEM
13-116-6	OEM
13-117-6	1662
13-118-6	OEM
13-119-6	OEM
13-120-6	OEM
13-121-6	OEM
13-122-6	OEM
13-123-6	OEM
13-124-6	OEM
13-125-6	OEM
13-126-6	OEM
13-127-6	OEM
13-128-6	OEM
13-129-6	OEM
13-131-6	OEM
13-132-6	OEM
13-133-6	OEM
13-135-6	OEM
13-136-6	OEM
13-137-6	OEM
13-138-6	OEM
13-139-6	OEM
13-140-6	OEM
13-141-6	OEM
13-142-6	OEM
13-143-6	OEM
13-144-6	OEM
13-145-6	OEM
13-146-6	OEM
13-147-6	OEM
13-148-6	OEM
13-149-6	OEM
13-150-6	OEM
13-151-6	OEM
13-152-6	OEM
13-153-6	OEM
13-155-6	OEM
13-156-6	OEM
13-157-6	OEM
13-158-6	OEM
13-159-6	OEM
13-160-6	OEM
13-161-6	OEM
13-162-6	OEM
13-163-6	OEM
13-164-6	OEM
13-165-6	OEM
13-166-6	OEM
13-167-6	OEM
13-168-6	OEM
13-169-6	OEM
13-170-6	OEM
13-171-6	OEM
13-172-6	OEM
13-173-6	OEM
13-900-6	OEM

DEVICE TYPE	REPL CODE
13-901-6	OEM
13-902-6	OEM
13-903-6	OEM
13-905-6	OEM
13-906-6	OEM
13-907-6	OEM
13-908-6	OEM
13-912-6	OEM
13-915-6	OEM
13-917-6	OEM
13-920-6	OEM
13-922-6	OEM
13-923-6	OEM
13-925-6	OEM
13-926-6	OEM
13-928-6	OEM
13-931-6	OEM
13-932-6	OEM
13-933-6	OEM
13-935-6	OEM
13-936-6	OEM
13-937-6	OEM
13-938-6	OEM
13-939-6	OEM
13-941-6	OEM
13-945-6	OEM
13-946-6	OEM
13-949-6	OEM
13-950-6	OEM
13-951-6	OEM
13-952-6	OEM
13-954-6	OEM
13-956-6	OEM
13-957-6	OEM
13-959-6	OEM
13-960-6	OEM
13-961-6	OEM
13-963-6	OEM
13-964-6	OEM
13-965-6	OEM
13-967-6	OEM
13-968-6	OEM
13-970-6	OEM
13-971-6	OEM
13-972-6	OEM
13-973-6	OEM
13-974-6	OEM
13-975-6	OEM
13-977-6	OEM
13-979-6	OEM
13-981-6	OEM
13-982-6	OEM
13-984-6	OEM
13-985-6	OEM
13-986-6	OEM
13-987-6	OEM
13-1032-5	0144
13-1032-51	0224
13-1836-1	0016
13-1847-1	0419
13-2384-2	0007
13-6247-3	0015
13-10102-1	0015
13-10320-14	0007
13-10321-1	0144
13-10321-2	0144
13-10321-3	0015
13-10321-5	0144
13-10321-6	0007
13-10321-7	0144
13-10321-8	0144
13-10321-9	0144
13-10321-10	0007
13-10321-11	0007
13-10321-12	0144
13-10321-13	OEM
13-10321-14	0144
13-10321-15	0144
13-10321-16	0144
13-10321-17	0144
13-10321-20	0144
13-10321-21	0144
13-10321-24	0911
13-10321-26	0144
13-10321-29	0127
13-10321-30	0144
13-10321-31	0127
13-10321-32	0127
13-10321-34	2496
13-10321-35	0224
13-10321-36	0224
13-10321-37	0212
13-10321-41	0224
13-10321-42	0911
13-10321-43	0144
13-10321-46	0224
13-10321-47	0007
13-10321-48	0623
13-10321-50	0259
13-10321-51	0144
13-10321-52	OEM
13-10321-53	0212
13-10321-54	0133
13-10321-55	0133
13-10321-56	0111
13-10321-59	0079
13-10321-62	0224
13-10321-65	0127
13-10321-66	0224

DEVICE TYPE	REPL CODE
13-10321-67	0144
13-10321-70	2439
13-10321-71	0224
13-10321-72	0127
13-10321-75	0008
13-10321-76	0007
13-10321-79	0144
13-10321-151	OEM
13-10321-152	OEM
13-10321-153	2496
13-10321-154	1023
13-10321-155	OEM
13-10321-156	0224
13-10321-157	0224
13-10321-158	3562
13-10321-159	0367
13-10321-160	0127
13-10321-161	0367
13-12001-0	0123
13-12002-0	0143
13-12003-0	0019
13-13021-15	0127
13-13543-1	0142
13-13543-2	0142
13-14065-77	0079
13-14085-1	0144
13-14085-2	0144
13-14085-3	0127
13-14085-4	0127
13-14085-6	0016
13-14085-7	0016
13-14085-9	0004
13-14085-10	0004
13-14085-11	0164
13-14085-12	0164
13-14085-13	0037
13-14085-14	0396
13-14085-15	0016
13-14085-15A	0086
13-14085-16	0127
13-14085-17	0127
13-14085-18	0004
13-14085-23	0004
13-14085-24	0144
13-14085-25	0164
13-14085-26	0224
13-14085-27	0144
13-14085-28	0050
13-14085-29	0142
13-14085-30	0050
13-14085-31	0136
13-14085-32	0136
13-14085-33	0136
13-14085-34	0016
13-14085-35	0004
13-14085-41	0111
13-14085-49	0111
13-14085-50	0016
13-14085-54	0076
13-14085-60	0004
13-14085-71	0004
13-14085-72	0016
13-14085-74	0144
13-14085-75	0144
13-14085-76	0144
13-14085-77	0144
13-14085-83	0076
13-14085-84	0016
13-14085-85	0111
13-14085-86	1257
13-14085-87	0037
13-14085-88	0042
13-14085-89	0016
13-14085-91	0191
13-14085-92	0006
13-14085-93	0042
13-14085-94	0086
13-14085-95	0111
13-14085-96	0111
13-14085-97	0111
13-14085-121	0042
13-14085-122	0079
13-14085-125	0284
13-14085-126	1779
13-14094-1	0143
13-14094-2	0143
13-14094-3	0143
13-14094-5	0143
13-14094-8	0123
13-14094-9	0143
13-14094-11	0143
13-14094-12	0015
13-14094-13	0030
13-14094-14	0143
13-14094-15	0143
13-14094-16	0015
13-14094-17	0015
13-14094-24	0080
13-14094-31	0030
13-14094-33	0133
13-14094-35	OEM
13-14094-36	0139
13-14094-38	0015
13-14094-39	0015
13-14094-42	0015
13-14094-54	0015
13-14097-7	0133
13-14261-1	0015
13-14261-3	0015

DEVICE TYPE	REPL CODE
13-14278-1	0030
13-14278-2	0030
13-14279-1	0208
13-14604-1	0265
13-14605-1	0086
13-14606-1	0016
13-14627-1	0015
13-14627-4	0015
13-14735	0160
13-14735-1	0160
13-14735A	0160
13-14778-1	0265
13-14858-1	0015
13-14879-1	0002
13-14879-2	0137
13-14879-3	0002
13-14879-4	0644
13-14879-5	0416
13-14879-6	0526
13-14879-7	0526
13-14886-1	0136
13-14887-1	0136
13-14888-3	0211
13-14889-1	0136
13-14890-1	0143
13-15465-1	6404
13-15804-1	0016
13-15805-1	0211
13-15806-1	0160
13-15808-1	0076
13-15808-2	0016
13-15809-1	0233
13-15810-1	0007
13-15833-1	0086
13-15835-1	0224
13-15836-1	0211
13-15840-1	0016
13-15840-2	0016
13-15841-1	0076
13-15842-1	0320
13-15865-1	0016
13-16104-8	0015
13-16104-9	0015
13-16105-3	1293
13-16106-1	0769
13-16219-7	0196
13-16235-8	0143
13-16247-3	0015
13-16570-1	0037
13-16570-1A	0037
13-16570-2	0037
13-16570-2A	0037
13-16592-1	0969
13-16607-1	0969
13-16608-1	0969
13-16744-1	0144
13-16769-1	0016
13-17174-1	0071
13-17174-2	0015
13-17174-3	0015
13-17174-4	0087
13-17174-5	0071
13-17204	0162
13-17204-1	0133
13-17546-2	0133
13-17557-1	0015
13-17569	0469
13-17569-1	0599
13-17569-2	0133
13-17595-2	0133
13-17596-1	0469
13-17596-2	0124
13-17596-2(BIAS)	0911
13-17596-2(DET/AGC)	0133
13-17596-2(RECT)	0015
13-17596-3	0124
13-17596-4	0124
13-17596-5	0133
13-17596-6	0124
13-17596-7	0124
13-17596-8	0124
13-17596-9	0124
13-17596-10	0124
13-17607-1	0969
13-17607B	0969
13-17608-1	0969
13-17608-2	0969
13-17608B	0969
13-17608C	0969
13-17609-1	0969
13-17825-1	0015
13-17918-1	0103
13-18032-1	0004
13-18033-1	0004
13-18034	0160
13-18034-1	0160
13-18034A	0160
13-18087-1	0016
13-18087-2	0016
13-18158-1	0016
13-18198-1	0599
13-18282	0142
13-18282-1	0142
13-18304-1	0004
13-18359	0142
13-18359-1	0142
13-18359-3	0142
13-18359A	0142
13-18363	0198

If replacement code is OEM, contact original manufacturer for replacement.

DEVICE TYPE	REPL CODE
13-18363-1	0155
13-18363-1A	0198
13-18364-1	0016
13-18365-1	0111
13-18458-1	0015
13-18481-1	0242
13-18481-2	0110
13-18481-3	0242
13-18642-1	0599
13-18642-2	0599
13-18642-2D	0599
13-18642-2E	0599
13-18642-2F	0599
13-18642-3	0599
13-18642-3A	0599
13-18642-3B	0599
13-18642-20	0599
13-18654-1	0595
13-18671-1	0004
13-18671-1A	0004
13-18671-1B	0004
13-18671-1C	0004
13-18924-1	0934
13-18924-1(LARGE-CAS	1386
13-18924-1(SMALL-CAS	1129
13-18924-2	0340
13-18924-3	1129
13-18924-4	1129
13-18924-5	1129
13-18924-7	0058
13-18924-8	1129
13-18927-1	0284
13-18927-1A	0086
13-18944-1	0279
13-18944-2	0279
13-18946-1	0050
13-18946-2	0050
13-18947-1	0050
13-18948-1	0136
13-18948-2	0050
13-18949-1	0144
13-18950-1	0007
13-18950-2	0050
13-18951-1	0136
13-18951-2	0136
13-18956-2	0279
13-19776-1	0037
13-21606-1	0969
13-22017-0	0133
13-22154-0	0030
13-22154-500	0549
13-22156-0	0005
13-22319-0	0313
13-22452-0	0015
13-22463-0	0015
13-22463-1	0023
13-22581	0016
13-22581-1	0016
13-22582-1	0037
13-22582-1A	0037
13-22606-0	0124
13-22609-0	0015
13-22690-1	0321
13-22692-1	0321
13-22692-2	0321
13-22739-1	0160
13-22741	0160
13-22741-1	0265
13-23001-2	0224
13-23002-2	0224
13-23013-2	1136
13-23160-2	0326
13-23160-3	0127
13-23160-4	0079
13-23160-5	0127
13-23163-2	0113
13-23309-5	0076
13-23323-4	0079
13-23323-6	0144
13-23324-6	0079
13-23325-5	0079
13-23326-6	2039
13-23327-4	0111
13-23338-3	0079
13-23338-4	0111
13-23339-2	0111
13-23339-3	0284
13-23505-2	0086
13-23506-2	0431
13-23508-0	0455
13-23510-4	0018
13-23543-1	0142
13-23543-2	0142
13-23594-1	0103
13-23785-1	0004
13-23822	0008
13-23822-1	0008
13-23824	0079
13-23824-1	0008
13-23824-2	0007
13-23824-3	0326
13-23825-1	0233
13-23826-1	0037
13-23826-1A	0037
13-23826-2	0037
13-23826-2A	0037
13-23826-3	0037
13-23826-3A	0037

DEVICE TYPE	REPL CODE
13-23826-Q	0006
13-23840-1	0086
13-23892-5	0590
13-23916-1	0016
13-23917-1	0133
13-25226-1	0079
13-25343-1	0142
13-26009-1	0007
13-26377-1	0222
13-26377-2	2736
13-26386-1	0037
13-26386-1A	0037
13-26386-2	0037
13-26386-2A	0037
13-26386-3	0037
13-26386-4	0037
13-26576-1	0007
13-26576-2	0007
13-26577-1	0007
13-26577-2	0007
13-26577-3	0007
13-26614-1	0087
13-26666	0086
13-26666-1	0086
13-27050-1	0038
13-27404-1	0079
13-27404-2	0016
13-27432-1	0086
13-27432-2	0079
13-27433-1	0016
13-27443-1	0086
13-27596-5	0133
13-27974-1	0275
13-27974-2	0275
13-27974-3	0275
13-27974-4	0275
13-28222-1	1190
13-28222-2	0556
13-28222-3	0556
13-28222-4	0556
13-28336-1	0455
13-28336-2	0161
13-28336-20	1647
13-28386-1	0126
13-28391-1	0037
13-28391-1A	0037
13-28391-2	0037
13-28391-2A	0037
13-28392-1	0086
13-28392-2	0086
13-28392-3	0086
13-28392-5	0590
13-28393-1	0037
13-28393-1A	0037
13-28393-2	0037
13-28393-2A	0037
13-28393-3	0037
13-28394-1	0086
13-28394-2	0086
13-28394-3	0086
13-28394-4	0126
13-28394-4A	0126
13-28394-5	0126
13-28394-5A	0126
13-28394-6	0126
13-28432-1	0855
13-28432-2	0233
13-28469-2	0042
13-28471-1	0086
13-28471-1(METAL)	0086
13-28532-1	0556
13-28584	0144
13-28584-1	0144
13-28654-1	0321
13-28654-2	0321
13-28654-3	2861
13-28654-4	2861
13-28654-5	0321
13-29033-1	0079
13-29033-2	0079
13-29033-3	0079
13-29033-4	0111
13-29033-5	0079
13-29033-6	0079
13-29033-7	OEM
13-29165-1	0087
13-29165-2	0087
13-29392-2	0144
13-29432-1	0016
13-29437-1	0334
13-29656-1	0769
13-29663-1	0102
13-29687-2	0133
13-29775-1	0396
13-29775-2	0396
13-29775-3	0396
13-29776-1	0037
13-29776-1A	0037
13-29776-2	0037
13-29776-3	0037
13-29777-1	0030
13-29867-1	0133
13-29867-2	0133
13-29867-2(SUPP)	0015
13-29867-2(SW)	0133
13-29947-1	0079
13-29974-1	0007
13-29974-4	0275
13-30281	0143

DEVICE TYPE	REPL CODE
13-31013-1	0710
13-31013-1/2	0037
13-31013-2	0037
13-31013-3	0196
13-31013-4	0144
13-31013-5	0047
13-31013-6	0015
13-31013-7	0224
13-31013-8	0144
13-31013-9	0006
13-31013-10	0079
13-31013-11	0710
13-31013-13	0590
13-31013-17	1045
13-31013-18	1157
13-31013-19	0527
13-31013-20	0224
13-31013-24	0431
13-31013-25	0320
13-31013-26	0590
13-31013-27	0558
13-31013-28	0155
13-31013-30	0006
13-31013-43	2636
13-31013-44	0949
13-31013-45	0076
13-31013-49	0086
13-31013-50	0126
13-31013-52	0006
13-31013-53	1060
13-31013-54	0224
13-31013-59	1274
13-31014-1	0015
13-31014-2	0196
13-31014-3	0015
13-31014-4	0911
13-31014-6	0023
13-31014-7	0023
13-31014-32	0344
13-31014-41	0374
13-32362-1	0111
13-32363-1	OEM
13-32364-1	0037
13-32366-1	0144
13-32366-2	0144
13-32630-1	0079
13-32630-2	0590
13-32630-3	0086
13-32630-4	0590
13-32631	0786
13-32631-1	0037
13-32631-2	0786
13-32631-3	0126
13-32632-1	0546
13-32634-1	0555
13-32635-1	1257
13-32636-1	0042
13-32638-1	0161
13-32640-1	0042
13-32642-1	0161
13-33172-1	0182
13-33172-2	0102
13-33173-1	0843
13-33174-1	0283
13-33174-2	0283
13-33174-8	OEM
13-33175-1	0396
13-33175-2	0396
13-33176-1	0283
13-33177-1	0030
13-33178-1	0786
13-33179	OEM
13-33179-1	0245
13-33179-2	0002
13-33179-3	0213
13-33179-4	0170
13-33179-5	0526
13-33179-6	0137
13-33179-7	0186
13-33179-8	1596
13-33179-9	OEM
13-33179-12	2997
13-33179-14	0137
13-33180-1	0546
13-33181-1	0223
13-33181-2	0223
13-33181-3	0223
13-33182-1	0074
13-33182-2	0074
13-33183-0	1386
13-33183-1	6030
13-33184-1	0312
13-33185-1	0561
13-33186-1	0039
13-33187-1	0049
13-33187-2	0189
13-33187-3	0695
13-33187-4	0489
13-33187-5	0104
13-33187-6	0064
13-33187-7	0064
13-33187-8	0285
13-33187-9	0700
13-33187-10	0336
13-33187-11	0052
13-33187-12	0157
13-33187-13	0089
13-33187-14	0372
13-33187-15	0709

DEVICE TYPE	REPL CODE
13-33187-18	0681
13-33187-19	0274
13-33187-20	0213
13-33187-22	OEM
13-33187-23	0450
13-33187-26	0077
13-33187-27	1806
13-33187-28	OEM
13-33187-30	OEM
13-33187-31	0695
13-33187-34	0186
13-33187-38	0165
13-33187-39	0292
13-33188-2	0103
13-33189-1	0914
13-33190-1	0293
13-33350-1	0016
13-33376-1	0015
13-33595-1	0016
13-33595-2	0016
13-33595-3	0016
13-33742-1	0555
13-33742-1METAL	0086
13-33742-1PLASTIC	0546
13-33925-1	0161
13-33959-1	1129
13-34001-1	0396
13-34002-1	0419
13-34002-2	0419
13-34002-3	2969
13-34002-4	0419
13-34002-5	2969
13-34003-1	0218
13-34003-1(METAL)	0086
13-34004-1	0378
13-34004-1(METAL)	0126
13-34045-1	0144
13-34045-2	0144
13-34046-1	0555
13-34046-2	0555
13-34046-3	0555
13-34046-4	0555
13-34046-5	0236
13-34047-1	1257
13-34047-2	1257
13-34047-3	1257
13-34047-4	0676
13-34048-1	OEM
13-34056-1	0133
13-34057-1	0015
13-34089-2	0275
13-34089-4	0275
13-34338-1	OEM
13-34367-1	0037
13-34368-1	0242
13-34369-1	0150
13-34371-1	0086
13-34372-1	0264
13-34372-2	0555
13-34373-1	0378
13-34373-2	1257
13-34374-1	0130
13-34375-1	0321
13-34375-2	0321
13-34378-1	0321
13-34378-2	0321
13-34378-3	0321
13-34381	0079
13-34381-1	0111
13-34381-2	0111
13-34616-1	0419
13-34617-1	0848
13-34684-1	0130
13-34838-1	0419
13-34839-1	0848
13-34901-1	1277
13-34940-1	0037
13-35059-1	0167
13-35089-1	1698
13-35089-2	1698
13-35089-3	1698
13-35089-4	1698
13-35224-1	OEM
13-35226-1	0079
13-35257-1	0275
13-35257-2	0275
13-35257-3	0275
13-35257-4	0275
13-35324	3491
13-35324-1	2243
13-35550	0144
13-35550-1	0855
13-35621-1	0143
13-35792-1	0004
13-35807-1	0855
13-35807-2	0079
13-35894-4	0190
13-36386-1	0037
13-36444-3	0161
13-36445-3	0455
13-37526-1	0546
13-37527-1	0378
13-37708-1	0538
13-37833-2	OEM
13-37868-1	0023
13-37869-1	0710
13-37870-1	0065
13-37870-2	0065
13-37900-1	0931

DEVICE TYPE	REPL CODE
13-37905-1	0039
13-37933-1	OEM
13-37933-2	0374
13-39004-1	0042
13-39004-2	0042
13-39046-3	0555
13-39047-3	1257
13-39072-1	0182
13-39072-2	0182
13-39073-1	0102
13-39074-1	0236
13-39098-1	0555
13-39099-1	0042
13-39099-2	0419
13-39100-1	0919
13-39106-1	OEM
13-39114-1	0079
13-39114-2	0079
13-39114-3	0590
13-39115-1	0338
13-39115-2	0786
13-39115-3	0037
13-39146-1	0334
13-39174-1	0334
13-39607-4	4058
13-39678-1	4058
13-39678-3	4058
13-39678-4	4058
13-39819-1	0919
13-39819-2	0919
13-39851-1	0855
13-39860-1	0015
13-39863-1	0039
13-39867-2	0102
13-39884-1	0042
13-39884-2	0042
13-39884-3	0042
13-39970-1	0037
13-40083-1	0037
13-40083-2	0037
13-40312-1	0111
13-40340-1	2969
13-40341-1	0676
13-40342-1	2465
13-40343-1	1588
13-40344-1	0558
13-40345-1	0520
13-40346-1	0130
13-40347-1	1671
13-41122-1	0071
13-41122-2	0023
13-41122-4	0071
13-41123-2	0071
13-41123-4	0071
13-41628-2	0236
13-41628-3	0042
13-41628-5	0219
13-41629-4	0676
13-41738-1	0538
13-43005-1	0236
13-43112-1	0321
13-43250-1	0133
13-43382-1	0286
13-43463-1	0309
13-43463-2	0065
13-43633-1	0359
13-43634-1	0037
13-43635-1	0419
13-43766-1	0015
13-43773-1	0079
13-43777-1	0023
13-43777-2	0023
13-43790-1	0555
13-43791-1	1257
13-43956-1	1208
13-43956-2	1208
13-44290	0321
13-44291	0321
13-45016-1	0223
13-45018-1	1698
13-45147-3	0344
13-45321-1	0283
13-50385-1	0520
13-50482-1	0455
13-50484-1	0279
13-50486-1	0279
13-50528-1	0111
13-50631-1	0279
13-50944-1	0279
13-55009-1	0969
13-55009-2	0969
13-55010-1	0286
13-55018-4	0086
13-55020-1	0144
13-55029-1	0015
13-55030-1	0102
13-55031-1	0102
13-55031-2	0102
13-55031-3	0102
13-55046-1	0143
13-55061-1	0016
13-55061-1(AGC)	0086
13-55061-1(HOR-MUL)	0079
13-55061-1(SOUND)	0079
13-55061-2	0016
13-55061-2(SYL)	0079
13-55061-2(WARDS)	0086
13-55062-1	0233
13-55063-1	0144

DEVICE TYPE	REPL CODE
13-55064-1	0086
13-55064-1(SYL)	0178
13-55064-1(WARDS)	0590
13-55065-1	0144
13-55066-1	0016
13-55066-2	0016
13-55066-2(SYL)	0086
13-55066-2(WARDS)	0086
13-55067-1	0016
13-55068-1	0016
13-55069-1	0037
13-55069-1A	0037
13-55078-1	0102
13-55166-1	0143
13-55166-1/2439-	0143
13-55166-1/2439-2	0143
13-55323-1	OEM
13-55332-1	0137
13-55333-1	0907
13-67539-1	0276
13-67539-1/3464	0276
13-67544-1	0157
13-67583-5	0144
13-67583-6	0016
13-67584-4/3464	0007
13-67585-4	0016
13-67585-4/2439-	0855
13-67585-4/2439-2	0079
13-67585-5	0016
13-67585-5/2439-	0855
13-67585-5/2439-2	0144
13-67585-6/2439-	0079
13-67585-7	0079
13-67585-7/2439-	0855
13-67585-7/2439-2	0016
13-67586-3	0016
13-67590-1	0133
13-67590-1/2439-	0143
13-67590-1/2439-2	0143
13-67599-3	0004
13-67599-3/2439-	1293
13-67599-3/2439-2	0004
13-67599-9	0136
13-67600-3	0030
13-67600-4	OEM
13-67600-4/2439-2	0030
13-67600-5	0030
13-68617-1	0016
13-85943-1	0196
13-85943-2	0196
13-85943-3	0196
13-85962-1	0143
13-86416-1	0038
13-86420-1	0595
13-87433-1	0595
13-87539-4	0015
13-87539-4(REALTONE)	0276
13-94096-2	0004
13-100000	2535
13-100001	OEM
13-102001	0023
13-105698-1	0086
13-200003	OEM
13-200004	OEM
13-200005	OEM
13-200007	OEM
13-200008	OEM
13-200009	OEM
13-200010	OEM
13-200011	OEM
13-200013	OEM
13-200014	OEM
13-200015	OEM
13-200016	OEM
13-200017	OEM
13-200018	OEM
13-200019	OEM
13-200020	OEM
13-200021	OEM
13-200022	OEM
13-200023	OEM
13-200024	OEM
13-200025	OEM
13-200026	OEM
13-200028	OEM
13-200029	OEM
13-200030	OEM
13-200031	OEM
13-200032	OEM
13-200033	OEM
13-200034	OEM
13-200035	OEM
13-200036	OEM
13-200037	OEM
13-200038	OEM
13-200039	OEM
13-200040	OEM
13-200041	OEM
13-200042	OEM
13-200045	OEM
13-200050	OEM
13-200052	OEM
13-200056	OEM
13-200057	OEM
13-200058	OEM
13-200059	OEM
13-200060	OEM
13-200061	OEM
13-200062	OEM

DEVICE TYPE	REPL CODE
13-200068	OEM
13-200069	OEM
13-200070	OEM
13-200072	OEM
13-200073	OEM
13-200074	OEM
13-200076	OEM
13-200077	OEM
13-200078	OEM
13-200079	OEM
13-200080	OEM
13-200081	OEM
13-200083	OEM
13-200084	OEM
13-200085	OEM
13-200089	OEM
13-200090	OEM
13-200091	OEM
13-200092	OEM
13-200093	OEM
13-200094	OEM
13-200095	OEM
13-200096	OEM
13-200100	OEM
13-200101	OEM
13-200102	OEM
13-200103	OEM
13-200104	OEM
13-200114	OEM
13-200117	OEM
13-200118	OEM
13-200119	OEM
13-200122	OEM
13-200123	OEM
13-200124	OEM
13-200126	OEM
13-200133	OEM
13-200134	OEM
13-200136	OEM
13-200138	OEM
13-200139	OEM
13-200140	OEM
13-200143	OEM
13-200148	OEM
13-200154	OEM
13-200155	OEM
13-200162	OEM
13-200165	OEM
13-200172	OEM
13-200173	OEM
13-200176	OEM
13-200177	OEM
13-200178	OEM
13-200179	OEM
13-200180	OEM
13-200181	OEM
13-200182	OEM
13-200183	OEM
13-200184	OEM
13-200185	OEM
13-200186	OEM
13-200187	OEM
13-200188	OEM
13-200191	OEM
13-200192	OEM
13-200193	OEM
13-200194	OEM
13-200195	OEM
13-200197	OEM
13-200198	OEM
13-200199	OEM
13-200200	OEM
13-200201	OEM
13-200202	OEM
13-200203	OEM
13-200206	OEM
13-200207	OEM
13-200208	OEM
13-200210	OEM
13-200211	OEM
13-200216	OEM
13-200218	OEM
13-200220	OEM
13-200222	OEM
13-200223	OEM
13-200226	OEM
13-200227	OEM
13-200228	OEM
13-200229	OEM
13-200230	OEM
13-200231	OEM
13-200232	OEM
13-200238	OEM
13-200240	OEM
13-200244	OEM
13-200254	OEM
13-200263	OEM
13-200264	OEM
13-200265	OEM
13-350591	0167
13-1000000	2535
13-1000001	2535
13-3015121-1	0309
13-3015122-1	0079
13-3015123-1	0037
13-3015124-1	0434
13-3015125-1	1841
13-3015127-1	0468
13-3015128-1	0710

If replacement code is OEM, contact original manufacturer for replacement.

127

DEVICE TYPE	REPL CODE
13-3015132-1	0855
13-3015733-1	0037
13-3015735-1	2379
13-3015739-1	OEM
13-3017119-2	2011
13-3017148-1	4272
13-3017149-1	0079
13-3017150-1	0037
13-3017629-1	0264
13-3017630-1	0421
13A	0053
13A8	OEM
13A565	OEM
13B	0053
13B	0053
13B1	0053
13B2	0053
13B3	0053
13BKJ1	1293
13D1	OEM
13D2	OEM
13D4	0015
13DD02F	0170
13E1	OEM
13E2	OEM
13E10	OEM
13E20A	OEM
13E35	OEM
13E60	OEM
13E100	OEM
13F64	OEM
13J2	0015
13J2F	0015
13K3	OEM
13M85	OEM
13N1	0053
13N2	0053
13P1	0015
13P2	0133
13P2(RECTIFIER)	0071
13PT030	0902
13R2	OEM
13RC2	3246
13RC5	0726
13RC10	0707
13RC15	0464
13RC20	0464
13RC25	0716
13RC30	0716
13RC40	0717
13RC50	0720
13RC60	0720
13RC70	0674
13RC80	0674
13RECT-SI-1014	0023
13S	0201
13SD-1N60	0019
13SD-1N60S	0019
13SI-TMS3453N2L	OEM
13ST-2SC2073SO	1274
13T1	OEM
13T4	0142
13V64	OEM
13V66/LD932	OEM
13V92	OEM
13Y	0053
13Z4	OEM
13Z6	OEM
13Z6A	OEM
13Z6F	0451
13Z6FAF	OEM
13Z-1005	0143
14-0072-1	0015
14-0072-1(PHILCO)	0015
14-0072-2	0015
14-0072-2(PHILCO)	0015
14-0072-3	0015
14-0072-3(PHILCO)	0015
14-0104-1	0042
14-0104-2	0919
14-0104-3	0126
14-0104-4	0086
14-0104-5	0396
14-0104-7	0016
14-0110-1	0007
14-0110-2	0007
14-1	0016
14-2	0016
14-3	0016
14-201I-02	0368
14-501-01	0196
14-501-02	0196
14-502-01	0143
14-503-01	0479
14-503-02	0479
14-503-03	0479
14-503-04	0479
14-503-08	0479
14-504-01	0143
14-504-04	0479
14-507-01	0133
14-508-01	0030
14-509-01	0137
14-509-02	0162
14-510-01	0143
14-511-01	0143
14-512-01	0143
14-513-01	0143
14-514-01	0143
14-514-02	0133
14-514-03	0102
14-514-04	0123
14-514-04/64	0123
14-514-05	0143
14-514-06	0143
14-514-08	0143
14-514-09	0143
14-514-10	0143
14-514-11	0123
14-514-11/61	0123
14-514-12	0124
14-514-13	0123
14-514-13/63	0123
14-514-14	0102
14-514-15	0133
14-514-16	0123
14-514-16/66	0123
14-514-17	0133
14-514-18	0102
14-514-19	0133
14-514-20	1141
14-514-21	0143
14-514-22	0143
14-514-46	OEM
14-514-55	0143
14-514-61	0143
14-514-62	0124
14-514-64	0124
14-514-65	1141
14-514-66	0102
14-514-70	0133
14-514-72	0143
14-515-01	0137
14-515-02	0162
14-515-03	0137
14-515-04	0644
14-515-05	0490
14-515-06	0505
14-515-07	0002
14-515-08	0864
14-515-09	0002
14-515-11	0002
14-515-12	0012
14-515-13	0644
14-515-14	0490
14-515-15	0162
14-515-16	0012
14-515-17	0644
14-515-18	0789
14-515-19	0012
14-515-23	0681
14-515-24	0012
14-515-25	0137
14-515-26	0644
14-515-73	0002
14-557-10	0004
14-564-08	0164
14-566-08	0136
14-569-09	0050
14-572-10	0079
14-573-10	0160
14-574-10	0160
14-575-10	0016
14-576-10	0164
14-577-10	0004
14-578-10	0160
14-579-10	0160
14-580-01	0050
14-581-01	0050
14-582-01	0136
14-583-01	0016
14-584-01	0004
14-585-01	0050
14-586-01	0085
14-587-01	0050
14-588-01	0050
14-589-01	0160
14-590-01	0160
14-591-01	0050
14-593-01	1659
14-593-03	1659
14-600-01	0136
14-600-02	0136
14-600-04	0136
14-600-07	0143
14-600-10	0050
14-600-11	0050
14-600-13	0050
14-600-16	0136
14-600-19	0050
14-600-20	0050
14-600-22	0050
14-601-01	0160
14-601-02	0599
14-601-03	0160
14-601-04	0160
14-601-05	0160
14-601-06	0160
14-601-07	0160
14-601-08	0160
14-601-09	0160
14-601-10	0103
14-601-11	0160
14-601-12	0103
14-601-13	0103
14-601-14	0074
14-601-15	0103
14-601-15A	0103
14-601-16	0103
14-601-16A	0103
14-601-17	0161
14-601-18	0103
14-601-20	0103
14-602-01	0284
14-602-02	0016
14-602-03	0127
14-602-04	0004
14-602-05	0004
14-602-05A	0004
14-602-06	0164
14-602-07	0164
14-602-08	0164
14-602-09	0164
14-602-3	2839
14-602-10	0004
14-602-11	0037
14-602-11A	0037
14-602-12	0016
14-602-13	0037
14-602-14	0016
14-602-15	0004
14-602-16	0016
14-602-17	0016
14-602-18	0086
14-602-19	0233
14-602-20	0037
14-602-20A	0037
14-602-21	0208
14-602-22	0016
14-602-23	0016
14-602-24	0086
14-602-25	0111
14-602-26	0016
14-602-27	2839
14-602-28	0126
14-602-28A	0126
14-602-29	0086
14-602-30	0086
14-602-31	0007
14-602-32	0037
14-602-32A	0037
14-602-33	2839
14-602-34	0007
14-602-35	0016
14-602-36	0233
14-602-37	0233
14-602-38	2839
14-602-39	2839
14-602-40	2839
14-602-41	0144
14-602-42	0037
14-602-42A	0037
14-602-43	0086
14-602-44	0037
14-602-44A	0037
14-602-45	0007
14-602-46	0111
14-602-46A	0111
14-602-47	0037
14-602-47A	0037
14-602-48	0016
14-602-49	0079
14-602-50	0016
14-602-51	0164
14-602-52	0208
14-602-54	0786
14-602-54A	0037
14-602-55	0590
14-602-55A	0016
14-602-56	0037
14-602-56A	0037
14-602-57	4100
14-602-58	0037
14-602-58A	0037
14-602-59	0086
14-602-60	0126
14-602-61	0016
14-602-62	0016
14-602-63	0111
14-602-64	0688
14-602-65	0086
14-602-66	0126
14-602-67	0178
14-602-68	0037
14-602-69	0016
14-602-70	0590
14-602-71	0786
14-602-72	0086
14-602-73	0126
14-602-74	0590
14-602-75	0786
14-602-76	0168
14-602-77	0127
14-602-77B	0127
14-602-78	0016
14-602-79	0126
14-602-79A	0126
14-602-80	0016
14-602-81	0016
14-602-85	0126
14-602-580	0037
14-602-600	0037
14-603-01	0086
14-603-02	0007
14-603-02A	0086
14-603-03	0007
14-603-04	0016
14-603-05	0127
14-603-05-2	0127
14-603-06	0127
14-603-07	0086
14-603-08	0007
14-603-09	0007
14-603-3	OEM
14-603-10	0016
14-603-11	0016
14-603-12	0144
14-603-13	0007
14-604-01	2736
14-604-02	0222
14-604-03	3502
14-604-07	0160
14-604-08	0160
14-607-29	0126
14-607-29A	0126
14-608-01	0161
14-608-02	0161
14-608-02A	0419
14-609-01	0334
14-609-01A	0334
14-609-02	0283
14-609-02A	0334
14-609-03	0042
14-609-03A	0419
14-609-04	0042
14-609-05	0334
14-609-49A	0144
14-700-01	0321
14-700-02	0321
14-700-03	0321
14-700-04	0321
14-700-05	0321
14-800-32	0016
14-801-23	0111
14-802-12	0016
14-803-12	0037
14-804-12	0037
14-805-12	0016
14-807-12	0150
14-808-12	0037
14-850-12	0007
14-851-12	0007
14-853-23	0016
14-854-12	0016
14-856-23	0037
14-857-12	0037
14-858-12	0016
14-862-32	0016
14-863-23	0037
14-865-12	0016
14-866-32	0016
14-867-32	0037
14-901-12	0283
14-2000-01	0396
14-2000-02	0396
14-2000-03	0396
14-2000-04	0396
14-2000-05	0396
14-2002-01	0321
14-2007	2147
14-2007-00	2147
14-2007-00B	0748
14-2007-01	0748
14-2007-02	2147
14-2007-03	0748
14-2008-01	0659
14-2010-01	0661
14-2010-03	0345
14-2011-01	0368
14-40325A	0103
14-40363A	0103
14-40369A	0103
14-40421A	0103
14-40464A	0103
14-40465A	0103
14-40466A	0103
14-40471	0103
14-40934-1	0103
14-60237	0283
14-SAM	1881
14A	0160
14A0	0160
14A1	0160
14A1-A82	0160
14A2	0160
14A3	0160
14A4	0160
14A5	0160
14A6	0160
14A7	0160
14A8	0160
14A8-1	0050
14A8-1-12	0050
14A9	0160
14A10	0160
14A10R	0160
14A11	0160
14A12	0160
14A13	0160
14A13P	0160
14A14	0160
14A14-7	0160
14A14-7B	0160
14A15	0160
14A15L	0160
14A16	0160
14A16-5	0160
14A17	0160
14A17-1	0160
14A18	0160
14A19	0160
14A19G	0160
14A502	OEM
14B338-001	OEM
14B348-003	1061
14B348-1	1061
14B348-2	1061
14B348-3	1061
14B348-4	1061
14B348-5	1061
14DM8	OEM
14E20A	OEM
14E30	OEM
14E50	OEM
14E100	OEM
14J2	0015
14J2F	0015
14L0035	3684
14LN033	2559
14LN034	2570
14LQ007	0574
14MW69	0004
14P1	OEM
14P2	0015
14R2	OEM
14SI-HEF4011UBP	OEM
14SP-LT-3211B	OEM
14T-009-003	OEM
14T1	OEM
14T4	0179
14T4S	OEM
14Z4	OEM
14Z6	OEM
14Z6A	OEM
14Z6F	0528
14Z6FAF	OEM
15	OEM
15-0075603-04X	OEM
15-033-0	0015
15-082019	0079
15-085002	0143
15-085003	0143
15-085004	0196
15-085005	0133
15-085006	0015
15-085007	0015
15-085008	0133
15-085009	0143
15-085015	0015
15-085016	0015
15-085018	0911
15-085027	0143
15-085032	0143
15-085033	0071
15-085037	0143
15-085038	0196
15-085039	0196
15-085040	0015
15-085041	0071
15-085042	0918
15-085043	0015
15-085047	0196
15-085061	0143
15-088002	0037
15-088002A	0037
15-088003	0127
15-088004	0144
15-1	0016
15-2	0016
15-2R51-1	0696
15-3	0037
15-4	0037
15-5	0037
15-15	OEM
15-19CC19	0028
15-20A70	0123
15-20A90	0123
15-20A-90M	0143
15-30	0037
15-40	0037
15-50	0037
15-166N	0127
15-5016T/IC7313AP	0358
15-5021/ICLM8363	1238
15-7142C-1	0696
15-14504-1	3346
15-26587-1	0627
15-31015-1	6515
15-31015-7	0167
15-31015-13	OEM
15-33201-1	0167
15-33201-2	0167
15-34005-1	2507
15-34048	1929
15-34048-1	0659
15-34049-1	0696
15-34049-3	0696
15-34202-1	2507
15-34379-1	0438
15-34401-1	2266
15-34408-1	0659
15-34452	0673
15-34452-1	0673
15-34502-1	0356
15-34502-2	0356
15-34502-3	0356
15-34503	0696
15-34503-1	0696
15-34503-2	0696
15-34906-1	1601
15-35059	0167
15-35059-1	0167
15-35059-2	0167
15-36446-1	1385
15-36647-1	3898
15-36994-1	2728
15-36995-1	1411
15-37534-1	3346
15-37534-2	3346
15-37700-1	2153
15-37701-1	2032
15-37701-2	2032
15-37702-1	0348
15-37703-1	0350
15-37704-1	0345
15-37833-2	1695
15-39060-1	1797
15-39061-1	3166
15-39075-1	0850
15-39098-1	0555
15-39207-1	2584
15-39208-1	2663
15-39209-1	1327
15-39600-1	3346
15-39600-2	3346
15-40140-2	0330
15-40183-1	0514
15-41545-1	3346
15-41627-1	2804
15-41627-2	2804
15-41627-3	2804
15-41764-1	2785
15-41764-2	2785
15-41856-1	3166
15-43098-1	1867
15-43251-1	1797
15-43251-2	1797
15-43312-1	2790
15-43312-2	2790
15-43636-1	1162
15-43637-1	4580
15-43638-1	2716
15-43703-1	0850
15-43704-1	2218
15-43705-1	0215
15-43706-1	2368
15-45141-1	0215
15-45184-1	1946
15-45185-1	1135
15-45186-1	0620
15-45300-1	0167
15-45693-1	3924
15-53201-1	1929
15-53201-2	1929
15-71420-1	0696
15-100001	0015
15-100002	0015
15-100003	2117
15-100004	0015
15-103022	0015
15-108001	2875
15-108002	0196
15-108003	0015
15-108004	0015
15-108005	0015
15-108006	0015
15-108007	0469
15-108008	0133
15-108009	0196
15-108010	0015
15-108011	0015
15-108012	0769
15-108013	0102
15-108014	0469
15-108015	0015
15-108016	0015
15-108017	0769
15-108020	4993
15-108021	0015
15-108022	0015
15-108023	0196
15-108024	0015
15-108025	0133
15-108026	0102
15-108027	0102
15-108028	1293
15-108029	0102
15-108030	0201
15-108031	0015
15-108032	0015
15-108033	0644
15-108034	0015
15-108035	0102
15-108036	0015
15-108037	0015
15-108038	0469
15-108039	OEM
15-108040	0102
15-108041	0102
15-108042	0133
15-108043	0102
15-108044	0102
15-108045	0201
15-108046	0071
15-108047	0102
15-108048	0102
15-108049	0015
15-108050	0015
15-108107	0769
15-123060	1048
15-123065	0042
15-123100	0820
15-123101	0133
15-123102	0023
15-123103	0102
15-123104	0286
15-123105	0015
15-123106	0644
15-123202	0236
15-123230	1142
15-123231	0286
15-123242	0023
15-123243	0023
15-123300	0015
15-123303	1045
15-123353	OEM
15-123412	0388
15-123413	OEM
15-123425	0080
15-301513-1	1042
15-392007-1	2584
15-2210921	0050
15-2221011	0004
15-3012472-01X	OEM
15-3013086-01X	OEM
15-3013885-01X	OEM
15-3013886-01X	OEM
15-3013887-01X	OEM
15-3013888-01X	OEM
15-3015129-1	0516
15-3015130-1	0375
15-3015131-1	3666
15-3015131-2	3665
15-3015131-3	3666
15-3015132-1	0617
15-3015569-1	0473
15-3015570-1	3566
15-3015734-1	0069
15-3015740-1	5597
15-3015807-1	OEM
15-3015808-1	OEM
15-3017045-1	1051
15-3017119-1	2011
15-3017119-2	2011
15-3017148-1	OEM
15-3017630-1	0421
15-22210111	0004
15-22210131	0050
15-22210300	0050
15-22210921	0050
15-22211021	0050
15-22211200	0004
15-22211328	0004
15-22211921	0050
15-22214400	0050
15-22214411	0050
15-22214435	0050
15-22214821	0050
15-22214831	0050
15-22216500	0004
15-22216600	0050
15-22217400	0050
15-22223720	0016
15-30115734-1	OEM
15A1HA1	OEM
15A1HS0	OEM
15A1HS1	OEM
15A1PA1	OEM
15A1PS0	OEM
15A1PS1	OEM
15A2HA2	OEM
15A2HS0	OEM
15A2HS1	OEM
15A2PA2	OEM
15A2PS0	OEM
15A2PS1	OEM
15A3HA3	OEM
15A3HS0	OEM
15A3HS1	OEM
15A3PA3	OEM
15A3PS0	OEM
15A3PS1	OEM
15A4HA4	OEM
15A4HS0	OEM
15A4HS1	OEM
15A4PA4	OEM
15A4PS0	OEM
15A4PS1	OEM
15A5HA5	OEM
15A5HS0	OEM
15A5HS1	OEM
15A5PA5	OEM
15A5PS0	OEM
15A5PS1	OEM
15A6HS0	OEM
15A6HS1	OEM
15A6PS0	OEM
15A6PS1	OEM
15A7HS0	OEM
15A7HS1	OEM
15A7PS0	OEM
15A7PS1	OEM
15A8HS0	OEM

If replacement code is OEM, contact original manufacturer for replacement.

DEVICE TYPE	REPL CODE	DEVICE TYPE	REPL CODE	DEVICE TYPE	REPL CODE	DEVICE TYPE	REPL CODE	DEVICE TYPE	REPL CODE	DEVICE TYPE	REPL CODE	DEVICE TYPE	REPL CODE
15A8HS1	OEM	15F8	0811	15KP160A	OEM	15L130	OEM	15PK40A	OEM	16	OEM	16C35C	0717
15A8PS0	OEM	15F10	0916	15KP170	OEM	15L140	OEM	15PK43A	0563	16-2	0015	16C40	0717
15A8PS1	OEM	15F15E1	OEM	15KP170A	OEM	15L150	OEM	15PK45A	OEM	16-17	0321	16C40B	0717
15A9HS0	OEM	15F15E2	OEM	15KP180	OEM	15L160	OEM	15PK48A	OEM	16-19(SYMPHONIC)	0126	16C40C	0735
15A9HS1	OEM	15F15E3	OEM	15KP180A	OEM	15L170	OEM	15PK51A	OEM	16-20(SYMPHONIC)	0086	16C40R	OEM
15A9PS0	OEM	15FC11	OEM	15KP200	OEM	15L180	OEM	15PK54A	OEM	16-500	0769	16C45	0720
15A9PS1	OEM	15FD11	OEM	15KP200A	OEM	15L190	OEM	15PK58A	0825	16-736	0144	16C45B	0720
15A10HS0	OEM	15FT1N	OEM	15KP220	OEM	15L200	OEM	15PK60A	OEM	16-3006	0077	16C45C	0720
15A10HS1	OEM	15FT2N	OEM	15KP220A	OEM	15L210	OEM	15PK64A	OEM	16-21426	0007	16C50	0720
15A10PS0	OEM	15FT3N	OEM	15KP240	OEM	15L220	OEM	15PK70A	OEM	16-147191229	0016	16C50B	0720
15A10PS1	OEM	15FT4N	OEM	15KP240A	OEM	15L230	OEM	15PK75A	OEM	16-171191368	0016	16C50C	3260
15A11HS0	OEM	15FT5N	OEM	15KP260	OEM	15L240	OEM	15PK78A	OEM	16-207190405	0004	16C60	0720
15A11HS1	OEM	15FT6N	OEM	15KP260A	OEM	15L250	OEM	15PK85A	OEM	16-501190016	0071	16C60B	0720
15A11PS0	OEM	15FWJ11	OEM	15KP280	OEM	15L260	OEM	15PK90A	OEM	16A1	0038	16C60C	0759
15A11PS1	OEM	15G4B41	5303	15KP280A	OEM	15L270	OEM	15PK100A	OEM	16A1(FLEETWOOD)	0016	16C70	0674
15A12HS0	OEM	15GQJ11	OEM	15KS17	OEM	15L280	OEM	15PK110A	OEM	16A2	0038	16C70B	0674
15A12HS1	OEM	15GS1	OEM	15KS17A	OEM	15L290	OEM	15PK120A	OEM	16A2(FLEETWOOD)	0016	16C70C	2848
15A12PS0	OEM	15GS2	OEM	15KS18	OEM	15L300	OEM	15PK130A	OEM	16A132	OEM	16C80	0674
15A12PS1	OEM	15GS4	OEM	15KS18A	OEM	15LC11	OEM	15PK150A	OEM	16A545-7	0016	16C80B	0674
15A50	OEM	15GS6	OEM	15KS20	OEM	15M3PN	0984	15PK160A	OEM	16A667-GRN	0111	16C80C	0761
15A100	OEM	15GS8	OEM	15KS20A	OEM	15M4N	OEM	15PK170A	1395	16A667-ORG	0111	16C90	0674
15A200	OEM	15GS10	OEM	15KS22	OEM	15M45	0681	15Q3	1241	16A667-RED	0111	16C90B	0674
15A400	OEM	15GS12	OEM	15KS22A	OEM	15MA300	OEM	15R0/18	OEM	16A667-YEL	0111	16C90C	0674
15A600	OEM	15GWJ11	OEM	15KS24	OEM	15MA400	OEM	15R1/18	OEM	16A667G	0079	16C100	0674
15A800	OEM	15H3P	0983	15KS24A	OEM	15MLA160	OEM	15R1/52	OEM	16A667R	0086	16C100B	0674
15A14663	6655	15H3PN	0984	15KS26	OEM	15MLA180	OEM	15R2	OEM	16A667Y	0079	16C100C	0674
15A14664	0261	15IP005	OEM	15KS26A	OEM	15MLA200	OEM	15R2/4	OEM	16A668-GRN	0111	16C110	0674
15A14665	OEM	15IP005D	OEM	15KS28	OEM	15MQ20	1590	15R2/66	OEM	16A668-ORG	0111	16C110B	0674
15A14724	OEM	15IP005N	OEM	15KS28A	OEM	15MQ30	1590	15R2B	OEM	16A668-YEL	0111	16C110C	0674
15A14741	5403	15IP01	OEM	15KS30	OEM	15MQ40	1590	15R2S	OEM	16A668G	0079	16C120	0674
15A14742	5403	15IP01D	OEM	15KS30A	OEM	15MT15ZK	OEM	15R3/4	OEM	16A668Y	0079	16C120B	0674
15A17125	0527	15IP01N	OEM	15KS33	OEM	15MT20ZA	OEM	15R3B	OEM	16A669-GRN	0111	16C120C	0674
15A17126	1533	15IP02	OEM	15KS33A	OEM	15N02F1	OEM	15R3S	OEM	16A669-YEL	0111	16E08	OEM
15AGD	OEM	15IP02D	OEM	15KS36	OEM	15N05M1	OEM	15R4/3	OEM	16A669G	0079	16E4	OEM
15AK60	OEM	15IP02N	OEM	15KS36A	OEM	15N1	0015	15R4/3C	OEM	16A787	0211	16E5	OEM
15AK80	OEM	15IP04	OEM	15KS40	OEM	15N2	0097	15R4/4	OEM	16A1938	0016	16E6	OEM
15AK100	OEM	15IP04D	OEM	15KS40A	OEM	15N2(POWER)	0097	15R4/59	OEM	16A6670	0086	16E16A	OEM
15AN20	OEM	15IP04N	OEM	15KS43	OEM	15N3	0097	15R4C	OEM	16A6680	0086	16E35	OEM
15AN30	OEM	15IP06	OEM	15KS43A	OEM	15N3(POWER)	0097	15R4S	OEM	16A14692	0133	16E50	OEM
15AN40	OEM	15IP06D	OEM	15KS45	OEM	15N10K1	OEM	15R5/3	OEM	16A14693	0124	16E90	OEM
15AN50	OEM	15IP06N	OEM	15KS45A	OEM	15N15A	OEM	15R5/3D	OEM	16A14694	0133	16E1330	0079
15AN60	OEM	15IP08	OEM	15KS48	OEM	15N15A9	OEM	15R5/5	OEM	16A14695	OEM	16E1330(GE)	0016
15AN80	OEM	15IP08D	OEM	15KS48A	OEM	15N20A	OEM	15R5/61	OEM	16A14696	OEM	16F5	5417
15AN90	OEM	15IP08N	OEM	15KS51	OEM	15N20A9	OEM	15R5C	OEM	16A14697	OEM	16F5R	2275
15AN100	OEM	15IP10	OEM	15KS51A	OEM	15N25A	OEM	15R5S	OEM	16A14698	OEM	16F10	5482
15AN120	OEM	15IP10D	OEM	15KS54	OEM	15N25A9	OEM	15R6/3	OEM	16A14699	OEM	16F10B	2872
15AN140	OEM	15IP10N	OEM	15KS54A	OEM	15N30A	OEM	15R6/3D	OEM	16A14721	OEM	16F10R	2275
15AN160	OEM	15J2	0015	15KS58	OEM	15N30A9	OEM	15R6/5	OEM	16A14739	OEM	16F15	2872
15B011	OEM	15J2F	0015	15KS58A	OEM	15N35A	OEM	15R6/61	OEM	16A17050	OEM	16F20	2872
15B1	0947	15J4B41	5305	15KS60	OEM	15N35A9	OEM	15R6C	OEM	16A17051	OEM	16F20R	2275
15B1(ZENER)	0873	15KP17	OEM	15KS60A	OEM	15N40A	OEM	15R6S	OEM	16A17052	0023	16F30	5483
15B2	OEM	15KP17A	OEM	15KS64	OEM	15N40A9	OEM	15R7/3	OEM	16A17130	OEM	16F30R	0471
15B2(1WATT)	0002	15KP18	OEM	15KS64A	OEM	15N45A	OEM	15R7/3D	OEM	16A17131	OEM	16F40	3705
15B2(ZENER)	0873	15KP18A	OEM	15KS70	OEM	15N45A9	OEM	15R7/5	OEM	16A17132	OEM	16F40R	0471
15B2	0681	15KP20	OEM	15KS70A	OEM	15N50A	OEM	15R7/61	OEM	16A17133	OEM	16F50	3711
15B3	0681	15KP20A	OEM	15KS75	OEM	15N50A9	OEM	15R7CD	OEM	16A17134	OEM	16F50R	0471
15B3(ZENER)	1097	15KP22	OEM	15KS75A	OEM	15N55A	OEM	15R7S	OEM	16A17135	OEM	16F60	1104
15B3(ZENER)	0681	15KP22A	OEM	15KS78	OEM	15N55A9	OEM	15R8/3	OEM	16A17136	OEM	16F60R	0471
15B4	0535	15KP24	OEM	15KS78A	OEM	15N60A	OEM	15R8/3D	OEM	16A17137	OEM	16F80	1600
15B4B41	0319	15KP24A	OEM	15KS85	OEM	15N60A9	OEM	15R8/5	OEM	16ATCRA	0464	16F80R	0444
15B6	0959	15KP26	OEM	15KS85A	OEM	15N65A	OEM	15R8/63	OEM	16ATCRB	0464	16F100	2982
15B8	0811	15KP26A	OEM	15KS90	OEM	15N65A9	OEM	15R8CD	OEM	16ATCRC	0464	16F100R	0444
15B10	0916	15KP28	OEM	15KS90A	OEM	15N70A	OEM	15R8S	OEM	16ATCRD	0464	16F120	OEM
15BC11	OEM	15KP28A	OEM	15KS100	OEM	15N70A9	OEM	15R52	OEM	16ATCRE	0464	16F-B1	OEM
15BD11	0015	15KP30	OEM	15KS100A	OEM	15N75A	OEM	15R0/18	OEM	16ATCRF	0717	16FCRA	OEM
15BD11(FA-1)	OEM	15KP30A	OEM	15KS110	OEM	15N75A9	OEM	15S05	0110	16ATCRG	0717	16FCRB	OEM
15BG15	OEM	15KP33	OEM	15KS110A	OEM	15N80A	OEM	15S1	0947	16ATCRH	0717	16FCRC	OEM
15BL11	OEM	15KP33A	OEM	15KS120	OEM	15N80A9	OEM	15S2	0242	16ATCRI	0720	16FCRD	OEM
15C05	0110	15KP36	OEM	15KS120A	OEM	15N85A	OEM	15S4	0535	16ATCRJ	0720	16FCRE	OEM
15C1	0947	15KP36A	OEM	15KS130	OEM	15N85A9	OEM	15S6	0959	16ATCRK	0674	16FCRF	OEM
15C2	0242	15KP40	OEM	15KS130A	OEM	15N90A	OEM	15SB03S	1590	16ATCRL	0674	16FCRG	OEM
15C2D	0242	15KP40A	OEM	15KS150	OEM	15N90A9	OEM	15SB04M	OEM	16B1	0855	16FCRH	OEM
15C4	0535	15KP43	OEM	15KS150A	OEM	15N95A	OEM	15SB04S	1590	16B1(ZENER)	0440	16FCRI	OEM
15C6	0959	15KP43A	OEM	15KS160	OEM	15N95A9	OEM	15SI-CA3064E	0797	16B2	0079	16FCRJ	OEM
15C8	0811	15KP45	OEM	15KS160A	OEM	15N100A	OEM	15SM6	OEM	16B20	OEM	16FCRK	OEM
15C10	0916	15KP45A	OEM	15KS170	OEM	15N100A9	OEM	15SM15	OEM	16B40	OEM	16FCRL	OEM
15C12	OEM	15KP48	OEM	15KS170A	OEM	15N110A	OEM	15SM25	OEM	16B670-GRN	0396	16FDC	OEM
15C14	OEM	15KP48A	OEM	15KS180	OEM	15N120A	OEM	15SM40	OEM	16B670-RED	0855	16FL5S02	OEM
15C16	OEM	15KP51	OEM	15KS180A	OEM	15N130A	OEM	15SM55	OEM	16B670-YEL	0855	16FL5S05	OEM
15CC11	OEM	15KP51A	OEM	15KS200	OEM	15N140A	OEM	15SM70	OEM	16B670R	0710	16FL5S10	OEM
15CD11	OEM	15KP54	OEM	15KS200A	OEM	15N160A	OEM	15SM100	OEM	16B670Y	0710	16FL10S02	OEM
15CG11	OEM	15KP54A	OEM	15KS220	OEM	15N170A	OEM	15SM150	OEM	16C025	0464	16FL10S05	OEM
15CG15	OEM	15KP58	OEM	15KS220A	OEM	15N180A	OEM	15SM200	OEM	16C025B	0464	16FL10S10	OEM
15CL11	OEM	15KP58A	OEM	15KS240	OEM	15N190A	OEM	15SP-005	OEM	16C025C	3275	16FL20S02	OEM
15D02M1	OEM	15KP60	OEM	15KS240A	OEM	15N200A	OEM	15SP-01	OEM	16C050	0464	16FL20S05	OEM
15D05M1	OEM	15KP60A	OEM	15KS260	OEM	15N210A	OEM	15SP-02	OEM	16C050B	0464	16FL20S10	OEM
15D4B41	5301	15KP64	OEM	15KS260A	OEM	15N220A	OEM	15SP-04	OEM	16C050C	2174	16FL40S02	OEM
15D4D41	OEM	15KP64A	OEM	15KS280	OEM	15N230A	OEM	15SP-06	OEM	16C-4	0015	16FL40S10	OEM
15D10K1	OEM	15KP70	OEM	15KS280A	OEM	15N240A	OEM	15SP-08	OEM	16C4	0015	16FL60S02	OEM
15D48B41	OEM	15KP70A	OEM	15L15	OEM	15N250A	OEM	15SP-10	OEM	16C4B1P	0276	16FL60S05	OEM
15DD02F	0170	15KP75	OEM	15L20	OEM	15N260A	OEM	15ST-2SB561C(AU)E	0431	16C-4P	0276	16FL60S10	OEM
15DF4	0023	15KP75A	OEM	15L25	OEM	15P02F1-A	OEM	15SZ-RD24EB	0489	16C10	0464	16FL80S05	OEM
15DF6	0023	15KP78	OEM	15L30	OEM	15P05M1-A	OEM	15T1	OEM	16C10B	0464	16FL80S10	OEM
15DF8	OEM	15KP78A	OEM	15L35	OEM	15P1	OEM	15T4	OEM	16C10C	0562	16FL100S05	OEM
15DF15E1	OEM	15KP85	OEM	15L40	OEM	15P2	0133	15TB050	OEM	16C15	0464	16FL100S10	OEM
15DF15E2	OEM	15KP85A	OEM	15L45	OEM	15P2(POWER)	0097	15TB100	OEM	16C15B	0464	16FR10	2327
15DF15E3	OEM	15KP90	OEM	15L50	OEM	15P3	0097	15TB200	OEM	16C15C	3227	16FR20	1232
15DG15	OEM	15KP90A	OEM	15L55	OEM	15P3(POWER)	0097	15TB400	OEM	16C20	0464	16FR30	OEM
15DL11	OEM	15KP100	OEM	15L60	OEM	15P10K1	OEM	15TB600	OEM	16C20B	0464	16FR40	2349
15E	2296	15KP100A	OEM	15L65	OEM	15PK17A	3171	15V66	OEM	16C20C	0757	16FR60	2360
15E6	0959	15KP110	OEM	15L70	OEM	15PK18A	OEM	15W71	OEM	16C20R	OEM	16FR80	1255
15E7	0811	15KP110A	OEM	15L75	OEM	15PK20A	OEM	15Y	0681	16C25	0717	16FR100	0444
15E8	0811	15KP120	OEM	15L80	OEM	15PK22A	1904	15Z3	0037	16C25B	0717	16G010F	OEM
15E10	0916	15KP120A	OEM	15L85	OEM	15PK24A	OEM	15Z4	OEM	16C25C	3237	16G011F	OEM
15E20A	OEM	15KP130	OEM	15L90	OEM	15PK26A	OEM	15Z6	OEM	16C30	0717	16G011L	OEM
15E40	OEM	15KP130A	OEM	15L95	OEM	15PK28A	OEM	15Z6A	OEM	16C30B	0717	16G2	0016
15E60	OEM	15KP150	OEM	15L100	OEM	15PK30A	OEM	15Z6AF	0446	16C30C	3240	16G5	0015
15E100	OEM	15KP150A	OEM	15L110	OEM	15PK33A	OEM	15Z6F	0446	16C35	0717	16G27	0321
15F6	0959	15KP160	OEM	15L120	OEM	15PK36A	OEM	15Z6FAF	OEM	16C35B	0717	16G28	0133

If replacement code is OEM, contact original manufacturer for replacement. 129

DEVICE TYPE	REPL CODE
16G28A	0133
16GN	0127
16J1	0144
16J2	0144
16J2(DIODE)	0015
16J2F	0015
16J3	0079
16K1	0144
16K2	0144
16K3	0144
16KPR	OEM
16KQ30	OEM
16KQ30B	OEM
16KQ40	OEM
16KQ40B	OEM
16KQ50	OEM
16KQ50B	OEM
16KQ60	OEM
16KQ60B	OEM
16KQ90	OEM
16KQ90B	OEM
16KQ100	OEM
16KQ100B	OEM
16KZ	OEM
16L2	0144
16L3	0144
16L4	0111
16L5	0144
16L22	0144
16L23	0144
16L24	0111
16L25	0111
16L42	0016
16L43	0016
16L44	0016
16L45	0111
16L62	0016
16L63	0016
16L64	0127
16L65	0111
16M10	OEM
16M11	OEM
16M12	OEM
16MQ30	OEM
16MQ30(B)	OEM
16MQ40	OEM
16MQ40(B)	OEM
16MQ50	OEM
16MQ50(B)	OEM
16MQ60	OEM
16MQ60(B)	OEM
16MS1	OEM
16MS1A	OEM
16MS1B	OEM
16MS1C	OEM
16MS1D	OEM
16N2	0416
16NT100	OEM
16P1	OEM
16P2	2117
16P2881	0396
16P3367	0396
16PCRA	1641
16PCRB	1641
16PCRC	1641
16PCRD	1641
16PCRE	1641
16PCRF	1574
16PCRG	1574
16PCRH	1574
16PCRI	1655
16PCRJ	1655
16PCRK	OEM
16PCRL	OEM
16PCRNA	OEM
16PCRNB	OEM
16PCRNC	OEM
16PCRND	OEM
16PCRNE	OEM
16PCRNF	OEM
16PCRNG	OEM
16PCRNH	OEM
16PCRNI	OEM
16PCRNJ	OEM
16PCRNK	OEM
16PCRNL	OEM
16PCRSA	2497
16PCRSB	2497
16PCRSC	0736
16PCRSD	0740
16PCRSE	0740
16PCRSF	0742
16PCRSG	0742
16PCRSH	0742
16PCRSI	0747
16PCRSJ	0747
16PCRSK	OEM
16PCRSL	OEM
16RC2	0717
16RC2A	3246
16RC5	0717
16RC5A	0726
16RC10	0717
16RC10A	0707
16RC10AS24	0799
16RC15	0717
16RC15A	0464
16RC20	0717
16RC20A	0464
16RC20AS24	0799
16RC25	0717
16RC25A	0716
16RC30	0717
16RC30A	0717
16RC30AS24	0799
16RC40	0717
16RC40A	0717
16RC40AS24	0799
16RC50A	0773
16RC50AS24	OEM
16RC60	0720
16RC60A	0720
16RC60AS24	0799
16RC70	OEM
16RC70A	OEM
16RC80	OEM
16RC80A	0745
16RC90	OEM
16RC90A	OEM
16RC100	OEM
16RC100A	OEM
16RC110A	0674
16RC120A	OEM
16RCF5A	OEM
16RCF10A	OEM
16RCF15A	OEM
16RCF20A	OEM
16RCF25A	OEM
16RCF30A	OEM
16RCF40A	OEM
16RCF50A	OEM
16RCF60A	OEM
16RCF70A	OEM
16RCF80A	OEM
16RIA10	0464
16RIA10M	OEM
16RIA20	0464
16RIA20M	OEM
16RIA30	OEM
16RIA40	0720
16RIA40M	OEM
16RIA60	0720
16RIA60M	OEM
16RIA80	0674
16RIA80M	OEM
16RIA100	0674
16RIA100M	OEM
16RIA110	0674
16RIA110M	OEM
16RIA120	0674
16RIA120M	OEM
16S2-AW01-11	0313
16SL107	OEM
16SL108	OEM
16ST-2SA733P	0006
16ST-2SC945Q	0076
16ST-2SC945Q/R	0076
16ST-2SC945Q/R(AU)E	0076
16ST-2SC945R	0076
16ST-2SD994	0055
16SZ-AW01-11	0313
16T1	OEM
16T4	0342
16T4S	OEM
16T17	OEM
16T20	OEM
16T37-RE00	OEM
16T40	OEM
16TCRA	0464
16TCRB	0464
16TCRC	0464
16TCRD	0464
16TCRE	0464
16TCRF	0717
16TCRG	0717
16TCRH	0720
16TCRI	0720
16TCRJ	0720
16TCRK	0674
16TCRL	0674
16U1	0079
16X	0440
16X1	0016
16X2	0016
16X39	0133
16Z4	0137
16Z6	0162
16Z6A	0162
16Z6F	0162
16Z6FAF	OEM
17-10	0015
17-410	0015
17-443	0086
17-451	0016
17-457	0079
17-458	0126
17-459	0037
17-459A	0037
17-12054-1	1812
17-12056-1	1035
17-12057-1	2086
17-12058-1	0141
17-12064-1	0557
17-12065-1	0081
17-12089-1	2067
17A4422-1	0160
17A17068	OEM
17E07	OEM
17E14A	OEM
17E33	OEM
17E45	OEM
17E75	OEM
17P1	OEM
17P2	0133
17RCG5	OEM
17REB60	OEM
17S04	OEM
17S06	OEM
17S08	1040
17S08R	1778
17S10	1040
17S10R	1778
17S12	OEM
17S14	OEM
17S16	OEM
17S50	0143
17SP-LT-3211B	OEM
17SP-P722-7R	OEM
17T1	OEM
17T4	0342
17T4S	OEM
17TB1	0562
17TB1-CE00	OEM
17TB1-CH00	OEM
17TB1-EE00	OEM
17TB1-EH00	OEM
17TB1-GE00	OEM
17TB1-GH00	OEM
17TB1-JE00	OEM
17TB1-JH00	OEM
17TB1-LE00	OEM
17TB1-LH00	OEM
17TB1-NE00	OEM
17TB1-NH00	OEM
17TB1-RE00	OEM
17TB2	0757
17TB2-CE00	OEM
17TB2-CH00	OEM
17TB2-EE00	OEM
17TB2-EH00	OEM
17TB2-GE00	OEM
17TB2-GH00	OEM
17TB2-JE00	OEM
17TB2-JH00	OEM
17TB2-LE00	OEM
17TB2-LH00	OEM
17TB2-NE00	OEM
17TB2-NH00	OEM
17TB2-RE00	OEM
17TB3	3240
17TB3-CE00	OEM
17TB3-CH00	OEM
17TB3-EE00	OEM
17TB3-EH00	OEM
17TB3-GE00	OEM
17TB3-GH00	OEM
17TB3-JE00	OEM
17TB3-JH00	OEM
17TB3-LE00	OEM
17TB3-LH00	OEM
17TB3-NE00	OEM
17TB3-NH00	OEM
17TB3-RE00	OEM
17TB4	0735
17TB4-CE00	OEM
17TB4-CH00	OEM
17TB4-EE00	OEM
17TB4-EH00	OEM
17TB4-GE00	OEM
17TB4-GH00	OEM
17TB4-JE00	OEM
17TB4-JH00	OEM
17TB4-LE00	OEM
17TB4-LH00	OEM
17TB4-NE00	OEM
17TB4-NH00	OEM
17TB4-RE00	OEM
17TB5	3260
17TB5-CH00	OEM
17TB5-EE00	OEM
17TB5-EH00	OEM
17TB5-GE00	OEM
17TB5-GH00	OEM
17TB5-JE00	OEM
17TB5-JH00	OEM
17TB5-LE00	OEM
17TB5-LH00	OEM
17TB5-NE00	OEM
17TB5-NH00	OEM
17TB5-RE00	OEM
17TB6	0759
17TB6-CE00	OEM
17TB6-CH00	OEM
17TB6-EE00	OEM
17TB6-EH00	OEM
17TB6-GE00	OEM
17TB6-GH00	OEM
17TB6-JE00	OEM
17TB6-JH00	OEM
17TB6-LE00	OEM
17TB6-LH00	OEM
17TB6-NE00	OEM
17TB6-NH00	OEM
17TB6-RE00	OEM
17TB7	2848
17TB7-CE00	OEM
17TB7-CH00	OEM
17TB7-EE00	OEM
17TB7-EH00	OEM
17TB7-GE00	OEM
17TB7-GH00	OEM
17TB7-JE00	OEM
17TB7-JH00	OEM
17TB7-LE00	OEM
17TB7-LH00	OEM
17TB7-NE00	OEM
17TB7-NH00	OEM
17TB7-RE00	OEM
17TB8	0761
17TB8-CE00	OEM
17TB8-CH00	OEM
17TB8-EE00	OEM
17TB8-EH00	OEM
17TB8-GE00	OEM
17TB8-GH00	OEM
17TB8-JE00	OEM
17TB8-JH00	OEM
17TB8-LE00	OEM
17TB8-LH00	OEM
17TB8-NE00	OEM
17TB8-NH00	OEM
17TB8-RE00	OEM
17TB9	OEM
17TB10	OEM
17TB11	OEM
17TB12	OEM
17TB16-CH00	OEM
17TB16-GH00	OEM
17V10	OEM
17Z4	OEM
17Z6	0157
17Z6A	0157
17Z6AF	0157
17Z6F	0157
17Z6FAF	OEM
18-085001	0015
18-085002	0137
18-3	0371
18-607-2	0076
18-3539-1	0086
18A	0371
18A8-1	0050
18A8-1-12	0050
18A8-1-127	0050
18A8-1L	0050
18A8-1L8	0050
18AA-1-82	0160
18B1	0371
18BT03Z	OEM
18BT12Z	OEM
18DB2A	0287
18DB2A-C	0287
18DB4A	0293
18DB4A-C	0293
18DB6A	0299
18DB6A-C	0250
18DB8A	0250
18DB8A-C	0250
18DB10A	0250
18DB10A-C	0250
18E06	OEM
18E12A	OEM
18E27	OEM
18E40	OEM
18E55	OEM
18EB3	0371
18J2	0071
18J2F	0071
18L62	OEM
18NT100	OEM
18P2	1325
18P-2A82	0004
18RC2	3246
18RC5	0726
18RC10	0707
18RC15	0717
18RC20	0464
18RC25	0716
18RC30	0716
18RC40	0717
18RC50	0773
18RC60	0720
18RM90	OEM
18SI-SN76650N	0391
18ST-2SC1815Y(AP)	0076
18ST-2SC1815Y(AP)E	0076
18ST-2SC2371M	0275
18ST-2SD478C	0388
18ST-BU205-01	0065
18ST-MPSH81	0037
18T1	OEM
18Z6	0631
18Z6A	0631
18Z6AF	0631
18Z6F	0631
18Z6FAF	OEM
19-003935	0103
19-020-001	0136
19-020-002	0136
19-020-003	0004
19-020-005	0136
19-020-007	0004
19-020-015	0211
19-020-019	0040
19-020-031	0050
19-020-032	0050
19-020-033	0279
19-020-034	0004
19-020-035	0004
19-020-036	0004
19-020-037	0144
19-020-038	0086
19-020-043	5571
19-020-043A	0016
19-020-044	0007
19-020-045	0178
19-020-048	0007
19-020-052	0144
19-020-056	0042
19-020-058	0016
19-020-066	0042
19-020-070	0224
19-020-071	0127
19-020-072	0488
19-020-073	0016
19-020-074	0016
19-020-075	0086
19-020-076	0693
19-020-077	0693
19-020-079	0627
19-020-081	1659
19-020-44	0144
19-020-100	0126
19-020-101	0042
19-020-102	1257
19-020-111	2156
19-020-112	1966
19-020-114	0006
19-020-115	0321
19-040-002	0015
19-040-003	0015
19-040-004	0015
19-080-001	0133
19-080-002	0015
19-080-008	0133
19-080-009	0143
19-080-014	0041
19-090-007	0755
19-090-008	0313
19-090-008A	0170
19-090-014	0041
19-090-015	0188
19-05589	1394
19-09973-0	0268
19-076001	0574
19-085005	0143
19-085010	0015
19-085016	0030
19-085017	0644
19-085018	0143
19-085022	0015
19-1	0037
19-1-7	OEM
19-2	0037
19-3	0037
19-6-7	OEM
19-10	0037
19-20	0037
19-30	0037
19-130-004	0614
19-130-005	1199
19-3415	0164
19-3416	0164
19-3692	0086
19-3934-643	0086
19-3935-641	0264
19-8049	OEM
19-9072	OEM
19-10476-0	5241
19-100001	0071
19-C	1293
19A11552B-P1	0631
19A11644P1	0659
19A115024-P4	0015
19A115024-P6	0071
19A115056-P1	0969
19A115061-P1	0016
19A115061-P2	0016
19A115077-P1	0211
19A115077-P2	0211
19A115086-P1	0143
19A115087-P1	0136
19A115089	0097
19A115094-P1	0435
19A115098	0136
19A115098-P1	0136
19A115099-P1	0136
19A115100-P1	0015
19A115101	0160
19A115101-P1	0160
19A115102-P1	0016
19A115103-P1	0595
19A115108-P1	0016
19A115108-P2	0016
19A115123-P1	0016
19A115123-P2	0016
19A115129-2	0038
19A115129-P1	0038
19A115140-P1	0050
19A115140-P2	0050
19A115142-P1	0016
19A115142-P2	0016
19A115145-P3	0015
19A115145-P4	0015
19A115178-P1	0037
19A115178-P2	0037
19A115180-2	0126
19A115184-P1	0160
19A115192-P1	0050
19A115192-P2	0050
19A115200-P1	0042
19A115201-P1	0595
19A115201-P2	0595
19A115208	0279
19A115208-P1	0279
19A115208-P2	0279
19A115249-1	0144
19A115253-P1	0016
19A115253-P2	0016
19A115267P1	0160
19A115281-P1	0211
19A115300-1	0086
19A115300-2	0086
19A115300-P1	0555
19A115300-P2	0555
19A115300-P3	0555
19A115301-P1	0279
19A115301-P2	0279
19A115304-2	0086
19A115315-P1	0016
19A115315-P2	0016
19A115322	0911
19A115322-P1	0911
19A115328-P1	0016
19A115328-P2	0016
19A115341P1	0160
19A115342-1	0144
19A115342-P1	0016
19A115342-P2	0016
19A115359-P1	0016
19A115359-P2	0016
19A115361-P1	0160
19A115362-P1	0016
19A115362-P2	0016
19A115385-P1	0160
19A115410-P1	0016
19A115410-P2	0016
19A115440-1	0144
19A115441-1	0144
19A115458-P1	0037
19A115458-P2	0037
19A115460-P1	0717
19A115487-P1	0435
19A115527	0178
19A115527-P1	0178
19A115528-P3	0012
19A115531-P1	0969
19A115540-P1	0435
19A115546-P1	0595
19A115546-P2	0595
19A115548-P1	0279
19A115552-P1	0079
19A115552-P2	0079
19A115553-P1	0050
19A115554-P1	0050
19A115554-P2	0050
19A115556-P1	0279
19A115561	0160
19A115567-P1	0050
19A115567-P2	0050
19A115569-P1	0015
19A115569-P2	0015
19A115623-P1	0142
19A115623-P2	0142
19A115628-P1	0050
19A115628-P2	0050
19A115635-1	0050
19A115635-P1	0050
19A115636-P1	0050
19A115653-P1	0037
19A115653-P2	0037
19A115654-P1	0037
19A115654-P2	0037
19A115665-P1	0050
19A115665-P2	0050
19A115666-1	0144
19A115673-P1	0595
19A115673-P2	0595
19A115674-P1	0004
19A115674-P2	0004
19A115683-P1	0717
19A115683-P2	0717
19A115688-P1	0037
19A115688-P2	0037
19A115706-P1	0037
19A115706-P2	0037
19A115720-1	0016
19A115728-1	0016
19A115747-P1	0717
19A115768-P1	0037
19A115768-P2	0037
19A115786	0016
19A115786A	0016
19A115913-1	1812
19A115913-2	2067
19A115913-3	1035
19A115913-4	2086
19A115913-10	0354
19A115913-19	0141
19A115913-20	0557
19A115913P2	2067
19A115913P14	1820
19A116180-7	1018
19A116180-8	0738
19A116180-11	1193
19A116180-18	1358
19A116180-22	0381
19A116180-24	1199
19A116180-25	0974
19A116180-27	0828
19A116180-29	1477
19A116180-P13	1394
19A116180P1	0232
19A116180P2	0268
19A116180P3	0310
19A116180P4	0507
19A116180P5	0692
19A116180P7	1018
19A116180P8	0738
19A116180P11	1193
19A116180P15	1164
19A116180P16	1303
19A116180P18	1358
19A116180P20	0357
19A123160-1	0144
19A126813	0103
19A126813A	0103
19A126826-P2	0130
19AI15527-1	0178
19AR2	0015
19AR3	0143
19AR4	0479
19AR4-1	0479
19AR5	0015
19AR6-1	0208
19AR6-2	0208
19AR6-3	0208
19AR7-1	0004
19AR7-2	0004
19AR8	0123
19AR11	0015
19AR12	0015
19AR13-1	0050
19AR13-2	0050
19AR13-3	0050
19AR13-4	0050
19AR14-1	0004
19AR14-2	0004
19AR16-1	0004
19AR16-2	0004
19AR17	0015
19AR18	0050
19AR19-1	0004
19AR19-2	0004
19AR20	0016
19AR22	0123
19AR24	0050
19AR25	0004
19AR26	0004
19AR27	0004
19AR29	0196
19AR29-1	0196
19AR30	0769
19AR31	0160
19AR32	0004
19AR34	0015
19AR35	0142
19AR36	0016
19B200011-P1	0097
19B200011-P2	0097
19B200011-P3	0097
19B200011-P4	0097
19B200011-P5	0015
19B200054-P1	0004
19B200061-P1	0004
19B200061-P2	0004
19B200061-P3	0004
19B200061-P4	0004
19B200063-P1	0004
19B200065-P1	0595
19B200065-P2	0595
19B200129-P1	0279
19B200130-P1	0050
19B200130-P2	0050
19B200132-P1	0211
19B200132-P2	0211
19B200132-P3	0211
19B200132-P4	0211
19B200210-P1	0004
19B200210-P2	0004
19B200210-P3	0004
19B200248-P1	0934
19B200248-P2	0934
19B200248-P3	0934
19B200249-P1	0133
19B200249-P2	0133
19B200249-P3	0133
19B200379-P1	0012
19B2000129-P1	0279
19B2000130-P1	0050
19B2000130-P2	0050
19B2000132-P1	0004
19B2000132-P2	0004
19B2000132-P3	0004
19B2000132-P4	0004
19BA009	OEM
19C300LL5-1	0086
19C300073-P1	0211
19C300073-P2	0211
19C300073-P3	0211
19C300073-P4	0211
19C300073-P5	0211
19C300073-P6	0211

If replacement code is OEM, contact original manufacturer for replacement.

DEVICE TYPE	REPL CODE
19C300074-P2	0211
19C300076-P1	0015
19C300076-P2	0015
19C300076-P3	0015
19C300076-P4	0015
19C300076-P5	0015
19C300076-P6	0015
19C300113-P1	0160
19C300114-P1	0016
19C300114-P2	0016
19C300115-P1	0086
19C300128-P1	0211
19C300128-P2	0211
19C300128-P3	0211
19C300128-P4	0211
19C300128-P5	0211
19C300128-P6	0211
19C300128-P7	0211
19C300128-P8	0211
19C300138-P4	0211
19C300138-P8	0211
19C300216-P1	0050
19C300216-P2	0050
19C307022	0030
19C307022-P1	0030
19C3001414P2	0079
19CC19	0644
19E06	OEM
19E12A	OEM
19E15-1	3669
19E18-1	3781
19E19-2	3808
19E25	OEM
19E40	OEM
19E70	OEM
19L-4A82	0004
19P1	0133
19P2	1325
19SZ-WZ-120	0052
19Z6	OEM
19Z6A	OEM
19Z6AF	0025
19Z6F	0025
19Z6FAF	OEM
20	0262
20-0352	1843
20-08048-433	OEM
20-1	0144
20-1(ZENER)	0695
20-3	0695
20-16-3	0143
20-22-08	0015
20-1680-143	0015
20-1680-174	0086
20-1680-175	0143
20-1680-189	0164
20-9062	0110
20A0007	0004
20A0009	0004
20A0015	0004
20A0017	0160
20A0041	0160
20A0042	0160
20A0053	0016
20A0054	0015
20A0059	0378
20A0060	0378
20A0073	0016
20A0074	0160
20A0075	0126
20A0076	0086
20A05	0071
20A1	0947
20A2	0242
20A3	1736
20A4	0535
20A5	1760
20A6	0959
20A6F	0596
20A8	0811
20A8F	OEM
20A10	0916
20A10F	OEM
20A11	0133
20A12	OEM
20A13	0133
20A50	OEM
20A-70	0143
20A70	0143
20A79	0143
20A-90	0123
20A90	0123
20A-90H	0143
20A90H	0019
20A90HMP	0123
20A90LF	0143
20A-90M	0143
20A90M	0143
20A90MLF	0123
20A90Z	0123
20A100	OEM
20A200	OEM
20A400	OEM
20A600	OEM
20A800	OEM
20A10849	0016
20AS	0015
20B1	OEM
20B1M	0627
20B2FR	OEM
20B4FR	OEM
20B6FR	OEM
20B20	OEM
20B40	OEM
20B409	0162
20B410	0162
20BG2C11	6392
20BG2Z11	OEM
20BL2C41	2219
20BS	0015
20C	0015
20C05	0071
20C1	0947
20C1R10	OEM
20C1R20	OEM
20C1R30	OEM
20C1S10	OEM
20C1S20	OEM
20C1S30	OEM
20C2	0242
20C2R10	OEM
20C2R20	OEM
20C2R30	OEM
20C2S10	OEM
20C2S20	OEM
20C2S30	OEM
20C3	1736
20C4	0535
20C5	1760
20C6	0959
20C8	0959
20C9	0811
20C10	0811
20C12	OEM
20C14	OEM
20C16	OEM
20C18	OEM
20C71	0004
20C72	0004
20C2073BGSZ	OEM
20CL2C41	2219
20CS04FM	OEM
20CS04H	2219
20CS04M	1931
20CTQ30	OEM
20CTQ35	OEM
20CTQ40	OEM
20CTQ45	OEM
20D02M1	OEM
20D05	0071
20D05MA	OEM
20D1	OEM
20D2	0023
20D2FM	OEM
20D2L	0071
20D4	0071
20D4FM	OEM
20D6	0071
20D6FM	OEM
20D8	OEM
20D10	0071
20D10K1	OEM
20DCS10	0015
20DCS10R	0015
20E06	OEM
20E1	0071
20E1R20	OEM
20E1R40	OEM
20E1R60	OEM
20E1S20	OEM
20E1S40	OEM
20E1S60	OEM
20E2	0071
20E2R20	OEM
20E2R40	OEM
20E2R60	OEM
20E2S20	OEM
20E2S40	OEM
20E2S60	OEM
20E4	0071
20E4FD	OEM
20E6	0071
20E8	0071
20E10	0071
20E10FA13	0071
20E12A	OEM
20E20	OEM
20E40	OEM
20E-54-5411	2006
20E70	OEM
20E1114	1024
20EB	0695
20F1	0575
20F1R07	OEM
20F1R15	OEM
20F1S07	OEM
20F1S15	OEM
20F2R07	OEM
20F2R15	OEM
20F2S07	OEM
20F2S15	OEM
20F5	1590
20F5R	2275
20F10	5189
20F10R	2275
20F15	0865
20F20	0865
20F20R	2275
20F30	5190
20F30R	0471
20F40	0847
20F40R	0471
20F50	OEM
20F60	1599
20F80	1600
20F100	1604
20FQ020	0610
20FQ025	OEM
20FQ030	0610
20FQ035	0610
20FQ040	0610
20FQ045	0610
20FQS07	OEM
20FR5	4917
20FR10	5394
20FR20	1625
20FR30	5398
20FR40	1242
20FR50	5399
20FR60	1196
20FR80	2124
20FR100	2236
20FT1K	OEM
20FT1L	OEM
20FT2K	OEM
20FT2L	OEM
20FT3K	OEM
20FT3L	OEM
20FT4K	OEM
20FT4L	OEM
20FT5K	OEM
20FT5L	OEM
20FT6K	OEM
20FT6L	OEM
20FT7K	OEM
20FT8K	OEM
20G2C11	OEM
20G2Z11	OEM
20G3Z11	OEM
20GG2C11	5847
20GG2Z11	OEM
20H	0015
20H2	0097
20H3	0097
20H3N	2275
20H3P	0983
20H3PN	0984
20H260RT	OEM
20HA3	0315
20HB5	1590
20HB20	0865
20HB40	0847
20J2	0097
20J3P	0097
20JG2C11	2683
20JG2Z11	OEM
20JH3	2633
20K	0015
20L2C41	OEM
20L15	OEM
20L20	OEM
20L25	OEM
20L30	OEM
20L35	OEM
20L40	OEM
20L45	OEM
20L50	OEM
20L55	OEM
20L60	OEM
20L65	OEM
20L70	OEM
20L75	OEM
20L80	OEM
20L85	OEM
20L90	OEM
20L95	OEM
20L100	OEM
20L110	OEM
20L120	OEM
20L130	OEM
20L140	OEM
20L150	OEM
20L160	OEM
20L170	OEM
20L180	OEM
20L190	OEM
20L200	OEM
20L210	OEM
20L220	OEM
20L230	OEM
20L240	OEM
20L250	OEM
20L260	OEM
20L270	OEM
20L280	OEM
20L290	OEM
20L300	OEM
20LF	OEM
20M	0015
20M10	2629
20M15	OEM
20M20	2633
20M30	2639
20M40	1995
20M50	2652
20M60	2657
20M80	3846
20M100	2631
20MA10	2670
20MA20	2633
20MA30	1995
20MA40	1995
20MA60	2657
20MA80	3846
20MA100	3178
20MA120	OEM
20MA140	OEM
20MA160	OEM
20MC	0050
20MLA60	OEM
20MLA80	OEM
20MLA100	OEM
20MLA120	OEM
20N02F1	OEM
20N05M1	OEM
20N1	0015
20N2	0097
20N3	0097
20N10K1	OEM
20N15A	OEM
20N15A9	OEM
20N20A	OEM
20N20A9	OEM
20N25A	OEM
20N25A9	OEM
20N30A	OEM
20N30A9	OEM
20N35A	OEM
20N35A9	OEM
20N40A	OEM
20N40A9	OEM
20N45A	OEM
20N45A9	OEM
20N50A	OEM
20N50A9	OEM
20N55A	OEM
20N55A9	OEM
20N60A	OEM
20N60A9	OEM
20N65A	OEM
20N65A9	OEM
20N70A	OEM
20N70A9	OEM
20N75A	OEM
20N75A9	OEM
20N80A	OEM
20N80A9	OEM
20N85A	OEM
20N85A9	OEM
20N90A	OEM
20N90A9	OEM
20N95A	OEM
20N95A9	OEM
20N100A	OEM
20N100A9	OEM
20N110A	OEM
20N120A	OEM
20N130A	OEM
20N140A	OEM
20N150A	OEM
20N160A	OEM
20N170A	OEM
20N180A	OEM
20N190A	OEM
20N200A	OEM
20N210A	OEM
20N220A	OEM
20N230A	OEM
20N240A	OEM
20N250A	OEM
20N260A	OEM
20P02F1-A	OEM
20P05M1-A	OEM
20P1S	0464
20P1SG	0707
20P2	0097
20P2S	0464
20P2SG	0464
20P3	0097
20P3S	0716
20P3SG	0717
20P4S	0717
20P4SG	0717
20P5S	0773
20P5SG	0720
20P6S	0720
20P6SG	0720
20P8SG	0745
20P10K1	OEM
20P10SG	OEM
20P12SG	OEM
20PM10	OEM
20Q3	1232
20R2	3160
20R3	0321
20R3P	OEM
20RM60	OEM
20RM80	OEM
20RM100	OEM
20RM120	OEM
20RM150	OEM
20RM200	OEM
20RM220	OEM
20RM250	OEM
20S05	0071
20S1	OEM
20S1S03	OEM
20S1S04	OEM
20S2	OEM
20S2S03	OEM
20S2S04	OEM
20S2SC	OEM
20S3	0800
20S3P	OEM
20S3SC	OEM
20S4	0800
20S4SC	OEM
20S5	0575
20S5SC	OEM
20S6	OEM
20S6SC	OEM
20SI-TA7607AP	0906
20SS2SC	OEM
20SS3SC	OEM
20SS4SC	OEM
20SS5SC	OEM
20SS6SC	OEM
20T2FR	OEM
20T3P	OEM
20T4FR	OEM
20T6FR	OEM
20TB1	0707
20TB1-CE00	OEM
20TB1-CH00	OEM
20TB1-EE00	OEM
20TB1-EH00	OEM
20TB1-GE00	OEM
20TB1-GH00	OEM
20TB1-JH00	OEM
20TB1-LE00	OEM
20TB1-LH00	OEM
20TB1-NE00	OEM
20TB1-NH00	OEM
20TB1-RE00	OEM
20TB2	0464
20TB2-CE00	OEM
20TB2-CH00	OEM
20TB2-EE00	OEM
20TB2-EH00	OEM
20TB2-GH00	OEM
20TB2-JH00	OEM
20TB2-LE00	OEM
20TB2-LH00	OEM
20TB2-NE00	OEM
20TB2-NH00	OEM
20TB2-RE00	OEM
20TB3	0716
20TB3-CE00	OEM
20TB3-CH00	OEM
20TB3-EE00	OEM
20TB3-EH00	OEM
20TB3-GE00	OEM
20TB3-GH00	OEM
20TB3-JH00	OEM
20TB3-LE00	OEM
20TB3-LH00	OEM
20TB3-NE00	OEM
20TB3-NH00	OEM
20TB3-RE00	OEM
20TB4	0717
20TB4-CE00	OEM
20TB4-CH00	OEM
20TB4-EE00	OEM
20TB4-EH00	OEM
20TB4-GE00	OEM
20TB4-GH00	OEM
20TB4-JE00	OEM
20TB4-JH00	OEM
20TB4-LE00	OEM
20TB4-LH00	OEM
20TB4-NE00	OEM
20TB4-NH00	OEM
20TB4-RE00	OEM
20TB5	0773
20TB5-CE00	OEM
20TB5-CH00	OEM
20TB5-EH00	OEM
20TB5-GE00	OEM
20TB5-GH00	OEM
20TB5-JE00	OEM
20TB5-JH00	OEM
20TB5-LE00	OEM
20TB5-LH00	OEM
20TB5-NE00	OEM
20TB5-NH00	OEM
20TB5-RE00	OEM
20TB6	0720
20TB6-CE00	OEM
20TB6-CH00	OEM
20TB6-EE00	OEM
20TB6-EH00	OEM
20TB6-GE00	OEM
20TB6-GH00	OEM
20TB6-JE00	OEM
20TB6-JH00	OEM
20TB6-LE00	OEM
20TB6-LH00	OEM
20TB6-NE00	OEM
20TB6-NH00	OEM
20TB6-RE00	OEM
20TB7	OEM
20TB7-CE00	OEM
20TB7-CH00	OEM
20TB7-EE00	OEM
20TB7-EH00	OEM
20TB7-GE00	OEM
20TB7-GH00	OEM
20TB7-JE00	OEM
20TB7-JH00	OEM
20TB7-LE00	OEM
20TB7-LH00	OEM
20TB7-NE00	OEM
20TB7-NH00	OEM
20TB7-RE00	OEM
20TB8	OEM
20TB8-CE00	OEM
20TB8-CH00	OEM
20TB8-EE00	OEM
20TB8-EH00	OEM
20TB8-GE00	OEM
20TB8-GH00	OEM
20TB8-JE00	OEM
20TB8-JH00	OEM
20TB8-LE00	OEM
20TB8-LH00	OEM
20TB8-NE00	OEM
20TB8-NH00	OEM
20TB8-RE00	OEM
20TB9	OEM
20TB10	OEM
20TB11	OEM
20TB12	OEM
20TC05	OEM
20TC025	OEM
20TC10	OEM
20TC15	OEM
20TC20	OEM
20TC25	OEM
20TC30	OEM
20TC40	OEM
20TC50	OEM
20TC60	OEM
20TC70	OEM
20TC80	OEM
20TC90	OEM
20TC100	OEM
20TC110	OEM
20TC120	OEM
20TCA10	OEM
20TCA20	OEM
20TCA30	OEM
20TCA40	OEM
20TCA50	OEM
20TCA60	OEM
20TCA70	OEM
20TCA80	OEM
20TCA90	OEM
20TCA100	OEM
20TCA110	OEM
20TCA120	OEM
20V3P	OEM
20V10	OEM
20V-HG	0004
20V-MG	0279
20W3P	OEM
20X	0666
20X3P	OEM
20Y	0695
20Y3P	OEM
20Z6	OEM
20Z6A	OEM
20Z6AF	0644
20Z6F	0644
20Z6FAF	OEM
20Z8F	OEM
20ZB	OEM
21/3	0479
21/3.92	0479
21-0101	0590
21-1	0016
21-1AA	0312
21-1AA(MAGNAVOX)	0312
21-1L	0016
21-2	0127
21-4	0127
21-6	0127
21-7	0127
21-28	0160
21-32	0050
21-33	0050
21-34	0004
21-35	0142
21-36	0004
21-37	0004
21-810	0015
21-810-2	0015
21A001-000	0015
21A001-00	0015
21A002	0196
21A002-000	0196
21A003-016	0143
21A004-000	0102
21A005	0469
21A005-000	0004
21A006-000	0015
21A007-000	0015
21A008-000	0015
21A008-001	0015
21A008-002	0102
21A008-003	0015
21A008-008	0133
21A008-016	0469
21A009	0133
21A009-000	0143
21A009-002	0123
21A009-008	0133
21A009-009	0133
21A015-001	0004
21A015-002	2736
21A015-003	0222
21A015-004	0144
21A015-005	0208
21A015-006	0164
21A015-008	0150
21A015-008A	0037
21A015-009	0037
21A015-009A	0037
21A015-011	0037
21A015-011A	0037
21A015-012	0037
21A015-012A	0037
21A015-013	0050
21A015-014	0144
21A015-016	0144
21A015-018	0086
21A015-019	0086
21A015-020	0016
21A015-021	2736
21A015-022	0222
21A015-025	0037
21A015-026	0086
21A015-027	0016
21A020-001	0015
21A020-005	0143
21A020-006	0015
21A037-003	0137
21A037-006	0028
21A037-008	0137
21A037-009	0526
21A037-012	0165
21A037-016	0098
21A037-017	1639
21A037-018	0361
21A037-020	0313
21A037-021	0213
21A038-000	0004
21A039-000	0004
21A040-000	0004
21A040-001	0143
21A040-003	0144
21A040-004	0144
21A040-005	0004
21A040-007	0144
21A040-010	0144
21A040-014	0004
21A040-015	0735
21A040-016	0144
21A040-017	0144
21A040-019	0144
21A040-020	0016
21A040-021	0004
21A040-022	0004
21A040-023	0127
21A040-024	0127
21A040-025	0127
21A040-031	0136
21A040-032	0155
21A040-033	0016
21A040-033A	0016
21A040-034	0016
21A040-035	0841
21A040-036	0164
21A040-037	0016
21A040-045	0224
21A040-046	0326
21A040-047	0326
21A040-049	0126
21A040-050	0126
21A040-051	0086
21A040-052	0042
21A040-053	0224
21A040-054	0127
21A040-055	0127
21A040-056	0016
21A040-057	0004
21A040-058	0004
21A040-059	0037
21A040-060	0164
21A040-061	0164
21A040-063	0127
21A040-064	0111
21A040-065	0111
21A040-066	0111
21A040-067	0111
21A040-068	0465
21A040-077	0016
21A040-078	0016
21A040-079	0004
21A040-081	0164
21A040-082	0111
21A040-083	0111
21A040-091	0224
21A040-092	0016
21A040-36	0004
21A040-37	0016
21A040-44	0015
21A040-54	0224
21A041-002	0030
21A041-003	0030
21A045-000	0050
21A048-000	0050
21A048-00	OEM
21A049-000	0050

If replacement code is OEM, contact original manufacturer for replacement. 131

DEVICE TYPE	REPL CODE
21A050-000	0050
21A050-001	0050
21A050-004	0144
21A051-000	0279
21A053-000	0004
21A054-000	0004
21A055-000	0004
21A062-000	0150
21A063-000	0211
21A064-000	0160
21A074-000	0004
21A079-000	0015
21A097-000	0160
21A1	0469
21A2	0196
21A3	0769
21A4	1293
21A6	0015
21A7	0015
21A11-002	0139
21A13-041	0030
21A101-001	2549
21A101-001(IC)	2549
21A101-001(RECT)	0015
21A101-002	2689
21A101-004	2855
21A101-005	0523
21A101-006	0633
21A101-007	0668
21A101-008	0924
21A101-009	0940
21A101-010	0958
21A101-011	2859
21A101-012	2860
21A101-013	2862
21A101-015	1797
21A101-016	0350
21A101-017	0348
21A101-018	2864
21A101-14	OEM
21A102-001	0015
21A102-002	0250
21A103-005	0030
21A103-006	0123
21A103-007	0015
21A103-010	0143
21A103-011	0143
21A103-012	0071
21A103-013	0071
21A103-015	0071
21A103-016	0123
21A103-017	0143
21A103-018	0015
21A103-019	0143
21A103-021	0015
21A103-022	0143
21A103-043	1914
21A103-044	0015
21A103-045	0313
21A103-046	0143
21A103-047	0030
21A103-048	0123
21A103-049	0644
21A103-050	0015
21A103-052	0143
21A103-055	0143
21A103-057	OEM
21A103-058	0015
21A103-060	0030
21A103-064	0012
21A103-065	0133
21A103-069	0030
21A103-070	0015
21A103-104	0071
21A103-064	0012
21A105-001	0144
21A105-004	0086
21A105-006	0086
21A108-001	0133
21A108-002	0012
21A108-003	0133
21A108-004	0133
21A109-001	0143
21A109-002	0143
21A109-003	0123
21A109-022	0143
21A110-001	0015
21A110-002	0015
21A110-003	0015
21A110-004	0071
21A110-005	0102
21A110-006	0023
21A110-007	0015
21A110-008	0102
21A110-009	0102
21A110-012	0015
21A110-013	0102
21A110-014	0102
21A110-071	0023
21A110-072	0071
21A111-001	0133
21A111-002	0139
21A112-001	0037
21A112-002	0126
21A112-003	0006
21A112-004	0786
21A112-006	0102
21A112-007	0127
21A112-010	0007
21A112-013	0155
21A112-015	0016
21A112-017	0016
21A112-018	0016
21A112-019	1211
21A112-020	0076
21A112-023	0003
21A112-025	0142
21A112-029	0142
21A112-031	0074
21A112-033	0142
21A112-036	2040
21A112-045	0111
21A112-046	0076
21A112-047	0037
21A112-048	1257
21A112-049	0555
21A112-050	0016
21A112-058	0076
21A112-062	1211
21A112-063	1211
21A112-065	0037
21A112-070	0168
21A112-071	0168
21A112-074	0855
21A112-084	0224
21A112-085	0016
21A112-086	0144
21A112-087	0144
21A112-088	0016
21A112-089	0016
21A112-090	0016
21A112-091	0016
21A112-092	0016
21A112-093	0037
21A112-094	0919
21A112-095	0042
21A112-096	1200
21A112-098	0168
21A112-100	0037
21A112-101	0151
21A112-102	0006
21A112-103	0065
21A112-104	0016
21A112-120	1317
21A112-124	2112
21A112-125	0676
21A112-126	1638
21A113-002	0321
21A118-008	0168
21A118-029	0042
21A118-031	0018
21A118-032	0527
21A118-036	2040
21A118-049	0419
21A118-063	1274
21A118-096	0261
21A118-12	OEM
21A118-100	0949
21A118-114	0220
21A118-122	1638
21A118-124	2112
21A118-131	1795
21A118-137	0076
21A118-139	0006
21A118-140	0076
21A118-153	0275
21A118-201	0945
21A118-233	0555
21A118-234	0723
21A118-235	2253
21A118-236	1967
21A118-237	0161
21A118-238	5309
21A118-863	0085
21A119-005	0123
21A119-008	0053
21A119-030	0015
21A119-034	0999
21A119-038	0057
21A119-040	0120
21A119-041	0157
21A119-045	1319
21A119-049	0695
21A119-063	1274
21A119-064	0466
21A119-068	0023
21A119-073	0165
21A119-075	0015
21A119-077	2613
21A119-079	0015
21A119-080	0133
21A119-108	0041
21A119-123	0123
21A119-187	0023
21A119-189	0015
21A119-190	0023
21A120-001	0391
21A120-002	1797
21A120-008	0167
21A120-009	4561
21A120-016	0232
21A120-017	0462
21A120-044	1049
21A120-045	4560
21A120-049	0485
21A120-050	3997
21A120-051	0906
21A120-052	2601
21A120-071	2216
21A120-074	4469
21A120-099	0906
21A120-178	0762
21A120-185	2599
21A120-204	1420
21A120-208	4554
21A500	0469
21A500-000	0469
21A112095	0042
21B1AH	2438
21B1M	0649
21B1Z	0649
21B-14	0015
21B-17	0015
21D1FM	OEM
21D2FM	OEM
21D3FM	OEM
21D4FM	OEM
21D6FM	OEM
21DQ03	0031
21DQ04	0031
21DQ05	0031
21DQ06	0031
21DQ09	0031
21DQ10	0031
21E06	OEM
21E12A	OEM
21E18	OEM
21E38A	OEM
21E60	OEM
21ECG5123	3285
21F02-2F	OEM
21F02-2N	OEM
21F02-4F	OEM
21F02-4I	OEM
21F02-4N	OEM
21F02-21	OEM
21F02B	OEM
21F02F	OEM
21F02I	OEM
21F02N	OEM
21F1SC	0865
21F2SC	0865
21F3SC	0800
21FQ030	0610
21FQ035	0610
21FQ040	0610
21FQ045	0610
21J-23840	0015
21K60	0143
21L02-1B	OEM
21L02-1F	OEM
21L02-1I	OEM
21L02-1N	OEM
21L02-2F	OEM
21L02-2I	OEM
21L02-2N	OEM
21L02-3B	OEM
21L02-3F	OEM
21L02-3I	OEM
21L02-3N	OEM
21L02B	4886
21L02F	OEM
21L02FDC	OEM
21L02FFC	OEM
21L02FPC	OEM
21L02HDC	OEM
21L02HFC	OEM
21L02HPC	OEM
21L02I	OEM
21L02N	OEM
21L021DC	OEM
21L021FC	OEM
21L021PC	OEM
21L022DC	OEM
21L022FC	OEM
21L022PC	OEM
21M006	0136
21M007	0279
21M018	0030
21M020	0006
21M022	0037
21M025	2010
21M026	2010
21M027	1233
21M028	1257
21M084	0016
21M086	0016
21M091	0111
21M093	0224
21M094	0127
21M095	0111
21M099	0224
21M122	0016
21M123	0016
21M124	0111
21M125	0016
21M137	0111
21M138	0111
21M139	0016
21M140	0127
21M146	0016
21M149	0016
21M150	0016
21M151	0127
21M152	0127
21M153	0127
21M154	0127
21M160	0111
21M161	0111
21M174	0111
21M178	0127
21M179	0127
21M180	0555
21M181	0555
21M182	0127
21M183	0555
21M184	0555
21M185	0086
21M186	0016
21M188	0127
21M192	0218
21M193	0590
21M196	0683
21M200	0016
21M214	0012
21M224	0321
21M228	0086
21M248	0015
21M252	OEM
21M283	0015
21M286	0555
21M288	0143
21M289	0123
21M302	0015
21M307	0012
21M312	0015
21M315	0015
21M316	0030
21M317	0015
21M323	0143
21M325	0123
21M327	OEM
21M330	0133
21M345	0676
21M355	0037
21M369	0386
21M386	0015
21M387	0086
21M408	0111
21M417	0015
21M419	0015
21M430	OEM
21M431	OEM
21M432	0143
21M433	0015
21M434	0015
21M435	0015
21M436	0015
21M437	0015
21M443	1257
21M446	0111
21M448	0086
21M455	0086
21M459	1233
21M465	0455
21M466	0161
21M469	0015
21M485	1469
21M487	0015
21M488	0016
21M492	0030
21M493	0170
21M502	0030
21M506	1601
21M519	0015
21M520	0016
21M526	0030
21M532	1206
21M534	0321
21M541	0320
21M545	0015
21M556	0555
21M562	0133
21M563	0016
21M568	0123
21M577	0224
21M578	0016
21M579	0016
21M581	0037
21M582	4463
21M583	0030
21M584	0012
21M585	0012
21M586	1141
21M588	0696
21M594	0143
21M028	1257
21MW132	0211
21P560	OEM
21PT5	OEM
21PT10	OEM
21PT20	OEM
21PT40	OEM
21PT60	OEM
21R05S	3160
21R1S	2873
21R1SC	2873
21R2S	1116
21R2SC	1116
21R3S	1118
21R3SC	1118
21R4S	0800
21R5S	1186
21R6S	0315
21R8S	1124
21R10S	0045
21R12S	OEM
21R35	0800
21RC10	0562
21RC20	0757
21RC30	0735
21RC40	0735
21RC50	0759
21RC60	0759
21RC80	0761
21RC100	OEM
21RECT-SI-1039(AU)	0790
21SZ-RD13EB1	0053
21Z6	OEM
21Z6A	OEM
22-00920-000	OEM
22-001001	0016
22-001002	0144
22-001003	0144
22-001004	0144
22-001005	0144
22-001006	0016
22-001007	0016
22-001008	0178
22-001009	0178
22-001010	0037
22-002001	0222
22-002006	0211
22-002007	0004
22-002008	0222
22-002009	0222
22-004003	0143
22-004004	0071
22-1	0127
22-1(ZENER)	0700
22-1-005	0019
22-1-044	0133
22-1-075	0023
22-1-5	0019
22-1-70	0133
22-1-127	0030
22-1-129	0143
22-1-130	0030
22-1-131	0012
22-1-132	0091
22-1-138	0015
22-908-03A	OEM
22-908-03B	OEM
22-950-3B	OEM
22A50	OEM
22A100	OEM
22A200	OEM
22A400	OEM
22A600	OEM
22A800	OEM
22BC11	OEM
22BD11	OEM
22BH18M	OEM
22BH18P	OEM
22CC11	OEM
22CD11	OEM
22E05	OEM
22E8	0279
22E10A	OEM
22E15	OEM
22E30	OEM
22E50	OEM
22E89	0841
22FC11	OEM
22FD11	OEM
22MPG5	OEM
22MPS5	OEM
22NT100	OEM
22P1	OEM
22PB18M	OEM
22PD18M	OEM
22PD18P	OEM
22PH18M	OEM
22PS18M	OEM
22R2	0865
22R4	OEM
22R22	1116
22RC2	3246
22RC5	0726
22RC10	0707
22RC15	0464
22RC20	0464
22RC25	0716
22RC30	0716
22RC40	0717
22RC50	0773
22RC60	0720
22RC70	OEM
22RIA10	5760
22RIA10M	OEM
22RIA20	0464
22RIA20M	OEM
22RIA40	0717
22RIA40M	OEM
22RIA60	0720
22RIA60M	OEM
22RIA80	0745
22RIA80M	OEM
22RIA100	4771
22RIA100M	OEM
22RIA110	OEM
22RIA110M	OEM
22RIA120	0674
22RIA120M	OEM
22ST-2SA1015-0	0148
22ST-2SA1015O	0148
22ST-2SD1177C	0558
22V10	OEM
22Z6	0012
22Z6A	0012
22Z6AF	0012
22Z6F	0012
22Z6FAF	OEM
23	0016
23-0003	0242
23-0004	0015
23-0010	0015
23-0017	0015
23-0018	0015
23-1	0037
23-2	0037
23-3	0037
23-10	0037
23-20	0037
23-30	0037
23-5009	0599
23-5014	0004
23-5017	0004
23-5020	0155
23-5021	0155
23-5022	0155
23-5023	0155
23-5024	0155
23-5025	0155
23-5026	0155
23-5027	0155
23-5029	0155
23-5031	0178
23-5032	3502
23-5033	0016
23-5034	0841
23-5035	0103
23-5037	0086
23-5038	0103
23-5039	0086
23-5042	0160
23-5044	0396
23-5045	0126
23-5048	2839
23-5051	3249
23-5052	0079
23-6001-16	0164
23-6001-17	0164
23-6001-20	0164
23-6001-21	0164
23-6001-23	0164
23-PT274-120	0007
23-PT274-121	0016
23-PT274-122	0037
23-PT274-123	0007
23-PT274-125	0133
23-PT275-121	0007
23-PT275-122	0144
23-PT275-124	0911
23-PT283-122	0007
23-PT283-124	0007
23-PT283-125	0133
23-PT284-122	0050
23-PT284-123	0050
23-ST-2SA733Q(AU)E	0006
23B-210-025	0160
23B-210-230-2	0969
23B114044	0016
23B114053	0086
23B114054	0086
23B-210067-001	4391
23B-210067-002	4391
23B210679-1	0769
23BSC101	0015
23C05C	OEM
23C025	0464
23C025C	0464
23C050	0464
23C050C	0464
23C10	0464
23C10C	0464
23C15	0464
23C15C	0464
23C20	0464
23C20C	0464
23C25	0717
23C25C	0717
23C30	0717
23C30C	0717
23C35	0717
23C35C	0717
23C40	0717
23C40C	0717
23C45	0720
23C45C	0720
23C50	0720
23C50B	0720
23C50C	0720
23C60	0720
23C60B	0720
23C60C	0720
23C70	0674
23C70B	0745
23C70C	0674
23C80	0674
23C80B	0745
23C80C	0674
23C90B	OEM
23C100B	OEM
23C110B	OEM
23C120B	OEM
23C1000-1-539	OEM
23D	0396
23E001-1	0016
23E05	OEM
23E10A	OEM
23E20	OEM
23E30	OEM
23E60	OEM
23J2	0133
23J2C	OEM
23K3	OEM
23R2	OEM
23RA5	0464
23RA10	0464
23RA20	0464
23RA30	0720
23RA40	0720
23RA50	0720
23RA60	0720
23RA80	OEM
23SD-1SS151	0911
23SD-BAW62	0124
23ST-2SA733Q(AU)E	0006
23ST-2SA733R(AU)E	0006
23ST-MPS9682J	0037
23T1	OEM
23T2	OEM
23T3	OEM
23T4	OEM
23T5	OEM
23T6	OEM
23T7	OEM
23T8	OEM
23T9	OEM
23T10	OEM
23T11	OEM
23T12	OEM
23TB1	0707
23TB2	0464
23TB3	0716
23TB4	0717
23TB5	0773
23TB6	0720
23TB7	OEM
23TB8	OEM
23TB9	OEM
23TB10	OEM
23TB11	OEM
23TB12	OEM
23Z6	OEM
23Z6A	OEM
23Z6AF	0170
23Z6F	0170
23Z6FAF	OEM
24	OEM
24-002	0016
24-016	0127
24-016-001	0150
24-016-005	0127
24-2	0489
24-198	0015
24-602-25	0016
24-3564	0144
24-28201	0133
24-DP1	0015
24A	0016
24A-015-003	OEM
24A1	0144
24B	0016
24B(ZENER)	0489
24B1	0016
24B2	0489
24B4	0489
24C02AB1	OEM
24C02AIP	OEM
24C04B1	OEM
24CH1FM	OEM
24CH1FN	OEM
24CH2FM	OEM
24CH3FM	OEM
24CH4FM	OEM
24D400P1	OEM
24DP1	0015
24E-000	0030
24E-001	0133
24E-001C	0030
24E-002	0911
24E-002-0	0911
24E-002-C	0911
24E-005	OEM
24E005	OEM
24E-006	0133
24E05	OEM
24E-022	0911
24E10A	OEM
24E20	OEM
24E35	OEM
24E60	OEM
24F15E1	OEM
24J2	0133
24J2C	OEM
24K570S	OEM
24M	OEM
24MW11	0279
24MW15	0211
24MW16	0211
24MW27	0004

If replacement code is OEM, contact original manufacturer for replacement.

DEVICE TYPE	REPL CODE
24MW28	0004
24MW29	0211
24MW34	0004
24MW43	0211
24MW44	0050
24MW55	0050
24MW59	0050
24MW60	0211
24MW61	0136
24MW69	0211
24MW70	0211
24MW74	0136
24MW76	0030
24MW77	0279
24MW78	0211
24MW83	0211
24MW84	0211
24MW87	0143
24MW107	0211
24MW111	0004
24MW115	0211
24MW116	0211
24MW119	0076
24MW122	0123
24MW130	0038
24MW132	0211
24MW152	0136
24MW156	0211
24MW157	0050
24MW175	0229
24MW178	0004
24MW179	0004
24MW185	0004
24MW186	0211
24MW187	0004
24MW192	0276
24MW196	0229
24MW197	0015
24MW199	0143
24MW205	0136
24MW207	0644
24MW208	0015
24MW227	0015
24MW241	0015
24MW243	0143
24MW244	0123
24MW246	0071
24MW256	0164
24MW263	0211
24MW267	0015
24MW268	0015
24MW269	0015
24MW271	0136
24MW287	0127
24MW303	0136
24MW331	0012
24MW333	0016
24MW339	0050
24MW340	0050
24MW350	0050
24MW351	0050
24MW352	0136
24MW353	0136
24MW361	0127
24MW368	0136
24MW370	0004
24MW372	0016
24MW384	0004
24MW405	0050
24MW406	0050
24MW407	0050
24MW408	0211
24MW441	0004
24MW454	0016
24MW458	0016
24MW460	0016
24MW461	0016
24MW525	0050
24MW535	0127
24MW593	0127
24MW594	0127
24MW595	0127
24MW596	0127
24MW597	0127
24MW598	0004
24MW599	0004
24MW600	0004
24MW601	0004
24MW602	0071
24MW603	0143
24MW605	0071
24MW607	1073
24MW608	0004
24MW609	0016
24MW613	0004
24MW614	0004
24MW615	0004
24MW618	0816
24MW619	0015
24MW652	0683
24MW653	0127
24MW654	0151
24MW655	0531
24MW-656	0127
24MW656	0127
24MW657	0076
24MW658	0111
24MW659	0111
24MW660	0076
24MW661	0006
24MW662	0042
24MW663	0086
24MW664	0030
24MW665	0123
24MW667	0133
24MW669	0015
24MW670	1075
24MW671	0015
24MW673	0151
24MW674	0531
24MW675	0144
24MW676	0111
24MW677	0076
24MW700	0127
24MW714	1471
24MW721	0015
24MW723	0321
24MW724	0144
24MW725	0144
24MW726	0030
24MW727	0886
24MW734	0030
24MW736	0683
24MW737	0155
24MW738	0284
24MW739	0284
24MW740	0191
24MW741	0164
24MW742	0631
24MW743	0012
24MW744	1914
24MW746	0211
24MW747	0279
24MW748	0211
24MW760	0016
24MW763	0211
24MW764	0211
24MW765	0211
24MW768	0015
24MW771	0143
24MW772	0015
24MW773	0016
24MW774	0016
24MW775	0016
24MW776	0016
24MW777	0004
24MW778	0042
24MW779	0071
24MW780	0004
24MW781	0004
24MW782	0004
24MW783	0164
24MW785	0133
24MW789	0004
24MW790	0016
24MW793	0284
24MW795	0016
24MW796	0016
24MW797	0016
24MW799	0004
24MW801	0016
24MW805	0127
24MW807	0016
24MW808	0016
24MW809	0016
24MW812	0127
24MW813	0127
24MW814	0151
24MW815	0127
24MW816	0136
24MW817	0016
24MW818	0016
24MW819	0164
24MW820	0123
24MW823	0016
24MW824	0004
24MW825	0133
24MW826	0111
24MW827	0144
24MW828	0841
24MW829	0071
24MW851	0015
24MW852	0144
24MW853	0004
24MW854	0016
24MW855	0016
24MW856	0004
24MW857	0004
24MW858	0133
24MW860	0143
24MW861	0133
24MW862	0015
24MW863	0127
24MW864	0071
24MW865	0144
24MW867	0015
24MW871	0015
24MW874	0076
24MW892	0004
24MW893	0004
24MW894	0133
24MW895	0211
24MW896	0211
24MW899	0016
24MW924	0071
24MW950	0030
24MW953	0127
24MW954	0016
24MW955	0030
24MW956	0133
24MW957	0007
24MW958	0007
24MW961	0016
24MW964	0111
24MW965	0111
24MW967	0143
24MW973	0164
24MW974	0229
24MW975	0229
24MW976	0037
24MW977	0042
24MW978	0161
24MW988	0016
24MW989	0321
24MW990	0111
24MW991	0136
24MW992	0016
24MW994	0222
24MW995	0015
24MW996	2142
24MW997	3506
24MW998	0012
24MW1022	0111
24MW1023	0016
24MW1024	0016
24MW1025	0111
24MW1028	0574
24MW1029	0143
24MW1030	0143
24MW1031	0037
24MW1038	0144
24MW1040	0164
24MW1043	0143
24MW1049	0037
24MW1051	0143
24MW1052	0030
24MW1057	0127
24MW1058	0127
24MW1059	0016
24MW1060	0111
24MW1061	0006
24MW1062	5748
24MW1062(NPN)	OEM
24MW1062(PNP)	OEM
24MW1063	0030
24MW1065	0170
24MW1066	0015
24MW1067	0143
24MW1068	0016
24MW1069	0016
24MW1071	0015
24MW1081	0127
24MW1082	0144
24MW1083	0004
24MW1084	0004
24MW1089	0016
24MW1092	0143
24MW1096	0016
24MW1105	0715
24MW1106	0127
24MW1107	0446
24MW1108	0023
24MW1109	0133
24MW1110	4483
24MW1112	0030
24MW1113	0139
24MW1115	0004
24MW1116	2839
24MW1118	0087
24MW1120	0155
24MW1122	0212
24MW1123	0015
24MW1124	0023
24MW1125	0170
24MW1126	OEM
24MW1141	0016
24MW1143	0558
24MW1144	0015
24MW1146	0015
24MW1147	0016
24MW1152	0076
24MW1161	0086
24MW1162	0015
24MW7796	0079
24MY716	OEM
24P02F1-A	OEM
24P05M1-A	OEM
24P10K1	OEM
24R	0079
24R2	0800
24S04	OEM
24S06	OEM
24S08	OEM
24S10	2209
24S12	OEM
24S14	OEM
24S16	OEM
24SD-1SV70	1023
24ST-MPS9410AJ	0086
24ST-MPS9700G	0079
24SZ-HZ4B3	0036
24T-002	0144
24T002	0127
24T-011-008	0144
24T011-008	0144
24T-011-011	0037
24T011-012	0007
24T-011-013	0224
24T-011-015	0127
24T-013-003	0007
24T-013-005	0144
24T-015-013	0079
24T-016	0127
24T016	0127
24T-016-(016)	0111
24T-016-001	0007
24T-016-005	0144
24T-016-010	0127
24T-016-011	0144
24T-016-013	0144
24T-016-015	0144
24T-016-016	0144
24T-016-024	0127
24T-016-0B	0127
24T021	0007
24T-026-001	0321
24T-029	OEM
24T-029-001	OEM
24T013003	0127
24T013005	0127
24T016001	0127
24T016005	0127
24T1	OEM
24T2	OEM
24T3	OEM
24T4	OEM
24T5	OEM
24T6	OEM
24T7	OEM
24T8	OEM
24T9	OEM
24T10	OEM
24T11	OEM
24T12	OEM
24TB1	0562
24TB2	0757
24TB3	3240
24TB4	0735
24TB5	3260
24TB6	0759
24TB7	2848
24TB8	0761
24TB9	OEM
24TB10	OEM
24TB11	OEM
24TB12	OEM
24V10A	OEM
24V11	OEM
24Z6	OEM
24Z6A	OEM
24Z6F	0313
24Z6FAF	OEM
25	OEM
25-06D	0907
25-3	0143
25-5	0015
25-100015	0144
25-108550-03	OEM
25A	0144
25A1	0144
25A1ABG0	OEM
25A1ABG1	OEM
25A1PG0	OEM
25A1PG1	OEM
25A1QBG0	OEM
25A1QBG1	OEM
25A2	0016
25A2ABG0	OEM
25A2ABG2	OEM
25A2PG0	OEM
25A2PG2	OEM
25A2QBG0	OEM
25A2QBG2	OEM
25A3ABG0	OEM
25A3ABG3	OEM
25A3PG0	OEM
25A3PG3	OEM
25A3QBG0	OEM
25A3QBG3	OEM
25A4ABG0	OEM
25A4ABG4	OEM
25A4PG0	OEM
25A4PG4	OEM
25A4QBG0	OEM
25A4QBG4	OEM
25A5ABG0	OEM
25A5ABG5	OEM
25A5PG0	OEM
25A5PG5	OEM
25A5QBG0	OEM
25A5QBG5	OEM
25A6ABG0	OEM
25A6ABG6	OEM
25A6PG0	OEM
25A6PG6	OEM
25A6QBG0	OEM
25A6QBG6	OEM
25A7ABG0	OEM
25A7ABG7	OEM
25A7PG0	OEM
25A7PG7	OEM
25A7QBG0	OEM
25A7QBG7	OEM
25A8ABG0	OEM
25A8ABG8	OEM
25A8PG0	OEM
25A8PG8	OEM
25A8QBG0	OEM
25A8QBG8	OEM
25A9ABG0	OEM
25A9ABG9	OEM
25A9PG0	OEM
25A9PG9	OEM
25A9QBG0	OEM
25A9QBG9	OEM
25A10ABG0	OEM
25A10ABG10	OEM
25A10PG0	OEM
25A10PG10	OEM
25A10QBG0	OEM
25A10QBG10	OEM
25A11ABG0	OEM
25A11ABG11	OEM
25A11PG0	OEM
25A11PG11	OEM
25A11QBG0	OEM
25A11QBG11	OEM
25A12ABG0	OEM
25A12ABG12	OEM
25A12PG0	OEM
25A12PG12	OEM
25A12QBG0	OEM
25A12QBG12	OEM
25A13ABG0	OEM
25A13ABG13	OEM
25A13PG0	OEM
25A13PG13	OEM
25A13QBG0	OEM
25A13QBG13	OEM
25A14ABG0	OEM
25A14ABG14	OEM
25A14PG0	OEM
25A14PG14	OEM
25A14QBG0	OEM
25A14QBG14	OEM
25A15ABG0	OEM
25A15ABG15	OEM
25A15PG0	OEM
25A15PG15	OEM
25A15QBG0	OEM
25A15QBG15	OEM
25A16ABG0	OEM
25A16ABG16	OEM
25A16PG0	OEM
25A16PG16	OEM
25A16QBG0	OEM
25A16QBG16	OEM
25A17ABG0	OEM
25A17ABG17	OEM
25A17PG0	OEM
25A17PG17	OEM
25A17QBG0	OEM
25A17QBG17	OEM
25A18ABG0	OEM
25A18ABG18	OEM
25A18PG0	OEM
25A18PG18	OEM
25A18QBG0	OEM
25A18QBG18	OEM
25A19ABG0	OEM
25A19ABG19	OEM
25A19PG0	OEM
25A19PG19	OEM
25A19QBG0	OEM
25A19QBG19	OEM
25A20ABG0	OEM
25A20ABG20	OEM
25A20PG0	OEM
25A20PG20	OEM
25A20QBG0	OEM
25A20QBG20	OEM
25A321	0050
25A324	0050
25A440A	0050
25A473Y	0919
25A561Y	0037
25A1262-005	0144
25A1273-001	0016
25A1281-001	0144
25AC3SL	3123
25AC3SR	3123
25AC5SL	4038
25AC5SR	4038
25AC6SL	4038
25AC6SR	4038
25AK20	OEM
25AK30	OEM
25AK50	OEM
25AM624	0144
25AN20	OEM
25AN30	OEM
25AN40	OEM
25AN50	OEM
25AN60	OEM
25AN80	OEM
25AN100	OEM
25AN120	OEM
25AN140	OEM
25AN160	OEM
25ANS	OEM
25B	0144
25B05T	OEM
25B-1	0144
25B1	0144
25B1C	2716
25B1T	2716
25B2	0224
25B2C	2716
25B2T	2716
25B4B41	OEM
25B10T	OEM
25B20T	OEM
25B21	0079
25B40T	OEM
25B60T	OEM
25B186	0211
25B375A-NB	0969
25B378	0004
25B496	0279
25C05	3160
25C05R	1620
25C1	OEM
25C2	OEM
25C4	OEM
25C6	OEM
25C8	OEM
25C10	2873
25C10R	0254
25C12	OEM
25C14	OEM
25C15	1116
25C15R	1099
25C16	OEM
25C20	1116
25C30	1118
25C30R	0258
25C40	0800
25C40R	0258
25C50	1186
25C50R	1634
25C60	0315
25C60R	0267
25C70R	1111
25C80	1124
25C80R	1111
25C90	0045
25C90R	0280
25C100	0045
25C100R	0280
25C206	0144
25C536E	0004
25CC11	OEM
25CC13	1116
25CD13	1099
25CS58LGBM	0016
25D4B41	OEM
25D10	0071
25D15	OEM
25D20	OEM
25D25	OEM
25D30	OEM
25D40	OEM
25D50	OEM
25DC11	OEM
25DF10	OEM
25DF15	OEM
25DF20	OEM
25DF25	OEM
25DF30	OEM
25E05	OEM
25E10A	OEM
25E19	OEM
25E33	OEM
25E55	OEM
25F-B1F	0287
25FC11	OEM
25FC13	0800
25FCRA	OEM
25FCRB	OEM
25FCRC	OEM
25FCRD	OEM
25FCRE	OEM
25FCRF	OEM
25FCRG	OEM
25FCRH	OEM
25FCRI	OEM
25FCRJ	OEM
25FCRK	OEM
25FCRL	OEM
25FXF11	OEM
25FXF12	OEM
25G4B41	OEM
25G5	3716
25G5R	2640
25G10	2629
25G10R	2670
25G20	2633
25G20R	2741
25G40	1995
25G40R	2879
25G60	2657
25G80	3846
25G100	2631
25G120	OEM
25GC11	OEM
25GC12	1995
25H5	1551
25H5A	1551
25H10	1551
25H10A	1551
25H15	2813
25H15A	2813
25H20A	2813
25H25	4244
25H25A	4244
25H30	4244
25H30A	4244
25H40	2823
25H40A	2823
25H50	2844
25H50A	2844
25H60	2844
25H60A	2844
25H70	2806
25H70A	2806
25H80	2806
25H80A	2806
25H90	2454
25H90A	2454
25H100	2454
25H100A	2454
25HB5	3716
25HB10	2629
25HB15	2633
25HB20	2633
25HB25	2639
25HB30	2639
25HB35	1995
25HB40	1995
25HB50	2652
25HB60	2657
25HBR5	1772
25HBR10	1772
25HBR20	1772
25HBR30	1772
25HBR40	1772
25HBR50	1772
25HBR60	1772
25HC11	OEM
25HR5	1772
25HR5A	1772
25HR10	1772
25HR10A	1772
25HR15	1772
25HR15A	1772
25HR20	1772
25HR20A	1772
25HR30	1772
25HR30A	1772
25HR40	1772
25HR40A	1772
25HR50	1772
25HR50A	1772
25HR60	1772
25HR60A	1772
25HR80	1807
25HR80A	1807
25HR100	1807
25HR100A	1807
25IP005	OEM
25IP005D	OEM
25IP005N	OEM
25IP01	OEM
25IP01D	OEM
25IP01N	OEM
25IP02	OEM
25IP02D	OEM
25IP02N	OEM
25IP04	OEM
25IP04D	OEM
25IP04N	OEM
25IP06	OEM
25IP06D	OEM
25IP06N	OEM
25IP08	OEM
25IP08D	OEM
25IP08N	OEM
25IP10	OEM
25IP10D	OEM
25IP10N	OEM
25J2	0133
25J2C	0133
25J4B41	OEM
25JB1L	2347
25JB2L	2347
25JB4L	2353
25JC11	OEM
25JC12	2657
25K10	0071
25K20	OEM
25K30	OEM
25K40	OEM
25K50	OEM
25KB7	OEM
25KC11	OEM
25L01I	OEM
25L01N	OEM
25L15	OEM
25L20	OEM
25L25	OEM
25L30	OEM
25L35	OEM
25L40	OEM
25L45	OEM
25L50	OEM
25L55	OEM
25L60	OEM
25L65	OEM
25L70	OEM
25L75	OEM
25L80	OEM
25L85	OEM
25L90	OEM

If replacement code is OEM, contact original manufacturer for replacement.

DEVICE TYPE	REPL CODE
25L95	OEM
25L100	OEM
25L110	OEM
25L120	OEM
25L130	OEM
25L140	OEM
25L150	OEM
25L160	OEM
25L170	OEM
25L180	OEM
25L190	OEM
25L200	OEM
25L210	OEM
25L220	OEM
25L230	OEM
25L240	OEM
25L250	OEM
25L260	OEM
25L270	OEM
25L280	OEM
25L290	OEM
25L300	OEM
25LC11	OEM
25LC12	3846
25LF11	1111
25LS2521	OEM
25M10	OEM
25MC11	OEM
25N15	0002
25N15A	OEM
25N15A9	OEM
25N20A	OEM
25N20A9	OEM
25N25A	OEM
25N25A9	OEM
25N27	0436
25N30A	OEM
25N30A9	OEM
25N35A	OEM
25N35A9	OEM
25N40A	OEM
25N40A9	OEM
25N45A	OEM
25N45A9	OEM
25N50A	OEM
25N50A9	OEM
25N55A	OEM
25N55A9	OEM
25N60A	OEM
25N60A9	OEM
25N65A	OEM
25N65A9	OEM
25N70A	OEM
25N70A9	OEM
25N75A	OEM
25N75A9	OEM
25N80A	OEM
25N80A9	OEM
25N85A	OEM
25N85A9	OEM
25N90A	OEM
25N90A9	OEM
25N95A	OEM
25N95A9	OEM
25N100A	OEM
25N100A9	OEM
25N110A	OEM
25N120A	OEM
25N130A	OEM
25N140A	OEM
25N150A	OEM
25N160A	OEM
25N170A	OEM
25N180A	OEM
25N190A	OEM
25N200A	OEM
25N210A	OEM
25N220A	OEM
25N230A	OEM
25N240A	OEM
25N250A	OEM
25N260A	OEM
25NC12	2631
25NF11	0280
25P1	0143
25P1SG	OEM
25P2SG	OEM
25P3SG	OEM
25P4SG	OEM
25P5	OEM
25P6SG	OEM
25P8SG	OEM
25P10	OEM
25P12SG	OEM
25P20	OEM
25P20SG	OEM
25P30	OEM
25P40	OEM
25P50	OEM
25P60	OEM
25PCRA	1640
25PCRB	1640
25PCRC	1640
25PCRD	1640
25PCRE	1640
25PCRF	2623
25PCRG	2623
25PCRH	2623
25PCRI	2625
25PCRJ	2625
25PCRK	OEM
25PCRL	OEM
25PCRNA	OEM
25PCRNB	OEM
25PCRNC	OEM
25PCRND	OEM
25PCRNE	OEM
25PCRNF	OEM
25PCRNG	OEM
25PCRNH	OEM
25PCRNI	OEM
25PCRNJ	OEM
25PCRNK	OEM
25PCRNL	OEM
25PCRSA	2174
25PCRSB	2174
25PCRSC	0562
25PCRSD	0757
25PCRSE	0757
25PCRSF	0735
25PCRSG	0735
25PCRSH	0735
25PCRSI	0759
25PCRSJ	0759
25PCRSK	0761
25PCRSL	OEM
25PDU5M	OEM
25PW5	OEM
25PW10	OEM
25PW20	OEM
25PW30	OEM
25PW40	OEM
25PW50	OEM
25PW60	OEM
25QF11	OEM
25R	0144
25R2	OEM
25RIA10	OEM
25RIA10M	OEM
25RIA20	OEM
25RIA20M	OEM
25RIA40	OEM
25RIA40M	OEM
25RIA60	OEM
25RIA60M	OEM
25RIA80	OEM
25RIA80M	OEM
25RIA100	OEM
25RIA100M	OEM
25RIA110	OEM
25RIA110M	OEM
25RIA120	OEM
25RIA120M	OEM
25SD-1N60-TMS	0019
25SDG1	OEM
25SDG2	OEM
25SDG2JHKO	OEM
25SDG2JHNO	OEM
25SDG3	OEM
25SDG4	OEM
25SDG4JHKO	OEM
25SDG4JHNO	OEM
25SDG5	OEM
25SDG5JHKO	OEM
25SDG5JHNO	OEM
25SDG6	OEM
25SDG6JHKO	OEM
25SDG6JHNO	OEM
25SP005	OEM
25SP005D	OEM
25SP005N	OEM
25SP01	OEM
25SP01D	OEM
25SP01N	OEM
25SP02	OEM
25SP02D	OEM
25SP02N	OEM
25SP04	OEM
25SP04D	OEM
25SP04N	OEM
25SP-06	OEM
25SP06	OEM
25SP06D	OEM
25SP06N	OEM
25SP08	OEM
25SP08D	OEM
25SP08N	OEM
25SP10	OEM
25SP10D	OEM
25SP10N	OEM
25ST-2SC18150	0076
25ST-2SD781	0558
25T-002	0127
25T1	0211
25T2	OEM
25T3	OEM
25T4	OEM
25T5	OEM
25T6	OEM
25T7	OEM
25T8	OEM
25T9	OEM
25T10	OEM
25T11	OEM
25T12	OEM
25T20	OEM
25T40	OEM
25TB1-CE00	OEM
25TB1-CH00	OEM
25TB1-EE00	OEM
25TB1-EH00	OEM
25TB1-GE00	OEM
25TB1-GH00	OEM
25TB1-JE00	OEM
25TB1-LE00	OEM
25TB1-LH00	OEM
25TB1-NE00	OEM
25TB1-NH00	OEM
25TB1-RE00	OEM
25TB2-CE00	OEM
25TB2-CH00	OEM
25TB2-EE00	OEM
25TB2-EH00	OEM
25TB2-GE00	OEM
25TB2-GH00	OEM
25TB2-JE00	OEM
25TB2-JH00	OEM
25TB2-LE00	OEM
25TB2-LH00	OEM
25TB2-NE00	OEM
25TB2-NH00	OEM
25TB2-RE00	OEM
25TB3-CE00	OEM
25TB3-CH00	OEM
25TB3-EE00	OEM
25TB3-EH00	OEM
25TB3-GE00	OEM
25TB3-GH00	OEM
25TB3-JE00	OEM
25TB3-JH00	OEM
25TB3-LE00	OEM
25TB3-LH00	OEM
25TB3-NE00	OEM
25TB3-NH00	OEM
25TB3-RE00	OEM
25TB4-CE00	OEM
25TB4-CH00	OEM
25TB4-EH00	OEM
25TB4-GE00	OEM
25TB4-GH00	OEM
25TB4-JE00	OEM
25TB4-JH00	OEM
25TB4-LE00	OEM
25TB4-LH00	OEM
25TB4-NE00	OEM
25TB4-NH00	OEM
25TB4-RE00	OEM
25TB5-CE00	OEM
25TB5-CH00	OEM
25TB5-EE00	OEM
25TB5-EH00	OEM
25TB5-GE00	OEM
25TB5-GH00	OEM
25TB5-JE00	OEM
25TB5-JH00	OEM
25TB5-LE00	OEM
25TB5-LH00	OEM
25TB5-NE00	OEM
25TB5-NH00	OEM
25TB5-RE00	OEM
25TB6-CE00	OEM
25TB6-CH00	OEM
25TB6-EE00	OEM
25TB6-EH00	OEM
25TB6-GE00	OEM
25TB6-GH00	OEM
25TB6-JE00	OEM
25TB6-JH00	OEM
25TB6-LE00	OEM
25TB6-LH00	OEM
25TB6-NE00	OEM
25TB6-NH00	OEM
25TB6-RE00	OEM
25TB7-CE00	OEM
25TB7-EE00	OEM
25TB7-EH00	OEM
25TB7-GE00	OEM
25TB7-GH00	OEM
25TB7-JE00	OEM
25TB7-JH00	OEM
25TB7-LE00	OEM
25TB7-LH00	OEM
25TB7-NE00	OEM
25TB7-NH00	OEM
25TB7-RE00	OEM
25TB8-CE00	OEM
25TB8-CH00	OEM
25TB8-EE00	OEM
25TB8-EH00	OEM
25TB8-GE00	OEM
25TB8-GH00	OEM
25TB8-JE00	OEM
25TB8-JH00	OEM
25TB8-LE00	OEM
25TB8-LH00	OEM
25TB8-NE00	OEM
25TB8-NH00	OEM
25TB8-RE00	OEM
25TB9-CH00	OEM
25TB9-EE00	OEM
25TB9-EH00	OEM
25TB9-GE00	OEM
25TB9-GH00	OEM
25TB9-JE00	OEM
25TB9-JH00	OEM
25TB9-LE00	OEM
25TB9-NE00	OEM
25TB9-RE00	OEM
25TB10-CE00	OEM
25TB10-CH00	OEM
25TB10-EE00	OEM
25TB10-EH00	OEM
25TB10-GE00	OEM
25TB10-GH00	OEM
25TB10-JE00	OEM
25TB10-JH00	OEM
25TB10-LE00	OEM
25TB10-LH00	OEM
25TB10-NE00	OEM
25TB10-NH00	OEM
25TB10-RE00	OEM
25TB11-CE00	OEM
25TB11-CH00	OEM
25TB11-EE00	OEM
25TB11-EH00	OEM
25TB11-GE00	OEM
25TB11-GH00	OEM
25TB11-JE00	OEM
25TB11-JH00	OEM
25TB11-LE00	OEM
25TB11-LH00	OEM
25TB11-NE00	OEM
25TB11-NH00	OEM
25TB11-RE00	OEM
25TB12-CE00	OEM
25TB12-CH00	OEM
25TB12-EE00	OEM
25TB12-EH00	OEM
25TB12-GE00	OEM
25TB12-GH00	OEM
25TB12-JE00	OEM
25TB12-JH00	OEM
25TB12-LE00	OEM
25TB12-LH00	OEM
25TB12-NE00	OEM
25TB12-RE00	OEM
25TCRA	0464
25TCRB	0464
25TCRC	0464
25TCRD	0464
25TCRE	0464
25TCRF	0717
25TCRG	0717
25TCRH	0717
25TCRI	0720
25TCRJ	0720
25TCRK	0674
25TCRL	0674
25VC02	OEM
25VC05	OEM
25VC1	OEM
25VC2	OEM
25VC3	OEM
25VC4	OEM
25VC5	OEM
25VC6	OEM
25VC7	OEM
25VC8	OEM
25Z6	0137
25Z6A	0137
25Z6AF	0137
25Z6F	0137
25Z6FAF	OEM
26	OEM
26/P19503	0086
26-16162-1	1024
26-4701508	0071
26E04	OEM
26E08A	OEM
26E17	OEM
26E30	OEM
26E45	OEM
26G10	OEM
26G20	OEM
26G40	OEM
26G60	OEM
26G80	OEM
26G100	OEM
26G120	OEM
26J2	0133
26J2C	0133
26MB5A	OEM
26MB10A	5301
26MB20A	5301
26MB40A	3446
26MB60A	5305
26MB80A	6523
26MB100A	5948
26MB120A	OEM
26MW613	0004
260D15901	0111
26P1	OEM
26R2	0315
26R2S	0315
26ST-2SC383TM	0076
26ST-JE9014C	4811
26T1	0211
26T2	OEM
26T2C	OEM
26T3	OEM
26T4	OEM
26T5	OEM
26T6	OEM
26T7	OEM
26T8	OEM
26T9	OEM
26T10	OEM
26T11	OEM
26T12	OEM
26TB1-CE00	OEM
26TB1-CH00	OEM
26TB1-EE00	OEM
26TB1-EH00	OEM
26TB1-GE00	OEM
26TB1-GH00	OEM
26TB1-JE00	OEM
26TB1-JH00	OEM
26TB1-LE00	OEM
26TB1-LH00	OEM
26TB1-NE00	OEM
26TB1-NH00	OEM
26TB1-RE00	OEM
26TB2-CE00	OEM
26TB2-CH00	OEM
26TB2-EE00	OEM
26TB2-EH00	OEM
26TB2-GE00	OEM
26TB2-GH00	OEM
26TB2-JE00	OEM
26TB2-JH00	OEM
26TB2-LE00	OEM
26TB2-LH00	OEM
26TB2-NE00	OEM
26TB2-NH00	OEM
26TB2-RE00	OEM
26TB3-CE00	OEM
26TB3-CH00	OEM
26TB3-EE00	OEM
26TB3-EH00	OEM
26TB3-GE00	OEM
26TB3-GH00	OEM
26TB3-JE00	OEM
26TB3-JH00	OEM
26TB3-LE00	OEM
26TB3-LH00	OEM
26TB3-NE00	OEM
26TB3-NH00	OEM
26TB3-RE00	OEM
26TB4-CE00	OEM
26TB4-CH00	OEM
26TB4-EE00	OEM
26TB4-EH00	OEM
26TB4-GE00	OEM
26TB4-GH00	OEM
26TB4-JE00	OEM
26TB4-JH00	OEM
26TB4-LE00	OEM
26TB4-LH00	OEM
26TB4-NE00	OEM
26TB4-NH00	OEM
26TB4-RE00	OEM
26TB5-CE00	OEM
26TB5-CH00	OEM
26TB5-EE00	OEM
26TB5-EH00	OEM
26TB5-GE00	OEM
26TB5-GH00	OEM
26TB5-JE00	OEM
26TB5-JH00	OEM
26TB5-LE00	OEM
26TB5-LH00	OEM
26TB5-NE00	OEM
26TB5-NH00	OEM
26TB5-RE00	OEM
26TB6-CE00	OEM
26TB6-CH00	OEM
26TB6-EE00	OEM
26TB6-EH00	OEM
26TB6-GE00	OEM
26TB6-GH00	OEM
26TB6-JE00	OEM
26TB6-JH00	OEM
26TB6-LE00	OEM
26TB6-LH00	OEM
26TB6-NE00	OEM
26TB6-NH00	OEM
26TB6-RE00	OEM
26TB7-CE00	OEM
26TB7-CH00	OEM
26TB7-EH00	OEM
26TB7-GE00	OEM
26TB7-GH00	OEM
26TB7-JH00	OEM
26TB7-LE00	OEM
26TB7-LH00	OEM
26TB7-NH00	OEM
26TB7-RE00	OEM
26TB8-CE00	OEM
26TB8-CH00	OEM
26TB8-EE00	OEM
26TB8-EH00	OEM
26TB8-GE00	OEM
26TB8-GH00	OEM
26TB8-JH00	OEM
26TB8-LE00	OEM
26TB8-LH00	OEM
26TB8-NE00	OEM
26TB8-NH00	OEM
26TB8-RE00	OEM
26TB9-CE00	OEM
26TB9-CH00	OEM
26TB9-EH00	OEM
26TB9-GE00	OEM
26TB9-GH00	OEM
26TB9-JH00	OEM
26TB9-LE00	OEM
26TB9-LH00	OEM
26TB9-NE00	OEM
26TB9-NH00	OEM
26TB9-RE00	OEM
26TB10-CE00	OEM
26TB10-CH00	OEM
26TB10-EE00	OEM
26TB10-EH00	OEM
26TB10-GE00	OEM
26TB10-GH00	OEM
26TB10-JH00	OEM
26TB10-LE00	OEM
26TB10-LH00	OEM
26TB10-NE00	OEM
26TB10-NH00	OEM
26TB10-RE00	OEM
26TB11-CE00	OEM
26TB11-CH00	OEM
26TB11-EE00	OEM
26TB11-EH00	OEM
26TB11-GE00	OEM
26TB11-GH00	OEM
26TB11-JH00	OEM
26TB11-LE00	OEM
26TB11-LH00	OEM
26TB11-NE00	OEM
26TB11-NH00	OEM
26TB11-RE00	OEM
26TB12-CE00	OEM
26TB12-CH00	OEM
26TB12-EE00	OEM
26TB12-EH00	OEM
26TB12-GE00	OEM
26TB12-GH00	OEM
26TB12-JH00	OEM
26TB12-LE00	OEM
26TB12-NE00	OEM
26TB12-NH00	OEM
26TB12-RE00	OEM
26Z6	OEM
26Z6A	OEM
26Z6F	0361
26Z6FAF	OEM
27-0432-00-00	OEM
27-0435-00	OEM
27-0460-00	OEM
27-0473-01	OEM
27-0473-03	OEM
27-0501-00	OEM
27-0532-03	OEM
27-0554-01	OEM
27-0602-01	OEM
27-0605-00	OEM
27-0690-00	OEM
27-0692-00	OEM
27-06900000	OEM
27-226	0196
27-C226	0196
27A10446-101-11	0329
27B1(1WATT)	1596
27C226	0196
27C256-20	OEM
27C256-20FA	OEM
27C256-XX	OEM
27E04	OEM
27E08A	OEM
27E16	OEM
27E30	OEM
27E50	OEM
27J2	0133
27P1	0143
27ST-2SA673C	0148
27ST-2SD871	0055
27ST-LM2682	0079
27T1	OEM
27T2	OEM
27T3	OEM
27T4	OEM
27T5	OEM
27T6	OEM
27T7	OEM
27T8	OEM
27T9	OEM
27T10	OEM
27T11	OEM
27T12	OEM
27T401	0279
27T402	0279
27T403	0211
27T404	0211
27T405	0211
27T406	0160
27T407	0435
27T408	0595
27T409	0198
27T410	0038
27T411	0198
27T412	0136
27TB1	OEM
27TB1-CE00	OEM
27TB1-CH00	OEM
27TB1-EE00	OEM
27TB1-EH00	OEM
27TB1-GE00	OEM
27TB1-GH00	OEM
27TB1-JE00	OEM
27TB1-JH00	OEM
27TB1-LE00	OEM
27TB1-LH00	OEM
27TB1-NE00	OEM
27TB1-NH00	OEM
27TB1-RE00	OEM
27TB2	OEM
27TB2-CE00	OEM
27TB2-CH00	OEM
27TB2-EE00	OEM
27TB2-EH00	OEM
27TB2-GE00	OEM
27TB2-GH00	OEM
27TB2-JE00	OEM
27TB2-JH00	OEM
27TB2-LE00	OEM
27TB2-LH00	OEM
27TB2-NE00	OEM
27TB2-NH00	OEM
27TB2-RE00	OEM
27TB3	OEM
27TB3-CE00	OEM
27TB3-CH00	OEM
27TB3-EE00	OEM
27TB3-EH00	OEM
27TB3-GE00	OEM
27TB3-GH00	OEM
27TB3-JE00	OEM
27TB3-JH00	OEM
27TB3-LE00	OEM
27TB3-LH00	OEM
27TB3-NE00	OEM
27TB3-NH00	OEM
27TB3-RE00	OEM
27TB4	OEM
27TB4-CE00	OEM
27TB4-CH00	OEM
27TB4-EE00	OEM
27TB4-EH00	OEM
27TB4-GE00	OEM
27TB4-GH00	OEM
27TB4-JE00	OEM
27TB4-JH00	OEM
27TB4-LE00	OEM
27TB4-LH00	OEM
27TB4-NE00	OEM
27TB4-NH00	OEM
27TB4-RE00	OEM
27TB5	OEM
27TB5-CE00	OEM
27TB5-CH00	OEM
27TB5-EE00	OEM
27TB5-EH00	OEM
27TB5-GE00	OEM
27TB5-GH00	OEM
27TB5-JE00	OEM
27TB5-JH00	OEM
27TB5-LE00	OEM
27TB5-LH00	OEM
27TB5-NE00	OEM
27TB5-NH00	OEM
27TB5-RE00	OEM
27TB6	OEM
27TB6-CE00	OEM
27TB6-EE00	OEM
27TB6-EH00	OEM
27TB6-GE00	OEM
27TB6-GH00	OEM
27TB6-JE00	OEM
27TB6-JH00	OEM
27TB6-LE00	OEM
27TB6-LH00	OEM
27TB6-NE00	OEM
27TB6-NH00	OEM
27TB6-RE00	OEM
27TB7	OEM
27TB7-CE00	OEM
27TB7-CH00	OEM
27TB7-EE00	OEM
27TB7-EH00	OEM
27TB7-GE00	OEM
27TB7-GH00	OEM
27TB7-JE00	OEM
27TB7-JH00	OEM
27TB7-LE00	OEM
27TB7-LH00	OEM
27TB7-NE00	OEM
27TB7-NH00	OEM
27TB7-RE00	OEM
27TB8	OEM
27TB8-CE00	OEM
27TB8-CH00	OEM
27TB8-EE00	OEM
27TB8-EH00	OEM
27TB8-GE00	OEM
27TB8-GH00	OEM
27TB8-JH00	OEM
27TB8-LE00	OEM
27TB8-LH00	OEM
27TB8-NE00	OEM
27TB8-NH00	OEM
27TB8-RE00	OEM
27TB9	OEM
27TB9-CE00	OEM
27TB9-CH00	OEM
27TB9-EE00	OEM
27TB9-EH00	OEM
27TB9-GE00	OEM
27TB9-GH00	OEM
27TB9-JE00	OEM

134

If replacement code is OEM, contact original manufacturer for replacement.

DEVICE TYPE	REPL CODE
27TB9-JH00	OEM
27TB9-LE00	OEM
27TB9-LH00	OEM
27TB9-NE00	OEM
27TB9-NH00	OEM
27TB9-RE00	OEM
27TB10	OEM
27TB10-CE00	OEM
27TB10-CH00	OEM
27TB10-EE00	OEM
27TB10-EH00	OEM
27TB10-GE00	OEM
27TB10-GH00	OEM
27TB10-JE00	OEM
27TB10-JH00	OEM
27TB10-LE00	OEM
27TB10-LH00	OEM
27TB10-NE00	OEM
27TB10-NH00	OEM
27TB10-RE00	OEM
27TB11	OEM
27TB11-CE00	OEM
27TB11-CH00	OEM
27TB11-EE00	OEM
27TB11-EH00	OEM
27TB11-GE00	OEM
27TB11-GH00	OEM
27TB11-JE00	OEM
27TB11-JH00	OEM
27TB11-LE00	OEM
27TB11-LH00	OEM
27TB11-NE00	OEM
27TB11-NH00	OEM
27TB11-RE00	OEM
27TB12	OEM
27TB12-CE00	OEM
27TB12-CH00	OEM
27TB12-EE00	OEM
27TB12-EH00	OEM
27TB12-GE00	OEM
27TB12-GH00	OEM
27TB12-JH00	OEM
27TB12-LE00	OEM
27TB12-LH00	OEM
27TB12-NE00	OEM
27TB12-NH00	OEM
27TB12-RE00	OEM
27TB13	OEM
27TB14	OEM
27TB15	OEM
27X	0450
27Y	0450
27Z6	0100
27Z6A	0100
27Z6F	0100
27Z6FAF	OEM
28-1-01	0015
28-1-02	0015
28-6-01	0015
28-7-01	0015
28-13-01	0015
28-14-01	0015
28-15-01	0015
28-15-02	0015
28-18-01	0015
28-19-01	0015
28-20-01	0015
28-20-02	0015
28-21-01	0015
28-22-01	0015
28-22-02	0015
28-22-03	0015
28-22-04	0015
28-22-05	0015
28-22-06	0015
28-22-07	0015
28-22-10	0015
28-22-11	0087
28-22-12	0015
28-22-13	0102
28-22-14	0015
28-22-15	0015
28-22-16	0087
28-22-17	0015
28-22-18	0087
28-22-19	1293
28-22-19(ELECTROHOME	0102
28-22-20	0087
28-22-21	0015
28-22-22	0102
28-23-01	0769
28-24-01	1293
28-25-01	0015
28-26-01	0469
28-29-01	0015
28-31-00	1313
28-32-00	0190
28-32-0X	0190
28-32-OX	0190
28-33-01	0405
28-33-02	0405
28-35-00	1493
28-35-01	2777
28-37-00	1061
28-39-01	2524
28-65-01	0015
28-254566-1	0015
28A477	0136

DEVICE TYPE	REPL CODE
28A608E	0150
28BR2	OEM
28BR2S	OEM
28C16-15	OEM
28C620	OEM
28C774	OEM
28C777	OEM
28C1014	OEM
28CPQ030	1931
28CPQ040	1931
28CPQ050	OEM
28CPQ060	OEM
28E04	OEM
28E08A	OEM
28E15	OEM
28E30	OEM
28E50	OEM
28J2	1325
28J2C	0133
28L22	OEM
28M018	0030
28P1	0143
28R2	1124
28R25	1124
28ST-2SC1213C	0191
28ST-2SC2230AY	0261
28ST-2SD467(C)	0945
28ST-2SD467C	0945
28ST-MPS9633C	0079
28T1	OEM
28T2	OEM
28T3	OEM
28T4	OEM
28T5	OEM
28T6	OEM
28T7	OEM
28T8	OEM
28T9	OEM
28T10	OEM
28T11	OEM
28T12	OEM
28TB1-CE00	OEM
28TB1-CH00	OEM
28TB1-EE00	OEM
28TB1-EH00	OEM
28TB1-GE00	OEM
28TB1-GH00	OEM
28TB1-JE00	OEM
28TB1-JH00	OEM
28TB1-LE00	OEM
28TB1-LH00	OEM
28TB1-NE00	OEM
28TB1-RE00	OEM
28TB2-CE00	OEM
28TB2-CH00	OEM
28TB2-EE00	OEM
28TB2-EH00	OEM
28TB2-GE00	OEM
28TB2-GH00	OEM
28TB2-JE00	OEM
28TB2-JH00	OEM
28TB2-LE00	OEM
28TB2-LH00	OEM
28TB2-NE00	OEM
28TB2-RE00	OEM
28TB3-CE00	OEM
28TB3-CH00	OEM
28TB3-EE00	OEM
28TB3-EH00	OEM
28TB3-GE00	OEM
28TB3-GH00	OEM
28TB3-JE00	OEM
28TB3-JH00	OEM
28TB3-LE00	OEM
28TB3-LH00	OEM
28TB3-NE00	OEM
28TB3-RE00	OEM
28TB4-CE00	OEM
28TB4-CH00	OEM
28TB4-EE00	OEM
28TB4-EH00	OEM
28TB4-GE00	OEM
28TB4-GH00	OEM
28TB4-JE00	OEM
28TB4-JH00	OEM
28TB4-LE00	OEM
28TB4-LH00	OEM
28TB4-NE00	OEM
28TB4-RE00	OEM
28TB5-CE00	OEM
28TB5-CH00	OEM
28TB5-EE00	OEM
28TB5-EH00	OEM
28TB5-GE00	OEM
28TB5-GH00	OEM
28TB5-JE00	OEM
28TB5-LE00	OEM
28TB5-LH00	OEM
28TB5-NE00	OEM
28TB6-CE00	OEM
28TB6-CH00	OEM
28TB6-EE00	OEM
28TB6-EH00	OEM
28TB6-GE00	OEM
28TB6-GH00	OEM
28TB6-JE00	OEM
28TB6-JH00	OEM
28TB6-LE00	OEM
28TB6-LH00	OEM

DEVICE TYPE	REPL CODE
28TB6-NE00	OEM
28TB6-NH00	OEM
28TB6-RE00	OEM
28TB7-CE00	OEM
28TB7-CH00	OEM
28TB7-EE00	OEM
28TB7-EH00	OEM
28TB7-GE00	OEM
28TB7-GH00	OEM
28TB7-JE00	OEM
28TB7-JH00	OEM
28TB7-LE00	OEM
28TB7-LH00	OEM
28TB7-NE00	OEM
28TB7-NH00	OEM
28TB7-RE00	OEM
28TB8-CE00	OEM
28TB8-CH00	OEM
28TB8-EE00	OEM
28TB8-EH00	OEM
28TB8-GE00	OEM
28TB8-GH00	OEM
28TB8-JE00	OEM
28TB8-JH00	OEM
28TB8-LE00	OEM
28TB8-LH00	OEM
28TB8-NE00	OEM
28TB8-NH00	OEM
28TB8-RE00	OEM
28TB9-CH00	OEM
28TB9-EE00	OEM
28TB9-EH00	OEM
28TB9-GE00	OEM
28TB9-GH00	OEM
28TB9-JE00	OEM
28TB9-JH00	OEM
28TB9-LE00	OEM
28TB9-LH00	OEM
28TB9-NE00	OEM
28TB9-NH00	OEM
28TB9-RE00	OEM
28TB10-CE00	OEM
28TB10-CH00	OEM
28TB10-EE00	OEM
28TB10-EH00	OEM
28TB10-GE00	OEM
28TB10-GH00	OEM
28TB10-JE00	OEM
28TB10-JH00	OEM
28TB10-LE00	OEM
28TB10-LH00	OEM
28TB10-NE00	OEM
28TB10-NH00	OEM
28TB10-RE00	OEM
28TB11-CE00	OEM
28TB11-CH00	OEM
28TB11-EE00	OEM
28TB11-EH00	OEM
28TB11-GE00	OEM
28TB11-GH00	OEM
28TB11-JE00	OEM
28TB11-JH00	OEM
28TB11-LE00	OEM
28TB11-LH00	OEM
28TB11-NE00	OEM
28TB11-NH00	OEM
28TB11-RE00	OEM
28TB12-CE00	OEM
28TB12-CH00	OEM
28TB12-EE00	OEM
28TB12-EH00	OEM
28TB12-GE00	OEM
28TB12-GH00	OEM
28TB12-JE00	OEM
28TB12-JH00	OEM
28TB12-LE00	OEM
28TB12-LH00	OEM
28TB12-NE00	OEM
28TB12-NH00	OEM
28TB12-RE00	OEM
28TB13	OEM
28TB14	OEM
28TB15	OEM
28V12	OEM
28Z6	0002
28Z6A	0002
28Z6AF	0002
28Z6F	0002
28Z6FAF	OEM
29-178A	0733
29-178B	0733
29-178C	0733
29-178D	0733
29-178E	0733
29-178M	0733
29-178N	0733
29-178P	0733
29-178PA	0733
29-178PB	0733
29-178S	0733
29-178T	0733
29-180A	0733
29-180B	0733
29-180C	0733
29-180D	0733
29-180E	0733
29-180M	0733
29-180N	0733
29-180P	0733

DEVICE TYPE	REPL CODE
29-180PA	0733
29-180PB	0733
29-180S	0733
29-180T	0733
29-218A	0733
29-218B	0733
29-218C	0733
29-218D	0733
29-218F	0733
29-218H	0733
29-218K	0733
29-218M	0733
29-218P	0733
29-218S	0733
29-218V	0733
29-218Z	0733
29-218ZB	0733
29-218ZD	0733
29B1B	0345
29B1Z	0345
29D5R19	OEM
29D9R19GH	OEM
29M01201	OEM
29P1	0188
29ST-3SK80	0367
29SZ-RD11EB2	0181
29T1	OEM
29T2	OEM
29T2C	OEM
29T3	OEM
29T4	OEM
29T5	OEM
29T6	OEM
29T7	OEM
29T8	OEM
29T9	OEM
29T10	OEM
29T11	OEM
29T12	OEM
29TB1	OEM
29TB1-CE00	OEM
29TB1-CH00	OEM
29TB1-EE00	OEM
29TB1-EH00	OEM
29TB1-GE00	OEM
29TB1-GH00	OEM
29TB1-JE00	OEM
29TB1-JH00	OEM
29TB1-LH00	OEM
29TB1-RE00	OEM
29TB2	OEM
29TB2-CE00	OEM
29TB2-CH00	OEM
29TB2-EE00	OEM
29TB2-EH00	OEM
29TB2-GE00	OEM
29TB2-GH00	OEM
29TB2-JE00	OEM
29TB2-JH00	OEM
29TB2-LE00	OEM
29TB2-LH00	OEM
29TB2-RE00	OEM
29TB3	OEM
29TB3-CE00	OEM
29TB3-CH00	OEM
29TB3-EE00	OEM
29TB3-EH00	OEM
29TB3-GE00	OEM
29TB3-GH00	OEM
29TB3-JE00	OEM
29TB3-JH00	OEM
29TB3-LE00	OEM
29TB3-LH00	OEM
29TB3-RE00	OEM
29TB4	OEM
29TB4-CE00	OEM
29TB4-CH00	OEM
29TB4-EE00	OEM
29TB4-EH00	OEM
29TB4-GE00	OEM
29TB4-GH00	OEM
29TB4-JE00	OEM
29TB4-JH00	OEM
29TB4-LE00	OEM
29TB4-LH00	OEM
29TB4-RE00	OEM
29TB5	OEM
29TB5-CE00	OEM
29TB5-CH00	OEM
29TB5-EE00	OEM
29TB5-EH00	OEM
29TB5-GE00	OEM
29TB5-GH00	OEM
29TB5-JE00	OEM
29TB5-JH00	OEM
29TB5-LE00	OEM
29TB5-LH00	OEM
29TB5-RE00	OEM
29TB6	OEM
29TB6-CE00	OEM
29TB6-CH00	OEM
29TB6-EE00	OEM
29TB6-EH00	OEM
29TB6-GE00	OEM
29TB6-GH00	OEM
29TB6-JE00	OEM
29TB6-JH00	OEM
29TB6-LE00	OEM
29TB6-LH00	OEM

DEVICE TYPE	REPL CODE
29TB6-RE00	OEM
29TB7	OEM
29TB7-CE00	OEM
29TB7-CH00	OEM
29TB7-EE00	OEM
29TB7-EH00	OEM
29TB7-GE00	OEM
29TB7-GH00	OEM
29TB7-JE00	OEM
29TB7-JH00	OEM
29TB7-LE00	OEM
29TB7-LH00	OEM
29TB7-RE00	OEM
29TB8	OEM
29TB8-CE00	OEM
29TB8-CH00	OEM
29TB8-EE00	OEM
29TB8-EH00	OEM
29TB8-GE00	OEM
29TB8-GH00	OEM
29TB8-JE00	OEM
29TB8-JH00	OEM
29TB8-LE00	OEM
29TB8-LH00	OEM
29TB8-RE00	OEM
29TB9	OEM
29TB9-CE00	OEM
29TB9-CH00	OEM
29TB9-EE00	OEM
29TB9-EH00	OEM
29TB9-GE00	OEM
29TB9-GH00	OEM
29TB9-JE00	OEM
29TB9-JH00	OEM
29TB9-LE00	OEM
29TB9-LH00	OEM
29TB9-RE00	OEM
29TB10	OEM
29TB10-CE00	OEM
29TB10-CH00	OEM
29TB10-EE00	OEM
29TB10-EH00	OEM
29TB10-GE00	OEM
29TB10-GH00	OEM
29TB10-JE00	OEM
29TB10-JH00	OEM
29TB10-LE00	OEM
29TB10-LH00	OEM
29TB10-RE00	OEM
29TB11	OEM
29TB11-CE00	OEM
29TB11-CH00	OEM
29TB11-EE00	OEM
29TB11-EH00	OEM
29TB11-GE00	OEM
29TB11-GH00	OEM
29TB11-JE00	OEM
29TB11-JH00	OEM
29TB11-LE00	OEM
29TB11-LH00	OEM
29TB11-NE00	OEM
29TB11-RE00	OEM
29TB12	OEM
29TB12-CE00	OEM
29TB12-CH00	OEM
29TB12-EE00	OEM
29TB12-EH00	OEM
29TB12-GE00	OEM
29TB12-GH00	OEM
29TB12-JE00	OEM
29TB12-JH00	OEM
29TB12-LE00	OEM
29TB12-LH00	OEM
29TB12-NE00	OEM
29TB12-RE00	OEM
29TB13	OEM
29TB14	OEM
29TB15	OEM
29V008M01	0279
29V0038H03	0211
29V011H01	0279
29V012H01	0279
30	OEM
30-004-001	0599
30-007-0	0688
30-005072	0103
30-090	0161
30-30	OEM
30-219A	0463
30-219B	0463
30-219C	0463
30-219D	0463
30-219F	0463
30-219H	0463
30-219K	0463
30-219M	0463
30-219P	0463
30-219S	0463
30-219V	0463
30-219Z	0463
30-219ZB	0463
30-219ZD	0463
30-254A	0463
30-254B	0463
30-254C	0463
30-254D	0463
30-254E	0463
30-254F	0463
30-254K	0463

DEVICE TYPE	REPL CODE
30-254P	0463
30-254V	0463
30-254ZB	0463
30-576-4	OEM
30-8054-7	0015
30-8057-13	0907
30A6F	0596
30A8F	OEM
30A10F	OEM
30AD50	OEM
30AD100	OEM
30AD200	OEM
30AD400	OEM
30AD600	OEM
30AD800	OEM
30AS	0015
30AV60	OEM
30AV80	OEM
30AV100	OEM
30B	0195
30B2	0195
30B2C11	OEM
30B2FR	OEM
30B2Z11	OEM
30B3	0195
30B4FR	OEM
30B5	0015
30B6FR	OEM
30BG2C11	OEM
30BG2C15	OEM
30BG2Z11	OEM
30BG11	1522
30BG15	1522
30BL2C11	OEM
30BL11	OEM
30BS	0015
30C	0015
30C1	OEM
30C2	OEM
30C4	OEM
30C6	OEM
30C8	OEM
30C10	OEM
30C12	OEM
30C14	OEM
30C16	OEM
30CB	0015
30CG2C15	OEM
30CG15	OEM
30CL2C11	OEM
30CL11	OEM
30CS03F	OEM
30CS04F	OEM
30CTQ30	OEM
30CTQ35	OEM
30CTQ40	OEM
30CTQ45	OEM
30D1	0087
30D1FC	OEM
30D2	0071
30D2C11	OEM
30D2Z11	OEM
30D4	0087
30DF	0031
30DF1	0559
30DF2	0087
30DF2-FC	0087
30DF2-FIN	0031
30DF6	0031
30DF6-FC	0031
30DG2C11	OEM
30DG2C15	OEM
30DG2Z11	OEM
30DG11	1522
30DG15	OEM
30DL1	OEM
30DL2	OEM
30DL2C11	OEM
30DL4	OEM
30DL11	OEM
30E08A	OEM
30F1	0941
30FG11	0029
30FH05S	1512
30FH1S	1512
30FH2S	1512
30FH3S	1836
30FH4S	1836
30FQ030	0610
30FQ030A	0610
30FQ035	0610
30FQ035A	0610
30FQ040	0610
30FQ040A	0610
30FQ045	0610
30FQ045A	0610
30FWJ2C11	OEM
30FWJ2C12	0579
30FWJ11	OEM
30G2C11	OEM
30G6P41	OEM
30G6P42	OEM
30GC15	OEM
30GG2C11	OEM
30GG2Z11	OEM
30GG11	0029
30GWJ2C11	OEM
30GWJ2C12	0579
30GWJ11	OEM

DEVICE TYPE	REPL CODE
30H	0015
30H3	0097
30H3N	0471
30H3P	3697
30H3PN	0987
30HB050	5469
30HB100	5469
30HB200	1633
30HB400	5503
30HB600	1663
30HB800	1579
30J2	0097
30J2C11	OEM
30J2Z11	OEM
30J3P	0105
30J6P41	OEM
30J6P42	OEM
30JG2C11	OEM
30JG2Z11	OEM
30JG11	0596
30JH3	4244
30K	0015
30L6P41	OEM
30L15	OEM
30L20	OEM
30L25	OEM
30L29	OEM
30L30	OEM
30L35	OEM
30L40	OEM
30L45	OEM
30L50	OEM
30L55	OEM
30L60	OEM
30L65	OEM
30L70	OEM
30L75	OEM
30L80	OEM
30L85	OEM
30L90	OEM
30L95	OEM
30L100	OEM
30L110	OEM
30L120	OEM
30L130	OEM
30L140	OEM
30L150	OEM
30L160	OEM
30L170	OEM
30L180	OEM
30L190	OEM
30L200	OEM
30L210	OEM
30L220	OEM
30L230	OEM
30L240	OEM
30L250	OEM
30L260	OEM
30L270	OEM
30L280	OEM
30L290	OEM
30L300	OEM
30LF	OEM
30LSP42	OEM
30M	0015
30MF5	0029
30MF10	1522
30MF15	1522
30MF20	1522
30MF30	0029
30MF40	0029
30N2	0097
30N3	0097
30N15A	OEM
30N15A9	OEM
30N20A	OEM
30N20A9	OEM
30N25A	OEM
30N25A9	OEM
30N30A	OEM
30N30A9	OEM
30N35A	OEM
30N35A9	OEM
30N40A	OEM
30N40A9	OEM
30N45A	OEM
30N45A9	OEM
30N50A	OEM
30N50A9	OEM
30N55A	OEM
30N55A9	OEM
30N60A	OEM
30N60A9	OEM
30N65A	OEM
30N65A9	OEM
30N70A	OEM
30N70A9	OEM
30N75A	OEM
30N75A9	OEM
30N80A	OEM
30N80A9	OEM
30N85A	OEM
30N85A9	OEM
30N90A	OEM
30N90A9	OEM
30N95A	OEM
30N95A9	OEM
30N100A9	OEM
30N110A	OEM

If replacement code is OEM, contact original manufacturer for replacement.

135

DEVICE TYPE	REPL CODE
30N120A	OEM
30N130A	OEM
30N150A	OEM
30N160A	OEM
30N170A	OEM
30N180A	OEM
30N190A	OEM
30N200A	OEM
30N210A	OEM
30N220A	OEM
30N230A	OEM
30N240A	OEM
30N260A	OEM
30NS	OEM
30P1	0143
30P2	0097
30P3	0097
30P4	OEM
30Q3	1571
30Q6P42	OEM
30QHC030	OEM
30QHC045	OEM
30R1	0947
30R2	OEM
30R2SW	OEM
30R3	0535
30R3P	OEM
30R4	OEM
30R6	0959
30R8	0087
30R10	0087
30R12	OEM
30R25	0045
30RECT-SI-1020	0023
30RECT-SI-1044(AU)	0015
30RH05S	1522
30RH1S	1522
30RH2S	1522
30RH3S	0029
30RH4S	0029
30S05	0110
30S1	0947
30S1S03	OEM
30S1S04	OEM
30S2	1760
30S3	1736
30S3P	OEM
30S4	0535
30S5	1760
30S6	0959
30S8	0811
30S10	0916
30SB02S	1536
30SB02SA	1536
30SB03S	1536
30SB03SA	1536
30SB04S	1536
30SB04SA	1536
30SB025S	1536
30SP-LT-6540G	OEM
30ST-2SC2611	0275
30SZ-HZ5C1	0248
30T2	OEM
30T2FR	OEM
30T3P	OEM
30T4FR	OEM
30T6FR	OEM
30TB050	OEM
30TB100	OEM
30TB200	OEM
30TB400	OEM
30TB600	OEM
30TC10	OEM
30TC20	OEM
30TC30	OEM
30TC40	OEM
30TC50	OEM
30TC60	OEM
30TC70	OEM
30TC80	OEM
30TC90	OEM
30TC100	OEM
30TC110	OEM
30TC120	OEM
30TCA10	OEM
30TCA20	OEM
30TCA30	OEM
30TCA40	OEM
30TCA50	OEM
30TCA60	OEM
30TCA70	OEM
30TCA80	OEM
30TCA90	OEM
30TCA100	OEM
30TCA110	OEM
30TCA120	OEM
30U6P42	OEM
30V3P	OEM
30V10	OEM
30V11	OEM
30V12	OEM
30V-H6	0004
30V-HG	0004
30W3P	OEM
30X3P	OEM
30X5PV-CM	OEM
30X10PV-CM	OEM
30Y	0195
30Y3P	OEM

DEVICE TYPE	REPL CODE
30n140A	OEM
30n250A	OEM
31-0001	0050
31-0002	0050
31-0003	0050
31-0004	0050
31-0005	0136
31-0006	0004
31-0007	0016
31-0008	0004
31-0009	0016
31-002-0	0076
31-0010	0178
31-0012	0111
31-0013	0111
31-0015	0050
31-0016	0050
31-0017	0004
31-0018	0004
31-0025	0004
31-0026	0004
31-0033	0004
31-0035	0164
31-0041	0136
31-0042	0136
31-0048	0127
31-0049	0127
31-0050	0127
31-0051	0144
31-0052	0111
31-0053	0004
31-0054	0127
31-0055	0786
31-0065	0136
31-0066	0555
31-0068	0016
31-0069	0016
31-0070	0004
31-0075	0164
31-0080	0016
31-0081	0016
31-0082	0016
31-0083	0086
31-0084	0016
31-0085	0016
31-0097	0144
31-0098	0127
31-0099	0111
31-011	0133
31-015	0190
31-025	0211
31-025-0	0364
31-027-0	0376
31-058-0	2035
31-069-0	0833
31-091-3	0830
31-093	0133
31-0100	0111
31-0101	0218
31-0102	1233
31-0103	0144
31-0104	0016
31-0105	0164
31-0106	0016
31-0107	0004
31-0108	0136
31-0115	0016
31-0116	0016
31-0123	0050
31-0124	0050
31-0132	0136
31-0134	0136
31-0135	0136
31-0139	0136
31-0141	0136
31-0148	0004
31-0150	0050
31-0153	0004
31-0161	0136
31-0163	0136
31-0165	0050
31-0166	0050
31-0168	0050
31-0170	0050
31-0171	0136
31-0172	0004
31-0175	1004
31-0177	0007
31-0178	0136
31-0180	0050
31-0181	0050
31-0182	0164
31-0183	0164
31-0184	0136
31-0187	0016
31-0188	0004
31-0189	0164
31-0190	0136
31-0191	0136
31-0192	0222
31-0196	0969
31-0205	0211
31-0206	0050
31-0217	0136
31-0228	0136
31-0229	0164
31-0230	0016
31-0239	0016
31-0240	0160

DEVICE TYPE	REPL CODE
31-0241	0050
31-0241-1	0050
31-0242	0144
31-0243	0144
31-0246	0016
31-0247	0211
31-0248	0816
31-0253	0279
31-1	0016
31-1N914	0124
31-16	0016
31-101	OEM
31-194	0071
31-195	0015
31-2104733	0050
31-21004900	0050
31-21007744	0050
31-21024033	0050
31-21024044	0050
31-21047111	0050
31-21050611	0050
31-21050622	0050
31-22005400	0004
31DF1	0087
31DF2	0087
31DF3	1352
31DF4	1352
31DQ03	2520
31DQ04	0559
31DQ05	3559
31DQ06	3559
31DQ09	3559
31DQ10	OEM
31K111-002	OEM
31K111-02	OEM
31MQ30	OEM
31MQ40	OEM
31N2	OEM
31P1	OEM
31P4	OEM
31R2	1116
31SI-UPC1360C	1617
31ST-2SA733Q	0006
31ST-2SA733Q/R	0006
31ST-2SA733Q/R(AU)E	0006
31ST-2SA733R	0006
31ST-2SC1923-0	2666
31ST-2SC1923-8	OEM
31ST-2SC1923-O	2666
31Z6	0296
31Z6A	0296
32-0000	0143
32-0001	0143
32-0002	0143
32-0003	0143
32-0004	0143
32-0005	0012
32-0007	0123
32-0008	0143
32-006-0	0553
32-0013	0143
32-0022	0133
32-0023	0143
32-0025	0244
32-0026	0015
32-0029	0143
32-0033	1914
32-0035	0143
32-0036	0143
32-0037	0015
32-0038	0865
32-0039	0123
32-0042	0015
32-0043	0030
32-0044	0030
32-0045	0015
32-0046	0015
32-0047	0015
32-0048	0229
32-0049	0170
32-0050	0015
32-0057	0133
32-0059	0015
32-0060	0015
32-0061	0015
32-0062	0196
32-0063	0133
32-209A	0217
32-209B	0217
32-209C	0217
32-209D	0217
32-209F	0217
32-209H	0217
32-209K	0217
32-209M	0217
32-209P	0653
32-209S	0653
32-251A	0217
32-251B	0217
32-251C	0217
32-251D	0217
32-251F	0217
32-251H	0217
32-251K	0217
32-251M	0217
32-251P	0653
32-251S	0653
32-3305-1	0190
32-3305-4	0190

DEVICE TYPE	REPL CODE
32-13843-2	0016
32-16591	3004
32-16599	0265
32-18537	0143
32-18539	0123
32-20738	0016
32-20739	0037
32-23555-1	2600
32-23555-2	2600
32-23555-3	2600
32-23555-4	2600
32-29778	0190
32-29778-1	0190
32-29778-2	0190
32-29778-3	0190
32-29778-4	0190
32-33051-1	0190
32-33051-5	0190
32-33057-1	0190
32-33057-2	1493
32-33057-3	0190
32-33057-4	0190
32-33057-5	0190
32-33057-6	0190
32-33091-6	1061
32-33091-9	1061
32-33094-1	1493
32-33094-2	1493
32-33094-3	1493
32-33094-4	1493
32-33094-5	1493
32-33094-6	1493
32-35894-1	0190
32-35894-2	1493
32-35894-3	1493
32-35894-4	1493
32-35894-5	0190
32-35894-6	1493
32-35894-6X7	1493
32-35894-7	1493
32-39091-1	1061
32-39091-2	1061
32-39091-3	1696
32-39091-4	1061
32-39091-5	1061
32-39091-6	1061
32-39091-7	1696
32-39091-8	1696
32-39091-9	1061
32-39091-15	1061
32-39091-132-39091-5	OEM
32-39704-1	1493
32-39704-2	1493
32-43737-1	3621
32-3309094-5	OEM
32E07A	OEM
32E64	0126
32KBS	OEM
32N2	OEM
32P4	OEM
32R2	1116
32ST-HZ20-04(AU)	0695
32ST-JE9018H	0144
32SZ-HZ20-04	0695
32SZ-HZ20-04(AU)	0695
32Z6	0188
32Z6A	0188
33-0002	0015
33-0005	OEM
33-0006	0015
33-0023	0015
33-0024	0015
33-0025	0644
33-0026	0015
33-0029	0015
33-0030	0015
33-0031	0015
33-0033	0769
33-0036	0102
33-0039	0435
33-070	0016
33-071	0016
33-090	0161
33-096	0455
33-2N3906	0006
33-3H22P	OEM
33-4-3	1024
33-4-3A	1024
33-7-3	1024
33-8-3	1024
33-1000-00	0211
33-1001-00	0211
33-1002-00	0816
33-1004-00	0160
33-1009-01	0004
33-1019-00	0004
33-1020-00	0004
33-1021-00	0004
33A14666	OEM
33A14667	OEM
33A14668	3473
33A14670	OEM
33A14725	OEM
33A17056	4349
33A17057	4840
33A17058	1336
33A17059	6279
33A17060	OEM
33A17061	OEM

DEVICE TYPE	REPL CODE
33A17062	3897
33A17063	OEM
33B	0166
33B1	0195
33B1/1W	OEM
33B1/2.5W	OEM
33B2	0166
33BH05M	OEM
33BH05P	OEM
33C	0166
33D5R02	OEM
33D9R02GH	OEM
33G59019	0196
33G59024	0015
33G59113	1293
33G59121	0015
33G59122	0015
33H50	0144
33K3	OEM
33K59	0321
33M10	OEM
33P1	OEM
33PB05M	OEM
33PD05M	OEM
33PH05M	OEM
33RECT-SI-1066	0271
33SI-TA7335P	4336
33ST-2SC710D	0364
33ST-2SC2610	0261
33ST-2SD478A-01	0388
33ST-2SD748-01	3197
33ST-2SD748A-01	3197
33T1	OEM
33T2	OEM
33T3	OEM
33T4	OEM
33T5	OEM
33T6	OEM
33T7	OEM
33T8	OEM
33T9	OEM
33T10	OEM
33T11	OEM
33T12	OEM
33V10	OEM
33Y	0166
33Z6	0188
33Z6A	0188
34	0023
34-0012	1024
34-028-0	0019
34-029-0	0030
34-032-0	0124
34-0661-85	OEM
34-2N3563	0144
34-2N3904	0076
34-6	0050
34-6-16-47	0037
34-34-6015-43	0016
34-119	0050
34-220	0050
34-221	0050
34-298	0050
34-1000	0103
34-1000A	0103
34-1002	0042
34-1003	0919
34-1006	0275
34-1026	0178
34-1027	0899
34-1028	0103
34-1028A	0103
34-2001-1	0143
34-3022-7	0143
34-3057-48	OEM
34-5082-0012	0023
34-5170-0020	2821
34-5171-0016	0688
34-5172-0076	1212
34-5261-0141	0006
34-5262-0128	0284
34-6000-3	0050
34-6000-4	0004
34-6000-5	0004
34-6000-6	0004
34-6000-7	0004
34-6000-8	0004
34-6000-9	0050
34-6000-10	0050
34-6000-11	0050
34-6000-12	0050
34-6000-13	0050
34-6000-14	0050
34-6000-15	0004
34-6000-16	0050
34-6000-17	0050
34-6000-18	0050
34-6000-19	0050
34-6000-20	0050
34-6000-25	0050
34-6000-26	0050
34-6000-27	0004
34-6000-28	0004
34-6000-29	0004
34-6000-30	0004
34-6000-31	0004
34-6000-32	0004
34-6000-33	0004
34-6000-34	0004

DEVICE TYPE	REPL CODE
34-6000-50	OEM
34-6000-52	OEM
34-6000-54	OEM
34-6000-55	OEM
34-6000-56	OEM
34-6000-58	0050
34-6000-59	0050
34-6000-60	0050
34-6000-61	0050
34-6000-62	0050
34-6000-63	0050
34-6000-64	0016
34-6000-65	0050
34-6000-66	0050
34-6000-67	0050
34-6000-68	0050
34-6000-69	0144
34-6000-70	0144
34-6000-71	0848
34-6000-72	0326
34-6000-76	0050
34-6000-77	0050
34-6000-78	0050
34-6000-79	0050
34-6000-80	0050
34-6000-81	0050
34-6000-82	0050
34-6000-83	0050
34-6000-84	0050
34-6000-85	0050
34-6000-85HR52	OEM
34-6001-1	0085
34-6001-3	0144
34-6001-5	0016
34-6001-6	0144
34-6001-7	0004
34-6001-8	0004
34-6001-9	0004
34-6001-10	0004
34-6001-11	0004
34-6001-12	0004
34-6001-13	0004
34-6001-14	0004
34-6001-15	0037
34-6001-16	0004
34-6001-18	0004
34-6001-19	0004
34-6001-20	0004
34-6001-21	0004
34-6001-22	0004
34-6001-23	0004
34-6001-26	0004
34-6001-28	0164
34-6001-29	0004
34-6001-30	0004
34-6001-31	0004
34-6001-33	0004
34-6001-34	0016
34-6001-41	0004
34-6001-42	0004
34-6001-43	0004
34-6001-44	0004
34-6001-47	0004
34-6001-48	0016
34-6001-49	0016
34-6001-50	0016
34-6001-51	0086
34-6001-52	0016
34-6001-53	0079
34-6001-54	0136
34-6001-55	0079
34-6001-56	0079
34-6001-57	0079
34-6001-58	0079
34-6001-60	0079
34-6001-61	0050
34-6001-62	0016
34-6001-63	0016
34-6001-64	0144
34-6001-65	0233
34-6001-66	0164
34-6001-69	0016
34-6001-70	0016
34-6001-71	0198
34-6001-72	0004
34-6001-73	0111
34-6001-74	0016
34-6001-76	0004
34-6001-77	0016
34-6001-78	0086
34-6001-79	0160
34-6001-80	0086
34-6001-82	0086
34-6001-83	0086
34-6001-84	0208
34-6001-85	0086
34-6001-86	0126
34-6001-7434-6001-76	OEM
34-6002-1	0178
34-6002-2	0160
34-6002-3	0160
34-6002-4	0160
34-6002-5	0160
34-6002-6	0160
34-6002-7	0160
34-6002-8	0160
34-6002-9	0160
34-6002-10	0160
34-6002-11	0160

DEVICE TYPE	REPL CODE
34-6002-13	0160
34-6002-14	0160
34-6002-17	0085
34-6002-18	0160
34-6002-18A	0085
34-6002-19	0160
34-6002-20	0160
34-6002-21	0142
34-6002-22	0085
34-6002-22A	0085
34-6002-23	1671
34-6002-24	0969
34-6002-25	0918
34-6002-26	0142
34-6002-27	0103
34-6002-28	0178
34-6002-29	0178
34-6002-30	2002
34-6002-31	0969
34-6002-32	0103
34-6002-32A	0103
34-6002-33	0599
34-6002-34	0160
34-6002-35	0130
34-6002-37	0130
34-6002-41	0561
34-6002-42	1357
34-6002-43	0419
34-6002-45	0283
34-6002-46	0142
34-6002-49	0969
34-6002-54	0079
34-6002-55	0079
34-6002-56	0042
34-6002-57	0919
34-6002-58	0637
34-6002-61	0074
34-6002-62	0142
34-6002-63	0065
34-6002-64	0065
34-6005-1	0050
34-6005-2	0178
34-6005-3	0178
34-6006-1	0042
34-6007-1	0016
34-6007-2	0016
34-6007-3	0016
34-6007-4	0590
34-6007-5	0079
34-6007-6	0079
34-6007-7	0079
34-6007-8	0590
34-6007-9	0079
34-6007-10	0007
34-6007-11	0007
34-6007-12	0007
34-6007-13	0007
34-6007-14	0111
34-6008	0004
34-6009	0004
34-6010	4100
34-6015-1	0016
34-6015-2	0016
34-6015-3	0016
34-6015-4	0016
34-6015-5	0016
34-6015-6	0016
34-6015-7	0016
34-6015-8	0127
34-6015-9	0016
34-6015-10	0016
34-6015-11	0016
34-6015-12	0079
34-6015-13	0016
34-6015-14	0016
34-6015-15	0008
34-6015-15(PHILCO)	0007
34-6015-16	0008
34-6015-17	0008
34-6015-18	0007
34-6015-19	0008
34-6015-20	0016
34-6015-21	0016
34-6015-22	0007
34-6015-23	0086
34-6015-24	0086
34-6015-25	0079
34-6015-26	0037
34-6015-27	0224
34-6015-28	0334
34-6015-29	0008
34-6015-30	0086
34-6015-31	0007
34-6015-32	0050
34-6015-33	0050
34-6015-34	0050
34-6015-35	0050
34-6015-36	0050
34-6015-37	0326
34-6015-38	0326
34-6015-39	0050
34-6015-40	0050
34-6015-41	0016
34-6015-42	0037
34-6015-43	0079
34-6015-43A	0016
34-6015-44	0016
34-6015-46	0224
34-6015-47	0224

If replacement code is OEM, contact original manufacturer for replacement.

DEVICE TYPE	REPL CODE
34-6015-48	0224
34-6015-49	0144
34-6015-50	0127
34-6015-51	0086
34-6015-52	0224
34-6015-54	0016
34-6015-62	0326
34-6015-64	0283
34-6015-80	0016
34-6016-2	0016
34-6016-3	0016
34-6016-4	0016
34-6016-6	0079
34-6016-7	0016
34-6016-8	0016
34-6016-11	0004
34-6016-12	0126
34-6016-13	1257
34-6016-14	0016
34-6016-15	0037
34-6016-15A	0037
34-6016-16	0086
34-6016-17	0144
34-6016-18	0016
34-6016-19	0016
34-6016-22	0086
34-6016-23	0126
34-6016-23A	0126
34-6016-24	0016
34-6016-25	0016
34-6016-26	0086
34-6016-27	0086
34-6016-28	0050
34-6016-29	0050
34-6016-30	0086
34-6016-31	0561
34-6016-32	0037
34-6016-32A	0126
34-6016-33	0086
34-6016-41	0855
34-6016-44	0590
34-6016-45	0042
34-6016-46	0919
34-6016-47	0037
34-6016-49	0016
34-6016-49A	0016
34-6016-50	0004
34-6016-51	0590
34-6016-53	0561
34-6016-54	1357
34-6016-56	0855
34-6016-59	0786
34-6016-60	0037
34-6016-63	0016
34-6016-64	0688
34-6016-65	1257
34-6016-1734-6016-18	OEM
34-6017-3	0396
34-6018-2	0321
34-6075-46	0079
34-8001-43	0136
34-8002-1	0143
34-8002-2	0143
34-8002-3	0143
34-8002-4	0143
34-8002-5	0143
34-8002-6	0143
34-8002-7	0143
34-8002-22	OEM
34-8002-23	OEM
34-8002-27	OEM
34-8003	0015
34-8015-12	OEM
34-8022	0143
34-8022-1	0143
34-8022-2	0143
34-8022-3	0143
34-8022-4	0143
34-8022-5	0143
34-8022-6	0143
34-8022-6(PHILCO)	0123
34-8022-7	0143
34-8022-9	OEM
34-8022-77	0143
34-8024-24	0102
34-8024-25	0102
34-8026-1	0015
34-8026-2	0015
34-8026-3	0015
34-8026-4	0015
34-8027	0911
34-8028	1024
34-8034	0196
34-8034-1	0015
34-8034-2	0015
34-8034-3	0015
34-8034-4	0015
34-8034-7	0196
34-8036-1	0015
34-8036-2	0015
34-8036-3	0015
34-8036-4	0015
34-8037	0196
34-8037-1	0196
34-8037-2	0196
34-8037-3	0196
34-8037-4	0196
34-8040-2	0015
34-8042-1	0015

DEVICE TYPE	REPL CODE
34-8042-2	0015
34-8042-3	0015
34-8043-4	1024
34-8047-1	0907
34-8047-2	0015
34-8047-13	0143
34-8048-1	0015
34-8048-2	0229
34-8048-3	0015
34-8048-4	0015
34-8048-5	0015
34-8050-1	0015
34-8050-2	0015
34-8050-5	0015
34-8050-6	0015
34-8050-7	0015
34-8050-8	0015
34-8050-9	0015
34-8050-10	0071
34-8050-14	0015
34-8051	0015
34-8052-1	OEM
34-8053-2	0769
34-8053-3	0769
34-8053-4	0769
34-8053-6	OEM
34-8053-7	0769
34-8054-1	0015
34-8054-2	0015
34-8054-3	0015
34-8054-4	0015
34-8054-5	0015
34-8054-6	0015
34-8054-7	0015
34-8054-8	0102
34-8054-9	0015
34-8054-10	0015
34-8054-11	0015
34-8054-12	0015
34-8054-13	0015
34-8054-14	0015
34-8054-15	0015
34-8054-16	0914
34-8054-17	1208
34-8054-18	0015
34-8054-19	OEM
34-8054-23	0015
34-8054-25	0102
34-8054-27	0015
34-8055-2	0015
34-8055-3	2613
34-8056-1	1293
34-8057-1	0030
34-8057-2	OEM
34-8057-3	0123
34-8057-4	1639
34-8057-5	0133
34-8057-6	0133
34-8057-7	0162
34-8057-8	2488
34-8057-9	0644
34-8057-10	0025
34-8057-11	0015
34-8057-12	0002
34-8057-13	0133
34-8057-14	0137
34-8057-15	1293
34-8057-16	0644
34-8057-18	0015
34-8057-19	0030
34-8057-21	OEM
34-8057-22	0102
34-8057-23	0143
34-8057-24	0102
34-8057-25	0143
34-8057-26	0143
34-8057-27	0644
34-8057-28	0015
34-8057-29	0143
34-8057-30	0143
34-8057-31	0560
34-8057-32	0157
34-8057-33	0137
34-8057-34	0907
34-8057-36	OEM
34-8057-37	0162
34-8057-38	0039
34-8057-39	0102
34-8057-46	0322
34-8057-47	0256
34-8057-53	0137
34-8057-56	0313
34-8058	0469
34-8058-1	0469
34-8058-1#(2)	0469
34-8058-2	0469
34-8058-7	0469
34-8059-1	0015
34-8059-2	0015
34-8059-6	0095
34-8059-7	0095
34-8061-1	0201
34-8062-1	0752
34-8062-4	0374
34-9037-1	0196
34-9037-2	0907
34-11016	0201
34-60001-63	0079
34D5R02	OEM

DEVICE TYPE	REPL CODE
34D9R02GH	OEM
34E06A	OEM
34E3L	0144
34E31	0144
34G3098-2	0529
34GA	0979
34H31	0144
34ID	0983
34MT3	OEM
34MW117	OEM
34N2	OEM
34P1AA	0037
34P4	0133
34R2	0800
34SI-UPC1373HA	2015
34ST-2N6558	0638
34ST-2SD468C	0018
34ST-MPS9418AT	0320
34SZ-UZ-12B	0052
34SZ-UZ12B	0052
34TB4	OEM
34TB5	OEM
34TB6	OEM
34TB7	OEM
34TB8	OEM
34TB9	OEM
34TB10	OEM
34V12	OEM
34Z6	OEM
34Z6A	OEM
35	0023
35-003-001	0015
35-013-0	0005
35-43	OEM
35-44	OEM
35-1000	0071
35-1003	0071
35-1004	0015
35-1005	0015
35-1006	5417
35-1008	0242
35-1014	0133
35-1029	0071
35-210631-01	0571
35-210631-02	0571
35-39306001	0016
35-39306002	0016
35-39306003	0016
35AD50	OEM
35AD100	OEM
35AD200	OEM
35AD400	OEM
35AD600	OEM
35AD800	OEM
35B611	0287
35BL611	0287
35C	0010
35C05	3160
35C05B	OEM
35C05BF	OEM
35C05F	OEM
35C05R	1620
35C025	0636
35C025B	0636
35C025BF	0603
35C025F	0603
35C050	0636
35C050B	0636
35C050BF	0603
35C050F	0603
35C10	2873
35C10B	0636
35C10BF	0603
35C10F	0603
35C10R	0254
35C15	1116
35C15B	0636
35C15BF	0603
35C15F	0603
35C15R	1099
35C20	1116
35C20B	0636
35C20BF	0603
35C20F	0603
35C20R	1099
35C25	0217
35C25B	0217
35C25BF	0605
35C25F	0605
35C30	1118
35C30B	0217
35C30BF	0605
35C30F	0605
35C30R	0258
35C35	0463
35C35B	0463
35C35BF	OEM
35C35F	OEM
35C40	0800
35C40B	0217
35C40BF	0605
35C40F	0605
35C40R	0258
35C45	0463
35C45B	0463
35C45BF	OEM
35C45F	OEM
35C50	1186
35C50B	0217

DEVICE TYPE	REPL CODE
35C50BF	0605
35C50F	0605
35C50R	1634
35C60	0315
35C60B	0217
35C60BF	0605
35C60F	0605
35C60R	0267
35C70	1124
35C70(RECT.)	1124
35C70B	0653
35C70BF	0463
35C70F	0463
35C70R	1111
35C80	1124
35C80B	0653
35C80BF	0463
35C80F	0463
35C80R	1111
35C90	0045
35C90B	0653
35C90BF	0463
35C90F	0463
35C90R	0280
35C100	0045
35C100B	0653
35C100BF	0463
35C100F	0463
35C100R	0280
35C110	0653
35C110B	0653
35C110BF	0463
35C110F	0463
35C120	0653
35C120B	0653
35C120BF	0463
35C120F	0463
35D5R02	OEM
35D9R02GH	OEM
35E05A	OEM
35F70	OEM
35F80	OEM
35F90	OEM
35F100	OEM
35F110	OEM
35F120	OEM
35FCRA	OEM
35FCRB	OEM
35FCRC	OEM
35FCRD	OEM
35FCRE	OEM
35FCRF	OEM
35FCRG	OEM
35FCRH	OEM
35FCRI	OEM
35FCRJ	OEM
35FCRK	OEM
35FCRL	OEM
35H5	3160
35H10	1116
35H10R	1099
35H20	1116
35H30	0800
35H40	0800
35HR20	1099
35HR30	0258
35HR40	0258
35M10	OEM
35N2	OEM
35P1	0211
35P2	0211
35P2C	0211
35P4	0133
35PCRA	1640
35PCRB	1640
35PCRC	1640
35PCRD	1640
35PCRE	1640
35PCRF	2623
35PCRG	2623
35PCRH	2623
35PCRI	2625
35PCRJ	2625
35PCRK	OEM
35PCRL	OEM
35PCRNA	OEM
35PCRNB	OEM
35PCRNC	OEM
35PCRND	OEM
35PCRNE	OEM
35PCRNF	OEM
35PCRNG	OEM
35PCRNH	OEM
35PCRNI	OEM
35PCRNJ	OEM
35PCRNK	OEM
35PCRNL	OEM
35PCRSA	0726
35PCRSB	0726
35PCRSC	0707
35PCRSD	0464
35PCRSE	0464
35PCRSF	0717
35PCRSG	0717
35PCRSH	0717
35PCRSI	0720
35PCRSJ	0720
35PCRSK	0745
35PCRSL	0745

DEVICE TYPE	REPL CODE
35RCS10A	OEM
35RCS20A	OEM
35RCS30A	OEM
35RCS40A	OEM
35RCS50A	OEM
35RCS60A	OEM
35RCS80A	OEM
35RE60	OEM
35RE90	OEM
35RE100	OEM
35RE110	OEM
35RE120	OEM
35RE130	OEM
35SI-UPC574J	1319
35SI-UPC580C	1049
35SP005	OEM
35SP005D	OEM
35SP005N	OEM
35SP01	OEM
35SP01D	OEM
35SP01N	OEM
35SP02	OEM
35SP02D	OEM
35SP02N	OEM
35SP04	OEM
35SP04D	OEM
35SP04N	OEM
35SP06	OEM
35SP06D	OEM
35SP06N	OEM
35SP08	OEM
35SP08D	OEM
35SP08N	OEM
35SP10	OEM
35SP10D	OEM
35SP10N	OEM
35SZ-UPC574J	1319
35T1	0211
35T2	OEM
35T3	OEM
35T4	OEM
35T5	OEM
35T6	OEM
35T7	OEM
35T8	OEM
35T9	OEM
35T10	OEM
35T11	OEM
35T12	OEM
35TC4I	OEM
35TCRA	0464
35TCRB	0464
35TCRC	0464
35TCRD	0464
35TCRE	0464
35TCRF	0717
35TCRG	0717
35TCRH	0717
35TCRI	0720
35TCRJ	0720
35TCRK	0674
35TCRL	0674
35TE18	OEM
35TE20	OEM
35TE22	OEM
35TE24	OEM
35TE26	OEM
35TE28	OEM
35TE30	OEM
35TE35	OEM
35TE40	OEM
35V10	OEM
35V11	OEM
35V12	OEM
35Z6	0140
35Z6A	0140
36-0041	1469
36-0083	2845
36-6343	0137
36B2(2%)	OEM
36B3	0010
36D5R37	OEM
36D9R37GH	OEM
36D-32	0133
36D32	0133
36E004-1	0143
36GRA	0979
36J003-1	0004
36MB5A	OEM
36MB10A	2690
36MB20A	2773
36MB40A	2897
36MB60A	2897
36MB80A	3155
36MB100A	3155
36MB120A	OEM
36P1	0211
36P1C	0211
36P1F	0211
36P2F	0211
36P3	0211
36P3A	0211
36P3C	0211
36P4	0211
36P4C	0211
36P5	0211
36P5C	0211
36P7	0004
36P7C	0004

DEVICE TYPE	REPL CODE
36P7T	0004
36P8	0004
36P8C	0004
36R2	0315
36R2S	0315
36RA50	0463
36RA60	0463
36RA70	OEM
36RA80	0463
36RA90	OEM
36RA100	0463
36RA110	0463
36RA120	0463
36RA140	OEM
36RA150	OEM
36RA160	OEM
36RC10	0217
36RC10A	0217
36RC20	0217
36RC20A	0217
36RC30	0217
36RC30A	0217
36RC40	0217
36RC40A	0217
36RC50A	OEM
36RC60	0217
36RC60A	0217
36RC80	0463
36RC80A	0463
36RC100	0463
36RC100A	OEM
36RC110	0463
36RC110A	OEM
36RC120	0463
36RC120A	OEM
36RCS10A	OEM
36RCS20A	OEM
36RCS30A	OEM
36RCS40A	OEM
36RCS50A	OEM
36RCS60A	OEM
36RCS80A	OEM
36RE50	0463
36RE60	0463
36RE70	OEM
36RE80	0463
36RE90	OEM
36RE100	0463
36RE110	0463
36RE120	0733
36RE130	OEM
36RE130M	OEM
36REH60	0605
36REH80	0463
36REH100	0463
36REH120	0463
36REH130	OEM
36SI-CA3065E	0167
36SI-UPD1705C-012	OEM
36ST-2SB857C	2895
36T1	0211
36T2	OEM
36T3	OEM
36T4	OEM
36T5	OEM
36T6	OEM
36T7	OEM
36T8	OEM
36T9	OEM
36T10	OEM
36T11	OEM
36T12	OEM
36TB1-CE00	OEM
36TB1-CH00	OEM
36TB1-EE00	OEM
36TB1-EH00	OEM
36TB1-GE00	OEM
36TB1-GH00	OEM
36TB1-JE00	OEM
36TB1-JH00	OEM
36TB1-LE00	OEM
36TB1-LH00	OEM
36TB1-NE00	OEM
36TB1-NH00	OEM
36TB2-CE00	OEM
36TB2-CH00	OEM
36TB2-EE00	OEM
36TB2-EH00	OEM
36TB2-GE00	OEM
36TB2-GH00	OEM
36TB2-JH00	OEM
36TB2-LE00	OEM
36TB2-LH00	OEM
36TB2-NE00	OEM
36TB2-NH00	OEM
36TB2-RE00	OEM
36TB3-CE00	OEM
36TB3-CH00	OEM
36TB3-EE00	OEM
36TB3-EH00	OEM
36TB3-GE00	OEM
36TB3-GH00	OEM
36TB3-JH00	OEM
36TB3-LE00	OEM
36TB3-LH00	OEM
36TB3-NE00	OEM
36TB3-NH00	OEM
36TB3-RE00	OEM
36TB4-CE00	OEM

DEVICE TYPE	REPL CODE
36TB4-CH00	OEM
36TB4-EE00	OEM
36TB4-EH00	OEM
36TB4-GE00	OEM
36TB4-GH00	OEM
36TB4-JH00	OEM
36TB4-LE00	OEM
36TB4-LH00	OEM
36TB4-NE00	OEM
36TB4-NH00	OEM
36TB4-RE00	OEM
36TB5-CE00	OEM
36TB5-CH00	OEM
36TB5-EE00	OEM
36TB5-EH00	OEM
36TB5-GE00	OEM
36TB5-GH00	OEM
36TB5-JH00	OEM
36TB5-LE00	OEM
36TB5-LH00	OEM
36TB5-NE00	OEM
36TB5-NH00	OEM
36TB5-RE00	OEM
36TB6-CE00	OEM
36TB6-CH00	OEM
36TB6-EE00	OEM
36TB6-EH00	OEM
36TB6-GE00	OEM
36TB6-GH00	OEM
36TB6-JE00	OEM
36TB6-JH00	OEM
36TB6-LE00	OEM
36TB6-LH00	OEM
36TB6-NE00	OEM
36TB6-NH00	OEM
36TB6-RE00	OEM
36TB7-CE00	OEM
36TB7-CH00	OEM
36TB7-EE00	OEM
36TB7-EH00	OEM
36TB7-GE00	OEM
36TB7-GH00	OEM
36TB7-JE00	OEM
36TB7-JH00	OEM
36TB7-LE00	OEM
36TB7-LH00	OEM
36TB7-NH00	OEM
36TB8-CE00	OEM
36TB8-CH00	OEM
36TB8-EE00	OEM
36TB8-EH00	OEM
36TB8-GE00	OEM
36TB8-LE00	OEM
36TB8-LH00	OEM
36TB8-RE00	OEM
36TB9-CE00	OEM
36TB9-CH00	OEM
36TB9-EE00	OEM
36TB9-EH00	OEM
36TB9-GE00	OEM
36TB9-GH00	OEM
36TB9-JE00	OEM
36TB9-JH00	OEM
36TB9-LE00	OEM
36TB9-LH00	OEM
36TB9-RE00	OEM
36TB10-CE00	OEM
36TB10-CH00	OEM
36TB10-EE00	OEM
36TB10-EH00	OEM
36TB10-GE00	OEM
36TB10-GH00	OEM
36TB10-JE00	OEM
36TB10-JH00	OEM
36TB10-LE00	OEM
36TB10-LH00	OEM
36TB10-RE00	OEM
36TB11-CH00	OEM
36TB11-EE00	OEM
36TB11-EH00	OEM
36TB11-GE00	OEM
36TB11-GH00	OEM
36TB11-JE00	OEM
36TB11-JH00	OEM
36TB11-LE00	OEM
36TB11-LH00	OEM
36TB11-RE00	OEM
36TB12-CH00	OEM
36TB12-EE00	OEM
36TB12-EH00	OEM
36TB12-GE00	OEM
36TB12-GH00	OEM
36TB12-JE00	OEM
36TB12-JH00	OEM
36TB12-LH00	OEM
36TB13	OEM
36TBA-RE00	OEM
36V12	OEM
36W4A	2969
36Z6	0162
36Z6A	0162
36ZW38	OEM
37-8-01	1024
37-8-1	1024
37-210	2007
37H01	1392
37H02	1750
37H03	0663
37H04	0542

If replacement code is OEM, contact original manufacturer for replacement.

137

DEVICE TYPE	REPL CODE
37H05	2387
37H06	0864
37H07	0519
37H08	0505
37H09	0611
37P4	OEM
37RA60	0217
37RA80	0653
37RA100	0653
37RA120	0653
37RA140	OEM
37RA150	OEM
37RA160	OEM
37RC10	0217
37RC10A	0217
37RC20	0217
37RC20A	0217
37RC30	0217
37RC30A	0217
37RC40	0217
37RC40A	0217
37RC60A	0217
37RC70A	OEM
37RC80	0653
37RC80A	OEM
37RC100	0653
37RC100A	OEM
37RC110	0653
37RC110A	OEM
37RC120	0653
37RC120A	OEM
37RE60	0217
37RE70	0653
37RE80	0653
37RE90	0653
37RE100	OEM
37RE100M	OEM
37RE110	OEM
37RE120	OEM
37RE130	OEM
37RE130M	OEM
37REH60	0217
37REH80	0653
37REH100	0653
37REH120	0653
37REH130	OEM
37SE-RD10EB	0064
37SZ-BZ-120	0137
37SZ-RD10EB	0064
37T1	0136
37T2	OEM
37T3	OEM
37T4	OEM
37T5	OEM
37T6	OEM
37T7	OEM
37T8	OEM
37T9	OEM
37T10	OEM
37T11	OEM
37T12	OEM
37TB1-CE00	OEM
37TB1-CH00	OEM
37TB1-EE00	OEM
37TB1-EH00	OEM
37TB1-GE00	OEM
37TB1-GH00	OEM
37TB1-JE00	OEM
37TB1-JH00	OEM
37TB1-LE00	OEM
37TB1-LH00	OEM
37TB1-NE00	OEM
37TB1-NH00	OEM
37TB1-RE00	OEM
37TB2-CE00	OEM
37TB2-CH00	OEM
37TB2-EE00	OEM
37TB2-EH00	OEM
37TB2-GE00	OEM
37TB2-GH00	OEM
37TB2-JE00	OEM
37TB2-JH00	OEM
37TB2-LE00	OEM
37TB2-LH00	OEM
37TB2-NE00	OEM
37TB2-RE00	OEM
37TB3-CE00	OEM
37TB3-CH00	OEM
37TB3-EE00	OEM
37TB3-GE00	OEM
37TB3-GH00	OEM
37TB3-JE00	OEM
37TB3-JH00	OEM
37TB3-LE00	OEM
37TB3-LH00	OEM
37TB3-NE00	OEM
37TB3-NH00	OEM
37TB3-RE00	OEM
37TB4-CE00	OEM
37TB4-CH00	OEM
37TB4-EE00	OEM
37TB4-EH00	OEM
37TB4-GE00	OEM
37TB4-GH00	OEM
37TB4-JE00	OEM
37TB4-JH00	OEM
37TB4-LE00	OEM
37TB4-LH00	OEM
37TB4-NE00	OEM
37TB4-NH00	OEM
37TB4-RE00	OEM
37TB5-CE00	OEM
37TB5-CH00	OEM
37TB5-EE00	OEM
37TB5-EH00	OEM
37TB5-GE00	OEM
37TB5-GH00	OEM
37TB5-JE00	OEM
37TB5-JH00	OEM
37TB5-LE00	OEM
37TB5-LH00	OEM
37TB5-NE00	OEM
37TB5-NH00	OEM
37TB5-RE00	OEM
37TB6-CE00	OEM
37TB6-CH00	OEM
37TB6-EE00	OEM
37TB6-EH00	OEM
37TB6-GE00	OEM
37TB6-GH00	OEM
37TB6-JE00	OEM
37TB6-JH00	OEM
37TB6-LE00	OEM
37TB6-LH00	OEM
37TB6-NE00	OEM
37TB6-NH00	OEM
37TB6-RE00	OEM
37TB7-CE00	OEM
37TB7-CH00	OEM
37TB7-EE00	OEM
37TB7-EH00	OEM
37TB7-GE00	OEM
37TB7-GH00	OEM
37TB7-JE00	OEM
37TB7-JH00	OEM
37TB7-LE00	OEM
37TB7-LH00	OEM
37TB7-NE00	OEM
37TB7-NH00	OEM
37TB7-RE00	OEM
37TB8-CE00	OEM
37TB8-CH00	OEM
37TB8-EE00	OEM
37TB8-EH00	OEM
37TB8-GE00	OEM
37TB8-GH00	OEM
37TB8-JE00	OEM
37TB8-JH00	OEM
37TB8-LE00	OEM
37TB8-LH00	OEM
37TB8-NE00	OEM
37TB8-NH00	OEM
37TB8-RE00	OEM
37TB9-CE00	OEM
37TB9-CH00	OEM
37TB9-EE00	OEM
37TB9-EH00	OEM
37TB9-GE00	OEM
37TB9-GH00	OEM
37TB9-JE00	OEM
37TB9-JH00	OEM
37TB9-LE00	OEM
37TB9-LH00	OEM
37TB9-NE00	OEM
37TB9-NH00	OEM
37TB9-RE00	OEM
37TB10-CE00	OEM
37TB10-CH00	OEM
37TB10-EE00	OEM
37TB10-EH00	OEM
37TB10-GE00	OEM
37TB10-GH00	OEM
37TB10-JH00	OEM
37TB10-LE00	OEM
37TB10-LH00	OEM
37TB10-NE00	OEM
37TB10-NH00	OEM
37TB10-RE00	OEM
37TB11-CE00	OEM
37TB11-CH00	OEM
37TB11-EE00	OEM
37TB11-EH00	OEM
37TB11-GE00	OEM
37TB11-GH00	OEM
37TB11-JH00	OEM
37TB11-LE00	OEM
37TB11-LH00	OEM
37TB11-NE00	OEM
37TB11-NH00	OEM
37TB11-RE00	OEM
37TB12-CE00	OEM
37TB12-CH00	OEM
37TB12-EE00	OEM
37TB12-EH00	OEM
37TB12-GH00	OEM
37TB12-JH00	OEM
37TB12-LE00	OEM
37TB12-LH00	OEM
37TB12-NE00	OEM
37TB12-NH00	OEM
37TB12-RE00	OEM
37TB13	OEM
37TB14	OEM
37TB15	OEM
37TB16-JH00	OEM
37TB30EH00	OEM
37Z6	0157
37Z6A	0157
38-11016	0201
38A-64C	0644
38A64C	0644
38A4148-000	0128
38A4148-001	0128
38A4157-000	0128
38A4871-000	OEM
38A5576-000	0468
38A5577-000	0546
38A5578-000	0378
38E04A	OEM
38N2	OEM
38P1	0160
38P1C	0160
38R2	1124
38R2S	1124
38SI-SN76730N	OEM
38SI-UPC1373H	2015
38ST-2SA10150(AP)	0148
38ST-2SA10150(AP)B	0148
38ST-2SC1855	0224
38T1	0211
38T2	OEM
38T3	OEM
38T4	OEM
38T5	OEM
38T6	OEM
38T7	OEM
38T8	OEM
38T9	OEM
38T10	OEM
38T11	OEM
38T12	OEM
38TB1-CE00	OEM
38TB1-EE00	OEM
38TB1-EH00	OEM
38TB1-GE00	OEM
38TB1-GH00	OEM
38TB1-JE00	OEM
38TB1-JH00	OEM
38TB1-LE00	OEM
38TB1-LH00	OEM
38TB1-NE00	OEM
38TB1-NH00	OEM
38TB1-RE00	OEM
38TB2-CE00	OEM
38TB2-CH00	OEM
38TB2-EE00	OEM
38TB2-EH00	OEM
38TB2-GE00	OEM
38TB2-GH00	OEM
38TB2-JE00	OEM
38TB2-JH00	OEM
38TB2-LE00	OEM
38TB2-LH00	OEM
38TB2-NE00	OEM
38TB2-NH00	OEM
38TB2-RE00	OEM
38TB3-CE00	OEM
38TB3-CH00	OEM
38TB3-EE00	OEM
38TB3-EH00	OEM
38TB3-GE00	OEM
38TB3-GH00	OEM
38TB3-JE00	OEM
38TB3-JH00	OEM
38TB3-LE00	OEM
38TB3-LH00	OEM
38TB3-NE00	OEM
38TB3-NH00	OEM
38TB3-RE00	OEM
38TB4-CE00	OEM
38TB4-CH00	OEM
38TB4-EE00	OEM
38TB4-EH00	OEM
38TB4-GE00	OEM
38TB4-GH00	OEM
38TB4-JE00	OEM
38TB4-JH00	OEM
38TB4-LE00	OEM
38TB4-LH00	OEM
38TB4-NE00	OEM
38TB4-NH00	OEM
38TB4-RE00	OEM
38TB5-CE00	OEM
38TB5-EE00	OEM
38TB5-EH00	OEM
38TB5-GE00	OEM
38TB5-GH00	OEM
38TB5-JE00	OEM
38TB5-JH00	OEM
38TB5-LE00	OEM
38TB5-LH00	OEM
38TB5-NE00	OEM
38TB5-NH00	OEM
38TB5-RE00	OEM
38TB6-CE00	OEM
38TB6-EE00	OEM
38TB6-EH00	OEM
38TB6-GE00	OEM
38TB6-GH00	OEM
38TB6-JE00	OEM
38TB6-JH00	OEM
38TB6-LE00	OEM
38TB6-LH00	OEM
38TB6-NE00	OEM
38TB6-NH00	OEM
38TB6-RE00	OEM
38TB7-CE00	OEM
38TB7-EE00	OEM
38TB7-EH00	OEM
38TB7-GE00	OEM
38TB7-GH00	OEM
38TB7-JE00	OEM
38TB7-JH00	OEM
38TB7-LE00	OEM
38TB7-LH00	OEM
38TB7-NE00	OEM
38TB7-NH00	OEM
38TB7-RE00	OEM
38TB8-CE00	OEM
38TB8-CH00	OEM
38TB8-EE00	OEM
38TB8-EH00	OEM
38TB8-GE00	OEM
38TB8-GH00	OEM
38TB8-JH00	OEM
38TB8-LE00	OEM
38TB8-LH00	OEM
38TB8-NE00	OEM
38TB8-NH00	OEM
38TB8-RE00	OEM
38TB9-CE00	OEM
38TB9-CH00	OEM
38TB9-EE00	OEM
38TB9-EH00	OEM
38TB9-GE00	OEM
38TB9-GH00	OEM
38TB9-JE00	OEM
38TB9-JH00	OEM
38TB9-LE00	OEM
38TB9-LH00	OEM
38TB9-NE00	OEM
38TB9-NH00	OEM
38TB9-RE00	OEM
38TB10-CE00	OEM
38TB10-CH00	OEM
38TB10-EE00	OEM
38TB10-EH00	OEM
38TB10-GE00	OEM
38TB10-GH00	OEM
38TB10-JE00	OEM
38TB10-JH00	OEM
38TB10-LE00	OEM
38TB10-LH00	OEM
38TB10-NE00	OEM
38TB10-NH00	OEM
38TB10-RE00	OEM
38TB11-CE00	OEM
38TB11-CH00	OEM
38TB11-EE00	OEM
38TB11-EH00	OEM
38TB11-GE00	OEM
38TB11-GH00	OEM
38TB11-JE00	OEM
38TB11-JH00	OEM
38TB11-LE00	OEM
38TB11-LH00	OEM
38TB11-NE00	OEM
38TB11-NH00	OEM
38TB11-RE00	OEM
38TB12-CE00	OEM
38TB12-CH00	OEM
38TB12-EE00	OEM
38TB12-EH00	OEM
38TB12-GE00	OEM
38TB12-GH00	OEM
38TB12-JE00	OEM
38TB12-JH00	OEM
38TB12-LE00	OEM
38TB12-LH00	OEM
38TB12-NE00	OEM
38TB12-NH00	OEM
38TB12-RE00	OEM
38TB13	OEM
38Z6	0466
38Z6A	0466
39-033-0	2285
39-033-2	2285
39-047-1	1888
39-054-1	1775
39-059-0	0646
39-060-0	4563
39-060-1	1120
39-061-0	1532
39-062-0	OEM
39-076-0	1899
39-077-0	0176
39-11	OEM
39-13	0137
39A9	0211
39A69-2	0133
39B2	0528
39B3	OEM
39B6	OEM
39B-9E	OEM
39J2F	OEM
39N2	OEM
39P1	0160
39P1C	0160
39P1K	OEM
39P2C	0279
39PC1	0085
39R-26	0436
39RECT-SI-1006	0023
39SD-1N4140	OEM
39SD-1N4148	0124
39ST-2SD820	2040
39ST-2SD898B	0055
39SZ-RD12FB	0137
39T1	0211
39TB7	OEM
39TB9	OEM
39TB11	OEM
39TB13	OEM
39Z6	0062
39Z6A	0062
40	OEM
40-013-0	OEM
40-035-0	0215
40-063-0	2801
40-065-19-001	1848
40-065-19-002	0337
40-065-19-003	1833
40-065-19-004	1824
40-065-19-005	0033
40-065-19-006	1035
40-065-19-007	3365
40-065-19-008	2086
40-065-19-012	0554
40-065-19-013	0141
40-065-19-014	1472
40-065-19-016	1018
40-065-19-027	1423
40-065-19-029	1358
40-065-19-030	1477
40-0502	0229
40-601	0211
40-13184-3	0846
40A50	3160
40A100	2873
40A150	1116
40A200	1116
40A300	1118
40A400	0800
40A500	1186
40A600	0315
40AD50	OEM
40AD100	OEM
40AD200	OEM
40AD400	OEM
40AD600	OEM
40AD800	OEM
40AS	0015
40AV20	OEM
40AV30	OEM
40AV50	OEM
40AV60	OEM
40B05T	OEM
40B5	0015
40B10T	OEM
40B20T	OEM
40B40T	OEM
40B605	OEM
40BS	0015
40C	0015
40C05	3970
40C05B	3970
40C025	1694
40C025B	1694
40C050	1694
40C050B	1694
40C1	OEM
40C1R10	OEM
40C1R20	OEM
40C1R30	OEM
40C1S10	OEM
40C1S20	OEM
40C1S30	OEM
40C2	OEM
40C2FM	OEM
40C2PW8V1SP	0150
40C2R10	OEM
40C2R20	OEM
40C2R30	OEM
40C2R110	OEM
40C2S10	OEM
40C2S20	OEM
40C2S30	OEM
40C4	OEM
40C4FM	OEM
40C6	OEM
40C6FM	OEM
40C8	OEM
40C10	1694
40C10B	1694
40C12	OEM
40C14	OEM
40C15	1694
40C15B	1694
40C16	OEM
40C20	1694
40C20B	1694
40C25	3970
40C25B	3970
40C30	3970
40C30B	3970
40C35	3970
40C35B	3970
40C40	3970
40C40B	3970
40C45	3970
40C45B	3970
40C50	3970
40C50B	3970
40C60	3970
40C60B	3970
40C70	0674
40C70B	0674
40C80	0674
40C80B	0674
40C90	0674
40C90B	0674
40C100	0674
40C100B	0674
40C110	0674
40C110B	0674
40C120	0674
40C120B	0674
40CDQ020	OEM
40CDQ030	OEM
40CDQ035	OEM
40CDQ040	OEM
40CDQ045	OEM
40CPQ040	OEM
40CPQ045	OEM
40D1	3612
40D2	6837
40D4	6837
40D6	6838
40D8	6838
40D1547	0050
40D6665A03	0015
40E03A	OEM
40E1R20	OEM
40E1R40	OEM
40E1R60	OEM
40E1S20	OEM
40E1S40	OEM
40E1S60	OEM
40E2FM	OEM
40E2R20	OEM
40E2R40	OEM
40E2R60	OEM
40E2S20	OEM
40E2S40	OEM
40E2S60	OEM
40E4FM	OEM
40E6FM	OEM
40F05	OEM
40F1R07	OEM
40F1R15	OEM
40F1S07	OEM
40F1S15	OEM
40F2R07	OEM
40F2R15	OEM
40F2S07	OEM
40F2S15	OEM
40F10	OEM
40F15	OEM
40F20	OEM
40F25	OEM
40F30	OEM
40F35	OEM
40F40	OEM
40F45	OEM
40F50	OEM
40F60	OEM
40H	0015
40H000F	OEM
40H000P	OEM
40H002F	OEM
40H3	0097
40H3N	0471
40H3P	0197
40H3PN	0991
40HA10	OEM
40HA20	OEM
40HA40	OEM
40HA60	OEM
40HA80	OEM
40HA100	OEM
40HA120	OEM
40HA140	OEM
40HA160	OEM
40HC032F	OEM
40HF5	3160
40HF5R	0267
40HF10	2873
40HF10R	0267
40HF15	1116
40HF20	1116
40HF20R	0267
40HF30	1118
40HF30R	0267
40HF40	0800
40HF40R	0258
40HF50	1186
40HF50R	0267
40HF60	0315
40HF60R	0267
40HF70	1124
40HF80	1124
40HF80R	0280
40HF90	0045
40HF100	0045
40HF100R	0280
40HF120	OEM
40HF140	OEM
40HF160	OEM
40HFL5S02	1522
40HFL5S05	1522
40HFL10S02	1522
40HFL10S05	1522
40HFL10S10	4808
40HFL20S02	1522
40HFL20S05	1522
40HFL20S10	4808
40HFL40S02	0029
40HFL40S05	0029
40HFL40S10	6918
40HFL60S02	0596
40HFL60S05	0596
40HFL60S10	6083
40HFL80S05	OEM
40HFL80S10	OEM
40HFL100S05	OEM
40HFL100S10	OEM
40HFR5	1620
40HFR10	0254
40HFR15	1099
40HFR20	1099
40HFR30	1103
40HFR40	0258
40HFR50	1634
40HFR60	0267
40HFR70	1111
40HFR80	1111
40HFR90	0280
40HFR100	0280
40HFR120	OEM
40HFR140	OEM
40HFR160	OEM
40J	OEM
40J2	0015
40J2F	OEM
40J3P	0109
40JH3	2823
40JH3R	2177
40JP3	OEM
40JZ	0015
40K	0015
40KR	0015
40L15	OEM
40L20	OEM
40L25	OEM
40L30	OEM
40L35	OEM
40L40	OEM
40L45	OEM
40L50	OEM
40L55	OEM
40L60	OEM
40L65	OEM
40L70	OEM
40L75	OEM
40L80	OEM
40L85	OEM
40L90	OEM
40L95	OEM
40L100	OEM
40L110	OEM
40L120	OEM
40L130	OEM
40L140	OEM
40L150	OEM
40L160	OEM
40L170	OEM
40L180	OEM
40L190	OEM
40L200	OEM
40L210	OEM
40L220	OEM
40L230	OEM
40L240	OEM
40L250	OEM
40L260	OEM
40L270	OEM
40L280	OEM
40L290	OEM
40L300	OEM
40LF	OEM
40M	0015
40N1	0015
40N2	0097
40N3	0097
40N15A	OEM
40N15A9	OEM
40N20A	OEM
40N20A9	OEM
40N25A	OEM
40N25A9	OEM
40N30A	OEM
40N30A9	OEM
40N35A	OEM
40N35A9	OEM
40N40A	OEM
40N40A9	OEM
40N45A	OEM
40N45A9	OEM
40N50A	OEM
40N50A9	OEM
40N55A	OEM
40N55A9	OEM
40N60A	OEM
40N60A9	OEM
40N65A	OEM
40N65A9	OEM
40N70A	OEM
40N70A9	OEM
40N75A	OEM
40N75A9	OEM
40N80A	OEM
40N80A9A9	OEM
40N85A	OEM

138
If replacement code is OEM, contact original manufacturer for replacement.

DEVICE TYPE	REPL CODE	DEVICE TYPE	REPL CODE	DEVICE TYPE	REPL CODE	DEVICE TYPE	REPL CODE	DEVICE TYPE	REPL CODE	DEVICE TYPE	REPL CODE	DEVICE TYPE	REPL CODE
40N85A9	OEM	40TCA50	OEM	42-18310	0142	42-27372	0007	42TB3-LE00	OEM	42TB12-LH00	OEM	43N3	0198
40N90A	OEM	40TCA60	OEM	42-19642	0086	42-27373	0007	42TB3-LH00	OEM	42TB12-NE00	OEM	43N6	0198
40N90A9	OEM	40TCA70	OEM	42-19643	0126	42-27374	0079	42TB3-NE00	OEM	42TB12-NH00	OEM	43P1	0279
40N95A	OEM	40TCA80	OEM	42-19644	0198	42-27375	0079	42TB3-NH00	OEM	42TB12-RE00	OEM	43P2	0211
40N95A9	OEM	40TCA90	OEM	42-19645	0071	42-27376	0211	42TB3-RE00	OEM	42TB13-CE00	OEM	43P3	0279
40N100A	OEM	40TCA100	OEM	42-19670	0198	42-27377	0574	42TB4-CE00	OEM	42TB13-EE00	OEM	43P4	0211
40N100A9	OEM	40TCA110	OEM	42-19671	0004	42-27378	0143	42TB4-EE00	OEM	42TB13-EH00	OEM	43P4C	0211
40N110A	OEM	40TCA120	OEM	42-19681	0123	42-27379	0030	42TB4-EH00	OEM	42TB13-GE00	OEM	43P6	0211
40N120A	OEM	40V3P	OEM	42-19682	0050	42-27380	0143	42TB4-GE00	OEM	42TB13-GH00	OEM	43P6A	0211
40N130A	OEM	40V10	OEM	42-19683	0144	42-27381	0143	42TB4-GH00	OEM	42TB13-JE00	OEM	43P6C	0279
40N140A	OEM	40V12	OEM	42-19792	0050	42-27463	0015	42TB4-JE00	OEM	42TB13-JH00	OEM	43P7	0211
40N150A	OEM	40W3P	OEM	42-19840	0016	42-27529	1136	42TB4-JH00	OEM	42TB13-LE00	OEM	43P7A	0211
40N160A	OEM	40X3P	OEM	42-19862	0208	42-27530	0155	42TB4-LE00	OEM	42TB13-LH00	OEM	43P7C	0211
40N170A	OEM	40Y3P	0015	42-19862A	0164	42-27533	0155	42TB4-LH00	OEM	42TB13-NE00	OEM	43P13	0050
40N180A	OEM	40Z6	OEM	42-19863	0004	42-27534	0076	42TB4-NE00	OEM	42TB13-NH00	OEM	43R2	OEM
40N190A	OEM	40Z6A	OEM	42-19863A	0004	42-27535	0111	42TB4-NH00	OEM	42TB13-RE00	OEM	43ST-2SC535B	0127
40N200A	OEM	41-001	0469	42-19864	0004	42-27536	0006	42TB4-RE00	OEM	42TB14-CE00	OEM	43ST-2SC1514-05	1077
40N210A	OEM	41-0318	0103	42-19864A	0004	42-27537	0191	42TB5-CE00	OEM	42TB14-EE00	OEM	43ST-2SC1514-15	1077
40N220A	OEM	41-0318A	0103	42-19865	0015	42-27538	0919	42TB5-EE00	OEM	42TB14-EH00	OEM	43SZ-RD6.2E	0466
40N230A	OEM	41-0499	0016	42-20222	0004	42-27539	0042	42TB5-EH00	OEM	42TB14-GE00	OEM	43SZ-YZ-063	0466
40N240A	OEM	41-0500	0126	42-20738	0198	42-27540	0005	42TB5-GE00	OEM	42TB14-GH00	OEM	43SZ-YZ063	0466
40N250A	OEM	41-0500A	0126	42-20739	0126	42-27541	0137	42TB5-GH00	OEM	42TB14-JE00	OEM	43T1	OEM
40NJ	0015	41-0606	0168	42-20960	0178	42-27542	0133	42TB5-JE00	OEM	42TB14-JH00	OEM	43T2	OEM
40P1	0211	41-0905	0137	42-20961	0103	42-27543	0019	42TB5-JH00	OEM	42TB14-LE00	OEM	43T3	OEM
40P2	0211	41-0909	0178	42-20961A	0103	42-27544	0123	42TB5-LE00	OEM	42TB14-LH00	OEM	43T4	OEM
40P2(POWER)	0097	41-J2	0015	42-21232	0126	42-28056	0016	42TB5-LH00	OEM	42TB14-NE00	OEM	43T5	OEM
40P2RECT	0097	41B581014	0086	42-21233	0086	42-28057	0164	42TB5-NE00	OEM	42TB14-NH00	OEM	43T6	OEM
40P3	0097	41C1FM	OEM	42-21234	0016	42-28058	0015	42TB5-NH00	OEM	42TB14-RE00	OEM	43T7	OEM
40Q3	0847	41C2FM	OEM	42-21362	0123	42-28199	0143	42TB5-RE00	OEM	42TB15-CE00	OEM	43T8	OEM
40Q4	3705	41C3FM	OEM	42-21400	0015	42-28200	0030	42TB6-CE00	OEM	42TB15-EE00	OEM	43T9	OEM
40R2S	0045	41C4FM	OEM	42-21401	0007	42-28201	0133	42TB6-EE00	OEM	42TB15-EH00	OEM	43T10	OEM
40R3	0800	41C6FM	OEM	42-21402	0007	42-28202	0015	42TB6-EH00	OEM	42TB15-GE00	OEM	43TB1-JH00	OEM
40R3P	OEM	41C-402	4406	42-21403	0136	42-28203	0144	42TB6-GE00	OEM	42TB15-GH00	OEM	43TB1-LE00	OEM
40RCS5	1694	41C-405	OEM	42-21404	0208	42-28204	0144	42TB6-GH00	OEM	42TB15-JE00	OEM	43TB1-LH00	OEM
40RCS10	1694	41C-406	3232	42-21405	0164	42-28205	0016	42TB6-JE00	OEM	42TB15-JH00	OEM	43TB1-NE00	OEM
40RCS15	OEM	41C-407	0574	42-21406	0004	42-28206	0144	42TB6-JH00	OEM	42TB15-LE00	OEM	43TB1-RE00	OEM
40RCS20	1694	41C-409	2289	42-21407	0198	42-28207	0016	42TB6-LE00	OEM	42TB15-LH00	OEM	43TB2-JH00	OEM
40RCS25	OEM	41D5R03	OEM	42-21408	0015	42-28208	0037	42TB6-LH00	OEM	42TB15-NH00	OEM	43TB2-LE00	OEM
40RCS30	3970	41D9R03GH	OEM	42-21443	0265	42-28210	0016	42TB6-NE00	OEM	42TB15-RE00	OEM	43TB2-LH00	OEM
40RCS40	3970	41E1FM	OEM	42-21866	0015	42-28211	0037	42TB6-NH00	OEM	42X25	0015	43TB2-NE00	OEM
40RCS50	3970	41E2FM	OEM	42-22008	0037	42-30092	0111	42TB6-RE00	OEM	42X32	0015	43TB2-NH00	OEM
40RCS60	3970	41E3-1	0143	42-22008A	0037	42A11	0015	42TB7-CE00	OEM	42X210	0038	43TB2-RE00	OEM
40RCS70	0674	41E3FM	OEM	42-22009	0396	42A14	0143	42TB7-EE00	OEM	42X230	0004	43TB3-JH00	OEM
40RCS80	0674	41E4FM	OEM	42-22154	0590	42A23	0015	42TB7-EH00	OEM	42X233	0211	43TB3-LE00	OEM
40RCS90	0674	41E5R03	OEM	42-22158	0016	42B2	0015	42TB7-GE00	OEM	42X244	0015	43TB3-LH00	OEM
40RCS100	0674	41E6FM	OEM	42-22532	0127	42B16	0015	42TB7-GH00	OEM	42X244B	0015	43TB3-NE00	OEM
40RCS110	0674	41F1FM	OEM	42-22533	0016	42D5R03	OEM	42TB7-JE00	OEM	42X245	0015	43TB3-NH00	OEM
40RCS120	0674	41F2FM	OEM	42-22534	0004	42D9R03GH	OEM	42TB7-JH00	OEM	42X245B	0015	43TB4-JH00	OEM
40S2S03	OEM	41F3FM	OEM	42-22535	0164	42E03A	OEM	42TB7-LE00	OEM	42X308	0211	43TB4-LE00	OEM
40S2S04	OEM	41F4FM	OEM	42-22535Q	0211	42J	OEM	42TB7-LH00	OEM	42X309	0211	43TB4-LH00	OEM
40S3	0800	41F6FM	OEM	42-22536	0030	42J2	0015	42TB7-NE00	OEM	42X310	0038	43TB4-NE00	OEM
40S3P	OEM	41GJ298	OEM	42-22537	0143	42K	OEM	42TB7-NH00	OEM	42X311	0211	43TB4-NH00	OEM
40S5	0994	41HA40	OEM	42-22538	0133	42L	OEM	42TB7-RE00	OEM	42Z6	0057	43TB4-RE00	OEM
40SB02S	1536	41HA60	OEM	42-22539	0143	42N2	OEM	42TB8-CE00	OEM	42Z6A	0057	43TB5-JH00	OEM
40SB02SA	1536	41HA80	OEM	42-22540	1293	42NT100	OEM	42TB8-EE00	OEM	43	OEM	43TB5-LE00	OEM
40SB03S	1536	41HA100	OEM	42-22755	0143	42OT1	0164	42TB8-EH00	OEM	43-022861	0144	43TB5-LH00	OEM
40SB03SA	1536	41HF10	OEM	42-22778	0050	42P1	0279	42TB8-GE00	OEM	43-023190	0130	43TB5-NE00	OEM
40SB04SA	1536	41HF20	OEM	42-22779	0050	42P15	0050	42TB8-GH00	OEM	43-023212	0079	43TB5-NH00	OEM
40SB025S	1536	41HF40	OEM	42-22780	0050	42P83	0016	42TB8-JE00	OEM	43-023221	0016	43TB5-RE00	OEM
40SG1	4968	41HF60	OEM	42-22781	0050	42R2	0097	42TB8-JH00	OEM	43-023222	0126	43TB6-JH00	OEM
40SG2	0604	41HF80	OEM	42-22784	0050	42ST-2SC930E	2195	42TB8-LE00	OEM	43-023223	0086	43TB6-LE00	OEM
40SG3	0133	41HF100	OEM	42-22785	0144	42ST-2SD666C	1376	42TB8-LH00	OEM	43-023843	0103	43TB6-LH00	OEM
40SG4	0790	41HF120	OEM	42-22786	0016	42ST-LBC547C	OEM	42TB8-NE00	OEM	43-023844	0086	43TB6-NE00	OEM
40SG5	0790	41HF140	OEM	42-22787	0016	42T1	OEM	42TB8-NH00	OEM	43-025763	0144	43TB6-NH00	OEM
40SG6	0015	41HF160	OEM	42-22809	0016	42T2	OEM	42TB8-RE00	OEM	43-025764	0144	43TB6-RE00	OEM
40SG7	0369	41HFR10	OEM	42-22810	0037	42T3	OEM	42TB9-CE00	OEM	43-025765	0144	43TB7-JH00	OEM
40SG8	0369	41HFR20	OEM	42-22810A	0037	42T4	OEM	42TB9-EE00	OEM	43-025766	0016	43TB7-LE00	OEM
40SI-MC1364P	0797	41HFR40	OEM	42-22811	0016	42T5	OEM	42TB9-EH00	OEM	43-025767	0144	43TB7-LH00	OEM
40SI-UPB562C	OEM	41HFR60	OEM	42-22812	0016	42T6	OEM	42TB9-GE00	OEM	43-025834	0222	43TB7-NE00	OEM
40SL05	OEM	41HFR80	OEM	42-22834	0265	42T7	OEM	42TB9-GH00	OEM	43-0203845	0126	43TB7-NH00	OEM
40SL1	OEM	41HFR90	0280	42-22835	0015	42T8	OEM	42TB9-JE00	OEM	43-540012	0015	43TB7-RE00	OEM
40SL2	OEM	41HFR100	OEM	42-22847	0016	42T9	OEM	42TB9-JH00	OEM	43A144188-5	0147	43TB8-JH00	OEM
40SL3	OEM	41HFR120	OEM	42-23348	0016	42T10	OEM	42TB9-LE00	OEM	43A168135-1	1035	43TB8-LE00	OEM
40SL4	OEM	41HFR140	OEM	42-23349	0016	42T11	OEM	42TB9-LH00	OEM	43A168135-2	1812	43TB8-LH00	OEM
40SL5	OEM	41HFR160	OEM	42-23350	0015	42T12	OEM	42TB9-NE00	OEM	43A168135-3	2086	43TB8-NE00	OEM
40SL6	OEM	41J2	0015	42-23350A	0015	42T13	OEM	42TB9-NH00	OEM	43A168135-4	0141	43TB8-NH00	OEM
40SP-BP-104	OEM	41J2F	OEM	42-23459	0042	42T14	OEM	42TB9-RE00	OEM	43A168135-6	1820	43TB8-RE00	OEM
40ST-2SC2371L	0275	41MQ30	OEM	42-23541	0037	42T15	OEM	42TB10-CE00	OEM	43A168135-7	0033	43TB9-JH00	OEM
40T1	OEM	41MQ40	OEM	42-23541A	0037	42TB1-CE00	OEM	42TB10-EE00	OEM	43A168135-8	0081	43TB9-LE00	OEM
40T2	OEM	41MQ50	OEM	42-23542	0016	42TB1-EE00	OEM	42TB10-EH00	OEM	43A168135-9	0354	43TB9-LH00	OEM
40T3	OEM	41MQ60	OEM	42-23622	0004	42TB1-EH00	OEM	42TB10-GE00	OEM	43A168135-10	0557	43TB9-NE00	OEM
40T3P	OEM	41N	0007	42-23960	0127	42TB1-GE00	OEM	42TB10-GH00	OEM	43A223006P1	0677	43TB9-NH00	OEM
40T4	OEM	41N1	0144	42-23960P	0127	42TB1-GH00	OEM	42TB10-JE00	OEM	43A223007	0268	43TB9-RE00	OEM
40T5	OEM	41N2	0144	42-23961	0127	42TB1-JE00	OEM	42TB10-JH00	OEM	43A223008	5241	43TB10-JH00	OEM
40T6	OEM	41N2A	0144	42-23961P	0127	42TB1-JH00	OEM	42TB10-LE00	OEM	43A223009	0310	43TB10-LE00	OEM
40T7	OEM	41N2AA	0144	42-23962	0127	42TB1-LE00	OEM	42TB10-LH00	OEM	43A223012	0680	43TB10-LH00	OEM
40T8	OEM	41N2B	0144	42-23962P	0127	42TB1-LH00	OEM	42TB10-NE00	OEM	43A223015	0867	43TB10-NE00	OEM
40T9	OEM	41N3	0144	42-23963	0127	42TB1-NE00	OEM	42TB10-NH00	OEM	43A223017	0554	43TB10-NH00	OEM
40T10	OEM	41R1FM	OEM	42-23963P	0127	42TB1-NH00	OEM	42TB10-RE00	OEM	43A223018	0554	43TB10-RE00	OEM
40T11	OEM	41R2FM	OEM	42-23964	0016	42TB1-RE00	OEM	42TB11-CE00	OEM	43A223025	1164	43TB11-JH00	OEM
40T12	OEM	41R3FM	OEM	42-23964P	0016	42TB2-CE00	OEM	42TB11-EE00	OEM	43A223026P1	1303	43TB11-LE00	OEM
40T13	OEM	41R4FM	OEM	42-23965	0136	42TB2-EE00	OEM	42TB11-EH00	OEM	43A223028	1150	43TB11-LH00	OEM
40T14	OEM	41R6FM	OEM	42-23965P	0050	42TB2-EH00	OEM	42TB11-GE00	OEM	43A223029P1	1046	43TB11-NE00	OEM
40T15	OEM	41SI-HA1128	0167	42-23966	0016	42TB2-GE00	OEM	42TB11-GH00	OEM	43A223030	1477	43TB11-NH00	OEM
40TC10	OEM	41SI-LM3065N	0167	42-23966P	0016	42TB2-GH00	OEM	42TB11-JE00	OEM	43A223031	1705	43TB11-RE00	OEM
40TC20	OEM	41Z6	0165	42-23967	0164	42TB2-JE00	OEM	42TB11-JH00	OEM	43A223033P1	0117	43TB12-JH00	OEM
40TC30	OEM	41Z6A	0165	42-23967P	0164	42TB2-JH00	OEM	42TB11-LE00	OEM	43A223034P1	0564	43TB12-LE00	OEM
40TC40	OEM	42-051	0071	42-23968	0160	42TB2-LE00	OEM	42TB11-LH00	OEM	43B	0054	43TB12-LH00	OEM
40TC50	OEM	42-1	2462	42-23968P	0160	42TB2-LH00	OEM	42TB11-NE00	OEM	43C216408P1	0677	43TB12-NE00	OEM
40TC60	OEM	42-2	2453	42-23969	0143	42TB2-NE00	OEM	42TB11-NH00	OEM	43C216409P1	5241	43TB12-NH00	OEM
40TC70	OEM	42-7	0015	42-23970	0030	42TB2-NH00	OEM	42TB11-RE00	OEM	43C216410P1	1896	43TB12-RE00	OEM
40TC80	OEM	42-14027	0015	42-23972	0123	42TB2-RE00	OEM	42TB12-CE00	OEM	43C216411P1	3670	43TB13	OEM
40TC90	OEM	42-16599	0160	42-23975	0015	42TB3-CE00	OEM	42TB12-EE00	OEM	43C216414P1	1933	43TB13-JH00	OEM
40TC100	OEM	42-17143	0211	42-23977	0916	42TB3-EE00	OEM	42TB12-EH00	OEM	43C216447	1915	43TB13-LE00	OEM
40TC120	OEM	42-17443	0015	42-24263	0396	42TB3-EH00	OEM	42TB12-GE00	OEM	43C216447P1	1915	43TB13-LH00	OEM
40TCA10	OEM	42-17443A	0015	42-24387	0133	42TB3-GE00	OEM	42TB12-GH00	OEM	43D5R03	OEM	43TB13-NE00	OEM
40TCA20	OEM	42-17444	0198	42-27202	0015	42TB3-GH00	OEM	42TB12-JE00	OEM	43D9R03GH	OEM	43TB13-NH00	OEM
40TCA30	OEM	42-18109	0841	42-27277	0111	42TB3-JE00	OEM	42TB12-JH00	OEM	43J	OEM	43TB13-RE00	OEM
40TCA40	OEM	42-18111	0198	42-27278	0015	42TB3-JH00	OEM	42TB12-LE00	OEM	43K	OEM	43TB14-JH00	OEM

If replacement code is OEM, contact original manufacturer for replacement.

139

DEVICE TYPE	REPL CODE
43TB14-LE00	OEM
43TB14-LH00	OEM
43TB14-NE00	OEM
43TB14-NH00	OEM
43TB14-RE00	OEM
43TB15-CE00	OEM
43TB15-EE00	OEM
43TB15-EH00	OEM
43TB15-GE00	OEM
43TB15-GH00	OEM
43TB15-JE00	OEM
43TB15-JH00	OEM
43TB15-LE00	OEM
43TB15-LH00	OEM
43TB15-NE00	OEM
43TB15-NH00	OEM
43TB15-RE00	OEM
43X16A567	0198
43Z6	0170
43Z6A	0170
44	OEM
44-13	0136
44-530	0015
44-44886G01	0155
44A-1A5	0160
44A354637-001	0178
44A417779-001	0308
44B1	0850
44B1Z	0850
44BH05M	OEM
44BH05P	OEM
44D5R03	OEM
44D9R03GH	OEM
44E03A	OEM
44J	OEM
44K	OEM
44P1	0050
44PB05M	OEM
44PBF7C	OEM
44PD05M	OEM
44PD05P	OEM
44PH05M	OEM
44PH05P	OEM
44PS05M	OEM
44R2	0197
44R2R	0991
44SD-CDG00	0133
44SP-LD271	0511
44SP-LP271	OEM
44ST-2SB568C	1900
44ST-2SB649AC	0520
44SZ-WZ040	0036
44SZ-WZ-063	0466
44T1	OEM
44T-100-118	OEM
44T-100-120	1044
44T-300-91	0030
44T-300-92	0041
44T-300-93	0064
44T-300-94	0077
44T-300-95	0015
44T-300-96	0133
44T-300-97	0019
44T-300-98	OEM
44T-300-99	2046
44T-300-100	0083
44T-300-101	1888
44T-300-102	1044
44T-300-103	0151
44T-300-104	0076
44T-300-105	0321
44T-300-106	0076
44T-300-107	0161
44T-300-108	2684
44T-300-109	0930
44T-300-110	1060
44T-300-111	1212
44T-300-112	0076
44T-300-113	0321
44T-300-358	OEM
44T-300-359	4746
44TB7	OEM
44TB9	OEM
44TB11	OEM
45A2FX355	0015
45AN30	OEM
45AN40	OEM
45AN50	OEM
45AN60	OEM
45AN80	OEM
45AN100	OEM
45AN120	OEM
45AN140	OEM
45AN160	OEM
45ANS	OEM
45AR20	OEM
45AR30	OEM
45AR50	OEM
45AR60	OEM
45AR80	OEM
45AR100	OEM
45AR120	OEM
45AR140	OEM
45AR160	OEM
45AR4040	OEM
45ARS	OEM
45D5R03	OEM
45D9R03GH	OEM
45E03A	OEM
45F10	OEM
45F15	OEM
45F20	OEM
45F25	OEM
45F30	OEM
45F40	OEM
45F50	OEM
45F60	OEM
45F80	OEM
45J	OEM
45K	OEM
45L5	0594
45L5R	1337
45L10	0594
45L10R	1337
45L15	0594
45L15R	1337
45L20	0594
45L20R	1337
45L25	0594
45L25R	1337
45L30	0594
45L30R	1337
45L35	1975
45L35R	1894
45L40	1975
45L40R	1894
45L45	1975
45L45R	1894
45L50	1975
45L50R	1894
45L60	1975
45L60R	1894
45L70	0652
45L70R	0193
45L80	0652
45L80R	0193
45L90	0652
45L90R	0193
45L100	0652
45L100R	0193
45L120	OEM
45LK10A	0594
45LK10R	1337
45LK20A	0594
45LK20R	1337
45LK30A	0594
45LK30R	1337
45LK40A	1975
45LK40R	1894
45LK50A	1975
45LK50R	1894
45LK60A	1975
45LK60R	1894
45LK80A	0652
45LK80R	0193
45LK100A	0652
45LK100R	0193
45M10	0594
45M15	0594
45M20	0594
45M30	0594
45M40	0594
45M50	1975
45M60	1975
45M80	0652
45M100	0652
45MA10	1337
45MA20	1337
45MA30	1337
45MA40	1337
45MA60	1894
45MA80	0193
45MA100	0193
45MA120	0202
45MA140	0202
45MA160	OEM
45MLA60	OEM
45MLA80	OEM
45MLA100	OEM
45MLA120	OEM
45MN-1	OEM
45MR	OEM
45MR-1	OEM
45MS2	OEM
45N1	0038
45N2	0038
45N2A	0208
45N2M	0016
45N3	0016
45N4	0016
45N4M	0016
45NP	0144
45P1U5M	OEM
45R2	OEM
45R2S	OEM
45SD-W005M	0106
45ST-2SC454C	0076
45ST-2SC1106	0220
45SZ-RD5.1FB	0041
45TB7	OEM
45V10	OEM
45V12	OEM
45X1A502C	0211
45X1A520C	0004
45X2	0279
45X11PV-CM	OEM
45ZE1	OEM
46	OEM
46-06311-3	0127
46-4	0911
46-29-6	0167
46-34-3	0015
46-36-3	0015
46-86-3	0015
46-119-3	0007
46-163-3	0004
46-530-3	0010
46-840-3	0004
46-861-3	0911
46-862	0911
46-862-3	0050
46-864-3	0144
46-865-3	0050
46-866-3	0050
46-867-3	0233
46-868-3	1273
46-869-3	0004
46-1325-3	4133
46-1340-3	2689
46-1343-3	0574
46-1344-3	OEM
46-1346-3	2689
46-1347-3	0823
46-1348-3	0823
46-1352-3	0748
46-1354-3	OEM
46-1356-3	0823
46-1357-3	0872
46-1361-3	0167
46-1362-3	2610
46-1363-3	4502
46-1364-3	0399
46-1365-3	0391
46-1366-3	0784
46-1369-3	0872
46-1370-3	2615
46-1370-9	OEM
46-1382-3	OEM
46-1383-3	2457
46-1391-3	2644
46-1392-3	0858
46-1393-3	1316
46-1394-3	4514
46-1395-3	2921
46-1396-3	3859
46-1397-3	4515
46-1398-3	2216
46-1399-3	OEM
46-5002-1	0627
46-5002-3	3679
46-5002-4	0627
46-5002-5	0373
46-5002-6	2689
46-5002-7	0627
46-5002-8	0784
46-5002-11	0345
46-5002-12	0348
46-5002-13	0350
46-5002-15	0167
46-5002-16	0360
46-5002-19	0368
46-5002-21	0373
46-5002-23	0375
46-5002-26	0167
46-5002-27	0368
46-5002-28	0391
46-5002-31	0399
46-5290-0042	0358
46-5290-0178	2052
46-5291-0164	2279
46-6661-2	0229
46-6829	0127
46-8257-3	0016
46-8477-3	0111
46-8601-3	0015
46-8607-3	3017
46-8610-3	0004
46-8611	0004
46-8611-3	0004
46-8611-4	0196
46-8612-3	0050
46-8613	0911
46-8613-3	0136
46-8613-3(HOR-OUT)	0969
46-8613-3(SYNC)	0050
46-8614	0911
46-8614-3	0595
46-8615-3	0160
46-8616-3	0123
46-8617-3	0160
46-8619	0015
46-8619-3	0143
46-8620-3	0102
46-8621	0030
46-8621-3	0276
46-8622	0911
46-8622-3	0969
46-8623	0143
46-8623-3	0143
46-8624-3	0191
46-8625	0911
46-8625-1	0136
46-8625-2	0136
46-8625-3	0136
46-8625-4	0136
46-8625-5	0136
46-8625-6	0136
46-8627	0911
46-8629	0127
46-8630	0143
46-8631-3	0004
46-8634-3	0160
46-8634-9	OEM
46-8636-3	0136
46-8638	0321
46-8638-3	0160
46-8638P-3	0086
46-8642	0030
46-8643	0911
46-8643-3	0911
46-8644	0030
46-8644-3	0143
46-8645	OEM
46-8646	0212
46-8646-3	0143
46-8647	0127
46-8647-3	0015
46-8648	0321
46-8649	0321
46-8650	0127
46-8651	0079
46-8652	0127
46-8653	0127
46-8654	0127
46-8655	OEM
46-8656	OEM
46-8660-3	0004
46-8661	0015
46-8661-3	0015
46-8663-3	0911
46-8664-3	3511
46-8665-3	0004
46-8666-3	0004
46-8668-3	0004
46-8671-3	0208
46-8672-3	0007
46-8676-3	0133
46-8677-2	0144
46-8677-3	0259
46-8679-1	0004
46-8679-2	0004
46-8679-3	0004
46-8680-1	0004
46-8680-2	0004
46-8680-3	0004
46-8681-1	0004
46-8681-2	0004
46-8681-3	0164
46-8682-2	0016
46-8682-3	0111
46-8687-3	0015
46-8688-3	0911
46-8689-3	0015
46-8694-3	1073
46-8695-3	0016
46-8697-3	0015
46-13101-3	0849
46-13103-3	0043
46-13104-3	0385
46-13104-5	OEM
46-13105-3	0602
46-13110-3	OEM
46-13118-3	OEM
46-13119-3	0878
46-13120-3	OEM
46-13121-3	2268
46-13122-3	OEM
46-13123-3	OEM
46-13124-3	0850
46-13125-3	0880
46-13126-3	2647
46-13127-3	OEM
46-13128-3	OEM
46-13129-3	OEM
46-13130-3	OEM
46-13131-3	0837
46-13133-3	3115
46-13134-3	OEM
46-13142-3	OEM
46-13143-3	1049
46-13145-3	0167
46-13148-3	OEM
46-13149-3	OEM
46-13150-3	OEM
46-13152-3	3198
46-13153-3	3888
46-13154-3	2647
46-13155-3	OEM
46-13156-3	0457
46-13162-3	3662
46-13163-3	4162
46-13164-3	4178
46-13165-3	4197
46-13166-3	3652
46-13167-3	3909
46-13168-3	4230
46-13169-3	4255
46-13170-3	OEM
46-13171-3	3907
46-13172-3	2932
46-13173-3	1012
46-13174-3	3913
46-13174-9	OEM
46-13175-3	4360
46-13176-3	3216
46-13177-3	2279
46-13178-3	0308
46-13180-3	0910
46-13184-3	0846
46-13185-3	0851
46-13187-3	OEM
46-13188-3	0906
46-13190-3	4071
46-13193-3	OEM
46-13196-3	OEM
46-13197-3	OEM
46-13200-3	OEM
46-13203-3	OEM
46-13204-3	OEM
46-13208-3	0912
46-13212-3	OEM
46-13215-3	OEM
46-13216-3	2043
46-13217-3	OEM
46-13219-3	OEM
46-13221-3	OEM
46-13222-3	OEM
46-13223-3	0898
46-13225-3	5068
46-13227-3	OEM
46-13228-3	OEM
46-13230-3	OEM
46-13231-3	OEM
46-13232-3	OEM
46-13233-3	3911
46-13234-3	5531
46-13237-3	1437
46-13238-3	2043
46-13239-3	5612
46-13243-3	OEM
46-13244-3	OEM
46-13245-3	OEM
46-13246-3	OEM
46-13247-3	OEM
46-13248-3	OEM
46-13249-3	OEM
46-13250-3	OEM
46-13251-3	OEM
46-13252-3	OEM
46-13253-3	OEM
46-13254-3	OEM
46-13255-3	OEM
46-13256-3	OEM
46-13257-3	0328
46-13258-3	0215
46-13259-3	OEM
46-13260-3	OEM
46-13261-3	OEM
46-13262-3	OEM
46-13263-3	OEM
46-13264-3	5892
46-13267-3	0912
46-13268-3	OEM
46-13270-3	OEM
46-13271-3	OEM
46-13272-3	0473
46-13273-3	OEM
46-13274-3	OEM
46-13275-3	OEM
46-13279-3	0765
46-13290-3	OEM
46-13291-3	OEM
46-13292-3	OEM
46-13294-3	OEM
46-13295-3	OEM
46-13296-3	0101
46-13297-3	0765
46-13298-3	2838
46-13299-3	3916
46-13301-3	3923
46-13302-3	0859
46-13303-3	OEM
46-13304-3	OEM
46-13305-3	OEM
46-13306-3	OEM
46-13307-3	4876
46-13309-3	4075
46-13310-3	0356
46-13311-3	1311
46-13312-3	4669
46-13313-3	0409
46-13314-3	0056
46-13315-3	0409
46-13316-3	0297
46-13317-3	0473
46-13318-3	OEM
46-13319-3	0119
46-13320-3	OEM
46-13321-3	OEM
46-13322-3	2052
46-13323-3	0859
46-13324-3	4273
46-13326-3	OEM
46-13327-3	1020
46-13329-3	OEM
46-13334-3	OEM
46-13337-3	OEM
46-13338-3	5666
46-13339-3	5068
46-13340-3	0167
46-13341-3	3216
46-13342-3	OEM
46-13343-3	OEM
46-13344-3	OEM
46-13345-3	0356
46-13346-3	OEM
46-13349-3	OEM
46-13350-3	OEM
46-13351-3	OEM
46-13353-3	OEM
46-13354-3	OEM
46-13356-3	0658
46-13358-3	OEM
46-13359-3	OEM
46-13360-3	OEM
46-13361-3	OEM
46-13368-3	OEM
46-13371-3	OEM
46-13379-3	0859
46-13380-3	OEM
46-13381-3	OEM
46-13383-3	OEM
46-13384-3	OEM
46-13385-3	OEM
46-13386-3	OEM
46-13389-3	OEM
46-13392-3	2898
46-13393-3	OEM
46-13395-3	OEM
46-13398-3	OEM
46-13399-3	OEM
46-13400-3	OEM
46-13401-3	OEM
46-13402-3	OEM
46-13404-3	0356
46-13405-3	OEM
46-13406-3	OEM
46-13411	1437
46-13411-3	1437
46-13413-3	OEM
46-13414-3	OEM
46-13420-3	OEM
46-13421-3	OEM
46-13422-3	OEM
46-13423-3	OEM
46-13424-3	OEM
46-13427-3	OEM
46-13428-3	1437
46-13434-3	OEM
46-13435-3	OEM
46-13436-3	OEM
46-13437-3	OEM
46-13439-3	OEM
46-13440-3	OEM
46-13441-3	OEM
46-13442-3	OEM
46-13443-3	OEM
46-13444-3	OEM
46-13445-3	OEM
46-13446-3	OEM
46-13447-3	OEM
46-13448-3	3728
46-13449-3	OEM
46-13450-3	OEM
46-13452-3	OEM
46-13453-3	OEM
46-13454-3	OEM
46-13455-3	0973
46-13459-3	OEM
46-13461-3	OEM
46-13462-3	OEM
46-13463-3	OEM
46-13464-3	OEM
46-13465-3	OEM
46-13466-3	4212
46-13469-3	OEM
46-13473-3	OEM
46-13474-3	OEM
46-13478-3	OEM
46-13479-3	OEM
46-13480-3	OEM
46-13481-3	OEM
46-13482-3	OEM
46-13483-3	OEM
46-13484-3	2094
46-13485-3	OEM
46-13486-3	OEM
46-13487-3	2213
46-13488-3	OEM
46-13489-3	OEM
46-13491-3	2650
46-13493-3	4349
46-13494-3	OEM
46-13495-3	0624
46-13502-3	4875
46-13503-3	OEM
46-13504-3	OEM
46-13505-3	OEM
46-13507-3	OEM
46-13508-3	OEM
46-13509-3	OEM
46-13513-3	OEM
46-13514-3	5300
46-13515-3	OEM
46-13516-3	OEM
46-13517-3	OEM
46-13518-3	OEM
46-13519-3	OEM
46-13520-3	OEM
46-13521-3	OEM
46-13522-3	OEM
46-13523-3	OEM
46-13524-3	OEM
46-13527-3	0328
46-13528-3	4773
46-13531-3	OEM
46-13534-3	OEM
46-13537-3	OEM
46-13538-3	1192
46-13539-3	OEM
46-13540-3	OEM
46-13541-3	OEM
46-13542-3	OEM
46-13543-3	OEM
46-13545-3	OEM
46-13546-3	3476
46-13547-3	5742
46-13547-9	OEM
46-13548-3	1977
46-13550-3	3692
46-13551-3	2599
46-13552-3	5004
46-13554-3	OEM
46-13557-3	OEM
46-13558-3	OEM
46-13559-3	OEM
46-13561-3	2268
46-13567-3	OEM
46-13571-3	OEM
46-13572-3	OEM
46-13573-3	5954
46-13574-3	OEM
46-13575-3	OEM
46-13577-3	OEM
46-13580-3	OEM
46-13581-3	2641
46-13582-3	OEM
46-13583-3	OEM
46-13585-3	OEM
46-13586-3	OEM
46-13587-3	OEM
46-13588-3	3461
46-13588-9	3461
46-13590-3	3726
46-13591-3	OEM
46-13593-3	0243
46-13594-3	OEM
46-13595-3	OEM
46-13596-3	OEM
46-13597-3	OEM
46-13598-3	OEM
46-13599-3	OEM
46-13600-3	OEM
46-13601-3	OEM
46-13604	1977
46-13604--3	OEM
46-13604-3	1977
46-13607-3	OEM
46-13608-3	OEM
46-13609-3	OEM
46-13611-3	OEM
46-13612-3	OEM
46-13613-3	OEM
46-13616-3	OEM
46-13617-3	OEM
46-13618-3	OEM
46-13620-3	OEM
46-13621-3	OEM
46-13622-3	OEM
46-13623-3	OEM
46-13624-3	OEM
46-13625-3	OEM
46-13626-3	OEM
46-13627-3	OEM
46-13628-3	OEM
46-13629-3	OEM
46-13630-3	OEM
46-13631-3	OEM
46-13632-3	OEM
46-13633-3	OEM
46-13634-3	OEM
46-13639-3	OEM
46-13642-3	OEM
46-13643-3	OEM
46-13644-3	OEM
46-13645-3	4339
46-13646-3	OEM
46-13647-3	OEM
46-13648-3	OEM
46-13649-3	5124
46-13650-3	OEM
46-13651-3	OEM
46-13652-3	OEM
46-13653-3	OEM
46-13654-3	OEM
46-13659-3	OEM
46-13661-3	OEM
46-13662-3	0034
46-13663-3	OEM
46-13664-3	OEM
46-13665-3	OEM
46-13666-3	OEM
46-13667-3	OEM
46-13668-3	OEM
46-13669-3	OEM
46-13674-4	OEM
46-13675-3	OEM
46-13676-3	OEM
46-13679-3	OEM
46-13686-3	1022
46-13687-3	OEM
46-13688-3	OEM
46-13689-3	3776

140 If replacement code is OEM, contact original manufacturer for replacement.

DEVICE TYPE	REPL CODE
46-13690-3	OEM
46-13691-3	OEM
46-13692-3	OEM
46-13699-3	OEM
46-13700-3	OEM
46-13704-3	0328
46-13706-3	OEM
46-13708-3	OEM
46-13709-3	OEM
46-13714-3	OEM
46-13715-3	OEM
46-13719-3	OEM
46-13720-3	OEM
46-13727-3	OEM
46-13728-3	OEM
46-13729-3	OEM
46-13730-3	0024
46-13731-3	OEM
46-13732-3	OEM
46-13738-3	OEM
46-13739-3	OEM
46-13740-3	OEM
46-13741-3	OEM
46-13742-3	OEM
46-13743-3	OEM
46-13744-3	OEM
46-13745-3	OEM
46-13746-3	OEM
46-13747-3	OEM
46-13748-3	OEM
46-13749-3	OEM
46-13750-3	OEM
46-13751-3	OEM
46-13752-3	OEM
46-13753-3	OEM
46-13754-3	OEM
46-13755-3	OEM
46-13758-3	OEM
46-13759-3	OEM
46-13762-3	OEM
46-13763-3	OEM
46-13764-3	OEM
46-13766-3	OEM
46-13767-3	OEM
46-13768-3	OEM
46-13769-3	OEM
46-13771-3	4283
46-13773-3	OEM
46-13774-3	OEM
46-13775-3	OEM
46-13776-3	OEM
46-13780-3	OEM
46-13781-3	OEM
46-13782-3	OEM
46-13784-3	OEM
46-13785-3	OEM
46-13786-3	OEM
46-13787-3	OEM
46-13788-3	OEM
46-13789-3	OEM
46-13790-3	OEM
46-13791-3	OEM
46-13792-3	OEM
46-13793-3	OEM
46-13794-3	OEM
46-13795-3	OEM
46-13796-3	OEM
46-13797-3	OEM
46-13798-3	OEM
46-13799-3	OEM
46-13800-3	OEM
46-13801-3	OEM
46-13802-3	OEM
46-13803-3	OEM
46-13804-3	OEM
46-13805-3	OEM
46-13806-3	OEM
46-13807-3	OEM
46-13808-3	OEM
46-13809-3	OEM
46-13810-3	OEM
46-13815-3	2015
46-13816-3	0129
46-13817-3	OEM
46-13818-3	OEM
46-13819-3	OEM
46-13820-3	OEM
46-13827-3	OEM
46-13828-3	OEM
46-13829-3	4074
46-13830-3	1666
46-13832-3	OEM
46-13833-3	OEM
46-13834-3	OEM
46-13835-3	OEM
46-13839-3	4243
46-13840-3	OEM
46-13841-3	OEM
46-13842-3	OEM
46-13844-3	OEM
46-13845-3	OEM
46-13846-3	OEM
46-13847-3	OEM
46-13848-3	OEM
46-13849-3	OEM
46-13850-3	OEM
46-13851-3	OEM
46-13852-3	OEM
46-13853-3	OEM
46-13855-3	OEM
46-13856-3	OEM
46-13857-3	OEM
46-13858-3	OEM
46-13859-3	OEM
46-13860-3	OEM
46-13861-3	OEM
46-13862-3	OEM
46-13863-3	OEM
46-13869-3	OEM
46-13870-3	OEM
46-13871-3	OEM
46-13872-3	OEM
46-13873-3	OEM
46-13874-3	OEM
46-13875-3	OEM
46-13876-3	OEM
46-13877-3	4307
46-13879-3	OEM
46-13887-3	OEM
46-13888-3	OEM
46-13889-3	OEM
46-13890-3	OEM
46-13891-3	OEM
46-13892-3	OEM
46-13893-3	OEM
46-13894-3	OEM
46-13895-3	OEM
46-13896-3	OEM
46-13899-3	OEM
46-13900-3	OEM
46-13901-3	OEM
46-13902-3	OEM
46-13903-3	OEM
46-13904-3	OEM
46-13905-3	OEM
46-13906-3	OEM
46-13907-3	OEM
46-13908-3	OEM
46-13909-3	OEM
46-13910-3	OEM
46-13911-3	4569
46-13912-3	1433
46-13916-3	OEM
46-13917-3	OEM
46-13921-3	1521
46-13922-3	3860
46-13923-3	OEM
46-13924-3	4923
46-13925-3	6401
46-13926-3	OEM
46-13927-3	OEM
46-13928-3	OEM
46-13930-3	OEM
46-13931-3	OEM
46-13932-3	OEM
46-13933-3	OEM
46-13934-3	OEM
46-13935-3	OEM
46-13936-3	OEM
46-13937-3	OEM
46-13938-3	1977
46-13939-3	OEM
46-13941-3	OEM
46-13942-3	OEM
46-13943-3	OEM
46-13944-3	OEM
46-13946-3	OEM
46-13947-3	OEM
46-13949-3	OEM
46-13951-3	OEM
46-13953-3	OEM
46-13954-3	OEM
46-13956-3	OEM
46-13957-3	OEM
46-13958-3	OEM
46-13959-3	OEM
46-13960-3	OEM
46-13962-3	4040
46-13963-3	1977
46-13967-3	OEM
46-13969-3	3223
46-13970-9	OEM
46-13972-3	OEM
46-13973-3	OEM
46-13975-3	OEM
46-13977-3	OEM
46-13978-3	OEM
46-13979-3	OEM
46-13980-3	6822
46-13983-3	OEM
46-13984-3	OEM
46-13985-3	OEM
46-13986-3	OEM
46-13987-3	OEM
46-13988-3	OEM
46-13989-3	OEM
46-13990-3	OEM
46-13991-3	OEM
46-13992-3	OEM
46-13993-3	OEM
46-13994-3	OEM
46-13995-3	OEM
46-13996-3	OEM
46-13997-3	OEM
46-13998-3	OEM
46-13999-3	OEM
46-14367-3	0328
46-16261	0015
46-16261-3	0015
46-16428-3	OEM
46-16513-4	OEM
46-18583-3	OEM
46-25156-3	OEM
46-35986-3	OEM
46-37328-3	0551
46-61249-3	0015
46-61267-3	0133
46-61294-3	OEM
46-61307-3	0133
46-61951-3	0120
46-61961-3	0120
46-61992-3	OEM
46-67120A13	0015
46-80309-3	0133
46-81187-3	0283
46-83183-3	OEM
46-83395-3	OEM
46-83619-3	OEM
46-83648-3	OEM
46-83649-3	OEM
46-84120-3	0144
46-85285-3	0144
46-86101-3	0127
46-86102-3	0136
46-86104-3	0918
46-86104-9	OEM
46-86105-3	1293
46-86106-3	0102
46-86107-3	0007
46-86108-3	0007
46-86109-3	0127
46-86110-3	3568
46-86112-2	0007
46-86112-3	0184
46-86113-3	0007
46-86114-3	0007
46-86115-3	0208
46-86116-3	0077
46-86117-3	0007
46-86118-3	0007
46-86119-3	0007
46-86120-3	0127
46-86121-3	0016
46-86122-3	0016
46-86123-3	0050
46-86125-3	0222
46-86126-3	0127
46-86127-3	0127
46-86130-3	0178
46-86130-9	OEM
46-86131-3	0326
46-86132-3	0191
46-86133-3	0127
46-86134-3	0911
46-86135-3	0222
46-86135-9	OEM
46-86136-3	0160
46-86138-3	1293
46-86139-3	0015
46-86140-3	0144
46-86141-3	0071
46-86143-3	0016
46-86144-3	0016
46-86145-3	0016
46-86146-3	0071
46-86147-3	0071
46-86148	0071
46-86148-3	0015
46-86149-3	0015
46-86150-3	0229
46-86151-3	0229
46-86152-3	0016
46-86163-3	0004
46-86165-3	0004
46-86166-3	0211
46-86168-3	0133
46-86169-3	0016
46-86170-3	0037
46-86171-3	0016
46-86172-3	0127
46-86173-3	0233
46-86177-3	0015
46-86178-3	1141
46-86179-3	0102
46-86180-3	0769
46-86182-3	0233
46-86183-3	0233
46-86184	0133
46-86184-3	0133
46-86185-3	1073
46-86186-3	0133
46-86187-3	0133
46-86189-3	0178
46-86192-3	0191
46-86194-3	1075
46-86195-3	0004
46-86196-3	0164
46-86198-3	0841
46-86198-9	OEM
46-86199-3	0015
46-86200-3	0123
46-86201-3	0015
46-86201-3(CENTERING	0914
46-86207-3	0127
46-86208-3	0144
46-86209-3	0127
46-86210-3	0233
46-86211-3	0208
46-86212-3	0015
46-86213-3	0160
46-86214-3	0143
46-86220-3	0196
46-86224-3	0007
46-86225-3	0644
46-86226-3	0178
46-86227-3	0201
46-86228-3	0016
46-86229-3	0037
46-86229-3A	0037
46-86230-3	0037
46-86231-3	0016
46-86232-3	0233
46-86233-3	0086
46-86234-3	0161
46-86235-3	0455
46-86238-3	0037
46-86238-3A	0037
46-86239-3	0127
46-86240-3	0144
46-86244-3	0144
46-86247-2	0016
46-86247-3	0191
46-86249	0030
46-86249-3	0755
46-86250-3	0133
46-86251-3	0127
46-86252-3	0155
46-86253-3	0143
46-86254-3	0907
46-86256-1	0136
46-86256-2	0136
46-86256-3	0004
46-86257-3	0016
46-86261-3	0015
46-86262-3	0144
46-86264-3	0015
46-86265-3	0127
46-86266-3	0143
46-86267-3	0015
46-86268-3	0016
46-86269-3	0144
46-86270-3	0015
46-86271-3	0015
46-86272-3	0275
46-86274-3	0016
46-86279-3	0201
46-86280-3	0102
46-86281-3	0102
46-86282-3	0102
46-86283-3	0037
46-86284-3	OEM
46-86285-3	0007
46-86286-3	0911
46-86287-3	OEM
46-86288-3	0911
46-86289-3	0030
46-86290-3	0015
46-86291-3	0201
46-86292-3	0374
46-86293-3	0037
46-86294-3	0752
46-86295-3	0127
46-86296-3	0361
46-86297-3	0715
46-86298-3	0549
46-86299-3	0127
46-86300-3	0050
46-86301-3	0127
46-86302-3	0127
46-86303-3	0015
46-86304-3	0479
46-86305-3	0030
46-86307-3	0015
46-86308-3	0102
46-86309-3	0133
46-86309-3(ZENER)	0137
46-86310-3	0016
46-86311-3	0127
46-86312-3	0196
46-86313-3	0286
46-86314-3	0144
46-86314-3A	0144
46-86315-3	0086
46-86316-3	0321
46-86317-3	0042
46-86318-3	0233
46-86319-3	0275
46-86320-3	0102
46-86321-3	0015
46-86322-3	0015
46-86323-3	0170
46-86324-3	0102
46-86326-3	0015
46-86327-3	0283
46-86328-3	0102
46-86329-3	0371
46-86330-3	0128
46-86331-3	0102
46-86332-3	0196
46-86334-3	0374
46-86335-3	0042
46-86336-3	0196
46-86337-3	0015
46-86338-3	0133
46-86339-3	0015
46-86340-3	1293
46-86341-3	0100
46-86342-3	0150
46-86343-3	0133
46-86344-3	0283
46-86345-3	0066
46-86346-3	0283
46-86347-3	0419
46-86348-3	0042
46-86349-3	0178
46-86349-9	2345
46-86350-3	0178
46-86351-3	0015
46-86352-3	0127
46-86353-3	0111
46-86354-3	0127
46-86355-2	0015
46-86355-3	0015
46-86357-3	0144
46-86358-3	0015
46-86360-3	0555
46-86364-3	0015
46-86365-3	0023
46-86371-3	0086
46-86372-3	OEM
46-86373-3	0004
46-86374-3	0042
46-86375-3	0016
46-86376-3	0151
46-86377-3	0037
46-86378-3	0016
46-86379-3	0137
46-86380-3	0907
46-86381	0086
46-86381-3	0086
46-86382-3	3994
46-86383-3	0015
46-86384-3	0142
46-86386-3	0142
46-86387-3	0142
46-86388-3	0103
46-86388-9	OEM
46-86389-3	0065
46-86390-3	0003
46-86391-3	0102
46-86392-3	0490
46-86393-2	0102
46-86393-3	0102
46-86394-3	0631
46-86394-3(10)	0631
46-86395-3	0102
46-86396-3	0349
46-86397-3	0144
46-86398-3	0590
46-86399-3	0688
46-86400-3	0042
46-86401-3	0100
46-86402-3	0015
46-86403-3	0126
46-86404-3	0016
46-86405-3	0086
46-86406-3	0126
46-86407-3	0016
46-86408-3	0016
46-86409-3	0016
46-86411-3	0455
46-86412-3	0781
46-86414-3	OEM
46-86415-3	0065
46-86416-3	0015
46-86419-3	0016
46-86420-3	0015
46-86421-3	0012
46-86422-3	0133
46-86424-3	0037
46-86425-3	0126
46-86426-3	0086
46-86427-3	0086
46-86428-3	0133
46-86429-3	0203
46-86430-3	0004
46-86431-3	0133
46-86432-3	0098
46-86433-3	0015
46-86434-3	0111
46-86435-3	0127
46-86436-3	0133
46-86437-3	0015
46-86438-3	0015
46-86439-3	0142
46-86439-9	OEM
46-86440-3	0102
46-86442-3	0244
46-86444-3	1313
46-86445-3	0715
46-86446-3	0142
46-86446-9	0142
46-86447-3	1664
46-86448-3	3349
46-86451-3	0374
46-86452-3	OEM
46-86454-3	0374
46-86455-3	0220
46-86456-3	0644
46-86457-3	0466
46-86458-3	0313
46-86459-3	0018
46-86460-3	0091
46-86461-3	0065
46-86462-3	0313
46-86463-3	0015
46-86464-3	0002
46-86465-3	1319
46-86466-3	0949
46-86467-3	0098
46-86467-5	0098
46-86468-3	OEM
46-86469-3	0168
46-86472-9	OEM
46-86473-3	OEM
46-86474-3	1319
46-86475-3	0220
46-86476-3	0928
46-86476-9	0928
46-86477-3	2040
46-86478-3	OEM
46-86479-3	OEM
46-86481-3	0133
46-86482-3	0638
46-86483-3	0244
46-86484-3	0143
46-86485-3	0191
46-86486-3	0065
46-86487-3	0313
46-86488-3	1219
46-86489-3	0023
46-86492-3	1142
46-86492-9	OEM
46-86493-3	0074
46-86494	0071
46-86494-3	0071
46-86496-3	0178
46-86496-9	OEM
46-86497-3	0015
46-86498-3	OEM
46-86499-3	0071
46-86500-3	1274
46-86501-3	0466
46-86502-3	OEM
46-86503-3	0015
46-86504-3	0181
46-86505-3	0638
46-86505-9	0638
46-86506-3	0168
46-86507-3	0023
46-86508-3	0949
46-86509-3	0638
46-86511-3	0017
46-86512-3	0016
46-86513-3	0076
46-86513-4	0532
46-86514-3	0006
46-86515-3	0919
46-86516-3	0555
46-86517-3	0006
46-86518-3	1665
46-86518-9	OEM
46-86519-3	0023
46-86520-3	0286
46-86521-3	0077
46-86522-3	0074
46-86522-9	0220
46-86523-3	0137
46-86524-3	OEM
46-86525-1	0102
46-86525-3	0102
46-86526-3	0388
46-86529-3	0398
46-86530-3	0010
46-86530-3(RECT)	0344
46-86531-3	0836
46-86533-3	1274
46-86534-3	1900
46-86535-3	0836
46-86536-3	0532
46-86537-3	5505
46-86538-3	0224
46-86540-3	0155
46-86543-3	0547
46-86544-3	0127
46-86545-3	0590
46-86546-3	0006
46-86547-3	0374
46-86550-3	0191
46-86551-3	0006
46-86551-9	OEM
46-86552	0388
46-86552-3	0388
46-86553-3	0071
46-86554-3	0010
46-86555-3	OEM
46-86556-3	0949
46-86557-3	0309
46-86558-3	0087
46-86559-3	0091
46-86559-3(DIODE)	0133
46-86560-3	0344
46-86561-3	0270
46-86561-9	OEM
46-86562-3	0071
46-86563-3	2040
46-86565-3	1338
46-86566-3	0062
46-86567-3	0638
46-86568-3	0178
46-86569-3	0705
46-86569-9	OEM
46-86570-3	0052
46-86571-3	0312
46-86572-3	0066
46-86573-3	0338
46-86574-3	0527
46-86574-9	2589
46-86577-3	6065
46-86578-3	0006
46-86579-3	0532
46-86581-3	0676
46-86582-3	6108
46-86583-3	0546
46-86584-3	0378
46-86585-9	OEM
46-86587-3	0999
46-86589-3	6692
46-86590-3	0042
46-86591-3	0066
46-86592-3	OEM
46-86595-3	OEM
46-86596-3	0076
46-86598-3	6775
46-86599-3	1597
46-86600-3	3079
46-86602-3	0396
46-86605-3	0466
46-86606-3	OEM
46-86609-3	OEM
46-86610-3	0559
46-86612-3	2514
46-86614-3	0191
46-86615-3	OEM
46-86616-3	0419
46-86617-3	3284
46-86618-3	5890
46-86619-3	0041
46-86620-9	2636
46-86621-3	6946
46-86622-3	5104
46-86623-3	OEM
46-86625-3	0688
46-86626-3	0053
46-86627-3	0440
46-86628-3	0261
46-86629-3	0625
46-86630-3	0066
46-86631-3	OEM
46-86633-3	OEM
46-86634-3	OEM
46-86635-3	1084
46-86637-3	0203
46-86639-3	OEM
46-86641-3	OEM
46-86642-3	0140
46-86643-3	OEM
46-86644-3	OEM
46-86645-3	OEM
46-86646-3	1274
46-86646-9	1274
46-86647-3	0261
46-86648-3	0261
46-86649	0064
46-86649-3	0064
46-86652-3	OEM
46-86653-3	OEM
46-86654-3	0489
46-86660-3	0502
46-86663-9	OEM
46-86664-3	3295
46-86665-3	3335
46-86666-3	0257
46-86667-3	OEM
46-86668-3	OEM
46-86669-3	OEM
46-86670-3	0511
46-86671-3	0161
46-86672-3	3308
46-86673-3	1505
46-86674-3	0274
46-86677-3	0052
46-86678-3	0166
46-86679-3	0148
46-86680-3	2874
46-86681-3	0055
46-86681-9	0055
46-86682-3	0076
46-86683-3	0532
46-86684-3	2526
46-86687-3	2464
46-86689-3	OEM
46-86691-3	OEM
46-86693-3	OEM
46-86694-3	OEM
46-86695-3	OEM
46-86696-3	OEM
46-86700-3	0018
46-86701-3	OEM
46-86702-3	0873
46-86703-3	OEM
46-86704-3	OEM
46-86708-3	OEM
46-86709-3	0340
46-86710-3	OEM
46-86711-3	OEM
46-86712-3	0057
46-86713-3	OEM
46-86715-3	0919
46-86716-3	0710
46-86717-3	3672
46-86718-3	1202
46-86719-3	1338

If replacement code is OEM, contact original manufacturer for replacement.

141

DEVICE TYPE	REPL CODE
46-86720-3	4911
46-86721-3	0396
46-86722-3	1338
46-86724-3	0018
46-86725-3	0688
46-86726-3	1132
46-86727-3	0037
46-86728-3	3760
46-86729-3	0577
46-86730-3	1132
46-86732-3	OEM
46-86733-3	OEM
46-86734-3	0071
46-86735-3	0253
46-86736-3	0076
46-86737-3	0023
46-86738-3	0253
46-86739-3	0023
46-86740-3	0015
46-86741-3	0019
46-86742-3	0296
46-86743-3	0055
46-86744-3	0018
46-86746-3	5361
46-86747-3	OEM
46-86748-3	1900
46-86749-3	OEM
46-86750-3	OEM
46-86751-3	0261
46-86752-3	0282
46-86753-3	0055
46-86753-9	0055
46-86754-3	2589
46-86755-3	OEM
46-86756-3	0525
46-86760-3	OEM
46-86762-3	OEM
46-86763-3	OEM
46-86767-3	OEM
46-86768-3	OEM
46-86770-3	0456
46-86771-3	OEM
46-86772-3	OEM
46-86773-3	OEM
46-86774-3	0019
46-86774-4	0019
46-86778-3	OEM
46-86781-3	0681
46-86782-3	OEM
46-86783-3	OEM
46-86784-3	OEM
46-86786-3	OEM
46-86787-3	OEM
46-86788-3	OEM
46-86789-3	OEM
46-86791-3	OEM
46-86792-3	1157
46-86793-3	0546
46-86794-3	0466
46-86797-3	0062
46-86800-3	OEM
46-86801-3	OEM
46-86802-3	OEM
46-86803-3	OEM
46-86804-3	2882
46-86805-3	0006
46-86807-3	3017
46-86808-3	OEM
46-86809-3	OEM
46-86810-3	OEM
46-86811-3	6055
46-86813-3	OEM
46-86814-3	OEM
46-86815-3	OEM
46-86816-3	OEM
46-86817-3	OEM
46-86818-3	OEM
46-86820-3	1069
46-86823-3	0282
46-86825-3	OEM
46-86826-3	OEM
46-86827-3	OEM
46-86828-3	OEM
46-86830-3	0877
46-86831-3	2195
46-86832-3	OEM
46-86834-3	OEM
46-86835-3	OEM
46-86836-3	0064
46-86837-3	OEM
46-86838-3	OEM
46-86840-3	OEM
46-86841-3	OEM
46-86843-3	0520
46-86844-3	OEM
46-86845-3	OEM
46-86846-3	OEM
46-86847-3	OEM
46-86848-3	OEM
46-86849-9	OEM
46-86850-3	OEM
46-86852-3	OEM
46-86856-3	OEM
46-86858-3	OEM
46-86859-3	OEM
46-86860-3	0553
46-86861-3	OEM
46-86862-3	0111
46-86863-3	3017
46-86864-3	OEM
46-86865-3	OEM
46-86866-3	OEM
46-86867-3	0015
46-86870-3	0076
46-86872-3	OEM
46-86873-3	OEM
46-86874-3	OEM
46-86875-3	OEM
46-86877-3	OEM
46-86878-3	OEM
46-86879-3	0274
46-86880-3	OEM
46-86881-3	OEM
46-86883-3	0372
46-86884-3	OEM
46-86885-3	OEM
46-86886-3	OEM
46-86887-3	2464
46-86888-3	2047
46-86889-3	0018
46-86891-3	OEM
46-86893-3	OEM
46-86894-3	OEM
46-86895-3	OEM
46-86896-3	5082
46-86897-3	0118
46-86898-3	OEM
46-86899-3	OEM
46-86900-3	OEM
46-86901-3	OEM
46-86902-3	OEM
46-86903-3	OEM
46-86904-3	OEM
46-86906-3	0321
46-86906-9	OEM
46-86907-3	0525
46-86908-3	0688
46-86909-3	2529
46-86910-3	2533
46-86912-3	0253
46-86913-3	OEM
46-86914-3	5546
46-86915-3	0041
46-86916-3	6919
46-86917-3	4890
46-86918-3	0023
46-86919-3	OEM
46-86920-3	0819
46-86921-3	0062
46-86922-3	0181
46-86923-3	5381
46-86924-3	0006
46-86925-3	0062
46-86926-3	OEM
46-86927-3	OEM
46-86929-3	OEM
46-86930-3	0006
46-86931-3	0371
46-86932-3	OEM
46-86933-3	0466
46-86934-3	OEM
46-86935-3	OEM
46-86936-3	OEM
46-86937-3	0079
46-86938-3	0037
46-86940-3	OEM
46-86941-3	OEM
46-86942-3	0062
46-86944-3	OEM
46-86946-3	OEM
46-86948-3	OEM
46-86949-3	OEM
46-86950-3	2407
46-86951-3	0723
46-86952-3	2558
46-86953-3	0057
46-86954-3	0041
46-86955-3	OEM
46-86956-3	0527
46-86957-3	OEM
46-86958-3	OEM
46-86959-3	OEM
46-86961-3	OEM
46-86962-3	0219
46-86963-3	1045
46-86964-3	OEM
46-86965-3	OEM
46-86967-3	OEM
46-86968-3	0148
46-86969-3	3474
46-86970-3	OEM
46-86971-3	OEM
46-86972-3	OEM
46-86973-3	OEM
46-86974-3	OEM
46-86975-3	OEM
46-86976-3	OEM
46-86977-3	OEM
46-86978-3	OEM
46-86979-3	OEM
46-86980-3	OEM
46-86982-3	0242
46-86983-3	OEM
46-86984-3	OEM
46-86985-3	OEM
46-86986-3	OEM
46-86987-3	OEM
46-86988-3	OEM
46-86989-3	OEM
46-86990-3	OEM
46-86991-3	OEM
46-86992-3	OEM
46-86993-3	0431
46-86994-3	OEM
46-86995-3	OEM
46-86996-3	0062
46-86997-3	0466
46-86998-3	0041
46-86999-3	0371
46-88676-3	0178
46-96679-3	0148
46-101701-3	OEM
46-101910-3	OEM
46-131000-3	OEM
46-131008-3	OEM
46-131009-3	OEM
46-131012-3	OEM
46-131013-3	OEM
46-131014-3	0107
46-131015-3	OEM
46-131018-3	OEM
46-131019-3	OEM
46-131020-3	OEM
46-131021-3	OEM
46-131022-3	OEM
46-131023-3	OEM
46-131024-3	OEM
46-131025-3	OEM
46-131026-3	OEM
46-131027-3	OEM
46-131028-3	OEM
46-131029-3	OEM
46-131030-3	2172
46-131031-3	OEM
46-131032-3	OEM
46-131033-3	OEM
46-131034-3	OEM
46-131046-3	OEM
46-131047-3	OEM
46-131048-3	OEM
46-131050-3	OEM
46-131051-3	OEM
46-131052-3	OEM
46-131053-3	3480
46-131055-3	OEM
46-131058-3	OEM
46-131059-3	OEM
46-131060-3	2884
46-131065-3	OEM
46-131066-3	OEM
46-131067-3	OEM
46-131068-3	OEM
46-131070-3	OEM
46-131071-3	OEM
46-131072-3	OEM
46-131073-3	0356
46-131074-3	OEM
46-131075-3	OEM
46-131076-3	OEM
46-131077-3	OEM
46-131078-3	OEM
46-131079-3	OEM
46-131080-3	OEM
46-131081-3	OEM
46-131082-3	OEM
46-131083-3	OEM
46-131084-3	OEM
46-131085-3	OEM
46-131086-3	OEM
46-131087-3	OEM
46-131088-3	OEM
46-131089-3	OEM
46-131092-3	OEM
46-131093-3	OEM
46-131095-3	OEM
46-131096-3	OEM
46-131097-3	OEM
46-131098-3	4782
46-131099-3	4286
46-131100-3	4066
46-131101-3	OEM
46-131102-3	OEM
46-131103-3	OEM
46-131104-3	OEM
46-131105-3	OEM
46-131108-3	OEM
46-131110-3	OEM
46-131111-3	OEM
46-131112-3	OEM
46-131113-3	OEM
46-131114-3	OEM
46-131115-3	OEM
46-131116-3	OEM
46-131117-3	OEM
46-131118-3	OEM
46-131119-3	OEM
46-131120-3	OEM
46-131121-3	OEM
46-131122-3	OEM
46-131123-3	OEM
46-131124-3	OEM
46-131125-3	OEM
46-131126-3	0288
46-131127-3	OEM
46-131128-3	OEM
46-131129-3	OEM
46-131130-3	OEM
46-131131-3	4246
46-131132-9	OEM
46-131133-3	OEM
46-131134-3	OEM
46-131135-3	OEM
46-131136-3	5431
46-131137-3	OEM
46-131138-3	OEM
46-131139-3	OEM
46-131141-3	OEM
46-131142-3	OEM
46-131145-3	OEM
46-131146-3	OEM
46-131147-3	OEM
46-131148-3	OEM
46-131149-3	OEM
46-131152-3	OEM
46-131154-3	OEM
46-131155-3	OEM
46-131156-3	OEM
46-131158-3	5746
46-131171-3	OEM
46-131172-3	0024
46-131173-3	OEM
46-131174-3	OEM
46-131175-3	OEM
46-131176-3	OEM
46-131177-3	OEM
46-131178-3	OEM
46-131179-3	OEM
46-131180-3	OEM
46-131181-3	OEM
46-131182-3	OEM
46-131183-3	OEM
46-131185-3	OEM
46-131186-3	OEM
46-131187-3	OEM
46-131188-3	6005
46-131189-3	OEM
46-131190-3	OEM
46-131191-3	OEM
46-131192-3	OEM
46-131195-3	OEM
46-131196-3	OEM
46-131197-3	OEM
46-131198-3	OEM
46-131199-3	OEM
46-131200-3	OEM
46-131202-3	OEM
46-131203-3	4923
46-131204-3	4202
46-131205-3	OEM
46-131206-3	0534
46-131207-3	0552
46-131208-3	0727
46-131209-3	OEM
46-131210-3	OEM
46-131211-3	OEM
46-131212-3	OEM
46-131213-3	OEM
46-131214-3	OEM
46-131215-3	OEM
46-131216-3	OEM
46-131217-9	OEM
46-131219-3	OEM
46-131220-3	OEM
46-131221-3	OEM
46-131222-3	OEM
46-131224-3	OEM
46-131225-3	OEM
46-131226-3	OEM
46-131227-3	OEM
46-131228-3	OEM
46-131229-3	OEM
46-131230-3	0616
46-131231-3	OEM
46-131232-3	OEM
46-131233-3	OEM
46-131234-3	OEM
46-131235-3	OEM
46-131236-3	OEM
46-131237-3	3403
46-131238-3	0412
46-131239-3	OEM
46-131240-3	0057
46-131241-3	OEM
46-131242-3	OEM
46-131243-3	OEM
46-131245-3	4840
46-131246-3	OEM
46-131248-3	OEM
46-131249-3	OEM
46-131251-3	OEM
46-131252-3	OEM
46-131253-3	OEM
46-131254-3	OEM
46-131255-3	OEM
46-131256-3	OEM
46-131257-3	OEM
46-131258-3	OEM
46-131259-3	OEM
46-131260-3	OEM
46-131261-3	OEM
46-131262-3	0330
46-131263-3	OEM
46-131264-3	OEM
46-131265-3	4131
46-131266-3	5162
46-131267-3	OEM
46-131268-3	OEM
46-131269-3	OEM
46-131270-3	OEM
46-131271-3	OEM
46-131272-3	OEM
46-131273-3	OEM
46-131274-3	3130
46-131275-3	OEM
46-131276-3	OEM
46-131277-3	6727
46-131278-3	OEM
46-131279-3	OEM
46-131280-3	OEM
46-131281-3	OEM
46-131283-3	OEM
46-131284-3	OEM
46-131285-3	OEM
46-131286-3	OEM
46-131287-3	OEM
46-131288-3	OEM
46-131289-3	OEM
46-131290-3	OEM
46-131291-3	OEM
46-131292-3	OEM
46-131295-3	OEM
46-131296-3	OEM
46-131298-3	OEM
46-131299-3	OEM
46-131302-3	OEM
46-131304-3	OEM
46-131305-3	OEM
46-131306-3	OEM
46-131307-3	OEM
46-131308-3	OEM
46-131313-3	OEM
46-131314-3	OEM
46-131315-3	0387
46-131316-3	OEM
46-131321-3	OEM
46-131322-3	OEM
46-131323-3	OEM
46-131324-3	OEM
46-131326-3	OEM
46-131327-3	OEM
46-131328-3	OEM
46-131329-3	OEM
46-131330-3	OEM
46-131331-3	OEM
46-131332-3	OEM
46-131333-3	OEM
46-131334-3	OEM
46-131335-3	OEM
46-131336-3	OEM
46-131339-3	OEM
46-131340-3	OEM
46-131341-3	2929
46-131342-3	2998
46-131343-3	3068
46-131344-3	OEM
46-131345-3	OEM
46-131347-3	OEM
46-131348-3	OEM
46-131349-3	3333
46-131350-3	OEM
46-131351-3	3410
46-131352-3	OEM
46-131353-3	OEM
46-131354-3	OEM
46-131357-3	1561
46-131358-3	OEM
46-131360-3	OEM
46-131361-3	OEM
46-131362-3	OEM
46-131363-3	OEM
46-131364-3	OEM
46-131365-3	OEM
46-131366-3	OEM
46-131367-3	OEM
46-131368-3	OEM
46-131369-3	OEM
46-131370-3	OEM
46-131371-3	OEM
46-131373-3	OEM
46-131378-3	OEM
46-131382-3	OEM
46-131383-3	OEM
46-131384-3	OEM
46-131385-3	OEM
46-131386-3	OEM
46-131387-3	OEM
46-131388-3	OEM
46-131389-3	OEM
46-131390-3	OEM
46-131391-3	OEM
46-131393-3	OEM
46-131395-3	OEM
46-131396-3	1281
46-131398-3	OEM
46-131399-3	OEM
46-131400-3	OEM
46-131401-3	4310
46-131404-3	OEM
46-131405-3	OEM
46-131406-3	OEM
46-131407-3	OEM
46-131408-3	OEM
46-131409-3	OEM
46-131410-3	OEM
46-131411-3	OEM
46-131412-3	OEM
46-131413-3	OEM
46-131414-3	OEM
46-131415-3	OEM
46-131416-3	OEM
46-131418-3	OEM
46-131419-3	OEM
46-131420-3	OEM
46-131421-3	OEM
46-131423-3	OEM
46-131424-3	OEM
46-131428-3	OEM
46-131430-3	OEM
46-131431-3	OEM
46-131432-3	3206
46-131433-3	3902
46-131434-3	OEM
46-131435-3	OEM
46-131436-3	OEM
46-131438-9	3857
46-131439-3	OEM
46-131452-3	OEM
46-131453-3	OEM
46-131454-3	OEM
46-131455-3	OEM
46-131456-3	OEM
46-131457-3	OEM
46-131458-3	OEM
46-131459-3	OEM
46-131460-3	OEM
46-131461-3	OEM
46-131462-3	OEM
46-131463-3	OEM
46-131464-3	OEM
46-131465-3	OEM
46-131466-3	OEM
46-131467-3	OEM
46-131469-3	OEM
46-131470-3	OEM
46-131471-3	OEM
46-131472-3	OEM
46-131473-3	OEM
46-131474-3	OEM
46-131475-3	OEM
46-131476-3	OEM
46-131477-3	OEM
46-131478-3	OEM
46-131479-3	OEM
46-131480-3	OEM
46-131481-3	OEM
46-131482-3	OEM
46-131483-3	OEM
46-131484-3	OEM
46-131485-3	OEM
46-131486-3	OEM
46-131488-3	OEM
46-131491-3	OEM
46-131492-3	OEM
46-131493-3	OEM
46-131494-9	OEM
46-131495-3	OEM
46-131500-3	OEM
46-131503-3	OEM
46-131504-3	OEM
46-131505-3	OEM
46-131507-3	0387
46-131508-3	OEM
46-131509-3	OEM
46-131510-3	OEM
46-131511-3	OEM
46-131512-3	OEM
46-131513-3	OEM
46-131514-3	2843
46-131515-3	3054
46-131516-3	1775
46-131519-3	6242
46-131520-3	OEM
46-131521-3	OEM
46-131522-3	OEM
46-131523-3	OEM
46-131524-3	OEM
46-131525-3	OEM
46-131526-3	OEM
46-131531-3	OEM
46-131532-3	OEM
46-131533-3	OEM
46-131535-3	OEM
46-131536-3	OEM
46-131538-3	OEM
46-131539-3	OEM
46-131540-3	OEM
46-131541-3	OEM
46-131542-3	OEM
46-131543-3	OEM
46-131544-3	OEM
46-131545-3	OEM
46-131546-3	OEM
46-131547-3	OEM
46-131548-3	OEM
46-131549-3	OEM
46-131551-3	OEM
46-131552-3	OEM
46-131553-3	OEM
46-131554-3	OEM
46-131555-3	OEM
46-131561-3	OEM
46-131562-3	OEM
46-131563-3	OEM
46-131564-3	OEM
46-131565-3	OEM
46-131566-3	OEM
46-131567-3	OEM
46-131568-3	OEM
46-131569-3	OEM
46-131570-3	OEM
46-131571-3	OEM
46-131572-3	OEM
46-131573-3	OEM
46-131575-3	OEM
46-131576-3	OEM
46-131577-3	3344
46-131578-3	OEM
46-131579-3	OEM
46-131580-3	OEM
46-131581-3	OEM
46-131582-3	OEM
46-131583-3	OEM
46-131584-3	OEM
46-131585-3	1631
46-131586-3	OEM
46-131587-3	OEM
46-131588-3	OEM
46-131589-3	OEM
46-131590-3	OEM
46-131591-3	OEM
46-131592-3	OEM
46-131593-3	OEM
46-131594-3	OEM
46-131595-3	OEM
46-131596-3	OEM
46-131597-3	OEM
46-131598-3	OEM
46-131599-3	OEM
46-131600-3	OEM
46-131601-3	OEM
46-131602-3	OEM
46-131604-3	OEM
46-131605-3	OEM
46-131606-3	OEM
46-131609-3	OEM
46-131610-3	OEM
46-131611-3	OEM
46-131613-3	OEM
46-131614-3	OEM
46-131615-3	OEM
46-131616-3	OEM
46-131617-3	OEM
46-131618-3	OEM
46-131619-3	OEM
46-131620-3	OEM
46-131621-3	OEM
46-131622-3	OEM
46-131623-3	OEM
46-131624-3	OEM
46-131625-3	OEM
46-131626-3	OEM
46-131627-3	OEM
46-131629-3	2099
46-131631-3	OEM
46-131632-3	OEM
46-131633-3	OEM
46-131634-3	OEM
46-131635-3	OEM
46-131636-3	OEM
46-131637-3	OEM
46-131638-3	OEM
46-131639-3	OEM
46-131640-3	OEM
46-131641-3	OEM
46-131642-3	OEM
46-131644-3	OEM
46-131645-3	OEM
46-131646-3	OEM
46-131647-3	OEM
46-131648-3	OEM
46-131649-3	OEM
46-131650-3	OEM
46-131651-3	OEM
46-131652-3	OEM
46-131655-3	OEM
46-131656-3	0457
46-131658-3	OEM
46-131659-3	OEM
46-131660-3	OEM
46-131662-3	OEM
46-131664-3	OEM
46-131665-3	OEM
46-131666-3	OEM
46-131667-3	OEM
46-131669-3	OEM
46-131670-3	OEM
46-131671-3	OEM
46-131672-3	OEM
46-131675-3	OEM
46-131676-3	OEM
46-131677-3	OEM
46-131678-3	0034
46-131680-3	OEM
46-131681-3	OEM
46-131682-3	OEM
46-131683-3	2397
46-131685-3	OEM
46-131687-3	OEM
46-131688-3	OEM
46-131689-3	OEM
46-131693-3	OEM
46-131694-3	OEM
46-131695-3	OEM

If replacement code is OEM, contact original manufacturer for replacement.

DEVICE TYPE	REPL CODE	DEVICE TYPE	REPL CODE	DEVICE TYPE	REPL CODE	DEVICE TYPE	REPL CODE	DEVICE TYPE	REPL CODE	DEVICE TYPE	REPL CODE	DEVICE TYPE	REPL CODE
46-131696-3	OEM	46-131862-3	OEM	46-132039-3	OEM	46-132204-3	OEM	46-132348-3	OEM	46-132511-3	OEM	46-132666-3	OEM
46-131697-3	OEM	46-131863-3	OEM	46-132040-3	OEM	46-132205-3	OEM	46-132349-3	OEM	46-132512-3	OEM	46-132667-3	OEM
46-131699-3	OEM	46-131864-3	OEM	46-132041-3	OEM	46-132206-3	OEM	46-132350-3	OEM	46-132513-3	OEM	46-132668-3	OEM
46-131700-3	OEM	46-131865-3	OEM	46-132042-3	OEM	46-132207-3	OEM	46-132351-3	OEM	46-132514-3	OEM	46-132669-3	OEM
46-131701-3	OEM	46-131866-3	OEM	46-132043-3	OEM	46-132208-3	OEM	46-132352-3	OEM	46-132515-3	OEM	46-132670-3	OEM
46-131702-3	OEM	46-131868-3	OEM	46-132044-3	OEM	46-132209-3	OEM	46-132354-3	OEM	46-132517-3	OEM	46-132671-3	OEM
46-131703-3	OEM	46-131869-3	OEM	46-132045-3	OEM	46-132210-3	OEM	46-132355-3	OEM	46-132518-3	OEM	46-132672-3	OEM
46-131704-3	OEM	46-131870-3	OEM	46-132046-3	OEM	46-132211-3	OEM	46-132356-3	OEM	46-132519-3	OEM	46-132673-3	OEM
46-131705-3	OEM	46-131871-3	OEM	46-132048-3	OEM	46-132213-3	OEM	46-132358-3	OEM	46-132520-3	OEM	46-132674-3	OEM
46-131712-3	OEM	46-131872-3	OEM	46-132050-3	OEM	46-132214-3	OEM	46-132359-3	OEM	46-132521-3	OEM	46-132675-3	OEM
46-131713-3	OEM	46-131873-3	OEM	46-132051-3	OEM	46-132215-3	OEM	46-132360-3	OEM	46-132525-3	OEM	46-132677-3	OEM
46-131715-3	OEM	46-131874-3	OEM	46-132052-3	OEM	46-132216-3	OEM	46-132361-3	OEM	46-132526-3	OEM	46-132678-3	OEM
46-131716-3	OEM	46-131875-3	OEM	46-132053-3	OEM	46-132220-3	OEM	46-132362-3	OEM	46-132527-3	OEM	46-132679-3	OEM
46-131717-3	OEM	46-131876-3	OEM	46-132054-3	OEM	46-132221-3	OEM	46-132364-3	OEM	46-132528-3	OEM	46-132680-3	OEM
46-131718-3	OEM	46-131877-3	OEM	46-132056-3	OEM	46-132222-3	OEM	46-132365-3	OEM	46-132529-3	OEM	46-132681-3	OEM
46-131719-3	OEM	46-131878-3	OEM	46-132059-3	OEM	46-132228-3	OEM	46-132367-3	OEM	46-132532-3	OEM	46-132682-3	OEM
46-131721-3	OEM	46-131882-3	OEM	46-132061-3	OEM	46-132231-3	OEM	46-132368-3	OEM	46-132534-3	OEM	46-132683-3	OEM
46-131723-3	OEM	46-131885-3	OEM	46-132062-3	OEM	46-132232-3	OEM	46-132369-3	OEM	46-132535-3	OEM	46-132684-3	OEM
46-131724-3	OEM	46-131895-3	OEM	46-132063-3	OEM	46-132233-3	OEM	46-132371-3	OEM	46-132536-3	OEM	46-132689-3	OEM
46-131725-3	OEM	46-131896-3	OEM	46-132064-3	OEM	46-132234-3	OEM	46-132372-3	OEM	46-132539-3	OEM	46-132690-3	OEM
46-131726-3	OEM	46-131897-3	OEM	46-132065-3	OEM	46-132235-3	OEM	46-132373-3	OEM	46-132540-3	OEM	46-132691-3	OEM
46-131727-3	OEM	46-131898-3	OEM	46-132066-3	OEM	46-132237-3	OEM	46-132374-3	OEM	46-132542-3	OEM	46-132692-3	OEM
46-131729-3	OEM	46-131899-3	OEM	46-132067-3	OEM	46-132238-3	OEM	46-132375-3	OEM	46-132543-3	OEM	46-132694-3	OEM
46-131730-3	OEM	46-131900-3	OEM	46-132068-3	OEM	46-132242-3	OEM	46-132376-3	OEM	46-132544-3	OEM	46-132695-3	OEM
46-131734-3	OEM	46-131901-3	OEM	46-132069-3	OEM	46-132243-3	OEM	46-132377-3	OEM	46-132545-3	OEM	46-132697-3	OEM
46-131735-3	OEM	46-131902-3	OEM	46-132070-3	2318	46-132244-3	OEM	46-132378-3	OEM	46-132546-3	OEM	46-132698-3	OEM
46-131736-3	OEM	46-131903-3	OEM	46-132071-3	OEM	46-132245-3	OEM	46-132379-3	OEM	46-132547-3	OEM	46-132699-3	OEM
46-131737-3	OEM	46-131905-3	0678	46-132072-3	OEM	46-132246-3	OEM	46-132381-3	OEM	46-132548-3	OEM	46-132702-3	OEM
46-131739-3	OEM	46-131906-3	OEM	46-132075-3	OEM	46-132247-3	OEM	46-132382-3	OEM	46-132549-3	OEM	46-132703-3	OEM
46-131740-3	OEM	46-131914-3	OEM	46-132076-3	OEM	46-132248-3	OEM	46-132383-3	OEM	46-132550-3	OEM	46-132704-3	OEM
46-131741-3	OEM	46-131915-3	OEM	46-132077-3	OEM	46-132249-3	OEM	46-132386-3	OEM	46-132551-3	OEM	46-132705-3	OEM
46-131744-3	OEM	46-131916-3	OEM	46-132079-3	OEM	46-132250-3	OEM	46-132389-3	OEM	46-132552-3	OEM	46-132706-3	OEM
46-131745-3	0311	46-131917-3	OEM	46-132080-3	OEM	46-132252-3	OEM	46-132390-3	OEM	46-132553-3	OEM	46-132708-3	OEM
46-131746-3	OEM	46-131918-3	OEM	46-132083-3	OEM	46-132253-3	OEM	46-132391-3	OEM	46-132554-3	OEM	46-132709-3	OEM
46-131747-3	OEM	46-131919-3	OEM	46-132084-3	OEM	46-132256-3	OEM	46-132392-3	OEM	46-132555-3	OEM	46-132710-3	OEM
46-131751-3	OEM	46-131920-3	OEM	46-132085-3	OEM	46-132257-3	OEM	46-132393-3	OEM	46-132556-3	OEM	46-132711-3	OEM
46-131755-3	OEM	46-131921-3	OEM	46-132086-3	OEM	46-132259-3	OEM	46-132394-3	0101	46-132557-3	OEM	46-132712-3	OEM
46-131756-3	OEM	46-131922-3	OEM	46-132087-3	OEM	46-132260-3	OEM	46-132395-3	OEM	46-132558-3	OEM	46-132713-3	OEM
46-131757-3	OEM	46-131923-3	OEM	46-132088-3	OEM	46-132261-3	OEM	46-132396-3	OEM	46-132560-3	OEM	46-132714-3	OEM
46-131758-3	OEM	46-131924-3	OEM	46-132090-3	OEM	46-132263-3	OEM	46-132397-3	OEM	46-132561-3	OEM	46-132715-3	OEM
46-131759-3	OEM	46-131926-3	OEM	46-132092-3	OEM	46-132264-3	OEM	46-132398-3	2843	46-132562-3	OEM	46-132716-3	OEM
46-131760-3	OEM	46-131927-3	OEM	46-132093-3	OEM	46-132265-3	OEM	46-132399-3	OEM	46-132563-3	OEM	46-132717-3	OEM
46-131761-3	OEM	46-131928-3	OEM	46-132094-3	OEM	46-132266-3	OEM	46-132404-3	OEM	46-132564-3	OEM	46-132718-3	OEM
46-131762-3	OEM	46-131929-3	OEM	46-132099-3	OEM	46-132268-3	OEM	46-132405-3	OEM	46-132565-3	OEM	46-132719-3	OEM
46-131766-3	OEM	46-131931-3	OEM	46-132101-3	OEM	46-132269-3	OEM	46-132407-3	OEM	46-132566-3	OEM	46-132720-3	OEM
46-131767-3	OEM	46-131932-3	OEM	46-132104-3	OEM	46-132270-3	OEM	46-132408-3	OEM	46-132567-3	OEM	46-132721-3	OEM
46-131768-3	OEM	46-131933-3	OEM	46-132105-3	OEM	46-132271-3	OEM	46-132409-3	OEM	46-132568-3	OEM	46-132722-3	OEM
46-131770-3	OEM	46-131934-3	OEM	46-132106-3	OEM	46-132272-3	OEM	46-132411-3	OEM	46-132569-3	OEM	46-132726-3	OEM
46-131771-3	OEM	46-131935-3	OEM	46-132108-3	OEM	46-132273-3	OEM	46-132412-3	OEM	46-132572-3	OEM	46-132727-3	OEM
46-131772-3	4311	46-131937-3	OEM	46-132109-3	OEM	46-132274-3	OEM	46-132413-3	OEM	46-132574-3	OEM	46-132728-3	OEM
46-131773-3	OEM	46-131938-3	OEM	46-132111-3	OEM	46-132275-3	OEM	46-132415-3	OEM	46-132575-3	OEM	46-132729-3	OEM
46-131774-3	1158	46-131940-3	OEM	46-132112-3	OEM	46-132277-3	OEM	46-132416-3	OEM	46-132578-3	OEM	46-132730-3	OEM
46-131776-3	OEM	46-131941-3	OEM	46-132113-3	OEM	46-132279-3	OEM	46-132417-3	OEM	46-132579-3	OEM	46-132731-3	OEM
46-131777-3	OEM	46-131942-3	OEM	46-132115-3	OEM	46-132280-3	OEM	46-132418-3	OEM	46-132580-3	OEM	46-132732-3	OEM
46-131778-3	OEM	46-131943-3	OEM	46-132116-3	OEM	46-132281-3	OEM	46-132419-3	OEM	46-132582-3	OEM	46-132733-3	OEM
46-131779-3	OEM	46-131944-3	OEM	46-132117-3	OEM	46-132283-3	OEM	46-132420-3	OEM	46-132583-3	OEM	46-132734-3	OEM
46-131780-3	OEM	46-131946-3	OEM	46-132118-3	OEM	46-132284-3	OEM	46-132422-3	0034	46-132588-3	OEM	46-132735-3	OEM
46-131781-3	OEM	46-131947-3	OEM	46-132119-3	OEM	46-132285-3	OEM	46-132423-3	OEM	46-132589-3	OEM	46-132736-3	OEM
46-131782-3	OEM	46-131948-3	OEM	46-132120-3	OEM	46-132286-3	2079	46-132424-3	OEM	46-132590-3	OEM	46-132737-3	OEM
46-131783-3	OEM	46-131950-3	OEM	46-132122-3	OEM	46-132287-3	3896	46-132425-3	OEM	46-132593-3	OEM	46-132738-3	OEM
46-131785-3	OEM	46-131951-3	OEM	46-132124-3	OEM	46-132288-3	OEM	46-132426-3	OEM	46-132595-3	OEM	46-132739-3	OEM
46-131786-3	OEM	46-131952-3	OEM	46-132127-3	OEM	46-132289-3	OEM	46-132428-3	OEM	46-132598-3	OEM	46-132740-3	OEM
46-131787-3	3206	46-131954-3	OEM	46-132129-3	OEM	46-132290-3	OEM	46-132430-3	OEM	46-132600-3	OEM	46-132741-3	OEM
46-131788-3	OEM	46-131955-3	OEM	46-132130-3	OEM	46-132291-3	OEM	46-132433-3	OEM	46-132604-3	OEM	46-132744-3	OEM
46-131789-3	OEM	46-131956-3	OEM	46-132131-3	OEM	46-132293-3	OEM	46-132434-3	OEM	46-132605-3	OEM	46-132745-3	OEM
46-131790-3	OEM	46-131958-3	OEM	46-132132-3	OEM	46-132295-3	OEM	46-132435-3	OEM	46-132607-3	OEM	46-132747-3	OEM
46-131793-3	0619	46-131960-3	OEM	46-132133-3	OEM	46-132296-3	OEM	46-132437-3	OEM	46-132608-3	OEM	46-132748-3	OEM
46-131794-3	OEM	46-131962-3	OEM	46-132134-3	OEM	46-132298-3	OEM	46-132438-3	OEM	46-132609-3	OEM	46-132750-3	OEM
46-131798-3	OEM	46-131963-3	OEM	46-132135-3	OEM	46-132299-3	OEM	46-132440-3	OEM	46-132610-3	OEM	46-132751-3	OEM
46-131799-3	OEM	46-131964-3	OEM	46-132137-3	OEM	46-132300-3	OEM	46-132441-3	OEM	46-132611-3	OEM	46-132754-3	OEM
46-131800-3	OEM	46-131968-3	OEM	46-132139-3	OEM	46-132301-3	OEM	46-132442-3	OEM	46-132612-3	OEM	46-132758-3	OEM
46-131801-3	0619	46-131969-3	4054	46-132142-3	OEM	46-132302-3	OEM	46-132443-3	OEM	46-132617-3	OEM	46-132760-3	OEM
46-131802-3	OEM	46-131970-3	OEM	46-132143-3	OEM	46-132303-3	3645	46-132444-3	OEM	46-132618-3	OEM	46-132763-3	OEM
46-131804-3	OEM	46-131971-3	OEM	46-132149-3	OEM	46-132304-3	OEM	46-132445-3	OEM	46-132619-3	OEM	46-132765-3	OEM
46-131806-3	OEM	46-131972-3	OEM	46-132150-3	OEM	46-132305-3	4009	46-132446-3	OEM	46-132620-3	OEM	46-132766-3	OEM
46-131807-3	OEM	46-131974-3	OEM	46-132152-3	OEM	46-132307-3	OEM	46-132447-3	OEM	46-132621-3	OEM	46-132767-3	OEM
46-131808-3	OEM	46-131975-3	OEM	46-132153-3	OEM	46-132308-3	OEM	46-132448-3	OEM	46-132622-3	OEM	46-132768-3	OEM
46-131809-3	OEM	46-131976-3	OEM	46-132154-3	OEM	46-132309-3	OEM	46-132449-3	OEM	46-132623-3	OEM	46-132769-3	OEM
46-131812-3	OEM	46-131977-3	OEM	46-132155-3	OEM	46-132310-3	OEM	46-132450-3	OEM	46-132624-3	OEM	46-132770-3	OEM
46-131813-3	OEM	46-131978-3	OEM	46-132156-3	OEM	46-132311-3	OEM	46-132451-3	OEM	46-132625-3	OEM	46-132771-3	OEM
46-131814-3	OEM	46-131979-3	OEM	46-132157-3	OEM	46-132312-3	OEM	46-132452-3	OEM	46-132627-3	OEM	46-132772-3	OEM
46-131816-3	OEM	46-131980-3	OEM	46-132158-3	OEM	46-132313-3	OEM	46-132453-3	OEM	46-132628-3	OEM	46-132773-3	OEM
46-131817-3	OEM	46-131981-3	OEM	46-132159-3	OEM	46-132314-3	OEM	46-132454-3	OEM	46-132629-3	OEM	46-132774-3	OEM
46-131818-3	OEM	46-131982-3	OEM	46-132161-3	OEM	46-132315-3	OEM	46-132455-3	OEM	46-132630-3	OEM	46-132775-3	OEM
46-131822-3	OEM	46-131986-3	OEM	46-132162-3	OEM	46-132316-3	OEM	46-132456-3	OEM	46-132631-3	OEM	46-132778-3	OEM
46-131825-3	OEM	46-131987-3	OEM	46-132163-3	OEM	46-132317-3	OEM	46-132459-3	OEM	46-132634-3	OEM	46-132779-3	OEM
46-131826-3	OEM	46-131988-3	OEM	46-132164-3	OEM	46-132318-3	OEM	46-132460-3	OEM	46-132635-3	OEM	46-132781-3	OEM
46-131827-3	OEM	46-131989-3	OEM	46-132165-3	OEM	46-132320-3	OEM	46-132461-3	OEM	46-132636-3	OEM	46-132783-3	OEM
46-131828-3	OEM	46-131990-3	OEM	46-132166-3	OEM	46-132321-3	OEM	46-132462-3	OEM	46-132637-3	2104	46-132784-3	OEM
46-131831-3	OEM	46-131992-3	OEM	46-132167-3	OEM	46-132323-3	OEM	46-132463-3	OEM	46-132638-3	2109	46-132786-3	OEM
46-131832-3	OEM	46-131993-3	OEM	46-132169-3	OEM	46-132324-3	OEM	46-132464-3	OEM	46-132639-3	OEM	46-132787-3	OEM
46-131837-3	OEM	46-131994-3	OEM	46-132171-3	OEM	46-132325-3	OEM	46-132465-3	OEM	46-132640-3	OEM	46-132792-3	OEM
46-131838-3	OEM	46-131995-3	OEM	46-132172-3	OEM	46-132326-3	OEM	46-132473-3	OEM	46-132645-3	OEM	46-132793-3	OEM
46-131839-3	OEM	46-131996-3	OEM	46-132175-3	OEM	46-132327-3	OEM	46-132474-3	OEM	46-132647-3	4032	46-132794-3	OEM
46-131840-3	OEM	46-131997-3	OEM	46-132177-3	OEM	46-132328-3	OEM	46-132475-3	OEM	46-132648-3	2330	46-132796-3	OEM
46-131841-3	OEM	46-131998-3	OEM	46-132178-3	OEM	46-132329-3	OEM	46-132476-3	OEM	46-132649-3	4843	46-132797-3	OEM
46-131844-3	OEM	46-131999-3	OEM	46-132179-3	OEM	46-132330-3	OEM	46-132480-3	OEM	46-132650-3	OEM	46-132798-3	OEM
46-131847-3	OEM	46-132000-3	OEM	46-132180-3	OEM	46-132333-3	OEM	46-132483-3	OEM	46-132651-3	OEM	46-132799-3	OEM
46-131848-3	OEM	46-132001-3	OEM	46-132182-3	OEM	46-132334-3	OEM	46-132485-3	OEM	46-132652-3	OEM	46-132802-3	OEM
46-131849-3	OEM	46-132002-3	OEM	46-132183-3	OEM	46-132335-3	OEM	46-132489-3	OEM	46-132653-3	OEM	46-132803-3	OEM
46-131850-3	OEM	46-132003-3	OEM	46-132185-3	OEM	46-132336-3	OEM	46-132490-3	OEM	46-132654-3	OEM	46-132804-3	OEM
46-131851-3	OEM	46-132004-3	OEM	46-132188-3	OEM	46-132338-3	OEM	46-132498-3	OEM	46-132655-3	OEM	46-132805-3	OEM
46-131853-3	OEM	46-132005-3	OEM	46-132190-3	OEM	46-132339-3	OEM	46-132499-3	OEM	46-132657-3	OEM	46-132806-3	OEM
46-131854-3	OEM	46-132006-3	OEM	46-132191-3	OEM	46-132340-3	OEM	46-132500-3	OEM	46-132660-3	OEM	46-132810-3	OEM
46-131857-3	OEM	46-132007-3	OEM	46-132192-3	OEM	46-132341-3	OEM	46-132501-3	OEM	46-132661-3	OEM	46-132811-3	OEM
46-131858-3	OEM	46-132009-3	OEM	46-132193-3	OEM	46-132342-3	OEM	46-132502-3	OEM	46-132662-3	OEM	46-132812-3	OEM
46-131859-3	OEM	46-132022-3	OEM	46-132197-3	OEM	46-132343-3	OEM	46-132506-3	OEM	46-132663-3	OEM	46-132813-3	OEM
46-131860-3	OEM	46-132023-3	1796	46-132201-3	OEM	46-132344-3	OEM	46-132507-3	OEM	46-132664-3	OEM	46-132814-3	OEM
46-131861-3	OEM	46-132024-3	OEM	46-132203-3	OEM	46-132347-3	OEM	46-132510-3	OEM	46-132665-3	OEM	46-132815-3	OEM

If replacement code is OEM, contact original manufacturer for replacement.

DEVICE TYPE	REPL CODE
46-132816-3	OEM
46-132817-3	OEM
46-132820-3	OEM
46-132821-3	OEM
46-132826-3	OEM
46-132827-3	OEM
46-132828-3	OEM
46-132829-3	OEM
46-132830-3	OEM
46-132831-3	OEM
46-132832-3	OEM
46-132833-3	OEM
46-132834-3	OEM
46-132835-3	OEM
46-132836-3	OEM
46-132837-3	OEM
46-132838-3	OEM
46-132839-3	OEM
46-132840-3	OEM
46-132843-3	OEM
46-132844-3	OEM
46-132845-3	OEM
46-132846-3	OEM
46-132848-3	OEM
46-132849-3	OEM
46-132850-3	0619
46-132852-3	OEM
46-132853-3	OEM
46-132854-3	OEM
46-132855-3	OEM
46-132856-3	OEM
46-132857-3	OEM
46-132858-3	OEM
46-132859-3	OEM
46-132860-3	OEM
46-132865-3	OEM
46-132866-3	OEM
46-132867-3	OEM
46-132868-3	OEM
46-132869-3	OEM
46-132870-3	OEM
46-132871-3	OEM
46-132872-3	OEM
46-132873-3	OEM
46-132874-3	OEM
46-132875-3	OEM
46-132876-3	OEM
46-132877-3	OEM
46-132878-3	OEM
46-132879-3	OEM
46-132882-3	OEM
46-132883-3	OEM
46-132884-3	1644
46-132885-3	OEM
46-132886-3	4349
46-132888-3	OEM
46-132891-3	OEM
46-132893-3	OEM
46-132894-3	OEM
46-132895-3	OEM
46-132896-3	OEM
46-132897-3	OEM
46-132898-3	OEM
46-132899-3	OEM
46-132900-3	OEM
46-132902-3	OEM
46-132904-3	OEM
46-132906-3	OEM
46-132907-3	OEM
46-132908-3	OEM
46-132909-3	OEM
46-132912-3	OEM
46-132914-3	OEM
46-132915-3	OEM
46-132917-3	OEM
46-132918-3	OEM
46-132919-3	OEM
46-132920-3	OEM
46-132921-3	OEM
46-132922-3	OEM
46-132923-3	OEM
46-132924-3	OEM
46-132925-3	OEM
46-132929-3	OEM
46-132930-3	OEM
46-132931-3	3473
46-132932-3	OEM
46-132934-3	OEM
46-132935-3	OEM
46-132939-3	OEM
46-132940-3	OEM
46-132941-3	OEM
46-132943-3	OEM
46-132947-3	OEM
46-132949-3	OEM
46-132950-3	OEM
46-132951-3	OEM
46-132952-3	OEM
46-132953-3	OEM
46-132954-3	OEM
46-132955-3	OEM
46-132956-3	OEM
46-132957-3	OEM
46-132958-3	OEM
46-132959-3	OEM
46-132960-3	OEM
46-132961-3	OEM
46-132962-3	OEM
46-132963-3	OEM

DEVICE TYPE	REPL CODE
46-132964-3	OEM
46-132965-3	OEM
46-132966-3	OEM
46-132967-3	OEM
46-132968-3	OEM
46-132969-3	OEM
46-132970-3	OEM
46-132972-3	OEM
46-132973-3	OEM
46-132974-3	OEM
46-132975-3	OEM
46-132976-3	OEM
46-132977-3	OEM
46-132978-3	OEM
46-132979-3	OEM
46-132986-3	OEM
46-132988-3	OEM
46-132992-3	OEM
46-132997-3	OEM
46-133000-3	OEM
46-133001-3	OEM
46-133004-3	OEM
46-133005-3	OEM
46-133009-3	OEM
46-133010-3	OEM
46-133011-3	OEM
46-133012-3	OEM
46-133013-3	OEM
46-133017-3	OEM
46-133018-3	OEM
46-133019-3	OEM
46-133021-3	OEM
46-133022-3	OEM
46-133024-3	OEM
46-133025-3	OEM
46-133027-3	OEM
46-133028-3	OEM
46-133029-3	OEM
46-133034-3	OEM
46-133035-3	OEM
46-133036-3	OEM
46-133037-3	OEM
46-133038-3	OEM
46-133039-3	OEM
46-133040-3	OEM
46-133042-3	OEM
46-133043-3	OEM
46-133044-3	OEM
46-133045-3	OEM
46-133046-3	OEM
46-133047-3	OEM
46-133048-3	OEM
46-133050-3	OEM
46-133051-3	OEM
46-133052-3	OEM
46-133057-3	OEM
46-133058-3	OEM
46-133059-3	OEM
46-133061-3	OEM
46-133062-3	OEM
46-133063-3	OEM
46-133064-3	OEM
46-133066-3	OEM
46-133067-3	OEM
46-133068-3	OEM
46-133069-3	OEM
46-133071-3	OEM
46-133072-3	OEM
46-133073-3	OEM
46-133074-3	OEM
46-133075-3	OEM
46-133076-3	OEM
46-133077-3	OEM
46-133078-3	OEM
46-133079-3	OEM
46-133080-3	OEM
46-133081-3	OEM
46-133082-3	OEM
46-133083-3	OEM
46-133084-3	OEM
46-133085-3	OEM
46-133086-3	OEM
46-133087-3	OEM
46-133088-3	OEM
46-133089-3	OEM
46-133090-3	OEM
46-133091-3	OEM
46-133092-3	OEM
46-133093-3	OEM
46-133094-3	OEM
46-133095-3	OEM
46-133103-3	OEM
46-133105-3	OEM
46-133106-3	OEM
46-133107-3	OEM
46-133108-3	OEM
46-133109-3	OEM
46-133110-3	OEM
46-133111-3	OEM
46-133112-3	OEM
46-133113-3	OEM
46-133114-3	OEM
46-133116-3	OEM
46-133119-3	OEM
46-133120-3	OEM
46-133121-3	OEM
46-133122-3	OEM
46-133123-3	OEM
46-133124-3	OEM

DEVICE TYPE	REPL CODE
46-133125-3	OEM
46-133126-3	OEM
46-133127-3	OEM
46-133136-3	OEM
46-133137-3	OEM
46-133142-3	OEM
46-133143-3	OEM
46-133144-3	OEM
46-133145-3	OEM
46-133147-3	OEM
46-133148-3	OEM
46-133149-3	OEM
46-133154-3	OEM
46-133155-3	OEM
46-133156-3	OEM
46-133158-3	OEM
46-133159-3	OEM
46-133160-3	OEM
46-133161-3	OEM
46-133166-3	OEM
46-133169-3	OEM
46-133182-3	OEM
46-133183-3	OEM
46-133184-3	OEM
46-133185-3	OEM
46-133186-3	OEM
46-133187-3	OEM
46-133188-3	OEM
46-133190-3	OEM
46-133192-3	OEM
46-133193-3	OEM
46-133194-3	OEM
46-133195-3	OEM
46-133200-3	OEM
46-133201-3	OEM
46-133206-3	OEM
46-133207-3	OEM
46-133208-3	OEM
46-133209-3	OEM
46-133210-3	OEM
46-133211-3	OEM
46-133212-3	OEM
46-133213-3	OEM
46-133214-3	OEM
46-133216-3	OEM
46-133221-3	OEM
46-133240-3	OEM
46-133244-3	OEM
46-133245-3	OEM
46-133246-3	OEM
46-133253-3	OEM
46-133261-3	OEM
46-133262-3	OEM
46-133263-3	OEM
46-133270-3	OEM
46-133274-3	OEM
46-133275-3	2180
46-133276-3	OEM
46-133278-3	OEM
46-133283-3	OEM
46-133284-3	OEM
46-133285-3	OEM
46-133293-3	6043
46-133300-3	OEM
46-133301-3	OEM
46-133302-3	OEM
46-133304-3	OEM
46-133305-3	OEM
46-133306-3	OEM
46-133307-3	OEM
46-133315-3	OEM
46-133316-3	OEM
46-133321-3	OEM
46-133322-3	OEM
46-133323-3	OEM
46-133325-3	3406
46-133326-3	OEM
46-133327-3	OEM
46-133328-3	OEM
46-133329-3	OEM
46-133330-3	OEM
46-133331-3	OEM
46-133332-3	OEM
46-133333-3	OEM
46-133334-3	OEM
46-133336-3	OEM
46-133337-3	OEM
46-133339-3	OEM
46-133340-3	OEM
46-133341-3	OEM
46-133342-3	OEM
46-133343-3	OEM
46-133344-3	3473
46-133346-3	OEM
46-133347-3	OEM
46-133351-3	OEM
46-133352-3	OEM
46-133353-3	OEM
46-133354-3	OEM
46-133358-3	OEM
46-133359-3	OEM
46-133362-3	OEM
46-133363-3	OEM
46-133365-3	OEM
46-133367-3	OEM
46-133368-3	OEM
46-133371-3	OEM
46-133378-3	OEM
46-133379-3	OEM

DEVICE TYPE	REPL CODE
46-133380-3	OEM
46-133381-3	OEM
46-133382-3	OEM
46-133383-3	OEM
46-133384-3	OEM
46-133386-3	OEM
46-133387-3	OEM
46-133388-3	1158
46-133389-3	1281
46-133402-3	OEM
46-133403-3	OEM
46-133404-3	OEM
46-133405-3	OEM
46-133406-3	OEM
46-133407-3	OEM
46-133408-3	OEM
46-133409-3	OEM
46-133410-3	OEM
46-133411-3	OEM
46-133412-3	OEM
46-133413-3	OEM
46-133414-3	OEM
46-133415-3	OEM
46-133416-3	OEM
46-133417-3	OEM
46-133418-3	OEM
46-133419-3	OEM
46-133420-3	OEM
46-133421-3	OEM
46-133422-3	OEM
46-133423-3	OEM
46-133424-3	OEM
46-133425-3	OEM
46-133426-3	OEM
46-133427-3	OEM
46-133428-3	OEM
46-133430-3	OEM
46-133432-3	OEM
46-133437-3	OEM
46-133438-3	OEM
46-133441-3	OEM
46-133444-3	OEM
46-133445-3	OEM
46-133446-3	OEM
46-133447-3	OEM
46-133448-3	OEM
46-133449-3	OEM
46-133450-3	OEM
46-133451-3	OEM
46-133452-3	OEM
46-133453-3	OEM
46-133454-3	OEM
46-133455-3	OEM
46-133456-3	OEM
46-133458-3	OEM
46-133459-3	OEM
46-133460-3	OEM
46-133462-3	OEM
46-133463-3	OEM
46-133464-3	OEM
46-133465-3	OEM
46-133471-3	OEM
46-133472-3	OEM
46-133473-3	OEM
46-133475-3	OEM
46-133476-3	OEM
46-133477-3	OEM
46-133478-3	OEM
46-133479-3	OEM
46-133480-3	OEM
46-133481-3	OEM
46-133483-3	OEM
46-133489-3	OEM
46-133491-3	OEM
46-133492-3	OEM
46-133493-3	OEM
46-133495-3	OEM
46-133501-3	OEM
46-133503-3	OEM
46-133504-3	OEM
46-133506-3	OEM
46-133507-3	OEM
46-133508-3	OEM
46-133509-3	OEM
46-133510-3	OEM
46-133515-3	OEM
46-133517-3	OEM
46-133522-3	OEM
46-133523-3	OEM
46-133524-3	OEM
46-133528-3	OEM
46-133535-3	OEM
46-133537-3	OEM
46-133543-3	OEM
46-133544-3	OEM
46-133545-3	OEM
46-133546-3	OEM
46-133547-3	OEM
46-133548-3	OEM
46-133549-3	OEM
46-133550-3	OEM
46-133551-3	OEM
46-133552-3	OEM
46-133553-3	OEM
46-133554-3	OEM
46-133555-3	OEM
46-133558-3	OEM
46-133565-3	OEM
46-133566-3	OEM

DEVICE TYPE	REPL CODE
46-133570-3	OEM
46-133571-3	OEM
46-133578-3	OEM
46-133593-3	OEM
46-133691-3	OEM
46-133692-3	5596
46-133693-3	OEM
46-133694-3	OEM
46-133695-3	OEM
46-133696-3	OEM
46-133697-3	0311
46-133801-3	OEM
46-133831-3	1281
46-133832-3	OEM
46-133912-3	OEM
46-133967-3	OEM
46-134039-3	OEM
46-134041-3	OEM
46-351284-3	OEM
46-351285-3	OEM
46-353671-3	OEM
46-611117-3	1982
46-720336-3	OEM
46-721199-3	OEM
46-721209-3	OEM
46-721236-3	OEM
46-721243-3	OEM
46-721246-3	OEM
46-721267-3	OEM
46-721342-3	OEM
46-721344-3	OEM
46-721348-3	OEM
46-721352-3	OEM
46-721360-3	OEM
46-721806-3	OEM
46-721807-3	OEM
46-721809-3	OEM
46-721811-3	OEM
46-721813-3	OEM
46-721815-3	OEM
46-721821-3	OEM
46-721822-3	OEM
46-721823-3	OEM
46-721824-3	OEM
46-721826-3	OEM
46-721828-3	OEM
46-721829-3	OEM
46-721894-3	OEM
46-721898-3	OEM
46-721903-3	OEM
46-721905-3	OEM
46-721906-3	OEM
46-721908-3	OEM
46-721909-3	OEM
46-721910-3	OEM
46-721911-3	OEM
46-721913-3	OEM
46-721914-3	OEM
46-721916-3	OEM
46-721917-3	OEM
46-721924-3	OEM
46-721925-3	OEM
46-721926-3	OEM
46-721927-3	OEM
46-721928-3	OEM
46-721929-3	OEM
46-721930-3	OEM
46-721931-3	OEM
46-721933-3	OEM
46-721934-3	OEM
46-721936-3	OEM
46-721938-3	OEM
46-721940-3	OEM
46-721942-3	OEM
46-721945-3	OEM
46-721946-3	OEM
46-721947-3	OEM
46-721951-3	OEM
46-721952-3	OEM
46-721953-3	OEM
46-721954-3	OEM
46-721955-3	OEM
46-721964-3	OEM
46-721968-3	OEM
46-721969-3	OEM
46-721971-3	OEM
46-721972-3	OEM
46-721975-3	OEM
46-721982-3	OEM
46-722012-3	OEM
46-722013-3	OEM
46-722016-3	OEM
46-722017-3	OEM
46-722020-3	OEM
46-722021-3	OEM
46-722022-3	OEM
46-722023-3	OEM
46-722024-3	OEM
46-722025-3	OEM
46-722026-3	OEM
46-722029-3	OEM
46-722038-3	OEM
46-722039-3	OEM
46-722040-3	OEM
46-722042-3	OEM
46-722043-3	OEM
46-722044-3	OEM
46-722047-3	OEM
46-722050-3	OEM

DEVICE TYPE	REPL CODE
46-722051-3	OEM
46-722053-3	OEM
46-722054-3	OEM
46-722057-3	OEM
46-722059-3	OEM
46-722060-3	OEM
46-722062-3	OEM
46-722065-3	OEM
46-722066-3	1114
46-722068-3	OEM
46-722070-3	OEM
46-722071-3	OEM
46-722072-3	OEM
46-722073-3	OEM
46-722074-3	OEM
46-722076-3	OEM
46-722079-3	OEM
46-722080-3	OEM
46-722083-3	OEM
46-722086-3	OEM
46-722088-3	OEM
46-722089-3	OEM
46-722090-3	OEM
46-722091-3	OEM
46-722092-3	OEM
46-722093-3	OEM
46-722095-3	OEM
46-722096-3	OEM
46-722097-3	OEM
46-722098-3	OEM
46-722099-3	OEM
46-722100-3	OEM
46-722101-3	OEM
46-722104-3	OEM
46-722105-3	OEM
46-722106-3	OEM
46-722107-3	OEM
46-722108-3	OEM
46-722111-3	OEM
46-722112-3	OEM
46-722113-3	OEM
46-722114-3	OEM
46-722115-3	OEM
46-722116-3	OEM
46-722118-3	OEM
46-722121-3	OEM
46-722122-3	OEM
46-722123-3	OEM
46-722124-3	OEM
46-722126-3	OEM
46-722128-3	OEM
46-722129-3	OEM
46-722130-3	OEM
46-722131-3	OEM
46-722133-3	OEM
46-722134-3	OEM
46-722135-3	OEM
46-722420-3	OEM
46-722421-3	OEM
46-722540-3	OEM
46-722543-3	OEM
46-722547-3	OEM
46-722608-3	OEM
46-722633-3	OEM
46-750033-3	OEM
46-750034-3	OEM
46-750035-3	OEM
46-750036-3	OEM
46-750037-3	OEM
46-750038-3	OEM
46-750052-3	OEM
46-750055-3	OEM
46-750058-3	OEM
46-751270-3	OEM
46-751271-3	OEM
46-751633-3	OEM
46-751634-3	OEM
46-751652-3	OEM
46-751656-3	OEM
46-751657-3	OEM
46-751658-3	OEM
46-751659-3	OEM
46-751660-3	OEM
46-752091-3	OEM
46-752111-3	OEM
46-752113-3	OEM
46-752116-3	OEM
46-752117-3	OEM
46-752182-3	OEM
46-752183-3	OEM
46-752185-3	OEM
46-752189-3	OEM
46-753126-3	OEM
46-753127-3	OEM
46-753128-3	OEM
46-753129-3	OEM
46-753134-3	OEM
46-753135-3	OEM
46-753138-3	OEM
46-754471-3	OEM
46-754472-3	OEM
46-754547-3	OEM
46-754548-3	OEM
46-754549-3	OEM
46-754550-3	OEM
46-754552-3	OEM
46-754557-3	OEM
46-754559-3	OEM
46-754560-3	OEM

DEVICE TYPE	REPL CODE
46-754561-3	OEM
46-754562-3	OEM
46-754564-3	OEM
46-754565-3	OEM
46-754566-3	OEM
46-754567-3	OEM
46-754568-3	OEM
46-754569-3	OEM
46-754570-3	OEM
46-754571-3	OEM
46-754572-3	OEM
46-754573-3	OEM
46-754574-3	OEM
46-754575-3	OEM
46-754577-3	OEM
46-754579-3	OEM
46-754580-3	OEM
46-754581-3	OEM
46-754583-3	OEM
46-754584-3	OEM
46-754586-3	OEM
46-754587-3	OEM
46-754588-3	OEM
46-754589-3	OEM
46-754590-3	OEM
46-754591-3	OEM
46-754592-3	OEM
46-754593-3	OEM
46-754594-3	OEM
46-754595-3	OEM
46-754596-3	OEM
46-754599-3	OEM
46-754601-3	OEM
46-754602-3	OEM
46-754603-3	OEM
46-754605-3	OEM
46-754606-3	OEM
46-754607-3	OEM
46-754608-3	OEM
46-754610-3	OEM
46-754611-3	OEM
46-754612-3	OEM
46-754650-3	OEM
46-754661-3	OEM
46-754709-3	OEM
46-754710-3	OEM
46-754711-3	OEM
46-754712-3	OEM
46-754713-3	OEM
46-754714-3	OEM
46-754715-3	OEM
46-756047-3	OEM
46-756054-3	OEM
46-756055-3	OEM
46-756065-3	OEM
46-756085-3	OEM
46-756118-3	OEM
46-756127-3	OEM
46-756142-3	OEM
46-756148-3	OEM
46-756149-3	OEM
46-756157-3	OEM
46-756384-3	OEM
46-756385-3	OEM
46-756386-3	OEM
46-756388-3	OEM
46-756389-3	OEM
46-756390-3	OEM
46-756391-3	OEM
46-756392-3	OEM
46-756410-3	OEM
46-756411-3	OEM
46-756413-3	OEM
46-756414-3	OEM
46-756421-3	OEM
46-756484-3	OEM
46-756525-3	OEM
46-756527-3	OEM
46-756528-3	OEM
46-756529-3	OEM
46-756530-3	OEM
46-756533-3	OEM
46-756534-3	OEM
46-756688-3	OEM
46-756690-3	OEM
46-801344-3	OEM
46-801386-3	OEM
46-852644-3	OEM
46-861000-3	OEM
46-861002-3	OEM
46-861005-3	OEM
46-861007-3	OEM
46-861008-3	OEM
46-861009-3	1359
46-861010-3	0723
46-861011-3	0558
46-861012-3	0520
46-861014-3	5280
46-861015-3	0497
46-861016-3	0087
46-861017-3	0949
46-861018-3	0949
46-861019-3	2643
46-861020-3	0261
46-861021-3	0130
46-861022-3	0023
46-861023-3	0388
46-861024-3	OEM
46-861025-3	3827

If replacement code is OEM, contact original manufacturer for replacement.

DEVICE TYPE	REPL CODE
46-861027-3	3065
46-861028-3	OEM
46-861029-3	OEM
46-861030-3	OEM
46-861031-3	1900
46-861032-3	OEM
46-861034-3	OEM
46-861036-3	OEM
46-861037-2	0284
46-861037-3	3270
46-861038-3	0298
46-861039-3	1274
46-861040-3	1900
46-861041-3	0023
46-861042-3	2885
46-861043-3	0261
46-861044-3	OEM
46-861045-3	0466
46-861046-3	0057
46-861048-3	OEM
46-861049-3	OEM
46-861051-3	OEM
46-861053-3	OEM
46-861054-3	OEM
46-861055-3	OEM
46-861056-3	OEM
46-861057-3	OEM
46-861058-3	OEM
46-861059-3	OEM
46-861060-3	OEM
46-861061-3	OEM
46-861062-3	OEM
46-861063-3	OEM
46-861064-3	OEM
46-861065-3	OEM
46-861066-3	OEM
46-861067-3	0361
46-861068-3	OEM
46-861070-3	OEM
46-861071-3	OEM
46-861072-3	OEM
46-861074-3	OEM
46-861075-3	OEM
46-861076-3	OEM
46-861077-3	1157
46-861078-3	OEM
46-861080-3	OEM
46-861084-3	OEM
46-861086-3	OEM
46-861087-3	OEM
46-861088-3	OEM
46-861089-3	0140
46-861090-3	OEM
46-861091-3	OEM
46-861092-3	OEM
46-861094-3	0166
46-861095-3	OEM
46-861096-3	3017
46-861097-3	2058
46-861098-3	OEM
46-861102-3	OEM
46-861103-3	OEM
46-861107-3	OEM
46-861111-3	0012
46-861113-3	0253
46-861114-3	2882
46-861114-3(DIODE)	0282
46-861115-3	0719
46-861116-3	0077
46-861117-3	OEM
46-861118-3	0170
46-861119-3	0721
46-861120-3	OEM
46-861122-3	OEM
46-861123-3	OEM
46-861124-3	OEM
46-861125-3	OEM
46-861126-3	OEM
46-861128-3	OEM
46-861129-3	OEM
46-861130-3	OEM
46-861131-3	OEM
46-861132-3	OEM
46-861133-3	OEM
46-861134-3	OEM
46-861135-3	0681
46-861136-3	OEM
46-861137-3	OEM
46-861139-3	OEM
46-861140-3	OEM
46-861141-3	0195
46-861142-3	0282
46-861144-3	OEM
46-861145-3	0257
46-861146-3	OEM
46-861148-3	3609
46-861149-3	0102
46-861149-9	OEM
46-861151-3	0275
46-861153-3	OEM
46-861154-3	OEM
46-861155-3	OEM
46-861156-3	OEM
46-861157-3	OEM
46-861158-3	0064
46-861159-3	0057
46-861160-3	OEM
46-861161-3	2678
46-861162-3	OEM

DEVICE TYPE	REPL CODE
46-861163-3	OEM
46-861166-3	OEM
46-861168-3	OEM
46-861169-3	OEM
46-861170-3	0057
46-861171-3	OEM
46-861172-3	0064
46-861173-3	OEM
46-861174-3	2520
46-861175-3	3643
46-861176-3	0181
46-861178-3	2821
46-861179-3	0041
46-861180-3	OEM
46-861181-3	OEM
46-861182-3	OEM
46-861183-9	OEM
46-861184-3	OEM
46-861185-3	OEM
46-861186-3	0466
46-861187-3	0392
46-861188-3	OEM
46-861189-3	OEM
46-861190-3	OEM
46-861191-3	OEM
46-861192-3	OEM
46-861193-3	OEM
46-861194-3	OEM
46-861195-3	OEM
46-861196-3	OEM
46-861197-3	OEM
46-861199-3	OEM
46-861200-3	1123
46-861201-3	OEM
46-861202-3	OEM
46-861203-3	2514
46-861204-3	OEM
46-861205-3	OEM
46-861206-9	OEM
46-861207-3	OEM
46-861209-3	2961
46-861210-3	OEM
46-861211-3	0695
46-861212-3	0429
46-861214-3	OEM
46-861215-3	OEM
46-861216-3	1533
46-861217-3	OEM
46-861218-3	OEM
46-861219-3	OEM
46-861220-3	OEM
46-861222-3	2411
46-861222-9	2411
46-861223-3	OEM
46-861224-3	OEM
46-861225-3	OEM
46-861226-3	OEM
46-861227-3	OEM
46-861228-3	OEM
46-861229-3	OEM
46-861230-3	OEM
46-861231-3	0018
46-861232-3	OEM
46-861233-3	OEM
46-861235-3	OEM
46-861236-3	OEM
46-861237-3	OEM
46-861238-3	OEM
46-861239-3	OEM
46-861240-3	OEM
46-861241-3	OEM
46-861243-3	OEM
46-861244-3	OEM
46-861245-3	0892
46-861246-3	OEM
46-861247-3	OEM
46-861248-3	OEM
46-861249-3	OEM
46-861250-3	OEM
46-861251-3	OEM
46-861252-3	4334
46-861253-3	1533
46-861254-3	OEM
46-861255-3	OEM
46-861256-3	0511
46-861257-3	OEM
46-861258-3	OEM
46-861259-3	OEM
46-861261-3	OEM
46-861262-3	OEM
46-861263-3	OEM
46-861265-3	0023
46-861266-3	4790
46-861267-3	OEM
46-861268-3	OEM
46-861269-3	3450
46-861270-3	OEM
46-861271-3	1533
46-861272-3	0275
46-861274-3	0124
46-861275-3	OEM
46-861276-3	OEM
46-861277-3	OEM
46-861278-3	OEM
46-861279-3	OEM
46-861280-3	OEM
46-861281-3	0162
46-861282-3	OEM
46-861283-3	OEM

DEVICE TYPE	REPL CODE
46-861284-3	OEM
46-861285-3	0253
46-861286-3	OEM
46-861287-3	OEM
46-861288-3	OEM
46-861289-3	2171
46-861290-3	5040
46-861291-3	OEM
46-861292-3	OEM
46-861293-3	OEM
46-861294-3	0062
46-861295-3	2604
46-861296-3	5322
46-861297-3	5352
46-861298-3	5352
46-861299-3	0148
46-861300-3	OEM
46-861301-3	0881
46-861302-3	OEM
46-861303-3	OEM
46-861304-3	0071
46-861305-3	OEM
46-861306-3	1967
46-861307-3	OEM
46-861308-3	OEM
46-861309-3	OEM
46-861310-3	OEM
46-861311-3	OEM
46-861312-3	OEM
46-861313-3	OEM
46-861314-3	OEM
46-861315-3	OEM
46-861316-3	OEM
46-861317-3	0700
46-861318-3	OEM
46-861319-3	OEM
46-861320-3	OEM
46-861321-3	OEM
46-861323-3	OEM
46-861324-3	OEM
46-861325-3	OEM
46-861326-3	OEM
46-861327-3	1533
46-861328-3	OEM
46-861329-3	OEM
46-861330-3	OEM
46-861331-3	OEM
46-861332-3	0253
46-861333-3	0999
46-861336-3	5852
46-861337-3	OEM
46-861338-3	OEM
46-861339-3	OEM
46-861340-3	0053
46-861341-3	OEM
46-861342-3	OEM
46-861343-3	OEM
46-861344-3	5486
46-861345-3	1026
46-861346-3	5917
46-861347-3	OEM
46-861348-3	OEM
46-861349-3	OEM
46-861350-3	OEM
46-861352-3	OEM
46-861353-3	OEM
46-861354-3	OEM
46-861355-3	OEM
46-861356-3	OEM
46-861357-3	OEM
46-861359-3	OEM
46-861360-3	OEM
46-861361-3	OEM
46-861362-3	OEM
46-861363-3	OEM
46-861365-3	0826
46-861366-3	OEM
46-861367-3	0480
46-861368-3	OEM
46-861369-3	OEM
46-861370-3	OEM
46-861371-3	OEM
46-861372-3	OEM
46-861373-3	OEM
46-861374-3	OEM
46-861375-3	OEM
46-861376-3	OEM
46-861378-3	OEM
46-861379-3	1026
46-861380-3	OEM
46-861381-1	0052
46-861381-3	0053
46-861382-3	0166
46-861383-3	OEM
46-861384-3	OEM
46-861385-3	OEM
46-861386-3	OEM
46-861387-3	OEM
46-861388-3	OEM
46-861389-9	OEM
46-861390-3	OEM
46-861391-3	OEM
46-861392-3	OEM
46-861393-3	OEM
46-861394-3	OEM
46-861395-3	OEM
46-861396-3	0313
46-861397-3	0672
46-861398-3	OEM

DEVICE TYPE	REPL CODE
46-861401-3	OEM
46-861402-3	OEM
46-861403-3	OEM
46-861404-3	OEM
46-861405-3	OEM
46-861406-3	OEM
46-861407-3	0155
46-861408-3	OEM
46-861409-3	OEM
46-861410-3	0071
46-861411-3	OEM
46-861412-3	0284
46-861413-3	1533
46-861414-3	OEM
46-861415-3	OEM
46-861416-3	OEM
46-861417-3	OEM
46-861418-3	OEM
46-861419-3	OEM
46-861420-3	OEM
46-861421-3	OEM
46-861422-3	1533
46-861423-3	OEM
46-861424-3	OEM
46-861425-3	OEM
46-861426-3	OEM
46-861427-3	OEM
46-861428-3	OEM
46-861429-3	OEM
46-861430-3	OEM
46-861431-3	OEM
46-861432-3	OEM
46-861433-3	OEM
46-861434-3	OEM
46-861435-3	OEM
46-861436-3	OEM
46-861437-3	OEM
46-861438-3	OEM
46-861439-3	0151
46-861440-3	OEM
46-861441-3	OEM
46-861442-3	OEM
46-861443-3	OEM
46-861444-3	OEM
46-861445-3	0338
46-861446-3	0261
46-861447-3	OEM
46-861448-3	OEM
46-861449-3	OEM
46-861450-3	OEM
46-861451-3	OEM
46-861452-3	OEM
46-861453-3	0551
46-861454-3	OEM
46-861455-3	OEM
46-861456-3	OEM
46-861457-3	OEM
46-861458-3	OEM
46-861459-3	1075
46-861460-3	OEM
46-861461-3	5589
46-861462-3	3156
46-861463-3	1553
46-861464-3	3326
46-861465-3	0848
46-861466-3	0053
46-861467-3	0023
46-861468-3	OEM
46-861469-3	OEM
46-861470-3	OEM
46-861471-3	OEM
46-861472-3	OEM
46-861473-3	OEM
46-861474-3	OEM
46-861475-3	0551
46-861476-3	OEM
46-861477-3	OEM
46-861478-3	OEM
46-861479-3	OEM
46-861480-3	OEM
46-861481-3	OEM
46-861482-3	OEM
46-861483-3	OEM
46-861484-3	OEM
46-861485-3	OEM
46-861486-3	OEM
46-861487-3	OEM
46-861490-3	1514
46-861491-3	OEM
46-861492-3	OEM
46-861493-3	OEM
46-861494-3	OEM
46-861495-3	OEM
46-861496-3	OEM
46-861497-3	OEM
46-861498-3	OEM
46-861499-3	OEM
46-861500-3	0140
46-861501-3	OEM
46-861502-3	OEM
46-861503-3	OEM
46-861504-3	0666
46-861505-3	OEM
46-861506-3	OEM
46-861507-3	OEM
46-861508-3	0036
46-861510-3	OEM
46-861511-3	OEM
46-861513-3	OEM

DEVICE TYPE	REPL CODE
46-861514-3	OEM
46-861515-3	OEM
46-861516-3	OEM
46-861517-3	OEM
46-861518-3	OEM
46-861519-3	OEM
46-861520-3	OEM
46-861521-3	OEM
46-861522-3	OEM
46-861523-3	OEM
46-861524-3	OEM
46-861525-3	OEM
46-861527-3	OEM
46-861529-3	OEM
46-861530-3	OEM
46-861531-3	OEM
46-861532-3	OEM
46-861533-3	OEM
46-861534-3	OEM
46-861535-3	OEM
46-861536-3	OEM
46-861537-3	OEM
46-861538-3	0480
46-861540-3	OEM
46-861543-3	OEM
46-861544-3	OEM
46-861545-3	2824
46-861546-3	OEM
46-861547-3	0181
46-861548-3	OEM
46-861549-3	OEM
46-861550-3	OEM
46-861551-3	0372
46-861552-3	OEM
46-861553-3	OEM
46-861554-3	OEM
46-861555-3	0077
46-861556-3	OEM
46-861557-3	OEM
46-861558-3	OEM
46-861559-3	OEM
46-861560-3	0901
46-861561-3	OEM
46-861562-3	OEM
46-861565-3	OEM
46-861566-3	0901
46-861567-3	OEM
46-861568-3	OEM
46-861569-3	OEM
46-861570-3	OEM
46-861571-3	OEM
46-861572-3	OEM
46-861573-3	OEM
46-861574-3	0719
46-861575-3	OEM
46-861576-3	OEM
46-861577-3	OEM
46-861578-3	OEM
46-861579-3	OEM
46-861580-3	OEM
46-861581-3	OEM
46-861582-3	OEM
46-861583-3	OEM
46-861584-3	OEM
46-861585-3	OEM
46-861586-3	OEM
46-861587-3	OEM
46-861588-3	OEM
46-861589-3	OEM
46-861590-3	OEM
46-861592-3	OEM
46-861593-3	OEM
46-861594-3	OEM
46-861596-3	OEM
46-861597-3	OEM
46-861598-3	OEM
46-861600-3	1722
46-861603-3	OEM
46-861604-3	OEM
46-861605-3	0520
46-861606-1	5458
46-861606-3	0558
46-861607-3	OEM
46-861608-3	OEM
46-861609-3	OEM
46-861610-3	OEM
46-861611-3	OEM
46-861612-3	OEM
46-861613-3	OEM
46-861614-3	OEM
46-861615-3	OEM
46-861617-3	OEM
46-861618-3	OEM
46-861619-3	OEM
46-861621-3	OEM
46-861622-3	OEM
46-861627-3	1533
46-861628-3	OEM
46-861629-3	OEM
46-861630-3	OEM
46-861631-3	OEM
46-861632-3	OEM
46-861633-3	1864
46-861634-3	0023
46-861636-3	OEM
46-861637-3	OEM
46-861639-3	OEM
46-861642-3	OEM
46-861643-3	OEM

DEVICE TYPE	REPL CODE
46-861644-3	OEM
46-861645-3	3163
46-861646-3	0724
46-861647-3	5486
46-861648-3	1026
46-861649-3	2116
46-861650-3	OEM
46-861651-3	OEM
46-861652-3	5966
46-861653-3	OEM
46-861654-3	0124
46-861657-3	OEM
46-861659-3	OEM
46-861660-3	OEM
46-861661-3	OEM
46-861662-3	OEM
46-861664-3	OEM
46-861665-3	OEM
46-861666-3	OEM
46-861667-3	OEM
46-861668-3	OEM
46-861669-3	OEM
46-861672-3	OEM
46-861673-3	OEM
46-861677-3	OEM
46-861678-3	OEM
46-861680-3	0275
46-861684-3	1376
46-861685-3	OEM
46-861686-3	OEM
46-861687-3	OEM
46-861691-3	0009
46-861692-3	OEM
46-861693-3	OEM
46-861694-3	OEM
46-861695-3	OEM
46-861696-3	OEM
46-861699-3	0441
46-861700-3	OEM
46-861701-3	OEM
46-861702-3	OEM
46-861703-3	OEM
46-861704-3	OEM
46-861705-3	OEM
46-861707-3	OEM
46-861708-3	OEM
46-861709-3	OEM
46-861711-3	OEM
46-861712-3	0261
46-861713-3	OEM
46-861714-3	OEM
46-861716-3	OEM
46-861717-3	0023
46-861718-3	0031
46-861720-3	0372
46-861721-3	OEM
46-861722-3	OEM
46-861723-3	OEM
46-861724-3	OEM
46-861725-3	OEM
46-861728-3	OEM
46-861729-3	OEM
46-861730-3	OEM
46-861734-3	OEM
46-861735-3	OEM
46-861737-3	0790
46-861738-3	0403
46-861739-3	3273
46-861741-3	OEM
46-861744-3	OEM
46-861745-3	OEM
46-861747-3	OEM
46-861748-3	OEM
46-861752-3	OEM
46-861753-3	OEM
46-861754-3	OEM
46-861756-3	OEM
46-861757-3	OEM
46-861758-3	OEM
46-861759-3	OEM
46-861761-3	OEM
46-861762-3	OEM
46-861763-3	OEM
46-861767-3	OEM
46-861768-3	OEM
46-861773-3	OEM
46-861776-3	OEM
46-861777-3	OEM
46-861780-3	OEM
46-861781-3	OEM
46-861783-3	OEM
46-861786-3	OEM
46-861787-3	OEM
46-861788-3	OEM
46-861789-3	OEM
46-861790-3	OEM
46-861791-3	OEM
46-861801-3	OEM
46-861803-3	OEM
46-861807-3	OEM
46-861810-3	OEM
46-861811-3	OEM
46-861812-3	OEM
46-861816-3	OEM
46-861817-3	OEM
46-861825-3	OEM
46-861826-3	OEM
46-861829-3	OEM
46-861832-3	OEM

DEVICE TYPE	REPL CODE
46-861833-3	OEM
46-861834-3	OEM
46-861836-3	OEM
46-861837-3	OEM
46-861838-3	OEM
46-861839-3	OEM
46-861840-3	OEM
46-861842-3	OEM
46-861843-3	OEM
46-861845-3	OEM
46-861851-3	0042
46-861854-3	OEM
46-861857-3	0042
46-861861-3	1181
46-861862-3	OEM
46-861863-3	OEM
46-861864-3	4235
46-861865-3	OEM
46-861866-3	OEM
46-861867-3	2307
46-861868-3	2458
46-861869-3	1266
46-861870-3	0873
46-861871-3	OEM
46-861872-3	OEM
46-861874-3	OEM
46-861875-3	OEM
46-861878-3	OEM
46-861883-3	OEM
46-861884-3	OEM
46-861888-3	OEM
46-861889-3	OEM
46-861890-3	OEM
46-861891-3	OEM
46-861893-3	OEM
46-861895-3	OEM
46-861896-3	OEM
46-861897-3	OEM
46-861898-3	OEM
46-861899-3	OEM
46-861902-3	OEM
46-861904-3	OEM
46-861906-3	OEM
46-861907-3	OEM
46-861908-3	OEM
46-861909-3	OEM
46-861911-3	OEM
46-861912-3	0335
46-861913-3	0582
46-861914-3	OEM
46-861915-3	OEM
46-861916-3	OEM
46-861917-3	OEM
46-861918-3	OEM
46-861919-3	OEM
46-861920-3	OEM
46-861923-3	OEM
46-861924-3	0062
46-861925-3	OEM
46-861926-3	OEM
46-861927-3	OEM
46-861930-3	OEM
46-861931-3	OEM
46-861932-3	OEM
46-861933-3	OEM
46-861934-3	OEM
46-861935-3	OEM
46-861936-3	OEM
46-861937-3	OEM
46-861938-3	OEM
46-861940-3	OEM
46-861942-3	OEM
46-861943-3	OEM
46-861944-3	1376
46-861945-3	OEM
46-861946-3	OEM
46-861948-3	OEM
46-861949-3	OEM
46-861950-3	OEM
46-861951-3	OEM
46-861952-3	OEM
46-861954-3	OEM
46-861955-3	OEM
46-861957-3	OEM
46-861958-3	OEM
46-861959-3	OEM
46-861961-3	OEM
46-861962-3	OEM
46-861963-3	OEM
46-861964-3	OEM
46-861966-3	OEM
46-861967-3	OEM
46-861968-3	OEM
46-861969-3	OEM
46-861970-3	OEM
46-861971-3	OEM
46-861981-3	OEM
46-861982-3	OEM
46-861983-3	OEM
46-861984-3	OEM
46-861986-3	OEM
46-861987-3	OEM
46-861988-3	OEM
46-861989-3	OEM
46-861990-3	OEM
46-861991-3	OEM
46-861992-3	OEM
46-861993-3	OEM
46-861994-3	OEM

If replacement code is OEM, contact original manufacturer for replacement.

145

DEVICE TYPE	REPL CODE
46-861995-3	OEM
46-861997-3	OEM
46-861998-3	OEM
46-861999-3	OEM
46-862000-3	OEM
46-862001-3	OEM
46-862002-3	4686
46-862003-3	OEM
46-862004-3	OEM
46-862007-3	OEM
46-862009-3	OEM
46-862010-3	OEM
46-862012-3	OEM
46-862013-3	OEM
46-862014-3	OEM
46-862015-3	OEM
46-862016-3	OEM
46-862017-3	OEM
46-862019-3	OEM
46-862020-3	OEM
46-862021-3	OEM
46-862022-3	OEM
46-862023-3	OEM
46-862024-3	OEM
46-862025-3	OEM
46-862026-3	OEM
46-862027-3	OEM
46-862028-3	OEM
46-862029-3	OEM
46-862030-3	OEM
46-862031-3	OEM
46-862033-3	OEM
46-862034-3	OEM
46-862035-3	OEM
46-862036-3	OEM
46-862037-3	OEM
46-862038-3	OEM
46-862039-3	OEM
46-862040-3	OEM
46-862041-3	OEM
46-862042-3	OEM
46-862043-3	OEM
46-862045-3	0077
46-862046-3	OEM
46-862047-3	OEM
46-862048-3	OEM
46-862049-3	OEM
46-862055-3	OEM
46-862057-3	OEM
46-862058-3	OEM
46-862066-3	OEM
46-862067-3	OEM
46-862068-3	0155
46-862069-3	OEM
46-862070-3	OEM
46-862072-3	OEM
46-862073-3	OEM
46-862074-3	OEM
46-862075-3	OEM
46-862077-3	OEM
46-862078-3	OEM
46-862079-3	OEM
46-862080-3	OEM
46-862081-3	5322
46-862083-3	OEM
46-862087-3	OEM
46-862088-3	OEM
46-862089-3	0166
46-862090-3	OEM
46-862091-3	OEM
46-862092-3	1498
46-862094-3	OEM
46-862096-3	OEM
46-862097-3	1533
46-862098-3	OEM
46-862099-3	OEM
46-862100-3	1533
46-862103-3	OEM
46-862107-3	OEM
46-862108-3	OEM
46-862109-3	OEM
46-862111-3	OEM
46-862112-3	0031
46-862113-3	OEM
46-862116-3	OEM
46-862118-3	OEM
46-862119-3	OEM
46-862120-3	OEM
46-862121-3	0919
46-862122-3	OEM
46-862124-3	OEM
46-862125-3	OEM
46-862126-3	OEM
46-862129-3	OEM
46-862131-3	OEM
46-862132-3	OEM
46-862133-3	OEM
46-862134-3	OEM
46-862135-3	OEM
46-862136-3	OEM
46-862138-3	OEM
46-862139-3	OEM
46-862140-3	OEM
46-862142-3	OEM
46-862145-3	OEM
46-862146-3	OEM
46-862151-3	OEM
46-862152-3	0541
46-862153-3	0017
46-862155-3	OEM
46-862156-3	OEM
46-862157	OEM
46-862157-3	3990
46-862158-3	OEM
46-862159-3	OEM
46-862161-3	OEM
46-862162-3	OEM
46-862163-3	OEM
46-862164-3	OEM
46-862165-3	OEM
46-862166-3	OEM
46-862167-3	0102
46-862168-3	0023
46-862169-3	OEM
46-862170-3	2116
46-862173-3	OEM
46-862176-3	OEM
46-862177-3	OEM
46-862178-3	OEM
46-862179-3	OEM
46-862180-3	OEM
46-862181-3	OEM
46-862182-3	OEM
46-862183-3	OEM
46-862184-3	OEM
46-862186-3	OEM
46-862187-3	OEM
46-862188-3	OEM
46-862189-3	OEM
46-862191-3	OEM
46-862192-3	OEM
46-862193-3	OEM
46-862194-3	OEM
46-862195-3	OEM
46-862196-3	OEM
46-862209-3	OEM
46-862211-3	OEM
46-862212-3	OEM
46-862217-3	OEM
46-862219-3	OEM
46-862220-3	OEM
46-862221-3	OEM
46-862223-3	OEM
46-862224-3	OEM
46-862227-3	OEM
46-862228-3	OEM
46-862229-3	OEM
46-862230-3	OEM
46-862232-3	OEM
46-862233-3	OEM
46-862234-3	OEM
46-862236-3	OEM
46-862237-3	OEM
46-862238-3	OEM
46-862239-3	OEM
46-862240-3	OEM
46-862241-3	OEM
46-862244-3	OEM
46-862245-3	OEM
46-862248-3	OEM
46-862249-3	OEM
46-862253-3	OEM
46-862254-3	OEM
46-862255-3	OEM
46-862257-3	OEM
46-862259-3	OEM
46-862260-3	OEM
46-862262-3	OEM
46-862269-3	OEM
46-862270-3	OEM
46-862271-3	OEM
46-862276-3	OEM
46-862277-3	OEM
46-862282-3	OEM
46-862283-3	OEM
46-862286-3	OEM
46-862287-3	OEM
46-862288-3	OEM
46-862289-3	0079
46-862290-3	0168
46-862291-3	0638
46-862292-3	OEM
46-862293-3	OEM
46-862294-3	OEM
46-862295-3	1533
46-862297-3	OEM
46-862298-3	OEM
46-862299-3	OEM
46-862300-3	OEM
46-862301-3	0023
46-862302-3	OEM
46-862303-3	OEM
46-862304-3	OEM
46-862305-3	OEM
46-862306-3	OEM
46-862307-3	OEM
46-862308-3	OEM
46-862309-3	OEM
46-862318-3	0274
46-862321-3	1039
46-862322-3	0031
46-862323-3	0031
46-862325-3	OEM
46-862326-3	OEM
46-862327-3	OEM
46-862328-3	0275
46-862329-3	5365
46-862330-3	OEM
46-862331-3	OEM
46-862332-3	OEM
46-862333-3	OEM
46-862336-3	0261
46-862337-3	OEM
46-862339-3	OEM
46-862340-3	OEM
46-862341-3	OEM
46-862342-3	OEM
46-862343-3	OEM
46-862345-3	OEM
46-862346-3	OEM
46-862347-3	OEM
46-862348-3	OEM
46-862349-3	OEM
46-862350-3	0140
46-862351-3	OEM
46-862352-3	OEM
46-862353-3	OEM
46-862354-3	OEM
46-862355-3	OEM
46-862356-3	OEM
46-862359-3	OEM
46-862360-3	OEM
46-862361-3	OEM
46-862362-3	OEM
46-862363-3	OEM
46-862365-3	OEM
46-862367-3	OEM
46-862368-3	OEM
46-862369-3	OEM
46-862370-3	OEM
46-862371-3	OEM
46-862372-3	OEM
46-862373-3	OEM
46-862374-3	OEM
46-862375-3	OEM
46-862377-3	OEM
46-862378-3	OEM
46-862379-3	OEM
46-862380-3	OEM
46-862381-3	OEM
46-862391-3	OEM
46-862392-3	OEM
46-862393-3	OEM
46-862394-3	OEM
46-862395-3	OEM
46-862396-3	OEM
46-862398-3	OEM
46-862399-3	OEM
46-862401-3	OEM
46-862402-3	OEM
46-862406-3	OEM
46-862407-3	OEM
46-862408-3	OEM
46-862409-3	0031
46-862410-3	0466
46-862411-3	3069
46-862412-3	OEM
46-862413-3	2171
46-862414-3	OEM
46-862415-3	OEM
46-862425-3	OEM
46-862427-3	OEM
46-862429-3	OEM
46-862435-3	OEM
46-862436-3	OEM
46-862437-3	OEM
46-862438-3	OEM
46-862439-3	OEM
46-862441-3	OEM
46-862442-3	OEM
46-862446-3	1492
46-862447-3	OEM
46-862448-3	OEM
46-862449-3	OEM
46-862450-3	OEM
46-862452-3	OEM
46-862453-3	OEM
46-862456-3	0999
46-862459-3	OEM
46-862460-3	OEM
46-862461-3	OEM
46-862462-3	OEM
46-862463-3	OEM
46-862464-3	OEM
46-862465-3	OEM
46-862466-3	OEM
46-862467-3	OEM
46-862469-3	OEM
46-862470-3	OEM
46-862471-3	OEM
46-862472-3	OEM
46-862473-3	OEM
46-862474-3	OEM
46-862476-3	OEM
46-862477-3	OEM
46-862478-3	OEM
46-862479-3	OEM
46-862480-3	OEM
46-862481-3	OEM
46-862482-3	OEM
46-862483-3	OEM
46-862484-3	OEM
46-862491-3	OEM
46-862493-3	OEM
46-862494-3	OEM
46-862495-3	OEM
46-862497-3	OEM
46-862498-3	OEM
46-862500-3	OEM
46-862503-3	OEM
46-862504-3	OEM
46-862505-3	OEM
46-862506-3	OEM
46-862507-3	OEM
46-862508-3	OEM
46-862509-3	OEM
46-862510-3	OEM
46-862512-3	OEM
46-862515-3	OEM
46-862516-3	5579
46-862517-3	OEM
46-862522-3	2171
46-862528-3	4858
46-862529-3	5767
46-862530-3	0558
46-862532-3	5815
46-862541-3	OEM
46-862544-3	OEM
46-862550-3	OEM
46-862552-3	OEM
46-862553-3	OEM
46-862557-3	0049
46-862559-3	2712
46-862564-3	OEM
46-862565-3	OEM
46-862566-3	OEM
46-862567-3	OEM
46-862568-3	OEM
46-862569-3	OEM
46-862571-3	OEM
46-862573-3	OEM
46-862574-3	OEM
46-862575-3	OEM
46-862576-3	OEM
46-862577-3	OEM
46-862578-3	OEM
46-862579-3	OEM
46-862580-3	OEM
46-862581-3	OEM
46-862582-3	1533
46-862585-3	OEM
46-862586-3	OEM
46-862587-3	OEM
46-862588-3	OEM
46-862589-3	OEM
46-862590-3	OEM
46-862591-3	OEM
46-862593-3	OEM
46-862594-3	OEM
46-862595-3	2171
46-862598-3	OEM
46-862599-3	OEM
46-862600-3	OEM
46-862601-3	OEM
46-862602-3	OEM
46-862603-3	OEM
46-862604-3	OEM
46-862605-3	OEM
46-862606-3	OEM
46-862607-3	OEM
46-862608-3	OEM
46-862609-3	OEM
46-862611-3	0002
46-862612-3	0052
46-862614-3	0253
46-862615-3	0062
46-862616-3	0041
46-862620-3	OEM
46-862621-3	OEM
46-862622-3	OEM
46-862623-3	OEM
46-862624-3	OEM
46-862625-3	OEM
46-862630-3	OEM
46-862631-3	OEM
46-862633-3	1864
46-862634-3	0064
46-862639-3	0165
46-862642-3	0052
46-862650-3	OEM
46-862651-3	0062
46-862652-3	0077
46-862653-3	0036
46-862654-3	OEM
46-862655-3	OEM
46-862656-3	OEM
46-862657-3	OEM
46-862658-3	OEM
46-862659-3	OEM
46-862660-3	OEM
46-862661-3	OEM
46-862662-3	OEM
46-862663-3	OEM
46-862664-3	OEM
46-862665-3	OEM
46-862666-3	OEM
46-862667-3	OEM
46-862668-3	OEM
46-862669-3	OEM
46-862670-3	OEM
46-862671-3	OEM
46-862672-3	OEM
46-862673-3	OEM
46-862674-3	OEM
46-862676-3	OEM
46-862677-3	OEM
46-862678-3	OEM
46-862679-3	OEM
46-862680-3	OEM
46-862681-3	OEM
46-862682-3	OEM
46-862683-3	OEM
46-862684-3	OEM
46-862685-3	OEM
46-862686-3	OEM
46-862687-3	OEM
46-862688-3	OEM
46-862689-3	OEM
46-862690-3	OEM
46-862691-3	OEM
46-862693-3	OEM
46-862694-3	OEM
46-862695-3	OEM
46-862696-3	OEM
46-862697-3	OEM
46-862764-3	OEM
46-862770-3	OEM
46-862771-3	OEM
46-862772-3	OEM
46-862775-3	OEM
46-862776-3	OEM
46-862777-3	OEM
46-862778-3	OEM
46-862782-3	OEM
46-862784-3	OEM
46-862786-3	OEM
46-862787-3	OEM
46-862788-3	OEM
46-862791-3	OEM
46-862794-3	OEM
46-862795-3	OEM
46-862796-3	0195
46-862857-3	6014
46-862858-3	3454
46-862994-3	0031
46-866209	0309
46-961037-3	OEM
46-8691025-3	OEM
46AR1	0015
46AR2	0015
46AR3	0015
46AR4	0015
46AR5	0015
46AR6	0015
46AR7	0015
46AR8	0015
46AR9	0015
46AR10	0015
46AR11	0015
46AR12	0015
46AR13	0071
46AR15	0071
46AR16	0071
46AR18	0071
46AR21	0015
46AR27	0015
46AR28	0015
46AR29	0015
46AR35	0015
46AR50	0071
46AR52	0071
46AR59	0071
46AX1	0015
46AX2	0015
46AX3	0015
46AX4	0015
46AX5	0015
46AX7	0015
46AX8	0015
46AX9	0015
46AX10	0015
46AX11	0015
46AX12	0071
46AX13	0071
46AX14	0071
46AX16	0015
46AX17	0015
46AX19	0015
46AX21	0015
46AX30	0015
46AX34	0015
46AX52	0015
46AX54	0015
46AX55	0071
46AX56	0071
46AX59	0071
46AX70	0071
46AX82	0071
46AX84	0071
46AX85	0071
46B-3A5	0265
46BD1	0015
46BD2	0015
46BD5	0015
46BD8	0015
46BD9	0015
46BD11	0015
46BD12	0015
46BD14	0015
46BD19	0015
46BD25	0015
46BD27	0071
46BD30	0071
46BD32	0071
46BD33	0071
46BD34	0071
46BD38	0071
46BD39	0071
46BD52	0071
46BD101	0071
46BR5	0015
46BR7	0015
46BR9	0015
46BR10	0015
46BR11	0015
46BR15	0015
46BR17	0015
46BR18	0071
46BR21	0071
46BR27	0071
46BR62	0071
46BR63	0071
46BR64	0071
46BR68	0071
46BX2	0015
46BX3	0015
46C-42	0144
46D5R03	OEM
46D9R03GH	OEM
46J	OEM
46K	OEM
46R2	0122
46R2R	0510
46R2S	0204
46RECT-SI-1002	0023
46SI-SAF1039P	0944
46ST-MPS9700E	0079
46ST-MPS9700F	0079
46TB1-CE00	OEM
46TB1-CH00	OEM
46TB1-EE00	OEM
46TB1-EH00	OEM
46TB1-JH00	OEM
46TB1-LE00	OEM
46TB1-LH00	OEM
46TB1-NE00	OEM
46TB1-NH00	OEM
46TB2-CE00	OEM
46TB2-CH00	OEM
46TB2-EE00	OEM
46TB2-EH00	OEM
46TB2-JH00	OEM
46TB2-LE00	OEM
46TB2-LH00	OEM
46TB2-NE00	OEM
46TB2-NH00	OEM
46TB3-CE00	OEM
46TB3-CH00	OEM
46TB3-EE00	OEM
46TB3-EH00	OEM
46TB3-JH00	OEM
46TB3-LE00	OEM
46TB3-LH00	OEM
46TB3-NE00	OEM
46TB3-NH00	OEM
46TB4-CE00	OEM
46TB4-CH00	OEM
46TB4-EE00	OEM
46TB4-EH00	OEM
46TB4-JH00	OEM
46TB4-LE00	OEM
46TB4-LH00	OEM
46TB4-NE00	OEM
46TB4-NH00	OEM
46TB5-CE00	OEM
46TB5-CH00	OEM
46TB5-EE00	OEM
46TB5-EH00	OEM
46TB5-GH00	OEM
46TB5-JH00	OEM
46TB5-LE00	OEM
46TB5-LH00	OEM
46TB5-NE00	OEM
46TB5-NH00	OEM
46TB6-CE00	OEM
46TB6-CH00	OEM
46TB6-EE00	OEM
46TB6-EH00	OEM
46TB6-GH00	OEM
46TB6-JH00	OEM
46TB6-LE00	OEM
46TB6-LH00	OEM
46TB6-NE00	OEM
46TB6-NH00	OEM
46TB7-JE00	OEM
46TB7-JH00	OEM
46TB7-LE00	OEM
46TB7-LH00	OEM
46TB7-NE00	OEM
46TB7-NH00	OEM
46TB7-RE00	OEM
46TB8-CHG0	OEM
46TB8-JE00	OEM
46TB8-JH00	OEM
46TB8-LE00	OEM
46TB8-LH00	OEM
46TB8-NE00	OEM
46TB8-NH00	OEM
46TB8-RE00	OEM
46TB9-JE00	OEM
46TB9-JH00	OEM
46TB9-LE00	OEM
46TB9-LH00	OEM
46TB9-NE00	OEM
46TB9-NH00	OEM
46TB9-RE00	OEM
46TB10-JE00	OEM
46TB10-JH00	OEM
46TB10-LE00	OEM
46TB10-LH00	OEM
46TB10-NE00	OEM
46TB10-NH00	OEM
46TB10-RE00	OEM
46TB11-JE00	OEM
46TB11-JH00	OEM
46TB11-LE00	OEM
46TB11-LH00	OEM
46TB11-NE00	OEM
46TB11-NH00	OEM
46TB11-RE00	OEM
46TB12-JE00	OEM
46TB12-JH00	OEM
46TB12-LE00	OEM
46TB12-LH00	OEM
46TB12-NH00	OEM
46TB12-RE00	OEM
46TB13	OEM
46TB13-JH00	OEM
46TB13-LE00	OEM
46TB13-LH00	OEM
46TB13-NE00	OEM
46TB13-NH00	OEM
46TB13-RE00	OEM
46TB14-JH00	OEM
46TB14-LE00	OEM
46TB14-LH00	OEM
46TB14-NE00	OEM
46TB14-NH00	OEM
46TB14-RE00	OEM
46TB15-JH00	OEM
46TB15-LE00	OEM
46TB15-LH00	OEM
46TB15-NE00	OEM
46TB15-NH00	OEM
46TB15-RE00	OEM
47-1	0911
47-2	0911
47-2(DIO)	0911
47-2(XSTR)	0127
47-4	0911
47-866882-3	OEM
47B	0993
47C23-3	0150
47C221AF4241	OEM
47C231AN4943	OEM
47C232AN4989	OEM
47C337ANR801	OEM
47C420AF8582	OEM
47C432AN-8088	OEM
47C432AN-8088Z	OEM
47C432AN-8098	OEM
47C432AN-8497	OEM
47C432AN8693	OEM
47C432AN-8734	OEM
47C432AN8939	OEM
47C432AN8989	OEM
47C434N-3509Z	OEM
47C634N2427	OEM
47C634N2438	OEM
47C634N2453	OEM
47C634N-2454	OEM
47C634N2454	OEM
47C670N1264	OEM
47C870N4627	OEM
47C1638NU313	OEM
47D5R03	OEM
47D9R03GH	OEM
47P1	0160
47R2	OEM
47S155275	0312
47TB1-CE00	OEM
47TB1-CH00	OEM
47TB1-EE00	OEM
47TB1-JE00	OEM
47TB1-JH00	OEM
47TB1-LE00	OEM
47TB1-LH00	OEM
47TB1-NE00	OEM
47TB1-NH00	OEM
47TB2-CE00	OEM
47TB2-CH00	OEM
47TB2-EE00	OEM
47TB2-EH00	OEM
47TB2-JE00	OEM
47TB2-JH00	OEM
47TB2-LE00	OEM
47TB2-LH00	OEM
47TB2-NE00	OEM
47TB2-NH00	OEM
47TB3-CE00	OEM
47TB3-CH00	OEM
47TB3-EE00	OEM
47TB3-EH00	OEM
47TB3-JH00	OEM
47TB3-LE00	OEM
47TB3-LH00	OEM
47TB3-NE00	OEM
47TB3-NH00	OEM
47TB4-CE00	OEM
47TB4-CH00	OEM
47TB4-EE00	OEM
47TB4-EH00	OEM
47TB4-JH00	OEM

If replacement code is OEM, contact original manufacturer for replacement.

DEVICE TYPE	REPL CODE
47TB4-LE00	OEM
47TB4-LH00	OEM
47TB4-NE00	OEM
47TB4-NH00	OEM
47TB5-CE00	OEM
47TB5-CH00	OEM
47TB5-EE00	OEM
47TB5-EH00	OEM
47TB5-JH00	OEM
47TB5-LE00	OEM
47TB5-NE00	OEM
47TB5-NH00	OEM
47TB6-CE00	OEM
47TB6-CH00	OEM
47TB6-EE00	OEM
47TB6-EH00	OEM
47TB6-JH00	OEM
47TB6-LE00	OEM
47TB6-NE00	OEM
47TB6-NH00	OEM
47TB7	OEM
47TB7-CE00	OEM
47TB7-CH00	OEM
47TB7-EE00	OEM
47TB7-EH00	OEM
47TB7-JH00	OEM
47TB7-LE00	OEM
47TB7-NE00	OEM
47TB7-NH00	OEM
47TB8-CE00	OEM
47TB8-CH00	OEM
47TB8-EE00	OEM
47TB8-EH00	OEM
47TB8-JH00	OEM
47TB8-LE00	OEM
47TB8-NE00	OEM
47TB8-NH00	OEM
47TB9	OEM
47TB9-CE00	OEM
47TB9-CH00	OEM
47TB9-EE00	OEM
47TB9-EH00	OEM
47TB9-JH00	OEM
47TB9-LE00	OEM
47TB9-NE00	OEM
47TB9-NH00	OEM
47TB10-CE00	OEM
47TB10-CH00	OEM
47TB10-EE00	OEM
47TB10-EH00	OEM
47TB10-JH00	OEM
47TB10-LE00	OEM
47TB10-NE00	OEM
47TB10-NH00	OEM
47TB11	OEM
47TB11-CE00	OEM
47TB11-CH00	OEM
47TB11-EE00	OEM
47TB11-EH00	OEM
47TB11-JH00	OEM
47TB11-LE00	OEM
47TB11-NE00	OEM
47TB11-NH00	OEM
47TB12-CE00	OEM
47TB12-EE00	OEM
47TB12-EH00	OEM
47TB12-JH00	OEM
47TB12-LE00	OEM
47TB12-NE00	OEM
47TB12-NH00	OEM
47V10	OEM
47V11	OEM
47V12	OEM
47Z102536-P1	0133
48-00155077	0133
48-00155119	0155
48-00155128	0023
48-00155192	0999
48-00155222	0261
48-01	0015
48-01-041	1224
48-01-043	2156
48-01-048	1344
48-01-055	3528
48-01-094	1224
48-01+	0015
48-0305A01	OEM
48-03005A01	0133
48-03005A03	0143
48-03005A05	0133
48-03005A06	0124
48-03005A07	0015
48-03005A08	0030
48-03073A06	0244
48-03073A08	0925
48-03073A09	0012
48-03073A10	1266
48-21-0644-012	1189
48-35P1	0211
48-36P1	0211
48-36P3	0211
48-39P1	0160
48-39P3	0211
48-43P3	0211
48-43P4	0211
48-45N2	0111
48-56P1	0279
48-57B2	0160
48-57B42	0160
48-77	1024
48-110	0196
48-171-A06	0004
48-191A01	0015
48-191A01-9	0015
48-191A02	0015
48-191A03	0015
48-191A04	0015
48-191A05	0102
48-191A05A	0102
48-191A06	0015
48-191A07	0015
48-191A07A	0015
48-191A08	0015
48-191A09	0015
48-971-A95	0016
48-971A04	0144
48-971A05	0016
48-971A13	0142
48-971A203	0050
48-1005	0015
48-1050-SL12318	1812
48-1050-SL12319	1035
48-1050-SL12320	2086
48-1050-SL12321	1820
48-1050-SL12322	0033
48-1050-SL12323	0081
48-1050-SL12324	0141
48-1050-SL12325	0557
48-1050-SL12326	0354
48-1050-SL12327	0329
48-3003A02	0018
48-3003A03	0016
48-3003A04	0006
48-3003A05	0016
48-3003A06	0527
48-3003A09	0321
48-3003A10	0212
48-3003A11	0079
48-3003A12	0016
48-6712	0196
48-6712A02	0907
48-8213H07	0519
48-8213H08	0505
48-8375D02	0934
48-8613	0911
48-8613-3	0136
48-8619-3	0143
48-10001-A01	0015
48-10001-A03	0015
48-10001-A030-1	0015
48-10062A01	0015
48-10062A01A	0015
48-10062A02	0015
48-10062A04	0015
48-10062A05	0015
48-10062A05A	0015
48-10073A01	0004
48-10073A02	0211
48-10074A01	0004
48-10074A02	0211
48-10074A03	0004
48-10075A01	0265
48-10075A02	0265
48-10075A03	0265
48-10075A04	0265
48-10075A05	0265
48-10075A06	0265
48-10075A07	0265
48-10075A08	0265
48-10079A01	0050
48-10079A02	0050
48-10103A01	0265
48-10103A02	0265
48-10103A03	0265
48-10103A04	0265
48-10103A05	0265
48-10103A06	0085
48-10103A07	0265
48-10103A08	0265
48-10103A09	0265
48-10103A10	0265
48-10103A11	0085
48-10346A01	0162
48-10346A02	0914
48-10516C02	0030
48-10577A01	0133
48-10577A13	0133
48-12443	0004
48-13466	0038
48-13470	0144
48-13481	0016
48-13494A1G	0111
48-13707	0843
48-17162A06	0004
48-17162A10	0164
48-17162A13	0142
48-17162A17	0004
48-17162A22	0004
48-17271A03	0004
48-21598B01	0004
48-32000	0137
48-34816	0133
48-40004S05	2039
48-40004S06	0930
48-40118B01	0037
48-40118B01A	0037
48-40170-G01	0111
48-40170G01	0111
48-40171G01	0079
48-40172G01	0222
48-40235C02	OEM
48-40235G01	0015
48-40235G02	0023
48-40246-G01	0111
48-40246G01	0111
48-40246G02	0016
48-40247G01	0127
48-40247G02	0111
48-40458A04	0157
48-40458A06	0244
48-40458A064	0244
48-40516C01	0247
48-40516C02	0030
48-40734P01	0781
48-40738P01	0133
48-40739P01	0015
48-40764P01	2475
48-41508A01	0015
48-41508A02	0015
48-41763C01	0244
48-41763C02	0244
48-41763C03	0244
48-41768G01	0019
48-41784J03	1779
48-41784J04	1779
48-41785J03	0455
48-41785J04	0455
48-41815J02	0127
48-41816J01	0127
48-41816J02	0151
48-41873J02	0057
48-41873J03	0170
48-41884J03	0161
48-42098B01	0037
48-42098B01A	0037
48-42383A0	0030
48-42383A01	0030
48-42485B01	0030
48-42503P01	0005
48-42884P01	1581
48-42885P01	0930
48-42899J01	0139
48-43238G01	0037
48-43265G01	0015
48-43283A01	0030
48-43351A01	0004
48-43351A02	0127
48-43351A03	0144
48-43351A04	0144
48-43351A05	0144
48-43354A81	0016
48-43354A82	0016
48-43354A83	0164
48-43467J01	3017
48-43992J01	0224
48-44080J05	0012
48-44885G01	1211
48-44885G02	1211
48-44886G01	0155
48-45323G01	0715
48-47389C01	OEM
48-57120A01	0015
48-60022A13	0016
48-60022A14	0178
48-60022A97	0143
48-60022A98	0015
48-60077A06	0143
48-60154A01	0123
48-61074B01	0143
48-61767B01	0143
48-62334A01	0123
48-62334A02	0143
48-63005A66	0016
48-63005A72	0016
48-63006A56	0143
48-63026A45	0142
48-63026A46	0144
48-63026A47	0016
48-63026A48	0016
48-63029A16	0050
48-63029A17	0164
48-63029A18	0211
48-63029A19	0211
48-63029A20	0143
48-63029A60	0050
48-63029A90	0136
48-63029A91	0211
48-63029A92	0279
48-63029A93	0211
48-63029A94	0211
48-63044A05	0004
48-63075A72	0050
48-63075A73	0050
48-63075A74	0136
48-63075A75	0050
48-63075A76	0279
48-63075A78	0143
48-63076A52	0016
48-63076A81	0127
48-63076A82	0127
48-63076A83	0016
48-63077A03	0279
48-63077A10	0016
48-63077A11	0143
48-63077A29	0144
48-63077A30	0016
48-63077A31	0016
48-63077A32	0143
48-63078A52	0127
48-63078A54	0127
48-63078A59	0279
48-63078A60	0279
48-63078A61	0279
48-63078A62	0164
48-63078A63	0050
48-63078A64	0279
48-63078A65	0136
48-63078A66	0164
48-63078A68	0164
48-63078A69	0164
48-63078A70	0016
48-63078A71	0016
48-63078A86	2839
48-63079A97	0016
48-63081A82	0050
48-63082A15	0279
48-63082A16	0164
48-63082A24	0136
48-63082A25	0016
48-63082A26	0016
48-63082A27	0016
48-63082A45	0016
48-63082A71	0016
48-63084A03	0004
48-63084A04	0004
48-63084A05	0004
48-63084A06	0143
48-63086A16	0015
48-63086A19	0164
48-63090A01	0143
48-63590A01	0143
48-64169	0015
48-64978A10	0265
48-64978A11	0265
48-64978A24	0265
48-64978A27	0050
48-64978A28	0050
48-64978A29	0050
48-64978A39	0212
48-64978A40	0037
48-64978A40A	0037
48-64978A41	0037
48-64978A41A	0037
48-65108A23	0004
48-65108A62	0004
48-65112A65	0144
48-65112A67	0144
48-65112A68	0007
48-65112A73	0911
48-65113A84	0911
48-65113A88	0144
48-65118A64	0144
48-65123A67	0144
48-65123A94	0016
48-65123A95	0144
48-65132A79	0050
48-65144A72	0144
48-65145A74	0015
48-65146A61	0007
48-65146A62	0007
48-65146A63	0007
48-65147A72	0016
48-65173A78	0007
48-65174A24	0007
48-65177A77	0126
48-65177A77A	0126
48-65831A02	1073
48-65837A02	0143
48-65937A02	0143
48-66037A03	0015
48-66037A04	0015
48-66037A05	0015
48-66037A08	0015
48-66037A10	0015
48-66037A12	0015
48-66544A88	1024
48-66629A02	0015
48-66629A03	0015
48-66629A05	0015
48-66629A06	0015
48-66653A001	0015
48-66653A002	0015
48-66653A003	0769
48-66653A005	0769
48-66653A0053	0769
48-66653A02	0469
48-66653APT001	0469
48-66653APT015	0769
48-66653APT0U1	0469
48-66653APT1003	0769
48-66653APT0U1	0469
48-66654A02	0015
48-66865A01	1024
48-66865A02	4947
48-66865A03	4947
48-66865A04	4947
48-67020A11	0143
48-67120A01	0015
48-67120A02	0133
48-67120A03	0133
48-67120A04	0071
48-67120A05	3760
48-67120A06	0015
48-67120A07	0015
48-67120A08	1293
48-67120A09	0143
48-67120A0607	0015
48-67120A10	0071
48-67120A11	0133
48-67926A01	0015
48-68688A79	0015
48-68688A79B	0015
48-69394A01	0016
48-82137H01	1392
48-82137H02	1750
48-82137H03	0663
48-82137H04	0542
48-82137H05	2387
48-82137H06	0864
48-82137H09	0611
48-82256C33	0755
48-82292A03	0143
48-82732C04	1241
48-82965F	0571
48-83461E17	2847
48-83461E23	2073
48-83461E28	0305
48-83461E34	0870
48-83461E39	0262
48-83461E44	0827
48-83741C01	0705
48-83875D01	0442
48-83875D03	0464
48-83875D04	3252
48-83875D05	3253
48-83875D06	0934
48-84973CB1	0720
48-86148	0015
48-86168-3	0143
48-86193	0143
48-86200-3	0143
48-86289-3	0133
48-86343-3	0143
48-86376-3	0016
48-86444-2	1313
48-86797-3	0062
48-86904GF	0050
48-90066A01	0196
48-90068A01	0469
48-90158A01	0102
48-90165A01	0037
48-90165A01A	0037
48-90172A01	0016
48-90210A01	0143
48-90222A08	0143
48-90229A01	0015
48-90232A01	0007
48-90232A03	0144
48-90232A04	0144
48-90232A05	0016
48-90232A06	0126
48-90232A06A	0126
48-90232A07	0142
48-90232A08	0086
48-90232A09	0126
48-90232A09A	0126
48-90232A10	0144
48-90232A11	0016
48-90232A12	0126
48-90232A12A	0126
48-90232A13	0016
48-90232A14	0321
48-90232A15	0126
48-90232A15A	0126
48-90232A16	0142
48-90232A17	0007
48-90232A18	0007
48-90232A19	0144
48-90233A01	0143
48-90233A04	0015
48-90233A05	0911
48-90233A06	0143
48-90233A08	0143
48-90234A01	0015
48-90234A02	0229
48-90234A03	0469
48-90234A11	0928
48-90234A12	0102
48-90234A13	0155
48-90234A14	0006
48-90234A36	0558
48-90234A38	0688
48-90234A39	0321
48-90234A58	3407
48-90234A59	0151
48-90234A60	0715
48-90234A61	2847
48-90234A62	0091
48-90234A64	0111
48-90234A66	0911
48-90234A86	0168
48-90234A97	0140
48-90234A98	0371
48-90234A99	0688
48-90235A01	0196
48-90334A67	0133
48-90343A02	0127
48-90343A05	1211
48-90343A06	1211
48-90343A07	0203
48-90343A08	0203
48-90343A17	0155
48-90343A30	0181
48-90343A50	0076
48-90343A52	0065
48-90343A53	0102
48-90343A54	0182
48-90343A55	0162
48-90343A56	2017
48-90343A57	0261
48-90343A58	0338
48-90343A59	0203
48-90343A61	0388
48-90343A62	0071
48-90343A64	0023
48-90343A66	0143
48-90343A67	0155
48-90343A68	0006
48-90343A70	0520
48-90343A72	1211
48-90343A73	1211
48-90343A75	0113
48-90343A76	0219
48-90343A77	0155
48-90343A79	1212
48-90343A80	0151
48-90343A83	0155
48-90343A85	0558
48-90343A88	0139
48-90343A89	0120
48-90343A91	0015
48-90343A92	0015
48-90343A93	0015
48-90343A94	0466
48-90420A01	0577
48-90420A02	0676
48-90420A03	0124
48-90420A04	0133
48-90420A05	0527
48-90420A06	0919
48-90420A11	1211
48-90420A17	0036
48-90420A18	0052
48-90420A19	0577
48-90420A29	0355
48-90420A30	1211
48-90420A31	2208
48-90420A34	4076
48-90420A36	0151
48-90420A42	0819
48-90420A60	0525
48-90420A61	0042
48-90420A71	0133
48-90420A72	0715
48-90420A73	0261
48-90420A76	0023
48-90420A77	0023
48-90420A79	1791
48-90420A80	1089
48-90420A82	0275
48-90420A83	0643
48-90420A84	0388
48-90420A85	0015
48-90420A86	0015
48-90420A87	0015
48-90420A88	0450
48-90420A92	0275
48-90420A97	0023
48-90420A98	0023
48-90420A99	0155
48-90423A93	0284
48-90432A01	0155
48-90432A03	1009
48-90432A04	0199
48-90432A06	0006
48-90432A08	0520
48-90432A15	0023
48-90432A19	0124
48-90432A28	0781
48-90432A32	2208
48-90432A33	0558
48-90432A34	0577
48-90432A35	0667
48-90432A37	0577
48-90432A40	0057
48-90432A42	0253
48-90432A43	0466
48-90432A55	0819
48-90432A63	0036
48-90432A69	1077
48-90432A70	0388
48-90432A71	0949
48-90432A72	0344
48-90432A73	1603
48-90432A75	0313
48-90432A76	0219
48-90432A77	0819
48-90432A78	0062
48-90432A79	0023
48-90432A80	0071
48-90432A85	2411
48-90432A90	0527
48-90432A91	0111
48-90432A92	0284
48-90432A93	0284
48-90432A94	1593
48-90432A95	1211
48-90432A96	0124
48-90432A97	0124
48-90432A99	0100
48-90445A01	0039
48-90445A05	1211
48-90445A28	0321
48-90445A32	0450
48-90445A44	1260
48-90445A48	0275
48-90445A50	0091
48-90445A53	0261
48-90445A54	0558
48-90445A56	1274
48-90445A57	0781
48-90445A60	0017
48-90445A61	0071
48-90445A62	0676
48-90445A63	0470
48-90445A64	0127
48-90445A65	0275
48-90445A66	0681
48-90445A67	0436
48-90445A68	0203
48-90445A69	0638
48-90445A70	0275
48-90445A71	0275
48-90445A72	1211
48-90445A73	1211
48-90445A74	1211
48-90445A75	1211
48-90445A90	0853
48-90445A92	0597
48-90445A95	0071
48-90445A96	0023
48-90445A97	1319
48-97046A02	0004
48-97046A03	0004
48-97046A04	0144
48-97046A05	0127
48-97046A06	0127
48-97046A07	0127
48-97046A08	0136
48-97046A09	0136
48-97046A1S	0222
48-97046A10	0004
48-97046A14	0446
48-97046A15	0222
48-97046A16	0136
48-97046A17	0127
48-97046A18	0144
48-97046A20	0127
48-97046A21	0127
48-97046A22	0016
48-97046A23	0016
48-97046A24	0016
48-97046A25	0007
48-97046A26	0037
48-97046A27	0037
48-97046A28	0016
48-97046A29	0086
48-97046A30	0042
48-97046A31	0222
48-97046A32	0004
48-97046A33	0004
48-97046A34	0004
48-97046A36	0126
48-97046A37	0164
48-97046A38	0042
48-97046A39	0126
48-97046A40	0086
48-97046A42	0016
48-97046A43	0016
48-97046A45	0007
48-97046A46	0016
48-97046A47	0321
48-97046A48	0321
48-97046A50	0016
48-97046A51	0144
48-97046A52	0079
48-97046A53	0211
48-97046A54	0004
48-97046A55	0004
48-97046A56	0004
48-97046A57	0016
48-97048A01	0133
48-97048A02	0143
48-97048A04	0015
48-97048A05	0123
48-97048A06	0143
48-97048A07	0015
48-97048A08	0137
48-97048A10	0015
48-97048A16	0137
48-97048A17	0133
48-97048A18	0015
48-97048A19	0143
48-97048A20	0071
48-97127A01	0015
48-97127A02	0144
48-97127A03	0144
48-97127A04	0086
48-97127A05	0164
48-97127A06	0127
48-97127A09	0164
48-97127A012	0016
48-97127A013	0016
48-97127A015	0150
48-97127A018	0016
48-97127A019	0086
48-97127A12	0016
48-97127A13	0016
48-97127A15	0150
48-97127A18	0016
48-97127A19	0016
48-97127A20	0004
48-97127A22	0004

If replacement code is OEM, contact original manufacturer for replacement.

147

DEVICE TYPE	REPL CODE
48-97127A23	0164
48-97127A24	0016
48-97127A29	0016
48-97127A30	0004
48-97127A31	0004
48-97127A32	0211
48-97127A33	0016
48-97162A01	0144
48-97162A02	0144
48-97162A03	0136
48-97162A04	0016
48-97162A05	0016
48-97162A06	0164
48-97162A07	0164
48-97162A08	0164
48-97162A09	0016
48-97162A11	0004
48-97162A12	0079
48-97162A15	0016
48-97162A16	0004
48-97162A18	0004
48-97162A19	0004
48-97162A20	0004
48-97162A21	0016
48-97162A23	0016
48-97162A24	0004
48-97162A25	0004
48-97162A26	0127
48-97162A28	0007
48-97162A30	0007
48-97162A31	0007
48-97162A32	0007
48-97162A33	0016
48-97162A34	0164
48-97168A01	0143
48-97168A02	0015
48-97168A03	0123
48-97168A04	0143
48-97168A06	0015
48-97168A07	0143
48-97168A09	0143
48-97168A10	0015
48-97168A11	0015
48-97168A13	0143
48-97168A14	0015
48-97172A01	0015
48-97177A01	0321
48-97177A02	0007
48-97177A03	0007
48-97177A04	0144
48-97177A06	0321
48-97177A07	0144
48-97177A08	0144
48-97177A09	0016
48-97177A010	0455
48-97177A011	0455
48-97177A015	0143
48-97177A10	0546
48-97177A11	0378
48-97177A12	0016
48-97177A13	0016
48-97177A14	0037
48-97177A14A	0037
48-97177A15	0143
48-97177H01	0321
48-97221A01	0004
48-97221A02	0004
48-97221A03	0004
48-97221A04	0004
48-97221A05	0004
48-97222A01	0143
48-97222A02	0015
48-97238A01	0136
48-97238A02	0136
48-97238A03	0136
48-97238A04	0016
48-97238A05	0004
48-97238A06	0222
48-97238A07	0004
48-97239A01	0143
48-97270A01	0015
48-97270A02	0143
48-97271A01	0004
48-97271A02	0004
48-97271A03	0004
48-97271A04	0004
48-97271A05	0050
48-97271A06	0050
48-97271A3	0004
48-97271A4	0004
48-97271A5	0004
48-97271A6	0004
48-97305A02	0157
48-97305A03	0276
48-97305A05	0157
48-97762A02	0144
48-97768A06	0071
48-103083	0435
48-115107	0023
48-123173	0079
48-123522	0136
48-123536	0136
48-123802	0016
48-123803	0016
48-124158	0004
48-124159	0004
48-124175	0004
48-124204	0160
48-124216	0595

DEVICE TYPE	REPL CODE
48-124217	0595
48-124218	0595
48-124219	0211
48-124220	0595
48-124221	0595
48-124246	0160
48-124247	0160
48-124255	0136
48-124256	0136
48-124258	0164
48-124259	0164
48-124275	0164
48-124276	0164
48-124279	0164
48-124285	0160
48-124286	0211
48-124296	0050
48-124297	0211
48-124300	0164
48-124302	0160
48-124303	0211
48-124304	0211
48-124305	0136
48-124306	0211
48-124307	0279
48-124308	0279
48-124309	0211
48-124310	0136
48-124311	0136
48-124312	0136
48-124314	0279
48-124315	0279
48-124316	0136
48-124318	0211
48-124319	0211
48-124322	0164
48-124327	0279
48-124328	0279
48-124329	0435
48-124332	0160
48-124343	0279
48-124344	0279
48-124345	0279
48-124346	0136
48-124347	0136
48-124348	0136
48-124349	0136
48-124350	0136
48-124351	0136
48-124352	0136
48-124353	0211
48-124354	0211
48-124355	0211
48-124356	0160
48-124357	0279
48-124358	0279
48-124359	0279
48-124360	0136
48-124363	0050
48-124364	0136
48-124365	0136
48-124366	0136
48-124367	0136
48-124368	0050
48-124370	0279
48-124371	0279
48-124373	0004
48-124377	0136
48-124378	0279
48-124379	0279
48-124380	0279
48-124388	0136
48-124389	0279
48-124398	0279
48-124443	0279
48-124444	0279
48-124445	0279
48-124446	0279
48-124804	0144
48-124805	0144
48-124808	0144
48-125204	0160
48-125208	0160
48-125228	0136
48-125229	0279
48-125230	0279
48-125231	0279
48-125232	0279
48-125233	0595
48-125234	0595
48-125235	0595
48-125236	0595
48-125237	0279
48-125238	0279
48-125239	0279
48-125240	0279
48-125242	0279
48-125252	0435
48-125267	0160
48-125271	0164
48-125276	0164
48-125278	0136
48-125282	0004
48-125285	0004
48-125286	0435
48-125288	0160
48-125294	0004
48-125296	0279
48-125299	0435

DEVICE TYPE	REPL CODE
48-125332	0160
48-127021	0025
48-128093	0136
48-128094	0164
48-128095	0136
48-128096	0136
48-128219	0050
48-128239	0595
48-128303	0279
48-129934	0160
48-129935	0160
48-129936	0160
48-129937	0160
48-134101	0136
48-134145	0555
48-134173	0016
48-134190A1G	0007
48-134302	0160
48-134372	0136
48-134387	0143
48-134404	0136
48-134405	0136
48-134406	0136
48-134407	0164
48-134408	0004
48-134411	0050
48-134412	0050
48-134413	0050
48-134414	0136
48-134415	0279
48-134416	0279
48-134417	0279
48-134418	0279
48-134419	0279
48-134420	0279
48-134421	0279
48-134422	0279
48-134423	0279
48-134424	0279
48-134425	0279
48-134426	0279
48-134427	0279
48-134428	0279
48-134429	0279
48-134430	0435
48-134431	0841
48-134432	0279
48-134433	0279
48-134434	0136
48-134439	0050
48-134443	0279
48-134444	0279
48-134445	0279
48-134446	0279
48-134447	0160
48-134448	0160
48-134449	0160
48-134450	0279
48-134454	0136
48-134456	0136
48-134457	0136
48-134458	0279
48-134459	0969
48-134462	0279
48-134463	0160
48-134464	0016
48-134465	0016
48-134466	0279
48-134467	2872
48-134468	0279
48-134469	0279
48-134470	0279
48-134471	0279
48-134472	0279
48-134473	0279
48-134474	0279
48-134475	0279
48-134476	0279
48-134477	0279
48-134478	0126
48-134478A	0126
48-134479	0136
48-134480	0136
48-134481	0136
48-134482	0164
48-134483	0164
48-134484	0050
48-134485	0050
48-134486	0050
48-134487	0160
48-134488	0160
48-134493	0160
48-134494	0279
48-134495	0279
48-134496	0279
48-134499	0279
48-134500	0279
48-134501	0279
48-134504	0050
48-134506	0050
48-134507	0050
48-134508	0136
48-134509	0279
48-134510	0279
48-134512	0279
48-134514	0136
48-134519	0160
48-134520	0595
48-134521	0136

DEVICE TYPE	REPL CODE
48-134522	0136
48-134524	0050
48-134525	0037
48-134525A	0037
48-134526	0050
48-134535	0279
48-134536	0136
48-134537	0143
48-134538	0279
48-134539	0279
48-134540	0279
48-134541	0279
48-134542	0279
48-134543	0279
48-134544	0279
48-134545	0136
48-134547	0136
48-134552	0100
48-134553	0279
48-134554	0279
48-134555	0279
48-134556	0279
48-134557	0279
48-134558	0279
48-134559	0279
48-134560	0160
48-134561	0136
48-134562	0279
48-134563	0279
48-134564	0279
48-134565	0279
48-134567	0279
48-134570	0160
48-134572	0004
48-134573	0211
48-134574	0160
48-134575	0160
48-134576	0136
48-134577	0136
48-134578	0136
48-134579	0050
48-134584	0841
48-134585	0841
48-134587	0143
48-134588	0143
48-134591	0136
48-134592	0160
48-134600	0136
48-134601	0136
48-134602	0136
48-134603	0279
48-134604	0279
48-134605	0136
48-134606	0160
48-134610	0279
48-134611	0160
48-134612	0160
48-134613	0160
48-134621	0004
48-134622	0435
48-134623	0969
48-134625	0279
48-134626	0279
48-134631	0279
48-134632	0004
48-134633	0164
48-134634	0160
48-134635	0136
48-134636	0279
48-134637	0279
48-134638	0160
48-134639	0160
48-134640	0599
48-134641	0279
48-134644	0160
48-134645	0160
48-134646	0160
48-134647	0160
48-134648	0233
48-134649	0160
48-134651	0160
48-134652	0969
48-134653	0012
48-134654	0016
48-134655	0279
48-134656	0279
48-134657	0279
48-134659	0100
48-134663	0039
48-134664	0016
48-134665	0016
48-134666	0016
48-134667	0016
48-134668	0016
48-134669	0016
48-134670	0160
48-134672	0160
48-134673	0016
48-134674	0016
48-134675	0016
48-134676	0050
48-134677	0050
48-134678	0050
48-134679	0050
48-134680	0136
48-134681	0136
48-134682	0136
48-134683	0136
48-134684	0136

DEVICE TYPE	REPL CODE
48-134689	0086
48-134690	0016
48-134691	0016
48-134692	0599
48-134693	0050
48-134694	0050
48-134695	0599
48-134696	0160
48-134697	0136
48-134698	0162
48-134699	0327
48-134700	0595
48-134701	0103
48-134701A	0103
48-134702	0037
48-134702A	0037
48-134703	0016
48-134704	0327
48-134705	0016
48-134706	0144
48-134709	0144
48-134711	0136
48-134713	0144
48-134714	0016
48-134715	0103
48-134715A	0103
48-134717	0144
48-134718	0016
48-134719	0144
48-134720	0016
48-134721	0016
48-134722	0160
48-134723	0160
48-134724	0144
48-134725	0144
48-134726	0016
48-134727	0085
48-134728	0149
48-134729	0599
48-134730	0160
48-134731	0085
48-134732	0016
48-134733	0016
48-134733A	0016
48-134734	0016
48-134734A	0016
48-134737	0016
48-134738	0160
48-134739	0016
48-134739A	0142
48-134740	0599
48-134741	0599
48-134742	0599
48-134743	0599
48-134744	0160
48-134745	0037
48-134745A	0037
48-134746	0160
48-134747	0160
48-134748	0599
48-134749	0160
48-134750	0160
48-134751	0160
48-134752	0599
48-134753	0599
48-134756	0007
48-134757	0160
48-134758	0160
48-134759	0160
48-134760	0599
48-134761	0599
48-134763	0160
48-134764	0160
48-134765	0016
48-134766	0160
48-134767	0160
48-134768	0016
48-134769	0015
48-134772	0144
48-134773	0144
48-134774	0144
48-134775	0016
48-134776	0016
48-134777	0144
48-134779	0144
48-134780	0144
48-134781	0133
48-134782	0016
48-134783	0144
48-134784	0144
48-134785	0016
48-134786	0144
48-134787	0144
48-134788	0599
48-134789	0127
48-134790	0015
48-134791	0016
48-134792	1659
48-134795	0136
48-134796	0136
48-134797	0136
48-134798	0136
48-134800	0144
48-134801	0016
48-134802	0016
48-134803	0079
48-134804	0016
48-134805	0224
48-134806	0144

DEVICE TYPE	REPL CODE
48-134807	0016
48-134808	0079
48-134809	0016
48-134810	0710
48-134811	0016
48-134814	0144
48-134815	0037
48-134815A	0037
48-134816	0133
48-134817	0016
48-134818	0144
48-134819	0233
48-134820	0144
48-134821	0144
48-134822	0016
48-134823	0079
48-134824	0016
48-134825	0224
48-134826	0144
48-134827	0144
48-134828	0144
48-134829	0037
48-134829A	0037
48-134830	0037
48-134830A	0688
48-134831	0037
48-134831A	0688
48-134832	0037
48-134832A	0688
48-134833	0037
48-134833A	0037
48-134837	0144
48-134838	0086
48-134839	0016
48-134840	0016
48-134841	0016
48-134842	0016
48-134843	0233
48-134844	0016
48-134845	0127
48-134846	0710
48-134847	0016
48-134848	0016
48-134850	0789
48-134851	0789
48-134852	0016
48-134853	0233
48-134854	0016
48-134855	0144
48-134856	0841
48-134857	0224
48-134858	0039
48-134859	0136
48-134860	0136
48-134861	0136
48-134862	0136
48-134865	0037
48-134865A	0037
48-134866	0037
48-134866A	0037
48-134867	0037
48-134867A	0037
48-134868	0037
48-134868A	0037
48-134869	0037
48-134869A	0037
48-134870	0037
48-134870A	0037
48-134871	0037
48-134871A	0037
48-134872	0142
48-134879	0144
48-134880	0136
48-134882	0103
48-134884	0103
48-134885	0142
48-134888	0160
48-134889	0016
48-134891	0144
48-134892	0144
48-134893	0144
48-134894	0016
48-134895	0016
48-134896	0016
48-134897	0016
48-134898	0233
48-134899	0016
48-134900	0074
48-134901	0637
48-134902	0144
48-134903	0016
48-134904	0127
48-134904A1G	0127
48-134904F	0127
48-134905	0016
48-134906	0016
48-134907	0085
48-134908	0144
48-134909	0037
48-134909A	0037
48-134910	0037
48-134910A	0037
48-134910F	0037
48-134911	0037
48-134912	0244
48-134913	0037
48-134913A	0037
48-134914	0037
48-134914A	0037

DEVICE TYPE	REPL CODE
48-134915	0037
48-134915A	0037
48-134916	0907
48-134917	0907
48-134918	0016
48-134919	0233
48-134920	0142
48-134921	0102
48-134922	0127
48-134923	0127
48-134924	0127
48-134925	0127
48-134926	0127
48-134927	0233
48-134928	0016
48-134929	0016
48-134930	0160
48-134931	0595
48-134932	0326
48-134933	0016
48-134933E	0016
48-134934	0969
48-134935	0016
48-134936	0178
48-134937	0144
48-134938	0160
48-134939	0102
48-134940	0037
48-134940A	0037
48-134941	0086
48-134942	0016
48-134943	0037
48-134943A	0037
48-134944	0321
48-134945	0127
48-134946	0144
48-134947	0160
48-134948	0144
48-134949	0144
48-134950	0144
48-134951	0126
48-134951A	0126
48-134952	0016
48-134953	0086
48-134954	0123
48-134956	0279
48-134957	0012
48-134958	0015
48-134959	0015
48-134960	0144
48-134961	0127
48-134962	0127
48-134963	0127
48-134964	0127
48-134965	0127
48-134966	0127
48-134967	0037
48-134967A	0037
48-134969	0103
48-134970	0016
48-134972	0142
48-134973	0037
48-134973A	0037
48-134974	0160
48-134975	0037
48-134975A	0037
48-134977	0160
48-134978	0102
48-134979	0144
48-134980	0016
48-134981	0127
48-134982	0086
48-134983	0144
48-134985	0144
48-134987	0455
48-134988	0016
48-134989	0037
48-134989A	0037
48-134990	0015
48-134991	0162
48-134992	0016
48-134993	0157
48-134994	0016
48-134995	0637
48-134996	0016
48-134997	0111
48-134998	0275
48-136665	0016
48-137000	0361
48-137001	0969
48-137002	0233
48-137003	0016
48-137004	0144
48-137005	0086
48-137006	0144
48-137007	0016
48-137008	0103
48-137008A	0103
48-137010	0016
48-137011	0264
48-137013	0016
48-137014	0016
48-137015	0111
48-137017	0100
48-137019	0016
48-137020	0037
48-137020A	0037
48-137021	0037
48-137022	0016

If replacement code is OEM, contact original manufacturer for replacement.

DEVICE TYPE	REPL CODE
48-137023	0321
48-137024	1129
48-137025	0085
48-137026	0085
48-137027	0103
48-137027A	0103
48-137029	0015
48-137030	2969
48-137031	0160
48-137032	0037
48-137032A	0037
48-137033	0144
48-137034	0436
48-137035	0233
48-137036	0103
48-137036A	0103
48-137037	0161
48-137039	0841
48-137040	0127
48-137041	0086
48-137043	0016
48-137044	0016
48-137045	0037
48-137045A	0037
48-137046	0037
48-137047	0016
48-137048	0100
48-137053	0103
48-137053A	0103
48-137055	0144
48-137056	0016
48-137057	0016
48-137058	1659
48-137059	0127
48-137061	0037
48-137062	0450
48-137065	3298
48-137067	0037
48-137067A	0037
48-137068	0037
48-137068A	0037
48-137069	0037
48-137069A	0037
48-137070	0843
48-137071	0127
48-137072	0016
48-137073	0016
48-137074	0015
48-137075	0127
48-137076	0127
48-137077	0127
48-137078	0085
48-137079	0103
48-137079A	0103
48-137080	0419
48-137083	0016
48-137088	0086
48-137089	0016
48-137090	0037
48-137090A	0037
48-137091	0546
48-137092	0546
48-137093	0264
48-137096	0016
48-137098	0110
48-137101	0016
48-137102	0085
48-137104	0144
48-137105	0144
48-137106	0016
48-137107	0016
48-137108	0016
48-137109	0016
48-137110	0016
48-137111	0016
48-137112	0102
48-137115	0016
48-137116	0130
48-137118	0160
48-137119	0160
48-137120	0160
48-137121	0599
48-137122	0160
48-137123	0160
48-137124	0160
48-137125	0599
48-137126	0144
48-137127	0037
48-137127A	0037
48-137128	0161
48-137130	0012
48-137132	0436
48-137133	0914
48-137134	0637
48-137136	0144
48-137137	0016
48-137138	0016
48-137139	0016
48-137140	0144
48-137142	2255
48-137143	0015
48-137144	0144
48-137145	0161
48-137146	0161
48-137147	0161
48-137148	0161
48-137149	0546
48-137153	0455
48-137154	0455
48-137155	0455
48-137156	0455
48-137157	0455
48-137158	0144
48-137160	0378
48-137164	0012
48-137165	1659
48-137166	0144
48-137167	0907
48-137168	0378
48-137169	0546
48-137171	0079
48-137171D	0016
48-137172	0016
48-137173	0037
48-137173A	0037
48-137174	0016
48-137175	0103
48-137175A	0103
48-137176	0037
48-137176A	0037
48-137177	0137
48-137178	0969
48-137179	0637
48-137180	0103
48-137180A	0103
48-137183	0122
48-137184	2635
48-137190	0144
48-137191	0144
48-137192	0016
48-137193	0164
48-137194	0144
48-137195	0037
48-137196	0144
48-137197	0007
48-137198	0015
48-137199	0211
48-137200	0161
48-137202	0546
48-137203	0637
48-137205	0071
48-137206	0016
48-137207	0142
48-137208	0015
48-137212	0071
48-137213	0085
48-137214	0222
48-137215	0085
48-137216	0085
48-137217	0085
48-137218	0085
48-137219	0085
48-137220	0085
48-137234	0969
48-137235	0969
48-137238	0855
48-137239	0334
48-137240	0378
48-137251	0103
48-137256	0455
48-137257	0016
48-137258	0455
48-137259	0455
48-137260	0016
48-137265	0016
48-137266	0039
48-137267	0222
48-137268	0222
48-137269	0222
48-137270	0222
48-137271	0222
48-137272	0137
48-137279	0062
48-137280	1129
48-137281	0058
48-137282	1659
48-137290	0071
48-137291	0015
48-137295	0058
48-137299	0143
48-137300	0111
48-137301	0071
48-137302	0071
48-137303	0455
48-137304	0455
48-137306	0700
48-137307	0086
48-137308	0222
48-137309	0419
48-137310	0848
48-137311	2969
48-137312	3136
48-137314	0378
48-137315	0086
48-137316	0071
48-137318	0037
48-137319	0546
48-137320	0378
48-137321	0786
48-137322	0253
48-137324	0037
48-137325	0111
48-137326	0074
48-137327	0535
48-137329	0085
48-137330	0681
48-137331	0455
48-137333	0103
48-137336	0016
48-137338	2782
48-137339	0144
48-137340	0535
48-137341	0065
48-137342	0969
48-137343	0321
48-137344	0103
48-137347	0023
48-137348	0023
48-137349	4508
48-137350	0016
48-137351	0224
48-137352	0144
48-137353	0016
48-137354	0144
48-137355	0144
48-137364	0233
48-137366	0037
48-137367	0969
48-137368	0103
48-137369	2969
48-137370	3136
48-137371	0144
48-137372	0144
48-137373	0016
48-137374	0016
48-137375	0144
48-137376	0144
48-137377	0016
48-137378	0016
48-137379	0037
48-137380	0037
48-137381	0037
48-137382	0037
48-137383	0037
48-137384	0016
48-137385	0133
48-137388	0144
48-137390	0111
48-137391	0037
48-137392	0396
48-137393	0064
48-137394	0681
48-137395	0058
48-137396	0042
48-137398	0016
48-137399	0016
48-137400	0127
48-137421	0244
48-137437	0042
48-137472	0455
48-137473	0161
48-137483	0144
48-137487	0030
48-137488	0212
48-137491	0007
48-137495	0143
48-137501	0455
48-137502	0037
48-137504	0037
48-137505	0546
48-137506	0042
48-137507	0919
48-137509	0016
48-137514	0133
48-137526	2969
48-137527	3136
48-137531	2255
48-137540	0919
48-137549	0161
48-137550	0455
48-137552	0555
48-137553	1257
48-137554	OEM
48-137562	3136
48-137563	0361
48-137566	0919
48-137567	0212
48-137573	0133
48-137577	1075
48-137601	OEM
48-137605	0143
48-137606	OEM
48-137607	0644
48-137610	0378
48-137612	0127
48-137621	1075
48-137855	0016
48-137978	0160
48-137988	0086
48-155035	0006
48-155039	0019
48-155041	0080
48-155042	0219
48-155044	2085
48-155045	0203
48-155046	0155
48-155047	0124
48-155048	0313
48-155051	0261
48-155058	2040
48-155059	0949
48-155060	0133
48-155061	0143
48-155063	0293
48-155065	0203
48-155068	0588
48-155070	0275
48-155071	0284
48-155073	0284
48-155074	0219
48-155077	0133
48-155081	0181
48-155083	0071
48-155087	0224
48-155088	0016
48-155089	1211
48-155093	0284
48-155095	0006
48-155097	0219
48-155099	0023
48-155107	0023
48-155108	0102
48-155110	0949
48-155113	0058
48-155114	0019
48-155116	0676
48-155119	0155
48-155124	0223
48-155125	0102
48-155126	0023
48-155128	0023
48-155130	0638
48-155131	0120
48-155136	0023
48-155140	0130
48-155145	0041
48-155146	0631
48-155148	0139
48-155150	0155
48-155152	0344
48-155153	0168
48-155154	0155
48-155156	0006
48-155157	2422
48-155158	1258
48-155159	0124
48-155173	0139
48-155177	0015
48-155178	0023
48-155179	0023
48-155182	0490
48-155184	0466
48-155185	0041
48-155189	2040
48-155192	0999
48-155193	0015
48-155195	0023
48-155196	0137
48-155197	0065
48-155198	0071
48-155207	0041
48-155209	0638
48-155210	0052
48-155212	0023
48-155213	0638
48-155221	0130
48-155222	0261
48-155223	0102
48-155224	0065
48-155225	0298
48-155235	0015
48-155236	0015
48-155253	0497
48-155258	0124
48-155259	1077
48-155263	0002
48-155279	0120
48-155284	0203
48-155289	0182
48-155293	0577
48-155294	0819
48-155295	0025
48-155296	0023
48-155298	0064
48-155299	0877
48-155334	0124
48-155343	0819
48-355008	0123
48-355029	0058
48-355046	0139
48-355048	0023
48-355052	0224
48-355053	0151
48-355054	0275
48-355056	1740
48-355059	0042
48-443006A06	0313
48-644587	0143
48-644676	0050
48-644677	0050
48-644678	0004
48-644679	0164
48-644681	0143
48-645867	0050
48-646954	0015
48-647311	0143
48-647313	0143
48-647713	0143
48-647829	0015
48-660370A05	0015
48-674297U	0911
48-674970	0911
48-711052	0143
48-732230	1024
48-733746	0015
48-739300	0143
48-741255	0907
48-741280	0143
48-741656	0907
48-741724	0907
48-741752	0479
48-742698	0479
48-742970	0911
48-746831	0015
48-751656	0196
48-751724	1073
48-752497	0015
48-754153	0479
48-822321E07	1391
48-822321E08	1529
48-859248	0086
48-859428	0086
48-865539	0123
48-869001	0004
48-869087B	0085
48-869090	0969
48-869099B	0085
48-869138	0086
48-869148	0211
48-869170	0086
48-869182	0160
48-869184	0086
48-869198	0004
48-869205	0599
48-869206	1659
48-869225	0178
48-869228	0086
48-869237	0160
48-869244	0103
48-869248	0016
48-869249	0211
48-869253	0211
48-869254	0038
48-869256	2123
48-869259	0103
48-869263	0086
48-869264	1659
48-869266	0007
48-869273C	0637
48-869274	0178
48-869278	0103
48-869279C	0074
48-869282	0211
48-869283	0038
48-869301	0178
48-869302	0103
48-869306	1814
48-869308	0126
48-869321	0103
48-869337	0074
48-869380	0086
48-869393	0178
48-869400	0126
48-869408	0074
48-869426	0126
48-869427	0599
48-869450	0007
48-869464	0086
48-869475	0211
48-869475A	0211
48-869476	0038
48-869476A	0038
48-869481	0007
48-869561	6193
48-1370893	0455
48-8690468	0050
48-44885601	1211
48-46785104	0455
48-V34816	0133
48A40458A06	0165
48A40516C02	0030
48A41508A01	0015
48A41508A02	0015
48A42383A01	0030
48A62692A01	0143
48A90456A80	OEM
48A124315	0211
48AA0516C02	0030
48B41266G01	0102
48B41768G01	0019
48B43265G01	0015
48B62334A01	0143
48B63494A01	0030
48B63494H01	0030
48B66629A01	0143
48B66629A02	0143
48B66629A03	0015
48B66629A05	0015
48B67020A11	0143
48B90158A01	0535
48B732230	1024
48B7322230	1024
48C40235C01	0023
48C40235G01	0015
48C40235G02	0102
48C40235G1	0015
48C40524A02	0133
48C42428A01	0019
48C61074B01	0143
48C61767B01	0143
48C65831A02	1073
48C65831A03	0479
48C65832A02	0143
48C65837A01	0143
48C65837A02	0143
48C66037A03	0015
48C66037A04	0015
48C66037A05	0015
48C66037A10	0015
48C66037A12	0015
48C66629A02	0015
48C-66653A-001	0469
48C66653A02	0015
48C66865A01	1024
48C67120A01	0143
48C67120A02	0133
48C67120A05	0015
48C67926A01	0015
48C125233	0038
48C125235	0038
48C125236	0038
48C125237	0136
48C134587	0143
48C134816	0133
48C134840	0127
48C666534A02	0469
48C674970	0911
48C742970	0911
48C751656	0196
48D5R03	OEM
48D9R03GH	OEM
48D67	0133
48D6653APT.005	0769
48D8375D02	0934
48D60154A01	0143
48D63590A01	0143
48D66037A03	0015
48D66037A04	0015
48D66037A05	0015
48D66037A08	0015
48D66653-APT.00	0769
48D66653A02	0469
48D66653A05	0769
48D66653APT001	0469
48D66653APT003	0769
48D66653APT005	0769
48D66653APT015	0769
48D66653APT.005	0769
48D66654A02	0015
48D67120A01	0015
48D67120A02	0015
48D67120A05	0015
48D67120A06	0015
48D67120A07	0015
48D67120A08	1293
48D67120A09	0143
48D67120A011	0079
48D67120A11	0133
48D67120A11(DIO)	0143
48D67120A11(XSTR)	0079
48D67120A13	0133
48D67120A13(C)	0133
48D67120AB	0023
48D67120H02	0015
48D69723A01	1313
48D69723A02	1313
48D69723A02-185	1313
48D69723B01	1313
48D83875D01	0442
48D83875D03	0464
48D83875D04	3252
48D83875D05	3253
48D83875D06	0934
48D90068A01	0469
48D90210A01	0143
48DL7120A02	0907
48E03A	OEM
48E05A	OEM
48G10346A01	0143
48G10346A02	0133
48G13001A01	1021
48J	OEM
48K	OEM
48K35P1	0136
48K36P1	0136
48K36P3	0136
48K39P1	0085
48K43P3	0136
48K43P4	0136
48K45N2	0038
48K56P1	0211
48K57B2	0085
48K57B42	0085
48K64169	0015
48K125230	0085
48K134450	0211
48K134458	0211
48K134494	0050
48K134495	0050
48K134496	0050
48K134587	0143
48K134601	0050
48K134796	0050
48K134798	0050
48K544539	0019
48K640675	0019
48K644681	0019
48K646594	0015
48K646954	0015
48K647311	0143
48K647713	0143
48K647769	0143
48K647829	0015
48K741255	0196
48K741752	0479
48K742698	0479
48K746831	0015
48K751724	1073
48K752297	0015
48K752497	0015
48K754153	0479
48K865539	0123
48K869001	0279
48M355002	0224
48M355004	1211
48M355005	0638
48M355006	0203
48M355007	0006
48M355008	0143
48M355009	0019
48M355012	0261
48M355013	0102
48M355014	0133
48M355016	0023
48M355021	0182
48M355023	0023
48M355025	0080
48M355029	0058
48M355035	0124
48M355036	0120
48M355037	0155
48M355038	0949
48M355039	0219
48M355040	0042
48M355041	0861
48M355042	2085
48M355043	2040
48M355044	0949
48M355045	0015
48M355046	0139
48M355047	0752
48M355048	0102
48M355049	0015
48M355050	1596
48M355051	0074
48M355052	0224
48M355053	0151
48M355054	0275
48M355055	0520
48M355056	1740
48M355057	0275
48M355058	0338
48M355059	0042
48M355062	0313
48M355065	1823
48NSP1035	0160
48P1	0004
48P-2A5	0004
48P60022A97	0143
48P60022A98	0030
48P60077A06	0143
48P63005A72	0079
48P63006A56	0143
48P63076A81	0079
48P63076A82	0079
48P63077A03	0211
48P63077A11	0143
48P63077A31	0079
48P63077A32	0143
48P63077A52	0143
48P63078A52	0079
48P63078A62	0211
48P63078A69	0127
48P63078A70	0079
48P63078A71	0016
48P63078A86	6906
48P63079A97	0079
48P63082A24	0079
48P63082A25	0079
48P63082A26	0079
48P63082A27	0086
48P63082A45	0144
48P63082A71	0144
48P63082A74	OEM
48P63086A18	0079
48P64978A27	0050
48P64978A28	0050
48P64978A29	0050
48P65112A65	0079
48P65112A73	0911
48P65113A88	0079
48P65118A64	0079
48P65123A67	0007
48P65123A95	0127
48P65137A77	OEM
48P65144A72	0127
48P65145A74	OEM
48P65146A61	0127
48P65146A62	0127
48P65146A63	0144
48P65148A02	0005
48P65148A04	OEM
48P65173A77	0015
48P65173A78	0144
48P65174A24	0007
48P65175A12	0283
48P65175A24	OEM
48P65193A55	0911
48P65193A56	0127
48P65194A92	0127
48Q134722	0160
48R2	0206
48R2S	OEM

If replacement code is OEM, contact original manufacturer for replacement.

149

DEVICE TYPE	REPL CODE
48R25	0206
48R10001-A01	0015
48R10001-A03	0015
48R10001-A030-1	0015
48R10062A01	0015
48R10062A02	0015
48R10062A04	0015
48R10062A05	0015
48R10073A02	0136
48R10074A02	0136
48R100620A02	0015
48R100620A04	0015
48R100620A05	0015
48R134407	0211
48R134573	0211
48R134587	0143
48R134621	0004
48R134632	0004
48R134665	0038
48R134666	0086
48R134671	0015
48R134722	0160
48R660370A05	0015
48R859428	0086
48R869138	0086
48R869148	0211
48R869170	0086
48R869206	1659
48R869248	0079
48R869249	0211
48R869253	0211
48R869254	0038
48R869256	2123
48R869264	1659
48R869282	0211
48R869283	0038
48R869306	1814
48R869426	0150
48R869464	0086
48R869475	0211
48R869475A	0211
48R869476	0038
48R869476A	0038
48S00155035	0006
48S00155039	0019
48S00155060	0124
48S00155077	0133
48S00155087	0224
48S00155093	0284
48S00155114	0019
48S00155131	0120
48S00155137	0023
48S00155138	0015
48S00155144	1319
48S00155146	0466
48S00155160	0133
48S00155177	0015
48S00155222	0261
48S00155258	0124
48S00155284	0203
48S00155334	0124
48S00155343	0819
48S00155365	0284
48S00155400	0577
48S00155403	0577
48S00355052	0224
48S50	0899
48S191A02	0015
48S191A04	0015
48S191A04(A)	0015
48S191A05	0102
48S191A06	0015
48S191A07	0015
48S191A08	0102
48S191A11	0015
48S10062A01	0015
48S10062A02	0015
48S10062A05	0015
48S10062A05A	0015
48S10346A02	0143
48S10577A01	0133
48S10577A02	0133
48S10577A04	0102
48S10577A11	0133
48S10577A13	0133
48S10641D62	0631
48S32000	0137
48S40149P01	1212
48S40170G01	0076
48S40171G01	0086
48S40172G01	0222
48S40235G02	0015
48S40241G01	0111
48S40246G01	0127
48S40247G01	0111
48S40247G02	0079
48S40382J01	0555
48S40383J01	1257
48S40606G01	0079
48S40606G02	0111
48S40606J02	0111
48S40607G01	0111
48S40607J01	0111
48S40662G02	0228
48S40662G04	0042
48S40929P01	2176
48S41508A01	0015
48S43239G02	0233
48S43240G01	0042

DEVICE TYPE	REPL CODE
48S43241G01	0042
48S43467J01	3017
48S43991J01	0144
48S43992J01	0144
48S44883G01	0042
48S44884G01	0919
48S44885G01	0016
48S44885G02	0016
48S44886G01	0155
48S44887G01	0133
48S65123A67	0127
48S67120A11	0102
48S67120A13	0133
48S90158A01	0535
48S90233A01	0143
48S90233A02	0143
48S90233A04	0015
48S90233A06	0143
48S90233A07	0137
48S90233A08	0143
48S90234A01	0535
48S90234A02	0015
48S90234A03	0469
48S90235A01	0196
48S97048A04	0535
48S97127A01	0293
48S97168A01	0143
48S97168A04	0143
48S97168A07	0143
48S97172A01	0535
48S97305A02	0157
48S97305A03	0535
48S134404	0211
48S134405	0050
48S134406	0050
48S134407	0050
48S134408	0211
48S134458	0136
48S134587	0143
48S134666	0079
48S134695	0160
48S134718	0079
48S134719	0079
48S134720	0079
48S134721	0079
48S134732	0079
48S134733	0079
48S134733A	0079
48S134734	0016
48S134734A	0079
48S134736	0015
48S134737	0160
48S134739	0142
48S134739A	0142
48S134746	0160
48S134747	0160
48S134751	0160
48S134756	0127
48S134758	0160
48S134759	0160
48S134760	0160
48S134761	0160
48S134765	0079
48S134766	0160
48S134767	0160
48S134768	0079
48S134773	0079
48S134774	0079
48S134775	0079
48S134776	0079
48S134783	0079
48S134784	0079
48S134785	0079
48S134789	0079
48S134790	0015
48S134797	0136
48S134804	0144
48S134805	0079
48S134807	0016
48S134809	0079
48S134810	0079
48S134811	0079
48S134814	0037
48S134815	0037
48S134816	0133
48S134819	0233
48S134820	0007
48S134821	0150
48S134823	0079
48S134825	0127
48S134826	0079
48S134827	0079
48S134830	0037
48S134831	0037
48S134832	0037
48S134837	0079
48S134838	0233
48S134840	0079
48S134841	0079
48S134842	0079
48S134843	0283
48S134844	0079
48S134845	0144
48S134846	0079
48S134850	0137
48S134851	0012
48S134853	0086
48S134854	0016
48S134855	0144

DEVICE TYPE	REPL CODE
48S134857	0079
48S134858	0039
48S134860	0279
48S134861	0279
48S134862	0279
48S134872	0142
48S134879	0079
48S134888	0160
48S134889	0079
48S134894	0079
48S134898	0079
48S134899	0079
48S134900	0074
48S134901	0637
48S134902	0144
48S134903	0016
48S134904	0079
48S134905	0016
48S134906	0016
48S134908	0079
48S134909	0150
48S134910	0150
48S134912	0244
48S134913	0037
48S134915	0037
48S134916	0196
48S134917	0196
48S134918	0079
48S134919	0233
48S134920	0142
48S134921	0015
48S134922	0079
48S134923	0079
48S134924	0079
48S134925	0079
48S134926	0079
48S134927	0079
48S134932	0007
48S134933	0016
48S134934	0969
48S134935	0086
48S134936	0419
48S134937	0326
48S134938	0969
48S134939	0015
48S134941	0079
48S134942	0086
48S134943	0037
48S134944	0321
48S134945(A2C)	0079
48S134946	0144
48S134947	0085
48S134948	0144
48S134949	0007
48S134950	0144
48S134952	0079
48S134953	0086
48S134954	0143
48S134956	0050
48S134957	0012
48S134958	0015
48S134959	0015
48S134960	0144
48S134961	0079
48S134962	0079
48S134963	0079
48S134964	0079
48S134970	0144
48S134972	0142
48S134974	0085
48S134978	1293
48S134979	0144
48S134981	0127
48S134988	0016
48S134989	0037
48S134990	0015
48S134992	0079
48S134995	0637
48S134997	0016
48S134998	0142
48S137000	0137
48S137001	0969
48S137002	0283
48S137003	0079
48S137006	0016
48S137006(A3S)	0079
48S137007	0590
48S137014	0086
48S137015	0111
48S137017	0002
48S137021	0244
48S137021(10)	0244
48S137022	0086
48S137029	0015
48S137031	0160
48S137032	0037
48S137033	0079
48S137034	0436
48S137040	0015
48S137041	0016
48S137044	0079
48S137045	0037
48S137047	0086
48S137055	0144
48S137056	0016
48S137057	0016
48S137063	0039
48S137065	OEM
48S137070	0321

DEVICE TYPE	REPL CODE
48S137074	0015
48S137076	OEM
48S137081	0201
48S137082	0286
48S137093	0264
48S137094	OEM
48S137101	0143
48S137106	0086
48S137107	0016
48S137108	0016
48S137109	0079
48S137110	0016
48S137111	0079
48S137113	0334
48S137114	0752
48S137115	0016
48S137127	0037
48S137133	0133
48S137134	0637
48S137145	0555
48S137158	0127
48S137160	0378
48S137164	0012
48S137167	1141
48S137168	0378
48S137169	0546
48S137170	0631
48S137171	0079
48S137171(D)	0079
48S137172	0016
48S137173	0037
48S137174	0016
48S137190	0079
48S137191	0079
48S137192	0079
48S137203	0637
48S137206	0086
48S137207	0142
48S137208	0015
48S137260	0079
48S137266	0039
48S137270	0222
48S137272	0039
48S137281	0058
48S137295	0058
48S137299	0143
48S137300	0016
48S137308	0222
48S137309	0419
48S137310	0848
48S137311	0042
48S137312	3136
48S137314	0037
48S137315	0016
48S137321	0037
48S137323	0419
48S137330	0002
48S137331	1257
48S137337	OEM
48S137341	0637
48S137342	0969
48S137343	0321
48S137344	0103
48S137347	0023
48S137348	0023
48S137350	0079
48S137351	0079
48S137364	0334
48S137364(H)	0233
48S137369	2969
48S137370	3136
48S137386	0855
48S137387	0631
48S137389	0398
48S137397	1313
48S137415	0283
48S137415(I)	0233
48S137442	0560
48S137472	1257
48S137473	0555
48S137476	0334
48S137495	0143
48S137498	0016
48S137512	0079
48S137524	0359
48S137528	1021
48S137530	0016
48S137531	2255
48S137533	0102
48S137535	0178
48S137539	0065
48S137543	0016
48S137546	0102
48S137548	0074
48S137551	0102
48S137560	OEM
48S137572	0546
48S137855	0079
48S144258	0124
48S155001	0004
48S155002	0015
48S155005	0178
48S155006	0233
48S155013	0419
48S155014	0848
48S155030	0334
48S155034	0949
48S155035	0006
48S155037	0023

DEVICE TYPE	REPL CODE
48S155039	0019
48S155040	0023
48S155041	0080
48S155042	0219
48S155043	0638
48S155044	2085
48S155044(15)	0142
48S155045	0203
48S155046	0155
48S155047	0124
48S155048	0313
48S155050	0058
48S155051	0261
48S155052	0120
48S155053	0861
48S155054	0497
48S155054(ZENER)	0170
48S155056	0182
48S155057	0023
48S155058	2040
48S155059	0949
48S155060	0133
48S155061	0143
48S155062	0042
48S155063	0293
48S155066	0919
48S155067	0103
48S155068	0588
48S155069	0949
48S155070	0275
48S155071	0284
48S155072	0638
48S155073	0284
48S155074	0219
48S155075	2320
48S155076	0065
48S155077	0133
48S155078	0143
48S155079	0023
48S155080	0091
48S155081	0181
48S155082	5094
48S155083	0071
48S155084	0313
48S155085	0071
48S155086	0625
48S155087	0224
48S155087(SCR)	0058
48S155088	0016
48S155089	1211
48S155090	0223
48S155091	1274
48S155092	0058
48S155093	0284
48S155094	0284
48S155095	0006
48S155096	0638
48S155097	0219
48S155098	1257
48S155099	0023
48S155100	0023
48S155103	0137
48S155104	0002
48S155105	0042
48S155106	0015
48S155107	0023
48S155108	0102
48S155110	0638
48S155111	0219
48S155114	0019
48S155116	0676
48S155117	0155
48S155118	0820
48S155121	0018
48S155122	0527
48S155123	0218
48S155126	0023
48S155127	0446
48S155128	0023
48S155129	0124
48S155131	0120
48S155136	0023
48S155137	0023
48S155138	0023
48S155139	0344
48S155140	0130
48S155141	0079
48S155144	1319
48S155150	0155
48S155160	0133
48S155169	0140
48S155177	0015
48S155178	0023
48S155179	0023
48S155180	5131
48S155183	0124
48S155189	2040
48S155193	0023
48S155195	0023
48S155199	0388
48S155199(ZENER)	0466
48S155201	0023
48S155207	0041
48S155213	0638
48S155222	0261
48S155223	0102
48S155224	0065
48S155225	0298
48S155238	0015

DEVICE TYPE	REPL CODE
48S155239	1089
48S155241	2422
48S155242	0155
48S155252	4961
48S155258	0124
48S155259	1077
48S155267	5161
48S155275	0312
48S155279	0120
48S155280	0877
48S155281	0091
48S155282	0062
48S155284	0203
48S155285	0819
48S155286	0060
48S155287	0006
48S155289	0182
48S155292	0023
48S155293	0577
48S155294	0819
48S155295	0025
48S155296	0023
48S155298	0064
48S155299	0041
48S155302	0168
48S155305	0949
48S155307	0284
48S155310	0071
48S155311	0025
48S155312	0313
48S155313	0102
48S155314	0497
48S155317	0170
48S155320	0577
48S155323	0064
48S155324	0071
48S155325	0165
48S155333	0388
48S155336	0023
48S155337	0060
48S155343	0819
48S155349	0002
48S155366	0120
48S155376	0604
48S155377	0311
48S155378	0700
48S155380	0203
48S155382	1203
48S155383	2320
48S155387	0440
48S164844	OEM
48S317113	0233
48S317476	0233
48S623334A01	0143
48S1552132	0638
48SP134804	0079
48SP134826	0127
48SP134837	0127
48SP134855	0079
48SP134857	0127
48SP134894	0079
48SP134897	0079
48SP134903	0079
48SP134904	0127
48SP134905	0079
48SP134906	0079
48SP134933	0079
48SP134937	0127
48ST-2SD870	0055
48ST-2SD871	0055
48T43394P01	0525
48T43688P01	OEM
48T66544A88	1024
48V68629A40	OEM
48X00155093	OEM
48X90	OEM
48X9271A03	0211
48X90223A02	0155
48X90223A03	0091
48X90223A04	0466
48X90229A02	0667
48X90229A03	2452
48X90229A04	0261
48X90229A05	0055
48X90229A06	0018
48X90229A07	0615
48X90229A08	OEM
48X90229A09	0041
48X90229A15	0525
48X90229A16	1997
48X90229A17	0284
48X90229A18	0203
48X90229A19	1593
48X90229A20	0155
48X90229A36	0064
48X90229A37	0261
48X90229A38	0396
48X90229A45	0355
48X90229A46	6972
48X90229A47	0134
48X90229A48	0597
48X90229A52	0203
48X90229A56	0667
48X90229A61	0455
48X90229A66	2895
48X90229A67	0053
48X90229A68	0053
48X90229A69	0006
48X90229A70	0274

DEVICE TYPE	REPL CODE
48X90229A94	0525
48X90229A97	2208
48X90229A98	0118
48X90229A99	OEM
48X90232A01	0079
48X90232A02	0079
48X90232A03	0079
48X90232A04	0079
48X90232A05	0086
48X90232A06	0150
48X90232A07	0086
48X90232A08	0079
48X90232A09	0150
48X90232A10	0079
48X90232A11	0079
48X90232A12	0150
48X90232A13	0079
48X90232A14	0321
48X90232A15	0150
48X90232A16	0142
48X90232A17	0127
48X90232A18	0127
48X90232A19	0127
48X90232A20	0127
48X90232A40	1211
48X90232A47	0922
48X90232A67	0124
48X90232A68	0091
48X90232A69	0091
48X90232A72	0681
48X90232A74	0077
48X90232A75	2895
48X90232A76	OEM
48X90232A80	2047
48X90232A83	0124
48X90232A84	0631
48X90232A89	0873
48X90232A90	0339
48X90232A91	0489
48X90232A92	0165
48X90232A93	0137
48X90232A94	0071
48X90232A95	0017
48X90232A96	0041
48X90232A97	0755
48X90232A98	0700
48X90232A99	0261
48X90233A01	0143
48X90233A02	0143
48X90233A03	OEM
48X90233A04	0015
48X90233A05	0911
48X90233A06	0143
48X90233A07	0137
48X90233A08	0030
48X90233A09	0549
48X90233A17	0133
48X90233A25	0060
48X90233A26	0388
48X90233A27	0168
48X90233A28	0060
48X90233A39	0053
48X90233A40	0819
48X90233A41	0253
48X90233A50	0041
48X90233A55	1997
48X90233A67	0911
48X90234A01	0015
48X90234A02	0015
48X90234A03	0015
48X90234A05	0286
48X90234A59	0151
48X90234A66	0911
48X90234A67	0133
48X90235A01	0196
48X90235A05	0057
48X90235A09	0339
48X90235A70	0009
48X90235A72	0133
48X90237A18	0284
48X90237A19	0155
48X90237A20	0155
48X90237A62	0071
48X90237A63	0077
48X90237A64	0062
48X90237A65	0052
48X90237A66	0133
48X90343A02	0127
48X90343A07	0203
48X90343A39	0466
48X90343A54	0182
48X90343A83	0155
48X90380A03	0388
48X90380A04	0527
48X90380A05	0023
48X90380A06	0140
48X90380A07	0489
48X90380A08	0017
48X90380A09	0041
48X90380A10	0615
48X90380A29	0339
48X90380A30	0681
48X90380A46	0120
48X90380A74	0577
48X90380A76	0203
48X90380A77	0527
48X90380A78	0577
48X90380A80	0667
48X90380A85	0057

If replacement code is OEM, contact original manufacturer for replacement.

DEVICE TYPE	REPL CODE
48X90380A86	0071
48X90380A87	0163
48X90420A01	0577
48X90420A24	0577
48X90420A28	0819
48X90420A29	0355
48X90420A31	2208
48X90420A42	0819
48X90420A43	0018
48X90420A53	0120
48X90420A56	0060
48X90420A74	0949
48X90420A83	0643
48X90420A85	0015
48X90420A86	0015
48X90420A87	0015
48X90420A88	0450
48X90420A90	0309
48X90420A92	0275
48X90420A98	0023
48X90432A01	0155
48X90432A11	1767
48X90432A14	1593
48X90432A15	0023
48X90432A32	2208
48X90432A35	0667
48X90432A36	0667
48X90432A37	0577
48X90432A41	0873
48X90432A42	0253
48X90432A54	0355
48X90432A55	0819
48X90432A57	0577
48X90445A11	2208
48X90445A17	0577
48X90445A33	0127
48X90445A34	0151
48X90445A40	0296
48X90445A52	0181
48X90445A60	2506
48X90445A63	0042
48X90445A71	0275
48X90445A74	1211
48X90445A91	0667
48X90445A93	0553
48X90445A94	0440
48X90445A96	0023
48X90445A97	1319
48X90456A04	0355
48X90456A07	4282
48X90456A11	0667
48X90456A12	0111
48X90456A16	0253
48X90456A24	0124
48X90456A26	0124
48X90456A32	0690
48X90456A34	1319
48X90456A35	0667
48X90456A47	0284
48X90456A70	0023
48X90456A71	0052
48X90456A72	0133
48X90456A73	0993
48X90456A75	0949
48X90456A76	0161
48X90456A77	2636
48X90456A80	0695
48X90456A94	0023
48X90456A95	0023
48X90456A96	0062
48X90478A04	0577
48X90478A05	1260
48X90478A06	3136
48X90478A10	0023
48X90478A13	0062
48X90478A15	0853
48X90478A16	0853
48X90478A17	3136
48X90478A18	0643
48X90478A20	1203
48X90478A21	0155
48X90478A22	1203
48X90478A23	3096
48X90478A24	4796
48X90478A26	1404
48X90478A27	0071
48X90478A27(MI-152A)	OEM
48X90478A28	1009
48X90478A29	0053
48X90478A30	0041
48X90478A31	OEM
48X90478A45	0203
48X90478A46	0527
48X90478A47	0355
48X90478A48	0819
48X90478A50	0419
48X90478A51	0558
48X90478A52	0577
48X90478A53	0577
48X90478A54	0667
48X90478A55	0042
48X90478A57	0023
48X90478A60	0023
48X90478A61	0041
48X90478A68	0577
48X90478A69	0667
48X90478A70	0120
48X90478A71	0041
48X90478A72	0062
48X90478A73	0077
48X90478A75	0023
48X90478A77	0695
48X90478A78	0181
48X90478A91	0041
48X90478A94	4282
48X90478A98	0018
48X90488A01	0124
48X90488A16	0355
48X90488A17	0577
48X90488A42	0261
48X90488A44	0440
48X90488A45	0023
48X90488A46	0077
48X90488A47	0015
48X90488A48	0015
48X90488A49	0261
48X90488A50	0359
48X90488A51	2643
48X90488A61	1740
48X90488A62	0690
48X90488A63	0681
48X90488A66	2643
48X90488A68	0181
48X90488A69	0071
48X90488A71	OEM
48X90488A74	0355
48X90532A36	0667
48X97046A15	0222
48X97046A16	0136
48X97046A17	0079
48X97046A18	0079
48X97046A19	0151
48X97046A20	0151
48X97046A21	0151
48X97046A22	1211
48X97046A23	1211
48X97046A24	0111
48X97046A25	0079
48X97046A31	0222
48X97046A32	0435
48X97046A34	0211
48X97046A36	0203
48X97046A48	1056
48X97046A50	0079
48X97046A51	0144
48X97046A52	0086
48X97046A53	0004
48X97046A54	0004
48X97046A55	0004
48X97046A60	0016
48X97046A61	0016
48X97046A62	0016
48X97048A02	0143
48X97048A04	0015
48X97048A05	0143
48X97048A06	0143
48X97048A07	0015
48X97048A08	0137
48X97048A09	0030
48X97048A10	0015
48X97048A18	0079
48X97048A19	0143
48X97127A01	0015
48X97127A05	0211
48X97127A22	0211
48X97162A01	0144
48X97162A02	0144
48X97162A03	0050
48X97162A04	0144
48X97162A05	0016
48X97162A06	0004
48X97162A07	0004
48X97162A09	0144
48X97162A10	0144
48X97162A17	0211
48X97162A19	0211
48X97162A21	0016
48X97162A36	0164
48X97162A37	0164
48X97168A01	0143
48X97168A02	0030
48X97168A03	0143
48X97168A04	0143
48X97168A06	0015
48X97168A07	0143
48X97168A10	0015
48X97168A-11	OEM
48X97168A11	0030
48X97168A16	0015
48X97172A01	0015
48X97177A03	0079
48X97177A10	0546
48X97177A11	0378
48X97177A12	0086
48X97177A13	0079
48X97177A14	0150
48X97177A15	0143
48X97177H01	0321
48X97221A01	0211
48X97221A02	0050
48X97221A03	0211
48X97221A04	0211
48X97221A05	0211
48X97222A01	0143
48X97222A02	0015
48X97238A01	0136
48X97238A02	0136
48X97238A03	0136
48X97238A04	0016
48X97238A05	0211
48X97238A06	0816
48X97239A01	0143
48X97271A01	0015
48X97271A02	0143
48X97271A03	0211
48X97305A02	0157
48X97305A03	0782
48X134902	0127
48X134970	0079
48X155172	0819
48X155222	0261
48X155238	1791
48X155241	2422
48X355052	0224
48X644681	0143
48X9048844	OEM
49-1	0144
49-1042	0015
49-3112	0015
49-61963	2255
49-B-1-AH	OEM
49A0000	1423
49A0002-000	1164
49A0005-000	0507
49A0006-000	0692
49A0010	0033
49A0012-000	1303
49A0510	0033
49P1C	0160
49RECT-SI-154	0023
49ST-2SC1213D-24	0191
49X90232A05	0079
50	OEM
50-30307-01	OEM
50-30307-07	0527
50-30702-06	0006
50-30702-07	0006
50-30715-06	0148
50-30715-07	0148
50-30715-08	0148
50-30718-07	0527
50-30727-05	1900
50-30737-07	1514
50-30740-06	1638
50-40101-04	0127
50-40101-05	0144
50-40102-04	0127
50-40102-05	0079
50-40105-08	0284
50-40106-09	0037
50-40201-08	0016
50-40201-09	0076
50-40201-10	0079
50-40204-10	0150
50-40205-09	0037
50-40301-02	2643
50-40306-07	0018
50-40708-06	0076
50-40708-07	0076
50-40708-09	0076
50-40711-06	0066
50-40711-07	0066
50-40712-08	0860
50-40724-03	0055
50-40725-06	0309
50-40726-05	1274
50-40727-08	0261
50-40733-04	0261
50-40734-08	0270
50-40735-07	1553
50-40741-12	2058
50-40743-01	0551
50-40744-06	0388
50-41001-01	2636
50-41302-01	1485
50-50704-11	3017
50A	0015
50A52	0136
50A102	0136
50A103	0126
50A103K	0136
50AC40A	OEM
50AC60A	OEM
50AC80A	OEM
50AC100A	OEM
50AC120A	OEM
50AD50	OEM
50AD100	OEM
50AD200	OEM
50AD400	OEM
50AD600	OEM
50AD800	OEM
50AS	0015
50B5	0015
50B54	0004
50B173-C	0004
50B173-S	0004
50B173C	0211
50B175-B	0279
50B175A	0004
50B175B	0004
50B175C	0004
50B324	0164
50B364	0164
50B415	0164
50B423	0004
50BU75-C	0004
50C	0015
50C05	3716
50C05R	2640
50C5R	2168
50C6-7	OEM
50C6.5-7.5	OEM
50C10	2629
50C10R	2670
50C20	2633
50C20R	2741
50C30	2639
50C30R	2828
50C40	1995
50C40R	2879
50C50	2652
50C50R	2946
50C60	2657
50C60R	3022
50C70	3846
50C70R	3088
50C80	3846
50C80R	3088
50C90	2631
50C90R	3178
50C100	2631
50C100R	3178
50C371	0016
50C372	0016
50C373	0016
50C374	0016
50C380-0	0127
50C380-OR	0127
50C394-0	0127
50C394-R	0127
50C538	0016
50C644	0016
50C784	0144
50C784-R	0127
50C828	0016
50C829	0144
50C829B	0144
50C829C	0144
50C838	0016
50C1047	0144
50CJ139	0079
50CZ5.0	OEM
50CZ5.0A	OEM
50CZ5.0B	OEM
50CZ6.0	OEM
50CZ6.0A	OEM
50CZ6.0B	OEM
50CZ6.5	OEM
50CZ6.5A	OEM
50CZ6.5B	OEM
50CZ7.0	OEM
50CZ7.0A	OEM
50CZ7.0B	OEM
50CZ7.5	OEM
50CZ7.5A	OEM
50CZ7.5B	OEM
50CZ8.0	OEM
50CZ8.0A	OEM
50CZ8.0B	OEM
50CZ8.5	OEM
50CZ8.5A	OEM
50CZ8.5B	OEM
50CZ9.0	OEM
50CZ9.0A	OEM
50CZ9.0B	OEM
50CZ10	OEM
50CZ10A	OEM
50CZ10B	OEM
50CZ11	OEM
50CZ11A	OEM
50CZ11B	OEM
50CZ12	OEM
50CZ12A	OEM
50CZ12B	OEM
50CZ13	OEM
50CZ13A	OEM
50CZ13B	OEM
50CZ14	OEM
50CZ14A	OEM
50CZ14B	OEM
50CZ15	OEM
50CZ15A	OEM
50CZ15B	OEM
50CZ16	OEM
50CZ16A	OEM
50CZ16B	OEM
50CZ17	OEM
50CZ17A	OEM
50CZ17B	OEM
50CZ18	OEM
50CZ18A	OEM
50CZ18B	OEM
50CZ20	OEM
50CZ20A	OEM
50CZ20B	OEM
50CZ22	OEM
50CZ22A	OEM
50CZ22B	OEM
50CZ24	OEM
50CZ24A	OEM
50CZ24B	OEM
50CZ26	OEM
50CZ26A	OEM
50CZ26B	OEM
50CZ28	OEM
50CZ28A	OEM
50CZ28B	OEM
50CZ30	OEM
50CZ30A	OEM
50CZ30B	OEM
50CZ33	OEM
50CZ33A	OEM
50CZ33B	OEM
50CZ36	OEM
50CZ36A	OEM
50CZ36B	OEM
50CZ40	OEM
50CZ40A	OEM
50CZ40B	OEM
50CZ43	OEM
50CZ43A	OEM
50CZ43B	OEM
50CZ45	OEM
50CZ45A	OEM
50CZ45B	OEM
50CZ48	OEM
50CZ48A	OEM
50CZ48B	OEM
50CZ51	OEM
50CZ51A	OEM
50CZ51B	OEM
50CZ54	OEM
50CZ54A	OEM
50CZ54B	OEM
50CZ58	OEM
50CZ58A	OEM
50CZ58B	OEM
50CZ60	OEM
50CZ60A	OEM
50CZ60B	OEM
50CZ64	OEM
50CZ64A	OEM
50CZ64B	OEM
50CZ70	OEM
50CZ70A	OEM
50CZ70B	OEM
50CZ75	OEM
50CZ75A	OEM
50CZ75B	OEM
50CZ78	OEM
50CZ78A	OEM
50CZ78B	OEM
50CZ85	OEM
50CZ85A	OEM
50CZ85B	OEM
50CZ90	OEM
50CZ90A	OEM
50CZ90B	OEM
50CZ100	OEM
50CZ100A	OEM
50CZ100B	OEM
50CZ110	OEM
50CZ110A	OEM
50CZ110B	OEM
50D1	OEM
50D2	0015
50D4	0015
50D6	OEM
50D8	0071
50D10	0071
50D12	OEM
50D14	OEM
50D15	OEM
50D16	OEM
50D18	OEM
50D20	OEM
50D25	OEM
50D30	OEM
50D40	OEM
50D50	OEM
50E03A	OEM
50E05	0015
50E05A	OEM
50E1	0015
50E2	0015
50E3	0015
50E4	0015
50E5	0015
50E6	0015
50E7	0071
50E8	0071
50E10	0071
50E12	OEM
50E14	OEM
50E16	5254
50E18	OEM
50E20	OEM
50F1	2065
50F5	0200
50F20	OEM
50F30	OEM
50F40	OEM
50F50	OEM
50G6P41	OEM
50H3	OEM
50H3N	0471
50H3P	0200
50H3PN	0995
50HQ020	1536
50HQ030	1536
50HQ035	1536
50HQ040	1536
50HQ045	1536
50HV100AV10L	OEM
50J	OEM
50J1	1760
50J2P	0116
50J3P	0116
50J6P41	OEM
50JH3	2844
50K	OEM
50K10	OEM
50K20	OEM
50K30	OEM
50K40	OEM
50K50	OEM
50KZ5.0	OEM
50KZ5.0A	OEM
50KZ5.0B	OEM
50KZ6.0	OEM
50KZ6.0A	OEM
50KZ6.0B	OEM
50KZ6.5	OEM
50KZ6.5A	OEM
50KZ6.5B	OEM
50KZ7.0	OEM
50KZ7.0A	OEM
50KZ7.0B	OEM
50KZ7.5	OEM
50KZ7.5A	OEM
50KZ7.5B	OEM
50KZ8.0	OEM
50KZ8.0A	OEM
50KZ8.0B	OEM
50KZ8.5	OEM
50KZ8.5A	OEM
50KZ8.5B	OEM
50KZ9.0	OEM
50KZ9.0A	OEM
50KZ9.0B	OEM
50KZ10	OEM
50KZ10A	OEM
50KZ10B	OEM
50KZ11	OEM
50KZ11A	OEM
50KZ11B	OEM
50KZ12	OEM
50KZ12A	OEM
50KZ12B	OEM
50KZ13	OEM
50KZ13A	OEM
50KZ13B	OEM
50KZ14	OEM
50KZ14A	OEM
50KZ14B	OEM
50KZ15	OEM
50KZ15A	OEM
50KZ15B	OEM
50KZ16	OEM
50KZ16A	OEM
50KZ16B	OEM
50KZ17	OEM
50KZ17A	OEM
50KZ17B	OEM
50KZ18	OEM
50KZ18A	OEM
50KZ18B	OEM
50KZ20	OEM
50KZ20A	OEM
50KZ20B	OEM
50KZ22	OEM
50KZ22A	OEM
50KZ22B	OEM
50KZ24	OEM
50KZ24A	OEM
50KZ24B	OEM
50KZ26	OEM
50KZ26A	OEM
50KZ26B	OEM
50KZ28	OEM
50KZ28A	OEM
50KZ28B	OEM
50KZ30	OEM
50KZ30A	OEM
50KZ30B	OEM
50KZ33	OEM
50KZ33A	OEM
50KZ33B	OEM
50KZ36	OEM
50KZ36A	OEM
50KZ36B	OEM
50KZ40	OEM
50KZ40A	OEM
50KZ40B	OEM
50KZ43	OEM
50KZ43A	OEM
50KZ43B	OEM
50KZ45	OEM
50KZ45A	OEM
50KZ45B	OEM
50KZ48	OEM
50KZ48A	OEM
50KZ48B	OEM
50KZ51	OEM
50KZ51A	OEM
50KZ51B	OEM
50KZ54	OEM
50KZ54A	OEM
50KZ54B	OEM
50KZ58	OEM
50KZ58A	OEM
50KZ58B	OEM
50KZ60	OEM
50KZ60A	OEM
50KZ60B	OEM
50KZ64	OEM
50KZ64A	OEM
50KZ64B	OEM
50KZ70	OEM
50KZ70A	OEM
50KZ70B	OEM
50KZ75	OEM
50KZ75A	OEM
50KZ75B	OEM
50KZ78	OEM
50KZ78A	OEM
50KZ78B	OEM
50KZ85	OEM
50KZ85A	OEM
50KZ85B	OEM
50KZ90	OEM
50KZ90A	OEM
50KZ90B	OEM
50KZ100	OEM
50KZ100A	OEM
50KZ100B	OEM
50KZ110	OEM
50KZ110A	OEM
50KZ110B	OEM
50L6P41	OEM
50L15	OEM
50L20	OEM
50L25	OEM
50L30	OEM
50L35	OEM
50L40	OEM
50L45	OEM
50L50	OEM
50L55	OEM
50L60	OEM
50L65	OEM
50L70	OEM
50L75	OEM
50L80	OEM
50L85	OEM
50L90	OEM
50L95	OEM
50L100	OEM
50L110	OEM
50L120	OEM
50L130	OEM
50L140	OEM
50L150	OEM
50L160	OEM
50L170	OEM
50L180	OEM
50L190	OEM
50L200	OEM
50L210	OEM
50L220	OEM
50L230	OEM
50L240	OEM
50L250	OEM
50L260	OEM
50L270	OEM
50L280	OEM
50L290	OEM
50L300	OEM
50LA	OEM
50LF	OEM
50LF11	OEM
50M	0015
50M9.1SZ	OEM
50M9.1SZ5	0988
50M24Z5	0273
50M33Z5	0314
50M62Z5	0382
50MV80	OEM
50MV100	OEM
50MV120	OEM
50N15A	OEM
50N15A9	OEM
50N20A	OEM
50N20A9	OEM
50N25A	OEM
50N25A9	OEM
50N30A	OEM
50N30A9	OEM
50N35A	OEM
50N35A9	OEM
50N40A	OEM
50N40A9	OEM
50N45A	OEM
50N45A9	OEM
50N50A	OEM
50N50A9	OEM
50N55A	OEM
50N55A9	OEM
50N60A	OEM
50N60A9	OEM
50N65A	OEM
50N65A9	OEM
50N70A	OEM
50N70A9	OEM
50N75A	OEM
50N75A9	OEM
50N80A	OEM
50N80A9	OEM
50N85A	OEM
50N85A9	OEM
50N90A	OEM

If replacement code is OEM, contact original manufacturer for replacement.

151

DEVICE TYPE	REPL CODE
50N90A9	OEM
50N95A	OEM
50N95A9	OEM
50N100A	OEM
50N100A9	OEM
50N110A	OEM
50N120A	OEM
50N130A	OEM
50N140A	OEM
50N150A	OEM
50N160A	OEM
50N170A	OEM
50N180A	OEM
50N190A	OEM
50N200A	OEM
50N210A	OEM
50N220A	OEM
50N230A	OEM
50N240A	OEM
50NF11	OEM
50P1SP	OEM
50P2	0136
50P2SG	OEM
50P2SP	OEM
50P3	0136
50P3SP	OEM
50P4SG	OEM
50P4SP	OEM
50P5SP	OEM
50P6SG	OEM
50P6SP	OEM
50P8SG	OEM
50P8SP	OEM
50P10SG	OEM
50P10SP	OEM
50P12SP	OEM
50P16SP	OEM
50Q6P42	OEM
50QF11	OEM
50R2	OEM
50R2S	0583
50R3P	OEM
50RCS5	1694
50RCS5S60	1694
50RCS10	1694
50RCS10S60	1694
50RCS20	1694
50RCS20S60	1694
50RCS30	3970
50RCS30S60	3970
50RCS40	3970
50RCS40S60	3970
50RCS50	OEM
50RCS60	3970
50RCS60S60	3970
50RCS70	OEM
50RCS80	0674
50RCS80S60	0674
50RCS90	OEM
50RCS100	0674
50RCS100S60	0674
50RCS110	0674
50RCS110S60	0674
50RCS120	0674
50RCS120S60	0674
50RIA5	OEM
50RIA10	1694
50RIA10M	OEM
50RIA20	1694
50RIA20M	OEM
50RIA30	OEM
50RIA40	3970
50RIA40M	OEM
50RIA60	3970
50RIA60M	OEM
50RIA80	0674
50RIA80M	OEM
50RIA100	0674
50RIA100M	OEM
50RIA110	0674
50RIA110M	OEM
50RIA120	0674
50RIA120M	OEM
50S2SP	OEM
50S2.5-3.5	OEM
50S3P	OEM
50S3SP	OEM
50S3.4	OEM
50S4SP	OEM
50S5	2065
50S5SP	OEM
50S6SP	OEM
50S8SP	OEM
50S20	OEM
50S30	OEM
50S40	OEM
50S50	OEM
50SI-HA11446	2109
50SQ030	OEM
50SQ035	OEM
50SQ040	OEM
50SQ045	OEM
50SQ060	OEM
50SQ080	OEM
50SQ090	OEM
50SQ0100	OEM
50SS2SP	OEM
50SS3SP	OEM
50SS4SP	OEM

DEVICE TYPE	REPL CODE
50SS5SP	OEM
50SS6SP	OEM
50SS8SP	OEM
50ST-2SC945R	0076
50ST-2SD467(B)	0945
50ST-2SD467B	0945
50SZ-HZ12A2	0999
50T3P	OEM
50T6.8	0920
50T6.8A	0920
50T6.8B	0920
50T7.5	0938
50T7.5A	0938
50T7.5B	0938
50T8.2	0952
50T8.2A	0952
50T8.2B	0952
50T9.1	0988
50T9.1A	0988
50T9.1B	0988
50T10	1003
50T10A	1003
50T10B	1003
50T11	1013
50T11A	1013
50T11B	1013
50T12	0883
50T12A	0883
50T12B	0883
50T13	1043
50T13A	1043
50T13B	1043
50T15	0926
50T15A	0926
50T15B	0926
50T16	1072
50T16A	1072
50T16B	1072
50T18	1098
50T18A	1098
50T18B	1098
50T20	1127
50T20A	1127
50T20B	1127
50T22	1144
50T22A	1144
50T22B	1144
50T24	1156
50T24A	1156
50T24B	1156
50T27	1176
50T27A	1176
50T27B	1176
50T30	1201
50T30A	1201
50T30B	1201
50T33	1214
50T33A	1214
50T33B	1214
50T36	1223
50T36A	1223
50T36B	1223
50T39	1237
50T39A	1237
50T39B	1237
50T43	1256
50T43A	1256
50T43B	1256
50T45	1263
50T47	1280
50T47A	1280
50T47B	1280
50T51	1297
50T51A	1297
50T51B	1297
50T62	1343
50T62A	1343
50T62B	1343
50T68	1355
50T68A	1355
50T68B	1355
50T75	1374
50T75A	1374
50T75B	1374
50T82	1391
50T82A	1391
50T82B	1391
50T91	1402
50T91A	1402
50T91B	1402
50T100	1413
50T100A	1413
50T100B	1413
50T110	1435
50T110A	1435
50T110B	1435
50T120	1448
50T120A	1448
50T120B	1448
50T130	1461
50T130A	1461
50T130B	1461
50T150	1497
50T150A	1497
50T150B	1497
50T160	1513
50T160A	1513
50T160B	1513
50T180	1539

DEVICE TYPE	REPL CODE
50T180A	1539
50T180B	1539
50T200	1577
50T200A	1577
50T200B	1577
50T801	OEM
50U6P42	OEM
50V3P	OEM
50V10	OEM
50V11	OEM
50W3P	OEM
50X3P	OEM
50X7-8	OEM
50X7.5-8.5	OEM
50X8-9	OEM
50X8.5-9.5	OEM
50X9-10A	OEM
50XV	OEM
50Y3P	OEM
50Z6.2	0908
50Z6.2A	0908
50Z6.2B	0908
50Z6.8	0920
50Z6.8A	0920
50Z6.8B	0920
50Z7.5	0938
50Z7.5A	0938
50Z7.5B	0938
50Z8.2	0952
50Z8.2A	0952
50Z8.2B	0952
50Z9.1	0012
50Z9.1A	0012
50Z9.1B	0012
50Z9.1C	0012
50Z10	1003
50Z10A	1003
50Z10B	1003
50Z11	0789
50Z11A	0789
50Z11B	0789
50Z12	0137
50Z12A	0137
50Z12B	0137
50Z12C	0137
50Z13	1043
50Z13A	1043
50Z13B	1043
50Z14	0100
50Z14A	0100
50Z14B	0100
50Z15	0002
50Z15A	0002
50Z15B	0002
50Z15C	0002
50Z16	1072
50Z16A	1072
50Z16B	1072
50Z17	1088
50Z17A	1088
50Z17B	1088
50Z18	1098
50Z18A	1098
50Z18B	1098
50Z19	1115
50Z19A	1115
50Z19B	1115
50Z20	1127
50Z20A	1127
50Z20B	1127
50Z22	1144
50Z22A	1144
50Z22B	1144
50Z24	1156
50Z24A	1156
50Z24B	1156
50Z25	1166
50Z25A	1166
50Z25B	1166
50Z27	0436
50Z27A	0436
50Z27B	0436
50Z27C	0436
50Z30	1201
50Z30A	1201
50Z30B	1201
50Z33	0039
50Z33A	0039
50Z33B	0039
50Z33C	0039
50Z36	1223
50Z36A	1223
50Z36B	1223
50Z39	1237
50Z39A	1237
50Z39B	1237
50Z43	1256
50Z43A	1256
50Z43B	1256
50Z45	1263
50Z45A	1263
50Z45B	1263
50Z47	1280
50Z47A	1280
50Z47B	1280
50Z50	1289
50Z50A	1289
50Z50B	1289
50Z51	1297

DEVICE TYPE	REPL CODE
50Z51A	1297
50Z51B	1297
50Z52	1312
50Z52A	1312
50Z52B	1312
50Z52D	1312
50Z52D5	1312
50Z52D10	1312
50Z56	0778
50Z56A	0778
50Z56B	0778
50Z62	0778
50Z62A	0778
50Z62B	0778
50Z68	1355
50Z68A	1355
50Z68B	1355
50Z75	1374
50Z75A	1374
50Z75B	1374
50Z82	0327
50Z82A	0327
50Z82B	0327
50Z82C	0327
50Z91	1402
50Z91A	1402
50Z91B	1402
50Z100	1413
50Z100A	1413
50Z100B	1413
50Z105	OEM
50Z105A	OEM
50Z105B	OEM
50Z110	0149
50Z110A	0149
50Z110B	0149
50Z120	1448
50Z120A	1448
50Z120B	1448
50Z130	1461
50Z130A	1461
50Z130B	1461
50Z140	1475
50Z140A	1475
50Z140B	1475
50Z140D	1475
50Z140D10	1475
50Z150	1497
50Z150A	1497
50Z150B	1497
50Z160	1497
50Z160A	1497
50Z160B	1497
50Z175	1523
50Z175A	1523
50Z175B	1523
50Z175D	1523
50Z175D5	1523
50Z175D10	1523
50Z180	1539
50Z180A	1539
50Z180B	1539
50Z200	1577
50Z200A	1577
50Z200B	1577
50Z1040D5	OEM
51	0144
51-01003-04	0133
51-02004-12	0041
51-02006-12	0165
51-02007-12	0057
51-02008-12	0062
51-02020-05	0064
51-02025-04	0091
51-02029-04	0137
51-02032-04	0077
51-03007-06	0023
51-03009A02	0780
51-03015-02	0080
51-03017-01	0790
51-03020-02	0023
51-03021-02	0023
51-03024-02	0023
51-03025-04	0133
51-03026-04	0023
51-03029-04	0023
51-03030-04	0023
51-03035-04	0087
51-04001-01	0123
51-06002-00	0549
51-08001-05	0124
51-08001-11	0124
51-08004-06	0124
51-08006-02	0124
51-4	0275
51-903	1135
51-1059A01	1335
51-1375A05	OEM
51-3009A02	OEM
51-3009A07	OEM
51-10276A01	2600
51-10302A01	0627
51-10302A1	0627
51-10305A43	OEM
51-10422A01	0649
51-10422A02	0649
51-10437A01	0649
51-10534A01	2979
51-10534A03	2016

DEVICE TYPE	REPL CODE
51-10534A04	2979
51-10542A01	0618
51-10566A01	0696
51-10594A01	1335
51-10600A	6684
51-10600A01	4839
51-10611A09	2089
51-10611A10	OEM
51-10611A11	0232
51-10611A12	0357
51-10611A15	0738
51-10611A16	1423
51-10619A01	1335
51-10631A01	0659
51-10634A01	OEM
51-10636A	1969
51-10636A01	1969
51-10637A01	2720
51-10638A01	1832
51-10650A01	0356
51-10655A03	0850
51-10655A17	0473
51-10655A19	0409
51-10655A21	1135
51-10655B02	0784
51-10658A01	2728
51-10658A02	2728
51-10658A03	2728
51-10672A01	1748
51-10678A01	1832
51-10679A13	0784
51-10711A01	1385
51-10711A02	1385
51-10726A01	OEM
51-10726A02	OEM
51-10730A01	OEM
51-10740A02	OEM
51-13753-A19	0516
51-13753A01	1049
51-13753A04	3977
51-13753A10	3238
51-13753A11	0167
51-13753A18	3242
51-13753A19	0516
51-13753A20	2762
51-13753A21	3738
51-13753A22	2599
51-13753A23	4416
51-13753A24	5004
51-13753A25	3564
51-13753A26	3692
51-13753A27	4469
51-13753A28	2599
51-13753A29	3997
51-13753A35	3692
51-13753A39	3692
51-13753A40	1162
51-13753A46	2038
51-13753A47	3239
51-13753A48	3317
51-13753A49	3325
51-13753A50	3060
51-13753A52	3461
51-13753A53	3250
51-13753A54	2599
51-13753A55	1420
51-13763A22	3522
51-13763A27	2599
51-15066A01	0696
51-40000S08	1042
51-40000S09	OEM
51-40464P01	0514
51-40464P01	OEM
51-41850J01	6059
51-42211P01	2512
51-42211P01	OEM
51-42908J01	0514
51-43639B02	2016
51-43684B01	2979
51-43684B02	2016
51-43684B0P	2016
51-44789J01	2008
51-44789J02	2008
51-44837J04	3231
51-70177A07	0618
51-84320A09	1969
51-90305A04	0846
51-90305A05	0851
51-90305A6	0167
51-90305A17	OEM
51-90305A20	3973
51-90305A21	2932
51-90305A24	4004
51-90305A27	4017
51-90305A30	4091
51-90305A31	4095
51-90305A37	4678
51-90305A39	4663
51-90305A40	1570
51-90305A41	4677
51-90305A43	4666
51-90305A44	4670
51-90305A45	4981
51-90305A46	4099
51-90305A50	0391
51-90305A59	1319
51-90305A60	2559
51-90305A61	0167
51-90305A62	4665

DEVICE TYPE	REPL CODE
51-90305A72	2279
51-90305A73	4671
51-90305A77	4648
51-90305A78	1251
51-90305A87	0167
51-90305A88	4773
51-90305A89	1420
51-90305A90	0391
51-90305A91	0167
51-90305A92	3997
51-90433A07	3809
51-90433A08	2244
51-90433A09	1023
51-90433A10	0119
51-90433A11	0394
51-90433A12	1589
51-90433A13	1135
51-90433A27	2244
51-90433A30	2244
51-90433A32	1570
51-90433A33	1572
51-90433A34	1575
51-90433A35	4670
51-90433A36	OEM
51-90433A52	6704
51-90433A53	3564
51-90433A54	6707
51-90433A55	6011
51-90433A56	OEM
51-90433A60	3977
51-90433A63	2279
51-90433A64	OEM
51-90433A66	0851
51-90433A86	OEM
51-90433A87	0674
51-355051	OEM
51-10422801	0649
51-40000508	OEM
51-40000509	OEM
51-43639802	2016
51-44789302	OEM
51-44837504	OEM
51A	OEM
51B	OEM
51C43684B02	2016
51C436884B01	2016
51D170	0211
51D176	0004
51D188	0279
51D189	0279
51D70177A01	1742
51D70177A02	0784
51D70177A02(C)	2377
51D70177A07	0167
51D70177B02	0784
51G10679A03	0850
51G10679A13	0784
51G10679A14	OEM
51GX3	0469
51GX14	0469
51HQ045	1536
51HV100AV14L	OEM
51HV100AV16L	OEM
51IN60P	0143
51IS34S	0143
51LN60P	0143
51LS34S	0143
51M33801A01	3977
51M33801A04	1049
51M33801A05	3242
51M33801A06	2914
51M33801A07	3238
51M70177A01	1742
51M70177A03	0850
51M70177A05	0391
51M70177A07	0618
51M70177B02	0784
51N3M	1671
51P	OEM
51P2	0136
51P4	0136
51PB	OEM
51PBH	OEM
51PBHL	OEM
51PBL	OEM
51PL	OEM
51R8432A09	1969
51R84320A09	1969
51RC10	0603
51RC20	0603
51RC30	0605
51RC40	0605
51RC50	0605
51RC60	0605
51RC70	0463
51RC80	0463
51RC100	0463
51RC120	0463
51RCG5	OEM
51RCG10	OEM
51RCG15	OEM
51RCG20	OEM
51RCG25	OEM
51RCG30	OEM
51RCG40	OEM
51RCG50	OEM
51RCG80	OEM
51S02	OEM
51S1S34	0143

DEVICE TYPE	REPL CODE
51S105FA01	0696
51S137A48	3317
51S137A50	3060
51S1048A01	0167
51S1056GA01	0696
51S1059A01	0696
51S1373A40	1162
51S3753A48	3317
51S10276A01	2600
51S10302A01	0627
51S10382A	0649
51S10408A01	0823
51S10422A	0649
51S10422A01	0649
51S10432A01	3679
51S10437A01	0649
51S10534A01	2016
51S10534A03	2016
51S10566A01	0696
51S10585A01	OEM
51S10592A01	0696
51S10594A01	1335
51S10600A	2438
51S10600A01	3731
51S10611A09	2089
51S10611A10	OEM
51S10611A11	0232
51S10611A12	0357
51S10611A15	0738
51S10611A16	1423
51S10636A	1969
51S10636A01	1969
51S10638A01	1832
51S10655A01	1742
51S10655A15	OEM
51S10655A17	0473
51S10655A18	0215
51S10655A19	0409
51S10655B01	1742
51S10655B03	0850
51S10655B05	OEM
51S10655B13	0167
51S10655C05	0391
51S13747A03	2524
51S13749A46	2038
51S13752A47	3239
51S13753A01	1049
51S13753A02	3238
51S13753A03	2914
51S13753A06	3242
51S13753A07	0167
51S13753A08	2579
51S13753A09	0167
51S13753A10	3238
51S13753A11	0167
51S13753A23	4416
51S13753A28	2599
51S13753A37	5123
51S13753A39	3692
51S13753A40	1162
51S13753A46	2038
51S13753A47	3239
51S13753A48	3317
51S13753A49	3325
51S13753A50	3060
51S13753A52	3461
51S13753A53	3250
51S13753A55	1420
51S13753A56	2599
51S13753A60	6934
51S13753A64	3060
51S13753A65	2109
51S13753A66	OEM
51S13753A67	3860
51S13753A68	5116
51S23753A47	3239
51S33753A47	3239
51S44789J01	2008
51S44789J02	2008
51S90518A12	6623
51S1059401	1327
51SI13753A40	OEM
51SZ-UZ-4.0C	0274
51T40113T01	4846
51X2	OEM
51X9050A78	OEM
51X13753A24	5004
51X90226A72	OEM
51X90266A15	0624
51X90266A26	OEM
51X90266A45	0765
51X90305A21	2932
51X90305A41	4677
51X90305A45	4981
51X90305A46	4099
51X90305A59	1319
51X90305A61	0167
51X90305A88	4773
51X90433A12	1589
51X90433A28	4669
51X90433A33	1572
51X90433A35	4670
51X90433A47	OEM
51X90433A52	5101
51X90433A53	3564
51X90433A54	2008
51X90433A55	6011
51X90433A56	OEM
51X90433A99	5102

If replacement code is OEM, contact original manufacturer for replacement.

DEVICE TYPE	REPL CODE
51X90458A01	1575
51X90458A02	5449
51X90458A03	5134
51X90458A04	OEM
51X90458A05	5450
51X90458A06	5100
51X90458A07	0176
51X90458A15	2042
51X90458A30	3692
51X90458A32	OEM
51X90458A33	OEM
51X90458A34	OEM
51X90458A50	3692
51X90458A51	0167
51X90458A52	5003
51X90458A55	3462
51X90458A56	4678
51X90458A71	3045
51X90458A72	3055
51X90458A73	2008
51X90458A74	OEM
51X90458A75	3713
51X90458A76	OEM
51X90458A77	OEM
51X90458A78	5463
51X90458A79	OEM
51X90458A80	3707
51X90458A81	5132
51X90458A82	5077
51X90458A83	0356
51X90458A84	0356
51X90458A88	0101
51X90458A89	0915
51X90458A90	3168
51X90458A91	OEM
51X90458A92	OEM
51X90458A93	0176
51X90458A94	0176
51X90458A95	1339
51X90458A96	1197
51X90458A97	OEM
51X90458A98	0917
51X90480A02	OEM
51X90480A03	OEM
51X90480A07	0619
51X90480A08	0619
51X90480A09	0330
51X90480A16	0101
51X90480A17	0915
51X90480A18	2042
51X90480A20	0678
51X90480A32	3685
51X90480A41	3686
51X90480A46	0917
51X90480A49	OEM
51X90480A57	2599
51X90480A64	3698
51X90480A65	3701
51X90480A66	0330
51X90480A92	0484
51X90480A93	3713
51X90480A94	1162
51X90480A95	3462
51X90480A96	0970
51X90495A14	3462
51X90507A20	2008
51X90507A21	OEM
51X90507A24	0917
51X90507A28	2014
51X90507A29	2015
51X90507A30	OEM
51X90507A39	0765
51X90507A40	0765
51X90507A46	0694
51X90507A77	2055
51X90507A78	2056
51X90507A79	OEM
51X90507A80	2057
51X90507A81	OEM
51X90507A82	OEM
51X90507A83	2014
51X90507A84	0473
51X90507A85	0129
51X90507A86	OEM
51X90507A87	2062
51X90507A88	OEM
51X90507A91	OEM
51X90507A92	1008
51X90507A93	1946
51X90507A94	OEM
51X90507A95	OEM
51X90507A97	2044
51X90507A98	0493
51X90507A99	0119
51X90518A01	OEM
51X90518A02	OEM
51X90518A03	OEM
51X90518A07	0619
51X90518A08	0056
51X90518A09	5136
51X90518A13	5447
51X90518A19	2531
51X90518A28	3168
51X90518A34	2042
51X90518A35	1589
51X90518A36	0215
51X90518A55	OEM
51X90518A68	OEM
51X90518A69	0967
51X90518A71	0963
51X90518A72	OEM
51X90518A73	OEM
51X90518A74	OEM
51X90518A89	OEM
51X90518A90	OEM
51X90518A95	OEM
51X90518A97	5099
51X90580A41	OEM
51X90597A88	OEM
51X904080A96	0970
51X9048095	OEM
51Z6	0777
51Z6A	0777
52-010-106-0	0527
52-010-109-0	0338
52-010-151-0	0617
52-020-108-0	0016
52-020-166-0	0224
52-020-167-0	0224
52-020-169-0	0224
52-020-173-0	2039
52-025-004-0	0103
52-040-009-0	0574
52-040-010-0	1206
52-045-001-0	1226
52-050-021-0	0143
52-051-008-0	0143
52-051-009-0	0124
52-051-017-0	0143
52-052-004-0	0123
52-053-005-0	0039
52-053-013-0	0012
52-062-007-0	0139
52-1	0015
52-4	0275
52A011	0015
52A011-1	0071
52A15	0143
52A26	0631
52BBIA	0015
52BBLA	0015
52C04	0004
52D189	0164
52DS-18	0015
52GT	OEM
52HQ030	1536
52HQ035	1536
52HQ040	1536
52HQ045	1536
52HV100AV18L	OEM
52J	OEM
52L	OEM
52P	OEM
52PB	OEM
52PBH	OEM
52PBHL	OEM
52PBL	OEM
52PL	OEM
52RCG5	OEM
52RCG10	OEM
52RCG15	OEM
52RCG20	OEM
52RCG25	OEM
52RCG30	OEM
52RCG40	OEM
52RCG50	OEM
52RCG60	OEM
52SD-1	0015
52SD1	0015
52SI-SAA1061	OEM
52ST-2SD467C	0945
52ST-JE9018G	0144
52TA7611AP-S	0069
52X2	OEM
52Z4	OEM
52Z6	2381
52Z6A	2381
53-0051-2	0015
53-0082-3	0071
53-0082-1003	0229
53-0086-1	0015
53-0088-1	0015
53-0088-2	0229
53-0088-3	0071
53-0088-1002	0071
53-0088-1003	0071
53-0088-1004	0071
53-0094-1	0015
53-0095-1	0015
53-0098-1	0015
53-0099-1	0015
53-0099-3	0015
53-0099-4	0015
53-0106-1	0015
53-0106-1001	0071
53-0109-1	0015
53-0111-1	0229
53-0111-1001	0071
53-0113-1	0015
53-0120-1	0015
53-0122-1	0229
53-0136T	0071
53-1110	0016
53-1173	0396
53-1362	0555
53-1487	2145
53-1516	0037
53-1517	0934
53-1967	0555
53A001-1	0143
53A001-2	0143
53A001-3	0015
53A001-4	0071
53A001-5	0025
53A001-6	0030
53A001-9	0015
53A001-10	0137
53A001-12	0015
53A001-13	OEM
53A001-31	OEM
53A001-33	0100
53A001-34	0071
53A001-35	0015
53A006-1	0143
53A008-1	0143
53A009-1	0196
53A0016	0549
53A0081	0143
53A010-1	0087
53A011-1	0015
53A014-1	0102
53A015-1	0102
53A016-1	0098
53A017-1	0102
53A018-1	1141
53A019-1	0133
53A020-1	0133
53A022-1	0015
53A022-2	0143
53A022-3	0133
53A022-4	0015
53A022-5	0102
53A022-6	0012
53A022-7	0012
53A022-8	OEM
53A022-10	0201
53A030-1	0133
53B001-1	0143
53B001-2	0143
53B001-3	0143
53B001-5	0015
53B001-6	0015
53B001-7	0133
53B001-8	0030
53B001-9	0133
53B003-1	0015
53B003-2	0015
53B004-1	0143
53B004-2	0143
53B005-2	0143
53B006-1	0015
53B007-1	0143
53B008-1	0911
53B010-1	0196
53B010-2	0196
53B010-3	0015
53B010-4	0015
53B010-5	0087
53B010-6	0133
53B010-7	0123
53B010-8	0914
53B010-9	0914
53B010-10	0102
53B011-1	0015
53B011-2	0015
53B011-3	0769
53B012-1	0065
53B013-1	0133
53B014-1	0133
53B015-1	0062
53B017-1	0918
53B018-1	0276
53B019-1	0201
53B019-2	0015
53B019-3	0196
53B020-2	0015
53B020-3	0030
53C001	0143
53C001-1	0143
53C002-1	0299
53C003-1	0015
53C005-3	0015
53C006-1	0143
53C006-2	0143
53C006-52	0143
53C007-1	0015
53C008-1	0196
53C009-1	0015
53C009-2	0143
53C011-4	0201
53C012-1	0015
53C013-1	0188
53C014-1	0015
53C015-1	0182
53C016-1	0015
53C017-1	0102
53C020-1	0143
53C021-1	0299
53C022-1	0015
53CD01-1	0143
53D001-1	0030
53D002-1	0143
53D002-2	0143
53D003-1	0015
53D003-2	0015
53D5R08	OEM
53D9R08GH	OEM
53E001-1	0143
53E003-1	0133
53E003-2	0133
53E006-1	0143
53E009-1	0030
53E010-1	0015
53E011-1	0276
53E011-2	0631
53F001-1	0015
53F002-1	0015
53H001-1	0015
53H001-2	0143
53J001-1	0087
53J002-1	0087
53J002-2	0229
53J003-1	0015
53J003-2	0133
53J004-1	0631
53J004-2	0361
53J004-3	0644
53K001-2	0143
53K001-3	0030
53K001-4	0298
53K001-5	0143
53K001-6	0015
53K001-6(5,7)	0015
53K001-7	0015
53K001-7(6,8)	0015
53K001-9	0229
53K001-10	OEM
53K001-11	0015
53K001-13	OEM
53K001-14	0012
53K001-15	0030
53K001-16	OEM
53K001-18	0012
53L001-1	0123
53L001-5	0023
53L001-10	0019
53L001-14	0023
53L001-15	0133
53LS140J16	OEM
53LS140N16	OEM
53LS141J16	OEM
53LS141N16	OEM
53LS240J16	OEM
53LS240N16	OEM
53LS241J16	OEM
53LS241N16	OEM
53N001-1	0143
53N001-2	0015
53N001-3	0015
53N001-4	0560
53N001-5	0133
53N001-6	0030
53N001-7	0143
53N001-9	0398
53N002-2	0015
53N003-1	0143
53N003-2	0143
53N003-3	0123
53N004-1	0030
53N004-5	0143
53N004-6	0143
53N004-7	0015
53N004-8	0015
53N004-9	0015
53N004-10	0123
53N004-11	0143
53N004-12	0133
53N004-13	0030
53N004-14	0143
53N49	0435
53P151	0198
53P153	0160
53P157	0211
53P158	0198
53P159	0198
53P161	1212
53P162	1212
53P163	0198
53P165	0076
53P166	0006
53P169	0086
53P170	0126
53RA441J	OEM
53RA441N	OEM
53S080J	OEM
53S080N	OEM
53S081J	OEM
53S081N	OEM
53S140J16	OEM
53S140N16	OEM
53S141J16	OEM
53S141N16	OEM
53S240J16	OEM
53S240N16	OEM
53S241J16	OEM
53S241N16	OEM
53SC-15	0030
53ST-2SC2344	1274
53SZ-BZ-110	0313
53SZ-HZ9B3	0318
53SZ-RD11FB	0313
53T001-1	0143
53T001-2	0030
53T001-3	0015
53T001-4	0143
53T001-5	0143
53T001-6	0143
53T001-7	0133
53U001-1	0143
53U001-2	0133
53W001-6	0015
53W001-7	0124
53Y001-1	0015
53YT	OEM
53Z4	OEM
53Z6	2024
53Z6A	2024
53Z20D	OEM
53Z47D5	OEM
53Z62D	OEM
53Z62D10	OEM
53Z68D	OEM
53Z68D5	OEM
53Z68D10	OEM
53Z75D5	OEM
53Z110D	OEM
53Z130D5	OEM
54	0144
54-1	0016
54A	0079
54B	0016
54B2C	OEM
54BLK	0144
54BLU	0016
54BRN	0144
54C	0016
54CAY	OEM
54D	0016
54D5R08	OEM
54D9408GH	OEM
54E	0710
54F	0016
54F00DM	OEM
54F00FM	OEM
54F02DM	OEM
54F02FM	OEM
54F04DM	OEM
54F04FM	OEM
54F08DM	OEM
54F08FM	OEM
54F10DM	OEM
54F10FM	OEM
54F11DM	OEM
54F11FM	OEM
54F20DM	OEM
54F20FM	OEM
54F32DM	OEM
54F32FM	OEM
54F64DM	OEM
54F64FM	OEM
54F74DM	OEM
54F74FM	OEM
54F109DM	OEM
54F109FM	OEM
54F138DM	OEM
54F151DM	OEM
54F151FM	OEM
54F153DM	OEM
54F153FM	OEM
54F157DM	OEM
54F157FM	OEM
54F158DM	OEM
54F158FM	OEM
54F160DM	OEM
54F160FM	OEM
54F161DM	OEM
54F161FM	OEM
54F162DM	OEM
54F162FM	OEM
54F163DM	OEM
54F163FM	OEM
54F175DM	OEM
54F175FM	OEM
54F181DM	OEM
54F181FM	OEM
54F182DM	OEM
54F182FM	OEM
54F189DM	OEM
54F189FM	OEM
54F240DM	OEM
54F240FM	OEM
54F241DM	OEM
54F241FM	OEM
54F242DM	OEM
54F242FM	OEM
54F243DM	OEM
54F243FM	OEM
54F244DM	OEM
54F244FM	OEM
54F245DM	OEM
54F251DM	OEM
54F251FM	OEM
54F253DM	OEM
54F253FM	OEM
54F257DM	OEM
54F257FM	OEM
54F258DM	OEM
54F258FM	OEM
54F280DM	OEM
54F280FM	OEM
54F283DM	OEM
54F283FM	OEM
54F289DM	OEM
54F289FM	OEM
54F352DM	OEM
54F352FM	OEM
54F353DM	OEM
54F353FM	OEM
54F373DM	OEM
54F373FM	OEM
54F374DM	OEM
54F374FM	OEM
54F500DM	OEM
54F533DM	OEM
54F533FM	OEM
54F534DM	OEM
54F534FM	OEM
54F537DM	OEM
54F537FM	OEM
54F538DM	OEM
54F538FM	OEM
54F539DM	OEM
54F545DM	OEM
54F588DM	OEM
54GRN	0016
54H00DM	OEM
54H00FM	OEM
54H01DM	OEM
54H01FM	OEM
54H04DM	OEM
54H04FM	OEM
54H05DM	OEM
54H05FM	OEM
54H08DM	OEM
54H08FM	OEM
54H10DM	OEM
54H10FM	OEM
54H11DM	OEM
54H11FM	OEM
54H20DM	OEM
54H20FM	OEM
54H21DM	OEM
54H21FM	OEM
54H22DM	OEM
54H22FM	OEM
54H30DM	OEM
54H30FM	OEM
54H40DM	OEM
54H40FM	OEM
54H50DM	OEM
54H50FM	OEM
54H51DM	OEM
54H51FM	OEM
54H52DM	OEM
54H52FM	OEM
54H53DM	OEM
54H53FM	OEM
54H54DM	OEM
54H54FM	OEM
54H55FM	OEM
54H60FM	OEM
54H61DM	OEM
54H61FM	OEM
54H62FM	OEM
54H71FM	OEM
54H72DM	OEM
54H72FM	OEM
54H73DM	OEM
54H73FM	OEM
54H74DM	OEM
54H74FM	OEM
54H76FM	OEM
54H78FM	OEM
54H87DM	OEM
54H87FM	OEM
54H101FM	OEM
54H102FM	OEM
54H103DM	OEM
54H103FM	OEM
54H106DM	OEM
54H106FM	OEM
54H108DM	OEM
54H108FM	OEM
54H183FM	OEM
54HC00F	OEM
54HC02F	OEM
54HC08F	OEM
54HC20F	OEM
54HC30F	OEM
54HCT00F	OEM
54HCT02F	OEM
54HCT04F	OEM
54HCT08F	OEM
54HCT10F	OEM
54HCT11F	OEM
54HCT27F	OEM
54HCT30F	OEM
54HCT32F	OEM
54HCT74F	OEM
54HCT258F	OEM
54LS00DM	OEM
54LS00FM	OEM
54LS02	1550
54LS02DM	1550
54LS02FM	OEM
54LS03DM	OEM
54LS03FM	OEM
54LS04DM	OEM
54LS04FM	OEM
54LS05DM	OEM
54LS05FM	OEM
54LS08DM	OEM
54LS08FM	OEM
54LS09FM	OEM
54LS10DM	OEM
54LS10FM	OEM
54LS11DM	OEM
54LS11FM	OEM
54LS13DM	OEM
54LS13FM	OEM
54LS14DM	OEM
54LS14FM	OEM
54LS15FM	OEM
54LS20DM	OEM
54LS20FM	OEM
54LS21DM	OEM
54LS21FM	OEM
54LS22FM	OEM
54LS26DM	OEM
54LS26FM	OEM
54LS27DM	OEM
54LS27FM	OEM
54LS28DM	OEM
54LS28FM	OEM
54LS30DM	OEM
54LS30FM	OEM
54LS32DM	OEM
54LS32FM	OEM
54LS33FM	OEM
54LS37DM	OEM
54LS37FM	OEM
54LS38	OEM
54LS38DM	OEM
54LS38FM	OEM
54LS40DM	OEM
54LS40FM	OEM
54LS42DM	OEM
54LS42FM	OEM
54LS47DM	OEM
54LS47FM	OEM
54LS48DM	OEM
54LS48FM	OEM
54LS49DM	OEM
54LS49FM	OEM
54LS51DM	OEM
54LS51FM	OEM
54LS54FM	OEM
54LS55FM	OEM
54LS74DM	OEM
54LS74FM	OEM
54LS76DM	OEM
54LS76FM	OEM
54LS78DM	OEM
54LS78FM	OEM
54LS83ADM	OEM
54LS83AFM	OEM
54LS85DM	OEM
54LS85FM	OEM
54LS89DM	OEM
54LS89FM	OEM
54LS90FM	OEM
54LS92FM	OEM
54LS93DM	OEM
54LS93FM	OEM
54LS95BDM	OEM
54LS95BFM	OEM
54LS107DM	OEM
54LS107FM	OEM
54LS109DM	OEM
54LS109FM	OEM
54LS112DM	OEM
54LS112FM	OEM
54LS113FM	OEM
54LS114FM	OEM
54LS125A/BCBJA	OEM
54LS125A/BCBJC	OEM
54LS125ADM	OEM
54LS125AFM	OEM
54LS126DM	OEM
54LS126FM	OEM
54LS133DM	OEM
54LS133FM	OEM
54LS136DM	OEM
54LS136FM	OEM
54LS138DM	OEM
54LS138FM	OEM
54LS139DM	OEM
54LS139FM	OEM
54LS151DM	OEM
54LS151FM	OEM
54LS152FM	OEM
54LS153DM	OEM
54LS153FM	OEM
54LS155DM	OEM
54LS155FM	OEM
54LS156DM	OEM
54LS156FM	OEM
54LS157DM	OEM
54LS157FM	OEM
54LS158DM	OEM
54LS158FM	OEM
54LS160FM	OEM
54LS161DM	OEM
54LS161FM	OEM
54LS162FM	OEM
54LS163DM	OEM
54LS163FM	OEM
54LS164DM	OEM
54LS164FM	OEM
54LS165DM	OEM
54LS165FM	OEM
54LS168DM	OEM
54LS168FM	OEM

If replacement code is OEM, contact original manufacturer for replacement.

DEVICE TYPE	REPL CODE
54LS169DM	OEM
54LS169FM	OEM
54LS170DM	OEM
54LS170FM	OEM
54LS175DM	OEM
54LS175FM	OEM
54LS181FM	OEM
54LS189DM	OEM
54LS189FM	OEM
54LS190FM	OEM
54LS191DM	OEM
54LS191FM	OEM
54LS192DM	OEM
54LS192FM	OEM
54LS193FM	OEM
54LS194ADM	OEM
54LS194AFM	OEM
54LS195ADM	OEM
54LS195AFM	OEM
54LS196FM	OEM
54LS240DM	OEM
54LS240FM	OEM
54LS241DM	OEM
54LS241FM	OEM
54LS244DM	OEM
54LS244FM	OEM
54LS245DM	OEM
54LS245FM	OEM
54LS247DM	OEM
54LS247FM	OEM
54LS251DM	OEM
54LS251FM	OEM
54LS253DM	OEM
54LS253FM	OEM
54LS256DM	OEM
54LS256FM	OEM
54LS257DM	OEM
54LS257FM	OEM
54LS258ADM	OEM
54LS258AFM	OEM
54LS258DM	OEM
54LS258FM	OEM
54LS259DM	OEM
54LS259FM	OEM
54LS260DM	OEM
54LS260FM	OEM
54LS266DM	OEM
54LS266FM	OEM
54LS273DM	OEM
54LS273FM	OEM
54LS279DM	OEM
54LS279FM	OEM
54LS283DM	OEM
54LS283FM	OEM
54LS283J	OEM
54LS283W	OEM
54LS289DM	OEM
54LS289FM	OEM
54LS290DM	OEM
54LS290FM	OEM
54LS293DM	OEM
54LS293FM	OEM
54LS295ADM	OEM
54LS295AFM	OEM
54LS298DM	OEM
54LS298FM	OEM
54LS299DM	OEM
54LS299FM	OEM
54LS322DM	OEM
54LS322FM	OEM
54LS323DM	OEM
54LS323FM	OEM
54LS347DM	OEM
54LS347FM	OEM
54LS352DM	OEM
54LS352FM	OEM
54LS353DM	OEM
54LS353FM	OEM
54LS365ADM	OEM
54LS365AFM	OEM
54LS366ADM	OEM
54LS366AFM	OEM
54LS367ADM	OEM
54LS367AFM	OEM
54LS368ADM	OEM
54LS368AFM	OEM
54LS373DM	OEM
54LS373FM	OEM
54LS374DM	OEM
54LS374FM	OEM
54LS375DM	OEM
54LS375FM	OEM
54LS377DM	OEM
54LS377FM	OEM
54LS378DM	OEM
54LS378FM	OEM
54LS379DM	OEM
54LS379FM	OEM
54LS384DM	OEM
54LS384FM	OEM
54LS386DM	OEM
54LS386FM	OEM
54LS390DM	OEM
54LS390FM	OEM
54LS393DM	OEM
54LS393FM	OEM
54LS395DM	OEM
54LS395FM	OEM
54LS447DM	OEM
54LS447FM	OEM
54LS490DM	OEM
54LS490FM	OEM
54LS533DM	OEM
54LS533FM	OEM
54LS534DM	OEM
54LS534FM	OEM
54LS563DC	OEM
54LS563DM	OEM
54LS563FM	OEM
54LS563PC	OEM
54LS564DM	OEM
54LS564FM	OEM
54LS573DM	OEM
54LS573FM	OEM
54LS574DM	OEM
54LS574FM	OEM
54LS670DM	OEM
54LS670FM	OEM
54LS670W	OEM
54ORN	0144
54R	OEM
54RED	0144
54S00DM	OEM
54S00FM	OEM
54S03DM	OEM
54S04ADM	OEM
54S04AFM	OEM
54S04DM	OEM
54S04FM	OEM
54S05ADM	OEM
54S05AFM	OEM
54S05DM	OEM
54S05FM	OEM
54S09FM	OEM
54S10DM	OEM
54S10FM	OEM
54S11DM	OEM
54S11FM	OEM
54S15DM	OEM
54S15FM	OEM
54S20DM	OEM
54S20FM	OEM
54S22DM	OEM
54S22FM	OEM
54S30DM	OEM
54S30FM	OEM
54S32DM	OEM
54S32FM	OEM
54S40DM	OEM
54S40FM	OEM
54S51DM	OEM
54S51FM	OEM
54S64DM	OEM
54S64FM	OEM
54S65FM	OEM
54S74DM	OEM
54S74FM	OEM
54S86DM	OEM
54S86FM	OEM
54S109DM	OEM
54S109FM	OEM
54S112DM	OEM
54S112FM	OEM
54S113FM	OEM
54S114FM	OEM
54S132DM	OEM
54S132FM	OEM
54S133DM	OEM
54S133FM	OEM
54S134FM	OEM
54S135FM	OEM
54S137DM	OEM
54S137FM	OEM
54S138DM	OEM
54S138FM	OEM
54S139DM	OEM
54S139FM	OEM
54S140DM	OEM
54S140FM	OEM
54S151DM	OEM
54S151FM	OEM
54S153DM	OEM
54S153FM	OEM
54S157DM	OEM
54S157FM	OEM
54S158DM	OEM
54S158FM	OEM
54S175DM	OEM
54S175FM	OEM
54S181DM	OEM
54S181FM	OEM
54S182DM	OEM
54S182FM	OEM
54S189FM	OEM
54S194DM	OEM
54S194FM	OEM
54S253DM	OEM
54S253FM	OEM
54S258DM	OEM
54S258FM	OEM
54S260DM	OEM
54S260FM	OEM
54S280DM	OEM
54S280FM	OEM
54S289DM	OEM
54S289FM	OEM
54SC137C(A)	OEM
54SC138C(A)	OEM
54SC139C(A)	OEM
54SC237C(A)	OEM
54SC238C(A)	OEM
54SC239C(A)	OEM
54SC240C(A)	OEM
54SC241C(MA)	OEM
54SC242C(MA)	OEM
54SC243C(MA)	OEM
54SC244C(MA)	OEM
54SC245C(MA)	OEM
54SC540C(MA)	OEM
54SC541C(MA)	OEM
54SD-BA282	0163
54SI-TA7075P	0849
54SP-LT-527R	OEM
54ST-2SC1815Y	0076
54ST-2SC1815Y(AU)E	0076
54WHT	0016
54YEL	0016
54Z4	OEM
54Z6	2385
54Z6A	2385
55-0014	OEM
55-1	0143
55-641	0396
55-642	0086
55-643	0126
55-1016	0004
55-1026	0016
55-1027	0208
55-1029	0164
55-1031	0164
55-1032	0038
55-1034	0050
55-1082	0016
55-1083	0037
55-1083A	0037
55-1084	0086
55-1085	0037
55-1085A	0037
55C05	0217
55C05B	0217
55C05BF	0217
55C05F	0217
55C025	0217
55C025B	0217
55C025BF	0217
55C025F	0217
55C050	0603
55C050B	0603
55C050BF	0636
55C050F	0636
55C10	0217
55C10B	0217
55C10BF	0217
55C10F	0217
55C15	0217
55C15B	0217
55C15BF	0217
55C15F	0217
55C20	0217
55C20B	0217
55C20BF	0217
55C20F	0217
55C25	0217
55C25B	0217
55C25BF	0217
55C25F	0217
55C30	0217
55C30B	0217
55C30BF	0217
55C30F	0217
55C35	0217
55C35B	0463
55C35BF	0217
55C35F	0217
55C40	0217
55C40B	0463
55C40BF	0217
55C40F	0217
55C45	0217
55C45B	0463
55C45BF	0217
55C45F	0217
55C50	0217
55C50B	0463
55C50BF	0217
55C50F	0217
55C60	0217
55C60B	0463
55C60BF	0217
55C60F	0217
55C70	0217
55C70B	0463
55C70BF	0653
55C70F	0653
55C80	0463
55C80B	0463
55C80BF	0653
55C80F	0653
55C90	0463
55C90B	0463
55C90BF	0653
55C90F	0653
55C100	0463
55C100B	0463
55C100BF	0653
55C100F	0653
55C110	0463
55C110B	0463
55C110BF	0653
55C110F	0653
55C120	0463
55C120B	0463
55C120BF	0653
55C120F	0653
55C130	OEM
55C130B	OEM
55C130BF	OEM
55C130F	OEM
55C150	OEM
55C150B	OEM
55C150BF	OEM
55C150F	OEM
55C160	OEM
55C160B	OEM
55C160BF	OEM
55C160F	OEM
55C170	OEM
55C170B	OEM
55C170BF	OEM
55C170F	OEM
55C180	OEM
55C180B	OEM
55C180BF	OEM
55C180F	OEM
55C05BF	OEM
55D5R02	OEM
55D9R08GH	OEM
55E04A	OEM
55HQ015	OEM
55HQ020	OEM
55HQ025	OEM
55HQ030	OEM
55P	OEM
55P2	0136
55P3	0136
55PB	OEM
55PBH	OEM
55PBHL	OEM
55PBL	OEM
55PL	OEM
55SD-1N60S	0019
55SI-MC14011BCP	0215
55ST-2SD401AK	1274
55SZ-RD3.3EB	0296
55SZ-RD12EB	0999
55V10	OEM
55V11	OEM
55Z4	0170
55Z6	1429
55Z6A	1429
56-1	0143
56-2	0143
56-3	0143
56-4	0143
56-5	0133
56-6	0062
56-7	3638
56-8	0143
56-10	0143
56-11	0143
56-15	0102
56-16	0041
56-19	0012
56-20	0143
56-21	0911
56-23	0030
56-24	0133
56-25	0002
56-26	0143
56-27	0133
56-28	0133
56-31	0644
56-32	0361
56-33	0015
56-35	0016
56-36	0416
56-44	0162
56-45	0526
56-46	0012
56-47	0436
56-49	0030
56-51	0137
56-52	0015
56-53	0789
56-54	0244
56-55	0346
56-56	0124
56-57	0137
56-58	0466
56-59	0140
56-62	0012
56-63	0025
56-64	0721
56-66	0346
56-67	0170
56-68	1258
56-70	0188
56-71	0025
56-72	0925
56-73	0133
56-74	1266
56-78	0229
56-89	0143
56-93	0133
56-4780	OEM
56-4826	0151
56-4827	0111
56-4829	1211
56-4830	0018
56-4831	0527
56-4832	0133
56-4833	2573
56-4834	0514
56-4835	0030
56-4836	0139
56-4837	0052
56-4839	0015
56-4885	0244
56-4886	0123
56-8086	0127
56-8086A	0127
56-8086B	0127
56-8086C	0127
56-8087	0127
56-8087B	0127
56-8087C	0127
56-8088	0127
56-8088A	0127
56-8088C	0127
56-8089	0016
56-8089A	0016
56-8089C	0016
56-8090	0016
56-8090A	0016
56-8090C	0016
56-8091	0004
56-8091A	0004
56-8091B	0004
56-8091C	0004
56-8091D	0004
56-8092	0004
56-8092A	0004
56-8092B	0004
56-8093	0143
56-8094	2839
56-8095	0123
56-8096	0644
56-8097	0015
56-8098	0037
56-8098A	0037
56-8098B	0037
56-8098C	0037
56-8099	0164
56-8100	0208
56-8100A	0208
56-8100B	0208
56-8100C	0208
56-8100D	0208
56-8101	0164
56-8196	0111
56-8197	0111
56-8198	0015
56-8199	0015
56-861041-3	0023
56A1	0627
56A1-1	0627
56A3-1	0167
56A4-1	0348
56A5-1	0350
56A6-1	0345
56A7-1	0039
56A7-26	OEM
56A7-45	OEM
56A9-1	0784
56A11-1	0692
56A13-1	1074
56A14-1	1417
56A15-1	1199
56A16-1	1782
56A17-1	1327
56A19-1	0851
56A20-1	0797
56A21-1	2224
56A22-1	0016
56A23-1	0842
56A24-1	2032
56A25-1	0842
56A29-2	OEM
56A34-1	3865
56A42-1	4084
56A46-1	2438
56A49-1	3929
56A49-2	3929
56A53-1	OEM
56A55-1	1318
56A60-1	4131
56A65-1	1162
56A74-1	3692
56A74LS-00	OEM
56A75-1	0485
56A75-1A	0485
56A101-1	3416
56A102-1	4071
56A107-1	2799
56A111-05	OEM
56A111-1	OEM
56A112-1	OEM
56A113-1	1319
56A120-1	2511
56A121-1	0898
56A122-1	1051
56A123-1	OEM
56A124-1	OEM
56A125-1	OEM
56A126-1	OEM
56A127-1	OEM
56A128-1	OEM
56A137-1	0658
56A138-1	4047
56A141-1	3410
56A141-4	3896
56A161-1-2	OEM
56A161-2	OEM
56A221-1	0079
56A223-2	4470
56A232-1	OEM
56A234-1	OEM
56A236-1	OEM
56A249-1	OEM
56A250-1	OEM
56A265-1	0101
56A355-1	2641
56A357-1	OEM
56A359-1	4032
56A360-1	2330
56A402-L	1060
56A404-1	OEM
56A551	1318
56B74-1	3692
56B75-1	2599
56C1	0627
56C1-1	0627
56C7-1	0039
56C7-26	OEM
56C7-45	OEM
56C17-1	1327
56C49-1	3929
56D3-1	0167
56D4-1	0348
56D5-1	0350
56D5R08	OEM
56D6-1	0345
56D9-1	0784
56D9R08GH	OEM
56D17-1	1327
56D20-1	0797
56D49-1	3929
56D49-2	3929
56D53-1	OEM
56D65-1	1162
56D75-1	2599
56D75-1A	0485
56P1	0050
56P2	0050
56P3	0050
56P4	0050
56P4P	0050
56SI-TA7644BP	0658
56ST-LM2152	0079
56ST-MJE9742	0275
56SZ-WZ120	0052
56SZ-WZ120(AU)	0052
56TB13	OEM
56TB14	OEM
56TB15	OEM
56TB16	OEM
56TB16-CE00	OEM
56TB16-EE00	OEM
56TB16-JE00	OEM
56TB16-JH00	OEM
56TB16-LE00	OEM
56TB16-LH00	OEM
56TB16-NE00	OEM
56TB17	OEM
56TB17-CE00	OEM
56TB17-EE00	OEM
56TB17-EH00	OEM
56TB17-JE00	OEM
56TB17-JH00	OEM
56TB17-LE00	OEM
56TB17-LH00	OEM
56TB17-NE00	OEM
56TB18	OEM
56TB18-CE00	OEM
56TB18-CH00	OEM
56TB18-EE00	OEM
56TB18-EH00	OEM
56TB18-JE00	OEM
56TB18-JH00	OEM
56TB18-LE00	OEM
56TB18-NE00	OEM
56TB18-NH00	OEM
56TB19	OEM
56TB19-CE00	OEM
56TB19-CH00	OEM
56TB19-EE00	OEM
56TB19-JE00	OEM
56TB19-JH00	OEM
56TB19-LE00	OEM
56TB19-LH00	OEM
56TB19-NE00	OEM
56TB19-NH00	OEM
56TB20	OEM
56TB20-CE00	OEM
56TB20-CH00	OEM
56TB20-EE00	OEM
56TB20-EH00	OEM
56TB20-JE00	OEM
56TB20-JH00	OEM
56TB20-LE00	OEM
56TB20-NE00	OEM
56Z4	0137
56Z6	0437
56Z6A	0437
57-0006	0015
57-0004503	0016
57-0005452	0016
57-000901504	0016
57-00901504	0079
57-1	0064
57-2	0015
57-6	0015
57-12	0015
57-13	0015
57-15	0015
57-17	0015
57-18	3160
57-20	0015
57-21	0015
57-22	0015
57-23	0015
57-24	0015
57-25	0229
57-26	0229
57-27	0015
57-28	0015
57-29	0229
57-31	0015
57-32	0196
57-33	0015
57-36	0769
57-38	0015
57-39	0757
57-42	0087
57-42A	0087
57-43	0229
57-46	0015
57-49	0229
57-52	0290
57-55	0895
57-56	0290
57-58	0015
57-59	0015
57-60	0015
57-61	0061
57-62	2311
57-64	0071
57-65	0080
57-83	0405
57-90	3610
57-98	3610
57-100	0064
57-110	0181
57-120	0052
57-150	OEM
57-160	0440
57-200	0695
57-220	0700
57-249	1266
57-330	0166
57-439	0274
57-519	OEM
57-569	0253
57-629	0466
57-689	0062
57-829	0165
57-919	0057
57A1-55	1371
57A2-1	0136
57A2-4	0164
57A2-15	0004
57A2-19	0136
57A2-24	0004
57A2-49	2839
57A2.4	0004
57A3-1	1371
57A3-2	1371
57A3-3	2839
57A3-13	1371
57A5-1	0136
57A5-2	0136
57A5-3	0004
57A5-4	0136
57A5-5	0004
57A5-6	0144
57A5-7	0144
57A5-8	0144
57A6-1	0211
57A6-2	0160
57A6-3	0160
57A6-4	0016
57A6-5	0208
57A6-6	0038
57A6-7	0198
57A6-8	0160
57A6-9	0016
57A6-11	0016
57A6-12	0160
57A6-15	0126
57A6-18	1371
57A6-28	1371
57A6-34	4100
57A7-1	0144
57A10-1	0144
57A10A-8-6	0144
57A12-1	0233
57A12-2	0233
57A14-2	0086
57A15-2	0016
57A15-3	0016
57A19-1	0037
57A20-1	0144
57A20G14	0899

If replacement code is OEM, contact original manufacturer for replacement.

DEVICE TYPE	REPL CODE
57A21-2	0144
57A21-4	0144
57A21-5	0144
57A21-6	0144
57A21-7	0144
57A21-8	0016
57A21-9	0144
57A21-10	0144
57A21-11	0127
57A21-12	0127
57A21-13	0127
57A21-14	0127
57A21-15	0144
57A21-16	0007
57A21-17	0007
57A21-18	0007
57A21-20	OEM
57A21-21	0127
57A21-26	0127
57A21-45	0127
57A23-1	0126
57A23-2	0126
57A23-3	0126
57A24-1	0016
57A24-2	0016
57A24-3	0016
57A29-2	2549
57A30	OEM
57A31-1	0321
57A31-2	0683
57A31-3	0683
57A31-4	0321
57A32-1	0817
57A32-2	1469
57A32-3	1611
57A32-5	OEM
57A32-6	4490
57A32-7	OEM
57A32-8	OEM
57A32-9	OEM
57A32-10	0696
57A32-11	0465
57A32-12	0696
57A32-13	OEM
57A32-14	OEM
57A32-15	OEM
57A32-16	0696
57A32-17	4481
57A32-19	1983
57A32-21	1469
57A32-22	0438
57A32-25	4463
57A32-27	4463
57A32-28	1469
57A32-29	1469
57A32-32	0514
57A33-1	1371
57A63-11	0309
57A100-3	2839
57A100-5	2839
57A100-385	2839
57A101-4	0144
57A102-4	0007
57A103-4	0007
57A104-1	0233
57A104-2	0233
57A104-3	0233
57A104-4	0233
57A104-5	0233
57A104-6	0233
57A104-7	0233
57A104-8	0233
57A104-8-6	0086
57A105-12	0016
57A106-12	0037
57A107-1	0144
57A107-2	0144
57A107-3	0144
57A107-4	0144
57A107-5	0144
57A107-6	0144
57A107-8	0144
57A108-1	0150
57A108-2	0150
57A108-3	0150
57A108-4	0150
57A108-5	0150
57A108-6	0150
57A108-6-8	0126
57A108-7	0150
57A108-8	0150
57A111-9	4100
57A126-1	0111
57A126-12	0127
57A128-9	0086
57A129-9	0086
57A130-9	0126
57A131-10	0086
57A132-10	0126
57A133-12	0037
57A134-12	0144
57A135-12	0016
57A136-12	0016
57A137-12	0037
57A137-12A	0037
57A138-4	0008
57A138-4-6	0008
57A139-1	0007
57A139-2	0007
57A139-3	0007
57A139-4	0008
57A139-4-6	0144
57A140-12	0016
57A141-4	0007
57A142-4	0326
57A142-4(3RDLF)	0326
57A143-12	0111
57A144-12	0111
57A145-12	0037
57A145-12A	0037
57A146-12	0144
57A147-12	0037
57A148-12	0037
57A149-12	0321
57A150-12	0321
57A151-6	0144
57A152-12	0144
57A153-6	0016
57A153-9	0079
57A155-10	0178
57A156	0086
57A156-9	0016
57A157	0037
57A157-9	0037
57A158-10	0142
57A159	0037
57A159-2	OEM
57A159-12	0037
57A160-8	0233
57A164-4	0007
57A166-12	0016
57A167-9	0590
57A168-9	0786
57A169-12	0321
57A172-8	0264
57A174-8	0037
57A175-12	0037
57A177-12	0007
57A178-12	0037
57A179-4	0007
57A180-4	0326
57A181-12	0016
57A182-10	0079
57A182-12	0079
57A183-11	0233
57A184-11	0007
57A184-12	0016
57A185-11	0065
57A185-12	0037
57A186-11	0065
57A187-12	0236
57A188-12	0676
57A189-8	0037
57A190-12	OEM
57A191-12	0016
57A192-10	0142
57A193-11	0283
57A193-12	0079
57A194-1L	0233
57A194-11	0233
57A194-12	0058
57A195-10	0142
57A196-10	0270
57A196-11	0065
57A197-12	0037
57A198-11	0065
57A199-4	0016
57A200-12	0016
57A201-14	0037
57A202-13	0016
57A203-14	0016
57A204-14	0016
57A205-14	0723
57A206-14	0919
57A207-8	0233
57A208-8	0283
57A211-8	0264
57A213-11	0065
57A214-2	0161
57A214-12	0546
57A215-12	0037
57A216-12	0037
57A219-14	0155
57A220-14	0006
57A235-12	0037
57A236-11	0283
57A240-14	0006
57A241-14	0155
57A243-10	0058
57A244-14	0419
57A245-14	0848
57A249-4	0007
57A250-14	0042
57A251-14	0848
57A252-1	0016
57A253-14	0016
57A256-10	0103
57A258-8	0037
57A259-10	0058
57A261-10	0233
57A263-11	0309
57A264-12	OEM
57A265-4	0016
57A267-4	0212
57A268-9	0016
57A273-14	2220
57A274-14	0597
57A277-14	1638
57A278-14	1274
57A279-14	0042
57A280-14	0155
57A281-11	0233
57A281-14	0006
57A282-12	0016
57A283-11	0233
57A286-10	0042
57A290-12	0321
57A293-11	0233
57A294-12	0079
57A295-8	0283
57A296-10	0388
57A297-12	OEM
57A301-12	OEM
57A302-12	OEM
57A305-12	0037
57A309-12	2917
57A310-14	0676
57A311-14	0236
57A312	0309
57A312-11	0283
57A313-11	0065
57A401-11	0723
57A402-4	0007
57A402-L	1060
57A403-12	0037
57A404-12	0320
57A405-12	0431
57A411-1	OEM
57A411-3	3017
57A413-1	0261
57A419-GR	0076
57A419-GY	0076
57A419-Y	0076
57A420-GR	0148
57A420-Q	0148
57A421-11	0723
57A422-8	1317
57A423-8	0261
57A423-8T	0261
57A424-11	0055
57A428-12	1274
57A429-16	OEM
57A431-2	OEM
57A431-J	OEM
57A446-2	0860
57A458-0	0006
57A458-O	0006
57A459-Y	0261
57A460-11	3465
57A460-12	1533
57A460-15	1533
57A485-1	1638
57A493-10	0710
57B2-1	0050
57B2-2	0050
57B2-3	0164
57B2-4	0164
57B2-5	0038
57B2-6	0004
57B2-7	0164
57B2-8	0208
57B2-9	0050
57B2-10	0164
57B2-11	0050
57B2-12	0004
57B2-13	0050
57B2-14	0050
57B2-15	0164
57B2-16	0164
57B2-17	0050
57B2-18	0050
57B2-19	0050
57B2-20	0050
57B2-21	0164
57B2-22	0050
57B2-23	0004
57B2-24	0004
57B2-25	0164
57B2-26	0050
57B2-27	0016
57B2-28	0016
57B2-29	0004
57B2-30	0050
57B2-31	0050
57B2-32	0004
57B2-33	0004
57B2-34	0004
57B2-35	0050
57B2-36	0004
57B2-37	0050
57B2-38	0086
57B2-39	0004
57B2-40	0050
57B2-41	0050
57B2-42	0050
57B2-43	0004
57B2-44	0004
57B2-45	0004
57B2-46	0004
57B2-47	0178
57B2-48	0050
57B2-49	2839
57B2-50	0050
57B2-51	0050
57B2-52	0004
57B2-57	0086
57B2-58	0178
57B2-59	0016
57B2-60	0004
57B2-61	0164
57B2-62	0016
57B2-63	0016
57B2-64	0016
57B2-65	0050
57B2-66	0050
57B2-67	0050
57B2-68	0050
57B2-70	0037
57B2-70A	0037
57B2-71	0037
57B2-71A	0037
57B2-72	0004
57B2-73	0016
57B2-75	0050
57B2-77	0050
57B2-78	0004
57B2-79	0079
57B2-80	0050
57B2-83	0004
57B2-84	0178
57B2-85	0079
57B2-87	0016
57B2-88	0004
57B2-89	0050
57B2-90	0050
57B2-93	0050
57B2-97	0016
57B2-101	0016
57B2-102	0016
57B2-103	0016
57B2-104	0050
57B2-105	0050
57B2-113	0016
57B2-116	0016
57B2-126	0016
57B2-149	0050
57B2-153	0016
57B2-157	0050
57B2-158	0050
57B2-159	0050
57B2-192	0016
57B3-1	1371
57B3-2	1371
57B3-3	2839
57B3-4	0004
57B3-5	0004
57B3-6	0004
57B3-7	3004
57B3-8	3004
57B3-9	3004
57B3-10	3004
57B3-11	3004
57B3-12	0265
57B3-13	1371
57B3-105	0050
57B4-1	0160
57B4-2	0160
57B4-4	0160
57B5-6	0111
57B5-7	0111
57B5-8	0111
57B6	0211
57B6-4	0079
57B6-9	0079
57B6-11	0079
57B6-12	0085
57B6-19	0079
57B12-4	0086
57B21	0144
57B21-2	0144
57B21-4	0144
57B21-5	0144
57B21-6	0007
57B21-7	0007
57B21-9	0127
57B21-12	0144
57B21-13	0144
57B21-14	0144
57B21-15	0144
57B21-16	0144
57B21-17	0007
57B21-18	0144
57B27-2	0079
57B30-12	0127
57B31-14	0676
57B100-3	2839
57B100-5	2839
57B100-7	0004
57B100-11	0222
57B100-385	2839
57B101-4	0144
57B-102-4	0079
57B102-4	0007
57B103-4	0007
57B104-8	0233
57B105-12	0016
57B106-12	0037
57B107-8	0016
57B108-6	0037
57B108-6A	0037
57B109-9	0086
57B110-9	0126
57B111-9	4100
57B112-9	0126
57B112-9A	0126
57B113-9	0086
57B114-9	0126
57B114-9A	0126
57B115-9	0126
57B115-9A	0126
57B116-9	0126
57B116-9A	0126
57B117-9	0016
57B118-12	0016
57B119-2	0007
57B119-12	0016
57B120-12	0016
57B121-9	0016
57B122-9	0037
57B122-9A	0037
57B123-10	0178
57B124-10	0085
57B125-9	0016
57B126-12	0016
57B128-9	0086
57B129-9	0016
57B130-9	0037
57B130-9A	0037
57B131-10	0042
57B132-10	0919
57B133-12	0037
57B134-12	0144
57B135-12	0016
57B136-1	0233
57B136-2	0233
57B136-3	0233
57B136-4	0233
57B136-5	0233
57B136-6	0233
57B136-7	0233
57B136-8	0233
57B136-9	0233
57B136-10	0233
57B136-11	0233
57B136-12	0016
57B137-12	0037
57B137-12A	0037
57B138-4	0008
57B139-4	0008
57B140-12	0016
57B141-1	0144
57B141-2	0144
57B141-3	0144
57B141-4	0007
57B142-1	0144
57B142-2	0144
57B142-3	0144
57B142-4	0326
57B143-1	0144
57B143-2	0144
57B143-3	0144
57B143-4	0144
57B143-5	0144
57B143-6	0144
57B143-7	0144
57B143-8	0144
57B143-9	0144
57B143-10	0144
57B143-11	0144
57B143-12	0016
57B144-12	0016
57B145-12	0037
57B145-12A	0037
57B146-12	0016
57B147-12	0037
57B147-12A	0037
57B148-1	0126
57B148-2	0126
57B148-3	0126
57B148-4	0126
57B148-5	0126
57B148-6	0126
57B148-7	0126
57B148-8	0126
57B148-9	0126
57B148-10	0126
57B148-11	0126
57B148-12	0126
57B148-12A	0126
57B149-2	0321
57B149-12	0321
57B150-12	0321
57B151-6	0144
57B152-1	0016
57B152-2	0016
57B152-3	0016
57B152-4	0016
57B152-5	0016
57B152-6	0016
57B152-7	0016
57B152-8	0016
57B152-9	0016
57B152-10	0016
57B152-11	0016
57B152-12	0144
57B153-1	0016
57B153-2	0079
57B153-3	0016
57B153-4	0016
57B153-5	0016
57B153-6	0016
57B153-7	0016
57B153-8	0016
57B153-9	0016
57B155-10	0178
57B156-9	0016
57B157-9	0037
57B157-9A	0037
57B158-1	0142
57B158-2	0142
57B158-3	0142
57B158-4	0142
57B158-5	0142
57B158-6	0142
57B158-7	0142
57B158-8	0142
57B158-9	0142
57B158-10	0178
57B159-12	0037
57B159-12A	0037
57B160-1	0144
57B160-2	0144
57B160-3	0144
57B160-4	0144
57B160-5	0144
57B160-6	0144
57B160-7	0144
57B160-8	0144
57B162-12	0590
57B163-12	0126
57B163-12A	0126
57B166-12	0144
57B167-9	0086
57B168	0004
57B168-9	0126
57B169	0004
57B169-2	0321
57B169-12	0321
57B170	0004
57B170-9	0086
57B171-9	0126
57B175-9	0103
57B175-9A	0103
57B175-12	0037
57B179-4	0127
57B179-12	OEM
57B180	0050
57B181-12	0079
57B182-12	0076
57B184	0050
57B184-1	0079
57B184-12	0007
57B185-12	0037
57B186	0050
57B186-11	0065
57B187	0050
57B187-12	0456
57B188	0050
57B188-12	0676
57B191-12	0016
57B192-10	0142
57B192-11	0142
57B194-11	0016
57B196-10	0270
57B198-11	0065
57B208-8	0283
57B211-8	0264
57B213-11	0065
57B214-12	0546
57B243-10	0058
57B245-14	0848
57B258-8	0037
57B263-11	0309
57B277-14	1638
57B278-14	1274
57B279-4	1077
57B279-14	1077
57B280-14	0155
57B281-14	0006
57B282-12	0016
57B283-11	0233
57B286-10	0419
57B296-10	0388
57B310-14	0676
57B311-14	0236
57B312-11	0283
57B313-11	0055
57B316-10	2596
57B401-11	0723
57B402-4	1060
57B402-L	1060
57B404-12	0617
57B413-1	0710
57B418-10	2526
57B419-GR	0076
57B419-P	0076
57B419-Q	0076
57B420-GR	0148
57B420-P	0006
57B420-Q	0006
57B421-11	1157
57B423-8	0261
57B424-11	0055
57B425-F	OEM
57B426-F	OEM
57B427-1	0168
57B428-8	0388
57B428-12	1274
57B428-12-P	0388
57B428-12P	0388
57B429-8	1638
57B429-12	1900
57B429-12-P	1638
57B429-12P	1638
57B432-1	OEM
57B433-1	0279
57B434-1	0016
57B446-2	0860
57B459-Y	0261
57B460-12	1533
57B483-11	0233
57B1127	0004
57B1130	0050
57B1131	0050
57B1143	0004
57B1186	0050
57C5	0038
57C5-1	0136
57C5-2	0050
57C5-3	0004
57C5-4	0136
57C5-5	0004
57C5-6	0144
57C5-7	0144
57C5-8	0144
57C5-9	0136
57C5-10	0136
57C6-1	0211
57C6-2	0160
57C6-3	0160
57C6-4	0016
57C6-5	0208
57C6-6	0038
57C6-6A	0279
57C6-6B	0279
57C6-6C	0279
57C6-7	0198
57C6-8	0160
57C6-9	0016
57C6-10	0142
57C6-11	0016
57C6-12	0160
57C6-14	0142
57C6-15	0126
57C6-16	0136
57C6-17	0198
57C6-18	1371
57C6-19	0198
57C6-20	0208
57C6-21	0208
57C6-22	0211
57C6-23	0160
57C6-24	0142
57C6-25	0004
57C6-26	0126
57C6-26A	0126
57C6-27	0198
57C6-28	1371
57C6-29	0198
57C6-30	0198
57C6-31	0126
57C6-31A	0126
57C6-32	0198
57C6-33	0126
57C6-33A	0126
57C6-34	4100
57C7-1	0144
57C7-2	0144
57C7-3	0144
57C7-4	0144
57C7-5	0144
57C7-6	0144
57C7-7	0144
57C7-8	0086
57C7-9	0016
57C7-10	0016
57C7-15	0016
57C7-17	0016
57C7-18	0016
57C7-20	0016
57C9-2	0160
57C10-1	0144
57C10-2	0144
57C11-1	0016
57C12-1	0233
57C12-2	0233
57C12-3	0178
57C12-4	0086
57C12-5	0178
57C14-1	0086
57C14-2	0086
57C14-3	0086
57C15-1	0079
57C15-2	0016
57C15-3	0016
57C15-4	0016
57C15-5	0037
57C15-50	0037
57C16	0136
57C16-1	0016
57C19-1	0037
57C19-1A	0037
57C20-1	0144
57C22-1	0599
57C22-2	0599
57C23-1	0126
57C23-2	0126
57C23-3	0126
57C24-1	0016
57C24-2	0016
57C24-3	0016
57C24-4	0016
57C27-1	0016

If replacement code is OEM, contact original manufacturer for replacement.

DEVICE TYPE	REPL CODE
57C27-2	0144
57C28	2600
57C29-1	2549
57C29-2	2549
57C68	0004
57C104-8	0007
57C105-12	0079
57C109-9	0086
57C110-9	0126
57C121-9	0016
57C122-9	0126
57C142-4	0007
57C148-12	0126
57C148-12A	0126
57C156-9	0016
57C157-9	0037
57C157-90	0037
57C164-4	0007
57C179-4	1060
57C182-12	0079
57C191-12	0016
57C208-8	0261
57C279-14	0042
57C423-8	0261
57D1-1	0143
57D1-2	0143
57D1-3	0208
57D1-4	0208
57D1-5	0208
57D1-6	0208
57D1-7	0164
57D1-8	0004
57D1-9	0050
57D1-10	0050
57D1-11	0211
57D1-12	0050
57D1-13	0050
57D1-14	0004
57D1-15	0050
57D1-16	0050
57D1-17	0164
57D1-18	0164
57D1-19	0164
57D1-20	0164
57D1-21	0164
57D1-22	0050
57D1-23	0004
57D1-24	0050
57D1-25	0050
57D1-26	0004
57D1-27	0004
57D1-28	0004
57D1-30	0050
57D1-31	0050
57D1-32	0050
57D1-33	0050
57D1-34	0004
57D1-35	0050
57D1-36	0050
57D1-37	0050
57D1-38	0164
57D1-39	0050
57D1-40	0004
57D1-41	0050
57D1-42	0164
57D1-43	0004
57D1-44	0004
57D1-45	0050
57D1-46	0050
57D1-47	0050
57D1-48	0050
57D1-49	0050
57D1-50	0050
57D1-51	0016
57D1-52	0150
57D1-53	0004
57D1-54	0143
57D1-55	1371
57D1-56	0164
57D1-57	0050
57D1-58	0004
57D1-59	0004
57D1-60	0164
57D1-61	0050
57D1-62	0143
57D1-63	0229
57D1-64	0143
57D1-65	0911
57D1-66	0004
57D1-67	0050
57D1-68	0004
57D1-69	0050
57D1-70	0004
57D1-71	0004
57D1-72	0050
57D1-73	0050
57D1-74	0050
57D1-75	0016
57D1-76	0037
57D1-77	0164
57D1-78	0208
57D1-79	0004
57D1-80	0050
57D1-81	0050
57D1-82	0004
57D1-83	0004
57D1-84	0050
57D1-85	0050
57D1-86	0050

DEVICE TYPE	REPL CODE
57D1-87	0050
57D1-88	0050
57D1-89	0050
57D1-90	0004
57D1-91	0004
57D1-92	0004
57D1-93	0004
57D1-94	0050
57D1-95	0004
57D1-96	0050
57D1-97	0050
57D1-98	0050
57D1-99	0050
57D1-100	0050
57D1-101	0050
57D1-102	0050
57D1-103	0050
57D1-104	0004
57D1-105	0004
57D1-106	0004
57D1-107	0136
57D1-108	0050
57D1-109	0050
57D1-110	0050
57D1-111	0004
57D1-112	0050
57D1-113	0050
57D1-114	0136
57D1-115	0050
57D1-116	0004
57D1-117	0004
57D1-118	0004
57D1-119	0160
57D1-120	0050
57D1-121	0004
57D1-122	0233
57D1-123	0016
57D1-124	0016
57D3-6	0211
57D4-1	0160
57D4-2	0160
57D5-1	0136
57D5-2	0136
57D5-4	0136
57D5R21	OEM
57D6-4	0016
57D6-10	0142
57D6-12	0160
57D6-19	0198
57D9-1	0050
57D9-2	0160
57D9R21GH	OEM
57D14-1	0016
57D14-2	0016
57D14-3	0016
57D17-1	1327
57D19-1	0037
57D19-2	0037
57D19-3	0037
57D19-10	0037
57D19-20	0037
57D19-30	0037
57D24-1	0144
57D24-2	0144
57D24-3	0144
57D68	0211
57D107-8	0144
57D108-8	OEM
57D126	0211
57D127	0275
57D130	0136
57D131	0136
57D132	0136
57D132-9	0050
57D136-12	0016
57D143	0211
57D156	0211
57D159-12	0126
57D166-12	0144
57D169	0211
57D170	0211
57D180	0279
57D184	0279
57D186	0136
57D187	0136
57D188	0136
57D189	0211
57D1127	0211
57D1130	0050
57D1131	0050
57D1132	0050
57D1143	0211
57D1186	0050
57DG-23	0160
57DG-32	0160
57L1-1	0050
57L1-2	0050
57L1-3	0050
57L1-4	0050
57L1-5	0164
57L1-6	0004
57L1-7	0164
57L1-8	0004
57L1-9	0050
57L1-10	0050
57L1-11	0050
57L1-12	0050
57L2-1	0086
57L2-2	0016

DEVICE TYPE	REPL CODE
57L3-1	0016
57L3-4	0016
57L5-1	0085
57L106-9	0321
57LS300J	OEM
57LS301J	OEM
57LS304J	OEM
57LS306J	OEM
57LS307J	OEM
57LS376J	OEM
57LS380J	OEM
57M1-1	0050
57M1-2	0050
57M1-3	0050
57M1-4	0050
57M1-5	0004
57M1-6	0004
57M1-7	0164
57M1-8	0164
57M1-9	0050
57M1-10	0050
57M1-11	0050
57M1-12	0050
57M1-13	0126
57M1-13A	0126
57M1-14	0016
57M1-15	0016
57M1-16	0208
57M1-17	0050
57M1-18	0208
57M1-19	0016
57M1-20	0016
57M1-21	0126
57M1-21A	0126
57M1-22	0126
57M1-23	0016
57M1-24	0016
57M1-25	0126
57M1-25A	0126
57M1-26	0016
57M1-27	0016
57M1-28	0016
57M1-29	0016
57M1-30	0016
57M1-31	0016
57M1-32	0016
57M1-33	0086
57M1-34	0086
57M1-35	0164
57M2-1	0208
57M2-2	0208
57M2-3	0164
57M2-4	0164
57M2-6	0208
57M2-7	0086
57M2-8	0164
57M2-9	0208
57M2-10	0126
57M2-10A	0126
57M2-11	0086
57M2-14	0086
57M2-15	0126
57M2-15A	0126
57M2-16	0233
57M2-17	0233
57M2-18	0086
57M2-506	2839
57M3-1	0103
57M3-1A	0103
57M3-2	0103
57M3-3	0086
57M3-4	0103
57M3-4A	0103
57M3-5	0178
57M3-6	0103
57M3-6A	0103
57M3-7	0085
57M3-8	0085
57M3-9P	0222
57M3-10P	0222
57M3-12	0222
57P1	0211
57RECT-SI-154(AU)	0023
57RECT-SI-1021(AO)	OEM
57RECT-SI-1021(AU)	0023
57S-06	0298
57S300J	OEM
57S301J	OEM
57S304J	OEM
57S306J	OEM
57S307J	OEM
57S373J	OEM
57S374J	OEM
57S376J	OEM
57S378J	OEM
57S380J	OEM
57S382J	OEM
57SI-HA11423	1192
57ST-3SK60	2439
57TB11	OEM
57TB12	OEM
57TB13	OEM
57TB14	OEM
57TB15	OEM
57TB16	OEM
57TB16-CE00	OEM
57TB16-GE00	OEM
57TB16-RE00	OEM
57TB17	OEM

DEVICE TYPE	REPL CODE
57TB17-CE00	OEM
57TB17-GE00	OEM
57TB17-RE00	OEM
57TB18	OEM
57TB18-CE00	OEM
57TB18-GE00	OEM
57TB18-RE00	OEM
57TB19	OEM
57TB19-CE00	OEM
57TB19-GE00	OEM
57TB19-RE00	OEM
57TB20	OEM
57TB20-CE00	OEM
57TB20-GE00	OEM
57TB20-RE00	OEM
57X14	0015
57Z4	OEM
57Z6	1436
57Z6A	1436
58-01	1241
58-1	0224
58A290-12	0321
58B2-14	0050
58P	OEM
58PB	OEM
58PBH	OEM
58PBHL	OEM
58PBL	OEM
58PL	OEM
58SI-LM393N	0624
58SI-LM393P	0624
58ST-2SA1029C	0006
58ST-2SC2344E	1274
58ST-MPS9418AS	0320
58SZ-RD6.2EB3	0466
58TB9	OEM
58TB10	OEM
58TB11	OEM
58TB12	OEM
58TB13	OEM
58TB13-CE00	OEM
58TB13-GE00	OEM
58TB13-RE00	OEM
58TB14	OEM
58TB14-CE00	OEM
58TB14-GE00	OEM
58TB14-RE00	OEM
58TB15	OEM
58TB15-CE00	OEM
58TB15-GE00	OEM
58TB15-RE00	OEM
58TB16	OEM
58TB16-CE00	OEM
58TB16-GE00	OEM
58TB16-RE00	OEM
58TB17	OEM
58TB17-CE00	OEM
58TB17-GE00	OEM
58TB17-RE00	OEM
58TB18	OEM
58TB18-CE00	OEM
58TB18-GE00	OEM
58TB18-RE00	OEM
58TB19	OEM
58TB19-CE00	OEM
58TB19-GE00	OEM
58TB19-RE00	OEM
58TB20	OEM
58TB20-CE00	OEM
58TB20-GE00	OEM
58TB20-RE00	OEM
58Z6	2206
58Z6A	2206
59-1	0911
59-5035	OEM
59-5055	OEM
59-5635	OEM
59-5637	OEM
59-5655	OEM
59-5657	OEM
59-5735	OEM
59-5737	OEM
59-5755	OEM
59-5757	OEM
59-5800	OEM
59-5802	OEM
59-5804	OEM
59-5840	OEM
59-5842	OEM
59-5844	OEM
59B402781	OEM
59B402787	1063
59B402788	1799
59E001-1	0133
59SD-1N34A(AU)	0123
59SD-134A(AU)	OEM
59SI-LA1210	0598
59SI-LM393N	0624
59SI-UPA53C	4075
59SI-UPD1913C	OEM
59ST-BC548B	0079
59Z6	0205
59Z6A	0205
60	OEM
60-3	0015
60-20	OEM
60-1045	OEM
60-1046	OEM
60-1069	OEM

DEVICE TYPE	REPL CODE
60-3012	OEM
60-3013	OEM
60-3014	OEM
60-3015	OEM
60-3016	OEM
60-3039-4	OEM
60-3039-6	OEM
60-3039-12	OEM
60-3040-12	OEM
60-3040-24	OEM
60-3053-12	OEM
60-3053-24	OEM
60AC80	OEM
60BC15	2633
60C	0015
60CDQ020	OEM
60CDQ030	OEM
60CDQ035	OEM
60CDQ040	OEM
60CDQ045	OEM
60D	0015
60D5R05	OEM
60D9R05GH	OEM
60DC15	2633
60DE10	0071
60DE12	OEM
60DE16	OEM
60DE18	OEM
60DE20	OEM
60DE22	OEM
60DE24	OEM
60DE25	OEM
60DE1414	OEM
60EQ5A	OEM
60F1	2070
60F5	0204
60F80	OEM
60FC15	1995
60FWJ2C11	OEM
60FWJ11	OEM
60GC15	1995
60GWJ2C11	OEM
60GWJ11	OEM
60H	0015
60H3	OEM
60H3N	0471
60H3P	0204
60H3PN	0510
60HF5	3716
60HF10	2629
60HF10R	1772
60HF15	2633
60HF20	2633
60HF25	2639
60HF30	2639
60HF30R	1772
60HF35	1995
60HF40	1995
60HF40R	1772
60HF45	2652
60HF50	2652
60HF50R	1772
60HF60	2657
60HF60R	1772
60HF80	3846
60HF100	2631
60HF100R	1807
60HFR10	2741
60HFR20	2741
60HFR60	6389
60HQ030	OEM
60HQ035	OEM
60HQ045	OEM
60HQ060	OEM
60HQ080	OEM
60HQ090	OEM
60HQ100	OEM
60J1	0959
60J2	0015
60J2P	0122
60J3P	0122
60JC15	2657
60JH3	2844
60KS200C	OEM
60L15	OEM
60L20	6100
60L25	OEM
60L30	OEM
60L35	OEM
60L40	OEM
60L45	OEM
60L50	OEM
60L55	OEM
60L60	OEM
60L65	OEM
60L70	OEM
60L75	OEM
60L80	OEM
60L85	OEM
60L90	OEM
60L95	OEM
60L100	OEM
60L110	OEM
60L120	OEM
60L130	OEM
60L140	OEM
60L150	OEM
60L160	OEM
60L170	OEM

DEVICE TYPE	REPL CODE
60L180	OEM
60L190	OEM
60L200	OEM
60L210	OEM
60L220	OEM
60L230	OEM
60L240	OEM
60L250	OEM
60L260	OEM
60L270	OEM
60L280	OEM
60L290	OEM
60L300	OEM
60LA	0087
60LC15	3846
60LF	OEM
60M	0015
60N15A	OEM
60N15A9	OEM
60N20A	OEM
60N20A9	OEM
60N25A	OEM
60N25A9	OEM
60N30A	OEM
60N30A9	OEM
60N35A9	OEM
60N40A	OEM
60N40A9	OEM
60N45A	OEM
60N45A9	OEM
60N50A	OEM
60N50A9	OEM
60N55A	OEM
60N55A9	OEM
60N60A	OEM
60N60A9	OEM
60N65A	OEM
60N65A9	OEM
60N70A	OEM
60N70A9	OEM
60N75A	OEM
60N75A9	OEM
60N80A	OEM
60N80A9	OEM
60N85A	OEM
60N85A9	OEM
60N90A	OEM
60N90A9	OEM
60N95A	OEM
60N95A9	OEM
60N100A	OEM
60N100A9	OEM
60N110A	OEM
60N120A	OEM
60N130A	OEM
60N140A	OEM
60N150A	OEM
60N160A	OEM
60N170A	OEM
60N180A	OEM
60N190A	OEM
60N200A	OEM
60N220A	OEM
60N230A	OEM
60N240A	OEM
60N250A	OEM
60NC15	3846
60QC15	OEM
60R3P	OEM
60S05	1272
60S1	1272
60S2	1277
60S2D	1659
60S3	1277
60S3P	OEM
60S4	1277
60S4D	1277
60S5	2070
60S6	1282
60S6D	1282
60S8	1285
60S10	1285
60SB03S	1536
60SB04S	1536
60SP-PD-41P1	OEM
60SP-PD-41PI	OEM
60SP-RD-41PI	OEM
60SP-SD-41PI	OEM
60ST-2SC945R	0076
60SZ-RD9.1EB2	0057
60T3P	OEM
60T4	1129
60V3P	OEM
60V10	OEM
60V12	OEM
60W3P	OEM
60X3P	OEM
60Y3P	OEM
60Z6	0221
60Z6A	0221
61	OEM
61-259	0143
61-607	0004
61-608	0004
61-654	0004
61-655	0004
61-656	0004
61-746	0016
61-747	0086

DEVICE TYPE	REPL CODE
61-751	0016
61-754	0016
61-755	0016
61-756	0229
61-782	0160
61-813	0086
61-814	0016
61-815	0016
61-820	0229
61-926	0229
61-928	0004
61-929	0004
61-1053-1	0419
61-1130	0004
61-1131	0004
61-1215	0004
61-1320	0015
61-1400	0016
61-1401	0016
61-1402	0016
61-1403	0016
61-1404	0016
61-1763	0016
61-1764	0086
61-1765	0015
61-1906	0222
61-1907	0004
61-1934	0004
61-1935	0004
61-3096-90	0848
61-7728	0015
61-8968	1293
61-8968M	1293
61-8969	0769
61-8969M	0769
61-59395	0143
61-260039	0136
61-260039A	0136
61A0001-10	2246
61A0001-11	1469
61A0001-12	0428
61A001-10	2246
61A001-11	1469
61A001-12	0428
61A023-2	2377
61A030-6	0167
61A030-9	2827
61A0306	0167
61B002-1	0050
61B003-1	0136
61B004-1	0004
61B005-1	0004
61B006-1	0004
61B007-1	0144
61B007-2	0144
61B009-1	0004
61B0015-1	0004
61B015-1	0004
61B016-1	0004
61B017-1	0004
61B018-1	0004
61B019-1	0004
61B020-1	0004
61B021-1	0004
61B022-2	0004
61B022-3	0004
61B023-1	0004
61B026-1	0004
61B027-1	0164
61B042-9	0574
61B1C	0797
61C001-1	0198
61C001-2	3973
61C001-4	2932
61C001-7	4004
61C001-11	4017
61C001-12	1516
61C001-30	4663
61C001-32	1570
61C001-33	4677
61C001-34	4671
61C001-35	4666
61C001-36	4670
61C001-38	4665
61C002-1	0211
61C002-2	4678
61C002-3	4099
61C003-1	0211
61C004-1	0086
61C005-1	0160
61C66-1	2949
61C66-2	2949
61C66-3	2949
61C66-4	2949
61C66-5	2949
61C66-6	2949
61C66-7	2949
61C66-8	2949
61C66-9	2949
61C66-10	2949
61E17	2847
61E34	0870
61E39	0262
61E44	0827
61F1FM	OEM
61F2FM	OEM
61F3FM	OEM
61F4FM	OEM
61F6FM	OEM

If replacement code is OEM, contact original manufacturer for replacement.

DEVICE TYPE	REPL CODE
61H20B27F-8803	OEM
61H20B48F-8M1	OEM
61H20B56F	OEM
61J2	0015
61K001-8	OEM
61K001-9	0876
61K001-10	0514
61K001-12	0876
61K001-13	1470
61L001-3	4546
61L001-4	OEM
61L001-5	4560
61L001-6	4561
61L001-7	OEM
61L001-8	4556
61MQ30	OEM
61MQ40	OEM
61MQ50	OEM
61MQ60	OEM
61N004-18	OEM
61N004-19	OEM
61P1	0136
61P1D	0050
61P10	0136
61R1FM	OEM
61R2FM	OEM
61R3FM	OEM
61R4FM	OEM
61R6FM	OEM
61SI-SAB1018P	OEM
61SI-SN74145N	0614
61SP-LT-4234G	OEM
61ST-BC557B	0037
61SV	OEM
61T1	OEM
61T1C	OEM
61T2	OEM
61T2C	OEM
61T3	OEM
61T3C	OEM
61T4	0340
61T5	OEM
61T6	OEM
61T7	OEM
61T8	OEM
61T9	OEM
61T10	OEM
61T11	OEM
61T12	OEM
61T13	OEM
61T14	OEM
61T15	OEM
61T16	OEM
61T18	OEM
61T19	OEM
61T20	OEM
61T20-EE00	OEM
61T20-RE00	OEM
61T21	OEM
61T21-EE00	OEM
61T21-RE00	OEM
61T22	OEM
61T22-EE00	OEM
61T22-RE00	OEM
61T23	OEM
61T23-EE00	OEM
61T23-RE00	OEM
61T24	OEM
61T24-EE00	OEM
61T24-RE00	OEM
61T25-EE00	OEM
61T25-RE00	OEM
61T26	OEM
61T26-EE00	OEM
61T26-RE00	OEM
61T27-EE00	OEM
61T27-RE00	OEM
61T28	OEM
61T28-EE00	OEM
61T28-RE00	OEM
61T29-EE00	OEM
61T29-RE00	OEM
61T30	OEM
61T30-EE00	OEM
61T30-RE00	OEM
61T31-CE00	OEM
61T31-GE00	OEM
61T31-RE00	OEM
61T32	OEM
61T32-CE00	OEM
61T32-GE00	OEM
61T32-RE00	OEM
61T33-CE00	OEM
61T33-GE00	OEM
61T33-RE00	OEM
61T34	OEM
61T34-CE00	OEM
61T34-GE00	OEM
61T34-RE00	OEM
61T35-CE00	OEM
61T35-GE00	OEM
61T35-RE00	OEM
61T36	OEM
61T36-CE00	OEM
61T36-GE00	OEM
61T36-RE00	OEM
61T37	OEM
61T37-CE00	OEM
61T37-GE00	OEM

DEVICE TYPE	REPL CODE
61T38	OEM
61T38-CE00	OEM
61T38-GE00	OEM
61T38-RE00	OEM
61T39	OEM
61T39-CE00	OEM
61T39-GE00	OEM
61T39-RE00	OEM
61T40-CE00	OEM
61T40-GE00	OEM
61T40-RE00	OEM
61TB1-JH00	OEM
61TB2-JH00	OEM
61TB3-JH00	OEM
61TB4-JH00	OEM
61TB5-JH00	OEM
61TB6-JH00	OEM
61TB7	OEM
61TB7-JH00	OEM
61TB8-JH00	OEM
61TB9	OEM
61TB9-EE00	OEM
61TB9-RE00	OEM
61TB10-EE00	OEM
61TB10-RE00	OEM
61TB11	OEM
61TB11-EE00	OEM
61TB11-RE00	OEM
61TB12-EE00	OEM
61TB12-RE00	OEM
61TB13	OEM
61TB13-EE00	OEM
61TB13-RE00	OEM
61TB14-EE00	OEM
61TB14-RE00	OEM
61TB15	OEM
61TB15-EE00	OEM
61TB15-RE00	OEM
61TB16-EE00	OEM
61TB16-RE00	OEM
61TB17	OEM
61TB17-EE00	OEM
61TB17-RE00	OEM
61TB18-EE00	OEM
61TB18-RE00	OEM
61TB19	OEM
61TB19-EE00	OEM
61TB19-RE00	OEM
61TB20-EE00	OEM
61TB20-RE00	OEM
61TC	OEM
61Z6	0499
62-3597-1	0150
62-3597-2	0150
62-7567	0016
62-8555	0079
62-8781	0050
62-10234	0143
62-10655	0143
62-12034	0143
62-13258	0004
62-13259	0208
62-13261	0015
62-13477	0015
62-13494	0004
62-15318	0143
62-15483	0015
62-16013	0196
62-16711	0015
62-16712	0196
62-16769	0143
62-16841	0143
62-16905	0016
62-16918	0004
62-16919	0178
62-17232	0911
62-17390	0050
62-17391	0050
62-17550	0016
62-18135	0015
62-18337	0196
62-18415	0279
62-18416	0279
62-18417	0279
62-18418	0050
62-18419	0050
62-18420	0004
62-18421	0004
62-18422	0050
62-18423	0279
62-18424	0279
62-18425	0016
62-18426	0233
62-18427	0085
62-18428	0160
62-18429	0599
62-18430	0004
62-18431	0015
62-18434	0015
62-18435	0015
62-18436	0015
62-18438	0015
62-18641	0016
62-18642	0016
62-18643	0016
62-18782	0133
62-18828	0016
62-19115	0015
62-19260	0911

DEVICE TYPE	REPL CODE
62-19280	0016
62-19452	0037
62-19516	0016
62-19548	0016
62-19581	0127
62-19620	0911
62-19734	0196
62-19749	0015
62-19814	0015
62-19837	0016
62-19838	0016
62-19846	0143
62-20154	0037
62-20154A	0037
62-20155	0016
62-20223	0133
62-20240	0016
62-20241	0016
62-20242	0016
62-20243	0016
62-20244	0037
62-20244A	0037
62-20319	0133
62-20360	0016
62-20437	0133
62-20565	1293
62-20597	0133
62-20643	0002
62-21369	0015
62-21496	0016
62-21552	0133
62-21573	0363
62-21574	0490
62-21683	0150
62-21699	1024
62-22038	0016
62-22039	0016
62-22250	0016
62-22251	0016
62-22524	0150
62-22529	0150
62-26597	0133
62-26851	0050
62-109474	0196
62-112524	0143
62-113998	0015
62-114267	0127
62-118825	0071
62-125528	0133
62-126321	0133
62-126856	0015
62-127532	0911
62-128343	0279
62-129556	0911
62-129604	0127
62-130045	0133
62-130046	0133
62-130047	0012
62-130139	0150
62-130761	0002
62-130762	0002
62-132497	0150
62-134074	0911
62A01	0015
62A02	0015
62A04	0015
62A05	0015
62B40B20F-8752	OEM
62B40B32F-8810	OEM
62B40B32F-8827	OEM
62J2	0015
62LS141J16	OEM
62R2	OEM
62R2R	1241
62ST-2SC458	0076
62ST-2SC458C	0076
62ST-LBC547B	OEM
62SV	OEM
62T1	OEM
62T2	OEM
62T3	OEM
62T4	0568
62T5	OEM
62T6	OEM
62T7	OEM
62T8	OEM
62T9	OEM
62T10	OEM
62T11	OEM
62T12	OEM
62T13	OEM
62T14	OEM
62T15	OEM
62T16	OEM
62T17	OEM
62T18	OEM
62T19	OEM
62T20	OEM
62T20-LH00	OEM
62T21	OEM
62T21-LH00	OEM
62T22	OEM
62T22-LH00	OEM
62T23	OEM
62T23-LH00	OEM
62T24	OEM
62T24-LH00	OEM
62T25-LH00	OEM
62T26	OEM

DEVICE TYPE	REPL CODE
62T26-LH00	OEM
62T27-LH00	OEM
62T28	OEM
62T28-LH00	OEM
62T29-LH00	OEM
62T29-NH00	OEM
62T30	OEM
62T30-LH00	OEM
62T30-NH00	OEM
62T31-LH00	OEM
62T31-NH00	OEM
62T32	OEM
62T32-LH00	OEM
62T32-NH00	OEM
62T33-LH00	OEM
62T33-NH00	OEM
62T34	OEM
62T34-LH00	OEM
62T34-NH00	OEM
62T35-LH00	OEM
62T35-NH00	OEM
62T36	OEM
62T36-LH00	OEM
62T36-NH00	OEM
62T37	OEM
62T37-LH00	OEM
62T37-NH00	OEM
62T38	OEM
62T38-LH00	OEM
62T38-NH00	OEM
62T39-LH00	OEM
62T39-NH00	OEM
62T40	OEM
62T40-LH00	OEM
62T40-NH00	OEM
62TB7	OEM
62TB9	OEM
62TB11	OEM
62TB13	OEM
62TB15	OEM
62TB17	OEM
62TB19	OEM
62Z6	0679
62Z6A	0679
63-00-84381-2	0211
63-3954	0050
63-7246	0164
63-7247	0004
63-7248	0208
63-7396	0004
63-7397	0004
63-7398	0004
63-7399	0004
63-7420	0004
63-7421	0016
63-7433	0015
63-7538	0050
63-7541	0050
63-7547	0279
63-7548	0050
63-7549	0208
63-7564	0004
63-7565	0208
63-7567	0016
63-7579	0050
63-7580	0050
63-7581	0050
63-7582	0050
63-7596	0004
63-7660	0050
63-7670	0016
63-7871	0004
63-7872	0004
63-7873	0004
63-8119	0050
63-8120	0164
63-8376	0050
63-8377	0050
63-8378	0050
63-8379	0050
63-8380	0004
63-8381	0143
63-8473	0208
63-8512	0178
63-8555	0016
63-8590	0160
63-8685	0015
63-8699	0050
63-8700	0050
63-8701	0016
63-8702	0016
63-8703	0004
63-8704	0004
63-8705	0208
63-8706	0160
63-8707	0103
63-8707A	0103
63-8819	0229
63-8824	0015
63-8825	0244
63-8945	0178
63-8954	0050
63-8955	0143
63-9072	0050
63-9337	0016
63-9338	0016
63-9339	0016
63-9340	0208
63-9341	0016

DEVICE TYPE	REPL CODE
63-9516	0016
63-9517	0050
63-9518	0016
63-9519	0004
63-9520	0004
63-9521	0004
63-9522	0030
63-9523	0143
63-9659	0004
63-9664	0050
63-9665	0050
63-9782	0030
63-9783	0244
63-9787	0229
63-9829	0016
63-9830	0016
63-9831	0016
63-9832	0016
63-9833	0016
63-9847	0016
63-9876	0050
63-9877	0050
63-9941	0050
63-9942	0137
63-10035	0050
63-10036	0050
63-10037	0004
63-10038	0004
63-10062	0178
63-10064	0015
63-10145	0050
63-10146	0050
63-10147	0004
63-10148	0050
63-10149	0050
63-10150	0050
63-10151	0004
63-10152	0004
63-10153	0004
63-10154	0004
63-10156	0004
63-10158	0004
63-10159	0004
63-10188	0016
63-10195	0050
63-10196	0050
63-10200	0279
63-10235-64	OEM
63-10375	0050
63-10376	0050
63-10377	0016
63-10378	0160
63-10383	0208
63-10384	0164
63-10408	0004
63-10708	0016
63-10709	0015
63-10725	0016
63-10732	0016
63-10733	0016
63-10734	0016
63-10735	0016
63-10736	0016
63-10737	0016
63-10739	0143
63-10860	0016
63-11025	0016
63-11055	0050
63-11073	0164
63-11074	0143
63-11143	0016
63-11144	0004
63-11147	0025
63-11148	0287
63-11215	0229
63-11289	0016
63-11290	0178
63-11291	0015
63-11468	0016
63-11469	0016
63-11470	0016
63-11471	0016
63-11472	0016
63-11474	0004
63-11496	0050
63-11497	0164
63-11582	0050
63-11584	0050
63-11585	0279
63-11586	0004
63-11659	0025
63-11660	0016
63-11661	0004
63-11757	0016
63-11758	0016
63-11759	0016
63-11762	0071
63-11825	0079
63-11831	0016
63-11832	0016
63-11833	0016
63-11834	0030
63-11878	0178
63-11879	0143
63-11881	0015
63-11934	0016
63-11935	0016
63-11936	0086
63-11937	0016

DEVICE TYPE	REPL CODE
63-11938	0178
63-11957	0015
63-11989	0086
63-11991	0103
63-11991A	0103
63-12003	0016
63-12004	0016
63-12062	0016
63-12077	0229
63-12110	0025
63-12154	0037
63-12154A	0037
63-12156	0037
63-12156A	0037
63-12157	0037
63-12157A	0037
63-12158	0143
63-12272	0016
63-12273	0074
63-12287	0287
63-12316	0004
63-12317	0004
63-12366	0071
63-12605	0016
63-12607	0143
63-12608	0016
63-12609	0016
63-12610	0050
63-12641	0016
63-12642	0016
63-12645	0143
63-12669	0164
63-12670	0164
63-12696	0016
63-12697	0016
63-12698	0164
63-12706	0016
63-12707	0016
63-12750	0016
63-12751	0016
63-12752	0016
63-12753	0016
63-12754	0143
63-12755	0143
63-12756	0143
63-12757	0143
63-12874	0016
63-12875	0016
63-12876	0004
63-12877	0016
63-12878	0016
63-12879	0016
63-12880	0004
63-12881	0004
63-12933	0016
63-12940	0016
63-12941	0016
63-12942	0016
63-12943	0016
63-12944	0079
63-12945	0164
63-12946	0016
63-12947	0164
63-12948	0016
63-12949	0016
63-12950	0016
63-12951	0016
63-12952	0016
63-12953	0016
63-12954	0178
63-12989	0086
63-12990	0086
63-13025	0050
63-13080	0143
63-13214	0086
63-13215	0086
63-13216	0074
63-13322	0037
63-13322A	0037
63-13323	0164
63-13419	0016
63-13438	0016
63-13440	0016
63-13441	0016
63-13839	0050
63-13840	0004
63-13842	0143
63-13864	0016
63-13899	0050
63-13903	0015
63-13919	0015
63-13926	0321
63-13927	0016
63-13954	0074
63-14032	0016
63-14051	0016
63-14052	0016
63-14057	0016
63-14195	0015
63-15483	0015
63-16918	0004
63-17390	0050
63-18135	0229
63-18416	0279
63-18418	0050
63-18419	0050
63-18420	0004
63-18421	0004
63-18423	0050

DEVICE TYPE	REPL CODE
63-18424	0050
63-18426	0283
63-18427	0085
63-18430	0004
63-18643	0016
63-19173	0290
63-19280	0016
63-19282	0016
63-22724	0143
63-23041	0004
63-25179	0004
63-25180	0004
63-25181	0004
63-25182	0004
63-25261	0164
63-25281	0004
63-25282	0004
63-25342	0123
63-25720	0004
63-25726	0050
63-25727	0004
63-25728	0004
63-25729	0004
63-25933	0143
63-25942	0004
63-25944	0004
63-25946	0279
63-26382	0143
63-26597	0015
63-26849	0279
63-26850	0050
63-26851	0004
63-27278	0279
63-27279	0279
63-27280	0279
63-27281	0004
63-27366	0050
63-27367	0279
63-27483	0229
63-27500	0050
63-27622	0015
63-28250	0143
63-28348	0050
63-28358	0050
63-28390	0004
63-28399	0004
63-28426	0233
63-28888	0143
63-29383	0229
63-29451	0160
63-29459	0160
63-29461	0016
63-29661	0050
63-29662	0279
63-29663	0279
63-29664	0279
63-29665	0004
63-29666	0004
63-29819	0050
63-29820	0050
63-29821	0050
63-29862	0050
63-29863	0279
63-250128-2	0911
63-250128-8	0911
63-250128-12	0911
63-250128-14	0911
63-250128-16	0911
63-259128-3	OEM
63A03Y	OEM
63J2	0015
63LS10J16	OEM
63LS140N16	OEM
63LS141N16	OEM
63LS240J16	OEM
63LS240N16	OEM
63LS241J16	OEM
63LS241N16	OEM
63N1	0637
63N50	0435
63P3	0211
63R2	OEM
63RA441J	OEM
63RA441N	OEM
63RECT-SI-1021	0023
63S080J	OEM
63S080N	OEM
63S081J	OEM
63S081N	OEM
63S140J16	OEM
63S140N16	OEM
63S141J16	OEM
63S141N16	OEM
63S240J16	OEM
63S240N16	OEM
63S241J16	OEM
63S241N16	OEM
63ST-2SC1162C	0558
63Z6	0505
63Z6A	0505
64-1	0143
64-8054-6	0015
64-J2	0015
64EPA	OEM
64EPB	OEM
64J2	0015
64KZ	OEM
64N1	0074
64R2	0109

If replacement code is OEM, contact original manufacturer for replacement.

157

DEVICE TYPE	REPL CODE
64RECT-SI-1001(AU)	0790
64RECT-U-1012	1999
64SP-LT-6740R	OEM
64T1	0279
64T4	0058
64Z6	0686
64Z6A	0686
65	0015
65-08001	0816
65-080001	1851
65-085002	0143
65-085003	0143
65-085004	0137
65-085010	0143
65-085012	0143
65-085013	0015
65-1	0016
65-1-70	0050
65-1-70-12	0050
65-1-70-12-7	0050
65-1A	0050
65-1A0	0050
65-1A0R	0050
65-1A1	0050
65-1A2	0050
65-1A3	0050
65-1A3P	0050
65-1A4	0050
65-1A4-7	0050
65-1A4-7B	0050
65-1A5	0050
65-1A5L	0050
65-1A6	0050
65-1A6-5	0050
65-1A7	0050
65-1A7-1	0050
65-1A8	0050
65-1A9	0050
65-1A9G	0050
65-1A19	0050
65-1A21	0050
65-1A82	0050
65-2	0208
65-2-70	0208
65-2-70-12	0208
65-2-70-12-7	0208
65-2A	0208
65-2A0	0208
65-2A0R	0208
65-2A1	0208
65-2A2	0208
65-2A3	0208
65-2A3P	0208
65-2A4	0208
65-2A4-7	0208
65-2A4-7B	0208
65-2A5	0208
65-2A5L	0208
65-2A6	0208
65-2A6-1	0208
65-2A7	0208
65-2A7-1	0208
65-2A8	0208
65-2A9	0208
65-2A9G	0208
65-2A19	0208
65-2A21	0208
65-2A82	0208
65-4	0595
65-4-70	0595
65-4-70-12	0595
65-4-70-12-7	0595
65-4A	0595
65-4A0	0595
65-4A0R	0595
65-4A1	0595
65-4A2	0595
65-4A3	0595
65-4A3P	0595
65-4A4	0595
65-4A4-7	0595
65-4A4-7B	0595
65-4A5	0595
65-4A5L	0595
65-4A6	0595
65-4A6-2	0595
65-4A7	0595
65-4A7-1	0595
65-4A8	0595
65-4A9	0595
65-4A9G	0595
65-4A19	0595
65-4A21	0595
65-4A82	0595
65-10	0050
65-11	0050
65-12	0050
65-13	0050
65-14	0050
65-15	0050
65-16	0050
65-17	0050
65-18	0050
65-19	0050
65-20	0208
65-21	0208
65-22	0208
65-23	0208
65-24	0208

DEVICE TYPE	REPL CODE
65-25	0208
65-26	0208
65-27	0208
65-28	0208
65-29	0208
65-40	0595
65-41	0595
65-42	0595
65-43	0595
65-44	0595
65-45	0595
65-46	0595
65-47	0595
65-48	0595
65-49	0595
65-11137-23	2728
65-11502-03	0079
65-20820-00	3946
65-22009-00	OEM
65-27328-01	4734
65-33361-00	1251
65-37323-164	0794
65-45402-00	2279
65-45430-00	OEM
65-48629-00	OEM
65-80001	1004
65-250128-12	0911
65-744238	0479
65A	0037
65A0	0050
65A1	0050
65A2	0050
65A3	0050
65A4	0050
65A5	0050
65A6	0050
65A7	0050
65A8	0050
65A9	0050
65A10	0050
65A10R	0050
65A12	0050
65A13	0050
65A13P	0050
65A14	0050
65A14-7	0050
65A14-7B	0050
65A15	0050
65A15L	0050
65A16	0050
65A16-3	0050
65A17	0050
65A17-1	0050
65A18	0050
65A19	0050
65A19G	0050
65A-70	0050
65A-70-12	0050
65A-70-12-7	0050
65A119	0050
65A121	0050
65A182	0050
65B	0037
65B0	0136
65B1	0136
65B3	0136
65B4	0136
65B5	0136
65B6	0136
65B7	0136
65B8	0136
65B9	0136
65B10	0136
65B10R	0136
65B11	0136
65B12	0136
65B13	0136
65B13P	0136
65B14	0136
65B14-7	0136
65B14-7B	0136
65B15	0136
65B15L	0136
65B16	0136
65B16-2	0136
65B17	0136
65B17-1	0136
65B18	0136
65B19	0136
65B19G	0136
65B-70	0136
65B-70-12	0136
65B-70-12-7	0136
65B119	0136
65B121	0136
65B182	0136
65BO	0136
65C	0037
65C0	0160
65C01	0050
65C02	0050
65C02A	OEM
65C03	0050
65C1	0037
65C2	0160
65C3	0160
65C4	0160
65C5	0160
65C6	0160

DEVICE TYPE	REPL CODE
65C7	0160
65C8	0160
65C9	0160
65C10	0160
65C10R	0160
65C11	0160
65C12	0160
65C13	0160
65C13P	0160
65C14	0160
65C14-7	0160
65C14-7B	0160
65C15	0160
65C15L	0160
65C16	0160
65C16-4	0160
65C17	0160
65C17-1	0160
65C18	0160
65C19	0160
65C19G	0160
65C22	OEM
65C-70	0160
65C-70-12	0160
65C-70-12-7	0160
65C119	0160
65C121	0160
65C182	0160
65D	0037
65D1	0037
65D5R09	OEM
65D9R09GH	OEM
65E	0037
65E05A	OEM
65E1	0037
65F	0037
65F1	0037
65J2	0015
65P117	0015
65P124	0015
65P124-1	0015
65P124-2	0015
65P153	0015
65P155	0015
65P206	0015
65P284	0015
65P297	0015
65R2	OEM
65R2S	OEM
65SI-HA11580	1049
65ST-2SC454B	0076
65ST-2SC535B	0127
65T1	0004
65Z6	0864
65Z6A	0864
66-1	0004
66-1-70	0004
66-1-70-12	0004
66-1-70-12-7	0004
66-1A	0004
66-1A0	0004
66-1A0R	0004
66-1A1	0004
66-1A2	0004
66-1A3	0004
66-1A3P	0004
66-1A4	0004
66-1A4-7	0004
66-1A4-7B	0004
66-1A5	0004
66-1A5L	0004
66-1A6	0004
66-1A6-3	0004
66-1A7	0004
66-1A7-1	0004
66-1A8	0004
66-1A9	0004
66-1A9G	0004
66-1A19	0004
66-1A21	0004
66-1A82	0004
66-2	0004
66-2-70	0004
66-2-70-12	0004
66-2-70-12-7	0004
66-2A	0004
66-2A0	0004
66-2A0R	0004
66-2A1	0004
66-2A2	0004
66-2A3	0004
66-2A3P	0004
66-2A4	0004
66-2A4-7	0004
66-2A4-7B	0004
66-2A5	0004
66-2A5L	0004
66-2A6	0004
66-2A6-4	0004
66-2A7	0004
66-2A7-1	0004
66-2A8	0004
66-2A9	0004
66-2A9G	0004
66-2A19	0004
66-2A21	0004
66-2A82	0004
66-3	0004
66-3-70	0004

DEVICE TYPE	REPL CODE
66-3-70-12	0004
66-3-70-12-7	0004
66-3A	0004
66-3A0	0004
66-3A0R	0004
66-3A1	0004
66-3A2	0004
66-3A3	0004
66-3A3P	0004
66-3A4	0004
66-3A4-7	0004
66-3A4-7B	0004
66-3A5	0004
66-3A5L	0004
66-3A6	0004
66-3A6C	0004
66-3A7	0004
66-3A7-1	0004
66-3A8	0004
66-3A9	0004
66-3A9G	0004
66-3A19	0004
66-3A21	0004
66-3A82	0004
66-10	0004
66-11	0004
66-12	0004
66-13	0004
66-14	0004
66-15	0004
66-16	0004
66-17	0004
66-18	0004
66-19	0004
66-20	0004
66-21	0004
66-22	0004
66-23	0004
66-24	0004
66-25	0004
66-26	0004
66-27	0004
66-28	0004
66-29	0004
66-30	0004
66-31	0004
66-32	0004
66-33	0004
66-34	0004
66-35	0004
66-36	0004
66-37	0004
66-38	0004
66-2246	0015
66-6023	0004
66-6023-00	0004
66-6024-00	0004
66-6025-00	0004
66-6026-00	0004
66-6027-00	0004
66-6028-00	0004
66-6030-00	0015
66-6031-00	0015
66-6033	0004
66-8504	0071
66-11502-02	0079
66-11502-03	0079
66-11702-11	0079
66-18050-03	OEM
66-19013-07J	0079
66-19014-03J	4811
66-19014-035	4811
66-19400-00	0161
66-19400-01	0161
66-20324-00	0802
66-20438-00	0919
66-29015-03J	0037
66-29015-035	0037
66-F29-1	0016
66-P11I20	0037
66-P1120	0037
66A52	OEM
66A96-1	0190
66B-020A	2474
66C0039-001	OEM
66F-001	0015
66F001	0015
66F-001-1	0015
66F001-1	0015
66F-010	0042
66F016-1	0133
66F016-2	0133
66F017	0907
66F018	0133
66F020-1	0275
66F020-2	0275
66F021-1	0007
66F022-1	0007
66F023-1	0037
66F024-1	0037
66F025-1	0086
66F026-1	0111
66F027-1	0016
66F028-1	0016
66F029-1	0016
66F039-1	0396
66F041-1	0037
66F042-1	0007
66F-054-1	1493

DEVICE TYPE	REPL CODE
66F-054-2	1493
66F-054-3	1493
66F054-3	0190
66F054-4	0190
66F057-1	0016
66F057-2	0016
66F058-2	0546
66F074-1	0283
66F074-2	0283
66F074-3	0283
66F074-4	0283
66F-084-1	0321
66F-112-1	1493
66F112-1	1493
66F-112-2	1493
66F112-2	1493
66F125-1	2153
66F136-1	2032
66F159-1	1061
66F159-2	1061
66F159-3	1061
66F175-1	2584
66F176-1	2663
66F-181-1	1493
66F181-1	1493
66F1271	0345
66F1551	0850
66F1751	2584
66F1761	2663
66J2	0015
66R2	0122
66R2S	0810
66ST-2SC1514BK	1077
66ST-2SD819	2643
66SZ-RD10EB3	0064
66WM8	OEM
66X0003	1024
66X0003-001	1024
66X0003-1	1024
66X002-001	0907
66X0020-000	0143
66X0020-001	0143
66X0023-001	0015
66X0023-002	2613
66X0023-003	0229
66X0023-004	0015
66X0023-005	0015
66X0023-006	0015
66X0023-007	0015
66X0023-008	0015
66X0023-009	0071
66X0023-1	0015
66X0024-000	0196
66X0025-000	0196
66X0025-000-001	0196
66X0025-000,001	0196
66X0025-001	0196
66X0028-001	0015
66X0028-008	0071
66X0033-000	0015
66X0033-001	0015
66X0035-000	0769
66X0035-001	0769
66X0036-001	1293
66X0036-002	0102
66X0037-001	0015
66X0038-001	0102
66X0039-001	0143
66X0040-001	OEM
66X0040-003	0631
66X0040-004	0721
66X0040-005	0064
66X0040-007	0398
66X0040-008	0028
66X0040-009	0002
66X0040-011	0528
66X0040-012	0778
66X0040-019	0036
66X0040-020	0057
66X0040-021	0152
66X0041-001	0469
66X0043-001	0133
66X0044-001	0133
66X0044-100	0133
66X0045-001	0128
66X0046-001	0124
66X0047-001	0143
66X0047-901	0143
66X0048-001	0015
66X0049-001	0855
66X0049-001(DIODE)	0123
66X0049-002	0143
66X0049-004	0028
66X0049-100	0123
66X0050-001	0030
66X0051-001	0143
66X0053-001	1208
66X0054-001	1208
66X0054-002	1208
66X0055-001	1208
66X0056-001	0133
66X0060-001	1493
66X0060-002	1493
66X0061-001	0128
66X0062-001	0133
66X0067-002	OEM
66X0068-002	0102
66X0069-001	0133
66X0070-001	0124

DEVICE TYPE	REPL CODE
66X0071-001	0023
66X0073-001	0087
66X002000	0143
66X041-001	0015
66X053-001	0015
66X060-001	OEM
66X14	0015
66X14-C	0015
66X14C	0015
66X16	0015
66X17	0015
66X19	0015
66X20	0143
66X21	0196
66X23	0015
66X24	0015
66X25	0196
66X25-0	0196
66X26	0015
66X29	0133
66X41-1	0469
66X45-1	0128
66X218	0196
66XZ18	0196
66Z6	0237
66Z6A	0237
67-01603-01	2852
67-1000-00	0015
67-1003-00	0015
67-10430-01	1319
67-20315-01	OEM
67-30201-05	0030
67-30321-05	3643
67-31043-05	0549
67-31212-04	0052
67-31603-01	OEM
67-31703-01	OEM
67-32009-01	0658
67-32109-02	4047
67-32706-03	OEM
67-32706-04	OEM
67-32720-01	2013
67-32720-02	1938
67-32720-03	OEM
67-32720-04	OEM
67-32808-02	4923
67-33105-01	OEM
67-33215-01	3344
67-34002-06	0080
67-34003-06	0023
67-34148-07	0124
67-35402-06	0242
67-39221-04P	0057
67-40060-01	0019
67-40060-02	0019
67-51703-02	3809
67-53315-01	1521
67-90430-01	1319
67-93401-01	3331
67-93501-01	3830
67-RECT-U-1002	OEM
67C015H20LSS	OEM
67C024H20LSS	OEM
67C030H20LSS	OEM
67C050H20LSS	OEM
67C075H20LSS	OEM
67C100H20LSS	OEM
67C120H20LSS	OEM
67C150H20LSS	OEM
67C200H20LSS	OEM
67C250H20LSS	OEM
67C300H20LSS	OEM
67C400H20LSS	OEM
67C500H20LSS	OEM
67C750H20LSS	OEM
67D006H53PNN	OEM
67D010H53PNN	OEM
67D015H53PNN	OEM
67D015H55FNN	OEM
67D018H55FNN	OEM
67D020H53PNN	OEM
67D024H55FNN	OEM
67D030H53PNN	OEM
67D036H55FNN	OEM
67D048H55FNN	OEM
67D050H04TNN	OEM
67D050H20TTS	OEM
67D050H53PNN	OEM
67D050H55FNN	OEM
67D075H04TNN	OEM
67D075H20TTS	OEM
67D075H55FNN	OEM
67D080H53PNN	OEM
67D100H04TNN	OEM
67D100H20TTS	OEM
67D100H53PNN	OEM
67D100H55FNN	OEM
67D120H04TNN	OEM
67D120H20TTS	OEM
67D120H53PNN	OEM
67D120H55FNN	OEM
67D150H04TNN	OEM
67D150H20TTS	OEM
67D150H53PNN	OEM
67D150H55FNN	OEM
67D200H04TNN	OEM
67D200H20TTS	OEM
67D200H53PNN	OEM
67D200H55FNN	OEM

DEVICE TYPE	REPL CODE
67D250H20TTS	OEM
67D250H53PNN	OEM
67D250H55FNN	OEM
67D300H04TNN	OEM
67D300H20TTS	OEM
67D300H53PNN	OEM
67D300H55FNN	OEM
67D400H04TNN	OEM
67D400H20TTS	OEM
67D400H55FNN	OEM
67D500H20TTS	OEM
67D500H55FNN	OEM
67D600H20TTS	OEM
67D750H20TTS	OEM
67J2	0071
67J2A	0071
67LS300J	OEM
67LS301J	OEM
67LS304J	OEM
67LS306J	OEM
67LS307J	OEM
67LS376J	OEM
67LS380J	OEM
67P1	0160
67P2	0160
67P3	0160
67R2	OEM
67RECT-U-1002	OEM
67S300J	OEM
67S301J	OEM
67S304J	OEM
67S306J	OEM
67S307J	OEM
67S373J	OEM
67S374J	OEM
67S376J	OEM
67S378J	OEM
67S380J	OEM
67S382J	OEM
67SD-1N34A	0123
67Z6	1387
67Z6A	1387
68-A-8318-P1	0037
68A831-P1	0037
68A7349-D32	1035
68A7349-D46	0141
68A7349-D62	0557
68A7349-PD32	1035
68A7349PD30	1812
68A7349PD36	1820
68A7349PD45	0081
68A7349PD46	0141
68A7349PD62	0557
68A7652P1	1340
68A7652P2	2871
68A8225P001	0411
68A9025	0232
68A9026	0677
68A9027	0310
68A9028	0357
68A9030	0507
68A9031	0680
68A9032	1197
68A9033	0692
68A9034	3429
68A9035	0867
68A9036	3478
68A9037	0990
68A9038	0738
68A9040	1265
68A9041	1423
68A9042	1150
68A9047	5159
68A9048	1487
68A9049	1531
68HDS	OEM
68P1	0160
68P1B	0160
68PB08M	OEM
68PBF9C	OEM
68PD08M	OEM
68PH08M	OEM
68PS08M	OEM
68R2	0131
68R2S	0131
68SP-CQY89A	OEM
68ST-2SD819	2643
68ST-MPS9700E	0079
68SZ-RD12FB3	0137
68X0003	1024
68X0003-001	1024
68X003-001	1024
68X0040-004	0721
68X0040-005	0170
68Z6	0247
68Z6A	0247
69-001	0239
69-01014-01	OEM
69-02005-01	OEM
69-02006-02	0112
69-02007-01	OEM
69-1810	0079
69-1811	0079
69-1812	0079
69-1813	0079
69-1814	0086
69-1815	0150
69-1816	0111
69-1817	0150

If replacement code is OEM, contact original manufacturer for replacement.

DEVICE TYPE	REPL CODE
69-1818	0161
69-1819	0455
69-1820	0143
69-1821	0030
69-1822	0133
69-1823	0015
69-2246	0015
69-2922	0019
69-3116	2535
69AJ110	0899
69B1M	0350
69N1	0144
69SP112	0126
69ST-2SD313F	0042
69SZ-HZ12A3(AU)	0999
69V097H62	0079
70	OEM
70ATB7	OEM
70ATB9	OEM
70ATB11	OEM
70B1C	0348
70B1Z	0348
70BN20	OEM
70BN30	OEM
70BN40	OEM
70BN50	OEM
70BN60	OEM
70BN80	OEM
70BN100	OEM
70BN120	OEM
70BN140	OEM
70BN160	OEM
70BNS	OEM
70C05	OEM
70C05B	OEM
70C05BF	OEM
70C05C	OEM
70C05CF	OEM
70C05F	OEM
70C025	0217
70C025B	0217
70C025BF	0217
70C025F	0217
70C050	0217
70C050B	0217
70C050BF	0217
70C050F	0217
70C10	0217
70C10B	0217
70C10BF	0217
70C10C	OEM
70C10CF	OEM
70C10F	0217
70C15	0217
70C15B	0217
70C15BF	0217
70C15C	OEM
70C15CF	OEM
70C15F	0217
70C20	0217
70C20B	0217
70C20BF	0217
70C20C	OEM
70C20CF	OEM
70C20F	0217
70C25	0217
70C25B	0217
70C25BF	0217
70C25C	OEM
70C25CF	OEM
70C25F	0217
70C30	0217
70C30B	0217
70C30BF	0217
70C30C	OEM
70C30CF	OEM
70C30F	0217
70C35	0217
70C35B	0463
70C35BF	0217
70C35C	0217
70C35CF	OEM
70C35F	0217
70C40	0217
70C40B	0463
70C40BF	0217
70C40C	OEM
70C40CF	OEM
70C40F	0217
70C45	0217
70C45B	0463
70C45BF	0217
70C45C	OEM
70C45CF	OEM
70C45F	0217
70C50	0217
70C50B	0463
70C50BF	0217
70C50C	OEM
70C50CF	OEM
70C50F	0217
70C60	0217
70C60B	0463
70C60BF	0217
70C60C	OEM
70C60CF	OEM
70C60F	0217
70C70	0463
70C70B	0463
70C70BF	0653
70C70C	OEM
70C70CF	OEM
70C70F	0653
70C80	0463
70C80B	0463
70C80BF	0653
70C80C	OEM
70C80CF	OEM
70C80F	0653
70C90	0463
70C90B	0463
70C90BF	0653
70C90C	OEM
70C90CF	OEM
70C90F	0653
70C100	0463
70C100B	0463
70C100BF	0653
70C100C	OEM
70C100CF	OEM
70C100F	1714
70C110	0463
70C110B	0463
70C110BF	0653
70C110C	OEM
70C110CF	OEM
70C110F	0653
70C120	0463
70C120B	0463
70C120BF	0653
70C120C	OEM
70C120CF	OEM
70C120F	0653
70C130	OEM
70C130B	OEM
70C130BF	OEM
70C130F	OEM
70C140	OEM
70C140B	OEM
70C140BF	OEM
70C140F	OEM
70C150	OEM
70C150B	OEM
70C150BF	OEM
70C150F	OEM
70C160	OEM
70C160B	OEM
70C160BF	OEM
70C160F	OEM
70C170	OEM
70C170B	OEM
70C170BF	OEM
70C170F	OEM
70C180	OEM
70C180B	OEM
70C180BF	OEM
70C180F	OEM
70D5R10	OEM
70D9R10GH	OEM
70E04A	OEM
70F10	OEM
70F15	OEM
70F20	OEM
70F25	OEM
70F30	OEM
70F40	0015
70F50	OEM
70F60	OEM
70F100	OEM
70H5	1551
70H5A	1551
70H5AR	2165
70H5R	2165
70H10	1551
70H10A	1551
70H10AR	2165
70H10R	2165
70H15	2813
70H15A	2813
70H15AR	2168
70H15R	2168
70H20	2813
70H20A	2813
70H20AR	2168
70H20R	2168
70H25	4244
70H25A	4244
70H25AR	3556
70H25R	3556
70H30	4244
70H30A	4244
70H30AR	3556
70H30R	3556
70H40	2823
70H40A	2823
70H40AR	2177
70H40R	2177
70H50	2844
70H50A	2844
70H50AR	2183
70H50R	2183
70H60	2844
70H60A	2844
70H60AR	2183
70H60R	2183
70H70	2806
70H70A	2806
70H70AR	2202
70H70R	2202
70H80	2806
70H80A	2806
70H80AR	2202
70H80R	2202
70H90	2454
70H90A	2454
70H90AR	2324
70H90R	2324
70H100	2454
70H100A	2454
70H100AR	2324
70H100R	2324
70H120A	2619
70HA40	OEM
70HA60	OEM
70HA80	OEM
70HA100	OEM
70HA120	OEM
70HA140	OEM
70HA160	OEM
70HF10	1551
70HF20	2813
70HF40	2823
70HF60	2844
70HF60A	OEM
70HF80	2806
70HF80T	2818
70HF100	2454
70HF100A	OEM
70HF100T	2818
70HF120	2619
70HF140	OEM
70HF160	OEM
70HFL5S02	4148
70HFL5S05	4148
70HFL5S10	4148
70HFL10S02	4148
70HFL10S05	4148
70HFL10S10	4148
70HFL20S02	4148
70HFL20S05	4148
70HFL20S10	4148
70HFL40S02	OEM
70HFL40S05	OEM
70HFL40S10	OEM
70HFL60S02	5521
70HFL60S05	5521
70HFL60S10	5521
70HFL80S05	OEM
70HFL80S10	OEM
70HFL100S05	OEM
70HFL100S10	OEM
70HFR10	2165
70HFR20	2168
70HFR30	OEM
70HFR40	2177
70HFR50	OEM
70HFR60	2183
70HFR80	2202
70HFR80T	1807
70HFR100	2324
70HFR100T	1807
70HFR120	5229
70HFR140	OEM
70HFR160	OEM
70HG10	OEM
70HG20	OEM
70HG40	OEM
70HG60	OEM
70HG80	OEM
70HG100	OEM
70HG120	OEM
70HR5A	1734
70HR10A	1734
70HR15	2168
70HR15A	2168
70HR20	2168
70HR20A	2168
70HR30A	1772
70HR40	2177
70HR40A	2177
70HR50	2183
70HR50A	2183
70HR60	2183
70HR60A	2183
70HR90	2454
70HR90A	2454
70HR100	2454
70HR100A	2454
70HR120A	5229
70KS200C	OEM
70M10	1017
70M15	1017
70M20	1017
70M30	1017
70M40	1017
70M50	1040
70M60	1030
70M80	1040
70M100	1040
70MA10	0496
70MA20	0496
70MA30	0496
70MA40	0496
70MA60	1766
70MA80	2805
70MA100	1778
70MA120	3138
70MA140	3138
70MA160	OEM
70MLA60	OEM
70MLA80	OEM
70MLA100	OEM
70MLA120	OEM
70MLAB160	OEM
70MLAB180	OEM
70MLAB200	OEM
70MLAB250	OEM
70N1	0016
70N1M	0111
70N2	0198
70N3	0127
70N4	0016
70R2	OEM
70R2S	0145
70RC2	OEM
70RC5	OEM
70RC10	OEM
70RC15	OEM
70RC20	OEM
70RC30	OEM
70RC40	OEM
70RC50	OEM
70RC50A	OEM
70RC60	OEM
70RC60A	OEM
70RC70A	OEM
70RC80A	OEM
70RCF5A	OEM
70RCF10A	OEM
70RCF15A	OEM
70RCF20A	OEM
70RCF25A	OEM
70RCF30A	OEM
70RCF40A	OEM
70RCF60A	OEM
70RCF70A	OEM
70RCF80A	OEM
70RCS10A	OEM
70RCS20A	OEM
70RCS30A	OEM
70RCS40A	OEM
70RCS50A	OEM
70RCS60A	OEM
70RE60	0463
70RE60A	0463
70RE70	0463
70RE70A	0463
70RE80	0463
70RE80A	0463
70RE90	0463
70RE90A	0463
70RE100	0463
70RE100A	0463
70RE110	0463
70RE110A	0463
70RE120	0463
70RE120A	0463
70RE130	OEM
70REB60	0463
70REB70	0463
70REB80	0463
70REB90	0463
70REB100	0463
70REB110	0463
70REB120	0463
70REB130	OEM
70S5	OEM
70S10	OEM
70S15	OEM
70S25	OEM
70S30	OEM
70S35	OEM
70S40	0015
70S45	OEM
70S50	OEM
70S60	OEM
70S70	OEM
70S2020	OEM
70SD-1SV124	0623
70ST-2SC945Q	0076
70STB7	OEM
70STB9	OEM
70STB11	OEM
70STB13	OEM
70T1	OEM
70T2	OEM
70T3	OEM
70T4	OEM
70T5	OEM
70T6	OEM
70T7	OEM
70T8	OEM
70T9	OEM
70T10	OEM
70T11	OEM
70T12	OEM
70T13	OEM
70T14	OEM
70T15	OEM
70T16	OEM
70T17	OEM
70T18	OEM
70T19	OEM
70T20	OEM
70T25	OEM
70T30	OEM
70T35	OEM
70T40	0015
70T45	OEM
70T50	OEM
70T60	OEM
70T70	OEM
70TB1	OEM
70TB1-CE00	OEM
70TB1-CH00	OEM
70TB1-GH00	OEM
70TB1-JE00	OEM
70TB1-JH00	OEM
70TB1-LE00	OEM
70TB1-LH00	OEM
70TB1-NE00	OEM
70TB1-NH00	OEM
70TB1-RE00	OEM
70TB2	OEM
70TB2-CE00	OEM
70TB2-CH00	OEM
70TB2-GH00	OEM
70TB2-JE00	OEM
70TB2-JH00	OEM
70TB2-LE00	OEM
70TB2-LH00	OEM
70TB2-NE00	OEM
70TB2-NH00	OEM
70TB2-RE00	OEM
70TB3	OEM
70TB3-CE00	OEM
70TB3-CH00	OEM
70TB3-GH00	OEM
70TB3-JE00	OEM
70TB3-JH00	OEM
70TB3-LE00	OEM
70TB3-LH00	OEM
70TB3-NE00	OEM
70TB3-NH00	OEM
70TB3-RE00	OEM
70TB4	OEM
70TB4-CE00	OEM
70TB4-CH00	OEM
70TB4-GE00	OEM
70TB4-GH00	OEM
70TB4-JE00	OEM
70TB4-JH00	OEM
70TB4-LE00	OEM
70TB4-LH00	OEM
70TB4-NE00	OEM
70TB4-NH00	OEM
70TB4-RE00	OEM
70TB5	OEM
70TB5-CE00	OEM
70TB5-CH00	OEM
70TB5-GE00	OEM
70TB5-GH00	OEM
70TB5-JE00	OEM
70TB5-JH00	OEM
70TB5-LE00	OEM
70TB5-LH00	OEM
70TB5-NE00	OEM
70TB5-NH00	OEM
70TB6	OEM
70TB6-CE00	OEM
70TB6-CH00	OEM
70TB6-GE00	OEM
70TB6-GH00	OEM
70TB6-JE00	OEM
70TB6-JH00	OEM
70TB6-LE00	OEM
70TB6-LH00	OEM
70TB6-NE00	OEM
70TB6-NH00	OEM
70TB6-RE00	OEM
70TB7	OEM
70TB7-CH00	OEM
70TB7-GE00	OEM
70TB7-GH00	OEM
70TB7-JE00	OEM
70TB7-JH00	OEM
70TB7-LE00	OEM
70TB7-LH00	OEM
70TB7-NE00	OEM
70TB7-NH00	OEM
70TB7-RE00	OEM
70TB8	OEM
70TB8-CE00	OEM
70TB8-CH00	OEM
70TB8-GH00	OEM
70TB8-JE00	OEM
70TB8-JH00	OEM
70TB8-LE00	OEM
70TB8-LH00	OEM
70TB8-NE00	OEM
70TB8-NH00	OEM
70TB8-RE00	OEM
70TB9	OEM
70TB9-CE00	OEM
70TB9-CH00	OEM
70TB9-GH00	OEM
70TB9-JE00	OEM
70TB9-JH00	OEM
70TB9-LE00	OEM
70TB9-LH00	OEM
70TB9-NE00	OEM
70TB9-NH00	OEM
70TB9-RE00	OEM
70TB10	OEM
70TB10-CE00	OEM
70TB10-CH00	OEM
70TB10-GH00	OEM
70TB10-JE00	OEM
70TB10-JH00	OEM
70TB10-LE00	OEM
70TB10-LH00	OEM
70TB10-NE00	OEM
70TB10-NH00	OEM
70TB10-RE00	OEM
70TB11	OEM
70TB11-CE00	OEM
70TB11-CH00	OEM
70TB11-GH00	OEM
70TB11-JE00	OEM
70TB11-JH00	OEM
70TB11-LE00	OEM
70TB11-LH00	OEM
70TB11-NE00	OEM
70TB11-NH00	OEM
70TB12	OEM
70TB12-CE00	OEM
70TB12-CH00	OEM
70TB12-GH00	OEM
70TB12-JE00	OEM
70TB12-JH00	OEM
70TB12-LE00	OEM
70TB12-LH00	OEM
70TB12-NE00	OEM
70TB12-NH00	OEM
70TB12-RE00	OEM
70TB13	OEM
70TB13-CE00	OEM
70TB13-CH00	OEM
70TB13-GH00	OEM
70TB13-JE00	OEM
70TB13-JH00	OEM
70TB13-LH00	OEM
70TB13-NE00	OEM
70TB13-NH00	OEM
70TB13-RE00	OEM
70TB14	OEM
70TB14-CE00	OEM
70TB14-CH00	OEM
70TB14-GH00	OEM
70TB14-JE00	OEM
70TB14-JH00	OEM
70TB14-LE00	OEM
70TB14-LH00	OEM
70TB14-NE00	OEM
70TB14-NH00	OEM
70TB14-RE00	OEM
70TB15	OEM
70TB15-CE00	OEM
70TB15-CH00	OEM
70TB15-GH00	OEM
70TB15-JE00	OEM
70TB15-JH00	OEM
70TB15-LE00	OEM
70TB15-LH00	OEM
70TB15-NE00	OEM
70TB15-NH00	OEM
70TB15-RE00	OEM
70TB16	OEM
70TB16-CE00	OEM
70TB16-CH00	OEM
70TB16-GH00	OEM
70TB16-JE00	OEM
70TB16-JH00	OEM
70TB16-LE00	OEM
70TB16-LH00	OEM
70TB16-NE00	OEM
70TB16-NH00	OEM
70TB16-RE00	OEM
70TB17	OEM
70TB17-CE00	OEM
70TB17-CH00	OEM
70TB17-GH00	OEM
70TB17-JE00	OEM
70TB17-JH00	OEM
70TB17-LE00	OEM
70TB17-LH00	OEM
70TB17-NE00	OEM
70TB17-NH00	OEM
70TB17-RE00	OEM
70TB18	OEM
70TB19	OEM
70TB20	OEM
70U5	1017
70U5R	0496
70U10	1017
70U10R	0496
70U15	1017
70U15A	1017
70U15AR	0496
70U15R	0496
70U20	1017
70U20R	0496
70U25	1017
70U25A	1017
70U25AR	0496
70U25R	0496
70U30	1017
70U30R	0496
70U35	1030
70U35R	1766
70U40	1017
70U40R	0496
70U45	1030
70U45R	1766
70U50	1030
70U50R	1766
70U60	1030
70U60R	1766
70U70	1040
70U70A	1040
70U70AR	1778
70U70R	1778
70U80	1040
70U80R	1778
70U90	1040
70U90A	1040
70U90AR	1778
70U90R	1778
70U100	1040
70U100R	1778
70U120	OEM
70UW15	1017
70UW15R	0496
70UW25	1017
70UW25R	0496
70UW35	1017
70UW35R	0496
70UW45	1030
70UW45R	1766
70UW65	1040
70UW65R	1778
70V10	OEM
70V10A	OEM
70V11A	OEM
70.00.730	0136
70.01.704	0016
71-126268	0016
71HA60	OEM
71HF5	OEM
71HF10	OEM
71HF20	OEM
71HF40	OEM
71HF60	OEM
71HF80	OEM
71HF100	OEM
71HF120	OEM
71HF140	OEM
71HF160	OEM
71HFR10	OEM
71HFR20	OEM
71HFR40	OEM
71HFR60	OEM
71HFR80	OEM
71HFR100	OEM
71HFR120	OEM
71HFR140	OEM
71HFR160	OEM
71N1	0142
71N1B	0016
71N1T	0142
71N2	0142
71N2T	0142
71RA30	0463
71RA50	0463
71RA60	0463
71RA80	0463
71RA100	0463
71RA110	0463
71RA120	0463
71RA140	OEM
71RA150	OEM
71RA160	OEM
71RB50	0463
71RB60	0463
71RB80	0463
71RB100	0463
71RB110	0463
71RB120	0463
71RB140	OEM
71RB150	OEM
71RB160	OEM
71RC2B	OEM
71RC5A	0217
71RC5B	0603
71RC10	OEM
71RC10A	0217
71RC10B	0603
71RC15A	0217
71RC20	OEM
71RC20A	0217
71RC20B	0603
71RC25A	0217
71RC30	OEM
71RC30A	0217
71RC30AS60	0217
71RC30B	0605
71RC40	OEM
71RC40A	0217
71RC40B	0605
71RC50	OEM
71RC50A	0217
71RC50B	OEM
71RC60	OEM
71RC60A	0217
71RC60AS50	0217
71RC60B	OEM
71RC80	OEM
71RC80A	0463
71RC80AS50	0463
71RC100	OEM
71RC100A	OEM
71RC110A	OEM
71RC120	OEM

If replacement code is OEM, contact original manufacturer for replacement.

DEVICE TYPE	REPL CODE
71RC120A	OEM
71RCF70A	OEM
71RCF80A	OEM
71RCG10	OEM
71RCG15	OEM
71RCG20	OEM
71RCG25	OEM
71RCG30	OEM
71RCG40	OEM
71RCG50	OEM
71RCG60	OEM
71RCS10A	OEM
71RCS20A	OEM
71RCS30A	OEM
71RCS40A	OEM
71RCS50A	OEM
71RCS60A	OEM
71RCS80A	OEM
71RE60	0463
71RE70	0463
71RE80	0463
71RE90	0463
71RE90A	OEM
71RE100	0463
71RE100A	OEM
71RE110	0463
71RE120	0463
71RE130	OEM
71RE130A	OEM
71REA50	0463
71REA60	0463
71REA70	OEM
71REA80	0463
71REA90	OEM
71REA100	0463
71REA110	0463
71REA120	0463
71REA130	OEM
71REB50	0463
71REB60	0463
71REB70	OEM
71REB80	0463
71REB90	OEM
71REB100	0463
71REB110	0463
71REB120	0463
71REB130	OEM
71RECT-SI-1019	0344
71REH60	0605
71REH80	0463
71REH100	0463
71REH110	0463
71REH120	0463
71REH130	OEM
71RIA10	OEM
71RIA20	OEM
71RIA40	OEM
71RIA60	OEM
71RIA80	OEM
71RIA100	OEM
71RIA110	OEM
71RIA120	OEM
71ST-2SC1505L	0949
71SZ-RD12B(AU)	0052
71SZ-UZ-12AB(AU)	OEM
71SZ-UZ-12B(AU)	0052
71T1	OEM
71T1C	OEM
71T2	0283
71T2C	OEM
71T3	OEM
71T3C	OEM
71T4	OEM
71T5	OEM
71T6	OEM
71T7	OEM
71T8	OEM
71T9	OEM
71T10	OEM
71T11	OEM
71T12	OEM
71T13	OEM
71T14	OEM
71T15	OEM
71T16	OEM
71T17	OEM
71T18	OEM
71T19	OEM
71T20	OEM
71T20-CE00	OEM
71T20-CH00	OEM
71T20-EE00	OEM
71T20-EH00	OEM
71T20-GE00	OEM
71T20-GH00	OEM
71T20-JE00	OEM
71T20-JH00	OEM
71T20-LE00	OEM
71T20-LH00	OEM
71T20-NE00	OEM
71T20-NH00	OEM
71T20-RE00	OEM
71T21	OEM
71T21-CE00	OEM
71T21-CH00	OEM
71T21-EE00	OEM
71T21-EH00	OEM
71T21-GE00	OEM
71T21-GH00	OEM
71T21-JE00	OEM
71T21-JH00	OEM
71T21-LE00	OEM
71T21-LH00	OEM
71T21-NE00	OEM
71T21-NH00	OEM
71T21-RE00	OEM
71T22	OEM
71T22-CE00	OEM
71T22-CH00	OEM
71T22-EE00	OEM
71T22-EH00	OEM
71T22-GE00	OEM
71T22-GH00	OEM
71T22-JE00	OEM
71T22-JH00	OEM
71T22-LE00	OEM
71T22-LH00	OEM
71T22-NE00	OEM
71T22-NH00	OEM
71T22-RE00	OEM
71T23	OEM
71T23-CE00	OEM
71T23-CH00	OEM
71T23-EE00	OEM
71T23-EH00	OEM
71T23-GE00	OEM
71T23-GH00	OEM
71T23-JE00	OEM
71T23-JH00	OEM
71T23-LE00	OEM
71T23-LH00	OEM
71T23-NE00	OEM
71T23-NH00	OEM
71T23-RE00	OEM
71T24	OEM
71T24-CE00	OEM
71T24-CH00	OEM
71T24-EE00	OEM
71T24-EH00	OEM
71T24-GE00	OEM
71T24-GH00	OEM
71T24-JE00	OEM
71T24-JH00	OEM
71T24-LE00	OEM
71T24-LH00	OEM
71T24-NE00	OEM
71T24-NH00	OEM
71T24-RE00	OEM
71T25-CE00	OEM
71T25-CH00	OEM
71T25-EE00	OEM
71T25-EH00	OEM
71T25-GE00	OEM
71T25-GH00	OEM
71T25-JE00	OEM
71T25-JH00	OEM
71T25-LE00	OEM
71T25-LH00	OEM
71T25-NE00	OEM
71T25-NH00	OEM
71T25-RE00	OEM
71T26	OEM
71T26-CE00	OEM
71T26-CH00	OEM
71T26-EE00	OEM
71T26-EH00	OEM
71T26-GE00	OEM
71T26-GH00	OEM
71T26-JE00	OEM
71T26-JH00	OEM
71T26-LE00	OEM
71T26-LH00	OEM
71T26-NE00	OEM
71T26-NH00	OEM
71T26-RE00	OEM
71T27-CE00	OEM
71T27-CH00	OEM
71T27-EE00	OEM
71T27-EH00	OEM
71T27-GE00	OEM
71T27-GH00	OEM
71T27-JE00	OEM
71T27-JH00	OEM
71T27-LE00	OEM
71T27-LH00	OEM
71T27-NE00	OEM
71T27-NH00	OEM
71T27-RE00	OEM
71T28	OEM
71T28-CE00	OEM
71T28-CH00	OEM
71T28-EE00	OEM
71T28-EH00	OEM
71T28-GE00	OEM
71T28-GH00	OEM
71T28-JE00	OEM
71T28-JH00	OEM
71T28-LE00	OEM
71T28-LH00	OEM
71T28-NE00	OEM
71T28-NH00	OEM
71T28-RE00	OEM
71T29-CE00	OEM
71T29-CH00	OEM
71T29-EE00	OEM
71T29-EH00	OEM
71T29-GE00	OEM
71T29-GH00	OEM
71T29-JE00	OEM
71T29-JH00	OEM
71T29-LE00	OEM
71T29-LH00	OEM
71T29-NE00	OEM
71T29-NH00	OEM
71T29-RE00	OEM
71T30-CE00	OEM
71T30-CH00	OEM
71T30-EE00	OEM
71T30-EH00	OEM
71T30-GE00	OEM
71T30-GH00	OEM
71T30-JE00	OEM
71T30-JH00	OEM
71T30-LE00	OEM
71T30-LH00	OEM
71T30-NE00	OEM
71T30-NH00	OEM
71T30-RE00	OEM
71T31-CE00	OEM
71T31-CH00	OEM
71T31-EE00	OEM
71T31-EH00	OEM
71T31-GE00	OEM
71T31-GH00	OEM
71T31-JE00	OEM
71T31-JH00	OEM
71T31-LE00	OEM
71T31-LH00	OEM
71T31-NE00	OEM
71T31-NH00	OEM
71T31-RE00	OEM
71T32	OEM
71T32-CE00	OEM
71T32-CH00	OEM
71T32-EE00	OEM
71T32-EH00	OEM
71T32-GE00	OEM
71T32-GH00	OEM
71T32-JE00	OEM
71T32-JH00	OEM
71T32-LE00	OEM
71T32-LH00	OEM
71T32-NE00	OEM
71T32-NH00	OEM
71T32-RE00	OEM
71T33-CE00	OEM
71T33-CH00	OEM
71T33-EE00	OEM
71T33-EH00	OEM
71T33-GE00	OEM
71T33-GH00	OEM
71T33-JE00	OEM
71T33-JH00	OEM
71T33-LE00	OEM
71T33-LH00	OEM
71T33-NE00	OEM
71T33-NH00	OEM
71T33-RE00	OEM
71T34	OEM
71T34-CE00	OEM
71T34-CH00	OEM
71T34-EE00	OEM
71T34-EH00	OEM
71T34-GE00	OEM
71T34-GH00	OEM
71T34-JE00	OEM
71T34-JH00	OEM
71T34-LE00	OEM
71T34-LH00	OEM
71T34-NE00	OEM
71T34-NH00	OEM
71T34-RE00	OEM
71T35-GE00	OEM
71T35-GH00	OEM
71T35-JE00	OEM
71T35-JH00	OEM
71T35-LE00	OEM
71T35-LH00	OEM
71T35-NE00	OEM
71T35-RE00	OEM
71T36	OEM
71T36-CE00	OEM
71T36-GE00	OEM
71T36-GH00	OEM
71T36-JE00	OEM
71T36-JH00	OEM
71T36-LE00	OEM
71T36-LH00	OEM
71T36-NE00	OEM
71T36-NH00	OEM
71T36-RE00	OEM
71T37	OEM
71T37-CE00	OEM
71T37-GE00	OEM
71T37-GH00	OEM
71T37-JE00	OEM
71T37-JH00	OEM
71T37-LE00	OEM
71T37-LH00	OEM
71T37-NE00	OEM
71T37-NH00	OEM
71T37-RE00	OEM
71T38	OEM
71T38-CE00	OEM
71T38-GE00	OEM
71T38-GH00	OEM
71T38-JE00	OEM
71T38-JH00	OEM
71T38-LE00	OEM
71T38-LH00	OEM
71T38-NE00	OEM
71T38-NH00	OEM
71T38-RE00	OEM
71T39	OEM
71T39-CE00	OEM
71T39-CH00	OEM
71T39-GE00	OEM
71T39-GH00	OEM
71T39-JE00	OEM
71T39-JH00	OEM
71T39-LE00	OEM
71T39-LH00	OEM
71T39-NE00	OEM
71T39-NH00	OEM
71T39-RE00	OEM
71T40-CE00	OEM
71T40-CH00	OEM
71T40-GE00	OEM
71T40-GH00	OEM
71T40-JE00	OEM
71T40-JH00	OEM
71T40-LE00	OEM
71T40-LH00	OEM
71T40-NE00	OEM
71T40-NH00	OEM
71T40-RE00	OEM
71TB1-CE00	OEM
71TB1-CH00	OEM
71TB1-EE00	OEM
71TB1-EH00	OEM
71TB1-GE00	OEM
71TB1-GH00	OEM
71TB1-JE00	OEM
71TB1-JH00	OEM
71TB1-LE00	OEM
71TB1-LH00	OEM
71TB1-RE00	OEM
71TB2-CE00	OEM
71TB2-CH00	OEM
71TB2-EE00	OEM
71TB2-EH00	OEM
71TB2-GE00	OEM
71TB2-GH00	OEM
71TB2-JE00	OEM
71TB2-JH00	OEM
71TB2-LH00	OEM
71TB2-RE00	OEM
71TB3-CE00	OEM
71TB3-CH00	OEM
71TB3-EE00	OEM
71TB3-EH00	OEM
71TB3-GE00	OEM
71TB3-GH00	OEM
71TB3-JE00	OEM
71TB3-JH00	OEM
71TB3-LE00	OEM
71TB3-LH00	OEM
71TB3-RE00	OEM
71TB4-CE00	OEM
71TB4-CH00	OEM
71TB4-EE00	OEM
71TB4-EH00	OEM
71TB4-GE00	OEM
71TB4-GH00	OEM
71TB4-JE00	OEM
71TB4-JH00	OEM
71TB4-LE00	OEM
71TB4-LH00	OEM
71TB4-RE00	OEM
71TB5-CE00	OEM
71TB5-CH00	OEM
71TB5-EH00	OEM
71TB5-GE00	OEM
71TB5-GH00	OEM
71TB5-JE00	OEM
71TB5-JH00	OEM
71TB5-LE00	OEM
71TB5-LH00	OEM
71TB5-RE00	OEM
71TB6-CE00	OEM
71TB6-CH00	OEM
71TB6-EE00	OEM
71TB6-EH00	OEM
71TB6-GE00	OEM
71TB6-GH00	OEM
71TB6-JE00	OEM
71TB6-JH00	OEM
71TB6-LE00	OEM
71TB6-LH00	OEM
71TB7	OEM
71TB7-CE00	OEM
71TB7-CH00	OEM
71TB7-EE00	OEM
71TB7-EH00	OEM
71TB7-GE00	OEM
71TB7-GH00	OEM
71TB7-JE00	OEM
71TB7-JH00	OEM
71TB7-LE00	OEM
71TB7-LH00	OEM
71TB8-CE00	OEM
71TB8-CH00	OEM
71TB8-EE00	OEM
71TB8-EH00	OEM
71TB8-GE00	OEM
71TB8-GH00	OEM
71TB8-JE00	OEM
71TB8-JH00	OEM
71TB8-LE00	OEM
71TB8-LH00	OEM
71TB9	OEM
71TB9-CE00	OEM
71TB9-CH00	OEM
71TB9-EE00	OEM
71TB9-EH00	OEM
71TB9-GE00	OEM
71TB9-GH00	OEM
71TB9-JE00	OEM
71TB9-JH00	OEM
71TB9-LH00	OEM
71TB10-CE00	OEM
71TB10-CH00	OEM
71TB10-EE00	OEM
71TB10-EH00	OEM
71TB10-GE00	OEM
71TB10-GH00	OEM
71TB10-JE00	OEM
71TB10-JH00	OEM
71TB10-LE00	OEM
71TB10-LH00	OEM
71TB11	OEM
71TB11-CE00	OEM
71TB11-CH00	OEM
71TB11-EE00	OEM
71TB11-EH00	OEM
71TB11-GE00	OEM
71TB11-GH00	OEM
71TB11-JE00	OEM
71TB11-JH00	OEM
71TB11-LE00	OEM
71TB11-LH00	OEM
71TB12-CE00	OEM
71TB12-CH00	OEM
71TB12-EE00	OEM
71TB12-EH00	OEM
71TB12-GE00	OEM
71TB12-GH00	OEM
71TB12-JE00	OEM
71TB12-JH00	OEM
71TB12-LE00	OEM
71TB12-LH00	OEM
71TB13	OEM
71TB13-CE00	OEM
71TB13-CH00	OEM
71TB13-EE00	OEM
71TB13-EH00	OEM
71TB13-GE00	OEM
71TB13-GH00	OEM
71TB13-JE00	OEM
71TB13-JH00	OEM
71TB13-LE00	OEM
71TB13-LH00	OEM
71TB13-NE00	OEM
71TB13-NH00	OEM
71TB13-RE00	OEM
71TB14-CE00	OEM
71TB14-CH00	OEM
71TB14-EE00	OEM
71TB14-EH00	OEM
71TB14-GE00	OEM
71TB14-GH00	OEM
71TB14-JE00	OEM
71TB14-JH00	OEM
71TB14-LE00	OEM
71TB14-LH00	OEM
71TB14-NE00	OEM
71TB14-NH00	OEM
71TB14-RE00	OEM
71TB15	OEM
71TB15-CE00	OEM
71TB15-CH00	OEM
71TB15-EE00	OEM
71TB15-EH00	OEM
71TB15-GE00	OEM
71TB15-GH00	OEM
71TB15-JE00	OEM
71TB15-JH00	OEM
71TB15-LE00	OEM
71TB15-LH00	OEM
71TB15-NE00	OEM
71TB15-NH00	OEM
71TB15-RE00	OEM
71TB16-CE00	OEM
71TB16-EE00	OEM
71TB16-EH00	OEM
71TB16-GE00	OEM
71TB16-GH00	OEM
71TB16-JE00	OEM
71TB16-JH00	OEM
71TB16-LE00	OEM
71TB16-LH00	OEM
71TB16-NE00	OEM
71TB16-NH00	OEM
71TB16-RE00	OEM
71TB17	OEM
71TB17-CE00	OEM
71TB17-CH00	OEM
71TB17-EE00	OEM
71TB17-EH00	OEM
71TB17-GE00	OEM
71TB17-GH00	OEM
71TB17-JE00	OEM
71TB17-JH00	OEM
71TB17-LE00	OEM
71TB17-LH00	OEM
71TB17-NE00	OEM
71TB17-NH00	OEM
71TB17-RE00	OEM
71TB18-CE00	OEM
71TB18-CH00	OEM
71TB18-EE00	OEM
71TB18-EH00	OEM
71TB18-GE00	OEM
71TB18-GH00	OEM
71TB18-JE00	OEM
71TB18-JH00	OEM
71TB18-LE00	OEM
71TB18-LH00	OEM
71TB18-NE00	OEM
71TB18-NH00	OEM
71TB18-RE00	OEM
71TB19	OEM
71TB19-CE00	OEM
71TB19-CH00	OEM
71TB19-EH00	OEM
71TB19-GE00	OEM
71TB19-GH00	OEM
71TB19-JE00	OEM
71TB19-JH00	OEM
71TB19-LE00	OEM
71TB19-LH00	OEM
71TB19-NE00	OEM
71TB19-RE00	OEM
71TB20-CE00	OEM
71TB20-CH00	OEM
71TB20-EE00	OEM
71TB20-EH00	OEM
71TB20-GE00	OEM
71TB20-GH00	OEM
71TB20-JE00	OEM
71TB20-JH00	OEM
71TB20-LE00	OEM
71TB20-LH00	OEM
71TB20-NE00	OEM
71TB20-RE00	OEM
71TC	OEM
71Z6	OEM
71Z6A	OEM
72-6	OEM
72-9	0102
72-11	0015
72-14	OEM
72-15	0015
72-18	0133
72B1Z	0746
72HG10	OEM
72HG20	OEM
72HG40	OEM
72HG60	OEM
72HG80	OEM
72HG100	OEM
72HG120	OEM
72N1	0144
72N1B	0086
72N2	0144
72N2B	0016
72R2S	OEM
72RA30	OEM
72RA50	0217
72RA60	0217
72RA80	0653
72RA100	0653
72RA120	0653
72RA140	OEM
72RA150	OEM
72RA160	OEM
72RB50	0217
72RB60	0217
72RB80	0653
72RB100	0653
72RB120	0653
72RB140	OEM
72RB150	OEM
72RB160	OEM
72RC2B	0653
72RC5A	0217
72RC5B	0636
72RC10A	0217
72RC10B	0636
72RC15A	0217
72RC20A	0217
72RC20B	0636
72RC25A	0217
72RC30A	0217
72RC30AS60	0217
72RC30B	0217
72RC40A	0217
72RC40B	0217
72RC50A	0217
72RC50B	OEM
72RC60A	0217
72RC60AS50	0217
72RC60B	OEM
72RC80A	0653
72RC80AS50	OEM
72RC100A	OEM
72RC110A	OEM
72RC120A	OEM
72RCF70A	OEM
72RCF80A	OEM
72RCG5	OEM
72RCG10	OEM
72RCG15	OEM
72RCG20	OEM
72RCG25	OEM
72RCG30	OEM
72RCG40	OEM
72RCG50	OEM
72RCG60	OEM
72REA60	OEM
72REA70	OEM
72REA80	OEM
72REA90	OEM
72REA100	OEM
72REA110	OEM
72REA120	OEM
72REA130	OEM
72REB60	OEM
72REB70	OEM
72REB80	OEM
72REB90	OEM
72REB100	OEM
72REB110	OEM
72REB120	OEM
72REB130	OEM
72REH60	0217
72REH80	0653
72REH100	0653
72REH110	0653
72REH120	0653
72REH130	OEM
72RIA10	OEM
72RIA20	OEM
72RIA40	OEM
72RIA60	OEM
72RIA80	OEM
72RIA100	OEM
72RIA110	OEM
72RIA120	OEM
72SI-TA7074P	0391
72ST-2SD900B	0055
72ST-MPS9750F	0037
72ST-MPS9750G	0037
72T1	OEM
72T2	0236
72T3	OEM
72T4	OEM
72T6	OEM
72T7	OEM
72T8	OEM
72X7377ESD	OEM
72X7385	OEM
72X7437	OEM
72X8287ESD	OEM
72X8290	OEM
72X8299	OEM
72X8319	OEM
72Z	0015
72Z4	OEM
72Z6	OEM
72Z6A	OEM
73-15	0002
73-17	0416
73-22	0490
73-31	0157
73-44	0253
73-125-B-003	OEM
73A01	0841
73A02	0841
73A03	0136
73A60-11	0102
73C180475	0167
73C180476-5	0167
73C180837-1	0661
73C180837-2	0661
73C180837-3	0661
73C180843	0797
73C180843-1	0797
73C180843-2	0797
73C180843-3	0797
73C180843-4	0797
73C181254	1493
73C182051	1493
73C182051-1	1493
73C182051-2	1493
73C182051-3	1493
73C182186	0167
73C182763-1	0746
73C182763-2	0746
73C182764-1	0850
73C182764-2	0850
73C182764-4	0850
73N1	0007
73N1B	0016
73N51	0435
73SI-MC1353P	0849
73SI-MC1358P	0167
73ST-2SC945R(AU)E	0076
73ST-2SC1921-03	0261
73T1	OEM
73T2	0283
73T3	OEM
73T4	OEM
73T5	OEM
73T6	OEM
73T7	OEM
73T8	OEM
73T9	OEM
73T10	OEM
73T11	OEM
73T12	OEM
73T13	OEM
73T14	OEM
73T15	OEM
73T16	OEM

160

If replacement code is OEM, contact original manufacturer for replacement.

DEVICE TYPE	REPL CODE
73T17	OEM
73T18	OEM
73T19	OEM
73T20	OEM
73T20-CE00	OEM
73T20-CH00	OEM
73T20-EE00	OEM
73T20-EH00	OEM
73T20-GE00	OEM
73T20-GH00	OEM
73T20-JE00	OEM
73T20-JH00	OEM
73T20-LE00	OEM
73T20-RE00	OEM
73T21	OEM
73T21-CE00	OEM
73T21-CH00	OEM
73T21-EE00	OEM
73T21-EH00	OEM
73T21-GE00	OEM
73T21-GH00	OEM
73T21-JE00	OEM
73T21-JH00	OEM
73T21-LE00	OEM
73T21-RE00	OEM
73T22	OEM
73T22-CE00	OEM
73T22-CH00	OEM
73T22-EE00	OEM
73T22-EH00	OEM
73T22-GE00	OEM
73T22-GH00	OEM
73T22-JE00	OEM
73T22-JH00	OEM
73T22-LE00	OEM
73T22-RE00	OEM
73T23	OEM
73T23-CE00	OEM
73T23-CH00	OEM
73T23-EE00	OEM
73T23-EH00	OEM
73T23-GE00	OEM
73T23-GH00	OEM
73T23-JE00	OEM
73T23-JH00	OEM
73T23-LE00	OEM
73T23-RE00	OEM
73T24	OEM
73T24-CE00	OEM
73T24-CH00	OEM
73T24-EE00	OEM
73T24-EH00	OEM
73T24-GE00	OEM
73T24-GH00	OEM
73T24-JE00	OEM
73T24-JH00	OEM
73T24-LE00	OEM
73T24-RE00	OEM
73T25-CE00	OEM
73T25-CH00	OEM
73T25-EE00	OEM
73T25-EH00	OEM
73T25-GE00	OEM
73T25-GH00	OEM
73T25-JE00	OEM
73T25-JH00	OEM
73T25-LE00	OEM
73T25-LH00	OEM
73T25-RE00	OEM
73T26	OEM
73T26-CE00	OEM
73T26-CH00	OEM
73T26-EE00	OEM
73T26-EH00	OEM
73T26-GE00	OEM
73T26-GH00	OEM
73T26-JE00	OEM
73T26-JH00	OEM
73T26-LE00	OEM
73T26-LH00	OEM
73T26-RE00	OEM
73T27-CE00	OEM
73T27-CH00	OEM
73T27-EE00	OEM
73T27-EH00	OEM
73T27-GE00	OEM
73T27-GH00	OEM
73T27-JE00	OEM
73T27-JH00	OEM
73T27-LE00	OEM
73T27-LH00	OEM
73T27-RE00	OEM
73T28	OEM
73T28-CE00	OEM
73T28-CH00	OEM
73T28-EE00	OEM
73T28-EH00	OEM
73T28-GE00	OEM
73T28-GH00	OEM
73T28-JE00	OEM
73T28-JH00	OEM
73T28-LE00	OEM
73T28-LH00	OEM
73T28-RE00	OEM
73T29-CE00	OEM
73T29-CH00	OEM
73T29-EE00	OEM
73T29-EH00	OEM
73T29-GE00	OEM
73T29-GH00	OEM
73T29-JE00	OEM
73T29-JH00	OEM
73T29-LE00	OEM
73T29-LH00	OEM
73T29-RE00	OEM
73T30-CE00	OEM
73T30-CH00	OEM
73T30-EE00	OEM
73T30-EH00	OEM
73T30-GE00	OEM
73T30-GH00	OEM
73T30-JE00	OEM
73T30-JH00	OEM
73T30-L300	OEM
73T30-LH00	OEM
73T30-RE00	OEM
73TB1-CE00	OEM
73TB1-CH00	OEM
73TB1-EE00	OEM
73TB1-EH00	OEM
73TB1-GE00	OEM
73TB1-GH00	OEM
73TB1-JE00	OEM
73TB1-JH00	OEM
73TB1-LE00	OEM
73TB1-LH00	OEM
73TB1-NE00	OEM
73TB1-NH00	OEM
73TB1-RE00	OEM
73TB2-CE00	OEM
73TB2-CH00	OEM
73TB2-EE00	OEM
73TB2-EH00	OEM
73TB2-GE00	OEM
73TB2-GH00	OEM
73TB2-JE00	OEM
73TB2-JH00	OEM
73TB2-LE00	OEM
73TB2-LH00	OEM
73TB2-NE00	OEM
73TB2-NH00	OEM
73TB2-RE00	OEM
73TB3-CE00	OEM
73TB3-CH00	OEM
73TB3-EE00	OEM
73TB3-EH00	OEM
73TB3-GE00	OEM
73TB3-GH00	OEM
73TB3-JE00	OEM
73TB3-JH00	OEM
73TB3-LE00	OEM
73TB3-LH00	OEM
73TB3-NE00	OEM
73TB3-NH00	OEM
73TB3-RE00	OEM
73TB4-CE00	OEM
73TB4-CH00	OEM
73TB4-EE00	OEM
73TB4-EH00	OEM
73TB4-GE00	OEM
73TB4-GH00	OEM
73TB4-JE00	OEM
73TB4-JH00	OEM
73TB4-LE00	OEM
73TB4-LH00	OEM
73TB4-NE00	OEM
73TB4-NH00	OEM
73TB4-RE00	OEM
73TB5-CE00	OEM
73TB5-CH00	OEM
73TB5-EE00	OEM
73TB5-EH00	OEM
73TB5-GE00	OEM
73TB5-GH00	OEM
73TB5-JE00	OEM
73TB5-JH00	OEM
73TB5-LE00	OEM
73TB5-LH00	OEM
73TB5-NE00	OEM
73TB5-NH00	OEM
73TB5-RE00	OEM
73TB6-CE00	OEM
73TB6-CH00	OEM
73TB6-EE00	OEM
73TB6-EH00	OEM
73TB6-GE00	OEM
73TB6-GH00	OEM
73TB6-JE00	OEM
73TB6-JH00	OEM
73TB6-LE00	OEM
73TB6-LH00	OEM
73TB6-NE00	OEM
73TB6-NH00	OEM
73TB6-RE00	OEM
73TB7	OEM
73TB7-CE00	OEM
73TB7-CH00	OEM
73TB7-EE00	OEM
73TB7-EH00	OEM
73TB7-GH00	OEM
73TB7-JE00	OEM
73TB7-JH00	OEM
73TB7-LE00	OEM
73TB7-LH00	OEM
73TB7-NE00	OEM
73TB7-NH00	OEM
73TB7-RE00	OEM
73TB8-CH00	OEM
73TB8-EE00	OEM
73TB8-EH00	OEM
73TB8-GE00	OEM
73TB8-GH00	OEM
73TB8-JE00	OEM
73TB8-JH00	OEM
73TB8-LE00	OEM
73TB8-LH00	OEM
73TB8-NE00	OEM
73TB8-NH00	OEM
73TB8-RE00	OEM
73TB9	OEM
73TB9-CE00	OEM
73TB9-CH00	OEM
73TB9-EE00	OEM
73TB9-EH00	OEM
73TB9-GE00	OEM
73TB9-GH00	OEM
73TB9-JE00	OEM
73TB9-JH00	OEM
73TB9-LE00	OEM
73TB9-LH00	OEM
73TB9-NH00	OEM
73TB9-RE00	OEM
73TB10-CE00	OEM
73TB10-CH00	OEM
73TB10-EE00	OEM
73TB10-EH00	OEM
73TB10-GE00	OEM
73TB10-GH00	OEM
73TB10-JE00	OEM
73TB10-JH00	OEM
73TB10-LE00	OEM
73TB10-LH00	OEM
73TB10-NE00	OEM
73TB10-NH00	OEM
73TB10-RE00	OEM
73TB11	OEM
73TB11-CE00	OEM
73TB11-CH00	OEM
73TB11-EE00	OEM
73TB11-EH00	OEM
73TB11-GE00	OEM
73TB11-GH00	OEM
73TB11-JE00	OEM
73TB11-JH00	OEM
73TB11-LE00	OEM
73TB11-LH00	OEM
73TB11-NE00	OEM
73TB11-NH00	OEM
73TB11-RE00	OEM
73TB12-CE00	OEM
73TB12-CH00	OEM
73TB12-EE00	OEM
73TB12-EH00	OEM
73TB12-GE00	OEM
73TB12-GH00	OEM
73TB12-JE00	OEM
73TB12-JH00	OEM
73TB12-LE00	OEM
73TB12-LH00	OEM
73TB12-NE00	OEM
73TB12-NH00	OEM
73TB12-RE00	OEM
73TB13	OEM
73TB13-CE00	OEM
73TB13-CH00	OEM
73TB13-EE00	OEM
73TB13-EH00	OEM
73TB13-GE00	OEM
73TB13-GH00	OEM
73TB13-JE00	OEM
73TB13-JH00	OEM
73TB13-LE00	OEM
73TB13-LH00	OEM
73TB13-NE00	OEM
73TB13-NH00	OEM
73TB13-RE00	OEM
73TB14-CE00	OEM
73TB14-CH00	OEM
73TB14-EE00	OEM
73TB14-EH00	OEM
73TB14-GE00	OEM
73TB14-GH00	OEM
73TB14-JE00	OEM
73TB14-JH00	OEM
73TB14-LE00	OEM
73TB14-LH00	OEM
73TB14-NE00	OEM
73TB14-NH00	OEM
73TB14-RE00	OEM
73TB15	OEM
73TB15-CE00	OEM
73TB15-CH00	OEM
73TB15-EE00	OEM
73TB15-EH00	OEM
73TB15-GE00	OEM
73TB15-GH00	OEM
73TB15-JE00	OEM
73TB15-JH00	OEM
73TB15-LE00	OEM
73TB15-LH00	OEM
73TB15-NE00	OEM
73TB15-NH00	OEM
73TB15-RE00	OEM
73TB16-CE00	OEM
73TB16-CH00	OEM
73TB16-EE00	OEM
73TB16-EH00	OEM
73TB16-GE00	OEM
73TB16-GH00	OEM
73TB16-JE00	OEM
73TB16-LE00	OEM
73TB16-LH00	OEM
73TB16-NE00	OEM
73TB16-NH00	OEM
73TB16-RE00	OEM
73TB17	OEM
73TB17-CE00	OEM
73TB17-CH00	OEM
73TB17-EE00	OEM
73TB17-EH00	OEM
73TB17-GE00	OEM
73TB17-GH00	OEM
73TB17-JE00	OEM
73TB17-JH00	OEM
73TB17-LE00	OEM
73TB17-LH00	OEM
73TB17-NE00	OEM
73TB17-NH00	OEM
73TB17-RE00	OEM
73TB18-CE00	OEM
73TB18-CH00	OEM
73TB18-EE00	OEM
73TB18-EH00	OEM
73TB18-GE00	OEM
73TB18-GH00	OEM
73TB18-JE00	OEM
73TB18-JH00	OEM
73TB18-LE00	OEM
73TB18-LH00	OEM
73TB18-NE00	OEM
73TB18-NH00	OEM
73TB18-RE00	OEM
73TB19	OEM
73TB19-CE00	OEM
73TB19-CH00	OEM
73TB19-EE00	OEM
73TB19-EH00	OEM
73TB19-GE00	OEM
73TB19-GH00	OEM
73TB19-JE00	OEM
73TB19-JH00	OEM
73TB19-LE00	OEM
73TB19-LH00	OEM
73TB19-NE00	OEM
73TB19-NH00	OEM
73TB19-RE00	OEM
73TB20-CE00	OEM
73TB20-CH00	OEM
73TB20-EE00	OEM
73TB20-EH00	OEM
73TB20-GE00	OEM
73TB20-GH00	OEM
73TB20-JH00	OEM
73TB20-LE00	OEM
73TB20-LH00	OEM
73TB20-NE00	OEM
73TB20-NH00	OEM
73TB20-RE00	OEM
73W00124	0462
73Z4	OEM
73Z6	0809
73Z6A	0809
74	0144
74-3	0279
74-3-70	0279
74-3-70-12	0279
74-3-70-12-7	0279
74-3A	0279
74-3A0	0279
74-3A0R	0279
74-3A1	0279
74-3A2	0279
74-3A3	0279
74-3A3P	0279
74-3A4	0279
74-3A4-7	0279
74-3A4-7B	0279
74-3A5	0279
74-3A5L	0279
74-3A6	0279
74-3A6-3	0279
74-3A7	0279
74-3A7-1	0279
74-3A8	0279
74-3A9	0279
74-3A9G	0279
74-3A19	0279
74-3A21	0279
74-3A82	0279
74-30	0279
74-31	0279
74-32	0279
74-33	0279
74-34	0279
74-35	0279
74-36	0279
74-37	0279
74-38	0279
74-39	0279
74A01	0841
74A02	0841
74A03	0841
74ACT00E	OEM
74ACT04E	OEM
74ACT04M	OEM
74ACT05E	OEM
74ACT08E	OEM
74ACT32E	OEM
74ACT32M	OEM
74ACT193M	OEM
74ALS00	OEM
74ALS00A	OEM
74ALS00AD(SM)	OEM
74ALS00AN	OEM
74ALS02	OEM
74ALS02D(SM)	OEM
74ALS02N	OEM
74ALS04A	OEM
74ALS04AN	OEM
74ALS04BD(SM)	OEM
74ALS08	OEM
74ALS08D(SM)	OEM
74ALS08N	OEM
74ALS09	OEM
74ALS10	OEM
74ALS10AD(SM)	OEM
74ALS10N	OEM
74ALS11AD(SM)	OEM
74ALS27	OEM
74ALS27N	OEM
74ALS32	OEM
74ALS32D(SM)	OEM
74ALS32N	OEM
74ALS38	OEM
74ALS74	OEM
74ALS74A	OEM
74ALS74AD(SM)	OEM
74ALS74AN	OEM
74ALS109	OEM
74ALS109AN	OEM
74ALS138	OEM
74ALS138N	OEM
74ALS174D(SM)	OEM
74ALS175	OEM
74ALS175N	OEM
74ALS240ADW(SM)	OEM
74ALS244A	OEM
74ALS244ADW(SM)	OEM
74ALS244AN	OEM
74ALS245A	OEM
74ALS245ADW(SM)	OEM
74ALS257	OEM
74ALS373	OEM
74ALS573	OEM
74ALS573BDW(SM)	OEM
74ALS573N	OEM
74ALS652DW(SM)	OEM
74AS573DW(SM)	OEM
74AS646DW(SM)	OEM
74AS760DW(SM)	OEM
74C04	2930
74CH646EN	OEM
74CH648EN	OEM
74CH7038EN	OEM
74F00	OEM
74F00(SM)	OEM
74F00DC	OEM
74F00N	OEM
74F00PC	OEM
74F02DC	OEM
74F02PC	OEM
74F04	OEM
74F04(SM)	OEM
74F04DC	OEM
74F04PC	OEM
74F08	OEM
74F08(SM)	OEM
74F08DC	OEM
74F08N	OEM
74F08PC	OEM
74F10	OEM
74F10(SM)	OEM
74F10DC	OEM
74F10N	OEM
74F10PC	OEM
74F11	OEM
74F11DC	OEM
74F11N	OEM
74F11PC	OEM
74F20	OEM
74F20DC	OEM
74F20N	OEM
74F20PC	OEM
74F27N	OEM
74F30D(SM)	OEM
74F32	OEM
74F32(SM)	OEM
74F32DC	OEM
74F32PC	OEM
74F64DC	OEM
74F64PC	OEM
74F74	OEM
74F74(SM)	OEM
74F74DC	OEM
74F74N	OEM
74F74PC	OEM
74F86PC	OEM
74F109	OEM
74F109DC	OEM
74F109PC	OEM
74F125(SM)	OEM
74F138(SM)	OEM
74F138DC	OEM
74F138PC	OEM
74F139	OEM
74F139DC	OEM
74F139N	OEM
74F139PC	OEM
74F151	OEM
74F151DC	OEM
74F151FC	OEM
74F151PC	OEM
74F153	OEM
74F153DC	OEM
74F153FC	OEM
74F153PC	OEM
74F157DC	OEM
74F157FC	OEM
74F157PC	OEM
74F158	OEM
74F158A	OEM
74F158A(SM)	OEM
74F158APC	OEM
74F158DC	OEM
74F158FC	OEM
74F158N	OEM
74F158PC	OEM
74F160DC	OEM
74F160PC	OEM
74F161DC	OEM
74F161PC	OEM
74F162DC	OEM
74F162PC	OEM
74F163DC	OEM
74F163PC	OEM
74F174	OEM
74F174(SM)	OEM
74F174N	OEM
74F174PC	OEM
74F175	OEM
74F175DC	OEM
74F175N	OEM
74F175PC	OEM
74F181DC	OEM
74F181PC	OEM
74F182DC	OEM
74F182PC	OEM
74F189DC	OEM
74F189FC	OEM
74F189PC	OEM
74F191PC	OEM
74F240DC	OEM
74F240FC	OEM
74F240PC	OEM
74F241	OEM
74F241DC	OEM
74F241FC	OEM
74F241N	OEM
74F241PC	OEM
74F242DC	OEM
74F242FC	OEM
74F242PC	OEM
74F243DC	OEM
74F243FC	OEM
74F243PC	OEM
74F244(SM)	OEM
74F244DC	OEM
74F244FC	OEM
74F244PC	OEM
74F245	OEM
74F245(SM)	OEM
74F245DC	OEM
74F245PC	OEM
74F251DC	OEM
74F251FC	OEM
74F251PC	OEM
74F253DC	OEM
74F253FC	OEM
74F253PC	OEM
74F257	OEM
74F257DC	OEM
74F257FC	OEM
74F257N	OEM
74F257PC	OEM
74F258DC	OEM
74F258FC	OEM
74F258PC	OEM
74F280(SM)	OEM
74F280DC	OEM
74F280PC	OEM
74F283(SM)	OEM
74F283DC	OEM
74F283PC	OEM
74F289DC	OEM
74F289FC	OEM
74F289PC	OEM
74F352DC	OEM
74F352FC	OEM
74F352PC	OEM
74F353DC	OEM
74F353FC	OEM
74F353PC	OEM
74F373DC	OEM
74F373PC	OEM
74F374	OEM
74F374DC	OEM
74F374PC	OEM
74F379	OEM
74F500DC	OEM
74F500PC	OEM
74F533DC	OEM
74F533PC	OEM
74F534DC	OEM
74F534PC	OEM
74F537DC	OEM
74F537FC	OEM
74F537PC	OEM
74F538DC	OEM
74F538FC	OEM
74F538PC	OEM
74F539DC	OEM
74F539FC	OEM
74F539PC	OEM
74F545PC	OEM
74F588DC	OEM
74F588PC	OEM
74H00DC	0677
74H00PC	0677
74H01DC	5241
74H01PC	5241
74H04DC	1896
74H04PC	1896
74H05DC	3221
74H05PC	3221
74H08PC	5258
74H10DC	0680
74H10PC	0680
74H11DC	2382
74H11PC	2382
74H20DC	3670
74H20PC	3670
74H21DC	4772
74H21PC	4772
74H22	4516
74H22/9H22	4516
74H22/94H22	4516
74H22DC	4516
74H22PC	4516
74H30DC	5284
74H30PC	5284
74H40DC	0554
74H40PC	0554
74H50DC	1781
74H50FC	1781
74H50PC	1781
74H51DC	1933
74H51PC	1933
74H52DC	2009
74H52PC	2009
74H53DC	2090
74H53PC	2090
74H54DC	2158
74H54PC	2158
74H55DC	3129
74H55PC	3129
74H60DC	5312
74H60PC	5312
74H61DC	2638
74H61PC	2638
74H62DC	2705
74H62PC	2705
74H71DC	3233
74H71PC	3233
74H72DC	3281
74H72PC	3281
74H73DC	2444
74H73PC	2444
74H74DC	2472
74H74PC	2472
74H76DC	5208
74H76PC	5208
74H78DC	5320
74H78PC	5320
74H87DC	2557
74H87PC	2557
74H101DC	5424
74H101PC	5424
74H102DC	5426
74H102PC	5426
74H103DC	2941
74H103PC	2941
74H106DC	5159
74H106PC	5159
74H108DC	0180
74H108PC	0180
74H183DC	4329
74H183PC	4329
74HC00	OEM
74HC00/FP	OEM
74HC00D	OEM
74HC00N	2328
74HC02	OEM
74HC02D	OEM
74HC02N	1443
74HC03D	OEM
74HC03N	1444
74HC04	OEM
74HC04AP	1446
74HC04D	OEM
74HC04N	1552
74HC05	OEM
74HC08	OEM
74HC08D	OEM
74HC08M	OEM
74HC08N	2393
74HC10	OEM
74HC10D	OEM
74HC10N	2413
74HC11D	OEM
74HC11N	2418
74HC14	OEM
74HC14AP	OEM
74HC14D	OEM

If replacement code is OEM, contact original manufacturer for replacement.

161

DEVICE TYPE	REPL CODE
74HC14N	2447
74HC20D	OEM
74HC20N	1466
74HC21D	OEM
74HC21N	1468
74HC27	OEM
74HC27D	OEM
74HC27N	1476
74HC30	OEM
74HC30D	OEM
74HC30N	1480
74HC32	OEM
74HC32D	OEM
74HC32N	2586
74HC42D	OEM
74HC42N	1507
74HC58D	OEM
74HC58N	OEM
74HC73D	OEM
74HC73N	1549
74HC74	OEM
74HC74D	OEM
74HC74N	1552
74HC75D	OEM
74HC75N	1555
74HC85D	OEM
74HC85E	OEM
74HC85N	1573
74HC86	OEM
74HC86D	OEM
74HC86N	2971
74HC93D	OEM
74HC93N	1584
74HC107D	OEM
74HC107N	4611
74HC109D	OEM
74HC109N	6179
74HC112D	OEM
74HC112N	0214
74HC123D	OEM
74HC123N	3851
74HC125D	OEM
74HC125N	6189
74HC126D	OEM
74HC126N	6191
74HC132D	OEM
74HC132N	6194
74HC137D	OEM
74HC137N	0779
74HC138	OEM
74HC138D	OEM
74HC138N	6197
74HC139	OEM
74HC139D	OEM
74HC139N	3893
74HC147D	OEM
74HC147N	0932
74HC151D	OEM
74HC151N	6202
74HC153D	OEM
74HC153N	6204
74HC154	OEM
74HC154D	OEM
74HC154EN	OEM
74HC154N	6205
74HC157	OEM
74HC157D	OEM
74HC157N	OEM
74HC158D	OEM
74HC158N	1080
74HC160D	OEM
74HC160N	1109
74HC161D	OEM
74HC161N	1121
74HC162D	OEM
74HC162N	1134
74HC163D	OEM
74HC163N	3995
74HC164D	OEM
74HC164N	6212
74HC165D	OEM
74HC165N	6214
74HC166	OEM
74HC166D	OEM
74HC166N	4660
74HC173D	OEM
74HC173N	6223
74HC174D	OEM
74HC174N	6226
74HC175D	OEM
74HC175N	6227
74HC181D	OEM
74HC181N	4667
74HC182D	OEM
74HC182N	4668
74HC190D	OEM
74HC190N	4672
74HC191D	OEM
74HC191N	4673
74HC192D	OEM
74HC192N	4674
74HC193D	OEM
74HC193N	4675
74HC194D	OEM
74HC194N	1548
74HC195D	OEM
74HC195N	1568
74HC221D	OEM
74HC221N	4693

DEVICE TYPE	REPL CODE
74HC237D	OEM
74HC237N	1947
74HC238D	OEM
74HC238N	4702
74HC240D	OEM
74HC240N	1968
74HC241D	OEM
74HC241N	1979
74HC242D	OEM
74HC242N	1985
74HC243D	OEM
74HC243N	1990
74HC244	OEM
74HC244D	OEM
74HC244N	4709
74HC245D	OEM
74HC245N	2003
74HC251D	OEM
74HC251N	2054
74HC253D	OEM
74HC253N	4717
74HC257D	OEM
74HC257N	4718
74HC258D	OEM
74HC258N	4720
74HC259	OEM
74HC259D	OEM
74HC259N	4722
74HC273	OEM
74HC273D	OEM
74HC273N	4738
74HC280D	OEM
74HC280N	4738
74HC283D	OEM
74HC283N	4744
74HC297D	OEM
74HC297N	4759
74HC299D	OEM
74HC299N	6308
74HC354D	OEM
74HC354N	4776
74HC356D	OEM
74HC356N	4777
74HC365D	OEM
74HC365N	2853
74HC366D	OEM
74HC366N	2858
74HC367	OEM
74HC367D	OEM
74HC367N	2867
74HC368	OEM
74HC368(SM)	OEM
74HC368D	OEM
74HC368N	2870
74HC373	OEM
74HC373D	OEM
74HC373N	4388
74HC374	OEM
74HC374D	OEM
74HC374N	6420
74HC377D	OEM
74HC377N	6422
74HC390D	OEM
74HC390N	6436
74HC393D	OEM
74HC393N	6440
74HC423D	OEM
74HC423N	4789
74HC533D	OEM
74HC533N	3632
74HC534D	OEM
74HC534N	3636
74HC540D	OEM
74HC540N	4801
74HC541D	OEM
74HC541N	4802
74HC563D	OEM
74HC563N	4805
74HC564D	OEM
74HC564N	4806
74HC573D	OEM
74HC573N	6604
74HC574D	OEM
74HC574N	6606
74HC583D	OEM
74HC583N	4812
74HC597D	OEM
74HC597N	4814
74HC640D	OEM
74HC640N	4825
74HC643D	OEM
74HC643N	4827
74HC646D	OEM
74HC646N	4828
74HC648D	OEM
74HC648N	4829
74HC670D	OEM
74HC670N	4832
74HC688D	OEM
74HC688N	4836
74HC4002D	OEM
74HC4002N	5391
74HC4015D	OEM
74HC4015N	5409
74HC4016D	OEM
74HC4016M	OEM
74HC4016N	5410
74HC4017D	OEM
74HC4017N	5414

DEVICE TYPE	REPL CODE
74HC4020D	OEM
74HC4020N	5415
74HC4024D	OEM
74HC4024N	5418
74HC4040D	OEM
74HC4040N	5434
74HC4046AD	OEM
74HC4046AN	5061
74HC4046AP	OEM
74HC4049D	OEM
74HC4049N	5441
74HC4050D	OEM
74HC4050N	5443
74HC4051D	OEM
74HC4051N	5446
74HC4052D	OEM
74HC4052N	5448
74HC4053	OEM
74HC4053AP	OEM
74HC4053D	OEM
74HC4053N	5451
74HC4059D	OEM
74HC4059N	5459
74HC4060D	OEM
74HC4060N	5462
74HC4066	OEM
74HC4066D	OEM
74HC4066N	5471
74HC4066S	OEM
74HC4067D	OEM
74HC4067N	5472
74HC4075D	OEM
74HC4075N	5476
74HC4094AP	OEM
74HC4094D	OEM
74HC4094N	5495
74HC4316D	OEM
74HC4316N	5818
74HC4351D	OEM
74HC4351N	5843
74HC4352D	OEM
74HC4352N	5844
74HC4353D	OEM
74HC4353N	5846
74HC4510D	OEM
74HC4510N	5949
74HC4511D	OEM
74HC4511N	5950
74HC4514D	OEM
74HC4514N	5955
74HC4515D	OEM
74HC4515N	5956
74HC4516D	OEM
74HC4516N	5959
74HC4518D	OEM
74HC4518N	5964
74HC4520D	OEM
74HC4520N	5968
74HC4538D	OEM
74HC4538N	5987
74HC4543D	OEM
74HC4543N	5998
74HC7030D	OEM
74HC7030N	5422
74HC7038EN	OEM
74HC7046AD	OEM
74HC7046AN	5057
74HC7046D	OEM
74HC7046N	5057
74HC7266D	OEM
74HC7266N	5754
74HC7597D	OEM
74HC7597N	OEM
74HC40102D	OEM
74HC40102N	4982
74HC40103D	OEM
74HC40103N	4983
74HC40104D	OEM
74HC40104N	4984
74HC40105D	OEM
74HC40105N	5947
74HCT00D	OEM
74HCT00N	6743
74HCT02	4823
74HCT02D	OEM
74HCT02N	4823
74HCT03D	OEM
74HCT03N	5781
74HCT04	3265
74HCT04D	OEM
74HCT04N	3265
74HCT08	3268
74HCT08D	OEM
74HCT08N	3268
74HCT10D	OEM
74HCT10N	5782
74HCT11D	OEM
74HCT11N	5783
74HCT14	3269
74HCT14D	OEM
74HCT14N	3269
74HCT20D	OEM
74HCT20N	5785
74HCT21D	OEM
74HCT21N	5786
74HCT27D	OEM
74HCT27N	5787
74HCT30D	OEM
74HCT30N	5789

DEVICE TYPE	REPL CODE
74HCT32	3274
74HCT32D	OEM
74HCT32N	3274
74HCT42D	OEM
74HCT42N	5792
74HCT73D	OEM
74HCT73N	5796
74HCT74D	OEM
74HCT74N	5797
74HCT75D	OEM
74HCT75N	5798
74HCT85D	OEM
74HCT85N	5799
74HCT86D	OEM
74HCT86N	5800
74HCT93D	OEM
74HCT93N	5802
74HCT107D	OEM
74HCT107N	6454
74HCT109D	OEM
74HCT109N	6455
74HCT112D	OEM
74HCT112N	6456
74HCT123D	OEM
74HCT123N	6460
74HCT125D	OEM
74HCT125N	6461
74HCT126D	OEM
74HCT126N	6462
74HCT132D	OEM
74HCT132N	6466
74HCT137D	OEM
74HCT137N	4328
74HCT138	5952
74HCT138D	OEM
74HCT138N	5952
74HCT139D	OEM
74HCT139N	6471
74HCT147D	OEM
74HCT147N	6487
74HCT151D	OEM
74HCT151N	6492
74HCT153D	OEM
74HCT153N	6494
74HCT154D	OEM
74HCT154EN	OEM
74HCT154N	4956
74HCT157D	OEM
74HCT157N	6499
74HCT158D	OEM
74HCT158N	5957
74HCT160D	OEM
74HCT161N	6504
74HCT162D	OEM
74HCT162N	6505
74HCT163D	OEM
74HCT163N	6508
74HCT164D	OEM
74HCT164N	6510
74HCT165D	OEM
74HCT165N	6511
74HCT166D	OEM
74HCT166N	6513
74HCT173D	OEM
74HCT173N	6517
74HCT174D	OEM
74HCT174N	6518
74HCT175D	OEM
74HCT175N	6519
74HCT181D	OEM
74HCT181N	6522
74HCT182D	OEM
74HCT182N	5981
74HCT190D	OEM
74HCT190N	6528
74HCT191D	OEM
74HCT191N	6529
74HCT192D	OEM
74HCT192N	6532
74HCT193D	OEM
74HCT193N	6533
74HCT194D	OEM
74HCT194N	6535
74HCT195	5962
74HCT195D	OEM
74HCT195N	5962
74HCT221D	OEM
74HCT221N	6562
74HCT237D	OEM
74HCT237N	6573
74HCT238D	OEM
74HCT238N	6574
74HCT240-2N	OEM
74HCT240D	OEM
74HCT240N	3988
74HCT241D	OEM
74HCT241N	6577
74HCT242D	OEM
74HCT242N	6578
74HCT243D	OEM
74HCT243N	6581
74HCT244	5969
74HCT244(SM)	OEM
74HCT244D	OEM
74HCT244N	5969
74HCT245	4013
74HCT245-2N	OEM
74HCT245D	OEM
74HCT245N	4013

DEVICE TYPE	REPL CODE
74HCT251D	OEM
74HCT251N	6588
74HCT253D	OEM
74HCT253N	6590
74HCT257D	OEM
74HCT257N	6592
74HCT258D	OEM
74HCT258N	6593
74HCT259D	OEM
74HCT259N	6595
74HCT273-2N	OEM
74HCT273D	OEM
74HCT273N	4063
74HCT280D	OEM
74HCT280N	6618
74HCT283D	OEM
74HCT283N	6621
74HCT297D	OEM
74HCT297N	6631
74HCT299D	OEM
74HCT299N	6632
74HCT354D	OEM
74HCT354N	0785
74HCT356D	OEM
74HCT356N	0807
74HCT365D	OEM
74HCT365N	6658
74HCT366D	OEM
74HCT366N	6661
74HCT367D	OEM
74HCT367N	6662
74HCT368D	OEM
74HCT368N	6663
74HCT373D	OEM
74HCT373N	5984
74HCT374	OEM
74HCT374-2N	OEM
74HCT374D	OEM
74HCT374N	4247
74HCT374P	OEM
74HCT377D	OEM
74HCT377N	6670
74HCT390D	OEM
74HCT390N	6675
74HCT393D	OEM
74HCT393N	6679
74HCT423D	OEM
74HCT423N	4386
74HCT533D	OEM
74HCT533N	5614
74HCT534D	OEM
74HCT534N	5632
74HCT540D	OEM
74HCT540N	6791
74HCT541D	OEM
74HCT541N	6792
74HCT563D	OEM
74HCT563N	6799
74HCT564D	OEM
74HCT564N	6800
74HCT573D	OEM
74HCT573N	6805
74HCT574D	OEM
74HCT574N	6038
74HCT583D	OEM
74HCT583N	6813
74HCT597D	OEM
74HCT597N	6818
74HCT640D	OEM
74HCT640N	6859
74HCT643D	OEM
74HCT643N	6866
74HCT646D	OEM
74HCT646N	6869
74HCT648D	OEM
74HCT648N	4428
74HCT670D	OEM
74HCT670N	6898
74HCT688D	OEM
74HCT688N	3378
74HCT4002D	OEM
74HCT4002N	3330
74HCT4015D	OEM
74HCT4015N	3371
74HCT4016D	OEM
74HCT4016N	3375
74HCT4017D	OEM
74HCT4017N	3383
74HCT4020D	OEM
74HCT4020N	3396
74HCT4024D	OEM
74HCT4024N	3413
74HCT4040D	OEM
74HCT4040N	3464
74HCT4046AD	OEM
74HCT4046AN	5054
74HCT4051D	OEM
74HCT4051N	3512
74HCT4052D	OEM
74HCT4052N	3514
74HCT4053D	OEM
74HCT4053N	3520
74HCT4059D	OEM
74HCT4059N	3560
74HCT4060D	OEM
74HCT4060N	3569
74HCT4066D	OEM
74HCT4066N	3584
74HCT4067D	OEM

DEVICE TYPE	REPL CODE
74HCT4067N	3588
74HCT4075D	OEM
74HCT4075N	3620
74HCT4094D	OEM
74HCT4094N	3691
74HCT4316D	OEM
74HCT4316N	4259
74HCT4351D	OEM
74HCT4351N	4322
74HCT4352D	OEM
74HCT4352N	4324
74HCT4353D	OEM
74HCT4353N	4326
74HCT4510D	OEM
74HCT4510N	4804
74HCT4511D	OEM
74HCT4511N	4807
74HCT4514D	OEM
74HCT4514N	4816
74HCT4515D	OEM
74HCT4515N	4821
74HCT4516D	OEM
74HCT4516N	4822
74HCT4518D	OEM
74HCT4518N	4826
74HCT4520D	OEM
74HCT4520N	4831
74HCT4538D	OEM
74HCT4538N	4871
74HCT4543D	OEM
74HCT4543N	4892
74HCT7030D	OEM
74HCT7030N	3427
74HCT7038N	OEM
74HCT7046AD	OEM
74HCT7046AN	3485
74HCT7046D	OEM
74HCT7046N	3485
74HCT7266D	OEM
74HCT7266N	4184
74HCT7597D	OEM
74HCT7597N	OEM
74HCT40102D	OEM
74HCT40102N	4977
74HCT40103D	OEM
74HCT40103N	4978
74HCT40104D	OEM
74HCT40104N	4979
74HCT40105D	OEM
74HCT40105N	4980
74HCU04	OEM
74HCU04A	OEM
74HCU04AP	OEM
74HCU04D	OEM
74HCU04N	4522
74L03	1569
74LS00	1519
74LS00CH	1519
74LS00DC	1519
74LS00J	1519
74LS00N	1519
74LS00NA	1519
74LS00PC	1519
74LS00W	1519
74LS02	1550
74LS02CH	1550
74LS02DC	1550
74LS02J	1550
74LS02N	1550
74LS02PC	1550
74LS02W	1550
74LS03	1569
74LS03CH	1569
74LS03DC	1569
74LS03J	1569
74LS03P	1569
74LS03PC	1569
74LS03W	1569
74LS04	1585
74LS04(SM)	OEM
74LS04DC	1585
74LS04N	6039
74LS04NA	1585
74LS04P	1585
74LS04PC	1585
74LS05	1598
74LS05(SM)	OEM
74LS05DC	1598
74LS05N	6040
74LS05PC	1598
74LS06	OEM
74LS06(MIN)	OEM
74LS06(SM)	OEM
74LS07	OEM
74LS08	1623
74LS08CH	1623
74LS08DC	1623
74LS08J	1623
74LS08N	1623
74LS08NA	1623
74LS08PC	1623
74LS08W	1623
74LS09	1632
74LS09N	OEM
74LS09PC	1632
74LS10	1652
74LS10(SM)	OEM
74LS10CH	1652
74LS10DC	1652

DEVICE TYPE	REPL CODE
74LS10J	1652
74LS10N	1652
74LS10PC	1652
74LS10W	1652
74LS11	1657
74LS11CH	1657
74LS11DC	1657
74LS11J	1657
74LS11N	1657
74LS11PC	1657
74LS11W	1657
74LS12	1669
74LS13DC	1678
74LS13N	1678
74LS13PC	1678
74LS14	1688
74LS14(SM)	OEM
74LS14D(SM)	OEM
74LS14DC	1688
74LS14N	1688
74LS14PC	1688
74LS14PF	1688
74LS15	1697
74LS15PC	1697
74LS16-1	OEM
74LS17	OEM
74LS20	0035
74LS20CH	0035
74LS20DC	0035
74LS20J	0035
74LS20N	0035
74LS20PC	0035
74LS20W	0035
74LS21	1752
74LS21DC	1752
74LS21PC	1752
74LS22	1764
74LS22PC	1764
74LS26	1372
74LS26DC	1372
74LS26PC	1372
74LS27	0183
74LS27CH	0183
74LS27DC	0183
74LS27J	0183
74LS27N	6879
74LS27PC	0183
74LS27W	0183
74LS28	OEM
74LS28DC	0467
74LS28PC	0467
74LS30	0822
74LS30CH	0822
74LS30DC	0822
74LS30J	0822
74LS30N	6886
74LS30PC	0822
74LS30W	0822
74LS32	0088
74LS32(SM)	OEM
74LS32CH	0088
74LS32DC	0088
74LS32J	0088
74LS32L	0088
74LS32N	0088
74LS32P	0088
74LS32PC	0088
74LS32W	0088
74LS33	1821
74LS33PC	1821
74LS37	1719
74LS37DC	1719
74LS37FC	1719
74LS37PC	1719
74LS38	1828
74LS38-1	1828
74LS38CH	1828
74LS38DC	1828
74LS38FC	1828
74LS38J	1828
74LS38N	1828
74LS38PC	1828
74LS38W	1828
74LS40DC	0135
74LS40PC	0135
74LS42	1830
74LS42CH	1830
74LS42DC	1830
74LS42J	1830
74LS42PC	1830
74LS42W	1830
74LS47DC	1834
74LS47PC	1834
74LS48DC	1838
74LS48PC	1838
74LS49DC	1839
74LS49PC	1839
74LS51	1027
74LS51CH	1027
74LS51DC	1027
74LS51J	1027
74LS51PC	1027
74LS51W	1027
74LS54DC	1846
74LS54PC	1846
74LS55PC	0452
74LS73	1856
74LS73CH	1856
74LS73J	1856

162

If replacement code is OEM, contact original manufacturer for replacement.

DEVICE TYPE	REPL CODE
74LS73W	1856
74LS74	0243
74LS74A	0243
74LS74AN	0243
74LS74ANB	OEM
74LS74APC	0243
74LS74CH	0243
74LS74J	0243
74LS74PC	0243
74LS74W	0243
74LS75	1859
74LS75(SM)	OEM
74LS75CH	1859
74LS75J	1859
74LS75N	6922
74LS75W	1859
74LS76	2166
74LS76DC	2166
74LS76PC	2166
74LS77	1861
74LS83ACH	2204
74LS83ADC	2204
74LS83AJ	2204
74LS83APC	2204
74LS83AW	2204
74LS85	0426
74LS85CH	0426
74LS85DC	0426
74LS85J	0426
74LS85PC	0426
74LS85W	0426
74LS86	0288
74LS86CH	0288
74LS86DC	0288
74LS86J	0288
74LS86N	0288
74LS86PC	0288
74LS86W	0288
74LS89DC	OEM
74LS89FC	OEM
74LS89PC	OEM
74LS90	1871
74LS90DC	1871
74LS90PC	1871
74LS91	1874
74LS92	1876
74LS92PC	1876
74LS93	1877
74LS93CH	1877
74LS93DC	1877
74LS93J	1877
74LS93N	1877
74LS93PC	1877
74LS93W	1877
74LS95	OEM
74LS95BDC	0766
74LS95BFC	0766
74LS95BPC	0766
74LS95N	OEM
74LS107	6844
74LS107CH	1592
74LS107DC	1592
74LS107J	1592
74LS107PC	1592
74LS107W	1592
74LS109	1895
74LS109A	4885
74LS109CH	1895
74LS109DC	1895
74LS109J	1895
74LS109PC	1895
74LS109W	1895
74LS112	2115
74LS112A	OEM
74LS112DC	2115
74LS112PC	2115
74LS113PC	2241
74LS114PC	2286
74LS122	4994
74LS122N	4994
74LS123	0973
74LS123CH	0973
74LS123J	0973
74LS123N	0973
74LS123W	0973
74LS125	0075
74LS125A	0075
74LS125AD(SM)	OEM
74LS125ADC	0075
74LS125AM	OEM
74LS125AN	0075
74LS125APC	0075
74LS126	2850
74LS126A	OEM
74LS126AN	OEM
74LS126DC	2850
74LS126PC	2850
74LS132	1615
74LS132DC	1615
74LS132N	1615
74LS132PC	1615
74LS133DC	3366
74LS133PC	3366
74LS136CH	1618
74LS136DC	1618
74LS136J	1618
74LS136PC	1618
74LS136W	1618
74LS138	0422
74LS138DC	0422
74LS138N	0422
74LS138NA	OEM
74LS138P	0422
74LS138PC	0422
74LS139	0153
74LS139A	OEM
74LS139AN	OEM
74LS139DC	0153
74LS139N	0153
74LS139PC	0153
74LS145	1554
74LS145PC	OEM
74LS148	3856
74LS151	1636
74LS151DC	1636
74LS151N	5044
74LS151PC	1636
74LS152	OEM
74LS153	0953
74LS153DC	0953
74LS153N	0953
74LS153NB	OEM
74LS153PC	0953
74LS154	4956
74LS155	0209
74LS155DC	0209
74LS155N	4142
74LS155NA	4142
74LS155PC	0209
74LS156	1644
74LS156DC	1644
74LS156N	1644
74LS156PC	1644
74LS157	1153
74LS157DC	1153
74LS157N	1153
74LS157PC	1153
74LS158	1646
74LS158DC	1646
74LS158PC	1646
74LS160PC	0831
74LS161	0852
74LS161A	5074
74LS161AN	0852
74LS161APC	5074
74LS161CH	0852
74LS161DC	0852
74LS161J	0852
74LS161PC	0852
74LS161W	0852
74LS162	OEM
74LS162N	OEM
74LS162PC	0874
74LS163	0887
74LS163CH	0887
74LS163DC	0887
74LS163J	0887
74LS163N	5092
74LS163PC	0887
74LS163W	0887
74LS164	4274
74LS164DC	4274
74LS164FC	4274
74LS164N	4274
74LS164PC	4274
74LS165DC	4289
74LS165FC	4289
74LS165PC	4289
74LS166	4301
74LS166A	OEM
74LS168DC	0961
74LS168PC	0961
74LS169DC	0980
74LS169PC	0980
74LS170DC	2605
74LS170FC	2605
74LS170PC	2605
74LS173A	5125
74LS174	0260
74LS174B	OEM
74LS174N	0260
74LS174NA	OEM
74LS174PC	0260
74LS175	1662
74LS175DC	1662
74LS175N	1662
74LS175PC	1662
74LS181PC	1668
74LS189DC	OEM
74LS189FC	OEM
74LS189PC	OEM
74LS190PC	1676
74LS191	6856
74LS191CH	1677
74LS191DC	1677
74LS191J	1677
74LS191PC	1677
74LS191W	1677
74LS192	1679
74LS192DC	1679
74LS192PC	1679
74LS193	1682
74LS193CH	1682
74LS193DC	1682
74LS193J	1682
74LS193N	1682
74LS193PC	1682
74LS193W	1682
74LS194	1294
74LS194ADC	1294
74LS194AFC	1294
74LS194APC	1294
74LS195	1511
74LS195ADC	1305
74LS195AFC	1305
74LS195APC	1305
74LS195N	1511
74LS196	2807
74LS196PC	2807
74LS197	2450
74LS197DC	2450
74LS197N	OEM
74LS197PC	2450
74LS221	1230
74LS221CH	1230
74LS221J	1230
74LS221PC	OEM
74LS221W	1230
74LS240	0447
74LS240DC	0447
74LS240N	0447
74LS240PC	0447
74LS241	1715
74LS241DC	1715
74LS241N	1715
74LS241PC	1715
74LS242	1717
74LS242DC	1717
74LS242PC	1717
74LS243	6868
74LS243APC	OEM
74LS243DC	0900
74LS243N	0900
74LS243PC	0900
74LS244	0453
74LS244(SM)	OEM
74LS244DC	0453
74LS244N	0453
74LS244PC	0453
74LS245	0458
74LS245DC	0458
74LS245N	0458
74LS245NA	0458
74LS245PC	0458
74LS247DC	1721
74LS247PC	1721
74LS248DC	1721
74LS248PC	1723
74LS249DC	1724
74LS249PC	1724
74LS251(SM)	OEM
74LS251DC	1726
74LS251PC	1726
74LS253DC	1728
74LS253PC	1728
74LS256DC	OEM
74LS256PC	OEM
74LS257	1733
74LS257A	1733
74LS257AN	1733
74LS257APC	1733
74LS257DC	1733
74LS257N	1733
74LS257PC	1733
74LS258	1735
74LS258APC	1735
74LS258DC	1735
74LS258N	1735
74LS258PC	1735
74LS259	3175
74LS259DC	3175
74LS259PC	3175
74LS260DC	5859
74LS260PC	5859
74LS266	0587
74LS266CH	0587
74LS266DC	0587
74LS266J	0587
74LS266PC	0587
74LS266W	0587
74LS273	0888
74LS273DC	0888
74LS273N	0888
74LS273PC	0888
74LS279	5302
74LS279DC	3259
74LS279N	5302
74LS279PC	3259
74LS280	1762
74LS283	1768
74LS283DC	1768
74LS283N	OEM
74LS283PC	1768
74LS289DC	OEM
74LS289PC	OEM
74LS290	4352
74LS290DC	4352
74LS290PC	4352
74LS293	0082
74LS293DC	0082
74LS293PC	0082
74LS295ADC	2212
74LS295AFC	2212
74LS295APC	2212
74LS298DC	3337
74LS298PC	3337
74LS299DC	4353
74LS299FC	4353
74LS322	1794
74LS322A	OEM
74LS322DC	1794
74LS322FC	1794
74LS322PC	1794
74LS323DC	OEM
74LS323FC	OEM
74LS323PC	OEM
74LS324	5864
74LS327	5866
74LS347DC	OEM
74LS347PC	OEM
74LS352	0756
74LS352DC	0756
74LS352PC	0756
74LS353DC	0768
74LS353PC	0768
74LS365	0937
74LS365A	0937
74LS365ADC	0937
74LS365AN	OEM
74LS365APC	0937
74LS366ADC	0950
74LS366APC	0950
74LS367	0971
74LS367A	0971
74LS367ADC	0971
74LS367APC	0971
74LS368	0985
74LS368A	0985
74LS368ADC	0985
74LS368AN	0985
74LS368APC	0985
74LS373	0704
74LS373DC	0704
74LS373N	0704
74LS373PC	0704
74LS374	0708
74LS374DC	0708
74LS374N	0708
74LS374P	0708
74LS374PC	0708
74LS375	OEM
74LS375DC	OEM
74LS375N	OEM
74LS375PC	OEM
74LS377DC	1112
74LS377PC	1112
74LS378	1125
74LS378DC	1125
74LS378FC	1125
74LS378PC	1125
74LS379DC	1143
74LS379FC	1143
74LS379PC	1143
74LS390	1278
74LS390DC	1278
74LS390PC	1278
74LS393	0813
74LS393DC	0813
74LS393N	0813
74LS393NA	0813
74LS393PC	0813
74LS395A	1320
74LS395DC	1320
74LS395FC	1320
74LS395PC	1320
74LS447DC	OEM
74LS447PC	OEM
74LS471	OEM
74LS490	2199
74LS490PC	2199
74LS502DC	OEM
74LS502PC	OEM
74LS503DC	OEM
74LS503PC	OEM
74LS504DC	OEM
74LS504PC	OEM
74LS533DC	5614
74LS533PC	5614
74LS534DC	5632
74LS534PC	5632
74LS540DC	2519
74LS540PC	2519
74LS541	2525
74LS541DC	2525
74LS541N	2525
74LS541PC	2525
74LS574PC	6038
74LS590	OEM
74LS590N	OEM
74LS612	OEM
74LS612N	OEM
74LS624	3112
74LS629	OEM
74LS629N	3146
74LS645	0770
74LS646	OEM
74LS646NT	OEM
74LS670	1122
74LS670DC	1122
74LS670FC	1122
74LS670N	OEM
74LS670PC	1122
74LS688	3378
74LS783	OEM
74LS785	OEM
74LS2578C	OEM
74LSP14APC	1294
74N1	0016
74P1	0037
74P1M	0126
74Q1262	0050
74Q22881	1851
74S00	0699
74S00DC	0699
74S00N	0699
74S00PC	0699
74S02	2223
74S02PC	2223
74S03DC	2203
74S03PC	2203
74S04	2248
74S04ADC	2248
74S04APC	2248
74S04DC	2248
74S04N	6058
74S04PC	2248
74S05	2305
74S05ADC	2305
74S05APC	2305
74S05D(SM)	OEM
74S05DC	2305
74S05N	OEM
74S05PC	2305
74S08	2547
74S08DC	2547
74S08N	OEM
74S08PC	2655
74S09DC	2642
74S09PC	2642
74S10	2426
74S10DC	2426
74S10N	OEM
74S10PC	2426
74S11	2428
74S11DC	2428
74S11N	6063
74S11PC	2428
74S15DC	2432
74S15PC	2432
74S20	5646
74S20DC	1011
74S20N	5646
74S20PC	1011
74S21	OEM
74S22DC	2442
74S22PC	2442
74S30DC	3681
74S30PC	3681
74S32	3795
74S32DC	OEM
74S32N	3795
74S32PC	3795
74S37	5648
74S38	0775
74S40	2456
74S40DC	OEM
74S40PC	2456
74S51	4241
74S51DC	4241
74S51N	OEM
74S51NA	4241
74S51PC	4241
74S64	2476
74S64DC	2476
74S64PC	2476
74S65	2477
74S65DC	2477
74S65PC	2477
74S74	2483
74S74DC	2483
74S74PC	2483
74S85	5664
74S86	2489
74S86DC	2489
74S86PC	2489
74S109DC	OEM
74S109PC	OEM
74S112	1607
74S112A	1607
74S112DC	1607
74S112N	1607
74S112PC	1607
74S113DC	1613
74S113PC	1613
74S114DC	1619
74S114PC	1619
74S132	2121
74S132DC	2121
74S132PC	2121
74S133	OEM
74S133DC	1808
74S133N	OEM
74S133PC	1808
74S134DC	1816
74S134PC	1816
74S135PC	OEM
74S137DC	OEM
74S137PC	OEM
74S138	2125
74S138DC	2125
74S138N	OEM
74S138PC	2125
74S139	OEM
74S139DC	OEM
74S139PC	OEM
74S140DC	1875
74S140PC	1875
74S151	1944
74S151DC	1944
74S151N	OEM
74S151PC	1944
74S153	2138
74S153DC	2138
74S153PC	2138
74S157	1685
74S157DC	1685
74S157PC	1685
74S158	OEM
74S158DC	2141
74S158N	OEM
74S158PC	2141
74S163	0887
74S163N	OEM
74S174	2119
74S174N	2119
74S174NA	2119
74S174PC	2119
74S175	2128
74S175DC	2128
74S175N	2128
74S175PC	2128
74S181DC	2151
74S181PC	2151
74S182	2152
74S182DC	2152
74S182PC	2152
74S189DC	OEM
74S189FC	OEM
74S189PC	OEM
74S194DC	1920
74S194FC	1920
74S194PC	1920
74S195	OEM
74S195A	OEM
74S240	OEM
74S240DC	2456
74S240PC	OEM
74S241	OEM
74S241DC	OEM
74S241N	OEM
74S241PC	OEM
74S251DC	2184
74S253DC	OEM
74S253PC	OEM
74S257DC	OEM
74S257PC	OEM
74S258	OEM
74S258DC	2191
74S258PC	2191
74S280	2205
74S280PC	OEM
74S288	2161
74S289DC	OEM
74S289FC	OEM
74S289PC	OEM
74S299	OEM
74S373	2249
74S374	2251
74SC137C(A)	OEM
74SC137D(A)	OEM
74SC137P(A)	OEM
74SC138C(A)	OEM
74SC138D(A)	OEM
74SC138P(A)	OEM
74SC139C(A)	OEM
74SC139D(A)	OEM
74SC139P(A)	OEM
74SC237C(A)	OEM
74SC237P(A)	OEM
74SC238C(A)	OEM
74SC238D(A)	OEM
74SC239C(A)	OEM
74SC239D(A)	OEM
74SC239P(A)	OEM
74SC240C(MA)	OEM
74SC240D(MA)	OEM
74SC240P(MA)	OEM
74SC241C(MA)	OEM
74SC241D(MA)	OEM
74SC241P(MA)	OEM
74SC242C(MA)	OEM
74SC242D(MA)	OEM
74SC242P(MA)	OEM
74SC243C(MA)	OEM
74SC243D(MA)	OEM
74SC243P(MA)	OEM
74SC244C(MA)	OEM
74SC244D(MA)	OEM
74SC244P(MA)	OEM
74SC540C(MA)	OEM
74SC540D(MA)	OEM
74SC540P(MA)	OEM
74SC541C(MA)	OEM
74SC541D(MA)	OEM
74SC541P(MA)	OEM
74SL258ADC	OEM
74SL266DC	OEM
74SL299PC	OEM
74ST-2SA10150(AU)E	0148
74ST-2SC763D	0127
74ST-2SC785-O	1136
74ST-2SC1906(AP)	0127
74ST-2SD1138C	0388
74T1	OEM
74T2	0236
74T3	OEM
74T4	OEM
74T5	OEM
74T6	OEM
74T7	OEM
74T8	OEM
74T9	OEM
74T10	OEM
74T11	OEM
74T12	OEM
74T13	OEM
74T14	OEM
74T15	OEM
74T20	OEM
74T20-CE00	OEM
74T20-CH00	OEM
74T20-EE00	OEM
74T20-GE00	OEM
74T20-GH00	OEM
74T20-JE00	OEM
74T20-JH00	OEM
74T20-LE00	OEM
74T20-LH00	OEM
74T20-NE00	OEM
74T20-NH00	OEM
74T20-RE00	OEM
74T21	OEM
74T21-CE00	OEM
74T21-CH00	OEM
74T21-EE00	OEM
74T21-GH00	OEM
74T21-JE00	OEM
74T21-JH00	OEM
74T21-LE00	OEM
74T21-LH00	OEM
74T21-NE00	OEM
74T21-NH00	OEM
74T21-RE00	OEM
74T22	OEM
74T22-CE00	OEM
74T22-CH00	OEM
74T22-EE00	OEM
74T22-GE00	OEM
74T22-GH00	OEM
74T22-JE00	OEM
74T22-JH00	OEM
74T22-LE00	OEM
74T22-LH00	OEM
74T22-NE00	OEM
74T22-NH00	OEM
74T22-RE00	OEM
74T23	OEM
74T23-CE00	OEM
74T23-CH00	OEM
74T23-EE00	OEM
74T23-EH00	OEM
74T23-GE00	OEM
74T23-GH00	OEM
74T23-JE00	OEM
74T23-JH00	OEM
74T23-LE00	OEM
74T23-LH00	OEM
74T23-NE00	OEM
74T23-NH00	OEM
74T23-RE00	OEM
74T24	OEM
74T24-CE00	OEM
74T24-CH00	OEM
74T24-EE00	OEM
74T24-EH00	OEM
74T24-GE00	OEM
74T24-GH00	OEM
74T24-JE00	OEM
74T24-JH00	OEM
74T24-LE00	OEM
74T24-LH00	OEM
74T24-NE00	OEM
74T24-NH00	OEM
74T24-RE00	OEM
74T25-CE00	OEM
74T25-CH00	OEM
74T25-EE00	OEM
74T25-EH00	OEM
74T25-GE00	OEM
74T25-GH00	OEM
74T25-JE00	OEM
74T25-LE00	OEM
74T25-LH00	OEM
74T25-NE00	OEM
74T25-NH00	OEM
74TB1-CE00	OEM
74TB1-CH00	OEM
74TB1-EE00	OEM
74TB1-GE00	OEM
74TB1-GH00	OEM
74TB1-JE00	OEM
74TB1-LE00	OEM
74TB1-LH00	OEM
74TB1-NE00	OEM
74TB1-NH00	OEM
74TB1-RE00	OEM
74TB2-CE00	OEM
74TB2-CH00	OEM
74TB2-GE00	OEM
74TB2-JE00	OEM
74TB2-JH00	OEM
74TB2-LE00	OEM
74TB2-LH00	OEM

If replacement code is OEM, contact original manufacturer for replacement.

163

DEVICE TYPE	REPL CODE
74TB2-NE00	OEM
74TB2-NH00	OEM
74TB2-RE00	OEM
74TB3-CE00	OEM
74TB3-CH00	OEM
74TB3-EE00	OEM
74TB3-GE00	OEM
74TB3-GH00	OEM
74TB3-JE00	OEM
74TB3-JH00	OEM
74TB3-LE00	OEM
74TB3-LH00	OEM
74TB3-NE00	OEM
74TB3-NH00	OEM
74TB3-RE00	OEM
74TB4-CE00	OEM
74TB4-CH00	OEM
74TB4-EE00	OEM
74TB4-GE00	OEM
74TB4-GH00	OEM
74TB4-JE00	OEM
74TB4-JH00	OEM
74TB4-LE00	OEM
74TB4-LH00	OEM
74TB4-NE00	OEM
74TB4-NH00	OEM
74TB4-RE00	OEM
74TB5-CE00	OEM
74TB5-CH00	OEM
74TB5-EE00	OEM
74TB5-GE00	OEM
74TB5-GH00	OEM
74TB5-JE00	OEM
74TB5-JH00	OEM
74TB5-LE00	OEM
74TB5-LH00	OEM
74TB5-NE00	OEM
74TB5-NH00	OEM
74TB5-RE00	OEM
74TB6-CE00	OEM
74TB6-CH00	OEM
74TB6-EE00	OEM
74TB6-GE00	OEM
74TB6-GH00	OEM
74TB6-JE00	OEM
74TB6-JH00	OEM
74TB6-LE00	OEM
74TB6-NE00	OEM
74TB6-NH00	OEM
74TB6-RE00	OEM
74TB7-CE00	OEM
74TB7-CH00	OEM
74TB7-EE00	OEM
74TB7-GE00	OEM
74TB7-GH00	OEM
74TB7-JE00	OEM
74TB7-JH00	OEM
74TB7-LE00	OEM
74TB7-LH00	OEM
74TB7-NE00	OEM
74TB7-NH00	OEM
74TB7-RE00	OEM
74TB8-CE00	OEM
74TB8-CH00	OEM
74TB8-EE00	OEM
74TB8-GE00	OEM
74TB8-GH00	OEM
74TB8-JE00	OEM
74TB8-JH00	OEM
74TB8-LE00	OEM
74TB8-LH00	OEM
74TB8-NE00	OEM
74TB8-NH00	OEM
74TB8-RE00	OEM
74TB9-CE00	OEM
74TB9-CH00	OEM
74TB9-EE00	OEM
74TB9-GE00	OEM
74TB9-GH00	OEM
74TB9-JE00	OEM
74TB9-JH00	OEM
74TB9-LE00	OEM
74TB9-LH00	OEM
74TB9-NE00	OEM
74TB9-NH00	OEM
74TB9-RE00	OEM
74TB10-CE00	OEM
74TB10-CH00	OEM
74TB10-EE00	OEM
74TB10-GE00	OEM
74TB10-GH00	OEM
74TB10-JE00	OEM
74TB10-JH00	OEM
74TB10-LE00	OEM
74TB10-LH00	OEM
74TB10-NE00	OEM
74TB10-NH00	OEM
74TB10-RE00	OEM
74TB11-CE00	OEM
74TB11-CH00	OEM
74TB11-EE00	OEM
74TB11-GE00	OEM
74TB11-GH00	OEM
74TB11-JE00	OEM
74TB11-JH00	OEM
74TB11-LE00	OEM
74TB11-LH00	OEM
74TB11-NE00	OEM
74TB11-NH00	OEM
74TB11-RE00	OEM
74TB12-CE00	OEM
74TB12-CH00	OEM
74TB12-EE00	OEM
74TB12-GE00	OEM
74TB12-GH00	OEM
74TB12-JE00	OEM
74TB12-JH00	OEM
74TB12-LE00	OEM
74TB12-LH00	OEM
74TB12-NE00	OEM
74TB12-NH00	OEM
74TB12-RE00	OEM
74TB13	OEM
74TB13-CE00	OEM
74TB13-CH00	OEM
74TB13-EE00	OEM
74TB13-GE00	OEM
74TB13-GH00	OEM
74TB13-JE00	OEM
74TB13-JH00	OEM
74TB13-LE00	OEM
74TB13-LH00	OEM
74TB13-NE00	OEM
74TB13-NH00	OEM
74TB13-RE00	OEM
74TB14-CE00	OEM
74TB14-CH00	OEM
74TB14-EE00	OEM
74TB14-GE00	OEM
74TB14-GH00	OEM
74TB14-JE00	OEM
74TB14-JH00	OEM
74TB14-LE00	OEM
74TB14-LH00	OEM
74TB14-NE00	OEM
74TB14-NH00	OEM
74TB14-RE00	OEM
74TB15	OEM
74TB15-CE00	OEM
74TB15-CH00	OEM
74TB15-EE00	OEM
74TB15-GE00	OEM
74TB15-GH00	OEM
74TB15-JE00	OEM
74TB15-JH00	OEM
74TB15-LE00	OEM
74TB15-LH00	OEM
74TB15-NE00	OEM
74TB15-NH00	OEM
74TB15-RE00	OEM
74TB16-CE00	OEM
74TB16-CH00	OEM
74TB16-EE00	OEM
74TB16-GE00	OEM
74TB16-GH00	OEM
74TB16-JE00	OEM
74TB16-JH00	OEM
74TB16-LE00	OEM
74TB16-LH00	OEM
74TB16-NE00	OEM
74TB16-NH00	OEM
74TB16-RE00	OEM
74TB17	OEM
74TB17-CH00	OEM
74TB17-EE00	OEM
74TB17-GE00	OEM
74TB17-GH00	OEM
74TB17-JE00	OEM
74TB17-JH00	OEM
74TB17-LE00	OEM
74TB17-LH00	OEM
74TB17-NE00	OEM
74TB17-NH00	OEM
74TB17-RE00	OEM
74TB18-CE00	OEM
74TB18-CH00	OEM
74TB18-GE00	OEM
74TB18-GH00	OEM
74TB18-JE00	OEM
74TB18-LE00	OEM
74TB18-LH00	OEM
74TB18-NE00	OEM
74TB18-NH00	OEM
74TB18-RE00	OEM
74TB19	OEM
74TB19-CE00	OEM
74TB19-CH00	OEM
74TB19-EE00	OEM
74TB19-GE00	OEM
74TB19-GH00	OEM
74TB19-JE00	OEM
74TB19-JH00	OEM
74TB19-LE00	OEM
74TB19-LH00	OEM
74TB19-NE00	OEM
74TB19-NH00	OEM
74TB19-RE00	OEM
74TB20-CE00	OEM
74TB20-CH00	OEM
74TB20-EE00	OEM
74TB20-GE00	OEM
74TB20-GH00	OEM
74TB20-JE00	OEM
74TB20-JH00	OEM
74TB20-LE00	OEM
74TB20-LH00	OEM
74TB20-NE00	OEM
74TB20-NH00	OEM
74TB20-RE00	OEM
74Z4	OEM
74Z6	0821
74Z6A	0821
75	0015
75(HEP)	0488
75-0-010	OEM
75-30	OEM
75-30-01	OEM
75-30-02	OEM
75-31	OEM
75-31-01	OEM
75-31-02	OEM
75-43	OEM
75-100-001	0124
75-461	0004
75A198-11	0065
75B3	OEM
75BV50H	OEM
75BV100H	OEM
75BV150H	OEM
75D01	0442
75D02	0934
75D03	0464
75D04	3252
75D05	3253
75D06	0934
75D1	0015
75D2	0015
75D4	OEM
75D6	OEM
75D8	0071
75D10	0071
75D12	OEM
75D14	OEM
75D16	OEM
75D18	OEM
75D20	OEM
75E03A	OEM
75E1	0015
75E2	0015
75E3	0015
75E4	0015
75E5	0015
75E6	0015
75E7	0071
75E8	0071
75E10	0071
75E12	OEM
75E14	OEM
75E16	OEM
75E18	OEM
75E20	1017
75E211	0486
75F05	0015
75F545DC	OEM
75G6P41	OEM
75HQ030	OEM
75HQ035	OEM
75HQ040	OEM
75HQ045	OEM
75J6P41	OEM
75L6P41	OEM
75N1	0233
75N5	0002
75N5AA	0016
75N5.1	0162
75N5.6	0157
75N6.2	0631
75N12	0137
75N27	0436
75R1B	0015
75R2B	0015
75R3B	0015
75R4B	0015
75R5B	0015
75R6B	0015
75R7B	0071
75R8B	0071
75R9B	0071
75R10B	0071
75R11B	0102
75R12B	0102
75R13B	0102
75R14B	0102
75R15B	OEM
75R16B	OEM
75R18B	OEM
75R20B	OEM
75R22B	OEM
75R24B	OEM
75R26B	OEM
75R28B	OEM
75R30B	OEM
75R32B	OEM
75R34B	OEM
75R36B	OEM
75R38B	OEM
75R40B	OEM
75R42B	OEM
75R44B	OEM
75R46B	OEM
75R48B	OEM
75R50B	OEM
75S107F	OEM
75S107N	OEM
75S108F	OEM
75S108N	OEM
75S207F	OEM
75S207N	OEM
75S208F	OEM
75S208N	OEM
75ST-2SC2229Y	0066
75ST-2SD467C(AU)E	0945
75ST-BC547B	0079
75SZ-HZ6C3	0466
75TE3.9	OEM
75TE3.9A	OEM
75TE4.7	OEM
75TE4.7A	OEM
75TE5.6	OEM
75TE5.6A	OEM
75TE6.8	OEM
75TE6.8A	OEM
75TE8.2	OEM
75TE8.2A	OEM
75TE10	OEM
75TE10A	OEM
75TE12	OEM
75TE12A	OEM
75TE15	OEM
75TE15A	OEM
75TE18	OEM
75TE18A	OEM
75TE22	OEM
75TE22A	OEM
75TE27	OEM
75TE27A	OEM
75TE33	OEM
75TE33A	OEM
75TE39	OEM
75TE39A	OEM
75TE47	OEM
75TE47A	OEM
75TE56	OEM
75TE56A	OEM
75W-005	0106
75W005	0106
75Z05	OEM
75Z4	OEM
75Z6	0840
75Z6A	0840
75Z6.8	0025
75Z6.8A	0025
75Z6.8B	0025
75Z6.8C	OEM
75Z7.5	0644
75Z7.5A	0644
75Z7.5B	0644
75Z7.5C	OEM
75Z8.2	0244
75Z8.2A	0244
75Z8.2B	0244
75Z8.2C	OEM
75Z9.1	0012
75Z9.1A	0012
75Z9.1B	0012
75Z9.1C	0012
75Z10	0170
75Z10A	0170
75Z10B	0170
75Z10C	OEM
75Z11	0789
75Z11A	0789
75Z11B	0789
75Z11C	0789
75Z12	0137
75Z12A	0137
75Z12B	0137
75Z12C	0137
75Z13	0361
75Z13A	0361
75Z13B	0361
75Z13C	0361
75Z14	0100
75Z14A	0100
75Z14B	0100
75Z14C	0100
75Z15	0002
75Z15A	0002
75Z15B	0002
75Z15C	0002
75Z16	0416
75Z16A	0416
75Z16B	0416
75Z16C	OEM
75Z17	1639
75Z18	0490
75Z18A	0490
75Z18B	0490
75Z18C	OEM
75Z19	0943
75Z19A	0943
75Z19B	0943
75Z19C	OEM
75Z20	0526
75Z20A	0526
75Z20B	0526
75Z20C	OEM
75Z22	0560
75Z22A	0560
75Z22B	0560
75Z22C	OEM
75Z24	0398
75Z24A	0398
75Z24B	0398
75Z24C	OEM
75Z25	1596
75Z25A	1596
75Z25B	1596
75Z25C	OEM
75Z27	0436
75Z27A	0436
75Z27B	0436
75Z27C	0436
75Z30	0721
75Z30A	0721
75Z30B	0721
75Z30C	OEM
75Z33	0039
75Z33A	0039
75Z33B	0039
75Z33C	0039
75Z36	0814
75Z36A	0814
75Z36B	0814
75Z36C	OEM
75Z39	0346
75Z39A	0346
75Z39B	0346
75Z39C	OEM
75Z43	0925
75Z43A	0925
75Z43B	0925
75Z43C	OEM
75Z45	OEM
75Z45A	OEM
75Z45B	OEM
75Z45C	OEM
75Z47	0993
75Z47A	0993
75Z47B	0993
75Z47C	OEM
75Z50	OEM
75Z50A	OEM
75Z50B	OEM
75Z50C	OEM
75Z51	0497
75Z51A	0497
75Z51B	0497
75Z51C	OEM
75Z52	OEM
75Z52A2A	OEM
75Z52B	OEM
75Z52C	OEM
75Z56	1823
75Z56A	1823
75Z56B	1823
75Z56C	1823
75Z62	0778
75Z62A	0778
75Z62B	0778
75Z62C	0778
75Z68	2144
75Z68A	2144
75Z68B	2144
75Z68C	OEM
75Z71A	OEM
75Z71B	OEM
75Z71C	OEM
75Z75	1181
75Z75A	1181
75Z75B	1181
75Z75C	OEM
75Z82	0327
75Z82A	0327
75Z82B	0327
75Z82C	0327
75Z91	1301
75Z91A	1301
75Z91B	1301
75Z91C	OEM
75Z100	0098
75Z100A	0098
75Z100B	0098
75Z100C	OEM
75Z105	OEM
75Z105A	OEM
75Z105B	OEM
75Z105C	OEM
75Z110	0149
75Z110A	0149
75Z110B	0149
75Z110C	0149
75Z120	0186
75Z120A	0186
75Z120B	0186
75Z120C	OEM
75Z130	0213
75Z130A	0213
75Z130B	0213
75Z130C	OEM
75Z140	0245
75Z140A	0245
75Z140B	0245
75Z140C	OEM
75Z150	0028
75Z150A	0028
75Z150B	0028
75Z150C	OEM
75Z160	0255
75Z160A	0255
75Z160B	0255
75Z160C	OEM
75Z175	OEM
75Z175A	OEM
75Z175B	OEM
75Z175C	OEM
75Z180	0363
75Z180A	0363
75Z180B	0363
75Z180C	OEM
75Z200	0417
75Z200A	0417
75Z200B	0417
75Z200C	OEM
76	0136
76-005-003	1598
76-005-005	1372
76-005-007	0243
76-005-013	0971
76-0105	0178
76-1	0086
76-100-001	1110
76-120-001	0967
76-140-001	2302
76-190-001	2732
76-500-001	1126
76-1400-001	OEM
76-11770	0085
76-13570-37	OEM
76-13570-39	0144
76-13570-59	0144
76-13570-63	OEM
76-13570-65	0911
76-13570-85	0911
76-13848-23	0911
76-13866-17	0144
76-13866-18	0076
76-13866-19	0144
76-13866-19(VHF)	0127
76-13866-20	0144
76-13866-59	0144
76-13866-62	0007
76-14090-1	0086
76-14196-1	0123
76-14327-1	0190
76-14327-2	0190
76-14327-3	0190
76-14327-4	0190
76-14327-5	0190
76-14327-6	0190
76-14327-7	0190
76-14327-8	0190
76-I(SYLVANIA)	0037
76-L(SYLVANIA)	0037
76G1450J	0015
76N1	0016
76N1(REMOTE)	0079
76N1(VID)	0111
76N1B	0086
76N1M	0016
76N2	0016
76N2B	0086
76N3B	0086
76RECT-SI-176	0091
76SD-1N4148(AU)	0124
76SI-HD14011BP	0215
76SK-1N4148(AU)	0124
76SO-1N4148(AU)	0124
76ST-2SC1514-15	1077
76ST-2SC1815GR	0076
76X0076-001	OEM
76X0077-001	OEM
76Z4	0052
76Z6	0862
76Z6A	0862
77	0279
77(DIO)	0790
77-001	0239
77-27166-2	0050
77-270877-2	0160
77-270878-2	0160
77-270993-1	0229
77-271025-1	0004
77-271026-1	0004
77-271027-1	0004
77-271029-1	0050
77-271029-2	0050
77-271031-1	0143
77-271032-1	0143
77-271036-1	0004
77-271037-1	0004
77-271038-1	0050
77-271039-1	0004
77-271166-2	0050
77-271166-3	0050
77-271334-1	0015
77-271374-1	0015
77-271453-1	0016
77-271490	0086
77-271490-1	0086
77-271491-1	0160
77-271798-1	0161
77-271798-3	0161
77-271818-1	0126
77-271967-1	0016
77-272913-1	0042
77-272914-1	0919
77-272999-1	0086
77-273001-2	0016
77-273001-3	0050
77-273004-1	0164
77-273715-1	0042
77-273716-1	0919
77-273738-1	0042
77-273739-1	0919
77A	0435
77A0	0435
77A01	0133
77A02	0133
77A1	0435
77A2	0435
77A3	0435
77A4	0435
77A5	0435
77A6	0435
77A7	0435
77A8	0435
77A9	0435
77A10	0435
77A10R	0435
77A11	0133
77A12	0435
77A13	0133
77A13P	0435
77A14	0435
77A14-7	0435
77A14-7B	0435
77A15	0435
77A15L	0435
77A16	0435
77A16-1	0435
77A17	0435
77A17-1	0435
77A18	0435
77A19	0435
77A19G	0435
77A-70	0435
77A-70-12	0435
77A-70-12-7	0435
77A119	0435
77A121	0435
77A182	0435
77B0	0265
77B2C	OEM
77C	0160
77C0	0160
77C1	0160
77C2	0160
77C3	0160
77C4	0160
77C5	0160
77C6	0160
77C7	0160
77C8	0160
77C9	0160
77C10	0160
77C10R	0160
77C11	0160
77C12	0160
77C13	0160
77C13P	0160
77C14	0160
77C14-7	0160
77C14-7B	0160
77C15	0160
77C15L	0160
77C16	0160
77C16-3	0160
77C17	0160
77C17-1	0160
77C18	0160
77C19	0160
77C19G	0160
77C-70	0160
77C-70-12	0160
77C-70-12-7	0160
77C119	0160
77C121	0160
77C182	0160
77C800-005	1812
77C800-007	1035
77C800-008	0141
77C813-002	0081
77N1	0016
77N2	0016
77N2B	0086
77N3	0198
77N4	0016
77N5	0016
77N6	0016
77SS-2N5062	0895
77ST-2SD669AC	0558
77ST-2SD869	0055
77Z4	OEM
77Z6	0879
77Z6A	0879
78-001	0061
78-900-001	OEM
78-900-002	0006
78-900-003	0378
78-900-004	4265
78-5009	0160
78-254566-1	0015
78-254566-4	0015
78-271030-1	0229
78-271031-1	0123
78-271032-2	0123
78-271143-1	0015
78-271199-1	0143
78-271228-1	0143
78-271383-1	0137
78-271383-2	0436
78-271383-3	0002

If replacement code is OEM, contact original manufacturer for replacement.

DEVICE TYPE	REPL CODE	DEVICE TYPE	REPL CODE	DEVICE TYPE	REPL CODE	DEVICE TYPE	REPL CODE	DEVICE TYPE	REPL CODE	DEVICE TYPE	REPL CODE	DEVICE TYPE	REPL CODE
78-271383-4	0002	78M05CDB	OEM	79M15DB	OEM	80L250	OEM	80T20-CH00	OEM	80TF10	OEM	81R3FMA	OEM
78-272160-1	0015	78M05CU	OEM	79M18CDB	OEM	80L260	OEM	80T20-EE00	OEM	80TF10A	OEM	81RK10	OEM
78-272212-1	0160	78M05DB	OEM	79M18CU	OEM	80L270	OEM	80T20-EH00	OEM	80TF12	OEM	81RK10M	OEM
78-273002-1	0143	78M05E	OEM	79M18DB	OEM	80L280	OEM	80T21	OEM	80TF12A	OEM	81RK20	OEM
78-273008	0015	78M05HC	OEM	79M24CDB	OEM	80L290	OEM	80T21-CE00	OEM	80TF15	OEM	81RK20M	OEM
78-273008-1	0015	78M05HF	0619	79M24CU	OEM	80L300	OEM	80T21-CH00	OEM	80TF15A	OEM	81RK40	OEM
78-273085	0015	78M06CDB	OEM	79M24DB	OEM	80N9A	OEM	80T21-EE00	OEM	80TF18	OEM	81RK40M	OEM
78A200010P4	0232	78M06CU	OEM	79P1	0004	80N15A	OEM	80T21-EH00	OEM	80TF18A	OEM	81RK60	OEM
78BLK	0279	78M06DB	OEM	79SI-UPC393C	0624	80N15A9	OEM	80T22	OEM	80TF22	OEM	81RK60M	OEM
78C01	0144	78M08	1187	79Z4	OEM	80N20A	OEM	80T22-CE00	OEM	80TF22A	OEM	81RK80	OEM
78C02	0144	78M08CDB	OEM	79Z6	0920	80N20A9	OEM	80T22-CH00	OEM	80TF27	OEM	81RK80M	OEM
78D5R10	OEM	78M08CU	OEM	79Z6A	0920	80N25A	OEM	80T22-EE00	OEM	80TF27A	OEM	81RK100	OEM
78D9R10GH	OEM	78M08DB	OEM	80	1208	80N25A9	OEM	80T22-EH00	OEM	80TF33	OEM	81RK120	OEM
78D56	OEM	78M09	1775	80-001300	0071	80N30A	OEM	80T23	OEM	80TF33A	OEM	81RK120M	OEM
78EP	OEM	78M09A	OEM	80-001400	0071	80N30A9	OEM	80T23-CE00	OEM	80TF39	OEM	81RK140	OEM
78GRN	0279	78M09E	OEM	80-0256-18	OEM	80N35A	OEM	80T23-CH00	OEM	80TF39A	OEM	81RK140M	OEM
78H05-KC	2836	78M12	0330	80-050100	0016	80N35A9	OEM	80T23-EE00	OEM	80TF47	OEM	81RK160	OEM
78H05KC	2836	78M12A	OEM	80-050300	0208	80N40A	OEM	80T23-EH00	OEM	80TF47A	OEM	81RK160M	OEM
78H12	OEM	78M12CDB	OEM	80-050400	0050	80N40A9	OEM	80T24	OEM	80TF56	OEM	81RL10	0521
78HO5KC	2836	78M12CU	OEM	80-050500	0050	80N45A	OEM	80T24-CH00	OEM	80TF56A	OEM	81RL20	0521
78HV05CDA	1905	78M12DB	OEM	80-050600	0208	80N45A9	OEM	80T24-EE00	OEM	80V10A	OEM	81RL30	0521
78HV05CU	0619	78M12KC	0330	80-050700	0160	80N50A	OEM	80T24-EH00	OEM	80V11	OEM	81RL40	0521
78HV05DA	OEM	78M13A	OEM	80-051500	0016	80N50A9	OEM	80T25-CH00	OEM	80X8-8.5	OEM	81RL50	0521
78HV06CDA	OEM	78M15CDB	OEM	80-051600	0126	80N55A	OEM	80T25-EE00	OEM	80X8.5-9	OEM	81RL60	0521
78HV06CU	OEM	78M15CU	OEM	80-052102	0016	80N55A9	OEM	80T25-EH00	OEM	80X9-9.5	OEM	81RL80	0108
78HV06DA	OEM	78M15DB	OEM	80-052202	0016	80N60A	OEM	80TB1-NE00	OEM	80X9.5-10	OEM	81RL100	0108
78HV08CDA	OEM	78M15H	OEM	80-052302	0016	80N60A9	OEM	80TB1-NH00	OEM	80Z4	OEM	81RL110	0108
78HV08CU	OEM	78M18A	2244	80-052402	0103	80N65A	OEM	80TB1-RE00	OEM	80Z6	0938	81RL120	0108
78HV08DA	OEM	78M18M	OEM	80-052600	0016	80N65A9	OEM	80TB2-NE00	OEM	80Z6A	0938	81RLA50	0605
78HV12CDA	6585	78M20CDB	OEM	80-052700	0126	80N70A	OEM	80TB2-NH00	OEM	81-1007	OEM	81RLA60	0605
78HV12CU	3445	78M20CU	OEM	80-052800	0208	80N70A9	OEM	80TB2-RE00	OEM	81-23860400-3	0546	81RLA80	0463
78HV12DA	OEM	78M20DB	OEM	80-053001	0016	80N75A	OEM	80TB3-NE00	OEM	81-23860400A	0546	81RLA100	0463
78HV14CDA	OEM	78M24CDB	OEM	80-053300	0086	80N75A9	OEM	80TB3-NH00	OEM	81-23860400B	0546	81RLA120	0463
78HV14CU	OEM	78M24CU	OEM	80-053400	0016	80N80A	OEM	80TB3-RE00	OEM	81-27123100-3	0015	81RLA140	OEM
78HV14DA	OEM	78M24DB	OEM	80-053600	0144	80N80A9	OEM	80TB4-NE00	OEM	81-27123150-8	0143	81RLA160	OEM
78HV15CDA	OEM	78M93D	OEM	80-053702	1506	80N85A	OEM	80TB4-NH00	OEM	81-27123300-3	0015	81RLB50	0521
78HV15CU	OEM	78MHV05CDB	OEM	80-60-1	0143	80N85A9	OEM	80TB4-RE00	OEM	81-27123307-3	0015	81RLB60	0521
78HV15DA	OEM	78MHV05CU	OEM	80-308-2	0016	80N90A9	OEM	80TB5-NE00	OEM	81-27125140-7	0016	81RLB80	0108
78HV18CDA	OEM	78MHV05DB	OEM	80-1059	0139	80N95A	OEM	80TB5-NH00	OEM	81-27125140-7A	0016	81RLB100	0108
78HV18CU	OEM	78MHV06CDB	OEM	80-4464-04	OEM	80N95A9	OEM	80TB5-RE00	OEM	81-27125140-7B	0016	81RLB110	0108
78HV18DA	OEM	78MHV06CU	OEM	80-104900	0136	80N100A	OEM	80TB6-NE00	OEM	81-27125160-5	0016	81RLB120	0108
78HV24CDA	OEM	78MHV06DB	OEM	80-105200	0136	80N100A9	OEM	80TB6-NH00	OEM	81-27125160-5A	0016	81RM10	0521
78HV24CU	OEM	78MHV08CDB	OEM	80-105300	0136	80N110A	OEM	80TB6-RE00	OEM	81-27125160-5B	0016	81RM30	0521
78HV24DA	OEM	78MHV08CU	OEM	80-205400	0004	80N120A	OEM	80TB7-CE00	OEM	81-27125270-2	0016	81RM40	0521
78L02AA	OEM	78MHV08DB	OEM	80-205600	0004	80N130A	OEM	80TB7-CH00	OEM	81-27125270-2A	0016	81RM50	0521
78L05	1288	78MHV12CDB	OEM	80-236400	0004	80N140A	OEM	80TB7-EE00	OEM	81-27125270-2B	0016	81RM60	0521
78L05-AN	1288	78MHV12DB	OEM	80-236430	0004	80N150A	OEM	80TB7-EH00	OEM	81-27125300-7	0016	81RM70	0108
78L05-AV	1288	78MHV13CU	OEM	80-243900	0004	80N160A	OEM	80TB8-CE00	OEM	81-27125530-9	0546	81RM80	0108
78L05A	1288	78MHV15CDB	OEM	80-318250	0016	80N170A	OEM	80TB8-CH00	OEM	81-27125530-9A	0546	81RM90	0108
78L05ACP	1288	78MHV15CU	OEM	80-337390	0016	80N180A	OEM	80TB8-EE00	OEM	81-27125530-9B	0546	81RM100	0108
78L05AV	1288	78MHV15DB	OEM	80-338030	0144	80N190A	OEM	80TB8-EH00	OEM	81-27126100-0	0546	81SD-FV1043	0549
78L05AVP	1288	78MHV18CU	OEM	80-338040	0144	80N200A	OEM	80TB9-CE00	OEM	81-27126130-7	0160	81ST-2SA1015O(AU)B	0148
78L05CLP	OEM	78MHV20CDB	OEM	80-339430	0144	80N210A	OEM	80TB9-CH00	OEM	81-27126130-7A	0160	81ST-2SA1050(AU)B	0148
78L05H	OEM	78MHV20DB	OEM	80-339440	0144	80N220A	OEM	80TB9-EE00	OEM	81-27126130-7B	0160	81ST-2SB561C	0431
78L05J	1288	78MHV24CDB	OEM	80-383840	0144	80N230A	OEM	80TB9-EH00	OEM	81-46123001-3	0143	81SV-KB262	0120
78L05V	1288	78MHV24CU	OEM	80-383930	0144	80N240A	OEM	80TB10-CE00	OEM	81-46123002-1	0030	81T1	OEM
78L06	2285	78MHV24DB	OEM	80-383940	0016	80N250A	OEM	80TB10-CH00	OEM	81-46123004-5	0015	81T2	0086
78L06A	2285	78N1	0016	80-389910	0016	80P1	0004	80TB10-EE00	OEM	81-46123004-7	0015	81T3	OEM
78L06AC	2285	78N2B	0016	80-389930	0016	80P1,610080-1	0004	80TB10-EH00	OEM	81-46123005	0015	81T4	OEM
78L06C	2285	78RED	0279	80-414120	0103	80P1SP	OEM	80TB11-CE00	OEM	81-46123006-2	0143	81T5	OEM
78L06CLP	OEM	78SZ-UZP-12B	0137	80-414130	0103	80P2	0126	80TB11-CH00	OEM	81-46123010-4	2255	81T6	OEM
78L08	0083	78YEL	0279	80-421980	0016	80P2B	0126	80TB11-EE00	OEM	81-46123013-8	0143	81T7	OEM
78L08A	0083	78Z4	OEM	80-2226314	0004	80P2SP	OEM	80TB11-EH00	OEM	81-46123014-6	0015	81T8	OEM
78L08AC	0083	78Z6	0908	80A5	0071	80P3	0126	80TB12-CE00	OEM	81-46123015-3	0143	81T9	OEM
78L08AWC	0083	78Z6A	0908	80AS	0071	80P3B	0126	80TB12-CH00	OEM	81-46123018-7	0015	81T10	OEM
78L09	1775	79F015	0143	80B1AM	OEM	80P3SP	OEM	80TB12-EH00	OEM	81-46123029-4	0143	81T11	OEM
78L09A	1775	79F114-1	0086	80B-US	OEM	80P4SP	OEM	80TB13	OEM	81-46125001-1	0136	81T12	OEM
78L09CLP	1775	79F114-2A	0126	80C48C098	OEM	80P5SP	OEM	80TB13-CE00	OEM	81-46125002-9	0004	81T20	OEM
78L09K	OEM	79F114-3	0086	80C51FV568	OEM	80P6SP	OEM	80TB13-CH00	OEM	81-46125003-7	0004	81T20-NE00	OEM
78L010AP	OEM	79F114-4	0126	80C88	OEM	80P8SP	OEM	80TB13-EH00	OEM	81-46125004-5	0004	81T20-NH00	OEM
78L12	1817	79F114-4A	0126	80C97	3151	80P10SP	OEM	80TB14-CH00	OEM	81-46125005-2	0164	81T20-RE00	OEM
78L12A	1817	79F150	1024	80C888-2	OEM	80P12SP	OEM	80TB14-EH00	OEM	81-46125006-0	0144	81T21	OEM
78L12ACDB	OEM	79F150-2	1024	80E-US	OEM	80P16SP	OEM	80TB15	OEM	81-46125007-8	0127	81T21-NE00	OEM
78L12ACS	OEM	79F153	0469	80H	0071	80S0030	OEM	80TB15-CE00	OEM	81-46125009-4	0004	81T21-NH00	OEM
78L12ACZ	1817	79L05	4429	80H3	0206	80S2SP	OEM	80TB15-CH00	OEM	81-46125010-2	0004	81T21-RE00	OEM
78L12CDB	OEM	79L05AC	4429	80H3N	0444	80S3SP	OEM	80TB15-EE00	OEM	81-46125011-0	0004	81T22	OEM
78L12CLP	OEM	79L05CLP	OEM	80H3P	2982	80S4SP	OEM	80TB15-EH00	OEM	81-46125012-8	0127	81T22-NE00	OEM
78L12CS	OEM	79L12	1825	80L15	OEM	80S5SP	OEM	80TB16-CE00	OEM	81-46125013-6	0127	81T22-NH00	OEM
78L15A	OEM	79L12CLP	OEM	80L20	6100	80S6SP	OEM	80TB16-CH00	OEM	81-46125016-9	0016	81T22-RE00	OEM
78L15ACDB	OEM	79L15	OEM	80L25	OEM	80S8SP	OEM	80TB16-EE00	OEM	81-46125018-5	0164	81T23	OEM
78L15ACS	OEM	79L15CLP	OEM	80L30	OEM	80SI-M51358B	0906	80TB16-EH00	OEM	81-46125019-3	0016	81T23-NE00	OEM
78L15CDB	OEM	79L18CZ	OEM	80L35	OEM	80SI-M51358P	0906	80TB17	OEM	81-46125026-8	0016	81T23-NH00	OEM
78L15CLP	OEM	79LL05	OEM	80L40	OEM	80SI-MAB8021	OEM	80TB17-CE00	OEM	81-46125027-6	0016	81T23-RE00	OEM
78L15CS	OEM	79LS05	OEM	80L45	OEM	80SQ030	OEM	80TB17-CH00	OEM	81-46125028-4	0160	81T24	OEM
78L18CLP	OEM	79M05	1275	80L50	OEM	80SQ035	OEM	80TB17-EE00	OEM	81-46125029-2	0004	81T24-NE00	OEM
78L18J	OEM	79M05A	OEM	80L55	OEM	80SQ040	OEM	80TB17-EH00	OEM	81-46125030-0	0127	81T24-NH00	OEM
78L24	OEM	79M05C	1275	80L60	OEM	80SQ045	OEM	80TB18-CE00	OEM	81-46125032-6	0127	81T24-RE00	OEM
78L24CLP	OEM	79M05CDB	OEM	80L65	OEM	80SS2SP	OEM	80TB18-CH00	OEM	81-46125033-4	0127	81T25-NE00	OEM
78L56	OEM	79M05CT	1275	80L70	OEM	80SS3SP	OEM	80TB18-EE00	OEM	81-46125034-2	0004	81T25-NH00	OEM
78L62	2285	79M05CU	OEM	80L75	OEM	80SS4SP	OEM	80TB18-EH00	OEM	81-46125036-7	0004	81T25-RE00	OEM
78L62AC	2285	79M05DB	OEM	80L80	OEM	80SS5SP	OEM	80TB19	OEM	81-46125065-6	0321	81TB1-CE00	OEM
78L62AWC	2285	79M05.2CDB	OEM	80L85	OEM	80SS6SP	OEM	80TB19-CE00	OEM	81-46128001-8	3232	81TB1-CH00	OEM
78L62WV	2285	79M05.2CU	OEM	80L90	OEM	80SS8SP	OEM	80TB19-CH00	OEM	81-46128002-6	2289	81TB1-EE00	OEM
78L82AC	0083	79M05.2DB	OEM	80L95	OEM	80ST-2SC2271E	0261	80TB19-EE00	OEM	81-46143002-7	0120	81TB1-LE00	OEM
78L82AWC	OEM	79M06CDB	OEM	80L100	OEM	80ST-2SC2753	1498	80TB19-EH00	OEM	81A4-1	OEM	81TB1-LH00	OEM
78LO2ACDB	OEM	79M06CU	OEM	80L110	OEM	80T1	OEM	80TB20-CE00	OEM	81A5-2	OEM	81TB1-NE00	OEM
78LO2ACS	OEM	79M06DB	OEM	80L120	OEM	80T2	0018	80TB20-CH00	OEM	81BUS	OEM	81TB2-CE00	OEM
78LO2CDB	OEM	79M08CDB	OEM	80L130	OEM	80T3	OEM	80TB20-EE00	OEM	81F1FM	OEM	81TB2-CH00	OEM
78LO2CS	OEM	79M08CU	OEM	80L140	OEM	80T4	OEM	80TB20-EH00	OEM	81F1FMA	OEM	81TB2-EE00	OEM
78LO5ACDB	OEM	79M08DB	OEM	80L150	OEM	80T5	OEM	80TF3.9	OEM	81F2FM	OEM	81TB2-LE00	OEM
78LO5ACS	OEM	79M12	1827	80L160	OEM	80T6	OEM	80TF3.9A	OEM	81F2FMA	OEM	81TB2-LH00	OEM
78LO5CDB	OEM	79M12A	OEM	80L170	OEM	80T7	OEM	80TF4.7	OEM	81F3FM	OEM	81TB2-NE00	OEM
78LO5CS	OEM	79M12C	1827	80L180	OEM	80T8	OEM	80TF4.7A	OEM	81F3FMA	OEM	81TB3-CE00	OEM
78LO6ACS	OEM	79M12CDB	OEM	80L190	OEM	80T9	OEM	80TF5.6	OEM	81P3	0126	81TB3-CH00	OEM
78LO6CS	OEM	79M12CKC	1827	80L200	OEM	80T10	OEM	80TF5.6A	OEM	81R1FM	OEM	81TB3-EE00	OEM
78M05	0619	79M12CU	OEM	80L210	OEM	80T11	OEM	80TF6.8	OEM	81R1FMA	OEM	81TB3-LE00	OEM
78M05(SM)	OEM	79M12DB	OEM	80L220	OEM	80T12	OEM	80TF6.8A	OEM	81R2FM	OEM	81TB3-LH00	OEM
78M05A	0619	79M15CDB	OEM	80L230	OEM	80T20	OEM	80TF8.2	OEM	81R2FMA	OEM	81TB3-NE00	OEM
78M05C	0619	79M15CU	OEM	80L240	OEM	80T20-CE00	OEM	80TF8.2A	OEM	81R3FM	OEM	81TB4-CE00	OEM

If replacement code is OEM, contact original manufacturer for replacement.

165

DEVICE TYPE	REPL CODE
81TB4-CH00	OEM
81TB4-EE00	OEM
81TB4-LE00	OEM
81TB4-LH00	OEM
81TB4-NE00	OEM
81TB5-CE00	OEM
81TB5-CH00	OEM
81TB5-EE00	OEM
81TB5-LE00	OEM
81TB5-LH00	OEM
81TB5-NE00	OEM
81TB6-CE00	OEM
81TB6-CH00	OEM
81TB6-EE00	OEM
81TB6-LE00	OEM
81TB6-LH00	OEM
81TB6-NE00	OEM
81TB7	OEM
81TB7-CE00	OEM
81TB7-CH00	OEM
81TB7-EE00	OEM
81TB7-LE00	OEM
81TB7-LH00	OEM
81TB7-NE00	OEM
81TB8-CE00	OEM
81TB8-CH00	OEM
81TB8-EE00	OEM
81TB8-LE00	OEM
81TB8-LH00	OEM
81TB8-NE00	OEM
81TB9	OEM
81TB9-CE00	OEM
81TB9-CH00	OEM
81TB9-LE00	OEM
81TB9-LH00	OEM
81TB9-NE00	OEM
81TB10-NH00	OEM
81TB10-RE00	OEM
81TB11	OEM
81TB11-NH00	OEM
81TB11-RE00	OEM
81TB12-NH00	OEM
81TB12-RE00	OEM
81TB13	OEM
81TB13-NH00	OEM
81TB13-RE00	OEM
81TB14-NH00	OEM
81TB14-RE00	OEM
81TB15	OEM
81TB15-NH00	OEM
81TB15-RE00	OEM
81TB16-NH00	OEM
81TB16-RE00	OEM
81TB17	OEM
81TB17-NH00	OEM
81TB17-RE00	OEM
81TB18-NH00	OEM
81TB18-RE00	OEM
81TB19	OEM
81TB19-NH00	OEM
81TB19-RE00	OEM
81TB20-NE00	OEM
81TB20-NH00	OEM
81TB20-RE00	OEM
81X0042-100	1647
81Z6	0952
81Z6A	0952
82	0049
82-2	OEM
82-3	OEM
82-4	0015
82-409501	0016
82-410300	0126
82A205	OEM
82HM181CJG	OEM
82HM181CPG	OEM
82HM181MJG	OEM
82HM191CJG	OEM
82HM191CPG	OEM
82HM191MJG	OEM
82M432B2	1545
82N1	0127
82P3	OEM
82RECT-SI-154(AU)	0023
82RL10	0650
82RL20	0650
82RL30	0650
82RL40	0650
82RL50	0650
82RL60	0650
82RL80	0020
82RL100	0020
82RL110	0020
82RL120	0020
82RLA50	0217
82RLA60	0217
82RLA80	0653
82RLA100	0653
82RLA110	0653
82RLA120	0653
82RLA130	OEM
82RLA140	OEM
82RLA150	OEM
82RLA160	OEM
82RLB50	0650
82RLB60	0650
82RLB80	0650
82RLB100	0020
82RLB110	0020

DEVICE TYPE	REPL CODE
82RLB120	0020
82RM10	0650
82RM20	0650
82RM30	0650
82RM40	0650
82RM50	0650
82RM60	0650
82RM70	OEM
82RM80	0020
82RM90	OEM
82RM100	0020
82S100	OEM
82S100N	OEM
82S100N/7700	OEM
82S123	2161
82S210F	OEM
82S210N	OEM
82SP-LT-211	OEM
82ST-2SC288A	1332
82T2	0042
82Z6	0952
82Z6A	0952
83	0126
83-1	0037
83-2	0102
83-11	0375
83-28	2030
83-43-3	0769
83-829	0015
83-880	0015
83-1056	0160
83A30-1	0015
83A40-1	1293
83B38-1	0143
83C6V8	0025
83C30-1	0015
83C40-1	1293
83D5R11	OEM
83D9R11GH	OEM
83N52	0435
83P1	0037
83P1A	0037
83P1B	0037
83P1BC	0037
83P1M	0037
83P1MC	0037
83P2	0037
83P2A	0037
83P2AA	0037
83P2AA1	0037
83P2B	0126
83P2M	0037
83P2M1	0037
83P2N	0037
83P3	0037
83P3A	0037
83P3AA	0037
83P3AA1	0037
83P3B	0037
83P3B1	0037
83P3M	0037
83P3M1	0037
83P4	0037
83X3202	OEM
83Z6	1003
83Z6A	1003
84	0160
84-44-3	0769
84A	0160
84A0	0160
84A1	0160
84A2	0160
84A3	0160
84A4	0160
84A5	0160
84A6	0160
84A7	0160
84A8	0160
84A9	0160
84A10	0160
84A10R	0160
84A12	0160
84A13	0160
84A13P	0160
84A14	0160
84A14-7	0160
84A14-7B	0160
84A15	0160
84A15L	0160
84A16	0160
84A16B	0160
84A17	0160
84A17-1	0160
84A18	0160
84A19	0160
84A19G	0160
84A20	0133
84A-70	0160
84A-70-12	0160
84A-70-12-7	0160
84A121	0160
84A182	0160
84AA1	0160
84AA19	0160
84B	0160
84C01	0275
84D5R11	OEM
84D9R11GH	OEM
84G01	0275

DEVICE TYPE	REPL CODE
84S157PC	1685
84SZ-BZV46-1VR	OEM
84SZ-RD12EB3	0052
84TB1-JH00	OEM
84TB1-LE00	OEM
84TB1-LH00	OEM
84TB1-NE00	OEM
84TB1-NH00	OEM
84TB2-CE00	OEM
84TB2-CH00	OEM
84TB2-EE00	OEM
84TB2-EH00	OEM
84TB2-LH00	OEM
84TB2-NE00	OEM
84TB2-NH00	OEM
84TB3-CE00	OEM
84TB3-CH00	OEM
84TB3-EH00	OEM
84TB3-LH00	OEM
84TB3-NE00	OEM
84TB3-NH00	OEM
84TB4-CE00	OEM
84TB4-CH00	OEM
84TB4-EE00	OEM
84TB4-EH00	OEM
84TB4-LH00	OEM
84TB4-NE00	OEM
84TB4-NH00	OEM
84TB5-CE00	OEM
84TB5-CH00	OEM
84TB5-EE00	OEM
84TB5-EH00	OEM
84TB5-LH00	OEM
84TB5-NE00	OEM
84TB5-NH00	OEM
84TB6-CE00	OEM
84TB6-CH00	OEM
84TB6-EE00	OEM
84TB6-EH00	OEM
84TB6-LH00	OEM
84TB6-NE00	OEM
84TB6-NH00	OEM
84TB7	OEM
84TB7-CE00	OEM
84TB7-CH00	OEM
84TB7-EE00	OEM
84TB7-EH00	OEM
84TB7-LH00	OEM
84TB7-NE00	OEM
84TB8-CE00	OEM
84TB8-CH00	OEM
84TB8-EE00	OEM
84TB8-EH00	OEM
84TB8-LH00	OEM
84TB8-NE00	OEM
84TB9	OEM
84TB9-CE00	OEM
84TB9-CH00	OEM
84TB9-EE00	OEM
84TB9-EH00	OEM
84TB9-LH00	OEM
84TB9-NE00	OEM
84TB10-CE00	OEM
84TB10-CH00	OEM
84TB10-EE00	OEM
84TB10-EH00	OEM
84TB10-LH00	OEM
84TB10-NE00	OEM
84TB11	OEM
84TB11-CE00	OEM
84TB11-CH00	OEM
84TB11-EE00	OEM
84TB11-LH00	OEM
84TB11-NE00	OEM
84TB12-CE00	OEM
84TB12-CH00	OEM
84TB12-EE00	OEM
84TB12-LH00	OEM
84TB12-NE00	OEM
84TB13	OEM
84TB13-CE00	OEM
84TB13-CH00	OEM
84TB13-EE00	OEM
84TB13-LH00	OEM
84TB13-NE00	OEM
84TB14-CE00	OEM
84TB14-CH00	OEM
84TB14-EE00	OEM
84TB14-LH00	OEM
84TB14-NE00	OEM
84TB15-CE00	OEM
84TB15-CH00	OEM
84TB15-EE00	OEM
84TB15-LH00	OEM
84TB15-NE00	OEM
84Z6	OEM
84Z6A	OEM
85	0604
85-5	0015
85-370-2-BLU	0160
85-557-2	OEM
85A500161	0411
85D5R11	OEM
85D9R11GH	OEM
85HA40	OEM
85HA60	OEM
85HA80	OEM
85HA100	OEM
85HA120	OEM

DEVICE TYPE	REPL CODE
85HA140	OEM
85HA160	OEM
85HF10	2751
85HF20	2751
85HF30	OEM
85HF30A	OEM
85HF40	2786
85HF60	2786
85HF60A	OEM
85HF80	2818
85HF100	2818
85HF100A	OEM
85HF120	2619
85HF140	OEM
85HF160	OEM
85HFL10S02	OEM
85HFL10S05	OEM
85HFL10S10	OEM
85HFL20S02	OEM
85HFL20S05	OEM
85HFL20S10	OEM
85HFL40S02	OEM
85HFL40S05	OEM
85HFL40S10	OEM
85HFL60S02	OEM
85HFL60S05	OEM
85HFL60S10	OEM
85HFL80S02	OEM
85HFL80S05	OEM
85HFL80S10	OEM
85HFL100S05	OEM
85HFL100S10	OEM
85HFR10	1734
85HFR20	1734
85HFR30	OEM
85HFR30A	OEM
85HFR40	1772
85HFR50	OEM
85HFR60	1772
85HFR60A	OEM
85HFR80	1807
85HFR100	1807
85HFR100A	OEM
85HFR120	5229
85HFR140	OEM
85HFR160	OEM
85HQ030	OEM
85HQ035	OEM
85HQ040	OEM
85HQ045	OEM
85P1	OEM
85ST-2SA733Q	0006
85ST-2SC458C(AU)E	0076
85Z6	0883
85Z6A	0883
86	0023
86-0001	0030
86-0002	0143
86-0005	0012
86-0006	0015
86-0007	1073
86-0007-004	0016
86-0008	0019
86-0016-01	0015
86-0022-001	0016
86-0029-001	0016
86-0031-001	0016
86-0033-007	0816
86-0036-001	0037
86-0046-001	OEM
86-0509	0030
86-0510	0062
86-0511	0015
86-0513	0123
86-0514	0030
86-0515	0139
86-0516	0080
86-0518	0005
86-0519	0133
86-0520	0139
86-0521	0052
86-0522	0133
86-1-3	0015
86-3-1	0479
86-3-3	0015
86-4-1	0015
86-4-2	0595
86-5-2	0208
86-6-2	0208
86-7-1	0015
86-8-2	0160
86-9-1	0196
86-9-3	0015
86-10-01	0143
86-10-1	0143
86-10-2	0595
86-11-2	0595
86-12-1	0911
86-12-2	0595
86-12-3	0911
86-13-2	0208
86-14-1	0123
86-14-2	0208
86-15-1	0123
86-16-2	0004
86-18-1	0196
86-18-1A	0196
86-18-2	0050
86-19-2	0160

DEVICE TYPE	REPL CODE
86-20-1	0143
86-20-2	0050
86-21-1	0015
86-21-2	0004
86-22-1	0143
86-22-2	0004
86-22-3	0015
86-23-1	0914
86-23-2	0004
86-23-3	0015
86-24-2	0208
86-25-1	0137
86-25-2	0208
86-26-1	0015
86-26-2	0595
86-27-1	0133
86-27-2	0004
86-28-2	0004
86-28-3	0015
86-29-2	0004
86-30-1	0015
86-30-2	0004
86-30-3	0015
86-31-1	0137
86-31-2	0595
86-32-1	0015
86-32-2	0004
86-33-2	0004
86-34-3	0015
86-35-1	0012
86-35-2	0208
86-35-3	0015
86-36-1	0015
86-36-2	0050
86-37-1	6405
86-37-2	0050
86-37-3	0469
86-37-18	OEM
86-38-1	0015
86-38-2	0050
86-39-1	OEM
86-39-2	0004
86-40-3	0015
86-41-1	1141
86-42-3	0015
86-43-1	0479
86-43-3	0015
86-44-2	0595
86-44-3	6650
86-45-1	0143
86-45-2	0004
86-45-3	1293
86-46-2	0004
86-46-3	0015
86-47-2	0004
86-47-3	0469
86-48-1	0123
86-48-2	0004
86-49-1	0143
86-49-2	0004
86-49-3	0015
86-50-2	0004
86-50-3	0015
86-51-2	0015
86-51-3	0015
86-52-1	0015
86-52-9	OEM
86-53-3	0133
86-54-2	0004
86-54-3	0015
86-55-3	0469
86-56-3	0469
86-56-3B	0469
86-56-3C	0469
86-56-3F	0469
86-57-3	0015
86-58-1	0012
86-58-2	0016
86-58-3	0015
86-59-1	0015
86-59-2	0004
86-59-3	0015
86-60-1	0143
86-60-2	0004
86-60-3	0015
86-61-1	0137
86-61-2	0004
86-62-1	0133
86-62-2	0160
86-62-3	0015
86-63-2	0160
86-63-3	0015
86-64-1	0143
86-65-1	0137
86-65-3	0015
86-65-4	0133
86-65-9	0015
86-66-1	0526
86-67-0	0015
86-67-1	0361
86-67-2	0071
86-67-3	0023
86-67-8	0015
86-67-9	0015
86-68-3	6809
86-68-3A	0276
86-70-1	0133
86-72-2	0004
86-72-3	0071

DEVICE TYPE	REPL CODE
86-73-1	0526
86-73-2	0004
86-74-1	0133
86-74-2	0004
86-74-9	0133
86-75-1	0398
86-75-2	0004
86-75-3	0015
86-75-3(SEARS)	0015
86-76-1	0133
86-76-2	0208
86-77-1	0133
86-77-2	0004
86-78-1	0133
86-78-2	0004
86-78-3	0015
86-79-2	0004
86-80-1	0015
86-80-2	0004
86-80-3	0015
86-81-2	0208
86-82-2	0004
86-83-2	0004
86-84-1	0015
86-84-2	0004
86-85-1	0137
86-86-2	0050
86-87-2	0050
86-87-3	0030
86-88-1	0526
86-88-2	0050
86-88-3	0143
86-89-1	0015
86-89-2	0050
86-89-3	0015
86-90-2	0050
86-91-1	0398
86-91-2	0050
86-92-1	0137
86-92-2	0050
86-93-1	0416
86-93-2	0004
86-93-3	OEM
86-94-1	0039
86-95-1	0273
86-95-2	0004
86-96-1	0600
86-96-3	0469
86-97-1	0196
86-98-2	0004
86-99-2	0050
86-100-2	0050
86-101-2	0050
86-102-2	0050
86-102-3	0340
86-103-2	0004
86-103-3	0857
86-103-9	3370
86-104-3	0182
86-105-3	0102
86-106-1	1493
86-106-2	1493
86-106-3	1493
86-106-3-1	1493
86-106-3-2	1493
86-106-3-3	1493
86-106-3-4	1493
86-106-3-5	1493
86-106-4	1493
86-106-5	1493
86-107-2	0050
86-108-2	0136
86-109-1	0446
86-109-2	0136
86-109-3	0567
86-109-5	OEM
86-110-01	OEM
86-110-1	3428
86-110-2	0016
86-110-3	0895
86-111-1	0560
86-111-2	0136
86-111-3	0015
86-112-2	0050
86-113-1	0398
86-113-2	OEM
86-113-3	3368
86-114-1	0244
86-114-2	0004
86-114-3	1313
86-115-2	0004
86-115-3	OEM
86-116-1	0030
86-116-2	0136
86-116-3	0023
86-117-1	1596
86-117-2	0050
86-117-3	0102
86-118-1	0170
86-118-3	0102
86-119-1	0814
86-119-2	0016
86-120-2	0160
86-121-2	0086
86-123-2	0016
86-125-1	0143
86-126-2	0004
86-126-3	0559
86-127-2	0160

DEVICE TYPE	REPL CODE
86-127-3	2524
86-128-2	0004
86-128-3	0559
86-129-2	0004
86-130-2	0004
86-131-2	0004
86-132-2	0004
86-133-2	0004
86-135-1	0244
86-135-2	0050
86-136-2	0050
86-138-2	0144
86-138-3	0127
86-139-1	0526
86-139-2	0016
86-139-3	0015
86-141-1	OEM
86-141-2	0160
86-142-2	0160
86-143-2	0016
86-144-2	0016
86-145-1	0644
86-146-1	0143
86-146-2	0160
86-146-3	0015
86-147-1	0015
86-147-2	0160
86-147-3	0015
86-148-1	0256
86-149-1	0993
86-149-2	0050
86-150-1	OEM
86-150-2	0050
86-150-3	0098
86-151-2	0050
86-152-1	OEM
86-152-2	0004
86-153-1	OEM
86-155-2	0016
86-156-2	0004
86-156-2A	0211
86-157-2	0079
86-158-2	0016
86-159-2	0004
86-160-2	0126
86-161-2	0086
86-162-2	0050
86-163-2	0050
86-164-2	0050
86-164-9	OEM
86-165-2	0275
86-166-2	0016
86-169-2	0004
86-170-2	0086
86-171-2	0016
86-172-2	0004
86-173-2	0160
86-173-9	0160
86-175-2	0016
86-176-2	0004
86-177-2	0275
86-178-2	0037
86-178-20	0037
86-179-2	0050
86-180-2	0050
86-181-2	0050
86-182-2	0016
86-183-2	0037
86-183-20	0037
86-185-2	0007
86-186-2	0007
86-188-2	0016
86-189-2	0016
86-191-2	0016
86-192-2	0016
86-194-2	0016
86-195-2	0016
86-196-2	0016
86-198-2	0016
86-199-2	0016
86-201-2	0016
86-202-2	0016
86-204-2	0007
86-205-2	0007
86-207-2	0086
86-208-2	0086
86-210-2	0086
86-211-2	0086
86-213-2	0233
86-214-2	0233
86-215-2	0233
86-217-2	0037
86-217-20	0037
86-218-2	0037
86-218-20	0037
86-219-2	0037
86-221-2	0637
86-222-2	0637
86-224-2	0637
86-224-9	OEM
86-225-2	0637
86-227-2	0142
86-228-2	0275
86-230-2	0160
86-231-2	0160
86-232-2	0160
86-233-2	0037
86-234-2	0086
86-235-2	0160

If replacement code is OEM, contact original manufacturer for replacement.

DEVICE TYPE	REPL CODE
86-236-2	0142
86-237-2	0016
86-238-2	0016
86-243-2	0144
86-244-2	0144
86-245-2	0144
86-246-2	0037
86-246-20	0037
86-247-2	0016
86-248-2	0160
86-249-2	0004
86-249-9	0142
86-250-2	0016
86-251-2	0037
86-251-20	0037
86-253-2	0050
86-254-2	0050
86-255-2	0016
86-256-2	0016
86-257-2	0275
86-259-2	0142
86-260-2	0142
86-261-2	0142
86-262-2	0007
86-262-9	0065
86-263-2	0007
86-264-2	0016
86-265-2	0016
86-266-2	0086
86-267-2	0086
86-271-2	0178
86-272-2	0178
86-273-2	0086
86-275-2	0142
86-276-2	0037
86-276-20	0037
86-277-2	0016
86-278-2	0050
86-279-2	0050
86-280-2	0136
86-281-2	0136
86-282-2	0136
86-283-2	0004
86-284-2	0546
86-286-2	0037
86-286-20	0037
86-287-2	0275
86-287-9	OEM
86-289-2	0007
86-290-2	0007
86-291-2	0086
86-291-7	OEM
86-291-9	0016
86-292-2	0969
86-293-2	0016
86-294-2	0037
86-294-20	0037
86-295-2	0004
86-296-2	0050
86-297-2	0004
86-298-2	0037
86-298-20	0037
86-300-2	0004
86-301-2	0208
86-303-2	0004
86-304-2	0004
86-305-2	0004
86-306-2	0086
86-308-2	0016
86-309-2	0016
86-310-2	0016
86-311-2	0136
86-312-2	0050
86-313-2	0160
86-316-2	0233
86-317-2	0160
86-319-2	0160
86-320-2	0050
86-321-2	0050
86-322-2	0050
86-323-2	0016
86-324-2	0016
86-327-2	0016
86-328-2	0016
86-329-2	0126
86-330-2	0086
86-334-2	0126
86-336-2	0086
86-339-2	0016
86-339-9	0016
86-340-2	0037
86-340-20	0037
86-342-2	0016
86-344-2	0161
86-344-9	OEM
86-347-2	0050
86-347-7	0050
86-348-2	0050
86-353-2	0160
86-354-2	0160
86-359-2	0016
86-362-2	0016
86-363-2	0050
86-365-2	0016
86-366-2	0050
86-367-2	0050
86-368-2	0050
86-370-2	0599
86-370-2YEL	0160

DEVICE TYPE	REPL CODE
86-373-2	0050
86-374-2	0050
86-376-2	0050
86-379-2	0016
86-381-2	0224
86-386-2	0144
86-389-2	0198
86-390-2	0016
86-391-2	0016
86-392-2	0004
86-393-2	0086
86-396-2	0455
86-396-9	OEM
86-399-2	0016
86-399-9	0016
86-400-2	1212
86-403-2	0016
86-406-2	0037
86-407-2	0037
86-412-2	0178
86-416-2	0144
86-417-2	0144
86-419-2	0004
86-420-2	0016
86-421-2	0004
86-422-2	0018
86-422-3	0546
86-423-2	0527
86-423-3	0378
86-428-2	0086
86-428-9	0086
86-431-2	0126
86-431-9	0126
86-440-2	0086
86-441-2	0086
86-442-2	0007
86-444-2	0111
86-445-2	0016
86-449-2	0136
86-449-9	0050
86-452-2	0086
86-455-3	0359
86-457-2	0016
86-458-2	0016
86-459-2	0037
86-460-2	0016
86-461-2	0016
86-462-2	0016
86-463-2	3392
86-463-3	0086
86-464-2	0212
86-465-2	0079
86-467-2	0144
86-472-2	0016
86-475-2	0037
86-476-2	0004
86-477-2	0321
86-479-2	OEM
86-480-9	0222
86-481-1	0016
86-481-2	0016
86-482-2	0037
86-483-2	0016
86-483-3	0016
86-484-2	0016
86-485-2	0016
86-486-2	0016
86-486-9	OEM
86-487-2	0142
86-487-3	0142
86-488-2	0144
86-490-2	0144
86-491-2	0144
86-493-2	0016
86-494-2	0016
86-495-2	0016
86-496-2	0016
86-497-2	0004
86-500-2	0321
86-501-2	0037
86-502-2	0016
86-506-2	0161
86-507-2	0455
86-509-2	0004
86-510-2	0086
86-511-9	0047
86-512-2	0435
86-513-2	0326
86-515-2	0855
86-515-2(SEARS)	0016
86-520-2	0016
86-521-2	0855
86-525-2	0127
86-526-2	0111
86-527-2	0037
86-528-2	0037
86-529-2	0042
86-530-2	0919
86-533-2	0006
86-534-2	0016
86-536-2	0079
86-537-2	0079
86-538-2	0079
86-540-2	0349
86-541-2	0396
86-547-2	0037
86-549-2	0396
86-550-2	0855
86-551-2	0016

DEVICE TYPE	REPL CODE
86-552-2	0037
86-554-2	0016
86-555-2	0006
86-556-2	0283
86-557-2	0855
86-558-2	0396
86-561-2	0016
86-563-2	0065
86-563-9	0065
86-564-2	0359
86-564-3	0065
86-564-9	0065
86-565-1	OEM
86-565-2	0016
86-566-2	0855
86-567-2	0086
86-568-2	0419
86-568-9	0042
86-569-2	OEM
86-570-2	0006
86-570-3	0006
86-572-2	0312
86-572-3	0312
86-573-2	0016
86-574-2	0133
86-590-2	6668
86-593-2	0224
86-593-9	1136
86-594-2	0224
86-595-2	0016
86-596-2	0127
86-597-2	0127
86-598-2	0016
86-599-2	0016
86-600-2	0037
86-601-2	0590
86-601-9	OEM
86-602-2	0786
86-602-9	OEM
86-604-2	0042
86-605-2	0212
86-606-2	0212
86-607-02	0076
86-607-2	0191
86-608-2	0688
86-609-2	0218
86-609-9	0320
86-610-2	0431
86-610-9	0006
86-611-2	0855
86-612-2	0233
86-613-2	0236
86-614-2	0676
86-615-2	0855
86-619-2	0224
86-620-2	0224
86-621-2	0224
86-622-2	0037
86-624-2	0142
86-624-9	0142
86-625-2	0212
86-626-2	0309
86-626-9	0065
86-628-2	0283
86-628-9	5915
86-629-2	0233
86-629-9	OEM
86-630-2	0855
86-631-2	0283
86-632-2	0212
86-633-2	0065
86-633-9	0309
86-646-2	0016
86-648-2	0168
86-649-2	0855
86-650-2	0086
86-651-2	0710
86-653-2	0283
86-655-2	0198
86-659-2	0527
86-660-2	0546
86-661-2	0016
86-663-2	0042
86-664-2	0283
86-664-9	2987
86-665-2	0103
86-665-9	0103
86-668-2	2123
86-668-9	OEM
86-669-2	0037
86-670-2	OEM
86-671-2	2220
86-672-2	0283
86-673-2	0561
86-674-2	0086
86-675-2	0086
86-702-2	0016
86-801-2	OEM
86-802-2	OEM
86-803-2	OEM
86-804-9	1274
86-805-2	OEM
86-807-2	OEM
86-809-2	OEM
86-810-9	1274
86-900-2	OEM
86-901-2	OEM
86-902-2	OEM
86-903-2	OEM

DEVICE TYPE	REPL CODE
86-904-2	OEM
86-905-2	OEM
86-906-2	OEM
86-907-2	OEM
86-909-2	OEM
86-910-2	OEM
86-911-2	OEM
86-912-2	OEM
86-914-2	OEM
86-916-2	OEM
86-918-2	OEM
86-920-2	OEM
86-922-2	OEM
86-923-2	OEM
86-925-2	OEM
86-926-2	OEM
86-927-2	OEM
86-928-2	OEM
86-929-2	OEM
86-931-2	OEM
86-932-2	OEM
86-933-2	OEM
86-934-2	OEM
86-936-2	OEM
86-937-2	OEM
86-1392	0016
86-5000-2	0004
86-5000-3	0015
86-5001-2	0004
86-5001-3	0015
86-5002-3	0015
86-5003-2	0208
86-5003-3	0015
86-5004-2	0208
86-5005-2	0208
86-5006-2	0004
86-5006-3	0015
86-5007-2	0208
86-5007-3	0143
86-5008-2	0208
86-5009-2	0618
86-5009-3	0015
86-5010-3	0133
86-5011-2	0208
86-5011-3	0133
86-5012-2	0208
86-5012-3	0015
86-5013-2	0208
86-5015-2	0208
86-5015-3	0133
86-5016-2	0208
86-5017-2	0208
86-5018-2	0016
86-5024-3	0015
86-5026-2	0208
86-5027-2	0004
86-5027-3	0133
86-5028-3	0242
86-5029-2	0208
86-5029-3	0015
86-5032-3	0242
86-5034-2	0208
86-5037-3	0133
86-5039-2	0160
86-5040-2	0016
86-5041-2	0016
86-5042-2	0004
86-5043-2	0160
86-5044-2	0016
86-5045-2	0016
86-5046-2	0016
86-5047-2	0208
86-5048-2	0208
86-5049-2	0016
86-5050-2	0016
86-5051-2	0016
86-5052-2	0164
86-5055-2	0016
86-5056-2	0016
86-5057-2	0160
86-5058-2	0160
86-5060-2	0208
86-5061-2	0208
86-5062-2	0208
86-5063-2	0004
86-5064-2	0126
86-5064-2A	0126
86-5065-2	0198
86-5067-2	0004
86-5070-2	0086
86-5073-2	0086
86-5074-2	0086
86-5075-2	0590
86-5079-2	0037
86-5080-2	0208
86-5081-2	0016
86-5082-2	0126
86-5082-2A	0126
86-5083-2	0160
86-5084-2	0103
86-5084-2A	0103
86-5085-2	0178
86-5086-2	0208
86-5087-2	0208
86-5088-2	0160
86-5089-2	0160
86-5090-2	0160
86-5091-2	0004
86-5093-2	0086

DEVICE TYPE	REPL CODE
86-5095-2	0321
86-5096-2	0321
86-5097-2	0016
86-5099-2	0016
86-5100-2	0161
86-5101-2	0103
86-5101-2A	0103
86-5102-2	0042
86-5103-2	0016
86-5104-2	0786
86-5105-2	0396
86-5106-2	0178
86-5107-2	0042
86-5108-2	0042
86-5109-2	0086
86-5110-2	0016
86-5111-2	0016
86-5112-2	0103
86-5113-2	0160
86-5114-2	0016
86-5122-2	0321
86-5125-2	0160
86-5911-3	0015
86-5943-2	0160
86-10003	0224
86-86525-3	0344
86-86560-3	0344
86-100002	0224
86-100003	0079
86-100004	0224
86-100005	0016
86-100006	0224
86-100007	0224
86-100008	0016
86-100009	0037
86-100010	0018
86-100011	0527
86-100012	0030
86-100013	0133
86-100014	0133
86-200003	OEM
86-200055	OEM
86A318	0004
86A327	0111
86A332	0103
86A338	0178
86A339	0899
86C04	0455
86HF10	OEM
86HF20	OEM
86HF40	OEM
86HF60	OEM
86HF80	OEM
86HF100	OEM
86HF120	OEM
86HF140	OEM
86HF160	OEM
86HFR10	OEM
86HFR20	OEM
86HFR40	OEM
86HFR60	OEM
86HFR80	OEM
86HFR100	OEM
86HFR120	OEM
86HFR140	OEM
86HFR160	OEM
86SI-74145N	0614
86ST-MPS9750D	0037
86X0006-001	0076
86X0007-001	1212
86X0007-004	0144
86X0007-104	0016
86X0007-204	0144
86X0008-001	0016
86X0009-001	0160
86X00011-001	0211
86X006-001	0016
86X007-004	0016
86X007-034	0016
86X0011-001	0136
86X0012-001	0111
86X0013-001	0136
86X0014-001	0050
86X0015-001	0160
86X0016-001	0037
86X0016-001A	0037
86X0017-001	0004
86X0018-001	0164
86X0019-001	0016
86X0022-001	0016
86X0024-001	2600
86X0025-001	0198
86X0025-001(AFO)	0142
86X0025-001(TIK)	0079
86X0027-001	2600
86X0028-001	0142
86X0029-001	0016
86X0030-001	0265
86X0031-001	0016
86X0031-002	0016
86X0031-003	0016
86X0032-001	0016
86X0033-001	0222
86X0033-01	0222
86X0034-001	0326
86X0035-001	0086
86X0036-001	0037
86X0036-001(DIODE)	0102
86X0036-001(TRANSIST	0037

DEVICE TYPE	REPL CODE
86X0036-001A	0037
86X0037-001	2839
86X0037-002	0004
86X0037-100	2839
86X0038-001	0007
86X0040-00	0016
86X0040-001	0016
86X0041-001	0037
86X0041-001A	0037
86X0042-001	3136
86X0042-002	2969
86X0042-100	1647
86X0043-001	0144
86X0044-001	0037
86X0044-001A	0037
86X0045-001	0016
86X0046-001	0037
86X0047-001	0037
86X0048-001	0016
86X0049-001	0076
86X0050-001	0016
86X0051-001	0079
86X0052-001	0224
86X0053-001	0167
86X0054-00	0079
86X0054-001	0016
86X0055-001	2527
86X0056-001	0324
86X0056-002	0324
86X0058-001	0198
86X0058-002	0198
86X0058-003	0198
86X0059-001	0161
86X0059-002	0556
86X0060-001	0127
86X0061-001	0127
86X0062-001	0127
86X0063-001	0016
86X0064-001	1601
86X0065-001	0283
86X0066-001	0006
86X0066-003	0006
86X0067-001	2313
86X0067-002	4526
86X0068-001	1702
86X0068-002	4534
86X0069-001	0239
86X0070-001	0312
86X0071-001	0079
86X0072-001	0037
86X0073-001	0546
86X0073-002	0558
86X0074-001	0161
86X0075-001	0455
86X0075-002	0919
86X0076-001	1698
86X0077-001	0239
86X0077-002	0061
86X0078-001	0061
86X0080-001	3136
86X0080-002	2969
86X0080-100	3687
86X0081-001	0095
86X0081-002	0095
86X0082-001	0516
86X0083-001	0161
86X0084-001	0842
86X0085-001	OEM
86X0086-001	2759
86X0087-001	OEM
86X0088-001	OEM
86X0089-001	0396
86X0090-001	1212
86X037-001	0038
86X0113-001	0076
86X0114-001	0006
86X0115-001	0283
86X0116-001	0283
86X0123-001	3820
86X0124-001	3853
86X0127-001	0855
86X0128-001	0723
86X0129-001	4183
86X2	0599
86X3	0279
86X6	0016
86X6-1	0016
86X6-4-518	0016
86X7-2	0016
86X7-3	0016
86X7-4	0016
86X7-6	0127
86X7-6013	0144
86X8-1	0016
86X8-2	0016
86X8-3	0016
86X8-4	0016
86X34-1	0016
86X46	0037
86X47	0037
86X53	OEM
86X53-1	0167
86X56-2	0324
86X65-1	0283
86X74-1	0161
86X75-2	0919
86X82-1	0516
86X86-1	2759
86X87-1	OEM

DEVICE TYPE	REPL CODE
86X88-1	6947
86X115	0283
86X483-2	0086
86X6029-001	0144
86Z6	1043
86Z6A	1043
87	0023
87-0001	1202
87-0002	1204
87-0002-1	2195
87-0003	1060
87-0004	1206
87-0005	0076
87-0006	0218
87-0009	1212
87-0013	0547
87-0014	0076
87-0015	0628
87-0016	0136
87-0017	0628
87-0018	0004
87-0019	0004
87-0020	0004
87-0021	0004
87-0022	1226
87-0023-7	0224
87-0023-T	1211
87-0027	0127
87-0028	1233
87-0029	0218
87-0203-1	0155
87-0212-1	0111
87-0216	1469
87-0217	1470
87-0218-U	1212
87-0227	0424
87-0228	1488
87-0229	1490
87-0230	0111
87-0230-1	0111
87-0233	1501
87-0234	0514
87-0235	0151
87-0235-C	0224
87-0235A	0151
87-0235B	0151
87-0235C	0151
87-0236-Q	0018
87-0236-R	0018
87-0236-S	0018
87-0236Q	0018
87-0236R	0018
87-0236S	0018
87-0237-R	0527
87-0237-S	0527
87-0238	0111
87-0239-A	0018
87-0246	1516
87-5-3	0469
87-10-0	0143
87-10-1	0143
87-56-3	0469
87-67-3	0023
87-71	OEM
87-104-3	0182
87-218-U	0111
87-423-2	0006
87-593-2	1136
87-724-375-01	0155
87A	0023
87B	OEM
87B02	0546
87C48	OEM
87C201-25-T	OEM
87RECT-SI-154	0023
87RECT-SI-154(AU)	0023
87SI-TA7680AP	4047
87Z6	1052
87Z6A	1052
88	OEM
88-2	OEM
88-3	0015
88-125	0015
88-831	0015
88-832	0015
88-833	0015
88-9132	4506
88-9132F	4506
88-9302	1411
88-9302RS	1411
88-9302S	1411
88-9574	1434
88-9774	OEM
88-9774F	OEM
88-9779	1748
88-9779F	1748
88-9824R	OEM
88-9841	OEM
88-9841R	1832
88-9842	OEM
88-9842F	1335
88-9842R	1335
88-9842RS	1335
88-9842S	1335
88-18920	2111
88-20372	2728
88-20404	0514
88-98302	OEM
88-98302R	OEM

If replacement code is OEM, contact original manufacturer for replacement.

167

DEVICE TYPE	REPL CODE
88-1250108	0111
88-1250109	0016
88-B-7-258	0673
88-B-7258	0673
88A752271	2530
88B	0050
88B0	0050
88B1	0050
88B2	0050
88B3	0050
88B4	0050
88B5	0050
88B6	0050
88B7	0050
88B8	0050
88B9	0050
88B10	0050
88B10R	0050
88B11	0050
88B12	0050
88B13	0050
88B13P	0050
88B14	0050
88B14-7	0050
88B14-7B	0050
88B15	0050
88B15L	0050
88B16	0050
88B16E	0050
88B17	0050
88B17-1	0050
88B18	0050
88B19	0050
88B19G	0050
88B-70	0050
88B-70-12	0050
88B-70-12-7	0050
88B119	0050
88B121	0050
88B182	0050
88B7258	0673
88C	0279
88C0	0279
88C1	0279
88C2	0279
88C3	0279
88C4	0279
88C5	0279
88C6	0279
88C7	0279
88C8	0279
88C9	0279
88C10	0279
88C10R	0279
88C11	0279
88C12	0279
88C13	0279
88C13P	0279
88C14	0279
88C14-7	0279
88C14-7B	0279
88C15	0279
88C15L	0279
88C16	0279
88C16D	0279
88C17	0279
88C17-1	0279
88C18	0279
88C19	0279
88C19G	0279
88C-70	0279
88C-70-12	0279
88C-70-12-7	0279
88C119	0279
88C121	0279
88C182	0279
88CC-70-12	0279
88ST-2SA1015Y	0148
88SZ-RD12FB2	0137
88X0053-001	2377
88X8841	OEM
88Z6	0926
88Z6A	0926
89-REST-U-1081	OEM
89RECT-U-1001	OEM
89ST-MPS9410AK	0086
89WJ75/46N	0143
90-30	0076
90-31	0155
90-32	0076
90-33	1212
90-35	2608
90-36	0905
90-37	2046
90-38	0219
90-39	1303
90-45	0007
90-46	1332
90-47	1332
90-48	0076
90-49	0544
90-50	3672
90-54	0050
90-55	3672
90-56	0191
90-57	0076
90-58	0349
90-59	0050
90-60	1136

DEVICE TYPE	REPL CODE
90-61	0191
90-62	3672
90-65	0076
90-66	0155
90-67	1303
90-68	0268
90-69	0076
90-70	1212
90-71	0191
90-72	2608
90-73	0905
90-74	2046
90-75	0386
90-140	0076
90-175	4144
90-176	0386
90-177	1967
90-178	0212
90-179	3672
90-180	0151
90-181	1211
90-450	0833
90-451	0386
90-452	0076
90-453	0076
90-454	1967
90-455	0326
90-456	0076
90-457	0076
90-458	0076
90-459	0076
90-600	0228
90-601	0076
90-602	0364
90-603	0111
90-604	1136
90-605	0076
90-606	3672
90-607	1270
90-608	1270
90-609	0833
90-610	0830
90-612	0076
90-613	3672
90-614	1212
90-1648	OEM
90T2	0127
90T112-1	OEM
90V10A	OEM
90V11	OEM
90X9.5-10.5	OEM
91-3	0143
91-4	0050
91-46	0143
91-50	0030
91-US	OEM
91A	0144
91A01	0015
91A02	0015
91A03	0015
91A04	0071
91A05	0015
91A06	0015
91A08	0102
91A018	0015
91A11	0015
91AJ150	0178
91B	0144
91B(ZENER)	1301
91BGRN	0144
91C	0016
91C-US	OEM
91D	0016
91D5R11	OEM
91D9R11GH	OEM
91E	0016
91F	0144
91H	OEM
91L11PC	OEM
91N1	0123
91N1B	0007
91RC5	0603
91RC10	0603
91RC20	0603
91RC30	0605
91RC40	0605
91RC60	0605
91RC80	0463
91RC100	0463
91RC110	0463
91RC120	0463
91RL10	OEM
91RL20	OEM
91RL30	OEM
91RL40	OEM
91RL50	OEM
91RL60	OEM
91RM10	OEM
91RM20	OEM
91RM30	OEM
91RM40	OEM
91RM50	OEM
91RM60	OEM
91T1	OEM
91T2	OEM
91T3	OEM
91T4	OEM
91T5	OEM
91T6	0111

DEVICE TYPE	REPL CODE
91TB1-JE00	OEM
91TB1-JH00	OEM
91TB1-LE00	OEM
91TB1-LH00	OEM
91TB1-NE00	OEM
91TB1-NH00	OEM
91TB2-JE00	OEM
91TB2-JH00	OEM
91TB2-LE00	OEM
91TB2-LH00	OEM
91TB2-NE00	OEM
91TB2-NH00	OEM
91TB3-JE00	OEM
91TB3-JH00	OEM
91TB3-LE00	OEM
91TB3-LH00	OEM
91TB3-NE00	OEM
91TB3-NH00	OEM
91TB4-JE00	OEM
91TB4-JH00	OEM
91TB4-LE00	OEM
91TB4-LH00	OEM
91TB4-NE00	OEM
91TB4-NH00	OEM
91TB5-JE00	OEM
91TB5-JH00	OEM
91TB5-LE00	OEM
91TB5-LH00	OEM
91TB5-NE00	OEM
91TB5-NH00	OEM
91TB6-JE00	OEM
91TB6-JH00	OEM
91TB6-LE00	OEM
91TB6-LH00	OEM
91TB6-NE00	OEM
91TB6-NH00	OEM
91TB7	OEM
91TB7-JE00	OEM
91TB7-JH00	OEM
91TB7-LE00	OEM
91TB7-LH00	OEM
91TB7-NE00	OEM
91TB7-NH00	OEM
91TB8-JE00	OEM
91TB8-JH00	OEM
91TB8-LE00	OEM
91TB8-LH00	OEM
91TB8-NE00	OEM
91TB8-NH00	OEM
91TB9	OEM
91TB9-JE00	OEM
91TB9-JH00	OEM
91TB9-LE00	OEM
91TB9-LH00	OEM
91TB9-NE00	OEM
91TB9-NH00	OEM
91TB10-JE00	OEM
91TB10-JH00	OEM
91TB10-LE00	OEM
91TB10-LH00	OEM
91TB10-NE00	OEM
91TB10-NH00	OEM
91TB11	OEM
91TB11-JE00	OEM
91TB11-JH00	OEM
91TB11-LE00	OEM
91TB11-LH00	OEM
91TB11-NE00	OEM
91TB11-NH00	OEM
91TB12-JE00	OEM
91TB12-JH00	OEM
91TB12-LE00	OEM
91TB12-LH00	OEM
91TB12-NE00	OEM
91TB12-NH00	OEM
92	OEM
92-1	0143
92-1-70	0435
92-1-70-12	0435
92-1-70-12-7	0435
92-1A	0435
92-1A0	0435
92-1A0R	0435
92-1A1	0435
92-1A2	0435
92-1A3	0435
92-1A3P	0435
92-1A4	0435
92-1A4-7	0435
92-1A4-7B	0435
92-1A5	0435
92-1A5L	0435
92-1A6	0435
92-1A6-1	0435
92-1A7	0435
92-1A7-1	0435
92-1A8	0435
92-1A9	0435
92-1A9G	0435
92-1A19	0435
92-1A21	0435
92-1A82	0435
92-2	OEM
92-10	0435
92-11	0435
92-11-1	0015
92-12	0435
92-13	0435
92-14	0435

DEVICE TYPE	REPL CODE
92-15	0435
92-16	0435
92-17	0435
92-18	0435
92-19	0435
92-64-1	0907
92-1001	0143
92A11-1	0015
92B12-2	0015
92BIC	1335
92BLC	1335
92D5R11	OEM
92D7R11	OEM
92D9R11GH	OEM
92GU01	4945
92GU01A	4945
92GU05	4945
92GU06	4945
92GU45	3749
92GU45A	3749
92GU51	1587
92GU51A	1587
92GU55	1587
92GU56	1587
92L102-2	0015
92N1	0144
92N1B	0144
92PE37A	3882
92PE37B	3882
92PE37C	3882
92PE77A	4468
92PE77B	4468
92PE77C	4468
92PE487	0261
92PE488	0261
92PE489	0261
92PU01	4939
92PU01A	4939
92PU05	4945
92PU06	5995
92PU07	4945
92PU10	0261
92PU36	3718
92PU36A	3718
92PU36B	3718
92PU36C	3718
92PU45	5002
92PU45A	5002
92PU51	1587
92PU51A	1587
92PU55	1587
92PU56	1587
92PU57	1587
92PU100	4945
92PU200	1587
92PU391	3708
92PU392	3708
92PU393	3708
92RC5	OEM
92RC10	OEM
92RC20	OEM
92RC30	0217
92RC40	OEM
92RC60	0217
92RC80	OEM
92RC100	OEM
92RC110	OEM
92RC120	OEM
92RL10	OEM
92RL20	OEM
92RL30	OEM
92RL40	OEM
92RL50	OEM
92RL60	OEM
92RM10	OEM
92RM20	OEM
92RM30	OEM
92RM40	OEM
92RM50	OEM
92RM60	OEM
92T6	0111
93-13	0133
93-188	2004
93-302	0015
93A1-20	0015
93A1-21	0015
93A1D-1	0015
93A2	0229
93A3D-2	0015
93A4-2	0015
93A4-4	0015
93A5-2	0196
93A5-8	0196
93A5-9	0196
93A5-10	0196
93A6-1	0015
93A6-2	0015
93A8-1	0143
93A8-4	OEM
93A9	0211
93A9-1	0004
93A9-2	0004
93A9-3	0279
93A9-4	0279
93A10-1	0015
93A11	0015
93A12	0015
93A12-1	0015
93A12-3	0015

DEVICE TYPE	REPL CODE
93A15-1	0229
93A15-10	0196
93A25-1	0143
93A25-2	0123
93A25-3	0143
93A25-B	0143
93A27-1	0143
93A27-2	0015
93A27-3	0133
93A27-8	0133
93A30-1	0015
93A30-3	0015
93A31-1	0133
93A33-1	0143
93A36-1	0030
93A38-1	0143
93A39-1	0398
93A39-2	0157
93A39-3	0012
93A39-5	0526
93A39-6	0170
93A39-7	0526
93A39-8	0398
93A39-11	0025
93A39-12	0137
93A39-13	0313
93A39-14	1596
93A39-15	0016
93A39-17	0127
93A39-19	0157
93A39-21	OEM
93A39-24	0002
93A39-25	0778
93A39-26	0157
93A39-28	0213
93A39-30	0170
93A39-31	0361
93A39-34	0451
93A39-35	0346
93A39-37	0213
93A39-40	0039
93A39-43	0137
93A39-44	0313
93A39-45	0398
93A39-48	1639
93A39-49	0296
93A39-50	0416
93A40-1	0102
93A40-2	OEM
93A41-2	0019
93A41-5	0143
93A42-1	0015
93A42-2	0015
93A42-7	0015
93A42-8	0015
93A43-1	0911
93A43-2	0911
93A43-4	0911
93A44-2	0911
93A45-1	0015
93A45-2	0015
93A47	0015
93A48-1	0133
93A48-2	0015
93A51-3	0015
93A52-1	0015
93A52-2	0133
93A52-7	0102
93A53-1	0469
93A53-2	0469
93A53-3	0015
93A55-1	0313
93A56-1	0015
93A57-1	0769
93A58-1	0015
93A59-1	0911
93A59-2	0911
93A59-10	OEM
93A60-1	0102
93A60-2	0015
93A60-3	0102
93A60-5	0133
93A60-6	0133
93A60-7	0023
93A60-8	0015
93A60-9	0015
93A60-10	0102
93A60-11	0102
93A60-14	0015
93A60-80	0015
93A61-1	OEM
93A61-2	OEM
93A63-1	0030
93A63-2	0911
93A63-3	OEM
93A63-4	OEM
93A64-1	0133
93A64-2	0133
93A64-3	0133
93A64-4	OEM
93A64-5	0133
93A64-7	0133
93A64-8	0133
93A65-1	OEM
93A67-1	0015
93A68	OEM
93A69-1	0102
93A69-2	0133
93A70-1	OEM

DEVICE TYPE	REPL CODE
93A71-1	0102
93A75-1	0469
93A76-1	0030
93A76-6	OEM
93A77-1	0143
93A78-1	0015
93A79-6	0071
93A80-1	0137
93A83-1	0123
93A91-1	1493
93A91-2	1493
93A91-3	1493
93A91-4	1493
93A93-1	0374
93A93-2	0374
93A96-1	0190
93A96-2	0190
93A96-3	0190
93A97-1	0015
93A97-3	0015
93A98-1	2956
93A99-2	2956
93A99-3	2956
93A99-7	1048
93A99-8	1048
93A102-2	0361
93A104-1	0015
93A104-2	4350
93A105-1	0143
93A106-1	OEM
93A106-2	OEM
93A106-3	OEM
93A107-2	0149
93A110-1	0143
93A111-1	6429
93A112-1	0071
93A120	0015
93A664-2	0133
93B1-1	0015
93B1-2	0015
93B1-3	0015
93B1-4	0015
93B1-5	0015
93B1-6	0015
93B1-7	0015
93B1-8	0015
93B1-9	0015
93B1-10	0015
93B1-11	0015
93B1-12	0015
93B1-13	0015
93B1-14	0015
93B1-15	0015
93B1-16	0015
93B1-17	0015
93B1-18	0015
93B1-20	0015
93B1-21	0015
93B2-1	0015
93B3-3	1024
93B3-3,4	1024
93B3-4	1024
93B5	0196
93B5-1	0196
93B5-2	0196
93B5-3	0196
93B5-3-6	0196
93B5-3-8	0196
93B5-3-9	0196
93B5-4	0196
93B5-5	0196
93B5-6	0196
93B5-7	0196
93B5-8	0196
93B5-9	0196
93B5-10	0196
93B6	0196
93B8	0196
93B8-1	0143
93B9	0196
93B12	0015
93B12-1	0015
93B12-2	0015
93B12-3	0015
93B15-1	0229
93B19-1	0469
93B20-1	0229
93B20-2	0229
93B20-3	0229
93B21-5	OEM
93B22-3	1024
93B24-1	0015
93B24-2	0015
93B24-3	0015
93B25-1	0143
93B25-2	0143
93B25-3	0143
93B27-1	0143
93B27-2	0015
93B27-3	0123
93B27-4	0133
93B27-5	0133
93B30-1	0015
93B30-3	0015
93B34-2	0015
93B36-1	0030
93B38-1	0143
93B38-5	0143
93B39-1	0012

DEVICE TYPE	REPL CODE
93B39-2	0162
93B39-3	0012
93B39-4	0436
93B39-5	0526
93B39-6	0170
93B39-7	0526
93B39-12	0137
93B39-13	0137
93B39-31	0361
93B41	0143
93B41-1	0143
93B41-2	0143
93B41-3	0143
93B41-4	0015
93B41-5	0030
93B41-6	0015
93B41-8	0015
93B41-12	0015
93B41-14	0015
93B41-15	0030
93B41-20	0229
93B41-29	0143
93B42-1	0015
93B42-2	0015
93B42-3	0015
93B42-4	0015
93B42-5	0015
93B42-6	0015
93B42-7	0015
93B42-8	0015
93B42-9	0015
93B42-10	0015
93B42-11	0015
93B42-12	0015
93B44-1	0911
93B45-1	0023
93B45-2	0015
93B45-3	0071
93B46-1	0143
93B47-1	0015
93B48-1	0133
93B48-2	0133
93B48-3	0133
93B48-4	0133
93B51-3	0015
93B52-1	0102
93B52-1-55	OEM
93B52-2	0102
93B52-27	0072
93B53-1	0015
93B53-2	0469
93B57-1	0769
93B58-1	0102
93B59-1	0911
93B60-3	0102
93B60-8	0133
93B60-10	0102
93B60-11	0102
93B63-1	OEM
93B63-2	OEM
93B64-1	0133
93B64-2	0133
93B65-1	0071
93B65-2	0071
93B67-1	0102
93B68-14	0911
93B71-1	0071
93B77-1	0143
93B91-1	1493
93B96-1	0190
93B96-2	0190
93B97-1	0015
93B122	0015
93B123	0015
93B130-1	OEM
93BLC	2242
93C	3032
93C1-20	0015
93C1-21	0015
93C1-2021	0469
93C2-6	0143
93C5-1	0479
93C5-2	0479
93C5-3	0479
93C5-4	0479
93C5-5	0196
93C5-6	0196
93C5-7	0196
93C5-8	0196
93C5-9	0196
93C5-10	0196
93C6-7	0196
93C6-9	0196
93C7-1	0143
93C7-2	0133
93C7-3	0133
93C8-1	0143
93C12-1	0015
93C12-2	0015
93C12-3	0015
93C16-2	0015
93C18-1	0071
93C18-2	0071
93C19-1	0015
93C21-1	0143
93C21-2	0143
93C21-3	0143
93C21-4	0143
93C21-5	0143

168 If replacement code is OEM, contact original manufacturer for replacement.

DEVICE TYPE	REPL CODE
93C21-6	0143
93C21-7	0143
93C21-8	0143
93C22-1	1024
93C22-3	1024
93C24-1	0015
93C24-2	0015
93C24-3	0015
93C24-4	0015
93C25-2	0123
93C25-3	0143
93C25-4	0015
93C26-1	0015
93C26-2	0015
93C26-3	0015
93C26-4	0015
93C26-5	0015
93C26-6	1073
93C26-7	0196
93C26-7,9	0196
93C26-8	0015
93C26-9	0196
93C26-10	0196
93C26-11	0196
93C27-1	0143
93C27-2	0133
93C27-3	0133
93C27-4	0015
93C27-5	0143
93C27-6	0143
93C27-7	0133
93C28-4	0015
93C30-1	0015
93C30-3	0015
93C39-1	0188
93C39-2	0052
93C39-3	0012
93C39-4	0436
93C39-5	0526
93C39-6	0137
93C39-7	0526
93C39-8	0398
93C39-9	0644
93C39-10	0644
93C39-11	0198
93C39-12	0137
93C39-13	0137
93C39-14	0644
93C39-19	0157
93C39-24	0002
93C39-25	0778
93C39-28	0213
93C39-43	0137
93C39-45	0398
93C39-49	0296
93C39-51	0466
93C39-52	OEM
93C39-58	0398
93C39-77	0041
93C39-79	0466
93C39-80	0057
93C39-106	OEM
93C40	1293
93C40-1	1293
93C42-2	0015
93C42-7	0015
93C46	OEM
93C46AN	OEM
93C46N	OEM
93C51-3	0479
93C52-1	0102
93C52-1-55	OEM
93C52-5	0015
93C52-9	0015
93C52-9-52T	0015
93C52-9-55	0071
93C52-10	0015
93C52-14	0023
93C52-15	0015
93C52-27	0071
93C52-952T	OEM
93C53-2	0469
93C55-1	0143
93C59	0196
93C59-2	0196
93C60-3	0102
93C60-5	0133
93C60-6	0133
93C60-7	0023
93C60-9	0031
93C60-9-55	0023
93C60-10	0102
93C60-21	0023
93C60-21-52T	0023
93C60-21-55	0023
93C60-21-64	0023
93C60-26	0023
93C60-27	0023
93C60-27-52T	0023
93C64-1	0124
93C64-2	0124
93C64-3	0124
93C64-5	0133
93C64-10	0023
93C64-11	0124
93C64-11H	0124
93C64-11H-52T	0124
93C65-11H	OEM
93C69-1	0102
93C77-1	0143
93C91-2	1493
93C93-1	0374
93C97-1	0015
93C112-1	0497
93C118-1	0071
93C118-2	0071
93C218	0143
93C267	0479
93CG9-1	0102
93D8-1	0143
93D39-7	0526
93D39-43	0137
93D39-43-52T	0137
93D39-51	0466
93D39-52-52T	OEM
93D39-54	0053
93D39-54-52T	0053
93D39-67	OEM
93D39-73	0157
93D39-77-52T	0041
93D39-79-52T	0466
93D39-80	0057
93D39-80-52T	0057
93D39-106-52T	OEM
93D52-1	0015
93D60-7	0023
93D60-21-52T	0023
93D60-21-55	0023
93D60-21-64	0023
93D60-27-52T	0023
93D64-2	0124
93D91-1	1493
93D91-2	1493
93D91-3	1493
93D91-4	1493
93D91-5	1493
93D91-6	1493
93D96-1	0190
93D96-2	0190
93D96-3	0190
93D98-1	2956
93D99-1	2956
93D99-2	2956
93D99-3	2956
93D99-4	2956
93D99-5	1048
93D99-6	1048
93D99-7	1048
93D99-8	1048
93D99-9	2956
93D112-57	0911
93ERH-1X1128	0167
93ERH-DX0155//	0023
93ERH-DX0156//	0015
93EVHD1N4148//	0124
93H00DC	OEM
93H00DM	OEM
93H00FC	OEM
93H00FM	OEM
93H00PC	OEM
93H72DC	OEM
93H72DM	OEM
93H72FC	OEM
93H72FM	OEM
93H72PC	OEM
93H87DC	2557
93H87PC	2557
93H183DC	4329
93H193PC	4329
93K2-1	0196
93L00DC	1305
93L00DM	1305
93L00FC	OEM
93L00FM	OEM
93L00PC	1511
93L01DC	OEM
93L01FM	OEM
93L01PC	OEM
93L02DM	OEM
93L08DC	2114
93L08DM	2114
93L08FM	OEM
93L08PC	2114
93L09DC	OEM
93L09DM	OEM
93L09FM	OEM
93L09PC	OEM
93L3-1	0229
93L3-2	0229
93L5-1	0015
93L5-2	0229
93L5-3	0087
93L5-4	0015
93L5-5	0087
93L5-6	0015
93L5-7	0015
93L5-8	0087
93L10DC	OEM
93L10DM	OEM
93L10FM	OEM
93L10PC	OEM
93L11DC	OEM
93L11DM	OEM
93L11FM	OEM
93L12DC	OEM
93L12DM	OEM
93L12FM	OEM
93L12PC	OEM
93L14DC	OEM
93L14DM	OEM
93L14FM	OEM
93L14PC	OEM
93L16DC	2660
93L16DM	OEM
93L16FM	OEM
93L16PC	2660
93L18DC	OEM
93L18DM	OEM
93L18FM	OEM
93L18PC	OEM
93L21DC	OEM
93L21DM	OEM
93L21FM	OEM
93L21PC	OEM
93L22DC	OEM
93L22DM	OEM
93L22FM	OEM
93L22PC	OEM
93L24DC	OEM
93L24DM	OEM
93L24FM	OEM
93L24PC	OEM
93L28DC	OEM
93L28DM	OEM
93L28FC	OEM
93L28FM	OEM
93L28PC	OEM
93L34DC	OEM
93L34DM	OEM
93L34FM	OEM
93L34PC	OEM
93L38DC	OEM
93L38DM	OEM
93L38FC	OEM
93L38FM	OEM
93L38PC	OEM
93L40DC	OEM
93L40DM	OEM
93L40FM	OEM
93L40PC	OEM
93L41DC	OEM
93L41DM	OEM
93L41FM	OEM
93L41PC	OEM
93L60DC	OEM
93L60DM	OEM
93L60FM	OEM
93L60PC	OEM
93L66DC	OEM
93L66DM	OEM
93L66FM	OEM
93L66PC	OEM
93L101-2	0015
93L102-2	0015
93L103-4	0015
93L104-5	0087
93L107-2	0015
93L415DC	OEM
93L415DM	OEM
93L415FC	OEM
93L415FM	OEM
93L415PC	OEM
93L422A	OEM
93L422DC	OEM
93L422DM	OEM
93L422FC	OEM
93L422FM	OEM
93L422N	OEM
93L425DC	OEM
93L425DM	OEM
93L425FM	OEM
93L425PC	OEM
93M8-1	0229
93N9-1	1493
93P1AA	0037
93S00DC	OEM
93S00DM	OEM
93S00FC	OEM
93S00FM	OEM
93S00PC	OEM
93S10DC	OEM
93S10DM	OEM
93S10FM	OEM
93S10PC	OEM
93S12DC	OEM
93S12DM	OEM
93S12FM	OEM
93S12PC	OEM
93S16DC	OEM
93S16DM	OEM
93S16FM	OEM
93S16PC	OEM
93S21DC	OEM
93S21DM	OEM
93S21FM	OEM
93S21PC	OEM
93S41DC	OEM
93S41DM	OEM
93S41FM	OEM
93S41PC	OEM
93S42DC	OEM
93S42DM	OEM
93S42FM	OEM
93S42PC	OEM
93S43DC	OEM
93S43DM	OEM
93S43FM	OEM
93S43PC	OEM
93S46DC	OEM
93S46DM	OEM
93S46FM	OEM
93S46PC	OEM
93S47DC	OEM
93S47DM	OEM
93S47FM	OEM
93S47PC	OEM
93S48DC	OEM
93S48DM	OEM
93S48FM	OEM
93S48PC	OEM
93S62DC	OEM
93S62DM	OEM
93S62FM	OEM
93S62PC	OEM
93S153DC	2138
93S157DC	1685
93S157PC	1685
93S158DC	2141
93S158PC	2141
93S174DC	2119
93S174PC	2119
93S175DC	2128
93S175PC	2128
93S194DC	1920
93S194PC	1920
93SC165	0103
93SC165133	0103
93SC165133A	0103
93SE165	0130
93T6	0111
93T4100203100	0151
93T4105002132	0456
93T4120265210	0057
93T4120280156	0143
93T4120290136	0143
93T4120482210	0030
93T4125005150	0999
93T4130060052	0015
93T4150133000	4084
93T4150182072	2052
93X60-9	OEM
93Z510DC	OEM
93Z510DM	OEM
93Z510FC	OEM
93Z510FM	OEM
93Z510LC	OEM
93Z510LM	OEM
93Z510PC	OEM
93Z511DC	OEM
93Z511DM	OEM
93Z511FC	OEM
93Z511FM	OEM
93Z511LM	OEM
93Z511PC	OEM
93.20.709	0287
93.20.714	0287
93.24.401	0143
93.24.601	0143
93.24.604	0143
94-42-9	0143
94-1066-1	0015
94A-1A6-4	0160
94A60-3	OEM
94A64-1	OEM
94A80-1	0137
94BLC	0817
94N1	0016
94N1B	0016
94N1R	0016
94N1V	0086
94N2	0016
94T1	0279
94T2	OEM
94T3	OEM
94T4	OEM
94T5	OEM
94TB1-JH00	OEM
94TB1-LE00	OEM
94TB1-NE00	OEM
94TB1-NH00	OEM
94TB2-JE00	OEM
94TB2-JH00	OEM
94TB2-LE00	OEM
94TB2-LH00	OEM
94TB2-NE00	OEM
94TB2-NH00	OEM
94TB3-JE00	OEM
94TB3-JH00	OEM
94TB3-LE00	OEM
94TB3-LH00	OEM
94TB3-NE00	OEM
94TB3-NH00	OEM
94TB4-JE00	OEM
94TB4-JH00	OEM
94TB4-LE00	OEM
94TB4-LH00	OEM
94TB4-NH00	OEM
94TB5-JE00	OEM
94TB5-JH00	OEM
94TB5-LE00	OEM
94TB5-LH00	OEM
94TB5-NE00	OEM
94TB5-NH00	OEM
94TB6-JE00	OEM
94TB6-JH00	OEM
94TB6-LE00	OEM
94TB6-LH00	OEM
94TB6-NE00	OEM
94TB6-NH00	OEM
94TB7	OEM
94TB7-JE00	OEM
94TB7-JH00	OEM
94TB7-LE00	OEM
94TB7-LH00	OEM
94TB7-NE00	OEM
94TB7-NH00	OEM
94TB8-JE00	OEM
94TB8-JH00	OEM
94TB8-LE00	OEM
94TB8-LH00	OEM
94TB8-NE00	OEM
94TB8-NH00	OEM
94TB9	OEM
94TB9-JE00	OEM
94TB9-JH00	OEM
94TB9-LE00	OEM
94TB9-LH00	OEM
94TB9-NE00	OEM
94TB9-NH00	OEM
94TB10-JE00	OEM
94TB10-JH00	OEM
94TB10-LE00	OEM
94TB10-LH00	OEM
94TB10-NE00	OEM
94TB10-NH00	OEM
95	0124
95/1016	OEM
95/1032	OEM
95/4000/2	OEM
95/4000/4	OEM
95/4005/2	OEM
95/4005/3	OEM
95/5032	OEM
95/6011	OEM
95/6110	OEM
95/6440	OEM
95-108	0050
95-110	0050
95-111	0136
95-112	0595
95-113	0595
95-114	0595
95-116	0050
95-117	0050
95-118	0050
95-119	0050
95-120	0050
95-120A	0279
95-121	0050
95-122	0050
95-123	0050
95-124	0050
95-125	0144
95-126	0144
95-127	0144
95-128	0144
95-129	0144
95-130	0144
95-131	0144
95-201	0004
95-202	0208
95-203	0004
95-204	0004
95-208	0004
95-209	0004
95-212	0004
95-213	0004
95-214	0004
95-216	0016
95-217	0004
95-218	0004
95-220	0086
95-221	0016
95-222-1	0004
95-222-2	0208
95-223	0144
95-224-1	0004
95-224-2	0208
95-225	0016
95-226-003	0126
95-226-004	0086
95-226-1	0126
95-226-2	0016
95-226-3	0126
95-226-4	0086
95-227	0016
95-250	0160
95-251	0160
95-252	0142
95-252-1	0142
95-252-2	0142
95-252-3	0142
95-252-4	0142
95-296	0016
95-11410100	0004
95-11410200	0004
95-11410900	0004
95-11413500	0004
95-11414000	0211
95-11511500	0071
95A5-10	OEM
95B5-8	0196
95ERRMCG044115	OEM
95ERRMCG044117	OEM
95ERRMCG044118	OEM
95ERRMCG044119	OEM
95ERRMCG526A15	OEM
95ERRMCG526A17	0133
95ERRMCG526A18	OEM
95ERRMCG526A21	0860
95ERRMCG575A15	OEM
95ERRMCG575A17	0133
95ERRMCG575A18	OEM
95ERRMCG575A21	0860
95G	0023
95H00DC	OEM
95KUAB0015AM	0676
95KUAC0004AZ	0076
95KUAD0031SZ	1203
95KUAD0036MZ	3107
95KUB0429BZ	OEM
95KUBC0112AZ	0015
95KUBC0150BZ	0015
95KUBC0215BK	0080
95KUBC0215BZ	0080
95KUBC0216CZ	OEM
95KUBC112AZ	0015
95KUBC216CZ	OEM
95KUBD0115AZ	0253
95KUBD0128AZ	0371
95KUBD0429BZ	3854
95KUBDAC5R6B	5304
95KUBDAS5R6B	3854
95KUCB0027AZ	0619
95KUCC0013DZ	OEM
95KUCZ0051ZZ	OEM
95KUCZ0097ZZ	OEM
96-0008	0143
96-138-2	0144
96-5005-01	0283
96-5007-01	0143
96-5007-02	0123
96-5022-01	0015
96-5022-1	0015
96-5023-01	0015
96-5026-01	0160
96-5032-01	0004
96-5033-01	0004
96-5033-02	0004
96-5033-03	0004
96-5033-04	0004
96-5045-01	0160
96-5046-01	0015
96-5059-01	0143
96-5062-01	0050
96-5064-01	0160
96-5076-01	0164
96-5080-02	0016
96-5081-01	0160
96-5082-01	0015
96-5085-01	0004
96-5085-02	0004
96-5086-02	0160
96-5088-01	0015
96-5091-01	0137
96-5093-01	0123
96-5093-02	0123
96-5093-03	0123
96-5094-01	0123
96-5094-01(TRANSISTO	0136
96-5095-01	0050
96-5096-01	0015
96-5098-01	0004
96-5099-01	0050
96-5100-01	0160
96-5101-01	0004
96-5102-01	0004
96-5103-01	0015
96-5106-01	0242
96-5107-01	0086
96-5107-02	0086
96-5109-01	0015
96-5109-02	0015
96-5110-02	0002
96-5110-03	0002
96-5112-01	0087
96-5113-01	0015
96-5115-01	0016
96-5115-02	0016
96-5115-03	0016
96-5115-04	0016
96-5115-05	0016
96-5116-01	0170
96-5117-01	0103
96-5117-91	0103
96-5118-01	0133
96-5120-01	0299
96-5124-02	0644
96-5125-01	0160
96-5131-01	0007
96-5132-01	0142
96-5133-01-02	0137
96-5133-02	0137
96-5135-01	0142
96-5138-01	0050
96-5139-01	0050
96-5140-01	0050
96-5141-01	0050
96-5143-01	0160
96-5143-02	0160
96-5148-01	0160
96-5149-01	0242
96-5152-01	0016
96-5152-03	0016
96-5153-01	0016
96-5153-03	0016
96-5155-01	0160
96-5161-01	0590
96-5162-03	0103
96-5162-04	0103
96-5163-01	0007
96-5164-02	0103
96-5164-03	0103
96-5165-01	0126
96-5166-01	0015
96-5170-01	0086
96-5174-01	0007
96-5175-01	0007
96-5176-01	0126
96-5177-01	0016
96-5178-01	0071
96-5180-01	0086
96-5180-02	0086
96-5184-01	0242
96-5187-01	0016
96-5190-01	0178
96-5191-01	0178
96-5192-01	0160
96-5193-01	0087
96-5194-01	0087
96-5195-01	0916
96-5196-01	0015
96-5198-01	0007
96-5199-01	0007
96-5201-01	0103
96-5203-01	0086
96-5204-01	0086
96-5205-01	0208
96-5207-01	0103
96-5208-01	0086
96-5209-01	0126
96-5213-01	0016
96-5214-01	1129
96-5215-01	0037
96-5219-01	0283
96-5220-01	4100
96-5228-01	0016
96-5229-01	0016
96-5231-01	0086
96-5235-01	0007
96-5236-01	0007
96-5237-01	0016
96-5238-01	0627
96-5238-02	0627
96-5241-01	0916
96-5244-01	0086
96-5246-01	1116
96-5248-04	0137
96-5248-09	0451
96-5248-11	0451
96-5249-01	0234
96-5249-02	0205
96-5249-03	0256
96-5250-01	0234
96-5250-03	0305
96-5250-06	0247
96-5250-07	0225
96-5252-01	0086
96-5254-01	0133
96-5255-01	0016
96-5256-01	0086
96-5257-01	0016
96-5258-01	0688
96-5259-01	0007
96-5260-01	0007
96-5269-01	2123
96-5284-01	0074
96-5334-04	0256
96-5334-05	0262
96-5344-02	0864
96-5344-03	0247
96-51430-02	0160
96E1S953	0133
96E1S2076A	0124
96E2SA733	0006
96E2SC945	0076
96E2SC1213	0191
96E2SC2827	0723
96EP	OEM
96ERD5.6EB2	0253
96ESM-1A-04FR	0023
96ESM-3-02FR	0031
96L02	1459
96L02DC	1459
96L02DM	1459
96L02FM	OEM
96L02PC	1459
96LS02DC	2906
96LS02DM	2906
96LS02FM	OEM
96LS02PC	2906
96LS32DC	OEM
96LS32DM	OEM
96LS32FM	OEM
96LS32PC	OEM
96LS42DC	OEM
96LS42DM	OEM
96LS42PC	OEM
96N(AIRLINE)	0144
96N1	0142
96N927	0144
96N932	0144
96NPT	0144

If replacement code is OEM, contact original manufacturer for replacement.

169

DEVICE TYPE	REPL CODE
96S02DC	4228
96S02PC	4228
96XZ0778-44N	0143
96XZ0868/15X	0143
96XZ077844N	0143
96XZ778/21N	0143
96XZ778/27N	0196
96XZ778/44N	0143
96XZ801/06N	0160
96XZ801/10N	0160
96XZ801/14N	0016
96XZ801/34X	0160
96XZ801/37N	0050
96XZ801/50N	0004
96XZ6050/25N	0007
96XZ6051-28N	0136
96XZ6051-35N	0136
96XZ6051-36N	0136
96XZ6052/52N	0016
96XZ6052-52N	0079
96XZ6053/11N	0016
96XZ6053/24N	0164
96XZ6053/27N	0004
96XZ6053/35N	0016
96XZ6053/36N	0016
96XZ6053/38N	0086
96XZ6053/51N	0004
96XZ6053-09N	0211
96XZ6053-10N	0136
96XZ6053-11N	0079
96XZ6053-24N	0136
96XZ6053-27N	0211
96XZ6053-51N	0164
96XZ6054/45X	0816
97	OEM
97-3	1293
97A83	0085
97A283-11	OEM
97EPA	OEM
97EPB	0595
97N2	0595
97N2U	0208
97P1	0211
97P1U	0164
98-1	0004
98-2	0004
98-3	0004
98-4	0004
98-5	0004
98-6	0004
98-7	0004
98-301	0015
98-302	0229
98A40-2	OEM
98A40-7	OEM
98A40-17	OEM
98A12518	0015
98B5-4	0479
98DM	OEM
98M2SA1162Y/G	1731
98M2SC1318-R/	0155
98M2SC2712Y/G	0719
98M2SD601A//	0719
98M2SD601A///	0719
98MDT144EK//	3439
98M-HSM2838C/	OEM
98M-IMT1/////	OEM
98MMA157/////	OEM
98MMA223/////	OEM
98N2P	2736
98P1P	0222
98T2	0079
99-101	0136
99-102	0136
99-103	0136
99-104	0004
99-105	0050
99-106	0050
99-107	0050
99-108	0050
99-109-1	0016
99-109-2	0016
99-120	0050
99-121	0050
99-201	0004
99-202	0004
99-203	0004
99-PWR	0085
99AT6	0211
99B5	0211
99BA6	0279
99BE6	0279
99E16-1	3384
99K7	0595
99L-4A6-1	0004
99L6	0038
99L6(SHARP)	0086
99P1	0037
99P1M	0037
99P2	0126
99P2B	0126
99P3AA	0004
99P6	0688
99P10	0037
99P117	0126
99PLM	0126
99S001	0160
99S002	0004
99S003	0004

DEVICE TYPE	REPL CODE
99S004	0164
99S004A	0004
99S005	0004
99S006	0050
99S007	0050
99S07	0595
99S010	0004
99S010A	0004
99S011	0004
99S011A	0004
99S012	0016
99S012A	0016
99S012E	0016
99S014	0160
99S014A	0160
99S015	0160
99S016	0144
99S016-1	0144
99S017	0144
99S018	0144
99S018A	0144
99S019	0144
99S019A	0144
99S019B	0144
99S020	0198
99S022	0627
99S025	0155
99S025A	0016
99S031	0007
99S032	0007
99S032(3RD-LF)	0326
99S033	0111
99S033-40	1371
99S034	0855
99S035	0016
99S036	0016
99S036(TELEDYNE)	0086
99S037	0144
99S038	0016
99S039	0037
99S040	0855
99S041	0212
99S042	0823
99S044	0007
99S045	0349
99S045A	0212
99S046	0212
99S047	0178
99S049	2593
99S053	0696
99S055	0224
99S056	0224
99S057	0599
99S060-1	0855
99S061-1	0855
99S063-1	1698
99S067-1	0212
99S070-1	0855
99S073	0126
99S074	0086
99S075	0419
99S077-1	0855
99S079	0065
99S079-1	0065
99S082-1	0167
99S083-1	0419
99S084-1	0037
99S085	0016
99S087-1	0233
99S090-1	0144
99S091-1	0546
99S092-1	0378
99S094-1	0348
99S095-1	0350
99S096-1	0661
99S097-1	0797
99S099-1	0919
99S0102-1	0283
99S100-1	0042
99S101-1	0233
99S102-1	0264
99S103-1	0130
99S103-2	0130
99S103-3	0130
99S105-1	0161
99SA7	0208
99SK5	0595
99SK7	0595
99S022	0627
99SQ7	0595
100-001-01/2228-3	0229
100-003-40/228-3	0143
100-003-40/2228-3	0143
100-007-10/2228/3	0133
100-007-13/228-3	0143
100-007-13/2228-3	0143
100-008-53/2228-3	0030
100-0051	0143
100-00310-09	0133
100-00340-00	0143
100-00910-07	0019
100-00914-10	0123
100-011-20	0133
100-011-50/2228-3	0133
100-0110-01	OEM
100-0124	0143
100-0125	0143
100-0495-15	0006
100-0673-04	0148

DEVICE TYPE	REPL CODE
100-01110-01	0133
100-01120-09	0133
100-1	0546
100-1A	OEM
100-5	OEM
100-10	0091
100-11	0133
100-12	0019
100-13	0015
100-14	0012
100-15	0015
100-120	0133
100-125	0133
100-130	0133
100-132-00	0015
100-135	0091
100-136	0019
100-137	0133
100-138	0015
100-139	0012
100-140	OEM
100-180	0019
100-181	0123
100-184	0133
100-215	0019
100-216	0133
100-217	0023
100-218	0025
100-219	0244
100-435	0133
100-436	0019
100-437	0062
100-438	0023
100-439	0143
100-520	0023
100-521	0165
100-522	0012
100-523	0012
100-524	0139
100-525	0398
100-526	0030
100-527	0023
100-914-10	OEM
100-929-60/2228-3	OEM
100-10121-05	0015
100-10132-00	0015
100-22363-08	0030
100A	0015
100B63	0211
100C	0071
100C05	1076
100C05B	1076
100C025	0733
100C025B	0733
100C050	0733
100C050B	0733
100C3.8-4.4	OEM
100C-4R	0015
100C4.4-5	OEM
100C4.8-5.4	OEM
100C5.4-5.9	OEM
100C5.9-6.4	OEM
100C6-7	OEM
100C6B	OEM
100C6.2-6.8	OEM
100C6.8-7.4	OEM
100C10	0733
100C10B	0733
100C15	0733
100C15B	0733
100C20	0733
100C20B	0733
100C25	0733
100C25B	0733
100C30	0733
100C30B	0733
100C35	0733
100C35B	0733
100C40	0733
100C40B	0733
100C45	0733
100C45B	0733
100C50	0733
100C50B	0733
100C60	0733
100C60B	0733
100C70	0733
100C70B	0733
100C80	0733
100C80B	0733
100C90	0733
100C90B	0733
100C100	0733
100C100B	0733
100C110	0733
100C110B	0733
100C120	0733
100C120B	0733
100C130	1878
100C130B	1878
100C140	1878
100C140B	1878
100C150	1878
100C150B	1878
100C160	1878
100C160B	1878
100C170	OEM
100C170B	OEM
100C180	OEM

DEVICE TYPE	REPL CODE
100C180B	OEM
100D10	0071
100D20	OEM
100D30	OEM
100D40	OEM
100EXD21	OEM
100F20	OEM
100F30	OEM
100F40	OEM
100F50	OEM
100H3	OEM
100HF20	OEM
100HF20F	OEM
100HF20M	OEM
100HF40	OEM
100HF40F	OEM
100HF40M	OEM
100HF60	OEM
100HF60F	OEM
100HF60M	OEM
100HF80	OEM
100HF80F	OEM
100HF80M	OEM
100HF100	OEM
100HF100F	OEM
100HF100M	OEM
100HF120	OEM
100HF120F	OEM
100HF120M	OEM
100HF140	OEM
100HF140F	OEM
100HF140M	OEM
100HF160	OEM
100HF160F	OEM
100HF160M	OEM
100HHFR20	OEM
100HHFR20HFR	OEM
100HHFR20M	OEM
100HHFR40	OEM
100HHFR40HFR	OEM
100HHFR40M	OEM
100HHFR60	OEM
100HHFR60HFR	OEM
100HHFR60M	OEM
100HHFR80	OEM
100HHFR80HFR	OEM
100HHFR80M	OEM
100HHFR100	OEM
100HHFR100HFR	OEM
100HHFR100M	OEM
100HHFR120	OEM
100HHFR120HFR	OEM
100HHFR120M	OEM
100HHFR140	OEM
100HHFR140HFR	OEM
100HHFR140M	OEM
100HHFR160	OEM
100HHFR160HFR	OEM
100HHFR160M	OEM
100J6P41	OEM
100JB05L	5695
100JB1L	5695
100JB2L	5919
100JB4L	5920
100JB6L	5923
100JB8L	5924
100JB10L	4813
100JB12L	OEM
100JD12	OEM
100JH21	OEM
100K10	0071
100K10A	0594
100K10R	1337
100K20	OEM
100K20A	0594
100K20R	1337
100K30	OEM
100K30A	0594
100K30R	1337
100K40A	1975
100K40R	1894
100K50A	1975
100K50R	1894
100K60A	1975
100K60R	1894
100K80A	0652
100K80R	0193
100K100A	0652
100K100R	0193
100KF10	OEM
100KF20	OEM
100KF30	OEM
100L1-1.2	OEM
100L1.05-1.25	OEM
100L1.05-2.5	OEM
100L1.5-1.8	OEM
100L1.6-2	OEM
100L1.25-1.5	OEM
100L6P41	OEM
100L15	OEM
100L20	0344
100L25	OEM
100L30	OEM
100L35	OEM
100L40	OEM
100L45	OEM
100L50	OEM
100L55	OEM
100L60	OEM

DEVICE TYPE	REPL CODE
100L65	OEM
100L70	OEM
100L75	OEM
100L80	OEM
100L85	OEM
100L90	OEM
100L95	OEM
100L100	OEM
100L110	OEM
100L120	OEM
100L130	OEM
100L140	OEM
100L150	OEM
100L160	OEM
100L170	OEM
100L180	OEM
100L190	OEM
100L200	OEM
100L210	OEM
100L220	OEM
100L230	OEM
100L240	OEM
100L250	OEM
100L260	OEM
100L270	OEM
100L280	OEM
100L290	OEM
100L300	OEM
100MAB180	OEM
100MAB200	OEM
100MAB250	OEM
100MLAB160	OEM
100MLAB180	OEM
100MLAB200	OEM
100N1	0007
100N1AS	0007
100N1P	0007
100N1P(SOUND)	0079
100N1P(VID)	0007
100N3	0008
100N3P	0007
100N15A	OEM
100N15A(	OEM
100N20A	OEM
100N20A9	OEM
100N25A	OEM
100N25A9	OEM
100N30A	OEM
100N30A9	OEM
100N35A	OEM
100N35A9	OEM
100N39	OEM
100N40A	OEM
100N40A9	OEM
100N45A9	OEM
100N50A	OEM
100N50A9	OEM
100N55A	OEM
100N55A9	OEM
100N60A	OEM
100N60A9	OEM
100N65A	OEM
100N65A9	OEM
100N70A	OEM
100N70A9	OEM
100N75A	OEM
100N75A9	OEM
100N80A	OEM
100N80A9	OEM
100N85A	OEM
100N85A9	OEM
100N90A	OEM
100N90A9	OEM
100N95A	OEM
100N95A9	OEM
100N100A	OEM
100N100A9	OEM
100N110A	OEM
100N120A	OEM
100N130A	OEM
100N140A	OEM
100N150A	OEM
100N160A	OEM
100N170A	OEM
100N180A	OEM
100N190A	OEM
100N200A	OEM
100N210A	OEM
100N220A	OEM
100N230A	OEM
100N240A	OEM
100N250A	OEM
100P4H	OEM
100P6H	OEM
100P8H	OEM
100P10H	OEM
100P12H	OEM
100P16H	OEM
100PBH	OEM
100PIN-BNC	OEM
100PIN-PP	OEM
100PIN-RM	OEM
100PV-BNC	OEM
100PV-PP	OEM
100PV-RM	OEM
100Q6P41	OEM
100QD21	OEM
100QH21	OEM
100Q-PIN-RM	OEM

DEVICE TYPE	REPL CODE
100R1B	0015
100R2B	0015
100R3B	0015
100R4B	0015
100R5B	0015
100R6B	0015
100R7B	0071
100R8B	0071
100R9B	0071
100R10B	0071
100R11B	0102
100R12B	0102
100R13B	0102
100R14B	0102
100R15B	0017
100R16B	0344
100R18B	0344
100R20B	0344
100R22B	OEM
100R24B	OEM
100R26B	OEM
100R28B	OEM
100R30B	OEM
100R32B	OEM
100R34B	OEM
100R36B	OEM
100R38B	OEM
100R40B	OEM
100R42B	OEM
100R44B	OEM
100R46B	OEM
100R48B	OEM
100R50B	OEM
100S2-2.6	OEM
100S2.5-3	OEM
100S3-3.5	OEM
100S3.2-3.8	OEM
100S5SP	OEM
100S6SP	OEM
100S8SP	OEM
100S10SP	OEM
100S12SP	OEM
100S20	OEM
100S30	OEM
100S40	OEM
100S50	OEM
100SS3-07DC	OEM
100SS3-07SC	OEM
100SS4-07SC	OEM
100SS5-07SC	OEM
100SS5SP	OEM
100SS6SP	OEM
100SS8SP	OEM
100SS10SP	OEM
100SS12SP	OEM
100Series	OEM
100T2	0103
100T2A	0103
100U6P41	OEM
100UV-PV-RM	OEM
100V10A	OEM
100V11	OEM
100W1	0144
100X6	0103
100X6A	0103
100X7-8	OEM
100X7.4-8.0	OEM
100X8-9	OEM
100X9-10	OEM
100YD21	OEM
100Z4	OEM
100d15	OEM
100d25	OEM
101-0373-00	0076
101-2(ADMIRAL)	0144
101-3(ADMIRAL)	0144
101-4(ADMIRAL)	0144
101-12	0279
101-15	0004
101-6742	0595
101-6742(RCA)	0290
101-6744(RCA)	0290
101A	0050
101A1AX1	OEM
101A1AY1	OEM
101A1AYF1	OEM
101A1EX1	OEM
101A1EY1	OEM
101A1EYF1	OEM
101A2AX2	OEM
101A2AY2	OEM
101A2AYF2	OEM
101A2EX2	OEM
101A2EY2	OEM
101A2EYF2	OEM
101A3AX3	OEM
101A3AY3	OEM
101A3AYF3	OEM
101A3EX3	OEM
101A3EY3	OEM
101A3EYF3	OEM
101A4AX4	OEM
101A4AY4	OEM
101A4AYF4	OEM
101A4EX4	OEM
101A4EY4	OEM
101A4EYF4	OEM
101A5AX5	OEM
101A5AY5	OEM

DEVICE TYPE	REPL CODE
101A5AYF5	OEM
101A5EX5	OEM
101A5EY5	OEM
101A5EYF5	OEM
101B	0050
101B1-11	OEM
101B1-12	OEM
101B1-13	OEM
101B1-14	OEM
101B1-26	OEM
101B1-27	OEM
101B1-31	OEM
101B1-32	OEM
101B1-41	OEM
101B1-42	OEM
101B1-51	OEM
101B1-52	OEM
101B3-11	OEM
101B3-12	OEM
101B3-13	OEM
101B3-14	OEM
101B3-26	OEM
101B3-27	OEM
101B3-31	OEM
101B3-32	OEM
101B3-41	OEM
101B3-42	OEM
101B3-51	OEM
101B6	0015
101B7-11	OEM
101B7-12	OEM
101B7-13	OEM
101B7-14	OEM
101B7-26	OEM
101B7-27	OEM
101B7-31	OEM
101B7-32	OEM
101B7-41	OEM
101B7-42	OEM
101B7-51	OEM
101B7-52	OEM
101BE-52	OEM
101F1-11	OEM
101F1-12	OEM
101F1-13	OEM
101F1-14	OEM
101F1-26	OEM
101F1-27	OEM
101F1-31	OEM
101F1-32	OEM
101F1-41	OEM
101F1-42	OEM
101F1-51	OEM
101F1-52	OEM
101F1FM	OEM
101F1S	1337
101F2FM	OEM
101F2S	1337
101F3-11	OEM
101F3-12	OEM
101F3-13	OEM
101F3-14	OEM
101F3-26	OEM
101F3-27	OEM
101F3-31	OEM
101F3-32	OEM
101F3-41	OEM
101F3-42	OEM
101F3-51	OEM
101F3-52	OEM
101F3FM	OEM
101F3S	1337
101F4S	1894
101F5S	1894
101F6S	1894
101F7-11	OEM
101F7-12	OEM
101F7-13	OEM
101F7-14	OEM
101F7-26	OEM
101F7-27	OEM
101F7-31	OEM
101F7-32	OEM
101F7-41	OEM
101F7-42	OEM
101F7-51	OEM
101F7-52	OEM
101F8S	0193
101F10S	0193
101F12S	0202
101KL20S15	OEM
101KL20S20	OEM
101KL40S10	OEM
101KL40S15	OEM
101KL40S20	OEM
101KL60S10	OEM
101KL60S15	OEM
101KL60S20	OEM
101KL80S10	OEM
101KL80S15	OEM
101KL80S20	OEM
101KL80S25	OEM
101KL100S10	OEM
101KL100S15	OEM
101KL100S20	OEM
101KL100S25	OEM
101KL100S30	OEM
101KL120S10	OEM
101KL120S15	OEM

170 If replacement code is OEM, contact original manufacturer for replacement.

DEVICE TYPE	REPL CODE
101KL120S20	OEM
101KL120S25	OEM
101KL120S30	OEM
101KL130S10	OEM
101KL130S15	OEM
101KL130S20	OEM
101KL130S30	OEM
101KL140S10	OEM
101KL140S15	OEM
101KL140S20	OEM
101KL140S25	OEM
101KL140S30	OEM
101KL150S10	OEM
101KL150S15	OEM
101KL150S20	OEM
101KL150S25	OEM
101KL150S30	OEM
101KL160S10	OEM
101KL160S15	OEM
101KL160S20	OEM
101KL160S25	OEM
101KL160S30	OEM
101KLR40S10	OEM
101KLR40S15	OEM
101KLR40S20	OEM
101KLR40S25	OEM
101KLR40S30	OEM
101KLR60S10	OEM
101KLR60S15	OEM
101KLR60S20	OEM
101KLR60S25	OEM
101KLR60S30	OEM
101KLR80S10	OEM
101KLR80S15	OEM
101KLR80S20	OEM
101KLR80S25	OEM
101KLR80S30	OEM
101KLR100S10	OEM
101KLR100S15	OEM
101KLR100S20	OEM
101KLR100S25	OEM
101KLR100S30	OEM
101KLR120S10	OEM
101KLR120S15	OEM
101KLR120S20	OEM
101KLR120S25	OEM
101KLR120S30	OEM
101KLR130S10	OEM
101KLR130S15	OEM
101KLR130S20	OEM
101KLR130S25	OEM
101KLR130S30	OEM
101KLR140S10	OEM
101KLR140S15	OEM
101KLR140S20	OEM
101KLR140S25	OEM
101KLR140S30	OEM
101KLR150S10	OEM
101KLR150S15	OEM
101KLR150S20	OEM
101KLR150S25	OEM
101KLR150S30	OEM
101KLR160S10	OEM
101KLR160S15	OEM
101KLR160S20	OEM
101KLR160S25	OEM
101KLR160S30	OEM
101LLS	OEM
101M	0050
101P1	0037
101P10	0037
101R1FM	OEM
101R1S	OEM
101R2FM	OEM
101R2S	OEM
101R3FM	OEM
101R3S	OEM
101R4S	OEM
101RA10	0733
101RA20	0733
101RA30	0733
101RA50	0733
101RA60	0733
101RA80	0733
101RA100	0733
101RA110	0733
101RA120	0733
101RA130	1878
101RC10	0733
101RC20	0733
101RC30	0733
101RC40	0733
101RC50	0733
101RC60	0733
101RC80	0733
101RC120	OEM
101RE50	0733
101RE60	0733
101RE60M	OEM
101RE70	OEM
101RE70M	OEM
101RE80	0733
101RE80M	OEM
101RE90	OEM
101RE90M	OEM
101RE100	0733
101RE100M	OEM
101RE110	0733
101RE110M	OEM

DEVICE TYPE	REPL CODE
101RE120	0733
101RE120M	OEM
101RE130	OEM
101RE130M	OEM
101S1AX0	OEM
101S1AX1	OEM
101S1AY0	OEM
101S1AY1	OEM
101S1AYF0	OEM
101S1AYF1	OEM
101S1EX0	OEM
101S1EX1	OEM
101S1EY0	OEM
101S1EY1	OEM
101S1EYF0	OEM
101S1EYF1	OEM
101S2AX0	OEM
101S2AX1	OEM
101S2AY0	OEM
101S2AY1	OEM
101S2AYF0	OEM
101S2AYF1	OEM
101S2EX0	OEM
101S2EX1	OEM
101S2EY0	OEM
101S2EY1	OEM
101S2EYF0	OEM
101S2EYF1	OEM
101S3AX0	OEM
101S3AX1	OEM
101S3AY0	OEM
101S3AY1	OEM
101S3AYF0	OEM
101S3AYF1	OEM
101S3EX0	OEM
101S3EX1	OEM
101S3EY0	OEM
101S3EY1	OEM
101S3EYF0	OEM
101S3EYF1	OEM
101S4AX0	OEM
101S4AX1	OEM
101S4AY0	OEM
101S4AY1	OEM
101S4AYF0	OEM
101S4AYF1	OEM
101S4EX0	OEM
101S4EX1	OEM
101S4EY0	OEM
101S4EY1	OEM
101S4EYF0	OEM
101S4EYF1	OEM
101S5AX0	OEM
101S5AX1	OEM
101S5AY0	OEM
101S5AY1	OEM
101S5AYF0	OEM
101S5AYF1	OEM
101S5EX0	OEM
101S5EX1	OEM
101S5EY0	OEM
101S5EY1	OEM
101S5EYF0	OEM
101S5EYF1	OEM
101S6AX0	OEM
101S6AX1	OEM
101S6AY0	OEM
101S6AY1	OEM
101S6AYF0	OEM
101S6AYF1	OEM
101S6EX0	OEM
101S6EX1	OEM
101S6EY0	OEM
101S6EY1	OEM
101S6EYF0	OEM
101S6EYF1	OEM
101S7AX0	OEM
101S7AX1	OEM
101S7AY0	OEM
101S7AY1	OEM
101S7AYF0	OEM
101S7AYF1	OEM
101S7EX0	OEM
101S7EX1	OEM
101S7EY0	OEM
101S7EY1	OEM
101S7EYF0	OEM
101S7EYF1	OEM
101S8AX0	OEM
101S8AX1	OEM
101S8AY0	OEM
101S8AY1	OEM
101S8AYF0	OEM
101S8AYF1	OEM
101S8EX0	OEM
101S8EX1	OEM
101S8EY0	OEM
101S8EY1	OEM
101S8EYF0	OEM
101S8EYF1	OEM
101S9AX0	OEM
101S9AX1	OEM
101S9AY0	OEM
101S9AY1	OEM
101S9AYF0	OEM
101S9AYF1	OEM
101S9EX0	OEM
101S9EX1	OEM
101S9EY0	OEM

DEVICE TYPE	REPL CODE
101S9EY1	OEM
101S9EYF0	OEM
101S9EYF1	OEM
101S10AX0	OEM
101S10AX1	OEM
101S10AY0	OEM
101S10AY1	OEM
101S10AYF0	OEM
101S10AYF1	OEM
101S10EX0	OEM
101S10EY0	OEM
101S10EYF0	OEM
101S11AX0	OEM
101S11AX1	OEM
101S11AY0	OEM
101S11AY1	OEM
101S11AYF0	OEM
101S11AYF1	OEM
101S12AX0	OEM
101S12AX1	OEM
101S12AY0	OEM
101S12AY1	OEM
101S12AYF0	OEM
101S12AYF1	OEM
101SS2-07DC	OEM
101SS2-07SC	OEM
101SS5-07SC	OEM
101XLS	OEM
102-02	0143
102-0145-16	OEM
102-0373-00	0076
102-0394--25	OEM
102-0394-25	0155
102-0454-02	0076
102-0460-02	0151
102-0461-02	0151
102-0495-00	0781
102-0495-20	0781
102-0535-02	0127
102-0732-28	0111
102-0735-02	0191
102-0735-25	0191
102-0828-17	1211
102-0945-16	0076
102-0945-17	0076
102-0945-38	0076
102-0945-39	0076
102-4	0007
102-207	0143
102-339	0133
102-412	0124
102-1047-03	0113
102-1061-01	0042
102-1166-25	0728
102-1317-18	0155
102-1335-04	1212
102-1342-02	0127
102-1343-02	0171
102-1384-17	0018
102-1675-02	0224
102-1675-11	0076
102-1675-12	0076
102-1678-00	2475
102A1AX1	OEM
102A1AY1	OEM
102A1AYF1	OEM
102A1EX1	OEM
102A1EY1	OEM
102A1EYF1	OEM
102A2AX2	OEM
102A2AY2	OEM
102A2AYF2	OEM
102A2EX2	OEM
102A2EY2	OEM
102A2EYF2	OEM
102A3AX3	OEM
102A3AY3	OEM
102A3AYF3	OEM
102A3EX3	OEM
102A3EY3	OEM
102A3EYF3	OEM
102A4AX4	OEM
102A4AY4	OEM
102A4AYF4	OEM
102A4EX4	OEM
102A4EY4	OEM
102A4EYF4	OEM
102A5AX5	OEM
102A5AY5	OEM
102A5AYF5	OEM
102A5EX5	OEM
102A5EY5	OEM
102A5EYF5	OEM
102B1-11	OEM
102B1-12	OEM
102B1-13	OEM
102B1-14	OEM
102B1-26	OEM
102B1-27	OEM
102B1-31	OEM
102B1-32	OEM
102B1-41	OEM
102B1-42	OEM
102B1-51	OEM
102B1-52	OEM
102B3-11	OEM
102B3-12	OEM
102B3-13	OEM
102B3-14	OEM

DEVICE TYPE	REPL CODE
102B3-26	OEM
102B3-27	OEM
102B3-31	OEM
102B3-32	OEM
102B3-41	OEM
102B3-42	OEM
102B3-51	OEM
102B3-52	OEM
102B6	0015
102B7-11	OEM
102B7-12	OEM
102B7-13	OEM
102B7-14	OEM
102B7-26	OEM
102B7-27	OEM
102B7-31	OEM
102B7-32	OEM
102B7-41	OEM
102B7-42	OEM
102B7-51	OEM
102B7-52	OEM
102D	0015
102DE14020	0578
102F1-11	OEM
102F1-12	OEM
102F1-13	OEM
102F1-14	OEM
102F1-26	OEM
102F1-27	OEM
102F1-31	OEM
102F1-32	OEM
102F1-41	OEM
102F1-42	OEM
102F1-51	OEM
102F1-52	OEM
102F3-11	OEM
102F3-12	OEM
102F3-13	OEM
102F3-14	OEM
102F3-26	OEM
102F3-27	OEM
102F3-31	OEM
102F3-32	OEM
102F3-41	OEM
102F3-42	OEM
102F3-51	OEM
102F3-52	OEM
102F7-11	OEM
102F7-12	OEM
102F7-13	OEM
102F7-14	OEM
102F7-26	OEM
102F7-27	OEM
102F7-31	OEM
102F7-32	OEM
102F7-41	OEM
102F7-42	OEM
102F7-51	OEM
102F7-52	OEM
102G1BX0	OEM
102G1BX1	OEM
102G1BY0	OEM
102G1BY1	OEM
102G1BYF0	OEM
102G1BYF1	OEM
102G1EX0	OEM
102G1EX1	OEM
102G1EY0	OEM
102G1EY1	OEM
102G1EYF0	OEM
102G1EYF1	OEM
102G2BX0	OEM
102G2BX2	OEM
102G2BY0	OEM
102G2BY2	OEM
102G2BYF0	OEM
102G2BYF2	OEM
102G2EX0	OEM
102G2EX2	OEM
102G2EY0	OEM
102G2EY2	OEM
102G2EYF0	OEM
102G2EYF2	OEM
102G3BX0	OEM
102G3BX3	OEM
102G3BY0	OEM
102G3BY3	OEM
102G3BYF0	OEM
102G3BYF3	OEM
102G3EX0	OEM
102G3EX3	OEM
102G3EY0	OEM
102G3EY3	OEM
102G3EYF0	OEM
102G3EYF3	OEM
102G4BX0	OEM
102G4BX4	OEM
102G4BY0	OEM
102G4BY4	OEM
102G4BYF0	OEM
102G4BYF4	OEM
102G4EX0	OEM
102G4EX4	OEM
102G4EY0	OEM
102G4EY4	OEM
102G4EYF0	OEM
102G4EYF4	OEM
102G5BX0	OEM
102G5BX5	OEM

DEVICE TYPE	REPL CODE
102G5BY0	OEM
102G5BY5	OEM
102G5BYF0	OEM
102G5BYF5	OEM
102G5EX0	OEM
102G5EX5	OEM
102G5EY0	OEM
102G5EY5	OEM
102G5EYF0	OEM
102G5EYF5	OEM
102G6BX0	OEM
102G6BX6	OEM
102G6BY0	OEM
102G6BY6	OEM
102G6BYF0	OEM
102G6BYF6	OEM
102G6EX0	OEM
102G6EX6	OEM
102G6EY0	OEM
102G6EY6	OEM
102G6EYF0	OEM
102G6EYF6	OEM
102G7BX0	OEM
102G7BX7	OEM
102G7BY0	OEM
102G7BY7	OEM
102G7BYF0	OEM
102G7BYF7	OEM
102G7EX0	OEM
102G7EX7	OEM
102G7EY0	OEM
102G7EY7	OEM
102G7EYF0	OEM
102G7EYF7	OEM
102G8BX0	OEM
102G8BX8	OEM
102G8BY0	OEM
102G8BY8	OEM
102G8BYF0	OEM
102G8BYF8	OEM
102G8EX0	OEM
102G8EX8	OEM
102G8EY0	OEM
102G8EY8	OEM
102G8EYF0	OEM
102G8EYF8	OEM
102G9BX0	OEM
102G9BX9	OEM
102G9BY0	OEM
102G9BY9	OEM
102G9BYF0	OEM
102G9BYF9	OEM
102G9EX0	OEM
102G9EY0	OEM
102G9EYF0	OEM
102G10BX0	OEM
102G10BX10	OEM
102G10BY0	OEM
102G10BY10	OEM
102G10BYF0	OEM
102G10BYF10	OEM
102G10EX0	OEM
102G10EY0	OEM
102G10EYF0	OEM
102G11BX0	OEM
102G11BX11	OEM
102G11BY0	OEM
102G11BY11	OEM
102G11BYF0	OEM
102G11BYF11	OEM
102G11EX0	OEM
102G11EY0	OEM
102G11EYF0	OEM
102G12BX0	OEM
102G12BX12	OEM
102G12BY0	OEM
102G12BY12	OEM
102G12BYF0	OEM
102G12BYF12	OEM
102G12EX0	OEM
102G12EY0	OEM
102G12EYF0	OEM
102G13BX0	OEM
102G13BX13	OEM
102G13BY0	OEM
102G13BY13	OEM
102G13BYF0	OEM
102G13BYF13	OEM
102G13EX0	OEM
102G13EY0	OEM
102G13EYF0	OEM
102G14BX0	OEM
102G14BX14	OEM
102G14BY0	OEM
102G14BY14	OEM
102G14BYF0	OEM
102G14BYF14	OEM
102G14EX0	OEM
102G14EY0	OEM
102G14EYF0	OEM
102G15BX0	OEM
102G15BX15	OEM
102G15BY0	OEM
102G15BY15	OEM
102G15BYF0	OEM
102G15BYF15	OEM
102G15EX0	OEM
102G15EY0	OEM
102G15EYF0	OEM

DEVICE TYPE	REPL CODE
102G16BX0	OEM
102G16BX16	OEM
102G16BY0	OEM
102G16BY16	OEM
102G16BYF0	OEM
102G16BYF16	OEM
102G16EX0	OEM
102G16EY0	OEM
102G16EYF0	OEM
102G17BX17	OEM
102G17BY17	OEM
102G17BYF17	OEM
102G18BX18	OEM
102G18BY18	OEM
102G18BYF18	OEM
102G19BX19	OEM
102G19BY19	OEM
102G19BYF19	OEM
102G20BX20	OEM
102G20BY20	OEM
102G20BYF20	OEM
102P1	0037
102P10	0037
102S1AX0	OEM
102S1AX1	OEM
102S1AY0	OEM
102S1AY1	OEM
102S1AYF0	OEM
102S1AYF1	OEM
102S1EX0	OEM
102S1EX1	OEM
102S1EY0	OEM
102S1EY1	OEM
102S1EYF0	OEM
102S1EYF1	OEM
102S2AX0	OEM
102S2AX1	OEM
102S2AY0	OEM
102S2AY1	OEM
102S2AYF0	OEM
102S2AYF1	OEM
102S2EX0	OEM
102S2EX1	OEM
102S2EY0	OEM
102S2EY1	OEM
102S2EYF0	OEM
102S2EYF1	OEM
102S3AX0	OEM
102S3AX1	OEM
102S3AY0	OEM
102S3AY1	OEM
102S3AYF0	OEM
102S3AYF1	OEM
102S3EX0	OEM
102S3EX1	OEM
102S3EY0	OEM
102S3EY1	OEM
102S3EYF0	OEM
102S3EYF1	OEM
102S4AX0	OEM
102S4AX1	OEM
102S4AY0	OEM
102S4AY1	OEM
102S4AYF0	OEM
102S4AYF1	OEM
102S4EX0	OEM
102S4EX1	OEM
102S4EY0	OEM
102S4EY1	OEM
102S4EYF0	OEM
102S4EYF1	OEM
102S5AX0	OEM
102S5AX1	OEM
102S5AY0	OEM
102S5AY1	OEM
102S5AYF0	OEM
102S5AYF1	OEM
102S5EX0	OEM
102S5EX1	OEM
102S5EY0	OEM
102S5EY1	OEM
102S5EYF0	OEM
102S5EYF1	OEM
102S6AX0	OEM
102S6AX1	OEM
102S6AY0	OEM
102S6AY1	OEM
102S6AYF0	OEM
102S6AYF1	OEM
102S6EX0	OEM
102S6EX1	OEM
102S6EY0	OEM
102S6EY1	OEM
102S6EYF0	OEM
102S6EYF1	OEM
102S7AX0	OEM
102S7AX1	OEM
102S7AY0	OEM
102S7AY1	OEM
102S7AYF0	OEM
102S7AYF1	OEM
102S7EX0	OEM
102S7EX1	OEM
102S7EY0	OEM
102S7EY1	OEM
102S7EYF0	OEM
102S7EYF1	OEM
102S8AX0	OEM
102S8AX1	OEM

DEVICE TYPE	REPL CODE
102S8AY0	OEM
102S8AY1	OEM
102S8AYF0	OEM
102S8AYF1	OEM
102S8EX0	OEM
102S8EX1	OEM
102S8EY0	OEM
102S8EY1	OEM
102S8EYF0	OEM
102S8EYF1	OEM
102S9AX0	OEM
102S9AX1	OEM
102S9AY0	OEM
102S9AY1	OEM
102S9AYF0	OEM
102S9AYF1	OEM
102S9EX0	OEM
102S9EX1	OEM
102S9EY0	OEM
102S9EY1	OEM
102S9EYF0	OEM
102S9EYF1	OEM
102S10AX0	OEM
102S10AX1	OEM
102S10AY0	OEM
102S10AY1	OEM
102S10AYF0	OEM
102S10AYF1	OEM
102S10EX0	OEM
102S10EY0	OEM
102S10EYF0	OEM
102S11AX0	OEM
102S11AX1	OEM
102S11AY0	OEM
102S11AY1	OEM
102S11AYF0	OEM
102S11AYF1	OEM
102S12AX0	OEM
102S12AX1	OEM
102S12AY0	OEM
102S12AY1	OEM
102S12AYF0	OEM
102S12AYF1	OEM
102SD13780	2031
103	OEM
103-00315-06	OEM
103-0227-18	1409
103-0235-85	0228
103-0461-02	OEM
103-0571-11	1967
103-0571-12	1935
103-1	OEM
103-3	0143
103-4	0144
103-9	OEM
103-15	OEM
103-18	OEM
103-19	0143
103-20	0196
103-21	OEM
103-22	0025
103-23	0143
103-23-01	0143
103-23-1	0143
103-24	OEM
103-28	1024
103-29	0015
103-30	OEM
103-31	0143
103-32	0196
103-34	0143
103-39	0030
103-42	0133
103-43	0196
103-44	0143
103-46	OEM
103-47	0030
103-47-01	0030
103-49	0911
103-50	OEM
103-51	0133
103-59	0015
103-60	0911
103-61	0911
103-62	0911
103-65	0911
103-70	1024
103-71	1024
103-72	OEM
103-73	0143
103-74	0143
103-76	0015
103-79	0143
103-82	0015
103-83	0361
103-84	0100
103-85	0361
103-87	0143
103-89	1024
103-90	0123
103-93	0918
103-96	0023
103-96-01	0361
103-101	2875
103-102	0123
103-104	0030
103-105	0398
103-105-01	0398
103-111	0072

If replacement code is OEM, contact original manufacturer for replacement.

171

DEVICE TYPE	REPL CODE
103-112	0102
103-114	0143
103-123	OEM
103-126	0560
103-128	OEM
103-131	0133
103-135	0814
103-136	0002
103-137	0560
103-140	0296
103-140A	0062
103-141	0124
103-141-01	6706
103-142	0133
103-142-01	0133
103-144	0273
103-144-01	0273
103-144-03	0305
103-145	0133
103-145-01	0015
103-146	0030
103-150	0436
103-151	0305
103-152	1024
103-152-01	1024
103-157	0417
103-158	0137
103-159	0133
103-160	0102
103-166	OEM
103-176	0030
103-176-01	0715
103-176-01A	1023
103-178	0133
103-178-02	0133
103-178-02A	0133
103-179	OEM
103-185	0015
103-189	0030
103-191	0015
103-192	5235
103-193	0102
103-193-01	0023
103-194	0077
103-196	0102
103-196-01	OEM
103-197	OEM
103-202	0143
103-202-01	0911
103-202-GE	0911
103-203	0015
103-206	1246
103-207	0213
103-208	0213
103-211	5237
103-212	0560
103-212-76	0023
103-212-B	OEM
103-214	0102
103-215	1313
103-216	0015
103-219	0030
103-222	0133
103-222-01	0133
103-227	OEM
103-228	0015
103-231	0440
103-235	0030
103-235-01	0030
103-235-01A	OEM
103-236	0039
103-237	1319
103-238	1870
103-239	0286
103-239-01	0286
103-239-02	0374
103-239-02B	0374
103-239-02103-240	OEM
103-240	0133
103-244	0102
103-245	0015
103-246	0313
103-247	0102
103-248	0398
103-249	OEM
103-251	1596
103-252	0490
103-253	OEM
103-253-01	OEM
103-253-02	OEM
103-254	0015
103-254-01	0015
103-255	OEM
103-256	0237
103-257	OEM
103-258	0752
103-259	OEM
103-260	2847
103-261	0015
103-261-02	0344
103-261-02A	0015
103-261-03	0182
103-261-04	0023
103-261-04A	0023
103-263	0102
103-263A	0102
103-266	OEM
103-266-01	OEM
103-266-02#	OEM

DEVICE TYPE	REPL CODE
103-269	OEM
103-269-01	OEM
103-269-02	OEM
103-270	0346
103-271	0019
103-272	0012
103-274	OEM
103-275	0286
103-275-01	0286
103-276	0398
103-278	0560
103-278-01	OEM
103-279	1266
103-279-01	0137
103-279-02	0755
103-279-03	0672
103-279-04	0118
103-279-05	0289
103-279-06	0188
103-279-07	0451
103-279-08	0528
103-279-08A	0274
103-279-09	0140
103-279-09A	0140
103-279-10	0162
103-279-10A	0041
103-279-11	0157
103-279-11A	0253
103-279-12	0091
103-279-12A	0091
103-279-13	0466
103-279-13A	0466
103-279-14	0025
103-279-14A	0062
103-279-14R	0062
103-279-15	0644
103-279-15A	0644
103-279-16	0165
103-279-16A	0165
103-279-17	1075
103-279-18	0012
103-279-19	0064
103-279-19A	0064
103-279-20	0313
103-279-20A	0181
103-279-21	0137
103-279-21A	0052
103-279-22	0053
103-279-22A	0053
103-279-23	0100
103-279-23A	0873
103-279-24	0681
103-279-24A	0681
103-279-25	0416
103-279-26	1639
103-279-26A	0210
103-279-27	0490
103-279-28	0943
103-279-28A	0943
103-279-29	0695
103-279-29A	0695
103-279-30	0560
103-279-31	0398
103-279-31A	0466
103-279-32	1596
103-279-33	0436
103-279-34	0257
103-279-35	0721
103-279-36	0814
103-279-36A	0814
103-279-37	0814
103-279-37A	0814
103-279-38	0346
103-279-39	0925
103-279-40	0993
103-279-41	0497
103-279-42	0863
103-279-43	1148
103-279-43A	1148
103-279-44	0778
103-279-45	2144
103-279-46	1181
103-279-46A	1181
103-279-47	0327
103-279-48	2997
103-279-49	1301
103-279-50	0098
103-279-51	0149
103-279-52	0186
103-279-53	0213
103-279-54	0245
103-279-55	0028
103-279-56	0255
103-279-57	0871
103-279-58	0363
103-279-59	2831
103-279-60	0417
103-279A	1266
103-280	OEM
103-280-01	OEM
103-280-02	0023
103-280-03	OEM
103-281	1023
103-284	0023
103-284A	0023
103-285	0374
103-287	0102
103-288	0039
103-288-01	0039

DEVICE TYPE	REPL CODE
103-289	0398
103-290	0162
103-292	0398
103-293	1023
103-293-02	0374
103-295	0023
103-295-01	0133
103-295-01A	0133
103-295-02	0133
103-295-02A	0133
103-295-03	0023
103-295A	0133
103-298-04	OEM
103-298-05	0023
103-298-05A	0023
103-301	OEM
103-301-09	0025
103-301-13	0012
103-301-13A	0012
103-301-17A	0361
103-301-19A	0002
103-301-22	0526
103-301-22A	0526
103-301-24	0398
103-301-24A	0489
103-301-27	OEM
103-304-08	OEM
103-305	0344
103-305A	0344
103-306	5254
103-306A	3295
103-308	0052
103-308A	0052
103-309-01	0064
103-309-01A	0064
103-312	0031
103-315-01	0015
103-315-01A	0015
103-315-03	0015
103-315-03A	0015
103-315-04	0015
103-315-06	0015
103-315-06A	0015
103-316-04	0017
103-317	OEM
103-326	0023
103-326A	0023
103-327	OEM
103-328	OEM
103-328-01	OEM
103-328-03	OEM
103-329	OEM
103-330	0790
103-330A	0790
103-334	0195
103-336-11	0253
103-336-15	0077
103-336-15A	0077
103-336-18	0057
103-336-18A	0057
103-336-19	0064
103-336-19A	0064
103-339	0102
103-339-01	0031
103-339-01A	0031
103-339-02A	0031
103-339-03	0102
103-339-04	0102
103-339-04A	0031
103-339-4	0102
103-339A	0031
103-344	0015
103-344-01	0015
103-344-01A	0015
103-344-02	0015
103-344-02A	0015
103-344-05	OEM
103-344-06	0015
103-344-06A	0015
103-344A	0015
103-345-06	0015
103-347-03A	OEM
103-350	OEM
103-352-01	OEM
103-355-06	0071
103-355-06A	0071
103-360-01	OEM
103-361	OEM
103-368-03	0023
103-372	OEM
103-376-02	OEM
103-376-02A	OEM
103-380	OEM
103-381	OEM
103-387	OEM
103-387B	OEM
103-389	OEM
103-389A	OEM
103-392	OEM
103-393	OEM
103-394	0017
103-398	OEM
103-398A	OEM
103-399-12	OEM
103-399-29	OEM
103-402-03	OEM
103-404	OEM
103-408	0466
103-408A	0466

DEVICE TYPE	REPL CODE
103-409	0137
103-409A	0052
103-410	OEM
103-412	5277
103-412A	OEM
103-417-02	OEM
103-417-03	0031
103-417-03A	0031
103-417-04	0023
103-417-04A	0031
103-417-05	0031
103-417-05A	0031
103-417A	0031
103-429	OEM
103-433	0124
103-433A	OEM
103-443	OEM
103-447	OEM
103-461	OEM
103-461A	OEM
103-462	OEM
103-462-01	OEM
103-462-03	OEM
103-467A	OEM
103-469A	OEM
103-471-01	OEM
103-471A	OEM
103-472A	OEM
103-475A	OEM
103-476-15A	OEM
103-476-16A	OEM
103-476-18A	OEM
103-476-19A	OEM
103-476-20A	OEM
103-598	OEM
103-765-01	0037
103-902	OEM
103-1344	OEM
103-29000	OEM
103-Z9000	0398
103-Z9001	0143
103-Z9002	0644
103-Z9003	0137
103-Z9004	0039
103-Z9005	0188
103-Z9006	0162
103-Z9007	0157
103-Z9008	0631
103-Z9009	0062
103-Z9010	0170
103-Z9011	0789
103-Z9012	0361
103-Z9013	0002
103-Z9014	0436
103-Z9015	0863
103-Z9016	0778
103-Z9017	0327
103-Z9018	0149
103-Z9019	0165
103-Z9020	0025
103-Z9021	0244
103-Z9022	0490
103-Z9023	0526
103-Z9024	0721
103-Z9025	0497
103-Z9026	0173
103-Z9027	0186
103-Z9028	0225
103-Z9029	0234
103-Z9030	0247
103-Z9031	0256
103-Z9032	0269
103-Z9033	0291
103-Z9034	0314
103-Z9035	0316
103-Z9036	0343
103-Z9037	0263
103-Z9038	2847
103-Z9039	0139
103-Z9040	3638
103-Z9041	0528
103-Z9042	0313
103-Z9043	1172
103-Z9044	0120
103-Z9045	1914
103A1AX1	OEM
103A1AY1	OEM
103A1AYF1	OEM
103A1EX1	OEM
103A1EY1	OEM
103A1EYF1	OEM
103A2AX2	OEM
103A2AY2	OEM
103A2AYF2	OEM
103A2EX2	OEM
103A2EY2	OEM
103A2EYF2	OEM
103A3AX3	OEM
103A3AY3	OEM
103A3AYF3	OEM
103A3EX3	OEM
103A3EY3	OEM
103A3EYF3	OEM
103A4AX4	OEM
103A4AY4	OEM
103A4AYF4	OEM
103A4EX4	OEM
103A4EY4	OEM
103A4EYF4	OEM

DEVICE TYPE	REPL CODE
103A5AX5	OEM
103A5AY5	OEM
103A5AYF5	OEM
103A5EX5	OEM
103A5EY5	OEM
103A5EYF5	OEM
103B1-11	OEM
103B1-12	OEM
103B1-13	OEM
103B1-14	OEM
103B1-26	OEM
103B1-27	OEM
103B1-31	OEM
103B1-32	OEM
103B1-41	OEM
103B1-42	OEM
103B1-51	OEM
103B1-52	OEM
103B3-11	OEM
103B3-12	OEM
103B3-13	OEM
103B3-14	OEM
103B3-26	OEM
103B3-27	OEM
103B3-31	OEM
103B3-32	OEM
103B3-41	OEM
103B3-42	OEM
103B3-51	OEM
103B3-52	OEM
103B6	1325
103B7-11	OEM
103B7-12	OEM
103B7-13	OEM
103B7-14	OEM
103B7-26	OEM
103B7-27	OEM
103B7-31	OEM
103B7-32	OEM
103B7-41	OEM
103B7-42	OEM
103B7-51	OEM
103B7-52	OEM
103B98M090	1775
103B98N060	0917
103D079400	0678
103DE75200	0534
103DE76710	OEM
103EP	OEM
103F1-11	OEM
103F1-12	OEM
103F1-13	OEM
103F1-14	OEM
103F1-26	OEM
103F1-27	OEM
103F1-31	OEM
103F1-32	OEM
103F1-41	OEM
103F1-42	OEM
103F1-51	OEM
103F1-52	OEM
103F3-11	OEM
103F3-12	OEM
103F3-13	OEM
103F3-14	OEM
103F3-26	OEM
103F3-27	OEM
103F3-31	OEM
103F3-32	OEM
103F3-41	OEM
103F3-42	OEM
103F3-51	OEM
103F3-52	OEM
103F7-11	OEM
103F7-12	OEM
103F7-13	OEM
103F7-14	OEM
103F7-26	OEM
103F7-27	OEM
103F7-31	OEM
103F7-32	OEM
103F7-41	OEM
103F7-42	OEM
103F7-51	OEM
103F7-52	OEM
103G3125	0015
103G3125A	0015
103LLS	OEM
103MLA60	OEM
103MLA80	OEM
103MLA100	OEM
103MLA120	OEM
103P(AIRLINE)	0037
103PJLA160	OEM
103PJLA180	OEM
103PJLA200	OEM
103PJLA250	OEM
103S1AX0	OEM
103S1AX1	OEM
103S1AY0	OEM
103S1AY1	OEM
103S1AYF0	OEM
103S1AYF1	OEM
103S1EX0	OEM
103S1EX1	OEM
103S1EY0	OEM
103S1EY1	OEM
103S1EYF0	OEM
103S1EYF1	OEM

DEVICE TYPE	REPL CODE
103S2AX0	OEM
103S2AX1	OEM
103S2AY0	OEM
103S2AY1	OEM
103S2AYF0	OEM
103S2AYF1	OEM
103S2EX0	OEM
103S2EX1	OEM
103S2EY0	OEM
103S2EY1	OEM
103S2EYF0	OEM
103S2EYF1	OEM
103S3AX0	OEM
103S3AX1	OEM
103S3AY0	OEM
103S3AY1	OEM
103S3AYF0	OEM
103S3AYF1	OEM
103S3EX0	OEM
103S3EX1	OEM
103S3EY0	OEM
103S3EY1	OEM
103S3EYF0	OEM
103S3EYF1	OEM
103S4AX0	OEM
103S4AX1	OEM
103S4AY0	OEM
103S4AY1	OEM
103S4AYF0	OEM
103S4AYF1	OEM
103S4EX0	OEM
103S4EX1	OEM
103S4EY0	OEM
103S4EY1	OEM
103S4EYF0	OEM
103S4EYF1	OEM
103S5AX0	OEM
103S5AX1	OEM
103S5AY0	OEM
103S5AY1	OEM
103S5AYF0	OEM
103S5AYF1	OEM
103S5EX0	OEM
103S5EX1	OEM
103S5EY0	OEM
103S5EY1	OEM
103S5EYF0	OEM
103S5EYF1	OEM
103S6AX0	OEM
103S6AX1	OEM
103S6AY0	OEM
103S6AY1	OEM
103S6AYF0	OEM
103S6AYF1	OEM
103S6EX0	OEM
103S6EX1	OEM
103S6EY0	OEM
103S6EY1	OEM
103S6EYF0	OEM
103S6EYF1	OEM
103S7AX0	OEM
103S7AX1	OEM
103S7AY0	OEM
103S7AY1	OEM
103S7AYF0	OEM
103S7AYF1	OEM
103S7EX0	OEM
103S7EX1	OEM
103S7EY0	OEM
103S7EY1	OEM
103S7EYF0	OEM
103S7EYF1	OEM
103S8AX0	OEM
103S8AX1	OEM
103S8AY0	OEM
103S8AY1	OEM
103S8AYF0	OEM
103S8AYF1	OEM
103S8EX0	OEM
103S8EX1	OEM
103S8EY0	OEM
103S8EY1	OEM
103S8EYF0	OEM
103S8EYF1	OEM
103S9AX0	OEM
103S9AX1	OEM
103S9AY0	OEM
103S9AY1	OEM
103S9AYF0	OEM
103S9AYF1	OEM
103S9EX0	OEM
103S9EX1	OEM
103S9EY0	OEM
103S9EY1	OEM
103S9EYF0	OEM
103S9EYF1	OEM
103S10AX0	OEM
103S10AX1	OEM
103S10AY0	OEM
103S10AY1	OEM
103S10AYF0	OEM
103S10AYF1	OEM
103S10EX0	OEM
103S10EY0	OEM
103S10EYF0	OEM
103S11AX0	OEM
103S11AX1	OEM
103S11AY0	OEM
103S11AY1	OEM

DEVICE TYPE	REPL CODE
103S11AYF0	OEM
103S11AYF1	OEM
103S12AX0	OEM
103S12AX1	OEM
103S12AY0	OEM
103S12AY1	OEM
103S12AYF0	OEM
103S12AYF1	OEM
103SD78370	2330
103TB7	OEM
103TB9	OEM
103TB11	OEM
104-1	0030
104-2	OEM
104-17	0136
104-17(RCA)	0037
104-19	0136
104-21	0136
104A1AX1	OEM
104A1AY1	OEM
104A1AYF1	OEM
104A1EX1	OEM
104A1EY1	OEM
104A1EYF1	OEM
104A2AX2	OEM
104A2AY2	OEM
104A2AYF2	OEM
104A2EX2	OEM
104A2EY2	OEM
104A2EYF2	OEM
104A3AX3	OEM
104A3AY3	OEM
104A3AYF3	OEM
104A3EX3	OEM
104A3EY3	OEM
104A3EYF3	OEM
104A4AX4	OEM
104A4AY4	OEM
104A4AYF4	OEM
104A4EX4	OEM
104A4EY4	OEM
104A4EYF4	OEM
104A5AX5	OEM
104A5AY5	OEM
104A5AYF5	OEM
104A5EX5	OEM
104A5EY5	OEM
104A5EYF5	OEM
104AHU7K	OEM
104B1-11	OEM
104B1-12	OEM
104B1-13	OEM
104B1-14	OEM
104B1-26	OEM
104B1-27	OEM
104B1-31	OEM
104B1-32	OEM
104B1-41	OEM
104B1-42	OEM
104B1-51	OEM
104B1-52	OEM
104B3-11	OEM
104B3-12	OEM
104B3-13	OEM
104B3-14	OEM
104B3-26	OEM
104B3-27	OEM
104B3-31	OEM
104B3-32	OEM
104B3-41	OEM
104B3-42	OEM
104B3-51	OEM
104B3-52	OEM
104B6	0015
104B7-11	OEM
104B7-12	OEM
104B7-13	OEM
104B7-14	OEM
104B7-26	OEM
104B7-27	OEM
104B7-31	OEM
104B7-32	OEM
104B7-41	OEM
104B7-42	OEM
104B7-51	OEM
104B7-52	OEM
104F1-11	OEM
104F1-12	OEM
104F1-13	OEM
104F1-14	OEM
104F1-26	OEM
104F1-27	OEM
104F1-31	OEM
104F1-32	OEM
104F1-41	OEM
104F1-42	OEM
104F1-51	OEM
104F1-52	OEM
104F3-11	OEM
104F3-12	OEM
104F3-13	OEM
104F3-14	OEM
104F3-26	OEM
104F3-27	OEM
104F3-31	OEM
104F3-32	OEM
104F3-41	OEM
104F3-42	OEM
104F3-51	OEM

172 If replacement code is OEM, contact original manufacturer for replacement.

DEVICE TYPE	REPL CODE
104F3-52	OEM
104F7-11	OEM
104F7-12	OEM
104F7-13	OEM
104F7-14	OEM
104F7-26	OEM
104F7-27	OEM
104F7-31	OEM
104F7-32	OEM
104F7-41	OEM
104F7-42	OEM
104F7-51	OEM
104F7-52	OEM
104H01	0086
104K	OEM
104S1AX0	OEM
104S1AX1	OEM
104S1AY0	OEM
104S1AY1	OEM
104S1AYF0	OEM
104S1AYF1	OEM
104S1EX0	OEM
104S1EX1	OEM
104S1EY0	OEM
104S1EY1	OEM
104S1EYF0	OEM
104S1EYF1	OEM
104S2AX0	OEM
104S2AX1	OEM
104S2AY0	OEM
104S2AY1	OEM
104S2AYF0	OEM
104S2AYF1	OEM
104S2EX0	OEM
104S2EX1	OEM
104S2EY0	OEM
104S2EY1	OEM
104S2EYF0	OEM
104S2EYF1	OEM
104S3AX0	OEM
104S3AX1	OEM
104S3AY0	OEM
104S3AY1	OEM
104S3AYF0	OEM
104S3AYF1	OEM
104S3EX0	OEM
104S3EX1	OEM
104S3EY0	OEM
104S3EY1	OEM
104S3EYF0	OEM
104S3EYF1	OEM
104S4AX0	OEM
104S4AX1	OEM
104S4AY0	OEM
104S4AY1	OEM
104S4AYF0	OEM
104S4AYF1	OEM
104S4EX0	OEM
104S4EX1	OEM
104S4EY0	OEM
104S4EY1	OEM
104S4EYF0	OEM
104S4EYF1	OEM
104S5AX0	OEM
104S5AX1	OEM
104S5AY0	OEM
104S5AY1	OEM
104S5AYF0	OEM
104S5AYF1	OEM
104S5EX0	OEM
104S5EX1	OEM
104S5EY0	OEM
104S5EY1	OEM
104S5EYF0	OEM
104S5EYF1	OEM
104S6AX0	OEM
104S6AX1	OEM
104S6AY0	OEM
104S6AY1	OEM
104S6AYF0	OEM
104S6AYF1	OEM
104S6EX0	OEM
104S6EX1	OEM
104S6EY0	OEM
104S6EY1	OEM
104S6EYF0	OEM
104S6EYF1	OEM
104S7AX0	OEM
104S7AX1	OEM
104S7AY0	OEM
104S7AY1	OEM
104S7AYF0	OEM
104S7AYF1	OEM
104S7EX0	OEM
104S7EX1	OEM
104S7EY0	OEM
104S7EY1	OEM
104S7EYF0	OEM
104S7EYF1	OEM
104S8AX0	OEM
104S8AX1	OEM
104S8AY0	OEM
104S8AY1	OEM
104S8AYF0	OEM
104S8AYF1	OEM
104S8EX0	OEM
104S8EX1	OEM
104S8EY0	OEM
104S8EY1	OEM

DEVICE TYPE	REPL CODE
104S8EYF0	OEM
104S8EYF1	OEM
104S9AX0	OEM
104S9AX1	OEM
104S9AY0	OEM
104S9AY1	OEM
104S9AYF0	OEM
104S9AYF1	OEM
104S9EX0	OEM
104S9EX1	OEM
104S9EY0	OEM
104S9EY1	OEM
104S9EYF0	OEM
104S9EYF1	OEM
104S10AX0	OEM
104S10AX1	OEM
104S10AY0	OEM
104S10AY1	OEM
104S10AYF0	OEM
104S10AYF1	OEM
104S10EX0	OEM
104S10EY0	OEM
104S10EYF0	OEM
104S11AX0	OEM
104S11AX1	OEM
104S11AY0	OEM
104S11AY1	OEM
104S11AYF0	OEM
104S11AYF1	OEM
104S12AX0	OEM
104S12AX1	OEM
104S12AY0	OEM
104S12AY1	OEM
104S12AYF0	OEM
104S12AYF1	OEM
104T2	0103
104TB7	OEM
104TB9	OEM
104TB11	OEM
104Z4	OEM
105	0143
105(ADMIRAL)	0016
105-001-04	0079
105-001-05	0079
105-001-07	0326
105-001-08	0144
105-005-04/2228-3	0144
105-005-12	0144
105-006-08	0016
105-008-04/2228-3	0144
105-009-21/2228-3	0144
105-00106-00	0144
105-00107-09	0127
105-00108-07	0144
105-060-09	0016
105-085-33	0016
105-02004-09	0144
105-02005-07	0127
105-02006-05	0127
105-02008-01	0127
105-06004-00	0144
105-06007-05	0016
105-08243-05	0079
105-110	OEM
105-114	OEM
105-904-85	0079
105-904-86	0079
105-904-87	0079
105-931-91/2228-3	0016
105-941-97/2228-3	0144
105-24191-04	0144
105-28196-07	0016
105B6	0015
105B7-11	OEM
105B7-12	OEM
105B7-13	OEM
105B7-14	OEM
105B7-26	OEM
105B7-27	OEM
105B7-31	OEM
105B7-32	OEM
105B7-41	OEM
105B7-42	OEM
105B7-51	OEM
105B7-52	OEM
105DE87820	OEM
105S925080	2180
105T4	OEM
105V10	OEM
105Z4	OEM
106	0015
106-001	0113
106-002	0076
106-003	0076
106-004	0386
106-005	0781
106-006	2475
106-007	0133
106-008	0019
106-009	0139
106-010	0057
106-011	0023
106-012	5025
106-013	0087
106-1	0015
106-120	0037
106-351	1060
106A	0442
106B	0934

DEVICE TYPE	REPL CODE
106B6	0015
106B7-11	OEM
106B7-12	OEM
106B7-13	OEM
106B7-14	OEM
106B7-26	OEM
106B7-27	OEM
106B7-31	OEM
106B7-32	OEM
106B7-41	OEM
106B7-42	OEM
106B7-51	OEM
106B7-52	OEM
106C	1213
106D	OEM
106E	OEM
106F	2084
106F4	1250
106KB0	0126
106KBA	0126
106LL2	OEM
106M	0321
106P1	0160
106P1AG	0160
106P1T	0160
106Q	2084
106RED	0037
106Y	2084
106Z4	OEM
107-0021-00	1659
107-1	OEM
107-2	OEM
107-3	OEM
107-4	OEM
107-8	0016
107-3088	0079
107A	0050
107A(SCR)	0442
107B	0050
107B(SCR)	0934
107B6	0015
107B7-11	OEM
107B7-12	OEM
107B7-13	OEM
107B7-14	OEM
107B7-26	OEM
107B7-27	OEM
107B7-31	OEM
107B7-32	OEM
107B7-41	OEM
107B7-42	OEM
107B7-51	OEM
107B7-52	OEM
107BRN	0016
107C	1213
107D	0095
107E	OEM
107F	2084
107M	0050
107N1	0086
107N2	0016
107P341	0571
107Q	2084
107Y	2084
107Z4	OEM
108	0015
108(FARFISA)	0143
108-0049-08	0321
108-0068-12	0321
108-1	0050
108-2	0050
108-3	0050
108-4	0050
108-6	0037
108-60	0037
108-74	0143
108-116	OEM
108A	0442
108A4	0015
108B	0934
108B1-11	OEM
108B1-12	OEM
108B1-13	OEM
108B1-14	OEM
108B1-26	OEM
108B1-27	OEM
108B1-31	OEM
108B1-32	OEM
108B1-41	OEM
108B1-42	OEM
108B1-51	OEM
108B1-52	OEM
108B3-11	OEM
108B3-12	OEM
108B3-13	OEM
108B3-14	OEM
108B3-26	OEM
108B3-27	OEM
108B3-31	OEM
108B3-32	OEM
108B3-41	OEM
108B3-42	OEM
108B3-51	OEM
108B3-52	OEM
108B4	0015
108B6	0015
108B7-11	OEM
108B7-12	OEM
108B7-13	OEM

DEVICE TYPE	REPL CODE
108B7-14	OEM
108B7-26	OEM
108B7-27	OEM
108B7-31	OEM
108B7-32	OEM
108B7-41	OEM
108B7-42	OEM
108B7-51	OEM
108B7-52	OEM
108C	1213
108D	0095
108E-E2	0015
108F	1250
108F1-11	OEM
108F1-12	OEM
108F1-13	OEM
108F1-14	OEM
108F1-26	OEM
108F1-27	OEM
108F1-31	OEM
108F1-32	OEM
108F1-41	OEM
108F1-42	OEM
108F1-51	OEM
108F1-52	OEM
108F3-11	OEM
108F3-12	OEM
108F3-13	OEM
108F3-14	OEM
108F3-26	OEM
108F3-31	OEM
108F3-32	OEM
108F3-41	OEM
108F3-42	OEM
108F3-51	OEM
108F3-52	OEM
108F7-11	OEM
108F7-12	OEM
108F7-13	OEM
108F7-14	OEM
108F7-26	OEM
108F7-27	OEM
108F7-31	OEM
108F7-32	OEM
108F7-41	OEM
108F7-42	OEM
108F7-51	OEM
108F7-52	OEM
108GRN	0037
108Q	1386
108T2	2465
108Y	1386
108Z4	OEM
109	0016
109-036500	0143
109-1	0079
109-1(RCA)	0016
109-192	0143
109A949CE	2004
109A949CM-P1	0407
109B6	0015
109B7-11	OEM
109B7-12	OEM
109B7-13	OEM
109B7-14	OEM
109B7-26	OEM
109B7-27	OEM
109B7-31	OEM
109B7-32	OEM
109B7-41	OEM
109B7-42	OEM
109B7-51	OEM
109B7-52	OEM
109LL2	OEM
109SLS	OEM
109T2	2465
109UA	OEM
109UB	OEM
109UC	OEM
109UD	OEM
109WA	OEM
109WB	OEM
109WC	OEM
109WD	OEM
109XA	OEM
109XB	OEM
109XC	OEM
109XD	OEM
109Z4	OEM
110	0037
110-01563-00	0004
110-629	0015
110-635	0015
110-636	0071
110-672	0015
110-684	0015
110-763	0143
110-US	OEM
110B6	0071
110BH1	0769
110LL2	OEM
110P	OEM
110P1	0037
110P1AA	0037
110P1M	0037
110P2	0150
110PB	OEM
110PB9M	OEM
110PBF9	OEM

DEVICE TYPE	REPL CODE
110PBHL	OEM
110PBL	OEM
110PBM	OEM
110PD9M	OEM
110PH9M	OEM
110PL	OEM
110PS9M	OEM
110T4	OEM
110Z4	OEM
111-0-9170-00700	OEM
111-4-2020-0860	0143
111-4-2020-04600	0167
111-4-2020-05600	0123
111-4-2020-06100	0133
111-4-2020-06200	0102
111-4-2020-08000	0015
111-4-2020-08600	0143
111-4-2020-11300	0025
111-4-2020-11500	0313
111-4-2020-13300	0814
111-4-2020-14400	0102
111-4-2020-14500	0015
111-4-2020-14600	0016
111-4-2020-15100	0102
111-4-2060-0400	0167
111-4-2060-02300	0872
111-4-2060-02400	0872
111-4-2060-03900	0849
111-4-2060-04000	0167
111-4-2060-05100	0875
111-4-2060-05200	0878
111-731	0321
111-6191	0720
111-6510	0208
111-6910	0050
111-6935	0136
111N1	0486
111N2	0103
111N4	0103
111N4A	0103
111N4B	0103
111N5	OEM
111P1	0486
111P3B	0899
111P7	0486
111RK10	OEM
111RK10M	OEM
111RK20	OEM
111RK20M	OEM
111RK40	OEM
111RK40M	OEM
111RK60	OEM
111RK60M	OEM
111RK80	OEM
111RK80M	OEM
111RK100	OEM
111RK100M	OEM
111RK120	OEM
111RK120M	OEM
111RLA60	OEM
111RLA80	OEM
111RLA100	OEM
111RLA120	OEM
111T2	0233
111Z4	3874
112-000172	0037
112-000185	0037
112-000187	0037
112-000267	0050
112-001	0279
112-002	0136
112-003	0211
112-004	0211
112-0011-A	0079
112-034923	0004
112-1A82	0016
112-2	0126
112-2A	0126
112-3	3653
112-7	0037
112-8	0037
112-10	0037
112-361	0086
112-362	0626
112-363	0103
112-500-0-50	0133
112-500-0-501	0133
112-520	0144
112-521	0144
112-522	0144
112-523	0016
112-524	0160
112-525	0086
112-601-0-102	0015
112-826	0015
112-200525	0004
112-202147	0160
112-203053	0086
112-203055	0103
112-203391	0111
112-7292955	0599
112P1	OEM
112RLA60	OEM
112RLA80	OEM
112RLA100	OEM
112RLA120	OEM
113-039	0015
113-118	0198
113-321	0015

DEVICE TYPE	REPL CODE
113-392	0015
113-398	0144
113-938	0144
113-998	0229
113A7739	0015
113N1	OEM
113N1AG	0396
113N2	0396
113Z4	OEM
114-013	0015
114-1	0079
114-4-2020-14500	0015
114-118	0144
114-267	0144
114N4P	0208
114P3P	0164
115	3282
115-039	0015
115-063	0160
115-1	0198
115-4	0198
115-13	0079
115-225	0016
115-227	0050
115-228	0050
115-229	0050
115-268	0160
115-269	0160
115-275	0136
115-559	0015
115-599	0015
115-867	0229
115-875	0016
115B7T	OEM
115E	3282
115E(2SA1115E)	3282
115F	3282
115T4	OEM
115UA	OEM
115UB	OEM
115UC	OEM
115UD	OEM
115UE	OEM
115UF	OEM
115WA	OEM
115WB	OEM
115WC	OEM
115WD	OEM
115XA	OEM
115XB	OEM
115XC	OEM
115XD	OEM
115YA	OEM
115YB	OEM
115YC	OEM
115YD	OEM
115Z4	0002
116-052	0015
116-068	0969
116-072	0136
116-073	0144
116-074	0016
116-075	0142
116-078	0016
116-079	0144
116-080	0144
116-082	0144
116-083	0144
116-085	0016
116-086	0969
116-087	0969
116-088	0969
116-089	0969
116-091	0004
116-092	0016
116-1	3792
116-198	0144
116-199	0144
116-200	0144
116-201	0004
116-202	0050
116-203	0004
116-206	0004
116-207	0050
116-208	0050
116-209	0050
116-687	0208
116-756	0136
116-757	0004
116-875	0016
116-997	0004
116BT300R	OEM
116BT500R	OEM
117-1	0142
117-2	0164
117-6	2839
117-9	1647
117-134-11	0015
117-A40	0374
118-1	0144
118-2	0144
118-3	0144
118-4	0144
118-7470	OEM
118J2	OEM
118UA	OEM
118UB	OEM
118UC	OEM
118UD	OEM

DEVICE TYPE	REPL CODE
118XA	OEM
118XB	OEM
118XC	OEM
118XD	OEM
119-0016	0435
119-0054	0016
119-0055	0037
119-0056	0016
119-0068	0178
119-0075	0130
119-0077	0086
119-6511	0015
120-000190	0050
120-00-19	0211
120-001-300	0015
120-00190	0136
120-00195	0004
120-00213	0136
120-001190	0050
120-001192	0279
120-001195	0211
120-001300	0015
120-001301	0123
120-001795	0211
120-001798	0693
120-002012	0004
120-002013	0004
120-002014	0004
120-002213	0050
120-002214	0050
120-002216	0050
120-002513	0136
120-002515	0136
120-002518	0136
120-002520	0164
120-002521	0004
120-002656	0136
120-002748	0004
120-003147	0133
120-003148	0015
120-003149	0071
120-003150	0222
120-003151	0693
120-004048	0136
120-004061	0071
120-004480	0016
120-004482	0016
120-004483	0016
120-004492	0136
120-004493	0164
120-004494	0164
120-004495	0164
120-004496	0144
120-004497	0144
120-004498	0143
120-004499	0143
120-004503	0015
120-004629	0907
120-004722	0050
120-004723	0144
120-004724	0144
120-004725	0144
120-004727	0004
120-004728	0164
120-004729	0004
120-004730	0143
120-004877	0133
120-004878	0015
120-004879	0012
120-004880	0016
120-004881	0144
120-004882	0016
120-004883	0016
120-004884	0334
120-004887	0222
120-004888	0595
120-005291	0144
120-005292	0144
120-005293	0144
120-005294	0144
120-005295	0144
120-005296	0144
120-005297	0144
120-005298	0144
120-005299	0143
120-005300	0030
120-006604	0037
120-01193	0004
120-02213	0050
120-1	0016
120-2	0016
120-3	0016
120-7	0016
120-8	0016
120-8A	0016
120-190	0004
120-7396	0031
120A11	0133
120BLU	0016
120P1	0037
120P1M	0037
120T4	OEM
120V10	OEM
121	0212
121(DIO)	0023
121(SEARS)	0016
121-1	0037
121-1RED	0037
121-6	0208

If replacement code is OEM, contact original manufacturer for replacement.

173

DEVICE TYPE	REPL CODE
121-7	0208
121-8	0208
121-9	0004
121-10	0004
121-11	0004
121-12	0004
121-14	0279
121-14(COLUMBIA)	0086
121-14(ZENITH)	0015
121-15	0595
121-16	0595
121-17	0595
121-18	0142
121-18(ZENITH)	0164
121-19	0004
121-21	0595
121-22	0595
121-24	0595
121-25	0595
121-26	0595
121-27	0211
121-31	0143
121-33	0004
121-34	0004
121-43	0004
121-44	0136
121-45	0136
121-46	0004
121-47	0004
121-48	0050
121-49	0050
121-50	0595
121-51	0595
121-52	0004
121-53	0279
121-54	0136
121-59	0208
121-60	0208
121-61	0004
121-62	0136
121-63	0050
121-64	0004
121-65	0136
121-66	0136
121-67	0136
121-68	0004
121-69	0004
121-70	0595
121-71	0595
121-72	0004
121-73	0050
121-74	0050
121-75	0050
121-76	0050
121-78	0050
121-79	0050
121-80	0279
121-81	0279
121-82	0279
121-83	0279
121-84	0279
121-85	0279
121-86	0279
121-87	0279
121-88	0279
121-89	0279
121-90	0279
121-91	0279
121-92	0279
121-93	0279
121-94	0279
121-95	0211
121-96	0211
121-99-1A	OEM
121-100	0595
121-101	0050
121-102	0050
121-103	0050
121-104	0050
121-105	0050
121-106	0211
121-107	0211
121-113	0144
121-119	0050
121-120	0164
121-128	0279
121-132	0050
121-134	0050
121-135	0050
121-136	0050
121-137	0050
121-138	0050
121-139	0050
121-145	0279
121-146	0279
121-147	0279
121-148	0004
121-150	0136
121-151	0004
121-152	0004
121-153	0136
121-154	0136
121-157	0050
121-160	0279
121-161	0136
121-162	0136
121-163	0004
121-164	0004
121-165	0595
121-166	0595
121-167	0164
121-170	0037
121-171	0160
121-179	0050
121-180	0050
121-181	0050
121-184	0004
121-185	0050
121-186	0136
121-187	0136
121-189	0136
121-190	0004
121-191	0004
121-192	0004
121-193	0004
121-195B	0016
121-200	0211
121-205	0279
121-206	0279
121-207	0279
121-208	0279
121-209	0279
121-210	0279
121-211	0279
121-212	0279
121-213	0279
121-219	0279
121-220	0279
121-221	0279
121-222	0279
121-225	0279
121-226	0004
121-227	0004
121-228	0136
121-229	0136
121-230	0136
121-231	0136
121-232	0136
121-233	0136
121-234	0279
121-235	0279
121-236	0279
121-237	0208
121-238	0208
121-239	0004
121-240	0004
121-240X	0004
121-241	0136
121-241(ZENITH)	0136
121-242	0050
121-243	0050
121-244	0050
121-245	0004
121-246	0004
121-247	0208
121-247BLK	0208
121-247VIL	0595
121-247VIO	0595
121-247WHT	0595
121-248	0208
121-248BLU	0208
121-248VIL	0595
121-248VIO	0595
121-254	0279
121-256	0136
121-257	0050
121-258	0050
121-259	0050
121-260	0050
121-261	0136
121-262	0136
121-263	0136
121-266	0211
121-267	0211
121-268	0050
121-269	0050
121-270	0160
121-271	0160
121-272	0004
121-273	0004
121-274	0004
121-275	0004
121-276	0198
121-277	0198
121-278	0198
121-279	0086
121-283	0007
121-284	0050
121-286	0079
121-287	0004
121-288	0079
121-289	0136
121-290	0136
121-291	0004
121-292	0136
121-293	0136
121-294	0050
121-295	0050
121-296	0136
121-297	0136
121-298	0050
121-299	0136
121-300	0004
121-301	0004
121-302	0595
121-303	0007
121-304	0136
121-305	0004
121-306	0004
121-307	0004
121-308	0160
121-309	0004
121-310	0004
121-311	0164
121-311B	0164
121-311C	0164
121-311D	0164
121-311E	0164
121-311F	0164
121-312	0050
121-313	0050
121-314	0004
121-315	0142
121-316	0144
121-317	0144
121-318	0144
121-318L	0144
121-319	0004
121-320	0004
121-321	0144
121-327	0004
121-328	0004
121-329	0050
121-330	0050
121-331	0050
121-332	0050
121-333	0050
121-334	0050
121-335	0050
121-336	0050
121-345	0144
121-347	0136
121-348	0004
121-349	0050
121-350	0136
121-351	5250
121-352	0136
121-353	0136
121-354	0279
121-356	0050
121-357	0050
121-358	0050
121-359	0050
121-360	0841
121-361	0233
121-362	0279
121-363	0160
121-364	0016
121-365	0038
121-366	0016
121-367	0016
121-368	0050
121-369	0076
121-370	0969
121-370-X	OEM
121-371	0160
121-372	0211
121-373	0164
121-373B	0164
121-373C	0164
121-373C(ORANGE)	0164
121-373D	0164
121-373D(RED)	0164
121-373E	0164
121-373E(ORANGE)	0164
121-373F	0164
121-373F(YELLOW)	0164
121-373G	0164
121-373H	0164
121-373H(YELLOW)	0164
121-373I	0164
121-373J	0164
121-373J(YELLOW)	0164
121-373K	0164
121-373K(GREEN)	0164
121-373L	0164
121-373M	0164
121-373M(GREEN)	0164
121-373N	0164
121-373N(BLUE)	0164
121-373O	0164
121-373P	0164
121-373P(BLUE)	0164
121-373Q	0164
121-373Q(VIOLET)	0164
121-374	0004
121-375	0004
121-377	0007
121-378	0007
121-379	0007
121-380	0007
121-381	0136
121-382	0160
121-383	0050
121-384	0050
121-385	0136
121-388	0841
121-389	0160
121-389-X	OEM
121-395	0004
121-395-X	OEM
121-396	0004
121-397	0279
121-398	0160
121-399	0004
121-400	0164
121-401	0841
121-401BROWN	0841
121-401ORANGE	0841
121-401RED	0841
121-401YELLOW	0841
121-403	0164
121-404	0016
121-406	0599
121-408	0004
121-409	0004
121-410	0004
121-411	0050
121-412	0050
121-413	0050
121-414	0050
121-415	0050
121-415B	0050
121-416	0211
121-417	0037
121-418	0599
121-418BLUE	0599
121-418GREEN	0599
121-418ORANGE	0599
121-418VIOLET	0599
121-418YELLOW	0599
121-419	0006
121-420	0004
121-421	0164
121-422	0198
121-423	0016
121-425	0164
121-425A	0164
121-425A(BROWN)	0164
121-425B	0164
121-425B(RED)	0164
121-425C	0164
121-425D	0164
121-425D(RECT)	0164
121-425E	0164
121-425E(ORANGE)	0164
121-425F	0164
121-425F(YELLOW)	0164
121-425G	0164
121-425G(ORANGE)	0164
121-425H	0164
121-425H(YELLOW)	0164
121-425I	0164
121-425I(GREEN)	0164
121-425J	0164
121-425J(YELLOW)	0164
121-425K	0164
121-425K(GREEN)	0164
121-425L	0164
121-425L(BLUE)	0164
121-425M	0164
121-425M(GREEN)	0164
121-425N	0164
121-425N(BLUE)	0164
121-425O	0164
121-425P	0164
121-425Q	0164
121-425Q(VIOLET)	0164
121-426	0050
121-427	0050
121-428	0050
121-429	0050
121-430	0086
121-430B	0079
121-430CL	0079
121-431	0086
121-432	0136
121-433	0079
121-433A	0079
121-433CL	0079
121-434	0079
121-434H	0079
121-435	0079
121-436	0142
121-437	0004
121-441	0037
121-442	0079
121-443	OEM
121-443A	OEM
121-444	0006
121-445	0233
121-446	0006
121-447	0079
121-447-04	OEM
121-448	0016
121-449	0309
121-450	0016
121-451	0142
121-452	0074
121-453	0016
121-460	0136
121-461	0007
121-462	0007
121-470	0006
121-471	0007
121-472	0144
121-473	0233
121-477	OEM
121-480	0144
121-481	0007
121-482	0127
121-483	0144
121-490	0004
121-491	0136
121-492	0136
121-493	0136
121-494	0136
121-495	0037
121-496	0006
121-497	0037
121-497WHT	0006
121-498	0079
121-499	0079
121-499-01	0079
121-499-01A	0079
121-499-01C	0079
121-499-1A	0079
121-499A	0079
121-500	0086
121-501	0224
121-502	0224
121-503	0224
121-504	0079
121-505	0144
121-506	0144
121-507	0224
121-508	0007
121-509	0016
121-510	0144
121-520	0076
121-521	0224
121-521(MOTOROLA)	0079
121-521(ZENITH)	0224
121-522	0076
121-523	0016
121-524	0016
121-524A	0224
121-526	0007
121-538	0050
121-538B	0050
121-539	0050
121-540	0050
121-540B	0050
121-541	0050
121-541B	0050
121-542	0050
121-542B	0050
121-543	0004
121-544	0004
121-546	0224
121-546B	0144
121-547	0224
121-551	0224
121-552	0050
121-553	0050
121-554	0136
121-555	0136
121-557	0208
121-558	0208
121-560	0144
121-580	0007
121-581	0016
121-582	0142
121-582GREEN	0142
121-583	0144
121-585	0259
121-585B	0259
121-587	0144
121-588	0178
121-600	0079
121-600(ZENITH)	0079
121-601	0050
121-602	0037
121-603	0037
121-610	0016
121-612	0144
121-612-16	0144
121-613	0144
121-613-16	0144
121-614	0144
121-614-9	0144
121-615	0150
121-616	0144
121-617	OEM
121-619	OEM
121-620	OEM
121-622	OEM
121-626	OEM
121-627	OEM
121-630	0899
121-632	0004
121-633	0004
121-634	0004
121-635	0004
121-636	0004
121-636B	0004
121-636C	0004
121-636D	0004
121-637	0144
121-638	0144
121-638B	0144
121-639	0016
121-639CL	0086
121-640	0004
121-641	0208
121-641BLU	0208
121-641GRN	0208
121-641ORN	0208
121-641RED	0208
121-641YEL	0208
121-642	0006
121-643	0006
121-644	0144
121-645	0144
121-646	0016
121-647	0016
121-648	0016
121-649	0016
121-650	0038
121-651	0144
121-652	0016
121-653	0144
121-654	0037
121-655	0076
121-656	0076
121-657	0016
121-658	0144
121-661	0037
121-662	0076
121-663	0211
121-664	0037
121-665	0103
121-667	0006
121-668	0076
121-671	0076
121-672	0016
121-673	0208
121-674	0211
121-675	1212
121-676	0076
121-677	1212
121-678	0155
121-678GREEN	0155
121-678YELLOW	0155
121-679	0037
121-679GREEN	0037
121-679YELLOW	0037
121-680	0037
121-681	0037
121-682	0037
121-683	0037
121-684	0076
121-687	0079
121-692	0007
121-695	0079
121-697	0050
121-698	0050
121-699	0037
121-699-01	0037
121-699-02	0037
121-699A	0037
121-701	0079
121-702	0076
121-703	0076
121-704	0006
121-705	0211
121-706	0079
121-707	0455
121-708	0161
121-709	0455
121-710	0161
121-711	0076
121-712	0275
121-713	0142
121-714	0037
121-716	0037
121-719	0042
121-722	0086
121-723	0007
121-725	0006
121-726	0103
121-726A	0103
121-730	0144
121-731	0321
121-732	0144
121-733	0076
121-734	0130
121-735	0127
121-737	0086
121-737CL	0086
121-739	0127
121-741	0259
121-742	0127
121-743	0233
121-743-01	0334
121-743-01(T05)	0233
121-743-01(X51)	0334
121-744	0233
121-745	0016
121-746	0037
121-748	0007
121-751	0016
121-752	3749
121-753	0144
121-754	0224
121-755	0264
121-756	0321
121-758	0003
121-758-X	0003
121-758X	0003
121-759	1142
121-759X	0065
121-760	0007
121-761	0007
121-762	0595
121-762CL	0208
121-764	0016
121-765	0126
121-765-01	0037
121-766	0086
121-766-01	0590
121-767	0111
121-767CL	0016
121-768	0111
121-768CL	0016
121-770	0419
121-770-X	0042
121-770CL	0419
121-770X	0042
121-772	0042
121-772CL	0419
121-773	0079
121-773CL	0086
121-774	0037
121-774CL	0126
121-775	0007
121-776	0187
121-777	0187
121-777-01	0233
121-779	0127
121-782	0212
121-783	0212
121-784	0212
121-785	0212
121-786	0212
121-787	0212
121-787-01	0079
121-792	0187
121-793	0160
121-801	0037
121-802	0007
121-803	0676
121-804	0042
121-805	0161
121-806	0042
121-807	0144
121-808	0161
121-809	0236
121-812	0016
121-819	0144
121-819-01	0855
121-821	0003
121-822	0283
121-823	0007
121-824	0007
121-825	0079
121-826	0212
121-827	0144
121-828	OEM
121-829	0103
121-830	0279
121-831	0065
121-831-X	0065
121-834	0127
121-835	0076
121-836	0079
121-840	0224
121-841	0144
121-843	0264
121-843A	0590
121-844	0086
121-845	0126
121-846	0076
121-847	0007
121-848	0144
121-849	0127
121-850	0079
121-851	0144
121-853	0419
121-853-X	OEM
121-853X	0555
121-854	0042
121-855	0224
121-855-01	0224
121-856	0016
121-857	0144
121-858	0321
121-859	OEM
121-860	0321
121-861	0037
121-862	0079
121-863	0079
121-865	0037
121-866	OEM
121-868	0283
121-868-01	0283
121-868-02	0283
121-869	0144
121-871	0855
121-872	0224
121-873	0919
121-875	0037
121-876	0111
121-877	0079
121-878	0086
121-879	0037
121-880	0419
121-880-X	OEM
121-881	0016
121-883	0016
121-884	0144
121-885	0224
121-886	0919
121-887	0228
121-888	0079
121-889	0016
121-895	0079
121-895A	0079
121-896	0037
121-897	OEM
121-899	0144
121-900	0076
121-906	0224

If replacement code is OEM, contact original manufacturer for replacement.

DEVICE TYPE	REPL CODE
121-907	0224
121-908	0224
121-909	0144
121-910	0144
121-911	0187
121-911X	0187
121-912	5311
121-913	0016
121-914	0016
121-915	0016
121-916	0016
121-921	OEM
121-921-01	0042
121-921-02	OEM
121-924	0224
121-925	0144
121-926	0919
121-926-01	0919
121-926-02	OEM
121-927	0042
121-927-01	0042
121-927-02	OEM
121-928	0111
121-929	0224
121-930	0224
121-931	0079
121-932	0144
121-933	1021
121-943	0224
121-944	0079
121-945	0224
121-946	0127
121-950	0224
121-950-01	0224
121-951	0224
121-952	0037
121-953	0212
121-954	0224
121-956	0042
121-957	0015
121-958	0144
121-964	OEM
121-965	OEM
121-966	0042
121-966-01	0042
121-966-02	0042
121-966-03	0042
121-967	0419
121-968	0144
121-969	0919
121-969-01	OEM
121-969-02	0919
121-970	0042
121-970-02	0236
121-972	0079
121-972-01	0079
121-973	0037
121-973A	0037
121-974	0127
121-975	0079
121-975A	0079
121-976	0042
121-976-01	0042
121-977	0919
121-977-01	0848
121-978	0037
121-978-01	0037
121-978-01A	5807
121-978-03	0037
121-978-03A	0037
121-978-03C	0037
121-978A	0037
121-980	0378
121-980-01	0378
121-982	0079
121-983	0127
121-984	0127
121-984-01	OEM
121-985	0065
121-985-01	OEM
121-985-X	OEM
121-986	0037
121-986A	0037
121-987	0236
121-987-01	2969
121-987-02	0419
121-987-03	0763
121-988	0676
121-988-01	OEM
121-988-02	0848
121-988-03	0919
121-989	0283
121-990	0283
121-992	0236
121-992-01	0236
121-993	1021
121-994	0676
121-995	0127
121-996	0637
121-997	0919
121-998	0911
121-999	0470
121-1001	0224
121-1002	0127
121-1003	0309
121-1004	0079
121-1005	0037
121-1006	0042
121-1007	0378
121-1008	0236
121-1008-01	0424
121-1009	0676
121-1010	0144
121-1012	0597
121-1013	1203
121-1014	0334
121-1015	0065
121-1016	0006
121-1017	0155
121-1018	0127
121-1019	0037
121-1019-01	0037
121-1019-01A	0037
121-1019-01C	0037
121-1019A	0037
121-1020	0855
121-1020A	0855
121-1021	0431
121-1023	0224
121-1024	0212
121-1026	OEM
121-1027	1506
121-1028	1021
121-1028-01	0388
121-1029	0065
121-1029-01	0065
121-1029-02	0065
121-1030	0212
121-1031	0178
121-1032	0211
121-1033	0309
121-1034	0283
121-1034-01	0283
121-1034-1	0283
121-1034A	0283
121-1035	0320
121-1035A	0320
121-1036	0431
121-1037	0283
121-1040	0079
121-1040-01	0079
121-1040-01A	0079
121-1040A	0079
121-1042	3838
121-1042-01	3838
121-1042A	3838
121-1043	0037
121-1043A	0037
121-1044	0127
121-1045	0284
121-1048	0321
121-1049	0236
121-1051	0532
121-1059	0037
121-1059A	0037
121-1060	OEM
121-1061	0236
121-1061-01	0388
121-1062	0037
121-1063	0283
121-1064	0037
121-1064A	0037
121-1065	0079
121-1065A	0079
121-1066	0367
121-1070	0723
121-1072	0236
121-1072-01	0236
121-1082-02	0042
121-1084	0079
121-1084A	0079
121-1086-01	2880
121-1089	OEM
121-1090	OEM
121-1091	OEM
121-1092	0065
121-1094	OEM
121-1096	0079
121-1101	0338
121-1101-02	0037
121-1101A	0037
121-1102	0006
121-1102A	0006
121-1103	OEM
121-1109	2880
121-1109-01	2880
121-1110	OEM
121-1112	0676
121-1112-01	0676
121-1112-1	OEM
121-1114	0055
121-1124	0160
121-1125	OEM
121-1125-01	OEM
121-1125-01A	OEM
121-1125B	OEM
121-1126	OEM
121-1126A	OEM
121-1127-01	OEM
121-1127-01A	OEM
121-1128	OEM
121-1130	OEM
121-1130A	OEM
121-1130B	OEM
121-1133	1731
121-1133A	1741
121-1133B	OEM
121-1134	0160
121-1136-01	OEM
121-1136-1	4376
121-1139A	OEM
121-1140	0261
121-1140A	0261
121-1140C	0261
121-1141	1533
121-1141-01	1533
121-1141-02	1533
121-1145	0006
121-1145A	0006
121-1146	0710
121-1146A	0079
121-1148	1533
121-1153	1492
121-1158	1795
121-1158A	1795
121-1160	OEM
121-1162-01A	OEM
121-1167	3472
121-1167-01	OEM
121-1169	OEM
121-1190	OEM
121-1201	OEM
121-1210	OEM
121-1216-01	OEM
121-1225-01	OEM
121-1226B	OEM
121-1227A	OEM
121-1232	0079
121-1232A	0079
121-1237	OEM
121-1256	OEM
121-1256A	OEM
121-1256Z	OEM
121-1262A	OEM
121-1263	OEM
121-1263A	OEM
121-1264	OEM
121-1264-01	OEM
121-1264-01A	OEM
121-1264A	OEM
121-1290	OEM
121-1291-01	OEM
121-1292	0079
121-1299	OEM
121-1300A	OEM
121-1301A	OEM
121-1330	0279
121-1350	0279
121-1360	0279
121-1390	0279
121-1400	0279
121-1410	0595
121-5065	0016
121-9003	0431
121-505501	0016
121-Z9000	0079
121-Z9000-A	0016
121-Z9000A	0016
121-Z9001	0309
121-Z9002	0455
121-Z9003	0037
121-Z9004	0004
121-Z9005	0126
121-Z9006	0160
121-Z9007	0164
121-Z9008	0555
121-Z9009	0969
121-Z9010	0178
121-Z9011	0103
121-Z9012	0142
121-Z9013	0136
121-Z9014	0218
121-Z9015	0208
121-Z9016	0275
121-Z9017	0222
121-Z9018	0074
121-Z9019	1233
121-Z9020	0150
121-Z9021	0224
121-Z9022	0637
121-Z9023	2736
121-Z9024	0396
121-Z9025	0599
121-Z9026	0556
121-Z9027	0693
121-Z9028	0168
121-Z9029	0004
121-Z9030	0208
121-Z9031	0038
121-Z9032	0160
121-Z9033	0435
121-Z9034	0130
121-Z9035	0161
121-Z9036	0546
121-Z9037	0626
121-Z9038	3477
121-Z9039	0930
121-Z9040	0830
121-Z9041	1401
121-Z9042	0177
121-Z9043	0538
121-Z9044	0003
121-Z9045	0710
121-Z9046	0338
121-Z9047	0236
121-Z9048	0676
121-Z9049	1698
121-Z9050	0037
121-Z9051	0841
121-Z9052	1671
121-Z9053	0378
121-Z9054	0264
121-Z9055	0561
121-Z9056	1357
121-Z9057	0899
121-Z9058	0486
121-Z9059	0597
121-Z9060	2243
121-Z9061	3336
121-Z9062	2002
121-Z9063	1588
121-Z9064	1401
121-Z9065	0076
121-Z9066	0018
121-Z9067	0527
121-Z9068	0320
121-Z9069	1935
121-Z9070	0259
121-Z9071	0312
121-Z9072	0040
121-Z9073	2411
121-Z9074	2262
121-Z9075	3339
121-Z9076	3340
121-Z9077	2422
121-Z9078	2415
121-Z9079	1384
121-Z9080	2429
121-Z9081	3483
121-Z9082	3484
121-Z9083	0553
121-Z9084	2869
121-Z9085	1203
121-Z9086	2220
121-Z9087	2222
121-Z9088	0414
121-Z9089	0177
121-Z9090	0359
121-Z9091	0538
121-Z9092	2005
121-Z9093	0259
121-Z9094	0886
121-Z9095	1471
121-Z9096	2465
121-Z9097	2675
121-Z9098	0050
121-Z9099	1190
121-Z9100	1025
121-Z9101	0349
121-Z9102	3249
121-Z9103	0431
121-Z9104	1421
121-Z9105	0520
121-Z9106	0388
121-Z9107	1077
121-Z9108	2200
121-Z9109	1740
121-Z9110	2085
121-Z9111	0723
121-Z9112	0055
121-Z9113	3052
121-Z9114	0853
121-Z9115	1638
121-Z9119	0853
121A	0023
121A-US	OEM
121G1241	0102
121G3019	0016
121G3020	0016
121GI241	0102
121GL241	0102
121N1	OEM
121S2	0312
121T2	0144
121U1	OEM
121U2	OEM
121U2AT	0312
121U3AC	0312
122	0023
122-1	0016
122-2	0079
122-2(DIO)	0071
122-2N1B	0359
122-3	OEM
122-6	0016
122-80	0015
122-229	0279
122-522	1489
122-1028	0435
122-1028A	0435
122-1625	0160
122-1648	0136
122-1962	0038
122-A484	0144
122A	0023
122A-US	OEM
122GRN	0037
122N2	0359
122T2	0144
122YEL	0037
123-001	0817
123-002	0212
123-003	0321
123-004	0016
123-005	0111
123-007	0111
123-008	0830
123-009	0833
123-010	0016
123-011	0219
123-011A	0219
123-012	0155
123-015	0143
123-016	0133
123-017	0396
123-017(DIODE)	0124
123-018	0102
123-019	0244
123-020	0012
123-021	0015
123-022	0133
123-024	0124
123-025	0133
123A-US	OEM
123B-001	0103
123B-002	0219
123B-003	0133
123B-004	0244
123B-005	0631
123B-006	0416
123N1	0003
123S425	0086
123S-437	0086
123T2	0144
124	0023
124-0028	0071
124-0165	0315
124-0178	0015
124-1	0160
124-N16	0595
124A	0023
124J490	0015
124N1	0595
124N16	0016
125-1	0150
125-4	0969
125-4(RCA)	0969
125-121	0086
125-402	0160
125-403	0160
125-410	0178
125-425C	0164
125-655	0224
125-A000-F01	0810
125-B415	0042
125A	OEM
125A000F01	0810
125A134	0004
125A137	0086
125A137A	0086
125AS251	0178
125B	OEM
125B132	0016
125B133	0037
125B139	0086
125B410	0178
125BN20	OEM
125BN30	OEM
125BN40	OEM
125BN50	OEM
125BN60	OEM
125BN80	OEM
125BN100	OEM
125BN120	OEM
125BN140	OEM
125BN160	OEM
125BNS	OEM
125C3	2674
125C3RB	2674
125C211	0016
125CN30	OEM
125CN40	OEM
125CN50	OEM
125CN60	OEM
125CN80	OEM
125CN100	OEM
125CN120	OEM
125CN140	OEM
125CN160	OEM
125CNS	OEM
125P1	0037
125P1M	0037
125P116	0037
125PALB**	0761
125PAM**	0761
125PI	0037
125PL	0037
125PL50	OEM
125PL60	OEM
125PL80	OEM
125PL100	OEM
125PLB50	OEM
125PLB60	OEM
125PLB80	OEM
125PLB100	OEM
125PLB110	OEM
125PLB120	OEM
125PM10	OEM
125PM20	OEM
125PM30	OEM
125PM40	OEM
125PM50	OEM
125PM60	OEM
125PM80	OEM
125PM100	OEM
125T1	OEM
125T4	OEM
125UA	OEM
125UB	OEM
125UC	OEM
125UD	OEM
125UE	OEM
125UF	OEM
125V10	OEM
125WA	OEM
125WB	OEM
125WC	OEM
125WD	OEM
125XA	OEM
125XB	OEM
125XC	OEM
125XD	OEM
125YA	OEM
125YB	OEM
125YC	OEM
125YD	OEM
126	0023
126-1	2799
126-4	0015
126-7	0015
126-7(ARVIN)	0015
126-12	0016
126-40	1291
126A	0023
126N1	0208
126N2	0208
126P1	0164
126T1	OEM
127	0016
127-001	0855
127-1	0468
127-7	0595
127-115	0111
127A905F01	0267
127T1	OEM
128	0144
128-853	0555
128-9050	0103
128A157F01	0267
128A157F02	0267
128C212H01	2067
128C213H01	1786
128C830H05	0564
128N2	0086
128N3	OEM
128N4	0144
128WHT	0016
129-4	0164
129-5	0160
129-6	0085
129-7	0085
129-8	0004
129-8-1	0004
129-8-1A	0004
129-8-2	0004
129-9	0160
129-10	0160
129-11	0136
129-13	0160
129-14	0198
129-15	0198
129-16	0079
129-17	0208
129-18	0164
129-20	0037
129-21	0016
129-23	0178
129-27	0007
129-28	0086
129-29	0126
129-30	0208
129-31	0004
129-32	0004
129-33	0042
129-33(PILOT)	0016
129-34	0037
129-34(PILOT)	0037
129BRN	0016
129N1	0007
129WHT	0016
130	0127
130-04	OEM
130-06	OEM
130-08	OEM
130-013	2006
130-10	OEM
130-104	0160
130-105	0398
130-138	0144
130-144	2194
130-146	0103
130-149	0037
130-150	2194
130-152	0259
130-152-00	0259
130-172	2194
130-174	2194
130-185	0007
130-185-98	0259
130-240	0007
130-245	1390
130-338-00	0015
130-398-99	0015
130-30189	0133
130-30192	0015
130-30256	0071
130-30261	0276
130-30265	0133
130-30266	0133
130-30274	0133
130-30281	0143
130-30301	0143
130-30313	0015
130-30702	0133
130-40089	0595
130-40095	0004
130-40096	0208
130-40214	0016
130-40215	0016
130-40216	0111
130-40229	0143
130-40236	0004
130-40294	0016
130-40304	0144
130-40311	0016
130-40312	0016
130-40313	0016
130-40314	0208
130-40315	0037
130-40317	0016
130-40318	0016
130-40347	0208
130-40349	3502
130-40352	0004
130-40357	0016
130-40362	0144
130-40421	0144
130-40429	0037
130-40439	3502
130-40456	0164
130-40459	0144
130-40883	0111
130-40896	0016
130-40901	0111
130-40922	0016
130-V10	0127
130-VLO	0127
130A17268	0015
130HF20	OEM
130HF20F	OEM
130HF20M	OEM
130HF40	OEM
130HF40F	OEM
130HF40M	OEM
130HF60	OEM
130HF60F	OEM
130HF60M	OEM
130HF80	OEM
130HF80F	OEM
130HF80M	OEM
130HF120	OEM
130HF120F	OEM
130HF120M	OEM
130HF130	OEM
130HF130F	OEM
130HF130M	OEM
130HF140	OEM
130HF140F	OEM
130HF140M	OEM
130HF160	OEM
130HF160F	OEM
130HF160M	OEM
130HHFR20	OEM
130HHFR20HFR	OEM
130HHFR20M	OEM
130HHFR40	OEM
130HHFR40HFR	OEM
130HHFR40M	OEM
130HHFR60	OEM
130HHFR60HFR	OEM
130HHFR60M	OEM
130HHFR80	OEM
130HHFR80HFR	OEM
130HHFR80M	OEM
130HHFR120	OEM
130HHFR120HFR	OEM
130HHFR120M	OEM
130HHFR130	OEM
130HHFR130HFR	OEM
130HHFR130M	OEM
130HHFR140	OEM
130HHFR140HFR	OEM
130HHFR140M	OEM
130HHFR160	OEM
130HHFR160HFR	OEM
130HHFR160M	OEM
130ORN	0127
130P4	OEM
130T4	OEM
130YE	0015
131-2	0555
131A	0196
131A246F01	0267
131A246F02	0267
131N2	0334
131N2G	0042
131P4	OEM
132-001	0004
132-002	0016
132-003	0283
132-004	0016
132-005	0016
132-007	0126

If replacement code is OEM, contact original manufacturer for replacement.

175

DEVICE TYPE	REPL CODE
132-008	0007
132-009	0007
132-010	0004
132-011	0016
132-014	0283
132-015	0144
132-017	0016
132-018	0016
132-019	0050
132-020	0050
132-021	0016
132-021B	0086
132-022	0086
132-023	0016
132-024	0455
132-025	0074
132-026	0016
132-027	0050
132-028	0142
132-029	0688
132-030	0016
132-031	0688
132-032	0126
132-033	0142
132-038	0086
132-039	0126
132-041	0016
132-042	0016
132-045	0349
132-047	0349
132-048	0843
132-049	0321
132-050	0016
132-051	0016
132-052A	0396
132-054	0016
132-055	0016
132-056	0037
132-057	0016
132-059	0142
132-062	0016
132-063	0016
132-065	0178
132-066	0086
132-069	0016
132-070	0103
132-072	0161
132-074	0037
132-075	0016
132-076	0007
132-077	0016
132-078	0275
132-082	0007
132-085	0103
132-087	0007
132-090	0004
132-3	0042
132-5	0419
132-90	0004
132-185	0007
132-501	0016
132-502	0016
132-503	0016
132-504	0016
132-515	0142
132-516	0142
132-521	0142
132-522	0142
132-523	0142
132-524	0142
132-525	0142
132-526	0142
132-539	0016
132-540	0016
132-541	0103
132-542	1506
132-B3511	0196
132B3511	0196
132N1	0086
132P4	OEM
133-002	0823
133-0021-0	1843
133-1	0546
133-3	0042
133P100	1340
134-1	0378
134-1P	0150
134-4P	0037
134B1038-4	0111
134B1038-8	0111
134B1038-13	0111
134B1038-21	0079
134B1038-22	0111
134B1040-7	0590
134P1	0688
134P1(REMOTE)	0786
134P1(VID)	0150
134P1A	0037
134P1AA	0126
134P1M	0037
134P2	0126
134P4	0037
134P4AA	0037
134P4M	0037
134P6	0150
135-3	0015
135B1N	4156
135C	0604
135C4L	0604
135H1M	0283
135N1	0233
135N1M	0233
135P4	0229
136-000100	1024
136-000200	1024
136-000300	1024
136-12	0086
136P1	0150
136P4	OEM
136RED	0016
137	0150
137-003	2007
137-12	0150
137-684	0071
137-718	0015
137-737	0242
137-759	0002
137-824	0143
137-828	0071
137P4	OEM
137Q31	0190
138-4	0016
139-4	0144
139N1	0224
139N1D	0224
140-013	0015
140BV50H	OEM
140BV100H	OEM
140BV150H	OEM
140N1	0103
140N2	0103
140PL10	OEM
140PL20	OEM
140PL30	OEM
140PL40	OEM
140PL50	OEM
140PL60	OEM
140PM10	OEM
140PM20	OEM
140PM30	OEM
140PM40	OEM
140PM50	OEM
140PM60	OEM
140T4	OEM
141-003	0143
141-4	0079
141-402	0007
141-430	0079
142	0133
142-001	0016
142-002	0111
142-003	0111
142-004	0042
142-005	0155
142-006	0219
142-007	0617
142-008	0042
142-009	0133
142-010	0133
142-011	0143
142-012	0012
142-014	0015
142-015	0416
142-016	0025
142-3	0016
142-4	0016
142N1	0155
142N1P	0007
142N3	0079
142N3P	0079
142N3T	0016
142N4	0016
142N5	0016
142N6	0144
142N7	OEM
142N8	OEM
142N10	OEM
143	0222
143-12	0079
144-3	0133
144-4	0233
144-6	OEM
144-12	0079
144A-1	0160
144A-1-12	0160
144A-1-12-3	0160
144A-1-12-8	0160
144N1	0283
144N1G	0283
144N1G(AMP)	0283
144N1G(VID)	0283
144N1P	0283
144N2	0283
144N3	0283
144N4	0233
145-2	0283
145-6	OEM
145-12	0150
145-100	0170
145-470	0993
145-2023DN	OEM
145-2023DNT	OEM
145-2023SN	OEM
145-2023SNT	OEM
145-2025	OEM
145-2051	OEM
145-2068	OEM
145-2071	OEM
145-2071R	OEM
145-2072-1	OEM
145-2072-2	OEM
145-2072-4	OEM
145-2073	OEM
145-2076	OEM
145-T1B	0136
145A9254	0015
145A9786	0015
145N1	0007
145N1(LAST-LF)	0326
145N1P	0007
145NIP	0079
145T1B	0050
146-1	0283
146-12	0079
146-T1	0160
146D-1	0133
146D1	2117
146D1B112	0907
146N3	0016
146N5	0016
146T1	0085
147-7031-01	0079
147-7040-01	1239
147-7043-01	1042
147-T1	0160
147N1	0018
147P2	0527
147T1	0085
148-1	0086
148-3	0102
148-3(XSTR)	0079
148-12	0150
148-134622	0435
148N1	0086
148N2	0016
148N3	0086
148N212	0016
148P-2	0004
148P-2-12	0004
148P-2-12-8	0004
149-3	OEM
149-4	0042
149-10	0042
149-12	0321
149-142-G1	0133
149L-4	0004
149L-4-12	0004
149L-4-12-8	0004
149N1	0161
149N2	0161
149N2B	2969
149N2D	0042
149N4B	2969
149N2002D	0042
149N2004	0042
149N20020	3103
149P1	0455
149P1B	3136
149P1D	0042
149P4B	3136
149P2001D	0919
149P2003	0919
149P20010	OEM
150	0015
150-001-9-005	0019
150-001-9-007	0143
150-002-9-001	0143
150-004-9-001	0143
150-005-9-001	0143
150-006-9-001	0143
150-012-9-001	0019
150-013-7-001	OEM
150-013-9-001	0019
150-014-9-001	0019
150-014-9001	OEM
150-015-9-001	0123
150-016-9-001	0143
150-018-9-001	0015
150-022-9-001	0015
150-066-9-001	0124
150-1	0079
150-2	OEM
150-12	0321
150BC15	0594
150C05	OEM
150C05B	OEM
150C025	0733
150C025B	0733
150C050	0733
150C050B	0733
150C4.7-5.3	OEM
150C6.2-6.8	OEM
150C10	0733
150C10B	0733
150C15	0733
150C15B	0733
150C20	0733
150C20B	0733
150C25	0733
150C25B	0733
150C30	0733
150C30B	0733
150C35	0733
150C35B	0733
150C40	0733
150C40B	0733
150C45	0733
150C45B	0733
150C50	0733
150C50B	0733
150C60	0733
150C60B	0733
150C70	0733
150C70B	0733
150C80	0733
150C80B	0733
150C90	0733
150C90B	0733
150C100	0733
150C100B	0733
150C110	0733
150C110B	0733
150C120	0733
150C120B	0733
150C130	1878
150C130B	1878
150C140	1878
150C140B	1878
150C150	1878
150C150B	1878
150C160	1878
150C160B	1878
150C170	OEM
150C170B	OEM
150C180	OEM
150C180B	OEM
150D	0002
150DC15	0594
150FC15	0594
150GC15	0594
150JC15	1975
150K**	0594
150K40A	OEM
150K5A	0594
150K5R	1337
150K10A	0594
150K10AM	OEM
150K10R	1337
150K15A	0594
150K15R	1337
150K20A	0594
150K20AM	OEM
150K20R	1337
150K25A	0594
150K25R	1337
150K30A	0594
150K30AM	OEM
150K30R	1337
150K40A	0594
150K40AM	OEM
150K40R	1894
150K50A	1975
150K50R	1894
150K60A	1975
150K60AM	OEM
150K60R	1894
150K70A	0652
150K70R	0193
150K80A	0652
150K80AM	OEM
150K80R	0193
150K90A	3188
150K100A	0652
150K100AM	OEM
150K100R	0193
150K120A	3277
150K120AM	OEM
150K140A	OEM
150KR5A	4891
150KR10A	1337
150KR10AM	OEM
150KR20A	1337
150KR20AM	OEM
150KR30A	1337
150KR30AM	OEM
150KR40A	1337
150KR40AM	OEM
150KR50A	6923
150KR60A	1894
150KR60AM	OEM
150KR80A	0193
150KR80AM	OEM
150KR100A	0193
150KR100AM	OEM
150KR120A	OEM
150KR120AM	OEM
150KS5	OEM
150KS10	OEM
150KS15	OEM
150KS20	OEM
150KS25	OEM
150KS30	OEM
150KS40	OEM
150KS50	OEM
150KS60	OEM
150KS70	OEM
150KS80	OEM
150KS90	OEM
150KS100	OEM
150KS120	OEM
150L5A	0594
150L5R	1337
150L10A	0594
150L10R	1337
150L15A	0594
150L15R	1337
150L20A	0594
150L20R	1337
150L25A	0594
150L25R	1337
150L30A	0594
150L30R	1337
150L40A	1975
150L40R	1894
150L50A	1975
150L50R	1894
150L60A	1975
150L60R	1894
150L70A	0652
150L70R	0193
150L80A	0652
150L80R	0193
150L90A	0652
150L90R	0193
150L100A	0652
150L100R	0193
150L120A	3277
150L140A	OEM
150LC15	0652
150LD11	1778
150LD13	OEM
150MA60	OEM
150MA80	OEM
150MA100	OEM
150MA120	OEM
150MA140	OEM
150MA160	OEM
150MA180	OEM
150MLAB160	OEM
150MLAB180	OEM
150MLAB200	OEM
150MLAB250	OEM
150N1	0007
150N2	0016
150N3	0007
150N15A	OEM
150N15A9	OEM
150N20A	OEM
150N20A9	OEM
150N25A	OEM
150N25A9	OEM
150N30A	OEM
150N30A9	OEM
150N35A	OEM
150N35A9	OEM
150N40A	OEM
150N40A9	OEM
150N45A	OEM
150N45A9	OEM
150N50A	OEM
150N50A9	OEM
150N55A	OEM
150N55A9	OEM
150N60A	OEM
150N60A9	OEM
150N65A	OEM
150N65A9	OEM
150N70A	OEM
150N70A9	OEM
150N75A	OEM
150N75A9	OEM
150N80A	OEM
150N80A9	OEM
150N85A	OEM
150N85A9	OEM
150N90A	OEM
150N90A9	OEM
150N95A	OEM
150N95A9	OEM
150N100A	OEM
150N100A9	OEM
150N110A	OEM
150N120A	OEM
150N130A	OEM
150N140A	OEM
150N150A	OEM
150N160A	OEM
150N170A	OEM
150N180A	OEM
150N190A	OEM
150N200A	OEM
150N210A	OEM
150N220A	OEM
150N230A	OEM
150N240A	OEM
150N250A	OEM
150NC15	0652
150ND13	OEM
150P1SP	OEM
150P2SP	OEM
150P3SP	OEM
150P4SP	OEM
150P5SP	OEM
150P6SP	OEM
150P8SP	OEM
150P10SP	OEM
150P12SP	OEM
150P16SP	OEM
150QC15	3277
150QD13	OEM
150R1B	0087
150R2B	0242
150R3B	1736
150R4B	0535
150R5B	0959
150R6B	0959
150R7B	0811
150R8B	0087
150R9B	0087
150R10B	0087
150R11B	OEM
150R12B	OEM
150R13B	OEM
150R14B	OEM
150R15B	OEM
150R16B	OEM
150R18B	OEM
150R20B	OEM
150R22B	OEM
150R24B	OEM
150R26B	OEM
150R28B	OEM
150R30B	OEM
150R32B	OEM
150R34B	OEM
150R36B	OEM
150R38B	OEM
150R40B	OEM
150R42B	OEM
150R44B	OEM
150R46B	OEM
150R48B	OEM
150R50B	OEM
150RC5	OEM
150RC10	0733
150RC15	OEM
150RC20	0733
150RC25	OEM
150RC30	0733
150RC35	OEM
150RC40	0733
150RC50	0733
150RC60	0733
150RC60A	OEM
150RC70	0733
150RC70A	OEM
150RC80	0733
150RC80A	OEM
150RE50	0733
150RE60	0733
150RE80	0733
150RE90	OEM
150RE100	0733
150RE110	0733
150RE120	0733
150RE130	OEM
150S2SP	OEM
150S3SP	OEM
150S4SP	OEM
150S6SP	OEM
150S8SP	OEM
150S10H	OEM
150S12H	OEM
150SS2SP	OEM
150SS3SP	OEM
150SS4SP	OEM
150SS5SP	OEM
150SS6SP	OEM
150SS8SP	OEM
150SS10H	OEM
150SS12H	OEM
150T4	OEM
150TD13	OEM
150X9-9.75	OEM
150YD13	OEM
151	0023
151-001-9-001	0133
151-002-9-001	0133
151-006-9-001	0039
151-0021-9-001	OEM
151-04SPC	OEM
151-06SPC	OEM
151-08SPC	OEM
151-011-9-001	0133
151-011-9-011	0015
151-013-9-001	0907
151-014-9-001	0914
151-015-9-001	0124
151-018-9-001	0015
151-021-001	0133
151-021-9-001	0133
151-022-9-001	0133
151-023-9-001	0015
151-024-9-001	0133
151-025-9-001	0229
151-029-9-003	0015
151-030-9-001	0133
151-030-9-002	1141
151-030-9-003	0631
151-030-9-004	0030
151-030-9-005	0023
151-030-9-006	0133
151-031-9-001	0631
151-031-9-006	0012
151-032-004	0133
151-032-9-001	0133
151-032-9-002	0133
151-032-9-004	0133
151-034-9-001	0133
151-035-9-001	0133
151-035-9-004	0133
151-039-9-003	0030
151-040-7-003	0023
151-040-9-001	0133
151-040-9-002	0133
151-040-9-003	0023
151-045-9-001	0015
151-045-9-003	0102
151-049-9-001	0133
151-049-9-002	0133
151-051-9-001	0133
151-059-9-001	0133
151-060-9-001	0124
151-061-9-001	0133
151-062-9-001	1023
151-064-9-001	0133
151-064-9-002	0133
151-066-9-001	0124
151-067-9-001	0133
151-069-9-001	0124
151-072-9-001	0163
151-0l49	0178
151-1	0023
151-3	0023
151-4	0023
151-6	0079
151-9	0344
151-10SPC	OEM
151-12SPC	OEM
151-14SPC	OEM
151-16SPC	OEM
151-18SPC	OEM
151-20SPC	OEM
151-22SPC	OEM
151-26SPC	OEM
151-28SPC	OEM
151-30SPC	OEM
151-32-9-004	0133
151-267-9-001	0133
151A	0023
151F1FM	OEM
151F2FM	OEM
151F3FM	OEM
151M11	0144
151MQ30	OEM
151MQ40	OEM
151N1	0144
151N2	0016
151N4	0016
151N5	0079
151N11	0144
151N116	0144
151R1FM	OEM
151R2FM	OEM
151R3FM	OEM
151RA10	0733
151RA20	0733
151RA30	0733
151RA40	0733
151RA50	0733
151RA60	0733
151RA80	0733
151RA100	0733
151RA110	0733
151RA120	0733
151RA140	1878
151RA150	1878
151RA160	1878
151RB10	0733
151RB20	0733
151RB30	0733
151RB40	0733
151RB50	0733
151RB60	0733
151RB80	0733
151RB100	0733
151RB110	0733
151RB120	0733
151RB140	1878
151RB150	1878
151RB160	1878
151RC10	1076
151RC10A	0733
151RC15	OEM
151RC15A	OEM
151RC20	1076
151RC20A	0733
151RC30	1078
151RC30A	0733
151RC40	1078
151RC40A	0733
151RC50	1078
151RC50A	0733
151RC60	1078
151RC60A	0733
151RC80	1094
151RC80A	0733
151RC100	OEM
151RC120	OEM
151RCF15A	OEM
151RCF25A	OEM
151RCF60A	OEM
151RCF70A	OEM
151RCF80A	OEM
151RE50	0733
151RE60	0733
151RE80	0733
151RE100	0733
151RE110	0733
151RE120	0733
151REA50	0733
151REA60	0733

If replacement code is OEM, contact original manufacturer for replacement.

DEVICE TYPE	REPL CODE
151REA70	OEM
151REA80	0733
151REA90	OEM
151REA100	0733
151REA110	0733
151REA120	0733
151REA130	OEM
151REB50	0733
151REB60	0733
151REB70	OEM
151REB80	0733
151REB90	OEM
151REB100	0733
151REB110	0733
151REB120	0733
151REB130	OEM
151RL50	0423
151RL60	0423
151RL80	1860
151RL100	1860
151RL110	1860
151RL120	1860
151RM10	0423
151RM20	0423
151RM30	0423
151RM40	0423
151RM50	0423
151RM60	0423
151RM80	1860
151RM100	1860
152	0023
152-006-9-001	0039
152-008-7-001	0030
152-008-9-001	0012
152-0047	0535
152-0047-00	0535
152-04SPC	OEM
152-06SPC	OEM
152-08SPC	OEM
152-012-9-001	0012
152-019-9-001	0631
152-021-9-001	0789
152-029-9-002	0039
152-042-9-001	0410
152-042-9-001(FET)	0212
152-042-9-002	0025
152-047	0015
152-047-9-001	0466
152-047-9-004	0466
152-051-9-001	0012
152-051-9-002	0631
152-052-9-002	0091
152-054-9-001	0244
152-057-9-001	0416
152-079-001	0162
152-079-9-001	0041
152-079-9-002	0631
152-079-9-003	0091
152-079-9-004	0644
152-082-9-001	0012
152-0154	1403
152-10SPC	OEM
152-12	OEM
152-12SPC	OEM
152-14SPC	OEM
152-16SPC	OEM
152-18SPC	OEM
152-20SPC	OEM
152-22SPC	OEM
152-26SPC	OEM
152-28SPC	OEM
152-30SPC	OEM
152A	OEM
152CB	0411
152ET	OEM
152K5A	OEM
152K10A	OEM
152K10AM	OEM
152K15A	OEM
152K20A	OEM
152K20AM	OEM
152K25A	OEM
152K30A	OEM
152K30AM	OEM
152K40A	OEM
152K40AM	OEM
152K50A	OEM
152K60A	OEM
152K60AM	OEM
152K70A	OEM
152K80A	OEM
152K80AM	OEM
152K90A	OEM
152K100A	OEM
152K100AM	OEM
152K120A	OEM
152K120AM	OEM
152L5A	OEM
152L10A	OEM
152L15A	OEM
152L20A	OEM
152L25A	OEM
152L30A	OEM
152L40A	OEM
152L50A	OEM
152L60A	OEM
152L70A	OEM
152L80A	OEM
152L90A	OEM

DEVICE TYPE	REPL CODE
152L100A	OEM
152L120A	OEM
152N-2	0130
152N2C	0130
152P1B	0899
152PJA180	OEM
152PJA200	OEM
152PJA250	OEM
152PJAL60	OEM
152PJAL80	OEM
152PJAL100	OEM
152PJAL120	OEM
152SC711(D)	0025
153-004-9-001	0030
153-008-9-001	0715
153-008-9-002	0139
153-04	3470
153-04SPC	OEM
153-05	3470
153-06	3470
153-06SPC	OEM
153-07	3470
153-08	3470
153-08SPC	OEM
153-09	3470
153-011-9-001	0120
153-9	0086
153-10	3470
153-10SPC	OEM
153-12	3470
153-12SPC	OEM
153-14	3470
153-14SPC	OEM
153-16	3449
153-16SPC	OEM
153-18	3449
153-18SPC	OEM
153-20SPC	OEM
153-22SPC	OEM
153-24SPC	OEM
153-26SPC	OEM
153-28SPC	OEM
153-30SPC	OEM
153E	OEM
153N1	0419
153N5	OEM
153N5C	0042
154	0023
154-001-9-001	0030
154-004-9-001	0030
154-04	3470
154-04SPC	OEM
154-05	3470
154-06	3470
154-06SPC	OEM
154-07	3470
154-08	3470
154-08SPC	OEM
154-09	3470
154-10	3470
154-10SPC	OEM
154-12	3470
154-12SPC	OEM
154-14	3470
154-16	3449
154-16SPC	OEM
154-18	3449
154-18SPC	OEM
154-20SPC	OEM
154-22SPC	OEM
154-24SPC	OEM
154-26SPC	OEM
154-28SPC	OEM
154-30SPC	OEM
154A	0023
154A3675-105	0211
154A3676	0136
154A3676-205	0211
154A3677	0136
154A3679	0211
154A3679-5110	0136
154A3680	0160
154A3992	0015
154A5943	0142
154A5943-1	0142
154A5944-410	0079
154A5944-413	0111
154A5945-519	0111
154A5946	0016
154A5946-622	0086
154A5946-624	0079
154A5946-667	0126
154A5947-7732	0150
154A8681	0211
154E	OEM
154K5A	OEM
154K10A	OEM
154K10AM	OEM
154K15A	OEM
154K20A	OEM
154K20AM	OEM
154K25A	OEM
154K30A	OEM
154K30AM	OEM
154K40A	OEM
154K40AM	OEM
154K50A	OEM
154K60A	OEM
154K60AM	OEM

DEVICE TYPE	REPL CODE
154K70A	OEM
154K80A	OEM
154K80AM	OEM
154K90A	OEM
154K100A	OEM
154K100AM	OEM
154K120A	OEM
154K120AM	OEM
154L5A	OEM
154L10A	OEM
154L15A	OEM
154L20A	OEM
154L25A	OEM
154L30A	OEM
154L40A	OEM
154L50A	OEM
154L51	OEM
154L60A	OEM
154L70A	OEM
154L80A	OEM
154L90A	OEM
154L100A	OEM
154L120A	OEM
154T1	0050
154T1A	0050
154T1B	0050
154WA	2189
154WK	0689
155D06010B	OEM
155N1	0419
155T1	0050
156	0016
156(DIO)	0023
156-0011-00	1063
156-0012-00	OEM
156-0017	2515
156-0017-00	2515
156-04	0130
156-06	0130
156-08	0130
156-032	0103
156-043	0103
156-043A	0103
156-044	0103
156-053	0103
156-063	0103
156-064	0103
156-083	0130
156-084	0130
156-0148-00	0357
156-0151-00	1545
156-0176-00	1911
156-10	1955
156-104	0130
156-123	0130
156-124	0130
156-143	OEM
156A	0023
156B	OEM
156C	OEM
156D	OEM
156E	OEM
156T1	0050
156WHT	0016
157	0037
157-009-9-001	0165
157-100	0064
157-120	0052
157-180	0371
157-439	0274
157-829	OEM
157-870	0327
157-1120	0052
157A	OEM
157B	OEM
157C	OEM
157D	OEM
157E	OEM
157N3	0546
157P4	0378
157T1	0050
157T1A	0050
157YEL	0037
158-3	0037
158-10	0142
158P1	0126
158P1M	0126
158P2	0037
158P2M	0037
158P3	0037
159-12	0150
159T1	0050
160-8	0079
160E15	OEM
160F15	OEM
160G2G41	OEM
160J2G41	OEM
160L2G41	OEM
160Q2G41	OEM
160T1	0050
160U2G41	OEM
161-001I	0079
161-006-0001	3669
161-006-0002	3669
161-009I	0079
161-009J	0079
161-011-0001	3808
161-011-0002	3808
161-011H	0284

DEVICE TYPE	REPL CODE
161-011J	0079
161-012-0002	4172
161-012H	0037
161-012J	0037
161-014H	0076
161-015G	0037
161-015H	0338
161-015I	0338
161-016(H)	0079
161-016H	0079
161-016K	0016
161-017I	0284
161-017J	0284
161-017K	0284
161-037H	0079
161-037J	0284
161-039G	0079
161-039H	0079
161-039I	0079
161-039J	0079
161-040G	0168
161-040H	0338
161-040I	0338
161-040J	0338
161-041H	0710
161-041I	0079
161-041J	0079
161-042G	0042
161-042H	0042
161-043G	0919
161-043H	0919
161-044D	0388
161-044E	0388
161-046G	0168
161-046H	0168
161-046I	0168
161-047(H)	0042
161-047G	0456
161-047H	0456
161-050G	0037
161-050H	0037
161-051G	0261
161-051H	0261
161-053G	1077
161-053H	0261
161-054A	0388
161-061H	0079
161-0161	0079
161-0161H	0079
161-1	OEM
161-5	0419
161-118-0001	1248
161-152-0101	1063
161-152-0102	1063
161-LNC	0103
161N2	1506
161N4C	0103
161RL10	OEM
161RL20	OEM
161RL30	OEM
161RL40	OEM
161RL50	OEM
161RL60	OEM
161RM10	OEM
161RM20	OEM
161RM30	OEM
161RM40	OEM
161RM50	OEM
161RM60	OEM
161T1	0050
161T2	0144
162-005A	0023
162-028A	0511
162-038A	OEM
162-041A	OEM
162-045A	2384
162-047A	OEM
162-3	3294
162-4	OEM
162-10	OEM
162-12	OEM
162-16	OEM
162-18	0311
162-18-0	0311
162-26-01	OEM
162J2	0015
162N2	0161
162P1	0455
162T1	0050
162T2	0144
163-04	3470
163-04A	OEM
163-04SPC	OEM
163-05	3470
163-06	3470
163-06A	OEM
163-06SPC	OEM
163-07	3470
163-08	3470
163-08A	OEM
163-08SPC	OEM
163-09	3470
163-10	3470
163-10SPC	OEM
163-12	3470
163-12A	OEM
163-12SPC	OEM
163-14	3470
163-14A	OEM

DEVICE TYPE	REPL CODE
163-14SPC	OEM
163-16	3449
163-16A	OEM
163-18	3449
163-18A	OEM
163-18SPC	OEM
163-20A	OEM
163-20SPC	OEM
163-22A	OEM
163-22SPC	OEM
163-24SPC	OEM
163-28SPC	OEM
163-30SPC	OEM
163J2	0015
164-003A	0120
164-006A	OEM
164-04	3470
164-04A	OEM
164-04SPC	OEM
164-05	3470
164-06	3470
164-06A	OEM
164-06SPC	OEM
164-07	3470
164-08	3470
164-08A	OEM
164-08SPC	OEM
164-09	3470
164-10	3470
164-10A	OEM
164-10SPC	OEM
164-12	3470
164-12A	OEM
164-12SPC	OEM
164-14	3470
164-14A	OEM
164-14SPC	OEM
164-16	3449
164-16A	OEM
164-18	3449
164-18A	OEM
164-20A	OEM
164-20SPC	OEM
164-22A	OEM
164-22SPC	OEM
164-24SPC	OEM
164-26SPC	OEM
164-28SPC	OEM
164-30SPC	OEM
164J2	0015
165	0196
165-1A82	0050
165-2A82	0208
165-4A82	0595
165-432-2-48-1	0124
165A-182	0050
165B-182	0050
165C-182	0160
165J2	0015
165N1	0079
166	1073
166-1A82	0004
166-2A82	0004
166-3A82	0004
166J2	0015
167-001B	0167
167-006A	1319
167-006B	1319
167-013A	0391
167-014A	1797
167-018A	0167
167-019A	0167
167-024B	OEM
167-028A	OEM
167-030A	OEM
167-035A	OEM
167-9	0590
167J2	0071
167N1	0016
167N2	0016
168-9	0786
168J2	0087
168N1	0016
169-257	0142
169-284	0142
169J2	OEM
170(RCA)	0007
170-1	0133
170-9	0086
170J2	OEM
171-001-9-001	0160
171-003-9-001	0142
171-015-9-001	0160
171-016-9-001	0222
171-1	0155
171-2	0604
171-3	OEM
171-4	OEM
171-9	0126
171J	OEM
171K	OEM
171RC10A	OEM
171RC10AM	OEM
171RC20A	OEM
171RC20AM	OEM
171RC40A	OEM
171RC40AM	OEM
171RC60A	OEM
171RC60AM	OEM

DEVICE TYPE	REPL CODE
171RC80A	OEM
171RC80AM	OEM
171RK80A	OEM
171RK80AM	OEM
171RK100A	OEM
171RK100AM	OEM
171RK120A	OEM
171RK120AM	OEM
171RK140A	OEM
171RK140AM	OEM
171RK160A	OEM
171RK160AM	OEM
172-001-9-001	0626
172-003-9-001	0103
172-003-9-001A	0103
172-006-9-001	0555
172-007-9-001	1401
172-008-9-001	1401
172-009-9-001	1401
172-010-9-001	0228
172-011-9-001	0219
172-013-9-001	0830
172-014-9-001	0042
172-014-9-002	2280
172-014-9-003	0042
172-024-9-004	0386
172-028-9-001	2475
172-028-9-002	1935
172-031-9-003	0228
172-038-9-001	0884
172-038-9-002	0930
172-038-9-003	0386
172-044-9-001	0042
173-1	0321
173-1(SYLVANIA)	0321
173-15	0416
173A419-2	0160
173A3936	0160
173A3963	0160
173A3970	0211
173A3981	0015
173A3981-1	0015
173A4348	0004
173A4349	0004
173A4389-1	0004
173A4390	0004
173A4391	0086
173A4393	0015
173A4394	0102
173A4394-1	0133
173A4399	0016
173A4416	0016
173A4419	0160
173A4419-1	0160
173A4419-2	0160
173A4419-3	0160
173A4419-4	0160
173A4419-5	0160
173A4419-6	0160
173A4419-7	0160
173A4419-8	0160
173A4419-9	0160
173A4419-10	0160
173A4420	0160
173A4420-1	0160
173A4420-5	0160
173A4421-1	0160
173A4422-1	0160
173A4424	0469
173A4436	0160
173A4469	0160
173A4470-11	0016
173A4470-13	0079
173A4470-32	0016
173A4473-5	0111
173A4489-2	0086
173A4490-2	0555
173A4490-5	0086
173A4490-7	0042
173A4491-2	0103
173A4491-2A	0103
173H	OEM
174-002-9-001	0208
174-1	0015
174-2	0015
174-3	0015
174-3A82	0279
174-25566-01	0126
174A4424	0469
175-006-9-001	1056
175-007-9-001	0004
175-008-9-001	0004
175-010-9-001	0919
175-2	0396
175-8349	0339
175E15	OEM
175F15	OEM
175PA50	0159
175PA60	0159
175PA80	0096
175PA100	0096
175PA110	0096
175PA120	0096
175PA130	OEM
175PA140	OEM
175PA150	OEM
175PA160	OEM
175PAK50	OEM
175PAK60	OEM

DEVICE TYPE	REPL CODE
175PAK80	OEM
175PAK100	OEM
175PAK110	OEM
175PAK120	OEM
175PAK130	OEM
175PAK140	OEM
175PAK150	OEM
175PAK160	OEM
175RA60	1889
175RA80	0733
175RA100	0733
175RA110	0733
175RA120	0733
175RA140	OEM
175RA150	OEM
175RA160	OEM
175RC10	1889
175RC20	1889
175RC30	1889
175RC40	1889
175RC60	1889
175RC80	0733
176-003	0144
176-003-9-001	0144
176-004	0086
176-004-9-001	0144
176-004-9-002	0833
176-005	0144
176-005-9-001	0144
176-006	0144
176-006-9-001	0144
176-007	0144
176-007-9-001	0144
176-008-9-001	0016
176-014-9-001	0016
176-016-9-001	0155
176-017-9-001	0016
176-018-9-001	1390
176-024-9-001	0016
176-024-9-002	0833
176-025-9-001	0076
176-025-9-002	0127
176-026-9-001	0224
176-029-9-001	0155
176-029-9-002	1390
176-029-9-003	1390
176-029-9-004	1581
176-031-9-001	0155
176-031-9-002	0111
176-037-9-001	0224
176-037-9-002	0728
176-037-9-003	0111
176-040-9-001	2534
176-042-9-001	0155
176-042-9-002	0076
176-042-9-003	0076
176-042-9-004	0111
176-042-9-005	0219
176-042-9-006	0191
176-042-9-007	0228
176-043-9-002	0076
176-044-9-001	0830
176-044-9-002	0544
176-047-9-001	0191
176-048-9-002	0076
176-049-9-002	0076
176-054-9-001	0076
176-055-9-004	2276
176-056-9-001	1136
176-056-9-003	1136
176-056-9-005	0728
176-060-9-001	2195
176-060-9-002	0076
176-060-9-003	0076
176-060-9-004	2787
176-062-9-001	0076
176-065-9-001	0076
176-070-9-001	1973
176-072-9-005	0151
176-073-9-001	0127
176-073-9-002	0830
176-073-9-003	0018
176-073-9-012	0830
176-074-9-001	0171
176-074-9-002	1581
176-074-9-003	0930
176-074-9-004	0945
176-075-9-001	0113
176-075-9-003	0151
176-075-9-004	1211
176-075-9-006	0781
176-075-9-008	0781
176-087-9-001	0833
176-087-9-002	0830
176T1	OEM
176T2	OEM
176T3	OEM
176T4	OEM
176T5	OEM
176T6	OEM
176T7	OEM
176T8	OEM
176T9	OEM
176T10	OEM
176T11	OEM
176T12	OEM
177-001	0126
177-001-9-001	0126
177-006-9-001	0006

If replacement code is OEM, contact original manufacturer for replacement.

177

DEVICE TYPE	REPL CODE
177-006-9-002	0006
177-007-9-001	0203
177-012-9-001	0006
177-018-9-001	0006
177-019-9-003	0006
177-020-9-001	0006
177-023-9-001	0919
177-025-9-001	0148
177-025-9-002	0688
177A07	0618
177E	OEM
179-1	0133
179-2	0133
179-4	0170
179-16	OEM
179-46444-01	1248
179-46444-02	1063
179-46444-04	OEM
179-46444-05	3847
179-46445-01	1035
179-46445-02	2086
179-46445-03	1824
179-46445-05	3365
179-46445-06	1833
179-46445-08	1848
179-46445-09	0337
179-46445-10	1622
179-46447-21	1545
179N2	5368
179P1	5371
180-1	0015
180-253	OEM
180N1	0326
180N1P	0224
180P1SP	OEM
180P2SP	OEM
180P3SP	OEM
180P4SP	OEM
180P5SP	OEM
180P6SP	OEM
180P8SP	OEM
180P10SP	OEM
180P12SP	OEM
180P16SP	OEM
180T2	0103
180T2A	0103
180T2B	0103
180T2C	0103
181(WORKMAN)	0190
181-000100	2089
181-000200	0649
181-003-9-001	2704
181-1	0133
181-1F	0133
181-2	0124
181-2F	OEM
181-3	0124
181-1002	0124
181-1003	0124
181N1	0007
181N1D	0007
181N2	0007
181N2D	0007
181T2	0130
181T2A	0103
181T2B	0177
181T2C	0103
182-009-9-001	0683
182-014-9-002	3017
182-014-9-003	0321
182-015-9-001	3126
182-029-9-001	0683
182-037-9-001	0683
182-038-9-001	0410
182-039-9-001	0683
182-044-1-001	OEM
182-044-9-001	3308
182-044-9-002	0321
182-045-9-001	0321
182-046-9-001	3308
182-056-9-001	0683
182-138-9-001	0410
182-144-9-002	OEM
182T2A	0538
182T2B	0538
182T2C	0538
183-1(SYLVANIA)	6030
183P1	0126
183T2A	0359
183T2B	0359
184-1	0102
184-1G033	1073
184-2	0102
184A-1	0160
184A-1-12	0160
184A-1-12-7	0160
184A-1L	0160
184A-1L8	0160
184T2A	0359
184T2B	0359
184T2C	0074
185-008	2280
185-009-01	OEM
185-4	OEM
185-5	OEM
185-6	0015
185-6(RECT)	0015
185-6-01	OEM
185-8	0500
185-9	0016
185-9-01	0571
185-9-02	0569
185-9-1	OEM
185-16	OEM
185-84	OEM
185-736	0178
185-Z9000	2320
185-Z9001	3903
185-Z9002	0061
185-Z9003	0759
185-Z9004	1129
185-Z9005	0340
185-Z9006	0895
185-Z9007	0058
185-Z9008	0934
185-Z9009	0500
185-Z9010	0705
185-Z9011	3651
185-Z9012	0720
185-Z9013	1642
185-Z9014	1641
185-Z9015	1640
185-Z9016	1702
185-Z9017	2313
185-Z9018	2313
185-Z9019	1780
185-Z9020	1673
185-Z9021	1494
185-Z9022	0857
185T2A	0359
185T2B	0359
186-001	0155
186-002	0076
186-003	0076
186-004	0076
186-005	0111
186-006	0191
186-007	0076
186-008	0386
186-009	0219
186-011	0133
186-012	0133
186-013	0143
186-015	0133
186-016	0012
186-1	1135
186N1	0007
187-1	0327
187-6	0170
187-7	0398
188-5	0147
188-68-35	0469
188-70-48	0469
188-826	0160
188B-1-82	0050
188C-1-82	0279
188P-2	0004
188P-2-12	0004
188P-2-127	0004
188P-2L	0004
188P-2L8	0004
189	0144
189-1	0065
189L-4	0004
189L-4-12	0004
189L-4-127	0004
189L-4L	0004
189L-4L8	0004
189N1	0309
189N1G	0309
190N1	0264
190N1C	0161
190N1D	0264
190N3	0161
190N3C	0161
190V039H18	0769
192-1A82	0435
192-120	0137
192-156	OEM
192-160	OEM
192-200	0137
192-330	0039
192-519	OEM
192-569	0157
192-1120	0137
192N2	0065
194N1	0065
194N1D	1955
195N1	0042
195N1C	0042
195N1D	0042
195N3	0042
195P2	0919
195P2C	0848
195P4	0919
196-654	0015
199-POWER	0160
200	0015
200-007	0144
200-010	0144
200-011	0086
200-015	0144
200-016	0198
200-018	0178
200-052	0037
200-053	0321
200-055	0144
200-056	0144
200-057	0016
200-058	0016
200-064	0321
200-076	0042
200-846	0016
200-856	2839
200-862	0016
200-863	0016
200-3172-208	OEM
200-3174-006	OEM
200-4302	OEM
200-6582	0087
200-6582-22	0229
200A	0038
200A#	0733
200B	0733
200B40	OEM
200B45	OEM
200B50	OEM
200BN20	OEM
200BN30	OEM
200BN40	OEM
200BN50	OEM
200BN60	OEM
200BN80	OEM
200BN100	OEM
200BN120	OEM
200BN140	OEM
200BN160	OEM
200BNS	OEM
200C	0733
200C4.7-5.3	OEM
200CNQ020	OEM
200CNQ030	OEM
200CNQ035	OEM
200CNQ040	OEM
200CNQ045	OEM
200D	0733
200E	0733
200EXD21	OEM
200F	0733
200H	0733
200JH21	OEM
200K	0733
200M	0733
200MAB180	OEM
200MAB200	OEM
200MAB250	OEM
200N15A	OEM
200N15A9	OEM
200N20A	OEM
200N20A9	OEM
200N25A	OEM
200N25A9	OEM
200N30A	OEM
200N30A9	OEM
200N35A	OEM
200N35A9	OEM
200N40A	OEM
200N40A9	OEM
200N45A	OEM
200N45A9	OEM
200N50A	OEM
200N50A9	OEM
200N55A	OEM
200N55A9	OEM
200N60A	OEM
200N60A9	OEM
200N65A	OEM
200N65A9	OEM
200N70A	OEM
200N70A9	OEM
200N75A	OEM
200N75A9	OEM
200N80A	OEM
200N80A9	OEM
200N85A	OEM
200N85A9	OEM
200N90A	OEM
200N90A9	OEM
200N95A	OEM
200N95A9	OEM
200N100A	OEM
200N100A9	OEM
200N110A	OEM
200N120A	OEM
200N130A	OEM
200N140A	OEM
200N150A	OEM
200N160A	OEM
200N170A	OEM
200N180A	OEM
200N190A	OEM
200N200A	OEM
200N210A	OEM
200N220A	OEM
200N230A	OEM
200N240A	OEM
200N250A	OEM
200PIN-BNC	OEM
200PIN-PP	OEM
200PIN-RM	OEM
200PV-BNC	OEM
200PV-PP	OEM
200PV-RM	OEM
200QD1	OEM
200QD21	OEM
200QH21	OEM
200R1B	0087
200R2B	2621
200R3B	1736
200R4B	5470
200R5B	1760
200R6B	0959
200R7B	0087
200R8B	0087
200R9B	0087
200R10B	0087
200R11B	OEM
200R12B	OEM
200R13B	OEM
200R14B	OEM
200R15B	OEM
200R16B	OEM
200R18B	OEM
200R20B	OEM
200R22B	OEM
200R24B	OEM
200R26B	OEM
200R28B	OEM
200R30B	OEM
200R32B	OEM
200R34B	OEM
200R36B	OEM
200R38B	OEM
200R40B	OEM
200R42B	OEM
200R44B	OEM
200R46B	OEM
200R48B	OEM
200R50B	OEM
200RB4	0535
200RS45	OEM
200RS50	OEM
200S	0733
200S2-2.65	OEM
200S40	OEM
200S45	OEM
200S50	OEM
200UB5	1017
200UB5R	0496
200UB10	1017
200UB10R	0496
200UB20	1017
200UB20R	0496
200UB30	1017
200UB30R	0496
200UB40	1030
200UB40R	1766
200UB50	1030
200UB50R	1766
200X2100-022	0872
200X2110-269	0167
200X2120-012	0391
200X2120-033	0849
200X2174-006	0151
200X2300-033	1192
200X2501-708	1049
200X2600-103	OEM
200X2600-183	3462
200X3110-607	0220
200X3145-404	0220
200X3151-432	1077
200X3162-538	0236
200X3172-208	1077
200X3174-006	0151
200X3174-014	0151
200X3174-021	0151
200X3189-304	2643
200X3190-604	0127
200X3192-101	0261
200X3206-800	0638
200X3207-306	1274
200X3222-907	0066
200X3223-025	0261
200X3224-007	2118
200X3224-204	1077
200X4049-081	1490
200X4082-614	0037
200X4085-415	1338
200X4094-001	1900
200X4101-500	0148
200X4547-806	0388
200X4547-814	0388
200X4589-802	0055
200X8000-026	0019
200X8010-094	0133
200X8010-102	0120
200X8010-165	0133
200X8100-130	0023
200X8130-171	0344
200X8220-531	0681
200X8220-851	0057
200X8220-878	0057
200X9120-224	0023
200YD21	OEM
201	0037
201-15	0004
201-25-4343-12	0144
201-211	OEM
201-254323-12	0144
201-254323-13	0144
201-254343-12	0144
201-254343-13	0127
201-254343-34	0007
201-254343-49	0144
201-283818-1	0212
201-283818-2	0212
201-283818-3	0212
201A	0050
201A#	0464
201A0723	0244
201AP	OEM
201B	0050
201B#	0464
201C	0757
201CNQ020	OEM
201CNQ030	OEM
201CNQ035	OEM
201CNQ040	OEM
201CNQ045	OEM
201D	0757
201E	3237
201F	3240
201H	3260
201K	3260
201M	0759
201P	2848
201S	0761
201U	2174
201UL140S20	OEM
201V	4771
201X2000-118	0019
201X2010-131	0124
201X2010-144	0124
201X2010-159	0124
201X2010-165	0133
201X2100-119	0344
201X2100-126	0023
201X2100-164	0344
201X2120-009	0023
201X2130-234	0023
201X2220-118	0057
201X2220-878	0057
201X2230-042	0298
201X3120-255	0023
201X3130-109	0071
201Z	4771
201ZB	OEM
201ZD	OEM
201ZF	OEM
201ZH	OEM
201ZK	OEM
202	0164
202(RECT)	2872
202-1	3217
202-2	0149
202-3	OEM
202-5-1260-32123	3643
202-5-2300-01710	0196
202-5-2300-01810	0023
202-5-2300-01910	0604
202-5-2450-13540	0023
202-5-3200-03010	0118
202-5-3210-05110	0041
202-5-3210-06220	0466
202-5-3210-13020	0053
202-5-3220-30010	0195
202-5-3220-36010	0010
202-5-9110-18820	0143
202-5-9531-01010	0133
202-207	OEM
202-237	OEM
202A	0038
202A#	0464
202B	0736
202C	0740
202D	0740
202E	0742
202F	0742
202H	0742
202K	0747
202M	0759
202N1	0378
2020(RECT)	2872
202P	2848
202P1	0378
202S	0761
202S03	OEM
202U	2497
202V	4771
202Z	4771
202ZB	OEM
202ZD	OEM
202ZF	OEM
202ZH	OEM
202ZK	OEM
203	0015
203(ZENER)	0695
203-1	0212
203-2	0015
203-3	0604
203-4	0212
203-5-4570-73452	1505
203-5-4570-73462	1505
203-5-4921-01270	5275
203-5-5000-53660	0532
203-5-5000-53664	0532
203-5-5083-33160	0018
203-5-5100-53660	0532
203-5-5251-57069	0111
203-5-5251-57079	0111
203-5-6580-40050	2882
203-5-6850-40050	2882
203-5-7000-92970	0688
203-5-8620-32550	0555
203-6	0212
203A	3073
203A6137	0631
203B	0736
203C	0740
203D	0740
203E	0742
203F	0742
203H	0742
203J	OEM
203JPLA160	OEM
203JPLA180	OEM
203JPLA200	OEM
203JPLA250	OEM
203K	0747
203M	0759
203P	2848
203S	0761
203S4D	0212
203U	3073
203V	4771
203X3189-408	0309
203Z	4771
203ZB	OEM
203ZD	OEM
203ZF	OEM
203ZH	OEM
203ZK	OEM
204A	OEM
204A(SCR)	2174
204B	OEM
204C	OEM
204D	OEM
204F	OEM
204H	OEM
204K	OEM
204M	OEM
204Z4	OEM
205	OEM
205-5-9040-44210	0133
205A2-333	0155
205Z4	OEM
206-5-0131-22210	0616
206-5-0723-20110	2550
206-5-0783-21011	2052
206-5-0824-10110	2590
206-5-0834-10214	3161
206-5-1384-192210	OEM
206-5-2341-41610	4216
206A	OEM
206B	OEM
206C	OEM
206D	OEM
206E	OEM
206F	OEM
206H	OEM
206K	OEM
206M	OEM
206Z4	OEM
207A	0050
207A(SCR)	1102
207A1	0050
207A3	0004
207A7	0004
207A9	0144
207A10	0016
207A16	0178
207A16A	0178
207A20	0085
207A20A	0085
207A26	0160
207A31	0079
207A32-B	1403
207B	0050
207B(SCR)	2904
207C	OEM
207C(SCR)	0957
207D	OEM
207D(SCR)	0957
207E	OEM
207E(SCR)	2905
207H	OEM
207H(SCR)	0671
207K	OEM
207K(SCR)	2782
207M	0050
207M(SCR)	0332
207V073C04	0037
207Z4	OEM
208M	OEM
208Z4	OEM
209-1	0037
209-30	0042
209-31	0143
209-32	0133
209-846	0016
209-856	2839
209-862	0016
209-863	0016
209A	OEM
209B	OEM
209B-FLAG	0217
209B-FLEX	0217
209C	OEM
209D-FLAG	0217
209D-FLEX	0217
209F-FLAG	0217
209F-FLEX	0217
209H	OEM
209H-FLAG	0217
209H-FLEX	0217
209K	OEM
209K-FLAG	0217
209K-FLEX	0217
209M	OEM
209M-FLAG	0217
209M-FLEX	0217
209P	OEM
209S	OEM
209S-FLAG	0653
209S-FLEX	0463
209V	OEM
209Z	OEM
209Z4	OEM
210X2100-126	OEM
210Z4	OEM
211-58	0535
211-141	OEM
211A	0279
211A6381-I	0178
211B	0279
211B-FLAG	0217
211B-FLEX	0217
211C	0279
211D	0279
211D-FLAG	0217
211D-FLEX	0217
211E	0279
211F	0279
211F-FLAG	0217
211F-FLEX	0217
211H	OEM
211H-FLAG	0217
211H-FLEX	0217
211K	OEM
211K-FLAG	0217
211K-FLEX	0217
211M	OEM
211M-FLAG	0217
211M-FLEX	0217
211P	OEM
211S	OEM
211S-FLAG	0653
211S-FLEX	0463
211V	OEM
211Z	OEM
211Z4	0789
212-00102	0190
212-00104	0190
212-012	0190
212-013	0190
212-2	OEM
212-4	OEM
212-5	OEM
212-7	0015
212-18	0015
212-21	0015
212-22	0015
212-23	0015
212-25	0015
212-26	OEM
212-27	0015
212-33	0015
212-35	0015
212-36	0015
212-37	0015
212-38	0015
212-39	0015
212-40	0575
212-41	0015
212-42	0015
212-46	0469
212-47	0015
212-48	0015
212-49	0015
212-50	0015
212-51	0015
212-57	0015
212-58	0015
212-59	0015
212-60	0023
212-61	0015
212-62	0703
212-63	0469
212-64	0015
212-65	0015
212-66	0201
212-68	0102
212-70	0015
212-71	0015
212-72	0015
212-75	0015
212-76	0015
212-76-02	0015
212-77	0015
212-79	0015
212-80	0102
212-85	0769
212-85B	0769
212-86	0102
212-90	0374
212-92	0015
212-93	1780
212-94	0015
212-94B	0015
212-95	0374
212-96	0790
212-102	3805
212-103	3805

DEVICE TYPE	REPL CODE
212-104	3805
212-105	3805
212-106	3805
212-108	0128
212-109	0128
212-110	0128
212-128	3805
212-129	3805
212-130	3805
212-130-X	0128
212-130X	3805
212-131	3805
212-132	3805
212-133	3805
212-134	3805
212-135	3805
212-136	3805
212-137	3805
212-138	3805
212-139	3805
212-139-01	3805
212-139-02	3805
212-139-03	1493
212-140	3805
212-140-01	3805
212-141	1061
212-141-01	1061
212-141-02	1696
212-141-03	1696
212-141-04	1696
212-141-1	OEM
212-142	1493
212-142-01	1493
212-142-02	1061
212-143	3610
212-144	3610
212-145	2097
212-145-01	1061
212-145-02	1061
212-146	2097
212-146-01	2097
212-146-02	2097
212-147	1061
212-148	1061
212-148-01	3324
212-149	1061
212-150	1061
212-151	1493
212-192	0015
212-241	1061
212-245	1061
212-505	0079
212-507	0079
212-695	0016
212-699	0037
212-741-005	2635
212-Z9000	0087
212-Z9001	0299
212-Z9002	0250
212-Z9003	1293
212-Z9004	0290
212-Z9005	0258
212-Z9006	0800
212-Z9007	1208
212-Z9008	0286
212-Z9009	OEM
212-Z9010	0344
212-Z9011	0533
212-Z9012	0122
212-Z9013	0131
212-Z9014	0145
212-Z9015	0315
212-Z9016	1017
212-Z9017	2347
212-Z9018	4346
212-Z9019	0960
212-Z9020	0572
212-Z9021	2371
212-Z9500A	0190
212-Z9521	2955
212-Z9522	1493
212-Z9523	1061
212-Z9526A	1696
212-Z9529	2524
212-Z9530	3610
212-Z9531	2777
212-Z9532	0405
212-Z9533	1700
212-Z9534	2954
212-Z9535	2957
212-Z9536-A	1986
212-Z9537	1188
212-Z9538	2956
212-Z9539	1048
212A	OEM
212B	OEM
212C	OEM
212D	OEM
212E	OEM
212F	OEM
212M	OEM
212P	OEM
212R2S	OEM
212S	OEM
212Z4	OEM
213-1	0086
213A	OEM
213B	OEM
213C	OEM

DEVICE TYPE	REPL CODE
213D	OEM
213E	OEM
213F	OEM
213H	OEM
213K	OEM
213M	OEM
213Z4	OEM
214H	OEM
215-51	0015
215-58	0015
215-76(GE)	0015
215-76GE	0015
215T4	OEM
215Z4	0002
217-1	0144
217-76-02	0015
217N1	0637
217N1D	0177
217N2	0637
217N2C	0177
217N4	0637
218-22	0016
218-23	0016
218-24	0016
218-25	0016
218-26	0086
218-A-464-PM	2006
218A	OEM
218A4164P1M	2006
218B	0733
218D	0733
218F	0733
218H	0733
218K	0733
218M	0733
218P	0733
218S	0733
218V	0733
218Z	0733
218ZB	0733
218ZD	0733
218ZF	OEM
218ZH	OEM
219-103-2006	0167
219-303-4305	OEM
219B-FLAG	0217
219B-FLEX	0217
219BLY-A	OEM
219D-FLAG	0217
219D-FLEX	0217
219F-FLAG	0217
219F-FLEX	0217
219H	OEM
219H-FLAG	0217
219H-FLEX	0217
219K-FLAG	0217
219K-FLEX	0217
219M-FLAG	0217
219M-FLEX	0217
219S-FLAG	0653
219S-FLEX	0463
219ZB-FLEX	0463
219ZD-FLEX	0463
219Z-FLEX	0463
220-001001	0016
220-001002	0016
220-001011	0144
220-001012	0144
220-002001	0222
220-003001	0015
220-008001	0321
220C	OEM
220T4	OEM
221	0560
221-0048	0167
221-00267	OEM
221-00563	OEM
221-00586	OEM
221-00590	OEM
221-00707	OEM
221-31	0627
221-32	0627
221-34	0659
221-35	OEM
221-36	2147
221-37	0748
221-39	0748
221-40	0406
221-41	0748
221-42	0348
221-43	0350
221-45	2438
221-45-01	2438
221-46	0661
221-48	0167
221-48-01	0167
221-62	0345
221-64	2453
221-64(IC)	2462
221-64(RECT)	0102
221-65	0696
221-69	1327
221-69-01	1327
221-76	0618
221-76-01	0618
221-77	2460
221-78	1327
221-79	0696
221-79-01	0696

DEVICE TYPE	REPL CODE
221-80	2462
221-81	OEM
221-82	0661
221-83	OEM
221-83-01	OEM
221-84	OEM
221-84-01	OEM
221-86	2473
221-87	0348
221-87-01	2803
221-89	1748
221-90	1335
221-91	0514
221-91-01	0514
221-92	OEM
221-93	0308
221-94	2478
221-95	2478
221-96	2480
221-96C	2480
221-97	2481
221-97-01	2481
221-98	1162
221-98-05	1162
221-98A05	1162
221-100	OEM
221-101-01	0330
221-102	OEM
221-102-01	5755
221-102A	OEM
221-103	3739
221-103-01A	OEM
221-103A	3739
221-104	3674
221-104D	6273
221-105	3675
221-105-01	3675
221-106	2774
221-106-01	2774
221-107	1411
221-108	2728
221-111-02	OEM
221-116	3866
221-121	0176
221-129	0620
221-129A-01	0620
221-130	OEM
221-131	2947
221-132	3933
221-134	OEM
221-134-01	OEM
221-140	3921
221-141	0842
221-143	OEM
221-144	OEM
221-146	6207
221-147	6208
221-148	OEM
221-149	OEM
221-149-01	OEM
221-153	OEM
221-154	OEM
221-155	OEM
221-155-01	OEM
221-157-02	OEM
221-158	1051
221-158-01	1051
221-158-02	1051
221-158-03	1051
221-158-02001	1051
221-159	OEM
221-166	0619
221-166-00	0619
221-166-0	1801
221-166-02	1187
221-166-04	0330
221-166-09	OEM
221-166-4	0330
221-166-9	OEM
221-167-01	1288
221-167-04	OEM
221-167-05	1817
221-171	3347
221-175	3945
221-175-01	3945
221-177	3666
221-178	4210
221-179-01	2095
221-179-01-E-01	2095
221-179-02	2095
221-179-03	2095
221-179-05	OEM
221-179-1	2095
221-182	OEM
221-182-01	1946
221-187	5123
221-187A	5123
221-188	0620
221-190	1415
221-190-01	1096
221-190-01A	1096
221-190-E-01	1096
221-193	3739
221-193A	3739
221-201	OEM
221-201-03	OEM
221-202	3949
221-213	0619
221-213-00	0619

DEVICE TYPE	REPL CODE
221-213-02	1187
221-213-04	0330
221-213-4	0330
221-217	6213
221-230	3726
221-240	0356
221-241	OEM
221-242-01	OEM
221-250-02	5464
221-250-03	OEM
221-261	3951
221-261-01	3951
221-261B03	3951
221-264	OEM
221-267	OEM
221-285-01	OEM
221-285-02	OEM
221-285-03	OEM
221-290	OEM
221-290-01	OEM
221-291	4126
221-296	OEM
221-296-00	OEM
221-296-04	0330
221-297	OEM
221-300	OEM
221-302	OEM
221-303	3403
221-313-01	OEM
221-314	OEM
221-316	4646
221-343	OEM
221-346	6024
221-347	4314
221-347-01	4314
221-347A01	OEM
221-348	OEM
221-364	0518
221-364-01	OEM
221-365	OEM
221-365-01	OEM
221-365-02	OEM
221-366	OEM
221-369	OEM
221-370	OEM
221-371-01	OEM
221-371-02	OEM
221-373-02	OEM
221-376	OEM
221-377-01	OEM
221-383	4009
221-384A01	OEM
221-394	OEM
221-418	OEM
221-418-01	OEM
221-418-02	OEM
221-419	OEM
221-422-01	3665
221-446	OEM
221-446-00	OEM
221-465	OEM
221-466	OEM
221-467	3206
221-468	6239
221-473	OEM
221-475	3054
221-475C	3054
221-476	2843
221-476D	2843
221-479-06	OEM
221-482	OEM
221-493	OEM
221-496-01	OEM
221-516	3590
221-517-01	OEM
221-517-1	OEM
221-518	OEM
221-522	OEM
221-524	OEM
221-524-01	OEM
221-528	OEM
221-537	OEM
221-538	OEM
221-539	OEM
221-540	OEM
221-544	OEM
221-544-01	OEM
221-550	OEM
221-550-01	OEM
221-554-01	OEM
221-556	OEM
221-560	OEM
221-561	4032
221-563	OEM
221-565	OEM
221-566	OEM
221-568	OEM
221-569	OEM
221-570	OEM
221-571	OEM
221-571-01	OEM
221-572	OEM
221-573	OEM
221-578	OEM
221-579	OEM
221-580-04	OEM
221-586	OEM
221-587	OEM
221-589	OEM

DEVICE TYPE	REPL CODE
221-590	OEM
221-598	OEM
221-600	OEM
221-604	OEM
221-604-02	OEM
221-605	OEM
221-628	OEM
221-636	OEM
221-637	OEM
221-637-01	OEM
221-648	OEM
221-650	OEM
221-650-03	OEM
221-652-01	OEM
221-656	OEM
221-679	4261
221-679-01	OEM
221-682-01	OEM
221-683	OEM
221-683A	OEM
221-684-01	OEM
221-685	OEM
221-685-02	OEM
221-701	OEM
221-703	OEM
221-704	OEM
221-705	OEM
221-707	OEM
221-708	OEM
221-708-01	OEM
221-776	OEM
221-776-01	OEM
221-782	OEM
221-791	OEM
221-796	6264
221-806	OEM
221-812	OEM
221-4757D04	3054
221-4767D02	2843
221-Z9000	2600
221-Z9001	2549
221-Z9002	0673
221-Z9003	0823
221-Z9004	2689
221-Z9005	0649
221-Z9006	0438
221-Z9007	2527
221-Z9008	0324
221-Z9009	2716
221-Z9010	0850
221-Z9011	1385
221-Z9012	0784
221-Z9013	0391
221-Z9014	0360
221-Z9015	1832
221-Z9016	2535
221-Z9017	1291
221-Z9018	1686
221-Z9019	1183
221-Z9020	0026
221-Z9021	0574
221-Z9022	0872
221-Z9023	0905
221-Z9024	1469
221-Z9025	2593
221-Z9026	1206
221-Z9027	0514
221-Z9028	0780
221-Z9029	1797
221-Z9030	0718
221-Z9031	3346
221-Z9032	0746
221-Z9033	3690
221-Z9034	0356
221-Z9035	5564
221-Z9036	0797
221-Z9037	2728
221-Z9038	2153
221-Z9039	2032
221-Z9040	3166
221-Z9041	0516
221-Z9042	0967
221-Z9043	0619
221-Z9044	1288
221-Z9045	0083
221-Z9046	0858
221-Z9047	0523
221-Z9048	2615
221-Z9049	3946
221-Z9050	2921
221-Z9051	1044
221-Z9052	2914
221-Z9053	3238
221-Z9054	3242
221-Z9055	2038
221-Z9056	2759
221-Z9057	2762
221-Z9058	0880
221-Z9059	0846
221-Z9060	0851
221-Z9061	1532
221-Z9062	3286
221-Z9063	1805
221-Z9064	1049
221-Z9065	4160
221-Z9066	2008
221-Z9067	4006
221-Z9068	3980
221-Z9069	4010

DEVICE TYPE	REPL CODE
221-Z9070	3763
221-Z9071	1120
221-Z9072	2061
221-Z9073	2218
221-Z9074	0001
221-Z9075	0232
221-Z9076	0357
221-Z9077	0692
221-Z9078	0564
221-Z9079	1812
221-Z9080	1035
221-Z9081	1820
221-Z9082	2598
221-Z9083	0081
221-Z9084	0141
221-Z9085	0557
221-Z9086	1149
221-Z9087	1335
221-Z9088	2902
221-Z9089	3189
221-Z9090	2016
221-Z9091	5573
221-Z9092	OEM
221-Z9093	1601
221-Z9094	3715
221-Z9095	3717
221-Z9096	0842
221-Z9097	1070
221-Z9098	0413
221-Z9099	2247
221-Z9100	4481
221-Z9101	4485
221-Z9102	4486
221-Z9103	4031
221-Z9104	1611
221-Z9105	4490
221-Z9106	4491
221-Z9107	2111
221-Z9108	2560
221-Z9109	2576
221-Z9110	2580
221-Z9111	2568
221-Z9112	0465
221-Z9113	4502
221-Z9114	2289
221-Z9115	1239
221-Z9116	4348
221-Z9117	4514
221-Z9118	4515
221-Z9119	3332
221-Z9120	4520
221-Z9121	0875
221-Z9122	0878
221-Z9123	4084
221-Z9124	2579
221-Z9125	4331
221-Z9126	2771
221-Z9127	4325
221-Z9128	4535
221-Z9129	4025
221-Z9130	4024
221-Z9131	3961
221-Z9132	1251
221-Z9133	0215
221-Z9134	5578
221-Z9135	2845
221-Z9136	2264
221-Z9137	3859
221-Z9138	4463
221-Z9139	2674
221-Z9140	3720
221-Z9141	1843
221-Z9142	2680
221-Z9143	1786
221-Z9144	0406
221-Z9145	1964
221-Z9146	4084
221-Z9147	2352
221-Z9148	2342
221-Z9149	3318
221-Z9150	0917
221-Z9151	2559
221-Z9152	3254
221-Z9153	1867
221-Z9154	2804
221-Z9155	2785
221-Z9156	0668
221-Z9157	0633
221-Z9158	3973
221-Z9159	2579
221-Z9160	1470
221-Z9161	1516
221-Z9162	2932
221-Z9163	0394
221-Z9164	0101
221-Z9165	OEM
221-Z9166	0910
221-Z9167	2790
221-Z9168	5582
221-Z9169	3363
221-Z9170	3919
221-Z9171	3920
221-Z9172	2011
221-Z9173	2796
221-Z9174	3239
221-Z9175	3780
221-Z9176	3060
221-Z9177	2216
221-Z9178	5585

DEVICE TYPE	REPL CODE
221-Z9179	4554
221-Z9180	4004
221-Z9181	4017
221-Z9182	5463
221A	OEM
221C	OEM
221E	OEM
221G3114	2515
221G3114-1	2515
222-1	0267
222-2	0267
222A	OEM
222B	OEM
222C	OEM
222D	OEM
222F	OEM
222H	OEM
222K	OEM
222M	OEM
222N1	0546
222P	OEM
222S	OEM
222V	OEM
222Z	OEM
223	0144
223-1	0037
223-3	OEM
223-4	OEM
223-5	OEM
223-6	OEM
223-10-01	OEM
223-18	3461
223-18-01	3897
223-20-01	OEM
223-28	3530
223-40	2348
223-Z9000	2827
223-Z9001	2830
223-Z9002	2832
223-Z9003	2834
223-Z9004	2610
223-Z9005	2608
223-Z9006	1983
223-Z9007	2046
223-Z9008	2837
223A	OEM
223B	OEM
223D	OEM
223F	OEM
223H	OEM
223K	OEM
223M	OEM
223P	OEM
223P1	0037
223P1AA	0037
223S	OEM
223U	OEM
223Z	OEM
223ZB	OEM
223ZD	OEM
224-1	0111
224B007-1	OEM
224N1	0111
225	OEM
225A6946-P000	0232
225A6946-P003	0331
225A6946-P004	0357
225A6946-P010	0507
225A6946-P020	0692
225A6946-P050	0738
225A6946-P093	0564
225A6976-P095	1477
225ITTN	OEM
225T4	OEM
226-1	0079
226-1(SYLVANIA)	0016
226-2	0079
226-2(DIO)	OEM
226-2(DIODE)	0102
226-3	3653
226-4	3392
226-8	OEM
226N1	0079
226P10601	0912
226P30104	OEM
227-3	3294
227-2000D1	0196
227-200001	0196
228-1	0818
228A	OEM
228B	OEM
228D	OEM
228F	OEM
228H	OEM
228ITTJ	OEM
228K	OEM
228M	OEM
228N1	0546
228N5	0818
228P	OEM
228S	OEM
228V	OEM
228Z	OEM
228ZB	OEM
228ZD	OEM
228ZF	OEM
228ZH	OEM
228ZK	OEM
229-0011	0196

If replacement code is OEM, contact original manufacturer for replacement. 179

DEVICE TYPE	REPL CODE
229-0014	0143
229-0026	0050
229-0027	0164
229-0028	0164
229-0029	0164
229-0030	0164
229-0030-8	OEM
229-0035	0143
229-0037	0143
229-0038	0050
229-0041	0164
229-0049	0143
229-0050-8	OEM
229-0050-13	0016
229-0050-14	0016
229-0050-15	0016
229-0055	0164
229-0056	0164
229-0057	0143
229-0062	0164
229-0077	0050
229-0079	0050
229-0080	0164
229-0082	0050
229-0083	0050
229-0085	0164
229-0086	0050
229-0087	0050
229-0088	0164
229-0089	0050
229-0090	0050
229-0091	0164
229-0092	0164
229-0093	0143
229-0095	0050
229-0096	0030
229-0097	0164
229-0098	0050
229-0099	0050
229-0-180-33	0127
229-0-180-34	0127
229-0100	0164
229-0102	0015
229-0105	0143
229-0106	0050
229-0107	0143
229-0108	0143
229-0110	0050
229-0111	0050
229-0112	0050
229-0114	0911
229-0116	0085
229-0117	0015
229-0119	0015
229-0120	0015
229-0121	0050
229-0122	2839
229-0122-20	0321
229-0123	0050
229-0124	0164
229-0125	0164
229-0129	0050
229-0130	0164
229-0131	0050
229-0132	0050
229-0133	0164
229-0134	2839
229-0135	0015
229-0136	0050
229-0137	0164
229-0138	0164
229-0139	0164
229-0140	0164
229-0141	0143
229-0142	0164
229-0143	0164
229-0144	0079
229-0145	0050
229-0146	0164
229-0147	0015
229-0149	0079
229-0150	0079
229-0151	0079
229-0151-3	0144
229-0152	0079
229-0154	0079
229-0156-12	OEM
229-0162	0015
229-0180-26	OEM
229-0180-31	OEM
229-0180-32	0007
229-0180-33	0007
229-0180-34	0144
229-0180-119	0007
229-0180-123	0016
229-0180-124	0144
229-0180-130	OEM
229-0180-149	0144
229-0182-65	0143
229-0185-2	0144
229-0185-3	0144
229-0190-29	0144
229-0190-30	0007
229-0190-31	0127
229-0190-90	0016
229-0191-29	0127
229-0191-30	0127
229-0191-31	OEM
229-0192-18	0212

DEVICE TYPE	REPL CODE
229-0192-19	0144
229-0192-20	0321
229-0204-4	0144
229-0204-6	0007
229-0204-6(VHF)	0007
229-0204-23	0144
229-0210-14	0144
229-0210-19	0127
229-0214-17	OEM
229-0214-40	0144
229-0214-41	OEM
229-0220-9	0144
229-0220-14	0911
229-0220-19	0144
229-0240-19	OEM
229-0240-20	0911
229-0240-25	0007
229-0248-45	0144
229-0248-46	OEM
229-0250-10	0144
229-0250-11	0911
229-0260-18	0127
229-180-32	0007
229-485-2	0127
229-1054-5	0015
229-1054-9	0015
229-1054-47	OEM
229-1054-52	OEM
229-1054-82	0015
229-1054-85	0015
229-1200-29	0911
229-1200-36	0016
229-1301-21	1129
229-1301-32	0326
229-1301-39	3346
229-1301-40	3690
229-1301-41	0345
229-1301-42	1797
229-1301-43	3166
229-1301-44	0850
229-1513-46	0086
229-5100-15U	0144
229-5100-15V	0144
229-5100-31V	0007
229-5100-32	0007
229-5100-32V	0007
229-5100-33V	0144
229-5100-164	0911
229-5100-224	0144
229-5100-225	0144
229-5100-226	0144
229-5100-227	0136
229-5100-228	0144
229-5100-231	0143
229-5100-232	0015
229-5100-233	0015
229-5100-234	0015
229-5100-235	0102
229-6011	0086
229-9191-31	OEM
229A	OEM
229B	OEM
229D	OEM
229F	OEM
229H	OEM
229K	OEM
229M	OEM
229P	OEM
229S	OEM
229V	OEM
229Z	OEM
229ZB	OEM
229ZD	OEM
229ZF	OEM
229ZH	OEM
229ZK	OEM
230-0006	0019
230-006	0143
230-0014	0133
230-0023	0057
230H	OEM
230T4	OEM
231-0000-01	0164
231-0004	0103
231-0004-01	0111
231-0004-03	0111
231-0006-03	0599
231-0006B	0160
231-0008	0178
231-0009	0004
231-006B	0160
231-0011	0160
231-0013	0086
231-0015	0160
231RC10A	OEM
231RC10AM	OEM
231RC20A	OEM
231RC20AM	OEM
231RC40A	OEM
231RC40AM	OEM
231RC60A	OEM
231RC60AM	OEM
231RC80A	OEM
231RC80AM	OEM
231RK80A	OEM
231RK100A	OEM
231RK100AM	OEM
231RK120A	OEM
231RK120AM	OEM

DEVICE TYPE	REPL CODE
231TB7	OEM
232	OEM
232-0001	0015
232-0007	0743
232-0008	0254
232-0012	0686
232-0014	0097
232-1	0079
232-2	0076
232-1006	0015
232-1009	0015
232-1011	0015
232B2	0079
232N1	0079
232N2	0079
232TB7	OEM
233(SEARS)	0086
233J	OEM
233K	OEM
233L	OEM
233TB7	OEM
234-1	2436
234J	OEM
234K	OEM
234L	OEM
234TB7	OEM
235	0279
235-1	OEM
235H	OEM
235J	OEM
235K	OEM
235L	OEM
236-0002	1035
236-0003	0141
236-0005	0232
236-0006	0331
236-0007	0357
236-0008	0381
236-0009	1164
236-0012	0956
236-0017	0557
239	OEM
240-US	OEM
240A	0464
240B	0464
240C	0464
240D	0464
240E	0717
240E15	OEM
240F	0717
240F15	OEM
240H	0717
240K	0720
240M	0720
240P	0674
240PAC10	OEM
240PAC20	OEM
240PAC30	OEM
240PAC40	OEM
240PAC50	OEM
240PAC60	OEM
240PAC70	OEM
240PAC80	OEM
240PAC90	OEM
240PAC100	OEM
240PAL50	0454
240PAL60	0454
240PAL80	0584
240PAL100	0584
240PAL110	0584
240PAL120	0584
240PAM10	0454
240PAM20	0454
240PAM30	0454
240PAM40	0454
240PAM50	0454
240PAM60	0454
240PAM80	0584
240PAM100	0584
240S	0674
240T4	OEM
240U	0464
240V	0674
240Z	0674
240ZB	0674
240ZD	0674
241-15A	0050
241C025	OEM
241C025B	OEM
241C25	OEM
241C25B	OEM
241C30	OEM
241C30B	OEM
241C35	OEM
241C35B	OEM
241C40	OEM
241C40B	OEM
241C45	OEM
241C45B	OEM
241C50	OEM
241C50B	OEM
241C60	OEM
241C60B	OEM
241C70	OEM
241C70B	OEM
241C80	OEM
241C80B	OEM
241C90	OEM
241C90B	OEM

DEVICE TYPE	REPL CODE
241C100	OEM
241C100B	OEM
241C110	OEM
241C110B	OEM
241C120	OEM
241C120B	OEM
241TB7	OEM
241UA	OEM
241UB	OEM
241UC	OEM
241UD	OEM
241UF	OEM
241UH	OEM
241UK	OEM
241UM	OEM
241WA	OEM
241WB	OEM
241WC	OEM
241WD	OEM
241WF	OEM
241WH	OEM
241WK	OEM
241WM	OEM
242	0489
242-1	OEM
242-997	2123
242B7	OEM
242H	OEM
242XB	OEM
242XD	OEM
242XF	OEM
242XH	OEM
242XK	OEM
242XM	OEM
242XP	OEM
242XS	OEM
242YB	OEM
242YD	OEM
242YF	OEM
242YH	OEM
242YK	OEM
242YM	OEM
242YP	OEM
242YS	OEM
242ZB	OEM
242ZD	OEM
242ZF	OEM
242ZH	OEM
242ZK	OEM
242ZM	OEM
242ZP	OEM
242ZS	OEM
243A-US	OEM
244	OEM
244H	OEM
244TB7	OEM
245N1B	0637
245N2B	0637
246-3	OEM
246H	OEM
246P1	0037
246P463060	0057
246P463070	0057
246P464030	0064
246P464060	0064
247-1	0911
247-257	0016
247-621	0015
247-623	0004
247-624	0160
247-625	0086
247-626	0086
247-629	0016
248-38104-1	0086
249-1L	0224
249-140	OEM
249-160	OEM
249-399	OEM
249-519	0041
249-569	0877
249-629	0292
249-759	0077
249-7867-3331-504	OEM
249-7868-3331-504	OEM
249-7869-3331-504	OEM
249-7870-3331-504	OEM
249-7871-3331-504	OEM
249-7872-3331-504	OEM
249-7967-3332-504	OEM
249-7968-3332-504	OEM
249-7969-3332-504	OEM
249-7970-3332-504	OEM
249-7971-3332-504	OEM
249-7972-3332-504	OEM
249-8067-3333-504	OEM
249-8068-3333-504	OEM
249-8069-3333-504	OEM
249-8070-3333-504	OEM
249-8071-3333-504	OEM
249-8072-3333-504	OEM
249-N1	OEM
249H	OEM
249HA	OEM
249N1	0224
250-0359	1597
250-0373	0076
250-0380	0284
250-0700	0111
250-0711	0376

DEVICE TYPE	REPL CODE
250-0712	0076
250-1	0283
250-3	0283
250-4	OEM
250-1213	0191
250-1312	1212
250A-FLAG	0217
250A-FLEX	0217
250B35	OEM
250BC15	1017
250B-FLAG	0217
250B-FLEX	0217
250DC15	1017
250D-FLAG	0217
250D-FLEX	0217
250FC15	1017
250F-FLAG	0217
250F-FLEX	0217
250GC15	1017
250GD15	OEM
250H	OEM
250H-FLEX	0463
250JB05L	2347
250JB1L	2347
250JB2L	2347
250JB3L	2353
250JB4L	2353
250JB5L	2354
250JB6L	2354
250JB8L	2356
250JB10L	4813
250JB12L	OEM
250JC15	1030
250K-FLEX	0463
250LC15	1040
250MA60	OEM
250MA80	OEM
250MA100	OEM
250MA120	OEM
250MA140	OEM
250MA160	OEM
250MA180	OEM
250M-FLEX	0463
250MLAB160	OEM
250MLAB180	OEM
250MLAB200	OEM
250MLAB250	OEM
250N3	0283
250N15A	OEM
250N15A9	OEM
250N20A	OEM
250N20A9	OEM
250N25A	OEM
250N25A9	OEM
250N30A	OEM
250N30A9	OEM
250N35A	OEM
250N35A9	OEM
250N40A	OEM
250N40A9	OEM
250N45A	OEM
250N45A9	OEM
250N50A	OEM
250N50A9	OEM
250N55A	OEM
250N55A9	OEM
250N60A	OEM
250N60A9	OEM
250N65A	OEM
250N65A9	OEM
250N70A	OEM
250N70A9	OEM
250N75A	OEM
250N75A9	OEM
250N80A	OEM
250N80A9	OEM
250N85A	OEM
250N85A9	OEM
250N90A	OEM
250N90A9	OEM
250N95A	OEM
250N95A9	OEM
250N100A	OEM
250N100A9	OEM
250N110A	OEM
250N120A	OEM
250N130A	OEM
250N140A	OEM
250N150A	OEM
250N160A	OEM
250N170A	OEM
250N180A	OEM
250N190A	OEM
250N200A	OEM
250N210A	OEM
250N220A	OEM
250N230A	OEM
250N240A	OEM
250N250A	OEM
250NC15	1040
250P4H	OEM
250P6H	OEM
250P8H	OEM
250P10H	OEM
250P12H	OEM
250P16H	OEM
250PA60	0159
250PA80	0096
250PA100	0096

DEVICE TYPE	REPL CODE
250PA120	0096
250PA140	OEM
250PA150	OEM
250PA160	OEM
250PAC10	0192
250PAC20	0192
250PAC30	0159
250PAC40	0159
250PAC50	0159
250PAC60	0159
250PAL10	0454
250PAL20	0454
250PAL30	0454
250PAL40	0454
250PAL50	0454
250PAL60	0454
250PAM10	0454
250PAM20	0454
250PAM30	0454
250PAM40	0454
250PAM50	0454
250PAM60	0454
250P-FLEX	0463
250R1B	0947
250R2B	0242
250R3B	1736
250R4B	0535
250R5B	1760
250R6B	0959
250R7B	0811
250R8B	0811
250R9B	0916
250R10B	0916
250R11B	OEM
250R12B	OEM
250R13B	OEM
250R14B	OEM
250R15B	OEM
250R16B	OEM
250R18B	OEM
250R20B	OEM
250R22B	OEM
250R24	OEM
250R24B	OEM
250R26	OEM
250R26B	OEM
250R28	OEM
250R28B	OEM
250R30	OEM
250R30B	OEM
250R32	OEM
250R32B	OEM
250R34	OEM
250R34B	OEM
250R36	OEM
250R36B	OEM
250R38	OEM
250R38B	OEM
250R40	OEM
250R40B	OEM
250R42	OEM
250R42B	OEM
250R44	OEM
250R44B	OEM
250R46	OEM
250R46B	OEM
250R48	OEM
250R48B	OEM
250R50	OEM
250R50B	OEM
250RA10	1889
250RA20	1889
250RA30	1889
250RA40	0733
250RA50	0733
250RA60	0733
250RA70	OEM
250RA80	0733
250RA100	0733
250RA110	0733
250RA120	0733
250RA140	OEM
250RA150	OEM
250RA160	OEM
250RA170	OEM
250RA180	OEM
250RA190	OEM
250RA200	OEM
250RC5	OEM
250RC10	OEM
250RC15	OEM
250RC20	OEM
250RC30	OEM
250RC40	OEM
250RC50	OEM
250RC60	OEM
250RL60	0341
250RL80	1690
250RL100	0341
250RL110	0341
250RL120	0341
250RM60	1690
250RM80	0341
250RM100	0341
250RM110	0341
250RM120	0341
250RM130	OEM
250RM140	OEM
250RM150	OEM

DEVICE TYPE	REPL CODE
250RM160	OEM
250RM170	OEM
250RS35	OEM
250RS40	OEM
250S2H	OEM
250S4H	OEM
250S6H	OEM
250S30	OEM
250S35	OEM
250S40	OEM
250S-FLEX	0463
250T4	OEM
250V-FLEX	0463
250ZB-FLEX	0463
250ZD-FLEX	0463
250Z-FLEX	0463
251-2	0124
251-250-03	OEM
251A-FLAG	0217
251A-FLEX	0217
251B-FLAG	0217
251B-FLEX	0217
251D-FLAG	0217
251D-FLEX	0217
251F2S	OEM
251F3S	OEM
251F4S	1766
251F5S	1766
251F6S	1766
251F8S	1778
251F10S	1778
251F12S	OEM
251F-FLAG	0217
251F-FLEX	0217
251H	OEM
251H-FLEX	0463
251K-FLEX	0463
251M	OEM
251M1	0038
251M-FLEX	0463
251R2S	OEM
251R3S	OEM
251R4S	OEM
251RA10	OEM
251RA20	OEM
251RA30	OEM
251RA40	OEM
251RA60	1889
251RA80	0733
251RA100	0733
251RA120	0733
251RA140	OEM
251RA150	OEM
251RA160	OEM
251RA180	OEM
251RA190	OEM
251RA200	OEM
251RC10	1889
251RC20	1889
251RC30	1889
251RC40	1889
251RC50	1889
251RC60	1889
251RC80	0733
251RC100	OEM
251RC120	OEM
251RL60	1690
251RL80	0341
251RL100	0341
251RL110	0341
251RL120	0341
251RM60	1690
251RM80	0341
251RM100	0341
251RM110	0341
251RM120	0341
251RM130	OEM
251RM140	OEM
251RM150	OEM
251RM160	OEM
251RM170	OEM
251S-FLEX	0463
251UL20S10	OEM
251UL20S15	OEM
251UL40S10	OEM
251UL40S15	OEM
251UL40S20	OEM
251UL60S10	OEM
251UL60S15	OEM
251UL60S20	OEM
251UL80S10	OEM
251UL80S15	OEM
251UL80S20	OEM
251UL100S10	OEM
251UL100S15	OEM
251UL100S20	OEM
251UL100S25	OEM
251UL100S30	OEM
251UL120S20	OEM
251UL120S25	OEM
251UL120S30	OEM
251UL130S20	OEM
251UL130S30	OEM
251UL140S20	OEM
251UL140S25	OEM
251UL140S30	OEM
251UL150S30	OEM
251UL160S25	OEM
251UL160S30	OEM

180 If replacement code is OEM, contact original manufacturer for replacement.

DEVICE TYPE	REPL CODE
251UL180S25	OEM
251UL180S30	OEM
251UL260S30	OEM
251ZB-FLEX	0463
251ZD-FLEX	0463
251Z-FLEX	0463
252-2	0133
252GT	OEM
253-5	0526
253B	OEM
253PJA60	OEM
253PJA80	OEM
253PJA100	OEM
253PJA120	OEM
253PJA140	OEM
253PJA160	OEM
253PJLA60	OEM
253PJLA80	OEM
253PJLA100	OEM
253PJLA120	OEM
253RA10	OEM
253RA20	OEM
253RA30	OEM
253RA40	OEM
253RA60	OEM
253RA80	OEM
253RA100	OEM
253RA120	OEM
253RA140	OEM
253RA150	OEM
253RA160	OEM
253RA170	OEM
253RA180	OEM
253RA190	OEM
253RA200	OEM
253RL60	OEM
253RL80	OEM
253RL100	OEM
253RL110	OEM
253RL120	OEM
253RM60	OEM
253RM80	OEM
253RM100	OEM
253RM110	OEM
253RM120	OEM
254-0102-139	0144
254-10	0336
254-11	0052
254-27	3889
254-34	OEM
254-36	0371
254A-FLAG	0217
254A-FLEX	0217
254B-FLAG	0217
254B-FLEX	0217
254D-FLAG	0217
254D-FLEX	0217
254F-FLAG	0217
254F-FLEX	0217
254G	OEM
254GI	0015
254H	OEM
254H-FLAG	0217
254H-FLEX	0217
254K-FLAG	0217
254K-FLEX	0217
254M-FLAG	0217
254M-FLEX	0217
254P-FLAG	0653
254P-FLEX	0653
254S-FLAG	0217
254S-FLEX	0217
254V-FLEX	0463
254ZB-FLEX	0463
254ZD-FLEX	0463
254Z-FLEX	0463
255B7-CH00	OEM
255P13701	OEM
256M	OEM
256M11	OEM
256TB7	OEM
257-1	0489
257-IF	OEM
257A-US	OEM
258-1	OEM
258-2	0378
258TB7	OEM
259	OEM
260	OEM
260-00301	OEM
260-2	0023
260-10-006	0683
260-10-016	0006
260-10-020	0076
260-10-021	0191
260-10-031	0030
260-10-033	0023
260-10-036	0905
260-10-039	0216
260-10-042	0111
260-10-044	0165
260-10-046	0631
260-10-048	0123
260-10-049	0139
260-10-050	0229
260-10-052	0728
260-10-053	0930
260-10-054	0042
260-10-055	0830
260-10-056	0544
260-61-011	0133
260-61-047	0133
260-P10305	OEM
260C33801	0513
260D00401	0004
260D00402	0004
260D00403	0004
260D00404	0004
260D00507	0143
260D0404	0136
260D02501	0004
260D02601	0004
260D02701	0164
260D04501	0136
260D04701	0164
260D05701	0144
260D05704	0127
260D05707	0144
260D05709	0079
260D07201	0233
260D07412	0016
260D07901	0086
260D08013	0127
260D08201	0079
260D08214	0561
260D08514	0004
260D08601	0086
260D08701	0086
260D08801	0016
260D08912	0164
260D09001	0016
260D09301	0103
260D09314	0016
260D09413	0004
260D09612	0086
260D106A1	0016
260D13701	0111
260D13702	0016
260D13704	0004
260D15901	0076
260D15902	0191
260J	OEM
260K	OEM
260P0770	0079
260P01209	0160
260P02903	0079
260P02903A	0079
260P02908	0079
260P03001	0164
260P03201	0007
260P03201A	0007
260P04001	0079
260P04002	0079
260P04003	0076
260P04004	0079
260P04502	0079
260P04503	0079
260P04505	0079
260P05402	0127
260P05402A	0127
260P05801	0144
260P05901	0007
260P05901A	0007
260P06901	0144
260P06902	0144
260P06903	0144
260P06904	0079
260P07001	0079
260P07002	0079
260P07004	0144
260P07301	0079
260P07502	0222
260P07601	0164
260P07701	0079
260P07702	0079
260P07703	0076
260P07704	0079
260P07705	0076
260P07707	0079
260P07901	0144
260P08001	0144
260P08201	0037
260P08401	0144
260P08601	0178
260P08801	0079
260P08801A	0079
260P08901	0065
260P08908	0820
260P09201	0007
260P09402	0142
260P09501	0003
260P09508	0003
260P09701	0065
260P09902	0079
260P045040	0124
260P106A1	0155
260P1003	0086
260P1030	0233
260P1060	0144
260P1601	0007
260P1610	0007
260P1760	0127
260P4002	0079
260P10003	0086
260P10003A	0086
260P10005	0076
260P10301	0233
260P10403	0144
260P10501	0144
260P10502	0144
260P10601	0007
260P10602	0144
260P10707	0590
260P10801	2359
260P11101	0144
260P11101A	0144
260P11102	0326
260P11209	0065
260P11302	0079
260P11303	0079
260P11304	0016
260P11305	0016
260P11403	0037
260P11502	0079
260P11503	0079
260P11504	0079
260P11505	0079
260P12001	0079
260P12002	0079
260P12401	0086
260P12701	0042
260P13001	0136
260P13604	0945
260P13701	0079
260P13702	0079
260P13704	0431
260P14101	0076
260P14102	0016
260P14103	0016
260P14104	0086
260P14202	0419
260P14407	1274
260P15100	0142
260P15108	0142
260P15201	0037
260P15202	0037
260P15203	0037
260P15701	0376
260P16009	0178
260P16101	0047
260P16202	0142
260P16208	0142
260P16301	0144
260P16302	0144
260P16304	0945
260P16502	0006
260P16503	0006
260P16504	0006
260P16603	0148
260P16802	0431
260P17002	0086
260P17101	0364
260P17102	0079
260P17103	0079
260P17104	0016
260P17105	0364
260P17106	0364
260P17201	0144
260P17501	0376
260P17502	0376
260P17503	0376
260P17601	0127
260P17602	0144
260P17603	0127
260P17701	0376
260P17702	0007
260P17704	0376
260P19009	0074
260P19101	0016
260P19108	0003
260P19208	0103
260P19501	0016
260P19503	0111
260P19909	0074
260P20101	0178
260P21001	0279
260P21002	0279
260P21102	0555
260P21106	0561
260P21208	0142
260P21308	0555
260P21608	0065
260P21901	0074
260P21908	0220
260P22001	0321
260P22002	0321
260P22003	3126
260P22004	3126
260P22101	0233
260P22203	0283
260P22204	0283
260P22801	0386
260P24008	0103
260P24308	0003
260P24408	0637
260P24803	0178
260P24901	0007
260P25504	1338
260P25601	3282
260P25604	3282
260P26201	0338
260P26301	0676
260P28107	0191
260P28401	0042
260P28701	0555
260P30701	0261
260P31303	0155
260P31402	0076
260P33108	0065
260P33408	0003
260P33802	0513
260P33803	0513
260P33804	0513
260P33805	0513
260P33806	0513
260P34008	2636
260P34202	0388
260P34602	1077
260P35101	1077
260P35301	0710
260P35401	0949
260P35601	0127
260P35908	2636
260P36001	0006
260P36003	0006
260P36501	0224
260P37108	0236
260P38501	0066
260P38701	2882
260P41604	0155
260P41605	0155
260P41802	0558
260P41904	0191
260P41905	0191
260P42002	1274
260P42201	0261
260P42502	0275
260P42504	0275
260P42706	0419
260P42807	1274
260P43201	0055
260P43501	0055
260P44501	OEM
260P44701	1533
260P45902	1747
260P46901	0338
260P52301	0261
260P57101	0275
260P58201	OEM
260P60401	0881
260P60601	2116
260P70403	0144
260P70501	0144
260P70502	0144
260P141103	0016
260P166040	0148
260P254010	3282
260P255040	1338
260P256010	3282
260P256030	3282
260P256040	3282
260P325030	0018
260P338040	0513
260P338050	0513
260P356010	0127
260P360030	0006
260P385010	0066
260P387010	2882
260P387030	2882
260P416020	0155
260P416030	0155
260P416040	0155
260P419030	0191
260P419040	0191
260P422010	0261
260P428020	1274
260P428070	1274
260P469010	0338
260P469020	0338
260P559010	0151
260P559030	0151
260P559050	0151
260P560040	0148
260P560050	0148
260P561010	OEM
260P571010	0275
260P573020	1638
260P574020	0388
260P582010	OEM
260P603010	1026
260P604010	0881
260P606010	2116
260P607010	2116
260P608010	2116
260P632010	0881
260P641030	OEM
260P654020	0284
260P664010	OEM
260P664030	OEM
260Z00109	0144
260Z00209	0144
260Z00309	0144
260Z00401	0191
260Z00402	0016
260Z00407	OEM
260Z00703	0164
260Z01201	0164
261-02	OEM
261-03	OEM
261A	0733
261B	0733
261C	0733
261D	0733
261F	0733
261H	0733
261J	OEM
261K	0733
261M	0733
261S	0733
261Z	0733
261ZB	0733
261ZD	0733
262-1	2506
263H	OEM
263P05209	0024
263P06602	0101
263P17402	1542
263P82401	OEM
263P82501	OEM
263P89601	OEM
263P142030	OEM
263P142040	OEM
263P170030	OEM
263P228040	OEM
263P228050	OEM
263P229010	OEM
263P229020	OEM
263P299010	6769
263P545020	OEM
263P546010	OEM
263P548010	OEM
263P684010	OEM
263P701010	3755
263P755020	OEM
263P757010	OEM
263P792020	OEM
263P798010	OEM
263P872040	3479
264-701508	0071
264D00101	0133
264D00209	0133
264D00503	0030
264D00505	0015
264D00507	0298
264D00612	0143
264D00701	0143
264D00801	0123
264D00901	0143
264D0701	0123
264D01001	0143
264D01112	0015
264D02602	OEM
264H	OEM
264P0080	0143
264P00401	0143
264P00501	0196
264P00502	0196
264P00506	0196
264P00601	0015
264P00602	0071
264P00801	0123
264P01011	0015
264P01012	0015
264P01301	0143
264P01305	0143
264P01306	0123
264P01350	0143
264P01508	1293
264P01701	0102
264P02001	0015
264P02104	0769
264P02301	0102
264P02402	0102
264P02501	0162
264P02502	0165
264P02503	0057
264P03001	0015
264P03301	0298
264P03302	0313
264P03303	0137
264P03401	0911
264P03501	OEM
264P03601	0102
264P03603	0102
264P03604	0017
264P03605	0102
264P03606	0102
264P03607	0015
264P03701	0015
264P03703	0087
264P03802	0143
264P04003	0002
264P04005	0157
264P04108	OEM
264P04109	OEM
264P04206	0374
264P04301	0015
264P04303	0071
264P04402	0015
264P04501	0133
264P04502	0124
264P04504	0133
264P04507	0133
264P04701	0102
264P04702	0015
264P04703	0015
264P04705	0102
264P04801	0015
264P04901	0015
264P05001	0015
264P05002	0015
264P05404	0124
264P05501	OEM
264P05902	0030
264P06301	0004
264P06601	0015
264P06603	0102
264P06606	0015
264P08002	0015
264P08801	0023
264P08901	0201
264P08902	0286
264P09001	0071
264P09101	0102
264P09301	0137
264P09501	0102
264P09707	0451
264P045040	0124
264P045080	0124
264P10F02	0313
264P10102	0023
264P10103	0102
264P10105	0015
264P10201	0023
264P10202	0635
264P10308	0681
264P10403	0248
264P10502	0313
264P10906	0416
264P11003	0062
264P11007	0010
264P11009	0195
264P12303	0911
264P13002	0102
264P14002	0286
264P14701	0071
264P17401	0062
264P17402	0052
264P19303	0041
264P19304	0118
264P19305	0118
264P19306	0052
264P19307	0371
264P19308	0057
264P20006	0319
264P20301	0835
264P22001	0062
264P22006	0064
264P22008	0036
264P22103	0052
264P22104	0489
264P22105	0091
264P22202	0873
264P22203	0292
264P22205	0064
264P22206	0721
264P22208	0064
264P22404	OEM
264P22501	OEM
264P22601	OEM
264P23101	0023
264P24401	3417
264P27202	OEM
264P28501	0015
264P29004	0052
264P29009	OEM
264P29101	0489
264P29102	0091
264P29104	0062
264P29205	0091
264P29206	0372
264P29209	0372
264P33004	0100
264P33009	0100
264P34109	0140
264P34202	OEM
264P34206	1266
264P34702	4262
264P39401	OEM
264P39402	OEM
264P39802	0106
264P46004	0140
264P46006	0041
264P46106	0091
264P46302	0165
264P46402	0064
264P46502	0052
264P47003	0195
264P50203	0582
264P51201	0737
264P102020	0635
264P157010	0344
264P157040	0017
264P203020	OEM
264P225020	OEM
264P231010	0023
264P244010	3417
264P244020	1319
264P285010	0015
264P295020	0023
264P295030	0017
264P341020	0064
264P341090	0140
264P358040	0102
264P358070	0031
264P358090	0541
264P389010	0911
264P457080	0296
264P458050	OEM
264P460040	0140
264P460050	0140
264P460060	0041
264P460090	0041
264P461040	0253
264P462020	0062
264P462080	0165
264P463010	0077
264P463020	0165
264P463050	0057
264P463060	0057
264P463080	0057
264P463090	0057
264P464060	0064
264P465010	0052
264P465060	0053
264P467090	0700
264P469050	0450
264P469080	OEM
264P470040	0166
264P471010	0010
264P471020	0166
264P483080	0041
264P484020	0157
264P485050	OEM
264P485060	0644
264P486020	0244
264P486080	OEM
264P487070	0137
264P487090	0137
264P488020	0053
264P488080	0002
264P490040	OEM
264P491090	0721
264P501040	0672
264P501050	0118
264P501090	OEM
264P502010	OEM
264P502030	0582
264P508010	0241
264P512010	0737
264P512020	0737
264P512030	0724
264P521030	0023
264P521040	0023
264P522010	0023
264P528010	OEM
264P528020	OEM
264P535010	OEM
264P543010	0790
264P544010	0106
264P544090	0106
264P550010	0835
264P566010	OEM
264P613010	OEM
264P825010	0023
264PA71010	0062
264Z00103	0030
264Z00201	0015
264Z00701	0143
265-1	0016
265D00702	0133
265H	OEM
265P03301	0139
265Z00101	0133
266-1	0133
266-1F	0133
266A30N	OEM
266P00101	2600
266P00101(XSTR)	0079
266P00102	2600
266P00103	OEM
266P00301	1624
266P00602	4196
266P00801	1624
266P0501	3325
266P01002	1319
266P01102	OEM
266P01802	OEM
266P03901	OEM
266P05201	OEM
266P05202	OEM
266P05301	OEM
266P05302	OEM
266P016010	1022
266P037010	OEM
266P064010	OEM
266P305A1	OEM
266P10101	0391
266P10103	0391
266P10201	1797
266P10202	1797
266P10601	0912
266P11301	0906
266P11501	OEM
266P11601	0069
266P12101	0534
266P13003	OEM
266P13401	OEM
266P13501	OEM
266P13701	OEM
266P15401	0624
266P16201	4057
266P19201	2641
266P19701	OEM
266P19801	4307
266P20402	4591
266P21401	OEM
266P21409	OEM
266P21501	4040
266P22101	OEM
266P24901	OEM
266P28101	3403
266P30102	0167

If replacement code is OEM, contact original manufacturer for replacement.

DEVICE TYPE	REPL CODE
266P30103	0167
266P30109	0167
266P30201	0465
266P30501	OEM
266P30601	2247
266P30706	1983
266P30801	OEM
266P32301	0167
266P32302	0167
266P32402	1120
266P32501	1532
266P32801	2728
266P35001	0412
266P35801	1602
266P36402	5404
266P38802	1521
266P41801	OEM
266P50101	3325
266P57001	2852
266P59201	OEM
266P60301	OEM
266P60304	4133
266P60502	0850
266P61401	4319
266P62103	0308
266P63001	0658
266P67301	OEM
266P68801	OEM
266P71301	0687
266P71401	OEM
266P75201	2696
266P82803	OEM
266P87803	OEM
266P92304	1288
266P93402	0330
266P130030	OEM
266P154010	0624
266P197010	OEM
266P922010	0619
266P922020	0619
266P923010	4403
266P923020	1775
266P931010	1775
266P934020	0330
266P934040	0330
266P934060	0619
266P963030	OEM
267-3	OEM
267P90201	OEM
267P90202	3461
267P90205	3462
267P90206	OEM
267P91002	2348
267P91003	3897
267P91006	2348
267P916020	OEM
267P925010	OEM
268H	OEM
268P02902	OEM
268P03301	0112
268P033010	0112
268P058010	OEM
269M01201	0133
269P33804	0513
269P559030	OEM
269V004-H01	0196
270-Y30B60	0733
270-Y30B70	0733
270-Y30B80	0733
270-Y30B90	0733
270-Y30C100	0733
270-Y30C110	0733
270-Y30C120	0733
270PAF10V20	OEM
270PAF10V25	OEM
270PAF10V30	OEM
270PAF20V20	OEM
270PAF20V25	OEM
270PAF20V30	OEM
270PAF40V20	OEM
270PAF40V25	OEM
270PAF40V30	OEM
270PAF60V20	OEM
270PAF60V25	OEM
270PAF60V30	OEM
270PAF80V20	OEM
270PAF80V25	OEM
270PAF80V30	OEM
270PAF100V20	OEM
270PAF100V25	OEM
270PAF100V30	OEM
270PAF120V20	OEM
270PAF120V25	OEM
270PAF120V30	OEM
270PE2-35	OEM
270XY5-35SC00	OEM
271H	OEM
271XY5-35SC00	OEM
272H	OEM
272K	OEM
272P01302	OEM
272P01401	3830
272P026010	2099
272P13801	OEM
272P13901	OEM
272P14001	3068
272P15901	4840
272P132010	OEM
272P138010	OEM
272P139010	OEM
272P140010	3068
272P165030	OEM
272P181010	OEM
272P184010	OEM
272P187010	OEM
272P188010	OEM
272P189010	OEM
272P237010	OEM
272P238010	4032
272P238020	4032
272P239010	2330
272P239020	OEM
272P239030	OEM
272P239040	OEM
272P240010	OEM
272P255010	OEM
272P255020	OEM
272P351010	OEM
272P351020	OEM
272P394010	OEM
272P440010	OEM
272P460010	OEM
272P461010	3473
272P469010	OEM
272P490010	OEM
272P491010	OEM
272P492010	OEM
272P493010	OEM
272P628010	OEM
272P629010	OEM
272P630010	OEM
272P631010	OEM
272P648010	OEM
272P657010	OEM
272P658010	OEM
272P837020	OEM
272P860010	OEM
274-54-B-IC	OEM
274-69BIC	0350
274P008030	OEM
274P008040	OEM
274P157010	OEM
274P177010	OEM
275-0-3110-04600	OEM
275A-US	OEM
275H	OEM
275J	OEM
275K	OEM
275L	OEM
275RF5	OEM
275RF10	OEM
275RF20	OEM
275RF30	OEM
275RF40	OEM
275RF50	OEM
275RF60	OEM
275U5A	1017
275U5AR	0496
275U10A	1017
275U10AR	0496
275U15A	1017
275U15AR	0496
275U20A	1017
275U20AR	0496
275U25A	1030
275U25AR	1766
275U30A	1030
275U30AR	1766
275U40A	1030
275U40AR	1766
275U50A	1030
275U50AR	1766
275U60A	1030
275U60AR	1766
275U70A	2805
275U70AR	1778
275U80A	2805
275U80AR	1778
275U90A	2805
275U90AR	1778
275U100A	2805
275U100AR	1778
276-007	0308
276-009	1183
276-010	0406
276-018	5560
276-019	1767
276-021	0856
276-022	4598
276-025	2181
276-026	2990
276-030	4928
276-033	5024
276-035	5287
276-036	3965
276-036B	3965
276-037	0835
276-038	0356
276-041	1951
276-053	4902
276-065	4236
276-066	4240
276-066A	4240
276-068	6977
276-069	6978
276-070	3990
276-073	OEM
276-075	4786
276-081	5062
276-0225	OEM
276-0707	OEM
276-113	6980
276-116	OEM
276-124	6980
276-130	5031
276-134	4961
276-142	6981
276-143	6711
276-145	4918
276-561	0631
276-562	0012
276-563	0137
276-564	0002
276-565	0162
276-568	0824
276-569	OEM
276-570	0832
276-571	0834
276-572	0644
276-703	1042
276-705	1044
276-706	0375
276-1000	6925
276-1001	0588
276-1002	0588
276-1003	0588
276-1020	6929
276-1050	2704
276-1067	6932
276-1079	1386
276-1089	2084
276-1090	2078
276-1101	0023
276-1102	0023
276-1103	0790
276-1104	0015
276-1114	0087
276-1122	0124
276-1123	0123
276-1124	0911
276-1141	0110
276-1142	0947
276-1143	0242
276-1144	0535
276-1146	6936
276-1151	0276
276-1152	0276
276-1161	4129
276-1165	0730
276-1171	6937
276-1172	1404
276-1173	6938
276-1180	6939
276-1181	5588
276-1185	5386
276-1251	0806
276-1252	OEM
276-1301	OEM
276-1302	OEM
276-1303	OEM
276-1307	OEM
276-1308	OEM
276-1337	OEM
276-1603	0076
276-1604	0006
276-1617	0016
276-1656	OEM
276-1704	OEM
276-1705	3033
276-1707	3039
276-1708	3040
276-1709	3042
276-1710	OEM
276-1711	0620
276-1712	0176
276-1713	2232
276-1714	3357
276-1715	3695
276-1717	2692
276-1718	0580
276-1720	3347
276-1721	3733
276-1723	0967
276-1725	0375
276-1728	3254
276-1729	2264
276-1731	3034
276-1735	2071
276-1737	3050
276-1740	0026
276-1743	1534
276-1748	OEM
276-1749	OEM
276-1750	OEM
276-1757	0438
276-1758	0780
276-1759	0167
276-1762	5187
276-1763	OEM
276-1764	OEM
276-1767	OEM
276-1770	0619
276-1771	0330
276-1772	1311
276-1773	1275
276-1774	1827
276-1777	2811
276-1778	2541
276-1782	OEM
276-1783	OEM
276-1784	OEM
276-1786	OEM
276-1787	OEM
276-1792	3743
276-1795	OEM
276-1796	OEM
276-1797	OEM
276-1801	0232
276-1802	0357
276-1803	1164
276-1805	1100
276-1808	1199
276-1811	0310
276-1813	1150
276-1818	1303
276-1822	0462
276-1828	0614
276-1835	0971
276-1915	0088
276-2001	0595
276-2001/RS2001	0595
276-2002	0595
276-2002/RS2002	0595
276-2003	0050
276-2003/RS2003	0050
276-2004	0004
276-2004/RS2004	0004
276-2005	0208
276-2005/RS2005	0208
276-2006	0085
276-2006/RS2006	0085
276-2007	0211
276-2007/RS2007	0164
276-2008	0710
276-2008/RS2008	0710
276-2009	0079
276-2009/RS2009	0079
276-2010	0127
276-2010/RS2010	0079
276-2011	0144
276-2011/RS2011	0144
276-2012	0710
276-2012/RS2012	0710
276-2013	0016
276-2013/RS2013	0016
276-2014	0079
276-2014/RS2014	0079
276-2015	0144
276-2015/RS2015	0144
276-2016	4305
276-2016/RS2016	0079
276-2017	0042
276-2017/RS2017	0042
276-2018	0561
276-2018/RS2018	0561
276-2019	1351
276-2019/RS2019	1351
276-2020	0477
276-2021	0150
276-2021/RS2021	0150
276-2022	0037
276-2022/RS2022	0037
276-2023	0037
276-2023/RS2023	0037
276-2024	0037
276-2024/RS2024	0037
276-2025	0919
276-2025/RS2025	0919
276-2026	1357
276-2026/RS2026	1357
276-2027	0919
276-2027/RS2027	1359
276-2028	0321
276-2029	1882
276-2030	0076
276-2030/RS2030	0079
276-2031	0326
276-2031/RS2031	0326
276-2032	0006
276-2032/RS2032	0037
276-2033	0079
276-2033/RS2033	0079
276-2034	0037
276-2034/RS2034	0037
276-2035	0321
276-2036	0321
276-2038	0414
276-2038/RS2038	0414
276-2039	0177
276-2039/RS2039	0177
276-2040	2002
276-2040/RS2040	2002
276-2041	0103
276-2041/RS2041	0103
276-2042	1384
276-2042/RS2042	3339
276-2043	0486
276-2043/RS2043	0486
276-2044	2978
276-2048	0042
276-2051	0076
276-2055	0309
276-2057	0076
276-2058	0076
276-2059	0079
276-2060	0396
276-2061	0710
276-2062	1382
276-2068	2220
276-2072	2325
276-2073	OEM
276-2074	OEM
276-2329	OEM
276-2334	0301
276-2335	OEM
276-2336	OEM
276-2337	OEM
276-2401	0473
276-2411	0215
276-2413	0409
276-2417	0508
276-2423	0515
276-2449	0001
276-2466	0101
276-2481	0621
276-2503	0518
276-2505	0518
276-2520	0503
276-2521	0506
276H	OEM
277-14	1900
277-221	OEM
277-1012	OEM
277A	OEM
277G	OEM
277H	OEM
277J	OEM
277K	OEM
278-2	0623
278-14	1274
278H	OEM
279-02	OEM
279-14ITT	0064
279-22ITT744	OEM
279H	OEM
280-0001	0905
280-0002	0514
280-07	0720
280H	OEM
281	0016
283H	OEM
284H	OEM
284J	OEM
285H	OEM
285J	OEM
285K	OEM
285L	OEM
286-1BFY	OEM
286H	OEM
286HM	OEM
286HP	OEM
286J	OEM
287H	OEM
288(SEARS)	0015
288-0550R	4064
288H	OEM
288HC	OEM
289H	OEM
289J	OEM
289K	OEM
289L	OEM
290-1003	0133
290A	OEM
290V02H69	0144
290V034C01	0071
291-04	0015
291-20	0015
291H	OEM
292-10	0015
292A	OEM
292H	OEM
293H	OEM
294	0037
294-42-9	0019
294-92-2	0079
294H	OEM
295	OEM
295-01	0133
295-03	0023
295-1	0133
295-95-1	0176
295H	OEM
295L001H01	0015
295L001M01	0015
295L001M02	0015
295L002H01	0015
295L002M03	0229
295L003M01	0015
295V002H01	0015
295V003H01	0769
295V003M01	0769
295V005H02	0015
295V005H03	0143
295V006H01	0015
295V006H02	0015
295V006H03	0015
295V006H05	0015
295V006H06	0229
295V006H07	0015
295V006H08	0229
295V006H09	0015
295V007H02	0015
295V008H01	0015
295V012H01	0015
295V012H02	0015
295V012H03	0015
295V012H06	0015
295V014H01	0015
295V014H04	0015
295V014H7	0015
295V015H02	0015
295V016H01	0015
295V017H01	0015
295V020B01	0015
295V020H01	0015
295V023H01	0015
295V027C01	0015
295V027C01-1	0015
295V028C01	0015
295V028C02	0015
295V028C03	0015
295V028C04	0071
295V029C01	0015
295V029C02	0015
295V031B	1293
295V031B02	0469
295V031C02	0469
295V033B01	0769
295V034C01	1293
295V035C01	0015
295V041H04	0160
296	2498
296-18-9	0004
296-19-9	0004
296-42-9	0019
296-46-9	0050
296-50-9	0016
296-51-9	0016
296-55-9	0532
296-56-9	0016
296-58-9	0086
296-59-9	0016
296-60-9	0004
296-61-9	0222
296-62-9	0004
296-64-9-1	0164
296-77-9	0155
296-81-9	1390
296-86	0224
296-98-9	0076
296H	OEM
296L002B01	0124
296L003B01	0137
296V001H01	1024
296V001M01	1024
296V002H01	0143
296V002H02	0143
296V002H05	0143
296V002H06	0143
296V002H07	0143
296V002H08	0143
296V002M01	0143
296V004H01	0196
296V006H02	0143
296V006H03	0015
296V006H07	0015
296V007H02	0143
296V011H03	0361
296V012H01	0143
296V015B01	0143
296V015H01	0143
296V017H01	0137
296V018B01	0137
296V018B02	0644
296V019B01	0137
296V019B04	0789
296V020B01	0133
296V020B02	0015
296V024B01	0143
296V024B02	0133
296V034C01	1293
297C011H01	0050
297H	OEM
297L001H01	0208
297L001H02	0208
297L001H03	0004
297L001M01	0208
297L001M02	0004
297L001M03	0004
297L002H01	0004
297L005H01	0004
297L006H01	0016
297L006H02	0016
297L007C02	0016
297L007H01	0016
297L007H02	0016
297L007H03	0016
297L007H03/C03	0079
297L008C02	0086
297L008H01	0086
297L010C01	0688
297L012C01	0037
297L013B01	0016
297L013B02	0037
297V002H03	0208
297V002H04	0208
297V002H05	0208
297V002M04	0208
297V002M05	0208
297V003	0211
297V003H02	0004
297V003H03	0211
297V003H06	0004
297V003H08	0004
297V003H09	0004
297V003M01	0211
297V003M07	0211
297V004H01	0004
297V004H03	0004
297V004H04	0004
297V004H06	0004
297V004H08	0004
297V004H09	0004
297V004H010	0211
297V004H10	0211
297V004H11	0004
297V004H14	0211
297V004H15	0211
297V004H16	0211
297V004M01	0211
297V005H01	0004
297V008H01	0279
297V008M01	0050
297V07K01	OEM
297V010H01	0004
297V010M01	0004
297V011	0279
297V011H01	0136
297V011H02	0279
297V012	0279
297V012H01	0136
297V012H02	0279
297V012H03	0279
297V012H04	0050
297V012H05	0279
297V012H06	0279
297V012H07	0050
297V012H08	0279
297V012H09	0279
297V012H10	0136
297V012H11	0050
297V012H12	0050
297V012H13	0050
297V012H14	0211
297V012H15	0136
297V017H01	0279
297V017H02	0279
297V018H01	0004
297V019B01	0279
297V019B04	0789
297V019H01	0279
297V020H01	0050
297V020H02	0279
297V020M01	0279
297V021H01	0279
297V021H02	0279
297V021H03	0279
297V022H01	0279
297V024H01	0050
297V024H03	0050
297V025H02	0211
297V025H03	0004
297V025H04	0211
297V025H05	0211
297V025H15	0211
297V026H01	0136
297V026H03	0279
297V027C01	0015
297V027H01	0211
297V032H01	0211
297V033H01	0211
297V034H01	0136
297V035H01	0136
297V036H01	0136
297V036H02	0136
297V037B02	0004
297V037H01	0211
297V037H02	0211
297V038H01	0279
297V038H02	0050
297V038H03	0050
297V038H04	0050
297V038H05	0279
297V038H06	0136
297V038H07	0211
297V038H09	0279
297V038H10	0136
297V038H11	0136
297V038H12	0136
297V040H01	0211
297V040H08	0211
297V040H09	0164
297V040H10	0211
297V040H11	0211
297V040H12	0211
297V040H13	0211
297V040H15	0160
297V040H16	0211
297V041H01	0265
297V041H02	0160
297V041H03	0160
297V041H04	0160
297V041H05	0085
297V041H06	0160
297V041H07	0085
297V041H15	0085
297V042C01	0211
297V042C02	0211
297V042C03	0211
297V042C04	0211
297V042H01	0211
297V042H02	0211
297V042H03	0136

If replacement code is OEM, contact original manufacturer for replacement.

DEVICE TYPE	REPL CODE
297V042H04	0136
297V043H01	0211
297V044H01	0279
297V045H01	0136
297V045H02	0136
297V049H01	0198
297V049H03	0198
297V049H04	0198
297V049H05	0016
297V049H06	0086
297V050C02	0004
297V050H01	0469
297V050H02	0469
297V050H03	0211
297V051C03	0211
297V051C04	0211
297V051H01	0211
297V051H02	0211
297V051H03	0211
297V051H04	0004
297V052C01	0211
297V052H01	0004
297V052H02	0211
297V052H04	0004
297V053C01	0211
297V053H01	0004
297V053H02	0004
297V054C01	0279
297V054C02	0279
297V054H01	0136
297V054H02	0136
297V055C01	0279
297V055H01	0136
297V057H01	0164
297V057H02	0164
297V059H01	0198
297V059H02	0198
297V059H03	0198
297V060H01	0142
297V060H02	0142
297V060H03	0142
297V061C01	0103
297V061C01A	0103
297V061C02	0103
297V061C02A	0103
297V061C03	0198
297V061C04	0198
297V061C05	0086
297V061C06	0198
297V061C07	0016
297V061H01	0016
297V061H02	0016
297V061H03	0016
297V062C01	0160
297V062C05	0160
297V062C06	0086
297V063C01	0136
297V063H01	0050
297V064B01	0050
297V064H01	0050
297V065C01	0136
297V065C02	0136
297V065C03	0136
297V065H01	0279
297V065H02	0279
297V065H03	0279
297V068C01	OEM
297V069C01	0637
297V070C01	0136
297V070H49	0144
297V071C02	OEM
297V071C03	0142
297V071H03	0142
297V072C01	0144
297V072C03	0144
297V072C04	0144
297V072C05	0086
297V072C06	0016
297V073C01	0126
297V073C02	0126
297V073C03	0037
297V073C04	0037
297V074C01	0007
297V074C02	0198
297V074C03	0198
297V074C04	0198
297V074C05	OEM
297V074C06	0016
297V074C07	0016
297V074C08	0076
297V074C09	0144
297V074C10	0086
297V074C11	0126
297V074C12	0086
297V075C01	OEM
297V076B01	0211
297V076C01	0211
297V077C01	0136
297V078C01	0144
297V078C02	0144
297V080C01	0126
297V081C01	0004
297V082B01	0086
297V082B02	0126
297V082B03	0126
297V083C01	0037
297V083C02	0016
297V083C03	0126
297V083C04	0086

DEVICE TYPE	REPL CODE
297V084C01	0275
297V085C01	0016
297V085C02	0016
297V085C03	0016
297V085C04	0016
297V086C01	0037
297V086C02	0016
297V086C03	0016
297V086C04	0455
297V087B02	0546
297V86C02	OEM
298H	OEM
299-POWER	0435
299B09001	0124
299D09001	0124
299D09002	0041
299D09005	0124
299D13101	0873
299H	OEM
299POWER	0435
300	0211
300A	0594
300AR	1337
300B	0594
300BR	1337
300C	0594
300CR	1337
300D	0594
300DR	1337
300E	0594
300ER	1337
300EXD13	OEM
300EXH21	OEM
300F	0594
300FR	1337
300FXD13	OEM
300G	1975
300GR	1894
300H	1975
300HR	1894
300JB05L	4089
300JB1L	4089
300JB2L	4089
300JB3L	4096
300JB4L	4096
300JB5L	4096
300JB6L	4096
300JH21	OEM
300K	1975
300KR	1894
300LD11A	OEM
300LD13	OEM
300M	1975
300MR	1894
300N15A	OEM
300N15A9	OEM
300N20A	OEM
300N20A9	OEM
300N25A	OEM
300N25A9	OEM
300N30A	OEM
300N30A9	OEM
300N35A	OEM
300N35A9	OEM
300N40A	OEM
300N40A9	OEM
300N45A	OEM
300N45A9	OEM
300N50A	OEM
300N50A9	OEM
300N55A	OEM
300N55A9	OEM
300N60A	OEM
300N60A9	OEM
300N65A	OEM
300N65A9	OEM
300N70A	OEM
300N70A9	OEM
300N75A	OEM
300N75A9	OEM
300N80A	OEM
300N80A9	OEM
300N85A	OEM
300N85A9	OEM
300N90A	OEM
300N90A9	OEM
300N95A	OEM
300N95A9	OEM
300N100A	OEM
300N100A9	OEM
300N110A	OEM
300N120A	OEM
300N130A	OEM
300N140A	OEM
300N150A	OEM
300N160A	OEM
300N170A	OEM
300N180A	OEM
300N190A	OEM
300N200A	OEM
300N210A	OEM
300N220A	OEM
300N230A	OEM
300N240A	OEM
300N250A	OEM
300ND11A	OEM
300ND13	OEM
300P2S	OEM
300PA50	OEM

DEVICE TYPE	REPL CODE
300PA60	0159
300PA80	0096
300PA100	0096
300PA120	0096
300PA140	OEM
300PA150	OEM
300PA160	OEM
300PAC10	0192
300PAC20	0192
300PAC30	0159
300PAC40	0159
300PAC50	0159
300PAC60	0159
300QD13	OEM
300QH21	OEM
300R1B	0947
300R2B	0242
300R3B	1736
300R4B	OEM
300R5B	1760
300R6B	2621
300R7B	0811
300R8B	0811
300R9B	2621
300R10B	OEM
300R11B	OEM
300R12B	OEM
300R13B	OEM
300R14B	OEM
300R15B	OEM
300R16B	OEM
300R18B	OEM
300R20B	OEM
300R22B	OEM
300R24B	OEM
300R26B	OEM
300R28B	OEM
300R30B	OEM
300R32B	OEM
300R34B	OEM
300R36B	OEM
300R38B	OEM
300R40B	OEM
300R42B	OEM
300R44B	OEM
300R46B	OEM
300R48B	OEM
300R50B	OEM
300RA10	1889
300RA20	1889
300RA30	1889
300RA40	1889
300RA50	0733
300RA60	0733
300RA80	0733
300RA100	0733
300RA110	0733
300RA120	0733
300RA130	OEM
300RA140	OEM
300RA150	OEM
300RA160	OEM
300RA170	OEM
300RA180	OEM
300RA190	OEM
300RA200	OEM
300RB10	1889
300RB20	1889
300RB30	1889
300RB40	0733
300RB50	0733
300RB60	0733
300RB70	OEM
300RB80	0733
300RB90	OEM
300RB100	0733
300RB110	0733
300RB120	0733
300RB130	OEM
300RB140	OEM
300RB150	OEM
300RB160	OEM
300RB170	OEM
300RB180	OEM
300RB190	OEM
300RB200	OEM
300RC5	OEM
300RC10	OEM
300RC15	OEM
300RC20	OEM
300RC30	OEM
300RC40	OEM
300RC60	OEM
300S5H	OEM
300S6H	OEM
300S8H	OEM
300S10H	OEM
300S12H	OEM
300SS5H	OEM
300SS6H	OEM
300SS8H	OEM
300SS10H	OEM
300SS12H	OEM
300TD11A	OEM
300TD13	OEM
300U5	1017
300U5A	1017
300U5AR	0496

DEVICE TYPE	REPL CODE
300U5R	0496
300U10	1017
300U10A	1017
300U10AR	0496
300U10R	0496
300U15	1017
300U15A	1017
300U15AR	0496
300U15R	0496
300U20	1017
300U20A	1017
300U20AR	0496
300U20R	0496
300U25	1017
300U25A	1017
300U25AR	0496
300U25R	0496
300U30	1017
300U30A	1017
300U30AR	0496
300U30R	0496
300U40	1030
300U40A	1017
300U40AR	0496
300U40R	1766
300U50	1030
300U50A	1030
300U50AR	1766
300U50R	1766
300U60	1030
300U60A	1030
300U60AR	1766
300U60R	1766
300U70	1040
300U70A	1040
300U70AR	1778
300U70R	1778
300U80	1040
300U80A	1040
300U80AR	1778
300U80R	1778
300U90	1040
300U90A	1040
300U90AR	1778
300U90R	1778
300U100	1040
300U100A	1040
300U100AR	1778
300U100R	1778
300U120A	3872
300UR20A	0496
300UR30A	0496
300UR40A	0496
300UR60A	1766
300UR80A	1778
300UR100A	1778
300UR120A	6569
300WD11A	OEM
300WD13	OEM
300YD13	OEM
301	0211
301-1	0469
301-576-2	0461
301-576-3	0659
301-576-4	0232
301-576-6	0086
301-576-14	0375
301-679-1	1902
301-680-1	3731
301-695-1	1224
301-696-1	1344
301AL	6311
301C025	OEM
301C025B	OEM
301C25	OEM
301C25B	OEM
301C30	OEM
301C30B	OEM
301C35	OEM
301C35B	OEM
301C40	OEM
301C40B	OEM
301C45	OEM
301C45B	OEM
301C50	OEM
301C50B	OEM
301C60	OEM
301C60B	OEM
301C70	OEM
301C70B	OEM
301C80	OEM
301C80B	OEM
301C90	OEM
301C90B	OEM
301C100	OEM
301C100B	OEM
301C110	OEM
301C110B	OEM
301C120	OEM
301C120B	OEM
301CL	6559
301F1FM	OEM
301F2FM	OEM
301F3FM	OEM
301R1FM	OEM
301R2FM	OEM
301R3FM	OEM
301RA10	OEM
301RA20	OEM

DEVICE TYPE	REPL CODE
301RA30	OEM
301RA40	OEM
301RA60	1889
301RA80	0733
301RA100	0733
301RA120	0733
301RA130	OEM
301RA140	OEM
301RA150	OEM
301RA160	OEM
301RA170	OEM
301RA180	OEM
301RA190	OEM
301RA200	OEM
301RB10	OEM
301RB20	OEM
301RB30	OEM
301RB40	OEM
301RB50	OEM
301RB60	OEM
301RB80	OEM
301RB100	OEM
301RB110	OEM
301RB120	OEM
301RB130	OEM
301RB140	OEM
301RB150	OEM
301RB160	OEM
301RB170	OEM
301RB180	OEM
301RB190	OEM
301RB200	OEM
301RC10	1889
301RC20	1889
301RC30	5607
301RC40	1889
301RC50	1889
301RC60	1889
301RC80	1889
301RC100	OEM
301RC120	OEM
301U80	1040
301U100	1040
301U120	3872
301U120A	4478
301U140	2805
301U160	OEM
301U160A	OEM
301U180	OEM
301U200	OEM
301U210	OEM
301U220	OEM
301U230	OEM
301U240	OEM
301U250	OEM
301UR120	3489
301UR140	3138
301UR160	OEM
301UR160A	OEM
301UR180	OEM
301UR200	OEM
302	0211
302(OPTO)	OEM
302-2	0253
302-679-1	2039
302-680	2039
302-681	OEM
302-K	0315
302A	1116
302AL	6312
302AR	0267
302B	2873
302BR	0267
302C	1116
302CL	6312
302CR	0267
302D	1116
302DR	0267
302E	1118
302E-RT	OEM
302F	1118
302FR	0267
302G	0800
302GR	0267
302G-RT	OEM
302H	0800
302HR	0267
302K	1186
302KR	0267
302M	0315
302MR	0267
302P	1124
302S	1124
302U5A	OEM
302U10A	OEM
302U15A	OEM
302U20A	OEM
302U25A	OEM
302U30A	OEM
302U40A	OEM
302U50A	OEM
302U60A	OEM
302U70A	OEM
302U80A	OEM
302U90A	OEM
302U100A	OEM
302U120A	OEM
302V	0045
302Z	0045

DEVICE TYPE	REPL CODE
303-1	0037
303-1(IC)	0485
303-2	0126
303-4	OEM
303-5	OEM
303-7	OEM
303-K	0315
303A	1116
303AL	6313
303AR	0267
303B	2873
303BR	0267
303C	1116
303CL	6313
303CR	0267
303D	1116
303DR	0267
303E	1118
303E-RT	OEM
303F	1118
303FR	0267
303G	0800
303GR	0267
303G-RT	OEM
303H	0800
303HR	0267
303K	1186
303KR	0267
303M	0315
303MR	0267
303P	1124
303PJA180	OEM
303PJA200	OEM
303PJA250	OEM
303RA10	OEM
303RA20	OEM
303RA30	OEM
303RA40	OEM
303RA60	OEM
303RA80	OEM
303RA100	OEM
303RA120	OEM
303RA130	OEM
303RA140	OEM
303RA150	OEM
303RA170	OEM
303RA180	OEM
303RA190	OEM
303RA200	OEM
303RB10	OEM
303RB20	OEM
303RB30	OEM
303RB40	OEM
303RB60	OEM
303RB80	OEM
303RB100	OEM
303RB120	OEM
303RB130	OEM
303RB140	OEM
303RB150	OEM
303RB160	OEM
303RB170	OEM
303RB180	OEM
303RB190	OEM
303RB200	OEM
303S	1124
303U80	OEM
303U100	OEM
303U120	OEM
303U140	OEM
303U160	OEM
303U180	OEM
303U200	OEM
303U210	OEM
303U220	OEM
303U230	OEM
303U240	OEM
303U250	OEM
303V	0045
303Z	0045
303Z4	OEM
304	OEM
304A	0097
304AL	6314
304AR	2275
304B	0090
304BR	2275
304C	0109
304CL	6314
304CR	2275
304D	0109
304DR	2275
304F	0105
304FR	0471
304H	0109
304HR	0471
304K	0116
304KR	0471
304M	0122
304MR	0471
304P	0131
304PR	0444
304RA60	OEM
304RA80	OEM
304RA100	OEM
304RA120	OEM
304RA130	OEM
304RA140	OEM
304RA150	OEM

DEVICE TYPE	REPL CODE
304RA160	OEM
304RA170	OEM
304S	0131
304SR	0444
304V	0145
304Z	0145
304Z4	OEM
305-1	3707
305-2	OEM
305-3	OEM
305-4	OEM
305A	0703
305AR	2275
305B	4077
305BR	2275
305C	0575
305CR	2275
305D	0575
305DR	2275
305F	2049
305FR	0471
305GI418C	0344
305H	0994
305HR	0471
305K	2065
305KR	0471
305M	2070
305MR	0471
305P	2077
305PR	0444
305S	2077
305SR	0444
305T4	OEM
305U80	OEM
305U100	OEM
305U120	OEM
305U140	OEM
305U160	OEM
305U180	OEM
305U200	OEM
305U210	OEM
305U220	OEM
305U230	OEM
305U240	OEM
305U250	OEM
305V	0607
305Z	0607
305Z4	OEM
305ZR	0444
306-1	0016
306-8	0079
306-12	OEM
306AL	6315
306CL	6315
306Z4	OEM
307-005-9-001	0574
307-007-9-001	0905
307-007-9-002	2608
307-008-9-001	0817
307-029-1-001	0905
307-047-9-001	0413
307-059-9-001	0229
307-095-9-001	OEM
307-095-9-002	0215
307-095-9-003	1288
307-095-9-004	2238
307-107-9-001	4552
307-107-9-002	OEM
307-107-9-003	1044
307-107-9-004	4543
307-107-9-005	4539
307-107-9-006	4619
307-108-9-001	2364
307-112-9-001	1805
307-112-9-002	1288
307-112-9-003	1288
307-112-9-005	0413
307-112-9-006	4145
307-112-9-007	2246
307-112-9-009	2238
307-113-9-001	0215
307-113-9-002	2290
307-113-9-003	1288
307-113-9-004	4145
307-115-9-001	2246
307-120-9-001	4006
307-128-9-002	OEM
307-131-9-001	2290
307-131-9-002	1120
307-131-9-003	4563
307-131-9-005	OEM
307-131-9-006	0701
307-131-9001	2290
307-133-9-004	1532
307-133-9-005	4567
307-133-9001	4567
307-143-9-001	4564
307-143-9-002	3980
307-143-9-003	4571
307-143-9-004	0321
307-143-9-007	OEM
307-145-9-001	2312
307-152-9-001	OEM
307-152-9-004	0621
307-152-9-005	2807
307-152-9-007	1519
307-152-9-008	OEM
307-152-9-009	1877
307-152-9-010	6337

If replacement code is OEM, contact original manufacturer for replacement.

183

DEVICE TYPE	REPL CODE
307-152-9-011	OEM
307-152-9-012	0215
307A	0015
307AL	6316
307B	0015
307C	0015
307CL	6316
307D	0015
307F	0015
307H	0015
307K	0015
307M	0015
307Z4	OEM
308-1	OEM
308A	2872
308AR	2275
308B	2872
308BR	2275
308C	2872
308CR	2275
308D	2872
308DR	2275
308F	1104
308FR	0471
308H	1104
308HR	0471
308K	1104
308KR	0471
308Z4	OEM
309-01ITT	0064
309-033-0	2285
309-3	OEM
309-4	OEM
309-6	OEM
309-324-616	0143
309-327-601	0644
309-327-608	0644
309-327-802	0644
309-327-803	0071
309-327-910	0015
309-327-916	0143
309-327-926	0016
309-327-927	0015
309-327-931	0004
309-327-932	0015
309U10	OEM
309U80	OEM
309U100	OEM
309U120	OEM
309U140	OEM
309U160	OEM
309U180	OEM
309U200	OEM
309U210	OEM
309U220	OEM
309U230	OEM
309U240	OEM
309U250	OEM
309Z4	OEM
310	0015
310-068	0136
310-4	0015
310-68	0136
310-123	0136
310-124	0136
310-139	0136
310-187	0016
310-188	0004
310-189	0164
310-190	0136
310-191	0050
310-192	0222
310-8028-001	0735
310J	OEM
310L	OEM
310T4	OEM
310VF	OEM
310Z4	OEM
311AL	6318
311CL	6318
311Z4	0789
312A12	OEM
312AJ	6319
312AL	6319
312CJ	6319
312CL	6319
312J	OEM
312K	OEM
312L	OEM
312R2S	OEM
312Z4	OEM
313AJ	OEM
313AL	OEM
313CJ	OEM
313CL	OEM
313Z4	OEM
314-6006	0178
314-6007-1	0016
314-6007-2	0016
314-6007-3	0016
314-6010-3	0079
315	0015
315-01A	OEM
315-6CGI	0015
315S02	OEM
315T4	OEM
315Z4	OEM
316Z4	OEM
317-2627-1	0141
317K	2811
317T	2541
317Z4	OEM
318-1	5897
318-2	3047
318-3	OEM
318-7	OEM
319A	0594
319B	0594
319D	0594
319E	0594
319F	0594
319G	1975
319G06	OEM
319H	1975
319K	1975
319Z4	OEM
320	OEM
320A	0015
320B	0015
320C	0015
320D	0015
320F	0015
320H	0015
320K	0015
320M	0015
320P	0071
320S	0071
320T4	OEM
320VF	OEM
320Z	0071
320Z4	OEM
321	1713
321-919	OEM
321A	OEM
321AJ	6322
321AL	6322
321CJ	6322
321CL	6322
321Z4	OEM
322	OEM
322-0147	0015
322-1	0178
322A	OEM
322AJ	6323
322AL	6323
322CJ	6323
322CL	6323
322E	OEM
322G	OEM
322T1	0004
323AJ	6324
323AL	6324
323CJ	6324
323CL	6324
323T1	0004
324	0004
324(DIO)	OEM
324(IC)	0620
324-0011	0196
324-0012	1024
324-0014	0143
324-0015	0469
324-0016	0050
324-0026	0050
324-0027	0136
324-0028	0136
324-0029	0004
324-0030	0164
324-0035	0143
324-0037	0143
324-0038	0136
324-0041	0004
324-0049	0143
324-0055	0211
324-0056	0164
324-0057	0143
324-0062	0164
324-0074	0004
324-0077	0050
324-0079	0136
324-0080	0164
324-0082	0050
324-0083	0050
324-0085	0164
324-0086	0050
324-0087	0050
324-0088	0211
324-0089	0004
324-0090	0279
324-0091	0004
324-0092	0004
324-0093	0004
324-0093(PHILCO)	0143
324-0095	0050
324-0097	0164
324-0098	0136
324-0099	0136
324-012	0050
324-019	0086
324-0100	0004
324-0102	0229
324-0105	0143
324-0106	0136
324-0107	0123
324-0107-01	0143
324-0108	0143
324-0110	0050
324-0111	0050
324-0112	0050
324-0113	0911
324-0114	0911
324-0115	0599
324-0116	0969
324-0117	0015
324-0118	2872
324-0119	0015
324-0120	0015
324-0121	0136
324-0122	0208
324-0123	0050
324-0124	0164
324-0125	0164
324-0126	0222
324-0128	0969
324-0129	0050
324-0130	0136
324-0131	0050
324-0132	0050
324-0133	0211
324-0134	0038
324-0135	0015
324-0136	0050
324-0137	0628
324-0138	0628
324-0139	0004
324-0140	0164
324-0141	0143
324-0142	0004
324-0143	0211
324-0144	0211
324-0145	0136
324-0146	0211
324-0147	0015
324-0149	0144
324-0150	0144
324-0151	0198
324-0152	0198
324-0154	0198
324-0155	0050
324-0160	0143
324-0162	0015
324-0166	OEM
324-0187	0050
324-0611	4100
324-1	0144
324-132	0050
324-144	0211
324-6005-5	0016
324-6011	0086
324-6013	0086
324A	OEM
324AL	6325
324CL	6325
324T1	0004
324T2	0004
325-0025-327	0143
325-0025-329	0004
325-0025-330	0004
325-0025-331	0004
325-0028-79	0004
325-0028-80	0004
325-0028-81	0004
325-0028-82	0136
325-0028-83	0004
325-0028-84	0144
325-0028-85	0050
325-0028-86	0143
325-0028-87	0143
325-0028-89	0015
325-0030-315	0004
325-0030-317	0004
325-0030-318	0004
325-0030-319	0004
325-0031-303	0016
325-0031-304	0198
325-0031-305	0198
325-0031-306	0164
325-0031-310	0016
325-0031-335	0143
325-0031-338	0015
325-0036-536	0004
325-0036-562	0143
325-0036-564	0136
325-0036-565	0136
325-0042-311	0276
325-0042-351	0016
325-0047-516	0004
325-0047-517	0015
325-0054-310	0004
325-0054-311	0004
325-0054-312	0015
325-0076-306	0016
325-0076-307	0016
325-0076-308	0016
325-0076-315	0015
325-0081-100	0016
325-0081-101	0016
325-0081-102	0164
325-0081-109	0287
325-0081-110	0015
325-0135-B	0015
325-0137-6	0004
325-0141-23	0015
325-0500-12	0111
325-0500-13	0111
325-0574-30	0016
325-0574-31	0016
325-0574-32	0030
325-0670	0004
325-0670-1	0004
325-0670-7	0004
325-0670-16	0015
325-0670A	0004
325-1370-18	0004
325-1370-19	0016
325-1370-20	0016
325-1375-10	0136
325-1375-11	0136
325-1375-12	0136
325-1376-53	0004
325-1376-54	0136
325-1376-55	0136
325-1376-56	0004
325-1376-57	0004
325-1376-58	0004
325-1376-60	0143
325-1378-18	0127
325-1378-19	0127
325-1378-20	0004
325-1378-21	0164
325-1378-22	0004
325-1441-10	0015
325-1441-11	0015
325-1442-8	0211
325-1442-9	0142
325-1446-26	0086
325-1446-27	0086
325-1446-28	0233
325-1446-29	0015
325-1513-29	0198
325-1513-30	0198
325-1513-46	0086
325-1771-15	0016
325-1771-16	0127
325-4610-100	0071
325AJ	6326
325AL	6326
325CJ	6326
325CL	6326
325EQ	OEM
325L	OEM
325PAH50	OEM
325PAH60	OEM
325PAH80	OEM
325PAH100	OEM
325PAH110	OEM
325PAH120	OEM
325RA5	OEM
325RA10	OEM
325RA20	OEM
325RA30	OEM
325RA40	OEM
325RA50	OEM
325RA60	OEM
325T1	0004
325T4	OEM
326	OEM
326A	OEM
326AJ	6327
326AL	6327
326CJ	6327
326CL	6327
326T1	0004
327-1	4521
327-3	OEM
328-3	OEM
329-1	3668
329-100	OEM
329-130	OEM
329-200	OEM
329-629	OEM
329A	1017
329AR	0496
329B	1017
329BR	0496
329C	1017
329CR	0496
329D	1017
329DR	0496
329E	1017
329ER	0496
329F	1017
329FR	0496
329G	1030
329GR	1766
329H	1030
329HR	1766
329K	1030
329KR	1766
329M	1030
329MR	1766
329P	1040
329PR	1778
329S	1040
329SR	1778
329V	1040
329VR	1778
329Z	1040
329ZR	1778
330-2	OEM
330-5	OEM
330-10	OEM
330-11	OEM
330D05P	OEM
330GI	0133
330T4	OEM
330VF	OEM
331-1	0419
331AL	OEM
331CL	6328
331H-15	OEM
331TB7	OEM
331TB9	OEM
331TB11	OEM
331TB13	OEM
332AJ	6329
332AL	6329
332TB7	OEM
332TB9	OEM
332TB11	OEM
332TB13	OEM
333-1	0150
333-2	OEM
333AJ	6330
333AL	6330
333CJ	6330
333CL	6330
333TB7	OEM
333TB9	OEM
333TB11	OEM
333TB13	OEM
334-1	OEM
334-377	0074
334AL	6331
334CL	6331
334TB7	OEM
334TB9	OEM
334TB11	OEM
335-1	0065
335A	1620
335AJ	6332
335AL	6332
335B	0254
335C	1099
335CJ	6332
335CL	6332
335D	1099
335F	1103
335G	0267
335H	0258
335K	1634
335M	0267
335P	1111
335S	1111
335V	0280
335Z	0280
336A	1620
336B	0254
336C	1099
336D	1099
336F	1103
336G	0267
336H	0258
336K	1634
336M	0267
336S	1111
336V	0280
336Z	0280
337-120	OEM
337-220	OEM
337-330	OEM
337-829	OEM
337-919	OEM
337A	0529
337B	0743
337C	0533
337D	0533
337F	0772
337H	0533
337K	0796
337M	0810
337P	0540
337S	0540
337V	0545
337Z	0545
338-6551-A	OEM
339	0176
339-04	0102
339-5	OEM
339-6	2022
339-7	OEM
339-529-001	0143
339-529-002	0170
339A	1017
339AR	0496
339B	1017
339BR	0496
339C	1017
339CR	0496
339D	1017
339DR	0496
339E	1017
339ER	0496
339F	1017
339FR	0496
339G	1030
339GI	OEM
339GR	1766
339H	1030
339HR	1766
339K	1030
339KR	1766
339M	1030
339MR	1766
339P	1040
339PR	1778
339S	1040
339SR	1778
339V	1040
339VR	1778
339Z	1040
339ZR	1778
340-3	OEM
340RA10	5607
340RA20	5607
340RA30	5607
340RA40	5607
340RA60	5607
340T4	OEM
341-0127-A	OEM
341-0128-A	OEM
341A	0964
341AR	2275
341B	3688
341BR	2275
341C	0983
341CR	2275
341D	0983
341DR	2275
341F	3697
341FR	0471
341H	3697
341HR	0471
341K	0200
341KR	0471
341M	0204
341MR	0471
341P	0206
341PR	0444
341S	0206
341SR	0444
341V	0583
341Y	0583
341Z	0583
342-0132-B	OEM
342-0133-A	OEM
342-0134-B	OEM
342-0135-B	OEM
342-0265-A	OEM
342-0272-A	OEM
342-1	0086
342AJ	6333
342AL	6333
342CJ	6333
342CL	6333
343-1001	OEM
343-1002	OEM
343AJ	6334
343AL	6334
343CJ	6334
343CL	6334
343RA10	OEM
343RA20	OEM
343RA30	OEM
343RA40	OEM
343RA60	OEM
344-0010-B	OEM
344-0011	OEM
344-0020-A	OEM
344-0021	OEM
344-0041-A	OEM
344-1	0086
344-6000-2	0016
344-6000-3	0144
344-6000-3A	0144
344-6000-4	0016
344-6000-5	0016
344-6000-5A	0016
344-6001-1	0086
344-6001-2	0086
344-6002-3	0016
344-6005-1	0016
344-6005-2	0079
344-6005-5	0016
344-6005-6	0133
344-6005-7	OEM
344-6005-8	OEM
344-6006-6	0143
344-6011-1	0086
344-6011-2	0086
344-6012-1	0126
344-6013-1B	0086
344-6013-4	0086
344-6014-1B	0126
344-6015-7	0144
344-6015-7A	0144
344-6015-8	0127
344-6015-9	0127
344-6015-10	0144
344-6015-11	0144
344-6017-1	0037
344-6017-2	0016
344-6017-3	0126
344-6017-4	0086
344-6017-5	0016
344-6017-6	0144
344AL	OEM
344CL	OEM
344TB7	OEM
344TB9	OEM
345-2	0086
346-3	0079
346-4	0079
346A	0979
346B	0904
346C	0984
346D	0984
346F	0987
346H	0987
346K	0995
346M	0510
346P	1002
346S	1002
346V	0942
346Z	0942
347-2	OEM
347-4	OEM
347AL	6336
347CL	OEM
349-1	0086
349-2	0079
349-7	OEM
349-113-011	1812
349-113-012	1035
349-113-013	0081
349-113-014	0141
349-113-015	2067
349-113-022	0081
349-113-024	2595
349-113-025	2598
349AL	OEM
349CL	OEM
350	0279
350-1	OEM
350-2	OEM
350-3	OEM
350-4	OEM
350-5	OEM
350B20	OEM
350B25	OEM
350B30	OEM
350D7216	0076
350D7217	0076
350J	OEM
350K	OEM
350K3516	0006
350K3517	0006
350K5717	0148
350L	OEM
350P	OEM
350P2SP	OEM
350P4SP	OEM
350P6SP	OEM
350P8SP	OEM
350P10SP	OEM
350P12SP	OEM
350P16SP	OEM
350PAF10V08	OEM
350PAF10V10	OEM
350PAF10V12	OEM
350PAF20V08	OEM
350PAF20V10	OEM
350PAF20V12	OEM
350PAF40V08	OEM
350PAF40V10	OEM
350PAF40V12	OEM
350PAF60V08	OEM
350PAF60V10	OEM
350PAF60V12	OEM
350R1B	OEM
350R2B	OEM
350R3B	OEM
350R4B	OEM
350R5B	OEM
350R6B	OEM
350R7B	OEM
350R8B	OEM
350R9B	OEM
350R10B	OEM
350R11B	OEM
350R12B	OEM
350R13B	OEM
350R14B	OEM
350R15B	OEM
350R16B	OEM
350R18B	OEM
350R20B	OEM
350R22B	OEM
350R24B	OEM
350R26B	OEM
350R28B	OEM
350R30B	OEM
350R32B	OEM
350R34B	OEM
350R36B	OEM
350R38B	OEM
350R40B	OEM
350R42B	OEM
350R44B	OEM
350R46B	OEM
350R48B	OEM
350R50B	OEM
350RA10	1889
350RA20	1889
350RA30	1889
350RA40	1889
350RA60	1889
350RA80	0733
350RA100	0733
350RA120	0733
350RA130	OEM
350RA140	OEM
350RA150	OEM

If replacement code is OEM, contact original manufacturer for replacement.

DEVICE TYPE	REPL CODE
350RA160	OEM
350RA170	OEM
350RA180	OEM
350RB50	OEM
350RB60	OEM
350RB70	OEM
350RB80	OEM
350RB90	OEM
350RB100	OEM
350RB110	OEM
350RB120	OEM
350RC10	OEM
350RC20	OEM
350RC30	OEM
350RC40	OEM
350RC60	OEM
350RS25	OEM
350RS30	OEM
350S20	OEM
350S25	OEM
350S30	OEM
350T4	OEM
351	0031
351-07	OEM
351-029-020	0406
351-2	OEM
351-3006	1063
351-3031	0133
351-7008-010	1248
351-7008-020	3847
351-7011-020	3384
351-7011-030	3808
351-7011-040	3808
351-7011-050	3669
351-7011-060	3669
351-7011-070	1248
351-7011-080	1248
351-7011-090	1354
351-7011-100	1063
351-7011-110	1063
351-7011-120	1063
351-7011-150	3303
351-7011-160	3303
351-7011-170	OEM
351-7011-180	OEM
351-7015-010	3793
351-7015-020	3797
351-7015-030	1248
351-7015-040	1354
351-7015-050	3843
351-7015-060	3847
351-7015-070	3303
351-7025-010	4172
351-7025-020	1063
351-7026-010	3793
351-7026-030	1248
351-7026-060	3847
351-7026-070	3303
351-7121-010	OEM
351-7121-020	1063
351-7206-080	3793
351-7206-090	3797
351-7206-100	1248
351-7206-110	1354
351-7206-140	3303
351-7206-150	3793
351-7206-160	3797
351-7206-170	1248
351-7206-180	1354
351-7206-190	3843
351-7206-200	3847
351-7206-210	3303
351-7577-010	1340
351A	0031
351RA10	OEM
351RA20	OEM
351RA30	OEM
351RA40	OEM
351RA60	1889
351RA80	0733
351RA100	0733
351RA120	0733
351RA130	OEM
351RA140	OEM
351RA150	OEM
351RA160	OEM
351RA170	OEM
351RA180	OEM
352	0211
352(DIO)	0031
352-0023-001	1035
352-0197-000	0016
352-0677-040	0103
352-0677-051	0103
352-5	0546
352-6	0561
352-7	OEM
352A	0031
352AR	2275
352B	2275
352BR	2275
352C	2275
352CR	2275
352D	2275
352DR	2275
352F	0471
352FR	0471
352H	0471
352HR	0471
352K	0471
352KR	0471
352M	0471
352MR	0471
352YT	OEM
353	0211
353(IC)	3695
353-6	OEM
353-9001-001	0136
353-9001-002	0136
353-9001-003	0136
353-9002-002	0136
353-9008-001	0126
353-9012-001	0004
353-9201-001	0265
353-9203-001	0042
353-9301-001	0086
353-9301-002	0050
353-9301-004	0126
353-9304-001	0037
353-9304-004	0126
353-9306-001	0016
353-9306-002	0016
353-9306-003	0016
353-9310-001	0016
353-9312-001	0004
353-9314-001	0016
353-9315-001	0016
353-9317-001	0126
353-9318-001	0111
353-9318-002	0111
353-9319-001	0016
353-9319-002	0016
353-9502-001	0042
353PJLA160	OEM
353PJLA180	OEM
353PJLA200	OEM
353PJLA250	OEM
353RA10	OEM
353RA20	OEM
353RA30	OEM
353RA40	OEM
353RA60	OEM
353RA80	OEM
353RA100	OEM
353RA120	OEM
353RA130	OEM
353RA140	OEM
353RA150	OEM
353RA160	OEM
353RA170	OEM
353RA180	OEM
353Y	OEM
354	0031
354(CHRYSLER)	1335
354-3052	0211
354-9001-001	0019
354-9101-002	0123
354-9101-006	0015
354-9102-001	0015
354-9110-001	0015
354A	0031
354Y	OEM
355	OEM
355AJ	OEM
355AL	OEM
355CJ	OEM
355CL	OEM
355D6	0007
355D7	0212
355D8	0007
355D9	0016
356	0031
356A	0031
357A-10	2156
357A-22	1224
358-03	OEM
358MHZ	1024
358P007A1	OEM
359A	0015
359B	0015
359C	0015
359D	0015
359F	0015
359H	0015
359K	0015
359M	0015
359P	0071
359S	0071
359V	0071
359Z	0071
360-1	0224
360-2	0338
360-32	0133
360BM	OEM
360J	OEM
360K	OEM
360K1010	0133
360K1015	0124
360K1027	0124
360K3039	0052
360K3068	0253
360K3098	0052
360K3100	0041
360K3106	0466
360K3121	0062
360K3139	0253
360K7160	0015
360M	OEM
361-1	0555
361K7086	0790
361K7090	0015
361K7091	0071
361K7093	0015
361K7094	0015
361K7160	0015
361K7287	0023
361Q8003	0106
362-1	2987
362-1R	OEM
362-3	0283
362-6	0283
362-7	2987
363A	OEM
363AL	6340
363B	OEM
363CL	6340
363D	OEM
363F	OEM
363H	OEM
363M	OEM
363S	OEM
363Z	OEM
364-1	0037
364-1(SYLVANIA)	0037
364-3	OEM
364-2001	0019
364-10048	0321
364-B12	0720
364B14	0682
365	OEM
365-1	0016
365L	OEM
365T	0279
365T1	0279
366-1	0079
366-1(SYLVANIA)	0144
366-2	0079
366-2(SYLVANIA)	0144
366A	0964
366A-RT	OEM
366B	3688
366B-RT	OEM
366C	0983
366C-RT	OEM
366D	0983
366D-RT	OEM
366F	3697
366F-RT	OEM
366H	0197
366H-RT	OEM
366K	0200
366K-RT	OEM
366M	0204
366M-RT	OEM
366P	0258
366RA	0979
366RB	0904
366RC	0984
366RD	0984
366RF	0987
366RH	0991
366RK	0995
366RM	0510
366RP	1002
366RS	1002
366RV	0942
366RZ	0942
366S	0206
366V	0583
366Z	0583
367A	0097
367A-RT	OEM
367B	0090
367B-RT	OEM
367C	0109
367C-RT	OEM
367D	0109
367D-RT	OEM
367F	0105
367F-RT	OEM
367H	0109
367H-RT	OEM
367K	0116
367K-RT	OEM
367M	0122
367M-RT	OEM
367P	0131
367RA	0760
367RB	0743
367RC	0533
367RD	0533
367RF	0772
367RH	0533
367RK	0796
367RM	0810
367RP	0540
367RS	0540
367RV	0545
367RZ	0545
367S	0131
367V	0145
367Z	0145
368A	5417
368B	5482
368BPY	OEM
368C	2872
368D	2872
368F	5483
368H	3705
368K	3711
368M	1104
368P	3722
368RA	1229
368RB	1231
368RC	1232
368RD	1232
368RF	1236
368RH	1242
368RK	1244
368RM	1196
368RP	1255
368RS	1255
368RV	0444
368RZ	0444
368S	3722
368V	2982
368Z	2982
369-2	0015
369-3	0015
369HHD	4236
370	OEM
370-1	0065
370-2	0347
370AJ	1284
370AL	1284
370CJ	1284
370CL	1284
370J	OEM
370K	OEM
370L	OEM
371A	3160
371AJ	1406
371AL	1406
371B	2873
371C	1116
371CJ	1406
371CL	1406
371D	1116
371F	1118
371H	0800
371K	1186
371M	0315
371P	1124
371RA	1620
371RB	0254
371RC	1099
371RD	1099
371RF	1103
371RH	0258
371RK	1634
371RM	0267
371RP	1111
371RS	1111
371RV	0280
371RY	0280
371RZ	0280
371S	1124
371V	0045
371Z	0045
372AL	1547
372CL	1547
372Z	0545
373AL	OEM
373CL	OEM
374-1	0321
374A	OEM
374AL	OEM
374B	OEM
374C	OEM
374CL	OEM
374D	OEM
374F	OEM
374H	OEM
374K	OEM
374M	OEM
375CQY	OEM
375RA5	OEM
375RA10	OEM
375RA20	OEM
375RA30	OEM
375RA40	OEM
375RA50	OEM
375RA60	OEM
376-0062	0844
376A	OEM
376B	OEM
376C	OEM
376D	OEM
376E	OEM
376F	OEM
376G	OEM
376H	OEM
376K	OEM
376M	OEM
377-1	OEM
377A	OEM
377B	OEM
377C	OEM
377D	OEM
377E	OEM
377F	OEM
377G	OEM
377H	OEM
377K	OEM
377M	OEM
377Y	OEM
378-1	0321
378-44	0103
378-44A	0103
380	OEM
380(IC)	0375
380-2	0309
380-3	OEM
380A/C	0375
380B/M	0375
380H61	0015
380J	OEM
380K	OEM
383	0050
383(IC)	1042
384A	0015
384B	0015
384C	0015
384D	0015
384F	0015
384H	0015
384K	0071
384M	0071
384P	0071
384S	0071
384V	0071
384Z	0071
385A	0015
385B	0015
385C	0015
385D	0015
385F	0015
385H	0015
385K	0015
385KW	0015
385M	0015
385P	0071
385S	0071
385Z	0071
386	3034
386-1	0037
386-1(SYLVANIA)	0037
386-1AY	0015
386-1CY	0015
386-1FY	0015
386-7118P1	0144
386-7178P1	0016
386-7183P1	0103
386-7183P1A	0103
386-7184P1	0126
386-7185P1	0016
386-7188P1	0144
386-7243-P001	0007
386AK	0015
386AW	0015
386AX	0015
386AY	0015
386BW	0015
386BY	0015
386CW	0015
386CX	0015
386CY	0015
386D	OEM
386DW	0015
386DY	0015
386FW	0015
386FX	0015
386FY	0015
386K	0015
386KX	0015
386KY	0015
386MW	0015
386MY	0015
387-1	OEM
387E	OEM
388A	0914
388B	0102
388C	1082
388D	1082
388F	OEM
388H	OEM
388K	OEM
388M	OEM
388S	OEM
388Z	OEM
389-1	OEM
389C	OEM
389E	OEM
390-1	0802
390-1	0037
390J	OEM
390K	OEM
392-1	0144
392-1(SYLVANIA)	0086
392-2	0309
393-1	0786
393-1(SYLVANIA)	0126
394-1	0069
394-2	2799
394-3074-2	0211
394-3074-5	0211
394-3097-1	0211
394-3097-2	0211
394-3102-1	0595
394-3127-1	0086
394-3127-2	0086
394-3127-3	0086
394-3135	0162
394-3135A	0103
396-7178P1	0144
398-2	OEM
398-8418-1	3781
398-8972-1	1265
398-13223-1	0232
398-13224-1	0357
398-13225-1	0381
398-13226-1	0268
398-13632-1	0357
398B	0947
398P	6806
398V	0921
398Z	0087
399-3	3103
399-4	3103
399-5	0236
399-8	0236
399A	0110
399B	0242
399C	0242
399D	0242
400-2	OEM
400-1735	3845
400-1736	3868
400A	0143
400B	0594
400C	0594
400C-11958	0015
400D	0143
400E	OEM
400E15	OEM
400E120	0744
400EXD21	OEM
400F	0594
400F15	OEM
400G	OEM
400H	1975
400K	1975
400M	1975
400MAB180	OEM
400MAB200	OEM
400MAB250	OEM
400P	0652
400P4SP	OEM
400P6SP	OEM
400P8SP	OEM
400P12S	OEM
400PIN-RM	OEM
400PV-RM	OEM
400QD21	OEM
400R1B	OEM
400R2B	OEM
400R3B	OEM
400R4B	OEM
400R5B	OEM
400R6B	OEM
400R7B	OEM
400R8B	OEM
400R9B	OEM
400R10B	OEM
400R11B	OEM
400R12B	OEM
400R13B	OEM
400R14B	OEM
400R15B	OEM
400R16B	OEM
400R18B	OEM
400R20B	OEM
400R22B	OEM
400R24B	OEM
400R26B	OEM
400R28B	OEM
400R30B	OEM
400R32B	OEM
400R34B	OEM
400R36B	OEM
400R38B	OEM
400R40B	OEM
400R42B	OEM
400R44B	OEM
400R46B	OEM
400R48B	OEM
400R50B	OEM
400S	0652
400S2-2.6	OEM
400S2SP	OEM
400S3SP	OEM
400S4SP	OEM
400S5SP	OEM
400S6SP	OEM
400S8SP	OEM
400SS2SP	OEM
400SS3SP	OEM
400SS4SP	OEM
400SS5SP	OEM
400SS6SP	OEM
400SS8SP	OEM
400V	0652
400YD21	OEM
400Z	0652
401-041-6507	0275
401A	0594
401B	0594
401C	0594
401D	0594
401F	0594
401H	1975
401K	1975
401M	1975
401P	0652
401PDA20L15	OEM
401PDA40L15	OEM
401PDA40L20	OEM
401PDA60L15	OEM
401PDA60L20	OEM
401PDA80L15	OEM
401PDA80L20	OEM
401PDA100L20	OEM
401PDA100L25	OEM
401PDA100L30	OEM
401PDA120L20	OEM
401PDA120L25	OEM
401PDA120L30	OEM
401PDA130L20	OEM
401PDA130L30	OEM
401PDA140L20	OEM
401PDA140L25	OEM
401PDA140L30	OEM
401PDA160L25	OEM
401PDA160L30	OEM
401PDA180L25	OEM
401PDA180L30	OEM
401PDL40S15	OEM
401PDL40S20	OEM
401PDL60S15	OEM
401PDL60S20	OEM
401PDL80S15	OEM
401PDL80S20	OEM
401PDL100S20	OEM
401PDL100S30	OEM
401PDL120S20	OEM
401PDL120S30	OEM
401PDL130S20	OEM
401PDL130S30	OEM
401PDL140S30	OEM
401PDL150S30	OEM
401PDL160S30	OEM
401S	0652
401V	0652
401Z	0652
402	OEM
402A	3160
402B	2873
402C	1116
402D	1116
402F	1118
402H	0800
402K	1186
402M	0315
402P	1124
402S	1124
402V	0045
402Z	0045
403-009/07	0103
403-1	3284
403-2	OEM
403-4	0911
403-6	OEM
403A	3160
403B	1116
403C	1116
403D	1116
403F	1118
403H	0800
403K	1186
403M	0315
403P	1124
403PJA60	OEM
403PJA80	OEM
403PJA100	OEM
403PJA120	OEM
403PJA140	OEM
403PJA160	OEM
403S	1124
403V	0045
403Z	0045
404	OEM
404-1(SYL)	0079
404-2	0127
404-2(SYLVANIA)	0016
404A	0097
404B	0090
404B(NCR)	0126
404C	0109
404CM	OEM
404D	0109
404F	0105
404H	0109
404K	0116
404M	0122
404P	0131
404S	0131
404V	0145
404VM	OEM
404Z	0145
405-000-4407	0881
405-000-6104	0892
405-000-6302	0892
405-000-9907	2083
405-001-7407	0148
405-001-7605	0148
405-004-3109	0203
405-004-3208	0203
405-004-4205	0006
405-004-4502	0006
405-004-4601	0006
405-004-4809	0006
405-004-5004	0006
405-004-5103	0006

If replacement code is OEM, contact original manufacturer for replacement. 185

DEVICE TYPE	REPL CODE
405-006-1103	0148
405-006-1202	0148
405-006-1301	0148
405-006-1707	0148
405-006-1806	0148
405-006-4906	1900
405-006-5101	1900
405-006-6702	0006
405-007-5308	0472
405-007-6701	3760
405-010-6507	0261
405-010-6606	0261
405-010-6705	0261
405-011-7305	0151
405-011-7404	0151
405-011-7503	0151
405-011-7513	0151
405-011-8401	0151
405-011-8500	0151
405-011-8609	0151
405-012-2002	0076
405-012-2101	0076
405-012-2309	0076
405-012-7908	0945
405-012-8004	0945
405-013-2001	1274
405-013-2209	1274
405-013-4500	0261
405-013-4609	0261
405-013-6207	0261
405-013-6306	0261
405-013-6801	0155
405-013-7006	0155
405-014-2406	1553
405-014-2505	1553
405-014-8408	0275
405-014-8409	0275
405-014-8507	0275
405-014-8606	0275
405-014-9207	2824
405-015-2900	0009
405-015-3006	0009
405-016-1100	0151
405-016-6204	0284
405-016-6402	0284
405-016-6600	0284
405-016-8109	0275
405-016-9403	OEM
405-017-1901	0155
405-017-9501	2926
405-018-2501	0892
405-018-2600	2307
405-018-7100	1376
405-018-7209	1376
405-019-1909	0532
405-019-2708	0532
405-019-2807	0532
405-019-2817	0532
405-019-3804	0532
405-019-4504	0532
405-019-4505	0532
405-019-6706	0532
405-019-6805	0532
405-020-2001	OEM
405-020-5200	0076
405-020-5220	0076
405-020-5705	0076
405-020-6900	0076
405-020-7501	0076
405-020-7709	0076
405-020-7907	0076
405-021-5605	0396
405-022-0005	1492
405-022-4409	1533
405-022-6601	1533
405-022-6700	1533
405-022-6809	0551
405-023-4903	2882
405-023-5009	2882
405-023-5306	2882
405-024-9907	1505
405-025-0200	1505
405-027-0604	OEM
405-027-0802	3017
405-027-1007	3017
405-031-1000	OEM
405-033-1701	OEM
405-039-3303	0155
405-039-3402	0155
405-039-8001	1492
405-040-6102	1317
405-041-6507	0275
405-041-6705	0275
405-053-0504	0274
405-056-8701	1533
405-056-8800	1533
405-058-0208	OEM
405-058-0802	0203
405-058-4800	1498
405-059-9804	0042
405-059-9903	0042
405-064-7307	0919
405-064-7406	0919
405-066-4304	0275
405-082-2407	2116
405-083-1300	2171
405-095-9004	2171
405-2	0224
405-3	OEM

DEVICE TYPE	REPL CODE
405-4	OEM
405-114-6700	2098
405-114-6908	6274
405-114-7103	0558
405-114-7301	0558
405A	1991
405AR	0267
405B	1241
405BR	0267
405C	1241
405CR	0267
405D	1241
405DR	0267
405E	0315
405ER	0267
405F	0315
405FR	0267
405H	0315
405HR	0471
406	OEM
406-000-2806	0558
406-000-2905	0558
406-000-3001	0558
406-000-3100	0558
406-000-3209	0520
406-000-3308	0520
406-000-3407	0520
406-000-3506	0520
406-000-3605	0275
406-000-5302	0066
406-000-5708	1274
406-000-6309	1274
406-000-6804	0148
406-000-7108	1900
406-000-7603	1900
406-001-0900	0275
406-001-7404	6439
406-001-7503	6439
406-001-7602	6452
406-001-7701	6452
406-004-9702	1498
406-006-2701	2171
406-006-6504	0006
406-3	OEM
407-002-6809	1158
407-002-9602	1158
407-004-8306	0071
407-004-9105	0023
407-005-2303	0023
407-005-4208	0133
407-005-4505	0124
407-005-7605	0071
407-005-8602	0023
407-006-0407	0023
407-006-0902	0023
407-006-3903	0023
407-006-4108	0023
407-006-5709	0559
407-006-6706	0282
407-007-6605	0023
407-007-6606	0023
407-007-6903	0023
407-007-7405	0023
407-007-7603	0023
407-007-9904	0124
407-008-0207	0133
407-008-6001	0901
407-008-6704	0124
407-009-8905	0282
407-009-9100	0031
407-011-3004	0023
407-011-3103	0023
407-011-4308	0023
407-011-4407	0023
407-012-4208	0124
407-012-4406	0133
407-012-5809	0133
407-012-6202	0901
407-012-6212	0901
407-013-1008	0133
407-013-1206	0133
407-013-1909	0023
407-013-2609	0143
407-013-3200	0023
407-013-4207	0133
407-013-4306	0124
407-013-6508	0124
407-013-7109	0133
407-016-0107	2678
407-016-7205	2678
407-018-4202	OEM
407-020-6607	OEM
407-026-8407	OEM
407-027-4606	5082
407-027-5207	5040
407-028-2205	OEM
407-028-8900	OEM
407-028-9105	3990
407-029-1207	OEM
407-029-7308	OEM
407-030-2507	1069
407-031-0205	OEM
407-031-7204	OEM
407-033-1507	OEM
407-040-2009	OEM
407-040-4003	OEM
407-042-7309	3134
407-043-0200	4791
407-048-1103	0041

DEVICE TYPE	REPL CODE
407-048-1130	0041
407-048-1608	0041
407-048-2001	0253
407-048-3206	0062
407-048-3404	0062
407-048-3503	0062
407-048-3701	0077
407-048-4005	0077
407-048-4203	0077
407-048-5101	0057
407-048-5200	0057
407-048-5606	0064
407-048-5903	0064
407-048-6603	0181
407-048-6900	0053
407-048-7105	0053
407-048-7303	0052
407-048-7600	0053
407-048-7808	0053
407-048-7907	0372
407-048-8003	0873
407-049-2901	1075
407-049-3403	0137
407-049-8507	OEM
407-050-2501	0166
407-051-5303	0489
407-051-6409	0274
407-051-6706	OEM
407-052-3506	0010
407-053-0702	0582
407-053-4700	0489
407-053-6001	0582
407-054-0008	0064
407-054-3306	0052
407-054-4709	0053
407-054-4808	0053
407-054-5805	0873
407-055-7907	0372
407-056-7906	0041
407-056-8002	0041
407-057-4102	0062
407-057-4201	0062
407-057-6304	0077
407-057-9602	0057
407-057-9701	0057
407-057-9800	0057
407-059-3400	0137
407-065-0905	OEM
407-070-8408	0057
407-075-3903	OEM
407-075-9509	0062
407-076-2608	0102
407-076-3803	OEM
407-079-2605	0031
407-088-6011	0901
407-088-6502	0023
407-095-8001	0102
407-096-9809	0466
407-102-6006	0143
407-102-6501	OEM
407-102-6600	OEM
407-103-1604	0541
407-103-2502	OEM
407-103-2601	OEM
407-103-6500	0031
407-104-2204	1158
407-104-2402	1158
407-124-5209	1483
407-124-5506	0023
407-124-5605	1082
407-124-5803	1483
407-124-6404	0023
407-124-6406	0023
407-124-6503	OEM
407-143-2708	0166
407-147-5705	OEM
407A	0964
407AR	2872
407B	3688
407BR	2275
407C	0983
407CR	2872
407D	0983
407DR	2275
407F	3697
407FR	0471
407H	0197
407HR	0471
407K	0200
407KR	1104
407M	0204
407MR	0471
407P	0206
407RA	0979
407RB	0904
407RC	0984
407RD	0984
407RF	0987
407RH	0991
407RK	0995
407RM	0510
407RP	1002
407RS	1002
407RV	0942
407RZ	0942
407S	0206
407V	0583
407Z	0583
408	OEM

DEVICE TYPE	REPL CODE
408-000-0301	1281
408-008-2406	0124
408-008-8606	0071
408-009-3501	OEM
408-009-3600	OEM
408-009-3709	OEM
408-009-3808	OEM
408-009-9008	0023
408-009-9107	0140
408-009-9206	0031
408-009-9305	0023
408-009-9404	0080
408-010-0902	0062
408-014-8408	0275
408-1	OEM
408-5	OEM
408A	0097
408AR	2872
408B	0090
408BR	2275
408C	0109
408CR	2275
408D	0109
408DR	2275
408F	0105
408FR	0471
408H	0109
408HR	0471
408K	0116
408KR	0471
408M	0122
408MR	0471
408P	0131
408RA	0760
408RB	0743
408RC	0760
408RD	0533
408RF	0772
408RH	0772
408RK	0796
408RM	0810
408RP	0540
408RS	0540
408RV	0545
408RZ	0545
408S	0131
408V	0145
408Z	0145
409-001-0604	1521
409-004-5705	3054
409-004-8102	OEM
409-004-8409	2843
409-006-0203	1644
409-009-2709	0034
409-011-1608	OEM
409-015-1208	OEM
409-017-7208	3223
409-017-7505	3068
409-018-9706	OEM
409-019-0801	4202
409-019-1709	OEM
409-019-3109	0534
409-019-4205	0457
409-019-4700	0328
409-019-5608	0727
409-019-5707	2929
409-019-6209	2641
409-019-6407	4307
409-019-6605	4310
409-022-2205	OEM
409-032-3407	OEM
409-036-0105	2099
409-037-5406	OEM
409-040-8401	OEM
409-042-9000	1644
409-046-7705	OEM
409-047-5601	5705
409-047-8602	3857
409-047-9104	1631
409-047-9203	3410
409-051-2801	0024
409-051-3006	0034
409-052-4408	OEM
409-053-7309	4923
409-058-4105	OEM
409-063-4206	OEM
409-067-3304	OEM
409-074-9900	OEM
409-083-0103	5891
409-093-3804	OEM
409-107-6708	OEM
409-108-0200	OEM
409-108-2402	OEM
409-108-2600	OEM
409-109-4108	OEM
409-109-4405	OEM
409-110-4807	OEM
409-111-3106	OEM
409-117-9607	3645
409-118-2102	OEM
409-121-4209	OEM
409-121-4407	OEM
409-132-7800	OEM
409-132-7909	0034
409-135-5407	OEM
409-135-5506	4843
409-142-4905	OEM
409-145-6500	OEM
409-146-7001	4032

DEVICE TYPE	REPL CODE
409-147-9905	OEM
409-151-7904	OEM
409-156-6605	4032
409-169-5305	OEM
409-169-5800	OEM
409-172-8003	OEM
409-172-8102	OEM
409-173-2703	OEM
409-173-2802	OEM
409-173-5209	OEM
409-174-1408	OEM
409-184-9807	OEM
409-185-0803	OEM
409-187-7701	OEM
409-193-2905	OEM
409-194-8401	OEM
409-199-5306	OEM
409-219-9406	OEM
409-220-8009	OEM
409-225-9704	OEM
409-228-5604	OEM
409-242-6007	OEM
409-243-0806	2348
409-246-8809	OEM
409-272-3205	OEM
409-274-3302	OEM
409-289-3403	OEM
409-301-2803	OEM
409-301-9604	OEM
409A	5417
409AR	2275
409B	5482
409BR	2275
409C	2872
409CR	2275
409D	2872
409DR	2275
409F	5483
409FR	0471
409H	3705
409HR	0471
409K	3711
409KR	0471
409M	1104
409MR	0471
409P	3722
409RA	1229
409RB	1231
409RC	1232
409RD	1232
409RF	1236
409RH	2349
409RK	1244
409RM	1196
409RP	1255
409RS	1255
409RV	0444
409RY	2236
409RZ	0444
409S	3722
409V	2982
409Z	2982
410	0359
410-012-0150	0004
410-013-0240	0004
410-015-2409	OEM
410-019-4706	OEM
410-022-6506	OEM
410-024-9307	OEM
410-051-5808	1644
410-067-3300	1644
410-070-2000	OEM
410-070-9801	OEM
410-2	OEM
410-165-3202	OEM
410A	0594
410AR	1337
410B	0594
410BR	1337
410C	0594
410CR	1337
410D	0594
410DR	1337
410E	0594
410ER	1337
410F	0594
410FR	1337
410H	1975
410HR	1894
410K	1975
410KF	OEM
410KR	1894
410M	1975
410MR	1894
410PE2-35	OEM
410XY5-35SC00	OEM
411	0359
411-1	OEM
411-6	OEM
411-237	0086
411A	OEM
411B	OEM
411C	OEM
411D	OEM
411E	OEM
411F	OEM
411H	1975
411HR	1894
411K	1975

DEVICE TYPE	REPL CODE
411KR	1894
411M	1975
411MR	1894
411P	0652
411PR	0193
411S	0652
411SR	0193
411V	0652
411VR	0193
411Z	0652
411ZD	OEM
411ZH	OEM
411ZR	0193
412	0279
412-1A5	0016
412-2	3132
412H	OEM
413	0359
414	0079
414-2	OEM
414A-15	0160
414H	OEM
415	OEM
415C01111P	OEM
415T4	OEM
416	0518
416-1D400-26	OEM
416-1D400-115	OEM
416A	1551
416AR	1772
416B	1551
416BR	1772
416C	2813
416CR	1772
416D	2813
416F	4244
416FR	1772
416H	2823
416K	2844
416KR	1772
416M	2844
416P	2806
416PR	1807
416RA	1551
416RB	1551
416RC	2168
416RD	2168
416RF	2177
416RH	2177
416RK	2183
416RM	2183
416RP	2202
416RS	2202
416RV	2324
416RZ	2324
416S	2806
416SR	1807
416V	2454
416VR	1807
416Z	2454
416ZR	1807
417-1	3827
417-2	0050
417-5	0004
417-6	0164
417-7	0016
417-11	0050
417-12	0050
417-13	0050
417-14	0050
417-16	0050
417-17	0004
417-18	0164
417-19	0127
417-20	0160
417-21	0164
417-22	0050
417-23	0050
417-25	0050
417-27	0050
417-28	0164
417-29	0599
417-29BLK	0599
417-29GRN	0599
417-29WHT	0599
417-30	0160
417-31	0050
417-32	0160
417-33	0050
417-35	0050
417-36	0050
417-37	0050
417-38	0050
417-39	0050
417-40	0004
417-41	0004
417-42	0599
417-43	0126
417-44	0160
417-45	0160
417-46	0160
417-47	0004
417-48	0004
417-49	0086
417-50	0050
417-51	0164
417-52	0004
417-53	0050
417-54	0050

DEVICE TYPE	REPL CODE
417-56	0050
417-57	0050
417-58	0050
417-59	0086
417-60	0050
417-62	0085
417-66	0050
417-67	0076
417-68	0050
417-69	0016
417-70	0050
417-71	0050
417-72	0050
417-73	0050
417-74	0004
417-75	0004
417-76	0050
417-77	0076
417-78	0004
417-79	0136
417-81	1659
417-84	0144
417-85	0144
417-87	0086
417-88	0086
417-89	0086
417-90	0160
417-91	0111
417-92	0016
417-93	0016
417-94	0155
417-99	0160
417-101	0103
417-102	0150
417-103	0004
417-105	0007
417-106	0007
417-107	0144
417-108	0016
417-109	0076
417-110	0016
417-111	0126
417-112	0969
417-113	0969
417-114	0076
417-115	0233
417-116	0037
417-118	0155
417-119	2600
417-120	0599
417-121	0208
417-122	0164
417-124	0144
417-125	0144
417-126	0016
417-127	0198
417-128	0086
417-129	0016
417-132	0037
417-133	0007
417-134	0079
417-135	0155
417-136	0126
417-137	0086
417-138	0126
417-139	0130
417-139A	0103
417-140	0321
417-141	0160
417-142	0599
417-143	0050
417-144	0161
417-145	0455
417-146	0004
417-147	0164
417-148	0164
417-149	0164
417-150	0164
417-151	0164
417-152	0004
417-153	0037
417-153-13431	0688
417-154	0016
417-155	0086
417-158	0074
417-159	0275
417-160	0222
417-161	0396
417-167	0321
417-168	0037
417-169	0321
417-170	0126
417-171	0079
417-172	0016
417-175	0042
417-176	0037
417-177	0435
417-182	0037
417-183	1659
417-184	0037
417-185	0016
417-187	1659
417-190	0007
417-192	0016
417-194	0321
417-195	0275
417-196	0037
417-197	0016
417-199	0178

If replacement code is OEM, contact original manufacturer for replacement.

DEVICE TYPE	REPL CODE
417-200	0037
417-201	0037
417-203	0556
417-204	0074
417-205	0127
417-206	0843
417-207	0843
417-211	0321
417-212	0103
417-212A	0103
417-213	0111
417-215	0103
417-216	0160
417-217	0016
417-218	0016
417-219	0079
417-220	0264
417-221	1357
417-222	0396
417-223	0212
417-224	0018
417-226-1	0016
417-228	0016
417-229	0016
417-231	0321
417-233	0016
417-235	0037
417-237	0086
417-237-13163	0086
417-239	0637
417-240	0212
417-241	0321
417-243	0007
417-244	0016
417-245	0283
417-246	0321
417-247	0086
417-248	0637
417-250	0086
417-252	0321
417-253	0321
417-254	0130
417-255	0126
417-257	0086
417-258	0007
417-260	0126
417-262	0007
417-272	2243
417-282	0538
417-283	0079
417-284	0150
417-286	0177
417-294	0710
417-298	1274
417-801	0198
417-811	0076
417-821	0079
417-822	0037
417-823	0312
417-834	0334
417-836	0338
417-852	0042
417-863	0212
417-864	0086
417-865	0037
417-874	0006
417-875	0076
417-923	0309
417-926	0546
417-932	0556
417-937	0079
417A	1116
417B	2873
417C	1116
417D	1116
417F	1118
417H	0800
417HD	OEM
417K	1186
417M	0315
417P	1124
417RA	1099
417RB	0254
417RC	1099
417RD	1099
417RF	1103
417RH	0258
417RK	1634
417RM	0267
417RP	1111
417RS	1111
417RV	0280
417RZ	0280
417S	1124
417V	0045
417Z	0045
418A	1116
418B	2873
418C	1116
418D	1116
418E	0800
418F	1118
418H	0800
418K	1186
418M	0315
418P	1124
418RA	1099
418RB	0254
418RC	1099

DEVICE TYPE	REPL CODE
418RD	1099
418RF	1103
418RH	0258
418RK	1634
418RM	0267
418RP	1111
418RS	1111
418RV	0280
418RZ	0280
418S	1124
418V	0045
418Z	0045
419-1	2293
419-2	3881
419-3	OEM
419A	1116
419B	2873
419C	1116
419D	1116
419F	1118
419H	0800
419K	1186
419M	0315
419P	1124
419RA	1099
419RB	0254
419RC	1099
419RD	1099
419RF	1103
419RH	0258
419RK	1634
419RM	0267
419RP	1111
419RS	1111
419RV	0280
419S	1124
419V	0045
420	OEM
420-1	0037
420-301	OEM
420-2003-173	0071
420-2005-000	0196
420-2104-570	0071
420KF	OEM
420PA40	OEM
420PB30	1754
420PB50	1754
420PB60	1754
420PB80	1803
420PB100	5222
420PB110	6421
420PB120	1803
420PB130	5223
420PB140	5223
420PB150	5223
420PB160	5223
420PB170	OEM
420PB180	OEM
420PB190	OEM
420PB200	OEM
420PBL50	0764
420PBL60	0764
420PBL80	0478
420PBL100	0478
420PBL110	0478
420PBL120	0478
420PBM50	0764
420PBM60	0764
420PBM80	0478
420PBM100	0478
420PBM110	0478
420PBM120	0478
420PL60	OEM
420PL80	OEM
420PL100	OEM
420PL110	OEM
420PL120	OEM
420PM60	OEM
420PM80	OEM
420PM100	OEM
420PM110	OEM
420PM120	OEM
420PM130	OEM
420PM140	OEM
420PM150	OEM
420PM160	OEM
420PM170	OEM
420T1	0004
420T4	OEM
421	OEM
421-1	0042
421-2	0919
421-3	0042
421-4	0919
421-5	0477
421-6	0050
421-6B	0050
421-7	0050
421-7B	0050
421-8	0050
421-8(MAG)	1359
421-8B	0050
421-9	0004
421-10	0004
421-11	0004
421-11B	0004
421-12	0004
421-12B	0004
421-13	0004

DEVICE TYPE	REPL CODE
421-13B	0004
421-13C	0211
421-14	0004
421-14B	0004
421-15	0004
421-15B	0004
421-16	0050
421-17	0050
421-18	0142
421-19	0004
421-20	0136
421-20B	0136
421-21	0136
421-21B	0136
421-22	0136
421-22B	0136
421-24	0160
421-25	0160
421-26	0136
421-4027	0015
421-6599	0160
421-7143	0004
421-7443	0015
421-7443A	0015
421-7444	0016
421-8109	0004
421-8111	0016
421-8310	0142
421-9644	0016
421-9670	0016
421-9671	0004
421-9682	0279
421-9683	0144
421-9792	0050
421-9840	0016
421-9862	0208
421-9862A	0004
421-9863	0004
421-9863A	0004
421-9864	0004
421-9864A	0004
421-9865	0015
421T1	0004
422	OEM
422-0222	0004
422-0738	0016
422-0739	0126
422-0960	0178
422-0961	0103
422-1232	0126
422-1233	0086
422-1234	0016
422-1362	0015
422-1401	0144
422-1402	0144
422-1403	0136
422-1404	0086
422-1405	0126
422-1406	0004
422-1407	0016
422-1408	0071
422-1443	0265
422-1866	0015
422-2008	0126
422-2158	0086
422-2532	0144
422-2533	0016
422-2534	0016
422-2535	0004
422-2540	0015
422-2778	0050
422-2779	0050
422-2780	0050
422B	OEM
423	4097
423-1	OEM
423-800-235	2086
423-800175	1035
423-800176	0557
423-800177	1035
423-800178	0141
423-800194	1833
423-800202	1820
423-800223	1472
423-800234	1812
423-800236	0354
423AB1A11	OEM
423AB1AB1	0276
423AB1AF1	OEM
423AB1AI1	OEM
423AC1A11	OEM
423AC1AI1	OEM
423AF1AH1	OEM
423BB1A11	OEM
423BB1AB1	0287
423BB1AF1	OEM
423BB1AI1	OEM
423BC1A11	OEM
423BC1AI1	OEM
423BF1AH1	OEM
423DB1A11	OEM
423DB1AB1	0293
423DB1AF1	OEM
423DB1AI1	OEM
423DC1A11	OEM
423DC1AI1	OEM
423DF1AH1	OEM
423EB2AF1	OEM
423EF2AH1	OEM

DEVICE TYPE	REPL CODE
423EF3AH1	OEM
423FB1AB1	0276
423FB1AF1	OEM
423FB1AI1	OEM
423FC1A11	OEM
423FC1AI1	OEM
423FF1AH1	OEM
423MB1A11	OEM
423MB1AB1	0299
423MB1AF1	OEM
423MB1AI1	OEM
423MB2A11	OEM
423MB2AI1	OEM
423MB6AH1	OEM
423MC1A11	OEM
423MC1AI1	OEM
423MC2A11	OEM
423MC2AI1	OEM
423MC5AE1	OEM
423MC6AH1	OEM
423MC11AH1	OEM
423MD5AE1	OEM
423MD6AH1	OEM
423MD11AH1	OEM
423MF1AH1	OEM
423MH5AE1	OEM
423MH6AH1	OEM
423MH10AE1	OEM
423MH11AH1	OEM
423NB1A11	OEM
423NB1AB1	0250
423NB1AF1	OEM
423NB1AI1	OEM
423NB2AF1	OEM
423NB2AI1	OEM
423NC1A11	OEM
423NC1AI1	OEM
423NC2A11	OEM
423NC2AI1	OEM
423NC7AE1	OEM
423NC17AH1	OEM
423ND17AH1	OEM
423NF1AH1	OEM
423NF2AH1	OEM
423NH10AE1	OEM
423NH16AE1	OEM
423NH26AH1	OEM
423PB1AB1	0250
423PB10AH1	OEM
423PC8AE1	OEM
423PC10AE1	OEM
423PC13AE1	OEM
423PC15AE1	OEM
423PD8AE1	OEM
423PD10AE1	OEM
423PD13AE1	OEM
423PD15AE1	OEM
423PH5AS1	OEM
423PH8AS1	OEM
423PH10AE1	OEM
423PH10AS1	OEM
423PH13AS1	OEM
423PH15AE1	OEM
423PH15AS1	OEM
423PH20AS1	OEM
423PH25AS1	OEM
423SC14AH1	OEM
423SD14AH1	OEM
423SH14AH1	OEM
423SH19AH1	OEM
423SH24AH1	OEM
423TB8AH1	OEM
424	OEM
424AB1AB1	OEM
424AB1AF1	OEM
424AF1AH1	OEM
424BB1AB1	OEM
424BB1AF1	OEM
424BF1AH1	OEM
424DB1AB1	OEM
424DB1AF1	OEM
424DF1AH1	OEM
424DF2AH1	OEM
424EF2AH1	OEM
424EF3AH1	OEM
424FB1AB1	OEM
424FB1AF1	OEM
424FF1AH1	OEM
424K	OEM
424M	OEM
424MB1AB1	OEM
424MB1AF1	OEM
424MC5AE1	OEM
424MC10AE1	OEM
424MC13AE1	OEM
424MD5AE1	OEM
424MD10AE1	OEM
424MD13AE1	OEM
424MF1AH1	OEM
424MH5AE1	OEM
424MH5AS1	OEM
424MH9AS1	OEM
424MH10AE1	OEM
424MH13AE1	OEM
424MH13AS1	OEM
424MH17AE1	OEM
424MH17AS1	OEM
424MH21AE1	OEM
424MH21AS1	OEM

DEVICE TYPE	REPL CODE
424MH25AE1	OEM
424PFE1	OEM
424PFS1	OEM
425	OEM
425K	OEM
425M	OEM
425NH9AB1	OEM
425NH10AB1	OEM
425NH14AB1	OEM
425NH17AB1	OEM
425Q	OEM
425SH2AB1	0182
425SH3AB1	OEM
425SH4AB1	0344
425SH6AB1	OEM
425SH8AB1	OEM
425SH23AB1	OEM
425SH29AB1	OEM
425SH38AB1	OEM
425T	OEM
425T4	OEM
426	OEM
426-1	1955
426EH2AB1	0017
426EH3AB1	0017
426EH4AB1	OEM
426EH6AB1	OEM
426EH8AB1	OEM
426EH10AB1	OEM
426EH12AB1	OEM
426EH16AB1	OEM
426EH20AB1	OEM
427	OEM
427-1	0264
427-2	0561
427-3	0561
427N2	0264
428	OEM
428-1	0818
428-2	0818
428N2	0818
429	OEM
429-0092-1	0050
429-0092-2	0004
429-0092-3	0004
429-0092-56	0143
429-0093-69	0136
429-0093-71	0071
429-0094-39	0136
429-0910-50	0050
429-0910-51	0004
429-0910-52	0004
429-0910-53	0123
429-0910-54	0143
429-0958-41	0276
429-0958-42	0016
429-0958-43	0631
429-0981-12	0127
429-0985-12	0127
429-0986-12	0144
429-0989-68	0015
429-10001-0A	0084
429-10002-0A	0097
429A	1017
429AR	0496
429B	1017
429BR	0496
429C	1017
429CR	0496
429D	1017
429DR	0496
429E	1017
429ER	0496
429F	1017
429FR	0496
429G	1030
429GR	1766
429H	1030
429HR	1766
429K	1030
429M	1030
429MR	1766
429RR	1766
430	0079
430-31	0015
430-85	0164
430-86	0016
430-87	0016
430-22861	0144
430-23190	0130
430-23212	0016
430-23221	0016
430-23222	0126
430-23223	0086
430-23843	0103
430-23844	0086
430-25762	0321
430-25763	0144
430-25764	0144
430-25765	0144
430-25766	0016
430-25767	0144
430-25834	0222
430-203845	0126
430CL	0016
430KF	OEM
430T4	OEM
431	4097
431-1B400-26	OEM

DEVICE TYPE	REPL CODE
431-1B400-26R	OEM
431-1B400-115	OEM
431-1B400-115R	OEM
431-2A60-26	OEM
431-2A60-26R	OEM
431-2A60-26SR	OEM
431-2A60-115	OEM
431-2A60-115R	OEM
431-2A60-115SR	OEM
431-2A400-26	OEM
431-2A400-26R	OEM
431-2A400-26SR	OEM
431-2A400-115R	OEM
431-2A400-115SR	OEM
431-2B60-26	OEM
431-2B60-26R	OEM
431-2B60-26SR	OEM
431-2B60-115	OEM
431-2B60-115R	OEM
431-2B60-115SR	OEM
431-3A400-26R	OEM
431-3A400-115R	OEM
431-3B60-115	OEM
431-3B400-26	OEM
431-3B400-115	OEM
431-26551A	0696
431L	OEM
432	OEM
432-1	0086
433	0079
433(ZENITH)	0016
433-1	1260
433-1(SYLVANIA)	0079
433-2	1533
433-2	1533
433-4	OEM
433-5	OEM
433B	OEM
433CL	0016
433J	OEM
433M852	0126
434	0111
434-1	0037
434-1	0037
434-2	OEM
434-3	OEM
434-4	0037
434A	OEM
434B	OEM
434TS1	OEM
435-1	0079
435-1	0079
435-2	0079
435-2	0079
435-4	OEM
435-21026-0A	0232
435-21027-0A	0310
435-21028-0A	0357
435-21029-0A	0462
435-21030-0A	0507
435-21033-0A	0692
435-21034-0A	1160
435-21035-0A	1358
435-23006-0A	1164
435-23007-0A	1303
435-40012	0015
435A	1620
435B	0254
435C	1099
435D	1099
435F	1103
435H	0258
435J	OEM
435K	1634
435L	OEM
435M	0267
435P	2202
435S	2202
435V	2324
435Z	2324
436-10010-0A	0828
436-10011-0A	1705
436A	1620
436B	1099
436C	1099
436D	1099
436F	0258
436H	0258
436K	0267
436M	0267
436P	1111
436S	1111
436V	0280
436Z	0280
437-1	0261
437A	0529
437B	0743
437C	0533
437D	0533
437F	0772
437H	0533
437K	0796
437M	0810
437P	0131
437S	0131
437V	0145
437Z	0444
438-1	OEM
439A	1017

DEVICE TYPE	REPL CODE
439AR	0496
439B	1017
439BR	0496
439C	1017
439CR	0496
439D	1017
439DR	0496
439E	1017
439ER	0496
439F	1017
439FR	0496
439G	1030
439GR	1766
439H	1030
439HR	1766
439K	1030
439KR	1766
439M	1030
439MR	1766
440	OEM
440C-C	OEM
440C-E	OEM
440KF	OEM
440T4	OEM
441	OEM
441-1	OEM
441A	0964
441B	3688
441C	0983
441D	0983
441F	3697
441H	0197
441K	0200
441M	0204
441P	0206
441S	0206
441V	0583
441Z	0583
442-1	0008
442-2	1695
442-5	0360
442-9	0438
442-10	2147
442-16	0696
442-18	0780
442-22	0308
442-24	2155
442-25	2207
442-28	0659
442-30	1911
442-30-2897	1911
442-33	0661
442-39	1290
442-48	OEM
442-50	OEM
442-54	0619
442-57	0348
442-58	0350
442-60	2224
442-63	1311
442-66	2231
442-71	2232
442-73	OEM
442-74	0368
442-75	2093
442-82	0661
442-96	0413
442-99	1135
442-602	0620
442-604	3684
442-612	3034
442-613	3777
442-615	0687
442-622	OEM
442-623	2755
442-624	OEM
442-630	1275
442-635	3915
442-636	4716
442-640	2721
442-644	1817
442-647	3394
442-648	2495
442-650	OEM
442-651	2836
442-654	3347
442-655	OEM
442-659	3864
442-663	0330
442-664	1827
442-665	4429
442-672	4045
442-673	4715
442-674	0330
442-675	1827
442-676	OEM
442-677	4646
442-682	3839
442-686	0375
442-687	OEM
442-688	3733
442-691	1187
442-693	OEM
442-702	1905
442-703	OEM
442-704	2541
442-705	2709
442-713	1042
442-715	2755

If replacement code is OEM, contact original manufacturer for replacement.

187

DEVICE TYPE	REPL CODE
442-728	0765
442C-A	OEM
442C-D	OEM
442J	OEM
442K	OEM
442L	OEM
442R	0991
442TB1	OEM
442TB2	OEM
442TB3	OEM
442TB4	OEM
442TB5	OEM
442TB6	OEM
442TB7	OEM
442TB8	OEM
442TB9	OEM
442TB10	OEM
442TB11	OEM
442TB12	OEM
442TB13	OEM
442TB14	OEM
442TB15	OEM
442TB16	OEM
442TB17	OEM
443-1	0232
443-2	0692
443-3	0867
443-4	1417
443-5	1164
443-6	1303
443-7	1199
443-7-16088	1199
443-9	OEM
443-10	OEM
443-11	OEM
443-12	0507
443-13	1423
443-15	0738
443-16	1150
443-17	1367
443-18	0357
443-21	OEM
443-22	0175
443-23	1131
443-25	1487
443-26	0699
443-27	0354
443-32	0175
443-34	0828
443-35	1032
443-36	1100
443-42	1607
443-43	5426
443-44	1432
443-44-2854	1432
443-45	0462
443-46	0310
443-53	1046
443-54	0331
443-58	2382
443-59	5680
443-60	0493
443-61	1135
443-62	0011
443-65	0812
443-66	1910
443-67	2252
443-68	0680
443-70	2941
443-71	0677
443-72	1342
443-73	1339
443-74	1253
443-77	0990
443-87	0614
443-89	0487
443-90	1149
443-162	1915
443-603	0215
443-604	2819
443-606	1938
443-607	0409
443-612	1915
443-622	1442
443-623	0522
443-623-51644	0522
443-625	1261
443-628	1939
443-629	1199
443-640	0564
443-642	0381
443-680	1477
443-683	OEM
443-698	1358
443-703	0473
443-704	2044
443-706	0129
443-707	3555
443-708	2331
443-709	2163
443-711	1721
443-712	2061
443-713	2213
443-717	1184
443-718	1305
443-719	0587
443-720	3151
443-721	OEM
443-722	2252
443-727	1459
443-728	1519
443-729	1678
443-730	0243
443-731	4352
443-732	0822
443-733	0082
443-737	1037
443-738	3397
443-745	1569
443-751	0621
443-752	1662
443-753	OEM
443-754	0447
443-755	1585
443-757	0852
443-760	0056
443-762	4467
443-764	2037
443-777	3566
443-778	2368
443-779	1550
443-780	1623
443-781	1859
443-782	0209
443-783	1247
443-784	0495
443-785	3018
443-792	1615
443-794	0503
443-795	0506
443-797	1652
443-798	0035
443-799	1153
443-800	0183
443-801	2807
443-802	1733
443-804	3175
443-805	0888
443-807	1830
443-811	0075
443-813	1871
443-815	1682
443-816	1632
443-817	1679
443-818	1598
443-819	OEM
443-822	0153
443-824	1715
443-827	0384
443-828	1856
443-829	2166
443-836	1542
443-837	0704
443-839	0900
443-840	4118
443-841	1108
443-842	OEM
443-843	0443
443-854	3259
443-855	1768
443-856	OEM
443-857	0971
443-858	2228
443-860	OEM
443-863	0708
443-864	1657
443-871	1819
443-872	1688
443-874	OEM
443-875	0088
443-877	0422
443-879	0260
443-881	3441
443-884	1717
443-885	0458
443-886	0493
443-887	0515
443-888	3721
443-889	1554
443-891	0288
443-892	4301
443-893	1278
443-896	2223
443-897	2248
443-898	0775
443-899	2477
443-900	2483
443-904	0518
443-906	OEM
443-909	0516
443-912	3856
443-913	OEM
443-915	2489
443-916	3566
443-919	2850
443-920	0426
443-921	1278
443-927	3276
443-928	0982
443-929	0508
443-930	2315
443-934	0887
443-935	2138
443-942	0973
443-948	2115
443-951	1027
443-955	0953
443-958	0146
443-961	1752
443-964	1685
443-965	OEM
443-971	3378
443-972	2249
443-973	0813
443-974	5648
443-976	2547
443-979	2251
443-981	2125
443-982	2456
443-983	2128
443-999	3112
444-1	0055
444-1(IC)	2164
444-229-8	1628
444T20	OEM
444T21	OEM
444T22	OEM
444T23	OEM
444T24	OEM
444T26	OEM
444T28	OEM
444TB7	OEM
444TB9	OEM
444TB11	OEM
444TB13	OEM
444TB15	OEM
444TB17	OEM
444TB19	OEM
445-0028-P1	0720
445-0028-P2	0720
445-0300P3	0411
445-0303-001	1403
445-0303-002	1403
445-1	1533
445N1	OEM
446A	0979
446B	0983
446C	0984
446D	0984
446F	0991
446H	0991
446K	0995
446M	0510
446P	0206
446S	0206
446V	0583
446Z	0583
447	0079
447(ZENITH)	0016
447-1	0008
448A662	0086
449	0161
449-1	3481
450	OEM
450-1	0079
450-2	0111
450-3	OEM
450-4	OEM
450-5	OEM
450E15	OEM
450E120	OEM
450F15	OEM
450J	OEM
450K	OEM
450KF	OEM
450PF5	OEM
450PF10	OEM
450PF20	OEM
450PF30	OEM
450PF50	OEM
450PF60	OEM
450Pf40	OEM
450R1B	OEM
450R2B	OEM
450R3B	OEM
450R4B	OEM
450R5B	OEM
450R6B	OEM
450R7B	OEM
450R8B	OEM
450R9B	OEM
450R10B	OEM
450R11B	OEM
450R12B	OEM
450R13B	OEM
450R14B	OEM
450R15B	OEM
450R16B	OEM
450R18B	OEM
450R20B	OEM
450R22B	OEM
450R24B	OEM
450R26B	OEM
450R28B	OEM
450R30B	OEM
450R32B	OEM
450R34B	OEM
450R36B	OEM
450R38B	OEM
450R40B	OEM
450R42B	OEM
450R44B	OEM
450R46B	OEM
450R48B	OEM
450R50B	OEM
450T4	OEM
450VB5A	OEM
450VB10A	OEM
450VB15A	OEM
450VB20A	OEM
450VB25A	OEM
450VB30A	OEM
450VB40A	OEM
450VB50A	OEM
451	OEM
451-3	0037
451D	1241
451J	OEM
451K	OEM
451L	OEM
451PF5	OEM
451PF10	OEM
451PF20	OEM
451PF30	OEM
451PF40	OEM
451PF50	OEM
451PF60	OEM
453J	OEM
453K	OEM
453L	OEM
454-A2534-1	0015
454-A2534-10	0015
454A104	0086
454J	OEM
454K	OEM
454L	OEM
455-1	1273
456-1	OEM
456-2	0079
456J	OEM
456K	OEM
456T20	OEM
456T21	OEM
456T22	OEM
456T23	OEM
456T24	OEM
456TB7	OEM
456TB9	OEM
456TB11	OEM
456TB13	OEM
456TB15	OEM
456TB17	OEM
456TB19	OEM
458-1	OEM
458-3	0590
458J	OEM
458K	OEM
458L	OEM
458T20	OEM
458T21	OEM
458T22	OEM
458T23	OEM
458T24	OEM
458TB7	OEM
458TB9	OEM
458TB11	OEM
458TB13	OEM
458TB15	OEM
458TB17	OEM
458TB19	OEM
460	OEM
460-1	0037
460J	OEM
460K	OEM
460KF	OEM
460L	OEM
462-1	OEM
462-3	0419
462-11	OEM
462TB7	OEM
462TB9	OEM
462TB11	OEM
462TB13	OEM
464-1	3326
464-100-19	0143
464-103-19	0143
464-106-19	0143
464-110-19	0123
464-111-19	0143
464-113-19	0143
464-119-19	0123
464-280-19	0229
464-285-15	0015
464-285-19	0229
464-311-19	0170
464TB7	OEM
464TB9	OEM
464TB11	OEM
464.062.15	0631
465-005-19	0004
465-032-19	0050
465-036-19	0004
465-042-19	0050
465-045-19	0050
465-049-19	0050
465-061-19	0050
465-067-19	0164
465-072-19	0004
465-073-19	0004
465-075-19	0004
465-080-19	0004
465-082-19	0004
465-086-19	0050
465-1	OEM
465-1A5	0050
465-2A5	0208
465-4A5	0595
465-106-19	0016
465-108-19	0164
465-115-19	0004
465-132-19	0004
465-137-19	0222
465-146-19	0050
465-163-19	0004
465-165-19	0004
465-166-19	0816
465-181-19	0127
465-191-15	0004
465-199-19	0012
465-206-19	0222
465-223-19	0050
465-260-15	3502
465A-15	0050
465B-15	0050
465C-15	0160
466-1A5	0004
466-2A5	0004
466-3A5	0004
466TB7	OEM
466TB9	OEM
467C	0431
468-1	1698
469-1	OEM
470	OEM
470KF	OEM
470PB30	1754
470PB40	OEM
470PB50	1754
470PB60	1754
470PB80	1803
470PB100	1803
470PB110	1803
470PB120	5222
470PB130	5223
470PB140	5223
470PB150	5223
470PB160	5223
470PB170	OEM
470PB180	OEM
470PB190	OEM
470PB200	OEM
470PDA10	2146
470PDA20	2146
470PDA40	2146
470PDA60	2146
470PDA80	0474
470PDA100	0474
470PDAR10	OEM
470PDAR20	OEM
470PDAR40	OEM
470PDAR60	OEM
471-010	0015
471-1	0283
471-1(IC)	OEM
471-1(METAL)	0086
471-1(PLASTIC)	0546
471PD140	OEM
471PD160	OEM
471PD180	OEM
471PD200	OEM
471PDA120	1195
471PDA140	OEM
471PDA150	OEM
471PDA160	OEM
471PDA180	OEM
471PDA200	OEM
471PDA210	OEM
471PDA220	OEM
471PDA230	OEM
471PDA240	OEM
471PDA250	OEM
472-1	OEM
472-H12	OEM
472US1	OEM
473-1	OEM
473A31	0160
473B5	0004
473B6-2	0211
473B6-2A	0211
473B6-4	0211
473B6-5	0211
473B6-7	0211
474	OEM
474-004	0015
474-025	0015
474-1	0079
474-3A5	0279
475	OEM
475-018	0242
475-1	0037
476-1	0434
476T1	OEM
476T2	OEM
476T3	OEM
476T4	OEM
476T5	OEM
476T6	OEM
476T7	OEM
476T8	OEM
476T9	OEM
476T10	OEM
476T11	OEM
476T12	OEM
477-054-5805	4446
477-0375-001	1035
477-0377-001	1812
477-0379-001	0557
477-0380-001	0081
477-0381-001	0141
477-0412-004	1164
477-0415-002	0738
477-0417-002	1177
477-1	1841
477-2	OEM
477A15	0435
478-1	OEM
478C	0097
478E	OEM
479-1	0710
479-1006-002	0759
479-1066	0759
479C	OEM
479E	OEM
479K	OEM
479M	OEM
480	OEM
480-1	0855
480-9(SEARS)	0222
480KF	OEM
482-1	0037
482-US1	OEM
482US2	OEM
484A15	0160
488B15	0050
488C15	0279
490	OEM
490-2(SEARS)	0144
491-2(SEARS)	0144
491A948	0086
492-1A5	0435
499	0079
499-1	0016
500-1	0079
500-4	0079
500B10	0071
500B15	OEM
500B20	OEM
500EXH21	OEM
500F	OEM
500HXD25	OEM
500P8H	OEM
500P12H	OEM
500P16H	OEM
500P20H	OEM
500P25H	OEM
500PA5	OEM
500PA10	OEM
500PA20	OEM
500PA30	OEM
500PA40	OEM
500PA50	OEM
500PA60	OEM
500R1B	OEM
500R2B	OEM
500R3B	OEM
500R4B	OEM
500R5B	OEM
500R6B	OEM
500R7B	OEM
500R8B	OEM
500R9B	OEM
500R10B	OEM
500R11B	OEM
500R12B	OEM
500R13B	OEM
500R14B	OEM
500R15B	OEM
500R16B	OEM
500R18B	OEM
500R20B	OEM
500R22B	OEM
500R24B	OEM
500R26B	OEM
500R28B	OEM
500R30B	OEM
500R32B	OEM
500R34B	OEM
500R36B	OEM
500R38B	OEM
500R40B	OEM
500R42B	OEM
500R44B	OEM
500R46B	OEM
500R48B	OEM
500R50B	OEM
500RS20	0344
500S2.8-3.2	OEM
500S10	0071
500S10H	OEM
500S12H	OEM
500S15	0182
500S20	0344
500SS10H	OEM
500SS12H	OEM
500V5A	OEM
500V10A	OEM
500V20A	OEM
500V30A	OEM
500V40A	OEM
500V50A	OEM
500V60A	OEM
501	OEM
501-363-2	0242
501ES001M	0144
501P	OEM
501PA5	OEM
501PA10	OEM
501PA20	OEM
501PA30	OEM
501PA40	OEM
501PA50	OEM
501PA60	OEM
501PBA60	OEM
501PBQ50	OEM
501PBQ70	OEM
501PBQ80	OEM
501PBQ90	OEM
501PBQ100	OEM
501PBQ110	OEM
501PBQ120	OEM
501T1	0050
501V60	4957
501V60B	4957
501V60S	OEM
501V80	0744
501V80B	0744
501V100	0744
501V100B	0744
501V120	0744
501V120B	0744
501V140	OEM
501V140B	OEM
501V160	OEM
501V180	OEM
501V200	OEM
501V210	OEM
501V220	OEM
501V230	OEM
501V240	OEM
501V250	OEM
501VF60B	OEM
501VF80B	OEM
501VF100B	OEM
501VF120	OEM
501VF120B	OEM
501VF140	OEM
501VF140B	OEM
501VF160	OEM
501VF180	OEM
501VF200	OEM
501VF210	OEM
501VF220	OEM
501VF230	OEM
501VF240	OEM
501VR60B	2299
501VR80B	2765
501VR100B	2765
501VR120	2765
501VR120B	2765
501VR140	OEM
501VR140B	OEM
501VR160	OEM
501VR180	OEM
501VR200	OEM
501VR210	OEM
501VR220	OEM
501VR230	OEM
501VR240	OEM
502	0079
502V5A	OEM
502V10A	OEM
502V20A	OEM
502V30A	OEM
502V40A	OEM
502V50A	OEM
502V60A	OEM
503	OEM
503-T10192	0087
503-T21271	0143
503-T21472	0143
503-T21651	0030
503PJA180	OEM
503PJA200	OEM
503PJA250	OEM
503PJLA60	OEM
503PJLA80	OEM
503PJLA100	OEM
503PJLA120	OEM
503T1	0050
503V60	OEM
503V60B	OEM
503V80	OEM
503V80B	OEM
503V100	OEM
503V100B	OEM
503V120	OEM
503V120B	OEM
503V140	OEM
503V140B	OEM
503V160	OEM
503V180	OEM
503V200	OEM
503V210	OEM
503V220	OEM
503V230	OEM
503V240	OEM
503V250	OEM
504T1	0050
505ES105	0841
505T1	0050
506T1	0050
507-4756-3331-500	OEM
507-4757-3331-500	5854

188

If replacement code is OEM, contact original manufacturer for replacement.

DEVICE TYPE	REPL CODE
507-4758-3331-500	5854
507-4759-3331-500	OEM
507-4760-3331-500	OEM
507-4761-3331-500	OEM
507-4856-3332-500	OEM
507-4857-3332-500	2682
507-4858-3332-500	2682
507-4859-3332-500	OEM
507-4860-3332-500	OEM
507-4861-3332-500	OEM
507-4956-3333-500	OEM
507-4957-3333-500	2726
507-4958-3333-500	2726
507-4959-3333-500	OEM
507-4960-3333-500	OEM
507-4961-3333-500	OEM
507T1	0050
508	OEM
508-1(IC)	OEM
508ES020P	0150
508ES021P	0150
508T1	0050
509	0079
509-01	OEM
509-1	0309
509-10	OEM
509-50	OEM
509ES025P	0211
510A-90	0143
510A90	0143
510ED46	0143
510ES030M	0590
510ES031M	0590
510IN60	0143
510IS34	0143
510LN60	0143
510LS34	0143
511-1	2833
511-3	0761
511-515	0198
511-519	0198
511-898	0015
511ES035P	0590
511ES036P	0590
511S345	0143
512ES040P	0841
512M	OEM
512M11	OEM
512RED	0016
513-891	0479
513-1500-067	OEM
513ES045P	0841
514-048	1865
514-053	0718
515	0198
515-074	0693
515-299	0015
515-521	0144
515ES045M	0150
515ES046M	0150
516	0198
516ES047M	0150
516ES048M	0150
517-0021	0015
517-0025	0015
517-0031	0015
517-0033	0015
517-1	4376
517-3	OEM
517-518	0198
518	OEM
518-499	0015
519-1	0079
519-528A43	OEM
519ES067M	0079
519ES068M	0079
520ES070M	0150
521-081	0123
521-094	0015
521-145	0143
521-9165	OEM
521-9166	OEM
521-9173	OEM
521-9174	OEM
521-9175	OEM
521-9176	OEM
521-9177	OEM
521-9178	OEM
521-9180	OEM
521-9181	OEM
521-9183	OEM
521-9184	OEM
521-9185	1970
521-9186	1978
521-9189	2990
521-9190	OEM
521-9195	1978
521-9200	OEM
521-9206	0835
521-9207	3095
521-9208	OEM
521-9210	OEM
521-9211	OEM
521-9212	OEM
521-9214	OEM
521-9215	OEM
521-9216	OEM
521-9217	1348
521-9222	OEM

DEVICE TYPE	REPL CODE
521-9223	OEM
521-9224	1767
521-9225	3128
521-9240	OEM
521-9246	1951
521-9247	OEM
521-9248	3128
521-9249	1951
521-9250	1767
521-9251	OEM
521-9253	OEM
521-9254	OEM
521-9256	1951
521-9258	3128
521-9260	1767
521-9264	OEM
521-9265	OEM
521-9266	OEM
521ES071M	0150
521T1	0279
522	0079
522(ZENITH)	0127
522-726	0015
522-893	0196
522-958	0250
522ES075M	0590
522ES076M	0590
523	OEM
523-0001-002	0015
523-0001-003	0015
523-0006-002	0124
523-0007-001	0124
523-0009-041	0549
523-0009-049	0030
523-006-002	0124
523-0013-002	0015
523-0013-201	0071
523-0017-001	0087
523-0501-002	0023
523-1000-001	0015
523-1000-067	0143
523-1000-295	0143
523-1000-326	2467
523-1000-881	0015
523-1000-882	0015
523-1000-883	0015
523-1002-326	6396
523-1500-067	0143
523-1500-803	0124
523-1500-881	0015
523-1500-883	0124
523-2001-100	0170
523-2003-001	0143
523-2003-100	0170
523-2003-150	0002
523-2003-519	0162
523-2004-100	0225
523-2005-100	0170
523-2005-279	1302
523-2503-100	0170
523-2503-150	0002
523-2503-519	0162
523-2503-689	0025
523-2509-100	0170
523-4001-001	0087
523AB1A11	OEM
523AB1AF1	OEM
523AB1AI1	OEM
523AC1A11	OEM
523AC1AD1	OEM
523AC1AI1	OEM
523AD1AD1	OEM
523BB1A11	OEM
523BB1AF1	OEM
523BB1AI1	OEM
523BC1A11	OEM
523BC1AD1	OEM
523BC1AI1	OEM
523BD1AD1	OEM
523DB1A11	OEM
523DB1AF1	OEM
523DB1AI1	OEM
523DC1A11	OEM
523DC1AD1	OEM
523DC1AI1	OEM
523DD1AD1	OEM
523ES077M	0590
523ES078M	0590
523FB1A11	OEM
523FB1AF1	OEM
523FB1AI1	OEM
523FC1A11	OEM
523FC1AD1	OEM
523FC1AI1	OEM
523FD1AD1	OEM
523MB1A11	OEM
523MB1AF1	OEM
523MB1AI1	OEM
523MB2A11	OEM
523MB2AI1	OEM
523MC1A11	OEM
523MC1AD1	OEM
523MC1AI1	OEM
523MC2A11	OEM
523MC2AI1	OEM
523MD1AD1	OEM
523MH5AE1	OEM
523MH5AS1	OEM
523MH9AS1	OEM

DEVICE TYPE	REPL CODE
523MH10AE1	OEM
523MH13AS1	OEM
523MH17AS1	OEM
523MH21AS1	OEM
523MH25AS1	OEM
523NB1A11	OEM
523NB1AF1	OEM
523NB1AI1	OEM
523NB2A11	OEM
523NB2AI1	OEM
523NC1A11	OEM
523NC1AD1	OEM
523NC1AI1	OEM
523NC2A11	OEM
523NC2AI2	OEM
523NC4AE1	OEM
523NC7AE1	OEM
523NC10AE1	OEM
523ND1AD1	OEM
523ND4AE1	OEM
523ND7AE1	OEM
523ND10AE1	OEM
523NH10AE1	OEM
523NH13AE1	OEM
523NH16AE1	OEM
523NH20AE1	OEM
523R	OEM
524-457	0143
524AB1AF1	OEM
524AC1AD1	OEM
524AD1AD1	OEM
524BB1AF1	OEM
524BC1AD1	OEM
524BD1AD1	OEM
524DB1AF1	OEM
524DC1AD1	OEM
524DD1AD1	OEM
524FB1AF1	OEM
524FC1AD1	OEM
524FD1AD1	OEM
524MB1AF1	OEM
524MC1AD1	OEM
524MC5AE1	OEM
524MC10AE1	OEM
524MD1AD1	OEM
524MD5AE1	OEM
524MD10AE1	OEM
524MH5AE1	OEM
524MH5AS1	OEM
524MH9AS1	OEM
524MH10AE1	OEM
524MH13AE1	OEM
524MH13AS1	OEM
524MH17AE1	OEM
524MH17AS1	OEM
524MH21AE1	OEM
524MH21AS1	OEM
524MH25AS1	OEM
524WHT	0016
525	OEM
525-24	0015
525-212	0071
525-498	0015
525-877	0143
525BF	0240
526	OEM
526-1	0527
526-376	0015
527-062	0196
527-1	OEM
527-798	0229
528-325	0229
528BSY	OEM
529-01-1	OEM
529-01-5	OEM
529-1	0224
529-2-1	OEM
529-2-5	OEM
530	0015
530-073-31	0157
530-082-3	0071
530-082-4	0071
530-082-1003	0229
530-086-1	0015
530-088-1	0015
530-088-2	0229
530-088-3	0071
530-088-1002	0071
530-088-1003	0071
530-088-1004	0071
530-094-1	0015
530-095-1	0015
530-098-1	0015
530-099-1	0015
530-099-3	0015
530-099-4	0015
530-106-1	0015
530-106-1001	0071
530-109-1	0015
530-111-1	0015
530-111-1001	0071
530-113-1	0015
530-120-1	0015
530-122-1	0229
530-136-T	0071
530-165-8	2954
531	OEM
531US	OEM
532-1	1503

DEVICE TYPE	REPL CODE
532-3	1503
532-5	OEM
532-341	0015
532-341A	0015
532BXY	OEM
535-1	5929
536	OEM
536-1	0007
536-2	0007
536DP	0224
536FS	0016
536FU	0016
536GT	0111
536J2F	0015
537FS	0144
537J2F	0015
538J2F	0015
539-003-1	OEM
539-003-5	OEM
539-005-1	OEM
539-005-5	OEM
539-01-1	OEM
539-01-5	OEM
539J2F	0015
540-008	0535
540-010	0015
540-013	0100
540-014	0071
540-015	0242
540J2F	0015
540PB30	OEM
540PB50	OEM
540PB60	OEM
543H	OEM
544-0003-043	3914
544-1	OEM
544-2002-004	2593
544-2002-008	1686
544-2003-002	0784
544-2003-005	1311
544-2003-006	OEM
544-2004-001	4506
544-2006-001	1239
544-2006-011	1042
544-2006-11	3723
544-2007-001	0030
544-2008-001	OEM
544-2009-555	0967
544-2020-002	0620
544-3001-001	2840
544-3001-002	OEM
544-3001-003	OEM
544-3001-102	OEM
544-3001-103	0473
544-3001-117	0508
544-3001-140	0001
544-3001-143	1535
544-3001-201	3550
544-3001-213	OEM
544H	OEM
545-1	4945
545-2	OEM
545-3	OEM
545-5	OEM
545-6	OEM
546	0144
546-1	1587
547-2001	OEM
547-2002	OEM
547-2003	OEM
547-2004	OEM
547-2005	OEM
547-2006	OEM
547-2007	OEM
547-2008	OEM
547J2F	0071
548D	OEM
549-0101	OEM
549-0104	OEM
549-0201	OEM
549-0301	OEM
549-1	0150
549-2	0037
549-4001-002	OEM
550	OEM
550-0204	OEM
550-0205	OEM
550-0206	OEM
550-0206-004	OEM
550-0304	OEM
550-0305	OEM
550-0306	OEM
550-0306-004	OEM
550-0404	OEM
550-0405	OEM
550-0406	OEM
550-0406-004	OEM
550-0504	OEM
550-0505	OEM
550-0506	OEM
550-0604	OEM
550-0605	OEM
550-0606	OEM
550-2204	OEM
550-2205	OEM
550-2206	OEM
550-2304	OEM
550-2305	OEM
550-2306	OEM

DEVICE TYPE	REPL CODE
550-2404	OEM
550-2405	OEM
550-2406	OEM
550-3004	OEM
550E	OEM
550H	OEM
550P4H	OEM
550P6H	OEM
550P8H	OEM
550P10H	OEM
550P12H	OEM
550P16H	OEM
550PA5	2816
550PA10	2816
550PA20	2816
550PA30	1754
550PA40	1754
550PA50	1754
550PA60	1754
550PB30	1754
550PB50	1754
550PB60	1754
550PB80	1803
550PB100	1803
550PB120	1803
550PB140	6673
550PB150	5223
550PB160	5223
550PB180	OEM
550R1B	OEM
550R2B	OEM
550R3B	OEM
550R4B	OEM
550R5B	OEM
550R6B	OEM
550R7B	OEM
550R8B	OEM
550R9B	OEM
550R10B	OEM
550R11B	OEM
550R12B	OEM
550R13B	OEM
550R14B	OEM
550R15B	OEM
550R16B	OEM
550R18B	OEM
550R20B	OEM
550R22B	OEM
550R24B	OEM
550R26B	OEM
550R28B	OEM
550R30B	OEM
550R32B	OEM
550R34B	OEM
550R36B	OEM
550R38B	OEM
550R40B	OEM
550R42B	OEM
550R44B	OEM
550R46B	OEM
550R48B	OEM
550R50B	OEM
551	0144
551-0002	0272
551-006	0718
551-010-00	0141
551-013-00	0081
551-0205	OEM
551-0305	OEM
551-0405	OEM
551-0505	OEM
551A	1865
551B	OEM
551E	OEM
551F	OEM
551H	OEM
551M	0224
551PA5	OEM
551PA10	OEM
551PA20	OEM
551PA30	OEM
551PA40	OEM
551PA50	OEM
551PA60	OEM
552	0839
552E	OEM
552F	OEM
552H	OEM
553	OEM
553E	OEM
553F	OEM
553H	OEM
554-1	0261
554E	OEM
554F	OEM
554H	OEM
555	0967
555-3	0086
555-2001	OEM
555-2002	OEM
555-2003	OEM
555-2004	OEM
555-2005	OEM
555-2006	OEM
555-2007	OEM
555-2008	OEM
555-2301	OEM
555-2303	OEM
555-2401	OEM

DEVICE TYPE	REPL CODE
555-3001	OEM
555-3002	OEM
555-3003	OEM
555-3004	OEM
555-3005	OEM
555-3006	OEM
555-3007	OEM
555-3008	OEM
555-4001	OEM
555-4003	OEM
555-4007	OEM
555-4301	OEM
555-4303	OEM
555-4401	OEM
555-4403	OEM
555D	0967
555H	OEM
555PB	OEM
556	3254
556-1	OEM
556D	3254
556E	OEM
556F	OEM
556H	OEM
558-0101-001	OEM
558-0101-003	OEM
558-0101-004	OEM
558-0101-005	OEM
558-0101-006	OEM
558-0101-007	OEM
558-0102-001	OEM
558-0102-003	OEM
558-0102-004	OEM
558-0102-005	OEM
558-0102-006	OEM
558-0102-007	OEM
558-0201-001	OEM
558-0201-003	OEM
558-0201-004	OEM
558-0201-005	OEM
558-0201-006	OEM
558-0201-007	OEM
558-0202-001	OEM
558-0202-003	OEM
558-0202-004	OEM
558-0202-005	OEM
558-0202-006	OEM
558-0202-007	OEM
558-0301-001	OEM
558-0301-003	OEM
558-0301-004	OEM
558-0301-005	OEM
558-0301-006	OEM
558-0301-007	OEM
558-0302-001	OEM
558-0302-003	OEM
558-0302-004	OEM
558-0302-005	OEM
558-0302-006	OEM
558-0302-007	OEM
558CP	3748
558E	OEM
558F	OEM
558H	OEM
559-0101-001	OEM
559-0101-003	OEM
559-0101-004	OEM
559-0101-005	OEM
559-0101-006	OEM
559-0101-007	OEM
559-0102-001	OEM
559-0102-003	OEM
559-0102-004	OEM
559-0102-005	OEM
559-0102-006	OEM
559-0102-007	OEM
559-0103-001	OEM
559-0103-003	OEM
559-0103-004	OEM
559-0103-005	OEM
559-0103-006	OEM
559-0103-007	OEM
559-0201-001	OEM
559-0201-003	OEM
559-0201-004	OEM
559-0201-005	OEM
559-0201-006	OEM
559-0201-007	OEM
559-0202-001	OEM
559-0202-003	OEM
559-0202-004	OEM
559-0202-006	OEM
559-0202-007	OEM
559-0301-001	OEM
559-0301-003	OEM
559-0301-004	OEM
559-0301-005	OEM
559-0301-006	OEM
559-0301-007	OEM
559-0302-001	OEM
559-0302-003	OEM
559-0302-004	OEM
559-0302-005	OEM
559-0302-006	OEM
559-0302-007	OEM
559-1	0037
559-1492-001	1354
559-1493-001	3303
559-1494-001	3847

DEVICE TYPE	REPL CODE
559-1495-001	3797
559-1496-001	1248
559-2101-001	OEM
559-2101-003	OEM
559-2101-004	OEM
559-2101-005	OEM
559-2101-006	OEM
559-2101-007	OEM
559-2201-001	OEM
559-2201-003	OEM
559-2201-004	OEM
559-2201-005	OEM
559-2201-006	OEM
559-2201-007	OEM
559-2301-001	OEM
559-2301-003	OEM
559-2301-004	OEM
559-2301-005	OEM
559-2301-006	OEM
559-2301-007	OEM
559-3001-001	OEM
559-3001-003	OEM
559H	OEM
560	OEM
560-0101	OEM
560-0102	OEM
560-0103	OEM
560-0104	OEM
560-0105	OEM
560-0106	OEM
560-0107	OEM
560-0108	OEM
560-0201	OEM
560-0202	OEM
560-0203	OEM
560-0204	OEM
560-0205	OEM
560-0206	OEM
560-0207	OEM
560-0208	OEM
560-0301	OEM
560-0302	OEM
560-0304	OEM
560-0305	OEM
560-0306	OEM
560-0307	OEM
560-0308	OEM
560-0401	OEM
560-0402	OEM
560-0403	OEM
560-0404	OEM
560-0405	OEM
560-0406	OEM
560-0407	OEM
560-0408	OEM
560-0501	OEM
560-0502	OEM
560-0503	OEM
560-0504	OEM
560-0505	OEM
560-0506	OEM
560-0507	OEM
560-0508	OEM
560-0601	OEM
560-0602	OEM
560-0603	OEM
560-0604	OEM
560-0605	OEM
560-0606	OEM
560-0607	OEM
560-0608	OEM
560-2	0016
560E	OEM
560F	OEM
560H	OEM
561	OEM
561-0884-006	1789
561-0884-041	1964
561-0884-043	0308
561-0884-047	2342
561-1	1503
561-2	OEM
561-4	OEM
561-2511-106	0143
561-2511-120	0143
561-2511-190	0143
561-2511-210	0143
561-2511-240	0143
561-2511-290	0143
561-2511-400	0143
561-2511-503	0143
561-2511-510	0143
561-2511-530	0143
561-2511-535	0015
561-2511-538	0143
561-2511-540	0143
561-2511-544	0143
561-2511-555	0143
561-2511-558	0143
561-2511-564	0104
561-2511-570	0143
561-2511-575	0143
561-2511-580	0133
561-2511-700	0036
561-2511-900	0062
561-2554-560	0133
561-2554-570	0133
561-2554-571	0133
561-2554-577	0133

If replacement code is OEM, contact original manufacturer for replacement. 189

DEVICE TYPE	REPL CODE
561-2554-578	0133
561-2554-610	0133
561-2554-620	0133
561-2554-820	0133
561-2554-821	0133
561-2554-824	0133
561-2554-830	0133
561-2554-841	0133
561-2554-842	0133
561-2554-850	0133
561-2554-880	0102
561-2556-250	0133
561-2556-270	0133
561-2556-290	0133
561-2556-360	0143
561-2556-450	0015
561-2556-590	0133
561-2556-620	0133
561-2556-950	0143
561-2557-032	0372
561-2557-042	0036
561-2557-050	0140
561-2557-060	0091
561-2557-062	0205
561-2557-070	0062
561-2557-092	0631
561-2557-142	0170
561-2557-152	0247
561-2557-161	0137
561-2557-191	0416
561-2560-460	0296
561-2560-461	0289
561-2560-480	0451
561-2560-491	0528
561-2560-501	0446
561-2560-520	0157
561-2560-522	0157
561-2560-530	0466
561-2560-531	0631
561-2560-680	0666
561-2560-754	0025
561-2560-755	0077
561-2560-756	0244
561-2560-757	0012
561-2560-758	0170
561-2560-816	0298
561-2560-820	0631
561-2560-823	0631
561-2560-825	0631
561-2560-914	0124
561-2560-915	0133
561-2560-935	0012
561-2560-957	0025
561-2560-958	0644
561-2560-961	0170
561-2560-962	0170
561-2560-963	0137
561-2560-964	0436
561-2560-966	0371
561-2560-967	0371
561-2560-969	0560
561-2560-970	0398
561-2560-971	0436
561-2561-313	0318
561-2561-321	0032
561-2561-322	0068
561-2561-358	1707
561-2561-359	1712
561-2561-370	0263
561-2561-590	1890
561-2561-604	0986
561-2561-766	0631
561-2561-776	0416
561-2561-780	0526
561-2561-788	0497
561-2568-191	1071
561-2568-280	1185
561-2568-300	0132
561-2568-312	0207
561-2573-260	3638
561-2579-707	1591
561-2580-003	0731
561-2580-040	0433
561-2580-152	0663
561-2580-392	0778
561-2583-110	0883
561-2583-141	0926
561-2583-606	0133
561-2583-608	0133
561-2583-791	0234
561-2583-793	0234
561-2588-092	0401
561-2588-185	0528
561-2588-930	0437
561-2589-930	0542
561-2589-971	1890
561-2590-090	0133
561-2591-480	0124
561-2591-540	0124
561-2593-701	1266
561-2594-480	0124
561-2597-180	0256
561-2597-280	0289
561-2597-291	0188
561-2597-310	0528
561-2597-321	0446
561-2597-341	0157
561-2597-350	0631
561-2597-351	0631

DEVICE TYPE	REPL CODE
561-2597-361	0025
561-2597-381	0244
561-2597-383	0012
561-2597-420	0137
561-2597-421	0137
561-2597-440	0002
561-2597-441	0002
561-2597-464	0490
561-2597-471	0526
561-2597-570	0497
561-2598-000	0296
561-2598-250	0041
561-2599-340	0102
561-2599-360	0102
561-2600-230	0012
561-2602-210	1266
561-2602-300	0041
561-2602-310	0012
561-2602-350	0025
561-2602-430	0361
561-2602-440	0100
561-2603-383	0437
561-2603-530	0251
561-2654-756	0091
561-2706-000	0102
561-2707-770	0124
561-2709-560	0863
561-4800-350	0154
561-4800-402	0154
561-4800-403	0147
561-4800-425	0571
561-4800-440	2337
561-4800-442	2337
561-4800-443	2340
561-4800-445	2006
561-4800-446	0571
561-4800-448	2337
561-4800-452	0154
561-4800-502	0154
561-4800-520	4169
561-5004-412	0015
561-5005-360	0015
561-5005-380	0015
561-5005-390	0015
561-5005-400	0015
561-5005-470	0015
561-5005-890	0133
561-5006-460	0015
561-5006-470	0015
561-5008-810	0015
561-5010-820	0015
561-5010-840	0015
561-5010-950	0015
561-5010-960	0015
561-5011-190	2070
561-5011-200	2070
561-5011-842	1116
561-5011-850	1116
561-5011-860	1116
561-5011-870	0800
561-5011-876	0258
561-5011-880	0800
561-5011-900	0315
561-5011-902	0315
561-5011-970	0315
561-5011-976	1099
561-5012-021	0097
561-5012-027	0760
561-5012-042	0109
561-5012-180	0015
561-5012-210	0015
561-5012-220	0015
561-5013-422	0983
561-5013-432	0983
561-5015-660	0535
561-5015-662	0015
561-5015-860	2070
561-5016-140	0983
561-5016-160	0510
561-5016-920	0015
561-5016-930	0015
561-5016-940	0015
561-5016-950	0015
561-5016-960	0015
561-5017-640	0015
561-5020-690	0015
561-5020-700	0015
561-5020-701	0015
561-5020-710	0015
561-5021-292	2633
561-5021-576	0258
561-5021-600	0315
561-5024-830	0015
561-5026-100	0015
561-5026-130	0015
561-5031-930	0015
561-5031-940	0015
561-5031-950	0015
561-5032-080	1991
561-5032-086	1992
561-5032-090	1241
561-5032-140	1576
561-5032-530	0015
561-5032-770	0015
561-5032-790	0015
561-5032-890	1337
561-5032-891	0594
561-5032-930	1975
561-5034-951	0133

DEVICE TYPE	REPL CODE
561-5037-400	1030
561-5037-680	0045
561-5040-010	0015
561-5040-020	0015
561-5040-030	0015
561-5040-040	0015
561-5040-050	0015
561-5040-060	0071
561-5040-070	0071
561-5040-440	1017
561-5040-480	1017
561-5040-600	0015
561-5040-821	0535
561-5040-830	0015
561-5040-850	0015
561-5045-270	0315
561-5047-210	0242
561-5053-970	0959
561-5106-830	0562
561-5106-880	0735
561-5106-890	0759
561-5106-900	0759
561-5106-920	0761
561-5117-750	0671
561-5138-980	0735
561-5138-990	0720
561-5141-720	0671
561-5144-420	2255
561-5144-440	3370
561-5150-600	1129
561-5150-610	0340
561-5150-620	0895
561-6160-368	1590
561-6160-550	0276
561-6160-650	0319
561-6160-680	0340
561-6161-090	0947
561-6162-030	0240
561-6162-246	0287
561-6162-247	0087
561-6162-248	0934
561-6162-250	0240
561-6162-252	0015
561-6162-295	0464
561-6163-025	0015
561-6163-047	0800
561-6163-050	0735
561-6163-070	0800
561-6163-072	0258
561-6163-080	2823
561-6163-094	0735
561-6164-002	0468
561-6164-003	0015
561-6164-025	0015
561-6164-160	0682
561-6164-180	0109
561-6164-185	0847
561-6164-250	0800
561-6164-252	0717
561-6164-253	0267
561-6164-255	2823
561-6164-275	0015
561-6164-280	0015
561-6164-295	1634
561-6164-297	2844
561-6164-410	1599
561-6164-420	1196
561-6165-080	0332
561-6165-085	0735
561-6166-010	0015
561-6166-020	0959
561-6168-800	3613
561-6561-860	0015
561-6800-035	0208
561-6800-109	0004
561-6800-123	0279
561-6800-167	0595
561-6800-169	0595
561-6800-170	0595
561-6800-174	0435
561-6800-176	0085
561-6800-188	0211
561-6800-212	0208
561-6800-214	0208
561-6800-215	0004
561-6800-217	0004
561-6800-228	0208
561-6800-241	0211
561-6800-242	0085
561-6800-250	0085
561-6800-270	0211
561-6800-277	0435
561-6800-301	0160
561-6800-327	0279
561-6800-335	0198
561-6800-336	0198
561-6800-337	0127
561-6800-362	0211
561-6800-376	0085
561-6800-380	0085
561-6800-396	0279
561-6800-404	0004
561-6800-405	0211
561-6800-406	0004
561-6800-414	0279
561-6800-441	0435
561-6800-444	0038
561-6800-456	0085
561-6800-466	0211

DEVICE TYPE	REPL CODE
561-6800-472	0086
561-6800-482	0016
561-6800-484	0016
561-6800-495	0016
561-6800-497	0086
561-6800-503	0279
561-6800-508	0211
561-6800-519	0279
561-6800-520	0279
561-6800-524	0211
561-6800-526	0211
561-6800-541	0198
561-6800-555	0160
561-6800-586	0279
561-6800-591	0004
561-6800-597	0279
561-6800-600	0279
561-6800-652	0211
561-6800-656	0086
561-6800-657	0086
561-6800-662	0841
561-6800-669	0160
561-6800-679	0595
561-6800-685	0595
561-6800-687	0735
561-6800-696	0198
561-6800-697	0086
561-6800-700	0050
561-6800-706	0144
561-6800-718	0144
561-6800-741	0050
561-6800-914	0144
561-6800-916	0144
561-6800-929	0016
561-6800-930	0016
561-6801-007	0211
561-6801-008	0211
561-6801-034	0126
561-6801-038	0841
561-6801-040	0085
561-6801-100	0279
561-6801-102	0208
561-6801-136	0160
561-6801-175	0211
561-6801-178	0050
561-6801-182	0841
561-6801-183	0841
561-6801-184	0841
561-6801-185	0279
561-6801-301	0050
561-6801-303	0164
561-6801-304	0595
561-6801-305	0164
561-6801-308	0595
561-6801-309	0279
561-6801-311	0595
561-6801-363	0160
561-6801-365	0160
561-6801-370	0211
561-6801-372	0211
561-6801-373	0211
561-6801-378	0211
561-6801-379	0211
561-6801-381	0211
561-6801-404	0211
561-6801-415	0211
561-6801-420	0086
561-6801-502	0085
561-6801-537	0160
561-6801-542	0599
561-6801-544	0599
561-6801-545	0599
561-6801-556	0599
561-6801-557	0599
561-6801-592	0127
561-6801-605	0595
561-6801-606	0595
561-6801-613	0086
561-6801-623	0126
561-6801-666	0160
561-6801-670	1659
561-6801-711	0086
561-6801-755	0085
561-6801-922	0126
561-6801-926	0004
561-6801-990	0086
561-6801-997	0279
561-6801-998	0279
561-6802-076	0435
561-6802-078	0435
561-6802-137	0085
561-6802-147	0085
561-6802-153	0432
561-6802-156	0432
561-6802-188	0050
561-6802-218	0198
561-6802-221	0016
561-6802-223	0016
561-6802-270	0086
561-6802-369	0016
561-6802-375	0211
561-6802-382	0050
561-6802-484	0016
561-6802-501	0016
561-6802-564	0211
561-6802-646	2123
561-6802-714	0127
561-6802-869	0160
561-6802-904	0126

DEVICE TYPE	REPL CODE
561-6802-905	0126
561-6802-907	0037
561-6802-908	0037
561-6802-923	0111
561-6802-924	0111
561-6802-925	0111
561-6802-996	0050
561-6803-011	0016
561-6803-012	0037
561-6803-013	0016
561-6803-053	0086
561-6803-054	0178
561-6803-055	0103
561-6803-115	0016
561-6803-133	0126
561-6803-135	0037
561-6803-214	0160
561-6803-215	0160
561-6803-250	0037
561-6803-300	0488
561-6803-371	0050
561-6803-391	0111
561-6803-393	0111
561-6803-397	0111
561-6803-403	0218
561-6803-416	0155
561-6803-417	0155
561-6803-440	0187
561-6803-441	1021
561-6803-442	0538
561-6803-448	0103
561-6803-460	0321
561-6803-502	0126
561-6803-504	0037
561-6803-565	0079
561-6803-566	0079
561-6803-567	0320
561-6803-568	0086
561-6803-569	0086
561-6803-585	0142
561-6803-638	0037
561-6803-639	0037
561-6803-644	0037
561-6803-645	0126
561-6803-646	0079
561-6803-702	0037
561-6803-703	0037
561-6803-705	0320
561-6803-711	0111
561-6803-715	0103
561-6803-721	0127
561-6803-732	0969
561-6803-739	0142
561-6803-766	0178
561-6803-771	0130
561-6803-772	0130
561-6803-773	0538
561-6803-789	0486
561-6803-819	0321
561-6803-822	3104
561-6803-858	0111
561-6803-902	0359
561-6803-903	0079
561-6803-904	0079
561-6803-905	0037
561-6803-906	0037
561-6804-030	0126
561-6804-037	0126
561-6804-092	1147
561-6804-123	0079
561-6804-124	0079
561-6804-125	0037
561-6804-126	0037
561-6804-234	0126
561-6804-235	0126
561-6804-237	0086
561-6804-240	0142
561-6804-249	0037
561-6804-275	0144
561-6804-348	0177
561-6804-356	0037
561-6804-360	2959
561-6804-387	0919
561-6804-389	0919
561-6804-400	0079
561-6804-401	0079
561-6804-402	0037
561-6804-403	0037
561-6804-424	0155
561-6804-851	2123
561-6804-855	1147
561-6804-905	2002
561-6804-921	0161
561-6804-946	0086
561-6805-190	0161
561-6805-195	0455
561-6805-240	0359
561-6805-247	0321
561-6805-294	0042
561-6805-296	0042
561-6805-302	0130
561-6805-308	0396
561-6805-320	0086
561-6805-322	0126
561-6805-354	0037
561-6805-415	0434
561-6805-485	1382
561-6805-486	0321
561-6805-670	0177

DEVICE TYPE	REPL CODE
561-6805-830	0710
561-6806-027	0312
561-6806-028	0312
561-6806-307	0359
561-6901-000	0279
561-6901-006	0595
561-6901-008	0038
561-6901-010	0969
561-6901-110	0969
561-6901-410	0359
561-6901-411	1955
561-6901-440	0065
561-6901-473	0786
561-6901-527	0272
561-6901-826	2411
561-6901-850	0178
561-6902-105	1190
561-6902-521	0161
561-6936-220	0103
561-6940-251	0178
561-6940-347	0086
561-6952-923	0016
561-6953/020	0016
561-6953-003	0004
561-6953-004	0004
561-6953-006	0050
561-6953-007	0050
561-6953-009	0160
561-6953-010	0208
561-6953-011	0595
561-6953-020	0016
561-6953-021	0142
561-6953-024	0086
561-6953-025	0126
561-6953-041	0042
561-6954-030	0676
561-6954-099	0127
561-6955-935	0321
561-6956-373	0969
561-6956-515	0155
561-6956-531	0127
561-6956-534	0037
561-6956-550	0320
561-6956-553	0396
561-6956-555	0037
561-6956-602	0546
561-6956-651	0378
561-6956-652	0378
561-6956-740	2243
561-6956-942	0555
561-6958-405	0378
561C	0320
561E	OEM
561F	OEM
561H	OEM
562	OEM
562-1	0143
562E	OEM
562F	OEM
562H	OEM
564HD	OEM
564HDS	OEM
565	3347
565-072	0076
565-073	2035
565-074	0016
565-075	1401
565-076	1401
565-1	0086
567	3733
568H	OEM
569-0320-809	0406
569-0320-813	0687
569-0320-814	0354
569-0320-815	1918
569-0320-818	1820
569-0320-820	0141
569-0320-821	0557
569-0320-822	0141
569-0320-826	1820
569-0320-831	0026
569-0540-355	0967
569-0540-358	0356
569-0540-623	0026
569-0541-000	0613
569-0541-006	2964
569-0541-014	3037
569-0541-018	2417
569-0541-024	0078
569-0541-030	4101
569-0541-031	4107
569-0541-036	4112
569-0541-037	4115
569-0541-038	3016
569-0541-041	4124
569-0541-042	4128
569-0541-043	4132
569-0542-744	0011
569-0544-300	1812
569-0544-304	1035
569-0544-305	2086
569-0544-308	1820
569-0544-312	1168
569-0544-318	0033
569-0544-322	0141
569-0544-328	0329
569-0544-348	0557
569-0690-300	2662
569-0690-301	1686

DEVICE TYPE	REPL CODE
569-0690-500	0473
569-0690-501	0215
569-0690-502	0409
569-0690-550	0394
569-0690-681	2722
569-0773-600	0967
569-0773-610	0356
569-0773-800	0232
569-0773-811	0522
569-0880-430	1812
569-0880-444	0033
569-0880-445	0081
569-0880-446	0141
569-0880-450	2595
569-0880-458	0461
569-0880-462	0557
569-0881-801	5241
569-0881-804	1896
569-0881-810	0680
569-0881-811	2382
569-0881-820	3670
569-0881-821	4772
569-0881-822	4516
569-0881-830	5284
569-0881-840	0554
569-0881-850	1781
569-0881-851	1933
569-0881-852	2009
569-0881-853	2090
569-0881-855	3129
569-0881-860	5312
569-0881-874	2472
569-0881-908	0180
569-0882-600	0232
569-0882-601	0268
569-0882-602	0310
569-0882-603	0331
569-0882-604	0357
569-0882-605	0381
569-0882-606	1197
569-0882-607	1329
569-0882-608	0462
569-0882-609	0487
569-0882-610	0507
569-0882-612	2227
569-0882-613	1432
569-0882-614	2228
569-0882-616	1339
569-0882-617	1342
569-0882-620	0692
569-0882-625	3438
569-0882-627	0812
569-0882-630	0867
569-0882-632	0893
569-0882-633	4130
569-0882-637	3478
569-0882-638	0990
569-0882-640	1018
569-0882-641	1032
569-0882-642	1046
569-0882-647	1100
569-0882-650	0738
569-0882-651	1160
569-0882-653	1177
569-0882-654	1193
569-0882-660	1265
569-0882-672	1417
569-0882-673	1164
569-0882-674	1303
569-0882-675	1423
569-0882-676	1150
569-0882-680	1527
569-0882-682	1564
569-0882-685	0370
569-0882-686	1358
569-0882-689	5358
569-0882-690	1199
569-0882-692	0828
569-0882-693	0564
569-0882-696	1705
569-0882-707	0936
569-0882-709	0962
569-0882-721	0175
569-0882-722	1131
569-0882-723	1149
569-0882-726	1184
569-0882-732	1261
569-0882-741	1367
569-0882-745	0614
569-0882-750	1484
569-0882-751	1487
569-0882-753	1531
569-0882-754	1546
569-0882-755	1566
569-0882-760	1621
569-0882-761	1635
569-0882-764	0729
569-0882-765	1675
569-0882-774	1759
569-0882-775	1776
569-0882-776	1784
569-0882-777	1792
569-0882-779	1809
569-0882-780	1818
569-0882-781	1831
569-0882-782	1845
569-0882-790	1901
569-0882-791	1906
569-0882-792	1910

If replacement code is OEM, contact original manufacturer for replacement.

DEVICE TYPE	REPL CODE
569-0882-793	1915
569-0882-796	1939
569-0882-797	1945
569-0883-200	0699
569-0883-203	2203
569-0883-204	2248
569-0883-205	2305
569-0883-210	2426
569-0883-211	2428
569-0883-215	2432
569-0883-220	1011
569-0883-222	2442
569-0883-240	2456
569-0883-264	2476
569-0883-265	2477
569-0883-274	2483
569-0883-312	1607
569-0883-338	2125
569-0883-340	1875
569-0883-353	2138
569-0883-357	1685
569-0883-358	2141
569-0883-374	2119
569-0885-850	1222
569-0885-853	1262
569-0885-854	1253
569-0886-031	1929
569-0886-800	0243
569-0964-001	1695
569-0964-002	1290
569-0965-006	1033
569-1000-020	0870
569-2142-100	0015
569-8800-090	0042
569-9440-102	4900
570-004503	0016
570-005503	0016
570-1	0037
570H	OEM
571-844	0103
571-844A	0103
572-0040-051	0160
572-1	0079
572-683	0016
573-469	0016
573-472	0144
573-474	0144
573-474A	0144
573-475	0144
573-479	0016
573-480	0016
573-481	0016
573-491	0144
573-494	0144
573-495	0144
573-507	0144
573-509	0144
573-515	0142
573-518	0050
573-529	0004
573-532	0086
574	0037
574-1	0150
574-844	0074
575-028	0015
575-042	0015
575-048	0015
575-050	0015
576-0001-002	0037
576-0001-002(SEARS)	0004
576-0001-003	0004
576-0001-004	0198
576-0001-005	0198
576-0001-006	0144
576-0001-008	0016
576-0001-009	0004
576-0001-012	0016
576-0001-013	0037
576-0001-014	0079
576-0002-001	2969
576-0002-002	0160
576-0002-003	0103
576-0002-004	0004
576-0002-005	0160
576-0002-006	0016
576-0002-008	0037
576-0002-009	0435
576-0002-010	0435
576-0002-011	0161
576-0002-012	0004
576-0002-013	0208
576-0002-026	2969
576-0002-029	2969
576-0003-001	0144
576-0003-002	0144
576-0003-003	0144
576-0003-004	0144
576-0003-005	0144
576-0003-006	0144
576-0003-007	0144
576-0003-008	0136
576-0003-009	0136
576-0003-010	0050
576-0003-011	0079
576-0003-012	0150
576-0003-013	0136
576-0003-014	0136
576-0003-015	0136
576-0003-017	0037

DEVICE TYPE	REPL CODE
576-0003-018	0144
576-0003-019	0037
576-0003-020	0144
576-0003-021	0144
576-0003-022	0111
576-0003-023	0007
576-0003-024	0136
576-0003-026	0007
576-0003-027	0144
576-0003-028	0144
576-0003-029	0127
576-0003-12	1371
576-0003-224	0212
576-0004-004	0321
576-0004-005	0626
576-0004-006	2338
576-0004-007	2675
576-0004-008	0488
576-0004-009	2675
576-0004-010	0016
576-0004-011	2675
576-0004-012	2675
576-0004-013	0693
576-0004-021	2296
576-0004-035	0264
576-0004-035(IC)	3946
576-0004-051	1189
576-0004-053	2296
576-0004-104	2675
576-0004-105	0930
576-0005-001	1659
576-0005-004	0086
576-0006-003	0321
576-0006-011	0144
576-0006-221	0349
576-0006-222	0212
576-0006-227	0212
576-0007-001	0396
576-001	0004
576-001-013	0150
576-002-001	0555
576-002-004	0211
576-003-009	0050
576-004-051	1189
576-005	0004
576-0036-212	0693
576-0036-213	0693
576-0036-847	0198
576-0036-913	0693
576-0036-916	0016
576-0036-917	0016
576-0036-918	0144
576-0036-919	0144
576-0036-920	0016
576-0036-921	0016
576-0040-051	0160
576-0040-251	0103
576-0040-253	0004
576-0040-254	0160
576-1	0326
576-14	0375
576-2000-278	0435
576-2000-990	0136
576-2000-993	0136
576-2001-970	0435
577B196	0571
577R819H01	0086
579-0001-009	0279
580-029	0015
580H	OEM
581B83-7	2007
586-2	0016
586-151	1812
586-152	1820
586-153	0141
586-154	0329
586-155	0557
586-187	0081
586-303	1035
586-308	1824
586-331	0939
586-412	1033
586-415	1424
586-425	0354
586-442	0461
586-517	0913
586-528	0882
586-546	0844
586-547	0976
586-780	1005
587-033	1711
588-40-202	1469
588U	0321
589H	OEM
590	1070
591	OEM
592	OEM
592-027	1248
592-028	1354
592-029-0	1063
592-032-0	OEM
592-032-1	OEM
592-079-0	OEM
592-081-0	1063
594-1	OEM
595-1	0016
595-1(SYLVANIA)	0016
595-2	0016
595-2(SYLVANIA)	0016

DEVICE TYPE	REPL CODE
596-2	0133
596-5	0133
597-1	0150
597-2	OEM
598H	OEM
600	0015
600/8EDA-XX01-4	OEM
600/11DA-1A01-4	OEM
600/11DA-1C01-4	OEM
600/11DA-1D01-4	OEM
600/11DA-2A01-4	OEM
600/11DA-2B01-4	OEM
600/11DA-2C01-4	OEM
600/11DA-2D01-4	OEM
600/11DA-3A01-4	OEM
600/11DA-3B01-4	OEM
600/11DA-3C01-4	OEM
600/11DA-3D01-4	OEM
600/11DA-4A01-4	OEM
600/11DA-4B01-4	OEM
600/11DA-4C01-4	OEM
600/11DA-4D01-4	OEM
600-104-308	1056
600-207-801	0076
600-224-605	1212
600-229-201	0191
600-301-801	1409
600C	0133
600HT1U	3699
600HT2U	3699
600HT3U	3699
600HT4U	3699
600HT6U	3699
600HT8U	3734
600HT10U	5642
600PBQ120	OEM
600PBQ130	OEM
600PBQ140	OEM
600PBQ150	OEM
600PBQ160	OEM
600PBQ170	OEM
600PBQ180	OEM
600PIN-RM	OEM
600PV-RM	OEM
600R1B	OEM
600R2B	OEM
600R3B	OEM
600R4B	OEM
600R5B	OEM
600R6B	OEM
600R7B	OEM
600R8B	OEM
600R9B	OEM
600R10B	OEM
600R11B	OEM
600R12B	OEM
600R13B	OEM
600R14B	OEM
600R15B	OEM
600R16B	OEM
600R18B	OEM
600R20B	OEM
600R22B	OEM
600R24B	OEM
600R26B	OEM
600R28B	OEM
600R30B	OEM
600R32B	OEM
600R34B	OEM
600R36B	OEM
600R38B	OEM
600R40B	OEM
600R42B	OEM
600R44B	OEM
600R46B	OEM
600R48B	OEM
600R50B	OEM
600X0091-086	0016
600X0092-086	0144
600X0093-086	0007
600X0094-086	0007
600X0095-086	0037
600X0096-066	0143
600X0097-066	0143
600X0098-066	0196
600X0099-066	0015
600X0100-066	0133
600X0101-066	0137
600X0141-000	0127
600X0143-000	0127
600X0175-000	0127
600X0186-000	0911
600X0195-000	0127
601	0015
601-0226-0666	0361
601-0100865	1432
601-1	0016
601-2	0016
601C	0133
601X0048-066	0087
601X0049-066	0015
601X0149-086	0016
601X0150-066	0143
601X0151-066	0143
601X0152-066	0015
601X0224-066	0133
601X0225-066	0133
601X0226-066	0361
601X0226-0666	0137

DEVICE TYPE	REPL CODE
601X0227-066	0015
601X0375-006	0102
601X0402-038	0361
601X0417-086	0037
601X0432-066	OEM
602	OEM
602-032	0160
602-040	0004
602-075	0050
602-56	0037
602-60	0037
602-61	0144
602-113	0144
602X0006-000	OEM
602X0008-002	0111
602X-0018-000	OEM
602X0018-000	0016
602X0018-002	0111
602X0019-000	0015
603	0513
603-020	0050
603-030	0050
603-040	0050
603-5	OEM
603-113	0144
603E	0513
603F	0513
603G	0513
603G(2SC2603G)	0513
604	0016
604-030	0050
604-080	0050
604-3	0396
604-113	0144
604B	0015
604C	0133
605	0198
605-030	0004
605-113	0144
606-020	0004
606-113	0015
606AJ24	OEM
606C	OEM
606J	OEM
606K	OEM
606L	OEM
606M	OEM
607-030	0016
607-113	0015
607AJ24	OEM
608	0015
608-030	0015
608-2	0086
608-3	0086
608-101	0015
608-112	0969
608-113	0015
608C	OEM
609-020	0050
609-030	0015
609-0371923	OEM
609-112	0016
609-113	0015
609-2497000	OEM
609-2497001	OEM
610	0015
610-001-103	0015
610-009-2402	0057
610-017-706	0133
610-035	0004
610-035-1	0004
610-036	0004
610-036-1	0004
610-036-2	0004
610-036-3	0004
610-036-4	0004
610-036-5	0004
610-036-7	0004
610-036-8	0004
610-039	0160
610-039-1	0160
610-039-103	OEM
610-040	0004
610-040-1	0004
610-040-2	0004
610-041	0144
610-041-1	0144
610-041-2	0144
610-041-3	0144
610-042	0144
610-042-1	0144
610-043	0004
610-043-1	0004
610-043-2	0004
610-043-3	0004
610-043-4	0004
610-043-6	0004
610-043-7	0004
610-045	0144
610-045-1	0144
610-045-2	0144
610-045-3	0016
610-045-4	0016
610-046-7	0004
610-050	0050
610-050-1	0050
610-050-2	0050
610-050-3	0050
610-051	0050

DEVICE TYPE	REPL CODE
610-051-1	0050
610-051-2	0050
610-051-4	0050
610-052	0136
610-052-1	0136
610-053	0050
610-053-1	0050
610-053-2	0050
610-055	0050
610-055-1	0050
610-055-2	0050
610-055-3	0050
610-056	0136
610-056-1	0136
610-056-2	0136
610-056-3	0136
610-056-4	0136
610-067	0160
610-067-1	0160
610-067-2	0160
610-067-3	0160
610-068	0160
610-068-1	0160
610-069	0144
610-069-1	0144
610-070	0016
610-070-1	0016
610-070-2	0016
610-070-3	0016
610-071	0142
610-071-1	0142
610-072	0144
610-072-1	0144
610-072-2	0144
610-073	0144
610-073-1	0144
610-074	0136
610-074-1	0136
610-076	0016
610-076-1	0016
610-076-2	0016
610-077	0016
610-077-1	0016
610-077-2	0016
610-077-3	0016
610-077-4	0016
610-077-5	0016
610-078	0016
610-078-1	0016
610-079	0004
610-079-1	0004
610-080	0004
610-080-1	0004
610-083	0126
610-083-1	0126
610-083-2	0126
610-083-3	0126
610-11	OEM
610BB	OEM
610C	0015
610N	OEM
612	0015
612-1	0555
612-16	0079
612-16(ZENITH)	0144
612-16A	0144
612-60039	0136
612-60039A	0136
612C	0133
613	0079
613(ZENITH)	0144
613-4	0233
613-72	0144
614	0015
614(ZENITH)	0144
614-1	0086
614-2	0079
614-3	0016
614-12	0144
614-118	0133
614A-1-5L	0160
614A1-5L	0160
614C	0133
614H	OEM
614X	OEM
614X1	0004
614X2	0004
614X3	0004
614X4	0004
614X5	0004
614X6	0004
614X7	0004
614X8	0208
614X9	0004
614X10	0004
615-1	0127
616	0015
616-1	0150
616-501B	OEM
616C	0133
617-7	OEM
617-10	0016
617-15	0143
617-17	0143
617-46	0015
617-50	0004
617-52	0004
617-53	0015
617-54	0050

DEVICE TYPE	REPL CODE
617-55	0050
617-56	0136
617-57	0050
617-58	0050
617-62	0015
617-63	0016
617-64	0016
617-65	0007
617-66	0015
617-67	0016
617-68	0016
617-69	0164
617-70	0004
617-71	0016
617-87	0198
617-117	0042
617-156	0143
617-161	0016
617-162	0015
617-163	0015
618	0015
618C	0133
619	1403
619-2	1403
619-3	2378
619-3(RCA)	2378
620	0015
620-1	0037
620-2	0037
620-56	0150
620C	0133
622	0015
622-1	0086
622-1(RCA)	0086
622C	0133
622H	OEM
623(RCA)	0042
623-1	0555
624	0015
624(RCA)	0919
624-0005	0196
624-0006	0196
624-0007	0196
624-0009	0015
624-0010	0015
624-0011	0143
624-1	0455
624C	0133
625-1	0079
625-1(RCA)	0086
626	0016
626-1	0016
626N002A	OEM
627-1	0037
628-3	0546
629-3	0378
629A02	0015
630-002	0143
630-002-801	0102
630-052	0015
630-076	0016
630-077	0170
630-079	0143
631-1	0126
631-3(SYLVANIA)	0126
632	OEM
632-1(SYLVANIA)	0546
632-3	0419
634	2064
634-1	0127
634H	OEM
635	0037
635-1	0212
635-1(RCA)	0349
635H	OEM
636H	OEM
637	0003
637-1	0074
637-1(RCA)	0074
638	0016
638-1	0086
638H	0178
638HJ	0178
639	0079
639(ZENITH)	0016
639CL	0086
639H	OEM
640-1(SYLVANIA)	0042
640H	OEM
641H	OEM
642-028	0143
642-068	0196
642-098	0123
642-102	0143
642-116	0050
642-117	0004
642-119	0143
642-126	0133
642-132	0143
642-147	0050
642-150	0004
642-151	0164
642-152	0222
642-173	0050
642-174	0016
642-176	0160
642-186	0644
642-199	0143
642-202	0050

DEVICE TYPE	REPL CODE
642-206	0085
642-207	0050
642-216	0276
642-217	0222
642-219	0015
642-221	0143
642-229	0127
642-230	0127
642-236	0025
642-242	0016
642-246	0016
642-254	0127
642-255	0002
642-260	0127
642-261	0161
642-264	0085
642-266	0455
642-268	0127
642-269	0127
642-270	0127
642-271	0265
642-272	0160
642-274	0127
642-275	0133
642-277	0208
642-279	0123
642-280	0030
642-281	0133
642-304	0229
642-306	0086
642-316	0085
642-319	0127
642AS4076-101	0127
643RLX	0786
644-1	0455
644-405E	0284
646H	OEM
647-1	0065
648	OEM
648HD	OEM
649-1	0065
649-3	5675
650	0143
650-1	OEM
650-105	0211
650-106	0211
650-107	0211
650-108	0211
650-109	0038
650-110	0015
650C	OEM
650C0	0372
650C1	0036
650C2	0036
650C3	OEM
650C4	OEM
650C5	0274
650C6	0274
650C7	OEM
650PBQ50	OEM
650PBQ60	OEM
650PBQ70	OEM
650PBQ80	OEM
650PBQ90	OEM
650PBQ100	OEM
650PBQ110	OEM
650PBQ120	OEM
651	0140
651-001C	0019
651-022A	0143
651-023A	0143
651C	OEM
651C0	0140
651C1	0140
651C2	0140
651C3	0140
651C4	0041
651C5	0041
651C6	0041
651C7	0041
651C8	0041
651C9	0253
651PDB40L20	OEM
651PDB40L25	OEM
651PDB50L20	OEM
651PDB50L25	OEM
651PDB60L20	OEM
651PDB60L25	OEM
651PDB80L20	OEM
651PDB80L25	OEM
651PDB80L30	OEM
651PDB100L25	OEM
651PDB100L30	OEM
651PDB110L25	OEM
651PDB120L25	OEM
651PDB120L30	OEM
651PDB130L30	OEM
651PDB140L30	OEM
651PDB160L30	OEM
652	0091
652-003A	0023
652-005A	0023
652-005B	0080
652-013A	0106
652-015B	0133
652C	OEM
652C0	0157
652C1	0253
652C2	0253

If replacement code is OEM, contact original manufacturer for replacement.

191

DEVICE TYPE	REPL CODE
652C3	0091
652C4	0091
652C5	0091
652C6	0091
652C7	0466
652C8	0466
652C9	OEM
653	OEM
653-010A	OEM
653-022A	1605
653-023A	1767
653-2	OEM
653-2F	OEM
653-3	OEM
653-3F	OEM
653-4	OEM
653-4F	OEM
653-5	OEM
653-503A	OEM
653C	OEM
653C0	OEM
653C1	0062
653C2	0062
653C3	0062
653C4	0062
653C5	OEM
653C6	0077
653C7	0077
653C8	OEM
653C9	0165
654-1	0321
654-1(SYLVANIA)	0321
654-202B	0631
654-215A	0631
654-222A	0398
654-401A	0030
654-404A	OEM
654-411B	0361
654C9	0057
655-60CP20	OEM
655-60MP20	OEM
655-CP4	OEM
655-MP4	OEM
655-MP5	OEM
655-NV-90C	OEM
655-NV-90C-P883	OEM
655-NV-90M	OEM
655C9	0064
655NV-60C	OEM
655NV-60C-P883	OEM
655NV-60M	OEM
655NV-60M-P883	OEM
655NV-90M-883	OEM
655NV-400C	OEM
655NV-400C-P883	OEM
655NV-400M	OEM
655NV-400M-883	OEM
656-1	0283
656-2	0556
656-136	0004
656-137	0004
656-138	0164
656-139	0004
656-141	0015
656-142	0143
657-010A	OEM
657H	OEM
658H	OEM
660-126	0016
660-127	0144
660-128	0086
660-131	0016
660-134	0198
660-145	0086
660-220	0016
660-221	0016
660-222	0016
660-224	0164
660-225	0016
660-227	0004
660-228	0208
660-230	0015
660B	0211
662-009R	0079
662-010E	0037
662-039C	OEM
662-048B	0079
662-048C	OEM
662HA	OEM
662N004S	0037
662N007B	0079
662N009S	0079
662N010I	0037
662N031B	6547
662N033C	0710
662N046A	OEM
662N047A	OEM
662N607C	OEM
662T26	OEM
662T28	OEM
662T30	OEM
662T32	OEM
662T34	OEM
663-1	OEM
663-3	OEM
664-015B	2969
664-016B	0728
664-409B	0111
664-410C	0111
664-410D	0111
664-412C	0191
664-413B	1136
664-420C	0224
664-423B	0006
664-614B	1136
664-615B	0111
664H	OEM
664N427B	OEM
665-1A5L	0050
665-2A5L	0208
665-4A5L	0595
665-833B	0431
665A-1-5L	0050
665B-1-5L	0136
665C-1-5L	0160
666/BL60	OEM
666-1	0037
666-1-A-5L	0004
666-2-A-5L	0004
666-3A-5L	0004
666T20	OEM
666T21	OEM
666T22	OEM
666T23	OEM
666T24	OEM
666TB19	OEM
667-004B	0683
667-008B	0212
667-009A	1202
667-012A	OEM
668-009A	2728
668-028B	1561
668-032A	OEM
668-033A	0514
668-037A	3436
668-045A	0176
668-056A	OEM
668-160B	OEM
668-606A	OEM
668-614A	0646
668-616A	1602
668TB7	OEM
668TB9	OEM
668TB11	OEM
668TB13	OEM
668TB15	OEM
669	0037
669-1	0637
669A464H01	1035
669A471H01	1417
669A492H01	0557
670HA	OEM
671A290H01	1812
671A291H01	0033
671A292H01	0081
671A293H01	0141
673-1	OEM
673-1S	OEM
673-2	OEM
673-2S	OEM
673-3	OEM
673-3S	OEM
673-4	OEM
673-4S	OEM
673-5	OEM
673-5S	OEM
673-6	OEM
673-6S	OEM
673-7	OEM
673-8	OEM
673-9	OEM
673-10	OEM
673-11	OEM
673-12	OEM
673-75	OEM
673-85	OEM
674-3A5L	0279
675-153	0164
675-154	0004
675-155	0004
675-156	0004
675-158	0143
675-206	0816
676-1	0326
676-1(DIO)	OEM
676-1S	OEM
676-2	OEM
676-2S	OEM
676-3	OEM
676-3S	OEM
676-4	OEM
676-4S	OEM
676-5	OEM
676-5S	OEM
676-6	OEM
676-6S	OEM
676-12	OEM
676-18	OEM
676-24	OEM
676-30	OEM
676-36	OEM
676-42	OEM
676-48	OEM
676-50	OEM
676-RS	OEM
676H	OEM
677A-1-5L	0435
677H	OEM
678-1	OEM
678-2	OEM
678-3	OEM
678-4	OEM
678-5	OEM
678-6	OEM
679-1	1674
679-1(DIO)	1633
679-2	1633
679-3	1663
679-4	1663
679-5	1663
679-6	1663
680-1	0007
680-1(DIO)	1633
680-1(IC)	3731
680-2	1633
680-3	OEM
680-4	OEM
680-5	OEM
680-6	OEM
681-1D	OEM
681-1N	OEM
681-1P	OEM
681-2D	OEM
681-2N	OEM
681-2P	OEM
681-3D	OEM
681-3N	OEM
681-3P	OEM
681-4D	OEM
681-4N	OEM
681-4P	OEM
681-5D	OEM
681-5N	OEM
681-5P	OEM
681-6D	OEM
681-6N	OEM
681-6P	OEM
682-1	OEM
682-2	OEM
682-3	OEM
682-4	OEM
682-5	OEM
682-6	OEM
683	OEM
683-1	OEM
683-2	OEM
683-3	OEM
683-4	OEM
683-5	OEM
683-6	OEM
684-1	2081
684-2	OEM
684-3	OEM
684-4	OEM
684-5	OEM
684-6	OEM
684-652423-1	0015
684A-1-5L	0160
686-0012	0086
686-0112	0086
686-0130	0086
686-0210	0178
686-0243	0103
686-143	0103
686-143A	0103
688-1	0058
688-10	OEM
688-12	OEM
688-15	OEM
688-18	OEM
688-20	OEM
688-25	OEM
688-255A	OEM
688B-1-5L	0050
688C	OEM
688C-1-5L	0279
689-1	OEM
689-1D	OEM
689-1N	OEM
689-1P	OEM
689-2D	OEM
689-2N	OEM
689-2P	OEM
689-3D	OEM
689-3N	OEM
689-3P	OEM
689-4D	OEM
689-4N	OEM
689-4P	OEM
689-5D	OEM
689-5N	OEM
689-5P	OEM
689-6D	OEM
689-6N	OEM
689-6P	OEM
690C092H88	0015
690L270H02	0160
690L297H01	0050
690L297H02	0160
690V02H69	0144
690V08H36	0079
690V010H40	0007
690V010H41	0144
690V010H42	0136
690V010H43	0030
690V028H28	0144
690V028H48	0144
690V028H49	0911
690V028H69	0007
690V028H89	0144
690V031H33	0015
690V034H29	0136
690V034H30	0004
690V034H31	0004
690V034H32	0143
690V034H39	0211
690V034H74	0143
690V037H91	0143
690V037H92	0469
690V038H22	0087
690V038H23	0196
690V039H17	1293
690V039H18	0769
690V039H22	0087
690V039H52	0015
690V039H54	0469
690V040H56	0050
690V040H57	0136
690V040H58	0136
690V040H59	0136
690V040H60	0136
690V040H61	0211
690V040H62	0211
690V040H63	0143
690V041H08	0015
690V043H62	0164
690V043H63	0164
690V047H54	0136
690V047H55	0136
690V047H56	0279
690V047H57	0279
690V047H58	0211
690V047H59	0004
690V047H60	0211
690V047H61	0143
690V047H97	0016
690V049H81	0144
690V052H23	0211
690V052H24	0211
690V052H50	0143
690V052H63	0050
690V052H68	0143
690V053H57	0015
690V054H20	0004
690V054H21	0211
690V056H27	0050
690V056H29	0050
690V056H30	0050
690V056H31	0050
690V056H32	0050
690V056H33	0004
690V056H34	0004
690V056H89	0136
690V056H90	0211
690V057H25	0050
690V057H27	0211
690V057H28	0211
690V057H59	0136
690V057H62	0136
690V059H20	0004
690V059H21	0164
690V059H52	0004
690V059H55	0004
690V059H63	0143
690V060H58	0144
690V060H59	0144
690V061H98	0211
690V061H99	0211
690V062H47	0004
690V063H14	0136
690V063H15	0136
690V063H16	0211
690V063H17	0211
690V063H50	0004
690V063H51	0211
690V066H44	0050
690V066H45	0136
690V066H46	0004
690V066H47	0004
690V066H48	0143
690V066H49	0136
690V066H89	0050
690V067H09	0143
690V067H35	0208
690V067H69	OEM
690V068H29	0136
690V068H30	0211
690V068H31	0211
690V068H32	0143
690V069H39	0015
690V070H49	0144
690V070H98	0144
690V073H59	0136
690V073H60	0143
690V073H61	0030
690V073H85	0136
690V075H62	0086
690V075H68	0144
690V077H34	0136
690V077H35	0136
690V077H36	0136
690V077H37	0211
690V077H73	0004
690V080H36	0007
690V080H37	0136
690V080H38	0233
690V080H39	0211
690V080H40	0136
690V080H41	0198
690V080H42	0969
690V080H43	0969
690V080H44	0211
690V080H45	0637
690V080H47	0015
690V080H49	0102
690V080H50	0102
690V080H51	0102
690V080H52	0015
690V080H53	0287
690V080H54	0087
690V080H91	0015
690V081H07	0144
690V081H08	0050
690V081H09	0160
690V081H40	0276
690V081H91	0102
690V081H92	0002
690V081H96	0208
690V081H97	0085
690V082H40	0015
690V082H47	0164
690V083H89	0143
690V084H60	0136
690V084H61	0004
690V084H62	0016
690V084H63	0004
690V084H94	0144
690V084H95	0144
690V084H96	0144
690V085	0164
690V085H42	0136
690V085H44	0164
690V086H39	0211
690V086H51	0016
690V086H52	0144
690V086H86	0037
690V086H87	0144
690V086H88	0016
690V086H89	0126
690V086H90	0086
690V086H91	0015
690V086H92	0015
690V086H94	0007
690V086H95	0007
690V086H96	0144
690V088H20	0133
690V088H44	0144
690V088H45	0144
690V088H46	0127
690V088H47	0127
690V088H48	0144
690V088H49	0127
690V088H50	0016
690V088H51	0016
690V088H52	0004
690V089H46	0127
690V089H86	0127
690V089H89	0016
690V089H90	0004
690V089H91	0015
690V092H52	0016
690V092H54	0016
690V092H81	0016
690V092H84	0016
690V092H85	0143
690V092H88	0229
690V092H96	0016
690V092H97	0016
690V094H17	0103
690V094H18	0004
690V094H20	0004
690V094H21	0016
690V094H35	0015
690V097H59	0004
690V097H62	0016
690V098H48	0016
690V098H49	0016
690V098H50	0016
690V098H51	0222
690V098H52	0143
690V098H53	0015
690V099H59	0164
690V099H79	0016
690V0103H27	0016
690V06199	0279
690V38H25	1024
690V68H32	0143
690V73H60	0143
690V102H39	0208
690V102H40	0133
690V102H71	0016
690V102H72	0030
690V102H96	0136
690V103H23	0144
690V103H24	0144
690V103H25	0144
690V103H26	0144
690V103H27	0144
690V103H28	0127
690V103H29	0079
690V103H30	0086
690V103H31	0016
690V103H32	0079
690V103H33	0016
690V103H53	0137
690V103H54	0143
690V104H53	0004
690V104H54	0004
690V105H19	0151
690V105H-21	0050
690V105H21	0136
690V105H-22	0079
690V105H22	1471
690V105H-24	0136
690V105H24	0004
690V105H-25	0079
690V105H25	0076
690V105H26	0136
690V105H27	0284
690V105H28	1136
690V105H29	1136
690V105H30	0030
690V105H31	0015
690V105H32	0012
690V109H44	0015
690V109H46	0127
690V109H72	0030
690V110H30	0144
690V110H31	0144
690V110H32	0144
690V110H33	0144
690V110H34	0086
690V110H36	0086
690V110H55	0126
690V110H88	0143
690V110H89	0555
690V111H63	0030
690V114H29	0144
690V114H30	0016
690V114H31	0144
690V114H33	0016
690V114H36	0015
690V116H19	0144
690V116H20	0127
690V116H21	0016
690V116H22	0321
690V116H23	0037
690V116H24	0086
690V116H25	0455
690V116H26	0161
690V116H40	0137
690V116H41	0015
690V118H57	0133
690V118H58	0015
690V118H59	0144
690V118H60	0037
690V118H61	0037
690V118H62	0004
690V119H13	0030
690V119H14	0015
690V119H15	0133
690V119H54	0164
690V119H94	0136
690V119H95	0050
690V119H96	0050
690V119H97	0050
690V120H89	0079
690V037H91	0143
692-0014-00	OEM
692-0016-00	2840
692-0020-00	3395
693EP	0016
693FS	0016
693G	0016
693GT	0016
694D	0016
694E	0016
695-1	OEM
695-2	OEM
695-3	OEM
695-4	OEM
695-5	2856
695-6	OEM
695C	OEM
695M	OEM
696-1	OEM
696-2	OEM
696-3	OEM
696-4	OEM
696-5	OEM
696-6	OEM
697-1	OEM
697-2	OEM
697-3	OEM
697-4	OEM
697-5	OEM
697-6	OEM
697-15CP2	OEM
697-CP4	OEM
697NV-400C	OEM
697NV-400C-P883	OEM
697NV-400M	OEM
697NV-400M-P883	OEM
698-1	OEM
698-2	OEM
698-3	OEM
698-4	OEM
698-5	OEM
698-6	OEM
698V102H39	0038
699	0016
700	OEM
700-04	0321
700-1	OEM
700-2	OEM
700-3	OEM
700-4	OEM
700-5	OEM
700-6	OEM
700-110	0086
700-113	0103
700-133	0037
700-134	0079
700-135	0079
700-136	0126
700-137	0015
700-154	0284
700-155	0111
700-156	0079
700-159	0012
700-325	0284
700A858-249	OEM
700A858-285	0015
700A858-286	0015
700A858-318	0076
700A858-319	0076
700A858-322	0133
700A858-328	0111
700M	OEM
700PA50	4085
700PA60	4085
700PA80	1714
700PA100	1714
700PA110	1714
700PA120	1714
700PA130	OEM
700PA140	OEM
700PA150	OEM
700PA160	OEM
700PA170	OEM
700PA180	OEM
700PA190	OEM
700PA200	OEM
700PA210	OEM
700PBQ10	OEM
700PBQ20	OEM
700PBQ30	OEM
700PBQ40	OEM
700PBQ50	OEM
700PBQ60	OEM
700PK50	4085
700PK60	4085
700PK80	1714
700PK100	1714
700PK120	1714
700PK140	OEM
700PK150	OEM
700PK160	OEM
700PK180	OEM
700PK200	OEM
700PK210	OEM
700PK220	OEM
700PK230	OEM
700PK240	OEM
700PK250	OEM
700PK260	OEM
700PK270	OEM
700PK280	OEM
700PK290	OEM
700PK300	OEM
700PKL160S686	OEM
700PKL160T60	OEM
700PKL160T606	OEM
700PKL160T626	OEM
700PKL160T663	OEM
700PKL160T673	OEM
700PKL160T683	OEM
700PKL180S686	OEM
700PKL180T60	OEM
700PKL180T606	OEM
700PKL180T626	OEM
700PKL180T663	OEM
700PKL180T673	OEM
700PKL180T683	OEM
700PKL190S686	OEM
700PKL190T60	OEM
700PKL190T606	OEM
700PKL190T626	OEM
700PKL190T663	OEM
700PKL190T673	OEM
700PKL190T683	OEM
700PKL200S686	OEM
700PKL200T60	OEM
700PKL200T606	OEM
700PKL200T626	OEM
700PKL200T663	OEM
700PKL200T673	OEM
700PKL200T683	OEM
700PKL210S686	OEM
700PKL210T60	OEM
700PKL210T606	OEM
700PKL210T626	OEM
700PKL210T663	OEM
700PKL210T673	OEM
700PKL210T683	OEM
700PKL220S686	OEM
700PKL220T60	OEM
700PKL220T606	OEM
700PKL220T626	OEM
700PKL220T663	OEM
700PKL220T673	OEM
700PKL220T683	OEM
700U	OEM

If replacement code is OEM, contact original manufacturer for replacement.

DEVICE TYPE	REPL CODE
700UM	OEM
701	OEM
701-1	OEM
701-2	OEM
701-3	OEM
701-4	OEM
701-5	OEM
701-6	OEM
701F6S	OEM
701F8S	OEM
701F10S	OEM
701F12S	OEM
701F14S	OEM
701F16S	OEM
701F18S	OEM
702-810	0196
703-056-(4)	0079
703-1	0086
703-2	0086
703A	OEM
703B	0086
703C	OEM
703D	OEM
703F	OEM
703H	OEM
703PJA60	OEM
703PJA80	OEM
703PJA100	OEM
703PJA120	OEM
703PJA140	OEM
703PJA160	OEM
704-15K36	OEM
704-15K36T	OEM
704-34	OEM
704-34A	OEM
704-34B	OEM
704-45A	OEM
704-56A	OEM
704-190A	OEM
704-1549	OEM
705-600007	0588
705A	OEM
706-1	OEM
707	2969
708-1	OEM
708-2	OEM
708-6	OEM
708-13	OEM
709CE	1291
710	0015
710-0	OEM
710-0300-015	OEM
710-0300-025	OEM
710-0300-075	OEM
710-0301-015	OEM
710-0301-025	OEM
710-0301-075	OEM
710-0302-015	OEM
710-0302-025	OEM
710-0302-075	OEM
710-0304-015	OEM
710-0304-025	OEM
710-0304-075	OEM
710-0305-015	OEM
710-0305-025	OEM
710-0305-075	OEM
710-1	3568
710-2	OEM
710-3	OEM
710A	1017
710AR	0496
710B	1017
710BR	0496
710C	1017
710CE	1786
710CR	0496
710D	1017
710DR	0496
710E	1017
710ER	0496
710F	1017
710FR	0496
710H	1030
710HR	1766
710K	1030
710KR	1766
710M	1030
710MR	1766
710P	1040
710PR	1778
710S	1040
710SR	1778
710V	1040
710VR	1778
710Z	1040
710ZR	1778
711	OEM
711-1	OEM
711-6	OEM
713-2	OEM
713A	0315
713AR	0267
713B	0315
713BR	0267
713C	0315
713CR	0267
713D	0315
713DR	0267
713F	0315
713FR	0267
713H	0315
713HR	0267
713K	0315
713KR	0267
713M	0315
713MR	0267
713PC	OEM
714A	0315
714AR	0267
714B	0315
714BR	0267
714C	0315
714CR	0267
714D	0315
714DR	0267
714F	0315
714FR	0267
714H	0315
714HR	0267
714K	0315
714KR	0267
714M	0315
714MR	0267
715EN	0016
715FB	0127
715HC	1545
717A	1017
717B	1017
717C	1017
717D	1017
717E	1017
717F	1017
717H	1030
717K	1030
717M	1030
717P	1040
717S	1040
717V	1040
717Z	1040
718-1	OEM
719-1	OEM
719H	OEM
720-35019	0211
720DC	1411
722	OEM
723	0026
723A/B	OEM
723BE	1183
723C	0026
723CE	1183
723CJ	0026
724	OEM
724C	0191
724D	0191
725A	OEM
725H	OEM
726B	OEM
726C	OEM
729-3	0086
730	OEM
730-6001	OEM
730-6002	OEM
730-6004	OEM
730-6005	OEM
730-6006	OEM
730-6007	OEM
730-6009	OEM
730-6010	OEM
730-6011	OEM
730-6012	OEM
730-6014	OEM
730-6016	OEM
730-6020	OEM
730-6023	OEM
730-6025	OEM
730-6029	OEM
730-6030	OEM
730-6031	OEM
733-1	OEM
733W00024	1812
733W00025	1035
733W00026	2086
733W00027	1820
733W00028	0141
733W00029	0557
733W00030	0354
733W00039	1199
733W00042	0232
733W00043	0692
733W00048	1824
733W00049	1833
733W00050	0337
733W00064	0357
733W00065	0507
733W00067	1303
733W00068	1358
733W00069	1150
733W00076	1915
733W00126	0893
733W00133	0564
733W00183	1484
733W00211	0215
734EU	0321
735	OEM
735DAC	OEM
736	OEM
737	0079
737(ZENITH)	0016
737-1-1	OEM
737-1-2	OEM
737-1-3	OEM
737-1-4	OEM
737-1-5	OEM
739	0687
739-0261-601	OEM
739-0261-602	OEM
739-0361-601	OEM
739-0361-602	OEM
739-0461-601	OEM
739-0461-602	OEM
739-0561-601	OEM
739-0561-602	OEM
739-0661-601	OEM
739-0661-602	OEM
739-0761-601	OEM
739-0761-602	OEM
739-0861-601	OEM
739-0861-602	OEM
739-0961-601	OEM
739-0961-602	OEM
739-2-1	OEM
739-2-2	OEM
739-2-3	OEM
739-2-4	OEM
739-2-5	OEM
739-3-1	OEM
739-3-2	OEM
739-3-3	OEM
739-3-4	OEM
739-3-5	OEM
739-4-1	OEM
739-4-2	OEM
739-4-3	OEM
739-4-4	OEM
739-4-5	OEM
739-52-1	OEM
739-52-2	OEM
739-52-3	OEM
739-52-4	OEM
739-52-5	OEM
739-53-1	OEM
739-53-3	OEM
739-53-4	OEM
739-53-5	OEM
739-54-1	OEM
739-54-2	OEM
739-54-3	OEM
739-54-4	OEM
739-54-5	OEM
739-1061-601	OEM
739-1061-602	OEM
739DC	0687
739H01	0016
740	OEM
740-56-2-1	OEM
740-56-5-1	OEM
740-937-120	1012
740-1003-150	2142
740-2001-110	0351
740-2001-306	2247
740-2001-307	0696
740-2002-111	0659
740-2003-150	2142
740-2007-120	1012
740-3006	OEM
740-3012	OEM
740-3014	OEM
740-5853-350	OEM
740-5903-301	1206
740-8120-160	2546
740-8160-190	0574
740-9000-554	1469
740-9000-566	0428
740-9000-754	1469
740-9003-301	1206
740-9003-350	0412
740-9007-046	1383
740-9007-205	1044
740-9011-322	4031
740-9016-105	0438
740-9017-092	4477
740-9037-120	1012
740-9037-204	3332
740-9607-205	1044
741	0308
741-3-1	OEM
741-3-2	OEM
741-3-3	OEM
741-3-4	OEM
741-3-5	OEM
741-4-1	OEM
741-4-2	OEM
741-4-3	OEM
741-4-4	OEM
741-4-5	OEM
741C	0308
742	0143
742-1	0546
742-58-2-1	OEM
742-58-5-1	OEM
743	0233
744	0086
745-0005	OEM
745-0007	OEM
745-0008	OEM
745-0009	OEM
745-0017	OEM
745-0018	OEM
745H	OEM
746H	OEM
746HC	0748
748	0079
748(ZENITH)	0016
749-1501	OEM
749-1601	OEM
749-1701	OEM
749-1801	OEM
749-1901	OEM
749-2001	OEM
749-8160-190	0574
749DHC	2530
750	OEM
750-045	0178
750-137	0211
750-138	0211
750-139	0211
750-140	0211
750-141	0015
750-35019	0004
750A858-285	0023
750A858-319	0079
750A858-328	0111
750A858-448	0042
750C838-123	0016
750C838-124	0016
750C838-125	0016
750D858-211	0071
750D858-212	0016
750D858-213	0144
750H	OEM
750M63-104	0050
750M63-105	0164
750M63-115	0004
750M63-116	0050
750M63-117	0050
750M63-119	0016
750M63-120	0016
750M63-146	0016
750M63-147	0164
750M63-148	0164
750M63-149	0015
751-2001-212	0015
751-4000-88	0143
751-6300-001	0015
751H	OEM
752-1	OEM
752RT	OEM
753-0100-699	1257
753-0101-047	0144
753-0101-226	0555
753-0160-699	1257
753-1303-801	0284
753-1372-100	0076
753-1644-100	0111
753-1828-001	0016
753-2000-003	0016
753-2000-004	0016
753-2000-006	0178
753-2000-007	0151
753-2000-008	0016
753-2000-009	0016
753-2000-011	0016
753-2000-100	0111
753-2000-101	0037
753-2000-107	0086
753-2000-460	0127
753-2000-463	0816
753-2000-535	0224
753-2000-710	0144
753-2000-711	0376
753-2000-735	0016
753-2000-870	0016
753-2000-871	0016
753-2001-173	0042
753-2100-001	0016
753-2100-002	0222
753-2100-008	0016
753-3000-535	0224
753-4000-010	0111
753-4000-011	0016
753-4000-024	0321
753-4000-101	0016
753-4000-537	0016
753-4000-668	0127
753-4000-929	0127
753-4001-474	1004
753-4001-932	0042
753-4004-248	0037
753-5751-359	0151
753-5851-359	0151
753-6000--002	OEM
753-6000-002	1211
753-6000-019	0683
753-8400-230	0111
753-8500-380	0076
753-8510-470	0086
753-9000-019	0683
753-9000-839	0076
753-9000-922	0931
753-9001-674	1060
753-9001-675	0076
753-9010-021	1659
753-9010-235	0042
753-9020-784	1136
753-9050-785	1136
753R	OEM
754-0102-139	0005
754-1003-030	0143
754-2000-001	0133
754-2000-002	0015
754-2000-005	0015
754-2000-009	0143
754-2000-011	0133
754-2009-150	0133
754-2509-150	0133
754-2720-007	0062
754-2720-021	0133
754-2900-105	OEM
754-2900-106	OEM
754-4000-088	0143
754-4000-188	0143
754-4000-410	0143
754-4000-553	0755
754-5000-021	0015
754-5700-282	0244
754-5710-219	0244
754-5750-282	0244
754-5750-283	0133
754-5750-284	0015
754-5900-090	0143
754-8130-140	0005
754-9000-082	0165
754-9000-351	0030
754-9000-473	0133
754-9001-124	0139
754-9002-687	0715
754-9030-009	1075
754-9052-473	0133
754-9053-090	0012
754R	OEM
755N	OEM
755P	OEM
756	0015
756-1	OEM
756H	OEM
757N	OEM
757P	OEM
759H	OEM
759P	OEM
760H	OEM
761	OEM
762-2	0061
765-1	OEM
767	0079
767(ZENITH)	0016
767CL	0016
767H	OEM
768	2174
768-1	OEM
770-045	0042
770A	1017
770B	1017
770DC	1017
770D	1017
770E	1017
770F	1017
770H	1030
770K	1030
770M	1030
770P	1040
770S	1040
770V	1040
770Z	1040
771-12	OEM
771-14	OEM
771-16	OEM
771A	0496
771B	0496
771C	0496
771D	0496
771E	0496
771F	0496
771H	1766
771HD	OEM
771HDS	OEM
771K	1766
771M	1766
771P	1778
771S	1778
771V	1778
772-724	0211
772A	0127
772B	0127
772B1	0127
772BJ	0127
772BL	0127
772BM	0127
772BN	0127
772BY	0127
772C	0127
772CC	0127
772D	0127
772D1	0127
772DC	0127
772DG	0127
772E	0127
772EH	0127
772F	0127
772FE	0127
772G	0127
773	0079
773(ZENITH)	0016
773-3000-535	OEM
773CL	0086
773RED	0144
774	0150
774(ZENITH)	0037
774CL	0126
774H	OEM
775-1	0396
775-1(SYLVANIA)	0396
775BRN	0144
776-1	0126
776-1(SYLVANIA)	0037
776-2	0037
776-3	0037
776GRN	0016
777-2	0023
777R	OEM
778-1	5281
779-1	OEM
779BLU	0144
780-4	OEM
780-6	OEM
780-7	5297
780DA	OEM
780WHT	0016
781-1	1379
781D	OEM
781H	OEM
783B	OEM
783D	OEM
783F	OEM
783H	OEM
783K	OEM
783M	OEM
783RED	0144
783S	OEM
783Z	OEM
783ZD	OEM
783ZH	OEM
783ZM	OEM
783ZS	OEM
783ZZ	OEM
784A	OEM
784B	OEM
784C	OEM
784D	OEM
784E	OEM
784F	OEM
784H	OEM
784K	OEM
784M	OEM
784ORN	0144
784S	OEM
784Z	OEM
784ZB	OEM
784ZD	OEM
785H	OEM
785YEL	0016
786	0144
786H	OEM
787BLU	0144
788A	1017
788AR	0496
788B	1017
788BR	0496
788C	1017
788CR	0496
788D	1017
788DR	0496
788F	1017
788FR	0496
788H	1030
788HR	1766
788K	1030
788KR	1766
788M	1030
788MR	1766
788S	1040
788SR	1778
788Z	1040
788ZR	1778
790	OEM
790H	OEM
791	0016
792-238	0015
792-286	0211
792-287	0211
792-288	0211
792-289	0211
792-290	0211
792-292	0143
792-414	0023
792H	OEM
796H	OEM
800	OEM
800-000-025	0190
800-002-00	0123
800-003-00	0143
800-004-00	0137
800-005-00	0143
800-006-00	0015
800-007-00	0196
800-008-00	0469
800-0016	1339
800-010-00	0087
800-011-00	1293
800-012-00	0769
800-013-00	0015
800-014-00	0015
800-014-01	0015
800-016-00	0133
800-017-00	0015
800-018-00	0087
800-018-02	0087
800-020-00	0143
800-021-00	0133
800-022-00	0143
800-023-00	0137
800-024-00	0015
800-028-00	0416
800-029-30	0102
800-030-00	0025
800-032-00	0015
800-034-00	0205
800-035-00	0137
800-036-00	0133
800-037-00	0087
800-038-00	0015
800-039-00	0143
800-040-00	0133
800-041-00	0015
800-042-00	0133
800-043-00	0087
800-045-00	3575
800-046-00	0015
800-050-00	0087
800-051-00	0087
800-01300-504	0015
800-01400	0015
800-1	OEM
800-2	OEM
800-3	OEM
800-4	OEM
800-5	OEM
800-6	OEM
800-122	0142
800-158	0142
800-172	0142
800-180	0142
800-181	0142
800-196	3004
800-198	OEM
800-203	0142
800-204	0142
800-205	0164
800-208	2839
800-219	2839
800-245	4100
800-250-102	0198
800-253	0265
800-256	0142
800-256(METAL)	0142
800-256(PLASTIC)	0275
800-270	1647
800-282	0102
800-284	0126
800-289	1647
800-292	0126
800-294	4100
800-305	4100
800-310	2839
800-310(CP)	OEM
800-310CP	0208
800-315	4100
800-321	0142
800-328	4100
800-329	0085
800-356	OEM
800-362	3687
800-364	OEM
800-366	3687
800-398	OEM
800-401	0142
800-501-00	0076
800-501-01	0016
800-501-02	0016
800-501-03	0016
800-501-04	0016
800-501-11	0016
800-501-22	0016
800-502-00	0004
800-503-00	2839
800-504-00	0136
800-505-00	0164
800-506-00	0595
800-507-00	0160
800-508-00	0016
800-509-00	0076
800-510-00	0103
800-510-01	0103
800-511-00	0126
800-512-00	0086
800-513-00	0086
800-514-00	0016
800-515-00	0086
800-516-00	0126
800-517-00	0143
800-518-00	0160
800-521-01	0016
800-521-02	0086
800-521-03	0086
800-522-01	0016
800-522-02	0016
800-522-03	0086
800-522-04	0016
800-523-01	0037
800-523-02	0037
800-524-02	0103
800-524-02A	0103
800-524-03	0103
800-524-03A	0103

If replacement code is OEM, contact original manufacturer for replacement.

193

DEVICE TYPE	REPL CODE
800-524-04A	0103
800-525-03	0126
800-525-04	0037
800-525-04A	0103
800-526-00	0016
800-527-00	0037
800-528	0208
800-528-00	0208
800-529-00	0016
800-530-00	0016
800-530-01	0016
800-533-00	0042
800-534-00	0016
800-534-00(DIO)	0030
800-534-00(XSTR)	0079
800-534-01	0016
800-535-00	0321
800-535-01	0321
800-536-00	0144
800-537-01	0208
800-537-02	1506
800-537-03	0164
800-538-00	0016
800-544-00	0016
800-544-00(U.J.T.)	1659
800-544-10	0016
800-544-20	0016
800-544-30	0016
800-546-00	0042
800-547-00	0037
800-548-00	0016
800-550-00	0074
800-550-10	0637
800-552-00	0334
800-557-00	0007
800-601	OEM
800-608	OEM
800-619	2460
800-669B	3863
800-670	OEM
800-670B	4020
800-671B	OEM
800-672	1371
800-672-B	OEM
800-763	0065
800-764	0065
800-765	OEM
800-766	OEM
800-767	1581
800-771	0919
800-791	3805
800-817	OEM
800-818	6088
800-50100	0016
800-50300	0208
800-50400	0050
800-50500	0136
800-50600	0208
800-50700	0160
800-51500	0016
800-51600	0126
800-52102	0016
800-52202	0016
800-52302	0016
800-52402	0103
800-52600	0016
800-52700	0126
800-52800	0208
800-53001	0198
800-53300	0086
800-53400	0016
800-53600	0144
800-53702	1506
800EXD25	OEM
800EXD26	OEM
800EXH21	OEM
800FXD25	OEM
800FXD26	OEM
800HB1U	5633
800HB2U	5633
800HB3U	5633
800HB4U	5633
800HB6U	5633
800P12H	OEM
800PDB10	OEM
800PDB20	OEM
800PDB30	OEM
800PDB40	OEM
800PDB50	OEM
800PDB60	OEM
800PIN-RM	OEM
800PV-RM	OEM
800UD25	OEM
800UD26	OEM
800YD25	OEM
800YD26	OEM
800YKD25	OEM
800YKD26	OEM
801	OEM
801-04900	0136
801-05200	0136
801-05300	0136
801-1	OEM
801-2	OEM
801-3	OEM
801-4	OEM
801-5	OEM
801-6	OEM
801B	0016

DEVICE TYPE	REPL CODE
801F8H	OEM
801F12H	OEM
801F16H	OEM
801F20H	OEM
801F25H	OEM
801F30H	OEM
801PDB60B	2146
801PDB80B	0474
801PDB100B	0474
801PDB120	0474
801PDB120B	0474
801PDB140	OEM
801PDB140B	OEM
801PDB160	OEM
801PDB180	OEM
801PDB200	OEM
801PDB210	OEM
801PDB220	OEM
801PDB230	OEM
801PDB240	OEM
801PDB250	OEM
801PJA250	OEM
801PJA300	OEM
801PJA400	OEM
802	OEM
802-0027	0183
802-0038	1828
802-0245	0458
802-0260	5859
802-0266	0587
802-05400	0004
802-05600	0004
802-1	OEM
802-2	OEM
802-3	OEM
802-4	OEM
802-22631U	0004
802-36400	0004
802-36430	0004
802-43900	0004
802CPY	OEM
803-0073	1528
803-1	OEM
803-2	OEM
803-3	OEM
803-4	OEM
803-18250	0016
803-37390	0016
803-38030	0144
803-38040	0144
803-39430	0144
803-39440	0144
803-83840	0144
803-83930	0144
803-83940	0016
803-89910	0016
803-89930	0016
804	0016
804-1D	OEM
804-1N	OEM
804-1P	OEM
804-2D	OEM
804-2N	OEM
804-2P	OEM
804-3D	OEM
804-3N	OEM
804-3P	OEM
804-4D	OEM
804-4N	OEM
804-4P	OEM
804-14120	0103
804-14130	0103
804-21980	0016
804A765-2	0916
805-1060	0143
805-10600	0143
807-1	0086
808-3	OEM
808-206	0015
808-304	0004
808-305	0004
808-306	0004
808-307	0004
808-308	0004
808-309	0208
808-310	0004
808-311	0004
808-312	0143
809-1	OEM
809A	OEM
809B	OEM
809B-FLAG	0217
809B-FLEX	0217
809C	OEM
809D	OEM
809D-FLAG	0217
809D-FLEX	0217
809E	OEM
809F	OEM
809F-FLAG	0217
809F-FLEX	0217
809H-FLAG	0217
809H-FLEX	0217
809K	OEM
809K-FLAG	0217
809K-FLEX	0217
809M-FLAG	0217
809M-FLEX	0217
809P	OEM

DEVICE TYPE	REPL CODE
809S	OEM
809S-FLAG	0653
809S-FLEX	0463
810	2728
810-4	OEM
810-6	OEM
810-8	OEM
812H	OEM
813H	OEM
814	OEM
814H	OEM
815-003	0735
815-181D	0211
815-1810	0004
818WHT	0016
819H	OEM
820H	OEM
821	OEM
821CXYA	OEM
821CXYB	OEM
821CXYC	OEM
821CXYD	OEM
822	0016
822-1	0015
822-1(SYLVANIA)	0007
822-2	1219
822-3	0015
822-4	0015
822-5	1219
822A	0016
822ABLU	0016
822B	0016
823-1	OEM
823B	0016
823WHT	0016
824-09501	0016
824-1	0086
824-1(SYLVANIA)	0008
824-10300	0126
825CPY	OEM
826	0042
826-1	2022
826BAY	OEM
827BRN	0016
828GRN	0016
829	0037
829A	0037
829B	0037
829C	0037
829D	0037
829DE	0037
829E	0037
829F	0037
830	0004
830H	OEM
832-1	OEM
832H	OEM
833	0037
833-3	OEM
835-300-0002	0720
835H	OEM
837-1	OEM
837H	OEM
838-1	OEM
838H	OEM
839H	OEM
840PE2-98	OEM
840XY2-35SC	OEM
845H	OEM
846H	OEM
848	4103
848HA	OEM
848HD	OEM
848HDS	OEM
850PA50	6177
850PA60	6177
850PA80	6029
850PA100	1714
850PA110	1714
850PA120	1714
850PA130	OEM
850PA140	OEM
850PA150	OEM
850PA160	OEM
850PA170	OEM
850PA180	OEM
850PA190	OEM
850PA200	OEM
850PK50	4085
850PK60	4085
850PK80	1714
850PK100	1714
850PK120	1714
850PK140	OEM
850PK150	OEM
850PK160	OEM
850PK180	OEM
850PK200	OEM
850PK210	OEM
850PK220	OEM
850PK230	OEM
850PK240	OEM
851-0372-130	0015
851H	OEM
851PDE40L20	OEM
851PDE40L25	OEM
851PDE40L30	OEM
851PDE50L20	OEM
851PDE50L25	OEM

DEVICE TYPE	REPL CODE
851PDE50L30	OEM
851PDE60L20	OEM
851PDE60L25	OEM
851PDE60L30	OEM
851PDE80L20	OEM
851PDE80L25	OEM
851PDE80L30	OEM
851PDE100L20	OEM
851PDE100L25	OEM
851PDE100L30	OEM
851PDE120L20	OEM
851PDE120L25	OEM
851PDE120L30	OEM
851PDE130L20	OEM
851PDE130L25	OEM
851PDE130L30	OEM
851PDE140L20	OEM
851PDE140L25	OEM
851PDE140L30	OEM
851PDE160L20	OEM
851PDE160L25	OEM
851PDE160L30	OEM
852-92-43	0455
853-0300-632	0016
853-0300-634	1257
853-0300-643	0786
853-0300-644	0111
853-0300-900	0016
853-0300-923	0016
853-0301-096	0386
853-0301-317	0155
853-0373-110	0016
854-0372-020	0015
854H	OEM
856H	OEM
857-1	OEM
858GS	0016
859GK	0111
860-022-01	0130
860-1GI	OEM
861H	OEM
862-1	OEM
863-1	OEM
863-254B	0133
863-567B	0133
863-776B	0133
863H	OEM
866-6	0103
866-6(BENDIX)	0103
866H	OEM
868-1	OEM
868A-01	OEM
868A-02	OEM
868A-09	OEM
868A-10	OEM
868A-11	OEM
868A-12	OEM
868A-14	OEM
868A-15	OEM
868A-16	OEM
868A-18	OEM
868A-20	OEM
868A-21	OEM
868A-22	OEM
868A-23A	OEM
868A-23B	OEM
868A-23C	OEM
868A-24A	OEM
868A-25	OEM
868A-27	OEM
868A-32	OEM
868A-33	OEM
868A-40	OEM
868A-41	OEM
868A-58	OEM
868A-59	OEM
868A-60	OEM
868A-61	OEM
868A-62	OEM
868A-63	OEM
868A-64	OEM
868A-65	OEM
868A-67	OEM
868A-68	OEM
868A-69	OEM
868A-70	OEM
868A-71	OEM
868A-80	OEM
868G-50	OEM
868G-51	OEM
868G-55	OEM
868G-56	OEM
868G-57	OEM
869-1	OEM
869H	OEM
870H	OEM
873-1	OEM
874H	OEM
876H	OEM
880	OEM
880-1	OEM
880-2	OEM
880-101-00	0627
880-102-00	2593
880-103-00	1063
880-207-000	0015
880-250-001	0160
880-250-010	0160
880-250-011	0161

DEVICE TYPE	REPL CODE
880-250-102	0016
880-250-107	0126
880-250-108	0016
880-250-109	0016
880-250108	0111
881-1	OEM
881-250-102	0016
881-250-107	0126
881-250-108	0016
881-250-109	0016
881-250108	0111
881H	OEM
882-1	OEM
884-250-001	0160
884-250-010	0160
884-250-011	0161
885-1	OEM
885B	OEM
886	OEM
886-1	OEM
887	OEM
895	0079
895-1	OEM
898	1822
900C	OEM
900HC	3384
901-000-6-51	0004
901-5553-7	0755
901F	0079
901SS1-07SC	OEM
902	OEM
902-000-2-04	1212
902-000-8-04	0076
902-001-7-18	1136
902-002-3-06	0376
902-003-0-012	0076
902-003-0-12	0076
902-003-3-17	0076
902-003-6-006	1212
902-003-6-06	1212
902-2	OEM
903	0007
903-00390	0143
903-00391	0549
903-00393	0133
903-00394	0015
903-1B	0030
903-3	0016
903-3G	0016
903-8B	0123
903-9B	0143
903-10B	0143
903-11	0030
903-12B	0143
903-13	OEM
903-13B	0229
903-14B	0015
903-15B	0015
903-16	OEM
903-16B	0143
903-17	0087
903-17A	0087
903-17B	0087
903-17C	0087
903-18	0143
903-18B	0143
903-19B	0030
903-20	0133
903-22	OEM
903-23	0143
903-23A	0143
903-23B	0143
903-23C	0143
903-23D	0143
903-23E	0143
903-25B	0133
903-26B	0188
903-27	0019
903-27B	0019
903-28	OEM
903-28B	0015
903-29B	0143
903-30B	0143
903-32	0015
903-33	OEM
903-34	0143
903-34A	0143
903-34B	0143
903-34C	0143
903-34D	0143
903-34E	0143
903-35	OEM
903-35B	0071
903-36	0071
903-36A	0071
903-36B	0071
903-36C	0071
903-36D	0071
903-36F	0071
903-37B	0143
903-39	0015
903-40	0143
903-41B	0133
903-42	OEM
903-42B	0133
903-43#	OEM
903-43B	0143
903-45B	0143
903-46	0015

DEVICE TYPE	REPL CODE
903-47	0755
903-47B	0715
903-48	OEM
903-48B	0133
903-49	0015
903-49B	0015
903-50	0015
903-51	0143
903-51B	0143
903-52	0015
903-52B	0015
903-54	OEM
903-54B	0143
903-56	OEM
903-58	0133
903-58B	0133
903-59	0015
903-63	OEM
903-65	0143
903-65B	0143
903-67	0549
903-67B	0030
903-68	0015
903-68B	0102
903-69	0015
903-69B	0015
903-70	OEM
903-71B	0030
903-72	OEM
903-72B	0133
903-73	0015
903-73B	0053
903-77	OEM
903-79B	0015
903-80	OEM
903-80B	0030
903-82	0133
903-82B	0133
903-83	OEM
903-83B	0143
903-84B	0133
903-85B	0030
903-86	OEM
903-91	0015
903-92	OEM
903-92B	0143
903-93	OEM
903-95B	0133
903-96B	0030
903-97	OEM
903-97B	0137
903-99	0549
903-99B	0030
903-100B	0133
903-101	OEM
903-101B	0030
903-102	0015
903-103	OEM
903-103B	0143
903-104B	0015
903-105	OEM
903-105B	0015
903-108	0143
903-108B	0143
903-109	0015
903-110B	0005
903-112B	0133
903-113B	0143
903-114	OEM
903-114B	0143
903-115	OEM
903-116B	0133
903-117	0015
903-117B	0015
903-118	0133
903-118B	0133
903-119	0012
903-119B	0012
903-120B	0157
903-121	0133
903-121B	0133
903-123B	0030
903-125	0015
903-126	OEM
903-128	OEM
903-129	0015
903-130	OEM
903-133	0133
903-136B	0133
903-137	0549
903-137B	0030
903-138	OEM
903-139	OEM
903-140	OEM
903-141B	0030
903-142	OEM
903-142B	1978
903-146	0015
903-149	0015
903-150	OEM
903-152	OEM
903-154	0015
903-155	OEM
903-156	0015
903-156B	0015
903-157	0015
903-163	0030
903-163B	0623
903-164	0015

DEVICE TYPE	REPL CODE
903-164B	0015
903-166	OEM
903-166B	0025
903-167	OEM
903-167B	0019
903-168	OEM
903-168B	0019
903-169B	0023
903-171B	0030
903-172	OEM
903-173	OEM
903-174	OEM
903-176	OEM
903-177B	0133
903-178	0133
903-179	0012
903-180	0025
903-185	OEM
903-193	OEM
903-197	0023
903-198	0015
903-200	OEM
903-206	0442
903-208	0106
903-212	0143
903-303	0015
903-304	1272
903-305	6488
903-306	1272
903-311	0133
903-318	OEM
903-321	OEM
903-325	1767
903-326	1605
903-327	0019
903-330	0023
903-331	0631
903-332	0124
903-333	0253
903-334	0535
903-335	0062
903-337	0064
903-341	0019
903-342	OEM
903-343	OEM
903-345	OEM
903-347	0023
903-348	0087
903-349	0019
903-351	OEM
903-352	OEM
903-353	OEM
903-355	0019
903-356	0087
903-357	0052
903-358	OEM
903-359	OEM
903-360	OEM
903-361	OEM
903-362	OEM
903-363	OEM
903-365	OEM
903-366	OEM
903-375	1605
903-378	1767
903-380	OEM
903-385	1767
903-386	OEM
903-389	OEM
903-391	OEM
903-394	OEM
903-397	0133
903-407	0143
903-408	OEM
903-412	0087
903-413	OEM
903-414	OEM
903-415	6842
903-417	OEM
903-418	OEM
903-419	OEM
903-424	OEM
903-425	OEM
903-426	0015
903-427	0361
903-428	OEM
903-429	OEM
903-430	OEM
903-435	0123
903-438	0015
903-440	1605
903-440B	0030
903-443	0644
903-444	0071
903-445	0023
903-447	OEM
903-448	0466
903-449	0181
903-450	0015
903-451	0087
903-453	0062
903-454	0755
903-455	0086
903-456	0053
903-457	0015
903-463	0023
903-465	OEM
903-466	OEM
903-467	0124

If replacement code is OEM, contact original manufacturer for replacement.

DEVICE TYPE	REPL CODE
903-468	OEM
903-470	OEM
903-472	OEM
903-473	OEM
903-474	OEM
903-475	0911
903-476	0143
903-477	OEM
903-479	0053
903-480	0036
903-481	0041
903-482	0041
903-483	1319
903-484	OEM
903-486	0133
903-487	0077
903-492	0064
903-494	OEM
903-495	0165
903-496	0253
903-502	OEM
903-507	0123
903-508	0124
903-509	0057
903-510	0015
903-511	0028
903-512	0015
903-513	0041
903-519	0124
903-523	0124
903-528	0124
903-529	OEM
903-531	0289
903-532	0023
903-533	0052
903-534	0124
903-535	2520
903-537	0188
903-538	OEM
903-539	OEM
903-540	OEM
903-541	0199
903-542	OEM
903-543	OEM
903-544	0052
903-545	0137
903-546	0450
903-556	0143
903-557	0133
903-558	0623
903-559	0298
903-560	0298
903-561	0110
903-562	0023
903-568	OEM
903-574	OEM
903-575	OEM
903-579	OEM
903-583	OEM
903-600	OEM
903-606	OEM
903-630	OEM
903-631	OEM
903-632	OEM
903-639	OEM
903-652	OEM
903-655	OEM
903-664	OEM
903-665	OEM
903-667	OEM
903-669	OEM
903-670	OEM
903-671	OEM
903-680	OEM
903-684	OEM
903-734	0124
903-753	OEM
903-754	OEM
903-756	OEM
903-760	OEM
903-762	OEM
903-764	OEM
903-800	0339
903-827	OEM
903-830	0015
903-852	0582
903-864	0133
903-869	0124
903-878	OEM
903-885	1319
903-970	0319
903-976	0133
903-984	0253
903-1008	OEM
903-1010	OEM
903-1018	OEM
903-1022	0582
903-1071	0064
903-1081	0877
903-1084	OEM
903-1088	OEM
903-1089	OEM
903-1113	OEM
903-1124	0339
903-1128	0041
903-1200	2419
903-1202	OEM
903-1203	OEM
903-1204	OEM

DEVICE TYPE	REPL CODE
903-1205	OEM
903-1206	0041
903-1207	0041
903-1208	OEM
903-1209	0248
903-1210	OEM
903-1211	OEM
903-1213	OEM
903-1214	0041
903-1216	OEM
903-1217	OEM
903-1218	OEM
903-1220	0901
903-1229	OEM
903-1233	OEM
903-1241	OEM
903-1242	OEM
903-1243	OEM
903-1270	0140
903-1271	0466
903-1273	OEM
903-1275	0064
903HC	3808
903HM	OEM
903J	0079
903Y00212	0229
903Y00228	0012
903Y002149	0016
903Y002150	0111
903Y-002151	0378
903Y002151	1257
903Y002152	0555
904	0007
904-95	0016
904-95A	0016
904-95B	0111
904-96B	0079
904-97B	0143
904A	0007
904HC	3781
905	0007
905-00066	2279
905-00160	1385
905-00161	3513
905-5	3506
905-5B	OEM
905-7	OEM
905-9-B	2849
905-9B	OEM
905-13	2554
905-13B	2554
905-17B	OEM
905-18	OEM
905-19	OEM
905-19B	OEM
905-20	OEM
905-23	OEM
905-24B	0696
905-27	2535
905-28	2535
905-30	OEM
905-38B	0696
905-39B	0465
905-40	OEM
905-41	OEM
905-44B	OEM
905-46B	0696
905-47	OEM
905-48	OEM
905-55	1929
905-58	OEM
905-59	1239
905-66	2279
905-69	2279
905-77	OEM
905-78	OEM
905-80	OEM
905-100	OEM
905-101	3916
905-102	1199
905-103	3913
905-104	4360
905-105	0872
905-106	3891
905-107	4197
905-108	3652
905-109	3907
905-110	3909
905-111	4230
905-112	3918
905-113	OEM
905-114	3662
905-115	3911
905-116	4178
905-118	2279
905-118-01	2279
905-120	2728
905-121	0412
905-122	1561
905-123	4320
905-124	OEM
905-125	0473
905-126	0215
905-127	OEM
905-131	6027
905-136	OEM
905-137	4145
905-138	1561
905-139	1602

DEVICE TYPE	REPL CODE
905-140	OEM
905-141	0514
905-142	OEM
905-144	1602
905-145	OEM
905-147	1008
905-151	OEM
905-152	0837
905-154	OEM
905-155	0646
905-156	3081
905-157	OEM
905-158	OEM
905-159	OEM
905-161	4308
905-162	OEM
905-164	OEM
905-165	0898
905-166	OEM
905-170	4145
905-171	1602
905-172	4155
905-173	2512
905-174	OEM
905-175	OEM
905-177	1012
905-178	0646
905-180	OEM
905-181	OEM
905-182	OEM
905-184	OEM
905-185	OEM
905-186	0409
905-189	3943
905-190	1319
905-191	0872
905-193	OEM
905-194	OEM
905-195	OEM
905-196	OEM
905-197	OEM
905-198	4050
905-199	OEM
905-200	1938
905-201	1012
905-202	2093
905-203	OEM
905-204	2702
905-205	OEM
905-206	OEM
905-208	OEM
905-209	3742
905-210	2279
905-211	OEM
905-212	OEM
905-213	OEM
905-214	2590
905-215	OEM
905-216	OEM
905-217	0678
905-218	2218
905-219	1288
905-220	0328
905-221	0963
905-222	OEM
905-223	3891
905-226	3946
905-227	OEM
905-229	4846
905-231	OEM
905-232	OEM
905-233	2930
905-234	3891
905-235	2052
905-236	OEM
905-237	OEM
905-238	2724
905-239	5901
905-240	OEM
905-241	3168
905-242	0330
905-243	3742
905-244	1239
905-246	OEM
905-247	OEM
905-248	OEM
905-249	OEM
905-250	OEM
905-251	OEM
905-252	OEM
905-253	1251
905-254	3161
905-255	0356
905-256	3899
905-257	OEM
905-259	OEM
905-260	6034
905-261	OEM
905-262	2650
905-263	OEM
905-264	OEM
905-265	2650
905-266	OEM
905-267	1288
905-268	0621
905-269	OEM
905-270	OEM
905-271	OEM
905-275	OEM

DEVICE TYPE	REPL CODE
905-276	OEM
905-277	OEM
905-278	OEM
905-279	OEM
905-280	OEM
905-281	OEM
905-282	OEM
905-283	OEM
905-284	0358
905-286	OEM
905-287	4770
905-288	0176
905-289	2052
905-291	3161
905-293	OEM
905-294	OEM
905-295	OEM
905-298	3946
905-299	OEM
905-301	2702
905-303	OEM
905-308	OEM
905-310	OEM
905-311	OEM
905-323	OEM
905-324	OEM
905-325	0701
905-326	4747
905-327	OEM
905-328	OEM
905-329	4746
905-338	OEM
905-340	OEM
905-344	0243
905-347	2094
905-349	OEM
905-354	0034
905-360	OEM
905-368	1192
905-369	0101
905-375	OEM
905-380	0362
905-384	OEM
905-387	OEM
905-388	OEM
905-391	OEM
905-407	OEM
905-408	OEM
905-409	OEM
905-414	OEM
905-416	OEM
905-417	OEM
905-418	OEM
905-424	OEM
905-442	OEM
905-454	3753
905-463	0023
905-465	4216
905-488	OEM
905-491	OEM
905-492	OEM
905-529	OEM
905-537	OEM
905-538	OEM
905-539	OEM
905-540	OEM
905-585	OEM
905-645	OEM
905-658	0765
905-659	0624
905-662	0409
905-717	0409
905-738	OEM
905-830	OEM
905-920	OEM
905-922	0624
905-923	OEM
905-940	3590
905-1085	0624
905-1087	OEM
905-1106	0473
905-1123	4202
905-1126	0101
905-1141	OEM
905-1224	2402
905-1225	OEM
905-1226	OEM
905-1227	0620
905-1228	OEM
905-1229	OEM
905-1230	OEM
905-1231	OEM
905-1233	OEM
905-1233-01	OEM
905-1234	OEM
905-1235	OEM
905-1236	OEM
905-1238	0765
905-1239	0409
905-1240	0409
905-1247	OEM
905-1247-01	OEM
905-1248	OEM
905-1289	3172
905-1298	OEM
905-1339	OEM
905-1366	OEM
905-1372	2715
905-1373	0409

DEVICE TYPE	REPL CODE
905-1376	OEM
905-1377	OEM
905-1378	OEM
905-1482	OEM
905HC	3669
905HM	OEM
906	OEM
906HC	4170
907	OEM
907HC	4172
907HM	OEM
908	OEM
908D1	0143
908HC	3793
909	OEM
909-27125-140	0016
909-27125-160	0127
909HC	3797
909HM	OEM
910	0007
910H	OEM
910HC	1248
910HM	OEM
910X1	0164
910X2	0164
910X3	0004
910X4	0004
910X5	0004
910X6	0004
910X7	0164
910X8	0164
910X10	0164
911H	OEM
911HC	1354
911HM	OEM
912-1A6A	0016
912H	OEM
912HC	3843
913H	OEM
913HC	3847
913HM	OEM
914	0133
914-000-2-00	0133
914-000-4-00	0019
914-000-6-00	0133
914-000-7-00	0715
914-001-1-00	0139
914-001-7-00	0123
914A-1-6-5	0160
914F298-1	0086
914HC	1063
914HM	OEM
915	OEM
915H	OEM
915HC	3845
915HM	OEM
916-000-4-00	OEM
916-31001-1	0004
916-31001-1B	0004
916-31001-7B	0004
916-31003-5B	0004
916-31007-5	0004
916-31007-5B	0004
916-31012-6	0004
916-31012-6B	0004
916-31019-3	0136
916-31019-3B	0136
916-31024-3	0016
916-31024-3B	0127
916-31024-5	0127
916-31024-5B	0144
916-31025-4	0007
916-31025-4B	0007
916-31025-5	0016
916-31025-5B	0127
916-31026-9B	0004
916-32000-7	0143
916-32003-2	0143
916-32006-2	0143
916-33003-2	0015
917-1201-0	0574
917-12010	0574
918H-1	OEM
918H-2	OEM
919-00-1445	0157
919-00-1445-001	0644
919-00-1445-002	0137
919-00-1445-1	0644
919-00-1445-2	0137
919-00-1449-1	0087
919-00-2440-1	0015
919-00-2440-2	0015
919-00-3309	0526
919-00-3309-2	0234
919-00-3309-3	0251
919-00-4326	0133
919-00-4799	0133
919-00-5045	0229
919-00-7109	0229
919-00-7349	0162
919-00-7394	0133
919-00-7766	0015
919-00-7776	0015
919-00-9929	0133
919-001172	0133
919-001172-1	0133
919-001445-2	0137
919-001449	0242
919-001449-1	0242

DEVICE TYPE	REPL CODE
919-001449-3	0242
919-002240-1	0242
919-002440	0087
919-002440-1	0087
919-002440-2	0535
919-003309	0526
919-003309-1	0490
919-004326	0133
919-004799	0015
919-005045	0242
919-007109	0015
919-007394	0015
919-007776	0947
919-008862	0242
919-01-0459	0015
919-01-0623	0015
919-01-0829	0229
919-01-0829-1	0229
919-01-0867	0143
919-01-0873	0133
919-01-1172-1	0133
919-01-1211	0015
919-01-1212	0015
919-01-1213	0012
919-01-1214	0244
919-01-1215	0133
919-01-1307	0133
919-01-1339	0229
919-01-1340	0234
919-01-3035	0012
919-01-3058	0162
919-01-3072	0133
919-03036	0087
919-010459	0242
919-010623	0242
919-010829	0947
919-010829-1	0242
919-010867	0143
919-010873	0133
919-011211	0947
919-011212	0015
919-011215	0133
919-011307	0133
919-011339	0087
919-011340	0864
919-013036	0947
919-013044	0015
919-013058	0137
919-013059	0133
919-013060	0133
919-013061	0087
919-013067	0133
919-013072	0015
919-013079	0087
919-013081	0133
919-013082	0133
919-015618-1	0526
919-017406-011	0269
919-017406-013	0247
919-017406-056	0256
919-017406-057	0225
919-72-2	1403
920	OEM
920B03003	OEM
920B04201	OEM
920B05301	OEM
920B3003	OEM
920B19803	OEM
920B19804	OEM
920B19808	OEM
921	OEM
921-01122	0016
921-01123	0079
921-01124	0079
921-01125	0527
921-01127	0079
921-01128	3477
921-01129	0396
921-01130	0527
921-01131	0161
921-1A	0050
921-1B	0050
921-2A	0050
921-2B	0050
921-3A	0050
921-3B	0050
921-4	0004
921-4A	0050
921-4B	0136
921-5A	0208
921-5B	0208
921-6A	0208
921-6B	0208
921-7	0016
921-7B	0208
921-8	0016
921-9	0004
921-9B	0050
921-10	0050
921-10B	0050
921-11	OEM
921-11B	0050
921-12	0004
921-12B	0050
921-13	0004
921-13B	0050
921-14	0004
921-14B	0004
921-15	0050

DEVICE TYPE	REPL CODE
921-15B	0050
921-16	0050
921-16B	0050
921-17	0050
921-17B	0050
921-19	0050
921-20	0144
921-20A	0144
921-20B	0144
921-20BK	0016
921-21	0144
921-21A	0144
921-21B	0144
921-21BK	0144
921-22	0144
921-22A	0144
921-22B	0144
921-22BG	0016
921-23	0144
921-23A	0144
921-23B	0144
921-23BK	0016
921-24#	OEM
921-24B	0004
921-25B	0050
921-26	0016
921-26A	0016
921-26B	0050
921-27	0004
921-27A	0004
921-27B	0016
921-28	0016
921-28-BX	OEM
921-28A	0016
921-28B	0016
921-28BLU	0016
921-29B	0037
921-30	0144
921-30A	0144
921-30B	0144
921-31	0144
921-31A	0144
921-31B	0144
921-32	0144
921-32A	0144
921-32B	0144
921-33	0144
921-33B	0144
921-34	0144
921-34A	0144
921-34B	0144
921-35	0004
921-35A	0004
921-35B	0004
921-36	OEM
921-36B	0004
921-37B	0004
921-38	0004
921-38A	0004
921-38B	0004
921-39	0004
921-39A	0004
921-39B	0004
921-40	0004
921-40A	0004
921-40B	0004
921-41	OEM
921-41B	0004
921-43B	0016
921-43E	0079
921-44B	0164
921-45	0004
921-45A	0004
921-45B	0004
921-46	0016
921-46A	0016
921-46B	0208
921-46BK	0016
921-47	0016
921-47A	0016
921-47B	0126
921-47BL	0016
921-48	OEM
921-49B	0016
921-50	OEM
921-50B	0016
921-51	0004
921-51B	0004
921-52	0004
921-52B	0004
921-53	OEM
921-53B	0164
921-54	OEM
921-54B	0208
921-55B	0007
921-56B	0007
921-57B	0007
921-58B	0007
921-59B	0127
921-60B	0086
921-61	0142
921-61B	0142
921-62	0127
921-62A	0127
921-62B	0127
921-63	0127
921-63A	0127
921-63B	0127
921-64	0127

If replacement code is OEM, contact original manufacturer for replacement.

195

DEVICE TYPE	REPL CODE
921-64A	0127
921-64B	0127
921-64C	0127
921-65	0136
921-65A	0136
921-65B	0136
921-66	0136
921-66A	0136
921-66B	0136
921-67	0004
921-67A	0004
921-67B	0004
921-68	0004
921-68A	0004
921-68B	0004
921-69	0164
921-69A	0164
921-69B	0164
921-70	0037
921-70A	0037
921-70B	0037
921-71	0208
921-71A	0208
921-71B	0208
921-72B	0144
921-73B	0016
921-77B	0016
921-80	OEM
921-81	0279
921-84	0127
921-84A	0127
921-84B	0127
921-85	0127
921-85A	0127
921-85B	0127
921-86	0127
921-86A	0127
921-86B	0127
921-88	0142
921-88A	0142
921-88B	0142
921-89	OEM
921-91	OEM
921-92B	0111
921-93B	0016
921-97B	0144
921-98	OEM
921-98B	0144
921-99B	0016
921-100	3511
921-100B	0004
921-101	OEM
921-102	0127
921-102A	0127
921-102B	0127
921-103B	0150
921-104	0150
921-105B	0164
921-106B	0111
921-107	OEM
921-108	OEM
921-109B	0016
921-110B	0126
921-111B	0111
921-112B	0150
921-113	OEM
921-114	0224
921-114B	0111
921-115	0224
921-115B	2195
921-116	0224
921-116B	0111
921-117	OEM
921-117B	0016
921-118B	0164
921-119	0111
921-119B	0127
921-120B	0016
921-121	OEM
921-123B	0016
921-124B	0016
921-125B	0016
921-126B	0321
921-127	OEM
921-127B	1060
921-128B	0016
921-129B	0127
921-130	0127
921-133	0076
921-133B	0076
921-140B	0164
921-141B	0127
921-142B	0127
921-143B	0127
921-144	OEM
921-145	0007
921-145B	0127
921-147B	0004
921-148B	0004
921-150B	0004
921-151	OEM
921-152	OEM
921-152B	0111
921-153	OEM
921-153B	0004
921-154	OEM
921-154B	0111
921-155	OEM
921-155B	0111

DEVICE TYPE	REPL CODE
921-156B	0142
921-157B	0843
921-158B	0144
921-159	OEM
921-159B	0016
921-160B	0037
921-161B	0016
921-163B	0555
921-164	0555
921-164B	OEM
921-165	0555
921-167	0555
921-170	OEM
921-170B	0144
921-171B	0144
921-172B	0144
921-173	OEM
921-173B	0144
921-174B	0144
921-176	0224
921-176B	0127
921-177	0144
921-177B	0127
921-179	OEM
921-181B	0127
921-182B	0126
921-188B	0086
921-189B	0016
921-191B	0016
921-193	OEM
921-194	OEM
921-195B	0016
921-196	0111
921-196B	0111
921-197B	0037
921-198	3103
921-198BX	1647
921-200B	0016
921-201	OEM
921-202	0224
921-202B	2195
921-203	OEM
921-203B	0321
921-204	OEM
921-204B	0127
921-205B	0111
921-206	0111
921-206B	0111
921-207	1212
921-207B	0111
921-208B	0111
921-209	0284
921-209B	0076
921-210B	0127
921-211B	0127
921-212B	0144
921-213B	0127
921-214B	0016
921-215B	0016
921-216B	0004
921-217B	0004
921-222B	0004
921-223B	0004
921-224	OEM
921-224B	0164
921-225B	0016
921-226	0127
921-226B	0127
921-227B	0164
921-228B	0016
921-229B	0016
921-230B	0590
921-231B	0321
921-232	OEM
921-232B	0127
921-233	OEM
921-233B	0127
921-234	OEM
921-234B	0016
921-235B	0127
921-236B	0086
921-237	OEM
921-237B	0191
921-238B	0004
921-239	OEM
921-239B	0111
921-240B	0111
921-241B	0086
921-242B	0164
921-243	OEM
921-243B	1056
921-244	OEM
921-244B	0164
921-250	OEM
921-252B	0016
921-253	OEM
921-254B	0037
921-255B	0016
921-256	OEM
921-256X	0164
921-257B	0111
921-258B	0111
921-262	OEM
921-263	OEM
921-264B	0079
921-265	0144
921-265B	0224
921-266	0144
921-266B	0144

DEVICE TYPE	REPL CODE
921-267	0144
921-267B	0144
921-268B	0016
921-269	OEM
921-269B	0016
921-270	OEM
921-270B	0126
921-271	OEM
921-272B	1211
921-273B	0004
921-274B	0004
921-275B	0155
921-276B	0155
921-281B	0111
921-282B	0164
921-283	0016
921-288	0016
921-289	OEM
921-290	OEM
921-291B	0079
921-292	0037
921-292B	0037
921-293	OEM
921-294	OEM
921-296	OEM
921-296B	0037
921-301	0224
921-301B	0224
921-304	OEM
921-304B	0079
921-305	OEM
921-305B	0016
921-306B	0079
921-307	0079
921-307B	0079
921-308	0037
921-308B	0037
921-309	0079
921-310	OEM
921-311	OEM
921-312	OEM
921-312B	0079
921-313B	0144
921-314	0079
921-314B	0016
921-315B	0126
921-316	OEM
921-317	OEM
921-318B	0004
921-319	OEM
921-319B	0004
921-324	OEM
921-325B	0144
921-326B	0127
921-327B	0164
921-330	OEM
921-331	OEM
921-332B	0037
921-333B	2461
921-333P	2461
921-334	OEM
921-334B	0144
921-335	OEM
921-335B	0144
921-336	OEM
921-336B	0144
921-337B	0111
921-338B	0144
921-340	0086
921-341	OEM
921-345	0079
921-345B	0016
921-346	0338
921-347	0710
921-348B	0037
921-349	0224
921-350B	0224
921-351	0079
921-351B	0079
921-352	OEM
921-352B	0079
921-353	0079
921-353B	0079
921-354B	0079
921-355	0079
921-355B	0079
921-356	OEM
921-357	OEM
921-357B	2039
921-358	OEM
921-359	OEM
921-360B	0079
921-362	OEM
921-366	OEM
921-367	OEM
921-369	0016
921-370	OEM
921-371	OEM
921-372	OEM
921-376	OEM
921-377	0710
921-378	0320
921-379	0224
921-382	3492
921-383	3493
921-387	OEM
921-388	OEM
921-389	6088
921-389(PNP)	OEM

DEVICE TYPE	REPL CODE
921-393	OEM
921-394	OEM
921-395	OEM
921-396	OEM
921-398	OEM
921-399	OEM
921-400	OEM
921-401	OEM
921-402	OEM
921-403	0396
921-404	3477
921-405	0037
921-407	0079
921-408	0079
921-409	OEM
921-410	0018
921-411	0309
921-412	6088
921-414	OEM
921-416	OEM
921-421	OEM
921-422	OEM
921-424	0309
921-425	1581
921-426	OEM
921-428	0144
921-429	0236
921-430	0676
921-431	0042
921-432	0919
921-433	0919
921-434	0042
921-436	OEM
921-437	OEM
921-438	OEM
921-439	OEM
921-446	OEM
921-449	0079
921-450	0079
921-451	OEM
921-452	3477
921-453	1943
921-462	0079
921-463	0079
921-464	0079
921-465	OEM
921-467	0236
921-468	OEM
921-469	OEM
921-470	0079
921-472	1943
921-473	1943
921-474	OEM
921-476	2127
921-477	OEM
921-478	OEM
921-481	OEM
921-497	OEM
921-538	OEM
921-548	OEM
921-732	OEM
921-931	0042
921-1000	OEM
921-1001	OEM
921-1002	OEM
921-1005	2441
921-1006	0264
921-1007	0037
921-1008	1967
921-1009	0042
921-1010	1967
921-1011	0861
921-1013	0155
921-1014	0224
921-1015	0076
921-1016	0006
921-1017	0076
921-1018	1935
921-1019	1747
921-1020	0264
921-1021	0378
921-1022	0155
921-1026	OEM
921-1028	0076
921-1031	3308
921-1034	OEM
921-1037	OEM
921-1043	OEM
921-1045	0079
921-1047	0042
921-1049	0079
921-1051	0079
921-1052	0264
921-1053	0111
921-1055	0111
921-1059	0144
921-1060	0079
921-1062	0079
921-1063	0079
921-1065	0079
921-1067	2861
921-1068	0127
921-1069	0284
921-1070	0006
921-1071	0284
921-1072	0079
921-1073	0284
921-1074	0111
921-1075	0284

DEVICE TYPE	REPL CODE
921-1076	0275
921-1077	0284
921-1078	0284
921-1080	OEM
921-1083	OEM
921-1084	OEM
921-1086	OEM
921-1090	0617
921-1093	OEM
921-1095	OEM
921-1102	OEM
921-1103	0079
921-1105	OEM
921-1108	OEM
921-1111	OEM
921-1114	1376
921-1115	0472
921-1116	OEM
921-1118	OEM
921-1119	OEM
921-1120	OEM
921-1121	OEM
921-1122	0079
921-1123	OEM
921-1125	OEM
921-1126	OEM
921-1127	OEM
921-1128	OEM
921-1129	OEM
921-1132	OEM
921-1133	OEM
921-1134	0037
921-1135	OEM
921-1142	0079
921-1143	0919
921-1147	OEM
921-1148	OEM
921-1149	OEM
921-1150	3043
921-1152	0284
921-1153	OEM
921-1154	OEM
921-1156	OEM
921-1157	OEM
921-1163	OEM
921-1164	OEM
921-1165	OEM
921-1166	OEM
921-1168	0284
921-1169	0042
921-1171	0006
921-1176	OEM
921-1177	OEM
921-1180	0006
921-1182	0006
921-1185	0284
921-1186	OEM
921-1187	OEM
921-1188	0356
921-1191	0688
921-1192	OEM
921-1195	0079
921-1196	0079
921-1197	0037
921-1199	0419
921-1200	0688
921-1201	0321
921-1202	0018
921-1203	1935
921-1204	0076
921-1205	3672
921-1206	1747
921-1207	0037
921-1208	0527
921-1209	0155
921-1210	0042
921-1211	OEM
921-1214	0037
921-1216	OEM
921-1219	OEM
921-1220	OEM
921-1227	OEM
921-1228	OEM
921-1229	0321
921-1231	OEM
921-1234	OEM
921-1236	OEM
921-1237	OEM
921-1239	OEM
921-1240	OEM
921-1241	OEM
921-1244	0224
921-1245	OEM
921-1247	OEM
921-1249	OEM
921-1250	2019
921-1251	2539
921-1252	1132
921-1253	0037
921-1255	0321
921-1257	OEM
921-1258	OEM
921-1259	OEM
921-1261	OEM
921-1262	0037
921-1263	0079
921-1267	OEM
921-1268	OEM
921-1269	OEM

DEVICE TYPE	REPL CODE
921-1270	OEM
921-1271	OEM
921-1273	OEM
921-1279	0284
921-1280	OEM
921-1281	0037
921-1282	1212
921-1283	OEM
921-1284	0076
921-1285	0321
921-1286	0931
921-1287	0076
921-1288	0161
921-1289	OEM
921-1290	0546
921-1291	0037
921-1292	0284
921-1293	0144
921-1294	0224
921-1295	0079
921-1298	OEM
921-1299	OEM
921-1301	OEM
921-1303	0111
921-1304	OEM
921-1305	0320
921-1307	OEM
921-1308	OEM
921-1309	3658
921-1310	0009
921-1311	3580
921-1312	0018
921-1313	0013
921-1314	0076
921-1315	0076
921-1316	4043
921-1317	0249
921-1318	OEM
921-1319	1298
921-1320	0150
921-1321	0321
921-1322	1045
921-1323	OEM
921-1324	OEM
921-1325	0086
921-1326	3580
921-1327	2019
921-1334	OEM
921-1335	0144
921-1336	0144
921-1337	0144
921-1338	0079
921-1339	0079
921-1340	0037
921-1341	0006
921-1342	OEM
921-1355	OEM
921-1356	OEM
921-1358	OEM
921-1362	0284
921-1370	OEM
921-1384	OEM
921-1400	OEM
921-1420	OEM
921-1427	OEM
921-1468	OEM
921-1469	OEM
921-1470	OEM
921-1471	OEM
921-1478	OEM
921-1483	0224
921-1509	OEM
921-1515	0819
921-1516	OEM
921-1544	0018
921-1550	0826
921-1560	0355
921-1564	0127
921-1612	OEM
921-1632	0719
921-1689	4067
921-1690	OEM
921-1693	4109
921-1701	1376
921-1704	OEM
921-1799	0881
921-1801	1026
921-1803	OEM
921-1824	OEM
921-1838	0892
921-1866	OEM
921-1867	0006
921-1868	OEM
921-1869	OEM
921-1869(2SD1449T)	OEM
921-1870	2926
921-1871	2926
921-1872	0013
921-1873	0013
921-1874	0151
921-1875	0892
921-1876	1026
921-1877	0013
921-1878	1233
921-1879	0148
921-1880	0826
921-1882	OEM
921-1883	2926
921-1884	OEM

DEVICE TYPE	REPL CODE
921-1885	0018
921-1886	0527
921-1887	0013
921-1888	2926
921-1889	1747
921-1890	0429
921-1891	0013
921-1892	2926
921-1893	0155
921-1894	OEM
921-1895	OEM
921-1896	2895
921-1897	0151
921-1898	OEM
921-1899	OEM
921-1900	0826
921-1924	1553
921-1946	0151
921-1947	OEM
921-1988X	1647
921-3558	0079
921HC	3303
921HM	OEM
922	OEM
923	OEM
923HC	OEM
923HM	OEM
924-2209	0396
924-16598	0004
924-17945	0160
925	OEM
925-1	OEM
925-2	3494
926	OEM
926FM	OEM
926HC	3868
926HM	OEM
927HC	4154
930(0V)	0111
930B	0111
930DC	1812
930DM	OEM
930DZ	0127
930FM	OEM
930HM	OEM
930PC	1812
930X1	0016
930X2	0016
930X3	0016
930X4	0144
930X5	0144
930X6	0136
930X7	0004
930X8	0004
930X9	0004
930X10	0004
931	0133
931DC	3032
931FM	OEM
931PC	3032
932	OEM
932DC	1035
932DM	OEM
932FM	OEM
932HM	OEM
932PC	1035
933DC	2086
933DM	OEM
933FM	OEM
933HM	OEM
933PC	2086
934	OEM
934Q5FC	OEM
935-1	2235
935DC	1168
935PC	1168
936-10	0015
936-20	0015
936-NPN	0161
936DC	1820
936PC	1820
937DC	1824
937PC	1824
940	OEM
941	OEM
941DC	2598
941DM	OEM
941FM	OEM
941HM	OEM
941PC	2598
941T1	0841
942	OEM
942-002	0718
942-337	OEM
942-341	OEM
943	OEM
944	OEM
944DC	0033
944DM	OEM
944FM	OEM
944H	OEM
944HM	OEM
944PC	0033
945	1659
945DC	0081
945DM	OEM
945FM	OEM
945HM	OEM
945PC	0081

If replacement code is OEM, contact original manufacturer for replacement.

DEVICE TYPE	REPL CODE
946	OEM
946-8620-3	0015
946DC	0141
946DM	OEM
946FM	OEM
946PC	0141
947	OEM
947-1	0079
948-10300	0720
948DC	3365
948FM	OEM
948HM	OEM
948PC	3365
949	OEM
949DC	1833
949DM	OEM
949FM	OEM
949PC	1833
950	OEM
950-D10	OEM
950DC	2595
950DM	OEM
950FM	OEM
950H	OEM
950H1-S	OEM
950HA-1	OEM
950HM	OEM
950PC	2595
951	0018
951-1	0211
951-1(SYLVANIA)	0136
951DC	2067
951DM	OEM
951FM	OEM
951HM	OEM
951PC	2067
952	0086
952DC	OEM
953	0086
953DC	OEM
953H	0037
954	OEM
954DC	OEM
955	OEM
955-1	0050
955-2	0050
955-3	0050
955DC	OEM
956	OEM
956DC	OEM
957	OEM
957-7656-0	1129
957DC	OEM
958	OEM
958DC	OEM
958HM	OEM
960DC	OEM
961DC	1848
961PC	1848
962DC	0557
962DM	OEM
962FM	OEM
962PC	0557
963DC	0337
963FM	OEM
963PC	0337
964-2073B	0016
964-2209	0396
964-16598	0136
964-16599	0085
964-17142	0211
964-17443	0015
964-17444	0016
964-17887	0085
964-17945	0160
964-19862	2839
964-19862A	0004
964-19863	0004
964-19864	0004
964-19865	0015
964-20738	0016
964-20739	0126
964-21866	0015
964-22008	0126
964-22009	0396
964-22158	0086
964-24387	0086
964-24584	0016
964-25046	0086
964-27986	0561
964-174443	0015
964DC	OEM
965-1A6-5	0050
965-2A6-1	0208
965-4A6-2	0595
965A16-3	0050
965B16-2	0136
965C-16-4	0160
965T1	0211
966-1A6-3	0004
966-2A6-4	0004
966-3A6C	0004
966DC	OEM
967-MP4	OEM
967D	OEM
970	OEM
971-11	OEM
971-12	OEM
971DC	OEM
972-659E-0	0006
972-659E-O	0338
972D7	0015
972X1	0050
972X2	0050
972X3	0050
972X4	0050
972X5	0050
972X6	0136
972X7	0136
972X8	0136
972X9	0004
972X10	0004
972X11	0004
972X12	0004
973	OEM
974-1(SYLVANIA)	0275
974-2	0283
974-2(SYLVANIA)	0275
974-3	0275
974-3A6-3	0275
974-4	0283
974-4(SYLVANIA)	0275
974HC	1799
975	0079
976-0036-921	0133
977-1	0133
977-2	0015
977-2B	0015
977-3B	0071
977-4	0015
977-4B	0276
977-5	0015
977-6B	0276
977-8	0015
977-8B	0015
977-9	0015
977-10	0015
977-10B	0015
977-11	0015
977-11B	0015
977-12	0015
977-13	0015
977-13B	0015
977-14	OEM
977-14B	0196
977-15	OEM
977-16	0015
977-17	0015
977-18	0015
977-18B	0015
977-19	0023
977-19B	0023
977-20	0015
977-20B	0015
977-22	0015
977-22B	0015
977-23	0015
977-23B	0015
977-24B	0276
977-25B	0015
977-26	0015
977-27B	0015
977-28	0015
977-28B	0015
977-30	0769
977-31	3805
977-32	3805
977-33	3805
977-34	1061
977-34-01	1061
977-35	1061
977-35-02	1696
977-35-03	1061
977-36	1696
977-37	1696
977-38	1493
977-39	1493
977-40	3610
977-41	2097
977-42	2097
977-43	2097
977-44	OEM
977-45	3819
977-46	OEM
977-52	2955
977-218	0276
977-Z9500A	0190
977-Z9521	3805
977-Z9522	1493
977-Z9523	1061
977-Z9526A	1696
977-Z9529	2524
977-Z9530	3610
977-Z9531	2777
977-Z9532	0405
977-Z9533	1700
977-Z9534	2954
977-Z9535	2957
977-Z9536	1986
977-Z9536A	1986
977-Z9537	1188
977-Z9538	2956
977-Z9539	1048
977A1-6-1	0435
978-1923	0126
980H	OEM
981H	OEM
982H	OEM
983H	OEM
984A-1-6B	0160
985H	OEM
986M	0037
987T1	0211
988T1	0211
989DC	OEM
989HM	OEM
989T1	0211
990-110	OEM
990-130	OEM
990-150	OEM
990-160	OEM
990-170	OEM
990-180	OEM
990-190	OEM
990T1	0211
991-00-1172	0133
991-00-1172-1	0133
991-00-1219	0016
991-00-1221	0004
991-00-1222	0004
991-00-1449	0229
991-00-1449-1	0229
991-00-2232	0016
991-00-2248	0016
991-00-2298	0016
991-00-2356	0016
991-00-2356/K	0016
991-00-2440	0229
991-00-2440-1	0229
991-00-2440-2	0229
991-00-2873	0016
991-00-2888	0086
991-00-3144	0016
991-00-3304	0016
991-00-7394	0015
991-00-7776	0015
991-00-8393	0016
991-00-8393A	0016
991-00-8393M	0016
991-00-8394	0016
991-00-8394A	0016
991-00-8394AH	0016
991-00-8395	0016
991-002232	0155
991-002298	0111
991-002356	0111
991-002873	0111
991-003304	0155
991-008393	0155
991-01-0098	0037
991-01-0099	0160
991-01-0461	0396
991-01-0462	0037
991-01-1216	0160
991-01-1217	0164
991-01-1219	0016
991-01-1220	0016
991-01-1221	0004
991-01-1222	0004
991-01-1223	0004
991-01-1224	0004
991-01-1225	0037
991-01-1305	0086
991-01-1306	0016
991-01-1312	0016
991-01-1314	0086
991-01-1315	0126
991-01-1316	0127
991-01-1317	0103
991-01-1318	0016
991-01-1319	0037
991-01-1705	0016
991-01-1706	0321
991-01-2328	0037
991-01-2686	0126
991-01-3044	0016
991-01-3055	0321
991-01-3056	0016
991-01-3057	0016
991-01-3058	0037
991-01-3063	0103
991-01-3068	0016
991-01-3170	0419
991-01-3543	0396
991-01-3544	0016
991-01-3599	0037
991-01-3683	0016
991-01-3740	0016
991-01-5001	0419
991-01-5063	0419
991-010098	0037
991-010462	0155
991-011217	0164
991-011219	0016
991-011220	0016
991-011221	0004
991-011222	0004
991-011223	0004
991-011225	0037
991-011305	0086
991-011306	0016
991-011312	0016
991-011313	0016
991-011314	0086
991-011318	0016
991-011319	0037
991-011576	0321
991-011706	0321
991-012686	0079
991-013044	0155
991-013056	0155
991-013057	0155
991-013058	0037
991-013063	0042
991-013068	0155
991-013543	0396
991-013544	0111
991-015587	0016
991-015614	0006
991-015615	0155
991-015663	0396
991-015942	0718
991-016274	0155
991-019542-1	1865
991-025515	0215
991-025515-001	0215
991-025515-002	0215
991-025517	0621
991-026005	0495
991-026022	1938
991-026022-00	1938
991-026025	0473
991-026605	0515
991-026609	1008
991-026615	0508
991-027358	0409
991-027358-001	0409
991-028650-001	0394
991-028679-001	1135
991-028680-001	1517
991-028681-001	1946
991-028682-001	2061
991-029866	1738
991T1	0211
992-00-1192	0085
992-00-2271	0103
992-00-2298	0016
992-00-3139	0103
992-00-3139A	0103
992-00-3144	0016
992-00-3172	0142
992-00-4091	0103
992-00-4092	0103
992-00-8870	0160
992-00-8890	0599
992-00-8890L	0599
992-008-890	0265
992-00271	0103
992-00271A	0103
992-001192	0160
992-002271	0103
992-003139	0103
992-003172	0424
992-004091	0103
992-008870	0599
992-008890	0160
992-01-1216	0160
992-01-1218	0160
992-01-1317	0103
992-01-3684	0233
992-01-3705	0178
992-01-3738	0016
992-02271	0103
992-011216	0160
992-011218	0085
992-011317	0042
992-017169	0103
992-020054	2411
992-1A6-1	0435
992-10	0015
992-531-01	0276
992T1	0004
995-01-6130	0919
995-01-6131	0042
1000	OEM
1000-0948	OEM
1000-0963	OEM
1000-06971	OEM
1000-12	0012
1000-17	0143
1000-23	1385
1000-25	0627
1000-129	0015
1000-130	0133
1000-131	0143
1000-132	0012
1000-135	0151
1000-136	0076
1000-137	0076
1000-138	2035
1000-139	1390
1000-139*	0693
1000-140	2039
1000-141	1401
1000-142	0042
1000-2640	0137
1000-6914	0062
1000-6948	1251
1000-6963	5080
1000-6971	4302
1000-6989	1382
1000-7052	1505
1000-7227	3764
1000-7334	1505
1000-7359	0106
1000-9959	1060
1000DS10	OEM
1000EXD22	OEM
1000FXD22	OEM
1000HB1U	5634
1000HB2U	5634
1000HB3U	5634
1000HB4U	5634
1000HB6U	5634
1000HT1U	5631
1000HT2U	5631
1000HT3U	5631
1000HT4U	5631
1000HT6U	5631
1000HT8U	5631
1000PA50	6177
1000PA60	6177
1000PA80	6029
1000PA100	6029
1000PA110	6029
1000PA120	6029
1000PA130	OEM
1000PA140	OEM
1000PA150	OEM
1000PK50	OEM
1000PK60	OEM
1000PK80	OEM
1000PK100	OEM
1000PK120	6029
1000PK140	OEM
1000PK150	OEM
1000PK160	OEM
1000PK170	OEM
1000PK180	OEM
1000PKL60S65	OEM
1000PKL60S646	OEM
1000PKL60S656	OEM
1000PKL60S666	OEM
1000PKL60S676	OEM
1000PKL60S683	OEM
1000PKL60T603	OEM
1000PKL60T623	OEM
1000PKL60T663	OEM
1000PKL80S65	OEM
1000PKL80S646	OEM
1000PKL80S656	OEM
1000PKL80S666	OEM
1000PKL80S676	OEM
1000PKL80S683	OEM
1000PKL80T603	OEM
1000PKL80T623	OEM
1000PKL80T663	OEM
1000PKL100S65	OEM
1000PKL100S646	OEM
1000PKL100S656	OEM
1000PKL100S666	OEM
1000PKL100S676	OEM
1000PKL100S683	OEM
1000PKL100T603	OEM
1000PKL100T623	OEM
1000PKL100T663	OEM
1000PKL110S65	OEM
1000PKL110S646	OEM
1000PKL110S656	OEM
1000PKL110S666	OEM
1000PKL110S676	OEM
1000PKL110S683	OEM
1000PKL110T603	OEM
1000PKL110T623	OEM
1000PKL110T663	OEM
1000PKL120S65	OEM
1000PKL120S646	OEM
1000PKL120S656	OEM
1000PKL120S666	OEM
1000PKL120S676	OEM
1000PKL120S683	OEM
1000PKL120T603	OEM
1000PKL120T623	OEM
1000PKL120T663	OEM
1000PKL130S65	OEM
1000PKL130S646	OEM
1000PKL130S656	OEM
1000PKL130S666	OEM
1000PKL130S676	OEM
1000PKL130S683	OEM
1000PKL130T603	OEM
1000PKL130T623	OEM
1000PKL140S65	OEM
1000PKL140S646	OEM
1000PKL140S656	OEM
1000PKL140S666	OEM
1000PKL140S676	OEM
1000PKL140S683	OEM
1000PKL140T603	OEM
1000PKL140T623	OEM
1000PKL140T663	OEM
1000PKL1305663	OEM
1000YKD22	OEM
1001	6607
1001(EF-JOHNSON)	2840
1001(TRANS)	0086
1001-0014	0143
1001-0036	0438
1001-01	0086
1001-02	0191
1001-03	0364
1001-04	0376
1001-05	0155
1001-06	0783
1001-07	0693
1001-08	1401
1001-09	0236
1001-012	0012
1001-0158	OEM
1001-0478	0120
1001-5	1403
1001-6	1403
1001-10	0143
1001-11	0015
1001-12	0012
1001-13	0102
1001-1179	0079
1001-4975	OEM
1001-5600	0120
1001-5659	0143
1001-5667	0015
1001-5683	0023
1001-5709	OEM
1001-5717	0261
1001-5766	0037
1001-5816	0919
1001-5824	0919
1001-5832	0055
1001-5840	0168
1001-5865	0079
1001-5915	0284
1001-5949	0076
1001-5956	2511
1001-5972	0167
1001-6657	0456
1001-6699	0071
1001-6731	0023
1001-6806	0133
1001-6848	0286
1001-6863	0062
1001-6939	0261
1001-6947	0710
1001-6962	0338
1001-7005	OEM
1001-7044	0079
1001-7069	0079
1001-7077	0079
1001-7085	0338
1001-7119	0388
1001-7135	0079
1001-7150	0846
1001-7168	0851
1001-7877	OEM
1001-9552	0133
1001-9602	0143
1001-9610	0023
1001-9628	0261
1001-9636	0155
1001-9644	0284
1001-9651	0388
1001-9677	0846
1001-9685	0851
1001-9693	0167
1001-9727	1420
1001-9735	1319
1001-9958	0224
1001-9966	0079
1001-9974	0079
1001-9990	0079
1001PDE120	OEM
1001PDE140	OEM
1001PDE160	OEM
1001PDE180	OEM
1001PDE200	OEM
1001PDE210	OEM
1001PDE220	OEM
1001PDE230	OEM
1001PDE240	OEM
1001PDE250	OEM
1002	0688
1002-0006	0574
1002-0014	0143
1002-01	0321
1002-02	2195
1002-02A	0144
1002-03	0016
1002-04	0016
1002-04-1	0144
1002-05	0004
1002-07	0021
1002-08	0143
1002-09	0143
1002-0219	0293
1002-0345	0358
1002-0402	0079
1002-0436	0919
1002-0519	0582
1002-17	0143
1002-17(DIODE)	0143
1002-68	2195
1002-345	OEM
1002-4404	0137
1002-4891	0037
1002-5567	0224
1002-5591	0676
1002-5625	0079
1002-5690	0077
1002-6219	0293
1002-9296	0120
1002-9668	0100
1002A	OEM
1002A(JULIETTE)	0127
1002A-1	0126
1002A-2	0086
1003	0004
1003(E.F.-JOHNSON)	0004
1003(JULIETTE)	0136
1003(TRANS)	0881
1003-01	0127
1003-02	2377
1003-0284	OEM
1003-0518	1638
1003-0567	1049
1003-11	0133
1003-13	0015
1003-2084	0298
1003-3116	0358
1003-6754	0111
1003A	OEM
1003PJA250	OEM
1003PJA300	OEM
1004	0198
1004(2SC537)	0016
1004(DIODE)	0143
1004(G.E.)	0007
1004(JULIETTE)	0144
1004(JULIETTE)*	0144
1004(TRANS)	0892
1004-01	0164
1004-02	1390
1004-03	0016
1004-0392	0037
1004-0434	0224
1004-0558	0313
1004-0780	1212
1004-0798	0239
1004-3	OEM
1004-17	0144
1004-25	OEM
1004-1986	1238
1004-1994	1251
1004-2042	1308
1004A	OEM
1005	0016
1005(2SC537)	0016
1005(JULIETTE)	0004
1005(JULIETTE)*	0004
1005(JULIETTERECTIFI	0015
1005-17	0004
1005-20	0015
1005A	OEM
1006	0224
1006(DIODE)	0143
1006(G.E.)	0007
1006(JULIETTE)	0079
1006(JULIETTE)*	0004
1006(JULIETTE-RECTIF	0015
1006/0945	0064
1006-0887	1251
1006-0895	1505
1006-0903	2052
1006-0937	0419
1006-0945	0064
1006-17	0071
1006-21	0151
1006-24	0015
1006-48	0151
1006-78	0050
1006-93	0004
1006-1737	0002
1006-2594	0006
1006-5977	0030
1006-5985	0170
1006-7445	3666
1006-9292	0019
1006A	OEM
1007	0143
1007(JULIETTE)*	0136
1007(JULIETTE-RECTIF	0015
1007-0951	0790
1007-17	0004
1007-1124	0143
1007-3054	0224
1007-3062	0224
1007-3088	0224
1007-3153	0076
1007-3229	0710
1007-3344	0396
1007-5869	0284
1007-5901	0140
1007-5919	0549
1007-6537	3925
1008	0086
1008(E.F.-JOHNSON)	0004
1008(E.F.JOHNSON)	0164
1008(JULIETTE)	0222
1008(POWER)	0222
1008-02	0016
1008-17	0085
1009	0004
1009(E.F.-JOHNSON)	0004
1009(G.E.)	0007
1009(JULIETTE-RECTIF	0015
1009-01	1270
1009-01*	0212
1009-02	0155
1009-03	1390
1009-03*	0693
1009-03-17	0086
1009-04	1401
1009-04-17	0693
1009-05	2035
1009-05A	0419

If replacement code is OEM, contact original manufacturer for replacement.

Original Device Types

DEVICE TYPE	REPL CODE
1009-06	0025
1009-06(10)	0644
1009-07	0015
1009-08	0133
1009-09	0015
1009-2	0079
1009-11	0507
1009-17	0016
1009-127	0683
1009-8403	1274
1010	0170
1010(20A90)	0123
1010/8033	0037
1010-0866	0079
1010-14	1390
1010-17	1390
1010-17(R.F.)	0693
1010-78	0050
1010-87	0050
1010-89	0136
1010-143	0133
1010-145	0143
1010-3417	0023
1010-7738	0037
1010-7928	0016
1010-7936	0419
1010-7951	0181
1010-7985	0065
1010-7993	0086
1010-8009	0006
1010-8025	0065
1010-8033	0203
1010-8041	0086
1010-8066	0326
1010-8082	0016
1010-8090	0016
1010-8116	0102
1010-8132	0560
1010-8165	0124
1010-8173	0143
1010-9486	0023
1010-9494	0017
1010-9932	0850
1010-9940	0167
1010-9965	0797
1010-9973	0661
1010A	0124
1011	0143
1011-01	0693
1011-02	0025
1011-0302	0124
1011-11	0334
1011-11(R.F.)	0144
1012	0015
1012(GE)	0037
1012(G.E.)	0037
1012-17	0143
1012-17(POWER)	0097
1012A1PGBP	OEM
1012A3PGAO	OEM
1012A10	OEM
1012B30	OEM
1012C1PGAO	OEM
1012D3PGBP	OEM
1012GE	0150
1013	0143
1013-15	2195
1013-16	0004
1014	0079
1014(E.F.-JOHNSON)	0004
1014-25	0627
1014AO	OEM
1014AP	OEM
1014BO	OEM
1014BP	OEM
1014CO	OEM
1014CP	OEM
1015	0002
1015-0518	OEM
1016	0688
1016(GE)	0037
1016-17	0015
1016-77	0143
1016-78	0015
1016-79	0015
1016-80	0627
1016-81	0042
1016-83	0144
1016-84	0144
1016-85	0470
1018-25	1826
1018-1048	0819
1018-1063	0076
1018-2400	0019
1018-3259	0133
1018-4943	0008
1018-6278	0170
1018-6963	0015
1018-7961	0071
1018-9884	0133
1019-0569	0361
1019-25	2142
1019-74	0004
1019-1203	0326
1019-1385	0102
1019-3852	0016
1019-6699	0143
1019M	0037
1020	0015
1020-01	OEM
1020-17	0016
1020-25	0465
1020G	0127
1021	0321
1021-17	0211
1021-25	0905
1021A	OEM
1022	OEM
1022-0911	0036
1022-1976	0165
1022-5548	0015
1023-17	0211
1023A	OEM
1023AD8DIA3	OEM
1023AD8DIB3	OEM
1023AD8DIC3	OEM
1023AD8DID3	OEM
1023AD16PDA3	OEM
1023AD16PDB3	OEM
1023AD16PDC3	OEM
1023AD16PDD3	OEM
1023AD16SEA3	OEM
1023AD16SEB3	OEM
1023AD16SEC3	OEM
1023AD16SED3	OEM
1023EX16DI005	OEM
1023EX16DI16AOP	OEM
1023EX16DI16BOP	OEM
1023EX32DI00P	OEM
1023EX32DI16AOP	OEM
1023EX32DI16BOP	OEM
1023EX32PD00P	OEM
1023EX32PD16AOP	OEM
1023EX32PD16BOP	OEM
1023EX32SE00P	OEM
1023EX32SE16AOP	OEM
1023EX32SE16BOP	OEM
1023G	0016
1023G(GE)	0016
1023M	OEM
1024	0015
1024-17	0085
1024G	0079
1024M11	OEM
1025	OEM
1025-2712	0167
1025-4172	0167
1025-4712	0167
1025G	0079
1026	0127
1026G	0016
1027	0436
1027(G.E.)	0144
1027-4231	0765
1027-4264	5126
1027-4389	3848
1027-4454	OEM
1027-4462	5167
1027-4850	5168
1027-4959	5169
1027-5006	4838
1027-5113	5178
1027-5394	OEM
1027-5535	5170
1027-5816	OEM
1027-5881	OEM
1027-6244	3130
1027-6319	OEM
1027-6459	OEM
1027-6533	0819
1027-6624	0643
1027-7259	1157
1027-7291	1157
1027-7366	0018
1027-7986	0429
1027-8042	0018
1027-8059	0667
1027-9974	0023
1027-9982	0604
1027-9990	0041
1027G	0086
1028	0079
1028-0006	0253
1028-0014	0253
1028-0030	0064
1028-0048	0064
1028-0055	0023
1028-0063	1767
1028-0071	0124
1028-0089	0124
1028-0097	0041
1028-0105	0062
1028-1079	OEM
1028-3984	0133
1028-4297	0111
1028-4305	2461
1028-4313	0144
1028-6680	0005
1028-6755	0023
1028A	OEM
1028G	0016
1029	0079
1029(G.E.)	0016
1029-02	0065
1029-1788	OEM
1029G	0016
1030	0037
1030(G.E.)	0065
1030-8DIA300P	OEM
1030-8DIB300P	OEM
1030-8DIC300P	OEM
1030-8DID300P	OEM
1030-16DIA300P	OEM
1030-16DIC300P	OEM
1030-16DID300P	OEM
1030-16PDA300P	OEM
1030-16PDB300P	OEM
1030-16PDC300P	OEM
1030-16PDD300P	OEM
1030-16SEA300P	OEM
1030-16SEB300P	OEM
1030-16SEC300P	OEM
1030-16SED300P	OEM
1030-17	0143
1030-25	1164
1030-32DIA300P	OEM
1030-32DIB300P	OEM
1030-32DIC300P	OEM
1030-32DID300P	OEM
1030-32PDA300P	OEM
1030-32PDB300P	OEM
1030-32PDC300P	OEM
1030-32PDD300P	OEM
1030-32SEA300P	OEM
1030-32SEB300P	OEM
1030-32SEC300P	OEM
1030-32SED300P	OEM
1030-64PDA300P	OEM
1030-64PDB300P	OEM
1030-64PDC300P	OEM
1030-64PDD300P	OEM
1030-64SEA300P	OEM
1030-64SEB300P	OEM
1030-64SEC300P	OEM
1030-64SED300P	OEM
1030-5530	0060
1031-17	0087
1031-25	0268
1032	0211
1032-25	2845
1032-3467	0139
1032-3475	0139
1032-3483	0139
1032-8243	0305
1032R40	OEM
1033	0137
1033-0911	0133
1033-0983	0133
1033-0991	0133
1033-1	0136
1033-2	0136
1033-3	0136
1033-4	0136
1033-5	0211
1033-6	0038
1033-7	0211
1033-8	0015
1033-17	0015
1033-1007	0124
1033-1247	2056
1033-1262	2057
1033-1270	0058
1033-1338	0484
1033-1874	2062
1033-1916	0019
1033-4340	0101
1033-4985	0203
1033-5313	0355
1033-5537	0355
1033-6204	0819
1033-6451	0155
1033-6493	0155
1033-6949	0284
1033-6956	0284
1033-7079	2208
1033-7400	0577
1033-7426	0577
1033-7699	0667
1033-7905	0577
1034	0164
1034-17	0016
1034-43	0595
1035	0164
1035-02	OEM
1035-80	1211
1035-7564	0619
1035Z4	OEM
1036	0164
1036A	OEM
1037	OEM
1037-0575	2395
1037-65	1211
1037-7174	3764
1038	0142
1038(G.E.)	0086
1038/9922	0203
1038-1	0079
1038-1-10	0016
1038-6	0016
1038-6CL	0016
1038-8	0016
1038-10	0016
1038-15	0016
1038-15CL	0016
1038-18	0016
1038-18CL	0016
1038-21	0016
1038-23	0016
1038-23CL	0016
1038-24	0016
1038-1697	0080
1038-1721	0015
1038-1788	0182
1038-1804	0523
1038-1853	0168
1038-1861	0625
1038-9922	0016
1039-0060	0006
1039-01	0076
1039-0433	0219
1039-0441	0155
1039-0458	0155
1039-0461	1211
1039-0482	1653
1039-0515	0168
1039-0516	0638
1039-0888	0127
1039-0961	1211
1039-1290	2040
1039-9772	0836
1040	0015
1040-01	1212
1040-02	0178
1040-03	0016
1040-04	1390
1040-05	1401
1040-06	OEM
1040-08	0143
1040-09	0181
1040-0968	OEM
1040-2	0016
1040-7	0086
1040-10	0015
1040-11	0086
1040-59	0050
1040-80	0208
1040-81	0015
1040-155	0155
1040-1373	OEM
1040-9068	0006
1040-9332	0023
1040-9373	0489
1041-63	0023
1041-66	0133
1041-68	0138
1041-69	2390
1041-71	0155
1041-72	0076
1041-76	2039
1041-77	0693
1041-4950	0577
1041-4951	0577
1041-6949	0148
1042-01	0212
1042-02	3017
1042-03	0076
1042-04	0076
1042-05	0191
1042-06	0006
1042-07	0364
1042-08	0833
1042-09	0830
1042-10	1004
1042-11	0817
1042-12	0019
1042-13	0123
1042-14	0143
1042-15	0133
1042-16	0124
1042-17	0015
1042-18	0012
1042-19	0165
1042-20	0143
1042-23	0120
1042-7938	0391
1043-0049	0133
1043-07	0076
1043-1195	0212
1043-1229	0155
1043-1260	0127
1043-1278	0037
1043-1286	0042
1043-1294	0919
1043-1310	0455
1043-1328	0546
1043-1344	0696
1043-1534	0137
1043-1583	0120
1043-7069	OEM
1043-7267	OEM
1043-7275	3726
1043-7309	0142
1043-7358	0168
1043-7374	0037
1043-7382	0015
1044	0015
1044-0295	0037
1044-6888	0431
1044-7035	3239
1044-7043	2038
1044-7049	2038
1044-7878	0419
1044-8983	0133
1044-9544	0086
1045-0518	0015
1045-0534	0015
1045-2761	0167
1045-2951	0016
1045-3082	0086
1045-4676	0037
1045-7802	0133
1045-7828	0042
1045-7836	0919
1045-7844	0103
1045-7851	0103
1045Z4	OEM
1047-25	0428
1047-715	OEM
1047-1571	0080
1047-7115	0006
1048-1307	0080
1048-6408	OEM
1048-6421	0133
1048-7361	0261
1048-9839	0244
1048-9870	0019
1048-9888	0123
1048-9904	0224
1048-9912	0079
1048-9920	0076
1048-9938	0030
1048-9946	0015
1048-9953	0139
1048-9987	0133
1048-9995	0015
1049-0035	0527
1049-0060	0151
1049-0092	0111
1049-0100	1211
1049-0167	0018
1049-1744	0076
1049-3435	0023
1050	0015
1050-5816	0644
1050B	0150
1051-5559	0123
1052-0229	0148
1052-17	0004
1052-6390	2914
1052-6408	3238
1052-6416	3242
1054-8295	1313
1055-7726	0224
1055Z4	OEM
1056-4417	0023
1056-8269	0419
1056-8376	OEM
1056-8384	4511
1056-8392	OEM
1057-17	0004
1057-2071	0284
1057-9140	0313
1058	0283
1058-3227	3294
1058-3664	0818
1059-2848	0102
1059-7805	0139
1059-7961	0071
1059-9140	0313
1059M	0037
1060	0015
1060-17	0004
1060-17(DRIVER)	0164
1060-17(PRE-AMP)	0211
1060-3553	0143
1060-6564	0006
1060-8149	0113
1060-9428	0261
1061-4667	0143
1061-5972	0167
1061-6274	1142
1061-6282	0220
1061-6290	0017
1061-7090	OEM
1061-8312	0006
1061-8320	0076
1061-8321	OEM
1061-8338	1274
1061-8346	0638
1061-8353	0638
1061-8361	0071
1061-8379	0023
1061-8387	0023
1061-8668	0638
1061-8807	0006
1061-8908	0638
1061-8916	0023
1061-8924	0023
1061-8932	0999
1061-9068	0006
1061-9153	3859
1061-9161	2921
1061-9526	4174
1061-9666	1316
1061-9856	2216
1062-0615	0144
1062-0706	OEM
1062-1414	OEM
1062-6018	0037
1062-6414	0006
1062-7511	2643
1062GE	0133
1063-79	0015
1063-3553	0143
1063-4145	0025
1063-4806	2313
1063-4814	1702
1063-4939	2759
1063-5019	0516
1063-5027	OEM
1063-5142	0283
1063-5209	0039
1063-5381	0016
1063-5399	0079
1063-5423	0037
1063-5431	0037
1063-5449	0037
1063-5646	1638
1063-5688	1274
1063-5704	0949
1063-6454	0025
1063-6926	0037
1063-7247	OEM
1063-7411	OEM
1063-7916	0283
1063-8369	0220
1063-8435	0203
1063-8591	0019
1063-8799	OEM
1063-8963	0191
1063-8971	0071
1063-8989	0466
1064-6461	0532
1064-6545	0873
1064M	0037
1065-2055	3242
1065-2212	2015
1065-2543	2604
1065-2642	2604
1065-3225	0042
1065-3525	0042
1065-4861	0232
1065-6775	0497
1065-9928	0023
1065-9936	0949
1065-9944	2085
1065Z4	OEM
1066-9666	1316
1067	0233
1068-17	4144
1069	0042
1069-7032	0861
1070	0071
1070(XSTR)	2985
1070-0623	0023
1070-0631	0949
1070-4781	1700
1070-5481	0039
1070-8576	2195
1071	0919
1071-2081	0118
1071-4186	1298
1071-4251	1779
1071-4913	0155
1072-1	0236
1072-6677	OEM
1072-8491	0320
1072G	0786
1072K	0786
1073-6361	2784
1073-6486	0006
1074	0309
1074-117	0103
1074-120	0012
1074-1582	0037
1075	0326
1075-5122	0466
1075-6146	0388
1075Z4	OEM
1076-0999	0527
1076-1377	0007
1076-1484	0133
1076-1559	0283
1076-1674	0017
1076-4801	0637
1076-5196	0037
1077	0661
1077-07	0016
1077-0261	0080
1077-240Z	OEM
1077-2309	0018
1077-2325	0143
1077-2333	0005
1077-2341	0133
1077-2358	0120
1077-2366	0015
1077-2374	0895
1077-2382	0574
1077-2390	1206
1077-2408	0428
1077-2760	0143
1077-3828	1274
1077-3836	0015
1077-3844	1561
1077-9270	0005
1077-9296	0123
1077H11	OEM
1077H12	OEM
1078-7372	0196
1079	0797
1079-5110	0144
1079-9928	0525
1079-9955	0023
1079-9963	0023
1080	0071
1080-03	0042
1080-05	0617
1080-06	0219
1080-07	0191
1080-08	0023
1080-20	0284
1080-21	0076
1080-130	0042
1080-9978	OEM
1080G	0126
1081-1511	0320
1081-3087	0320
1081-3186	0039
1081-3285	3651
1081-3293	0340
1081-3301	0016
1081-3319	0016
1081-3343	0309
1081-3350	0264
1081-3368	0042
1081-3475	0079
1081-3541	2759
1081-3558	3060
1081-3624	0398
1081-4000	0037
1081-4010	0037
1081-4739	2515
1081-8581	0037
1081-9464	0016
1082-1056	0079
1082-1403	0079
1082-2211	0023
1082-4803	1188
1082-6717	0015
1082-6915	2925
1082-9208	0911
1082-9240	0968
1083-17	0164
1084	0071
1084(GE)	0144
1085(GE)	1493
1085-8967	0144
1085Z4	OEM
1086	1493
1086(GE)	1493
1086(G.E.)	0190
1086-1227	1023
1086-3967	0710
1086-4080	0124
1086-9931	2279
1087	0086
1087-01	2039
1087-02	0076
1087-1606	0224
1087-1630	0148
1087-1648	0688
1087-1663	0148
1087-1713	0133
1087-2901	0076
1088-1	OEM
1088-9517	0133
1089-1	OEM
1089-7619	0428
1089-9938	1900
1090	0071
1090-0033	0023
1090-0071	0133
1090-0827	0157
1090-1	OEM
1090-1981	0133
1090-19801	0133
1090A	OEM
1091	0560
1091-0826	0057
1091-1	OEM
1091-3549	0181
1092	0130
1093	0079
1093-2697	0143
1093-3034	0127
1093-3059	0284
1093A41-165	OEM
1094-7877	0042
1094Z4	OEM
1095	0037
1095-01	0321
1095-2638	0006
1095-2679	0062
1095-6324	0253
1095J2F	0015
1095Z4	OEM
1096-11	0693
1096-12	0532
1096J2F	0015
1097	0797
1097-85	0006
1098-14	1597
1098-15	0693
1098-16	OEM
1098-1975	0041
1098-8665	2506
1099-0950	0086
1099-1214	1274
1099-2949	0701
1099-2972	0023
1099-3616	1482
1099-3624	3050
1099-6346	2379

If replacement code is OEM, contact original manufacturer for replacement.

DEVICE TYPE	REPL CODE
1099-6395	3741
1099-6544	2800
1099-6981	0344
1099-9050	0079
1099-9100	0219
1099-9175	1274
1099-9183	0168
1099-9217	0079
1100	1257
1100-01A	OEM
1100-75	0693
1100-1179	0079
1100-3951	0284
1100-3985	0065
1100-6962	0140
1100-9446	3756
1100-9453	0127
1100-9461	0076
1100-9479	0284
1100-9487	0124
1100-9750	0358
1100I	OEM
1101	1302
1101/01A	OEM
1101-01A	OEM
1101-1640	1359
1101-9072	3240
1101A	OEM
1101ADM	OEM
1101PDK120	OEM
1101PDK140	OEM
1101PDK160	OEM
1101PDK180	OEM
1101PDK200	OEM
1101PDK220	OEM
1101PDK240	OEM
1101PDK260	OEM
1101PDK280	OEM
1101PDK300	OEM
1102	0188
1102-17	0164
1102-17A	0004
1102-63	0595
1102-6853	0023
1102-9568	0623
1103	0188
1103-88	0015
1103-3669	1319
1103-3727	0133
1103-5557	0236
1103-7751	1049
1103I	OEM
1103N	OEM
1104	0140
1104/01A	OEM
1104-01A	OEM
1104-94	0004
1104-95	0208
1104-96	0015
1104-5960	0261
1105	0253
1105-15	0160
1105-2750	0023
1105-3063	0066
1105-4558	1211
1105Z4	OEM
1106	0062
1106-29	0015
1106-36	0015
1106-97	0144
1106-99	0086
1107	0077
1107B-938N78	OEM
1108	0165
1109	0057
1110	0064
1110-86	0015
1111	0181
1111-17	0050
1111-18	0050
1111P	0383
1112	0052
1112-8	0037
1112-78	0086
1112-79	0693
1113	0873
1113-03	0016
1113-13	0050
1113AD-A-CJ-O	OEM
1113ADACJO	OEM
1113AD-A-CJ-P	OEM
1113ADACJP	OEM
1113AD-A-OO-O	OEM
1113ADAOOO	OEM
1113AD-A-OO-P	OEM
1113ADAOOP	OEM
1113AD-B-CJ-O	OEM
1113ADBCJO	OEM
1113AD-B-CJ-P	OEM
1113ADBCJP	OEM
1113AD-B-OO-O	OEM
1113ADBOOO	OEM
1113AD-B-OO-P	OEM
1113ADBOOP	OEM
1113EX8C	OEM
1113EX16C	OEM
1113EX16T	OEM
1113EX80	OEM
1113EX160	OEM

DEVICE TYPE	REPL CODE
1113SX8C	OEM
1113SX16C	OEM
1113SX16T	OEM
1113SX80	OEM
1113SX85	OEM
1113SX160	OEM
1114	OEM
1114-4458	2559
1114E1	OEM
1114Z4	0052
1115	0065
1115-16	0015
1116	0210
1116-42	0015
1116-3243	0079
1116-4027	0016
1116-4035	0079
1116-4084	0037
1116-4092	0037
1116-4100	0079
1116-4118	0079
1116-4126	0037
1116-4365	0133
1116-5016	0037
1116-6691	0851
1116-7004	0431
1117(MC)	0079
1117-76	0015
1117-1857	0079
1117-4422	0079
1117-5353	0066
1118	0371
1118-17	0143
1118-20	0015
1119	0283
1119-54	0050
1119-55	0050
1119-56	0050
1119-57	0004
1119-58	0208
1119-59	0004
1119-9254	2666
1120	0695
1120-17	0133
1120-18	0015
1120-6034	OEM
1120-6364	0275
1121	OEM
1121-1	1417
1121-17	0015
1122	0700
1122-96	0136
1122-2403	0079
1122-2411	0037
1122-2430	0527
1122-2437	0527
1122-8863	0358
1122Z4	OEM
1123-55	0144
1123-56	0144
1123-57	0144
1123-58	0144
1123-59	0144
1123-60	0016
1123-1388	0309
1123-1719	0162
1123-2624	OEM
1124	0160
1124-0017	0162
1124-0239	0906
1124-7234	2083
1124A	0160
1124B	0160
1124C	0085
1125	0555
1125/2582	0037
1125-1188	1338
1125-2582	0037
1125-2590	0549
1125-2608	0062
1125-7722	0143
1125Z4	OEM
1126-0023	0577
1126-0031	0053
1126-0049	0023
1126-0239	0906
1126-0304	0819
1126-0312	0819
1126-0320	0819
1126-0352	0577
1126-0353	0577
1126-0395	0124
1126-5170	1338
1126-7127	0203
1126-7150	0151
1126-7226	0006
1126-7234	2083
1126-8851	0079
1127	0436
1127-8454	0577
1127-8470	0015
1127-8488	0466
1128	0037
1128-17	0004
1128-4239	4773
1128-4304	1260
1128-4437	0015
1128-7540	0164
1128-7547	0005

DEVICE TYPE	REPL CODE
1129	1739
1129-8015	0148
1133	0039
1133-0289	2520
1133-0305	0253
1133-0321	0064
1135-3646	0037
1135-7076	0320
1135-8066	0023
1135-8074	0039
1135-9098	0344
1135-9254	0309
1135-9262	0283
1135Z4	OEM
1136-4064	0133
1137	0661
1137-7058	0057
1137-7215	0124
1138	0015
1138-0789	2011
1138-0979	0069
1138-4757	0270
1138-9442	0391
1138-9459	OEM
1138-9467	0203
1138-9640	0042
1138-9657	0015
1139-17	0015
1140	OEM
1140-17	0004
1140-2302	0846
1140-2310	0212
1140-2328	0079
1140-2864	0079
1140-2898	0210
1140-3193	0079
1140-3195	OEM
1140-3201	0079
1140-3219	0388
1140-3391	0058
1140-3409	0681
1140-4118	4469
1140-4126	0181
1140-4233	3881
1140-4258	0561
1140-4597	0721
1140-7673	0023
1141-3119	1162
1143-0584	1938
1143-0741	0355
1143-0956	0730
1143-1046	0133
1143-1049	0124
1143-2903	0577
1143-4784	1951
1144-1482	0819
1144-3876	0006
1144-5749	0023
1144-9261	0042
1145	0279
1145-17	0004
1145-2695	0052
1145-2703	0079
1145-2711	0224
1145-2729	0561
1145-2737	0037
1145-2745	0079
1145-2752	0079
1145-2778	0042
1145-2786	0906
1145-2794	3920
1145-3156	0079
1145-3164	0037
1145-3370	0559
1145-4071	0212
1145-4188	1023
1145-4253	0037
1145-4741	3494
1145-4949	0079
1145-5011	1382
1145-5037	OEM
1146	0279
1146-0888	0124
1146-0896	0005
1146-0912	0019
1146-5200	0133
1146S	0181
1147	0150
1147-07	OEM
1147-08	0619
1147-09	0215
1147-0249	OEM
1147-0523	0041
1147-0531	1767
1147-10	2232
1147-11	2218
1147-12	1535
1147-161	3763
1147-161(VARACTOR)	0005
1147-3204	0062
1147-3220	0695
1147-3238	0181
1147-4738	OEM
1147-6249	0148
1147-7673	0023
1147-8815	5103
1148-0956	0730
1148-17	0164
1148-7944	0023

DEVICE TYPE	REPL CODE
1148-9499	3045
1148-9523	3055
1148-9556	2008
1148-9580	OEM
1148-9648	1260
1148-9671	3136
1149-0182	0062
1149-0224	0023
1149-0729	0167
1149-0740	1587
1149-0760	0037
1149-0794	0079
1149-2253	OEM
1149-2469	0037
1149-2477	0144
1149-2493	0949
1149-2501	2636
1149-2527	0019
1149-2535	0124
1149-2543	0790
1149-2576	0133
1149-4332	0076
1149-4374	0338
1149-4390	0076
1149-4408	1317
1149-4424	0161
1149-6729	0167
1150	0095
1150-7746	0076
1150-7753	1505
1150-7761	0064
1150-8504	1212
1150-9098	2208
1151	0391
1151-3736	0076
1151-5442	OEM
1153-0128	1376
1154	6622
1154-5563	1202
1154-5613	0006
1154-5696	3990
1154-6199	0076
1154-6561	0210
1154-6579	0388
1154-6587	0006
1154-7072	0625
1154-9680	0528
1154-9880	0528
1154-9938	0176
1155	2279
1155-1785	0037
1155-1934	3903
1155-5562	0598
1155-5570	0701
1155-5588	4803
1155-5596	0076
1155-5604	0558
1155-5612	0143
1155-5620	0124
1155-5636	0064
1155-6560	0006
1155-6578	2279
1155-8228	1060
1155-8236	0076
1155-8764	0212
1155-9259	2898
1155GE	0102
1155Z4	OEM
1156	1313
1156(TC)	1805
1156-1644	0133
1157	0086
1157-0165	0437
1157-2096	0547
1157-2104	2195
1157-4712	2195
1157-4720	OEM
1157-4738	2279
1157-4746	0143
1157-4753	0143
1157-4761	0133
1157-4779	0005
1157-4787	0023
1157-4795	0124
1157-4829	0527
1157-4837	0079
1157-4845	0016
1157-4852	0079
1157-4860	0710
1157-4878	4811
1157-4886	0144
1157-8564	0215
1157-8572	2170
1157-8580	0388
1157-8598	0676
1157-8606	0127
1157-8622	0076
1157-8630	0191
1157-8648	0148
1157-8655	0133
1157-8663	2217
1157-8671	0023
1157-8689	1319
1157-8697	0274
1157-8705	0181
1157-8929	0139
1157-8937	1914
1157-8945	0120
1158	OEM

DEVICE TYPE	REPL CODE
1159	OEM
1159-2318	5249
1159-2342	3926
1160	OEM
1160-7009	0466
1160-7611	0253
1160-7629	0057
1160-8015	0023
1160H	OEM
1161-2926	0253
1161-7719	0224
1163-4110	0057
1163-4243	0076
1163-5423	OEM
1163-7907	OEM
1163-9507	1357
1163-9572	0006
1163-9960	OEM
1164-4762	4432
1164-4804	0037
1164-4812	OEM
1164B	2633
1164D	1995
1164F	2657
1164H	3846
1164K	2631
1165(GE)	0167
1166	0142
1166-3829	3920
1166-3879	3920
1166-3887	0239
1166-5197	5675
1166-5205	4521
1168-2754	0143
1168-2788	0137
1168-7944	0023
1169	0233
1169-2076	0167
1169-4478	0062
1169-7653	0676
1170-0036	2868
1171-8309	OEM
1172-0026	0859
1172-0034	1192
1172-0036	2868
1172-0042	0330
1172-1396	0055
1172-1494	0016
1172-1936	OEM
1172-5157	2008
1172-5272	0819
1172-5306	0922
1172-5330	0577
1172-5413	0053
1172-5504	0124
1172-9811	0127
1172-9829	0037
1172-9837	0284
1172-9845	0079
1172-9852	0284
1172-9860	0018
1172-9878	0358
1172-9886	1308
1172-9894	2702
1172-9902	0549
1172-9910	0062
1173-1171	0127
1173-1494	0079
1173-2575	3756
1173-4613	4336
1173-4639	4339
1173-6824	0079
1173-6832	OEM
1173-8192	1981
1173-8200	0264
1173-8220	0264
1173-8291	0133
1173-8309	0023
1173-8317	0814
1173-8325	0023
1173-8556	0064
1174	0391
1175-0056	0794
1175-0064	0284
1175-5659	OEM
1175-7879	0694
1175-7903	0754
1175-7911	0765
1175-7937	0624
1175-7945	0577
1175-8000	0765
1175-8018	0624
1175-8026	0667
1175-8190	0819
1175-8281	0577
1175-8299	0577
1175-8349	0339
1175-8364	0296
1176-5005	3713
1176-5013	1211
1176-5039	0041
1176-6367	0224
1176-7126	0079
1176-7134	0037
1176-7142	0076
1176-7159	1274
1176-7167	0261
1176-7175	0055
1176-7183	0261

DEVICE TYPE	REPL CODE
1176-7191	3474
1176-7209	0066
1176-7217	0023
1176-7225	0023
1176-7233	0466
1176-7241	0023
1176-7258	OEM
1176-7266	0658
1176-7274	2268
1176-7645	0023
1176-8819	0836
1176-8827	0006
1176-72167	0023
1177	0244
1177-1144	3692
1177-1151	2599
1177-1169	5004
1177-1177	0261
1177-1185	2643
1177-1193	0275
1177-1201	0388
1177-1219	0023
1177-1227	0023
1177-1235	0023
1177-1243	0133
1177-1250	0091
1177-1268	0436
1177-1276	0999
1177-1284	0440
1177-1292	0705
1177H01	OEM
1177H02	OEM
1177H03	OEM
1177H04	OEM
1177H09	OEM
1178	0167
1178-3842	0168
1178-3859	0079
1178-4291	0261
1178-7066	OEM
1178-7209	0066
1178-7454	0906
1178-7462	0658
1178-7470	0037
1178-7488	0006
1178-7491	0638
1178-7496	0638
1178-7512	0079
1178-7520	0836
1178-7538	1274
1178-7546	1638
1178-7553	0710
1178-7561	0270
1178-7579	0055
1178-7587	0055
1178-7603	0023
1178-7611	0133
1178-7637	0494
1178-7645	0023
1178-7652	0071
1178-7660	0023
1178-7678	0023
1178-7686	0466
1178-7694	0466
1178-7696	OEM
1178-7812	OEM
1178-7868	0466
1179	6624
1179-0334	0759
1179-1308	1045
1179-1324	1157
1179-1332	0723
1179-1340	0080
1179-1357	0023
1179-1365	0015
1179-2256	0076
1179-2264	0590
1179-2306	0312
1179-2330	0511
1179-9186	0124
1179A	OEM
1180	OEM
1180-1	OEM
1180-1859	0124
1180-1867	0006
1180-1875	0015
1180-1883	0895
1180-1891	OEM
1180-1909	0023
1180-1917	1900
1180-1925	0055
1180-1933	0041
1180-1941	2040
1180-1958	0284
1180-1966	2411
1180-1974	3017
1180-1982	0431
1180-1990	2058
1180-2006	0076
1180-2014	3104
1180-2022	0728
1180-2030	0166
1180-2048	0062
1180-2055	1666
1180-2063	OEM
1180-2071	5124
1180-2089	3726
1180-2881	0127
1180-4457	0052

DEVICE TYPE	REPL CODE
1180-5520	0041
1180-5959	OEM
1180-5991	2109
1180-6296	0436
1180-6429	OEM
1180-6445	5412
1180-6734	0466
1180-6858	OEM
1180-6866	OEM
1180-9446	OEM
1181-3201	0701
1181-3268	0170
1181-3396	1382
1181-3409	0127
1181-3417	0111
1181-3425	0111
1181-3433	2882
1181-3458	0532
1181-3466	0558
1181-3474	2882
1181-3565	5070
1181-3739	0261
1181-3763	0658
1181-3771	0076
1181-3789	0261
1181-3797	0066
1181-3805	0168
1181-3813	1274
1181-3821	0023
1181-3912	0638
1181-3920	0949
1181-4472	0919
1181-4910	6676
1181-4928	1135
1181-4944	OEM
1181-5263	0052
1181-7103	0133
1181-7111	0023
1181-7129	3692
1181-7137	2599
1181-7145	0167
1181-7152	0388
1181-7160	0638
1181-7194	1319
1181-7228	0638
1183-0494	0118
1183-17	0693
1183-1633	2759
1183-2052	0133
1183-2060	0676
1183-3258	0055
1183-3266	0999
1183-3274	0790
1183-3282	0102
1183-3290	0023
1183-3308	0468
1183-3314	0015
1183-3316	0015
1183-3340	OEM
1183-3458	0133
1183-3548	0133
1183-8216	0371
1184-4	OEM
1184-5109	0014
1184-5641	1732
1184-5658	0064
1184-5666	0064
1184-5682	0023
1184-5708	0124
1184-5716	0124
1184-5732	0181
1184-8108	0485
1184-8728	1420
1184-9056	1795
1184-9064	0999
1184-9098	0790
1184G	0126
1185-0161	2531
1185-0260	0203
1185-5	OEM
1186	0037
1186-1	0030
1186-3	0030
1186-4	0030
1186-5	0911
1186-6	OEM
1186-5573	0023
1186-5581	0489
1186-5672	2868
1186-5839	3718
1186-5888	0859
1186-5912	5117
1186-5953	0895
1186-5987	0275
1186-5995	0275
1186-6035	0283
1187	0086
1188-0101	0181
1188-0333	2604
1188-3097	0577
1188-6306	0080
1190	0065
1190-9983	0023
1190H	OEM
1191-3290	OEM
1191-3308	OEM
1191-3316	OEM
1191-3340	1934
1191-3357	0409

If replacement code is OEM, contact original manufacturer for replacement.

199

DEVICE TYPE	REPL CODE
1191-3365	0121
1191-3373	1338
1191-3381	2208
1191-3399	0060
1191-3415	0071
1191-3423	0071
1191-3431	0140
1191-3449	0140
1191-4769	0127
1191-4793	0723
1191-4819	0133
1191-4991	4284
1191-7860	0168
1191-8547	5210
1191-8869	2678
1192	0211
1192(IC)	2377
1192(XSTR)	0211
1192-7837	0120
1192-7845	0123
1192-7852	2511
1192-7860	0168
1192-7878	0076
1192-7886	0042
1192-9288	0168
1193-0054	2845
1193-0062	0155
1193-0070	0168
1193-0083	0076
1193-0096	0527
1193-0104	1157
1193-0112	0041
1193-0120	OEM
1193-4148	OEM
1193-4163	1157
1193-4171	0064
1193-4189	0730
1193-4197	0466
1193-4205	0118
1193-8503	OEM
1193-8511	0640
1193-8529	OEM
1193-8537	0689
1195-2679	0062
1195-4455	0559
1195-6372	0091
1195-6380	0133
1195-6398	0133
1195-6406	0023
1195-6414	0023
1195-6422	0023
1195-6430	0181
1195-6448	0120
1195-6455	0559
1195-6463	1982
1195-6497	0261
1195-6505	0284
1195-6513	1274
1195-6521	0949
1195-6539	0261
1195-6547	3250
1195-6562	1420
1195-6570	0485
1195-6893	0057
1195-6901	0275
1195-6943	0065
1195-6950	0130
1197-0027	0064
1197-1645	OEM
1197-1686	0819
1197-1777	0577
1197-1793	0053
1197-1819	0165
1197-5055	OEM
1197-5505	OEM
1197-6024	0041
1197-6032	3680
1197-6040	4441
1198-4143	0006
1198-4176	0261
1198-4200	0261
1198-4267	5041
1198-4291	0860
1198-4325	0261
1198-4358	0148
1198-4382	0124
1198-4388	0124
1198-4853	0719
1198-4887	OEM
1198-4911	OEM
1198-5181	0719
1199-7822	0023
1199-7830	0313
1199-7848	0167
1199-7855	1192
1199-7855(ZE)	0313
1199-7863	0037
1199-7871	0261
1200	2453
1200/1	OEM
1200/2	OEM
1200/11	OEM
1200/12	OEM
1200/22	OEM
1200-1913	0006
1200-2036	1900
1200-2093	0155
1200-2148	0023
1200-2184	0023
1200-2200	2079
1200-2242	0361
1200-2267	OEM
1200-2358	0970
1200-2366	OEM
1200-2382	1319
1200-2416	0176
1200-2440	3476
1200-2531	0284
1200-3412	0166
1200-3422	OEM
1200-3430	3860
1200-3448	2109
1200-3463	2641
1200-3489	OEM
1200-3497	0024
1200-3505	1349
1200-3513	OEM
1200-3530	3860
1200-3539	0006
1200-3547	0945
1200-3554	0275
1200-3562	0275
1200-3588	0055
1200-3596	3912
1200-3604	1747
1200-3612	0166
1200-3620	0124
1200-3638	0023
1200-3646	0031
1200-3653	0106
1200-3661	OEM
1200-3679	OEM
1200-4099	OEM
1200-4123	OEM
1200-4156	OEM
1200-4883	OEM
1200-4925	4226
1200-5112	OEM
1200-8336	0309
1200-9437	1722
1200-9460	1597
1200-9494	1376
1200-9528	0124
1200-9551	5082
1200-9585	0140
1200H	OEM
1200PDE10	OEM
1200PDE20	OEM
1200PDE30	OEM
1200PDE40	OEM
1200PDE50	OEM
1200PDE60	OEM
1200PN50	OEM
1200PN60	OEM
1200PN80	OEM
1200PN100	OEM
1200PN120	OEM
1200PN140	OEM
1200PN150	OEM
1200PN160	OEM
1200PN180	OEM
1200PN200	OEM
1200PN210	OEM
1200PN220	OEM
1200PN230	OEM
1200PN240	OEM
1200PN250	OEM
1200XY2-35SC	OEM
1201	OEM
1201(TRANS)	OEM
1201-4114	0015
1201-4148	0313
1201-4171	0023
1201-4205	0790
1201-7331	0127
1201-7349	0079
1201-7372	0527
1201-7406	3990
1201-7430	0092
1201-7737	OEM
1201-7760	OEM
1201-8156	0338
1201-8180	0076
1201-8214	0284
1201-8248	0099
1201-8271	OEM
1201-9618	5707
1201-W1K	OEM
1201PDE20	OEM
1201PDE30	OEM
1201PDE40	OEM
1201PDE60	OEM
1201PDE80	OEM
1201PDE100	OEM
1201PDE120	OEM
1201PDE140	OEM
1201SS1-07SC	OEM
1202	0826
1202(SWITCH)	0826
1202(TRANS)	0826
1202-0229	0148
1202-7678	0014
1202-7702	2189
1202-7710	1083
1202-7751	0181
1202-7769	0053
1202-W4K	OEM
1202-W8K	OEM
1202H	OEM
1202M	0079
1202XY2-35SC	OEM
1203	0809
1203(TRANS)	0881
1203-6323	0355
1203-6380	0873
1203-6406	0339
1203-6414	0053
1203-7362	0143
1203-7370	0790
1203-7388	0071
1203-7396	0031
1203-7412	0224
1203-7420	0836
1203-7438	0079
1203-7446	0148
1203-7453	0284
1203-7461	1488
1203-7479	1490
1203-7487	0006
1203-7495	0284
1203-WAP	OEM
1204	0892
1204(TRANS)	0892
1204-0010	0006
1204-0028	2420
1204-W1KAP	OEM
1205	0015
1205-7790	0053
1205-7816	0261
1205-7832	0906
1205-7840	0066
1205-7845	0006
1205-7857	0155
1205-7865	0006
1205-7873	1614
1205-7899	0261
1205-7907	3476
1205-7923	0023
1205A	0015
1206	6625
1206(TRANS)	OEM
1206-17	0123
1206-6667	OEM
1206-W1KAP	OEM
1207	0938
1207-17	0143
1207-4543	0023
1207-4553	OEM
1207-4707	1938
1207-4758	0018
1207-6519	OEM
1207-6543	0023
1207-6576	OEM
1207-6600	0133
1207-6634	0015
1207-6667	0015
1207-6691	0041
1207-6725	1274
1207-6758	0018
1207-6782	0558
1207-6816	0168
1207-6873	0445
1207-6907	1938
1207-6931	0034
1207-6964	0520
1207-7673	0018
1207-WAP	OEM
1208	0952
1208-3853	0064
1208-3861	0140
1209	0988
1209-0445	0261
1209-3027	0023
1209-3035	0181
1209-3042(DIO)	OEM
1209-3043	0181
1209-3043(DIO)	0023
1209-5873	0066
1209-7143	1614
1210	1003
1210-17	0470
1210-17(MIXER)	0079
1210-17(OSC)	0079
1210-17B	0016
1210-W23K	OEM
1210-W46K	OEM
1211	1013
1211-9327	OEM
1211-W46K	OEM
1211-W92K	OEM
1212	0883
1212(ROSS)	0133
1212-4	0930
1212-5009	0023
1213	1043
1213-6446	0133
1213-6453	OEM
1214	0037
1214-1560	OEM
1214-4915	0148
1214-4945	0906
1214-4952	0148
1214-4957	0148
1214-4960	0148
1214-4978	0860
1214-4986	0261
1214-4994	0023
1214-5009	0023
1214-5017	0091
1214-5024	0071
1214-5025	0071
1214-7952	0148
1214-W1K	OEM
1215	0015
1215-3839	0015
1215-4274	0017
1215-5693	0031
1215-5701	0041
1215-5719	OEM
1215-5727	OEM
1215-8663	4246
1215-8671	4126
1215-9620	OEM
1215RA	2275
1216	OEM
1216-2541	0246
1216-2575	3499
1217-0536	0037
1217-0544	0261
1217-2284	4569
1217-2383	0261
1217-5164	0014
1217-8554	OEM
1217-8562	1132
1217-8570	1132
1217-8588	0155
1217-8596	0155
1217-8604	0284
1217-8612	0284
1217-8620	2464
1217-8935	4306
1217-8943	6182
1217-8950	5165
1217-8968	5166
1217-8976	5166
1217-8992	3869
1217-9008	5168
1217-9016	5169
1217-9024	0765
1217-9032	OEM
1217-9040	5170
1217-9057	OEM
1217-9065	3130
1217-9073	OEM
1217-9081	0112
1217-9099	2464
1217-9107	0643
1217-9115	1132
1217-9123	2041
1217-9131	0723
1217-9149	0723
1217-9156	0060
1217-9164	0014
1217-9172	0060
1217-9180	0023
1217-9198	0182
1217-9206	0041
1217-9214	0041
1217-9222	0253
1217-9230	0253
1217-9248	0064
1217-9255	0064
1217-9271	0031
1217-9289	0446
1217-9297	0023
1217-9305	0339
1217-9313	0062
1217-9321	0064
1217-9339	0053
1217-9347	0053
1217-9362	0282
1217-9370	0293
1217-9388	0635
1217-9396	0293
1218	OEM
1218H	OEM
1219-8685	OEM
1220	OEM
1220-3055	OEM
1220H	OEM
1221	OEM
1221-1021	OEM
1222	OEM
1222-6684	0006
1222-7104	0079
1222H	OEM
1223	0752
1223-1924	0440
1223-2229	0018
1223-2237	2351
1223-2245	0076
1223-2252	0031
1223-2260	0041
1223-2278	0023
1223-2286	0371
1223-2294	0700
1224	OEM
1224-3804	OEM
1224H	OEM
1225-4975	0101
1226H	OEM
1227	OEM
1227-0187	0076
1227-17	0016
1227-4296	0155
1227-4304	0155
1227-4312	0284
1227-4320	0284
1227-4338	1157
1227-6457	OEM
1227-8495	OEM
1227-8610	0970
1227-9142	1614
1227-9741	0551
1228-17	0016
1228-4017	0076
1228-4022	1779
1228-4410	0658
1228-4428	0836
1228-4451	1533
1228-4469	1533
1228H	OEM
1229-0862	5703
1229-1134	4768
1229-1159	4109
1229-1167	1026
1229-1175	0826
1229-1183	0881
1229-1191	0892
1229-1308	0057
1229-4617	OEM
1229-4625	2884
1229-4633	0129
1229-4641	OEM
1229-4658	0129
1229-4690	5207
1229-4724	0819
1229-4799	0721
1229-4807	0077
1229-4815	0077
1229-6133	OEM
1229-6141	OEM
1229-8170	2869
1229-8477	0076
1229-8485	0076
1229-8709	0052
1229-8725	1319
1229-8733	0041
1229-8766	0133
1229H	0144
1230	6627
1230-9266	0165
1231-0082	OEM
1231-0108	OEM
1231-0116	2055
1231-0132	0356
1231-0140	0356
1231-0157	3776
1231-0165	2884
1231-0181	OEM
1231-0207	4417
1231-0215	4312
1231-0256	0548
1231-0280	OEM
1231-0314	OEM
1231-0348	2464
1231-0355	0819
1231-0363	2208
1231-0371	0577
1231-0389	1967
1231-0397	0060
1231-0405	0057
1231-0421	OEM
1231-0447	0057
1231-3185	0148
1231-4720	0860
1231-4787	0148
1231-8325	3776
1231-8333	0624
1231-8341	0678
1231-8358	6026
1231-8366	0624
1231-8374	OEM
1231-8390	OEM
1231-8408	1132
1231-8416	0355
1231-8424	0695
1231-8432	0695
1231-8440	0023
1231-8788	1767
1231-8903	OEM
1232-2889	0681
1232-7284	OEM
1232-7292	1521
1232-7300	3860
1232-7409	0949
1232-7573	4959
1232-7730	2770
1232-7755	3104
1232-7805	0468
1232-7862	OEM
1232-7946	1485
1233	OEM
1233H	OEM
1234-1095	1379
1234-1674	4923
1234-5849	2961
1234-5856	OEM
1234-5864	0076
1234-5880	0781
1234-5898	0023
1234-5906	0023
1234-5914	0695
1234-5922	4074
1234-5930	OEM
1234-5948	4923
1234-5955	1542
1234-5963	5162
1234H	OEM
1235-2126	2770
1235-7943	0017
1235H	OEM
1236	OEM
1236H	OEM
1237-5473	0071
1237-5739	0079
1237-6042	0037
1237-6208	OEM
1237-7912	2015
1237-9467	0041
1238-9730	0527
1238-9748	0023
1238-9755	0041
1238-9763	0006
1238-9771	1274
1238H	OEM
1239	OEM
1239-4755	0124
1239-6537	1521
1239-6545	2109
1239-6552	0015
1239-6560	0133
1239-7766	0101
1239-7774	1638
1239-7782	0148
1239-7808	0071
1239-7824	0023
1240	OEM
1240-3432	3581
1240-3440	3168
1240-3457	0508
1240H	OEM
1241	0279
1241A	0211
1241H	OEM
1242-1814	OEM
1242-7522	4407
1243	OEM
1243H	OEM
1244-3834	1533
1244H	OEM
1245H	OEM
1247	OEM
1247-7097	OEM
1247-7121	0015
1247-7139	OEM
1247-7147	OEM
1247-9523	1533
1247H	OEM
1248	0004
1248-4010	0140
1248H	OEM
1250	OEM
1250-1326	0313
1250-4320	OEM
1250-4346	0042
1250-4478	OEM
1250-4486	OEM
1250-4643	0877
1250-4650	0695
1250-5210	0024
1250-5228	OEM
1250-5855	0079
1251-1-1	0212
1252-4906	0023
1253-5F	OEM
1253-6	OEM
1253-6F	OEM
1253-7	OEM
1253-7F	OEM
1253-8	OEM
1253-8F	OEM
1253-9	OEM
1253-10	OEM
1253H	OEM
1254	0150
1254-1025	1082
1254-1074	0031
1254-1082	0102
1254-1090	0023
1254-1108	0118
1254-1413	0018
1254-1694	0330
1254-1942	1157
1254-1959	1157
1254-2106	2164
1254-2171	OEM
1254-2593	2470
1254-3583	2273
1254-3591	OEM
1254-5661	OEM
1254-5869	0517
1254-5877	OEM
1254-5885	4040
1254-5893	OEM
1254-7170	OEM
1254-7295	OEM
1254H	OEM
1255-1063	4306
1255-1081	5228
1255-1099	5232
1255-1107	OEM
1255-1123	3869
1255-1131	4054
1255-1164	OEM
1255-1198	3130
1255-1206	0112
1255-1214	1059
1255-1222	0826
1255-1289	0124
1255-1297	5261
1255-2626	0052
1255H	OEM
1256-1213	4078
1256-1221	OEM
1256-1478	OEM
1256-1486	OEM
1256-1494	OEM
1256H	OEM
1257-15	OEM
1257-3812	0638
1257-4497	OEM
1257-4505	OEM
1257-4521	OEM
1257-4537	3479
1257-4539	3479
1257-4547	OEM
1257-4554	OEM
1257-4562	OEM
1257-4570	0681
1257-4596	0023
1257-4612	0700
1257-4620	0057
1257-4638	0631
1258-2352	0091
1258-2532	0466
1258-2540	0071
1258-9198	0023
1259-12	OEM
1259-2713	OEM
1259-2721	OEM
1259-2739	1026
1259-2747	0881
1259-2754	3460
1259-2804	2219
1259-4917	3726
1259-4941	OEM
1259-4958	2015
1259-4966	4417
1259-4974	OEM
1259-5005	0495
1259-5021	OEM
1259-5039	OEM
1259-5047	1533
1259-5054	0253
1259-5062	0466
1259-5070	0124
1259-5096	0041
1259-5104	0064
1259-5112	0091
1259-5120	OEM
1259-5138	0015
1259-5146	0282
1259-5153	OEM
1259-5161	OEM
1259-5179	3844
1259-5187	3844
1259-6516	2845
1259-6524	0534
1259-6532	0107
1259-6565	0076
1259-6581	0275
1259-6615	OEM
1259-6623	2604
1259-6631	OEM
1259-7702	2189
1263A	0015
1263B	OEM
1264	0345
1264H	OEM
1266-0268	0079
1266-2053	1319
1266-2219	0006
1266-2227	0148
1266-2243	0284
1266-2250	0219
1266-2268	0079
1266-2276	0124
1266-2284	1967
1266-2292	0388
1266-2300	0055
1266-2318	0124
1266-2326	0137
1266-2334	0181
1266-2342	0023
1266-2359	0023
1266-2367	0023
1266-2375	0023
1266-2383	OEM
1266-2383(DS2(LED))	OEM
1266-2391	0080
1266-2409	0023
1266-2417	0790
1266-2425	0678
1266-2433	2079
1266-2441	2092
1266-2458	2104
1266-2466	2109
1266-2471	0790
1266-2953	1319
1266-5201	0456
1266H	OEM
1268H	OEM

If replacement code is OEM, contact original manufacturer for replacement.

DEVICE TYPE	REPL CODE
1270-1751	4035
1270-1769	3331
1270-1777	3830
1270-1785	4312
1270-1793	0062
1270-1801	0023
1270-4797	5627
1270-4805	0039
1270-4813	0053
1270-4821	0466
1270-4839	OEM
1270-4847	3397
1270-5208	0006
1270-5214	0261
1270-5216	0261
1270-5224	0284
1270-5232	0261
1270-5240	0284
1270-5257	1533
1270-5265	0023
1270-5273	0023
1270-5281	0124
1270-5299	4083
1270-5588	0140
1270-6701	0790
1270-7014	0124
1270-7030	0133
1270-7048	0133
1271-2972	0638
1271-3111	3896
1272	0016
1272H	OEM
1273-8480	0023
1275-3034	0261
1276-1292	0372
1276H	OEM
1277-17	0004
1277-7074	OEM
1277-7264	OEM
1277-7272	OEM
1277-7280	OEM
1277-9302	0446
1277A	4150
1278	0391
1278(GE)	0391
1279-3147	0253
1282	0555
1285	1257
1287-5670	3494
1287-7049	0079
1287-7239	0017
1287-7247	0031
1287-7254	OEM
1287-7262	OEM
1287-7304	OEM
1287-7668	0695
1287-7734	OEM
1287-7908	3940
1287-7916	3331
1287-7924	3830
1287-7932	0001
1287-7940	3726
1287-8989	3940
1287-9987	0631
1287-9995	0157
1288-0134	0181
1288-0175	OEM
1288-0183	2541
1288-0357	OEM
1288-0779	0064
1288-0787	OEM
1288-0795	OEM
1288-0803	0002
1288-1389	0077
1288H	OEM
1289	0015
1289A	OEM
1290-3613	1317
1290-6798	OEM
1290-6806	OEM
1290-6814	0041
1290-6848	1614
1290-6855	1614
1290-6863	0037
1290-6871	0037
1290-6885	1614
1290-6954	OEM
1290-7010	OEM
1292H	OEM
1294	0150
1294-9624	0638
1294H	OEM
1296-1892	0534
1296-1900	0457
1296-1918	0101
1296-1926	3900
1296-1934	0261
1296-1942	0551
1296-1959	0551
1296-2718	1281
1296-2742	0261
1297-1404	1533
1297-1412	1533
1298-0439	OEM
1298-0447	OEM
1298-0777	0534
1298-0785	0970
1298-0793	0552
1298-0801	0079
1298-0819	0037
1298-0827	0023
1298-0835	0261
1298-0961	OEM
1298-0967	OEM
1298-3391	0144
1298-3409	0330
1298-3425	OEM
1298-3888	0330
1298-3896	OEM
1298-3904	OEM
1298-3920	5179
1298-3995	OEM
1298-6923	2217
1298-6931	0079
1298-6949	OEM
1299-7862	0330
1300PKL20S63	OEM
1300PKL20S625	OEM
1300PKL20S635	OEM
1300PKL20S645	OEM
1300PKL20S655	OEM
1300PKL20S663	OEM
1300PKL20S673	OEM
1300PKL20S683	OEM
1300PKL20T603	OEM
1300PKL30S63	OEM
1300PKL30S625	OEM
1300PKL30S635	OEM
1300PKL30S645	OEM
1300PKL30S655	OEM
1300PKL30S663	OEM
1300PKL30S673	OEM
1300PKL30S683	OEM
1300PKL30T603	OEM
1300PKL40S63	OEM
1300PKL40S625	OEM
1300PKL40S635	OEM
1300PKL40S645	OEM
1300PKL40S655	OEM
1300PKL40S666	OEM
1300PKL40S673	OEM
1300PKL40S683	OEM
1300PKL40T603	OEM
1300PKL50S63	OEM
1300PKL50S625	OEM
1300PKL50S645	OEM
1300PKL50S655	OEM
1300PKL50S666	OEM
1300PKL50S676	OEM
1300PKL50S683	OEM
1300PKL50T603	OEM
1300PKL60S63	OEM
1300PKL60S625	OEM
1300PKL60S635	OEM
1300PKL60S645	OEM
1300PKL60S655	OEM
1300PKL60S666	OEM
1300PKL60S673	OEM
1300PKL60S683	OEM
1300PKL60T603	OEM
1300PKL502635	OEM
1300RN	0127
1301	OEM
1302	0777
1303	0801
1303-1802	0388
1303-2479	0053
1304	OEM
1305	0870
1306	0205
1307	0475
1307H	0696
1308	0499
1308-1802	0388
1309	0679
1309-0915	0999
1309-1004	1542
1309-1020	OEM
1310	0225
1310-4997	0261
1310-8253	0006
1310-8261	0261
1310-8287	0836
1310-8295	0284
1310-8303	0582
1310-8311	1533
1310-8352	0057
1310-8378	OEM
1310-8386	OEM
1310-8394	0534
1310-8395	0284
1310-8402	0552
1310-8410	0727
1310-8522	0057
1310-8586	OEM
1311	0230
1311-8641	1934
1312	0234
1313	1387
1313-5496	5437
1313-5538	1900
1313-5546	2348
1313-5553	0457
1313-5561	1519
1313-5652	0168
1313-5785	OEM
1313-5793	0034
1314	0037
1314-1718	1274
1315	0016
1315-9967	2116
1315-9975	OEM
1315-9983	0638
1316	0016
1316-0908	0261
1316-0916	0042
1316-0924	0338
1316-0932	0261
1316-0951	3726
1316-0963	4126
1316-0973	3054
1316-0981	2843
1316-17	0004
1316-1003	3590
1316-1005	3590
1316-1013	2929
1316-1021	OEM
1316-1039	0517
1316-1047	OEM
1316-1054	OEM
1316-1062	OEM
1316-3167	0006
1316-3175	0023
1316-3183	0253
1316-3191	OEM
1316-3217	0034
1316-3225	0311
1316-3233	OEM
1316-3241	OEM
1316-3258	0457
1316-6137	OEM
1316-7887	3765
1316-7895	1977
1316-7903	OEM
1316-7911	1319
1316-7929	1319
1316-7937	2253
1316-7945	0723
1316-7952	0723
1316-7960	0071
1316-7978	0023
1316-7986	0071
1316-7994	0023
1317-17	0004
1318	OEM
1318-5996	0551
1318-6275	0261
1319	OEM
1319BB	OEM
1319M	OEM
1319MF	OEM
1320	0211
1321	0065
1321-01	OEM
1321-1461	0137
1321-1917	1533
1321-1925	OEM
1321-4051	0267
1322	OEM
1322-01	OEM
1323	OEM
1324	0236
1325-1186	4349
1325-1418	OEM
1327	OEM
1327-1291	2109
1327-1309	1192
1327-4922	0006
1327-4980	0261
1327-5029	0261
1327-5045	OEM
1327-5052	OEM
1327-5060	1533
1327-5078	0041
1327-5110	0019
1327-5136	0023
1327-5144	0031
1328-0003	0071
1328-0011	0053
1328-0037	OEM
1329	0211
1330	0211
1330-5313	0481
1330-5339	0053
1330-8937	0124
1330-8945	0466
1330-8952	0041
1330-8960	0023
1330-8978	0062
1330-8994	0053
1330-9018	0466
1330-9026	0023
1330-9034	0091
1330-9059	0023
1330-9067	0023
1330-9075	0041
1330-9083	0023
1330-9091	0344
1330-9109	0257
1330-9117	0195
1330-9125	0071
1330-9141	0140
1330-9158	0023
1330-9174	0124
1330-9182	OEM
1330-9190	3871
1330-9208	4177
1330-9216	4066
1330-9224	0330
1330-9232	1631
1330-9240	1689
1330-9256	0118
1330-9257	1521
1330-9265	2843
1330-9273	3054
1330-9281	3860
1330-9299	OEM
1331-7532	0819
1331-7540	0577
1331-7565	0577
1331-7573	2208
1331-7581	0819
1331-7607	0275
1331-7615	0168
1331-7623	3574
1331-7672	0781
1331-9272	0077
1332	OEM
1333	OEM
1333-0535	OEM
1336	OEM
1339	0103
1340	0279
1343	OEM
1344-6448	0253
1344-8253	0023
1344-8287	0023
1344-8477	0261
1345	1581
1346-6347	4470
1346-8897	OEM
1346-8905	2641
1346-8913	OEM
1346-8921	4032
1346-8939	2330
1346-8947	3897
1346-8954	3017
1346-8962	0248
1346-8970	0137
1346-8988	0057
1346-8996	0253
1346-9002	0057
1346-9010	0466
1346-9028	0072
1347	0746
1347-17	0004
1347-7112	2384
1348	0746
1348-1429	0037
1348-1437	0079
1348-1445	0133
1348-1452	0039
1348-1593	2164
1348-4969	0527
1348-4977	0155
1348-4985	0041
1348-4993	0057
1348-5008	0181
1348-5016	0195
1348-5024	2348
1348-5032	3473
1348-5040	OEM
1348-5057	OEM
1348A12H01	1342
1348A14H01	1150
1348A30H01	1812
1348A32H01	1035
1348A36H01	1820
1348A44H01	0033
1348A45H01	0081
1348A46H01	0141
1348A62H01	0557
1349-17	0208
1350	0279
1351	0850
1352	0485
1352-9870	1533
1355-3086	0023
1356A	OEM
1358	1581
1359-0161	0330
1359-3827	0577
1359-3835	0577
1360	0211
1362-17	0004
1362-17A	0004
1364-17	0004
1365-4991	OEM
1365-5113	0034
1365-5121	OEM
1365-6939	0041
1365-6947	OEM
1365-7192	2217
1368-1747	0031
1368-1754	0102
1368-1762	0372
1368-1796	OEM
1368-1804	OEM
1368-1812	OEM
1368-1838	OEM
1368-1846	3223
1368-1853	1022
1368-1861	OEM
1368-1879	OEM
1368-2638	1319
1368C/D	0016
1370-7229	0023
1370-7237	OEM
1370-7245	0372
1370-7252	OEM
1370-7260	OEM
1370-7351	1376
1370-7369	3454
1370-7377	0713
1371-17	0208
1371-5404	0052
1371-5412	1207
1371-5420	OEM
1373-17	0151
1373-17A	0127
1373-17AL	0144
1374-17	0155
1374-17A	0155
1374-17AC	0016
1374-6714	0339
1374-6722	0133
1374-6730	1123
1374-6748	0165
1374-6755	0091
1374-6763	0023
1374-6771	OEM
1374-6789	0162
1374-6797	OEM
1374-6813	0071
1374-6821	2330
1374-6839	OEM
1374-6847	2348
1374-6854	OEM
1374-6896	0284
1374-6920	0261
1374-7019	0261
1374-7605	OEM
1376	OEM
1376-001	2007
1376-002	2007
1376-2257	0041
1376-6456	0165
1377-2637	0023
1377-2645	0031
1377-2652	4049
1377-2660	OEM
1377-2678	0077
1377-2686	0057
1377-2694	OEM
1377-2710	OEM
1377-2728	OEM
1377-2736	OEM
1377-2744	3310
1377-2751	OEM
1377-2769	OEM
1377-2777	6827
1377-3775	OEM
1377-3783	OEM
1377-3791	4440
1377-3809	0006
1377-3817	1376
1377-3825	OEM
1377-3833	6933
1377-3841	1084
1377-3858	0284
1377-3866	0527
1377-4591	OEM
1377-4609	OEM
1377-6208	0023
1377-6224	OEM
1377-6232	OEM
1377-6349	0472
1377-6356	OEM
1378-8633	OEM
1378-8658	OEM
1380-4679	OEM
1380-4687	4246
1380-4695	OEM
1380-4729	1775
1380-5601	0023
1380-5650	OEM
1380-5668	OEM
1380-5676	OEM
1380-5692	OEM
1380-5700	OEM
1380-5726	OEM
1380-5734	0271
1380-5742	OEM
1380-6054	0071
1380-6062	0023
1380-6070	1631
1380-6146	OEM
1380-6179	1731
1380-6187	1741
1380-6195	OEM
1380-6203	1533
1380-6211	0719
1384-3263	4344
1384-3271	OEM
1384-3289	0023
1384-3909	OEM
1384-4972	OEM
1384-5029	OEM
1384-5185	OEM
1384S1	OEM
1390	0279
1390-6417	OEM
1392	OEM
1396	0595
1400	0279
1401-1225	OEM
1401-1405	OEM
1401-1407	OEM
1401-1410	OEM
1401-1415	OEM
1401-1420	OEM
1401-1425	OEM
1402	0016
1402A	OEM
1402B	0016
1402C	0079
1402CD	0079
1402D	0079
1402E	0079
1402E/D	OEM
1403A	OEM
1404A	OEM
1405-17	0015
1405A	OEM
1406T	OEM
1407T	OEM
1410	0279
1410-102	0133
1410-102(ROGERS)	0229
1410-167	0015
1410-169	0124
1410-169(ROGERS)	0133
1410-171	0143
1411	OEM
1411-130	0025
1411-134	1254
1411-135	0137
1411-136	0170
1411-137	0631
1412-1	0016
1412-1-12	0016
1412-1-12-8	0016
1412-170	0015
1412-177	1386
1412-182	0242
1412-190	0242
1412DA1AP	OEM
1412DA1BP	OEM
1412DA1CP	OEM
1412DA1DP	OEM
1412DA1EP	OEM
1412DA2AP	OEM
1412DA2BP	OEM
1412DA2CP	OEM
1412DA2DP	OEM
1412DA2EP	OEM
1412DA3AP	OEM
1412DA3BP	OEM
1412DA3CP	OEM
1412DA3DP	OEM
1412DA3EP	OEM
1412DA4AP	OEM
1412DA4BP	OEM
1412DA4CP	OEM
1412DA4DP	OEM
1412DA4EP	OEM
1413-159	0040
1413-160	0211
1413-168	0599
1413-172	0599
1413-175	0211
1413-178	0160
1414-157	0086
1414-158	0037
1414-158(ROGERS)	0037
1414-173	0079
1414-174	0155
1414-176	0037
1414-179	3483
1414-180	2411
1414-183	0155
1414-184	0086
1414-185	0126
1414-186	0086
1414-187	0126
1414-188	0130
1414-189	0086
1414A	0160
1414A-12	0160
1414A-12-8	0160
1415	0016
1416	0086
1417	0224
1417-177	0435
1420-1-1	0127
1420-2-2	0007
1423	0127
1431	OEM
1434	0236
1436-17	0004
1438B	OEM
1438B-83	OEM
1439	OEM
1441-0415	OEM
1441-0420	OEM
1441-0425	OEM
1441-0615	OEM
1441-0620	OEM
1441-0625	OEM
1441-0815	OEM
1441-0820	OEM
1441-0825	OEM
1441-1015	OEM
1441-1020	OEM
1441-1025	OEM
1441-1215	OEM
1441-1220	OEM
1441-1225	OEM
1441-1415	OEM
1441-1420	OEM
1441-1425	OEM
1443D	OEM
1443D-83	OEM
1444	OEM
1445	OEM
1446-17	OEM
1452N1	OEM
1453G	OEM
1455-7-4	0127
1458	0356
1459	0211
1461C	OEM
1461C-83	OEM
1462	1149
1464-607-7	0405
1464-607-8	0405
1465	0016
1465-1	0050
1465-1-12	0050
1465-1-12-8	0050
1465-2	0208
1465-2-12	0208
1465-2-12-8	0208
1465-4	0595
1465-4-12	0595
1465-4-12-8	0595
1465A	0050
1465A-12	0050
1465A-12-8	0050
1465B	0136
1465B-12	0136
1465B-12-8	0136
1465C	0160
1465C-12	0160
1465C-12-8	0160
1466-1	0004
1466-1-12	0004
1466-1-12-8	0004
1466-2	0004
1466-2-12	0004
1466-2-12-8	0004
1466-3	0004
1466-3-12	0004
1466-3-12-8	0004
1471-4356	1820
1471-4364	0141
1471-4372	0557
1471-4380	1812
1471-4398	0033
1471-4729	0267
1471-9860	1820
1473	0006
1474-3	0279
1474-3-12	0279
1474-3-12-8	0279
1476-17	0004
1476-17-6	0004
1477-3436	1843
1477A	0435
1477A-12	0435
1477A-12-8	0435
1478-6982	1918
1479-0224	1824
1479-0240	0677
1479-0257	4772
1479-0265	3670
1479-7971	1896
1480B	OEM
1480B-83	OEM
1482	0016
1482-17	1390
1483	0102
1483(XSTR)	0086
1483E209	OEM
1483E419	0102
1484A	0160
1484A-12	0160
1484A-12-8	0160
1485-9896	1609
1486-4	OEM
1486-8780	0680
1487-17	4144
1488(SEARS)	0015
1488B	0050
1488B-12	0050
1488B-12-8	0050
1488C	0279
1488C-12	0279
1488C-12-8	0279
1489-17	0143
1490	OEM
1492-1	0435
1492-1-12	0435
1492-1-12-8	0435
1493-17	0016
1496	3751
1499-009-0202	OEM
1499-009-0309	OEM
1499-009-0901	OEM
1500PJA10	OEM
1500PJA20	OEM
1500PJA30	OEM
1500PJA40	OEM

If replacement code is OEM, contact original manufacturer for replacement.

201

DEVICE TYPE	REPL CODE
1501	0224
1502-0229	0148
1502B	0079
1502C	0079
1502CH	OEM
1502D	0224
1502M	OEM
1502MH833	5675
1504	OEM
1505	0015
1505A	0015
1506T	OEM
1507T	OEM
1512	0143
1512,-36/1-01-883	OEM
1512C-16/1-01	OEM
1512C-36/1-01	OEM
1512C-1601	OEM
1512C-160212	OEM
1512C-160312H	OEM
1512C-160612HP	OEM
1512M-16/1-01-883	OEM
1512M-16/1-06	OEM
1512M-36/1-01	OEM
1512M-160712HP833	OEM
1512M-161112HP833	OEM
1514	0127
1515	0079
1517	OEM
1518	OEM
1521B	0899
1524	0198
1524(PNP)	OEM
1526	0050
1526(RECT)	OEM
1526/802	OEM
1527	OEM
1527-5282	1035
1527-5308	0081
1540	0016
1542	0614
1542(GE)	0614
1548-17	0178
1550	0143
1550-17	0361
1553-17	0037
1559	0569
1559(GE)	0588
1559-17	0160
1559-17A	0160
1561-0403	0103
1561-0404	0103
1561-0408	0130
1561-0410	0130
1561-0604	0103
1561-0608	0130
1561-0610	0130
1561-0615	0130
1561-0803	0130
1561-0804	0130
1561-0805	0130
1561-0808	0130
1561-0810	0130
1561-0815	0130
1561-17	0160
1561-1004	0130
1561-1005	0130
1561-1008	0130
1561-1010	0130
1561-1015	0130
1561-1208	1841
1561-1210	1841
1561-1215	1841
1561-1404	0177
1561-1410	1841
1561-1415	1841
1561-1608	1841
1561-1610	1841
1561-1615	1841
1561A603	0103
1561A608	0130
1561A615	0130
1562	0015
1567	0016
1567-0	0016
1567-2	0016
1571-0401	0178
1571-0402	0178
1571-0420	0178
1571-0425	0178
1571-0601	0178
1571-0602	0178
1571-0620	0178
1571-0801	0178
1571-0802	0178
1571-0820	0178
1571-0825	0178
1571-32	0178
1571-33	0178
1571-34	OEM
1571-35	OEM
1571-36	OEM
1571-41	0178
1571-42	0178
1571-43	0178
1571-44	OEM
1571-46	OEM
1571-1001	0178
1571-1002	0178

DEVICE TYPE	REPL CODE
1571-1020	0178
1571-1025	0178
1571-1220	0178
1571-1225	0178
1571-1425	0178
1582	0037
1582-0403	0103
1582-0404	0103
1582-0405	0103
1582-0408	0130
1582-0410	0130
1582-0415	0130
1582-0508	0130
1582-0510	0130
1582-0603	0103
1582-0604	0103
1582-0605	0103
1582-0608	0130
1582-0610	0130
1582-0615	0130
1582-0803	0130
1582-0804	0130
1582-0805	0130
1582-0808	0130
1582-0810	0130
1582-0815	0130
1582-1003	0130
1582-1004	0130
1582-1005	0130
1582-1008	0130
1582-1010	0130
1582-1015	0130
1582-1208	0130
1582-1210	0130
1582-1215	0130
1582-1810	0130
1600EXD24	OEM
1600FD26	OEM
1600FXD24	OEM
1600GXD21	OEM
1600PN50	OEM
1600PN60	OEM
1600PN80	OEM
1600PN100	OEM
1600PN120	OEM
1600PN140	OEM
1600PN150	OEM
1600PN160	OEM
1601GPT	OEM
1601PDK120	2126
1601PDK140	OEM
1601PDK160	OEM
1601PDK180	OEM
1601PDK200	OEM
1601PDK210	OEM
1601PDK220	OEM
1601PDK230	OEM
1601PDK240	OEM
1601PDK250	OEM
1602	0006
1602E	OEM
1603	OEM
1604/OPI	OEM
1604/POC	OEM
1605	OEM
1606	OEM
1607	OEM
1607-6812	OEM
1607A80	1197
1608	OEM
1609	0065
1611-17	0015
1612SK24E	0321
1614	OEM
1615C	0196
1616	OEM
1616/MIC	OEM
1616/OII	OEM
1616/OIO	OEM
1616C	0479
1616CCI	OEM
1616HCO	OEM
1617	OEM
1617C	1073
1619	OEM
1620	OEM
1620BB	OEM
1620DMA	OEM
1620M	OEM
1620MF	OEM
1620TTL	OEM
1627-1413	2871
1627-2064	0354
1634-17	0470
1634-17-14A	0144
1642	OEM
1643	0619
1652H	OEM
1653H	OEM
1654H	OEM
1655H	OEM
1663C-01D	OEM
1663C-02D	OEM
1663M-01D	OEM
1663M-02D	OEM
1664TTL	OEM
1666C-01A12	OEM
1666C-02B12H	OEM
1666C-03C12HP	OEM

DEVICE TYPE	REPL CODE
1666C-06A12HP833	OEM
1666M-07B	OEM
1666M-11C12	OEM
1666M-15A12H	OEM
1667M-6D	OEM
1672	OEM
1673M-5B	OEM
1674-17	0015
1682	OEM
1687-17	0470
1699-17	0133
1700	OEM
1700-5182	2515
1701	OEM
1701-01	OEM
1702	0198
1702-0	0079
1702-01	OEM
1702-O	0079
1702K	0079
1702M	0018
1702MNO	0079
1703	0103
1703-01	OEM
1706-3B	OEM
1710	0155
1710-1	1135
1710-2	4087
1710-3	OEM
1711-0402	OEM
1711-0405	OEM
1711-0602	OEM
1711-0605	OEM
1711-0802	OEM
1711-0805	OEM
1711-17	0016
1711-1002	OEM
1711-1005	OEM
1711-1202	OEM
1711-1205	OEM
1711-1402	OEM
1711-1405	OEM
1711-1602	OEM
1711-1605	OEM
1711-1802	OEM
1712-17	0016
1713-0402	OEM
1713-0405	OEM
1713-0602	OEM
1713-0605	OEM
1713-0802	OEM
1713-0805	OEM
1713-17	0015
1713-1002	OEM
1713-1005	OEM
1713-1202	OEM
1713-1205	OEM
1713-1402	OEM
1713-1405	OEM
1713-1602	OEM
1713-1605	OEM
1713-1802	OEM
1714-0402	0424
1714-0405	0424
1714-0602	0424
1714-0605	0424
1714-0802	0424
1714-0805	0424
1714-2	OEM
1714-1002	0424
1714-1005	0424
1714-1202	0424
1714-1205	0424
1714-1402	0424
1714-1405	0424
1714-1602	0424
1714-1605	0424
1714-1802	0424
1714-1805	0424
1715-3	OEM
1716-0402	OEM
1716-0405	OEM
1716-2	5508
1716-1805	OEM
1717	OEM
1717-0402	OEM
1717-0405	OEM
1717-0602	OEM
1717-0605	OEM
1717-0802	OEM
1717-0805	OEM
1717-1002	OEM
1717-1005	OEM
1717-1202	OEM
1717-1205	OEM
1717-1402	OEM
1717-1405	OEM
1717-1602	OEM
1717-1605	OEM
1717-1802	OEM
1719-1	5536
1720	OEM
1720-5	OEM
1720-6	OEM
1720R	OEM
1723-0405	2465
1723-0410	2465
1723-0605	2465
1723-0610	2465

DEVICE TYPE	REPL CODE
1723-0805	2465
1723-0810	2465
1723-17	0016
1723-1005	2465
1723-1010	2465
1723-1205	2465
1723-1210	2465
1723-1405	2465
1723-1410	2465
1723-1605	2465
1723-1610	2465
1723-1805	0130
1723-1810	0130
1723R	OEM
1725	OEM
1726	OEM
1726-0405	OEM
1726-0410	OEM
1726-0605	OEM
1726-0610	OEM
1726-0805	OEM
1726-0810	OEM
1726-1005	OEM
1726-1010	OEM
1726-1205	OEM
1726-1210	OEM
1726-1405	OEM
1726-1410	OEM
1726-1605	OEM
1726-1610	OEM
1726-1805	OEM
1726-1810	OEM
1727	OEM
1731	OEM
1732	OEM
1736R	OEM
1737R	4902
1738R	4786
1739R	OEM
1740R	OEM
1741-0051	0232
1741-0069	0677
1741-0085	0268
1741-0119	0310
1741-0143	0357
1741-0150	1896
1741-0176	0381
1741-0184	3221
1741-0200	0462
1741-0234	0507
1741-0242	0680
1741-0275	2382
1741-0291	1342
1741-0325	0692
1741-0333	3670
1741-0366	4516
1741-0416	0867
1741-0424	5284
1741-0440	3478
1741-0473	1018
1741-0481	0554
1741-0564	1160
1741-0572	1933
1741-0598	1177
1741-0606	2090
1741-0622	1193
1741-0630	2158
1741-0663	3129
1741-0689	1265
1741-0697	5312
1741-0721	2472
1741-0747	1423
1741-0770	0117
1741-0804	1358
1741-0895	0564
1741-0952	1477
1741-1018	0936
1741-1042	1484
1741-1075	1487
1741-1133	0522
1741-1190	1032
1741-1224	1046
1741-1257	0175
1741-1299	4772
1741-1323	4329
1741-1349	1818
1741-1380	2009
1743-0610	2465
1743-0620	OEM
1743-0630	2465
1743-0810	OEM
1743-0820	2465
1743-0830	OEM
1743-1010	2465
1743-1020	OEM
1743-1030	2465
1743-1210	OEM
1743-1220	2465
1743-1230	OEM
1743-1410	2465
1743-1420	2465
1743-1430	2465
1743-1610	OEM
1743-1620	2465
1743-1630	OEM
1743-1810	2416
1743R	OEM
1748-0620	OEM
1748-1020	OEM

DEVICE TYPE	REPL CODE
1748-1420	OEM
1750	OEM
1750-00-0-0	OEM
1750-00-WXX-WXX	OEM
1750-01-0-0	OEM
1750-01-WXX-WXX	OEM
1750-02-0-0	OEM
1750-02-WXX-WXX	OEM
1751	6229
1751-17	1211
1751G036	0016
1753-1	OEM
1753-2	OEM
1754	OEM
1754-1	0656
1754-3	0620
1755	OEM
1756-1	0906
1756-17	0133
1757	OEM
1757-7	OEM
1760-1	5996
1760-2	5996
1760-3	OEM
1761	OEM
1761-1	6004
1761-17	0144
1762	OEM
1762-2	OEM
1763	OEM
1763-0415	0130
1763-0420	0130
1763-0425	0130
1763-0615	0130
1763-0620	0130
1763-0625	0130
1763-0815	0130
1763-0820	2187
1763-0825	0130
1763-1015	0130
1763-1020	0130
1763-1025	0130
1763-1215	0130
1763-1220	0130
1763-1225	0130
1763-1415	0130
1763-1420	0130
1763-1425	0130
1763-1615	OEM
1763-1625	OEM
1763-1815	OEM
1764	OEM
1765	OEM
1766	0137
1768	OEM
1768-0415	OEM
1768-0420	OEM
1768-0425	OEM
1768-0615	OEM
1768-0625	OEM
1768-0815	OEM
1768-0825	OEM
1768-1015	OEM
1768-1025	OEM
1768-1215	OEM
1768-1225	OEM
1768-1415	OEM
1768-1425	OEM
1768-1625	OEM
1768-1815	OEM
1771-0440	OEM
1771-0450	OEM
1771-0460	OEM
1771-0640	OEM
1771-0650	OEM
1771-0660	OEM
1771-0840	OEM
1771-0850	OEM
1771-0860	OEM
1771-1040	OEM
1771-1050	OEM
1771-1060	OEM
1771-1240	OEM
1771-1250	OEM
1771-1260	OEM
1771-1440	OEM
1771-1450	OEM
1771-1460	OEM
1771-1640	OEM
1772	OEM
1773-3	OEM
1774-2	OEM
1775-2	OEM
1776-0450	OEM
1776-0650	OEM
1776-1050	OEM
1776-1250	OEM
1776-1450	OEM
1777-1	OEM
1777-17	0004
1778-17	0143
1780-1	2029
1780-2	OEM
1785	OEM
1787	OEM
1788	OEM
1789-17	0086
1791	OEM
1792-17	0144

DEVICE TYPE	REPL CODE
1793	OEM
1794	OEM
1794-17	1075
1794-17(10)	0012
1795	OEM
1798	OEM
1799-17	0016
1800	2840
1800-17	0016
1800DC	0844
1800PC	0844
1800XY2-35SC	OEM
1801DC	0868
1801PC	0868
1801SS1-07SC	OEM
1802-01	OEM
1802DC	0882
1802L	0527
1802M	0527
1802PC	0882
1802XY2-35SC	OEM
1803-1	3535
1803DC	0894
1803PC	0894
1804	0718
1804-17	0233
1804DC	0913
1804PC	0913
1805	0268
1805DC	0923
1805PC	0923
1806	0357
1806-17	0103
1806-17A	0103
1806DC	0939
1806PC	0939
1807	1046
1807DC	0956
1807PC	0956
1808	1199
1808-8	OEM
1808DC	0976
1808PC	0976
1809	0133
1809(I.C.)	0718
1809DC	0992
1809PC	0992
1810	OEM
1810DC	1005
1811	OEM
1811/4K	OEM
1811/16K	OEM
1811-110-10111	0911
1811DC	1019
1811PC	1019
1812-1	0016
1812-1-12	0016
1812-1-127	0016
1812-1L	0016
1812-1L8	0016
1812DC	1033
1812PC	1033
1813	OEM
1813DC	4458
1813PC	4458
1814	OEM
1814/4K	OEM
1814/16K	OEM
1814A	0160
1814A-12	0160
1814A-127	0160
1814AL	0160
1814AL-8	0160
1814DC	4461
1814PC	4461
1815	OEM
1816CMOS-8L	OEM
1816CMOS-8S	OEM
1816CMOS-16L	OEM
1816CMOS-16S	OEM
1816R	OEM
1817R	OEM
1818	0133
1818(I.C.)	0718
1818-1	OEM
1820	OEM
1820-0054	0232
1820-0055	1199
1820-0063	1160
1820-0068	0507
1820-0069	0692
1820-0070	0867
1820-0075	1164
1820-0077	1303
1820-0087	2595
1820-0095	3365
1820-0099	0564
1820-0122	0354
1820-0174	0357
1820-0214	1046
1820-0261	0175
1820-0301	1423
1820-0304	1417
1820-0328	0310
1820-0341	1622
1820-0352	1843
1820-0430	1911
1820-0476	1545
1820-0495	0522

DEVICE TYPE	REPL CODE
1820-0512	2472
1820-0861	0141
1820-0862	3365
1820-0863	0461
1820-0864	0331
1820-0865	0033
1820-0869	1168
1820-0870	0462
1820-0894	0357
1820-1064	0729
1820-1068	5284
1820-1111	1018
1820-1172	1339
1820R	OEM
1821	OEM
1821-1	OEM
1821R	OEM
1826-1	0024
1827-17	0004
1833	OEM
1834	OEM
1835	OEM
1835-17	0191
1839-2	OEM
1840-17	0222
1841	OEM
1841-17	0016
1842	OEM
1843	OEM
1843-17	0007
1844-17	0037
1845-17	0007
1846	OEM
1846-17	0133
1847	OEM
1848-17	0015
1849	0015
1849R	0015
1850	0015
1850-2	OEM
1850-17	0037
1850R	0015
1851-17	0229
1852-17	0144
1853-0045	0126
1854-0003	0016
1854-17	0015
1855-17	0015
1858	0595
1858-1	OEM
1858-1/KIT	OEM
1858A	0012
1859	OEM
1859-14	0160
1859-16	0160
1859-17	0321
1859R	0015
1861	3079
1862	OEM
1862-001	OEM
1862-002	OEM
1865-1	0050
1865-1-12	0050
1865-1-127	0050
1865-1L	0050
1865-2	0208
1865-2-12	0208
1865-2L	0208
1865-2L8	0208
1865-4	0595
1865-4-12	0595
1865-4-127	0595
1865-4L	0595
1865-4L8	0595
1865A	0050
1865A-12	0050
1865A-127	0050
1865AL8	0050
1865B	0136
1865B-12	0136
1865B-127	0136
1865BL	0136
1865BL8	0136
1865C	0160
1865C-12	0160
1865C-127	0160
1865CL	0160
1865CL8	0160
1866-1	0004
1866-1-12	0004
1866-1-127	0004
1866-1L	0004
1866-1L8	0004
1866-2	0004
1866-2-12	0004
1866-2-127	0004
1866-2L	0004
1866-2L8	0004
1866-3	0004
1866-3-12	0004
1866-3-127	0004
1866-3L	0004
1866-3L8	0004
1866-17	0016
1867-17	0037
1868	OEM
1868-001	OEM
1868-002	OEM
1871	OEM

If replacement code is OEM, contact original manufacturer for replacement.

DEVICE TYPE	REPL CODE
1872	OEM
1874-2	OEM
1874-3	0279
1874-3-12	0279
1874-3-127	0279
1874-3L	0279
1874-3L8	0279
1877A	0435
1877A-12	0435
1877A-127	0435
1877AL	0435
1877AL8	0435
1879-17	0155
1879-17A	0086
1880-17	0144
1881-17	0144
1882-17	0016
1883-17	0016
1884-17	0016
1884A	0160
1884A-12	0160
1884A-127	0160
1884AL	0160
1884AL8	0160
1885-17	0233
1886-17	OEM
1888B	0050
1888B-12	0050
1888B-127	0050
1888BL	0050
1888BL8	0050
1888C	0279
1888C-12	0279
1888C-127	0279
1888CL	0279
1888CL8	0279
1889-17	1471
1890-17	0144
1892-1	0435
1892-1-12	0435
1892-1-127	0435
1892-1L	0435
1892-1L8	0435
1893	OEM
1893-17	0016
1894	OEM
1895	OEM
1900	OEM
1901-0028	0535
1901-0036	0535
1901-0045	0242
1901-0388	0535
1901-0389	0535
1901-0557	2673
1906-17	0208
1915-17	0155
1915A	OEM
1916-17	1390
1917-17	0004
1919-17	0004
1919-17A	0004
1922-00	OEM
1923-17	0144
1923-17-1	0144
1925-17	0151
1929-17	0016
1931-17	0127
1931-17A	0144
1932-17	0016
1933-17	0086
1934-17	0321
1935-17	0203
1936-17	0178
1937-17	0133
1940-17	0037
1941-17	0023
1943-430	0079
1945-17	0222
1946-17	0004
1947-17	0123
1948-17	0914
1949-17	0023
1950	OEM
1950-17	0015
1951-17	0136
1952-17	0007
1954-17	0004
1955-17	0222
1956-17	0143
1957	OEM
1957-2	OEM
1958-17	0208
1960-17	0004
1961-17	0076
1966-17	0016
1968-17	2035
1969-17	0042
1970-16	0015
1970-17	0015
1971-17	0071
1972-17	0086
1973-17	0004
1974-17	0004
1977-17	0143
1979-17	0133
1980-17	0143
1981/1904	OEM
1981/1908	OEM
1981/1912	OEM

DEVICE TYPE	REPL CODE
1981/1916	OEM
1981/1920	OEM
1981-17	0133
1982/1904	OEM
1982-17	0015
1983/1908	OEM
1983/1912	OEM
1983/1916	OEM
1983-17	0144
1985/1	OEM
1985/2	OEM
1998-17	0127
1999	0016
1999-17	0127
2000-001	2238
2000-002	0215
2000-003	2290
2000-004	1288
2000-005	1805
2000-006	4145
2000-007	2246
2000-008	1288
2000-009	3751
2000-01	OEM
2000-010	4405
2000-011	4405
2000-017	1532
2000-029	4564
2000-030	OEM
2000-031	3980
2000-032	4571
2000-033	4567
2000-034	0321
2000-035	2801
2000-036	2312
2000-037	4227
2000-038	OEM
2000-052	4558
2000-053	OEM
2000-101	0321
2000-102	0410
2000-103	0410
2000-104	3308
2000-105	0321
2000-107	0321
2000-108	0683
2000-111	0683
2000-125	0133
2000-201	0148
2000-202	0688
2000-203	1056
2000-204	0151
2000-205	0127
2000-206	2787
2000-207	1581
2000-208	0930
2000-209	0945
2000-210	0076
2000-211	0833
2000-212	0830
2000-213	0076
2000-214	0127
2000-215	0018
2000-216	2276
2000-218	0006
2000-221	2421
2000-235	0076
2000-240	1060
2000-241	0781
2000-242	0830
2000-245	0076
2000-258	0284
2000-265	0006
2000-266	0376
2000-267	0127
2000-268	0364
2000-269	0018
2000-270	0884
2000-271	0930
2000-275	0284
2000-276	0018
2000-301	0019
2000-302	0124
2000-303	0133
2000-304	0023
2000-305	0012
2000-308	0012
2000-309	0030
2000-312	0416
2000-317	0133
2000-318	0123
2000-320	0015
2000-321	0041
2000-322	0091
2000-323	0715
2000-324	0091
2000-325	0077
2000-326	0416
2000-327	0012
2000-328	0091
2000-329	0631
2000-330	0319
2000-331	0139
2000-332	0133
2000-333	0041
2000-339	0139
2000-341	0163
2000-342	0120
2000-344	0030

DEVICE TYPE	REPL CODE
2000-345	0133
2000-348	0087
2000-367	0165
2001	0042
2001(DIO)	OEM
2001(E.F.JOHNSON)	0042
2001-17	0016
2001-303	0133
2001A	OEM
2001PDK60	3846
2001PDK80	2126
2001PDK100	2126
2001PDK120	2126
2001PDK140	OEM
2001PDK160	OEM
2002	0160
2002(DIO)	OEM
2002A	OEM
2003	0103
2003(DIO)	OEM
2003-01	OEM
2003-17	0016
2004	0164
2004-01	0931
2004-02	2195
2004-03	0931
2004-04	0076
2004-05	1409
2004-06	0006
2004-14	0076
2004-67	0124
2004-68	0120
2004-69	5024
2004-70	0215
2005	OEM
2005(TRANS)	OEM
2006	0016
2006-17	0053
2007-01	0160
2008	0178
2008-17	0016
2009	0435
2010	0435
2010(RECT.)	5189
2010-17	0321
2011	0161
2012	0211
2014	OEM
2014I	0168
2015	0050
2015(RECT)	5189
2015-00	0136
2015-1	0103
2015-1A	0103
2015-2	0103
2015-2A	0103
2015-3	0103
2015-3A	0103
2016	1887
2016P	1887
2017-108	0386
2017-109	0228
2017-111	0139
2017-113	0298
2017-114	0015
2017-115	0076
2018	OEM
2018-003-106	0006
2018-01	0532
2018-12	OEM
2018-401-10	0076
2018-411-100	0076
2018-413-10	0076
2018-4140102	1136
2019-40	1025
2019-45	0124
2020	0050
2020(RECT)	2872
2020(RECT.)	2872
2020-00	0136
2020-01	1382
2020-02	1146
2020-03	0544
2020-04	0321
2020-05	0532
2020-06	1409
2020-07	0006
2020-08	0005
2020-6	OEM
2020-7	OEM
2020-8	OEM
2020-9	OEM
2020R	1232
2021	0050
2021-00	0136
2021-05	0023
2022	OEM
2022-01	0150
2022-03	0076
2022-04	0930
2022-05	0016
2022-06	0212
2022-07	0143
2022-08	0015
2022-244	0076
2023	OEM
2023-34	OEM
2023-41	0012
2025	5190

DEVICE TYPE	REPL CODE
2025-1	2716
2025-2	2716
2025-3	2716
2025-9110-18810	0143
2026	0016
2026-00	0016
2026-4	2969
2026-5	2969
2027	0079
2027-00	0693
2027R.F.	0079
2028	0144
2028-00	0144
2030	5190
2030R	5398
2031-17	0023
2032-33	1060
2032-34	1060
2032-35	0006
2032-36	1270
2032-37	0076
2032-38	0215
2032-40	1409
2035	0847
2035-83	OEM
2035-5100-53660	0532
2035-5100-69372	0547
2039-2	0595
2040	0847
2040-17	0170
2041-01	0151
2041-02	0155
2041-03	0219
2041-04	0930
2041-05	0133
2041-06	0012
2042-1	2462
2042-2	2453
2042-17	0004
2043	OEM
2043-17	0037
2044-17	0198
2045	5192
2045-17	0015
2045Z4	OEM
2047-52	4588
2049-01	OEM
2049-03	1288
2049-32	0030
2050	5192
2052	0015
2055A100-50	2265
2056-04	2246
2056-05	0413
2056-06	3650
2056-10	0006
2056-75	0321
2056-105	2238
2057-305	OEM
2057A2-22	OEM
2057A2-27	0079
2057A2-28	0211
2057A2-37	0136
2057A2-48	0142
2057A2-49	0050
2057A2-60	0136
2057A2-62	0016
2057A2-64	0016
2057A2-65	0136
2057A2-66	0136
2057A2-80	0136
2057A2-81	0142
2057A2-84	0142
2057A2-87	0224
2057A2-103	0016
2057A2-109	0127
2057A2-110	0127
2057A2-113	0016
2057A2-116	0127
2057A2-117	0127
2057A2-117(OSC)	0079
2057A2-117(RF-AMP)	0079
2057A2-119	0127
2057A2-120	0127
2057A2-121	0016
2057A2-122	0076
2057A2-127	0144
2057A2-128	0127
2057A2-131	0076
2057A2-133	0160
2057A2-143	0079
2057A2-145	0016
2057A2-146	0016
2057A2-147	0004
2057A2-148	0004
2057A2-149	0050
2057A2-150	0786
2057A2-151	0086
2057A2-152	0016
2057A2-153	0016
2057A2-154	0016
2057A2-155	0016
2057A2-156	0086
2057A2-157	0007
2057A2-158	0007
2057A2-159	0050
2057A2-163	0151
2057A2-165	0004
2057A2-166	0050

DEVICE TYPE	REPL CODE
2057A2-167	0208
2057A2-175	OEM
2057A2-179	0144
2057A2-180	0007
2057A2-181	0007
2057A2-182	0037
2057A2-183	0037
2057A2-184	0016
2057A2-185	0007
2057A2-187	0007
2057A2-192	0007
2057A2-193	0007
2057A2-195	0007
2057A2-196	0007
2057A2-197	0007
2057A2-198	0037
2057A2-199	0086
2057A2-200	0150
2057A2-201	0144
2057A2-202	0007
2057A2-203	0150
2057A2-204	0007
2057A2-205	0050
2057A2-206	0211
2057A2-207	0007
2057A2-208	0016
2057A2-209	0016
2057A2-210	0004
2057A2-211	0222
2057A2-212	2039
2057A2-215	0016
2057A2-216	1136
2057A2-217	0127
2057A2-218	1136
2057A2-219	0113
2057A2-220	0284
2057A2-221	0127
2057A2-222	0016
2057A2-223	0142
2057A2-224	0144
2057A2-225	0151
2057A2-226	0016
2057A2-227	0076
2057A2-228	0191
2057A2-229	0006
2057A2-230	0086
2057A2-231	0050
2057A2-232	0050
2057A2-234	0086
2057A2-237	0127
2057A2-241	0004
2057A2-249	0111
2057A2-251	0007
2057A2-252	0050
2057A2-253	OEM
2057A2-254	OEM
2057A2-255	OEM
2057A2-256	0144
2057A2-257	0111
2057A2-258	0007
2057A2-259	0127
2057A2-260	0111
2057A2-261	0233
2057A2-262	0111
2057A2-263	0136
2057A2-264	0016
2057A2-265	0969
2057A2-272	0111
2057A2-273	0111
2057A2-274	0111
2057A2-275	0111
2057A2-276	0016
2057A2-277	0037
2057A2-278	0016
2057A2-279	0016
2057A2-280	0016
2057A2-281	0016
2057A2-284	0086
2057A2-285	0016
2057A2-288	0004
2057A2-289	0076
2057A2-289(4TH-LF)	0326
2057A2-290	0111
2057A2-294	0016
2057A2-295	0086
2057A2-296	0016
2057A2-297	0016
2057A2-298	0148
2057A2-300	0016
2057A2-301	0042
2057A2-302	0085
2057A2-303	0016
2057A2-304	0127
2057A2-305	0127
2057A2-306	0076
2057A2-307	0037
2057A2-309	0144
2057A2-310	0144
2057A2-311	0144
2057A2-312	OEM
2057A2-313	0144
2057A2-314	0144
2057A2-315	OEM
2057A2-316	0016
2057A2-317	0164
2057A2-318	OEM
2057A2-319	0079
2057A2-320	OEM
2057A2-322	0127

DEVICE TYPE	REPL CODE
2057A2-323	0127
2057A2-324	0016
2057A2-325	0127
2057A2-326	0127
2057A2-329	0004
2057A2-331	0127
2057A2-332	0016
2057A2-333	0111
2057A2-334	0111
2057A2-341	0016
2057A2-342	0144
2057A2-343	0037
2057A2-352	0111
2057A2-353	0037
2057A2-356	0320
2057A2-359	0037
2057A2-370	1212
2057A2-373	0111
2057A2-374	0016
2057A2-385	0111
2057A2-386	0144
2057A2-387	0016
2057A2-390	0016
2057A2-391	0111
2057A2-392	0144
2057A2-393	0144
2057A2-394	0144
2057A2-395	0127
2057A2-396	0016
2057A2-397	0037
2057A2-398	0016
2057A2-399	0016
2057A2-400	0037
2057A2-401	0016
2057A2-402	0144
2057A2-403	0037
2057A2-404	0111
2057A2-405	0111
2057A2-406	0037
2057A2-412	0016
2057A2-427	0155
2057A2-428	0111
2057A2-429	OEM
2057A2-430	0037
2057A2-432	0224
2057A2-433	0016
2057A2-434	0016
2057A2-436	1211
2057A2-445	0683
2057A2-446	0006
2057A2-448	0144
2057A2-449	0016
2057A2-452	0191
2057A2-454	0111
2057A2-457	0037
2057A2-463	0016
2057A2-464	0016
2057A2-465	0151
2057A2-466	0592
2057A2-468	0155
2057A2-475	0111
2057A2-477	0127
2057A2-478	0151
2057A2-479	0592
2057A2-480	0148
2057A2-483	0224
2057A2-484	0018
2057A2-486	0155
2057A2-487	0016
2057A2-489	0037
2057A2-501	0127
2057A2-502	0111
2057A2-503	0127
2057A2-504	0144
2057A2-505	0144
2057A2-507	0224
2057A2-508	0224
2057A2-509	0144
2057A2-510	0016
2057A2-511	0016
2057A2-518	0111
2057A2-524	0155
2057A2-526	0224
2057A2-527	0224
2057A2-529	0688
2057A2-530	0086
2057A2-539	0127
2057A2-540	0127
2057A2-541	0127
2057A2-542	0547
2057A2-543	0547
2057A2-558	0284
2057A2-559	0079
2057A2-560	0079
2057A2-561	0037
2057A10-64	0016
2057A32-25	4463
2057A32-26	1469
2057A32-33	0514
2057A100	0103
2057A100-4	2839
2057A100-8	0004
2057A100-9	0004
2057A100-10	0136
2057A100-13	2839
2057A100-14	2839
2057A100-15	0211
2057A100-16	1506
2057A100-17	0086
2057A100-18	2839

DEVICE TYPE	REPL CODE
2057A100-21	0004
2057A100-23	0164
2057A100-24	0004
2057A100-26	1506
2057A100-30	2839
2057A100-31	OEM
2057A100-32	OEM
2057A100-33	OEM
2057A100-34	0164
2057A100-35	2839
2057A100-40	5748
2057A100-41	0164
2057A100-44	0164
2057A100-45	4033
2057A100-47	1647
2057A100-48	0164
2057A100-49	0161
2057A100-50	4033
2057A100-51	0037
2057A100-53	0127
2057A100-55	0004
2057A100-58	1647
2057A100-60	OEM
2057A100-62	3863
2057A100-66	1647
2057A100-67	0320
2057A100-69	3644
2057A100-72	1371
2057A100-72(NPN)	OEM
2057A100-72(PNP)	OEM
2057A-288	0211
2057A289	0086
2057A-429	0144
2057A-430	0150
2057B0-3	2839
2057B-2	0279
2057B2-4	0211
2057B2-14	0144
2057B2-23	0004
2057B2-27	0470
2057B2-28	0470
2057B2-29	0004
2057B2-32	0211
2057B2-34	0211
2057B2-35	0136
2057B2-37	0136
2057B2-38	0016
2057B2-41	0136
2057B2-42	0136
2057B2-43	0211
2057B2-44	0211
2057B2-45	0211
2057B2-46	0038
2057B2-47	0142
2057B2-48	0628
2057B2-49	0004
2057B2-50	0136
2057B2-51	0136
2057B2-52	0004
2057B2-57	0211
2057B2-58	0142
2057B2-59	0284
2057B2-60	0628
2057B2-61	0164
2057B2-62	0076
2057B2-63	0111
2057B2-64	0127
2057B2-65	0136
2057B2-66	0136
2057B2-67	0136
2057B2-68	0136
2057B2-69	0016
2057B2-70	0136
2057B2-71	0136
2057B2-72	0211
2057B2-73	0198
2057B2-77	0136
2057B2-78	0211
2057B2-79	0136
2057B2-80	0136
2057B2-81	0136
2057B2-83	0211
2057B2-84	0142
2057B2-85	0144
2057B2-86	0211
2057B2-87	0144
2057B2-88	0136
2057B2-89	0050
2057B2-90	0050
2057B2-93	0050
2057B2-94	0004
2057B2-97	0016
2057B2-99	0004
2057B2-101	0127
2057B2-102	0127
2057B2-103	0144
2057B2-104	0136
2057B2-105	0136
2057B2-107	0004
2057B2-108	0144
2057B2-109	0144
2057B2-110	0144
2057B2-111	0144
2057B2-112	0144
2057B2-113	0016
2057B2-114	0127
2057B2-115	0127
2057B2-116	0127
2057B2-117	0127

If replacement code is OEM, contact original manufacturer for replacement.

203

DEVICE TYPE	REPL CODE
2057B2-118	0136
2057B2-119	0144
2057B2-120	0144
2057B2-121	0016
2057B2-122	0016
2057B2-123	0016
2057B2-124	0004
2057B2-125	0127
2057B2-127	0144
2057B2-128	0144
2057B2-129	0004
2057B2-130	0016
2057B2-133	0160
2057B2-134	0969
2057B2-135	0004
2057B2-136	0969
2057B2-137	0004
2057B2-138	0007
2057B2-139	0007
2057B2-140	0233
2057B2-141	0136
2057B2-142	0004
2057B2-143	0127
2057B2-149	0050
2057B2-150	0919
2057B2-151	0042
2057B2-152	0016
2057B2-153	0016
2057B2-154	0016
2057B2-155	0016
2057B2-157	0050
2057B2-158	0050
2057B2-159	0050
2057B2-160	0144
2057B2-161	0144
2057B2-162	0144
2057B2-192	0007
2057B2-206	0004
2057B2A2-118	0050
2057B45-14	0004
2057B-59	0111
2057B-84	0142
2057B-85	0016
2057B100-1	0004
2057B100-3	2839
2057B100-4	0208
2057B100-5	2839
2057B100-6	0004
2057B100-7	0211
2057B100-8	0004
2057B100-9	0004
2057B100-11	0222
2057B100-12	0144
2057B100-13	0004
2057B100-16	1506
2057B100-17	0086
2057B101-4	0016
2057B102-4	0016
2057B103-4	0016
2057B104-8	0233
2057B106-12	0037
2057B107-8	0086
2057B108-6	0037
2057B109-9	0086
2057B110-9	0126
2057B111-9	4100
2057B112-9	0126
2057B-113	0144
2057B113-9	0086
2057B114-9	0126
2057B115-9	0126
2057B116-9	0126
2057B117-9	0016
2057B118-12	0016
2057B119-2	0016
2057B120-12	0016
2057B121-9	0126
2057B122-9	0126
2057B123-10	0142
2057B124-10	0160
2057B125-9	0016
2057B126-12	0086
2057B129-9	0086
2057B141-4	0016
2057B142-4	0016
2057B143-12	0016
2057B144-12	0086
2057B145-12	0126
2057B146-12	0016
2057B147-12	0037
2057B149-12	0321
2057B151-6	0016
2057B152-12	0016
2057B153-9	0086
2057B155-10	0178
2057B156-9	0086
2057B157-9	0074
2057B158-10	0178
2057B159-12	0037
2057B163-12	0126
2057B168	0004
2057B169	0004
2057B175-9	0074
2057B186	0050
2057B206	0004
2058	0006
2058-02	3308
2058D	OEM
2060	1599

DEVICE TYPE	REPL CODE
2060-024	0015
2061-42	1288
2061-44	0133
2061-45	0030
2061A45-38	0133
2061A45-47	0211
2061A45-72	0015
2061B45-14	0164
2061B45-35	0015
2062-17	1401
2063-17	0076
2063-17-12	0016
2064	0079
2064(CROWN)	0016
2064(IC)	OEM
2064-17	0244
2064C	OEM
2065-03	0076
2065-04	0076
2065-06	0930
2065-07	2787
2065-08	0124
2065-17	0133
2065-50	4541
2065-51	0215
2065-52	1288
2065-53	2238
2065-54	0076
2065-55	0410
2066-17	0133
2068-018-104	0514
2068-022-108	2728
2068DD	OEM
2070	1600
2074	OEM
2074-17	0683
2074AD	OEM
2075	OEM
2075-3	OEM
2076	0133
2077-07	0143
2077-2	2728
2079-40	1025
2079-41	OEM
2079-42	0165
2079-93	0012
2079-129	OEM
2080	1600
2081	OEM
2081-6	0919
2081-17	0386
2082	OEM
2082-6	0042
2084-17	0015
2085-17	0161
2085Z4	OEM
2087-46	0012
2090	0283
2090(CROWN)	0233
2090A43-1	0911
2090A53-2	0469
2091-02	6196
2091-03	2684
2091-49	1206
2091-50	2546
2091-51	0076
2091A41-81	OEM
2093	OEM
2093/1097	3232
2093A2-289	0144
2093A3D-2	0229
2093A3D-20	0222
2093A4-2	0229
2093A5-2	0479
2093A5-10	0196
2093A6-1	0229
2093A6-2	0229
2093A8-1	0143
2093A9-3	0279
2093A9-4	0279
2093A12-1	0015
2093A25-3	0143
2093A33-1	0143
2093A38-1	0143
2093A38-4	0015
2093A38-5	0143
2093A38-8	0030
2093A38-10	0143
2093A38-11	0133
2093A38-13	0015
2093A38-14	0143
2093A38-15	0143
2093A38-16	0012
2093A38-21	0143
2093A38-22	0123
2093A38-23	0211
2093A38-24	0086
2093A38-27	0143
2093A38-28	0015
2093A38-29	0030
2093A38-30	0143
2093A38-31	0143
2093A38-32	0143
2093A38-33	0143
2093A38-34	0143
2093A38-35	0123
2093A38-37	0133
2093A38-40	0143
2093A39-12	0137

DEVICE TYPE	REPL CODE
2093A41	0143
2093A41-2	0143
2093A41-5	0030
2093A41-6	0071
2093A41-8	0015
2093A41-14	0143
2093A41-16	0012
2093A41-23	0030
2093A41-24	0012
2093A41-24A	0012
2093A41-25	0030
2093A41-27	0030
2093A41-28	0071
2093A41-29	0123
2093A41-37	OEM
2093A41-38	0143
2093A41-40	0211
2093A41-41	0211
2093A41-42	0071
2093A41-43	0071
2093A41-45	0015
2093A41-49	0015
2093A41-50	0143
2093A41-51	0015
2093A41-53	0644
2093A41-54	0015
2093A41-55	0015
2093A41-56	0137
2093A41-57	0015
2093A41-58	1073
2093A41-59	0143
2093A41-60	0137
2093A41-61	0015
2093A41-62	0015
2093A41-63	0162
2093A41-65	0023
2093A41-66	0015
2093A41-67	0102
2093A41-68	0143
2093A41-69	0102
2093A41-70	0025
2093A41-71	OEM
2093A41-72	0102
2093A41-73	0102
2093A41-74	0286
2093A41-75	0015
2093A41-76	0133
2093A41-77	0023
2093A41-78	0015
2093A41-79	0030
2093A41-80	OEM
2093A41-81	0015
2093A41-82	0053
2093A41-84	0015
2093A41-85	0526
2093A41-86	0015
2093A41-87	0164
2093A41-88	0015
2093A41-89	0015
2093A41-90	0162
2093A41-91	0030
2093A41-92	0143
2093A41-94	OEM
2093A41-95	0030
2093A41-96	0015
2093A41-101	0030
2093A41-102	0139
2093A41-103	0015
2093A41-104	0015
2093A41-105	0133
2093A41-108	0015
2093A41-110	0015
2093A41-112	0287
2093A41-113	0053
2093A41-115	0023
2093A41-116	0015
2093A41-117	0030
2093A41-125	0012
2093A41-126	6509
2093A41-129	0133
2093A41-130	0030
2093A41-131	0015
2093A41-139	0015
2093A41-141	0143
2093A41-155	0133
2093A41-156	0133
2093A41-157	0005
2093A41-158	0133
2093A41-159	0012
2093A41-161	0005
2093A41-162	0030
2093A41-163	0012
2093A41-164	0133
2093A41-165	0133
2093A41-166	0030
2093A41-167	0143
2093A41-169	0143
2093A41-171	0133
2093A41-172	0133
2093A41-173	0015
2093A41-180	0015
2093A41-181	0143
2093A41-182	0015
2093A41-185	0015
2093A41-186	0012
2093A41-187	0143
2093A41-188	0005
2093A41-189	0015
2093A41-193	0030

DEVICE TYPE	REPL CODE
2093A41-194	0162
2093A41-196	0019
2093A41-197	0015
2093A41-198	OEM
2093A41-200	0005
2093A42-7	0015
2093A43-2	0911
2093A52-1	0071
2093A59-1	0911
2093A69-1	0071
2093A71-1	0071
2093A75-1	0469
2093A77-1	0143
2093A78-1	0071
2093A79-6	0071
2093A80-1	0137
2093B4-6	0015
2093B11-21	0123
2093B38-4	0133
2093B38-9	0911
2093B38-14	0015
2093B41-6	0015
2093B41-8	0015
2093B41-9	0015
2093B41-10	0015
2093B41-11	0143
2093B41-12	0015
2093B41-14	0071
2093B41-15	OEM
2093B41-16	0012
2093B41-18	0015
2093B41-20	0015
2093B41-21	0015
2093B41-22	0015
2093B41-23	0030
2093B41-24	0012
2093B41-25	0015
2093B41-27	0030
2093B41-28	0015
2093B41-29	0123
2093B41-32	0015
2093B41-33	0918
2093B41-34	0015
2093B41-35	0015
2093B41-37	0015
2093B41-62	0015
2094	OEM
2095	OEM
2095Z4	OEM
2097	OEM
2097/1114	4506
2098	OEM
2101	0111
2101(DIO)	OEM
2101A	OEM
2101A-2F	OEM
2101A-2N	OEM
2101A-4F	OEM
2101A-4N	OEM
2101AF	OEM
2101AN	OEM
2101N	OEM
2102	0015
2102-010	0143
2102-014	0015
2102-017	0015
2102-025	0143
2102-028	0143
2102-029	0124
2102-031	0030
2102-032	0057
2102-074	0015
2102-1DC	OEM
2102-1DL	OEM
2102-1DM	OEM
2102-1FC	OEM
2102-1FL	OEM
2102-1FM	OEM
2102-1PC	OEM
2102-2DC	OEM
2102-2DL	OEM
2102-2DM	OEM
2102-2FC	OEM
2102-2FL	OEM
2102-2FM	OEM
2102-2PC	OEM
2102-120	0050
2102-124	0050
2102A	4886
2102A(DIO)	OEM
2102AN-4L	4886
2102DC	OEM
2102FDC	4886
2102FDL	OEM
2102FDM	OEM
2102FFC	OEM
2102FFL	OEM
2102FFM	OEM
2102FPC	4886
2102HDC	OEM
2102HDL	OEM
2102HDM	OEM
2102HFC	OEM
2102HFL	OEM
2102HFM	OEM
2102HPC	OEM
2102L1DC	OEM
2102L1DL	OEM
2102L1DM	OEM

DEVICE TYPE	REPL CODE
2102L1FC	OEM
2102L1FL	OEM
2102L1FM	OEM
2102L2DC	OEM
2102L2DL	OEM
2102L2DM	OEM
2102L2FC	OEM
2102L2FL	OEM
2102L2FM	OEM
2102L2PC	OEM
2102LFDC	OEM
2102LFDL	OEM
2102LFDM	OEM
2102LFFC	OEM
2102LFFL	OEM
2102LFFM	OEM
2102LFPC	OEM
2102LHDC	OEM
2102LHDL	OEM
2102LHDM	OEM
2102LHFC	OEM
2102LHFL	OEM
2102LHFM	OEM
2102LHPC	OEM
2103	OEM
2103A	OEM
2104	4887
2105	0030
2105Z4	OEM
2106	OEM
2106-17	0298
2106-119	0004
2106-120	0050
2106-121	0004
2106-122	0004
2106-123	0004
2106-124	0143
2106AF001	OEM
2107	4815
2108	OEM
2109	OEM
2109-101-0064	OEM
2109-101-0066	OEM
2109-101-0204	OEM
2109-101-0709	OEM
2109-101-1005	OEM
2109-101-1403	OEM
2109-101-5304	2599
2109-102-5304	2599
2109-102-5401	5004
2109-103-2006	0167
2109-103-2200	0906
2109-103-3001	0658
2109-104-9800	OEM
2109-110-1407	OEM
2109-301-0707	1519
2109-301-6008	2015
2109-301-6600	2079
2109-301-6707	4706
2109-401-1400	OEM
2110	0865
2110N-41	0133
2110N-42	0015
2110N-132	0007
2110N-133	0007
2110N-134	0178
2111-11	OEM
2111A	0659
2111A-2F	OEM
2111A-2N	OEM
2111A-4F	OEM
2111A-4N	OEM
2111AF	OEM
2111AN	OEM
2112	OEM
2112-17	0004
2112A-2F	OEM
2112A-2N	OEM
2112A-4F	OEM
2112A-4N	OEM
2112AF	OEM
2112AN	OEM
2113	0196
2114	2037
2114-0	0233
2114-17	0164
2114-30L	2037
2114L	2037
2114L-3	2037
2114L-30	2037
2115	0865
2115R	1625
2115Z4	OEM
2116-17	0015
2117	0518
2118	OEM
2118-004-10	0023
2118-3	OEM
2118-4	OEM
2118-7	OEM
2118-201-10	OEM
2119	OEM
2119-101-0500	0167
2119-101-1204	0872
2119-101-1301	3859
2119-101-1408	2921
2119-101-1505	2268
2119-101-1602	1049
2119-101-2607	0906

DEVICE TYPE	REPL CODE
2119-101-3204	0176
2119-101-4306	0167
2119-101-5107	3692
2119-101-5204	0485
2119-101-9408	0906
2119-101-9602	0658
2119-101-9709	0658
2119-102-0309	0167
2119-102-0503	0534
2119-102-0600	0552
2119-102-0907	0534
2119-102-1003	0552
2119-102-2600	0906
2119-102-3003	0970
2119-102-4008	OEM
2119-102-4309	4959
2119-102-5100	3692
2119-102-5401	5004
2119-102-5702	0970
2119-102-7304	1521
2119-102-7401	3860
2119-102-7605	0330
2119-103-0603	1319
2119-103-1006	OEM
2119-103-2302	3397
2119-201-1300	0176
2119-201-3009	3397
2119-202-0803	2845
2119-401-1201	OEM
2119-601-2709	3476
2119-601-5005	4569
2119-601-5209	3476
2119-901-0201	3900
2119-901-1109	0330
2120-17	0416
2121	OEM
2121-17	0076
2122-3	0396
2122-17	0143
2124	OEM
2125	5190
2125Z4	OEM
2127-17	1136
2130	5190
2132	0555
2132-17	1212
2133	OEM
2134-17	0470
2135	0847
2135E	2979
2135Z4	OEM
2137-103-2803	0037
2137-103-4308	0037
2137-301-0106	0261
2137-301-0504	0144
2137-301-1800	0079
2137-301-5305	0261
2137-301-5402	0261
2137-301-5509	1614
2137-301-5606	1614
2137-301-7208	0079
2137-401-5304	0037
2138-17	0007
2139-101-4005	0006
2139-101-4102	0006
2139-101-4209	0148
2139-101-5301	0006
2139-103-2807	0037
2139-103-3307	0006
2139-103-3802	0006
2139-103-4001	0006
2139-103-4302	0037
2139-103-5705	0676
2139-103-7006	1587
2139-103-7103	0037
2139-103-8807	0284
2139-103-8904	0284
2139-103-9006	0284
2139-103-9307	0006
2139-103-9404	0261
2139-103-9501	0261
2139-103-9608	0148
2139-103-9705	0006
2139-301-0401	0144
2139-301-0508	0144
2139-301-0809	0836
2139-301-0906	0836
2139-301-1406	0261
2139-301-2304	0168
2139-301-2314	0168
2139-301-2401	0168
2139-301-2410	0638
2139-301-5105	0261
2139-301-5202	0261
2139-301-5309	0261
2139-301-5406	0261
2139-301-5503	1614
2139-301-5600	1614
2139-301-6508	5041
2139-301-7202	0079
2139-301-7707	0076
2139-301-8508	0155
2139-301-8702	0155
2139-301-9100	1614
2139-301-9202	0168
2139-301-9804	0079
2139-301-9901	0079
2139-302-3603	2351
2139-302-6006	0018

DEVICE TYPE	REPL CODE
2139-302-6501	0076
2139-302-7406	0076
2139-302-7409	0079
2139-302-7506	0076
2139-302-8103	1274
2139-302-8501	0191
2139-302-8608	0191
2139-303-320	2195
2139-304-5609	0860
2139-304-5706	0860
2139-305-3408	0261
2139-305-9204	0066
2139-305-9301	0066
2139-307-2603	0224
2139-308-0305	0224
2139-401-0701	1485
2139-401-1007	1533
2139-401-1104	1533
2139-401-1308	1533
2139-401-5308	0037
2139-401-8507	2643
2139-401-9609	0065
2139-401-9808	0261
2141	OEM
2141-UCB	OEM
2141-UCE	OEM
2145	5192
2145-401-3502	0055
2148-027-10	0019
2148-033-10	0087
2148-034-10	0052
2148-17	0015
2148H	OEM
2148H-3	OEM
2148HL	OEM
2148HL-3	OEM
2149-040-0200	0055
2149-101-0505	0676
2149-101-8505	1900
2149-101-9005	1338
2149-101-9102	0527
2149-101-9500	0037
2149-201-4504	1638
2149-201-4601	1900
2149-202-0400	0527
2149-203-0607	3476
2149-301-0202	1274
2149-301-0309	0066
2149-301-0406	1533
2149-301-0503	0551
2149-301-409	OEM
2149-301-510	0066
2149-301-1401	2770
2149-301-1406	0261
2149-301-1605	0103
2149-301-4202	5041
2149-301-4309	0079
2149-301-4804	0309
2149-301-4901	0103
2149-301-5100	0066
2149-301-8105	1274
2149-301-8202	0066
2149-301-8901	0066
2149-301-9100	0155
2149-301-9508	0155
2149-302-7307	0949
2149-302-7404	0638
2149-302-7501	0949
2149-302-9103	0638
2149-302-9109	0638
2149-302-9608	0638
2149-302-9802	0949
2149-303-4305	2636
2149-303-5805	0275
2149-303-7300	0388
2149-303-8004	0275
2149-303-8402	0949
2149-304-3109	0625
2149-401-0405	1533
2149-401-0502	0551
2149-401-6007	0388
2149-401-6104	1157
2149-401-6308	1157
2149-401-8201	0079
2149-401-8308	0590
2149-401-9303	0388
2149-401-9808	0261
2149-401-9905	0261
2149-404-0103	0270
2149-404-0200	0055
2149-404-0307	0055
2149H	OEM
2149H-2	OEM
2149H-3	OEM
2149HL-3	OEM
2150	5192
2150-17	0012
2151-17	0123
2152	0015
2153	OEM
2153NS	OEM
2154	OEM
2155Z4	OEM
2156	OEM
2157-301-1703	0079
2159-101-0607	0148
2159-301-0207	0076
2159-301-0304	0261
2159-301-1707	0079

If replacement code is OEM, contact original manufacturer for replacement.

DEVICE TYPE	REPL CODE
2159-301-1804	0079
2159-301-2096	0261
2159-301-2906	0261
2159-302-1707	0079
2159-401-2604	3104
2159-701-0207	0076
2160	1659
2160-17	0219
2161-17	0244
2163-17	0178
2164A-15	OEM
2164A-20	OEM
2165	0167
2167-17	1897
2167-201-0704	0023
2167-206-1102	0023
2167-208-5108	0023
2167-301-6305	0023
2167-401-6304	0053
2167-401-8003	0253
2167-401-8100	0466
2167-406-4804	0124
2167-408-0509	0140
2167-408-0606	0053
2167-408-0800	0466
2168-17	0386
2169	OEM
2169-101-0602	0019
2169-101-0806	0123
2169-101-1306	2217
2169-102-2605	0015
2169-103-0608	0133
2169-103-1807	0124
2169-103-2006	0167
2169-103-2608	0468
2169-201-0106	OEM
2169-201-0601	0080
2169-201-0708	0023
2169-201-0805	0790
2169-201-0902	0015
2169-201-2601	0790
2169-201-2708	0015
2169-202-1900	0143
2169-202-2002	0133
2169-202-2109	0133
2169-202-2206	0023
2169-202-2303	0102
2169-202-2400	0023
2169-202-2604	0133
2169-205-0700	0133
2169-205-0807	0124
2169-205-1006	0057
2169-205-1103	0999
2169-205-3307	0023
2169-205-3404	0494
2169-206-1009	0023
2169-206-1106	0023
2169-206-1203	0023
2169-207-0201	0023
2169-207-1109	0071
2169-207-1206	0017
2169-208-1708	0023
2169-208-5102	0023
2169-208-5306	0071
2169-208-5704	0023
2169-208-5706	0023
2169-209-1105	0080
2169-210-5808	0071
2169-213-1102	0071
2169-213-1108	0071
2169-218-1307	0023
2169-218-1404	0023
2169-218-1501	0023
2169-219-3106	0023
2169-219-4207	0023
2169-219-4208	0023
2169-219-5106	0023
2169-220-1508	0023
2169-301-0207	0076
2169-301-1100	0133
2169-301-2901	0133
2169-301-2907	0133
2169-301-6105	0031
2169-301-6309	0023
2169-304-0104	0023
2169-304-1109	0023
2169-304-1400	0023
2169-308-0504	0023
2169-401-0900	0057
2169-401-1206	0999
2169-401-4104	0298
2169-401-5808	1319
2169-401-7604	0440
2169-403-2304	0700
2169-403-2401	0436
2169-403-5600	0466
2169-403-6508	0371
2169-403-7503	0999
2169-403-7707	0440
2169-403-8508	0039
2169-404-0103	0077
2169-404-0307	0313
2169-404-1100	0313
2169-404-1807	0466
2169-404-1904	0077
2169-404-2006	0041
2169-404-4006	0041
2169-404-4404	0361
2169-406-4804	0124

DEVICE TYPE	REPL CODE
2169-406-4808	0124
2169-408-0600	0053
2169-408-0707	OEM
2169-408-0804	0466
2169-408-5704	0023
2169-501-1603	OEM
2169-503-6401	OEM
2169-901-0303	OEM
2170	1600
2176	OEM
2177	OEM
2179-001-0200	0705
2179-001-1302	0312
2179-301-9207	0023
2180-17	0143
2180-151	0144
2180-152	0144
2180-153	0016
2180-154	0016
2180-155	0178
2181-17	0155
2189-106-0500	0339
2189-301-0906	0836
2189-301-9804	0079
2195	OEM
2195-17	0111
2196-17	0123
2197-17	0127
2199-17	0015
2199-101-9408	0906
2200-17	0015
2201	OEM
2201(DIO)	OEM
2201A	OEM
2202	4109
2202(DIO)	OEM
2202-17	0386
2202A	OEM
2203	0244
2203-17	0244
2203A	OEM
2204	4067
2204-17	0198
2205	0030
2205-17	0030
2206	0015
2206(TRANS)	OEM
2206-17	0015
2207	OEM
2207-17	0111
2208	OEM
2208-17	0086
2208-21	OEM
2209	OEM
2209-17	0133
2209-21	OEM
2210-17	0919
2211-17	0555
2211B	0015
2212	OEM
2212-17	0111
2213	OEM
2213-17	0127
2213-21	OEM
2214	OEM
2214-17	2195
2215	0424
2215-17	0050
2215-21	OEM
2217	OEM
2217-21	OEM
2218	OEM
2218-17	0030
2218-21	OEM
2220-17	0037
2220-29	OEM
2221	4945
2221A	4945
2222	0016
2222A	0016
2223	OEM
2223-21	OEM
2224-17	0224
2225-17	0224
2226-17	0224
2231	0037
2231-17	1141
2231A	OEM
2231B	OEM
2231D	OEM
2231F	OEM
2231H	OEM
2231K	OEM
2231M	OEM
2231P	OEM
2231S	OEM
2232-17	0143
2232A	OEM
2232B	OEM
2232D	OEM
2232F	OEM
2232H	OEM
2232K	OEM
2232M	OEM
2232P	OEM
2232S	OEM
2232V	OEM
2232Z	OEM
2233-17	0015

DEVICE TYPE	REPL CODE
2243	0160
2243-21	OEM
2244-1	0676
2245-17	0236
2246-17	0218
2252	0015
2261	0079
2263	0016
2269	0037
2270	0016
2271	0111
2272	0037
2275-1	1888
2275-17	0016
2280-13	0143
2281-13	0143
2282-13	0143
2282-17(RAT.DET)	0123
2283-13	0143
2284-13	0143
2284-17	0127
2289-13	0907
2290-13	0143
2290-17	0016
2291-17	0127
2295	0178
2301	OEM
2301A	OEM
2302	0015
2302(VARACTOR)	OEM
2302-17	0151
2302A	OEM
2303	OEM
2303A	OEM
2304	0133
2304-1	1016
2305	OEM
2306	OEM
2307	OEM
2308	OEM
2309	0012
2309-110-0013	OEM
2309-110-4208	OEM
2309-110-4305	OEM
2309-110-7601	OEM
2309-115-0319	0511
2309-115-3101	0511
2309-115-6106	OEM
2309-201-0032	OEM
2309D	OEM
2312	OEM
2312-2	OEM
2312-3	OEM
2313	OEM
2314	OEM
2314K80AM	OEM
2315	OEM
2315-046	0015
2316B-3CJ	OEM
2316B-3CK	OEM
2316B-4CK	OEM
2320-17	0076
2321	OEM
2321-17	0155
2322	0079
2322-17	1967
2323-17	0157
2324-010-10	OEM
2328-17	0139
2330-021	0644
2330-191	0071
2330-201	0071
2330-252	0071
2331	OEM
2332-3CJ	OEM
2332-3CK	OEM
2332-4CJ	OEM
2332-4CK	OEM
2332-20F	OEM
2332-20I	OEM
2332-20N	OEM
2332-25F	OEM
2332-25I	OEM
2332-25N	OEM
2332-30F	OEM
2332-30N	OEM
2332-45F	OEM
2332-45I	OEM
2332-45N	OEM
2332A	OEM
2332B	OEM
2332E20F	OEM
2332E20I	OEM
2332E20N	OEM
2332E25F	OEM
2332E25I	OEM
2332E25N	OEM
2332E30F	OEM
2332E30I	OEM
2332E30N	OEM
2332E45F	OEM
2332E45I	OEM
2332E45N	OEM
2332M25F	OEM
2332M25I	OEM
2332M30F	OEM
2332M30I	OEM
2332M45F	OEM
2332M45I	OEM

DEVICE TYPE	REPL CODE
2334-17	0386
2336-17	3672
2337-17	0076
2338-17	0076
2339-17	0244
2340-17	1967
2341-17	0025
2344	OEM
2355D	OEM
2359-17	0212
2360-17	0015
2361-17	0155
2362-1	0079
2362-1(SYLVANIA)	0144
2362-17	0157
2364	OEM
2364-3CJ	OEM
2364-4CK	OEM
2364-5CJ	OEM
2364-5CK	OEM
2364-20F	OEM
2364-20I	OEM
2364-20N	OEM
2364-25F	OEM
2364-25I	OEM
2364-25N	OEM
2364-30F	OEM
2364-30N	OEM
2364-35F	OEM
2364-35N	OEM
2364-45F	OEM
2364-130	OEM
2364A	OEM
2364E20F	OEM
2364E20N	OEM
2364E25F	OEM
2364E25N	OEM
2364E30F	OEM
2364E30N	OEM
2364E45F	OEM
2364E45N	OEM
2364M25F	OEM
2364M30F	OEM
2364M45F	OEM
2365	OEM
2365S	OEM
2381-17	0037
2382-17	0042
2392	OEM
2396-17	0002
2399-17	0833
2400	OEM
2400-17	0133
2400-23	0015
2400-27	0015
2401	OEM
2401A	OEM
2402	0015
2402(VARACTOR)	OEM
2402-17	0030
2402-453	0004
2402-454	0004
2402-455	0004
2402-456	0222
2402-457	0004
2402-459	0143
2402-461	0015
2402-462	0015
2402-463	0015
2402A	OEM
2403	0133
2403A	OEM
2405	0133
2405-453	0004
2405-454	0004
2405-455	0004
2405-456	0004
2405-457	0004
2405-458	0143
2405-459	0015
2405-462	0015
2405-463	0015
2408-17	0555
2408-326	0004
2408-328	0004
2408-329	0164
2408-330	0143
2408-331	0015
2411-17	0023
2413	OEM
2413-21	OEM
2414-1	OEM
2415	OEM
2415-21	OEM
2416	OEM
2417	0142
2418-17	1401
2419	OEM
2419-21	OEM
2420M54532P	OEM
2420NPEP159	OEM
2420SLM339N	0176
2420SN07406	1197
2420SN07407	1329
2420SN75188	0503
2420SN75189	0506
2420SNLS151	1636
2420SNNE555	0967
2420SNS412N	1849

DEVICE TYPE	REPL CODE
2420T78005P	0619
2420TMM16P2	1887
2421T05Z24Y	0489
2421T05Z39X	0036
2421T1Z1300	0361
2421T1Z1500	0002
2421T1Z2000	0526
2421T2B4B41	0319
2421T5B4B41	0319
2421TS5277B	0023
2422TA1015Y	0148
2422TC1815Y	0076
2422TD14380	3658
2422TD71700	3052
2427	0127
2427(RCA)	0144
2432	0823
2434	0823
2437-17	0830
2443	0127
2443(RCA)	0016
2444	0142
2444(RCA)	0142
2445	0144
2446	0079
2446(RCA)	0016
2447	0079
2447(RCA)	0016
2448	0127
2448(RCA)	0037
2448-17	0364
2449-17	0111
2450	0079
2450(RCA)	0144
2450-17	1270
2450S	OEM
2451-17	0165
2452-17	0012
2453-17	0293
2454-17	0031
2460	OEM
2460-13	0015
2470-1724	5241
2470-1732	3221
2473	0079
2473(RCA)	0144
2473-2109	0462
2474	0233
2474(RCA)	0233
2475	0127
2475(RCA)	0016
2476	0079
2476(RCA)	0144
2477	0079
2477(RCA)	0144
2478	0136
2478A	0136
2478B	0136
2482	0136
2482(RCA)	0126
2484	0016
2487B	0050
2488	0136
2488A	0136
2489	0136
2489A	0050
2490	0004
2490A	0004
2491	0142
2491A	0142
2491B	0142
2494	0969
2494(RCA)	0969
2495	0086
2495(RCA)	0016
2495-012	0136
2495-013	0136
2495-014	0004
2495-078	0050
2495-079	0050
2495-080	0004
2495-082	0050
2495-166-1	0144
2495-166-2	0016
2495-166-4	0144
2495-166-8	0144
2495-166-9	0144
2495-200	0136
2495-376	0050
2495-377	0050
2495-378	0050
2495-388	0004
2495-488-1	0050
2495-488-2	0050
2495-489	0071
2495-520	0144
2495-521	0144
2495-522-1	0144
2495-522-4	0016
2495-523-1	0144
2495-529	0016
2495-567-2	0004
2495-567-3	0004
2495-586-2	0004
2496	0969
2497-473	0004
2497-496	0004
2498-163	0086
2498-507-2	0144

DEVICE TYPE	REPL CODE
2498-507-3	0144
2498-508-2	0144
2498-508-3	0144
2498-513	0071
2498-903-2	0144
2498-903-3	0144
2500	0969
2500(RCA)	0969
2501	OEM
2501(IC)	OEM
2501A	OEM
2501PDK20	OEM
2501PDK30	OEM
2501PDK40	OEM
2501PDK60	OEM
2501PDN120	OEM
2501PDN140	OEM
2501PDN160	OEM
2501PDN180	OEM
2501PDN200	OEM
2501PDN210	OEM
2501PDN220	OEM
2501PDN230	OEM
2501PDN240	OEM
2501PDN250	OEM
2502	0126
2502(RCA)	0004
2502A	OEM
2503	OEM
2503A	OEM
2503V	OEM
2505K	OEM
2510-31	0143
2510-32	0015
2510-101	0224
2510-102	0224
2510-103	0111
2510-104	0016
2510-105	0555
2513IXCM2140	OEM
2513IXCMXXXX	OEM
2514	1963
2514NXCMXXXX	OEM
2516	0167
2516(EPROM)	OEM
2516-1	0167
2516JL-45	5485
2516N	OEM
2517	OEM
2518	OEM
2522	0015
2523	0015
2524N	OEM
2529N	OEM
2531A	OEM
2540	OEM
2546	0127
2546(RCA)	0016
2554-1(RCA)	2716
2554-2(RCA)	2716
2554-3	2716
2554-3(RCA)	2716
2554-4	2716
2554-4(RCA)	2716
2559	2527
2559-1	2527
2560	0324
2560(J.C.PENNEY)	0324
2560-1	0324
2584	0198
2601	OEM
2601A	OEM
2601PDN120	OEM
2601PDN140	OEM
2601PDN160	OEM
2601PDN180	OEM
2601PDN200	OEM
2601PDN210	OEM
2601PDN220	OEM
2601PDN230	OEM
2601PDN240	OEM
2601PDN250	OEM
2602	OEM
2602A	OEM
2603	0513
2603-180	0004
2603-181	0004
2603-182	0004
2603-183	0136
2603-184	0016
2603-186	0143
2603A	OEM
2603E	0513
2603F	0513
2605A	OEM
2605B	OEM
2605D	OEM
2605F	OEM
2605H	OEM
2605K	OEM
2605M	OEM
2606-286	0004
2606-287	0004
2606-288	0841
2606-291	0004
2606-292	0136
2606-294	0144
2606-295	0050
2606-296	0143

DEVICE TYPE	REPL CODE
2606-297	0030
2606-299	0015
2606-303	0446
2607-45F	OEM
2607-45I	OEM
2607-45N	OEM
2608I	OEM
2609-0011	OEM
2612	0004
2613-15F	OEM
2613-15I	OEM
2613-15N	OEM
2613-20F	OEM
2613-20I	OEM
2613-20N	OEM
2613-25F	OEM
2613-25I	OEM
2613-25N	OEM
2613-45F	OEM
2613-45I	OEM
2613-45N	OEM
2614-15F	OEM
2614-15I	OEM
2614-15N	OEM
2614-20F	OEM
2614-20I	OEM
2614-20N	OEM
2614-25F	OEM
2614-25I	OEM
2614-25N	OEM
2614-45F	OEM
2614-45I	OEM
2614-45N	OEM
2615A	OEM
2615B	OEM
2615D	OEM
2615F	OEM
2615H	OEM
2615K	OEM
2615M	OEM
2616-30F	OEM
2616-30I	OEM
2616-30N	OEM
2616-35F	OEM
2616-35I	OEM
2616-35N	OEM
2616-45F	OEM
2616-45I	OEM
2616-45N	OEM
2616A20F	OEM
2616A20I	OEM
2616A20N	OEM
2616A25F	OEM
2616A25I	OEM
2616A25N	OEM
2616A30F	OEM
2616A30I	OEM
2616A30N	OEM
2616A45F	OEM
2616A45I	OEM
2616A45N	OEM
2616AE20F	OEM
2616AE20I	OEM
2616AE20N	OEM
2616AE25F	OEM
2616AE25I	OEM
2616AE25N	OEM
2616AE30F	OEM
2616AE30I	OEM
2616AE30N	OEM
2616AE45F	OEM
2616AE45I	OEM
2616AE45N	OEM
2616AM20F	OEM
2616AM20I	OEM
2616AM25F	OEM
2616AM25I	OEM
2616AM30F	OEM
2616AM30I	OEM
2616AM45F	OEM
2616AM45I	OEM
2616E-35F	OEM
2616E-35I	OEM
2616E-45F	OEM
2616E-45I	OEM
2617-45F	OEM
2617-45I	OEM
2617-45N	OEM
2620	0233
2621	OEM
2622	OEM
2626-1	1686
2632-35F	OEM
2632-35N	OEM
2632-45F	OEM
2632-45I	OEM
2632-45N	OEM
2632A20F	OEM
2632A20I	OEM
2632A20N	OEM
2632A25F	OEM
2632A25I	OEM
2632A25N	OEM
2632A-30F	OEM
2632A30F	OEM
2632A-30I	OEM
2632A30I	OEM
2632A-30N	OEM
2632A30N	OEM

If replacement code is OEM, contact original manufacturer for replacement.

205

DEVICE TYPE	REPL CODE
2632A45F	OEM
2632A45I	OEM
2632A45N	OEM
2632AE20F	OEM
2632AE20I	OEM
2632AE20N	OEM
2632AE25F	OEM
2632AE25I	OEM
2632AE25N	OEM
2632AE30F	OEM
2632AE30I	OEM
2632AE30N	OEM
2632AE45F	OEM
2632AE45I	OEM
2632AE45N	OEM
2632AM25F	OEM
2632AM25I	OEM
2632AM30F	OEM
2632AM30I	OEM
2632AM45F	OEM
2632AM45I	OEM
2632E-45F	OEM
2632E-45I	OEM
2633(RCA)	0144
2634	0127
2634(RCA)	0144
2634-1	0144
2635	OEM
2636	0144
2637	OEM
2637I	OEM
2637N	OEM
2641N	OEM
2650A1I	OEM
2650A1N	OEM
2650AI	OEM
2650AN	OEM
2650B1I	OEM
2650B1N	OEM
2650BI	OEM
2650BN	OEM
2651I	OEM
2651N	OEM
2652	OEM
2652-1I	OEM
2652-1N	OEM
2652I	OEM
2652N	OEM
2653I	OEM
2653N	OEM
2655	OEM
2656	OEM
2657	OEM
2661-1I	OEM
2661-1N	OEM
2661-2I	OEM
2661-2N	OEM
2661-3I	OEM
2661-3N	OEM
2661E	OEM
2663E	OEM
2664-45F	OEM
2664-45I	OEM
2664-45N	OEM
2664A20F	OEM
2664A20I	OEM
2664A20N	OEM
2664A25F	OEM
2664A25I	OEM
2664A25N	OEM
2664A-30F	OEM
2664A-30I	OEM
2664A-30N	OEM
2664A-45F	OEM
2664A-45I	OEM
2664A-45N	OEM
2664AE20F	OEM
2664AE20I	OEM
2664AE20N	OEM
2664AE25F	OEM
2664AE25I	OEM
2664AE25N	OEM
2664AE30F	OEM
2664AE30I	OEM
2664AE30N	OEM
2664AE45F	OEM
2664AE45I	OEM
2664AE45N	OEM
2664AM25F	OEM
2664AM25I	OEM
2664AM30F	OEM
2664AM30I	OEM
2664AM45F	OEM
2664AM45I	OEM
2664E	OEM
2664E-50F	OEM
2664E-50I	OEM
2665	OEM
2665E	OEM
2666E	OEM
2667	0006
2668E	OEM
2670I	OEM
2670N	OEM
2671	0160
2671I	OEM
2671N	OEM
2671R	4262
2672I	OEM
2672N	OEM
2673AI	OEM
2673AN	OEM
2673I	OEM
2673N	OEM
2673R	4266
2674R	4267
2675R	4268
2676R	2192
2678R	2185
2684-0002	OEM
2700	0050
2701	OEM
2701A	OEM
2702	0124
2702A	OEM
2703	OEM
2703-384	0004
2703-385	0004
2703-386	0004
2703-387	0841
2703-388	0164
2703-389	0143
2703-390	0015
2703A	OEM
2704	0143
2704-384	0004
2704-385	0004
2704-386	0004
2704-387	0164
2704-388	0143
2704-389	0015
2706	OEM
2716	2263
2716-SA2-A0	2263
2716-SC2-A1	2263
2732	2672
2732/2332	2672
2732A	2672
2732A-2	2672
2732A-2-QGE-1	OEM
2732A-3	OEM
2732A-4	OEM
2732A-20	OEM
2732A-25	OEM
2732A-30	2672
2732D	2672
2735	OEM
2737	OEM
2745B	0085
2755	OEM
2757	OEM
2762	0111
2763	0015
2764	0806
2764-2	0806
2764-25	0806
2764-30	0806
2764-250	0806
2764-450	0806
2764-FA4-A2	0806
2764-FA5-A3	0806
2764-FC5-A3	0806
2764-RX8-R1	OEM
2764-RX8-R2	OEM
2764A-2	OEM
2765	OEM
2766	0015
2767	OEM
2774	0162
2777	0015
2779	0015
2780	0160
2780-3	0265
2780-4	0160
2780-5	0160
2781	0211
2784	0015
2786	0015
2787	0016
2789	0143
2791	0050
2792	0050
2794	0015
2795A	0012
2796	0155
2797	0050
2798	0037
2799	0006
2799-1	1832
2799-2	1832
2800	OEM
2801	OEM
2801A	OEM
2802	0071
2802(VARACTOR)	OEM
2802A	OEM
2802A(VARACTOR)	OEM
2803	OEM
2803A	OEM
2804	OEM
2805	OEM
2816	OEM
2816-3	OEM
2816-4	OEM
2840	OEM
2842	OEM
2844	OEM
2845	OEM
2853	0555
2853-1	0555
2853-2	0042
2853-3	0555
2854	0016
2854-1	0555
2854-2	0042
2854-3	0555
2855-1	0555
2855-2	0042
2855-3	0555
2856-1	0555
2856-2	0042
2856-3	0555
2900-007	0144
2901	2715
2901(MIN)	OEM
2901(SM)	2715
2901-010	0160
2903D	0624
2904-003	0079
2904-008	0160
2904-014	0160
2904-016	0136
2904-029	0136
2904-030	0626
2904-032	0086
2904-033	0079
2904-034	0198
2904-035	0198
2904-037	0693
2904-038	0037
2904-038H05	0279
2904-045	0079
2904-053	0079
2904-054	0079
2904-057	0161
2904-058	0546
2904-059	0693
2904-061	1581
2904D	0765
2906	OEM
2906-004	2592
2906-005	0780
2906A	OEM
2907	0037
2907A	OEM
2910A	OEM
2910A-1	OEM
2910A-2	OEM
2910A-4	OEM
2911A	OEM
2911A-1	OEM
2911A-2	OEM
2911A-4	OEM
2912A(A)	OEM
2913(A)	OEM
2914(A)	OEM
2920	OEM
2920-6	OEM
2920-8	OEM
2920-16	OEM
2920-18	OEM
2921(A)	OEM
2925	0016
2925(E.F.-JOHNSON)	0079
2936	OEM
2957A100-25	0178
2979DRAEB	OEM
3000	OEM
3000BD21	OEM
3000D11A	OEM
3000PJA10	OEM
3001	0144
3001-201	3550
3001A	0015
3001F	0759
3001G	2848
3001H	0761
3001PDN60	OEM
3001PDN80	OEM
3001PDN100	OEM
3001PDN120	OEM
3001PDN140	OEM
3002	0144
3003	0127
3003(SEARS)	0127
3004(SEARS)	0127
3004-856	0004
3005	2514
3005(SEARS)	0016
3005-861	0016
3006	2514
3006(SEARS)	0079
3007	2514
3007(SEARS)	0016
3008	0050
3008(E.F.-JOHNSON)	0050
3009	0050
3009(E.F.-JOHNSON)	0050
3009(SEARS)	0004
3010	0136
3010(SEARS)	0004
3011	0079
3011(E.F.-JOHNSON)	0079
3011(E.F.JOHNSON)	0016
3012	0150
3012(EFJOHNSON)	0150
3012(SEARS)	0841
3013	0211
3013(SEARS)	0841
3014	0211
3014(SEARS)	0004
3015FBM	OEM
3015FBM10	OEM
3015FBM15	OEM
3015FBM20	OEM
3015FBN	OEM
3015FBN10	OEM
3015FBN15	OEM
3015FBN20	OEM
3015G	OEM
3015G10	OEM
3016B	0139
3017	0037
3018	0144
3018(E.F.-JOHNSON)	0144
3018(E.F.JOHNSON)	0144
3019	0037
3019(EFJOHNSON)	0136
3020	0144
3021	0144
3022	0086
3023	0007
3026	0079
3027	0007
3028	0144
3029	0127
3030	OEM
3034	0086
3034(RCA)	0086
3035Z4	OEM
3037	OEM
3040	OEM
3041	OEM
3045Z4	OEM
3050	OEM
3052P	5199
3052V	2517
3054	0178
3055Z4	OEM
3064TC	0360
3065Z4	OEM
3066DC	2527
3066F	OEM
3067DC	0324
3067F	OEM
3068	0079
3069	0015
3069(ARVIN)	0015
3069-1	OEM
3074A21	0015
3075DC	1335
3075Z4	OEM
3085Z4	OEM
3095Z4	OEM
3100-48	OEM
3101E	OEM
3102	OEM
3103	OEM
3104	OEM
3105	3160
3105Z4	OEM
3107-103-40501	OEM
3107-105-40501	2097
3107-108-4040X	3610
3107-108-4050X	1061
3107-108-40401	3610
3107-108-40404	3610
3107-108-40501	1061
3107-204-9000	0016
3107-204-90010	0016
3107-204-90020	0016
3107-204-90070	0160
3107-204-90080	0144
3107-204-90100	0127
3107-204-90140	0085
3107-204-90150	0111
3107-204-90190	0085
3110	2873
3110R	0254
3111	0016
3112	0004
3113	0016
3115	1116
3115R	1099
3115Z4	OEM
3119-901-110	0330
3120	1116
3120R	1099
3122P	4264
3122V	OEM
3124	OEM
3124-45	OEM
3125	1118
3125R	1103
3125Z4	OEM
3126	OEM
3130	1118
3130-0000-014	0083
3130-3167-909	0765
3130-3169-909	OEM
3130-3193-512	2242
3130-3248-801	1239
3130-3268-100	OEM
3130R	1103
3135	0800
3135/709	0659
3135Z4	OEM
3136/5072A	0244
3137-103-4308	0037
3140	0800
3140R	0258
3145	1186
3146-977	0103
3150	1186
3150R	1634
3151	OEM
3152-159	0178
3152-170	0103
3153GM1	3239
3155Z4	OEM
3160	0315
3161	0112
3161R	0112
3161R99	OEM
3165Z4	OEM
3170	1124
3175Z4	OEM
3180	1124
3182	3047
3189	OEM
3195Z4	OEM
3198-0009	OEM
3198-0045	OEM
3202	3392
3202-5H01	0086
3202-51-01	0086
3203	OEM
3204	OEM
3205	6742
3205A	OEM
3205Z4	OEM
3206	OEM
3212	OEM
3213	3718
3214	OEM
3215	6744
3222	0126
3225	2639
3225R	2828
3227-E	0144
3233-9	OEM
3235	0800
3245	1186
3255-9-7K	OEM
3256-9-7K	OEM
3257-9-7C	OEM
3258-9-7K	OEM
3260-91-7R	OEM
3260-92-7R	OEM
3270	1124
3271/25	OEM
3280	1124
3283-00160-000	2273
3291	OEM
3291/14	OEM
3292/14	OEM
3293/14	OEM
3301(SEARS)	0127
3302	0037
3306	OEM
3307-4-5F	OEM
3322-6	0143
3324-30	OEM
3325-0500-13	OEM
3326-4-5E	OEM
3329/03	OEM
3329-9-5F	OEM
3330-9-5F	OEM
3331	OEM
3331-9-5F	OEM
3333-9-7K	OEM
3334	OEM
3341-9-7K	OEM
3342	OEM
3347	OEM
3348	OEM
3349	OEM
3353	OEM
3354/25	OEM
3355/25	OEM
3356/25	OEM
3367	0396
3370	0144
3373	0130
3374-3	1024
3377	0015
3383-9-5F	OEM
3391	0111
3391(SEARS)	0111
3391A	0111
3391A(SEARS)	0111
3400-2412-3	2515
3401DM	OEM
3402	4774
3402-110	OEM
3402-210	OEM
3402-312	OEM
3402-313	OEM
3402B	OEM
3403	5345
3403(RCA)	0079
3404-110	OEM
3404-210	OEM
3404-312	OEM
3404-313	OEM
3411	OEM
3414	OEM
3417	OEM
3420	OEM
3421	OEM
3425	0279
3430J	OEM
3430K	OEM
3431J	OEM
3431K	OEM
3434	0279
3435	0279
3450	3511
3451	3511
3452	OEM
3455	OEM
3456A	OEM
3456B	OEM
3458	0050
3461	0079
3462	OEM
3475	4192
3476	0233
3476(RCA)	0007
3491	OEM
3492	0079
3500	0279
3500A	OEM
3500B	OEM
3500C	OEM
3500E	OEM
3500MP	OEM
3500R	OEM
3500S	OEM
3500T	OEM
3500U(M)	OEM
3501	0086
3501-9-6G	OEM
3501A	OEM
3501B	OEM
3501C	OEM
3501R	OEM
3501S	OEM
3501T	OEM
3503	0142
3503(RCA)	0142
3504	0211
3504(RCA)	0050
3505	0143
3505(AIRLINE)	0907
3505(RCA)	0016
3505A	OEM
3506	0361
3506(RCA)	0016
3507	0086
3507(RCA)	0004
3507(SEARS)	0127
3507(WARDS)	0079
3507-9-6G	OEM
3507J	OEM
3508	0086
3508(RCA)	0079
3508(SEARS)	0007
3508(WARDS)	0144
3508J	OEM
3509	0144
3509(SEARS)	0079
3509(WARDS)	0079
3510	0079
3510(RCA)	0079
3510(SEARS)	0144
3510(WARDS)	0144
3510AM	OEM
3510BM	OEM
3510CM	OEM
3510SM	OEM
3510VM(M)	OEM
3511	0144
3511(SEARS)	0321
3511(WARDS)	0321
3512	0160
3512(RCA)	0321
3512(SEARS)	0321
3512(WARDS)	0321
3512-9-6G	OEM
3512-9-7C	OEM
3513	0037
3513(RCA)	0079
3513(SEARS)	0037
3513(WARDS)	0037
3513-9-7C	OEM
3514	0160
3514(RCA)	0969
3514(SEARS)	0127
3514(WARDS)	0079
3514-91-7R	OEM
3514-92-7R	OEM
3515	0085
3515(RCA)	0160
3516	0160
3516(RCA)	0007
3516(WARDS)	0144
3517	0004
3518	0127
3518(RCA)	0007
3519	0016
3519(RCA)	0016
3519-1	0016
3519-2	0016
3520	0137
3520(DIO)	0137
3520(RCA)	0142
3520(WARDS)	0137
3520(XSTR)	0142
3520-1	0142
3520-6	OEM
3520-7	OEM
3520-8	OEM
3520-9	OEM
3521	0086
3521(SEARS)	0079
3521-1	0127
3521H	OEM
3521J	OEM
3521K	OEM
3521L	OEM
3521R	OEM
3522	0150
3522(SEARS)	0037
3522J	OEM
3522K	OEM
3522L	OEM
3522S	OEM
3523	0590
3523(RCA)	0126
3523(SEARS)	0079
3523J	OEM
3523K	OEM
3523L	OEM
3524	0786
3524(RCA)	0144
3524(SEARS)	0037
3524-1	0144
3524-2	0127
3525	1257
3525(RCA)	0016
3526	0555
3526(RCA)	0016
3527	0079
3527(RCA)	0144
3527-1	0127
3527AM	OEM
3527BM	OEM
3527CM	OEM
3528AM	OEM
3528BM	OEM
3528CM	OEM
3529	0015
3529A	0087
3529B	0087
3529C	0087
3530	0127
3530(RCA)	0144
3530-1	0127
3530-2	0127
3531	0259
3531-021-000	1432
3531-022-000	1901
3531-023-000	1367
3531-033-000	2453
3532	0233
3532(RCA)	0079
3532-1	0086
3532-9A-7K	OEM
3532-9B-7K	OEM
3533	0696
3533(RCA)	0126
3533-1	0126
3534	0050
3534(RCA)	0050
3534-9-7T	OEM
3535	0008
3535(RCA)	0007
3536	0079
3536-1	0079
3536-2	0079
3537	0079
3537(RCA)	0144
3538	0079
3538(RCA)	0016
3538-7	0239
3538-8	0061
3539	0086
3539(RCA)	0144
3539-1CD	OEM
3539-1CP	OEM
3539-2CP	OEM
3539-307-001	0144
3539-307-002	0144
3539DC	2618
3539UCP	OEM
3540	0150
3540#	0463
3540(RCA)	0037
3540-1	0037
3541	0086
3541(RCA)	0016
3542J	OEM
3542S	OEM
3543	0079
3543(RCA)	0016
3544	0004
3544(RCA)	0086
3544-1	0079
3545	0233
3545(RCA)	0233
3546	0079
3546(RCA)	0016

206

If replacement code is OEM, contact original manufacturer for replacement.

DEVICE TYPE	REPL CODE
3546-1(RCA)	0016
3546-2(RCA)	0016
3547	0283
3548	0079
3548(RCA)	0016
3549	0150
3549(RCA)	0037
3549-1	0150
3549-1(RCA)	0037
3549-2	0150
3550	0164
3550J	OEM
3550K	OEM
3550S	OEM
3551	0136
3551(RCA)	0016
3551A	0016
3551A-BLU	0136
3551A-GRN	0136
3551J	OEM
3551S	OEM
3552	3249
3552(RCA)	0233
3552-1	0233
3552-1(RCA)	0334
3553	3249
3553AM	OEM
3554	0086
3554(RCA)	0016
3554AM	OEM
3554BM	OEM
3554CM	OEM
3554SM	OEM
3555	0086
3555-01	0720
3555-02	0720
3555-03	0720
3555-3	0086
3556	0086
3557	OEM
3558	0079
3558(RCA)	0016
3559	0150
3559(RCA)	0037
3559-1	0037
3560	0079
3560-1	0086
3560-1(RCA)	0127
3560-2	0086
3561	0079
3561-1	0086
3562	0150
3562(RCA)	0037
3563	0150
3563(RCA)	0037
3564	0136
3564(RCA)	0074
3565	0142
3565(RCA)	0086
3565-1	0079
3566	0142
3566(RCA)	0086
3567	0142
3567(RCA)	0142
3567-2	0042
3567-2(RCA)	0275
3568	0007
3568(RCA)	0144
3568(WARDS)	0144
3569	0007
3569(RCA)	0016
3569-1	0079
3570	0037
3570(RCA)	0037
3570-1	0037
3570P	0037
3571	0086
3571(RCA)	0079
3571-1	0007
3571AM	OEM
3571R	0079
3572	0127
3572(RCA)	0016
3572-3	0144
3572AM	OEM
3573AM	OEM
3574	0037
3574(RCA)	0037
3574-1	0126
3574-1(RCA)	0037
3576	0326
3576(RCA)	0144
3577	0079
3577(RCA)	0079
3577-1	0079
3578-1	0004
3579	0007
3579(RCA)	0007
3580-9-6G	OEM
3580J	OEM
3580JM	OEM
3581	0150
3581(RCA)	0037
3581J	OEM
3581JM	OEM
3582	3249
3582(RCA)	0233
3582J	OEM
3582JM	OEM
3583	0535
3583(RCA)	0969
3583AM	OEM
3583JM	OEM
3584	0142
3584(RCA)	0142
3584-9-6G	OEM
3584JM	OEM
3585	OEM
3585-5	0239
3585-6	0061
3585-7	0239
3585-8	0061
3586	0136
3586(RCA)	0016
3586-2	0007
3588	0016
3588(RCA)	0212
3588-2	0212
3589	0016
3590	0126
3591	0086
3592(RCA)	0126
3597	0037
3597-1	0037
3597-2	0037
3598(RCA)	0144
3598-2	0126
3600	0211
3600-01-020-25722-01	OEM
3600-01-020-25722-02	OEM
3600-01-020-25722-04	OEM
3600-01-020-25722-05	OEM
3600-01-020-25722-07	OEM
3600-01-020-25722-10	OEM
3600-02-040-25383-01	OEM
3600-02-040-25383-02	OEM
3600-02-040-25383-04	OEM
3600-02-040-25383-05	OEM
3600-02-040-25383-07	OEM
3600-02-040-25383-10	OEM
3600-03-080-25711-01	OEM
3600-03-080-25711-02	OEM
3600-03-080-25711-04	OEM
3600-03-080-25711-05	OEM
3600-03-080-25711-07	OEM
3600-03-080-25711-10	OEM
3600-04-080-25712-01	OEM
3600-04-080-25712-02	OEM
3600-04-080-25712-04	OEM
3600-04-080-25712-05	OEM
3600-04-080-25712-07	OEM
3600-04-080-25712-10	OEM
3600-06-240-25713-01	OEM
3600-06-240-25713-02	OEM
3600-06-240-25713-04	OEM
3600-06-240-25713-05	OEM
3600-06-240-25713-07	OEM
3600-06-240-25713-10	OEM
3600-14-020-25722-01	OEM
3600-14-020-25722-02	OEM
3600-14-020-25722-04	OEM
3600-14-020-25722-05	OEM
3600-14-020-25722-07	OEM
3600-14-020-25722-10	OEM
3600-20-040-25383-01	OEM
3600-20-040-25383-02	OEM
3600-20-040-25383-04	OEM
3600-20-040-25383-05	OEM
3600-20-040-25383-07	OEM
3600-20-040-25383-10	OEM
3600-21-020-26542-01	OEM
3600-21-020-26542-02	OEM
3600-21-020-26542-04	OEM
3600-21-020-26542-05	OEM
3600-21-020-26542-07	OEM
3600-21-020-26542-10	OEM
3601	0086
3601(RCA)	0079
3601-1	0079
3602	OEM
3603	0050
3603-1	0079
3604	0396
3604(RCA)	0144
3604-1	0396
3604-3	0079
3606-210	OEM
3606-312	OEM
3606-313	OEM
3606AG	OEM
3606AM	OEM
3606BG	OEM
3606GM	OEM
3607	0595
3607-210	OEM
3607-312	OEM
3607-313	OEM
3607BG	OEM
3608(RCA)	0086
3608-1	0086
3608-1(RCA)	0264
3608-2	0086
3608-2(J.C.-PENNEY)	0086
3608-2(J.C.PENNEY)	0086
3608-2(RCA)	0086
3608-210	OEM
3608-312	OEM
3608-313	OEM
3609	0595
3610	0127
3610(RCA)	0144
3611	0555
3612	0555
3612(RCA)	0042
3612-210	OEM
3612-312	OEM
3612-313	OEM
3613	0334
3613(RCA)	0283
3613-2	0283
3613-3	0334
3613-3(RCA)	0334
3613-210	OEM
3613-312	OEM
3613-313	OEM
3614	OEM
3614-1	0079
3614-3	0079
3614-210	OEM
3614-312	OEM
3614-313	OEM
3615	0086
3615(RCA)	0086
3615-1	0086
3616	0150
3616-1	0037
3616-1(RCA)	0126
3617	0050
3618	0349
3618(RCA)	0144
3618-0010	OEM
3618-0020	OEM
3618-1	0160
3619-1	2367
3619-2	1403
3619-3	1403
3620	0150
3620(RCA)	0037
3620-1	0037
3621(RCA)	0042
3622-1	0086
3622-2	0086
3624-06	OEM
3624-1	0455
3624-2	0455
3624-16	OEM
3624-22	OEM
3624-23	OEM
3624-24	OEM
3624-25	OEM
3624-26	OEM
3624-27	OEM
3624-28	OEM
3625	0079
3625(RCA)	0016
3626	0016
3626AP	OEM
3626BP	OEM
3626CP	OEM
3627	0037
3627(RCA)	0037
3627AM	OEM
3627BM	OEM
3628	0208
3628-2(RCA)	0283
3628-3	0546
3628A-3	OEM
3628A-4	OEM
3629	OEM
3629-3	0378
3629AM	OEM
3629AP	OEM
3629BM	OEM
3629BP	OEM
3629CM	OEM
3629CP	OEM
3629SM	OEM
3630AM	OEM
3630BM	OEM
3630CM	OEM
3630SM	OEM
3631	0037
3631-1	0016
3631-1(RCA)	0042
3632	OEM
3632-1	0419
3632-2(RCA)	0555
3633-1	0823
3633-1(IC)	0823
3634	0074
3634-1	0637
3635	0212
3635(RCA)	0212
3635-1	0212
3635-2	0212
3636	0142
3636B-2	OEM
3637	0136
3637(RCA)	0074
3637-1	0103
3638	0178
3638-1	0899
3640(RCA)	0419
3646-2(RCA)	0144
3647	0074
3648(RCA)	0969
3649	0637
3650	OEM
3650-6	OEM
3650-7	OEM
3650-8	OEM
3650-9	OEM
3650HG	OEM
3650JG	OEM
3650KG	OEM
3650MG	OEM
3651	0150
3652	0050
3652HG	OEM
3652JG	OEM
3652MG	OEM
3653	OEM
3656AG	OEM
3656BG	OEM
3657-1	0224
3657-2	0224
3665	0103
3666	0150
3666(RCA)	0086
3666-1	0037
3669	0065
3669-2	0637
3676	0326
3676-1	0007
3679	0334
3679-1	0334
3680-1	0007
3681	0042
3681-1	1843
3682	0919
3682(RCA)	0455
3683	0103
3686	0136
3686(RCA)	0004
3686-1	0167
3687	0233
3687-1	0283
3688	0058
3688-1	0058
3693(ARVINE)	0144
3697-1	0037
3700-01-010-26295-01	OEM
3700-01-010-26295-02	OEM
3700-01-010-26295-03	OEM
3700-01-010-26295-04	OEM
3700-01-010-26295-07	OEM
3700-01-010-26295-10	OEM
3700-02-012-26296-01	OEM
3700-02-012-26296-02	OEM
3700-02-012-26296-03	OEM
3700-02-012-26296-04	OEM
3700-02-012-26296-07	OEM
3700-02-012-26296-10	OEM
3700-03-016-26297-01	OEM
3700-03-016-26297-02	OEM
3700-03-016-26297-03	OEM
3700-03-016-26297-04	OEM
3700-03-016-26297-07	OEM
3700-03-016-26297-10	OEM
3700-04-016-26297-01	OEM
3700-04-016-26297-02	OEM
3700-04-016-26297-03	OEM
3700-04-016-26297-04	OEM
3700-04-016-26297-10	OEM
3700-05-020-25722-01	OEM
3700-05-020-25722-02	OEM
3700-05-020-25722-03	OEM
3700-05-020-25722-04	OEM
3700-05-020-25722-07	OEM
3700-05-020-25722-10	OEM
3700-06-020-25722-01	OEM
3700-06-020-25722-02	OEM
3700-06-020-25722-03	OEM
3700-06-020-25722-04	OEM
3700-06-020-25722-07	OEM
3700-06-020-25722-10	OEM
3700-153	0015
3702-210	OEM
3702-312	OEM
3702-313	OEM
3703	0631
3714H1	0103
3714H1A	0103
3736-8	OEM
3736-18	OEM
3746	0279
3755-1	0062
3755-2	0062
3793	0720
3798NS	OEM
3800-4-6H	OEM
3800-9-6H	OEM
3801	1056
3801-4-6H	OEM
3801-9-6H	OEM
3801-210	OEM
3801-312	OEM
3801-313	OEM
3802	OEM
3802-210	OEM
3802-312	OEM
3802-313	OEM
3803	OEM
3803-210	OEM
3803-312	OEM
3803-313	OEM
3804	3511
3804-210	OEM
3804-312	OEM
3804-313	OEM
3805	OEM
3805-210	OEM
3805-312	OEM
3805-313	OEM
3806	5121
3806-210	OEM
3806-312	OEM
3806-313	OEM
3807	OEM
3807-210	OEM
3807-312	OEM
3807-313	OEM
3808-210	OEM
3808-312	OEM
3808-313	OEM
3809	OEM
3810	OEM
3811	OEM
3812	OEM
3819	0321
3819(RCA)	0321
3851	0136
3852	0279
3867	0016
3868	0693
3878	0233
3881	0007
3888A-D13	0062
3888A-D17	0062
3900	2232
3900-01	OEM
3900-05	OEM
3900-06	OEM
3901-01	OEM
3901-05	OEM
3901-06	OEM
3902-210	OEM
3902-312	OEM
3902-313	OEM
3903-01	OEM
3903-05	OEM
3903-06	OEM
3906-110	OEM
3906-210	OEM
3906-312	OEM
3906-313	OEM
3907	0211
3907(2N404A)	0136
3907/2N404A	0050
3907-01	OEM
3907-05	OEM
3907-06	OEM
3908-01	OEM
3908-05	OEM
3908-06	OEM
3909	3033
3909-210	OEM
3909-312	OEM
3909-313	OEM
3912-01	OEM
3912-05	OEM
3912-06	OEM
3913-01	OEM
3913-05	OEM
3915-01	OEM
3915-05	OEM
3915-06	OEM
3918-110	OEM
3918-210	OEM
3918-312	OEM
3918-313	OEM
3919-01	OEM
3919-05	OEM
3919-06	OEM
3920-01	OEM
3920-05	OEM
3920-06	OEM
3921	OEM
3922-01	OEM
3922-05	OEM
3922-06	OEM
3926-01	OEM
3926-05	OEM
3926-06	OEM
3927-110	OEM
3927-210	OEM
3927-312	OEM
3927-313	OEM
3929-210	OEM
3929-312	OEM
3929-313	OEM
3930-210	OEM
3930-312	OEM
3930-313	OEM
3931-01	OEM
3931-05	OEM
3931-06	OEM
3935-01	OEM
3935-05	OEM
3935-06	OEM
3937-01	OEM
3937-05	OEM
3937-06	OEM
3938-01	OEM
3938-05	OEM
3938-06	OEM
3939-01	OEM
3939-05	OEM
3939-06	OEM
3940-01	OEM
3940-05	OEM
3940-06	OEM
3947-210	OEM
3947-312	OEM
3947-313	OEM
3961	0136
3961(G.E.)	0050
3970	0279
3970(G.E.)	0004
3970-01	OEM
3970-05	OEM
3970-06	OEM
3970CL	0004
3999	0016
4000	2013
4000(IC)	2013
4001	0233
4001(IC)	0473
4001(MODULE)	4363
4001-151	0071
4001-222	0050
4001-223	0050
4001-224	0004
4001-225	0004
4001-226	0004
4001-228	0264
4001-230	0143
4001B	0233
4001BDC	0473
4001BDM	0473
4001BFC	0473
4001BFM	0473
4001BPC	0473
4001PDR60	OEM
4001PDR80	OEM
4001PDR100	OEM
4001PDR120	OEM
4001PDR140	OEM
4001PDR160	OEM
4001PDR180	OEM
4001PDR200	OEM
4002	6801
4002(IC)	2044
4002A	2044
4002BDC	2044
4002BDM	2044
4002BFC	2044
4002BFM	2044
4002BPC	2044
4003	OEM
4003(SEARS)	0143
4003E	0079
4004	0693
4004(E.F.JOHNSON)	0693
4004(PENNCREST)	0004
4004(SEARS)	0143
4005	0626
4005(E,F,JOHNSON)	0693
4005(E-F-JOHNSON)	0693
4005(E.F.-JOHNSON)	0626
4005(SEARS)	0143
4006	2675
4006(E.F.JOHNSON)	0086
4006(SEARS)	0143
4006BDC	0641
4006BDM	OEM
4006BFC	OEM
4006BFM	OEM
4006BPC	6575
4007	0693
4007(IC)	2819
4007(SEARS)	0143
4007UBDC	2819
4007UBDM	OEM
4007UBFC	OEM
4007UBPC	2819
4008	0488
4008(E-F-JOHNSON)	0488
4008(E.F.-JOHNSON)	0488
4008(SEARS)	0143
4008B	0488
4008BDC	0982
4008BDM	0982
4008BFC	0982
4008BFM	0982
4008BPC	0982
4009	6802
4009(IC)	1988
4009(PENNCREST)	0164
4009(SEARS)	0143
4010	0016
4010(PENNCREST)	0143
4010(SEARS)	0143
4011	0037
4011(IC)	0215
4011(SEARS)	0143
4011-PC	0215
4011A	0215
4011BDC	0215
4011BDM	0215
4011BFC	0215
4011BFM	0215
4011BPC	0215
4011PC	0215
4012	0086
4012(IC)	0493
4012A	0493
4012BDC	0493
4012BDM	0493
4012BFC	0493
4012BFM	0493
4012BPC	0493
4013	0626
4013(IC)	0409
4013(RECTIFIER)	0015
4013B	0409
4013BDC	0409
4013BDM	0409
4013BFC	0409
4013BFM	0409
4013BPC	0409
4014	0015
4014-000-10160	0004
4014-200-30110	0133
4014BDC	0854
4014BDM	OEM
4014BFC	OEM
4014BFM	OEM
4014BPC	0854
4015	1008
4015(IC)	1008
4015BDC	1008
4015BDM	OEM
4015BFC	OEM
4015BFM	OEM
4015BPC	1008
4016	1135
4016(IC)	1135
4016(RAM)	1887
4016BDC	1135
4016BDM	OEM
4016BFC	OEM
4016BFM	OEM
4016BPC	1135
4016CX	1887
4017	0508
4017(IC)	0508
4017BDC	0508
4017BDM	0508
4017BFC	0508
4017BFM	0508
4017BP	OEM
4017BPC	0508
4018BDC	1381
4018BDM	1381
4018BFC	1381
4018BFM	1381
4018BPC	1381
4019	1517
4019(IC)	1517
4019BDC	4300
4019BDM	OEM
4019BFC	OEM
4019BFM	OEM
4019BPC	1517
4020	2681
4020(CMOS)	1651
4020(IC)	1651
4020-8	OEM
4020-9	OEM
4020BDC	1651
4020BDM	1651
4020BFC	1651
4020BFM	1651
4020BPC	1651
4021	0016
4021(IC)	1738
4021BDC	1738
4021BDM	OEM
4021BFC	OEM
4021BFM	OEM
4021BPC	1738
4022	0079
4022BDC	1247
4022BDM	1247
4022BFC	1247
4022BFM	1247
4022BPC	1247
4023	0515
4023(IC)	0515
4023-25	OEM
4023A	0515
4023BDC	0515
4023BDM	0515
4023BFC	0515
4023BFM	0515
4023BPC	0515
4024	1946
4024(IC)	1946
4024BDC	1946
4024BDM	1946
4024BFC	1946
4024BFM	1946
4024BPC	1946
4024D	OEM
4024D(SM)	OEM
4025	2061
4025(IC)	2061
4025A	2061
4025BDC	2061
4025BDM	2061
4025BFC	2061

If replacement code is OEM, contact original manufacturer for replacement.

DEVICE TYPE	REPL CODE
4025BFM	2061
4025BPC	2061
4027	1938
4027(IC)	1938
4027B	1938
4027BDC	1938
4027BDM	1938
4027BFC	1938
4027BFM	1938
4027BPC	1938
4028BDC	2213
4028BDM	2213
4028BFC	2213
4028BFM	2213
4028BPC	2213
4029	2218
4029BDC	2218
4029BDM	2218
4029BFC	2218
4029BFM	2218
4029BPC	2218
4030	0495
4030(IC)	0495
4030BDC	0495
4030BDM	0495
4030BFC	0495
4030BFM	0495
4030BPC	0495
4031BDC	2943
4031BDM	OEM
4031BFC	OEM
4031BFM	OEM
4031BPC	2943
4034BDC	3570
4034BDM	OEM
4034BFC	OEM
4034BFM	OEM
4034BPC	3570
4034L	0555
4034S	0555
4035	0693
4035BDC	2750
4035BDM	OEM
4035BFC	OEM
4035BFM	OEM
4035BPC	2750
4036	0126
4040	0056
4040(IC)	0056
4040BDC	0056
4040BDM	0056
4040BFC	0056
4040BFM	0056
4040BPC	0056
4041(IC)	OEM
4041-000-1018	0143
4041-000-10150	0015
4041-000-10160	0004
4041-000-20120	0004
4041-000-30180	0004
4041-000-40270	0127
4041-000-40300	0127
4041-000-60170	0127
4041-000-60200	0127
4041-000-80100	0136
4041-200-10180	0143
4041-200-30110	0162
4041-200-40100	0143
4041BDC	3145
4041BDM	OEM
4041BFC	OEM
4041BFM	OEM
4041BPC	3145
4042	0121
4042(IC)	0121
4042BDC	0121
4042BDM	0121
4042BFC	0121
4042BFM	0121
4042BPC	0121
4043BDC	1544
4043BDM	1544
4043BFC	1544
4043BFM	1544
4043BPC	1544
4044BDC	2292
4044BDM	2292
4044BFC	2292
4044BFM	2292
4044BPC	2292
4044D	OEM
4044D(SM)	OEM
4046(SEARS)	0016
4047BDC	2315
4047BDM	2315
4047BFC	2315
4047BFM	2315
4047BPC	2315
4049	0001
4049(IC)	0001
4049B	0001
4049BDC	0001
4049BDM	0001
4049BFC	OEM
4049BFM	OEM
4049BPC	0001
4050	0394
4050(IC)	0394
4050BDC	0394
4050BDM	0394
4050BFC	OEM
4050BFM	OEM
4050BPC	0394
4051	0362
4051(IC)	0362
4051-300-10150	0015
4051BDC	0362
4051BDM	0362
4051BFC	OEM
4051BFM	OEM
4051BPC	0362
4052	0024
4052(IC)	0024
4052(RCA)	0224
4052BDC	0024
4052BDM	0024
4052BFC	0024
4052BFM	OEM
4052BPC	0024
4053	0034
4053BDC	0034
4053BDM	0034
4053BFC	OEM
4053BFM	OEM
4053BPC	0034
4053BS	OEM
4055	3272
4055(IC)	3272
4057	0016
4060DJRC8686	OEM
4066	0079
4066(IC)	0101
4066BDC	0101
4066BDM	0101
4066BFC	OEM
4066BFM	OEM
4066BPC	0101
4067-12	OEM
4067-15	OEM
4067BDC	3696
4067BDM	3696
4067BFC	OEM
4067BFM	OEM
4067BPC	3696
4068	6807
4068-83	OEM
4068BDC	2482
4068BDM	2482
4068BFC	2482
4068BFM	2482
4068BPC	2482
4069UBDC	0119
4069UBDM	0119
4069UBFC	OEM
4069UBFM	OEM
4069UBPC	0119
4070BDC	2494
4070BDM	2494
4070BFC	2494
4070BFM	2494
4070BPC	2494
4071BDC	0129
4071BDM	0129
4071BFC	0129
4071BFM	0129
4071BPC	0129
4072BDC	2502
4072BDM	2502
4072BFC	2502
4072BFM	2502
4072BPC	2502
4073BDC	1528
4073BDM	1528
4073BFC	1528
4073BFM	1528
4073BPC	1528
4075BDC	2518
4075BDM	2518
4075BFC	2518
4075BFM	2518
4075BPC	2518
4076BDC	3455
4076BDM	3455
4076BFC	OEM
4076BFM	OEM
4076BPC	3455
4077	OEM
4077BDC	2536
4077BDM	2536
4077BFC	2536
4077BFM	2536
4077BPC	2536
4078BDC	0915
4078BDM	0915
4078BFC	0915
4078BFM	0915
4078BPC	0915
4080	0321
4080-187-0507	0086
4080-838-0001	0178
4080-838-2	0178
4080-838-3	0178
4080-866-0006	0419
4080-866-1	0178
4080-866-2	0178
4080-879-0001	0419
4081	0621
4081(IC)	0621
4081BDC	0621
4081BDM	0621
4081BFC	0621
4081BFM	0621
4081BPC	0621
4082-03	OEM
4082-501-0001	0160
4082-748-0002	0157
4082BDC	0297
4082BDM	0297
4082BFC	0297
4082BFM	0297
4082BPC	0297
4085	0016
4085BDC	0300
4085BDM	0300
4085BFC	0300
4085BFM	0300
4085BM	OEM
4085BPC	0300
4085KG	OEM
4085SM	OEM
4086	0037
4086BDC	0530
4086BDM	0530
4086BFC	0530
4086BFM	0530
4086BPC	0530
4087	0037
4092BFM	OEM
4093BDC	2368
4093BDM	2368
4093BFC	OEM
4093BPC	OEM
4099A	0378
4100	OEM
4101	OEM
4101-685	0015
4102	4886
4103	OEM
4104	2675
4104BDC	OEM
4104BDM	OEM
4104BFC	OEM
4104BFM	OEM
4104BPC	OEM
4104UMC	OEM
4104USC	OEM
4115	OEM
4115-04	OEM
4116	0518
4117	OEM
4120-9	OEM
4124	0926
4125	1088
4126	1098
4127	1127
4127JG	OEM
4127KG	OEM
4128	1144
4129	1166
4130	1176
4131	1201
4132	1214
4133	1223
4134	1237
4135	1256
4136	1280
4137	1297
4138	1321
4140	1355
4141	1374
4142	1391
4143	1402
4144	1413
4145	1975
4145(RECTIFIER)	1975
4145(ZENER)	1435
4146	1448
4148	1497
4148(DIO)	0124
4149	1513
4150	1539
4151	1577
4161	0236
4162	OEM
4163	OEM
4164	2341
4164-2	2341
4164C	2341
4164P1M	2006
4165	OEM
4167	0079
4167(AIRLINE)	0007
4167(PENNCREST)	0007
4167(SEARS)	0144
4168	0079
4168(PENNCREST)	0007
4168(SEARS)	0144
4168(WARDS)	0007
4169	0079
4169(PENNCREST)	0007
4169(SEARS)	0144
4169(WARDS)	0007
4170	OEM
4189	OEM
4189-83(M)	OEM
4201	OEM
4203J	OEM
4203K	OEM
4203S	OEM
4203SQ	OEM
4204J	OEM
4204K	OEM
4204S	OEM
4205J	OEM
4205K	OEM
4205S	OEM
4206J	OEM
4206K	OEM
4207	OEM
4207-S	OEM
4208-3268-000	2039
4213AM	OEM
4213BM	OEM
4213SM	OEM
4214AP	OEM
4214BP	OEM
4214RM	OEM
4214SM	OEM
4220	1003
4220-A	OEM
4220-AS	OEM
4220-B	OEM
4220-B5	OEM
4221	1013
4221-S	OEM
4222	0883
4223	1043
4224	0926
4225	1088
4226	1098
4227	1127
4228	1144
4229	1166
4230	1176
4231	1201
4232	1214
4233	1223
4234	1237
4235	1256
4236	1280
4237	1297
4238	1321
4240	1355
4241	1374
4242	1391
4243	1402
4244	1413
4245	1435
4246	1448
4247	0085
4248	1497
4249	1513
4250	1539
4251	1577
4253	OEM
4264-15	OEM
4264-20	OEM
4295-1	1178
4295-1(RCA)	1178
4295-2	1178
4295-2(RCA)	2266
4300ACD	OEM
4300ACP	OEM
4301	OEM
4302	OEM
4309(AIRLINE)	0016
4310(AIRLINE)	0037
4310-(AIRLINE)	0037
4312	0142
4312(RCA)	0142
4313	0211
4315	0211
4320	1003
4321	1013
4322	0883
4323	1043
4324	0926
4325	1088
4326	1098
4327	1127
4328	1144
4329	1166
4330	1176
4331	0160
4331(ZENER)	1201
4332	1214
4333	1223
4334	1237
4335	1256
4336	1280
4337	1297
4338	1321
4340	1355
4341	1374
4342	1391
4343	1402
4344	1413
4345	1435
4346	1448
4347	0085
4348	0211
4348(ZENER)	1497
4349	0211
4349(ZENER)	1513
4350	1539
4351	1577
4351.0012	0143
4351.0013	0143
4351.0031	0143
4354	0143
4354.0012	0015
4354.0013	0030
4357	OEM
4358	OEM
4360D	0042
4362	OEM
4363	0136
4363BLU	0136
4363GRN	0136
4363ORN	0136
4363WHT	0136
4364	0136
4364(IC)	OEM
4365	0136
4366	0136
4367	0136
4368	0050
4381P1	1063
4398	0211
4400	OEM
4400Y	2179
4403	0015
4404	OEM
4416	OEM
4419-4	1671
4420	1003
4421	1013
4422	0883
4423	1043
4424	0926
4425	1088
4426	1098
4427	1127
4428	1144
4429	1166
4430	1176
4431	1201
4432	1214
4433	1223
4434	1237
4435	1256
4436	1280
4437	1297
4437-3	2242
4438	1321
4438-3	2728
4439-1	1832
4439-1(RCA)	1832
4439-2	1832
4439-2(RCA)	1832
4440	1355
4441	1374
4442	0037
4442(ZENER)	1391
4442-3	0546
4442-366	0419
4443	1402
4444	1413
4445	1435
4446	1448
4448	1497
4449	1513
4450	0211
4450(ZENER)	1539
4451	0279
4451(ZENER)	1577
4453	OEM
4454	0136
4456	0136
4457	0136
4459	0969
4460-2	1832
4460-3	1832
4462	0211
4463	0160
4464	0198
4464G-20L	OEM
4465	0198
4466	0279
4466ORN	0211
4467	0841
4467(RECT)	1241
4467(RECTIFIER)	1241
4468BRN	0211
4469RED	0211
4470	0198
4470-31	0198
4470-32	0198
4470-33	0198
4470-ORN	0841
4470M-32	0198
4471	0279
4471ORN	0211
4471YEL	0211
4472	0279
4472GRN	0211
4473	0004
4473-1	0144
4473-2	0144
4473-3	0144
4473-4	0016
4473-5	0016
4473-5X	0016
4473-6	0144
4473-7	0144
4473-8	0144
4473-9	0016
4473-11	0144
4473-12	0016
4473-M-3	0079
4473-M3	0086
4473-M-12	0086
4473-N	0086
4474	0279
4474YEL	0211
4475	0279
4475GRN	0211
4476	0279
4476BLU	0211
4477	0279
4477PUR	0211
4477V10	0004
4478	0126
4483	0086
4484	0279
4484-1	0150
4484-2	0150
4485	0279
4485-1	0150
4486	0279
4491-6	0161
4491-9	0161
4501	0136
4506	3721
4509	0136
4510	0211
4510BDC	1952
4510BDM	1952
4510BFC	1952
4510BFM	1952
4510BPC	1952
4511	1535
4511BDC	1535
4511BDM	1535
4511BFC	OEM
4511BFM	OEM
4511BPC	1535
4512BDC	2108
4512BDM	2108
4512BFC	OEM
4512BFM	OEM
4512BPC	2108
4514BDC	1819
4514BDM	1819
4514BFC	OEM
4514BFM	OEM
4514BPC	1819
4515BDC	3555
4515BDM	3555
4515BFC	OEM
4515BFM	OEM
4515BPC	3555
4516BDC	2331
4516BDM	2331
4516BFC	2331
4516BFM	2331
4516BPC	2331
4518	1037
4518(IC)	1037
4518BDC	1037
4518BDM	1037
4518BFC	1037
4518BFM	1037
4518BPC	1037
4519BDC	OEM
4519BDM	OEM
4519BFC	OEM
4519BFM	OEM
4519BPC	OEM
4520BDC	2650
4520BDM	2650
4520BFC	2650
4520BFM	2650
4520BPC	2650
4528BDC	1037
4528BDM	3168
4528BFC	OEM
4528BFM	OEM
4528BPC	3168
4531BDC	3292
4531BDM	3292
4531BFC	OEM
4531BFM	OEM
4531BPC	3292
4532BDC	1010
4532BDM	1010
4532BFC	OEM
4532BFM	OEM
4532BPC	1010
4539BDC	3611
4539BDM	3611
4539BFC	OEM
4539BFM	OEM
4539BPC	3611
4543BDC	4932
4543BDM	4932
4543BFC	OEM
4543BFM	OEM
4543BPC	4932
4545	0136
4545BLU	0136
4545WHT	0136
4552	0100
4552-01	OEM
4553	0279
4553-01	OEM
4553BLU	0211
4553BRN	0211
4553GRN	0211
4553ORN	0211
4553RED	0211
4553V10	0004
4553YEL	0211
4554	OEM
4554-01	OEM
4555BDC	2910
4555BDM	2910
4555BFC	OEM
4555BFM	OEM
4555BPC	2910
4556BDC	3397
4556BDM	3397
4556BFC	OEM
4556BFM	OEM
4556BPC	3397
4557BDC	OEM
4557BDM	OEM
4557BFC	OEM
4557BFM	OEM
4557BPC	OEM
4558	3974
4558C	0356
4558D	0356
4558DD	0356
4558DV	0356
4560D	OEM
4562	0211
4563	0211
4564	0211
4565	0211
4567	0211
4570	6841
4572-01	OEM
4572-05	OEM
4572-06	OEM
4573	0435
4582BDC	4579
4582BDM	4579
4582BFC	OEM
4582BFM	OEM
4582BPC	4579
4582BRN	0160
4583BDC	1286
4583BDM	1286
4583BFC	OEM
4583BFM	OEM
4583BPC	1286
4583RED	0160
4584GRN	0160
4586	0136
4587	0144
4589	0136
4590	0150
4594	0198
4595	0136
4596	0211
4597	0435
4597GRN	0435
4597RED	0435
4603	0136
4604	0136
4605	0136
4605RED	0136
4607	0211
4608	0160
4620GRN	0160
4621	0136
4622	0435
4623	0969
4624	0198
4627	0211
4630	0198
4632	0136
4633BN9503	OEM
4640	0599
4640P	0599
4648	0233
4649	0160
4652	0969
4653	0012
4663	0039
4677	0136
4684-120-3	0144
4685-285-3	0144
4685S	OEM
4686-81-2	0004
4686-81-3	0004
4686-82-3	0016
4686-87-3	0229
4686-89-3	0071
4686-95-3	0144
4686-97-3	0071
4686-105-3	0071
4686-106-3	0071
4686-107-3	0144
4686-108-3	0144
4686-112-3	0144
4686-114-3	0144
4686-116-3	0229
4686-118-3	0144
4686-119-3	0144
4686-120-3	0144
4686-126-3	0144

If replacement code is OEM, contact original manufacturer for replacement.

DEVICE TYPE	REPL CODE
4686-127-3	0144
4686-130-3	0178
4686-131-3	0144
4686-132-3	0016
4686-139-3	0071
4686-140-3	0144
4686-143-3	0016
4686-144-3	0016
4686-147-3	0229
4686-148-3	0229
4686-149-3	0015
4686-150-3	0229
4686-151-3	0229
4686-163-3	0004
4686-169-3	0144
4686-170-3	0126
4686-171-3	0144
4686-172-3	0144
4686-173-3	0016
4686-177-3	0229
4686-179-3	0071
4686-182-3	0086
4686-183-3	0016
4686-184-3	0071
4686-186-3	0071
4686-189-3	0071
4686-195-3	0004
4686-196-3	0004
4686-199-3	0071
4686-201-3	0071
4686-207-3	0144
4686-208-3	0144
4686-209-3	0144
4686-212-3	0071
4686-213-3	0160
4686-224-3	0144
4686-226-3	0178
4686-227-3	0201
4686-228-3	0144
4686-229-3	0126
4686-230-3	0126
4686-231-3	0016
4686-232-3	0233
4686-234-3	0419
4686-235-3	0126
4686-238-3	0126
4686-244-3	0144
4686-251-3	0144
4686-252-3	0334
4686-256-1	0136
4686-256-2	0136
4686-256-3	0136
4686-257-3	0016
4689	0086
4699	0327
4700	0595
4701	0103
4702	0599
4703	OEM
4704	0327
4705	0198
4705-01	OEM
4706	0144
4707	OEM
4708	OEM
4709	0144
4709-02	OEM
4713	OEM
4714	0198
4715	0103
4715-01	OEM
4715A	0103
4719	OEM
4719-01	OEM
4720BDC	OEM
4720BDM	OEM
4720BFC	OEM
4720BFM	OEM
4720BPC	OEM
4721	OEM
4721BDC	OEM
4721BDM	OEM
4721BFC	OEM
4721BFM	OEM
4721BPC	OEM
4722	0160
4722BLU	0160
4722GRN	0160
4722ORN	0160
4722PUR	0160
4722RED	0160
4722YEL	0160
4723	OEM
4723BDC	OEM
4723BDM	OEM
4723BFC	OEM
4723BFM	OEM
4723BPC	OEM
4724BDC	OEM
4724BDM	OEM
4724BFC	OEM
4724BFM	OEM
4724BPC	OEM
4725	OEM
4725BDC	OEM
4725BDM	OEM
4725BFC	OEM
4725BFM	OEM
4725BPC	OEM
4727	0160
4727-01	OEM
4727BDC	OEM
4727BDM	OEM
4727BFM	OEM
4727BPC	OEM
4729	0599
4730	0160
4731	OEM
4731-83	OEM
4731BDC	OEM
4731BDM	OEM
4731BFC	OEM
4731BFM	OEM
4731BPC	OEM
4732	0016
4732-83	OEM
4733	0016
4733-83	OEM
4734	0016
4734-83	OEM
4734BDC	OEM
4734BDM	OEM
4734BPC	OEM
4735	OEM
4735-83	OEM
4735BDC	OEM
4735BDM	OEM
4735BFC	OEM
4735BFM	OEM
4735BPC	OEM
4736B	OEM
4736B-83	OEM
4736BDC	OEM
4736BDM	OEM
4736BFC	OEM
4736BFM	OEM
4736BPC	OEM
4737	0016
4737BDC	OEM
4737BDM	OEM
4737BFC	OEM
4737BFM	OEM
4737BPC	OEM
4740	0225
4741BDC	OEM
4741BDM	OEM
4741BFC	OEM
4741BFM	OEM
4741BPC	OEM
4745	0419
4746	0127
4756	0007
4765	0016
4768	0016
4778-8(RCA)	0087
4780D	OEM
4789	0127
4792	1659
4800-200	0004
4800-220	0004
4800-221	0004
4800-222	0004
4800-223	0816
4800-224	0914
4801-0000-001	0037
4801-0000-003	0111
4801-0000-010	0079
4801-0000-016	0008
4801-0000-035	0144
4801-0000-060	0037
4801-00154	0133
4801-00628	0143
4801-00629	0143
4801-00801	0012
4801-1100-0011	0079
4801-1100-011	0160
4802-0000-002	0161
4802-00002	0144
4802-00003	0016
4802-00004	0037
4802-00005	0103
4802-00005A	0103
4802-00006	0016
4802-00007	0693
4802-00008	1401
4802-00009	0016
4802-00010	0321
4802-00012	0016
4802-00014	0155
4802-00015	0016
4802-00016	2035
4802-00017	0693
4802-00019	1401
4802-3268-000	2039
4802-3274-200	0556
4804-3267-901	2039
4805-1241-200	0124
4806-0000-004	0080
4806-0000-005	0087
4808-0000-037	0863
4809-0000-001	0549
4811-0000-025	0321
4811-0000-039	3387
4815	0037
4816B	OEM
4819	0233
4820	0144
4820-0201	0124
4821	0144
4821-0000-027	1224
4821-0644-011	1224
4821-0644-012	1963
4822-130-30132	0025
4822-130-30192	0015
4822-130-30193	0157
4822-130-30256	0015
4822-130-30259	0015
4822-130-30261	0287
4822-130-30264	0162
4822-130-30281	0143
4822-130-30284	0446
4822-130-30287	0644
4822-130-30301	0143
4822-130-30311	0143
4822-130-30312	0143
4822-130-30414	0276
4822-130-40095	0164
4822-130-40096	0208
4822-130-40132	0103
4822-130-40182	0133
4822-130-40184	0016
4822-130-40212	2736
4822-130-40213	0222
4822-130-40214	0127
4822-130-40215	0127
4822-130-40216	0127
4822-130-40229	0143
4822-130-40233	0085
4822-130-40235	0004
4822-130-40236	0004
4822-130-40252	0050
4822-130-40255	0050
4822-130-40304	0007
4822-130-40311	0127
4822-130-40312	0127
4822-130-40313	0127
4822-130-40314	0208
4822-130-40315	0037
4822-130-40317	0127
4822-130-40318	0127
4822-130-40319	2839
4822-130-40333	0079
4822-130-40348	0150
4822-130-40354	0016
4822-130-40356	0086
4822-130-40361	0016
4822-130-40369	0150
4822-130-40385	3502
4822-130-40441	0050
4822-130-40454	0016
4822-130-40456	0164
4822-130-40477	0150
4822-130-40508	0150
4822-130-40537	0161
4822-130-40614	0150
4822-130-41275	0071
4822-130-50221	0015
4822-130-50228	0293
4822-130-60588	0826
4822-130-81053	OEM
4825	0224
4826	0144
4827	OEM
4828-4	0143
4835-13-47796	OEM
4835-109-87542	OEM
4835-110-57006	OEM
4835-111-17023	OEM
4835-130-370-37	OEM
4835-130-7058	OEM
4835-130-27065	OEM
4835-130-27066	OEM
4835-130-37001	OEM
4835-130-37003	OEM
4835-130-37005	5593
4835-130-37007	5594
4835-130-37008	OEM
4835-130-37009	0031
4835-130-37011	0124
4835-130-37016	OEM
4835-130-37045	0666
4835-130-37046	0166
4835-130-37047	0023
4835-130-37048	0124
4835-130-37049	0053
4835-130-37052	0031
4835-130-37053	0023
4835-130-37054	5605
4835-130-37056	OEM
4835-130-37057	5607
4835-130-37058	1082
4835-130-37059	0031
4835-130-37061	0031
4835-130-37062	0124
4835-130-37063	0700
4835-130-37064	0489
4835-130-37065	OEM
4835-130-37066	OEM
4835-130-37067	0012
4835-130-37068	0877
4835-130-37069	OEM
4835-130-37074	OEM
4835-130-37081	0695
4835-130-37082	0195
4835-130-37084	0253
4835-130-37085	0165
4835-130-37086	0057
4835-130-37088	OEM
4835-130-37089	2604
4835-130-37091	0450
4835-130-37092	0010
4835-130-37094	0031
4835-130-37095	OEM
4835-130-37096	0057
4835-130-37098	OEM
4835-130-37099	0031
4835-130-37101	OEM
4835-130-37112	OEM
4835-130-37113	OEM
4835-130-37116	0015
4835-130-37121	0292
4835-130-37126	OEM
4835-130-37145	0124
4835-130-37182	5628
4835-130-37203	5637
4835-130-37235	0124
4835-130-37304	0140
4835-130-37328	0124
4835-130-37329	0253
4835-130-37332	0133
4835-130-37334	0604
4835-130-37335	0195
4835-130-37336	0466
4835-130-37337	0023
4835-130-37355	OEM
4835-130-37389	OEM
4835-130-37397	OEM
4835-130-37399	0466
4835-130-37402	0057
4835-130-37404	0440
4835-130-37405	0077
4835-130-37423	5677
4835-130-37433	OEM
4835-130-37471	1404
4835-130-37472	1404
4835-130-37491	1654
4835-130-37501	5683
4835-130-37502	5685
4835-130-37503	5686
4835-130-37516	OEM
4835-130-37529	OEM
4835-130-37535	OEM
4835-130-37536	OEM
4835-130-37541	OEM
4835-130-37544	5696
4835-130-37547	OEM
4835-130-37548	5697
4835-130-37549	OEM
4835-130-37551	4501
4835-130-37552	OEM
4835-130-37553	OEM
4835-130-37555	OEM
4835-130-37556	OEM
4835-130-37557	OEM
4835-130-37558	OEM
4835-130-37559	OEM
4835-130-37561	OEM
4835-130-37562	5696
4835-130-37563	1654
4835-130-37663	OEM
4835-130-37664	OEM
4835-130-37679	OEM
4835-130-37738	OEM
4835-130-37739	OEM
4835-130-37741	OEM
4835-130-47042	6534
4835-130-47048	2245
4835-130-47049	0037
4835-130-47051	0079
4835-130-47052	0079
4835-130-47053	0037
4835-130-47054	0037
4835-130-47055	0079
4835-130-47056	0111
4835-130-47058	3749
4835-130-47059	0261
4835-130-47061	1533
4835-130-47062	OEM
4835-130-47063	OEM
4835-130-47064	0079
4835-130-47065	1722
4835-130-47066	1741
4835-130-47067	0551
4835-130-47068	OEM
4835-130-47072	6537
4835-130-47073	0261
4835-130-47083	OEM
4835-130-47084	1359
4835-130-47085	OEM
4835-130-47086	1722
4835-130-47087	1741
4835-130-47088	4410
4835-130-47089	0236
4835-130-47091	2116
4835-130-47092	OEM
4835-130-47094	OEM
4835-130-47095	1722
4835-130-47096	4410
4835-130-47097	2116
4835-130-47098	OEM
4835-130-47099	0261
4835-130-47101	1157
4835-130-47107	6539
4835-130-47112	6540
4835-130-47116	OEM
4835-130-47117	1518
4835-130-47126	0037
4835-130-47137	0151
4835-130-47173	6542
4835-130-47191	6545
4835-130-47235	0151
4835-130-47243	1026
4835-130-47244	0881
4835-130-47275	0284
4835-130-47353	0881
4835-130-47358	0076
4835-130-47397	1026
4835-130-47413	4061
4835-130-47422	0013
4835-130-47424	0006
4835-130-47425	3154
4835-130-47426	0472
4835-130-47427	0018
4835-130-47428	2307
4835-130-47429	0532
4835-130-47431	3882
4835-130-47432	3064
4835-130-47433	2882
4835-130-47434	OEM
4835-130-47435	0151
4835-130-47436	0151
4835-130-47439	3114
4835-130-47441	0151
4835-130-47442	0148
4835-130-47458	OEM
4835-130-47479	0892
4835-130-47503	2666
4835-130-47525	3950
4835-130-47536	OEM
4835-130-47537	OEM
4835-130-47538	OEM
4835-130-47543	1338
4835-130-47544	OEM
4835-130-47545	2895
4835-130-47575	0148
4835-130-47576	1338
4835-130-47639	3850
4835-130-47705	OEM
4835-130-47744	0261
4835-130-47749	5437
4835-130-47751	2333
4835-130-47755	OEM
4835-130-47756	0860
4835-130-47757	0860
4835-130-47758	OEM
4835-130-47759	0261
4835-130-47761	3474
4835-130-47762	1533
4835-130-47763	OEM
4835-130-47764	0161
4835-130-47765	0148
4835-130-47768	4944
4835-130-47769	0275
4835-130-47771	OEM
4835-130-47796	OEM
4835-130-47892	OEM
4835-130-47896	4944
4835-130-47897	OEM
4835-130-47931	OEM
4835-130-57003	1234
4835-130-57004	OEM
4835-130-87001	OEM
4835-130-87055	OEM
4835-130-87056	OEM
4835-130-87263	1338
4835-130-97005	0311
4835-130-97006	1281
4835-130-97042	5596
4835-130-97043	OEM
4835-209-07822	OEM
4835-209-1702	OEM
4835-209-8708	OEM
4835-209-8752	OEM
4835-209-8755	OEM
4835-209-17001	OEM
4835-209-17002	OEM
4835-209-17003	OEM
4835-209-17004	1578
4835-209-17005	3755
4835-209-17021	OEM
4835-209-17024	OEM
4835-209-17026	OEM
4835-209-17027	OEM
4835-209-17033	0034
4835-209-17148	3132
4835-209-17314	OEM
4835-209-17315	OEM
4835-209-17339	OEM
4835-209-17345	OEM
4835-209-17352	OEM
4835-209-17355	OEM
4835-209-17368	OEM
4835-209-17369	OEM
4835-209-17432	OEM
4835-209-17433	OEM
4835-209-47005	OEM
4835-209-47006	OEM
4835-209-47007	OEM
4835-209-47008	OEM
4835-209-47009	OEM
4835-209-47013	OEM
4835-209-47015	OEM
4835-209-47017	OEM
4835-209-47026	OEM
4835-209-47053	OEM
4835-209-47054	OEM
4835-209-47056	2348
4835-209-47058	OEM
4835-209-47059	OEM
4835-209-47061	OEM
4835-209-47062	OEM
4835-209-47063	OEM
4835-209-47064	OEM
4835-209-47071	OEM
4835-209-47072	OEM
4835-209-47073	OEM
4835-209-47074	OEM
4835-209-47076	OEM
4835-209-47091	OEM
4835-209-47101	OEM
4835-209-47106	OEM
4835-209-47107	OEM
4835-209-47108	OEM
4835-209-47109	OEM
4835-209-47111	OEM
4835-209-47112	OEM
4835-209-47113	OEM
4835-209-47808	OEM
4835-209-87057	OEM
4835-209-87065	0347
4835-209-87066	3453
4835-209-87067	0619
4835-209-87068	OEM
4835-209-87069	0727
4835-209-87071	5693
4835-209-87072	OEM
4835-209-87073	2929
4835-209-87074	1022
4835-209-87075	OEM
4835-209-87079	0765
4835-209-87081	0624
4835-209-87082	1602
4835-209-87083	OEM
4835-209-87084	OEM
4835-209-87085	3068
4835-209-87086	OEM
4835-209-87087	OEM
4835-209-87088	OEM
4835-209-87089	4201
4835-209-87091	5712
4835-209-87092	OEM
4835-209-87094	0552
4835-209-87105	0101
4835-209-87114	4078
4835-209-87252	1288
4835-209-87259	0619
4835-209-87261	2753
4835-209-87262	2894
4835-209-87263	0176
4835-209-87264	1319
4835-209-87266	OEM
4835-209-87268	5694
4835-209-87269	OEM
4835-209-87271	0124
4835-209-87272	OEM
4835-209-87273	OEM
4835-209-87274	0619
4835-209-87275	2244
4835-209-87277	0024
4835-209-87278	OEM
4835-209-87283	0330
4835-209-87323	OEM
4835-209-87342	3479
4835-209-87398	OEM
4835-209-87399	OEM
4835-209-87406	4349
4835-209-87531	OEM
4835-209-87541	OEM
4835-209-87552	4427
4835-209-87553	OEM
4835-209-87554	OEM
4835-209-87556	OEM
4835-209-87557	OEM
4835-209-87559	OEM
4835-209-87561	OEM
4835-209-87562	OEM
4835-209-87563	OEM
4835-209-87564	OEM
4835-209-87565	OEM
4835-209-87605	OEM
4835-209-87612	0970
4835-209-87712	OEM
4835-209-87741	OEM
4835-209-87801	OEM
4835-209-87803	1813
4835-209-87806	OEM
4835-209-87807	OEM
4835-209-87808	OEM
4835-209-87821	1288
4835-209-87826	OEM
4835-209-87827	0330
4835-209-87834	5693
4835-209-87835	3453
4835-209-87836	OEM
4835-209-87837	OEM
4835-209-87838	OEM
4835-209-87904	OEM
4835-209-87947	OEM
4835-209-87948	OEM
4835-209-87949	OEM
4835-209-87982	OEM
4835-209-88002	OEM
4835-209-88003	4291
4835-209-88004	OEM
4835-209-88005	OEM
4835-209-88023	OEM
4835-209-88025	OEM
4835-209-88106	OEM
4835-209-88107	OEM
4835-209-88108	OEM
4835-209-88109	OEM
4835-209-88114	OEM
4835-210-27002	OEM
4835-210-27003	OEM
4835-218-27004	OEM
4836-130-37333	0062
4836-209-87531	OEM
4837	0144
4838	0233
4839	0016
4840	0016
4841	0016
4842	0016
4843	0233
4844	0037
4845	0144
4851	0127
4852	0016
4853	0233
4854	0016
4855	0144
4856	OEM
4857	0224
4858	0039
4872	0142
4882	0103
4888A	0160
4888B	0160
4904	0111
4907-976	0004
4927	0079
4935	0590
4937	0111
4943	0006
4989	0006
5000	1865
5001	1659
5001-002	0364
5001-010	2035
5001-014	0076
5001-020	0076
5001-021	0191
5001-032	0155
5001-037	0151
5001-038	0076
5001-043	0376
5001-044	2039
5001-046	0212
5001-047	3017
5001-050	0833
5001-064	0386
5001-068	0617
5001-070	0155
5001-074	0076
5001-080	0143
5001-083	0133
5001-089	0023
5001-107	0133
5001-112	0139
5001-117	0023
5001-125	0012
5001-128	0133
5001-135	0015
5001-141	0019
5001-142	0062
5001-144	0133
5001-152	0012
5001-156	0133
5001-160	0157
5001-161	0019
5001-162	0133
5001-163	0080
5001-164	0133
5001-165	0120
5001-196	0030
5001-197	0041
5001-508	0103
5001-509	0037
5001-510	0144
5001-511	1212
5001-512	0208
5001-513	0781
5001-514	2475
5001-517	1935
5001-539	0155
5001-540	0155
5001-541	0151
5001-542	0224
5001-543	0113
5001-544	0151
5001-545	1211
5002	OEM
5002(THOMAS)	0718
5002-030	1704
5002-031	1044
5003	OEM
5003P	OEM
5004	OEM
5005	1865
5005(THOMAS)	1865
5007	1865
5007(THOMAS)	1865

If replacement code is OEM, contact original manufacturer for replacement.

209

DEVICE TYPE	REPL CODE
5009	0618
5009(THOMAS)	0618
5025S	OEM
5035	OEM
5051-300-10150	0015
5052	0211
5055	OEM
5055J18	OEM
5056H-116	OEM
5065	0079
5070	OEM
5070A	OEM
5082-2835	0911
5082-4350	1281
5082-4420	OEM
5082-4480	OEM
5082-4483	OEM
5082-4486	OEM
5082-4520	OEM
5082-4550	3128
5082-4550A	OEM
5082-4555	OEM
5082-4587	OEM
5082-4620	OEM
5082-4650	1951
5082-4650A	OEM
5082-4655	OEM
5082-4687	OEM
5082-4787	OEM
5082-4920	OEM
5082-4950	1767
5082-4950A	OEM
5082-4955	OEM
5082-4987	OEM
5082-7650	OEM
5082-7651	OEM
5082-7653	OEM
5082-7730	4902
5082-7731	4783
5082-7736	OEM
5082-7740	4127
5082-7750	OEM
5082-7751	OEM
5082-7760	OEM
5085	0050
5086J24	OEM
5087J24	OEM
5090A	OEM
5093	0144
5096	0321
5101N60	0019
5101S34	0143
5104	OEM
5107	OEM
5116-1JC	OEM
5116JC	OEM
5120A90	0143
5120L	OEM
5122	0137
5124	0002
5130	0436
5132	0039
5133	OEM
5136	OEM
5142	0327
5151DC	OEM
5151JC	OEM
5152	OEM
5153	OEM
5155J18	OEM
5156JC	OEM
5157	OEM
5158	6912
5158-1	0516
5159	OEM
5160	OEM
5161	OEM
5162	OEM
5163	OEM
5164	OEM
5165	OEM
5166	OEM
5167	OEM
5168	OEM
5169	OEM
5170	OEM
5171	OEM
5172	OEM
5173	OEM
5174	OEM
5175	OEM
5176	OEM
5201-5	OEM
5201-6	OEM
5201A-5	OEM
5201A-6	OEM
5203N1	2488
5203RNI	1073
5203RNL	1073
5205NI	0015
5205NL	0015
5210DC-1	0947
5213	OEM
5213-4000	0122
5217	0133
5218	OEM
5220	OEM
5222	0137
5224	0002
5224(SCR)	0735
5226-1	0037
5226-2	0016
5228B(ZENER)	0036
5230	0436
5230A	0140
5232	0039
5233-7100	0522
5242	0327
5253	0085
5255-1J24	OEM
5256-1J24	OEM
5260-1J24	OEM
5261-1J24	OEM
5275-1J24	OEM
5276-1J24	OEM
5280-1J24	OEM
5280-2J24	OEM
5281-1J24	OEM
5281-2J24	OEM
5282-1J24	OEM
5283-1J24	OEM
5291	OEM
5300-1J16	OEM
5300-2	0411
5300-3	0411
5300-82-3	0071
5300-82-4	0071
5300-82-1003	0229
5300-86-1	0015
5300-88-1	0015
5300-88-2	0229
5300-88-3	0071
5300-88-1002	0071
5300-88-1003	0071
5300-88-1004	0071
5300-94-1	0015
5300-95-1	0015
5300-98-1	0015
5300-99-1	0015
5300-99-3	0015
5300-99-4	0015
5301-06-1	0015
5301-06-1001	0071
5301-09-1	0015
5301-1J16	OEM
5301-5	OEM
5301-6	OEM
5301-11-1	0229
5301-11-1001	0071
5301-13-1	0015
5301-20-1	0015
5301-22-1	0229
5301-36-T	0071
5301A-5	OEM
5301A-6	OEM
5303-1	1403
5303-2	1403
5305-1J16	OEM
5306-1J16	OEM
5308-1J20	OEM
5309-1J20	OEM
5310	2599
5320	OEM
5320-003	0178
5321	OEM
5322	OEM
5323	OEM
5324	0247
5326	0256
5327	0262
5328	0269
5330	0291
5330-1J16	OEM
5331	0305
5331-1J16	OEM
5332	0314
5333	0316
5334	0322
5335	0333
5336	0343
5337	0027
5340	0401
5340-1J24	OEM
5340-2J	OEM
5340-2JS	OEM
5341	0421
5341-1J24	OEM
5341-2J	OEM
5341-2JS	OEM
5342	0439
5343	0238
5344	1172
5345(ZENER)	1182
5345-2	5865
5346	1198
5348	0642
5348-1J20	OEM
5349-1J20	OEM
5350	1269
5350-1J18	OEM
5351	0600
5351-1J18	OEM
5351-31	OEM
5352-1J18	OEM
5353-1J18	OEM
5361-1N60P	0123
5371	OEM
5380-1J24	OEM
5380-2J	OEM
5380-2JS	OEM
5380-21	0015
5380-71	0016
5380-72	0016
5380-73	0086
5380-73(POWER)	0178
5381-1J24	OEM
5381-2J	OEM
5381-2JS	OEM
5388-1J	OEM
5389-1J	OEM
5389-2J	OEM
5400DM	OEM
5400FM	OEM
5401	OEM
5401DM	OEM
5401FM	OEM
5402DM	OEM
5402FM	OEM
5403	OEM
5403-MS	0012
5403DM	OEM
5403FM	OEM
5404DM	OEM
5404FM	OEM
5405DM	OEM
5405FM	OEM
5406DM	OEM
5406FM	OEM
5407DM	OEM
5407FM	OEM
5408DM	OEM
5408FM	OEM
5409DM	OEM
5409FM	OEM
5410DM	OEM
5410FM	OEM
5411DM	OEM
5411FM	OEM
5412DM	OEM
5412FM	OEM
5413DM	OEM
5413FM	OEM
5414DM	OEM
5414FM	OEM
5416	0015
5416DM	OEM
5416FM	OEM
5417DM	OEM
5417F	0155
5417FM	OEM
5417G	0155
5417H	0155
5419G	OEM
5420DM	OEM
5420FM	OEM
5421DM	OEM
5421FM	OEM
5422DM	OEM
5422FM	OEM
5423FM	OEM
5425DM	OEM
5425FM	OEM
5427DM	OEM
5427FM	OEM
5430DM	OEM
5430FM	OEM
5432DM	OEM
5432FM	OEM
5437DM	OEM
5437FM	OEM
5438DM	OEM
5438FM	OEM
5439DM	OEM
5439FM	OEM
5440DM	OEM
5440FM	OEM
5442ADM	OEM
5442AFM	OEM
5443AFM	OEM
5444AFM	OEM
5445DM	OEM
5445FM	OEM
5446-4	OEM
5446ADM	OEM
5446AFM	OEM
5447ADM	OEM
5447AFM	OEM
5448DM	OEM
5448FM	OEM
5450DM	OEM
5450FM	OEM
5451DM	OEM
5451FM	OEM
5453DM	OEM
5453FM	OEM
5454DM	OEM
5454FM	OEM
5459	0321
5460DM	OEM
5460FM	OEM
5464	0004
5470FM	OEM
5472DM	OEM
5472FM	OEM
5473DM	OEM
5473FM	OEM
5474DM	OEM
5474FM	OEM
5475DM	OEM
5475FM	OEM
5476DM	OEM
5476FM	OEM
5477FM	OEM
5480FM	OEM
5482FM	OEM
5483ADM	OEM
5483AFM	OEM
5485DM	OEM
5485FM	OEM
5486DM	OEM
5486FM	OEM
5487-1	OEM
5487-3	OEM
5488-1	OEM
5488-3	OEM
5489DM	OEM
5489FM	OEM
5490ADM	OEM
5490AFM	OEM
5490DM	OEM
5491ADM	OEM
5491AFM	OEM
5492ADM	OEM
5492AFM	OEM
5493ADM	OEM
5493AFM	OEM
5494DM	OEM
5494FM	OEM
5495ADM	OEM
5495AFM	OEM
5496DM	OEM
5496FM	OEM
5506	0755
5507	0118
5508	0296
5510	0036
5512	0140
5513	0041
5514	0253
5516	0062
5520	0064
5522	0052
5522-8	0242
5524	1608
5525	0440
5526	0371
5528	0700
5528DM	OEM
5530	0450
5532	0166
5532P	OEM
5540	6935
5540	0161
5555E	OEM
5556E	OEM
5557E	OEM
5558E	OEM
5586	OEM
5601-MS	0015
5601-NI	0015
5601-NL	0015
5607	4346
5609	OEM
5609A	OEM
5610	OEM
5611-628(F)	0150
5611-673	0037
5611-673D	0037
5611-695	0786
5611-695C	0786
5611-933(R)	0148
5611-950(Y)	1338
5611-1015(Y)	0148
5611-6370	0279
5611-6730	0150
5611-RN2206	OEM
5612-75(C)	0279
5612-77(C)	2839
5612-77C	2839
5612-370	0004
5612-370C	0004
5613-458	0155
5613-458B	0155
5613-458C	0155
5613-458D	0076
5613-458LGC	0155
5613-460	0127
5613-460A	0127
5613-460B	0127
5613-460C	0127
5613-461	0224
5613-461(B)	0079
5613-461C	0224
5613-535	0127
5613-535(B)	0079
5613-535A	0127
5613-535B	0127
5613-535C	0127
5613-710B	0364
5613-711(E)	0079
5613-711E	0376
5613-828(S)	1211
5613-828S	1211
5613-870(F)	0079
5613-871(F)	0111
5613-1047(B)	0113
5613-1162	0561
5613-1209	0590
5613-1209C	0590
5613-1213	0710
5613-1213D	0086
5613-1317NC(Q)	0155
5613-1327(T)	1212
5613-1327T	1212
5613-1335	0079
5613-1335(E)	0111
5613-1335D	0079
5613-1342	0224
5613-1342C	0127
5613-1359(B)	0151
5613-1359(C)	0151
5613-1359B	0151
5613-1383NC(R)	0018
5613-1473A(R)	0261
5613-1573A(R)	0261
5613-1573B(R)	0261
5613-1684(Q)	0155
5613-1684(R)	0155
5613-1684(T)	0155
5613-1684H(R)	0155
5613-1684T	0155
5613-1740(R)	0151
5613-1788(R)	0155
5613-1788R	0155
5613-1815(GR)	0076
5613-1846(Q)	0781
5613-1846Q	0781
5613-1923(Y)	2666
5613-3153	2757
5613-3620	0275
5613-4581	0007
5613-4581C	0079
5613-C114YS	OEM
5613-RN1206	OEM
5614-330(E)	1597
5614-350C	1597
5614-360D	0042
5614-882(P)	0161
5614-1197	1563
5614-1397	1533
5614-1398	1533
5614-1846	2116
5614-3600	OEM
5617-7	4293
5622-TPS703A	OEM
5623	OEM
5626-31	OEM
5629-6	5691
5631-0A90	0019
5631-0A90M	0143
5631-1N34A	0123
5631-1N60	0019
5631-1N60P	0123
5631-1S2076	0133
5631-1S2473	0133
5631-20A90	0123
5631-20A90H	0019
5631-20A90H(1)	0123
5631-MA150	0133
5632-1S2226	0015
5632-1S2227	0015
5632-AN217(BB)	2559
5632-DFA1A4	0023
5632-DFM1A4	0023
5632-ERB24-04	0023
5632-ERB24-06	0023
5632-ERB28-04	0023
5632-ERC04-04	0071
5632-HZ11A	0170
5632-S1B01-02	0015
5632-S5566B	0015
5632-S5566G	0790
5632-SIB01-02	0080
5632-U06G	0959
5632-W03B	0023
5632-W06A	0015
5632-W06B	0023
5633-1S85	0715
5633-1S85Y	0030
5633-1S2790W	0623
5633-152790W	0549
5633-SD115	0755
5635	OEM
5635-HZ11	0181
5635-HZ11A	0170
5635-HZ15	0681
5635-HZT33	3417
5635-RD4R7EB	0140
5635-RD4R7EB2	0140
5635-RD5R1EB	0041
5635-RD6R8EB	0062
5635-RD6R8EB2	0062
5635-RD7R5EB2	0077
5635-RD8R2EB	0165
5635-RD8R2EB2	0165
5635-RD9R1EB	0057
5635-RD9R1EB1	0057
5635-RD9R1EB2	0057
5635-RD10EB	0064
5635-RD11EB2	0181
5635-RD13EB	0053
5635-RD15EB	0873
5635-RD20EB3	0210
5635-RD30EB	0195
5635-RD36EB	0010
5635-ZB1-10	0170
5636-1SS133	0133
5636-RD5R1EB	0041
5636-RD6R8EB	0062
5637	OEM
5637-1N25D	OEM
5637-4	5788
5637-GL31AR	2990
5637-LN250RP	OEM
5637-LT9223A	OEM
5638-10	6966
5638-10KIT	OEM
5641-MV11	0015
5642	OEM
5644	OEM
5648-1	5884
5651-2	OEM
5651-C6B3	OEM
5652-AN217	2559
5652-AN217(BB)	2559
5652-AN217BB	2559
5652-AN5316	4958
5652-AN5436	3701
5652-AN5512	0970
5652-AN7218	2898
5652-AN7410	1308
5652-AN7410NS	1308
5652-BA527	2761
5652-BA5402	2772
5652-BA6124	5070
5652-BA7001	OEM
5652-EA6124	OEM
5652-HA1156	0514
5652-HA1325	3961
5652-LA4265	OEM
5652-LA7520	0534
5652-LA7911	OEM
5652-M51513L	4559
5652-TA78L005	1288
5652-TA7230P	4302
5652-TA7658P	5080
5652-UPC1018C	2898
5652-UPC1373H	2015
5653-AN5156K	OEM
5653-AN5265	4349
5653-C1870CA1	OEM
5653-M5278L56	OEM
5653-PST520G	OEM
5653-TA7777N	3206
5653-TA8207K	OEM
5653-TA78012A	0330
5654-D1709C	OEM
5654-HD38991A	2702
5654-M50433-1	OEM
5654-M50442-1	OEM
5654-M50442-2	OEM
5654-M58473P	OEM
5654-M58659P	OEM
5654-UPD6104C	OEM
5655	OEM
5657	OEM
5661-C6B3	1129
5662-HA1325	3961
5665	OEM
5667	OEM
5680	0126
5685-D2SBA40	0293
5701	0037
5702	OEM
5710	OEM
5719	OEM
5720	OEM
5721	0016
5722-3000	0050
5735	OEM
5737	OEM
5755	OEM
5757	2720
5765	OEM
5766-25	0211
5767	OEM
5780	OEM
5789	OEM
5792	OEM
5792/MSA16	OEM
5793	OEM
5793/MSA17	OEM
5795	OEM
5800	OEM
5802	OEM
5804	OEM
5805	OEM
5832-32	OEM
5836	OEM
5837	OEM
5840	0931
5842	OEM
5844	OEM
5845	OEM
5847	0042
5853	OEM
5853/MST23	OEM
5862	0007
5864-ATR321	OEM
5865	OEM
5865/MCT32	OEM
5865/TR361	OEM
5866/MST15	OEM
5872-0010	OEM
5872-0020	OEM
5877	OEM
5883	OEM
5900	OEM
5921	OEM
5921/MSA18	OEM
5922	OEM
5922/MSA29	OEM
5923	0947
5927	OEM
5927/MST21	OEM
5932	1832
5939A	OEM
5976	OEM
5981	OEM
6000-015	OEM
6001	1239
6001-061	OEM
6002	OEM
6003	0321
6008	0050
6011	0321
6013	0321
6019	0133
6022	OEM
6022/MCA13	OEM
6024	OEM
6024/ATR387	OEM
6024/MSA20	OEM
6027	OEM
6027H	OEM
6033	OEM
6033YF	2514
6034	OEM
6041	OEM
6043	OEM
6050	OEM
6055JA8	OEM
6056	1282
6056J24	OEM
6072J24	OEM
6080-002-304	OEM
6080-004-304	OEM
6080-005-304	OEM
6080-900-304	OEM
6081	OEM
6081/ATR408	OEM
6081/MCA11	OEM
6081-900-304	OEM
6082-002-304	OEM
6082-004-304	OEM
6082-005-304	OEM
6086J24	OEM
6087J24	OEM
6099-2	0419
6100	0164
6100-35	0164
6101	OEM
6102	1141
6115	0244
6115A	OEM
6116	OEM
6116ASP-20	OEM
6117	OEM
6117/MST11	OEM
6133	OEM
6136	0016
6143H827	0079
6151	0086
6151(RCA)	0086
6154	0136
6155	0136
6155J18	OEM
6156J24	OEM
6158	0144
6158-3	0144
6161J24	OEM
6162	0136
6162/ATR388	OEM
6163	OEM
6167	OEM
6171-17	0102
6171-18	0102
6171J24	OEM
6172J34	OEM
6177A	OEM
6181-1	0233
6185-3	0144
6214	OEM
6221	0349
6227	0212
6229	OEM
6230	OEM
6233	OEM
6236	OEM
6255-1J24	OEM
6256-1J24	OEM
6260	OEM
6260-1J24	OEM
6261-1J24	OEM
6264	OEM
6264-150	OEM
6264LP-15	OEM
6264P-150	OEM
6271	OEM
6275-1J24	OEM
6276	OEM
6276-1J24	OEM
6280-1J24	OEM

210 If replacement code is OEM, contact original manufacturer for replacement.

DEVICE TYPE	REPL CODE
6280-2J24	OEM
6281-1J24	OEM
6281-2J24	OEM
6283-1J24	OEM
6290J24	OEM
6291J24	OEM
6292J24	OEM
6293J24	OEM
6300-1J16	OEM
6300-1N	1907
6301-1J16	OEM
6304	OEM
6304/BL43	OEM
6305	OEM
6305-1J16	OEM
6306-1J16	OEM
6308-1J20	OEM
6309-1J20	OEM
6310	OEM
6310/MXK14	OEM
6312	OEM
6312/MXK15	OEM
6313	0050
6314	OEM
6314/MXK16	OEM
6315	OEM
6316	OEM
6322	OEM
6322/BL25	OEM
6322/MLT11	OEM
6330-1J16	OEM
6331-1J16	OEM
6334	OEM
6334-BL27	OEM
6335-1J24	OEM
6336-1J24	OEM
6340-001-505A	OEM
6340-002-505R	OEM
6340-005-505G	OEM
6340-1J24	OEM
6340-2J	OEM
6340-2JS	OEM
6340-301-505A	OEM
6340-302-505R	OEM
6340-305-505G	OEM
6341-1J24	OEM
6342-001-505A	OEM
6342-002-505R	OEM
6342-005-505G	OEM
6342-301-505A	OEM
6342-302-505R	OEM
6342-305-505G	OEM
6343-1	0016
6344	OEM
6344-QKH235	OEM
6344A	OEM
6348-1J20	OEM
6348-2J	OEM
6349-1J20	OEM
6349-2J	OEM
6350-1J18	OEM
6351	0212
6351-1J18	OEM
6352-1J18	OEM
6353-1J18	OEM
6367-1	0079
6378	OEM
6378/BL62	OEM
6378/MXT20	OEM
6380-1	0103
6380-1J24	OEM
6380-2J	OEM
6380-2JS	OEM
6381-1	0178
6381-1J24	OEM
6381-2J	OEM
6381-2JS	OEM
6388-1J	OEM
6389-1J	OEM
6389-2J	OEM
6390	OEM
6393	OEM
6406A	OEM
6410	OEM
6410A	OEM
6417	OEM
6421S	OEM
6432-3	0012
6440	0211
6445	0279
6450CX-506	OEM
6452	0211
6455	OEM
6455/MCA12	OEM
6458D	0356
6464	OEM
6500-1	OEM
6500-4	OEM
6502	3036
6502A	3036
6502AD	3036
6502B	3036
6502B/2MHZ	OEM
6502C	3036
6504	OEM
6504B	OEM
6507	3041
6507(AIRLINE)	0144
6509R4	OEM

DEVICE TYPE	REPL CODE
6510	OEM
6510A	OEM
6510CBM	OEM
6514	0076
6517	0079
6522	OEM
6523-34	0015
6523A	OEM
6525B	OEM
6526	OEM
6526A	OEM
6526A-1	OEM
6529B	OEM
6531	0127
6532	1962
6533	OEM
6543	OEM
6543A	OEM
6550	OEM
6551	0696
6551A	OEM
6552	0356
6558S	OEM
6560-101	OEM
6562	0765
6564	OEM
6564/BL71	OEM
6565	OEM
6567	OEM
6567R9	OEM
6568/MCT17	OEM
6569	OEM
6570	0308
6570-036	OEM
6572	0356
6581	OEM
6581R4AR	OEM
6584/OMK7000/TK69	OEM
6589	OEM
6591/MCA10	OEM
6592	OEM
6592/MCC10	OEM
6593	OEM
6593/MXC11	OEM
6594	OEM
6594/MCC1	OEM
6595	OEM
6596	OEM
6596/BL317	OEM
6597	OEM
6599	OEM
6601	OEM
6602	OEM
6602/MSC10	OEM
6604	4887
6605	4815
6605/MLT23	OEM
6613/BL324	OEM
6613PM	OEM
6615	OEM
6615/BL312	OEM
6616	OEM
6624	OEM
6624/MCT18	OEM
6629	0071
6629-A05	0071
6630	OEM
6631	OEM
6632	OEM
6632/MLT24	OEM
6633	OEM
6633/MLT17	OEM
6634/MLT25	OEM
6635	OEM
6635/MST18	OEM
6636	OEM
6636/BL87	OEM
6636/MST24	OEM
6637	OEM
6637/MST29	OEM
6638/MST30	OEM
6639	OEM
6639/BL46	OEM
6639/MCT14	OEM
6640	OEM
6640/BL60	OEM
6640/MCT16	OEM
6641	OEM
6641/BL86	OEM
6642	OEM
6644	OEM
6644/BL95	OEM
6645	OEM
6645/BL95H	OEM
6645/MXT61	OEM
6646	OEM
6646/MXT70	OEM
6647	OEM
6648	OEM
6649	OEM
6650	OEM
6651-486	0086
6664	4251
6685	OEM
6762	0037
6780	OEM
6780/MXK47	OEM
6781	OEM
6781/MXK11	OEM

DEVICE TYPE	REPL CODE
6795	OEM
6795A/MXT12	OEM
6800	0384
6802	0389
6804	OEM
6805	OEM
6810	OEM
6818	0435
6821	0443
6838	0484
6840	OEM
6842	OEM
6844	OEM
6845	OEM
6850	0509
6851	OEM
6861	OEM
6889	0576
6890	OEM
6890/BL650	OEM
6900K91-002	0033
6900K91-003	0141
6900K91-004	0557
6900K91-006	1820
6900K91-007	1035
6900K91-009	1424
6900K93-001	2067
6900K93-002	2598
6900K95-001	0329
6900K95-002	0354
6904	OEM
6905	OEM
6905/BL613	OEM
6905/MCT10	OEM
6906	OEM
6906/BL643	OEM
6906/MCT26	OEM
6914	0624
6915	OEM
6941/CONCEPT48	OEM
6942/CONCEPT48	OEM
6950	OEM
6950JR	OEM
6959	OEM
6962/BL665	OEM
6967A	OEM
6975	OEM
6975/MXK21	OEM
7000	OEM
7001	0079
7001(E.F.-JOHNSON)	0079
7002	0079
7005G(LOWREY)	0016
7006	0079
7008	OEM
7014	0079
7015	0079
7016	OEM
7016-L	OEM
7021	0696
7025	OEM
7031	0160
7058	OEM
7088	OEM
7090	OEM
7108	0016
7109	0224
7110	OEM
7110-1(A)	OEM
7110-2(A)	OEM
7111	OEM
7112	0133
7113	0079
7115	0144
7116	0224
7117	0079
7118	0144
7122	0144
7122-5	0079
7123	0144
7124	0144
7125	0144
7126	0144
7127	0144
7128	0144
7129	0079
7130A	1739
7131	0144
7132	0144
7133	0144
7134	0144
7149A	0167
7152	OEM
7152/MOT16B	OEM
7156	OEM
7161	0512
7161(WURLITZER)	0512
7163	OEM
7166	OEM
7166/BL933	OEM
7166/MLT10	OEM
7171	0079
7172	0079
7172-54	0435
7173	0144
7174	0144
7175	0144
7176	0079
7177	0144

DEVICE TYPE	REPL CODE
7178	0144
7182	OEM
7204A	2535
7206-0	0469
7208	OEM
7208B	OEM
7209A	0469
7211-9	0015
7212-3	0015
7212-3A	0015
7213	0042
7213-0	0229
7213-7	0015
7214	0144
7214(LOWREY)	0103
7214-6	0071
7214A	0103
7214S	0015
7215	0144
7215-0	0004
7215-1	0071
7215-2	0071
7216	0144
7217	0144
7218	0144
7219	0144
7219-3	0222
7220	0144
7220-1(A)	OEM
7221	0144
7221A	0167
7225	OEM
7228	OEM
7230	OEM
7232	OEM
7233	0224
7233S	0224
7234	0144
7235	0144
7236	0224
7236S	0224
7237	0144
7238	0144
7239	0211
7242	OEM
7247-A137	OEM
7250	OEM
7252	0042
7253	0283
7253(LOWREY)	0233
7254	OEM
7256	OEM
7258	OEM
7261	0224
7262	0144
7263	0224
7264	0224
7270P	OEM
7300/MPT26	OEM
7301	OEM
7302	0079
7303	0150
7303-1	0037
7303-3	0037
7306-1	0079
7306-7	0079
7306-8	0079
7306-13	0079
7308	OEM
7309/BL693	OEM
7310	0142
7310(G.E.)	0142
7311	0142
7312	0178
7313	0661
7316	0546
7316-1	0555
7317	0142
7317-1	1257
7318	0079
7318-1	0079
7318-2	3047
7318-6	0079
7320	OEM
7321	0855
7321-1	0079
7322	0178
7322-1	0142
7324/MPT11	OEM
7335-1	0065
7346-3	0079
7349	OEM
7349-2	0079
7349-5	0079
7351	0455
7358-00	OEM
7360R7	OEM
7362-3	0283
7362-6	0283
7363-1	0037
7364-1	0419
7364-6053P1	0693
7366-1	0065
7372-1	0212
7381/BL979	OEM
7387	OEM
7393	OEM
7394	OEM
7398-6117P1	0016

DEVICE TYPE	REPL CODE
7398-6118P1	0016
7398-6119P1	0016
7398-6120P	2035
7398-6120P1	2035
7400	0232
7400/9N00	0232
7400-6A	0232
7400-9A	0232
7400A	0232
7400DC	0232
7400N	2649
7400PC	0232
7401-6A	0268
7401-9A	0268
7401DC	0268
7401PC	0268
7402	0310
7402-6A	0310
7402-9A	0310
7402DC	0310
7402N	0310
7402PC	0310
7403	OEM
7403-6A	0331
7403-9A	0331
7403DC	0331
7403N	0331
7403PC	0331
7404	0357
7404-6A	0357
7404-9A	0357
7404A	0357
7404DC	0357
7404N	0357
7404PC	0357
7405	0381
7405-6A	0381
7405-9A	0381
7405DC	0381
7405PC	0381
7406	1197
7406DC	0381
7406N	1197
7406PC	1197
7407	1329
7407A	1329
7407DC	1329
7407N	1329
7407PC	1329
7408	0462
7408-6A	0462
7408-9A	0462
7408A	0462
7408DC	0462
7408N	0462
7408PC	0462
7409DC	0487
7409PC	0487
7410	0507
7410-6A	0507
7410-9A	0507
7410DC	0507
7410N	0507
7410PC	0507
7411-6A	0522
7411-9A	0522
7411DC	0522
7411PC	0522
7412DC	2227
7412PC	2227
7413	0161
7413(IC)	1432
7413DC	1432
7413PC	1432
7414	0042
7414(IC)	2228
7414DC	2228
7414N	4385
7414PC	2228
7415	OEM
7416	1339
7416DC	1339
7416N	1339
7416NA	0973
7416PC	1339
7417	1342
7417DC	1342
7417N	1342
7417NA	1342
7417PC	1342
7419	0659
7420	0919
7420(IC)	0692
7420-6A	0692
7420-9A	0692
7420DC	0692
7420PC	0692
7421	1347
7421DC	1347
7421PC	1347
7422DC	4523
7422PC	4523
7423	0042
7423DC	3429
7423PC	3429
7425	1353
7425DC	3438
7425PC	3438
7426	OEM

DEVICE TYPE	REPL CODE
7426DC	0798
7426PC	0798
7427	0144
7427(IC)	0812
7427DC	0812
7427PC	0812
7428	0144
7429	0016
7430	1360
7430-6A	0867
7430-9A	0867
7430DC	0867
7430N	1360
7430PC	0867
7431	0016
7432	1366
7432(IC)	0893
7432DC	0893
7432PC	0893
7433	0079
7437	0546
7437(IC)	3478
7437DC	3478
7437PC	3478
7438	0990
7438DC	0990
7438N	0990
7438PC	0990
7439DC	5722
7439PC	5722
7440-6A	1018
7440-9A	1018
7440DC	5868
7440PC	1018
7441	1032
7441-6A	1032
7441-9A	1032
7441DC	1032
7441PC	1032
7442ADC	1046
7442APC	1046
7442DC	1046
7442PC	1046
7443	1054
7443ADC	1054
7443APC	1054
7443DC	1054
7443PC	1054
7444	1066
7444ADC	1066
7444APC	1066
7444DC	1066
7444PC	1066
7445	1074
7445DC	1074
7445PC	1074
7446	1090
7446ADC	1090
7446APC	1090
7446PC	1090
7447	1100
7447/BL325A	OEM
7447/MCT30	OEM
7447ADC	1100
7447APC	1100
7447BDC	1100
7447BPC	1100
7447DC	1100
7447PC	1100
7448	1117
7448DC	1117
7448PC	1117
7449A	OEM
7450-6A	0738
7450-9A	0738
7450DC	0738
7450PC	0738
7451	1160
7451-6A	1160
7451-9A	1160
7451DC	1160
7451N	4453
7451PC	1160
7452A	OEM
7453-6A	1177
7453-9A	1177
7453DC	1177
7453PC	1177
7454-6A	1193
7454-9A	1193
7454DC	1193
7454PC	1193
7460	1265
7460-6A	1265
7460-9A	1265
7460DC	1265
7460PC	1265
7461	OEM
7470	1418
7470-6A	1394
7470-9A	1394
7470DC	1394
7470PC	1394
7472	1417
7472-6A	1417
7472-9A	1417
7472DC	1417
7472PC	1417
7473	1164

DEVICE TYPE	REPL CODE
7473-6A	1164
7473-9A	1164
7473DC	1164
7473F	1164
7473PC	1164
7474	1303
7474/9N74	1303
7474-6A	1303
7474-9A	1303
7474DC	1303
7474F	1303
7474N	1303
7474PC	1303
7475	1423
7475-6A	1423
7475-9A	1423
7475DC	1423
7475PC	1423
7476	1150
7476-6A	1150
7476-9A	1150
7476DC	1150
7476N	1150
7476PC	1150
7480DC	1527
7480PC	1527
7482-6A	1564
7482-9A	1564
7482DC	1564
7482PC	1564
7483ADC	3092
7483APC	3092
7483DC	0117
7483PC	0117
7484A	OEM
7485	0370
7485DC	0370
7485PC	0370
7486	1358
7486DC	1358
7486PC	1358
7489DC	5358
7489FC	OEM
7489PC	5358
7490	1199
7490-6A	1199
7490-9A	1199
7490ADC	1199
7490APC	1199
7490DC	1199
7490PC	1199
7491ADC	0974
7491AFC	OEM
7491APC	0974
7491DC	0974
7491PC	0974
7492	0828
7492-6A	0828
7492-9A	0828
7492ADC	0828
7492APC	0828
7492DC	0828
7492PC	0828
7493	0564
7493/9393	0564
7493-6A	0564
7493-9A	0564
7493ADC	0564
7493APC	0564
7493DC	0564
7493PC	0564
7494DC	1692
7494FC	OEM
7494PC	1692
7495	1445
7495ADC	1477
7495AFC	OEM
7495APC	1477
7495DC	1477
7495PC	1477
7496DC	1705
7496FC	OEM
7496PC	1705
7501	0155
7501R1	OEM
7502	0111
7503	0037
7504	OEM
7504-1	OEM
7505	0155
7506	0016
7507	0086
7508	OEM
7508A02	OEM
7508A37	OEM
7509	0111
7510	0424
7510(TRANSISTOR)	0178
7511	0155
7513	0086
7514	0103
7515	0016
7516	0016
7517	0016
7517S	4774
7518	0016
7519	0155
7520F	OEM
7520N	OEM

If replacement code is OEM, contact original manufacturer for replacement.

DEVICE TYPE	REPL CODE	DEVICE TYPE	REPL CODE	DEVICE TYPE	REPL CODE	DEVICE TYPE	REPL CODE	DEVICE TYPE	REPL CODE	DEVICE TYPE	REPL CODE	DEVICE TYPE	REPL CODE
7521B	OEM	7715-15X	OEM	7906CK	OEM	8000-00004-301	0076	8000-0005-007	0016	8000-00043-065	2475	8051AHL5220123	OEM
7522F	OEM	7715-18	OEM	7906CU	2624	8000-00004-303	0018	8000-0005-008	0103	8000-00043-067	0041	8051C	OEM
7522N	OEM	7715-20	OEM	7906DA	OEM	8000-00004-305	0627	8000-0005-009	0016	8000-00043-068	0318	8051CPU-001	OEM
7523B	OEM	7715-20X	OEM	7908	OEM	8000-00004-306	2377	8000-0005-010	0086	8000-00045-004	1635	8052ALR	OEM
7524F	OEM	7715-30	OEM	7908CDA	OEM	8000-00004-307	0465	8000-0005-011	1401	8000-00047-002	3573	8052ALY	OEM
7524N	OEM	7715-30X	OEM	7908CK	OEM	8000-00004-308	2142	8000-0005-015	0143	8000-00047-003	3565	8053ALB	OEM
7525B	OEM	7715-40	OEM	7908CT	OEM	8000-00004-P079	0016	8000-0005-016	0143	8000-00047-006	2285	8054	OEM
7527-5A	0644	7715-40X	OEM	7908CU	2764	8000-00004-P081	0321	8000-0005-017	0143	8000-00049-010	0080	8054ALB	OEM
7528F	OEM	7715-50	OEM	7908DA	OEM	8000-00004-P082	0086	8000-0005-018	0143	8000-00049-020	0030	8055	OEM
7528N	OEM	7715-50X	OEM	7909	OEM	8000-00004-P083	1401	8000-0005-019	0644	8000-00049-021	0041	8058	OEM
7529	OEM	7717	0475	7911/ACIA	OEM	8000-00004-P084	1401	8000-0005-020	0631	8000-00049-025	3763	8070-4	0004
7547	OEM	7719	0679	7911/BP2	OEM	8000-00004-P085	0155	8000-0005-021	0012	8000-00049-026	2395	8071-4	0004
7554	0012	7720	0225	7911/CP1-701	OEM	8000-00004-P086	0155	8000-0005-022	0015	8000-00049-053	0076	8072-4	0004
7555	1534	7721	0230	7911/CP3-01	OEM	8000-00004-P088	0004	8000-0005-023	0143	8000-00049-054	0076	8073-4	0004
7568	0015	7722	0030	7911/CP3-03	OEM	8000-00004-P089	0037	8000-0009-089	0076	8000-00049-055	0151	8074-4	0016
7574	0644	7724	0247	7911/CP9/B/	OEM	8000-00005-001	0683	8000-00010-017	0321	8000-00049-056	0037	8075-4	0016
7577	OEM	7726	0256	7911/CRC-4K	OEM	8000-00005-002	0076	8000-00010-109	0133	8000-00049-057	0151	8080A	4467
7585	0079	7727	0262	7911/CRC-8K	OEM	8000-00005-004	0111	8000-00011-004	0364	8000-00049-058	1967	8085	OEM
7586	0079	7728	0269	7911/DSC	OEM	8000-00005-005	0076	8000-00011-0048	0007	8000-00049-059	2798	8087	OEM
7587	0079	7730	0291	7911/PIA	OEM	8000-00005-007	1409	8000-00011-041	0023	8000-00049-060	2475	8087-2	OEM
7588	0079	7732	0314	7911/RPC	OEM	8000-00005-009	1390	8000-00011-042	0133	8000-00049-061	0018	8088	OEM
7589	0016	7733	0316	7911/RPC-16	OEM	8000-00005-010	1390	8000-00011-043	0012	8000-00049-062	1270	8098	0391
7590	0016	7733(XSTR)	2039	7911/RPC-16A	OEM	8000-00005-011	1401	8000-00011-044	0015	8000-00053-004	0780	8099/MST38	OEM
7601	OEM	7734	0322	7911/RPC-16C	OEM	8000-00005-013	1581	8000-00011-045	0139	8000-00053-005	OEM	8100	OEM
7602	OEM	7735	0333	7911/RPC-32	OEM	8000-00005-015	0143	8000-00011-046	0143	8000-00057-007	OEM	8100-00-00	OEM
7603	0164	7736	0343	7911/RPC-32A	OEM	8000-00005-016	0143	8000-00011-047	0364	8000-00057-008	OEM	8100-00-01	OEM
7604	OEM	7737	0027	7911/RPC-32C	OEM	8000-00005-017	0143	8000-00011-048	0364	8000-00057-009	1535	8100-00-10	OEM
7605	OEM	7738	0266	7911/SMC	OEM	8000-00005-018	0143	8000-00011-049	0076	8000-00057-011	0012	8100-00-11	OEM
7619	OEM	7739	0382	7911/SP9	OEM	8000-00005-019	0644	8000-00011-050	0042	8000-00058-003	0091	8100-01-00	OEM
7625	1624	7740	0401	7911/SP9/B/	OEM	8000-00005-020	0631	8000-00011-051	1390	8000-00058-004	0006	8100-01-01	OEM
7626	0037	7741	0421	7911/SP80	OEM	8000-00005-021	0012	8000-00011-052	1897	8000-00058-006	0780	8100-01-10	OEM
7628LA	OEM	7753	1748	7911/SP80/A/	OEM	8000-00005-022	0015	8000-00011-053	0410	8000-00058-008	4563	8100-01-11	OEM
7635	0006	7753DMP	0103	7911-CP80/A/	OEM	8000-00005-023	0143	8000-00011-054	3126	8000-00058-009	1532	8100-10-00	OEM
7636	1637	7801	OEM	7912	1827	8000-00005-055	0076	8000-00011-055	3126	8000-004-P061	0071	8100-10-01	OEM
7637	0016	78010BC	OEM	7912C	1827	8000-00005-152	0015	8000-00011-064	0012	8000-004-P063	0143	8100-10-10	OEM
7638	0527	7802	OEM	7912CDA	3030	8000-00006-001	1390	8000-00011-103	0644	8000-004-P064	0071	8100-10-11	OEM
7639	0527	7803	OEM	7912CU	3038	8000-00006-002	1401	8000-00011-104	0015	8000-004-P067	0071	8100-11-00	OEM
7640	1645	7804	OEM	7912DA	3030	8000-00006-003	0364	8000-00011-116	OEM	8000-004-P068	0071	8100-11-01	OEM
7641	0016	7805	0619	7915C	3777	8000-00006-004	0037	8000-00011-166	0030	8000-004-P089	0126	8100-11-10	OEM
7642	0144	7805A	0619	7915CU	3190	8000-00006-005	0889	8000-00012-038	0133	8000-0016-127	0905	8100-11-11	OEM
7646IT	OEM	7805C	0619	7915DA	3184	8000-00006-006	2766	8000-00012-039	0076	8000-0016-129	0905	8100FMP	OEM
7662	OEM	7805CDA	1911	7918CDA	OEM	8000-00006-007	0019	8000-00012-040	0218	8000-0028-042	0357	8101-01A	OEM
7663	OEM	7805CK	OEM	7918CK	OEM	8000-00006-008	0133	8000-00012-041	4039	8000-0030-009	0208	8102-206	0015
7666	0167	7805CT	0619	7918CU	3312	8000-00006-009	0012	8000-00016-127	0905	8000-0058-006	0780	8102-207	0079
7675	0016	7805H	0619	7918DA	OEM	8000-00006-010	0039	8000-00028-037	0155	8000-0095-010	0693	8102-208	0191
7692	OEM	7806CDA	OEM	7920	OEM	8000-00006-011	1226	8000-00028-038	0191	8000-028-206	OEM	8102-209	0016
7700-01D	OEM	7806CK	OEM	7920A	OEM	8000-00006-146	0091	8000-00028-039	0042	8001	OEM	8102-210	0816
7700-010	OEM	7806CU	0917	7921	0242	8000-00006-147	0023	8000-00028-040	0919	8002	OEM	8103	OEM
7701	0071	7806DA	OEM	7924CDA	OEM	8000-00006-190	0861	8000-00028-041	0228	8003	1954	8104-0-0	OEM
7701-1.5A	OEM	7808C	1187	7924CK	OEM	8000-00006-201	0080	8000-00028-042	0357	8003-114	0016	8104-16-1	OEM
7701-2A	OEM	7808CDA	OEM	7924CU	3554	8000-00006-230	4070	8000-00028-043	0564	8003-115	0015	8104-32-0	OEM
7701-2X	OEM	7808CK	OEM	7924DA	OEM	8000-00006-231	0015	8000-00028-044	0614	8004	1954	8104-32-1	OEM
7701-3A	OEM	7808CU	1187	7950	OEM	8000-00006-232	0012	8000-00028-045	0139	8005	OEM	8104-64-1	OEM
7701-3X	OEM	7808DA	OEM	7950.2DA	OEM	8000-00006-278	0781	8000-00028-046	0143	8005(PENNCREST)	0130	8106-207	0007
7701-4A	OEM	7809A	OEM	7962	0015	8000-00006-279	2526	8000-00028-047	0064	8006	OEM	8108-85/88	OEM
7701-4X	OEM	7810	0144	7977	OEM	8000-00006-280	0076	8000-00028-048	0023	8007	OEM	8110	OEM
7701-5B	OEM	7810(IC)	OEM	7991	0111	8000-00006-281	0133	8000-00028-206	0076	8008	OEM	8111	OEM
7701-5X	OEM	7810G	OEM	7992	0079	8000-00009-089	0076	8000-00029-006	0076	8010	OEM	8112S	OEM
7701-6A	OEM	7810H	OEM	7993	0164	8000-00009-174	0191	8000-00029-007	0945	8010-51	0030	8113	OEM
7701-6X	OEM	7811	0144	8000-00001-068	0004	8000-00009-177	0127	8000-00030-007	0155	8010-52	0133	8114	2037
7701-7A	OEM	7812	0144	8000-00003-004	0006	8000-00009-178	0683	8000-00030-008	1967	8010-53	0143	8115	OEM
7701-7X	OEM	7812(IC)	0330	8000-00003-033	0364	8000-00009-280	2440	8000-00030-009	0208	8010-171	2377	8116	0518
7701-8X	OEM	7812A	0330	8000-00003-034	0151	8000-0004-004	0037	8000-00030-010	0080	8010-172	2020	8120-00-0	OEM
7701-9A	OEM	7812C	1341	8000-00003-035	0076	8000-0004-086	0208	8000-00032-025	0076	8010-173	0321	8120-00-1	OEM
7701-9X	OEM	7812CDA	3359	8000-00003-036	0076	8000-0004-P060	0143	8000-00032-026	1146	8010-174	0007	8120-01-0	OEM
7701-10B	OEM	7812CT	0330	8000-00003-037	0006	8000-0004-P-061	0015	8000-00032-027	0208	8010-175	0007	8120-01-1	OEM
7701-10X	OEM	7812CU	0330	8000-00003-038	0004	8000-0004-P061	0133	8000-00032-028	0830	8010-176	0016	8120-10-0	OEM
7701-12A	OEM	7812DA	5405	8000-00003-039	0004	8000-0004-P062	0133	8000-00032-029	OEM	8011	OEM	8120-10-1	OEM
7701-12X	OEM	7812P	0330	8000-00003-040	0222	8000-0004-P063	0143	8000-00032-030	2111	8012	OEM	8120-11-1	OEM
7701-15A	OEM	7813	0144	8000-00003-041	2039	8000-0004-P064	0133	8000-00032-031	0817	8016	OEM	8121B	OEM
7701-15X	OEM	7814	OEM	8000-00003-042	2039	8000-0004-P065	0012	8000-00034-010	0015	8016-L	OEM	8121C	OEM
7701-18A	OEM	7815	1311	8000-00003-043	2039	8000-0004-P066	0133	8000-00035-001	0133	8020-202	0133	8121D	OEM
7701-18X	OEM	7815(IC)	1311	8000-00003-044	0015	8000-0004-P067	0015	8000-00035-002	0023	8020-203	0015	8121E	OEM
7701-20B	OEM	7815CDA	1989	8000-00003-045	0143	8000-0004-P068	0015	8000-00035-003	0127	8020-204	0111	8121F	OEM
7701-20X	OEM	7815CU	1311	8000-00003-046	0139	8000-0004-P079	0364	8000-00038-001	0930	8020-205	0016	8123B	OEM
7702	OEM	7815DA	1299	8000-00004-003	0008	8000-0004-P080	0321	8000-00038-002	0011	8020-206	0042	8123C	OEM
7702-1A	0071	7816	0016	8000-00004-004	0037	8000-0004-P081	0683	8000-00038-003	1635	8021B	OEM	8123D	OEM
7704	OEM	7817	0016	8000-00004-060	0123	8000-0004-P082	0783	8000-00038-004	0232	8021C	OEM	8123E	OEM
7704-1	0071	7818	0016	8000-00004-061	0139	8000-0004-P083	1401	8000-00038-005	4516	8021D	OEM	8123F	OEM
7705	OEM	7818CDA	OEM	8000-00004-062	0133	8000-0004-P084	1401	8000-00038-006	0564	8021E	OEM	8128	1887
7706-1	0071	7818CU	2244	8000-00004-063	0123	8000-0004-P085	0076	8000-00038-007	1303	8021F	OEM	8131	OEM
7707	1703	7818DA	OEM	8000-00004-064	0133	8000-0004-P086	0076	8000-00038-008	0133	8023B	OEM	8131-01	OEM
7708	0777	7821	OEM	8000-00004-065	0057	8000-0004-P088	0595	8000-00038-009	0143	8023C	OEM	8131-10	OEM
7708-1	0071	7821/MPT12	OEM	8000-00004-066	0120	8000-0004-P089	0037	8000-00038-010	0005	8023D	OEM	8131-11	OEM
7709	0791	7823/MLT13	OEM	8000-00004-067	0139	8000-0004-P090	0817	8000-00041-015	0143	8023E	OEM	8132	OEM
7710	0791	7824CDA	OEM	8000-00004-068	0023	8000-0004-P185	0219	8000-00041-016	0143	8023F	OEM	8135-0	OEM
7710-1	0071	7824CU	2224	8000-00004-079	0079	8000-0004-P060	0143	8000-00041-017	0139	8025MJP	OEM	8142	OEM
7711	0815	7824DA	OEM	8000-00004-080	3017	8000-0004-P061	0133	8000-00041-018	0012	8031	OEM	8143	OEM
7711-1	0071	7829A	OEM	8000-00004-081	0683	8000-0004-P062	0133	8000-00041-019	0133	8032	OEM	8149	OEM
7712	0827	7849/BTR140	OEM	8000-00004-082	0783	8000-0004-P063	0143	8000-00041-040	2195	8035	OEM	8150-00	OEM
7712-1	0071	7849/MCT23	OEM	8000-00004-083	1401	8000-0004-P064	0133	8000-00041-041	0076	8035MJP	OEM	8150-01	OEM
7713-1	0071	7850CU	OEM	8000-00004-084	1401	8000-0004-P065	0012	8000-00041-042	0076	8039-6I	OEM	8150-10	OEM
7714	0870	7874	1865	8000-00004-085	0359	8000-0004-P066	0133	8000-00041-043	0386	8039-6N	OEM	8150-11	OEM
7715	0185	7874(WURLITZER)	0512	8000-00004-086	0208	8000-0004-P067	0015	8000-00041-044	0833	8039I	OEM	8154	OEM
7715-3	OEM	7880	OEM	8000-00004-087	2035	8000-0004-P068	0015	8000-00041-046	0076	8039N	OEM	8155	OEM
7715-3X	OEM	7885	OEM	8000-00004-088	0004	8000-0004-P079	0016	8000-00041-047	2684	8040	OEM	8155-P	OEM
7715-4	OEM	7889	OEM	8000-00004-089	0037	8000-0004-P080	0321	8000-00042-007	0124	8041	OEM	8175-7937	0624
7715-4X	OEM	7893	OEM	8000-00004-85	0016	8000-0004-P081	0321	8000-00042-008	0232	8041A	OEM	8198	OEM
7715-5	OEM	7901/MPT13	OEM	8000-00004-184	0002	8000-0004-P082	0016	8000-00042-009	0507	8042	OEM	8199	OEM
7715-5X	OEM	7902/MPT17	OEM	8000-00004-185	0219	8000-0004-P083	0086	8000-00042-010	OEM	8042-105	OEM	8200	OEM
7715-6	OEM	7905	1275	8000-00004-236	OEM	8000-0004-P084	0086	8000-00042-011	1915	8042-139	OEM	8200-202	0111
7715-7	OEM	7905CDA	1993	8000-00004-239	0091	8000-0004-P085	0016	8000-00042-012	OEM	8042AH	OEM	8200-203	0111
7715-7X	OEM	7905CU	1275	8000-00004-241	0615	8000-0004-P086	0208	8000-00042-013	0410	8045	OEM	8200-204	1004
7715-8	OEM	7905DA	1993	8000-00004-242	0191	8000-0004-P088	0004	8000-00042-014	0312	8048	OEM	8201	OEM
7715-9	OEM	7905UC	1275	8000-00004-243	0191	8000-0004-P089	0037	8000-00042-015	0340	8049	OEM	8202	OEM
7715-10	OEM	7905.2CDA	OEM	8000-00004-248	0030	8000-0005-001	0321	8000-00043-019	1136	8049HC150	OEM	8210	OEM
7715-10X	OEM	7905.2CU	OEM	8000-00004-298	1136	8000-0005-002	0127	8000-00043-020	1056	8050	0155	8211	OEM
7715-12	OEM	7906C	2624	8000-00004-299	0127	8000-0005-003	0127	8000-00043-021	0012	8050C	0155	8212	1849
7715-15	OEM	7906CDA	OEM	8000-00004-300	0076	8000-0005-004	0076	8000-00043-064	1165	8051	OEM	8220	OEM

If replacement code is OEM, contact original manufacturer for replacement.

DEVICE TYPE	REPL CODE
8221	OEM
8222	OEM
8223	OEM
8225P1	0411
8230	OEM
8231	OEM
8232	OEM
8235	OEM
8235-041-00330	OEM
8235-041-00390	OEM
8235-041-01100	OEM
8235-041-04130	OEM
8235-041-04131	OEM
8235-041-04180	OEM
8237A	OEM
8237A-5	OEM
8237A5	OEM
8239	OEM
8242	2136
8245	OEM
8247	OEM
8249	OEM
8250	OEM
8251A	OEM
8252	OEM
8253	OEM
8253-5	OEM
8253C-5	OEM
8254-2	OEM
8255A	0051
8255A-5	0051
8255A5	OEM
8255AC-5	0051
8258	OEM
8259A	OEM
8266	OEM
8272/MLT41	OEM
8280	2159
8281-1	0079
8281H	OEM
8284A	OEM
8288	OEM
8290	OEM
8300-8	0015
8301	0037
8302	0079
8303	0126
8304	0086
8310	OEM
8313/MPT16	OEM
8318	OEM
8318A	OEM
8323	OEM
8326	OEM
8332	OEM
8332A	OEM
8333	OEM
8340X7	OEM
8341	OEM
8345	OEM
8346	OEM
8347	OEM
8348	OEM
8348WMA	OEM
8356	OEM
8360R1	OEM
8360R2	OEM
8362R8	OEM
8364R7	OEM
8366	OEM
8370	OEM
8394	0111
8400-1	0126
8400-1A	0126
8400-1B	0126
8405	0037
8406X	OEM
8409-07004	0148
8409-07004-1	0148
8409-07004-2	0148
8409-07004-3	0148
8409-07100	0527
8409-07100-1	1514
8409-07211	0076
8409-07211-1	0076
8409-07211-2	0151
8409-07211-3	0284
8409-07213	0728
8409-07219	0018
8409-07220	0723
8409-07221	3323
8409-07223	2880
8409-07318	3107
8409-07319	2822
8409-07320-1	1376
8409-07321	1055
8409-07321-1	1055
8409-07502	1158
8409-07503	4449
8409-08004	1585
8409-08006	OEM
8409-08007	OEM
8409-7320	5411
8409-10061	OEM
8409-10062	OEM
8409-10064	OEM
8409-10130	OEM
8409-10136	OEM
8409-10468	OEM

DEVICE TYPE	REPL CODE
8409-10710	OEM
8409-10718	OEM
8409-11102	0133
8409-11103	0124
8409-11138	0124
8409-11151	0023
8409-11152	0133
8409-11206	1864
8409-11303	1082
8409-11303-1	1082
8409-11308	OEM
8409-11309	1325
8409-11332	0541
8409-11346	0541
8409-11389	0541
8409-11403	0015
8409-12023	0274
8409-12023-1	0140
8409-12122	2876
8409-12317	0999
8409-12417	0721
8409-12480	0253
8409-12483	0052
8409-12493	0450
8410	0507
8411	0522
8412	2227
8413	1432
8414	2228
8415	OEM
8416	1339
8417	1342
8423	OEM
8440-121	1270
8440-122	0931
8440-123	0076
8440-124	0155
8440-126	0076
8467	OEM
8468	OEM
8471	0555
8474	1303
8475	1423
8475A	OEM
8476	1150
8477	OEM
8477A	OEM
8478	OEM
8481/BLT032	OEM
8482	0911
8493/F2913	OEM
8496PT	OEM
8500-201	0004
8500-202	0004
8500-203	0004
8500-204	0222
8500-206	0015
8500R3	OEM
8501R1	OEM
8502	OEM
8502H	OEM
8502R0	OEM
8502RO	OEM
8503	0127
8504	0016
8507H	OEM
8508H	OEM
8510	2272
8510H	OEM
8511	OEM
8511H	OEM
8512	OEM
8513A	0102
8513H	OEM
8514	OEM
8514A	OEM
8515H	OEM
8516	OEM
8516C	OEM
8516H	OEM
8517H	OEM
8517HA	OEM
8518H	OEM
8519H	OEM
8520	1042
8520A-1	OEM
8520A1	OEM
8520H	OEM
8520R4	OEM
8521	0079
8522H	OEM
8523H	0079
8524E	OEM
8530	1199
8540	0037
8550	0320
8550C	0006
8554-9	0086
8563-R7	OEM
8563R9	OEM
8563R9B	OEM
8564-1	2313
8564-2	1702
8564-3	2313
8564-4	1702
8564-R4	OEM
8564R4	OEM
8564R5C	OEM
8564R6V6	OEM

DEVICE TYPE	REPL CODE
8568	OEM
8574/MXT132	OEM
8578/MST60	OEM
8580R5	OEM
8582	OEM
8582A	OEM
8599/MKT39	OEM
8601	0037
8602	0155
8606	0144
8607	0144
8609	0144
8610	OEM
8611	0144
8612	OEM
8614-007-0	0079
8616MDJ	OEM
8618	OEM
8622/MST52	OEM
8622MBV	OEM
8644	OEM
8682	OEM
8691	OEM
8701	OEM
8701-4586-21	OEM
8701C	OEM
8710	OEM
8710-51	0030
8710-52	0133
8710-53	0143
8710-54	0012
8710-55	0015
8710-161	0321
8710-162	0931
8710-163	0016
8710-164	0076
8710-165	0076
8710-166	0076
8710-167	0016
8710-168	1409
8710-169	0037
8710-170	0555
8712	OEM
8713H	OEM
8715H	OEM
8721-R3	OEM
8721R3	OEM
8722-R1	OEM
8722H	OEM
8722R2	OEM
8730H	OEM
8736H	OEM
8740	OEM
8741H	OEM
8744A	OEM
8748	OEM
8753H	OEM
8754H	OEM
8757H	OEM
8763	OEM
8764	OEM
8770/BTR546	OEM
8798	OEM
8800-201	0015
8800-202	0016
8800-203	0016
8800-204	0016
8800-205	0042
8800-206	0015
8805	OEM
8806	OEM
8813	OEM
8813BA	OEM
8821	OEM
8824	OEM
8825	OEM
8826	OEM
8835	OEM
8836	OEM
8837	OEM
8840	OEM
8840-51	0015
8840-52	0030
8840-53	0133
8840-54	0019
8840-55	0057
8840-56	0139
8840-121	1270
8840-122	0931
8840-123	0076
8840-124	0155
8840-126	0076
8840-161	0321
8840-162	0127
8840-163	0076
8840-164	0076
8840-165	0076
8840-166	0076
8840-167	0079
8840-168	0079
8840-169	0555
8840-171	1469
8848	OEM
8849	OEM
8852	OEM
8855	OEM
8864-1	0015
8867	0037
8868-6	0086

DEVICE TYPE	REPL CODE
8868-7	0111
8868-8	0079
8880	OEM
8880-3	0086
8883-2	0160
8883-4	0086
8886-2	0079
8895	OEM
8896	OEM
8898	OEM
8899	OEM
8900	OEM
8902	OEM
8908	OEM
8910-51	0030
8910-52	0133
8910-53	0019
8910-54	0244
8910-55	0139
8910-141	0321
8910-142	0931
8910-143	0076
8910-144	0076
8910-145	1409
8910-146	0386
8910-147	0905
8910-148	1469
8934	OEM
8945	OEM
8947	OEM
8948	OEM
8949	OEM
8955	OEM
8956	OEM
8979	OEM
8999-115	0085
8999-201	0015
8999-202	0004
8999-203	0164
8999-205	0015
8999A-1333	OEM
9000-0061	OEM
9000-0080	OEM
9000-0150	OEM
9000-0151	OEM
9000-0152	OEM
9000-0153	OEM
9000-0870	OEM
9000-0871	OEM
9000-1151	OEM
9000-1152	OEM
9000-1153	OEM
9000-1154	OEM
9000-1155	OEM
9000-1156	OEM
9000-1157	OEM
9000-1158	OEM
9000DC	OEM
9000DM	OEM
9000FM	OEM
9001	OEM
9001-0601	OEM
9001DC	OEM
9001DM	OEM
9001FM	OEM
9002	2649
9002DC	OEM
9002DM	OEM
9002FM	OEM
9003	2651
9003-0631	OEM
9003-0636	OEM
9003DC	OEM
9003DM	OEM
9003FM	OEM
9004	2653
9004DC	OEM
9004DM	OEM
9004FM	OEM
9005	0627
9005-0	0160
9005-0151	OEM
9005-0162	OEM
9005DC	OEM
9005DM	OEM
9005FM	OEM
9006	0627
9006DC	OEM
9006DM	OEM
9006FM	OEM
9007	OEM
9007DC	OEM
9007DM	OEM
9007FM	OEM
9008	2656
9008DC	OEM
9008DM	OEM
9008FM	OEM
9009DC	OEM
9009DM	OEM
9009FM	OEM
9010	0780
9010-1101	OEM
9010-1111	OEM
9010-1140	OEM
9010-1200	OEM
9010-1210	OEM
9010-1230	OEM
9010-1324	OEM

DEVICE TYPE	REPL CODE
9010-1332	OEM
9010-1334	OEM
9010-2101	OEM
9010-2410	OEM
9010-2500	OEM
9010-2550	OEM
9010-3000	OEM
9010-3100	OEM
9010-5301	OEM
9010-5302	OEM
9010-6030	OEM
9010-6040	OEM
9010-6050	OEM
9010-6070	OEM
9010-6080	OEM
9010-6085	OEM
9010-6090	OEM
9010-6210	OEM
9010-6220	OEM
9010-6320	OEM
9010-7010	OEM
9011	0224
9011(G)	0079
9011E	0224
9011F	0079
9011G	0079
9011H	0224
9012	1359
9012-001	OEM
9012DC	OEM
9012DM	OEM
9012FM	OEM
9012G	0037
9012H	0037
9012HE	0004
9012HF	0004
9012HG	0150
9012O	OEM
9013	0079
9013G	0079
9013H	0079
9013HF	0079
9013HG	0079
9013HH	0079
9014	0079
9014(D)	0079
9014B	0079
9014C	0079
9014DC	OEM
9014DM	OEM
9014FM	OEM
9014N	OEM
9015	0037
9015C	0006
9015D	0006
9015DC	OEM
9015DM	OEM
9015FM	OEM
9016	0224
9016(F)	0079
9016(G)	0079
9016D	0224
9016DC	OEM
9016DM	OEM
9016E	0224
9016F	0224
9016FM	OEM
9017FM	OEM
9018	0224
9018D	0224
9018E	0224
9018F	0144
9018G	0144
9018H	0144
9019-6215	OEM
9019-6421	OEM
9019-6422	OEM
9019-7224	OEM
9019-7225	OEM
9020DC	OEM
9020DM	OEM
9020FM	OEM
9020H-04	OEM
9021	OEM
9022	OEM
9022DC	OEM
9022DM	OEM
9022FM	OEM
9024DC	OEM
9024DM	OEM
9024FM	OEM
9030DC	OEM
9033	0079
9033-1	0079
9033-2	0111
9033-3	0111
9033-4	0111
9033-5	0111
9033G	0086
9033G(SYLVANIA)	0079
9033GREEN	0111
9033ORANGE	0111
9033Q	0111
9033RED	0111
9033WHITE	0111
9040H-02	OEM
9040H-03	OEM
9042B	0710
9050	OEM

DEVICE TYPE	REPL CODE
9081	OEM
9093-1-6A	0354
9093-9-6A	0354
9093-9-7A	0354
9093BC	OEM
9093DC	0354
9093DM	OEM
9093FC	OEM
9093FM	OEM
9093PC	0354
9094-1-6A	1622
9094-9-6A	1622
9094-9-7A	1622
9094BC	OEM
9094DC	1622
9094DM	OEM
9094FC	OEM
9094FM	OEM
9094PC	1622
9097-1-6A	1472
9097-9-6A	1472
9097-9-7A	1472
9097BC	OEM
9097DC	1472
9097DM	OEM
9097FC	OEM
9097FM	OEM
9097PC	1472
9099-1-6A	0329
9099-9-6A	0329
9099-9-7A	0329
9099BC	OEM
9099DC	0329
9099DM	OEM
9099FC	OEM
9099FM	OEM
9099PC	0329
9100-1	0015
9109DC	1340
9109DM	OEM
9110	OEM
9110DC	2871
9111	OEM
9111DC	2931
9111DM	OEM
9111FM	OEM
9112	2022
9112DC	1918
9112DM	OEM
9123	OEM
9128DS-1411	OEM
9135PC	1609
9137-C-1004	0081
9137-C-1020	0557
9157PC	1424
9158PC	0461
9170	OEM
9200	OEM
9201	OEM
9202	OEM
9203-8	0071
9210H-02	OEM
9216	OEM
9225H-04	OEM
9240H02	OEM
9242G	OEM
9300	0144
9300-5	0015
9300-6	0015
9300-7	0015
9300A	0144
9300B	0144
9300DC	OEM
9300DM	OEM
9300FC	OEM
9300FM	OEM
9300PC	4203
9300Z	0144
9301-1	0015
9301DC	2182
9301DM	OEM
9301FM	OEM
9301PC	2182
9302-2	0229
9302-2A	0229
9302-3	0015
9302FM	OEM
9304DC	OEM
9304DM	OEM
9304FM	OEM
9304PC	OEM
9305FM	OEM
9305PC	OEM
9306DC	OEM
9306DM	OEM
9306FM	OEM
9306PC	OEM
9307DC	OEM
9307DM	OEM
9307FM	OEM
9307PC	1117
9308DC	1064
9308DM	OEM
9308FM	OEM
9308PC	1064
9309DC	5430
9309DM	OEM
9309FM	OEM
9309PC	5430

DEVICE TYPE	REPL CODE
9310DC	OEM
9310DM	OEM
9310FM	OEM
9310PC	1621
9311DC	OEM
9311DM	OEM
9311FM	OEM
9311PC	1546
9312DC	OEM
9312DM	OEM
9312FM	OEM
9312PC	OEM
9313DC	OEM
9313DM	OEM
9313FM	OEM
9313PC	OEM
9314	0144
9314DC	2468
9314DM	OEM
9314FM	OEM
9314PC	2468
9315DC	1032
9315DM	OEM
9315FM	OEM
9315PC	1032
9316/74161	1635
9316B	OEM
9316DC	5820
9316DM	6503
9316FM	OEM
9316PC	6514
9317BDC	1090
9317BDM	1090
9317BFM	OEM
9317BPC	1090
9317CDC	1090
9317CDM	1090
9317CFM	OEM
9318DC	4082
9318DM	OEM
9318FM	OEM
9318PC	4082
9319FM	OEM
9319PC	OEM
9320FM	OEM
9321DC	5821
9321DM	OEM
9321FM	OEM
9321PC	5821
9322DC	OEM
9322DM	1595
9322FM	OEM
9322PC	1595
9324DC	OEM
9324DM	OEM
9324PC	OEM
9328DC	5822
9328DM	OEM
9328FC	OEM
9328FM	OEM
9328PC	5822
9330-006-11112	0015
9330-011-70112	0004
9330-092-90112	0631
9330-228-60112	0133
9330-229-20112	0015
9330-229-60112	0127
9330-229-70112	0127
9330-688-30112	0111
9330-767-60112	0037
9330-908-10112	0037
9334DC	1733
9334DM	1733
9334FM	OEM
9334PC	3175
9338DC	OEM
9338DM	OEM
9338FC	OEM
9338FM	OEM
9338PC	OEM
9339-560-70112	OEM
9339-841-90112	OEM
9340DC	OEM
9340DM	OEM
9340FM	OEM
9340PC	OEM
9341DC	1831
9341DM	OEM
9341FM	OEM
9341PC	1831
9342DC	1845
9342DM	OEM
9342FM	OEM
9342PC	OEM
9344FM	OEM
9345DC	1074
9345PC	1074
9348-3	0015
9348DC	OEM
9348DM	OEM
9348FM	OEM
9348PC	OEM
9352DC	1046
9352FM	OEM
9352PC	1046
9353DC	1054
9353PC	1054
9354DC	1066
9354PC	1066

If replacement code is OEM, contact original manufacturer for replacement.

DEVICE TYPE	REPL CODE
9357A	1090
9357ADC	1090
9357APC	1090
9357B	1100
9357BDC	1100
9357BPC	1100
9358	1117
9358DC	1117
9358PC	1117
9360DC	1910
9360DM	OEM
9360FM	OEM
9360PC	1910
9366DC	1915
9366DM	OEM
9366FM	OEM
9366PC	1915
9367-1	0086
9368DC	5825
9368PC	5825
9370DC	5826
9370PC	5826
9374DC	5827
9374PC	5827
9375DC	1423
9375PC	1423
9377	2912
9380DC	1527
9380PC	1527
9382DC	1564
9382PC	1564
9383DC	0117
9383PC	0117
9385DC	0370
9385PC	0370
9386DC	0587
9386DM	0587
9386FM	OEM
9386PC	0587
9390	0211
9390DC	1199
9390PC	1199
9391	0211
9391DC	0974
9391PC	0974
9392DC	0828
9392PC	0828
9393	0564
9393DC	0564
9393PC	0564
9394DC	1692
9394PC	1692
9395DC	1477
9395PC	1477
9396DC	1705
9396PC	1705
9400-8	0004
9400-9	0004
9400CJ	OEM
9400CN	OEM
9401-7	0004
9401CJ	OEM
9401CN	OEM
9402CJ	OEM
9402CN	OEM
9403-2	0160
9403-3	0050
9403-6	0050
9403-7	0004
9403-8	0136
9403-9	0004
9403DC	OEM
9403DM	OEM
9404-0	0160
9404-2	0086
9404-3	0693
9404-9	0178
9405-0	0086
9405-1	0086
9405-2	0126
9406	0497
9409-4	0178
9409DC	OEM
9409DM	OEM
9409PC	OEM
9410A	0079
9412	OEM
9423DC	OEM
9423FC	OEM
9423PC	OEM
9426B	0144
9426B,C	0144
9426C	0144
9440	0133
9445	OEM
9464C-0839	OEM
9491A	OEM
9491AJ	OEM
9491AM	OEM
9491BJ	OEM
9491BM	OEM
9495AE	OEM
9495BE	OEM
9495CE	OEM
9495CJ	OEM
9495DE	OEM
9495DJ	OEM
9495EE	OEM
9495HE	OEM
9495HJ	OEM
9496AE	OEM
9496BE	OEM
9496CE	OEM
9496CJ	OEM
9496DE	OEM
9496DJ	OEM
9496EE	OEM
9496HE	OEM
9496HJ	OEM
9501	0111
9502	0111
9502DC	OEM
9503DC	OEM
9504DC	OEM
9510	OEM
9510-1	0050
9510-2	0050
9510-3	0136
9510-7	0050
9511	OEM
9513	0144
9517A-5PC	OEM
9520	OEM
9521	0696
9534DC	OEM
9550	OEM
9550-1	1888
9564	0004
9586-102/120	OEM
9586-121/124	OEM
9591-102/120	OEM
9591-121/124	OEM
9600	0079
9600-5	0079
9600A	OEM
9600C	0144
9600DC	6320
9600DM	6320
9600F	0144
9600FM	OEM
9600G	0144
9600H	0144
9600PC	6320
9601	0144
9601-12	0144
9601DC	2252
9601DM	OEM
9601FM	OEM
9601PC	2252
9602	2270
9602DC	2270
9602DM	6369
9602FM	OEM
9602PC	2270
9604E	6948
9604F	0144
9605	OEM
9606	0062
9607	0077
9609	OEM
9611	OEM
9614C	OEM
9614DC	OEM
9614DM	OEM
9614FM	OEM
9614PC	OEM
9615C	OEM
9615DC	5220
9615DM	5220
9615FM	OEM
9615PC	5220
9616	OEM
9616DC	OEM
9616DM	OEM
9616EDC	OEM
9616EPC	OEM
9616PC	OEM
9617K	0086
9618	0224
9619(A)	OEM
9620	OEM
9620-2	OEM
9620A	OEM
9622	OEM
9622-2	OEM
9623	0079
9623F	0144
9623G	0144
9623H	0144
9625F	0144
9625H	0144
9627DC	OEM
9627DM	OEM
9627PC	OEM
9629	OEM
9629-8	OEM
9629-16	OEM
9629-24	OEM
9629A	OEM
9629A-16	OEM
9629A-24	OEM
9630C	0144
9631U	1943
9632	0079
9636ARC	OEM
9636ARM	OEM
9636ATC	OEM
9637	OEM
9637-8	OEM
9637ARC	OEM
9637ARM	OEM
9637ATC	OEM
9638	OEM
9638-32	OEM
9638-48	OEM
9638-56	OEM
9638RC	OEM
9638RM	OEM
9638TC	OEM
9640-2	OEM
9640A	OEM
9640DC/26S10	OEM
9640DM/26S10	OEM
9640PC/26S10	OEM
9643TC	OEM
9645DC/3245	OEM
9645PC/3245	OEM
9650-001	0015
9650-1DC	OEM
9650-1DM	OEM
9650-2DC	OEM
9650-2DM	OEM
9650-3DC	OEM
9650-3DM	OEM
9650A	OEM
9650A-2	OEM
9654-0330.31	3687
9654-0331.31	3687
9664PC	6873
9665PC	0839
9666DC	1001
9666PC	1001
9667DC	1126
9667PC	1126
9668DC	1252
9668PC	1252
9682	0037
9690A	OEM
9696H	0086
9697	OEM
9699	OEM
9725	OEM
9740	OEM
9740H02	OEM
9803	0133
9804	OEM
9808	OEM
9817	OEM
9818	OEM
9826	OEM
9861B-43	0143
9864DS-1176	OEM
9903HC	OEM
9905HC	OEM
9906	OEM
9907HC	OEM
9908	OEM
9909	OEM
9910	OEM
9914HC	OEM
9915	OEM
9915HC	OEM
9916	OEM
9917	OEM
9920-3-6	0071
9920-4	0004
9920-5	0004
9920-6-1	0016
9920-6-2	0016
9920-7-2	0016
9921-7	0004
9921-8	0004
9923(REGENCY)	OEM
9923-U8A99238X	OEM
9923-U8A-992328X	OEM
9925-0	0160
9925-2	0142
9925-2-1	0142
9925-2-2	0142
9926HM	OEM
9930BC	OEM
9930DC	OEM
9930DM	OEM
9930FC	OEM
9930FM	OEM
9932BC	OEM
9932DC	OEM
9932DM	OEM
9932FC	OEM
9932FM	OEM
9933BC	OEM
9933DC	OEM
9933DM	OEM
9933FC	OEM
9933FM	OEM
9934BC	OEM
9934DC	OEM
9934FC	OEM
9942PC	1845
9944BC	OEM
9944DC	OEM
9944DM	OEM
9944FC	OEM
9944FM	OEM
9945BC	OEM
9945DC	OEM
9945DM	OEM
9945FC	OEM
9945FM	OEM
9946BC	OEM
9946DC	OEM
9946DM	OEM
9946FC	OEM
9948BC	OEM
9948DC	OEM
9948DM	OEM
9948FC	OEM
9948FM	OEM
9951BC	OEM
9951DC	OEM
9951DM	OEM
9951FC	OEM
9951FM	OEM
9962BC	OEM
9962DC	OEM
9962DM	OEM
9962FC	OEM
9962FM	OEM
9970	0118
9973	0041
9981	0791
9982	0815
9983	0437
9984	0185
9992	0821
9993	0862
9994	0908
10003	0130
10010	0084
10010IOF	OEM
10014DC	OEM
10031	0196
10032	0004
10032A	OEM
10036	0004
10036-001	0126
10037	0004
10038	0004
10039	0004
10060	OEM
10060-0	2245
10100	0071
10100B	OEM
10100BD	OEM
10100F	OEM
10101B	OEM
10101F	OEM
10101G0A	OEM
1010100A	OEM
10102B	OEM
10102F	OEM
10102G0A	OEM
1010200A	OEM
10103B	OEM
10103F	OEM
10103G0A	OEM
1010300A	OEM
10104B	OEM
10104F	OEM
10104G0A	OEM
1010400A	OEM
10105B	OEM
10105F	OEM
10105G0A	OEM
1010500A	OEM
10106B	OEM
10106F	OEM
10106G0A	OEM
1010600A	OEM
10107B	OEM
10107F	OEM
10108B	OEM
10108F	OEM
10109B	OEM
10109F	OEM
10110B	OEM
10110F	OEM
10111B	OEM
10111F	OEM
10112B	OEM
10112F	OEM
10113B	OEM
10113F	OEM
10114	OEM
10114DC	OEM
10115	OEM
10115DC	OEM
10116	OEM
10116DC	OEM
10117B	OEM
10117F	OEM
10118B	OEM
10118F	OEM
10119B	OEM
10119F	OEM
10121B	OEM
10121F	OEM
10123DC	OEM
10124B	OEM
10124DC	OEM
10124F	OEM
10124N	OEM
10125B	OEM
10125DC	OEM
10125F	OEM
10125N	OEM
10129F	OEM
10129N	OEM
10130F	OEM
10131F	OEM
10132F	OEM
10132N	OEM
10133F	OEM
10134DC	OEM
10134F	OEM
10134N	OEM
10135F	OEM
10136F	OEM
10137F	OEM
10139F	OEM
10139N	OEM
10140F	OEM
10142F	OEM
10142I	OEM
10145F	OEM
10145I	OEM
10148F	OEM
10149F	OEM
10150BD	OEM
10151F	OEM
10155F	OEM
10155N	OEM
10158F	OEM
10159F	OEM
10159N	OEM
10160F	OEM
10161DC	OEM
10161F	OEM
10162DC	OEM
10162F	OEM
10162N	OEM
10164DC	OEM
10164F	OEM
10164N	OEM
10165DC	OEM
10165F	OEM
10165N	OEM
10170F	OEM
10171DC	OEM
10171F	OEM
10171N	OEM
10172DC	OEM
10172F	OEM
10172N	OEM
10173DC	OEM
10173F	OEM
10173N	OEM
10174DC	OEM
10174F	OEM
10174N	OEM
10175F	OEM
10176F	OEM
10180	0015
10181	0143
10181F	OEM
10188F	OEM
10188N	OEM
10189F	OEM
10189N	OEM
10190F	OEM
10191F	OEM
10192DC	OEM
10200BD	OEM
10210B	OEM
10210F	OEM
10211B	OEM
10211F	OEM
10212B	OEM
10212F	OEM
10231B	OEM
10231F	OEM
10250BD	OEM
10300	0037
10300-12	0126
10300BD	OEM
10302-01	0867
10302-02	0692
10302-03	0507
10302-04	0232
10302-05	1160
10302-06	0381
10350	OEM
10350BD	OEM
10400BD	OEM
10410-N0B013	OEM
10410-N0B013-1	OEM
10410-N0B013-2	OEM
10410-N0B013-3	OEM
10410-N0B013-4	OEM
10410-N0B013-5	OEM
10410-N0B013-6	OEM
10410-V0B011	OEM
10410-V0B011-1	OEM
10410-V0B011-2	OEM
10410-V0B011-3	OEM
10410-V0B011-4	OEM
10410-V0B011-5	OEM
10410-V0B011-6	OEM
10410-V0B011-7	OEM
10410-V0B011-8	OEM
10415AF	OEM
10415BF	OEM
10415F	OEM
10422AF	OEM
10422BF	OEM
10422F	OEM
10450BD	OEM
10470AF	OEM
10470F	OEM
10474AF	OEM
10474F	OEM
10508	0150
10514DM	OEM
10514FM	OEM
10515DM	OEM
10515FM	OEM
10516DM	OEM
10516FM	OEM
10523DM	OEM
10523FM	OEM
10524DM	OEM
10524FM	OEM
10525DM	OEM
10525FM	OEM
10534DM	OEM
10534FM	OEM
10541DM	OEM
10561DM	OEM
10562DM	OEM
10562FM	OEM
10564DM	OEM
10564FM	OEM
10565DM	OEM
10565FM	OEM
10571DM	OEM
10571FM	OEM
10572DM	OEM
10572FM	OEM
10573DM	OEM
10573FM	OEM
10574DM	OEM
10574FM	OEM
10592DM	OEM
10592FM	OEM
10650A01	0356
10655A01	1742
10655A03	0850
10655A05	0391
10655A13	0784
10655A15	OEM
10655B01	1742
10655B02	0784
10655B03	0850
10655B13	0167
10655B14	3908
10655C05	0391
10795-5	0081
10795-6	0141
10795-8	0557
10795-9	0354
10795-10	0329
10900-7359	0106
10909	0015
10912A	OEM
10912AZ	OEM
10912B	OEM
10912C	OEM
10912D	OEM
10912E	OEM
10912F	OEM
10912Z	OEM
10938	OEM
11005	OEM
11112	0162
11200-1	0507
11202-1	0357
11203-1	0564
11204-1	1915
11205-1	0692
11206-1	1394
11207-1	0310
11208-1	0867
11209-1	0117
11211-1	0487
11213-1	1303
11214-1	1018
11216-1	0232
11229	0414
11233-2	1193
11236-1	0086
11236-3	0103
11252	0143
11252-0	0144
11252-1	0144
11252-2	0144
11252-3	0016
11252-4	0160
106951	0086
11252-5	0086
106952	0626
11252-6	0626
11273-1	0175
11274-1	0331
11276-1	1705
11303-9	0015
11332-1	0015
11339-2	0015
11339-8	0144
11393-8	0144
11399-8	0229
11401-3	0015
11426-7	0144
11457-4829	0527
11503-9	0015
11506-3	0160
11522-5	0016
11522-7	0050
11522-8	0050
11522-9	0050
11526-8	0160
11526-9	0160
11527-5	0136
11555-9	0015
11559-9	0015
11586-7	0229
11587-5	0016
11605-2	0015
11606-8	0969
11607-2	0136
11607-3	0144
11607-4	0016
11607-5	0142
11607-8	0016
11607-9	0144
11608-0	0144
11608-2	0144
11608-3	0144
11608-5	0016
11608-6	0969
11608-7	0969
11608-8	0969
11608-9	0969
11609-1	0004
11609-2	0016
11619-8	0144
11619-9	0144
11620-0	0144
11620-1	0144
11620-2	0050
11620-3	0004
11620-6	0004
11620-7	0050
11620-8	0050
11620-9	0050
11658-8	0016
11668-3	0050
11668-4	0050
11668-5	0004
11668-6	0004
11668-7	0208
11675-6	0136
11675-7	0004
11687-5	0016
11699-7	0004
11746	0015
12061-0013	1189
12110-0	0279
12110-3	0279
12110-4	0279
12110-5	0279
12110-6	0004
12110-7	0004
12112-0	0004
12112-8	0279
12112-C	0016
12112-D	0079
12112-E	0016
12112-F	0016
12112C	0079
12112D	0079
12112E	0079
12112F	0079
12113-5	0050
12113-7	0050
12113-8	0050
12113-9	0050
12114-8	0004
12115-0	0050
12115-7	0050
12116-1	0279
12116-2	0279
12116-4	0004
12117-9	0279
12118-0	0279
12118-4	0004
12118-6	0279
12118-9	0136
12119-0	0050
12119-1	0004
12119-2	0004
12122-5	0004
12122-6	0004
12122-7	0004
12122-8	0050
12122-9	0050
12123-0	0050
12123-1	0050
12123-2	0004
12123-3	0050
12123-4	0279
12123-5	0279
12123-6	0279
12124-0	0279
12124-1	0279
12124-2	0136
12124-3	0136
12124-4	0136
12124-6	0004
12125-4	0279
12125-6	0050
12125-7	0136
12125-8	0050
12125-9	0050

If replacement code is OEM, contact original manufacturer for replacement.

DEVICE TYPE	REPL CODE
12126-0	0050
12126-6	0004
12126-7	0004
12127-0	0160
12127-1	0160
12127-2	0004
12127-3	0279
12127-4	0004
12127-5	0279
12127-6	0016
12127-7	0016
12127-8	0016
12127-9	0016
12128-9	0279
12163	0085
12173	0279
12174	0279
12175	0279
12176	0279
12178	0085
12180	0136
12183	0279
12191	0279
12192	0279
12193	0279
12195	0004
12196	0004
12294B-11	OEM
12296B11	OEM
12429	0769
12536	0103
12536A	0103
12537	0486
12538	0178
12539	0161
12546	0233
12550	0087
12560	0790
12593	0016
12594	0037
12602	0015
12634	0015
12716	OEM
12720	0015
12732	OEM
12736	0015
12746	0015
12764	OEM
12768	0015
12786	0015
12788	0015
12803	0015
12808	0143
12837	0015
12844	0015
12850	0143
12871	0196
12888	0037
12901	0188
12951-1	1843
13100BD2	OEM
13100BD4	OEM
13100BD8	OEM
13100BD16	OEM
13150BD2	OEM
13150BD4	OEM
13150BD8	OEM
13150BD16	OEM
13150L	0133
13184	OEM
13200BD2	OEM
13200BD4	OEM
13200BD8	OEM
13200BD16	OEM
13298	0103
13300BD8	OEM
13300BD16	OEM
13400BD	OEM
13782	0015
14027	0015
14126-1	0015
14173I8	0855
14207	2352
14303	0016
14305	0619
14308	1187
14511	1535
14526	OEM
14529	4451
14568	OEM
14573	0435
14588-9	0015
14753A	OEM
14778-5	OEM
15009	0004
15021	OEM
15021Z	OEM
15024	0160
15027	0160
15101GOA	OEM
1510100A	OEM
15102GOA	OEM
1510200A	OEM
15103GOA	OEM
1510300A	OEM
15104GOA	OEM
1510400A	OEM
15105GOA	OEM
1510500A	OEM

DEVICE TYPE	REPL CODE
15106GOA	OEM
1510600A	OEM
15122	0133
15240	0037
15352R	0030
15354-3	0085
15405-1	0141
15405-2	1833
15405-4	1035
15486	0086
15607GWF	OEM
15607GXF	OEM
15607HWF	OEM
15607HXF	OEM
15608GWF	OEM
15608GXF	OEM
15608HWF	OEM
15608HXF	OEM
15609GWF	OEM
15609GXF	OEM
15609HWF	OEM
15609HXF	OEM
15610GWF	OEM
15610GXF	OEM
15610HWF	OEM
15610HXF	OEM
15611GWF	OEM
15611GXF	OEM
15611HWF	OEM
15611HXF	OEM
15612GWF	OEM
15612GXF	OEM
15612HWF	OEM
15612HXF	OEM
15808-1	OEM
15809-1	0198
15810-1	0079
15820-1	0198
15835-1	0198
15840-1	0016
15841-1	0016
15901GPF	OEM
15901GRF	OEM
15901GUF	OEM
15901HPF	OEM
15901HRF	OEM
15901HUF	OEM
15902GPF	OEM
15902GRF	OEM
15902GUF	OEM
15902HPF	OEM
15902HRF	OEM
15902HUF	OEM
15903GPF	OEM
15903GRF	OEM
15903GUF	OEM
15903HPF	OEM
15903HRF	OEM
15903HUF	OEM
15904GPF	OEM
15904GRF	OEM
15904GUF	OEM
15904HPF	OEM
15904HRF	OEM
15904HUF	OEM
15905GPF	OEM
15905GRF	OEM
15905GUF	OEM
15905HPF	OEM
15905HRF	OEM
15905HUF	OEM
15906GPF	OEM
15906GRF	OEM
15906GUF	OEM
15906HPF	OEM
15906HRF	OEM
15906HUF	OEM
15907GRF	OEM
15907GUF	OEM
15908GRF	OEM
15908GUE	OEM
15908GUF	OEM
15909GRF	OEM
15909GUF	OEM
15910GRF	OEM
15910GUF	OEM
15911GRF	OEM
15911GUF	OEM
15912GRF	OEM
15912GUF	OEM
15927	0085
15942	0718
15942-1	1865
16002-039	0143
16073	2371
16088	1199
16111	0571
16162	0411
16170	0571
16208	0571
16238	0147
16266	0103
16289	0571
16291	0571
16598	0164
16599	0160
16605	0748
16681	0015
16778	2438

DEVICE TYPE	REPL CODE
16958	0211
16959	0160
17002	0015
17011-1	0720
17042	0279
17043	0279
17047-1	0211
17142	0004
17143	0004
17144	0198
17246-33	1403
17401GOA	1076
17402GOA	1076
17403GOA	1078
17404GOA	1078
17405GOA	1078
17406GOA	1078
17407GOA	1094
17408GOA	1094
17409GOA	1094
17411GOA	1094
17412-5	0016
17412GOA	1094
17413GOA	OEM
17414GOA	OEM
17443	0015
17444	0076
17607IWA	OEM
17607IXA	OEM
17608IWA	OEM
17608IXA	OEM
17609IWA	OEM
17609IXA	OEM
17610IWA	OEM
17610IXA	OEM
17611IWA	OEM
17611IXA	OEM
17612IWA	OEM
17612IXA	OEM
17887	0160
17901HRA	OEM
17901HUA	OEM
17902HRA	OEM
17902HUA	OEM
17903HRA	OEM
17903HUA	OEM
17904HRA	OEM
17904HUA	OEM
17905HRA	OEM
17905HUA	OEM
17906HRA	OEM
17906HUA	OEM
17945	0085
18031	OEM
18109	0004
18112	0079
18310	0142
18410-41	0030
18410-42	0123
18410-43	0165
18410-141	1270
18410-142	0931
18410-143	0076
18410-144	0155
18410-145	0076
18410-146	1409
18410-147	0386
18410-148	2728
18493	0050
18509	0016
18529	0279
18530	0211
18540	0050
18541	0050
18555	0076
18600-51	0030
18600-52	0133
18600-53	0019
18600-54	0165
18600-151	0931
18600-152	0076
18600-153	0076
18600-155	1469
18600-156	2111
18600-I51	0127
18601	0211
18611	0164
18731	0211
18818R3383	OEM
18820S3367	OEM
19042	0015
19278	0142
19420	0144
19645	0079
19865	0015
20013	OEM
20013A	OEM
20014A	OEM
20061	OEM
20082	OEM
20082-0	OEM
20100	OEM
20106	OEM
20112	2843
20125	OEM
20129	OEM
20133	OEM
20139	OEM
20174	OEM

DEVICE TYPE	REPL CODE
20180	OEM
20187	OEM
20192	OEM
20294	2969
20295	2969
20333	OEM
20452	OEM
20453	OEM
20454	OEM
20505S	1099
20572-307	OEM
20637	OEM
20738	0198
20739	0126
20810-21	0015
20810-22	0015
20810-91	0111
20810-92	0111
20810-93	0086
20810-94	0555
20881	OEM
20957	OEM
20969	OEM
21035H-177	OEM
21123	OEM
21157	OEM
22008	0037
22009	0396
22158	0016
22881	1004
22939	0168
23100BD	OEM
23114-046	0016
23114-050	0126
23114-051	0126
23114-052	0233
23114-053	0016
23114-054	0016
23114-056	0144
23114-057	0144
23114-060	0144
23114-061	0004
23114-070	0103
23114-078	0144
23114-082	0016
23114-095	0016
23114-097	0969
23114-104	0144
23115-042	0071
23115-057	0016
23115-058	0016
23115-072	0071
23115-085	0087
23125-037	0144
23128	OEM
23128-25I	OEM
23128-25N	OEM
23128-30I	OEM
23128-30N	OEM
23128-45I	OEM
23128-45N	OEM
23128B	OEM
23128E25I	OEM
23128E25N	OEM
23128E30I	OEM
23128E30N	OEM
23128E45I	OEM
23128E45N	OEM
23128M30I	OEM
23128M45I	OEM
23150BD	OEM
23200BD	OEM
23209-110-760	OEM
23300BD	OEM
23311-006	0160
23350BD	OEM
23400BD	OEM
23402N	OEM
23450BD	OEM
23555	OEM
23606	0321
23754	0042
23762	0103
23785	0136
23785-1	0136
23826	0037
23826(SYLVANIA)	0037
23879	0759
24001GOF	0192
24001IOF	OEM
24002	0127
24002GOF	0096
24002IOF	OEM
24003GOF	0096
24003IOF	OEM
24004GOF	0096
24004IOF	OEM
24005GOF	0159
24005IOF	OEM
24006GOF	0159
24006IOF	OEM
24007GOF	0096
24007IOF	OEM
24008GOF	0096
24008IOF	OEM
24009GOF	0096
24009IOF	OEM
24010GOF	0096
24010IOF	OEM

DEVICE TYPE	REPL CODE
24011GOF	0096
24011IOF	OEM
24012GOF	0096
24012IOF	OEM
24013GOF	OEM
24013IOF	OEM
24014GOF	OEM
24014IOF	OEM
24198	0136
24198(RECT.)	0015
25114-101	0004
25114-102	0004
25114-103	0004
25114-104	0004
25114-116	0016
25114-121	0144
25114-130	0016
25114-143	0142
25114-161	0079
25115-115	0015
25201-001	0143
25202-002	0015
25211-200	0644
25260-61-067	0133
25642-020	0136
25642-030	0136
25642-031	0136
25642-040	0136
25642-041	0136
25642-110	0136
25642-115	0136
25642-120	0136
25651-020	0004
25651-021	0004
25651-033	0004
25655-055	0004
25655-056	0004
25657-050	0004
25658-120	0222
25658-121	0222
25661-020	0160
25661-022	0085
25671-020	0007
25671-021	0007
25671-023	0007
25672-016	0233
25810-51	0015
25810-52	0133
25810-53	0143
25810-54	0165
25810-55	0143
25810-107	1152
25810-161	0076
25810-162	0076
25810-163	0076
25810-164	0905
25810-165	1469
25810-167	1152
25840-51	0015
25840-52	0133
25840-53	0143
25840-54	0244
25840-55	0143
25840-161	0016
25840-162	0111
25840-163	0076
25840-165	1469
25840-167	1152
26011B-575	OEM
26011C-699	OEM
26011D-717	OEM
26011D-718	OEM
26012B-840	OEM
26128A-35F	OEM
26128A-35I	OEM
26128A-35N	OEM
26128A-45F	OEM
26128A-45I	OEM
26128A-45N	OEM
26810-51	0123
26810-52	0064
26810-151	0076
26810-151(1)	0007
26810-152	0006
26810-153	0155
26810-154	0076
26810-155	0018
26810-156	2008
26810-157	0514
26810-158	0428
26810-159	1044
27113-100	0015
27123-050	0015
27123-070	0015
27123-100	0015
27123-120	0015
27125-080	0016
27125-090	0016
27125-110	0086
27125-120	0004
27125-140	0016
27125-150	0004
27125-160	0016
27125-170	0004
27125-270	0016
27125-300	0016
27125-310	0208
27125-330	0004
27125-340	0004

DEVICE TYPE	REPL CODE
27125-350	0004
27125-360	0279
27125-370	0016
27125-380	0086
27125-460	0111
27125-470	0111
27125-480	0004
27125-490	0208
27125-500	0016
27125-530	0016
27125-540	0004
27125-550	0004
27126-060	0222
27126-090	0160
27126-100	0103
27127-550	0016
27128	1628
27128A	1628
27128G-250	1628
27256	OEM
27256/R09-32015	OEM
27256/R09-32017	OEM
27256-1	OEM
27256-2FXI-A5	OEM
27256-200	OEM
27256-200(JR15C1)	OEM
27256-200(JR15C2)	OEM
27256-200(JR15M)	OEM
27256-250	OEM
27256-XX	OEM
27256D	OEM
27512	OEM
27512-150NS	OEM
27840-41	0015
27840-42	0143
27840-43	0143
27840-161	0079
27840-162	0079
27840-164	1152
27901IXF	OEM
27902IXF	OEM
27903IXF	OEM
27904IXF	OEM
27905IXF	OEM
27906IXF	OEM
27907IWF	OEM
27908IWF	OEM
27909IWF	OEM
27910IWF	OEM
27911IWF	OEM
27912IWF	OEM
27913-14200	0411
28287	0143
28311	0233
28778	OEM
28810-61	0015
28810-62	0030
28810-63	0133
28810-64	0123
28810-65	0244
28810-171	0321
28810-172	0127
28810-173	0079
28810-174	0079
28810-175	2246
28810-176	1469
28810-177	0428
28810-178	1152
29611ADC	2373
29611ADM	OEM
29611AFM	OEM
29611DC	2373
29611DM	OEM
29611FM	OEM
29613ADC	OEM
29613ADM	OEM
29613AFM	OEM
29613DC	OEM
29613DM	OEM
29613FM	OEM
29621ADC	2304
29621ADM	OEM
29621AFM	OEM
29621DC	2304
29621DM	OEM
29621FM	OEM
29623ADC	OEM
29623ADM	OEM
29623AFM	OEM
29623DC	OEM
29623DM	OEM
29623FM	OEM
29631ADC	2881
29631ADM	OEM
29631AFM	OEM
29631DC	2881
29631DM	OEM
29631FM	OEM
29633ADC	OEM
29633ADM	OEM
29633AFM	OEM
29633DC	OEM
29633DM	OEM
29633FM	OEM
29641ADC	OEM
29641ADM	OEM
29641AFM	OEM
29641DC	OEM
29641DM	OEM

DEVICE TYPE	REPL CODE
29641FM	OEM
29643ADC	OEM
29643ADM	OEM
29643AFM	OEM
29643DC	OEM
29643DM	OEM
29643FM	OEM
29651ADC	3137
29651ADM	OEM
29651AFM	OEM
29651DC	3137
29651DM	OEM
29651FM	OEM
29653ADC	OEM
29653ADM	OEM
29653AFM	OEM
29653DC	OEM
29653DM	OEM
29653FM	OEM
29671ADC	OEM
29671ADM	OEM
29671AFM	OEM
29671DC	OEM
29671DM	OEM
29671FM	OEM
29673DC	OEM
29673DM	OEM
29673FM	OEM
29681ADC	OEM
29681ADM	OEM
29681AFM	OEM
29681ASC	OEM
29681ASM	OEM
29681DC	OEM
29681DM	OEM
29681FM	OEM
29681SC	OEM
29681SM	OEM
29683ADC	OEM
29683ADM	OEM
29683AFM	OEM
29683ASC	OEM
29683ASM	OEM
29683DC	OEM
29683DM	OEM
29683FM	OEM
29683SC	OEM
29683SM	OEM
29693DC	OEM
29693DM	OEM
29693FM	OEM
29810-63	0143
29810-173	0016
29810-178	0219
29810-179	2728
29810-180	0514
30001GOF	0192
30001IOF	OEM
30002GOF	0192
30002IOF	OEM
30003GOF	4164
30003IOF	OEM
30004GOF	4164
30004IOF	OEM
30005GOF	0159
30005IOF	OEM
30006GOF	0159
30006IOF	OEM
30007GOF	0096
30007IOF	OEM
30008GOF	0096
30008IOF	OEM
30009GOF	0096
30009IOF	OEM
30010GOF	0096
30011GOF	0096
30011IOF	OEM
30012GOF	0096
30012IOF	OEM
30013GOF	OEM
30013IOF	OEM
30014GOF	OEM
30014IOF	OEM
30201	0164
30202	0164
30203	0160
30204	0211
30206	0211
30207	0211
30208	0841
30208-1	0004
30208-2	0211
30210	0076
30211	0160
30213	0050
30214	0050
30215	0136
30215(RCA)	0160
30216	0211
30216(RCA)	0160
30217	0136
30218	0211
30218(RCA)	0050
30219	0198
30221	0136
30222	0136
30223	0136
30224	0198
30226	0198

If replacement code is OEM, contact original manufacturer for replacement.

215

DEVICE TYPE	REPL CODE
30227	0016
30228	0016
30229	0016
30230	0136
30231	0279
30234	0142
30235	0111
30236	0178
30238	0050
30239	0050
30240	0050
30241	0079
30242	0016
30243	0079
30244	0211
30245	0142
30246	0160
30246A	0160
30247	0136
30248	0198
30253	0016
30254	0178
30256	0178
30257	0142
30259	0198
30263	0004
30267	2839
30268	0016
30269	0016
30270	0037
30271	0455
30272	0161
30273	0050
30274	0136
30276	0103
30278	0126
30289	0079
30290	0037
30291	4100
30292	0144
30293	0004
30294	0042
30302	0085
30302(RCA)	0004
30498	OEM
30510	0071
30613	0079
30613(RCA)	0079
30710	0167
30901HRF	OEM
30901HUF	OEM
30902HRF	OEM
30902HUF	OEM
30903HRF	OEM
30903HUF	OEM
30904HRF	OEM
30904HUF	OEM
30905HRF	OEM
30905HUF	OEM
30906HRF	OEM
30906HUF	OEM
31001	0016
31003	0016
31004	OEM
31013-11	0710
31013E	OEM
31018-277-530	0037
31018-277-560	0466
31450	0242
32040	OEM
32109-101-005	OEM
32109-101-006	5936
32109-101-020	OEM
32109-101-070	OEM
32109-101-100	OEM
32109-101-140	OEM
32109-101-300	OEM
32109-101-310	OEM
32109-101-440	OEM
32109-101-490	OEM
32109-101-550	OEM
32109-110-007	OEM
32109-110-011	OEM
32109-110-084	OEM
32109-301-070	1519
32109-301-610	4246
32109-301-890	0034
32109-410-270	0101
32109-410-280	0101
32109-1001-100	OEM
32117-401-120	OEM
32117-901-110	0330
32119-101-080	3333
32119-101-640	4040
32119-101-870	OEM
32119-101-880	OEM
32119-101-940	0906
32119-102-010	0457
32119-102-020	0481
32119-102-040	0517
32119-102-050	0534
32119-102-060	0552
32119-102-090	0534
32119-102-100	0552
32119-102-120	OEM
32119-102-260	0906
32119-102-300	0970
32119-102-420	OEM
32119-102-570	0970
32119-102-730	1521
32119-102-760	0330
32119-103-100	OEM
32119-103-110	5179
32119-103-420	2164
32119-110-010	OEM
32119-110-016	2164
32119-110-018	OEM
32119-110-050	4291
32119-110-098	OEM
32119-201-180	OEM
32119-201-190	OEM
32119-201-310	0034
32119-201-360	0425
32119-401-010	4126
32119-401-120	OEM
32119-401-200	OEM
32119-401-210	OEM
32119-710-019	OEM
32119-801-130	2348
32119-901-020	3900
32119-901-110	0330
32119-901-130	2348
32119-901-220	OEM
32119-910-013	OEM
32137-103-280	0037
32137-103-430	0037
32137-301-010	0261
32137-301-050	0144
32137-301-080	1084
32137-301-090	6501
32137-301-110	3882
32137-301-180	0079
32137-301-530	0261
32137-301-540	0261
32137-301-550	1614
32137-301-560	1614
32137-301-720	0079
32137-401-530	0037
32139-101-420	0148
32139-101-530	0006
32139-301-090	0836
32139-301-140	0261
32139-301-230	0168
32139-301-240	0168
32139-301-350	0168
32139-301-510	0261
32139-302-350	0168
32139-302-810	1274
32139-304-560	0860
32139-304-570	0860
32139-401-100	1533
32139-401-110	1533
32139-401-130	1533
32139-410-006	0638
32147-301-020	1274
32149-101-850	1900
32149-101-860	1900
32149-201-450	1638
32149-301-010	3499
32149-301-020	1274
32149-301-040	1533
32149-301-050	0551
32149-301-090	1157
32149-301-140	2770
32149-301-190	0638
32149-401-040	1533
32149-401-050	0551
32149-401-150	OEM
32149-403-020	5437
32149-404-020	0055
32149-404-030	0055
32157-301-170	0079
32159-201-010	OEM
32159-210-002	1533
32159-210-003	0551
32159-210-005	0551
32159-210-006	1533
32159-301-020	0076
32159-301-030	0261
32159-301-170	0079
32159-301-180	0079
32159-301-230	3320
32159-301-290	0261
32159-701-020	0076
32167-101-130	2217
32167-103-080	0023
32167-110-002	0071
32167-201-070	0023
32167-201-110	OEM
32167-201-160	0015
32167-201-170	0023
32167-201-180	0015
32167-201-250	OEM
32167-206-110	0023
32167-206-670	0023
32167-207-120	3058
32167-208-510	0023
32167-208-520	1082
32167-208-550	0023
32167-208-570	0023
32167-208-580	0071
32167-218-130	0023
32167-301-630	0023
32167-301-670	OEM
32167-401-630	0053
32167-401-800	0253
32167-401-860	OEM
32167-401-870	0118
32167-401-880	OEM
32167-402-070	0023
32167-403-560	0466
32167-403-850	0039
32167-405-480	0124
32167-406-040	OEM
32167-406-080	0041
32167-406-110	0023
32167-406-130	0057
32167-406-190	OEM
32167-406-480	0124
32167-406-630	0053
32167-407-480	0124
32167-408-060	6210
32167-408-080	0466
32167-441-011	0062
32169-101-050	0102
32169-101-080	0123
32169-101-090	1119
32169-101-100	1039
32169-101-130	2217
32169-101-180	0023
32169-101-220	0959
32169-201-200	0017
32169-201-230	0031
32169-201-240	0102
32169-202-220	0023
32169-206-110	0023
32169-207-110	0071
32169-208-510	0023
32169-208-530	0071
32169-208-570	0023
32169-208-580	0071
32169-218-130	0023
32169-221-002	3833
32169-301-020	0076
32169-301-090	0102
32169-301-610	0031
32169-301-630	0023
32169-301-670	0017
32169-401-070	0023
32169-403-560	0466
32169-403-850	0039
32169-403-920	0094
32169-404-200	0041
32169-408-080	0466
32169-408-570	0023
32189-106-120	OEM
32199-101-020	OEM
32199-411-090	OEM
32199-500-000	OEM
32199-500-001	OEM
32199-901-200	2273
32309-024-010	1281
32309-024-020	OEM
32309-024-040	OEM
32309-101-090	OEM
32309-101-100	OEM
32309-110-001	0595
32309-110-230	OEM
32309-110-420	OEM
32309-110-430	OEM
32309-110-760	OEM
32309-201-003	OEM
32309-202-003	OEM
32310	OEM
32310ZD	OEM
32980	0673
33010	0037
33011	0037
33137-103-430	0037
33324	0030
33511DC	OEM
33512DC	OEM
33563	0016
33571	OEM
33572	OEM
33952	0030
34001PC	0473
34002PC	2044
34011PC	0215
34012PC	0493
34013PC	0409
34014DC	0854
34014FC	OEM
34014FM	OEM
34014PC	0854
34015DC	1008
34015DM	1008
34015FC	OEM
34015FM	OEM
34015PC	1008
34016PC	1135
34017PC	0508
34019PC	1517
34020PC	1651
34021DC	5831
34021DM	OEM
34021FC	OEM
34021FM	OEM
34021PC	1738
34022	0160
34023PC	0515
34025PC	2061
34027PC	1938
34028PC	2213
34029PC	2218
34030PC	0495
34035DC	OEM
34035DM	OEM
34035FC	OEM
34035FM	OEM
34035PC	OEM
34040PC	0056
34042PC	0121
34049PC	0001
34050PC	0394
34051PC	0362
34052PC	0024
34055PC	3272
34066PC	0101
34068PC	2482
34069PC	0119
34070PC	2494
34071PC	0129
34077PC	2536
34078PC	0915
34081PC	0621
34085PC	0300
34086PC	0530
34098	0136
34099	0136
34099PC	3297
34100	0136
34101	0735
34118	0050
34119	0279
34174	0015
34201	0087
34219	0279
34220	0279
34221	0279
34298	0160
34315	0160
34342	0050
34389	0050
34394	0015
34401-1	OEM
34405	0242
34423	0050
34425	0160
34512PC	2108
34518PC	1037
34519-992-010	OEM
34520PC	2650
34527PC	3116
34539PC	3611
34553	0050
34555PC	2910
34556PC	3397
34715	0085
34720DC	OEM
34720DM	OEM
34720FC	OEM
34720FM	OEM
34720PC	OEM
34725DC	OEM
34725DM	OEM
34725FC	OEM
34725FM	OEM
34725PC	OEM
34894	0015
34923	0164
34942	0050
35004	0144
35044	0160
35045	0211
35059-2	0167
35070	0050
35084	0085
35086	0211
35144	0160
35168	0136
35169	0050
35170	0050
35201	0085
35218	0841
35219	0137
35231	0160
35242	0079
35259	0127
35260	0085
35287	0015
35287A	0015
35289	0015
35306	0015
35333	0071
35349	0160
35391DC	OEM
35392DC	2618
35405	0178
35449	0144
35452-2	0164
35454	0211
35454-1	0164
35454-2	0164
35454-3	0164
35500	0015
35590	0004
35604	0535
35628	0004
35677	0004
35678	0004
35682-104-620	2273
35683-112-220	2164
35684-107-534	0330
35684-114-010	0638
35684-116-010	1157
35684-117-710	OEM
35684-119-710	0638
35728	0160
35792	0004
35815	0136
35816	0004
35817	0004
35818	0136
35819	0164
35820	0211
35820-1	0164
35820-2	0164
35820-3	0164
35824	0004
35824-	OEM
35860	0015
35885A	0160
35885B	0160
35950	0211
35951	0160
35952	0211
35953	0211
35954	0211
35955	0211
36091R	0810
36147	0242
36201	0015
36203	0160
36212	0144
36212V1	0144
36213	0546
36303	0160
36304	0160
36304-4	0160
36312	0160
36316	OEM
36344	0142
36387	0086
36395	0160
36446-2	1385
36477	0160
36503	0015
36503(AIRCASTLE)	0015
36508	0143
36534	0841
36535	0229
36537	0229
36539	0137
36549	0015
36554	0015
36555	0015
36557	0164
36558	0004
36559	0050
36560	0050
36563	0136
36564	0015
36577	0126
36578	0144
36579	0086
36580	0016
36581	0144
36582	0321
36591	0242
36634	0142
36810-151	OEM
36816	0279
36847	0144
36854A	OEM
36896	0085
36910	0160
36913	0169
36917	0016
36918	0144
36919	0144
36920	0016
36921	0016
37126-1	0015
37278	0050
37279	0208
37334	0007
37383	0144
37384	0144
37464	0086
37510-51	OEM
37510-52	0133
37510-53	0123
37510-54	0244
37510-161	0111
37510-162	0079
37510-163	0079
37510-164	0905
37510-165	3952
37510-166	0428
37510-167	1152
37549	0004
37550	0004
37551	0004
37552	0208
37584	0142
37585	0198
37649	0086
37680	0015
37682	0720
37694	0086
37730	0142
37800	0086
37847	0086
37884	0016
37987	0015
37992	0759
38052	0242
38074	0535
38091	0164
38095	0037
38120	0233
38121	0233
38122	0693
38175	0038
38176	0004
38177	0211
38178	0198
38207	0144
38208	0144
38209	0279
38246	0007
38270	0086
38271	0086
38272	0103
38332	0411
38378	0843
38385	0959
38448	0555
38510-51	0715
38510-52	0123
38510-53	0064
38510-54	0139
38510-161	1270
38510-162	0931
38510-163	0076
38510-164	0155
38510-165	0218
38510-166	0076
38510-167	1409
38510-168	0219
38510-169	2728
38510-170	0514
38510-171	1012
38510-330	0133
38510-331	0157
38510-350	0111
38511	0144
38563	0212
38608	0720
38609	0720
38716	0042
38731(KALOF)	0103
38785	0144
38786	0144
38787	0007
38788	0016
38789	0693
38840	0411
38881-D13	0062
38885	0735
38890	0411
38897	0103
38920	0144
38921	0144
38927	0411
38927-00000	2673
38970	0759
38976	0735
39005	0720
39039	0411
39096	0016
39119	0735
39209-1	1327
39264	2704
39299	0735
39458	0161
39510	0275
39542	1403
39558	2006
39669	0411
39750	0042
39763	2704
39767	0042
39804	0242
39805	0411
39811	1403
39830	0720
39840	0411
39901-0001	0435
39902	2255
39952	2006
40004	0050
40005	0050
40006	0050
40014BDC	OEM
40014BDM	OEM
40014BFC	OEM
40014BFM	OEM
40014BPC	OEM
40022	0160
40024	0015
40024VM	0015
40034	0004
40034-1	0004
40034-2	0004
40034-3	0004
40034VM	0004
40035	0004
40035-1	0004
40035-2	0004
40035-3	0004
40036	0004
40036-1	0004
40036-2	0004
40036-3	0004
40037	0208
40037-1	0208
40037-2	0208
40037-3	0208
40037VM	0208
40038	0004
40038-1	0004
40038-2	0004
40038-3	0004
40038VM	0004
40039T	OEM
40040T	OEM
40041T	OEM
40042	OEM
40043	OEM
40044	OEM
40049	OEM
40050	0160
40051	0160
40051-2	0160
40053	0086
40078	OEM
40080	0086
40081	1401
40082	2675
40082A	0693
40084	0016
40085BDC	3415
40085BDM	3415
40085BFC	3415
40085BFM	3415
40085BPC	3415
40097BDC	5871
40097BDM	OEM
40097BFC	OEM
40097BFM	OEM
40097BPC	5871
40098BDC	0427
40098BDM	OEM
40098BFC	OEM
40098BFM	OEM
40098BPC	0427
40108	0084
40108R	0529
40109	0090
40109R	0743
40110	0097
40110R	0533
40111	0105
40111R	0772
40112	0109
40112R	0533
40113	0116
40113R	0796
40114	1104
40114R	0810
40115	0131
40115R	0540
40143	0015
40160BDC	1349
40160BDM	1349
40160BFC	1349
40160BFM	1349
40160BPC	1349
40161BDC	1363
40161BDM	1363
40161BFC	1363
40161BFM	1363
40161BPC	1363
40162BDC	1378
40162BDM	1378
40162BFC	1378
40162BFM	1378
40162BPC	1378
40163BDC	1397
40163BDM	1397
40163BFC	1397
40163BFM	1397
40163BPC	1397
40192BDC	1753
40192BDM	1753
40192BFC	1753
40192BFM	1753
40192BPC	1753
40193BDC	1765
40193BDM	1765
40193BFC	1765
40193BFM	1765
40193BPC	1765
40194BDC	6453
40194BDM	OEM
40194BFC	OEM
40194BFM	OEM
40194BPC	1758
40195BDC	1773
40195BDM	OEM
40195BFC	OEM
40195BFM	OEM
40195BPC	1773
40208	3160
40208R	1620
40209	0800
40209R	0254
40210	1116
40210R	1099
40211	1118
40211R	1103

If replacement code is OEM, contact original manufacturer for replacement.

DEVICE TYPE	REPL CODE
40212	0800
40212R	0258
40213	1186
40213R	1634
40214	0315
40214R	0267
40216	0720
40217	0016
40218	0016
40219	0016
40220	0016
40221	0016
40222	0016
40231	0007
40232	0007
40233	0007
40234	0007
40235	0007
40236	0007
40237	0007
40238	0007
40238-3GT	0015
40239	0007
40240	0007
40242	0007
40243	0007
40244	0007
40245	0007
40246	0007
40250	0424
40250V1	0178
40251	0103
40253	0004
40254	0085
40255	3249
40256	0334
40259	0007
40259(RECT)	0122
40260	0007
40261	0050
40262	0050
40263	0004
40263(RCA)	0050
40264	0142
40264V1	0142
40265	0015
40266	0947
40267	0242
40268	0136
40269	0279
40279	0555
40280	2030
40280R	0267
40281	3289
40282	3290
40283	0016
40290	3293
40291	0419
40292	0042
40294	0007
40295	0259
40296	0259
40305	0555
40306	0555
40307	0042
40309	0086
40309L	0626
40309S	0626
40309V1	0086
40309V2	0086
40310	0178
40310V1	0178
40311	0086
40311A	0546
40311B	0546
40311L	0626
40311S	0626
40312	0178
40312V1	0178
40313	0142
40314	0086
40314L	0626
40314S	0626
40314V1	0546
40314V2	0546
40315	0086
40315L	0626
40315S	0626
40315V1	0546
40315V2	0546
40316	0178
40317	0086
40317L	0590
40317S	0590
40317V1	0546
40317V2	0546
40318	0142
40319	0126
40319L	0786
40319S	0126
40319V1	0546
40319V2	0546
40320	0086
40320L	0590
40320S	0590
40320V1	0546
40320V2	0546
40321	0187
40321L	0168

DEVICE TYPE	REPL CODE
40321V1	0187
40321V2	0187
40322	1021
40323	0086
40323L	0626
40323S	0626
40323V1	0546
40323V2	0546
40324	0178
40325	0103
40326	0086
40326L	0590
40326S	0590
40326V2	0546
40327	0434
40327L	0168
40327V2	0546
40328	0142
40329	0004
40346	0187
40346L	0168
40346S	1967
40346V1	0334
40346V2	3249
40347	1471
40347L	0626
40347S	0018
40347V1	0555
40347V2	3249
40348	0168
40348V1	0419
40348V2	3249
40349	0168
40349V2	3249
40350	0007
40351	0007
40352	0007
40354	0233
40355	0233
40359	0004
40360	0086
40360L	0626
40360S	0626
40360V1	0546
40360V2	0546
40361	0086
40361L	0626
40361V1	3392
40361V2	0546
40361V3	0546
40362	0126
40362S	0126
40362V1	0378
40362V2	0378
40363	0103
40364	0178
40366	0086
40366L	0168
40366S	0626
40367	1471
40368	0042
40369	0103
40372	0178
40373	0178
40374	0142
40375	3328
40378	1478
40379	0735
40383	0015
40385	0187
40385L	0168
40385V1	0546
40385V2	0546
40389	0555
40390	0334
40391	0126
40392	0086
40394	0527
40395	0004
40396	0038
40396/N	0208
40396/P	0164
40396N	0208
40396P	0004
40397	0016
40398	0016
40399	0016
40400	0016
40403	0211
40404	0414
40405	0016
40406	0126
40406L	0786
40406S	0126
40407	0086
40407L	0590
40407S	0590
40408	0126
40408L	0626
40408S	0626
40409	0086
40410	0126
40411	0130
40412	0187
40412L	0168
40412S	OEM
40412V1	0168
40412V2	0187
40413	0144

DEVICE TYPE	REPL CODE
40414	0144
40414V2	OEM
40421	0160
40422	0142
40423	0142
40424	0178
40425	0142
40426	0142
40427	0142
40428	OEM
40429	0739
40430	3349
40437V1	0546
40437V2	0546
40438V1	0264
40438V2	0264
40439	0334
40439V1	0334
40439V2	0334
40440	0969
40442	0969
40444	2465
40446	0626
40450	0590
40451	0590
40452	0590
40453	0590
40454	0590
40455	0590
40456	0590
40457	0086
40458	0086
40459	0233
40460	OEM
40461	0321
40461-2	0086
40462	0085
40464	0103
40465	0103
40466	0103
40467A	0843
40468	0321
40468A	0843
40469	0488
40470	0144
40471	0488
40472	0007
40473	0016
40474	0016
40475	0007
40476	0007
40477	0016
40478	0007
40479	0007
40480	0144
40481	0007
40482	0144
40485	2378
40487	0050
40488	0136
40489	0050
40490	0004
40491	0142
40500	0016
40501	0086
40502	0407
40503	0411
40504	2255
40505	3368
40506	3370
40507	2255
40508	3368
40509	0407
40510	0411
40511	0407
40512	0411
40513	0103
40514	0103
40517	0198
40518	0198
40519	0016
40525	2336
40526	2337
40527	2340
40528	2336
40529	2337
40530	2340
40531	2367
40532	2337
40533	1403
40534	2336
40535	2378
40536	1403
40537	0126
40537L	0126
40537S	0126
40538	0126
40538L	0126
40538S	0126
40539	0086
40539A	OEM
40539L	0086
40539S	0086
40542	0103
40543	0103
40544	3249
40546	0142
40547	0142
40553	0239

DEVICE TYPE	REPL CODE
40554	0239
40555	0239
40559	0843
40559A	0843
40561	OEM
40562	OEM
40563	OEM
40564	OEM
40565	OEM
40566	OEM
40567	OEM
40568	OEM
40569	OEM
40570	OEM
40571	OEM
40572	OEM
40573	OEM
40574	OEM
40577	0016
40578	0086
40581	2675
40582	0626
40583	2137
40594	0546
40595	0886
40598	OEM
40598A	OEM
40600	0349
40601	0349
40602	0349
40603	0349
40604	0349
40605	0555
40608	0414
40611	0086
40611S	0626
40612	0160
40613	0042
40616	0086
40616L	0626
40616S	0626
40618	0042
40621	0042
40622	0042
40623	0265
40624	0419
40625	0086
40626	0160
40627	0419
40628	0086
40629	0042
40630	0042
40631	0042
40632	0419
40633	0103
40634	0126
40634L	0378
40634S	0378
40635	0086
40635L	0626
40635S	0626
40636	0538
40637	0016
40637A	0018
40638	0407
40639	0411
40640	0239
40641	0061
40642	1208
40643	1208
40644	1208
40650	0283
40654	2084
40655	0705
40662	2004
40663	2006
40664	0178
40665	0042
40666	0555
40667	3434
40668	3435
40669	0571
40672	2007
40673	0212
40675	OEM
40680	1837
40681	1837
40682	1844
40683	3185
40684	2367
40685	2378
40686	1403
40687	2371
40689	2007
40690	2007
40691	2337
40692	2340
40696	2367
40697	2378
40698	1403
40702	2004
40703	2006
40704	2007
40707	2004
40708	2006
40710	2007
40713	0154
40714	0147
40716	0147

DEVICE TYPE	REPL CODE
40719	0154
40720	0147
40721	0588
40722	0571
40724	OEM
40731	3451
40732	0411
40733	0016
40734	0411
40735	0799
40736R	OEM
40737	1641
40738	1641
40739	1574
40740	1655
40741	2430
40742	0430
40743	1478
40744	0682
40745	3458
40746	1837
40747	1844
40748	3185
40749	1640
40750	1641
40751	1574
40752	1655
40753	0736
40754	0740
40755	0154
40756	0759
40757	1837
40758	1640
40759	2623
40760	0759
40763	0004
40766	2336
40769	2337
40770	2371
40771	2378
40777	0154
40778	0147
40781	0154
40782	0147
40785	0154
40786	0147
40789	3121
40790	2007
40793	2004
40794	2006
40796	0278
40798	0278
40801	0278
40808	0071
40809	0071
40814	0086
40815	0126
40816	0556
40819	2439
40820	2439
40821	2439
40822	2439
40823	0212
40828	0004
40829	0899
40833	0857
40836	0264
40837	0264
40841	0349
40842	0572
40843R	OEM
40844R	OEM
40850	0142
40852	0359
40852(VM)	0004
40853	0359
40853(VM)	0164
40854	0637
40867	2078
40868	0500
40869	0705
40871	0236
40872	0676
40874	0320
40875	0556
40877	0556
40878	1190
40880	0239
40881	0060
40882	1298
40884	3516
40885	1698
40886	1698
40887	1698
40888	0239
40889	0061
40890	1208
40891	1208
40892	1208
40894	0259
40895	0259
40896	0259
40897	0259
40899	0061
40900	0566
40901	0588
40902	0571
40910	0178
40911	0178

DEVICE TYPE	REPL CODE
40912	0142
40913	3509
40915	0855
40934-1	0103
40938	0745
40953	0693
40954	0886
40955	3012
40964	0414
40965	0684
40967	3516
40968	1410
40970	3545
40971	2841
40972	3387
40973	1224
40974	1966
40975	0693
40976	0693
40977	3543
40979	OEM
40980	OEM
41001-4	0015
41004	OEM
41008	0414
41008A	3516
41009	0414
41009A	3516
41010	1410
41012	3510
41013	3510
41014	0588
41015	0571
41020(RCA)	1702
41020-618	0071
41021(RCA)	1702
41023(RCA)	1702
41023-224	0071
41023-225	0071
41051	0016
41052	0126
41053	0086
41178	0161
41179	0455
41201	OEM
41257-P-15	OEM
41342	0455
41344	0161
41464-15	OEM
41500	0042
41501	0848
41502	0086
41503	0126
41504	0042
41505	1698
41506	0074
41508	3770
41616	0015
41689	0144
41694	0144
42020	0143
42020-737	0170
42021	0071
42025-850	0137
42065	0178
42221	0015
42302	0136
42304	0164
42305	0004
42311	0136
42321	0841
42322	0004
42323	0142
42324	0211
42342	0178
42396	0321
42464	0079
42942	0042
43021-017	0016
43021-198	0086
43022-860	0144
43044	0016
43046	0160
43054	0111
43055	0111
43060	0103
43062	0133
43074	0599
43095	0103
43104	0538
43200	0232
43200-8	OEM
43201	0357
43202	0462
43205	1164
43256	OEM
43296	0321
43959	0143
43992-2	0595
44001	0071
44002	0124
44003	0071
44004	0071
44005	0071
44006	0071
44007	0071
44011-PC	OEM
44221	OEM
44465-3	0015

DEVICE TYPE	REPL CODE
44465-4	0015
44465-5	0015
44465-6	0015
44616-1	0211
44763	0546
44764	0378
44765	4499
44766	0321
44933	1208
44934	1208
44935	1208
44936	1208
44936(RCA)	1208
44937	0015
44937(RCA)	1208
44938	0015
44938(RCA)	1208
44967-2	0211
45190	0060
45191	0556
45192	0556
45193	1298
45194	1298
45195	1190
45299	2673
45380	0649
45381	0696
45390	1385
45393	2535
45394	0375
45395	2535
45411	2137
45495-2	0595
45810-51	0015
45810-52	0715
45810-53	0019
45810-54	0064
45810-161	1270
45810-162	0931
45810-163	0076
45810-164	0155
45810-165	0218
45810-166	0076
45810-167	2728
45810-168	0514
45810-169	1012
45810-170	1044
46140-2	0015
46287-4	0123
46490-2	0595
46590-2	0038
46591-2	0038
46592-2	0038
46593-2	0038
46631-2	0595
46774-1	0595
46775-2	0595
46914	0242
47126	0015
47126-003	0015
47126-1	0015
47126-1A	0015
47126-2	0015
47126-3	0015
47126-3A	0015
47126-4	0015
47126-4A	0015
47126-6	0015
47126-7	0015
47126-8	0087
47126-9	0015
47126-10	0087
47126-12	0015
47127-3	0015
47394-2	0211
47645-2	0038
47737-2	0211
48106	0299
48159	OEM
48287	0143
48287-4	0123
48385-2	0038
48751-028	0150
48902A0A10	OEM
48937-2	0136
48939-2	0136
49058-2	0038
49138-2	0595
49139-2	0211
49751-163	0222
49939-2	0050
50006G0F	OEM
5000600F	OEM
50011G0F	OEM
50027	0710
50028	0338
50029	0037
50137-2	0086
50210-2	1035
50210-7	1622
50210-8	0557
50447-4	0160
50464	OEM
50464CP-12	OEM
50477-4	0160
50505-01	0143
50745-01	0015
50745-02	0015
50745-03	0087

If replacement code is OEM, contact original manufacturer for replacement.

217

DEVICE TYPE	REPL CODE
50745-04	0087
50745-05	0087
50745-06	0015
50745-07	0015
50745-08	0015
50957-03	0144
51009	OEM
51102-01A	OEM
51194	0086
51194-01	0086
51194-02	0086
51194-03	0086
51202L	OEM
51213	0016
51213-01	0016
51213-02	0016
51213-03	0016
51213-2	0016
51428-01	0016
51429-02	0016
51429-03	0016
51429-3	0016
51441	0016
51441-01	0016
51441-02	0016
51441-03	0016
51442	0016
51442-01	0016
51442-02	0016
51442-03	0016
51545	0016
51547	0016
51650	0160
51750	0406
52000-030	1812
52000-032	1035
52000-033	2086
52000-036	1820
52000-037	1824
52000-044	0033
52000-046	0141
52000-048	3365
52000-049	1833
52000-052	0329
52000-055	1472
52000-057	1424
52000-058	0461
52000-061	1848
52000-062	0557
52000-063	0337
53004-1716	0133
53007-2	0071
53009-1	0030
53016	0133
53016R	0133
53088-4	0071
53092-1	0143
53093-1	0196
53099-1	0015
53099-3	0015
53110P-15	OEM
53200-22	0016
53200-23	0016
53200-51	0016
53200-74	0111
53201-01	0004
53201-11	0004
53203-72	0086
53300-31	0071
53300-41	0015
53301-01	0071
53400-01	0016
53704D	0239
54107DM	OEM
54107FM	OEM
54121DM	OEM
54121FM	OEM
54122DM	OEM
54122FM	OEM
54123DM	OEM
54123FM	OEM
54125DM	OEM
54125FM	OEM
54126DM	OEM
54126FM	OEM
54132DM	OEM
54132FM	OEM
54136	OEM
54145DM	OEM
54145FM	OEM
54150DM	OEM
54150FM	OEM
54151ADM	OEM
54151AFM	OEM
54152AFM	OEM
54153DM	OEM
54153FM	OEM
54154DM	OEM
54154FM	OEM
54155DM	OEM
54155FM	OEM
54156DM	OEM
54156FM	OEM
54157DM	OEM
54157FM	OEM
54160DM	OEM
54160FM	OEM
54161DM	OEM
54161FM	OEM

DEVICE TYPE	REPL CODE
54162FM	OEM
54163DM	OEM
54163FM	OEM
54164DM	OEM
54164FM	OEM
54165DM	OEM
54165FM	OEM
54166DM	OEM
54166FM	OEM
54167FM	OEM
54170DM	OEM
54170FM	OEM
54175DM	OEM
54175FM	OEM
54176DM	OEM
54176FM	OEM
54177DM	OEM
54177FM	OEM
54178DM	OEM
54178FM	OEM
54179DM	OEM
54179FM	OEM
54180DM	OEM
54180FM	OEM
54190FM	OEM
54191DM	OEM
54191FM	OEM
54192DM	OEM
54192FM	OEM
54193DM	OEM
54193FM	OEM
54194DM	OEM
54194FM	OEM
54195DM	OEM
54195FM	OEM
54196DM	OEM
54196FM	OEM
54197DM	OEM
54197FM	OEM
54198DM	OEM
54198FM	OEM
54199DM	OEM
54199FM	OEM
54298DM	OEM
54298FM	OEM
54806P1	0720
55001	0232
55002	0310
55002GOF	OEM
55003	0357
55003GOF	OEM
55004	0381
55005	0507
55006	0692
55007	0867
55008	1046
55009	1100
55010	0738
55011	1303
55012	1150
55017	4329
55017HOF	OEM
55021	0487
55022	2227
55023	4523
55024	1339
55027	1432
55029	1193
55032	0268
55034	1018
55035	1329
55036	1197
55107ADM	OEM
55107AFM	OEM
55107BDM	OEM
55107BFM	OEM
55108BDM	OEM
55108BFM	OEM
55110ADM	OEM
55166	0143
55170	OEM
55170-1	0224
55200-500	0015
55325F	OEM
55450ADM	OEM
55450BDM	OEM
55451ARM	OEM
55451BRM	OEM
55452ARM	OEM
55452BRM	OEM
55453ARM	OEM
55453BRM	OEM
55491DM	OEM
55492ADM	OEM
55606	0016
55810-51	0143
55810-52	0143
55810-53	0139
55810-161	0007
55810-162	0079
55810-163	0007
55810-164	0007
55810-165	0079
55810-166	0178
55810-167	0627
55810-168	2377
55810-169	1226
55810-170	2020
55975-1	0081

DEVICE TYPE	REPL CODE
55976-1	0141
55977	1812
55978-1	0033
55979-1	2067
55980	2086
55982-1	1035
55987-1	0557
56016	OEM
56519	0141
56552	0354
56553	1812
56557	1820
56558	0081
56571	0557
57000-5452	0144
57000-5503	0198
57174	1403
57202	0411
57401AJ	OEM
57401F	OEM
57401J	OEM
57401J16	OEM
57402AF	OEM
57402F	OEM
57402J	OEM
57508	OEM
57516	OEM
57518	OEM
57558	OEM
57558-1	OEM
57558-1F42	OEM
57558-1J40	OEM
57558F42	OEM
57558J40	OEM
58321S	OEM
58810-80	0015
58810-81	0030
58810-82	0133
58810-83	0143
58810-85	0015
58810-86	0170
58810-160	0321
58810-161	0127
58810-162	0079
58810-163	0079
58810-164	0111
58810-165	0079
58810-166	0079
58810-167	0111
58810-168	0079
58810-169	0555
58810-170	0905
58810-171	1469
58819	OEM
58840-111	0015
58840-112	0030
58840-113	0133
58840-114	0019
58840-116	0139
58840-117	0170
58840-191	0321
58840-192	0931
58840-193	0079
58840-194	0079
58840-195	0079
58840-196	0079
58840-197	0079
58840-198	0079
58840-199	0079
58840-200	0386
58840-201	0905
58840-203	1012
59395	0143
59395(RCA)	0143
59557-48	0004
59557-49	0015
59625-1	0037
59625-2	0037
59625-3	0037
59625-4	0037
59625-5	0037
59625-6	0037
59625-7	0037
59625-8	0037
59625-9	0037
59625-10	0037
59625-11	0037
59625-12	0037
59840	0133
59840-1	0124
59844-1	0015
59844-2	0015
59844-3	0015
59987-1	0004
59988-1	0086
59989-1	0126
59990-1	0160
59991-1	0137
60034	2006
60045	1403
60059	1403
60108	0720
60132	0555
60133	0042
60136	0411
60182	1403
60202	0411
60213(1C)	2593
60215-1	0143

DEVICE TYPE	REPL CODE
60245	0411
60246	0411
60256	0240
60259	1403
60270	2337
60304	3260
60306	0407
60317	1403
60319	1403
60322	2004
60323	1403
60327	0155
60337	0349
60341	2340
60360	0571
60373	1208
60401	OEM
60402	OEM
60406	OEM
60407	0555
60408	0042
60409	5525
60410	0588
60413	0555
60415	0571
60416	0419
60424	0147
60451	0411
60466	0588
60478	2371
60496	0147
60510	0344
60533	0147
60550	2371
60572	0588
60579	0411
60582	1403
60594	2004
60613	0411
60615	2371
60650	0411
60663	0411
60667	0147
60673	1403
60694	0411
60732	0411
60733	0411
60741	1403
60793	0843
60806	1403
60816	0571
60817	0571
60833	0571
60879	2371
60908	2704
60916	0571
60968	0147
60987	0042
60998	2371
61003-4	0164
61008-8	0004
61008-8-1	0004
61008-8-2	0004
61009-1	0144
61009-1-1	0144
61009-1-2	0144
61009-2	0144
61009-2-1	0144
61009-4	0016
61009-4-1	0016
61009-6	0144
61009-6-1	0144
61009-9	0126
61009-9-1	0126
61009-9-2	0126
61009-9-3	0004
61010-0	0144
61010-0-1	0144
61010-2-1	0136
61010-6	0160
61010-6-1	0144
61010-7-1	0144
61010-7-2	0016
61011-0	0126
61011-0-1	0126
61011-2	0015
61011-3-2	0016
61012-4-1	0595
61012-5-1	0050
61013-2-1	0016
61013-4-1	0126
61013-9-1	0144
61015-0-1	0144
61025	OEM
61050	OEM
61075	OEM
61088	0947
61093	1403
61096	1403
61100	0571
61102-0	0136
61104	2371
61122	0759
61134	2371
61157	1403
61158	1403
61189	0147
61190	1403
61224	1403

DEVICE TYPE	REPL CODE
61229-1	OEM
61239	1257
61242	0042
61244	0126
61249-1	0356
61260	0682
61291	1403
61292-1	OEM
61294-1	OEM
61295	0147
61364PD06	OEM
61366	0079
61376	0571
61384	2006
61399	0411
61408	0759
61436	0087
61452	0571
61532	0147
61566	0696
61596	0147
61612	2007
61613	2007
61652	2007
61664	1403
61762	0588
61770	1403
61807	0242
61819	0720
61831	0571
61832	2007
61865	0919
61866	0042
61872	0571
61926	0419
61932	0147
61957	0759
62025	OEM
62075	0759
62102	3770
62104	6656
62169-403-832	0144
62191	0571
62193	2007
62207	1403
62211	0571
62212	0147
62221	0161
62222	0264
62232	1403
62238	0571
62274	1403
62282	0759
62334	0147
62342	0571
62410G	OEM
62457	1403
62676	0042
62680	2371
62746	2371
62950	0555
63282	0037
63722(BOSTON-GEAR)	0109
63723(BOSTON-GEAR)	0122
63728(BOSTON-GEAR)	3815
63729(BOSTON-GEAR)	0735
63730(BOSTON-GEAR)	0759
64071-1	0211
64074	0378
64075	0919
64076	0042
64090	0239
64197	0919
65050	OEM
65075	OEM
65100	OEM
65256BLFP-15T	OEM
65804-62	0050
65804-63	0004
66007-4	0086
66008-2	0004
66009-5	0160
66010-3	0160
66405B	0284
66526	4526
66527	4534
66600	0030
66682-42	0015
67055	0133
67193-82	0279
67193-85	0211
67401	1079
67401AJ	OEM
67401J	OEM
67401J16	OEM
67402AJ	OEM
67402J	OEM
67402J18	OEM
67508	OEM
67516	OEM
67518	OEM
67544	0157
67558	OEM
67558-1	OEM
67558-1J40	OEM
67558-F42	OEM
67558F42	OEM
67558J40	OEM
67586	0079

DEVICE TYPE	REPL CODE
67590	0143
67599	0164
67802	0144
68001	OEM
68006	OEM
68007	OEM
68177	0015
68177A	0015
68504-62	0136
68504-63	0004
68504-77	0143
68504-78	0015
68595-13	0279
68617	0016
68645-03	0015
68895-13	0004
68995-1	1340
69011	OEM
69107-42	0136
69107-43	0050
69107-44	0136
69107-45	0211
69111	0015
69213-78	0023
70008-0	0103
70008-3	0103
70019-1	0178
70019-5	0178
70023-0-00	0016
70023-1-00	0016
70064-7	0015
70066-3	0015
70066-4	0015
70158-9-00	0126
70167-8-00	0144
70177A01	1742
70177A02	0784
70177A07	0618
70177B02	0784
70205-8A	0071
70231	0144
70260-11	0144
70260-12	0144
70260-13	0144
70260-14	0016
70260-15	0016
70260-16	0016
70260-18	0103
70260-19	0126
70260-20	0016
70260-29	0126
70270-05	0071
70270-23	0015
70270-38	0071
70372-2	0015
70398-1	0079
70399-1	1659
70399-2	2123
70432-16	0015
70434	0160
70511	0016
70581-1	1293
70622(RCA)	0438
71006-30	0015
71037-2	OEM
71037-4	OEM
71060-4	OEM
71060-6	OEM
71100-4	OEM
71119-1	0133
71119-2	0124
71193-2	0004
71226-1	0155
71226-2	0155
71226-3	0155
71226-4	0155
71226-5	0155
71226-6	0155
71226-10	0016
71226-15	0155
71266-4	0016
71411-1	0789
71411-2	0137
71411-3	0490
71411-4	0526
71412-4	0155
71412-5	0155
71447-1	0218
71447-2	0218
71447-3	0218
71448	0160
71448-1	0160
71448-2	0160
71448-3	0160
71448-4	0160
71448-5	0160
71448-6	0160
71448-7	0160
71449	0242
71449-1	0947
71467-1	0133
71488-4	0160
71488-5	0160
71488-6	0160
71588-1	0015
71588-2	0015
71588-5	0015
71588-6	0015
71667-1	0133

DEVICE TYPE	REPL CODE
71686-4	2922
71686-5	3104
71686-6	3104
71687	0037
71687-1	0037
71687-101	0037
71748-1	0321
71778	0143
71779	0015
71783	0299
71794	0087
71818-1	0037
71819-1	0016
71963-1	0111
72003	0841
72004	0841
72006	0841
72013	0143
72017	0196
72020	1024
72025	0015
72026	0015
72027	0196
72036	1073
72041	0015
72053	0196
72054-1	0396
72058	0015
72058A	0015
72059	1024
72060	0143
72080	0143
72089	0143
72097	0015
72101	0015
72103	0015
72104	0143
72106	0030
72109	0015
72110	0769
72111	1293
72113	0015
72113A	0015
72114	0016
72115	0016
72116	0016
72117	0004
72119	0015
72123	0015
72123A	0015
72128	0123
72128A	0143
72129	0143
72129A	0143
72130	0015
72130-1	0015
72132-1	1888
72133-1	0618
72133-2	0618
72135	0644
72135-C	0644
72137	0102
72145	0015
72146	0133
72147	0133
72148	0196
72150	0004
72151	0016
72151(RECTIFIER)	0087
72152	1141
72158	0015
72161-1	0102
72162-1	1493
72162-2	0023
72163-1	1141
72165-1	0186
72165-3	0528
72165-5	0245
72165-6	0255
72168-2	0398
72168-3	0631
72171-1	0015
72172-1	0071
72173-1	0500
72174-1	0276
72176	0015
72180	1061
72181	0175
72185	1150
72190	0164
72191	0208
72193	0222
72204	0016
72206	0016
72207	0016
72784-21	0279
72784-22	0004
72784-23	0004
72797-80	0136
72797-81	0050
72799-41	0004
72813-10	0004
72847-51	0004
72856-63	0160
72874-52	0016
72879-39	0136
72879-40	0136
72923-08	0050
72941-33	0004

218 If replacement code is OEM, contact original manufacturer for replacement.

DEVICE TYPE	REPL CODE	DEVICE TYPE	REPL CODE	DEVICE TYPE	REPL CODE	DEVICE TYPE	REPL CODE	DEVICE TYPE	REPL CODE	DEVICE TYPE	REPL CODE	DEVICE TYPE	REPL CODE
72949-10	0144	74180PC	1818	75453BTC	1262	80416C	0160	81506-9B	0004	88510-175	0079	93419ADC	OEM
72951-95	0144	74181DC	1831	75454BN	1279	80501	0079	81506-9C	0004	88510-176	0555	93419APC	OEM
72951-96	0144	74181PC	1831	75454BT	1279	80540	0016	81507-0	0004	88510-177	0905	93419DC	OEM
72963-14	0016	74182DC	1845	75461TC	OEM	80544	0016	81507-0A	0004	88510-178	1469	93419DM	OEM
72979-80	0144	74182PC	1845	75462TC	OEM	80545	0016	81507-0B	0004	88641	0015	93419PC	OEM
73100-9	0004	74190DC	1901	75468	1126	80551	0037	81507-0C	0004	88686	0198	93422ADC	OEM
74021-1	5284	74190PC	1901	75471TC	OEM	80710	0167	81507-0D	0004	88687	0016	93422ADM	OEM
74107	4364	74191DC	1906	75472TC	OEM	80813VM	0016	81507-4	0004	88688	0016	93422AFC	OEM
74107DC	0936	74191PC	1906	75474P	OEM	80814VM	0016	81507-5	0208	88700	0841	93422AFM	OEM
74107PC	0936	74192	1910	75477	OEM	80815VM	0016	81507-6	0208	88710S	OEM	93422ALC	OEM
74108ADC	OEM	74192DC	1910	75478	OEM	80816VM	0016	81510-3	0279	88738	OEM	93422ALM	OEM
74116	4365	74192PC	1910	75491PC	1718	80817VM	0208	81510-4	0004	88796-1-1	0759	93422APC	OEM
74120	1108	74193	1915	75492PC	1729	80818VM	0004	81510-5	0279	88832	0160	93422DC	OEM
74121DC	0175	74193DC	1915	75654-1	0259	80829	1832	81511-4	0004	88834	0086	93422DM	OEM
74121N	0175	74193PC	1915	75700-03-01	0160	80910-147	0905	81511-5	0279	88862	0016	93422FC	OEM
74121PC	0175	74194DC	OEM	75700-04	0016	81404-4A	0004	81511-6	0279	89028-2	0081	93422FM	OEM
74122DC	1131	74194FC	OEM	75700-04-01	0016	81500-3	0004	81511-7	0279	89028-3	0033	93422LC	OEM
74122PC	1131	74194PC	OEM	75700-05	0016	81501-5	0004	81511-8	0004	89028-4	0141	93422LM	OEM
74123	1149	74195	4203	75700-05-01	0016	81502-0	0279	81512-0	0004	89028-4-1-4	0141	93422PC	OEM
74123DC	1149	74195DC	1932	75700-05-02	0016	81502-0A	0279	81512-0A	0004	89028-6	2086	93425ADC	OEM
74123PC	1149	74195FC	OEM	75700-05-03	0016	81502-0B	0279	81512-0B	0004	90050	0160	93425APC	OEM
74125	4368	74195N	1932	75700-08	0016	81502-1	0279	81512-0C	0004	90203-6	0015	93425DC	OEM
74125DC	1174	74195PC	1932	75700-08-02	0016	81502-1A	0279	81512-0D	0004	91001	0015	93425DM	OEM
74125N	1174	74196	1939	75700-09-01	0016	81502-1B	0279	81512-0E	0004	91021	0595	93425FM	OEM
74125PC	1174	74196DC	1939	75700-09-21	0016	81502-2	0004	81513-3	0016	91605	0079	93425PC	OEM
74126DC	1184	74196PC	1939	75700-13-01	0126	81502-2A	0004	81513-6	0004	93005	0015	93431DC	OEM
74126PC	1184	74197	4383	75700-14-02	0015	81502-2B	0004	81513-7	0160	93006	0015	93431DM	OEM
74132DC	1261	74197DC	1945	75700-14-05	0071	81502-3B	0004	81513-8	0015	93007	0015	93431FC	OEM
74132PC	1261	74197PC	1945	75700-22-01	0178	81502-4	0004	81513-9	0004	93011	0015	93431FM	OEM
74139	OEM	74198DC	1953	75700-24-02	0071	81502-4A	0004	81514-2	0015	93012	0015	93432DC	OEM
74141DC	1367	74198FC	OEM	75702-15-21	0015	81502-4B	0004	81515-8	0004	93018	0244	93432DM	OEM
74141PC	1367	74198PC	1953	75702-15-24	0229	81502-5	0004	81516-0	0004	93022	0015	93432FC	OEM
74145	0614	74199DC	1960	75702-15-34	0071	81502-5A	0279	81516-0A	0004	93022A	0015	93432FM	OEM
74145DC	0614	74199FC	OEM	75960CH	0211	81502-5B	0279	81516-0B	0004	93023	0015	93432PC	OEM
74145N	0614	74199PC	1960	76162-2	0190	81502-6	0595	81516-0C	0004	93027	0229	93438DM	2308
74145PC	0614	74200-8	0015	76281A	OEM	81502-6A	0595	81516-0D	0004	93028	0015	93438FC	OEM
74148	1455	74200-9	0015	76361A	OEM	81502-6B	0595	81516-0E	0004	93030	0170	93438FM	OEM
74148N	1455	74221	1230	76496	OEM	81502-6C	0595	81516-0F	0004	93091-4	1493	93438PC	2308
74150	1484	74221N	2129	76600P	0780	81502-6D	0595	81516-0G	0004	93096-1	0190	93441DC	OEM
74150DC	1484	74273	OEM	76675	0143	81502-7	0279	81516-0H	0004	93141DC	1367	93441DM	OEM
74150PC	1484	74279	OEM	76675A	0143	81502-7A	0279	81516-0J	0004	93141PC	1367	93441FC	OEM
74151ADC	1487	74279DC	OEM	76675B	0143	81502-7B	0279	82716	0144	93145DC	0614	93441FM	OEM
74151APC	1487	74279PC	OEM	77001	0239	81502-7C	0279	82965F	0571	93145PC	0614	93441PC	OEM
74151DC	1487	74283	OEM	77018A	OEM	81502-8	0279	83008	0015	93150DC	1484	93442DC	OEM
74151PC	1487	74283DC	OEM	77027-1	0354	81502-8A	0279	83741C01	0705	93150PC	1484	93442DM	OEM
74152DC	1509	74283PC	OEM	77027-2	0354	81502-8B	0279	84001	0126	93151DC	1487	93442FC	OEM
74152PC	1509	74290PC	6262	77032-8	OEM	81502-8C	0279	84001A	0126	93151PC	1487	93442FM	OEM
74153	4370	74293PC	2620	77052-3	0004	81502-9	0004	84001B	0126	93152DC	1509	93442PC	OEM
74153DC	1531	74298DC	OEM	77052-4	0004	81502-9A	0004	84011	0215	93152PC	1509	93448DC	2306
74153N	4370	74298PC	OEM	77053-2	0004	81502-9B	0004	84011U	0215	93153DC	1531	93448DM	2306
74153PC	1531	74374	OEM	77068-3170756	0142	81502-9C	0004	84323	3032	93153PC	1531	93448FC	OEM
74154	1546	74390	3210	77190-7	0015	81503-0	0004	84324	0557	93154DC	1546	93448FM	OEM
74154DC	1546	75107ADC	OEM	77190-8	0071	81503-0A	0004	84353-2	4154	93154PC	1546	93448PC	2306
74154PC	1546	75107APC	OEM	77271-3	0015	81503-0B	0004	84626	1063	93155DC	1566	93450DC	2835
74155DC	1566	75107BDC	OEM	77271-4	0071	81503-1	0004	84626-1	1063	93155PC	1566	93450DM	2835
74155PC	1566	75107BPC	OEM	77271-8	0050	81503-1A	0004	84626-2	1063	93156DC	1582	93450FC	OEM
74156DC	1582	75108BDC	OEM	77272-0	0004	81503-1B	0004	84626-3	1063	93156PC	1582	93450PC	2835
74156PC	1582	75108BPC	OEM	77272-1	0004	81503-3	0004	84626-4	1063	93164DC	0729	93451DC	2881
74157	4371	75110ADC	OEM	77272-5	0004	81503-3A	0004	84628	3303	93164PC	0729	93451DM	2881
74157DC	1595	75110APC	OEM	77272-7	0004	81503-4	0004	84628-1	3303	93165DC	1675	93451FC	OEM
74157PC	1595	75150	OEM	77272-9	0004	81503-4A	0004	84628-2	3303	93165PC	1675	93451PC	2881
74158	4372	75150D(SM)	OEM	77273-2	0004	81503-4B	0004	84628-3	3303	93166DC	0231	93452DC	2374
74160DC	1621	75150DC	OEM	77273-3	0004	81503-4C	0004	84628-4	3303	93166PC	0231	93452DM	2374
74160PC	1621	75150PC	OEM	77273-6	0004	81503-6	0279	84630	3384	93170DC	1711	93452PC	2374
74161	4373	75150RC	OEM	77273-7	0004	81503-6A	0279	84630-1	3384	93170PC	1711	93453DM	2374
74161AN	OEM	75150TC	OEM	77489	0911	81503-6B	0279	84630-2	3384	93174DC	1759	93453PC	2376
74161DC	1635	75154	OEM	78001	0061	81503-6C	0279	84630-3	3384	93174PC	1759	93454DC	OEM
74161N	4373	75154DC	OEM	78005AP	1288	81503-7	0279	84631	1799	93175DC	1776	93454DM	OEM
74161PC	1635	75154PC	OEM	78009AP	OEM	81503-7A	0279	84631-1	1799	93175PC	1776	93454FC	OEM
74162	4374	75170-2	OEM	78010AP	2779	81503-7B	0279	84631-2	1799	93176DC	1784	93454FM	OEM
74162PC	1007	75188	0503	78010BB	OEM	81503-7C	0279	84631-3	1799	93176PC	1784	93454PC	OEM
74163	4375	75188N	0503	78010BC	OEM	81503-8	0279	84631-4	1799	93177DC	1792	93458DC	OEM
74163DC	1656	75189	0506	78012AP	0330	81503-8B	0004	85000-ORG	0042	93177PC	1792	93458DM	OEM
74163N	1656	75189A	0506	78106C	2285	81503-8C	0004	85549	0016	93178DC	1802	93459DC	OEM
74163PC	1656	75189AN	0506	78331	0037	81504-1	0279	86345	OEM	93178PC	1802	93459DM	OEM
74164DC	0729	75212ACW	OEM	78524-39-01	0071	81504-1A	0279	86394GL6	1981	93179DC	1809	93470DC	OEM
74164FC	OEM	75230-9	0015	78527-75-01	0004	81504-1B	0279	86452	0211	93179PC	1809	93470DM	OEM
74164PC	0729	75232F	OEM	78527-76-01	0004	81504-1C	0279	86812	0198	93180DC	1818	93471DC	OEM
74165	1675	75232N	OEM	78527-78-01	0004	81504-3	0279	86822	0198	93180PC	1818	93471DM	OEM
74165DC	1675	75234F	OEM	78527-79-01	0004	81504-3A	0279	86832	0211	93190DC	1901	93471PC	OEM
74165FC	OEM	75234N	OEM	78606C	2285	81504-3B	0279	86842	0211	93190PC	1901	93475DC	OEM
74165PC	1675	75324F	OEM	78894	0015	81504-3C	0279	86848	0279	93191DC	1906	93475DM	OEM
74166	4377	75324N	OEM	78896	1024	81505-8	0004	87322-04	2453	93191PC	1906	93475FC	OEM
74166DC	0231	75325F	OEM	78972	0911	81505-8A	0004	87532	0086	93196DC	1939	93475FM	OEM
74166FC	OEM	75325N	OEM	79408	0012	81505-8B	0004	87756	0133	93196PC	1939	93475PC	OEM
74166N	0231	75450ADC	OEM	79855	0144	81505-8C	0004	87757	0079	93197DC	1945	93475PM	OEM
74166PC	0231	75450APC	1222	79856	0144	81505-8X	0004	87758	0037	93197PC	1945	94000	0004
74167PC	OEM	75450BDC	1222	79922	0178	81506-4	0136	87759	0037	93198DC	1953	94001	0004
74170DC	1711	75450BF	OEM	79949	1823	81506-4A	0136	88060-51	0030	93198PC	1953	94002	0004
74170FC	OEM	75450BN	1222	79985	0143	81506-4B	0136	88060-52	0133	93199DC	1960	94003	0164
74170PC	1711	75450BPC	1222	79992	0042	81506-4C	0136	88060-53	0123	93199PC	1960	94004	0085
74174	1759	75451ARC	OEM	80011	OEM	81506-5	0279	88060-54	0244	93403DC	OEM	94005	0164
74174DC	1759	75451ATC	5944	80021	OEM	81506-5A	0279	88060-55	0133	93403DM	OEM	94006	0004
74174PC	1759	75451BN	1235	80050	0160	81506-5B	0279	88060-141	0321	93403FM	OEM	94007	0050
74175	1776	75451BRC	1235	80053	2600	81506-5C	0279	88060-142	0224	93403PC	OEM	94008	0004
74175DC	1776	75451BT	1235	80070	2600	81506-6	0279	88060-143	0079	93407ADC	OEM	94009	0164
74175PC	1776	75451BTC	1235	80071	2600	81506-6A	0279	88060-144	0111	93407AFC	OEM	94010	0599
74176DC	1784	75452	1253	80073	2600	81506-6B	0279	88060-145	0086	93407BDC	OEM	94013	0050
74176PC	1784	75452ARC	OEM	80074	2600	81506-6C	0279	88060-146	0555	93407BDM	OEM	94014	0004
74177	1792	75452ATC	4445	80081	2593	81506-7	0136	88060-147	0905	93407BFC	OEM	94015	0004
74177DC	1792	75452BN	1253	80083	2600	81506-7A	0136	88510-51	0030	93407BFM	OEM	94016	0004
74177PC	1792	75452BRC	1253	80090	2600	81506-7B	0136	88510-52	0133	93410ADC	OEM	94017	0164
74178DC	1802	75452BT	1253	80094	2600	81506-7C	0136	88510-53	0123	93415ADC	OEM	94018	0164
74178FC	OEM	75452BTC	1253	80114	2549	81506-8	0136	88510-54	0244	93415AFC	OEM	94019	0164
74178PC	1802	75453ARC	OEM	80249-910787	0637	81506-8A	0136	88510-55	0133	93415APC	OEM	94020	0164
74179DC	1809	75453ATC	6090	80286	OEM	81506-8B	0136	88510-171	0321	93415DC	OEM	94021	0164
74179FC	OEM	75453BN	1262	80287	2549	81506-8C	0136	88510-172	0127	93415DM	OEM	94022	0164
74179PC	1809	75453BRC	1262	80287(CO-PROC)	OEM	81506-9	0004	88510-173	0079	93415FM	OEM	94023	0208
74180DC	1818	75453BT	1262	80287(IC)	OEM	81506-9A	0004	88510-174	0111	93415PC	OEM	94024	0160

If replacement code is OEM, contact original manufacturer for replacement.

219

DEVICE TYPE	REPL CODE
94025	0160
94026	0160
94027	0016
94028	0050
94029	0208
94030	0004
94032	0160
94033	0050
94034	0160
94035	0050
94036	0050
94037	0037
94037(EICO)	0004
94038	0136
94038(EICO)	0004
94039	0004
94040	0160
94041	0086
94042	0086
94043	0693
94044	0144
94047	0016
94048	0016
94049	0178
94050	0086
94051	0086
94051(EICO)	0233
94052	0086
94062	0590
94063	0126
94064	0126
94065	0103
94065A	0103
94066	0086
94067	0126
94068	0126
94070	0086
94094	0178
94094(EICO)	0103
94132B-2131	OEM
94152	0462
94325	1824
94327	0033
94331	2086
94333	1035
95000	0143
95000DC	OEM
95001	0143
95002	0143
95003	0133
95004	0143
95007	0143
95008	0143
95012	0133
95014	0143
95015	0015
95015(EICO)	0133
95016	0229
95017	0143
95018	0143
95101	0050
95102	0050
95103	0050
95107	0050
95108	0050
95109	0681
95110	0050
95111	0050
95112	0595
95113	0595
95114	0595
95115	0595
95115DC	OEM
95116	0136
95116DC	OEM
95117	0595
95118	0136
95119	0136
95120	0136
95120A	0279
95121	0050
95122	0136
95123	0136
95124	0050
95124DC	OEM
95125	0144
95126	0144
95127	0144
95128	0144
95129	0144
95130	0144
95131	0144
95132	0212
95133	2922
95150	OEM
95151	0050
95169-1	OEM
95170-1	0224
95170-2	0224
95170-2(DIO)	0143
95170-2(XSTR)	0224
95171-1	0155
95171-2	0155
95171-3	0076
95171-4	0155
95172-2	0004
95173-1	0004
95173-2	OEM
95176-4	OEM
95180-1	OEM
95181-1	OEM
95182-1	OEM
95186-1	OEM
95187-1	OEM
95191	OEM
95192	OEM
95195	OEM
95196	OEM
95201	0211
95202	0038
95203	0211
95204	0211
95208	0211
95209	0211
95211	0595
95212	0211
95213	0211
95214	0211
95216	0198
95216RED	0198
95216YEL	0198
95217	0211
95218	0211
95219	0211
95220	0086
95221	0037
95222-1	0211
95222-2	0038
95223	0079
95224-1	0004
95224-2	0208
95224-3	0004
95224-4	0208
95225	0198
95226-003	0786
95226-004	0590
95226-1	0086
95226-2	0198
95226-3	0338
95226-4	0320
95226-8	OEM
95227	0037
95227-1	0037
95228	0321
95231	0321
95232	0037
95233	0086
95235	1129
95239-1	0037
95240-1	0037
95241-1	0006
95241-3	0527
95242-1	0144
95246-3	OEM
95250	0160
95250-1	0160
95251	0160
95252	0142
95252-1	0142
95252-2	0142
95252-3	0142
95252-4	0142
95253	0160
95257	3004
95258-1	0546
95258-2	0378
95262-1	0161
95262-2	0455
95263-1	0161
95263-2	0455
95265-2	OEM
95266-1	OEM
95266-2	OEM
95269-1	OEM
95273-1	OEM
95273-2	OEM
95275-1	OEM
95277-1	OEM
95277-3	OEM
95285-2	OEM
95285-4	OEM
95286	1385
95286-3	OEM
95287	2728
95287-2	OEM
95291	0696
95294	0696
95296	0396
95301-1	OEM
95306-3	OEM
95306-9	OEM
95307-1	OEM
95400DC	OEM
95401DC	OEM
96101DC	OEM
96101DM	OEM
96101PC	OEM
96103	OEM
96103DC	OEM
96103DM	OEM
96106DC	OEM
96106DM	OEM
96106FM	OEM
96106PC	OEM
96147-001	0147
96148-001	0147
96702	OEM
97072	OEM
97073	OEM
97074	OEM
97081-001	OEM
97081-016	OEM
97081-116	OEM
97096-001	OEM
97098	OEM
97099	OEM
97100	0581
97101	OEM
97102	OEM
97103-108	OEM
97103-208	OEM
97112	OEM
97114	OEM
97202-222	0490
98496-001	0147
98497-001	0147
99023-3	0015
99101	0136
99102	0136
99103	0050
99104	0050
99105	0050
99106	0050
99107	0050
99108	0050
99109-1	1212
99109-2	0198
99116-1	OEM
99120	0136
99121	0136
99131-2	OEM
99171-1	OEM
99173-1	OEM
99176-1	OEM
99180-1	OEM
99195-1	0024
99195-3	0024
99201	0004
99201-110	0137
99201-128	0166
99201-208	0631
99201-210	0157
99201-211	0631
99201-212	0631
99201-216	0170
99201-219	0137
99201-221	0002
99201-242	0186
99201-312	0025
99201-316	0170
99201-325	0398
99201-331	0925
99202	0004
99202-22	0002
99202-128	0039
99202-220	0361
99202-221	0416
99202-222	0490
99202-226	0436
99202-228	0039
99202-233	0327
99203	0004
99203-005	0015
99203-006	0015
99203-1	6238
99203-3	0549
99203-4	0015
99203-5	0015
99203-6	0015
99203-6(RCA)	0015
99203-7	0071
99203-8	0071
99203-203	0604
99203-206	0790
99204	0004
99205	0004
99206-1	0016
99206-2	0016
99207-2	0016
99210-204	0188
99210-210	0157
99212-1	OEM
99217	0211
99218	0211
99241-2	OEM
99243-1	OEM
99244-1	OEM
99250	0160
99250-1	0160
99251	OEM
99252	0142
99252-1	0142
99252-2	0142
99252-2(METAL)	0142
99252-2(PLASTIC)	0275
99252-3	0142
99252-4	0042
99261-1	OEM
99287-24	OEM
99287-115	OEM
100017	0019
100101D	OEM
100101F	OEM
100102D	OEM
100102F	OEM
100107D	OEM
100107F	OEM
100112D	OEM
100112DC	OEM
100112F	OEM
100112FC	OEM
100114DC	OEM
100114FC	OEM
100117D	OEM
100117F	OEM
100118D	OEM
100118F	OEM
100122D	OEM
100122DC	OEM
100122F	OEM
100122FC	OEM
100123DC	OEM
100123FC	OEM
100130FC	OEM
100136D	OEM
100136F	OEM
100145D	OEM
100145F	OEM
100150FC	OEM
100155DC	OEM
100155FC	OEM
100166D	OEM
100166F	OEM
100180D	OEM
100180F	OEM
100181D	OEM
100412	0015
100415BF	OEM
100415F	OEM
100422AF	OEM
100422BF	OEM
100422F	OEM
100422N	OEM
100449	1024
100451AF	OEM
100470AF	OEM
100470F	OEM
100471	0196
100474AF	OEM
100474F	OEM
100520	0015
100581	0196
100617	0015
100624	0015
100678	0136
100693	0004
100768	2174
100802	0079
100844	0143
101010A	OEM
101010G	OEM
101015A	OEM
101020A	OEM
101025A	OEM
101030A	OEM
101040A	OEM
101050A	OEM
101050G	OEM
101078	0050
101087	0050
101089	0136
101100A	OEM
101100G	OEM
101154	0133
101403	0015
101434	0144
101435	0086
101436	0693
101615	0015
101678	0595
101973	0004
101974	0004
102005	1199
102050A	OEM
102050G	OEM
102100A	OEM
102100G	OEM
102249	1024
102510A	OEM
102515A	OEM
102520A	OEM
102525A	OEM
102530A	OEM
102540A	OEM
102989	0143
103318	0015
103443	0595
103508-2	1063
103508-3	3845
103521	0079
103562	0004
103705	0141
103717	0557
103729	1812
103731	1035
103743	1820
103755	0081
103872	0196
104009	0136
104059	0136
104080	0208
104081	0015
104152	0143
104213	0015
104273	0015
104325	0015
104444	0004
104510A	OEM
104510G	OEM
104515A	OEM
104515G	OEM
104520A	OEM
104520G	OEM
104525A	OEM
104525G	OEM
104530A	OEM
104530G	OEM
104540A	OEM
104540G	OEM
104550G	OEM
104615	0015
104648D	2672
104825	2550
104830	1812
104833	2086
104836	1820
104844	0033
104846	0141
104862	0557
104925	2590
105010A	OEM
105010G	OEM
105050A	OEM
105064	0446
105100A	OEM
105100G	OEM
105330	1024
105412(5	3032
105517	0143
106010G	OEM
106015G	OEM
106020G	OEM
106025G	OEM
106030G	OEM
106040G	OEM
106050G	OEM
106379	0229
106525	1704
106625	2754
106719	2289
107225	1532
107255	2008
107268	1073
107510G	OEM
107515G	OEM
107520G	OEM
107525G	OEM
107530G	OEM
107540	0015
107540G	OEM
107550G	OEM
107625	2008
107628	1073
107729	0911
107739	0211
108568	OEM
109308	0196
109328	0196
109474	0196
110008-01	OEM
110010-01	OEM
110043	0015
110075	0693
110240-005	3365
110242-003	0557
110242-004	0557
110263	0164
110388	0015
110472-003	0033
110494	0164
110495	0208
110496	0015
110515	0085
110610	0143
110629	0015
110636	0015
110669	0086
110697	0016
110699	0086
110873	0015
110957	0004
110958	0208
110959	0004
111010A	OEM
111015A	OEM
111020A	OEM
111025A	OEM
111030A	OEM
111040A	OEM
111086	0015
111117	0050
111118	0050
111207	0143
111278	0086
111279	0693
111303	0016
111313	0050
111516	0015
111605	0143
111642	0015
111725	0555
111776	0015
111820	0015
111825	2285
111954	0050
111955	0050
111956	0050
111957	0004
111958	0208
111959	0004
112017	0015
112018	0015
112027	OEM
112296	0050
112297	0004
112329	0015
112329(AMPHENOL)	0133
112330	0143
112355	0144
112356	0016
112357	0016
112358	0016
112359	0016
112360	0086
112361	0086
112475	0015
112510A	OEM
112515A	OEM
112520	0016
112520A	OEM
112521	0016
112522	0016
112523	0016
112524	0019
112525	0546
112525A	OEM
112526	0143
112527	0626
112528	0087
112529	0143
112529(AMPHENOL)	0133
112530	0012
112530A	OEM
112531	0015
112540A	OEM
112826	0015
112986	0037
112998	OEM
112999	OEM
113039	0015
113182	0037
113321	0015
113348	0016
113363	0071
113391	1293
113392	2613
113397	0769
113398	0016
113438	0016
113938	0144
113997	0769
113998	0015
114013	0015
114267	0212
114401	0759
114510A	OEM
114510G	OEM
114515A	OEM
114515G	OEM
114520A	OEM
114520G	OEM
114525	0144
114525A	OEM
114525G	OEM
114530A	OEM
114530G	OEM
114540A	OEM
114540G	OEM
114550G	OEM
115039	0015
115063	0160
115099	0030
115101	0143
115123	0644
115225	0079
115227	0050
115228	0050
115229	0050
115268	0160
115269	0160
115275	0136
115281	0160
115282	0160
115283	0160
115284	0160
115304	0693
115436	0030
115524	0071
115529	0071
115559	0015
115559A	0015
115599	0015
115792	0919
115867	0914
115875	0016
115910	0144
116010G	OEM
116015G	OEM
116020G	OEM
116021	0133
116021(SEARS)	0133
116025G	OEM
116030G	OEM
116040G	OEM
116048	0143
116050	0123
116050G	OEM
116051	0535
116052	0015
116054	0015
116068	0969
116072	0136
116073	0127
116074	0127
116075	0127
116076	0016
116077	0016
116078	0127
116078(RCA)	0037
116079	0079
116080	0144
116081	0233
116082	0079
116083	0079
116084	0136
116085	0016
116086	0969
116087	0086
116088	0969
116089	0969
116090	0283
116091	0126
116092	0127
116093	0160
116119	0144
116148	0198
116198	0144
116199	0144
116200	0144
116201	0004
116202	0050
116203	0004
116204	0208
116205	0004
116206	0004
116207	0050
116208	0050
116209	0050
116273	0143
116279	0142
116284	0126
116286	0004
116314	0911
116413	2633
116445	0659
116588	0076
116623	1686
116628	0004
116683	0050
116684	0050
116685	0004
116686	0004
116687	0208
116756	0136
116757	0004
116761	0855
116875	0016
116988	0164
116997	0004
116998	0004
117145	0015
117145A	0015
117208	0004
117209	0004
117210	0004
117510G	OEM
117515G	OEM
117520G	OEM
117525G	OEM
117530G	OEM
117540G	OEM
117550G	OEM
117616	0279
117617	0279
117618	0050
117658	0050
117659	0143
117724	0136
117725	0050
117726	0050
117727	0004
117728	0004
117729	0715
117730	0143
117760	0143
117823	0144
117824	0136
117866	0050
117867	0164
118125	0144
118200	0016
118244	0015
118279	0142
118284	0037
118358	0644
118361	2600
118686	0142
118713	0016
118822	0127
118825	0015
118873	0015
119013	0050
119035	4706

If replacement code is OEM, contact original manufacturer for replacement.

DEVICE TYPE	REPL CODE
119119(PAIR)	0123
119199	0143
119412	0127
119414	0144
119526	0136
119554	0007
119555	0007
119556	0007
119557	0007
119594	0170
119596	0133
119597	0133
119609	2600
119635	0079
119636	0079
119650	0142
119661	0030
119662	0911
119719	0918
119721	0160
119722	0969
119723	0969
119724	0016
119725	0016
119726	0016
119727	0164
119728	0086
119730	0037
119822	0086
119823	0007
119824	0007
119825	0007
119919	0143
119956	0133
119982	0016
119983	0126
120073	0016
120074	0016
120075	0004
120143	0004
120144	0004
120481	0016
120482	0016
120483	0016
120503	0015
120504	0137
120544	0015
120545	0004
120546	0004
120617	0143
120818	0290
120909-24.4	0004
121151	0004
121152	0004
121153	0279
121154	0279
121180	0242
121243	0160
121244	0599
121467	0037
121468	0015
121655	0016
121658	0016
121659	0037
121660	0016
121661	4100
121661(RCA)	0016
121662	0016
121663	0016
121664	0198
121680	0015
122074	0016
122129	0015
122166	0143
122199	2600
122243	0004
122244	0004
122517	0144
122518	0144
122519	0111
122519(SW)	0079
122520	0143
122524	0143
122664	0016
122665	0016
122725	0136
122781	OEM
122788	0015
122792	0160
122901	0004
122902	0127
122904	0127
123004	0015
123139	0086
123215	0142
123244	0136
123274	0155
123275	0142
123275-14	0142
123276	0030
123296	0015
123375	0142
123379	0004
123429	0144
123430	0144
123431	0144
123511	0136
123555-01	0720
123555-02	0720
123555-03	0720
123702	4350
123703	0086
123726	0030
123791	0004
123792	0160
123804	0015
123804-1	0015
123805	0004
123805(DIODE)	0133
123806	1588
123807	0016
123808	0222
123809	0004
123813	0133
123852	0488
123877	0004
123940	0086
123941	0079
123944	0126
123971	0037
123991	0037
124024	0127
124047	0037
124097	0136
124098	0015
124263	0144
124412	0144
124616	0126
124623	0127
124624	0127
124625	0050
124626	0004
124753	0079
124754	0079
124755	0037
124756	0079
124757	0008
124759	0016
124812	0015
125020	0496
125105	0015
125126	0137
125127	0015
125135	0079
125137	0144
125138	0144
125139	0079
125140	0079
125141	0079
125142	0126
125143	0079
125144	0224
125217	OEM
125261	0911
125263	0144
125264	0144
125329	0127
125330	0136
125389	0127
125389-14	0016
125390	0127
125392	0144
125394	0127
125397	0133
125399	0715
125458	0015
125458(HV-23)	0535
125471	0015
125474	0127
125475	0127
125475-14	0144
125488	0102
125499	0313
125519	0155
125528	0133
125529	0102
125549	0015
125588	0133
125703	0160
125707	0126
125757	OEM
125761	0160
125787	0276
125790	0050
125835	0015
125844	0102
125856	0015
125884	0133
125944	0144
125964	0015
125972	0050
125992	0644
125993	0015
125994	0151
125994(RCA)	0127
125994-14	0144
125995	0127
126023	0144
126024	0144
126025	0007
126093	0004
126093-1	0004
126093-2	0004
126093-3	0004
126093-4	0004
126131	0015
126138	0142
126148	0015
126149	0715
126150	0079
126156	0079
126176	0015
126177	0143
126184	0050
126185	0136
126186	0050
126187	0004
126188	0142
126276	0004
126320	0015
126321	0133
126331	0079
126334	0079
126413	0276
126424	0111
126524	0037
126525	0079
126526	0079
126527	0102
126582	0002
126604	2689
126670	0144
126697	0004
126698	0144
126699	0016
126700	0037
126701	0016
126702	0016
126703	0086
126704	0016
126705	0233
126706	0016
126707	0037
126708	0016
126709	0233
126710	0233
126711	0016
126712	0079
126713	0079
126714	0016
126715	0037
126716	0079
126717	0079
126718	0037
126719	0037
126720	0079
126721	0086
126722	0142
126724	0126
126725	0086
126726	0142
126772	0142
126849	0287
126850	OEM
126851	0025
126852	0002
126853	0363
126854	0149
126855	0015
126856	0102
126857	1208
126858	1208
126859	1208
126860	0769
126861	0015
126862	2506
126863	0313
126864	0039
126871	0823
126885	0071
126898	0061
126899	0239
126900	0074
126945	0004
127017	0143
127102	0015
127112	0004
127114	0004
127128	1628
127166	2681
127176	0015
127177	0313
127214	0321
127263	0016
127297	0004
127303	0004
127350A	OEM
127350AZ	OEM
127350B	OEM
127350C	OEM
127350D	OEM
127350E	OEM
127350F	OEM
127350Z	OEM
127351A	OEM
127351AZ	OEM
127351B	OEM
127351C	OEM
127351D	OEM
127351E	OEM
127351F	OEM
127351Z	OEM
127354	0079
127355	0111
127376	0086
127379	0071
127382	0002
127393	0079
127396	0015
127397	0164
127474	0133
127529	0079
127532	0911
127533	0911
127589	0004
127590	0841
127693	0144
127695	0015
127712	0233
127767	2736
127784	0143
127792	0144
127793	0144
127794	0144
127798	0042
127828	0599
127835	0087
127845	0086
127899	0079
127905F02	0267
127933	0124
127962	0004
127978	0161
127980	0212
127992	0015
127993	0133
128056	0042
128057	0919
128256	0015
128343	0004
128474	0133
128899	0086
128938	0136
128940	0004
129028	0143
129029	0015
129029(DIO)	0015
129029(XSTR)	0079
129049	0079
129050	0144
129051	0086
129095	0968
129144	0144
129145	0224
129146	0155
129147	0079
129157	0143
129158	0143
129203	0374
129213	0015
129241	0299
129251	0050
129286	0004
129289	0050
129334	0015
129347	0050
129348	0071
129348(DIO)	0143
129348(XSTR)	0211
129359	0715
129375	0133
129389	0050
129392	0127
129392-14	0144
129393	0127
129393-14	0144
129394	0127
129394-14	0144
129424	1382
129425	0111
129474	0143
129475	0139
129494	0015
129507	0164
129508	0164
129509	0111
129510	0111
129511	0111
129512	0111
129513	0111
129556	0911
129571	0127
129572	0079
129573	0127
129574	0127
129604	0470
129697	0037
129698	0079
129699	0037
129759	0015
129802	0004
129821	1843
129871	0823
129897	0079
129899	0079
129903	0188
129904	0012
129930	OEM
129938	0631
129940	0361
129946	0002
129979	0127
129980	0212
130013	0079
130013(TRIAC)	2006
130026	1986
130040	0396
130044	0170
130045	0133
130046	1996
130047	0170
130052	0015
130096	1823
130110	0071
130130	0360
130132	0490
130139	0037
130200-00	0004
130200-02	0004
130215	0037
130278	0144
130328	0137
130338-01	0015
130380	0137
130389-00	0015
130400-95	0004
130400-96	0208
130402-36	0004
130403-04	0144
130403-13	0016
130403-17	0016
130403-18	0016
130403-47	0208
130403-52	0004
130403-62	0144
130404-21	0144
130404-29	0126
130404-59	0144
130474	0546
130536	0037
130537	0016
130607	0015
130751	0167
130761	0416
130762	0002
130793	0127
131005	0735
131006	0735
131050	0015
131075	0042
131139	0283
131140	0079
131161	0419
131214	0911
131221	0144
131239	0419
131240	0079
131241	0037
131242	0037
131242-12	0126
131243	0079
131243-12	0079
131245	0015
131257	0130
131300	1812
131301	1035
131303	1820
131304	0033
131305	0081
131306	0141
131308	0557
131311	0079
131312	0354
131318	0102
131346	0239
131347	0061
131454	0079
131475	0102
131476	0102
131501	0549
131502	0133
131502(RCA)	0015
131543	0007
131544	0144
131545	0144
131647	0037
131648	0144
131789	0037
131814	0030
131815	0087
131815(RCA)	0911
131844	0144
131848	0224
131848(RCA)	0042
131849	0042
131941	OEM
131950	0015
132148	0102
132149	0015
132175	0086
132176	0037
132180	0086
132313	2716
132314	2527
132315	0324
132325	0239
132326	2311
132327	0086
132328	0086
132329	0079
132416	0137
132418	0102
132445	0546
132446	0546
132447	0378
132448	0848
132478	0688
132488	0378
132492	0778
132495	0161
132498	0037
132499	0042
132500	0086
132501	0102
132509	0102
132547	0102
132548	0102
132549	0102
132558	3466
132571	0455
132573	0042
132574	0848
132616	0025
132634	1986
132642	0155
132643	0155
132645	0133
132650	1882
132776	0161
132813	0042
132814	0015
132815	0087
132823	0079
132824	0039
132830	0037
132865	0157
132912	0143
132915	0143
132966	0286
132995	1190
133026	0286
133171	0007
133176	0590
133177	0086
133178	0079
133182	0037
133218	0079
133249	0079
133253	0037
133265	0283
133266	0015
133275	0079
133276	0007
133390	0133
133390(PWR.-RECT)	0015
133439	0018
133440	0338
133442	OEM
133543	0015
133573	0555
133600	2716
133615	0102
133616	0102
133690	0079
133696	0016
133743	0016
133950	0015
134050	OEM
134074	0911
134142	0144
134143	0079
134144	0144
134144-1	0127
134155	0086
134180	0143
134195-001	1812
134196-001	1035
134197-001	0081
134198-001	0141
134254-001	2595
134263	0144
134264	0911
134279	0455
134280	0161
134281	1671
134282	0130
134335	0053
134340	2266
134342	1403
134411	0086
134415	1023
134417	0224
134419	0144
134442	0396
134444	0002
134445	1023
134450	0212
134509	1178
134587	0143
134771	0419
134772	0283
134773	0637
134774	0546
134777	0752
134989	0086
134993	0157
135029	2378
135244	0286
135281	0015
135284	0015
135286	0037
135297	0144
135320	0290
135324	0349
135341	0102
135351	0899
135352	0074
135362	0006
135380	0102
135386	1208
135406	0186
135531	0052
135532	0053
135571	0133
135631	0405
135691	0190
135716	0283
135734	0102
135735	0419
135739	0419
135744	0969
135872	0019
135932	0290
135963	0349
136066	0233
136145	2242
136146	2728
136147	1832
136162	0133
136163	0133
136164	0030
136165	0079
136168	0224
136239	0079
136240	0224
136334	OEM
136355	0720
136423	0126
136424	0086
136430	0079
136601	0455
136605	0071
136634	0361
136635	0015
136648	0042
136688	0133
136696	0086
136721	0039
136766	0050
137031	0405
137065	0378
137066	0546
137075	0102
137093	0004
137127	0224
137155	0037
137161	0512
137241	0086
137245	0360
137276	OEM
137277	OEM
137338	0224
137339	0079
137340	0037
137341	0769
137352	0637
137369	0161
137383	0016
137388	0224
137527	0042
137606	0023
137607	0065
137613	0479
137614	0079
137646	0190
137647	0446
137648	0086
137652	0015
137655	0398
137693	0405
137699	OEM
137718	0637
137736	0478
137780	1023
137783	OEM
137833	OEM
137855	0286
137875	0079
137876	1403
137997	0259
138010	0405
138019	0190
138032	2313
138032(RCA)	2313
138033	1702
138033(RCA)	1702
138107	0778
138121	0378
138171	OEM
138172	0015
138173	0023
138174	0436
138175	0015
138191	0079
138192	0042
138193	0455
138194	0103
138195	0538
138196	0133
138218	0155
138310	OEM
138311	0232
138312	0268

If replacement code is OEM, contact original manufacturer for replacement.

221

DEVICE TYPE	REPL CODE
138313	0310
138314	0357
138315	0462
138317	0522
138318	0692
138319	1347
138320	1915
138380	1832
138380(IC)	1832
138381	0893
138403	1164
138421	0190
138429	0058
138609	5072
138681	2530
138699	0516
138736	0344
138752	0190
138763	0079
138907	0190
138945	0715
138946	0136
138974	0631
139001	0190
139017	0334
139044	0264
139045	OEM
139061	OEM
139064	0455
139065	0133
139069	0455
139266	0546
139267	0378
139268	3047
139269	0855
139270	0178
139295	0065
139328	0133
139343	0162
139362	0079
139366	5249
139455	0037
139569	0079
139618	0396
139634	0143
139696	0086
139706	0133
139899	OEM
140110	OEM
140129	0546
140130	0378
140259	0283
140290	0037
140365	2317
140501	0086
140503	0102
140506	0556
140525	0016
140600-02	OEM
140602-58	OEM
140715	0752
140763	0239
140764	0061
140971	0023
140972	0023
140973	0002
140976	0065
140977	0065
140979	0419
140995	0286
141003	0018
141008	0079
141018	0037
141019	0855
141020	0419
141134	3239
141135	2038
141187	0490
141227	0037
141254	1700
141255	2313
141256	1702
141259	0516
141270	2759
141279	0516
141280	2762
141290	2771
141295	0283
141302	0039
141330	0079
141331	0079
141332	0212
141335	0086
141343	0037
141344	0037
141345	0037
141355	0086
141367	0065
141370	0144
141421	0037
141429	0137
141464	1700
141489	3494
141558	0079
141581	0137
141711	0037
141719	OEM
141767	0079
141783	0079

DEVICE TYPE	REPL CODE
141849	0015
141872-1	0023
141872-6	0015
141873	2925
141967	0925
142007-2	0748
142137	1319
142190	0037
142251	0546
142251(IC)	1969
142294	0718
142341	3780
142417	0490
142569	2784
142670	0039
142671	0283
142681	0239
142682	0340
142683	0079
142684	0079
142686	0079
142689	0065
142690	0264
142691	0042
142692	0463
142711	0079
142717	0463
142718	2759
142719	3060
142728	1188
142738	0398
142771	2430
142811	0079
142814	0405
142838	0037
142839	0037
142903	3780
143033	2759
143041	5737
143041(IC)	1545
143041(XSTR)	0855
143042	0079
143062	1340
143162	0911
143316	0079
143594	0344
143595	0015
143690	2379
143696	3741
143753	0631
143766	2800
143777	0560
143790	0500
143791	0037
143792	0079
143793	0016
143794	0079
143795	0079
143796	0079
143797	0320
143798	0086
143802	0037
143803	0037
143804	0079
143805	0079
143806	0037
143807	0037
143808	3239
143821	2038
143822	3060
143837	0133
143847	0398
143913	1700
143940	0079
143963	0037
143964	0264
144004	0015
144011	3973
144012	2932
144015	4004
144017	4162
144018	4017
144022	4095
144024	4665
144026	0167
144028	2083
144030	0203
144031	0006
144033	0037
144034	0111
144035	1211
144037	0113
144039	0155
144040	1212
144043	0155
144044	0155
144045	0558
144047	0155
144050	0071
144051	0071
144052	0015
144054	0019
144056	0466
144057	0120
144072-2	0330
144076	0919
144182	0558
144581	0133
144582	0151

DEVICE TYPE	REPL CODE
144585	0143
144612	4678
144691	0133
144761	0006
144848	4663
144849	1570
144850	4677
144851	4671
144852	4666
144853	4670
144854	4981
144855	4099
144856	0558
144857	0919
144858	0688
144859	0321
144860	0023
144861	0466
144863	0688
144920	3809
144921	2244
144922	0451
144923	1319
144966	0218
144967	1589
144968	0215
144969	1135
144970	0394
144971	0119
144973	1593
144974	0133
145113	1319
145172	0378
145173	0079
145174	OEM
145208	1188
145258	0086
145395	0079
145398	0079
145410	0037
145513	0340
145585	OEM
145586	0409
145648	0309
145660	0133
145671	0065
145683	0030
145687	0144
145718	1700
145730	OEM
145776	0037
145803	1318
145817	0313
145818	0215
145833	0079
145838	0155
145839	0023
145840	0527
145847	OEM
145966	0203
146027	0124
146052	2759
146081	0919
146136	0023
146137	0023
146138	1319
146139	0042
146141	0079
146142	0037
146143	0264
146149	3919
146150	3735
146151	3780
146152	3060
146164	1482
146173	0123
146260	0057
146261	0210
146264	0416
146273	0157
146301	0079
146316	0344
146320	0162
146359	0037
146364-1	1986
146416	OEM
146460-2	1832
146484	0079
146512	0577
146514	4670
146521	0212
146522	0151
146569	1045
146570	0667
146571	0124
146572	0111
146575	0143
146576	0124
146595	4669
146596	0558
146631	0053
146641	0141
146642	0557
146643	1812
146644	0081
146732	3429
146742	0893
146823	0309
146826	0283

DEVICE TYPE	REPL CODE
146846	0052
146847	0079
146848	0224
146849	0561
146850	0037
146851	0710
146854	0079
146855	0042
146856	0042
146857	0906
146858	3920
146893	1570
146894	1572
146895	1575
146896	0167
146897	0143
146899	0355
146900	0819
146902	1603
146903	0577
146904	0667
146908	0253
146911	1319
146912	0124
146933-503	0374
147007-3	0015
147015	3494
147111	OEM
147112-7	0126
147171-11	1208
147187-2-14	0071
147213	0133
147214	0143
147215	2520
147216	0015
147218	0133
147219	0165
147220	0181
147221	0062
147232	2632
147234	0215
147242	0577
147243	0148
147245	0191
147245-0-1	0144
147246	0558
147250	0520
147256	0033
147312	0018
147339	5093
147340	5067
147351-4-1	0969
147351-5-1	0160
147352-0-1	0142
147353-0-1	0007
147356-9-1	0144
147357-0-1	0126
147357-1-1	0016
147357-2-1	0144
147357-4-1	0126
147357-7-1	0016
147357-9-1	0144
147359-0-1	0126
147360-1	0079
147363-1	0016
147389	0688
147399	OEM
147400	OEM
147406	0053
147437	4700
147438	0167
147464	1319
147477-2	0681
147477-7	0436
147477-7-1	0170
147477-8-2	0071
147477-8-3	0071
147477-8-7	0071
147477-8-8	0071
147477-8-10	0071
147478	0101
147478-8-2	0229
147499	0076
147546	0053
147549-1	0037
147549-2	0037
147555-1	0016
147617-12	0102
147639	OEM
147663	0037
147664	0079
147665	0037
147672	5691
147676-1	0326
147687	0004
147693	0071
147704	0144
147704-6-4	0137
147735	0681
147757	OEM
147886	0144
147887	0409
147888	0674
147922-2	0911
147924	0819
147943	1023
147974	0558
147975	0555
147993	0559

DEVICE TYPE	REPL CODE
148056	OEM
148061	0079
148062	OEM
148070	1382
148085	0212
148123	0143
148124	3460
148132	2632
148134	3279
148146	1132
148229	0755
148235	0356
148236	0001
148237	0688
148246	0015
148256	0076
148257	0253
148259	0582
148272	0163
148295	0057
148446	OEM
148507	5094
148509	OEM
148529	0062
148531	0057
148533	2208
148664	OEM
148684	0888
148690	0346
148711	2208
148712	1009
148714	0199
148715	5463
148716	1808
148717	3707
148718	5137
148719	5102
148720	1575
148721	5132
148722	5077
148723	5133
148724	0356
148725	5134
148726	3686
148727	5450
148728	0356
148729	5100
148730	0215
148731	0493
148732	2061
148733	0001
148734	0101
148735	0915
148736	2042
148737	3168
148738	2449
148739	4930
148740	0176
148741	0678
148742	1339
148743	0861
148744	3692
148745	0619
148746	0853
148747	3136
148748	0643
148749	4282
148750	0018
148751	0419
148751-147	0144
148752	0558
148753	2208
148754	1203
148755	0667
148756	0577
148757	0690
148758	1203
148759	3096
148760	0060
148761	0111
148762	0525
148763	0023
148764	0091
148765	1404
148766	0440
148769	0085
148770	3004
148771	0124
148772	0150
148777	0005
148778	0549
148779	0079
148780	0144
148781	0244
148782	0525
148801	0388
148803	0120
148804	0041
148805	1319
148875	OEM
148907	0079
148919	0388
148952	3486
148953	3487
148954	5753
148955	1203
148956	0917
148957	0062
148958	0695

DEVICE TYPE	REPL CODE
148959	1593
148964	0309
148968	0212
148970	OEM
148984	0065
148991	1918
148995	0037
148996	0079
148997	0079
148998	0055
148999	0042
149007	1882
149014	OEM
149015	0470
149016	6229
149017	0619
149018	0620
149019	0673
149020	OEM
149033	OEM
149034	6004
149035	5996
149036	5996
149037	1508
149038	1311
149039	OEM
149040	0037
149041	0037
149042	6234
149249	OEM
149251	0239
149252	0167
149253	3940
149254	3920
149255	0026
149433	0339
149434	0120
149488	0667
149539	0080
149540	0053
149544	0224
149546	3349
149585	3686
149586	4194
149594	OEM
149598	0917
149599	4282
149615	0124
149616	0440
149676	0911
149729	OEM
149730	0143
149731	0790
149751	0316
149797	0437
149849	0577
149864	0667
149870	3926
149882	4961
149930	0052
149938	1651
149982	1951
150006	OEM
150009	OEM
150038	1341
150068	OEM
150069	OEM
150070	OEM
150117	0076
150156	OEM
150322	0667
150325	0906
150330	0819
150340	2094
150342	4678
150344	0037
150363	0137
150364	0388
150365	1319
150366	0037
150368	5675
150369	4521
150371	1686
150373	1370
150374	2024
150400	OEM
150401	2983
150402	1449
150403	1449
150404	1591
150405	1591
150410	1481
150414	2406
150415	OEM
150416	2408
150417	2408
150418	0176
150419	2910
150420	OEM
150428B	OEM
150430	2094
150431	0864
150440	0422
150447	1392
150448	OEM
150513	0076
150514	0151
150515	3308
150516	1132

DEVICE TYPE	REPL CODE
150517	2464
150518	0037
150519	0191
150521	0819
150522	1338
150523	0148
150524	0355
150527	0318
150528	0023
150529	0124
150530	0124
150531	0118
150533	0041
150534	0253
150535	0466
150536	1132
150573	0133
150644	OEM
150645	OEM
150646	2717
150651	0023
150671	0071
150703	1323
150704	OEM
150705	0437
150706	OEM
150711	OEM
150764	0527
150767	OEM
151010A	OEM
151010G	OEM
151050A	OEM
151050G	OEM
151056	0624
151100A	OEM
151100G	OEM
151241	0133
151245	OEM
151263	0037
151326	0224
151329	0378
151332	1505
151333	0678
151334	0041
151335	0052
151342	OEM
151343	OEM
151344	OEM
151345	OEM
151476	0102
151544	1035
151548	0329
151579	OEM
151693	0144
151974	0037
152050A	OEM
152050G	OEM
152051	3920
152052	0012
152069	0715
152100A	OEM
152100G	OEM
152124	0276
152185	0148
152213	0062
152214	0151
152284	0133
152284(LED)	OEM
152286	0143
152329	0181
152348	0919
152363	OEM
152364	0176
152375	0681
152407	0873
152472	0181
152473K	0133
152500	4432
152544	0151
152545	1077
152546	OEM
152547	OEM
152548	0015
152550	0143
152551	0019
152623	0700
152624	0489
152625	0472
152626	0009
152627	0057
152672	OEM
152682	1664
152750	0253
152766	0050
152793	0440
152805	OEM
152835	0062
152841	0911
152854	0361
152855	0253
152857	0162
152869	0010
152887	0511
152898	2520
152920	1589
152921	0765
152923	0215
152929	3168
152935	0119

If replacement code is OEM, contact original manufacturer for replacement.

DEVICE TYPE	REPL CODE
152970	0006
152971	1593
152972	2208
152978	0062
152981	OEM
153129	0367
153233	0037
153259	2208
153260	0127
153265	0623
153312	0161
153321	0050
153325	0037
153334	0155
153342	OEM
153350	0919
153351	0144
153399	0079
153433	2464
153443	2464
153444	OEM
153445	0036
153456	0176
153489	0144
153493	0124
153512	OEM
153518	0041
153519	0057
153534	0364
153535	0364
153545	1137
153568	0765
153612	2779
153630	OEM
153632	1449
153633	OEM
153634	OEM
153661	0819
153672	0023
153673	0489
153676	0546
153677	3718
153678	0055
153679	0042
153680	0283
153682	0895
153684	2759
153685	3920
153712	2015
153716	OEM
153826	0052
153844	0071
153875	3940
153882	0203
153937	0215
154002	0681
154027	1135
154192	0472
154197	OEM
154201	OEM
154202	OEM
154222	6676
154223	OEM
154224	OEM
154225	OEM
154228	OEM
154230	OEM
154231	OEM
154505	0700
154515	3940
154564	1973
154572	2056
154573	OEM
154574	2057
154575	0037
154576	0694
154577	2055
154578	0911
154579	0009
154580	OEM
154581	0765
154582	0233
154583	0018
154584	0016
154587	0037
154588	0037
154589	0037
154590	0062
154646	0144
154647	0144
154648	2042
154649	0101
154650	0855
154651	0276
154652	2062
154653	0667
154654	0553
154655	0253
154656	0681
154704	0188
154730	2014
154736	OEM
154749	1997
154752	0015
154753	0484
154754	2008
154755	OEM
154756	0253
154765	0203
154766	0577
154767	2044
154768	0493
154770	0129
154771	1008
154772	1946
154773	0056
154774	0473
154782	0619
154783	2895
154784	5253
154785	0922
154807	0191
154812	0016
154822	2015
154831	0079
154832	0922
154856	0140
154988	0819
155001	OEM
155010A	OEM
155010G	OEM
155033	0667
155050A	OEM
155050G	OEM
155100A	OEM
155100G	OEM
155131	0719
155276	0080
155331	1073
155335	OEM
155339	1795
155444	0643
155495	1731
155508	2531
155509	2531
155519	0693
155520	OEM
155522	0077
155523	0440
155525	0930
155527	OEM
155556	0484
155558	0181
155565	0041
155566	0120
155568	0577
155632	2042
155677	0224
155678	0133
155679	2891
155680	0367
155681	2602
155682	0549
155683	1023
155684	0124
155708	1484
155709	1546
155710	1910
155711	0963
155712	0967
155713	OEM
155714	0597
155727	OEM
155732	0071
155810	0466
155822	0053
155829	0911
155836	0253
155837	0181
155838	0118
155841	2895
155842	0455
155892	2859
155893	0466
155911	3606
156018	2991
156023	0007
156025	1239
156026	0367
156027	0124
156029	0715
156254	0014
156262	OEM
156297	0450
156313	0305
156317	0023
156369	0789
156372	0734
156468	0002
156477	0167
156545	2884
156546	2172
156548	0006
156549	3282
156567	OEM
156570	OEM
156571	2409
156580	5681
156581	OEM
156582	OEM
156583	OEM
156584	0249
156591	OEM
156592	OEM
156593	OEM
156594	OEM
156616	OEM
156637	0162
156688	0050
156689	0140
156708	OEM
156712	0877
156725	2062
156727	0133
156728	OEM
156729	OEM
156730	2641
156731	OEM
156733	1967
156736	1132
156790	0091
156791	0031
156795	2678
156800	0873
156801	0700
156891	OEM
156892	0004
156893	OEM
156894	5238
156895	2094
156896	0191
156897	0688
156910	0023
156911	3460
156912	5679
156914	OEM
156915	2409
156916	OEM
156917	0688
156918	5681
156919	0006
156920	0877
156928	0279
156931	0144
156932	1689
156933	2350
156934	0006
156935	0161
156936	0210
156937	0053
156938	0057
156939	0582
156942	OEM
156943	0595
156944	0148
156945	0681
156947	0133
156955	0319
156956	0241
156960	0484
156969	0120
156970	OEM
157068	4173
157142	0549
157246	OEM
157301	0133
157306	0710
157309	OEM
157424	0133
157425	1505
157427	1075
157437	OEM
157564	1545
157575	1911
157627	1157
157633	0126
157635	0855
157637	1348
157652	OEM
157653	1420
157654	0409
157662	OEM
157663	OEM
157668	OEM
157669	1203
157677	1022
157679	0124
157681	6943
157688	OEM
157689	4336
157694	0319
157805	OEM
157806	2292
157808	0037
157815	OEM
157816	OEM
157832	0253
157833	0079
157835	OEM
157951	0881
157958	0525
157959	0881
157970	0087
157971	4194
157972	4075
157973	OEM
157975	1026
158040	0083
158061	0493
158062	OEM
158063	0493
158064	OEM
158066	0354
158075	0355
158077	0371
158078	OEM
158153	0064
158238	0121
158240	1544
158242	1132
158249	3682
158313	0133
158344	0071
158381	OEM
158387	OEM
158390	1731
158391	OEM
158487	3703
158578	1319
158584	6546
158624	1054
158625	1066
158626	1066
158705	OEM
158768	OEM
158770	OEM
158773	OEM
158836	0497
158837	0500
158869	OEM
159019	OEM
159020	OEM
159021	OEM
159036	OEM
159042	OEM
159044	OEM
159064	0897
159065	0901
159066	OEM
159069	OEM
159216	OEM
159234	OEM
159238	0062
159240	OEM
159242	0151
159249	1159
159250	0133
159277	OEM
159355	1288
159362	0111
159369	0450
159425	1369
159426	0681
159429	0248
159430	1375
159433	1379
159434	0436
159435	0621
159446	OEM
159475	0901
159483	OEM
159490	OEM
159582	OEM
159588	1601
159649	0017
159890	0052
159945	0139
159946	OEM
159947	0428
159948	OEM
159949	OEM
159950	0643
159951	0151
159959	1927
159960	1203
159961	0210
159962	OEM
159963	0052
159970	1934
159971	1663
159972	OEM
159973	1132
159974	1319
160063	OEM
160069	OEM
160082	1955
160083	2022
160084	OEM
160085	0042
160087	OEM
160088	OEM
160089	OEM
160090	0313
160091	0077
160092	0631
160094	2029
160175	2094
160180	OEM
160251	OEM
160302	1967
160362	OEM
160364	0631
160385	OEM
160386	OEM
160387	OEM
160412	OEM
160423	OEM
160426	OEM
160432	OEM
160433	OEM
160434	OEM
160435	OEM
160521	OEM
160545	OEM
160547	0006
160553	OEM
160554	1057
160555	OEM
160556	OEM
160557	1505
160562	OEM
160568	OEM
160569	OEM
160574	0015
160575	OEM
160576	2323
160577	OEM
160578	OEM
160589	OEM
160696	0079
160719	OEM
160740	OEM
160741	2323
160747	OEM
160752	1531
160753	1484
160763	2469
160764	1910
160768	OEM
160830	OEM
160831	OEM
160832	0765
160836	0089
160837	OEM
160838	OEM
160839	0285
160844	2517
160851	OEM
160852	0140
160869	2015
160872	OEM
160879	OEM
160890	1338
160972	0016
160973	0079
160979	0079
161001	0123
161006	0143
161015	0123
161016	0143
161016H	0079
161021	0133
161022	0361
161027	0911
161029	0015
161030	0015
161031	0015
161032	0102
161033	0102
161034	0911
161037	0015
161038	0143
161046	0244
161066	0721
161077	0079
161078	OEM
161079	0024
161080	0053
161081	0877
161117	OEM
161120	0151
161123	0151
161149	0133
161193	0428
161194	0525
161195	0643
161199	0631
161247	0037
161249	0695
161265	OEM
161325	1594
161326	2254
161362	OEM
161392	2928
161419	OEM
161437	OEM
161447	OEM
161558	0719
161571	0016
161572	0016
161573	3051
161579	0016
161585	OEM
161586	OEM
161588	0719
161669	OEM
161705	0004
161714	0041
161715	3130
161717	0208
161719	OEM
161727	OEM
161728	OEM
161732	0129
161733	3144
161734	0037
161736	0016
161737	0016
161738	0016
161739	OEM
161743	0356
161745	0319
161746	OEM
161748	OEM
161749	OEM
161752	0016
161756	3156
161757	3156
161869	0361
161870	0274
161871	0002
161872	0002
161877	0490
161878	0526
161879	OEM
161880	OEM
161896	0925
161906	0778
161912	OEM
161919	OEM
161920	1505
161921	OEM
161935	OEM
161936	2452
161937	OEM
161976	OEM
161994	0644
161995	0446
161998	OEM
162002-039	0143
162002-040	0136
162002-041	0136
162002-042	0136
162002-062	0160
162002-062A	0160
162002-090	0144
162002-095	0160
162002-39	0143
162002-40	0136
162002-41	0136
162021	0181
162037	0356
162039	0009
162163	OEM
162201	1024
162259	OEM
162297	OEM
162394	OEM
162446	OEM
162451	2266
162505	0018
162506	OEM
162507	OEM
162511	OEM
162512	OEM
162514	OEM
162665	OEM
162669	OEM
162673	OEM
162674	2014
162675	OEM
162677	0151
162682	0292
162706	0848
162735	0124
162736	0133
162737	OEM
162739	OEM
162740	OEM
162745	0456
162772	OEM
162845	OEM
162846	OEM
162850	OEM
162851	OEM
162871	OEM
162902	OEM
162909	0052
162921	1250
162922	0328
162929	0148
162931	1386
163033	0631
163060	0892
163064	OEM
163198	0945
163199	0755
163202	OEM
163348	0124
163353	0124
163355	OEM
163397	0030
163434	0620
163441	0133
163443	OEM
163506	OEM
163512	OEM
163629	OEM
163755	0101
163793	OEM
163794	1288
163795	OEM
163804	OEM
163805	OEM
163806	OEM
163807	0041
163816	OEM
163818	0030
163822	OEM
163823	2369
163891	OEM
163892	OEM
163893	0688
163916	OEM
163917	0061
163924	OEM
163925	OEM
163926	OEM
163938	OEM
164030	OEM
164035	OEM
164049	0015
164053	OEM
164058	3104
164061	OEM
164062	OEM
164064	OEM
164114	OEM
164115	3104
164116	1796
164185	0782
164203	OEM
164204	OEM
164214	OEM
164215	OEM
164216	OEM
164230	OEM
164231	OEM
164242	OEM
164253	4067
164323	OEM
164324	OEM
164326	OEM
164327	OEM
164328	OEM
164343	OEM
164344	OEM
164345	OEM
164351	OEM
164353	0892
164354	1212
164492	OEM
164493	OEM
164494	OEM
164502	OEM
164547	0188
164588	0124
164589	0017
164590	0031
164591	0162
164593	1266
164594	0446
164595	0181
164599	OEM
164600	OEM
164601	OEM
164602	2541
164660	OEM
164705	OEM
164707	OEM
164708	OEM
164717	0124
164719	0015
164733	OEM
164739	OEM
164742	OEM
164743	OEM
164744	OEM
164747	OEM
164748	OEM
164750	OEM
164751	OEM
164752	OEM
164753	OEM
164767	OEM
164771	OEM
164819	OEM
164840	OEM
164847	OEM
164874	0133
164959	0148
164964	3104
164981	1168
164982	1820
164984	0215
164985	OEM
165358	0137
165392	0127
165572	0143
165597	0015
165667	0136
165668	0016
165735	0086
165736	0086
165737	0688
165738	0178
165739	0015
165740	0100
165827	0016
165828	0016
165931	0127
165932	0127
165976	0004
165995	0144
166040	0015
166272	0144
166273	0143
166400	0164
166593	0023
166726	0023
166881	0015
166882	0004
166883	0004

If replacement code is OEM, contact original manufacturer for replacement.

DEVICE TYPE	REPL CODE
166906	0127
166907	2582
166908	0136
166909	0136
166917	0086
166918	0161
166919	0455
166920	0015
166921	0012
166922	0015
166985	0361
166997	0164
166999	0050
167034	0015
167235	0222
167263	0127
167285	0222
167413	0015
167540	0155
167541	0111
167542	1581
167543	0015
167544	0015
167562	0143
167569	0016
167572	0123
167679	0004
167680	0164
167688	0016
167690	0037
167691	0042
167956	0111
167957	0111
167958	0178
167998	0004
167999	0004
168339	0015
168405	0111
168567	0127
168606	0720
168651	0111
168652	0030
168653	0631
168657	0144
168658	0144
168659	0144
168660	0086
168692	0120
168692(VARISTOR)	0120
168706	0133
168717	0050
168906	0164
168907	0004
168910	0143
168953	0208
168954	0004
168983	0004
168984	0164
169113	0015
169114	0133
169115	0143
169116	0015
169117	0133
169175	0164
169194	0127
169195	0144
169196	0127
169197	0016
169198	0030
169199	0157
169216	0142
169359	0004
169360	0004
169361	0004
169362	0143
169363	0015
169403	1303
169501	0143
169505	0127
169558	0133
169565	0015
169570	0015
169574	0127
169590	0023
169679	0076
169680	0076
169765	0015
169771	1211
169773	0004
170090-1	OEM
170128	0688
170132-1	2839
170133	0015
170287-1	3502
170294	0079
170297	0015
170307-1	0160
170308	0155
170338	0127
170370	0133
170373	0123
170376	0160
170376-1	0160
170388	0127
170407-1	0160
170479-1	0160
170576	0079
170577	OEM
170580	0079

DEVICE TYPE	REPL CODE
170666-1	0160
170668-1	0160
170733-1	1141
170750	0015
170753-1	0007
170756-1	0007
170783-1	2839
170783-3	0208
170794	2195
170827-1	3502
170850-1	0265
170856	0015
170857	0133
170890-1	3502
170891-1	6257
170906	0007
170906-1	0007
170953	0111
170954	4491
170955	0111
170956	0696
170963	0111
170964	4481
170965	0015
170966-1	0015
170967	1791
170967(TRAN)	1212
170967-1	0079
170968-1	0079
170970-1	0015
170993	OEM
170994-1	1647
171003	0599
171003(SEARS)	0144
171003(TOSHIBA)	0079
171004	0160
171005	0208
171005(TOSHIBA)	0208
171009	0127
171009(SEARS)	0144
171009(TOSHIBA)	0079
171010-1	2839
171015	0233
171015(TOSHIBA)	0142
171016	0136
171016(SEARS)	0004
171017	0004
171018	0004
171019	0015
171026	0076
171026(SEARS)	0004
171026(TOSHIBA)	0079
171027	0079
171028	0144
171029	0007
171029(SEARS)	0144
171029(TOSHIBA)	0127
171030	0007
171030(SEARS)	0144
171030(TOSHIBA)	0016
171031	0007
171031(SEARS)	0144
171031(TOSHIBA)	0127
171032	0144
171032-1	2839
171033	0144
171033-1	3849
171033-1(MAGNAVOX)	1647
171033-2	3687
171033-4	3850
171033-5	OEM
171034	0127
171038	0086
171039	0050
171039(SEARS)	0050
171039(TOSHIBA)	0050
171040	0079
171040(SEARS)	0079
171040(TOSHIBA)	0079
171042	OEM
171044	0184
171044(SEARS)	0086
171044(TOSHIBA)	0079
171045	0184
171046	0076
171047	0168
171047(TOSHIBA)	0074
171048	0544
171049	0004
171052	0184
171053-1	1671
171054	0836
171057	OEM
171088-1	OEM
171090-1	0144
171091-1	OEM
171092-1	0002
171139-1	0144
171140-1	0144
171141-1	0144
171142-1	OEM
171143-1	OEM
171144-1	0127
171149-016	0139
171149-017	0133
171149-024	0139
171154	0376
171162-004	0111
171162-005	0016

DEVICE TYPE	REPL CODE
171162-006	0016
171162-008	0016
171162-009	0016
171162-026	0590
171162-027	0144
171162-039	0005
171162-042	0143
171162-072	0164
171162-073	0164
171162-074	0004
171162-075	0004
171162-076	0004
171162-080	0004
171162-081	0164
171162-082	0160
171162-083	0222
171162-086	0160
171162-089	0222
171162-090	0816
171162-095	0547
171162-100	0111
171162-108	0841
171162-113	0532
171162-118	0007
171162-119	0016
171162-120	0004
171162-121	0004
171162-124	0233
171162-125	0233
171162-126	0233
171162-128	0144
171162-129	0144
171162-130	0144
171162-131	0144
171162-132	0016
171162-143	0016
171162-161	0016
171162-162	0016
171162-163	0086
171162-164	0561
171162-169	0050
171162-172	0644
171162-180	0076
171162-186	0224
171162-187	0224
171162-188	0155
171162-190	0016
171162-191	0016
171162-192	OEM
171162-193	0126
171162-195	1357
171162-196	0133
171162-197	0133
171162-202	0076
171162-204	0547
171162-235	2005
171162-247	5374
171162-252	0015
171162-265	0555
171162-269	0143
171162-270	0143
171162-271	0133
171162-272	0012
171162-278	1136
171162-279	1136
171162-280	0284
171162-282	0030
171162-285	1212
171162-286	0076
171162-287	2035
171162-288	0111
171162-291	1597
171162-292	0012
171162-1188	0710
171174-1	1506
171174-2	3342
171174-3	0419
171175-1	1647
171175-2	1647
171179-027	2018
171179-028	2020
171179-036	0574
171179-038	OEM
171179-045	1012
171179-051	1206
171179-070	2051
171206-1	0144
171206-2	0144
171206-4	0144
171206-5	0144
171206-6	0212
171206-7	0007
171206-8	0224
171206-9	0127
171206-10	0127
171206-11	0127
171206-12	OEM
171206-13	0127
171206-14	OEM
171207-1	0144
171207-2	0144
171207-3	0127
171207-4	0321
171207-5	OEM
171207-6	OEM
171207-7	OEM
171212-2	OEM
171217-2	OEM
171217-3	0224

DEVICE TYPE	REPL CODE
171217-4	0133
171268-1	OEM
171304	1017
171305	0015
171318	0470
171319	0470
171320	0127
171338-1	0127
171338-2	0127
171338-3	0127
171369-1	OEM
171416	0015
171522	0004
171553	0376
171554	0111
171555	0006
171556	0431
171557	0076
171558	0076
171559	0151
171560	0170
171561	0015
171657	0015
171676	0111
171677	0111
171678	0111
171814	0005
171840	0133
171841	0133
171842	0157
171843	0133
171894	0030
171915	0127
171916	0004
171917	0004
171982	2568
171983	0127
171984	0030
172201	0133
172252	0574
172253	0133
172254	0030
172272	1206
172318	5284
172336	0126
172463	0042
172547	0133
172551	0015
172721	0023
172722	0133
172722(AFC)	0030
172761	0007
172762	0527
172763	0018
172816	0164
172856	0623
173078	OEM
173082	0164
173083	0164
173115	OEM
173116	3051
173117	OEM
173217	OEM
173219	0160
173331	3104
173346	OEM
173350	OEM
173357	OEM
173425	OEM
173426	OEM
173427	OEM
173428	OEM
173461	OEM
173590	OEM
173598	0975
173752	4378
173780	0127
173901	OEM
173904	OEM
173906	OEM
173928	OEM
174025	OEM
174098	OEM
174130	OEM
174160	OEM
174169	OEM
174183	OEM
174222	OEM
174223	OEM
174283	0094
174285	0094
174370	0631
174372	1954
174373	0734
174374	OEM
174375	OEM
174376	OEM
174377	OEM
174378	OEM
174381	OEM
174431	0871
174449	OEM
174450	0002
174486	OEM
174489	0133
174576	0124
174631	OEM
174632	OEM
174633	OEM

DEVICE TYPE	REPL CODE
174640	0719
174641	3439
174643	OEM
174660	OEM
174819	OEM
174858	0124
174863	0124
174994	OEM
175006-181	0050
175006-182	0050
175006-183	0050
175006-184	0050
175006-185	0050
175006-186	0004
175006-187	0144
175006-355	0030
175007-275	0016
175007-276	0016
175007-277	0086
175027-021	0016
175027-022	0085
175037	OEM
175043-023	0160
175043-058	0016
175043-059	0016
175043-060	0016
175043-062	0144
175043-063	0144
175043-064	0144
175043-065	0222
175043-066	0143
175043-068	0143
175043-069	0244
175043-081	0816
175043-81	0160
175043-100	0144
175043-107	0144
175341	0064
175342	OEM
175343	OEM
175344	0002
175382	OEM
175393	OEM
175394	OEM
175401	0144
175424	0695
175663	0016
175704	OEM
175705	OEM
175722	OEM
175886	0160
175910	4067
176144	OEM
176145	OEM
176146	OEM
176147	OEM
176148	OEM
176149	OEM
176150	OEM
176154	OEM
176155	OEM
176156	OEM
176157	OEM
176181	OEM
176222	3940
176223	3331
176224	3830
176225	0001
176226	3726
176258	0212
176296	3494
176363	0224
176383	OEM
176666	0681
176743	0142
176746	0253
176748	OEM
176751	0142
176852	OEM
176853	2929
176854	3206
176873	4312
176911	0137
176921	OEM
176925	0553
176980	0079
177092	0124
177095	OEM
177097	OEM
177098	OEM
177099	OEM
177101	OEM
177102	OEM
177105	0211
177106	6079
177107	OEM
177108	OEM
177109	OEM
177110	5486
177111	OEM
177112	2926
177113	OEM
177114	OEM
177117	OEM
177118	0062
177121	1319
177122	OEM
177189	OEM
177286	OEM

DEVICE TYPE	REPL CODE
177361-1	0111
177383	OEM
177384	OEM
177388	OEM
177389	OEM
177390	OEM
177523	0077
177547	OEM
177549	OEM
177607	OEM
177612	3220
177613	OEM
177619	2397
177773	OEM
177788	1553
177789	1514
177791	1533
177807	0025
177850	OEM
177857	3940
177901	OEM
177963	OEM
177967	OEM
177972	OEM
177976	OEM
177978	0133
178032	OEM
178063	1026
178064	0881
178200	OEM
178274	OEM
178291	OEM
178295	OEM
178296	OEM
178297	OEM
178387	OEM
178388	OEM
178389	OEM
178392	OEM
178393	OEM
178448	OEM
178452	OEM
178476	1022
178514	OEM
178515	OEM
178519	OEM
178520	OEM
178525	0133
178526	0527
178541	OEM
178576	OEM
178577	OEM
178581	0292
178626	0064
178627	0790
178628	6198
178629	0023
178630	0023
178631	0023
178632	0700
178633	0695
178634	0023
178635	0052
178636	0049
178637	0031
178638	0181
178639	1864
178640	0999
178641	0077
178642	1337
178643	1337
178644	0755
178645	0137
178646	0041
178647	0127
178648	0076
178649	0148
178650	2882
178651	0018
178653	2047
178654	0945
178655	0148
178656	0638
178660	0095
178690	2845
178692	2031
178693	2180
178694	3206
178695	2641
178696	0594
178697	4843
178737	2248
178738	1197
178739	0798
178740	1623
178741	0356
178742	4246
178743	1618
178744	1230
178745	1288
178746	1022
178901	OEM
179047	OEM
179123	OEM
179320	OEM
179473	OEM
179509	OEM
179547	OEM
179603	0151

DEVICE TYPE	REPL CODE
179627	OEM
179726	3127
179728	OEM
179729	OEM
179730	OEM
179732	OEM
179733	OEM
179734	OEM
179737	OEM
179740	1722
179741	1741
179743	3326
179744	OEM
179751	0916
179862	OEM
179866	OEM
179868	OEM
179890	OEM
179901	OEM
179925	OEM
180010-001	1686
180020	0814
180057	OEM
180060	1796
180113	OEM
180137	1533
180197	0124
180198	0489
180199	0626
180200	3249
180201	0151
180211	OEM
180212	OEM
180213	OEM
180214	0617
180215	5096
180217	1689
180218	0006
180219	0148
180221	0140
180223	OEM
180242	OEM
180323	1954
180330	OEM
180338	0644
180518	OEM
180519	OEM
180520	OEM
180528	OEM
180530	OEM
180533	OEM
180545	OEM
180546	OEM
180547	OEM
180548	OEM
180549	OEM
180550	OEM
180551	OEM
180552	OEM
180554	OEM
180555	OEM
180556	OEM
180557	OEM
180558	OEM
180559	OEM
180560	OEM
180570	0124
180617	0015
180762	OEM
180763	OEM
180764	OEM
180765	OEM
180766	OEM
180767	OEM
180768	OEM
180769	OEM
180770	OEM
180771	OEM
180772	OEM
180773	OEM
180774	OEM
180775	OEM
180776	OEM
180777	OEM
180778	OEM
180780	OEM
180781	OEM
180783	OEM
180784	OEM
180785	OEM
180786	OEM
180787	OEM
180788	OEM
180789	OEM
180817	OEM
180831	OEM
180851	OEM
180872	OEM
180873	6206
180876	OEM
180877	OEM
180878	OEM
180880	OEM
180881	OEM
180884	OEM
180885	OEM
180887	6403
180889	OEM
180892	OEM

If replacement code is OEM, contact original manufacturer for replacement.

DEVICE TYPE	REPL CODE
180893	2307
180894	5991
180895	0195
180896	0582
180961	OEM
180968	OEM
181003-7	0144
181003-8	0144
181003-9	0144
181012	0111
181015	0037
181018	OEM
181023	0016
181030	0037
181034	0037
181038	0486
181039	0050
181039(IC)	OEM
181040	OEM
181073	0133
181151	OEM
181165	OEM
181178	0195
181181	OEM
181183	0624
181214	0016
181239	OEM
181256	OEM
181257	OEM
181281	OEM
181282	OEM
181283	OEM
181284	OEM
181285	OEM
181286	OEM
181287	OEM
181291	OEM
181292	OEM
181295	OEM
181296	OEM
181297	OEM
181298	OEM
181299	OEM
181300	OEM
181311	OEM
181312	OEM
181314	OEM
181315	5109
181316	OEM
181317	OEM
181324	OEM
181325	OEM
181326	OEM
181327	OEM
181328	OEM
181329	OEM
181330	OEM
181331	OEM
181335	OEM
181336	OEM
181337	OEM
181338	OEM
181362	OEM
181363	OEM
181440	OEM
181465	OEM
181466	OEM
181467	OEM
181468	OEM
181475	OEM
181476	OEM
181477	OEM
181478	OEM
181479	OEM
181498	OEM
181503-6	0144
181503-7	0144
181503-9	0144
181504-1	0144
181504-2	0016
181504-7	0144
181506	OEM
181506-7	0144
181507	OEM
181515-4	0086
181515-6	0086
181515-7	0086
181515-9	0086
181516	OEM
181519	1266
181520	0292
181522	0873
181523	OEM
181524	OEM
181526	0133
181530	1731
181533	0698
181553	OEM
181615	OEM
181616	OEM
181619	0124
181654	OEM
181655	OEM
181681	0133
181765	OEM
181772	OEM
181773	OEM
181774	OEM
181775	OEM

DEVICE TYPE	REPL CODE
181778	OEM
181779	OEM
181780	OEM
181795	OEM
181797	OEM
181826	OEM
181827	OEM
181828	OEM
181829	OEM
181836	OEM
181860	0101
181874	OEM
181876	OEM
181910	OEM
181911	OEM
181912	OEM
181913	OEM
181914	OEM
181915	OEM
181917	OEM
181931	OEM
181940	OEM
181959	OEM
181966	0292
181991	OEM
181993	OEM
182027	OEM
182028	OEM
182029	OEM
182030	OEM
182031	OEM
182032	OEM
182033	OEM
182034	OEM
182035	OEM
182036	OEM
182037	OEM
182038	OEM
182040	OEM
182041	OEM
182042	OEM
182072	OEM
182073	OEM
182075	OEM
182076	OEM
182100	OEM
182101	OEM
182107	OEM
182115	OEM
182267	OEM
182268	OEM
182301	OEM
182302	OEM
182304	0023
182323	OEM
182324	OEM
182325	OEM
182349	OEM
182350	OEM
182352	OEM
182353	OEM
182354	OEM
182355	OEM
182356	OEM
182357	OEM
182358	OEM
182406	OEM
182407	OEM
182444	OEM
182503	3670
182510	0990
182603	OEM
182604	OEM
182605	OEM
182606	OEM
182607	OEM
182610	OEM
182611	OEM
182612	OEM
182613	OEM
182739	OEM
182753	OEM
182754	OEM
182755	OEM
182756	OEM
182757	1722
182758	OEM
182759	OEM
182760	OEM
182761	OEM
182762	OEM
182763	OEM
182764	OEM
182825	OEM
182827	0041
182838	1386
182898	OEM
182919	OEM
183013	0649
183014	0696
183015	0127
183016	0127
183017	0079
183018	0127
183019	0127
183030	0079
183031	0079
183032	0037

DEVICE TYPE	REPL CODE
183033	0133
183034	0218
183035	1233
183044	2535
183045	OEM
183046	OEM
183050	OEM
183051	OEM
183052	0165
183053	OEM
183056	OEM
183071	OEM
183072	OEM
183073	OEM
183074	1338
183086	OEM
183087	OEM
183096	OEM
183097	OEM
183098	OEM
183104	OEM
183107	2678
183189	OEM
183405	2535
183532	0406
183896	3954
183898	2083
184073	0640
184074	5584
184078	6669
184086	3703
184087	0897
184093	6671
184106	0041
184574	OEM
184576	OEM
184577	OEM
184578	OEM
184579	OEM
184580	OEM
184581	OEM
184582	OEM
184583	OEM
184585	OEM
184586	OEM
184589	OEM
184591	OEM
184592	OEM
184593	OEM
184615	OEM
184627	OEM
184631	OEM
184632	OEM
184633	OEM
184638	OEM
184640	OEM
184642	OEM
184643	OEM
184644	OEM
184753	OEM
184757	OEM
184779	OEM
184798	0124
184812	OEM
184830	1017
184918	OEM
184920	OEM
184921	OEM
184922	OEM
184929	0242
184985	OEM
185001	OEM
185022	0102
185095	OEM
185104	OEM
185105	OEM
185107	OEM
185118	OEM
185147	OEM
185200	2678
185202	0023
185206	0023
185207	4042
185231	4078
185233	0101
185236	0079
185237	1864
185335	0124
185411	0133
185436	0102
185628	0511
185704	0015
185878	2496
185879	0071
185880	0023
185881	1404
185882	0064
185883	0140
185884	0253
185885	0005
185895	3765
185896	1977
185897	4284
185898	1319
185899	4955
185900	3680
185901	5136
185915	0076
185916	0127

DEVICE TYPE	REPL CODE
185917	0006
185918	1553
185919	1505
185920	0723
185921	1779
185922	1298
185923	0076
186001	OEM
186050	OEM
186065	OEM
186070	OEM
186112	OEM
186311	OEM
186342A	0086
186383	OEM
186404	0901
186499	5556
186512	0892
186544	0279
186545	0279
186584	0892
186599	OEM
186600	OEM
186610	0037
186611	0279
186642	0079
186645	0079
186648	0041
186650	OEM
186659	0004
186660	4067
186670	OEM
186671	1319
186687	OEM
186703	OEM
186741	0279
186742	0031
186773	0330
186797	3426
186801	0013
187064	OEM
187217	0037
187218	0016
187267	0790
187278	OEM
187553	OEM
187583	2058
187628	OEM
187640	OEM
187659	0881
187660	1026
187749	0826
187774	OEM
187775	OEM
187784	OEM
187901	OEM
187963	OEM
188056	0124
188086	0727
188158	OEM
188165	0103
188180	0037
188211	OEM
188226	0126
188232	0002
188233	0062
188234	0023
188235	0091
188236	0023
188237	0158
188238	0071
188240	0032
188241	0257
188242	3871
188243	4349
188244	4281
188245	0050
188246	4066
188271	1154
188272	0275
188273	0168
188274	3574
188400-34	0720
188551	2926
188660-01	0406
188960	0050
188961	0050
188962	0050
188963	0050
188964	0023
188965	0023
188966	0050
188972	0050
188973	0750
189123	OEM
189124	OEM
189148	OEM
189149	OEM
189150	OEM
189151	OEM
189152	1022
189153	OEM
189154	OEM
189155	OEM
189309	OEM
189310	OEM
189311	OEM
189312	OEM
189313	OEM

DEVICE TYPE	REPL CODE
189314	OEM
189315	OEM
189316	OEM
189319	OEM
189322	OEM
189327	OEM
189328	OEM
189330	OEM
189333	OEM
189424	OEM
189852	OEM
189853	OEM
189972	OEM
189988	OEM
189998	0126
189999	OEM
190206	1082
190208	0064
190224	0112
190227	OEM
190233	OEM
190253	OEM
190277	OEM
190404	0170
190425	0160
190425A	0160
190426	2235
190427	0050
190428	0016
190429	2022
190482	OEM
190483	2116
190484	OEM
190486	0150
190540	OEM
190681	0062
190692	OEM
190714	0007
190715	0016
190716	0143
190718	OEM
190719	OEM
190724	0486
190994	1722
191142	2116
191205	OEM
191208	OEM
191290	OEM
191291	OEM
191292	OEM
191293	OEM
191294	OEM
191295	OEM
191296	0624
191297	0619
191298	OEM
191299	0619
191300	0042
191313	OEM
191316	OEM
191318	OEM
191319	OEM
191328	OEM
191387	OEM
191407	0720
191490	OEM
191491	OEM
191556	OEM
191726	OEM
191729	OEM
191747	OEM
191862	0495
191868	0356
191869	0624
191870	0720
191985	0621
191986	0621
191989	0621
192027	0057
192062	2650
192063	2650
192064	2650
192066	2810
192067	OEM
192068	2810
192069	2810
192105	0736
192113	OEM
192135	OEM
192144	OEM
192229	0012
192271	0361
192272	OEM
192276	3355
192277	OEM
192285	0330
192339	OEM
192344	OEM
192351	OEM
192448	OEM
192450	OEM
192544	OEM
192681	1731
192689	0617
192696	OEM
192702	OEM
192703	OEM
192742	2929
192743	OEM

DEVICE TYPE	REPL CODE
192782	OEM
192789	OEM
192828	OEM
192848	0057
192849	OEM
192902	OEM
192903	OEM
192904	OEM
192909	0284
192963	OEM
192965	0079
193022	0461
193057	1205
193058	1376
193082	3206
193083	OEM
193084	OEM
193159	0490
193207	0406
193228	OEM
193230	OEM
193309	3765
193333	3776
193625	OEM
193626	OEM
193717	0133
193832	0719
194086-3	0841
194168	OEM
194169	OEM
194170	OEM
194171	OEM
194172	OEM
194188	OEM
194189	OEM
194222	OEM
194223	OEM
194225	OEM
194226	OEM
194233	OEM
194234	OEM
194239	OEM
194241	OEM
194243	0086
194244	OEM
194285	0330
194305	0619
194320	OEM
194474-8	0160
194561	0023
194765	OEM
194899	OEM
194907	0919
194917	0023
194929	OEM
195040	OEM
195143	OEM
195288	OEM
195319	0071
195320	0124
195322	OEM
195323	OEM
195336	1779
195478	0077
195492	OEM
195494	OEM
195495	OEM
195496	OEM
195510	0013
195511	0097
195601-6	0004
195606	0765
195617	0123
195648-6	0015
195703	0541
195736	OEM
195768	OEM
195791	4340
195827	OEM
195841	OEM
195857	OEM
195877	OEM
195880	0292
195881	0292
195885	OEM
195889	OEM
195927	2801
195928	4018
195946	OEM
195955	OEM
196000	OEM
196002	OEM
196023-1	0016
196023-2	0016
196058-4	0160
196062	0124
196064-3	0004
196117	0076
196121	1251
196122	4009
196129	OEM
196148-0	0160
196176	2078
196183-5	0160
196183-7	0004
196184-3	0015
196187	4416
196188	4417
196189	OEM

DEVICE TYPE	REPL CODE
196190	OEM
196192	1672
196193	OEM
196200	2058
196201	3882
196211	OEM
196212	OEM
196220	OEM
196221	0911
196259-4	0015
196296	OEM
196317	OEM
196330	OEM
196331	4444
196333	4067
196337	OEM
196374	1566
196388	OEM
196392	0079
196393	0126
196414	4457
196432	1772
196436	OEM
196496	0733
196501-7	0160
196511	OEM
196512	OEM
196514	OEM
196515	OEM
196516	0733
196517	1203
196582	OEM
196584	OEM
196597	0071
196598	1722
196607-9	0160
196634	0680
196639	1248
196779-9	0086
196779-9-1	0086
196780-1	0086
196961	OEM
197323	1636
197372	0124
197374	0062
197376	0587
197381	3259
197464	0124
197591	1981
197646	OEM
197648	OEM
197666	0081
197713	OEM
197878	OEM
197890	OEM
197935	0826
197936	OEM
198003-1	0016
198003-2	0016
198005-1	0693
198007-3	0016
198010-1	0136
198013-P1	0016
198014-1	0086
198020-1	0086
198020-2	0086
198020-3	0086
198023-1	0016
198023-2	0086
198023-3	0016
198023-4	0016
198023-5	0016
198024	0037
198030	0016
198030-2	0016
198030-3	0016
198030-4	0016
198030-6	0016
198030-7	0016
198031-1	0016
198031-2	0016
198034-1	0103
198034-2	0103
198034-3	0103
198034-4	0103
198034-5	0103
198035-1	0086
198035-3	0086
198036-1	0037
198038-1	0178
198038-3	0178
198038-4	0178
198039-0507	0103
198039-1	0178
198039-3	0178
198039-6	0103
198039-7	0103
198039-501	0178
198039-503	0178
198039-506	0103
198039-507	0103
198042-2	0016
198042-3	0016
198045-4	0086
198047-1	0086
198047-2	0086
198047-3	0086
198047-5	0086
198047-6	0086

If replacement code is OEM, contact original manufacturer for replacement. 225

DEVICE TYPE	REPL CODE
198048-1	0086
198048-2	0086
198049-1	0178
198050	0037
198051-1	0016
198051-2	0016
198051-3	0016
198051-4	0016
198063-1	0919
198064-1	0130
198065-1	0126
198065-3	0126
198067-1	0016
198072-1	0086
198074-1	0126
198075-1	0168
198077-1	0086
198078-1	0126
198079-1	0130
198079-2	0103
198400	1291
198409-1	1833
198409-5	0033
198409-6	1035
198409-11	0141
198409-12	0557
198409-13	1812
198409-14	1820
198410-1	1291
198581-1	0016
198581-2	0016
198581-3	0016
198589	0124
198590	5058
198591	OEM
198592	OEM
198593	OEM
198594	OEM
198595	OEM
198596	OEM
198597	0015
198598	OEM
198599	0790
198600	OEM
198601	OEM
198602	OEM
198603	0292
198606	OEM
198607	OEM
198609	4644
198743	0079
198744	OEM
198745	0037
198746	0079
198747	0037
198748	0320
198749	0037
198750	0111
198751	0434
198752	OEM
198763	0710
198763-1	0084
198763-2	0529
198763-3	0097
198763-4	0760
198763-5	0097
198763-6	0760
198763-7	0097
198763-8	0760
198763-9	0105
198763-10	0772
198763-11	0109
198763-12	0533
198763-13	0116
198763-14	0796
198763-15	0122
198763-16	0810
198764-5	1116
198764-6	1099
198764-13	0315
198765-1	3160
198765-2	1620
198765-3	2873
198765-4	0254
198765-5	1116
198765-6	1099
198765-7	1118
198765-8	1103
198765-9	0800
198765-10	0258
198765-11	1186
198765-12	1634
198765-13	0315
198765-14	0267
198766-1	0759
198766-2	0759
198766-3	0759
198766-5	0759
198766-7	0759
198766-8	0759
198773-1	0124
198774	0248
198775-1	0124
198776-1	0124
198779-1	0124
198785	0124
198785-1	0124
198785-2	0124
198794	OEM

DEVICE TYPE	REPL CODE
198794-1	0595
198799-4	0124
198800-1	0411
198801-1	2673
198802	0720
198809-1	0133
198810-1	0124
198813-1	0124
198816	1403
198818	0411
198936-2	0147
199596	0133
199662	0193
199807	0855
199919	0287
199985	0015
200028-7-28	0004
200062-5-31	0004
200062-5-32	0004
200062-5-33	0004
200062-5-34	0004
200062-5-36	0015
200062-6-32	0015
200064-6-103	0144
200064-6-104	0050
200064-6-105	0144
200064-6-106	0050
200064-6-107	0079
200064-6-108	0004
200064-6-109	0969
200064-6-110	0969
200064-6-111	0004
200064-6-115	0015
200064-6-119	0015
200064-6-120	0015
200067	0037
200076	0016
200137	3473
200155	OEM
200156	OEM
200157	0137
200158	OEM
200165	3468
200167	5333
200168	OEM
200200	0111
200200-700	0111
200208	0030
200220	0037
200251-5377	0016
200252	0086
200259-700	0899
200419	OEM
200420	2093
200433	0037
200471	OEM
200472	OEM
200553	OEM
200554	OEM
200555	OEM
200556	OEM
200557	OEM
200558	OEM
200566	OEM
200567	OEM
200574	OEM
200648-26	0143
200781-702	0142
200838	5183
201034	0142
201133	OEM
201146	OEM
201963	0674
202048	OEM
202055	0217
202066	OEM
202315	0143
202315(THOMAS)	0133
202463	0015
202609-0713	0016
202617	1211
202862-518	0124
202862-947	0016
202907-047P1	0016
202909-577	0037
202909-587	0037
202909-827	0103
202911-737	0037
202913-057	0086
202914-010	1812
202914-010/250-060	0081
202914-010/250-070	1168
202914-010/250-100	1820
202914-020	0141
202914-030	0557
202914-040	1035
202914-050	0033
202914-417	0016
202915-627	0016
202917-137	0126
202920-150	0974
202922-237	0016
202922-280	3677
202925-047	0486
203364	0037
203718	0126
203743	2860
203751	1624
203780	3859

DEVICE TYPE	REPL CODE
203781	1316
203793	OEM
203811	OEM
204117	0076
204201-001	0086
204210-002	0016
204211-001	0103
204280	OEM
204290	OEM
204292	1701
204969	0016
205032	0037
205048	0037
205049	0037
205367	0037
205702	0050
205782-97	0079
205782-103	0079
205919	5985
206017	OEM
206038	OEM
206049	OEM
206050	0895
206180	0242
206185	0242
206190	0242
206395	OEM
206617	0133
206730	OEM
206889	0097
207119	0142
207125	0283
207417	0683
207484	1534
207826	OEM
207827	2679
207828	OEM
207831	OEM
207871	2213
207878	1544
207887	OEM
207890	0119
208434	3870
209185-962	0160
209417-0714	0144
209919	0072
210074	0016
210076	0037
210226	OEM
210227	OEM
210236	0079
210533	OEM
210543	OEM
210548	OEM
210646	OEM
210783	OEM
210786	OEM
211040-1	0130
211083	0124
212465	OEM
212717	1136
213217	1212
214105	0015
214396	0160
215002	0050
215008	0050
215031	0050
215038	0050
215053	0164
215071	0816
215072	0016
215074	0198
215075	0086
215081	0079
215089	0222
215487	OEM
215488	OEM
215489	OEM
215490	OEM
215491	OEM
215495	OEM
215496	OEM
215524	OEM
215525	OEM
215526	OEM
215527	OEM
215528	OEM
215529	OEM
215530	OEM
215531	4314
215532	OEM
215533	OEM
215534	OEM
215669	0015
215861	OEM
216001	0143
216003	0123
216014	0015
216020	0015
216024	0244
216099	OEM
216434	OEM
216435	OEM
216445-2	0016
216449	0015
216817	0015
216986	0160
217119	0435
217230	0435

DEVICE TYPE	REPL CODE
217306	OEM
217309	OEM
217320	OEM
217321	OEM
217654	OEM
217657	OEM
217658	OEM
217892	0160
218012DS	0085
218398	OEM
218401	OEM
218402	OEM
218403	OEM
218502	0004
218503	0004
218511	0086
218537	0126
218612	0015
219016	0595
219245	0229
219301	0160
219361	0160
219412	OEM
219440	0160
219832	OEM
219935	0015
219940	0160
220114	OEM
220536	OEM
220637	OEM
220638	OEM
220673	0455
220674	0079
220675	2375
221128	0015
221158	0086
221600	0016
221601	0595
221602	0160
221605	0160
221856	0136
221857	0016
221897	0016
221918	0016
221924	0595
221940	0160
221941	0160
222131	0016
222509	0004
222611	0015
222867	0071
222915	0160
223083	OEM
223124	0004
223215	0015
223216	0015
223323	0015
223357	0071
223358	0015
223365	0160
223366	0004
223367	0595
223368	0595
223369	0050
223370	0595
223371	0004
223372	0279
223462	0015
223467	0015
223473	0279
223474	0050
223475	0279
223482	0208
223483	0004
223484	0004
223485	0004
223486	0004
223487	0136
223489	0229
223490	0160
223576	0160
223684	0595
223720	0229
223724	0015
223753	0015
223810	0004
224159	0015
224503	0160
224506	0016
224584	0279
224586	0050
224587	0050
224597	0015
224696	0004
224774	0015
224780	0137
224820	0208
224857	0004
224873	0160
225200	0015
225265	0315
225267	0229
225300	0208
225301	0157
225311	0050
225316	0157
225410	0143
225592	0015
225593	0004

DEVICE TYPE	REPL CODE
225594	0050
225594A	0136
225595	0160
225596	0160
225600	0050
225925	0160
225927	0160
226058	0015
226181	0279
226182	0015
226237	0015
226334	0143
226338	0279
226344	0143
226441	0595
226517	3017
226546	0015
226634	0160
226788	0015
226789	0435
226791	0208
226922	0071
226924	0004
226999	0160
227000	0144
227015	0229
227348	0015
227517	0364
227565	0015
227566	0160
227567	OEM
227675	0122
227676	0315
227720	0015
227724	0122
227744	0015
227752	0279
227801	0122
227804	0160
227917	0004
228007	0170
228229	0160
228230	0160
228287	0004
228417	0151
228558	0160
228560	0071
229017	0364
229042	0122
229045	0435
229088	0315
229133	0050
229392	0144
229522	0015
229805	0087
230084	0178
230199-4	2949
230208	0160
230209	0595
230214	0086
230218	0015
230225-2	3381
230233	0086
230253	0004
230256	0595
230259	0004
230523	0160
230524	0004
230525	0004
230756	0315
230768	0759
230773	0122
231017	0155
231140-01	0144
231140-04	0969
231140-07	0144
231140-09	0969
231140-11	0160
231140-15	0016
231140-21	0004
231140-23	0144
231140-26	0969
231140-28	0233
231140-31	0144
231140-33	0160
231140-34	0144
231140-36	0007
231140-37	0007
231140-43	0007
231140-44	0144
231140-45	0208
231150	0015
231161	0248
231339	0015
231374	0016
231375	0086
231378	0103
231588	0279
231665	0015
231669	0015
231672	0160
231706	0004
231797	0160
231923	0015
232017	0076
232021	0055
232194	0160
232203	0015
232268	0178

DEVICE TYPE	REPL CODE
232359	0103
232359A	0103
232519	0122
232520	0315
232674	0160
232675	0160
232676	0050
232678	0016
232680	0050
232681	0136
232840	0144
232841	0086
232949	0595
233011	0015
233025	0102
233117	0155
233150	0002
233305	0435
233307	0435
233507	0279
233508	0435
233509	0160
233561	0015
233597	0015
233735	0086
233944	0086
233945	0279
233969	0126
234015	0050
234024	0086
234076	0004
234077	0160
234078	0435
234178	0160
234552	0015
234553	0071
234565	0015
234566	0160
234611	0015
234612	0016
234630	0004
234631	0050
234758	0016
234761	0015
234763	0016
235157	0122
235192	0016
235194	0004
235200	0050
235205	0016
235206	0016
235299	0315
235312	0160
235313	0015
235382	0071
235541	0087
235543	0015
235546	0015
235997	0074
236039	0007
236251	0144
236265	0595
236266	0012
236282	0233
236285	0016
236286	0016
236287	0086
236288	0969
236433	0126
236706	0144
236709	0004
236854	0130
236907	0144
236935	0160
237020	0144
237021	0144
237024	0144
237025	0016
237026	0144
237028	1390
237070	0087
237075	0334
237223	0016
237227	0015
237421	0087
237450	0142
237452	0160
237453	0015
237509	0315
237785	0144
237840	0144
237929	0015
238368	0016
238417	0004
238418	0004
239097	0087
239219	0644
239221	0015
239429	0071
239517	0042
239612	0086
239713	0130
239917	0833
239970	0016
240003	0004
240006	0004
240055	0087
240076	0087
240077	0315

DEVICE TYPE	REPL CODE
240388	0142
240401	0016
240402	0126
240403	0969
240404	0074
240456	0015
240564	0133
240594	0015
240603	0015
241052	0126
241184	0030
241249	0144
241295	0071
241302	0071
241420	0315
241517	0006
241657	0103
241778	0144
241960	0144
242029	0015
242141	0071
242183	0160
242221	0004
242226	0015
242422	0126
242460	0126
242590	0144
242758	0016
242759	0016
242838	0160
242958	0126
242960	0144
243115	0087
243168	0969
243215	0435
243318	0144
243364	0015
243645	0144
243815	0435
243837	0208
243843	1403
243939	0004
244007	0279
244357	0142
244817	0364
245078-3	0144
245117	0165
245217	0057
245489	OEM
245517	0143
245568-2	0841
245917	1935
248017	0018
248717	2684
248817	0133
248917	0080
249217	0080
249508-3	0133
249588	0136
250031	OEM
250032	0296
250062	OEM
250066	OEM
250400	0208
251026	0319
251026-01	1404
251026-02	1194
251026-03	1194
251104-04	OEM
251527-01	OEM
251527-03	OEM
251535-01	OEM
251535-02	OEM
251536-01	OEM
251536-02	OEM
251538-02	OEM
251640-03	OEM
251641-02	OEM
251715-01	OEM
251819-07	0133
251819-16	0124
251828-01	OEM
251828-03	OEM
251829-01	OEM
251853-02	OEM
251871-01	OEM
251913-01	OEM
251968-03	OEM
252034-02	OEM
252308-01	OEM
252333-02	OEM
252371-03	OEM
252372-01	OEM
252817	0023
253704	0435
255728	0004
255903	0315
256068	0160
256071	0160
256122	0315
256126	0279
256127	0595
256217	0151
256317	0006
256319	0006
256417	0151
256480	0435
256517	0224
256617	0113

226

If replacement code is OEM, contact original manufacturer for replacement.

DEVICE TYPE	REPL CODE
256717	0030
256728	0315
256729	0122
256730	0315
256817	0076
256917	0076
257017	0151
257242	0435
257243	0435
257340	0004
257341	0160
257385	0595
257403	0160
257470	0279
257473	0004
257534	0435
257536	0160
257540	0144
258017	0410
258882	0015
258884	0315
258990	0160
258993	0595
259315	0015
259368	0015
259878	0015
260116-699	OEM
260429	0015
260468	0595
260565	0144
261401	0435
261463	0015
261488	0435
261586	0050
261596	0015
261898	0015
261970	0160
261975	0015
262066	0016
262111	0170
262112	0015
262113	0004
262114	0160
262116	0178
262309	0435
262310	0315
262370	0160
262546	0170
262638	0126
262648	0122
262872	0015
263424	0170
263561	0142
263807	0122
263856	0160
263857	0142
265074	0144
265115	0315
265164	0015
265217	0139
265235	0015
265236	0229
265240	0016
265241	0144
265634	0015
265771	0050
266583	0229
266685	0016
266686	0004
266702	0279
267272	0436
267791	0103
267797	0144
267878	0130
267898	0016
267899	0016
268717	0688
269367	0208
269374	0004
270642	0071
270744	0160
270745	0160
270746	0160
270779	0122
270780	0160
270781	0595
270785	0160
270786	0759
275131	0016
275612	0160
275831	0071
275845	0969
276097	0015
276160	0086
276331	0016
276413	0086
276415	0086
279317	0208
279417	0079
279517	0042
279617	1581
279717	0930
279817	0553
279917	0151
280017	0124
280117	0139
280217	0071
280317	0012
280417	0005

DEVICE TYPE	REPL CODE
281917	0644
282217	2766
282317	0155
282601	0015
290458LGD	0079
291509	0130
293118	1675
297065C03	0050
297074C11	0126
297240-1	0004
300233	0015
300312	0315
300315	0015
300486	0595
300524	0015
300532	0122
300536	0595
300538	0004
300540	0004
300541	0004
300542	0595
300550	0015
300732	0170
300733	0315
300735	0122
300774	0595
301586	0015
301591	0016
301606	0086
302342	0016
304581B	0016
309004	0718
309316-01	OEM
309412	0160
309421	0004
309504	1403
310017	0004
310030	0050
310035	0004
310132	0050
310157	0628
310158	0628
310159	0004
310160	0004
310162	0050
310201	0164
310204	0050
310221	0050
310223	0136
310224	0004
310225	0004
310254	0462
310389-01	OEM
310651-01	OEM
310654-02	OEM
310654-03	OEM
310654-05	OEM
312558-01	OEM
312558-02	OEM
314849-01	OEM
314858-01	OEM
315009-01	OEM
315012-01	OEM
315014-01	OEM
315014-04	OEM
315020-01	OEM
315092-01	OEM
315093-01	OEM
317053-01	OEM
317054-01	OEM
317093	2857
317208	0137
318004-01	OEM
318004-03	OEM
318005-01	OEM
318005-03	OEM
318005-04	OEM
318006-01	OEM
318011-03	OEM
318012-01	OEM
318013-01	OEM
318018-02	OEM
318018-04	OEM
318019-02	OEM
318019-04	OEM
318020-03	OEM
318020-05	OEM
318022-02	OEM
318023-02	OEM
318087-01	OEM
318091-01	OEM
320007	0143
321119-901-020	OEM
322968-17	0004
322968-140	0160
322968-141	0969
322968-167	0004
325302-01	OEM
325341-08	OEM
325502-01	6041
325502-03	1887
325505-01	0296
325505-02	0372
325506-01	0041
325572-01	OEM
326830	1812
326832	1035
326833	2086
326836	1820

DEVICE TYPE	REPL CODE
326844	0033
326845	0081
326846	0141
326852	0329
326853	0354
326862	0557
329814	0081
330003	0015
330018	0015
330019	0015
331378	1035
336637-20	3384
336638-21	OEM
339002	0677
339003	0680
339009	0554
339300	0232
339300-2	0232
339486	1358
339868	0264
340085DC	OEM
340085DM	OEM
340085FC	OEM
340085FM	OEM
340085PC	3415
340097PC	4367
340098PC	0427
340160PC	1349
340161PC	1363
340162PC	1378
340163PC	1397
340174DC	1542
340174DM	1542
340174FC	OEM
340174FM	OEM
340174PC	1542
340175DC	1520
340175DM	1520
340175FC	OEM
340175FM	OEM
340175PC	1520
340192PC	1753
340193PC	1765
340194DC	1758
340194DM	1758
340194FC	OEM
340194FM	OEM
340194PC	1758
340195DC	1773
340195DM	1773
340195FC	OEM
340195FM	OEM
340195PC	1773
341181	0079
346015-15	0144
346015-16	0144
346015-17	0144
346015-18	0144
346015-19	0144
346015-20	0144
346015-21	0144
346015-22	0144
346015-23	0086
346015-24	0016
346015-25	0144
346015-30	0086
346015-37	0144
346016-1	0004
346016-11	0004
346016-14	0016
346016-16	0086
346016-17	0086
346016-18	0016
346016-19	0016
346016-25	0016
346016-26	0016
346016-27	0086
346016-63	0334
348048-2	0015
348053-3	0015
348054-1	0015
348054-2	0015
348054-5	0015
348054-6	0229
348054-7	0071
348054-9	0015
348054-10	0015
348054-11	0229
348054-14	0229
348054-15	0071
348055-2	0015
348055-3	0015
348057-8	0071
348057-9	0071
348057-17	0157
348058-2	0071
350171-1002	0015
361317-1	0123
373003	0004
373117	0004
373119	0004
373401-1	0232
373404-1	0357
373405-1	0507
373406-1	0692
373407-1	0867
373408-1	1018
373409-1	1303
373410-1	1358

DEVICE TYPE	REPL CODE
373411-1	1394
373412-1	0117
373413-1	1675
373414-1	1150
373423-1	0487
373424-1	1417
373427-1	1199
373428-1	1705
373429-1	1197
373708-1	1809
373712-1	0828
373713-1	1423
373714-1	1177
373714-2	1193
373715-1	1160
373716-1	1564
373718-1	0564
373721-1	1329
374109-1	0462
374110-1	1265
380049	0461
380205-01	OEM
380259-01	OEM
390059-01	OEM
390089-01	OEM
390302-01	OEM
390303-01	OEM
390304-01	OEM
390308-01	OEM
390309-02	OEM
390317-01	OEM
390318-01	OEM
390319-01	OEM
390341-01	OEM
400931	1168
401003-001-0	0037
401113-1	0141
401113-2	1812
401113-3	1035
401113-4	0081
401113-5	0557
401182	2067
405919-35AD	0122
405919-45AD	0810
405965-30A	0599
405965-35A	0126
410221(RCA)	1702
414020	OEM
424863	0124
433836	0016
437476	0042
442077	0873
442079	0053
442085	0041
443070	0527
452077	0321
454549	0279
454760	0050
455947	0101
463984-1	1018
464010	0015
464070	0015
475018	0242
476171-18	0102
480235A57	0137
480235AS7	OEM
485752-090	0911
489043A06	0006
489751-001	0143
489751-020	0911
489751-025	0079
489751-026	0079
489751-027	0144
489751-028	0037
489751-029	0079
489751-030	0079
489751-031	0037
489751-032	0919
489751-033	0042
489751-037	0086
489751-038	0086
489751-039	0007
489751-040	0016
489751-041	0016
489751-042	0037
489751-043	0142
489751-044	0042
489751-045	0004
489751-047	0007
489751-048	0127
489751-049	0127
489751-052	0127
489751-058	0127
489751-097	0037
489751-107	0016
489751-108	0004
489751-109	0004
489751-113	0004
489751-114	0004
489751-115	0969
489751-119	0103
489751-120	0127
489751-121	0007
489751-122	0016
489751-123	0079
489751-124	0037
489751-125	0016
489751-127	0007
489751-128	0007

DEVICE TYPE	REPL CODE
489751-129	0086
489751-130	0037
489751-131	0144
489751-137	0144
489751-143	0144
489751-144	0086
489751-145	0144
489751-146	0037
489751-147	0144
489751-148	0144
489751-162	0144
489751-163	0222
489751-164	0079
489751-165	0144
489751-166	0016
489751-167	0144
489751-168	0144
489751-169	0144
489751-171	0144
489751-172	0079
489751-173	0127
489751-174	0178
489751-175	0523
489751-206	0144
489751-208	0321
489752-001	0143
489752-003	0143
489752-004	0907
489752-005	0015
489752-08	0143
489752-013	0015
489752-014	0015
489752-015	0015
489752-016	0102
489752-017	0479
489752-020	0911
489752-022	0015
489752-025	0015
489752-026	0102
489752-027	0015
489752-028	0015
489752-029	0087
489752-031	0143
489752-035	0015
489752-036	0123
489752-037	0015
489752-038	0276
489752-040	0170
489752-041	0002
489752-042	0143
489752-043	0015
489752-044	0196
489752-045	0137
489752-049	0143
489752-050	0015
489752-051	0015
489752-052	0911
489752-053	OEM
489752-054	0286
489752-066	0015
489752-072	0469
489752-073	0015
489752-088	0030
489752-089	0911
489752-090	0911
489752-091	0313
489752-092	0015
489752-094	0015
489752-095	0007
489752-096	0102
489752-097	0015
489752-108	0015
489752-109	0170
489752-123	0015
489752-124	0162
489752-125	0123
489752-127	0030
489752-169	0030
489765-005	0196
489850-004	0143
500001	0123
500003	0071
500009G	0143
500859	0015
500904	OEM
501010	0015
501152	0015
501170	OEM
501193	OEM
501343	OEM
501697	OEM
501783	OEM
502382	OEM
502394	OEM
502395	OEM
502616	OEM
502617	OEM
502754	OEM
502823	OEM
502824	OEM
503146-1	0907
504720	0133
504833	0575
505254	2598
505287	0086
506911	0242
508590	0357
510007	0004
511534S	0123

DEVICE TYPE	REPL CODE
511994-4	OEM
512021	OEM
513031S	2534
514023	0079
514045	0127
514067S	0126
514068S	0786
514072S	0126
515039S	0086
515041S	0364
515043S	0079
515045S	0079
516009S	0321
518005(0)	OEM
518022S	1469
520120-1001	OEM
530015-2	0143
530019-1002	0124
530042-1	OEM
530043-1	0196
530045-1	0479
530045-2	0479
530045-3	0479
530045-4	0479
530051-1	0015
530051-2	0015
530051-4	OEM
530057-1	0015
530060-1	OEM
530063-1	0123
530063-2	0143
530063-4	0143
530063-6	0015
530063-7	0015
530063-10	0143
530063-11	0015
530063-12	0015
530063-13	0133
530063-14	0123
530065-1	0123
530065-2	0143
530065-3	0143
530065-1002	0143
530065-1002A	0143
530065-1003	0143
530070-1	OEM
530070-4	OEM
530071-1	0242
530071-2	0015
530071-3	0015
530071-1011	0133
530072-1	0015
530072-2	0015
530072-4	0015
530072-5	0015
530072-6	0015
530072-7	0143
530072-8	0133
530072-9	0015
530072-10	0015
530072-11	0015
530072-14	0015
530072-15	0015
530072-18	0133
530072-1001	0123
530072-1002	0133
530072-1006	0124
530072-1008	0133
530072-1009	0133
530072-1010	0133
530072-1011	0133
530072-1014	0087
530072-1015	0133
530072-1017	0015
530072-1019	0015
530073-0030	0256
530073-2	0700
530073-3	0170
530073-4	0631
530073-5	0631
530073-6	0137
530073-8	0071
530073-9	0002
530073-12	0002
530073-13	0137
530073-14	0137
530073-15	0416
530073-16	0417
530073-17	0002
530073-18	0436
530073-20	0814
530073-21	0526
530073-22	0490
530073-23	0100
530073-24	0398
530073-26	0416
530073-28	0526
530073-30	0490
530073-31	0157
530073-32	0234
530073-40	0162
530073-1013	0137
530073-1015	0416
530073-1016	0417
530073-1017	0002
530073-1021	0262
530073-1022	OEM
530073-1023	0100
530073-1024	0398

DEVICE TYPE	REPL CODE
530073-1025	0245
530073-1028	0526
530073-1029	0273
530073-1030	0256
530073-1031	0631
530073-1034	0025
530073-1035	OEM
530073-1044	0253
530082-1	0015
530082-2	0071
530082-3	0133
530082-4	0087
530082-1002	0071
530082-1003	0015
530082-1004	0015
530084-4	0015
530085-2	0143
530086-1	0015
530087-2	0469
530088-1	0071
530088-2	0071
530088-3	0087
530088-4	0015
530088-1002	0276
530088-1003	0015
530088-1004	0015
530089-2	1024
530091-1	3688
530092-1	0143
530092-2	0143
530092-1001	0143
530092-1002	0133
530093-1	0196
530093-2	0479
530093-3	0479
530093-1001	0015
530094-1	0015
530095-1	0015
530096	0769
530096(-1)	0769
530096-1	1293
530096-2	0469
530096-3	1293
530097-1	OEM
530097-2	0469
530097-3	0102
530098-1	0015
530098-1001	0015
530099-1	0015
530099-3	0015
530099-4	0015
530099-5	0196
530099-6	0015
530101-1001	0133
530104-1	0030
530104-2	0030
530104-2(8)	0030
530104-1001	0030
530105-1	0143
530105-1001	0123
530105-1002	OEM
530106-001	0023
530106-1	0914
530106-1001	0914
530109-1	0015
530111-1	0015
530111-1001	0015
530111-1002	0071
530112-1	0015
530113-1	0396
530113-2	0071
530113-1001	0102
530115-1001	0143
530116-1	0286
530116-3	0133
530116-1001	0133
530116-1003	0015
530118-2	0137
530119-1	0286
530119-5	0286
530119-7	0752
530119-8	0374
530119-9	0752
530120-1	0276
530122-1	0015
530122-2	0102
530123-1	0143
530123-3	0102
530123-4	0102
530123-5	0023
530123-7	0102
530124-1	0015
530124-2	0752
530124-3	0015
530126-1	0015
530127-1	0143
530127-4	0015
530127-5	0196
530127-6	0015
530128-1	1024
530129-1	0188
530132	0769
530132-1	0769
530135-1	0071
530135-2	0124
530135-3	0015
530135-1003	0015
530136-1	1293
530140-1	0030

If replacement code is OEM, contact original manufacturer for replacement.

227

DEVICE TYPE	REPL CODE	DEVICE TYPE	REPL CODE	DEVICE TYPE	REPL CODE	DEVICE TYPE	REPL CODE	DEVICE TYPE	REPL CODE	DEVICE TYPE	REPL CODE	DEVICE TYPE	REPL CODE
530140-1(8)	0030	530192-120	0137	573371	0050	604030	0050	610061-1	0050	610124-1	0595	610216-2	0065
530142-7	OEM	530192-1120	0137	573398	0050	604040	0050	610063-1	0637	610125-1	0037	610216-3	0065
530142-8	0030	530192-1180	0490	573402	0136	604080	0050	610064-1	0074	610126-1	0004	610217-1	0177
530144-1	0133	530192-1200	0137	573405	0050	604112	0136	610067	0160	610126-2	0208	610217-2	0177
530144-3	0133	530192-1240	0681	573406	0050	604113	3356	610067-1	0160	610128-2	0111	610217-5	0637
530144-1001	0124	530210-1001	0012	573422	0004	604122	0016	610067-2	0160	610128-4	0144	610222-5	OEM
530144-1002	0133	530221-1	0811	573428	0136	604407	0133	610067-3	0265	610129-1	0126	610223-1	0037
530144-1003	0133	530222-1	0071	573432	0004	605020	OEM	610068	0160	610129-D	0224	610223-2	OEM
530144-1004	0124	530224-3	0200	573467	0016	605030	0004	610068-1	0265	610131-2	0334	610224-1	0111
530145-100	0170	530226-1	0015	573468	0016	605112	0136	610069	0144	610132	0016	610224-9001	0111
530145-120	0137	530226-2	0102	573469	0016	605113	0531	610069-1	0144	610132-1	0016	610226-1	0111
530145-130	0053	530226-1002	0102	573471	0136	605122	0222	610070	0016	610134-1	0688	610226-2	0111
530145-339	0188	530248-1	OEM	573472	0144	605131	0769	610070-1	0016	610134-2	0688	610226-5	0111
530145-369	OEM	530257-1	0489	573474	0144	606020	0164	610070-2	0016	610134-4	0688	610226-6	0111
530145-569	0157	530300-1	OEM	573475	0079	606112	0004	610070-3	0016	610134-6	0688	610227-1	0378
530145-689	0025	530303-1	OEM	573479	0016	606113	0015	610070-4	0079	610135-1	0233	610227-3	OEM
530145-1100	0170	530306-3	OEM	573480	0016	606131	0015	610071	0142	610136-1	0150	610228-1	0546
530145-1470	0993	530551-6	0015	573481	0016	607020	OEM	610071-1	0142	610139-1	0224	610228-3	1165
530145-1569	0157	530972-14	0102	573494	0144	607030	0208	610071-2	0142	610139-2	0144	610228-4	1165
530146-1	1141	532003	0178	573495	0144	607101	0196	610072	0144	610140-1	0103	610228-5	0818
530146-2	1141	533013	0133	573501	0233	607112	0969	610072-1	0144	610141-2	0016	610232-1	0079
530148-3	0102	533034	0015	573515	0142	607113	1293	610072-2	0144	610142-1	0155	610232-2	0076
530148-4	0102	534001H	0133	573518	0136	607122	0142	610073	0144	610142-2	0016	610232-9001	0076
530148-1003	0102	535007H	OEM	573529	0004	608020	OEM	610073-1	0007	610142-3	0079	610232-9002	0079
530148-1004	0102	535151-1001	0015	573532	0086	608030	0015	610073-13	0137	610142-4	0016	610233-1	3009
530149-9	0752	537200	0004	574003	0004	608101	0015	610073-1013	OEM	610142-5	0079	610234-1	OEM
530150-1	0133	537428	0050	575001	0143	608112	0969	610074	0136	610142-6	0144	610241-1	0065
530151-1	0133	539148-1004	0102	575002	0143	608112(SHARP)	0599	610074-1	0037	610142-7	0079	610242-1	0065
530151-1001	0023	539157-569	0253	575005	0143	608113	0015	610074-2	0279	610142-8	0079	610245-1	0177
530151-1003	0023	540204	0007	575009	0143	608122	0086	610075-1	0233	610142-10	OEM	610245-2	0270
530152-1	0276	540205	0233	575019	0143	609020	0136	610076	0016	610144-1	0283	610246-1	0037
530153-1	1493	543995	0037	575024	0030	609030	0015	610076-1	0016	610144-2	0283	610249-1	0224
530154-1	0133	551015	0004	575028	0015	609112	0711	610076-2	0016	610144-3	0233	610250-1	0283
530157-130	0361	551026	0015	575037	0911	609113	0015	610077	0016	610144-4	0233	610250-3	0283
530157-569	0157	551034	0535	575042	0015	610002-011	1657	610077-1	0016	610144-6	0233	610291	OEM
530157-689	0025	551051	0004	575047	0102	610002-014	1688	610077-2	0016	610144-101	0283	610356-5	0111
530157-870	2997	552005	0071	575048	6718	610002-026	1372	610077-3	0079	610145-1	0326	610358-1	0212
530157-950	5590	552006	0015	575049	0102	610002-038	0990	610077-4	0079	610146-1	0079	610358-2	0212
530157-1100	0170	552007	0102	575050	0015	610002-074	0243	610077-5	0079	610146-3	0079	610358-3	0212
530157-1101	0170	552010	0015	575051	0015	610002-086	0288	610077-6	0079	610146-5	0079	610360-2	0037
530157-1120	0052	552308	0016	575091	0143	610002-123	0973	610078	0016	610147-1	0079	610361-1	1357
530157-1131	OEM	552503	0037	575995	0469	610010-413	1126	610078-1	0016	610147-2	0037	610361-5	1357
530157-1150	0002	558479P	OEM	576001	0004	610010-470	2732	610079	0004	610148-1	0086	610370-1	OEM
530157-1200	0526	558875	0232	576005	0004	610020	0015	610079-1	0004	610148-2	0079	610386-1	0144
530157-1220	0700	558876	0310	576054	0133	610020-917	2302	610079-2	0111	610148-2A	0079	610392-1	0144
530157-1390	0346	558877	0507	576063	0143	610024-1	0150	610080	0004	610148-3	0086	610392-2	0309
530157-1569	0157	558878	0692	580029	0015	610030	0123	610080-1	0004	610148-4	0086	610395-1	0236
530157-1829	0244	558879	0867	581070	0103	610035	0004	610083	0037	610149-3	0919	610395-2	0676
530157-1919	0057	558880	1018	581078	2378	610035-1	0279	610083-1	0688	610150-1	0224	610397-1	0919
530157-1950	0098	558881	1164	581078-1	2378	610035-2	0211	610083-2	0688	610150-2	0079	610397-2	0042
530160-1	0279	558882	1303	586343-1	1224	610036	0004	610083-3	0037	610150-3	0007	610419-1	0224
530162-1	0015	558883	1199	586344-1	1344	610036-1	0279	610083-4	0688	610151-1	0111	610421-3	0042
530162-1001	0015	558885	0564	599995	1024	610036-2	0279	610083-5	OEM	610151-2	0079	610421-4	0919
530163-120	0137	559507	0268	600008-001	0064	610036-3	0279	610083-6	0037	610151-3	0111	610421-7	OEM
530165	2957	559509	0738	600080-413-001	0016	610036-4	0211	610083-9001	0037	610151-4	0079	610427-2	0264
530165-1	1493	559510	1265	601030	0143	610036-5	0004	610088	0004	610151-5	0111	610427-3	OEM
530165-2	1493	559613	1177	601032	0050	610036-6	0211	610088-1	0004	610153-1	0042	610428-2	0818
530165-3	1493	560004	0265	601040	0050	610036-7	0211	610088-2	0004	610153-3	0042	610433-4	OEM
530165-4	1493	560020S	0087	601052	0050	610036-8	0004	610091	0144	610153-5	0042	610435-1	OEM
530165-5	2954	560165-20	3622	601054	0136	610039	0160	610091-1	0123	610153-6	0042	610435-2	OEM
530165-6	2524	561103	0345	601054(SHARP)	0435	610039-1	0160	610091-2	0144	610155-1	0419	610517-3	OEM
530165-7	1048	564171	OEM	601065	0208	610040	0004	610092	0144	610157-3	0546	610525-2	OEM
530165-8	2954	567312	0198	601113	0007	610040-1	0004	610092-1	0144	610157-4	0378	610540-1	OEM
530165-9	1048	568101	0143	601122	0079	610040-2	0004	610092-2	0144	610158-2	0037	610559-1	OEM
530165-10	2954	570000-5452	0016	602032	0160	610041	0144	610093-1	0037	610158-3	0037	610569-1	6428
530165-11	2524	570000-5503	0016	602040	0164	610041-1	0144	610094	0079	610161-1	0103	611001-3	2336
530165-12	1048	570004-503	0016	602051	0164	610041-2	0144	610094-1	0079	610161-4	0103	611001-4	2337
530165-13	2524	570005-452	0016	602060-76	OEM	610041-3	0144	610094-2	0079	610162-3	3294	611001-5	1403
530165-14	2957	570005-503	0016	602061-73	OEM	610042	0007	610094-3	0111	610162-4	0042	611001-6	1403
530165-15	2954	570009-01-504	0016	602070-05	OEM	610042-1	0144	610096	0144	610162-7	0919	611002-3	OEM
530165-16	2954	570029	0103	602075	0050	610043	0004	610096-1	0144	610162-8	0042	611003-3	0058
530165-17	2524	570030	0455	602081	0012	610043-1	0004	610099	0126	610164-1	0321	611003-4	0058
530165-18	2957	570031	0161	602113	0144	610043-2	0004	610099-1	0126	610165-1	0079	611003-5	0058
530165-20	3622	573001	0004	602113(SHARP)	0016	610043-3	0004	610099-2	0126	610166-1	0212	611004-3	0712
530165-21	1048	573003	0004	602122	0086	610043-4	0004	610099-3	0004	610167-1	0079	611004-4	0712
530166-1004	0631	573005	0004	602190-01	OEM	610043-6	0211	610099-5	0126	610167-2	0079	611013-1	4272
530166-1005	0186	573011	0004	602190-03	OEM	610043-7	0211	610099-6	0037	610167-4	0016	611018-1	1213
530166-1006	0269	573012	0004	602190-06	OEM	610044-3	OEM	610100	0144	610168-1	0079	611019-1	0612
530166-1007	0186	573018	0004	602190-34	OEM	610044-4	OEM	610100-1	0007	610168-2	0079	611020	0004
530166-1013	0186	573022	0004	602190-38	OEM	610045	0144	610100-3	0144	610174-1	0144	611064	0381
530166-1017	0162	573024	0143	602190-39	OEM	610045-1	0144	610102-1	0150	610180-1	0224	611065	1423
530167-1	0039	573029	0004	602190-40	OEM	610045-2	0144	610104-2	OEM	610181-1	0008	611066	1358
530167-1001	0166	573034	0143	602190-44	OEM	610045-3	0016	610106	0160	610181-2	0007	611071	1046
530170-1	0133	573036	0004	602190-45	OEM	610045-4	0016	610106-1	0160	610181-4	OEM	611111	0015
530171-1	0023	573037	0208	602191-58	OEM	610045-5	0016	610107-1	0144	610186-1	0007	611112	OEM
530171-3	0015	573101	0144	602191-59	OEM	610046-7	0144	610107-2	0086	610189-1	0309	611132	0196
530171-1001	0155	573103	0004	602210-03	OEM	610050	0050	610110	0126	610190-1	0264	611563	0232
530171-1002	0015	573110	0004	602210-05	OEM	610050-1	0050	610110-1	0037	610190-3	0161	611564	0310
530171-1003	0015	573114	0004	602210-06	OEM	610050-2	0050	610110-2	0037	610190-4	0264	611565	0357
530171-1569	0253	573117	0004	602210-07	OEM	610050-3	0050	610111	0196	610194-1	0065	611566	0507
530176-1	1319	573118	0211	602210-08	OEM	610051	0050	610111-1	0196	610194-2	0637	611567	0692
530179-1	0133	573119	0004	602210-09	OEM	610051-1	0050	610112	0015	610194-3	0065	611568	1018
530179-1001	0133	573125	0004	602210-10	OEM	610051-2	0050	610112-1	0919	610195-1	0419	611569	0738
530179-1002	0133	573142	0004	602210-18	OEM	610051-4	0050	610113-1	0396	610195-2	0848	611570	1177
530179-1003	0015	573152	0004	602210-26	OEM	610052	0136	610113-2	0396	610195-3	0042	611571	1303
530180-1001	0015	573153	0004	602909-2A	0016	610052-1	0004	610120-1	0037	610195-4	0919	611572	1199
530181-1	0133	573166	0160	602909-3A	0126	610053	0050	610121-1	0312	610195-2002	OEM	611573	0828
530181-3	0124	573184	0004	602909-7A	0086	610053-1	0050	610121-1(PUT)	0312	610195-2003	OEM	611730	1915
530181-1001	0133	573199	0969	603020	0050	610053-2	0050	610121-1(SCR)	0312	610202-1	0378	611731	1910
530181-1002	0124	573200	0004	603030	0050	610055	0050	610121-2	0312	610202-2	0378	611844	1358
530181-1003	0124	573212	0969	603031	0160	610055-1	0050	610121-2(BISW)	4169	610203-1	0212	611845	0381
530181-9001	0133	573303	0136	603040	0050	610055-2	0050	610121-2(PUT)	0312	610203-2	0212	611870	1150
530181-9003	0133	573328	0004	603112	0050	610055-3	0050	610121-3	0312	610203-3	0212	611872	0936
530182-1	OEM	573329	0136	603113	0007	610056	0136	610122	0170	610203-4	0212	611878	3129
530184-2	0102	573330	0136	603114	0015	610056-1	0050	610122-1	4447	610203-5	0212	611900	0936
530184-1001	0102	573335	0050	603122	0016	610056-2	0050	610122-2	0359	610203-6	0212	611901	1818
530184-1002	0102	573336	0050	603312	0050	610056-3	0050	610122-3	0309	610209-1	0037	612003-1	OEM
530185-1	0468	573356	0279	604020	OEM	610056-4	0050	610122-6	0309	610213-1	0086	612004-1	OEM
530191-5	3249	573366	0136	604022-75	OEM	610056-456P4	0143	610123-1	0003	610213-2	0086	612005-1	0167

228

If replacement code is OEM, contact original manufacturer for replacement.

DEVICE TYPE	REPL CODE	DEVICE TYPE	REPL CODE	DEVICE TYPE	REPL CODE	DEVICE TYPE	REPL CODE	DEVICE TYPE	REPL CODE	DEVICE TYPE	REPL CODE	DEVICE TYPE	REPL CODE
612005-2	0167	612305	1051	652072	0155	740470	0016	757004	OEM	772738	0127	811791	0141
612006-1	0696	612305-1	1051	652085	0160	740471	0222	757008-02	0016	772739	0127	811793	0557
612006-1M	0696	612305-2	1051	652086	0160	740502	3625	757024	OEM	772740	0123	811794	1035
612006-1Z	0696	612306-3	OEM	652091	0155	740538	1983	757030	OEM	772768	0136	812200	OEM
612007	0659	612308-1	1856	652092	0015	740543	3625	757044	OEM	785278-01	0143	812201	OEM
612007-1	0659	612310-3	OEM	652230	0155	740570	0015	757080	OEM	785278-101	0079	814044A	0004
612007-2	0659	612318-2	OEM	652231	0086	740583	1983	757085	OEM	785897-01	0050	815003	0004
612007-3	0659	612319-1	OEM	652321	0233	740622	0438	757090	OEM	793356-1	0103	815015	0004
612008-2	0687	612330-4	OEM	652615	0015	740628	0025	757095	OEM	800020-001	0692	815020	0279
612009-2	OEM	612331-2	2790	654000	0155	740629	0907	757097	OEM	800021-001	0867	815020A	0279
612010-2	OEM	612332-1	3665	654001	2123	740630	0015	757098	OEM	800022-001	1018	815020B	0279
612011-2	OEM	612332-6	3666	654032	0479	740781	4031	757182	OEM	800023-001	0507	815021	0279
612012-2	OEM	612334-1	0516	654420	0242	740782	5393	757302	OEM	800024-001	0232	815021A	0279
612013	OEM	612336-1	OEM	655319	0160	740828	0133	757306	OEM	800025-001	1177	815021B	0279
612014-2	OEM	612337-5	OEM	656064	1882	740855	1659	757307	OEM	800026-001	0738	815022	0004
612015-2	OEM	612338-3	2785	656204	0016	740856	0042	757308	OEM	800033-1	0759	815022A	0004
612016-2	OEM	612347-1	2804	656524	0155	740857	0155	757309	OEM	800073-6	0086	815022B	0004
612017-2	OEM	612351-1	0167	656719	0155	740885	0841	757310	OEM	800073-7	0086	815023	0004
612018-2	OEM	612352-1	3924	656746	0155	740946	0136	757311	OEM	800080-001	0310	815023A	0004
612019-2	OEM	612353-1	OEM	657161	0512	740947	0136	757312	OEM	800382-001	1423	815023B	0004
612020	0599	612380-1	OEM	657179	0455	740948	0136	757322	OEM	800383-001	0117	815024	0004
612020-1	0627	612412-2	6748	657180	0161	740949	0127	757326	OEM	800385-001	1046	815024A	0004
612021-1	0649	612438-1	OEM	657181	0455	740950	0127	757361	OEM	800386-001	1915	815024B	0004
612022	OEM	612448	0619	657874	0718	740951	0127	757362	OEM	800387-001	0357	815025	0279
612024-1	2438	612449-1	OEM	658577	0079	741050	0004	759500	0071	800400-001	1303	815025A	0279
612024-3	2438	612472-1	OEM	658578	0079	741051	0715	760005	0212	800491-001	0175	815025B	0279
612025-1	2716	612479-1	0619	658657	0155	741052	0715	760006	0030	800651-001	1197	815026	0595
612025-2	2716	612479-3	OEM	660030	0004	741098	1206	760007	0133	800806-001	1329	815026A	0595
612025-3	2716	612479-4	OEM	660031	0265	741100	0133	760011	0232	801500	0211	815026B	0595
612029-1	0345	612479-5	1311	660059	0004	741101	0015	760013	1199	801501	0211	815026C	0595
612029-3	0345	612480	OEM	660060	0004	741114	0376	760014	OEM	801507	0279	815026D	0595
612042-1	2462	612485-2	OEM	660064	0050	741115	0386	760015	1150	801509	0211	815027	0279
612042-2	2453	612493-1	0034	660070	0086	741116	0091	760018	0486	801510	0211	815027A	0279
612044-1	0850	612494-1	0356	660072	0004	741473	2512	760019	OEM	801511	0211	815027B	0279
612045-1	2535	612496-1	2815	660074	0086	741518	2246	760021	0486	801512	0155	815027C	0279
612048-4	2267	612541-1	OEM	660077	0160	741519	0514	760037	0124	801513	0155	815028	0279
612049-1	OEM	612554-1	OEM	660082	0004	741673	3650	760048	0350	801514	0155	815028A	0279
612054-2	2696	612556-2	OEM	660084	0050	741686	1704	760051	0321	801515	0155	815028B	0279
612061-1	0797	612565-1	OEM	660085	0050	741687	1044	760077	OEM	801516	0155	815028C	0279
612063-1	OEM	612566-1	OEM	660094	0160	741689	0030	760101-0005	0143	801517	0155	815029	0004
612067	0350	612576-1	OEM	660095	0160	741726	0364	760101-0006	0143	801518	0160	815029A	0004
612069-1	0350	612577-1	OEM	660097	0160	741729	0006	760104	OEM	801519	0085	815029B	0004
612070-1	0348	612587-1	OEM	660103	0160	741731	0224	760105	1888	801520	0004	815029C	0004
612072-1	0746	612593-2	OEM	660138	0899	741732	0833	760106	1535	801522	0160	815030	0004
612074-1	0409	612599-0003	OEM	660144	0435	741737	1211	760109	OEM	801523	0599	815030A	0004
612075-1	0514	612626-5	OEM	660144A	0435	741738	0162	760142	0079	801524	0155	815030B	0004
612075-3	0514	612658-0003	OEM	661010	0196	741739	0057	760202-0003	0080	801525	2123	815031	0004
612076-1	3690	612664-2	OEM	670850	0265	741740	0023	760204-0001	0549	801527	0218	815031A	0004
612076-2	3690	612668-0002	OEM	670850-1	0265	741741	0133	760204-0002	0005	801529	0155	815031B	0004
612076-4	3690	612669-0002	OEM	671077-6	0079	741852	2246	760205-0006	0015	801530	0155	815033	0211
612077-2	2728	612731-0001	OEM	699739	0015	741853	1826	760211-0006	0037	801531	2123	815034	0211
612080-1	2232	612771-1	OEM	700021-00	0769	741854	2111	760212-0002	OEM	801532	0155	815034A	0004
612082-1	0842	612792-1	OEM	700043-00	0015	741855	0151	760212-0114	OEM	801533	0396	815034B	0004
612082-2	0842	613020	0015	700055-00	0196	741856	0155	760213-0002	0079	801534	0155	815034C	0004
612082-3	0842	613031	OEM	700063-00	0015	741857	0155	760213-0005	0127	801535	0312	815036	0279
612091-1	2227	613112	0144	700080	0103	741858	0018	760213-0097	0144	801536	0155	815036A	0279
612092-1	1303	613128P	OEM	700080A	0103	741859	0930	760213-0100	0079	801537	0103	815036B	0279
612100-1	1100	613128P(TECEC-0913)	OEM	700083	0103	741860	0349	760213-0104	OEM	801538	0599	815036C	0279
612103-3	0619	613130	0015	700083A	0103	741861	0155	760213-0106	0224	801540	0037	815037	0279
612103-4	2224	613132	1293	700180-00	0143	741862	0113	760215-0001	3477	801541	0283	815037A	0279
612105-1	OEM	614010	0015	700191	0178	741863	0203	760215-0002	2770	801543	0155	815037B	0279
612106-1	OEM	614012	OEM	700195	0178	741864	0133	760215-0006	OEM	801545	3575	815037C	0279
612107-2	2224	614020	0143	700230-00	0016	741865	0015	760251	0155	801707	0015	815038	0004
612107-4	0619	614033-3	OEM	700231-00	0016	741866	0143	760253	0144	801711	0015	815038A	0004
612112	0015	614112	0911	700647	0015	741867	0064	760269	0006	801712	0133	815038B	0004
612113-1	0356	615004-8	0133	700663	0015	741868	0030	760275	0555	801714	0015	815038C	0004
612114-1	OEM	615010	0143	700664	0015	741869	0244	760276	1257	801715	0071	815041	0279
612120-1	3363	615130	1024	701584-00	0037	741870	0244	760284	0488	801716	0015	815041A	0279
612123-3	OEM	616010	0196	701589-00	0037	742004	0143	760298	0162	801722	0143	815041B	0279
612124-1	OEM	617020	OEM	701662-00	0133	742008	0015	760304	0137	801723	0071	815041C	0279
612125-1	OEM	617871-1	0160	701678-00	0007	742009	0015	760309	0437	801724	0124	815043	0279
612126	0906	618020	OEM	702407-00	0086	742362	0701	760522-0002	0696	801726	0012	815043A	0279
612126-1	0906	618139-1	0160	702415-00	0561	742363	1012	760522-0004	OEM	801728	0133	815043B	0279
612130	0015	618580	0321	703227-1	OEM	742364	1044	760522-0008	1385	801729	0155	815043C	0279
612130-1	OEM	619009-1	0178	703639-1	3690	742510	1532	760522-0012	3946	801730	0242	815055	0279
612132	0015	619020	OEM	703639-2	3690	742512	0076	761113	0015	801731	0137	815056	0279
612144-1	2535	619094	0411	705269	OEM	742513	1212	762200-14	0354	801800	2840	815057	0279
612159-1	1197	619130	0015	717126-505	1896	742537	1653	765722	0143	801804	0718	815058	0004
612160-1	OEM	619256	2007	717136-1	0699	742546	0006	770339	2089	801805	0268	815058A	0004
612160-3	OEM	619256-1	2006	717136-15	1011	742547	0113	770523	0004	801806	0357	815058B	0004
612175-1	OEM	619550-1	1888	717399-22	1340	742548	0151	770524	0004	801807	1046	815058C	0004
612183-1	0798	630002-001	0076	717399-73	1918	742549	0151	770525	0164	801808	1199	815058X	0211
612184-1	1835	630003-110	4265	720240	0079	742705	0364	770730	0004	801809	0718	815064	0136
612185-1	0381	630006-001	4253	720453	0110	742723	1251	770768-3170756	0142	802008	0124	815064A	0136
612186-1	1135	630007-001	2022	720454	0947	742724	OEM	771907	0015	802032-2	0004	815064B	0136
612187-1	OEM	630008-907	2022	720455	0242	742725	1303	771908	0276	802032-4	0004	815064C	0136
612188-1	1074	630063	0242	720456	0535	742726	1288	771909	0143	802033-3	0004	815065	0279
612189-1	3627	633977	0196	720457	0959	742727	2232	771910	0143	802054-0	0004	815065A	0279
612189-2	3627	650196	0211	720458	0535	742728	2787	771911	0143	802056-0	0004	815065B	0279
612191-1	OEM	650845	0133	720463	0959	742729	0018	772712	0143	802189-7	0004	815065C	0279
612192-1	2075	650854	0133	731009	0004	742730	0123	772713	0015	802189-8	0004	815066	0279
612194-1	0088	650859-1	0211	733293	0165	742732	0030	772714	0276	802263-0	0004	815066A	0279
612195-1	3856	650859-2	0211	740183	0015	742920	0065	772716	0050	802263-1	0004	815066B	0279
612197-1	0937	650859-3	0211	740247	0816	742922	1075	772717	0050	802389-2	0004	815066C	0279
612199-1	1519	650860	0595	740289	0015	742970	0830	772718	0004	802415-2	0004	815067	0050
612200-1	0243	650970	0160	740306	0111	742986	0111	772719	0050	802425-0	0969	815067A	0050
612230-1	1644	651012	0211	740402	0143	743655	0577	772720	0004	802439-0	0004	815067B	0050
612236-2	OEM	651030	0015	740417	0004	743949	0181	772721	0004	802560	0211	815067C	0050
612247-2	0944	651038	0015	740437	0079	744002	0196	772722	0004	803182-5	0016	815068	0136
612261-1	1519	651202	0160	740438	0111	744006	0196	772723	0004	803369-6	0016	815068A	0136
612272-1	2038	651236	0211	740439	0111	744275	0577	772724	0004	803372-0	0016	815068B	0136
612273-1	3239	651891	0155	740440	0111	746003	0015	772725	0004	803373-0	0016	815068C	0136
612275-1	1888	651955-1	0155	740441	0079	746004	0015	772727	0004	803696	0111	815069	0004
612289-1	OEM	651955-2	0155	740442	0111	750397	OEM	772728	0004	803733-0	0016	815069A	0004
612291-1	1877	651955-3	0155	740443	0816	750746A	1024	772729	0004	803733-3	0016	815069B	0004
612294-1	3741	651956	0086	740461	0155	751007	OEM	772732	0164	803735-3	0016	815069C	0004
612298-1	OEM	651995-1	0016	740462	0155	752309	0015	772733	0164	810002-269	1812	815070	0004
612303-1	0485	651995-2	0016	740463	0155	752314	0769	772736	0004	810002-475	0759	815070A	0004
612304-1	1016	651995-3	0016	740466	0016	756985	OEM	772737	0004	811790	1812	815070B	0004

If replacement code is OEM, contact original manufacturer for replacement.

DEVICE TYPE	REPL CODE
815070C	0004
815070D	0004
815074	0004
815075	0208
815076	0208
815082	0004
815083	0004
815101	0279
815103	0279
815104	0004
815105	0279
815107	0279
815108	0279
815109	0279
815114	0004
815115	0279
815116	0279
815117	0279
815118	0004
815120	0004
815120A	0004
815120B	0004
815120C	0004
815120D	0004
815120E	0004
815122	0004
815133	0079
815134	0079
815135	OEM
815136	0004
815137	0265
815137B	0160
815137Y	0160
815138	0015
815139	0004
815142	0015
815158	0004
815160	0004
815160-C	0211
815160-I	0004
815160-J	0004
815160-K	0004
815160-L	0004
815160-O	0004
815160-P	0004
815160-Q	0004
815160A	0004
815160B	0004
815160C	0004
815160D	0004
815160E	0004
815160F	0004
815160H	0004
815164	0144
815165	0144
815166	0142
815166-4	0142
815167-3	0142
815170	0144
815171	0016
815171D	0016
815172	0144
815172A	0144
815173	0111
815173A	0144
815173C	0144
815173F	0144
815174	0016
815174L	0016
815175	0142
815175H	0142
815177	0004
815178	0004
815179	0004
815180-3	0142
815180-4	0142
815180-7	0142
815181	0004
815181-B	0211
815181A	0004
815181B	0004
815181C	0004
815181D	0004
815182	0016
815183	0016
815184	0016
815184E	0016
815185	0126
815185E	0126
815186	0016
815186C	0016
815186L	0079
815189	0004
815190	0016
815191	0016
815193	0050
815195	0004
815196	0004
815197	0050
815198	0079
815199	0037
815199-6	0037
815201	0079
815202	0079
815203-3	0265
815203-5	0265
815206	0007
815209	0144
815210	0079

DEVICE TYPE	REPL CODE
815211	0037
815212	0079
815213	0037
815218-3	0004
815218-4	0208
815227	0079
815228	4499
815228A	0004
815228A01	0211
815228A1	0004
815228B1	0004
815229	0037
815232	2839
815233	0079
815234	0050
815236	0037
815237	0079
815240	OEM
815243	1371
815247	0037
815308	0279
815308A	0279
816135	0142
817020	0914
817032	0143
817036	1024
817042	0015
817043	0015
817044	0015
817053	0015
817062	1024
817062(CRYSTAL)	0479
817064	0015
817066	0015
817067	0015
817068	0015
817068P	0015
817074	0196
817077	0143
817079	0015
817082	0143
817088	0015
817104	0015
817109	0015
817111	0015
817112	0015
817114	0015
817117	0015
817120	0914
817121	0015
817122	0015
817123	0769
817124	1293
817125	0143
817126	0196
817127	0196
817128	0015
817129	1024
817130	0015
817133	0015
817134	0015
817135	0015
817138	0015
817140	0015
817141	0015
817143	0015
817147	1024
817148	0015
817149	0469
817155	0137
817156	0015
817157	0015
817158	0143
817159	0143
817160	0123
817161	0015
817164	0015
817166	0015
817167	0015
817172	0133
817173	0162
817175	1024
817177	0123
817178	0004
817179	0087
817179A	0087
817180	0015
817190	0133
817193	0071
817194	0143
817195	0015
817197	0012
817199	0143
817208	0137
817209	0087
817962	0479
824960-0	0144
829704-6	4772
829704-7	4772
852158-7-1	0015
852158-7.1	0015
853640	0050
853864-0	0050
860003-99	0033
860003-101	1812
860003-111	3032
860003-121	1035
860003-141	0081
860003-151	0081

DEVICE TYPE	REPL CODE
860003-161	1820
860011	0133
862200-16	0354
862209-16	0557
870233	1501
870246	1516
871125	0143
880092	0222
881916	1303
889132	4506
889302	1411
889304	2535
894876	0079
900750-01	0023
900750-02	0080
900755-01	OEM
900756-01	0276
900757-01	OEM
900850-01	0124
900850-05	0133
900850-16	0124
900927-01	0062
900927-02	0062
900941-01	0077
900948-06	0296
900948-11	0041
901225-01	OEM
901226-01	OEM
901227-02	OEM
901227-03	OEM
901229-03	OEM
901229-05	OEM
901237-01	OEM
901246-01	OEM
901251-30	1688
901337-01	OEM
901342-01	OEM
901343-01	OEM
901401-01	OEM
901435-01	3036
901435-02	OEM
901435-03	OEM
901436-01	OEM
901437-01	OEM
901438-01	OEM
901439-03	OEM
901447-10	OEM
901447-20	OEM
901447-29	OEM
901453-01	2037
901455-01	OEM
901458-01	1962
901460-03	OEM
901465-03	OEM
901465-20	OEM
901465-21	OEM
901465-22	OEM
901465-23	OEM
901466-04	OEM
901468-06	OEM
901468-14	OEM
901468-15	OEM
901468-16	OEM
901472-07	OEM
901474-03	OEM
901479-02	OEM
901482-07	OEM
901483-03	OEM
901483-04	OEM
901484-05	OEM
901486-01	OEM
901486-06	OEM
901486-07	OEM
901491-01	OEM
901499-01	OEM
901502-01	0101
901505-01	2341
901510-01	2270
901521-01	1519
901521-02	1585
901521-03	1623
901521-06	0243
901521-17	1830
901521-18	0153
901521-20	0075
901521-21	1550
901521-22	0183
901521-26	1682
901521-29	0704
901521-30	1688
901521-32	0288
901521-34	1662
901521-54	2450
901521-57	1733
901521-58	1735
901521-68	3146
901522-01	1342
901522-03	1792
901522-04	0232
901522-06	1197
901522-30	1329
901523-01	0967
901523-03	3254
901523-04	1804
901523-08	1110
901527-01	0330
901527-02	0619
901528-03	1911
901528-04	3906

DEVICE TYPE	REPL CODE
901640-01	OEM
901885-04	OEM
901887-01	OEM
901888-01	OEM
901895-01	OEM
901895-02	OEM
902521	0050
902652-01	0076
902653-01	0061
902658-01	0076
902671	0076
902679	0945
902682	0860
902686-01	0079
902693-01	0076
902694-01	0456
902717	0006
902720	0148
902744-01	0148
906103-02	0755
906107-01	OEM
906108-01	OEM
906108-02	OEM
906108-08	OEM
906109-02	OEM
906109-04	OEM
906111-01	OEM
906112-01	OEM
906114-01	OEM
906114-02	OEM
906128-01	0011
906129-01	1864
906140-01	OEM
906144-01	OEM
906145-02	OEM
906150-02	OEM
910050-2	0004
910062-1	0004
910070-6	0004
910094-4	0004
910799	0144
910952	0455
912002	0718
913112	OEM
916002	1470
916009	0079
916028	0076
916029	0191
916030	0079
916031	1212
916031(CARTAPE)	0111
916031(PENNYS)	0079
916033	0076
916034	0086
916046	0555
916049	0127
916050	0076
916051	0037
916052	0076
916055	1212
916060	0144
916061	2247
916062	0037
916063	2300
916064	2377
916067	1983
916068	0127
916069	0144
916070	1469
916072	1206
916081	0858
916082	0321
916083	1152
916084	0428
916091	0079
916092	2300
916098	1152
916100	0321
916101	4348
916102	1470
916103	OEM
916104	OEM
916105	2046
916106	2512
916108	OEM
916109	3332
916110	1044
916111	0780
916112	0673
916113	0514
916114	0161
916118	0930
916119	1581
916121	2008
916125	1805
916138	1635
916149	OEM
916150	1288
916154	OEM
916155	0701
916157	4355
921608	0015
922021	0143
922092	0015
922183	0015
922214	0005
922311	0015
922358	0012
922359	0030

DEVICE TYPE	REPL CODE
922360	0015
922433	0124
922502	OEM
922503	OEM
922504	OEM
922505	OEM
922524	0057
922545	OEM
922603	0012
922604	0143
922607	OEM
922693	0137
922799	0015
922860	0023
922873	0133
922878	2990
922883	OEM
922896	0279
922903	OEM
922950	0313
922969	0015
923147	0133
923233	0181
924605-3	0015
924801-5	0015
924805-5	0015
924805-8	0015
925297	0124
928510-1	2067
928510-101	2067
928512-101	1812
928514-1	0141
928514-101	0141
928515-101	0081
928517-101	2086
928533-101	0557
928560-1	0033
928560-101	0033
928571-1	0033
930347-1	0692
930347-2	0692
930347-3	0232
930347-4	1417
930347-5	1018
930347-6	1193
930347-7	1164
930347-9	0974
930347-10	0692
930347-11	0310
930347-12	1160
930347-13	0357
930347-15	0381
932292-1C	1812
933044-2D	1035
934362-3	0283
936001	1024
942677-1	0143
942677-2	0143
942677-3	0143
942677-4	0143
942677-6	0143
942677-7	0143
944148	2006
945820-4	0015
952851	OEM
962685	0911
964158	0911
964298	0143
964634	0144
964688	2839
964713	0144
964864	OEM
964999	0911
965000	0016
965073	0911
965074	0144
965632	0007
965633	0144
965634	0144
965854	OEM
965936	0911
966116	OEM
966117	OEM
966368	OEM
970046	0144
970046-1	0144
970046-2	0144
970046A	0144
970047	0911
970150-07	OEM
970153-08	OEM
970244	0144
970245	0144
970246	0037
970247	0079
970248	0037
970249	0144
970250	0079
970251	0037
970252	0016
970253	0321
970254	0037
970255	0142
970257	OEM
970309	0144
970309-1	0144
970309-2	0144
970309-3	0144
970309-4	0144

DEVICE TYPE	REPL CODE
970309-5	0144
970309-12	0144
970310	0144
970310-1	0144
970310-2	0144
970310-3	0144
970310-4	0144
970310-5	0144
970310-12	0144
970311	0127
970332	0144
970332-12	0144
970565	OEM
970659	0079
970660	0016
970661	0016
970662	0079
970663	0037
970759	0911
970762	0037
970762-6	0126
970787	OEM
970905	OEM
970911	0144
970916	0016
970916-6	0016
970939	0127
970940	0079
970962	0127
970963	0911
970964	OEM
971035	0127
971036	0911
971059	0037
971457	0015
971458	0015
971459	0007
971460	0111
971477	0211
971526	0127
971836	OEM
971904	0007
971905	0037
971906	OEM
972155	0079
972156	0079
972214	0016
972215	0016
972216	0015
972217	0526
972258-1	0143
972258-2	0143
972258-3	0143
972258-4	0143
972258-5	0143
972258-6	0143
972258-8	0143
972259-8	0143
972305	0007
972306	0127
972307	0127
972416	OEM
972417	0127
972418	0127
972419	0127
972420	0127
972571	1293
972571-1	1293
972571-2	1293
972571-3	1293
972571-4	0015
972571-5	0071
972571-6	0015
972571-7	0015
973918-2	0015
973935-20	0015
973936-1	0015
973936-2	0015
973936-3	0015
973936-4	0015
973936-5	0015
973936-6	0015
973936-7	0015
973936-8	0015
973936-9	0015
973936-10	0015
973936-11	0015
973936-12	0015
973936-13	0015
973936-14	0015
973936-15	0015
973936-16	0015
973936-17	0015
973936-18	0015
973936-19	0015
973936-20	0071
973936-21	0015
973962-1	0015
973973-6	OEM
980028	OEM
980052	0435
980052A	0435
980132	0160
980134	0160
980135	0160
980136	0279
980138	0144
980139	0144
980140	0050

DEVICE TYPE	REPL CODE
980142	0050
980143	0015
980144	0004
980146	0050
980147	0016
980148	0004
980149	0004
980150	0969
980153	0004
980155	0160
980164	0015
980316	0279
980372	0136
980373	0136
980374	0136
980375	0004
980376	0004
980426	0279
980432	0279
980434	0279
980435	0050
980437	0160
980438	0279
980439	0279
980440	0016
980441	0050
980462	0435
980462A	0435
980463	0435
980463A	0435
980505	0050
980506	0050
980507	0050
980508	0004
980509	0050
980510	0004
980511	0004
980514	0143
980514A	0050
980540	0015
980545A	0050
980626	0136
980636A	0050
980833	0136
980834	0136
980835	0136
980836	0004
980837	0004
980958	0136
980959	0050
980960	0004
980961	0004
980964	0015
981143	0050
981144	0050
981145	0050
981146	0050
981147	0004
981148	0004
981149	0004
981150	0143
981151	0030
981153	0143
981203	0136
981204	0136
981206	0004
981207	0143
981248	0769
981249	1293
981371	0469
981445	0015
981522	0143
981672	0004
981673	0004
981674	0004
981675	0004
981676	0143
981739	0015
981952	0015
981953	0015
981954	0015
981955	0015
981956	0015
981959	0050
981969	0435
981969A	0435
982065	0143
982150	0136
982151	0004
982152	0004
982214	0015
982231	0016
982244	0004
982253	0015
982254	0012
982267	0136
982268	0144
982269	0144
982270	0123
982271	0123
982275	0143
982283	0004
982284	0004
982285	0004
982289	0136
982290	0143
982300	0086
982307	0222
982321	0144

If replacement code is OEM, contact original manufacturer for replacement.

DEVICE TYPE	REPL CODE
982322	0050
982324	0030
982361	0196
982363	0196
982374	0050
982376	0142
982377	0015
982497	0050
982510	0079
982511	0079
982512	0016
982523	0178
982526	0015
982528	0142
982531	0004
982532	0004
982601	OEM
982815	0144
982816	0144
982817	0144
982818	0144
982819	0144
982820	0211
982822	0143
982823	0015
983011	0644
983012	0841
983036	0160
983095	0144
983096	0144
983097	0016
983099	0143
983101	0015
983233	0127
983234	0127
983235	0127
983236	0136
983237	0004
983238	0004
983239	0143
983271	0136
983272	0136
983405	0004
983406	0004
983407	0004
983408	0004
983409	0004
983411	0004
983413	0015
983689	0133
983742	0127
983743	0016
983744	0907
983795	0160
983874	0160
983945	0435
983975	0160
983995	0769
984156	0144
984158	0144
984159	0144
984160	0004
984161	0164
984162	0133
984163	0143
984182	0015
984183	0015
984184	0015
984189	0015
984191	0007
984192	0007
984193	0037
984194	0144
984195	0144
984196	0086
984197	0016
984198	0016
984200	0143
984221	0004
984222	0016
984224	0016
984225	OEM
984226	0143
984227	0233
984228	0004
984229	0086
984252	0644
984254	0015
984259	0103
984259A	0103
984260	0102
984261	0160
984286	0016
984431	0160
984521	0222
984522	0015
984577	0144
984590	0016
984591	0016
984593	0016
984594	0015
984608	0142
984666	0143
984667	0143
984685	0136
984686	0016
984687	0016
984688	2839
984690	0276

DEVICE TYPE	REPL CODE
984713	0015
984743	0144
984744	0144
984745	0016
984746	0211
984794	0087
984795	0087
984851	0144
984852	0144
984853	0144
984854	0016
984875	0144
984876	0127
984877	0127
984878	0127
984879	0016
984880	0133
984881	0123
984882	0015
984932	0142
985036	0160
985087	0079
985096	0144
985097	0144
985098	0016
985099	0016
985100	0079
985101	0079
985102	0016
985103	0222
985104	0015
985105	0015
985106	0133
985175	0321
985215	0144
985216	0004
985217	0211
985218	0015
985431	0160
985432	0435
985442	0127
985442A	0144
985443	0160
985443A	0144
985444	0127
985444A	0144
985445	0136
985445A	0050
985446	0136
985446A	0050
985447	0160
985448	0644
985449	0160
985453	0160
985455	0160
985468	0004
985468A	0004
985469	0004
985469A	0004
985470	0164
985470A	0004
985471	0164
985472	0015
985543	0016
985609	0004
985610	0004
985611	0136
985619	0127
985621	0143
985686	0160
985715	0321
985735	0208
985735A	0208
985957	0030
985961	0053
986302	0004
986305	0164
986414	0015
986542	0016
986543	0164
986576	0127
986577	0133
986578	0162
986634	0144
986635	0144
986636	0016
986637	0015
986693	0127
986694	0127
986766	0004
986767	1293
986779	0164
986930	0212
986931	0126
986932	0555
986933	1257
986934	0133
986935	0015
986997	OEM
988000	0144
988001	0144
988002	0144
988003	0016
988005	0164
988048	0030
988049	0229
988050	0170
988051	0015
988080	0160

DEVICE TYPE	REPL CODE
988336	0160
988413	0160
988414	0435
988468	0160
988977	0435
988985	0144
988986	0144
988987	0144
988988	0144
988989	0144
988990	0037
988991	0016
988992	0786
988993	0086
988994	0143
988995	0133
988996	0133
988997	0143
988998	0143
989171	0435
989387	0160
989615	0435
989692	0435
989693	0435
991064	0071
991129	0071
991421	0071
991422	0071
991429	0071
992052	0076
992066	0076
992108	1136
992129	0076
992143	0019
992150	0133
992171	0080
992289	0211
994634	0144
995001	0160
995002	0004
995003	0004
995012	0855
995014	0160
995015	0160
995016	0016
995017	0016
995022	0627
995025	0855
995029	0855
995030	0142
995042	0823
995053	0696
995053-1	0696
995081-1	0661
998280-930	1812
998280-945	0081
998280-962	0557
1000100	0828
1000100-000	0828
1000101	0564
1000101-000	0564
1005191	OEM
1006661REV.C	OEM
1043176-1	0015
1043176-2	0015
1043176-3	0015
1043176-4	0015
1043176-5	0015
1045013	0015
1045154-1	0015
1045154-2	0015
1045154-3	0015
1045154-4	0071
1045154-5	0087
1045154-6	0087
1045494-1	0479
1107832-6	1073
1107832-7	0196
1107832-8	0196
1107832-9	0196
1107832-10	0196
1107832-11	0196
1107863-1	1024
1107863-2	1024
1107863-3	1024
1142415-2	0143
1195397	0907
1221028	0435
1221615	0160
1221625	0085
1221648	0279
1221649	0279
1221900	0244
1221962	0016
1222123	0016
1222133	0016
1222136	0050
1222314	0050
1222371	0050
1222424	0016
1222463	0144
1223770	0143
1223771	0124
1223772	0015
1223773	0170
1223781	0144
1223782	0079
1223783	2969
1223784	0693

DEVICE TYPE	REPL CODE
1223785	1390
1223786	0626
1223909	1704
1223910	2754
1223911	0364
1223912	0151
1223913	0155
1223914	0006
1223915	0151
1223916	0224
1223917	1935
1223918	2475
1223919	0113
1223920	0076
1223921	0019
1223925	0030
1223926	0162
1223927	0057
1223928	0023
1223929	0023
1223930	0133
1223931	0019
1224031	0006
1224076	1532
1224275	3515
1224276	OEM
1224277	OEM
1258444	0015
1303256	0087
1310505	OEM
1317303-1	0037
1320004	OEM
1320031	OEM
1320135	0016
1320135A	0016
1320135BC	0016
1320135C	0016
1321341	OEM
1322966	0286
1330021-0	1843
1330021-1	1843
1331409	5766
1337915	OEM
1340051	OEM
1343041	OEM
1344401	OEM
1353271	OEM
1353331	OEM
1360071	OEM
1360081	OEM
1360271	OEM
1360331	OEM
1360391	OEM
1361192	OEM
1361201	OEM
1371162	OEM
1371174	OEM
1378204	OEM
1401092	OEM
1401100	OEM
1401101(LED)	OEM
1407205-1	0160
1408615-1	0144
1408640-1	0144
1408649-1	0143
1408694-1	0212
1415721-1	0102
1415762-1	0239
1415762-2	0061
1417302-1	0431
1417303-1	0126
1417303-2	0126
1417306-1	0079
1417306-4	0079
1417306-5	0079
1417316-1	0546
1417317-1	0378
1417318-1	0079
1417318-2	0320
1417320-1	0103
1417321	0079
1417321-1	0855
1417322-1	0178
1417324-1	0079
1417325-1	0590
1417330-3	0037
1417330-4	0037
1417331-1	0065
1417335-1	0065
1417338-5	0086
1417339-1	0037
1417340-2	0079
1417342-1	0079
1417344-1	0086
1417345-2	0086
1417347-1	0037
1417349-2	0320
1417352-5	0546
1417354-1	4873
1417356-2	0103
1417358-1	0042
1417359-1	0455
1417362-1	0283
1417362-4	0283
1417363-1	0037
1417364-1	0419
1417366-1	0065
1417370-1	0065
1417372-1	0212

DEVICE TYPE	REPL CODE
1417380-1	0309
1417381-2	0079
1417399-8	2498
1417400-1	0079
1417872-11	0124
1420427-1	0004
1420427-2	0004
1420427-3	0004
1421207-1	1141
1421729-7	OEM
1421734-1	6207
1421763-2	OEM
1421896-104	OEM
1421896-106	OEM
1421896-107	OEM
1421899-6	OEM
1440614-9	OEM
1440977	0769
1440977-1	0769
1440990	0469
1442415-2	0911
1442415-3	0911
1443200-3	0004
1443223-1	0030
1444875-1	0137
1445470-2	0286
1445470-50	0201
1445470-501	0286
1445470-502	0102
1445470-503	0286
1445470-504	0374
1445740-502	0201
1445829-501	0378
1445829-502	0378
1445829-503	0546
1445829-504	0546
1449098-1	0233
1457061-16	OEM
1460607-9	OEM
1462434-1	0823
1462445-1	2689
1462455-1	OEM
1462506-1	0324
1462516	0167
1462516-001	0167
1462516-1	0167
1462554	2716
1462554-1	2716
1462554-2	2716
1462554-3	2716
1462554-4	2716
1462559-1	2527
1462560-001	0324
1462560-1	0324
1462599-1	OEM
1463641-1	1986
1463641-2	1986
1463677-1	0360
1463677-2	0360
1463677-3	0360
1463681-1	1843
1463686-1	0167
1463695-2	OEM
1464295-1	1178
1464295-2	2266
1464437-2	2242
1464437-3	2242
1464438-2	2728
1464438-3	2728
1464439-2	1832
1464460-2	1832
1464460-3	1832
1464607-1	0405
1464607-2	0405
1464607-3	0405
1464607-4#	OEM
1464607-5	0405
1464607-6	0405
1464607-7	2777
1464607-8	2777
1464607-9	1700
1464607-10	1700
1464609-3	OEM
1464778-9	0914
1464846-1	2530
1464846-2	2530
1464865-1	0405
1464984-1	0405
1464984-2	0405
1465158-1	0516
1465158-2	0516
1465188-1	2527
1465316-1	3239
1465345-1	2038
1465615	2762
1465615-1	2762
1465615-2	2762
1465617-2	2759
1465651-1	OEM
1465819-1	2317
1466701-1	2771
1466860-1	0405
1466860-2	1188
1466862-2	2777
1466865-1	0405
1470872-6	0133
1470990	0469
1470990-1	0469
1471036-14	0160

DEVICE TYPE	REPL CODE
1471036-20	0160
1471072-4	0133
1471100-1	0004
1471100-8	0004
1471100-9	0004
1471101-2	0004
1471101-3	0004
1471101-4	0004
1471101-15	0004
1471104-5	0136
1471104-6	0136
1471104-7	0136
1471104-8	0136
1471112-7	0037
1471112-8	0037
1471112-8-9	0126
1471112-9	0150
1471112-10	0688
1471112-12	0126
1471113-2	0016
1471114-1	0037
1471115-13	0079
1471115-14	0144
1471117-1	0142
1471120-7	0079
1471120-8	0079
1471120-8-9	0079
1471120-14	0086
1471120-15	0079
1471122-6	0111
1471122-7	0111
1471123-3	0086
1471123-4	0086
1471124-5	0599
1471125-3	0969
1471132-002	0419
1471132-2	0161
1471132-3	0419
1471132-4	0042
1471132-5	0419
1471132-6	0130
1471133-1	0546
1471134-1	0378
1471135-001	0103
1471135-1	0103
1471135-2	0130
1471136-3	0396
1471139-1	1671
1471140-1	0161
1471141-1	0455
1471393-4	0287
1471405-1	0087
1471777-11	0873
1471822-11	0123
1471839-1	0715
1471839-2	OEM
1471839-3	OEM
1471839-5	0715
1471858	2938
1471858-1	0015
1471872-001	0015
1471872-004	0015
1471872-006	0015
1471872-008	0015
1471872-1	0133
1471872-2	0133
1471872-3	0102
1471872-4	0133
1471872-5	0124
1471872-6	0015
1471872-7	0133
1471872-8	0133
1471872-10	0133
1471872-11	0124
1471872-12	0133
1471872-13	0133
1471872-14	0133
1471872-15	0143
1471872-16	0133
1471872-17	0143
1471872-18	0133
1471876-6	1141
1471878-3	0025
1471893-3	OEM
1471893-4	0778
1471898-3	0631
1471898-4	0778
1471898-5	0157
1471908-1	0290
1471908-4	2622
1471922-1	0911
1471922-2	0911
1471922-4	0911
1472164-6	OEM
1472171-32	0015
1472450-1	0144
1472460-1	0229
1472460-2	0133
1472460-3	0133
1472460-4	0229
1472460-5	0229
1472460-6	0133
1472460-7	0133
1472460-8	0133
1472460-9	0918
1472460-13	0102
1472460-14	0087
1472460-16	0015
1472460-18	0479

DEVICE TYPE	REPL CODE
1472474-2	0233
1472482-1	0004
1472634-1	0144
1472654-1	0224
1472872-4	0133
1473503-1	0142
1473508-1	0086
1473514-1	0969
1473515-1	0160
1473516-1	0126
1473519-1	0079
1473520-1	0142
1473521-1	0127
1473523-2	OEM
1473524-1	0127
1473524-2	0144
1473524-3	0127
1473527-1	0016
1473528-1	2681
1473528-2	2681
1473529-1	0127
1473530-1	0144
1473530-2	0144
1473531-1	0259
1473532-1	0016
1473533-1	0144
1473535-1	0007
1473535-1(RCA)	0007
1473536-001	0079
1473536-1	0079
1473536-2	0007
1473537-1	0144
1473538-1	0016
1473539-1	0079
1473540-1	0037
1473541-1	0233
1473543-1	0007
1473544	0855
1473544-1	0127
1473545-1	0086
1473546-1	0016
1473546-2	0016
1473547-1	0086
1473549-1	0037
1473549-2	0037
1473551-1	0016
1473552-1	0233
1473553-1	0086
1473554-1	0016
1473555-1	0016
1473555-2	0016
1473555-3	0086
1473555-I	0086
1473556-1	0016
1473557-1	0016
1473558-1	0127
1473559-001	0037
1473559-1	0037
1473560	0086
1473560-002	0079
1473560-1	0086
1473560-2	0086
1473561-001	0079
1473561-1	0086
1473561-Y	0079
1473562-1	0037
1473563-1	0037
1473564-1	0074
1473565-001	0086
1473565-1	0086
1473566-1	0086
1473567-1	0142
1473567-2	0161
1473567-4	0042
1473568-1	0144
1473569-1	0016
1473570-1	0037
1473571	0283
1473571-1	0007
1473572-1	0079
1473572-3	0086
1473573-1	0208
1473574	0855
1473574-1	0037
1473576	0007
1473576-1	0326
1473577-1	0007
1473578-1	0004
1473579-1	0007
1473581-1	0037
1473582-1	0016
1473583-7	0239
1473583-8	0239
1473584-1	0142
1473585-1	0061
1473585-5	0239
1473585-6	0061
1473585-7	0239
1473585-8	0061
1473586	0007
1473586-2	0079
1473587-1	OEM
1473588-2	0349
1473588-8	0212
1473589-1	0016
1473590-1	0149
1473591-1	0037
1473592-1	0126
1473593-1	0086

If replacement code is OEM, contact original manufacturer for replacement.

231

DEVICE TYPE	REPL CODE
1473595-1	0016
1473597	0150
1473597-1	0037
1473597-2	0037
1473597-7	0150
1473598-1	0136
1473598-2	0004
1473601	0637
1473601-001	0079
1473601-1	0079
1473601-2	0079
1473602	0855
1473603-1	0144
1473604-1	0396
1473604-3	0144
1473606-1	0144
1473608-002	0086
1473608-1	0086
1473608-2	0086
1473608-3	0086
1473610-1	0127
1473611-1	0042
1473612-1	0419
1473612-11	0042
1473613-2	0334
1473613-3	0334
1473613-4	0283
1473614-1	0079
1473614-3	0079
1473615-1	0086
1473616-1	0126
1473617-1	0144
1473617-2	0127
1473618-1	0212
1473619-1	2340
1473619-2	2378
1473619-3	2378
1473620-001	0037
1473620-1	0037
1473620-2	0037
1473621-1	0419
1473622-002	0086
1473622-1	0016
1473622-2	0086
1473623-1	0419
1473624-1	0848
1473624-2	0455
1473625-001	0590
1473625-1	0086
1473626-1	0079
1473627-1	0037
1473628-1	0546
1473628-2	0283
1473628-3	0546
1473629-3	0378
1473631-1	0079
1473632-1	0283
1473632-2	0555
1473632-3	0419
1473633-1	0283
1473634-1	0065
1473635	0212
1473635-1	0212
1473635-2	0349
1473636-1	0142
1473637-1	0074
1473638-1	0899
1473640-1	0419
1473641-2	OEM
1473647-1	0065
1473648-1	0969
1473649-1	0065
1473650-2	OEM
1473651-1	0150
1473652-1	0144
1473656-1	0556
1473656-2	0556
1473656-4	0233
1473657-1	0224
1473657-2	0224
1473665-2	0103
1473666-1	0126
1473669-1	0065
1473669-2	0065
1473676-1	0326
1473676-1(3RD-LF)	0326
1473677-3	0360
1473679-1	0086
1473679-2	0233
1473680-1	0007
1473681-1	0042
1473681-I	0042
1473682-1	0455
1473683-1	0103
1473686-1	0136
1473687-1	0334
1473688-1	0058
1473777-2	0002
1474178-10	0015
1474613-2	0283
1474717-2	0002
1474777-002	0002
1474777-1	0137
1474777-2	0002
1474777-3	0363
1474777-4	0039
1474777-7	0778
1474777-8	0015
1474777-11	0100

DEVICE TYPE	REPL CODE
1474778	0015
1474778-013	0087
1474778-2	0015
1474778-3	0015
1474778-4	0087
1474778-5	0102
1474778-6	0102
1474778-7	0015
1474778-8	0087
1474778-9	0914
1474778-10	0015
1474778-11	0015
1474778-13	0087
1474778-14	0102
1474778-16	0133
1474778-21	0102
1474788-10	0015
1474872-1	0133
1475721-1	0071
1476049-2	0102
1476161-12	0102
1476161-13	0015
1476171-1	0015
1476171-8	0015
1476171-11	0015
1476171-11(TRANS)	0085
1476171-11(TRANSISTO	0085
1476171-12	1208
1476171-13	0102
1476171-13(TRANSISTO	0085
1476171-14	1208
1476171-15	1208
1476171-17	0102
1476171-18	0102
1476171-19	1208
1476171-20	1208
1476171-21	0087
1476171-22	0102
1476171-24	1208
1476171-25	0102
1476171-26	0102
1476171-27	1208
1476171-28	0015
1476171-29	0015
1476171-30	0023
1476171-31	0015
1476171-32	0102
1476171-33	0133
1476171-34	0102
1476171-35	1208
1476171-36	0344
1476172-12	0102
1476179-001	0143
1476179-1	0143
1476179-3	0143
1476183-2	0102
1476183-3	0286
1476183-4	0752
1476183-5	0102
1476183-6	0102
1476183-8	1293
1476188-1	0016
1476689-1	0030
1476690-1	0133
1476690-2	0133
1476778-5	OEM
1476930	0752
1476933-501	0752
1476933-503	0752
1477022	0162
1477022-1	0163
1477046-1	0002
1477046-4	0137
1477046-5	0814
1477046-10	0490
1477069-1	1023
1477074-1	1023
1477080-501	0002
1477081-501	0002
1477949-1	1023
1477949-2	OEM
1478023-1	0769
1478164-1	0039
1478564-1	2313
1478564-2	1702
1478564-5	2313
1478564-6	1702
1501824	OEM
1503085	OEM
1503135	OEM
1522237-20	0016
1604236	OEM
1642606B1	0162
1642606B4	0631
1642606B6	0157
1662258-6	1099
1700001	0037
1700008	0079
1700019	0079
1700020	0224
1700032	0224
1700033	0224
1700034	0037
1700035	0488
1700036	0042
1700037	0693
1700038	0693

DEVICE TYPE	REPL CODE
1771872-12	0124
1773599-1	0006
1773631-1	0079
1800002	0143
1800006	0015
1800009	0124
1800012	0157
1800013	0170
1800017	0087
1800018	0015
1800019	2144
1800020	0814
1810037	0144
1810038	0144
1810039	0144
1811119	0015
1815036	0144
1815037	0144
1815039	0144
1815041	0016
1815042	0016
1815043	0016
1815045	0144
1815047	0144
1815054	0016
1815067	0144
1815068	0144
1815139	0038
1815153	0086
1815154	0016
1815154/7	0590
1815154-9	0086
1815156	0086
1815157	0086
1815157-9	0086
1815159	0086
1817004	0144
1817005	0016
1817005-3	0144
1817006	0086
1817006-3	0144
1817007	0016
1817008	0144
1817017	0208
1817045	0144
1817108	0016
1819045	0144
1820657	0769
1826065-1	0405
1826065-2	0405
1826065-3	2777
1826860-1	0405
1827322	0126
1846282-1	0016
1851490	0267
1887048	0469
1895989-1	1622
1895991-1	0141
1895992-1	0557
1895993-1	1812
1895994-1	1035
1895995-1	2086
1914062-1	1820
1944748	0599
1956016	0004
1956197	0244
1956486	0015
1960584	0160
1960632	0599
1960642	0149
1960643	0004
1961479	0160
1961480	0160
1961835	0160
1961837	0004
1961843	0015
1962326	0599
1962594	0015
1965016	0126
1965017	0160
1965019	0012
1966079	0160
1966808	0015
1967799	0086
1967799-1	0086
1967801	0086
1967813	0015
1969497	0015
2000261	OEM
2000287-28	0004
2000391	OEM
2000433-150	0143
2000521	0741
2000625-31	0004
2000625-32	0004
2000625-33	0004
2000625-34	0004
2000625-36	0015
2000626-32	0015
2000646-103	0216
2000646-104	0050
2000646-105	0233
2000646-106	0136
2000646-107	0016
2000646-108	0004
2000646-109	0160
2000646-110	0969
2000646-111	0164
2000646-112	0615

DEVICE TYPE	REPL CODE
2000646-113	0160
2000646-115	0015
2000646-119	0015
2000646-120	0015
2000648-21	0050
2000648-22	0050
2000648-23	0136
2000648-26	0143
2000648-120	0015
2000752-80	0086
2000757	0196
2000757-18	0143
2000757-19	0907
2000757-74	0196
2000757-79	0196
2000757-80	0144
2000804-7	0144
2000804-8	0144
2000804-9	0004
2001221	OEM
2001222	OEM
2001225	OEM
2001372	OEM
2001533	OEM
2001653	0004
2001653-20	0136
2001653-21	0136
2001653-22	0279
2001653-23	0004
2001653-24	0004
2001653-58	0050
2001653-59	0050
2001786-134	0143
2001786-139	1073
2001786-141	0015
2001786-142	0071
2001786-169	1024
2001786-207	0015
2001809-47	0004
2001809-48	0004
2001809-48A	0004
2001809-48B	0004
2001812-65	0279
2001822	OEM
2002151-020	0143
2002151-18	0050
2002151-18A	0050
2002151-19	0004
2002151-20	0143
2002152-14	0004
2002153-58	0050
2002153-59	0050
2002153-60	0136
2002153-71	0004
2002153-76	0050
2002153-77	0016
2002153-78	0004
2002153-83	0208
2002207	0030
2002207-2	0030
2002209-1	0012
2002209-3	OEM
2002209-4	0631
2002209-5	0170
2002209-7	0490
2002209-9	0170
2002209-10	0137
2002209-11	0244
2002210-110	0004
2002211-24	0004
2002211-25	0004
2002331-46	0361
2002332-53	0144
2002332-54	0144
2002332-55	0144
2002332-56	0144
2002332-57	0015
2002332-58	0015
2002336-12	OEM
2002336-19	0136
2002336-20	0143
2002336-115	0015
2002402	0133
2002402-29	0015
2002403-19	0136
2002620-18	0144
2002620-19	0144
2002621-2	0016
2003069	0071
2003069-1	0071
2003069-2	0133
2003069-4	0143
2003069-5	0139
2003069-6	0133
2003073-0701	0016
2003073-0702	0037
2003073-8	0004
2003073-9	0016
2003073-10	0016
2003073-11	0050
2003073-12	0628
2003073-13	0050
2003073-14	0004
2003073-15	0004
2003073-16	0208
2003073-67	0015
2003073-68	0015
2003073-91	0042
2003073-91A	0103

DEVICE TYPE	REPL CODE
2003168-135	0016
2003168-136	0016
2003229-25	0016
2003239-65	0016
2003251	0619
2003255	OEM
2003271	OEM
2003311	OEM
2003321	3202
2003342-109	0144
2003342-244	0127
2003351	OEM
2003501	OEM
2003779-22	0127
2003779-23	0127
2003779-24	0127
2003779-25	0127
2003779-26	0012
2003811	OEM
2003981	OEM
2004107-40	0196
2004357-106	0143
2004358-123	0004
2004358-142	0015
2004358-168	0004
2004746-87	0142
2004746-114	0144
2004746-115	0144
2004746-116	0126
2004746-117	0126
2005300	0122
2005779-26	0644
2006226-14	0004
2006227-51	0016
2006334-31	0164
2006334-115	0016
2006334-155	0086
2006422-132	0143
2006422-133	0015
2006431-44	0144
2006431-45	0016
2006431-46	0016
2006431-49	0016
2006431-50	0143
2006436-35	0555
2006436-36	0555
2006436-37	0126
2006436-38	0015
2006436-40	0086
2006436-89	0015
2006441-91	0015
2006441-113	0004
2006441-122	0143
2006441-123	0030
2006441-132	0133
2006463-89	0015
2006512-40	0015
2006512-79	0196
2006512-80	0196
2006513-19	0144
2006513-39	0127
2006513-133	0164
2006514-59	0222
2006514-60	0016
2006514-61	0693
2006582	0015
2006582-20	0143
2006582-21	0071
2006582-22	0015
2006582-23	0015
2006582-24	0015
2006582-25	0016
2006582-101	0007
2006607-59	0160
2006607-60	0016
2006607-61	0693
2006607-63	0644
2006613-77	0016
2006623-47	0321
2006623-48	0133
2006623-49	0015
2006623-88	0161
2006623-128	0693
2006623-145	0016
2006623-148	0086
2006627-54	0133
2006681-93	0127
2006681-94	0127
2006681-95	0127
2006681-96	0016
2006681-97	0030
2006681-120	0164
2008292-56	0127
2008292-87	0136
2008292-88	0133
2008292-89	0015
2008293-109	0211
2008293-111	0164
2008299-1	0127
2008299-2	0143
2008299-3	0015
2008302-41	0015
2010088-49	0079
2010494-3	0007
2010494-4	0079
2010499-52	0079
2010952-14	0208
2010957-49	0015
2010967-82	0030

DEVICE TYPE	REPL CODE
2010967-83	0133
2010967-84	0157
2013019-117	0015
2020341	OEM
2024794-3	OEM
2024794-6	OEM
2024794-8	OEM
2024794-115	OEM
2024794-127	OEM
2024794-140	OEM
2024794-143	OEM
2024794-152	OEM
2024794-187	OEM
2024794-188	OEM
2024794-189	OEM
2024794-190	OEM
2024794-192	OEM
2024794-193	OEM
2024794-194	OEM
2024794-218	OEM
2024794-330	OEM
2024794-364	OEM
2024794-366	OEM
2024794-367	OEM
2026387-1	OEM
2026392-1	OEM
2029655-7	OEM
2057013-0004	0037
2057013-0007	0037
2057013-0008	0037
2057013-0012	0037
2057013-0701	0037
2057013-0702	0037
2057013-0703	0037
2057062-0702	0015
2057100-62	OEM
2057199-070BA	0103
2057199-0700	0103
2057199-0701	0103
2057323-0500	0103
2057323-0501	0103
2060041	0015
2068491-704	0349
2068510-0701	1820
2068510-0702	0141
2068510-0703	0557
2068510-0704	0354
2068510-0705	0329
2076393	0136
2076403	0050
2076403-0703	0050
2076945-0701	0004
2090056-1	0085
2090056-5	0085
2090056-27	0085
2090924-0008	0004
2090924-008	0004
2090924-6	0004
2090924-8	0004
2090924-8A	0004
2091211-0014	0279
2091214-0005	0050
2091217-0014	0050
2091241-0005	0050
2091241-005	0136
2091241-0013	0279
2091241-0014	0279
2091241-0015	0279
2091241-0018	0004
2091241-0719	0136
2091241-1	0279
2091241-2	0279
2091241-3	0279
2091241-4	0279
2091241-5	0136
2091241-5A	0136
2091241-6	0279
2091241-7	0279
2091241-8	0279
2091241-9	0004
2091241-10	0279
2091241-11	0279
2091241-12	0279
2091241-13	0279
2091241-13A	0279
2091241-14	0279
2091241-15	0279
2091241-15A	0279
2091247-005	0050
2091260	0038
2091260-1	2839
2091260-2	2839
2091260-3	0038
2091578-0702	0211
2091578-1	0211
2091858-0712	0160
2091858-0715	0079
2091858-11	0160
2091859-0008	0085
2091859-0011	0160
2091859-0025	0085
2091859-0711	0144
2091859-0712	0160
2091859-0713	0085
2091859-0714	0085
2091859-0715	0160
2091859-0716	0160
2091859-0717	0160
2091859-0718	0160

DEVICE TYPE	REPL CODE
2091859-0720	0085
2091859-0723	0160
2091859-2	0085
2091859-4	0085
2091859-6	0085
2091859-8	0085
2091859-9	0160
2091859-10	0085
2091859-11	0085
2091859-16	0160
2091859-25	0160
2091959-16	0160
2092055-0001	0143
2092055-0002	0244
2092055-0003	0030
2092055-0004	0446
2092055-0005	0644
2092055-0007	0123
2092055-001	0143
2092055-0010	0143
2092055-0016	0157
2092055-0017	0244
2092055-0018	0025
2092055-0024	1596
2092055-0027	0244
2092055-0708	0911
2092055-0710	0025
2092055-0711	0143
2092055-0712	0244
2092055-0713	0143
2092055-0714	0016
2092055-0714(DIODE)	0133
2092055-1	0143
2092055-3	0030
2092055-4	0446
2092055-5	0644
2092055-7	0143
2092117-0018	0127
2092160-3	2839
2092405-7	0143
2092417-005	0050
2092417-0017	0127
2092417-0018	0127
2092417-0019	0127
2092417-0704	0050
2092417-0707	0050
2092417-0708	0050
2092417-0709	0050
2092417-0710	0050
2092417-0711	0007
2092417-0712	0007
2092417-0713	0007
2092417-0714	0007
2092417-0715	0007
2092417-0716	0007
2092417-0717	0050
2092417-0719	0016
2092417-0720	0016
2092417-0721	0016
2092417-0724	0079
2092417-0725	0079
2092417-1	0050
2092417-2	0050
2092417-3	0050
2092417-4	0050
2092417-5	0050
2092417-6	0050
2092417-7	0050
2092417-8	0050
2092417-9	0050
2092417-17	0079
2092417-18	0079
2092417-19	0079
2092418-0022	0007
2092418-0023	0007
2092418-0024	0007
2092418-071	0050
2092418-0708	0050
2092418-0710	0050
2092418-0711	0595
2092418-0712	0050
2092418-0715	0144
2092418-0716	0007
2092418-0717	0007
2092418-0718	0007
2092418-0719	0007
2092418-0720	0007
2092418-0721	0007
2092418-0724	0144
2092418-1	0050
2092418-2	0050
2092418-5	0050
2092418-6	0050
2092418-7	0050
2092418-8	0050
2092418-10	0050
2092418-11	0050
2092605-0705	0079
2092608-22	0079
2092609-0001	0079
2092609-0002	0079
2092609-001	0079
2092609-0022	0079
2092609-0023	0079
2092609-0024	0079
2092609-0025	0037
2092609-0026	0079
2092609-0027	0079
2092609-0028	0079

If replacement code is OEM, contact original manufacturer for replacement.

DEVICE TYPE	REPL CODE
2092609-0705	0016
2092609-0706	0016
2092609-0707	0016
2092609-0713	0016
2092609-0715	0016
2092609-0718	0016
2092609-0720	0079
2092609-0721	0079
2092609-1	0016
2092609-2	0016
2092609-3	0016
2092609-5	0016
2092693-0724	0127
2092693-0725	0127
2092693-1	0004
2092693-2	0050
2092693-3	0050
2092693-4	0050
2092693-8	0004
2092693-9	0050
2093308-070	0144
2093308-0700	0144
2093308-0701	0016
2093308-0702	0016
2093308-0703	0016
2093308-0704	0127
2093308-0704A	0144
2093308-0705	0127
2093308-0706	0127
2093308-0706A	0144
2093308-0708	0016
2093308-0725	0127
2093308-1	0144
2093308-2	0144
2093308-3	0144
2093308-8708	0079
2095083	0143
2097013-0702	0086
2120144	0127
2139103-4001	OEM
2146516	0196
2231154	0052
2234494	3384
2234496	1063
2234497	3868
2243255-1	0004
2295361	0557
2300439-00B	OEM
2300440-00A	OEM
2300441-00A	OEM
2311345	OEM
2312371	3664
2312501	OEM
2312522	OEM
2312532	OEM
2312561	OEM
2312651	OEM
2312771	OEM
2312772	OEM
2312872	OEM
2312873	OEM
2314009	0969
2314381	0472
2314391	1376
2315272	OEM
2315471	OEM
2316177	0127
2318365	0919
2319990	3859
2320011	0004
2320022	0016
2320031	0127
2320041	0151
2320041H	0007
2320042	0127
2320043	0127
2320051	0233
2320051(BRADFORD)	0283
2320051H	0233
2320052	0086
2320062	0144
2320063	0144
2320073	0144
2320083	0042
2320084	0178
2320092	0222
2320111	0016
2320123	0016
2320141	0127
2320141H	0127
2320143	0127
2320154	0279
2320161	0037
2320161(RCA)	0050
2320162	0037
2320191	0711
2320201	0599
2320221	0142
2320222	0142
2320223	0142
2320233	0086
2320242	0126
2320243	0126
2320261	0004
2320271	0074
2320273	0074
2320281	0003
2320291	0065
2320299	0065

DEVICE TYPE	REPL CODE
2320302	0004
2320302H	0004
2320331	0208
2320413	0016
2320415	OEM
2320422	0164
2320422-1	0004
2320423	0004
2320432	0042
2320441	0016
2320471	0127
2320471-1	0127
2320471H	0127
2320482	0042
2320482H	0042
2320483	0042
2320485	0042
2320486	0042
2320492	0004
2320512	0279
2320513	0004
2320514	0050
2320514-1	0279
2320541	0160
2320563	0127
2320591	0076
2320591-1	0079
2320594	0076
2320595	0076
2320596	0076
2320598	0076
2320602	0042
2320631	0148
2320632	0148
2320635	0148
2320637	0148
2320643	0191
2320644	0191
2320646	0191
2320646-1	0155
2320647	0191
2320647-1	0155
2320651	0042
2320652	0042
2320663	0191
2320664	0191
2320681	0148
2320682	0148
2320696	0016
2320696-1	0016
2320843	0558
2320845	0558
2320846	0558
2320855	0520
2320884	0919
2320913	OEM
2320914	OEM
2320931	0142
2320946	0086
2320961	0637
2320994	0142
2321001	0142
2321095	0168
2321101	0338
2321111	0338
2321112	0338
2321121	2420
2321151	0710
2321154	0052
2321221	1077
2321241	0359
2321264	0934
2321281	0919
2321291	0142
2321301	1274
2321302	0338
2321306	1274
2321321	0688
2321351	0688
2321372	2596
2321374	0074
2321381	1638
2321403	0142
2321411	1077
2321412	1077
2321433	0388
2321438	0388
2321439	0388
2321472	0261
2321511	0224
2321521	0643
2321522	0643
2321541	0151
2321551	2643
2321561	2636
2321563	2636
2321581	0424
2321591	1274
2321621	0151
2321647	0191
2321652	0171
2321693	0388
2321699	0388
2321703	1900
2321751	0006
2321763	0676
2321764	0676
2321791	0388
2321803	3320

DEVICE TYPE	REPL CODE
2321871	1967
2321881	0018
2321882	0018
2321891	0527
2321982	0018
2321984	0018
2321991	0261
2321992	0261
2321993	0261
2322163	0705
2322191	0151
2322223	0723
2322561	0275
2322562	0275
2322851	0055
2322943	0095
2323021	0055
2323102	0111
2323112	0388
2323114	0388
2323123	0236
2323351	2464
2323352	0819
2323411	0388
2323431	5910
2323432	2047
2323434	2047
2323521	2539
2323522	2539
2323523	2539
2323526	2539
2323541	0638
2323642	OEM
2323771	OEM
2323782	0058
2323931	0388
2323941	1638
2324082	1747
2324084	1747
2324171	0558
2324292	0060
2324322	0261
2324411	1533
2324412	1533
2324414	1533
2324471	3683
2325702	1338
2325725	0151
2326022	1505
2326214	0558
2326216	0558
2326218	0558
2326611	0275
2326631	OEM
2326661	0275
2326991	0142
2327022	0086
2327023	0016
2327031	0015
2327041	0015
2327052	0103
2327053	0103
2327061	0142
2327071	0137
2327073	0398
2327074	0053
2327075	0721
2327076	0039
2327077	0416
2327078	0313
2327111	0212
2327122	0016
2327132	0321
2327134	OEM
2327135	OEM
2327142	0321
2327142(JFET)	0321
2327142(MOSFET)	0212
2327152	0555
2327153	0555
2327172	0103
2327182	0142
2327192	0899
2327203	0555
2327206	0042
2327232	0212
2327262	0037
2327282	0126
2327283	0126
2327292	0086
2327293	0086
2327301	OEM
2327302	0627
2327311	1611
2327312	1611
2327332	0086
2327363	0547
2327387	0037
2327393	OEM
2327403	0086
2327411	4490
2327421	0438
2327422	0438
2327431	0212
2327501	2116
2327502	2116
2327504	2116
2327505	2116
2327751	0013

DEVICE TYPE	REPL CODE
2327771	2926
2327772	OEM
2327773	2926
2327783	OEM
2327844	3454
2327883	1514
2327931	0095
2328012	OEM
2328451	OEM
2328454	OEM
2328455	OEM
2330011	0276
2330011H	0276
2330021	0644
2330032	0752
2330034	0374
2330191	0102
2330192	0344
2330201	0015
2330211	0102
2330235	0023
2330241	0137
2330251	0023
2330251(POWER)	0087
2330251H	0015
2330252	0023
2330253	0023
2330254	0023
2330256	0023
2330302	0025
2330302H	0644
2330305	0100
2330307	0244
2330332	0087
2330341	0196
2330351	0133
2330352	0124
2330353	0124
2330354	0023
2330361	0276
2330362	0015
2330381	0374
2330533	0023
2330551	0023
2330553	0023
2330561	0015
2330562	0015
2330564	0023
2330611	0120
2330612	0015
2330631	0062
2330632	0062
2330633	0077
2330634	0062
2330643	0025
2330721	0023
2330741	0318
2330743	0057
2330752	0918
2330771	0087
2330773	0087
2330791	0025
2330921	0201
2331001	0582
2331121	0102
2331141	0015
2331142	0015
2331152	0137
2331154	0052
2331155	0052
2331161	0181
2331164	0248
2331165	0181
2331172	0248
2331173	0313
2331174	0313
2331201	0604
2331351	0124
2331381	0182
2331441	0123
2331481	0015
2331491	0446
2331493	0041
2331495	0253
2331497	0466
2331502	0087
2331546	0372
2331582	0489
2331773	OEM
2331775	0118
2331781	0372
2331782	0372
2331785	0036
2331797	0582
2331799	0582
2331801	0877
2331802	0253
2331804	0877
2331805	0157
2331806	0091
2331807	0091
2331809	0292
2331814	0062
2331815	0062
2331816	0062
2331817	0077
2331819	0077
2331821	0165
2331823	0165

DEVICE TYPE	REPL CODE
2331826	0318
2331827	0057
2331829	0057
2331831	0064
2331834	0064
2331835	0181
2331841	0999
2331842	0999
2331843	0052
2331844	0999
2331845	0053
2331849	0999
2331851M	OEM
2331857	0372
2331912	0023
2331913	0133
2331941	0102
2331991	0559
2332004	0010
2332031	OEM
2332032	OEM
2332121	0344
2332141	0023
2332142	0023
2332152	0102
2332221	0091
2332242	0023
2332251	0023
2332431	2604
2332483	0755
2332491	3990
2332492	1123
2332501	0010
2332791	0106
2332792	2384
2332794	2384
2332841	0181
2332851	0023
2332891	0511
2332892	0511
2333003	0023
2333011	0023
2333101	0015
2333173	0123
2333201	0023
2333231	0071
2333262	OEM
2333855	0489
2333972	OEM
2334011	OEM
2334021	OEM
2334052	0755
2334061	0118
2334122	0041
2334142	0091
2334243	0440
2334244	0440
2334283	0489
2334303	0195
2334304	OEM
2334305	0195
2334312	0195
2334324M	OEM
2334471	3683
2334581	0023
2334592	0023
2334671	OEM
2334672	OEM
2334881	0124
2335041	0700
2335042	0700
2335181	0695
2335182	0695
2335461	0489
2335462	0489
2335982	0559
2335991	3417
2336291	0023
2336381	OEM
2336612	0282
2336911	OEM
2337011	0133
2337063	0560
2337065	0416
2337071	0015
2337101	0137
2337293	0057
2337372	0106
2338031	1654
2338161	0023
2338162	0023
2338171	OEM
2338321	0133
2338531	0017
2338871	0031
2338902	0023
2338932	OEM
2338941	1119
2338944	OEM
2338971	1560
2339011	0877
2339021	OEM
2339021M	OEM
2339023	OEM
2339031	OEM
2339032	OEM
2339052	OEM
2339053	OEM
2339091	OEM

DEVICE TYPE	REPL CODE
2339091M	OEM
2339093	OEM
2339102M	OEM
2339121M	OEM
2339142	0999
2339151	OEM
2339152	OEM
2339152M	OEM
2339191M	OEM
2339201	OEM
2339203	0700
2339211	0489
2339212	OEM
2339222	0450
2339223	0709
2339232	OEM
2339242	OEM
2339251	0010
2339252	0010
2339481	0023
2339491	0015
2339531	OEM
2339602	OEM
2339691	OEM
2339692	OEM
S-M	OEM
2339801M	OEM
2339812M	OEM
2339814	OEM
2339817	OEM
2339822	OEM
2339825	OEM
2339832	OEM
2339833M	OEM
2339835M	OEM
2339837	OEM
2339839	OEM
2339845	2974
2339846	OEM
2339847	OEM
2339849	OEM
2339851	OEM
2339852	OEM
2339854M	OEM
2339857	OEM
2339867	OEM
2339868	OEM
2339868M	OEM
2339872M	OEM
2339873	OEM
2339874	OEM
2339876	OEM
2339885	OEM
2339885M	2405
2339886M	OEM
2339887M	OEM
2339889	2414
2339921	OEM
2339943M	OEM
2339971	OEM
2339972M	OEM
2339981	OEM
2339991	0672
2340211	OEM
2340283	1914
2340331	0120
2340332	0139
2340511	OEM
2340521	OEM
2343961	0023
2344071	4323
2347021	0015
2348062	OEM
2348103	OEM
2348121	OEM
2348141	OEM
2348163	OEM
2348181	OEM
2348183	OEM
2348252	OEM
2348291	OEM
2348391	0241
2348431	1082
2348511	OEM
2360021	2560
2360042	0167
2360141	0872
2360151	4546
2360171	0872
2360181	OEM
2360192	OEM
2360201	0167
2360212	OEM
2360221	0043
2360231	0385
2360241	OEM
2360252	OEM
2360253	OEM
2360254	OEM
2360261	OEM
2360271	4561
2360281	4556
2360291	4560
2360331	0167
2360351	OEM
2360361	0872
2360391	0167
2360401	0872
2360431	1049

DEVICE TYPE	REPL CODE
2360441	1049
2360501	2109
2360501(SIF)	0167
2360511	0872
2360561	0936
2360611	2170
2360631	4546
2360681	OEM
2360691	1420
2360741	0232
2360751	1920
2360761	OEM
2360782	4700
2360851	0215
2360951	1585
2361251	1197
2361281	0485
2361301	2079
2361461	0330
2361571	4705
2361572	4705
2362051	1623
2362301	0088
2362492	OEM
2362541	5090
2362605	0356
2362991	4742
2363001	6693
2363191	0101
2363261	4705
2364131	3462
2364134	OEM
2364172	2511
2364181	1192
2365021	3728
2365061	2109
2365062	2109
2365411	0176
2365452	0624
2366151	5676
2366201	3410
2366392	1521
2366411	OEM
2366571	OEM
2366591	1042
2366621	2641
2366631	5123
2366721	4959
2368211	1813
2368271	OEM
2368282	1433
2368283	OEM
2368291	OEM
2368292	OEM
2368451	OEM
2368501	2031
2368671	OEM
2368692	OEM
2368913	1158
2369151	0445
2369582	OEM
2370061	OEM
2370152	OEM
2370873	1631
2371806	OEM
2372161	OEM
2380131	OEM
2380391	OEM
2380426	0330
2380661	OEM
2380662	OEM
2381111	OEM
2381344	OEM
2381471	OEM
2381832	OEM
2381862	OEM
2382952	OEM
2383191	OEM
2383341	OEM
2383342	OEM
2383421	OEM
2390022	0058
2398511	OEM
2398611	0124
2485076-2	0086
2485076-3	0086
2485077-2	0086
2485077-3	0086
2485078-1	0016
2485078-2	0016
2485078-2(PENNCREST)	0079
2485078-2(SEARS)	0079
2485078-3	0016
2485079-1	0016
2485079-2	0016
2485079-3	0016
2485080	0133
2485080(DIODE)	0143
2486836	0015
2487340	0037
2487341	0037
2487424	0590
2495012	0136
2495013	0136
2495014	0004
2495078	0050
2495079	0050
2495080	0004

If replacement code is OEM, contact original manufacturer for replacement.

233

DEVICE TYPE	REPL CODE
2495082	0050
2495083	0123
2495083-2	0143
2495084	0143
2495166-1	0144
2495166-2	0016
2495166-4	0016
2495166-8	0016
2495166-9	0016
2495200	0136
2495376	0050
2495377	0050
2495378	0136
2495379	0136
2495380	0143
2495383	0143
2495388	0004
2495388-1	0004
2495388-2	0004
2495488-1	0136
2495488-2	0136
2495520	0007
2495521	0007
2495521-1	0016
2495522-1	0007
2495522-4	0016
2495523-1	0007
2495529	0143
2495529(ARVIN)	0086
2495529(DIODE)	0143
2495567-2	0004
2495567-3	0004
2495568	0164
2495568-2	0004
2496125-2	0016
2496436	0143
2497094-1	0007
2497094-2	0007
2497473	0004
2497473-1	0004
2497496	0004
2497888	0164
2498163	0086
2498456-2	0127
2498457-2	0016
2498482-2	0127
2498507-1	0144
2498507-2	0144
2498507-3	0144
2498508-2	0127
2498508-3	0127
2498512	0037
2498513	0015
2498530	0143
2498837	0050
2498837-4	0004
2498902-1	0127
2498902-2	0127
2498903-1	0127
2498903-2	0224
2498903-3	0127
2498904-3	0016
2498904-4	0016
2498904-6	0016
2499048	0030
2499950	0111
2500389-432	1035
2500389-444	0033
2500390-435	1168
2500390-436	1820
2500390-437	1824
2500390-446	0141
2500390-449	1833
2500390-461	1848
2500390-462	0557
2500391-445	0081
2500747	1035
2501337-433	2086
2501557-430	1812
2501557-436	1820
2501557-437	1824
2501557-446	0141
2501557-449	1833
2501557-461	1848
2501557-462	0557
2520063	0016
2552007	0087
2610783	0310
2610784	1705
2610786	0232
2610788	0175
2650238A	OEM
2652613	0033
2652614	0081
2656211-1	1812
2656212	0141
2656212-1	0141
2656213	0033
2656213-1	0033
2656214	0081
2656214-1	0081
2656747	0033
2656748	0141
2666293	1564
2666294-1	0117
2709759	1911
2711904	0823
2712080	0016
2729789	0841

DEVICE TYPE	REPL CODE
2780312	1024
2808577	1035
2811925-002	3494
2855296-01	0004
2868536-1	1303
2880661	OEM
2898431-2	0141
2899000-00	0141
2899001-00	0557
2899002-00	1812
2899003-00	1820
2899004-00	0081
2902798-2	1545
2903993-I	0037
2904014	0160
2910011	0552
2910012	0387
2910021	0727
2910932	OEM
2910941	OEM
2911481	3403
2911491	OEM
2911501	0412
2911511	OEM
2912175	3857
2912176	3857
2912177	2348
2912178	3857
2912561	3068
2912961	4040
2913081	4111
2913091	OEM
2913891	0311
2913941	OEM
2913945	OEM
2913981	4066
2914912	OEM
2914921	OEM
2914931	2843
2914941	3054
2914951	4444
2914961	4452
2915191	OEM
2915192	0517
2916242	OEM
2916321	OEM
2916631	OEM
2916633	OEM
2916634	OEM
2916671	OEM
2916681	4964
2917221	OEM
2917222	OEM
2917301	OEM
2917361	4964
2917591	OEM
2917601	2998
2917611	1022
2917621	OEM
2917711	OEM
2917721	OEM
2917731	OEM
2917741	OEM
2917742	OEM
2917802	OEM
2917803	OEM
2970038H05	0279
3004856	0004
3005300	0122
3005861	0016
3007359-00	1824
3007359-01	1833
3007359-02	0337
3007359-03	1035
3007472-00	0081
3007473-00	1035
3007473-01	1035
3007474-00	1812
3007474-01	1812
3007475-00	0557
3007475-01	0557
3007476-00	0141
3007476-01	0141
3007477-00	1820
3007477-01	1820
3007572-00	2086
3007573-00	0354
3007604-00	1609
3008321-00	1911
3020061	0151
3034725-1	2515
3100001	0026
3100002	2232
3100004	0619
3100017	0002
3100021	0560
3100026	0814
3102006	1519
3102007	1550
3102008	1585
3102009	1598
3102010	1657
3102011	0035
3102013	0822
3102014	0088
3102015	0243
3102016	1876
3102017	1877
3102018	1615

DEVICE TYPE	REPL CODE
3102019	0953
3102020	1153
3102021	4301
3102022	0260
3102023	1662
3102024	0971
3102025	0985
3102026	2100
3102027	2930
3102028	1644
3106001	OEM
3106002	1253
3108001	OEM
3108002	4886
3108003	2291
3108009	0518
3110001	3441
3130057	0178
3130058	0103
3146977	0103
3146977A	0103
3152159	0178
3152170	0103
3152170A	0103
3170717	0233
3170757	0233
3172626	2086
3172627-2	1833
3172629-1	1812
3172629-2	1848
3172630	0033
3172631	3365
3172632-1	0557
3172638	2595
3176135-1	1820
3176135-2	1824
3177200	1035
3230591	OEM
3267390-01	0554
3403787	0016
3404520-601	0349
3412004-1912	0321
3412951	1843
3412986-1	2515
3430063	0015
3430063-1	0535
3430063-I	0535
3457845-1	2030
3457964-1	1224
3457964-2	1224
3457964-3	1224
3457964-4	1224
3459332-1	0007
3460553-2	0160
3460553-4	0160
3460758-2	0947
3462221-1	0160
3462306-1	0160
3463098-1	0084
3463098-2	0529
3463604-1	0178
3463604-2	0178
3463609-2	0007
3468068-1	0007
3468068-2	0007
3468068-3	0007
3468068-4	0007
3520025-001	1820
3520041-001	0232
3520042-001	0507
3520043-001	1164
3520044-001	1018
3520045-001	1160
3520046-001	1303
3520047-001	0867
3520048-001	0357
3520050-001	1417
3539307-001	0007
3539307-002	0007
3596061	0133
3596062	0143
3596063	0037
3596067	0144
3596068	0144
3596069	0144
3596070	0144
3596071	0144
3596072	0144
3596091	0419
3596092	0419
3596100	0848
3596101	0848
3596116	0086
3596117	0079
3596118	0037
3596128	0037
3596242	0030
3596260	0144
3596261	0144
3596316	OEM
3596317	OEM
3596338	0079
3596339	0079
3596340	0126
3596341	0126
3596353	1748
3596354	1335
3596398	0025
3596401	1897

DEVICE TYPE	REPL CODE
3596402	0212
3596435	0030
3596440	0127
3596446	0042
3596447	0042
3596448	0042
3596449	0042
3596451	0919
3596452	0919
3596453	0919
3596454	0919
3596570	0016
3596803	OEM
3596808	2593
3596809	1832
3596810	2728
3597049	1239
3597103	0144
3597104	0144
3597114	0127
3597260	0144
3597261	0144
3597280	1239
3598173	1239
3610001-001	OEM
3610003	1063
3610005	3384
3650238A	0006
3670724H	0076
3671857E	0142
3673351K	0191
3673354G	0191
3680322-3	1186
3720923-1	1963
3720923-2	1963
3720923-3	1963
3720923-4	1963
3731313-1	0160
3939307-002	0007
4003000	OEM
4013373-0701	1799
4036392-P2	0170
4036598-P1	0160
4036598-P2	0004
4036612-P1	0279
4036612-P2	0279
4036707-P1	0279
4036707-P2	0279
4036715-P1	0050
4036715-P2	0050
4036733-P1	0160
4036749-P1	0595
4036749-P2	0595
4036754-P1	0038
4036754-P2	0038
4036831-P1	0435
4036832-P1	0435
4036887-P8	0016
4036923-P1	0050
4036923-P2	0050
4036924-P1	0016
4036924-P2	0016
4036937-P1	0279
4036937-P2	0279
4036962-P1	0050
4036962-P2	0050
4036963-P1	0050
4036963-P2	0050
4036965-P1	0050
4036965-P2	0050
4037145-P1	0004
4037145-P2	0004
4037289-P1	0595
4037289-P2	0595
4037325-P1	0015
4037410-P1	0050
4037410-P2	0050
4037413-P1	0631
4037586-P1	0016
4037586-P2	0016
4037594-P1	0160
4037607-P1	0160
4037647-P1	0555
4037647-P2	0555
4037764-P1	0050
4037764-P2	0050
4037800-P1	0016
4037800-P2	0016
4037804-P1	0004
4037804-P2	0004
4037839-P1	0595
4037839-P2	0595
4037993-P1	0279
4037993-P2	0279
4038256-P1	0208
4038256-P2	0208
4038260-P1	0279
4038260-P2	0279
4038264-P1	0595
4038264-P2	0595
4038359-P1	0050
4038359-P2	0050
4038406-P1	0050
4038406-P2	0050
4041200-30110	0133
4041200-40100	0143
4080187-0502	0042
4080187-0504	0103
4080187-0506	0419

DEVICE TYPE	REPL CODE
4080187-0507	0419
4080320-050B	0103
4080320-0501	0103
4080320-0504	0103
4080627-0501	0178
4080835-0002	0419
4080838-0001	0178
4080838-0002	0178
4080838-002	0419
4080838-2	0178
4080838-3	0178
4080865-0012	0161
4080866-0006	0555
4080866-0006(PLASTIC	0042
4080866-0007	0178
4080866-000A	0103
4080866-0012	0419
4080866-0013	0042
4080866-1	0178
4080866-2	0178
4080866-8006	0103
4080873-0001	0161
4080879-0001	0042
4080879-0006	0419
4080879-0015	0178
4082501-0001	3004
4082501-0001A	0160
4082501-001	0085
4082626-0001	1686
4082664-0001	2593
4082665	1335
4082665-0001	1335
4082665-0002	1335
4082665-0003	1335
4082671-0002	0396
4082748-0002	0157
4082799-0001	1832
4082799-0002	1832
4082799-1	1832
4082799-2	1832
4082802-0001	2720
4082802-0002	2720
4082873-0001	0848
4082886-0002	0161
4084114-0001	0212
4084114-0002	0212
4084117-0001	2530
4084117-0002	2530
4090187-0502	1506
4090605-1	2535
4101685	0015
4361620	0103
4420022-P1	0267
4420022-P2	0267
4450028-P1	0720
4450028-P2	0720
4450028P4	0720
4450300-1	0147
4450300P2	0411
4450300P3	0411
4450303-001	1403
4450303-002	1403
4511424	0893
4613443	4406
4663001A905	1303
4663001A909	0357
4663001A911	1018
4663001A912	0507
4663001A915	0867
4663001D907	0232
4800002	0124
4800021	0631
4800022	0041
4800023	0287
4800026	0094
4800037	0137
4800045	1344
4800062	2296
4804427	2675
4806080	2156
4806095	2156
4813466	0016
4820004	0042
4822001	0076
4822003	0037
4824002	0919
4824003	0486
4890210A03	1154
4890210A06	0124
4890210A10	2739
4890210A12	0181
4890210A13	0372
4890210A14	0261
4890210A16	0643
4890210A17	1157
4890210A18	0018
4890210A19	0023
4890210A20	0604
4890210A21	0041
4890210A23	0181
4890210A24	0064
4890210A25	0124
4890210A26	0124
4890210A28	0062
4890210A29	0253
4890210A30	0181
4890210A31	0060
4890210A32	0466
4890210A53	1338

DEVICE TYPE	REPL CODE
4890210A54	1157
4890210A55	0023
4890210A56	0730
4890210A57	0041
4890210A59	0064
4890210A61	0018
4890210A62	0667
4890210A76	0466
4890210A92	OEM
4890210A96	0077
4890223A07	1767
4890223A39	2604
4890223A61	1154
4890223A62	1203
4890223A63	3574
4890223A64	0023
4890223A65	0023
4890223A66	0166
4890223A67	0091
4890223A68	0750
4890223A88	0170
4890223A89	0015
4890223A90	0248
4890223A92	0071
4890223A93	1533
4890223A94	0355
4890223A95	0577
4890223A96	0113
4890223A97	0261
4890223A98	0261
4890223A99	0118
4890229A10	OEM
4890229A30	2604
4890229A49	0124
4890229A51	0023
4890229A53	0275
4890229A59	0118
4890229A86	0023
4890232A40	1211
4890232A67	0124
4890232A78	0023
4890232A94	0071
4890232A99	0261
4890233A53	0019
4890233A97	0450
4890234A30	0284
4890234A31	0155
4890234A83	0203
4890235A09	0339
4890235A14	0023
4890235A24	0023
4890235A25	0023
4890235A45	OEM
4890235A51	1981
4890235A52	0819
4890235A53	0168
4890235A54	1154
4890235A55	0023
4890235A56	0248
4890235A57	0137
4890235A58	0032
4890235A59	0165
4890235A60	0017
4890235A61	0055
4890235A62	0604
4890235A71	0064
4890235A89	0203
4890237A60	0690
4890237A80	0018
4890343A49	0155
4890343A81	0018
4890343A87	2083
4890420A01	0577
4890420A19	0577
4890420A24	0577
4890420A29	0355
4890420A42	0819
4890420A83	0643
4890420A84	0388
4890420A85	0015
4890420A86	0015
4890420A87	0015
4890432A02	0558
4890432A06	0006
4890432A15	0023
4890432A42	0118
4890432A55	0819
4890432A56	0819
4890432A65	1767
4890445A09	2208
4890445A17	0577
4890445A51	0181
4890445A52	0181
4890448A32	0023
4890456A24	0124
4890456A30	1951
4890456A85	0057
4890478A30	0041
4890478A47	0355
4890478A51	0558
4890478A52	0577
4890478A53	0577
4890478A68	0577
4890478A69	0667
4890478A83	0203
4890488A01	0019
4890488A06	1951
4890488A19	0667
4890488A32	0023

DEVICE TYPE	REPL CODE
4890488A67	0071
4890488A77	0339
4890543A15	0158
4890549A20	OEM
4890549A22	0023
4890549A25	OEM
4890549A64	0511
4890549A71	0018
4890549A99	0077
4890562A02	0015
4890562A04	0019
4890562A29	0071
4907976	0004
4914296	4170
4915702	1339
4915705	0522
4999774	0160
4999885	0432
4999887	0004
5000027	OEM
5073004	0004
5076054	0133
5076204	0699
5076205BZ	1011
5113753A37	5123
5113753A67	3860
5113753A68	5116
5120134	OEM
5120850	OEM
5165440	1820
5175460	0462
5190266A68	3848
5190458A07	0176
5190480A92	0484
5190480A96	0970
5190495A88	5902
5190495A89	OEM
5190495A90	3800
5190507A20	2008
5190507A39	0765
5190507A40	0765
5190507A46	0694
5190507A60	0754
5190507A78	2056
5190507A87	2062
5190518A19	2531
5190528A01	0765
5190528A02	4281
5190528A28	3800
5190528A29	0330
5190528A30	5823
5190528A30(TNH11304)	OEM
5190528A41	1631
5190528A43	4131
5190528A44	OEM
5190528A48	OEM
5190528A50	OEM
5190528A53	6106
5190528A54	OEM
5190528A55	5167
5190528A56	5168
5190528A57	5169
5190528A58	4838
5190528A59	5178
5190528A60	OEM
5190528A61	5170
5190528A62	OEM
5190528A63	OEM
5190528A64	3130
5190528A65	OEM
5190528A66	OEM
5190538A18	1938
5190538A20	3848
5190538A20(AN5125M)	OEM
5190538A22	0330
5190538A98	4349
5190555A50	1521
5190555A53	3800
5190555A60	0034
5261001A	OEM
5261071	OEM
5262063	OEM
5262081	OEM
5300073-15	0002
5300113-1	0015
5301181	OEM
5301341	OEM
5301571	OEM
5305582	OEM
5306567	OEM
5320003	0178
5320004	0076
5320011	0004
5320022	0076
5320023	0076
5320023H	0079
5320024	0079
5320026	0079
5320031	0843
5320032	0321
5320042H	0037
5320043H	0037
5320051	0127
5320064	0076
5320064H	0079
5320067	0076
5320069	0076
5320074	0016
5320101	0004

If replacement code is OEM, contact original manufacturer for replacement.

DEVICE TYPE	REPL CODE
5320111	0126
5320141	0004
5320151	1401
5320241	0016
5320295	0004
5320295H	0208
5320296	0004
5320305	0208
5320305H	0004
5320306	0208
5320326	0016
5320326H	0127
5320328	0144
5320361	0208
5320372	0016
5320372H	0016
5320373	0079
5320386	0038
5320422H	0042
5320432	5435
5320433	0042
5320475	0208
5320485	0004
5320492H	0042
5320501	0693
5320511	1401
5320583	0321
5320592	0006
5320593	0006
5320612	0086
5320613	0191
5320622	0590
5320632	1257
5320642	0555
5320643	0161
5320651	0076
5320671	0042
5320702	0321
5320723	0455
5320731	0143
5320772	0224
5320791	0930
5320813	0076
5320851	0079
5320861	0127
5320872	0004
5320921	1779
5320942	0321
5320943	0321
5321183	0431
5321184	0431
5321204	0527
5321213	0018
5321214	0018
5321235	0386
5321251	0688
5321252	0688
5321253	0688
5321255	0006
5321261	0016
5321291	0151
5321301	0042
5321311	2684
5321321	0930
5321422	1270
5321431	0127
5321501	3308
5321502	3308
5321662	1132
5321663	1132
5321901	0224
5322216	1505
5322733	0006
5323071	0553
5323561	0881
5323562	1026
5323704	3104
5323903	0151
5324051	3104
5324111	OEM
5324631	OEM
5326244	OEM
5327011	0151
5327021	0006
5327031	0148
5327163	OEM
5328193	OEM
5330001	0015
5330011	0057
5330012	0012
5330031	0015
5330041	0023
5330041(HR-5A)	0071
5330041H	0015
5330042	0015
5330051	0025
5330054	0053
5330054H	0053
5330059	0560
5330101	0015
5330101H	0015
5330102	0015
5330102H	0015
5330104	0023
5330104H	0015
5330131	0133
5330132	0124
5330133	0124
5330135	0124
5330201	0030
5330212H	0133
5330261	0133
5330261H	0133
5330312	0062
5330315	0077
5330322	0012
5330325	0165
5330328	0057
5330331	0143
5330332	0143
5330334	0133
5330335	0143
5330336	0015
5330341	0023
5330371	0015
5330372	0015
5330381	0015
5330392	0253
5330431	0023
5330521	0005
5330532	0053
5330541	0681
5330542	0681
5330551	0064
5330552	0181
5330571	0124
5330572	0133
5330573	0133
5330661	0623
5330712	0118
5330714	0274
5330721	0123
5330731	0019
5330732	0143
5330761	0124
5330842	0041
5330852	0030
5331001	0133
5331017	0582
5331051	0143
5331102	0319
5331271	0371
5331511	3460
5331521	0319
5331591	0133
5331592	0133
5331931	0319
5332192	0023
5333341	OEM
5339002	0133
5339021	0133
5339351	OEM
5340001	0133
5340001(TRANSISTOR)	0079
5340001H	0133
5340021	0015
5340022	0120
5340022H	0133
5340051	0133
5340082	0030
5340111	0133
5340113	0139
5340202	0120
5350051	OEM
5350081	OEM
5350121	2247
5350132	4481
5350136	4481
5350141	4482
5350151	4483
5350152	4483
5350161	4484
5350182	0465
5350211	4320
5350231	2111
5350251	2632
5350321	4331
5350481	OEM
5350491	4331
5350591	OEM
5350604	2884
5350611	1319
5350702	3167
5350961	2632
5351021	1611
5351031	4491
5351041	0696
5351042	0696
5351051	4490
5351061	2568
5351062	2568
5351351	0167
5351361	0872
5351411	4721
5351501	5088
5351521	5569
5351541	OEM
5351551	5091
5351601	OEM
5351621	OEM
5352631	2094
5352791	OEM
5353002	OEM
5353021	OEM
5353023	OEM
5353031	OEM
5353033	OEM
5353041	OEM
5353061	OEM
5353081	OEM
5353091	OEM
5353101	OEM
5353111	OEM
5353112	OEM
5353121	OEM
5353591	2369
5354511	OEM
5354523	OEM
5354531	OEM
5354541	OEM
5354601	OEM
5354611	OEM
5355262	2015
5355611	2641
5355751	OEM
5356011	OEM
5356211	OEM
5356251	OEM
5356341	OEM
5357351	OEM
5357531	OEM
5357561	0103
5359031	0232
5359251	2592
5359261	3763
5359262	3763
5359271	0564
5359281	0083
5359451	OEM
5359522	4869
5359592	OEM
5359701	2279
5359841	5089
5361071	OEM
5361671	OEM
5362055	OEM
5362121	OEM
5362291	OEM
5362382	OEM
5362741	0215
5362862	OEM
5362882	OEM
5362883	OEM
5362912	OEM
5362914	OEM
5362931	OEM
5364091	3051
5364201	3130
5364306	OEM
5364309	OEM
5364601	1288
5364602	OEM
5364631	OEM
5364642	OEM
5364651	OEM
5364881	OEM
5364902	OEM
5364911	OEM
5364923	OEM
5364971	OEM
5366401	OEM
5366581	OEM
5367061	OEM
5368931	OEM
5369181	1689
5369431	1022
5369911	1927
5369914	OEM
5370031	OEM
5374053	OEM
5374291	OEM
5374302	OEM
5376912	OEM
5377132	OEM
5377551	OEM
5377561	OEM
5377562	OEM
5378641	OEM
5380031	OEM
5380051	0015
5380052	1348
5380131	OEM
5380132	OEM
5381211	OEM
5381214	OEM
5381661	OEM
5381662	OEM
5381681	5589
5381682	3156
5382051	OEM
5382092	OEM
5390191	OEM
5391032	0484
5406665-P2	0004
5406665-P5	0004
5490307-P2	0170
5490307-P3	0137
5490307-P4	0002
5490415-P4	0015
5490459-P1	0015
5490459-P2	0015
5490459-P3	0015
5490459-P4	0015
5490804-P1	0015
5490804-P2	0015
5490804-P3	0015
5490804-P4	0015
5490804-P5	0015
5490804-P6	0015
5491236-P1	0143
5491236-P2	0143
5491263-P1	0143
5491338-P1	0162
5492153-1	0435
5492153-P1	0435
5492639-P1	0038
5492639-P2	0038
5492653-P1	0595
5492653-P2	0595
5492655-P1	0595
5492655-P2	0595
5492655-P3	0595
5492655-P4	0595
5492655-P5	0595
5492655-P6	0595
5492659-P1	0595
5492659-P2	0595
5493158-1	0160
5493158-P1	0160
5493159-P1	0097
5493957-P1	0050
5493957-P2	0050
5493957-P3	0050
5493957-P4	0050
5493957-P5	0050
5493957-P6	0050
5494922-P1	0015
5494922-P2	0015
5494922-P3	0015
5494922-P4	0015
5494922-P5	0015
5494922-P6	0015
5494922-P7	0015
5494922-P8	0015
5495178-P1	0097
5495912-P2	0436
5495922-P1	0097
5495922-P2	0097
5495922-P3	0097
5495923-P1	0717
5496438-P1	0436
5496663-P1	0160
5496665-P1	0211
5496665-P2	0211
5496665-P3	0211
5496665-P4	0211
5496665-P5	0211
5496665-P6	0211
5496666-P1	0211
5496666-P2	0211
5496666-P3	0211
5496666-P4	0211
5496666-P5	0211
5496666-P6	0211
5496666-P7	0211
5496666-P8	0211
5496667-P1	0211
5496667-P2	0211
5496668-P1	0435
5496774-P1	0211
5496774-P2	0211
5496774-P3	0211
5496774-P4	0211
5496774-P5	0211
5496774-P6	0211
5496839-P1	0211
5496939-P1	0160
5496939-P2	0160
5496947-P3	0436
5518017	0843
5729031	0435
5955748	0004
5955749	0015
5958539	0841
5960904	OEM
5983945A	0435
5985432	0435
5988414	0435
5988977	0435
5989171	0435
5989615	0435
5989692	0435
5989693	0435
6100724-2	0279
6105590K01	OEM
6125070K01	OEM
6126150K01	5292
6127784(SM)	OEM
6127893(SM)	OEM
6142190	0810
6207159	4553
6208839	0076
6212096	0042
6212839	0079
6212922	0144
6218945	0076
6510053-2	0050
6710223-1	0037
6846503	0015
6846812	0469
6879847	OEM
6920802	OEM
6920900	OEM
7011200-02	2086
7011201-02	1833
7011203-02	1423
7011203-03	1423
7012128	1820
7012128-02	1820
7012130	1340
7012131	1918
7012132	1564
7012133-02	0117
7012142-03	1915
7012166	0310
7012167-02	1199
7023416-00	0015
7026011	0007
7026012	0144
7026013	0144
7026014	0016
7026015	0016
7026016	0016
7026018	0177
7026019	0126
7026020	0079
7026024	0042
7026036	0030
7027002	0015
7027005	0015
7027007	0102
7027023	0015
7027031	0139
7027033	0182
7027036	0196
7027038	0015
7027039	0015
7030105	0004
7043130A	OEM
7043216	0015
7043261	0015
7070692	0015
7071021	0079
7071031	0079
7100460	0143
7100628	0015
7100630	0015
7116060	0019
7129386-P2	0143
7200351	0030
7200953	0124
7201090	0244
7201212	0139
7202782	0244
7220132	OEM
7269847	0208
7274653	0160
7276211	0279
7276605	0435
7277066	0208
7278421	0279
7278422	0004
7278423	0004
7279003	0435
7279005	0435
7279007	0435
7279009	0435
7279011	0435
7279013	0435
7279017	0435
7279025	0435
7279027	0435
7279031	0435
7279033	0435
7279035	0435
7279039	0085
7279049	0085
7279069	0599
7279073	0435
7279076	0435
7279281	0841
7279293	0435
7279298	0435
7279379	0279
7279497	0015
7279566	0435
7279779	0136
7279779(G.M.)	0016
7279780	0050
7279781	0050
7279782	0279
7279788	0279
7279789	0279
7279793	0435
7279893	0143
7279940	0279
7279941	0004
7280281	0435
7281307	0279
7281308	0279
7281309	0279
7281310	0004
7281891	0279
7282315	0435
7282358	0143
7283377	0123
7284137	0016
7284513	0050
7284751	0004
7285354	2873
7285663	0160
7285774	0085
7285776	0160
7285778	0085
7286858	0016
7287079	0244
7287107	0599
7287110	0160
7287112	0599
7287117	0599
7287452	0016
7287940	0136
7288019	0030
7288072	0435
7288073	0435
7288076	0435
7288079	0435
7289041	0160
7289047	0085
7289079	0160
7289097	0599
7290593	0160
7290594	0085
7291252	0085
7292308	0050
7292683	0599
7292684	0969
7292689	0599
7292690	0160
7292955	0160
7293818	0074
7293819	0074
7294133	0004
7294796	0160
7294910	0007
7295195	0144
7295196	0144
7295197	0016
7296314	0016
7296476	0244
7297043	0085
7297053	0016
7297054	0016
7297092	0085
7297093	0085
7297347	0599
7297348	0969
7297358	0012
7297980	0007
7298079	0160
7299325	0015
7299720	0435
7299780	0599
7301660	0599
7301661	0599
7301664	0074
7301665	0074
7301666	0074
7302340	0229
7303105	0004
7303120	0016
7303304	0074
7304149	0637
7304971	3575
7305469	0244
7305783	0160
7306982	0103
7311325	0673
7313568	2264
7420683	OEM
7440006	0196
7492377-5	0137
7492377-P1	0162
7492377-P5	0137
7492377-P10	0162
7520136	OEM
7528046-P4	1035
7528048-P4	0141
7528153-P4	3365
7528156-P3	1248
7528158-P4	1248
7528159-P4	0033
7528160-P4	2067
7528374P3	2067
7570003	0160
7570003-01	0160
7570004	0016
7570004-01	0016
7570005	0016
7570005-01	0016
7570005-02	0016
7570005-03	0016
7570008	0016
7570008-02	0016
7570009	0086
7570009-01	0016
7570009-21	0016
7570011-01	0071
7570011-02	0071
7570013-01	0037
7570014	0242
7570014-02	0143
7570014-05	0015
7570014-34	0015
7570015-34	0015
7570016	0143
7570016-02	0143
7570016-03	0143
7570021-12	0436
7570021-21	0436
7570022-01	0178
7570024-02	0015
7570030-01	0455
7570031-01	0042
7570032-01	0126
7570215-21	0133
7570215-24	0015
7570215-34	0015
7571329-01	0276
7576004-01	0037
7576015-01	0016
7582438-01	0019
7582439-01	0143
7777146-P2	0143
7777146-P3	0143
7777146-P4	0143
7777146-P23	0143
7820135	OEM
7835297-01	0279
7851316-01	0004
7851323	0050
7851325	0016
7851326	0016
7851327	0016
7851328-01	0299
7851329-01	0276
7851379-01	0016
7851380-01	0016
7851441-01	0015
7851442-01	0446
7851467-01	0208
7851650-01	0007
7851651-01	0007
7851652-01	0037
7851654-01	0143
7851655-01	0143
7851657-01	0015
7851947-01	0143
7851949-01	0016
7851950-01	0016
7851952-01	0016
7851953-01	0683
7851954-01	0037
7851955-01	3502
7851956-01	0086
7852223-01	0143
7852223-01A	0143
7852264-01	0015
7852438-0	0143
7852438-01	0143
7852439-01	0143
7852452-01	0076
7852454	0016
7852454-01	0111
7852455-01	0016
7852457-01	0191
7852459-01	0016
7852460-01	1139
7852577-01	0276
7852775-01	0004
7852776-01	0004
7852778-01	0004
7852779-01	0004
7852781-01	0076
7852782-01	0143
7852897-01	0050
7852899-01	0136
7852900-01	0050
7852902-01	0123
7852903-01	0030
7852904-01	0162
7852907-01	0015
7853090-01	0683
7853091-01	0191
7853092-01	0191
7853093-01	0284
7853094-01	0076
7853098-01	0276
7853351-01	0004
7853352-01	0004
7853354-01	0004
7853356-01	0004
7853357-01	0143
7853358-01	0015
7853463-01	0076
7853464-01	0016
7853465-01	0016
7855282	0143
7855282-01	0143
7855283-01	0133
7855283-01(AMPEX)	0004
7855284-01	0015
7855291-01	0016
7855292-01	0016
7855293-01	0016
7855294-01	0016
7855295-01	0222
7855296-01	0004
7855297-01	0004
7855298-01	0042
7855352-01	0143
7855357-01	0143
7910070-01	0004
7910071-01	0004
7910072-01	0160
7910073-01	0161
7910076-01	0015
7910108-01	0007
7910111-01	0244
7910134-01	0321
7910267-01	0419
7910268-01	0683

If replacement code is OEM, contact original manufacturer for replacement. 235

DEVICE TYPE	REPL CODE
7910269-01	0151
7910270-01	0151
7910271-01	0111
7910272-01	0111
7910273-01	0218
7910274-01	0086
7910275-01	0015
7910276-01	0030
7910278-01	0012
7910584-01	0016
7910585-01	0016
7910586-01	0016
7910587-01	0016
7910588-01	0004
7910589-01	0004
7910590-01	0015
7910780-01	0144
7910781-01	0127
7910783-01	0136
7910784-01	0030
7910801-01	0004
7910803-01	0164
7910804-01	0016
7910805-01	0015
7910872-01	0015
7910873-01	0015
7910875-01	0126
7913605	0074
7914009-01	0127
7914010-01	0127
7914011-01	0015
7914014-01	0133
7914015-01	0030
7932367	1929
7932638	0133
7932980	0673
7938318	0321
8000016	1339
8000017	1342
8000736	0086
8000737	0086
8002494B	0240
8010490	0136
8010520	0279
8010530	0136
8014711	0050
8014712	0279
8015613	0126
8020134	OEM
8020244	0453
8020245	0458
8020322	0004
8020324	0004
8020333	0004
8020334	0004
8020373	0704
8020540	0004
8020560	0004
8021897	0004
8021898	0004
8022630	0004
8022631	0004
8023643	0004
8023892	0004
8024152	0164
8024250	0969
8024390	0050
8024390(AIWA)	0004
8024400	0004
8026002	4823
8026004	3265
8026008	3268
8026014	3269
8026032	3274
8026138	5952
8026195	5962
8026244	5969
8026245	4013
8026373	5984
8030529	4451
8031825	0144
8031836	0144
8031837	0470
8031839	0470
8033690	0016
8033696	0016
8033720	0076
8033730	0016
8033803	0144
8033804	0144
8033943	0144
8033944	0016
8034903	0042
8036683	0127
8037330	0016
8037332	0016
8037333	0016
8037343	0086
8037353	0016
8037722	1136
8037723	1136
8040048	OEM
8040216	OEM
8040253	OEM
8040259	OEM
8040272	OEM
8040316B	OEM
8040328	OEM
8040332	OEM

DEVICE TYPE	REPL CODE
8040364B	OEM
8040464	OEM
8040496	OEM
8040517	OEM
8040541	OEM
8040542	OEM
8040543	OEM
8040544	OEM
8040545	OEM
8040665	OEM
8040684	OEM
8041016	2291
8041016A	2291
8041088	OEM
8041364	OEM
8042364A	OEM
8044316	OEM
8044364	OEM
8044732	OEM
8045364A	OEM
8046670	OEM
8049008	OEM
8050339	0176
8050358	0765
8050386	3034
8050526	OEM
8050527	OEM
8051060	0019
8052192	0062
8052446	0143
8052805	1288
8075068	OEM
8075069	OEM
8075306	OEM
8075711	OEM
8079015	OEM
8100906	0006
8110014	0321
8110904	0076
8111230	0037
8112023	0004
8112027	0004
8112071	0004
8112090	0004
8112143	0222
8112146	0004
8112162	0004
8113034	0016
8113323	0191
8113327	0376
8114057	0018
8115009	0037
8120126	0133
8120133	0015
8120164	0139
8150148	0124
8150235	0062
8190005	1275
8190104	OEM
8220136	OEM
8249600	0007
8362309	OEM
8362311	OEM
8362312	OEM
8362535N	OEM
8362536	OEM
8362550	OEM
8484771-1	0084
8484771-3	0090
8484771-7	0097
8484771-8	0760
8484771-10	0772
8484894	OEM
8505870-1	1248
8508309	0126
8508331RB	2515
8518237-1	0084
8518237-2	0090
8518237-3	0097
8518237-9	0743
8518237-10	0760
8518382-1	3160
8518382-2	2873
8518382-3	1116
8518382-9	0254
8518382-10	1099
8518383-10	0204
8518383P1	1991
8518383P2	1241
8518383P3	1241
8521587-1	0015
8521587-101	0242
8521587-102	0535
8521692-1	0240
8538640	0050
8620211	OEM
8620815	OEM
8729902XX	OEM
8759602XX	OEM
8975158-1	0004
8981399-1	0015
8981399-2	0015
9001345-02	0564
9001346	0522
9001349-02	1358
9001349-03	1358
9001549-02	1018
9001551-02	0357
9001551-03	0357

DEVICE TYPE	REPL CODE
9001567	1424
9001567-02	1424
9001570-02	0331
9002097-03	0936
9003091-02	0507
9003091-03	0507
9003096-02	0738
9003096-03	0738
9003097-02	0936
9003148	1812
9003148-01	1812
9003148-02	1812
9003149	0141
9003149-02	0141
9003150	0557
9003150-02	0557
9003150-03	0557
9003151	0232
9003151-03	0232
9003152	1303
9003152-01	1303
9003234-04	0990
9003398-03	0462
9003398-04	0462
9003420-03	1705
9003445-03	0828
9003642-03	0867
9003911	1035
9003911-01	1035
9003911-03	1035
9004075-03	0268
9004076	0692
9004076-03	0692
9004076-04	0692
9004093-03	1164
9004300-03	1150
9004360-03	1193
9004896-04	1177
9004898-04	0522
9100502	0004
9100621	0004
9100706	0004
9100944	0004
9101600	1545
9246055	0015
9248015	0015
9248055	0015
9248058	0015
9320152	OEM
9320170	OEM
9320220	OEM
9330006	0015
9730150	OEM
9739636-20	0015
10112563	3384
10176209	1063
10541284	1248
10541285	3032
10638971	OEM
10658276	1812
10658278	1820
10658279	0033
10658280	0081
10658281	0141
10658282	2067
10674068	1403
11019072	3240
11050925	0006
11056225	0006
11069934A	0103
11113005	1605
11113006	2604
11113007	OEM
11113014	OEM
11113025	OEM
11113035	OEM
11114027	0388
11114035	0042
11114044	0006
11114044T	0006
11114045	0006
11114045T	0006
11114047	0527
11114048	0006
11114048T	0006
11114049	0006
11114049T	0148
11114050	0144
11114055	0284
11114056	0284
11114056T	0284
11114060	0284
11114062	0155
11114063	0261
11114063T	0261
11114064	0261
11114064T	0261
11114066	0284
11114066T	0284
11114068	0284
11114073	6046
11114077	0284
11114087	0638
11114088	0638
11114089	0066
11114089T	0066
11114090	0261
11114091	0261
11114091T	0261

DEVICE TYPE	REPL CODE
11114092	0388
11114093	1900
11114095	0261
11114096	0261
11114103	0224
11114106	1533
11114107	0055
11114112	0388
11114113	3474
11114114	1533
11114119	0016
11114127	0060
11114133	2058
11114134	3505
11114135	1376
11114149T	1514
11114181	3437
11114225T	1553
11114236	OEM
11114237	OEM
11114281T	6093
11114282T	1514
11114284	OEM
11114306	0551
11114307	1533
11114333T	OEM
11115001	0080
11115002	0023
11115002T	0023
11115003	0790
11115003T	0790
11115004	0466
11115014	0023
11115017	0133
11115020	0071
11115024	0124
11115024T	0124
11115025	0133
11115026	0133
11115027	0133
11115029	2217
11115030	0137
11115040	0895
11115043	0023
11115046	0877
11115059	0023
11115060	0182
11115061	0296
11115062	0019
11115063	0023
11115064	0466
11115065	0023
11115066	0087
11115071	0999
11115075	0023
11115089	0466
11115090	0253
11115095	0087
11115096	0166
11115097	0057
11115121	0023
11115155	0023
11115188	0466
11115223	0023
11115223T	0023
11115225T	1553
11115358T	0041
11115364T	0466
11115376T	0057
11115386T	4820
11115446	0535
11116191	0720
11119016	6458
11119023	0167
11119024	4773
11119025	5101
11119026	3564
11119027	2008
11119028	OEM
11119029	OEM
11119030	0358
11119031	3680
11119032	0678
11119033	2079
11119034	2015
11119035	OEM
11119077	OEM
11119112	0727
11119113	3860
11119114	1521
11119117	OEM
11119118	4074
11119120	OEM
11119123	OEM
11119139	2843
11119140	3054
11119144	OEM
11119225	4032
11119226	2330
11119256	OEM
11119257	OEM
11119260	OEM
11119399	3473
11119446	OEM
11210016/7825	0143
11220009/7825	0004
11220018/7611	0004
11220022/7611	0004
11220046/7825	0016

DEVICE TYPE	REPL CODE
11220061/7825	0164
11220076/7825	0004
11220106/7611	0164
11253588	3843
11292312	0677
11292313	0554
11292314	1933
11292315	2158
11369564	3221
11790334	0759
12090924-4	0004
12901503	0037
13020000	0004
13020002	0004
13030189	0133
13030192	0015
13030256	0071
13030266	0133
13030274	0133
13030285	0165
13030301	0143
13030312	0143
13030313	0015
13030401	0361
13033801	0015
13037215	0076
13038115	0113
13038900	0015
13040089	0208
13040095	0004
13040096	0208
13040216	0016
13040229	0143
13040236	0004
13040304	0144
13040313	0016
13040317	0016
13040318	0016
13040329	0208
13040347	2839
13040349	0222
13040352	0004
13040357	0016
13040362	0144
13040421	0144
13040429	0126
13040456	0164
13040459	0144
13050221	0015
13069306	0547
13073525	0191
13083908	0076
13093003	2195
13093004	2195
13093005	2195
13094517	0076
13214051	0267
13411386	0124
13411398	3163
13411409	3460
13419261-00	OEM
13419323	OEM
13421244	0006
13421268	OEM
13428129	4870
13428179	5486
13442206-00	OEM
13442430-00	OEM
13447562	OEM
14001376-01	2007
14001376-02	2007
14001376-03	2007
14388917-1	OEM
14500001-001	0141
14500001-002	1833
14500001-003	0337
14500001-004	1848
14500004-001D	1820
14500004-001P	1820
14500004-002	1824
14500004-003	1168
14500005-001	0033
14636723	0360
14700990	0469
14714729	0267
14769302	0752
14956180	OEM
15105300	1911
15108046	0071
15109200	2248
16103860	3034
16173130	0358
16233010	1206
16271033	1820
16271041	1820
16371420	OEM
16453160	2702
16483610	2279
16483611	2279
16906600-01	0037
17100901	0143
17100902	0143
17101881	0143
17101882	0143
17184600	0381
17200000	0133
17200240	0015
17201160	0005
17201350	0023

DEVICE TYPE	REPL CODE
17210010	0023
17210430	0549
17240010	0023
17241480	0124
18022090	OEM
18080510	OEM
18901105	0079
18901106	0079
18901107	0016
18901402	0111
18901607	0144
18901807	0144
18911202	0037
18955002	0527
19080002	0015
19166123	1848
19901403	0111
19901503	2461
19901606	0079
19901607	0127
19901806	0144
19901807	0144
20001786-134	0143
20001786-139	0479
20001786-141	0015
20001786-142	0015
20025153-77	0531
20030703-0701	0016
20030703-0702	0037
20052600	0016
20080127	0124
20115070	0143
20130109	0559
20502055Z4	OEM
20602065Z4	OEM
20702075Z4	OEM
20912578-1	0841
20918596-2	0160
22114209	OEM
22114210	0590
22114225	0555
22114253	0037
22114254	1257
22114468	0688
22114594	0356
22114626	3671
22114634	0804
22114676	0919
22114677	2261
22115174	0012
22115175	0030
22115181	0143
22115182	0143
22115183	0015
22115184	OEM
22115192	0143
22115304	0623
22115405	0015
22115427	0199
22692012	0133
22901513	0144
22902046	0144
23111006	0160
23113056	0079
23114001	0144
23114004	0969
23114007	0233
23114009	0969
23114011	0160
23114015	0191
23114017	0155
23114021	0004
23114023	0144
23114026	0969
23114028	0233
23114031	0144
23114033	0160
23114034	0144
23114036	0144
23114037	0007
23114038	0178
23114043	0144
23114044	0326
23114045	0208
23114046	0079
23114050	0037
23114051	0037
23114052	0233
23114053	0233
23114054	0233
23114056	0144
23114057	0144
23114058	0086
23114060	0144
23114061	0004
23114070	0103
23114070A	0103
23114071	0103
23114072	OEM
23114074	0102
23114078	0836
23114081	0006
23114082	0144
23114083	0178
23114084	0178
23114086	0178
23114087	0079
23114088	0178
23114090	OEM

DEVICE TYPE	REPL CODE
23114095	0233
23114097	0969
23114100	0103
23114104	0326
23114108	0103
23114109	0144
23114112	0127
23114118	0079
23114119	0079
23114124	0037
23114125	0233
23114126	0127
23114127	0144
23114131	0455
23114132	0161
23114133	0455
23114134	0161
23114136	0037
23114137	0006
23114138	0037
23114148	0127
23114155	0016
23114157	0127
23114163	0184
23114164	0007
23114165	0184
23114171	0144
23114172	0144
23114180	0144
23114181	0144
23114195	0086
23114208	0074
23114211	0004
23114212	0079
23114213	0079
23114214	0079
23114215	0079
23114216	0111
23114217	0111
23114218	0079
23114219	OEM
23114220	0178
23114221	0178
23114226	OEM
23114232	0086
23114238	0144
23114248	0168
23114249	0283
23114250	0283
23114251	0283
23114253	0228
23114254	0228
23114255	0079
23114258	0111
23114259	0155
23114260	0155
23114261	0155
23114262	0006
23114264	OEM
23114265	OEM
23114266	0168
23114267	0079
23114268	0142
23114275	0079
23114276	0076
23114277	0142
23114280	0284
23114282	0284
23114293	0006
23114296	0079
23114297	0191
23114299	0191
23114300	0006
23114301	0006
23114302	0006
23114313	0786
23114314	0155
23114315	0142
23114317	0074
23114321	0065
23114323	0309
23114325	0037
23114326	0065
23114344	0638
23114347	0006
23114349	0076
23114420	3902
23114454	5310
23114457	OEM
23114528	0151
23114530	0148
23114544	5365
23114550	0037
23114552	0284
23114662	0076
23114733	0018
23114735	0429
23114758	0270
23114768	0055
23114821	0076
23114864	0615
23114867	0625
23114900	0638
23114915	0076
23114918	1900
23114919	0103
23114923	1274
23114939	0848
23114941	0638

236 If replacement code is OEM, contact original manufacturer for replacement.

DEVICE TYPE	REPL CODE
23114944	0220
23114945	0309
23114961	1139
23114962	1142
23114966	0191
23114969	1274
23114974	0168
23114975	0638
23114982	0638
23114983	0264
23114992	0676
23114993	0168
23114994	0155
23114995	0006
23114999	0168
23115012	0071
23115016	0918
23115019	0015
23115022	0769
23115023	0015
23115025	0911
23115038	OEM
23115042	0015
23115044	0015
23115046	0015
23115049	0133
23115050	0133
23115051	0914
23115052	0015
23115057	0016
23115058	0016
23115064	0133
23115065	0133
23115068	0133
23115070	0143
23115071	0133
23115072	0133
23115074	0907
23115076	0012
23115077	OEM
23115078	1073
23115079	0196
23115080	0133
23115085	0015
23115088	0143
23115094	0102
23115098	0071
23115102	0143
23115103	OEM
23115104	OEM
23115108	0133
23115109	0133
23115113	0911
23115115	0143
23115116	0143
23115117	0071
23115118	0071
23115120	0015
23115121	0911
23115129	0143
23115130	0071
23115131	0102
23115140	0015
23115145	0102
23115157	0201
23115168	0631
23115185	0015
23115192	0102
23115194	0133
23115199	0015
23115200	0015
23115201	0015
23115215	0374
23115227	0911
23115238	0398
23115249	0133
23115250	0023
23115263	0015
23115273	0023
23115277	0244
23115285	0133
23115292	0398
23115294	0023
23115296	0023
23115301	0721
23115321	1313
23115322	OEM
23115328	0398
23115334	1313
23115337	0023
23115338	0023
23115366	OEM
23115367	OEM
23115374	0244
23115377	0023
23115455	0041
23115486	0489
23115532	0023
23115535	0019
23115549	0695
23115585	0242
23115621	0023
23115622	OEM
23115665	0466
23115690	0023
23115774	0466
23115797	0023
23115800	2604
23115809	0133
23115810	0023
23115822	1319
23115878	1319
23115884	1596
23115888	0023
23115889	0023
23115897	0133
23115903	0312
23115908	0062
23115909	0023
23115910	0023
23115912	0023
23115913	0023
23115914	0102
23115919	0052
23115921	0041
23115922	1319
23115924	OEM
23115931	0466
23115935	OEM
23115938	0374
23115939	OEM
23115940	0999
23115947	0071
23115948	OEM
23115949	0143
23115960	0017
23115965	0344
23115966	0071
23115979	0253
23115981	0102
23115984	0644
23115986	1313
23115987	0244
23115990	0721
23115994	0071
23115999	0102
23118052	0031
23118060	1082
23118094	0023
23118123	OEM
23118173	1039
23118186	0335
23118186(MA700A)	OEM
23118338	0031
23118339	5408
23118450	0071
23118536	0140
23118538	0466
23118634	0118
23118642	OEM
23118708	OEM
23118714	OEM
23118822	0023
23118850	0466
23118859	0133
23118943	1137
23118977	0031
23119003	2689
23119004	0823
23119005	2689
23119007	0823
23119011	2610
23119012	0872
23119013	2615
23119014	1797
23119016	4502
23119017	0399
23119019	0391
23119022	2610
23119023	2615
23119025	0784
23119032	2615
23119033	2615
23119039	OEM
23119060	OEM
23119142	4066
23119144	OEM
23119167	OEM
23119180	OEM
23119182	OEM
23119208	OEM
23119209	OEM
23119210	OEM
23119228	4009
23119259	OEM
23119319	OEM
23119330	OEM
23119336	OEM
23119345	OEM
23119348	OEM
23119355	3206
23119363	OEM
23119450	OEM
23119456	OEM
23119489	3403
23119501	OEM
23119526	OEM
23119548	4840
23119566	5162
23119664	OEM
23119702	OEM
23119710	1521
23119723	4246
23119742	1372
23119763	3860
23119796	0658
23119880	5971
23119901	0906
23119905	OEM
23119920	OEM
23119950	0167
23119960	0564
23119961	2051
23119966	1049
23119971	4174
23119978	2268
23119981	3859
23119988	2216
23119989	2921
23119990	3859
23119992	OEM
23119993	1316
23119994	4515
23119995	4514
23119998	OEM
23119999	0784
23124037	0144
23126177	0127
23126183	0007
23126184	0079
23126240	OEM
23126251	OEM
23126252	OEM
23126253	OEM
23126254	OEM
23126289	0127
23126290	0127
23126291	0127
23126577	0911
23126620	0144
23126622	0715
23200596-1	0086
23205955	0076
23205981	0076
23206375	0148
23206471	0191
23206631	0191
23212215	1077
23213515	0688
23219925	0261
23225889	0023
23244121	1533
23284521	OEM
23302565	0023
23303515	0133
23303525	0124
23303531	0124
23311006	0085
23311066	0160
23311545	0052
23311555	0052
23313515	0133
23314055	0203
23314068	3273
23314158	3310
23314162	OEM
23314197	0275
23314356	OEM
23314357	OEM
23314361	OEM
23314511	OEM
23314525	0456
23314699	OEM
23316003	OEM
23316184	1119
23316250	OEM
23316275	OEM
23316288	OEM
23316302	OEM
23316306	OEM
23316309	OEM
23316312	OEM
23316313	OEM
23316325	OEM
23316332	OEM
23316339	OEM
23316370	OEM
23316380	0182
23316391	0732
23316399	1082
23316406	1171
23316411	3417
23316412	OEM
23316471	OEM
23317975	0041
23318051	OEM
23318075	0091
23318086	2099
23318132	OEM
23318135	OEM
23318137	OEM
23318147	OEM
23318151	0062
23318208	OEM
23318241	OEM
23318242	OEM
23318244	OEM
23318271	0057
23318299	OEM
23318361	OEM
23318409	4246
23318466	OEM
23318468	OEM
23318495	OEM
23318627	OEM
23318759	OEM
23318860	OEM
23318861	OEM
23318862	OEM
23318918	OEM
23319002	OEM
23319003	OEM
23319202	4794
23319307	OEM
23319308	OEM
23319364	OEM
23319448	OEM
23319459	OEM
23319497	OEM
23319502	OEM
23319592	OEM
23319637	OEM
23319802	0765
23319870	OEM
23319911	0071
23319929	OEM
23319985	OEM
23320315	OEM
23373411	0124
23381625	0023
23383211	0133
23383215	0133
23389311	1654
23390511	OEM
23391411	OEM
23394811	0023
23394815	0023
23394821	0023
23394911	0015
23394915	0015
23399911	0672
23600042	OEM
23683115	OEM
23685015	2031
23687415	OEM
23691515	0445
23904234	OEM
23904381	OEM
23904398	OEM
23996971	OEM
23996981	4226
23996991	OEM
23997001	OEM
23997011	OEM
23997021	OEM
23997031	OEM
23997041	0719
23997051	OEM
23997061	0719
23997071	1722
23997081	1597
23997091	1376
23997101	0124
23997111	5082
23997121	0140
24000097	OEM
24000255	OEM
24561601-E	0267
24561602-E	0267
24561603	0267
24561604-E	0267
24850078-3	OEM
25114101	0004
25114102	0004
25114103	0004
25114104	0004
25114116	0016
25114121	0016
25114130	0233
25114143	0142
25114161	0144
25115102	0143
25115108	0015
25115115	0015
26010006	0683
26010010	0191
26010011	0914
26010016	0006
26010020	0076
26010021	0191
26010022	1401
26010023	0111
26010024	0042
26010026	1136
26010027	0006
26010028	0133
26010029	0631
26010030	0133
26010031	0143
26010032	0139
26010033	0015
26010041	0320
26010044	0244
26010046	0631
26010047	0133
26010050	OEM
26010051	0224
26010052	0320
26010053	0830
26010056	0144
26010057	0133
26010058	0693
26010059	0042
26010062	1023
26411007	OEM
26417402	OEM
26630109	0167
27113100	0015
27123050	0015
27123070	0015
27123100	0015
27123100A	0015
27123120	0015
27123150	0143
27123220	0015
27123240	0143
27123270	0143
27123290	0015
27125080	0016
27125090	0016
27125110	0004
27125120	0004
27125140	0016
27125150	0016
27125160	0016
27125170	0164
27125210	0470
27125220	0470
27125230	0136
27125240	0136
27125250	0470
27125260	0211
27125270	0016
27125300	0016
27125310	0208
27125330	0004
27125340	0004
27125350	0004
27125360	0004
27125370	0016
27125380	0016
27125460	0016
27125470	0016
27125480	0164
27125490	0208
27125500	0016
27125540	0841
27125550	0004
27126060	3502
27126090	0160
27126100	0103
27126130	0160
27126130(TRANSISTOR)	0160
27126130-12	0160
27126220	0144
27420170	OEM
27430040	OEM
27430050	OEM
27430080	OEM
27430090	OEM
27430100	OEM
27430130	OEM
27430150	OEM
27430160	OEM
27430220	OEM
27430240	OEM
27430300	OEM
27430301	OEM
27430360	OEM
27430510	OEM
27430520	OEM
30000010	0136
30000021	0628
30000032	OEM
30200033	0042
30200053	0076
30200061	0151
30200062	0151
30200091	0151
30200101	2048
30400021	0683
30400131	0321
30400152	1747
30400171	0212
30600010	0019
30600020	0123
30600040	0015
30600090	0139
30600140	0137
30601371	0106
30601971	0319
30602521	0276
30602711	0124
30900361	0356
30900460	0646
30900530	4746
30900540	4719
30900720	2237
30900740	0356
30900741	0356
30900900	OEM
30901020	OEM
30901050	1288
30901080	1830
30901090	OEM
30901100	OEM
30901110	OEM
30901120	2237
30901140	OEM
30901150	5211
30901160	OEM
30901170	OEM
30901190	OEM
30901200	OEM
30901350	0484
31210049-00	0050
31210077-44	0050
31210240-33	0050
31210240-44	0050
31210471-11	0050
31210506-11	0050
31210506-22	0050
31220054-00	0004
32119401-200	OEM
32510001	0015
34002412	2515
34002412-3	2515
35002711	0150
35002712	0150
35002713	0150
35002912	0786
35003517	0006
35004112	0338
35004411	0006
35024812	0676
35025012	0527
35025212	1638
35026317	0520
35026712	2869
35044100	0007
35044396	0007
35044397	0007
35044398	0007
35044399	0007
35045402	OEM
35045416	0079
35045502	0079
35045708	0079
35045712	0079
35046506	0003
35046611	0142
35046612	0142
35046613	0142
35046811	0142
35046812	0142
35046813	0142
35046911	0103
35046912	0103
35046913	0103
35047216	0076
35047217	0076
35047218	0079
35047219	0079
35049311	0042
35053012	1317
35053212	0945
35053700	1795
35053811	0275
35053812	0275
35056311	0275
35056312	0275
35056313	0275
35063411	1274
35063412	1274
35063512	0018
35065417	0161
35065700	0055
35065911	0018
35065912	0018
35066100	0055
35066617	0558
35067000	1533
35067212	3658
35067300	0309
35067600	1533
35081400	0168
35120718	1747
35393060-01	0016
35393060-02	0016
35393060-03	0016
36001004	0133
36001008	0170
36001009	0143
36001010	0133
36001015	0133
36001027	0124
36002003	0143
36003007	0098
36003034	0244
36003039	0999
36003049	1319
36003061	0062
36003066	0313
36003096	0012
36003098	0052
36003100	0041
36003106	0466
36003118	0064
36003121	0062
36003122	0253
36003125	0053
36003152	0166
36003154	0052
36003157	0041
36003174	0091
36003175	OEM
36107051	0015
36107062	0015
36107085	0015
36107086	0790
36107094	0023
36107152	0102
36107153	0133
36107154	0102
36107160	0015
36107167	0102
36107169	0023
36107175	0023
36107178	0282
36107253	0102
36107255	0102
36107263	0023
36107286	0071
36107287	0023
36107289	0031
36108003	0106
36108009	0468
36108025	0253
36108026	0041
36108030	OEM
36108031	OEM
36108054	3844
36108055	3844
36186200	1424
36188000	1423
36188700	0677
36501009	OEM
36502004	OEM
36771100	0142
36801061	OEM
36801062	OEM
36801080	OEM
36801081	OEM
36801103	OEM
36801104	OEM
36801118	OEM
36803003	2604
36803009	OEM
37000918	0019
37001003	2855
37001034	2868
37001039	3726
37001040	2845
37001046	OEM
37001047	3860
37001059	1521
37001064	4035
37001065	3331
37001066	3830
37003001	0133
37003001(IC)	0633
37003012	0485
37003020	2599
37003023	0445
37003027	2109
37003029	2109
37005043	OEM
37005064	OEM
37007014	0859
37007021	0534
37009010	1420
37009016	5117
37011020	2015
37011036	4312
37011039	2641
37011041	4417
37011060	OEM
37011063	0107
37051036	0101
37051100	0495
37051246	1938
37051310	0215
37051378	0034
37051523	OEM
37053002	0024
37053003	1349
37058002	OEM
37058026	OEM
37058045	OEM
37246602	0133
37246711	0133
37275350	0133
37568200	0182
37568250	0023
37568800	0023
37582000	0182
38102023	OEM
38112013	OEM
39502017T	OEM
40306312	0784
40306400	0391
40306604	2615
40760211-002	2006
40760211-P2	2006
41013566	0015
41015030AG	3017
41020618	0015
41020687	0087
41021007	0015
41023224	0015
41023225	0015
41025773	0071
41025849	0015
41027063	0015
41027612	0143
41027613	0143
41027991	0023
41027992	0143
41029009	0123
41029290	0123
41029498	0195
41029499	0071
41030618	0087

If replacement code is OEM, contact original manufacturer for replacement. 237

DEVICE TYPE	REPL CODE
41514016	OEM
41520419	0015
41522875	0123
41527380	0019
41527570	0120
41622859	0124
41624836	0143
41627989	0139
42020414	0170
42020737	0170
42023425	0361
42024925	0062
42027065	0864
42027092	0416
42029566	0053
43020731	0086
43020735	OEM
43021017	0016
43021067	0127
43021083	0016
43021168	0126
43021198	0086
43021415	0086
43021579	OEM
43021771	OEM
43022055	0050
43022134	0321
43022860	0155
43022861	0016
43023190	0130
43023212	0016
43023221	0016
43023222	0126
43023223	0086
43023843	0103
43023844	0016
43023845	0037
43024216	0103
43024218	0161
43024219	0455
43024225	0321
43024306	0264
43024833	0136
43024834	0628
43024859	0111
43024873	0111
43024878	0079
43024879	0018
43024880	0148
43025055	0076
43025056	0076
43025059	0191
43025538	0111
43025539	0590
43025620	0050
43025762	0321
43025832	0321
43025972	0218
43026284	0086
43026285	0126
43026932	OEM
43027155	OEM
43027213	0236
43027214	0042
43027379	0076
43027571	0781
43027614	0144
43027615	0144
43027616	0144
43027617	0144
43027618	0127
43027619	0150
43027620	0016
43027872	0079
43027987	0042
43029471	0151
43029472	0151
43029483	0547
43029484	0320
43029485	0431
43029486	0236
43100103	0143
43122874	2593
43126551	0696
43126551-A	0696
43126561	OEM
43200103	0143
43300203	0143
43540012	0015
43550009	OEM
43600101	0015
44007301	0144
44008401	0144
44011001	0016
44079004	0111
44089001	0127
44090004	0016
44211001	0164
46861453-3	OEM
46862200	OEM
48134666	0016
48134842	0016
48137195A	0037
48869715	0130
50210600-00-VF	0037
50210700-01-VF	0111
50210710-10-VF	0111
50211500-01VF	0037
50254200	1197

DEVICE TYPE	REPL CODE
50254400	1545
50254600	0699
50254700	2426
50254900	1011
50255000	1613
51310000	1035
51310001	2086
51310002	1820
51310003	0033
51310004	0141
51310005	3365
51310006	0557
51310007	1622
51320000	0232
51320001	0310
51320002	0357
51320003	0507
51320004	0692
51320005	1018
51320006	1711
51320008	1417
51320009	0331
51320010	0798
51320011	0867
51320012	0232
51320016	1160
51320017	0381
51320018	1358
51330005	0462
51510422A01	0649
51510566A01	0696
51513753A09	0167
51544789J01	2008
51544789J02	2008
51565600-VF	0079
51577500	1812
51577600	1035
51577700	2086
51577800	0033
51577900	0141
51578000	3365
51578100	0557
51624200	0033
51717000	1622
51717100	1472
52335500	1477
52335600	1896
52335600HL	1896
52335700	3670
52335800	1781
52335800HL	1781
52335900	2472
52335900HL	2472
53015201	0087
53020612	0086
53223463	0060
54967774-P5	0211
55330007-001	0914
55335005-001	0084
55919603	OEM
55920301	OEM
57000901-504	0016
57276605	0435
57279005	0435
57279007	0435
57279011	0435
57279017	0435
57279025	0435
57279027	0435
57279033	0435
57279073	0435
57279076	0435
57279293	0435
57279298	0435
57279566	0435
57279793	0435
57280281	0435
57282315	0435
57288072	0435
57288073	0435
57288076	0435
57288079	0435
57299720	0435
60674003	OEM
60674015	OEM
60674016	OEM
60674017	OEM
60674025	OEM
61260039	0136
61260039A	0136
62020911	0535
62045035	2313
62049219	0004
62057957	0004
62113480	0004
62118970	0211
62119292	0279
62154543	0123
62381620	0123
62488131	0916
62525932	OEM
62737654	0784
62771232	0058
62995793	OEM
63000061	1024
63354880	OEM
63551996	OEM
63735248	OEM
63862290	OEM

DEVICE TYPE	REPL CODE
63962600	OEM
65600500	1812
65600600	1035
65600700	0141
65600800	0354
65600900	0329
65611000	1622
65611100	1472
70114087	1747
70114088	1747
70114113	1935
70114117	3104
70114347	OEM
70115421	OEM
70119023	2932
70119034	4197
70119036	3907
70119037	3909
70119041	4008
70119048	3662
70119049	3913
70119058	OEM
70119060	OEM
70119062	0215
70119063	2213
70119064	0394
70119512	OEM
70119514	OEM
70119517	OEM
70119518	OEM
70119526	2843
70119527	3054
70119561	OEM
70119581	OEM
70119583	OEM
70119627	OEM
70119743	OEM
70119751	OEM
70119767	OEM
70119775	OEM
70119776	OEM
70135052	OEM
70260450	0127
70260490	0030
70260540	0012
70270050	0015
70270250	0133
70270390	0015
70270490	0340
70270500	2255
70270700	OEM
70270710	OEM
70270720	0015
70270740	4406
70270770	4990
70370050	0015
71700901	OEM
71773660	0123
72045600	2871
72729031	0435
76276722	0080
80000900	1024
80001300	0015
80001400	0015
80002400	0015
80050100	0016
80050300	0208
80050400	0050
80050500	0136
80050600	0126
80050700	0160
80051001	0103
80051500	0016
80051600	0126
80052101	0111
80052102	0016
80052201	0086
80052202	0016
80052301	0086
80052302	0016
80052402	0103
80052600	0016
80052700	0126
80052800	0208
80053001	0016
80053300	0042
80053400	0016
80053500	OEM
80053501	0321
80053600	0144
80053702	1506
80104900	0136
80105200	0136
80105300	0136
80146620	0050
80146630	0050
80203350	0004
80205400	0004
80205600	0004
80222631U	0004
80226310	0004
80236400	0164
80236430	0164
80243900	0004
80285400	0841
80318250	0016
80337390	0086
80338030	0144
80338040	0144

DEVICE TYPE	REPL CODE
80339430	0144
80339440	0144
80339460	OEM
80366830	0127
80366840	0127
80383840	0016
80383930	0016
80383940	0016
80389910	0016
80414120	0103
80414130	0103
80421980	0086
80510600	0143
80521881	0143
80523520	0030
81063405	0676
81073304	0006
82073206	0111
82409501	0016
82410300	0126
83037204	0076
83038004	0284
83039404	0155
83073205	0016
83073206	0016
83073304	0016
83073305	0016
83073306	0111
83073504	0016
83078402	1136
83093005	0127
83094502	0016
83167403	0224
83167405	0224
83167503	0224
83167505	0224
84026103	0218
86401000	0016
87045030	OEM
87096010	0023
87100600	0143
87100605	0019
87201881	0019
87204260	0123
87205530	0030
87219410	0015
87221394	0005
87227880	0133
87227881	0124
87291320	OEM
87291330	OEM
87301620	1914
87302650	0139
87400020	0015
87500620	0123
87500720	0015
87500920	0012
87600920	0012
87996010	0030
88125010-9	0016
88901010	0806
88902010	0806
88921010	0806
88922010	2672
88922040	OEM
88922060	OEM
88940010	2672
88941010	2672
88942010	2672
88942040	OEM
88942060	OEM
88962010	0806
88962040	OEM
88962060	OEM
89941008	0086
89942601	0224
89942702	0224
89946008	0126
89960404	0224
89962306	0016
89962307	0079
89962308	0079
89962404	0224
89963008	0016
89963009	0016
90200090	1206
90200100	2845
90270020	0240
90270060	0023
90270080	0934
90308040	OEM
90500160	1385
91056140	0037
91190032	0015
92005600	0004
93037230	0016
93037240	0016
93038040	0079
93039440	0079
93063240	0016
93063270	0016
93063280	0016
93063470	0016
93064440	0111
93064450	0016
93073260	0111
93073340	0079
93073350	0086
93073440	0233

DEVICE TYPE	REPL CODE
93073540	0016
93078420	0127
93082830	0016
93082840	0016
93082920	0127
93097120	0086
93938040	0016
93939440	0127
94029220	0142
94810300	0720
94825000-05	0354
94825000-11	1820
94846400-00	2006
94846400-01	2006
94846400-02	2006
95114101-00	0004
95114102-00	0004
95114109-00	0004
95114135-00	0004
95114140-00	0160
95115115-00	0071
96421866	0071
120001190	0050
120001192	0279
120001195	0004
120001300	0015
120002013	0004
120002014	0004
120002213	0050
120002214	0050
120002216	0050
120002513	0050
120002515	0050
120002518	0050
120002520	0050
120002521	0004
120002656	0050
120002748	0004
120004492	0050
120004493	0004
120004494	0004
120004495	0004
120004496	0144
120004497	0144
120004880	0144
120004881	0144
120004882	0144
120004883	0016
120004884	1390
120004887	0160
123561011	OEM
123578311	OEM
123578411	OEM
123596211	OEM
123596311	OEM
123597111	OEM
152221011	0004
152221483	0050
153260500	OEM
153263700	OEM
153267521	OEM
153268600	OEM
176069002	0364
178204004	OEM
180690121	OEM
180696711	OEM
180701811	OEM
180730511	OEM
180750911	OEM
180751111	OEM
180768911	OEM
180768931	OEM
180791321	OEM
180839211	OEM
181515417	0590
200215358	OEM
200315428	1077
211300732	OEM
213119180	OEM
226021014	0144
229005013	0016
229005014	0016
229005015	0016
229018032	0144
229018033	0144
229018034	0144
229020423	0144
229021014	0144
229025010	0144
229510015V	0144
229510031V	0144
229510032V	0144
229510033V	0144
231150050	0143
233119336	OEM
233164471	OEM
266910202	OEM
312104732	0050
312104733	0050
351054000	OEM
370010011	0167
381079051	OEM
386008040	OEM
387040350	OEM
390000250	OEM
390000460	OEM
390000850	OEM
390001050	OEM
390001450	OEM

DEVICE TYPE	REPL CODE
390002750	OEM
390003050	OEM
390008650	OEM
390013850	OEM
390015450	OEM
390015750	OEM
390016650	OEM
390024450	OEM
390025950	OEM
390027350	OEM
390037450	OEM
391808881	OEM
391974880	OEM
394110070	OEM
394110140	OEM
395008190	OEM
399015090	OEM
402003173	0229
410000608F	0006
410000733P	0006
410000733Q	0006
410001015Y	0148
410001249R	0520
410001249S	0520
410020536G	0532
410020945K	0076
410020945P	0076
410020945Q	0076
410021568R	1779
410021568S	1779
410021674K	1060
410021674L	1060
410021730L	0127
410021815Y	0076
410022001L	1505
410022228A	1317
410022271D	0261
410022271E	0261
410022274E	0155
410022274F	0155
410022334L	2253
410022373K	0723
410022909R	0261
410022909S	0261
410023117R	0558
410023117S	0558
410023568K	0723
410023568L	0723
410091402C	0016
410091502B	0127
410091502C	3756
410091502D	0127
410091702M	0079
410091702N	0284
410091802M	0527
410149042B	0710
410149042C	0710
412050010A	0057
412051091M	0057
412614135	OEM
415100574J	1319
415101379C	4284
415200050	2849
415207530	3765
415207530N	3765
415207601W	1977
415307313P	0358
415307368P	OEM
415401160	0514
415901220B	OEM
415950445P	OEM
415950453P	OEM
430203845	0126
440008401	0015
440009905	0124
440011001	0079
450010201	0144
450010701	0007
485134922	0016
485134923	0016
485134924	0016
485134925	0016
485134926	0016
485134956	0050
485134997	0111
500000060	0019
530177001	OEM
530239038	6200
530990180	0188
532390017	1997
539100020	OEM
570004503	0016
570005452	0016
570005503	0016
600000060	0019
600000150	0133
601100001	0057
601100002	0466
602000002	0023
603000002	0623
610480003	0086
610497001	OEM
612160030	5299
612303001	3522
619000970	OEM
630000003	0042
632000001	2684
632000002	0833
632037218	0076

DEVICE TYPE	REPL CODE
632039418	0155
632049514	0203
632049518	0006
632073518	0191
632122617	0219
632197406	0830
640000002	1532
640000003	1042
640000403	OEM
640580700	OEM
661000001	0139
662100200	0178
662400200	OEM
722114299	3684
765232011	OEM
800000029-006	0007
802026310	0211
815992449	OEM
871322000	OEM
871900006	OEM
871900069	OEM
871900090	OEM
871901029	OEM
871901423	OEM
871902221	OEM
871910003	OEM
871910005	OEM
871910016	OEM
871910017	OEM
871910043	OEM
871910044	OEM
871910086	OEM
871910103	OEM
871910104	OEM
871910108	OEM
871910123	OEM
871910138	OEM
871910158	OEM
871910260	OEM
871910271	OEM
871910273	OEM
871910274	OEM
871910275	OEM
871910276	OEM
871910278	OEM
871910280	OEM
871910289	OEM
871910290	OEM
871910291	OEM
871910297	OEM
871910298	OEM
871910306	OEM
871910671	OEM
871910782	OEM
871910794	OEM
871910795	OEM
871910804	OEM
871910968	OEM
871910974	OEM
871910983	OEM
871910984	OEM
871910985	OEM
871910989	OEM
871910990	OEM
871910997	OEM
871911016	OEM
871911017	OEM
871911031	OEM
871911036	OEM
871911048	OEM
871911053	OEM
871911078	OEM
871911434	OEM
871911829	OEM
871919000	OEM
871919104	OEM
871920002	OEM
871920023	OEM
871920077	OEM
871920080	OEM
871920082	OEM
871930033	OEM
871930057	OEM
871930059	OEM
871930065	OEM
871930071	OEM
871930076	OEM
871930082	OEM
871930118	OEM
871930129	OEM
871930138	OEM
871930152	OEM
871930160	OEM
871930213	OEM
871930238	OEM
871930243	OEM
871930245	OEM
871930252	OEM
871930262	OEM
871930267	OEM
871930274	OEM
871930300	OEM
871930313	OEM
871930333	OEM
871930359	OEM
871930437	OEM
871930463	OEM
871930507	OEM
871930515	OEM

If replacement code is OEM, contact original manufacturer for replacement.

DEVICE TYPE	REPL CODE
871931123	OEM
871931187	OEM
871931320	OEM
871950026	OEM
871950306	OEM
871951001	OEM
871971393	OEM
871975143	OEM
871976871	OEM
871980034	OEM
871980076	OEM
871980083	OEM
871980148	OEM
871980155	OEM
871980170	OEM
871981585	OEM
871990019	OEM
871990023	OEM
871990026	OEM
871990057	OEM
871990058	OEM
871990065	OEM
871990133	OEM
871990198	OEM
871990279	OEM
871990290	OEM
871990309	OEM
871990328	OEM
871990329	OEM
871990339	OEM
871990492	OEM
871990644	OEM
871990658	OEM
871990730	OEM
871990798	OEM
871990857	OEM
871991017	OEM
871991025	OEM
871991062	OEM
871991065	OEM
871991068	OEM
871991072	OEM
871991106	OEM
871991155	OEM
871991165	OEM
871991302	OEM
871991355	OEM
871991359	OEM
871991552	OEM
871991845	OEM
871991865	OEM
871991866	OEM
871991877	OEM
871992153	OEM
871992223	OEM
871992364	OEM
871992774	OEM
871992777	OEM
871992808	OEM
871993105	OEM
871993130	OEM
871993336	OEM
871993341	OEM
871993368	OEM
871993370	OEM
871993377	OEM
871993423	OEM
871993683	OEM
871993696	OEM
871993749	OEM
871993796	OEM
871993849	OEM
871993872	OEM
871993875	OEM
871993884	OEM
871993911	OEM
871993923	OEM
871994045	OEM
871994076	OEM
871994081	OEM
871994134	OEM
871994137	OEM
871994146	OEM
871994214	OEM
871994215	OEM
871994217	OEM
871994580	OEM
871995062	OEM
871995111	OEM
871996990	OEM
871997019	OEM
871998101	OEM
871998204	OEM
872910005	OEM
872910075	OEM
872910101	OEM
872910107	OEM
872910162	OEM
872910278	OEM
872910343	OEM
872910372	OEM
872910418	OEM
872910426	OEM
872910491	OEM
872910493	OEM
872910529	OEM
872910553	OEM
872910660	OEM
872910668	OEM

DEVICE TYPE	REPL CODE
872910725	OEM
872910726	OEM
872910753	OEM
872910777	OEM
872910798	OEM
872910799	OEM
872910805	OEM
872910806	OEM
872910814	OEM
872910953	OEM
872911129	OEM
872911155	OEM
872911167	OEM
872911297	OEM
872911313	OEM
872911366	OEM
872911512	OEM
872911530	OEM
872911577	OEM
872911579	OEM
872911642	OEM
872911657	OEM
872911853	OEM
872912263	OEM
872912753	OEM
872914055	OEM
872915483	OEM
872917313	OEM
872917723	OEM
872917732	OEM
872917742	OEM
872917743	OEM
872917863	OEM
872918092	OEM
872918093	OEM
872919053	OEM
872919457	OEM
872919523	OEM
872919992	OEM
872920017	OEM
872920132	OEM
872920152	OEM
872920178	OEM
872920184	OEM
872920196	OEM
872920202	OEM
872920253	OEM
872920258	OEM
872920267	OEM
872920305	OEM
872920419	OEM
872920483	OEM
872920502	OEM
872920643	OEM
872920915	OEM
872920960	OEM
872921202	OEM
872921311	OEM
872921312	OEM
872921632	OEM
872922093	OEM
872922462	OEM
872923832	OEM
872924583	OEM
872926693	OEM
872928803	OEM
872930022	OEM
872930036	OEM
872930090	OEM
872930156	OEM
872930182	OEM
872930187	OEM
872930429	OEM
872930432	OEM
872930450	OEM
872930492	OEM
872930692	OEM
872930906	OEM
872930908	OEM
872931142	OEM
872931342	OEM
872931382	OEM
872932278	OEM
872932611	OEM
872935352	OEM
872937884	OEM
872937891	OEM
872938262	OEM
872938263	OEM
872938303	OEM
872938612	OEM
872940016	OEM
872960012	OEM
872960027	OEM
872960094	OEM
872960330	OEM
872960632	OEM
872960633	OEM
872966347	OEM
872967242	OEM
872967243	OEM
872969792	OEM
872980080	OEM
872980083	OEM
872980183	OEM
872980193	OEM
872980222	OEM
872980234	OEM
872980250	OEM

DEVICE TYPE	REPL CODE
872980525	OEM
872980539	OEM
872980541	OEM
872980543	OEM
872980545	OEM
872980565	OEM
872980567	OEM
872980569	OEM
872980616	OEM
872980620	OEM
872980628	OEM
872980630	OEM
872980634	OEM
872980638	OEM
872980703	OEM
872980707	OEM
872980872	OEM
872980876	OEM
872981124	OEM
872983133	OEM
872988391	OEM
872988392	OEM
872988402	OEM
872990036	OEM
872990038	OEM
872990045	OEM
872990061	OEM
872990063	OEM
872990065	OEM
872990067	OEM
872990074	OEM
872990080	OEM
872990083	OEM
872990085	OEM
872990089	OEM
872990103	OEM
872990105	OEM
872990210	OEM
872990239	OEM
872990330	OEM
872990410	OEM
872990427	OEM
872990648	OEM
872992008	OEM
872992091	OEM
872996522	OEM
872996732	OEM
874110029	OEM
874113170	OEM
874113980	OEM
874115050	OEM
874901601	OEM
874990008	OEM
874990015	OEM
874990036	OEM
874990080	OEM
874990135	OEM
874990149	OEM
874992003	OEM
874992059	OEM
874992081	OEM
874993035	OEM
874994121	OEM
874994152	OEM
874995610	OEM
874995830	OEM
875101870	OEM
875200141	OEM
875200610	OEM
875200730	OEM
875201080	OEM
875201090	OEM
875201120	OEM
875201290	OEM
875201330	OEM
875201390	OEM
875201870	OEM
875201920	OEM
875201930	OEM
875203026	OEM
875203028	OEM
875203093	OEM
875203165	OEM
875203167	OEM
875203180	OEM
875203229	OEM
875203230	OEM
875203232	OEM
875203233	OEM
875203314	OEM
875203334	OEM
875203338	OEM
875203340	OEM
875203354	OEM
875203355	OEM
875203361	OEM
875203440	OEM
875203528	OEM
875203552	OEM
875203554	OEM
875232011	OEM
875232044	OEM
875232118	OEM
875232165	OEM
875232232	OEM
875232608	OEM
875232618	OEM
875232872	OEM
875233331	OEM

DEVICE TYPE	REPL CODE
875233406	OEM
875280016	OEM
875280061	OEM
875280603	OEM
875280878	OEM
875281065	OEM
875794800	OEM
875847000	OEM
875885200	OEM
875900105	OEM
875900868	OEM
875903017	OEM
875903035	OEM
875903148	OEM
875903163	OEM
875903528	OEM
875910060	OEM
875910075	OEM
875910093	OEM
875910155	OEM
875910212	OEM
875910228	OEM
875910233	OEM
875910237	OEM
875910307	OEM
875910325	OEM
875910405	OEM
875910559	OEM
875910582	2031
875910641	OEM
875910645	OEM
875910768	OEM
875910777	OEM
875910785	OEM
875911037	OEM
875911168	OEM
875911188	OEM
875911293	OEM
875912556	OEM
875913240	OEM
875914001	OEM
875914011	OEM
875914017	OEM
875914026	OEM
875914051	OEM
875914053	OEM
875914069	OEM
875914071	OEM
875914337	OEM
875914454	OEM
875914582	OEM
875914634	OEM
875915740	OEM
875917012	OEM
875917812	OEM
875917912	OEM
875920079	OEM
875920123	OEM
875920201	OEM
875920213	OEM
875920245	OEM
875920387	OEM
875920388	OEM
875920430	OEM
875920441	OEM
875920581	OEM
875920582	OEM
875920673	OEM
875920726	OEM
875920776	OEM
875920810	OEM
875920814	OEM
875920882	OEM
875920896	OEM
875920953	OEM
875923026	OEM
875923049	OEM
875923123	OEM
875923426	OEM
875923435	OEM
875924011	OEM
875924012	OEM
875924024	OEM
875924069	OEM
875924071	OEM
875924075	OEM
875924081	OEM
875927630	OEM
875930390	OEM
875931441	OEM
875932040	OEM
875934053	OEM
875940012	OEM
875940088	OEM
875940235	OEM
875940365	OEM
875942001	OEM
875960005	OEM
875960013	OEM
875960035	OEM
875960043	OEM
875960046	OEM
875960102	OEM
875960103	OEM
875960106	OEM
875960141	OEM
875960143	OEM
875960145	OEM
875960148	OEM

DEVICE TYPE	REPL CODE
875960201	OEM
875960247	OEM
875960254	OEM
875960265	OEM
875960270	OEM
875960271	OEM
875960287	OEM
875960320	OEM
875960328	OEM
875960342	OEM
875960394	OEM
875960400	OEM
875960405	OEM
875960430	OEM
875960431	OEM
875960433	OEM
875960449	OEM
875960463	OEM
875960475	OEM
875960484	OEM
875960486	OEM
875960490	OEM
875960493	OEM
875960539	OEM
875960543	OEM
875960545	OEM
875963021	OEM
875963082	OEM
875963139	OEM
875963140	OEM
875963201	OEM
875963254	OEM
875963261	OEM
875963289	OEM
875964519	OEM
875965142	OEM
875965214	OEM
875970000	OEM
875970006	OEM
875970011	OEM
875970020	OEM
875970024	OEM
875970040	OEM
875970043	OEM
875970050	OEM
875970075	OEM
875970089	OEM
875970112	OEM
875970121	OEM
875970124	OEM
875970192	OEM
875971004	OEM
875974556	OEM
875974564	OEM
875980012	OEM
875980015	OEM
875980018	OEM
875980036	OEM
875980071	OEM
875980101	OEM
875980112	OEM
875980123	OEM
875980173	OEM
875980180	OEM
875980185	OEM
875980198	OEM
875980208	OEM
875980234	OEM
875980239	OEM
875980252	OEM
875980261	OEM
875980274	OEM
875980285	OEM
875980324	OEM
875980329	OEM
875980333	OEM
875980364	OEM
875980472	OEM
875980506	OEM
875980518	OEM
875980534	OEM
875980535	OEM
875980550	OEM
875981290	OEM
875982007	OEM
875982009	OEM
875982010	OEM
875982022	OEM
875982049	OEM
875982051	OEM
875982062	OEM
875982091	OEM
875982145	OEM
875982193	OEM
875982194	OEM
875987802	OEM
875990070	OEM
875990072	OEM
875990239	OEM
875990515	OEM
875990602	OEM
875990716	OEM
875990808	OEM
875990816	OEM
875990817	OEM
875990823	OEM
875990881	OEM
875990889	OEM
875990906	OEM

DEVICE TYPE	REPL CODE
875990949	OEM
875990950	OEM
875991018	OEM
875991039	OEM
875991252	OEM
875991255	OEM
875991282	OEM
875991311	OEM
875991372	OEM
875991379	OEM
875991380	OEM
875991444	OEM
875991531	OEM
875991554	OEM
875991742	OEM
875991829	OEM
875991876	OEM
875991992	OEM
875992015	OEM
875992027	OEM
875992081	OEM
875992219	OEM
875992341	OEM
875992397	OEM
875992425	OEM
875992426	OEM
875992449	OEM
875992482	OEM
875992564	OEM
875992751	OEM
875992962	OEM
875992965	OEM
875993736	OEM
875993756	OEM
875993795	OEM
875994062	OEM
875994079	OEM
875994088	OEM
875994517	OEM
875994600	OEM
875994662	OEM
875994702	OEM
875994703	OEM
875994761	OEM
875997080	OEM
875997140	OEM
875997152	OEM
875997193	OEM
875997243	OEM
875997249	OEM
875997421	OEM
875997771	OEM
875997834	OEM
875998058	OEM
875998169	OEM
875998210	OEM
875998466	OEM
875999082	OEM
876362300	OEM
876934001	OEM
881250108	0016
881250109	0016
884814411	OEM
885540026-3	0692
885540031-2	4772
910678870	0037
998615901	OEM
1039956300	1319
1522210111	0004
1522210131	0136
1522210300	0004
1522210921	0136
1522211021	0136
1522211200	0004
1522211221	0004
1522211328	0004
1522211921	0050
1522214400	0050
1522214411	0136
1522214435	0136
1522214821	0136
1522214831	0050
1522216500	0004
1522216600	0136
1522217400	0050
1522223720	0016
1522270100	0143
1522270101	0143
1522270208	0143
1523270105	0015
1611190553	0030
1611819064	0016
1716580001	OEM
1760099001	0376
1760579001	0376
1760589001	0376
1760607001	OEM
1760609001	0364
1760609002	0127
1760609003	0376
1760829001	0364
1760979001	0364
1760979002	0364
2002010061	0564
2002010072	1164
2002020066	0034
2002020077	0101
2002030027	OEM
2002100022	0872

DEVICE TYPE	REPL CODE
2002110206	0167
2002110269	0167
2002110332	3728
2002110345	2868
2002110415	OEM
2002110542	OEM
2002120012	0391
2002120022	0872
2002120033	0849
2002120046	2511
2002120051	0906
2002120067	0069
2002120080	OEM
2002300012	0898
2002300023	1192
2002300029	1420
2002300033	1192
2002300046	2031
2002300067	OEM
2002300078	OEM
2002400617	0514
2002400638	3726
2002400641	OEM
2002400752	4047
2002400779	3590
2002501006	0348
2002501300	1327
2002501708	1049
2002502202	0067
2002502317	0445
2002502338	0492
2002502341	0498
2002502385	0578
2002600107	1319
2002600122	0039
2002600149	1319
2002600183	3462
2002600198	3417
2002600213	1631
2002610039	2254
2002610042	1594
2002610086	3331
2002610091	3830
2002610109	4302
2002620151	OEM
2002700101	5124
2002700130	OEM
2002700158	2015
2002700175	4923
2002700187	OEM
2002800034	0308
2002800112	0356
2002800133	0624
2002800146	0624
2002800178	0624
2002900042	4456
2002900138	OEM
2002900395	0107
2002900408	0963
2002900437	OEM
2002900455	OEM
2002900710	OEM
2003018812	OEM
2003028813	1332
2003028829	0836
2003037227	0076
2003037309	0076
2003038092	0284
2003038208	0184
2003038812	0836
2003038829	0836
2003049501	0781
2003049519	0781
2003049526	0781
2003049614	0781
2003049621	0781
2003055813	4841
2003064314	1142
2003073517	0191
2003082823	1211
2003082837	1211
2003094515	0076
2003094522	0076
2003094536	0076
2003094554	0076
2003094560	0076
2003098316	0066
2003110607	0220
2003117044	1142
2003121216	0558
2003134410	0547
2003134427	0547
2003144795	0638
2003145404	0220
2003150702	0949
2003150710	0949
2003150727	0949
2003151428	1077
2003151432	1077
2003162538	0236
2003162700	0728
2003172208	1077
2003172216	1077
2003172305	1077
2003173009	0127
2003173017	0127
2003174006	0151
2003174014	0151
2003174021	0151

If replacement code is OEM, contact original manufacturer for replacement.

239

DEVICE TYPE	REPL CODE
2003174105	1505
2003174113	1505
2003181508	0076
2003181516	0076
2003181523	0076
2003181537	0076
2003184100	0525
2003184502	0525
2003185506	0224
2003189023	OEM
2003189025	0525
2003189109	0223
2003189304	2643
2003189408	0309
2003190604	0127
2003190612	0127
2003194135	1317
2003195906	0284
2003195914	0284
2003200100	1505
2003200118	1505
2003200125	1505
2003200320	0284
2003206800	0638
2003206818	0638
2003207306	1274
2003212007	0860
2003212015	0860
2003212204	0359
2003222907	0066
2003222915	0066
2003223000	0261
2003223018	0261
2003223039	0261
2003223312	1530
2003237331	0723
2003238316	1553
2003238323	1553
2003245819	0076
2003245826	0076
2003245830	0076
2003245843	0076
2003246703	2978
2003248119	0558
2003248126	0558
2003248164	0558
2003248175	0558
2003248217	0261
2003251204	0224
2003251212	0224
2003261019	0261
2003278549	0249
2003278554	0249
2003290117	0388
2003340091	0275
2003340271	0558
2003340283	0558
2004047310	0919
2004049081	1490
2004049514	0006
2004056215	0006
2004056260	0006
2004060858	0006
2004067350	0148
2004073315	0006
2004073322	0006
2004073336	0006
2004073354	0006
2004074304	0520
2004082606	0037
2004082614	0037
2004085415	1338
2004085422	1338
2004085436	1338
2004093316	0148
2004093323	0148
2004094001	1900
2004095005	1338
2004095013	1338
2004095210	0006
2004095227	0006
2004101500	0148
2004101512	0148
2004101518	0148
2004101525	0148
2004104814	0013
2004104821	0013
2004104835	0013
2004120026	0919
2004302210	0164
2004305600	0004
2004305618	0004
2004341519	0164
2004356122	0431
2004356220	0527
2004356234	0527
2004356801	1900
2004503018	0208
2004546819	0018
2004546826	0018
2004547806	0388
2004547814	0388
2004568902	0055
2004581809	2636
2004586902	0055
2004587002	0055
2004588008	0456
2004588016	0456
2004589802	0055

DEVICE TYPE	REPL CODE
2004590007	0055
2004613904	0388
2004645306	1533
2004645503	1533
2004700108	3079
2007000015	OEM
2007100149	3017
2007100154	3017
2007100171	3104
2007100213	3308
2007110124	0367
2007110138	0367
2007110190	OEM
2007110215	OEM
2007200000	0312
2007200173	0826
2007200236	0826
2008000001	0019
2008000019	0123
2008000026	0019
2008000064	0143
2008000075	0918
2008010028	0133
2008010094	0133
2008010102	0120
2008010110	0133
2008010127	0124
2008010131	0124
2008010165	0133
2008010218	0133
2008010225	0124
2008010263	0133
2008010307	0124
2008100027	0023
2008100093	0344
2008100130	0023
2008110103	0023
2008120009	0023
2008120017	0023
2008120056	0494
2008130084	0023
2008130171	0344
2008130198	0023
2008130234	0023
2008130252	0023
2008140021	0031
2008150011	0031
2008160106	0031
2008209102	OEM
2008220125	0057
2008220174	0999
2008220531	0681
2008220698	0140
2008220703	0140
2008220851	0057
2008220895	0466
2008220970	0041
2008220997	0253
2008221014	0091
2008221048	0062
2008221097	0077
2008221113	0165
2008221168	0064
2008221211	0053
2008221522	0166
2008221772	0466
2008221824	0062
2008221890	0077
2008221975	0057
2008222052	0052
2008222582	0166
2008230039	0162
2008230042	0298
2008230057	0644
2008300017	0715
2008300038	OEM
2008300056	1023
2008300062	OEM
2008300085	OEM
2008310019	0715
2008310092	0715
2008310157	OEM
2008310163	0623
2008310186	OEM
2008310208	0715
2008310216	0715
2008310237	OEM
2008310240	OEM
2008400055	0163
2008400072	0124
2008400084	OEM
2008406103	OEM
2008409101	OEM
2008600011	0911
2008600032	0911
2008607108	OEM
2008609107	OEM
2008700022	2604
2008700036	OEM
2009120101	0023
2009120187	0015
2009120209	0023
2009120224	0023
2009120241	0015
2009120256	0015
2009120262	0015
2009120370	0023
2009130075	0071
2009130100	0559

DEVICE TYPE	REPL CODE
2009130118	0559
2009700063	0201
2011300055	OEM
2011300183	OEM
2011300469	OEM
2011320047	OEM
2011800017	OEM
2012000092	0019
2012000100	0019
2012000118	0019
2012010028	0133
2012010144	0133
2012010159	0133
2012010165	0133
2012010176	0023
2012010218	0133
2012010225	0124
2012010263	0133
2012100119	0344
2012100126	0023
2012100158	0023
2012100164	0344
2012110103	0071
2012120009	0023
2012120038	0023
2012120056	0023
2012130234	0102
2012220104	0077
2012220139	0064
2012220174	0999
2012220368	0681
2012220851	0057
2012220867	0440
2012220935	0140
2012220970	0041
2012220982	0041
2012221006	0253
2012221014	0077
2012221053	0466
2012221070	0062
2012221120	0165
2012221152	0057
2012221168	0064
2012221179	0064
2012221196	0181
2012221203	0181
2012221228	0999
2012221245	0053
2012221250	0053
2012221294	0681
2012221522	0195
2012221693	0140
2012221723	0041
2012221737	0041
2012221784	0253
2012221817	0466
2012221862	0062
2012221890	0077
2012222005	0057
2012222013	0057
2012222020	0064
2012222052	0064
2012222079	0064
2012222096	0052
2012222129	0052
2012222227	0873
2012222244	0681
2012222570	0195
2012222754	0181
2012222760	0053
2012222861	0053
2012223529	0372
2012230042	0298
2012230109	0137
2012230312	0137
2012400061	0163
2013120208	0023
2013120216	0015
2013120223	0015
2013120255	0015
2013120313	0015
2013120334	0015
2013120347	0604
2013200021	0148
2013200035	0148
2013200048	0148
2013200069	1514
2013200070	1514
2013200082	1514
2013200179	0013
2013200181	0013
2013200196	0013
2013200363	0006
2013200779	0013
2013500037	1553
2013500040	1553
2013500084	0076
2013500099	0076
2013500107	0127
2013500115	0261
2013500136	0151
2013500149	0151
2013500154	0151
2013500213	0249
2013500268	0076
2013500279	0076
2013500281	0076
2013500302	0076
2013500310	0076

DEVICE TYPE	REPL CODE
2013500327	0076
2013500359	2118
2013500365	2118
2013500388	0836
2013500470	2882
2013500482	0261
2013800027	0826
2013800059	4109
2013800088	0826
2013800119	4109
2013800126	4109
2013800143	4109
2018206110	OEM
2018211100	OEM
2018213100	OEM
2028106109	OEM
2028406113	OEM
2028406123	OEM
2029420295	OEM
2058599104	OEM
2058599109	OEM
2058599120	OEM
2058819107	OEM
2102400203	0356
2102400429	0356
2102400451	6341
2103500327	0076
2104000602	0148
2130309103	OEM
2138009101	OEM
2138010101	OEM
2138022101	OEM
2138307122	OEM
2168013105	OEM
2168017131	OEM
2168017134	OEM
2168022105	OEM
2168411105	OEM
2168411106	OEM
2168600106	OEM
2168601105	OEM
2208406113	OEM
2208622106	OEM
2290180119	0144
2295100224	0144
2295100225	0144
2295100226	0144
2295100227	0050
2295100228	0144
2295100232	0229
2295100233	0071
2295100234	0229
2295100235	0229
2302250002	3381
2302550002	3381
2302880023	OEM
2307890127	0120
2308220130	OEM
2308220507	OEM
2308270603	OEM
2309100000	OEM
2309100100	OEM
2309100200	OEM
2309100300	OEM
2309100400	OEM
2338179923	OEM
2505015301	OEM
2723100413	0023
2805015301	0163
2805015302	0163
2805025301	OEM
2805035301	OEM
2805045301	0911
2805055301	OEM
2805066101	OEM
2805076101	0802
2805086121	OEM
2805316101	OEM
2805326101	OEM
2805336101	OEM
2805346101	OEM
3071339004	1532
3071459001	2312
3071511002	OEM
3071517001	OEM
3071519001	4227
3071519002	OEM
3111007300	0143
3112006000	0143
3121004900	0050
3121007744	0050
3121024033	0050
3121024044	0050
3121047111	0050
3121050611	0050
3121050622	0050
3122005400	0004
3539306001	0016
3539306002	0016
3539306003	0016
3618020001	OEM
3630020001	OEM
4004056260	0006
4004085415	1338
4004095210	0006
4100005620	0006
4100006285	0006
4100009870	0006
4100010157	0148

DEVICE TYPE	REPL CODE
4100104753	0164
4100105440	0527
4100108240	1298
4100204602	0151
4100204603	0151
4100205352	0127
4100206443	0111
4100208271	0007
4100208283	0224
4100208291	0007
4100208292	0224
4100208293	0224
4100210472	0224
4100213421	0127
4100213591	0007
4100217172	0155
4100217177	OEM
4100218157	0076
4100221200	0860
4100222301	0261
4100222710	0261
4100224820	0261
4100230380	2985
4100230420	2171
4100304000	2882
4100308230	1157
4100313980	1533
4100314270	1533
4100900102	0364
4100900103	0364
4100900104	0364
4100900116	0376
4100903554	0018
4100905254	0527
4100907633	0127
4101154010	0338
4101155510	0076
4101490420	0710
4102100220	0164
4104007193	0006
4104007380	0455
4104103242	0164
4104204602	0127
4104204603	0151
4104204612	0151
4104204613	0151
4104205352	0127
4104206440	0111
4104213173	0155
4104213421	0127
4104215684	1779
4104548119	OEM
4104673030	OEM
4108296047	0079
4108296238	0079
4108296255	0079
4108296257	0224
4109208280	1211
4109208284	0016
4109213174	0155
4109213354	0111
4120100090	0143
4120100600	0019
4120100603	0019
4120141480	0124
4120200090	0143
4120200602	0123
4120400260	0120
4120500395	0036
4120500475	0140
4120500565	0253
4120500622	0466
4120500625	0466
4120500685	0062
4120501005	0064
4120501200	0052
4120501205	0052
4120501505	0681
4120501805	0371
4120502405	0489
4120504742	0137
4120505105	0092
4120510513	0248
4120510625	0091
4120511105	0099
4120520513	0041
4120520603	0466
4120521305	0053
4120601550	3990
4120622345	OEM
4120900010	0133
4120900020	0023
4120903100	OEM
4120910010	0023
4120910430	0549
4120922220	0133
4121141480	0124
4121200051	0041
4122510600	0253
4128100020	0023
4129100600	0019
4129100602	0123
4129104002	0080
4129121392	0005
4129200602	0123
4129200857	0030
4129227907	0623
4129301329	0030
4129321292	0030

DEVICE TYPE	REPL CODE
4129400003	0133
4129501200	0052
4130060010	0023
4130100012	0023
4130100015	0023
4130100021	0023
4130101011	0015
4130104002	0080
4130104006	0072
4130120020	0071
4130151550	0031
4130202040	0071
4130202060	0071
4130508240	1356
4130800060	1036
4131000220	1227
4138104002	0080
4138151520	0071
4138200020	0071
4139000005	0015
4139104002	0080
4150002031	2554
4150003770	2535
4151005753	2845
4151005768	OEM
4151014908	4470
4152032010	2550
4152041000	2590
4152056300	1319
4152075300	3765
4152076200	0552
4152076550	4032
4152078300	0727
4152078350	2330
4152079100	2641
4152085600	3925
4154011370	2728
4154011510	3606
4154011560	0514
4154013890	OEM
4157013102	0514
4158003780	OEM
4159009560	OEM
4159256100	OEM
4159301230	3897
4202003173	0015
4202003500	0143
4202003900	0102
4202005000	0196
4202005600	0123
4202006100	0124
4202006200	0133
4202007600	0102
4202007800	5510
4202007801	0102
4202007806	OEM
4202007860	OEM
4202008000	0102
4202008500	5608
4202008600	0143
4202008700	0023
4202009200	0490
4202011400	0062
4202011500	0181
4202012501	0313
4202012700	0002
4202012800	0490
4202013300	0010
4202013600	0133
4202014400	0080
4202014500	0080
4202014600	0959
4202015100	0182
4202015600	0133
4202016000	0133
4202016200	0133
4202017200	0344
4202017600	0023
4202018500	0023
4202018700	0133
4202019400	0010
4202019500	0010
4202020100	0091
4202020200	0071
4202020300	0559
4202020500	0023
4202020900	0344
4202021000	0023
4202021100	0087
4202021700	0466
4202021900	0133
4202022300	0023
4202022500	0124
4202022700	0124
4202022900	0344
4202023000	0102
4202023100	0023
4202023200	0023
4202023300	0344
4202023400	0015
4202024200	0062
4202024300	0062
4202093599	0123
4202104170	0287
4202104470	0071
4202104570	0102
4202104770	0004
4202104870	0102
4202105000	OEM

DEVICE TYPE	REPL CODE
4202105070	0918
4202105470	0644
4202106270	0752
4202106970	0102
4202107270	0286
4202107370	0286
4202107470	0133
4202107570	0374
4202107670	0124
4202107970	0102
4202107971	OEM
4202108070	0752
4202108170	0752
4202108270	0015
4202108570	0560
4202109070	0313
4202109370	0023
4202110270	0023
4202110370	0015
4202110470	0102
4202110670	0080
4202110770	0023
4202110870	0313
4202111070	0077
4202115870	0023
4202116370	0077
4202116670	0313
4202970330	0100
4203970101	0076
4206002400	0872
4206002600	0849
4206003900	0849
4206004000	0167
4206004400	0872
4206004600	0167
4206005200	0878
4206007500	0875
4206009100	4133
4206009200	0850
4206009700	0850
4206009800	0880
4206012500	0910
4206042400	0872
4206064400	OEM
4206104970	0167
4206105170	0391
4206105370	2615
4206105470	0167
4206105670	0837
4206105770	0167
4206105870	0167
4206970020	3684
4227920320	OEM
4253401360	OEM
4704020001	OEM
4800155039	0019
4800155047	0124
4800155059	0949
4800155060	0133
4800155073	0284
4800155077	0133
4800155093	0284
4800155094	0284
4800155144	1319
4800155166	0025
4800155172	0819
4800155177	0015
4800155179	0023
4800155258	0124
4800155293	0577
4800155294	0819
4800155296	0023
4800155307	0284
4800155322	4262
4800155330	0002
4800155334	0124
4800155349	0002
4800155364	0018
4800155372	0577
4800155380	0203
4800155400	0577
4800155401	0577
4800155402	0577
4890155343	0819
5023500177	OEM
5147013102	0514
5300731044	0253
5300731045	0062
5300731045	0062
5301271120	0052
5301481003	0102
5301511001	0023
5301511003	0023
5301511004	0023
5301570629	0466
5301570689	0062
5301571001	0155
5301571100	0064
5301571100	0064
5301571110	0181
5301571120	0052
5301571130	0053
5301571150	0681
5301571160	0440
5301571180	0371
5301571200	0695
5301571220	0700
5301571249	1266
5301571270	0450

240 If replacement code is OEM, contact original manufacturer for replacement.

DEVICE TYPE	REPL CODE
5301571300	0195
5301571330	0166
5301571369	0372
5301571399	0036
5301571439	0274
5301571439	0274
5301571519	0041
5301571569	0253
5301571629	0466
5301571689	0062
5301571829	0165
5301571919	0057
5301591100	0012
5301670001	OEM
5301710001	0155
5301711001	0023
5301711001	0604
5301711002	0604
5301711569	0253
5301791001	0133
5301791002	OEM
5301810001	0133
5301810002	0124
5301811001	0133
5301811002	0124
5301811003	0124
5301819001	0124
5301840001	5850
5301840001	0023
5301840002	0102
5301841001	0102
5301880005	OEM
5301881005	OEM
5301890001	OEM
5301890002	OEM
5301920569	OEM
5301920629	0631
5301921120	0137
5301921180	0490
5301921200	0526
5301921240	0398
5301921300	0721
5301921330	0039
5301921919	0012
5301940003	OEM
5301941003	0911
5301950005	OEM
5301951005	OEM
5301990479	0140
5301990689	0062
5301990919	0057
5302050003	0163
5302051003	0163
5302200001	0124
5302261002	0102
5302300002	OEM
5302300003	OEM
5302301003	OEM
5302301004	OEM
5302350001	2604
5302390002	1997
5302390008	1767
5302390011	0071
5302390017	1997
5302390019	0041
5302390020	0023
5302390021	0023
5302390022	0790
5302390023	0023
5302390024	5877
5302390025	0023
5302390026	0023
5302390027	6198
5302390028	6659
5302390029	0271
5302390030	0053
5302390031	0642
5302390032	0700
5302390033	0814
5302390034	OEM
5302390037	6199
5302390038	6200
5302390043	0581
5302390056	0041
5302390057	1982
5302390059	OEM
5302390061	0730
5302390066	0999
5302390086	3417
5302390146	0124
5302390150	OEM
5302390161	0023
5302390168	OEM
5302390182	OEM
5302390187	3460
5302390200	0934
5302390209	0071
5302390210	OEM
5302390252	0023
5302390254	OEM
5302410049	OEM
5302470001	0911
5302471001	0911
5302471001(247-1)	OEM
5302480001	OEM
5302491130	OEM
5302491140	OEM
5302491160	0440
5302491200	OEM
5302491270	4239
5302491300	0195
5302491519	0041
5302491569	0877
5302491629	0292
5302491689	OEM
5302491759	0077
5302491829	OEM
5302511001	0133
5302511002	0124
5302521001	0133
5302521002	0133
5302531005	0526
5302531014	0137
5302531016	OEM
5302541010	0336
5302541011	0052
5302541012	0253
5302541021	0053
5302541027	3889
5302541031	0695
5302541032	0296
5302541034	OEM
5302541036	0371
5302541038	0165
5302541039	0466
5302551001	0015
5302561002	0071
5302570001	0489
5302570001(257-1)	OEM
5302591001	OEM
5302600001	0031
5302600002	0031
5302600004	OEM
5302601001	0031
5302601001	0023
5302601002	0023
5302601002	0023
5302601003	0102
5302610001	0023
5302611001	0023
5302611001	0023
5302620001	0071
5302621001	0071
5302621002	0023
5302641001	1208
5302641002	1208
5302650001	OEM
5302660001	0133
5302661001	0133
5302670002	0271
5302671002	0023
5302680001	OEM
5302681001	0124
5302681002	0124
5302740001	0511
5302740002	5605
5302751001	0344
5302751002	0344
5302751003	0344
5302761003	OEM
5302771001	0143
5302781001	2379
5302781005	0437
5302781006	0864
5302781008	0041
5302801001	0421
5302840001	0468
5302850001	0511
5302860001	2604
5302970001	OEM
5302970002	OEM
5302970003	OEM
5302980001	0311
5302990001	1082
5302990002	1082
5302991001	1082
5302991002	0790
5303000001	0311
5303010002	OEM
5303011001	OEM
5303011002	5890
5303011002	OEM
5303011003	OEM
5303020002	0253
5303020003	0999
5303020006	OEM
5303021002	0253
5303021002	0253
5303021003	0052
5303021003	0052
5303021006	0064
5303030001	OEM
5303040001	OEM
5303040003	OEM
5303046001	OEM
5303047001	OEM
5303050002	0023
5303050003	0023
5303051002	0031
5303051002	0023
5303051003	0031
5303051003	0023
5303060001	OEM
5303061001	0947
5303100001	0031
5303100003	0031
5303101001	0023
5303101002	0023
5303101003	0031
5303101004	0702
5303121001	2077
5303130001	0163
5303130002	0163
5303131001	OEM
5303131002	OEM
5303150001	OEM
5303150002	OEM
5303150003	OEM
5303176001	OEM
5303177001	OEM
5303200001	OEM
5303200002	OEM
5303211919	0012
5303230001	OEM
5303240001	OEM
5303250001	OEM
5303260003	0541
5303261003	0541
5303277001	OEM
5303287001	OEM
5303291100	6705
5303291130	OEM
5303291160	OEM
5303291200	OEM
5303291330	5909
5303291519	6677
5303291569	3854
5303291629	0292
5303300629	OEM
5303340001	1281
5303371120	0052
5303371220	0700
5303371249	OEM
5303371330	0166
5303371399	0036
5303371479	0140
5303371689	0062
5303371829	0165
5303371919	0057
5303381859	0057
5303390001	OEM
5303410001	0031
5303411001	1483
5310200010	2714
5310200051	0079
5310200053	0006
5310200102	0006
5310200141	0076
5310200142	0076
5310200210	0836
5310200311	0191
5310200482	0638
5310200875	0074
5310200901	0638
5310200902	0638
5310200910	0066
5310200911	0066
5310200920	0261
5310200930	1274
5310200940	0860
5310200950	2643
5310400011	1900
5310400030	0220
5310400050	1274
5310400090	0638
5310400100	2643
5320200050	0167
5320200150	0906
5320200160	2043
5320200170	4071
5320500090	OEM
5320500100	3239
5320500120	2038
5320600070	0516
5320600080	OEM
5329500060	0167
5340100010	0019
5340200040	0133
5340200070	0182
5340200080	0023
5340200430	0124
5340200591	0494
5340200600	0133
5340200601	0133
5340200720	0023
5340200721	0015
5340200722	0071
5340200723	0143
5340200724	0071
5340200741	0071
5340200901	0023
5340200902	0023
5340200950	0344
5340300230	0244
5340300350	0053
5340300370	0466
5340300380	0631
5340300430	0528
5340300450	0466
5390100919	0057
5390120949	0057
5390140249	1266
5390150479	0140
5390150519	0041
5390160309	0118
5390190040	0253
5390190060	OEM
5390190090	OEM
5390190230	0077
5390190949	0057
5390620331	0166
5390620399	0036
5390620829	0165
5390750309	0118
5390750519	0041
5390760111	0181
5390760121	0052
5390760131	0053
5390760271	0450
5390760689	0062
5390990150	OEM
5390990180	0188
5390990200	OEM
5390990230	0339
5390990280	0057
5391100060	0124
5391100260	0031
5391100341	0124
5391100460	0124
5391100630	0133
5391100640	0102
5391100650	OEM
5391200020	2520
5391200030	0023
5391200110	0559
5391200302	0023
5391200380	0023
5391200390	0541
5391200420	0541
5391200500	OEM
5391200510	0023
5391200520	0015
5391200530	0071
5391300010	1864
5391300240	0689
5391300380	0199
5391300390	1009
5391400020	3703
5391500170	0242
5391500200	0023
5391500210	0031
5391500270	0133
5391500320	0124
5391500330	0031
5391500390	0023
5391500400	0087
5391500432	0023
5391500440	OEM
5391500460	0344
5391500610	0031
5391510040	0403
5391510050	0031
5391900100	0057
5392000011	OEM
5392000410	OEM
5392100120	OEM
5392200011	OEM
5392400050	OEM
5392400051	OEM
5392400100	2678
5392400110	OEM
5392500860	OEM
5393100131	OEM
5393200010	OEM
5393200040	OEM
5393200050	OEM
5530315001	OEM
5700045452	0198
6020232250	OEM
6020234220	OEM
6040120025	OEM
6060102002	OEM
6100830001	0037
6100830005	0037
6100830006	0037
6100839001	0037
6100839005	0037
6100839006	0037
6100940004	0111
6101220003	OEM
6101480003	0079
6101489003	0079
6101490010	0042
6101580003	0037
6102130001	0086
6102230001	0037
6102239001	0037
6102240001	0079
6102249001	0111
6102260001	0079
6102270003	3294
6102280005	0818
6102300003	OEM
6102320001	0079
6102320002	0076
6102329001	0079
6102329002	0076
6102330001	6391
6102340001	2436
6102340001(234-1)	OEM
6102349001	OEM
6102460001	0037
6102460002	OEM
6102500003	0261
6102500004	OEM
6103600001	0338
6103600002	0338
6103609001	0224
6103620001	6310
6103620001(362-1)	OEM
6103680001	0546
6103680002	0079
6103690001	0037
6103699001	0127
6103700001	0079
6103720002	0037
6103900001	0802
6103900001	0037
6103902001	0802
6103909001	0802
6103920001	0309
6103920002	0309
6104150001	0261
6104190002	2293
6104190003	2293
6104210001	0042
6104210002	0919
6104210003	0042
6104210004	0919
6104210005	0477
6104210006	4094
6104210008	1359
6104270002	0561
6104270003	0561
6104280002	0818
6104330001	3326
6104330002	1533
6104330002	1533
6104330003	3326
6104330004	3472
6104330005	1533
6104340001	0037
6104340001	0037
6104340002	OEM
6104340003	OEM
6104340004	0037
6104342001	0037
6104342004	0037
6104349001	0037
6104349002	0037
6104349004	0037
6104350001	0079
6104350001	0079
6104350002	0079
6104350002	0079
6104350004	0111
6104352001	0079
6104352002	0079
6104359001	0079
6104359002	0079
6104359004	0111
6104360001	2985
6104370001	0261
6104379001	0710
6104380001	1045
6104390001	0275
6104400023	0015
6104400117	0527
6104400118	2895
6104400119	OEM
6104400120	0076
6104400121	1157
6104400122	2926
6104400123	0148
6104410001	0037
6104420001	0008
6104429001	0008
6104430001	3749
6104440001	0055
6104470001	0008
6104490001	0037
6104500001	0079
6104500002	0037
6104509001	0079
6104510002	0037
6104510003	0037
6104570002	0419
6104570003	0419
6104580003	0590
6104600001	0037
6104609001	0037
6104620001	0555
6104620003	0419
6104630002	0309
6104631002	0309
6104640001	3326
6104650001	0079
6104680001	1698
6104710001	0283
6104730001	0309
6104740001	0079
6104750001	0037
6104760001	0434
6104770001	1841
6104790001	0710
6104800001	0855
6104809001	0855
6104820001	0037
6104860001	0079
6104870001	0037
6104880001	0264
6104980001	0037
6104989001	0037
6104990001	0016
6104999001	OEM
6105000001	0079
6105000004	0079
6105009001	0079
6105009004	0079
6105020001	OEM
6105030001	OEM
6105040001	0367
6105070002	1722
6105077001	1722
6105077002	1722
6105080001	5292
6105090001	0309
6105100001	1491
6105107001	1741
6105110001	2833
6105112001	5526
6105119001	2833
6105120001	0477
6105150002	OEM
6105157002	OEM
6105170001	4376
6105170002	4376
6105170003	4376
6105190001	OEM
6105210001	OEM
6105216001	OEM
6105260001	0527
6105269001	0527
6105270001	OEM
6105270002	OEM
6105272001	0472
6105279001	OEM
6105280001	0520
6105292001	0224
6105299001	OEM
6105309001	OEM
6105310001	0168
6105320001	1503
6105320003	1503
6105330001	3179
6105350003	OEM
6105352001	1376
6105359001	OEM
6105360001	0719
6105366001	OEM
6105380002	2833
6105382002	2833
6105389002	0079
6105390001	1157
6105442001	OEM
6105450001	4945
6105459001	OEM
6105460001	1587
6105469001	OEM
6105490001	OEM
6105497001	OEM
6105500001	OEM
6105507001	1426
6105510001	2985
6105520001	1553
6105529001	1553
6105530001	1514
6105539001	1514
6105540001	0261
6105549001	0261
6105550001	1533
6105569001	OEM
6105580001	1518
6105589001	0079
6105590001	OEM
6105590003	OEM
6105607001	OEM
6105610001	1503
6105630001	OEM
6105650001	1157
6105660001	2739
6105670001	0079
6105680001	0037
6105690001	6266
6105767001	OEM
6105807001	OEM
6105847001	OEM
6105869001	0261
6110130001	4272
6110130001(013-1)	OEM
6110130003	6104
6110150001	1129
6110160001	3651
6110180001	1213
6110190001	0612
6110210001	OEM
6120480004	0308
6120720001	OEM
6120750003	0514
6121260001	2799
6121260001(DSD84)	OEM
6121630001	0620
6121860001	1135
6121860001(186-1)	OEM
6122470002	0944
6122500001	0119
6122750001	1888
6122850001	2894
6122850003	2894
6122940001	OEM
6123030001	0485
6123040001	1016
6123050001	3707
6123180001	5743
6123190001	OEM
6123270001	4521
6123280001	5106
6123290001	3668
6123300011	OEM
6123300012	OEM
6123300013	OEM
6123300022	OEM
6123300023	3640
6123300024	5739
6123300025	2031
6123300026	OEM
6123300027	5741
6123300028	OEM
6123300037	OEM
6123300039	OEM
6123300040	OEM
6123300047	OEM
6123300052	OEM
6123300061	OEM
6123300064	OEM
6123300067	OEM
6123300068	OEM
6123300069	OEM
6123300070	OEM
6123300071	OEM
6123300072	OEM
6123300086	OEM
6123300087	OEM
6123300100	OEM
6123300101	4047
6123300102	0578
6123300103	OEM
6123300104	OEM
6123300120	OEM
6123300140	4284
6123300215	3130
6123300218	OEM
6123300224	OEM
6123300227	OEM
6123300229	OEM
6123300230	OEM
6123300231	OEM
6123300232	OEM
6123300293	OEM
6123300320	OEM
6123300332	OEM
6123300334	1977
6123300417	OEM
6123300418	3765
6123300419	OEM
6123300476	OEM
6123300478	OEM
6123300500	OEM
6123300502	OEM
6123300509	OEM
6123300512	OEM
6123300518	OEM
6123300522	OEM
6123300524	OEM
6123310002	2790
6123320001	3665
6123320003	3665
6123320006	3666
6123340001	0516
6123350001	1672
6123360001	3934
6123370003	3937
6123370005	3937
6123380002	2785
6123380003	2785
6123390001	0069
6123410001	OEM
6123420001	5727
6123470002	2804
6123500001	0215
6123510001	0167
6123520001	3924
6123540001	0375
6123590001	3627
6123600001	0619
6123620001	1051
6123620002	1051
6123630001	2011
6123630005	2011
6123700001	0347
6123700002	0347
6123800001	3602
6123940001	0069
6123940002	2799
6123999001	1288
6124120002	3132
6124140001	1114
6124140001(STK4021M)	OEM
6124140002	OEM
6124160001	OEM
6124160002	OEM
6124160003	3546
6124190001	OEM
6124220001	OEM
6124230001	OEM
6124240001	3352
6124260003	OEM
6124260004	OEM
6124340001	OEM
6124400001	OEM
6124410004	OEM
6124410005	OEM

If replacement code is OEM, contact original manufacturer for replacement.

241

DEVICE TYPE	REPL CODE
6124420001	OEM
6124440001	2164
6124450001	5106
6124470001	OEM
6124470001(LA7810)	OEM
6124480001	0619
6124490001	3481
6124490001(TDA2546A)	OEM
6124490002	OEM
6124500001	5155
6124500002	5668
6124670001	3453
6124680001	1698
6124680001(468-1)	OEM
6124690001	OEM
6124690001(469-1)	OEM
6124710001	OEM
6124720001	OEM
6124730001	OEM
6124740001	0024
6124760001	OEM
6124770002	OEM
6124780001	OEM
6124790001	0619
6124790003	1187
6124790004	3445
6124790005	1311
6124800001	3357
6124830001	OEM
6124840001	OEM
6124840002	OEM
6124850001	OEM
6124850002	OEM
6124860002	OEM
6124870002	OEM
6124870003	OEM
6124880001	OEM
6124890001	3403
6124890001(AN5291)	OEM
6124920001	1126
6124930001	0034
6124940001	0356
6124960001	2815
6124980001	OEM
6124990001	OEM
6124990002	OEM
6125020004	OEM
6125030001	OEM
6125040001	5636
6125070001	3015
6125080001	5292
6125354053	OEM
6125390001	3357
6125410001	OEM
6125420002	OEM
6125450001	3352
6125510004	OEM
6125520001	OEM
6125530001	OEM
6125540001	OEM
6125560002	OEM
6125570001	OEM
6125580003	OEM
6125590001	OEM
6125600002	OEM
6125610001	OEM
6125610002	OEM
6125610004	OEM
6125620001	OEM
6125630001	3331
6125640001	3830
6125650001	OEM
6125660001	2044
6125670004	OEM
6125680003	OEM
6125710001	3675
6125740001	2929
6125750001	3309
6125760001	OEM
6125770001	OEM
6125770002	OEM
6125780001	OEM
6125790001	OEM
6125830001	OEM
6125840002	OEM
6125840003	OEM
6125840004	OEM
6125840005	OEM
6125840007	OEM
6125860001	3897
6125860002	2348
6125870001	OEM
6125880001	OEM
6125890001	OEM
6125900001	OEM
6125910001	OEM
6125920001	OEM
6125930002	OEM
6125960001	3278
6125990001	OEM
6125990002	OEM
6125990003	OEM
6126010001	OEM
6126010002	OEM
6126050001	OEM
6126060001	4009
6126100002	OEM
6126120001	3015
6126150001	5292

DEVICE TYPE	REPL CODE
6126190001	OEM
6126210004	OEM
6126210008	OEM
6126210153	OEM
6126210393	OEM
6126210574	OEM
6126210590	OEM
6126214078	OEM
6126217001	OEM
6126250001	0727
6126260005	OEM
6126270001	OEM
6126280001	3068
6126290001	OEM
6126300001	OEM
6126300002	OEM
6126310001	OEM
6126310002	OEM
6126320001	OEM
6126380001	OEM
6126520001	OEM
6126570001	OEM
6126580003	OEM
6126600001	OEM
6126610001	OEM
6126620001	OEM
6126630001	OEM
6126630003	OEM
6126630004	OEM
6126640001	5693
6126670001	OEM
6126680001	OEM
6126680002	OEM
6126690002	OEM
6126710001	0619
6126730001	OEM
6126760001	6485
6126780001	OEM
6126810001	1022
6126820001	OEM
6126830001	OEM
6126830002	OEM
6126860001	OEM
6126880001	5711
6126900001	OEM
6126920001	OEM
6126940001	OEM
6126950001	OEM
6127040001	OEM
6127060001	OEM
6127070001	OEM
6127080001	OEM
6127090001	OEM
6127100001	OEM
6127140001	OEM
6127280001	OEM
6127290001	OEM
6127330001	OEM
6127340002	OEM
6127410001	OEM
6127450001	OEM
6155077002	OEM
6155107001	OEM
6190000080	0577
6190000160	OEM
6190000170	OEM
6190000190	0355
6190000200	0308
6190000210	0412
6190000290	0577
6190000340	0667
6190000433	0826
6190000450	0111
6190000460	0881
6190000462	0881
6190000470	0892
6190000480	OEM
6190000490	0922
6190000500	0014
6190000520	0667
6190000530	0577
6190000540	0836
6190000731	0076
6190000751	OEM
6190001002	0261
6190001230	0076
6190001231	0076
6190001451	1505
6190001470	1132
6190001520	2041
6190001580	0066
6190001620	2118
6190001711	1553
6190001733	0076
6190001740	0261
6190001743	0261
6190001900	0249
6190001902	0249
6190002000	OEM
6190002020	OEM
6190002030	2351
6190002200	1503
6190002420	0836
6190002450	1533
6190002510	OEM
6190002750	0640
6190002960	0014
6190003240	OEM
6190003350	0042

DEVICE TYPE	REPL CODE
6190003700	OEM
6190003782	1779
6190003900	0161
6190003910	0261
6190003920	3181
6190004020	0723
6190004030	OEM
6190004270	OEM
6190004412	2666
6190004520	2833
6190004530	2739
6190004560	0922
6190004810	OEM
6190004860	OEM
6190004940	1317
6190004950	1779
6190004960	0723
6190005200	3950
6190005440	0127
6190005460	OEM
6190005560	OEM
6190005570	OEM
6190005600	0860
6190005610	0161
6190005920	OEM
6190005950	OEM
6190005960	OEM
6190005970	OEM
6190007060	OEM
6190007070	OEM
6190090770	OEM
6190090810	OEM
6190100010	0802
6190100100	OEM
6190100122	1026
6190100151	4109
6190100402	0006
6190100450	OEM
6190100550	2464
6190100660	0148
6190100661	0148
6190100663	0148
6190100664	OEM
6190100770	OEM
6190100780	OEM
6190100940	5276
6190100950	0819
6190100960	0819
6190101340	4067
6190101480	0006
6190101481	0037
6190101482	OEM
6190101710	0919
6190101720	0006
6190101750	0676
6190101780	0037
6190101860	4067
6190102040	OEM
6190102070	1298
6190102160	4062
6190102180	OEM
6190102200	OEM
6190102320	OEM
6190102330	OEM
6190102420	0148
6190102500	OEM
6190102560	OEM
6190102570	OEM
6190102780	OEM
6190102790	OEM
6190700021	2083
6191400010	0857
6192000040	6107
6192000080	OEM
6192000101	OEM
6192000150	5707
6192000160	6144
6192000170	OEM
6192000180	OEM
6192000910	OEM
6192000920	OEM
6192000930	OEM
6192000940	OEM
6192000950	OEM
6192000960	OEM
6192000980	OEM
6192000990	4009
6192001020	OEM
6192001060	OEM
6192001270	OEM
6192001330	4349
6192020160	4955
6192020190	3680
6192020400	0534
6192020620	OEM
6192020630	OEM
6192040031	5169
6192040040	5170
6192040260	0552
6192060090	0970
6192060140	0727
6192060190	OEM
6192080080	4306
6192080200	OEM
6192080250	2031
6192100070	OEM
6192100150	2884
6192100170	OEM
6192100380	OEM

DEVICE TYPE	REPL CODE
6192120071	OEM
6192120110	4309
6192120120	OEM
6192120250	OEM
6192120300	OEM
6192120302	OEM
6192120360	OEM
6192120370	OEM
6192120380	OEM
6192130070	OEM
6192130130	OEM
6192140020	1319
6192140060	OEM
6192140080	0619
6192140081	1288
6192140170	1631
6192140210	4959
6192140400	3448
6192140620	3417
6192149480	0619
6192160030	3869
6192180010	5228
6192180061	2055
6192180080	3130
6192180110	4054
6192180120	3479
6192180130	4078
6192180150	OEM
6192180160	3869
6192180170	OEM
6192180180	OEM
6192180190	OEM
6192180200	OEM
6192180210	OEM
6192180220	OEM
6192180510	OEM
6192180550	OEM
6192180560	OEM
6192180570	OEM
6192180580	OEM
6192180590	OEM
6192180600	OEM
6192180610	OEM
6192180630	OEM
6192181750	OEM
6192181870	OEM
6192181890	OEM
6192200150	OEM
6192220190	OEM
6192220740	OEM
6192220870	OEM
6192240040	4306
6192240110	OEM
6192240130	OEM
6192240140	5232
6192240150	OEM
6192240151	OEM
6192240160	OEM
6192240580	6181
6192240590	OEM
6192240600	OEM
6192240610	OEM
6192260030	OEM
6192260090	OEM
6192260100	OEM
6192440130	OEM
6193000570	OEM
6193000760	OEM
6193100070	OEM
6193140360	OEM
6193140370	OEM
6193160130	OEM
6193160150	OEM
6193160160	OEM
6193160350	OEM
6193160360	OEM
6193160370	OEM
6193160380	OEM
6193160460	OEM
6193160690	OEM
6193160700	OEM
6193160750	OEM
6193160760	OEM
6193160770	OEM
6193160810	OEM
6193180190	OEM
6193220010	4838
6193240020	OEM
6193300110	OEM
6194000030	0112
6194000031	OEM
6194000040	4791
6194030050	4312
6195010740	OEM
6196990020	OEM
6196990030	OEM
6196990040	OEM
6196990051	OEM
6196990060	OEM
6196990080	OEM
6196990160	OEM
6611000900	0182
6611001000	0023
6611001100	0023
6611001200	0102
6611001500	0023
6611001501	0023
6611001700	0023
6611001800	0023

DEVICE TYPE	REPL CODE
6611002300	0182
6611003000	0201
6611003200	0133
6611003701	0071
6611004601	0023
6611004602	0023
6611004803	0023
6611005100	0106
6611007300	0023
6612002200	0023
6612004000	0019
6612005800	0133
6612005900	0133
6612006000	0133
6612006101	0494
6612009000	0123
6612009002	0143
6613002200	5104
6613003000	0124
6615000100	0091
6615000101	0466
6615000200	0313
6615000600	0644
6615001701	0077
6615002603	0466
6615002788	0274
6615005000	0057
6615005500	1596
6615005600	0440
6621000200	1274
6621000600	2643
6621000700	0638
6621000701	0638
6621001000	0191
6621001100	0142
6621001401	0103
6621001800	0638
6621002000	0178
6621002300	0220
6621002400	1142
6621002800	1274
6621003100	0076
6621003200	0076
6621003400	0076
6621003500	0191
6621004000	0184
6621005000	0836
6621005001	0836
6621005003	0836
6621006200	0066
6621007200	0228
6621007403	0860
6621008100	0191
6621009100	0151
6621009600	0309
6621010001	0625
6621014601	0066
6621015602	0261
6621016000	0155
6621016100	0079
6622000100	0945
6622000300	0079
6622000401	0079
6622005100	0042
6622005400	0388
6623001100	0006
6623001900	0006
6623001902	0006
6623002000	0006
6623002026	0148
6623002100	0006
6623002200	0006
6623002300	0006
6623002304	0006
6623002700	1900
6624001000	0037
6624001100	0431
6624002000	0006
6624003100	0919
6624003200	0076
6631000100	0705
6631000200	0312
6631001200	0312
6640000410	0619
6644000100	0167
6644001100	3859
6644001200	OEM
6644001400	2921
6644001500	2216
6644001700	4514
6644001800	4515
6644001900	1316
6644002100	OEM
6644004202	0167
6644004301	1049
6644004400	0872
6644012500	0906
6644012602	2043
6644012700	4071
6644014900	OEM
6645003400	OEM
6647006400	OEM
7044260991	5155
9511410100	0004
9511410200	0004
9511410900	0004
9511413500	0004
9511414000	0222
9511510200	0143

DEVICE TYPE	REPL CODE
9511511500	0071
12613740490	0211
12618740490	0211
13480085512	1626
13480085513	0070
16000190201	0136
16004191050	0037
16009090545	0786
16100190668	0144
16102190693	0016
16102190929	0144
16102190930	0016
16102190931	0555
16103190668	0144
16103190930	0127
16104190668	0127
16104191168	0016
16104191225	0144
16104191226	0144
16105190536	0016
16105191229	0086
16106190537	0016
16106190772	0079
16108190536	0111
16108290536	0086
16109190536	0111
16109209536	0016
16112190710	0127
16112190772	0079
16114190772	0079
16116190634	0016
16118190634	0079
16147191229	0016
16156197229	0086
16171190693	0016
16171190858	0016
16171191368	0016
16172190693	0016
16172190858	0016
16200190186	0211
16201190022	0004
16201190186	0211
16201190187	0164
16204190457	0164
16207190405	0164
16208190187	0164
16211190022	0164
16212190022	0164
16256197228	0126
16304190031	1973
16304191350	0111
16304197001	0079
16304198000	4389
16304199400	0161
16307190632	0016
16343190142	0555
16356179229	0086
16377190632	0016
16400690060	0143
16401190188	0143
16405990022	0133
16411190188	0143
16411992473	0133
16412190410	0143
16415490000	0143
16419990032	0143
16471190188	OEM
16501090016	0015
16501190005	0015
16501190016	0015
16505090005	0015
16515991002	0015
16516390010	0229
16602990107	0062
16602995856	0064
16611190553	0030
16613190555	0030
16629291210	0015
16669990103	OEM
16740135809	3506
16790036081	OEM
21192010402	2728
21192021701	OEM
21192021706	0514
21192050103	1602
21194010400	OEM
21391018005	0079
21393010508	0224
21393018508	0191
21393026501	0284
21393027409	0079
21393033402	2195
21393043405	0127
21393046604	0079
21394015201	0079
21396010204	0683
21396014602	0410
21396015500	OEM
21492019606	1359
21493051102	0723
21494012609	0419
21691010301	0019
21691031603	0143
21692010504	0023
21692010708	0023
21692011305	1736
21692011307	0071
21692011509	0535
21692090100	OEM

DEVICE TYPE	REPL CODE
21694020505	0137
21694040608	0137
21694040705	0273
21694041700	0100
21695010608	OEM
21695011603	OEM
23091014501	OEM
44202007800	0344
48350947009	OEM
48513047141	OEM
53017101001	0124
53023000003	OEM
53026000001	OEM
57000901504	0016
61250700001	3015
66113002200	0023
66211002300	OEM
66211002800	OEM
66310001000	0705
134800855677	0227
134800863350	0989
134800864205	1145
134800865539	0123
134800868504	1185
134800868825	0686
134800868907	0063
134804204101	0015
134882137801	1392
134882137802	1750
134882137803	0663
134882137804	0542
134882137805	2387
134882137806	0864
134882137807	0519
134882137808	0505
134882137809	0611
134882256333	0755
134882321507	1391
134882321508	1529
134882732304	1241
134883461511	1596
134883461517	2847
134883461528	0305
134883461534	0870
134883461539	0262
134883727201	1745
134883875401	0442
134883875402	0934
134883875403	0464
134883875404	3252
134883875405	3253
134883875406	0934
134884461544	0827
167900306081	0574
260010628057	0006
260010695041	0431
260020176168	0004
260030710037	0364
260030711052	0376
260032878001	3065
260040467037	0945
260040468025	0018
270000600008	0019
270041480007	0124
271026380009	0005
273000068221	0062
273000082221	0165
300003220005	2572
300007313167	0358
300012026007	1251
300012413001	3764
301003450375	3925
301720490201	0143
310720490000	0016
310720490010	0016
310720490020	0016
310720490070	0160
310720490080	0144
310720490100	0016
310720490150	0016
310720490190	0265
310720490201	0143
400100010160	0004
400100020120	0004
404100030180	0164
404100900160	0016
404120010180	0143
404120030100	0143
404120030110	0133
404130010150	0015
482213033019	OEM
482213033637	OEM
482213041457	OEM
482213041559	OEM
482213041907	OEM
482213081086	OEM
482213090606	OEM
482220960038	OEM
482220960039	OEM
482220960502	OEM
482220961344	OEM
482220970674	OEM
482220972744	OEM
482220973667	OEM
483513037031	0064
483513037051	0253
483513037084	OEM
483513037094	OEM
483513037134	0490

If replacement code is OEM, contact original manufacturer for replacement.

DEVICE TYPE	REPL CODE
483513037136	0124
483513037137	2458
483513037138	0490
483513037139	0582
483513037141	0062
483513037142	0062
483513037143	0124
483513037144	2458
483513037145	0124
483513037146	0124
483513037147	1082
483513037148	1864
483513037149	4042
483513037151	0790
483513037153	0581
483513037209	0023
483513037226	0077
483513037229	0023
483513037231	0440
483513037232	4999
483513037234	0023
483513037244	OEM
483513037254	3703
483513037256	0897
483513037326	1951
483513037355	0031
483513037378	OEM
483513047002	OEM
483513047006	OEM
483513047023	OEM
483513047025	3637
483513047035	3678
483513047036	OEM
483513047052	OEM
483513047066	OEM
483513047072	OEM
483513047127	6726
483513047128	3439
483513047129	0719
483513047133	0577
483513047134	0355
483513047135	5584
483513047137	0151
483513047141	0719
483513047142	0719
483513047144	0355
483513047145	1741
483513047146	1731
483513047147	1731
483513047148	2083
483513047226	0553
483513047238	3954
483513047259	0826
483513047261	1132
483513047263	3987
483513047264	OEM
483513047265	0014
483513047266	3629
483513047268	OEM
483513047269	3241
483513047471	0892
483513047481	1881
483513047482	OEM
483513047483	OEM
483513047485	OEM
483513047486	6752
483513047488	1731
483513047493	OEM
483513087016	0511
483520917144	OEM
483520917272	OEM
483520917274	OEM
483520917279	0119
483520917287	OEM
483520947002	OEM
483520947003	OEM
483520947005	OEM
483520947007	OEM
483520947008	OEM
483520947009	OEM
483520947011	OEM
483520947013	OEM
483520947014	OEM
483520947017	OEM
483520947081	OEM
483520947083	0034
483520987033	OEM
483520987057	OEM
483520987058	OEM
483520987063	OEM
483520987111	5575
483520987112	4195
483520987113	4195
483520987114	4078
483520987115	OEM
483520987116	OEM
483520987118	OEM
483520987119	OEM
483520987121	0112
483520987171	OEM
483520987189	OEM
483520987196	OEM
483520987197	OEM
483520987198	OEM
483520987199	OEM
483520987202	OEM
483520987342	3479
483520987415	OEM
483520987416	OEM

DEVICE TYPE	REPL CODE
483520987425	OEM
483520987543	OEM
483520987544	OEM
483520987545	OEM
505130010150	0015
515104221401	0649
933000611112	0015
933001170112	0004
933022960012	0144
933022960112	0016
933022970112	0144
933076760112	0334
1110917004200	OEM
1110917004204	2647
1110917005200	2647
1110991010200	0949
2025911018810	0143
2035510069362	0547
20225230001701	0023
20252300018101	0015
A00001B	OEM
A00005B	OEM
A0000.5B	OEM
A00010B	OEM
A00020B	OEM
A00050B	OEM
A00	0232
A001A0A	OEM
A001A0B	OEM
A001A0C	OEM
A001A0D	OEM
A003	OEM
A007H	0164
A00100B	OEM
A00200B	OEM
A00500A	OEM
A00500B	OEM
A00500C	OEM
A00500D	OEM
A01	0133
A01(MOTOROLA)	0133
A01(TRANSISTOR)	0050
A02	0133
A02(I.C.)	0331
A03	0357
A-04	0015
A04	0015
A04(I.C.)	0381
A05	0015
A05(I.C.)	0507
A05G	0023
A06	0015
A06(I.C.)	0692
A06-1-12	0016
A07	0143
A08	0102
A08(I.C.)	0867
A09	1018
A-025	0299
A025	OEM
A040B250C700	OEM
A054-103	0143
A054-105	0143
A054-108	0016
A054-109	0126
A054-114	0016
A054-115	0016
A054-119	0030
A054-142	0843
A054-148	0127
A054-149	0087
A054-150	0015
A054-151	0137
A054-154	0103
A054-155	0016
A054-156	0086
A054-157	0144
A054-158	0144
A054-159	0144
A054-160	0086
A054-163	0144
A054-164	0144
A054-165	0627
A054-170	0127
A054-173	0079
A054-175	0016
A054-186	0086
A054-187	0143
A054-195	0016
A054-206	0086
A054-221	0016
A054-222	0016
A054-223	0037
A054-224	0178
A054-225	0016
A054-226	0123
A054-228	0133
A054-229	0087
A054-230	0015
A054-231	0361
A054-232	0526
A054-233	0016
A054-234	0016
A054-470	0144
A059-100	0050
A059-101	0050
A059-102	0050
A059-103	0050
A059-104	0136

DEVICE TYPE	REPL CODE
A059-105	0136
A059-106	0004
A059-107	0004
A059-108	0160
A059-109	0016
A059-110	0086
A059-111	0626
A059-114	0015
A059-115	0085
A059-116	0004
A059-117	0644
A059-118	0071
A060-100	0127
A061-105	0127
A061-106	0127
A061-107	0136
A061-108	0127
A061-109	0127
A061-110	0136
A061-111	0136
A061-112	0127
A061-114	0004
A061-115	0004
A061-116	0222
A061-118	0015
A061-119	0012
A065-101	0015
A065-102	0016
A065-103	0016
A065-104	0016
A065-105	0164
A065-106	0004
A065-108	0016
A065-109	0016
A065-110	0016
A065-111	0222
A065-112	0164
A065-113	0016
A066-12	0133
A066-109	0076
A066-110	0683
A066-111	1136
A066-112	0016
A066-113	0037
A066-113(2SC7321)	0079
A066-113A	0037
A066-113AB	0037
A066-114	0228
A066-115	0191
A066-116	1583
A066-117	1401
A066-118	0037
A066-118A	0037
A066-119	0143
A066-119(1S1555)	0133
A066-119(GE)	0143
A066-119(SI)	0133
A066-120	0143
A066-121	0143
A066-124	0015
A066-125	1843
A066-143	0111
A068-100	0015
A068-101	0143
A068-102	0015
A068-103	0012
A068-104	0071
A068-106	0321
A068-107	0321
A068-108	0016
A068-109	0037
A068-109A	0037
A068-111	0144
A068-112	0144
A068-113	0016
A068-114	0178
A069-101	0127
A069-102	0127
A069-102/103	0016
A069-103	0127
A069-104	0016
A069-104/106	0016
A069-105	0004
A069-106	0016
A069-107	0164
A069-109	0143
A069-111	0123
A069-112	0015
A069-114	0127
A069-115	0143
A069-116	0127
A069-118	0123
A069-119	0127
A069-120	0016
A069-121	0136
A069-122	0016
A076F	0050
A081C	0164
A090	0143
A098R	0050
A-0205	0250
A0205	0299
A0375	0015
A0377	0015
A0500.5B	OEM
A0503B20C700	OEM
A0506B40C700	OEM
A0512B80C700	OEM
A0526B160C700	OEM

DEVICE TYPE	REPL CODE
A0540B250C700	OEM
A0553B320C700	OEM
A03004	0411
A04021	1024
A04049	0015
A04049-B	0015
A04049B	0015
A04091A	0015
A04092	0015
A04092-A	0015
A04092-B	0015
A04092A	0015
A04092B	0015
A04093	0015
A04093-A	0102
A04093-X	0102
A04093A2	0102
A04093X	0102
A04099-E	OEM
A04166-2	0002
A04201	0321
A04201(JVC)	0196
A04210-A	0276
A04212-A	0071
A04212-B	0071
A04212A	0015
A04212B	0015
A04226	0015
A04230	0102
A04230-A	0102
A04231-A	0276
A04233	0015
A04234-2	0012
A04241-A	0102
A04242	0015
A04284-A	0276
A04294	0102
A04294-1	0102
A04299-002	OEM
A04299-201	0201
A04299-202	0286
A04299-251	0286
A04331-021	0023
A04331-023	0015
A04332-007	0644
A04334-00A	OEM
A04344-007	0644
A04344-026	1596
A04350-022	0015
A04710	1293
A04716	0276
A04727	0469
A04731	0015
A04735-A	0769
A04901A	0015
A05001B	OEM
A05005B	OEM
A05010B	OEM
A05050B	OEM
A0710500D	OEM
A08010B	OEM
A08010D	OEM
A042313	0015
A072133-001	0618
A0311400	3859
A0354805	2043
A0847905	0055
A1	1708
A1-44	0103
A1A	0233
A1A1	0015
A1A5	0015
A1A9	0015
A1A205A	OEM
A1A210A	OEM
A1A215A	OEM
A1A405A	OEM
A1A410A	OEM
A1A605A	OEM
A1A610A	OEM
A1B	0016
A1B1	0015
A1B5	0015
A1B9	0015
A1B205A	OEM
A1B210A	OEM
A1B215A	OEM
A1B220A	OEM
A1B405A	OEM
A1B410A	OEM
A1B415A	OEM
A1B420A	OEM
A1B425A	OEM
A1B610A	OEM
A1B615A	OEM
A1B620A	OEM
A1B625A	OEM
A1B630A	OEM
A1C	0074
A1C1	0015
A1C5	0015
A1C9	0015
A1D	0637
A1D1	0015
A1D5	0015
A1D9	0015
A1DI	0637
A1DJ	0637
A1E	0007

DEVICE TYPE	REPL CODE
A1E1	0015
A1E5	0015
A1E9	0015
A1E207A	OEM
A1E210A	OEM
A1E215A	OEM
A1E220A	OEM
A1E250A	OEM
A1E307A	OEM
A1E310A	OEM
A1E315A	OEM
A1E320A	OEM
A1E407A	OEM
A1E410A	OEM
A1E415A	OEM
A1E420A	OEM
A1E507A	OEM
A1E515A	OEM
A1E520A	OEM
A1EK510A	OEM
A1F	0016
A1F1	0015
A1F5	0015
A1F9	0015
A1G	0127
A1G-1	0127
A1G1	0015
A1G-1A	0144
A1G5	0015
A1G9	0015
A1G205A	OEM
A1G205D	OEM
A1G210A	OEM
A1G210D	OEM
A1G215A	OEM
A1G215D	OEM
A1G220D	OEM
A1G225D	OEM
A1G230D	OEM
A1G240D	OEM
A1G250D	OEM
A1G405A	OEM
A1G405D	OEM
A1G410A	OEM
A1G410D	OEM
A1G415A	OEM
A1G415D	OEM
A1G420D	OEM
A1G425D	OEM
A1G430D	OEM
A1G440D	OEM
A1G450D	OEM
A1G605A	OEM
A1G605D	OEM
A1G610A	OEM
A1G610D	OEM
A1G615A	OEM
A1G615D	OEM
A1G620A	OEM
A1G620D	OEM
A1G625A	OEM
A1G625D	OEM
A1G630D	OEM
A1G640D	OEM
A1G650D	OEM
A1H	0016
A1H(MOTOROLA)	0637
A1H001A	OEM
A1H003A	OEM
A1H005A	OEM
A1H010A	OEM
A1H020A	OEM
A1H1	0071
A1H5	0071
A1H9	0071
A1H200A	OEM
A1J	0016
A1K	0144
A1K1	0071
A1K5	0071
A1K9	0071
A1L	0016
A1M	0233
A1M-1	0127
A1M1	0071
A1M5	0071
A1M9	0071
A1N	0142
A1N1	OEM
A1N5	OEM
A1N9	OEM
A1P	0127
A1P/4922	0127
A1P-/4923	0144
A1P/4923	0127
A1P/4923-1	0144
A1P-1	0127
A1P-1A	0127
A1P-5	0144
A1QH3020S	OEM
A1R	0127
A1R/4924	0127
A1R/4925	0127
A1R/4925A	0144
A1R/4926	0127
A1R/4926A	0144
A1R001A	OEM
A1R003A	OEM
A1R005A	OEM

DEVICE TYPE	REPL CODE
A1R010A	OEM
A1R020A	OEM
A1R050A	OEM
A1R-1	0127
A1R-1A	0144
A1R-2	0127
A1R-2A	0144
A1R-5	0144
A1R100A	OEM
A1R200A	OEM
A1R-24926	0144
A1S	0233
A1T	0016
A1T-1	0016
A1U	0007
A1U(LAST-IF)	0326
A1V	0016
A1VE	0016
A1W	0016
A1Y	0419
A1Z	0326
A-1.5-01	0015
A2	OEM
A2A	0233
A2A1	0015
A2A4	0015
A2A5	0015
A2A9	0015
A2B	0016
A2B0002	OEM
A2B0003	OEM
A2B0005	OEM
A2B1	0015
A2B4	0015
A2B5	0015
A2B9	0015
A2BRN	0016
A2C	0144
A2C1	0015
A2C4	0015
A2C5	0015
A2C9	0015
A2D	0144
A2D1	0015
A2D4	0015
A2D5	0015
A2D9	0015
A2E	0103
A2E1	0015
A2E-2	0103
A2E4	0015
A2E5	0015
A2E9	0015
A2EBLK	0103
A2EBRN	0103
A2EBRN-1	0103
A2F	0144
A2F1	0015
A2F4	0015
A2F5	0015
A2F9	0015
A2FGRN	0016
A2G	0007
A2G1	0015
A2G4	0015
A2G5	0015
A2G9	0015
A2G132	OEM
A2G133	OEM
A2G172	OEM
A2G173	OEM
A2H	0144
A2H1	0071
A2H4	0071
A2H5	0071
A2H9	0071
A2J	0016
A2K	0233
A2K1	0071
A2K4	0071
A2K5	0071
A2K9	0071
A2L	0144
A2M	0127
A2M-1	0127
A2M1	0071
A2M4	0071
A2M5	0071
A2M9	0126
A2MA	0087
A2N	0127
A2N-1	0127
A2N1	OEM
A2N-2	0127
A2N-2A	0144
A2N4	OEM
A2N5	OEM
A2N9	OEM
A2N2156	0432
A2P	0127
A2P-5	0144
A2S	0103
A2S009	OEM
A2S014	OEM
A2S024	OEM
A2S029	OEM
A2S031	OEM
A2S050	OEM
A2S087	OEM

DEVICE TYPE	REPL CODE
A2S097	OEM
A2S-3	0103
A2S101	OEM
A2S103	OEM
A2S106	OEM
A2S108	OEM
A2S120	OEM
A2S121	OEM
A2S122	OEM
A2S123	OEM
A2S124	OEM
A2S128	OEM
A2S201	OEM
A2S202	OEM
A2S206	OEM
A2S207	OEM
A2S220	OEM
A2S250	OEM
A2S251	OEM
A2S252	OEM
A2S253	OEM
A2S254	OEM
A2S255	OEM
A2S257	OEM
A2S258	OEM
A2S259	OEM
A2S262	OEM
A2S263	OEM
A2S264	OEM
A2S270	OEM
A2S271	OEM
A2S272	OEM
A2S273	OEM
A2S274	OEM
A2S275	OEM
A2S276	OEM
A2S301	OEM
A2S302	OEM
A2S303	OEM
A2S305	OEM
A2S306	OEM
A2S308	OEM
A2S312	OEM
A2S313	OEM
A2S350	OEM
A2S356	OEM
A2S370	OEM
A2S396	OEM
A2S400	OEM
A2S401	OEM
A2S520	OEM
A2S565	OEM
A2S566	OEM
A2S611	OEM
A2S612	OEM
A2S613	OEM
A2S614	OEM
A2S615	OEM
A2S621	OEM
A2S622	OEM
A2S623	OEM
A2S624	OEM
A2S625	OEM
A2S630	OEM
A2S631	OEM
A2S633	OEM
A2S634	OEM
A2S637	OEM
A2S638	OEM
A2S701	OEM
A2S702	OEM
A2S703	OEM
A2S711	OEM
A2S713	OEM
A2S714	OEM
A2S720	OEM
A2S721	OEM
A2S722	OEM
A2S723	OEM
A2S730	OEM
A2S731	OEM
A2S733	OEM
A2S734	OEM
A2S737	OEM
A2S738	OEM
A2S740	OEM
A2S741	OEM
A2S742	OEM
A2S743	OEM
A2S744	OEM
A2S745	OEM
A2S781	OEM
A2S782	OEM
A2S783	OEM
A2S791	OEM
A2S792	OEM
A2S793	OEM
A2S800	OEM
A2S804	OEM
A2S805	OEM
A2S807	OEM
A2S810	OEM
A2S811	OEM
A2S813	OEM
A2S814	OEM
A2S815	OEM
A2S817	OEM
A2S818	OEM
A2S819	OEM

If replacement code is OEM, contact original manufacturer for replacement.

243

DEVICE TYPE	REPL CODE
A2S821	OEM
A2S822	OEM
A2S823	OEM
A2S824	OEM
A2S825	OEM
A2S826	OEM
A2S827	OEM
A2S828	OEM
A2S835	OEM
A2S838	OEM
A2S839	OEM
A2S860	OEM
A2S861	OEM
A2S862	OEM
A2S863	OEM
A2S864	OEM
A2S865	OEM
A2S866	OEM
A2S900	OEM
A2S912	OEM
A2S970	OEM
A2SA550P	0037
A2SA564F	0203
A2SA564FR	0203
A2SA666PQR	0006
A2SB240A	0050
A2SB242A	0164
A2SB248A	0085
A2SC538PQR	0079
A2SC538R	0079
A2SD2260P	0178
A2SD226PQ	0178
A2SD2260P	0178
A2T	0144
A2T682	0208
A2T919	0144
A2U	0142
A2V	0144
A2W	0144
A2Y	0127
A2Z	0233
A-3	4830
A3	OEM
A3A	0144
A3A1	0015
A3A3	0015
A3A5	0015
A3A9	0015
A3B1	0015
A3B3	0015
A3B5	0015
A3B9	0015
A3C	0144
A3C1	0015
A3C3	0015
A3C5	0015
A3C9	0015
A3D	0144
A3D1	0015
A3D3	0015
A3D5	0015
A3D9	0015
A3E	0016
A3E1	0015
A3E3	0015
A3E5	0015
A3E9	0015
A3F	0016
A3F1	0015
A3F3	0015
A3F5	0015
A3F9	0015
A3G	0016
A3G1	0015
A3G3	0015
A3G5	0015
A3G9	0015
A3H	0144
A3H-1	0637
A3H1	0071
A3H3	0071
A3H5	0071
A3H9	0071
A3J	0111
A3K	0111
A3K1	0071
A3K3	0071
A3K5	0071
A3K9	0071
A3L	0275
A3M	0233
A3M1	0071
A3M3	0071
A3M5	0071
A3M9	0071
A3MA	0233
A3N	0016
A3N1	OEM
A3N3	OEM
A3N5	OEM
A3N9	OEM
A3N71	0144
A3N72	0144
A3N73	0144
A3P	0144
A3R	0144
A3S	0016
A3SB	0144
A3T	0016
A3T201	0595
A3T203	0595
A3T918	0007
A3T929	0016
A3T930	0016
A3T2221	0016
A3T2221A	0016
A3T2222	0016
A3T2222A	0016
A3T2484	0590
A3T2894	0037
A3T2906	0037
A3T2906A	0037
A3T2907	0037
A3T2907A	0786
A3T3011	0016
A3TE120	0103
A3TE230	0103
A3TE240	0103
A3TX003	0103
A3TX004	0103
A3U	0103
A3U-4	0103
A3W	0016
A3Y	0142
A3Z	0016
A-4	4830
A4A	0016
A4A1	0015
A4A-1-70	0160
A4A-1-705	0160
A4A-1A9G	0160
A4A5	0015
A4A9	0015
A4B	0111
A4B1	0015
A4B5	0015
A4B9	0015
A4C1	0015
A4C5	0015
A4C9	0015
A4D1	0015
A4D5	0015
A4D9	0015
A4E	0127
A4E1	0015
A4E-5	0144
A4E5	0015
A4E9	0015
A4F	0111
A4F1	0015
A4F5	0015
A4F9	0015
A4G	0144
A4G1	0015
A4G5	0015
A4G9	0015
A4H	0233
A4H1	0071
A4H5	0071
A4H9	0071
A4I7014	0130
A4J	0103
A4JBLK	0103
A4JBRN	0103
A4JD3B1	0595
A4JRED-1	0103
A4JX2A822	0208
A4K	0071
A4K1	0071
A4K5	0071
A4K9	0071
A4L	0208
A4M	0016
A4M1	0071
A4M5	0071
A4M9	0071
A4N	0016
A4N1	OEM
A4N5	OEM
A4N9	OEM
A4P	0016
A4P10	OEM
A4R	0016
A4S	0103
A4S008	OEM
A4S015	OEM
A4S017	OEM
A4S020	OEM
A4S021	OEM
A4S-1	0103
A4S112	OEM
A4S151	OEM
A4S153	OEM
A4S180	OEM
A4S312	OEM
A4S316	OEM
A4S317	OEM
A4S318	OEM
A4S360	OEM
A4S360J	OEM
A4S360K	OEM
A4S365	OEM
A4S370	OEM
A4S370I	OEM
A4S370J	OEM
A4S374	OEM
A4S375	OEM
A4S375I	OEM
A4S375J	OEM
A4S376	OEM
A4S386	OEM
A4T	0144
A4U	0016
A4V	0016
A4Y-1	0127
A4Y-1A	0144
A4Y-2	0016
A4Z	0103
A-5	5181
A5	OEM
A5-SAM	0901
A5A	0419
A5A-1	0161
A5A1	0015
A5A-2	0161
A5A2	0015
A5A-3	0161
A5A-4	0161
A5A-5	0161
A5A5	0015
A5A9	0015
A5A-IB	0042
A5B	0086
A5B1	0015
A5B2	0071
A5B5	0015
A5B9	0015
A5C	0016
A5C1	0015
A5C2	0015
A5C5	0015
A5C9	0015
A5D1	0015
A5D2	0015
A5D5	0015
A5D9	0015
A5E	0546
A5E1	0015
A5E2	0015
A5E5	0015
A5E9	0015
A5F	0264
A5F1	0015
A5F2	0015
A5F5	0015
A5F9	0015
A5F15T2	OEM
A5F40R2	OEM
A5F500U2-1	OEM
A5F500U2-2	OEM
A5F500U2-3	OEM
A5F500U2-4	OEM
A5F500U2-5	OEM
A5F500U2-6	OEM
A5F500U2-7	OEM
A5FF	0264
A5G	0161
A5G1	0015
A5G2	0015
A5G5	0015
A5G9	0015
A5H	0016
A5H1	0071
A5H2	0071
A5H5	0071
A5H9	0071
A5J	0144
A5K	0016
A5K1	0071
A5K2	0071
A5K5	0071
A5K9	0071
A5L	0016
A5M	0016
A5M1	0071
A5M2	0071
A5M5	0071
A5M9	0071
A5N	0016
A5N1	OEM
A5N2	OEM
A5N5	OEM
A5N9	OEM
A5P	0016
A5R	0016
A5R4027	OEM
A5S	0016
A5S001	OEM
A5S005	OEM
A5S012	OEM
A5S013	OEM
A5S025	OEM
A5S034	OEM
A5S045	OEM
A5S085	OEM
A5S090	OEM
A5S091	OEM
A5S092	OEM
A5S093	OEM
A5S100	OEM
A5S105	OEM
A5S107	OEM
A5S110	OEM
A5S113	OEM
A5S115	OEM
A5S125	OEM
A5S127	OEM
A5S138	OEM
A5S139	OEM
A5S152	OEM
A5S161	OEM
A5S163	OEM
A5S165	OEM
A5S168	OEM
A5S188	OEM
A5S301	OEM
A5S302	OEM
A5S303	OEM
A5S339	OEM
A5S342	OEM
A5S350	OEM
A5S377	OEM
A5S400	OEM
A5S401	OEM
A5S402	OEM
A5S403	OEM
A5S420	OEM
A5T	0334
A5T-1	0334
A5T3707	0086
A5T404	0037
A5T404A	0037
A5T2192	0086
A5T2193	0086
A5T2222	0016
A5T2222A	1645
A5T2243	0617
A5T2604	0037
A5T2605	0037
A5T2907	0037
A5T2907A	2245
A5T3391	0079
A5T3391A	0079
A5T3392	0079
A5T3496	0037
A5T3497	0434
A5T3504	0037
A5T3505	0037
A5T3565	0079
A5T3571	0414
A5T3572	0414
A5T3638	0037
A5T3638A	0037
A5T3644	0037
A5T3645	0037
A5T3707	0079
A5T3708	0079
A5T3709	0079
A5T3710	0079
A5T3711	0079
A5T3751	0086
A5T3821	2922
A5T3824	OEM
A5T3903	0016
A5T3904	0016
A5T3905	0037
A5T3906	0037
A5T4026	0472
A5T4027	0037
A5T4028	0472
A5T4029	0037
A5T4058	0688
A5T4059	0338
A5T4060	0338
A5T4061	0688
A5T4062	0688
A5T4123	0079
A5T4124	0079
A5T4125	0037
A5T4126	0037
A5T4248	0037
A5T4249	0037
A5T4250	0037
A5T4260	0037
A5T4402	0037
A5T4403	0037
A5T4409	0086
A5T4410	0617
A5T4416	OEM
A5T4416A	OEM
A5T4621	0037
A5T5058	0710
A5T5059	0710
A5T5086	0037
A5T5087	0037
A5T5172	0079
A5T5209	0086
A5T5210	0086
A5T5219	0079
A5T5220	0079
A5T5221	0037
A5T5223	0079
A5T5225	0079
A5T5226	0037
A5T5227	0037
A5T5400	0434
A5T5401	0434
A5T5447#	0037
A5T5448#	0037
A5T5450#	0320
A5T5550	0710
A5T5551	0710
A5T6222	0018
A5T6461	0710
A5T6462	0710
A5T6463	0710
A5T6464	0710
A5T6538	0734
A5T6539	0734
A5T6540	1645
A5T6541	1645
A5TA	0334
A5U	0016
A5V	0130
A5W	0016
A5Y	0161
A-6	5181
A6-5002-9	0649
A6A	0637
A6A1	0087
A6A5	0087
A6A9	0087
A6AK	0087
A6B	0144
A6B1	0087
A6B5	0087
A6B9	0087
A6C	0161
A6C-1	0161
A6C1	0087
A6C-1-RED	0161
A6C-2	0161
A6C-2-BLACK	0161
A6C-3	0161
A6C-3-WHITE	0161
A6C-4	0161
A6C5	0087
A6C9	0087
A6C-GREEN	0161
A6D	0546
A6D-1	0546
A6D1	0087
A6D-2	0546
A6D-3	0546
A6D5	0087
A6D9	0087
A6E	0144
A6E1	0087
A6E5	0087
A6E9	0087
A6EA6G	OEM
A6F	0144
A6F1	0087
A6F5	0087
A6F9	0087
A6F10	OEM
A6F60	OEM
A6F80	OEM
A6F100	OEM
A6FK	0087
A6G	0546
A6G1	0087
A6G5	0087
A6G9	0087
A6H	0079
A6H1	0087
A6H5	0087
A6H9	0087
A6HD	0016
A6J	0016
A6K	0016
A6K1	0087
A6K5	0087
A6K9	0087
A6L	0103
A6LBLK	0103
A6LBLK-1	0103
A6LBRN	0103
A6LBRN-1	0103
A6LRED	0103
A6LRED-1	0103
A6M	0637
A6M1	0087
A6M5	0087
A6M9	0087
A6N	0103
A6N1	0102
A6N5	0102
A6N-6	0103
A6N9	0102
A6P	0144
A6R	0016
A6S	0016
A6T	0144
A6T5222	0079
A6U	0144
A6V	0127
A6V-5	0144
A6W	0161
A6Y	0264
A6Z	0637
A6ZH	0637
A7-12	0103
A7-13	0103
A7A	0016
A7A1	0087
A7A5	0087
A7A9	0087
A7A30	0144
A7A31	0144
A7A32	0144
A7B	0142
A7B(MOTOROLA)	0142
A7B1	0087
A7B5	0087
A7B9	0087
A7C	0015
A7C(MOTOROLA)	0161
A7C1	0087
A7C5	0087
A7C7	0087
A7C9	0087
A7D	0015
A7D1	0087
A7D5	0087
A7D9	0087
A7E	0015
A7E(TRANSISTOR)	0016
A7E1	0087
A7E5	0087
A7E9	0087
A7F	0264
A7F1	0087
A7F5	0087
A7F9	0087
A7G	0015
A7G1	0087
A7G5	0087
A7G9	0087
A7H1	0087
A7H5	0087
A7H9	0087
A7K1	0087
A7K5	0087
A7K9	0087
A7M	0103
A7M1	0087
A7M5	0087
A7M-5(TRANSISTOR)	0103
A7M9	0087
A7M42394B39	2016
A7M42894B39	2016
A7N	0144
A7N1	0102
A7N5	0102
A7N9	0102
A7P	0144
A7R	0016
A7S	0016
A7T	0016
A7T3391	0155
A7T3391A	0155
A7T3392	0155
A7T5172	0155
A7T6027	0312
A7T6028	0312
A7U	0144
A7V	0144
A7W	0144
A7Y	0016
A7Z	0161
A8-1	0050
A8-1-70	0050
A8-1-70-1	0050
A8-1-70-12-7	0050
A8-1A	0050
A8-1A0	0050
A8-1A0R	0050
A8-1A1	0050
A8-1A2	0050
A8-1A3	0050
A8-1A3P	0050
A8-1A4	0050
A8-1A4-7	0050
A8-1A4-7B	0050
A8-1A5	0050
A8-1A5L	0050
A8-1A6	0050
A8-1A6-4	0050
A8-1A7	0050
A8-1A7-1	0050
A8-1A8	0050
A8-1A9	0050
A8-1A9G	0050
A8-1A19	0050
A8-1A21	0050
A8-1A82	0050
A8-10	0050
A8-11	0050
A8-12	0050
A8-13	0050
A8-14	0050
A8-15	0050
A8-16	0050
A8-17	0050
A8-18	0050
A8-19	0050
A8A	0855
A8B	0016
A8C	0455
A8D	0086
A8E	0419
A8F	2969
A8G	0016
A8J	0546
A8K	0419
A8L	0016
A8M	0074
A8N	0855
A8R	0103
A8P-2-70	0004
A8P-2-705	0004
A8P-2A9G	0004
A8P404-ORN	0160
A8P404F	0160
A8R	0111
A8S	0144
A8T	0637
A8T404	0037
A8T404A	0037
A8T3391	0079
A8T3391A	0079
A8T3392	0079
A8T3644	2245
A8T3645	2245
A8T3702	0037
A8T3703	0037
A8T3704	0018
A8T3705	0018
A8T3706	0079
A8T3707	0079
A8T3708	0079
A8T3709	0079
A8T3710	0079
A8T3711	0079
A8T4026	0527
A8T4027	0037
A8T4028	0527
A8T4029	0037
A8T4058	0037
A8T4059	0037
A8T4060	0037
A8T4061	0037
A8T4062	0037
A8T5172	0079
A8U	0103
A8V	0233
A8VA	0233
A8W	0103
A8Y	2969
A8Z	0855
A9A	0144
A9B	0016
A9C	0396
A9D	0144
A9E	0016
A9F	0016
A9G	0016
A9G100AN	OEM
A9G100AR	OEM
A9G100BN	OEM
A9G100BR	OEM
A9G200AN	OEM
A9G200AR	OEM
A9G200BN	OEM
A9G200BR	OEM
A9G250AN	OEM
A9G250AR	OEM
A9G250BN	OEM
A9G250BR	OEM
A9G500AN	OEM
A9G500AR	OEM
A9G500BN	OEM
A9G500BR	OEM
A9G1000AN	OEM
A9G1000AR	OEM
A9G1000BN	OEM
A9G1000BR	OEM
A9H	0016
A9J	0016
A9K	0074
A9L-4-70	0004
A9L-4-705	0004
A9L-4A9G	0004
A9M	0334
A9N	0130
A9P	0074
A9R	0637
A9S	0016
A9S161A	OEM
A9S162A	OEM
A9S163A	OEM
A9S164A	OEM
A9S165A	OEM
A9S166A	OEM
A9T	2235
A9U	0016
A9V	0042
A9W	0016
A9Y	0016
A10	0554
A10A	0015
A10B	0015
A10C	0015
A10D	0015
A10E	0015
A10G05-010-A	0016
A10G05-011-A	0016
A10G05-015-D	0016
A10M	0015
A10N	0071
A10P	0071
A11	0907
A11CA	OEM
A11CF	OEM
A11DA	OEM
A12	0004
A12(I.C.)	1160
A12-02	OEM
A12-1-70	0016
A12-1-705	0016
A12-1A9G	0016
A12-2	3249

If replacement code is OEM, contact original manufacturer for replacement.

DEVICE TYPE	REPL CODE
A12A	0004
A12B	0004
A12C	0004
A12D	0004
A12D36R2-H	OEM
A12F6	OEM
A12F8	OEM
A12F10	OEM
A12F12T2	OEM
A12F36R2	OEM
A12F36R2-H	OEM
A12F60	OEM
A12F80	OEM
A12F100	OEM
A12F500U2-1	OEM
A12F500U2-2	OEM
A12F500U2-3	OEM
A12F500U2-4	OEM
A12F500U2-5	OEM
A12F500U2-6	OEM
A12F500U2-7	OEM
A12H	0004
A12V	0004
A13	0004
A13(TRANS)	0050
A13-0032	0103
A13-17918-1	0103
A13-23594-1	0103
A13-33188-2	0103
A13-86416-1	0208
A13-86420-1	0595
A13-87433-1	0595
A13-SAM	0124
A13A	0050
A13A2	0015
A13AA2	0015
A13B	0050
A13B2	0015
A13C	0050
A13C2	0015
A13D	0050
A13D2	0015
A13E2	0015
A13F2	0015
A13G	0050
A13L	0050
A13M	0050
A13M2	0015
A13N1	0016
A13OR	0050
A13R	0050
A13X	0050
A13Y	0050
A14	0182
A14(TRANS)	0050
A14-586-01	0160
A14-601-10	0103
A14-601-12	0103
A14-601-13	0103
A14-602-63	0144
A14-603-05	0144
A14-603-06	0144
A14-1001	0136
A14-1002	0136
A14-1003	0136
A14-1004	0004
A14-1005	0004
A14-1006	0004
A14-1007	0004
A14-1008	0004
A14-1009	0004
A14-1010	0004
A14A	0071
A14A(TRANS)	0050
A14A-70	0160
A14A-705	0160
A14B	0015
A14B(TRANS)	0050
A14C	0015
A14C(TRANS)	0050
A14D	0015
A14D(TRANS)	0050
A14E	0015
A14E(TRANS)	0050
A14E2	0015
A14F	0015
A14G	0050
A14L	0050
A14M	0015
A14M(TRANS)	0050
A14N	0071
A14OR	0050
A14P	0071
A14PD1	OEM
A14PD2	0102
A14PD3	0102
A14R	0050
A14T	OEM
A14U	1325
A14X	0050
A14Y	0050
A15	1303
A15(TRANS)	0004
A15-2	OEM
A15-6	0004
A15-1001	0136
A15-1002	0136
A15-1003	0136
A15-1004	0004
A15-1005	0004
A15-1007	0143
A15-1008	0015
A15A	0947
A15A(TRANS)	0004
A15B	0242
A15B(TRANS)	0004
A15BK(2S)	0004
A15C	1736
A15C(TRANS)	0004
A15D	0535
A15D(TRANS)	0004
A15D30R2-H	OEM
A15E	1760
A15E(TRANS)	0004
A15F	0110
A15F(TRANS)	0004
A15F15T2	OEM
A15F30R2	OEM
A15F30R2-H	OEM
A15F500U2-1	OEM
A15F500U2-2	OEM
A15F500U2-3	OEM
A15F500U2-4	OEM
A15F500U2-5	OEM
A15F500U2-6	OEM
A15F500U2-7	OEM
A15G	0004
A15H(2S)	0004
A15K(2S)	0004
A15L	0004
A15M	0959
A15M(TRANS)	0004
A15N	0811
A15OR	0004
A15R(2S)	0004
A15RD	0004
A15U	0087
A15U(DIODE)	0110
A15U(RECTIFIER)	0110
A15U(TRANS)	0004
A15V(2S)	0004
A15VR(2S)	0004
A15X	0004
A15Y(2S)	0004
A16(2S)	0004
A16A	0004
A16A1	0208
A16A2	0208
A16B	0004
A16C	0004
A16D	0004
A16E	0004
A16F	0004
A16L	0004
A16M	0004
A16OR	0004
A16R	0004
A16X	0004
A16Y	0004
A17(2S)	0050
A17(I.C.)	1199
A17A	0050
A17B	0050
A17C	0050
A17D	0050
A17E	0050
A17F	0050
A17G	0050
A17H(2S)	0050
A17L	0050
A17OR	0050
A17R	0050
A17X	0050
A17Y	0050
A-18	0103
A18	0050
A18(I.C.)	0564
A18-4	0103
A18A	0050
A18B	0050
A18C	0050
A18D	0050
A18E	0050
A18F	0050
A18F500U2-1	OEM
A18F500U2-2	OEM
A18F500U2-3	OEM
A18F500U2-4	OEM
A18F500U2-5	OEM
A18F500U2-6	OEM
A18F500U2-7	OEM
A18G	0050
A18H(2S)	0050
A18L	0050
A18M	0050
A18OR	0050
A18R	0050
A18X	0050
A18Y	0050
A19(2S)	0164
A19(I.C.)	1477
A19-020-072	0144
A19A	0164
A19B	0164
A19C	0164
A19D	0164
A19E	0164
A19F	0164
A19G	0164
A19L	0164
A19M	0164
A19OR	0164
A19R	0164
A19X	0164
A19Y	0164
A20	0143
A20(2S)	0164
A20A	0164
A20B	0164
A20C	0164
A20D	0164
A20E	0164
A20F	0164
A20G	0628
A20G(2S)	0164
A20H	OEM
A20K	0037
A20KA	0037
A20L	0164
A20M	0164
A20OR	0164
A20R	0164
A20X	0164
A20Y	0164
A21(2S)	0164
A21-02	OEM
A21-04	OEM
A21A	0164
A21B	0164
A21C	0164
A21D	0164
A21E	0164
A21F	0164
A21G	0164
A21L	0164
A21M	0164
A21OR	0164
A21R	0164
A21X	0164
A21Y	0164
A22	0050
A22B	0087
A22B1	0087
A22D	0087
A22D1	0087
A22M	0087
A23	0015
A23(TRANS)	0050
A23-1101-01A	3206
A23B	0575
A23B1	0575
A23D	OEM
A23D1	OEM
A23M	OEM
A24	0050
A24F12T2	OEM
A24F36R2	OEM
A24F36R2-H	OEM
A24F500U2-1	OEM
A24F500U2-2	OEM
A24F500U2-3	OEM
A24F500U2-4	OEM
A24F500U2-5	OEM
A24F500U2-6	OEM
A24F500U2-7	OEM
A24MW594	0144
A24MW595	0144
A24MW596	0144
A24MW597	0144
A24T-016-01L	0144
A24T-016-016	0144
A25	0050
A25-12	3525
A25-1001	0136
A25-1002	0136
A25-1003	0136
A25-1004	0004
A25-1005	0004
A25-1006	0004
A25-1007	0143
A25-1008	0015
A25A	OEM
A25B	OEM
A25D	OEM
A25M	OEM
A25N	OEM
A25P	OEM
A25PB	OEM
A25Q	OEM
A26(2S)	0050
A26(W)	0133
A26A	0050
A26B	0050
A26C	0050
A26D	0050
A26E	0050
A26F	0050
A26G	0050
A26L	0050
A26M	0050
A26OR	0050
A26R	0050
A26X	0050
A26Y	0050
A27	0142
A27(2S)	0050
A27BR1200	OEM
A27DR521A	OEM
A27DR521B	OEM
A27DR521M	OEM
A27DR1200	OEM
A27MR1200	OEM
A28	0050
A28A	1557
A28A(TRANS)	0050
A28B	1557
A28B(TRANS)	0050
A28BR1200	OEM
A28BR1201	OEM
A28C	2140
A28C(TRANS)	0050
A28D	2140
A28D(TRANS)	0050
A28DR1201	OEM
A28E	0050
A28F	1557
A28F(TRANS)	0050
A28G	0050
A28L	0050
A28M	0050
A28OR	0050
A28X	0050
A28Y	0050
A29(2S)	0164
A29A	1538
A29A(TRANS)	0164
A29B	1538
A29B(TRANS)	0164
A29C	3110
A29C(TRANS)	0164
A29D	3110
A29D(TRANS)	0164
A29E	0164
A29F	1538
A29F(TRANS)	0164
A29G	0164
A29L	0164
A29M	0164
A29R	0164
A29V082B03	0126
A29X	0164
A29Y	0164
A30	0004
A30(2S)	0136
A30A	0136
A30B	0136
A30C	0136
A30D	0136
A30E	0136
A30F	0136
A30G	0136
A30L	0136
A30M	0136
A30OR	0136
A30X	0136
A30Y	0136
A31	0004
A31(2S)	0279
A31-0206	0144
A31A	0279
A31B	0279
A31C	0279
A31D	0279
A31E	0279
A31F	0279
A31G	0279
A31L	0279
A31M	0279
A31OR	0279
A31X	0279
A31Y	0279
A32(2S)	0050
A32A	0050
A32B	0050
A32C	0050
A32D	0050
A32E	0050
A32F	0050
A32G	0050
A32L	0050
A32M	0050
A32OR	0050
A32X	0050
A32Y	0050
A33	0004
A33(2S)	0004
A34	OEM
A34-6001-1	0160
A34-6002-17	0160
A35	0004
A35(2S)	0004
A35A	0004
A35B	0004
A35C	0004
A35D	0004
A35E	0004
A35F	0004
A35G	0004
A35L	0004
A35M	0004
A35OR	0004
A35X	0004
A35Y	0004
A36	0004
A36A	0050
A36B	0050
A36C	0050
A36D	0050
A36E	0050
A36F	0050
A36G	0050
A36L	0050
A36M	0050
A36OR	0050
A36R	0050
A36X	0050
A36Y	0050
A37(2S)	0050
A37A	0050
A37B	0050
A37C	0050
A37D	0050
A37E	0050
A37F	0050
A37G	0050
A37L	0050
A37M	0050
A37OR	0050
A37R	0050
A37X	0050
A37Y	0050
A38	0050
A38A	0050
A38B	0050
A38BR1200	OEM
A38BR1202	OEM
A38C	0050
A38D	0050
A38DR019A	OEM
A38DR019B	OEM
A38DR019M	OEM
A38DR1200	OEM
A38DR1202	OEM
A38E	0050
A38F	0050
A38G	0050
A38L	0050
A38M	0050
A38MR1200	OEM
A38OR	0050
A38R	0050
A38X	0050
A38Y	0050
A39(2S)	0050
A39A	0050
A39B	0050
A39C	0050
A39D	0050
A39E	0050
A39F	0050
A39G	0050
A39L	0050
A39M	0050
A39OR	0050
A39R	0050
A39X	0050
A39Y	0050
A40	0004
A40(2S)	0279
A40-6704	0196
A40-6722	0196
A40A	0585
A40A(TRANS)	0279
A40B	1241
A40B(TRANS)	0279
A40C	5487
A40C(TRANS)	0279
A40D	1571
A40D(TRANS)	0279
A40E	5487
A40E(TRANS)	0279
A40F	1991
A40F(TRANS)	0279
A40G	0279
A40L	0279
A40M	1576
A40M(TRANS)	0279
A40OR	0279
A40R	0279
A40X	0279
A40Y	0279
A41	0050
A41(2S)	0050
A41A	1567
A41A(TRANS)	0050
A41B	1567
A41B(TRANS)	0050
A41C	1103
A41C(TRANS)	0050
A41D	3251
A41D(TRANS)	0050
A41E	1186
A41E(TRANS)	0050
A41F	1992
A41F(TRANS)	0050
A41G	0050
A41L	0050
A41M	3263
A41M(TRANS)	0050
A41OR	0050
A41R	0050
A41X	0050
A41Y	0050
A42(2S)	0050
A42X00022-01	0575
A42X00373-01(TRANSIS	0211
A42X00454-01	1392
A42X210	0208
A43(2S)	0136
A44(2S)	0136
A44A	4938
A44A(TRANS)	0136
A44B	4938
A44B(TRANS)	0136
A44C	4938
A44C(TRANS)	0136
A44D	4938
A44D(TRANS)	0136
A44E	2591
A44E(TRANS)	0136
A44F	4938
A44F(TRANS)	0136
A44G	0136
A44L	0136
A44M	2591
A44M(TRANS)	0136
A44OR	0136
A44R	0136
A44X	0136
A44Y	0136
A45	0136
A45(2S)	0136
A45-1(2S)	0136
A45-2(2S)	0136
A45-3(2S)	0136
A45A	2537
A45B	2537
A45C	2537
A45E	2544
A45F	2537
A45J	OEM
A45K	OEM
A46	0279
A46-867-3	0233
A46-8614-3	0595
A46-86101-3	0127
A46-86109-3	0127
A46-86110-3	0127
A46-86133-3	0127
A46-86301-3	0127
A46-86302-3	0127
A46-86303-3	0127
A47	0050
A48	0790
A48(TRANS)	0050
A48-40247G01	0144
A48-43351A02	0144
A48-63078A52	0143
A48-97046A05	0144
A48-97046A06	0144
A48-97046A07	0144
A48-97127A06	0144
A48-97127A12	0144
A48-97127A18	0144
A48-124216	0595
A48-124217	0595
A48-124218	0595
A48-124220	0595
A48-124221	0595
A48-125233	0595
A48-125234	0595
A48-125235	0595
A48-125236	0595
A48-128239	0595
A48-134520	0595
A48-134700	0595
A48-134727	0160
A48-134731	0160
A48-134789	0144
A48-134819	0233
A48-134837	0144
A48-134843	0233
A48-134845	0144
A48-134853	0233
A48-134898	0233
A48-134902	0144
A48-134904	0144
A48-134907	0160
A48-134919	0233
A48-134922	0144
A48-134923	0144
A48-134924	0144
A48-134925	0144
A48-134926	0144
A48-134927	0233
A48-134931	0595
A48-134945	0144
A48-134961	0144
A48-134962	0144
A48-134963	0144
A48-134964	0144
A48-134965	0144
A48-134966	0144
A48-134981	0144
A48-137002	0233
A48-137035	0233
A48-137071	0144
A48-137075	0144
A48-137076	0144
A48-137077	0144
A48-137102	0160
A48-137155	0144
A48-137197	0144
A48-137213	0160
A48-137214	0160
A48-137215	0160
A48-137216	0160
A48-137217	0160
A48-137218	0160
A48-137219	0160
A48-137220	0160
A48-869254	0208
A48-869283	0208
A48-869476	0208
A48-869476A	0208
A49(2S)	0628
A49A	0628
A49B	0628
A49C	0628
A49D	0628
A49E	0628
A49F	0628
A49G	0628
A49L	0628
A49M	0628
A49OR	0628
A49R	0628
A49X	0628
A49Y	0628
A50	0015
A50(RECTIFIER)	0015
A50(TRANS)	0050
A50(TRANSISTOR)	0004
A50A	0050
A50B	0050
A50C	0050
A50D	0050
A50E	0050
A50F	0050
A50G	0050
A50L	0050
A50M	0050
A50OR	0050
A50R	0050
A50X	0050
A50Y	0050
A51	0136
A51(2S)	0136
A51A	0136
A51B	0136
A51C	0136
A51D	0136
A51E	0136
A51F	0136
A51G	0136
A51L	0136
A51M	0136
A51OR	0136
A51R	0136
A51X	0136
A51Y	0136
A52(2S)	0136
A52A	0136
A52B	0136
A52C	0136
A52D	0136
A52E	0136
A52F	0136
A52G	0136
A52L	0136
A52M	0136
A52OR	0136
A52R	0136
A52X	0136
A52Y	0136
A53(2S)	0628
A53A	0628
A53B	0628
A53C	0628
A53D	0628
A53E	0628
A53F	0628
A53G	0628
A53L	0628
A53M	0628
A53OR	0628
A53R	0628
A53X	0628
A53Y	0628
A54	0050
A54-3	0042
A54A	0050
A54B	0050
A54C	0050
A54D	0050
A54E	0050
A54F	0050
A54G	0050
A54L	0050
A54M	0050
A54OR	0050
A54R	0050
A54X	0050
A54Y	0050
A55(2S)	0136
A55A	0136
A55B	0136
A55C	0136
A55D	0136
A55E	0136
A55F	0136
A55G	0136

If replacement code is OEM, contact original manufacturer for replacement.

DEVICE TYPE	REPL CODE
A55L	0136
A55M	0136
A55OR	0136
A55R	0136
A55X	0136
A55Y	0136
A56(2S)	0136
A56A	0136
A57(2S)	0136
A57A	0136
A57A144-12	0144
A57A145-12	0144
A57B	0136
A57B124-10	0160
A57C	0136
A57C5	0208
A57C12-1	0233
A57C12-2	0233
A57D	0136
A57D1-122	0233
A57E	0136
A57F	0136
A57G	0136
A57L	0136
A57L5-1	0160
A57M	0136
A57M2-16	0233
A57M2-17	0233
A57M3-7	0160
A57M3-8	0160
A57OR	0136
A57R	0136
A57X	0136
A57Y	0136
A58(2S)	0050
A58A	0050
A58B	0050
A58C	0050
A58D	0050
A58E	0050
A58F	0050
A58G	0050
A58H	0050
A58J	0050
A58K	0050
A58L	0050
A58M	0050
A58OR	0050
A58R	0050
A58X	0050
A58Y	0050
A59(2S)	0050
A59A	0050
A59B	0050
A59C	0050
A59D	0050
A59E	0050
A59F	0050
A59G	0050
A59L	0050
A59M	0050
A59OR	0050
A59R	0050
A59X	0050
A59Y	0050
A60(2S)	0050
A60A	0050
A60B	0050
A60C	0050
A60D	0050
A60E	0050
A60F	0050
A60G	0050
A60H	0050
A60K	0050
A60L	0050
A60M	0050
A60OR	0050
A60R	0050
A60X	0050
A60Y	0050
A61(2S)	0050
A61A	0050
A61C	0050
A61D	0050
A61E	0050
A61G	0050
A61K	0050
A61L	0050
A61OR	0050
A61R	0050
A61X	0050
A61Y	0050
A62	0143
A62-18427	0160
A62-19581	0144
A63	0057
A63-18426	0233
A63-18427	0160
A64(2S)	0164
A64A	0164
A64B	0164
A64C	0164
A64D	0164
A64E	0164
A64F	0164
A64G	0164
A64GN	0164
A64H	0164
A64J	0164
A64K	0164
A64L	0164
A64M	0164
A64OR	0164
A64R	0164
A64X	0164
A64Y	0164
A65(2S)	0050
A65/40-0100	OEM
A65/40-1000	OEM
A65/40-7020	OEM
A65/40-7050	OEM
A65-09-220	0006
A65-1-1A9G	0050
A65-1-70	0050
A65-1-705	0050
A65-2-70	0208
A65-2-705	0208
A65-2A9G	0208
A65-4-70	0595
A65-4-705	0595
A65-4A9G	0595
A65-901	OEM
A65-P11305-0001A	0124
A65-P11324-0001	0124
A65A	0050
A65A19G	0050
A65A-70	0050
A65A-705	0050
A65B	0050
A65B19G	0136
A65B-70	0136
A65B-705	0136
A65C	0050
A65C-19G	0160
A65C-70	0160
A65C-705	0160
A65D	0050
A65E	0050
A65F	0050
A65G	0050
A65K	0050
A65L	0050
A65M	0050
A65OR	0050
A65R	0050
A65X	0050
A65Y	0050
A66(2S)	0050
A66-1-70	0004
A66-1-705	0004
A66-1A9G	0004
A66-2-70	0004
A66-2-705	0004
A66-2A9G	0004
A66-3-3A9G	0004
A66-3-70	0004
A66-3-705	0004
A66-3A9G	0004
A66A	0050
A66B	0050
A66C	0050
A66D	0050
A66E	0050
A66F	0050
A66G	0050
A66K	0050
A66L	0050
A66M	0050
A66OR	0050
A66R	0050
A66X	0050
A66Y	0050
A67(2S)	0004
A67-07-244	0076
A67-08-760	0544
A67-15-280	1583
A67-33-340	0111
A67-33-540	0155
A67-37-940	1136
A67-76-200	0830
A67A	0004
A67B	0004
A67C	0004
A67D	0004
A67E	0004
A67F	0004
A67G	0004
A67H	0004
A67K	0004
A67L	0004
A67OR	0004
A67R	0004
A67X	0004
A67Y	0004
A68	0050
A68-23-560	0228
A69(2S)	0136
A69A	0136
A69B	0136
A69C	0136
A69D	0136
A69E	0136
A69F	0136
A69G	0136
A69H	0136
A69IM4	0133
A69K	0136
A69L	0136
A69M	0136
A69OR	0136
A69R	0136
A69X	0136
A69Y	0136
A70(2S)	0050
A70-08	0050
A70-0B	0050
A70-OB	0050
A70A	0594
A70A(TRANS)	0050
A70B	0594
A70B(TRANS)	0050
A70C	0594
A70C(TRANS)	0050
A70D	0594
A70D(TRANS)	0050
A70E	1975
A70E(TRANS)	0050
A70F(2S)	0050
A70G	0050
A70H	0050
A70K	0050
A70L(2S)	0050
A70M	1975
A70MA(2S)	0050
A70N	0652
A70OA	0050
A70OR	0050
A70P	0652
A70PA	OEM
A70PB	OEM
A70R	0050
A70S	0652
A70T	0652
A70X	0050
A70Y	0050
A71(2S)	0050
A71A	0050
A71A(2S)	0050
A71A(RECTIFIER)	1337
A71AB(2S)	0050
A71AC(2S)	0050
A71B	0050
A71B(2S)	0050
A71B(RECTIFIER)	1337
A71BS(2S)	0050
A71C	1337
A71C(TRANS)	0050
A71D	0050
A71D(2S)	0050
A71E	1894
A71E(TRANS)	0050
A71F	0050
A71G	0050
A71H	0050
A71K	0050
A71L	0050
A71M	1894
A71M(TRANS)	0050
A71N	0193
A71OR	0050
A71P	0193
A71PA	OEM
A71PB	OEM
A71R	0050
A71S	0193
A71T	0193
A71X	0050
A71Y(2S)	0050
A71YA	0050
A72(2S)	0136
A72-49-600	0133
A72-83-300	2704
A72-86-700	0165
A72A	OEM
A72B	OEM
A72BLU(2S)	0136
A72BRN(2S)	0136
A72D	OEM
A72M	OEM
A72N	OEM
A72ORN(2S)	0136
A72P	OEM
A72PA	OEM
A72PB	OEM
A72S	0136
A72WHT(2S)	0136
A73(2S)	0050
A73-16-179	0139
A73A	0050
A73B	0050
A73C	0050
A73D	0050
A73E	0050
A73F	0050
A73G	0050
A73H	0050
A73K	0050
A73L	0050
A73M	0050
A73OR	0050
A73PA	OEM
A73PB	OEM
A73R	0050
A73X	0050
A73Y	0050
A74	0136
A74(2S)	0136
A74-3-70	0279
A74-3-705	0279
A74A	0136
A74B	0136
A74C	0136
A74D	0136
A74E	0136
A74F	0136
A74G	0136
A74H	0136
A74K	0136
A74L	0136
A74M	0136
A74OR	0136
A74R	0136
A74X	0136
A74Y	0136
A75(2S)	0136
A75-68-500	0015
A75A	0136
A75B(2S)	0136
A75C	0136
A75D	0136
A75E	0136
A75F	0136
A75G	0136
A75H	0136
A75K	0136
A75L	0136
A75M	0136
A75OR	0136
A75R	0136
A75X	0136
A75Y	0136
A76(2S)	0050
A76-11770	0160
A76A	0050
A76B	0050
A76C	0050
A76D	0050
A76E	0050
A76F	0050
A76G	0050
A76H	0050
A76K	0050
A76L	0050
A76OR	0050
A76R	0050
A76X	0050
A76Y	0050
A77(2S)	0628
A77A	5532
A77A(2S)	0628
A77A19G	0435
A77A-70	0435
A77A-705	0435
A77B	5532
A77B(2S)	0628
A77C(2S)	0628
A77C19G	0160
A77C-70	0160
A77C-705	0160
A77D	5532
A77D(2S)	0628
A77E	0628
A77F	0628
A77G	0628
A77H	0628
A77K	0628
A77L	0628
A77M	0628
A77M(DIO)	OEM
A77N	OEM
A77OR	0628
A77P	OEM
A77PB	OEM
A77R	0628
A77X	0628
A77Y	0628
A78(2S)	0004
A79(2S)	0004
A80(2S)	0164
A80-12	OEM
A80-12G	OEM
A80A	0164
A80B	0164
A80D	0164
A80E	0164
A80F	0164
A80G	0164
A80H	0164
A80K	0164
A80L	0164
A80M	0164
A80OR	0164
A80R	0164
A80X	0164
A80Y	0164
A81(2S)	0050
A81-04F	OEM
A82	0628
A82(2S)	0164
A82A	0164
A82B	0164
A82C	0164
A82D	0164
A82E	0164
A82F	0164
A82G	0164
A82H	0164
A82K	0164
A82M	0164
A82OR	0164
A82R	0164
A82X	0164
A82Y	0164
A83	0628
A83(2S)	0050
A83A	0050
A83B	0050
A83C	0050
A83D	0050
A83E	0050
A83F	0050
A83G	0050
A83H	0050
A83K	0050
A83L	0050
A83M	0050
A83OR	0050
A83P2B	0126
A83R	0050
A83X	0050
A83Y	0050
A84(2S)	0050
A84A	0050
A84A19G	0160
A84A-70	0160
A84A-705	0160
A84B	0050
A84C	0050
A84D	0050
A84E	0050
A84F	0050
A84G	0050
A84H	0050
A84K	0050
A84L	0050
A84M	0050
A84OR	0050
A84R	0050
A84X	0050
A84Y	0050
A85(2S)	0136
A85L	0136
A86(2S)	0050
A-86-3-1	0479
A86-3-1	1073
A-86-4-1	0479
A86-4-1	0479
A-86-9-1	0907
A86-9-1	0196
A86-10-2	0595
A86-44-2	0595
A86-213-2	0233
A86-214-2	0233
A86-215-2	0233
A86-316-2	0233
A87(2S)	0050
A87A	0050
A87B	0050
A87C	0050
A87D	0050
A87E	0050
A87F	0050
A87G	0050
A87H	0050
A87K	0050
A87L	0050
A87M	0050
A87OR	0050
A87R	0050
A87X	0050
A87Y	0050
A88	0050
A88-70	0050
A88-705	0050
A88B19G	0050
A88C19G	0279
A88C-70	0279
A88C-705	0279
A89(2S)	0050
A90	0136
A90A	1017
A90B	1017
A90C	1017
A90D	1017
A90E	1030
A90M	1030
A90N	1040
A90P	1040
A90PA	3872
A90PB	3872
A90S	1040
A90T	1040
A90T2	0144
A91A	0496
A91B	0496
A91C	0496
A91D	0496
A91E	1766
A91M	1766
A91N	1778
A91P	1778
A91PA	0496
A91PB	3489
A91S	1778
A91T	1778
A92(2S)	0050
A92-1-70	0435
A92-1-705	0435
A92-1A9G	0435
A92A	0050
A92B	0050
A92C	0050
A92D	0050
A92E	0050
A92F	0050
A92G	0050
A92H	0050
A92K	0050
A92L	0050
A92M	0050
A92OR	0050
A92R	0050
A92X	0050
A92Y	0050
A93	0628
A93(2S)	0050
A93A	0050
A93B	0050
A93C	0050
A93E	0050
A93F	0050
A93G	0050
A93H	0050
A93K	0050
A93L	0050
A93M	0050
A93OR	0050
A93R	0050
A93X	0050
A93Y	0050
A94	0628
A94(2S)	0164
A94A	0164
A94C	0164
A94D	0164
A94E	0164
A94F	0164
A94G	0164
A94H	0164
A94K	0164
A94L	0164
A94M	0164
A94OR	0164
A94R	0164
A94X	0164
A94Y	0164
A95	0628
A95(2S)	0050
A95-5280	0196
A95-5281	0015
A95-5285	0015
A95-5286	1024
A95-5289	0015
A95-5292	1293
A95-5294	0015
A-95-5295	1293
A95-5295	1293
A95-5296	0769
A95-5297	0196
A-95-5314	0190
A95-5314	0190
A96	0050
A96A	OEM
A96B	OEM
A96C	OEM
A96D	OEM
A96E	OEM
A96M	OEM
A96N	OEM
A96P	OEM
A96S	OEM
A96T	OEM
A97	0050
A97A83	0160
A97AA97B	OEM
A97C	OEM
A97D	OEM
A97E	OEM
A97M	OEM
A97N	OEM
A97P	OEM
A97S	OEM
A97T	OEM
A98	0050
A99	0628
A99(2S)	0050
A99S07	0595
A99SK5	0595
A99SK7	0595
A100	0015
A100(TRANS)	0136
A100A(2S)	0136
A100B(2S)	0136
A100C(2S)	0136
A100D	0136
A100E	0136
A100F	0136
A100G	0136
A100H	0136
A100J	0136
A100K	0136
A100M	0136
A100OR	0136
A100R	0136
A100U	OEM
A100X	0136
A100Y	0136
A101	0136
A101(2S)	0136
A101(IC)	OEM
A101-A	0015
A101-OR	0136
A101A	0136
A101AA(2S)	0136
A101AY(2S)	0136
A101B(2S)	0136
A101BA(2S)	0136
A101BB(2S)	0136
A101BC(2S)	0136
A101BX(2S)	0136
A101C(2S)	0136
A101CA(2S)	0136
A101CV(2S)	0136
A101CX(2S)	0136
A101D	0136
A101E(2S)	0136
A101F	0136
A101G	0136
A101H	0136
A101K	0136
A101L	0136
A101M	0136
A101OR	0136
A101QA(2S)	0136
A101R	0136
A101X(2S)	0136
A101XBX	0136
A101Y(2S)	0136
A101YA	0136
A101Z(2S)	0136
A102	0136
A102(2S)	0136
A102-OR	0136
A102A(2S)	0136
A102AA(2S)	0136
A102AB(2S)	0136
A102B(2S)	0136
A102BA(2S)	0136
A102BN(2S)	0136
A102C	0136
A102CA(2S)	0136
A102D	0136
A102E	0136
A102F	0136
A102G	0136
A102H	0136
A102K	0136
A102L	0136
A102M	0136
A102OR	0136
A102TV(2S)	0136
A102X	0136
A102Y	0136
A103	0136
A103(2S)	0136
A103A(2S)	0136
A103B(2S)	0136
A103C(2S)	0136
A103CA(2S)	0136
A103CAK(2S)	0136
A103CB	0136
A103CG(2S)	0136
A103D	0136
A103DA(2S)	0136
A103E	0136
A103F	0136
A103G	0136
A103GA	0136
A103K	0136
A103L	0136
A103M	0136
A103OR	0136
A103R	0136
A103X	0136
A103Y	0136
A104	0050
A104(2S)	0050
A104A	0628
A104A(2S)	0050
A104B	0050
A104C	0050
A104D(2S)	0050
A104E	0050
A104F	0050
A104G	0050
A104H	0050
A104K	0050
A104L	0050
A104M	0050
A104OR	0050
A104P(2S)	0050
A104R	0050
A104X	0050
A104Y	0050
A105(2S)	0136
A105A	0136
A105B	0136
A105C	0136
A105D	0136
A105E	0136
A105G	0136
A105H	0136

If replacement code is OEM, contact original manufacturer for replacement.

DEVICE TYPE	REPL CODE
A105K	0136
A105L	0136
A105M	0136
A105OR	0136
A105R	0136
A105X	0136
A105Y	0136
A-106	0079
A106	0136
A106(2S)	0136
A106A	0136
A106B	0136
A106C	0136
A106D	0136
A106E	0136
A106F	0136
A106G	0136
A106H	0136
A106K	0136
A106L	0136
A106M	0136
A106OR	0136
A106R	0136
A106X	0136
A106Y	0136
A107	0136
A107(2S)	0136
A107A	0136
A107B	0136
A107C	0136
A107D	0136
A107E	0136
A107F	0136
A107G	0136
A107H	0136
A107K	0136
A107L	0136
A107M	0136
A107OR	0136
A107R	0136
A107X	0136
A107Y	0136
A108	0016
A108(2S)	0136
A108A	0136
A108B	0136
A108C	0136
A108D	0136
A108E	0136
A108F	0136
A108G	0136
A108H	0136
A108K	0136
A108L	0136
A108M	0136
A108OR	0136
A108R	0136
A108X	0136
A108Y	0136
A109	0136
A109A	0136
A109B	0136
A109C	0136
A109D	0136
A109E	0136
A109F	0136
A109G	0136
A109K	0136
A109L	0136
A109M	0136
A109OR	0136
A109R	0136
A109X	0136
A109Y	0136
A110	0111
A110(2S)	0136
A110A	0136
A110B	0136
A110C	0136
A110D	0136
A110E	0136
A110F	0136
A110G	0136
A110K	0136
A110L	0136
A110M	0136
A110OR	0136
A110R	0136
A110X	0136
A110Y	0136
A111	0016
A111(2S)	0136
A111A	0136
A111B	0136
A111C	0136
A111D	0136
A111E	0136
A111F	0136
A111G	0136
A111K	0136
A111L	0136
A111M	0136
A111OR	0136
A111R	0136
A111T2	0233
A111X	0136
A111Y	0136
A112(2S)	0136
A112-000172	0037
A112-000185	0037
A112-000187	0037
A112A	0136
A112B	0136
A112C	0136
A112D	0136
A112E	0136
A112F	0136
A112G	0136
A112GN	0136
A112H	0136
A112K	0136
A112L	0136
A112M	0136
A112OR	0136
A112R	0136
A112X	0136
A112Y	0136
A113(2S)	0136
A113A	0136
A113B	0136
A113C	0136
A113D	0136
A113E	0136
A113F	0136
A113G	0136
A113GN	0136
A113H	0136
A113J	0136
A113L	0136
A113M	0136
A113R	0136
A113X	0136
A113Y	0136
A114	0136
A114A	0023
A114A(TRANS)	0136
A114B	0023
A114B(TRANS)	0136
A114C	0071
A114C(TRANS)	0136
A114D	0023
A114D(TRANS)	0136
A114E	0023
A114E(TRANS)	0136
A114ES	4109
A114F	0914
A114F(TRANS)	0136
A114G	0136
A114H	0136
A114K	0136
A114L	0136
A114M	0023
A114M(TRANS)	0136
A114OR	0136
A114R	0136
A114X	0136
A114Y	0136
A115	0136
A115(2S)	0136
A115A	0031
A115A(TRANS)	0136
A115B	0031
A115B(TRANS)	0136
A115C	0031
A115C(TRANS)	0136
A115D	0031
A115D(TRANS)	0136
A115E	0031
A115E(TRANS)	0136
A115F	0031
A115F(TRANS)	0136
A115G	0136
A115GN	0136
A115H	0136
A115J	0136
A115K	0136
A115L	0136
A115M	0031
A115M(TRANS)	0136
A115OR	0136
A115R	0136
A115X	0136
A115Y	0136
A116	0136
A116(2S)	0136
A116A	0136
A116B	0136
A116C	0136
A116D	0136
A116E	0136
A116F	0136
A116G	0136
A116GN	0136
A116H	0136
A116J	0136
A116K	0136
A116L	0136
A116M	0136
A116OR	0136
A116R	0136
A116X	0136
A116Y	0136
A117	0136
A117(2S)	0136
A117A	0136
A117B	0136
A117C	0136
A117D	0136
A117E	0136
A117F	0136
A117G	0136
A117GN	0136
A117H	0136
A117J	0136
A117K	0136
A117L	0136
A117M	0136
A117OR	0136
A117R	0136
A117T	OEM
A117X	0136
A117Y	0136
A118	0136
A118A	0136
A118B	0136
A118C	0136
A118D	0136
A118E	0136
A118F	0136
A118G	0136
A118GN	0136
A118H	0136
A118J	0136
A118K	0136
A118L	0136
A118M	0136
A118OR	0136
A118R	0136
A118X	0136
A118Y	0136
A119	0126
A120	0126
A120A	0126
A120P1	0037
A120UF	OEM
A121(2S)	0136
A121-1	0037
A121-1RED	0037
A121-15	0595
A121-16	0595
A121-17	0595
A121-21	0595
A121-50	0595
A121-361	0233
A121-444	0037
A121-446	0037
A121-480	0144
A121-495	0037
A121-496	0037
A121-497	0037
A121-497WHT	0037
A121-585	0127
A121-585B	0127
A121-602	0037
A121-603	0037
A121-679	0037
A121-687	0127
A121-699	0037
A121-746	0037
A121-762	0595
A121-774	0037
A121-1410	0595
A121A	0136
A121B	0136
A121C	0136
A121D	0136
A121E	0136
A121F	0136
A121G	0136
A121GN	0136
A121H	0136
A121J	0136
A121K	0136
A121L	0136
A121M	0136
A121OR	0136
A121R	0136
A121X	0136
A121Y	0136
A122	0050
A122(2S)	0136
A122-1962	0208
A122A	0136
A122B	0136
A122C	0136
A122D	0136
A122E	0136
A122F	0136
A122G	0136
A122GN	0136
A122GRN	0037
A122H	0136
A122K	0136
A122L	0136
A122M	0136
A122OR	0136
A122R	0136
A122X	0136
A122Y	0136
A122YEL	0037
A123	0136
A123(2S)	0136
A123-7	0015
A123A	0136
A123B	0136
A123C	0136
A123D	0136
A123E	0136
A123F	0136
A123G	0136
A123GN	0136
A123H	0136
A123J	0136
A123K	0136
A123L	0136
A123M	0136
A123OR	0136
A123R	0136
A123X	0136
A123Y	0136
A124	0136
A124(2S)	0136
A124A	0136
A124B	0136
A124C	0136
A124D	0136
A124E	0136
A124EF(DTA124EF)	OEM
A124F	0136
A124G	0136
A124GN	0136
A124H	0136
A124J	0136
A124K	0136
A124L	0136
A124M	0136
A124OR	0136
A124R	0136
A124X	0136
A124Y	0136
A125	0136
A125(2S)	0136
A125A	0136
A125B	0136
A125C	0136
A125D	0136
A125E	0136
A125F	0136
A125G	0136
A125GN	0136
A125H	0136
A125J	0136
A125K	0136
A125L	0136
A125M	0136
A125OR	0136
A125R	0136
A125X	0136
A125Y	0136
A126	0136
A126(2S)	0136
A127	0050
A127(2S)	0136
A-128	0079
A128	0016
A128(2S)	0164
A128A	0164
A128B	0164
A128C	0164
A128D	0164
A128E	0164
A128F	0164
A128G	0164
A128GN	0164
A128H	0164
A128J	0164
A128K	0164
A128L	0164
A128M	0164
A128OR	0164
A128R	0164
A128X	0164
A128Y	0164
A129	0164
A129-30	0595
A129-34	0037
A129A	0164
A129B	0164
A129C	0164
A129D	0164
A129E	0164
A129E(2S)	0164
A129F	0164
A129G	0164
A129GN	0164
A129H	0164
A129J	0164
A129K	0164
A129L	0164
A129M	0164
A129M(2S)	0164
A129N	OEM
A129OR	0164
A129P	OEM
A129PB	OEM
A129R	0164
A129X	0164
A129Y	0164
A130	0233
A130(2S)	0050
A130-149	0037
A130-40315	0037
A130-40429	0037
A130-ORN	0233
A130-V10	0233
A130A	0050
A130B	0050
A130C	0050
A130D	0050
A130E	0050
A130F	0050
A130G	0050
A130GN	0050
A130H	0050
A130J	0050
A130K	0050
A130L	0050
A130M	0050
A130OR	0050
A130R	0050
A130X	0050
A130Y	0050
A131	0136
A131(2S)	0136
A131A	0136
A131B	0136
A131C	0136
A131D	0136
A131E	0136
A131F	0136
A131G	0136
A131GN	0136
A131H	0136
A131J	0136
A131K	0136
A131L	0136
A131M	0136
A131OR	0136
A131R	0136
A131X	0136
A131Y	0136
A132	0015
A132(TRANS)	0136
A132-1	0015
A132A	0136
A132B	0136
A132C	0136
A132D	0136
A132E	0136
A132F	0136
A132G	0136
A132H	0136
A132J	0136
A132K	0136
A132L	0136
A132M	0136
A132OR	0136
A132X	0136
A132Y	0136
A133	0855
A133(2S)	0136
A133A	0136
A133B	0136
A133C	0136
A133D	0136
A133E	0136
A133F	0136
A133G	0136
A133GN	0136
A133H	0136
A133J	0136
A133K	0136
A133L	0136
A133M	0136
A133OR	0136
A133R	0136
A133X	0136
A133Y	0136
A134	0136
A134(2S)	0136
A134A	0136
A134B	0136
A134C	0136
A134D	0136
A134E	0136
A134F	0136
A134G	0136
A134H	0136
A134J	0136
A134K	0136
A134L	0136
A134OR	0136
A134R	0136
A134X	0136
A134Y	0136
A135	0076
A135(2S)	0050
A135A	0050
A135B	0050
A135C	0050
A135D	0050
A135E	0050
A135F	0050
A135G	0050
A135GN	0050
A135H	0050
A135J	0050
A135K	0050
A135L	0050
A135M	0050
A135OR	0050
A135R	0050
A135X	0050
A135Y	0050
A136	0628
A136(2S)	0050
A136A	0050
A136B	0050
A136C	0050
A136D	0050
A136E	0050
A136F	0050
A136G	0050
A136GN	0050
A136H	0050
A136J	0050
A136K	0050
A136L	0050
A136M	0050
A136OR	0050
A136R	0050
A136X	0050
A136Y	0050
A137	1371
A137(2S)	0136
A137A	0136
A137B	0136
A137C	0136
A137D	0136
A137E	0136
A137F	0136
A137G	0136
A137GN	0136
A137H	0136
A137J	0136
A137K	0136
A137L	0136
A137M	0136
A137OR	0136
A137R	0136
A137X	0136
A137Y	0136
A138	0111
A138(2S)	0004
A139	0111
A139(2S)	0136
A139A	0136
A139B	0136
A139C	0136
A139D	0136
A139E	1186
A139E(TRANS)	0136
A139F	0136
A139G	0136
A139GN	0136
A139J	0136
A139K	0136
A139L	0136
A139M	0315
A139M(TRANS)	0136
A139N	1124
A139OR	0136
A139P	0045
A139PB	OEM
A139R	0136
A139RE	1634
A139RM	0267
A139RN	1111
A139RP	0280
A139X	0136
A139Y	0136
A141	0004
A141(2S)	0136
A141A	0136
A141B(2S)	0136
A141C(2S)	0136
A141D	0136
A141E	0136
A141F	0136
A141G	0136
A141GN	0136
A141H	0136
A141K	0136
A141L	0136
A141M	0136
A141OR	0136
A141R	0136
A141X	0136
A141Y	0136
A142	0004
A142(2S)	0136
A142A(2S)	0136
A142B(2S)	0136
A142C(2S)	0136
A142D	0136
A142E	0136
A142F	0136
A142G	0136
A142GN	0136
A142H	0136
A142J	0136
A142K	0136
A142L	0136
A142M	0136
A142OR	0136
A142R	0136
A142X	0136
A142Y	0136
A143	0004
A143(2S)	0136
A143A	0136
A143B	0136
A143C	0136
A143D	0136
A143E	0136
A143E(DT)	OEM
A143F	0136
A143G	0136
A143GN	0136
A143H	0136
A143J	0136
A143K	0136
A143L	0136
A143M	0136
A143OR	0136
A143R	0136
A143X	0136
A143XA	OEM
A143Y	0136
A144(2S)	0136
A-144-3078	0720
A144A	0136
A144A-1	0160
A144A-19	0160
A144B	0136
A144C(2S)	0136
A144D	0136
A144E	0136
A144F	0136
A144G	0136
A144GN	0136
A144H	0136
A144J	0136
A144K	0136
A144L	0136
A144M	0136
A144OR	0136
A144R	0136
A144X	0136
A144Y	0136
A145(2S)	0136
A145A(2S)	0136
A145B	0136
A145C(2S)	0136
A145D	0136
A145E	0136
A145G	0136
A145GN	0136
A145K	0136
A145M	0136
A145OR	0136
A145R	0136
A145X	0136
A145Y	0136
A146(2S)	0136
A146A	0136
A146B	0136
A146C	0136
A146D	0136
A146E	0136
A146F	0136
A146G	0136
A146GN	0136
A146H	0136
A146J	0136
A146K	0136
A146L	0136
A146M	0136
A146OR	0136
A146X	0136
A146Y	0136
A147(2S)	0136
A147A	0136
A147B	0136
A147C	0136
A147D	0136
A147E	0136
A147F	0136
A147G	0136
A147H	0136
A147J	0136
A147K	0136
A147L	0136
A147M	0136
A147OR	0136
A147R	0136
A147X	0136
A147Y	0136
A148(2S)	0136
A148A	0136
A148A(2S)	0136
A148B	0136
A148B(2S)	0136
A148C	0136
A148C(2S)	0136
A148D	0136
A148E	0136
A148F	0136
A148G	0136
A148GN	0136
A148H	0136
A148J	0136
A148K	0136
A148L	0136
A148M	0136
A148OR	0136
A148P2	0004
A148P2-29	0004
A148R	0136
A148X	0136
A148Y	0136
A149(2S)	0136
A149A	0136

If replacement code is OEM, contact original manufacturer for replacement.

247

DEVICE TYPE	REPL CODE
A149B	0136
A149C	0136
A149D	0136
A149E	0136
A149F	0136
A149G	0136
A149GN	0136
A149H	0136
A149J	0136
A149K	0136
A149L	0136
A149L-4	0004
A149L-49	0004
A149M	0136
A149OR	0136
A149R	0136
A149X	0136
A149Y	0136
A150(2S)	0136
A150A	0136
A150B	0136
A150C	0136
A150D	0136
A150E	0136
A150F	0136
A150G	0136
A150GN	0136
A150H	0136
A150J	0136
A150K	0136
A150L	0136
A150M	0136
A150OR	0136
A150R	0136
A150X	0136
A150Y	0136
A151	0136
A151(2S)	0136
A151A	0136
A151B	0136
A151C	0136
A151D	0136
A151E	0136
A151F	0136
A151G	0136
A151GN	0136
A151H	0136
A151J	0136
A151K	0136
A151L	0136
A151M	0136
A151OR	0136
A151R	0136
A151X	0136
A151Y	0136
A152	0136
A152(2S)	0136
A152A	0136
A152B	0136
A152C	0136
A152D	0136
A152E	0136
A152F	0136
A152G	0136
A152GN	0136
A152H	0136
A152J	0136
A152K	0136
A152L	0136
A152M	0136
A152OR	0136
A152R	0136
A152X	0136
A152Y	0136
A153	0016
A153(2S)	0136
A153(JAPAN)	0136
A153A	0136
A153B	0136
A153C	0136
A153D	0136
A153E	0136
A153F	0136
A153G	0136
A153GN	0136
A153H	0136
A153J	0136
A153K	0136
A153L	0136
A153M	0136
A153OR	0136
A153R	0136
A153X	0136
A153Y	0136
A154	0224
A154(2S)	0136
A154A	0136
A154B	0136
A154C	0136
A154D	0136
A154E	0136
A154F	0136
A154G	0136
A154GN	0136
A154H	0136
A154J	0136
A154K	0136
A154L	0136
A154M	0136
A154OR	0136
A154R	0136
A154X	0136
A154Y	0136
A155	0224
A155(2S)	0136
A155A	0136
A155B	0136
A155C	0136
A155D	0136
A155E	0136
A155F	0136
A155G	0136
A155GN	0136
A155H	0136
A155J	0136
A155K	0136
A155L	0136
A155M	0136
A155OR	0136
A155R	0136
A155X	0136
A155Y	0136
A-156	0016
A156	0016
A156(2S)	0136
A156A	0136
A156B	0136
A156C	0136
A156D	0136
A156E	0136
A156F	0136
A156G	0136
A156GN	0136
A156H	0136
A156J	0136
A156K	0136
A156L	0136
A156M	0136
A156OR	0136
A156R	0136
A156X	0136
A156Y	0136
A157	0016
A157(2S)	0136
A157A	0016
A157A(2S)	0136
A157B	0016
A157B(2S)	0136
A157C	0016
A157C(2S)	0136
A157D	0136
A157E	0136
A157F	0136
A157G	0136
A157GN	0136
A157H	0136
A157J	0136
A157K	0136
A157L	0136
A157M	0136
A157OR	0136
A157R	0136
A157X	0136
A157Y(2S)	0136
A158	0016
A158A	0016
A158B	0079
A158C	0016
A159	0016
A159(2S)	0136
A159A	0136
A159B	0016
A159B(2S)	0136
A159C	0016
A159C(2S)	0136
A159D	0136
A159E	0136
A159F	0136
A159G	0136
A159GN	0136
A159H	0136
A159J	0136
A159K	0136
A159L	0136
A159M	0136
A159OR	0136
A159R	0136
A159X	0136
A159Y	0136
A160	0136
A160(2S)	0136
A160A	0136
A160B	0136
A160C	0136
A160D	0136
A160E	0136
A160F	0136
A160GN	0136
A160H	0136
A160J	0136
A160K	0136
A160L	0136
A160M	0136
A160OR	0136
A160R	0136
A160UF	OEM
A160X	0136
A160Y	0136
A161	0037
A161(2S)	0136
A161A	0136
A161B	0136
A161C	0136
A161D	0136
A161E	0136
A161F	0136
A161G	0136
A161GN	0136
A161H	0136
A161J	0136
A161K	0136
A161L	0136
A161M	0136
A161OR	0136
A161R	0136
A161X	0136
A161Y	0136
A162	0037
A162(2S)	0136
A162A	0136
A162B	0136
A162C	0136
A162D	0136
A162E	0136
A162F	0136
A162G	0136
A162GN	0136
A162H	0136
A162J	0136
A162K	0136
A162L	0136
A162M	0136
A162OR	0136
A162R	0136
A162X	0136
A162Y	0136
A163	0136
A163A	0136
A163B	0136
A163C	0136
A163D	0136
A163E	0136
A163F	0136
A163G	0136
A163GN	0136
A163H	0136
A163J	0136
A163K	0136
A163L	0136
A163M	0136
A163OR	0136
A163R	0136
A163X	0136
A163Y	0136
A164	0224
A164(2S)	0136
A164A	0136
A164B	0136
A164C	0136
A164D	0136
A164E	0136
A164F	0136
A164G	0136
A164GN	0136
A164H	0136
A164J	0136
A164K	0136
A164L	0136
A164M	0136
A164OR	0136
A164R	0136
A164X	0136
A164Y	0136
A165	0224
A165(2S)	0136
A165A	0136
A165B	0136
A165C	0136
A165D	0136
A165E	0136
A165F	0136
A165G	0136
A165GN	0136
A165H	0136
A165J	0136
A165K	0136
A165L	0136
A165M	0136
A165OR	0136
A165R	0136
A165X	0136
A165Y	0136
A166(2S)	0136
A166A	0136
A166B	0136
A166C	0136
A166D	0136
A166E	0136
A166F	0136
A166G	0136
A166GN	0136
A166H	0136
A166J	0136
A166K	0136
A166L	0136
A166M	0136
A166OR	0136
A166R	0136
A166X	0136
A166Y	0136
A167(2S)	0279
A167A	0279
A167B	0279
A167C	0279
A167D	0279
A167E	0279
A167F	0279
A167G	0279
A167GN	0279
A167H	0279
A167J	0279
A167K	0279
A167L	0279
A167M	0279
A167OR	0279
A167R	0279
A167X	0279
A167Y	0279
A168	0279
A168A(2S)	0279
A168B	0279
A168C	0279
A168D	0279
A168E	0279
A168F	0279
A168G	0279
A168GN	0279
A168H	0279
A168J	0279
A168K	0279
A168L	0279
A168M	0279
A168OR	0279
A168R	0279
A168X	0279
A168Y	0279
A169(2S)	0279
A169A	0279
A169B	0279
A169C	0279
A169D	0279
A169E	0279
A169F	0279
A169G	0279
A169GN	0279
A169H	0279
A169J	0279
A169K	0279
A169L	0279
A169M	0279
A169OR	0279
A169R	0279
A169X	0279
A169Y	0279
A170	0126
A170(2S)	0279
A170A	0594
A170A(TRANS)	0279
A170AR	1337
A170B	0594
A170B(TRANS)	0279
A170BR	1337
A170C	0594
A170C(TRANS)	0279
A170CR	1337
A170D	0594
A170D(TRANS)	0279
A170DR	1894
A170E	1975
A170E(TRANS)	0279
A170ER	1894
A170F	0279
A170G	0279
A170GN	0279
A170H	0279
A170J	0279
A170K	0279
A170L	0279
A170M	1975
A170M(TRANS)	0279
A170MR	1894
A170N	0652
A170NR	0193
A170OR	0279
A170P	0652
A170PA	3277
A170PB	3277
A170PC	3277
A170PD	3277
A170PE	OEM
A170PR	0193
A170R	0279
A170RA	1337
A170RB	1337
A170RC	1337
A170RD	1337
A170RE	1894
A170RM	1894
A170RN	0193
A170RP	0193
A170RPA	0202
A170RPB	0202
A170RPC	0202
A170RPD	0202
A170RPE	OEM
A170RS	0193
A170RT	0193
A170S	0652
A170SR	0193
A170T	0652
A170TR	0193
A170X	0279
A170Y	0279
A171	0037
A171(2S)	0279
A171A	0279
A171B	0279
A171C	0279
A171D	0279
A171E	0279
A171F	0279
A171G	0279
A171GN	0279
A171H	0279
A171J	0279
A171K	0279
A171L	0279
A171M	0279
A171OR	0279
A171R	0279
A171X	0279
A171Y	0279
A172(2S)	0279
A172A(2S)	0279
A172B	0279
A172C	0279
A172D	0279
A172E	0279
A172F	0279
A172G	0279
A172GN	0279
A172H	0279
A172J	0279
A172K	0279
A172L	0279
A172M	0279
A172OR	0279
A172R	0279
A172X	0279
A172Y	0279
A173(2S)	0004
A173A	0004
A173B(2S)	0004
A173C	0004
A173D	0004
A173E	0004
A173F	0004
A173G	0004
A173GN	0004
A173H	0004
A173J	0004
A173K	0004
A173L	0004
A173M	0004
A173OR	0004
A173R	0004
A173X	0004
A173Y	0004
A174(2S)	0211
A174A	0211
A174B	0211
A174C	0211
A174D	0211
A174E	0211
A174F	0211
A174G	0211
A174GN	0211
A174H	0211
A174J	0211
A174K	0211
A174L	0211
A174M	0211
A174OR	0211
A174R	0211
A174X	0211
A174Y	0211
A175(2S)	0136
A175A	0136
A175B	0136
A175C	0136
A175D	0136
A175E	0136
A175F	0136
A175G	0136
A175GN	0136
A175H	0136
A175J	0136
A175K	0136
A175L	0136
A175M	0136
A175OR	0136
A175R	0136
A175X	0136
A175Y	0136
A176(2S)	0136
A176-025-9-002	0144
A176A	0136
A176B	0136
A176C	0136
A176D	0136
A176E	0136
A176F	0136
A176G	0136
A176GN	0136
A176H	0136
A176J	0136
A176K	0136
A176L	0136
A176M	0136
A176OR	0136
A176R	0136
A176X	0136
A176Y	0136
A177	0037
A177(A)	0037
A177A	0037
A177A(DIO)	OEM
A177AB	0037
A177B	0594
A177C	0594
A177D	0594
A177E	1975
A177M	1975
A177N	0652
A177P	0652
A177PA	3277
A177PB	3277
A177PC	3277
A177PD	3277
A177PE	OEM
A177RA	1337
A177RB	1337
A177RC	1337
A177RD	1337
A177RE	1894
A177RM	1894
A177RN	0193
A177RP	0193
A177RPA	0202
A177RPB	0202
A177RPC	0202
A177RPD	0202
A177RPE	OEM
A177RS	0193
A177RT	0193
A177S	0652
A177T	0652
A178	0050
A178A	0037
A178AB	0037
A178B	0037
A178BA	0037
A179A	0037
A179AC	0037
A179B	0037
A179BB	0037
A180(2S)	0136
A180A	1017
A180A(TRANS)	0136
A180AR	1337
A180B	1017
A180B(TRANS)	0136
A180BR	1337
A180C	1017
A180C(TRANS)	0136
A180CR	1337
A180D	1017
A180D(TRANS)	0136
A180DR	1894
A180E	1030
A180E(TRANS)	0136
A180ER	1894
A180F	0136
A180G	0136
A180GN	0136
A180H	0136
A180J	0136
A180K	0136
A180L	0136
A180M	1030
A180M(TRANS)	0136
A180MR	1894
A180N	1040
A180NR	0193
A180OR	0136
A180P	1040
A180PA	2805
A180PB	2805
A180PC	2805
A180PD	2805
A180PE	OEM
A180PR	0193
A180R	0136
A180RA	0496
A180RB	0496
A180RC	0496
A180RD	0496
A180RE	1766
A180RM	1766
A180RN	1778
A180RP	1778
A180RPA	3138
A180RPB	3138
A180RPC	3138
A180RPD	3138
A180RPE	OEM
A180RS	1778
A180RT	1778
A180S	1040
A180SR	0193
A180T	1040
A180TR	0193
A180X	0136
A180Y	0136
A181(2S)	0136
A181A	0136
A181B	0136
A181C	0136
A181D	0136
A181E	0136
A181F	0136
A181G	0136
A181GN	0136
A181H	0136
A181J	0136
A181K	0136
A181L	0136
A181M	0136
A181OR	0136
A181R	0136
A181X	0136
A181Y	0136
A182(2S)	0050
A182A	0050
A182B	0050
A182C	0050
A182D	0050
A182E	0050
A182F	0050
A182G	0050
A182GN	0050
A182H	0050
A182J	0050
A182K	0050
A182L	0050
A182M	0050
A182OR	0050
A182R	0050
A182X	0050
A182Y	0050
A183(2S)	0136
A183A	0136
A183B	0136
A183C	0136
A183D	0136
A183E	0136
A183F	0136
A183G	0136
A183GN	0136
A183H	0136
A183J	0136
A183K	0136
A183L	0136
A183M	0136
A183OR	0136
A183R	0136
A183X	0136
A183Y	0136
A184	0050
A185	OEM
A186	OEM
A186(2S)	0164
A187A	1017
A187B	1017
A187C	1017
A187D	1017
A187E	1030
A187M	1030
A187N	1040
A187P	1040
A187PA	2805
A187PB	2805
A187PC	2805
A187PD	2805
A187PE	4222
A187RA	0496
A187RB	0496
A187RC	0496
A187RD	0496
A187RE	1766
A187RM	1766
A187RN	1778
A187RP	1778
A187RPA	3138
A187RPB	3138
A187RPC	3138
A187RPD	3138
A187RPE	4221
A187RS	1778
A187RT	1778
A187S	1040
A187T	1040
A187TV(2S)	0004
A188	0136
A188(2S)	0136
A188A	0136
A188B	0136
A188C	0136
A188D	0136
A188E	0136
A188F	0136
A188G	0136
A188GN	0136
A188H	0136
A188J	0136
A188K	0136
A188L	0136
A188M	0136
A188OR	0136
A188R	0136
A188X	0136
A188Y	0136
A189(2S)	0136

If replacement code is OEM, contact original manufacturer for replacement.

Original Device Types

DEVICE TYPE	REPL CODE
A189A	0136
A189B	0136
A189C	0136
A189D	0136
A189E	0136
A189F	0136
A189G	0136
A189GN	0136
A189H	0136
A189J	0136
A189K	0136
A189L	0136
A189M	0136
A189OR	0136
A189R	0136
A189X	0136
A189Y	0136
A190	5121
A190(2S)	0050
A190A	1017
A190AR	0496
A190B	1017
A190BR	0496
A190C	1017
A190CR	0496
A190D	1017
A190DR	1766
A190E	1030
A190ER	1766
A190M	1030
A190MR	1766
A190N	1040
A190NR	1778
A190P	1040
A190PA	3872
A190PB	3872
A190PC	2805
A190PD	2805
A190PE	4222
A190PR	1778
A190RA	0496
A190RB	0496
A190RC	0496
A190RD	0496
A190RE	1766
A190RM	1766
A190RN	1778
A190RP	1778
A190RPA	3138
A190RPB	3138
A190RPC	3138
A190RPD	3138
A190RPE	4221
A190RS	1778
A190RT	1778
A190S	1040
A190SR	1778
A190T	1040
A190TR	1778
A191	5121
A191(2S)	0050
A192	0321
A192(2S)	0050
A193	0164
A193(2S)	0050
A194	0321
A194(2S)	0050
A195	0321
A195(2S)	0050
A-195C	0037
A196	0321
A196(2S)	0050
A197	0136
A197(2S)	0136
A197/197RPB	3138
A197/197RPE	4221
A197A	1017
A197A(TRANS)	0136
A197B	1017
A197B(TRANS)	0136
A197C	1017
A197C(TRANS)	0136
A197D	1017
A197D(TRANS)	0136
A197E	1030
A197E(TRANS)	0136
A197F	0136
A197G	0136
A197GN	0136
A197H	0136
A197J	0136
A197K	0136
A197L	0136
A197M	1030
A197M(TRANS)	0136
A197N	1040
A197OR	0136
A197P	1040
A197PA	2805
A197PB	2805
A197PC	2805
A197PD	2805
A197PE	4222
A197R	0136
A197RA	0496
A197RB	0496
A197RC	0496
A197RD	0496
A197RE	1766

DEVICE TYPE	REPL CODE
A197RM	1766
A197RN	1778
A197RP	1778
A197RPA	3138
A197RPB	3138
A197RPC	3138
A197RPD	3138
A197RPE	4221
A197RS	1778
A197RT	1778
A197S	1040
A197T	1040
A197X	0136
A197Y	0136
A198	0004
A198(2S)	0050
A198A	1017
A198A(TRANS)	0050
A198B	1017
A198B(TRANS)	0050
A198C	1017
A198C(TRANS)	0050
A198D	1017
A198D(TRANS)	0050
A198E	1030
A198E(TRANS)	0050
A198F	0050
A198G	0050
A198GN	0050
A198H	0050
A198J	0050
A198K	0050
A198L	0050
A198M	1030
A198M(TRANS)	0050
A198N	1040
A198OR	0050
A198P	1040
A198PA	2805
A198PB	2805
A198PC	2805
A198PD	2805
A198PE	4222
A198R	0050
A198RA	0496
A198RB	0496
A198RC	0496
A198RD	0496
A198RE	1766
A198RM	1766
A198RN	1778
A198RP	1778
A198RPA	3138
A198RPB	3138
A198RPC	3138
A198RPD	3138
A198RPE	4221
A198RS	1778
A198RT	1778
A198S	1040
A198T	1040
A198X	0050
A198Y	0050
A199	0628
A199(2S)	0050
A200	0015
A200(TRANS)	0136
A200-052	0037
A200UF	OEM
A201	0136
A201(2S)	0136
A201-0(2S)	0136
A201-N	0136
A201-O	0136
A201-OR	0136
A201A(2S)	0136
A201B(2S)	0136
A201CL	0136
A201D	0136
A201E(2S)	0136
A201F	0136
A201G	0136
A201GN	0136
A201H	0136
A201J	0136
A201K	0136
A201L	0136
A201M	0136
A201N	0136
A201O	0136
A201OR	0136
A201R	0136
A201TV	0136
A201TVO	0136
A201X	0136
A201Y	0136
A202	0136
A202(2S)	0628
A202-OR	0628
A202A(2S)	0628
A202AP	0628
A202B(2S)	0628
A202C(2S)	0628
A202D(2S)	0628
A202D-4	0628
A202E	0628
A202F	0628
A202G	0628
A202GN	0628

DEVICE TYPE	REPL CODE
A202H	0628
A202J	0628
A202K	0628
A202L	0628
A202M	0628
A202OR	0628
A202R	0628
A202X	0628
A202Y	0628
A203	0004
A203(2S)	0628
A203A(2S)	0628
A203AA(2S)	0628
A203B(2S)	0628
A203C	0628
A203D	0628
A203P(2S)	0628
A204(2S)	0279
A204A	0279
A204B	0279
A204C	0279
A204D	0279
A204E	0279
A204F	0279
A204G	0279
A204GN	0279
A204H	0279
A204J	0279
A204K	0279
A204L	0279
A204M	0279
A204OR	0279
A204R	0279
A204X	0279
A204Y	0279
A205	0279
A205A	0279
A205B	0279
A205C	0279
A205D	0279
A205E	0279
A205F	0279
A205G	0279
A205GN	0279
A205H	0279
A205J	0279
A205K	0279
A205L	0279
A205M	0279
A205OR	0279
A205R	0279
A205X	0279
A205Y	0279
A206	0279
A206A	0279
A206B	0279
A206C	0279
A206D	0279
A206E	0279
A206F	0279
A206G	0279
A206GN	0279
A206H	0279
A206J	0279
A206K	0279
A206L	0279
A206M	0279
A206OR	0279
A206R	0279
A206X	0279
A206Y	0279
A207	0279
A207A	0279
A207B	0279
A207C	0279
A207D	0279
A207E	0279
A207F	0279
A207G	0279
A207GN	0279
A207H	0279
A207J	0279
A207K	0279
A207L	0279
A207M	0279
A207OR	0279
A207R	0279
A207X	0279
A207Y	0279
A208	0841
A208(2S)	0841
A208A	0841
A208B	0841
A208C	0841
A208D	0841
A208E	0841
A208F	0841
A208G	0841
A208GN	0841
A208H	0841
A208J	0841
A208K	0841
A208L	0841
A208M	0841
A208OR	0841
A208R	0841
A208X	0841
A208Y	0841
A209	0841

DEVICE TYPE	REPL CODE
A209(2S)	0841
A209A	0841
A209B	0841
A209C	0841
A209D	0841
A209E	0841
A209F	0841
A209G	0841
A209GN	0841
A209H	0841
A209J	0841
A209K	0841
A209L	0841
A209M	0841
A209OR	0841
A209R	0841
A209X	0841
A209Y	0841
A210	0841
A210(2S)	0841
A210A	0841
A210B	0841
A210C	0841
A210D	0841
A210E	0841
A210F	0841
A210G	0841
A210GN	0841
A210H	0841
A210J	0841
A210K	0841
A210L	0841
A210M	0841
A210OR	0841
A210R	0841
A210X	0841
A210Y	0841
A211	0555
A211(2S)	0279
A211A	0279
A211B	0279
A211C	0279
A211D	0279
A211E	0279
A211F	0279
A211G	0279
A211GN	0279
A211H	0279
A211J	0279
A211K	0279
A211L	0279
A211M	0279
A211OR	0279
A211R	0279
A211X	0279
A211Y	0279
A212	0279
A212(2S)	0050
A212A	0050
A212B	0050
A212C	0050
A212D	0050
A212E	0050
A212F	0050
A212G	0050
A212GN	0050
A212H	0050
A212J	0050
A212K	0050
A212L	0050
A212M	0050
A212OR	0050
A212R	0050
A212X	0050
A212Y	0050
A213	0136
A213(2S)	0136
A213A	0136
A213B	0136
A213C	0136
A213D	0136
A213E	0136
A213F	0136
A213G	0136
A213GN	0136
A213H	0136
A213J	0136
A213K	0136
A213L	0136
A213M	0136
A213OR	0136
A213R	0136
A213X	0136
A213Y	0136
A214	0136
A214(2S)	0136
A214A	0136
A214B	0136
A214C	0136
A214D	0136
A214E	0136
A214F	0136
A214G	0136
A214GN	0136
A214H	0136
A214J	0136
A214K	0136
A214L	0136
A214M	0136

DEVICE TYPE	REPL CODE
A214OR	0136
A214R	0136
A214X	0136
A214Y	0136
A215	0136
A215(2S)	0136
A215A	0136
A215B	0136
A215C	0136
A215D	0136
A215E	0136
A215F	0136
A215G	0136
A215GN	0136
A215H	0136
A215J	0136
A215K	0136
A215L	0136
A215M	0136
A215OR	0136
A215R	0136
A215X	0136
A215Y	0136
A216(2S)	0136
A216A	0136
A216B	0136
A216C	0136
A216D	0136
A216E	0136
A216F	0136
A216G	0136
A216GN	0136
A216H	0136
A216J	0136
A216K	0136
A216L	0136
A216M	0136
A216OR	0136
A216R	0136
A216X	0136
A216Y	0136
A217(2S)	0279
A217A	0279
A217B	0279
A217C	0279
A217D	0279
A217E	0279
A217F	0279
A217G	0279
A217GN	0279
A217H	0279
A217J	0279
A217K	0279
A217L	0279
A217M	0279
A217OR	0279
A217R	0279
A217X	0279
A217Y	0279
A218(2S)	0050
A218A	0050
A218B	0050
A218C	0050
A218D	0050
A218E	0050
A218F	0050
A218G	0050
A218GN	0050
A218H	0050
A218J	0050
A218K	0050
A218L	0050
A218M	0050
A218OR	0050
A218R	0050
A218X	0050
A218Y	0050
A219(2S)	0136
A219A	0136
A219B	0136
A219C	0136
A219D	0136
A219E	0136
A219F	0136
A219G	0136
A219GN	0136
A219H	0136
A219J	0136
A219K	0136
A219L	0136
A219M	0136
A219OR	0136
A219R	0136
A219X	0136
A219Y	0136
A220	0136
A220A	0136
A220B	0136
A220C	0136
A220D	0136
A220E	0136
A220F	0136
A220G	0136
A220GN	0136
A220H	0136
A220J	0136
A220K	0136
A220L	0136
A220M	0136

DEVICE TYPE	REPL CODE
A220OR	0136
A220R	0136
A220X	0136
A220Y	0136
A221	0136
A221(2S)	0136
A221-OR	0136
A221A	0136
A221B	0136
A221C	0136
A221D	0136
A221E	0136
A221F	0136
A221G	0136
A221GN	0136
A221H	0136
A221J	0136
A221K	0136
A221L	0136
A221M	0136
A221OR	0136
A221R	0136
A221X	0136
A221Y	0136
A222(2S)	0136
A222A	0136
A222B	0136
A222C	0136
A222D	0136
A222E	0136
A222F	0136
A222G	0136
A222GN	0136
A222H	0136
A222J	0136
A222K	0136
A222L	0136
A222M	0136
A222OR	0136
A222R	0136
A222X	0136
A222Y	0136
A223(2S)	0136
A223A	0136
A223B	0136
A223C	0136
A223D	0136
A223E	0136
A223F	0136
A223G	0136
A223GN	0136
A223H	0136
A223J	0136
A223K	0136
A223L	0136
A223M	0136
A223OR	0136
A223R	0136
A223X	0136
A223Y	0136
A224(2S)	0050
A224A	0050
A224B	0050
A224C	0050
A224D	0050
A224E	0050
A224F	0050
A224G	0050
A224GN	0050
A224H	0050
A224J	0050
A224K	0050
A224L	0050
A224M	0050
A224OR	0050
A224R	0050
A224X	0050
A224Y	0050
A225	0136
A225(2S)	0628
A-225-1	0050
A225A	0628
A225B	0628
A225C	0628
A225D	0628
A225E	0628
A225F	0628
A225G	0628
A225GN	0628
A225H	0628
A225J	0628
A225K	0628
A225L	0628
A225M	0628
A225OR	0628
A225R	0628
A225X	0628
A225Y	0628
A226	0050
A226(2S)	0050
A227(2S)	0050
A227A	0050
A227B	0050
A227C	0050
A227D	0050
A227E	0050
A227F	0050
A227G	0050
A227GN	0050

DEVICE TYPE	REPL CODE
A227H	0050
A227J	0050
A227K	0050
A227L	0050
A227M	0050
A227OR	0050
A227R	0050
A227X	0050
A227Y	0050
A228(2S)	0050
A229(2S)	0050
A229A	0050
A229B	0050
A229C	0050
A229D	0050
A229E	0050
A229F	0050
A229G	0050
A229GN	0050
A229H	0050
A229J	0050
A229K	0050
A229L	0050
A229OR	0050
A229R	0050
A229X	0050
A229Y	0050
A230	0050
A230(2S)	0050
A230A	0050
A230B	0050
A230C	0050
A230D	0050
A230E	0050
A230F	0050
A230G	0050
A230GN	0050
A230H	0050
A230J	OEM
A230J(2S)	0050
A230K	OEM
A230K(2S)	0050
A230L	OEM
A230L(2S)	0050
A230M	0050
A230OR	0050
A230R	0050
A230X	0050
A230Y	0050
A-231	0023
A231(2S)	0841
A-231-47049	OEM
A232(2S)	0841
A233	0050
A233(2S)	0050
A-233-2032	OEM
A233A(2S)	0050
A233B(2S)	0050
A233C(2S)	0050
A233D	0050
A233E	0050
A233F	0050
A233G	0050
A233GN	0050
A233H	0050
A233J	0050
A233K	0050
A233L	0050
A233M	0050
A233OR	0050
A233R	0050
A233X	0050
A233Y	0050
A234(2S)	0050
A234A(2S)	0050
A234B	0050
A234C	0050
A234D	0050
A234E	0050
A234F	0050
A234G	0050
A234GN	0050
A234H	0050
A234J	0050
A234K	0050
A234L	0050
A234M	0050
A234OR	0050
A234R	0050
A234X	0050
A234Y	0050
A235	0050
A235(2S)	0050
A235A	0050
A235B(2S)	0050
A235C	0050
A235D	0050
A235E	0050
A235F	0050
A235G	0050
A235GN	0050
A235H	0050
A235K	0050
A235M	0050
A235OR	0050
A235R	0050
A235X	0050
A235Y	0050
A236(2S)	0136

If replacement code is OEM, contact original manufacturer for replacement.

DEVICE TYPE	REPL CODE
A236A	0136
A236B	0136
A236C	0136
A236D	0136
A236E	0136
A236F	0136
A236G	0136
A236GN	0136
A236H	0136
A236J	0136
A236K	0136
A236L	0136
A236M	0136
A236OR	0136
A236R	0136
A236X	0136
A236Y	0136
A237	0136
A237(2S)	0136
A237A	0136
A237B	0136
A237C	0136
A237D	0136
A237E	0136
A237F	0136
A237G	0136
A237GN	0136
A237H	0136
A237J	0136
A237K	0136
A237L	0136
A237M	0136
A237OR	0136
A237R	0136
A237X	0136
A237Y	0136
A238	0136
A238(2S)	0136
A238A	0136
A238B	0136
A238C	0136
A238D	0136
A238E	0136
A238F	0136
A238G	0136
A238GN	0136
A238H	0136
A238J	0136
A238K	0136
A238L	0136
A239(2S)	0050
A239A	0050
A239B	0050
A239C	0050
A239D	0050
A239E	0050
A239F	0050
A239G	0050
A239GN	0050
A239GREEN	0050
A239H	0050
A239J	0050
A239K	0050
A239L	0050
A239M	0050
A239OR	0050
A239R	0050
A239RED	0050
A239X	0050
A239Y	0050
A240	0050
A240(2S)	0050
A240A(2S)	0050
A240B(2S)	0050
A240B2(2S)	0050
A240BL(2S)	0050
A240C	0050
A240D	0050
A240E	0050
A240F	0050
A240G	0050
A240GN	0050
A240GREEN	0050
A240H	0050
A240J	0050
A240K	0050
A240L	0050
A240M	0050
A240OR	0050
A240R	0050
A240RED	0050
A240X	0050
A240Y	0050
A241	0050
A241(2S)	0050
A241A	0050
A241B	0050
A241C	0050
A241D	0050
A241E	0050
A241F	0050
A241G	0050
A241GN	0050
A241H	0050
A241J	0050
A241K	0050
A241L	0050
A241M	0050
A241OR	0050

DEVICE TYPE	REPL CODE
A241R	0050
A241X	0050
A241Y	0050
A242(2S)	0050
A243(2S)	0050
A243A	0050
A244	0050
A244(AMC)	0007
A244A	0050
A245	0144
A245(2S)	0050
A245(AMC)	0144
A246	0016
A246(2S)	0136
A246(AMC)	0016
A246A	0136
A246B	0136
A246C	0136
A246D	0136
A246E	0136
A246F	0136
A246G	0136
A246GN	0136
A246H	0136
A246J	0136
A246K	0136
A246L	0136
A246M	0136
A246OR	0136
A246R	0136
A246V(2S)	0136
A246X	0136
A246Y	0136
A247	0233
A247(2S)	0136
A247(AMC)	0233
A247A	0136
A247B	0136
A247C	0136
A247D	0136
A247E	0136
A247F	0136
A247G	0136
A247GN	0136
A247H	0136
A247J	0136
A247K	0136
A247L	0136
A247M	0136
A247OR	0136
A247R	0136
A247X	0136
A247Y	0136
A248	0004
A248(AMC)	0079
A248A	0004
A248B	0004
A248C	0004
A248D	0004
A248E	0004
A248F	0004
A248G	0004
A248GN	0004
A248H	0004
A248J	0004
A248K	0004
A248L	0004
A248M	0004
A248OR	0004
A248R	0004
A248X	0004
A248Y	0004
A249	0016
A249(2S)	0164
A249(AMC)	0086
A250(2S)	0136
A250A	0136
A250B	0136
A250C	0136
A250D	0136
A250E	0136
A250F	0136
A250G	0136
A250GN	0136
A250H	0136
A250J	0136
A250L	0136
A250M	0136
A250OR	0136
A250X	0136
A250Y	0136
A251(2S)	0136
A251A	0136
A251B	0136
A251C	0136
A251D	0136
A251E	0136
A251F	0136
A251G	0136
A251H	0136
A251J	0136
A251K	0136
A251L	0136
A251M	0136
A251OR	0136
A251R	0136
A251X	0136
A251Y	0136
A252(2S)	0136

DEVICE TYPE	REPL CODE
A252A	0136
A252B	0136
A252C	0136
A252D	0136
A252E	0136
A252F	0136
A252G	0136
A252H	0136
A252J	0136
A252K	0136
A252L	0136
A252M	0136
A252OR	0136
A252R	0136
A252X	0136
A252Y	0136
A253	0555
A253(2S)	0136
A253A	0136
A253B	0136
A253C	0136
A253D	0136
A253E	0136
A253F	0136
A253G	0136
A253GN	0136
A253H	0136
A253J	0136
A253K	0136
A253L	0136
A253M	0136
A253OR	0136
A253R	0136
A253X	0136
A253Y	0136
A254(2S)	0136
A254A	0136
A254B	0136
A254C	0136
A254D	0136
A254E	0136
A254F	0136
A254G	0136
A254H	0136
A254J	0136
A254K	0136
A254L	0136
A254M	0136
A254OR	0136
A254R	0136
A254X	0136
A254Y	0136
A255(2S)	0136
A255A	0136
A255B	0136
A255C	0136
A255D	0136
A255E	0136
A255F	0136
A255G	0136
A255GN	0136
A255H	0136
A255J	0136
A255K	0136
A255L	0136
A255M	0136
A255OR	0136
A255R	0136
A255X	0136
A255Y	0136
A256(2S)	0136
A256A	0136
A256B	0136
A256C	0136
A256D	0136
A256E	0136
A256F	0136
A256G	0136
A256GN	0136
A256H	0136
A256J	0136
A256K	0136
A256L	0136
A256M	0136
A256OR	0136
A256R	0136
A256X	0136
A256Y	0136
A257(2S)	0136
A257A	0136
A257B	0136
A257C	0136
A257D	0136
A257E	0136
A257F	0136
A257G	0136
A257GN	0136
A257H	0136
A257J	0136
A257K	0136
A257L	0136
A257OR	0136
A257R	0136
A257X	0136
A257Y	0136
A258(2S)	0136
A-258-1	0628
A258A	0136
A258B	0136

DEVICE TYPE	REPL CODE
A258C	0136
A258D	0136
A258E	0136
A258F	0136
A258G	0136
A258GN	0136
A258H	0136
A258J	0136
A258K	0136
A258L	0136
A258M	0136
A258OR	0136
A258R	0136
A258X	0136
A258Y	0136
A-259	OEM
A259(2S)	0136
A259B	0136
A259C	0136
A259D	0136
A259E	0136
A259F	0136
A259G	0136
A259GN	0136
A259H	0136
A259J	0136
A259L	0136
A259M	0136
A259OR	0136
A259R	0136
A259X	0136
A259Y	0136
A260(2S)	0050
A260A	0050
A260B	0050
A260C	0050
A260D	0050
A260E	0050
A260F	0050
A260G	0050
A260GN	0050
A260H	0050
A260J	0050
A260K	0050
A260L	0050
A260M	0050
A260OR	0050
A260R	0050
A260X	0050
A260Y	0050
A261(2S)	0050
A261A	0050
A261B	0050
A261C	0050
A261D	0050
A261E	0050
A261F	0050
A261G	0050
A261GN	0050
A261H	0050
A261J	OEM
A261K	OEM
A261K(2S)	0050
A261L	0050
A261M	0050
A261OR	0050
A261R	0050
A261X	0050
A261Y	0050
A262(2S)	0050
A262A	0050
A262B	0050
A262C	0050
A262D	0050
A262E	0050
A262F	0050
A262G	0050
A262GN	0050
A262H	0050
A262J	0050
A262K	0050
A262L	0050
A262M	0050
A262OR	0050
A262R	0050
A262X	0050
A262Y	0050
A263(2S)	0050
A263A	0050
A263B	0050
A263C	0050
A263D	0050
A263E	0050
A263F	0050
A263G	0050
A263GN	0050
A263H	0050
A263J	0050
A263K	0050
A263L	0050
A263M	0050
A263OR	0050
A263R	0050
A263X	0050
A263Y	0050
A264(2S)	0050
A264A	0050
A264B	0050
A264C	0050

DEVICE TYPE	REPL CODE
A264D	0050
A264E	0050
A264F	0050
A264G	0050
A264GN	0050
A264H	0050
A264K	0050
A264L	0050
A264M	0050
A264OR	0050
A264R	0050
A264X	0050
A264Y	0050
A265(2S)	0050
A265A	0050
A265B	0050
A265C	0050
A265D	0050
A265E	0050
A265F	0050
A265G	0050
A265GN	0050
A265H	0050
A265J	0050
A265K	0050
A265L	0050
A265M	0050
A265OR	0050
A265R	0050
A265X	0050
A265Y	0050
A266(2S)	0136
A266A	0136
A266B	0136
A266C	0136
A266D	0136
A266E	0136
A266F	0136
A266G	0136
A266GN	0136
A266GREEN	0136
A266H	0136
A266J	0136
A266K	0136
A266L	0136
A266M	0136
A266OR	0136
A266R	0136
A266X	0136
A266Y	0136
A267	0136
A267(2S)	0136
A267A	0136
A267B	0136
A267C	0136
A267D	0136
A267E	0136
A267F	0136
A267G	0136
A267GN	0136
A267H	0136
A267J	0136
A267K	0136
A267L	0136
A267M	0136
A267OR	0136
A267R	0136
A267X	0136
A267Y	0136
A268(2S)	0136
A268A	0136
A268B	0136
A268C	0136
A268D	0136
A268E	0136
A268F	0136
A268G	0136
A268GN	0136
A268H	0136
A268J	0136
A268K	0136
A268L	0136
A268M	0136
A268OR	0136
A268R	0136
A268X	0136
A268Y	0136
A-269	0628
A269(2S)	0136
A269A	0136
A269B	0136
A269C	0136
A269D	0136
A269E	0136
A269F	0136
A269GN	0136
A269H	0136
A269J	0136
A269K	0136
A269L	0136
A269M	0136
A269OR	0136
A269X	0136
A269Y	0136
A270	0693
A270(2S)	0136
A270A	0136
A270B	0136
A270C	0136

DEVICE TYPE	REPL CODE
A270D	0136
A270E	0136
A270F	0136
A270G	0136
A270GN	0136
A270H	0136
A270J	0136
A270K	0136
A270L	0136
A270M	0136
A270OR	0136
A270R	0136
A270X	0136
A270Y	0136
A271	0555
A271(2)	0136
A271(2S)	0136
A271(3)	0136
A271A	0136
A271B	0136
A271C	0136
A271D	0136
A271E	0136
A271F	0136
A271G	0136
A271GN	0136
A271H	0136
A271J	0136
A271K	0136
A271L	0136
A271M	0136
A271OR	0136
A271R	0136
A271X	0136
A271Y	0136
A272	0042
A272(2S)	0136
A272A	0136
A272B	0136
A272C	0136
A272D	0136
A272E	0136
A272F	0136
A272G	0136
A272GN	0136
A272H	0136
A272J	0136
A272K	0136
A272L	0136
A272M	0136
A272OR	0136
A272R	0136
A272X	0136
A272Y	0136
A273	0042
A273(2S)	0136
A273A	0136
A273B	0136
A273C	0136
A273D	0136
A273E	0136
A273F	0136
A273G	0136
A273GN	0136
A273H	0136
A273J	0136
A273K	0136
A273L	0136
A273M	0136
A273OR	0136
A273X	0136
A273Y	0136
A274	OEM
A274(2S)	0136
A274A	0136
A274B	0136
A274C	0136
A274D	0136
A274E	0136
A274F	0136
A274G	0136
A274GN	0136
A274H	0136
A274J	0136
A274K	0136
A274L	0136
A274M	0136
A274OR	0136
A274R	0136
A274X	0136
A274Y	0136
A275	0555
A275(2S)	0136
A275A	0136
A275B	0136
A275C	0136
A275D	0136
A275E	0136
A275F	0136
A275G	0136
A275GN	0136
A275H	0136
A275J	0136
A275L	0136
A275M	0136
A275OR	0136
A275R	0136
A275X	0136
A275Y	0136

DEVICE TYPE	REPL CODE
A276	0042
A276(2S)	0050
A277	0042
A277(2S)	0279
A277A	0279
A277B	0279
A277C	0279
A277D	0279
A277E	0279
A277F	0279
A277G	0279
A277GN	0279
A277H	0279
A277J	0279
A277K	0279
A277L	0279
A277M	0279
A277OR	0279
A277X	0279
A277Y	0279
A278	0279
A278A	0279
A278B	0279
A278C	0279
A278D	0279
A278E	0279
A278F	0279
A278G	0279
A278GN	0279
A278J	0279
A278K	0279
A278L	0279
A278M	0279
A278OR	0279
A278R	0279
A278X	0279
A278Y	0279
A279	0279
A279A	0279
A279B	0279
A279C	0279
A279D	0279
A279E	0279
A279F	0279
A279G	0279
A279GN	0279
A279H	0279
A279J	0279
A279K	0279
A279L	0279
A279OR	0279
A279R	0279
A279X	0279
A279Y	0279
A280(2S)	0279
A280A	0279
A280B	0279
A280C	0279
A280D	0279
A280E	0279
A280F	0279
A280G	0279
A280GN	0279
A280H	0279
A280J	0279
A280K	0279
A280L	0279
A280M	0279
A280OR	0279
A280R	0279
A280X	0279
A280Y	0279
A281(2S)	0279
A281A	0279
A281B	0279
A281C	0279
A281D	0279
A281E	0279
A281F	0279
A281G	0279
A281GN	0279
A281H	0279
A281J	0279
A281K	0279
A281L	0279
A281M	0279
A281OR	0279
A281R	0279
A281X	0279
A281Y	0279
A282(2S)	0004
A282A	0004
A282B	0004
A282C	0004
A282D	0004
A282E	0004
A282F	0004
A282G	0004
A282GN	0004
A282H	0004
A282J	0004
A282K	0004
A282L	0004
A282M	0004
A282OR	0004
A282R	0004
A282X	0004
A282Y	0004
A283(2S)	0279

If replacement code is OEM, contact original manufacturer for replacement.

DEVICE TYPE	REPL CODE	DEVICE TYPE	REPL CODE	DEVICE TYPE	REPL CODE	DEVICE TYPE	REPL CODE	DEVICE TYPE	REPL CODE	DEVICE TYPE	REPL CODE	DEVICE TYPE	REPL CODE
A283A	0279	A289K	0136	A295B	OEM	A300(TRANS)	0050	A309E	1774	A314R	0136	A324D	0136
A283B	0279	A289L	0136	A295B(TRANS)	0136	A300PA	OEM	A309F	1774	A314X	0136	A324E	0136
A283C	0279	A289M	0136	A295C	0136	A301	0016	A309G	1774	A314Y	0136	A324F	0136
A283D	0279	A289OR	0136	A295C(TRANS)	0136	A301(2S)	0164	A309GN	1774	A315(2S)	0136	A324G	0136
A283E	0279	A289R	0136	A295D	0136	A301(JAPAN)	0136	A309H	1774	A315-GREEN	0136	A324GN	0136
A283F	0279	A289X	0136	A295D(TRANS)	0136	A301A	0164	A309J	1774	A315-RED	0136	A324H	0136
A283G	0279	A289Y	0136	A295E	0136	A301B	0164	A309K	1774	A315-YELLOW	0136	A324K	0136
A283GN	0279	A290(2S)	0136	A295E(TRANS)	0136	A301C	0164	A309L	1774	A315A	0136	A324L	0136
A283H	0279	A290A	0136	A295F	0136	A301D	0164	A309M	1774	A315A(DIO)	OEM	A324M	0136
A283J	0279	A290B	0136	A295G	0136	A301E	0164	A309OR	1774	A315B	0136	A324OR	0136
A283K	0279	A290C	0136	A295GN	0136	A301F	0164	A309R	1774	A315B(DIO)	OEM	A324R	0136
A283L	0279	A290D	0136	A295H	0136	A301G	0164	A309X	1774	A315C	0136	A324X	0136
A283M	0279	A290E	0136	A295J	0136	A301GN	0164	A309Y	1774	A315D	0136	A324Y	0136
A283OR	0279	A290F	0136	A295K	0136	A301H	0164	A310	0233	A315E	0136	A325(2S)	0136
A283R	0279	A290G	0136	A295L	0136	A301J	0164	A310(2S)	0136	A315F	0136	A325A	0136
A283X	0279	A290GN	0136	A295M	OEM	A301K	0164	A310A	0136	A315F(DIO)	OEM	A325B	0136
A283Y	0279	A290H	0136	A295N	OEM	A301L	0164	A310B	0136	A315G	0136	A325D	0136
A284(2S)	0279	A290J	0136	A295OR	0136	A301M	0164	A310C	0136	A315G(DIO)	OEM	A325E	0136
A284A	0279	A290K	0136	A295P	OEM	A301OR	0164	A310D	0136	A315GN	0136	A325G	0136
A284B	0279	A290L	0136	A295PA	OEM	A301R	0164	A310E	0136	A315H	0136	A325GN	0136
A284C	0279	A290M	0136	A295PB	OEM	A301X	0164	A310F	0136	A315J	0136	A325H	0136
A284D	0279	A290OR	0136	A295PC	OEM	A301Y	0164	A310G	0136	A315K	0136	A325J	0136
A284E	0279	A290R	0136	A295PD	OEM	A302	0004	A310GN	0136	A315L	0136	A325K	0136
A284F	0279	A290X	0136	A295PE	OEM	A302(2S)	0004	A310H	0136	A315M	0136	A325L	0136
A284G	0279	A290Y	0136	A295PM	OEM	A303	0004	A310J	0136	A315OR	0136	A325M	0136
A284GN	0279	A291	0136	A295PN	OEM	A303(2S)	0004	A310K	0136	A315R	0136	A325OR	0136
A284J	0279	A291A	0136	A295PS	OEM	A304(2S)	0279	A310L	0136	A315X	0136	A325R	0136
A284K	0279	A291B	0136	A295R	0136	A304-GREEN	0279	A310M	0136	A315Y	0136	A325X	0136
A284L	0279	A291C	0136	A295S	OEM	A304-RED	0279	A310OR	0136	A316(2S)	0136	A325Y	0136
A284M	0279	A291D	0136	A295T	OEM	A304-YELLOW	0279	A310R	0136	A316-GREEN	0136	A326(2S)	0136
A284OR	0279	A291E	0136	A295Y	0136	A304A	0279	A310X	0136	A316-RED	0136	A326A	0136
A284R	0279	A291F	0136	A296(2S)	0136	A304B	0279	A310Y	0136	A316-YELLOW	0136	A326B	0136
A284X	0279	A291G	0136	A296A	0136	A304C	0279	A311	0004	A316A	0136	A326C	0136
A284Y	0279	A291GN	0136	A296B	OEM	A304D	0279	A311(2S)	0004	A316B	0136	A326D	0136
A285(2S)	0050	A291H	0136	A296B(TRANS)	0136	A304F	0279	A311A	0004	A316C	0136	A326E	0136
A285B	0050	A291J	0136	A296C	OEM	A304G	0279	A311B	0004	A316D	0136	A326F	0136
A285C	0050	A291K	0136	A296C(TRANS)	0136	A304GN	0279	A311C	0004	A316E	0136	A326G	0136
A285E	0050	A291L	0136	A296D	0136	A304J	0279	A311D	0004	A316F	0136	A326GN	0136
A285F	0050	A291M	0136	A296D(TRANS)	0136	A304K	0279	A311E	0004	A316G	0136	A326H	0136
A285G	0050	A291OR	0136	A296E	0136	A304L	0279	A311F	0004	A316GN	0136	A326J	0136
A285GN	0050	A291PC	OEM	A296E(TRANS)	0136	A304M	0279	A311G	0004	A316H	0136	A326K	0136
A285H	0050	A291PD	OEM	A296F	0136	A304OR	0279	A311GN	0004	A316J	0136	A326L	0136
A285J	0050	A291PE	OEM	A296G	0136	A304R	0279	A311H	0004	A316K	0136	A326M	0136
A285L	0050	A291PM	OEM	A296GN	0136	A304X	0279	A311J	0004	A316L	0136	A326OR	0136
A285M	0050	A291PN	OEM	A296H	0136	A304Y	0279	A311K	0004	A316M	0136	A326R	0136
A285OR	0050	A291PS	OEM	A296J	0136	A305(2S)	0279	A311L	0004	A316OR	0136	A326X	0136
A285R	0050	A291R	0136	A296K	0136	A305-GREEN	0279	A311M	0004	A316R	0136	A326Y	0136
A285X	0050	A291X	0136	A296L	0136	A305-RED	0279	A311OR	0004	A316X	0136	A327	0050
A285Y	0050	A291Y	0136	A296M	OEM	A305-YELLOW	0279	A311R	0004	A316Y	0136	A327A	OEM
A286(2S)	0050	A292(2S)	0136	A296M(TRANS)	0136	A305A	0279	A311X	0004	A321	0004	A327A2	OEM
A286A	0050	A292A	0136	A296N	OEM	A305B	0279	A311Y	0004	A321(2S)	0004	A327B	OEM
A286B	0050	A292B	0136	A296OR	0136	A305C	0279	A312(2S)	0004	A321-1	0004	A327B2	OEM
A286C	0050	A292C	0136	A296P	OEM	A305D	0279	A312A	0004	A321A	0004	A327C	OEM
A286D	0050	A292D	0136	A296PA	OEM	A305E	0279	A312B	0004	A321B	0004	A327C2	OEM
A286E	0050	A292E	0136	A296PB	OEM	A305F	0279	A312C	0004	A321C	0004	A327F	OEM
A286F	0050	A292F	0136	A296PC	OEM	A305G	0279	A312D	0004	A321D	0004	A327F2	OEM
A286G	0050	A292G	0136	A296PD	OEM	A305GN	0279	A312E	0004	A321E	0004	A328	0279
A286GN	0050	A292GN	0136	A296PE	OEM	A305H	0279	A312F	0004	A321F	0004	A329(2S)	0136
A286H	0050	A292H	0136	A296PM	OEM	A305J	0279	A312G	0004	A321G	0004	A329A(2S)	0136
A286K	0050	A292J	0136	A296PN	OEM	A305K	0279	A312GN	0004	A321GN	0004	A329B(2S)	0136
A286M	0050	A292K	0136	A296PS	OEM	A305L	0279	A312H	0004	A321H	0004	A329C	0136
A286OR	0050	A292L	0136	A296R	0136	A305M	0279	A312J	0004	A321J	0004	A329D	0136
A286R	0050	A292M	0136	A296S	OEM	A305OR	0279	A312K	0004	A321K	0004	A329E	0136
A286X	0050	A292OR	0136	A296T	OEM	A305R	0279	A312L	0004	A321L	0004	A329F	0136
A286Y	0050	A292PC	OEM	A296X	0136	A305X	0279	A312M	0004	A321M	0004	A329G	0136
A287(2S)	0050	A292PD	OEM	A296Y	0136	A305Y	0279	A312OR	0004	A321OR	0004	A329GN	0136
A287A	0050	A292PE	OEM	A297(2S)	0136	A306	0016	A312R	0004	A321R	0004	A329H	0136
A287B	0050	A292PM	OEM	A297A	0136	A306(2S)	0050	A312X	0004	A321X	0004	A329J	0136
A287C	0050	A292PN	OEM	A297B	0136	A307	0016	A312Y	0004	A321Y	0004	A329K	0136
A287D	0050	A292PS	OEM	A297C	0136	A307(2S)	0050	A313(2S)	0136	A322	0004	A329L	0136
A287E	0050	A292R	0136	A297D	0136	A307A	0050	A313-BLUE	0136	A322(2S)	0004	A329M	0136
A287F	0050	A292X	0136	A297E	0136	A307B	0050	A313-GREEN	0136	A322A	0004	A329OR	0136
A287G	0050	A292Y	0136	A297F	0136	A307C	0050	A313-RED	0136	A322B	0004	A329R	0136
A287GN	0050	A293(2S)	0136	A297G	0136	A307D	0050	A313-YELLOW	0136	A322C	0004	A329X	0136
A287H	0050	A293A	0136	A297H	0136	A307E	0050	A313A	0136	A322D	0004	A329Y	0136
A287J	0050	A293B	0136	A297J	0136	A307F	0050	A313B	0136	A322E	0004	A330(2S)	0136
A287K	0050	A293C	0136	A297K	0136	A307G	0050	A313C	0136	A322F	0004	A330A	0136
A287L	0050	A293D	0136	A297L	0136	A307GN	0050	A313D	0136	A322G	0004	A330B	0136
A287M	0050	A293E	0136	A297L012C01	0037	A307J	0050	A313E	0136	A322GN	0004	A330C	0136
A287OR	0050	A293G	0136	A297M	0136	A307K	0050	A313F	0136	A322H	0004	A330D	0136
A287X	0050	A293GN	0136	A297OR	0136	A307L	0050	A313G	0136	A322K	0004	A330E	OEM
A287Y	0050	A293H	0136	A297R	0136	A307M	0050	A313GN	0136	A322L	0004	A330E(TRANS)	0136
A288(2S)	0136	A293J	0136	A297V073C01	0126	A307OR	0050	A313H	0136	A322M	0004	A330F	0136
A288A	0136	A293K	0136	A297V073C02	0126	A307R	0050	A313J	0136	A322OR	0004	A330G	0136
A288B	0136	A293L	0136	A297V073C03	0037	A307X	0050	A313K	0136	A322R	0004	A330GN	0136
A288C	0136	A293M	0136	A297V073C04	0037	A307Y	0050	A313L	0136	A322X	0004	A330H	0136
A288D	0136	A293OR	0136	A297X	0136	A308(2S)	0136	A313M	0136	A322Y	0004	A330J	0136
A288E	0136	A293R	0136	A297Y	0136	A308A	0136	A313OR	0136	A323	0016	A330K	0136
A288F	0136	A293X	0136	A298	0050	A308B	0136	A313R	0136	A323(2S)	0050	A330L	0136
A288G	0136	A293Y	0136	A298(2S)	0050	A308C	0136	A313X	0136	A323A	0050	A330M	OEM
A288GN	0136	A294(2S)	0136	A298A	0050	A308D	0136	A313Y	0136	A323B	0050	A330M(TRANS)	0136
A288J	0136	A294A	0136	A298B	0050	A308E	0136	A314(2S)	0136	A323C	0050	A330N	OEM
A288K	0136	A294B	0136	A298C	0050	A308F	0136	A314-GREEN	0136	A323D	0050	A330OR	0136
A288L	0136	A294C	0136	A298D	0050	A308G	0136	A314-RED	0136	A323E	0050	A330P	OEM
A288M	0136	A294D	0136	A298E	0050	A308GN	0136	A314-YELLOW	0136	A323F	0050	A330PA	OEM
A288OR	0136	A294E	0136	A298F	0050	A308H	0136	A314A	0136	A323G	0050	A330PB	OEM
A288X	0136	A294F	0136	A298G	0050	A308J	0136	A314B	0136	A323GN	0050	A330PC	OEM
A288Y	0136	A294GN	0136	A298GN	0050	A308K	0136	A314C	0136	A323J	0050	A330PD	OEM
A289(2S)	0136	A294H	0136	A298H	0050	A308L	0136	A314D	0136	A323K	0050	A330PE	OEM
A289A	0136	A294J	0136	A298J	0050	A308M	0136	A314E	0136	A323L	0050	A330S	OEM
A289B	0136	A294K	0136	A298K	0050	A308OR	0136	A314F	0136	A323M	0050	A330T	OEM
A289C	0136	A294L	0136	A298L	0050	A308R	0136	A314G	0136	A323R	0050	A330X	0136
A289D	0136	A294M	0136	A298M	0050	A308X	0136	A314GN	0136	A323X	0050	A330Y	0136
A289E	0136	A294OR	0136	A298OR	0050	A308Y	0136	A314H	0136	A323Y	0050	A331(2S)	0136
A289F	0136	A294R	0136	A298R	0050	A309(2S)	1774	A314J	0136	A324	0136	A331A	0136
A289G	0136	A294X	0136	A298X	0050	A309A	1774	A314K	0136	A324(2S)	0136	A331B	0136
A289GN	0136	A294Y	0136	A298Y	0050	A309B	1774	A314L	0136	A324A	0136	A331C	0136
A289H	0136	A295(2S)	0136	A299	0279	A309C	1774	A314M	0136	A324B	0136	A331D	0136
A289J	0136	A295A	0136	A300	0015	A309D	1774	A314OR	0136	A324C	0136	A331E	0136

If replacement code is OEM, contact original manufacturer for replacement.

DEVICE TYPE	REPL CODE
A331F	0136
A331G	0136
A331GN	0136
A331H	0136
A331J	0136
A331K	0136
A331L	0136
A331M	0136
A331OR	0136
A331R	0136
A331X	0136
A331Y	0136
A332(2S)	0050
A332A	0050
A332B	0050
A332C	0050
A332D	0050
A332E	0050
A332F	0050
A332G	0050
A332GN	0050
A332H	0050
A332J	0050
A332K	0050
A332L	0050
A332M	0050
A332OR	0050
A332R	0050
A332X	0050
A332Y	0050
A333	5121
A334	5121
A335(2S)	0136
A335A	0136
A335B	0136
A335C	0136
A335D	0136
A335E	0136
A335F	0136
A335G	0136
A335GN	0136
A335H	0136
A335J	0136
A335K	0136
A335L	0136
A335M	0136
A335OR	0136
A335R	0136
A335X	0136
A335Y	0136
A336	0050
A337(2S)	0136
A337A	OEM
A337A(TRANS)	0136
A337B	OEM
A337B(TRANS)	0136
A337C	OEM
A337C(TRANS)	0136
A337D	OEM
A337D(TRANS)	0136
A337E	OEM
A337E(TRANS)	0136
A337F	0136
A337G	0136
A337GN	0136
A337H	0136
A337J	0136
A337K	0136
A337L	0136
A337M	OEM
A337M(TRANS)	0136
A337N	OEM
A337OR	0136
A337P	OEM
A337PA	OEM
A337PB	OEM
A337PC	OEM
A337PD	OEM
A337PE	OEM
A337R	0136
A337S	OEM
A337T	OEM
A337X	0136
A337Y	0136
A338(2S)	0136
A338A	0136
A338B	0136
A338C	0136
A338D	0136
A338E	0136
A338F	0136
A338G	0136
A338GN	0136
A338H	0136
A338J	0136
A338K	0136
A338L	0136
A338M	0136
A338OR	0136
A338R	0136
A338X	0136
A338Y	0136
A339(2S)	0136
A339A	0136
A339B	0136
A339C	0136
A339D	0136
A339E	0136
A339F	0136

DEVICE TYPE	REPL CODE
A339G	0136
A339GN	0136
A339H	0136
A339J	0136
A339K	0136
A339L	0136
A339M	0136
A339OR	0136
A339R	0136
A339Y	0136
A340(2S)	0050
A340A	OEM
A340A2	OEM
A340B	OEM
A340B2	OEM
A340C	OEM
A340C2	OEM
A340F	OEM
A340F2	OEM
A341(2S)	0050
A341-OA	0050
A341-OB(2S)	0050
A341A	0050
A341B	0050
A341C	0050
A341E	0050
A341F	0050
A341G	0050
A341GN	0050
A341H	0050
A341J	0050
A341K	0050
A341L	0050
A341M	0050
A341OR	0050
A341R	0050
A341X	0050
A341Y	0050
A342(2S)	0050
A342A(2S)	0050
A342B	0050
A342C	0050
A342D	0050
A342E	0050
A342F	0050
A342G	0050
A342GN	0050
A342H	0050
A342J	0050
A342K	0050
A342L	0050
A342M	0050
A342OR	0050
A342R	0050
A342X	0050
A342Y	0050
A343(2S)	0050
A343A	0050
A343B	0050
A343C	0050
A343D	0050
A343E	0050
A343F	0050
A343G	0050
A343H	0050
A343J	0050
A343K	0050
A343L	0050
A343M	0050
A343OR	0050
A343R	0050
A343X	0050
A343Y	0050
A344	0016
A344(2S)	0136
A344A	0136
A344B	0136
A344C	0136
A344D	0136
A344E	0136
A344F	0136
A344G	0136
A344GN	0136
A344H	0136
A344J	0136
A344K	0136
A344L	0136
A344M	0136
A344OR	0136
A344R	0136
A344X	0136
A344Y	0136
A345	0016
A345(2S)	0050
A346	0016
A346(2S)	0050
A347(2S)	0050
A348(2S)	0050
A348A	0050
A348B	0050
A348C	0050
A348D	0050
A348E	0050
A348F	0050
A348G	0050
A348GN	0050
A348H	0050
A348J	0050
A348K	0050

DEVICE TYPE	REPL CODE
A348L	0050
A348M	0050
A348OR	0050
A348R	0050
A348X	0050
A348Y	0050
A349(2S)	0050
A350(2S)	0136
A350A	0136
A350AV	0136
A350B	0136
A350BK	0136
A350C(2S)	0136
A350D	0136
A350E	0136
A350F	0136
A350G	0136
A350GN	0136
A350H(2S)	0136
A350J	0136
A350K	0136
A350L	0136
A350M	0136
A350OR	0136
A350R(2S)	0136
A350T(2S)	0136
A350TY(2S)	0136
A350X	0136
A350Y(2S)	0136
A351(2S)	0136
A351A(2S)	0136
A351A-2	0136
A351B(2S)	0136
A351C	0136
A351D	0136
A351E	0136
A351F	0136
A351G	0136
A351GN	0136
A351GR	0136
A351K	0136
A351L	0136
A351M	0136
A351OR	0136
A351R	0136
A351X	0136
A351Y	0136
A352(2S)	0136
A352A(2S)	0136
A352B(2S)	0136
A352C	0136
A352D	0136
A352E	0136
A352F	0136
A352G	0136
A352GN	0136
A352H	0136
A352J	0136
A352K	0136
A352L	0136
A352M	0136
A352OR	0136
A352R	0136
A352X	0136
A352Y	0136
A353(2S)	0136
A353-9008-001	0126
A353-AC	0136
A353A(2S)	0136
A353AL	0136
A353B	0136
A353C(2S)	0136
A353CL	0136
A353D	0136
A353E	0136
A353F	0136
A353G	0136
A353GN	0136
A353H	0136
A353J	0136
A353K	0136
A353L	0136
A353M	0136
A353OR	0136
A353R	0136
A353X	0136
A353Y	0136
A354(2S)	0136
A354-B	0136
A354A(2S)	0136
A354B	0136
A354BK	0136
A354C	0136
A354D	0136
A354E	0136
A354F	0136
A354G	0136
A354GN	0136
A354H	0136
A354J	0136
A354K	0136
A354L	0136
A354M	0136
A354OR	0136
A354R	0136
A354X	0136
A354Y	0136
A355(2S)	0136
A355A(2S)	0136

DEVICE TYPE	REPL CODE
A355B	0136
A355C	0136
A355D	0136
A355E	0136
A355F	0136
A355G	0136
A355H	0136
A355J	0136
A355K	0136
A355L	0136
A355M	0136
A355OR	0136
A355R	0136
A355X	0136
A355Y	0136
A356(2S)	0136
A356A	0136
A356B	0136
A356C	0136
A356D	0136
A356E	0136
A356F	0136
A356G	0136
A356GN	0136
A356H	0136
A356J	0136
A356K	0136
A356L	0136
A356M	0136
A356OR	0136
A356R	0136
A357(2S)	0136
A357A	0136
A357B	0136
A357C	0136
A357D	0136
A357E	0136
A357F	0136
A357G	0136
A357GN	0136
A357H	0136
A357J	0136
A357K	0136
A357L	0136
A357M	0136
A357OR	0136
A357R	0136
A357X	0136
A357Y	0136
A358(2S)	0136
A358-3	0136
A358A	0136
A358B	0136
A358C	0136
A358D	0136
A358E	0136
A358F	0136
A358G	0136
A358GN	0136
A358H	0136
A358J	0136
A358K	0136
A358L	0136
A358M	0136
A358OR	0136
A358R	0136
A358X	0136
A358Y	0136
A359(2S)	0136
A359A	0136
A359B	0136
A359C	0136
A359D	0136
A359E	0136
A359F	0136
A359G	0136
A359GN	0136
A359H	0136
A359J	0136
A359K	0136
A359L	0136
A359M	0136
A359OR	0136
A359R	0136
A359X	0136
A359Y	0136
A360(2S)	0050
A360A	0050
A360B	0050
A360C	0050
A360E	0050
A360F	0050
A360G	0050
A360GN	0050
A360H	0050
A360J	0050
A360K	0050
A360L	0050
A360M	0050
A360OR	0050
A360R	0050
A360X	0050
A360Y	0050
A361(2S)	0050
A361A	0050
A361B	0050
A361C	0050
A361D	0050
A361E	0050

DEVICE TYPE	REPL CODE
A361F	0050
A361G	0050
A361GN	0050
A361H	0050
A361J	0050
A361K	0050
A361L	0050
A361M	0050
A361OR	0050
A361R	0050
A361X	0050
A361Y	0050
A362(2S)	0050
A363(2S)	0050
A364(2S)	0136
A364A	0136
A364B	0136
A364C	0136
A364D	0136
A364E	0136
A364F	0136
A364G	0136
A364GN	0136
A364H	0136
A364J	0136
A364K	0136
A364L	0136
A364M	0136
A364OR	0136
A364R	0136
A364X	0136
A364Y	0136
A365(2S)	0136
A365A	0136
A365B	0136
A365C	0136
A365D	0136
A365E	0136
A365F	0136
A365G	0136
A365GN	0136
A365H	0136
A365J	0136
A365K	0136
A365L	0136
A365M	0136
A365OR	0136
A365R	0136
A365X	0136
A365Y	0136
A366(2S)	0136
A366A	0136
A366B	0136
A366C	0136
A366D	0136
A366E	0136
A366F	0136
A366G	0136
A366GN	0136
A366H	0136
A366J	0136
A366K	0136
A366L	0136
A366M	0136
A366OR	0136
A366R	0136
A366X	0136
A366Y	0136
A367(2S)	0136
A367A	0136
A367B	0136
A367C	0136
A367D	0136
A367E	0136
A367F	0136
A367G	0136
A367GN	0136
A367H	0136
A367J	0136
A367K	0136
A367L	0136
A367M	0136
A367OR	0136
A367R	0136
A367X	0136
A367Y	0136
A368(2S)	0136
A368A	0136
A368B	0136
A368C	0136
A368D	0136
A368E	0136
A368F	0136
A368G	0136
A368GN	0136
A368H	0136
A368J	0136
A368K	0136
A368L	0136
A368M	0136
A368OR	0136
A368R	0136
A368X	0136
A368Y	0136
A369(2S)	0136
A369A	0136
A369B	0136
A369C	0136
A369D	0136

DEVICE TYPE	REPL CODE
A369E	0136
A369F	0136
A369G	0136
A369GN	0136
A369H	0136
A369J	0136
A369K	0136
A369L	0136
A369M	0136
A369OR	0136
A369R	0136
A369X	0136
A369Y	0136
A370	0164
A371	0164
A372(2S)	0050
A373(2S)	0004
A373A	0004
A374(2S)	0004
A375(2S)	0004
A375A	0004
A375B	0004
A375C	0004
A375D	0004
A375E	0004
A375F	0004
A375G	0004
A375GN	0004
A375H	0004
A375J	0004
A375K	0004
A375L	0004
A375M	0004
A375OR	0004
A375R	0004
A375X	0004
A375Y	0004
A376	0136
A376A	0136
A376B	0136
A376C	0136
A376D	0136
A376E	0136
A376F	0136
A376GN	0136
A376H	0136
A376J	0136
A376K	0136
A376L	0136
A376OR	0136
A376R	0136
A376X	0136
A376Y	0136
A377(2S)	0050
A377A	0050
A377B	0050
A377C	0050
A377D	0050
A377E	0050
A377F	0050
A377G	0050
A377GN	0050
A377H	0050
A377J	0050
A377K	0050
A377L	0050
A377M	0050
A377OR	0050
A377R	0050
A377X	0050
A377Y	0050
A378(2S)	0050
A379(2S)	0050
A380(2S)	0136
A380A	0136
A380B	0136
A380C	0136
A380D	0136
A380E	0136
A380F	0136
A380G	0136
A380GN	0136
A380H	0136
A380J	0136
A380K	0136
A380L	0136
A380M	0136
A380OR	0136
A380R	0136
A380X	0136
A380Y	0136
A381(2S)	0136
A381A	0136
A381B	0136
A381D	0136
A381E	0136
A381F	0136
A381G	0136
A381GN	0136
A381H	0136
A381K	0136
A381L	0136
A381M	0136
A381OR	0136
A381R	0136
A381X	0136
A381Y	0136
A382(2S)	0136
A382A	0136

DEVICE TYPE	REPL CODE
A382B	0136
A382C(2S)	0136
A382D	0136
A382E	0136
A382F	0136
A382G	0136
A382GN	0136
A382H	0136
A382J	0136
A382K	0136
A382L	0136
A382M	0136
A382OR	0136
A382R	0136
A382X	0136
A382Y	0136
A383(2S)	0136
A383A	0136
A383B	0136
A383C	0136
A383D	0136
A383E	0136
A383F	0136
A383G	0136
A383GN	0136
A383H	0136
A383J	0136
A383K	0136
A383L	0136
A383M	0136
A383OR	0136
A383R	0136
A383X	0136
A383Y	0136
A384(2S)	0136
A384A	0136
A384B	0136
A384C	0136
A384D	0136
A384E	0136
A384F	0136
A384G	0136
A384GN	0136
A384H	0136
A384J	0136
A384K	0136
A384L	0136
A384M	0136
A384OR	0136
A384R	0136
A384X	0136
A384Y	0136
A385(2S)	0136
A385A(2S)	0136
A385B	0136
A385C	0136
A385D(2S)	0136
A385E	0136
A385F	0136
A385G	0136
A385GN	0136
A385H	0136
A385J	0136
A385K	0136
A385L	0136
A385M	0136
A385OR	0136
A385R	0136
A385X	0136
A385Y	0136
A386	0050
A387	0050
A387A	OEM
A387B	OEM
A387C	OEM
A387D	OEM
A387E	OEM
A387M	OEM
A387N	OEM
A387P	OEM
A387PA	OEM
A387PB	OEM
A387S	OEM
A387T	OEM
A389	0050
A390	OEM
A390(2S)	0050
A390A	1217
A390B	1217
A390C	1217
A390D	1217
A390E	1217
A390M	1217
A390N	1195
A390P	1195
A390PA	1195
A390PB	1195
A390PC	OEM
A390PD	OEM
A390PE	OEM
A390S	1195
A390T	1195
A391(2S)	0279
A391A	0279
A391B	0279
A391C	0279
A391D	0279
A391E	0279
A391F	0279

If replacement code is OEM, contact original manufacturer for replacement.

DEVICE TYPE	REPL CODE
A391G	0279
A391GN	0279
A391H	0279
A391J	0279
A391K	0279
A391L	0279
A391M	0279
A391OR	0279
A391R	0279
A391X	0279
A391Y	0279
A392	0279
A392(2S)	0279
A392A	0279
A392B	0279
A392C	0279
A392D	0279
A392E	0279
A392F	0279
A392G	0279
A392GN	0279
A392H	0279
A392J	0279
A392K	0279
A392L	0279
A392M	0279
A392OR	0279
A392R	0279
A392X	0279
A392Y	0279
A393(2S)	0279
A393A(2S)	0279
A394(2S)	0279
A394A	0279
A394B	0279
A394C	0279
A394D	0279
A394E	0279
A394F	0279
A394G	0279
A394GN	0279
A394H	0279
A394J	0279
A394K	0279
A394L	0279
A394M	0279
A394OR	0279
A394R	0279
A394X	0279
A394Y	0279
A395(2S)	0279
A395A	0279
A395B	0279
A395C	0279
A395D	0279
A395E	0279
A395F	0279
A395G	0279
A395GN	0279
A395H	0279
A395J	0279
A395K	0279
A395L	0279
A395M	0279
A395OR	0279
A395R	0279
A395X	0279
A395Y	0279
A396	0211
A396A	OEM
A396B	OEM
A396C	OEM
A396D	OEM
A396E	OEM
A396M	OEM
A396N	OEM
A396P	OEM
A396S	OEM
A396T	OEM
A397(2S)	0211
A397A	1217
A397B	1217
A397C	1217
A397D	1217
A397E	1217
A397M	1217
A397N	1195
A397P	1195
A397PA	1195
A397PB	1195
A397PC	OEM
A397PD	OEM
A397PE	OEM
A397S	1217
A397T	1195
A398(2S)	0211
A398A	1217
A398A(TRANS)	0211
A398B	1217
A398B(TRANS)	0211
A398C	1217
A398C(TRANS)	0211
A398D	1217
A398D(TRANS)	0211
A398E	1217
A398E(TRANS)	0211
A398F	0211
A398G	0211
A398GN	0211

DEVICE TYPE	REPL CODE
A398H	0211
A398J	0211
A398K	0211
A398L	0211
A398M	1217
A398M(TRANS)	0211
A398N	1195
A398OR	0211
A398P	1195
A398PA	1195
A398PB	1195
A398PC	OEM
A398PD	OEM
A398PE	OEM
A398S	1195
A398T	1195
A398X	0211
A398Y	0211
A399(2S)	0211
A399A	0211
A399B	0211
A399C	0211
A399D	0211
A399E	OEM
A399E(TRANS)	0211
A399F	0211
A399G	0211
A399GN	0211
A399H	0211
A399J	0211
A399K	0211
A399L	0211
A399M	OEM
A399M(TRANS)	0211
A399N	OEM
A399OR	0211
A399P	OEM
A399PA	OEM
A399PB	OEM
A399PC	OEM
A399PD	OEM
A399S	OEM
A399T	OEM
A399X	0211
A399Y	0211
A400	0015
A400(TRANS)	0136
A400A	0136
A400B	0136
A400C	0136
A400D	0136
A400E	0136
A400F	0136
A400G	0136
A400GN	0136
A400H	0136
A400J	0136
A400K	0136
A400L	0136
A400M	0136
A400OR	0136
A400R	0136
A400X	0136
A400Y	0136
A401	0136
A401(2S)	0136
A402(2S)	0037
A402DA	OEM
A402DB	OEM
A402DC	OEM
A402DD	OEM
A402DE	OEM
A402DM	OEM
A402DN	OEM
A402DP	OEM
A402DS	OEM
A402DT	OEM
A402EA	OEM
A402EB	OEM
A402EC	OEM
A402ED	OEM
A402EE	OEM
A402EM	OEM
A402EP	OEM
A403	0050
A403(2S)	0050
A403A	0050
A403B	0050
A403C	0050
A403D	0050
A403E	0050
A403F	0050
A403G	0050
A403GN	0050
A403H	0050
A403J	0050
A403K	0050
A403L	0050
A403M	0050
A403OR	0050
A403R	0050
A403X	0050
A403Y	0050
A404(2S)	0050
A404A	0050
A404B	0050
A404C	0050
A404D	0050
A404E	0050

DEVICE TYPE	REPL CODE
A404F	0050
A404G	0050
A404GN	0050
A404H	0050
A404K	0050
A404L	0050
A404M	0050
A404OR	0050
A404R	0050
A404X	0050
A404Y	0050
A405(2S)	0050
A405-O	0050
A406	0004
A406(2S)	0004
A406A	0004
A406B	0004
A406C	0004
A406D	0004
A406E	0004
A406G	0004
A406GN	0004
A406H	0004
A406J	0004
A406K	0004
A406L	0004
A406M	0004
A406OR	0004
A406R	0004
A406X	0004
A406Y	0004
A407(2S)	0004
A407A	0004
A407B	0004
A407C	0004
A407D	0004
A407E	0004
A407F	0004
A407G	0004
A407GN	0004
A407H	0004
A407J	0004
A407K	0004
A407L	0004
A407M	0004
A407OR	0004
A407R	0004
A407X	0004
A407Y	0004
A408(2S)	0136
A408A	0136
A408B	0136
A408D	0136
A408E	0136
A408F	0136
A408GN	0136
A408H	0136
A408J	0136
A408K	0136
A408L	0136
A408M	0136
A408OR	0136
A408R	0136
A408X	0136
A408Y	0136
A409(2S)	0136
A409A	0136
A409B	0136
A409C	0136
A409D	0136
A409E	0136
A409F	0136
A409G	0136
A409GN	0136
A409H	0136
A409J	0136
A409K	0136
A409L	0136
A409M	0136
A409OR	0136
A409R	0136
A409X	0136
A409Y	0136
A410(2S)	0050
A411	0050
A411(2S)	0050
A412(2S)	0136
A412A	0136
A412B	0136
A412C	0136
A412D	0136
A412E	0136
A412F	0136
A412G	0136
A412GN	0136
A412H	0136
A412J	0136
A412K	0136
A412L	0136
A412M	0136
A412OR	0136
A412R	0136
A412X	0136
A412Y	0136
A413(2S)	0050
A414(2S)	0279
A414A	0279
A414B	0279
A414C	0279

DEVICE TYPE	REPL CODE
A414D	0279
A414E	0279
A414F	0279
A414G	0279
A414GN	0279
A414H	0279
A414J	0279
A414K	0279
A414L	0279
A414M	0279
A414OR	0279
A414R	0279
A414X	0279
A-415	0079
A415	0016
A415(2S)	0279
A415A	0279
A415B	0279
A415C	0279
A415D	0279
A415E	0279
A415F	0279
A415G	0279
A415H	0279
A415J	0279
A415K	0279
A415L	0279
A415M	0279
A415OR	0279
A415R	0279
A415X	0279
A415Y	0279
A416(2S)	0160
A416A	0160
A416B	0160
A416C	0160
A416D	0160
A416E	0160
A416F	0160
A416G	0160
A416GN	0160
A416H	0160
A416J	0160
A416K	0160
A416L	0160
A416M	0160
A416OR	0160
A416R	0160
A416X	0160
A416Y	0160
A417	0211
A417(2S)	0211
A417-19	0007
A417-43	0126
A417-62	0160
A417-115	0233
A417-116	0037
A417-132	0037
A417-138	0126
A417-153	0037
A417-154	0127
A417-170	0126
A417-176	0037
A417-182	0037
A417-184	0037
A417-190	0127
A417-196	0037
A417-200	0037
A417-201	0037
A417-205	0127
A417-234	0126
A417-235	0037
A418	0144
A419	0144
A419(2S)	0050
A420	0144
A420(2S)	0050
A420A	0050
A420B	0050
A420C	0050
A420D	0050
A420E	0050
A420F	0050
A420G	0050
A420H	0050
A420J	0050
A420K	0050
A420L	0050
A420M	0050
A420OR	0050
A420R	0050
A420X	0050
A420Y	0050
A421(2S)	0050
A422(2S)	0050
A422-A	0015
A423	0279
A424	5484
A424(2S)	0279
A425(2S)	0050
A426(2S)	0050
A426GN	0050
A427	0144
A427(2S)	0136
A427A	0136
A427B	0136
A427C	0136
A427D	0136
A427E	0136

DEVICE TYPE	REPL CODE
A427F	0136
A427G	0136
A427GN	0136
A427H	0136
A427J	0136
A427K	0136
A427L	0136
A427M	0136
A427OR	0136
A427R	0136
A427X	0136
A427Y	0136
A428(2S)	0136
A428A	0136
A428B	0136
A428C	0136
A428D	0136
A428E	0136
A428F	0136
A428G	0136
A428GN	0136
A428H	0136
A428J	0136
A428K	0136
A428L	0136
A428M	0136
A428OR	0136
A428R	0136
A428X	0136
A428Y	0136
A429(2S)	2714
A429-0981-12	0007
A429-O(2S)	2714
A429A	2714
A429B	2714
A429C	2714
A429D	2714
A429E	2714
A429F	2714
A429G	2714
A429GN	2714
A429G-O	2714
A429G-R	2714
A429G-Y	2714
A429H	2714
A429J	2714
A429K	2714
A429L	2714
A429M	2714
A429OR	2714
A429R(2S)	2714
A429X	2714
A430	0259
A430(2S)	0050
A430A	3722
A430B	3722
A430C	2146
A430D	2146
A430E	2146
A430M	2146
A430N	0474
A430P	0474
A430PA	0474
A430PB	0474
A430PC	OEM
A430PD	OEM
A430PE	OEM
A430PM	OEM
A430PS	OEM
A430S	0474
A430T	0474
A431	0050
A431(2S)	0050
A431A(2S)	0050
A432(2S)	0050
A432A(2S)	0050
A432B	0050
A432C	0050
A432D	0050
A432E	0050
A432F	0050
A432G	0050
A432GN	0050
A432H	0050
A432K	0050
A432L	0050
A432L(DIO)	OEM
A432LA	OEM
A432LB	OEM
A432LC	OEM
A432LD	OEM
A432LE	OEM
A432LM	OEM
A432M	0050
A432OR	0050
A432PM	OEM
A432PN	OEM
A432PT	OEM
A432R	0050
A432X	0050
A432Y	0050
A433(2S)	0050
A433A	0050
A433B	0050
A433C	0050
A433CA	OEM
A433CB	OEM
A433CP	OEM
A433D	0050

DEVICE TYPE	REPL CODE
A433E	0050
A433F	0050
A433G	0050
A433GN	0050
A433H	0050
A433K	0050
A433L	0050
A433L(DIO)	OEM
A433LB	OEM
A433LD	OEM
A433LM	OEM
A433LN	OEM
A433LS	OEM
A433LT	OEM
A433M	0050
A433OR	0050
A433PM	OEM
A433PN	OEM
A433PS	OEM
A433PT	OEM
A433R	0050
A433X	0050
A433Y	0050
A434(2S)	0050
A434A	0050
A434B	0050
A434C	0050
A434D	0050
A434E	0050
A434F	0050
A434G	0050
A434GN	0050
A434H	0050
A434J	0050
A434K	0050
A434L	0050
A434M	0050
A434OR	0050
A434R	0050
A434X	0050
A434Y	0050
A435	0050
A435(2S)	0050
A435A(2S)	0050
A435B(2S)	0050
A435C	0050
A435D	0050
A435E	0050
A435F	0050
A435G	0050
A435GN	0050
A435H	0050
A435J	0050
A435L	0050
A435M	0050
A435OR	0050
A435R	0050
A435X	0050
A435Y	0050
A436(2S)	0136
A436A	0136
A436B	0136
A436C	0136
A436D	0136
A436E	0136
A436F	0136
A436G	0136
A436GN	0136
A436H	0136
A436J	0136
A436K	0136
A437(2S)	0136
A437A	2146
A437A(TRANS)	0136
A437B	2146
A437B(TRANS)	0136
A437C	2146
A437C(TRANS)	0136
A437D	2146
A437D(TRANS)	0136
A437E	2146
A437E(TRANS)	0136
A437F	0136
A437G	0136
A437GN	0136
A437H	0136
A437J	0136
A437K	0136
A437L	0136
A437M	2146
A437M(TRANS)	0136
A437N	0474
A437OR	0136
A437P	0474
A437PA	0474
A437PB	0474
A437PC	OEM
A437PD	OEM
A437PE	OEM
A437R	0136
A437S	0474
A437T	0474
A437X	0136
A437Y	0136
A438(2S)	0136
A438A	0136
A438B	0136
A438C	0136
A438D	0136

DEVICE TYPE	REPL CODE
A438E	0136
A438F	0136
A438G	0136
A438GN	0136
A438H	0136
A438J	0136
A438K	0136
A438L	0136
A438M	0136
A438OR	0136
A438R	0136
A438X	0136
A438Y	0136
A440	0050
A440(2S)	0050
A440A(2S)	0050
A440AL	0050
A440B	0050
A440C	0050
A440D	0050
A440E	0050
A440F	0050
A440G	0050
A440GN	0050
A440H	0050
A440J	0050
A440K	0050
A440L	0050
A440M	0050
A440N	OEM
A440OR	0050
A440P	OEM
A440PA	OEM
A440PB	OEM
A440PC	OEM
A440PD	OEM
A440PE	OEM
A440R	0050
A440S	OEM
A440T	OEM
A440X	0050
A440Y	0050
A441	OEM
A441(2S)	0050
A442CA	OEM
A442CB	OEM
A442CP	OEM
A442L	OEM
A442LA	OEM
A442LB	OEM
A442LC	OEM
A442LD	OEM
A442LE	OEM
A442LM	OEM
A442LN	OEM
A442LS	OEM
A442LT	OEM
A442PM	OEM
A442PN	OEM
A442PT	OEM
A443	0004
A444	0004
A445	0004
A446(2S)	0211
A446A	0211
A446B	0211
A446C	0211
A446D	0211
A446E	0211
A446F	0211
A446G	0211
A446GN	0211
A446H	0211
A446J	0211
A446K	0211
A446L	0211
A446M	0211
A446OR	0211
A446R	0211
A446X	0211
A446Y	0211
A447(2S)	0136
A447A	OEM
A447A(2S)	0136
A447B	OEM
A447B(2S)	0136
A447C	OEM
A447C(2S)	0136
A447D	OEM
A447D(2S)	0136
A447E	OEM
A447E(2S)	0136
A447F	0136
A447G	0136
A447GN	0136
A447H	0136
A447J	0136
A447K	0136
A447L	0136
A447M	OEM
A447M(2S)	0136
A447N	OEM
A447OR	0136
A447P	OEM
A447PA	OEM
A447PB	OEM
A447PC	OEM
A447PD	OEM
A447PE	OEM

If replacement code is OEM, contact original manufacturer for replacement.

253

DEVICE TYPE	REPL CODE
A447R	0136
A447S	OEM
A447T	OEM
A447X	0136
A447Y	0136
A448(2S)	0050
A449	0136
A450(2S)	0050
A450H(2S)	0050
A451	0050
A451(2S)	0050
A451H(2S)	0050
A452(2S)	0050
A452H(2S)	0050
A453(2S)	0136
A453A	0136
A453B	0136
A453C	0136
A453D	0136
A453E	0136
A453F	0136
A453G	0136
A453GN	0136
A453H	0136
A453J	0136
A453K	0136
A453L	0136
A453M	0136
A453OR	0136
A453R	0136
A453X	0136
A453Y	0136
A454	0016
A454(2S)	0136
A454A	0136
A454B	0136
A454C	0136
A454D	0136
A454E	0136
A454F	0136
A454G	0136
A454GN	0136
A454H	0136
A454J	0136
A454K	0136
A454L	0136
A454OR	0136
A454R	0136
A454X	0136
A454Y	0136
A455	0673
A455(2S)	0136
A455A	0136
A455B	0136
A455C	0136
A455D	0136
A455E	0136
A455F	0136
A455G	0136
A455GN	0136
A455H	0136
A455J	0136
A455K	0136
A455L	0136
A455M	0136
A455OR	0136
A455R	0136
A455X	0136
A455Y	0136
A456(2S)	0136
A456A	0136
A456B	0136
A456C	0136
A456D	0136
A456E	0136
A456F	0136
A456G	0136
A456GN	0136
A456H	0136
A456J	0136
A456K	0136
A456L	0136
A456M	0136
A456OR	0136
A456R	0136
A456X	0136
A456Y	0136
A457(2S)	0136
A457A	0136
A457B	0136
A457C	0136
A457D	0136
A457E	0136
A457F	0136
A457G	0136
A457GN	0136
A457H	0136
A457J	0136
A457K	0136
A457L	0136
A457M	0136
A457OR	0136
A457R	0136
A457X	0136
A457Y	0136
A458	1056
A458C	1056
A459	0004
A459Y	0004
A460(2S)	0050
A461(2S)	0050
A462(2S)	0050
A463(2S)	0050
A463C	0050
A464(2S)	0050
A465	0150
A465-181-19	0007
A466	0086
A466(2S)	0136
A466-2(2S)	0136
A466-3(2S)	0136
A466A	0136
A466B	0136
A466BLK(2S)	0136
A466BLU(2S)	0136
A466C	0136
A466D	0136
A466E	0136
A466F	0136
A466G	0136
A466GN	0136
A466H	0136
A466J	0136
A466K	0136
A466L	0136
A466M	0136
A466OR	0136
A466R	0136
A466X	0136
A466Y	0136
A466YEL(2S)	0136
A467	0006
A467(2S)	0006
A467A	0006
A467B	0006
A467C	0006
A467D	0006
A467E	0006
A467F	0006
A467G(2S)	0006
A467GN	0006
A467G-O(2S)	0006
A467G-R(2S)	0006
A467G-Y(2S)	0006
A467H	0006
A467J	0006
A467K	0006
A467L	0006
A467M	0006
A467OR	0006
A467R	0006
A467X	0006
A467Y	0006
A468(2S)	0136
A468A	0136
A468B	0136
A468C	0136
A468D	0136
A468E	0136
A468F	0136
A468G	0136
A468GN	0136
A468H	0136
A468J	0136
A468K	0136
A468L	0136
A468M	0136
A468OR	0136
A468R	0136
A468X	0136
A468Y	0136
A469(2S)	0136
A469A	0136
A469B	0136
A469C	0136
A469D	0136
A469E	0136
A469F	0136
A469G	0136
A469GN	0136
A469H	0136
A469J	0136
A469K	0136
A469L	0136
A469M	0136
A469OR	0136
A469R	0136
A469X	0136
A469Y	0136
A470(2S)	0136
A470A	0136
A470B	0136
A470C	0136
A470D	0136
A470E	0136
A470F	0136
A470G	0136
A470GN	0136
A470H	0136
A470J	0136
A470K	0136
A470L	0136
A470M	0136
A470OR	0136
A470R	0136
A470X	0136
A470Y	0136
A471(2S)	0136
A471-1(2S)	0136
A471-2(2S)	0136
A471-3(2S)	0136
A471A	0136
A471B	0136
A471C	0136
A471D	0136
A471E	0136
A471F	0136
A471G	0136
A471GN	0136
A471H	0136
A471J	0136
A471K	0136
A471L	0136
A471M	0136
A471OR	0136
A471R	0136
A471X	0136
A471Y	0136
A472	0079
A472(2S)	0136
A472-1	0136
A472-2	0136
A472-3	0136
A472-4	0136
A472-5	0136
A472-6	0136
A472A(2S)	0136
A472B(2S)	0136
A472C(2S)	0136
A472D(2S)	0136
A472E(2S)	0136
A472F	0136
A472G	0136
A472GN	0136
A472H	0136
A472J	0136
A472K	0136
A472L	0136
A472M	0136
A472OR	0136
A472R	0136
A472X	0136
A472Y	0136
A-473	0224
A473	0144
A473(2S)	0919
A473-GR(2S)	0919
A473-O(2S)	0919
A473-O(KOREA)	0919
A473-R(2S)	0919
A473-Y(2S)	0919
A473B	0919
A473D	0919
A473GR	0919
A473R	0919
A473Y(2S)	0919
A474(2S)	0136
A474-G	0136
A474A	0136
A474B	0136
A474C	0136
A474D	0136
A474E	0136
A474F	0136
A474G	0136
A474GN	0136
A474H	0136
A474J	0136
A474K	0136
A474L	0136
A474M	0136
A474OR	0136
A474R	0136
A474X	0136
A474Y	0136
A475	0050
A476(2S)	0136
A476A	0136
A476B	0136
A476C	0136
A476D	0136
A476E	0136
A476F	0136
A476G	0136
A476GN	0136
A476H	0136
A476J	0136
A476K	0136
A476L	0136
A476M	0136
A476OR	0136
A476R	0136
A476X	0136
A476Y	0136
A477(2S)	0136
A477A	0136
A477B	0136
A477C	0136
A477D	0136
A477E	0136
A477F	0136
A477G	0136
A477GN	0136
A477H	0136
A477J	0136
A477K	0136
A477L	0136
A477M	0136
A477OR	0136
A477R	0136
A477X	0136
A477Y	0136
A478(2S)	0004
A478-G	0004
A478A	0004
A478B	0004
A478C	0004
A478D	0004
A478E	0004
A478F	0004
A478G	0004
A478GN	0004
A478H	0004
A478J	0004
A478K	0004
A478L	0004
A478M	0004
A478OR	0004
A478R	0004
A478X	0004
A478Y	0004
A479(2S)	0004
A479-G	0004
A479A	0004
A479B	0004
A479C	0004
A479D	0004
A479E	0004
A479F	0004
A479G	0004
A479GN	0004
A479H	0004
A479J	0004
A479K	0004
A479L	0004
A479M	0004
A479OR	0004
A479R	0004
A479X	0004
A479Y	0004
A480	0144
A480(2S)	0037
A480-OR	0037
A480A	0037
A480B	0037
A480C	0037
A480D	0037
A480E	0037
A480F	0037
A480G	0037
A480GN	0037
A480H	0037
A480J	0037
A480K	0037
A480L	0037
A480M	0037
A480OR	0037
A480R	0037
A480X	0037
A480Y	0037
A481	0007
A482	0007
A482(2S)	0037
A482A	0037
A482B	0037
A482C	0037
A482D	0037
A482E	0037
A482F	0037
A482G	0037
A482GN	0037
A482H	0037
A482J	0037
A482K	0037
A482L	0037
A482M	0037
A482OR	0037
A482R	0037
A482X	0037
A482Y	0037
A483	0899
A483(2S)	0899
A483-O(2S)	0899
A483-R	0899
A483-Y	0899
A484	0007
A484(2S)	0886
A484(ADMIRAL)	0007
A484-BL	0886
A484-R	0886
A484-Y	0886
A485	0259
A485(2S)	0886
A485-BL	0886
A485-BLU	0886
A485-R	0886
A485-RED	0886
A485-Y	0886
A485-YEL	0886
A485Y	0886
A486	0007
A486(2S)	0886
A486-BL	0886
A486-BLU	0886
A486-R	0886
A486-RED	0886
A486-Y	0886
A486-YEL	0886
A488-A0060	0124
A489	0007
A489(2S)	0919
A489-O(2S)	0919
A489-R(2S)	0919
A489-Y(2S)	0919
A490	0007
A490(2S)	1490
A490-O	1490
A490-R	1490
A490-Y	1490
A490A	1490
A490B	1490
A490C	1490
A490D	1490
A490E	1490
A490F	1490
A490G	1490
A490GN	1490
A490H	1490
A490J	1490
A490K	1490
A490L	1490
A490M	1490
A490OR	1490
A490R	1490
A490X	1490
A490Y(2S)	1490
A490YA	1490
A492	0007
A493(2S)	0006
A493-GR	0006
A493-O(2S)	0006
A493-Y	0006
A493A	0006
A493B	0006
A493C	0006
A493D	0006
A493E	0006
A493F	0006
A493G	0006
A493G-GR	0006
A493GN	0006
A493G-Y	0006
A493H	0006
A493J	0006
A493K	0006
A493L	0006
A493M	0006
A493OR	0006
A493R	0006
A493X	0006
A493Y(2S)	0006
A-494	0079
A494	0688
A494(2S)	0688
A494-GR(2S)	0688
A494-GR-1	0688
A494-O(2S)	0688
A494-OR	0688
A494-Y(2S)	0688
A494A	0688
A494B	0688
A494C	0688
A494D	0688
A494E	0688
A494F	0688
A494G	0688
A494GN	0688
A494GR	0688
A494H	0688
A494J	0688
A494K	0688
A494L	0688
A494M	0688
A494O	0688
A494OR	0688
A494R	0688
A494X	0688
A494Y	0688
A495	0127
A495(2S)	0006
A495-O	0006
A495-1	0006
A495-GN	0006
A495-O(2S)	0006
A495-OF	0006
A495-OR	0006
A495-ORG	0006
A495-ORG-G	0006
A495-Q	0006
A495-R(2S)	0006
A495-RD	0006
A495-RED	0006
A495-RED-G	0006
A495-Y(2S)	0006
A495-YEL	0006
A495-YEL-G	0006
A495-YL	0006
A495A	0006
A495B	0006
A495C	0006
A495D(2S)	0006
A495E	0006
A495F	0006
A495G	0006
A495G-GR(2S)	0006
A495GN	0006
A495G-O(2S)	0006
A495G-R(2S)	0006
A495G-Y(2S)	0006
A495H	0006
A495J	0006
A495K	0006
A495L	0006
A495M	0006
A495O	0006
A495OF	0006
A495OR	0006
A495R	0006
A495RD	0006
A495RED	0006
A495RED-G	0006
A495RO	0006
A495W(2S)	0006
A495W1	0006
A495WI	0006
A495X	0006
A495Y(2S)	0006
A495YEL	0006
A495YEL-G	0006
A495YL	0006
A496	0006
A496(2S)	0520
A496-O(2S)	0520
A496-ORG	0520
A496-R(2S)	0520
A496-RED	0520
A496-Y(2S)	0520
A496-YEL	0520
A496O	0520
A496ORG	0520
A496R	0520
A496RED	0520
A496Y(2S)	0520
A496YEL	0520
A497	0144
A497(2S)	0126
A497-O	0126
A497-ORG	0126
A497-R	0126
A497-RED	0126
A497-Y	0126
A497-YEL	0126
A497R	0126
A497RED	0126
A497Y	0126
A498	OEM
A498(2S)	0126
A498(F.E.T.)	0212
A498-O	0126
A498-ORG	0126
A498-R	0126
A498-RED	0126
A498-Y	0126
A498-YEL	0126
A498R	0126
A498RED	0126
A498Y(2S)	0126
A499(2S)	0150
A499-O(2S)	0150
A499-ORG	0150
A499-R(2S)	0150
A499-RED	0150
A499-Y(2S)	0150
A499-YEL	0150
A499A	0150
A499B	0150
A499C	0150
A499D	0150
A499E	0150
A499F	0150
A499G	0150
A499GN	0150
A499H	0150
A499J	0150
A499K	0150
A499L	0150
A499M	0150
A499O	0150
A499OR	0150
A499R	0150
A499X	0150
A499Y	0150
A500	0150
A500(2S)	0150
A500-O(2S)	0150
A500-OR	0150
A500-ORG	0150
A500-R(2S)	0150
A500-RED	0150
A500-Y(2S)	0150
A500-YEL	0150
A500A	0150
A500B	0150
A500C	0150
A500D	0150
A500E	0150
A500F	0150
A500G	0150
A500GN	0150
A500H	0150
A500J	0150
A500K	0150
A500L	OEM
A500L(TRANS)	0150
A500LA	OEM
A500LB	OEM
A500LC	OEM
A500LD	OEM
A500LE	OEM
A500LM	OEM
A500LN	OEM
A500LP	OEM
A500LS	OEM
A500LT	OEM
A500M	0150
A500O	0150
A500OR	0150
A500P	OEM
A500PA	OEM
A500PB	OEM
A500PC	OEM
A500PD	OEM
A500PE	OEM
A500PM	OEM
A500PN	OEM
A500PS	OEM
A500PT	OEM
A500R	0150
A500X	0150
A500Y	0150
A501	0126
A501(2S)	0126
A502(2S)	0006
A502-O	0006
A502-OR	0006
A502-R	0006
A502-Y	0006
A502A	0006
A502B	0006
A502C	0006
A502D	0006
A502E	0006
A502F	0006
A502G	0006
A502GE	OEM
A502GN	0006
A502H	0006
A502J	0006
A502K	0006
A502L	0006
A502M	0006
A502OR	0006
A502R	0006
A502X	0006
A502Y	0006
A503	0126
A503(2S)	0126
A503-GR	0126
A503-GRN	0126
A503-O(2S)	0126
A503-ORG	0126
A503-R(2S)	0126
A503-Y(2S)	0126
A503-YEL	0126
A503G	0126
A503GE	OEM
A503O	0126
A503Y	0126
A504	0126
A504(2S)	0126
A504-GR	0126
A504-GRN	0126
A504-O	0126
A504-ORG	0126
A504-R(2S)	0126
A504-Y(2S)	0126
A504-YEL	0126
A504G	0126
A504GE	OEM
A504O	0126
A504Y	0126
A505(2S)	0520
A505-O(2S)	0520
A505-ORG	0520
A505-R(2S)	0520
A505-RED	0520
A505-Y(2S)	0520
A505-YEL	0520
A505O	0520
A505ORG	0520
A505R	0520
A505RED	0520
A505Y	0520
A505YEL	0520
A506(2S)	0050
A507(2S)	0050
A507A	0050
A507B	0050
A507C	0050
A507D	0050
A507E	0050
A507F	0050
A507G	0050
A507GN	0050
A507H	0050
A507J	0050
A507K	0050
A507L	0050
A507OR	0050
A507R	0050
A507X	0050
A507Y	0050
A508(2S)	0050

254

If replacement code is OEM, contact original manufacturer for replacement.

DEVICE TYPE	REPL CODE
A508D	0050
A508F	0050
A509(2S)	0006
A509-0	0006
A509-O(2S)	0006
A509-OR	0006
A509-R	0006
A509-RD	0006
A509-Y(2S)	0006
A509-YE	0006
A509A	0006
A509B	0006
A509BL	0006
A509C	0006
A509D	0006
A509E	0006
A509F	0006
A509G	0006
A509GN	0006
A509G-O	0006
A509GR(2S)	0006
A509GR-1	0006
A509G-Y	0006
A509H	0006
A509J	0006
A509K	0006
A509L	0006
A509M	0006
A509OR	0006
A509Q	0006
A509R(2S)	0006
A509RD	0006
A509T	0006
A509V	0006
A509X	0006
A509Y(2S)	0006
A509YE	0006
A510	0886
A510(2S)	0886
A510-O(2S)	0886
A510-OR	0886
A510-ORG	0886
A510-R(2S)	0886
A510-RD	0886
A510-RED	0886
A510A	0886
A510B	0886
A510C	0886
A510D	0886
A510E	0886
A510F	0886
A510G	0886
A510GN	0886
A510H	0886
A510J	0886
A510K	0886
A510L	0886
A510M	0886
A510OR	0886
A510R	0886
A510X	0886
A510Y	0886
A511	0886
A511(2S)	0886
A511-G	0886
A511-O(2S)	0886
A511-OR	0886
A511-ORG	0886
A511-R(2S)	0886
A511-RD	0886
A511-RED	0886
A511A	0886
A511B	0886
A511C	0886
A511D	0886
A511E	0886
A511F	0886
A511G	0886
A511GN	0886
A511H	0886
A511J	0886
A511K	0886
A511L	0886
A511M	0886
A511OR	0886
A511R	0886
A511X	0886
A511Y	0886
A512(2S)	0886
A512-O(2S)	0886
A512-OR	0886
A512-OR1	0886
A512-ORG	0886
A512-R(2S)	0886
A512-RD	0886
A512-RED	0886
A512A	0886
A512B	0886
A512C	0886
A512D	0886
A512E	0886
A512F	0886
A512G	0886
A512GN	0886
A512H	0886
A512J	0886
A512K	0886
A512L	0886
A512M	0886
A512OR	0886
A512R	0886
A512X	0886
A512Y	0886
A513(2S)	0886
A513-O(2S)	0886
A513-OR	0886
A513-ORG	0886
A513-R(2S)	0886
A513-RD	0886
A513-RED	0886
A513A	0886
A513B	0886
A513C	0886
A513D	0886
A513E	0886
A513F	0886
A513G	0886
A513GN	0886
A513H	0886
A513J	0886
A513K	0886
A513L	0886
A513M	0886
A513OR	0886
A513R	0886
A513X	0886
A513Y	0886
A514-022057	0143
A514-023553	0595
A514-023626	0015
A514-025607	0015
A514-027662	0279
A514-027757	0015
A514-028072	0015
A514-028073	0015
A514-032815	0279
A514-033338	0155
A514-033903	0015
A514-035596	0015
A514-038984	0087
A514-040296	0321
A514-042791	0133
A514-044910	0037
A514-047830	0419
A514-0339903	0015
A515	0103
A516	0886
A516(2S)	0886
A516A(2S)	0886
A517	0136
A517(2S)	0136
A518(2S)	0136
A518-G	0136
A518A	0136
A518B	0136
A518C	0136
A518D	0136
A518E	0136
A518F	0136
A518G	0136
A518GN	0136
A518H	0136
A518J	0136
A518K	0136
A518L	0136
A518M	0136
A518OR	0136
A518R	0136
A518X	0136
A518Y	0136
A520	OEM
A521	OEM
A522	0103
A522(2S)	0037
A522-3	0103
A522A(2S)	0037
A522AL	0037
A522B	0037
A522C	0037
A522D	0037
A522E	0037
A522F	0037
A522G	0037
A522GN	0037
A522H	0037
A522J	0037
A522K	0037
A522L	0037
A522M	0037
A522OR	0037
A522R	0037
A522X	0037
A522Y	0037
A523	0103
A523(2S)	0126
A523A	0126
A524	0037
A525(2S)	0050
A525A(2S)	0050
A525B(2S)	0050
A525C	0050
A525D	0050
A525E	0050
A525F	0050
A525GN	0050
A525H	0050
A525J	0050
A525K	0050
A525L	0050
A525M	0050
A525OR	0050
A525R	0050
A525X	0050
A525Y	0050
A526	0037
A527(2S)	0126
A528(2S)	0126
A529	0126
A530(2S)	0037
A530A	0037
A530B	0037
A530C	0037
A530D	0037
A530E	0037
A530F	0037
A530G	0037
A530GN	0037
A530GR	0037
A530H(2S)	0037
A530H1	0037
A530HA	0037
A530HB	0037
A530HC	0037
A530J	0037
A530K	0037
A530L	0037
A530M	0037
A530OR	0037
A530R	0037
A530X	0037
A530Y	0037
A532(2S)	0126
A532A(2S)	0126
A532B(2S)	0126
A532C(2S)	0126
A532D(2S)	0126
A532E(2S)	0126
A532F(2S)	0126
A535	0037
A536	0050
A537(2S)	0126
A537A(2S)	0126
A537AA(2S)	0126
A537AB(2S)	0126
A537AC(2S)	0126
A537AH(2S)	0126
A537AHA	0126
A537AHB	0126
A537AHC	0126
A537H(2S)	0126
A537HA	0126
A537HB	0126
A537HC	0126
A537K	0126
A537L	0126
A538(2S)	0004
A538-G	0004
A538G	0004
A539(2S)	0006
A539A	0006
A539B	0006
A539C	0006
A539D	0006
A539E	0006
A539F	0006
A539G	0006
A539GN	0006
A539H	0006
A539J	0006
A539K	0006
A539L(2S)	0006
A539M	0006
A539OR	0006
A539R	0006
A539X	0006
A539Y	0006
A539Y(EBC)	2022
A539Y(KOREA)	0037
A540A	OEM
A540B	OEM
A540C	OEM
A540D	OEM
A540E	OEM
A540L	OEM
A540LA	OEM
A540LB	OEM
A540LC	OEM
A540LD	OEM
A540LE	OEM
A540LM	OEM
A540M	OEM
A540N	OEM
A540P	OEM
A540PA	OEM
A540PB	OEM
A540PC	OEM
A540PD	OEM
A540PE	OEM
A540PM	OEM
A540PN	OEM
A540PS	OEM
A540PT	OEM
A540S	OEM
A540T	OEM
A542(2S)	0037
A542A	0037
A542B	0037
A542C	0037
A542D	0037
A542E	0037
A542F	0037
A542G	0037
A542GN	0037
A542H	0037
A542J	0037
A542K	0037
A542L	0037
A542M	0037
A542OR	0037
A542R	0037
A542X	0037
A542Y	0037
A543(2S)	0688
A544(2S)	0126
A544A	0126
A544B	0126
A544C	0126
A544D	0126
A544E	0126
A544F	0126
A544G	0126
A544GN	0126
A544H	0126
A544J	0126
A544K	0126
A544L	0126
A544M	0126
A544OR	0126
A544R	0126
A544X	0126
A544Y	0126
A545(2S)	0786
A545A	0786
A545B	0786
A545C	0786
A545D	0786
A545E	0786
A545F	0786
A545G	0786
A545GN	0786
A545H	0786
A545J	0786
A545K(2S)	0786
A545KLM(2S)	0786
A545L(2S)	0786
A545LM(2S)	0786
A545M	0786
A545OR	0786
A545R	0786
A545X	0786
A545Y	0786
A546(2S)	0126
A546A(2S)	0126
A546B(2S)	0126
A546E(2S)	0126
A546H(2S)	0126
A547(2S)	0786
A547A(2S)	0786
A548(2S)	0150
A548G	0150
A548GN	0150
A548H	0150
A548HA	0150
A548HB	0150
A548HC	0150
A548OR	0150
A548R	0150
A548Y	0150
A549	0338
A549A(2S)	0338
A549AH(2S)	0338
A550(2S)	0037
A550A(2S)	0037
A550AB	0037
A550AQ(2S)	0037
A550AR	0037
A550AS	0037
A550B	0037
A550BC	0037
A550BL	0037
A550C	0037
A550D	0037
A550P	0037
A550Q(2S)	0037
A550R(2S)	0037
A550S(2S)	0037
A550Y	0037
A551	0126
A551(2S)	0126
A551C(2S)	0126
A551D(2S)	0126
A551E(2S)	0126
A552(2S)	0126
A553	0037
A554	0037
A554A	0037
A555	0006
A556	0006
A556-142	0143
A557	0150
A558	0037
A559	0037
A559A	0037
A560	0126
A560A	0126
A561	0006
A561(2S)	0006
A561-0	0006
A561-GR	0006
A561-GRN	0006
A561-O(2S)	0006
A561-OR	0006
A561-ORG	0006
A561-R(2S)	0006
A561-RD	0006
A561-RED	0006
A561-Y(2S)	0006
A561-YEL	0006
A561-YL	0006
A561GRN	0006
A561R	0006
A561RD	0006
A561RED	0006
A561Y	0006
A561YEL	0006
A561YL	0006
A562	0006
A562-0	0006
A562-GR	0006
A562-GRN	0006
A562-O	0006
A562-O(2S)	0006
A562-O(JAPAN)	0006
A562-O(KOREA)	0006
A562-OR	0006
A562-ORG	0006
A562-R(2S)	0006
A562-RD	0006
A562-RED	0006
A562-Y(2S)	0006
A562-YE	0006
A562-YEL	0006
A562D	0006
A562E	0006
A562G(2S)	0006
A562GR(2S)	0006
A562GRN	0006
A562O	0006
A562Q	0006
A562R(2S)	0006
A562RD	0006
A562RED	0006
A562T	0006
A562TM	0006
A562TM-0	0006
A562TM-O	0006
A562TMO	0006
A562TM-OFA	0006
A562TM-Y	0006
A562TM-YFA	0006
A562TO	0006
A562TQ	0006
A562V	0006
A562VO	0006
A562Y	0006
A562Y(2S)	0006
A562Y(JAPAN)	0006
A562Y(KOREA)	0006
A562YE	0006
A562YEL	0006
A562Y-TM	0006
A564	0203
A564-0(2S)	0203
A564-1	0203
A564-O(2S)	0203
A564-OGD	0203
A564-OR	0203
A564-P	0203
A564-Q	0203
A564-R	0203
A564A(2S)	0203
A564A(JAPAN)	0203
A564ABQ-1	0203
A564AG	0203
A564AK	0203
A564AL	0203
A564AP(2S)	0203
A564A-Q	0203
A564AQ(2S)	0203
A564A-R	0203
A564AR	0203
A564AR(JAPAN)	0203
A564A-S	0203
A564AS(2S)	0203
A564B	0203
A564C	0203
A564D	0203
A564E	0203
A564F(2S)	0203
A564FQ(2S)	0203
A564FQ-1	0203
A564FR-1	0203
A564G	0203
A564GN	0203
A564H	0203
A564J(2S)	0203
A564K	0203
A564L	0203
A564M	0203
A564OR	0203
A564P(2S)	0203
A564P.A	0203
A564Q	0203
A564Q(2S)	0203
A564QP	0203
A564QR(2S)	0203
A564QRS	0203
A564R	0203
A564S(2S)	0203
A564T(2S)	0203
A564X	0203
A564XL	0203
A564Y	0203
A565(2S)	0037
A565A(2S)	0037
A565AB	0037
A565B(2S)	0037
A565BA	0037
A565C(2S)	0037
A565D(2S)	0037
A565E	0037
A565F	0037
A565G	0037
A565GN	0037
A565H	0037
A565J	0037
A565K(2S)	0037
A565L	0037
A565M	0037
A565OR	0037
A565R	0037
A565X	0037
A565Y	0037
A566(2S)	0899
A566A(2S)	0899
A566B(2S)	0899
A566C(2S)	0899
A566H	0899
A-567	0038
A567	0037
A567A	0037
A567B	0037
A567C	0037
A567D	0037
A567E	0037
A567F	0037
A567G	0037
A567GN	0037
A567GR	0037
A567H	0037
A567J	0037
A567K	0037
A567L	0037
A567M	0037
A567OR	0037
A567R	0037
A567X	0037
A567Y	0037
A568(2S)	0006
A568-OR	0006
A568A	0006
A568B	0006
A568C	0006
A568D	0006
A568E	0006
A568F	0006
A568G	0006
A568GN	0006
A568H	0006
A568J	0006
A568K	0006
A568L	0006
A568M	0006
A568OR	0006
A568R	0006
A568X	0006
A568Y	0006
A569	0006
A569(2S)	0006
A569A	0006
A569B	0006
A569C	0006
A569D	0006
A569E	0006
A569F	0006
A569G	0006
A569GN	0006
A569H	0006
A569J(2S)	0006
A569K	0006
A569L	0006
A569M	0006
A569OR	0006
A569R	0006
A569X	0006
A569Y	0006
A570	5505
A570(2S)	0006
A570A	4835
A570A(TRANS)	0006
A570B	4835
A570B(TRANS)	0006
A570C	4835
A570C(TRANS)	0006
A570D	4835
A570D(TRANS)	0006
A570E	4835
A570E(TRANS)	0006
A570F	0006
A570G	0006
A570GN	0006
A570H	0006
A570J	0006
A570K	0006
A570L	0006
A570M	4835
A570M(TRANS)	0006
A570N	OEM
A570OR	0006
A570P	OEM
A570R	0006
A570S	OEM
A570T	OEM
A570X	0006
A570Y	0006
A571(2S)	0126
A572	0103
A572(2S)	0688
A572-1	0103
A572Y	0688
A573	0006
A574	0431
A575	0006
A576	0150
A576-0001-002	0037
A576-0001-013	0037
A577	0431
A578(2S)	0688
A579(2S)	0688
A580	0126
A580-040215	0130
A580-040315	0130
A580-040515	0130
A580-080215	0130
A580-080315	0130
A580-080515	0130
A581	0126
A590	OEM
A591	OEM
A593	0016
A594(2S)	0126
A594-O(2S)	0126
A594-R(2S)	0126
A594-Y(2S)	0126
A594N	0126
A595	0004
A596M	OEM
A596N	OEM
A596P	OEM
A596PA	OEM
A596PB	OEM
A596PC	OEM
A596PD	OEM
A596PE	OEM
A596S	OEM
A596T	OEM
A597	0126
A599	0786
A599Y	0786
A600	0015
A600(RECTIFIER)	0015
A601	OEM
A602	OEM
A603	0037
A603(2S)	0037
A603A	0037
A603B	0037
A603C	0037
A603D	0037
A603E	0037
A603F	0037
A603G	0037
A603GN	0037
A603H	0037
A603J	0037
A603K	0037
A603L	0037
A603M	0037
A603OR	0037
A603R	0037
A603X	0037
A603Y	0037
A604	0126
A604(2S)	0126
A605	OEM
A605(2S)	0126
A606	0126
A606(2S)	0126
A607	0126
A607(2S)	4920
A607A	1543
A607B	1543
A607C	1543
A607D	1543
A607E	1543
A607F	1543
A607G	1543
A607GN	1543
A607H	1543
A607J	1543
A607K	4920
A607L	4920
A607M	4920
A607OR	1543
A607R	1543
A607S	4920
A607SA	1543
A607SB	1543
A607SC	1543
A607SD	1543
A607X	1543
A607Y	1543
A608	0006

If replacement code is OEM, contact original manufacturer for replacement.

DEVICE TYPE	REPL CODE
A608(2S)	0006
A608-0	0006
A608-C(2S)	0006
A608-E(2S)	0006
A608-F(2S)	0006
A608-O	0006
A608-OR	0006
A608A(2S)	0006
A608AE	0006
A608AF	0006
A608B(2S)	0006
A608BL	0006
A608C(2S)	0006
A608D(2S)	0006
A608E	0006
A608E(2S)	0006
A608E(JAPAN)	0006
A608F	0006
A608F(2S)	0006
A608F(JAPAN)	0006
A608G(2S)	0006
A608GN	0006
A608H	0006
A608J	0006
A608K	0006
A608KE	0006
A608KF	0006
A608KF(JAPAN)	0006
A608L	0006
A608M	0006
A608NP	0006
A608OR	0006
A608P	0006
A608R	0006
A608SP	0006
A608X	0006
A608Y	0006
A609(2S)	0037
A609A(2S)	0037
A609B(2S)	0037
A609C(2S)	0037
A609D(2S)	0037
A609E(2S)	0037
A609F(2S)	0037
A609G(2S)	0037
A609GN	0037
A609J	0037
A609K	0037
A609L	0037
A609M	0037
A609OR	0037
A609R	0037
A609Y	0037
A610	0006
A610(2S)	0006
A610L	OEM
A610S	OEM
A611	0006
A611(2S)	0006
A611L	OEM
A611S	OEM
A612	OEM
A612(2S)	0126
A613(2S)	0899
A614(2S)	0899
A615-1008	0050
A615-1009	0050
A615-1010	0004
A615-1011	0004
A615-1012	0143
A616(1)	0899
A616(2)	0899
A616(2S)	0899
A617	0338
A617K(2S)	0338
A618	0338
A618K(2S)	0338
A620	0006
A620CA	OEM
A620CB	OEM
A620CC	OEM
A620CD	OEM
A620CE	OEM
A620CM	OEM
A620CN	OEM
A620CS	OEM
A620CT	OEM
A620DA	OEM
A620DC	OEM
A620DD	OEM
A620DP	OEM
A620LP	OEM
A620PC	OEM
A621	0037
A621A	OEM
A621B	OEM
A621C	OEM
A621D	OEM
A621E	OEM
A621M	OEM
A621N	OEM
A621P	OEM
A621PA	OEM
A621PB	OEM
A621S	OEM
A621T	OEM
A622	3477
A623(2S)	1421
A623-O(2S)	1421

DEVICE TYPE	REPL CODE
A624(2S)	1421
A625	0126
A626(2S)	3459
A626L	3459
A627(2S)	3459
A628(2S)	0006
A628-O	0006
A628-OR	0006
A628A(2S)	0006
A628A(JAPAN)	0006
A628AA	0006
A628AD	0006
A628A-E	0006
A628AE	0006
A628A-F	0006
A628B	0006
A628C	0006
A628D(2S)	0006
A628E(2S)	0006
A628EF	0006
A628F(2S)	0006
A628G	0006
A628GN	0006
A628H	0006
A628J	0006
A628K	0006
A628L	0006
A628M	0006
A628OR	0006
A628R	0006
A628X	0006
A628Y	0006
A629(2S)	0688
A629A	0688
A629B	0688
A629C	0688
A629D	0688
A629E	0688
A629F	0688
A629G	0688
A629GN	0688
A629H	0688
A629J	0688
A629K	0688
A629L	0688
A629M	0688
A629OR	0688
A629R	0688
A629X	0688
A629Y	0688
A633	1045
A633A	1045
A634(2S)	0676
A634(4)K	0676
A634(4)L	0676
A634-O(KOREA)	1045
A634A(2S)	0676
A634K(2S)	0676
A634L(2S)	0676
A634M(2S)	0676
A635	0378
A636(2S)	2010
A636(4)K	2010
A636(4)L	2010
A636-4K	2010
A636-4L	2010
A636A(2S)	2010
A636B(2S)	2010
A636C(2S)	2010
A636D(2S)	2010
A636K(2S)	2010
A636L(2S)	2010
A636M(2S)	2010
A637(2S)	0338
A637C	0338
A637D	0338
A638(2S)	0338
A638E	0338
A638F	0338
A638S	0338
A639(2S)	0338
A639L	0338
A639S	0338
A640	0688
A640(2S)	0688
A640A(2S)	0688
A640B(2S)	0688
A640C(2S)	0688
A640D(2S)	0688
A640L	0688
A640LA	OEM
A640M(2S)	0688
A640P	OEM
A640PA	OEM
A640PB	OEM
A640PC	OEM
A640PD	OEM
A640PE	OEM
A640PM	OEM
A640PN	OEM
A640PS	OEM
A640PT	OEM
A640S	0688
A640T	OEM
A641	0688
A641(2S)	0688
A641(PBP)	0688
A641A(2S)	0688
A641B(2S)	0688

DEVICE TYPE	REPL CODE
A641BL	0688
A641C(2S)	0688
A641D(2S)	0688
A641G	0688
A641GR	0688
A641K	0688
A641L	0688
A641L(2S)	0688
A641L(DIO)	OEM
A641LA	OEM
A641LB	OEM
A641LC	OEM
A641LD	OEM
A641LE	OEM
A641LM	OEM
A641M(2S)	0688
A641O	0688
A641OR	0688
A641PD	OEM
A641PE	OEM
A641PM	OEM
A641PN	OEM
A641PS	OEM
A641PT	OEM
A641R	0688
A641S	0688
A641Y	0688
A642	0006
A642(2S)	0006
A642-254	0144
A642-260	0144
A642-268	0144
A642-O	0037
A642-O(EBC)	0037
A642A(2S)	0006
A642B(2S)	0006
A642C(2S)	0006
A642D(2S)	0006
A642E(2S)	0006
A642F(2S)	0006
A642G	0006
A642GN	0006
A642H	0006
A642J	0006
A642K	0006
A642L	0006
A642L(2S)	0006
A642M	0006
A642OR	0006
A642R	0006
A642S	0006
A642S(2S)	0006
A642V	0006
A642W(2S)	0006
A642X	0006
A642Y	0006
A643(2S)	1233
A643L	1233
A643R(2S)	1233
A643S	1233
A643V(2S)	1233
A643W(2S)	1233
A644L	0111
A644S	0111
A645(2S)	1357
A645L	0111
A645S	0111
A646	1357
A646(2S)	1357
A647	0126
A648(2S)	2002
A649	2002
A649A	2002
A649L	0016
A649S	0016
A650	2002
A651	2002
A652	0787
A653	0787
A653L	0787
A656(2S)	3459
A656A	3459
A656L(2S)	3459
A656M(2S)	3459
A657	3459
A657A	3459
A658(2S)	3459
A658A	3459
A659(2S)	0006
A659A	0006
A659B	0006
A659D(2S)	0006
A659E(2S)	0006
A659F(2S)	0006
A659G	0006
A659L	0006
A659P	0006
A659R	0006
A659Y	0006
A661(2S)	0006
A661-GR	0006
A661-O(2S)	0006
A661-R	0006
A661-Y	0006
A661Y(2S)	0006
A663(2S)	0486
A663-BL	0486
A663-R	0486
A663-Y	0486

DEVICE TYPE	REPL CODE
A664	0527
A666(2S)	0006
A666A(2S)	0006
A666B	0006
A666BL	0006
A666C	0006
A666D	0006
A666E	0006
A666H(2S)	0006
A666HR(2S)	0006
A666I	0006
A666IQRS(2S)	0006
A666QRS	0006
A666R(2S)	0006
A666S(2S)	0006
A666Y	0006
A667-G	0079
A667-GRN	0111
A667-O	0086
A667-ORG	0111
A667-RED	0111
A667-Y	0079
A667-YEL	0111
A667RED	0144
A668	0126
A668-G	0079
A668-GRN	0111
A668-O	0086
A668-ORG	0111
A668-Y	0079
A668-YEL	0111
A669	0338
A669-G	0079
A669-GRN	0111
A669-Y	0079
A669-YEL	0111
A670(2S)	0919
A670A(2S)	0919
A670B(2S)	0919
A670C(2S)	0919
A671	1298
A671A	1298
A671B	1298
A671C	1298
A671K	1298
A671KA	1298
A671KB	1298
A671KC	1298
A671TD	1298
A672	0037
A672A(2S)	0037
A672B(2S)	0037
A672C(2S)	0037
A673(2S)	0148
A673-C	0148
A673-D	0148
A673-O	0148
A673-OR	0148
A673A	0148
A673A(2S)	0148
A673A(JAPAN)	0148
A673AB(2S)	0148
A673AC(2S)	0148
A673AC(JAPAN)	0148
A673AD(2S)	0148
A673AK	0148
A673AKA	0148
A673AKB	0148
A673AKC	0148
A673AKD	0148
A673AS(2S)	0148
A673B(2S)	0148
A673C	0148
A673C(2S)	0148
A673C(JAPAN)	0148
A673C2(2S)	0148
A673D	0148
A673D(2S)	0148
A673D(JAPAN)	0148
A673E	0148
A673F	0148
A673G	0148
A673GN	0148
A673H	0148
A673J	0148
A673K	0148
A673L	0148
A673M	0148
A673OR	0148
A673R	0148
A673X	0148
A673Y	0148
A675(2S)	0006
A676-60C-1	OEM
A676-60M-1	OEM
A676-90C	OEM
A676-90M	OEM
A676R-60C-1	OEM
A676R-60M1	OEM
A676R-90C	OEM
A676R-90M	OEM
A677(2S)	0006
A677-0	0006
A677-O	0006
A677-OR	0006
A677A	0006
A677B	0006
A677C	0006
A677D	0006

DEVICE TYPE	REPL CODE
A677E	0006
A677F	0006
A677G	0006
A677GN	0006
A677H	0006
A677HL	0006
A677J	0006
A677K	0006
A677L	0006
A677M	0006
A677OR	0006
A677R	0006
A677X	0006
A677Y	0006
A678(2S)	0006
A678-O	0006
A678-OR	0006
A678A	0006
A678B	0006
A678C	0006
A678D	0006
A678E	0006
A678F	0006
A678G	0006
A678GN	0006
A678H	0006
A678J	0006
A678K	0006
A678L	0006
A678M	0006
A678OR	0006
A678R	0006
A678X	0006
A678Y	0006
A679(2S)	2002
A679-R	2002
A679-Y	2002
A680(2S)	2002
A680-R	2002
A680-Y	2002
A681	0126
A682	0520
A682-O	0520
A682-Y	0520
A682O	0520
A683(2S)	0527
A683NC	0527
A683O	0527
A683P	0527
A683Q(2S)	0527
A683R(2S)	0527
A683S	0527
A683.4	0527
A684(2S)	0527
A684NC	0527
A684Q(2S)	0527
A684R(2S)	0527
A684S	0527
A685	0006
A689C	OEM
A689M	OEM
A690V081H97	0160
A691M4	0133
A691M5	0133
A691M5-2	0133
A692T5	0015
A692T5-O	0015
A692X13-4	0143
A692X16-O	0015
A693	0006
A693C	0006
A694X1	0053
A694X1-0A	0053
A694X1-OA	0361
A695	0431
A695C(2S)	0431
A695D(2S)	0431
A696#	OEM
A696(2S)	0006
A696D(2S)	0006
A696L	OEM
A696PE	OEM
A696PM	OEM
A696PN	OEM
A696PS	OEM
A696PT	OEM
A697(2S)	0006
A697C(2S)	0006
A698	0676
A699	0676
A699(H)	0676
A699A	0676
A699AP(2S)	0676
A699AQ(2S)	0676
A699AR(2S)	0676
A699CF(2S)	0676
A699P(2S)	0676
A699Q(2S)	0676
A699R(2S)	0676
A700(2S)	0919
A700B(2S)	0919
A700Y(2S)	0919
A701	0037
A701F(2S)	0037
A701FO	0037
A701FJ(2S)	0037
A701FO(2S)	0037
A702	0074
A702(2S)	0688

DEVICE TYPE	REPL CODE
A703(2S)	1421
A704	0006
A704A	0006
A704B	0006
A704C	0006
A704D	0006
A704E	0006
A704F	0006
A704G	0006
A704GN	0006
A704H	0006
A704J	0006
A704K	0006
A704L	0006
A704M	0006
A704OR	0006
A704R	0006
A704X	0006
A704Y	0006
A705	0006
A705(2S)	0006
A705A	0006
A705B	0006
A705C	0006
A705D	0006
A705E	0006
A705F	0006
A705G	0006
A705GN	0006
A705H	0006
A705J	0006
A705K	0006
A705L	0006
A705M	0006
A705OR	0006
A705R	0006
A705X	0006
A705Y	0006
A706	0378
A706-2	0378
A706-3	0378
A706-3A	OEM
A706-3C	OEM
A706-3D	OEM
A706-3E	OEM
A706-3F	OEM
A706-3G	OEM
A706-3H	OEM
A706-3I	OEM
A706-3J	OEM
A706-3K	OEM
A706-3L	OEM
A706-3M	OEM
A706-3N	OEM
A706-4	0378
A706-4A	OEM
A706-4B	OEM
A706-4C	OEM
A706-4D	OEM
A706-4E	OEM
A706-4F	OEM
A706-4G	OEM
A706-4H	OEM
A706-4I	OEM
A706-4J	OEM
A706-4K	OEM
A706-4L	OEM
A706-4M	OEM
A706-5A	OEM
A706-5B	OEM
A706-5C	OEM
A706-5D	OEM
A706-5E	OEM
A706-5F	OEM
A706-5G	OEM
A706-5H	OEM
A706-5I	OEM
A706-5J	OEM
A706-5K	OEM
A706-5L	OEM
A706-5M	OEM
A706-6A	OEM
A706-6B	OEM
A706-6C	OEM
A706-6D	OEM
A706-6E	OEM
A706-6F	OEM
A706-6G	OEM
A706-6H	OEM
A706-6I	OEM
A706-6J	OEM
A706-6K	OEM
A706-6L	OEM
A706-7A	OEM
A706-7B	OEM
A706-7C	OEM
A706-7D	OEM
A706-7E	OEM
A706-7F	OEM
A706-7G	OEM
A706-7H	OEM
A706-7I	OEM
A706-7J	OEM
A706-8A	OEM
A706-8B	OEM
A706-8C	OEM
A706-8D	OEM
A706-8E	OEM
A706-8F	OEM

DEVICE TYPE	REPL CODE
A706-8G	OEM
A706-8H	OEM
A706H	0378
A706J	0378
A707	OEM
A707(2S)	0431
A707(V)	0431
A707-3A	OEM
A707-3B	OEM
A707-3C	OEM
A707-3D	OEM
A707-3E	OEM
A707-3F	OEM
A707-3G	OEM
A707-3H	OEM
A707-3I	OEM
A707-3J	OEM
A707-3K	OEM
A707-3L	OEM
A707-3M	OEM
A707-4A	OEM
A707-4B	OEM
A707-4C	OEM
A707-4D	OEM
A707-4E	OEM
A707-4F	OEM
A707-4G	OEM
A707-4H	OEM
A707-4I	OEM
A707-4J	OEM
A707-4K	OEM
A707-4L	OEM
A707-5A	OEM
A707-5B	OEM
A707-5C	OEM
A707-5D	OEM
A707-5E	OEM
A707-5F	OEM
A707-5G	OEM
A707-5H	OEM
A707-5I	OEM
A707-5J	OEM
A707-5K	OEM
A707-5L	OEM
A707-6A	OEM
A707-6B	OEM
A707-6C	OEM
A707-6D	OEM
A707-6E	OEM
A707-6F	OEM
A707-6G	OEM
A707-6H	OEM
A707-6I	OEM
A707-6J	OEM
A707-6K	OEM
A707-7A	OEM
A707-7B	OEM
A707-7C	OEM
A707-7D	OEM
A707-7E	OEM
A707-7F	OEM
A707-7G	OEM
A707-7H	OEM
A707-7I	OEM
A707-8A	OEM
A707-8B	OEM
A707-8C	OEM
A707-8D	OEM
A707-8E	OEM
A707-8F	OEM
A707-8G	OEM
A708(2S)	0126
A708-3A	OEM
A708-3B	OEM
A708-3C	OEM
A708-3D	OEM
A708-3E	OEM
A708-3F	OEM
A708-3G	OEM
A708-3H	OEM
A708-3I	OEM
A708-3J	OEM
A708-3K	OEM
A708-4A	OEM
A708-4B	OEM
A708-4C	OEM
A708-4D	OEM
A708-4E	OEM
A708-4F	OEM
A708-4G	OEM
A708-4H	OEM
A708-4I	OEM
A708-5A	OEM
A708-5B	OEM
A708-5C	OEM
A708-5D	OEM
A708-5E	OEM
A708-5F	OEM
A708-5G	OEM
A708-5H	OEM
A708-5I	OEM
A708-5J	OEM
A708-6A	OEM
A708-6B	OEM
A708-6C	OEM
A708-6D	OEM
A708-6E	OEM
A708-6F	OEM
A708-6G	OEM

If replacement code is OEM, contact original manufacturer for replacement.

DEVICE TYPE	REPL CODE	DEVICE TYPE	REPL CODE	DEVICE TYPE	REPL CODE	DEVICE TYPE	REPL CODE	DEVICE TYPE	REPL CODE	DEVICE TYPE	REPL CODE	DEVICE TYPE	REPL CODE
A708-6H	OEM	A711-5C	OEM	A725EH16AB1	OEM	A755(2S)	0919	A800-516-00	0126	A848(2S)	0434	A909-1015	0143
A708-6I	OEM	A711-5D	OEM	A725EH20AB1	OEM	A755B(2S)	0919	A800-523-01	0037	A849	0434	A909-1016	0123
A708-7A	OEM	A711-6A	OEM	A725Y	0688	A755C(2S)	0919	A800-523-02	0037	A849(2S)	0434	A909-1017	0143
A708-7B	OEM	A711-6B	OEM	A726(2S)	0688	A756(2S)	3459	A800-527-00	0037	A850	0006	A909-1018	0015
A708-7C	OEM	A711-6C	OEM	A726Y	0688	A757	3459	A807	3459	A854	1338	A909-1019	0015
A708-7D	OEM	A711-8A	OEM	A728	0006	A757(2S)	3459	A808	3459	A854-Q	1338	A909-27125-160	0144
A708-7E	OEM	A711-8B	OEM	A728A	0006	A757N	OEM	A808A	3459	A854G	1338	A912	0338
A708-7F	OEM	A712	0434	A730	1233	A758	2002	A809	0338	A854Q	1338	A912Q	0338
A708-7G	OEM	A712-3A	OEM	A730L	OEM	A758(2S)	2002	A810	0338	A854Q(JAPAN)	1338	A912R	0338
A708-8A	OEM	A712-3B	OEM	A730LA	OEM	A758A	2002	A811	0037	A854QE	1338	A912S	0338
A708-8B	OEM	A712-3C	OEM	A730LB	OEM	A758B	2002	A811A	0037	A854R	1338	A913	1638
A708-8C	OEM	A712-3D	OEM	A730LC	OEM	A759	0855	A811C5	0037	A855	0688	A913AQ	1638
A708-8D	OEM	A712-4A	OEM	A730LD	OEM	A759(2S)	0037	A811C6	0037	A856	0688	A914	0520
A708-8E	OEM	A712-4B	OEM	A730P	5205	A759A	0037	A811C7	0037	A856-16	OEM	A915	0338
A708-8F	OEM	A712-4C	OEM	A730PA	OEM	A759B	0037	A811C8	0037	A856A	0688	A916	0338
A708-J	OEM	A712-5A	OEM	A730PB	OEM	A760	0688	A812	1731	A857	0338	A916-31025-58	0144
A708A(2S)	0126	A712-5B	OEM	A730PC	OEM	A761	0126	A812M3	1731	A858	0338	A916K	0338
A709	0037	A712-5C	OEM	A730PD	OEM	A761-1	0126	A812M4	1731	A859	0037	A916L	0338
A709-3A	OEM	A712-6A	OEM	A730PE	OEM	A761-2	0126	A812M5	1731	A860	0338	A916M	0338
A709-3B	OEM	A712-6B	OEM	A730PM	OEM	A762	0787	A812M6	1731	A861	1045	A917	0472
A709-3C	OEM	A712-7A	OEM	A730PN	OEM	A762-1	0787	A812M7	1731	A861(3)	1045	A918	0150
A709-3D	OEM	A712-7B	OEM	A730PS	OEM	A762-2	0787	A813	0150	A861JK	1045	A920	3712
A709-3E	OEM	A712-8A	OEM	A730PT	OEM	A763	0688	A813S2	0150	A866	0037	A921	0643
A709-3F	OEM	A713	3477	A731	1233	A764(2S)	0899	A813S3	0150	A866V	0037	A921-59B	0144
A709-3G	OEM	A713-3A	OEM	A731(2S)	1233	A765	0899	A813S4	0150	A866VG	0037	A921-62B	0144
A709-3H	OEM	A713-3B	OEM	A732	0126	A765(RECT.)	0916	A814	0676	A867	0150	A921-63B	0144
A709-3I	OEM	A713-3C	OEM	A733	0006	A766	1638	A814-O	0676	A867-14-1	OEM	A921-64B	0144
A709-3J	OEM	A713-3D	OEM	A733(2S)	0006	A766S	1638	A814-Y	0676	A868	0037	A921-70B	0037
A709-4A	OEM	A713-4A	OEM	A733-P	0006	A767	0037	A815	0676	A869	0037	A921A	0643
A709-4B	OEM	A713-4B	OEM	A733-Q	0006	A768	0919	A815-O	0676	A870	0037	A921AS	0643
A709-4C	OEM	A713-4C	OEM	A733A(2S)	0006	A768G	0919	A815-Y	0676	A871	5270	A922	0126
A709-4D	OEM	A713-5A	OEM	A733AK	0006	A768O	0919	A816	1638	A872	0643	A923	0338
A709-4E	OEM	A713-5B	OEM	A733AP	0006	A768Y	0919	A816-0	1638	A872A	0643	A923-1	0338
A709-4F	OEM	A713-5C	OEM	A733AP(JAPAN)	0006	A769	0848	A816-O	1638	A872AD	0643	A923-2	0338
A709-4G	OEM	A713-6A	OEM	A733AQ	0006	A770	0848	A816-Y	1638	A872AE	0643	A925	0150
A709-4H	OEM	A713-6B	OEM	A733AQ(JAPAN)	0006	A771	1359	A817	0431	A872AF	0643	A925-1	0150
A709-5A	OEM	A713-7A	OEM	A733H(2S)	0006	A772(2S)	0527	A817-Y	0431	A872C	0643	A925-2	0150
A709-5B	OEM	A713-7B	OEM	A733IO	0006	A772-1	0527	A817A	0431	A872D	0643	A927	0006
A709-5C	OEM	A713-8A	OEM	A733IQ(2S)	0006	A772-2	0527	A817AY	0431	A872E	0643	A929	0688
A709-5D	OEM	A713A	3477	A733J	OEM	A772-23	0527	A817Y(JAPAN)	0431	A872F	0643	A929G	0688
A709-5E	OEM	A714	2002	A733P	0006	A772B1	0127	A818	0676	A873	0150	A929H	0688
A709-5F	OEM	A714-L	2002	A733P(2S)	0006	A772EH	0127	A818-O	0676	A876HA	0037	A930	0688
A709-5G	OEM	A714L	2002	A733PQ	0006	A772FE	0127	A818-Y	0676	A876HB	0037	A931	5547
A709-5H	OEM	A715(2S)	0520	A733Q	0006	A772J	0527	A825(2S)	0006	A876HC	0037	A932	5270
A709-6A	OEM	A715B(2S)	0520	A733Q(2S)	0006	A773	2027	A825Q	0006	A877	3459	A933	0148
A709-6B	OEM	A715C(2S)	0520	A733Q1P(2S)	0006	A773-1	2027	A825R	0006	A878	3459	A933AQ	0148
A709-6C	OEM	A715D(2S)	0520	A733QP	0006	A773-2	2027	A825S	0006	A879	0338	A933AR	0148
A709-6D	OEM	A715WBP(2S)	0520	A733R(2S)	0006	A773H	2027	A826	0037	A879NC	0338	A933Q	0148
A709-6E	OEM	A715WT	0520	A733Y(KOREA)	0006	A774	0688	A826P	0037	A879P	0338	A933Q(JAPAN)	0148
A709-6F	OEM	A715WTB(2S)	0520	A734	OEM	A774A	0688	A826Q	0037	A879Q	0338	A933QL	0148
A709-6G	OEM	A715WTBC	0520	A734(2S)	0126	A775	0676	A826R	0037	A880	0688	A933QY	0148
A709-7A	OEM	A715WTC(2S)	0520	A735	0037	A775A	0676	A826S	0037	A880-250-107	0126	A933R	0148
A709-7B	OEM	A717(2S)	0126	A736(2S)	0126	A775AA	0676	A828A	0527	A881Q	0006	A933R(JAPAN)	0148
A709-7C	OEM	A718(2S)	0037	A738	0455	A775AB	0676	A829	0037	A881Q(JAPAN)	0006	A933RZ	0148
A709-7D	OEM	A719(2S)	0006	A738(B)	0455	A775AC	0676	A829A	0037	A882	2002	A933S	0148
A709-7E	OEM	A719-Q	0006	A738A	0455	A775B	0676	A829B	0037	A883	0527	A933S(JAPAN)	0148
A709-7F	OEM	A719K	0006	A738C(2S)	0455	A775C	0676	A829C	0037	A884	0527	A933SRR	0148
A709-8A	OEM	A719NC	0006	A738D(2S)	0455	A776	0150	A829D	0037	A885	0520	A933SSJ	0148
A709-8B	OEM	A719O	0006	A739	3561	A776A	0150	A829E	0037	A886	0520	A933SSK	0148
A709-8C	OEM	A719PQR	0006	A740	1638	A777	0431	A829F	0037	A886V	0520	A934(JAPAN)	0527
A709-8D	OEM	A719Q(2S)	0006	A740A	1638	A777(2S)	0431	A833	0037	A886VQ	0520	A935	0431
A709-8E	OEM	A719R(2S)	0006	A740AB	1638	A777NC	0431	A835	0338	A886VR	0520	A935R	0431
A710	0150	A719S(2S)	0006	A740P	OEM	A777Q	0431	A835H	0338	A887	1257	A935R(JAPAN)	0431
A710-3A	OEM	A720(2S)	0006	A740PA	OEM	A778	0338	A836(2S)	0688	A887P	1257	A937	2464
A710-3B	OEM	A720-G	0006	A740PB	OEM	A778(2S)	0338	A836C	0688	A887Q	1257	A937-1	0016
A710-3C	OEM	A720-O	0006	A740PC	OEM	A778A	0338	A836D(2S)	0688	A888	0037	A937-3	0016
A710-3D	OEM	A720-Q	0006	A740PD	OEM	A778A(2S)	0338	A836E(2S)	0688	A889	0037	A937-Q	2464
A710-3E	OEM	A720-R	0006	A740PE	OEM	A778AF-02	0338	A836F	0688	A890	0037	A937R	2464
A710-3F	OEM	A720A	0006	A740PM	OEM	A778AK	0338	A837(2S)	3459	A891	0037	A937R(JAPAN)	2464
A710-3G	OEM	A720B	0006	A740PN	OEM	A778AK(2S)	0338	A838	5280	A892	0597	A939	4402
A710-3H	OEM	A720C	0006	A740PS	OEM	A778AK-02	0338	A838B	5280	A893	0643	A940	1900
A710-4A	OEM	A720D	0006	A741	0150	A778K(2S)	0338	A838C	5280	A893A	0643	A940(JAPAN)	1900
A710-4B	OEM	A720L	0006	A741H	0150	A778K-02	0338	A839	1638	A893AC	0643	A940-Z	1900
A710-4C	OEM	A720NC	0006	A742	0126	A779	1257	A839-O	1638	A893AD	0643	A940AD	1900
A710-4D	OEM	A720Q(2S)	0006	A742H	0126	A779(2S)	1045	A839-R	1638	A893AE	0643	A940AE(JAPAN)	1900
A710-4E	OEM	A720QR	0006	A743(2S)	0520	A779K(2S)	1045	A839-Y	1638	A893AF	0643	A940D	1900
A710-4F	OEM	A720R	0006	A743A(2S)	0520	A779KB(2S)	1045	A840(2S)	1638	A893D	0643	A940E	1900
A710-5A	OEM	A720R(2S)	0006	A743AB(2S)	0520	A780	0659	A840H	1638	A893E	0643	A940GL2	1900
A710-5B	OEM	A720S(2S)	0006	A743AC(2S)	0520	A780(TRANS)	1357	A840JC	1638	A894	0431	A940LB	1900
A710-5C	OEM	A720Y	0006	A743C(2S)	0520	A780A	1357	A840JM	1638	A895	0150	A940R	1900
A710-5D	OEM	A721(2S)	0688	A744(2S)	0486	A780AK(2S)	1357	A840K	1638	A896	0338	A940RD	1900
A710-5E	OEM	A721Q	0688	A745	2002	A780AKB(2S)	1357	A841	0688	A896-1	0338	A940RE	1900
A710-5F	OEM	A721R	0688	A745A	2002	A781	0350	A841(2S)	0688	A896-2	0338	A941	0006
A710-6A	OEM	A721S(2S)	0688	A746(2S)	2002	A781(TRAN)	0150	A841-BL	0688	A897	0643	A942	0006
A710-6B	OEM	A721T(2S)	0688	A747	2002	A781(TRANS)	0150	A841-GR	0688	A898	0520	A945	0164
A710-6C	OEM	A721U(2S)	0688	A747(2S)	2002	A781K	0150	A842	0688	A899	3658	A945-0	0164
A710-6D	OEM	A722(2S)	0688	A747A	2002	A782	0037	A842(2S)	0688	A900	0520	A945-Q	0164
A710-6E	OEM	A722S(2S)	0688	A747A(2S)	2002	A783	0148	A842-BL	0688	A900(2S)	0520	A948	0126
A710-7A	OEM	A723(2S)	0006	A747B	0111	A784	3477	A842-GR	0688	A901	0688	A948E	0126
A710-7B	OEM	A723EH3AB1	OEM	A747C	OEM	A785	4971	A843	5370	A902	0688	A949	0472
A710-7C	OEM	A723EH4AB1	OEM	A748	0919	A786	0037	A843(2S)	1638	A903	0688	A949Y	0472
A710-7D	OEM	A723EH5AB1	OEM	A748(2S)	0676	A786-Q	0037	A844	0688	A904	0643	A950	1338
A710-7E	OEM	A723EH6AB1	OEM	A748B	0016	A786Q	0037	A844(2S)	0006	A904(2S)	0643	A950-0	1338
A710-8A	OEM	A723EH7AB1	OEM	A748C	0111	A786QL	0037	A844C	0688	A904A	0643	A950-O	1338
A710-8B	OEM	A723EH8AB1	OEM	A748Q(2S)	0676	A786R	0037	A844C(JAPAN)	0688	A905	0334	A950-Y	1338
A710-8C	OEM	A723EH9AB1	OEM	A749	0016	A787	0688	A844D	0688	A905(2S)	0643	A950FA	1338
A710-8D	OEM	A723EH10AB1	OEM	A749(2S)	0338	A788	0037	A844D(2S)	0688	A906	0688	A950Y	1338
A711	0150	A723EH11AB1	OEM	A749A	0338	A789	0148	A844D(JAPAN)	0688	A906(2S)	0688	A950Y(JAPAN)	1338
A711-3A	OEM	A723EH12AB1	OEM	A749B	0016	A790	0630	A844E	0688	A907	1671	A950Y(KOREA)	0527
A711-3B	OEM	A723R	0006	A749C	0111	A791	3477	A844E(2S)	0688	A907(2S)	1671	A951	0676
A711-3C	OEM	A724	0148	A750	0688	A793	0126	A844F	0688	A908	1588	A951-10	0676
A711-3D	OEM	A725(2S)	0688	A751(2S)	0472	A794	0520	A845	0338	A908(2S)	1588	A951KA	0676
A711-3E	OEM	A725EH2AB1	0071	A751(P)	0472	A794A	0520	A845AH	0338	A909	1588	A951KD	0676
A711-4A	OEM	A725EH3AB1	OEM	A751Q(2S)	0472	A795	0520	A845H	0338	A909-1008	0050	A951LC	0676
A711-4B	OEM	A725EH4AB1	OEM	A751R(2S)	0472	A796	3477	A846	OEM	A909-1009	0136	A951M	0676
A711-4C	OEM	A725EH6AB1	OEM	A752(2S)	0472	A798	0688	A847	0643	A909-1010	0136	A951MU	0676
A711-4D	OEM	A725EH8AB1	OEM	A753(2S)	2002	A799	0126	A847(2S)	0643	A909-1011	0004	A952	0006
A711-5A	OEM	A725EH10AB1	OEM	A753-4004-248	0037	A800	0071	A847A	0643	A909-1012	0004	A952(JAPAN)	0006
A711-5B	OEM	A725EH12AB1	OEM	A754(2S)	0919	A800(TRANS)	3562	A848	0434	A909-1013	0004	A952K	0006

If replacement code is OEM, contact original manufacturer for replacement.

DEVICE TYPE	REPL CODE
A952L	0006
A952L(JAPAN)	0006
A952M(JAPAN)	0006
A953	1338
A954	0006
A955	OEM
A956	0150
A956H3	0150
A956H4	0150
A956H5	0150
A956H6	0150
A957	1638
A957(JAPAN)	1638
A958	1900
A958Y	1900
A962	0378
A963	0520
A964	3712
A964-17887	0160
A964A	3712
A-965	OEM
A965	5233
A966	0527
A966-O(JAPAN)	0527
A966AY(KOREA)	3552
A966Y	0527
A968	1638
A968A	1638
A968B	1638
A970	0006
A971	1588
A973	0688
A-975	OEM
A978	0688
A979	4967
A980	2002
A981	2002
A982	2002
A984	0006
A984(JAPAN)	0006
A984E	0006
A984K	0006
A984KF(JAPAN)	0006
A985	5288
A985A	5288
A987	0006
A988	0643
A990	0688
A991	0688
A991-01-0098	0037
A991-01-1225	0037
A991-01-1316	0144
A991-01-1319	0037
A991-01-3058	0037
A992	0643
A992-00-1192	0160
A993	0037
A995	4969
A999	0006
A999L	0006
A1000	0071
A1001	2002
A1002	2002
A1003	1588
A1003-3	OEM
A1004	0037
A1005	0037
A1006	3500
A1006A	3500
A1007	1588
A1007A	1588
A1008	3501
A1010	1359
A1010-3	OEM
A1010L(JAPAN)	1359
A1010V	1359
A1011	1638
A1011(IC)	3054
A1011(IC-SM)	OEM
A1011(SM)	4444
A1011D	1638
A1011E	1638
A1012	3505
A1012-Y	3505
A1012Y(JAPAN)	3505
A1013	1514
A1013-0	1514
A1013-O	1514
A1013-O(JAPAN)	1514
A1013-R	1514
A1013R	1514
A1013R(JAPAN)	1514
A1015	0148
A1015-0	0148
A1015-O	0148
A1015-O(JAPAN)	0148
A1015-O(KOREA)	0006
A1015-OFA	0148
A1015-Y	0148
A1015-YFA	0148
A1015FA	0148
A1015G	0148
A1015GR	0148
A1015GR(JAPAN)	0148
A1015O	0148
A1015Y	0148
A1015Y(JAPAN)	0148
A1015Y(KOREA)	0148
A1016	0688
A1016K	0688
A1017	0338
A1018	0338
A1019	0643
A1020	0429
A1020-3	OEM
A1020-O	0429
A1020Y	0429
A1020Y(JAPAN)	0429
A1021	0520
A1021(JAPAN)	0520
A1021-O	0520
A1021-R	0520
A1021R	2533
A1021Y	0520
A1023	1593
A1023P	1593
A1023Q	1593
A1024	0911
A1025D	0037
A1025E	0037
A1026	0006
A1026(2S)	0006
A1027	0527
A1027(2S)	0037
A1027R	0037
A1028	2002
A1029	0006
A1029B	0006
A1029C	0006
A1029D	0006
A1030	0006
A1030B	0006
A1030C	0006
A1031B	0037
A1031C	0037
A1032B	0037
A1032C	0037
A1035	OEM
A1040	0006
A1041	1588
A1042	0486
A1043	1671
A1044	1671
A1045	0486
A1046	0486
A1047	0520
A1048	0013
A1048(JAPAN)	0013
A1048-GR	0013
A1048-O	0013
A1048-O(JAPAN)	0013
A1048GR	0013
A1048GR(JAPAN)	0013
A10480	0013
A1048Y	0013
A1049	0006
A1050	0148
A1060	0853
A1061	0853
A1061P	0853
A1061Q	0853
A1061R	0853
A1062	3527
A1064	1588
A1065	1588
A1066	0472
A1067	1588
A1068	1588
A1069	3533
A1069C	3533
A1072	1588
A1073	1588
A1075	3537
A1076	3537
A1077	0713
A1078	3541
A1080	0676
A1081D	0037
A1081E	0037
A1082D	0037
A1082E	0037
A1083D	0037
A1083E	0037
A1084D	1587
A1084E	1587
A1085D	1587
A1085E	1587
A1086	0079
A1087	0079
A1090	0037
A1091	0338
A1091-O	0338
A1091R	0338
A1092	0688
A1093	3527
A1094	3537
A1095	3537
A1096	0520
A1100	0006
A1100D	0006
A1100F	0006
A1100L	0006
A1101	OEM
A1102	0853
A1103	0853
A1104	3082
A1105	3082
A1106	3082
A1109	0144
A1110	0520
A1111	1638
A1111(IC)	OEM
A1112	1638
A1114-1002	0050
A1115	3282
A1115-E	3282
A1115-F	3282
A1115E	3282
A1116	3561
A1117	3561
A1120	0520
A1123	1514
A1124	1514
A1124C	0160
A1125	1638
A1127NC	0688
A1128	0006
A1133	1900
A1135	0853
A1144	0136
A1145	1514
A1146	3527
A1150	0006
A1150Y	0006
A1151	0527
A1152	0037
A1153	3572
A1154	0527
A1158	0431
A1160	0527
A1164	0037
A1169	3537
A1170	0144
A1170(2S)	3601
A1173	1514
A1174	0688
A1175	3580
A1175(JAPAN)	3580
A1175-F	3580
A1175E	3580
A1175F	3580
A1175F(JAPAN)	3580
A1175FH	3580
A1175H	3580
A1175H(JAPAN)	3580
A1175J	3580
A1180	1588
A1184	0520
A1185	0853
A1186	3527
A1186N	OEM
A1187	3585
A1188D	0472
A1188E	0472
A1189D	0472
A1189E	0472
A1190D	0472
A1190E	0472
A1191D	0472
A1191E	0472
A1193K	3836
A1194K	2869
A1195	1045
A1195-O	1045
A11950	1045
A1195R	1045
A1198A	OEM
A1201	0574
A1201-H45	2377
A1201-H-75	0167
A-1201B	0574
A1201B	0574
A1205	3082
A1206K	5365
A1207	1514
A1208	1514
A1210	0520
A1214	0037
A1215	3537
A1216	3601
A1217	0520
A1220	0050
A1220(2S)	0520
A1220A	0520
A1221	0520
A1238	0111
A1243	0279
A1246	3609
A1246R	3609
A1246S	3609
A1246S(JAPAN)	3609
A1246T	3609
A1246U	3609
A1261L(JAPAN)	1190
A1263	3082
A1264	3082
A1264T	3082
A1265	3082
A1277	1298
A1278	3500
A1301	3628
A1314	0086
A1318S(JAPAN)	OEM
A1320	0338
A1321	0338
A1341	0086
A1357N	0859
A1364N	0872
A1365	0167
A1368	0850
A1369	3660
A1377	0050
A1378	0050
A1379	0016
A1380	0016
A1381	OEM
A1383	0136
A1384	0136
A1390C	0013
A1392	OEM
A1396	0595
A1408	0520
A1409	0233
A1412-1	0016
A1414A	0160
A1414A9	0160
A1418	0144
A1423BC1AB1	OEM
A1423DC1AB1	OEM
A1423MC1AB1	OEM
A1423MC2AB1	OEM
A1423MC3AB1	OEM
A1423MC4AB1	OEM
A1423MC5AB1	OEM
A1423MC6AB1	OEM
A1423MH2AB1	OEM
A1423MH3AB1	OEM
A1423MH4AB1	OEM
A1423MH5AB1	OEM
A1423MH6AB1	OEM
A1423MH7AB1	OEM
A1423MH8AB1	OEM
A1423MH9AB1	OEM
A1423MH10AB1	OEM
A1423MH11AB1	OEM
A1423MH12AB1	OEM
A1423PBC1AB1	OEM
A1423PBC3AB1	OEM
A1423PBC4AB1	OEM
A1423PBC5AB1	OEM
A1423PBC6AB1	OEM
A1423PBH2AB1	OEM
A1423PBH4AB1	OEM
A1423PBH5AB1	OEM
A1423PBH6AB1	OEM
A1423PBH7AB1	OEM
A1423PBH8AB1	OEM
A1423PBH9AB1	OEM
A1423PCB2AB1	OEM
A1425MH8AB1	OEM
A1441L	5388
A1450	0472
A1450S	0472
A1450T	0472
A1460	0111
A1462	0144
A1462-19	0050
A1465-1	0050
A1465-4	0595
A1465-19	0050
A1465-29	0208
A1465-49	0595
A1465A	0050
A1465A9	0050
A1465B	0050
A1465B9	0050
A1465C	0160
A1465C9	0160
A1466-1	0004
A1466-2	0004
A1466-3	0004
A1466-19	0004
A1466-19-	0004
A1466-29	0004
A1466-39	0004
A1469	1298
A1469R	OEM
A1472-19	0198
A1474-3	0279
A1474-39	0279
A1477A	0435
A1477A9	0435
A1477C	0160
A1477C9	0160
A1480	OEM
A1484A	0160
A1484A9	0160
A1488B	0050
A1488B9	0050
A1488C	0279
A1488C9	0279
A1492-1	0435
A1492-19	0435
A1501	0015
A1507S	5767
A1518	0144
A1519	0144
A1520	0144
A1521	0144
A1558-17	0037
A1560P	OEM
A-1567	0016
A1567	0016
A1567-1	0016
A1606E	0713
A1618	OEM
A1618M	OEM
A1624E	0338
A1844-17	0037
A-1854-0492-1	0016
A1854-0533	0855
A1858	0595
A1867-17	0037
A1884-0209	2007
A1884-0218	2007
A1946	0015
A2003-3	OEM
A2010-3	OEM
A2011	OEM
A2020-3	OEM
A2039-2	0595
A2057A2-198	0037
A2057B2-115	0127
A2057B104-8	0233
A2057B106-12	0037
A2057B108-6	0037
A2057B110-9	0126
A2057B112-9	0126
A2057B114-9	0126
A2057B115-9	0126
A2057B116-9	0126
A2057B121-9	0126
A2057B122-9	0126
A2057B145-12	0126
A2057B163-12	0126
A2090	0233
A2202	0023
A2332	0007
A2410	0016
A2411	0016
A2412	0016
A2413	0016
A2414	0164
A2415	0178
A2416	1390
A2417	0637
A2418	0103
A2419	0019
A2420	0143
A2421	0102
A2422	0015
A2423	0015
A2424	0918
A2428	0037
A2434	0016
A2448	0037
A2458	1293
A2459	0769
A2460	0015
A2461	0023
A2462	0102
A2464	0007
A2465	0007
A2466	0016
A2468	0016
A2469	0016
A2470	0016
A2471	0086
A2473	0143
A2474	0137
A2475	0196
A2476	0143
A2479	0007
A2480	0007
A2481	0015
A2485	0015
A2498	0144
A2499	0016
A2511	OEM
A2585	OEM
A2620	0233
A2652-919	0321
A2746	0007
A2798	0037
A3003-3	OEM
A3010-3	OEM
A3101	OEM
A3103BX2	OEM
A3300	2546
A3301	1206
A3350	0412
A3410A	0050
A3410B	0050
A3511	OEM
A3512	OEM
A3513	0037
A3523	0126
A3533	0126
A3533-1	0126
A3540	0037
A3549	0037
A3559	0037
A3562	0037
A3563	0037
A3574	0037
A3581	0037
A3607	0595
A3609	0595
A3616-1	0126
A4000	OEM
A4012-0154	OEM
A4030	2991
A4086	0037
A4087	0037
A4126	0037
A4201	0196
A4212-A	0015
A4212A	0071
A4237M	OEM
A4247	0160
A4310	0037
A4347	0160
A4442	0037
A4478	0126
A4648	0233
A4700	0595
A4745	0037
A4789	0144
A4802-00004	0037
A4815	0037
A4819	0233
A4822-130-40348	0037
A4838	0233
A4843	0233
A4844	0037
A4851	0144
A4853	0233
A5003-3	OEM
A5010-3	OEM
A5027	OEM
A5029	OEM
A5226-1	0037
A5253	0160
A5640R	0688
A6181-1	0233
A6230-AH	1404
A6358S	3202
A6393S	OEM
A6458S	2884
A7011	OEM
A7012	OEM
A7013	OEM
A7014	OEM
A7016	1022
A7205	2438
A7233H2AB1	OEM
A7253	0233
A7520(IC)	0534
A7530N	3765
A8015T	OEM
A8400	OEM
A8402	OEM
A8404	OEM
A8405	0037
A8495	OEM
A8540	0037
A-8865-03	OEM
A-8865-04	OEM
A-8865-05	OEM
A8867	0037
A9218	0124
A9228-3	0124
A-9982	1051
A-9982-02	OEM
A9982-02	4210
A-9982-02A	4210
A-9982-07	1051
A9982-07	4211
A-9982A	1051
A10003A	OEM
A10003D	OEM
A10005D	OEM
A10010D	OEM
A10020D	OEM
A10075A	OEM
A10075D	OEM
A10105	0015
A10113	0015
A10118	0015
A10164	0015
A10165	0015
A-10167	0283
A10169	0015
A11744	0321
A11745	0321
A-11885	OEM
A12010A	OEM
A12010D	OEM
A12163	0160
A12178	0160
A12546	0233
A12594	0037
A-12791	0042
A12888	0037
A-13099	OEM
A-13284	3461
A-13414	OEM
A13658A3	OEM
A13658E3	3567
A-14343-06	OEM
A-14343-09	OEM
A-14343-9	OEM
A14665-2	0208
A14743	0178
A15003A	OEM
A15003D	OEM
A15005D	OEM
A15010D	OEM
A15020D	OEM
A15075A	OEM
A15075D	OEM
A15927	0160
A-16926	OEM
A19040-B	OEM
A19108-A	OEM
A20005D	OEM
A20010D	OEM
A20020D	OEM
A20371	0143
A20372	0016
A21268	0644
A22008	0037
A24015	0133
A24031	OEM
A24060	OEM
A24100	0016
A25005D	OEM
A25010D	OEM
A25020D	OEM
A25762-010	0233
A25762-012	0233
A29035-E	0025
A30005D	OEM
A30010D	OEM
A30020D	OEM
A30270	0037
A30278	0126
A30290	0037
A30302	0160
A34715	0160
A35084	0160
A35201	0160
A35260	0160
A36508	0143
A36539	0137
A36577	0126
A36896	0160
A40005D	OEM
A40010D	OEM
A40020D	OEM
A40410	0126
A41440	0037
A42946	0196
A42946B	0196
A48727	OEM
A49488-B	OEM
A49491-B	OEM
A50020B	OEM
A-54806-A	0720
A59625-1	0037
A59625-2	0037
A59625-3	0037
A59625-4	0037
A59625-5	0037
A59625-6	0037
A59625-7	0037
A59625-8	0037
A59625-9	0037
A59625-10	0037
A59625-11	0037
A59625-12	0037
A71687-1	0037
A75680	0015
A78331	0037
A81004	0730
A82930-6	OEM
A82930-8	OEM
A94004	0160
A94037	0037
A94063	0126
A95115	0595
A95211	0595
A95227	0037
A95232	0037
A112363	0103
A-113110	0037
A-113335	0585
A-113367(DIODE)	0124
A116078	0037
A116081	0233
A116084	0126
A116284	0126
A-118038	0071
A118284	0037
A119730	0037
A119983	0126
A-120018	0086
A-120077	0052
A-120125(PWR.RECT.)	0071
A120150	OEM
A-120278	0016
A-120304	0178
A-120327	0103
A-120407	0864
A-120417	0037
A-120420	0296
A121467	0037
A121659	0037
A124047	0037
A124623	0144
A124624	0144
A124755	0037
A-125278	0466
A125329	0144
A-125332	0016
A126524	0037
A126700	0037
A126705	0233
A126707	0037
A126715	0037
A126718	0037
A126719	0037
A126724	0126

If replacement code is OEM, contact original manufacturer for replacement.

DEVICE TYPE	REPL CODE
A127712	0233
A129509	0144
A129510	0144
A129511	0144
A129512	0144
A129513	0144
A129571	0144
A129572	0144
A129573	0144
A129574	0144
A129697	0037
A129699	0037
A130139	0037
A-132591	0242
A-134166-2	0137
A190187T	OEM
A190429	0037
A198794-1	0595
A218012DS	0160
A242361	OEM
A251283	OEM
A297074C11	0126
A489751-028	0037
A489751-031	0037
A573501	0233
A610074-1	0037
A610075-1	0233
A610083	0037
A610083-1	0037
A610083-2	0037
A610083-3	0037
A610110-1	0037
A610120-1	0037
A631790L	0309
A650232E	0006
A650235G	0006
A650238A	0006
A650372D	0006
A650923F	0006
A650925H	0006
A660097	0160
A670720K	0076
A670722D	0076
A670729B	0076
A671656A	0781
A671656K	0781
A673351K	0191
A673354K	0191
A673355H	0191
A673355K	0191
A675313F	0066
A675315F	0066
A675318A	0066
A675419H	0111
A678760A	0638
A678760C	0638
A678971C	0638
A678971D	0638
A701584-00	0037
A701589-00	0037
A711002	0041
A720657	0720
A758011	0071
A759500	0071
A772738	0144
A772739	0144
A815185	0126
A815185E	0126
A815199	0037
A815199-6	0037
A815211	0037
A815213	0037
A815229	0037
A815247	0037
A853702	OEM
A970246	0037
A970248	0037
A970251	0037
A970254	0037
A984193	0037
A1471114-1	0037
A1473549-1	0126
A1473563-1	0037
A1473570-1	0037
A1473574-1	0037
A1473590-1	0037
A1473591-1	0037
A1473597-1	0037
A1473616-1	0126
A2006681-95	0144
A2057013-0004	0037
A2057013-0701	0037
A2057013-0702	0037
A2057013-0703	0037
A2090056-1	0160
A2090056-5	0160
A2090056-27	0160
A2091859-0025	0160
A2091859-0720	0160
A2091859-10	0160
A2091859-11	0160
A2092418	0595
A2092418-0711	0595
A2092693-0724	0144
A2092693-0725	0144
A2498512	0037
A3011112	0086
A3115621	0023
A3115690	0023
A3170717	0233
A4037764-2	0126
A5010005	0124
A5320111	0037
A5768475	0023
A6000010	OEM
A6000020	0826
A6000030	0881
A6000040	0892
A6002010	OEM
A6002020	0826
A6002030	0881
A6002040	0892
A6002050	OEM
A6002060	OEM
A6010030	1026
A6010050	OEM
A6010060	OEM
A6012010	OEM
A6012020	6867
A6012030	OEM
A6012040	4067
A6012060	OEM
A6041840	3104
A6041848	3104
A6041876	3104
A6041880	3104
A6048403	3017
A6090130	OEM
A6235070	0261
A6314340	0236
A6314440	0728
A6314446	0728
A6316440	OEM
A6317420	0076
A6317440	0076
A6317460	0076
A6317480	0076
A6317499	0076
A6317520	0076
A6317526	0076
A6317540	0076
A6317547	0076
A6317560	0076
A6317562	0076
A6317567	0076
A6317581	0076
A6317764	0076
A6317800	2643
A6317802	2643
A6317900	0309
A6317901	0309
A6319300	0284
A6319302	0284
A6319400	0638
A6319403	0638
A6319500	1274
A6319550	1274
A6319560	1274
A6319576	1274
A6321241	0860
A6324920	0066
A6324922	0066
A6324942	0066
A6324961	0066
A6325060	0261
A6325070	0261
A6325077	0261
A6328328	1553
A6328333	1553
A6330000	0261
A6330004	0261
A6330059	0261
A6330069	0261
A6333310	0018
A6333320	0018
A6333346	0018
A6333751	0309
A6342200	3065
A6358055	0194
A6359135	OEM
A6360250	0261
A6363200	0275
A6365232	OEM
A6502380	0006
A6502460	0520
A6509120	0006
A6509121	0006
A6509140	0006
A6509141	0006
A6509154	5817
A6531140	0431
A6532300	1338
A6532320	1900
A6532841	0472
A6532853	0472
A6532921	1338
A6532941	1338
A6533240	OEM
A6533730	3505
A6533750	1514
A6533760	1514
A6534020	0148
A6534021	0148
A6534036	5055
A6534040	0148
A6534045	0148
A6534053	0148
A6534060	0148
A6534063	0148
A6534120	0429
A6534125	0429
A6534135	0429
A6534145	0429
A6534430	OEM
A6546025	3082
A6546665	OEM
A6547300	0338
A6610160	0919
A6623870	1359
A6625365	3082
A6633620	3459
A6639320	OEM
A6707244	0076
A6707298	0076
A6708303	0076
A6708850	0836
A6708861	0836
A6708871	0836
A6716560	0781
A6716660	0520
A6733280	0111
A6733340	0191
A6733560	0191
A6734590	0546
A6734592	0546
A6738701	0220
A6754194H	0111
A6771373	1142
A6773802	0103
A6773812	0103
A6789710	0638
A6823565	0228
A6836940	0538
A6841063	3333
A6841420	4183
A6841440	4183
A6841905	OEM
A6842185	4800
A6843401	0178
A6846008	0270
A6846701	2643
A6846801	2040
A6846806	2040
A6846860	2040
A6847905	0055
A6848004	0055
A6848103	0055
A6848520	0456
A6848908	2058
A6852901	3474
A6852961	OEM
A6852981	3474
A6862752	2411
A6862754	2411
A6865553	0309
A6867051	2961
A6867061	2961
A6867970	OEM
A6868654	1533
A6868673	1533
A6868702	1533
A6868706	1533
A6868757	1533
A6868767	1533
A6871242	5951
A6883056	OEM
A6907751	OEM
A6907752	OEM
A6907753	OEM
A7000900	0143
A7001800	0143
A7001957	0143
A7102001	0494
A7109202	OEM
A7109304	0296
A7109395	0036
A7109396	OEM
A7109432	0274
A7109433	0274
A7109473	0140
A7109890	0466
A7110015	0062
A7110016	0041
A7110017	0253
A7110018	0253
A7110023	0041
A7110040	0041
A7110041	0041
A7110055	0091
A7110076	0466
A7110077	0466
A7110114	0062
A7110115	0062
A7110116	0062
A7110159	5876
A7110160	0077
A7110207	0244
A7110209	0057
A7110263	0057
A7110359	5816
A7110360	0181
A7110410	0999
A7110411	0137
A7110412	0361
A7110461	0053
A7110462	OEM
A7110508	0873
A7110509	0681
A7110563	0440
A7110604	0490
A7110633	0666
A7110634	0695
A7110645	0700
A7110663	0666
A7110743	0166
A7115315	OEM
A7115414	OEM
A7115415	OEM
A7115605	OEM
A7115615	0755
A7116105	0274
A7116115	0274
A7116205	0582
A7116215	0140
A7116225	OEM
A7116305	0041
A7116315	0582
A7116405	0041
A7116415	0253
A7116505	0292
A7116515	0466
A7116615	0062
A7116625	0062
A7116705	0062
A7116715	OEM
A7116725	0077
A7116805	0077
A7116825	0165
A7116915	0057
A7116925	0057
A7117005	0057
A7117015	OEM
A7117025	OEM
A7117205	0999
A7117215	0999
A7117305	OEM
A7117415	OEM
A7117425	0681
A7117715	0666
A7118115	OEM
A7118305	OEM
A7118425	OEM
A7118925	0057
A7150041	0133
A7150258	0133
A7150351	0124
A7152800	OEM
A7160590	OEM
A7246602	0133
A7246653	0133
A7246700	0133
A7246703	0133
A7246711	0133
A7246727	0133
A7249601	0124
A7272130	1181
A7272143	1181
A7275400	0023
A7279039	0160
A7279049	0160
A7283550	0124
A7285774	0160
A7285778	0160
A7285900	0253
A7286100	0466
A7286107	0466
A7286120	0466
A7286201	0025
A7286500	0077
A7286700	0165
A7287500	0052
A7287513	0052
A7288504	0489
A7289000	0005
A7289047	0160
A7290594	0160
A7291252	0160
A7297043	0160
A7297092	0160
A7297093	0160
A7509201	0015
A7547053	0015
A7568160	0023
A7568250	0023
A7568300	0023
A7568460	0023
A7568475	0023
A7568480	0023
A7568487	0023
A7568500	0023
A7568521	0023
A7568700	0023
A7568719	0023
A7568752	0023
A7568754	0790
A7570013-01	0037
A7572100	0023
A7572200	0023
A7576004-01	0037
A7579500	0071
A7580111	0071
A7580310	0559
A7580656	0023
A7580658	OEM
A7580660	0023
A7580910	0017
A7582000	0182
A7671002	0319
A7682012	0196
A7682052	0015
A7801021	0895
A7801166	0403
A7801233	0403
A7803610	0705
A7811055	OEM
A7950540	1272
A7978850	0023
A7978855	0023
A7978950	0023
A7986480	0790
A8015613	0126
A8600606	OEM
A8603110	OEM
A8603140	4686
A8605671	OEM
A8606430	OEM
A8606431	OEM
A8606630	OEM
A8606660	3450
A8608780	OEM
A8608781	OEM
A8612100	OEM
A8612101	OEM
A8612360	OEM
A8620900	OEM
A8626050	OEM
A8626220	OEM
A8632853	0472
A8636410	OEM
A8636690	OEM
A8641063	3333
A8641301	1281
A8641302	1281
A8641303	1281
A8643100	0112
A8643135	0112
A8652035	2604
A11159761	0124
A-11790169	0124
A20030703-0702	0037
A23114050	0037
A23114051	0037
A23114130	0233
A23114550	0037
A25114130	0233
A43023843	0103
A43023845	0037
A67531140	0431
A71909304	0296
A75779500	0071
A80052402	0103
A80414120	0103
A80414130	0103
A86087881	OEM
AA015	0911
AA-07077	0004
AA-07089	0016
AA1	0279
AA1A4M	OEM
AA1L3M	OEM
AA1L3Z	OEM
AA1L4M	OEM
AA2	0595
AA2SB240A	0160
AA3	0050
AA4	0160
AA5	0435
AA8-1-70	0050
AA8-1-705	0050
AA8-1A9G	0050
AA10	0039
AA10-1	0039
AA50	0015
AA100	0015
AA101	0895
AA102	0058
AA103	OEM
AA104	OEM
AA107	0340
AA108	0895
AA109	0895
AA110	OEM
AA111	0143
AA111A	OEM
AA112	0143
AA112A	OEM
AA112B	OEM
AA112P	0143
AA113	0143
AA113P	0143
AA114	0143
AA115	0895
AA116	0143
AA116(SRC)	0058
AA117	0143
AA118	0143
AA118P	0143
AA119	0143
AA119P	0143
AA120	0143
AA121	0143
AA123	0143
AA129	OEM
AA130	0143
AA131	0143
AA132	0143
AA133	3249
AA134	0143
AA135	0143
AA136	0143
AA137	0143
AA138	0143
AA139	0143
AA140	0143
AA142	0143
AA143	0143
AA144	0143
AA200	0015
AA210	0143
AA218	0143
AA300	0015
AA310	3249
AA400	0015
AA401	OEM
AA500	0015
AA600	0015
AA779	0143
AA800	0071
AA1000	0071
AA5534S	OEM
AAIA4M	OEM
AAR	OEM
AAV-039	OEM
AAV039	OEM
AAV11A	OEM
AAV1043	OEM
AAV1051	OEM
AAY10-120	0090
AAY11	0124
AAY12	0143
AAY13	OEM
AAY14	0143
AAY15	0019
AAY18	0143
AAY21	OEM
AAY22	0143
AAY27	0143
AAY28	0143
AAY30	0143
AAY32	0143
AAY33	0143
AAY34	OEM
AAY39	OEM
AAY39A	OEM
AAY39R	OEM
AAY40	OEM
AAY42	0143
AAY43	OEM
AAY46	0143
AAY48	0143
AAY49	0143
AAY50	OEM
AAY50R	OEM
AAY51	OEM
AAY51R	OEM
AAY52	OEM
AAY52R	OEM
AAY53	0143
AAY54	0143
AAY55	0143
AAY56	OEM
AAY56R	OEM
AAY59	OEM
AAY60	OEM
AAY139	0143
AAZ10	0143
AAZ13	OEM
AAZ14	OEM
AAZ15	0143
AAZ17	0143
AAZ18	0143
AAZ18D	0015
AB1-9	0012
AB1-11	0181
AB1-35	0039
AB50	0087
AB100	0087
AB107	OEM
AB110	OEM
AB120	OEM
AB200	0087
AB207	OEM
AB210	OEM
AB220	OEM
AB300	0087
AB307	OEM
AB310	OEM
AB320	OEM
AB400	0087
AB407	OEM
AB410	OEM
AB420	OEM
AB500	0087
AB507	OEM
AB510	OEM
AB520	OEM
AB600	0087
AB700	0087
AB800	0087
AB800-20	OEM
AB801-20	OEM
AB802-20	OEM
AB803-20	OEM
AB803-51	OEM
AB810-20	OEM
AB810A20	OEM
AB811-20	OEM
AB811A20	OEM
AB812-20	OEM
AB812A20	OEM
AB813A20	OEM
AB813A51	OEM
AB820-20	OEM
AB822-20	OEM
AB822-51	OEM
AB1000	0087
A-B1000-139	0911
A-B1000-162	0911
A-B1002-16	OEM
AB2027	0436
AB4164ANP-12	2341
AB4164ANP-15	2341
AB7543GKN	OEM
ABD100A	OEM
ABD250A	OEM
ABDX25A	OEM
ABDX50A	OEM
ABF	0161
AC02BGM	OEM
AC02BT	OEM
AC02BTR	OEM
AC02DGM	OEM
AC02DT	OEM
AC02DTR	OEM
AC03BGML	2284
AC03BGMR	2284
AC03DGML	2284
AC03DGMR	2284
AC03EGML	OEM
AC03EGMR	OEM
AC03FGML	OEM
AC03FGMR	OEM
AC04BGML	OEM
AC04BGMR	OEM
AC04DGML	OEM
AC04DGMR	OEM
AC04EGML	OEM
AC04EGMR	OEM
AC04FGML	OEM
AC04FGMR	OEM
AC06B	OEM
AC06BS	OEM
AC06BSR	0154
AC06BT	0767
AC06D	OEM
AC06DR	OEM
AC06DS	OEM
AC06DSR	0147
AC06DT	0739
AC08BGML	0588
AC08BGMR	OEM
AC08BIML	OEM
AC08BIMR	OEM
AC08D	OEM
AC08DGML	0571
AC08DGMR	0571
AC08DIML	OEM
AC08DIMR	OEM
AC08EGML	0589
AC08EGMR	0589
AC08EIML	OEM
AC08EIMR	OEM
AC08FGML	0589
AC08FGMR	0589
AC08FIML	OEM
AC08FIMR	OEM
AC031	OEM
AC032	OEM
AC060	OEM
AC061	OEM
AC068BR	OEM
AC0V8BGM	OEM
AC0V8DGM	OEM
AC0V8FGM	OEM
AC10B	OEM
AC10BGML	0588
AC10BGMR	0588
AC10BIML	OEM
AC10BIMR	OEM
AC10BR	OEM
AC10BS	OEM
AC10BSR	0154
AC10BT	0767
AC10D	OEM
AC10DGML	OEM
AC10DGMR	0571
AC10DIML	OEM
AC10DIMR	OEM
AC10DR	OEM
AC10DS	OEM
AC10DSR	5051
AC10DT	0739
AC10EGML	0589
AC10EGMR	0589
AC10EIML	OEM
AC10EIMR	OEM
AC10FGML	0589
AC10FGMR	0589
AC10FIML	OEM
AC10FIMR	OEM
AC12BGML	0767
AC12BGMR	0739
AC12BIML	OEM

If replacement code is OEM, contact original manufacturer for replacement.

DEVICE TYPE	REPL CODE
AC12BIMR	OEM
AC12DGML	0739
AC12DGMR	0739
AC12DIML	OEM
AC12DIMR	OEM
AC12EGML	0739
AC12EGMR	0612
AC12EIML	OEM
AC12EIMR	OEM
AC12FGML	0612
AC12FGMR	0612
AC12FIML	OEM
AC12FIMR	OEM
AC14V	OEM
AC16BGML	OEM
AC16BGMR	OEM
AC16BIFL	OEM
AC16BIFR	OEM
AC16DGML	OEM
AC16DGMR	OEM
AC16DIFL	OEM
AC16DIFR	OEM
AC16EGML	OEM
AC16EGMR	OEM
AC16EIFL	OEM
AC16EIFR	OEM
AC16FGML	OEM
AC16FGMR	OEM
AC16FIFL	OEM
AC16FIFR	OEM
AC18M/U	0208
AC25BIFL	OEM
AC25BIFR	OEM
AC25DIFL	OEM
AC25DIFR	OEM
AC25EIFL	OEM
AC25EIFR	OEM
AC25FIFL	OEM
AC25FIFR	OEM
AC28V	OEM
AC30	0087
AC42V	OEM
AC50	0087
AC50(DIODE)	0133
AC50(RECTIFIER)	0110
AC56V	OEM
AC100	0087
AC105	0004
AC106	0004
AC107	0050
AC107M	0050
AC107N	0050
AC108	0004
AC109	0004
AC110	0004
AC113	0004
AC-113A	0004
AC-114	0004
AC114	0004
AC115	0004
AC116	0004
AC116-G	0279
AC116-GRN	0279
AC116-Y	0279
AC116-YEL	0279
AC117	0004
AC117A	0004
AC117B	0004
AC117P	0004
AC118	0004
AC119	0004
AC120	0004
AC121	0004
AC121-IV	0004
AC121-V	0004
AC121-VI	0004
AC121-VII	0004
AC121IV	0164
AC121V	0004
AC121VI	0004
AC121VII	0004
AC122	0004
AC122/30-GRN	0279
AC122/30-RED	0279
AC122/30-YEL	0279
AC122-30	0004
AC122-G	0279
AC122-GRN	0164
AC122-R	0279
AC122-RED	0164
AC122-V	0279
AC122-VIO	0164
AC122-Y	0279
AC122-YEL	0164
AC122GRN	0004
AC122RED	0004
AC122YEL	0004
AC123	0004
AC123-GRN	0279
AC123-YEL	0279
AC124	0004
AC125	0004
AC126	0164
AC127	0208
AC127/AC128-01	OEM
AC127/AC152	OEM
AC127-01	0208
AC127-132	0208
AC128	0164
AC128/01	0164
AC128/AC176	OEM
AC128-01	0164
AC128K	0164
AC129	0050
AC130	0595
AC130V	OEM
AC131	0004
AC131/30	0164
AC131-30	0164
AC132	0004
AC132-01	0004
AC133A	0004
AC134	0004
AC135	0004
AC136	0004
AC137	0004
AC138	0164
AC138H	OEM
AC139	0164
AC139/AC142	OEM
AC139K/AC142K	OEM
AC141	0208
AC-141B	2839
AC141B	0208
AC141H	OEM
AC141H-K	OEM
AC-141K	2839
AC141K	0208
AC142	0164
AC142H	OEM
AC142H-K	OEM
AC142K	0164
AC148	0160
AC150	0004
AC150-G	0279
AC150-GRN	0050
AC150-V	0279
AC150-VIO	0279
AC150-Y	0279
AC150-YEL	0050
AC150GRN	0004
AC150YEL	0004
AC151	0004
AC151-IV	0004
AC151-RIV	0004
AC151-RV	0004
AC151-RVI	0004
AC151-V	0004
AC151-VI	0004
AC151-VII	0004
AC151IV	0004
AC151R	0004
AC151RIV	0004
AC151RV	0004
AC151RVI	0004
AC151V	0004
AC151VI	0004
AC151VII	0004
AC152	0004
AC152-IV	0004
AC152-V	0004
AC152-VI	0004
AC152IV	0004
AC152V	0004
AC152VI	0004
AC153	0164
AC153K	0164
AC154	0164
AC154/AC157	OEM
AC155	0004
AC156	0004
AC157	0038
AC160	0004
AC160-G	0279
AC160-GRN	0050
AC160-R	1293
AC160-RED	0050
AC160-V	0279
AC160-VIO	0050
AC160-Y	1293
AC160-YEL	0050
AC160A	0004
AC160B	0004
AC160GRN	0004
AC160RED	0004
AC160YEL	0004
AC161	0004
AC162	0004
AC163	0004
AC164	0136
AC165	0004
AC166	0164
AC166/AC168	OEM
AC167	0164
AC168	0004
AC169	0136
AC170	0004
AC171	0004
AC172	0208
AC173	0004
AC175	0208
AC175A	0208
AC175B	0208
AC175P	0208
AC176	0208
AC176K	0164
AC177	0279
AC178	0164
AC179	0208
AC180	0164
AC180K	0164
AC180KL	OEM
AC181	0208
AC181K	0208
AC181KL	OEM
AC182	0004
AC-183	2839
AC183	0208
AC184	0004
AC185	0208
AC-186	2839
AC186	0208
AC187	0208
AC187/01	0595
AC187/AC188	OEM
AC187-01	4192
AC187K	0208
AC187R	0208
AC188	0164
AC188/01	0164
AC188-01	OEM
AC188-01/AC187-01	OEM
AC188K	0164
AC191	0004
AC192	0004
AC193	0164
AC193K	0164
AC194	0208
AC194K	0208
AC200	0087
AC250V	OEM
AC300	0535
AC400	0535
AC500	0959
AC600	0959
AC800	0811
AC1000	0916
AC4045NL	2037
AC5945	OEM
AC5945N	OEM
AC5947	OEM
AC5947N	OEM
AC5947NF	OEM
AC9082	0037
AC9083	0037
AC9084	0037
AC9085	0037
AC12801	0164
AC18701	0208
AC18801	0164
ACDC9000-1	0037
ACIA-534-200	OEM
ACIA-534-201	OEM
ACIA-534-300	OEM
ACIA-534-301	OEM
ACMB81416-15	OEM
ACR-10	OEM
ACR25U04LG	OEM
ACR25U06LG	OEM
ACR25U08LG	OEM
ACR25U10LG	OEM
ACR35U06LG	OEM
ACR83-1001	0136
ACR83-1002	0136
ACR83-1003	0136
ACR83-1004	0279
ACR83-1005	0279
ACR83-1006	0279
ACR83-1007	0143
ACR83-1008	0015
ACR810-101	0136
ACR810-102	0136
ACR810-103	0136
ACR810-104	0279
ACR810-105	0279
ACR810-106	0279
ACR810-107	0143
ACR810-108	0015
ACS02	OEM
ACS04	OEM
ACS09	OEM
ACS09B	OEM
ACS09OEM	OEM
ACS12-PRO	OEM
ACS14PRO	OEM
ACS15	OEM
ACS19	OEM
ACS64	OEM
ACS65	OEM
ACS120EM	OEM
ACS140EM	OEM
ACY11	OEM
ACY14	OEM
ACY16	0160
ACY-17	0004
ACY17	0004
ACY-18	0004
ACY18	0004
ACY-19	0004
ACY19	0004
ACY20	0004
ACY20-1	0004
ACY-21	0004
ACY21	0004
ACY21-1	0004
ACY22	0004
ACY22-1	0004
ACY23	0004
ACY23-V	0004
ACY23-VI	0004
ACY23V	0004
ACY23VI	0004
ACY24	0050
ACY27	0004
ACY28	0004
ACY29	0004
ACY30	0004
ACY31	0004
ACY32	0004
ACY32-V	0004
ACY32-VI	0004
ACY32V	0004
ACY32VI	0004
ACY33	0164
ACY33-VI	0164
ACY33-VII	0164
ACY33-VIII	0164
ACY33VI	0164
ACY33VII	0164
ACY34	0004
ACY35	0004
ACY36	0004
ACY38	0004
ACY39	0841
ACY40	0211
ACY41	0211
ACY41-1	0004
ACY44	0004
ACY44-1	0004
ACZ	0050
ACZ21	0050
AD04	OEM
AD-2	0811
AD2	OEM
AD8	0102
AD10	0015
AD27	OEM
AD-29	0102
AD29	0087
AD-29A	0102
AD-29B	0102
AD-29S	0102
AD30	0133
AD50	0015
AD58DTH	OEM
AD100	0015
AD100(DIODE)	0133
AD101	OEM
AD101AH	0093
AD102	OEM
AD103	0599
AD104	0599
AD105	0599
AD107	OEM
AD108	OEM
AD109	OEM
AD110	OEM
AD110A	0133
AD111	OEM
AD114	OEM
AD115	OEM
AD116	OEM
AD117	OEM
AD118	OEM
AD130	0160
AD131	0160
AD132	0160
AD133	0599
AD138	0160
AD138/50	0160
AD-139	0222
AD139	0085
AD-140	0160
AD140	0160
AD142	0599
AD143	0160
AD143B	0160
AD143R	0160
AD145	0160
AD-148	0160
AD148	0160
AD-149	0160
AD149	0085
AD149-01	0160
AD149-02	0160
AD149B	0160
AD149C	0160
AD-150	0160
AD150	0160
AD150(DIODE)	0133
AD-152	0222
AD152	0222
AD153	0160
AD155	0222
AD-156	0222
AD156	0222
AD-157	2736
AD157	2736
AD-159	0160
AD159	0160
AD160	0178
AD161	2736
AD161/AD162	OEM
AD-162	0222
AD162	0222
AD163	0969
AD164	0222
AD165	2736
AD166	0969
AD167	0969
AD169	0222
AD200	0015
AD200(DIODE)	0133
AD201AH	0093
AD201AN	OEM
AD201H	0093
AD262	0222
AD263	0222
AD301AH	0093
AD301ALH	OEM
AD301ALN	OEM
AD301AN	2267
AD346JD	OEM
AD346SD(M)	OEM
AD360SD	OEM
AD380JH	OEM
AD380KH	OEM
AD380LH	OEM
AD381JH	OEM
AD381KH	OEM
AD381LH	OEM
AD382JH	OEM
AD382KH	OEM
AD382LH	OEM
AD411	0133
AD503J	OEM
AD503JH	OEM
AD503K	OEM
AD503KH	OEM
AD503S	OEM
AD503SH	OEM
AD504JH	OEM
AD504KH	OEM
AD504LH	OEM
AD504MH	OEM
AD504SH	OEM
AD506KH	OEM
AD506LH	OEM
AD506SH	OEM
AD507JH	OEM
AD507KH	OEM
AD507SH	OEM
AD509JH	OEM
AD509KH	OEM
AD509SH	OEM
AD510JH	OEM
AD510KH	OEM
AD510LH	OEM
AD515JH	OEM
AD515KH	OEM
AD515LH	OEM
AD516A	OEM
AD516B	OEM
AD517J	OEM
AD517JH	OEM
AD517K	OEM
AD517KH	OEM
AD517LH	OEM
AD517SH	OEM
AD518J	OEM
AD518JH	OEM
AD518K	OEM
AD518KH	OEM
AD521JD	OEM
AD521K	OEM
AD521KD	OEM
AD521LD	OEM
AD522AD	OEM
AD522BD	OEM
AD523JH	OEM
AD523KH	OEM
AD523LH	OEM
AD524A	OEM
AD524B	OEM
AD524C	OEM
AD528J	OEM
AD528K	OEM
AD528S	OEM
AD530JD	OEM
AD530JH	OEM
AD530KD	OEM
AD530KH	OEM
AD530LD	OEM
AD530LH	OEM
AD530SD	OEM
AD530SH	OEM
AD531JD	OEM
AD531KD	OEM
AD531LD	OEM
AD531SD	OEM
AD532J	OEM
AD532JD	OEM
AD532JH	OEM
AD532K	OEM
AD532KD	OEM
AD532KH	OEM
AD532SD	OEM
AD532SH	OEM
AD533JD	OEM
AD533JH	OEM
AD533KD	OEM
AD533KH	OEM
AD533LD	OEM
AD533SD	OEM
AD533SH	OEM
AD534J	OEM
AD534JH	OEM
AD534K	OEM
AD534KH	OEM
AD534LH	OEM
AD534SH	OEM
AD534TH	OEM
AD535JD	OEM
AD535JH	OEM
AD535KD	OEM
AD535KH	OEM
AD536AJD	OEM
AD536AJH	OEM
AD536AKD	OEM
AD536AKH	OEM
AD537JD	OEM
AD537JH	OEM
AD537KD	OEM
AD537KH	OEM
AD537SD	OEM
AD537SH	OEM
AD539JD	OEM
AD539SD	OEM
AD540JH	OEM
AD540KH	OEM
AD542JH	OEM
AD542KH	OEM
AD542LH	OEM
AD544JH	OEM
AD544KH	OEM
AD544LH	OEM
AD545JH	OEM
AD545KH	OEM
AD545LH	OEM
AD545MH	OEM
AD547JH	OEM
AD547KH	OEM
AD547LH	OEM
AD558JH	OEM
AD558JN	OEM
AD558KD	OEM
AD558KN	OEM
AD558SD	OEM
AD558TD	OEM
AD559KD	OEM
AD559SD	OEM
AD561JD	OEM
AD561KD	OEM
AD561SD	OEM
AD561TD	OEM
AD562A	OEM
AD562AD/BCD	OEM
AD562AD/BIN	OEM
AD562KD/BCD	OEM
AD562KD/BIN	OEM
AD562SD/BCD	OEM
AD562SD/BIN	OEM
AD563JD/BCD	OEM
AD563JD/BIN	OEM
AD563KD/BIN	OEM
AD563KD-BCD	OEM
AD563SD/BCD	OEM
AD563SD/BIN	OEM
AD563TD/BCD	OEM
AD563TD/BIN	OEM
AD564KN	OEM
AD565AJD	OEM
AD565AKD	OEM
AD565ASD	OEM
AD565ATD	OEM
AD565JD	OEM
AD565JN	OEM
AD565KD	OEM
AD565KN	OEM
AD565SD	OEM
AD565TD	OEM
AD566AJD	OEM
AD566AKD	OEM
AD566ASD	OEM
AD566ATD	OEM
AD566JD	OEM
AD566JN	OEM
AD566KN	OEM
AD566SD	OEM
AD566TD	OEM
AD567JD	OEM
AD567JN	OEM
AD567KD	OEM
AD567SD	OEM
AD567TD	OEM
AD570JD	OEM
AD570SD	OEM
AD571JD	OEM
AD571KD	OEM
AD571SD	OEM
AD574AJD	OEM
AD574AKD	OEM
AD574ALD	OEM
AD574ASD	OEM
AD574ATD	OEM
AD574AUD	OEM
AD574JD	OEM
AD574KD	OEM
AD574LD	OEM
AD574SD	OEM
AD574TD	OEM
AD574UD	OEM
AD578JD	OEM
AD578KD	OEM
AD578S	OEM
AD580JH	OEM
AD580KH	OEM
AD580LH	OEM
AD580MH	OEM
AD581JH	OEM
AD581KH	OEM
AD581LH	OEM
AD581SH	OEM
AD581TH	OEM
AD581UH(M)	OEM
AD582KD	OEM
AD582KH	OEM
AD582SD	OEM
AD582SH	OEM
AD583KD	OEM
AD584K	OEM
AD584KH	OEM
AD584LH	OEM
AD584SH	OEM
AD585JD	OEM
AD585SD	OEM
AD589JH	OEM
AD589KH	OEM
AD589LH	OEM
AD589MH	OEM
AD589SH	OEM
AD589TH	OEM
AD589UH	OEM
AD590IF	OEM
AD590IH	OEM
AD590JF	OEM
AD590JH	OEM
AD590KF	OEM
AD590KH	OEM
AD590LF	OEM
AD590LH	OEM
AD590MF	OEM
AD590MH	OEM
AD594AD	OEM
AD594CD	OEM
AD611A	OEM
AD611B	OEM
AD611C	OEM
AD630JD	OEM
AD636JH	OEM
AD636KD	OEM
AD636KH	OEM
AD636SD	OEM
AD637J	OEM
AD637K	OEM
AD642JH	OEM
AD642KH	OEM
AD642LH	OEM
AD642SH	OEM
AD647JH	OEM
AD647KH	OEM
AD647LH	OEM
AD647SH	OEM
AD650JN	OEM
AD650JQ	OEM
AD650KN	OEM
AD650KQ	OEM
AD650SQ	OEM
AD741	0406
AD741C	0406
AD741CH	0406
AD741CN	1964
AD741H	0406
AD741JH	OEM
AD741JN	6086
AD741KH	0406
AD741KN	0308
AD741LH	4198
AD741LN	6086
AD741SH	OEM
AD810	OEM
AD811	OEM
AD812	OEM
AD813	OEM
AD814	OEM
AD815	OEM
AD816	OEM
AD818	OEM
AD820	OEM
AD821	OEM
AD822	OEM
AD830	OEM
AD831	OEM
AD832	OEM
AD833	OEM
AD833A	OEM
AD840	OEM
AD841	OEM
AD842	OEM
AD1000	OEM
AD1403AN	OEM
AD1403N	OEM
AD1408-7D	4252
AD1408-8D	OEM
AD1408-9D	OEM
AD1508-8D	OEM
AD1508-9D	OEM
AD1600	OEM
AD2700JD	OEM
AD2700LD	OEM
AD2701JD	OEM
AD2701LD	OEM
AD2701S	OEM

If replacement code is OEM, contact original manufacturer for replacement.

DEVICE TYPE	REPL CODE	DEVICE TYPE	REPL CODE	DEVICE TYPE	REPL CODE	DEVICE TYPE	REPL CODE	DEVICE TYPE	REPL CODE	DEVICE TYPE	REPL CODE	DEVICE TYPE	REPL CODE
AD2702JD	OEM	AD7521KD	OEM	AD7542SD	OEM	ADC1001CCD	OEM	ADP1640/DF	OEM	AEY29	OEM	AF181	0050
AD2702LD	OEM	AD7521KJN	OEM	AD7542TD	OEM	ADC1001CCN	OEM	ADP1640/SH	OEM	AEY29R	OEM	AF182	0050
AD2710KN	OEM	AD7521KN	OEM	AD7543AD	OEM	ADC1001CD	OEM	ADP1642	OEM	AEY30A	OEM	AF185	0050
AD2710LN	OEM	AD7521KPN	OEM	AD7543BD	OEM	ADC1021BCD	OEM	ADSHC85	OEM	AEY30B	OEM	AF186	0050
AD2712KN	OEM	AD7521LD	OEM	AD7543GBD	OEM	ADC1021BCN	OEM	ADSHC85ET	OEM	AEY30C	OEM	AF186G	0050
AD2712LN	OEM	AD7521LJN	OEM	AD7543GTD	OEM	ADC1021BD	OEM	ADV11A	OEM	AEY30D	OEM	AF186W	0050
AD2720AH	OEM	AD7521LN	OEM	AD7543JN	OEM	ADC1021CCD	OEM	ADVEFC32BH	OEM	AEY31	OEM	AF187	0004
AD2720BH	OEM	AD7521LPN	OEM	AD7543KN	OEM	ADC1021CCN	OEM	ADVFC32KN	OEM	AEY31A	OEM	AF188	0004
AD2720SH	OEM	AD7521SD	OEM	AD7543SD	OEM	ADC1021CD	OEM	ADVFC32SH	OEM	AEY32	OEM	AF192	0595
AD2720TH	OEM	AD7521SJN	OEM	AD7543TD	OEM	ADC1080HCD	OEM	ADX0214	0631	AEY39S	OEM	AF193	0050
AD3554AH	OEM	AD7521TD	OEM	AD7544AD	OEM	ADC1210HCD	OEM	ADX1103	0094	AF1(DIODE)	0102	AF200	0050
AD3954	OEM	AD7521TJN	OEM	AD7544BD	OEM	ADC1210HD	OEM	ADX1148	0080	AF4F	OEM	AF200U	0050
AD3954A	OEM	AD7521UD	OEM	AD7544GBD	OEM	ADC1211HCD	OEM	ADX1152	0124	AF63LA	OEM	AF201	0050
AD3954BH	OEM	AD7521UJN	OEM	AD7544GKN	OEM	ADC1211HD	OEM	ADX1364	0124	AF63LB	OEM	AF201C	0050
AD3955	OEM	AD7522JD	OEM	AD7544GTD	OEM	ADC1280HCD	OEM	ADX1473	0036	AF63LBA	OEM	AF201U	0050
AD3956	OEM	AD7522JN	OEM	AD7544JN	OEM	ADC3511CC	OEM	ADX1474	0947	AF68-3	OEM	AF202	0050
AD3958	OEM	AD7522KD	OEM	AD7544KN	OEM	ADC3711CC	OEM	ADX1518	0755	AF99	OEM	AF202L	0050
AD4001	0015	AD7522KN	OEM	AD7544SD	OEM	ADC7109C	OEM	ADY10	OEM	AF101	0050	AF202S	0050
AD4002	0071	AD7522LD	OEM	AD7544TD	OEM	ADC7109M	OEM	ADY11	OEM	AF101CJ	OEM	AF239	0050
AD4003	0071	AD7522LN	OEM	AD7545AQ	OEM	ADC7109R	OEM	ADY12	OEM	AF102	0050	AF239S	0050
AD4004	0071	AD7522SD	OEM	AD7545BQ	OEM	ADC-EK8B	OEM	ADY13	OEM	AF102CJ	OEM	AF240	0050
AD4005	0071	AD7522TD	OEM	AD7545CQ	OEM	ADC-EK10B	OEM	ADY18	OEM	AF103CJ	OEM	AF251	0050
AD4006	0071	AD7522UD	OEM	AD7545GCQ	OEM	ADC-EK12B	OEM	ADY20	OEM	AF104CJ	OEM	AF252	0050
AD4007	0071	AD7523AD	OEM	AD7545GLN	OEM	ADC-EK12DC	OEM	ADY22	0160	AF105	0136	AF253	0050
AD5010KD	OEM	AD7523BD	OEM	AD7545GUD	OEM	ADC-EK12DM	OEM	ADY23	0160	AF105A	0050	AF254	OEM
AD5201BD	OEM	AD7523CD	OEM	AD7545JN	OEM	ADC-EK12DR	OEM	ADY24	0160	AF105CJ	OEM	AF256	0050
AD5201TD	OEM	AD7523JN	OEM	AD7545KN	OEM	ADC-ET8BC	OEM	ADY25	OEM	AF-106	0050	AF267	0050
AD5202BD	OEM	AD7523KN	OEM	AD7545LN	OEM	ADC-ET8BM	OEM	ADY-26	0435	AF106	0050	AF279	0050
AD5202TD	OEM	AD7523LN	OEM	AD7545SD	OEM	ADC-ET10BC	OEM	ADY26	0040	AF106A	0050	AF279S	0050
AD5204BD	OEM	AD7523SD	OEM	AD7545TD	OEM	ADC-ET10BM	OEM	ADY27	0160	AF107	0050	AF280	0160
AD5204TD	OEM	AD7523TD	OEM	AD7545UD	OEM	ADC-ET12BC	OEM	ADY28	0160	AF108	0136	AF280S	OEM
AD5205BD	OEM	AD7523UD	OEM	AD7546AD	OEM	ADC-ET12BM	OEM	ADY30	OEM	AF109	0050	AF306	0050
AD5205TD	OEM	AD7524AD	OEM	AD7546BD	OEM	ADC-ET12BR	OEM	ADY32	OEM	AF109R	0050	AF367	0050
AD6020KD	OEM	AD7524BD	OEM	AD7546JN	OEM	ADC-MC8BC	OEM	ADZ11	0435	AF110	0050	AF369	0050
AD7420LPE	OEM	AD7524CD	OEM	AD7546KN	OEM	ADC-MC8BM	OEM	ADZ12	0435	AF110CJ	OEM	AF699	0037
AD7501JD	OEM	AD7524JN	OEM	AD7550BD	OEM	ADD3501	5732	AE1A	0087	AF111	0050	AF3570	0037
AD7501JN	OEM	AD7524KN	OEM	AD7552KN	OEM	ADDAC08AD	OEM	AE1B	0087	AF111CJ	OEM	AF3590	0037
AD7501KD	OEM	AD7524LN	OEM	AD7555BD	OEM	ADDAC08CD	OEM	AE1C	0087	AF112	0050	AF21490	0037
AD7501KN	OEM	AD7524SD	OEM	AD7555KN	OEM	ADDAC08D	OEM	AE1D	0087	AF112CJ	OEM	AF16672587	0341
AD7501SD	OEM	AD7524TD	OEM	AD7570J	OEM	ADDAC08ED	OEM	AE1E	0087	AF113	0050	AFC3527	0079
AD7502JD	OEM	AD7524UD	OEM	AD7570L	OEM	ADDAC08HD	OEM	AE1F	0087	AF113CJ	OEM	AFCS1170F	0037
AD7502JN	OEM	AD7525BD	OEM	AD7574AD	OEM	ADDAC80Z-CB1-1	OEM	AE1G	0087	AF114	0136	AFE428F003X3	OEM
AD7502KD	OEM	AD7525CD	OEM	AD7574BD	OEM	ADDAC80Z-CBI-I	OEM	AE3A	0110	AF114CJ	OEM	AFE436F003X1	OEM
AD7502KN	OEM	AD7525KN	OEM	AD7574JN	OEM	ADDAC80Z-CBI-V	OEM	AE3B	0947	AF114N	0050	AFL89WB20000C3	OEM
AD7502SD	OEM	AD7525LN	OEM	AD7574KN	OEM	ADDAC80Z-CCD-I	OEM	AE3C	0242	AF115	0136	AFS-160-1017	0143
AD7503JD	OEM	AD7525TD	OEM	AD7574SD	OEM	ADDAC80Z-CCD-V	OEM	AE3D	0535	AF115N	0050	AFS-160-1020	0123
AD7503JN	OEM	AD7525UD	OEM	AD7574TD	OEM	ADG200AA	OEM	AE3E	0959	AF116	0136	AFS-160-1021	0015
AD7503KD	OEM	AD7527BD	OEM	AD7583KN	OEM	ADG200AP	OEM	AE3F	0811	AF116N	0050	AFS-760-1017	0143
AD7503KN	OEM	AD7527CD	OEM	AD8007C	OEM	ADG200BA	OEM	AE3G	0916	AF117	0136	AFS24226	0037
AD7503SD	OEM	AD7527GCD	OEM	AD13850	0160	ADG200BP	OEM	AE10	0133	AF117C	0050	AFT0019M	0037
AD7506JD	OEM	AD7527GLN	OEM	AD51640/10	OEM	ADG200CJ	OEM	AE30	0133	AF117N	0050	AFT052	0037
AD7506KD	OEM	AD7527GUD	OEM	ADADC85C-12	OEM	ADG201AP	OEM	AE-50	0004	AF118	0050	AFT857P05L	OEM
AD7506KN	OEM	AD7527KN	OEM	ADB1200PCN	OEM	ADG201BP	OEM	AE50	0133	AF119	0050	AFT1341	0037
AD7506SD	OEM	AD7527LN	OEM	ADC0800PCD	OEM	ADG201CJ	OEM	AE100	0133	AF120	0136	AFT1746	0037
AD7506TD	OEM	AD7527TD	OEM	ADC0800PCN	OEM	ADH03011-8-3	OEM	AE150	0133	AF120CH	OEM	AFT2031	OEM
AD7507JD	OEM	AD7527UD	OEM	ADC0800PD	OEM	ADH03011-12-3	OEM	AE200	0133	AF120H	OEM	AFT2032	OEM
AD7507JN	OEM	AD7528AQ	OEM	ADC0801	3743	ADLC-540-200	OEM	AE304	1385	AF121	0050	AFT4231	OEM
AD7507KD	OEM	AD7528BQ	OEM	ADC0801LCD	OEM	ADLC-540-201	OEM	AE623	OEM	AF121-1CJ	OEM	AFT4232	OEM
AD7507KN	OEM	AD7528CQ	OEM	ADC0801LCN	OEM	ADLC-540-300	OEM	AE900	2688	AF121-2CJ	OEM	AFT6231	OEM
AD7507SD	OEM	AD7528JN	OEM	ADC0801LD	OEM	ADLC-540-301	OEM	AE904	1385	AF121S	0050	AFT6232	OEM
AD7507TD	OEM	AD7528KN	OEM	ADC0802	3743	ADO26B	OEM	AE-904-03	1385	AF122	0050	AFT8431	OEM
AD7510DIJD	OEM	AD7528LN	OEM	ADC0802LCD	3743	ADO27B	OEM	AE904-04	1385	AF122-1CJ	OEM	AFT8432	OEM
AD7510DIJN	OEM	AD7528SD	OEM	ADC0802LCN	3743	ADO29B	OEM	AE904-4	1385	AF122-2CJ	OEM	AFT12631	OEM
AD7510DIKD	OEM	AD7528TD	OEM	ADC0802LD	OEM	ADO32	OEM	AE904-6	1385	AF124	0136	AFT12632	OEM
AD7510DIKN	OEM	AD7528UD	OEM	ADC0803	OEM	ADO44	OEM	AE904-51	1385	AF125	0136	AFT18632	OEM
AD7510DISD	OEM	AD7530JD	OEM	ADC0803LCD	3743	ADO45	OEM	AE906	2593	AF126	0136	AFT18832	OEM
AD7511DIJD	OEM	AD7530JN	OEM	ADC0803LCN	3743	ADO60	OEM	AE-907	1434	AF127	0136	AFY10	0136
AD7511DIJN	OEM	AD7530JPE	OEM	ADC0803LD	OEM	ADO72A	OEM	AE907	1434	AF127/01	0050	AFY11	0136
AD7511DIKD	OEM	AD7530KD	OEM	ADC0804	OEM	ADOP07AH	OEM	AE907-51	1434	AF128	0050	AFY12	0050
AD7511DIKN	OEM	AD7530KN	OEM	ADC0804LCD	3743	ADOP07C	OEM	AE907	1335	AF129	0136	AFY14	0050
AD7511DISD	OEM	AD7530KPE	OEM	ADC0804LCN	3743	ADOP07CH	OEM	AE908	1832	AF130	0136	AFY15	0050
AD7511DITD	OEM	AD7530LD	OEM	ADC0805	OEM	ADOP07CN	OEM	AE908-51	1832	AF131	0136	AFY16	0050
AD7512DIJD	OEM	AD7530LN	OEM	ADC0808	OEM	ADOP07D	OEM	AE909	OEM	AF132	0136	AFY18	0136
AD7512DIJN	OEM	AD7530LPE	OEM	ADC0808CCJ	OEM	ADOP07DH	OEM	AE915	3050	AF133	0136	AFY18C	0050
AD7512DIKD	OEM	AD7530SD	OEM	ADC0808CCN	OEM	ADOP07DN	OEM	AE920	1042	AF134	0136	AFY18D	0050
AD7512DIKN	OEM	AD7530TD	OEM	ADC0808N	OEM	ADOP07EH	OEM	AE921	OEM	AF134-1CJ	OEM	AFY18E	0050
AD7512DISD	OEM	AD7530UD	OEM	ADC0809	OEM	ADOP07EN	OEM	AE922	OEM	AF134-2CJ	OEM	AFY19	0136
AD7512DITD	OEM	AD7531JD	OEM	ADC0809CCN	OEM	ADOP07H	OEM	AEIC50723202	OEM	AF135	0136	AFY34	0050
AD7513JH	OEM	AD7531JN	OEM	ADC0809N	OEM	ADP550	OEM	AEICC4277224	OEM	AF136	0136	AFY37	0050
AD7513JN	OEM	AD7531JPN	OEM	ADC0816	OEM	ADP560	OEM	AEL10	OEM	AF-137	0050	AFY39	0050
AD7513KH	OEM	AD7531KD	OEM	ADC0816CCJ	OEM	ADP560AC	OEM	AEL10H	OEM	AF137	0136	AFY40	0050
AD7513KN	OEM	AD7531KN	OEM	ADC0816CCN	OEM	ADP560AP	OEM	AEL13	OEM	AF137A	0050	AFY40K	0050
AD7513SH	OEM	AD7531KPN	OEM	ADC0816CJ	OEM	ADP560AT	OEM	AEL14	OEM	AF138	0136	AFY40R	0050
AD7513TH	OEM	AD7531LD	OEM	ADC0816N	OEM	ADP560ATC	OEM	AEL16	OEM	AF138/20	0050	AFY41	0050
AD7516JN	1135	AD7531LN	OEM	ADC0817CCN	OEM	ADP560ATP	OEM	AEL1009	OEM	AF139	0050	AFY42	0050
AD7516SD	OEM	AD7531LPN	OEM	ADC0817N	OEM	ADP560C	OEM	AEL1015	OEM	AF142	0050	AFZ11	0050
AD7516TD	OEM	AD7531SD	OEM	ADC08041	OEM	ADP560P	OEM	AEL1024	OEM	AF143	0050	AFZ12	0050
AD7519JN	OEM	AD7531TD	OEM	ADC11	OEM	ADP560TC	OEM	AEL1038	OEM	AF144	0136	AFZ23	0279
AD7520JD	OEM	AD7531UD	OEM	ADC12	OEM	ADP560TP	OEM	AEL1039	OEM	AF146	0050	AG01	OEM
AD7520JJE	OEM	AD7533AD	OEM	ADC-32	OEM	ADP590	OEM	AEL1044	OEM	AF147	0050	AG056	OEM
AD7520JN	OEM	AD7533BD	OEM	ADC-224-200	OEM	ADP590AC	OEM	AEL1053	OEM	AF148	0050	AG6	0546
AD7520JPE	OEM	AD7533CD	OEM	ADC-224-300	OEM	ADP590AP	OEM	AEL1062	OEM	AF149	0050	AG30	0133
AD7520KD	OEM	AD7533JN	OEM	ADC-228-200	OEM	ADP590ATC	OEM	AEL1067	OEM	AF150	0050	AG100	OEM
AD7520KJE	OEM	AD7533KN	OEM	ADC-228-201	OEM	ADP590ATP	OEM	AEL1075	OEM	AF150-1CJ	OEM	AG100D	0015
AD7520KN	OEM	AD7533LN	OEM	ADC-228-300	OEM	ADP590C	OEM	AEL1077	OEM	AF150-2CJ	OEM	AG100G	0015
AD7520KPE	OEM	AD7533SD	OEM	ADC-228-301	OEM	ADP590P	OEM	AEL-A51D	OEM	AF151-1CJ	OEM	AG100J	0015
AD7520LD	OEM	AD7533TD	OEM	ADC830	OEM	ADP590TC	OEM	AEY11	OEM	AF151-2CJ	OEM	AG106	OEM
AD7520LJE	OEM	AD7533UD	OEM	ADC833	OEM	ADP590TP	OEM	AEY12	OEM	AF164	0050	AG134	0136
AD7520LN	OEM	AD7541AD	OEM	ADC833BCD	OEM	ADP1010	OEM	AEY13	OEM	AF165	0050	AG150	OEM
AD7520SD	OEM	AD7541BD	OEM	ADC833BCN	OEM	ADP1015	OEM	AEY14	OEM	AF166	0050	AG206	OEM
AD7520SJE	OEM	AD7541JN	OEM	ADC833BD	OEM	ADP1020	OEM	AEY15	OEM	AF167	0050	AG406	OEM
AD7520TD	OEM	AD7541KN	OEM	ADC833CCD	OEM	ADP1400	OEM	AEY16	OEM	AF168	0050	AG466	OEM
AD7520TJE	OEM	AD7541LN	OEM	ADC833CCN	OEM	ADP1416	OEM	AEY17	OEM	AF169	0050	AG606	OEM
AD7520UD	OEM	AD7541SD	OEM	ADC833CD	OEM	ADP1500	OEM	AEY23	OEM	AF170	0050	AGC330	OEM
AD7520UJE	OEM	AD7541TD	OEM	ADC856C	OEM	ADP1520	OEM	AEY24	OEM	AF171	0050	AGH-001	4545
AD7521JD	OEM	AD7542AD	OEM	ADC856M	OEM	ADP1560	OEM	AEY25	OEM	AF172	0050	AGO512	0315
AD7521JJN	OEM	AD7542BD	OEM	ADC1001BCD	OEM	ADP1620/1	OEM	AEY26	OEM	AF178	0050	AGO1012	0315
AD7521JN	OEM	AD7542JN	OEM	ADC1001BCN	OEM	ADP1620/2	OEM	AEY27	OEM	AF179	0050	AGO1512	0315
AD7521JPN	OEM	AD7542KN	OEM	ADC1001BD	OEM	ADP1640/12	OEM	AEY28	OEM	AF180	0050	AGO2012	0315

DEVICE TYPE	REPL CODE
AGO2512	0315
AGO3012	0315
AGO3512	0315
AGO4012	0315
AGO5012	0315
AGO6012	0315
AGP15-200	0071
AGP15-400	0071
AGP15-600	0071
AGP15-800	0071
AH0010F(A)	OEM
AH0013CA	OEM
AH0013CB	OEM
AH0013MA	OEM
AH0013MB	OEM
AH0014CD	OEM
AH0014CN	OEM
AH0014D	OEM
AH0015CN	OEM
AH0015D	OEM
AH0019CD	OEM
AH0019CN	OEM
AH0019D	OEM
AH0126CD	OEM
AH0126D	OEM
AH0129CD	OEM
AH0129D	OEM
AH0133CD	OEM
AH0133CN	OEM
AH0133D	OEM
AH0134CD	OEM
AH0134CN	OEM
AH0134D	OEM
AH0139CD	OEM
AH0139D	OEM
AH0140CD	OEM
AH0140D	OEM
AH0141CD	OEM
AH0141D	OEM
AH0142CD	OEM
AH0142D	OEM
AH0143CD	OEM
AH0143D	OEM
AH0144CD	OEM
AH0144D	OEM
AH0145CD	OEM
AH0145D	OEM
AH0146CD	OEM
AH0146D	OEM
AH0151CD	OEM
AH0151CN	OEM
AH0151D	OEM
AH0152CD	OEM
AH0152CN	OEM
AH0152D	OEM
AH0153CD	OEM
AH0153D	OEM
AH0154CD	OEM
AH0154D	OEM
AH0161CD	OEM
AH0161D	OEM
AH0162CD	OEM
AH0162D	OEM
AH0163CD	OEM
AH0163D	OEM
AH0164CD	OEM
AH0164D	OEM
AH1	OEM
AH3	OEM
AH5	OEM
AH7	OEM
AH9	OEM
AH11	OEM
AH11-1	OEM
AH11-2	OEM
AH15	OEM
AH17	OEM
AH18	OEM
AH19	OEM
AH23	OEM
AH24	OEM
AH25	OEM
AH27	OEM
AH28	OEM
AH29	OEM
AH31	OEM
AH33	OEM
AH35	OEM
AH37	OEM
AH39	OEM
AH53	OEM
AH54	OEM
AH55	OEM
AH56	OEM
AH57-1	OEM
AH58	OEM
AH59	OEM
AH59-1	OEM
AH60	OEM
AH63	OEM
AH64	OEM
AH65	OEM
AH74	OEM
AH74-1	OEM
AH75	OEM
AH75-2	OEM
AH76	OEM
AH77	OEM
AH77-1	OEM
AH79	OEM
AH401	OEM
AH402	OEM
AH403	OEM
AH404	OEM
AH521	OEM
AH522	OEM
AH591	OEM
AH592	OEM
AH593	OEM
AH594	OEM
AH805	0071
AH810	0071
AH814	0071
AH815	0071
AH1005	0071
AH1010	0071
AH1015	0071
AH1020	0315
AH1510	0315
AH1520	0315
AH2010	0315
AH2020	0315
AH2114CG	OEM
AH2114G	OEM
AH2510	0315
AH2520	0315
AH4013	OEM
AH4077	OEM
AH4229	OEM
AH4230	OEM
AH5009CN	OEM
AH5010CN	OEM
AH5011CN	OEM
AH5012CN	OEM
AH5013CN	OEM
AH5014CN	OEM
AH5015CN	OEM
AH5016CN	OEM
AHB040	OEM
AHD554	OEM
AHD555	OEM
AHD557	OEM
AHD559	OEM
AHD560	OEM
AHD561	OEM
AHO510	0315
AHO520	0315
AHV8401	OEM
AHV8402	OEM
AHV8403	OEM
AHV8501	OEM
AHV8502	OEM
AHV8503	OEM
AHV8601	OEM
AHV8602	OEM
AHV8603	OEM
AHV8701	OEM
AHV8702	OEM
AHV8703	OEM
AHV8801	OEM
AHV8802	OEM
AHV8803	OEM
AHV9001	OEM
AHV9001A	OEM
AHV9002	OEM
AHV9002A	OEM
AHV9004	OEM
AHV9102	OEM
AHV9103A	OEM
AHV9104	OEM
AHV9201	OEM
AHV9201A	OEM
AHV9202	OEM
AHV9202A	OEM
AHV9204	OEM
AHV9301	OEM
AHV9301A	OEM
AHV9302	OEM
AHV9302A	OEM
AHV9304	OEM
AHV9401	OEM
AHV9401A	OEM
AHV9402	OEM
AHV9402A	OEM
AHV9404	OEM
AHV9501	OEM
AHV9501A	OEM
AHV9502	OEM
AHV9502A	OEM
AHV9504	OEM
AHV9801	OEM
AHV9801A	OEM
AHV9802	OEM
AHV9802A	OEM
AHV9803	OEM
AHV9803A	OEM
AHV9804	OEM
AHY10A	OEM
AHY10B	OEM
AHY10C	OEM
AHY10D	OEM
AIE	0007
AIH100A	OEM
AIM-12	OEM
AIM-12B	OEM
AJ5	0015
AJ10	0015
AJ15	0015
AJ20	0015
AJ25	0015
AJ30	0015
AJ35	0015
AJ40	0015
AJ50	0015
AJ60	0015
AJ103	0599
AJ7010	OEM
AJZ61	OEM
AK03	0730
AK1	1404
AK261	0143
AK10182-F20	OEM
AKBP02	0287
AKBP04	0293
AKBP06	0299
AKBP08	0250
AKBPC102	OEM
AKBPC104	OEM
AKBPC106	OEM
AKBPC108	OEM
AKBPC602	OEM
AKBPC604	OEM
AKBPC606	OEM
AKBPC608	OEM
AKBPC802	OEM
AKBPC804	OEM
AKBPC806	OEM
AKBPC808	OEM
AL-0010	OEM
AL01Z	1082
AL1C	0196
AL-10-5	2347
AL-10-10	2347
AL-10-20	2347
AL-10-30	2353
AL-10-40	2353
AL-10-50	2354
AL-10-60	2354
AL-10-70	2356
AL-10-80	2356
AL-10-90	2357
AL-10-100	2357
AL-10-120	OEM
AL-12-5	2347
AL-12-10	2347
AL-12-20	2347
AL-12-30	2353
AL-12-40	2353
AL-12-50	2354
AL-12-60	2354
AL-12-70	2356
AL-12-80	2356
AL-12-90	2357
AL-12-100	2357
AL-12-120	OEM
AL-15-5	2347
AL-15-10	2347
AL-15-20	2347
AL-15-30	2353
AL-15-40	2353
AL-15-50	2354
AL-15-60	2354
AL-15-70	2356
AL-15-80	2356
AL-15-90	2357
AL-15-100	2357
AL-15-120	OEM
AL-20-5	2347
AL-20-10	2347
AL-20-20	2347
AL-20-30	2353
AL-20-40	2353
AL-20-50	2354
AL-20-60	2354
AL-20-70	2356
AL-20-80	2356
AL-20-90	2357
AL-20-100	2357
AL-20-120	OEM
AL-25-5	2347
AL-25-10	2347
AL-25-20	2347
AL-25-30	2353
AL-25-40	2353
AL-25-50	2354
AL-25-60	2354
AL-25-70	2356
AL-25-80	2356
AL-25-90	2357
AL-25-100	2357
AL-25-120	OEM
AL-30-5	1633
AL-30-10	1633
AL-30-20	1633
AL-30-30	1663
AL-30-40	1663
AL-30-50	1663
AL-30-60	1663
AL-30-70	1579
AL-30-80	1579
AL-30-90	1579
AL-30-100	1579
AL-30-120	OEM
AL100	0969
AL101	0160
AL102	0969
AL102A	OEM
AL102B	OEM
AL102V	OEM
AL103	0969
AL103A	OEM
AL103B	OEM
AL106A	OEM
AL106B	OEM
AL106V	OEM
AL107A	OEM
AL107B	OEM
AL109A	OEM
AL112	0969
AL112A	OEM
AL112B	OEM
AL112D	OEM
AL112E	OEM
AL112G	OEM
AL112I	OEM
AL112SZ	OEM
AL112V	OEM
AL113	0599
AL113A	OEM
AL113B	OEM
AL113D	OEM
AL113E	OEM
AL113G	OEM
AL113I	OEM
AL113K	OEM
AL113L	OEM
AL113M	OEM
AL113N	OEM
AL113R	OEM
AL113S	OEM
AL113SZ	OEM
AL113V	OEM
AL210	0050
AL304A	OEM
AL304B	OEM
AL304G	OEM
AL304V	OEM
AL307	OEM
AL309A	OEM
AL309B	OEM
AL309D	OEM
AL309E	OEM
AL309G	OEM
AL309I	OEM
AL309K	OEM
AL309SZ	OEM
AL309V	OEM
AL80240	OEM
ALC1	0196
ALC1A	0196
ALCI	0196
ALD980	OEM
ALF1025	OEM
ALF3003	OEM
ALR450	OEM
ALS00A(SM)	OEM
ALS02(SM)	OEM
ALS08(SM)	OEM
ALS27(SM)	OEM
ALS38A(SM)	OEM
ALS74A(SM)	OEM
ALS244A	OEM
ALS244A(SM)	OEM
ALS245A	OEM
ALS257	OEM
ALS311A	OEM
ALS311B	OEM
ALS311G	OEM
ALS311V	OEM
ALS313A5	OEM
ALS374	OEM
ALS573B	OEM
ALS-8922	0016
ALT-512	OEM
ALTR-2480	OEM
ALZ10	0279
AM	0086
AM005	0015
AM01	0015
AM01M	0015
AM01Z	0015
AM010	0015
AM020	0015
AM025	0015
AM030	0015
AM035	0015
AM040	0015
AM050	0015
AM060	0015
AM06200012	0062
AM06200013	0133
AM06200014	0023
AM06200017	0143
AM06200065	0071
AM06200076	0286
AM1	0703
AM1S25610	OEM
AM2	0703
AM3	0015
AM4	0703
AM5	0703
AM9	0233
AM11	0575
AM12	0575
AM13	0015
AM21	0575
AM22	0575
AM23	0015
AM24	0575
AM25L02DC	OEM
AM25L02DM	OEM
AM25L02FM	OEM
AM25L02PC	OEM
AM25L02XC	OEM
AM25L02XM	OEM
AM25L03DC	OEM
AM25L03DM	OEM
AM25L03FM	OEM
AM25L03PC	OEM
AM25L03XC	OEM
AM25L03XM	OEM
AM25L04DC	OEM
AM25L04DM	OEM
AM25L04FM	OEM
AM25L04PC	OEM
AM25L04XC	OEM
AM25L04XM	OEM
AM25L05DC	OEM
AM25L05DM	OEM
AM25L05FM	OEM
AM25L05PC	OEM
AM25L06DC	OEM
AM25L06DM	OEM
AM25L06FM	OEM
AM25L06PC	OEM
AM25LS07DC	OEM
AM25LS07DM	OEM
AM25LS07FM	OEM
AM25LS07PC	OEM
AM25LS08DC	OEM
AM25LS08DM	OEM
AM25LS08FM	OEM
AM25LS08PC	OEM
AM25LS09DC	OEM
AM25LS09DM	OEM
AM25LS09FM	OEM
AM25LS09PC	OEM
AM25LS14DC	OEM
AM25LS14DM	OEM
AM25LS14FM	OEM
AM25LS14PC	OEM
AM25LS15DC	OEM
AM25LS15DM	OEM
AM25LS15FM	OEM
AM25LS15PC	OEM
AM25LS22DC	OEM
AM25LS22DM	OEM
AM25LS22FM	OEM
AM25LS22PC	OEM
AM25LS23DC	OEM
AM25LS23DM	OEM
AM25LS23FM	OEM
AM25LS23PC	OEM
AM25LS138DC	OEM
AM25LS138DM	OEM
AM25LS138FM	OEM
AM25LS138PC	OEM
AM25LS138XC	OEM
AM25LS138XM	OEM
AM25LS139DC	OEM
AM25LS139DM	OEM
AM25LS139FM	OEM
AM25LS139PC	OEM
AM25LS139XC	OEM
AM25LS139XM	OEM
AM25LS151PC	1636
AM25LS160DC	OEM
AM25LS160DM	OEM
AM25LS160FM	OEM
AM25LS160PC	OEM
AM25LS161DC	OEM
AM25LS161DM	OEM
AM25LS161FM	OEM
AM25LS161PC	OEM
AM25LS162DC	OEM
AM25LS162DM	OEM
AM25LS162FM	OEM
AM25LS162PC	OEM
AM25LS163DC	OEM
AM25LS163DM	OEM
AM25LS163FM	OEM
AM25LS163PC	OEM
AM25LS164DC	OEM
AM25LS164DM	OEM
AM25LS164FM	OEM
AM25LS164PC	OEM
AM25LS174DC	OEM
AM25LS174DM	OEM
AM25LS174FM	OEM
AM25LS174PC	OEM
AM25LS175DC	OEM
AM25LS175DM	OEM
AM25LS175FM	OEM
AM25LS175PC	OEM
AM25LS181DC	OEM
AM25LS181DM	OEM
AM25LS181FM	OEM
AM25LS181PC	OEM
AM25LS190DC	OEM
AM25LS190DM	OEM
AM25LS190FM	OEM
AM25LS190PC	OEM
AM25LS191DC	OEM
AM25LS191DM	OEM
AM25LS191FM	OEM
AM25LS191PC	OEM
AM25LS192DC	OEM
AM25LS192DM	OEM
AM25LS192FM	OEM
AM25LS192PC	OEM
AM25LS193DC	OEM
AM25LS193DM	OEM
AM25LS193FM	OEM
AM25LS193PC	OEM
AM25LS194ADC	OEM
AM25LS194ADM	OEM
AM25LS194AFM	OEM
AM25LS194APC	OEM
AM25LS195ADC	OEM
AM25LS195ADM	OEM
AM25LS195AFM	OEM
AM25LS195APC	OEM
AM25LS273DC	OEM
AM25LS273DM	OEM
AM25LS273FM	OEM
AM25LS273PC	OEM
AM25LS299DC	OEM
AM25LS299DM	OEM
AM25LS299FM	OEM
AM25LS299PC	OEM
AM25LS373DC	OEM
AM25LS373DM	OEM
AM25LS373FM	OEM
AM25LS373PC	OEM
AM25LS373XC	OEM
AM25LS373XM	OEM
AM25LS374DC	OEM
AM25LS374DM	OEM
AM25LS374FM	OEM
AM25LS374PC	OEM
AM25LS377BDC	OEM
AM25LS377BDM	OEM
AM25LS377BFM	OEM
AM25LS377BPC	OEM
AM25LS377DC	OEM
AM25LS377DM	OEM
AM25LS377FM	OEM
AM25LS377PC	OEM
AM25LS381DC	OEM
AM25LS381DM	OEM
AM25LS381FM	OEM
AM25LS381PC	OEM
AM25LS533DC	OEM
AM25LS533DM	OEM
AM25LS533FM	OEM
AM25LS533PC	OEM
AM25LS533XC	OEM
AM25LS2513DC	OEM
AM25LS2513DM	OEM
AM25LS2513FM	OEM
AM25LS2513PC	OEM
AM25LS2513XC	OEM
AM25LS2513XM	OEM
AM25LS2516DC	OEM
AM25LS2516DM	OEM
AM25LS2517DC	OEM
AM25LS2517DM	OEM
AM25LS2517FM	OEM
AM25LS2517PC	OEM
AM25LS2519DC	OEM
AM25LS2519DM	OEM
AM25LS2519FM	OEM
AM25LS2519PC	OEM
AM25LS2520DC	OEM
AM25LS2520DM	OEM
AM25LS2520PC	OEM
AM25LS2521PC	OEM
AM25LS2521PC-B	OEM
AM25LS2548DC	OEM
AM25LS2548DM	OEM
AM25LS2548FM	OEM
AM25LS2548PC	OEM
AM25LS2568DC	OEM
AM25LS2568DM	OEM
AM25LS2568FM	OEM
AM25LS2568PC	OEM
AM25LS2569DC	OEM
AM25LS2569DM	OEM
AM25LS2569FM	OEM
AM25LS2569PC	OEM
AM25S05DC	OEM
AM25S05DM	OEM
AM25S05FM	OEM
AM25S05PC	OEM
AM25S07DC	OEM
AM25S07DM	OEM
AM25S07FM	OEM
AM25S07PC	OEM
AM25S08DC	OEM
AM25S08DM	OEM
AM25S08FM	OEM
AM25S08PC	OEM
AM25S09DC	OEM
AM25S09DM	OEM
AM25S09FM	OEM
AM25S09PC	OEM
AM25S10DC	OEM
AM25S10DM	OEM
AM25S10FM	OEM
AM25S10PC	OEM
AM25S18DC	OEM
AM25S18DM	OEM
AM25S18FM	OEM
AM25S18PC	OEM
AM25S557DC	OEM
AM25S557DM	OEM
AM25S558DC	OEM
AM25S558DM	OEM
AM26L02DC	OEM
AM26L02DM	OEM
AM26L02FM	OEM
AM26L02PC	6698
AM26LS30PC	OEM
AM26LS31	OEM
AM26LS31CJ	OEM
AM26LS31CN	OEM
AM26LS31DC	OEM
AM26LS31DM	OEM
AM26LS31FM	OEM
AM26LS31J	OEM
AM26LS31MH	OEM
AM26LS31N	OEM
AM26LS31PC	OEM
AM26LS31XC	OEM
AM26LS31XM	OEM
AM26LS32	OEM
AM26LS32A	OEM
AM26LS32ACJ	OEM
AM26LS32ACN	OEM
AM26LS32AM	OEM
AM26LS32DC	OEM
AM26LS32DM	OEM
AM26LS32FM	OEM
AM26LS32J	OEM
AM26LS32N	OEM
AM26LS32PC	OEM
AM26LS32SM	OEM
AM26LS32XC	OEM
AM26LS33A	OEM
AM26LS33ACJ	OEM
AM26LS33ACN	OEM
AM26LS33AM	OEM
AM26LS33DC	OEM
AM26LS33DM	OEM
AM26LS33FM	OEM
AM26LS33PC	OEM
AM26LS33XC	OEM
AM26LS33XM	OEM
AM26S02DC	OEM
AM26S02DM	OEM
AM26S02FM	OEM
AM26S02PC	OEM
AM26S10C	OEM
AM26S10CJ	OEM
AM26S10CN	OEM
AM26S10DC	OEM
AM26S10DM	OEM
AM26S10FM	OEM
AM26S10M	OEM
AM26S10MJ	OEM
AM26S10MN	OEM
AM26S10PC	OEM
AM26S10XC	OEM
AM26S10XM	OEM
AM26S11C	OEM
AM26S11CJ	OEM
AM26S11CN	OEM
AM26S11DC	OEM
AM26S11DM	OEM
AM26S11FM	OEM
AM26S11MJ	OEM
AM26S11MN	OEM
AM26S11PC	OEM
AM26S11XC	OEM
AM26S11XM	OEM
AM26S12ADC	OEM
AM26S12ADM	OEM
AM26S12AFM	OEM
AM26S12APC	OEM
AM26S12AXC	OEM
AM26S12AXM	OEM
AM26S12DC	OEM
AM26S12DM	OEM
AM26S12FM	OEM
AM26S12PC	OEM
AM26S12XC	OEM
AM26S12XM	OEM
AM27LS00DC	OEM
AM27LS00DM	OEM
AM27LS00FM	OEM
AM27LS00PC	OEM
AM27LS01DC	OEM
AM27LS01DM	OEM
AM27LS01FM	OEM
AM27LS01PC	OEM
AM27LS02ADC	OEM
AM27LS02ADM	OEM
AM27LS02AFM	OEM
AM27LS02APC	OEM
AM27LS02DC	OEM
AM27LS02DM	OEM
AM27LS02FM	OEM
AM27LS02PC	OEM
AM27LS03DC	OEM
AM27LS03DM	OEM
AM27LS03FM	OEM
AM27LS03PC	OEM
AM27LS18DC	OEM
AM27LS18DM	OEM
AM27LS18FM	OEM
AM27LS19DC	OEM
AM27LS19DM	OEM
AM27LS19FM	OEM

If replacement code is OEM, contact original manufacturer for replacement.

DEVICE TYPE	REPL CODE
AM27S02DC	OEM
AM27S02DM	OEM
AM27S02FM	OEM
AM27S02PC	OEM
AM27S03ADC	OEM
AM27S03ADM	OEM
AM27S03AFM	OEM
AM27S03APC	OEM
AM27S03DC	OEM
AM27S03DM	OEM
AM27S03FM	OEM
AM27S03PC	OEM
AM27S08DC	OEM
AM27S08DM	OEM
AM27S09DC	OEM
AM27S09DM	OEM
AM27S10DC	OEM
AM27S10DM	OEM
AM27S11DC	OEM
AM27S11DM	OEM
AM27S12DC	2372
AM27S12DM	OEM
AM27S12FM	OEM
AM27S13DC	2373
AM27S13DM	OEM
AM27S13FM	OEM
AM27S15DC	OEM
AM27S15DM	OEM
AM27S18DC	3139
AM27S18DM	OEM
AM27S18FM	OEM
AM27S19DC	2161
AM27S19DM	OEM
AM27S19FM	OEM
AM27S20DC	1907
AM27S20DM	OEM
AM27S20FM	OEM
AM27S21DC	2209
AM27S21DM	OEM
AM27S21FM	OEM
AM27S25DC	OEM
AM27S25DM	OEM
AM27S26DC	OEM
AM27S26DM	OEM
AM27S27DC	OEM
AM27S27DM	OEM
AM27S28DC	3257
AM27S28DM	OEM
AM27S29DC	2304
AM27S29DM	OEM
AM27S30DC	2308
AM27S30DM	OEM
AM27S31DC	2306
AM27S31DM	OEM
AM27S32DC	2374
AM27S32DM	OEM
AM27S32PC	OEM
AM27S33DC	2376
AM27S33DM	OEM
AM27S33PC	OEM
AM27S80DC	OEM
AM27S80DM	OEM
AM27S80XX	OEM
AM27S81DC	OEM
AM27S81DM	OEM
AM27S81XX	OEM
AM27S180DC	2835
AM27S180DM	OEM
AM27S181DC	2881
AM27S181DM	OEM
AM27S184DC	OEM
AM27S184DM	OEM
AM27S185DC	3137
AM27S185DM	OEM
AM31	2049
AM31L01DC	OEM
AM31L01E	OEM
AM31L01FM	OEM
AM31L01PC	OEM
AM31L02DM	OEM
AM31L013E	OEM
AM32	2049
AM-33	0015
AM33	0015
AM34	2049
AM41	0994
AM42	0994
AM43	0015
AM44	0994
AM51	2065
AM52	2065
AM53	0015
AM54	2065
AM54LS373J	OEM
AM54LS373W	OEM
AM54LS373X	OEM
AM54LS533J	OEM
AM54LS533W	OEM
AM54LS533X	OEM
AM54S194J	OEM
AM54S194W	OEM
AM54S195J	OEM
AM54S195W	OEM
AM62	0015
AM63	0015
AM64	2070
AM65	0015
AM66	0015
AM74LS373J	0704
AM74LS373N	0704
AM74LS373X	0704
AM74LS533J	OEM
AM74LS533N	OEM
AM74LS533X	OEM
AM74S194J	OEM
AM74S194N	1920
AM74S195J	OEM
AM74S195N	OEM
AM90L44BDC	OEM
AM90L44BDM	OEM
AM90L44BPC	OEM
AM90L44CDC	OEM
AM90L44CDM	OEM
AM90L44CPC	OEM
AM90L44DDC	OEM
AM90L44DPC	OEM
AM90L60CDC	OEM
AM90L60CPC	OEM
AM90L60DDC	OEM
AM90L60DPC	OEM
AM90L60EDC	OEM
AM90L60EPC	OEM
AM91L01ADC	OEM
AM91L01ADM	OEM
AM91L01AFM	OEM
AM91L01APC	OEM
AM91L01BDC	OEM
AM91L01BDM	OEM
AM91L01BFM	OEM
AM91L01BPC	OEM
AM91L01CDC	OEM
AM91L01CDM	OEM
AM91L01CPC	OEM
AM91L02ADC	OEM
AM91L02ADM	OEM
AM91L02AFM	OEM
AM91L02APC	OEM
AM91L02BDC	OEM
AM91L02BDM	OEM
AM91L02BFM	OEM
AM91L02BPC	OEM
AM91L02CDC	OEM
AM91L02CDM	OEM
AM91L02CPC	OEM
AM91L02DC	OEM
AM91L02DM	OEM
AM91L02FM	OEM
AM91L02PC	OEM
AM91L0CDC	OEM
AM91L11ADC	OEM
AM91L11ADM	OEM
AM91L11AFM	OEM
AM91L11APC	OEM
AM91L11BDC	OEM
AM91L11BDM	OEM
AM91L11BFM	OEM
AM91L11BPC	OEM
AM91L11CDC	OEM
AM91L11CDM	OEM
AM91L11CPC	OEM
AM91L12ADC	OEM
AM91L12ADM	OEM
AM91L12AFM	OEM
AM91L12APC	OEM
AM91L12BDC	OEM
AM91L12BDM	OEM
AM91L12BFM	OEM
AM91L12BPC	OEM
AM91L12CDC	OEM
AM91L12CDM	OEM
AM91L12CPC	OEM
AM91L14BDC	OEM
AM91L14BDM	OEM
AM91L14BPC	OEM
AM91L14CDC	OEM
AM91L14CDM	OEM
AM91L14CPC	OEM
AM91L24BDC	OEM
AM91L24BDM	OEM
AM91L24BPC	OEM
AM91L24CDC	OEM
AM91L24CDM	OEM
AM91L24CPC	OEM
AM91L30ADC	OEM
AM91L30ADM	OEM
AM91L30APC	OEM
AM91L30BDC	OEM
AM91L30BDM	OEM
AM91L30BPC	OEM
AM91L30CDC	OEM
AM91L30CDM	OEM
AM91L30CPC	OEM
AM91L30DDC	OEM
AM91L30DPC	OEM
AM91L31ADC	OEM
AM91L31ADM	OEM
AM91L31BDC	OEM
AM91L31BDM	OEM
AM91L31CDC	OEM
AM91L31CDM	OEM
AM91L31DDC	OEM
AM91L40ADC	OEM
AM91L40ADM	OEM
AM91L40APC	OEM
AM91L40BDC	OEM
AM91L40BDM	OEM
AM91L40BPC	OEM
AM91L40CDM	OEM
AM91L40CPC	OEM
AM91L40DDC	OEM
AM91L40DPD	OEM
AM91L41DDC	OEM
AM92L44BDC	OEM
AM92L44BPC	OEM
AM92L44CDC	OEM
AM92L44CDM	OEM
AM92L44CPC	OEM
AM92L44DDC	OEM
AM92L44DPC	OEM
AM93L00DC	OEM
AM93L00FM	OEM
AM93L00PC	OEM
AM93L28DC	OEM
AM93L28DM	OEM
AM93L28FM	OEM
AM93L28PC	OEM
AM93L34DC	OEM
AM93L34DM	OEM
AM93L34FM	OEM
AM93L34PC	OEM
AM93L38DC	OEM
AM93L38DM	OEM
AM93L38FM	OEM
AM93L38PC	OEM
AM95-3310	OEM
AM95-4006	OEM
AM95-4010	OEM
AM95-4620	OEM
AM95-5032	OEM
AM95-5132	OEM
AM95-6011	OEM
AM95-6012	OEM
AM95-6110	OEM
AM95-6120	OEM
AM95-6220	OEM
AM95-6440	OEM
AM95-6450	OEM
AM95-6452	OEM
AM96-1000	OEM
AM96-4016	OEM
AM97C09CN	OEM
AM97C10CN	OEM
AM97C11CN	OEM
AM97C12CN	OEM
AM100A	OEM
AM100B	OEM
AM100C	OEM
AM101A	OEM
AM101B	OEM
AM102A	OEM
AM102B	OEM
AM103A	OEM
AM103B	OEM
AM124D	OEM
AM124F	OEM
AM201A	OEM
AM201B	OEM
AM201C	OEM
AM224D	0620
AM280HM	OEM
AM300	0133
AM300A	0133
AM301	0133
AM301A	0133
AM302	0133
AM302A	0133
AM303	0133
AM303A	0133
AM303B	0133
AM304	0133
AM304A	0133
AM305	0133
AM305A	0133
AM306	0133
AM306A	0133
AM307	0133
AM307A	0133
AM308	0133
AM308A	0133
AM324D	0620
AM324N	0620
AM405	0015
AM410	0015
AM410-2C	OEM
AM410-2M	OEM
AM411-2C	OEM
AM411-2M	OEM
AM414A	OEM
AM414B	OEM
AM414M	OEM
AM415	0015
AM420	0015
AM425	0015
AM430	0015
AM430A	OEM
AM430M	OEM
AM435	0015
AM440	0015
AM445	0015
AM450	0015
AM450-2	OEM
AM450-2M	OEM
AM452-2	OEM
AM452-2M	OEM
AM453-2C	OEM
AM453-2M	OEM
AM460	0015
AM460-2	OEM
AM460-2C	OEM
AM460-2M	OEM
AM462-1	OEM
AM462-1M	OEM
AM462-2	OEM
AM462-2M	OEM
AM464-2	OEM
AM464-2M	OEM
AM470-2C	OEM
AM470-2M	OEM
AM490-2A	OEM
AM490-2B	OEM
AM490-2C	OEM
AM490-2M	OEM
AM500GC	OEM
AM500MC	OEM
AM500MM	OEM
AM500MR	OEM
AM542AMC	OEM
AM542AMM	OEM
AM542AMR	OEM
AM543AMC	OEM
AM543AMM	OEM
AM543AMR	OEM
AM600	OEM
AM620	0133
AM620A	0133
AM626	0133
AM626A	0133
AM632	0133
AM632A	0133
AM670DM	OEM
AM681PC	OEM
AM685DL	OEM
AM685DM	OEM
AM685HL	OEM
AM685HM	OEM
AM686DC	OEM
AM686DM	OEM
AM686HC	OEM
AM686HM	OEM
AM687DL	OEM
AM723HM	1183
AM741HC	0406
AM747HC	2352
AM747HM	2352
AM748DC	2433
AM748DM	2433
AM748HC	2435
AM748HM	2435
AM904EPC	OEM
AM924BDC	OEM
AM1000H	OEM
AM1001H	OEM
AM1002H	OEM
AM1402A	OEM
AM1402A51E	OEM
AM1402A51F	OEM
AM1402A59F	OEM
AM1402ADM	OEM
AM1402APC	OEM
AM1403A	OEM
AM1403A51F	OEM
AM1403A51T	OEM
AM1403A59F	OEM
AM1403AHM	OEM
AM1403APC	OEM
AM1404A	OEM
AM1404A51F	OEM
AM1404A51T	OEM
AM1404A59F	OEM
AM1404AHM	OEM
AM1404APC	OEM
AM1406HM	OEM
AM1407HM	OEM
AM1408L6	OEM
AM1408L7	OEM
AM1408L8	OEM
AM1488XC	OEM
AM1489APC	OEM
AM1489AXC	OEM
AM1489PC	OEM
AM1489XC	OEM
AM1500DC	OEM
AM1500DL	OEM
AM1500DM	OEM
AM1500FM	OEM
AM1506HC	OEM
AM1507HC	OEM
AM1508L8	OEM
AM1660HC	OEM
AM1702A	OEM
AM1702A-1	OEM
AM1702A-2	OEM
AM1702AL	OEM
AM1702AL-1	OEM
AM1702AL-2	OEM
AM2009CD	OEM
AM2009CF	OEM
AM2009D	OEM
AM2009F	OEM
AM2501DC	OEM
AM2501DM	OEM
AM2502C/D	OEM
AM2502CJE	OEM
AM2502CPE	OEM
AM2502DC	OEM
AM2502DM	OEM
AM2502FM	OEM
AM2502M/D	OEM
AM2502MJE	OEM
AM2502PC	OEM
AM2502SM	OEM
AM2502XC	OEM
AM2503C/D	OEM
AM2503CJE	OEM
AM2503CPE	OEM
AM2503DC	OEM
AM2503DM	OEM
AM2503FM	OEM
AM2503M/D	OEM
AM2503MJE	OEM
AM2503PC	OEM
AM2503XC	OEM
AM2503XM	OEM
AM2504C/D	OEM
AM2504CJG	OEM
AM2504CPG	OEM
AM2504DC	OEM
AM2504DM	OEM
AM2504FM	OEM
AM2504M/D	OEM
AM2504MJG	OEM
AM2504PC	OEM
AM2504XC	OEM
AM2504XM	OEM
AM2505DC	OEM
AM2505DM	OEM
AM2505FM	OEM
AM2505PC	OEM
AM2506DC	OEM
AM2506DM	OEM
AM2506FM	OEM
AM2506PC	OEM
AM2600DC	OEM
AM2600DM	OEM
AM2600FM	OEM
AM2600PC	OEM
AM2602DC	OEM
AM2602DM	OEM
AM2602FM	OEM
AM2602PC	OEM
AM2708DC	4351
AM2708DM	OEM
AM2716DC	2263
AM2732ADC	5490
AM2764ADC	0806
AM2802DC	OEM
AM2802DM	OEM
AM2802PC	OEM
AM2803HC	OEM
AM2803HM	OEM
AM2803PC	OEM
AM2804HC	OEM
AM2804PC	OEM
AM2805HC	OEM
AM2805HM	OEM
AM2806HC	OEM
AM2806HM	OEM
AM2807PC	OEM
AM2808PC	OEM
AM2809HC	OEM
AM2809HM	OEM
AM2809PC	OEM
AM2810DC	OEM
AM2810DM	OEM
AM2812ADC	OEM
AM2812ADM	OEM
AM2812DC	OEM
AM2812DM	OEM
AM2813ADC	OEM
AM2813ADM	OEM
AM2813DC	OEM
AM2813DM	OEM
AM2814DC	OEM
AM2814DM	OEM
AM2814PC	OEM
AM2833DC	OEM
AM2833DM	OEM
AM2833PC	OEM
AM2841DC	OEM
AM2841DM	OEM
AM2855DC	OEM
AM2855DM	OEM
AM2855PC	OEM
AM2856HC	OEM
AM2856HM	OEM
AM2857DC	OEM
AM2857DM	OEM
AM2857PC	OEM
AM2901ADC	OEM
AM2901ADM	OEM
AM2901AFM	OEM
AM2901APC	OEM
AM2901AXC	OEM
AM2901BDC	OEM
AM2901BDM	OEM
AM2901BFM	OEM
AM2901BPC	OEM
AM2901CDC	OEM
AM2901CPC	OEM
AM2901DC	OEM
AM2901PC	OEM
AM2903A	OEM
AM2903DC	OEM
AM2903DM	OEM
AM2903FM	OEM
AM2961DC(M)	OEM
AM2961DC-B	OEM
AM2961DM(M)	OEM
AM2961DM-B(M)	OEM
AM2961FM(M)	OEM
AM2961FM-B(M)	OEM
AM2961XM(M)	OEM
AM2962DC(M)	OEM
AM2962DC-B	OEM
AM2962DM(M)	OEM
AM2962DM-B(M)	OEM
AM2962FM(M)	OEM
AM2962FM-B(M)	OEM
AM2962XC(M)	OEM
AM2962XM(M)	OEM
AM2964BDM	OEM
AM2964BFM	OEM
AM2964BPC	OEM
AM2964BXC	OEM
AM2965DC	OEM
AM2965DM	OEM
AM2965FM	OEM
AM2965PC	OEM
AM2965XC	OEM
AM2965XM	OEM
AM2966DC	OEM
AM2966DM	OEM
AM2966FM	OEM
AM2966PC	OEM
AM2966XC	OEM
AM2966XM	OEM
AM3010	0315
AM3020	0315
AM3101ADC	OEM
AM3101ADM	OEM
AM3101AFM	OEM
AM3101APC	OEM
AM3101DM	OEM
AM3101FM	OEM
AM3208SN	OEM
AM3235	0103
AM3341DC	OEM
AM3341DM	OEM
AM3341PC	OEM
AM3355DC	OEM
AM3355PC	OEM
AM3510	0315
AM3520	0315
AM3705CD	OEM
AM3705CF	OEM
AM3705CN	OEM
AM3705D	OEM
AM3705F	OEM
AM4010	0315
AM4020	0315
AM5005	0315
AM5010	0315
AM6005	0315
AM6010	0315
AM6012ADC	OEM
AM6012ADM	OEM
AM6012DC	OEM
AM6012DM	OEM
AM6070ADC	OEM
AM6070ADM	OEM
AM6070DC	OEM
AM6071ADC	OEM
AM6071ADM	OEM
AM6071DC	OEM
AM6071DM	OEM
AM6072DC	OEM
AM6072DM	OEM
AM6073DC	OEM
AM6073DM	OEM
AM6080ADC	OEM
AM6080ADM	OEM
AM6080APC	OEM
AM6080DC	OEM
AM6080DM	OEM
AM6080PC	OEM
AM6081ADC	OEM
AM6081ADM	OEM
AM6081APC	OEM
AM6081DC	OEM
AM6081DM	OEM
AM6112(A)	OEM
AM7600C	OEM
AM7600M	OEM
AM7600R	OEM
AM7601C	OEM
AM7601M	OEM
AM7601R	OEM
AM7605C	OEM
AM7605M	OEM
AM7605R	OEM
AM7606C	OEM
AM7606M	OEM
AM7606R	OEM
AM7611C	OEM
AM7611M	OEM
AM7612C	OEM
AM7612M	OEM
AM7613C	OEM
AM7613M	OEM
AM7614C	OEM
AM7614M	OEM
AM7615C	OEM
AM7615M	OEM
AM7831J	OEM
AM7831W	OEM
AM7831X	OEM
AM7832J	OEM
AM7832W	OEM
AM8085ACC	OEM
AM8085ADC	OEM
AM8085APC	OEM
AM8255A-5PC	0051
AM8510M	OEM
AM8510R	OEM
AM8520M	OEM
AM8520R	OEM
AM8530M	OEM
AM8530R	OEM
AM8831J	OEM
AM8831N	OEM
AM8831X	OEM
AM8832J	OEM
AM8832N	OEM
AM8832X	OEM
AM9016CDC	0518
AM9016CPC	0518
AM9016DDC	0518
AM9016DPC	0518
AM9016EDC	0518
AM9016EPC	0518
AM9016FDC	OEM
AM9016FPC	OEM
AM9044BDC	OEM
AM9044BDM	OEM
AM9044BPC	OEM
AM9044CDC	OEM
AM9044CDM	OEM
AM9044CPC	OEM
AM9044DDC	OEM
AM9044DDM	OEM
AM9044DPC	OEM
AM9044EDC	OEM
AM9050CDC	OEM
AM9050CPC	OEM
AM9050DDC	OEM
AM9050DPC	OEM
AM9050EDC	OEM
AM9050EPC	OEM
AM9060CDC	4815
AM9060CPC	4815
AM9060DDC	4815
AM9060DPC	4815
AM9060EDC	4815
AM9060EPC	4815
AM9080A1DC	OEM
AM9080A1PC	OEM
AM9080A2DC	OEM
AM9080A2DM	OEM
AM9080A2PC	OEM
AM9080A4DC	OEM
AM9080ADC	OEM
AM9080ADM	OEM
AM9080APC	OEM
AM9101	OEM
AM9101ADC	OEM
AM9101ADM	OEM
AM9101AFM	OEM
AM9101APC	OEM
AM9101BDC	OEM
AM9101BDM	OEM
AM9101BFM	OEM
AM9101BPC	OEM
AM9101CDC	OEM
AM9101CDM	OEM
AM9101CPC	OEM
AM9101DDC	OEM
AM9101DPC	OEM
AM9101EDC	OEM
AM9101EPC	OEM
AM9102ADC	4886
AM9102ADM	OEM
AM9102AFM	OEM
AM9102APC	4886
AM9102BDC	4886
AM9102BDM	OEM
AM9102BFM	OEM
AM9102BPC	4886
AM9102CDC	4886
AM9102CDM	OEM
AM9102CPC	4886
AM9102DC	4886
AM9102DDC	OEM
AM9102DM	OEM
AM9102DPC	OEM
AM9102EDC	OEM
AM9102EPC	OEM
AM9102FM	OEM
AM9102PC	4886
AM9111	OEM
AM9111ADC	OEM
AM9111ADM	OEM
AM9111AFM	OEM
AM9111APC	OEM
AM9111BDC	OEM
AM9111BDM	OEM
AM9111BFM	OEM
AM9111BPC	OEM
AM9111CDC	OEM
AM9111CDM	OEM
AM9111CPC	OEM
AM9111DDC	OEM
AM9111DPC	OEM
AM9111EDC	OEM

If replacement code is OEM, contact original manufacturer for replacement.

DEVICE TYPE	REPL CODE
AM9111EPC	OEM
AM9112	OEM
AM9112ADM	OEM
AM9112AFM	OEM
AM9112APC	OEM
AM9112BDC	OEM
AM9112BDM	OEM
AM9112BFM	OEM
AM9112BPC	OEM
AM9112CDC	OEM
AM9112CDM	OEM
AM9112CPC	OEM
AM9112DDC	OEM
AM9112DPC	OEM
AM9112EDC	OEM
AM9112EPC	OEM
AM9114	OEM
AM9114BDC	2037
AM9114BDM	OEM
AM9114BPC	2037
AM9114CDC	2037
AM9114CDM	OEM
AM9114CPC	2037
AM9114EDC	OEM
AM9114EPC	OEM
AM9124BDC	OEM
AM9124BDM	OEM
AM9124BPC	OEM
AM9124CDC	OEM
AM9124CDM	OEM
AM9124CPC	OEM
AM9124EDC	OEM
AM9124EPC	OEM
AM9130ADC	OEM
AM9130ADDM	OEM
AM9130BDC	OEM
AM9130BDM	OEM
AM9130BPC	OEM
AM9130CDC	OEM
AM9130CDM	OEM
AM9130CPC	OEM
AM9130DDC	OEM
AM9130DPC	OEM
AM9130EDC	OEM
AM9130EPC	OEM
AM9131ADC	OEM
AM9131ADM	OEM
AM9131BDC	OEM
AM9131BDM	OEM
AM9131CDC	OEM
AM9131CDM	OEM
AM9131DDC	OEM
AM9131EDC	OEM
AM9140ADC	OEM
AM9140ADM	OEM
AM9140APC	OEM
AM9140BDC	OEM
AM9140BDM	OEM
AM9140BPC	OEM
AM9140CDC	OEM
AM9140CDM	OEM
AM9140CPC	OEM
AM9140DDC	OEM
AM9140DPC	OEM
AM9140EDC	OEM
AM9140EPC	OEM
AM9208BDC	OEM
AM9208BDM	OEM
AM9208CDC	OEM
AM9214DC	OEM
AM9214DM	OEM
AM9216BDC	OEM
AM9216BDM	OEM
AM9216CDC	OEM
AM9217ADC	OEM
AM9217ADM	OEM
AM9217BDC	OEM
AM9217BDM	OEM
AM9218BCC	OEM
AM9218BDC	OEM
AM9218BDM	OEM
AM9218BPC	OEM
AM9218CCC	OEM
AM9218CDC	OEM
AM9218CPC	OEM
AM9232BCC	OEM
AM9232BDC	OEM
AM9232BDM	OEM
AM9232BPC	OEM
AM9232CCC	OEM
AM9232CDC	OEM
AM9232CPC	OEM
AM9233BCC	OEM
AM9233BDC	OEM
AM9233BDM	OEM
AM9233BPC	OEM
AM9233CCC	OEM
AM9233CDC	OEM
AM9233CPC	OEM
AM9244BDM	OEM
AM9244BPC	OEM
AM9244CDC	OEM
AM9244CDM	OEM
AM9244CPC	OEM
AM9244DDC	OEM
AM9244DDM	OEM
AM9244DPC	OEM
AM9244EDC	OEM
AM9244EPC	OEM
AM9300DC	OEM
AM9300DM	OEM
AM9300FM	OEM
AM9300PC	4203
AM9328DC	OEM
AM9328DM	OEM
AM9328FM	OEM
AM9328PC	OEM
AM9334DC	OEM
AM9334DM	OEM
AM9334FM	OEM
AM9334PC	OEM
AM9338DC	OEM
AM9338DM	OEM
AM9338FM	OEM
AM9338PC	OEM
AM9401DC	OEM
AM9401DM	OEM
AM9401PC	OEM
AM9404CDC	OEM
AM9404CDM	OEM
AM9404DDC	OEM
AM9404DDM	OEM
AM9404FDC	OEM
AM9517A-5PC	OEM
AM9702A-1HDC	OEM
AM9702AHDC	OEM
AM9702AL-1HDC	OEM
AM9702AL-2HDC	OEM
AM9702ALHDC	OEM
AM9709CN	OEM
AM9710CN	OEM
AM9711CN	OEM
AM9712CN	OEM
AM26123DC	OEM
AM26123DM	OEM
AM26123FM	OEM
AM26123PC	4748
AM27128DC	OEM
AM29203DC	OEM
AM29203DM	OEM
AM29203FM	OEM
AM29720DM	OEM
AM29720FM	OEM
AM29720PC	OEM
AM29721DC	OEM
AM29721DM	OEM
AM29721FM	OEM
AM29721PC	OEM
AM31013	OEM
AM35141DC	OEM
AM35142DC	OEM
AM97021-2HDC	OEM
AM161011H	0284
AM161011J	0079
AM161015H	0006
AM161016H	0079
AM161038H	0079
AM161039H	0079
AM161040H	0338
AM161041H	0710
AM161043H	0919
AM161044E	0388
AM161050H	0037
AM162005A	0015
AM164003A	OEM
AM167001A	0167
AM167013A	0391
AM167014A	1797
AM270059E	OEM
AM270059F	OEM
AM270159E	OEM
AM270159F	OEM
AMB4579	OEM
AMC8013AC	OEM
AMC8013AM	OEM
AMC8013BC	OEM
AMC8013BM	OEM
AMC8013CC	OEM
AMC8013CM	OEM
AMC40800	OEM
AMD-746	0661
AMD746	0345
AMD-780	0348
AMD780	0348
AMD-781	0350
AMD781	0350
AMF101	0556
AMF104	0103
AMF105	0103
AMF106	0637
AMF115	0103
AMF116	0103
AMF117	0103
AMF117A	0103
AMF118	0103
AMF118A	0103
AMF119	0103
AMF119A	0103
AMF120	0103
AMF120A	0103
AMF-121	0103
AMF201	0103
AMF201A	OEM
AMF201B	0130
AMF201C	0130
AMF201D	0615
AMF201E	0538
AMF210	0103
AMF210A	0103
AMF210B	0130
AMF210C	0074
AM-G-5	0015
AM-G-5A	0071
AM-G-5C	0071
AM-G-11	0250
AM-G-22	0015
AMI8025DAC	OEM
AMI8239MAQ	OEM
AMI8250MBK	OEM
AMI8314BLU	OEM
AMI8330YX	OEM
AMI8415AAB	OEM
AMI8431CN	OEM
AMI8503MFD	OEM
AMI8503MFX	OEM
AMI8524BT	OEM
AMI8524MAH	OEM
AMI8539MAV	OEM
AMIS25610	OEM
AMLM21D	OEM
AMLM101AH	0093
AMLM101H	0093
AMLM106	OEM
AMLM106F	OEM
AMLM108	OEM
AMLM108A	OEM
AMLM108AD	OEM
AMLM108AF	OEM
AMLM108D	OEM
AMLM108F	OEM
AMLM111	OEM
AMLM111D	2093
AMLM111F	OEM
AMLM112	OEM
AMLM112D	OEM
AMLM112F	OEM
AMLM118	OEM
AMLM118D	OEM
AMLM118F	OEM
AMLM119D	OEM
AMLM119F	OEM
AMLM119H	OEM
AMLM139AD	OEM
AMLM139AF	OEM
AMLM139D	OEM
AMLM139F	OEM
AMLM148D	OEM
AMLM201	0093
AMLM201A	0093
AMLM201AH	0093
AMLM201H	0093
AMLM206	OEM
AMLM207D	2267
AMLM207F	OEM
AMLM208	OEM
AMLM208A	OEM
AMLM208AD	OEM
AMLM208AF	OEM
AMLM208D	OEM
AMLM208F	OEM
AMLM211	OEM
AMLM216	OEM
AMLM216A	OEM
AMLM216AD	OEM
AMLM216D	OEM
AMLM218	OEM
AMLM218D	OEM
AMLM219D	OEM
AMLM219H	OEM
AMLM239AD	OEM
AMLM239D	OEM
AMLM248D	OEM
AMLM249D	OEM
AMLM301	0093
AMLM301A	0093
AMLM301AH	0093
AMLM306	OEM
AMLM307D	5928
AMLM308	OEM
AMLM308A	0890
AMLM308AD	OEM
AMLM308D	OEM
AMLM311	OEM
AMLM311D	2093
AMLM312	OEM
AMLM312D	OEM
AMLM316	OEM
AMLM316A	OEM
AMLM316AD	OEM
AMLM316D	OEM
AMLM318	OEM
AMLM318D	OEM
AMLM319D	OEM
AMLM319H	OEM
AMLM319N	2548
AMLM339AD	OEM
AMLM339AN	OEM
AMLM339D	OEM
AMLM339N	OEM
AMLM348D	OEM
AMLM348N	2796
AMLM349D	OEM
AMLM349N	OEM
AMPAL16L8PC	OEM
AMPAL16R8DC	OEM
AMS-D104	OEM
AMS-D105	OEM
AMS-D106	OEM
AMS-D126-A1	OEM
AMS-D127	OEM
AMS-D128	OEM
AMS-D218	OEM
AMS-D219	OEM
AMS-D220	OEM
AMS-D526	OEM
AMSSS725AJ	OEM
AMSSS725BJ	OEM
AMSSS725EJ	OEM
AMSSS741CJ	4198
AMSSS741J	OEM
AMSSS747CK	OEM
AMSSS747CP	OEM
AMSSS747K	OEM
AMSSS747M	OEM
AMSSS747P	OEM
AMS-SY52	OEM
AMSTRAD40044	OEM
AMU4L93L1851X	OEM
AMU5R7723312	1183
AMU6B930051X	OEM
AMU6B930059X	OEM
AMU6M93L1859X	OEM
AMU7B93L1851X	OEM
AMU7B93L1859X	OEM
AMU7B931851X	OEM
AMU7B931859X	OEM
AMX3548	0026
AMX3550	1519
AMX-3551	1550
AMX3551	1550
AMX3552	1585
AMX3553	1598
AMX3554	1657
AMX3555	0035
AMX3556	0822
AMX3557	0088
AMX3558	0243
AMX3560	1877
AMX3561	1615
AMX3562	0953
AMX3563	1153
AMX3564	4301
AMX3565	0260
AMX3566	1662
AMX3567	0971
AMX3568	0985
AMX3573	1253
AMX3582	0042
AMX3583	4305
AMX3584	0006
AMX3586	3441
AMX3655	0357
AMX-3675	1197
AMX3675	1197
AMX-3683	0990
AMX3683	0990
AMX3684	1329
AMX3688	1110
AMX3698	1623
AMX3701	0288
AMX3706	0813
AMX-3716	1688
AMX3716	1688
AMX3799	0486
AMX3800	0153
AMX3803	0973
AMX3804	1871
AMX3810	1230
AMX3864	0453
AMX3865	OEM
AMX3867	0503
AMX3868	0506
AMX3898	1652
AMX3921	OEM
AMX3955	1149
AMX4178	0076
AMX4181	2302
AMX4188	1827
AMX4200	0176
AMX4225	0447
AMX4227	0888
AMX4258	0308
AMX4260	1275
AMX4261	4437
AMX4263	0016
AMX4321	4445
AMX4321(MC75462P)	OEM
AMX4326	1110
AMX4327	2093
AMX4328	1828
AMX4329	OEM
AMX4330	0037
AMX4331	4265
AMX4470	0458
AMX4471	OEM
AMX4472	OEM
AMX4473	OEM
AMX4574	0808
AMX4575	OEM
AMX4577	0330
AMX4578	0443
AMX4579	OEM
AMX4582	1864
AMX4583	0422
AMX4584	0394
AMX4585	4451
AMX-4591	1197
AMX4642	OEM
AMX4658	0183
AMX4659	1554
AMX4660	0587
AMX4661	0356
AMX4663	3146
AMX4666	0056
AMX-4945	2248
AMX8001DC	OEM
AMZ8002DC	OEM
AMZ8036DM	OEM
AMZ8120	OEM
AMZ8121	OEM
AMZ8133	OEM
AMZ8136DC	OEM
AMZ8136DM	OEM
AMZ8136PC	OEM
AMZ8148DC	OEM
AMZ8148DM	OEM
AMZ8148PC	OEM
AMZ8173	OEM
AN0015CD	OEM
AN0120NA	OEM
AN0120NB	OEM
AN0120ND	OEM
AN0130NA	OEM
AN0130NB	OEM
AN0130ND	OEM
AN0140NA	OEM
AN0140NB	OEM
AN0140ND	OEM
AN-1	0015
AN3	OEM
AN29S	OEM
AN60P	OEM
AN74H72N	OEM
AN74LS107AN	1592
AN78L04	OEM
AN78L05	1288
AN78L05M-E1	OEM
AN78L06	4421
AN78L07	OEM
AN78L08	4422
AN78L09	1775
AN78L10	OEM
AN78L12	4424
AN78L15	4425
AN78L18	4427
AN78L20	OEM
AN78L24	4430
AN78M05	0619
AN78M05F	0619
AN78M05LB	0619
AN78M05R	OEM
AN78M08	1187
AN78M08R	OEM
AN78M09	1775
AN78M09-(LC)	1775
AN78M09F	OEM
AN78M10	2779
AN78M12	0330
AN78M12(LB)	0330
AN78M12-(LB)	0330
AN78M12-LB	0330
AN78M12LB	0330
AN78M15	1311
AN78M15(LB)	1311
AN78M15LB	1311
AN78N05	1288
AN78N08	OEM
AN78N12	OEM
AN79L04	OEM
AN79L05	4797
AN79L09	OEM
AN79L09-Y	OEM
AN79L15	4798
AN79L18	4799
AN79L20	OEM
AN79L24	1710
AN79M05	4818
AN79M06	4819
AN79N06	OEM
AN90B00	OEM
AN90B70	OEM
AN90C10	OEM
AN90C20	OEM
AN90C21	4838
AN90C22	5178
AN90C23	OEM
AN91A10S	OEM
AN91A14K	OEM
AN103	1532
AN103-0	1532
AN103G	1532
AN115	0701
AN136	2551
AN155	0039
AN158	0391
AN179	OEM
AN-203	2554
AN203	2554
AN203(C)	2554
AN203AA	2554
AN203BA	2554
AN203BB	2554
AN204D	OEM
AN205	OEM
AN-206	2555
AN206	2555
AN206AB	2555
AN206B	2555
AN206S	2555
AN208	3106
AN-210	2554
AN210	2556
AN210B	2556
AN210C	2556
AN-211	1826
AN211	1826
AN211A	1826
AN211AB	1826
AN211B	1826
AN213	3966
AN213-AB	3966
AN213AB	3966
AN-214	2111
AN214	2111
AN-214-G	2111
AN-214-P	2111
AN214-Q	OEM
AN214-QR	2111
AN214D	2111
AN-214P	2111
AN214P	2111
AN214PQR	2111
AN-214Q	5874
AN214Q	2111
AN214QR	2111
AN214R	2111
AN216	3968
AN217	2559
AN217(BB)	2559
AN217BB	2559
AN217CB	2559
AN217P	2559
AN217PBB	2559
AN220	2560
AN221	0167
AN222	0872
AN225	0399
AN227	2562
AN228V	2564
AN228W	2564
AN229	2563
AN230	2564
AN231	2565
AN234	2566
AN236	3973
AN238	3975
AN238S	0391
AN239	2914
AN239Q	2914
AN239QA	2914
AN239QB	2914
AN240	0167
AN240D	0167
AN240P	0167
AN240PD	0167
AN240PN	0167
AN240S	0167
AN241	3977
AN241A	3977
AN241B	3977
AN241C	3977
AN241D	3977
AN241P	3977
AN241PD	3977
AN242	3978
AN245	3238
AN-246	3238
AN246	3238
AN247	3242
AN247P	3242
AN249	OEM
AN252	2568
AN253	2568
AN253AB	2568
AN-253BB	2568
AN253BB	2568
AN253P	2568
AN255	OEM
AN259	3982
AN260	2569
AN262	2932
AN264	OEM
AN271	2570
AN271B	2570
AN271FB	2570
AN272	3985
AN274	2571
AN277	2573
AN277AB	2573
AN277B	2573
AN277BA	2573
AN278	3989
AN287	0107
AN287NT	0107
AN288	2576
AN289	3993
AN295	3997
AN295N	3997
AN298A	OEM
AN301	4000
AN302	4001
AN303	4002
AN304	1572
AN305	4004
AN313	4005
AN-315	4006
AN315	4006
AN316	4007
AN318	4008
AN320	OEM
AN321	OEM
AN326	4010
AN328	4014
AN331	2579
AN335	OEM
AN335F	OEM
AN337	4017
AN340	3216
AN340P	3216
AN342	2580
AN343	2580
AN345V	OEM
AN352	1251
AN353A	OEM
AN355	OEM
AN360	1516
AN362	1251
AN362L	1251
AN363N	0412
AN366	1501
AN370	OEM
AN374	4024
AN374P	4692
AN380	4025
AN521	OEM
AN605	OEM
AN607	OEM
AN608P	OEM
AN612	3980
AN614	OEM
AN616	OEM
AN640G	5463
AN660	OEM
AN705A	OEM
AN829	3074
AN829P	OEM
AN829S	3074
AN1201BR	0760
AN1339	0176
AN1339S	OEM
AN1358	0765
AN1358S	4195
AN1364	1162
AN1393	5210
AN1393S	OEM
AN1431	5204
AN1458	0356
AN1741	0308
AN2010S	OEM
AN2011S	OEM
AN2065	2555
AN2131	OEM
AN2140	OEM
AN2150S	OEM
AN2153NS	OEM
AN2154FAP	OEM
AN2240	OEM
AN2250S	OEM
AN2254FAP	OEM
AN2330	OEM
AN2340	OEM
AN2341	OEM
AN2350S	OEM
AN2410	OEM
AN2430	OEM
AN2450S	OEM
AN2510S	OEM
AN2512S	OEM
AN2513S	OEM
AN3120	OEM
AN3210K	4306
AN3211K	4306
AN3211NK	4306
AN3211S	OEM
AN3220K	OEM
AN3222	OEM
AN3223K	OEM
AN3224K	OEM
AN3230K	OEM
AN3230NK	OEM
AN3292NS	OEM
AN3292S	OEM
AN3294K	OEM
AN3296	OEM
AN3296S	OEM
AN3310K	5703
AN3311K	4306
AN3311NK	OEM
AN3312	6182
AN3313	5228
AN3313S	OEM
AN3316K	OEM
AN3320	OEM
AN3320K	5165
AN3320S	OEM
AN3321K	OEM
AN3330K	OEM
AN3334S	OEM
AN3346FAS	OEM
AN3394K	OEM
AN3396	OEM
AN3621K	OEM
AN3712K	OEM

If replacement code is OEM, contact original manufacturer for replacement.

DEVICE TYPE	REPL CODE
AN3720K	OEM
AN3790K	OEM
AN3791	OEM
AN3792	5232
AN3793	OEM
AN3794	OEM
AN3794N	OEM
AN3798NS	OEM
AN3810K	OEM
AN3812K	OEM
AN3813K	OEM
AN3813NK	OEM
AN3815K	OEM
AN3816SCR	OEM
AN3820	OEM
AN3821K	5166
AN3822K	5166
AN3824K	OEM
AN3824NK	OEM
AN3826K	OEM
AN3826NK	OEM
AN3830K	OEM
AN3840SR	OEM
AN3912	OEM
AN3920K	OEM
AN3925K	OEM
AN3928K	OEM
AN3990	OEM
AN3994K	OEM
AN4102	4647
AN5010	3809
AN5011	OEM
AN5013K	OEM
AN5015	4840
AN5015K	OEM
AN5019	OEM
AN5020	5123
AN5025K	OEM
AN5025KR	OEM
AN5036	OEM
AN5038	OEM
AN5070	5126
AN5071	OEM
AN5072	OEM
AN5079	OEM
AN5111	3692
AN5112	OEM
AN5120N	OEM
AN5125	3848
AN5125M	3848
AN5130	6623
AN5132	3698
AN5135K	3869
AN5135NK	3869
AN5136K	3871
AN5136K-R	3871
AN5136KR	3871
AN5137K	OEM
AN5138K	OEM
AN5138NK	OEM
AN5144	OEM
AN5150	OEM
AN5150N	OEM
AN5151	OEM
AN5151N	OEM
AN5153NK	3869
AN5156K	OEM
AN5156K-N	OEM
AN5156KN	OEM
AN5160NK	6388
AN5160NK)N	OEM
AN5160NK-N	6388
AN5179K	OEM
AN5180NK	OEM
AN5210	3738
AN5214S	OEM
AN5215	2008
AN5220	OEM
AN5221	OEM
AN5250	4662
AN5255	5116
AN5256	5116
AN5260	OEM
AN5262	4131
AN5265	4349
AN5291	OEM
AN5301K	4177
AN5301NK	4177
AN5302	OEM
AN5302K	OEM
AN5304K	OEM
AN5304NK	OEM
AN5310	2599
AN5310K	2599
AN5310KL	2599
AN5310L	2599
AN5310M	2599
AN5310N	2599
AN5310U	2599
AN5311	2599
AN5311KL	2599
AN5312	OEM
AN5313NK	OEM
AN5313NS	OEM
AN5314K	OEM
AN5315	5141
AN5316	4958
AN5316N	OEM
AN5318	5902
AN5318A	4281
AN5318N	4281
AN5320	4416
AN5321	OEM
AN5322NK	3645
AN5326	OEM
AN5330	4469
AN5332N	OEM
AN5340	3317
AN5341K	OEM
AN5342K	OEM
AN5352	4246
AN5352N	4246
AN5355	OEM
AN5356	OEM
AN5365	OEM
AN5371S	OEM
AN5372S	OEM
AN5410	2601
AN5411	5004
AN5416	3800
AN5421	OEM
AN5429	OEM
AN5430	OEM
AN5431N	OEM
AN5435	5003
AN5436	3701
AN5436N	3701
AN5437K	OEM
AN5437KR	OEM
AN5440	3325
AN5510	3997
AN5512	0970
AN5515	4840
AN5515X	4840
AN5520	3564
AN-5521	OEM
AN5521	4066
AN5530K	OEM
AN5531	OEM
AN5532	OEM
AN5551	OEM
AN5600K	OEM
AN5601NK	OEM
AN5610N	OEM
AN5612	OEM
AN5613	OEM
AN5615	OEM
AN5622	OEM
AN5625N	OEM
AN5630N	OEM
AN5632K	OEM
AN5633K	OEM
AN5635N	OEM
AN5700	4773
AN5701	OEM
AN5701N	OEM
AN5703	3707
AN5707NS	OEM
AN5710	5101
AN5712	3045
AN5720	3564
AN5722	3055
AN5730	2008
AN5732	2008
AN5733	OEM
AN5740	2760
AN5742	OEM
AN5743	OEM
AN5750	OEM
AN5752	3713
AN5753	3713
AN5760	OEM
AN5762	OEM
AN5763	OEM
AN5820	OEM
AN5822	OEM
AN5835	OEM
AN5836	1521
AN5837	OEM
AN5839	OEM
AN5855	OEM
AN5858K	OEM
AN5862	OEM
AN5862K	OEM
AN5900	6136
AN6040	OEM
AN6041	5137
AN6050	OEM
AN6135	OEM
AN6209	2055
AN6209K	2055
AN6209S	OEM
AN6249	OEM
AN6250	OEM
AN6251	OEM
AN6263	OEM
AN6263N	OEM
AN6290K	OEM
AN6291	3403
AN6291K	OEM
AN6291S	OEM
AN6295K	OEM
AN6295NK	OEM
AN6296	OEM
AN6300	4666
AN6306	2056
AN6306S	OEM
AN6307	2531
AN6310	5102
AN6320	4670
AN6320N	4670
AN6321	4981
AN6326	0694
AN6326N	0694
AN6327	OEM
AN6328	2057
AN6328S	OEM
AN6331	1575
AN6332	1575
AN6337	OEM
AN6340	1570
AN6341	4677
AN6341N	4677
AN6342	4678
AN6342N	4678
AN6343	5132
AN6344	1570
AN6345	5077
AN6346	OEM
AN6347	OEM
AN6350	5133
AN6352	0356
AN6354	OEM
AN6356N	5167
AN6357N	OEM
AN6359	5168
AN6359N	5168
AN6360	5134
AN6360S	OEM
AN6361	3686
AN6361N	3686
AN6361NS	OEM
AN6362	5450
AN6366	5169
AN6366K	5169
AN6366NK	5169
AN6366NS	OEM
AN6370	OEM
AN6387	0754
AN6390	5667
AN6391K	OEM
AN6391NK	OEM
AN6517S	OEM
AN6540	OEM
AN6541	OEM
AN6550	OEM
AN6551	2884
AN6552	0356
AN6552(F)	0356
AN6552S	OEM
AN6553	0356
AN6553F	OEM
AN6554	OEM
AN6554NS	OEM
AN6557	OEM
AN6557F	OEM
AN6557FLC	OEM
AN6558	0356
AN6561	3202
AN6562	0765
AN6564	0620
AN6564NS	OEM
AN6570	0308
AN6571	6694
AN6572	0356
AN6609N	OEM
AN6610	OEM
AN6612S	OEM
AN6638	OEM
AN6650-LF	OEM
AN6650S	OEM
AN6651	OEM
AN6652S	OEM
AN6660	OEM
AN6660K	OEM
AN6662	OEM
AN6663SP	OEM
AN6671K	OEM
AN6675	OEM
AN6677	5100
AN6683	OEM
AN6683N	OEM
AN6780	5447
AN6811	4671
AN6820	OEM
AN6821	4730
AN6855T	OEM
AN6873	2014
AN6873N	2014
AN6875	4736
AN6880	OEM
AN6884	5070
AN6886	OEM
AN6912	0176
AN6912N	0176
AN6912S	OEM
AN6913	4194
AN6914	0624
AN6914S	OEM
AN6915	OEM
AN7000	OEM
AN7025K	OEM
AN7062	5713
AN7070	OEM
AN7071	OEM
AN7072N	OEM
AN7074P	0391
AN7110	5136
AN7110E	5136
AN7111	OEM
AN7114	OEM
AN7115	4647
AN7115F	4647
AN7120	3167
AN7130	4633
AN7131	4635
AN7140	4635
AN7145	4648
AN7145H	4648
AN7145L	4648
AN7145M	4648
AN7146H	4637
AN7146M	4648
AN7147N	OEM
AN7148	OEM
AN7150	OEM
AN7154	4639
AN7155	OEM
AN7156N	4642
AN7158	3860
AN7158N	3860
AN7161N	6022
AN7163	OEM
AN7166	3860
AN7168	4035
AN7168N	4035
AN7171K	OEM
AN7205	OEM
AN7213	6693
AN7216	OEM
AN7218	2898
AN7218H	2898
AN7220	4226
AN7220A	4226
AN7220B	4226
AN7222	OEM
AN7223	OEM
AN7254	OEM
AN7266	OEM
AN7273	5719
AN7273A	OEM
AN7310	6753
AN7311	4682
AN7312	OEM
AN7351K	OEM
AN7375NS	OEM
AN7384	OEM
AN7410	1308
AN7410N	OEM
AN7410NS	1308
AN7411	OEM
AN7420	OEM
AN7470P	OEM
AN7805	0619
AN7805F	0619
AN7805LB	1801
AN7806	0917
AN7809	1336
AN7809F	OEM
AN7812	0330
AN7812F	0330
AN7815	6796
AN7818F	2244
AN7905T	1275
AN8003	OEM
AN8083SE2	OEM
AN8370S	OEM
AN8373S	OEM
AN8373SE2	OEM
AN8374S	OEM
AN8374SE2	OEM
AN8377	OEM
AN8387SE2	OEM
AN90800	OEM
ANAM1002	OEM
ANC7322	OEM
ANC7332	OEM
ANC-7345	OEM
ANC7345	OEM
ANC-7346	OEM
ANC7346	OEM
ANC-7708	OEM
ANC-7716	OEM
AND700	OEM
AND101R	OEM
AND101RG	3693
AND102G	3420
AND102GKB	OEM
AND102GKW	OEM
AND102R	OEM
AND102RKB	OEM
AND102RKW	OEM
AND103G	3420
AND103GK	OEM
AND103R	OEM
AND103RK	OEM
AND104R	5024
AND104RK	OEM
AND105G	3421
AND105GK	OEM
AND105R	5025
AND105RK	OEM
AND106R	OEM
AND106RK	OEM
AND107G	OEM
AND107GK	OEM
AND107R	OEM
AND107RK	OEM
AND108G	OEM
AND108GKB	OEM
AND108GKW	OEM
AND108R	OEM
AND108RKB	OEM
AND108RKW	OEM
AND109R	OEM
AND109RKB	OEM
AND109RKW	OEM
AND110R	OEM
AND110RK	OEM
AND113G	OEM
AND113R	3153
AND113S	OEM
AND113Y	OEM
AND114G	1767
AND114R	1605
AND114S	OEM
AND114Y	3128
AND115G	OEM
AND115R	OEM
AND116R	OEM
AND120R	OEM
AND121G	OEM
AND121R	1970
AND122G	1972
AND122R	5020
AND123G	OEM
AND123R	2990
AND123S	OEM
AND123Y	OEM
AND124G	0835
AND124R	OEM
AND124S	OEM
AND124Y	3095
AND132G	OEM
AND1320	OEM
AND132Y	OEM
AND202G	OEM
AND202R	OEM
AND205G	OEM
AND205R	OEM
AND205Y	OEM
AND206G	OEM
AND206R	OEM
AND206Y	OEM
AND207G	OEM
AND207R	OEM
AND207Y	OEM
AND208G	OEM
AND208R	OEM
AND208Y	OEM
AND226G	OEM
AND226R	OEM
AND226Y	OEM
AND324G	OEM
AND324R	OEM
AND325G	OEM
AND325R	OEM
AND326G	OEM
AND326R	OEM
AND327G	OEM
AND327R	OEM
AND352G	OEM
AND352R	OEM
AND353G	OEM
AND353R	OEM
AND370G	OEM
AND370R	OEM
AND371G	OEM
AND371R	OEM
AND516	OEM
AND600G	OEM
AND600R	OEM
AND622	OEM
AND651	OEM
AND700A	OEM
AND700G	OEM
AND700H	OEM
AND7000	OEM
AND700P	OEM
AND700R	OEM
AND700Y	OEM
AND703A	OEM
AND703G	OEM
AND703H	OEM
AND7030	OEM
AND703P	OEM
AND703R	OEM
AND703Y	OEM
AND704A	OEM
AND704G	OEM
AND704H	OEM
AND704P	OEM
AND704R	OEM
AND704Y	OEM
AND706A	OEM
AND706G	OEM
AND706H	OEM
AND7060	OEM
AND706P	OEM
AND706R	OEM
AND706Y	OEM
AND708H	OEM
AND710A	OEM
AND710G	OEM
AND710H	OEM
AND7100	OEM
AND710P	OEM
AND710R	OEM
AND710Y	OEM
AND713A	OEM
AND713G	OEM
AND713H	OEM
AND7130	OEM
AND713P	OEM
AND713R	OEM
AND713Y	OEM
AND714A	OEM
AND714G	OEM
AND714H	OEM
AND7140	OEM
AND714P	OEM
AND714R	OEM
AND714Y	OEM
AND716A	OEM
AND716G	OEM
AND716H	OEM
AND7160	OEM
AND716P	OEM
AND716R	OEM
AND716Y	OEM
AND718H	OEM
AND720A	OEM
AND720G	OEM
AND720H	OEM
AND7200	OEM
AND720P	OEM
AND720R	OEM
AND720Y	OEM
AND723A	OEM
AND723G	OEM
AND723H	OEM
AND7230	OEM
AND723P	OEM
AND723R	OEM
AND723Y	OEM
AND724A	OEM
AND724G	OEM
AND724H	OEM
AND7240	OEM
AND724P	OEM
AND724R	OEM
AND724Y	OEM
AND726A	OEM
AND726G	OEM
AND726H	OEM
AND7260	OEM
AND726P	OEM
AND726R	OEM
AND726Y	OEM
AND728H	OEM
AND740A	OEM
AND740G	OEM
AND740H	OEM
AND7400	OEM
AND740P	OEM
AND740R	OEM
AND743A	OEM
AND743G	OEM
AND743H	OEM
AND7430	OEM
AND743P	OEM
AND743R	OEM
AND744A	OEM
AND744G	OEM
AND744H	OEM
AND7440	OEM
AND744P	OEM
AND744R	OEM
AND744Y	OEM
AND746A	OEM
AND746G	OEM
AND746H	OEM
AND7460	OEM
AND746P	OEM
AND746R	OEM
AND746Y	OEM
AND748H	OEM
AND750A	OEM
AND750G	OEM
AND750H	OEM
AND7500	OEM
AND750P	OEM
AND750R	OEM
AND750Y	OEM
AND753A	OEM
AND753G	OEM
AND753H	OEM
AND7530	OEM
AND753P	OEM
AND753R	OEM
AND753Y	OEM
AND754A	OEM
AND754G	OEM
AND754H	OEM
AND7540	OEM
AND754P	OEM
AND754R	OEM
AND754Y	OEM
AND756A	OEM
AND756G	OEM
AND756H	OEM
AND7560	OEM
AND756P	OEM
AND756R	OEM
AND756Y	OEM
AND758H	OEM
AND1230	OEM
AND1240	OEM
AND1811	OEM
AND1861	OEM
AND3005GAL	OEM
AND3005GCL	OEM
AND3005HAL	OEM
AND3005HCL	OEM
AND30050AL	OEM
AND30050CL	OEM
AND3005RAL	OEM
AND3005RCL	OEM
AND3005YAL	OEM
AND3005YCL	OEM
AND3010GAL	OEM
AND3010GCL	OEM
AND3010HAL	OEM
AND3010HCL	OEM
AND30100AL	OEM
AND30100CL	OEM
AND3010RAL	OEM
AND3010RCL	OEM
AND3010YAL	OEM
AND3010YCL	OEM
AND3020GAL	OEM
AND3020GCL	OEM
AND3020HAL	OEM
AND3020HCL	OEM
AND30200AL	OEM
AND30200CL	OEM
AND3020RAL	OEM
AND3020RCL	OEM
AND3020YAL	OEM
AND3020YCL	OEM
AND4115R	OEM
AND4125R	OEM
AND4135G	OEM
AND4135R	OEM
AND4145G	OEM
AND4145R	OEM
AND4305GAL	OEM
AND4305GCL	OEM
AND4305HAL	OEM
AND4305HCL	OEM
AND43050AL	OEM
AND43050CL	OEM
AND4305RAL	OEM
AND4305RCL	OEM
AND4305YAL	OEM
AND4305YCL	OEM
AND4310GAL	OEM
AND4310GCL	OEM
AND4310HAL	OEM
AND4310HCL	OEM
AND43100AL	OEM
AND43100CL	OEM
AND4310RAL	OEM
AND4310RCL	OEM
AND4310YAL	OEM
AND4310YCL	OEM
AND5005GAL	OEM
AND5005GCL	OEM
AND5005HAL	OEM
AND5005HCL	OEM
AND50050AL	OEM
AND50050CL	OEM
AND5005RAL	OEM
AND5005RCL	OEM
AND5005YAL	OEM
AND5005YCL	OEM
AND5010GAJB	OEM
AND5010GAL	OEM
AND5010GCJB	OEM
AND5010GCL	OEM
AND5010HAL	OEM
AND50100AL	OEM
AND50100CL	OEM
AND5010RAJB	OEM
AND5010RAL	OEM
AND5010RCJB	OEM
AND5010RCL	OEM
AND5010YAL	OEM
AND5010YCL	OEM
AND5015GAL	OEM
AND5015GAL1	OEM
AND5015GCL	OEM
AND5015GCL1	OEM
AND5015HAL	OEM
AND5015HAL1	OEM
AND5015HCL	OEM
AND5015HCL1	OEM
AND50150AL	OEM
AND50150AL1	OEM
AND50150CL	OEM
AND50150CL1	OEM
AND5015RAL	OEM
AND5015RAL1	OEM
AND5015RCL	OEM
AND5015RCL1	OEM
AND5015YAL	OEM
AND5015YAL1	OEM
AND5015YCL	OEM
AND5015YCL1	OEM
AND5020GAL	OEM
AND5020GAL1	OEM
AND5020GCL	OEM
AND5020GCL1	OEM

If replacement code is OEM, contact original manufacturer for replacement.

265

DEVICE TYPE	REPL CODE
AND5020HAL	OEM
AND5020HAL1	OEM
AND5020HCL	OEM
AND5020HCL1	OEM
AND50200AL	OEM
AND50200AL1	OEM
AND50200CL	OEM
AND50200CL1	OEM
AND5020RAL	OEM
AND5020RAL1	OEM
AND5020RCL	OEM
AND5020RCL1	OEM
AND5020YAL	OEM
AND5020YAL1	OEM
AND5020YCL	OEM
AND5020YCL1	OEM
AND8101G	OEM
AND8101M	OEM
AND8101R	OEM
AND8102M	OEM
AND8152M	OEM
AND8202M	OEM
AND18035RCJ	OEM
AND18040RCJ	OEM
ANDBG05GAJ	OEM
ANDBG05RAJ	OEM
ANDBG10GAJ	OEM
ANDBG10MAJ	OEM
ANDBG10RAJ	OEM
ANDBG20MAJ	OEM
ANDBG30MAJ	OEM
ANDBG40MAJ	OEM
A01	0136
A07	0595
A04091A	0136
A04092	0015
A04092A	0015
A04092B	0015
A04093	0015
A04093-A	0015
A04093-X	0102
A04093A	0015
A04166-2	0002
A04201	0196
A04210A	0015
A04212-A	0015
A04212-B	0015
A04230-A	0102
A04233	0015
A04234-2	0012
A04241-A	0102
A04710	1293
A04716	0015
A04727	0469
A04735-A	0769
A04901A	0015
AOF-1050	OEM
AOF-1052	OEM
AOF-1300	OEM
AOM-12	OEM
AOTMS4416-15	OEM
AP0120NA	OEM
AP0120NB	OEM
AP0120ND	OEM
AP0130NA	OEM
AP0130NB	OEM
AP0130ND	OEM
AP0140NA	OEM
AP0140NB	OEM
AP0140ND	OEM
AP3.3A	0366
AP3.3B	0366
AP3.6A	0188
AP3.6B	0188
AP3.9A	0451
AP3.9B	0451
AP4.3A	0528
AP4.3B	0528
AP4.7A	0446
AP4.7B	0446
AP5.1A	0162
AP5.1B	0162
AP5.6A	0157
AP5.6B	0157
AP6.0A	0298
AP6.0B	0298
AP6.2A	0631
AP6.2B	0631
AP6.8A	0025
AP6.8B	0025
AP7.5A	0644
AP7.5B	0644
AP8.2A	0244
AP8.2B	0244
AP9.1A	0012
AP9.1B	0012
AP10.0A	0170
AP10.0B	0170
AP11.0A	0313
AP11.0B	0313
AP12.0A	0137
AP12.0B	0137
AP13.0A	0361
AP13.0B	0361
AP14.0A	0100
AP14.0B	0100
AP15-12	OEM
AP15.0A	0002
AP15.0B	0002
AP16.0A	0416
AP16.0B	0416
AP17.0A	1639
AP17.0B	1639
AP18.0A	0490
AP18.0B	0490
AP19.0A	0943
AP19.0B	0943
AP20.0A	0526
AP20.0B	0526
AP22.0A	0560
AP22.0B	0560
AP24.0A	0398
AP24.0B	0398
AP26.0A	0436
AP26.0B	0436
AP28.0A	1664
AP28.0B	1664
AP30-12	OEM
AP30-12L	OEM
AP30.0A	0721
AP30.0B	0721
AP33.0A	0039
AP33.0B	0039
AP36.0A	0814
AP36.0B	0814
AP39.0A	0346
AP39.0B	0346
AP413	OEM
AP414	OEM
AP433	OEM
AP623	OEM
AP2361	OEM
AP3897	OEM
AP3898	OEM
AP4023S	OEM
AP4156	OEM
AP4157	OEM
AP4829	OEM
AP4830	OEM
AP5179	OEM
AP5317	OEM
APB-11A-1001	0050
APB-11A-1004	0050
APB-11A-1008	0004
APB-11H-1001	0050
APB-11H-1004	0050
APB-11H-1007	0136
APB-11H-1008	0211
APB-11H-1010	0004
APD3.3A	0289
APD3.3B	0289
APD3.6A	0188
APD3.6B	0188
APD3.9A	0451
APD3.9B	0451
APD4C2003I	OEM
APD4C2003M	OEM
APD4C2008I	OEM
APD4C2008M	OEM
APD4C2028I	OEM
APD4C2028M	OEM
APD4C3003I	OEM
APD4C3003M	OEM
APD4C3008I	OEM
APD4C3008M	OEM
APD4C3028I	OEM
APD4C3028M	OEM
APD4C4003I	OEM
APD4C4003M	OEM
APD4C4008M	OEM
APD4C4028I	OEM
APD4C4028M	OEM
APD4C5003I	OEM
APD4C5003M	OEM
APD4C5008I	OEM
APD4C5008M	OEM
APD4C5028I	OEM
APD4C5028M	OEM
APD4C20003I	OEM
APD4C20003M	OEM
APD4C20008I	OEM
APD4C20008M	OEM
APD4C20028I	OEM
APD4C20028M	OEM
APD4.3A	0528
APD4.3B	0528
APD4.7A	0446
APD4.7B	0446
APD5.1A	0162
APD5.1B	0162
APD5.6A	0157
APD5.6B	0157
APD6.2A	0631
APD6.2B	0631
APD6.8A	0025
APD6.8B	0025
APD7.5A	0644
APD7.5B	0644
APD8.2A	0244
APD8.2B	0244
APD9.1A	0012
APD9.1B	0057
APD10.0A	0170
APD10.0B	0170
APD11.0A	0313
APD11.0B	0313
APD12.0A	0137
APD12.0B	0137
APD13.0A	0361
APD13.0B	0361
APD15.0A	0002
APD15.0B	0002
APD16.0A	0416
APD16.0B	0416
APD18.0A	0490
APD18.0B	0490
APD20.0A	0526
APD20.0B	0526
APD22.0A	0560
APD22.0B	0560
APD24.0A	0398
APD24.0B	0398
APD27.0A	0436
APD27.0B	0436
APD30.0A	0721
APD30.0B	0721
APD33.0A	0039
APD33.0B	0039
APD36.0A	0814
APD36.0B	0814
APD39.0A	0346
APD39.0B	0346
APD103	OEM
APD200	OEM
APD203	OEM
APD300	OEM
APD303	OEM
APD400	OEM
APD3595	0604
APLA722	OEM
APX43201/202(A)	OEM
APY10/I	OEM
APY10/II	OEM
APY11/I	OEM
APY11/II	OEM
APY12/I	OEM
APY12/II	OEM
APY12/III	OEM
APY13/I	OEM
APY13/II	OEM
APY13/III	OEM
AQ2	0086
AQ2(PHILCO)	0015
AQ3	0086
AQ3(PHILCO)	0015
AQ4	0198
AQ5	0086
AQ6	0198
AR01550	OEM
AR02550	OEM
AR03550	OEM
AR04501	OEM
AR04502	OEM
AR04550	OEM
AR05550	OEM
AR06550	OEM
AR06701	OEM
AR07700	OEM
AR09450	OEM
AR012000	OEM
AR061000	OEM
AR-4	0160
AR4	0085
AR-5	0160
AR5	0085
AR-6	0160
AR6	0085
AR-7	0160
AR7	0085
AR7C	0015
AR-8	0160
AR8	0160
AR8P404R	0160
AR-9	0160
AR9	0160
AR-10	0160
AR10	0160
AR-11	0160
AR11	0160
AR-12	0160
AR12	0160
AR-13	0160
AR13	0160
AR-14	0160
AR14	0160
AR-15	0142
AR15	0103
AR16	0015
AR-17	0042
AR17	0178
AR17(PHILCO)	0178
AR17A	0178
AR17B	0178
AR17GREY	0042
AR-18	0142
AR18	0178
AR18(PHILCO)	0178
AR19	0015
AR20	0015
AR21	0015
AR-22	OEM
AR22	0015
AR-22(DIO)	0015
AR22(RECTIFIER)	0015
AR22(TRANSISTOR)	0161
AR-22(XSTR)	0042
AR-23	OEM
AR23	0071
AR-23(DIO)	0071
AR23(RECTIFIER)	0811
AR23(TRANSISTOR)	0455
AR-23(XSTR)	0919
AR-24	0071
AR24	0071
AR24(PHILCO)	0555
AR24(RECTIFIER)	0811
AR24(TRANSISTOR)	0161
AR24(XSTR)	0419
AR24RED	0419
AR-25	0919
AR25	0848
AR25(G)	0919
AR25A	OEM
AR25B	OEM
AR25D	OEM
AR25F	OEM
AR25G	1257
AR25G(DIO)	OEM
AR25H	OEM
AR25J	OEM
AR25K	OEM
AR25M	OEM
AR26	1357
AR27	0848
AR27GREEN	0919
AR28	0419
AR28RED	0419
AR-29	1257
AR29	1357
AR-30	0419
AR30	0419
AR35	0419
AR37	0848
AR37GREEN	0919
AR38	0419
AR38RED	0419
AR44	0919
AR102	0164
AR-103	0004
AR103	0050
AR-104	0004
AR104	0050
AR-105	0004
AR105	0050
AR107	0016
AR108	0016
AR-200	0016
AR200	0144
AR200(W)	0079
AR200W	0144
AR200WHITE	0079
AR-201	0016
AR201	0144
AR201(Y)	0079
AR201Y	0144
AR201YELLOW	0079
AR-202	0016
AR202	0144
AR202G	0144
AR202GREEN	0079
AR203	0086
AR-203(R)	0590
AR203(R)	0590
AR203R	0086
AR203RED	0590
AR204	0016
AR205	0016
AR206	0016
AR207	0590
AR208	0016
AR209	0007
AR210	0007
AR211	0007
AR212	0144
AR213	0007
AR213(V)	0111
AR213V	0007
AR213VIOLET	0111
AR218	0224
AR218(RO)	0111
AR218ORANGE	0590
AR218RED	0590
AR218RO	0007
AR219	0007
AR219(YY)	0007
AR219YY	0127
AR220	0007
AR220(GY)	0007
AR220GREEN	0007
AR220GY	0127
AR220YELLOW	0007
AR221	0144
AR222	0007
AR222(BY)	0007
AR222BLUE	0007
AR222BY	0127
AR222YELLOW	0007
AR224	0127
AR224WHITE	0007
AR224YELLOW	0007
AR244	0919
AR303	0079
AR304	0126
AR304GREEN	0786
AR304RED	0786
AR306	0016
AR306BLUE	0086
AR306ORANGE	0086
AR308	0126
AR308VIOLET	0126
AR313	0144
AR343	0079
AR401P11	OEM
AR402P01	OEM
AR402P02	OEM
AR402P03	OEM
AR402P04	OEM
AR402P05	OEM
AR402P06	OEM
AR402P07	OEM
AR402P08	OEM
AR402P09	OEM
AR402P10	OEM
AR402P11	OEM
AR402P12	OEM
AR402S01	OEM
AR402S02	OEM
AR402S03	OEM
AR402S04	OEM
AR402S05	OEM
AR402S06	OEM
AR402S07	OEM
AR402S08	OEM
AR402S09	OEM
AR402S10	OEM
AR402S11	OEM
AR402S12	OEM
AR405P06	OEM
AR501	0212
AR502	0212
AR882	0015
AR904P02	OEM
AR904P03	OEM
AR904P04	OEM
AR904P05	OEM
AR904P06	OEM
AR904P07	OEM
AR904P08	OEM
AR904P09	OEM
AR904P10	OEM
AR904P11	OEM
AR904P12	OEM
AR904P13	OEM
AR904P14	OEM
AR904P15	OEM
AR904P16	OEM
AR904P17	OEM
AR904P18	OEM
AR904P19	OEM
AR904P20	OEM
AR904P21	OEM
AR904P22	OEM
AR904P23	OEM
AR904P24	OEM
AR904P25	OEM
AR904P26	OEM
AR904P27	OEM
AR904P28	OEM
AR904P29	OEM
AR904S02	OEM
AR904S03	OEM
AR904S04	OEM
AR904S05	OEM
AR904S06	OEM
AR904S07	OEM
AR904S08	OEM
AR904S09	OEM
AR904S10	OEM
AR904S11	OEM
AR904S12	OEM
AR904S13	OEM
AR904S14	OEM
AR904S15	OEM
AR904S16	OEM
AR904S17	OEM
AR904S18	OEM
AR904S19	OEM
AR904S20	OEM
AR904S21	OEM
AR904S22	OEM
AR904S23	OEM
AR904S24	OEM
AR904S25	OEM
AR904S26	OEM
AR904S27	OEM
AR904S28	OEM
AR904S29	OEM
AR912P25	OEM
AR912P26	OEM
AR912P27	OEM
AR912P28	OEM
AR912P29	OEM
AR912P30	OEM
AR912P31	OEM
AR912P32	OEM
AR912P33	OEM
AR912P34	OEM
AR912P35	OEM
AR912P36	OEM
AR912P37	OEM
AR912P38	OEM
AR912P39	OEM
AR912P40	OEM
AR912P41	OEM
AR912P42	OEM
AR912P43	OEM
AR912P44	OEM
AR912P45	OEM
AR912P46	OEM
AR912P47	OEM
AR912P48	OEM
AR912P49	OEM
AR912P50	OEM
AR912P51	OEM
AR912P52	OEM
AR912P53	OEM
AR912P54	OEM
AR912P55	OEM
AR912P56	OEM
AR912S25	OEM
AR912S26	OEM
AR912S27	OEM
AR912S28	OEM
AR912S29	OEM
AR912S30	OEM
AR912S31	OEM
AR912S32	OEM
AR912S33	OEM
AR912S34	OEM
AR912S35	OEM
AR912S36	OEM
AR912S37	OEM
AR912S38	OEM
AR912S39	OEM
AR912S40	OEM
AR912S41	OEM
AR912S42	OEM
AR912S43	OEM
AR912S44	OEM
AR912S45	OEM
AR912S46	OEM
AR912S47	OEM
AR912S48	OEM
AR912S49	OEM
AR912S50	OEM
AR912S51	OEM
AR912S52	OEM
AR912S53	OEM
AR912S54	OEM
AR912S55	OEM
AR912S56	OEM
AR1101P01	OEM
AR1101P02	OEM
AR1101P03	OEM
AR1101P04	OEM
AR1101P05	OEM
AR1101P06	OEM
AR1101P07	OEM
AR1101P08	OEM
AR1101P09	OEM
AR1101P10	OEM
AR1101S01	OEM
AR1101S02	OEM
AR1101S03	OEM
AR1101S04	OEM
AR1101S05	OEM
AR1101S06	OEM
AR1101S07	OEM
AR1101S08	OEM
AR1101S09	OEM
AR1101S10	OEM
AR1104P10	OEM
AR1104P11	OEM
AR1104P12	OEM
AR1104P13	OEM
AR1104P14	OEM
AR1104P15	OEM
AR1104P16	OEM
AR1104P17	OEM
AR1104P18	OEM
AR1104P19	OEM
AR1104P20	OEM
AR1104P21	OEM
AR1104P22	OEM
AR1104P23	OEM
AR1104P24	OEM
AR1104P25	OEM
AR1104P26	OEM
AR1104P27	OEM
AR1104P28	OEM
AR1104P29	OEM
AR1104S10	OEM
AR1104S11	OEM
AR1104S12	OEM
AR1104S13	OEM
AR1104S14	OEM
AR1104S15	OEM
AR1104S16	OEM
AR1104S17	OEM
AR1104S18	OEM
AR1104S19	OEM
AR1104S20	OEM
AR1104S21	OEM
AR1104S22	OEM
AR1104S23	OEM
AR1104S24	OEM
AR1104S25	OEM
AR1104S26	OEM
AR1104S27	OEM
AR1104S28	OEM
AR1104S29	OEM
AR1107P24	OEM
AR1107P25	OEM
AR1107P26	OEM
AR1107P27	OEM
AR1107P28	OEM
AR1107P29	OEM
AR1107P30	OEM
AR1107P31	OEM
AR1107P32	OEM
AR1107P33	OEM
AR1107P34	OEM
AR1107P35	OEM
AR1107P36	OEM
AR1107S24	OEM
AR1107S25	OEM
AR1107S26	OEM
AR1107S27	OEM
AR1107S28	OEM
AR1107S29	OEM
AR1107S30	OEM
AR1107S31	OEM
AR1107S32	OEM
AR1107S33	OEM
AR1107S34	OEM
AR1107S35	OEM
AR1107S36	OEM
AR1109P30	OEM
AR1109P31	OEM
AR1109P32	OEM
AR1109P33	OEM
AR1109P34	OEM
AR1109P35	OEM
AR1109P36	OEM
AR1109P37	OEM
AR1109P38	OEM
AR1109P39	OEM
AR1109P40	OEM
AR1109P41	OEM
AR1109P42	OEM
AR1109P43	OEM
AR1109P44	OEM
AR1109S30	OEM
AR1109S31	OEM
AR1109S32	OEM
AR1109S33	OEM
AR1109S34	OEM
AR1109S35	OEM
AR1109S36	OEM
AR1109S37	OEM
AR1109S38	OEM
AR1109S39	OEM
AR1109S40	OEM
AR1109S41	OEM
AR1109S42	OEM
AR1109S43	OEM
AR1109S44	OEM
AR2004P06	OEM
AR2004P07	OEM
AR2004P08	OEM
AR2004P09	OEM
AR2004P10	OEM
AR2004P11	OEM
AR2004P12	OEM
AR2004P13	OEM
AR2004P14	OEM
AR2004P15	OEM
AR2004P16	OEM
AR2004P17	OEM
AR2004P18	OEM
AR2004P19	OEM
AR2004P20	OEM
AR2004P21	OEM
AR2004P22	OEM
AR2004P23	OEM
AR2004P24	OEM
AR2004S06	OEM
AR2004S07	OEM
AR2004S08	OEM
AR2004S09	OEM
AR2004S10	OEM
AR2004S11	OEM
AR2004S12	OEM
AR2004S13	OEM
AR2004S14	OEM
AR2004S15	OEM
AR2004S16	OEM
AR2004S17	OEM
AR2004S18	OEM
AR2004S19	OEM
AR2004S20	OEM
AR2004S21	OEM
AR2004S22	OEM
AR2004S23	OEM
AR2004S24	OEM
AR2009P24	OEM
AR2009P25	OEM
AR2009P26	OEM
AR2009P27	OEM
AR2009P28	OEM
AR2009P29	OEM
AR2009P30	OEM
AR2009P31	OEM
AR2009P32	OEM
AR2009P33	OEM
AR2009P34	OEM
AR2009P35	OEM
AR2009P36	OEM
AR2009P37	OEM
AR2009P38	OEM
AR2009P39	OEM
AR2009P40	OEM
AR2009P41	OEM

266

If replacement code is OEM, contact original manufacturer for replacement.

DEVICE TYPE	REPL CODE
AR2009P42	OEM
AR2009P43	OEM
AR2009P44	OEM
AR2009PFS	OEM
AR2009S24	OEM
AR2009S25	OEM
AR2009S26	OEM
AR2009S27	OEM
AR2009S28	OEM
AR2009S29	OEM
AR2009S30	OEM
AR2009S31	OEM
AR2009S32	OEM
AR2009S33	OEM
AR2009S34	OEM
AR2009S35	OEM
AR2009S36	OEM
AR2009S37	OEM
AR2009S38	OEM
AR2009S39	OEM
AR2009S40	OEM
AR2009S41	OEM
AR2009S42	OEM
AR2009S43	OEM
AR2009S44	OEM
AR2400	OEM
AR2401	OEM
AR2402	OEM
AR2404	OEM
AR2406	OEM
AR2432B	OEM
AR3007P16	OEM
AR3007P17	OEM
AR3007P18	OEM
AR3007P19	OEM
AR3007P20	OEM
AR3007P21	OEM
AR3007P22	OEM
AR3007P23	OEM
AR3007P24	OEM
AR3007P25	OEM
AR3007P26	OEM
AR3007P27	OEM
AR3007P28	OEM
AR3007P29	OEM
AR3007P30	OEM
AR3007S16	OEM
AR3007S17	OEM
AR3007S18	OEM
AR3007S19	OEM
AR3007S20	OEM
AR3007S21	OEM
AR3007S22	OEM
AR3007S23	OEM
AR3007S24	OEM
AR3007S25	OEM
AR3007S26	OEM
AR3007S27	OEM
AR3007S28	OEM
AR3007S29	OEM
AR3007S30	OEM
AR3433S	OEM
AR11450	OEM
AR11452	OEM
AR20500	OEM
ARA25N	OEM
ARA25N-H	OEM
ARA25P	OEM
ARA25P-H	OEM
ARA46P	OEM
ARF612P01	OEM
ARF612P02	OEM
ARF612P03	OEM
ARF612P04	OEM
ARF612P05	OEM
ARF612P06	OEM
ARF612P07	OEM
ARF612P08	OEM
ARF612P09	OEM
ARF612P10	OEM
ARF612P11	OEM
ARF612P12	OEM
ARF612P13	OEM
ARF612P14	OEM
ARF612P15	OEM
ARF612S01	OEM
ARF612S02	OEM
ARF612S03	OEM
ARF612S04	OEM
ARF612S05	OEM
ARF612S06	OEM
ARF612S07	OEM
ARF612S08	OEM
ARF612S09	OEM
ARF612S10	OEM
ARF612S11	OEM
ARF612S12	OEM
ARF612S13	OEM
ARF612S14	OEM
ARF612S15	OEM
ARF912P01	OEM
ARF912P02	OEM
ARF912P03	OEM
ARF912P04	OEM
ARF912P05	OEM
ARF912P06	OEM
ARF912P07	OEM
ARF912P08	OEM
ARF912P09	OEM

DEVICE TYPE	REPL CODE
ARF912P10	OEM
ARF912P11	OEM
ARF912P12	OEM
ARF912P13	OEM
ARF912P14	OEM
ARF912P15	OEM
ARF912P16	OEM
ARF912P17	OEM
ARF912P18	OEM
ARF912P19	OEM
ARF912P20	OEM
ARF912P21	OEM
ARF912P22	OEM
ARF912P23	OEM
ARF912P24	OEM
ARF912P25	OEM
ARF912P26	OEM
ARF912S01	OEM
ARF912S02	OEM
ARF912S03	OEM
ARF912S04	OEM
ARF912S05	OEM
ARF912S06	OEM
ARF912S07	OEM
ARF912S08	OEM
ARF912S09	OEM
ARF912S10	OEM
ARF912S11	OEM
ARF912S12	OEM
ARF912S13	OEM
ARF912S14	OEM
ARF912S15	OEM
ARF912S16	OEM
ARF912S17	OEM
ARF912S18	OEM
ARF912S19	OEM
ARF912S20	OEM
ARF912S21	OEM
ARF912S22	OEM
ARF912S23	OEM
ARF912S24	OEM
ARF912S25	OEM
ARF912S26	OEM
ARF2012P01	OEM
ARF2012P02	OEM
ARF2012P03	OEM
ARF2012P04	OEM
ARF2012P05	OEM
ARF2012P06	OEM
ARF2012P07	OEM
ARF2012P08	OEM
ARF2012P09	OEM
ARF2012P10	OEM
ARF2012P11	OEM
ARF2012P12	OEM
ARF2012P13	OEM
ARF2012P14	OEM
ARF2012P15	OEM
ARF2012P16	OEM
ARF2012P17	OEM
ARF2012P18	OEM
ARF2012P19	OEM
ARF2012P20	OEM
ARF2012P21	OEM
ARF2012P22	OEM
ARF2012P23	OEM
ARF2012P24	OEM
ARF2012P25	OEM
ARF2012P26	OEM
ARF2012S01	OEM
ARF2012S02	OEM
ARF2012S03	OEM
ARF2012S04	OEM
ARF2012S05	OEM
ARF2012S06	OEM
ARF2012S07	OEM
ARF2012S08	OEM
ARF2012S09	OEM
ARF2012S10	OEM
ARF2012S11	OEM
ARF2012S12	OEM
ARF2012S13	OEM
ARF2012S14	OEM
ARF2012S15	OEM
ARF2012S16	OEM
ARF2012S17	OEM
ARF2012S18	OEM
ARF2012S19	OEM
ARF2012S20	OEM
ARF2012S21	OEM
ARF2012S22	OEM
ARF2012S23	OEM
ARF2012S24	OEM
ARF2012S25	OEM
ARF2012S26	OEM
ARS25A	OEM
ARS25B	OEM
ARS25D	OEM
ARS25G	OEM
ARS25J	OEM
ARS25K	OEM
ARS25M	OEM
ART2739	OEM
ART2895	OEM
AS01	0023
AS01V	0023
AS01V0	0023
AS01Z	0023
AS03250	OEM

DEVICE TYPE	REPL CODE
AS-2	0015
AS2	0015
AS-3	0015
AS3	0015
AS3A	0110
AS3B	0947
AS3C	0242
AS3D	0535
AS3E	0959
AS3F	0811
AS-4	0015
AS4	0015
AS-5	0015
AS5	0015
AS6	0015
AS11	0015
AS-14	0015
AS-15	0015
AS15	0015
AS80C40	OEM
AS100C40	OEM
AS120C40	OEM
AS215	0160
AS250C40	OEM
AS477	0841
AS3428	0595
AS5040C	OEM
AS5040M	OEM
AS5041C	OEM
AS5041M	OEM
AS5042C	OEM
AS5042M	OEM
AS5043C	OEM
AS5043M	OEM
AS5044C	OEM
AS5044M	OEM
AS5045C	OEM
AS5045M	OEM
AS5046C	OEM
AS5046M	OEM
AS5047C	OEM
AS5047M	OEM
AS5048C	OEM
AS5048M	OEM
AS5049C	OEM
AS5049M	OEM
AS5050C	OEM
AS5050M	OEM
AS5051C	OEM
AS5051M	OEM
AS5140C	OEM
AS5140M	OEM
AS5141C	OEM
AS5141M	OEM
AS5142C	OEM
AS5142M	OEM
AS5143C	OEM
AS5143M	OEM
AS5144C	OEM
AS5144M	OEM
AS5145C	OEM
AS5145M	OEM
AS10400	OEM
AS33867	0004
AS33868	0164
AS34280	0208
ASA2	OEM
ASA31	OEM
ASA51	OEM
ASA1000	OEM
ASA1001	OEM
ASA1003	OEM
ASA1004	OEM
ASBC-65	OEM
ASC/68	OEM
ASC/80	OEM
ASC/88	OEM
ASC/Z80	OEM
ASD25	0595
ASEC50	OEM
ASY12	OEM
ASY12-1	0164
ASY12-2	0164
ASY13	OEM
ASY13-1	0164
ASY13-2	0164
ASY14	0164
ASY14-1	0164
ASY14-2	0164
ASY14-3	0164
ASY-24	0050
ASY24	0004
ASY24B	0004
ASY26	0279
ASY26-RT	0050
ASY27	0279
ASY28	0595
ASY28-RT	0595
ASY29	0595
ASY29-RT	0595
ASY30	0136
ASY31	0004
ASY32	0004
ASY48	0004
ASY48-IV	0004
ASY48-V	0004
ASY48-VI	0004
ASY49	0004
ASY50	0004

DEVICE TYPE	REPL CODE
ASY51	0004
ASY52	0004
ASY53	0595
ASY54	0004
ASY55	0004
ASY56	0004
ASY56N	0279
ASY57	0136
ASY57N	0279
ASY58	0136
ASY58N	0279
ASY59	0136
ASY60	OEM
ASY61	0208
ASY61/TK33	OEM
ASY62	0208
ASY63	0050
ASY63N	0050
ASY64	OEM
ASY66	OEM
ASY67	0050
ASY70	0004
ASY70-IV	0004
ASY70-V	0016
ASY70-VI	0004
ASY70IV	0164
ASY70V	0164
ASY70VI	0164
ASY71	0164
ASY72	0595
ASY73	0595
ASY73-RT	0208
ASY74	0595
ASY74-RT	0208
ASY75	0595
ASY76	0279
ASY76-RT	0841
ASY77	0279
ASY80	0279
ASY80-RT	0841
ASY81	0841
ASY82	0004
ASY83	OEM
ASY84	0004
ASY85	OEM
ASY86	0595
ASY87	0595
ASY88	0595
ASY89	0595
ASY90	0004
ASY91	0004
ASZ10	0136
ASZ10(DIO)	0170
ASZ11	0136
ASZ12	0137
ASZ15	0002
ASZ16	0160
ASZ17	0160
ASZ18	0160
ASZ20	0050
ASZ20N	0050
ASZ21	0136
ASZ30	0136
ASZ1015	OEM
ASZ1016	OEM
ASZ1017	OEM
ASZ1018	OEM
AT/AF1	0211
AT/AF2	0211
AT/RF1	0050
AT/RF2	0050
AT/S13	0050
AT0017	0155
AT0017A	OEM
AT0025	0155
AT0025A	0155
AT0045	0155
AT0801ATI	OEM
AT-1	0050
AT-2	0050
AT-3	0050
AT-4	0050
AT4	0050
AT-5	0279
AT5	0050
AT-6	0050
AT6	0004
AT-6A	0004
AT6A	0004
AT-7	0086
AT7	0590
AT-8	0050
AT-9	0050
AT-10	0103
AT10H	0004
AT10M	0004
AT10N	0004
AT-11	0037
AT11	0150
AT-12	0086
AT12	0086
AT-12(PHILCO)	0086
AT13	0050
AT-14	0050
AT14	0050
AT15	0050
AT16	0050
AT17	0050
AT20H	0004

DEVICE TYPE	REPL CODE
AT20M	0004
AT20N	0004
AT24C01A	OEM
AT30H	0004
AT30M	0004
AT30N	0004
AT50	0004
AT52	0595
AT53	0595
AT71	0595
AT72	0595
AT73R	0595
AT74	0004
AT74S	0004
AT75R	0595
AT76R	0595
AT77	0595
AT100H	0004
AT100M	0004
AT100N	0004
AT110	0969
AT111	0969
AT112	0969
AT113	0969
AT128	OEM
AT200	0969
AT209	OEM
AT210	OEM
AT270	OEM
AT275	OEM
AT310	0127
AT311	0127
AT312	0127
AT313	0127
AT314	0127
AT315	0127
AT316	0127
AT318	0127
AT319	0127
AT321	0127
AT322	0127
AT323	0127
AT324	0127
AT325	0127
AT326	0127
AT327	0127
AT328	0127
AT329	0016
AT330	0127
AT331	0037
AT331A	0037
AT332	0037
AT332A	0037
AT333	0037
AT335	0016
AT335A	0037
AT336	0016
AT337	0016
AT338	0127
AT339	0086
AT340	0007
AT341	0007
AT342	0007
AT343	0007
AT344	0007
AT345	0007
AT346	0007
AT347	0016
AT348	0016
AT349	0016
AT350	0233
AT351	0233
AT353	0016
AT354	0016
AT355	0007
AT356	0007
AT360	OEM
AT361	OEM
AT362	OEM
AT363	OEM
AT364	OEM
AT365	OEM
AT366	OEM
AT367	OEM
AT368	OEM
AT370	0016
AT380	0086
AT381	0086
AT382	0086
AT383	0086
AT384	0086
AT385	0086
AT386	0086
AT387	0086
AT388	0086
AT390	0126
AT391	0126
AT392	0126
AT393	0126
AT394	0126
AT395	0126
AT396	0126
AT397	0126
AT398	0126
AT399	OEM
AT400	0016
AT401	0016
AT402	0016
AT403	0016

DEVICE TYPE	REPL CODE
AT403P01	OEM
AT403P02	OEM
AT403P03	OEM
AT403P04	OEM
AT403P05	OEM
AT403P06	OEM
AT403S01	OEM
AT403S02	OEM
AT403S03	OEM
AT403S04	OEM
AT403S05	OEM
AT403S06	OEM
AT404	0016
AT405	0016
AT405P01	OEM
AT405P02	OEM
AT405P03	OEM
AT405P04	OEM
AT405P05	OEM
AT405P06	OEM
AT405P07	OEM
AT405P08	OEM
AT405P09	OEM
AT405P10	OEM
AT405P11	OEM
AT405P12	OEM
AT405S01	OEM
AT405S02	OEM
AT405S03	OEM
AT405S04	OEM
AT405S05	OEM
AT405S06	OEM
AT405S07	OEM
AT405S08	OEM
AT405S09	OEM
AT405S10	OEM
AT405S11	OEM
AT405S12	OEM
AT406	0016
AT407	0016
AT410	0037
AT410-1	0037
AT412	0037
AT412-1	0037
AT413	0037
AT413-1	0037
AT414	0037
AT414-1	0037
AT415	0037
AT415-1	0037
AT416	0037
AT416-1	0037
AT417	0037
AT417-1	0037
AT418	0037
AT418-1	0037
AT419	0037
AT419-1	0037
AT420	0016
AT421	0016
AT422	0016
AT423	0016
AT424	0016
AT425	0016
AT426	0016
AT427	0016
AT430	0037
AT430-1	0037
AT431	0037
AT431-1	0037
AT432	0037
AT432-1	0037
AT433	0037
AT433-1	0037
AT434	0037
AT434-1	0037
AT435	0037
AT435-1	0037
AT436	0037
AT436-1	0037
AT437	0037
AT437-1	0037
AT438	0037
AT438-1	0037
AT440	0086
AT441	0086
AT442	0086
AT443	0086
AT444	0086
AT445	0086
AT446	0086
AT447	OEM
AT448	OEM
AT450	OEM
AT451	0037
AT451-1	0037
AT452	0037
AT452-1	0037
AT453	0037
AT453-1	0037
AT454	0037
AT454-1	0037
AT455	0037
AT455-1	0037
AT460	0126
AT461	0126
AT462	0126
AT463	0126
AT464	0126

DEVICE TYPE	REPL CODE
AT465	0126
AT466	0126
AT467	0126
AT468	0126
AT470	0086
AT471	0086
AT472	0086
AT473	0086
AT474	0086
AT475	0086
AT476	0086
AT477	0086
AT478	0086
AT479	0086
AT480	0126
AT481	0126
AT482	0126
AT483	0126
AT484	0126
AT485	0126
AT490	0016
AT491	0016
AT492	0016
AT493	0016
AT494	0016
AT495	0016
AT504	OEM
AT505P01	OEM
AT505P02	OEM
AT505P03	OEM
AT505P04	OEM
AT505P05	OEM
AT505P06	OEM
AT505P07	OEM
AT505P08	OEM
AT505P09	OEM
AT505P10	OEM
AT505P11	OEM
AT505P12	OEM
AT505P13	OEM
AT505P14	OEM
AT505P15	OEM
AT505S01	OEM
AT505S02	OEM
AT505S03	OEM
AT505S04	OEM
AT505S05	OEM
AT505S06	OEM
AT505S07	OEM
AT505S08	OEM
AT505S09	OEM
AT505S10	OEM
AT505S11	OEM
AT505S12	OEM
AT505S13	OEM
AT505S14	OEM
AT505S15	OEM
AT520	0144
AT521	0595
AT551	0595
AT704P01	OEM
AT704P02	OEM
AT704P03	OEM
AT704P04	OEM
AT704P05	OEM
AT704P06	OEM
AT704P07	OEM
AT704P08	OEM
AT704P09	OEM
AT704P10	OEM
AT704P11	OEM
AT704P12	OEM
AT704P13	OEM
AT704P14	OEM
AT704P15	OEM
AT704P16	OEM
AT704S01	OEM
AT704S02	OEM
AT704S03	OEM
AT704S04	OEM
AT704S05	OEM
AT704S06	OEM
AT704S07	OEM
AT704S08	OEM
AT704S09	OEM
AT704S10	OEM
AT704S11	OEM
AT704S12	OEM
AT704S13	OEM
AT704S14	OEM
AT704S15	OEM
AT704S16	OEM
AT804P01	OEM
AT804P02	OEM
AT804P03	OEM
AT804P04	OEM
AT804P05	OEM
AT804P06	OEM
AT804P07	OEM
AT804P08	OEM
AT804P09	OEM
AT804P10	OEM
AT804P11	OEM
AT804P12	OEM
AT804P13	OEM
AT804P14	OEM
AT804P15	OEM
AT804P16	OEM
AT804S01	OEM

If replacement code is OEM, contact original manufacturer for replacement.

DEVICE TYPE	REPL CODE	DEVICE TYPE	REPL CODE	DEVICE TYPE	REPL CODE	DEVICE TYPE	REPL CODE	DEVICE TYPE	REPL CODE	DEVICE TYPE	REPL CODE	DEVICE TYPE	REPL CODE
AT804S02	OEM	AT1007P16	OEM	AT4519	OEM	ATF587S06L	OEM	ATF860S10B	OEM	ATS21H1	OEM	AV108	OEM
AT804S03	OEM	AT1007P17	OEM	AT4520	OEM	ATF587S07L	OEM	ATF860S11B	OEM	ATS21J	OEM	AV109	OEM
AT804S04	OEM	AT1007P18	OEM	AT4521	OEM	ATF587S08L	OEM	ATF860S12B	OEM	ATS22H1	OEM	AV110	1777
AT804S05	OEM	AT1007P19	OEM	AT4642	OEM	ATF587S09L	OEM	ATF880P01P	OEM	ATS22J	OEM	AV111	OEM
AT804S06	OEM	AT1007P20	OEM	AT4680	OEM	ATF587S10L	OEM	ATF880P02P	OEM	ATS23J	OEM	AV112	OEM
AT804S07	OEM	AT1007P21	OEM	AT4690	OEM	ATF587S11L	OEM	ATF880P03P	OEM	ATS24J	OEM	AV113	OEM
AT804S08	OEM	AT1007P22	OEM	AT4841	OEM	ATF587S12L	OEM	ATF880P04P	OEM	ATS30	OEM	AV114	OEM
AT804S09	OEM	AT1007P23	OEM	AT4842	OEM	ATF827P01L	OEM	ATF880P05P	OEM	ATS40	OEM	AV115	OEM
AT804S10	OEM	AT1007P24	OEM	AT4880	OEM	ATF827P02L	OEM	ATF880P06P	OEM	ATS50	OEM	AV116	0433
AT804S11	OEM	AT1007S01	OEM	AT4890	OEM	ATF827P03L	OEM	ATF880P07P	OEM	ATS60	OEM	AV117	OEM
AT804S12	OEM	AT1007S02	OEM	AT5156	0126	ATF827P04L	OEM	ATF880P08P	OEM	ATY450	OEM	AV118	OEM
AT804S13	OEM	AT1007S03	OEM	AT6006	OEM	ATF827P05L	OEM	ATF880P09P	OEM	AU01	0023	AV119	OEM
AT804S14	OEM	AT1007S04	OEM	AT6007	OEM	ATF827P06L	OEM	ATF880P10P	OEM	AU01-07	0205	AV2010	OEM
AT804S15	OEM	AT1007S05	OEM	AT6008	OEM	ATF827P07L	OEM	ATF880P11P	OEM	AU01-08	0499	AV2011	OEM
AT804S16	OEM	AT1007S06	OEM	AT6009	OEM	ATF827P08L	OEM	ATF880P12P	OEM	AU01-09	0679	AV2012	0137
AT807P01	OEM	AT1007S07	OEM	AT6010	OEM	ATF827P09L	OEM	ATF880P13P	OEM	AU01-10	0225	AV2013	OEM
AT807P02	OEM	AT1007S08	OEM	AT6011	OEM	ATF827P09M	OEM	ATF880P14P	OEM	AU01-11	0230	AV2014	OEM
AT807P03	OEM	AT1007S09	OEM	AT6012	OEM	ATF827P09N	OEM	ATF880P15P	OEM	AU01-12	0234	AV2015	0002
AT807P04	OEM	AT1007S10	OEM	AT6013	OEM	ATF827P09P	OEM	ATF880P16P	OEM	AU01-13	0237	AV2016	OEM
AT807P05	OEM	AT1007S11	OEM	AT6014	OEM	ATF827P10L	OEM	ATF880P17P	OEM	AU01-15	0247	AV2017	OEM
AT807P06	OEM	AT1007S12	OEM	AT6015	OEM	ATF827P11L	OEM	ATF880P18P	OEM	AU01-16	0251	AV2018	OEM
AT807P07	OEM	AT1007S13	OEM	AT6016	OEM	ATF827P12L	OEM	ATF880P19P	OEM	AU01-18	0256	AV2019	OEM
AT807P08	OEM	AT1007S14	OEM	AT6017	OEM	ATF827P13L	OEM	ATF880S01P	OEM	AU01-20	0262	AV2020	OEM
AT807P09	OEM	AT1007S15	OEM	AT6018	OEM	ATF827P14L	OEM	ATF880S02P	OEM	AU01-22	0269	AV2021	OEM
AT807P10	OEM	AT1007S16	OEM	AT6019	OEM	ATF827S01L	OEM	ATF880S03P	OEM	AU01-24	0273	AV2022	OEM
AT807P11	OEM	AT1007S17	OEM	AT6020	OEM	ATF827S02L	OEM	ATF880S04P	OEM	AU01-27	0291	AV2023	OEM
AT807P12	OEM	AT1007S18	OEM	AT6021	OEM	ATF827S03L	OEM	ATF880S05P	OEM	AU01-30	0305	AV2024	OEM
AT807P13	OEM	AT1007S19	OEM	AT7510	OEM	ATF827S04L	OEM	ATF880S06P	OEM	AU01-33	0314	AV2025	OEM
AT807P14	OEM	AT1007S20	OEM	AT8040	OEM	ATF827S05L	OEM	ATF880S07P	OEM	AU01V0	OEM	AV2026	OEM
AT807P15	OEM	AT1007S21	OEM	AT8041	OEM	ATF827S06L	OEM	ATF880S08P	OEM	AU01Z	0023	AV2027	0436
AT807P16	OEM	AT1007S22	OEM	AT8060	OEM	ATF827S07L	OEM	ATF880S09P	OEM	AU02	0023	AV2027A	0436
AT807P17	OEM	AT1007S23	OEM	AT8110	OEM	ATF827S08L	OEM	ATF880S10P	OEM	AU02V0	0023	AV2028	OEM
AT807P18	OEM	AT1007S24	OEM	AT8111	OEM	ATF827S09L	OEM	ATF880S11P	OEM	AU02Z	0023	AV2029	OEM
AT807P19	OEM	AT1010S32	OEM	AT8140	OEM	ATF827S09M	OEM	ATF880S12P	OEM	AU100N	0164	AV2030	OEM
AT807P20	OEM	AT1018P20	OEM	AT8141	OEM	ATF827S09N	OEM	ATF880S13P	OEM	AU101	0969	AV2031	OEM
AT807P21	OEM	AT1018P21	OEM	AT8150	OEM	ATF827S09P	OEM	ATF880S14P	OEM	AU102	0160	AV2032	OEM
AT807P22	OEM	AT1018P22	OEM	AT8151	OEM	ATF827S10L	OEM	ATF880S15P	OEM	AU103	0969	AV2033	0039
AT807P23	OEM	AT1018P23	OEM	AT8160	OEM	ATF827S11L	OEM	ATF880S16P	OEM	AU104	0969	AV2034	OEM
AT807P24	OEM	AT1018P24	OEM	AT8161	OEM	ATF827S12L	OEM	ATF880S17P	OEM	AU105	0969	AV2035	OEM
AT807S01	OEM	AT1018P25	OEM	AT8250	OEM	ATF827S13L	OEM	ATF880S18P	OEM	AU106	0969	AV2036	OEM
AT807S02	OEM	AT1018P26	OEM	AT8251	OEM	ATF827S14L	OEM	ATF880S19P	OEM	AU107	0969	AV2037	OEM
AT807S03	OEM	AT1018P27	OEM	AT9006	OEM	ATF854P01N	OEM	ATF887P01L	OEM	AU108	0969	AV2038	OEM
AT807S04	OEM	AT1018P28	OEM	AT9007	OEM	ATF854P02N	OEM	ATF887P02L	OEM	AU110	0969	AV2039	OEM
AT807S05	OEM	AT1018P29	OEM	AT9008	OEM	ATF854P03N	OEM	ATF887P03L	OEM	AU111	0969	AV2040	OEM
AT807S06	OEM	AT1018P30	OEM	AT9009	OEM	ATF854P04N	OEM	ATF887P04L	OEM	AU112	0969	AV2041	OEM
AT807S07	OEM	AT1018P31	OEM	AT9010	OEM	ATF854P05N	OEM	ATF887P05L	OEM	AU113	0969	AV2042	OEM
AT807S08	OEM	AT1018P32	OEM	AT9011	OEM	ATF854P06N	OEM	ATF887P06L	OEM	AU206	0969	AV2043	OEM
AT807S09	OEM	AT1018P33	OEM	AT9012	OEM	ATF854P07N	OEM	ATF887P07L	OEM	AU210	0969	AV2044	OEM
AT807S10	OEM	AT1018P34	OEM	AT9013	OEM	ATF854P08N	OEM	ATF887P08L	OEM	AU213	0969	AV2045	OEM
AT807S11	OEM	AT1018P35	OEM	AT9014	OEM	ATF854P09N	OEM	ATF887P09L	OEM	AU2012	0137	AV2046	OEM
AT807S12	OEM	AT1018P36	OEM	AT9015	OEM	ATF854P10N	OEM	ATF887P10L	OEM	A-U2569	1929	AV2047	OEM
AT807S13	OEM	AT1018S20	OEM	AT9016	OEM	ATF854P11N	OEM	ATF887P11L	OEM	AUY10	0160	AV2048	OEM
AT807S14	OEM	AT1018S21	OEM	AT9017	OEM	ATF854P12N	OEM	ATF887P12L	OEM	AUY19	0160	AV2049	OEM
AT807S15	OEM	AT1018S22	OEM	AT9018	OEM	ATF854S01N	OEM	ATF887P13L	OEM	AUY20	0160	AV2050	OEM
AT807S16	OEM	AT1018S23	OEM	AT9019	OEM	ATF854S02N	OEM	ATF887P14L	OEM	AUY-21	0160	AV2051	OEM
AT807S17	OEM	AT1018S24	OEM	AT9020	OEM	ATF854S03N	OEM	ATF887S01L	OEM	AUY21	0085	AV2052	OEM
AT807S18	OEM	AT1018S25	OEM	AT9021	OEM	ATF854S04N	OEM	ATF887S02L	OEM	AUY21A	0160	AV2053	OEM
AT807S19	OEM	AT1018S26	OEM	AT10650-1	OEM	ATF854S05N	OEM	ATF887S03L	OEM	AUY22	0085	AV2054	OEM
AT807S20	OEM	AT1018S27	OEM	AT12570-5	OEM	ATF854S06N	OEM	ATF887S04L	OEM	AUY22A	0160	AV2055	1823
AT807S21	OEM	AT1018S28	OEM	ATAF1	0004	ATF854S07N	OEM	ATF887S05L	OEM	AUY24	OEM	AV2056	OEM
AT807S22	OEM	AT1018S29	OEM	ATAF2	0004	ATF854S08N	OEM	ATF887S06L	OEM	AUY26	OEM	AV2057	OEM
AT807S23	OEM	AT1018S30	OEM	ATC-SR-3	0087	ATF854S09N	OEM	ATF887S07L	OEM	AUY27	OEM	AV2058	OEM
AT807S24	OEM	AT1018S31	OEM	ATC-TR-4	0086	ATF854S10N	OEM	ATF887S08L	OEM	AUY28	0969	AV2059	OEM
AT874	0004	AT1018S33	OEM	ATC-TR-5	0160	ATF854S11N	OEM	ATF887S09L	OEM	AUY29	0599	AV2060	OEM
AT1004P01	OEM	AT1018S34	OEM	ATC-TR-6	0160	ATF854S12N	OEM	ATF887S10L	OEM	AUY30	0160	AV2061	OEM
AT1004P02	OEM	AT1018S35	OEM	ATC-TR-7	0086	ATF857P01L	OEM	ATF887S11L	OEM	AUY31	0160	AV2062	0778
AT1004P03	OEM	AT1018S36	OEM	ATC-TR-13	0086	ATF857P02L	OEM	ATF887S12L	OEM	AUY32	0160	AV2063	OEM
AT1004P04	OEM	AT1138	0599	ATC-TR-14	0160	ATF857P03L	OEM	ATF887S13L	OEM	AUY33	0160	AV2064	OEM
AT1004P05	OEM	AT1138A	0599	ATC-TR-15	0103	ATF857P06L	OEM	ATF887S14L	OEM	AUY34	0969	AV2065	OEM
AT1004P06	OEM	AT1138B	0599	ATC-TR-19	0042	ATF857P07L	OEM	ATF1047P01M	OEM	AUY37	0599	AV2066	OEM
AT1004P07	OEM	AT1825	OEM	ATF585P01B	OEM	ATF857P08L	OEM	ATF1047P02M	OEM	AUY38	0969	AV2067	OEM
AT1004P08	OEM	AT1833	0599	ATF585P02B	OEM	ATF857P09L	OEM	ATF1047P03M	OEM	AUZ11	OEM	AV2068	OEM
AT1004P09	OEM	AT1834	0599	ATF585P03B	OEM	ATF857P0L	OEM	ATF1047P04M	OEM	AV/5R4GY	OEM	AV2069	OEM
AT1004P10	OEM	AT1845	OEM	ATF585P04B	OEM	ATF857P10L	OEM	ATF1047P05M	OEM	AV0000105-0	0133	AV2070	OEM
AT1004P11	OEM	AT1845A	OEM	ATF585P05B	OEM	ATF857P11L	OEM	ATF1047P06M	OEM	AV03-04	1071	AV2071	OEM
AT1004P12	OEM	AT-1856	0103	ATF585P06A	OEM	ATF857P12L	OEM	ATF1047P07M	OEM	AV03-08	1481	AV2072	OEM
AT1004P13	OEM	AT1856	0103	ATF585P06B	OEM	ATF857S01L	OEM	ATF1047P08M	OEM	AV03-10	0505	AV2073	OEM
AT1004P14	OEM	AT2848	0126	ATF585P06L	OEM	ATF857S02L	OEM	ATF1047P09M	OEM	AV03-12	0864	AV2074	OEM
AT1004P15	OEM	AT3006	OEM	ATF585P06M	OEM	ATF857S03L	OEM	ATF1047P09N	OEM	AV03-15	1264	AV2075	OEM
AT1004S01	OEM	AT3007	OEM	ATF585P07B	OEM	ATF857S04L	OEM	ATF1047P09P	OEM	AV03-18	1071	AV2076	OEM
AT1004S02	OEM	AT3008	OEM	ATF585P08B	OEM	ATF857S05L	OEM	ATF1047P09R	OEM	AV03-22	1712	AV2077	OEM
AT1004S03	OEM	AT3009	OEM	ATF585S01B	OEM	ATF857S06L	OEM	ATF1047P10M	OEM	AV03-27	1750	AV2078	OEM
AT1004S04	OEM	AT3010	OEM	ATF585S02B	OEM	ATF857S07L	OEM	ATF1047P11M	OEM	AV2	OEM	AV2079	OEM
AT1004S05	OEM	AT3011	OEM	ATF585S03B	OEM	ATF857S08L	OEM	ATF1047P12M	OEM	AV3B28	OEM	AV2080	OEM
AT1004S06	OEM	AT3012	OEM	ATF585S04B	OEM	ATF857S09L	OEM	ATF1047P13M	OEM	AV4	OEM	AV2081	OEM
AT1004S07	OEM	AT3013	OEM	ATF585S05B	OEM	ATF857S10L	OEM	ATF1047P14M	OEM	AV4B32	OEM	AV2082	0327
AT1004S08	OEM	AT3014	OEM	ATF585S06A	OEM	ATF857S11L	OEM	ATF1047S01M	OEM	AV5	0137	AV2083	OEM
AT1004S09	OEM	AT3015	OEM	ATF585S06B	OEM	ATF857S12L	OEM	ATF1047S02M	OEM	AV6	OEM	AV2084	OEM
AT1004S10	OEM	AT3016	OEM	ATF585S06L	OEM	ATF860P01B	OEM	ATF1047S03M	OEM	AV7	OEM	AV2085	OEM
AT1004S11	OEM	AT3017	OEM	ATF585S06M	OEM	ATF860P02B	OEM	ATF1047S04M	OEM	AV8	OEM	AV2086	OEM
AT1004S12	OEM	AT3018	OEM	ATF585S07B	OEM	ATF860P03B	OEM	ATF1047S05M	OEM	AV9	OEM	AV2087	OEM
AT1004S13	OEM	AT3019	OEM	ATF585S08B	OEM	ATF860P04B	OEM	ATF1047S06M	OEM	AV10	0039	AV2088	OEM
AT1004S14	OEM	AT3020	OEM	ATF587P01L	OEM	ATF860P05B	OEM	ATF1047S07M	OEM	AV11	OEM	AV2089	OEM
AT1004S15	OEM	AT3021	OEM	ATF587P02L	OEM	ATF860P06B	OEM	ATF1047S08M	OEM	AV12	OEM	AV2090	OEM
AT1007P01	OEM	AT3260	0103	ATF587P03L	OEM	ATF860P07B	OEM	ATF1047S09M	OEM	AV13	OEM	AV2091	OEM
AT1007P02	OEM	AT3850	OEM	ATF587P04L	OEM	ATF860P08B	OEM	ATF1047S09N	OEM	AV14	OEM	AV2092	OEM
AT1007P03	OEM	AT4506	OEM	ATF587P05L	OEM	ATF860P09B	OEM	ATF1047S09P	OEM	AV15	OEM	AV2093	OEM
AT1007P04	OEM	AT4507	OEM	ATF587P06L	OEM	ATF860P10B	OEM	ATF1047S09R	OEM	AV16	OEM	AV2094	OEM
AT1007P05	OEM	AT4508	OEM	ATF587P07L	OEM	ATF860P11B	OEM	ATF1047S10M	OEM	AV17	OEM	AV2095	OEM
AT1007P06	OEM	AT4509	OEM	ATF587P08L	OEM	ATF860P12B	OEM	ATF1047S11M	OEM	AV18	OEM	AV2096	OEM
AT1007P07	OEM	AT4510	OEM	ATF587P09L	OEM	ATF860S01B	OEM	ATF1047S12M	OEM	AV19	OEM	AV2097	OEM
AT1007P08	OEM	AT4511	OEM	ATF587P10L	OEM	ATF860S02B	OEM	ATF1047S13M	OEM	AV102	OEM	AV2098	OEM
AT1007P09	OEM	AT4512	OEM	ATF587P11L	OEM	ATF860S03B	OEM	ATF1047S14M	OEM	AV104	0505	AV2099	OEM
AT1007P10	OEM	AT4513	OEM	ATF587P12L	OEM	ATF860S04B	OEM	ATGP	0004	AV104(ZENER)	0505	AV2100	OEM
AT1007P11	OEM	AT4514	OEM	ATF587S01L	OEM	ATF860S05B	OEM	ATM88A	OEM	AV105	0160	AV2105	OEM
AT1007P12	OEM	AT4515	OEM	ATF587S02L	OEM	ATF860S06B	OEM	ATRF1	0136	AV105(ZENER)	0864	AV2110	0149
AT1007P13	OEM	AT4516	OEM	ATF587S03L	OEM	ATF860S07B	OEM	ATRF2	0136	AV106	OEM	AV2115	OEM
AT1007P14	OEM	AT4517	OEM	ATF587S04L	OEM	ATF860S08B	OEM	ATS13	0136	AV107	1071	AV2120	OEM
AT1007P15	OEM	AT4518	OEM	ATF587S05L	OEM	ATF860S09B	OEM	ATS20J	OEM	AV107(ZENER)	1071	AV2125	OEM

268

If replacement code is OEM, contact original manufacturer for replacement.

DEVICE TYPE	REPL CODE	DEVICE TYPE	REPL CODE	DEVICE TYPE	REPL CODE	DEVICE TYPE	REPL CODE	DEVICE TYPE	REPL CODE	DEVICE TYPE	REPL CODE	DEVICE TYPE	REPL CODE
AV2130	OEM	AV8078	OEM	AV51076	OEM	AW08-13B	0361	AY5-9559	OEM	B00050C	OEM	B060010B	OEM
AV2135	OEM	AV8079	OEM	AV51077	OEM	AW08-15A	0002	AY102	0969	B00	1046	B060010C	OEM
AV2140	OEM	AV8080	OEM	AV51078	OEM	AW08-15B	0002	AY103K	OEM	B004B	0276	B060010D	OEM
AV2145	OEM	AV8081	OEM	AV51079	OEM	AW08-16A	0416	AY104	OEM	B004C	0287	B060010E	OEM
AV2150	OEM	AV8082	0352	AV51080	OEM	AW08-16B	0416	AY104K	OEM	B004E	0293	B060020A	OEM
AV2155	OEM	AV8083	OEM	AV51081	OEM	AW08-18A	0490	AY105K	OEM	B006001D	OEM	B060020B	OEM
AV2160	OEM	AV8084	OEM	AV51082	OEM	AW08-18B	0490	AY106	OEM	B006001E	OEM	B060020C	OEM
AV2165	OEM	AV8085	OEM	AV51083	OEM	AW08-20A	0526	AY3427S	OEM	B006001F	OEM	B060020D	OEM
AV2170	OEM	AV8086	OEM	AV51084	OEM	AW08-20B	0526	AY3600931PRO	OEM	B006001G	OEM	B090010A	OEM
AV2175	OEM	AV8087	OEM	AV51085	OEM	AW08-22A	0560	AYA7104	OEM	B006001H	OEM	B090010B	OEM
AV2180	OEM	AV8088	OEM	AV51086	OEM	AW08-22B	0560	AYA7203	OEM	B006004D	OEM	B090010C	OEM
AV2185	OEM	AV8089	OEM	AV51087	OEM	AW08-24A	0398	AYA7204	OEM	B006004E	OEM	B090010D	OEM
AV2190	OEM	AV8090	OEM	AV51088	OEM	AW08-24B	0398	AYA7206	OEM	B006004F	OEM	B090020A	OEM
AV2195	OEM	AV8091	OEM	AV51089	OEM	AW08-27A	0436	AYA7216	OEM	B006004G	OEM	B090020B	OEM
AV2200	OEM	AV8092	OEM	AV51090	OEM	AW08-27B	0436	AYA7218	OEM	B006004H	OEM	B090020C	OEM
AV7104	OEM	AV8093	OEM	AV51091	OEM	AW08-30A	0721	AYA7226	OEM	B006010D	OEM	B0100115	OEM
AV7203	OEM	AV8094	OEM	AV51092	OEM	AW08-30B	0721	AYA7228	OEM	B006010E	OEM	B0100117	OEM
AV7204	OEM	AV8095	OEM	AV51093	OEM	AW08-33A	0039	AYA7236	OEM	B006010F	OEM	B0272050	5124
AV7206	OEM	AV8096	OEM	AV51094	OEM	AW08-33B	0039	AYA7238	OEM	B006010G	OEM	B0272054	5124
AV7216	OEM	AV8097	OEM	AV51095	OEM	AW08M	2384	AYA7403	OEM	B0075660	1164	B0272120	4923
AV7218	OEM	AV8098	OEM	AV51096	OEM	AW09	0012	AYA7413	OEM	B01	1423	B0272490	4923
AV7224	OEM	AV8099	OEM	AV51097	OEM	AW0110	0170	AYA7433	OEM	B01-02	0015	B0272632	OEM
AV7226	OEM	AV8100	OEM	AV51098	OEM	AW0113	0137	AYA7803	OEM	B01-2	0133	B0305401	4552
AV7228	OEM	AV8105	OEM	AV51099	OEM	AW0122	0560	AYA7813	OEM	B02	1150	B0306000	0872
AV7236	OEM	AV8110	OEM	AV51100	OEM	AWOL-13	0361	AYA7823	OEM	B03	5208	B0306004	0872
AV7238	OEM	AV8115	OEM	AV51105	OEM	AWOL-13	0053	AYA71203	OEM	B071	0644	B0311000	1012
AV7248	OEM	AV8120	OEM	AV51110	OEM	AX-7	0644	AYA71211	OEM	B090	0012	B0311006	1012
AV7403	OEM	AV8125	OEM	AV51115	OEM	AX12	0137	AYA71221	OEM	B094	0170	B0311007	1012
AV7413	OEM	AV8130	OEM	AV51120	OEM	AX1600	OEM	AYA78018	OEM	B0102	0604	B0311008	1012
AV7433	OEM	AV8135	OEM	AV51125	OEM	AX91770	0144	AYA78118	OEM	B0102V	0604	B0311400	3859
AV7443	OEM	AV8140	OEM	AV51130	OEM	AXX3021	0518	AYAP2000	OEM	B01030	OEM	B0311402	3859
AV7453	OEM	AV8145	OEM	AV51140	OEM	AXX3037	OEM	AYY10-120	3688	B01031	OEM	B0311405	3859
AV7803	OEM	AV8150	OEM	AV51145	OEM	AXX3038	2037	AZ3.3	0289	B01032	OEM	B0312100	OEM
AV7813	OEM	AV8155	OEM	AV51150	OEM	AXX3039	OEM	AZ3.6	0188	B01057	OEM	B0313300	2921
AV7823	OEM	AV8160	OEM	AV51160	OEM	AXX3040	OEM	AZ3.9	0451	B01058	OEM	B0313400	2216
AV7843	OEM	AV8165	OEM	AV51165	OEM	AXX3041	OEM	AZ4.3	0528	B01077	OEM	B0313500	2921
AV7871	OEM	AV8170	OEM	AV51170	OEM	AXX3044	4887	AZ4.7	0446	B01078	OEM	B0313600	4514
AV7872	OEM	AV8175	OEM	AV51175	OEM	AXX3051	2105	AZ5.1	0162	B01097	OEM	B0313700	4515
AV8010	OEM	AV8180	OEM	AV51180	OEM	AXX3052	OEM	AZ5.6	0157	B01098	OEM	B0313800	1316
AV8011	OEM	AV8185	OEM	AV51185	OEM	AXX3054	OEM	AZ6.2	0631	B03010	OEM	B0315500	4174
AV8012	OEM	AV8190	OEM	AV51190	OEM	AXX3055	0518	AZ6.8	0062	B03011	OEM	B0316403	2268
AV8013	OEM	AV8195	OEM	AV51195	OEM	AY1-0212	4691	AZ7	0100	B03012	OEM	B0316451	0167
AV8014	OEM	AV8200	OEM	AV51200	OEM	AY1-1313	OEM	AZ7.5	0644	B04010	OEM	B0318920	1049
AV8015	1264	AV51010	OEM	AV71202	OEM	AY1-1320	OEM	AZ8.2	0244	B04011	OEM	B0319200	1044
AV8015(ZENER)	1264	AV51011	OEM	AV71211	OEM	AY1-5050	OEM	AZ9.1	0012	B04012	OEM	B0319960	0794
AV8016	OEM	AV51012	OEM	AV71221	OEM	AY3-0214	OEM	AZ10	0170	B04030	OEM	B0320240	OEM
AV8017	OEM	AV51013	OEM	AV71241	OEM	AY3-0215	OEM	AZ11	0313	B04031	OEM	B0320440	OEM
AV8018	1071	AV51014	OEM	AV71251	OEM	AY3-1015D	OEM	AZ12	0137	B04032	OEM	B0320500	OEM
AV8018(ZENER)	1071	AV51015	OEM	AV71261	OEM	AY3-1270	OEM	AZ13	0361	B05001	OEM	B0320635	OEM
AV8019	OEM	AV51016	OEM	AV71826	OEM	AY-3-1350	OEM	AZ15	0002	B05007	OEM	B0325046	OEM
AV8020	OEM	AV51017	OEM	AV78018	OEM	AY3-1350	OEM	AZ18	0371	B05008	OEM	B0325125	4734
AV8021	OEM	AV51018	OEM	AV78118	OEM	AY3-4592	OEM	AZ22	0700	B05027	OEM	B0325270	4336
AV8022	1712	AV51019	OEM	AV78318	OEM	AY-3-8110	OEM	AZ27	0436	B05028	OEM	B0325290	OEM
AV8022(ZENER)	1712	AV51020	OEM	AW01	0137	AY3-8211	OEM	AZ97B	0054	B05047	OEM	B0325350	4339
AV8023	OEM	AV51021	OEM	AW01-0	0298	AY3-8470	OEM	AZ-110	0313	B05048	OEM	B0325355	4339
AV8024	OEM	AV51022	OEM	AW01-02	OEM	AY3-8475	OEM	AZ748	0036	B015001D	OEM	B0325490	OEM
AV8025	OEM	AV51023	OEM	AW01-06	0298	AY3-8500	OEM	AZ748A	0451	B015001E	OEM	B0325512S	OEM
AV8026	OEM	AV51024	OEM	AW-01-07	0025	AY3-8500-1	OEM	AZ752	0253	B015001F	OEM	B0325536	OEM
AV8027	1750	AV51025	OEM	AW01-07	0025	AY-3-8500-1F	OEM	AZ752A	0157	B015001G	OEM	B0325570	OEM
AV8028	OEM	AV51026	OEM	AW-01-08	0244	AY3-8550-1	OEM	AZ754	0062	B015001H	OEM	B0345450	0308
AV8029	OEM	AV51027	OEM	AW01-08	0244	AY3-8603	OEM	AZ754A	0025	B015004D	OEM	B0345710	0906
AV8030	OEM	AV51028	OEM	AW01-08J	0244	AY3-8603-1	OEM	AZ758	0064	B015004E	OEM	B0347230	OEM
AV8031	OEM	AV51029	OEM	AW-01-09	0012	AY3-8606	OEM	AZ758A	0170	B015004F	OEM	B0347500	0765
AV8032	OEM	AV51030	OEM	AW01-09	0012	AY3-8606-1	OEM	AZ759	0052	B015004G	OEM	B0349250	OEM
AV8033	OEM	AV51031	OEM	AW01-7	0025	AY3-8607	OEM	AZ759A	0137	B015004H	OEM	B0350000	0356
AV8034	OEM	AV51032	OEM	AW01-9	0012	AY3-8607-1	OEM	AZ957	0062	B015010D	OEM	B0350500	0356
AV8035	OEM	AV51033	OEM	AW01-9/CP3112030	0012	AY3-8610	OEM	AZ957A	0062	B015010E	OEM	B0350510	OEM
AV8036	OEM	AV51034	OEM	AW01-9V	0012	AY3-8610-1	OEM	AZ957B	0025	B015010F	OEM	B0350602	0356
AV8037	OEM	AV51035	OEM	AW-01-10	0170	AY3-8765	OEM	AZ958B	0644	B015010G	OEM	B0351500	0823
AV8038	OEM	AV51036	OEM	AW01-10	0313	AY-3-8900-1	OEM	AZ961	0064	B015020C	OEM	B0354700	0906
AV8039	OEM	AV51037	OEM	AW01-11	0313	AY-3-8910	OEM	AZ961A	0064	B024004D	OEM	B0354710	0906
AV8040	OEM	AV51038	OEM	AW-01-12	0137	AY3-8910	OEM	AZ961B	0170	B024004E	OEM	B0354804	2043
AV8041	OEM	AV51039	OEM	AW01-12	0137	AY-3-8910A	OEM	AZ963	0052	B024004F	OEM	B0354805	2043
AV8042	OEM	AV51040	OEM	AW-01-12C	0137	AY-3-8912	OEM	AZ963A	0052	B024004G	OEM	B0354806	2043
AV8043	OEM	AV51041	OEM	AW01-12C	0137	AY3-8912	OEM	AZ963B	0137	B024004H	OEM	B0354830	2043
AV8044	OEM	AV51042	OEM	AW01-12V	0137	AY-3-8914	OEM	AZ965	0681	B024010C	OEM	B0354832	2043
AV8045	OEM	AV51043	OEM	AW01-13	0053	AY-3-8914A	OEM	AZ965A	0681	B024010D	OEM	B0354833	2043
AV8046	OEM	AV51044	OEM	AW01-15	0002	AY-3-8915	OEM	AZ965B	0002	B024010E	OEM	B0354901	4071
AV8047	OEM	AV51045	OEM	AW01-16	0416	AY3-8915	OEM	AZ966	0440	B024010F	OEM	B0355431	5113
AV8048	OEM	AV51046	OEM	AW01-18	0490	AY3-8917	OEM	AZ966A	0440	B024020C	OEM	B0355810	OEM
AV8049	OEM	AV51047	OEM	AW01-20	0526	AY3-9400	OEM	AZ966B	0416	B024020D	OEM	B0356190	3726
AV8050	OEM	AV51048	OEM	AW-01-22	0560	AY3-9410	OEM	AZ967	0371	B024020E	OEM	B0356221	5971
AV8051	OEM	AV51049	OEM	AW01-22	0560	AY3-9710	OEM	AZ967A	0371	B027490	OEM	B0356227	5971
AV8052	OEM	AV51050	OEM	AW01-24	0398	AY3-9725	OEM	AZ967B	0490	B030004C	OEM	B0356260	OEM
AV8053	OEM	AV51051	OEM	AW01-27	0436	AY-3-9735	OEM	AZ969	0700	B030004E	OEM	B0356265	OEM
AV8054	OEM	AV51052	OEM	AW01-30	0721	AY5-1230	OEM	AZ969A	0700	B030004F	OEM	B0356385	3680
AV8055	OEM	AV51053	OEM	AW-01-33	0039	AY5-1231	OEM	AZ969B	0560	B030004G	OEM	B0356446	0658
AV8056	0207	AV51054	OEM	AW01-33	0039	AY5-1232	OEM	AZ971	0450	B030010C	OEM	B0356448	0658
AV8057	OEM	AV51055	OEM	AW02M	0106	AY-5-1317A	OEM	AZ971A	0450	B030010D	OEM	B0356602	4074
AV8058	OEM	AV51056	OEM	AW03-02	OEM	AY5-1317A	OEM	AZ971B	0436	B030010E	OEM	B0356620	6282
AV8059	OEM	AV51057	OEM	AW03-03	1703	AY-5-3600-PRO	OEM	AZ973	0166	B030010F	OEM	B0356640	1666
AV8060	OEM	AV51058	OEM	AW03-04	0451	AY-5-8116	OEM	AZ973A	0166	B030020B	OEM	B0356641	1666
AV8061	OEM	AV51059	OEM	AW03-05	0446	AY5-8116	OEM	AZ973B	0039	B030020C	OEM	B0356690	4441
AV8062	OEM	AV51060	OEM	AW04M	0106	AY5-8116T	OEM	AZC1028	OEM	B030020D	OEM	B0356711	2268
AV8063	OEM	AV51061	OEM	AW06M	1999	AY5-8136	OEM	AZC1045	OEM	B030020E	OEM	B0356784	OEM
AV8064	OEM	AV51062	OEM	AW08-7.5A	0644	AY5-8136T	OEM	AZC1046	OEM	B038420	OEM	B0357640	OEM
AV8065	OEM	AV51063	OEM	AW08-7.5B	0644	AY5-8320	OEM	AZC1048	OEM	B045004C	OEM	B0357650	OEM
AV8066	OEM	AV51064	OEM	AW08-8.2A	0244	AY5-8321	OEM	AZC1049	OEM	B045004D	OEM	B0358130	OEM
AV8067	OEM	AV51065	OEM	AW08-8.2B	0244	AY5-8450	OEM	AZC1050	OEM	B045004E	OEM	B0358265	2843
AV8068	OEM	AV51066	OEM	AW08-9.1A	0012	AY5-8460	OEM	AZC1051	OEM	B045004F	OEM	B0358268	3206
AV8069	OEM	AV51067	OEM	AW08-9.1B	0012	AY5-9151A	OEM	AZC1052	OEM	B045010B	OEM	B0358272	3206
AV8070	OEM	AV51068	OEM	AW08-10A	0170	AY5-9151B	OEM	AZC1053	OEM	B045010C	OEM	B0358280	OEM
AV8071	OEM	AV51069	OEM	AW08-10B	0170	AY5-9152	OEM	AZC1054	OEM	B045010D	OEM	B0364710	0906
AV8072	OEM	AV51070	OEM	AW08-11A	0313	AY5-9152B	OEM	AZC1055	OEM	B045010E	OEM	B0372540	0619
AV8073	OEM	AV51071	OEM	AW08-11B	0313	AY5-9153A	OEM	AZC1056	OEM	B045010F	OEM	B0372900	OEM
AV8074	OEM	AV51072	OEM	AW08-12	0137	AY5-9153B	OEM	AZG	0127	B045020B	OEM	B0372960	4403
AV8075	OEM	AV51073	OEM	AW08-12A	0137	AY5-9154	OEM	AZQQ001GEA	2746	B045020C	OEM	B0373060	OEM
AV8076	OEM	AV51074	OEM	AW08-12B	0137	AY5-9154A	OEM	AZY	0127	B045020D	OEM	B0373230	0330
AV8077	OEM	AV51075	OEM	AW08-13A	0361	AY5-9158	OEM	B	OEM	B060010A	OEM	B0376795	OEM

DEVICE TYPE	REPL CODE	DEVICE TYPE	REPL CODE	DEVICE TYPE	REPL CODE	DEVICE TYPE	REPL CODE	DEVICE TYPE	REPL CODE	DEVICE TYPE	REPL CODE	DEVICE TYPE	REPL CODE
B0376855	OEM	B1T	0359	B3E1	0015	B5K9	0071	B15E	0164	B21M	0969	B25DS120	OEM
B0376856	OEM	B1U	2969	B3E5	0015	B5M1	0071	B16	0435	B210R	0969	B25E	0160
B0376887	OEM	B1U148	0161	B3E9	0015	B5M5	0071	B16A(2S)	0435	B21R	0969	B25F	0160
B0377890	OEM	B1V	1021	B3F1	0015	B5M9	0071	B16B	0435	B21X	0969	B25G	0160
B0379017	OEM	B1W	0016	B3F5	0015	B5N1	0017	B16C	0435	B21Y	0969	B25GN	0160
B0379023	OEM	B1Z	0178	B3F9	0015	B5N5	0017	B16D	0435	B22(2S)	0164	B25H	0160
B0379045	OEM	B2	0144	B3FM1202	OEM	B5N9	0017	B16E	0435	B-22-3	0004	B25J	0160
B0379065	OEM	B2A	0037	B3G1	0015	B5P	0334	B16F	0435	B22-3	0004	B25JS10	OEM
B0379070	OEM	B2A1	0015	B3G5	0015	B6A1	0087	B16G	0435	B-22-4	0004	B25JS20	OEM
B0379090	OEM	B2A5	0015	B3G9	0015	B6A5	0087	B16GN	0435	B22-4	0004	B25JS40	OEM
B0379115	OEM	B2A9	0015	B3H1	0071	B6A9	0087	B16H	0435	B22A(2S)	0164	B25JS60	OEM
B0379190	OEM	B2B	0178	B3H5	0071	B6B1	0087	B16J	0435	B22B(2S)	0164	B25JS80	OEM
B0379200	OEM	B2B1	0015	B3H9	0071	B6B5	0087	B16K	0435	B22C	0164	B25JS100	OEM
B0379220	OEM	B2B5	0015	B-3K	OEM	B6B9	0087	B16L	0435	B22D	0164	B25JS120	OEM
B0379240	OEM	B2B9	0015	B3K1	0071	B6C1	0087	B16M	0435	B22E	0164	B25K	0160
B0379400	3206	B2C1	0015	B3K5	0071	B6C5	0087	B16OR	0435	B22F	0164	B25L	0160
B0383100	3473	B2C5	0015	B3K9	0071	B6C9	0087	B16R	0435	B22G	0164	B25M	0160
B0383111	3473	B2C9	0015	B3M1	0071	B6D1	0087	B16X	0435	B22GN	0164	B25N	0160
B0383530	OEM	B2D	0016	B3M5	0071	B6D5	0087	B16Y	0435	B22H	0164	B25OR	0160
B0383700	OEM	B2D1	0015	B3M9	0071	B6D9	0087	B17	0077	B22I(2S)	0164	B25R	0160
B0383720	OEM	B2D5	0015	B3N1	0102	B6E1	0087	B17(TRANS)	0435	B22J	0164	B25Y	0160
B0383995	OEM	B2D9	0015	B3N5	0102	B6E5	0087	B17A(2S)	0435	B22K	0164	B-26	0004
B0383996	OEM	B2D746A	OEM	B3N9	0102	B6E9	0087	B17B	0435	B22L	0164	B26	0085
B0384095	OEM	B2D747A	OEM	B-3P	0143	B6F1	0087	B17D	0435	B22M	0164	B-26-1	0004
B0384695	OEM	B2D748A	OEM	B3SD0106	OEM	B6F5	0087	B17E	0435	B220R	0164	B26A(2S)	0085
B0384703	OEM	B2D749A	OEM	B4	0144	B6F9	0087	B17F	0435	B22P	0164	B26B	0085
B0402108	OEM	B2D750A	OEM	B4A1	0015	B6G1	0087	B17G	0435	B22R(2S)	0164	B26C	0085
B0403506	OEM	B2D751A	OEM	B4A5	0015	B6G5	0087	B17GN	0435	B22X	0164	B26D	0085
B0403774	OEM	B2D752A	OEM	B4A9	0015	B6G9	0087	B17H	0435	B22Y(2S)	0164	B26E	0085
B0406236	OEM	B2D753A	0466	B4B1	0015	B6H1	0087	B17J	0435	B-23	0004	B26F	0085
B0406803	OEM	B2D754A	OEM	B4B5	0015	B6H5	0087	B17K	0435	B23	0004	B26G	0085
B0406806	OEM	B2D755A	OEM	B4B9	0015	B6H9	0087	B17L	0435	B-23-1	0004	B26GN	0085
B0410022	OEM	B2D757A	0057	B4C1	0015	B6K1	0087	B17M	0435	B23-1	0004	B26H	0085
B0428410	OEM	B2D758A	OEM	B4C5	0015	B6K5	0087	B17OR	0435	B23-2	0004	B26J	0085
B0455010	OEM	B2D759A	0052	B4C9	0015	B6K9	0087	B17R	0435	B23A	0004	B26K	0085
B0470016	3214	B2D914	OEM	B4D1	0015	B6M1	0087	B17X	0435	B23B	0004	B26L	0085
B0470116	5756	B2D914F	OEM	B4D5	0015	B6M5	0087	B17Y	0435	B23C	0004	B26M	0085
B0470130	0409	B2D914T	OEM	B4D9	0015	B6M9	0087	B18	0435	B23D	0004	B26OR	0085
B0470303	OEM	B2D3600	OEM	B4E1	0015	B6N1	0102	B18A(2S)	0435	B23E	0004	B26R	0085
B0470494	0001	B2D3600F	OEM	B4E5	0015	B6N5	0102	B18B	0435	B23F	0004	B26X	0085
B0470522	0024	B2D3600T	OEM	B4E9	0015	B6N9	0102	B18C	0435	B23G	0004	B26Y	0085
B0470532	0034	B2D4148	OEM	B4F1	0015	B6P	0079	B18D	0435	B23GN	0004	B27(2S)	0085
B0470662	0101	B2D4148F	OEM	B4F5	0015	B6RC0911	OEM	B18E	0435	B23H	0004	B27A	0085
B0470932	2368	B2D4148T	OEM	B4F9	0015	B7A1	0087	B18F	0435	B23J	0004	B27B	0085
B0471000	OEM	B2E	0037	B4G1	0015	B7A5	0087	B18G	0435	B23K	0004	B27C	0085
B0474370	1542	B2E1	0015	B4G5	0015	B7B1	0087	B18GN	0435	B23L	0004	B27D	0085
B0487098	OEM	B2E5	0015	B4G9	0015	B7B5	0087	B18H	0435	B23M	0004	B27E	0085
B0487885	OEM	B2E9	0015	B4H1	0071	B7B9	0087	B18J	0435	B230R	0004	B27F	0085
B0526815	OEM	B2F1	0015	B4H5	0071	B7C1	0087	B18K	0435	B23R	0004	B27G	0085
B0589082	OEM	B2F5	0015	B4H9	0071	B7C5	0087	B18LA	0435	B23X	0004	B27GN	0085
B0589085	OEM	B2F9	0015	B4K1	0071	B7C9	0087	B18M	0435	B23Y	0004	B27H	0085
B0589530	OEM	B2F10	OEM	B4K5	0071	B7D1	0087	B18OR	0435	B24(2S)	0164	B27J	0085
B0589580	OEM	B2G	0037	B4K9	0071	B7D5	0087	B18R	0435	B24-06B	0071	B27K	0085
B03544710	0906	B2G1	0015	B4M1	0071	B7D9	0087	B18X	0435	B24-06C	0102	B27L	0085
B1	1713	B2G5	0015	B4M5	0071	B7E1	0087	B18Y	0435	B24-06D	0071	B27M	0085
B1-8.2	0244	B2G9	0015	B4M9	0071	B7E5	0087	B19(2S)	0969	B-24-1	0004	B27OR	0085
B1-12	0015	B2H	0074	B4N5	0017	B7E9	0087	B19A	0969	B24-1	0004	B27R	0085
B1A	0556	B2H1	0071	B4N9	0017	B7F1	0087	B19B	0969	B24A	0164	B27X	0085
B1A1	0015	B2H5	0071	B4TD0204	OEM	B7F5	0087	B19C	0969	B24B	0164	B27Y	0085
B1A5	0015	B2H9	0071	B4Y1-560M	OEM	B7F9	0087	B19D	0969	B24C	0164	B-28	0143
B1A9	0015	B2J	0161	B4Y2-140M	OEM	B7G1	0087	B19E	0969	B24D	0164	B28	0085
B1B	0015	B2K	0555	B4Y2-280M	OEM	B7G5	0087	B19F	0969	B24E	0164	B28A	0085
B1B1	0015	B2K1	0071	B4Y2-560M	OEM	B7G9	0087	B19G	0969	B24F	0164	B28B	0085
B1B5	0015	B2K5	0071	B4Y5-140M	OEM	B7H1	0087	B19GN	0969	B24G	0164	B28C	0085
B1B9	0015	B2K9	0071	B4Y5-280M	OEM	B7H5	0087	B19H	0969	B24GN	0164	B28D	0085
B1C	0161	B2M	0546	B4Y5-420M	OEM	B7H9	0087	B19J	0969	B24H	0164	B28E	0085
B1C1	0015	B2M1	0071	B4Y5-560M	OEM	B7K	OEM	B19K	0969	B24J	0164	B28F	0085
B1C-2	0161	B2M5	0071	B4Y10-140M	OEM	B7K1	0087	B19L	0969	B24K	0164	B28G	0085
B1C5	0015	B2M9	0071	B4Y10-280M	OEM	B7K5	0087	B19M	0969	B24L	0164	B28GN	0085
B1C9	0015	B2N1	0017	B4Y20-350M	OEM	B7K9	0087	B19OR	0969	B24M	0164	B28H	0085
B1D	0042	B2N5	0017	B4Y20-420M	OEM	B7M1	0087	B19R	0969	B240R	0164	B28J	0085
B1D-1	0161	B2N9	0017	B-5	0841	B7M5	0087	B19X	0969	B24R	0164	B28K	0085
B1D1	0015	B2P	1021	B5	0004	B7M9	0087	B19Y	0969	B24X	0164	B28L	0085
B1D5	0015	B2Q90	OEM	B5-31S	1129	B7N1	0102	B20	0085	B24Y	0164	B28M	0085
B1D9	0015	B2SB241	0164	B5-B	OEM	B7N5	0102	B20(2S)	0969	B25(2S)	0160	B28OR	0085
B1E	0334	B2SB244	0969	B5A	0004	B7N9	0102	B20-001	0160	B25-12	1966	B28R	0085
B1E-1	0334	B2V	0161	B5A1	0015	B8-12	OEM	B20A	0969	B25-28	3543	B28X	0085
B1E1	0015	B2Z	0127	B5A5	0015	B8A5	0102	B20B	0969	B25-N	0160	B28Y	0085
B1E5	0015	B3	0144	B5A9	0015	B8B5	0102	B20C	0969	B25A	0160	B29(2S)	0085
B1E9	0015	B3-12	1963	B5B1	0015	B8C5	0102	B20D	0969	B25B(2S)	0160	B29A	0085
B1F	0161	B3A1	0015	B5B5	0015	B8D5	0102	B20E	0969	B25C	0160	B29B	0085
B1F1	0015	B3A5	0015	B5B9	0015	B8E5	0102	B20F	0969	B25CS10	OEM	B29C	0085
B1F5	0015	B3A9	0015	B5C	0178	B8F5	0102	B20G	0969	B25CS20	OEM	B29D	0085
B1F9	0015	B3B1	0015	B5C1	0015	B8G5	0102	B20GN	0969	B25CS40	OEM	B29E	0085
B1G	0334	B3B5	0015	B5C5	0015	B8H5	0102	B20H	0969	B25CS60	OEM	B29F	0085
B1G1	0015	B3B9	0015	B5C9	0015	B8K5	0102	B20J	0969	B25CS80	OEM	B29G	0085
B1G5	0015	B3C1	0015	B5D	0233	B8M5	0102	B20K	0969	B25CS100	OEM	B29GN	0085
B1G9	0015	B3C5	0015	B5D1	0015	B8N5	0102	B20L	0969	B25CS120	OEM	B29H	0085
B1H	0007	B3C9	0015	B5D5	0015	B8P-2A21	0004	B20M	0969	B25D	0160	B29J	0085
B1H(DIODE)	0015	B3D1	0015	B5D9	0015	B9L-4A21	0004	B20OR	0969	B25DA10	OEM	B29K	0085
B1H(XSTR)	0007	B3D5	0015	B5E	0419	B9TUI	OEM	B20R	0969	B25DA20	OEM	B29L	0085
B1H1	0071	B3D9	0015	B5E1	0015	B10	OEM	B20S	OEM	B25DA40	OEM	B29M	0085
B1H5	0071	B3D746A	OEM	B5E5	0015	B10M	OEM	B20X	0969	B25DA60	OEM	B290R	0085
B1H9	0071	B3D747A	OEM	B5E9	0015	B12	0150	B20Y	0969	B25DA80	OEM	B29R	0085
B1J	0037	B3D748A	OEM	B5F	0236	B12(DIO)	0604	B21(2S)	0969	B25DA100	OEM	B29X	0085
B1K	0016	B3D749A	OEM	B5F1	0015	B12(RECT)	0023	B21A	0969	B25DA120	OEM	B29Y	0085
B1K1	0071	B3D750A	OEM	B5F5	0015	B12(RECT)	0071	B21B	0969	B25DC10	OEM	B-30	0143
B1K5	0071	B3D751A	OEM	B5F9	0015	B12-02	0015	B21C	0969	B25DC20	OEM	B30	0143
B1K9	0071	B3D752A	OEM	B5G	0142	B12-02R	0023	B21D	0969	B25DC40	OEM	B30(TRANS)	0085
B1M	0546	B3D753A	0466	B5G1	0015	B12-02RK	0604	B21E	0969	B25DC60	OEM	B30-12	4946
B1M1	0071	B3D754A	OEM	B5G5	0015	B12-1A21	0016	B21F	0969	B25DC80	OEM	B30A	0085
B1M5	0071	B3D755A	OEM	B5G9	0015	B12-12	1224	B21GN	0969	B25DC100	OEM	B30B	0085
B1M9	0071	B3D756A	OEM	B5H1	0071	B13	0004	B21H	0969	B25DC120	OEM	B30B250KP	0293
B1N	0016	B3D757A	0057	B5H5	0071	B14	0050	B21J	0969	B25DS10	OEM	B30C	0085
B1N1	0017	B3D758A	OEM	B5H9	0071	B14A-1-21	0160	B21K	0969	B25DS20	OEM	B30C50KP	0287
B1N5	0017	B3D759A	0052	B5J	0016	B15	0164	B21L	0969	B25DS40	OEM	B30C250	0015
B1N9	0017	B3D914	OEM	B5K1	0071	B15-12	1224			B25DS60	OEM	B30C250-1	0015
B1P	0637	B3D3600	OEM	B5K5	0071	B15D	0164			B25DS80	OEM	B30C250KP	0287
B1R	2422									B25DS100	OEM		

If replacement code is OEM, contact original manufacturer for replacement.

DEVICE TYPE	REPL CODE
B30C350-1	0015
B30C500	0015
B30C600	0015
B30C600CB	0015
B30C1000	0276
B30D	0085
B30E	0085
B30F	0085
B30G	0085
B30GN	0085
B30H	0085
B30J	0085
B30K	0085
B30L	0085
B30M	0085
B30OR	0085
B-30P	0143
B30R	0085
B30X	0085
B30Y	0085
B-31	0015
B31	0015
B31(TRANS)	0085
B31A	0085
B31B	0085
B31C	0085
B31D	0085
B31E	0085
B31F	0085
B31G	0085
B31GN	0085
B31H	0085
B31J	0085
B31K	0085
B31L	0085
B31M	0085
B31OR	0085
B31R	0085
B31X	0085
B31Y	0085
B32(2S)	0004
B32(3)	0004
B32(N)	0004
B32-0(2S)	0004
B32-1(2S)	0004
B32-2(2S)	0004
B32-4(2S)	0004
B32A	0004
B32B	0004
B32C	0004
B32D	0004
B32E	0004
B32F	0004
B32G	0004
B32GN	0004
B32H	0004
B32J	0004
B32K	0004
B32M	0004
B32OR	0004
B32R	0004
B32X	0004
B32Y	0004
B33	0004
B33(3)	0004
B33(4)	0004
B33(5)	0004
B33-4(2S)	0004
B33-5	0004
B33A	0004
B33B	0004
B33BK	0004
B33C(2S)	0004
B33D(2S)	0004
B33E(2S)	0004
B33F(2S)	0004
B33G	0004
B33GN	0004
B33H	0004
B33J	0004
B33K	0004
B33L	0004
B33M	0004
B33OR	0004
B33R	0004
B33X	0004
B33Y	0004
B34(2S)	0211
B34A	0211
B34B	0211
B34C	0211
B34D	0211
B34E	0211
B34F	0211
B34G	0211
B34GN	0211
B34H	0211
B34J	0211
B34K	0211
B34L	0211
B34M	0211
B34N(2S)	0211
B34OR	0211
B34R	0211
B34X	0211
B34Y	0211
B35	0164
B35-0262	OEM
B35A	0164

DEVICE TYPE	REPL CODE
B35B	0164
B35C	0164
B35C600	0015
B35D	0164
B35E	0164
B35F	0164
B35G	0164
B35GN	0164
B35H	0164
B35J	0164
B35K	0164
B35L	0164
B35M	0164
B35OR	0164
B35R	0164
B35X	0164
B35Y	0164
B37(2S)	0004
B37A(2S)	0004
B37B(2S)	0004
B37C(2S)	0004
B37D	0004
B37E(2S)	0004
B37F(2S)	0004
B37G	0004
B37GN	0004
B37H	0004
B37J	0004
B37K	0004
B37L	0004
B37M	0004
B37OR	0004
B37R	0004
B37X	0004
B37Y	0004
B38(2S)	0211
B38A	0211
B38B	0211
B38C	0211
B38D	0211
B38E	0211
B38F	0211
B38G	0211
B38GN	0211
B38H	0211
B38J	0211
B38K	0211
B38L	0211
B38M	0211
B38OR	0211
B38R	0211
B38X	0211
B38Y	0211
B39(2S)	0004
B39A	0004
B39B	0004
B39C	0004
B39D	0004
B39E	0004
B39F	0004
B39G	0004
B39GN	0004
B39H	0004
B39J	0004
B39K	0004
B39L	0004
B39M	0004
B39OR	0004
B39R	0004
B39X	0004
B39Y	0004
B40(2S)	0004
B40-12	1963
B40-12A	OEM
B40-28	2485
B40A	0004
B40A10	OEM
B40A20	OEM
B40A40	OEM
B40A60	OEM
B40A80	OEM
B40A100	OEM
B40A120	OEM
B40B	0004
B40C	0004
B40C800	0106
B40C800A	OEM
B40C800D	0241
B40C800D1	0241
B40C800DM	0241
B40C800M	0106
B40C800W	0106
B40C1000	0106
B40C1000A	2758
B40C1000M	0106
B40C1000W	0106
B40C1200S	4011
B40C1200W	0106
B40C1500	0106
B40C1500/1000	OEM
B40C1500/1000SI	OEM
B40C1500/1000SIC	OEM
B40C1500R	0106
B40C1500W	0106
B40C2000/1500	4787
B40C3700/2200	2994
B40C3700/2200SI	0724
B40C3700/2200SIC	0724
B40C5000/3300	1036

DEVICE TYPE	REPL CODE
B40C5000/3300SI	0724
B40C5000/3300SIC	2994
B40C7500-5000	OEM
B40D	0004
B40E	0004
B40F	0004
B40G	0004
B40GN	0004
B40H	0004
B40J	0004
B40K	0004
B40L	0004
B40M	0004
B40OR	0004
B40R	0004
B40X	0004
B40Y	0004
B41(2S)	0085
B41-04	0023
B41A	0085
B41B	0085
B41C	0085
B41D	0085
B41E	0085
B41F	0085
B41G	0085
B41GN	0085
B41H	0085
B41J	0085
B41K	0085
B41L	0085
B41M	0085
B41OR	0085
B41R	0085
B41X	0085
B41Y	0085
B42(2S)	0085
B42-04	0023
B42A	0085
B42B	0085
B42C	0085
B42D	0085
B42E	0085
B42F	0085
B42G	0085
B42GN	0085
B42H	0085
B42J	0085
B42K	0085
B42L	0085
B42M	0085
B42OR	0085
B42R	0085
B42X	0085
B42Y	0085
B43(2S)	0004
B43-04	0023
B43A(2S)	0004
B43B	0004
B43C	0004
B43D	0004
B43E	0004
B43F	0004
B43G	0004
B43GN	0004
B43H	0004
B43J	0004
B43K	0004
B43L	0004
B43M	0004
B43OR	0004
B43R	0004
B43X	0004
B43Y	0004
B44(2S)	0004
B44A	0004
B44B	0004
B44C	0004
B44D	0004
B44E	0004
B44F	0004
B44G	0004
B44GN	0004
B44H	0004
B44J	0004
B44K	0004
B44L	0004
B44M	0004
B44OR	0004
B44R	0004
B44X	0004
B44Y	0004
B45-12	OEM
B46(2S)	0004
B-46-110	2875
B46-110	0196
B46A	0004
B46B	0004
B46C	0004
B46D	0004
B46E	0004
B46F	0004
B46G	0004
B46GN	0004
B46H	0004
B46J	0004
B46K	0004
B46L	0004
B46M	0004

DEVICE TYPE	REPL CODE
B46OR	0004
B46R	0004
B46X	0004
B46Y	0004
B47(2S)	0004
B47A	0004
B47B	0004
B47C	0004
B47D	0004
B47E	0004
B47F	0004
B47G	0004
B47GN	0004
B47H	0004
B47J	0004
B47K	0004
B47L	0004
B47M	0004
B47OR	0004
B47R	0004
B47X	0004
B47Y	0004
B48(2S)	0211
B48A	0211
B48B	0211
B48C	0211
B48D	0211
B48E	0211
B48F	0211
B48G	0211
B48GN	0211
B48H	0211
B48J	0211
B48K	0211
B48L	0211
B48M	0211
B48OR	0211
B48R	0211
B48X	0211
B48Y	0211
B49	0211
B49A	0211
B49B	0211
B49C	0211
B49D	0211
B49E	0211
B49F	0211
B49G	0211
B49GN	0211
B49H	0211
B49J	0211
B49K	0211
B49L	0211
B49M	0211
B49OR	0211
B49R	0211
B49X	0211
B49Y	0211
B50(2S)	0211
B50A	0211
B50B	0211
B50C	0211
B50C800D	0241
B50C800D1	0241
B50D	0211
B50E	0211
B50F	0211
B50G	0211
B50GN	0211
B50H	0211
B50J	0211
B50K	0211
B50L	0211
B50M	0211
B50OR	0211
B50R	0211
B50X	0211
B50Y	0211
B51	0015
B51(TRANS)	0211
B51A	0211
B51B	0211
B51C	0211
B51D	0211
B51E	0211
B51F	0211
B51G	0211
B51GN	0211
B51H	0211
B51J	0211
B51K	0211
B51L	0211
B51M	0211
B51OR	0211
B51R	0211
B51X	0211
B51Y	0211
B52(2S)	0211
B52A	0211
B52B	0211
B52C	0211
B52D	0211
B52E	0211
B52F	0211
B52G	0211
B52GN	0211
B52H	0211
B52J	0211
B52K	0211

DEVICE TYPE	REPL CODE
B52L	0211
B52M	0211
B52OR	0211
B52R	0211
B52X	0211
B52Y	0211
B53(2S)	0211
B53A	0211
B53B	0211
B53C	0211
B53D	0211
B53E	0211
B53F	0211
B53G	0211
B53GN	0211
B53H	0211
B53J	0211
B53K	0211
B53L	0211
B53M	0211
B53OR	0211
B53R	0211
B53X	0211
B53Y	0211
B54(2S)	0004
B54A	0004
B54B(2S)	0004
B54BA	0004
B54C	0004
B54D	0004
B54E(2S)	0004
B54F(2S)	0004
B54G	0004
B54GN	0004
B54H	0004
B54J	0004
B54K	0004
B54L	0004
B54L1	0004
B54M	0004
B54OR	0004
B54R	0004
B54X	0004
B54Y(2S)	0004
B55	0004
B55A	0004
B55B	0004
B55C	0004
B55D	0004
B55E	0004
B55F	0004
B55G	0004
B55GN	0004
B55H	0004
B55J	0004
B55K	0004
B55L	0004
B55M	0004
B55OR	0004
B55R	0004
B55X	0004
B55Y	0004
B56(2S)	0004
B56-15	0242
B56-33	0947
B56A(2S)	0004
B56B(2S)	0004
B56C(2S)	0004
B56CK	0004
B56D	0004
B56E	0004
B56F	0004
B56G	0004
B56GN	0004
B56H	0004
B56J	0004
B56K	0004
B56L	0004
B56OR	0004
B56R	0004
B56X	0004
B56Y	0004
B57(2S)	0004
B57A	0004
B57B	0004
B57C	0004
B57D	0004
B57E	0004
B57F	0004
B57G	0004
B57GN	0004
B57H	0004
B57J	0004
B57K	0004
B57L	0004
B57M	0004
B57OR	0004
B57R	0004
B57X	0004
B57Y	0004
B58(2S)	0164
B59(2S)	0004
B59A	0004
B59B	0004
B59C	0004
B59D	0004
B59E	0004
B59F	0004
B59G	0004

DEVICE TYPE	REPL CODE
B59GN	0004
B59J	0004
B59K	0004
B59L	0004
B59M	0004
B59OR	0004
B59R	0004
B59X	0004
B59Y	0004
B60(2S)	0004
B60A(2S)	0004
B60B	0004
B60C	0004
B60C300	0015
B60C800W	0106
B60C1000W	0106
B60C1200S	1194
B60C1200W	0106
B60C1500W	0106
B60D	0004
B60E	0004
B60F	0004
B60G	0004
B60GN	0004
B60H	0004
B60J	0004
B60K	0004
B60L	0004
B60M	0004
B60OR	0004
B60R	0004
B60X	0004
B60Y	0004
B61(2S)	0004
B61A	0004
B61B	0004
B61C	0004
B61D	0004
B61E	0004
B61F	0004
B61G	0004
B61GN	0004
B61H	0004
B61J	0004
B61K	0004
B61L	0004
B61M	0004
B61OR	0004
B61R	0004
B61X	0004
B61Y	0004
B62(2S)	1004
B62A	1004
B62B	1004
B62C	1004
B62D	1004
B62E	1004
B62F	1004
B62G	1004
B62GN	1004
B62H	1004
B62J	1004
B62K	1004
B62L	1004
B62M	1004
B62OR	1004
B62R	1004
B62X	1004
B62Y	1004
B63(2S)	0222
B63A	0222
B63B	0222
B63C	0222
B63D	0222
B63E	0222
B63F	0222
B63G	0222
B63GN	0222
B63H	0222
B63K	0222
B63L	0222
B63M	0222
B63OR	0222
B63R	0222
B63X	0222
B63Y	0222
B64(2S)	0969
B64A	0969
B64B	0969
B64C	0969
B64D	0969
B64E	0969
B64F	0969
B64G	0969
B64H	0969
B64J	0969
B64K	0969
B64L	0969
B64M	0969
B64OR	0969
B64R	0969
B64X	0969
B64Y	0969
B65(2S)	0004
B65-1A21	0050
B65-2A21	0208
B65-4A21	0595
B65A	0004
B65A-1-21	0050

DEVICE TYPE	REPL CODE
B65B	0004
B65B-1-21	0050
B65C	0004
B65C-1-21	0160
B65D	0004
B65F	0004
B65G	0004
B65GN	0004
B65H	0004
B65J	0004
B65K	0004
B65L	0004
B65M	0004
B65OR	0004
B65R	0004
B65X	0004
B65Y	0004
B-66	0079
B66(2S)	0004
B66-1A21	0004
B66-2A21	0004
B66-3A21	0004
B66A	0004
B66B	0004
B66C	0004
B66D	0004
B66E	0004
B66F	0004
B66G	0004
B66GN	0004
B66H(2S)	0004
B66J	0004
B66K	0004
B66L	0004
B66M	0004
B66OR	0004
B66R	0004
B66X	0004
B66X0033-00	0015
B66X0035-001	0769
B66X0036	1293
B66X0036-001	1293
B66X0041-001	0469
B66Y	0004
B67(2S)	0004
B67A(2S)	0004
B67AH	0004
B67B	0004
B67C	0004
B67D	0004
B67E	0004
B67F	0004
B67G	0004
B67GN	0004
B67H	0004
B67J	0004
B67K	0004
B67L	0004
B67M	0004
B67OR	0004
B67R	0004
B67X	0004
B67Y	0004
B68	0004
B68A	0004
B68B	0004
B68C	0004
B68D	0004
B68E	0004
B68F	0004
B68G	0004
B68GN	0004
B68H	0004
B68J	0004
B68K	0004
B68L	0004
B68M	0004
B68OR	0004
B68R	0004
B68X	0004
B68Y	0004
B69(2S)	0160
B69A	0160
B69B	0160
B69C	0160
B69D	0160
B69E	0160
B69F	0160
B69G	0160
B69GN	0160
B69H	0160
B69J	0160
B69K	0160
B69L	0160
B69M	0160
B69OR	0160
B69R	0160
B69X	0160
B69Y	0160
B70	0164
B70-28	OEM
B70H40	OEM
B70H60	OEM
B70H80	OEM
B70H100	OEM
B71(2S)	0004
B71A	0004
B71B	0004
B71C	0004

If replacement code is OEM, contact original manufacturer for replacement. 271

DEVICE TYPE	REPL CODE
B71D	0004
B71E	0004
B71F	0004
B71G	0004
B71GN	0004
B71H	0004
B71J	0004
B71K	0004
B71L	0004
B71M	0004
B71OR	0004
B71R	0004
B71X	0004
B71Y	0004
B72(2S)	0211
B72A	0211
B72B	0211
B72C	0211
B72D	0211
B72E	0211
B72F	0211
B72G	0211
B72GN	0211
B72H	0211
B72J	0211
B72K	0211
B72L	0211
B72M	0211
B72OR	0211
B72R	0211
B72X	0211
B72Y	0211
B73(2S)	0004
B73A(2S)	0004
B73A-1	0004
B73B(2S)	0004
B73C(2S)	0004
B73D	0004
B73E	0004
B73F	0004
B73G	0004
B73GN	0004
B73GR(2S)	0004
B73H	0004
B73J	0004
B73K	0004
B73L	0004
B73M	0004
B73OR	0004
B73R	0004
B73S	0004
B73X	0004
B73Y	0004
B74(2S)	0164
B74A	0164
B74B	0164
B74C	0164
B74D	0164
B74E	0164
B74F	0164
B74G	0164
B74GN	0164
B74H	0164
B74J	0164
B74K	0164
B74L	0164
B74M	0164
B74OR	0164
B74R	0164
B74X	0164
B74Y	0164
B75(2S)	0004
B75A	0004
B75AH(2S)	0004
B75B	0004
B75C(2S)	0004
B75C1	0004
B75C-4	0004
B75D	0004
B75E	0004
B75F(2S)	0004
B75G	0004
B75GN	0004
B75H(2S)	0004
B75J	0004
B75L	0004
B75LB(2S)	0004
B75M	0004
B75OR	0004
B75R	0004
B75X	0004
B75Y	0004
B76(2S)	0004
B76A	0004
B76B	0004
B76C	0004
B76D	0004
B76E	0004
B76F	0004
B76G	0004
B76GN	0004
B76H	0004
B76J	0004
B76K	0004
B76L	0004
B76M	0004
B76OR	0004
B76R	0004
B76X	0004

DEVICE TYPE	REPL CODE
B76Y	0004
B77(2S)	0004
B77-A	0004
B77-C	0004
B77-OR	0004
B77A(2S)	0004
B77A-1-21	0435
B77AA(2S)	0004
B77AB(2S)	0004
B77AC(2S)	0004
B77AD(2S)	0004
B77AH(2S)	0004
B77AP(2S)	0004
B77B(2S)	0004
B77B-1-21	0160
B77B2	0004
B77B-11(2S)	0004
B77C	0004
B77D(2S)	0004
B77D0016-1	0147
B77E	0004
B77F	0004
B77G	0004
B77GN	0004
B77H(2S)	0004
B77K	0004
B77L	0004
B77M	0004
B77OR	0004
B77P	0004
B77PD	0004
B77R	0004
B77RED	0004
B77T0049	1063
B77V(2S)	0004
B77VRED(2S)	0004
B77X	0004
B77Y	0004
B78(2S)	0004
B78A	0004
B78B	0004
B78C	0004
B78D	0004
B78E	0004
B78F	0004
B78G	0004
B78GN	0004
B78H	0004
B78J	0004
B78K	0004
B78L	0004
B78M	0004
B78OR	0004
B78R	0004
B78X	0004
B78Y	0004
B79(2S)	0004
B79A	0004
B79B	0004
B79C	0004
B79D	0004
B79E	0004
B79F	0004
B79G	0004
B79GN	0004
B79H	0004
B79J	0004
B79K	0004
B79L	0004
B79M	0004
B79OR	0004
B79R	0004
B79X	0004
B79Y	0004
B80(2S)	0222
B80A	0222
B80B	0222
B80C	0222
B80C800	0106
B80C800A	OEM
B80C800D	0241
B80C800D1	0241
B80C800DM	0241
B80C800M	0106
B80C800W	0106
B80C1000	0106
B80C1000A	0106
B80C1000M	0106
B80C1000W	0106
B80C1200S	1194
B80C1200W	0106
B80C1500	0106
B80C1500/1000	OEM
B80C1500/1000SI	OEM
B80C1500/1000SIC	OEM
B80C1500R	0106
B80C1500W	0106
B80C2000/1500	2215
B80C3700/2200	6206
B80C3700/2200SI	0724
B80C3700/2200SIC	2994
B80C5000/3300	2994
B80C5000/3300SI	0724
B80C5000/3300SIC	2994
B80C7500-5000	OEM
B80D	0222
B80E	0222
B80F	0222
B80G	0222

DEVICE TYPE	REPL CODE
B80GN	0222
B80H	0222
B80J	0222
B80K	0222
B80L	0222
B80M	0222
B80OR	0222
B80R	0222
B80X	0222
B80Y	0222
B81(2S)	0969
B81-004	2520
B81A	0969
B81B	0969
B81C	0969
B81D	0969
B81E	0969
B81F	0969
B81GN	0969
B81H	0969
B81J	0969
B81K	0969
B81L	0969
B81M	0969
B81OR	0969
B81R	0969
B81X	0969
B81Y	0969
B82(2S)	0969
B82-004	2493
B82A	0969
B82B	0969
B82C	0969
B82D	0969
B82E	0969
B82F	0969
B82G	0969
B82GN	0969
B82H	0969
B82J	0969
B82K	0969
B82L	0969
B82M	0969
B82OR	0969
B82R	0969
B82X	0969
B82Y	0969
B83(2S)	0969
B83-7	2007
B83A	0969
B83B	0969
B83C	0969
B83D	0969
B83E	0969
B83F	0969
B83G	0969
B83GN	0969
B83H	0969
B83J	0969
B83K	0969
B83L	0969
B83M	0969
B83OR	0969
B83R	0969
B83X	0969
B83Y	0969
B84(2S)	0085
B84A	0085
B84A-1-21	0160
B84B	0085
B84C	0085
B84D	0085
B84E	0085
B84F	0085
B84G	0085
B84GN	0085
B84H	0085
B84J	0085
B84K	0085
B84L	0085
B84M	0085
B84OR	0085
B84R	0085
B84X	0085
B84Y	0085
B85(2S)	0164
B85A	0164
B85B	0164
B85C	0164
B85D	0164
B85E	0164
B85F	0164
B85G	0164
B85GN	0164
B85H	0164
B85J	0164
B85K	0164
B85L	0164
B85M	0164
B85OR	0164
B85R	0164
B85X	0164
B85Y	0164
B86	0160
B87(2S)	0164
B87A	0164
B87B	0164
B87C	0164
B87D	0164

DEVICE TYPE	REPL CODE
B87E	0164
B87F	0164
B87G	0164
B87GN	0164
B87H	0164
B87J	0164
B87K	0164
B87L	0164
B87M	0164
B87OR	0164
B87R	0164
B87X	0164
B87Y	0164
B88	0969
B88B-1-21	0050
B88C-1-21	0279
B89(2S)	0004
B89A(2S)	0004
B89AH(2S)	0004
B89C	0004
B89D	0004
B89E	0004
B89F	0004
B89G	0004
B89GN	0004
B89H(2S)	0004
B89J	0004
B89K	0004
B89L	0004
B89M	0004
B89OR	0004
B89R	0004
B89X	0004
B89Y	0004
B90(2S)	0004
B90A	0004
B90B	0004
B90C	0004
B90D	0004
B90E	0004
B90F	0004
B90G	0004
B90GN	0004
B90H	0004
B90J	0004
B90K	0004
B90L	0004
B90M	0004
B90OR	0004
B90R	0004
B90X	0004
B90Y	0004
B91(2S)	0004
B91A	0004
B91B	0004
B91C	0004
B91D	0004
B91E	0004
B91F	0004
B91G	0004
B91GN	0004
B91H	0004
B91J	0004
B91K	0004
B91L	0004
B91M	0004
B91OR	0004
B91R	0004
B91X	0004
B91Y	0004
B92(2S)	0004
B92-1A21	0435
B92-UA21	0435
B92A	0004
B92B	0004
B92C	0004
B92D	0004
B92E	0004
B92F	0004
B92G	0004
B92GN	0004
B92H	0004
B92J	0004
B92K	0004
B92L	0004
B92M	0004
B92X	0004
B92Y	0004
B93	0004
B94(2S)	0004
B94A	0004
B94B	0004
B94C	0004
B94D	0004
B94E	0004
B94F	0004
B94G	0004
B94GN	0004
B94H	0004
B94J	0004
B94K	0004
B94M	0004
B94OR	0004
B94R	0004
B94X	0004
B94Y	0004
B95(2S)	0004
B95A	0004
B95B	0004

DEVICE TYPE	REPL CODE
B95C	0004
B95D	0004
B95E	0004
B95F	0004
B95G	0004
B95GN	0004
B95H	0004
B95J	0004
B95L	0004
B95M	0004
B95OR	0004
B95R	0004
B95X	0004
B95Y	0004
B96	0211
B97(2S)	0004
B97A	0004
B97B	0004
B97C	0004
B97D	0004
B97F	0004
B97G	0004
B97GN	0004
B97H	0004
B97K	0004
B97L	0004
B97M	0004
B97OR	0004
B97R	0004
B97X	0004
B97Y	0004
B98(2S)	0211
B98A	0211
B98B	0211
B98C	0211
B98D	0211
B98E	0211
B98F	0211
B98G	0211
B98GN	0211
B98H	0211
B98J	0211
B98K	0211
B98L	0211
B98M	0211
B98OR	0211
B98R	0211
B98X	0211
B98Y	0211
B99	0164
B99A	0164
B99B	0164
B99C	0164
B99D	0164
B99E	0164
B99F	0164
B99G	0164
B99GN	0164
B99H	0164
B99J	0164
B99K	0164
B99L	0164
B99M	0164
B99OR	0164
B99R	0164
B99X	0164
B99Y	0164
B100	0211
B100A	0211
B100B	0211
B100C	0211
B100D	0211
B100E	0211
B100F	0211
B100G	0211
B100GN	0211
B100H	0211
B100J	0211
B100K	0211
B100L	0211
B100M	0211
B100OR	0211
B100R	0211
B100X	0211
B100Y	0211
B101(2S)	0211
B101A	0211
B101B	0211
B101C	0211
B101D	0211
B101E	0211
B101F	0211
B101G	0211
B101GN	0211
B101H	0211
B101J	0211
B101K	0211
B101L	0211
B101M	0211
B101OR	0211
B101R	0211
B101X	0211
B101Y	0211
B102(2S)	0211
B102A	0211
B102B	0211
B102C	0211
B102D	0211
B102E	0211

DEVICE TYPE	REPL CODE
B102F	0211
B102G	0211
B102GN	0211
B102H	0211
B102J	0211
B102K	0211
B102L	0211
B102M	0211
B102OR	0211
B102R	0211
B102X	0211
B102Y	0211
B103(2S)	0211
B103A	0211
B103B	0211
B103C	0211
B103D	0211
B103E	0211
B103F	0211
B103G	0211
B103GN	0211
B103H	0211
B103J	0211
B103K	0211
B103L	0211
B103M	0211
B103OR	0211
B103R	0211
B103X	0211
B103Y	0211
B104(2S)	0164
B104A	0164
B104B	0164
B104C	0164
B104D	0164
B104E	0164
B104F	0164
B104G	0164
B104GN	0164
B104H	0164
B104J	0164
B104K	0164
B104L	0164
B104M	0164
B104OR	0164
B104R	0164
B104X	0164
B104Y	0164
B105(2S)	0164
B105A	0164
B105B	0164
B105C	0164
B105D	0164
B105E	0164
B105F	0164
B105G	0164
B105GN	0164
B105H	0164
B105K	0164
B105L	0164
B105M	0164
B105OR	0164
B105R	0164
B105X	0164
B105Y	0164
B106(2S)	0164
B107(2S)	0160
B107A(2S)	0160
B107B	0160
B107C	0160
B107D	0160
B107E	0160
B107F	0160
B107G	0160
B107GN	0160
B107H	0160
B107J	0160
B107K	0160
B107L	0160
B107M	0160
B107OR	0160
B107R	0160
B107X	0160
B107Y	0160
B108(2S)	0164
B108A(2S)	0164
B108B(2S)	0164
B108C	0164
B108D	0164
B108E	0164
B108F	0164
B108G	0164
B108GN	0164
B108H	0164
B108J	0164
B108K	0164
B108L	0164
B108M	0164
B108OR	0164
B108X	0164
B108Y	0164
B109(2S)	0164
B109A	0164
B109B	0164
B110	0004
B110A	0004
B110B	0004
B110C	0004
B110D	0004

DEVICE TYPE	REPL CODE
B110E	0004
B110F	0004
B110G	0004
B110GN	0004
B110H	0004
B110J	0004
B110K	0004
B110L	0004
B110M	0004
B110OR	0004
B110R	0004
B110X	0004
B110Y	0004
B111(2S)	0004
B111A	0004
B111B	0004
B111C	0004
B111D	0004
B111E	0004
B111F	0004
B111G	0004
B111GN	0004
B111H	0004
B111J	0004
B111K(2S)	0004
B111L	0004
B111M	0004
B111OR	0004
B111R	0004
B111X	0004
B111Y	0004
B112(2S)	0004
B112A	0004
B112B	0004
B112C	0004
B112D	0004
B112E	0004
B112F	0004
B112G	0004
B112H	0004
B112J	0004
B112K	0004
B112L	0004
B112M	0004
B112OR	0004
B112R	0004
B112X	0004
B112Y	0004
B113	0004
B113(2S)	0004
B113A	0004
B113B	0004
B113C	0004
B113D	0004
B113E	0004
B113F	0004
B113G	0004
B113GN	0004
B113H	0004
B113J	0004
B113K	0004
B113L	0004
B113M	0004
B113OR	0004
B113R	0004
B113X	0004
B113Y	0004
B114	0004
B114(2S)	0004
B114A	0004
B114B	0004
B114C	0004
B114D	0004
B114E	0004
B114F	0004
B114G	0004
B114GN	0004
B114H	0004
B114J	0004
B114K	0004
B114L	0004
B114M	0004
B114OR	0004
B114R	0004
B114X	0004
B114Y	0004
B115	0004
B115A	0004
B115B	0004
B115C	0004
B115D	0004
B115E	0004
B115F	0004
B115G	0004
B115GN	0004
B115H	0004
B115J	0004
B115K	0004
B115L	0004
B115M	0004
B115OR	0004
B115R	0004
B115X	0004
B115Y	0004
B116(2S)	0004
B116A	0004
B116B	0004
B116C	0004
B116D	0004

If replacement code is OEM, contact original manufacturer for replacement.

DEVICE TYPE	REPL CODE
B116E	0004
B116F	0004
B116G	0004
B116GN	0004
B116H	0004
B116J	0004
B116K	0004
B116L	0004
B116M	0004
B116OR	0004
B116R	0004
B116X	0004
B116Y	0004
B117	0004
B117A	0004
B117B	0004
B117C	0004
B117D	0004
B117E	0004
B117F	0004
B117G	0004
B117GN	0004
B117H	0004
B117J	0004
B117K(2S)	0004
B117L	0004
B117M	0004
B117OR	0004
B117R	0004
B117X	0004
B117Y	0004
B118	0164
B119(2S)	0160
B119A(2S)	0160
B119B	0160
B119C	0160
B119D	0160
B119E	0160
B119F	0160
B119G	0160
B119GN	0160
B119H	0160
B119J	0160
B119K	0160
B119L	0160
B119M	0160
B119OR	0160
B119R	0160
B119X	0160
B119Y	0160
B120(2S)	0004
B120A	0004
B120B	0004
B120C	0004
B120D	0004
B120E	0004
B120F	0004
B120G	0004
B120GN	0004
B120H	0004
B120J	0004
B120K	0004
B120L	0004
B120M	0004
B120OR	0004
B120R	0004
B120X	0004
B120Y	0004
B121	OEM
B122(2S)	0004
B122A	0160
B122B	0160
B122C	0160
B122D	0160
B122E	0160
B122F	0160
B122G	0160
B122GN	0160
B122H	0160
B122J	0160
B122K	0160
B122L	0160
B122M	0160
B122OR	0160
B122R	0160
B122X	0160
B122Y	0160
B123	0085
B123A(2S)	0085
B123B	0085
B123C	0085
B123D	0085
B123E	0085
B123F	0085
B123G	0085
B123GN	0085
B123H	0085
B123J	0085
B123K	0085
B123L	0085
B123M	0085
B123OR	0085
B123R	0085
B123X	0085
B123Y	0085
B124	0160
B124A	0160
B124B	0160
B124C	0160
B124D	0160
B124E	0160
B124F	0160
B124G	0160
B124H	0160
B124J	0160
B124K	0160
B124L	0160
B124M	0160
B124OR	0160
B124R	0160
B124X	0160
B124Y	0160
B125	0599
B125C800	0106
B125C800A	OEM
B125C800D	4501
B125C800D1	4501
B125C800DM	4501
B125C800M	0106
B125C800W	0106
B125C1000	0106
B125C1000A	2758
B125C1000M	0241
B125C1000W	0106
B125C1200S	5659
B125C1200W	0106
B125C1500	0782
B125C1500/1000	5911
B125C1500/1000SIC	OEM
B125C1500R	2758
B125C1500W	1999
B125C2000/1500	5911
B125C3700/2200	1039
B125C3700/2200SI	0724
B125C3700/2200SIC	3006
B125C5000/3300	1039
B125C5000/3300SI	OEM
B125C5000/3300SIC	3006
B126(2S)	0160
B126A(2S)	0160
B126AA	0160
B126AB	0160
B126AC	0160
B126AD	0160
B126AE	0160
B126AF	0160
B126AG	0160
B126AH	0160
B126B	0160
B126C	0160
B126D	0160
B126E	0160
B126F(2S)	0160
B126FV	0160
B126G	0160
B126GN	0160
B126H	0160
B126J	0160
B126K	0160
B126L	0160
B126M	0160
B126OR	0160
B126P	0160
B126R	0160
B126V(2S)	0160
B126X	0160
B126Y	0160
B127(2S)	0160
B127A(2S)	0160
B127B	0160
B127C	0160
B127D	0160
B127E	0160
B127F	0160
B127G	0160
B127GN	0160
B127H	0160
B127J	0160
B127K	0160
B127L	0160
B127M	0160
B127OR	0160
B127R	0160
B127X	0160
B127Y	0160
B128(2S)	0969
B128A(2S)	0969
B128B	0969
B128C	0969
B128D	0969
B128E	0969
B128F	0969
B128G	0969
B128GN	0969
B128H	0969
B128J	0969
B128K	0969
B128L	0969
B128M	0969
B128OR	0969
B128R	0969
B128V(2S)	0969
B128X	0969
B128Y	0969
B129(2S)	0969
B129A	0969
B129B	0969
B129C	0969
B129D	0969
B129E	0969
B129F	0969
B129G	0969
B129GN	0969
B129H	0969
B129J	0969
B129K	0969
B129L	0969
B129M	0969
B129OR	0969
B129R	0969
B129X	0969
B129Y	0969
B130	0222
B130A(2S)	0222
B130B	0222
B130C	0222
B130D	0222
B130E	0222
B130F	0222
B130G	0222
B130GN	0222
B130H	0222
B130J	0222
B130K	0222
B130L	0222
B130M	0222
B130OR	0222
B130R	0222
B130X	0222
B130Y	0222
B131	0160
B131A(2S)	0160
B131B	0160
B131C	0160
B131D	0160
B131E	0160
B131F	0160
B131G	0160
B131GN	0160
B131H	0160
B131J	0160
B131K	0160
B131L	0160
B131M	0160
B131OR	0160
B131R	0160
B131X	0160
B131Y	0160
B132	0160
B132A(2S)	0160
B132B	0160
B132C	0160
B132D	0160
B132E	0160
B132F	0160
B132G	0160
B132GN	0160
B132H	0160
B132J	0160
B132L	0160
B132M	0160
B132OR	0160
B132R	0160
B132X	0160
B132Y	0160
B134	0160
B134(2S)	0004
B134A	0160
B134A(2S)	0004
B134B	OEM
B134B(2S)	0004
B134C	0004
B134D	0004
B134E	0004
B134F	0004
B134G	0004
B134GN	0004
B134H	0004
B134J	0004
B134K	0004
B134L	0004
B134M	0004
B134OR	0004
B134R	0004
B134X	0004
B134Y	0004
B135(2S)	0004
B135A	0004
B135B(2S)	0004
B135C(2S)	0004
B135D	0004
B135E(2S)	0004
B135F	0004
B135G	0004
B135GN	0004
B135H	0004
B135J	0004
B135K	0004
B135L	0004
B135M	0004
B135OR	0004
B135R	0004
B135X	0004
B135Y	0004
B136(2S)	0004
B136A(2S)	0004
B136B(2S)	0004
B136C(2S)	0004
B136D	0004
B136E	0004
B136F	0004
B136G	0004
B136GN	0004
B136H	0004
B136J	0004
B136K	0004
B136L	0004
B136M	0004
B136OR	0004
B136R	0004
B136U(2S)	0004
B136X	0004
B137(2S)	0160
B137A	0160
B137B	0160
B137C	0160
B137D	0160
B137E	0160
B137F	0160
B137G	0160
B137GN	0160
B137H	0160
B137K	0160
B137L	0160
B137OR	0160
B137R	0160
B137X	0160
B137Y	0160
B138(2S)	0160
B138A	0160
B138B	0160
B138C	0160
B138D	0160
B138E	0160
B138G	0160
B138GN	0160
B138H	0160
B138J	0160
B138K	0160
B138L	0160
B138M	0160
B138OR	0160
B138R	0160
B138X	0160
B138Y	0160
B140	0100
B140(TRANS)	0085
B140A	0085
B140B	0085
B140C	0085
B140D	0085
B140E	0085
B140F	0085
B140G	0085
B140GN	0085
B140H	0085
B140J	0085
B140K	0085
B140L	0085
B140M	0085
B140OR	0085
B140X	0085
B140Y	0085
B141(2S)	0085
B142(2S)	0085
B142A	0085
B142B(2S)	0085
B142C(2S)	0085
B142D	0085
B142E	0085
B142F	0085
B142G	0085
B142GN	0085
B142H	0085
B142J	0085
B142K	0085
B142L	0085
B142M	0085
B142OR	0085
B142R	0085
B142X	0085
B142Y	0085
B143(2S)	0085
B143A	0085
B143B	0085
B143C	0085
B143D	0085
B143E	0085
B143F	0085
B143G	0085
B143GN	0085
B143H	0085
B143J	0085
B143K	0085
B143L	0085
B143M	0085
B143OR	0085
B143P(2S)	0085
B143X	0085
B143Y	0085
B144(2S)	0085
B144A	0085
B144B	0085
B144C	0085
B144D	0085
B144E	0085
B144F	0085
B144G	0085
B144GN	0085
B144H	0085
B144J	0085
B144K	0085
B144L	0085
B144M	0085
B144OR	0085
B144P(2S)	0085
B144R	0085
B144X	0085
B144Y	0085
B145(2S)	0085
B145A	0085
B145B	0085
B145C	0085
B145D	0085
B145E	0085
B145F	0085
B145G	0085
B145GN	0085
B145H	0085
B145J	0085
B145K	0085
B145L	0085
B145M	0085
B145OR	0085
B145R	0085
B145X	0085
B145Y	0085
B146(2S)	0085
B146A	0085
B146B	0085
B146C	0085
B146D	0085
B146E	0085
B146F	0085
B146G	0085
B146GN	0085
B146H	0085
B146J	0085
B146K	0085
B146L	0085
B146M	0085
B146OR	0085
B146R	0085
B146X	0085
B146Y	0085
B147(2S)	0085
B147A	0085
B147B	0085
B147C	0085
B147D	0085
B147E	0085
B147F	0085
B147G	0085
B147H	0085
B147J	0085
B147K	0085
B147L	0085
B147M	0085
B147OR	0085
B147X	0085
B147Y	0085
B148	0599
B149	0085
B149-N	0085
B149A	0085
B149B	0085
B149C	0085
B149D	0085
B149E	0085
B149F	0085
B149G	0085
B149GN	0085
B149H	0085
B149J	0085
B149K	0085
B149L	0085
B149M	0085
B149OR	0085
B149R	0085
B149X	0085
B149Y	0085
B150	0002
B150(2S)	0164
B150A	0164
B150B	0164
B150C	0164
B150D	0164
B150E	0164
B150F	0164
B150G	0164
B150GN	0164
B150H	0164
B150J	0164
B150K	0164
B150L	0164
B150M	0164
B150OR	0164
B150R	0164
B150X	0164
B150Y	0164
B151	OEM
B151(2S)	0969
B151A	0969
B151B	0969
B151C	0969
B151D	0969
B151E	0969
B151F	0969
B151G	0969
B151GN	0969
B151H	0969
B151J	0969
B151K	0969
B151L	0969
B151M	0969
B151OR	0969
B151R	0969
B151X	0969
B151Y	0969
B152	5317
B152(2S)	0969
B152A	0969
B152B	0969
B152C	0969
B152D	0969
B152E	0969
B152F	0969
B152G	0969
B152GN	0969
B152H	0969
B152J	0969
B152K	0969
B152L	0969
B152M	0969
B152OR	0969
B152R	0969
B152X	0969
B152Y	0969
B153(2S)	0004
B153A	0004
B153B	0004
B153C	0004
B153D	0004
B153E	0004
B153F	0004
B153G	0004
B153GN	0004
B153H	0004
B153J	0004
B153K	0004
B153L	0004
B153M	0004
B153OR	0004
B153R	0004
B153X	0004
B153Y	0004
B154(2S)	0004
B154A	0004
B154B	0004
B154C	0004
B154D	0004
B154E	0004
B154F	0004
B154G	0004
B154GN	0004
B154H	0004
B154J	0004
B154K	0004
B154L	0004
B154M	0004
B154OR	0004
B154R	0004
B154X	0004
B154Y	0004
B155	0004
B155A(2S)	0004
B155B(2S)	0004
B155C	0004
B155D	0004
B155E	0004
B155F	0004
B155G	0004
B155GN	0004
B155H	0004
B155J	0004
B155K	0004
B155L	0004
B155M	0004
B155OR	0004
B155R	0004
B155X	0004
B155Y	0004
B156(2S)	0004
B156-A	0004
B156A(2S)	0004
B156AA(2S)	0004
B156AB(2S)	0004
B156AC(2S)	0004
B156AD	0004
B156B(2S)	0004
B156B3	0004
B156BK	0004
B156C(2S)	0004
B156D(2S)	0004
B156E	0004
B156F	0004
B156G	0004
B156GN	0004
B156H	0004
B156J	0004
B156K	0004
B156L	0004
B156M	0004
B156OR	0004
B156P(2S)	0004
B156R	0004
B156X	0004
B156Y	0004
B157(2S)	0136
B157A	0136
B157B	0136
B157C	0136
B157D	0136
B157E	0136
B157F	0136
B157G	0136
B157GN	0136
B157H	0136
B157J	0136
B157K	0136
B157L	0136
B157M	0136
B157OR	0136
B157R	0136
B157X	0136
B157Y	0136
B158(2S)	0136
B158A	0136
B158B	0136
B158C	0136
B158D	0136
B158E	0136
B158F	0136
B158G	0136
B158GN	0136
B158H	0136
B158J	0136
B158K	0136
B158L	0136
B158M	0136
B158OR	0136
B158R	0136
B158X	0136
B158Y	0136
B159(2S)	0136
B159A	0136
B159B	0136
B159C	0136
B159D	0136
B159E	0136
B159F	0136
B159G	0136
B159GN	0136
B159H	0136
B159J	0136
B159K	0136
B159L	0136
B159M	0136
B159OR	0136
B159R	0136
B159X	0136
B159Y	0136
B160(2S)	0136
B160A	0136
B160B	0136
B160C	0136
B160D	0136
B160E	0136
B160F	0136
B160G	0136
B160GN	0136
B160H	0136
B160J	0136
B160K	0136
B160L	0136
B160M	0136
B160OR	0136
B160R	0136
B160X	0136
B160Y	0136
B161(2S)	0211
B161A	0211
B161B	0211
B161C	0211
B161D	0211
B161E	0211
B161F	0211
B161G	0211
B161GN	0211
B161H	0211
B161J	0211
B161K	0211
B161L	0211
B161M	0211
B161OR	0211
B161R	0211
B161X	0211
B161Y	0211
B162(2S)	0004
B162A	0004
B162B	0004
B162C	0004
B162D	0004
B162E	0004
B162F	0004
B162G	0004
B162GN	0004
B162H	0004
B162J	0004
B162K	0004
B162L	0004
B162M	0004
B162OR	0004

If replacement code is OEM, contact original manufacturer for replacement.

DEVICE TYPE	REPL CODE
B162R	0004
B162X	0004
B162Y	0004
B163(2S)	0211
B163A	0211
B163B	0211
B163C	0211
B163D	0211
B163E	0211
B163F	0211
B163G	0211
B163GN	0211
B163H	0211
B163J	0211
B163K	0211
B163L	0211
B163M	0211
B163OR	0211
B163R	0211
B163X	0211
B163Y	0211
B164(2S)	0211
B164A	0211
B164B	0211
B164C	0211
B164D	0211
B164E	0211
B164F	0211
B164G	0211
B164GN	0211
B164H	0211
B164J	0211
B164L	0211
B164M	0211
B164OR	0211
B164R	0211
B164X	0211
B164Y	0211
B165(2S)	0211
B165A	0211
B165B	0211
B165C	0211
B165D	0211
B165E	0211
B165F	0211
B165G	0211
B165GN	0211
B165H	0211
B165J	0211
B165K	0211
B165M	0211
B165OR	0211
B165R	0211
B165X	0211
B165Y	0211
B166(2S)	0004
B166A	0004
B166B	0004
B166C	0004
B166D	0004
B166E	0004
B166F	0004
B166G	0004
B166GN	0004
B166H	0004
B166J	0004
B166K	0004
B166L	0004
B166M	0004
B166OR	0004
B166R	0004
B166X	0004
B166Y	0004
B167(2S)	0164
B167A	0164
B167B	0164
B167BK	0164
B167C	0164
B167D	0164
B167E	0164
B167F	0164
B167G	0164
B167GN	0164
B167H	0164
B167J	0164
B167K	0164
B167L	0164
B167M	0164
B167OR	0164
B167R	0164
B167X	0164
B167Y	0164
B168(2S)	0004
B168A	0004
B168B	0004
B168C	0004
B168D	0004
B168E	0004
B168F	0004
B168G	0004
B168GN	0004
B168H	0004
B168J	0004
B168K	0004
B168L	0004
B168M	0004
B168OR	0004
B168R	0004
B168X	0004
B168Y	0004
B169	0004
B169A	0004
B169B	0004
B169C	0004
B169D	0004
B169E	0004
B169F	0004
B169G	0004
B169GN	0004
B169H	0004
B169J	0004
B169K	0004
B169L	0004
B169M	0004
B169OR	0004
B169R	0004
B169X	0004
B169Y	0004
B170(2S)	0004
B170A	0004
B170B	0004
B170C	0004
B170D	0004
B170E	0004
B170F	0004
B170G	0004
B170GN	0004
B170H	0004
B170J	0004
B170K	0004
B170L	0004
B170M	0004
B170OR	0004
B170R	0004
B170X	0004
B170Y	0004
B171	0004
B171A(2S)	0004
B171B(2S)	0004
B171C	0004
B171D	0004
B171E	0004
B171F	0004
B171G	0004
B171GN	0004
B171H	0004
B171J	0004
B171K	0004
B171L	0004
B171M	0004
B171OR	0004
B171X	0004
B171Y	0004
B172(2S)	0004
B172-5	0087
B172-10	0087
B172-20	0087
B172-30	0087
B172-40	0087
B172-50	0087
B172-60	0087
B172-70	0087
B172-80	0087
B172-90	0087
B172-100	0087
B172-110	1749
B172-120	1749
B172A(2S)	0004
B172A-1	0004
B172A-F	0004
B172AF(2S)	0004
B172AL	0004
B172B(2S)	0004
B172C(2S)	0004
B172D(2S)	0004
B172E(2S)	0004
B172F(2S)	0004
B172FN	0004
B172G	0004
B172GN	0004
B172H(2S)	0004
B172J	0004
B172K	0004
B172L	0004
B172M	0004
B172OR	0004
B172P(2S)	0004
B172R(2S)	0004
B172X	0004
B172Y	0004
B173(2S)	0004
B173A(2S)	0004
B173B(2S)	0004
B173BL	0004
B173C(2S)	0004
B173CL	0004
B173D	0004
B173E	0004
B173F	0004
B173G	0004
B173GN	0004
B173H	0004
B173J	0004
B173K	0004
B173L(2S)	0004
B173M	0004
B173OR	0004
B173R	0004
B173X	0004
B173Y	0004
B174(2S)	0004
B174A	0004
B174B	0004
B174C	0004
B174D	0004
B174E	0004
B174F	0004
B174G	0004
B174GN	0004
B174H	0004
B174K	0004
B174L	0004
B174M	0004
B174OR	0004
B174R	0004
B174X	0004
B174Y	0004
B175(2S)	0004
B175A(2S)	0004
B175B(2S)	0004
B175B-1	0004
B175BL	0004
B175C(2S)	0004
B175CL	0004
B175D	0004
B175E(2S)	0004
B175F	0004
B175G	0004
B175GN	0004
B175H	0004
B175L	0004
B175M	0004
B175OR	0004
B175R	0004
B175X	0004
B175Y	0004
B176(2S)	0004
B176-O(2S)	0004
B176-P(2S)	0004
B176-PR(2S)	0004
B176A	0004
B176B(2S)	0004
B176C	0004
B176D	0004
B176E	0004
B176F	0004
B176G	0004
B176GN	0004
B176H	0004
B176J	0004
B176K	0004
B176L	0004
B176M(2S)	0004
B176O	0004
B176OR	0004
B176P(2S)	0004
B176PL	0004
B176PR	0004
B176PRC(2S)	0004
B176R(1)	0004
B176R(2S)	0004
B176RG	0004
B176X	0004
B176Y	0004
B177	0004
B177(2S)	0004
B177A	0004
B177B	0004
B177C	0004
B177D	0004
B177E	0004
B177F	0004
B177G	0004
B177GN	0004
B177H	0004
B177K	0004
B177L	0004
B177M	0004
B177OR	0004
B177R	0004
B177X	0004
B177Y	0004
B178	0004
B178(2S)	0004
B178-O(2S)	0004
B178-OR	0004
B178-S(2S)	0004
B178A(2S)	0004
B178B	0004
B178C(2S)	0004
B178D(2S)	0004
B178E	0004
B178F	0004
B178G	0004
B178GN	0004
B178H	0004
B178J	0004
B178K	0004
B178L	0004
B178M(2S)	0004
B178N(2S)	0004
B178OR	0004
B178R	0004
B178S	0004
B178T(2S)	0004
B178TC	0004
B178TS	0004
B178U(2S)	0004
B178V(2S)	0004
B178X(2S)	0004
B178Y(2S)	0004
B179	0160
B179(2S)	0050
B180(2S)	0164
B180A(2S)	0164
B181(2S)	0164
B181A(2S)	0164
B182	0050
B183(2S)	0004
B183A	0004
B183B	0004
B183C	0004
B183D	0004
B183E	0004
B183F	0004
B183G	0004
B183GN	0004
B183H	0004
B183J	0004
B183K	0004
B183L	0004
B183M	0004
B183OR	0004
B183R	0004
B183X	0004
B183Y	0004
B184(2S)	0004
B184A	0004
B184B	0004
B184C	0004
B184D	0004
B184E	0004
B184F	0004
B184G	0004
B184GN	0004
B184H	0004
B184J	0004
B184K	0004
B184L	0004
B184M	0004
B184OR	0004
B184R	0004
B184X	0004
B184Y	0004
B185(2S)	0004
B185-O	0004
B185A	0004
B185AA(2S)	0004
B185B	0004
B185C	0004
B185D	0004
B185E	0004
B185F(2S)	0004
B185G	0004
B185GN	0004
B185H	0004
B185I	0004
B185J	0004
B185L	0004
B185M	0004
B185OR	0004
B185P(2S)	0004
B185R	0004
B185X	0004
B185Y	0004
B186	0004
B186(SANYO)	0004
B186-1(2S)	0004
B186-7	0004
B186-K(2S)	0004
B186-O	0004
B186-OR	0004
B186A(2S)	0004
B186AG(2S)	0004
B186B(2S)	0004
B186BY(2S)	0004
B186C	0004
B186D	0004
B186E	0004
B186F	0004
B186G(2S)	0004
B186GN	0004
B186H(2S)	0004
B186J	0004
B186K	0004
B186L(2S)	0004
B186M	0004
B186OR	0004
B186R	0004
B186X	0004
B186Y(2S)	0004
B187	0004
B187(SANYO)	0004
B187-1	0004
B187-OR	0004
B187A	0004
B187AA(2S)	3511
B187B(2S)	3511
B187BK	0004
B187C(2S)	0004
B187D(2S)	0004
B187E	0004
B187F	0004
B187G(2S)	0004
B187GN	0004
B187H	0004
B187K(2S)	0004
B187L	0004
B187M	0004
B187OR	0004
B187R(2S)	0004
B187S	0004
B187TV	0004
B187X	0004
B187Y(2S)	0004
B188(2S)	0004
B188A	0004
B188B	0004
B188C	0004
B188D	0004
B188E	0004
B188F	0004
B188G	0004
B188GN	0004
B188H	0004
B188J	0004
B188K	0004
B188L	0004
B188M	0004
B188OR	0004
B188R	0004
B188X	0004
B188Y	0004
B189(2S)	0004
B189A	0004
B189B	0004
B189C	0004
B189D	0004
B189E	0004
B189F	0004
B189G	0004
B189GN	0004
B189H	0004
B189J	0004
B189K	0004
B189L	0004
B189M	0004
B189OR	0004
B189R	0004
B189X	0004
B189Y	0004
B190	0164
B191	0279
B191-5	1991
B191-10	OEM
B191-20	OEM
B191-30	OEM
B191-40	OEM
B191-50	OEM
B191-60	OEM
B191-70	OEM
B191-80	OEM
B191-90	OEM
B191-100	OEM
B191-120	OEM
B192	0164
B193	0164
B193F	OEM
B194	0164
B195	0164
B196	0164
B197	0164
B198	0164
B199(2S)	0211
B199A	0211
B199B	0211
B199C	0211
B199D	0211
B199E	0211
B199F	0211
B199G	0211
B199GN	0211
B199H	0211
B199J	0211
B199L	0211
B199M	0211
B199OR	0211
B199R	0211
B199X	0211
B199Y	0211
B200	0004
B200(2S)	0004
B200A(2S)	0004
B200B	0004
B200C	0004
B200C40	0015
B200D	0004
B200E	0004
B200F	0004
B200G	0004
B200GN	0004
B200H	0004
B200J	0004
B200K	0004
B200L	0004
B200M	0004
B200OR	0004
B200R	0004
B200X	0004
B200Y	0004
B201	0004
B202(2S)	0004
B202A	0004
B202B	0004
B202C	0004
B202D	0004
B202E	0004
B202F	0004
B202G	0004
B202GN	0004
B202H	0004
B202J	0004
B202L	0004
B202M	0004
B202OR	0004
B202R	0004
B202X	0004
B202Y	0004
B203	0599
B203A	0599
B203AA(2S)	0599
B203B	0599
B203C	0599
B203D	0599
B203E	0599
B203F	0599
B203G	0599
B203GN	0599
B203H	0599
B203J	0599
B203K	0599
B203L	0599
B203M	0599
B203OR	0599
B203R	0599
B203X	0599
B203Y	0599
B204(2S)	0599
B205(2S)	0599
B206(2S)	0599
B207	0599
B207A	0599
B208	0599
B208A	0599
B209	0599
B210	0599
B211	0599
B212	0599
B213	0599
B213A	0599
B214	0599
B214A	0599
B215(2S)	0969
B215A	0969
B215B	0969
B215C	0969
B215D	0969
B215E	0969
B215F	0969
B215G	0969
B215GN	0969
B215H	0969
B215J	0969
B215K	0969
B215L	0969
B215M	0969
B215OR	0969
B215R	0969
B215X	0969
B215Y	0969
B216(2S)	0160
B216A(2S)	0160
B216B	0160
B216C	0160
B216D	0160
B216E	0160
B216F	0160
B216G	0160
B216GN	0160
B216H	0160
B216J	0160
B216K	0160
B216L	0160
B216M	0160
B216OR	0160
B216R	0160
B216X	0160
B216Y	0160
B217(2S)	0160
B217A(2S)	0160
B217B	0160
B217C	0160
B217D	0160
B217E	0160
B217F	0160
B217G(2S)	0160
B217GN	0160
B217H	0160
B217K	0160
B217L	0160
B217M	0160
B217OR	0160
B217R	0160
B217U(2S)	0160
B217X	0160
B217Y	0160
B218(2S)	0211
B218A	0211
B218B	0211
B218C	0211
B218D	0211
B218E	0211
B218F	0211
B218G	0211
B218GN	0211
B218H	0211
B218J	0211
B218K	0211
B218L	0211
B218M	0211
B218OR	0211
B218R	0211
B218X	0211
B218Y	0211
B219(2S)	0211
B219A	0211
B219B	0211
B219E	0211
B219F	0211
B219G	0211
B219H	0211
B219J	0211
B219K	0211
B219L	0211
B219R	0211
B219X	0211
B219Y	0211
B220(2S)	0211
B220A(2S)	0211
B220B	0211
B220C	0211
B220D	0211
B220E	0211
B220F	0211
B220GN	0211
B220H	0211
B220J	0211
B220K	0211
B220L	0211
B220M	0211
B220OR	0211
B220R	0211
B220X	0211
B220Y	0211
B221(2S)	0211
B221A(2S)	0211
B221B	0211
B221C	0211
B221D	0211
B221E	0211
B221F	0211
B221G	0211
B221GN	0211
B221H	0211
B221J	0211
B221K	0211
B221L	0211
B221M	0211
B221OR	0211
B221R	0211
B221X	0211
B221Y	0211
B222(2S)	0211
B222A	0211
B222B	0211
B222C	0211
B222D	0211
B222E	0211
B222F	0211
B222G	0211
B222GN	0211
B222H	0211
B222J	0211
B222K	0211
B222L	0211
B222M	0211
B222OR	0211
B222R	0211
B222X	0211
B222Y	0211
B223(2S)	0211
B223-10	0087
B223-20	0344
B223-30	0087
B223-40	0087
B223-50	0087
B223-60	0087
B223A	0211
B223B	0211
B223C	0211
B223D	0211
B223E	0211
B223F	0211
B223G	0211
B223Y	0211
B224	0004
B224A	0004
B224B	0004
B224C	0004
B224D	0004
B224E	0004
B224F	0004
B224G	0004
B224GN	0004
B224H	0004
B224K	0004
B224L	0004
B224M	0004
B224OR	0004
B224R	0004
B224X	0004
B224Y	0004
B225(2S)	0211

If replacement code is OEM, contact original manufacturer for replacement.

DEVICE TYPE	REPL CODE
B225A	0211
B225B	0211
B225C	0211
B225D	0211
B225E	0211
B225F	0211
B225G	0211
B225GN	0211
B225H	0211
B225K	0211
B225L	0211
B225M	0211
B225OR	0211
B225R	0211
B225X	0211
B225Y	0211
B226(2S)	0211
B226A	0211
B226B	0211
B226C	0211
B226D	0211
B226E	0211
B226F	0211
B226G	0211
B226GN	0211
B226J	0211
B226K	0211
B226L	0211
B226M	0211
B226OR	0211
B226R	0211
B226X	0211
B226Y	0211
B227(2S)	0004
B227A	0004
B227B	0004
B227C	0004
B227D	0004
B227E	0004
B227F	0004
B227G	0004
B227GN	0004
B227H	0004
B227J	0004
B227K	0004
B227L	0004
B227M	0004
B227OR	0004
B227R	0004
B227X	0004
B227Y	0004
B228(2S)	0969
B228A	0969
B228B	0969
B228C	0969
B228D	0969
B228E	0969
B228F	0969
B228G	0969
B228GN	0969
B228H	0969
B228J	0969
B228K	0969
B228L	0969
B228M	0969
B228OR	0969
B228R	0969
B228X	0969
B228Y	0969
B229(2S)	0969
B229A	0969
B229B	0969
B229C	0969
B229D	0969
B229E	0969
B229F	0969
B229G	0969
B229GN	0969
B229J	0969
B229K	0969
B229L	0969
B229M	0969
B229OR	0969
B229R	0969
B229X	0969
B229Y	0969
B230(2S)	0969
B230A	0969
B230B	0969
B230C	0969
B230D	0969
B230E	0969
B230F	0969
B230G	0969
B230GN	0969
B230H	0969
B230J	0969
B230K	0969
B230L	0969
B230M	0969
B230OR	0969
B230R	0969
B230X	0969
B230Y	0969
B231(2S)	0969
B231A	0969
B231B	0969
B231C	0969
B231D	0969

DEVICE TYPE	REPL CODE
B231E	0969
B231F	0969
B231G	0969
B231GN	0969
B231H	0969
B231J	0969
B231K	0969
B231L	0969
B231M	0969
B231OR	0969
B231R	0969
B231X	0969
B231Y	0969
B232(2S)	0969
B232A	0969
B232B	0969
B232C	0969
B232D	0969
B232E	0969
B232F	0969
B232G	0969
B232GN	0969
B232H	0969
B232K	0969
B232L	0969
B232M	0969
B232OR	0969
B232R	0969
B232X	0969
B232Y	0969
B233(2S)	0969
B233A	0969
B233B	0969
B233C	0969
B233D	0969
B233E	0969
B233F	0969
B233G	0969
B233GN	0969
B233H	0969
B233J	0969
B233K	0969
B233L	0969
B233M	0969
B233OR	0969
B233R	0969
B233X	0969
B233Y	0969
B234(2S)	0969
B234A	0969
B234B	0969
B234C	0969
B234D	0969
B234E	0969
B234F	0969
B234G	0969
B234GN	0969
B234H	0969
B234J	0969
B234K	0969
B234L	0969
B234M	0969
B234N(2S)	0969
B234OR	0969
B234R	0969
B234X	0969
B234Y	0969
B235(2S)	0040
B235A(2S)	0432
B235B	0432
B235C	0432
B235D	0432
B235E	0432
B235F	0432
B235G	0432
B235GN	0432
B235H	0432
B235L	0432
B235M	0432
B235OR	0432
B235R	0432
B235X	0432
B235Y	0432
B236(2S)	0435
B236A	0435
B236B	0435
B236C	0435
B236D	0435
B236E	0435
B236F	0435
B236G	0435
B236GN	0435
B236H	0435
B236J	0435
B236K	0435
B236L	0435
B236M	0435
B236OR	0435
B236R	0435
B236X	0435
B236Y	0435
B237(2S)	0435
B237-12A(2S)	0435
B237-12B(2S)	0435
B237A	0435
B237B	0435
B237C	0435
B237D	0435
B237E	0435

DEVICE TYPE	REPL CODE
B237F	0435
B237G	0435
B237GN	0435
B237H	0435
B237J	0435
B237K	0435
B237L	0435
B237M	0435
B237OR	0435
B237R	0435
B237X	0435
B237Y	0435
B238(2S)	0164
B238-12A(2S)	0164
B238-12B(2S)	0164
B238-12C(2S)	0164
B238A	0164
B238B	0164
B238C	0164
B238C18	0079
B238D	0164
B238E	0164
B238F	0164
B238G	0164
B238GN	0164
B238H	0164
B238J	0164
B238K	0164
B238L	0164
B238M	0164
B238OR	0164
B238R	0164
B238X	0164
B238Y	0164
B239(2S)	0160
B239A(2S)	0160
B239B	0160
B239C	0160
B239D	0160
B239E	0160
B239F	0160
B239G	0160
B239GN	0160
B239H	0160
B239J	0160
B239K	0160
B239L	0160
B239M	0160
B239OR	0160
B239R	0160
B239X	0160
B239Y	0160
B240	0273
B240(2S)	0050
B240A(2S)	0050
B240B	0050
B240C	0050
B240D	0050
B240E	0050
B240F	0050
B240GN	0050
B240H	0050
B240J	0050
B240K	0050
B240L	0050
B240M	0050
B240OR	0050
B240R	0050
B240X	0050
B240Y	0050
B241(2S)	0164
B241A	0164
B241B	0164
B241C	0164
B241D	0164
B241E	0164
B241F	0164
B241G	0164
B241GN	0164
B241H	0164
B241J	0164
B241K	0164
B241L	0164
B241M	0164
B241OR	0164
B241R	0164
B241V	0164
B241X	0164
B241Y	0164
B242	0164
B242A	0164
B242B	0164
B242C	0164
B242D	0164
B242E	0164
B242F	0164
B242G	0164
B242GN	0164
B242H	0164
B242J	0164
B242K	0164
B242L	0164
B242M	0164
B242OR	0164
B242R	0164
B242X	0164
B242Y	0164
B243	0969
B243A	0969

DEVICE TYPE	REPL CODE
B243B	0969
B243C	0969
B243D	0969
B243E	0969
B243F	0969
B243G	0969
B243GN	0969
B243H	0969
B243J	0969
B243K	0969
B243L	0969
B243M	0969
B243OR	0969
B243R	0969
B243X	0969
B243Y	0969
B244	0969
B244A	0969
B244B	0969
B244C	0969
B244D	0969
B244E	0969
B244F	0969
B244G	0969
B244GN	0969
B244H	0969
B244J	0969
B244K	0969
B244L	0969
B244M	0969
B244OR	0969
B244R	0969
B244X	0969
B244Y	0969
B245	0969
B245A	0969
B245B	0969
B245C	0969
B245D	0969
B245E	0969
B245F	0969
B245G	0969
B245H	0969
B245J	0969
B245L	0969
B245M	0969
B245OR	0969
B245R	0969
B245X	0969
B245Y	0969
B246(2S)	0085
B246A	0085
B246B	0085
B246C	0085
B246D	0085
B246E	0085
B246F	0085
B246G	0085
B246GN	0085
B246H	0085
B246J	0085
B246K	0085
B246L	0085
B246M	0085
B246OR	0085
B246R	0085
B246X	0085
B246Y	0085
B247(2S)	0160
B247A	0160
B247B	0160
B247C	0160
B247D	0160
B247E	0160
B247F	0160
B247G	0160
B247GN	0160
B247H	0160
B247J	0160
B247K	0160
B247L	0160
B247M	0160
B247OR	0160
B247R	0160
B247X	0160
B247Y	0160
B248(2S)	0085
B248A(2S)	0085
B248B	0085
B248C	0085
B248D	0085
B248E	0085
B248F	0085
B248G	0085
B248GN	0085
B248H	0085
B248J	0085
B248K	0085
B248L	0085
B248M	0085
B248OR	0085
B248R	0085
B248X	0085
B248Y	0085
B249(2S)	0599
B249A(2S)	0599
B249B	0599
B249C	0599
B249D	0599

DEVICE TYPE	REPL CODE
B249E	0599
B249F	0599
B249G	0599
B249GN	0599
B249H	0599
B249J	0599
B249K	0599
B249L	0599
B249M	0599
B249OR	0599
B249X	0599
B249Y	0599
B250(2S)	0085
B250A(2S)	0085
B250B	0085
B250C7K4S	0015
B250C75	0015
B250C75K4	0015
B250C75K5	0015
B250C75K41	0015
B250C75K45	0015
B250C100	0015
B250C100TD	0015
B250C125	0015
B250C125K4	0015
B250C125N2	0015
B250C125X4	0015
B250C150	0015
B250C150K4	0015
B250C800	1999
B250C800A	2175
B250C800D	1864
B250C800D1	1864
B250C800DM	1864
B250C800M	0106
B250C800W	1999
B250C1000	1999
B250C1000A	2175
B250C1000M	0106
B250C1000W	1999
B250C1200S	3380
B250C1200W	1999
B250C1500	1999
B250C1500/1000	5925
B250C1500/1000SIC	OEM
B250C1500R	0299
B250C1500W	1999
B250C2000/1500	OEM
B250C3700/2200	1039
B250C3700/2200SIC	3006
B250C5000/3300	1039
B250C5000/3300SI	OEM
B250C5000/3300SIC	3006
B250D	0085
B250E	0085
B250F	0085
B250G	0085
B250GN	0085
B250H	0085
B250K	0085
B250L	0085
B250M	0085
B250OR	0085
B250X	0085
B250Y	0085
B251(2S)	0969
B251A(2S)	0969
B251B	0969
B251C	0969
B251D	0969
B251E	0969
B251F	0969
B251G	0969
B251GN	0969
B251H	0969
B251J	0969
B251K	0969
B251L	0969
B251M	0969
B251OR	0969
B251R	0969
B251X	0969
B252(2S)	0969
B252A(2S)	0969
B252B	0969
B252C	0969
B252D	0969
B252E	0969
B252F	0969
B252G	0969
B252GN	0969
B252H	0969
B252J	0969
B252L	0969
B252M	0969
B252OR	0969
B252R	0969
B252X	0969
B252Y	0969
B253(2S)	0969
B253A(2S)	0969
B253B	0969
B253C	0969
B253D	0969
B253E	0969
B253F	0969
B253G	0969
B253GN	0969
B253H	0969

DEVICE TYPE	REPL CODE
B253K	0969
B253L	0969
B253M	0969
B253OR	0969
B253X	0969
B253Y	0969
B254(2S)	1004
B254A	1004
B254B	1004
B254C	1004
B254D	1004
B254E	1004
B254F	1004
B254G	1004
B254GN	1004
B254H	1004
B254J	1004
B254K	1004
B254L	1004
B254M	1004
B254OR	1004
B254R	1004
B254X	1004
B254Y	1004
B255(2S)	1004
B255A	1004
B255B	1004
B255C	1004
B255D	1004
B255E	1004
B255F	1004
B255G	1004
B255GN	1004
B255H	1004
B255J	1004
B255K	1004
B255L	1004
B255M	1004
B255OR	1004
B255R	1004
B255X	1004
B255Y	1004
B256(2S)	1004
B256A	1004
B256B	1004
B256C	1004
B256D	1004
B256E	1004
B256F	1004
B256G	1004
B256GN	1004
B256H	1004
B256J	1004
B256L	1004
B256M	1004
B256OR	1004
B256R	1004
B256X	1004
B256Y	1004
B257(2S)	0004
B257A	0004
B257B	0004
B257C	0004
B257D	0004
B257E	0004
B257F	0004
B257G	0004
B257GN	0004
B257H	0004
B257K	0004
B257L	0004
B257M	0004
B257OR	0004
B257R	0004
B257X	0004
B257Y	0004
B258(2S)	0432
B258A	0432
B258B	0432
B258C	0432
B258D	0432
B258E	0432
B258F	0432
B258G	0432
B258GN	0432
B258H	0432
B258J	0432
B258K	0432
B258L	0432
B258M	0432
B258OR	0432
B258R	0432
B258X	0432
B258Y	0432
B259(2S)	0432
B259A	0432
B259B	0432
B259C	0432
B259D	0432
B259E	0432
B259F	0432
B259GN	0432
B259H	0432
B259J	0432
B259K	0432
B259L	0432
B259OR	0432
B259R	0432
B259X	0432

DEVICE TYPE	REPL CODE
B259Y	0432
B260(2S)	0040
B260A	0432
B260B	0432
B260C	0432
B260D	0432
B260E	0432
B260F	0432
B260G	0432
B260GN	0432
B260H	0432
B260J	0432
B260K	0432
B260L	0432
B260M	0432
B260OR	0432
B260R	0432
B260X	0432
B260Y	0432
B261(2S)	0004
B261A	0004
B261B	0004
B261C	0004
B261D	0004
B261E	0004
B261F	0004
B261G	0004
B261GN	0004
B261H	0004
B261J	0004
B261K	0004
B261L	0004
B261M	0004
B261N	0004
B261OR	0004
B261R	0004
B261X	0004
B261Y	0004
B262(2S)	0004
B262A	0004
B262B	0004
B262C	0004
B262D	0004
B262E	0004
B262F	0004
B262G	0004
B262GN	0004
B262H	0004
B262J	0004
B262K	0004
B262L	0004
B262M	0004
B262OR	0004
B262R	0004
B262X	0004
B262Y	0004
B263(2S)	0004
B263A	0004
B263B	0004
B263C	0004
B263D	0004
B263E	0004
B263F	0004
B263G	0004
B263GN	0004
B263H	0004
B263J	0004
B263K	0004
B263L	0004
B263M	0004
B263OR	0004
B263R	0004
B263X	0004
B263Y	0004
B264(2S)	0004
B264A	0004
B264B	0004
B264C	0004
B264D	0004
B264E	0004
B264F	0004
B264G	0004
B264GN	0004
B264H	0004
B264J	0004
B264K	0004
B264L	0004
B264M	0004
B264OR	0004
B264R	0004
B264X	0004
B264Y	0004
B265(2S)	0004
B265A	0004
B265B	0004
B265C	0004
B265D	0004
B265E	0004
B265F	0004
B265G	0004
B265GN	0004
B265H	0004
B265J	0004
B265K	0004
B265L	0004
B265M	0004
B265OR	0004
B265X	0004
B265Y	0004

If replacement code is OEM, contact original manufacturer for replacement.

DEVICE TYPE	REPL CODE
B266(2S)	0004
B266A	0004
B266B	0004
B266C	0004
B266D	0004
B266E	0004
B266F	0004
B266G	0004
B266GN	0004
B266H	0004
B266J	0004
B266K	0004
B266L	0004
B266M	0004
B266OR	0004
B266P(2S)	0004
B266Q(2S)	0004
B266R	0004
B266X	0004
B266Y	0004
B267(2S)	0004
B267A	0004
B267B	0004
B267C	0004
B267D	0004
B267E	0004
B267F	0004
B267G	0004
B267GN	0004
B267H	0004
B267J	0004
B267K	0004
B267L	0004
B267M	0004
B267OR	0004
B267R	0004
B267X	0004
B267Y	0004
B268(2S)	0004
B268A	0004
B268B	0004
B268C	0004
B268D	0004
B268E	0004
B268F	0004
B268G	0004
B268GN	0004
B268H	0004
B268J	0004
B268K	0004
B268L	0004
B268M	0004
B268OR	0004
B268R	0004
B268X	0004
B268Y	0004
B269(2S)	0004
B269A	0004
B269C	0004
B269D	0004
B269E	0004
B269F	0004
B269G	0004
B269GN	0004
B269J	0004
B269K	0004
B269L	0004
B269M	0004
B269OR	0004
B269R	0004
B269X	0004
B269Y	0004
B270(2S)	0004
B270A(2S)	0004
B270B(2S)	0004
B270C(2S)	0004
B270D(2S)	0004
B270E(2S)	0004
B270F	0004
B270G	0004
B270GN	0004
B270H	0004
B270J	0004
B270K	0004
B270L	0004
B270M	0004
B270OR	0004
B270R	0004
B270X	0004
B270Y	0004
B271(2S)	0004
B272(2S)	0004
B272-5	OEM
B272-10	OEM
B272-20	OEM
B272-30	OEM
B272-40	OEM
B272-50	OEM
B272-60	OEM
B272-70	OEM
B272-80	OEM
B272-90	OEM
B272-100	OEM
B272-120	OEM
B272A	0004
B272B	0004
B272C	0004
B272D	0004
B272E	0004

DEVICE TYPE	REPL CODE
B272F	0004
B272G	0004
B272GN	0004
B272J	0004
B272K	0004
B272L	0004
B272M	0004
B272OR	0004
B272R	0004
B272X	0004
B272Y	0004
B273(2S)	0004
B273A	0004
B273B	0004
B273C	0004
B273D	0004
B273E	0004
B273F	0004
B273G	0004
B273GN	0004
B273H	0004
B273J	0004
B273K	0004
B273L	0004
B273M	0004
B273OR	0004
B273R	0004
B273X	0004
B273Y	0004
B274	0969
B274(SYLVANIA)	0086
B274A	0969
B274B	0969
B274C	0969
B274D	0969
B274E	0969
B274F	0969
B274G	0969
B274H	0969
B274J	0969
B274K	0969
B274L	0969
B274M	0969
B274OR	0969
B274R	0969
B274V	0969
B274X	0969
B274Y	0969
B275(2S)	0969
B275A	0969
B275B	0969
B275C	0969
B275D	0969
B275E	0969
B275F	0969
B275G	0969
B275GN	0969
B275H	0969
B275J	0969
B275K	0969
B275L	0969
B275M	0969
B275OR	0969
B275R	0969
B275X	0969
B275Y	0969
B276(2S)	0969
B276A	0969
B276B	0969
B276C	0969
B276D	0969
B276E	0969
B276F	0969
B276G	0969
B276GN	0969
B276H	0969
B276J	0969
B276K	0969
B276L	0969
B276M	0969
B276OR	0969
B276R	0969
B276X	0969
B276Y	0969
B277	0050
B278	0164
B279	0164
B280	0004
B280C800	OEM
B281	0527
B281C	0527
B282(2S)	0599
B282A	0599
B282B	0599
B282C	0599
B282D	0599
B282E	0599
B282G	0599
B282GN	0599
B282H	0599
B282J	0599
B282K	0599
B282L	0599
B282M	0599
B282OR	0599
B282R	0599
B282X	0599
B282Y	0599
B283(2S)	0160

DEVICE TYPE	REPL CODE
B283A	0160
B283B	0160
B283C	0160
B283D	0160
B283E	0160
B283F	0160
B283G	0160
B283GN	0160
B283H	0160
B283J	0160
B283K	0160
B283L	0160
B283M	0160
B283OR	0160
B283R	0160
B283X	0160
B283Y	0160
B284(2S)	0160
B284A	0160
B284B	0160
B284C	0160
B284D	0160
B284E	0160
B284F	0160
B284G	0160
B284H	0160
B284J	0160
B284K	0160
B284L	0160
B284M	0160
B284OR	0160
B284R	0160
B284X	0160
B284Y	0160
B285(2S)	0969
B285-5	0276
B285-10	0276
B285-20	0287
B285-30	0293
B285-40	0293
B285-50	0299
B285-60	0299
B285-70	0250
B285-80	0250
B285-90	0250
B285-100	0250
B285-120	OEM
B285A	0969
B285B	0969
B285C	0969
B285D	0969
B285E	0969
B285F	0969
B285G	0969
B285GN	0969
B285H	0969
B285J	0969
B285K	0969
B285L	0969
B285M	0969
B285OR	0969
B285R	0969
B285X	0969
B285Y	0969
B286	0969
B287	0969
B288	0050
B289	0050
B290(2S)	0279
B290-GREEN	0279
B290-YELLOW	0279
B290A	0279
B290A-BLUE	0279
B290B	0279
B290C	0279
B290D	0279
B290E	0279
B290F	0279
B290G	0279
B290GN	0279
B290H	0279
B290J	0279
B290K	0279
B290L	0279
B290M	0279
B290OR	0279
B290R	0279
B290X	0279
B290Y	0279
B291(2S)	0279
B291-5	OEM
B291-10	OEM
B291-20	OEM
B291-30	OEM
B291-40	OEM
B291-50	OEM
B291-60	OEM
B291-70	OEM
B291-80	OEM
B291-90	OEM
B291-100	OEM
B291-120	OEM
B291-GREEN	0279
B291-RED	0279
B291-YELLOW	0279
B291A	0279
B291B	0279
B291C	0279
B291D	0279

DEVICE TYPE	REPL CODE
B291E	0279
B291F	0279
B291G	0279
B291GN	0279
B291H	0279
B291J	0279
B291K	0279
B291L	0279
B291M	0279
B291OR	0279
B291R	0279
B291X	0279
B291Y	0279
B292(2S)	0279
B292-BLUE	0279
B292-GREEN	0279
B292-ORANGE	0279
B292-RED	0279
B292-YELLOW	0279
B292A(2S)	0279
B292A-BLUE	0279
B292A-GREEN	0279
B292A-ORANG	0279
B292A-RED	0279
B292A-YELLO	0279
B292B	0279
B292C	0279
B292D	0279
B292E	0279
B292F	0279
B292G	0279
B292GN	0279
B292H	0279
B292J	0279
B292K	0279
B292L	0279
B292M	0279
B292OR	0279
B292R	0279
B292X	0279
B292Y	0279
B293(2S)	0004
B293A	0004
B293B	0004
B293C	0004
B293D	0004
B293E	0004
B293F	0004
B293G	0004
B293GN	0004
B293H	0004
B293J	0004
B293K	0004
B293L	0004
B293M	0004
B293OR	0004
B293R	0004
B293X	0004
B293Y	0004
B294	0015
B294(TRANS)	0004
B294A	0004
B294B	0004
B294C	0004
B294D	0004
B294E	0004
B294F	0004
B294G	0004
B294GN	0004
B294H	0004
B294J	0004
B294K	0004
B294L	0004
B294M	0004
B294OR	0004
B294R	0004
B294X	0004
B294Y	0004
B295(2S)	0969
B295A	0969
B295B	0969
B295C	0969
B295D	0969
B295E	0969
B295F	0969
B295G	0969
B295GN	0969
B295H	0969
B295J	0969
B295K	0969
B295L	0969
B295M	0969
B295OR	0969
B295R	0969
B295X	0969
B295Y	0969
B296(2S)	0969
B296A	0969
B296B	0969
B296C	0969
B296D	0969
B296E	0969
B296F	0969
B296G	0969
B296GN	0969
B296H	0969
B296J	0969
B296K	0969
B296L	0969

DEVICE TYPE	REPL CODE
B296M	0969
B296OR	0969
B296R	0969
B296X	0969
B296Y	0969
B299(2S)	0004
B299A	0004
B299B	0004
B299C	0004
B299D	0004
B299E	0004
B299F	0004
B299G	0004
B299GN	0004
B299H	0004
B299J	0004
B299K	0004
B299L	0004
B299M	0004
B299OR	0004
B299R	0004
B299X	0004
B299Y	0004
B300(2S)	0969
B300A	0969
B300B	0969
B300C	0969
B300D	0969
B300E	0969
B300F	0969
B300G	0969
B300GN	0969
B300H	0969
B300J	0969
B300K	0969
B300L	0969
B300M	0969
B300R	0969
B300X	0969
B300Y	0969
B301	0969
B301A	0969
B301B	0969
B301C	0969
B301D	0969
B301E	0969
B301F	0969
B301G	0969
B301GN	0969
B301H	0969
B301J	0969
B301L	0969
B301M	0969
B301OR	0969
B301R	0969
B301X	0969
B301Y	0969
B302(2S)	0004
B302A	0004
B302B	0004
B302C	0004
B302D	0004
B302E	0004
B302F	0004
B302G	0004
B302J	0004
B302K	0004
B302L	0004
B302M	0004
B302OR	0004
B302R	0004
B302X	0004
B302Y	0004
B303	0004
B303(0)	0004
B303-0(2S)	0004
B303A(2S)	0004
B303B(2S)	0004
B303BK	0004
B303C(2S)	0004
B303D	0004
B303E	0004
B303F	0004
B303G	0004
B303GN	0004
B303H(2S)	0004
B303J	0004
B303K(2S)	0004
B303L	0004
B303M	0004
B303OR	0004
B303R	0004
B303X	0004
B303Y	0004
B304(2S)	0164
B304A(2S)	0164
B304B	0164
B304C	0164
B304D	0164
B304E	0164
B304F	0164
B304G	0164
B304GN	0164
B304H	0164
B304J	0164
B304K	0164
B304L	0164
B304M	0164
B304OR	0164

DEVICE TYPE	REPL CODE
B304R	0164
B304X	0164
B304Y	0164
B309(2S)	0969
B309A	0969
B309B	0969
B309C	0969
B309D	0969
B309E	0969
B309F	0969
B309G	0969
B309GN	0969
B309H	0969
B309K	0969
B309L	0969
B309M	0969
B309OR	0969
B309R	0969
B309X	0969
B309Y	0969
B310	0969
B310A	0969
B310B	0969
B310C	0969
B310D	0969
B310E	0969
B310F	0969
B310G	0969
B310GN	0969
B310H	0969
B310J	0969
B310K	0969
B310L	0969
B310M	0969
B310OR	0969
B310R	0969
B310X	0969
B310Y	0969
B311(2S)	0969
B311A	0969
B311B	0969
B311C	0969
B311D	0969
B311E	0969
B311F	0969
B311G	0969
B311GN	0969
B311H	0969
B311J	0969
B311K	0969
B311L	0969
B311M	0969
B311OR	0969
B311R	0969
B311X	0969
B311Y	0969
B312A	0969
B312B	0969
B312C	0969
B312D	0969
B312E	0969
B312F	0969
B312G	0969
B312GN	0969
B312H	0969
B312J	0969
B312K	0969
B312L	0969
B312M	0969
B312X	0969
B312Y	0969
B313(2S)	0969
B313A	0969
B313B	0969
B313C	0969
B313D	0969
B313E	0969
B313F	0969
B313G	0969
B313GN	0969
B313H	0969
B313J	0969
B313K	0969
B313L	0969
B313M	0969
B313OR	0969
B313R	0969
B313X	0969
B313Y	0969
B314(2S)	0279
B314A	0279
B314B	0279
B314C	0279
B314D	0279
B314E	0279
B314F	0279
B314GN	0279
B314H	0279
B314J	0279
B314K	0279
B314L	0279
B314M	0279
B314OR	0279
B314R	0279
B314X	0279
B314Y	0279
B315(2S)	0004
B-315-1	0164
B315A	0004

DEVICE TYPE	REPL CODE
B315B	0004
B315C	0004
B315D	0004
B315E	0004
B315F	0004
B315G	0004
B315GN	0004
B315H	0004
B315J	0004
B315L	0004
B315M	0004
B315OR	0004
B315R	0004
B315X	0004
B315Y	0004
B316(2S)	0004
B316A	0004
B316B	0004
B316C	0004
B316D	0004
B316E	0004
B316F	0004
B316G	0004
B316GN	0004
B316H	0004
B316OR	0004
B316R	0004
B316X	0004
B316Y	0004
B317(2S)	0004
B318(2S)	0969
B318A	0969
B318B	0969
B318C	0969
B318D	0969
B318E	0969
B318F	0969
B318G	0969
B318GN	0969
B318H	0969
B318J	0969
B318K	0969
B318L	0969
B318M	0969
B318OR	0969
B318R	0969
B318X	0969
B318Y	0969
B319(2S)	0969
B319A	0969
B319B	0969
B319C	0969
B319D	0969
B319E	0969
B319F	0969
B319G	0969
B319GN	0969
B319H	0969
B319J	0969
B319K	0969
B319L	0969
B319M	0969
B319OR	0969
B319R	0969
B319X	0969
B319Y	0969
B320(2S)	0969
B320A	0969
B320B	0969
B320C	0969
B320D	0969
B320E	0969
B320F	0969
B320G	0969
B320GN	0969
B320H	0969
B320J	0969
B320K	0969
B320L	0969
B320M	0969
B320OR	0969
B320R	0969
B320X	0969
B320Y	0969
B321(2S)	0004
B322(2S)	0004
B323(2S)	0004
B-324	0164
B324	1056
B324-OR	1056
B324A(2S)	1056
B324B(2S)	1056
B324C	1056
B324D(2S)	1056
B324E(2S)	1056
B324E-1(2S)	1056
B324E-L	1056
B324F(2S)	1056
B324G(2S)	1056
B324GN	1056
B324H(2S)	1056
B324I(2S)	1056
B324J(2S)	1056
B324K(2S)	1056
B324L	1056
B324M	1056
B324N(2S)	1056
B324OR	1056
B324P(2S)	1056

If replacement code is OEM, contact original manufacturer for replacement.

DEVICE TYPE	REPL CODE
B324R	1056
B324S(2S)	1056
B324V(2S)	1056
B324X	1056
B324Y	1056
B326(2S)	0004
B326A	0004
B326B	0004
B326C	0004
B326D	0004
B326E	0004
B326F	0004
B326G	0004
B326GN	0004
B326H	0004
B326J	0004
B326K	0004
B326L	0004
B326M	0004
B326OR	0004
B326R	0004
B326X	0004
B326Y	0004
B327(2S)	0004
B327A	0004
B327B	0004
B327C	0004
B327D	0004
B327E	0004
B327F	0004
B327G	0004
B327GN	0004
B327H	0004
B327J	0004
B327K	0004
B327L	0004
B327M	0004
B327OR	0004
B327R	0004
B327X	0004
B327Y	0004
B328(2S)	0211
B328A	0211
B328B	0211
B328C	0211
B328D	0211
B328E	0211
B328F	0211
B328G	0211
B328GN	0211
B328H	0211
B328J	0211
B328K	0211
B328L	0211
B328M	0211
B328OR	0211
B328R	0211
B328X	0211
B328Y	0211
B329(2S)	0004
B329A	0004
B329B	0004
B329C	0004
B329D	0004
B329E	0004
B329F	0004
B329G	0004
B329GN	0004
B329H	0004
B329J	0004
B329K(2S)	0004
B329L	0004
B329M	0004
B329OR	0004
B329R	0004
B329X	0004
B329Y	0004
B331(2S)	0040
B331A	0432
B331B	0432
B331C	0432
B331D	0432
B331E	0432
B331F	0432
B331G	0432
B331GN	0432
B331H(2S)	0040
B331J	0432
B331K	0432
B331L	0432
B331M	0432
B331OR	0432
B331R	0432
B331X	0432
B331Y	0432
B332(2S)	0040
B332A	0432
B332B	0432
B332C	0432
B332D	0432
B332E	0432
B332F	0432
B332G	0432
B332GN	0432
B332H(2S)	0040
B332J	0432
B332K	0432
B332L	0432
B332M	0432
B332OR	0432
B332R	0432
B332X	0432
B332Y	0432
B333(2S)	0040
B333A	0432
B333B	0432
B333D	0432
B333E	0432
B333F	0432
B333G	0432
B333GN	0432
B333H	0432
B333HA	0432
B333HB	0432
B333J	0432
B333K	0432
B333L	0432
B333M	0432
B333OR	0432
B333R	0432
B333X	0432
B333Y	0432
B334	0435
B334-OR	0435
B334A	0435
B334B	0435
B334C	0435
B334D	0435
B334E	0435
B334F	0435
B334G	0435
B334GN	0435
B334H	0435
B334J	0435
B334K	0435
B334L	0435
B334M	0435
B334OR	0435
B334R	0435
B334X	0435
B334Y	0435
B335(2S)	0211
B336(2S)	0004
B337(2S)	0160
B337-B	0160
B337-OR	0160
B337A(2S)	0160
B337B(2S)	0160
B337BK(2S)	0160
B337C	0160
B337D	0160
B337E	0160
B337F	0160
B337G	0160
B337GN	0160
B337H(2S)	0160
B337J	0160
B337K	0160
B337L	0160
B337LB	0160
B337M	0160
B337OR	0160
B337R	0160
B337X	0160
B337Y	0160
B338(2S)	0160
B338A	0160
B338B	0160
B338C	0160
B338D	0160
B338E	0160
B338F	0160
B338G	0160
B338GN	0160
B338H(2S)	0160
B338HA(2S)	0160
B338HB(2S)	0160
B338J	0160
B338K	0160
B338L	0160
B338M	0160
B338OR	0160
B338R	0160
B338X	0160
B338Y	0160
B339(2S)	0599
B339H(2S)	0599
B340(2S)	0599
B340H(2S)	0599
B341(2S)	0969
B341A	0969
B341B	0969
B341C	0969
B341D	0969
B341E	0969
B341F	0969
B341G	0969
B341GN	0969
B341H(2S)	0969
B341J	0969
B341K	0969
B341L	0969
B341M	0969
B341OR	0969
B341R	0969
B341S	0969
B341V(2S)	0969
B341V(S)	0969
B341X	0969
B341Y	0969
B342(2S)	0969
B342A	0969
B342B	0969
B342C	0969
B342D	0969
B342E	0969
B342F	0969
B342G	0969
B342GN	0969
B342H	0969
B342J	0969
B342K	0969
B342L	0969
B342M	0969
B342OR	0969
B342R	0969
B342X	0969
B342Y	0969
B343(2S)	0969
B343A	0969
B343B	0969
B343C	0969
B343D	0969
B343E	0969
B343F	0969
B343G	0969
B343GN	0969
B343H	0969
B343J	0969
B343K	0969
B343L	0969
B343M	0969
B343OR	0969
B343R	0969
B343X	0969
B343Y	0969
B345(2S)	0004
B345A	0004
B345B	0004
B345C	0004
B345D	0004
B345E	0004
B345F	0004
B345G	0004
B345GN	0004
B345H	0004
B345J	0004
B345K	0004
B345L	0004
B345M	0004
B345OR	0004
B345R	0004
B345X	0004
B345Y	0004
B346(2S)	0004
B346A	0004
B346B	0004
B346C	0004
B346D	0004
B346E	0004
B346F	0004
B346G	0004
B346GN	0004
B346H	0004
B346J	0004
B346K(2S)	0004
B346L	0004
B346M	0004
B346OR	0004
B346Q(2S)	0004
B346R	0004
B346X	0004
B346Y	0004
B347(2S)	0004
B347A	0004
B347B	0004
B347C	0004
B347D	0004
B347E	0004
B347F	0004
B347G	0004
B347GN	0004
B347H	0004
B347J	0004
B347K	0004
B347L	0004
B347M	0004
B347OR	0004
B347R	0004
B347X	0004
B347Y	0004
B348(2S)	0004
B348A	0004
B348B	0004
B348C	0004
B348D	0004
B348E	0004
B348F	0004
B348G	0004
B348GN	0004
B348H	0004
B348J	0004
B348K	0004
B348L	0004
B348M	0004
B348OR	0004
B348Q(2S)	0004
B348R(2S)	0004
B348X	0004
B348Y	0004
B349(2S)	0004
B350(2S)	0211
B350A	0211
B350B	0211
B350C	0211
B350D	0211
B350E	0211
B350F	0211
B350G	0211
B350GN	0211
B350H	0211
B350J	0211
B350K	0211
B350L	0211
B350M	0211
B350OR	0211
B350R	0211
B350X	0211
B350Y	0211
B351(2S)	0435
B351A	0435
B351B	0435
B351C	0435
B351D	0435
B351E	0435
B351F	0435
B351G	0435
B351GN	0435
B351H	0435
B351J	0435
B351K	0435
B351L	0435
B351M	0435
B351OR	0435
B351R	0435
B351X	0435
B351Y	0435
B352(2S)	0040
B352A	0432
B352B	0432
B352C	0432
B352D(2S)	0040
B352E	0432
B352F	0432
B352G	0432
B352GN	0432
B352H	0432
B352J	0432
B352K	0432
B352L	0432
B352M	0432
B352OR	0432
B352R	0432
B352X	0432
B352Y	0432
B353(2S)	0040
B353A	0432
B353B	0432
B353C	0432
B353D	0432
B353E	0432
B353F	0432
B353G	0432
B353GN	0432
B353H	0432
B353J	0432
B353K	0432
B353L	0432
B353M	0432
B353OR	0432
B353R	0432
B353X	0432
B353Y	0432
B354(2S)	0432
B354A	0432
B354B	0432
B354C	0432
B354D	0432
B354E	0432
B354F	0432
B354G	0432
B354GN	0432
B354H	0432
B354J	0432
B354K	0432
B354L	0432
B354M	0432
B354OR	0432
B354R	0432
B354X	0432
B354Y	0432
B355(2S)	0085
B355A	0085
B355B	0085
B355C	0085
B355D	0085
B355E	0085
B355F	0085
B355G	0085
B355GN	0085
B355H	0085
B355J	0085
B355K	0085
B355L	0085
B355M	0085
B355OR	0085
B355R	0085
B355X	0085
B355Y	0085
B356(2S)	0085
B356A	0085
B356B	0085
B356C	0085
B356D	0085
B356E	0085
B356F	0085
B356G	0085
B356GN	0085
B356H	0085
B356J	0085
B356K	0085
B356L	0085
B356M	0085
B356OR	0085
B356R	0085
B356X	0085
B356Y	0085
B357(2S)	0969
B357A	0969
B357B	0969
B357C	0969
B357D	0969
B357E	0969
B357F	0969
B357G	0969
B357GN	0969
B357H	0969
B357J	0969
B357K	0969
B357L	0969
B357M	0969
B357OR	0969
B357R	0969
B357X	0969
B357Y	0969
B358(2S)	0969
B358A	0969
B358B	0969
B358C	0969
B358D	0969
B358E	0969
B358F	0969
B358G	0969
B358GN	0969
B358H	0969
B358J	0969
B358K	0969
B358L	0969
B358M	0969
B358OR	0969
B358R	0969
B358X	0969
B358Y	0969
B359(2S)	0969
B359A	0969
B359B	0969
B359C	0969
B359D	0969
B359E	0969
B359F	0969
B359G	0969
B359GN	0969
B359H	0969
B359J	0969
B359K	0969
B359L	0969
B359M	0969
B359OR	0969
B359R	0969
B359X	0969
B359Y	0969
B360	0969
B360A	0969
B360B	0969
B360C	0969
B360D	0969
B360E	0969
B360F	0969
B360G	0969
B360GN	0969
B360H	0969
B360J	0969
B360K	0969
B360L	0969
B360M	0969
B360OR	0969
B360R	0969
B360X	0969
B360Y	0969
B361(2S)	0969
B361A	0969
B361B	0969
B361C	0969
B361D	0969
B361E	0969
B361F	0969
B361G	0969
B361GN	0969
B361H	0969
B361J	0969
B361K	0969
B361L	0969
B361M	0969
B361OR	0969
B361R	0969
B361X	0969
B361Y	0969
B362(2S)	0969
B362A	0969
B362B	0969
B362C	0969
B362D	0969
B362E	0969
B362F	0969
B362G	0969
B362GN	0969
B362H	0969
B362J	0969
B362K	0969
B362L	0969
B362M	0969
B362OR	0969
B362R	0969
B362X	0969
B362Y	0969
B363	0848
B364(2S)	0164
B364-OR	0164
B364A	0164
B364B	0164
B364C	0164
B364D	0164
B364E	0164
B364F	0164
B364G	0164
B364GN	0164
B364H	0164
B364J	0164
B364K	0164
B364L	0164
B364M	0164
B364OR	0164
B364R	0164
B364X	0164
B364Y	0164
B365(2S)	0164
B365A	0164
B365B(2S)	0164
B365C	0164
B365D	0164
B365E	0164
B365F	0164
B365G	0164
B365GN	0164
B365H	0164
B365J	0164
B365K	0164
B365L	0164
B365M	0164
B365OR	0164
B365R	0164
B365X	0164
B365Y	0164
B366(2S)	0969
B366A	0969
B366B	0969
B366C	0969
B366D	0969
B366E	0969
B366F	0969
B366G	0969
B366GN	0969
B366H	0969
B366J	0969
B366K	0969
B366L	0969
B366M	0969
B366OR	0969
B366R	0969
B366X	0969
B366Y	0969
B367(2S)	0222
B367-4	0222
B367-5	0222
B367-OR	0222
B367A(2S)	0222
B367AL	0222
B367B(2S)	0222
B367B-2	0222
B367BL	0222
B367BP	0222
B367C(2S)	0222
B367D	0222
B367E	0222
B367F	0222
B367G	0222
B367H(2S)	0222
B367J	0222
B367K	0222
B367L	0222
B367M	0222
B367OR	0222
B367P	0222
B367R	0222
B367X	0222
B367Y	0222
B368(2S)	0222
B368-OR	0222
B368A(2S)	0222
B368B(2S)	0222
B368C	0222
B368D	0222
B368E	0222
B368F	0222
B368G	0222
B368GN	0222
B368H(2S)	0222
B368J	0222
B368K	0222
B368L	0222
B368M	0222
B368OR	0222
B368X	0222
B368Y	0222
B370(2S)	0004
B370-O	0004
B370A(2S)	0004
B370AA(2S)	0004
B370AB(2S)	0004
B370AC(2S)	0004
B370AH	0004
B370AHA(2S)	0004
B370AHB(2S)	0004
B370B(2S)	0004
B370C(2S)	0004
B370D(2S)	0004
B370E	0004
B370F	0004
B370G	0004
B370GN	0004
B370H	0004
B370J	0004
B370K	0004
B370L	0004
B370M	0004
B370OR	0004
B370P(2S)	0004
B370R	0004
B370V(2S)	0004
B370X	0004
B370Y	0004
B371(2S)	0004
B371A	0004
B371B	0004
B371C	0004
B371D(2S)	0004
B371E	0004
B371F	0004
B371G	0004
B371GN	0004
B371H	0004
B371J	0004
B371K	0004
B371L	0004
B371M	0004
B371OR	0004
B371R	0004
B371X	0004
B371Y	0004
B372(2S)	0841
B372-5	OEM
B372-10	OEM
B372-20	OEM
B372-30	OEM
B372-40	OEM
B372-50	OEM
B372-60	OEM
B372-70	OEM
B372-80	OEM
B372-90	OEM
B372-100	OEM
B372-120	OEM
B373(2S)	0841
B373A	0841
B373B	0841
B373C	0841
B373D	0841
B373E	0841
B373F	0841
B373G	0841
B373GN	0841
B373H	0841
B373K	0841
B373L	0841
B373M	0841
B373OR	0841
B373R	0841
B373X	0841
B373Y	0841
B374	0164
B375(2S)	1665
B375-2B(2S)	1665
B375-5B(2S)	1665
B375-OR	1665
B375A(2S)	1665
B375A-2B(2S)	1665
B375A-5B(2S)	1665
B375AL	1665
B375A-NB(2S)	1665
B375ATV	1665
B375B	1665
B375C	1665
B375D	1665
B375E	1665
B375F	1665
B375G	1665
B375GN	1665
B375H	1665
B375J	1665
B375K	1665
B375L	1665
B375M	1665
B375OR	1665

If replacement code is OEM, contact original manufacturer for replacement.

DEVICE TYPE	REPL CODE
B375R	1665
B375X	1665
B375Y	1665
B376(2S)	0004
B376-5	0106
B376-10	0106
B376-20	0106
B376-30	0106
B376-40	0106
B376-50	1999
B376-60	1999
B376-70	2384
B376-80	2384
B376-90	0782
B376-100	0782
B376-120	OEM
B376A	0004
B376B	0004
B376C	0004
B376D	0004
B376E	0004
B376F	0004
B376G(2S)	0004
B376GN	0004
B376J	0004
B376K	0004
B376L	0004
B376M	0004
B376OR	0004
B376R	0004
B376X	0004
B376Y	0004
B377(2S)	0211
B377B(2S)	0211
B378(2S)	0004
B378A(2S)	0004
B378B	0004
B378C	0004
B378D	0004
B378E	0004
B378F	0004
B378GN	0004
B378J	0004
B378K	0004
B378L	0004
B378M	0004
B378OR	0004
B378R	0004
B378X	0004
B378Y	0004
B379(2S)	0211
B379-2(2S)	0211
B379A(2S)	0211
B379B	0211
B379C	0211
B379D	0211
B379E	0211
B379F	0211
B379G	0211
B379GN	0211
B379H	0211
B379J	0211
B379K	0211
B379L	0211
B379M	0211
B379OR	0211
B379R	0211
B379Y	0211
B380(2S)	0211
B380A(2S)	0211
B380B	0211
B380BX555	OEM
B380C	0211
B380C800	0782
B380C800A	5620
B380C800D	3503
B380C800D1	3503
B380C800M	1999
B380C800W	1999
B380C1000	0782
B380C1000A	5620
B380C1000M	1999
B380C1000W	0782
B380C1200S	6699
B380C1200W	0782
B380C1500	0782
B380C1500/1000	5940
B380C1500/1000SIC	OEM
B380C1500R	0782
B380C1500W	0782
B380C2000/1500	0782
B380C3700/2200	4442
B380C3700/2200SIC	3021
B380C5000/3300	1763
B380D	0211
B380E	0211
B380F	0211
B380GN	0211
B380J	0211
B380K	0211
B380L	0211
B380OR	0211
B380R	0211
B380X	0211
B380Y	0211
B381(2S)	0004
B381A	0004
B381B	0004
B381C	0004

DEVICE TYPE	REPL CODE
B381D	0004
B381E	0004
B381F	0004
B381G	0004
B381GN	0004
B381H	0004
B381J	0004
B381K	0004
B381L	0004
B381M	0004
B381OR	0004
B381R	0004
B381X	0004
B381Y	0004
B382(2S)	0004
B382A	0004
B382B	0004
B382BK	0004
B382BN	0004
B382C	0004
B382D	0004
B382E	0004
B382F	0004
B382G	0004
B382GN	0004
B382H	0004
B382J	0004
B382K	0004
B382L	0004
B382OR	0004
B382R	0004
B382X	0004
B382Y	0004
B383(2S)	0004
B383-1(2S)	0004
B383-2(2S)	0004
B383A	0004
B383B	0004
B383C	0004
B383D	0004
B383E	0004
B383F	0004
B383G	0004
B383GN	0004
B383H	0004
B383J	0004
B383K	0004
B383L	0004
B383M	0004
B383OR	0004
B383R	0004
B383X	0004
B383Y	0004
B384(2S)	0004
B384A	0004
B384B	0004
B384C	0004
B384D	0004
B384E	0004
B384F	0004
B384G	0004
B384GN	0004
B384H	0004
B384J	0004
B384K	0004
B384L	0004
B384M	0004
B384OR	0004
B384R	0004
B384X	0004
B384Y	0004
B385(2S)	0004
B385A	0004
B385B	0004
B385C	0004
B385D	0004
B385E	0004
B385F	0004
B385G	0004
B385GN	0004
B385H	0004
B385J	0004
B385K	0004
B385L	0004
B385M	0004
B385OR	0004
B385R	0004
B385X	0004
B385Y	0004
B386(2S)	0004
B386A	0004
B386B	0004
B386C	0004
B386D	0004
B386E	0004
B386F	0004
B386G	0004
B386GN	0004
B386H	0004
B386K	0004
B386L	0004
B386M	0004
B386OR	0004
B386R	0004
B386X	0004
B386Y	0004
B387(2S)	0004
B387A	0004
B387B	0004

DEVICE TYPE	REPL CODE
B387D	0004
B387E	0004
B387F	0004
B387G	0004
B387GN	0004
B387H	0004
B387J	0004
B387K	0004
B387L	0004
B387M	0004
B387OR	0004
B387R	0004
B387X	0004
B387Y	0004
B389(2S)	0004
B389-0	0004
B389A	0004
B389B	0004
B389BK	0004
B389C	0004
B389D	0004
B389E	0004
B389F	0004
B389G	0004
B389GN	0004
B389H	0004
B389J	0004
B389K	0004
B389L	0004
B389M	0004
B389OR	0004
B389R	0004
B389X	0004
B389Y	0004
B390(2S)	0969
B390A	0969
B390B	0969
B390C	0969
B390D	0969
B390E	0969
B390F	0969
B390G	0969
B390GN	0969
B390H	0969
B390J	0969
B390K	0969
B390L	0969
B390M	0969
B390OR	0969
B390R	0969
B390X	0969
B390Y	0969
B391(2S)	0160
B391-5	OEM
B391-10	OEM
B391-20	OEM
B391-30	OEM
B391-40	OEM
B391-50	OEM
B391-60	OEM
B391-70	OEM
B391-80	OEM
B391-90	OEM
B391-100	OEM
B391-120	OEM
B391A	0160
B391B	0160
B391C	0160
B391D	0160
B391E	0160
B391F	0160
B391G	0160
B391GN	0160
B391H	0160
B391J	0160
B391K	0160
B391L	0160
B391M	0160
B391OR	0160
B391R	0160
B391X	0160
B391Y	0160
B392(2S)	0279
B392A	0279
B392B	0279
B392C	0279
B392D	0279
B392E	0279
B392F	0279
B392G	0279
B392GN	0279
B392H	0279
B392J	0279
B392K	0279
B392L	0279
B392M	0279
B392OR	0279
B392R	0279
B392X	0279
B392Y	0279
B393(2S)	0279
B393-5	0724
B393-10	0724
B393-20	0724
B393-30	0732
B393-40	0732
B393-50	0732
B393-60	0732
B393-70	0737

DEVICE TYPE	REPL CODE
B393-80	0737
B393-90	0737
B393-100	0737
B393-120	OEM
B393A	0279
B393B	0279
B393C	0279
B393D	0279
B393E	0279
B393F	0279
B393G	0279
B393GN	0279
B393H	0279
B393J	0279
B393K	0279
B393L	0279
B393M	0279
B393OR	0279
B393R	0279
B393X	0279
B393Y	0279
B394(2S)	0279
B394A	0279
B394B	0279
B394C	0279
B394D	0279
B394E	0279
B394F	0279
B394G	0279
B394GN	0279
B394H	0279
B394J	0279
B394K	0279
B394L	0279
B394M	0279
B394OR	0279
B394R	0279
B394X	0279
B394Y	0279
B395(2S)	0279
B395A	0279
B395B	0279
B395C	0279
B395D	0279
B395E	0279
B395F	0279
B395G	0279
B395GN	0279
B395H	0279
B395J	0279
B395K	0279
B395M	0279
B395OR	0279
B395R	0279
B395X	0279
B395Y	0279
B396(2S)	0211
B396A	0211
B396B	0211
B396C	0211
B396D	0211
B396E	0211
B396F	0211
B396G	0211
B396GN	0211
B396H	0211
B396J	0211
B396K	0211
B396L	0211
B396M	0211
B396OR	0211
B396R	0211
B396X	0211
B396Y	0211
B397	0050
B398	0164
B400(2S)	0004
B400A(2S)	0004
B400B(2S)	0004
B400BK	0004
B400C	0004
B400D	0004
B400E	0004
B400F	0004
B400G	0004
B400GN	0004
B400H	0004
B400J	0004
B400K(2S)	0004
B400L	0004
B400M	0004
B400OR	0004
B400R	0004
B400X	0004
B400Y	0004
B401	0279
B401A	0279
B401B	0279
B401C	0279
B401D	0279
B401E	0279
B401F	0279
B401G	0279
B401GN	0279
B401H	0279
B401K	0279
B401L	0279
B401M	0279
B401OR	0279
B401R	0279

DEVICE TYPE	REPL CODE
B401X	0279
B401Y	0279
B402(2S)	0279
B402A	0279
B402B	0279
B402C	0279
B402D	0279
B402E	0279
B402F	0279
B402G	0279
B402GN	0279
B402H	0279
B402J	0279
B402K	0279
B402L	0279
B402M	0279
B402OR	0279
B402R	0279
B402X	0279
B402Y	0279
B403(2S)	0279
B403A	0279
B403B	0279
B403C	0279
B403D	0279
B403E	0279
B403F	0279
B403G	0279
B403GN	0279
B403H	0279
B403J	0279
B403K	0279
B403L	0279
B403M	0279
B403OR	0279
B403R	0279
B403X	0279
B403Y	0279
B405	0164
B405-0	0164
B405-1	0164
B405-2C(2S)	0164
B405-3C(2S)	0164
B405-4C(2S)	0164
B405-O	0164
B405-OR	0164
B405-R	0164
B405A(2S)	0164
B405AG	0164
B405B(2S)	0164
B405C(2S)	0164
B405D(2S)	0164
B405DK	0164
B405E(2S)	0164
B405EK	0164
B405F	0164
B405G(2S)	0164
B405GN	0164
B405H(2S)	0164
B405J	0164
B405K(2S)	0164
B405L	0164
B405M	0164
B405OR	0164
B405R(2S)	0164
B405RE(2S)	0164
B405X	0164
B405Y	0164
B406	0969
B407(2S)	0160
B407-0(2S)	0160
B407-O	0160
B407-OR	0160
B407A	0160
B407B	0160
B407BK	0160
B407C	0160
B407D	0160
B407E	0160
B407F	0160
B407G	0160
B407GN	0160
B407H	0160
B407J	0160
B407K	0160
B407M	0160
B407OR	0160
B407R	0160
B407TV(2S)	0160
B407TV-2	0160
B407X	0160
B407Y	0160
B408(2S)	0004
B408A	0004
B408B	0004
B408C	0004
B408D	0004
B408E	0004
B408F	0004
B408G	0004
B408GN	0004
B408H	0004
B408J	0004
B408K	0004
B408L	0004
B408M	0004
B408OR	0004
B408R	0004
B408X	0004

DEVICE TYPE	REPL CODE
B408Y	0004
B409	0279
B410(2S)	0969
B411(2S)	0969
B411-1	OEM
B411-2	OEM
B411-C	OEM
B411F	OEM
B411S	OEM
B411TV	0969
B412	0969
B412-1	OEM
B412-2	OEM
B412-5-5	OEM
B412-5-10	OEM
B412-5-25	OEM
B412-7-5	OEM
B412-7-10	OEM
B412-7-25	OEM
B412-10-5	OEM
B412-10-10	OEM
B412-10-25	OEM
B412-12-5	0201
B412-12-10	OEM
B412-12-25	OEM
B412-15-5	0286
B412-15-10	OEM
B412-15-25	OEM
B412-20-5	0374
B412-20-10	OEM
B412-20-25	OEM
B412-25-5	OEM
B412-25-10	OEM
B412-25-25	OEM
B412-30-5	OEM
B412-30-10	OEM
B412-30-25	OEM
B412-40-5	OEM
B412-40-10	OEM
B412-40-25	OEM
B412-50-5	OEM
B412-50-10	OEM
B412-50-25	OEM
B412-C	OEM
B412F	OEM
B412S	OEM
B413(2S)	0222
B413-1	OEM
B413-2	OEM
B413-C	OEM
B413A	0222
B413B	0222
B413C	0222
B413D	0222
B413E	0222
B413F	OEM
B413F(2S)	0222
B413G	0222
B413GN	0222
B413H	0222
B413J	0222
B413K	0222
B413L	0222
B413M	0222
B413OR	0222
B413R	0222
B413S	OEM
B413X	0222
B413Y	0222
B414(2S)	1004
B414B	1004
B414C	1004
B414D	1004
B414E	1004
B414F	1004
B414G	1004
B414GN	1004
B414H	1004
B414J	1004
B414K	1004
B414L	1004
B414M	1004
B414OR	1004
B414R	1004
B414X	1004
B414Y	1004
B415(2S)	0164
B415-OR	0164
B415A(2S)	0164
B415B(2S)	0164
B415C	0164
B415D	0164
B415E	0164
B415F	0164
B415G	0164
B415GN	0164
B415H	0164
B415J	0164
B415K	0164
B415L	0164
B415M	0164
B415OR	0164
B415R	0164
B415X	0164
B415Y	0164
B416(2S)	0279
B416A	0279
B416B	0279
B416C	0279

DEVICE TYPE	REPL CODE
B416D	0279
B416E	0279
B416F	0279
B416G	0279
B416GN	0279
B416H	0279
B416J	0279
B416K	0279
B416L	0279
B416M	0279
B416OR	0279
B416R	0279
B416X	0279
B416Y	0279
B417(2S)	0279
B417A	0279
B417B	0279
B417C	0279
B417D	0279
B417E	0279
B417F	0279
B417G	0279
B417GN	0279
B417H	0279
B417J	0279
B417K	0279
B417L	0279
B417M	0279
B417OR	0279
B417R	0279
B417X	0279
B417Y	0279
B419	0222
B421(2S)	0004
B421-1	OEM
B421-2	OEM
B421-C	OEM
B421F	OEM
B421S	OEM
B422(2S)	0211
B422-1	OEM
B422-2	OEM
B422-C	OEM
B422A	0211
B422B	0211
B422C	0211
B422D	0211
B422E	0211
B422F	OEM
B422F(2S)	0211
B422G	0211
B422GN	0211
B422H	0211
B422J	0211
B422K	0211
B422L	0211
B422M	0211
B422OR	0211
B422R	0211
B422S	OEM
B422X	0211
B422Y	0211
B423(2S)	0004
B423-1	OEM
B423-2	OEM
B423-C	OEM
B423A	0004
B423B	0004
B423C	0004
B423D	0004
B423E	0004
B423F	OEM
B423F(2S)	0004
B423G	0004
B423GN	0004
B423H	0004
B423J	0004
B423K	0004
B423L	0004
B423M	0004
B423OR	0004
B423R	0004
B423S	OEM
B423X	0004
B423Y	0004
B424(2S)	0599
B424A	0599
B424B	0599
B424C	0599
B424D	0599
B424E	0599
B424F	0599
B424G	0599
B424GN	0599
B424H	0599
B424J	0599
B424K	0599
B424L	0599
B424M	0599
B424OR	0599
B424R	0599
B424X	0599
B424Y	0599
B425(2S)	0160
B425-BL	0160
B425-R	0160
B425-Y	0160
B425A	0160
B425B	0160

If replacement code is OEM, contact original manufacturer for replacement.

DEVICE TYPE	REPL CODE
B425C	0160
B425D	0160
B425E	0160
B425F	0160
B425G	0160
B425G-BL	0160
B425G-R	0160
B425G-Y	0160
B425H	0160
B425J	0160
B425K	0160
B425L	0160
B425M	0160
B425R	0160
B425X	0160
B425Y(2S)	0160
B426(2S)	0160
B426-BL	0160
B426-R	0160
B426-Y	0160
B426A	0160
B426B	0160
B426BL(2S)	0160
B426C	0160
B426D	0160
B426E	0160
B426F	0160
B426G	0160
B426G-BL	0160
B426GN	0160
B426G-R	0160
B426G-Y	0160
B426J	0160
B426K	0160
B426L	0160
B426M	0160
B426OR	0160
B426R(2S)	0160
B426X	0160
B426Y(2S)	0160
B427(2S)	0004
B427-10	0229
B427-15	0102
B427-20	0344
B427-25	OEM
B427-30	OEM
B427-35	OEM
B427-40	OEM
B427-45	OEM
B427-50	OEM
B427-55	OEM
B427-60	OEM
B427-65	OEM
B427-70	OEM
B427A	0004
B427B	0004
B427C	0004
B427D	0004
B427E	0004
B427F	0004
B427G	0004
B427GN	0004
B427H	0004
B427J	0004
B427K	0004
B427L	0004
B427M	0004
B427OR	0004
B427R	0004
B427X	0004
B427Y	0004
B428(2S)	0004
B428A	0004
B428B	0004
B428C	0004
B428D	0004
B428E	0004
B428F	0004
B428G	0004
B428GN	0004
B428H	0004
B428J	0004
B428K	0004
B428L	0004
B428M	0004
B428OR	0004
B428R	0004
B428X	0004
B428Y	0004
B429	0279
B430(2S)	0040
B431(2S)	0164
B431-1	OEM
B431-2	OEM
B431F	OEM
B431S	OEM
B432(2S)	0969
B432-1	OEM
B432-2	OEM
B432-C	OEM
B432A	0969
B432B	0969
B432C	0969
B432D	0969
B432E	0969
B432F	OEM
B432F(2S)	0969
B432G	0969
B432GN	0969

DEVICE TYPE	REPL CODE
B432H	0969
B432J	0969
B432K	0969
B432L	0969
B432M	0969
B432OR	0969
B432R	0969
B432S	OEM
B432X	0969
B432Y	0969
B433(2S)	5334
B433-1	OEM
B433-2	OEM
B433-C	OEM
B433F	OEM
B433S	OEM
B434(2S)	0919
B434-O	0919
B434-ORG	0919
B434-R(2S)	0919
B434-RED	0919
B434-Y(2S)	0919
B434-YEL	0919
B434G	0919
B434G-O	0919
B434G-R	0919
B434G-Y	0919
B434R	0919
B435(2S)	0919
B435-O(2S)	0919
B435-O	0919
B435-ORG	0919
B435-R(2S)	0919
B435-RED	0919
B435-Y(2S)	0919
B435-YEL	0919
B435G-O	0919
B435G-R	0919
B435G-Y	0919
B435O	0919
B435R	0919
B435RY	0919
B435Y	0919
B436	0050
B437	0050
B438	1056
B439(2S)	0004
B439A(2S)	0004
B439B	0004
B439C	0004
B439D	0004
B439E	0004
B439F	0004
B439G	0004
B439GN	0004
B439H	0004
B439J	0004
B439L	0004
B439M	0004
B439OR	0004
B439R	0004
B439X	0004
B439Y	0004
B440(2S)	0004
B440A	0004
B440B	0004
B440C	0004
B440E	0004
B440F	0004
B440G	0004
B440GN	0004
B440H	0004
B440K	0004
B440L	0004
B440M	0004
B440OR	0004
B440R	0004
B440X	0004
B440Y	0004
B441	0969
B441-1	OEM
B441-2	OEM
B441-C	OEM
B441F	OEM
B441S	OEM
B442	0969
B442-1	OEM
B442-2	OEM
B442-5	0276
B442-10	0276
B442-20	0287
B442-30	0293
B442-40	0293
B442-50	0299
B442-60	0299
B442-70	0250
B442-80	0250
B442-90	0250
B442-100	0250
B442-120	OEM
B442-C	OEM
B442F	OEM
B442S	OEM
B443(2S)	0004
B443-1	OEM
B443-2	OEM
B443-C	OEM
B443A(2S)	0004
B443B(2S)	0004

DEVICE TYPE	REPL CODE
B443C	0004
B443D	0004
B443E	0004
B443F	OEM
B443F(2S)	0004
B443G	0004
B443GN	0004
B443H	0004
B443J	0004
B443K	0004
B443L	0004
B443M	0004
B443OR	0004
B443R	0004
B443S	OEM
B443X	0004
B443Y	0004
B444(2S)	0136
B444A(2S)	0136
B444B(2S)	0136
B444C	0136
B444D	0136
B444E	0136
B444F	0136
B444G	0136
B444GN	0136
B444H	0136
B444K	0136
B444L	0136
B444M	0136
B444OR	0136
B444R	0136
B444X	0136
B444Y	0136
B445(2S)	1004
B445A	1004
B445B	1004
B445C	1004
B445D	1004
B445E	1004
B445F	1004
B445G	1004
B445GN	1004
B445H	1004
B445J	1004
B445K	1004
B445L	1004
B445M	1004
B445OR	1004
B445R	1004
B445X	1004
B445Y	1004
B446(2S)	1004
B446A	1004
B446B	1004
B446C	1004
B446D	1004
B446E	1004
B446F	1004
B446G	1004
B446GN	1004
B446H	1004
B446J	1004
B446K	1004
B446L	1004
B446M	1004
B446OR	1004
B446R	1004
B446X	1004
B446Y	1004
B447(2S)	0969
B447A	0969
B447B	0969
B447C	0969
B447D	0969
B447E	0969
B447F	0969
B447G	0969
B447GN	0969
B447H	0969
B447J	0969
B447K	0969
B447L	0969
B447OR	0969
B447R	0969
B447X	0969
B447Y	0969
B448(2S)	0222
B448A	0222
B448B	0222
B448C	0222
B448D	0222
B448E	0222
B448F	0222
B448G	0222
B448GN	0222
B448H	0222
B448K	0222
B448L	0222
B448M	0222
B448OR	0222
B448R	0222
B448X	0222
B448Y	0222
B449(2S)	0160
B449A	0160
B449B	0160
B449C	0160
B449D	0160

DEVICE TYPE	REPL CODE
B449E	0160
B449F(2S)	0160
B449G	0160
B449GN	0160
B449H	0160
B449J	0160
B449K	0160
B449L	0160
B449M	0160
B449OR	0160
B449P(2S)	0160
B449PG	0160
B449X	0160
B449Y	0160
B450(2S)	0164
B450A(2S)	0164
B451(2S)	0164
B451-1	OEM
B451-2	OEM
B451-C	OEM
B451F	OEM
B451S	OEM
B452(2S)	0164
B452-1	OEM
B452-2	OEM
B452-C	OEM
B452A(2S)	0164
B452F	OEM
B452S	OEM
B453(2S)	0164
B453-1	OEM
B453-2	OEM
B453-C	OEM
B453F	OEM
B453S	OEM
B454(2S)	0164
B455(2S)	0164
B456(2S)	0164
B457(2S)	0164
B457A	0164
B457AC	0164
B457B	0164
B457C	0164
B457D	0164
B457E	0164
B457F	0164
B457G	0164
B457GN	0164
B457H	0164
B457J	0164
B457K	0164
B457L	0164
B457M	0164
B457OR	0164
B457R	0164
B457X	0164
B457Y	0164
B458(2S)	0222
B458A(2S)	0222
B458B	0222
B458BC	0222
B458BL	0222
B458C	0222
B458D	0222
B458E	0222
B458F	0222
B458G	0222
B458GN	0222
B458H	0222
B458J	0222
B458K	0222
B458L	0222
B458M	0222
B458OR	0222
B458R	0222
B458X	0222
B458Y	0222
B459(2S)	0004
B459-O	0004
B459A(2S)	0004
B459B(2S)	0004
B459C(2S)	0004
B459C-2	0004
B459D(2S)	0004
B459E	0004
B459F	0004
B459G	0004
B459GN	0004
B459H	0004
B459J	0004
B459K	0004
B459L	0004
B459M	0004
B459OR	0004
B459R	0004
B459X	0004
B459Y	0004
B460(2S)	0004
B460A(2S)	0004
B460B(2S)	0004
B460C	0004
B460D	0004
B460E	0004
B460F	0004
B460G	0004
B460GN	0004
B460H	0004
B460J	0004
B460K	0004

DEVICE TYPE	REPL CODE
B460L	0004
B460M	0004
B460OR	0004
B460R	0004
B460X	0004
B460Y	0004
B461(2S)	0841
B461-1	OEM
B461-2	OEM
B461-C	OEM
B461A	0841
B461B	0841
B461BL	0841
B461C	0841
B461D	0841
B461E	0841
B461F	OEM
B461F(2S)	0841
B461G	0841
B461H	0841
B461J	0841
B461K	0841
B461L	0841
B461M	0841
B461OR	0841
B461R	0841
B461S	OEM
B461X	0841
B461Y	0841
B462(2S)	0222
B462-1	OEM
B462-2	OEM
B462-BL	0222
B462-BLU	0222
B462-BLU-G	0222
B462-C	OEM
B462-R	0222
B462-RED	0222
B462-RED-G	0222
B462-Y	0222
B462-YEL	0222
B462-YEL-G	0222
B462A	0222
B462B	0222
B462C	0222
B462D	0222
B462E	0222
B462F	OEM
B462F(2S)	0222
B462G	0222
B462G-BL	0222
B462GN	0222
B462G-R	0222
B462G-Y	0222
B462H	0222
B462K	0222
B462L	0222
B462M	0222
B462OR	0222
B462R	0222
B462S	OEM
B462X	0222
B462Y	0222
B463(1)	0222
B463(2S)	0222
B463-1	OEM
B463-2	OEM
B463-BL	0222
B463-BLU	0222
B463-BLU-G	0222
B463-C	OEM
B463-O	0222
B463-R	0222
B463-RED	0222
B463-RED-G	0222
B463-Y	0222
B463-YEL	0222
B463-YEL-G	0222
B463A	0222
B463B	0222
B463BL(2S)	0222
B463BLU	0222
B463BLU-G	0222
B463C	0222
B463D	0222
B463E(2S)	0222
B463F	OEM
B463F(2S)	0222
B463G	0222
B463G-BL	0222
B463GN	0222
B463G-R	0222
B463G-Y	0222
B463H	0222
B463J	0222
B463K	0222
B463L	0222
B463M	0222
B463OR	0222
B463R(2S)	5845
B463RED	0222
B463RED-G	0222
B463S	OEM
B463X	0222
B463XL	0222
B463Y(2S)	0222
B463YEL(2S)	0222
B463YEL-G(2S)	0222
B464(2S)	0969

DEVICE TYPE	REPL CODE
B464A	0969
B464B	0969
B464C	0969
B464D	0969
B464E	0969
B464F	0969
B464G	0969
B464GN	0969
B464H	0969
B464J	0969
B464K	0969
B464M	0969
B464OR	0969
B464X	0969
B464Y	0969
B465(2S)	0969
B465A	0969
B465B	0969
B465C	0969
B465D	0969
B465E	0969
B465F	0969
B465G	0969
B465GN	0969
B465H	0969
B465J	0969
B465K	0969
B465L	0969
B465M	0969
B465R	0969
B465X	0969
B465Y	0969
B466(2S)	1004
B466A	1004
B466B	1004
B466C	1004
B466D	1004
B466E	1004
B466F	1004
B466G	1004
B466GN	1004
B466H	1004
B466J	1004
B466K	1004
B466L	1004
B466M	1004
B466OR	1004
B466R	1004
B466X	1004
B466Y	1004
B467(2S)	1004
B467A	1004
B467C	1004
B467D	1004
B467E	1004
B467F	1004
B467G	1004
B467GN	1004
B467H	1004
B467J	1004
B467K	1004
B467L	1004
B467M	1004
B467OR	1004
B467X	1004
B467Y	1004
B468(2S)	0969
B468-OR	0969
B468A(2S)	0969
B468B(2S)	0969
B468B-5	0969
B468C(2S)	0969
B468D(2S)	0969
B468E	0969
B468F	0969
B468G	0969
B468GN	0969
B468H	0969
B468J	0969
B468K	0969
B468L	0969
B468OR	0969
B468X	0969
B468Y	0969
B470(2S)	0004
B470A	0004
B470B	0004
B470C	0004
B470D	0004
B470E	0004
B470F	0004
B470G	0004
B470GN	0004
B470H	0004
B470J	0004
B470K	0004
B470L	0004
B470M	0004
B470OR	0004
B470R	0004
B470X	0004
B470Y	0004
B471(2S)	0160
B471-1	OEM
B471-2	0160
B471-2(2S)	0160
B471-C	OEM
B471-O	0160
B471A(2S)	0160

DEVICE TYPE	REPL CODE
B471B(2S)	0160
B471C	0160
B471D	0160
B471E	0160
B471F	OEM
B471F(2S)	0160
B471G	0160
B471GN	0160
B471H	0160
B471J	0160
B471K	0160
B471L	0160
B471M	0160
B471OR	0160
B471R	0160
B471S	OEM
B471X	0160
B471Y	0160
B472(2S)	0599
B472-1	OEM
B472-2	OEM
B472-C	OEM
B472A	0599
B472B	0599
B472C	0599
B472D	0599
B472E	0599
B472F	OEM
B472F(2S)	0599
B472G	0599
B472GN	0599
B472H	0599
B472J	0599
B472K	0599
B472M	0599
B472OR	0599
B472S	OEM
B472X	0599
B472Y	0599
B473(2S)	0222
B473-1	OEM
B473-2	OEM
B473-C	OEM
B473A	0222
B473B	0222
B473C	0222
B473D(2S)	0222
B473E	0222
B473F	0222
B473F(2S)	0222
B473G	0222
B473GN	0222
B473H(2S)	0222
B473K	0222
B473L	0222
B473M	0222
B473S	OEM
B473X	0222
B473Y	0222
B474(2S)	1004
B474-2(2S)	1004
B474-3(2S)	1004
B474-4(2S)	1004
B474-6D(2S)	1004
B474-OR	1004
B474A	1004
B474B	1004
B474C	1004
B474D	1004
B474E	1004
B474F	1004
B474G	1004
B474GN	1004
B474H	1004
B474J	1004
B474K	1004
B474L	1004
B474M	1004
B474MP(2S)	1004
B474OR	1004
B474R	1004
B474S(2S)	1004
B474V4(2S)	1004
B474V10(2S)	1004
B474X	1004
B474Y(2S)	1004
B474YE1	1004
B474YEL	1004
B475(2S)	0004
B475A(2S)	0004
B475B(2S)	0004
B475C	0004
B475D(2S)	0004
B475E(2S)	0004
B475F(2S)	0004
B475G(2S)	0004
B475GN	0004
B475H	0004
B475J	0004
B475K	0004
B475L	0004
B475M	0004
B475OR	0004
B475P(2S)	0004
B475PL	0004
B475Q(2S)	0004
B475R	0004
B475X	0004
B475Y	0004

If replacement code is OEM, contact original manufacturer for replacement. 279

DEVICE TYPE	REPL CODE	DEVICE TYPE	REPL CODE	DEVICE TYPE	REPL CODE	DEVICE TYPE	REPL CODE	DEVICE TYPE	REPL CODE	DEVICE TYPE	REPL CODE	DEVICE TYPE	REPL CODE
B476(2S)	0841	B492(2S)	0841	B502A-R	0899	B533	0848	B562C(2S)	0527	B588-90	OEM	B642-QR	0819
B476S	0841	B492-1	OEM	B502A-Y	0899	B533-O	0848	B563	0899	B588-95	OEM	B642-R	0819
B476W	0841	B492-C	OEM	B503(2S)	0848	B533-C	OEM	B564	0527	B588-96	OEM	B642-R(JAPAN)	0819
B477	0435	B492A	0841	B503-O	0848	B533O	0848	B564(1)K	0527	B588-100	OEM	B642-S	0819
B477A	0435	B492B(2S)	0841	B503-R	0848	B533Y	0848	B564(1)L	0527	B588-110	OEM	B642P	0819
B477C	0435	B492C	0841	B503-Y	0848	B534(2S)	0004	B564L	0527	B588-120	OEM	B642Q	0819
B477D	0435	B492D	0841	B503A	0848	B534(A)	0004	B564M	0527	B588-130	OEM	B642R	0819
B477E	0435	B492E	0841	B503A-O	0848	B535(2S)	0164	B564Q	0527	B588-140	OEM	B642S	0819
B477F	0435	B492F	OEM	B503A-R	0848	B535G	0164	B564R	0527	B588-150	OEM	B643	0819
B477G	0435	B492F(2S)	0841	B503A-Y	0848	B536	0676	B564S	0527	B588-160	OEM	B643-O	0819
B477GN	0435	B492G	0841	B504	0126	B536K	0676	B565	0164	B588-170	OEM	B643-Q	0819
B477H	0435	B492GN	0841	B504A	0126	B536L	0676	B565A	0164	B588-180	OEM	B643-Q(JAPAN)	0819
B477J	0435	B492H	0841	B505	0676	B536M	0676	B565B	0164	B588-190	OEM	B643-R	0819
B477K	0435	B492J	0841	B506(2S)	3459	B537	0676	B565C	0164	B588-200	OEM	B643-R(JAPAN)	0819
B477L	0435	B492K	0841	B506A(2S)	3459	B537K	0676	B565D	0164	B589	2415	B643P	0819
B477M	0435	B492L	0841	B507(2S)	0676	B537L	0676	B565E	0164	B595	1359	B643Q	0819
B477OR	0435	B492M	0841	B507E	0676	B538	0599	B565F	0164	B595-Y	1359	B643QRS	0819
B477R	0435	B492OR	0841	B508(2S)	0919	B539(2S)	1588	B565G	0164	B596	0848	B643R	0819
B477X	0435	B492R	0841	B509(2S)	0919	B539A	1588	B565GN	0164	B596-0	0848	B643S	0819
B477Y	0435	B492X	0841	B510(2S)	0126	B539B	1588	B565H	0164	B596-O	0848	B644	0819
B478	0432	B492Y	0841	B510S(2S)	0126	B539C	1588	B565J	0164	B596R	0848	B644-Q	0819
B478BS	0432	B493	0164	B511(2S)	0919	B540	0164	B565K	0164	B596Y	0848	B644-R	0819
B479	0432	B493-1	OEM	B511-1	OEM	B541(2S)	3459	B565L	0164	B598	3760	B644-R(JAPAN)	0819
B480	0432	B493-2	OEM	B511-1(2S)	0919	B541-1	OEM	B565M	0164	B598E	3760	B644Q	0819
B481(2S)	0222	B493-C	OEM	B511-2	OEM	B541-2	OEM	B565OR	0164	B598F	3760	B644QR	0819
B481-1	OEM	B493F	OEM	B511-C	OEM	B541-C	OEM	B565R	0164	B600	3459	B644R	0819
B481-2	OEM	B493S	OEM	B511C(2S)	0919	B541F	OEM	B565X	0164	B601	0597	B644S	0819
B481-C	OEM	B493W	0164	B511D(2S)	0919	B541S	OEM	B565Y	0164	B601-1006	0050	B645E	1588
B481-OR	0222	B494(2S)	0164	B511E	0919	B542	0006	B566	0676	B601-1007	0050	B646	0472
B481A	0222	B495(2S)	0164	B511F	OEM	B542-1	OEM	B566A	0676	B601-1008	0050	B646A	0472
B481A2	OEM	B495A(2S)	0164	B511S	OEM	B542-2	OEM	B566AKB	0676	B601-1009	0004	B646AB	0472
B481B	0222	B495B	0164	B512(2S)	0919	B542-C	OEM	B566AKC	0676	B601-1010	0164	B646B	0472
B481B2	OEM	B495C(2S)	0164	B512-0	0919	B542D	0006	B566B	0676	B601-1011	0143	B646C	0472
B481C	0222	B495D(2S)	0164	B512-1	OEM	B542F	OEM	B566C	0676	B601-1012	0015	B646D	0472
B481C2	OEM	B495E	0164	B512-2	OEM	B542S	OEM	B566D	0676	B601K(JAPAN)	0597	B647	0472
B481D(2S)	0222	B495F	0164	B512-C	OEM	B543-1	OEM	B566K	0676	B604	0848	B647A	0472
B481D2	OEM	B495G	0164	B512-O	0919	B543-2	OEM	B566KB	0676	B605	0527	B647AB	0472
B481E(2S)	0222	B495GN	0164	B512A(2S)	0919	B543-C	OEM	B566KC	0676	B605K	0527	B647AC	0472
B481E2	OEM	B495H	0164	B512F	OEM	B543F	OEM	B567	3500	B606	0338	B647B	0472
B481F	0222	B495J	0164	B512P	0919	B543S	OEM	B568	1900	B607	0164	B647C	0472
B481F2	OEM	B495K	0164	B512S	OEM	B544(2S)	0527	B568-C	1900	B610-5	OEM	B647D	0472
B481G	0222	B495L	0164	B513(2S)	0919	B544D(2S)	0527	B568B	1900	B610-10	OEM	B648B	0520
B481GN	0222	B495M	0164	B513-1	OEM	B544E(2S)	0527	B568C	1900	B610-20	OEM	B648C	0520
B481H	0222	B495OR	0164	B513-2	OEM	B544E(JAPAN)	0527	B568D	1900	B610-30	OEM	B649	0520
B481J	0222	B495R	0164	B513-C	OEM	B544F(2S)	0527	B568HA	OEM	B610-40	OEM	B649A	0520
B481K	0222	B495T(2S)	0164	B513A(2S)	0919	B544P1(2S)	0527	B569	0455	B610-50	OEM	B649AB	0520
B481L	0222	B495X	0164	B513F	OEM	B544P2	0527	B570	0455	B610-60	OEM	B649AC	0520
B481M	0222	B495Y	0164	B513P	0919	B546	1638	B571	0455	B610-70	OEM	B649AD	0520
B481OR	0222	B496(2S)	0004	B513Q	0919	B546A	1638	B572	1045	B610-80	OEM	B649B	0520
B481R	0222	B496A	0004	B513R	0919	B546AK	1638	B573	1045	B610-90	OEM	B649C	0520
B481X	0222	B496B	0004	B513S	OEM	B546AK(JAPAN)	1638	B574	1045	B610-100	OEM	B649D	0520
B482(2S)	0004	B496C	0004	B514(2S)	0919	B546AL	1638	B575	0455	B610-120	OEM	B650H	2415
B482A	0004	B496D	0004	B515(2S)	0919	B546C	1638	B576	0455	B611	2002	B653	3459
B482A2	OEM	B496E	0004	B516	0004	B546E	1638	B577	0455	B611A	2002	B654	3459
B482B	0004	B496F	0004	B516C(2S)	0004	B546EX	1638	B578	1190	B612	1588	B654-5	0106
B482B2	OEM	B496G	0004	B516CD(2S)	0004	B546I	1638	B579	1190	B612A	1588	B654-10	0106
B482C	0004	B496GN	0004	B516D(2S)	0004	B546K	1638	B580	1190	B613	3561	B654-20	0106
B482C2	OEM	B496H	0004	B516P(2S)	0004	B546L	1638	B581	1190	B616	3527	B654-30	0106
B482D	0004	B496J	0004	B518	1671	B547	1638	B582	1190	B617	3527	B654-40	0106
B482D2	OEM	B496K	0004	B519	1671	B547A	1638	B583	1190	B617A	3527	B654-50	1999
B482E	0004	B496L	0004	B520	2002	B548	0520	B584	3488	B618	3527	B654-60	1999
B482E2	OEM	B496M	0004	B520-1	2002	B549	0520	B585	2262	B618A	3527	B654-70	2384
B482F	OEM	B496OR	0004	B520-2	2002	B549P	0520	B586	2262	B619	0164	B654-80	2384
B482F(2S)	0004	B496R	0004	B521	0848	B549Q	0520	B587	2415	B620	0150	B654-90	0782
B482F2	OEM	B496X	0004	B521-1	OEM	B549R	0520	B587-10	0124	B621	0527	B654-100	0782
B482G	0004	B496Y	0004	B521-2	OEM	B550(2S)	3459	B587-15	0102	B621A	0527	B654-120	OEM
B482GN	0004	B497(2S)	0004	B521-C	OEM	B551-1	OEM	B587-20	0344	B621A(JAPAN)	0527	B655	1588
B482H	0004	B497A	0004	B521F	OEM	B551-2	OEM	B587-25	OEM	B621C	0527	B656	1588
B482J	0004	B497B	0004	B521S	OEM	B551F	OEM	B587-30	OEM	B621N	0527	B668	0597
B482K	0004	B497C	0004	B522	0848	B551H	0899	B587-35	OEM	B621NC	0527	B669	0597
B482L	0004	B497D	0004	B522-1	0848	B551S	OEM	B587-40	OEM	B621Q	0527	B673	0597
B482M	0004	B497E	0004	B522-2	OEM	B552	1588	B587-45	OEM	B621R	0527	B674	0597
B482S	OEM	B497F	0004	B522-893	0196	B552-1	OEM	B587-50	OEM	B621S	0527	B675	0597
B482V	0004	B497G	0004	B522-C	OEM	B552-2	OEM	B587-55	OEM	B622	0434	B676-10C-2	OEM
B482X	0004	B497GN	0004	B522F	OEM	B552-C	OEM	B587-60	OEM	B626	1671	B676-10M-2	OEM
B482Y	0004	B497H	0004	B522S	OEM	B552F	OEM	B587-65	OEM	B627	3267	B676R-10M2	OEM
B483(2S)	0599	B497J	0004	B523	0919	B552S	OEM	B587-70	OEM	B628	1638	B679	0597
B483-1	OEM	B497K	0004	B523-1	OEM	B553	0713	B587-80	OEM	B628A	1638	B683	0848
B483-2	OEM	B497L	0004	B523-2	OEM	B553-1	OEM	B587-85	OEM	B631	0520	B683C	0848
B483F	OEM	B497M	0004	B523-C	OEM	B553-2	OEM	B587-90	OEM	B631K	0520	B683D	0848
B483S	OEM	B497OR	0004	B523F	OEM	B553-C	OEM	B587-95	OEM	B631KE	0520	B684	0527
B484(2S)	0599	B497R	0004	B523S	OEM	B553AC	OEM	B587-100	OEM	B632	0455	B686	0853
B485(2S)	0599	B497X	0004	B524	0919	B553F	OEM	B587-110	OEM	B632K	0455	B688	3082
B485B2	OEM	B497Y	0004	B525	0527	B553S	OEM	B587-120	OEM	B632K(JAPAN)	0455	B688-O	3082
B485C2	OEM	B498(2S)	0004	B525C	0527	B554(2S)	1588	B587-130	OEM	B633	5372	B688R	3082
B485D2	OEM	B498A	0004	B525D(2S)	0527	B555(2S)	2002	B587-140	OEM	B633E	5372	B689	0676
B486(2S)	0004	B498B	0004	B525E(2S)	0527	B555-O	2002	B587-150	OEM	B633P	5372	B690	0676
B486A	0004	B498C	0004	B526	0676	B555-R	2002	B587-160	OEM	B634Y	3459	B692X13	0143
B486B	0004	B498D	0004	B526C	0676	B555R	2002	B587-170	OEM	B635	0004	B696	3459
B486C	0004	B498E	0004	B527	0676	B556	2002	B587-180	OEM	B636	0004	B697	1588
B486D	0004	B498F	0004	B527-062	0196	B556-O	2002	B587-190	OEM	B637KC	0643	B697K	1588
B486E	0004	B498G	0004	B528	0676	B556-R	2002	B587-200	OEM	B637KD	0643	B698	0006
B486F	0004	B498GN	0004	B528E	0676	B557	2002	B588	2415	B637KE	0643	B698F	0006
B486G	0004	B498H	0004	B529	0919	B557-O	2002	B588-10	OEM	B638H	2415	B699	0919
B486GN	0004	B498J	0004	B530	2002	B557-R	2002	B588-15	OEM	B639H	2415	B699Q	0919
B486H	0004	B498K	0004	B531	2002	B558	2002	B588-20	0344	B640	0037	B700	3537
B486J	0004	B498L	0004	B531-1	OEM	B558-O	2002	B588-25	OEM	B641	0355	B702	3537
B486K	0004	B498M	0004	B531-2	OEM	B558-R	2002	B588-30	OEM	B641-Q	0355	B703	0676
B486L	0004	B498OR	0004	B531-C	OEM	B559	0455	B588-35	OEM	B641-Q(JAPAN)	0355	B703A	0676
B486M	0004	B498R	0004	B531-O	2002	B560(2S)	0472	B588-40	OEM	B641-QR	0355	B703Q	0676
B486OR	0004	B498X	0004	B531-R	2002	B561(2S)	0431	B588-45	OEM	B641-R	0355	B705	3537
B486R	0004	B498Y	0004	B531-Y	2002	B561B(2S)	0431	B588-50	OEM	B641P	0355	B705A	3537
B486X	0004	B500	OEM	B531F	OEM	B561B(JAPAN)	0431	B588-55	OEM	B641Q	0355	B705B	3537
B486Y	0004	B502(2S)	0899	B531S	OEM	B561C(2S)	0431	B588-60	OEM	B641R	0355	B707	0848
B491-1	OEM	B502-O	0899	B532(2S)	2002	B561C(JAPAN)	0431	B588-65	OEM	B641S	0355	B707K(JAPAN)	0848
B491-2	OEM	B502-R	0899	B532-1	OEM	B562(2S)	0527	B588-70	OEM	B642	0819	B708	0848
B491-C	OEM	B502-Y	0899	B532-2	OEM	B562-C	0527	B588-75	OEM	B642-O	0819	B709	1731
B491F	OEM	B502A	0899	B532F	OEM	B562AC	OEM	B588-80	OEM	B642-Q	0819	B709A	1731
B491S	OEM	B502A-O	0899	B532S	2002	B562B(2S)	0527	B588-85	OEM	B642-Q(JAPAN)	0819	B711	0597

If replacement code is OEM, contact original manufacturer for replacement.

DEVICE TYPE	REPL CODE
B712	0597
B713	5381
B714	0841
B715	0643
B716	0643
B716A	0643
B716AD	0643
B716D	0643
B716E	0643
B717B	5382
B717C	5382
B717D	5382
B719	1638
B721	0037
B723	1588
B726	1593
B726R	1593
B726S	1593
B726T	1593
B727(JAPAN)	OEM
B727K(JAPAN)	OEM
B731	0520
B733	0527
B733K	0527
B733O	0527
B733U	0527
B734	0527
B734K	0527
B734U	0527
B738B	0472
B738C	0472
B739B	0527
B739C	0527
B740	0472
B740-3	0472
B740B	0472
B740C	0472
B741	0472
B741B	0472
B741C	0472
B743Q	0520
B744	1603
B744A	1603
B744Q	1603
B744R	1603
B744S	1603
B745	4076
B745A	4076
B745AS	4076
B745S	4076
B745T	4076
B747	0848
B750	0597
B750A	0597
B751	0597
B751A	0597
B753	1359
B754	5381
B755	3537
B759	0643
B760	0713
B760A	0713
B761	3136
B761A	3136
B761P	3136
B761Q	3136
B761R	3136
B762	0713
B762A	0713
B762P	0713
B762Q	0713
B763	5381
B763A	5381
B764	0472
B765K	1957
B772	0455
B772Q	0455
B774	1603
B774Q	1603
B774R	1603
B774S	1603
B774S(JAPAN)	1603
B774T	1603
B775	5381
B776	5381
B788	0643
B788Q	0643
B788S	0643
B788T	0643
B788U	0643
B790	0148
B791(JAPAN)	OEM
B793	0472
B793A	0472
B793Q	0472
B793R	0472
B794	2869
B794K	2869
B794L	2869
B794L(JAPAN)	2869
B794M	2869
B795L	2869
B796	3561
B808	0006
B808F	0006
B808G1	0006
B810	0527
B811	0472
B812	0853

DEVICE TYPE	REPL CODE
B812A	0853
B816	3082
B817	3082
B819	4282
B819Q	4282
B819R	4282
B822	4043
B822Q	4043
B823	0848
B824R	1298
B825	0848
B825R	0848
B826	1298
B827	5381
B828	5381
B828S	5381
B833	4043
B833(Q)	4043
B834	0848
B834-O(JAPAN)	0848
B835	0527
B836	3457
B836L	3457
B837	2007
B837B	3457
B837C	3457
B837D	3457
B837LB	3457
B837LC	3457
B837LD	3457
B838B	3457
B839B	3457
B840B	3457
B840C	3457
B840LB	3457
B841C	3457
B841LB	3457
B841LC	3457
B849	5381
B849A	5381
B855A	5395
B855B	5395
B856B	0713
B856C	0713
B857B	2895
B857C	2895
B857D	2895
B858	0713
B858(JAPAN)	2895
B858B	2895
B858C	2895
B858D	2895
B859B	0676
B859C	0676
B860	1359
B861	1638
B861B	1638
B861C	1638
B861D	1638
B863	5381
B865	0630
B867	0713
B868	0676
B869	0713
B870	0713
B882	2222
B882(JAPAN)	2222
B883	0073
B884	0597
B885(JAPAN)	0597
B886	2222
B892S(JAPAN)	0472
B925Q(JAPAN)	OEM
B940P	1638
B941	2895
B941B	2895
B941P	2895
B941Q	2895
B955(K)	1957
B963L	OEM
B994	1298
B995	0713
B996	3136
B1001R	5062
B1012(K)	OEM
B1012/2/16K	OEM
B1012/2/32K	OEM
B1012K	OEM
B1013B	OEM
B1014	OEM
B1015	5378
B1016	4094
B1017	0160
B1018	5574
B1019	1298
B1020/32K	OEM
B1020/64K	OEM
B1020/96K	OEM
B1020/128K	OEM
B1022	0211
B1022-1	0004
B1023	OEM
B1025	OEM
B1026	OEM
B1058	0211
B1058-1	0004
B1085	0160
B1093	OEM
B1093L	OEM

DEVICE TYPE	REPL CODE
B1093Q	OEM
B1110	0160
B1135R	4062
B1151	0455
B1151A	0160
B1151B	0160
B1152	0160
B1152A	0160
B1152B	0160
B1154	0211
B1154-1	0004
B1165S	OEM
B1178	0969
B1181	0160
B1181MP	OEM
B1191	OEM
B1201	0015
B1202	0604
B1202V	0604
B1204	0071
B1210B60C1000-700	OEM
B1210L	OEM
B1215	0085
B1220B125C1000-700	OEM
B1220L	OEM
B1235	OEM
B1240B250C1000-700	OEM
B1240L	OEM
B1262	OEM
B1272	OEM
B1274	0160
B1274A	0160
B1274B	0160
B1274R	0919
B1280B500C1000-700	OEM
B1280L	OEM
B1310B60C2300-1400	OEM
B1310M	OEM
B1318	OEM
B1318L	OEM
B1320B125C2300-1400	OEM
B1320M	OEM
B1333	OEM
B-1338	0016
B1340B250C2300-1400	OEM
B1340M	OEM
B1359	OEM
B1364	0211
B1368	0160
B1368A	0160
B1368B	0160
B1368C	0160
B1368D	0160
B1368E	0160
B1368F	0160
B1380B500C2300-1400	OEM
B1380M	OEM
B1382	OEM
B1411-1	OEM
B1411-2	OEM
B1411-C	OEM
B1411F	OEM
B1411S	OEM
B1412-1	OEM
B1412-2	OEM
B1412-C	OEM
B1412F	OEM
B1412S	OEM
B1413-1	OEM
B1413-2	OEM
B1413-C	OEM
B1413F	OEM
B1413S	OEM
B1420	OEM
B-1421	0016
B1421-1	OEM
B1421-2	OEM
B1421-C	OEM
B1421F	OEM
B1421S	OEM
B1422-1	OEM
B1422-2	OEM
B1422-C	OEM
B1422F	OEM
B1422S	OEM
B1423-1	OEM
B1423-2	OEM
B1423-C	OEM
B1423F	OEM
B1423S	OEM
B-1426	0037
B1431-1	OEM
B1431-2	OEM
B1431-C	OEM
B1431F	OEM
B1431S	OEM
B1432-1	OEM
B1432-2	OEM
B1432-C	OEM
B1432F	OEM
B1432S	OEM
B-1433	0016
B1433-1	OEM
B1433-2	OEM
B1433-C	OEM
B1433F	OEM
B1433S	OEM
B1441-1	OEM
B1441-2	OEM

DEVICE TYPE	REPL CODE
B1441-C	OEM
B1441F	OEM
B1441S	OEM
B1442-1	OEM
B1442-2	OEM
B1442-C	OEM
B1442F	OEM
B1442S	OEM
B1443-1	OEM
B1443-2	OEM
B1443-C	OEM
B1443F	OEM
B1443S	OEM
B1451-1	OEM
B1451-2	OEM
B1451-C	OEM
B1451F	OEM
B1451S	OEM
B1452-1	OEM
B1452-2	OEM
B1452-C	OEM
B1452S	OEM
B1453-1	OEM
B1453-2	OEM
B1453-C	OEM
B1453F	OEM
B1453S	OEM
B1461-1	OEM
B1461-2	OEM
B1461-C	OEM
B1461F	OEM
B1461S	OEM
B1462-1	OEM
B1462-2	OEM
B1462-C	OEM
B1462F	OEM
B1462S	OEM
B1463-1	OEM
B1463-2	OEM
B1463-C	OEM
B1463F	OEM
B1463S	OEM
B1471-1	OEM
B1471-2	OEM
B1471-C	OEM
B1471F	OEM
B1471S	OEM
B1472-1	OEM
B1472-2	OEM
B1472-C	OEM
B1472F	OEM
B1472S	OEM
B1473-1	OEM
B1473-2	OEM
B1473-C	OEM
B1473F	OEM
B1473S	OEM
B1481-1	OEM
B1481-2	OEM
B1481-C	OEM
B1481F	OEM
B1482-1	OEM
B1482-2	OEM
B1482-C	OEM
B1482F	OEM
B1482S	OEM
B1483-2	OEM
B1483-C	OEM
B1483F	OEM
B1483S	OEM
B1491-1	OEM
B1491-2	OEM
B1491-C	OEM
B1491F	OEM
B1491S	OEM
B1492-1	OEM
B1492-2	OEM
B1492-C	OEM
B1492F	OEM
B1492S	OEM
B1493-1	OEM
B1493-2	OEM
B1493-C	OEM
B1493S	OEM
B-1501U	0015
B-1511	0160
B1511-1	OEM
B1511-2	OEM
B1511-C	OEM
B1511F	OEM
B1511S	OEM
B1512-1	OEM
B1512-2	OEM
B1512-C	OEM
B1512F	OEM
B1512S	OEM
B1513-1	OEM
B1513-2	OEM
B1513-C	OEM
B1513F	OEM
B1513S	OEM
B1521-1	OEM
B1521-2	OEM
B1521-C	OEM
B1521F	OEM
B1521S	OEM
B1522-1	OEM
B1522-2	OEM
B1522-C	OEM

DEVICE TYPE	REPL CODE
B1522F	OEM
B1522S	OEM
B1523-1	OEM
B1523-2	OEM
B1523-C	OEM
B1523F	OEM
B1523S	OEM
B1531-1	OEM
B1531-2	OEM
B1531-C	OEM
B1531F	OEM
B1531S	OEM
B1532-1	OEM
B1532-2	OEM
B1532F	OEM
B1532S	OEM
B1533-1	OEM
B1533-2	OEM
B1533-C	OEM
B1533F	OEM
B1533S	OEM
B1541-1	OEM
B1541-2	OEM
B1541-C	OEM
B1541S	OEM
B1542-1	OEM
B1542-2	OEM
B1542-C	OEM
B1542F	OEM
B1542S	OEM
B1543-1	OEM
B1543-2	OEM
B1543-C	OEM
B1543F	OEM
B1543S	OEM
B1551-1	OEM
B1551-2	OEM
B1551-C	OEM
B1551F	OEM
B1551S	OEM
B1552-1	OEM
B1552-2	OEM
B1552-C	OEM
B1552F	OEM
B1552S	OEM
B1553-1	OEM
B1553-2	OEM
B1553-C	OEM
B1553F	OEM
B1553S	OEM
B1561-1	OEM
B1561-2	OEM
B1561-C	OEM
B1561F	OEM
B1561S	OEM
B1562-1	OEM
B1562-2	OEM
B1562F	OEM
B1562S	OEM
B1563-1	OEM
B1563-2	OEM
B1563-C	OEM
B1563F	OEM
B1563S	OEM
B1571-1	OEM
B1571-2	OEM
B1571F	OEM
B1571S	OEM
B1572-C	OEM
B1573-1	OEM
B1573-2	OEM
B1573-C	OEM
B1573F	OEM
B1573S	OEM
B1581-1	OEM
B1581-2	OEM
B1581-C	OEM
B1581F	OEM
B1581S	OEM
B1582-1	OEM
B1582-2	OEM
B1582-C	OEM
B1582F	OEM
B1582S	OEM
B1583-1	OEM
B1583-2	OEM
B1583-C	OEM
B1583F	OEM
B1583S	OEM
B1591-1	OEM
B1591-2	OEM
B1591-C	OEM
B1591F	OEM
B1591S	OEM
B1592-1	OEM
B1592-2	OEM
B1592-C	OEM
B1592F	OEM
B1592S	OEM
B1593-1	OEM
B1593-2	OEM
B1593-C	OEM
B1593F	OEM
B-1599	0133
B-1666	0016
B1670C-01	OEM
B1670C-01T-1S	OEM
B1670C-02	OEM
B1670C-02T-1S	OEM

DEVICE TYPE	REPL CODE
B1670C-03	OEM
B1670C-03T-1S	OEM
B1670C-04	OEM
B1670C-04T-1S	OEM
B1670M-01	OEM
B1670M-01T-1S	OEM
B1670M-02	OEM
B1670M-02T-1S	OEM
B1670M-03	OEM
B1670M-03T-1S	OEM
B1670M-04	OEM
B1670M-04T-1S	OEM
B-1695	0455
B-1702	0133
B1760	0211
B1780	0164
B1780A	0164
B1780B	0164
B1780C	0164
B1780D	0164
B1780E	0164
B1780F	0164
B1780G	0164
B1780GN	0164
B1780H	0164
B1780J	0164
B1780K	0164
B1780L	0164
B1780M	0164
B1780OR	0164
B1780R	0164
B1780X	0164
B1780Y	0164
B1785	0211
B-1790	0161
B-1808	0244
B-1823	0042
B-1842	0016
B1851	0004
B1860	0211
B-1872	0016
B-1881U	0015
B-1882U	0015
B1904	0160
B1906B40C1500-1000	OEM
B1906L	OEM
B-1910	0111
B1912B80C1500-1000	OEM
B1912L	OEM
B1913	OEM
B-1914	0160
B1914	0160
B2000	OEM
B2090	0012
B2167-55(A)	OEM
B2404C	0023
B2404D	0023
B2406C	0023
B2406D	0023
B2411-1	OEM
B2411-2	OEM
B2411-C	OEM
B2411F	OEM
B2411S	OEM
B2412-1	OEM
B2412-2	OEM
B2412-C	OEM
B2412F	OEM
B2412S	OEM
B2413-1	OEM
B2413-2	OEM
B2413-C	OEM
B2413F	OEM
B2413S	OEM
B2421-1	OEM
B2421-2	OEM
B2421-C	OEM
B2421F	OEM
B2421S	OEM
B2422-1	OEM
B2422-2	OEM
B2422-C	OEM
B2422F	OEM
B2422S	OEM
B2423-1	OEM
B2423-2	OEM
B2423-C	OEM
B2423F	OEM
B2431-1	OEM
B2431-2	OEM
B2431F	OEM
B2431S	OEM
B2432-1	OEM
B2432-2	OEM
B2432-C	OEM
B2432F	OEM
B2432S	OEM
B2433-1	OEM
B2433-2	OEM
B2433-C	OEM
B2433F	OEM
B2433S	OEM
B2441-1	OEM
B2441-C	OEM
B2441F	OEM
B2441S	OEM
B2442-1	OEM
B2442-2	OEM
B2442-C	OEM

DEVICE TYPE	REPL CODE
B2442F	OEM
B2442S	OEM
B2443-1	OEM
B2443-2	OEM
B2443-C	OEM
B2443F	OEM
B2443S	OEM
B2451-1	OEM
B2451-2	OEM
B2451-C	OEM
B2451F	OEM
B2451S	OEM
B2452-1	OEM
B2452-2	OEM
B2452-C	OEM
B2452F	OEM
B2452S	OEM
B2453-1	OEM
B2453-2	OEM
B2453-C	OEM
B2453F	OEM
B2453S	OEM
B2491-1	OEM
B2491-2	OEM
B2491-C	OEM
B2491F	OEM
B2491S	OEM
B2492-1	OEM
B2492-2	OEM
B2492-C	OEM
B2492F	OEM
B2492S	OEM
B2493-1	OEM
B2493-2	OEM
B2493-C	OEM
B2493F	OEM
B2493S	OEM
B2511-1	OEM
B2511-2	OEM
B2511-C	OEM
B2511F	OEM
B2511S	OEM
B2512-1	OEM
B2512-2	OEM
B2512-C	OEM
B2512F	OEM
B2512S	OEM
B2513-1	OEM
B2513-2	OEM
B2513-C	OEM
B2513F	OEM
B2513S	OEM
B2521-1	OEM
B2521-2	OEM
B2521-C	OEM
B2521F	OEM
B2521S	OEM
B2522-1	OEM
B2522-2	OEM
B2522-C	OEM
B2522F	OEM
B2522S	OEM
B2523-1	OEM
B2523-2	OEM
B2523-C	OEM
B2523F	OEM
B2523S	OEM
B2531-1	OEM
B2531-2	OEM
B2531-C	OEM
B2531F	OEM
B2531S	OEM
B2532-1	OEM
B2532-2	OEM
B2532-C	OEM
B2532F	OEM
B2532S	OEM
B2533-2	OEM
B2533-C	OEM
B2533F	OEM
B2533S	OEM
B2541-1	OEM
B2541-2	OEM
B2541-C	OEM
B2541F	OEM
B2541S	OEM
B2542-1	OEM
B2542-2	OEM
B2542-C	OEM
B2542F	OEM
B2542S	OEM
B2543-1	OEM
B2543-2	OEM
B2543-C	OEM
B2543F	OEM
B2543S	OEM
B2551-1	OEM
B2551-2	OEM
B2551-C	OEM
B2551F	OEM
B2551S	OEM
B2552-1	OEM
B2552-C	OEM
B2552F	OEM
B2552S	OEM
B2553-1	OEM
B2553-2	OEM
B2553-C	OEM
B2553F	OEM
B2553S	OEM

If replacement code is OEM, contact original manufacturer for replacement. 281

DEVICE TYPE	REPL CODE
B2561-1	OEM
B2561-2	OEM
B2561-C	OEM
B2561F	OEM
B2561S	OEM
B2562-1	OEM
B2562-2	OEM
B2562-C	OEM
B2562F	OEM
B2562S	OEM
B2563-1	OEM
B2563-2	OEM
B2563-C	OEM
B2563F	OEM
B2563S	OEM
B2571-1	OEM
B2571-2	OEM
B2571-C	OEM
B2571F	OEM
B2571S	OEM
B2572-1	OEM
B2572-2	OEM
B2572-C	OEM
B2572F	OEM
B2572S	OEM
B2573-1	OEM
B2573-2	OEM
B2573-C	OEM
B2573F	OEM
B2573S	OEM
B2581-1	OEM
B2581-2	OEM
B2581-C	OEM
B2581F	OEM
B2581S	OEM
B2582-1	OEM
B2582-2	OEM
B2582-C	OEM
B2582F	OEM
B2582S	OEM
B2583-1	OEM
B2583-2	OEM
B2583-C	OEM
B2583F	OEM
B2583S	OEM
B2591-1	OEM
B2591-2	OEM
B2591-C	OEM
B2591F	OEM
B2591S	OEM
B2592-1	OEM
B2592-2	OEM
B2592-C	OEM
B2592F	OEM
B2592S	OEM
B2593-1	OEM
B2593-2	OEM
B2593-C	OEM
B2593F	OEM
B2593S	OEM
B2611-1	OEM
B2611-2	OEM
B2611-C	OEM
B2611F	OEM
B2611S	OEM
B2612-1	OEM
B2612-2	OEM
B2612-C	OEM
B2612F	OEM
B2612S	OEM
B2613-1	OEM
B2613-2	OEM
B2613-C	OEM
B2613F	OEM
B2613S	OEM
B2620	0102
B2621-1	OEM
B2621-2	OEM
B2621-C	OEM
B2621F	OEM
B2621S	OEM
B2622-1	OEM
B2622-2	OEM
B2622-C	OEM
B2622F	OEM
B2622S	OEM
B2623-1	OEM
B2623-2	OEM
B2623-C	OEM
B2623F	OEM
B2631-1	OEM
B2631-C	OEM
B2631F	OEM
B2631S	OEM
B2632-1	OEM
B2632-2	OEM
B2632-C	OEM
B2632F	OEM
B2632S	OEM
B2633-1	OEM
B2633-2	OEM
B2633-C	OEM
B2633F	OEM
B2633S	OEM
B2641-1	OEM
B2641-2	OEM
B2641F	OEM
B2641S	OEM
B2804D	0023

DEVICE TYPE	REPL CODE
B2806B40C900-600	OEM
B2812B80C900-600	OEM
B3015M	0017
B3030(2S)	0004
B3045	0236
B3046	0236
B3141	OEM
B3142	OEM
B3143	OEM
B3144	OEM
B3145	OEM
B3146	OEM
B3147	OEM
B3148	OEM
B3149	OEM
B3161	OEM
B3162	OEM
B3163	OEM
B3224E	0211
B3240	0164
B3240A	0164
B3240B	0164
B3240C	0164
B3240D	0164
B3240E	0164
B3240F	0164
B3240G	0164
B3240GN	0164
B3240H	0164
B3240J	0164
B3240K	0164
B3240L	0164
B3240M	0164
B3240OR	0164
B3240R	0164
B3240X	0164
B3240Y	0164
B3244	0279
B3465	0693
B3466	0419
B3468	0693
B3515	OEM
B3531	0555
B3533	0555
B3537	0555
B3538	0555
B3539	0419
B3540	0555
B3541	0555
B3542	0555
B3543	0419
B3544	0419
B3547	0042
B3548	0042
B3550	0042
B3551	0042
B3570	0555
B3576	0555
B3577	0042
B3578	0042
B3580	0042
B3584	0042
B3585	0042
B3586	0042
B3588	0042
B3589	0042
B3606	0555
B3607	0555
B3608	0555
B3609	0555
B3610	0555
B3611	0555
B3612	0555
B3613	0555
B3614	0555
B3746	0086
B3747	0555
B3748	0555
B3750	0555
B3783A	0164
B3783B	0164
B3783C	0164
B3783D	0164
B3783E	0164
B3783F	0164
B3783G	0164
B3783GN	0164
B3783H	0164
B3783J	0164
B3783K	0164
B3783L	0164
B3783M	0164
B3783OR	0164
B3783R	0164
B3783X	0164
B3783Y	0164
B3812A	0164
B3812B	0164
B3812C	0164
B3812D	0164
B3812F	0164
B3812G	0164
B3812GN	0164
B3812H	0164
B3812J	0164
B3812K	0164
B3812L	0164
B3812M	0164
B3812OR	0164

DEVICE TYPE	REPL CODE
B3812R	0164
B3812X	0164
B3812Y	0164
B3813A	0164
B3813B	0164
B3813C	0164
B3813D	0164
B3813E	0164
B3813F	0164
B3813G	0164
B3813GN	0164
B3813H	0164
B3813J	0164
B3813K	0164
B3813L	0164
B3813M	0164
B3813OR	0164
B3813R	0164
B3813X	0164
B3813Y	0164
B4002-0289	OEM
B4006R	OEM
B4008R	OEM
B4010R	OEM
B4012-0241	OEM
B4012R	OEM
B4014R	OEM
B4016R	OEM
B4018R	OEM
B4020R	OEM
B4022R	OEM
B4024R	OEM
B4026R	OEM
B4028R	OEM
B4030R	OEM
B4151	0211
B4151M	OEM
B4302	0023
B4304	0023
B4304V	0023
B4310C	OEM
B4340	0848
B4402	0023
B4404	0023
B4406	0023
B4440D	0164
B4631	0222
B5000	0042
B5000-GRN	0042
B5000-RED	0042
B5000-YEL	0042
B5001	0555
B5001-GRN	0042
B5001-ORG	0042
B5001-RED	0042
B5001-YEL	0042
B5002	0042
B5006R	OEM
B5008R	OEM
B5010R0R	OEM
B5012R	OEM
B5014R	OEM
B5016R	OEM
B5018R	OEM
B5020	0103
B5020R	OEM
B5021	0042
B5022	0042
B5022R	OEM
B5024R	OEM
B5026R	OEM
B5028R	OEM
B5030R	OEM
B5031	0042
B5032	0042
B-6001	0321
B-6002	0002
B6101C054	OEM
B6101C058	OEM
B6101C084	OEM
B6201/3	OEM
B7513	0279
B8313	OEM
B8507CK	OEM
B8555S	OEM
B8606	OEM
B9096	OEM
B9426	0144
B10060	OEM
B10061	OEM
B10062	OEM
B10063	OEM
B10064	0085
B10065	OEM
B10066	OEM
B10067	OEM
B10068	OEM
B10069	0085
B10142	0969
B10142A	0969
B10142B	0969
B10143	0969
B10143A	0969
B10143B	0969
B10144	OEM
B10144A	OEM
B10144B	OEM
B10162	0160
B10163	0160

DEVICE TYPE	REPL CODE
B10474	0160
B10475	0160
B10912	0160
B10913	0160
B17307	0103
B35016	0572
B36564	0015
B-75583-I02	0016
B81004	0110
B84009	OEM
B102000	0969
B102001	0969
B102002	0969
B102003	0969
B103000	0969
B103001	0969
B103002	0969
B103003	0969
B103004	0969
B113000	0599
B113000-BRN	0599
B113000-ORG	0599
B113000-RED	0599
B133001	0556
B133002	0556
B133003	0556
B133004	0556
B133005	0556
B133006	0556
B133007	0556
B133008	0556
B143000	0555
B143001	0555
B143003	0555
B143004	0042
B143009	0555
B143010	0555
B143011	0042
B143012	0042
B143015	0555
B143016	0555
B143018	0042
B143019	0042
B143024	0555
B143025	0555
B143026	0042
B143027	0042
B145000	0933
B170000	0103
B170000-B	0065
B170000-BLK	0615
B170000-BRN	0615
B170000-ORG	0103
B170000-ORN	0103
B170000-R	0103
B170000-RED	0103
B170000-Y	0103
B170000-YEL	0130
B170000BLK	0103
B170000BRN	0103
B170001	0103
B170001-B	0103
B170001-BLK	0103
B170001-BRN	0103
B170001-O	0103
B170001-ORG	0103
B170001-R	0103
B170001-RED	0103
B170001-Y	0103
B170001-YEL	0130
B170001BLK	0103
B170001BRN	0103
B170002	0103
B170002-BLK	0103
B170002-BRN	0103
B170002-O	0103
B170002-ORG	0103
B170002-R	0103
B170002-RED	0103
B170002-Y	0103
B170002-YEL	0130
B170003	0103
B170003-B	0065
B170003-BLK	0130
B170003-BRN	0130
B170003-O	0103
B170003-ORG	0130
B170003-R	0103
B170003-RED	0130
B170003-Y	0103
B170003-YEL	0130
B170004	0103
B170004-B	0103
B170004-BLK	0130
B170004-BRN	0130
B170004-O	0130
B170004-ORG	0130
B170004-R	0103
B170004-RED	0130
B170004-Y	0103
B170004-YEL	0130
B170005	0103
B170005-B	0103
B170005-BLK	0130
B170005-BRN	0130
B170005-O	0103
B170005-ORG	0130
B170005-R	0103
B170005-RED	0130

DEVICE TYPE	REPL CODE
B170005-Y	0103
B170005-YEL	0130
B170006	0103
B170006-B	0065
B170006-BLK	0130
B170006-BRN	0130
B170006-O	0074
B170006-ORG	0130
B170006-R	0074
B170006-RED	0130
B170006-Y	0074
B170006-YEL	0130
B170007	0103
B170007-B	0130
B170007-BLK	0130
B170007-BRN	0130
B170007-O	0074
B170007-ORG	0130
B170007-R	0074
B170007-RED	0130
B170007-Y	0074
B170007-YEL	0130
B170008	0074
B170008-BLK	0130
B170008-BRN	0130
B170008-ORG	0130
B170008-RED	0130
B170008-YEL	0130
B170009	0103
B170010	0103
B170011	0103
B170012	0103
B170013	0103
B170014	0103
B170015	0103
B170016	0103
B170017	0130
B170018	0103
B170019	0103
B170020	0103
B170021	0103
B170022	0103
B170023	0130
B170024	0103
B170025	0103
B170026	0130
B176000	0637
B176001	0074
B176002	0074
B176003	0074
B176004	0637
B176005	0637
B176006	0637
B176007	0637
B176009	0637
B176010	0637
B176011	0637
B176013	0637
B176014	0637
B176015	0637
B176024	0637
B176025	0637
B176026	0637
B176027	0637
B176028	0637
B176029	0637
B177000	0130
B232008	0142
B678760A	0638
B1045494P1	0479
B1760000	0359
B5493957-4	0126
B5493957-5	0126
B5493957-6	0126
B7579500	0071
B7978850	0023
B8400950	OEM
B507138054AQ	OEM
BA-075	0644
BA-07001	0143
BA-07007	0015
BA07018	OEM
BA07021	OEM
BA1A4M	OEM
BA1L4M	OEM
BA5A5	1325
BA5B5	0015
BA5C5	0015
BA5D5	0015
BA5E5	0015
BA5F5	0015
BA5G5	0015
BA5H5	0182
BA5K5	0182
BA5M5	0182
BA5N5	0182
BA5P5	0182
BA6	0164
BA6A	0164
BA8-1A-21	0050
BA10B	OEM
BA20	0468
BA40	0468
BA47	OEM
BA47F	OEM
BA50G	OEM
BA55B	OEM
BA60B	1404
BA60C	OEM

DEVICE TYPE	REPL CODE
BA65A	OEM
BA67	0016
BA70C	OEM
BA70X	OEM
BA71	0016
BA75C	OEM
BA80A	OEM
BA85A	OEM
BA85X	OEM
BA90A	OEM
BA95A	OEM
BA100	0015
BA100C	OEM
BA102	0030
BA102A	0623
BA102AA	0015
BA102B	OEM
BA102BA	0015
BA102C	0030
BA102CA	0015
BA102D	OEM
BA102DA	0015
BA102EA	0015
BA102FA	0015
BA102GA	0015
BA102HA	0015
BA102KA	0015
BA102MA	0015
BA102PA	0071
BA102RA	0071
BA102TA	0071
BA102VA	0071
BA103	0124
BA104	0080
BA105	0790
BA108	1325
BA109	0030
BA109G	0030
BA110	0030
BA110G	OEM
BA111	0030
BA112	OEM
BA114	0133
BA115	OEM
BA117	OEM
BA119	0015
BA120	0005
BA120A	OEM
BA121	0005
BA122	0133
BA124	0030
BA125	OEM
BA127	0015
BA127D	OEM
BA128	0015
BA129	0604
BA130	1325
BA132AA	0071
BA132BA	0071
BA132CA	0071
BA132DA	0071
BA132EA	0071
BA132FA	0071
BA132GA	0071
BA132HA	0071
BA132KA	0071
BA132MA	0071
BA132PA	0071
BA132RA	0071
BA132TA	0071
BA132VA	0071
BA133	0102
BA133F	0369
BA136	0133
BA136A	0110
BA-138	0030
BA138	OEM
BA139	OEM
BA140	OEM
BA-142	OEM
BA142	OEM
BA-142-01	0015
BA142-01	0015
BA143U	OEM
BA143V	OEM
BA145	0102
BA147	0133
BA148	0102
BA149	OEM
BA150	OEM
BA151	OEM
BA152	OEM
BA152A	0023
BA152PR	OEM
BA153	0015
BA154	0133
BA155	OEM
BA156	OEM
BA157	0017
BA157GP	0271
BA158	0017
BA158GP	0271
BA159	0017
BA159DGP	OEM
BA159GP	0524
BA160	OEM
BA161	OEM
BA162	OEM
BA163	OEM

DEVICE TYPE	REPL CODE
BA164	1325
BA165	OEM
BA166	0133
BA167	0133
BA168	0133
BA169	OEM
BA170	0133
BA171	OEM
BA172	1325
BA172-5	OEM
BA172-10	OEM
BA172-20	OEM
BA172-30	OEM
BA172-40	OEM
BA172-50	OEM
BA172-60	OEM
BA172-70	OEM
BA172-80	OEM
BA172-90	OEM
BA172-100	OEM
BA172-120	OEM
BA173	0271
BA174	0133
BA175	OEM
BA176	2491
BA177	0133
BA178	0110
BA180	1325
BA181	0133
BA182	2496
BA187	0133
BA188	0015
BA189	0015
BA190	0015
BA191	OEM
BA191-5	0319
BA191-10	0319
BA191-20	1404
BA191-30	0468
BA191-40	0468
BA191-50	0441
BA191-60	0441
BA191-70	1412
BA191-80	1412
BA191-90	2425
BA191-100	2425
BA191-120	OEM
BA192	OEM
BA193	OEM
BA194	OEM
BA195	OEM
BA196	OEM
BA197	OEM
BA198	OEM
BA199	OEM
BA199-250	OEM
BA199-350	OEM
BA199-450	OEM
BA199-550	OEM
BA200	0124
BA201	0124
BA202	0124
BA203	0124
BA204	0124
BA206	OEM
BA207	OEM
BA208	0065
BA209	OEM
BA210	OEM
BA211	OEM
BA212	OEM
BA213	OEM
BA214	OEM
BA215	OEM
BA216	0133
BA217	1325
BA218	1325
BA219	0133
BA220	0124
BA221	0124
BA222	2513
BA223	0124
BA223-10	4423
BA223-15	0102
BA223-20	0344
BA223-25	OEM
BA223-30	OEM
BA223-35	OEM
BA223-40	OEM
BA223-45	OEM
BA223-50	OEM
BA223-55	OEM
BA223-60	OEM
BA223-65	OEM
BA223-70	OEM
BA224	OEM
BA224-150	OEM
BA224-220	OEM
BA224-300	OEM
BA225	OEM
BA226	OEM
BA227	OEM
BA228	OEM
BA232-5	OEM
BA232-10	OEM
BA232-20	OEM
BA232-30	OEM
BA232-40	OEM
BA232-50	OEM

If replacement code is OEM, contact original manufacturer for replacement.

DEVICE TYPE	REPL CODE	DEVICE TYPE	REPL CODE	DEVICE TYPE	REPL CODE	DEVICE TYPE	REPL CODE	DEVICE TYPE	REPL CODE	DEVICE TYPE	REPL CODE	DEVICE TYPE	REPL CODE
BA232-60	OEM	BA682	OEM	BA5102A	2094	BA7212S	OEM	BAS16	3703	BAV29	OEM	BAV505	0109
BA232-70	OEM	BA682A	OEM	BA5102AL	OEM	BA7252S	OEM	BAS17	OEM	BAV30	OEM	BAV506	0116
BA232-80	OEM	BA683	OEM	BA5102S	OEM	BA7255S	OEM	BAS18	0023	BAV31	OEM	BAV507	0122
BA232-90	OEM	BA683A	OEM	BA5104A	OEM	BA7266S	OEM	BAS19	3841	BAV32	OEM	BAV508	0131
BA232-100	OEM	BA684A	OEM	BA5112	OEM	BA7274S	OEM	BAS20	3841	BAV33	OEM	BAV509	0131
BA232-120	OEM	BA685	OEM	BA5112LS	OEM	BA7280AS	OEM	BAS21	3841	BAV34	OEM	BAV515	0109
BA235	OEM	BA689	OEM	BA5114F	OEM	BA7280S	OEM	BAS27	OEM	BAV35	OEM	BAV516	0116
BA236	OEM	BA695	OEM	BA5114LS	OEM	BA7603F-T1	OEM	BAS28	OEM	BAV36	OEM	BAV517	0122
BA236A	OEM	BA704	OEM	BA5115	OEM	BA7603FTI	OEM	BAS29	3841	BAV37	OEM	BAV518	0131
BA236B	OEM	BA707	OEM	BA5115L	OEM	BA7604N	OEM	BAS31	OEM	BAV38	OEM	BAV519	0131
BA243	0549	BA707S	OEM	BA5116	OEM	BA7700K1	OEM	BAS32	OEM	BAV39	OEM	BAV525	0109
BA243A	0124	BA715	2884	BA5119S	OEM	BA7703K1	OEM	BAS32D	OEM	BAV40	OEM	BAV526	0116
BA243S	0133	BA718	2884	BA5204	OEM	BA7720S	OEM	BAS33	OEM	BAV41	OEM	BAV527	0122
BA244	0163	BA728	2894	BA5205F	OEM	BA7743S	OEM	BAS34	OEM	BAV42	OEM	BAV528	0131
BA244A	0133	BA728F	OEM	BA5206BF	OEM	BA7751LS	OEM	BAS35	4830	BAV44	OEM	BAV529	0131
BA244S	0124	BA751AA	0015	BA5302A	OEM	BA7755	OEM	BAS40	OEM	BAV45	OEM	BAV705	0197
BA280	OEM	BA751BA	0015	BA5402A	2772	BA7765AS	OEM	BAS40-01	OEM	BAV45A	OEM	BAV706	0200
BA281	OEM	BA751CA	0015	BA5404	OEM	BA7767AS	OEM	BAS40-02	OEM	BAV46	OEM	BAV707	0204
BA282	0163	BA751DA	0015	BA5406	6638	BA7767S	OEM	BAS40-03	OEM	BAV46D	OEM	BAV708	0206
BA282M3	OEM	BA751EA	0015	BA6104	OEM	BA8411	OEM	BAS40-04	OEM	BAV46E	OEM	BAV709	0206
BA283	0133	BA751FA	0015	BA6107	OEM	BA9101	OEM	BAS40-05	OEM	BAV46F	OEM	BAV715	0197
BA284	0124	BA751GA	0015	BA6109	OEM	BA9201	OEM	BAS40-06	OEM	BAV47	OEM	BAV716	0200
BA301	2051	BA751HA	0015	BA6109U	OEM	BA9221	OEM	BAS45	OEM	BAV48	OEM	BAV717	0204
BA301B	2051	BA751KA	0015	BA6110	OEM	BA10324	4191	BAS46	OEM	BAV49	OEM	BAV718	0206
BA306	OEM	BA751MA	0015	BA6118	OEM	BA10324F	OEM	BAS56	OEM	BAV50	OEM	BAV719	0206
BA308	0428	BA751PA	0071	BA6121	OEM	BA10339	2753	BAS70	OEM	BAV54	OEM	BAV725	0197
BA310	OEM	BA751RA	0071	BA6122	OEM	BA10358	OEM	BAS70-01	OEM	BAV54-30	OEM	BAV726	0200
BA311	2607	BA751TA	0071	BA6122A	5139	BA10358N	OEM	BAS70-02	OEM	BAV54-70	OEM	BAV727	0204
BA313	2609	BA751VA	0071	BA6122AF	OEM	BA10393	OEM	BAS70-03	OEM	BAV54-100	OEM	BAV728	0206
BA314	OEM	BA806	OEM	BA6124	5070	BA12003	1126	BAS70-04	OEM	BAV55	OEM	BAV729	0206
BA314A	OEM	BA820	OEM	BA6125	OEM	BA15218N	OEM	BAS70-05	OEM	BAV67	OEM	BAV805	0109
BA315	1914	BA841	OEM	BA6133	OEM	BAA6865	OEM	BAS70-06	OEM	BAV68	OEM	BAV806	0116
BA316	0124	BA842	OEM	BA6135	OEM	BAC-SHIMI	0124	BAS482	OEM	BAV69	OEM	BAV807	0122
BA317	0133	BA843	OEM	BA6137	OEM	BACSHIMI	0124	BASIC1	OEM	BAV70	0080	BAV808	0131
BA318	2614	BA845	OEM	BA6138	OEM	BACSIM1	0124	BASIC2	OEM	BAV71	OEM	BAV809	0131
BA328	2323	BA847	2983	BA6139	OEM	BAF1360	OEM	BASIC3	OEM	BAV72	OEM	BAV815	0109
BA328LN	2323	BA852	OEM	BA6144	5714	BAF5204	OEM	BASIC4	OEM	BAV74	1325	BAV816	0116
BA328MR	2512	BA857	OEM	BA6146	OEM	BAL0002-100	OEM	BAT10	OEM	BAV75	OEM	BAV817	0122
BA333	2052	BA858	OEM	BA6148	OEM	BAL0004-50	OEM	BAT11	OEM	BAV76	OEM	BAV818	0131
BA335	OEM	BA858B	OEM	BA6154	OEM	BAL0004-100	OEM	BAT13	OEM	BAV77	OEM	BAV819	0131
BA336	OEM	BA862	OEM	BA6200AL	OEM	BAL0101-150	OEM	BAT16-046	OEM	BAV79	OEM	BAV825	0109
BA337	OEM	BA867	OEM	BA6208	OEM	BAL0101-150A	OEM	BAT16-096	OEM	BAV80	OEM	BAV826	0116
BA338	2630	BA873	OEM	BA6209	3776	BAL0101-200	OEM	BAT17	OEM	BAV81	OEM	BAV827	0122
BA340	2632	BA885	OEM	BA6209K	OEM	BAL0105-50	OEM	BAT17-04	OEM	BAV82	OEM	BAV828	0131
BA343	OEM	BA1003	0396	BA6209N	0124	BAL0105-100	OEM	BAT17-05	OEM	BAV83	OEM	BAV829	0131
BA379	OEM	BA1102F	OEM	BA6209U	3776	BAL0204-50	OEM	BAT17-06	OEM	BAV84	OEM	BAV3308	2077
BA382	OEM	BA1104LS	OEM	BA6209U1	3776	BAL0204-125	OEM	BAT17DS	OEM	BAV85	OEM	BAV3309	2077
BA389	0124	BA1310	0701	BA6209U2	OEM	BAL0305-P300	OEM	BAT18	3842	BAV86	OEM	BAW10	OEM
BA401	2046	BA1310F	0701	BA6209U4	OEM	BAL0710-50	OEM	BAT19	OEM	BAV87	OEM	BAW10TF20	0133
BA402	0905	BA1320	1251	BA6209UI	3776	BAL0710-75	OEM	BAT21E	OEM	BAV88	OEM	BAW11	OEM
BA403	2668	BA1320F	OEM	BA6218	OEM	BAL74	OEM	BAT21J	OEM	BAV89	OEM	BAW11TF21	0133
BA404	2669	BA1330	0412	BA6219	6680	BAL99	OEM	BAT22E	OEM	BAV92	OEM	BAW12	OEM
BA423	0124	BA1332	OEM	BA6219B	5694	BAL6309	OEM	BAT22J	OEM	BAV93	OEM	BAW12TF22	0133
BA430-5	0724	BA1332L	OEM	BA6219B-U2	OEM	BAM40SR	OEM	BAT23G	OEM	BAV94	OEM	BAW13	OEM
BA430-10	0724	BA1335	OEM	BA6229	OEM	BAM80SR	OEM	BAT23J	OEM	BAV96A	OEM	BAW13TF23	0133
BA430-20	0724	BA1350	5105	BA6229W/MNT	OEM	BAM100SR	OEM	BAT24G	OEM	BAV96B	OEM	BAW14	OEM
BA430-30	0732	BA1351	OEM	BA6238A	4054	BAM120SR	OEM	BAT24H	OEM	BAV96C	OEM	BAW16	0133
BA430-40	0732	BA1355	OEM	BA6238AU	4054	BAM150	OEM	BAT25E	OEM	BAV96D	OEM	BAW17	0133
BA430-50	0732	BA1356	OEM	BA6238AU1	OEM	BAN62	0133	BAT25J	OEM	BAV97	OEM	BAW18	0133
BA430-60	0732	BA1360	OEM	BA6238AU4	4054	BAN805	OEM	BAT26E	OEM	BAV99	OEM	BAW19	OEM
BA430-70	0737	BA1360F	OEM	BA6239	OEM	BAR3S	OEM	BAT26J	OEM	BAV100	OEM	BAW21A	OEM
BA430-80	0737	BA1440	OEM	BA6239A	OEM	BAR10	OEM	BAT27G	OEM	BAV101	OEM	BAW21B	OEM
BA430-90	0737	BA1604	OEM	BA6239AN	OEM	BAR11	OEM	BAT27H	OEM	BAV102	OEM	BAW22	OEM
BA430-100	0737	BA2254F	OEM	BA6247	OEM	BAR12-1	OEM	BAT28G	OEM	BAV103	OEM	BAW23	OEM
BA430-120	OEM	BA2266	OEM	BA6247N	OEM	BAR12-2	OEM	BAT28H	OEM	BAV205	0994	BAW24	0133
BA479G	OEM	BA2435	OEM	BA6251	OEM	BAR12-3	OEM	BAT29	OEM	BAV206	2065	BAW25	0133
BA479S	OEM	BA3112	OEM	BA6256	OEM	BAR12-5	OEM	BAT31	OEM	BAV207	2070	BAW26	0133
BA481	2727	BA3302	OEM	BA6301	OEM	BAR13-1	OEM	BAT38	OEM	BAV208	2077	BAW27	0124
BA482	0163	BA3304	OEM	BA6302	OEM	BAR13-2	OEM	BAT39	OEM	BAV209	2077	BAW28	0080
BA483	0163	BA3304F	OEM	BA6302A	OEM	BAR13-3	OEM	BAT39A	OEM	BAV215	0994	BAW29	OEM
BA484	0163	BA3306	OEM	BA6303	OEM	BAR13-5	OEM	BAT41	OEM	BAV216	2065	BAW31	OEM
BA501	2737	BA3308	OEM	BA6303F	OEM	BAR14-1	OEM	BAT42	OEM	BAV217	2070	BAW32A	0133
BA501A	2737	BA3310N	OEM	BA6304	2409	BAR14-2	OEM	BAT43	OEM	BAV218	2077	BAW32B	0133
BA511	2746	BA3312N	OEM	BA6304A	2409	BAR14-3	OEM	BAT45	OEM	BAV219	2077	BAW32C	0080
BA511A	2746	BA3402	OEM	BA6304AL	2409	BAR14-5	OEM	BAT46	OEM	BAV225	0994	BAW32D	1325
BA514	2748	BA3404F	OEM	BA6304LA	OEM	BAR15-1	OEM	BAT47	OEM	BAV226	2065	BAW32E	1325
BA514A	2748	BA3404L	OEM	BA6305	OEM	BAR15-2	OEM	BAT48	OEM	BAV227	2070	BAW33	OEM
BA515	OEM	BA3416BL	OEM	BA6320L	OEM	BAR15-3	OEM	BAT49	OEM	BAV228	2077	BAW36	OEM
BA517	0124	BA3513	OEM	BA6321	OEM	BAR15-5	OEM	BAT50	OEM	BAV229	2077	BAW43	4919
BA518	OEM	BA3516	OEM	BA6328	OEM	BAR16-1	OEM	BAT51	OEM	BAV305	0994	BAW45	0133
BA521	2754	BA3702	OEM	BA6334	OEM	BAR16-2	OEM	BAT52	OEM	BAV306	2065	BAW46	OEM
BA521A	2754	BA3704	5070	BA6340	OEM	BAR16-3	OEM	BAT54	OEM	BAV307	2070	BAW47	OEM
BA521AX	2754	BA3707	OEM	BA6352S	OEM	BAR16-5	OEM	BAT59	OEM	BAV308	2077	BAW48	OEM
BA526	2760	BA3812L	OEM	BA6360	OEM	BAR18	OEM	BAT74	OEM	BAV309	2077	BAW49	OEM
BA527	2761	BA3822LS	OEM	BA6405	OEM	BAR19	OEM	BAT81	4858	BAV315	0994	BAW50	OEM
BA532	2767	BA3824LS	OEM	BA6418	OEM	BAR28	OEM	BAT82	4859	BAV316	2065	BAW51	OEM
BA532S	2767	BA4110	0460	BA6418N	OEM	BAR35	OEM	BAT83	4859	BAV317	2070	BAW52	OEM
BA534	OEM	BA4111	OEM	BA6431S	OEM	BAR42	OEM	BAT85	0730	BAV318	2077	BAW53	0133
BA535	OEM	BA4114	OEM	BA6455FS	OEM	BAR43	OEM	BAT86	4859	BAV319	2077	BAW54	OEM
BA536	2772	BA4210	OEM	BA6459P1	OEM	BAR43A	OEM	BAV10	OEM	BAV325	0994	BAW55	0124
BA546	2781	BA4220	3764	BA6459PI	OEM	BAR43C	OEM	BAV11	OEM	BAV326	2065	BAW56	0897
BA547	OEM	BA4224	OEM	BA6562	OEM	BAR43S	OEM	BAV12	OEM	BAV327	2070	BAW56G	OEM
BA579A	OEM	BA4232	OEM	BA6565A	OEM	BAR74	OEM	BAV13	OEM	BAV328	2077	BAW56GT	OEM
BA579C	OEM	BA4232AL	OEM	BA6581K	OEM	BAR99	OEM	BAV14	OEM	BAV329	2077	BAW57	OEM
BA579S	OEM	BA4233AL	OEM	BA6590S	OEM	BAR223-10	OEM	BAV15	OEM	BAV405	0197	BAW58	OEM
BA612	OEM	BA4236L	OEM	BA6805	OEM	BAR223-15	OEM	BAV16	OEM	BAV406	0200	BAW59	0133
BA614	2838	BA4403	OEM	BA6822S	OEM	BAR223-20	OEM	BAV17	0124	BAV407	0204	BAW60	OEM
BA614A	2838	BA4404	OEM	BA6993	0624	BAR223-25	OEM	BAV18	0124	BAV408	0206	BAW62	0124
BA616	OEM	BA4410	OEM	BA7001	OEM	BAR223-30	OEM	BAV19	0124	BAV409	0206	BAW63	OEM
BA618	OEM	BA4412	OEM	BA7004	OEM	BAR223-35	OEM	BAV20	0133	BAV415	0197	BAW63A	0133
BA631	OEM	BA4424N	OEM	BA7007	OEM	BAR223-40	OEM	BAV21	0133	BAV416	0200	BAW63B	0133
BA634	OEM	BA4558	0356	BA7021	OEM	BAR223-45	OEM	BAV22	OEM	BAV417	0204	BAW64	OEM
BA656	OEM	BA4558D	OEM	BA7050L	OEM	BAR223-50	OEM	BAV22R	OEM	BAV418	0206	BAW65	OEM
BA658	OEM	BA4558DX	0356	BA7055LS	OEM	BAR223-55	OEM	BAV23	OEM	BAV419	0206	BAW66	OEM
BA664	OEM	BA4558F	5433	BA7058LS	OEM	BAR223-60	OEM	BAV24	OEM	BAV425	0197	BAW67	OEM
BA668	OEM	BA4560F	OEM	BA7101	OEM	BAR223-65	OEM	BAV25	OEM	BAV426	0200	BAW68	OEM
BA668A	OEM	BA4561	OEM	BA7103	OEM	BAR223-70	OEM	BAV26	OEM	BAV427	0204	BAW69	OEM
BA679	OEM	BA5101	OEM	BA7116	OEM	BAS11	0023	BAV27	OEM	BAV428	0206	BAW70	OEM
BA681A	OEM	BA5102	2094	BA7125L	OEM	BAS15	0124	BAV28	OEM	BAV429	0206	BAW75	0133

If replacement code is OEM, contact original manufacturer for replacement.

283

DEVICE TYPE	REPL CODE
BAW76	0124
BAW77	OEM
BAW78A	OEM
BAW78B	OEM
BAW78C	OEM
BAW78D	OEM
BAW79A	OEM
BAW79B	OEM
BAW79C	OEM
BAW79D	OEM
BAW90	OEM
BAW91	OEM
BAW92	OEM
BAW93	OEM
BAW95C	OEM
BAW95D	OEM
BAW95E	OEM
BAW95F	OEM
BAW95G	OEM
BAW96	OEM
BAW99	0133
BAW100	OEM
BAW101	OEM
BAX11	OEM
BAX11II0	OEM
BAX11IIU	OEM
BAX12	0015
BAX12A	OEM
BAX-13	0124
BAX13	0124
BAX13A	OEM
BAX14	1082
BAX14A	OEM
BAX15	OEM
BAX-16	0133
BAX16	0133
BAX16A	OEM
BAX17	OEM
BAX17A	OEM
BAX18	1082
BAX18A	0080
BAX20	OEM
BAX21	OEM
BAX25	OEM
BAX26	OEM
BAX27	OEM
BAX28	0133
BAX30	0133
BAX32	OEM
BAX33	OEM
BAX34	OEM
BAX35	OEM
BAX36	OEM
BAX37	OEM
BAX38	OEM
BAX39	OEM
BAX40	OEM
BAX41	OEM
BAX42	OEM
BAX43	OEM
BAX44	OEM
BAX45	OEM
BAX46	OEM
BAX47	OEM
BAX48	OEM
BAX49	OEM
BAX50	OEM
BAX51	OEM
BAX52	OEM
BAX53	OEM
BAX54	OEM
BAX55	OEM
BAX56	OEM
BAX57	OEM
BAX58	OEM
BAX59	OEM
BAX60	OEM
BAX61	OEM
BAX62	OEM
BAX63	OEM
BAX64	OEM
BAX65	OEM
BAX66	OEM
BAX67	OEM
BAX68	OEM
BAX69	OEM
BAX70	OEM
BAX71	OEM
BAX72	OEM
BAX73	OEM
BAX74	0133
BAX78	OEM
BAX79C16	0440
BAX79C18	0371
BAX79C20	0695
BAX79C22	0700
BAX79C24	0489
BAX79C27	0450
BAX79C27A	0436
BAX81	OEM
BAX82	OEM
BAX83	OEM
BAX84	OEM
BAX85	OEM
BAX86A	OEM
BAX86B	OEM
BAX87	0133
BAX88	OEM
BAX88TF11	0133

DEVICE TYPE	REPL CODE
BAX89A	0133
BAX89B	OEM
BAX90A	OEM
BAX90B	OEM
BAX91A	OEM
BAX91B	OEM
BAX91C	OEM
BAX91C/TF102	0124
BAX92	OEM
BAX93	OEM
BAX94	OEM
BAX94C62	0778
BAX95TF600	0124
BAX96C2V7	0755
BAX96C3V3	0296
BAY15	0071
BAY16	0071
BAY17	0133
BAY18	0133
BAY19	0133
BAY20	0133
BAY21	0790
BAY23	0071
BAY24	OEM
BAY25	OEM
BAY26	OEM
BAY31	0133
BAY35	OEM
BAY36	0133
BAY38	0124
BAY41	0133
BAY42	0133
BAY43	0133
BAY44	1325
BAY45	0604
BAY46	0790
BAY52	0133
BAY60	0133
BAY61	0133
BAY63	0133
BAY64	0015
BAY66	OEM
BAY67	0133
BAY68	0133
BAY69	0133
BAY71	4953
BAY72	0133
BAY73	0133
BAY74	0392
BAY78	OEM
BAY79	OEM
BAY79III0	OEM
BAY79IIIU	OEM
BAY79IV0	OEM
BAY79IVU	OEM
BAY79V	OEM
BAY80	0182
BAY82	4953
BAY84	OEM
BAY85	OEM
BAY85S	OEM
BAY86	0015
BAY87	0015
BAY88	0581
BAY89	0581
BAY90	0071
BAY91	OEM
BAY91A	OEM
BAY92	0271
BAY93	0124
BAY94	OEM
BAY95	OEM
BAY96	OEM
BB	OEM
BB1	0102
BB1A	0015
BB-2	0015
BB2	0102
BB2A	0023
BB2A184	0015
BB2L	0023
BB2T	0023
BB3	OEM
BB3I	0023
BB3K	0023
BB-4	0023
BB4	0102
BB4-FC	0023
BB4A	OEM
BB4B	OEM
BB4C	5226
BB4T	0023
BB5	OEM
BB5A	OEM
BB5B	OEM
BB5C	OEM
BB-6	0023
BB6	0102
BB6S	0102
BB-8	0023
BB8	0102
BB-10	0102
BB10	0182
BB-10BB-10S	OEM
BB-10S	0102
BB10T	0102
BB12	OEM
BB14	OEM
BB18	OEM

DEVICE TYPE	REPL CODE
BB22	0030
BB-42-1B	2453
BB-42-2B	OEM
BB71	0016
BB100	1325
BB100GBE	OEM
BB100GRO	OEM
BB100GVE	OEM
BB101	OEM
BB102	OEM
BB102/15	OEM
BB102/16	OEM
BB102/17	OEM
BB102/18	OEM
BB102/19	OEM
BB102/20	OEM
BB103	0030
BB103B	OEM
BB103G	OEM
BB104	0030
BB104B	OEM
BB104G	OEM
BB105	0005
BB-105A	0030
BB105A	0005
BB105B	1023
BB105G	1023
BB106	0623
BB107	0015
BB-109	0015
BB109	1023
BB109G	0030
BB110	OEM
BB110B	OEM
BB110G	OEM
BB112	3142
BB113	OEM
BB117	0015
BB119	OEM
BB121	0715
BB121A	0715
BB121B	1023
BB122	0715
BB122GL	OEM
BB122S	OEM
BB125	0623
BB127	0015
BB130	OEM
BB138	0623
BB139	0030
BB141	OEM
BB141A	OEM
BB141B	OEM
BB142	0715
BB204	OEM
BB204B	2060
BB204G	2060
BB205A	OEM
BB205B	OEM
BB205G	0005
BB209	OEM
BB212	OEM
BB215	OEM
BB219	OEM
BB221	1023
BB222	OEM
BB229	OEM
BB304	OEM
BB304I	OEM
BB304II	OEM
BB304III	OEM
BB304IV	OEM
BB304V	OEM
BB305B	OEM
BB305G	OEM
BB312	OEM
BB313	OEM
BB314	OEM
BB329	OEM
BB329A	OEM
BB404	OEM
BB404A	OEM
BB404B	OEM
BB404C	OEM
BB404D	OEM
BB404E	OEM
BB405B	OEM
BB405G	OEM
BB406	OEM
BB409	OEM
BB417	OEM
BB503	OEM
BB504	OEM
BB505B	OEM
BB505G	OEM
BB510	OEM
BB515B	OEM
BB515G	OEM
BB521	OEM
BB523	OEM
BB529	OEM
BB531	OEM
BB601	OEM
BB609	OEM
BB609A	OEM
BB609B	OEM
BB610	OEM
BB619A	OEM
BB619B	OEM

DEVICE TYPE	REPL CODE
BB620	OEM
BB623	OEM
BB629	OEM
BB631	OEM
BB721	OEM
BB723	OEM
BB729	OEM
BB731	OEM
BB801	OEM
BB804	OEM
BB809	OEM
BB814	OEM
BB909A	OEM
BB909B	OEM
BBCC106	OEM
BBCC106B-1	OEM
BBCC106D-1	OEM
BBCC106E-1	OEM
BBCC106M-1	OEM
BBCS	OEM
BBIA	0015
BBY10	OEM
BBY11	OEM
BBY12	OEM
BBY13	OEM
BBY14	OEM
BBY15	OEM
BBY16	OEM
BBY17	0549
BBY18	OEM
BBY19	OEM
BBY20	OEM
BBY21	OEM
BBY22	OEM
BBY24	OEM
BBY24S1	OEM
BBY25	OEM
BBY25S1	OEM
BBY26	OEM
BBY26S1	OEM
BBY27	OEM
BBY27S1	OEM
BBY28	OEM
BBY29	OEM
BBY30	OEM
BBY31	0133
BBY32CB	OEM
BBY32DA	OEM
BBY32DB	OEM
BBY32EA	OEM
BBY32FA	OEM
BBY33DA2	OEM
BBY34A	OEM
BBY34B	OEM
BBY34C	OEM
BBY34D	OEM
BBY35F	OEM
BBY36	OEM
BBY37	OEM
BBY38	OEM
BBY39	OEM
BBY40	0133
BC10CM-BL	OEM
BC17LB-1	0037
BC45B	0079
BC-71	0016
BC71	0016
BC100	0233
BC103	0086
BC103C	0086
BC107	0016
BC107A	0016
BC107AP	0079
BC107B	0016
BC107BP	0079
BC108	0016
BC108A	0016
BC108AP	0079
BC-108B	0016
BC108B	0016
BC108BP	0079
BC108C	0016
BC108CP	0079
BC109	0016
BC-109B	0016
BC109B	0016
BC109BP	0079
BC109C	0016
BC109CP	0079
BC110	0016
BC111	0144
BC112	0144
BC113	0016
BC113A	OEM
BC114	0016
BC114A	OEM
BC114TR	0016
BC115	0016
BC116	0037
BC116A	0037
BC117	0086
BC118	0016
BC-119	0086
BC119	0086
BC120	0086
BC121	0127
BC122	0127
BC123	0127
BC125	0016

DEVICE TYPE	REPL CODE
BC125A	0016
BC125B	0016
BC126	0037
BC126A	0150
BC127	0111
BC128	0111
BC129	0016
BC129A	0079
BC129B	0079
BC130	0016
BC130A	0079
BC130B	0079
BC131	0016
BC131B	0079
BC132	0016
BC132A	0079
BC134	0016
BC135	0016
BC135A	0007
BC136	0016
BC137	0037
BC-138	0086
BC138	0086
BC139	0126
BC139A	0855
BC-140	0086
BC140	0086
BC140-06	0320
BC140-6	0086
BC140-10	0086
BC140-16	0086
BC140-25	0086
BC-140A	0086
BC140A	0086
BC-140B	0086
BC140B	0086
BC-140C	0086
BC140C	0086
BC-140D	0086
BC140D	0086
BC-141	0086
BC141	0086
BC141-06	0086
BC141-6	0086
BC141-10	0086
BC141-16	0086
BC141-25	0086
BC141A	OEM
BC141B	OEM
BC141C	OEM
BC-142	0086
BC142	0086
BC142-10	0086
BC142-16	0086
BC143	0126
BC144	0086
BC145	1471
BC146	0111
BC146-01	OEM
BC146-02	OEM
BC146-03	OEM
BC146G	0079
BC146R	0079
BC146Y	0079
BC147	0016
BC147A	0016
BC147B	0016
BC148	0016
BC-148A	0016
BC148A	0016
BC-148B	0016
BC148B	0016
BC-148C	0016
BC148C	0016
BC149	0016
BC149A	0016
BC149B	0016
BC149C	0016
BC149G	0016
BC150	0079
BC151	0079
BC152	0079
BC153	0688
BC154	0688
BC155	0127
BC155A	0144
BC155B	0079
BC155C	0111
BC156	0127
BC156A	0144
BC156B	0079
BC156C	0111
BC157	0037
BC157A	0037
BC157B	0037
BC157V1	OEM
BC157VI	0855
BC158	0037
BC158-1	0037
BC158A	0037
BC158A-1	0037
BC158B	0037
BC158C	0688
BC158V1	OEM
BC158VI	0855
BC159	0037
BC159A	0037
BC159B	0037
BC159C	0688

DEVICE TYPE	REPL CODE
BC160	0126
BC160-06	0527
BC160-6	0126
BC160-10	0126
BC160-16	0126
BC160-25	0126
BC160A	OEM
BC160B	OEM
BC160C	OEM
BC161	0126
BC161-06	0786
BC161-6	0126
BC161-10	0126
BC161-16	0126
BC161-25	0126
BC161A	OEM
BC161B	OEM
BC161C	OEM
BC167	0079
BC-167-B	0079
BC167A	0155
BC167B	0155
BC168	0079
BC168A	0155
BC168B	0155
BC168C	0155
BC169	0079
BC-169-C	0079
BC169A	0079
BC-169B	0079
BC169B	0079
BC-169C	0079
BC169C	0079
BC170	0111
BC170A	0111
BC170B	0111
BC170C	0111
BC171	0079
BC171A	0079
BC171B	0079
BC172	0079
BC172A	0079
BC172B	0079
BC172C	0079
BC173	0111
BC173,B	0086
BC173A	0111
BC173B	0111
BC173C	0111
BC174	0086
BC174A	0086
BC174B	0086
BC175	0079
BC177	0688
BC177-6	OEM
BC177A	0688
BC177B	0688
BC177C	OEM
BC177PA	OEM
BC177PAK	OEM
BC177PAL	OEM
BC177PAM	OEM
BC177PB	OEM
BC177PBK	OEM
BC177PBL	OEM
BC177PBM	OEM
BC177V	0037
BC177V1	0037
BC177VI	0150
BC178	0688
BC178A	0688
BC178B	0688
BC178C	0688
BC178D	0037
BC178P	OEM
BC178PA	OEM
BC178PAK	OEM
BC178PAL	OEM
BC178PAM	OEM
BC178PB	OEM
BC178PBK	OEM
BC178PBL	OEM
BC178PBM	OEM
BC178PC	OEM
BC178PCK	OEM
BC178PCL	OEM
BC178PCM	OEM
BC178V	0037
BC178V-1	0037
BC178V1	0037
BC178VI	0150
BC179	0688
BC179A	0688
BC179B	0688
BC179C	0688
BC179PB	OEM
BC179PBK	OEM
BC179PBL	OEM
BC179PBM	OEM
BC179PC	OEM
BC179PCK	OEM
BC179PCL	OEM
BC179PCM	OEM
BC179VI	OEM
BC180	0016
BC180B	0016
BC181	0037
BC181A	0037
BC182	0079

DEVICE TYPE	REPL CODE
BC182A	0155
BC182AP	0079
BC182B	0079
BC182BP	0079
BC182K	0111
BC182KA	0016
BC182KB	0016
BC182L	0155
BC182LA	0155
BC182P	0079
BC183	0079
BC183A	0079
BC183AP	0079
BC183B	0079
BC183BP	0079
BC183C	2833
BC183CP	OEM
BC183K	0111
BC183KA	0111
BC183KB	0016
BC183KC	0016
BC183L	0111
BC183LA	0155
BC183LB	0079
BC183P	0079
BC184	0079
BC184B	0079
BC184BP	0079
BC184C	0079
BC184CP	0079
BC184K	0016
BC184KB	0016
BC184KC	0016
BC184L	0111
BC184P	0079
BC185	0016
BC186	0037
BC187	0037
BC188	0127
BC189	0127
BC190	0079
BC190A	0590
BC190B	0016
BC192	0037
BC194	0144
BC194B	0144
BC195	0144
BC195CD	0144
BC196	0037
BC196A	0037
BC196B	0037
BC196V1	0037
BC196VI	0855
BC197	0016
BC197A	0016
BC197B	0016
BC198	0016
BC198A	0079
BC198B	0111
BC198C	0079
BC199	0016
BC199B	0111
BC199C	0079
BC200	0037
BC200-01	OEM
BC200-02	OEM
BC200-03	OEM
BC200G	0688
BC200R	0037
BC200Y	0037
BC201	0037
BC202	0037
BC203	0037
BC204	0688
BC204-6	0037
BC204A	0688
BC204B	0688
BC204V	0037
BC204V1	0037
BC204VI	0150
BC205	0037
BC205A	0037
BC205B	0688
BC205C	0688
BC205V	0037
BC205V1	0037
BC205VI	0037
BC206	0688
BC206A	0037
BC206B	0688
BC206C	0688
BC-207	0015
BC207	0079
BC207A	0079
BC207B	0079
BC208	0079
BC208A	0079
BC208B	0079
BC208C	0079
BC209	0079
BC209B	0079
BC209C	0079
BC210	0079
BC211	0086
BC211-6	OEM
BC211-10	OEM
BC211-16	OEM
BC211A	0086
BC211A-6	OEM

If replacement code is OEM, contact original manufacturer for replacement.

DEVICE TYPE	REPL CODE
BC211A-10	OEM
BC211A-16	OEM
BC212	0037
BC212A	0037
BC212AP	0037
BC212B	0037
BC212BP	0037
BC212K	0037
BC212KA	0037
BC212KB	0037
BC212L	0037
BC212LA	0037
BC212LB	0037
BC212P	0037
BC212V1	0037
BC212VI	0037
BC213	0037
BC213A	0037
BC213AP	0037
BC213B	0037
BC213BP	0037
BC213C	0527
BC213CP	OEM
BC213K	0037
BC213KA	0037
BC213KB	0037
BC213KC	0037
BC213L	0037
BC213LA	0037
BC213LB	0037
BC213LC	0037
BC213P	0037
BC214	0037
BC214A	0037
BC214B	0037
BC214BP	0037
BC214C	0527
BC214CP	0037
BC214K	0037
BC214KA	0037
BC214KB	0037
BC214KC	0037
BC214L	0037
BC214LA	0037
BC214LB	0037
BC214LC	0037
BC214P	0037
BC215	OEM
BC215A	0855
BC215B	0855
BC216	0086
BC216A	0086
BC216B	0086
BC220	0016
BC221	0037
BC222	0016
BC223	0191
BC223A	0079
BC223B	0079
BC224	0688
BC225	0688
BC226	0590
BC231	OEM
BC231A	0006
BC231B	0006
BC231M	0126
BC232	OEM
BC232A	0155
BC232B	0155
BC232M	0086
BC233A	0016
BC236	0855
BC237	0079
BC237(PHIN)	0111
BC237-5	OEM
BC237-18	0079
BC237A	0079
BC237A5	0079
BC237A18	0079
BC237B	0079
BC237B5	0079
BC237B18	0079
BC237C	2833
BC237C5	2833
BC237C18	2833
BC237PA	OEM
BC237PAK	OEM
BC237PAL	OEM
BC237PAM	OEM
BC237PB	OEM
BC237PBK	OEM
BC237PBL	OEM
BC237PBM	OEM
BC238	0079
BC238(PHIN)	0111
BC238-5	0079
BC238-16	0037
BC238-18	0079
BC238A	0079
BC238A5	0079
BC238A18	0079
BC238B	0079
BC238B5	0079
BC238B18	0079
BC238C	0111
BC238C5	0079
BC238C18	0079
BC238PA	OEM
BC238PAK	OEM

DEVICE TYPE	REPL CODE
BC238PAL	OEM
BC238PAM	OEM
BC238PB	OEM
BC238PBK	OEM
BC238PBL	OEM
BC238PBM	OEM
BC238PC	OEM
BC238PCK	OEM
BC238PCL	OEM
BC238PCM	OEM
BC239	0079
BC239(PHIN)	0111
BC239-5	0079
BC239-18	0079
BC239A	0111
BC239B	0111
BC239B5	0079
BC239B18	0079
BC239C	0079
BC239C5	2833
BC239C18	2833
BC239PB	OEM
BC239PBK	OEM
BC239PBL	OEM
BC239PBM	OEM
BC239PC	OEM
BC239PCK	OEM
BC239PCL	OEM
BC239PCM	OEM
BC250	0037
BC250A	0037
BC250B	0037
BC250C	0037
BC251	0037
BC251A	0037
BC251B	0037
BC251C	0037
BC252	0037
BC252A	0037
BC252B	0037
BC252C	0037
BC253	0037
BC253A	0037
BC253B	0037
BC253C	0037
BC254	0086
BC255	0086
BC256	0037
BC256A	0037
BC256B	0037
BC257	0037
BC257A	1233
BC257B	1233
BC257VI	0037
BC258	0037
BC258A	1233
BC258B	1233
BC258C	0688
BC258VI	0037
BC259	0037
BC259A	1233
BC259B	1233
BC259C	3477
BC260	0037
BC260A	0037
BC260B	0037
BC260C	0037
BC-261	0037
BC261	0037
BC261A	0037
BC261B	0037
BC261C	0037
BC262	0037
BC262A	0037
BC262B	0037
BC262C	0037
BC263	0037
BC263A	0037
BC263B	0037
BC263C	0037
BC264	2861
BC264A	2922
BC264B	0321
BC264C	0321
BC264D	OEM
BC264L	OEM
BC264LA	OEM
BC264LB	OEM
BC264LC	OEM
BC264LD	OEM
BC266	0037
BC266A	0037
BC266B	0037
BC267	0016
BC268	0016
BC269	0016
BC270	0016
BC271	0007
BC272	OEM
BC280	0016
BC280A	0016
BC280B	0016
BC280C	0016
BC281	0037
BC281A	0037
BC281B	0037
BC281C	0037
BC282	0079
BC283	0037

DEVICE TYPE	REPL CODE
BC284	0079
BC284A	0079
BC284B	0079
BC285	0016
BC286	0086
BC287	0126
BC288	0086
BC289	0016
BC289A	0016
BC289B	0016
BC290	0016
BC290B	0016
BC290C	0016
BC291	0037
BC291A	0037
BC291D	0037
BC292	0037
BC292A	0037
BC292B	OEM
BC292D	0037
BC294	0126
BC295	0144
BC297	0037
BC297-7	0037
BC298	0037
BC300	0617
BC300-4	0233
BC300-5	0233
BC300-6	0233
BC301	0086
BC301-4	0086
BC301-5	0086
BC301-6	0086
BC302-4	0086
BC302-5	0086
BC302-6	0086
BC303	0126
BC303-4	0126
BC303-5	0126
BC303-6	0855
BC304	0126
BC304-4	0786
BC304-5	0786
BC304-6	0786
BC-307	0015
BC307	0037
BC307(ALGG)	0037
BC307(PHIN)	0037
BC307-5	0037
BC307-18	0037
BC307A	0037
BC307A5	OEM
BC307A18	OEM
BC307B	0037
BC307B5	OEM
BC307B18	OEM
BC307C	0037
BC307PA	OEM
BC307PAK	OEM
BC307PAL	OEM
BC307PAM	OEM
BC307PB	OEM
BC307PBK	OEM
BC307PBL	OEM
BC307PBM	OEM
BC307PC	OEM
BC307V1	0037
BC307VI	0037
BC307VI5	0037
BC307VI18	OEM
BC307VII8	0037
BC308	0037
BC308(ALGG)	0006
BC308(SIEG)	3477
BC308-5	0037
BC308-18	0037
BC308A	0037
BC308A5	OEM
BC308A18	OEM
BC308B	0037
BC308B5	OEM
BC308B18	OEM
BC308C	0037
BC308PA	OEM
BC308PAK	OEM
BC308PAL	OEM
BC308PAM	OEM
BC308PB	OEM
BC308PBK	OEM
BC308PBL	OEM
BC308PBM	OEM
BC308PC	OEM
BC308PCK	OEM
BC308PCL	OEM
BC308PCM	OEM
BC308V1	0037
BC308VI	0855
BC308VI5	0037
BC308VI18	OEM
BC308VII8	0037
BC309	0037
BC309(ALGG)	0037
BC309(SIEG)	0037
BC309-5	0037
BC309-18	0037
BC309A	0037
BC309A5	OEM
BC309A18	OEM
BC309B	0037

DEVICE TYPE	REPL CODE
BC309B5	OEM
BC309B18	OEM
BC309C	0037
BC309PB	OEM
BC309PBK	OEM
BC309PBL	OEM
BC309PBM	OEM
BC309PC	OEM
BC309PCK	OEM
BC309PCL	OEM
BC309PCM	OEM
BC309VI	OEM
BC310	0086
BC311	0126
BC312	0086
BC313	0126
BC313-6	OEM
BC313-10	OEM
BC313-16	OEM
BC313A	0126
BC313A-6	OEM
BC313A-10	OEM
BC313A-16	OEM
BC315	0037
BC315L	OEM
BC317	0079
BC317A	0079
BC317B	0079
BC318	0079
BC318A	0079
BC318B	0079
BC318C	0079
BC319	0079
BC319B	0079
BC319C	0079
BC320	0037
BC320A	0688
BC320B	OEM
BC321	0688
BC321A	0688
BC321B	0688
BC322	0688
BC322B	0688
BC322C	0688
BC323	0617
BC324	0086
BC325	0037
BC325A	0037
BC326	0037
BC326A	0037
BC327	0037
BC327(25)	0037
BC327-01	OEM
BC327-5	0037
BC327-10	OEM
BC327-16	0431
BC327-18	0037
BC327-25	0431
BC327A	OEM
BC327A(16)	0786
BC327A16	OEM
BC327A25	OEM
BC327AP	0037
BC327BP	OEM
BC327CP	0037
BC328	0006
BC328/B338	OEM
BC328-01	OEM
BC328-5	0037
BC328-10	OEM
BC328-16	0431
BC328-18	0037
BC328-25	0431
BC328-40	OEM
BC328AP	0037
BC328BP	0037
BC328C	0037
BC328CP	0037
BC329B	OEM
BC330	OEM
BC330B	OEM
BC330C	OEM
BC331A	OEM
BC331B	OEM
BC331C	OEM
BC332	OEM
BC332A	OEM
BC332B	OEM
BC332C	OEM
BC333	OEM
BC334	OEM
BC335	OEM
BC336	0018
BC337	0546
BC337(16)	0018
BC337(25)	0018
BC337/BC327	OEM
BC337-01	OEM
BC337-5	0079
BC337-10	OEM
BC337-16	0079
BC337-16-5	OEM
BC337-16-18	OEM
BC337-18	0079
BC-337-25	OEM
BC337-25	0079
BC337-25-5	OEM
BC337-25-18	OEM
BC337-40	0111

DEVICE TYPE	REPL CODE
BC337A	OEM
BC337A-16	OEM
BC337A-25	OEM
BC337AP	0079
BC337BP	0079
BC337CP	0079
BC338	0079
BC338-01	OEM
BC338-5	0079
BC338-10	OEM
BC338-16	0079
BC338-16-5	OEM
BC338-16-18	OEM
BC338-18	OEM
BC338-20	OEM
BC338-25	0079
BC338-25-5	OEM
BC338-25-28	OEM
BC338-40	0079
BC338AP	OEM
BC338BP	OEM
BC338CP	OEM
BC340	OEM
BC340-06	0018
BC340-6	0086
BC340-10	0086
BC340-16	0086
BC341	OEM
BC341-06	0086
BC341-6	0086
BC341-10	0086
BC342	OEM
BC343	OEM
BC344	OEM
BC345	OEM
BC347	OEM
BC347A	OEM
BC347B	OEM
BC347L	OEM
BC348	OEM
BC348A	OEM
BC348B	OEM
BC348L	OEM
BC349	OEM
BC349A	OEM
BC349B	OEM
BC349L	OEM
BC350	0037
BC350A	0037
BC350B	0037
BC350L	0037
BC351	0037
BC351A	0037
BC351B	0037
BC351L	0037
BC352	0037
BC352A	0037
BC352B	0037
BC352L	0037
BC354	OEM
BC355	OEM
BC355A	OEM
BC355B	OEM
BC355C	OEM
BC357	OEM
BC358	OEM
BC358C	OEM
BC358VI	OEM
BC360	OEM
BC360-06	0527
BC360-6	0126
BC360-10	0126
BC360-16	0126
BC361	OEM
BC361-06	0786
BC361-6	0126
BC361-10	0126
BC362	OEM
BC363	OEM
BC364	OEM
BC365	0546
BC366	OEM
BC367	OEM
BC368	0320
BC368-25	0434
BC369	0527
BC369J	OEM
BC370	0786
BC370VI	0126
BC371	OEM
BC372C	OEM
BC375	3654
BC376	3655
BC377	0016
BC378	0016
BC381	0037
BC382	0016
BC382B	0079
BC382C	0079
BC382L	OEM
BC383	0016
BC383B	0079
BC383C	0016
BC383L	OEM
BC384	0016
BC384B	0079
BC384C	0111
BC384L	OEM
BC385	OEM

DEVICE TYPE	REPL CODE
BC385A	0111
BC385B	0111
BC386	OEM
BC386A	0111
BC386B	0111
BC387	OEM
BC388	OEM
BC389	OEM
BC390	OEM
BC391	OEM
BC393	0338
BC394	0233
BC395	0855
BC396	0126
BC400	0037
BC404	0037
BC404A	0126
BC404V1	0126
BC404VI	0037
BC405	0037
BC405A	0037
BC405B	0037
BC406	0786
BC406B	0037
BC407	0016
BC407A	0016
BC407B	0076
BC408	0016
BC408A	0111
BC408B	0111
BC408C	0111
BC409	0016
BC409B	0079
BC409C	0079
BC411	OEM
BC412	0693
BC413	0079
BC413B	0079
BC413BP	0079
BC413C	0079
BC414	0016
BC414B	0079
BC414BP	0079
BC414C	0079
BC414CP	2833
BC415	0150
BC415-6	0037
BC415A	0037
BC415AP	0037
BC415B	0037
BC415BP	0037
BC415C	0688
BC415CP	OEM
BC416	0150
BC416-6	0037
BC416A	0037
BC416AP	0037
BC416B	0037
BC416BP	0037
BC416C	0688
BC416CP	0688
BC417	0037
BC418	0037
BC418A	0037
BC418B	0527
BC419	0037
BC419A	0037
BC419B	0527
BC420VI	0338
BC424	OEM
BC425	OEM
BC426	OEM
BC427	OEM
BC429	0086
BC430	0546
BC431	0086
BC431B	0079
BC432	0037
BC437A	OEM
BC437B	OEM
BC438A	OEM
BC438B	OEM
BC438C	OEM
BC440	0617
BC441	0617
BC442	0127
BC445	0037
BC445-5	0037
BC445-18	0037
BC446	0037
BC446-5	0037
BC446-18	0037
BC447	0037
BC447-5	0037
BC447-18	0037
BC448	OEM
BC448-5	0037
BC448-18	OEM
BC449	0079
BC449-5	0037
BC449-18	0855
BC450	0472
BC450-5	0472
BC450-18	0037
BC451	OEM
BC452	0079
BC453	OEM
BC454	OEM
BC455	0079

DEVICE TYPE	REPL CODE
BC456	0224
BC460	0886
BC461	0886
BC461-4	0126
BC461-5	0126
BC461-6	0126
BC467A	OEM
BC467B	OEM
BC468A	OEM
BC468B	OEM
BC468C	OEM
BC469B	OEM
BC469C	OEM
BC477	0126
BC477A	0126
BC477V1	0126
BC477VI	0855
BC478	0037
BC478A	0037
BC478B	0037
BC479	0037
BC479B	0037
BC485	0037
BC485-5	0037
BC485-18	0037
BC485A	0037
BC485A5	0037
BC485A18	0037
BC485B	0037
BC485B5	0037
BC485B18	0037
BC485L	0037
BC485L5	0037
BC485L18	0037
BC486	0037
BC486-5	0037
BC486-18	0037
BC486A	0037
BC486A5	0037
BC486A18	0037
BC486B	0037
BC486B5	0037
BC486L	0037
BC486L5	0037
BC487	0037
BC487-5	0037
BC487-18	0037
BC487A	0037
BC487A5	0037
BC487A18	0037
BC487B	0037
BC487B5	0037
BC487B18	0037
BC487L	0037
BC487L5	0037
BC487L18	0037
BC488	0037
BC488-5	0037
BC488-18	0037
BC488A	0037
BC488A5	0037
BC488A18	0037
BC488B	0037
BC488B5	0037
BC488B18	0037
BC488L	0037
BC488L5	0037
BC488L18	0037
BC489	0037
BC489-5	0037
BC489-18	0037
BC489A	0037
BC489A5	0037
BC489A18	0037
BC489B	0037
BC489B5	0037
BC489B18	0037
BC489L	0037
BC489L5	0037
BC489L18	0037
BC490	0037
BC490-5	0037
BC490-18	0037
BC490A	0037
BC490A5	0037
BC490A18	0037
BC490B	OEM
BC490B5	0037
BC490B18	0037
BC490L	0037
BC490L5	0037
BC490L18	0037
BC507A	0016
BC507B	0016
BC508	0590
BC508A	0016
BC508B	0016
BC508C	0016
BC509	0590
BC509B	0016
BC509C	0016
BC510	0590
BC510B	0016
BC510C	0127
BC512	0037
BC512A	0037
BC512B	0786
BC513	0037
BC513A	0037

If replacement code is OEM, contact original manufacturer for replacement.
285

DEVICE TYPE	REPL CODE
BC513B	0786
BC513C	0527
BC514	0786
BC514A	0037
BC514B	0786
BC514C	0527
BC516	OEM
BC517	OEM
BC517-P	OEM
BC517W	OEM
BC526	OEM
BC527	0126
BC528	0126
BC530	OEM
BC531	OEM
BC532	0855
BC533	0855
BC534	0126
BC535	0086
BC537	0086
BC538	0086
BC546	0111
BC546A	0111
BC546AP	0079
BC546B	0111
BC546BP	0079
BC546VIP	0079
BC547	0079
BC547A	0079
BC547AP	0079
BC547B	0079
BC547BP	0079
BC547C	0079
BC547VI	0079
BC547VIP	0079
BC548	0079
BC548A	0111
BC548AP	0079
BC548B	0079
BC548BC	0079
BC548BP	0079
BC548C	0079
BC548CP	0111
BC548VI	0079
BC548VIP	0079
BC549	0079
BC549B	0079
BC549BP	0079
BC549C	0111
BC550	0079
BC550B	0079
BC550BP	0079
BC550C	0111
BC550CP	0111
BC556	0037
BC556A	0037
BC556B	0037
BC556PA	OEM
BC556PAK	OEM
BC556PAL	OEM
BC556PAM	OEM
BC556PB	OEM
BC556PBK	OEM
BC556PBL	OEM
BC556PBM	OEM
BC556PV1	OEM
BC556PV1K	OEM
BC556PV1L	OEM
BC556PV1M	OEM
BC556VI	0037
BC557	0037
BC557A	0037
BC557B	0037
BC557PA	OEM
BC557PAK	OEM
BC557PAL	OEM
BC557PAM	OEM
BC557PB	OEM
BC557PBK	OEM
BC557PBL	OEM
BC557PBM	OEM
BC557PV1	OEM
BC557PV1K	OEM
BC557PV1L	OEM
BC557PV1M	OEM
BC557VI	0037
BC558	0037
BC558(EUROPE)	2022
BC558A	0037
BC558B	0037
BC558B2	OEM
BC558C	5807
BC558PA	OEM
BC558PAK	OEM
BC558PAL	OEM
BC558PAM	OEM
BC558PB	OEM
BC558PBK	OEM
BC558PBL	OEM
BC558PBM	OEM
BC558PC	OEM
BC558PCK	OEM
BC558PCL	OEM
BC558PCM	OEM
BC558PV1	OEM
BC558PV1K	OEM
BC558PV1L	OEM
BC558PV1M	OEM
BC558VI	0037
BC559	0037
BC559A	0037
BC559B	0037
BC559C	3477
BC559PA	OEM
BC559PAK	OEM
BC559PAL	OEM
BC559PAM	OEM
BC559PB	OEM
BC559PBK	OEM
BC559PBL	OEM
BC559PBM	OEM
BC559PC	OEM
BC559PCK	OEM
BC559PCL	OEM
BC559PCM	OEM
BC560	0037
BC560A	0037
BC560B	0527
BC560C	0688
BC560PA	0037
BC560PAK	0037
BC560PAL	0037
BC560PAM	0037
BC560PB	0037
BC560PBK	0037
BC560PBL	0037
BC560PBM	0037
BC560PC	0688
BC560PCK	0688
BC560PCL	OEM
BC560PCM	0688
BC582	0079
BC582A	0079
BC582B	0079
BC583	0079
BC583A	0079
BC583B	0079
BC583C	0396
BC584	0590
BC584B	0396
BC584C	0396
BC585	OEM
BC586	OEM
BC586L18	OEM
BC612	OEM
BC612L	OEM
BC617	3749
BC618	3749
BC635	1376
BC635/636	OEM
BC636	0472
BC637	0320
BC637/638	OEM
BC638	0472
BC638-BC640	OEM
BC639	0086
BC639/640	OEM
BC640	0472
BC682	0086
BC727	0126
BC728	0126
BC737	0111
BC738	0111
BC807	1741
BC807-16	1491
BC807-25	1491
BC807-40	OEM
BC808	1741
BC808-16	1491
BC808-25	1491
BC808-40	OEM
BC817	1722
BC817-16	1426
BC817-25	1426
BC817-40	OEM
BC818	1722
BC818-16	1426
BC818-25	1426
BC818-40	OEM
BC846	0719
BC846A	0719
BC846B	5286
BC847A	0719
BC847B	0719
BC847C	OEM
BC848A	0719
BC848B	5286
BC848C	OEM
BC849B	5286
BC849C	OEM
BC850	0719
BC850B	5286
BC850C	OEM
BC856	1731
BC856A	1731
BC856B	1731
BC857	1731
BC857A	1731
BC857B	1731
BC857C	OEM
BC858	1731
BC858A	1731
BC858B	1731
BC858C	OEM
BC859	1731
BC859A	3832
BC859B	3832
BC859C	OEM
BC860	1731
BC860A	3832
BC860B	3832
BC860C	OEM
BC868	0662
BC869	3832
BC876	3836
BC877	3838
BC878	3836
BC879	3838
BC880	3836
BC968	OEM
BC-1072	0016
BC1073	0085
BC1073A	0085
BC1073B	OEM
BC-1082	0016
BC-1086	0016
BC-1096	0016
BC1096	0016
BC1274	0085
BC1274A	0085
BC1274B	0085
BC1473	0261
BC1478	0016
BC-1690	0016
BC2290	OEM
BC3337	0018
BC6500	0144
BC486518	OEM
BCD08	4927
BCD10	4927
BCD15	4927
BCD20	OEM
BCD25	OEM
BCD30	OEM
BCD35	OEM
BCD40	OEM
BCD45	OEM
BCD50	OEM
BCD4024BF3	OEM
BCF5	0229
BCF29	1731
BCF29R	OEM
BCF30	1731
BCF30R	OEM
BCF32	0719
BCF32R	OEM
BCF33	0719
BCF33R	OEM
BCF70	1731
BCF70R	OEM
BCF81	0719
BCF81R	OEM
BCK53	OEM
BCM15-60	OEM
BCM15-60E	OEM
BCM15-60J	OEM
BCM15-100	OEM
BCM15-100E	OEM
BCM15-100J	OEM
BCM15-200	OEM
BCM15-200E	OEM
BCM15-200J	OEM
BCM15-300	OEM
BCM15-300E	OEM
BCM15-300J	OEM
BCM1002-1	0050
BCM1002-2	0127
BCM1002-3	0164
BCM1002-4	0004
BCM1002-5	0004
BCM1002-6	0222
BCM1002-18	0164
BCM5101-4	OEM
BCP51	OEM
BCP52	OEM
BCP53	OEM
BCP54	OEM
BCP55	OEM
BCP56	OEM
BCP68	OEM
BCP69	OEM
BCR1AM4	OEM
BCR1AM6	OEM
BCR1AM8	OEM
BCR1AM10	OEM
BCR1AM12	OEM
BCR3AM4	OEM
BCR3AM8	OEM
BCR3AM10	OEM
BCR3AM12	OEM
BCR5A2	OEM
BCR5A4	OEM
BCR5A6	OEM
BCR5A8	OEM
BCR5B2	OEM
BCR5B4	OEM
BCR5B6	OEM
BCR5B8	OEM
BCR5C2	OEM
BCR5C4	OEM
BCR5C6	OEM
BCR5C8	OEM
BCR6AM4L	OEM
BCR6AM4R	OEM
BCR6AM6L	OEM
BCR6AM6R	OEM
BCR6AM8L	OEM
BCR6AM8R	OEM
BCR6AM10L	OEM
BCR6AM10R	OEM
BCR6AM12L	OEM
BCR6AM12R	OEM
BCR8A4L	OEM
BCR8A4R	OEM
BCR8A6L	OEM
BCR8A6R	OEM
BCR8A8L	OEM
BCR8A8R	OEM
BCR8A10L	OEM
BCR8A10R	OEM
BCR8CM4L	OEM
BCR8CM4R	OEM
BCR8CM6L	OEM
BCR8CM6R	OEM
BCR8CM8L	OEM
BCR8CM8R	OEM
BCR8CM10L	OEM
BCR8CM10R	OEM
BCR8CM12L	OEM
BCR8CM12R	OEM
BCR8DM	OEM
BCR8DM4L	OEM
BCR8DM4R	OEM
BCR8DM6L	OEM
BCR8DM6R	OEM
BCR8DM8L	OEM
BCR8DM8R	OEM
BCR8DM10L	OEM
BCR8DM10R	OEM
BCR8DM12L	OEM
BCR8DM12R	OEM
BCR10A2	OEM
BCR10A4	OEM
BCR10A6	OEM
BCR10A8	OEM
BCR10AM4L	OEM
BCR10AM4R	OEM
BCR10AM6L	OEM
BCR10AM6R	OEM
BCR10AM8L	0739
BCR10AM8R	0739
BCR10AM10L	0612
BCR10AM10R	0612
BCR10AM12L	OEM
BCR10AM12R	OEM
BCR10B2	OEM
BCR10B4	OEM
BCR10B6	OEM
BCR10B8	OEM
BCR10C2	OEM
BCR10C4	OEM
BCR10C6	OEM
BCR10C8	OEM
BCR10CM4L	OEM
BCR10CM4R	OEM
BCR10CM6L	OEM
BCR10CM6R	OEM
BCR10CM-8L	OEM
BCR10CM8R	OEM
BCR10CM10L	OEM
BCR10CM10R	OEM
BCR10CM12L	OEM
BCR10CM12R	OEM
BCR10DM4L	OEM
BCR10DM4R	OEM
BCR10DM6L	OEM
BCR10DM6R	OEM
BCR10DM8L	OEM
BCR10DM8R	OEM
BCR10DM10L	OEM
BCR10DM10R	OEM
BCR10DM12L	OEM
BCR10DM12R	OEM
BCR10EM4L	OEM
BCR10EM4R	OEM
BCR10EM6L	OEM
BCR10EM6R	OEM
BCR10EM8L	OEM
BCR10EM-10L	OEM
BCR10EM-10R	OEM
BCR10EM12L	OEM
BCR10EM12R	OEM
BCR10PM	OEM
BCR12AM4L	OEM
BCR12AM4R	OEM
BCR12AM6L	OEM
BCR12AM6R	OEM
BCR12AM8L	OEM
BCR12AM10L	OEM
BCR12AM10R	OEM
BCR12AM12L	OEM
BCR12AM12R	OEM
BCR12CM4L	OEM
BCR12CM4R	OEM
BCR12CM6L	OEM
BCR12CM6R	OEM
BCR12CM8L	OEM
BCR12CM8R	OEM
BCR12CM10L	OEM
BCR12CM10R	OEM
BCR12CM12L	OEM
BCR12CM12R	OEM
BCR12DM4L	OEM
BCR12DM4R	OEM
BCR12DM6L	OEM
BCR12DM6R	OEM
BCR12DM8L	OEM
BCR12DM8R	OEM
BCR12DM10L	OEM
BCR12DM10R	OEM
BCR12DM12L	OEM
BCR12DM12R	OEM
BCR12EM4L	OEM
BCR12EM4R	OEM
BCR12EM6L	OEM
BCR12EM6R	OEM
BCR12EM8L	OEM
BCR12EM8R	OEM
BCR12EM10L	OEM
BCR12EM10R	OEM
BCR12EM12L	OEM
BCR12EM12R	OEM
BCR16A4L	OEM
BCR16A4R	OEM
BCR16A6L	OEM
BCR16A6R	OEM
BCR16A8L	OEM
BCR16A8R	OEM
BCR16A10L	OEM
BCR16A10R	OEM
BCR16AM-4L	OEM
BCR16AM-4R	OEM
BCR16AM-6L	OEM
BCR16AM-6R	OEM
BCR16AM-8L	OEM
BCR16AM-8R	OEM
BCR16AM-10L	OEM
BCR16AM-10R	OEM
BCR16B4L	OEM
BCR16B4R	OEM
BCR16B6L	OEM
BCR16B6R	OEM
BCR16B8L	OEM
BCR16B8R	OEM
BCR16B10L	OEM
BCR16B10R	OEM
BCR16C4L	OEM
BCR16C4R	OEM
BCR16C6L	OEM
BCR16C6R	OEM
BCR16C8L	OEM
BCR16C8R	OEM
BCR16C10L	OEM
BCR16C10R	OEM
BCR16CM4L	OEM
BCR16CM4R	OEM
BCR16CM6L	OEM
BCR16CM6R	OEM
BCR16CM8L	OEM
BCR16CM8R	OEM
BCR16CM10L	OEM
BCR16CM10R	OEM
BCR16CM12L	OEM
BCR16CM12R	OEM
BCR16DM4L	OEM
BCR16DM4R	OEM
BCR16DM6L	OEM
BCR16DM6R	OEM
BCR16DM8L	OEM
BCR16DM8R	OEM
BCR16DM10L	OEM
BCR16DM10R	OEM
BCR16DM12L	OEM
BCR16E4L	OEM
BCR16E4R	OEM
BCR16E6L	OEM
BCR16E6R	OEM
BCR16E8L	OEM
BCR16E8R	OEM
BCR16E10L	OEM
BCR16E10R	OEM
BCR16EM-4L	OEM
BCR16EM-4R	OEM
BCR16EM-6L	OEM
BCR16EM-6R	OEM
BCR16EM-8L	OEM
BCR16EM-8R	OEM
BCR16EM-10L	OEM
BCR16EM-10R	OEM
BCR16FM-4L	OEM
BCR16FM-4R	OEM
BCR16FM-6L	OEM
BCR16FM-6R	OEM
BCR16FM-8L	OEM
BCR16FM-8R	OEM
BCR16FM-10L	OEM
BCR16FM-10R	OEM
BCR16GM-4L	OEM
BCR16GM-4R	OEM
BCR16GM-6L	OEM
BCR16GM-6R	OEM
BCR16GM-8L	OEM
BCR16GM-8R	OEM
BCR16GM-10L	OEM
BCR16GM-10R	OEM
BCR16HM4L	OEM
BCR16HM4R	OEM
BCR16HM6L	OEM
BCR16HM6R	OEM
BCR16HM8L	OEM
BCR16HM8R	OEM
BCR16HM10L	OEM
BCR16M-4L	OEM
BCR16M-4R	OEM
BCR16M-6L	OEM
BCR16M-6R	OEM
BCR16M-8L	OEM
BCR16M-8R	OEM
BCR16M-10L	OEM
BCR16M-10R	OEM
BCR20A4L	OEM
BCR20A4R	OEM
BCR20A6L	OEM
BCR20A6R	OEM
BCR20A8L	OEM
BCR20A8R	OEM
BCR20A10L	OEM
BCR20A10R	OEM
BCR20B4L	OEM
BCR20B4R	OEM
BCR20B6L	OEM
BCR20B6R	OEM
BCR20B8L	OEM
BCR20B8R	OEM
BCR20B10L	OEM
BCR20B10R	OEM
BCR20C4L	OEM
BCR20C4R	OEM
BCR20C6L	OEM
BCR20C6R	OEM
BCR20C8L	OEM
BCR20C8R	OEM
BCR20C10L	OEM
BCR20C10R	OEM
BCR20E4L	OEM
BCR20E4R	OEM
BCR20E6L	OEM
BCR20E6R	OEM
BCR20E8L	OEM
BCR20E8R	OEM
BCR20E10L	OEM
BCR20E10R	OEM
BCR25A4L	OEM
BCR25A4R	OEM
BCR25A6L	OEM
BCR25A6R	OEM
BCR25A8L	OEM
BCR25A8R	OEM
BCR25A10L	OEM
BCR25A10R	OEM
BCR25B4	0902
BCR25B4L	OEM
BCR25B4R	OEM
BCR25B6	0902
BCR25B6L	OEM
BCR25B6R	OEM
BCR25B8	OEM
BCR25B8L	OEM
BCR25B8R	OEM
BCR25B10	OEM
BCR25B10L	OEM
BCR25B10R	OEM
BCR30GM	OEM
BCR30GM4L	OEM
BCR30GM4R	OEM
BCR30GM6L	OEM
BCR30GM6R	OEM
BCR30GM8L	OEM
BCR30GM8R	OEM
BCR30GM10L	OEM
BCR30GM10R	OEM
BCR50A4	OEM
BCR50A6	OEM
BCR50A8	OEM
BCR50A12	OEM
BCR50A16	OEM
BCR70A4	OEM
BCR70A6	OEM
BCR70A8	OEM
BCR70A12	OEM
BCR70A16	OEM
BCR70A20	OEM
BCR70B4	OEM
BCR70B6	OEM
BCR70B8	OEM
BCR70B12	OEM
BCR70B16	OEM
BCR70B20	OEM
BCR70B24	OEM
BCR150A4	OEM
BCR150A6	OEM
BCR150A8	OEM
BCR150A12	OEM
BCR150A16	OEM
BCR150A20	OEM
BCR150A24	OEM
BCR150B4	OEM
BCR150B6	OEM
BCR150B8	OEM
BCR150B12	OEM
BCR150B16	OEM
BCR150B20	OEM
BCR150B24	OEM
BCR300A4	OEM
BCR300A6	OEM
BCR300A8	OEM
BCR300A12	OEM
BCR300A16	OEM
BCR300A20	OEM
BCR300A24	OEM
BCR300B4	OEM
BCR300B6	OEM
BCR300B8	OEM
BCR300B12	OEM
BCR300B16	OEM
BCR300B20	OEM
BCR300B24	OEM
BCS78-25	OEM
BCU75EPAK	OEM
BCV26	5268
BCV27	5267
BCV46	OEM
BCV47	OEM
BCV61	OEM
BCV62	OEM
BCV71	0719
BCV71R	OEM
BCV72	5286
BCV72R	OEM
BCW10	OEM
BCW11	OEM
BCW12	OEM
BCW13	OEM
BCW14	OEM
BCW15	OEM
BCW16	OEM
BCW17	OEM
BCW18	OEM
BCW19	OEM
BCW20	OEM
BCW21	OEM
BCW22	OEM
BCW23	OEM
BCW24	OEM
BCW25	OEM
BCW26	OEM
BCW29	0150
BCW29R	0150
BCW30	0150
BCW30R	0150
BCW31	1722
BCW31R	0144
BCW32	0144
BCW32R	0144
BCW33	0279
BCW33R	0279
BCW34	0016
BCW35	0037
BCW36	0016
BCW37	0037
BCW38C	OEM
BCW44	0086
BCW45	0037
BCW46	0086
BCW46A	0079
BCW46B	0079
BCW47	0086
BCW47A	0079
BCW47B	0079
BCW48	0086
BCW48A	0079
BCW48B	0079
BCW48C	0079
BCW49	0086
BCW49B	0079
BCW49C	0079
BCW50	0283
BCW51	0590
BCW52	0786
BCW56	0037
BCW56A	0037
BCW57	0037
BCW57A	0037
BCW57B	0527
BCW58	0037
BCW58A	0037
BCW58B	0037
BCW59	0037
BCW59A	0037
BCW59B	0688
BCW60	5286
BCW60A	0016
BCW60AA	0016
BCW60AB	0079
BCW60AC	0079
BCW60B	0079
BCW60C	0079
BCW60FF	OEM
BCW60FN	OEM
BCW60R	OEM
BCW61	0037
BCW61A	0786
BCW61B	0786
BCW61BA	0786
BCW61BB	0786
BCW61BC	0688
BCW61BD	0688
BCW61C	0037
BCW61D	0037
BCW61FF	OEM
BCW61FN	OEM
BCW61R	OEM
BCW62	0037
BCW62A	0037
BCW62B	0786
BCW63	0037
BCW63A	0037
BCW63B	0786
BCW63C	0527
BCW64	0786
BCW64A	0037
BCW64B	0786

286
If replacement code is OEM, contact original manufacturer for replacement.

DEVICE TYPE	REPL CODE
BCW64C	0527
BCW65	1722
BCW65A	1722
BCW65B	1722
BCW65C	OEM
BCW65EA	0079
BCW65EB	0079
BCW65EC	0018
BCW65R	OEM
BCW66	1722
BCW66EF	0018
BCW66EG	0018
BCW66EH	0018
BCW66EW	0018
BCW66F	1722
BCW66G	1722
BCW66H	1426
BCW66R	OEM
BCW67	1722
BCW67A	1722
BCW67B	1722
BCW67C	1722
BCW67DA	0527
BCW67DB	0527
BCW67DC	0527
BCW67R	OEM
BCW67RA	OEM
BCW68	1722
BCW68DF	0527
BCW68DG	0527
BCW68DH	0527
BCW68F	1722
BCW68G	1722
BCW68H	OEM
BCW68R	OEM
BCW68RH	OEM
BCW69	1731
BCW69R	0126
BCW70	1731
BCW70R	0786
BCW71	0719
BCW71R	0144
BCW72	0144
BCW72R	0144
BCW73	0016
BCW73-16	0590
BCW73-25	0016
BCW74	0016
BCW74-16	0590
BCW74-25	0016
BCW75	OEM
BCW75-10	0786
BCW75-16	0786
BCW75-25	0037
BCW76	OEM
BCW76-10	0786
BCW76-16	0786
BCW77	OEM
BCW77-16	0590
BCW77-25	0086
BCW78	0086
BCW78-16	0590
BCW78-25	0086
BCW79	OEM
BCW79-10	0037
BCW79-16	0037
BCW79-25	0126
BCW80	0126
BCW80-10	0037
BCW80-16	0037
BCW80-25	0126
BCW81	1722
BCW81R	OEM
BCW82	0590
BCW82A	0590
BCW82B	0590
BCW83	0016
BCW83A	0218
BCW83B	0590
BCW84	0590
BCW84B	0284
BCW85	0338
BCW86	0037
BCW87	0111
BCW88	0688
BCW89	2316
BCW89R	OEM
BCW90	0590
BCW90A	0018
BCW90B	0018
BCW90C	0018
BCW90K	0590
BCW90KA	0018
BCW90KB	0018
BCW90KC	0018
BCW91	0590
BCW91A	0590
BCW91B	0590
BCW91K	0590
BCW91KA	0590
BCW91KB	0590
BCW92	0786
BCW92A	0527
BCW92B	0527
BCW92K	0786
BCW92KA	0037
BCW92KB	0037
BCW93	0786
BCW93A	0037
BCW93B	0037
BCW93K	0786
BCW93KA	0037
BCW93KB	0037
BCW94	0079
BCW94A	0079
BCW94B	0079
BCW94C	0079
BCW94K	0590
BCW94KA	0079
BCW94KB	0079
BCW94KC	0079
BCW95	0086
BCW95A	0079
BCW95B	0079
BCW95K	0590
BCW95KA	0079
BCW95KB	0079
BCW96	0037
BCW96A	0037
BCW96B	0037
BCW96K	0786
BCW96KA	0037
BCW96KB	0037
BCW97	0037
BCW97A	0037
BCW97B	0037
BCW97K	0786
BCW97KA	0037
BCW97KB	0037
BCW98A	0111
BCW98B	0111
BCW98C	0111
BCW98D	0111
BCW99A	0527
BCW99B	0527
BCW99C	0527
BCW314	OEM
BCW601	OEM
BCX10	0126
BCX10A	2245
BCX17	0037
BCX17R	0037
BCX18	0338
BCX18R	0338
BCX19	0079
BCX19R	0079
BCX20	0079
BCX20R	0079
BCX21	OEM
BCX22	0233
BCX23	0472
BCX24	0233
BCX25	OEM
BCX26	0037
BCX27	OEM
BCX28	OEM
BCX29	OEM
BCX30	0472
BCX31	0086
BCX32	0320
BCX33	0320
BCX34	0320
BCX35	0037
BCX36	0037
BCX38A	OEM
BCX38B	OEM
BCX38C	OEM
BCX39	OEM
BCX41	OEM
BCX41R	OEM
BCX42	OEM
BCX42R	OEM
BCX45	0037
BCX46	0037
BCX47	1376
BCX48	OEM
BCX49	1376
BCX50	0037
BCX51	3600
BCX51-6	OEM
BCX51-10	OEM
BCX51-16	OEM
BCX52	3600
BCX52-6	OEM
BCX52-10	OEM
BCX53	5308
BCX53-6	OEM
BCX53-10	OEM
BCX54	0662
BCX54-6	OEM
BCX54-10	OEM
BCX54-16	OEM
BCX55	0662
BCX55-6	OEM
BCX55-10	OEM
BCX56	0662
BCX56-6	OEM
BCX56-10	OEM
BCX58	0079
BCX58IX	0018
BCX58VII	0079
BCX58VIII	0079
BCX58X	0018
BCX59	0079
BCX59IX	0018
BCX59VII	0018
BCX59VIII	0018
BCX59X	0018
BCX68	0662
BCX68-10	OEM
BCX68-16	OEM
BCX68-25	OEM
BCX69	3600
BCX69-10	OEM
BCX69-16	OEM
BCX69-25	OEM
BCX69R	OEM
BCX70	0719
BCX70AG	0079
BCX70AH	0079
BCX70AJ	0079
BCX70G	0719
BCX70H	0719
BCX70J	0719
BCX70K	OEM
BCX70R	OEM
BCX71	1731
BCX71BG	0786
BCX71BH	0786
BCX71BJ	0688
BCX71BK	0688
BCX71G	1731
BCX71H	1731
BCX71J	1731
BCX71K	OEM
BCX71R	OEM
BCX73	OEM
BCX73-16	0018
BCX73-25	0018
BCX73-40	0018
BCX74	OEM
BCX74-16	0018
BCX74-25	0018
BCX74-40	0018
BCX75	OEM
BCX75-16	0527
BCX75-25	0527
BCX75-40	0527
BCX76	OEM
BCX76-16	OEM
BCX76-25	0527
BCX76-40	0527
BCX78	2245
BCX78IX	0527
BCX78VII	0150
BCX78VIII	0527
BCX79	2245
BCX79IX	0527
BCX79VII	0150
BCX79VIII	0527
BCX94	OEM
BCY10	0037
BCY11	0037
BCY11S	OEM
BCY12	0037
BCY13	0016
BCY14	OEM
BCY15	0016
BCY16	0016
BCY17	0126
BCY18	0126
BCY19	0126
BCY20	OEM
BCY21	0126
BCY22	0126
BCY23	0126
BCY24	0126
BCY25	0126
BCY26	0126
BCY27	0126
BCY28	0126
BCY29	0126
BCY30	0126
BCY30A	OEM
BCY31	0126
BCY31A	OEM
BCY32	0126
BCY32A	OEM
BCY33	0126
BCY33A	OEM
BCY34	0126
BCY34A	0126
BCY35	0037
BCY36	0016
BCY37	0037
BCY38	0037
BCY39	0037
BCY40	0037
BCY42	0016
BCY43	0016
BCY46	0086
BCY47	0086
BCY48	0086
BCY49	0086
BCY50	0016
BCY50I	0050
BCY51	0016
BCY51I	0016
BCY54	0037
BCY55	0111
BCY56	0016
BCY57	0016
BCY58	0037
BCY58A	0016
BCY58B	0016
BCY58C	0016
BCY58D	0016
BCY58IX	0016
BCY58PA	OEM
BCY58PAK	OEM
BCY58PAL	OEM
BCY58PAM	OEM
BCY58PB	OEM
BCY58PBK	OEM
BCY58PBL	OEM
BCY58PBM	OEM
BCY58PC	OEM
BCY58PCK	OEM
BCY58PCL	OEM
BCY58PCM	OEM
BCY58PD	OEM
BCY58PDK	OEM
BCY58PDL	OEM
BCY58VII	0016
BCY58VIII	0016
BCY59	0016
BCY59-7	0016
BCY59-8	0016
BCY59-9	0016
BCY59-10	OEM
BCY59A	0016
BCY59B	0016
BCY59C	0016
BCY59D	0016
BCY59IX	0016
BCY59PA	OEM
BCY59PAK	OEM
BCY59PAL	OEM
BCY59PAM	OEM
BCY59PB	OEM
BCY59PBK	OEM
BCY59PBL	OEM
BCY59PBM	OEM
BCY59PC	OEM
BCY59PCK	OEM
BCY59PCL	OEM
BCY59PCM	OEM
BCY59PD	OEM
BCY59PDK	OEM
BCY59PDL	OEM
BCY59PDM	OEM
BCY59VII	0016
BCY59VIII	0016
BCY65	0086
BCY65E	0016
BCY65EA	OEM
BCY65EB	OEM
BCY65EC	OEM
BCY65EPA	OEM
BCY65EPAL	OEM
BCY65EPAM	OEM
BCY65EPB	OEM
BCY65EPBK	OEM
BCY65EPBL	OEM
BCY65EPBM	OEM
BCY65EPC	OEM
BCY65EPCK	OEM
BCY65EPCL	OEM
BCY65EPCM	OEM
BCY65EPD	OEM
BCY65EPDK	OEM
BCY65EPDL	OEM
BCY65EPDM	OEM
BCY65IX	0016
BCY65VII	0016
BCY65VIII	0016
BCY66	0086
BCY67	0126
BCY69	0016
BCY70	0037
BCY71	0037
BCY71A	0037
BCY72	0037
BCY72A	0037
BCY76	0016
BCY77	OEM
BCY77A	0037
BCY77B	0037
BCY77C	0037
BCY77PA	OEM
BCY77PAK	OEM
BCY77PAL	OEM
BCY77PAM	OEM
BCY77PB	OEM
BCY77PBK	OEM
BCY77PBL	OEM
BCY77PBM	OEM
BCY77PC	OEM
BCY77PCK	OEM
BCY77PCL	OEM
BCY77PCM	OEM
BCY77VII	0037
BCY77VIII	0037
BCY78	0688
BCY78-7	OEM
BCY78-8	OEM
BCY78-9	OEM
BCY78-10	OEM
BCY78A	0126
BCY78B	0126
BCY78C	0527
BCY78D	OEM
BCY78PA	OEM
BCY78PAK	OEM
BCY78PAL	OEM
BCY78PAM	OEM
BCY78PB	OEM
BCY78PBK	OEM
BCY78PBL	OEM
BCY78PBM	OEM
BCY78PC	OEM
BCY78PCK	OEM
BCY78PCL	OEM
BCY78PCM	OEM
BCY78PD	OEM
BCY78PDK	OEM
BCY78PDL	OEM
BCY78PDM	OEM
BCY78VII	0786
BCY78VIII	0786
BCY79	0037
BCY79-7	OEM
BCY79-8	OEM
BCY79-9	OEM
BCY79A	0786
BCY79B	0786
BCY79C	0527
BCY79PA	OEM
BCY79PAK	OEM
BCY79PAL	OEM
BCY79PAM	OEM
BCY79PB	OEM
BCY79PBK	OEM
BCY79PBL	OEM
BCY79PBM	OEM
BCY79PCK	OEM
BCY79PCL	OEM
BCY79PCM	OEM
BCY79VII	0037
BCY79VIII	0786
BCY84A	0016
BCY85	0086
BCY86	0086
BCY87	0144
BCY88	0144
BCY89	0144
BCY90	0037
BCY90B	0037
BCY91	0037
BCY91B	0037
BCY92	0037
BCY92B	0037
BCY93	0037
BCY93B	0037
BCY94	0037
BCY94B	0037
BCY95	0037
BCY95B	0037
BCY96	0126
BCY96B	0126
BCY97	0126
BCY97B	0126
BCY98	0037
BCY98B	0037
BCY443	0086
BCY501	0016
BCY511	0016
BCY771X	0037
BCZ6.8	OEM
BCZ6.8A	OEM
BCZ6.8B	OEM
BCZ7.5	OEM
BCZ7.5A	OEM
BCZ7.5B	OEM
BCZ8.2	OEM
BCZ8.2A	OEM
BCZ8.2B	OEM
BCZ9.1	OEM
BCZ9.1A	OEM
BCZ9.1B	OEM
BCZ10	0037
BCZ10(DIO)	OEM
BCZ10A	3079
BCZ10B	6249
BCZ11	0037
BCZ11(DIO)	OEM
BCZ11A	6249
BCZ11B	OEM
BCZ12	0037
BCZ12(DIO)	OEM
BCZ12A	6249
BCZ12B	6249
BCZ13	0037
BCZ13(DIO)	OEM
BCZ13A	6249
BCZ13B	6525
BCZ14	0037
BCZ15	OEM
BCZ15A	OEM
BCZ15B	OEM
BCZ16	OEM
BCZ16A	OEM
BCZ16B	OEM
BCZ18	OEM
BCZ18A	OEM
BCZ18B	OEM
BCZ20	OEM
BCZ20A	OEM
BCZ20B	OEM
BCZ22	OEM
BCZ22A	OEM
BCZ22B	OEM
BCZ24	OEM
BCZ24A	OEM
BCZ24B	OEM
BCZ27	OEM
BCZ27A	OEM
BCZ27B	OEM
BCZ30	OEM
BCZ30A	OEM
BCZ30B	OEM
BCZ33	OEM
BCZ33A	OEM
BCZ33B	OEM
BCZ36	OEM
BCZ36A	OEM
BCZ36B	OEM
BCZ39	OEM
BCZ39A	OEM
BCZ39B	OEM
BCZ43	OEM
BCZ43A	OEM
BCZ43B	OEM
BCZ47	OEM
BCZ47A	OEM
BCZ47B	OEM
BCZ51	OEM
BCZ51A	OEM
BCZ51B	OEM
BCZ56	OEM
BCZ56A	OEM
BCZ56B	OEM
BCZ62	OEM
BCZ62A	OEM
BCZ62B	OEM
BCZ66	OEM
BCZ66A	OEM
BCZ66B	OEM
BCZ75	OEM
BCZ75A	OEM
BCZ75B	OEM
BCZ82	OEM
BCZ82A	OEM
BCZ82B	OEM
BCZ91	OEM
BCZ91A	OEM
BCZ91B	OEM
BCZ100	OEM
BCZ100A	OEM
BCZ100B	OEM
BCZ110	OEM
BCZ110A	OEM
BCZ110B	OEM
BCZ120	OEM
BCZ120A	OEM
BCZ120B	OEM
BCZ130	OEM
BCZ130A	OEM
BCZ130B	OEM
BCZ150	OEM
BCZ150A	OEM
BCZ150B	OEM
BCZ160	OEM
BCZ160A	OEM
BCZ160B	OEM
BCZ180	OEM
BCZ180A	OEM
BCZ180B	OEM
BCZ200	OEM
BCZ200A	OEM
BCZ200B	OEM
BD-00072	0208
BD0A	0015
BD-1	OEM
BD1	0143
BD1-05	OEM
BD1-06	OEM
BD1-07	OEM
BD1-08	OEM
BD1-09	OEM
BD1-10	OEM
BD-1A	0015
BD1A	OEM
BD1B	OEM
BD-2	OEM
BD2	0143
BD-3	OEM
BD3	0143
BD3A-1B4	0276
BD-3A184	0276
BD3A-184	0229
BD3.6FB	0372
BD-4	OEM
BD4	0143
BD-5	OEM
BD5	0143
BD-6	OEM
BD6	0143
BD-7	OEM
BD7	0143
BD8-05	OEM
BD8-06	OEM
BD8-07	OEM
BD8-08	OEM
BD8-09	OEM
BD8-10	OEM
BD23B	OEM
BD23C	OEM
BD28	3298
BD61YA	OEM
BD71	0144
BD100	OEM
BD100C	OEM
BD101	OEM
BD102	OEM
BD106	0042
BD106A	0042
BD106B	0042
BD-107	0015
BD107	0555
BD107A	0042
BD107B	0042
BD109	0042
BD109-6	0042
BD111	0103
BD111A	0615
BD112	0615
BD113	0224
BD115	0233
BD116	0615
BD117	0538
BD118	0615
BD119	1021
BD120	1021
BD121	0160
BD123	0615
BD124	0042
BD124A	OEM
BD-127	0015
BD127	0275
BD128	0142
BD129	0142
BD130	0103
BD-131	2969
BD131	0161
BD-132	0455
BD132	0455
BD135	0161
BD135-6	0161
BD135-10	0161
BD135-16	0558
BD135-BD-136	OEM
BD135G	0555
BD136	0676
BD136-6	0455
BD136-10	0455
BD136-16	0520
BD136G	1257
BD137	0161
BD137-6	0161
BD137-10	0161
BD137-BD138	OEM
BD137G	0555
BD138	0455
BD138-6	0455
BD138-10	0455
BD138G	1257
BD139	0161
BD139-6	0161
BD139-10	0161
BD139-BD140	OEM
BD139G	0555
BD140	0455
BD140-6	0455
BD140-10	0455
BD140G	1257
BD141	0177
BD142	0103
BD144	0074
BD145	0615
BD148	0556
BD148-6	0556
BD148-10	0556
BD149	0161
BD149-6	0556
BD149-10	0556
BD150	OEM
BD151	0455
BD152	0455
BD153	0161
BD154	0161
BD155	0161
BD156	0455
BD157	0275
BD158	0275
BD160	0223
BD161	OEM
BD162	0042
BD163	0042
BD165	0161
BD166	0455
BD167	0161
BD168	0455
BD169	0161
BD170	0520
BD171	1698
BD172	1698
BD173	1698
BD175	0161
BD176	0455
BD177	0161
BD178	0455
BD179	0161
BD180	0455
BD181	0103
BD182	0103
BD183	0455
BD184	0538
BD185	0161
BD186	0455
BD187	0161
BD188	0455
BD189	0161

If replacement code is OEM, contact original manufacturer for replacement.

287

DEVICE TYPE	REPL CODE
BD190	0455
BD195	0556
BD196	1190
BD197	0556
BD198	1190
BD199	0556
BD200	1190
BD201	0477
BD201-BD202	OEM
BD202	1359
BD203	0477
BD203-BD204	OEM
BD204	1359
BD204M	OEM
BD205	0556
BD206	1190
BD207	0556
BD208	1190
BD213	OEM
BD213/45	0556
BD213/60	0556
BD213/80	0556
BD214	OEM
BD214/45	1190
BD214/60	1190
BD214/80	1190
BD214-45	1190
BD215	0275
BD216	0275
BD220	0042
BD221	0042
BD222	0042
BD223	0919
BD224	0919
BD225	0919
BD226	0161
BD227	0455
BD228	0161
BD228-BD229	OEM
BD229	0455
BD230-BD231	OEM
BD232	0275
BD232G	OEM
BD233	0161
BD233G	0236
BD234	0455
BD234G	0676
BD235	0161
BD235-BD236	OEM
BD235G	0236
BD236	0455
BD236G	0676
BD237	0558
BD237-BD238	OEM
BD237G	0236
BD238	0309
BD238G	0676
BD239	0236
BD239A	0236
BD239B	0236
BD240	0919
BD240A	0919
BD240B	0676
BD240C	0676
BD241	0042
BD241A	2969
BD241B	0236
BD241C	0236
BD242	0919
BD242A	0477
BD242B	0919
BD242C	0676
BD243	0042
BD243A	0556
BD243B	0042
BD244	0919
BD244A	0919
BD244B	0919
BD244C	1190
BD245	3052
BD245A	3052
BD245B	3052
BD245C	3052
BD246	3558
BD246A	3558
BD246B	3558
BD246C	3558
BD249	0130
BD249A	0130
BD249B	0130
BD249C	0130
BD250	1671
BD250A	1671
BD250B	1671
BD250C	1671
BD253	OEM
BD253A	OEM
BD253B	OEM
BD253C	OEM
BD260	OEM
BD261	OEM
BD262	2869
BD262(DARLINGTON)	2869
BD262A	2869
BD262A(DARLINGTON)	2869
BD262B	OEM
BD262C	OEM
BD262L	OEM
BD263	0553
BD263A	3487
BD263B	OEM
BD263C	OEM
BD263L	OEM
BD264	2222
BD264A	2222
BD264B	OEM
BD264L	OEM
BD265	2220
BD265A	OEM
BD265B	OEM
BD265L	OEM
BD266	2222
BD266A	2222
BD266B	6395
BD266L	OEM
BD267	2220
BD267A	2220
BD267B	5407
BD267L	OEM
BD271	0042
BD272	0919
BD273	0419
BD274	0676
BD275	0419
BD276	0848
BD277	0848
BD278	0419
BD278A	1351
BD278AE	0419
BD278E	0419
BD279	OEM
BD280	OEM
BD287	OEM
BD288	OEM
BD291	0419
BD292	0676
BD293	0419
BD294	0676
BD295	OEM
BD296	OEM
BD301	0556
BD302	1190
BD303	0556
BD304	1190
BD306A	0161
BD307A	0161
BD311	0177
BD312	0486
BD313	0177
BD314	1671
BD315	2398
BD316	1671
BD317	2398
BD318	1671
BD320A	OEM
BD320B	OEM
BD320C	OEM
BD321A	OEM
BD321B	OEM
BD321C	OEM
BD322A	OEM
BD322B	OEM
BD322C	OEM
BD323A	OEM
BD323B	OEM
BD323C	OEM
BD328	OEM
BD329	0558
BD330	0520
BD331	4015
BD332	4016
BD333	4015
BD334	4016
BD335	4015
BD336	4016
BD337	4015
BD338	4016
BD344	0520
BD345	0558
BD346	OEM
BD347	OEM
BD348	0520
BD349	0558
BD361	OEM
BD361A	OEM
BD362	OEM
BD362A	OEM
BD370A	OEM
BD370A-6	OEM
BD370A-10	OEM
BD370A-16	OEM
BD370B	OEM
BD370B-6	OEM
BD370B-10	OEM
BD370B-16	OEM
BD370C	OEM
BD370C-6	OEM
BD370C-10	OEM
BD370D	OEM
BD371	2503
BD371A	OEM
BD371A-6	OEM
BD371A-10	OEM
BD371A-16	OEM
BD371B	OEM
BD371B-6	OEM
BD371B-10	OEM
BD371B-16	OEM
BD371C	OEM
BD371C-6	OEM
BD371C-10	OEM
BD371D	OEM
BD372A	OEM
BD372A-6	OEM
BD372A-10	OEM
BD372A-16	OEM
BD372B	OEM
BD372B-6	OEM
BD372B-10	OEM
BD372B-16	OEM
BD372C-6	OEM
BD372C-10	OEM
BD372D	OEM
BD373A	OEM
BD373A-6	OEM
BD373A-10	OEM
BD373A-16	OEM
BD373B	OEM
BD373B-6	OEM
BD373B-10	OEM
BD373B-16	OEM
BD373C	OEM
BD373C-6	OEM
BD373C-10	OEM
BD373D	6491
BD375	0161
BD375-6	OEM
BD375-10	OEM
BD375-16	OEM
BD375-25	OEM
BD376	0455
BD376-6	OEM
BD376-10	OEM
BD376-16	OEM
BD376-25	OEM
BD377	0161
BD377-6	OEM
BD377-10	OEM
BD377-16	OEM
BD377-25	OEM
BD378	0455
BD378-6	OEM
BD378-10	OEM
BD378-16	OEM
BD378-25	OEM
BD379-6	OEM
BD379-10	OEM
BD379-16	OEM
BD379-25	OEM
BD380-6	OEM
BD380-10	OEM
BD380-16	OEM
BD380-25	OEM
BD401	OEM
BD-402	OEM
BD402	OEM
BD-403	OEM
BD403	OEM
BD-404	OEM
BD404	OEM
BD-405	OEM
BD405	OEM
BD-406	OEM
BD406	OEM
BD-407	OEM
BD407	OEM
BD415	0818
BD416	3294
BD417	0818
BD418	3294
BD424	OEM
BD424A	0130
BD424B	0130
BD427	OEM
BD429	OEM
BD430	OEM
BD-433	0042
BD433	0042
BD433-BD434	OEM
BD433A	0042
BD434	0919
BD434A	0919
BD435	0042
BD435-BD436	OEM
BD435A	0042
BD435C	OEM
BD436	0919
BD436A	0919
BD437	0042
BD437-BD438	OEM
BD438	0919
BD439	0042
BD440	0919
BD441	0419
BD442	0848
BD450	OEM
BD451	OEM
BD457	0080
BD457F	0080
BD457T	0080
BD458	OEM
BD458F	0604
BD458T	0604
BD461	0556
BD462	0455
BD463	0556
BD464	1190
BD466A	OEM
BD466B	OEM
BD477A	OEM
BD477B	OEM
BD483B	0080
BD483BF	0080
BD483BT	0080
BD487	OEM
BD488	OEM
BD497/01	0074
BD500	1190
BD500A	1190
BD500B	1190
BD501	0556
BD501A	0556
BD501B	0556
BD505	OEM
BD505-1	OEM
BD505-5	OEM
BD506	OEM
BD506-1	OEM
BD506-5	OEM
BD507	OEM
BD507-1	OEM
BD507-5	OEM
BD508	OEM
BD508-1	OEM
BD508-5	OEM
BD509	OEM
BD509-1	OEM
BD509-5	OEM
BD510	OEM
BD510-1	OEM
BD510-5	OEM
BD512	OEM
BD515	OEM
BD515-1	OEM
BD515-5	OEM
BD516	OEM
BD517	0546
BD517-1	OEM
BD517-5	OEM
BD518	OEM
BD519	OEM
BD519-1	OEM
BD519-5	OEM
BD520	OEM
BD522	OEM
BD524	0558
BD525	0546
BD525-1	0546
BD525-5	0546
BD526	0378
BD526-1	0378
BD526-5	0378
BD527	0546
BD527-1	0546
BD527-5	0546
BD528	0378
BD528-1	0378
BD528-5	0378
BD529	0546
BD529-1	0546
BD529-5	0546
BD530	0378
BD530-1	OEM
BD530-5	0378
BD533	0042
BD533J	OEM
BD533K	OEM
BD533L	OEM
BD534	0919
BD534J	OEM
BD534K	OEM
BD534L	0919
BD535	0042
BD535J	OEM
BD535K	OEM
BD536	0919
BD536J	OEM
BD536K	OEM
BD537	0419
BD538	0848
BD538J	OEM
BD538K	OEM
BD539	OEM
BD539A	OEM
BD539B	OEM
BD539C	OEM
BD539D	OEM
BD540	OEM
BD540A	OEM
BD540C	OEM
BD540D	OEM
BD543	1359
BD543A	1359
BD543B	1359
BD543C	1359
BD543D	3009
BD544	0477
BD544A	0477
BD544B	0477
BD544C	0477
BD544D	1157
BD545	OEM
BD545A	OEM
BD545B	OEM
BD545C	OEM
BD545D	OEM
BD546	OEM
BD546A	OEM
BD546B	OEM
BD546C	OEM
BD546D	OEM
BD550	4053
BD550A	6294
BD550B	4053
BD561	0161
BD562	0455
BD566	OEM
BD566A	OEM
BD567	OEM
BD567A	OEM
BD575	2969
BD576	3136
BD577	2969
BD578	3136
BD579	0419
BD580	3136
BD581	0556
BD582	1190
BD585	2969
BD586	3136
BD587	2969
BD588	3136
BD589	2969
BD590	3136
BD591	0419
BD592	1190
BD595	0556
BD596	0919
BD597	0556
BD598	1190
BD599	0556
BD600	1190
BD601	0556
BD605	0556
BD606	1190
BD607	0556
BD608	1190
BD609	0556
BD610	1190
BD611	OEM
BD612	OEM
BD613	OEM
BD614	OEM
BD615	OEM
BD616	OEM
BD617	OEM
BD618	OEM
BD619	OEM
BD620	OEM
BD633	0419
BD634	0676
BD635	0419
BD636	0676
BD637	0556
BD643	1203
BD644	2222
BD645	1203
BD646	0597
BD647	2220
BD648	0597
BD649	2220
BD649/BD650	OEM
BD650	2222
BD651	4015
BD652	1957
BD663	OEM
BD663A	0556
BD663B	0556
BD664	OEM
BD675	0553
BD675A	3343
BD676	2869
BD676A	3486
BD677	0553
BD677/678	OEM
BD677A	3343
BD678	2869
BD678A	3486
BD679	0553
BD679/680	OEM
BD679A	3343
BD680	2869
BD680A	3486
BD681	0553
BD681/682	OEM
BD683	OEM
BD683/684	OEM
BD684	OEM
BD695A	3487
BD696A	3488
BD697	0134
BD697A	3487
BD698	0073
BD698A	3488
BD699	3487
BD699A	3487
BD700	3488
BD700A	3488
BD701	3487
BD702	3488
BD705	0477
BD706	1359
BD707	0477
BD708	1359
BD709	0477
BD710	1359
BD711	0477
BD712	1359
BD733	0419
BD734	0676
BD735	0419
BD736	0676
BD737	0419
BD738	0676
BD743	OEM
BD743A	OEM
BD743B	OEM
BD743C	OEM
BD743D	OEM
BD744	OEM
BD744A	OEM
BD744B	OEM
BD744C	OEM
BD744D	OEM
BD745	OEM
BD745A	OEM
BD745B	OEM
BD745C	OEM
BD745D	OEM
BD746	OEM
BD746A	OEM
BD746B	OEM
BD746C	OEM
BD746D	OEM
BD750	4081
BD750A	4081
BD750B	4081
BD750C	4081
BD751	3656
BD751A	3656
BD751B	3656
BD751C	3656
BD795	2220
BD796	2222
BD797	2220
BD798	2222
BD799	2220
BD800	2222
BD801	0236
BD802	0676
BD805	4093
BD806	4094
BD807	4093
BD808	4094
BD813	OEM
BD814	OEM
BD815	OEM
BD816	OEM
BD817	OEM
BD818	OEM
BD825	OEM
BD825-6	OEM
BD825-10	OEM
BD825-16	OEM
BD826	1045
BD826-6	OEM
BD826-10	OEM
BD826-16	OEM
BD827	OEM
BD827-6	OEM
BD827-10	OEM
BD828	OEM
BD828-6	OEM
BD828-10	OEM
BD829	OEM
BD829-6	OEM
BD829-10	OEM
BD830	OEM
BD830-6	OEM
BD830-10	OEM
BD833	0555
BD834	1257
BD835	0555
BD836	1257
BD837	0555
BD838	1257
BD839	0219
BD840	1045
BD841	0818
BD842	3294
BD843	0818
BD844	3294
BD845	OEM
BD846	OEM
BD847	OEM
BD848	OEM
BD849	OEM
BD850	OEM
BD861	OEM
BD863	OEM
BD864	OEM
BD865	OEM
BD866	OEM
BD875	0553
BD876	2869
BD877	0553
BD878	4114
BD879	OEM
BD880	OEM
BD895	2220
BD895A	2220
BD896	2222
BD896A	2222
BD897	2220
BD897A	2220
BD898	2222
BD898A	2222
BD899	2220
BD899A	2220
BD900	2222
BD900A	2222
BD901	2220
BD902	2222
BD905	0477
BD906	1359
BD907	0477
BD908	1359
BD909	0477
BD910	1359
BD911	4121
BD912	1359
BD914	OEM
BD914F	OEM
BD914T	OEM
BD933	1157
BD934	0713
BD935	1157
BD936	0713
BD937	1157
BD938	0713
BD939	1157
BD940	0713
BD941	1157
BD941F	1157
BD942	0713
BD943	0042
BD944	0275
BD945	0042
BD946	0919
BD947	0042
BD948	0919
BD948F	OEM
BD949	0042
BD950	0919
BD951	0060
BD952	1298
BD953	1157
BD954	0477
BD955	1157
BD956	0713
BD975	OEM
BD976	OEM
BD979	OEM
BD980	OEM
BD1530	OEM
BD1540	OEM
BD1550	OEM
BD1560	OEM
BD2530	OEM
BD2540	OEM
BD2550	OEM
BD3595	OEM
BD3595F	0604
BD3595T	0604
BD3600	OEM
BD3600F	OEM
BD3600T	OEM
BD4148	OEM
BD4148F	OEM
BD4148T	OEM
BDF150S01L	OEM
BDF150S02L	OEM
BDF150S03L	OEM
BDF150S04L	OEM
BDF150S05L	OEM
BDF150S06L	OEM
BDF150S07L	OEM
BDF150S08L	OEM
BDF150S09L	OEM
BDF150S10L	OEM
BDF150S11L	OEM
BDF150S12L	OEM
BDF170S01B	OEM
BDF170S02B	OEM
BDF170S03B	OEM
BDF170S04B	OEM
BDF170S05B	OEM
BDF170S07B	OEM
BDF170S08B	OEM
BDM1615500	OEM
BDM1616500	OEM
BDM1617500	OEM
BDM1618500	OEM
BDN23R	OEM
BDOA	0276
BDS40832-200	OEM
BDS40832-201	OEM
BDS40832-206	OEM
BDS40832PD2	OEM
BDS40832S20	OEM
BDT20	OEM
BDT29	0236
BDT29A	0236
BDT29B	0236
BDT29C	1157
BDT30	0676
BDT30A	0676
BDT30B	0676
BDT30C	0713
BDT31	0236
BDT31A	0236
BDT31B	0236
BDT31C	0236

If replacement code is OEM, contact original manufacturer for replacement.

DEVICE TYPE	REPL CODE
BDT32	0676
BDT32A	0676
BDT32C	0676
BDT41	0477
BDT41A	0477
BDT41B	OEM
BDT41C	OEM
BDT42	1359
BDT42A	1359
BDT42B	OEM
BDT42C	OEM
BDT60	0597
BDT60A	0597
BDT60B	0597
BDT60C	1957
BDT61	1203
BDT61A	1203
BDT61B	1203
BDT61C	1948
BDT62	2222
BDT62A	2222
BDT62B	2222
BDT62C	1957
BDT63	2220
BDT63A	2220
BDT63B	2220
BDT63C	1948
BDT64	1957
BDT64A	1957
BDT64B	1957
BDT64C	1957
BDT65	1948
BDT65A	1948
BDT65B	1948
BDT65C	1948
BDT91	0477
BDT92	1359
BDT93	0477
BDT94	1359
BDT95	0477
BDT96	1359
BDV64	0073
BDV64A	0073
BDV64B	0073
BDV64C	OEM
BDV65	0134
BDV65A	0134
BDV65B	0134
BDV65C	OEM
BDV66	OEM
BDV66A	OEM
BDV66B	OEM
BDV66C	OEM
BDV67	OEM
BDV67A	OEM
BDV67B	OEM
BDV67C	OEM
BDV91	3052
BDV92	0853
BDV93	3052
BDV94	0853
BDV95	3052
BDV96	0853
BDW21	OEM
BDW21A	OEM
BDW21B	OEM
BDW21C	OEM
BDW22	OEM
BDW22A	OEM
BDW22B	OEM
BDW22C	OEM
BDW23	1203
BDW23A	1203
BDW23B	1203
BDW23C	1205
BDW24	0597
BDW24A	0597
BDW24B	0597
BDW24C	0597
BDW26	OEM
BDW32	OEM
BDW38	OEM
BDW51	0538
BDW51A	0538
BDW51B	0538
BDW51C	0538
BDW52	1588
BDW52A	1588
BDW52B	1588
BDW52C	1588
BDW53	OEM
BDW53A	OEM
BDW53B	OEM
BDW53C	OEM
BDW53D	OEM
BDW54	OEM
BDW54C	0597
BDW54D	OEM
BDW55	OEM
BDW56	OEM
BDW57	OEM
BDW58	OEM
BDW59	OEM
BDW60	OEM
BDW63	OEM
BDW63A	OEM
BDW63B	OEM
BDW63C	OEM
BDW63D	OEM

DEVICE TYPE	REPL CODE
BDW64	OEM
BDW64A	OEM
BDW64B	OEM
BDW64C	OEM
BDW64D	OEM
BDW73	OEM
BDW73A	OEM
BDW73B	OEM
BDW73C	OEM
BDW74	OEM
BDW74B	OEM
BDW74C	OEM
BDW74D	OEM
BDW83	OEM
BDW83A	OEM
BDW83B	OEM
BDW83C	OEM
BDW83D	OEM
BDW84	OEM
BDW84A	OEM
BDW84B	OEM
BDW84C	OEM
BDW84D	OEM
BDW91	OEM
BDW92	OEM
BDW93	1948
BDW93A	1948
BDW93B	1948
BDW93C	1948
BDW94	1957
BDW94A	1957
BDW94B	1957
BDW94C	1957
BDX10	0103
BDX10C	OEM
BDX11	0177
BDX12	0074
BDX13	0130
BDX13/40251	OEM
BDX18	0486
BDX18N	0486
BDX20	1588
BDX23	0538
BDX24	0177
BDX25	0236
BDX27	0919
BDX27-6	0919
BDX27-10	0919
BDX28	0919
BDX28-6	0919
BDX28-10	0919
BDX29	0236
BDX29-6	0236
BDX29-10	0236
BDX30	0236
BDX30-6	0236
BDX30-10	0236
BDX31	OEM
BDX32	0223
BDX33	2220
BDX33A	2220
BDX33B	2220
BDX33C	2220
BDX33D	2220
BDX33E	OEM
BDX34	2222
BDX34A	2222
BDX34B	2222
BDX34C	2225
BDX40	0538
BDX41	0538
BDX42	0553
BDX43	0553
BDX44	OEM
BDX45	2869
BDX46	2869
BDX47	OEM
BDX50	0538
BDX51	0538
BDX53	2220
BDX53A	2220
BDX53B	2220
BDX53C	2220
BDX53D	OEM
BDX53E	OEM
BDX53F	OEM
BDX53S	OEM
BDX54	2222
BDX54A	2222
BDX54B	2222
BDX54C	2222
BDX54D	OEM
BDX54E	OEM
BDX54F	OEM
BDX54S	OEM
BDX60	0538
BDX61	0130
BDX62	2262
BDX62/63	OEM
BDX62/63A	OEM
BDX62A	2262
BDX62B	2262
BDX62B/63B	OEM
BDX62C	2404
BDX62L	OEM
BDX63	2411
BDX63A	2411
BDX63B	2412
BDX63C	2412

DEVICE TYPE	REPL CODE
BDX63L	OEM
BDX64	2415
BDX64/65	OEM
BDX64A	2415
BDX64A/65	OEM
BDX64B	2415
BDX64B/65B	OEM
BDX64C	2404
BDX64L	OEM
BDX65	2422
BDX65A	2422
BDX65B	2422
BDX65C	2412
BDX65L	OEM
BDX66	2429
BDX66A	2429
BDX66B	2415
BDX66CBDX67	OEM
BDX66L	OEM
BDX67A	1384
BDX67B	1384
BDX67C	1384
BDX67L	OEM
BDX70	0419
BDX71	0419
BDX72	0419
BDX73	0419
BDX74	0042
BDX75	0042
BDX77	0477
BDX78	1359
BDX83	2422
BDX83A	2422
BDX83B	2422
BDX83C	2422
BDX85	2422
BDX85A	2422
BDX85B	2422
BDX85C	2415
BDX86	2415
BDX86A	2415
BDX86B	2415
BDX86C	2415
BDX87	2422
BDX87A	2422
BDX87B	2422
BDX87C	2422
BDX88	2415
BDX88A	2415
BDX88B	2415
BDX88C	2415
BDX91	0177
BDX92	2002
BDX93	0177
BDX94	2002
BDX95	0177
BDX96	1671
BDX331	OEM
BDY10	0103
BDY11	0103
BDY12	0042
BDY13	0042
BDY13-16	OEM
BDY15	2736
BDY15A	2736
BDY15B	2736
BDY15C	2736
BDY16	0178
BDY16A	2736
BDY16B	2736
BDY17	0103
BDY18	0538
BDY19	0538
BDY20	0103
BDY21	OEM
BDY22	OEM
BDY23	0177
BDY23A	0177
BDY23B	0177
BDY23C	0177
BDY24	0359
BDY25	0359
BDY26	0359
BDY27	0359
BDY28	0359
BDY29	2187
BDY34	0042
BDY37	0538
BDY37A	0130
BDY38	0103
BDY39	0103
BDY45	1841
BDY46	1841
BDY47	1841
BDY53	0103
BDY54	0177
BDY55	0538
BDY56	0177
BDY57	2465
BDY57A	2416
BDY58	2465
BDY58R	OEM
BDY60	0617
BDY61	0615
BDY62	0160
BDY63	0177
BDY65	0264
BDY66	0264
BDY69	2002

DEVICE TYPE	REPL CODE
BDY70	0126
BDY71	0178
BDY72	0178
BDY73	0103
BDY74	0538
BDY76	0130
BDY77	0538
BDY78	0424
BDY79	0424
BDY80	0042
BDY80A	OEM
BDY80B	OEM
BDY80C	OEM
BDY81	0236
BDY81A	OEM
BDY81B	OEM
BDY81C	OEM
BDY82	0919
BDY82A	OEM
BDY82B	OEM
BDY82C	OEM
BDY83	0919
BDY83A	OEM
BDY83B	OEM
BDY83C	OEM
BDY90	0615
BDY90A	3228
BDY91	0615
BDY92	0615
BDY93	0065
BDY93/01	0065
BDY94	0615
BDY95	0074
BDY96/01	OEM
BDY97	0074
BDY97/01	0074
BDY98	0074
BDY99	0074
BDY180T2	OEM
BDY181T2	OEM
BDY182T2	OEM
BDY183T2	OEM
BDY184T2	OEM
BDY185T2	OEM
BE6	0279
BE6A	0279
BE-55	0030
BE-66	0016
BE71	0086
BE107	0015
BE117	0015
BE127	0015
BE155	OEM
BE173	0127
BEL100N	OEM
BEL100P	OEM
BEL550A	OEM
BEL550B	OEM
BEL550C	OEM
BEL700	OEM
BEL1044	OEM
BES042	OEM
BES043	OEM
BES044	OEM
BES046	OEM
BES048	OEM
BES050	OEM
BES051	OEM
BES063	OEM
BF7-35	OEM
BF14-35	OEM
BF25-35	OEM
BF36C	OEM
BF40B8H	0724
BF50-35	OEM
BF60B8L	1034
BF60B9A	OEM
BF71	0016
BF100-35	OEM
BF108	0233
BF109	0233
BF110	0233
BF111	0233
BF114	0233
BF115	0079
BF117	0233
BF118	0233
BF119	0233
BF120	0233
BF121	0127
BF123	0127
BF125	0127
BF127	0127
BF137	0283
BF140	0233
BF140A	0233
BF140R	0233
BF140S	0233
BF152	0488
BF153	0488
BF154	0488
BF155	0007
BF155R	0233
BF155S	0233
BF156	0233
BF157	0233
BF157B	0233
BF158	0488
BF159	0488

DEVICE TYPE	REPL CODE
BF160	0488
BF161	0007
BF162	0144
BF163	0144
BF164	0144
BF165	0144
BF166	0007
BF167	0007
BF168	0007
BF169	0007
BF173	0007
BF173A	0144
BF174	0233
BF175	0007
BF176	0144
BF177	0086
BF178	0233
BF179	0233
BF179A	0233
BF179B	0233
BF179C	0233
BF-180	0079
BF180	0007
BF181	0007
BF182	0007
BF183	0007
BF183A	0016
BF184	0007
BF185	0007
BF186	0233
BF187	0144
BF188	0144
BF189	0016
BF194	0224
BF194A	0144
BF194B	0127
BF195	0224
BF195C	0127
BF195D	0127
BF196	0224
BF196-01	OEM
BF196P	OEM
BF197	0127
BF197-01	OEM
BF197P	OEM
BF-198	0224
BF198	0224
BF199	0224
BF200	0007
BF-200(PENNCREST)	0007
BF200(ZENITH)	0127
BF206	0007
BF207	0007
BF208	0007
BF209	0007
BF212	0007
BF213	0007
BF-214	0016
BF214	0007
BF214A	OEM
BF214B	OEM
BF-215	0016
BF215	0007
BF216	0127
BF217	0127
BF218	0127
BF219	0127
BF220	0127
BF222	0007
BF223	0144
BF224	0224
BF224J	0016
BF225	0224
BF225J	0016
BF-226	0016
BF226	0007
BF227	0007
BF228	0855
BF229	0127
BF230	0127
BF232	0007
BF233	0224
BF233-2	0224
BF233-3	0224
BF233-4	0144
BF233-5	0007
BF233-6	0224
BF234	0224
BF235	0144
BF236	0144
BF237	0079
BF238	0079
BF240	0224
BF240B	0224
BF241	0224
BF241C	0224
BF241D	0224
BF243	0688
BF244	0321
BF244A	0321
BF244B	0321
BF244C	0321
BF245	0321
BF245A	0321
BF245B	0321
BF245C	0321
BF246	0321
BF246A	OEM
BF246B	OEM

DEVICE TYPE	REPL CODE
BF246C	OEM
BF247	0321
BF247A	OEM
BF247B	OEM
BF247C	OEM
BF248	0016
BF249	0037
BF250	0016
BF251	0007
BF252	0007
BF253	0127
BF253-2	OEM
BF253-3	OEM
BF253-4	OEM
BF253-5	OEM
BF253-6	OEM
BF254	0224
BF254(ALGG)	0191
BF254(PHIN)	0191
BF254(SIEG)	0224
BF254B	0007
BF-255	0079
BF255	0224
BF255(ALGG)	0191
BF255(PHIN)	0191
BF255(SIEG)	0224
BF255C	0007
BF255D	0007
BF256	0321
BF256A	0321
BF256B	0321
BF256C	0321
BF256L	OEM
BF256LA	OEM
BF256LB	OEM
BF256LC	OEM
BF257	0187
BF258	0187
BF259	0233
BF260	0007
BF261	0007
BF262	0144
BF263	0144
BF264	0144
BF270	0007
BF271	0007
BF272	4359
BF273	0007
BF273C	0007
BF273D	0007
BF274	0007
BF274B	0007
BF274C	0007
BF279	0007
BF287	0007
BF288	0007
BF290	0007
BF291	0016
BF291A	0016
BF291B	0016
BF292	0233
BF292A	0233
BF292B	0233
BF292C	0233
BF293	0016
BF293A	0016
BF293D	0016
BF294	0233
BF297	0710
BF297-P	0264
BF297W	OEM
BF297W2	OEM
BF298	0710
BF298-P	0334
BF298W	OEM
BF298W2	OEM
BF299	0338
BF299-P	0334
BF299W	OEM
BF299W2	OEM
BF302	0007
BF303	0488
BF304	0007
BF305	0233
BF306	0007
BF308	0224
BF309	0414
BF310	0224
BF310(ALGG)	0259
BF311	0224
BF314	0224
BF314(ALGG)	0259
BF315	0150
BF316	0150
BF316A	OEM
BF320	OEM
BF320A	OEM
BF320B	OEM
BF320C	OEM
BF321	OEM
BF321A	0198
BF321B	0016
BF321C	0016
BF321D	0016
BF321E	0016
BF321F	0016
BF322	0086
BF323	0126
BF324	0802

DEVICE TYPE	REPL CODE
BF325	0414
BF327	OEM
BF329	0127
BF330	0414
BF332	0127
BF332B	OEM
BF333	0127
BF333C	0127
BF333D	0127
BF334	0127
BF335	0127
BF336	0233
BF337	0233
BF338	0233
BF339	0150
BF340	0037
BF341	3528
BF342	0037
BF343	0037
BF344	0007
BF345	0007
BF346A	OEM
BF346B	OEM
BF346C	OEM
BF347	OEM
BF348	0321
BF350	OEM
BF351	OEM
BF352	OEM
BF353	OEM
BF354	OEM
BF355	0233
BF357	0144
BF362	0007
BF363	0007
BF364	0224
BF365	0224
BF366	0086
BF367	0224
BF368	0079
BF368K	OEM
BF369	0079
BF369K	OEM
BF370	OEM
BF370R	OEM
BF371	2503
BF372	OEM
BF373	OEM
BF374	2503
BF375	2503
BF375C	2503
BF375D	2503
BF377	0414
BF378	0414
BF379	0037
BF380	OEM
BF380-1	OEM
BF380-5	OEM
BF381	OEM
BF381-5	OEM
BF382	OEM
BF382-1	OEM
BF382-5	OEM
BF384	0144
BF385	0144
BF387	0086
BF388	OEM
BF389B	OEM
BF389C	OEM
BF391	0710
BF391P	OEM
BF391W1	OEM
BF391W2	OEM
BF392	0710
BF392P	OEM
BF392W1	OEM
BF392W2	OEM
BF393	0710
BF393P	OEM
BF393W1	OEM
BF393W2	OEM
BF394	0018
BF394B	0018
BF395	0018
BF395C	0018
BF395D	0018
BF397	0338
BF397A	0338
BF398	0338
BF398A	0338
BF398B	0338
BF400	OEM
BF402	OEM
BF403	OEM
BF404	OEM
BF405	OEM
BF406	OEM
BF410	OEM
BF410A	OEM
BF410B	OEM
BF410C	OEM
BF410D	OEM
BF411	0855
BF412	0855
BF414	0037
BF415	0233
BF416	OEM
BF417	0233
BF418	OEM

If replacement code is OEM, contact original manufacturer for replacement. 289

DEVICE TYPE	REPL CODE	DEVICE TYPE	REPL CODE	DEVICE TYPE	REPL CODE	DEVICE TYPE	REPL CODE	DEVICE TYPE	REPL CODE	DEVICE TYPE	REPL CODE	DEVICE TYPE	REPL CODE
BF419	4393	BF693W2	OEM	BFF150S04L	OEM	BFR15A	OEM	BFS16F	0127	BFS97M	OEM	BFV51	0079
BF420	0261	BF694	OEM	BFF150S05B	OEM	BFR16	0016	BFS16G	0127	BFS98	0037	BFV52	0018
BF420A	OEM	BF694A	OEM	BFF150S05L	OEM	BFR17	0111	BFS17	0144	BFS98K	OEM	BFV53	0079
BF420L	OEM	BF694B	OEM	BFF150S06B	OEM	BFR18	0086	BFS17A	3338	BFS98L	OEM	BFV54	0079
BF421	0261	BF706	0037	BFF150S06L	OEM	BFR19	0086	BFS17R	OEM	BFS98M	OEM	BFV55	0079
BF421A	OEM	BF709	3562	BFF150S07B	OEM	BFR20	0086	BFS18	1722	BFS99	0283	BFV56	OEM
BF421L	OEM	BF715	0283	BFF150S08B	OEM	BFR21	0725	BFS18CA	0007	BFT10	OEM	BFV56A	OEM
BF422	0261	BF716	OEM	BFF150S08L	OEM	BFR22	0086	BFS18R	0127	BFT11	OEM	BFV57	OEM
BF422A	OEM	BF717	0283	BFF150S09L	OEM	BFR23	0126	BFS19	1722	BFT13	OEM	BFV57A	OEM
BF422L	OEM	BF718	OEM	BFF150S10L	OEM	BFR24	0126	BFS19CB	0079	BFT13A	OEM	BFV58	OEM
BF422W	OEM	BF720	OEM	BFF150S11L	OEM	BFR25	0111	BFS19R	0127	BFT14	OEM	BFV59	0007
BF422W3	OEM	BF721	OEM	BFF150S12L	OEM	BFR26	0016	BFS20	4410	BFT14A	OEM	BFV60	0007
BF423	0434	BF722	OEM	BFF170S01B	OEM	BFR27	OEM	BFS20R	0127	BFT15	OEM	BFV61	0007
BF423A	OEM	BF723	OEM	BFG16A	OEM	BFR28	0144	BFS21	0321	BFT16	OEM	BFV62	0111
BF423L	OEM	BF724	OEM	BFG17A	OEM	BFR29	OEM	BFS21A	0321	BFT17	OEM	BFV63	OEM
BF423W	OEM	BF739	OEM	BFG31	OEM	BFR30	OEM	BFS22	0693	BFT18	OEM	BFV63A	OEM
BF423W3	OEM	BF740	OEM	BFG33	OEM	BFR30R	OEM	BFS22A	0617	BFT18A	OEM	BFV63B	OEM
BF424	0802	BF757	OEM	BFG35	OEM	BFR31	OEM	BFS22B	OEM	BFT19	0434	BFV64	OEM
BF435	OEM	BF758	OEM	BFG55	OEM	BFR31R	OEM	BFS22R	OEM	BFT19A	0434	BFV64A	OEM
BF436	OEM	BF759	OEM	BFG67	OEM	BFR35A	0016	BFS23	0693	BFT20	0037	BFV64B	OEM
BF437	OEM	BF767	OEM	BFG92A	OEM	BFR36	0086	BFS23A	0177	BFT21	0037	BFV65	OEM
BF439	OEM	BF799	OEM	BFG93A	OEM	BFR37	0259	BFS23R	OEM	BFT22	0037	BFV65A	OEM
BF440	0037	BF800	OEM	BFG97	OEM	BFR38	0320	BFS26E	0037	BFT25	2891	BFV66	OEM
BF441	0037	BF801	OEM	BFG135	OEM	BFR39T05	0187	BFS26F	0037	BFT27	OEM	BFV66A	OEM
BF450	0037	BF802	OEM	BFG197	OEM	BFR40	0320	BFS26G	0037	BFT28	0434	BFV67	OEM
BF451	3572	BF805	OEM	BFG198	OEM	BFR40T05	0086	BFS27E	0007	BFT28A	0434	BFV68	OEM
BF456	0558	BF806	OEM	BFN16	OEM	BFR40T05	0086	BFS27F	0007	BFT28B	0434	BFV68A	OEM
BF457	0558	BF808	OEM	BFN17	OEM	BFR41	0320	BFS27G	0007	BFT28C	0434	BFV69	OEM
BF458	0275	BF810	OEM	BFN18	OEM	BFR41T05	0086	BFS28	0349	BFT29	0086	BFV69A	OEM
BF459	0275	BF811	OEM	BFN19	OEM	BFR41T05	0086	BFS28R	0349	BFT30	0086	BFV70	OEM
BF460	OEM	BF815	OEM	BFN20	OEM	BFR44A	OEM	BFS29	0086	BFT31	0086	BFV71	OEM
BF461	OEM	BF816	OEM	BFN21	OEM	BFR44B	OEM	BFS29P	0590	BFT33	0617	BFV72	OEM
BF462	OEM	BF817	OEM	BFN22	OEM	BFR44C	OEM	BFS30	0590	BFT34	0617	BFV72N	OEM
BF469	0275	BF818	OEM	BFN22R	OEM	BFR45	OEM	BFS30P	0590	BFT39	0086	BFV73	OEM
BF470	4402	BF819	0168	BFN23	OEM	BFR46	OEM	BFS31	0037	BFT40	0086	BFV73N	OEM
BF471	0275	BF819A	OEM	BFP10	OEM	BFR47	OEM	BFS31P	0016	BFT41	0086	BFV75	OEM
BF472	4402	BF820	3431	BFP11	OEM	BFR48	OEM	BFS32	0037	BFT42	0617	BFV75N	OEM
BF479T	OEM	BF821	3345	BFP12	OEM	BFR50	0320	BFS32P	0037	BFT43	0617	BFV76	OEM
BF480	0259	BF822	4462	BFP13	OEM	BFR51	0086	BFS33	0037	BFT46	OEM	BFV76N	OEM
BF481	OEM	BF823	4464	BFP14	OEM	BFR52	0086	BFS33P	0037	BFT47	OEM	BFV77	OEM
BF482	OEM	BF824	4410	BFP22	OEM	BFR53	2891	BFS34	0786	BFT48	OEM	BFV78	OEM
BF491	0338	BF-832	0037	BFP23	OEM	BFR54	OEM	BFS34P	0037	BFT49	OEM	BFV79	OEM
BF492	0338	BF840	4466	BFP25	OEM	BFR56	OEM	BFS36	0086	BFT50	OEM	BFV80	0007
BF493	0338	BF841	4466	BFP26	OEM	BFR57	0233	BFS36A	0016	BFT51	OEM	BFV81	0037
BF494	0224	BF847	OEM	BFP90	OEM	BFR58	0233	BFS37	0037	BFT53	0320	BFV81A	0037
BF494B	OEM	BF848	OEM	BFP91	OEM	BFR59	0233	BFS37A	0037	BFT54	0086	BFV81B	0037
BF495	0224	BF849	OEM	BFP96	OEM	BFR60	0431	BFS38	0016	BFT55	0016	BFV82	0037
BF496	OEM	BF858	OEM	BFQ10	OEM	BFR61	0786	BFS38A	0016	BFT57	0233	BFV82A	0037
BF497	0007	BF859	OEM	BFQ11	OEM	BFR62	0472	BFS39	0079	BFT59	0233	BFV82B	0037
BF502	OEM	BF869	0275	BFQ12	OEM	BFR63	0414	BFS40	0037	BFT60	0126	BFV82C	0037
BF503	OEM	BF870	4402	BFQ13	OEM	BFR64	0414	BFS40A	0037	BFT61	0126	BFV83	0144
BF505	0224	BF871	0275	BFQ14	OEM	BFR65	2059	BFS41	0037	BFT62	0126	BFV83A	0144
BF506	0037	BF872	4402	BFQ15	OEM	BFR77	0086	BFS42	0016	BFT69	0126	BFV83B	0016
BF506A	OEM	BF881	OEM	BFQ16	OEM	BFR78	0086	BFS43	0016	BFT70	0037	BFV83C	0016
BF507	0224	BF900	OEM	BFQ17	OEM	BFR79T05	0472	BFS44	0786	BFT71	0037	BFV85	0016
BF509S	OEM	BF905	OEM	BFQ18	OEM	BFR79T05	0472	BFS45	0786	BFT72	OEM	BFV85A	0016
BF510	OEM	BF907	OEM	BFQ18A	OEM	BFR80	0786	BFS46	OEM	BFT73	OEM	BFV85B	0016
BF511	OEM	BF910	OEM	BFQ19	OEM	BFR80T05	0472	BFS46A	OEM	BFT74	OEM	BFV85C	0016
BF512	OEM	BF914	OEM	BFQ22	OEM	BFR81	0527	BFS50	0488	BFT75	0126	BFV85D	0144
BF513	OEM	BF926	OEM	BFQ23	OEM	BFR81T05	0472	BFS51	0555	BFT79	0126	BFV85E	0144
BF516	0007	BF936	OEM	BFQ24	OEM	BFR81T05	0472	BFS55A	0111	BFT80	0126	BFV85F	0144
BF523	3562	BF939	3562	BFQ28	OEM	BFR84	OEM	BFS58	0144	BFT81	0126	BFV85G	0144
BF536	4410	BF960	0367	BFQ29	OEM	BFR86	0270	BFS59	0590	BFT91	OEM	BFV86	0037
BF540	0037	BF961	OEM	BFQ31	1426	BFR86A	OEM	BFS59K	OEM	BFT92	4419	BFV86A	0037
BF541	0037	BF963	OEM	BFQ31A	OEM	BFR86B	OEM	BFS59L	OEM	BFT93	4419	BFV86B	0037
BF542	0037	BF964	0367	BFQ31AR	OEM	BFR86T05	2523	BFS59M	OEM	BFT95	OEM	BFV86C	0037
BF550	0719	BF966	OEM	BFQ31R	OEM	BFR86T05	0187	BFS60	0590	BFT96	OEM	BFV87	0016
BF550R	OEM	BF967	OEM	BFQ32	OEM	BFR87A	OEM	BFS60K	OEM	BFT97	OEM	BFV88	0016
BF554	OEM	BF968	OEM	BFQ33	OEM	BFR87B	OEM	BFS60L	OEM	BFT98	OEM	BFV88A	OEM
BF562	OEM	BF970	OEM	BFQ34	OEM	BFR87T05	2523	BFS60M	OEM	BFT99	OEM	BFV88B	OEM
BF568	OEM	BF979	OEM	BFQ35	0126	BFR87T05	0187	BFS61K	OEM	BFV10	0079	BFV88C	0016
BF569	OEM	BF979S	OEM	BFQ36	0126	BFR88	0710	BFS61L	OEM	BFV11	0079	BFV88E	OEM
BF579	4419	BF980	OEM	BFQ37	0126	BFR88A	OEM	BFS61M	OEM	BFV12	0079	BFV89	0111
BF594	0224	BF981	OEM	BFQ41	OEM	BFR88B	OEM	BFS62	0007	BFV13	OEM	BFV89A	0111
BF595	0224	BF982	OEM	BFQ42	OEM	BFR88T05	2523	BFS64	OEM	BFV14	0018	BFV90A	OEM
BF596	0079	BF989	OEM	BFQ43	OEM	BFR88T05	0187	BFS65	OEM	BFV15	OEM	BFV90B	OEM
BF597	0111	BF990AR	OEM	BFQ51	OEM	BFR89	0710	BFS67	OEM	BFV17	0320	BFV91	OEM
BF597A	OEM	BF994	OEM	BFQ52	OEM	BFR89A	OEM	BFS67P	OEM	BFV19	OEM	BFV91N	OEM
BF597B	OEM	BF995	OEM	BFQ53	OEM	BFR89B	OEM	BFS68	0321	BFV20	0037	BFV92	OEM
BF599	1426	BF996	OEM	BFQ56	OEM	BFR89T05	2523	BFS68P	0321	BFV21	0037	BFV92N	OEM
BF606	3562	BF998R	OEM	BFQ57	OEM	BFR89T05	0187	BFS69	0037	BFV22	0037	BFV93	OEM
BF606A	OEM	BFAB3/800	OEM	BFQ58	OEM	BFR90	1332	BFS70	OEM	BFV23	OEM	BFV93A	OEM
BF615	OEM	BFC18/500	OEM	BFQ59	OEM	BFR90A	OEM	BFS71	OEM	BFV24	OEM	BFV93AN	OEM
BF616	OEM	BFC91	OEM	BFQ60	OEM	BFR91A	OEM	BFS72	OEM	BFV25	0037	BFV93N	OEM
BF617	OEM	BFD150S01L	OEM	BFQ63	OEM	BFR92	2891	BFS73	OEM	BFV26	0037	BFV94	OEM
BF618	OEM	BFD150S02L	OEM	BFQ64	OEM	BFR92A	2891	BFS74	OEM	BFV27	0007	BFV94N	OEM
BF620	4433	BFD150S03L	OEM	BFQ67	OEM	BFR93	2891	BFS75	OEM	BFV29	0037	BFV95	OEM
BF621	4435	BFD150S04L	OEM	BFQ68	OEM	BFR93A	2891	BFS76	OEM	BFV30	0037	BFV95N	OEM
BF622	3433	BFD150S05L	OEM	BFQ69	OEM	BFR94	2059	BFS77	OEM	BFV31	0037	BFV96	OEM
BF623	4435	BFD150S06L	OEM	BFQ70	OEM	BFR96S	OEM	BFS78	OEM	BFV32	0037	BFV96N	OEM
BF642	OEM	BFD150S08L	OEM	BFQ71	OEM	BFR98	2030	BFS79	OEM	BFV33	0037	BFV97	OEM
BF642W	OEM	BFD150S09L	OEM	BFQ72	OEM	BFR99	3562	BFS80	OEM	BFV34	0037	BFV97N	OEM
BF642W3	OEM	BFD150S10L	OEM	BFQ73	OEM	BFR106	OEM	BFS85	0414	BFV35	0338	BFV98	OEM
BF643	OEM	BFD150S11L	OEM	BFQ74	OEM	BFRC90	OEM	BFS88	0414	BFV36	0338	BFV98N	OEM
BF643W	OEM	BFD150S12L	OEM	BFQ78	OEM	BFRC91	OEM	BFS90	OEM	BFV37	0111	BFV99	OEM
BF643W3	OEM	BFD170S01B	OEM	BFQ86	OEM	BFRC96	OEM	BFS91	0111	BFV38	0111	BFW10	0321
BF657	0233	BFD170S02B	OEM	BFQ88	OEM	BFS10	OEM	BFS91A	0431	BFV39	OEM	BFW11	0321
BF658	0233	BFD170S03B	OEM	BFQ88A	OEM	BFS11	0007	BFS91B	0431	BFV40	0079	BFW12	0321
BF659	0233	BFD170S04B	OEM	BFQ88B	OEM	BFS12	OEM	BFS92	0126	BFV41	0079	BFW13	0321
BF660	OEM	BFD170S05B	OEM	BFQ89	OEM	BFS13E	0127	BFS93	0126	BFV42	0079	BFW16	0414
BF679T	OEM	BFD170S06B	OEM	BFQ98	OEM	BFS13F	0127	BFS94	0126	BFV43	0079	BFW16A	0414
BF689	0007	BFD170S07B	OEM	BFQ98B	OEM	BFS13G	0127	BFS95	0126	BFV44	0079	BFW17	0414
BF692	OEM	BFD170S08B	OEM	BFQ149	OEM	BFS14E	0127	BFS96	0037	BFV45	0079	BFW17A	0414
BF692-P	0434	BFF150S01L	OEM	BFR10	0007	BFS14F	0127	BFS96K	OEM	BFV46	0079	BFW19	0414
BF692W	OEM	BFF150S02B	0007	BFR11	0016	BFS14G	0127	BFS96L	OEM	BFV47	0079	BFW20	0037
BF692W2	OEM	BFF150S02L	OEM	BFR12	OEM	BFS15E	0127	BFS96M	OEM	BFV48	OEM	BFW21	0037
BF693	OEM	BFF150S03B	OEM	BFR14B	OEM	BFS15F	0127	BFS97	0037	BFV49	0079	BFW22	0037
BF693-P	0434	BFF150S03L	OEM	BFR14C	OEM	BFS15G	0127	BFS97K	OEM	BFV50	0079	BFW23	0037
BF693W	OEM	BFF150S04B	OEM			BFS16E	0127	BFS97L	OEM			BFW24	0617

DEVICE TYPE	REPL CODE
BFW25	0617
BFW26	0617
BFW29	0016
BFW30	0414
BFW31	0037
BFW32	0016
BFW33	0233
BFW34	OEM
BFW35	OEM
BFW36	0233
BFW37	0233
BFW38	OEM
BFW39	OEM
BFW39A	OEM
BFW40	OEM
BFW41	0007
BFW42	0488
BFW43	0338
BFW44	0126
BFW45	0233
BFW46	0016
BFW47	0414
BFW50	0276
BFW51	OEM
BFW51A	OEM
BFW52	OEM
BFW52A	OEM
BFW54	0321
BFW55	0321
BFW56	0321
BFW57	0855
BFW58	0855
BFW59	0016
BFW60	0016
BFW61	0321
BFW63	0007
BFW64	0144
BFW68	0016
BFW69	OEM
BFW70	1929
BFW71	OEM
BFW73	2503
BFW73A	2503
BFW74	2503
BFW75	OEM
BFW76	2503
BFW76A	2503
BFW77	2503
BFW77A	2503
BFW78	OEM
BFW79	OEM
BFW80	OEM
BFW87	0037
BFW88	0378
BFW89	0037
BFW90	0037
BFW91	0126
BFW92	0259
BFW92A	1506
BFW96	OEM
BFW97	OEM
BFW98	0414
BFW98G	OEM
BFW100	0276
BFW200	0287
BFW300	0293
BFW400	0293
BFW500	0299
BFW600	0299
BFW700	OEM
BFW800	0250
BFW1000	0250
BFX10	OEM
BFX11	2449
BFX12	0150
BFX13	0150
BFX14	OEM
BFX15	OEM
BFX16	OEM
BFX17	0086
BFX18	0144
BFX19	0144
BFX20	0144
BFX21	0144
BFX29	0037
BFX30	0037
BFX31	0007
BFX32	0127
BFX33	0488
BFX34	4161
BFX35	0037
BFX36	2449
BFX37	0688
BFX38	0126
BFX39	0126
BFX40	0126
BFX41	0126
BFX42	2503
BFX43	0016
BFX44	0016
BFX45	0144
BFX47	0007
BFX48	0150
BFX49G	OEM
BFX50	0086
BFX51	0086
BFX52	0086
BFX53	0590
BFX55	0414

DEVICE TYPE	REPL CODE
BFX59	0008
BFX59F	0016
BFX60	0007
BFX61	0086
BFX62	0007
BFX63	OEM
BFX65	0037
BFX66	0016
BFX67	OEM
BFX68	0086
BFX68A	0086
BFX69	0086
BFX69A	0086
BFX70	OEM
BFX71	OEM
BFX72	OEM
BFX73	0007
BFX74	0086
BFX74A	0126
BFX77	0007
BFX78	OEM
BFX79	OEM
BFX80	OEM
BFX81	OEM
BFX82	OEM
BFX83	OEM
BFX84	0086
BFX85	0086
BFX86	0086
BFX87	0126
BFX88	0126
BFX89	0007
BFX90	0338
BFX91B	OEM
BFX92	0016
BFX92A	0016
BFX93	0016
BFX93A	0111
BFX94	0016
BFX94A	OEM
BFX95	0016
BFX95A	0016
BFX95C	OEM
BFX95C1	OEM
BFX95C2	OEM
BFX96	0198
BFX96A	0086
BFX97	0086
BFX97A	0086
BFX98	0233
BFX99	0086
BFY10	0016
BFY11	0016
BFY12	0016
BFY13	0086
BFY14	0086
BFY15	0086
BFY16	0590
BFY16S	OEM
BFY17	0086
BFY18	0016
BFY19	0016
BFY20	OEM
BFY21	OEM
BFY22	0016
BFY23	0016
BFY23A	0016
BFY24	0016
BFY25	0016
BFY26	0016
BFY27	0086
BFY28	0016
BFY29	0016
BFY30	0016
BFY33	0016
BFY34	0086
BFY37	0016
BFY37I	0016
BFY39	0016
BFY39/1	0016
BFY39/2	0016
BFY39/3	0016
BFY39/11	0855
BFY39/I	0016
BFY39/II	0016
BFY39/III	0016
BFY39-1	0111
BFY39-2	0111
BFY39-3	0111
BFY39I	0016
BFY40	0086
BFY41	0233
BFY43	0233
BFY44	0086
BFY45	0233
BFY46	0086
BFY47	0127
BFY48	0127
BFY49	0127
BFY50	0086
BFY50E	OEM
BFY50I	OEM
BFY51	0086
BFY51(RTCF)	0018
BFY51I	0086
BFY52	0086
BFY53	0086
BFY55	0086
BFY55(RTCF)	0320

DEVICE TYPE	REPL CODE
BFY56	0086
BFY56A	0086
BFY56B	0086
BFY57	0233
BFY63	0488
BFY64	0126
BFY65	0233
BFY66	0086
BFY67	0086
BFY67A	0086
BFY67C	0086
BFY68	0086
BFY68A	0086
BFY69	0127
BFY69A	0127
BFY69B	0007
BFY70	0086
BFY72	0016
BFY73	0016
BFY74	0016
BFY75	0016
BFY76	0016
BFY77	0016
BFY78	0144
BFY79	0007
BFY80	0086
BFY81	2034
BFY82	2034
BFY83	OEM
BFY84	OEM
BFY85	0016
BFY85A	OEM
BFY85B	OEM
BFY86	0016
BFY86A	OEM
BFY86B	OEM
BFY87	0007
BFY87A	0007
BFY88	0007
BFY90	0488
BFY90(SIEG)	0016
BFY90B	0144
BFY91	OEM
BFY92	OEM
BFY94	0037
BFY99	0086
BFY167	0007
BFY371	0016
BFY391	0016
BFY501	0855
BFZ10	OEM
BG-07077	0012
BG08120K	OEM
BG-66	0016
BG71	0016
BG-94	0016
BG-190	OEM
BG2000-6164-004	OEM
BG2097-641	OEM
BG2097-642	OEM
BG3433S	OEM
BG4524K	OEM
BG5524C	OEM
BG5527S-1	OEM
BG5534S	1767
BG5628S	OEM
BG5725S-B3	OEM
BG12201-2	OEM
BG12203-2	OEM
BG12205-2	OEM
BG16101-2	OEM
BGX11-800TT	OEM
BGX11-1200CTT	OEM
BGX11-1200TT	OEM
BGX11-1400CTT	OEM
BGX12-600TT	OEM
BGX12-800TT	OEM
BGX12-1200CTT	OEM
BGX12-1200TT	OEM
BGX12-1400CTT	OEM
BGX13-600	4295
BGX13-600TT	OEM
BGX13-800	4295
BGX13-800TT	OEM
BGX13-1200	4295
BGX13-1200C	OEM
BGX13-1200CTT	OEM
BGX13-1200TT	OEM
BGX13-1400C-TT	OEM
BGX14-600TT	OEM
BGX14-800TT	OEM
BGX14-1200CTT	OEM
BGX14-1200TT	OEM
BGX14-1400CTT	OEM
BGX15-600	2966
BGX15-600TT	OEM
BGX15-800	2966
BGX15-800TT	OEM
BGX15-1200	2966
BGX15-1200C	OEM
BGX15-1200CTT	OEM
BGX15-1200TT	OEM
BGX15-1400C-TT	OEM
BGX17-600	2966
BGX17-600TT	OEM
BGX17-800	2966
BGX17-800TT	OEM
BGX17-1200	2966
BGX17-1200C	OEM

DEVICE TYPE	REPL CODE
BGX17-1200CTT	OEM
BGX17-1400C-TT	OEM
BGX50A	OEM
BGY12A	OEM
BGY12B	OEM
BGY13A	OEM
BGY13B	OEM
BGY14A	OEM
BGY14B	OEM
BGY15	OEM
BGY16	OEM
BGY17	OEM
BGY18	OEM
BGY19	OEM
BGY21	OEM
BGY22	OEM
BGY22A	OEM
BGY23	OEM
BGY23A	OEM
BGY24	OEM
BGY32	OEM
BGY33	OEM
BGY35	OEM
BGY36	OEM
BGY38	OEM
BH4R1	0015
BH4R2	OEM
BH4R3	OEM
BH4R4	OEM
BH4R5	OEM
BH4R6	0087
BH71	0016
BH200	OEM
BH300	OEM
BH400	OEM
BH500	OEM
BH-2401A	OEM
BH2401A	OEM
BHC0001	OEM
BHC0002	OEM
BHC0003	OEM
BHC0004	OEM
BHC0005	OEM
BHC4038AD	OEM
BHC4054AD	OEM
BH-DX0038CEZZ	0015
B-HQ	OEM
BI-07096	0315
BI71	0016
BI-82	0150
BIP7201	0198
BIP7301A	OEM
BIR	2422
BIW	0016
BJ-155	0030
BK-499	OEM
BK3903	OEM
BK3904	OEM
BKC300	OEM
BKC333	OEM
BKC400	OEM
BKC444	OEM
BKC600	OEM
BKC666	OEM
BKC900	OEM
BKC999	OEM
BKX13A	OEM
BKZ6.8	OEM
BKZ6.8A	OEM
BKZ6.8B	OEM
BKZ7.5	OEM
BKZ7.5A	OEM
BKZ7.5B	OEM
BKZ8.2	OEM
BKZ8.2A	OEM
BKZ8.2B	OEM
BKZ9.1	OEM
BKZ9.1A	OEM
BKZ9.1B	OEM
BKZ10	OEM
BKZ10A	OEM
BKZ10B	OEM
BKZ11	OEM
BKZ11A	OEM
BKZ11B	OEM
BKZ12	OEM
BKZ12A	OEM
BKZ12B	OEM
BKZ13	OEM
BKZ13B	OEM
BKZ15	OEM
BKZ15A	OEM
BKZ15B	OEM
BKZ16	OEM
BKZ16A	OEM
BKZ16B	OEM
BKZ18	OEM
BKZ18A	OEM
BKZ18B	OEM
BKZ20	OEM
BKZ20A	OEM
BKZ20B	OEM
BKZ22	OEM
BKZ22A	OEM
BKZ22B	OEM
BKZ24	OEM
BKZ24A	OEM
BKZ24B	OEM
BKZ27	OEM

DEVICE TYPE	REPL CODE
BKZ27A	OEM
BKZ27B	OEM
BKZ30	OEM
BKZ30A	OEM
BKZ30B	OEM
BKZ33	OEM
BKZ33A	OEM
BKZ33B	OEM
BKZ36	OEM
BKZ36A	OEM
BKZ36B	OEM
BKZ39	OEM
BKZ39A	OEM
BKZ39B	OEM
BKZ43	OEM
BKZ43A	OEM
BKZ43B	OEM
BKZ47	OEM
BKZ47A	OEM
BKZ47B	OEM
BKZ51	OEM
BKZ51A	OEM
BKZ51B	OEM
BKZ56	OEM
BKZ56A	OEM
BKZ56B	OEM
BKZ62	OEM
BKZ62A	OEM
BKZ62B	OEM
BKZ66	OEM
BKZ66A	OEM
BKZ66B	OEM
BKZ75	OEM
BKZ75A	OEM
BKZ75B	OEM
BKZ82	OEM
BKZ82A	OEM
BKZ82B	OEM
BKZ91	OEM
BKZ91A	OEM
BKZ91B	OEM
BKZ100	OEM
BKZ100A	OEM
BKZ100B	OEM
BKZ110	OEM
BKZ110A	OEM
BKZ110B	OEM
BKZ120	OEM
BKZ120A	OEM
BKZ120B	OEM
BKZ130	OEM
BKZ130A	OEM
BKZ130B	OEM
BKZ150	OEM
BKZ150A	OEM
BKZ150B	OEM
BKZ160	OEM
BKZ160A	OEM
BKZ160B	OEM
BKZ180	OEM
BKZ180A	OEM
BKZ180B	OEM
BKZ200	OEM
BKZ200A	OEM
BKZ200B	OEM
BL221	OEM
BL234C	OEM
BL244	OEM
BL245	OEM
BL246	OEM
BL246A	OEM
BL325	OEM
BL336	OEM
BL350	OEM
BL362	OEM
BL364	OEM
BL366	OEM
BL367A	OEM
BL397A	OEM
BL640	OEM
BL644	OEM
BL696	OEM
BL800A	OEM
BL803	OEM
BL807	OEM
BL814	OEM
BL825	OEM
BL829	OEM
BL843	OEM
BL844	OEM
BL847	OEM
BL849	OEM
BL934A	OEM
BL962	OEM
BL965	OEM
BL967A	OEM
BL970	OEM
BL973	OEM
BL982	OEM
BLA011	OEM
BLA012	OEM
BLA013	OEM
BLA019	OEM
BLA39B	OEM
BLC016	OEM
BLC032	OEM
BLC048	OEM
BLC0128	OEM
BLC0128A	OEM

DEVICE TYPE	REPL CODE
BLC0512	OEM
BLC80/05	OEM
BLC80/07	OEM
BLC80/10	OEM
BLC80/11	OEM
BLC80/11A	OEM
BLC80/11T	OEM
BLC80/12	OEM
BLC80/12A	OEM
BLC80/12T	OEM
BLC80/14	OEM
BLC80/14A	OEM
BLC80/14T	OEM
BLC80/116	OEM
BLC80/204	OEM
BLC80/316	OEM
BLC86/12B	OEM
BLC104	OEM
BLC116	OEM
BLC300	OEM
BLC406	OEM
BLC501	OEM
BLC508	OEM
BLC517	OEM
BLC519	OEM
BLC556	OEM
BLC8016	OEM
BLC8016A	OEM
BLC8016B	OEM
BLC8032A	OEM
BLC8032B	OEM
BLC8048A	OEM
BLC8048B	OEM
BLC8064A	OEM
BLC8064B	OEM
BLC8201	OEM
BLC8221	OEM
BLC8222	OEM
BLC8228	OEM
BLC8229	OEM
BLC8432	OEM
BLC8488	OEM
BLC8534	OEM
BLC8538	OEM
BLC8824	OEM
BLK001	OEM
BLK002	OEM
BLK003	OEM
BLK004	OEM
BLK005	OEM
BLK006	OEM
BLK007	OEM
BLK008	OEM
BLK010	OEM
BLK011	OEM
BLK012	OEM
BLK020	OEM
BLK022	OEM
BLK024	OEM
BLK829	OEM
BLM003	OEM
BLM006	OEM
BLM014	OEM
BLM017	OEM
BLM071	OEM
BLM076A	OEM
BLM086	OEM
BLM093	OEM
BLM095	OEM
BLM116	OEM
BLM127	OEM
BLM129	OEM
BLM136	OEM
BLM138	OEM
BLM143A	OEM
BLM148	OEM
BLM149A	OEM
BLM153	OEM
BLM154	OEM
BLM155	OEM
BLM162	OEM
BLM167	OEM
BLM176	OEM
BLM179	OEM
BLM181	OEM
BLM183	OEM
BLM184	OEM
BLM186	OEM
BLM188	OEM
BLM190	OEM
BLM192	OEM
BLM195	OEM
BLM196	OEM
BLM198	OEM
BLM199	OEM
BLM201	OEM
BLM203	OEM
BLM204	OEM
BLM205	OEM
BLM207	OEM
BLM211	OEM
BLM213	OEM
BLM256	OEM
BLM304	OEM
BLM306	OEM
BLM309	OEM
BLM310	OEM
BLM311	OEM
BLM312	OEM

DEVICE TYPE	REPL CODE
BLM313	OEM
BLP005D	OEM
BLP017D	OEM
BLP027D	OEM
BLP136D	OEM
BLP149D	OEM
BLP215	OEM
BLS032	OEM
BLS526	OEM
BLS530	OEM
BLS531	OEM
BLT028	OEM
BLT033	OEM
BLT036	OEM
BLT072	OEM
BLT074	OEM
BLT088	OEM
BLT101	OEM
BLT114A	OEM
BLT119	OEM
BLV10	OEM
BLV11	OEM
BLV20	OEM
BLV21	OEM
BLW10	OEM
BLW11	OEM
BLW12	OEM
BLW13	OEM
BLW14	OEM
BLW15	OEM
BLW16	2030
BLW17	OEM
BLW18	OEM
BLW19	OEM
BLW20	OEM
BLW21	OEM
BLW22	OEM
BLW23	OEM
BLW24	OEM
BLW25	2485
BLW29	OEM
BLW31	OEM
BLW32	OEM
BLW33	OEM
BLW34	OEM
BLW35	OEM
BLW36	OEM
BLW39	OEM
BLW42	OEM
BLW43	OEM
BLW44	OEM
BLW60	1189
BLW60C	OEM
BLW60F	OEM
BLW75	OEM
BLW76	OEM
BLW77	OEM
BLW78	OEM
BLW79	OEM
BLW80	OEM
BLW81	OEM
BLW82	OEM
BLW83	OEM
BLW84	OEM
BLW85	OEM
BLW86	OEM
BLW87	OEM
BLW89	OEM
BLW90	OEM
BLW92	OEM
BLW93	OEM
BLW94	OEM
BLW95	OEM
BLW96	OEM
BLW98	OEM
BLX10	OEM
BLX11	OEM
BLX12	OEM
BLX13C	OEM
BLX17	OEM
BLX18	OEM
BLX34	OEM
BLX35	OEM
BLX36	OEM
BLX37	OEM
BLX38	OEM
BLX39	OEM
BLX40	OEM
BLX41	OEM
BLX47	OEM
BLX48	OEM
BLX57	OEM
BLX65	0414
BLX67	3516
BLX68	2080
BLX69A	OEM
BLX82	OEM
BLX84	OEM
BLX85	OEM
BLX87	OEM
BLX88	0488
BLX91A	OEM
BLX92A	OEM
BLX93A	OEM
BLX94A	OEM
BLX94C	OEM
BLX281	OEM
BLX281A	OEM
BLX281B	OEM

If replacement code is OEM, contact original manufacturer for replacement.

291

Original Device Types

DEVICE TYPE	REPL CODE	DEVICE TYPE	REPL CODE	DEVICE TYPE	REPL CODE	DEVICE TYPE	REPL CODE	DEVICE TYPE	REPL CODE	DEVICE TYPE	REPL CODE	DEVICE TYPE	REPL CODE
BLX321	OEM	BM4006	OEM	BOD1-23L	OEM	BPA07420	OEM	BPX30	OEM	BR5K5	0017	BR351	1633
BLX331	OEM	BM4301A	OEM	BOD1-23LD	OEM	BPM5-250	OEM	BPX31	OEM	BR5M5	0017	BR352	1633
BLX332	OEM	BM4303	OEM	BOD1-23R	OEM	BPM5-250E	OEM	BPX32	OEM	BR5N5	0017	BR354	1663
BLX350	OEM	BM4304	OEM	BOD1-23RD	OEM	BPM5-250J	OEM	BPX35	OEM	BR5P5	0017	BR356	1663
BLX351	OEM	BM4601A	OEM	BOD1-24L	OEM	BPM5-500	OEM	BPX38I	OEM	BR31	0319	BR358	1579
BLY10	0103	BM4603B	OEM	BOD1-24LD	OEM	BPM5-500E	OEM	BPX38II	OEM	BR31G	0319	BR358F	1579
BLY11	0103	BM4603C	OEM	BOD1-24R	OEM	BPM5-500J	OEM	BPX38III	OEM	BR32	1404	BR358G	1579
BLY11S	OEM	BM4604	OEM	BOD1-24RD	OEM	BPM12-25D5	OEM	BPX38IV	OEM	BR32G	1404	BR412-5-5	OEM
BLY12	0615	BM4605	OEM	BOD1-25L	OEM	BPM12-25D12	OEM	BPX40	OEM	BR32J01	1404	BR412-5-10	OEM
BLY15	0830	BM4710	OEM	BOD1-25LD	OEM	BPM12-25D28	OEM	BPX41	OEM	BR34	0468	BR412-5-25	OEM
BLY15A	0178	BM4711	OEM	BOD1-25R	OEM	BPM12-60	OEM	BPX42	OEM	BR34G	0468	BR412-7-5	OEM
BLY16	OEM	BM4712	OEM	BOD1-25RD	OEM	BPM12-60E	OEM	BPX43-1	2297	BR36	0441	BR412-7-10	OEM
BLY17C	OEM	BM4717	OEM	BOD1-26L	OEM	BPM12-60J	OEM	BPX43-2	3825	BR36G	0441	BR412-7-25	OEM
BLY20	0555	BM8001	OEM	BOD1-26LD	OEM	BPM12-100	OEM	BPX43-3	3825	BR38	1412	BR412-10-5	OEM
BLY21	0042	BM8002	OEM	BOD1-26R	OEM	BPM12-100D5	OEM	BPX43-4	2297	BR38G	1412	BR412-10-10	OEM
BLY25	OEM	BM8003	OEM	BOD1-26RD	OEM	BPM12-100D12	OEM	BPX43I	OEM	BR42	0015	BR412-10-25	OEM
BLY26	OEM	BM8401A	OEM	BOD1-28L	OEM	BPM12-100D28	OEM	BPX43II	OEM	BR44	0015	BR412-12-5	OEM
BLY27	0079	BM8403	OEM	BOD1-28LD	OEM	BPM12-100E	OEM	BPX43III	OEM	BR46	0015	BR412-12-10	OEM
BLY28	0590	BM8404	OEM	BOD1-28R	OEM	BPM12-200	OEM	BPX43IV	OEM	BR47	0015	BR412-12-25	OEM
BLY29	OEM	BMM-128-200	OEM	BOD1-28RD	OEM	BPM12-200E	OEM	BPX47A	OEM	BR48	0015	BR412-15-5	OEM
BLY30	OEM	BMM-128-300	OEM	BOD1-30L	OEM	BPM12-200J	OEM	BPX47B-18	OEM	BR51	OEM	BR412-15-10	OEM
BLY33	0414	BN0335N5	OEM	BOD1-30LD	OEM	BPM12-210D5	OEM	BPX47B-20	OEM	BR52	0015	BR412-15-25	OEM
BLY34	0414	BN1L4M	OEM	BOD1-30R	OEM	BPM12-210D12	OEM	BPX47C36	OEM	BR54	OEM	BR412-20-5	OEM
BLY35	0233	BN12	OEM	BOD1-30RD	OEM	BPM12-210D28	OEM	BPX48	OEM	BR54-600	0304	BR412-20-10	OEM
BLY36	0042	BN-66	0016	BOD1-32R	OEM	BPM12-300	OEM	BPX58	OEM	BR-55	0030	BR412-20-25	OEM
BLY37	0555	BN74S301F	OEM	BOD1-34R	OEM	BPM12-300E	OEM	BPX59	3508	BR56	OEM	BR412-25-5	OEM
BLY38	0555	BN5040A	OEM	BOD1-36R	OEM	BPM12-300J	OEM	BPX60	OEM	BR58	OEM	BR412-25-10	OEM
BLY39	OEM	BN5111	3692	BOD1-38R	OEM	BPM12-420D5	OEM	BPX61	OEM	BR61	0319	BR412-25-25	OEM
BLY47	0177	BN5111A	3692	BOD1-40R	OEM	BPM12-420D12	OEM	BPX61P	OEM	BR61G	0319	BR412-30-5	OEM
BLY47A	0178	BN5111B	3692	BODI11LD	OEM	BPM12-420D28	OEM	BPX63	OEM	BR62	1404	BR412-30-10	OEM
BLY48	0177	BN5115	OEM	BOT521XXX	OEM	BPM15-25D5	OEM	BPX65	OEM	BR62G	1404	BR412-30-25	OEM
BLY48A	0178	BN5210	3738	BOT522XXX	OEM	BPM15-25D12	OEM	BPX66	OEM	BR64	0468	BR412-40-5	OEM
BLY49	0074	BN-5416	3800	BOV14S10K	OEM	BPM15-25D28	OEM	BPX66P	OEM	BR64G	0468	BR412-40-10	OEM
BLY49A	0178	BN5416	3800	BOV14S14K	OEM	BPM15-60	OEM	BPX68	OEM	BR-66	0016	BR412-40-25	OEM
BLY50	0074	BN5436N	3701	BOV30S10K	OEM	BPM15-60E	OEM	BPX70	OEM	BR66	0441	BR412-50-5	OEM
BLY53	0555	BN6111	OEM	BOV30S14K	OEM	BPM15-60J	OEM	BPX70C	OEM	BR66G	0441	BR412-50-10	OEM
BLY53AP	OEM	BN7133	0103	BOV60S05K	OEM	BPM15-100	OEM	BPX70D	OEM	BR67	0016	BR412-50-25	OEM
BLY53B	OEM	BN7168	0178	BOV60S07K	OEM	BPM15-100D5	OEM	BPX70E	OEM	BR68	1412	BR427-10	0017
BLY57	3289	BN7214	0103	BOV60S10K	OEM	BPM15-100D12	OEM	BPX71	OEM	BR68G	1412	BR427-15	0017
BLY58	3290	BN7253	0233	BOV60S14K	OEM	BPM15-100D28	OEM	BPX71-201	OEM	BR78	0259	BR427-20	OEM
BLY59	OEM	BN7517	0016	BOV60S20K	OEM	BPM15-100E	OEM	BPX71-202	OEM	BR81	0319	BR427-25	OEM
BLY60	OEM	BN7518	0016	BOV130S10K	OEM	BPM15-100J	OEM	BPX71-203	OEM	BR81D	0276	BR427-30	OEM
BLY61	0086	BN7551	0137	BOV130S14K	OEM	BPM15-150D5	OEM	BPX71-204	OEM	BR81DG	0276	BR427-35	OEM
BLY62	0555	BO-71	0127	BOV130S20K	OEM	BPM15-150D24	OEM	BPX72	OEM	BR81G	1412	BR427-40	OEM
BLY63	0042	BO-190	OEM	BOV150B32K	OEM	BPM15-150D28	OEM	BPX72C	OEM	BR-82	0037	BR427-45	OEM
BLY64	OEM	BO316415	0167	BOV150S05K	OEM	BPM15-165D12	OEM	BPX72D	OEM	BR82	1404	BR427-50	OEM
BLY65	OEM	BO319200	1044	BOV150S07K	OEM	BPM15-165D28	OEM	BPX72E	OEM	BR-82D	0287	BR427-55	OEM
BLY66	OEM	BO351500	0823	BOV150S10K	OEM	BPM15-165DS	OEM	BPX72F	OEM	BR82D	0287	BR427-60	OEM
BLY68	0236	BO354710	0906	BOV150S14K	OEM	BPM15-200	OEM	BPX79	OEM	BR82DG	0287	BR427-65	OEM
BLY70	OEM	BO354830	2043	BOV150S20K	OEM	BPM15-200E	OEM	BPX80	OEM	BR82G	1404	BR427-70	OEM
BLY72	OEM	BO356446	0658	BOV250B25K	OEM	BPM15-200J	OEM	BPX81I	OEM	BR84	0468	BR577-70	OEM
BLY74	OEM	BO356620	2043	BOV250S05K	OEM	BPM15-300	OEM	BPX81II	OEM	BR84D	0293	BR587-10	0017
BLY78	0555	BO470016	0473	BOV250S07K	OEM	BPM15-300E	OEM	BPX81III	OEM	BR84DG	0293	BR587-15	0017
BLY79	0042	BO470116	0215	BOV250S10K	OEM	BPM15-300J	OEM	BPX81IV	OEM	BR84G	0468	BR587-20	OEM
BLY82	OEM	BOD1-04	OEM	BOV250S14K	OEM	BPM15-330D5	OEM	BPX82	OEM	BR86	0441	BR587-25	OEM
BLY86	OEM	BOD1-05	OEM	BOV250S20K	OEM	BPM15-330D12	OEM	BPY11P	OEM	BR86D	0299	BR587-30	OEM
BLY87A	1966	BOD1-06	OEM	BOV275S05K	OEM	BPM15-330D28	OEM	BPY11P/I	OEM	BR86DG	0299	BR587-35	OEM
BLY87C	OEM	BOD1-07	OEM	BOV275S07K	OEM	BPM18-25D5	OEM	BPY11PIV	OEM	BR86G	0441	BR587-40	OEM
BLY88	0042	BOD1-08	OEM	BOV275S10K	OEM	BPM18-25D12	OEM	BPY11PV	OEM	BR88	1412	BR587-45	OEM
BLY88A	1224	BOD1-09	OEM	BOV275S14K	OEM	BPM18-25D28	OEM	BPY11PVI	OEM	BR88D	0250	BR587-50	OEM
BLY88C	OEM	BOD1-10	OEM	BOV275S20K	OEM	BPM18-100D6	OEM	BPY12	OEM	BR88DG	0250	BR587-55	OEM
BLY89	0042	BOD1-11L	OEM	BOV420B32K	OEM	BPM18-100D12	OEM	BPY15	OEM	BR88G	1412	BR587-60	OEM
BLY89A	1966	BOD1-11LD	OEM	BOV420S10K	OEM	BPM18-100D28	OEM	BPY20	OEM	BR100	2704	BR587-65	OEM
BLY89C	OEM	BOD1-11R	OEM	BOV420S14K	OEM	BPM18-140D5	OEM	BPY21	OEM	BR-100B	0555	BR587-70	OEM
BLY91	0555	BOD1-11RD	OEM	BOV420S20K	OEM	BPM18-140D12	OEM	BPY22	OEM	BR100B	0555	BR587-80	OEM
BLY91A	3542	BOD1-12L	OEM	BOV550S10K	OEM	BPM18-140D28	OEM	BPY43	OEM	BR101	OEM	BR587-85	OEM
BLY91C	OEM	BOD1-12LD	OEM	BOV550S14K	OEM	BPM18-280D5	OEM	BPY44	OEM	BR-101B	0042	BR587-90	OEM
BLY92	0042	BOD1-12R	OEM	BOV550S20K	OEM	BPM18-280D12	OEM	BPY45	OEM	BR101B	0042	BR587-95	OEM
BLY92A	2485	BOD1-12RD	OEM	BOV625S10K	OEM	BPM18-280D28	OEM	BPY46	OEM	BR102	OEM	BR587-100	OEM
BLY92C	OEM	BOD1-13L	OEM	BOV625S14K	OEM	BPM120-25	OEM	BPY47	OEM	BR103	1129	BR587-110	OEM
BLY93	3543	BOD1-13LD	OEM	BOV625S20K	OEM	BPM120-25E	OEM	BPY47P	OEM	BR104	OEM	BR587-120	OEM
BLY93A	2485	BOD1-13R	OEM	BP-0200	OEM	BPM120-25J	OEM	BPY48	OEM	BR106	OEM	BR587-130	OEM
BLY93C	OEM	BOD1-13RD	OEM	BP-0575	OEM	BPM150-20	OEM	BPY48P	OEM	BR108	OEM	BR587-140	OEM
BLY99	0414	BOD1-14L	OEM	BP2BC	OEM	BPM150-20E	OEM	BPY61I	OEM	BR151	2347	BR587-150	OEM
BM15-12	OEM	BOD1-14LD	OEM	BP5BC	OEM	BPM150-20J	OEM	BPY61II	OEM	BR151G	2347	BR587-160	OEM
BM25LE	OEM	BOD1-14R	OEM	BP8-12	OEM	BPM180-16	OEM	BPY61III	OEM	BR151W	OEM	BR587-170	OEM
BM30-12	5513	BOD1-14RD	OEM	BP15-12	OEM	BPM180-16E	OEM	BPY61IV	OEM	BR152	2347	BR587-180	OEM
BM45-12	OEM	BOD1-15L	OEM	BP30-12	OEM	BPM180-16J	OEM	BPY62	2297	BR152G	2347	BR587-190	OEM
BM70-12	3165	BOD1-15LD	OEM	BP30-12L	OEM	BPW10	OEM	BPY62-1	2297	BR152W	OEM	BR587-200	OEM
BM80-12	3062	BOD1-15R	OEM	BP50	OEM	BPW13A	OEM	BPY62-2	2297	BR154	2353	BR588-10	0017
BM80-28	OEM	BOD1-15RD	OEM	BP67	0016	BPW13B	OEM	BPY62-3	3825	BR154G	2353	BR588-15	0017
BM100-12	OEM	BOD1-16L	OEM	BP100P	OEM	BPW13C	OEM	BPY62I	OEM	BR154W	OEM	BR588-20	OEM
BM100-28	OEM	BOD1-16LD	OEM	BP103BI	OEM	BPW14A	OEM	BPY62II	OEM	BR156	2354	BR588-25	OEM
BM150-12	OEM	BOD1-16R	OEM	BP103BII	OEM	BPW14B	OEM	BPY62III	OEM	BR156G	2354	BR588-30	OEM
BM1002	OEM	BOD1-16RD	OEM	BP103BIII	OEM	BPW14C	OEM	BPY63	OEM	BR156W	OEM	BR588-35	OEM
BM1003	OEM	BOD1-17L	OEM	BP103BIV	OEM	BPW20	OEM	BPY63P	OEM	BR158	2356	BR588-40	OEM
BM1004	OEM	BOD1-17LD	OEM	BP103I	OEM	BPW21	OEM	BPY64	OEM	BR158G	2356	BR588-45	OEM
BM1005	OEM	BOD1-17R	OEM	BP103II	OEM	BPW21M	OEM	BPY64P	OEM	BR158W	OEM	BR588-50	OEM
BM1006	OEM	BOD1-17RD	OEM	BP103III	OEM	BPW22A	OEM	BPY66	OEM	BR-190	OEM	BR588-55	OEM
BM1026	OEM	BOD1-18L	OEM	BP103IV	OEM	BPW22A-I	OEM	BPY67	OEM	BR203	OEM	BR588-60	OEM
BM1027	OEM	BOD1-18LD	OEM	BP-104	OEM	BPW22A-II	OEM	BPY71	OEM	BR210	OEM	BR588-65	OEM
BM1028	OEM	BOD1-18R	OEM	BP104	OEM	BPW24	OEM	BPY72	OEM	BR220	OEM	BR588-70	OEM
BM1029	OEM	BOD1-18RD	OEM	BP-2190	OEM	BPW28	OEM	BQ	OEM	BR251	2347	BR588-80	OEM
BM1030	OEM	BOD1-19L	OEM	BP3371	OEM	BPW30	3508	BQ67	0016	BR251G	2347	BR588-85	OEM
BM1031	OEM	BOD1-19LD	OEM	BP5263	0050	BPW32	OEM	BQ-94	0016	BR251W	OEM	BR588-90	OEM
BM1032	OEM	BOD1-19R	OEM	BP336933	OEM	BPW33	OEM	BQA02-30A	0195	BR252	2347	BR588-95	OEM
BM1033	OEM	BOD1-19RD	OEM	BP336940	OEM	BPW34	OEM	B-R	OEM	BR252G	2347	BR588-100	OEM
BM1034	OEM	BOD1-20L	OEM	BP338978	OEM	BPW35	OEM	BR09250M	OEM	BR252W	OEM	BR588-110	OEM
BM1035	OEM	BOD1-20LD	OEM	BP338979	OEM	BPW36	OEM	BR09450	OEM	BR254	2353	BR588-120	OEM
BM1036	OEM	BOD1-20R	OEM	BP338986	OEM	BPW37	OEM	BR-1	0276	BR254W	OEM	BR588-130	OEM
BM1037	OEM	BOD1-20RD	OEM	BP338987	OEM	BPW38	OEM	BR1	0276	BR256	2354	BR588-140	OEM
BM1038	OEM	BOD1-21L	OEM	BP338995	OEM	BPW41	2604	BR5A5	0023	BR256W	OEM	BR588-150	OEM
BM1039	OEM	BOD1-21LD	OEM	BP338998	OEM	BPW41D	OEM	BR5B5	0023	BR258	2356	BR588-160	OEM
BM1040	OEM	BOD1-21R	OEM	BP372882	OEM	BPW44	OEM	BR5C5	0023	BR258W	OEM	BR588-170	OEM
BM4001	OEM	BOD1-21RD	OEM	BP879849	OEM	BPW45	OEM	BR5D5	0023	BR303	OEM	BR588-180	OEM
BM4002	OEM	BOD1-22L	OEM	BPA07347	OEM	BPW50	OEM	BR5E5	0023	BR305	0319	BR588-190	OEM
BM4003	OEM	BOD1-22LD	OEM	BPA07364	OEM	BPW71	OEM	BR5F5	0023	BR305G	0319	BR588-200	OEM
BM4004	OEM	BOD1-22R	OEM	BPA07374	OEM	BPX25	OEM	BR5G5	0023	BR310	2425	BR605	0319
BM4005	OEM	BOD1-22RD	OEM	BPA07403	OEM	BPX29	OEM	BR5H5	0017	BR310G	2425	BR605G	0319

If replacement code is OEM, contact original manufacturer for replacement.

DEVICE TYPE	REPL CODE
BR610	2425
BR805	0319
BR805D	0276
BR805DG	0276
BR805G	0319
BR810	2425
BR810D	0250
BR810DG	0250
BR810G	2425
BR-832	0037
BR1005	5201
BR1010	OEM
BR1505	2347
BR1505G	2347
BR1505W	OEM
BR1510	2357
BR1510F	2357
BR1510G	2357
BR1510W	OEM
BR1941L	OEM
BR1941M	OEM
BR2505	2347
BR2505G	2347
BR2505W	OEM
BR2510	2357
BR2510G	2357
BR2510W	OEM
BR2941L	OEM
BR3433S	OEM
BR3505	1633
BR3510	1579
BR5507S	OEM
BR5507S-1	OEM
BR13451	OEM
BR16252	OEM
BR16452	OEM
BR51400-1	0015
BR51401-2	0015
BRA40	0468
BRF151	0276
BRF152	0276
BRF153	0287
BRF154	0293
BRF155	0299
BRF156	0250
BRF157	0250
BRF201	0276
BRF202	0276
BRF203	0287
BRF204	0293
BRF205	0299
BRF206	0250
BRF207	0250
BRF251	0724
BRF252	0724
BRF253	0724
BRF254	0732
BRF255	0732
BRF256	0737
BRF257	0737
BRF401	0724
BRF402	0724
BRF403	0724
BRF404	0732
BRF405	0732
BRF406	0737
BRF407	0737
BRH1000	OEM
BRH1001	OEM
BRH1002	OEM
BRH1004	OEM
BRH1006	OEM
BRH2500	OEM
BRH2501	OEM
BRH2502	OEM
BRH2504	OEM
BRH2506	OEM
BRH3500	OEM
BRH3501	OEM
BRH3502	OEM
BRH3504	OEM
BRH3506	OEM
BRHV1502	OEM
BRHV1503	OEM
BRHV1504	OEM
BRHV1505	OEM
BRHV1506	OEM
BRR101	0106
BRR102	0106
BRR103	0106
BRR104	0106
BRR105	1999
BRR106	2384
BRR107	0782
BRR151	0106
BRR152	0106
BRR153	0106
BRR154	0106
BRR155	1999
BRR156	2384
BRR157	0782
BRS10-005	OEM
BRS10-01	OEM
BRS10-02	OEM
BRS10-04	OEM
BRS10-06	OEM
BRS10-08	OEM
BRS10-10	OEM
BRS12-005	OEM
BRS12-01	OEM
BRS12-02	OEM
BRS12-04	OEM
BRS12-06	OEM
BRS12-08	OEM
BRS12-10	OEM
BRS15-005	OEM
BRS15-01	OEM
BRS15-02	OEM
BRS15-04	OEM
BRS15-06	OEM
BRS15-08	OEM
BRS15-10	OEM
BRS25-005	OEM
BRS25-01	OEM
BRS25-02	OEM
BRS25-04	OEM
BRS25-06	OEM
BRS25-08	OEM
BRS25-10	OEM
BRS35-005	OEM
BRS35-01	OEM
BRS35-02	OEM
BRS35-04	OEM
BRS35-06	OEM
BRS35-08	OEM
BRS35-10	OEM
BRS101	1864
BRS102	1864
BRS103	1864
BRS104	1864
BRS105	1864
BRS106	3503
BRS107	3503
BRS301	0319
BRS302	0319
BRS303	1404
BRS304	0468
BRS305	0441
BRS306	1412
BRS307	2425
BRS601	0319
BRS602	0319
BRS603	1404
BRS604	0468
BRS605	0441
BRS606	1412
BRS607	2425
BRT60	OEM
BRT170S01	OEM
BRT170S02	OEM
BRT170S03	OEM
BRT170S04	OEM
BRT170S05	OEM
BRT170S06	OEM
BRT170S07	OEM
BRT170S08	OEM
BRT170S09	OEM
BRT170S10	OEM
BRT170S11	OEM
BRT170S12	OEM
BRT170S13	OEM
BRT170S14	OEM
BRT170S15	OEM
BRV615	OEM
BRV615T	OEM
BRX44	1129
BRX45	0340
BRX46	0895
BRX47	0058
BRX48	0403
BRX49	0403
BRX50	OEM
BRX51	OEM
BRX52	OEM
BRX53	OEM
BRX54	OEM
BRX55	OEM
BRX56	OEM
BRX60	0174
BRX61	3801
BRX62	3575
BRX63	OEM
BRX64	3291
BRX65	1494
BRX66	1494
BRY20	OEM
BRY23	OEM
BRY24	OEM
BRY25	OEM
BRY26	OEM
BRY28	OEM
BRY29	OEM
BRY30	OEM
BRY31	OEM
BRY32	OEM
BRY33	OEM
BRY34	OEM
BRY35	OEM
BRY36	OEM
BRY37	OEM
BRY39	4790
BRY39T	OEM
BRY42	OEM
BRY43	OEM
BRY44	OEM
BRY46	OEM
BRY49	OEM
BRY50	OEM
BRY51	OEM
BRY52	OEM
BRY53	OEM
BRY54	OEM
BRY54-100	0179
BRY54-100T	0179
BRY54-200	OEM
BRY54-200T	OEM
BRY54-300	0342
BRY54-300T	OEM
BRY54-400	3315
BRY54-400T	OEM
BRY54-500	3315
BRY54-500T	OEM
BRY54-600	3315
BRY54-600T	OEM
BRY54-1007	0179
BRY55	OEM
BRY55-30	1129
BRY55-60	0340
BRY55-100	0895
BRY55-200	0058
BRY55-300	0403
BRY55-400	OEM
BRY55M-300	OEM
BRY55M-400	OEM
BRY55M-600	OEM
BRY55M-800	OEM
BRY56	OEM
BRY56A	OEM
BRY56B	OEM
BRY56C	OEM
BRY57	OEM
BRY58-30	OEM
BRY58-60	OEM
BRY58-100	OEM
BRY58-200	OEM
BRY58-300	OEM
BRY61	OEM
BS	OEM
BS08A	4169
BS08H	2337
BS-1	0287
BS1	0015
BS2	0015
BS3-04CM1	OEM
BS3-06CM1	OEM
BS4	OEM
BS4-04FM5	OEM
BS4-06FM5	OEM
BS4-08FM5	OEM
BS5-04EM1	OEM
BS5-04FM5	OEM
BS5-06EM1	OEM
BS5-06FM5	OEM
BS5-08EM1	OEM
BS5-08FM5	OEM
BS6	OEM
BS6-01A	0154
BS6-01B	OEM
BS6-01E	1058
BS6-02A	0154
BS6-02B	OEM
BS6-02E	1058
BS6-03A	0147
BS6-03B	OEM
BS6-03E	1307
BS6-04A	0147
BS6-04B	OEM
BS6-04E	1307
BS6-05A	0278
BS6-05B	OEM
BS6-05E	1880
BS6-06A	0278
BS6-06B	OEM
BS6-06E	1880
BS6-07A	0869
BS6-07B	OEM
BS7-02A	0767
BS7-04A	0739
BS7-04FM1	OEM
BS7-05A	0612
BS7-06FM1	OEM
BS7-08FM1	OEM
BS8	OEM
BS8-01A	0154
BS8-01B	OEM
BS8-02A	0154
BS8-02B	OEM
BS8-03A	0147
BS8-03B	OEM
BS8-04A	0147
BS8-04B	OEM
BS8-05A	0278
BS8-05B	OEM
BS8-06A	0278
BS8-06B	OEM
BS8-07A	0869
BS8-07B	OEM
BS9-02A	0767
BS9-04A	0739
BS9-04FM5	OEM
BS9-04HR1	OEM
BS9-05A	0612
BS9-06FM5	OEM
BS9-06HR1	OEM
BS9-08FM5	OEM
BS9-08HR1	OEM
BS10	OEM
BS10-01A	0154
BS10-01B	OEM
BS10-02A	0154
BS10-02B	OEM
BS10-03A	0147
BS10-03B	OEM
BS10-04A	0147
BS10-04B	OEM
BS10-05A	0278
BS10-05B	OEM
BS10-06A	0278
BS10-06B	OEM
BS10-07A	OEM
BS10-07B	OEM
BS12-04HU1	OEM
BS12-04HU5	OEM
BS12-06HU1	OEM
BS12-06HU5	OEM
BS12-08HU1	OEM
BS12-08HU5	OEM
BS16-04HU1	OEM
BS16-06HU1	OEM
BS16-08HU1	OEM
BS29P	OEM
BS48	OEM
BS52	OEM
BS58	OEM
BS60	OEM
BS63	OEM
BS-66	0016
BS67	0016
BS68	0006
BS70	OEM
BS72	OEM
BS76	OEM
BS80	OEM
BS82	OEM
BS84	OEM
BS92	OEM
BS-94	0016
BS100D	OEM
BS102	OEM
BS104	OEM
BS107	OEM
BS107A	OEM
BS107P	OEM
BS110	OEM
BS112	OEM
BS114	OEM
BS116	OEM
BS118	OEM
BS128	OEM
BS138	OEM
BS142	OEM
BS148	OEM
BS156	OEM
BS158	OEM
BS162	OEM
BS166	OEM
BS170P	OEM
BS172	OEM
BS178	OEM
BS188	OEM
BS190	OEM
BS192	OEM
BS194	OEM
BS196	OEM
BS200	OEM
BS202	OEM
BS204	OEM
BS206	OEM
BS216	OEM
BS217	OEM
BS219	OEM
BS220	OEM
BS224	OEM
BS226	OEM
BS228	OEM
BS232	OEM
BS234	OEM
BS246	OEM
BS248	OEM
BS250	OEM
BS250P	OEM
BS256	OEM
BS258	OEM
BS260	OEM
BS262	OEM
BS264	OEM
BS276	OEM
BS277	OEM
BS280	OEM
BS286	OEM
BS310	OEM
BS314	OEM
BS316	OEM
BS320	OEM
BS324	OEM
BS342	OEM
BS344	OEM
BS384	OEM
BS386	OEM
BS390	OEM
BS412	OEM
BS426	OEM
BS430	OEM
BS440	OEM
BS450	OEM
BS452	OEM
BS454	OEM
BS462	OEM
BS466	OEM
BS475	0016
BS500	OEM
BS500A	OEM
BS500B	OEM
BS530UV	OEM
BS608A	OEM
BS608B	OEM
BS616A	OEM
BS616B	OEM
BS624A	OEM
BS624B	OEM
BS624C	OEM
BS624D	OEM
BS624E	OEM
BS624K	OEM
BS624L	OEM
BS624M	OEM
BS624N	OEM
BS624P	OEM
BS630	OEM
BS640	OEM
BS644	OEM
BS646	OEM
BS648	OEM
BS658	OEM
BS660	OEM
BS662	OEM
BS674	OEM
BS676	OEM
BS678	OEM
BS698	OEM
BS702	OEM
BS710	OEM
BS714	OEM
BS716	OEM
BS718	OEM
BS720	OEM
BS724	OEM
BS726	OEM
BS728	OEM
BS732	OEM
BS748	OEM
BS750	OEM
BS752	OEM
BS756	OEM
BS758	OEM
BS760	OEM
BS762	OEM
BS764	OEM
BS766	OEM
BS772	OEM
BS774	OEM
BS776	OEM
BS778	OEM
BS784	OEM
BS798	OEM
BS800	OEM
BS806A	OEM
BS806B	OEM
BS806C	OEM
BS806D	OEM
BS806E	OEM
BS806F	OEM
BS806G	OEM
BS806H	OEM
BS810	OEM
BS814	OEM
BS816	OEM
BS818	OEM
BS822	OEM
BS824	OEM
BS826	OEM
BS828	OEM
BS830	OEM
BS832	OEM
BS834	OEM
BS836	OEM
BS838	OEM
BS842	OEM
BS844	OEM
BS846	OEM
BS848	OEM
BS854	OEM
BS856	OEM
BS858	OEM
BS860	OEM
BS868	OEM
BS870	OEM
BS872	OEM
BS874	OEM
BS876	OEM
BS880	OEM
BS882	OEM
BS894	OEM
BS898	OEM
BS902	OEM
BS904	OEM
BS908	OEM
BS910	OEM
BS912	OEM
BS916	OEM
BS918	OEM
BS928	OEM
BS930	OEM
BS932	OEM
BS940	OEM
BS946	OEM
BS950	OEM
BS952	OEM
BS956	OEM
BS958	OEM
BS958D	OEM
BS959	OEM
BS960	OEM
BS962	OEM
BS966	OEM
BS968	OEM
BS969	OEM
BS970	OEM
BS974	OEM
BS975	OEM
BS976	OEM
BS986	OEM
BS990	OEM
BS994	OEM
BS9011G	0079
BS9301F019-8308	OEM
BS9301F019-8805	OEM
BS74154	1546
BSA01	0133
BSA02	0133
BSA11	0133
BSA12	OEM
BSA21	OEM
BSA31	OEM
BS-B1	0276
BS-B2	0287
BS-B4	0293
BSC01	OEM
BSC02	OEM
BSC03	OEM
BSC04	OEM
BSC05	OEM
BSC11	OEM
BSC12	OEM
BSC13	OEM
BSC14	OEM
BSC21	OEM
BSC22	OEM
BSC23	OEM
BSC24	OEM
BSC25	OEM
BSC26	OEM
BSC51	OEM
BSC52	OEM
BSC-256	OEM
BSC551	OEM
BSC552	OEM
BSC553	OEM
BSC554	OEM
BSC555	OEM
BSC556	OEM
BSC557	OEM
BSC1015	OEM
BSC1015A	OEM
BSC1015B	OEM
BSC1016	OEM
BSC1016A	OEM
BSC1016B	OEM
BSD10	OEM
BSD12	OEM
BSD212	OEM
BSD213	OEM
BSD214	OEM
BSD215	OEM
BSF17	OEM
BSJ111	3790
BSJ112	OEM
BSJ113	3791
BSJ174	OEM
BSJ175	OEM
BSJ176	OEM
BSJ177	OEM
BSM01	OEM
BSM02	OEM
BSM11	OEM
BSM12	OEM
BSM13	OEM
BSM21	OEM
BSM31	OEM
BSM41	OEM
BSM42	OEM
BSM51	OEM
BSM61	OEM
BSP15	OEM
BSP16	OEM
BSP19	OEM
BSP20	OEM
BSP30	OEM
BSP31	OEM
BSP32	OEM
BSP33	OEM
BSP40	OEM
BSP41	OEM
BSP42	OEM
BSP43	OEM
BSP50	OEM
BSP52	OEM
BSP60	OEM
BSP61	OEM
BSP62	OEM
BSR12	OEM
BSR12R	OEM
BSR13	1722
BSR13R	OEM
BSR14	1722
BSR14R	OEM
BSR15	1741
BSR15R	OEM
BSR16	1741
BSR16R	OEM
BSR17	1722
BSR17A	1426
BSR17R	OEM
BSR18	1491
BSR18A	1491
BSR19	5977
BSR19A	5977
BSR20	5269
BSR20A	5269
BSR30	3600
BSR31	3600
BSR32	3600
BSR33	3600
BSR40	0662
BSR41	0662
BSR42	0662
BSR43	0662
BSR50	6749
BSR51	6749
BSR52	3838
BSR56	OEM
BSR57	OEM
BSR58	OEM
BSR60	3836
BSR61	3836
BSR62	3836
BSR64	OEM
BSR65	OEM
BSR66	OEM
BSR67	OEM
BSR70	OEM
BSR72	OEM
BSR76	OEM
BSR78	OEM
BSR80	OEM
BSR81	OEM
BSR82	OEM
BSR89	OEM
BSR92	OEM
BSS10	0016
BSS13	0414
BSS14	0617
BSS15	0617
BSS16	0617
BSS17	0126
BSS18	0126
BSS19	0283
BSS20	0283
BSS21	0016
BSS22	0016
BSS23	0590
BSS24	OEM
BSS25	OEM
BSS26	0016
BSS28	0086
BSS29	0086
BSS30	0626
BSS32	0626
BSS33	0233
BSS34	OEM
BSS35	OEM
BSS36	OEM
BSS37	0338
BSS38	0855
BSS40	0086
BSS41	0086
BSS42	0617
BSS43	0617
BSS44	0126
BSS45	0538
BSS47	OEM
BSS48	OEM
BSS49	OEM
BSS50	OEM
BSS51	OEM
BSS52	OEM
BSS56	OEM
BSS58A	OEM
BSS58B	OEM
BSS60	OEM
BSS61	OEM
BSS62	OEM
BSS63	1495
BSS63R	OEM
BSS64	2316
BSS64R	OEM
BSS65	OEM
BSS65R	OEM
BSS66	OEM
BSS66R	OEM
BSS67	OEM
BSS67R	OEM
BSS68	0338
BSS69	OEM
BSS69R	OEM
BSS70	OEM
BSS70R	OEM
BSS71	OEM
BSS72	OEM
BSS74	OEM
BSS75	OEM
BSS79	OEM
BSS79B	1426

If replacement code is OEM, contact original manufacturer for replacement.

DEVICE TYPE	REPL CODE
BSS79C	1426
BSS80	OEM
BSS80B	OEM
BSS80C	OEM
BSS81	OEM
BSS81B	OEM
BSS81C	OEM
BSS82	OEM
BSS82B	1491
BSS82C	1491
BSS87	OEM
BSS89	OEM
BSS91	OEM
BSS93	OEM
BSS95	OEM
BSS97	OEM
BSS100	OEM
BSS101	OEM
BSS110	OEM
BSS123	OEM
BSS465	OEM
BST15	5274
BST16	5274
BST39	3433
BST40	3433
BST50	5272
BST51	5272
BST52	5272
BST60	5273
BST61	5273
BST62	5273
BST70A	OEM
BST72A	OEM
BST74A	OEM
BST76A	OEM
BST78	OEM
BST90	OEM
BST97	OEM
BST100	OEM
BST110	OEM
BST250	OEM
BSTA3026	OEM
BSTA3026M	OEM
BSTA3033	OEM
BSTA3033M	OEM
BSTA3040	OEM
BSTA3040J	OEM
BSTA3040K	OEM
BSTA3040L	OEM
BSTA3040M	OEM
BSTA3040MJ	OEM
BSTA3040MK	OEM
BSTA3040ML	OEM
BSTA3046	OEM
BSTA3046J	OEM
BSTA3046K	OEM
BSTA3046L	OEM
BSTA3046M	OEM
BSTA3046MJ	OEM
BSTA3046MK	OEM
BSTA3046ML	OEM
BSTA3053	OEM
BSTA3053M	OEM
BSTB0106	OEM
BSTB0113	OEM
BSTB0126	OEM
BSTB0140	OEM
BSTB0146	OEM
BSTB0206	OEM
BSTB0213	OEM
BSTB0226	OEM
BSTB0240	OEM
BSTB0246	OEM
BSTC0106	2471
BSTC0113	0240
BSTC0126	0671
BSTC0133	0332
BSTC0140	0332
BSTC0146	OEM
BSTC0206	OEM
BSTC0213	OEM
BSTC0226	OEM
BSTC0233	OEM
BSTC0240	OEM
BSTC0246	OEM
BSTC0313	0757
BSTC0313S6	OEM
BSTC0313S6+	0464
BSTC0326	0735
BSTC0326S6	OEM
BSTC0326S6+	0717
BSTC0340	0759
BSTC0340S6	OEM
BSTC0340S6+	0720
BSTC0353	0761
BSTC0353S6	4455
BSTC0353S6+	2025
BSTC0366	4455
BSTC0366S6	4455
BSTC0366S6+	2025
BSTC0380	OEM
BSTC0380S6	OEM
BSTC0380S6+	2025
BSTC0506	OEM
BSTC0506K	OEM
BSTC0506L	OEM
BSTC0513	OEM
BSTC0513K	OEM
BSTC0513L	OEM

DEVICE TYPE	REPL CODE
BSTC0526	OEM
BSTC0526K	OEM
BSTC0526L	OEM
BSTC0533	OEM
BSTC0533K	OEM
BSTC0533L	OEM
BSTC0540	0061
BSTC0540K	OEM
BSTC0540L	OEM
BSTC0546	OEM
BSTC0546K	OEM
BSTC0546L	OEM
BSTC0606	OEM
BSTC0613	OEM
BSTC0626	OEM
BSTC0626S6	OEM
BSTC0626S9	OEM
BSTC0633	OEM
BSTC0633H	OEM
BSTC0633S6	OEM
BSTC0633S9	OEM
BSTC0640	OEM
BSTC0640H	OEM
BSTC0640S6	OEM
BSTC0640S9	OEM
BSTC0643H	0239
BSTC0646	OEM
BSTC0646H	OEM
BSTC0646S6	OEM
BSTC0646S9	OEM
BSTC0653H	OEM
BSTC0706	OEM
BSTC0713	OEM
BSTC0726	OEM
BSTC0726T	OEM
BSTC0733	OEM
BSTC0733T	OEM
BSTC0740	OEM
BSTC0746	OEM
BSTC0926T92	OEM
BSTC0930T92	OEM
BSTC1026	OEM
BSTC1026M	OEM
BSTC1033	OEM
BSTC1033M	OEM
BSTC1040	OEM
BSTC1040B	OEM
BSTC1040C	OEM
BSTC1040D	OEM
BSTC1040M	OEM
BSTC1040MB	OEM
BSTC1040MC	OEM
BSTC1040MD	OEM
BSTC1040MS	OEM
BSTC1040MS1	OEM
BSTC1040S1	OEM
BSTC1040S2	OEM
BSTC1046	OEM
BSTC1046B	OEM
BSTC1046C	OEM
BSTC1046D	OEM
BSTC1046M	OEM
BSTC1046MB	OEM
BSTC1046MC	OEM
BSTC1046MD	OEM
BSTC1046MS1	OEM
BSTC1046MS2	OEM
BSTC1046S1	OEM
BSTC1046S2	OEM
BSTC1053	OEM
BSTC1053M	OEM
BSTC1226	OEM
BSTC1233	OEM
BSTC1240	OEM
BSTC1246	OEM
BSTC1250	OEM
BSTC3026	OEM
BSTC3033	OEM
BSTC3040	OEM
BSTC3040B	OEM
BSTC3040C	OEM
BSTC3040D	OEM
BSTC3040S1	OEM
BSTC3046	OEM
BSTC3046B	OEM
BSTC3046C	OEM
BSTC3046D	OEM
BSTC3046S1	OEM
BSTC3053	OEM
BSTC3126	OEM
BSTC3126M	OEM
BSTC3133	OEM
BSTC3133M	OEM
BSTC3140	OEM
BSTC3140B	OEM
BSTC3140C	OEM
BSTC3140D	OEM
BSTC3140M	OEM
BSTC3140MB	OEM
BSTC3140MC	OEM
BSTC3140MD	OEM
BSTC3140MS1	OEM
BSTC3140S1	OEM
BSTC3146	OEM
BSTC3146B	OEM
BSTC3146C	OEM
BSTC3146D	OEM
BSTC3146M	OEM
BSTC3146MB	OEM

DEVICE TYPE	REPL CODE
BSTC3146MC	OEM
BSTC3146MD	OEM
BSTC3146MS1	OEM
BSTC3146S1	OEM
BSTC3153M	OEM
BSTCC0126	OEM
BSTCC0126S6	OEM
BSTCC0126S9	OEM
BSTCC0126T91	OEM
BSTCC0130T91	OEM
BSTCC0133	OEM
BSTCC0133H	OEM
BSTCC0133S6	OEM
BSTCC0133S9	OEM
BSTCC0140	OEM
BSTCC0140H	OEM
BSTCC0140R	OEM
BSTCC0140S6	OEM
BSTCC0140S9	OEM
BSTCC0143	OEM
BSTCC0143H	OEM
BSTCC0143R	OEM
BSTCC0146	OEM
BSTCC0146S6	OEM
BSTCC0146S9	OEM
BSTCC0246H	OEM
BSTCC0246R	OEM
BSTCC0253	OEM
BSTCC0253H	OEM
BSTCC0253R	OEM
BSTD0220	OEM
BSTD0240	OEM
BSTD0260	OEM
BSTD0313	0757
BSTD0313S6	OEM
BSTD0313S6+	0464
BSTD0320	OEM
BSTD0326	0735
BSTD0326S6	OEM
BSTD0326S6+	0717
BSTD0340	0759
BSTD0340S6	OEM
BSTD0340S6+	0720
BSTD0353	0761
BSTD0353S6	4455
BSTD0353S6+	2025
BSTD0366	4455
BSTD0366S6	4455
BSTD0366S6+	0674
BSTD0380	OEM
BSTD0380S6	OEM
BSTD0380S6+	2025
BSTD1026	OEM
BSTD1026M	OEM
BSTD1033	OEM
BSTD1033M	OEM
BSTD1040	OEM
BSTD1040B	OEM
BSTD1040C	OEM
BSTD1040M	OEM
BSTD1040MB	OEM
BSTD1040MC	OEM
BSTD1040MD	OEM
BSTD1040MS1	OEM
BSTD1040MS2	OEM
BSTD1040S1	OEM
BSTD1040S2	OEM
BSTD1046	OEM
BSTD1046MC	OEM
BSTD1046MD	OEM
BSTD1046S1	OEM
BSTD1046S2	OEM
BSTD1053	OEM
BSTD1053M	OEM
BSTD1666M	OEM
BSTD1666P	OEM
BSTD1680M	OEM
BSTD1680P	OEM
BSTD3666M	OEM
BSTD3666N	OEM
BSTD3666P	OEM
BSTD3680M	OEM
BSTD3680N	OEM
BSTD3680P	OEM
BSTD4026M	OEM
BSTD4026MM	OEM
BSTD4033M	OEM
BSTD4033MM	OEM
BSTD4040M	OEM
BSTD4040MM	OEM
BSTD4040MN	OEM
BSTD4040N	OEM
BSTD4046M	OEM
BSTD4046MM	OEM
BSTD4046MN	OEM
BSTD4046N	OEM
BSTD4053M	OEM
BSTD4053MM	OEM
BSTD4126M	OEM
BSTD4126MM	OEM
BSTD4133M	OEM
BSTD4133MM	OEM
BSTD4140M	OEM
BSTD4140MM	OEM
BSTD4140MN	OEM
BSTD4140N	OEM
BSTD4146M	OEM
BSTD4146MM	OEM
BSTD4146MN	OEM

DEVICE TYPE	REPL CODE
BSTD4146N	OEM
BSTD4153M	OEM
BSTD4153MM	OEM
BSTE0240	OEM
BSTE0260	OEM
BSTE0280	OEM
BSTE0326	OEM
BSTE0326T81	OEM
BSTE0326T82	OEM
BSTE0326T83	OEM
BSTE0326T84	OEM
BSTE0326T85	OEM
BSTE0326T86	OEM
BSTE0330T81	OEM
BSTE0330T82	OEM
BSTE0330T83	OEM
BSTE0330T84	OEM
BSTE0330T86	OEM
BSTE0333	OEM
BSTE0340	OEM
BSTE0346	OEM
BSTE0426	OEM
BSTE0426T93	OEM
BSTE0426T94	OEM
BSTE0426T95	OEM
BSTE0426T96	OEM
BSTE0430T93	OEM
BSTE0430T95	OEM
BSTE0430T96	OEM
BSTE0433	OEM
BSTE0440	OEM
BSTE0446	OEM
BSTE0540	OEM
BSTE0580	OEM
BSTE4026MN	OEM
BSTE4026N	OEM
BSTE4033MN	OEM
BSTE4033N	OEM
BSTE4040MN	OEM
BSTE4040MP	OEM
BSTE4046MN	OEM
BSTE4046MP	OEM
BSTE4046N	OEM
BSTE4046P	OEM
BSTE4053MN	OEM
BSTE4053N	OEM
BSTE4126MN	OEM
BSTE4126N	OEM
BSTE4133MN	OEM
BSTE4133N	OEM
BSTE4140MN	OEM
BSTE4140MP	OEM
BSTE4140N	OEM
BSTE4140P	OEM
BSTE4146MN	OEM
BSTE4146MP	OEM
BSTE4146N	OEM
BSTE4146P	OEM
BSTE4153MN	OEM
BSTE4153N	OEM
BSTE05100	OEM
BSTF0320	OEM
BSTF0340	OEM
BSTF0360	OEM
BSTF0420	OEM
BSTF0420S1	OEM
BSTF0426	OEM
BSTF0426S1	OEM
BSTF0433	OEM
BSTF0433S1	OEM
BSTF0440S1	OEM
BSTF0446	OEM
BSTF0446S1	OEM
BSTF0455S7	OEM
BSTF0460S1	OEM
BSTF0460S7	OEM
BSTF0466	OEM
BSTF0466S1	OEM
BSTF0466S7	OEM
BSTF0520	OEM
BSTF0540	OEM
BSTF0560	OEM
BSTF0590	OEM
BSTF05110	OEM
BSTF2520+	3970
BSTF2540	3970
BSTF2540S1	OEM
BSTF2540S7	OEM
BSTF2540S9	OEM
BSTF2540S10	OEM
BSTF2553	OEM
BSTF2553+	0674
BSTF2553S1	OEM
BSTF2553S6	OEM
BSTF2553S7	OEM
BSTF2553S9	OEM
BSTF2553S10	OEM
BSTF2560	OEM
BSTF2560+	0674
BSTF2560S1	OEM
BSTF2560S6	OEM
BSTF2560S7	OEM
BSTF2560S9	OEM
BSTF2560S10	OEM
BSTF2566	OEM
BSTF2566+	0674
BSTF2566S1	OEM
BSTF2566S6	OEM
BSTF2566S7	OEM

DEVICE TYPE	REPL CODE
BSTF2566S9	OEM
BSTF2566S10	OEM
BSTF2580	OEM
BSTF2580+	0674
BSTF2580S1	OEM
BSTF2580S7	OEM
BSTF2580S9	OEM
BSTF2580S10	OEM
BSTF2590	OEM
BSTF2590S1	OEM
BSTF2590S6	OEM
BSTF2590S7	OEM
BSTF2590S9	OEM
BSTF2590S10	OEM
BSTF25100	OEM
BSTF25100S1	OEM
BSTF25100S6	OEM
BSTF25100S7	OEM
BSTF25100S9	OEM
BSTF25100S10	OEM
BSTF25110	OEM
BSTF25110S1	OEM
BSTF25110S6	OEM
BSTF25110S9	OEM
BSTF25110S10	OEM
BSTF35110	OEM
BSTG0220	OEM
BSTG0240	OEM
BSTG0260	OEM
BSTG0320	OEM
BSTG0340	OEM
BSTG0360	OEM
BSTG3540	OEM
BSTG3560	OEM
BSTG3590	OEM
BSTG35110	OEM
BSTH0420	OEM
BSTH0520	OEM
BSTH0540	OEM
BSTH0540S9	OEM
BSTH0540S10	OEM
BSTH0553	OEM
BSTH0553S9	OEM
BSTH0553S10	OEM
BSTH0560	OEM
BSTH0560S9	OEM
BSTH0560S10	OEM
BSTH0566	OEM
BSTH0566S9	OEM
BSTH0566S10	OEM
BSTH0580	OEM
BSTH0580S9	OEM
BSTH0580S10	OEM
BSTH0590	OEM
BSTH0590S9	OEM
BSTH0590S10	OEM
BSTH05100	OEM
BSTH05100S9	OEM
BSTH05100S10	OEM
BSTH05110	OEM
BSTH05110S9	OEM
BSTH05110S10	OEM
BSTH051120	OEM
BSTH3440I	OEM
BSTH3440IS9	OEM
BSTH3440K	OEM
BSTH3440KS9	OEM
BSTH3453I	OEM
BSTH3453IS9	OEM
BSTH3460K	OEM
BSTH3460KS9	OEM
BSTH3466I	OEM
BSTH3466IS9	OEM
BSTH3466K	OEM
BSTH3480I	OEM
BSTH3480IS9	OEM
BSTH3480K	OEM
BSTH3480KS9	OEM
BSTH3486IS9	OEM
BSTH3486K	OEM
BSTH3486KS9	OEM
BSTH3540	OEM
BSTH3540S9	OEM
BSTH3540S10	OEM
BSTH3553S9	OEM
BSTH3553S10	OEM
BSTH3560	OEM
BSTH3560S9	OEM
BSTH3566S9	OEM
BSTH3566S10	OEM
BSTH3580	OEM
BSTH3580S9	OEM
BSTH3580S10	OEM
BSTH3590	OEM
BSTH3590S9	OEM
BSTH3590S10	OEM
BSTH3733FS9	OEM
BSTH3733G	OEM
BSTH3733GS9	OEM
BSTH3740F	OEM
BSTH3740FS9	OEM
BSTH3740G	OEM
BSTH3740GS9	OEM
BSTH3746F	OEM
BSTH3746FS9	OEM
BSTH3746G	OEM
BSTH3746GS9	OEM
BSTH3753F	OEM
BSTH3753FS9	OEM

DEVICE TYPE	REPL CODE
BSTH3753G	OEM
BSTH3753GS9	OEM
BSTH3760FS9	OEM
BSTH3760G	OEM
BSTH3766FS9	OEM
BSTH3766G	OEM
BSTH3766GS9	OEM
BSTH3773F	OEM
BSTH4440I	OEM
BSTH4440K	OEM
BSTH4440KS9	OEM
BSTH4453I	OEM
BSTH4453K	OEM
BSTH4453KS9	OEM
BSTH4460I	OEM
BSTH4460K	OEM
BSTH4460KS9	OEM
BSTH4466I	OEM
BSTH4466KS9	OEM
BSTH4480I	OEM
BSTH4486I	OEM
BSTH4486K	OEM
BSTH4540	OEM
BSTH4540S9	OEM
BSTH4540S10	OEM
BSTH4553S9	OEM
BSTH4553S10	OEM
BSTH4560S9	OEM
BSTH4580S9	OEM
BSTH4590S9	OEM
BSTH4760GS9	OEM
BSTH4766F	OEM
BSTH4766GS9	OEM
BSTH6113F	OEM
BSTH6113FS9	OEM
BSTH6113G	OEM
BSTH6113GS9	OEM
BSTH6113Y	OEM
BSTH6120F	OEM
BSTH6120FS9	OEM
BSTH6120G	OEM
BSTH6120GS9	OEM
BSTH6120Y	OEM
BSTH6126F	OEM
BSTH6126FS9	OEM
BSTH6126Y	OEM
BSTH6133F	OEM
BSTH6133FS9	OEM
BSTH6133G	OEM
BSTH6133GS9	OEM
BSTH6133Y	OEM
BSTH6140F	OEM
BSTH6140FS9	OEM
BSTH6140G	OEM
BSTH6140GS9	OEM
BSTH34666KS9	OEM
BSTH35100	OEM
BSTH35100S9	OEM
BSTH35100S10	OEM
BSTH35110	OEM
BSTH35110S9	OEM
BSTH35110S10	OEM
BSTH45100S9	OEM
BSTH45110	OEM
BSTH45110S9	OEM
BSTK4560	OEM
BSTK4560S9	OEM
BSTK4560S10	OEM
BSTK4566	OEM
BSTK4566S9	OEM
BSTK4566S10	OEM
BSTK4580	OEM
BSTK4580S9	OEM
BSTK4580S10	OEM
BSTK4590	OEM
BSTK4590S9	OEM
BSTK4590S10	OEM
BSTK45100	OEM
BSTK45100S9	OEM
BSTK45100S10	OEM
BSTK45120	OEM
BSTK45120S9	OEM
BSTK45120S10	OEM
BSTL0220	OEM
BSTL0240	OEM
BSTL0260	OEM
BSTL0420	OEM
BSTL0440	OEM
BSTL0455	OEM
BSTL0460	OEM
BSTL0520	OEM
BSTL0540	OEM
BSTL0560	OEM
BSTL0590	OEM
BSTL05110	OEM
BSTL06140	OEM
BSTL06160	OEM
BSTL06180	OEM
BSTL2420	OEM
BSTL2440	OEM
BSTL2455	OEM
BSTL2460	OEM
BSTL2520	OEM
BSTL2540	OEM
BSTL2560	OEM
BSTL2580	OEM
BSTL2590	OEM
BSTL3440	OEM
BSTL3440IS9	OEM

DEVICE TYPE	REPL CODE
BSTL3440K	OEM
BSTL3440KS9	OEM
BSTL3446I	OEM
BSTL3446IS9	OEM
BSTL3446K	OEM
BSTL3446KS9	OEM
BSTL3453I	OEM
BSTL3453IS9	OEM
BSTL3453K	OEM
BSTL3453KS9	OEM
BSTL3460	OEM
BSTL3460I	OEM
BSTL3460IS9	OEM
BSTL3460K	OEM
BSTL3460KS9	OEM
BSTL3466I	OEM
BSTL3466IS9	OEM
BSTL3466K	OEM
BSTL3466KS9	OEM
BSTL3473IS9	OEM
BSTL3473K	OEM
BSTL3473KS9	OEM
BSTL3480	OEM
BSTL3480I	OEM
BSTL3480IS9	OEM
BSTL3480K	OEM
BSTL3480KS9	OEM
BSTL3486I	OEM
BSTL3486IS9	OEM
BSTL3486K	OEM
BSTL3486KS9	OEM
BSTL3520	OEM
BSTL3540	OEM
BSTL3540S9	OEM
BSTL3540S10	OEM
BSTL3553	OEM
BSTL3553S9	OEM
BSTL3560	OEM
BSTL3560S10	OEM
BSTL3566	OEM
BSTL3566S9	OEM
BSTL3566S10	OEM
BSTL3580	OEM
BSTL3580S10	OEM
BSTL3590	OEM
BSTL3590S10	OEM
BSTL3733G	OEM
BSTL3733GS9	OEM
BSTL3740G	OEM
BSTL3740GS9	OEM
BSTL3746F	OEM
BSTL3746G	OEM
BSTL3746GS9	OEM
BSTL3753F	OEM
BSTL3753G	OEM
BSTL3753GS9	OEM
BSTL3760F	OEM
BSTL3760G	OEM
BSTL3760GS9	OEM
BSTL3766F	OEM
BSTL3766G	OEM
BSTL3766GS9	OEM
BSTL4006	OEM
BSTL4020	OEM
BSTL4033	OEM
BSTL4440	OEM
BSTL4440I	OEM
BSTL4440K	OEM
BSTL4440KS9	OEM
BSTL4446I	OEM
BSTL4446K	OEM
BSTL4446KS9	OEM
BSTL4453I	OEM
BSTL4453IS9	OEM
BSTL4453K	OEM
BSTL4453KS9	OEM
BSTL4460	OEM
BSTL4460K	OEM
BSTL4460KS9	OEM
BSTL4460S9	OEM
BSTL4466I	OEM
BSTL4466K	OEM
BSTL4473I	OEM
BSTL4473K	OEM
BSTL4480	OEM
BSTL4480I	OEM
BSTL4480K	OEM
BSTL4486	OEM
BSTL4486I	OEM
BSTL4486K	OEM
BSTL4540	OEM
BSTL4540S9	OEM
BSTL4540S10	OEM
BSTL4553	OEM
BSTL4553S9	OEM
BSTL4553S10	OEM
BSTL4560	OEM
BSTL4560S9	OEM
BSTL4560S10	OEM
BSTL4566	OEM
BSTL4566S9	OEM
BSTL4566S10	OEM
BSTL4580	OEM
BSTL4580S9	OEM
BSTL4580S10	OEM
BSTL4590	OEM
BSTL4590S10	OEM
BSTL4733F	OEM
BSTL4733GS9	OEM

If replacement code is OEM, contact original manufacturer for replacement.

DEVICE TYPE	REPL CODE
BSTL4740F	OEM
BSTL4740GS9	OEM
BSTL4746F	OEM
BSTL4746GS9	OEM
BSTL4753F	OEM
BSTL4753GS9	OEM
BSTL4760F	OEM
BSTL4760GS9	OEM
BSTL4766F	OEM
BSTL4766GS9	OEM
BSTL6113	OEM
BSTL6113F	OEM
BSTL6113G	OEM
BSTL6113GS9	OEM
BSTL6120	OEM
BSTL6120F	OEM
BSTL6120G	OEM
BSTL6120GS9	OEM
BSTL6126	OEM
BSTL6126F	OEM
BSTL6126G	OEM
BSTL6126GS9	OEM
BSTL6133	OEM
BSTL6133F	OEM
BSTL6133G	OEM
BSTL6133GS9	OEM
BSTL6140F	OEM
BSTL6140G	OEM
BSTL6140GS9	OEM
BSTL25110	OEM
BSTL35100	OEM
BSTL35100S9	OEM
BSTL35100S10	OEM
BSTL35110	OEM
BSTL35110S9	OEM
BSTL35110S10	OEM
BSTL45100	OEM
BSTL45100S9	OEM
BSTL45100S10	OEM
BSTL45110	OEM
BSTL45110S9	OEM
BSTL45110S10	OEM
BSTL45120	OEM
BSTL45120S9	OEM
BSTL45120S10	OEM
BSTM4560	OEM
BSTM4560S9	OEM
BSTM4566S9	OEM
BSTM4580	OEM
BSTM4580S9	OEM
BSTM4590	OEM
BSTM4590S9	OEM
BSTM45100	OEM
BSTM45100S9	OEM
BSTM45110	OEM
BSTM45110S9	OEM
BSTM45120S9	OEM
BSTN0220	OEM
BSTN0240	OEM
BSTN0260	OEM
BSTN0320	OEM
BSTN0340	OEM
BSTN0360	OEM
BSTN0520	OEM
BSTN0540	OEM
BSTN0560	OEM
BSTN0590	OEM
BSTN05100	OEM
BSTN05110	OEM
BSTN4R80K	OEM
BSTN1520	OEM
BSTN1540	OEM
BSTN1560	OEM
BSTN1580	OEM
BSTN1590	OEM
BSTN2320	OEM
BSTN2340	OEM
BSTN2360	OEM
BSTN2520	OEM
BSTN2540	OEM
BSTN2560	OEM
BSTN2590	OEM
BSTN3440I	OEM
BSTN3440K	OEM
BSTN3446I	OEM
BSTN3446K	OEM
BSTN3453I	OEM
BSTN3453K	OEM
BSTN3460I	OEM
BSTN3460K	OEM
BSTN3466+	0733
BSTN3466I	OEM
BSTN3466K	OEM
BSTN3473I	OEM
BSTN3473IS9	OEM
BSTN3480I	OEM
BSTN3480IS9	OEM
BSTN3480K	OEM
BSTN3486I	OEM
BSTN3486IS9	OEM
BSTN3486K	OEM
BSTN3520	OEM
BSTN3540	OEM
BSTN3540S9	OEM
BSTN3540S10	OEM
BSTN3553S10	OEM
BSTN3560	OEM
BSTN3560+	0733
BSTN3560S9	OEM
BSTN3560S10	OEM
BSTN3566S9	OEM
BSTN3566S10	OEM
BSTN3580	OEM
BSTN3580+	0733
BSTN3580S9	OEM
BSTN3580S10	OEM
BSTN3590	OEM
BSTN3590S9	OEM
BSTN3590S10	OEM
BSTN3733G	OEM
BSTN3733GS9	OEM
BSTN3740G	OEM
BSTN3740GS9	OEM
BSTN3746G	OEM
BSTN3746GS9	OEM
BSTN3753F	OEM
BSTN3753G	OEM
BSTN3753GS9	OEM
BSTN3760G	OEM
BSTN3760GS9	OEM
BSTN3766F	OEM
BSTN3766G	OEM
BSTN3766GS9	OEM
BSTN4006	OEM
BSTN4020	OEM
BSTN4033	OEM
BSTN4440K	OEM
BSTN4460K	OEM
BSTN4473IS9	OEM
BSTN4480IS9	OEM
BSTN4486IS9	OEM
BSTN4486K	OEM
BSTN4520	OEM
BSTN4540	OEM
BSTN4540S9	OEM
BSTN4540S10	OEM
BSTN4553	OEM
BSTN4553S9	OEM
BSTN4553S10	OEM
BSTN4560	OEM
BSTN4560S9	OEM
BSTN4560S10	OEM
BSTN4566	OEM
BSTN4566S9	OEM
BSTN4566S10	OEM
BSTN4580	OEM
BSTN4580S9	OEM
BSTN4590	OEM
BSTN4590S9	OEM
BSTN4733F	OEM
BSTN4733G	OEM
BSTN4740F	OEM
BSTN4740G	OEM
BSTN4746F	OEM
BSTN4746G	OEM
BSTN4753	OEM
BSTN4753F	OEM
BSTN4753G	OEM
BSTN4760F	OEM
BSTN4766	OEM
BSTN4766F	OEM
BSTN4766GS9	OEM
BSTN5240S10	OEM
BSTN5253S10	OEM
BSTN5260S9	OEM
BSTN5260S10	OEM
BSTN5266S9	OEM
BSTN5266S10	OEM
BSTN5280S9	OEM
BSTN5280S10	OEM
BSTN5290S9	OEM
BSTN5290S10	OEM
BSTN5540	OEM
BSTN5540S9	OEM
BSTN5540S10	OEM
BSTN5553	OEM
BSTN5553S9	OEM
BSTN5553S10	OEM
BSTN5560S9	OEM
BSTN5560S10	OEM
BSTN5566S9	OEM
BSTN5566S10	OEM
BSTN5580S9	OEM
BSTN5580S10	OEM
BSTN5590S9	OEM
BSTN5590S10	OEM
BSTN6113	OEM
BSTN6113F	OEM
BSTN6113FS9	OEM
BSTN6113G	OEM
BSTN6113Y	OEM
BSTN6120	OEM
BSTN6120F	OEM
BSTN6120FS9	OEM
BSTN6120G	OEM
BSTN6120Y	OEM
BSTN6126	OEM
BSTN6126F	OEM
BSTN6126G	OEM
BSTN6126Y	OEM
BSTN6133	OEM
BSTN6133F	OEM
BSTN6133G	OEM
BSTN6133Y	OEM
BSTN6140F	OEM
BSTN6140G	OEM
BSTN6440IS9	OEM
BSTN6446IS9	OEM
BSTN6453IS9	OEM
BSTN6460IS9	OEM
BSTN6466IS9	OEM
BSTN6473IS9	OEM
BSTN6473K	OEM
BSTN6480IS9	OEM
BSTN6480K	OEM
BSTN6486IS9	OEM
BSTN6486K	OEM
BSTN15110	OEM
BSTN25100	OEM
BSTN25110	OEM
BSTN35100S9	OEM
BSTN35100S10	OEM
BSTN35110	OEM
BSTN35120	OEM
BSTN35120S9	OEM
BSTN35120S10	OEM
BSTN45100	OEM
BSTN45100S9	OEM
BSTN45110	OEM
BSTN45110S9	OEM
BSTN45120	OEM
BSTN45120S9	OEM
BSTN52100S9	OEM
BSTN52100S10	OEM
BSTN52110	OEM
BSTN52110S9	OEM
BSTN52110S10	OEM
BSTN52120	OEM
BSTN52120S9	OEM
BSTN52120S10	OEM
BSTP0220	OEM
BSTP0240	OEM
BSTP0260	OEM
BSTP0280	OEM
BSTP0320	OEM
BSTP0340	OEM
BSTP0360	OEM
BSTP0520	OEM
BSTP0540	OEM
BSTP0560	OEM
BSTP0590	OEM
BSTP05100	OEM
BSTP05110	OEM
BSTP1260	OEM
BSTP1520	OEM
BSTP1560S9	OEM
BSTP1560S10	OEM
BSTP1560T	OEM
BSTP1560TS9	OEM
BSTP1560TS10	OEM
BSTP1566	OEM
BSTP1566S9	OEM
BSTP1566S10	OEM
BSTP1566T	OEM
BSTP1566TS9	OEM
BSTP3520	OEM
BSTP4520	OEM
BSV01	OEM
BSV02	OEM
BSV11	OEM
BSV15	0126
BSV15-6	0126
BSV15-10	0126
BSV16	0126
BSV16-6	0126
BSV16-10	0126
BSV17	0126
BSV17-6	0126
BSV17-10	0126
BSV20	OEM
BSV20A	OEM
BSV21	0037
BSV22	OEM
BSV23	OEM
BSV24	OEM
BSV25	OEM
BSV26	OEM
BSV27	OEM
BSV28	OEM
BSV29	OEM
BSV33	OEM
BSV34	OEM
BSV34A	OEM
BSV35	0144
BSV35A	0016
BSV36	0470
BSV38	OEM
BSV38P	OEM
BSV39	OEM
BSV39P	OEM
BSV40	0016
BSV41	0016
BSV42	0037
BSV43A	0037
BSV43B	0786
BSV44A	0037
BSV44B	0786
BSV45A	0037
BSV45B	0786
BSV46	0037
BSV47A	0037
BSV47B	0786
BSV48A	0037
BSV48B	0786
BSV49A	0037
BSV49B	0786
BSV50E	OEM
BSV50F	OEM
BSV50G	OEM
BSV51	0086
BSV52	0144
BSV52R	0144
BSV53	0016
BSV53P	0127
BSV54	0016
BSV54P	0127
BSV55	0016
BSV55A	0037
BSV55AP	0037
BSV55P	0037
BSV56A	OEM
BSV56B	OEM
BSV56C	OEM
BSV57A	OEM
BSV57C	OEM
BSV58A	OEM
BSV58B	OEM
BSV59	0016
BSV60	5435
BSV61	OEM
BSV62	OEM
BSV63	OEM
BSV65FA	0079
BSV65FB	0079
BSV68	0338
BSV69	0086
BSV71	OEM
BSV74	OEM
BSV75	OEM
BSV76	OEM
BSV77	0007
BSV78	1147
BSV79	1147
BSV80	OEM
BSV81	OEM
BSV82	0126
BSV83	0126
BSV84	0086
BSV85	0018
BSV86	0079
BSV87	0079
BSV88	0016
BSV89	0016
BSV90	0016
BSV91	0016
BSV92	0224
BSV95	0414
BSV96	0037
BSV97	0037
BSV98	0037
BSV99	OEM
BSW10	0086
BSW11	0016
BSW12	0016
BSW13	0007
BSW17	OEM
BSW18	OEM
BSW19	0016
BSW19A	0338
BSW19VI	0338
BSW20	0037
BSW20A	0338
BSW20VI	0338
BSW21	0037
BSW21A	0037
BSW22	0037
BSW22A	0037
BSW23	0126
BSW24	0037
BSW25	3562
BSW26	0086
BSW27	0086
BSW28	0086
BSW29	0086
BSW30	OEM
BSW31	OEM
BSW32	0155
BSW33	0016
BSW34	0016
BSW35	0086
BSW36	OEM
BSW37	OEM
BSW38	OEM
BSW39	0016
BSW39-6	0086
BSW39-10	0086
BSW39-16	0086
BSW40	0126
BSW40-6	0126
BSW40-10	0126
BSW40-16	0126
BSW40-25	0126
BSW41	0016
BSW42	0016
BSW42A	0016
BSW42B	OEM
BSW43	0016
BSW43A	0016
BSW44	0037
BSW44A	0037
BSW45	0037
BSW45A	0037
BSW49	0086
BSW51	0016
BSW52	0016
BSW53	0016
BSW54	OEM
BSW58	0079
BSW59	0079
BSW61	OEM
BSW62	OEM
BSW63	OEM
BSW64	OEM
BSW65	0086
BSW66	0086
BSW67	6793
BSW-68	0187
BSW68	6793
BSW68A	OEM
BSW69	0187
BSW70	0233
BSW72	0037
BSW73	0037
BSW74	0037
BSW75	0037
BSW78	OEM
BSW79	OEM
BSW80	2503
BSW81	0037
BSW82	0016
BSW83	0016
BSW84	0016
BSW85	0016
BSW88	0016
BSW88A	0079
BSW88B	0079
BSW89	0016
BSW89A	0079
BSW89B	0079
BSW92	0016
BSW95	OEM
BSW95A	OEM
BSX12	0144
BSX12A	0086
BSX19	0016
BSX20	0488
BSX21	0855
BSX22	1390
BSX23	0086
BSX24	0016
BSX25	0016
BSX26	0144
BSX27	0144
BSX28	0488
BSX29	0150
BSX30	0016
BSX31	OEM
BSX32	0488
BSX33	0086
BSX34	OEM
BSX35	0144
BSX36	0037
BSX38	0016
BSX38A	0016
BSX38B	0016
BSX39	0488
BSX40	0126
BSX41	0126
BSX44	0016
BSX45	0086
BSX45-6	0086
BSX45-10	0086
BSX45-16	0086
BSX46	0086
BSX46-6	0086
BSX46-10	0086
BSX46-16	0086
BSX47	0086
BSX47-6	0086
BSX47-10	0086
BSX48	0016
BSX49	0016
BSX51	0016
BSX51A	0016
BSX51B	OEM
BSX52	0016
BSX52A	0016
BSX52B	OEM
BSX53	0016
BSX53A	OEM
BSX53B	OEM
BSX54	0016
BSX54A	OEM
BSX54B	OEM
BSX58	OEM
BSX59	0086
BSX60	0086
BSX61	0086
BSX62	0086
BSX62-10	0617
BSX62-16	0617
BSX62B	0086
BSX62C	0086
BSX62D	0086
BSX63	0639
BSX63-10	0617
BSX63B	0086
BSX63C	0086
BSX66	0016
BSX67	0016
BSX68	0016
BSX69	0016
BSX70	0086
BSX71	0086
BSX72	0086
BSX75	0016
BSX76	0016
BSX77	0016
BSX78	0016
BSX79	0016
BSX79A	0079
BSX79B	0079
BSX80	0016
BSX81	0016
BSX81A	0079
BSX81B	0079
BSX82	OEM
BSX83	OEM
BSX84	OEM
BSX85	OEM
BSX86	OEM
BSX87	0016
BSX87A	0488
BSX88	0016
BSX88A	0488
BSX89	0016
BSX90	0016
BSX91	0016
BSX92	0144
BSX93	0144
BSX94	OEM
BSX94A	0016
BSX95	0086
BSX96	0086
BSX97	0016
BSY10	0016
BSY11	0016
BSY17	0016
BSY18	0016
BSY19	0079
BSY20	0016
BSY21	0016
BSY22	0144
BSY23	0144
BSY24	0016
BSY25	0016
BSY26	0087
BSY27	0016
BSY28	0016
BSY29	0016
BSY32	OEM
BSY33	OEM
BSY34	OEM
BSY36	OEM
BSY38	0016
BSY38A	OEM
BSY39	0016
BSY39A	OEM
BSY40	0037
BSY41	0037
BSY42	OEM
BSY43	OEM
BSY44	0086
BSY45	0086
BSY46	0086
BSY47	OEM
BSY48	0016
BSY49	0016
BSY50	OEM
BSY51	0086
BSY52	0086
BSY53	0086
BSY54	0086
BSY55	0086
BSY56	0086
BSY58	0016
BSY59	0016
BSY61	0016
BSY62	0016
BSY62A	0016
BSY62B	0590
BSY63	0016
BSY68	0855
BSY70	0016
BSY71	0086
BSY72	0016
BSY73	0016
BSY74	0016
BSY75	0016
BSY76	0016
BSY77	0086
BSY78	0086
BSY79	0855
BSY80	0016
BSY81	0086
BSY82	0086
BSY83	0086
BSY84	0086
BSY85	0086
BSY86	0086
BSY87	0086
BSY88	0086
BSY89	0086
BSY90	0086
BSY91	0016
BSY92	0086
BSY93	0016
BSY95	0016
BSY95A	0016
BSY165	0016
BSY168	0016
BT67	0016
BT71	0016
BT82	0037
BT-94	0016
BT100A-300R	1213
BT100A-500R	OEM
BT101-300R	0671
BT101-500R	2782
BT102-300R	2635
BT102-500R	2782
BT106	OEM
BT106A	0442
BT106B	0934
BT106C	0095
BT106D	0095
BT107	2782
BT108	2782
BT109	OEM
BT109-500R	OEM
BT110	OEM
BT112-750R	OEM
BT113-700R	OEM
BT114	OEM
BT115	OEM
BT116	OEM
BT117	OEM
BT118	OEM
BT119	6280
BT120	0061
BT121	0239
BT123	OEM
BT124	OEM
BT126-750R	OEM
BT127-350R	OEM
BT127-750R	OEM
BT138	OEM
BT138-500	0612
BT138-500G	0612
BT138-600G	0612
BT138-800G	0869
BT138F-500	2188
BT138F-600	2188
BT138F-800	2188
BT139-500	1649
BT139-500E	OEM
BT139-500F	6481
BT139-500G	1649
BT139-600	1649
BT139-600E	OEM
BT139-600F	6481
BT139-600G	1649
BT139-800	1649
BT139-800E	OEM
BT139-800F	OEM
BT139-800G	1956
BT139F-500	2188
BT139F-600	2188
BT139F-800	2188
BT143-400R	OEM
BT146	OEM
BT148	OEM
BT149D	OEM
BT151	0857
BT151-500R	0857
BT929	0007
BT930	0259
B-T-1000-139	0127
BT8667	0683
BT151500R	1213
BTA08-200S	5835
BTA08-400S	5835
BTA08-600S	OEM
BTA08-700S	OEM
BTA08-800S	OEM
BTA41-200A	5509
BTA41-400A	5745
BTA41-600A	3663
BTA41-700A	OEM
BTA41-800A	OEM
BTA140-500	1649
BTA140-600	2188
BTA140-800	1956
BTB08-200S	5436
BTB08-400S	5436
BTB08-600S	OEM
BTB08-700S	0059
BTB08-800S	0059
BTB41-200A	3709
BTB41-400A	6012
BTB41-600A	3709
BTB41-700A	OEM
BTB41-800A	OEM
BTB50	OEM
BTB100	OEM
BTB200	OEM
BTB400	OEM
BTB600	OEM
BTB800	OEM
BTB1000	0087
BTB1200	OEM
BTD0105	2367
BTD0110	2367
BTD0120	0476
BTD0140	0480
BTD0305	2367
BTD0310	2367
BTD0320	0476
BTD0340	0480
BTD0360-1	OEM
BTD0360-2	OEM
BTD0360-3	OEM
BTD4	OEM

If replacement code is OEM, contact original manufacturer for replacement.

295

DEVICE TYPE	REPL CODE
BTD32B	OEM
BTL0405	OEM
BTL0410	OEM
BTL0420	OEM
BTL0440	OEM
BTL0460	OEM
BTL0605	OEM
BTL0610	OEM
BTL0620	OEM
BTL0640	OEM
BTL0660	OEM
BTL0805	OEM
BTL0810	OEM
BTL0820	OEM
BTL0840	OEM
BTL0860	OEM
BTL1005	OEM
BTL1010	OEM
BTL1020	OEM
BTL1040	OEM
BTL1060	OEM
BTL1605	OEM
BTL1610	OEM
BTL1620	OEM
BTL1640	OEM
BTL1660	OEM
BTM0405	OEM
BTM0410	OEM
BTM0420	OEM
BTM0440	OEM
BTM0460	OEM
BTM0605	OEM
BTM0610	OEM
BTM0620	OEM
BTM0640	OEM
BTM0660	OEM
BTM-50	0110
BTM50	0015
BTM100	OEM
BTM200	OEM
BTM400	OEM
BTM600	OEM
BTM800	OEM
BTM1000	0087
BTM1005	OEM
BTM1010	OEM
BTM1020	OEM
BTM1040	OEM
BTM1060	OEM
BTM1200	OEM
BTM1605	OEM
BTM1610	OEM
BTM1620	OEM
BTM1640	OEM
BTM1660	OEM
BTR0605	0767
BTR0610	0767
BTR0620	0767
BTR0640	0767
BTR0660	OEM
BTR170S15	OEM
BTR171	OEM
BTR174	OEM
BTR198A	OEM
BTR202	OEM
BTR209	OEM
BTR537	OEM
BTR540	OEM
BTR541	OEM
BTR545A	OEM
BTR547	OEM
BTR554	OEM
BTR570A	OEM
BTR574	OEM
BTR576	OEM
BTR583	OEM
BTR608	OEM
BTR614	OEM
BTR629A	OEM
BTR630	OEM
BTR632A	OEM
BTR633	OEM
BTR639	OEM
BTR640	OEM
BTR641	OEM
BTR647	OEM
BTR666	OEM
BTR1005	0588
BTR1010	0588
BTR1020	0588
BTR1040	OEM
BTR1060	OEM
BTS0605	1058
BTS0610	1058
BTS0620	1058
BTS0640	1307
BTS0660	1880
BTS95-500R	OEM
BTS1005	1058
BTS1010	1058
BTS1020	1058
BTS1040	1307
BTS1060	1880
BTS1605	1058
BTS1610	1058
BTS1620	1058
BTS1640	1307
BTS1660	OEM
BTS2505	1058

DEVICE TYPE	REPL CODE
BTS2510	1058
BTS2520	1058
BTS2540	1307
BTS2560	1880
BTS3500	0133
BTS3600	OEM
BTT24-1200R	OEM
BTT170S01	OEM
BTT170S02	OEM
BTT170S03	OEM
BTT170S04	OEM
BTT170S05	OEM
BTT170S06	OEM
BTT170S07	OEM
BTT170S08	OEM
BTT170S09	OEM
BTT170S10	OEM
BTT170S11	OEM
BTT170S12	OEM
BTT170S13	OEM
BTT170S14	OEM
BTT170S15	OEM
BTU0340	0278
BTU0405	0395
BTU0410	0404
BTU0420	0418
BTU0430	0418
BTU0440	0418
BTU0450	0418
BTU0460	0418
BTU0505	0154
BTU0510	0154
BTU0520	0154
BTU0530	0147
BTU0535	0278
BTU0540	0147
BTU0550	0278
BTU0560	0278
BTU0605	3118
BTU0630	3122
BTU0660	0278
BTU650	3124
BTU1005	0154
BTU1010	0154
BTU1020	0154
BTU1040	0902
BTU1060	0278
BTU1605	0154
BTU1610	0154
BTU1620	0154
BTU1640	0147
BTU1660	0278
BTU2505	2004
BTU2510	2004
BTU2520	2004
BTU2540	2006
BTU2560	2007
BTU3605	2007
BTV0405	3169
BTV0410	3169
BTV0420	3169
BTV0430	3177
BTV0440	3177
BTV0460	3192
BTV24-600R	3970
BTV24-800R	0682
BTV24-1400R	OEM
BTV34-600G	OEM
BTV34-600H	OEM
BTV34-800G	OEM
BTV34-800H	OEM
BTV34-1200G	OEM
BTV34-1200H	OEM
BTV34-1400G	OEM
BTV34-1400H	OEM
BTV58-600R	OEM
BTV58-850R	OEM
BTV58-1000R	OEM
BTW10-50	OEM
BTW10-100	OEM
BTW10-200	OEM
BTW10-300	OEM
BTW10-400	OEM
BTW10-500	OEM
BTW10-600	OEM
BTW11-50	OEM
BTW11-100	OEM
BTW11-200	OEM
BTW11-300	OEM
BTW11-400	OEM
BTW11-500	OEM
BTW11-600	OEM
BTW12-50	OEM
BTW12-100	OEM
BTW12-200	OEM
BTW12-300	OEM
BTW12-400	OEM
BTW12-500	OEM
BTW12-600	OEM
BTW13-50	0154
BTW13-100	0154
BTW13-200	0154
BTW13-300	0147
BTW13-400	0147
BTW13-500	0278
BTW13-600	0278
BTW14-50	0154
BTW14-100	0154
BTW14-200	0154

DEVICE TYPE	REPL CODE
BTW14-300	0147
BTW14-400	0147
BTW14-500	0278
BTW14-600	0278
BTW15-50	OEM
BTW15-100	OEM
BTW15-200	OEM
BTW15-300	OEM
BTW15-400	OEM
BTW15-500	OEM
BTW15-600	OEM
BTW16-50	0154
BTW16-100	0154
BTW16-200	0154
BTW16-300	0147
BTW16-400	0147
BTW16-500	0278
BTW16-600	0278
BTW17-100	OEM
BTW17-200	OEM
BTW17-300	OEM
BTW17-400	OEM
BTW17-500	OEM
BTW17-600	OEM
BTW18-50	OEM
BTW18-100	OEM
BTW18-200	OEM
BTW18-300	OEM
BTW18-400	OEM
BTW18-500	OEM
BTW18-600	OEM
BTW19-50	0154
BTW19-100	0154
BTW19-200	0154
BTW19-300	0147
BTW19-400	0147
BTW19-500	0278
BTW19-600	0278
BTW20-50	3118
BTW20-100	3119
BTW20-200	3121
BTW20-300	3123
BTW20-400	3123
BTW20-500	4038
BTW20-600	2007
BTW21-50	OEM
BTW21-100	OEM
BTW21-200	OEM
BTW21-300	OEM
BTW21-400	OEM
BTW21-500	OEM
BTW21-600	OEM
BTW23-600	OEM
BTW23-600RM	OEM
BTW23-700R	OEM
BTW23-800	OEM
BTW23-800R	OEM
BTW23-800RM	OEM
BTW23-1000	OEM
BTW23-1000R	OEM
BTW23-1000RM	OEM
BTW23-1200	OEM
BTW23-1200R	OEM
BTW23-1200RM	OEM
BTW23-1400	OEM
BTW23-1400R	OEM
BTW23-1400RM	OEM
BTW23-1600	OEM
BTW23-1600R	OEM
BTW23-1600RM	OEM
BTW24-600	OEM
BTW24-600R	OEM
BTW24-600RM	OEM
BTW24-700R	OEM
BTW24-800	OEM
BTW24-800R	OEM
BTW24-800RM	OEM
BTW24-1000	OEM
BTW24-1000R	OEM
BTW24-1000RM	OEM
BTW24-1200	OEM
BTW24-1200R	OEM
BTW24-1200RM	OEM
BTW24-1400	OEM
BTW24-1400R	OEM
BTW24-1400RM	OEM
BTW24-1600	OEM
BTW24-1600R	OEM
BTW24-1600RM	OEM
BTW26-150	OEM
BTW26-300	OEM
BTW26-400	OEM
BTW26-500	OEM
BTW26-600	OEM
BTW27-100R	OEM
BTW27-200R	OEM
BTW27-300R	OEM
BTW27-400R	OEM
BTW27-500R	OEM
BTW27-600R	OEM
BTW27S-200R	OEM
BTW27S-300R	OEM
BTW27S-400R	OEM
BTW27S-500R	OEM
BTW27SA-200R	OEM
BTW27SA-300R	OEM
BTW27SA-400R	OEM
BTW28-500R	OEM

DEVICE TYPE	REPL CODE
BTW28-600R	0747
BTW28-700R	OEM
BTW28-800R	OEM
BTW28A-500R	OEM
BTW28A500R	OEM
BTW28A-600R	0747
BTW28A600R	0747
BTW28A-700R	OEM
BTW28A700R	OEM
BTW28A-800R	OEM
BTW28A800R	OEM
BTW30-300	OEM
BTW30-300R	OEM
BTW30-300RM	0799
BTW30-400	OEM
BTW30-400R	OEM
BTW30-400RM	0799
BTW30-500	OEM
BTW30-500R	OEM
BTW30-500RM	0799
BTW30-600	0799
BTW30-600R	OEM
BTW30-600RM	0799
BTW30-800	OEM
BTW30-800R	OEM
BTW30-800RM	OEM
BTW30-800RS	OEM
BTW30-1000	OEM
BTW30-1000R	OEM
BTW30-1000RM	OEM
BTW30-1000RS	OEM
BTW30-1200	OEM
BTW30-1200R	OEM
BTW30-1200RM	OEM
BTW30-1200RS	OEM
BTW30-RM	OEM
BTW31-300	OEM
BTW31-300R	OEM
BTW31-300RM	0799
BTW31-400	OEM
BTW31-400R	OEM
BTW31-400RM	0799
BTW31-500	OEM
BTW31-500R	OEM
BTW31-500RM	OEM
BTW31-600	OEM
BTW31-600R	OEM
BTW31-600RM	OEM
BTW31-700R	OEM
BTW31-800	OEM
BTW31-800R	OEM
BTW31-800RM	OEM
BTW31-800RW	OEM
BTW31-1000	OEM
BTW31-1000R	OEM
BTW31-1000RM	OEM
BTW31-1000RW	OEM
BTW31-1200	OEM
BTW31-1200R	OEM
BTW31-1200RM	OEM
BTW31-1200RW	OEM
BTW31-RM	OEM
BTW32-300R	OEM
BTW32-400R	OEM
BTW32-500R	OEM
BTW32-600R	OEM
BTW32-600RU	OEM
BTW32-800R	OEM
BTW32-800RU	OEM
BTW32-1000R	OEM
BTW32-1000RU	OEM
BTW32-1200R	OEM
BTW32-1200RU	OEM
BTW32-6004	OEM
BTW32-RM	OEM
BTW33-600R	OEM
BTW33-600RM	OEM
BTW33-600RM10	OEM
BTW33-800R	OEM
BTW33-800RM	OEM
BTW33-800RM10	OEM
BTW33-1000R	OEM
BTW33-1000RM	OEM
BTW33-1200R	OEM
BTW33-1200RM	OEM
BTW33-RU	OEM
BTW34-600	OEM
BTW34-600G	OEM
BTW34-600H	OEM
BTW34-600M	OEM
BTW34-800	OEM
BTW34-800G	OEM
BTW34-800H	OEM
BTW34-1000	OEM
BTW34-1000G	OEM
BTW34-1000H	OEM
BTW34-1200	OEM
BTW34-1200G	OEM
BTW34-1200H	OEM
BTW34-1400	OEM
BTW34-1400G	OEM
BTW34-1400H	OEM
BTW34-1600	OEM
BTW34-1600G	OEM
BTW34-1600H	OEM
BTW35	OEM
BTW36-200RM	OEM
BTW36-400RM	OEM
BTW36-500RM	OEM

DEVICE TYPE	REPL CODE
BTW36-600RM	OEM
BTW37V600	OEM
BTW37V800	OEM
BTW37V1000	OEM
BTW37V1200	OEM
BTW38-600R	OEM
BTW38-800R	4991
BTW38-1000R	5860
BTW38-1200R	OEM
BTW38V600R	OEM
BTW38V800R	OEM
BTW38V1000R	OEM
BTW38V1200R	OEM
BTW39-50	0735
BTW39-50+	0464
BTW39-100	0562
BTW39-100+	0464
BTW39-200	0757
BTW39-200+	0464
BTW39-300	0735
BTW39-300+	0717
BTW39-400	0735
BTW39-400+	0717
BTW39-500	0759
BTW39-500+	0720
BTW39-600	0759
BTW39-600+	0720
BTW39-700	0761
BTW39-700+	2025
BTW39-800	0761
BTW39-800+	2025
BTW39-900	4455
BTW39-900+	2025
BTW39-1000	4455
BTW39-1000+	2025
BTW39-1100	OEM
BTW39-1100+	2025
BTW39-1200	OEM
BTW39-1200+	2025
BTW40-400R	0717
BTW40-400RM	OEM
BTW40-400RMT	OEM
BTW40-600R	0720
BTW40-600RM	OEM
BTW40-800R	0745
BTW41-500G	OEM
BTW41-500H	OEM
BTW41-600G	OEM
BTW41-600H	OEM
BTW41-800G	OEM
BTW41-800H	OEM
BTW42-600R	OEM
BTW42-800R	OEM
BTW42-1000R	OEM
BTW42-1200R	OEM
BTW43-600G	0418
BTW43-600H	OEM
BTW43-800G	6018
BTW43-800H	OEM
BTW43-1000G	3425
BTW43-1000H	OEM
BTW43-1200G	OEM
BTW43-1200H	OEM
BTW44-100	OEM
BTW44-200	OEM
BTW44-300	OEM
BTW44-400	OEM
BTW44-500	OEM
BTW44-600	OEM
BTW44-600R	OEM
BTW44-800R	OEM
BTW44-1000R	OEM
BTW44-1200R	OEM
BTW44-1400R	OEM
BTW44-1600R	OEM
BTW45-400R	0717
BTW45-400RM	OEM
BTW45-600R	0720
BTW45-600RM	OEM
BTW45-800R	0745
BTW45-1000R	OEM
BTW45-1200R	OEM
BTW46-200R	OEM
BTW46-400R	OEM
BTW46-500R	OEM
BTW46-600R	OEM
BTW47-100RM	OEM
BTW47-200RM	OEM
BTW47-200RU	OEM
BTW47-400RM	OEM
BTW47-400RU	OEM
BTW47-600	OEM
BTW47-600RM	OEM
BTW47-600RU	OEM
BTW47-600RU+	2025
BTW47-800	OEM
BTW47-800R	OEM
BTW47-800RM	OEM
BTW47-800RU	6465
BTW47-800RU+	2025
BTW47-1000	OEM
BTW47-1000R	OEM
BTW47-1000RM	OEM
BTW47-1000RU	4455
BTW47-1000RU+	2025
BTW47-1200	OEM
BTW47-1200R	OEM
BTW47-1200RM	OEM
BTW47-1200RU	OEM

DEVICE TYPE	REPL CODE
BTW47-1200RU+	2025
BTW47-1400	OEM
BTW47-1400R	OEM
BTW47-1400RM	OEM
BTW47-1400RU	OEM
BTW47-1600	OEM
BTW47-1600R	OEM
BTW47-1600RM	OEM
BTW47-1600RU	OEM
BTW47-RU	OEM
BTW48-200	1694
BTW48-200+	3970
BTW48-400	3970
BTW48-400+	3970
BTW48-600	3970
BTW48-600+	3970
BTW48-800	0674
BTW48-800+	0674
BTW48-1200	0674
BTW48-1200+	0674
BTW49-50	0799
BTW49-100	3374
BTW49-200	3374
BTW49-400	3374
BTW49-600	0799
BTW49-800	OEM
BTW50-100	1694
BTW50-200	1694
BTW50-400	3970
BTW50-600	3970
BTW50-800	0674
BTW50-1000	0674
BTW50-1200	0674
BTW58-1000R	OEM
BTW58-1300R	OEM
BTW58-1500R	OEM
BTW63-600RK	OEM
BTW63-600RN	OEM
BTW63-600RP	OEM
BTW63-800RK	OEM
BTW63-800RN	OEM
BTW63-800RP	OEM
BTW66-200N	OEM
BTW66-400	1526
BTW66-400N	OEM
BTW66-600	1526
BTW66-600N	OEM
BTW66-800	OEM
BTW66-800N	OEM
BTW66-1000	OEM
BTW66-1000N	OEM
BTW67-200	1526
BTW67-200N	OEM
BTW67-400	1526
BTW67-400N	OEM
BTW67-600	1526
BTW67-600N	OEM
BTW67-800	OEM
BTW67-800N	OEM
BTW67-1000	OEM
BTW67-1000N	OEM
BTW69-200	2665
BTW69-200N	2671
BTW69-400	2665
BTW69-400N	4988
BTW69-600	5836
BTW69-600N	3246
BTW69-800	5836
BTW69-800N	3246
BTW69-1000	OEM
BTW69-1000N	OEM
BTW69-1200	OEM
BTW69-1200N	OEM
BTW92	OEM
BTW92-200RM	OEM
BTW92-200RU	OEM
BTW92-400RM	OEM
BTW92-400RU	OEM
BTW92-600	OEM
BTW92-600R	OEM
BTW92-600RM	OEM
BTW92-600RU	OEM
BTW92-800	OEM
BTW92-800R	OEM
BTW92-800RM	OEM
BTW92-800RU	OEM
BTW92-1000	OEM
BTW92-1000R	OEM
BTW92-1000RM	OEM
BTW92-1000RU	OEM
BTW92-1200	OEM
BTW92-1200R	OEM
BTW92-1200RM	OEM
BTW92-1200RU	OEM
BTW92-1400	OEM
BTW92-1400R	OEM
BTW92-1400RM	OEM
BTW92-1400RU	OEM
BTW92-1600	OEM
BTW92-1600R	OEM
BTW92-1600RM	OEM
BTW92-1600RU	OEM
BTW338-600R	1050
BTX068	0016
BTX070	0004
BTX071	0208
BTX-094	0016
BTX-095	0016
BTX-096	0016

DEVICE TYPE	REPL CODE
BTX-097	0126
BTX0605	3169
BTX0610	3169
BTX0620	3169
BTX0640	3177
BTX0660	3192
BTX12/100R	OEM
BTX12/200R	OEM
BTX12/300R	OEM
BTX12/400R	OEM
BTX12/450R	OEM
BTX12/500R	OEM
BTX12/600R	OEM
BTX12/700R	OEM
BTX13/300R	OEM
BTX13/700R	OEM
BTX13-100R	OEM
BTX13-200R	OEM
BTX13-400R	OEM
BTX13-450R	OEM
BTX13-500R	OEM
BTX13-600R	OEM
BTX18-100	0179
BTX18-200	0179
BTX18-300	0342
BTX18-400	0342
BTX18-500	3315
BTX20	OEM
BTX21	OEM
BTX22	OEM
BTX23	OEM
BTX24	OEM
BTX25	OEM
BTX26	OEM
BTX29/1000R	OEM
BTX29-200R	OEM
BTX29-300R	OEM
BTX29-400R	OEM
BTX29-500R	OEM
BTX29-600R	OEM
BTX29-700R	OEM
BTX29-800R	OEM
BTX29-900R	OEM
BTX29-1200R	OEM
BTX29-1400R	OEM
BTX29-1600R	OEM
BTX29-1800R	OEM
BTX30-50	OEM
BTX30-100	0179
BTX30-200	0179
BTX30-300	0342
BTX30-400	0342
BTX30-500	3315
BTX30-600	3315
BTX31-50R	2430
BTX31-100	OEM
BTX31-100R	2430
BTX31-200	OEM
BTX31-200R	0430
BTX31-300R	1478
BTX31-400	OEM
BTX31-400R	1478
BTX31-500	OEM
BTX31-500R	0682
BTX31-600	OEM
BTX31-600R	0682
BTX31-700	OEM
BTX31-700R	OEM
BTX31-800	OEM
BTX31-800R	OEM
BTX31-900	OEM
BTX31-900R	OEM
BTX31-1000	OEM
BTX31-1000R	OEM
BTX31S50R	OEM
BTX31S100	OEM
BTX31S100R	OEM
BTX31S200	OEM
BTX31S200R	OEM
BTX31S300R	OEM
BTX31S400	OEM
BTX31S400R	OEM
BTX31S500	OEM
BTX31S500R	OEM
BTX31S600	OEM
BTX31S600R	OEM
BTX31S700	OEM
BTX31S700R	OEM
BTX31S800	OEM
BTX31S800R	OEM
BTX31S900	OEM
BTX31S900R	OEM
BTX31S1000	OEM
BTX31S1000R	OEM
BTX32-50R	2497
BTX32-100	OEM
BTX32-100R	0736
BTX32-200	OEM
BTX32-200R	0740
BTX32-300R	0742
BTX32-400	OEM
BTX32-400R	0742
BTX32-500	OEM
BTX32-500R	0747
BTX32-600	OEM
BTX32-600R	OEM
BTX32-700	OEM
BTX32-700R	OEM
BTX32-800	OEM

If replacement code is OEM, contact original manufacturer for replacement.

DEVICE TYPE	REPL CODE
BTX32-800R	OEM
BTX32-900	OEM
BTX32-900R	OEM
BTX32-1000	OEM
BTX32-1000R	OEM
BTX32S50R	OEM
BTX32S100	OEM
BTX32S100R	OEM
BTX32S200	OEM
BTX32S200R	OEM
BTX32S300R	OEM
BTX32S400	OEM
BTX32S400R	OEM
BTX32S500	OEM
BTX32S500R	OEM
BTX32S600	OEM
BTX32S600R	OEM
BTX32S700	OEM
BTX32S700R	OEM
BTX32S800	OEM
BTX32S800R	OEM
BTX32S900	OEM
BTX32S900R	OEM
BTX32S1000	OEM
BTX32S1000R	OEM
BTX33-50R	0726
BTX33-100	OEM
BTX33-100R	0707
BTX33-200	OEM
BTX33-200R	0464
BTX33-300R	0717
BTX33-400	OEM
BTX33-400R	0717
BTX33-500	OEM
BTX33-500R	0720
BTX33-600	OEM
BTX33-600R	0720
BTX33-700	OEM
BTX33-700R	OEM
BTX33-800	OEM
BTX33-800R	OEM
BTX33-900	OEM
BTX33-900R	OEM
BTX33-1000	OEM
BTX33-1000R	OEM
BTX33S50R	OEM
BTX33S100	OEM
BTX33S100R	OEM
BTX33S200	OEM
BTX33S200R	OEM
BTX33S300R	OEM
BTX33S400	OEM
BTX33S400R	OEM
BTX33S500	OEM
BTX33S500R	OEM
BTX33S600	OEM
BTX33S600R	OEM
BTX33S700	OEM
BTX33S700R	OEM
BTX33S800	OEM
BTX33S800R	OEM
BTX33S900	OEM
BTX33S900R	OEM
BTX33S1000	OEM
BTX33S1000R	OEM
BTX35-500R	OEM
BTX35-600R	OEM
BTX35-700R	OEM
BTX35-800R	OEM
BTX36-500R	OEM
BTX36-600R	OEM
BTX36-700R	OEM
BTX36-800R	OEM
BTX37-500R	OEM
BTX37-600R	OEM
BTX37-700R	OEM
BTX37-800R	OEM
BTX38-500R	OEM
BTX38-600R	OEM
BTX38-700R	OEM
BTX38-800R	OEM
BTX41/1800R	OEM
BTX41-200R	OEM
BTX41-300R	OEM
BTX41-400R	OEM
BTX41-500R	OEM
BTX41-600R	OEM
BTX41-700R	OEM
BTX41-800R	OEM
BTX41-900R	OEM
BTX41-1000R	OEM
BTX41-1200R	OEM
BTX41-1400R	OEM
BTX41-1600R	OEM
BTX44-200R	OEM
BTX44-300R	OEM
BTX44-400R	OEM
BTX44-500R	OEM
BTX44-600R	OEM
BTX44-700R	OEM
BTX44-800R	OEM
BTX44-900R	OEM
BTX44-1000R	OEM
BTX44-1200R	OEM
BTX44-1600R	OEM
BTX44-1800R	OEM
BTX45-200R	OEM
BTX45-300R	OEM
BTX45-400R	OEM
BTX45-500R	OEM
BTX45-600R	OEM
BTX45-700R	OEM
BTX45-800R	OEM
BTX45-900R	OEM
BTX45-1000R	OEM
BTX45-1200R	OEM
BTX45-1400R	OEM
BTX45-1600R	OEM
BTX45-1800R	OEM
BTX46-200R	OEM
BTX46-300R	OEM
BTX46-400R	OEM
BTX46-500R	OEM
BTX46-600R	OEM
BTX46-700R	OEM
BTX46-800R	OEM
BTX46-900R	OEM
BTX46-1000R	OEM
BTX46-1200R	OEM
BTX46-1400R	OEM
BTX46-1600R	OEM
BTX46-1800R	OEM
BTX47-1000R	OEM
BTX47-1200R	OEM
BTX47-1400R	OEM
BTX48-1000R	OEM
BTX48-1200R	OEM
BTX48-1400R	OEM
BTX49-600R	OEM
BTX49-700R	OEM
BTX49-800R	OEM
BTX49-900R	OEM
BTX49-1000R	OEM
BTX49-1100R	OEM
BTX49-1200R	OEM
BTX49-1400R	OEM
BTX50-600R	OEM
BTX50-700R	OEM
BTX50-800R	OEM
BTX50-900R	OEM
BTX50-1000R	OEM
BTX50-1100R	OEM
BTX50-1200R	OEM
BTX50-1400R	OEM
BTX51-500R	OEM
BTX51-600R	OEM
BTX51-700R	OEM
BTX51-800R	OEM
BTX52	OEM
BTX53	OEM
BTX54	OEM
BTX55	OEM
BTX57	OEM
BTX58	OEM
BTX59	OEM
BTX60	OEM
BTX64-100R	OEM
BTX64-200R	OEM
BTX64-300R	OEM
BTX64-400R	OEM
BTX64-500R	OEM
BTX64-600R	OEM
BTX65-100R	OEM
BTX65-200R	OEM
BTX65-300R	OEM
BTX65-400R	OEM
BTX65-500R	OEM
BTX65-600R	OEM
BTX66-100R	OEM
BTX66-200R	OEM
BTX66-300R	OEM
BTX66-400R	OEM
BTX66-500R	OEM
BTX66-600R	OEM
BTX67-100R	OEM
BTX67-200R	OEM
BTX67-300R	OEM
BTX67-400	OEM
BTX67-400R	OEM
BTX67-500	OEM
BTX67-500R	OEM
BTX67-600	OEM
BTX67-600R	OEM
BTX68-500R	0682
BTX68-600R	0682
BTX68-700R	OEM
BTX68-800R	OEM
BTX68-1000R	OEM
BTX70-100	OEM
BTX70-200	OEM
BTX70-400	OEM
BTX70-500	OEM
BTX70-600	OEM
BTX70-700	OEM
BTX70-800	OEM
BTX70-900	OEM
BTX70-1000	OEM
BTX70S100	OEM
BTX70S200	OEM
BTX70S400	OEM
BTX70S500	OEM
BTX70S600	OEM
BTX70S700	OEM
BTX70S800	OEM
BTX70S900	OEM
BTX70S1000	OEM
BTX71-50R	OEM
BTX71-100	OEM
BTX71-100R	OEM
BTX71-200	OEM
BTX71-200R	OEM
BTX71-300R	OEM
BTX71-400	OEM
BTX71-400R	OEM
BTX71-500	OEM
BTX71-500R	OEM
BTX71-600	OEM
BTX71-600R	OEM
BTX71-700	OEM
BTX71-700R	OEM
BTX71-800	OEM
BTX71-800R	OEM
BTX71-900	OEM
BTX71-900R	OEM
BTX71-1000	OEM
BTX71-1000R	OEM
BTX71S50R	OEM
BTX71S100	OEM
BTX71S100R	OEM
BTX71S200	OEM
BTX71S200R	OEM
BTX71S300R	OEM
BTX71S400	OEM
BTX71S400R	OEM
BTX71S500	OEM
BTX71S500R	OEM
BTX71S600	OEM
BTX71S600R	OEM
BTX71S700	OEM
BTX71S700R	OEM
BTX71S800	OEM
BTX71S800R	OEM
BTX71S900	OEM
BTX71S900R	OEM
BTX71S1000	OEM
BTX71S1000R	OEM
BTX72-50R	OEM
BTX72-100	OEM
BTX72-100R	OEM
BTX72-200	OEM
BTX72-200R	OEM
BTX72-300R	OEM
BTX72-400	OEM
BTX72-400R	OEM
BTX72-500	OEM
BTX72-500R	OEM
BTX72-600	OEM
BTX72-600R	OEM
BTX72-700	OEM
BTX72-700R	OEM
BTX72-800	OEM
BTX72-800R	OEM
BTX72-900	OEM
BTX72-900R	OEM
BTX72-1000	OEM
BTX72-1000R	OEM
BTX72S50R	OEM
BTX72S100	OEM
BTX72S100R	OEM
BTX72S200	OEM
BTX72S200R	OEM
BTX72S300R	OEM
BTX72S400	OEM
BTX72S400R	OEM
BTX72S500	OEM
BTX72S500R	OEM
BTX72S600	OEM
BTX72S600R	OEM
BTX72S700	OEM
BTX72S700R	OEM
BTX72S800	OEM
BTX72S800R	OEM
BTX72S900	OEM
BTX72S900R	OEM
BTX72S1000	OEM
BTX72S1000R	OEM
BTX73-50R	OEM
BTX73-100	OEM
BTX73-100R	OEM
BTX73-200	OEM
BTX73-200R	OEM
BTX73-300R	OEM
BTX73-400	OEM
BTX73-500	OEM
BTX73-500R	OEM
BTX73-600	OEM
BTX73-600R	OEM
BTX73-700	OEM
BTX73-700R	OEM
BTX73-800	OEM
BTX73-800R	OEM
BTX73-900	OEM
BTX73-900R	OEM
BTX73-1000	OEM
BTX73-1000R	OEM
BTX73A800	OEM
BTX73A900	OEM
BTX73A1000	OEM
BTX73A1100	OEM
BTX73A1200	OEM
BTX73A1300	OEM
BTX73AS800	OEM
BTX73AS900	OEM
BTX73AS1000	OEM
BTX73AS1100	OEM
BTX73AS1200	OEM
BTX73AS1300	OEM
BTX73B800	OEM
BTX73B900	OEM
BTX73B1000	OEM
BTX73B1100	OEM
BTX73B1200	OEM
BTX73B1300	OEM
BTX73BS800	OEM
BTX73BS900	OEM
BTX73BS1000	OEM
BTX73BS1100	OEM
BTX73BS1200	OEM
BTX73BS1300	OEM
BTX73S50R	OEM
BTX73S100	OEM
BTX73S100R	OEM
BTX73S200	OEM
BTX73S200R	OEM
BTX73S300R	OEM
BTX73S400	OEM
BTX73S500	OEM
BTX73S500R	OEM
BTX73S600	OEM
BTX73S600R	OEM
BTX73S700	OEM
BTX73S800	OEM
BTX73S800R	OEM
BTX73S900	OEM
BTX73S900R	OEM
BTX73S1000	OEM
BTX73S1000R	OEM
BTX74-100	OEM
BTX74-200	OEM
BTX74-400	OEM
BTX74-500	OEM
BTX74-600	OEM
BTX74-700	OEM
BTX74-800	OEM
BTX74-900	OEM
BTX74-1000	OEM
BTX74S100	OEM
BTX74S200	OEM
BTX74S400	OEM
BTX74S500	OEM
BTX74S600	OEM
BTX74S700	OEM
BTX74S800	OEM
BTX74S900	OEM
BTX74S1000	OEM
BTX75-100R	0562
BTX75-200R	0757
BTX75-300R	0735
BTX75-400R	0735
BTX76-100R	0707
BTX76-200R	0464
BTX76-300R	0717
BTX76-400R	0717
BTX81-100R	0707
BTX81-100RM	OEM
BTX81-100RU	OEM
BTX81-200R	0464
BTX81-200RM	OEM
BTX81-200RU	OEM
BTX81-300R	0716
BTX81-300RM	OEM
BTX81-300RU	OEM
BTX81-400R	0717
BTX81-400RM	OEM
BTX81-400RU	OEM
BTX81-500R	0773
BTX81-500RM	OEM
BTX81-500RU	OEM
BTX81-600R	0720
BTX81-600RM	OEM
BTX81-600RU	OEM
BTX81-700R	OEM
BTX81-700RM	OEM
BTX81-700RU	OEM
BTX81-800R	OEM
BTX81-800RM	OEM
BTX81-800RU	OEM
BTX82-100R	OEM
BTX82-100RM	OEM
BTX82-100RU	OEM
BTX82-200R	OEM
BTX82-200RM	OEM
BTX82-200RU	OEM
BTX82-300R	OEM
BTX82-300RM	OEM
BTX82-300RU	OEM
BTX82-400R	OEM
BTX82-400RM	OEM
BTX82-400RU	OEM
BTX82-500R	OEM
BTX82-500RM	OEM
BTX82-500RU	OEM
BTX82-600R	OEM
BTX82-600RM	OEM
BTX82-600RU	OEM
BTX82-700R	OEM
BTX82-700RM	OEM
BTX82-700RU	OEM
BTX82-800R	OEM
BTX82-800RM	OEM
BTX82-800RU	OEM
BTX92-600R	OEM
BTX92-800R	OEM
BTX92-900R	OEM
BTX92-1000R	OEM
BTX92-1100R	OEM
BTX92-1200R	OEM
BTX92-1400R	OEM
BTX92-1600R	OEM
BTX94-100	2004
BTX94-200	2004
BTX94-300	2006
BTX94-400	2006
BTX94-400H	2006
BTX94-400J	OEM
BTX94-500	2007
BTX94-600	2007
BTX94-600H	2007
BTX94-600J	OEM
BTX94-700	OEM
BTX94-800	OEM
BTX94-800H	OEM
BTX94-800J	OEM
BTX94-900	OEM
BTX94-1000	OEM
BTX94-1000H	OEM
BTX94-1000J	OEM
BTX94-1100	OEM
BTX94-1200	OEM
BTX94-1200H	OEM
BTX94-1200J	OEM
BTX95-500	OEM
BTX95-500R	OEM
BTX95-600	OEM
BTX95-600R	OEM
BTX95-700	OEM
BTX95-700R	OEM
BTX95-800	OEM
BTX95-800R	OEM
BTX1005	3169
BTX1010	3169
BTX1020	3169
BTX1040	3177
BTX1060	3192
BTX1605	0147
BTX1610	0154
BTX1620	0154
BTX1640	0147
BTX1660	3192
BTX-2367B	0016
BTX2367B	0016
BTX2505	2004
BTX2510	2004
BTX2520	2004
BTX2540	2006
BTX2560	3192
BTY10	OEM
BTY11	OEM
BTY13	OEM
BTY15	OEM
BTY16	OEM
BTY20	OEM
BTY21	OEM
BTY22	OEM
BTY23	OEM
BTY24	OEM
BTY25	OEM
BTY28	OEM
BTY29	OEM
BTY30	OEM
BTY31	OEM
BTY34	OEM
BTY34/300	OEM
BTY34/400	OEM
BTY34-100R	2430
BTY34-200R	0430
BTY34-300R	1478
BTY34-400R	1478
BTY35	OEM
BTY36	OEM
BTY37	OEM
BTY38	OEM
BTY39	OEM
BTY41	OEM
BTY43	OEM
BTY44	OEM
BTY46	OEM
BTY47	OEM
BTY50	OEM
BTY51	OEM
BTY52	OEM
BTY53	OEM
BTY54	OEM
BTY57	OEM
BTY58	OEM
BTY59	OEM
BTY60	OEM
BTY61	OEM
BTY62	OEM
BTY64	OEM
BTY65	OEM
BTY66	OEM
BTY67	OEM
BTY68	OEM
BTY69	OEM
BTY70	OEM
BTY79	OEM
BTY79-100	OEM
BTY79-100R	OEM
BTY79-100R05	OEM
BTY79-150R	OEM
BTY79-200	OEM
BTY79-200R	OEM
BTY79-200R05	OEM
BTY79-250R	OEM
BTY79-300	OEM
BTY79-300R	OEM
BTY79-400	OEM
BTY79-400R	0735
BTY79-400R05	OEM
BTY79-500	OEM
BTY79-500R	0759
BTY79-500R05	OEM
BTY79-600	OEM
BTY79-600R	0759
BTY79-700	OEM
BTY79-700R	OEM
BTY79-800	OEM
BTY79-800R	0761
BTY79-1000R	OEM
BTY79A-50	OEM
BTY79A-100	OEM
BTY79A-200	OEM
BTY79A-300	OEM
BTY79A-400	OEM
BTY79A-500	OEM
BTY80	OEM
BTY81	OEM
BTY84	OEM
BTY85	OEM
BTY86	OEM
BTY87	OEM
BTY87-100R	0736
BTY87-100R+	0464
BTY87-100RM	OEM
BTY87-100RU	OEM
BTY87-150R	OEM
BTY87-200R	0740
BTY87-200R+	0464
BTY87-200RM	OEM
BTY87-200RU	OEM
BTY87-250R	OEM
BTY87-300R	2889
BTY87-300R+	0717
BTY87-300RM	OEM
BTY87-300RU	OEM
BTY87-400R	0742
BTY87-400R+	0717
BTY87-400RM	OEM
BTY87-400RU	OEM
BTY87-500R	3213
BTY87-500R+	0720
BTY87-500RM	OEM
BTY87-500RU	OEM
BTY87-600R	0759
BTY87-600R+	0720
BTY87-600RM	OEM
BTY87-600RU	OEM
BTY87-700R	2848
BTY87-700R+	2025
BTY87-700RM	OEM
BTY87-700RU	OEM
BTY87-800R	0761
BTY87-800R+	2025
BTY87-800RM	OEM
BTY87-800RU	OEM
BTY88	OEM
BTY89	OEM
BTY90	OEM
BTY91	OEM
BTY91-100R	0562
BTY91-100R+	0464
BTY91-100RM	OEM
BTY91-100RU	OEM
BTY91-150R	OEM
BTY91-200R	0757
BTY91-200R+	0464
BTY91-200RM	OEM
BTY91-200RU	OEM
BTY91-250R	OEM
BTY91-300R	3240
BTY91-300R+	0717
BTY91-300RM	OEM
BTY91-300RU	OEM
BTY91-400R	0735
BTY91-400R+	0717
BTY91-400RM	OEM
BTY91-400RU	OEM
BTY91-500+	0720
BTY91-500R	3260
BTY91-500RM	OEM
BTY91-500RU	OEM
BTY91-600R	0759
BTY91-600R+	0720
BTY91-600RM	OEM
BTY91-600RU	OEM
BTY91-700R	2848
BTY91-700R+	2025
BTY91-800R	0761
BTY91-800R+	2025
BTY91-800RM	OEM
BTY91-800RU	OEM
BTY91-1000RM	OEM
BTY91-1000RU	OEM
BTY91-1200R	OEM
BTY91-1200RM	OEM
BTY91-1200RU	OEM
BTY94	OEM
BTY95	OEM
BTY95-250R	5759
BTY95-800R	0108
BTY98	OEM
BTY99	OEM
BTY99-150R	OEM
BTY99-250R	OEM
BTY99-800R	OEM
BTY-150R	OEM
BTZ10	OEM
BTZ11	OEM
BTZ12	OEM
BTZ13	OEM
BTZ15	OEM
BTZ16	OEM
BTZ18	OEM
BTZ19	OEM
BTZ21	OEM
BTZ35	OEM
BTZ36	OEM
BTZ37	OEM
BTZ38	OEM
BTZ39	OEM
BU029	0229
BU40	6218
BU67	0016
BU71	0016
BU74HC00	OEM
BU102	0359
BU104	0359
BU104D	OEM
BU104DP	OEM
BU104P	0723
BU105	0065
BU105-02	0065
BU106	0359
BU107	0074
BU108	0065
BU109	0637
BU109D	OEM
BU109DP	OEM
BU109P	0723
BU110	0359
BU111	0359
BU113	0359
BU114	0637
BU115	0065
BU118	OEM
BU120	0359
BU121	0359
BU122	0359
BU123	0359
BU124	OEM
BU124A	OEM
BU125	0617
BU125S	OEM
BU126	0637
BU129	0359
BU130	0074
BU131	0074
BU132	0637
BU133	0359
BU137	OEM
BU142	OEM
BU143	OEM
BU157	OEM
BU180	3719
BU180A	3719
BU181	OEM
BU181A	OEM
BU184	1503
BU189	1503
BU204	0065
BU205	0065
BU205-01	0065
BU206	0065
BU207	0309
BU207A	0637
BU208	0065
BU208A	0065
BU208B	0065
BU208D	0055
BU209	0065
BU209A	2820
BU210	0359
BU211	0359
BU212	0359
BU225	0065
BU226	2820
BU310	0359
BU311	0359
BU312	0359
BU322	1980
BU322A	OEM
BU323	1980
BU323A	OEM
BU324A	OEM
BU325	OEM
BU326	0309
BU326A	0309
BU326AP	OEM
BU326P	OEM
BU326R	0309
BU326S	0309
BU406	0723
BU406D	0723
BU406H	5577
BU407	0723
BU407D	0723
BU407H	5577
BU408	0723
BU408D	OEM
BU409	0723
BU426	4376
BU426A	4376

If replacement code is OEM, contact original manufacturer for replacement.

297

DEVICE TYPE	REPL CODE
BU433	4376
BU500	0309
BU508	3326
BU508A	3326
BU508D	5248
BU508DF	3326
BU508V	3326
BU522	OEM
BU522A	OEM
BU522B	OEM
BU526	0309
BU536	0309
BU546	0309
BU606	OEM
BU606D	OEM
BU607	OEM
BU607D	OEM
BU608	OEM
BU608D	OEM
BU626A	OEM
BU705	3326
BU800	0055
BU801	OEM
BU806	1503
BU807	1503
BU808	1503
BU810	OEM
BU810(A)	OEM
BU826	OEM
BU826A	OEM
BU902	3326
BU903	3326
BU908	3326
BU910	OEM
BU911	OEM
BU912	OEM
BU920	OEM
BU920P	5245
BU920P(A)	OEM
BU920PFI	6695
BU920T	OEM
BU921	OEM
BU921P	5245
BU921P(A)	OEM
BU921PFI	6695
BU921T	OEM
BU922	2602
BU922P	5245
BU922P(A)	OEM
BU922PFI	6695
BU922T	OEM
BU930	2602
BU931	2602
BU931R	2602
BU931RP	4269
BU932	2602
BU932R	2602
BU932RP	4269
BU2506DF	OEM
BU2508DF	OEM
BU2508DFLB	OEM
BU2702	OEM
BU2742S	OEM
BU2744S	OEM
BU2748S	OEM
BU2763S	OEM
BU3702F	OEM
BU4011B	0215
BU4013B	0409
BU4016B	OEM
BU4030B	OEM
BU4052B	0024
BU4053B	0034
BU4066B	0101
BU4066BF	OEM
BU4066BL	0101
BU4066BP	0101
BU4199	OEM
BU4538B	OEM
BU4551B	OEM
BU5702	OEM
BU5777F	OEM
BU8322F	OEM
BUC205	OEM
BUC208	OEM
BUC-97704-2	0079
BUF01AJ	OEM
BUF01AZ	OEM
BUF01AZ(M)	OEM
BUF01BJ	OEM
BUF01BZ	OEM
BUF01BZ(M)	OEM
BUF01EJ	OEM
BUF01EZ	OEM
BUF01FJ	OEM
BUF01FZ	OEM
BUF02AJ	OEM
BUF02AZ(M)	OEM
BUF02BJ	OEM
BUF02BZ(M)	OEM
BUF02EJ	OEM
BUF02EZ	OEM
BUF02FJ	OEM
BUF02FZ	OEM
BUF03AJ	OEM
BUF03BJ	OEM
BUF03EJ	OEM
BUF03FJ	OEM
BUF03G	OEM

DEVICE TYPE	REPL CODE
BUF03N	OEM
BUK417-500AE	OEM
BUK417-500BE	OEM
BUK426-800A	OEM
BUK426-800B	OEM
BUK426-1000A	OEM
BUK427-400A	OEM
BUK427-400B	OEM
BUK427-500A	OEM
BUK427-500B	OEM
BUK427-600A	OEM
BUK427-600B	OEM
BUK428-500A	OEM
BUK428-500B	OEM
BUK428-800A	OEM
BUK428-800B	OEM
BUK428-1000A	OEM
BUK428-1000B	OEM
BUK436-800A	OEM
BUK436-800B	OEM
BUK436-1000A	OEM
BUK436-1000B	OEM
BUK437-400A	OEM
BUK437-400B	OEM
BUK437-500A	OEM
BUK437-500B	OEM
BUK437-600A	OEM
BUK437-600B	OEM
BUK438-500A	OEM
BUK438-500B	OEM
BUK438-800A	OEM
BUK438-800B	OEM
BUK438-1000A	OEM
BUK438-1000B	OEM
BUK443-60B	OEM
BUK444-400A	OEM
BUK444-400B	OEM
BUK444-500A	OEM
BUK444-500B	OEM
BUK444-600A	OEM
BUK444-600B	OEM
BUK444-800A	OEM
BUK444-800B	OEM
BUK445-400A	OEM
BUK445-400B	OEM
BUK445-500A	OEM
BUK445-500B	OEM
BUK445-600A	OEM
BUK445-600B	OEM
BUK446-800A	3673
BUK446-800B	3673
BUK446-1000A	OEM
BUK446-1000B	OEM
BUK452-60A	OEM
BUK452-60B	OEM
BUK453-60A	OEM
BUK453-60B	OEM
BUK454-400A	OEM
BUK454-400B	OEM
BUK454-500A	OEM
BUK454-500B	OEM
BUK454-600A	OEM
BUK454-600B	OEM
BUK454-800A	OEM
BUK454-800B	OEM
BUK455-400A	OEM
BUK455-400B	OEM
BUK455-500A	OEM
BUK455-500B	OEM
BUK455-600A	OEM
BUK455-600B	OEM
BUK456-800A	5005
BUK456-800B	3673
BUK456-1000A	5005
BUK456-1000B	OEM
BUK457-400A	OEM
BUK457-400B	OEM
BUK457-500A	OEM
BUK457-500B	5661
BUK457-600A	OEM
BUK457-600B	OEM
BUK543-50A	OEM
BUK543-50B	OEM
BUK545-50A	OEM
BUK545-50B	OEM
BUK552-60A	OEM
BUK552-60B	OEM
BUK553-50A	OEM
BUK553-50B	OEM
BUK555-50A	OEM
BUK555-50B	OEM
BUKBUK426-1000B	OEM
BUP22A	OEM
BUP22B	3353
BUP22C	3353
BUP23A	OEM
BUP23B	OEM
BUP23C	OEM
BUP60	OEM
BUP61	OEM
BUP62	OEM
BUP63	OEM
BUP64	OEM
BUP65	OEM
BUP66	OEM
BUP67	OEM
BUP68	OEM
BUP69	OEM
BUP70	OEM

DEVICE TYPE	REPL CODE
BUP71	OEM
BUR10	OEM
BUR11	OEM
BUR12	OEM
BUR13	OEM
BUR20	OEM
BUR21	OEM
BUR22	OEM
BUR23	OEM
BUR24	OEM
BUR50	OEM
BUR51	OEM
BUR52	OEM
BUS11	4376
BUS11A	4376
BUS12	1498
BUS12A	1498
BUS13	6921
BUS13A	OEM
BUS14	OEM
BUS14A	OEM
BUS21A	3354
BUS21B	3354
BUS21C	3354
BUS22A	3354
BUS22B	3354
BUS22C	3354
BUS23A	3354
BUS23B	3354
BUS23C	3354
BUS47P	OEM
BUS133	OEM
BUS133A	OEM
BUS133H	OEM
BUT11	6007
BUT11A	6007
BUT11AF	2739
BUT11F	3305
BUT12	6007
BUT12A	4510
BUT13	OEM
BUT13P	3719
BUT18	6007
BUT18A	6007
BUT18AF	3426
BUT18F	3426
BUT21A	OEM
BUT21B	6007
BUT21C	6007
BUT22A	OEM
BUT22B	6007
BUT22C	2880
BUT54	6007
BUT56	6007
BUT56A	4510
BUT93	0037
BUT131	OEM
BUT131A	OEM
BUT131H	OEM
BUV11	1841
BUV18	OEM
BUV19	OEM
BUV20	2416
BUV21	OEM
BUV22	OEM
BUV23	OEM
BUV24	OEM
BUV25	OEM
BUV26	OEM
BUV27	5577
BUV28	5577
BUV30	OEM
BUV37	OEM
BUV46	6007
BUV47	1498
BUV47A	1498
BUV47B	1498
BUV48	1498
BUV48A	1498
BUV82	4376
BUV83	4376
BUV90	OEM
BUV90F	OEM
BUV93	OEM
BUV94	OEM
BUV95	OEM
BUV98	OEM
BUV98A	OEM
BUV98AV	OEM
BUV98V	OEM
BUV298AV	OEM
BUV298V	OEM
BUW11	4376
BUW11A	4376
BUW12	4376
BUW12A	4376
BUW13	1498
BUW13A	1498
BUW16	OEM
BUW17	OEM
BUW18	OEM
BUW19	OEM
BUW22	OEM
BUW23	OEM
BUW24	OEM
BUW25	OEM
BUW26	OEM
BUW32	OEM
BUW34	3009

DEVICE TYPE	REPL CODE
BUW35	3009
BUW36	6944
BUW38	OEM
BUW39	OEM
BUW40	OEM
BUW40A	6218
BUW40B	6218
BUW41	5577
BUW41A	5577
BUW41B	5577
BUW44	3354
BUW45	3354
BUW46	OEM
BUW48	OEM
BUW49	OEM
BUW57	OEM
BUW58	OEM
BUW64A	5445
BUW64B	5445
BUW64C	OEM
BUW66	OEM
BUW67	OEM
BUW70	OEM
BUW71	OEM
BUW72	OEM
BUW73	OEM
BUW74	1841
BUW75	1841
BUW76	1841
BUW77	OEM
BUW81	OEM
BUW81A	OEM
BUW84	6218
BUW85	6218
BUW86	1841
BUW132	3454
BUW132A	3454
BUW132H	3454
BUW133	OEM
BUW133A	OEM
BUW133H	OEM
BUX10	2465
BUX10A	6298
BUX11	2465
BUX11N	6299
BUX12	2465
BUX13	1841
BUX14	1841
BUX15	1841
BUX16	0359
BUX16A	0359
BUX16B	0359
BUX16C	0359
BUX17	1955
BUX17A	1955
BUX17B	1955
BUX17C	1955
BUX18	0074
BUX18A	0074
BUX18B	0074
BUX18C	1955
BUX20A	2416
BUX28	OEM
BUX29	1980
BUX30	OEM
BUX30AV	OEM
BUX30AVA	OEM
BUX30AVB	OEM
BUX30AVC	OEM
BUX31	OEM
BUX31A	OEM
BUX31B	OEM
BUX32	1498
BUX32A	1498
BUX32B	1498
BUX34	OEM
BUX37	OEM
BUX39	2465
BUX40	2465
BUX40A	OEM
BUX41	1331
BUX41N	6360
BUX42	0074
BUX43	1331
BUX44	1841
BUX46	0223
BUX46A	0223
BUX47	1498
BUX47A	1498
BUX47B	1498
BUX48	3354
BUX48A	3354
BUX49	OEM
BUX50	OEM
BUX51	OEM
BUX52	OEM
BUX53	OEM
BUX54	OEM
BUX55	OEM
BUX59	OEM
BUX60	OEM
BUX61	OEM
BUX62	OEM
BUX66	OEM
BUX66A	OEM
BUX66B	OEM
BUX66C	OEM
BUX67	2085
BUX67A	2085

DEVICE TYPE	REPL CODE
BUX67B	2085
BUX67C	2085
BUX69	OEM
BUX70	OEM
BUX77	OEM
BUX78	OEM
BUX80	1841
BUX81	1841
BUX82	1498
BUX83	1498
BUX84	2985
BUX84F	3504
BUX85	3504
BUX85F	3504
BUX86	3187
BUX87	3187
BUX97	1841
BUX97A	1841
BUX97B	1841
BUX98	OEM
BUX98A	OEM
BUX99	OEM
BUX238	OEM
BUY10	0103
BUY10S	OEM
BUY11	0103
BUY12	0074
BUY13	0074
BUY14	0556
BUY16	OEM
BUY17	OEM
BUY18S	0359
BUY19	OEM
BUY20	0074
BUY21	0074
BUY21A	0074
BUY22	0074
BUY24	0042
BUY26	OEM
BUY27	OEM
BUY28	OEM
BUY29	1331
BUY30	1331
BUY35	0359
BUY38	0424
BUY43	0130
BUY43-6	OEM
BUY43-10	OEM
BUY43-16	OEM
BUY44	0177
BUY46	0130
BUY46-4	OEM
BUY46-6	OEM
BUY50	OEM
BUY51A	2465
BUY52A	2465
BUY53A	2465
BUY54A	2465
BUY55	0074
BUY55-4	0074
BUY55-6	0074
BUY55-10	0074
BUY56	0074
BUY56-4	0074
BUY56-6	0074
BUY56-10	0074
BUY59	OEM
BUY60	OEM
BUY61	OEM
BUY62	OEM
BUY63	OEM
BUY64	OEM
BUY65	OEM
BUY66	OEM
BUY67	OEM
BUY69A	1498
BUY69B	0359
BUY69C	0359
BUY70A	1498
BUY70B	0359
BUY70C	0359
BUY71	2820
BUY72	0074
BUY72-4	0074
BUY72-6	0074
BUY72-10	0074
BUY88	OEM
BUY89	0309
BUY90	OEM
BUY91	OEM
BUY92	OEM
BUZ10	OEM
BUZ10A	OEM
BUZ11	OEM
BUZ11A	OEM
BUZ14	OEM
BUZ15	OEM
BUZ20	4970
BUZ21	OEM
BUZ23	OEM
BUZ24	5266
BUZ25	OEM
BUZ30	OEM
BUZ31	2162
BUZ32	5618
BUZ33	OEM
BUZ34	OEM
BUZ35	OEM
BUZ36	OEM

DEVICE TYPE	REPL CODE
BUZ40	1457
BUZ41	OEM
BUZ41A	1643
BUZ42	1643
BUZ43	OEM
BUZ44	OEM
BUZ44A	OEM
BUZ45	OEM
BUZ45A	OEM
BUZ46	6962
BUZ50	OEM
BUZ50A	OEM
BUZ50B	OEM
BUZ53	OEM
BUZ53A	OEM
BUZ54	OEM
BUZ54A	OEM
BUZ60	1456
BUZ63	OEM
BUZ64	OEM
BUZ71	4970
BUZ71A	4970
BUZ72A	4970
BUZ73A	4970
BUZ74	OEM
BUZ74A	6580
BUZ76	OEM
BUZ76A	OEM
BUZ80	3673
BUZ80A	3673
BUZ83	OEM
BUZ83A	OEM
BUZ84	5764
BUZ84A	5764
BUZ211	OEM
BUZ325	OEM
BV25	0015
BV67	0016
BV69	OEM
BV71	0016
BV100	OEM
BV110	OEM
BV120	OEM
BV130	OEM
BV140	OEM
BV150	OEM
BVDKBPC2502W	OEM
BVDPBM152	OEM
BVIANAM1002	OEM
BVILC7582B	OEM
BVISTK4231-5	OEM
BVX40-1000R	0545
BVX48/600	0122
BVX48-600	0122
BVY27-150	OEM
BW050	OEM
BW080	OEM
BW8T	OEM
BW67	0016
BW71	0016
BWALPHA	OEM
BWS1	OEM
BWS2	OEM
BWS66	0168
BWS67	0168
BWX5	OEM
BX090	0012
BX67	0016
BX71	0016
BX213	OEM
BX-324	0164
BX-342	OEM
BX342	OEM
BX-358	OEM
BX358	OEM
BX-360	OEM
BX360	OEM
BX-361	OEM
BX361	OEM
BX-364	OEM
BX364	OEM
BX-369	OEM
BX-376	OEM
BX376	OEM
BX-378	OEM
BX-379	OEM
BX-380	OEM
BX-383	OEM
BX383	OEM
BX-384	OEM
BX384	OEM
BX-384A	OEM
BX-393A	OEM
BX-495	0164
BX495(SONY)	0164
BX909	0012
BX-1013	OEM
BX-1013-1	OEM
BX-1016	OEM
BX-1038	OEM
BX1038	OEM
BX-1039	OEM
BX-1041	OEM
BX-1043	OEM
BX-1044	OEM
BX-1044-1	OEM
BX-1045	OEM
BX-1046	OEM
BX-1047	OEM

DEVICE TYPE	REPL CODE
BX-1083	OEM
BX-1084	OEM
BX-1086	OEM
BX-1087	OEM
BX-1088	OEM
BX-1090	OEM
BX-1091	OEM
BX-1092	OEM
BX-1093	OEM
BX-1094	OEM
BX-1095	OEM
BX-1153	OEM
BX-1317	OEM
BX1317	OEM
BX-1323	OEM
BX1323	OEM
BX-1357	OEM
BX1357	OEM
BX1387	OEM
BX-1393	OEM
BX1393	OEM
BX-1398	OEM
BX1398	OEM
BX1407	OEM
BX-1435B	OEM
BX1458	OEM
BX-1483	OEM
BX-3901	OEM
BX-3903	OEM
BX3903	OEM
BX-3904	OEM
BX-3912	OEM
BX-3921	OEM
BX-3943	OEM
BX-3945-1	OEM
BX-3946-1	OEM
BX-3947-2	OEM
BX-3948-1	OEM
BX-3949	OEM
BX-3950-1	OEM
BX-3951-2	OEM
BX-3952	OEM
BX-3953	OEM
BX-3954	OEM
BX-3955	OEM
BX-3956-1	OEM
BX-3958-1	OEM
BX-3959-1	OEM
BX-3960	OEM
BX-3969-1	OEM
BX-3969A	OEM
BX-3970-1	OEM
BX-3970A	OEM
BX-3971	OEM
BX-3971A	OEM
BX-3972	OEM
BX-3973	OEM
BX-3976	OEM
BX-3977	OEM
BX-3978	OEM
BX-3980	OEM
BX-3981	OEM
BX-3982-1	OEM
BX-3982-2	OEM
BX-3983	OEM
BX-3984	OEM
BX-3988	OEM
BX-3999	OEM
BX-3999-1	OEM
BX6224W	OEM
BX6238	OEM
BX6239	OEM
BX6240	OEM
BX6256	OEM
BX6259	OEM
BX6301	OEM
BX6302	OEM
BX6302A	OEM
BX6335	OEM
BX6410	OEM
BX7197W	OEM
BX7335	OEM
BX7385W	OEM
BX7403	OEM
BX7422F	OEM
BX7426	OEM
BX7426FA	OEM
BX7447	OEM
BX7483	OEM
BX7504A	OEM
BX7521	OEM
BX7580F	OEM
BX7596F	OEM
BX7645	OEM
BX7645A	OEM
BX7645F	OEM
BXB10125	OEM
BXC79C5V6	0253
BXD23/40636	OEM
BXW70-36	OEM
BXY10	0071
BXY10C	OEM
BXY10D	OEM
BXY11E	OEM
BXY11F	OEM
BXY13C	OEM
BXY13CA	OEM
BXY13D	OEM
BXY14E	OEM

If replacement code is OEM, contact original manufacturer for replacement.

DEVICE TYPE	REPL CODE
BXY14F	OEM
BXY15CA3	OEM
BXY15CA5	OEM
BXY18A2	OEM
BXY18AB	OEM
BXY18AB2	OEM
BXY18AB4	OEM
BXY18AB5	OEM
BXY18AB6	OEM
BXY19E	OEM
BXY19F	OEM
BXY19GB	OEM
BXY22G	OEM
BXY22H	OEM
BXY22J	OEM
BXY23	OEM
BXY27	OEM
BXY28	OEM
BXY29	OEM
BXY30-200	OEM
BXY30-500	OEM
BXY32	OEM
BXY35	OEM
BXY35A	OEM
BXY36	OEM
BXY36B	OEM
BXY36C	OEM
BXY36D	OEM
BXY36E	OEM
BXY37	OEM
BXY37B	OEM
BXY37C	OEM
BXY37D	OEM
BXY37E	OEM
BXY38	2621
BXY38B	OEM
BXY38C	OEM
BXY38D	OEM
BXY38E	OEM
BXY39	OEM
BXY39B	OEM
BXY39C	OEM
BXY39D	OEM
BXY39E	OEM
BXY40	OEM
BXY40B	OEM
BXY40C	OEM
BXY40D	OEM
BXY40E	OEM
BXY41	OEM
BXY41B	OEM
BXY41C	OEM
BXY41D	OEM
BXY41E	OEM
BXY42B	OEM
BXY42BA2	OEM
BXY42BA3	OEM
BXY42BA4	OEM
BXY42BA5	OEM
BXY42BA6	OEM
BXY43A	OEM
BXY43B	OEM
BXY43C	OEM
BXY44E	OEM
BXY50	OEM
BXY51	OEM
BXY52	OEM
BXY53	OEM
BXY54	OEM
BXY55	OEM
BXY56	OEM
BXY57	OEM
BXY58EA	OEM
BXY59D	OEM
BXY60	OEM
BXY63	0012
BY12-00	0071
BY54	0071
BY55	0071
BY56	0071
BY67	0016
BY71	0016
BY100	0071
BY100S	0071
BY101	0015
BY102	0015
BY103	0102
BY104	0071
BY105	0071
BY106	0015
BY107	0015
BY108	0071
BY109	0071
BY111	0015
BY112	0015
BY113	0015
BY114	0015
BY115	0015
BY116	0015
BY117	0015
BY118	0071
BY119	0071
BY121	0015
BY122	0276
BY123	0287
BY124	0015
BY125	0015
BY126	0015
BY126/50	0087
BY126/100	0087
BY126/200	0087
BY126/300	0087
BY126/400	0087
BY126MGP	0071
BY-127	0015
BY127	0102
BY127/500	0071
BY127/600	0071
BY127/700	0071
BY127/800	OEM
BY127MGP	0102
BY128	0071
BY129	0071
BY130	0015
BY133	0102
BY133GP	0102
BY134	0015
BY134GP	0071
BY135	0015
BY135GP	0015
BY137-400	OEM
BY137-800	OEM
BY138	OEM
BY139	OEM
BY140A	OEM
BY141	0015
BY142	OEM
BY143	OEM
BY147	OEM
BY151N	OEM
BY152N	OEM
BY153	0015
BY156	0087
BY157	0102
BY158	0102
BY159-50	0106
BY159-200	0106
BY159-400	0106
BY164	0276
BY165	OEM
BY166	OEM
BY167	OEM
BY172	0087
BY173	0087
BY174	OEM
BY176	OEM
BY179	0293
BY182	OEM
BY183-50	OEM
BY183-100	OEM
BY183-200	OEM
BY183-300	OEM
BY183-400	OEM
BY183-500	OEM
BY183-600	OEM
BY184	OEM
BY186	OEM
BY187	OEM
BY187-01	OEM
BY188	0071
BY188A	0015
BY188B	0015
BY188G	OEM
BY189	OEM
BY190	OEM
BY191-250	OEM
BY191-400	OEM
BY191P-250	OEM
BY191P-400	OEM
BY192	OEM
BY193	OEM
BY194	OEM
BY195	OEM
BY196	OEM
BY197	OEM
BY198	OEM
BY199	OEM
BY200	OEM
BY201	0535
BY201/2	0575
BY201/4	OEM
BY201/6	OEM
BY201-2	0575
BY201-200	0023
BY201-300	0023
BY201-400	0023
BY201-500	0023
BY201-600	0023
BY202	0575
BY203	0575
BY203/12	0344
BY203/12S	0344
BY203/16	0344
BY203/16S	0344
BY203/20	0344
BY203/20S	0344
BY203-12	0344
BY203-16	0344
BY203-20	0344
BY204	0959
BY204/4	0524
BY204/8	0524
BY204/10	0524
BY205	0994
BY206	0023
BY206GP	0023
BY207	0023
BY207GP	0023
BY-208	0811
BY208	0811
BY208-600	0017
BY208-800	0102
BY208-1000	0017
BY209	2077
BY210-400	0790
BY210-600	0023
BY210-800	OEM
BY211	0703
BY212	4077
BY212-750R	OEM
BY213	0575
BY213-700R	OEM
BY214	1272
BY214-50	1272
BY214-100	1272
BY214-200	1277
BY214-400	1277
BY214-600	1282
BY214-800	1285
BY214-1000	1285
BY215	0994
BY216	2065
BY217	0959
BY217-50	OEM
BY217-100	OEM
BY217-200	OEM
BY217-400	OEM
BY218	2077
BY218-13	OEM
BY218-15	OEM
BY218-100	OEM
BY218-200	OEM
BY218-400	OEM
BY218-600	OEM
BY219	2077
BY221	0703
BY222	4077
BY223	0575
BY224	1285
BY224-200	OEM
BY224-400	OEM
BY224-600	OEM
BY225	0994
BY225-100	1034
BY225-200	1034
BY226	1760
BY226MGP	0071
BY227	0071
BY227MGP	0071
BY228	2077
BY228/13	OEM
BY228/13S	OEM
BY228/15	OEM
BY228/15S	OEM
BY229	2077
BY229-200	1137
BY229-200F	OEM
BY229-200R	OEM
BY229-400	1137
BY229-400R	OEM
BY229-600	OEM
BY229-600F	OEM
BY229-600R	OEM
BY229-800	OEM
BY229-800R	OEM
BY229-1000	OEM
BY229-1000R	OEM
BY229F200	OEM
BY229F400	OEM
BY229F600	OEM
BY229F800	OEM
BY233-200	1119
BY233-400	1654
BY233-600	1654
BY239-200	OEM
BY239-400	OEM
BY239-600	OEM
BY239-800	OEM
BY239-1000	OEM
BY239-1250	OEM
BY246-600	OEM
BY246-1000	OEM
BY246-1200	OEM
BY249-300	5980
BY249-300R	OEM
BY249-600	1958
BY249-600R	OEM
BY250	OEM
BY251	0087
BY252	0087
BY253	0087
BY254	0087
BY255	0087
BY256	0276
BY257	0299
BY260-200	OEM
BY260-400	OEM
BY260-600	OEM
BY261-200	2347
BY261-400	2353
BY261-600	2354
BY268	0182
BY269	0182
BY277-600R	OEM
BY277-750R	OEM
BY289-150	OEM
BY289-200	OEM
BY289-300	OEM
BY289-400	OEM
BY289-450	OEM
BY289-600	OEM
BY289-900	OEM
BY289-1000	OEM
BY291-75	OEM
BY291-150	OEM
BY291-225	OEM
BY291-300	OEM
BY291-450	OEM
BY291-600	OEM
BY292-75	OEM
BY292-150	OEM
BY292-225	OEM
BY292-300	OEM
BY293-75	OEM
BY293-150	OEM
BY293-225	OEM
BY293-300	OEM
BY294-75	OEM
BY294-150	OEM
BY294-225	OEM
BY294-300	OEM
BY294-450	OEM
BY294-600	OEM
BY295-150	OEM
BY295-200	OEM
BY295-300	OEM
BY295-400	OEM
BY295-450	OEM
BY295-600	OEM
BY296	0102
BY296P	0102
BY297	0102
BY297P	0102
BY298	0102
BY298P	0102
BY299	0102
BY299P	0102
BY300-500	OEM
BY300-600	OEM
BY300-650	OEM
BY300-700	OEM
BY301	0703
BY302	4077
BY302-75	OEM
BY302-150	OEM
BY302-225	OEM
BY302-300	OEM
BY303	0575
BY304	3697
BY305	0994
BY306	2065
BY307	2070
BY308	2077
BY309	2077
BY311	0703
BY312	4077
BY313	0575
BY314	2049
BY315	0994
BY316	2065
BY317	2070
BY318	2077
BY318-100	0133
BY318-200	OEM
BY318-400	OEM
BY318-600	OEM
BY319	2077
BY321	0703
BY322	4077
BY323	0575
BY324	2049
BY325	0994
BY326	2065
BY327	2070
BY328	2077
BY329	2077
BY329-800	OEM
BY329-1000	OEM
BY329-1200	OEM
BY350-1300	OEM
BY350-1500	OEM
BY359-1000	OEM
BY359-1300	OEM
BY359-1500	OEM
BY360-600	OEM
BY396	0102
BY396P	0102
BY397	0102
BY397P	0031
BY398	0031
BY398P	0031
BY399	0102
BY399P	1362
BY399S	1362
BY401	0015
BY402	0015
BY403	0015
BY404	0015
BY405	0015
BY406	0023
BY406A	0200
BY407	0023
BY407A	0200
BY408	0206
BY409	0206
BY409A	OEM
BY410	1082
BY411	0964
BY412	3688
BY413	0983
BY414	3697
BY415	0197
BY416	0200
BY417	0204
BY418	0206
BY419	0206
BY421	0964
BY422	3688
BY423	0983
BY424	3697
BY425	0197
BY426	0200
BY427	0204
BY428	0206
BY429	0206
BY438	OEM
BY448	OEM
BY458	0102
BY476	OEM
BY476A	OEM
BY477	OEM
BY478	OEM
BY488	0097
BY500-100	1352
BY500-200	1352
BY500-400	1352
BY500-600	1362
BY500-800	1362
BY501	0084
BY502	0090
BY503	0097
BY504	0105
BY505	0109
BY506	0116
BY507	0122
BY508	0131
BY509	0131
BY510	OEM
BY511	0084
BY512	0090
BY513	0097
BY514	0105
BY515	0109
BY516	0116
BY517	0122
BY518	0131
BY519	0131
BY521	0084
BY522	0090
BY523	0097
BY524	0105
BY525	0109
BY526	0116
BY527	0122
BY528	0131
BY529	0131
BY550/50	OEM
BY550/100	OEM
BY550/200	OEM
BY550/400	OEM
BY550/600	OEM
BY550/800	OEM
BY584	OEM
BY588	0071
BY609	OEM
BY610	OEM
BY614	OEM
BY619	OEM
BY620	OEM
BY627	1208
BY701	0964
BY702	3688
BY703	0983
BY704	3697
BY705	0197
BY706	0200
BY707	0204
BY708	0206
BY709	0206
BY710	OEM
BY711	0964
BY712	3688
BY713	0983
BY714	3697
BY715	0197
BY716	0200
BY717	0204
BY718	0206
BY719	0206
BY721	0964
BY722	3688
BY723	0983
BY724	3697
BY725	0197
BY726	0200
BY727	0204
BY728	0206
BY729	0206
BY801	0084
BY802	0090
BY803	0097
BY804	0105
BY805	0109
BY806	0116
BY807	0122
BY808	0131
BY809	0131
BY811	0084
BY812	0090
BY813	0097
BY814	0105
BY815	0109
BY816	0116
BY817	0122
BY818	0131
BY819	0131
BY821	0084
BY822	0090
BY823	0097
BY824	0105
BY825	0109
BY826	0116
BY827	0122
BY828	0131
BY829	0131
BY1001	0071
BY1002	0071
BY1101	0071
BY1102	0071
BY1200	0071
BY1201	0071
BY1202	0071
BY2001	0607
BY2002	0607
BY2101	0607
BY2102	0607
BY2201	0607
BY2202	0607
BY3001	0607
BY3002	0607
BY3101	0607
BY3102	0607
BY3201	0607
BY3202	0607
BY4001	0583
BY4002	0583
BY4101	0583
BY4102	0583
BY4201	0583
BY4202	0583
BY5001	0145
BY5002	0145
BY5101	0145
BY5102	0145
BY5201	0145
BY5202	0145
BY6431	OEM
BY7001	0583
BY7002	0583
BY7101	0583
BY7102	0583
BY7201	0583
BY7202	0583
BY7637	OEM
BY8001	0145
BY8002	0145
BY8101	0145
BY8102	0145
BY8201	0145
BY8202	0145
BYD13D	0071
BYD13G	0071
BYD13J	0071
BYD13K	0071
BYD13M	0071
BYD14D	0071
BYD14G	0071
BYD14J	0071
BYD14K	0071
BYD14M	0071
BYD17D	0071
BYD17G	0071
BYD17J	0071
BYD17K	0071
BYD17M	0071
BYD33D	0023
BYD33DPH	OEM
BYD33G	0023
BYD33J	0031
BYD33JPH	OEM
BYD33K	0702
BYD33M	0702
BYD37D	0031
BYD37G	0031
BYD37J	0031
BYD37K	0702
BYD37M	0702
BYD73A	OEM
BYD73B	OEM
BYD73C	OEM
BYD73D	OEM
BYD73E	OEM
BYD73F	OEM
BYD73G	OEM
BYD74A	OEM
BYD74B	OEM
BYD74C	OEM
BYD74D	OEM
BYD74E	OEM
BYD74F	OEM
BYD74G	OEM
BYD77A	OEM
BYD77B	OEM
BYD77C	OEM
BYD77D	OEM
BYD77E	OEM
BYD77F	OEM
BYD77G	OEM
BYM05-50	OEM
BYM05-100	OEM
BYM05-200	OEM
BYM05-400	OEM
BYM05-600	OEM
BYM06-40	OEM
BYM06-50	OEM
BYM06-100	OEM
BYM06-200	OEM
BYM06-600	OEM
BYM10-50	OEM
BYM10-100	OEM
BYM10-200	OEM
BYM10-400	OEM
BYM10-600	OEM
BYM10-800	OEM
BYM10-1000	OEM
BYM11-50	OEM
BYM11-100	OEM
BYM11-200	OEM
BYM11-400	OEM
BYM11-600	OEM
BYM11-800	OEM
BYM11-1000	OEM
BYM12-50	OEM
BYM12-100	OEM
BYM12-150	OEM
BYM12-200	OEM
BYM12-300	OEM
BYM12-400	OEM
BYM26A	OEM
BYM26B	OEM
BYM26C	OEM
BYM26D	OEM
BYM26E	OEM
BYM36A	0541
BYM36B	OEM
BYM36C	OEM
BYM36D	OEM
BYM36E	OEM
BYM56A	OEM
BYM56B	OEM
BYM56C	OEM
BYM56D	OEM
BYM56E	OEM
BY0331	0031
BYP21-50	0903
BYP21-100	0903
BYP21-150	0903
BYP21-200	0903
BYP22-50	OEM
BYP22-100	OEM
BYP22-150	OEM
BYP22-200	OEM
BYQ28-50	1227
BYQ28-100	1227
BYQ28-150	1227
BYQ28-200	1227
BYR28-600	0966
BYR28-800	OEM
BYR29-600	1654
BYR29-700	OEM
BYR29-800	OEM
BYR34-600	OEM
BYR34-800	OEM
BYR79-600	OEM
BYR79-800	OEM
BYS15	OEM
BYS21	0080
BYS21-45	0080
BYS21-90	OEM
BYS22-45	OEM
BYS22-90	OEM
BYS24	OEM
BYS24-45	OEM
BYS24-90	OEM
BYS26	OEM
BYS26-45	OEM
BYS26-90	OEM
BYS27-45	OEM
BYS28	OEM
BYS28-45	OEM
BYS28-90	OEM
BYS30	OEM
BYS31	OEM
BYS32	OEM
BYS41	OEM
BYS42	OEM
BYS50	OEM
BYS51	OEM
BYS52-300	OEM
BYS71	OEM
BYS72	OEM
BYS76	OEM
BYS79	OEM
BYS80	OEM
BYS92-40	OEM
BYS92-45	OEM
BYS92-50	OEM
BYS93-40	OEM
BYS93-45	OEM
BYS93-50	OEM
BYS94	OEM
BYS95	OEM
BYS95-40	OEM

If replacement code is OEM, contact original manufacturer for replacement.
299

DEVICE TYPE	REPL CODE
BYS95-45	OEM
BYS95-50	OEM
BYS96	OEM
BYS97	OEM
BYS97-40	OEM
BYS97-45	OEM
BYS97-50	OEM
BYS98-40	OEM
BYS98-45	OEM
BYS98-50	OEM
BYT01-200	1082
BYT01-300	OEM
BYT01-400	OEM
BYT03-200	0541
BYT03-300	1352
BYT03-400	1352
BYT08P200	OEM
BYT08P300	OEM
BYT08P400	OEM
BYT08P1200	OEM
BYT08P1300	OEM
BYT08P1400	OEM
BYT11-600	1362
BYT11-800	1362
BYT11-1000	1362
BYT12-200	OEM
BYT12-300	OEM
BYT12-400	OEM
BYT12-600	OEM
BYT12-800	OEM
BYT12-1000	OEM
BYT12P600	OEM
BYT12P800	OEM
BYT12P1000	OEM
BYT12PI600	OEM
BYT13-600	1362
BYT13-800	1362
BYT13-1000	3411
BYT16P200	OEM
BYT16P300	OEM
BYT16P400	OEM
BYT28-300	0966
BYT28-400	0966
BYT28-500	0966
BYT30-200	OEM
BYT30-300	OEM
BYT30-400	OEM
BYT30-600	OEM
BYT30-800	OEM
BYT30-1000	OEM
BYT30P200	OEM
BYT30P300	OEM
BYT30P400	OEM
BYT30P600	OEM
BYT30P800	OEM
BYT30P1000	OEM
BYT30PI200	OEM
BYT30PI300	OEM
BYT30PI400	OEM
BYT30PI600	OEM
BYT30PI800	OEM
BYT30PI1000	OEM
BYT51A	0023
BYT51B	0023
BYT51D	0023
BYT51G	0023
BYT51J	0023
BYT51K	0017
BYT51M	0017
BYT52A	0023
BYT52B	0023
BYT52D	0023
BYT52G	0023
BYT52J	0023
BYT52K	0017
BYT52M	0017
BYT60-200	OEM
BYT60-300	OEM
BYT60-400	OEM
BYT60P200	OEM
BYT60P300	OEM
BYT60P400	OEM
BYT61-600	OEM
BYT61-800	OEM
BYT61-900	OEM
BYT61-1000	OEM
BYT61B-600	OEM
BYT61B-800	OEM
BYT61B-900	OEM
BYT61B-1000	OEM
BYT65-600	OEM
BYT65-800	OEM
BYT65-900	OEM
BYT65-1000	OEM
BYT65B-800	OEM
BYT65B-900	OEM
BYT65B-1000	OEM
BYT67-800	OEM
BYT67-1000	OEM
BYT71-100	OEM
BYT71-200	OEM
BYT71-400	OEM
BYT71-600	OEM
BYT71-800	OEM
BYT75-200	OEM
BYT75-400	OEM
BYT75-500	OEM
BYT75-600	OEM
BYT75-800	OEM
BYT75-1000	OEM
BYT77	1917
BYT78	OEM
BYT79-300	0966
BYT79-400	0966
BYT79-500	0966
BYT95A	0031
BYT95B	0031
BYT95C	0031
BYT95D	0017
BYT95E	0017
BYT230PI200	OEM
BYT230PI300	OEM
BYT230PI400	OEM
BYT230PI600	OEM
BYT230PI800	OEM
BYT230PI1000	OEM
BYT230PIV200	OEM
BYT230PIV300	OEM
BYT230PIV400	OEM
BYT230PIV600	OEM
BYT230PIV800	OEM
BYT230PIV1000	OEM
BYV10-20	0730
BYV10-20A	0730
BYV10-30	0730
BYV10-40	0730
BYV10-40A	OEM
BYV10-60	OEM
BYV12	0031
BYV13	0031
BYV14	0031
BYV15	OEM
BYV16	OEM
BYV18-30	OEM
BYV18-30A	OEM
BYV18-35	OEM
BYV18-35A	OEM
BYV18-40	OEM
BYV18-45	OEM
BYV18-45A	OEM
BYV19-30	OEM
BYV19-30A	OEM
BYV19-35	OEM
BYV19-35A	OEM
BYV19-40	OEM
BYV19-40A	OEM
BYV19-45	OEM
BYV19-45A	OEM
BYV20-30	0610
BYV20-30A	OEM
BYV20-35	0610
BYV20-35A	OEM
BYV20-40	0610
BYV20-40A	OEM
BYV20-45	0610
BYV20-45A	OEM
BYV21-30	0610
BYV21-30A	OEM
BYV21-35	0610
BYV21-35A	OEM
BYV21-40	0610
BYV21-40A	OEM
BYV21-45	0610
BYV21-45A	OEM
BYV22-30	0610
BYV22-30A	OEM
BYV22-35	1536
BYV22-35A	OEM
BYV22-40	1536
BYV22-40A	OEM
BYV22-45	1536
BYV22-45A	OEM
BYV23-30	OEM
BYV23-30A	OEM
BYV23-35	OEM
BYV23-35A	OEM
BYV23-40	OEM
BYV23-40A	OEM
BYV23-45	OEM
BYV23-45A	OEM
BYV24-800	OEM
BYV24-800R	OEM
BYV24-1000	OEM
BYV24-1000R	OEM
BYV25-800	OEM
BYV25-800R	OEM
BYV25-1000	OEM
BYV25-1000R	OEM
BYV26A	OEM
BYV26B	OEM
BYV26C	OEM
BYV26D	OEM
BYV26E	OEM
BYV27/50	OEM
BYV27/100	OEM
BYV27/150	OEM
BYV27/200	OEM
BYV27-15	0541
BYV27-50	0541
BYV27-100	0541
BYV27-150	0541
BYV27-200	0541
BYV28/50	OEM
BYV28/100	OEM
BYV28/150	OEM
BYV28/200	OEM
BYV28-50	0541
BYV28-100	0541
BYV28-150	0541
BYV28-200	0541
BYV29-300	1958
BYV29-400	1654
BYV29-500	1654
BYV30-200	1557
BYV30-300	2140
BYV30-400	2140
BYV30-500	OEM
BYV31-300	OEM
BYV31-400	OEM
BYV31-500	OEM
BYV32-50	OEM
BYV32-50F	OEM
BYV32-100	OEM
BYV32-100F	OEM
BYV32-150	OEM
BYV32-150F	OEM
BYV32-200	OEM
BYV32-200F	OEM
BYV32F50	OEM
BYV32F100	OEM
BYV32F150	OEM
BYV32F200	OEM
BYV33-30	2493
BYV33-30A	OEM
BYV33-30F	OEM
BYV33-35	2493
BYV33-35A	OEM
BYV33-35F	OEM
BYV33-40	2493
BYV33-40A	OEM
BYV33-40F	OEM
BYV33-45	2493
BYV33-45A	OEM
BYV33-45F	OEM
BYV33F-30	OEM
BYV33F-35	OEM
BYV33F-40	OEM
BYV33F-40A	OEM
BYV33F-45	OEM
BYV33J	0031
BYV34-300	OEM
BYV34-400	OEM
BYV34-500	OEM
BYV36A	OEM
BYV36B	OEM
BYV36C	OEM
BYV36D	OEM
BYV36E	OEM
BYV37	OEM
BYV38	OEM
BYV39-30	OEM
BYV39-30A	OEM
BYV39-35	OEM
BYV39-35A	OEM
BYV39-40	OEM
BYV39-40A	OEM
BYV39-45	OEM
BYV39-45A	OEM
BYV42-50	OEM
BYV42-100	OEM
BYV42-150	OEM
BYV42-200	OEM
BYV43-30	2493
BYV43-30A	OEM
BYV43-35	2493
BYV43-35A	OEM
BYV43-40	2493
BYV43-40A	OEM
BYV43-45	2493
BYV43-45A	OEM
BYV44-300	OEM
BYV44-400	OEM
BYV44-500	OEM
BYV52-50	2219
BYV52-100	2219
BYV52-150	2219
BYV52-200	2219
BYV54-50	OEM
BYV54-100	OEM
BYV54-150	OEM
BYV54-200	OEM
BYV54V50	OEM
BYV54V100	OEM
BYV54V150	OEM
BYV54V200	OEM
BYV61	OEM
BYV62	OEM
BYV63	OEM
BYV71-100	OEM
BYV71-400	OEM
BYV71-600	OEM
BYV71-800	OEM
BYV72-50	2219
BYV72-100	2219
BYV72-150	2219
BYV72-200	2219
BYV73-30	1931
BYV73-30A	OEM
BYV73-35	1931
BYV73-35A	OEM
BYV73-40	1931
BYV73-40A	OEM
BYV73-45	1931
BYV73-45A	OEM
BYV74-300	4409
BYV74-400	4409
BYV74-500	4409
BYV79-50	3507
BYV79-100	3507
BYV79-150	3507
BYV79-200	3507
BYV92-200	1522
BYV92-300	0029
BYV92-400	0029
BYV92-500	OEM
BYV93-300	OEM
BYV93-400	OEM
BYV93-500	OEM
BYV95A	0031
BYV95B	0031
BYV95C	0031
BYV96D	OEM
BYV96E	0702
BYV950	0023
BYW07-50	OEM
BYW07-100	OEM
BYW07-150	OEM
BYW07-150A	OEM
BYW07-200	OEM
BYW08-50	OEM
BYW08-100	OEM
BYW08-150	OEM
BYW08-200	OEM
BYW14-100	OEM
BYW14-200	OEM
BYW14-400	OEM
BYW14-600	OEM
BYW14-800	OEM
BYW15-100	OEM
BYW15-200	OEM
BYW15-400	OEM
BYW15-600	OEM
BYW15-800	OEM
BYW16-100	OEM
BYW16-200	OEM
BYW16-400	OEM
BYW16-600	OEM
BYW16-800	OEM
BYW17-100	OEM
BYW17-200	OEM
BYW17-400	OEM
BYW17-600	OEM
BYW17-800	OEM
BYW17-1000	OEM
BYW17-1200	OEM
BYW18-400	OEM
BYW18-600	OEM
BYW18-800	OEM
BYW18-1000	OEM
BYW19-800	OEM
BYW19-1000	OEM
BYW25	OEM
BYW25-800	OEM
BYW25-800R	OEM
BYW25-1000	OEM
BYW25-1000R	OEM
BYW27-50	1325
BYW27-100	0015
BYW27-200	0015
BYW27-400	0015
BYW27-600	0015
BYW27-800	0071
BYW27-1000	0071
BYW29-50	1119
BYW29-100	1119
BYW29-150	1119
BYW29-200	1119
BYW29F50	OEM
BYW29F100	OEM
BYW29F150	OEM
BYW29F200	OEM
BYW30-50	OEM
BYW30-100	OEM
BYW30-150	OEM
BYW30-200	OEM
BYW31-50	OEM
BYW31-100	OEM
BYW31-150	OEM
BYW31-200	OEM
BYW32	1137
BYW33	1137
BYW34	1137
BYW35	3147
BYW36	3147
BYW51-50	OEM
BYW51-100	1227
BYW51-150	1227
BYW51-200	1227
BYW52	0102
BYW53	0102
BYW54	0102
BYW55	0102
BYW56	0102
BYW72	1137
BYW73	1137
BYW74	1137
BYW75	1483
BYW76	0023
BYW77-50	OEM
BYW77-100	OEM
BYW77-150	OEM
BYW77-150A	OEM
BYW77-200	OEM
BYW77P50	OEM
BYW77P100	OEM
BYW77P150	OEM
BYW77P200	OEM
BYW77PI50	OEM
BYW77PI100	OEM
BYW77PI150	OEM
BYW77PI200	OEM
BYW78-50	OEM
BYW78-100	OEM
BYW78-150	OEM
BYW78-200	OEM
BYW80-50	1119
BYW80-150	1119
BYW80-150A	OEM
BYW80-200	1119
BYW81-50	OEM
BYW81-100	OEM
BYW81-150	OEM
BYW81-150A	OEM
BYW81-200	OEM
BYW81P50	OEM
BYW81P100	OEM
BYW81P150	OEM
BYW81P200	OEM
BYW81PI50	OEM
BYW81PI100	OEM
BYW81PI150	OEM
BYW81PI200	OEM
BYW82	0102
BYW83	0102
BYW84	0102
BYW85	0102
BYW86	0102
BYW88-50	0084
BYW88-100	0097
BYW88-200	0097
BYW88-300	0109
BYW88-400	0109
BYW88-500	0122
BYW88-600	0122
BYW88-800	0131
BYW88-1000	0145
BYW88-1200	OEM
BYW92-50	OEM
BYW92-100	OEM
BYW92-150	OEM
BYW92-150A	OEM
BYW92-200	OEM
BYW93-50	OEM
BYW93-100	OEM
BYW93-150	OEM
BYW93-200	OEM
BYW94-50	OEM
BYW94-50U	OEM
BYW94-100	OEM
BYW94-100U	OEM
BYW94-150	OEM
BYW94-150U	OEM
BYW94-200	OEM
BYW94-200U	OEM
BYW95	0031
BYW95A	0031
BYW95B	0031
BYW95C	0031
BYW96D	1917
BYW96E	1917
BYW98-50	3085
BYW98-100	0541
BYW98-150	0541
BYW98-200	0541
BYW99-50	OEM
BYW99-100	OEM
BYW99-150	OEM
BYW99P50	OEM
BYW99P100	OEM
BYW99P150	OEM
BYW99P200	OEM
BYW100-50	0541
BYW100-100	0541
BYW100-150	0541
BYW100-200	1082
BYW29100	OEM
BYW29200	OEM
BYW81150	OEM
BYX4-1000R	0545
BYX10	0071
BYX10G	1560
BYX10GP	OEM
BYX11	OEM
BYX12/400	0071
BYX13/500	OEM
BYX13/600	0071
BYX13/1000	1111
BYX13/1500	OEM
BYX13-400	0800
BYX13-600	0315
BYX13-800	OEM
BYX13-800R	OEM
BYX13-1000	0045
BYX13-1000R	OEM
BYX13-1200	OEM
BYX13-1200R	OEM
BYX13-1600	OEM
BYX14/500	OEM
BYX14-400	OEM
BYX14-600	OEM
BYX14-800	OEM
BYX14-1000	OEM
BYX14-1200	OEM
BYX15	1111
BYX16	1124
BYX20/200	OEM
BYX21/100	OEM
BYX21/200	OEM
BYX22/200	0015
BYX22/400	0015
BYX22/600	0015
BYX22/800	0071
BYX22-200	0015
BYX22-400	3855
BYX22-600	0015
BYX22-800	0071
BYX22-1200	0102
BYX23-400	OEM
BYX23-600	OEM
BYX23-800	OEM
BYX23-1000	OEM
BYX24	0293
BYX25-600	1599
BYX25-600R	1196
BYX25-800	1600
BYX25-800R	2124
BYX25-1000	1604
BYX25-1000R	2236
BYX25-1200	OEM
BYX25-1400	OEM
BYX26-60	0087
BYX27-400	OEM
BYX27-600	OEM
BYX27-800	OEM
BYX27-1000	OEM
BYX28/200	OEM
BYX28/200A	OEM
BYX28/200B	OEM
BYX28/400	OEM
BYX28/400A	OEM
BYX28/400B	OEM
BYX28/600	2070
BYX29-75	OEM
BYX29-100	OEM
BYX29-125	OEM
BYX29-150	OEM
BYX29-75000	OEM
BYX29-100000	OEM
BYX29-125000	OEM
BYX29-150000	OEM
BYX30/150	0242
BYX30-200	OEM
BYX30-200R	OEM
BYX30-300	OEM
BYX30-300R	OEM
BYX30-400	OEM
BYX30-400R	OEM
BYX30-500	OEM
BYX30-500R	OEM
BYX30-600	OEM
BYX30-600R	1894
BYX32/200	OEM
BYX32-400	OEM
BYX32-400R	OEM
BYX32-600	5939
BYX32-600R	1467
BYX32-800	0652
BYX32-800R	0193
BYX32-1000	0131
BYX32-1000R	0193
BYX32-1200	0145
BYX32-1200R	0545
BYX32-1600	OEM
BYX32-1600R	OEM
BYX33/200	OEM
BYX33-400	OEM
BYX33-600	OEM
BYX33-800	OEM
BYX33-1000	OEM
BYX33-1200	OEM
BYX33-1600	OEM
BYX34-200	OEM
BYX34-300	OEM
BYX34-400	OEM
BYX34-500	OEM
BYX35	OEM
BYX36-150	0087
BYX36-300	0015
BYX36-600	0015
BYX38	0087
BYX38/300	2049
BYX38/300R	1236
BYX38/600	2070
BYX38/600R	1006
BYX38/900	0607
BYX38/900R	1067
BYX38/1200	2077
BYX38/1200R	1130
BYX38-300	5483
BYX38-300+	1104
BYX38-300R	1236
BYX38-300R+	1104
BYX38-600	1599
BYX38-600+	1104
BYX38-600R	1196
BYX38-600R+	0471
BYX38-900	2982
BYX38-900+	2982
BYX38-900R	0444
BYX38-900R+	0444
BYX38-1200	2077
BYX38-1200R	1130
BYX39/600	0122
BYX39/800	0131
BYX39/1000	0145
BYX39-600	0122
BYX39-600+	1104
BYX39-600R	0810
BYX39-600R+	0471
BYX39-800	0131
BYX39-800+	2982
BYX39-800R	0540
BYX39-800R+	0444
BYX39-1000	0145
BYX39-1000+	2982
BYX39-1000R	0545
BYX39-1000R+	0444
BYX39-1200	OEM
BYX39-1400	OEM
BYX40-300+	1104
BYX40-300R+	0471
BYX40-600	0122
BYX40-600+	1104
BYX40-600R	0810
BYX40-600R+	0471
BYX40-800	0131
BYX40-800+	2982
BYX40-800R	0540
BYX40-800R+	0444
BYX40-1000	0145
BYX40-1000+	2982
BYX40-1000R	0545
BYX40-1000R+	0545
BYX40-8000R	0540
BYX42/300	0109
BYX42/600	0122
BYX42/900	0145
BYX42-300	0105
BYX42-300R	0533
BYX42-600	0122
BYX42-600+	1104
BYX42-600R	0810
BYX42-600R+	0471
BYX42-900	0145
BYX42-900+	2982
BYX42-900R	0545
BYX42-900R+	0444
BYX42-1200	OEM
BYX42-1200R	OEM
BYX45-200R	OEM
BYX45-400R	OEM
BYX45-600R	0087
BYX45-800R	0087
BYX45-1000R	0087
BYX45-1200R	OEM
BYX45-1400R	OEM
BYX46-200	0865
BYX46-200R	1625
BYX46-300	0847
BYX46-300R	1242
BYX46-400	0847
BYX46-400R	1242
BYX46-500	1599
BYX46-500R	1196
BYX46-600	1599
BYX46-600R	1196
BYX47	OEM
BYX48/300	0109
BYX48/600	0122
BYX48/900	0145
BYX48-300	0105
BYX48-300+	1104
BYX48-300R	0991
BYX48-300R+	0471
BYX48-600	0122
BYX48-600+	1104
BYX48-600R	0510
BYX48-600R+	0471
BYX48-900	0145
BYX48-900+	2982
BYX48-900R	0942
BYX48-900R+	0444
BYX48-1200	OEM
BYX48-1200R	OEM
BYX49-300	OEM
BYX49-300R	OEM
BYX49-600	OEM
BYX49-600R	OEM
BYX49-900	OEM
BYX49-900R	OEM
BYX49-1200	OEM
BYX49-1200R	OEM
BYX50-200	1557
BYX50-200R	1538
BYX50-300	2140
BYX50-300R	3110
BYX50-400	0197
BYX50-400R	0991
BYX50-500	0204
BYX50-500R	0510
BYX50-600	0204
BYX50-600R	0510
BYX51-100	5482
BYX52-300	1118
BYX52-300R	1103
BYX52-600	0315
BYX52-600R	0267
BYX52-900	0045
BYX52-900R	0280
BYX52-1200	OEM
BYX53	OEM
BYX54	OEM
BYX55	OEM

If replacement code is OEM, contact original manufacturer for replacement.

DEVICE TYPE	REPL CODE
BYX55-100	OEM
BYX55-200	OEM
BYX55-300	OEM
BYX55-350	0031
BYX55-350P	0031
BYX55-400	OEM
BYX55-500	OEM
BYX55-600	0031
BYX55-600P	0031
BYX56-600	0315
BYX56-600R	0267
BYX56-800	1124
BYX56-800R	1111
BYX56-1000	0045
BYX56-1000R	0280
BYX56-1200	OEM
BYX56-1400	OEM
BYX57-500	0102
BYX57-600	0102
BYX58-50	0133
BYX58-100	0133
BYX58-200	0133
BYX58-300	0023
BYX58-400	0023
BYX60-50	0015
BYX60-100	0015
BYX60-200	0015
BYX60-300	0015
BYX60-400	0015
BYX60-500	0015
BYX60-600	0015
BYX60-700	0071
BYX61-50	1557
BYX61-50U	OEM
BYX61-100	1557
BYX61-100U	OEM
BYX61-200	1557
BYX61-200U	OEM
BYX61-300	2140
BYX61-300U	OEM
BYX61-400	2140
BYX61-400U	OEM
BYX62-600	0706
BYX62-800	OEM
BYX62-1000	OEM
BYX63-600	0596
BYX63-800	OEM
BYX63-1000	OEM
BYX64-600	0596
BYX64-800	OEM
BYX64-1000	OEM
BYX65-50	1522
BYX65-50U	OEM
BYX65-100	1522
BYX65-100U	OEM
BYX65-200	1522
BYX65-200UBYX65-300	OEM
BYX65-300	0029
BYX65-300U	OEM
BYX65-400	0029
BYX65-400U	OEM
BYX66-400	0847
BYX66-500	0706
BYX66-600	0706
BYX66-700	OEM
BYX66-800	3722
BYX66-900	OEM
BYX66-1000	1604
BYX67-400	OEM
BYX67-500	0596
BYX67-600	0596
BYX67-700	OEM
BYX67-800	OEM
BYX67-900	OEM
BYX67-1000	OEM
BYX68	OEM
BYX69	OEM
BYX70-100	OEM
BYX70-300	OEM
BYX70-500	OEM
BYX70-600	OEM
BYX71-350	5779
BYX71-350R	OEM
BYX71-600	OEM
BYX71-600R	OEM
BYX72-150	OEM
BYX72-150R	OEM
BYX72-300	OEM
BYX72-300R	OEM
BYX72-500	OEM
BYX72-500R	OEM
BYX73S700R	OEM
BYX74-100	4787
BYX74-200	2215
BYX74-400	5911
BYX74-600	5925
BYX74-800	5940
BYX75	OEM
BYX76	OEM
BYX77	OEM
BYX78	OEM
BYX79	OEM
BYX80	OEM
BYX81	OEM
BYX82	0102
BYX82-50	OEM
BYX82-100	OEM
BYX82-200	OEM
BYX82-300	OEM

DEVICE TYPE	REPL CODE
BYX82-400	OEM
BYX83	0102
BYX84	0102
BYX85	0102
BYX86	0102
BYX87	OEM
BYX90	OEM
BYX90G	OEM
BYX91-90K	OEM
BYX91-120K	OEM
BYX91-150K	OEM
BYX91-180K	OEM
BYX91-190K	OEM
BYX92-50	2491
BYX92-100	2491
BYX92-200	2491
BYX92-300	1352
BYX92-400	1352
BYX96-100	OEM
BYX96-200	OEM
BYX96-300	OEM
BYX96-400	OEM
BYX96-600	OEM
BYX96-800	OEM
BYX96-900	OEM
BYX96-1000	OEM
BYX96-1200	OEM
BYX96-1400	OEM
BYX96-1600	OEM
BYX97-300	1995
BYX97-600	2657
BYX97-900	OEM
BYX97-1000	OEM
BYX97-1200	OEM
BYX97-1600	OEM
BYX98-300	0109
BYX98-600	0122
BYX98-900	0145
BYX98-1200	OEM
BYX99-300	3705
BYX99-600	1104
BYX99-900	OEM
BYX99-1200	OEM
BYX38900	0122
BYX39600	0122
BYX40600	0122
BYX42600	0122
BYX48600	0122
BYX55009	0071
BYY10	OEM
BYY15	OEM
BYY16	OEM
BYY20	OEM
BYY20/200	OEM
BYY21	OEM
BYY21/200	OEM
BYY22	OEM
BYY23	OEM
BYY24	OEM
BYY25	OEM
BYY27	OEM
BYY28	OEM
BYY29	OEM
BYY30	OEM
BYY31	0015
BYY32	0015
BYY33	0015
BYY34	0015
BYY35	0071
BYY36	0071
BYY37	0071
BYY38	OEM
BYY39	OEM
BYY39/200	OEM
BYY39/400	OEM
BYY39/600	OEM
BYY39/800	OEM
BYY39/800R	OEM
BYY39/1000R	OEM
BYY39/1200R	OEM
BYY39/1400R	OEM
BYY39/1600R	OEM
BYY39/1800R	OEM
BYY39/2000R	OEM
BYY39/2200R	OEM
BYY39/2400R	OEM
BYY39-800	OEM
BYY56	0524
BYY56/1200	OEM
BYY57/75H	OEM
BYY57/150H	OEM
BYY57/300H	OEM
BYY57/500H	OEM
BYY57/700H	OEM
BYY57-75	OEM
BYY57-150	OEM
BYY57-300	OEM
BYY57-450	OEM
BYY57-600	OEM
BYY58/75H	OEM
BYY58/150H	OEM
BYY58/300H	OEM
BYY58/500H	OEM
BYY58/700H	OEM
BYY58-75	OEM
BYY58-150	OEM
BYY58-300	OEM
BYY58-450	OEM
BYY58-600	OEM

DEVICE TYPE	REPL CODE
BYY59	OEM
BYY60	0087
BYY61	0087
BYY62	OEM
BYY67	OEM
BYY68	OEM
BYY69	OEM
BYY70	OEM
BYY71	OEM
BYY72	OEM
BYY73	OEM
BYY74	OEM
BYY75	OEM
BYY76	OEM
BYY77	OEM
BYY78	OEM
BYY88	0097
BYY89	0015
BYY90	OEM
BYY91	0071
BYY92	OEM
BYY93	OEM
BYY94	OEM
BYY95	OEM
BYY96	OEM
BYZ10	OEM
BYZ11	OEM
BYZ12	OEM
BYZ13	1241
BYZ14	OEM
BYZ15	OEM
BYZ16	OEM
BYZ17	OEM
BYZ18	OEM
BYZ19	OEM
BZ-050	0162
BZ050	0162
BZ-052	0162
BZ052	0157
BZ-054	0157
BZ054	0157
BZ-056	0157
BZ056	0157
BZ-058	0298
BZ058	0298
BZ-061	0631
BZ061	0631
BZ-063	0631
BZ063	0631
BZ-065	0025
BZ065	0025
BZ-067	0025
BZ067	0025
BZ-069	0025
BZ069	0025
BZ-071	0025
BZ071	0644
BZ-073	0644
BZ073	0644
BZ-075	0644
BZ075	0644
BZ-077	0644
BZ077	0644
BZ-079	0244
BZ079	0244
BZ-080	0012
BZ080	0244
BZ-081	0244
BZ081	0244
BZ-083	0244
BZ083	0244
BZ-085	1075
BZ085	0244
BZ-088	1075
BZ088	1075
BZ-090	0012
BZ090	0012
BZ090.1Z9	0012
BZ-092	0012
BZ092	0012
BZ-094	0012
BZ094	0012
BZ-096	0170
BZ096	0170
BZ-098	0170
BZ098	0170
BZ-0800	0244
BZ-0901	0012
BZ1-90	0012
BZ3.6	0296
BZ3.9	0036
BZ4.3	0274
BZ4.7	0140
BZ5.1	0041
BZ5.6	0253
BZ6.2	0466
BZ6.8	0062
BZ7.5	0077
BZ8.2	0165
BZ9.1	0057
BZ11FB	0313
BZ-12	0137
BZ12	0137
BZ55XC20	OEM
BZ67	0016
BZ71	0016
BZ79C10	0170
BZ88/C4V7	0157
BZ-100	0170

DEVICE TYPE	REPL CODE
BZ100	0170
BZ102	OEM
BZ102(0V7)	OEM
BZ102(1V4)	OEM
BZ102(2V1)	OEM
BZ102(2V8)	0672
BZ102(3V4)	0296
BZ102-0V7	OEM
BZ102-1V4	OEM
BZ102-2V1	OEM
BZ102-2V8	0672
BZ102-3V4	0296
BZ103	0062
BZ103A	0062
BZ104	0165
BZ104A	0165
BZ-105	0313
BZ105	0170
BZ105A	0064
BZ106	0052
BZ106A	0052
BZ107	0681
BZ107A	0681
BZ108	0371
BZ108A	0371
BZ109	0695
BZ109A	0695
BZ-110	0313
BZ110	0313
BZ110A	0489
BZ111	0195
BZ111A	0195
BZ112	0166
BZ112A	0166
BZ113	OEM
BZ-115	0789
BZ115	0789
BZ115-D12	OEM
BZ115-D22	OEM
BZ-120	0137
BZ120	0137
BZ-125	0361
BZ125	0361
BZ-130	0361
BZ130	0361
BZ-135	0100
BZ135	0100
BZ-140	0100
BZ140	0100
BZ-140LF	0100
BZ140LF	0100
BZ-145	0002
BZ145	0002
BZ147	0077
BZ148	0165
BZ-150	0002
BZ150	0002
BZ-157	0416
BZ157	0416
BZ-162	0416
BZ162	0416
BZ-167	1639
BZ167	1639
BZ-172	1639
BZ172	1639
BZ-177	0490
BZ177	0490
BZ-182	0490
BZ182	0490
BZ-187	0943
BZ187	0943
BZ-192	0943
BZ192	0943
BZ-197	0526
BZ197	0526
BZ-210	0526
BZ210	0526
BZ-220	0560
BZ220	0560
BZ-230	0398
BZ230	0560
BZ-240	0398
BZ240	0273
BZ-250	1596
BZ250	1596
BZ-260	0436
BZ260	0436
BZ-270	0436
BZ270	0436
BZ-280	1664
BZ280	1664
BZ-290	0721
BZ290	0721
BZ-300	0721
BZ300	0721
BZ-310	0039
BZ310	0721
BZ-320	0039
BZ320	0039
BZ-320LF	0039
BZ-330	0039
BZ330	0039
BZ-340	0814
BZ340	0039
BZ-350	0814
BZ350	0814
BZ688C5V6	OEM
BZ691C11	OEM
BZ752	OEM

DEVICE TYPE	REPL CODE
BZ752F	OEM
BZ752T	OEM
BZ758	OEM
BZ758F	OEM
BZ758T	OEM
BZ821T	0466
BZ821TF	0466
BZ821TT	0466
BZ963	0052
BZ963F	0052
BZ963T	0052
BZ965	0681
BZ965F	0681
BZ965T	0681
BZ969	OEM
BZ969F	OEM
BZ969T	OEM
BZ971	OEM
BZ971F	OEM
BZ971T	OEM
BZ1021V4	0133
BZ2090	0012
BZC88C8V2	OEM
BZD10C3V3	0777
BZD10C3V6	0791
BZD10C3V9	0801
BZD10C4V3	0815
BZD10C4V7	0827
BZD10C5V1	0437
BZD10C5V6	0870
BZD10C6V2	0185
BZD10C6V8	0205
BZD10C7V5	0475
BZD10C8V2	0499
BZD10C9V1	0679
BZD10C10	0225
BZD10C11	0230
BZD10C12	0234
BZD10C13	0237
BZD10C15	0247
BZD10C16	0251
BZD10C18	0256
BZD10C20	0262
BZD10C22	0269
BZD10C24	0273
BZD10C27	0291
BZD10C30	0305
BZD10C33	0314
BZD10C36	0316
BZD10C39	0322
BZD10C43	0333
BZD10C47	0343
BZD10C51	0027
BZD10C56	0266
BZD10C62	0382
BZD10C68	0401
BZD10C75	0421
BZD10C82	0439
BZD10C91	0238
BZD10C100	1172
BZD10C110	1182
BZD10C120	1198
BZD10C130	1209
BZD10C150	0642
BZD10C160	1246
BZD10C180	1269
BZD10C200	0600
BZD23C3V9	0451
BZD23C4V3	0528
BZD23C4V7	0446
BZD23C5V1	0162
BZD23C5V6	0157
BZD23C6V2	0631
BZD23C6V8	0025
BZD23C7V5	0644
BZD23C8V2	0244
BZD23C9V1	0012
BZD23C10	0170
BZD23C11	0313
BZD23C12	0137
BZD23C13	0361
BZD23C15	0002
BZD23C16	0416
BZD23C18	0490
BZD23C20	0526
BZD23C22	0560
BZD23C24	0398
BZD23C27	0436
BZD23C30	0721
BZD23C33	0039
BZD23C36	0814
BZD23C39	0346
BZD23C43	0925
BZD23C47	0993
BZD23C51	0497
BZD23C56	1823
BZD23C62	0778
BZD23C68	2144
BZD23C75	1181
BZD23C82	0327
BZD23C91	1301
BZD23C100	0149
BZD23C110	0149
BZD23C120	0186
BZD23C130	0213
BZD23C150	0028
BZD23C160	0255
BZD23C180	0363
BZD23C200	0417

DEVICE TYPE	REPL CODE
BZD23C220	OEM
BZD23C240	OEM
BZD23C270	OEM
BZD27C3V9	0451
BZD27C4V3	0528
BZD27C4V7	0446
BZD27C5V1	0162
BZD27C5V6	0157
BZD27C6V2	0631
BZD27C6V8	0025
BZD27C7V5	0644
BZD27C8V2	0244
BZD27C9V1	0012
BZD27C10	0170
BZD27C11	0313
BZD27C12	0137
BZD27C13	0361
BZD27C15	0002
BZD27C16	0416
BZD27C18	0490
BZD27C20	0526
BZD27C22	0560
BZD27C24	0398
BZD27C27	0436
BZD27C30	0721
BZD27C36	0814
BZD27C39	0346
BZD27C43	0925
BZD27C47	0993
BZD27C51	0497
BZD27C56	0863
BZD27C62	0778
BZD27C68	2144
BZD27C75	1181
BZD27C82	0327
BZD27C91	1301
BZD27C100	0098
BZD27C110	0149
BZD27C120	0186
BZD27C130	0213
BZD27C150	0028
BZD27C160	0255
BZD27C180	0363
BZD27C200	0417
BZD27C220	OEM
BZD27C240	OEM
BZD27C270	OEM
BZS2.7	0755
BZS3.3	0296
BZT03/D9V1	0679
BZT03/D10	0225
BZT03/D11	0230
BZT03/D12	0234
BZT03/D13	0237
BZT03/D15	0247
BZT03/D16	0251
BZT03/D18	0256
BZT03/D20	0262
BZT03/D22	0269
BZT03/D24	0273
BZT03/D27	0291
BZT03/D30	0305
BZT03/D33	0314
BZT03/D36	0316
BZT03/D39	0322
BZT03/D43	0333
BZT03/D47	0343
BZT03/D51	0027
BZT03/D56	0266
BZT03/D62	0382
BZT03/D68	0401
BZT03/D75	0421
BZT03/D82	0439
BZT03/D91	0238
BZT03/D100	1172
BZT03/D110	1182
BZT03/D120	1198
BZT03/D130	1209
BZT03/D150	0642
BZT03/D160	1246
BZT03/D180	1269
BZT03/D200	0600
BZT03/D220	OEM
BZT03/D240	OEM
BZT03/D270	OEM
BZT03C7V5	OEM
BZT03C8V2	OEM
BZT03C9V1	OEM
BZT03C10	OEM
BZT03C11	OEM
BZT03C12	OEM
BZT03C13	OEM
BZT03C15	OEM
BZT03C16	OEM
BZT03C18	OEM
BZT03C20	OEM
BZT03C22	OEM
BZT03C24	OEM
BZT03C27	OEM
BZT03C30	OEM
BZT03C33	OEM
BZT03C36	OEM
BZT03C39	OEM
BZT03C43	OEM
BZT03C47	OEM
BZT03C51	OEM
BZT03C56	OEM
BZT03C62	OEM
BZT03C68	OEM

DEVICE TYPE	REPL CODE
BZT03C75	OEM
BZT03C82	OEM
BZT03C91	OEM
BZT03C100	OEM
BZT03C110	OEM
BZT03C120	OEM
BZT03C130	OEM
BZT03C150	OEM
BZT03C160	OEM
BZT03C180	OEM
BZT03C200	OEM
BZT03C220	OEM
BZT03C240	OEM
BZT03C270	OEM
BZV10	OEM
BZV11	OEM
BZV12	OEM
BZV13	OEM
BZV14	OEM
BZV15-C10	OEM
BZV15-C11	OEM
BZV15-C12	OEM
BZV15-C13	OEM
BZV15-C15	OEM
BZV15-C16	OEM
BZV15-C18	OEM
BZV15-C20	OEM
BZV15-C22	OEM
BZV15-C24	OEM
BZV15-C27	OEM
BZV15-C30	OEM
BZV15-C33	OEM
BZV15-C36	OEM
BZV15-C39	OEM
BZV15-C43	OEM
BZV15-C47	OEM
BZV15-C51	OEM
BZV15-C56	OEM
BZV15-C62	OEM
BZV15-C68	OEM
BZV15-C75	OEM
BZV15C10	OEM
BZV15C11	OEM
BZV15C12	OEM
BZV15C13	OEM
BZV15C15	OEM
BZV15C16	OEM
BZV15C18	OEM
BZV15C20	5812
BZV15C22	5813
BZV15C24	OEM
BZV15C27	OEM
BZV15C30	OEM
BZV15C33	OEM
BZV15C36	OEM
BZV15C39	OEM
BZV15C43	OEM
BZV15C47	OEM
BZV15C51	OEM
BZV15C56	OEM
BZV15C62	OEM
BZV15C68	OEM
BZV15C75	OEM
BZV16-C6V8	0205
BZV16-C7V5	0475
BZV16-C8V2	0499
BZV16-C9V1	0679
BZV16-C10	0225
BZV16-C11	0230
BZV16-C12	0234
BZV16-C13	0237
BZV16-C15	0247
BZV16-C16	0251
BZV16-C18	0256
BZV16-C20	0262
BZV16-C22	0269
BZV16-C24	0273
BZV16-C27	0291
BZV16-C30	0305
BZV16-C33	0314
BZV16-C36	0316
BZV16-C39	0322
BZV16-C43	0333
BZV16-C47	0343
BZV16-C51	0027
BZV16-C56	0266
BZV16-C62	0382
BZV16-C68	0401
BZV16-C75	0421
BZV16-C82	0251
BZV16-C91	0238
BZV16-C100	1172
BZV16C3V3	0777
BZV16C3V6	0791
BZV16C3V9	0801
BZV16C4V3	0815
BZV16C4V7	0827
BZV16C5V1	0437
BZV16C5V6	0870
BZV16C6V2	0185
BZV16C6V8	0205
BZV16C7V5	0475
BZV16C8V2	0499
BZV16C9V1	0679
BZV16C10	0225
BZV16C11	0230
BZV16C12	0230
BZV16C13	0237
BZV16C15	0247

DEVICE TYPE	REPL CODE
BZV16C16	0251
BZV16C18	0256
BZV16C20	0262
BZV16C22	0269
BZV16C24	0273
BZV16C27	0291
BZV16C30	0305
BZV16C33	0314
BZV16C36	0316
BZV16C39	0322
BZV16C43	0333
BZV16C47	0343
BZV16C51	0027
BZV16C56	0266
BZV16C62	0382
BZV16C68	0401
BZV16C75	0421
BZV16C82	0256
BZV16C91	0238
BZV16C100	0225
BZV16C110	1182
BZV16C120	1198
BZV16C130	1209
BZV16C150	0642
BZV16C160	1246
BZV16C180	1269
BZV16C200	0600
BZV18C5V6	0157
BZV18C6V2	0631
BZV18C6V8	0025
BZV18C7V5	0644
BZV18C8V2	0244
BZV18C9V1	0012
BZV18C10	0170
BZV18C11	0313
BZV18C12	0137
BZV27	0466
BZV27A	0466
BZV28	0466
BZV28A	0466
BZV29	0466
BZV29A	0466
BZV30	0466
BZV30A	0466
BZV31	0466
BZV31A	0466
BZV32	0057
BZV32A	0057
BZV32B	0057
BZV33	0057
BZV33A	0057
BZV33B	0057
BZV34	0057
BZV34A	0057
BZV34B	0057
BZV35	0057
BZV35A	0057
BZV35B	0057
BZV36	0057
BZV36A	0057
BZV36B	0057
BZV37	OEM
BZV38	OEM
BZV40C3V3	0777
BZV40C3V6	0791
BZV40C3V9	0801
BZV40C4V3	0815
BZV40C4V7	0827
BZV40C5V1	0437
BZV40C5V6	0870
BZV40C6V2	0185
BZV40C6V8	0205
BZV40C7V5	0475
BZV40C8V2	0499
BZV40C8V7	3285
BZV40C9V1	0679
BZV40C10	0225
BZV40C11	0230
BZV40C12	0234
BZV40C13	0237
BZV40C14	1387
BZV40C15	0247
BZV40C16	0251
BZV40C17	1170
BZV40C18	0256
BZV40C19	2379
BZV40C20	0262
BZV40C22	0269
BZV40C24	0273
BZV40C25	2383
BZV40C27	0291
BZV40C28	1169
BZV40C30	0305
BZV40C33	0314
BZV40C36	0316
BZV40C39	0322
BZV40C43	0333
BZV40C47	0343
BZV40C51	0027
BZV40C56	0266
BZV40C60	2829
BZV40C62	0382
BZV40C68	0401
BZV40C75	0421
BZV40C82	0439
BZV40C87	2999
BZV40C91	0238
BZV40C100	1172
BZV40C110	1182
BZV40C120	1198
BZV40C130	1209
BZV40C140	1870
BZV40C150	0642
BZV40C160	1246
BZV40C170	2091
BZV40C180	1269
BZV40C190	2210
BZV40C200	0600
BZV41C2V7	1302
BZV41C3V0	1703
BZV41C3V3	0289
BZV41C3V6	0188
BZV41C3V9	0451
BZV41C4V3	0528
BZV41C4V7	0446
BZV41C5V1	0162
BZV41C5V6	0157
BZV41C6V2	0631
BZV41C6V8	0025
BZV41C7V5	0644
BZV41C8V2	0244
BZV41C9V1	0012
BZV41C10	0170
BZV41C12	0137
BZV41C13	0361
BZV41C15	0002
BZV41C16	0416
BZV41C18	0490
BZV41C20	0526
BZV41C22	0560
BZV41C24	0398
BZV41C27	0436
BZV41C30	0721
BZV41C33	0039
BZV41C36	0814
BZV41C39	0346
BZV41C43	0925
BZV41C47	0993
BZV43C	0152
BZV44C	0152
BZV45C	0152
BZV46	OEM
BZV46-1V5	OEM
BZV46-2V0	OEM
BZV46-C1V5	OEM
BZV46-C2V0	OEM
BZV46C1V5	OEM
BZV46C2V0	OEM
BZV47C3V3	0777
BZV47C3V6	0791
BZV47C3V9	0801
BZV47C4V3	0815
BZV47C4V7	0827
BZV47C5V1	0437
BZV47C5V6	0870
BZV47C6V2	0185
BZV47C6V8	0205
BZV47C7V5	0475
BZV47C8V2	0499
BZV47C9V1	0679
BZV47C10	0225
BZV47C11	0230
BZV47C12	0234
BZV47C13	0237
BZV47C15	0247
BZV47C16	0251
BZV47C18	0256
BZV47C20	0262
BZV47C22	0269
BZV47C24	0273
BZV47C27	0291
BZV47C30	0305
BZV47C33	0314
BZV47C36	0316
BZV47C39	0322
BZV47C43	0333
BZV47C47	0343
BZV47C51	0027
BZV47C56	0266
BZV47C62	0382
BZV47C68	0401
BZV47C75	0421
BZV47C82	0439
BZV47C91	0238
BZV47C100	1172
BZV47C110	1182
BZV47C120	1198
BZV47C130	1209
BZV47C150	0642
BZV47C160	1246
BZV47C180	1269
BZV47C200	0600
BZV48C3V3	0777
BZV48C3V6	0791
BZV48C3V9	0801
BZV48C4V3	0815
BZV48C4V7	0827
BZV48C5V1	0437
BZV48C5V6	0870
BZV48C6V2	0185
BZV48C6V8	0205
BZV48C7V5	0475
BZV48C8V2	0499
BZV48C8V7	3285
BZV48C9V1	0679
BZV48C10	0225
BZV48C11	0230
BZV48C12	0234
BZV48C13	0237
BZV48C15	0247
BZV48C16	0251
BZV48C18	0256
BZV48C20	0262
BZV48C22	0269
BZV48C24	0273
BZV48C27	0291
BZV48C30	0305
BZV48C33	0314
BZV48C36	0316
BZV48C39	0322
BZV48C43	0333
BZV48C47	0343
BZV48C51	0027
BZV48C56	0266
BZV48C62	0382
BZV48C68	0401
BZV48C75	0421
BZV48C82	0439
BZV48C91	0238
BZV48C100	1172
BZV48C110	1182
BZV48C120	1198
BZV48C130	1209
BZV48C150	0642
BZV48C160	1246
BZV48C180	1269
BZV48C200	0600
BZV49C0V8	OEM
BZV49C2V4	OEM
BZV49C2V7	OEM
BZV49C3V0	OEM
BZV49C3V3	OEM
BZV49C3V6	OEM
BZV49C3V9	OEM
BZV49C4V3	OEM
BZV49C4V7	OEM
BZV49C5V1	OEM
BZV49C5V6	OEM
BZV49C6V2	0466
BZV49C6V8	OEM
BZV49C7V5	OEM
BZV49C8V2	OEM
BZV49C9V1	0057
BZV49C10	OEM
BZV49C11	OEM
BZV49C12	0052
BZV49C13	OEM
BZV49C15	OEM
BZV49C16	OEM
BZV49C18	OEM
BZV49C20	OEM
BZV49C22	OEM
BZV49C24	OEM
BZV49C27	OEM
BZV49C30	OEM
BZV49C33	OEM
BZV49C36	OEM
BZV49C39	OEM
BZV49C43	OEM
BZV49C47	OEM
BZV49C51	OEM
BZV49C56	OEM
BZV49C62	OEM
BZV49C68	OEM
BZV49C75	OEM
BZV53A	OEM
BZV53B	OEM
BZV54A	OEM
BZV54B	OEM
BZV55C2V4	OEM
BZV55C2V7	OEM
BZV55C3V0	OEM
BZV55C3V3	OEM
BZV55C3V6	OEM
BZV55C3V9	OEM
BZV55C4V3	OEM
BZV55C4V7	OEM
BZV55C5V1	OEM
BZV55C5V6	OEM
BZV55C6V2	OEM
BZV55C6V8	OEM
BZV55C7V5	OEM
BZV55C8V2	OEM
BZV55C9V1	OEM
BZV55C10	OEM
BZV55C11	OEM
BZV55C12	OEM
BZV55C13	OEM
BZV55C15	OEM
BZV55C16	OEM
BZV55C18	OEM
BZV55C20	OEM
BZV55C22	OEM
BZV55C24	OEM
BZV55C27	OEM
BZV55C30	OEM
BZV55C33	OEM
BZV55C36	OEM
BZV55C39	OEM
BZV55C43	OEM
BZV55C47	OEM
BZV55C51	OEM
BZV55C56	OEM
BZV55C62	OEM
BZV55C68	OEM
BZV55C75	OEM
BZV58C3V3	0777
BZV58C3V6	0791
BZV58C3V9	0801
BZV58C4V3	0815
BZV58C4V7	0827
BZV58C5V1	0437
BZV58C5V6	0870
BZV58C6V2	0185
BZV58C6V8	0205
BZV58C7V5	0475
BZV58C8V2	0499
BZV58C9V1	0679
BZV58C10	0225
BZV58C11	0230
BZV58C12	0234
BZV58C13	0237
BZV58C15	0247
BZV58C16	0251
BZV58C18	0256
BZV58C20	0262
BZV58C22	0269
BZV58C24	0273
BZV58C27	0291
BZV58C30	0305
BZV58C33	0314
BZV58C36	0316
BZV58C39	0322
BZV58C43	0333
BZV58C47	0343
BZV58C51	0027
BZV58C56	0266
BZV58C62	0382
BZV58C68	0401
BZV58C75	0421
BZV58C82	0439
BZV58C91	0238
BZV58C100	1172
BZV58C110	1182
BZV58C120	1198
BZV58C130	1209
BZV58C150	0642
BZV58C160	1246
BZV58C180	1269
BZV58C200	0600
BZV60C2V4	1266
BZV60C2V7	0755
BZV60C3V0	0118
BZV60C3V3	0296
BZV60C3V6	0372
BZV60C3V9	0036
BZV60C4V3	0274
BZV60C4V7	0140
BZV60C5V1	0041
BZV60C5V6	0253
BZV60C6V2	0466
BZV60C6V8	0062
BZV60C7V5	0077
BZV60C8V2	0165
BZV60C9V1	0057
BZV60C10	0064
BZV60C11	0181
BZV60C12	0052
BZV60C13	0053
BZV60C15	0681
BZV60C16	0440
BZV60C18	0371
BZV60C20	0695
BZV60C22	0700
BZV60C24	0489
BZV60C27	0450
BZV60C30	0195
BZV60C33	0166
BZV60C36	0010
BZV60C39	0032
BZV60C43	0054
BZV60C47	0068
BZV60C51	0092
BZV60C56	0125
BZV60C62	0152
BZV60C68	0173
BZV60C75	0094
BZV69C8V2	0244
BZV-80	OEM
BZV-81	OEM
BZV85C3V6	0188
BZV85C3V9	0451
BZV85C4V3	0528
BZV85C4V7	0446
BZV85C5V1	0162
BZV85C5V6	0157
BZV85C6V2	0631
BZV85C6V8	0025
BZV85C7V5	0644
BZV85C8V2	0244
BZV85C9V1	0012
BZV85C10	0170
BZV85C11	0313
BZV85C12	0137
BZV85C13	0361
BZV85C15	0002
BZV85C16	0416
BZV85C18	0490
BZV85C20	0526
BZV85C22	0560
BZV85C24	0398
BZV85C27	0436
BZV85C30	0721
BZV85C33	1075
BZV85C36	0814
BZV85C39	0346
BZV85C43	0925
BZV85C47	0993
BZV85C51	0497
BZV85C56	0863
BZV85C62	0778
BZV85C68	2144
BZV85C75	1181
BZV461V5	OEM
BZW03/D7V5	OEM
BZW03/D8V2	OEM
BZW03/D9V1	OEM
BZW03/D10	OEM
BZW03/D11	OEM
BZW03/D12	OEM
BZW03/D13	OEM
BZW03/D15	OEM
BZW03/D16	OEM
BZW03/D18	OEM
BZW03/D20	OEM
BZW03/D22	OEM
BZW03/D24	OEM
BZW03/D27	OEM
BZW03/D30	OEM
BZW03/D33	OEM
BZW03/D36	OEM
BZW03/D39	OEM
BZW03/D43	OEM
BZW03/D47	OEM
BZW03/D51	OEM
BZW03/D56	OEM
BZW03/D62	OEM
BZW03/D68	OEM
BZW03/D75	OEM
BZW03/D82	OEM
BZW03/D91	OEM
BZW03/D100	OEM
BZW03/D110	OEM
BZW03/D120	OEM
BZW03/D130	OEM
BZW03/D150	OEM
BZW03/D160	OEM
BZW03/D180	OEM
BZW03/D200	OEM
BZW03/D220	OEM
BZW03/D240	OEM
BZW03/D270	OEM
BZW03C6V8	OEM
BZW03C7V5	OEM
BZW03C8V2	OEM
BZW03C9V1	OEM
BZW03C10	OEM
BZW03C11	OEM
BZW03C12	OEM
BZW03C13	OEM
BZW03C15	OEM
BZW03C16	OEM
BZW03C18	OEM
BZW03C20	OEM
BZW03C22	OEM
BZW03C24	OEM
BZW03C27	OEM
BZW03C30	OEM
BZW03C33	OEM
BZW03C36	OEM
BZW03C39	OEM
BZW03C43	OEM
BZW03C47	OEM
BZW03C51	OEM
BZW03C56	OEM
BZW03C62	OEM
BZW03C68	OEM
BZW03C75	OEM
BZW03C82	OEM
BZW03C91	OEM
BZW03C100	OEM
BZW03C110	OEM
BZW03C120	OEM
BZW03C130	OEM
BZW03C150	OEM
BZW03C160	OEM
BZW03C180	OEM
BZW03C200	OEM
BZW03C220	OEM
BZW03C240	OEM
BZW03C270	OEM
BZW04-5V5	3085
BZW04-5V8	OEM
BZW04-5V8B	OEM
BZW04-6V0	OEM
BZW04-6V0B	OEM
BZW04-6V4	OEM
BZW04-6V4B	OEM
BZW04-6V6	OEM
BZW04-6V6B	OEM
BZW04-7V0	OEM
BZW04-7V0B	OEM
BZW04-7V4	OEM
BZW04-7V4B	OEM
BZW04-7V8	OEM
BZW04-7V8B	OEM
BZW04-8V1	OEM
BZW04-8V1B	OEM
BZW04-8V5	OEM
BZW04-8V6	OEM
BZW04-8V6B	OEM
BZW04-8V9	OEM
BZW04-8V9B	OEM
BZW04-9V4	OEM
BZW04-9V4B	OEM
BZW04-9V7	OEM
BZW04-9V7B	OEM
BZW04-9V9	OEM
BZW04-9V9B	OEM
BZW04-10	3143
BZW04-10B	OEM
BZW04-11	OEM
BZW04-11B	OEM
BZW04-12	OEM
BZW04-12B	OEM
BZW04-12V5	OEM
BZW04-12V5B	OEM
BZW04-13	OEM
BZW04-13B	OEM
BZW04-13V5	OEM
BZW04-13V5B	OEM
BZW04-14	3162
BZW04-14B	OEM
BZW04-15	OEM
BZW04-15B	OEM
BZW04-16	3171
BZW04-16B	OEM
BZW04-17	OEM
BZW04-17B	OEM
BZW04-18	OEM
BZW04-18B	OEM
BZW04-18V5B	OEM
BZW04-18V15	OEM
BZW04-19	OEM
BZW04-19B	OEM
BZW04-20	OEM
BZW04-20B	OEM
BZW04-22	1904
BZW04-22B	OEM
BZW04-23	OEM
BZW04-23B	OEM
BZW04-24	OEM
BZW04-24B	OEM
BZW04-26	OEM
BZW04-26B	OEM
BZW04-27	OEM
BZW04-27B	OEM
BZW04-28	OEM
BZW04-28B	OEM
BZW04-29	OEM
BZW04-29B	OEM
BZW04-31	OEM
BZW04-31B	OEM
BZW04-32	OEM
BZW04-32B	OEM
BZW04-33	OEM
BZW04-33B	OEM
BZW04-35	OEM
BZW04-35B	OEM
BZW04-37	OEM
BZW04-37B	OEM
BZW04-38	OEM
BZW04-38B	OEM
BZW04-40	OEM
BZW04-40B	OEM
BZW04-41	0563
BZW04-41B	OEM
BZW04-44	OEM
BZW04-44B	OEM
BZW04-45	OEM
BZW04-45B	OEM
BZW04-47	OEM
BZW04-47B	OEM
BZW04-48	OEM
BZW04-48B	OEM
BZW04-50	OEM
BZW04-50B	OEM
BZW04-53	OEM
BZW04-53B	OEM
BZW04-55	0825
BZW04-55B	OEM
BZW04-58	OEM
BZW04-58B	OEM
BZW04-61	OEM
BZW04-61B	OEM
BZW04-64	OEM
BZW04-64B	OEM
BZW04-66	OEM
BZW04-66B	OEM
BZW04-70	OEM
BZW04-70B	OEM
BZW04-74	OEM
BZW04-74B	OEM
BZW04-78	OEM
BZW04-78B	OEM
BZW04-81	OEM
BZW04-81B	OEM
BZW04-85	OEM
BZW04-85B	OEM
BZW04-89	OEM
BZW04-89B	OEM
BZW04-94	OEM
BZW04-94B	OEM
BZW04-97	OEM
BZW04-97B	OEM
BZW04-102	OEM
BZW04-102B	OEM
BZW04-105	OEM
BZW04-105B	OEM
BZW04-111	OEM
BZW04-111B	OEM
BZW04-120	OEM
BZW04-120B	OEM
BZW04-121	OEM
BZW04-121B	OEM
BZW04-128	OEM
BZW04-128B	OEM
BZW04-130	OEM
BZW04-130B	OEM
BZW04-136	OEM
BZW04-136B	OEM
BZW04-138	OEM
BZW04-144	OEM
BZW04-145	OEM
BZW04-145B	OEM
BZW04-146	OEM
BZW04-154	OEM
BZW04-154B	OEM
BZW04-162	1395
BZW04-171	OEM
BZW04-171B	OEM
BZW04-188	OEM
BZW04-188B	OEM
BZW04-213	OEM
BZW04-213B	OEM
BZW04-239	OEM
BZW04-239B	OEM
BZW04-256	OEM
BZW04-256B	OEM
BZW04-273	OEM
BZW04-273B	OEM
BZW04-299	OEM
BZW04-299B	OEM
BZW04-342	OEM
BZW04-342B	OEM
BZW04-376	OEM
BZW04-376B	OEM
BZW04P5V8	OEM
BZW04P5V8B	OEM
BZW04P6V4	OEM
BZW04P6V4B	OEM
BZW04P7V0	OEM
BZW04P7V0B	OEM
BZW04P7V8	OEM
BZW04P7V8B	OEM
BZW04P8V5	OEM
BZW04P8V5B	OEM
BZW04P9V4	OEM
BZW04P9V4B	OEM
BZW04P10	OEM
BZW04P10B	OEM
BZW04P11	OEM
BZW04P11B	OEM
BZW04P13	OEM
BZW04P13B	OEM
BZW04P14	OEM
BZW04P14B	OEM
BZW04P15	OEM
BZW04P15B	OEM
BZW04P17	OEM
BZW04P17B	OEM
BZW04P19	OEM
BZW04P19B	OEM
BZW04P20	OEM
BZW04P20B	OEM
BZW04P23	OEM
BZW04P26	OEM
BZW04P26B	OEM
BZW04P28	OEM
BZW04P28B	OEM
BZW04P31	OEM
BZW04P31B	OEM
BZW04P33	OEM
BZW04P37	OEM
BZW04P37B	OEM
BZW04P40	OEM
BZW04P40B	OEM
BZW04P44	OEM
BZW04P44B	OEM
BZW04P48	OEM
BZW04P48B	OEM
BZW04P53	OEM
BZW04P53B	OEM
BZW04P58	OEM
BZW04P58B	OEM
BZW04P64	OEM
BZW04P64B	OEM
BZW04P70	OEM
BZW04P70B	OEM
BZW04P78	OEM
BZW04P78B	OEM
BZW04P85	OEM
BZW04P85B	OEM
BZW04P94	OEM
BZW04P94B	OEM
BZW04P102	OEM
BZW04P102B	OEM
BZW04P111	OEM
BZW04P111B	OEM
BZW04P128	OEM
BZW04P128B	OEM
BZW04P136	OEM
BZW04P136B	OEM
BZW04P145	OEM
BZW04P145B	OEM
BZW04P154	OEM
BZW04P154B	OEM
BZW04P171	OEM
BZW04P171B	OEM
BZW04P188	OEM
BZW04P188B	OEM
BZW04P213	OEM
BZW04P213B	OEM

If replacement code is OEM, contact original manufacturer for replacement.

DEVICE TYPE	REPL CODE
BZW04P239	OEM
BZW04P239B	OEM
BZW04P256	OEM
BZW04P256B	OEM
BZW04P273	OEM
BZW04P273B	OEM
BZW04P299	OEM
BZW04P299B	OEM
BZW04P342	OEM
BZW04P342B	OEM
BZW04P376	OEM
BZW04P376B	OEM
BZW05-10B	OEM
BZW05-35	OEM
BZW06-5V5	3085
BZW06-5V8	3085
BZW06-5V8B	OEM
BZW06-6V0	OEM
BZW06-6V4	OEM
BZW06-6V4B	OEM
BZW06-6V6	OEM
BZW06-7V0	OEM
BZW06-7V0B	OEM
BZW06-7V4	OEM
BZW06-7V8	OEM
BZW06-7V8B	OEM
BZW06-8V1	OEM
BZW06-8V5	OEM
BZW06-8V5B	OEM
BZW06-8V9	OEM
BZW06-9V4	OEM
BZW06-9V4B	OEM
BZW06-9V7	OEM
BZW06-10	3143
BZW06-10B	OEM
BZW06-10V5	OEM
BZW06-11	OEM
BZW06-11B	OEM
BZW06-12V1	OEM
BZW06-13	OEM
BZW06-13B	OEM
BZW06-13V1	OEM
BZW06-14	3162
BZW06-14B	OEM
BZW06-14V5	OEM
BZW06-15	OEM
BZW06-15B	OEM
BZW06-16V2	OEM
BZW06-17	OEM
BZW06-17B	OEM
BZW06-19	OEM
BZW06-19B	OEM
BZW06-19V4	OEM
BZW06-20	OEM
BZW06-20B	OEM
BZW06-21V8	OEM
BZW06-23	OEM
BZW06-23B	OEM
BZW06-24V3	OEM
BZW06-26	OEM
BZW06-26B	OEM
BZW06-26V8	OEM
BZW06-28	OEM
BZW06-28B	OEM
BZW06-29V1	OEM
BZW06-31	OEM
BZW06-31B	OEM
BZW06-31V6	OEM
BZW06-33	OEM
BZW06-33B	OEM
BZW06-34V8	OEM
BZW06-37	OEM
BZW06-37B	OEM
BZW06-38V1	OEM
BZW06-40	OEM
BZW06-40B	OEM
BZW06-41V3	OEM
BZW06-44	OEM
BZW06-44B	OEM
BZW06-45V4	OEM
BZW06-48	OEM
BZW06-48B	OEM
BZW06-50V2	OEM
BZW06-53	OEM
BZW06-53B	OEM
BZW06-58	OEM
BZW06-58B	OEM
BZW06-60V7	OEM
BZW06-64	OEM
BZW06-64B	OEM
BZW06-66V4	OEM
BZW06-70	OEM
BZW06-70B	OEM
BZW06-73V7	OEM
BZW06-78	OEM
BZW06-78B	OEM
BZW06-81	OEM
BZW06-85	OEM
BZW06-85B	OEM
BZW06-89V2	OEM
BZW06-94	OEM
BZW06-94B	OEM
BZW06-97V2	OEM
BZW06-102	OEM
BZW06-102B	OEM
BZW06-105	OEM
BZW06-111	OEM
BZW06-111B	OEM
BZW06-121	OEM
BZW06-128	OEM
BZW06-128B	OEM
BZW06-130	OEM
BZW06-136	OEM
BZW06-136B	OEM
BZW06-138	OEM
BZW06-145	OEM
BZW06-145B	OEM
BZW06-146	OEM
BZW06-154	OEM
BZW06-154B	OEM
BZW06-162	1395
BZW06-171	OEM
BZW06-171B	OEM
BZW06-188	OEM
BZW06-188B	OEM
BZW06-213	OEM
BZW06-213B	OEM
BZW06-239	OEM
BZW06-239B	OEM
BZW06-256	OEM
BZW06-256B	OEM
BZW06-273	OEM
BZW06-273B	OEM
BZW06-299	OEM
BZW06-299B	OEM
BZW06-342	OEM
BZW06-342B	OEM
BZW06-376	OEM
BZW06-376B	OEM
BZW06P5V8	OEM
BZW06P5V8B	OEM
BZW06P6V4	OEM
BZW06P6V4B	OEM
BZW06P7V0	OEM
BZW06P7V0B	OEM
BZW06P7V8	OEM
BZW06P7V8B	OEM
BZW06P8V5	OEM
BZW06P8V5B	OEM
BZW06P9V4	OEM
BZW06P9V4B	OEM
BZW06P10	OEM
BZW06P10B	OEM
BZW06P11	OEM
BZW06P11B	OEM
BZW06P13	OEM
BZW06P13B	OEM
BZW06P14	OEM
BZW06P14B	OEM
BZW06P15	OEM
BZW06P15B	OEM
BZW06P17	OEM
BZW06P17B	OEM
BZW06P19	OEM
BZW06P19B	OEM
BZW06P20	OEM
BZW06P20B	OEM
BZW06P23	OEM
BZW06P23B	OEM
BZW06P26	OEM
BZW06P26B	OEM
BZW06P28	OEM
BZW06P28B	OEM
BZW06P31	OEM
BZW06P31B	OEM
BZW06P33	OEM
BZW06P33B	OEM
BZW06P37	OEM
BZW06P37B	OEM
BZW06P40	OEM
BZW06P40B	OEM
BZW06P44	OEM
BZW06P44B	OEM
BZW06P48	OEM
BZW06P48B	OEM
BZW06P53	OEM
BZW06P53B	OEM
BZW06P58	OEM
BZW06P58B	OEM
BZW06P64	OEM
BZW06P64B	OEM
BZW06P70	OEM
BZW06P70B	OEM
BZW06P78	OEM
BZW06P78B	OEM
BZW06P85	OEM
BZW06P85B	OEM
BZW06P94	OEM
BZW06P94B	OEM
BZW06P102	OEM
BZW06P102B	OEM
BZW06P111	OEM
BZW06P111B	OEM
BZW06P128	OEM
BZW06P128B	OEM
BZW06P136	OEM
BZW06P136B	OEM
BZW06P145	OEM
BZW06P145B	OEM
BZW06P154	OEM
BZW06P154B	OEM
BZW06P171	OEM
BZW06P171B	OEM
BZW06P188	OEM
BZW06P188B	OEM
BZW06P213	OEM
BZW06P213B	OEM
BZW06P239	OEM
BZW06P239B	OEM
BZW06P256	OEM
BZW06P256B	OEM
BZW06P273	OEM
BZW06P273B	OEM
BZW06P299	OEM
BZW06P299B	OEM
BZW06P342	OEM
BZW06P342B	OEM
BZW06P376	OEM
BZW06P376B	OEM
BZW07-10	OEM
BZW07-10B	OEM
BZW07-27	OEM
BZW07-27B	OEM
BZW07-43	OEM
BZW07-43B	OEM
BZW07-110	OEM
BZW07-110B	OEM
BZW10-12	OEM
BZW10-15	OEM
BZW11-7V0	OEM
BZW11-7V8	OEM
BZW11-8V5	OEM
BZW11-9V4	OEM
BZW11-10	OEM
BZW11-10B	OEM
BZW11-11	OEM
BZW11-13	OEM
BZW11-14	OEM
BZW11-15	OEM
BZW11-17	OEM
BZW11-19	OEM
BZW11-20	OEM
BZW11-23	OEM
BZW11-26	OEM
BZW11-27	OEM
BZW11-27B	OEM
BZW11-28	OEM
BZW11-31	OEM
BZW11-33	OEM
BZW11-37	OEM
BZW11-40	OEM
BZW11-43	OEM
BZW11-43B	OEM
BZW11-44	OEM
BZW11-48	OEM
BZW11-53	OEM
BZW11-58	OEM
BZW11-64	OEM
BZW11-70	OEM
BZW11-78	OEM
BZW11-85	OEM
BZW11-94	OEM
BZW11-102	OEM
BZW11-110	OEM
BZW11-110B	OEM
BZW11-128	OEM
BZW11-136	OEM
BZW11-145	OEM
BZW11-154	OEM
BZW11-171	OEM
BZW12-11	OEM
BZW12-13	OEM
BZW12-18	OEM
BZW12-22	OEM
BZW12-27	OEM
BZW12-30	OEM
BZW12-36	OEM
BZW12-47	OEM
BZW12-56	OEM
BZW12-68	OEM
BZW12-82	OEM
BZW12-91	OEM
BZW12-110	OEM
BZW12-150	OEM
BZW12-180	OEM
BZW12-220	OEM
BZW12-270	OEM
BZW12-300	OEM
BZW12-360	OEM
BZW12-390	OEM
BZW13-11	OEM
BZW13-13	OEM
BZW13-18	OEM
BZW13-22	OEM
BZW13-27	OEM
BZW13-30	OEM
BZW13-36	OEM
BZW13-47	OEM
BZW13-56	OEM
BZW13-68	OEM
BZW13-82	OEM
BZW13-91	OEM
BZW13-110	OEM
BZW13-150	OEM
BZW13-180	OEM
BZW13-220	OEM
BZW13-270	OEM
BZW13-300	OEM
BZW13-360	OEM
BZW13-390	OEM
BZW14	OEM
BZW20	OEM
BZW22C1	OEM
BZW22C2V7	OEM
BZW22C3V0	OEM
BZW22C3V3	0777
BZW22C3V6	0791
BZW22C3V9	0801
BZW22C4V3	0815
BZW22C4V7	0827
BZW22C5V1	0437
BZW22C5V6	0870
BZW22C6V2	0185
BZW22C6V8	0205
BZW22C7V5	0475
BZW22C8V2	0499
BZW22C9V1	0679
BZW22C10	0225
BZW22C11	0230
BZW22C12	0234
BZW22C13	0237
BZW22C15	0247
BZW22C16	0251
BZW22C18	0256
BZW22C20	0262
BZW22C22	0269
BZW22C24	0273
BZW22C27	0291
BZW22C30	0305
BZW22C33	0314
BZW22C36	0316
BZW22C39	0322
BZW22C43	0333
BZW22C47	0343
BZW22C51	0027
BZW22C56	0266
BZW22C62	0382
BZW22C68	0401
BZW22C75	0421
BZW22C82	0439
BZW22C91	0238
BZW22C100	1172
BZW22C110	1182
BZW22C120	1198
BZW22C130	1209
BZW22C150	0642
BZW22C160	1246
BZW22C180	1269
BZW22C200	0600
BZW25-12	OEM
BZW25-12B	OEM
BZW25-24	OEM
BZW25-24B	OEM
BZW25-47	OEM
BZW25-47B	OEM
BZW25-120	OEM
BZW25-120B	OEM
BZW30-12	OEM
BZW30-13	OEM
BZW30-15	OEM
BZW30-16	OEM
BZW30-18	OEM
BZW30-19	OEM
BZW30-22	OEM
BZW30-24	OEM
BZW30-27	OEM
BZW30-29	OEM
BZW30-32	OEM
BZW30-35	OEM
BZW30-38	OEM
BZW30-41	OEM
BZW30-45	OEM
BZW30-47	OEM
BZW30-50	OEM
BZW30-55	OEM
BZW30-61	OEM
BZW30-66	OEM
BZW30-74	OEM
BZW30-81	OEM
BZW30-89	OEM
BZW30-97	OEM
BZW30-105	OEM
BZW30-120	OEM
BZW30-121	OEM
BZW30-130	OEM
BZW30-138	OEM
BZW30-146	OEM
BZW30-162	OEM
BZW30-175	OEM
BZW30-202	OEM
BZW30-243	OEM
BZW30-283	OEM
BZW30-324	OEM
BZW30-405	OEM
BZW30-486	OEM
BZW50-8V2	OEM
BZW50-10	OEM
BZW50-12	OEM
BZW50-12B	OEM
BZW50-15	OEM
BZW50-15B	OEM
BZW50-18	OEM
BZW50-18B	OEM
BZW50-22	OEM
BZW50-22B	OEM
BZW50-27	OEM
BZW50-27B	OEM
BZW50-33	OEM
BZW50-33B	OEM
BZW50-39	OEM
BZW50-39B	OEM
BZW50-47	OEM
BZW50-47B	OEM
BZW50-56	OEM
BZW50-56B	OEM
BZW50-68	OEM
BZW50-68B	OEM
BZW50-82	OEM
BZW50-82B	OEM
BZW50-100	OEM
BZW50-100B	OEM
BZW50-120	OEM
BZW50-120B	OEM
BZW50-150	OEM
BZW50-150B	OEM
BZW50-180	OEM
BZW50-180B	OEM
BZW70-3	OEM
BZW70-5V6	OEM
BZW70-6V2	OEM
BZW70-6V8	3085
BZW70-7V5	OEM
BZW70-8V2	OEM
BZW70-9V1	OEM
BZW70-10	OEM
BZW70-11	OEM
BZW70-12	OEM
BZW70-13	3143
BZW70-15	OEM
BZW70-16	3171
BZW70-18	3162
BZW70-20	3171
BZW70-22	OEM
BZW70-24	OEM
BZW70-27	1904
BZW70-30	OEM
BZW70-33	OEM
BZW70-36	OEM
BZW70-39	OEM
BZW70-43	OEM
BZW70-47	OEM
BZW70-51	0563
BZW70-56	OEM
BZW70-62	OEM
BZW86-7V5	OEM
BZW86-8V2	OEM
BZW86-9V1	OEM
BZW86-10	OEM
BZW86-11	OEM
BZW86-12	OEM
BZW86-13	OEM
BZW86-15	OEM
BZW86-16	OEM
BZW86-18	OEM
BZW86-20	OEM
BZW86-22	OEM
BZW86-24	OEM
BZW86-27	OEM
BZW86-30	OEM
BZW86-33	OEM
BZW86-36	OEM
BZW86-39	OEM
BZW86-43	OEM
BZW86-47	OEM
BZW86-51	OEM
BZW86-56	OEM
BZW86-62	OEM
BZW86-R	OEM
BZW86C7V5	OEM
BZW86C8V2	OEM
BZW86C9V1	OEM
BZW86C10	OEM
BZW86C11	OEM
BZW86C12	OEM
BZW86C13	OEM
BZW86C15	OEM
BZW86C16	OEM
BZW86C18	OEM
BZW86C20	OEM
BZW86C22	OEM
BZW86C24	OEM
BZW86C27	OEM
BZW86C30	OEM
BZW86C33	OEM
BZW86C36	OEM
BZW86C39	OEM
BZW86C43	OEM
BZW86C47	OEM
BZW86C51	OEM
BZW86C56	OEM
BZW91	OEM
BZW91-5V6	OEM
BZW91-6V2	OEM
BZW91-6V8	OEM
BZW91-7V5	OEM
BZW91-8V2	OEM
BZW91-9V1	OEM
BZW91-10	OEM
BZW91-11	OEM
BZW91-12	OEM
BZW91-13	OEM
BZW91-15	OEM
BZW91-16	OEM
BZW91-18	OEM
BZW91-20	OEM
BZW91-22	OEM
BZW91-24	OEM
BZW91-27	OEM
BZW91-30	OEM
BZW91-33	OEM
BZW91-36	OEM
BZW91-39	OEM
BZW91-43	OEM
BZW91-47	OEM
BZW91-51	OEM
BZW91-56	OEM
BZW91-62	OEM
BZW91-R	OEM
BZW93-5V6	OEM
BZW93-6V2	OEM
BZW93-6V8	OEM
BZW93-7V5	OEM
BZW93-8V2	OEM
BZW93-9V1	OEM
BZW93-10	OEM
BZW93-11	OEM
BZW93-12	OEM
BZW93-13	OEM
BZW93-15	OEM
BZW93-16	OEM
BZW93-18	OEM
BZW93-20	OEM
BZW93-22	OEM
BZW93-24	OEM
BZW93-27	OEM
BZW93-30	OEM
BZW93-33	OEM
BZW93-36	OEM
BZW93-39	OEM
BZW93-43	OEM
BZW93-47	OEM
BZW93-51	OEM
BZW93-56	OEM
BZW93-62	OEM
BZW93-R	OEM
BZW95-6V2	OEM
BZW95-6V8	OEM
BZW95-7V5	OEM
BZW95-8V2	OEM
BZW95-9V1	OEM
BZW95-10	OEM
BZW95-11	OEM
BZW95-12	OEM
BZW95-13	OEM
BZW95-15	OEM
BZW95-16	OEM
BZW95-18	OEM
BZW95-20	OEM
BZW95-22	OEM
BZW95-24	OEM
BZW95-27	OEM
BZW95-30	OEM
BZW95-33	OEM
BZW95-36	OEM
BZW95-39	OEM
BZW95-43	OEM
BZW95-47	OEM
BZW95-51	OEM
BZW95-56	OEM
BZW95-62	OEM
BZW96-3V9	OEM
BZW96-4V3	OEM
BZW96-4V7	OEM
BZW96-5V1	OEM
BZW96-5V6	OEM
BZW96-6V2	OEM
BZW96-6V8	OEM
BZW96-7V5	OEM
BZX9V1	OEM
BZX10	0466
BZX11	0062
BZX12	0077
BZX13	0165
BZX14	0057
BZX15	0064
BZX16	0181
BZX17	0052
BZX18	0053
BZX19	0681
BZX20	0440
BZX21	0371
BZX22	0695
BZX23	0700
BZX24	0700
BZX25	0436
BZX26	0257
BZX27	0039
BZX29-C5V1	0162
BZX29-C5V6	0157
BZX29-C6V2	0631
BZX29-C6V8	0025
BZX29-C7V5	0644
BZX29-C8V2	0244
BZX29-C9V1	0012
BZX29-C10	0170
BZX29-C11	0313
BZX29-C12	0137
BZX29-C15	0002
BZX29-C16	0416
BZX29-C18	0490
BZX29-C20	0526
BZX29-C22	0560
BZX29-C24	0398
BZX29-C27	0436
BZX29-C30	0721
BZX29-C33	0039
BZX29-C36	0814
BZX29-C39	0346
BZX29-C43	0925
BZX29-C47	0993
BZX29-C51	0497
BZX29-C56	0863
BZX29C4V7	0446
BZX29C5V1	0162
BZX29C5V6	0157
BZX29C6V2	0631
BZX29C6V8	0025
BZX29C7V5	0644
BZX29C8V2	0244
BZX29C9V1	0012
BZX29C10	0170
BZX29C11	0313
BZX29C12	0137
BZX29C13	0361
BZX29C15	0002
BZX29C16	0416
BZX29C18	0490
BZX29C20	0526
BZX29C22	0560
BZX29C24	0398
BZX29C27	0436
BZX29C30	0721
BZX29C33	0039
BZX29C36	0814
BZX29C39	0346
BZX29C43	0925
BZX29C47	0993
BZX29C51	0497
BZX29C56	0863
BZX29C82	0327
BZX29C100	0098
BZX30-C3V3	OEM
BZX30-C3V6	OEM
BZX30-C3V9	OEM
BZX30-C4V3	OEM
BZX30-C4V7	OEM
BZX30-C5V1	OEM
BZX30-C5V6	OEM
BZX30-C6V2	OEM
BZX30-C6V8	OEM
BZX30-C7V5	OEM
BZX30-C8V2	OEM
BZX30-C9V1	OEM
BZX30-C10	OEM
BZX30-C11	OEM
BZX30-C12	OEM
BZX30-C13	OEM
BZX30-C15	OEM
BZX30-C16	OEM
BZX30-C18	OEM
BZX30-C20	OEM
BZX30-C22	OEM
BZX30-C24	OEM
BZX30-C27	OEM
BZX30-D15	OEM
BZX30-D18	OEM
BZX30-D22	OEM
BZX30-D27	OEM
BZX31-C3V6	OEM
BZX31-C3V9	OEM
BZX31-C4V3	OEM
BZX33	OEM
BZX33-C4V7	OEM
BZX34	OEM
BZX34-C5V1	OEM
BZX35	OEM
BZX35-C5V6	OEM
BZX36	OEM
BZX36-C6V2	OEM
BZX36-C6V8	OEM
BZX36-C7V5	OEM
BZX36-C8V2	OEM
BZX36-C9V1	OEM
BZX43	OEM
BZX44	OEM
BZX45	OEM
BZX46-C2V7	0755
BZX46-C3V0	0118
BZX46-C3V3	0296
BZX46-C3V6	0372
BZX46-C3V9	0036
BZX46-C4V3	0274
BZX46-C4V7	0140
BZX46-C5V1	0041
BZX46-C5V6	0253
BZX46-C6V2	0466
BZX46-C6V8	0062
BZX46-C7V5	0077
BZX46-C8V2	0165
BZX46-C9V1	0057
BZX46-C10	0064
BZX46-C11	0181
BZX46-C12	0052
BZX46-C13	0053
BZX46-C15	0681
BZX46-C16	0440
BZX46-C18	0371
BZX46-C20	0695
BZX46-C22	0700
BZX46-C24	0489
BZX46-C27	0450
BZX46-C30	0195
BZX46-C33	0166
BZX46-C36	0010
BZX46-C39	0032
BZX46-C43	0054
BZX46-C47	0068
BZX46-C51	0092
BZX46-C56	0125
BZX46-C62	0152
BZX46C2V7	0755
BZX46C3V	0118
BZX46C3V0	0118

If replacement code is OEM, contact original manufacturer for replacement.

303

DEVICE TYPE	REPL CODE
BZX46C3V3	0296
BZX46C3V6	0372
BZX46C3V9	0036
BZX46C4V3	0274
BZX46C4V7	0140
BZX46C5V1	0041
BZX46C5V6	0253
BZX46C6V2	0466
BZX46C6V8	0062
BZX46C7V5	0077
BZX46C8V2	0165
BZX46C9V1	0057
BZX46C10	0064
BZX46C11	0181
BZX46C12	0052
BZX46C13	0053
BZX46C15	0681
BZX46C16	0440
BZX46C18	0371
BZX46C20	0695
BZX46C22	0700
BZX46C24	0489
BZX46C27	0450
BZX46C30	0195
BZX46C33	0166
BZX46C36	0010
BZX46C39	0032
BZX46C43	0054
BZX46C47	0068
BZX46C51	0092
BZX46C56	0125
BZX46C62	0152
BZX46C68	0173
BZX46C75	0094
BZX46C82	0049
BZX46C91	0156
BZX46C100	0189
BZX46C110	0099
BZX47	0062
BZX48	OEM
BZX49	OEM
BZX50	OEM
BZX51	0165
BZX52	0165
BZX53	0165
BZX54	0165
BZX55-C0V8	OEM
BZX55-C2V4	1266
BZX55-C2V7	0755
BZX55-C3V0	0118
BZX55-C3V3	0296
BZX55-C3V6	0372
BZX55-C3V9	0036
BZX55-C4V3	0274
BZX55-C4V7	0140
BZX55-C5V1	0041
BZX55-C5V6	0253
BZX55-C6V2	0466
BZX55-C6V8	0062
BZX55-C7V5	0077
BZX55-C8V2	0165
BZX55-C9V1	0057
BZX55-C10	0064
BZX55-C11	0181
BZX55-C12	0052
BZX55-C13	0053
BZX55-C15	0681
BZX55-C16	0440
BZX55-C18	0371
BZX55-C20	0695
BZX55-C22	0700
BZX55-C24	0489
BZX55-C27	0450
BZX55-C30	0195
BZX55-C33	0166
BZX55-C36	0010
BZX55-C39	0010
BZX55-C43	0054
BZX55-C47	0068
BZX55-C51	0092
BZX55-C56	0125
BZX55-C62	0152
BZX55C08V	OEM
BZX55C0V8	OEM
BZX55C2V4	1266
BZX55C2V7	0755
BZX55C3V	0118
BZX55C3V0	0118
BZX55C3V3	0296
BZX55C3V6	0372
BZX55C3V9	0036
BZX55C4V3	0274
BZX55C4V7	0140
BZX55C5V1	0041
BZX55C5V6	0253
BZX55C6V2	0466
BZX55C6V8	0062
BZX55C7V5	0077
BZX55C8V2	0165
BZX55C9V1	0057
BZX55C10	0064
BZX55C10V	0064
BZX55C11	0181
BZX55C11V	0181
BZX55C12	0052
BZX55C12V	0052
BZX55C13	0053
BZX55C13V	0053
BZX55C15	0681
BZX55C15V	0681
BZX55C16	0440
BZX55C16V	0440
BZX55C18	0371
BZX55C18V	0371
BZX55C20	0695
BZX55C20V	0695
BZX55C22	0700
BZX55C22V	0700
BZX55C24	0489
BZX55C24V	0489
BZX55C27	0450
BZX55C27V	0450
BZX55C30	0195
BZX55C30V	0195
BZX55C33	0166
BZX55C33V	0166
BZX55C36	0010
BZX55C39	0032
BZX55C43	2301
BZX55C47	0068
BZX55C51	0092
BZX55C56	0125
BZX55C62	0152
BZX55C68	0173
BZX55C75	0094
BZX55C82	0049
BZX55C91	0156
BZX55C100	0189
BZX55C110	0099
BZX55C120	0285
BZX55C130	0285
BZX55C150	0336
BZX55C160	0366
BZX55C180	0420
BZX55C200	1464
BZX55D5V6	0870
BZX55D6V8	0205
BZX55D8V2	0499
BZX55D10	0225
BZX55V36	OEM
BZX57	OEM
BZX58-C6V8	0062
BZX58-C7V5	0077
BZX58-C8V2	0165
BZX58-C9V1	0057
BZX58-C10	0064
BZX58C6V8	0062
BZX58C7V5	0077
BZX58C8V2	0165
BZX58C9V1	0057
BZX58C10	0064
BZX59-C11	0181
BZX59-C13	0053
BZX59-C15	0681
BZX59-C16	0440
BZX59-C18	0371
BZX59-C20	0695
BZX59-C22	0700
BZX59-C24	0489
BZX59-C27	0450
BZX59C11	0181
BZX59C12	0052
BZX59C13	0053
BZX59C15	0681
BZX59C16	0440
BZX59C18	0371
BZX59C20	0695
BZX59C22	0700
BZX59C24	0489
BZX59C27	0450
BZX60-C30	0195
BZX60-C33	0166
BZX60-C36	0010
BZX60-C39	0032
BZX60-C43	0054
BZX60-C47	0068
BZX60-C51	0092
BZX60-C56	0125
BZX60C30	0195
BZX60C33	0166
BZX60C36	0010
BZX60C39	0032
BZX60C43	0054
BZX60C47	0068
BZX60C51	0092
BZX60C56	0125
BZX61-C3V6	0188
BZX61-C3V9	0451
BZX61-C4V3	0528
BZX61-C4V7	0446
BZX61-C5V1	0162
BZX61-C5V6	0157
BZX61-C6V2	0631
BZX61-C6V8	0025
BZX61-C7V5	0644
BZX61-C8V2	0244
BZX61-C9V1	0012
BZX61-C10	0170
BZX61-C11	0313
BZX61-C12	0137
BZX61-C13	0361
BZX61-C15	0002
BZX61-C16	0416
BZX61-C18	0490
BZX61-C20	0526
BZX61-C22	0560
BZX61-C24	0398
BZX61-C27	0436
BZX61-C30	0721
BZX61-C33	0039
BZX61-C36	0814
BZX61-C39	0346
BZX61-C43	0925
BZX61-C47	0993
BZX61-C51	0497
BZX61-C56	0863
BZX61-C62	0778
BZX61-C68	2144
BZX61-C75	1181
BZX61-C82	0327
BZX61C3V6	0791
BZX61C3V9	0801
BZX61C4V3	0815
BZX61C4V7	0827
BZX61C5V1	0437
BZX61C5V6	0870
BZX61C6V2	0185
BZX61C6V8	0205
BZX61C7V5	0475
BZX61C8V2	0499
BZX61C9	0225
BZX61C9V1	0679
BZX61C10	0225
BZX61C11	0230
BZX61C12	0234
BZX61C13	0237
BZX61C15	0247
BZX61C16	0251
BZX61C18	0256
BZX61C20	0526
BZX61C22	0269
BZX61C24	0273
BZX61C27	0291
BZX61C30	0305
BZX61C33	0314
BZX61C36	0316
BZX61C39	0322
BZX61C43	0333
BZX61C47	0343
BZX61C51	0027
BZX61C56	0266
BZX61C62	0382
BZX61C68	0401
BZX61C75	0421
BZX61C82	0439
BZX61C91	0238
BZX61C100	1172
BZX61C110	1182
BZX61C120	1198
BZX61C130	1209
BZX61C150	0642
BZX61C160	1246
BZX61C180	1269
BZX61C200	0600
BZX62	OEM
BZX63	OEM
BZX63C8V2	0244
BZX63C9V1	0012
BZX64	OEM
BZX64C11	0313
BZX64C12	0137
BZX64C13	0361
BZX64C15	0002
BZX64C16	0416
BZX64C18	0416
BZX64C20	0526
BZX64C22	0560
BZX64C24	0398
BZX64C27	0436
BZX65	OEM
BZX65C30	0721
BZX65C33	0039
BZX65C36	0814
BZX65C39	0346
BZX65C43	0925
BZX65C47	0993
BZX65C51	0497
BZX65C56	0863
BZX66	0025
BZX67-C12	OEM
BZX67-C13	OEM
BZX67-C15	OEM
BZX67-C16	OEM
BZX67-C18	OEM
BZX67-C20	OEM
BZX67-C22	OEM
BZX67-C24	OEM
BZX67-C27	OEM
BZX67-C30	OEM
BZX67-C33	OEM
BZX67-C36	OEM
BZX67-C39	OEM
BZX67-C43	OEM
BZX67-C47	OEM
BZX67-C51	OEM
BZX67-C56	OEM
BZX67-C62	OEM
BZX67-C68	OEM
BZX67-C75	OEM
BZX67-C82	OEM
BZX67-C91	OEM
BZX67-C100	OEM
BZX67-C120	OEM
BZX67-C130	OEM
BZX67-C150	OEM
BZX67-C160	OEM
BZX67-C180	OEM
BZX67-C200	OEM
BZX67C12	OEM
BZX67C13	OEM
BZX67C15	OEM
BZX67C16	OEM
BZX67C18	OEM
BZX67C20	OEM
BZX67C22	OEM
BZX67C24	OEM
BZX67C27	OEM
BZX67C30	OEM
BZX67C33	OEM
BZX67C36	OEM
BZX67C39	OEM
BZX67C43	OEM
BZX67C47	OEM
BZX67C51	OEM
BZX67C56	OEM
BZX67C62	OEM
BZX67C68	OEM
BZX67C75	OEM
BZX67C82	OEM
BZX67C91	OEM
BZX67C100	OEM
BZX67C110	OEM
BZX67C120	OEM
BZX67C130	OEM
BZX67C150	OEM
BZX67C160	OEM
BZX67C180	OEM
BZX67C200	OEM
BZX68-62A	OEM
BZX68-62B	OEM
BZX68-62C	OEM
BZX68C62A	OEM
BZX68C62B	OEM
BZX68C62C	OEM
BZX69-C7V5	0077
BZX69-C8V2	0165
BZX69-C9V2	0057
BZX69-C10	0064
BZX69-C11	0181
BZX69-C12	0052
BZX69C7V5	0644
BZX69C10	0170
BZX69C11	0313
BZX69C12	0137
BZX70-C7V5	0475
BZX70-C8V2	0499
BZX70-C9V2	0679
BZX70-C10	0225
BZX70-C11	0230
BZX70-C12	0234
BZX70-C13	0237
BZX70-C15	0247
BZX70-C16	0251
BZX70-C18	0256
BZX70-C20	0262
BZX70-C22	0269
BZX70-C24	0273
BZX70-C27	0291
BZX70-C30	0305
BZX70-C33	0314
BZX70-C36	0316
BZX70-C39	0322
BZX70-C43	0333
BZX70-C47	0343
BZX70-C51	0027
BZX70-C56	0266
BZX70-C62	0382
BZX70-C68	0401
BZX70-C75	0421
BZX70C7V5	0475
BZX70C8V2	0499
BZX70C9V1	0679
BZX70C10	0225
BZX70C11	0230
BZX70C12	0234
BZX70C13	0237
BZX70C15	0247
BZX70C16	0251
BZX70C18	0256
BZX70C20	0262
BZX70C22	0269
BZX70C24	0273
BZX70C27	0291
BZX70C30	0305
BZX70C33	0314
BZX70C36	0316
BZX70C39	0322
BZX70C43	0333
BZX70C47	0343
BZX70C51	0027
BZX70C56	0266
BZX70C62	0382
BZX70C68	0401
BZX70C75	0421
BZX71-B5V1	0041
BZX71-B5V6	0253
BZX71-B6V2	0466
BZX71-B6V8	0062
BZX71-B7V5	0077
BZX71-B8V2	0165
BZX71-B9V1	0057
BZX71-B10	0064
BZX71-B11	0181
BZX71-B12	0052
BZX71-B13	0053
BZX71-B15	0681
BZX71-B16	0440
BZX71-B18	0371
BZX71-B20	0695
BZX71-B22	0700
BZX71-B24	0489
BZX71-C5V1	0041
BZX71-C5V6	0253
BZX71-C6V2	0466
BZX71-C6V8	0062
BZX71-C7V5	0077
BZX71-C8V2	0165
BZX71-C9V1	0057
BZX71-C10	0064
BZX71-C11	0181
BZX71-C12	0052
BZX71-C13	0053
BZX71-C15	0681
BZX71-C16	0440
BZX71-C18	0371
BZX71-C20	0695
BZX71-C22	0700
BZX71-C24	0489
BZX71B5V1	0087
BZX71B5V6	0253
BZX71B6V2	0466
BZX71B6V8	0062
BZX71B7V5	0077
BZX71B8V2	0165
BZX71B9V1	0057
BZX71B10	0064
BZX71B11	0181
BZX71B12	0052
BZX71B13	0053
BZX71B15	0681
BZX71B16	0440
BZX71B18	0371
BZX71B20	0695
BZX71B22	0700
BZX71B24	0489
BZX71C5V1	0041
BZX71C5V6	0253
BZX71C6V2	0466
BZX71C6V8	0062
BZX71C7V5	0077
BZX71C8V2	0165
BZX71C9V1	0057
BZX71C10	0064
BZX71C11	0181
BZX71C12	0052
BZX71C13	0053
BZX71C15	0681
BZX71C16	0440
BZX71C18	0371
BZX71C20	0695
BZX71C22	0700
BZX71C24	0489
BZX72	0057
BZX72A	0057
BZX72B	0057
BZX72C	0057
BZX74-C5V6	0253
BZX74-C6V2	0466
BZX74-C6V8	0062
BZX74-C7V5	0077
BZX74-C8V2	0165
BZX74-C9V1	0057
BZX74-C10	0064
BZX74-C11	0181
BZX74-C12	0052
BZX74C5V6	0253
BZX74C6V2	0466
BZX74C6V8	0062
BZX74C7V5	0077
BZX74C8V2	0165
BZX74C9V1	0057
BZX74C10	2107
BZX74C11	0181
BZX74C12	0052
BZX75/C2V1	OEM
BZX75-C1V4	OEM
BZX75-C2V1	OEM
BZX75-C2V8	0672
BZX75-C3V6	0372
BZX75C1V4	OEM
BZX75C1V4PN	OEM
BZX75C2V1	OEM
BZX75C2V8	6798
BZX75C3V6	0372
BZX76	0053
BZX77-D5V6	OEM
BZX77-D5V6P	OEM
BZX77-D6V2	OEM
BZX77-D6V2P	OEM
BZX77-D6V8	OEM
BZX77-D6V8P	OEM
BZX77-D7V5	OEM
BZX77-D7V5P	OEM
BZX77-D8V2	OEM
BZX77-D8V2P	OEM
BZX77-D9V1	OEM
BZX77-D9V1P	OEM
BZX78C5V1	OEM
BZX78C5V6	OEM
BZX78C6V2	0631
BZX78C6V8	OEM
BZX78C7V5	OEM
BZX78C8V2	OEM
BZX78C9V1	0012
BZX78C10	OEM
BZX78C11	OEM
BZX78C12	0137
BZX78C13	OEM
BZX78C15	0002
BZX78C16	OEM
BZX78C18	OEM
BZX78C20	OEM
BZX78C22	OEM
BZX78C24	OEM
BZX78C27	OEM
BZX78C30	OEM
BZX78C33	OEM
BZX78C36	OEM
BZX78C39	OEM
BZX78C43	OEM
BZX78C47	OEM
BZX78C51	OEM
BZX78C56	OEM
BZX78C62	OEM
BZX78C68	OEM
BZX78C75	OEM
BZX79/C5V6	0253
BZX79/C6.8	0025
BZX79/C9V1	0057
BZX79/C12	0137
BZX79/C18	0490
BZX79/C24	0398
BZX79-B	OEM
BZX79-C4V7	0140
BZX79-C5V1	0041
BZX79-C5V6	0253
BZX79-C6V2	0466
BZX79-C6V8	0062
BZX79-C7V5	0644
BZX79-C7VS	0077
BZX79-C8V2	0165
BZX79-C9V1	0057
BZX79-C10	0064
BZX79-C11	0181
BZX79-C12	0052
BZX79-C13	0053
BZX79-C15	0681
BZX79-C16	0440
BZX79-C18	0371
BZX79-C20	0695
BZX79-C22	0700
BZX79-C24	0489
BZX79-C27	0450
BZX79-C30	0195
BZX79-C33	0166
BZX79-C36	0010
BZX79-C39	0032
BZX79-C43	0054
BZX79-C47	0068
BZX79-C51	0092
BZX79-C56	0125
BZX79-C62	0152
BZX79-C68	0173
BZX79-C75	0094
BZX79B2V4	OEM
BZX79B2V7	OEM
BZX79B3V0	OEM
BZX79B3V3	OEM
BZX79B3V6	OEM
BZX79B3V9	OEM
BZX79B4V3	OEM
BZX79B4V7	OEM
BZX79B5V1	0582
BZX79B5V6	0877
BZX79B6V2	0292
BZX79B6V8	0062
BZX79B6VB	0062
BZX79B7V5	OEM
BZX79B8V2	3071
BZX79B9V1	0057
BZX79B10	0248
BZX79B11	OEM
BZX79B12	0999
BZX79B12PH	OEM
BZX79B13	OEM
BZX79B15	OEM
BZX79B16	4851
BZX79B18	OEM
BZX79B20	OEM
BZX79B22	4855
BZX79B24	OEM
BZX79B27	OEM
BZX79B30	OEM
BZX79B33	OEM
BZX79B36	OEM
BZX79B39	OEM
BZX79B43	OEM
BZX79B47	OEM
BZX79B51	OEM
BZX79B56	OEM
BZX79B62	OEM
BZX79B68	OEM
BZX79B75	OEM
BZX79C2V4	1266
BZX79C2V5	OEM
BZX79C2V7	0755
BZX79C3V	0118
BZX79C3V0	0118
BZX79C3V3	0296
BZX79C3V6	0372
BZX79C3V9	0036
BZX79C4V3	0274
BZX79C4V7	0140
BZX79C5V1	0041
BZX79C5V6	0253
BZX79C6V2	0466
BZX79C6V8	0062
BZX79C7V5	0077
BZX79C8V2	0165
BZX79C9V1	0057
BZX79C10	0064
BZX79C11	0181
BZX79C12	0052
BZX79C13	0053
BZX79C15	0681
BZX79C15V	0681
BZX79C16	0440
BZX79C18	0371
BZX79C20	0695
BZX79C22	0700
BZX79C24	0489
BZX79C27	0450
BZX79C30	0195
BZX79C33	0166
BZX79C36	0010
BZX79C39	0032
BZX79C43	0054
BZX79C47	0068
BZX79C51	0092
BZX79C56	0125
BZX79C62	0152
BZX79C68	0173
BZX79C75	0094
BZX80-C6V8	0025
BZX80-C7V5	0644
BZX80-C8V2	0244
BZX80-C9V1	0012
BZX80-C10	0170
BZX81-C11	0313
BZX81-C12	0137
BZX81-C13	0361
BZX81-C15	0002
BZX81-C16	0416
BZX81-C18	0490
BZX81-C20	0526
BZX81-C22	0560
BZX81-C24	0398
BZX81-C27	0436
BZX82-C30	0721
BZX82-C33	0039
BZX82-C36	0814
BZX82-C39	0346
BZX82-C43	0925
BZX82-C47	0993
BZX82-C51	0497
BZX82-C56	0863
BZX83(6.2V)	OEM
BZX83-C0V8	OEM
BZX83-C2V4	1266
BZX83-C2V7	0755
BZX83-C3V0	0118
BZX83-C3V3	0296
BZX83-C3V6	0372
BZX83-C3V9	0036
BZX83-C4V3	0274
BZX83-C4V7	0140
BZX83-C5V1	0041
BZX83-C5V6	0253
BZX83-C6V2	0466
BZX83-C6V8	0062
BZX83-C7V5	0062
BZX83-C8V2	0165
BZX83-C9V1	0057
BZX83-C10	0064
BZX83-C11	0181
BZX83-C13	0053
BZX83-C15	0681
BZX83-C16	0440
BZX83-C18	0371
BZX83-C20	0695
BZX83-C22	0700
BZX83-C24	0489
BZX83-C27	0450
BZX83-C30	0195
BZX83-C33	0166
BZX83-C36	0010
BZX83-C39	0032
BZX83-C43	0054
BZX83-C47	0068
BZX83-C51	0092
BZX83-C56	0125
BZX83-C62	0152
BZX83C048	OEM
BZX83C0V8	OEM
BZX83C2V4	1266
BZX83C2V7	0755
BZX83C3V0	0118
BZX83C3V3	0296
BZX83C3V6	0372
BZX83C3V9	0036
BZX83C4V3	0274
BZX83C4V7	0140
BZX83C5V1	0041
BZX83C5V6	0253
BZX83C6V2	0466
BZX83C6V8	0062
BZX83C7V5	0077
BZX83C8V2	0165
BZX83C9V1	0057
BZX83C10	0064
BZX83C10V	0170
BZX83C11	0181
BZX83C11V	0313

If replacement code is OEM, contact original manufacturer for replacement.

DEVICE TYPE	REPL CODE
BZX83C12	0052
BZX83C12V	0137
BZX83C13	0053
BZX83C13V	0361
BZX83C15	0681
BZX83C15V	0002
BZX83C16	0440
BZX83C16V	0416
BZX83C18	0371
BZX83C18V	0490
BZX83C20	0695
BZX83C20V	0526
BZX83C22	0700
BZX83C22V	0560
BZX83C24	0489
BZX83C24V	0398
BZX83C27	0450
BZX83C27V	0436
BZX83C30	0195
BZX83C30V	0721
BZX83C33	0166
BZX83C33V	0039
BZX83C36	0010
BZX83C39	0032
BZX83C43	0054
BZX83C47	0068
BZX83C51	0092
BZX83C56	0125
BZX83C62	0152
BZX83C68	0173
BZX83C75	0094
BZX84-C4V7	0140
BZX84-C5V1	0041
BZX84-C5V6	0253
BZX84-C6V2	0466
BZX84-C6V8	0062
BZX84-C7V5	0077
BZX84-C8V2	0165
BZX84-C9V1	0057
BZX84-C10	OEM
BZX84-C11	OEM
BZX84-C12	OEM
BZX84C2V4	1266
BZX84C2V7	0755
BZX84C3V0	0118
BZX84C3V3	0296
BZX84C3V6	0372
BZX84C3V9	0036
BZX84C4V3	0274
BZX84C4V7	0140
BZX84C5V1	0041
BZX84C5V6	0253
BZX84C6V2	0466
BZX84C6V8	0062
BZX84C7V5	0077
BZX84C8V2	0165
BZX84C9V1	0057
BZX84C10	OEM
BZX84C11	OEM
BZX84C12	0052
BZX84C13	OEM
BZX84C15	OEM
BZX84C16	OEM
BZX84C18	OEM
BZX84C20	OEM
BZX84C22	OEM
BZX84C24	OEM
BZX84C27	0450
BZX84C30	0195
BZX84C33	0166
BZX84C36	0166
BZX84C39	0032
BZX84C43	0054
BZX84C47	0068
BZX84C51	0092
BZX84C56	0125
BZX84C62	0152
BZX84C68	0173
BZX84C75	0094
BZX85-C2V7	1302
BZX85-C3V0	1703
BZX85-C3V3	0777
BZX85-C3V6	0791
BZX85-C3V9	0801
BZX85-C4V3	0815
BZX85-C4V7	0827
BZX85-C5V1	0437
BZX85-C5V6	0870
BZX85-C6V2	0185
BZX85-C6V8	0205
BZX85-C7V5	0475
BZX85-C8V2	0499
BZX85-C9V1	0679
BZX85-C10	0225
BZX85-C11	0230
BZX85-C12	0234
BZX85-C13	0237
BZX85-C15	0247
BZX85-C16	0251
BZX85-C18	0256
BZX85-C20	0262
BZX85-C22	0269
BZX85-C24	0273
BZX85-C27	0291
BZX85-C30	0305
BZX85-C33	0314
BZX85-C36	0316
BZX85-C39	0322
BZX85-C43	0333

DEVICE TYPE	REPL CODE
BZX85-C47	0343
BZX85-C51	0027
BZX85-C56	0266
BZX85-C62	0382
BZX85C2V7	1302
BZX85C3V0	1703
BZX85C3V3	0289
BZX85C3V6	0188
BZX85C3V8	0451
BZX85C3V9	0451
BZX85C4V3	0528
BZX85C4V7	0446
BZX85C5V1	0162
BZX85C5V6	0157
BZX85C6V2	0631
BZX85C6V8	0025
BZX85C7V5	0644
BZX85C8V1	0244
BZX85C8V2	0244
BZX85C9V1	0057
BZX85C10	0170
BZX85C11	0313
BZX85C11V	0230
BZX85C12	0137
BZX85C12V	0234
BZX85C13	0361
BZX85C13V	0237
BZX85C15	0002
BZX85C15V	0247
BZX85C16	0416
BZX85C16V	0251
BZX85C18	0490
BZX85C18V	0256
BZX85C20	0526
BZX85C20V	0262
BZX85C22	0560
BZX85C22V	0269
BZX85C24	0398
BZX85C24V	0273
BZX85C27	1596
BZX85C27V	0291
BZX85C30	0721
BZX85C30V	0305
BZX85C33	0039
BZX85C33V	0314
BZX85C36	0814
BZX85C39	0346
BZX85C43	0925
BZX85C47	0993
BZX85C51	0497
BZX85C56	0863
BZX85C62	0778
BZX85C68	2144
BZX85C75	1181
BZX85C82	0327
BZX85C91	1301
BZX85C100	0098
BZX85C110	0149
BZX85C120	0186
BZX85C130	0213
BZX85C150	0028
BZX85C160	0255
BZX85C180	0363
BZX85C200	0600
BZX86-E36	OEM
BZX87-C4V7	0827
BZX87-C5V1	0437
BZX87-C5V6	0870
BZX87-C6V2	0185
BZX87-C6V8	0205
BZX87-C7V5	0475
BZX87-C8V2	0499
BZX87-C9V1	0679
BZX87-C10	0225
BZX87-C11	0230
BZX87-C12	0234
BZX87-C13	0237
BZX87-C15	0247
BZX87-C16	0251
BZX87-C18	0256
BZX87-C20	0262
BZX87-C22	0269
BZX87-C24	0273
BZX87-C27	0291
BZX87-C30	0305
BZX87-C33	0314
BZX87-C36	0316
BZX87-C39	0322
BZX87-C43	0333
BZX87-C47	0343
BZX87-C51	0027
BZX87-C56	0266
BZX87-C62	0382
BZX87-C68	0401
BZX87-C75	0421
BZX87C5V1	0437
BZX87C5V6	0870
BZX87C6V2	0185
BZX87C6V8	0205
BZX87C7V5	0475
BZX87C8V2	0499
BZX87C9V1	0679
BZX87C10	0225
BZX87C11	0230
BZX87C12	0234
BZX87C13	0237
BZX87C15	0247
BZX87C16	0251
BZX87C18	0256

DEVICE TYPE	REPL CODE
BZX87C20	0262
BZX87C22	0269
BZX87C24	0273
BZX87C27	0291
BZX87C30	0305
BZX87C33	0314
BZX87C36	0316
BZX87C39	0322
BZX87C43	0333
BZX87C47	0343
BZX87C51	0027
BZX87C56	0266
BZX87C62	0382
BZX87C68	0401
BZX87C75	0421
BZX88-C4V7	0140
BZX88-C5V1	0041
BZX88-C5V6	0253
BZX88-C6V2	0466
BZX88-C6V8	0062
BZX88-C7V5	0077
BZX88-C8V2	0165
BZX88-C9V1	0057
BZX88-C10	OEM
BZX88-C11	OEM
BZX88-C12	OEM
BZX88C2V7	0755
BZX88C3V0	0118
BZX88C3V3	0296
BZX88C3V6	0372
BZX88C3V9	0036
BZX88C4V3	0274
BZX88C4V7	0140
BZX88C5V1	0041
BZX88C5V6	0253
BZX88C6V2	0466
BZX88C6V8	0062
BZX88C7V5	0077
BZX88C9V1	0057
BZX88C10	0064
BZX88C11	0181
BZX88C12	0052
BZX88C13	0053
BZX88C15	0681
BZX88C16	0440
BZX88C18	0371
BZX88C20	0695
BZX88C22	0700
BZX88C24	0489
BZX88C27	0450
BZX88C30	0195
BZX88C33	0166
BZX88C36	0010
BZX88C39	0032
BZX88C43	0054
BZX88C47	0068
BZX90	0062
BZX91	0062
BZX92	0062
BZX93	0062
BZX94	0062
BZX95-C5V6	0253
BZX95-C6V2	0466
BZX95-C6V8	0062
BZX95-C7V5	0077
BZX95-C8V2	0165
BZX95-C9V1	0057
BZX95-C10	0064
BZX95-C11	0181
BZX95-C12	0052
BZX95-C13	0053
BZX95C-4V7	0140
BZX95C-5V1	0041
BZX95C-5V6	0253
BZX95C-6V2	0466
BZX95C-6V8	0062
BZX95C-7V5	0077
BZX95C-8V2	0165
BZX95C-9V1	0057
BZX95C-10	0064
BZX95C-11	0181
BZX95C-12	0052
BZX95C-13	0053
BZX95C-15	0681
BZX95C-16	0440
BZX95C-18	0371
BZX95C-20	0695
BZX95C-22	0700
BZX95C-24	0489
BZX95C-27	0450
BZX95C-30	0195
BZX95C-33	0166
BZX95C-36	0010
BZX96-C2V7	0755
BZX96-C3	0118
BZX96-C3V3	0296
BZX96-C3V6	0372
BZX96-C3V9	0036
BZX96-C4V3	0274
BZX96-C4V7	0140
BZX96-C5V1	0041
BZX96-C5V6	0253
BZX96-C6V2	0466
BZX96-C6V8	0062
BZX96-C7V5	0077
BZX96-C8V2	0165
BZX96-C9V1	0057
BZX96-C10	0064
BZX96-C11	0181

DEVICE TYPE	REPL CODE
BZX96-C12	0052
BZX96-C13	0053
BZX96-C15	0681
BZX96-C16	0440
BZX96-C18	0371
BZX96-C20	0695
BZX96-C22	0700
BZX96-C24	0489
BZX96-C27	0450
BZX96-C30	0195
BZX96-C33	0166
BZX96C2V7	0755
BZX96C3	0118
BZX96C3V3	0296
BZX96C3V6	0188
BZX96C3V9	0036
BZX96C4V3	0274
BZX96C4V7	0140
BZX96C5V1	0041
BZX96C5V6	0253
BZX96C6V2	0466
BZX96C6V8	0062
BZX96C7V5	0077
BZX96C8V2	0165
BZX96C9V1	0057
BZX96C10	0064
BZX96C11	0181
BZX96C12	0052
BZX96C13	0053
BZX96C15	0681
BZX96C16	0440
BZX96C18	0371
BZX96C20	0695
BZX96C22	0700
BZX96C24	0489
BZX96C27	0450
BZX96C30	0195
BZX96C33	0166
BZX97-C0V8	OEM
BZX97-C2V4	1266
BZX97-C2V7	0755
BZX97-C3V0	0118
BZX97-C3V3	0296
BZX97-C3V6	0372
BZX97-C3V9	0036
BZX97-C4V3	0274
BZX97-C4V7	0140
BZX97-C5V1	0041
BZX97-C5V6	0253
BZX97-C6V2	0466
BZX97-C6V8	0062
BZX97-C7V5	0077
BZX97-C8V2	0165
BZX97-C9V1	0057
BZX97-C10	0064
BZX97-C11	0181
BZX97-C12	0052
BZX97-C13	0053
BZX97-C15	0681
BZX97-C16	0440
BZX97-C18	0371
BZX97-C20	0695
BZX97-C22	0700
BZX97-C24	0489
BZX97-C27	0450
BZX97-C30	0195
BZX97-C33	0166
BZX97C0V8	OEM
BZX97C2V4	1266
BZX97C2V7	0755
BZX97C3V0	0118
BZX97C3V3	0296
BZX97C3V6	0372
BZX97C3V9	0036
BZX97C4V3	0274
BZX97C4V7	0140
BZX97C5V1	0041
BZX97C5V6	0253
BZX97C6V2	0466
BZX97C6V8	0062
BZX97C7V5	0077
BZX97C8V2	0165
BZX97C9V1	0057
BZX97C10	0064
BZX97C11	0181
BZX97C12	0052
BZX97C13	0053
BZX97C15	0681
BZX97C16	0440
BZX97C18	0371
BZX97C20	0695
BZX97C22	0700
BZX97C24	0489
BZX97C27	0450
BZX97C30	0195
BZX97C33	0166
BZX97C36	0010
BZX97C39	0032
BZX97C43	0054
BZX97C47	0068
BZX98C3V9	OEM
BZX98C4V3	OEM
BZX98C4V7	OEM
BZX98C5V1	OEM
BZX98C5V6	OEM
BZX98C6V2	OEM
BZX98C6V8	OEM
BZX98C7V5	OEM
BZX98C8V2	OEM

DEVICE TYPE	REPL CODE
BZX98C9V1	OEM
BZX98C10	OEM
BZX98C11	OEM
BZX98C12	OEM
BZX98C13	OEM
BZX98C15	OEM
BZX98C16	OEM
BZX98C18	OEM
BZX98C20	1540
BZX98C22	OEM
BZX98C24	OEM
BZX98C27	OEM
BZX98C30	OEM
BZX98C33	OEM
BZX98C36	OEM
BZX98C39	OEM
BZX98C43	OEM
BZX98C47	OEM
BZX98C51	OEM
BZX98C56	OEM
BZX98C62	OEM
BZX98C68	OEM
BZX98C75	OEM
BZX98C82	OEM
BZX98C91	OEM
BZX98C100	OEM
BZX98C110	OEM
BZX98C120	OEM
BZX98C130	OEM
BZX98C150	OEM
BZX98C160	OEM
BZX98C180	OEM
BZX98C200	OEM
BZX79812	OEM
BZY16C6V8	0205
BZY16C7V5	0475
BZY16C8V2	0499
BZY16C9V1	0679
BZY16C10	0225
BZY16C11	0230
BZY16C12	0234
BZY16C13	0237
BZY16C15	0247
BZY16C16	0251
BZY16C18	0256
BZY16C20	0262
BZY16C22	0269
BZY16C24	0273
BZY16C27	0291
BZY16C30	0305
BZY16C33	0314
BZY16C36	0316
BZY16C39	0322
BZY16C43	0333
BZY16C47	0343
BZY16C51	0027
BZY16C56	0266
BZY16C62	0382
BZY16C68	0401
BZY16C75	0421
BZY16C82	0439
BZY16C91	0238
BZY16C100	1172
BZY17C5V6	0253
BZY17C6V2	0466
BZY17C6V8	0062
BZY17C7V5	0077
BZY17C8V2	0165
BZY17C9V1	0057
BZY17C10	0064
BZY17C11	0181
BZY17C12	0052
BZY17C13	0053
BZY17C15	0681
BZY17C16	0440
BZY17C18	0371
BZY17C20	0695
BZY17C22	0700
BZY17C24	0489
BZY17C27	0450
BZY17C30	0195
BZY17C33	0166
BZY17C36	0010
BZY17C39	0032
BZY17C43	0054
BZY17C47	0068
BZY17C51	0092
BZY17C56	0125
BZY18	0137
BZY18C5V6	0157
BZY18C6V2	0631
BZY18C6V8	0025
BZY18C7V5	0644
BZY18C8V2	0244
BZY18C9V1	0012
BZY18C10	0170
BZY18C11	0789
BZY18C12	0137
BZY19	0002
BZY22	0165
BZY23	0165
BZY24	0165
BZY25	0165
BZY29C33	0039
BZY56	0446
BZY57	0041
BZY58	0157
BZY59	0631
BZY60	0025

DEVICE TYPE	REPL CODE
BZY61	0644
BZY62	0244
BZY63	0012
BZY64	0274
BZY65	0041
BZY66	0466
BZY67	0077
BZY68	0057
BZY69	0052
BZY70	0165
BZY71	OEM
BZY74	0691
BZY75	1606
BZY76	0622
BZY78	0253
BZY78P	0253
BZY83/C5V1	0162
BZY83/C5V6	0157
BZY83/C10	0170
BZY83/C15	0002
BZY83/C16	0002
BZY83/D5V6	0157
BZY83/D10	0170
BZY83/D15	0002
BZY83-C4V7	0140
BZY83-C5V1	0041
BZY83-C5V6	0253
BZY83-C6V2	0466
BZY83-C6V8	0062
BZY83-C7V5	0077
BZY83-C8V2	0165
BZY83-C9V1	0057
BZY83-C10	0064
BZY83-C11	0181
BZY83-C12	0052
BZY83-C13	0053
BZY83-C15	0681
BZY83-C16	0440
BZY83-C18	0371
BZY83-C20	0695
BZY83-C22	0700
BZY83-C24	0489
BZY83-D1	OEM
BZY83-D4V7	0140
BZY83-D5V6	0253
BZY83-D6V8	0062
BZY83-D8V2	0165
BZY83-D10	0064
BZY83-D12	0052
BZY83-D15	0681
BZY83-D18	0371
BZY83-D22	0700
BZY83C4V7	0140
BZY83C5V1	0041
BZY83C5V6	0253
BZY83C6V2	0466
BZY83C6V8	0062
BZY83C7V5	0077
BZY83C8V2	0165
BZY83C9V1	0057
BZY83C10	0064
BZY83C11	0181
BZY83C12	0052
BZY83C13V5	0053
BZY83C15	0681
BZY83C16	0002
BZY83C16V5	0210
BZY83C18	0371
BZY83C20	0695
BZY83C22	0700
BZY83C24V5	0709
BZY83D1	OEM
BZY83D4V7	0140
BZY83D5V6	0253
BZY83D6V8	0062
BZY83D8V2	0165
BZY83D10	0064
BZY83D12	0052
BZY83D15	0681
BZY83D18	0371
BZY83D22	0700
BZY84D1	OEM
BZY84D5V6	1436
BZY84D6V8	1449
BZY84D8V2	1481
BZY84D10	1608
BZY84D12	0052
BZY85/C3V6	0188
BZY85/C5V1	0162
BZY85/C5V6	0157
BZY85/C10	0170
BZY85/C15	0002
BZY85/C27	0436
BZY85/D5V6	0157
BZY85/D10	0170
BZY85/D15	0002
BZY85-C4V7	0140
BZY85-C5V6	0253
BZY85-C6V1	0466
BZY85-C6V2	0466
BZY85-C6V8	0062
BZY85-C7V5	0077
BZY85-C8V2	0165
BZY85-C9V1	0057
BZY85-C10	0064
BZY85-C11	0181
BZY85-C12	0052
BZY85-C13	0053
BZY85-C15	0681

DEVICE TYPE	REPL CODE
BZY85-C16	0440
BZY85-C18	0371
BZY85-C20	0695
BZY85-C22	0700
BZY85-C24	0489
BZY85-D1	OEM
BZY85-D4V7	0140
BZY85-D5V6	0253
BZY85-D6V8	0062
BZY85-D8V2	0165
BZY85-D10	0064
BZY85-D12	0052
BZY85-D15	0681
BZY85-D18	0371
BZY85-D22	0700
BZY85B2V7	0755
BZY85B3	OEM
BZY85B3V3	0289
BZY85B3V6	OEM
BZY85B3V9	OEM
BZY85B4V3	OEM
BZY85B4V7	OEM
BZY85B5V6	OEM
BZY85B6V2	0466
BZY85B6V8	5898
BZY85B7V5	5907
BZY85B8V2	5912
BZY85B9V1	4171
BZY85B10	0248
BZY85B11	OEM
BZY85B12	0999
BZY85B13	OEM
BZY85B15	0681
BZY85B16	OEM
BZY85B18	OEM
BZY85B20	OEM
BZY85B22	OEM
BZY85B24	OEM
BZY85B27	OEM
BZY85B30	OEM
BZY85B33	OEM
BZY85C2V7	1302
BZY85C3	1703
BZY85C3V3	0289
BZY85C3V6	0188
BZY85C3V9	0451
BZY85C4V3	0528
BZY85C4V7	0446
BZY85C5V1	0041
BZY85C5V6	0157
BZY85C6V2	0466
BZY85C6V8	0062
BZY85C7V5	0077
BZY85C8V2	0165
BZY85C9V1	0057
BZY85C10	0064
BZY85C11	0181
BZY85C12	0052
BZY85C13	0053
BZY85C13V5	0053
BZY85C15	0681
BZY85C16	0440
BZY85C16V5	0440
BZY85C18	0371
BZY85C20	0695
BZY85C22	0700
BZY85C24	0398
BZY85C24V5	0489
BZY85C27	0436
BZY85C30	0721
BZY85C33	0166
BZY85D1	OEM
BZY85D4V7	0140
BZY85D5V6	0253
BZY85D6V8	0062
BZY85D8V2	0165
BZY85D10	0064
BZY85D12	0052
BZY85D15	0681
BZY85D18	0371
BZY85D22	0700
BZY87	OEM
BZY87-0V7	OEM
BZY87-1V4	OEM
BZY87-2V1	OEM
BZY87-2V8	0672
BZY87-3V4	0296
BZY88/C4V7	0157
BZY88/C5V1	0162
BZY88/C5V6	0157
BZY88/C6V2	0631
BZY88/C9V1	0012
BZY88/C9V5	0012
BZY88/C9V7	0162
BZY88-C1V3	OEM
BZY88-C2V7	0755
BZY88-C3V0	0118
BZY88-C3V3	0296
BZY88-C3V6	0372
BZY88-C3V9	0036
BZY88-C4V3	0274
BZY88-C4V7	0140
BZY88-C5V1	0041
BZY88-C5V6	0253
BZY88-C6V2	0466
BZY88-C6V8	0062
BZY88-C7V5	0077
BZY88-C8V2	0165
BZY88-C9V1	0057

If replacement code is OEM, contact original manufacturer for replacement.

305

DEVICE TYPE	REPL CODE
BZY88-C10	0064
BZY88-C11	0181
BZY88-C12	0052
BZY88-C13	0053
BZY88-C15	0681
BZY88-C16	0440
BZY88-C18	0371
BZY88-C20	0695
BZY88-C22	0700
BZY88-C24	0489
BZY88-C27	0450
BZY88-C30	0195
BZY88-C33	0166
BZY88C2V7	0755
BZY88C2V9	0672
BZY88C3V0	0118
BZY88C3V1	0118
BZY88C3V3	0296
BZY88C3V6	0372
BZY88C3V9	0036
BZY88C4V3	0274
BZY88C4V7	0140
BZY88C5V1	0041
BZY88C5V6	0253
BZY88C6V2	0466
BZY88C6V8	0062
BZY88C7V5	0077
BZY88C8V2	0165
BZY88C9V1	0057
BZY88C10	0064
BZY88C10V	0064
BZY88C11	0181
BZY88C11V	0181
BZY88C12	0137
BZY88C12V	0052
BZY88C13	0053
BZY88C13V	0053
BZY88C15	0681
BZY88C15V	0681
BZY88C16	0440
BZY88C16V	0440
BZY88C18	0371
BZY88C18V	0371
BZY88C20	0695
BZY88C20V	0695
BZY88C22	0700
BZY88C22V	0700
BZY88C24	0489
BZY88C24V	0489
BZY88C27	0450
BZY88C27V	0450
BZY88C30	0195
BZY88C30V	0195
BZY88C33	0166
BZY88C33V	0166
BZY91-4	OEM
BZY91-C7V5	OEM
BZY91-C8V2	OEM
BZY91-C9V1	OEM
BZY91-C10	OEM
BZY91-C11	OEM
BZY91-C12	OEM
BZY91-C13	OEM
BZY91-C15	OEM
BZY91-C16	OEM
BZY91-C18	OEM
BZY91-C20	OEM
BZY91-C22	OEM
BZY91-C24	OEM
BZY91-C27	OEM
BZY91-C30	OEM
BZY91-C33	OEM
BZY91-C36	OEM
BZY91-C39	OEM
BZY91-C43	OEM
BZY91-C47	OEM
BZY91-C51	OEM
BZY91-C56	OEM
BZY91-C62	OEM
BZY91-C68	OEM
BZY91-C75	OEM
BZY91C7V5	OEM
BZY91C8V2	OEM
BZY91C9V1	OEM
BZY91C10	OEM
BZY91C11	OEM
BZY91C12	OEM
BZY91C13	OEM
BZY91C15	OEM
BZY91C16	OEM
BZY91C18	OEM
BZY91C20	1540
BZY91C22	OEM
BZY91C24	OEM
BZY91C27	OEM
BZY91C30	OEM
BZY91C33	OEM
BZY91C36	OEM
BZY91C39	OEM
BZY91C43	OEM
BZY91C47	OEM
BZY91C51	OEM
BZY91C56	OEM
BZY91C62	OEM
BZY91C68	OEM
BZY91C75	OEM
BZY92/C5V1	0162
BZY92/C5V6	0157
BZY92/C15	0002
BZY92/C27	0436
BZY92-C3V9	0801
BZY92-C4V3	0815
BZY92-C4V7	0827
BZY92-C5V1	0437
BZY92-C5V6	0870
BZY92-C6V2	0185
BZY92-C6V8	0205
BZY92-C7V5	0475
BZY92-C8V2	0499
BZY92-C9V1	0679
BZY92-C10	0225
BZY92-C11	0230
BZY92-C12	0234
BZY92-C13	0237
BZY92-C15	0247
BZY92-C16	0251
BZY92-C18	0256
BZY92-C20	0262
BZY92-C22	0269
BZY92-C24	0273
BZY92-C27	0291
BZY92-C30	0305
BZY92-C33	0314
BZY92-C36	0316
BZY92C3V9	0451
BZY92C4V3	0528
BZY92C4V7	0446
BZY92C5V1	0162
BZY92C5V6	0157
BZY92C6V2	0631
BZY92C6V8	0025
BZY92C7V5	0644
BZY92C8V2	0244
BZY92C9V1	0012
BZY92C10	0170
BZY92C11	0313
BZY92C12	0137
BZY92C13	0361
BZY92C15	0002
BZY92C16	0416
BZY92C18	0490
BZY92C20	0526
BZY92C22	0560
BZY92C24	0398
BZY92C27	0436
BZY92C30	0721
BZY92C33	0039
BZY92C36	0814
BZY93-C4	OEM
BZY93-C7V5	OEM
BZY93-C8V2	OEM
BZY93-C9V1	OEM
BZY93-C10	OEM
BZY93-C11	OEM
BZY93-C12	OEM
BZY93-C13	OEM
BZY93-C15	OEM
BZY93-C16	OEM
BZY93-C18	OEM
BZY93-C20	OEM
BZY93-C22	OEM
BZY93-C24	OEM
BZY93-C27	OEM
BZY93-C30	OEM
BZY93-C33	OEM
BZY93-C36	OEM
BZY93-C39	OEM
BZY93-C43	OEM
BZY93-C47	OEM
BZY93-C51	OEM
BZY93-C56	OEM
BZY93-C62	OEM
BZY93-C68	OEM
BZY93-C75	OEM
BZY93C6V8	2713
BZY93C7V5	2717
BZY93C8V2	1216
BZY93C9V1	1228
BZY93C10	1243
BZY93C11	1259
BZY93C12	1267
BZY93C13	1283
BZY93C15	1292
BZY93C16	1300
BZY93C18	2719
BZY93C20	1323
BZY93C22	1334
BZY93C24	1346
BZY93C27	1361
BZY93C30	1377
BZY93C33	1396
BZY93C36	1405
BZY93C39	1419
BZY93C43	1431
BZY93C47	2749
BZY93C51	1452
BZY93C56	1465
BZY93C62	0608
BZY93C68	1502
BZY93C75	1515
BZY94/C12	0137
BZY94/C15	0002
BZY94-C10	0064
BZY94-C11	0181
BZY94-C12	0052
BZY94-C13	0053
BZY94-C15	0681
BZY94-C16	0440
BZY94-C18	0371
BZY94-C20	0695
BZY94-C22	0700
BZY94-C24	0489
BZY94-C27	0450
BZY94-C30	0195
BZY94-C33	0166
BZY94-C36	0010
BZY94-C39	0032
BZY94-C43	0054
BZY94-C47	0068
BZY94-C51	0092
BZY94-C56	0125
BZY94-C62	0152
BZY94-C68	0173
BZY94-C75	0094
BZY94C10	0064
BZY94C11	0181
BZY94C12	0052
BZY94C13	0053
BZY94C15	0681
BZY94C16	0440
BZY94C18	0371
BZY94C20	0695
BZY94C22	0700
BZY94C24	0489
BZY94C27	0450
BZY94C30	0195
BZY94C33	0166
BZY94C36	0010
BZY94C39	0032
BZY94C43	0054
BZY94C47	0068
BZY94C51	0099
BZY94C56	0125
BZY94C62	0152
BZY94C68	0173
BZY94C75	0094
BZY95-C10	0225
BZY95-C11	0230
BZY95-C12	0234
BZY95-C13	0237
BZY95-C15	0247
BZY95-C16	0251
BZY95-C18	0256
BZY95-C20	0262
BZY95-C22	0269
BZY95-C24	0273
BZY95-C27	0291
BZY95-C30	0305
BZY95-C33	0314
BZY95-C36	0343
BZY95-C39	0322
BZY95-C43	0333
BZY95-C47	0343
BZY95-C51	0027
BZY95-C56	0266
BZY95-C62	0382
BZY95-C68	0401
BZY95-C75	0421
BZY95C10	0225
BZY95C11	0230
BZY95C12	0234
BZY95C13	0237
BZY95C15	0247
BZY95C16	0251
BZY95C18	0256
BZY95C20	0262
BZY95C22	0269
BZY95C24	0273
BZY95C27	0291
BZY95C30	0305
BZY95C33	0314
BZY95C36	0316
BZY95C39	0322
BZY95C43	0333
BZY95C47	0343
BZY95C51	0027
BZY95C56	0266
BZY95C62	0382
BZY95C68	0401
BZY95C75	0421
BZY96-C4V7	0827
BZY96-C5V1	0437
BZY96-C5V6	0870
BZY96-C6V2	0185
BZY96-C6V8	0205
BZY96-C7V5	0475
BZY96-C8V2	0499
BZY96-C9V1	0679
BZY96-C10	0225
BZY96C4V7	0827
BZY96C5V1	0437
BZY96C5V6	0870
BZY96C6V2	0185
BZY96C6V8	0205
BZY96C7V5	0475
BZY96C8V2	0499
BZY96C9V1	0679
BZY96C10	0225
BZY96V9V1	OEM
BZY97C3V3	0777
BZY97C3V6	0791
BZY97C3V9	0801
BZY97C4V3	0815
BZY97C4V7	0827
BZY97C5V1	0437
BZY97C5V6	0870
BZY97C6V2	0185
BZY97C6V8	0205
BZY97C7V5	0475
BZY97C8V2	0499
BZY97C9V1	0679
BZY97C10	0225
BZY97C10V	0225
BZY97C11	0230
BZY97C11V	0230
BZY97C12	0234
BZY97C12V	0234
BZY97C13	0237
BZY97C13V	0237
BZY97C15	0247
BZY97C15V	0247
BZY97C16	0251
BZY97C16V	0251
BZY97C18	0256
BZY97C18V	0256
BZY97C20	0262
BZY97C20V	0262
BZY97C22	0269
BZY97C22V	0269
BZY97C24	0273
BZY97C24V	0273
BZY97C27	0291
BZY97C27V	0291
BZY97C30	0305
BZY97C30V	0305
BZY97C33	0314
BZY97C33V	0314
BZY97C36	0316
BZY97C36V	0316
BZY97C39	0322
BZY97C39V	0322
BZY97C43	0262
BZY97C43V	0262
BZY97C47	0269
BZY97C47V	0269
BZY97C51	0027
BZY97C51V	0027
BZY97C56	0266
BZY97C56V	0266
BZY97C62	0382
BZY97C62V	0382
BZY97C68	0401
BZY97C68V	0401
BZY97C75	0421
BZY97C75V	0421
BZY97C82	0439
BZY97C82V	0439
BZY97C91	0238
BZY97C91V	0238
BZY97C100	1172
BZY97C100V	1172
BZY97C110	1182
BZY97C110V	1182
BZY97C120	1198
BZY97C120V	1198
BZY97C130	1209
BZY97C130V	1209
BZY97C150	0642
BZY97C150V	0642
BZY97C160	1246
BZY97C160V	1246
BZY97C180	1269
BZY97C180V	1269
BZY97C200	0600
BZY97C200V	0600
BZZ10	0091
BZZ11	0062
BZZ12	0077
BZZ13	0165
BZZ14	1436
BZZ15	0691
BZZ16	1591
BZZ17	1606
BZZ18	1612
BZZ19	0622
BZZ20	0986
BZZ21	0989
BZZ22	1254
BZZ23	1240
BZZ24	1629
BZZ25	1693
BZZ26	1706
BZZ27	1720
BZZ28	0722
BZZ29	1745
C006001D	OEM
C006001E	OEM
C006001F	OEM
C006001G	OEM
C006001H	OEM
C006004D	OEM
C006004E	OEM
C006004F	OEM
C006004G	OEM
C006004H	OEM
C006010D	OEM
C006010E	OEM
C006010F	OEM
C006010G	OEM
C0-10750	1962
C0-10816	0394
C02	0244
C03	OEM
C05-03C	0196
C05-06A	OEM
C05-10	0071
C06C	0015
C08P1	0196
C08P1R	1073
C047-52	OEM
C049	0535
C055	OEM
C055P	OEM
C066	OEM
C066P	OEM
C0102	OEM
C0102L7	0071
C0406	0559
C0410	0071
C0410V	0071
C0508	0071
C0510	0071
C0615	0158
C-0799	OEM
C0900P	2542
C0901P	2964
C0902P	2417
C0903P	2986
C0904P	2334
C0905P	2574
C0906P	3003
C0907P	3010
C0908P	3016
C0909P	0078
C0910P	3025
C0911P	3037
C0912P	2964
C03051	OEM
C03069	OEM
C04075	OEM
C010174	6657
C010174-02	1686
C010444	OEM
C010444-22	OEM
C010444D-01	OEM
C010745-03	3041
C010745-12	3041
C010750-03	1962
C010750-12	OEM
C010816	0394
C010816-01	0394
C011298	OEM
C011299	OEM
C011299B-03	OEM
C011464	OEM
C012099	OEM
C012294	OEM
C012294-22	OEM
C012294-31	OEM
C012294B-01	OEM
C012295-03	OEM
C012296D-03	OEM
C012296D-22	OEM
C012298	OEM
C012399	OEM
C012399B-08	OEM
C012499	OEM
C012499B-01	OEM
C014311	OEM
C014312	OEM
C014313	5803
C014329	OEM
C014331-09	0518
C014332	OEM
C014333	OEM
C014336	0362
C014344	5655
C014345	1646
C014347	OEM
C014348	0619
C014349	OEM
C014351	OEM
C014361	OEM
C014362	OEM
C014363	OEM
C014377	6969
C014377-06	OEM
C014599	OEM
C014599B12	OEM
C014776	OEM
C014777	OEM
C014786	OEM
C014795	3036
C014795-12	OEM
C014805	OEM
C014805-01	OEM
C014805-22	OEM
C014805-31	OEM
C014806	3036
C014806-03	3036
C014806-12	OEM
C014806C-29	OEM
C014808-05	OEM
C014809	0037
C015001D	OEM
C015001E	OEM
C015001F	OEM
C015001G	OEM
C015001H	OEM
C015004D	OEM
C015004E	OEM
C015004F	OEM
C015004G	OEM
C015004H	OEM
C015020C	OEM
C015020D	OEM
C015020E	OEM
C015769	OEM
C016364	OEM
C016821	OEM
C017097	1623
C017101	OEM
C017950	OEM
C017951	OEM
C017956	OEM
C018094	OEM
C018991	0006
C019156	OEM
C019156-08	OEM
C021697	OEM
C021697-11	OEM
C024004D	OEM
C024004E	OEM
C024004F	OEM
C024004G	OEM
C024004H	OEM
C024010C	OEM
C024010D	OEM
C024010E	OEM
C024010F	OEM
C024020C	OEM
C024020D	OEM
C024020E	OEM
C024947A	OEM
C025953	OEM
C026028	OEM
C026160-001	OEM
C026162-001	OEM
C026163-001	OEM
C026164-001	OEM
C026165-001	OEM
C030004C	OEM
C030004E	OEM
C030004F	OEM
C030004G	OEM
C030010C	OEM
C030010D	OEM
C030010E	OEM
C030010F	OEM
C030020B	OEM
C030202C	OEM
C030202D	OEM
C030202E	OEM
C045004C	OEM
C045004D	OEM
C045004E	OEM
C045004F	OEM
C045010B	OEM
C045010C	OEM
C045010D	OEM
C045010E	OEM
C045010F	OEM
C045020B	OEM
C045020C	OEM
C045020D	OEM
C060010A	OEM
C060010B	OEM
C060010C	OEM
C060010D	OEM
C060010E	OEM
C060020A	OEM
C060020B	OEM
C060020D	OEM
C060202C	OEM
C060302	OEM
C060302A-29	OEM
C060472	OEM
C060474	1027
C060584	OEM
C060607	0124
C060609	OEM
C060612	2341
C060613	OEM
C060616	OEM
C060616B-05	OEM
C060617	OEM
C060619	OEM
C061428	0422
C061505	OEM
C061598	OEM
C061598B	OEM
C061598B-01	OEM
C061598B-22	OEM
C061618	OEM
C061618-16	OEM
C061702	0765
C061850	1688
C061922	OEM
C061991	OEM
C061991-29	OEM
C070024	OEM
C090010A	OEM
C090010B	OEM
C090010C	OEM
C090010D	OEM
C090020A	OEM
C090020B	OEM
C090020C	OEM
C096509	OEM
C0161991-29	OEM
C0C13000-1C	0590
C1/2-12	0414
C1-12	3516
C1A	1141
C1B	0015
C1D-02A	0196
C1H	0015
C1.0E02	0071
C2-0	OEM
C2AJ102	0015
C2C3.0	OEM
C2C3.3	0777
C2C3.6	0791
C2C3.9	0801
C2C4.3	0815
C2C4.7	0827
C2C5.1	0437
C2C5.6	0870
C2C6.2	0185
C2C6.8	0205
C2C7.5	0475
C2C8.2	0499
C2C9.1	0679
C2C10	0225
C2C11	0230
C2C12	0234
C2C13	0237
C2C15	0247
C2C16	0251
C2C18	0256
C2C20	0262
C2C22	0269
C2C24	0273
C2C27	0291
C2C30	0305
C2C33	0314
C2C36	0316
C2C39	0322
C2C43	0333
C2C47	0343
C2C51	0027
C2C56	0266
C2C62	0382
C2C68	0401
C2C75	0421
C2C82	0439
C2C91	0238
C2C100	1172
C2C110	1182
C2C120	1198
C2C130	1209
C2C150	0642
C2C160	1246
C2C180	1269
C2C200	0600
C2M50-2B	OEM
C2M50-28R	OEM
C2M60-28R	OEM
C2M70-28R	OEM
C2M100-28A	OEM
C3-1	OEM
C3-2B	OEM
C3-4	0720
C3A3.0	OEM
C3A3.3	OEM
C3A3.6	OEM
C3A3.9	OEM
C3A4.3	OEM
C3A4.7	OEM
C3A5.1	OEM
C3A5.6	OEM
C3A6.2	OEM
C3A6.8	OEM
C3A7.5	OEM
C3A8.2	OEM
C3A9.1	OEM
C3C3.0	OEM
C3C3.3	OEM
C3C3.6	OEM
C3C3.9	OEM
C3C4.3	OEM
C3C4.7	OEM
C3C5.1	OEM
C3C5.6	OEM
C3C6.2	OEM
C3C6.8	OEM
C3C7.5	OEM
C3C8.2	OEM
C3C9.1	OEM
C3C10	OEM
C3C11	OEM
C3C12	OEM
C3C13	OEM
C3C15	OEM
C3C16	OEM
C3C18	OEM
C3C20	OEM
C3C22	OEM
C3C24	OEM
C3C27	OEM
C3C30	OEM
C3C33	OEM
C3C36	OEM
C3C39	OEM
C3C43	OEM
C3C47	OEM
C3C51	OEM
C3C56	OEM
C3C62	OEM
C3C68	OEM
C3C75	OEM
C3C82	OEM
C3C91	OEM

306

If replacement code is OEM, contact original manufacturer for replacement.

DEVICE TYPE	REPL CODE
C3C100	OEM
C3C110	OEM
C3C120	OEM
C3C130	OEM
C3C150	OEM
C3C160	OEM
C3C180	OEM
C3C200	OEM
C3T225	OEM
C3T225A	OEM
C4C3.0	1703
C4C3.3	0289
C4C3.6	0372
C4C3.9	0451
C4C4.3	0528
C4C4.7	0446
C4C5.1	0162
C4C5.6	0157
C4C6.2	0631
C4C6.8	0025
C4C7.5	0644
C4C8.2	0244
C4C9.1	0012
C4C10	0170
C4C11	0313
C4C12	0137
C4C13	0361
C4C15	0002
C4C16	0416
C4C18	0490
C4C20	0526
C4C22	0560
C4C24	0398
C4C27	0436
C4C30	0721
C4C33	0039
C4C36	0814
C4C39	0346
C4C43	0925
C4C47	0993
C4C51	0497
C4C56	0863
C4C62	0778
C4C68	2144
C4C75	1181
C4C82	0327
C4C91	1301
C4C100	0098
C4C110	0149
C4C120	0186
C4C130	0213
C4C150	0028
C4C160	0255
C4C180	0363
C4C200	0417
C4LS374AP	0708
C4P03Q	1227
C4P04Q	1227
C4P05Q	1227
C4P06Q	1227
C4P09Q	1227
C4P10Q	1227
C5	1708
C5A	0340
C5AR1200	OEM
C5B	0058
C5BR1200	OEM
C5C	0403
C5C11	OEM
C5D	OEM
C5D459	OEM
C5D459CA	OEM
C5D459CC	OEM
C5D485	OEM
C5D485CA	OEM
C5D485CC	OEM
C5D914	OEM
C5D914CA	OEM
C5D914CC	OEM
C5D5226	OEM
C5D5227	OEM
C5D5228	OEM
C5D5229	OEM
C5D5230	OEM
C5D5231	OEM
C5D5232	OEM
C5D5233	OEM
C5D5234	0466
C5D5235	OEM
C5D5236	OEM
C5D5237	OEM
C5D5238	OEM
C5D5239	0057
C5D5240	OEM
C5D5241	OEM
C5D5242	0052
C5D5243	OEM
C5D5244	OEM
C5D5245	0681
C5D5246	OEM
C5D5247	OEM
C5D5248	OEM
C5D5249	OEM
C5D5250	OEM
C5D5251	OEM
C5D5252	OEM
C5D5253	OEM
C5D5254	OEM
C5D5255	OEM
C5D5256	OEM
C5D5257	OEM
C5DR1200	OEM
C5F	1129
C5G	OEM
C5H	OEM
C5U	OEM
C6	0309
C6A	0934
C6B	0934
C6B3	1129
C-6BX212	2123
C6C	0342
C6C3.6	OEM
C6C3.9	OEM
C6C4.3	OEM
C6C4.7	OEM
C6C5.1	OEM
C6C5.6	OEM
C6C6.2	OEM
C6C6.8	OEM
C6C7.5	OEM
C6C8.2	OEM
C6C9.1	OEM
C6C10	OEM
C6C11	OEM
C6C12	OEM
C6C13	OEM
C6C15	OEM
C6C16	OEM
C6C18	OEM
C6C20	OEM
C6C22	OEM
C6C24	OEM
C6C27	OEM
C6C30	OEM
C6C33	OEM
C6C36	OEM
C6C39	OEM
C6C43	OEM
C6C47	OEM
C6C51	OEM
C6C56	OEM
C6C62	OEM
C6C68	OEM
C6C75	OEM
C6C82	OEM
C6C91	OEM
C6C100	OEM
C6C110	OEM
C6C120	OEM
C6C130	OEM
C6C150	OEM
C6C160	OEM
C6C180	OEM
C6C200	OEM
C6D	0342
C6F	0934
C6G	OEM
C6P10FU	1227
C6P10FUR	1716
C6P20FU	1227
C6P20FUR	1716
C6U	0934
C7	0688
C7A	OEM
C7A4	0442
C7B	OEM
C7C	OEM
C7C3.0	OEM
C7C3.3	OEM
C7C3.6	OEM
C7C3.9	OEM
C7C4.3	OEM
C7C4.7	OEM
C7C5.1	OEM
C7C5.6	OEM
C7C6.2	OEM
C7C6.8	OEM
C7C7.5	OEM
C7C8.2	OEM
C7C9.1	OEM
C7C10	OEM
C7C11	OEM
C7C12	OEM
C7C13	OEM
C7C15	OEM
C7C16	OEM
C7C18	OEM
C7C20	OEM
C7C22	OEM
C7C24	OEM
C7C27	OEM
C7C30	OEM
C7C33	OEM
C7C36	OEM
C7C39	OEM
C7C43	OEM
C7C47	OEM
C7C51	OEM
C7C56	OEM
C7C62	OEM
C7C68	OEM
C7C75	OEM
C7C82	OEM
C7C91	OEM
C7C100	OEM
C7C110	OEM
C7C120	OEM
C7C130	OEM
C7C150	OEM
C7C160	OEM
C7C180	OEM
C7C200	OEM
C7C400	OEM
C7F	OEM
C7G	OEM
C7H	OEM
C7U	OEM
C8	0688
C8P03Q	1227
C8P04Q	1227
C8P05Q	1227
C8P06Q	1227
C8P04Q	OEM
C9A	OEM
C9B	OEM
C9C	OEM
C9F	OEM
C9G	OEM
C9H	OEM
C9U	OEM
C-10	0196
C10	0196
C10-04C	0196
C10-1B	0196
C10-2NA	0196
C10-12	OEM
C10-12A	2739
C10-13B	0196
C10-15B	0196
C10-15C	0196
C10-16A	0196
C10-16B	0196
C10-18B	0196
C-10-20A	1141
C10-20A	0907
C10-22C	1141
C10-31A	0196
C10-38C	0196
C10-47B	0196
C10A	2471
C10AR1200	OEM
C10B	0240
C10BR1200	OEM
C10C	2635
C10D	0671
C10D41200	OEM
C10F	1095
C10G	0240
C10H	2635
C10P03Q	2493
C10P04Q	2493
C10P05Q	OEM
C10P06Q	OEM
C10P09Q	OEM
C10P10F	OEM
C10P10FU	1227
C10P10FUR	1716
C10P10Q	OEM
C10P20F	OEM
C10P20FU	1227
C10P20FUR	1716
C10P30F	0966
C10P30FR	OEM
C10P40F	0966
C10P40FR	OEM
C10U	3385
C11	0208
C11(2S)	0208
C11A	2471
C11A(TRANS)	0208
C11AR1200	OEM
C11A-U	0240
C11B	0240
C11B(TRANS)	0208
C11BR1200	OEM
C11C	2635
C11C(TRANS)	0208
C11CA	OEM
C11CF	OEM
C11CJ	OEM
C11D	0671
C11D(TRANS)	0208
C11DA	OEM
C11DR700	OEM
C11DR1200	OEM
C11E	2782
C11E(TRANS)	0208
C11F	1095
C11F(TRANS)	0208
C11G	0240
C11G(TRANS)	0208
C11GN	0208
C11H	2635
C11H(TRANS)	0208
C11J	0208
C11K	0208
C11L	0208
C11M	0332
C11M(TRANS)	0208
C11OR	0208
C11R	0208
C11S1C1E1C	0015
C11U	1095
C11X	0208
C11Y	0208
C12	0086
C12-12	1410
C12A	OEM
C12A(TRANS)	0086
C12B	OEM
C12B(TRANS)	0086
C12C	OEM
C12C(TRANS)	0086
C12D	OEM
C12D(TRANS)	0086
C12E	0086
C12F	OEM
C12F(TRANS)	0086
C12G	OEM
C12G(TRANS)	0086
C12GN	0086
C12H	OEM
C12H(TRANS)	0086
C12J	0086
C12K	0086
C12L	0086
C12M	0086
C12OR	0086
C12R	0086
C12U	OEM
C12X	0086
C12Y	0086
C13	0595
C13A	0595
C13B	0595
C13C	0595
C13D	0595
C13E	0595
C13F	OEM
C13F(2S)	0595
C13G	0595
C13GN	0595
C13H	0595
C13J	0595
C13K	0595
C13L	0595
C13M	0595
C13OR	0595
C13R	0595
C13X	0595
C13Y	OEM
C13Y(2S)	0595
C14(2S)	0595
C14A	0595
C14B	0595
C14C	0595
C14D	0595
C14E	0595
C14F	0595
C14G	0595
C14GN	0595
C14H	0595
C14J	0595
C14K	0595
C14L	0595
C14M	0595
C14OR	0595
C14R	0595
C14X	0595
C14Y	0595
C15	0016
C15-0	0016
C15-1(2S)	0016
C15-2(2S)	0016
C15-3(2S)	0016
C15A	2471
C15A(TRANS)	0016
C15A-U	0240
C15B	0240
C15B(TRANS)	0016
C15C	2635
C15C(TRANS)	0016
C15D	0671
C15D(TRANS)	0016
C15E	2782
C15E(TRANS)	0016
C15F	1095
C15F(TRANS)	0016
C15G	0240
C15G(TRANS)	0016
C15GN	0016
C15H	0671
C15H(TRANS)	0016
C15J	0016
C15K	0016
C15L	0016
C15M	0332
C15M(TRANS)	0016
C15OR	0016
C15R	0016
C15U	1095
C15X	0016
C15Y	0016
C16(2S)	0016
C16A(2S)	0016
C16B	0016
C16C	0016
C16D	0016
C16E	0016
C16F	0016
C16G	0016
C16GN	0016
C16H	0016
C16J	0016
C16K	0016
C16L	0016
C16M	0016
C16OR	0016
C16P03Q	1931
C16P04Q	2219
C16P05Q	2219
C16P06Q	2219
C16P09Q	2219
C16P10F	2259
C16P10FU	2219
C16P10FUR	OEM
C16P10Q	2219
C16P20F	2259
C16P20FU	2219
C16P20FUR	OEM
C16P30F	4409
C16P30FR	OEM
C16P40F	4409
C16P40FR	OEM
C16R	0016
C16X	0016
C16Y	0016
C17(2S)	0016
C17A(2S)	0016
C17B	0016
C17C	0016
C17D	0016
C17E	0016
C17F	0016
C17G	0016
C17GN	0016
C17H	0016
C17J	0016
C17K	0016
C17L	0016
C17M	0016
C17OR	0016
C17R	0016
C17X	0016
C17Y	0016
C18(2S)	0079
C18A	0079
C18B	0079
C18C	0079
C18D	0079
C18E	0079
C18F	0079
C18G	0079
C18GN	0079
C18H	0079
C18J	0079
C18K	0079
C18L	0079
C18M	0079
C18OR	0079
C18R	0079
C18X	0079
C19(2S)	0086
C19A	0086
C19B	0086
C19C	0086
C19D	0086
C19E	0086
C19F	0086
C19G	0086
C19GN	0086
C19H	0086
C19J	0086
C19K	0086
C19L	0086
C19M	0086
C19OR	0086
C19R	0086
C19X	0086
C19Y	0086
C20(2S)	0086
C20A	2430
C20A(TRANS)	0086
C20A-U	0240
C20B	0430
C20B(TRANS)	0086
C20C	0717
C20C(TRANS)	0086
C20D	0682
C20D(TRANS)	0086
C20E	0720
C20E(TRANS)	0086
C20F	2430
C20F(TRANS)	0086
C20G	0086
C20GN	0086
C20H	0086
C20J	0086
C20K	0086
C20L	0086
C20M	0720
C20M(TRANS)	0086
C20OR	0086
C20R	0086
C20U	2430
C20X	0086
C20Y	0086
C21	0103
C21(2S)	0103
C21A	0103
C21B	0103
C21C	0103
C21D	0103
C21E	0103
C21F	0103
C21G	0103
C21GN	0103
C21H	0103
C21J	0103
C21K	0103
C21L	0103
C21M	0103
C21OR	0103
C21R	0103
C21X	0103
C21Y	0103
C22(2S)	0086
C22A	1641
C22A(TRANS)	0086
C22B	1641
C22B(TRANS)	0086
C22C	1574
C22D	1574
C22D(TRANS)	0086
C22E	1655
C22E(TRANS)	0086
C22F	1641
C22F(TRANS)	0086
C22G	0086
C22GN	0086
C22H	0086
C22J	0086
C22K	0086
C22L	0086
C22M	0086
C22OR	0086
C22R	0086
C22U	1641
C22X	0086
C22Y	0086
C23(2S)	0086
C23A	0086
C23B	0086
C23D	0086
C23E	0086
C23F	0086
C23G	0086
C23GN	0086
C23H	0086
C23H12B	0015
C23J	0086
C23K	0086
C23L	0086
C23M	0086
C23OR	0086
C23R	0086
C23X	0086
C23Y	0086
C24(2S)	0086
C24A	0086
C24B	0086
C24C	0086
C24D	0086
C24E	0086
C24F	0086
C24G	0086
C24GN	0086
C24H	0086
C24H5F	OEM
C24H10F	OEM
C24H15F	OEM
C24H20F	OEM
C24H30F	OEM
C24H40F	OEM
C24J	0086
C24K	0086
C24L	0086
C24M	0086
C24OR	0086
C24R	0086
C24X	0086
C24Y	0086
C25	1077
C25-06M	0282
C25P03Q	1931
C25P04Q	1931
C25P05Q	OEM
C25P06Q	OEM
C25P09Q	OEM
C25P10FU	2219
C25P10FUR	OEM
C25P10Q	OEM
C25P20FU	2219
C25P20FUR	OEM
C25P30F	4409
C25P30FR	OEM
C25P40F	4409
C25P40FR	OEM
C26(2S)	0016
C26A	0016
C26B	0016
C26C	0016
C26D	0016
C26E	0016
C26F	0016
C26G	0016
C26GN	0016
C26H	0016
C26J	0016
C26K	0016
C26L	0016
C26M	0016
C26OR	0016
C26R	0016
C26X	0016
C26Y	0016
C27(2S)	0016
C27A	0016
C27B	0016
C27D	0016
C27E	0016
C27F	0016
C27G	0016
C27GN	0016
C27H	0016
C27J	0016
C27K	0016
C27L	0016
C27M	0016
C27OR	0016
C27R	0016
C27X	0016
C27Y	0016
C28(2S)	0198
C28A	0198
C28B	0198
C28C	0198
C28D	0198
C28E	0198
C28F	0198
C28G	0198
C28GN	0198
C28H	0198
C28J	0198
C28K	0198
C28L	0198
C28M	0198
C28OR	0198
C28R	0198
C28X	0198
C28Y	0198
C29(2S)	0198
C29A	0198
C29B	0198
C29C	0198
C29D	0198
C29E	0198
C29F	0198
C29G	0198
C29GN	0198
C29H	0198
C29J	0198
C29K	0198
C29L	0198
C29M	0198
C29OR	0198
C29R	0198
C29X	0198
C29Y	0198
C30(2S)	0086
C30-1	0720
C30-2	0720
C30-5	0720
C30-12	OEM
C30-OR	0086
C30A	0562
C30A(TRANS)	0086
C30B	0757
C30B(TRANS)	0086
C30C	3240
C30C(TRANS)	0086
C30D	0735
C30D(TRANS)	0086
C30E	0747
C30E(TRANS)	0086
C30F	2174
C30F(TRANS)	0086
C30G	0086
C30GN	0086
C30H	0086
C30H03Q	OEM
C30H04Q	OEM
C30H05Q	OEM
C30H06Q	OEM
C30J	0086
C30L	0086
C30M	0720
C30M(TRANS)	0086
C30OR	0086
C30R	0086
C30U	3275
C30X	0086
C30Y	0086
C31(2S)	0086
C31A	OEM
C31A(TRANS)	0086
C31B	OEM
C31B(TRANS)	0086
C31C	5763
C31C(TRANS)	0086
C31D	OEM
C31D(TRANS)	0086
C31E	OEM
C31E(TRANS)	0086
C31F	OEM
C31F(TRANS)	0086
C31G	0086
C31GN	0086
C31H	0086
C31J	0086
C31K	0086
C31L	0086

If replacement code is OEM, contact original manufacturer for replacement.

DEVICE TYPE	REPL CODE
C31M	0086
C31OR	0086
C31R	0086
C31U	OEM
C31X	0086
C31Y	0086
C32(2S)	0086
C32A	0086
C32A(2S)	0086
C32B	1641
C32B(TRANS)	0086
C32C	1574
C32C(TRANS)	0086
C32D	OEM
C32D(TRANS)	0086
C32E	1655
C32E(TRANS)	0086
C32F	OEM
C32F(TRANS)	0086
C32G	0086
C32GN	0086
C32H	0086
C32J	0086
C32K	0086
C32L	0086
C32M	0086
C32OR	0086
C32R	0086
C32U	2497
C32X	0086
C32Y	0086
C33(2S)	0079
C33A	OEM
C33A(TRANS)	0079
C33B	OEM
C33B(TRANS)	0079
C33C	OEM
C33C(TRANS)	0079
C33D	OEM
C33D(TRANS)	0079
C33E	OEM
C33E(TRANS)	0079
C33F	OEM
C33F(TRANS)	0079
C33G	0079
C33GN	0079
C33H	0079
C33J	0079
C33K	0079
C33L	0079
C33M	0079
C33OR	0079
C33R	0079
C33U	OEM
C33X	0079
C33Y	0079
C34	0208
C34A	0208
C34A1	1640
C34A2	OEM
C34B1	1640
C34B2	OEM
C34C	0208
C34C1	2623
C34C2	1844
C34D	0208
C34D1	2623
C34D2	0735
C34E	0208
C34E1	2625
C34E2	0759
C34F	0208
C34F1	1640
C34F2	2174
C34G	0208
C34GN	0208
C34H	0208
C34J	0208
C34K	0208
C34L	0208
C34M	0208
C34OR	0208
C34R	0208
C34X	0208
C34Y	0208
C35	0208
C35A	0707
C35A(TRANS)	0208
C35AR1200	OEM
C35B	0464
C35B(TRANS)	0208
C35BR1200	OEM
C35C	0716
C35C(TRANS)	0208
C35D	0717
C35DR700	OEM
C35DR1200	OEM
C35E	0773
C35E(TRANS)	0208
C35ER1200	OEM
C35F	0726
C35F(TRANS)	0208
C35G	0464
C35G(TRANS)	0208
C35GN	0208
C35H	0716
C35H(TRANS)	0208
C35J	0208
C35K	0208

DEVICE TYPE	REPL CODE
C35L	0208
C35M	0720
C35M(TRANS)	0208
C35MR1200	OEM
C35N	0745
C35OR	0208
C35P	OEM
C35R	0208
C35S	0745
C35T	OEM
C35U	3246
C35X	0208
C35Y	0208
C36	0208
C36A	0736
C36B	0740
C36B(TRANS)	0208
C36C	2889
C36C(TRANS)	0208
C36D	0742
C36D(TRANS)	0208
C36E	3213
C36E(TRANS)	0208
C36F	2497
C36F(TRANS)	0208
C36G	3076
C36G(TRANS)	0208
C36GN	0208
C36H	3080
C36H(TRANS)	0208
C36J	0208
C36K	0208
C36L	0208
C36M	0720
C36M(TRANS)	0208
C36N	0674
C36OR	0208
C36R	0208
C36S	OEM
C36U	3073
C36X	0208
C36Y	0208
C37(2S)	0016
C37A	0562
C37A(TRANS)	0016
C37B	0757
C37B(TRANS)	0016
C37C	3240
C37C(TRANS)	0016
C37D	0735
C37D(TRANS)	0016
C37E	3260
C37E(TRANS)	0016
C37F	2174
C37F(TRANS)	0016
C37G	0717
C37G(TRANS)	0016
C37GN	0016
C37H	0016
C37J	0016
C37K	0016
C37L	0016
C37M	0759
C37M(TRANS)	0016
C37N	0761
C37OR	0016
C37R	0016
C37S	2848
C37U	3275
C37X	0016
C37Y	0016
C38	0079
C38(2S)	0016
C38A	0726
C38A(TRANS)	0016
C38B	0464
C38B(TRANS)	0016
C38BR1200	OEM
C38C	0716
C38C(TRANS)	0016
C38D	0717
C38D(TRANS)	0016
C38DR1200	OEM
C38E	0773
C38E(TRANS)	0016
C38F	0726
C38F(TRANS)	0016
C38G	0464
C38G(TRANS)	0016
C38H	0716
C38H(TRANS)	0016
C38HR1200	OEM
C38J	0016
C38K	0016
C38L	0016
C38M	0720
C38M(TRANS)	0016
C38OR	0016
C38R	0016
C38U	3246
C38X	0016
C38Y	0016
C39	0144
C39-207	0016
C39A(2S)	0144
C39B	0144
C39C	0144
C39D	0144
C39E	0144

DEVICE TYPE	REPL CODE
C39F	0144
C39G	0144
C39GN	0144
C39H	0144
C39J	0144
C39K	0144
C39L	0144
C39M	0144
C39OR	0144
C39R	0144
C39X	0144
C39Y	0144
C40(2S)	0144
C40A	OEM
C40A(TRANS)	0144
C40B	OEM
C40B(TRANS)	0144
C40C	OEM
C40C(TRANS)	0144
C40D	OEM
C40D(TRANS)	0144
C40E	OEM
C40E(TRANS)	0144
C40F	OEM
C40F(TRANS)	0144
C40G	3374
C40G(TRANS)	0144
C40GN	0144
C40H	OEM
C40H(TRANS)	0144
C40J	0144
C40K	0144
C40L	0144
C40M	OEM
C40N	OEM
C40OR	0144
C40R	0144
C40S	OEM
C40U	OEM
C40X	0144
C40Y	0144
C41(2S)	0615
C41B	0615
C41C	0615
C41F	0615
C41GN	0615
C41H	0615
C41J	0615
C41M	0615
C41OR	0615
C41R	0615
C41TV(2S)	0615
C41X	0615
C41Y	0615
C42(2S)	0074
C42A(2S)	0074
C42B	0074
C42C	0074
C42E	0074
C42F	0074
C42G	0074
C42GN	0074
C42H	0074
C42J	0074
C42K	0074
C42L	0074
C42M	0074
C42OR	0074
C42R	0074
C42X	0074
C42Y	0074
C43(2S)	0074
C44(2S)	0074
C44-04	0023
C45(2S)	0016
C45A	0217
C45B	0603
C45C	0605
C45C10	OEM
C45C12	OEM
C45D	0605
C45D1	OEM
C45D2	OEM
C45D3	OEM
C45D4	OEM
C45D5	OEM
C45D6	OEM
C45E	0605
C45F	0217
C45G	0217
C45H	0605
C45M	0605
C45N	0463
C45P	0463
C45PA	0463
C45PB	0463
C45S	0463
C45T	0463
C45U	0217
C46(2S)	0086
C46A	0217
C46A(TRANS)	0086
C46B	0636
C46B(TRANS)	0086
C46C	0217
C46C(TRANS)	0086
C46D	0217
C46DB	0086
C46E	0217

DEVICE TYPE	REPL CODE
C46E(TRANS)	0086
C46F	0217
C46F(TRANS)	0086
C46G	0217
C46G(TRANS)	0086
C46GN	0086
C46H	0217
C46H(TRANS)	0086
C46J	0086
C46K	0086
C46L	0086
C46M	0217
C46M(TRANS)	0086
C46N	0653
C46OR	0086
C46P	0653
C46PA	0653
C46PB	0653
C46S	0653
C46T	0653
C46U	0217
C46X	0086
C46Y	0086
C47(2S)	0086
C47A	0086
C47B	0086
C47C	0086
C47D	0086
C47E	0086
C47G	0086
C47GN	0086
C47H	0086
C47J	0086
C47K	0086
C47L	0086
C47M	0086
C47OR	0086
C47R	0086
C47X	0086
C47Y	0086
C48(2S)	0086
C48A	0086
C48B	0086
C48C(2S)	0086
C48D	0086
C48E	0086
C48F	0086
C48G	0086
C48GN	0086
C48H	0086
C48J	0086
C48K	0086
C48L	0086
C48M	OEM
C48M(TRANS)	0086
C48N	OEM
C48OR	0086
C48P	OEM
C48PA	OEM
C48PB	OEM
C48R	0086
C48S	OEM
C48T	OEM
C48X	0086
C48Y	0086
C49(2S)	0086
C49A	OEM
C49A(TRANS)	0086
C49A10	0521
C49A20	0521
C49B	OEM
C49B(TRANS)	0086
C49B10	0521
C49B20	0521
C49C	OEM
C49C(TRANS)	0086
C49C10	0521
C49C20	0521
C49D	OEM
C49D(TRANS)	0086
C49D10	0521
C49D20	0521
C49E	OEM
C49E(TRANS)	0086
C49E10	0521
C49E20	0521
C49F	0086
C49G	OEM
C49G(TRANS)	0086
C49GN	0086
C49H	0086
C49J	0086
C49K	0086
C49L	0086
C49M	OEM
C49M(TRANS)	0086
C49M10	0521
C49M20	0521
C49OR	0086
C49X	0086
C49Y(2S)	0086
C50	0595
C50A	0595
C50A(2S)	0595
C50AX500	OEM
C50B	0217
C50B(TRANS)	0595
C50BX500	OEM
C50C	0217

DEVICE TYPE	REPL CODE
C50C(TRANS)	0595
C50CX500	OEM
C50D	0217
C50DX500	OEM
C50E	0605
C50E(TRANS)	0595
C50EX500	OEM
C50F	0217
C50F(TRANS)	0595
C50G	0217
C50G(TRANS)	0595
C50GN	0595
C50H	0217
C50H(TRANS)	0595
C50J	0595
C50K	0595
C50L	0595
C50M	0605
C50M(TRANS)	0595
C50MX500	OEM
C50N	0463
C50OR	0595
C50P	0463
C50PA	0463
C50PB	0463
C50R	0595
C50S	0463
C50SX500	OEM
C50T	0463
C50U	0217
C50X	0595
C50Y	0595
C51(2S)	0086
C51A	0086
C51B	0086
C51C	0086
C51D	0086
C51E	0086
C51F	0086
C51G	0086
C51GN	0086
C51H	0086
C51J	0086
C51K	0086
C51L	0086
C51M	0086
C51OR	0086
C51PC	OEM
C51R	0086
C51X	0086
C51Y	0086
C52	0016
C52A	0217
C52A(TRANS)	0016
C52AX500	OEM
C52B	0217
C52B(TRANS)	0016
C52BX500	OEM
C52C	0217
C52C(TRANS)	0016
C52CX500	OEM
C52D	0217
C52D(TRANS)	0016
C52DX500	OEM
C52E	0217
C52E(TRANS)	0016
C52EX500	OEM
C52F	0217
C52F(TRANS)	0016
C52G	0217
C52G(TRANS)	0016
C52GN	0016
C52H	0217
C52H(TRANS)	0016
C52J	0016
C52K	0016
C52L	0016
C52M	0217
C52M(TRANS)	0016
C52MX500	OEM
C52N	0653
C52OR	0016
C52P	0653
C52PA	0653
C52PB	0653
C52S	0653
C52T	0653
C52U	0217
C52X	0016
C52Y	0016
C53	0016
C53A	0016
C53B	0016
C53C	0016
C53D	0016
C53E	0016
C53F	0016
C53G	0016
C53GN	0016
C53H	0016
C53J	0016
C53L	0016
C53OR	0016
C53R	0016
C53X	0016
C53Y	0016
C54(2S)	0016
C54A	0016
C54B	0016

DEVICE TYPE	REPL CODE
C54C	0016
C54D	0016
C54E	0016
C54F	0016
C54G	0016
C54GN	0016
C54H	0016
C54J	0016
C54K	0016
C54L	0016
C54M	0016
C54OR	0016
C54X	0016
C54Y	0016
C55(2S)	0016
C55A	OEM
C55A(TRANS)	0016
C55B	OEM
C55B(TRANS)	0016
C55C	OEM
C55C(TRANS)	0016
C55D	OEM
C55D(TRANS)	0016
C55E	OEM
C55E(TRANS)	0016
C55F	OEM
C55F(TRANS)	0016
C55G	OEM
C55G(TRANS)	0016
C55GN	0016
C55H	OEM
C55H(TRANS)	0016
C55J	0016
C55K	0016
C55L	0016
C55M	OEM
C55M(TRANS)	0016
C55N	OEM
C55OR	0016
C55R	0016
C55S	OEM
C55U	OEM
C55X	0016
C55Y	0016
C56(2S)	0127
C56A	OEM
C56A(TRANS)	0127
C56B	OEM
C56B(TRANS)	0127
C56C	OEM
C56C(TRANS)	0127
C56D	OEM
C56D(TRANS)	0127
C56E	OEM
C56E(TRANS)	0127
C56F	OEM
C56F(TRANS)	0127
C56G	OEM
C56G(TRANS)	0127
C56GN	0127
C56H	OEM
C56H(TRANS)	0127
C56J	0127
C56K	0127
C56L	0127
C56M	OEM
C56M(TRANS)	0127
C56N	OEM
C56OR	0127
C56R	0127
C56S	OEM
C56U	OEM
C56X	0127
C56Y	0127
C57	0590
C58(2S)	0233
C58A(2S)	0233
C58AC	0233
C58B	0233
C58D	0233
C58E	0233
C58F	0233
C58G	0233
C58GN	0233
C58H	0233
C58J	0233
C58K	0233
C58L	0233
C58M	0233
C58OR	0233
C58R	0233
C58X	0233
C58Y	0233
C59(2S)	0086
C59A	0086
C59B	0086
C59C	0086
C59D	0086
C59E	0086
C59F	0086
C59G	0086
C59GN	0086
C59H	0086
C59J	0086
C59K	0086
C59L	0086
C59M	0086
C59OR	0086
C59R	0086

DEVICE TYPE	REPL CODE
C59X	0086
C59Y	0086
C60	0208
C60A	OEM
C60A(TRANS)	0208
C60B	OEM
C60B(TRANS)	0208
C60C	OEM
C60C(TRANS)	0208
C60D	OEM
C60D(TRANS)	0208
C60E	OEM
C60E(TRANS)	0208
C60F	OEM
C60F(TRANS)	0208
C60G	OEM
C60G(TRANS)	0208
C60GN	0208
C60H	OEM
C60H(TRANS)	0208
C60H03Q	OEM
C60H04Q	OEM
C60H05Q	OEM
C60H06Q	OEM
C60J	0208
C60K	0208
C60L	0208
C60M	0208
C60OR	0208
C60R	0208
C60U	OEM
C60X	0208
C60Y	0208
C61(2S)	0086
C61A	0086
C61B	0086
C61C	0086
C61D	0086
C61E	0086
C61F	0086
C61G	0086
C61GN	0086
C61H	0086
C61J	0086
C61K	0086
C61L	0086
C61M	0086
C61OR	0086
C61R	0086
C61Y	0086
C62	0016
C62A	OEM
C62A(TRANS)	0016
C62B	OEM
C62B(TRANS)	0016
C62C	OEM
C62C(TRANS)	0016
C62D	OEM
C62D(TRANS)	0016
C62E	OEM
C62E(TRANS)	0016
C62F	OEM
C62F(TRANS)	0016
C62G	OEM
C62G(TRANS)	0016
C62GN	0016
C62H	OEM
C62H(TRANS)	0016
C62J	0016
C62L	0016
C62M	0016
C62OR	0016
C62R	0016
C62U	OEM
C62X	0016
C62Y	0016
C63	0016
C63(2S)	0144
C63A	0144
C63B	0144
C63D	0144
C63E	0144
C63F	0144
C63G	0144
C63GN	0144
C63H	0144
C63J	0144
C63K	0144
C63L	0144
C63M	0144
C63OR	0144
C63R	0144
C63X	0144
C63Y	0144
C64	0086
C64(2S)	0086
C64A	0086
C64B	0086
C64C	0086
C64D	0086
C64E	0086
C64F	0086
C64G	0086
C64GN	0086
C64H	0086
C64K	0086
C64L	0086
C64M	0086
C64OR	0086

If replacement code is OEM, contact original manufacturer for replacement.

DEVICE TYPE	REPL CODE	DEVICE TYPE	REPL CODE	DEVICE TYPE	REPL CODE	DEVICE TYPE	REPL CODE	DEVICE TYPE	REPL CODE	DEVICE TYPE	REPL CODE	DEVICE TYPE	REPL CODE
C64R	0086	C70H	0233	C74LS170P	2605	C79J	0224	C88M	0086	C97GN	0086	C103Y(2S)	0016
C64X	0086	C70J	0233	C74LS174P	0260	C79K	0224	C880R	0086	C97H	0086	C103YY	0340
C64Y	0086	C70K	0233	C74LS175P	1662	C79L	0224	C88R	0086	C97J	0086	C104	0016
C64Y-RST	0086	C70L	0233	C74LS181P	1668	C79M	0224	C88X	0086	C97K	0086	C104(2S)	0016
C65(2S)	0233	C70M	0233	C74LS190P	1676	C790R	0224	C88Y	0086	C97L	0086	C104A(2S)	0016
C65-0	0233	C700R	0233	C74LS191P	1677	C79R	0224	C89(2S)	0595	C97M	0086	C104B	0016
C65-OR	0233	C70R	0233	C74LS192P	1679	C79X	0224	C89A	0595	C970R	0086	C104C	0016
C65A	0233	C70X	0233	C74LS193P	1682	C79Y	0224	C89B	0595	C97R	0086	C104D	0016
C65B(2S)	0233	C70Y	0233	C74LS196P	2807	C80	0007	C89C	0595	C97X	0086	C104E	0016
C65C	0233	C71(2S)	0595	C74LS197P	2450	C80(2S)	0007	C89D	0595	C97Y	0086	C104F	0016
C65D	0233	C71A	0595	C74LS251P	1726	C80A	0733	C89E	0595	C98(2S)	0016	C104G	0016
C65E	0233	C71B	0595	C74LS253P	1728	C80A(TRANS)	0007	C89F	0595	C98A	0016	C104GN	0016
C65F	0233	C71C	0595	C74LS257P	1733	C80B	0733	C89G	0595	C98B	0016	C104H	0016
C65G	0233	C71D	0595	C74LS258P	1735	C80B(TRANS)	0007	C89GN	0595	C98C	0016	C104J	0016
C65GN	0233	C71E	0595	C74LS259P	3175	C80C	0733	C89H	0595	C98D	0016	C104K	0016
C65H	0233	C71F	0595	C74LS279P	3259	C80C(TRANS)	0007	C89J	0595	C98E	OEM	C104L	0016
C65K	0233	C71G	0595	C74LS298P	3337	C80C39	OEM	C89K	0595	C98E(2S)	0016	C104M	0016
C65L	0233	C71GN	0595	C74LS367P	0971	C80C49	OEM	C89L	0595	C98EG	OEM	C104OR	0016
C65M	0233	C71H	0595	C74LS368P	0985	C80D	0733	C89M	0595	C98ER	OEM	C104R	0016
C65N(2S)	0233	C71J	0595	C74LS670P	1122	C80D(TRANS)	0007	C890R	0595	C98F	0016	C104X	0016
C65OR	0233	C71M	0595	C74M	0198	C80E	0733	C89R	0595	C98G	0016	C104Y	0016
C65R	0233	C710R	0595	C74R	0198	C80E(TRANS)	0007	C89X	0595	C98GN	0016	C105(2S)	0016
C65X	0233	C71R	0595	C74X	0198	C80F	0733	C89Y	0595	C98H	0016	C105B	0016
C65Y(2S)	0233	C71X	0595	C74Y	0198	C80F(TRANS)	0007	C90(2S)	0595	C98J	0016	C106	0617
C65YA(2S)	0233	C72(2S)	0595	C75	0279	C80G	0007	C90A	0595	C98K	0016	C106(2S)	0617
C65YB(2S)	0233	C72A	0595	C75(2S)	0595	C80G(TRANS)	0007	C90B	0595	C98L	0016	C106A	0442
C65YTV(2S)	0233	C72B	0595	C75A	0595	C80GN	0007	C90C	0595	C98M	0016	C106A(2S)	0617
C65YTV1	0233	C72C	0595	C75B	0595	C80H	OEM	C90D	0595	C980R	0016	C106A1	0442
C66(2S)	0233	C72D	0595	C75B-1	0595	C80H(TRANS)	0007	C90E	0595	C98R	0016	C106A2	0442
C66A	0233	C72E	0595	C75C	0595	C80H03Q	OEM	C90F	0595	C98X	0016	C106A3	0442
C66B	0233	C72F	0595	C75E	0595	C80H04Q	OEM	C90G	0595	C98Y	0016	C106A4	0442
C66C	0233	C72GN	0595	C75F	0595	C80H05Q	OEM	C90GN	0595	C99(2S)	0016	C106A11	OEM
C66D	0233	C72H	0595	C75G	0595	C80H06Q	OEM	C90H	0595	C99A	0016	C106A12	OEM
C66E	0233	C72J	0595	C75GN	0595	C80J	0007	C90J	0595	C99B	0016	C106A21	OEM
C66EV	0233	C72K	0595	C75H	0595	C80K	0007	C90K	0595	C99C	0016	C106A32	OEM
C66F	0233	C72L	0595	C75J	0595	C80L	0007	C90L	0595	C99D	0016	C106A41	OEM
C66G	0233	C72M	0595	C75K	0595	C80M	0733	C90M	0595	C99E	0016	C106B	0934
C66GN	0233	C720R	0595	C75L	0595	C80M(TRANS)	0007	C900R	0595	C99F	0016	C106B(2S)	0617
C66H	0233	C72R	0595	C75M	0595	C80N	0733	C90R	0595	C99G	0016	C106B1	0934
C66J	0233	C72X	0595	C750R	0595	C800R	0007	C90X	0595	C99GN	0016	C106B2	0934
C66K	0233	C72Y	0595	C75R	0595	C80R	0007	C90Y	0595	C99H	0016	C106B3	0934
C66L	0233	C73	0279	C75X	0595	C80S	0733	C91	0038	C99J	0016	C106B4	0934
C66M	0279	C73(2S)	0595	C75Y	0595	C80U	OEM	C91(2S)	0595	C99K	0016	C106B11	OEM
C660R	0233	C73A	0595	C76	0279	C80X	0007	C91A	0595	C99L	0016	C106B12	OEM
C66R	0233	C73B	0595	C76(2S)	0595	C80Y	0007	C91B	0595	C99M	0016	C106B21	OEM
C66X	0233	C73C	0595	C76A	0595	C81	0018	C91C	0595	C990R	0016	C106B32	OEM
C66Y	0233	C73D	0595	C76B	0595	C81-004	4235	C91D	0595	C99R	0016	C106B41	OEM
C67(2S)	0016	C73E	0595	C76C	0595	C81A	0018	C91E	0595	C99X	0016	C106C	1213
C67A	0016	C73F	0595	C76D	0595	C81B	0018	C91F	0595	C99Y	0016	C106C(2S)	0617
C67B	0016	C73G	0595	C76E	0595	C81C	0018	C91G	0595	C100(2S)	0016	C106C1	1213
C67C	0016	C73GN	0595	C76F	0595	C81D	0018	C91GN	0595	C100-OY(2S)	0016	C106C2	1213
C67D	0016	C73H	0595	C76G	0595	C81E	0018	C91H	0595	C100A	0016	C106C3	1213
C67E	0016	C73J	0595	C76GN	0595	C81F	0018	C91J	0595	C100B	0016	C106C4	1213
C67F	0016	C73K	0595	C76H	0595	C81G	0018	C91K	0595	C100C	0016	C106C11	OEM
C67G	0016	C73L	0595	C76J	0595	C81GN	0018	C91L	0595	C100D	0016	C106C12	OEM
C67GN	0016	C73LBGL	0595	C76K	0595	C81H	0018	C91M	0595	C100E	0016	C106C21	OEM
C67H	0016	C73M	0595	C76L	0595	C81J	0018	C910R	0595	C100F	0016	C106C32	OEM
C67J	0016	C730R	0595	C76M	0595	C81K	0018	C91R	0595	C100G	0016	C106C41	OEM
C67K	0016	C73R	0595	C760R	0595	C81L	0018	C91X	0595	C100GN	0016	C106D	0095
C67L	0016	C73X	0595	C76R	0595	C81M	0018	C91Y	0595	C100J	0016	C106D1	0095
C67M	0016	C73Y	0595	C76X	0595	C810R	0018	C92	0617	C100L	0016	C106D2	0095
C67R	0016	C74(2S)	0198	C76Y	0595	C81R	0018	C92(2S)	0042	C100M	0016	C106D3	0095
C67X	0016	C74-GR	0198	C77(2S)	0595	C82	0127	C92-0025-R0	0817	C100OR	0016	C106D4	0095
C67Y	0016	C74-0	0198	C77A	0595	C82-004	1015	C93	0617	C100R	0016	C106D11	OEM
C68(2S)	0016	C74-R	0198	C77B	0595	C82BN	0127	C93(2S)	0042	C100X	0016	C106D12	OEM
C68A	0016	C74-Y	0198	C77C(2S)	0595	C82M	3235	C94	0617	C100Y	0016	C106D21	OEM
C68B	0016	C74A	0198	C77D	0595	C82R	0127	C94(2S)	0042	C101	0142	C106D32	OEM
C68C	0016	C74B	0198	C77F	0595	C82S	0144	C94A	OEM	C101(2S)	0074	C106D41	OEM
C68D	0016	C74C	0198	C77G	0595	C83	0127	C94AP	0042	C101A(2S)	0074	C106E	OEM
C68E	0016	C74D	0198	C77GN	0595	C83-829	0015	C94E	2922	C101B(2S)	0074	C106E1	0304
C68F	0016	C74E	0198	C77H	0595	C83-880	0015	C94EG	OEM	C101C	0074	C106E2	1234
C68G	0016	C74F	0198	C77J	0595	C84	OEM	C94ER	OEM	C101D	0074	C106E3	1234
C68GN	0016	C74G	0198	C77K	0595	C84(2S)	0595	C95	0086	C101E	0074	C106E4	1234
C68H	0016	C74GN	0198	C77L	0595	C84-009	3559	C95(2S)	0086	C101F	0074	C106E11	OEM
C68J	0016	C74H	0198	C77M	0595	C85	OEM	C95A	0086	C101G	0074	C106E12	OEM
C68K	0016	C74J	0198	C770R	0595	C85(2S)	0208	C95A(2S)	0086	C101GN	0074	C106E21	OEM
C68L	0016	C74K	0198	C77R	0595	C850	0208	C95B	0086	C101H	0074	C106E32	OEM
C68M	0016	C74L	0198	C77X	0595	C86	0208	C95C	0086	C101J	0074	C106F	1250
C680R	0016	C74LS00P	1519	C77Y	0595	C87(2S)	0016	C95D	0086	C101K	0074	C106F1	1250
C68R	0016	C74LS02P	1550	C77Z	0595	C87A	0016	C95E	OEM	C101L	0074	C106F2	1250
C68X	0016	C74LS03P	1569	C78(2S)	0595	C87B	0016	C95E(2S)	0086	C101M	0074	C106F3	1250
C68Y	0016	C74LS04P	1585	C78A	0595	C87C	0016	C95EG	OEM	C1010R	0074	C106F4	1250
C69(2S)	0086	C74LS05P	1598	C78B	0595	C87D	0016	C95F	0086	C101R	0074	C106F11	OEM
C69A	0086	C74LS08P	1623	C78C	0595	C87E	0016	C95GN	0086	C101X(2S)	0074	C106F12	OEM
C69B	0086	C74LS10P	1652	C78D	0595	C87F	0016	C95H	0086	C101XL	0074	C106F21	OEM
C69C	0086	C74LS11P	1657	C78E	0595	C87G	0016	C95J	0086	C101Y	0074	C106F32	OEM
C69D	0086	C74LS13P	1678	C78F	0595	C87H	0016	C95K	0086	C102	0126	C106F41	OEM
C69E	0086	C74LS14P	1688	C78GN	0595	C87J	0016	C95L	0086	C102R472	OEM	C106G	0617
C69F	0086	C74LS20P	0035	C78H	0595	C87K	0016	C95M	0086	C103	0016	C106G1	0934
C69G	0035	C74LS27P	0183	C78J	0595	C87L	0016	C950R	0086	C103(2S)	0016	C106G2	0934
C69GN	0086	C74LS30P	0822	C78K	0595	C87M	0016	C95R	0086	C103A	OEM	C106G3	0934
C69H	0086	C74LS32P	0088	C78L	0595	C870R	0016	C95X	0086	C103A(2S)	0016	C106G4	OEM
C69J	0086	C74LS42P	1830	C78M	0595	C87X	0016	C95Y	0086	C103A(SCR)	0895	C106GN	0617
C69K	0086	C74LS51P	1027	C78N05	OEM	C87Y	0016	C96	0079	C103B	0058	C106H	0617
C69L	0086	C74LS54P	1846	C780R	0595	C88(2S)	0086	C96E	OEM	C103B(2S)	0016	C106J	0617
C69M	0086	C74LS55P	0452	C78R	0595	C88A(2S)	0086	C96EG	OEM	C103C	0016	C106K	0617
C69OR	0086	C74LS74P	2483	C78X	0595	C88B	0086	C97	0086	C103D	0016	C106L	0617
C69R	0086	C74LS86P	0288	C78Y	0595	C88C	0086	C97(2S)	0086	C103E	0016	C106M	OEM
C69X	0086	C74LS90P	1871	C79(2S)	0224	C88D	0086	C97A(2S)	0086	C103F	0016	C106M(TRANS)	0617
C69Y	0086	C74LS93P	1877	C79A	0224	C88E	0086	C97B	0086	C103G	0016	C106M1	0304
C70(2S)	0233	C74LS109P	1895	C79B	0224	C88F	0086	C97C	0086	C103GN	0016	C106M2	1234
C70A	0233	C74LS136P	1618	C79C	0224	C88G	0086	C97D	0086	C103H	0016	C106M3	1234
C70B	0233	C74LS138P	0422	C79D	0224	C88GN	0086	C97E	0086	C103J	0016	C106M4	1234
C70C	0233	C74LS151P	1636	C79E	0224	C88H	0086	C97EG	OEM	C103K	0016	C106M11	OEM
C70D	0233	C74LS153P	0953	C79F	0224	C88J	0086	C97ER	OEM	C103L	0016	C106M12	OEM
C70E	0233	C74LS155P	0209	C79G	0224	C88K	0086	C97F	0086	C103M	0016	C106M21	OEM
C70F	0233	C74LS157P	1153	C79GN	0224	C88L	0086	C97G	0086	C103Q	1129	C106M32	OEM
C70G	0233	C74LS158P	1646	C79H	0224					C103X	0016	C106OR	0617
C70GN	0233									C103Y	1129	C106Q	1386

If replacement code is OEM, contact original manufacturer for replacement.

DEVICE TYPE	REPL CODE
C106Q1	1386
C106Q2	1386
C106Q3	1386
C106Q4	1386
C106Q11	OEM
C106Q12	OEM
C106Q21	OEM
C106Q32	OEM
C106Q41	OEM
C106R	0617
C106X	0617
C106Y	1386
C106Y(TRANS)	0617
C106Y1	1386
C106Y2	1386
C106Y3	1386
C106Y4	1386
C106Y11	OEM
C106Y12	OEM
C106Y21	OEM
C106Y32	OEM
C106Y41	OEM
C107	0042
C107A	0442
C107A1	0442
C107A2	0442
C107A3	0442
C107A4	OEM
C107A11	OEM
C107A12	OEM
C107A21	OEM
C107A32	OEM
C107A41	OEM
C107B	0934
C107B1	0934
C107B2	0934
C107B3	0934
C107B4	0934
C107B11	OEM
C107B12	OEM
C107B21	OEM
C107B32	OEM
C107B41	OEM
C107C	1213
C107C1	1213
C107C2	1213
C107C3	1213
C107C4	1213
C107C11	OEM
C107C12	OEM
C107C21	OEM
C107C32	OEM
C107C41	4354
C107D	0095
C107D1	0095
C107D2	0095
C107D3	0095
C107D4	0095
C107D11	OEM
C107D12	OEM
C107D21	OEM
C107D32	OEM
C107D41	OEM
C107E	OEM
C107E1	0304
C107E2	OEM
C107E3	OEM
C107E4	OEM
C107E11	OEM
C107E12	OEM
C107E21	OEM
C107E32	OEM
C107E41	OEM
C107F	1250
C107F1	1250
C107F2	1250
C107F3	1250
C107F4	1250
C107F11	OEM
C107F12	OEM
C107F21	OEM
C107F32	OEM
C107F41	OEM
C107G4	0042
C107G5	0042
C107G6	0042
C107M	OEM
C107M1	0304
C107M2	OEM
C107M3	OEM
C107M4	OEM
C107M11	OEM
C107M12	OEM
C107M21	OEM
C107M32	OEM
C107M41	OEM
C107Q	1386
C107Q1	1386
C107Q2	1386
C107Q3	1386
C107Q4	1386
C107Q11	OEM
C107Q12	OEM
C107Q21	OEM
C107Q32	OEM
C107Q41	OEM
C107Y	1386
C107Y1	1386
C107Y2	1386

DEVICE TYPE	REPL CODE
C107Y3	1386
C107Y4	1386
C107Y11	OEM
C107Y12	OEM
C107Y21	OEM
C107Y32	OEM
C107Y41	OEM
C108(2S)	0086
C108A	0442
C108A(TRANS)	0086
C108A1	0442
C108A2	0442
C108A3	0442
C108A4	0442
C108A11	OEM
C108A12	OEM
C108A21	OEM
C108A32	OEM
C108A41	OEM
C108A-0	0086
C108A-R	0086
C108B	0934
C108B(TRANS)	0086
C108B1	0934
C108B2	0934
C108B3	0934
C108B4	0934
C108B11	OEM
C108B12	OEM
C108B21	OEM
C108B32	OEM
C108B41	OEM
C108C	0095
C108C(TRANS)	0086
C108C1	0095
C108C2	0095
C108C3	0095
C108C4	0095
C108C11	OEM
C108C12	OEM
C108C21	OEM
C108C32	OEM
C108C41	OEM
C108D	0095
C108D(TRANS)	0086
C108D1	0095
C108D2	0095
C108D3	0095
C108D4	0095
C108D11	OEM
C108D12	OEM
C108D21	OEM
C108D32	OEM
C108D41	OEM
C108E	OEM
C108E(TRANS)	0086
C108E1	OEM
C108E2	1494
C108E3	1494
C108E4	1494
C108E11	OEM
C108E12	OEM
C108E21	OEM
C108E32	OEM
C108E41	OEM
C108F	1250
C108F(TRANS)	0086
C108F1	1250
C108F2	1250
C108F3	1250
C108F4	1250
C108F11	OEM
C108F12	OEM
C108F21	OEM
C108F32	OEM
C108F41	OEM
C108G	0086
C108GN	0086
C108H	0086
C108J	0086
C108K	0086
C108L	0086
C108M	OEM
C108M(TRANS)	0086
C108M1	OEM
C108M2	1494
C108M3	1494
C108M4	1494
C108M11	OEM
C108M12	OEM
C108M21	OEM
C108M32	OEM
C108M41	OEM
C108OR	0086
C108Q	OEM
C108Q1	OEM
C108Q2	1386
C108Q3	1386
C108Q4	1386
C108Q11	OEM
C108Q12	OEM
C108Q21	OEM
C108Q32	OEM
C108Q41	OEM
C108R	0086
C108X	0086
C108Y	OEM
C108Y(TRANS)	0086
C108Y1	OEM

DEVICE TYPE	REPL CODE
C108Y2	1386
C108Y3	1386
C108Y4	1386
C108Y11	OEM
C108Y12	OEM
C108Y21	OEM
C108Y32	OEM
C108Y41	OEM
C109(2S)	0086
C109A(2S)	0086
C109A-O	0086
C109A-R	0086
C109A-Y	0086
C109B	0086
C109C	0086
C109D	0086
C109E	0086
C109F	0086
C109G	0086
C109G1	0086
C109GN	0086
C109J	0086
C109K	0086
C109L	0086
C109OR	0086
C109R	0086
C109X	0086
C109Y	0086
C110(2S)	0016
C110A	0016
C110B	0016
C110C	0016
C110D	0016
C110E	0016
C110F	0016
C110G	0016
C110GN	0016
C110H	0016
C110J	0016
C110K	0016
C110L	0016
C110M	0016
C110OR	0016
C110R	0016
C110X	0016
C110Y	0016
C111(2S)	0016
C111A	0016
C111B	0144
C111B(TRANS)	0016
C111C	0016
C111D	0016
C111E	0016
C111E(TRANS)	0016
C111F	0016
C111G	0016
C111GN	0016
C111H	0016
C111J	0016
C111K	0016
C111L	0016
C111M	0016
C111OR	0016
C111R	0016
C111X	0016
C111Y	0016
C112	2214
C112(2S)	0086
C112A	0086
C112B	0086
C112C	0086
C112D	0086
C112E	0086
C112F	0086
C112G	0086
C112GN	0086
C112H	0086
C112J	0086
C112K	0086
C112L	0086
C112M	0086
C112OR	0086
C112R	0086
C112X	0086
C112Y	0086
C113(2S)	0086
C113A	0086
C113B	0086
C113C	0086
C113D	0086
C113E	0086
C113F	0086
C113G	0086
C113GN	0086
C113H	0086
C113J	0086
C113K	0086
C113L	0086
C113M	0086
C113OR	0086
C113R	0086
C113X	0086
C113Y	0086
C114(2S)	0086
C114A	0086
C114B	0086
C114C	0086
C114D	0086
C114E	0086

DEVICE TYPE	REPL CODE
C114E(DT)	0826
C114E(SWITCH)	OEM
C114EF	2088
C114ESB	OEM
C114ESC	OEM
C114ESN	0826
C114F	0086
C114G	0086
C114GN	0086
C114H	0086
C114J	0086
C114K	0086
C114L	0086
C114M	0086
C114OR	0086
C114R	0086
C114X	0086
C114Y	0086
C114YSR	OEM
C115(2S)	0086
C115-1	0086
C115-2	0086
C115-3	0086
C115-43	0086
C115A	0086
C115B	0086
C115C	0086
C115D	0086
C115E	0086
C115F	0086
C115G	0086
C115GN	0086
C115H	0086
C115J	0086
C115K	0086
C115L	0086
C115M	0086
C115OR	0086
C115R	0086
C115X	0086
C115Y	0086
C116(2S)	2050
C116-OR	2050
C116A	2078
C116A(TRANS)	2050
C116B	0500
C116B(TRANS)	2050
C116C	0705
C116C(TRANS)	2050
C116D	0705
C116D(TRANS)	2050
C116E	2050
C116F	2084
C116F(TRANS)	2050
C116G	2050
C116GN	2050
C116H	2050
C116J	2050
C116K	2050
C116L	2050
C116M(TRANS)	2050
C116OR	2050
C116R	2050
C116T(2S)	2050
C116X	2050
C116Y	2050
C117(2S)	0086
C117A	0086
C117B	0086
C117C	0086
C117D	0086
C117F	0086
C117G	0086
C117GN	0086
C117H	0086
C117J	0086
C117K	0086
C117L	0086
C117M	0086
C117OR	0086
C117R	0086
C117X	0086
C117Y	0086
C118	0126
C118(2S)	0086
C118A	OEM
C118A(TRANS)	0086
C118B	OEM
C118B(TRANS)	0086
C118C	OEM
C118C(TRANS)	0086
C118D	OEM
C118D(TRANS)	0086
C118E	OEM
C118E(TRANS)	0086
C118F	OEM
C118F(TRANS)	0086
C118G	0086
C118GN	0086
C118H	0086
C118J	0086
C118L	0086
C118M	OEM
C118M(TRANS)	0086
C118OR	0086
C118R	0086
C118X	0086
C118Y	0086
C119	0126

DEVICE TYPE	REPL CODE
C119(2S)	0086
C119A	0086
C119B	0086
C119C	0086
C119D	0086
C119E	0086
C119F	0086
C119G	0086
C119GN	0086
C119H	0086
C119J	0086
C119K	0086
C119L	0086
C119M	0086
C119OR	0086
C119R	0086
C119X	0086
C119Y	0086
C120(2S)	0016
C120A	0016
C120B	0016
C120C	0016
C120D	0016
C120E	0016
C120F	0016
C120G	0016
C120GN	0016
C120H	0016
C120H03Q	OEM
C120H04Q	OEM
C120H05Q	OEM
C120H06Q	OEM
C120J	0016
C120K	0016
C120M	0016
C120R	0016
C120Y	0016
C121(2S)	0086
C121A	0086
C121B	0086
C121C	0086
C121D	0086
C121E	0086
C121F	0086
C121G	0086
C121GN	0086
C121H	0086
C121J	0086
C121L	0086
C121M	0086
C121OR	0086
C121R	0086
C121X	0086
C121Y	0086
C122	0079
C122(2S)	0086
C122A	2078
C122A(TRANS)	0086
C122A1	2078
C122A2	2078
C122A3	2078
C122A4	2078
C122A5	2078
C122A6	2078
C122B	0500
C122B(TRANS)	0086
C122B1	2084
C122B2	0500
C122B3	0500
C122B4	0500
C122B5	0500
C122B6	2084
C122BB	0500
C122C	0705
C122C(TRANS)	0086
C122C1	0705
C122C2	0705
C122C3	0705
C122C4	0705
C122C5	0705
C122C6	0705
C122D	0705
C122D(TRANS)	0086
C122D1	0705
C122D2	0705
C122D3	0705
C122D4	0705
C122D5	0705
C122D6	0705
C122E	0857
C122E(TRANS)	0086
C122E1	0857
C122E2	OEM
C122E3	OEM
C122E4	OEM
C122E5	OEM
C122E6	OEM
C122F	2084
C122F(TRANS)	0086
C122F1	2084
C122F2	2084
C122F3	2084
C122F4	2084
C122F5	2084
C122F6	2084
C122G	0086
C122GN	0086
C122H	0086
C122J	0086

DEVICE TYPE	REPL CODE
C122K	0086
C122L	0086
C122M	0857
C122M(TRANS)	0086
C122M1	0857
C122M2	OEM
C122M3	OEM
C122M4	OEM
C122M5	OEM
C122M6	OEM
C122N1	0323
C122OR	0086
C122R	0086
C122S	OEM
C122UX5	2084
C122X	0086
C122Y	0086
C123	0086
C123A	0086
C123B	0086
C123C	0086
C123D	0086
C123E	0086
C123F	0086
C123G	0086
C123GN	0086
C123H	0086
C123IFD	OEM
C123J	0086
C123K	0086
C123L	0086
C123M	0086
C123MDD	OEM
C123MFD	OEM
C123OR	0086
C123R	0086
C123X	0086
C123Y	0086
C124(2S)	0086
C124A	2078
C124A(TRANS)	0086
C124B	0500
C124B(TRANS)	0086
C124C	0705
C124C(TRANS)	0086
C124D	0705
C124D(TRANS)	0086
C124E	0857
C124E(TRANS)	0086
C124EL	OEM
C124ES	0881
C124F	2084
C124F(TRANS)	0086
C124G	0086
C124GN	0086
C124H	0086
C124J	0086
C124K	0086
C124L	0086
C124M	0857
C124M(TRANS)	0086
C124OR	0086
C124R	0086
C124X	0086
C124Y	0086
C125(2S)	0086
C125AL	OEM
C126	0283
C126A	0393
C126A2	OEM
C126A3	OEM
C126A4	OEM
C126A5	OEM
C126A6	OEM
C126B	0393
C126B2	OEM
C126B3	OEM
C126B4	OEM
C126B5	OEM
C126B6	OEM
C126C	0606
C126C2	OEM
C126C3	OEM
C126C4	OEM
C126C5	OEM
C126C6	OEM
C126D	0606
C126D2	OEM
C126D3	OEM
C126D4	OEM
C126D5	OEM
C126D6	OEM
C126E	0946
C126E2	OEM
C126E3	OEM
C126E4	OEM
C126E5	OEM
C126E6	OEM
C126F	2499
C126F2	OEM
C126F3	OEM
C126F4	OEM
C126F5	OEM
C126F6	OEM
C126M	0946
C126M2	OEM
C126M3	OEM
C126M4	OEM
C126M5	OEM

DEVICE TYPE	REPL CODE
C126M6	OEM
C127(2S)	0016
C127A	0393
C127A(TRANS)	0016
C127B	0393
C127B(TRANS)	0016
C127C	0606
C127C(TRANS)	0016
C127D	0606
C127D(TRANS)	0016
C127E	0946
C127E(TRANS)	0016
C127F	2499
C127F(TRANS)	0016
C127G	0016
C127GN	0016
C127H	0016
C127J	0016
C127K	0016
C127L	0016
C127M	0946
C127M(TRANS)	0016
C127OR	0016
C127R	0016
C127X	0016
C127Y	0016
C128(2S)	0595
C128A	0595
C128B	0595
C128C	0595
C128D	0595
C128D/DOS	OEM
C128E	0595
C128F	0595
C128G	0595
C128GN	0595
C128H	0595
C128J	0595
C128K	0595
C128L	0595
C128M	0595
C128OR	0595
C128R	0595
C128X	0595
C128Y	0595
C129	0595
C129A	0595
C129B	0595
C129C	0595
C129D	0595
C129E	0595
C129F	0595
C129GN	0595
C129H	0595
C129J	0595
C129K	0595
C129L	0595
C129M	0595
C129OR	0595
C129R	0595
C129X	0595
C129Y	0595
C130(2S)	0086
C130A	0086
C130B	0086
C130C	0086
C130D	0086
C130E	0086
C130F	0086
C130GN	0086
C130H	0086
C130J	0086
C130K	0086
C130L	0086
C130M	0086
C130OR	0086
C130R	0086
C130X	0086
C130Y	0086
C131(2S)	0016
C131A	0016
C131B	0016
C131C	0016
C131D	0016
C131E	0016
C131F	0016
C131G	0016
C131GN	0016
C131H	0016
C131J	0016
C131L	0016
C131M	0016
C131OR	0016
C131R	0016
C131T	0016
C131Y	0016
C132(2S)	0016
C132A	0016
C132B	0016
C132C	0016
C132D	0016
C132E	0016
C132F	0016
C132G	0016
C132GN	0016
C132H	0016
C132J	0016
C132K	0016
C132L	0016

If replacement code is OEM, contact original manufacturer for replacement.

Original Device Types

DEVICE TYPE	REPL CODE
C132M	0016
C132OR	0016
C132R	0016
C132X	0016
C132Y	0016
C133(2S)	0016
C133A	0016
C133C	0016
C133D	0016
C133E	0016
C133F	0016
C133G	0016
C133GN	0016
C133H	0016
C133J	0016
C133K	0016
C133L	0016
C133M	0016
C133OR	0016
C133X	0016
C133Y	0016
C134(2S)	0016
C134A	0016
C134B(2S)	0016
C134C	0016
C134D	0016
C134E	0016
C134F	0016
C134G	0016
C134GN	0016
C134H	0016
C134J	0016
C134K	0016
C134L	0016
C134M	0016
C134OR	0016
C134R	0016
C134X	0016
C134Y	0016
C135(2S)	0016
C135A	0707
C135A(TRANS)	0016
C135B	0464
C135B(TRANS)	0016
C135C	0716
C135C(TRANS)	0016
C135D	0717
C135D(TRANS)	0016
C135E	0773
C135E(TRANS)	0016
C135F	0726
C135F(TRANS)	0016
C135G	0016
C135GN	0016
C135H	0016
C135J	0016
C135L	0016
C135M	0720
C135M(TRANS)	0016
C135N	0674
C135OR	0016
C135R	0016
C135S	0674
C135X	0016
C135Y	0016
C136(2S)	0016
C136D	OEM
C136D(2S)	0016
C136E	0720
C136M	0759
C136N	0745
C136S	OEM
C137	0016
C137A	0016
C137B	0016
C137C	0016
C137D	0016
C137E	0773
C137E(TRANS)	0016
C137ER1200	OEM
C137F	0016
C137G	0016
C137GN	0016
C137H	0016
C137J	0016
C137K	0016
C137L	0016
C137M	0720
C137M(TRANS)	0016
C137MR1200	OEM
C137N	0745
C137NR1200	OEM
C137OR	0016
C137P	OEM
C137PA	OEM
C137PB	0674
C137PBR1200	OEM
C137PR1200	OEM
C137R	0016
C137S	0745
C137T	0674
C137X	0016
C137Y	0016
C138	0016
C138A(2S)	0016
C138B	0016
C138C	0016
C138D	0016
C138E	0016
C138E10	OEM
C138E10E	0799
C138E20	OEM
C138E20E	3374
C138F	0016
C138G	0016
C138GN	0016
C138H	0016
C138J	0016
C138L	0016
C138M	0016
C138M10	OEM
C138M10M	0799
C138M20	OEM
C138M20M	0799
C138N10	OEM
C138N10M	OEM
C138N20	OEM
C138N20M	OEM
C138OR	0016
C138R	0016
C138S	0016
C138S10	OEM
C138S10A	OEM
C138S10M	OEM
C138S20	OEM
C138S20M	OEM
C138X	0016
C139	0016
C139A	0016
C139B	0016
C139C	0016
C139D	0016
C139E	0016
C139E10	OEM
C139E10E	0799
C139E20	OEM
C139E20E	3374
C139F	0016
C139G	0016
C139GN	0016
C139H	0016
C139J	0016
C139K	0016
C139M	0016
C139M1M0	OEM
C139M10	OEM
C139M10M	0799
C139M20	OEM
C139M20M	0799
C139N10	OEM
C139N10M	OEM
C139N20	OEM
C139N20M	OEM
C139OR	0016
C139R	0016
C139S10	OEM
C139S10M	OEM
C139S20	OEM
C139S20M	OEM
C139X	0016
C139Y	0016
C140	0086
C140A	0799
C140A(TRANS)	0086
C140B	0799
C140C	0799
C140C(TRANS)	0086
C140D	0799
C140D(TRANS)	0086
C140E	0086
C140F	0799
C140F(TRANS)	0086
C140G	0086
C140GN	0086
C140H	0086
C140J	0086
C140K	0086
C140L	0086
C140M	0086
C140OR	0086
C140R	0086
C140X	0086
C140Y	0086
C141	0079
C141A	0799
C141B	0799
C141C	0799
C141D	0799
C141F	0799
C142	0079
C143	0079
C143E(DT)	OEM
C144	0079
C144A	0079
C144E	0892
C144E(DT)	0892
C144E15	OEM
C144E15E	0799
C144E30	OEM
C144E30E	0799
C144ES	0892
C144ESD	0892
C144M15	OEM
C144M15M	0799
C144M30	OEM
C144M30M	0799
C144N15	OEM
C144N15M	OEM
C144N30	OEM
C144N30M	OEM
C144S15	OEM
C144S15M	OEM
C144S30	OEM
C144S30M	OEM
C145	0079
C145E	OEM
C145M	OEM
C145N	OEM
C145P	OEM
C145PA	OEM
C145PB	OEM
C145S	OEM
C146	0079
C146A	0396
C146A(2S)	0079
C146B	0016
C146C	OEM
C146D	OEM
C146E	OEM
C146F	OEM
C146M	OEM
C146N	OEM
C146P	OEM
C146S	OEM
C146T	OEM
C147(2S)	2338
C147A	1694
C147A(TRANS)	2675
C147B	1694
C147B(TRANS)	2675
C147C	3970
C147C(TRANS)	2675
C147D	3970
C147D(TRANS)	2675
C147E	3970
C147F	1694
C147F(TRANS)	2675
C147G	1694
C147G(TRANS)	2675
C147GN	2675
C147H	3970
C147H(TRANS)	2675
C147J	2675
C147K	2675
C147L	2675
C147M	3970
C147M(TRANS)	2675
C147N	0674
C147P	0674
C147PA	0674
C147PB	0674
C147R	2675
C147S	0674
C147T	0674
C147U	1694
C147X	2675
C147Y	2675
C148	0144
C148A	0144
C148B	0144
C148D	0144
C148E	0144
C148F	0144
C148G	0144
C148GN	0144
C148H	0144
C148J	0144
C148K	0144
C148L	0144
C148M	OEM
C148M(TRANS)	0144
C148M30	OEM
C148M40	OEM
C148N	OEM
C148N30	OEM
C148N40	OEM
C148OR	0144
C148P	OEM
C148P30	OEM
C148P40	OEM
C148PA	OEM
C148PA30	OEM
C148PA40	OEM
C148PB	OEM
C148PB30	OEM
C148PB40	OEM
C148R	0144
C148S	OEM
C148S30	OEM
C148S40	OEM
C148T	OEM
C148T30	OEM
C148T40	OEM
C148X	0144
C148Y	0144
C149	0086
C149A	OEM
C149A10	OEM
C149A20	OEM
C149B	OEM
C149B10	OEM
C149B20	OEM
C149C	OEM
C149C10	OEM
C149C20	OEM
C149D	OEM
C149D10	OEM
C149D20	OEM
C149E	OEM
C149E10	OEM
C149E20	OEM
C149G	OEM
C149M	OEM
C149M10	OEM
C149M20	OEM
C150(2S)	2361
C150-OR	2361
C150A	2361
C150B	2361
C150C	2361
C150D	2361
C150E	0605
C150E(TRANS)	2361
C150F	2361
C150G	2361
C150GN	2361
C150H	2361
C150J	2361
C150K	2361
C150L	2361
C150M	0605
C150M(TRANS)	2361
C150N	0463
C150OR	2361
C150P	0463
C150PA	0463
C150PB	0463
C150PC	OEM
C150R	2361
C150S	0463
C150T	0086
C150T(2S)	2361
C150T(SCR)	0463
C150X	2361
C150Y	2361
C151(2S)	0198
C151A	0198
C151B	0198
C151C	0198
C151D	0198
C151E	OEM
C151E(TRANS)	0198
C151G	0198
C151GN	0198
C151H	0198
C151HA	0198
C151HB	0198
C151HC	0198
C151J	0198
C151K	0198
C151L	0198
C151M	OEM
C151M(TRANS)	0198
C151N	OEM
C151OR	0198
C151P	OEM
C151PA	OEM
C151PB	OEM
C151R	0198
C151S	OEM
C151T	OEM
C151X	0198
C151Y	0198
C152	0198
C152A	0198
C152B	0198
C152C	0198
C152D	0198
C152E	0636
C152E(TRANS)	0198
C152F	0198
C152G	0198
C152GN	0198
C152H	0198
C152HA	0198
C152HB	0198
C152HC	0198
C152J	0198
C152K	0198
C152L	0198
C152M	0636
C152M(TRANS)	0198
C152N	0217
C152OR	0198
C152P	0653
C152PA	0653
C152PB	0653
C152PC	OEM
C152R	0198
C152S	0653
C152T	0653
C152X	0198
C152Y	0198
C153	0079
C153E	OEM
C153M	OEM
C153N	OEM
C153P	OEM
C153PA	OEM
C153PB	OEM
C153PC	OEM
C153T	OEM
C154(2S)	0711
C154-OR	0711
C154A	0521
C154A(TRANS)	0711
C154B	0042
C154B(SCR)	0521
C154B(TRANS)	0711
C154C	0233
C154C(SCR)	0521
C154C(TRANS)	0711
C154D	0521
C154D(TRANS)	0711
C154E	0521
C154E(TRANS)	0711
C154F	0711
C154G	0521
C154G(TRANS)	0711
C154GN	0711
C154H(2S)	0711
C154HA	0711
C154HB	0711
C154HC	0711
C154J	0711
C154K	0711
C154L	0711
C154M	0521
C154M(TRANS)	0711
C154OR	0711
C154R	0711
C154X	0711
C154Y	0711
C155	0127
C155(2S)	0127
C155A	0521
C155A(TRANS)	0127
C155B	0521
C155B(TRANS)	0127
C155C	0521
C155C(TRANS)	0127
C155D	0521
C155D(TRANS)	0127
C155E	0521
C155E(TRANS)	0127
C155F	0127
C155G	0521
C155GN	0127
C155H	0127
C155J	0127
C155K	0127
C155L	0127
C155M	0521
C155M(TRANS)	0127
C155OR	0127
C155P	OEM
C155R	0127
C155X	0127
C155Y	0127
C156(2S)	0127
C156A	0650
C156A(TRANS)	0127
C156B	0650
C156B(TRANS)	0127
C156C	0650
C156C(TRANS)	0127
C156D	0650
C156D(TRANS)	0127
C156E	0650
C156E(TRANS)	0127
C156F	0127
C156G	0650
C156G(TRANS)	0127
C156GN	0127
C156H	0127
C156J	0127
C156K	0127
C156L	0127
C156M	0650
C156M(TRANS)	0127
C156OR	0127
C156R	0127
C156X	0127
C156Y	0127
C157(2S)	0198
C157A	0650
C157A(TRANS)	0198
C157B	0650
C157B(TRANS)	0198
C157C	0650
C157C(TRANS)	0198
C157D	0650
C157D(TRANS)	0198
C157E	0650
C157E(TRANS)	0198
C157F	0198
C157G	0264
C157G(TRANS)	0198
C157GN	0198
C157J	0198
C157K	0198
C157L	0198
C157M	0650
C157M(TRANS)	0198
C157OR	0198
C157R	0198
C157Y	0198
C158(2S)	0198
C158A	0198
C158B	0198
C158C	0198
C158D	0198
C158E	0521
C158E(TRANS)	0198
C158F	0198
C158G(TRANS)	0198
C158GN	0198
C158H	0198
C158J	0198
C158K	0198
C158L	0198
C158M	0521
C158M(TRANS)	0198
C158N	0108
C158OR	0198
C158P	0108
C158PA	0108
C158PB	0108
C158R	0198
C158S	0108
C158T	0108
C158X	0198
C158Y	0198
C159(2S)	0016
C159A	0016
C159B	0016
C159C	0016
C159D	0016
C159E	0650
C159E(TRANS)	0016
C159F	0016
C159GN	0016
C159H	0016
C159J	0016
C159K	0016
C159L	0016
C159M	0020
C159M(TRANS)	0016
C159N	0020
C159OR	0016
C159P	0020
C159PA	0020
C159PB	0020
C159R	0016
C159S	0020
C159T	0020
C159X	0016
C159Y	0016
C160(2S)	0016
C160A	0016
C160B	0016
C160C	0016
C160D	0016
C160E	0016
C160F	0016
C160G	0016
C160GN	0016
C160H	0016
C160J	0016
C160K	0016
C160L	0016
C160M	0016
C160OR	0016
C160R	0016
C160X	0016
C160Y	0016
C161	0538
C162	0079
C163(2S)	0488
C163A	0488
C163B	0488
C163C	0488
C163D	0488
C163E	0488
C163F	0488
C163G	0488
C163GN	0488
C163H	0488
C163J	0488
C163K	0488
C163L	0488
C163M	0488
C163OR	0488
C163R	0488
C163X	0488
C163Y	0488
C164	0018
C164A	0521
C164A(TRANS)	0018
C164B	0521
C164B(TRANS)	0018
C164C	0521
C164C(TRANS)	0711
C164D	0521
C164D(TRANS)	0018
C164E	0521
C164E(TRANS)	0018
C164F	0018
C164G	0018
C164GN	0018
C164H	0018
C164J	0018
C164K	0018
C164L	0018
C164M	0521
C164OR	0018
C164R	0018
C164X	0018
C164Y	0018
C165	0590
C165A	0521
C165B	0521
C165C	0521
C165D	0521
C165E	0521
C165M	0521
C165N	0108
C165S	0108
C166	0016
C166(2S)	0016
C166A	0016
C166B	0016
C166C	0016
C166D	0016
C166E	0016
C166F	0016
C166G	0016
C166GN	0016
C166H	0016
C166J	0016
C166K	0016
C166L	0016
C166M	0016
C166OR	0016
C166P	OEM
C166R	0016
C166X	0016
C166Y	0016
C167(2S)	0016
C167A	0016
C167B	0016
C167C	0016
C167D	0016
C167E	0016
C167F	0016
C167G	0016
C167GN	0016
C167H	0016
C167K	0016
C167L	0016
C167M	0016
C167OR	0016
C167X	0016
C167Y	0016
C168	0079
C169	OEM
C169(2S)	0016
C170(2S)	0016
C170A	0016
C170B	0016
C170C	0016
C170D	0016
C170E	0016
C170F	0016
C170G	0016
C170GN	0016
C170H	0016
C170J	0016
C170K	0016
C170L	0016
C170M	0016
C170OR	0016
C170R	0016
C170X	0016
C170Y	0016
C171(2S)	0016
C171A	0016
C171B	0016
C171C	0016
C171D	0016
C171E	0016
C171F	0016
C171G	0016
C171GN	0016
C171H	0016
C171J	0016
C171K	0016
C171L	0016
C171M	0016
C171OR	0016
C171R	0016
C171X	0016
C171Y	0016
C172(2S)	0016
C172A(2S)	0016
C172B	0016
C172C	0016
C172D	0016
C172E	0016
C172F	0016
C172G	0016
C172GN	0016
C172H	0016
C172J	0016
C172K	0016
C172L	0016
C172M	0016
C172OR	0016
C172R	0016
C172Y	0016
C173(2S)	0595
C173A	0595
C173B	0595
C173C	0595
C173D	0595
C173E	0595
C173F	0595
C173G	0595
C173GN	0595
C173H	0595
C173J	0595
C173K	0595
C173L	0595

If replacement code is OEM, contact original manufacturer for replacement.
311

DEVICE TYPE	REPL CODE
C173M	0595
C1730R	0595
C173R	0595
C173X	0595
C173Y	0595
C174(2S)	0016
C174A(2S)	0016
C174B	0016
C174C	0016
C174D	0016
C174E	0016
C174F	0016
C174G	0016
C174GN	0016
C174H	0016
C174J	0016
C174K	0016
C174L	0016
C174M	0016
C1740R	0016
C174Q	0016
C174R	0016
C174S	0016
C174X	0016
C174Y	0016
C175(2S)	0595
C175A	0595
C175B(2S)	0595
C175BL	0595
C175C	0595
C175D	0595
C175E	0595
C175F	0595
C175G	0595
C175GN	0595
C175H	0595
C175J	0595
C175K	0595
C175L	0595
C175M	0595
C1750R	0595
C175R	0595
C175X	0595
C175Y	0595
C176(2S)	0595
C176A	0595
C176B	0595
C176C	0595
C176D	0595
C176E	0595
C176F	0595
C176G	0595
C176GN	0595
C176H	0595
C176J	0595
C176K	0595
C176L	0595
C1760R	0595
C176R	0595
C176X	0595
C176Y	0595
C177(2S)	0595
C177A	0595
C177B	0595
C177C	0595
C177D	0595
C177E	0595
C177F	0595
C177G	0595
C177GN	0595
C177H	0595
C177J	0595
C177K	0595
C177L	0595
C177M	0595
C1770R	0595
C177R	0595
C177X	0595
C177Y	0595
C178(2S)	0595
C178A	0733
C178A(TRANS)	0595
C178B	0733
C178B(TRANS)	0595
C178C	0733
C178C(TRANS)	0595
C178D	0733
C178D(TRANS)	0595
C178E	0733
C178E(TRANS)	0595
C178F	0595
C178G	0595
C178H	0595
C178J	0595
C178K	0595
C178L	0595
C178M	0733
C178M(TRANS)	0595
C178N	0733
C1780R	0595
C178P	0733
C178PA	0733
C178PB	0733
C178R	0595
C178S	0733
C178T	0733
C178X	0595
C178Y	0595
C179(2S)	0208

DEVICE TYPE	REPL CODE
C179A	0595
C179B	0208
C179C	0208
C179D	0208
C179E	0208
C179F	0208
C179G	0208
C179GN	0208
C179H	0208
C179J	0208
C179K	0208
C179L	0208
C179M	0208
C1790R	0208
C179R	0208
C179X	0208
C179Y	0208
C180	0208
C180A	0733
C180A(TRANS)	0208
C180AX500	1889
C180B	0733
C180B(TRANS)	0208
C180BX500	1889
C180C	0733
C180C(TRANS)	0208
C180CX500	1889
C180D	0733
C180D(TRANS)	0208
C180DX500	1889
C180E	1078
C180E(TRANS)	0208
C180EX500	1889
C180F	0208
C180G	0208
C180GN	0208
C180H	0208
C180J	0208
C180K	0208
C180L	0208
C180M	1078
C180M(TRANS)	0208
C180MX500	0733
C180N	1094
C1800R	0208
C180P	1094
C180PA	1094
C180PB	1094
C180PC	OEM
C180R	0208
C180S	1094
C180SX500	0733
C180T	1094
C180X	0208
C180Y	0208
C181(2S)	0208
C181A	0733
C181A(TRANS)	0208
C181B	0733
C181B(TRANS)	0208
C181C	0733
C181C(TRANS)	0208
C181D	0733
C181D(TRANS)	0208
C181E	0733
C181E(TRANS)	0208
C181F	0208
C181G	0208
C181GN	0208
C181H	0208
C181J	0208
C181L	0208
C181M	0733
C181M(TRANS)	0208
C181N	0733
C1810R	0208
C181P	0733
C181PA	0733
C181PB	0733
C181R	0208
C181S	0733
C181T	0733
C181X	0208
C181Y	0208
C182(2S)	0470
C182A	0470
C182B	0470
C182C	0470
C182D	0470
C182E	0470
C182F	0470
C182G	0470
C182GN	0470
C182H	0470
C182J	0470
C182K	0470
C182L	0470
C182M	0470
C182Q(2S)	0470
C182R	0470
C182V	0470
C182X	0470
C182Y	0470
C183(2S)	0470
C183-1	0470
C183-OR	0470
C183A	0470
C183AP	0470
C183B	0470

DEVICE TYPE	REPL CODE
C183BK	0470
C183C	0470
C183D	0470
C183E(2S)	0470
C183F	0470
C183G	0470
C183GN	0470
C183H	0470
C183J(2S)	0470
C183K(2S)	0470
C183L(2S)	0470
C183M(2S)	0470
C1830R	0470
C183P(2S)	0470
C183Q(2S)	0470
C183R(2S)	0470
C183S	0470
C183W(2S)	0470
C183X	0470
C183Y	0470
C184(2S)	0470
C184-OR	0470
C184A	OEM
C184A(TRANS)	0470
C184AP	0470
C184B	OEM
C184B(TRANS)	0470
C184BK	0470
C184C	OEM
C184C(TRANS)	0470
C184D	OEM
C184D(TRANS)	0470
C184E	OEM
C184E(TRANS)	0470
C184F	0470
C184G	0470
C184GN	0470
C184H(2S)	0470
C184J(2S)	0470
C184K	0470
C184L	0470
C184M	OEM
C184M(TRANS)	0470
C1840R	0470
C184P	0470
C184Q	0470
C184R	0470
C184X	0470
C184Y	0470
C185(2S)	0470
C185A	0470
C185A(2S)	0470
C185A(SCR)	OEM
C185B	OEM
C185B(TRANS)	0470
C185C	OEM
C185C(TRANS)	0470
C185D	OEM
C185E	OEM
C185E(TRANS)	0470
C185F	0470
C185G	0470
C185GN	0470
C185H	0470
C185J(2S)	0470
C185K	0470
C185L	0470
C185M	0470
C185M(2S)	0470
C185M(SCR)	OEM
C185N	OEM
C1850R	0470
C185Q(2S)	0470
C185R(2S)	0470
C185S	OEM
C185V(2S)	0470
C185X	0470
C185Y	0470
C186(2S)	0127
C186A	0127
C186B	0127
C186C	0127
C186D	0127
C186E	0127
C186F	0127
C186G	0127
C186GN	0127
C186H	0127
C186J	0127
C186K	0127
C186L	0127
C186M	0127
C1860R	0127
C186R	0127
C186X	0127
C186Y	0127
C187(2S)	0669
C187-OR	0669
C187A	0669
C187B	0669
C187C	0669
C187D	0669
C187E	0669
C187F	0669
C187G	0669
C187H	0669
C187I	0669
C187J	0669
C187K	0669

DEVICE TYPE	REPL CODE
C187L	0669
C187M	0669
C1870R	0669
C187R	0669
C187X	0669
C187Y	0669
C188(2S)	0086
C188A(2S)	0086
C188B	0086
C188C	0086
C188D	0086
C188E	0086
C188F	0086
C188G	0086
C188GN	0086
C188J	0086
C188K	0086
C188L	0086
C188M	0086
C1880R	0086
C188R	0086
C188X	0086
C188Y	0086
C189(2S)	0086
C189A	0086
C189B	0086
C189C	0086
C189D	0086
C189E	0086
C189F	0086
C189G	0086
C189GN	0086
C189H	0086
C189J	0086
C189K	0086
C189L	0086
C189M	0086
C1890R	0086
C189R	0086
C189X	0086
C189Y	0086
C190(2S)	0086
C190A	0086
C190B	0086
C190C	0086
C190D	0086
C190E	0086
C190F	0086
C190GN	0086
C190H	0086
C190J	0086
C190K	0086
C190L	0086
C190M	0086
C1900R	0086
C190R	0086
C190X	0086
C190Y	0086
C191(2S)	0016
C191A	0016
C191B	0016
C191C	0016
C191D	0016
C191E	0016
C191F	0016
C191G	0016
C191GN	0016
C191H	0016
C191J	0016
C191K	0016
C191L	0016
C191M	0016
C1910R	0016
C191R	0016
C191X	0016
C191Y	0016
C192(2S)	0016
C192A	0016
C192B	0016
C192C	0016
C192D	0016
C192E	0016
C192F	0016
C192G	0016
C192GN	0016
C192H	0016
C192J	0016
C192K	0016
C192L	0016
C192M	0016
C1920R	0016
C192R	0016
C192X	0016
C192Y	0016
C193(2S)	0016
C193A	0016
C193B	0016
C193C	0016
C193D	0016
C193E	0016
C193F	0016
C193G	0016
C193GN	0016
C193H	0016
C193J	0016
C193K	0016
C193L	0016
C193M	0016
C1930R	0016

DEVICE TYPE	REPL CODE
C193R	0016
C193X	0016
C194(2S)	0016
C194A	0016
C194B	0016
C194C	0016
C194D	0016
C194E	0016
C194F	0016
C194G	0016
C194GN	0016
C194H	0016
C194J	0016
C194K	0016
C194L	0016
C194M	0016
C1940R	0016
C194X	0016
C194Y	0016
C195(2S)	0016
C195A	0016
C195B	0016
C195C	0016
C195D	0016
C195E	0016
C195F	0016
C195G	0016
C195GN	0016
C195H	0016
C195J	0016
C195K	0016
C195L	0016
C195M	0016
C1950R	0016
C195R	0016
C195X	0016
C195Y	0016
C196(2S)	0016
C196A	0016
C196B	0016
C196C	0016
C196D	0016
C196E	0016
C196F	0016
C196G	0016
C196GN	0016
C196H	0016
C196J	0016
C196K	0016
C196L	0016
C196M	0016
C1960R	0016
C196R	0016
C196X	0016
C196Y	0016
C197(2S)	0016
C197A	0016
C197B	0016
C197C	0016
C197D	0016
C197E	0016
C197F	0016
C197G	0016
C197GN	0016
C197H	0016
C197J	0016
C197K	0016
C197L	0016
C197M	0016
C1970R	0016
C197R	0016
C197X	0016
C197Y	0016
C198(2S)	0525
C198A	0525
C198H	0525
C198S	0525
C198T	0525
C199(2S)	0016
C199A	0016
C199B	0016
C199C	0016
C199D	0016
C199E	0016
C199F	0016
C199G	0016
C199GN	0016
C199H	0016
C199J	0016
C199K	0016
C199L	0016
C199M	0016
C1990R	0016
C199R	0016
C199X	0016
C199Y	0016
C200	0016
C200(SCR)	1478
C200A	0016
C200B	0016
C200C	0016
C200D	0016
C200E	0016
C200F	0016
C200G	0016
C200GN	0016
C200H	0016
C200J	0016
C200K	0016

DEVICE TYPE	REPL CODE
C200L	0016
C200M	0016
C2000R	0016
C200R	0016
C200X	0016
C200Y	0016
C201	0126
C201(2S)	0016
C201A	0016
C201B	0016
C201C	0016
C201D	0016
C201E	0016
C201F	0016
C201G	0016
C201GN	0016
C201H	0016
C201J	0016
C201K	0016
C201L	0016
C201M	0016
C201R	0016
C201X	0016
C201Y	0016
C202	0004
C202(2S)	0016
C202A	0016
C202B	0016
C202C	0016
C202D	0016
C202E	0016
C202F	0016
C202G	0016
C202GN	0016
C202H	0016
C202J	0016
C202K	0016
C202L	0016
C202M	0016
C2020R	0016
C202R	0016
C202X	0016
C202Y	0016
C203(2S)	0590
C203A	0895
C203A(TRANS)	0590
C203AA	0590
C203B	0058
C203B(TRANS)	0590
C203C	0403
C203C(TRANS)	0590
C203D	0403
C203D(TRANS)	0590
C203E	0590
C203F	0590
C203G	0590
C203GN	0590
C203H	0590
C203J	0590
C203K	0590
C203L	0590
C203M	0590
C2030R	0590
C203Q	OEM
C203R	0590
C203X	0590
C203Y	1129
C203Y(TRANS)	0590
C203YY	0340
C204(2S)	0016
C204A	0016
C204B	0016
C204C	0016
C204D	0016
C204E	0016
C204F	0016
C204G	0016
C204GN	0016
C204H	0016
C204J	0016
C204K	0016
C204L	0016
C204M	0016
C2040R	0016
C204R	0016
C204X	0016
C204Y	0016
C205(2S)	0016
C205A	OEM
C205A(TRANS)	0016
C205B	OEM
C205B(TRANS)	0016
C205C	OEM
C205C(TRANS)	0016
C205D	OEM
C205D(TRANS)	0016
C205F	0016
C205G	0016
C205GN	0016
C205H	0016
C205J	0016
C205K	0016
C205L	0016
C205M	0016
C2050R	0016
C205Q	OEM
C205R	0016
C205X	0016
C205Y	OEM

DEVICE TYPE	REPL CODE
C205Y(TRANS)	0016
C205YY	OEM
C206(2S)	0216
C206-OR	0216
C206A	0216
C206B	0216
C206C	0216
C206D	0216
C206E	0216
C206G	0216
C206GN	0216
C206H	0216
C206J	0216
C206K	0216
C206L	0216
C206M	0216
C2060R	0216
C206R	0216
C206RED	0216
C206WHITE	0216
C206X	0216
C206Y	0216
C207	0259
C208(2S)	0007
C208A	0007
C208B	0007
C208C	0007
C208D	0007
C208E	0007
C208F	0007
C208G	0007
C208GN	0007
C208H	0007
C208J	0007
C208K	0007
C208L	0007
C208M	0007
C2080R	0007
C208R	0007
C208X	0007
C208Y	0007
C209	0259
C210	0086
C210(2S)	0086
C210A	0086
C210B	0086
C210C	0086
C210D	0086
C210E	0086
C210F	0086
C210G	0086
C210GN	0086
C210H	0086
C210J	0086
C210K	0086
C210L	0086
C210M	0086
C2100R	0086
C210R	0086
C210X	0086
C210Y	0086
C211(2S)	0086
C211A	0086
C211B	0086
C211C	0086
C211D	0086
C211F	0086
C211G	0086
C211GN	0086
C211H	0086
C211J	0086
C211K	0086
C211L	0086
C211M	0086
C2110R	0086
C211R	0086
C211X	0086
C211Y	0086
C212(2S)	0086
C212A	0086
C212B	0086
C212C	0086
C212D	0086
C212E	0086
C212F	0086
C212G	0086
C212GN	0086
C212H	0086
C212J	0086
C212K	0086
C212L	0086
C212M	0086
C2120R	0086
C212R	0086
C212X	0086
C212Y	0086
C213(2S)	0617
C213A	0617
C213B	0617
C213C	0617
C213D	0617
C213E	0617
C213F	0617
C213G	0617
C213GN	0617
C213H	0617
C213J	0617
C213K	0617
C213L	0617

If replacement code is OEM, contact original manufacturer for replacement.

DEVICE TYPE	REPL CODE
C213M	0617
C213OR	0617
C213R	0617
C213X	0617
C213Y	0617
C214(2S)	0617
C214A	0617
C214B	0617
C214C	0617
C214D	0617
C214E	0617
C214F	0617
C214G	0617
C214GN	0617
C214H	0617
C214J	0617
C214K	0617
C214L	0617
C214M	0617
C214OR	0617
C214X	0617
C214Y	0617
C215(2S)	0617
C215A	0617
C215B	0617
C215C	0617
C215E	0617
C215F	0617
C215G	0617
C215GN	0617
C215H	0617
C215J	0617
C215K	0617
C215L	0617
C215M	0617
C215OR	0617
C215R	0617
C215X	0617
C215Y	0617
C216(2S)	0086
C216A	0086
C216B	0086
C216C	0086
C216D	0086
C216E	0086
C216F	0086
C216G	0086
C216GN	0086
C216H	0086
C216J	0086
C216K	0086
C216L	0086
C216M	0086
C216OR	0086
C216R	0086
C216X	0086
C216Y	0086
C217(2S)	0086
C217A	0086
C217B	0086
C217C	0086
C217D	0086
C217E	0086
C217F	0086
C217G	0086
C217GN	0086
C217H	0086
C217J	0086
C217K	0086
C217L	0086
C217M	0086
C217OR	0086
C217R	0086
C217X	0086
C217Y	0086
C218(2S)	0086
C218A(2S)	0086
C218B	0086
C218C	0086
C218D	0086
C218E	0086
C218F	0086
C218G	0086
C218GN	0086
C218H	0086
C218J	0086
C218L	0086
C218M	0086
C218OR	0086
C218R	0086
C218T	OEM
C218X	0086
C218Y	0086
C219	0007
C220(2S)	0086
C220A	2430
C220A(TRANS)	0086
C220A2	1837
C220A3	OEM
C220A4	0226
C220A5	0226
C220A6	OEM
C220A7	OEM
C220A8	OEM
C220A9	OEM
C220B	0430
C220B(TRANS)	0086
C220B2	1837
C220B3	1837
C220B4	0226
C220B5	0226
C220B6	OEM
C220B7	OEM
C220B8	OEM
C220B9	OEM
C220C	1478
C220C(TRANS)	0086
C220C2	1844
C220C3	1844
C220C4	0226
C220C5	0226
C220C6	OEM
C220C7	OEM
C220C8	OEM
C220C9	OEM
C220D	1478
C220D(TRANS)	0086
C220D2	1844
C220D3	1844
C220D4	0226
C220D5	0226
C220D6	OEM
C220D7	OEM
C220D8	OEM
C220D9	OEM
C220E	0682
C220E(TRANS)	0086
C220E2	3185
C220E3	3185
C220E4	0226
C220E5	0226
C220E6	OEM
C220E7	OEM
C220E8	OEM
C220E9	OEM
C220F	2430
C220F(TRANS)	0086
C220F2	1837
C220F3	1837
C220F4	0226
C220F5	0226
C220F6	OEM
C220F7	OEM
C220F8	OEM
C220F9	OEM
C220G	0086
C220GN	0086
C220H	0086
C220K	0086
C220L	0086
C220M	0682
C220M(TRANS)	0086
C220M2	3185
C220M3	3185
C220M4	0226
C220M5	0226
C220M6	OEM
C220M7	OEM
C220M8	OEM
C220M9	OEM
C220OR	0086
C220R	0086
C220U	0464
C220U2	1837
C220U3	1837
C220U4	0226
C220U5	0226
C220U6	OEM
C220U7	OEM
C220U8	OEM
C220U9	OEM
C220X	0086
C220Y	0086
C221(2S)	0086
C221A	0086
C221B	0086
C221C	0086
C221D	0086
C221E	0086
C221F	0086
C221G	0086
C221GN	0086
C221H	0086
C221J	0086
C221K	0086
C221L	0086
C221M	0086
C221OR	0086
C221R	0086
C221X	0086
C221Y	0086
C222(2S)	0086
C222A	1641
C222A(TRANS)	0086
C222B	1641
C222B(TRANS)	0086
C222C	1574
C222C(TRANS)	0086
C222D	1574
C222D(TRANS)	0086
C222E	1655
C222E(TRANS)	0086
C222F	1641
C222F(TRANS)	0086
C222G	0086
C222GN	0086
C222H	0086
C222J	0086
C222L	0086
C222M	1655
C222M(TRANS)	0086
C222OR	0086
C222R	0086
C222U	1641
C222X	0086
C222Y	0086
C223	0617
C223A	0617
C223B	0617
C223C	0617
C223D	0617
C223E	0617
C223F	0617
C223G	0617
C223GN	0617
C223H	0617
C223J	0617
C223L	0617
C223M	0617
C223OR	0617
C223R	0617
C223X	0617
C223Y	0617
C224(2S)	0617
C224A	0617
C224B	0617
C224C	0617
C224D	0617
C224E	0617
C224F	0617
C224G	0617
C224GN	0617
C224GR-GL	0617
C224H	0617
C224J	0617
C224K	0617
C224L	0617
C224M	0617
C224OR	0617
C224R	0617
C224X	0617
C224Y	0617
C225(2S)	0086
C225A	0086
C225B	0086
C225C	0086
C225D	0086
C225E	0086
C225F	0086
C225G	0086
C225GN	0086
C225H	0086
C225J	0086
C225L	0086
C225M	0086
C225OR	0086
C225R	0086
C225X	0086
C225Y	0086
C226(2S)	0086
C226A	0086
C226B	0086
C226C	0086
C226D	0086
C226E	0086
C226F	0086
C226G	0086
C226GN	0086
C226H	0086
C226J	0086
C226K	0086
C226L	0086
C226M	0086
C226OR	0086
C226R	0086
C226X	0086
C226Y	0086
C227(2S)	0086
C227A	0086
C227B	0086
C227C	0086
C227D	0086
C227E	0086
C227F	0086
C227G	0086
C227GN	0086
C227H	0086
C227J	0086
C227K	0086
C227L	0086
C227M	0086
C227OR	0086
C227R	0086
C227X	0086
C227Y	0086
C228(2S)	0086
C228A	0707
C228A(TRANS)	0086
C228A2	1837
C228A3	1837
C228A4	0226
C228A5	0226
C228A7	OEM
C228A8	OEM
C228A9	OEM
C228B	0464
C228B(TRANS)	0086
C228B2	1837
C228B3	1837
C228B4	1837
C228B5	1837
C228B6	OEM
C228B7	OEM
C228B8	OEM
C228B9	OEM
C228C	0717
C228C(TRANS)	0086
C228C2	1844
C228C3	1844
C228C4	0226
C228C5	0226
C228C6	OEM
C228C7	OEM
C228C8	OEM
C228C9	OEM
C228D	2623
C228D(TRANS)	0086
C228D2	1844
C228D3	1844
C228D4	0226
C228D5	0226
C228D6	OEM
C228D7	OEM
C228D8	OEM
C228D9	OEM
C228E	0720
C228E(TRANS)	0086
C228E2	3185
C228E3	3185
C228E4	0226
C228E5	0226
C228E6	OEM
C228E7	OEM
C228E8	OEM
C228E9	OEM
C228F	0726
C228F(TRANS)	0086
C228F2	1837
C228F3	1837
C228F4	0226
C228F5	OEM
C228F6	OEM
C228F7	OEM
C228F8	OEM
C228F9	OEM
C228G	0086
C228GN	0086
C228H	0086
C228J	0086
C228K	0086
C228L	0086
C228M	0720
C228M(TRANS)	0086
C228M2	3185
C228M3	3185
C228M4	0226
C228M5	0226
C228M6	OEM
C228M7	OEM
C228M8	OEM
C228M9	OEM
C228OR	0086
C228R	0086
C228U	0464
C228U3	1837
C228U4	0226
C228U5	0226
C228U6	OEM
C228U7	OEM
C228U8	OEM
C228U9	OEM
C228X	0086
C228Y	0086
C229(2S)	0617
C229A	1640
C229A(TRANS)	0617
C229B	1640
C229B(TRANS)	0617
C229C	2623
C229C(TRANS)	0617
C229D	2623
C229D(TRANS)	0617
C229E	2625
C229E(TRANS)	0617
C229F	1640
C229F(TRANS)	0617
C229G	0617
C229GN	0617
C229H	0617
C229J	0617
C229K	0617
C229L	0617
C229M	2625
C229M(TRANS)	0617
C229OR	0617
C229R	0617
C229U	1640
C229X	0617
C229Y	0617
C230(2S)	2960
C230A	0226
C230A(TRANS)	0617
C230A2	1837
C230A3	1837
C230A4	0226
C230A5	0226
C230A6	OEM
C230A7	OEM
C230A8	OEM
C230A9	OEM
C230B	2623
C230B(TRANS)	0617
C230B2	1837
C230B3	1837
C230B4	0226
C230B5	0226
C230B6	OEM
C230B7	OEM
C230B8	OEM
C230B9	OEM
C230C	2623
C230C(TRANS)	0617
C230C2	1837
C230C3	1837
C230C4	0226
C230C5	0226
C230C6	OEM
C230C7	OEM
C230C8	OEM
C230C9	OEM
C230D	0735
C230D(TRANS)	0617
C230D2	1844
C230D3	1844
C230D4	0226
C230D5	0226
C230D6	OEM
C230D7	OEM
C230D8	OEM
C230D9	OEM
C230E	0747
C230E(TRANS)	0617
C230E2	3185
C230E3	3185
C230E4	0226
C230E5	0226
C230E6	OEM
C230E7	OEM
C230E8	OEM
C230E9	OEM
C230F	2497
C230F(TRANS)	0617
C230F2	1837
C230F3	1837
C230F4	0226
C230F5	0226
C230F6	OEM
C230F7	OEM
C230F8	OEM
C230F9	OEM
C230G	0617
C230GN	0617
C230H	0617
C230J	0617
C230K	0617
C230L	0617
C230M	0759
C230M(TRANS)	0617
C230M2	3185
C230M3	3185
C230M4	0226
C230M5	0226
C230M6	OEM
C230M7	OEM
C230M8	OEM
C230M9	OEM
C230OR	0617
C230R	0617
C230U	0464
C230U2	1837
C230U3	1837
C230U4	0226
C230U5	0226
C230U6	OEM
C230U7	OEM
C230U8	OEM
C230U9	OEM
C230X	0617
C230Y	0617
C231(2S)	2968
C231A	OEM
C231A(TRANS)	0617
C231A2	OEM
C231A3	OEM
C231A4	OEM
C231A5	OEM
C231A6	OEM
C231A7	OEM
C231A8	OEM
C231A9	OEM
C231B	OEM
C231B(TRANS)	0617
C231B2	OEM
C231B3	OEM
C231B4	OEM
C231B5	OEM
C231B6	OEM
C231B7	OEM
C231B8	OEM
C231B9	OEM
C231C	OEM
C231C(TRANS)	0617
C231C2	OEM
C231C3	OEM
C231C4	OEM
C231C5	OEM
C231C6	OEM
C231C7	OEM
C231C8	OEM
C231C9	OEM
C231D	2623
C231D(TRANS)	0617
C231D2	OEM
C231D3	OEM
C231D4	OEM
C231D5	OEM
C231D6	OEM
C231D7	OEM
C231D8	OEM
C231D9	OEM
C231E	OEM
C231E(TRANS)	0617
C231E2	OEM
C231E3	OEM
C231E4	OEM
C231E5	OEM
C231E6	OEM
C231E7	OEM
C231E8	OEM
C231E9	OEM
C231F	OEM
C231F(TRANS)	0617
C231F2	OEM
C231F3	OEM
C231F4	OEM
C231F5	OEM
C231F6	OEM
C231F7	OEM
C231F8	OEM
C231F9	OEM
C231G	0617
C231GN	0617
C231H	0617
C231J	0617
C231K	0617
C231L	0617
C231M	OEM
C231M(TRANS)	0617
C231M2	OEM
C231M3	OEM
C231OR	0617
C231R	0617
C231U	OEM
C231U2	OEM
C231U3	OEM
C231U4	OEM
C231U5	OEM
C231U6	OEM
C231U7	OEM
C231U8	OEM
C231U9	OEM
C231X	0617
C231Y	0617
C232(2S)	2968
C232A	1640
C232A(TRANS)	0617
C232B	1641
C232B(TRANS)	0617
C232C	1574
C232C(TRANS)	0617
C232D	2623
C232D(TRANS)	0617
C232E	1655
C232E(TRANS)	0617
C232F	1641
C232F(TRANS)	0617
C232G	0617
C232GN	0617
C232H	0617
C232J	0617
C232K	0617
C232L	0617
C232M	1655
C232M(TRANS)	0617
C232OR	0617
C232R	0617
C232U	2497
C232X	0617
C232Y	0617
C233(2S)	0617
C233A	1641
C233A(TRANS)	0617
C233B	OEM
C233B(TRANS)	0617
C233C	OEM
C233C(TRANS)	0617
C233D	1574
C233D(TRANS)	0617
C233E	OEM
C233F	1641
C233F(TRANS)	0617
C233G	0617
C233GN	0617
C233H	0617
C233J	0617
C233L	0617
C233M	1655
C233M(TRANS)	0617
C233OR	0617
C233R	0617
C233U	OEM
C233X	0617
C233Y	0617
C234(2S)	0086
C234A	0562
C234A(TRANS)	0086
C234A2	1837
C234A3	1837
C234A4	0226
C234A5	0226
C234A6	OEM
C234A7	OEM
C234A8	OEM
C234A9	OEM
C234B	0757
C234B(TRANS)	0086
C234B2	1837
C234B3	1837
C234B4	0226
C234B5	0226
C234B6	OEM
C234B7	OEM
C234B8	OEM
C234B9	OEM
C234C	0735
C234C(TRANS)	0086
C234C2	1844
C234C3	1844
C234C4	0226
C234C5	0226
C234C6	OEM
C234C7	OEM
C234C8	OEM
C234C9	OEM
C234D	0735
C234D(TRANS)	0086
C234D2	1844
C234D3	1844
C234D4	0226
C234D5	0226
C234D6	OEM
C234D7	OEM
C234D8	OEM
C234D9	OEM
C234E	0759
C234E(TRANS)	0086
C234E2	3185
C234E3	3185
C234E4	0226
C234E5	0226
C234E6	OEM
C234E7	OEM
C234E8	OEM
C234E9	OEM
C234F	2174
C234F(TRANS)	0086
C234F2	1837
C234F3	1837
C234F4	0226
C234F5	0226
C234F6	OEM
C234F7	OEM
C234F8	OEM
C234F9	OEM
C234G	0086
C234GN	0086
C234H	0086
C234J	0086
C234K	0086
C234L	0086
C234M	2625
C234M(TRANS)	0086
C234M2	3185
C234M3	3185
C234M4	0226
C234M5	0226
C234M6	OEM
C234M7	OEM
C234M8	OEM
C234M9	OEM
C234OR	0086
C234R	0086
C234U	OEM
C234U2	1837
C234U3	1837
C234U4	0226
C234U5	0226
C234U6	OEM
C234U7	OEM
C234U8	OEM
C234U9	OEM
C234X	0086
C234Y	0086
C235(2S)	0018
C235-0(2S)	0018
C235-O	0018
C235A	1640
C235A(TRANS)	0018
C235B	1640
C235B(TRANS)	0018
C235C	2623
C235C(TRANS)	0018
C235D	2623
C235D(TRANS)	0018
C235E	2625
C235E(TRANS)	0018
C235F	1640
C235F(TRANS)	0018
C235G	0018
C235GN	0018
C235H	0018
C235J	0018
C235K	0018

If replacement code is OEM, contact original manufacturer for replacement.

313

DEVICE TYPE	REPL CODE
C235L	0018
C235M	OEM
C235M(TRANS)	0018
C235OR	0018
C235R	0018
C235U	OEM
C235X	0018
C235Y	0018
C236(2S)	0086
C236A	0086
C236B	0086
C236C	0086
C236D	0086
C236E	0086
C236F	0086
C236G	0086
C236GN	0086
C236H	0086
C236J	0086
C236K	0086
C236L	0086
C236M	0086
C236OR	0086
C236R	0086
C236X	0086
C236Y	0086
C237(2S)	0016
C237A	0016
C237B	0016
C237C	0016
C237D	0016
C237E	0016
C237F	0016
C237G	0016
C237GN	0016
C237H	0016
C237J	0016
C237K	0016
C237L	0016
C237M	0016
C237OR	0016
C237R	0016
C237X	0016
C237Y	0016
C238(2S)	0016
C238A	0016
C238B	0016
C238C	0016
C238D	0016
C238E	0016
C238F	0016
C238G	0016
C238GN	0016
C238H	0016
C238J	0016
C238K	0016
C238L	0016
C238M	0016
C238OR	0016
C238R	0016
C238X	0016
C238Y	0016
C239(2S)	0016
C239A	0016
C239B	0016
C239C	0016
C239D	0016
C239E	0016
C239F	0016
C239G	0016
C239GN	0016
C239H	0016
C239J	0016
C239K	0016
C239L	0016
C239M	0016
C239OR	0016
C239R	0016
C239X	0016
C239Y	0016
C240(2S)	0103
C240A	0103
C240B	0103
C240C	0103
C240D	0103
C240E	0103
C240F	0103
C240G	0103
C240GN	0103
C240H	0103
C240J	0103
C240K	0103
C240L	0103
C240M	0103
C240OR	0103
C240R	0103
C240X	0103
C240Y	0103
C241(2S)	0103
C241A	0103
C241B	0103
C241C	0103
C241D	0103
C241E	0103
C241F	0103
C241G	0103
C241GN	0103
C241H	0103
C241K	0103
C241L	0103
C241M	0103
C241OR	0103
C241R	0103
C241X	0103
C241Y	0103
C242(2S)	0103
C242A	0103
C242B	0103
C242C	0103
C242D	0103
C242E	0103
C242F	0103
C242G	0103
C242GN	0103
C242H	0103
C242J	0103
C242K	0103
C242L	0103
C242M	0103
C242OR	0103
C242R	0103
C242X	0103
C242Y	0103
C243(2S)	0177
C244(2S)	1955
C244A	1955
C244B	1955
C244C	1955
C244D	1955
C244E	1955
C244F	1955
C244G	1955
C244GN	1955
C244J	1955
C244K	1955
C244L	1955
C244M	1955
C244OR	1955
C244R	1955
C244X	1955
C244Y	1955
C245(2S)	1955
C246(2S)	1955
C247(2S)	0086
C247A	0086
C247B	0086
C247C	0086
C247D	0086
C247E	0086
C247F	0086
C247G	0086
C247GN	0086
C247H	0086
C247J	0086
C247L	0086
C247M	0086
C247OR	0086
C247R	0086
C247X	0086
C247Y	0086
C248(2S)	0016
C248A	0016
C248B	0016
C248C	0016
C248D	0016
C248E	0016
C248F	0016
C248G	0016
C248J	0016
C248K	0016
C248L	0016
C248M	0016
C248OR	0016
C248R	0016
C248X	0016
C248Y	0016
C249(2S)	0086
C249A	0086
C249B	0086
C249C	0086
C249D	0086
C249E	0086
C249F	0086
C249G	0086
C249GN	0086
C249H	0086
C249J	0086
C249K	0086
C249L	0086
C249M	0086
C249OR	0086
C249R	0086
C249X	0086
C249Y	0086
C250(2S)	0016
C250A	0016
C250B	0016
C250C	0016
C250D	0016
C250E	0016
C250F	0016
C250G	0016
C250GN	0016
C250H	0016
C250J	0016
C250K	0016
C250L	0016
C250M	0016
C250OR	0016
C250R	0016
C250X	0016
C250Y	0016
C251(2S)	0259
C251A(2S)	0259
C251B	0259
C251C	0259
C251D	0259
C251E	0259
C251F	0259
C251G	0259
C251GN	0259
C251H	0259
C251J	0259
C251K	0259
C251L	0259
C251M	0259
C251OR	0259
C251R	0259
C251X	0259
C251Y	0259
C252(2S)	0259
C252A	0259
C252B	0259
C252C	0259
C252D	0259
C252E	0259
C252F	0259
C252G	0259
C252GN	0259
C252H	0259
C252J	0259
C252K	0259
C252L	0259
C252M	0259
C252OR	0259
C252R	0259
C252X	0259
C252Y	0259
C253(2S)	0259
C253A	0259
C253B	0259
C253C	0259
C253D	0259
C253E	0259
C253F	0259
C253G	0259
C253GN	0259
C253H	0259
C253J	0259
C253K	0259
C253L	0259
C253M	0259
C253OR	0259
C253R	0259
C253X	0259
C253Y	0259
C254(2S)	0086
C255	0086
C256	0086
C257	1973
C258	0264
C259	0264
C260	0590
C260D	0590
C260E	0590
C261(2S)	0693
C262	0590
C263(2S)	0144
C263A	0144
C263B	0144
C263C	0144
C263D	0144
C263E	0144
C263F	0144
C263G	0144
C263GN	0144
C263H	0144
C263J	0144
C263K	0144
C263L	0144
C263M	0144
C263OR	0144
C263R	0144
C263X	0144
C263Y	0144
C264	0079
C265	0079
C266	0470
C266(2S)	0470
C266A	0470
C266B	0470
C266C	0470
C266D	0470
C266E	0470
C266F	0470
C266G	0470
C266GN	0470
C266H	0470
C266J	0470
C266K	0470
C266L	0470
C266M	0470
C266OR	0470
C266P	OEM
C266R	0470
C266X	0470
C266Y	0470
C267(2S)	0016
C267A(2S)	0016
C267B	0016
C267C	0016
C267D	0016
C267E	0016
C267F	0016
C267G	0016
C267GN	0016
C267H	0016
C267J	0016
C267K	0016
C267L	0016
C267M	0016
C267OR	0016
C267R	0016
C267X	0016
C267Y	0016
C268(2S)	0086
C268-OR	0086
C268A(2S)	0086
C268B	0086
C268C	0086
C268D	0086
C268E	0086
C268F	0086
C268G	0086
C268GN	0086
C268H	0086
C268J	0086
C268K	0086
C268L	0086
C268M	0086
C268OR	0086
C268R	0086
C268X	0086
C268Y	0086
C269(2S)	0144
C269A	0144
C269B	0144
C269C	0144
C269D	0144
C269E	0144
C269F	0144
C269G	0144
C269GN	0144
C269H	0144
C269J	0144
C269K	0144
C269L	0144
C269M	0144
C269OR	0144
C269R	0144
C269X	0144
C269Y	0144
C270(2S)	0074
C271(2S)	0144
C271A	0144
C271B	0144
C271C	0144
C271D	0144
C271E	0144
C271F	0144
C271G	0144
C271GN	0144
C271H	0144
C271J	0144
C271K	0144
C271L	0144
C271M	0144
C271OR	0144
C271R	0144
C271X	0144
C271Y	0144
C272(2S)	0144
C272A	0144
C272B	0144
C272C	0144
C272D	0144
C272E	0144
C272F	0144
C272G	0144
C272GN	0144
C272H	0144
C272J	0144
C272K	0144
C272L	0144
C272M	0144
C272OR	0144
C272R	0144
C272X	0144
C272Y	0144
C273(2S)	0233
C277C(2S)	0208
C278-OR	0470
C280	0111
C280AO	0111
C280N	0733
C280P	0733
C280PA	0733
C280PB	0733
C280PC	OEM
C280PD	OEM
C280PE	OEM
C280PM	OEM
C280PS	OEM
C280S	0733
C280T	0733
C281(2S)	0531
C281-OR	0531
C281A(2S)	0531
C281B(2S)	0531
C281BL	0531
C281C(2S)	0531
C281C-EP(2S)	0531
C281D(2S)	0531
C281E	0531
C281EP(2S)	0531
C281F	0531
C281G	0531
C281GN	0531
C281H(2S)	0531
C281HB	0016
C281J	0531
C281K	0531
C281L	0531
C281M	0531
C281N	OEM
C281OR	0531
C281P	OEM
C281PA	OEM
C281PB	OEM
C281PC	OEM
C281PD	OEM
C281PE	OEM
C281PM	OEM
C281PN	OEM
C281PS	OEM
C281R	0531
C281S	OEM
C281X	0531
C281Y	0531
C282(2S)	0016
C282A	0016
C282A(TRANS)	0016
C282B	0016
C282B(TRANS)	0016
C282C	0016
C282C(TRANS)	0016
C282D	OEM
C282D(TRANS)	0016
C282E	OEM
C282E(TRANS)	0016
C282F	0016
C282G	0016
C282GN	0016
C282H(2S)	0016
C282J	0016
C282K	0016
C282L	0016
C282M	OEM
C282M(TRANS)	0016
C282N	OEM
C282OR	0016
C282P	OEM
C282PA	OEM
C282PB	OEM
C282PC	OEM
C282PD	OEM
C282PE	OEM
C282PM	OEM
C282PS	OEM
C282R	0016
C282S	OEM
C282T	OEM
C282X	0016
C282Y	0016
C283(2S)	1553
C283A	0016
C283A(TRANS)	1553
C283B	0016
C283B(TRANS)	1553
C283C	0016
C283C(TRANS)	1553
C283D	OEM
C283D(TRANS)	1553
C283E	OEM
C283E(TRANS)	1553
C283F	1553
C283G	1553
C283GN	1553
C283H	1553
C283J	1553
C283K	1553
C283L	1553
C283M	OEM
C283M(TRANS)	1553
C283N	OEM
C283OR	1553
C283P	OEM
C283PA	OEM
C283PB	OEM
C283PC	OEM
C283PD	OEM
C283PE	OEM
C283PM	OEM
C283PS	OEM
C283R	1553
C283S	OEM
C283T	OEM
C283X	1553
C283Y	1553
C284(2S)	0016
C284A	0016
C284B	0016
C284C	0016
C284D	0016
C284E	0016
C284F	0016
C284G	0016
C284GN	0016
C284H(2S)	0016
C284J	0016
C284K	0016
C284L	0016
C284M	0016
C284OR	0016
C284R	0016
C284X	0016
C284Y	0016
C285(2S)	0488
C285A(2S)	0488
C285B	0488
C285C	0488
C285D	0488
C285E	0488
C285F	0488
C285G	0488
C285GN	0488
C285H	0488
C285J	0488
C285K	0488
C285L	0488
C285M	0488
C285OR	0488
C285R	0488
C285X	0488
C285Y	0488
C286	0144
C286A	OEM
C286A(TRANS)	0144
C286B	0144
C286B(TRANS)	0144
C286C	OEM
C286C(TRANS)	0144
C286D	OEM
C286D(TRANS)	0144
C286E	0144
C286E(TRANS)	0144
C286F	0144
C286G	0144
C286GN	0144
C286H	0144
C286J	0144
C286K	0144
C286L	0144
C286M	OEM
C286M(TRANS)	0144
C286N	OEM
C286OR	0144
C286P	OEM
C286PA	OEM
C286PB	OEM
C286PC	OEM
C286PD	OEM
C286PE	OEM
C286PM	OEM
C286PS	OEM
C286R	0144
C286S	OEM
C286T	OEM
C286X	0144
C286Y	0144
C287	0470
C287-OR	0470
C287A	0470
C287A(2S)	0470
C287B	OEM
C287B(TRANS)	0470
C287C	OEM
C287C(TRANS)	0470
C287D	OEM
C287D(TRANS)	0470
C287E	OEM
C287E(TRANS)	0470
C287F	0470
C287G	0470
C287GN	0470
C287H	0470
C287J	0470
C287K	0470
C287L	0470
C287M	OEM
C287M(TRANS)	0470
C287N	OEM
C287OR	0470
C287P	OEM
C287PA	OEM
C287PB	OEM
C287PC	OEM
C287PD	OEM
C287PE	OEM
C287PM	OEM
C287PS	OEM
C287R	0470
C287S	OEM
C287T	OEM
C287X	0470
C287Y	0470
C288(2S)	1332
C288A(2S)	1332
C288A(5B)	1332
C288A1	1332
C288A1B	1332
C288A5-B	1332
C288AB	1332
C288B	1332
C288C	1332
C288D	1332
C288E	1332
C288F	1332
C288G	1332
C288GN	1332
C288H	1332
C288J	1332
C288K	1332
C288L	1332
C288M	1332
C288OR	1332
C288R	1332
C288X	1332
C288Y	1332
C289(2S)	0144
C289A	0144
C289B	0144
C289C	0144
C289D	0144
C289E	0144
C289F	0144
C289G	0144
C289GN	0144
C289H	0144
C289J	0144
C289K	0144
C289L	0144
C289M	0144
C289OR	0144
C289R	0144
C289X	0144
C289Y	0144
C290(2S)	0693
C290A	1889
C290B	1889
C290C	1889
C290D	0733
C290E	0733
C290F	OEM
C290G	OEM
C290H	OEM
C290J	OEM
C290M	0733
C290N	0733
C290P	0733
C290PA	0733
C290PB	0733
C290S	0733
C290T	0733
C291	0086
C291A	OEM
C291A(TRANS)	0086
C291B	OEM
C291B(TRANS)	0086
C291C	OEM
C291C(TRANS)	0086
C291D	0086
C291D(TRANS)	0086
C291E	OEM
C291E(TRANS)	0086
C291F	OEM
C291F(TRANS)	0086
C291G	OEM
C291G(TRANS)	0086
C291GN	0086
C291H	OEM
C291H(TRANS)	0086
C291J	OEM
C291J(TRANS)	0086
C291K	0086
C291M	OEM
C291M(TRANS)	0086
C291N	OEM
C291OR	0086
C291P	OEM
C291PA	OEM
C291PB	OEM
C291R	0086
C291S	OEM
C291T	OEM
C291X	0086
C291Y	0086
C292(2S)	0617
C292A	0617
C292B	0617
C292C	0617
C292D	0617
C292E	0617
C292F	0617
C292G	0617
C292GN	0617
C292H	0617
C292J	0617
C292K	0617
C292L	0617
C292M	0617
C292OR	0617
C292R	0617
C292X	0617
C292Y	0617
C293(2S)	0617
C293A	0617
C293B	0617
C293C	0617
C293D	0617
C293E	0617
C293F	0617
C293G	0617

If replacement code is OEM, contact original manufacturer for replacement.

DEVICE TYPE	REPL CODE
C293GN	0617
C293H	0617
C293J	0617
C293K	0617
C293L	0617
C293M	0617
C293OR	0617
C293R	0617
C293X	0617
C293Y	0617
C294	0283
C294X	0283
C295	0079
C296(2S)	0419
C297	0555
C298	0617
C298-4	0617
C299(2S)	3302
C299A	2298
C299B	2298
C299C	2298
C299D	2298
C299E	2298
C299F	2298
C299G	2298
C299GN	2298
C299H	2298
C299J	2298
C299K	2298
C299L	2298
C299M	2298
C299OR	2298
C299R	2298
C299X	2298
C299Y	2298
C300(2S)	0016
C300A	0016
C300B	0016
C300C	0016
C300D	0016
C300E	0016
C300F	0016
C300G	0016
C300GN	0016
C300H	0016
C300J	0016
C300K	0016
C300L	0016
C300M	0016
C300OR	0016
C300R	0016
C300X	0016
C300Y	0016
C301	0016
C301(2S)	0016
C301A	OEM
C301A(2S)	0016
C301B	0016
C301C	0016
C301D	0016
C301E	0016
C301F	0016
C301G	0016
C301GN	0016
C301H	0016
C301J	0016
C301K	0016
C301L	0016
C301M	0016
C301OR	0016
C301R	0016
C301X	0016
C301Y	0016
C302	0150
C302(2S)	0016
C302A	0016
C302B	0016
C302C	0016
C302D	0016
C302E	0016
C302F	0016
C302G	0016
C302GN	0016
C302H	0016
C302J	0016
C302K	0016
C302L	0016
C302M	0016
C302OR	0016
C302R	0016
C302X	0016
C302Y	0016
C303	0590
C304	0590
C305	0590
C305A	0590
C305B	0590
C305C	0590
C305C(IC)	2155
C305D	0590
C305E	0590
C305F	0590
C305G	0590
C305GN	0590
C305H	0590
C305J	0590
C305K	0590
C305L	0590
C305M	0590

DEVICE TYPE	REPL CODE
C305OR	0590
C305R	0590
C305X	0590
C305Y	0590
C306(2S)	0086
C306A	0086
C306B	0086
C306C	0086
C306D	0086
C306E	0086
C306F	0086
C306G	0086
C306GN	0086
C306H	0086
C306J	0086
C306K	0086
C306L	0086
C306M	0086
C306OR	0086
C306R	0086
C306X	0086
C306Y	0086
C307(2S)	0086
C307-OR	0086
C307A	0086
C307B	0086
C307C	0086
C307D	0086
C307E	0086
C307F	0086
C307G	0086
C307GN	0086
C307H	0086
C307J	0086
C307K	0086
C307L	0086
C307M	0086
C307OR	0086
C307R	0086
C307X	0086
C307Y	0086
C308	0086
C308A	0086
C308B	0086
C308C	0086
C308D	0086
C308E	0086
C308F	0086
C308G	0086
C308GN	0086
C308H	0086
C308J	0086
C308K	0086
C308L	0086
C308M	0086
C308OR	0086
C308R	0086
C308X	0086
C308Y	0086
C309(2S)	0086
C309A	0086
C309B	0086
C309C	0086
C309D	0086
C309E	0086
C309F	0086
C309G	0086
C309GN	0086
C309H	0086
C309J	0086
C309K	0086
C309L	0086
C309M	0086
C309OR	0086
C309R	0086
C309X	0086
C309Y	0086
C310	0617
C310(2S)	0086
C310A	0086
C310B	0086
C310C	0086
C310D	0086
C310E	0086
C310F	0086
C310G	0086
C310GN	0086
C310H	0086
C310J	0086
C310K	0086
C310L	0086
C310M	0086
C310OR	0086
C310R	0086
C310X	0086
C310Y	0086
C311	0693
C311(2S)	0693
C311A	OEM
C311B	0693
C311C	0693
C311D	0693
C311E	0693
C311F	0693
C311G	0693
C311GN	0693
C311H	0693
C311J	0693
C311K	0693

DEVICE TYPE	REPL CODE
C311L	0693
C311M	0693
C311OR	0693
C311R	0693
C311X	0693
C311Y	0693
C312	0626
C312(2S)	0626
C312A	0626
C312B	0626
C312C	0626
C312D	0626
C312E	0626
C312F	0626
C312G	0626
C312GN	0626
C312H	0626
C312J	0626
C312K	0626
C312L	0626
C312M	0626
C312OR	0626
C312R	0626
C312X	0626
C312Y	0626
C313	3356
C313-OR	3356
C313A	3356
C313B	3356
C313C(2S)	3356
C313D	3356
C313E	3356
C313F	3356
C313G	3356
C313GN	3356
C313H(2S)	3356
C313J	3356
C313K	3356
C313L	3356
C313M	3356
C313OR	3356
C313R	3356
C313X	3356
C313Y	3356
C314	0626
C315(2S)	0016
C315A	0016
C315B	0016
C315C	0016
C315D	0016
C315E	0016
C315F	0016
C315G	0016
C315GN	0016
C315H	0016
C315J	0016
C315K	0016
C315L	0016
C315M	0016
C315OR	0016
C315R	0016
C315X	0016
C315Y	0016
C316(2S)	0016
C316A	0016
C316B	0016
C316C	0016
C316D	0016
C316E	0016
C316F	0016
C316G	0016
C316GN	0016
C316H	0016
C316J	0016
C316K	0016
C316L	0016
C316M	0016
C316OR	0016
C316R	0016
C316X	0016
C316Y	0016
C317(2S)	0016
C317A	0016
C317B	0016
C317C(2S)	0016
C317D	0016
C317E	0016
C317F	0016
C317G	0016
C317GN	0016
C317H	0016
C317J	0016
C317K	0016
C317L	0016
C317M	0016
C317OR	0016
C317R	0016
C317X	0016
C317Y	0016
C318	0016
C318A(2S)	0016
C318AB	0016
C318B	0016
C318C	0016
C318D	0016
C318E	0016
C318F	0016
C318G	0016
C318GN	0016

DEVICE TYPE	REPL CODE
C318H	0016
C318J	0016
C318K	0016
C318L	0016
C318M	0016
C318OR	0016
C318R	0016
C318X	0016
C318Y	0016
C319(2S)	0488
C319A	0488
C319B	0488
C319C	0488
C319D	0488
C319E	0488
C319F	0488
C319G	0488
C319GN	0488
C319H	0488
C319J	0488
C319K	0488
C319L	0488
C319M	0488
C319OR	0488
C319R	0488
C319X	0488
C319Y	0488
C320(2S)	3387
C320A	3387
C320B	3387
C320C	3387
C320D	3387
C320E	3387
C320F	3387
C320G	3387
C320GN	3387
C320H	3387
C320J	3387
C320K	3387
C320L	3387
C320M	3387
C320OR	3387
C320R	3387
C320X	3387
C320Y	3387
C321	0016
C321A	0016
C321B	0016
C321C	0016
C321D	0016
C321E	0016
C321F	0016
C321G	0016
C321GN	0016
C321H(2S)	0016
C321HA(2S)	0016
C321HB(2S)	0016
C321HC(2S)	0016
C321J	0016
C321K	0016
C321L	0016
C321M	0016
C321OR	0016
C321R	0016
C321X	0016
C321Y	0016
C322	0079
C323(2S)	0016
C323A	0016
C323B	0016
C323C	0016
C323D	0016
C323E	0016
C323F	0016
C323G	0016
C323GN	0016
C323H	0016
C323J	0016
C323K	0016
C323L	0016
C323M	0016
C323OR	0016
C323R	0016
C323X	0016
C323Y	0016
C324(2S)	0016
C324A(2S)	0016
C324B	0016
C324C	0016
C324D	0016
C324E	0016
C324F	0016
C324G	0016
C324GN	0016
C324H(2S)	0016
C324HA(2S)	0016
C324J	0016
C324K	0016
C324L	0016
C324M	0016
C324OR	0016
C324R	0016
C324X	0016
C324Y	0016
C325(2S)	0259
C325C	0259
C326	0414
C327	0127
C327(EUROPE)	0037

DEVICE TYPE	REPL CODE
C328	0259
C328(EUROPE)	0006
C329(2S)	0259
C330	2817
C331	2817
C332	0079
C333	0016
C334	0016
C335(2S)	0531
C336	0016
C337	0016
C337(EUROPE)	0546
C338	0076
C338(EUROPE)	0079
C339	0079
C340	0470
C341	0320
C342	0079
C343	0016
C344	0127
C344Y	0127
C345	0320
C346	0016
C347	0016
C348(2S)	0016
C348A	0016
C348B	0016
C348C	0016
C348D	0016
C348E	0016
C348F	0016
C348G	0016
C348GN	0016
C348H	0016
C348J	0016
C348K	0016
C348L	0016
C348M	0016
C348OR	0016
C348X	0016
C348Y	0016
C349	0127
C349R	0127
C350	0016
C350A	OEM
C350A(TRANS)	0016
C350B	OEM
C350B(TRANS)	0016
C350C	OEM
C350C(TRANS)	0016
C350D	OEM
C350D(TRANS)	0016
C350E	0159
C350E(TRANS)	0016
C350F	0016
C350G	0016
C350GN	0016
C350H(2S)	0016
C350J	0016
C350K	0016
C350L	0016
C350M	0159
C350M(TRANS)	0016
C350N	0096
C350OR	0016
C350P	0096
C350PA	0096
C350PB	0096
C350PC	OEM
C350R	0016
C350S	0096
C350T	0096
C350X	0016
C350Y	0016
C351(2S)	0127
C351A	0127
C351B	0127
C351C	0127
C351D	0127
C351E	0127
C351F	0127
C351FA1	0127
C351G	0127
C351GN	0127
C351H	0127
C351J	0127
C351K	0127
C351L	0127
C351M	0127
C351OR	0127
C351R	0127
C351X	0127
C351Y	0127
C352	0449
C352-OR	0449
C352A	0449
C352AC	0449
C352B	0449
C352C	0449
C352D	0449
C352E	0449
C352F	0449
C352G	0449
C352GN	0449
C352H	0449
C352J	0449
C352K	0449
C352L	0449
C352M	0449

DEVICE TYPE	REPL CODE
C352OR	0449
C352R	0449
C352X	0449
C352Y	0449
C353(2S)	0086
C353A(2S)	0086
C353AC	0086
C353B	0086
C353C	0086
C353D	0086
C353E	0086
C353F	0086
C353G	0086
C353GN	0086
C353H	0086
C353J	0086
C353K	0086
C353L	0086
C353M	0086
C353OR	0086
C353R	0086
C353X	0086
C353Y	0086
C354	0930
C354A	3315
C354B	0454
C354C	0454
C354D	0454
C354E	0454
C354G	0454
C354M	0454
C355	0930
C355A	0454
C355B	0454
C355C	0454
C355D	0454
C355E	0454
C355G	0454
C355M	0454
C356(2S)	0079
C356A	0079
C356B	0079
C356C	0079
C356D	0079
C356E	0079
C356F	0079
C356G	0079
C356GN	0079
C356H	0079
C356J	0079
C356K	0079
C356L	0079
C356M	0079
C356OR	0079
C356R	0079
C356X	0079
C356Y	0079
C358C	0765
C358E	0454
C358M	0454
C358N	0584
C358P	0584
C358PA	0584
C358PB	0584
C358S	0584
C358T	0584
C360(2S)	0016
C360-OR	0016
C360A	0016
C360B	0016
C360C	0016
C360D(2S)	0016
C360E	0016
C360F	0016
C360G	0016
C360GN	0016
C360H	0016
C360J	0016
C360K	0016
C360L	0016
C360M	0016
C360OR	0016
C360R	0016
C360X	0016
C360Y	0016
C361(2S)	0155
C361A	0155
C361B	0155
C361C	0155
C361D	0155
C361E	0155
C361F	0155
C361G	0155
C361GN	0155
C361H	0155
C361J	0155
C361K	0155
C361L	0155
C361M	0155
C361OR	0155
C361R	0155
C361X	0155
C361Y	0155
C362(2S)	0155
C362A	0155
C362B	0155
C362C	0155
C362D	0155
C362E	0155

DEVICE TYPE	REPL CODE
C362F	0155
C362G	0155
C362GN	0155
C362H	0155
C362J	0155
C362K	0155
C362L	0155
C362M	0155
C362OR	0155
C362R	0155
C362X	0155
C362Y	0155
C363(2S)	0016
C363-OR	0016
C363A	0016
C363B	0016
C363C	0016
C363D	0016
C363E	0016
C363F	0016
C363G	0016
C363GN	0016
C363H	0016
C363J	0016
C363K	0016
C363L	0016
C363M	0016
C363OR	0016
C363R	0016
C363X	0016
C363Y	0016
C364	0525
C364A	0454
C364B	0454
C364C	0454
C364D	0454
C364E	0454
C364M	0454
C364N	OEM
C364S	OEM
C365A	0454
C365B	0454
C365C	0454
C365D	0454
C365E	0454
C365M	0454
C365N	0584
C365S	0584
C366	0284
C366(2S)	0284
C366-O	0284
C366A	0284
C366B	0284
C366C	0284
C366D	0284
C366E	0284
C366F	0284
C366G	0284
C366GN	0284
C366G-O	0284
C366G-R	0284
C366G-Y	0284
C366H	0284
C366J	0284
C366K	0284
C366L	0284
C366M	0284
C366OR	0284
C366X	0284
C367	0284
C367-O	0284
C367-R	0284
C367-Y	0284
C367A	0284
C367B	0284
C367C	0284
C367D	0284
C367E	0284
C367F	0284
C367G	0284
C367GN	0284
C367G-O	0284
C367G-R	0284
C367G-Y	0284
C367H	0284
C367J	0284
C367K	0284
C367L	0284
C367M	0284
C367OR	0284
C367R	0284
C367X	0284
C367Y	0284
C368(2S)	0111
C368-BL	0111
C368-GR	0111
C368A	0111
C368B	0111
C368C	0111
C368D	0111
C368E	0111
C368F	0111
C368G	0111
C368GN	0111
C368H	0111
C368J	0111
C368K	0111
C368L	0111
C368M	0111

If replacement code is OEM, contact original manufacturer for replacement.

315

DEVICE TYPE	REPL CODE
C368OR	0111
C368R	0111
C368V(2S)	0111
C368X	0111
C368Y	0111
C369(2S)	0111
C369-BL	0111
C369-GR	0111
C369-V	0111
C369A	0111
C369B	0111
C369BL(2S)	0111
C369C	0111
C369D	0111
C369E	0111
C369F	0111
C369G(2S)	0111
C369G-BL(2S)	0111
C369GBL(2S)	0111
C369G-GR(2S)	0111
C369GGR(2S)	0111
C369GN	0111
C369GR(2S)	0111
C369G-V(2S)	0111
C369H	0111
C369J	0111
C369K	0111
C369L	0111
C369M	0111
C369OR	0111
C369R	0111
C369V(2S)	0111
C369X	0111
C369Y	0111
C370(2S)	0155
C370-0	0155
C370-G	0155
C370-O	0155
C370-T	0155
C370A	0155
C370B	0155
C370C	0155
C370D	0155
C370E	0155
C370F(2S)	0155
C370G(2S)	0155
C370GN	0155
C370H(2S)	0155
C370I	0155
C370J(2S)	0155
C370K(2S)	0155
C370L	0155
C370M	0155
C370OR	0155
C370R	0155
C370X	0155
C370Y	0155
C371(2S)	0191
C371-0(2S)	0191
C371-O(2S)	0191
C371-OR	0191
C371-R(2S)	0191
C371-T	0191
C371A	0191
C371B(2S)	0191
C371C	0191
C371D	0191
C371E	0191
C371F	0191
C371G(2S)	0191
C371GN	0191
C371G-O	0191
C371G-R	0191
C371H	0191
C371J	0191
C371K	0191
C371L	0191
C371M	0191
C371O	0191
C371OR	0191
C371R(2S)	0191
C371R-1	0191
C371RED-G	0191
C371T	0191
C371X	0191
C371Y	0191
C372	0076
C372(H)	0076
C372-0(2S)	0076
C372-1(2S)	0076
C372-2(2S)	0076
C372-O(2S)	0076
C372-OR	0076
C372-ORG	0076
C372-Y(2S)	0076
C372A	0076
C372AR	0076
C372B	0076
C372C	0076
C372D	0076
C372E	0076
C372F	0076
C372G	0076
C372GN	0076
C372G-O	0076
C372G-Y	0076
C372J	0076
C372K	0076
C372L	0076
C372M	0076
C372O	0076
C372OR	0076
C372R	0076
C372X	0076
C372Y(2S)	0076
C372Y1	0076
C372YEL	0076
C372YEL-G	0076
C372Z	0076
C373(2S)	0076
C373-0	0076
C373-14	0076
C373-G	0076
C373-O	0076
C373-OR	0076
C373A	0076
C373AL	0076
C373B	0076
C373C	0076
C373D	0076
C373E	0076
C373F	0076
C373G	0076
C373GN	0076
C373GR(2S)	0076
C373H	0076
C373J	0076
C373K	0076
C373L	0076
C373M	0076
C373OR	0076
C373R	0076
C373W(2S)	0076
C373X	0076
C373Y	0076
C374(2S)	0547
C374-BL(2S)	0547
C374-OR	0547
C374-V(2S)	0547
C374A	0547
C374B	0547
C374BL	0547
C374BLK	0547
C374C	0547
C374D	0547
C374E	0547
C374F	0547
C374G	0547
C374GN	0547
C374H	0547
C374J	0547
C374K	0547
C374L	0547
C374M	0547
C374OR	0547
C374R	0547
C374V	0547
C374X	0547
C374Y	0547
C375(2S)	0127
C375-0(2S)	0127
C375-O(2S)	0127
C375-Y(2S)	0127
C375A	0127
C375B	0127
C375C	0127
C375D	0127
C375E	0127
C375F	0127
C375G	0127
C375GN	0127
C375H	0127
C375J	0127
C375K	0127
C375L	0127
C375M	0127
C375OR	0127
C375R	0127
C375X	0127
C376(2S)	0284
C376A	0284
C376B	0284
C376C	0284
C376D	0284
C376E	OEM
C376E(TRANS)	0284
C376E-PD	OEM
C376F	0284
C376G	0284
C376GN	0284
C376H	0284
C376J	0284
C376K	0284
C376L	0284
C376M	OEM
C376M(TRANS)	0284
C376N	OEM
C376OR	0284
C376P	OEM
C376PA	OEM
C376PB	OEM
C376PC	OEM
C376PD	OEM
C376R	0284
C376S	OEM
C376T	OEM
C376X	0284
C376Y	0284
C377(2S)	0076
C377(EUROPE)	OEM
C377-0	0076
C377-BN	0076
C377-BRN	0076
C377-O	0076
C377-OR	0076
C377-ORG	0076
C377-R	0076
C377-RED	0076
C377A	0076
C377B	0076
C377BN	0076
C377BRN	0076
C377C	0076
C377D	0076
C377E	OEM
C377E(TRANS)	0076
C377E-PE	OEM
C377F	0076
C377G	0076
C377GN	0076
C377H	0076
C377J	0076
C377K	0076
C377L	0076
C377M	OEM
C377M(TRANS)	0076
C377N	OEM
C377O	0076
C377OR	0076
C377P	OEM
C377PA	OEM
C377PB	OEM
C377PC	OEM
C377PD	OEM
C377R	0076
C377RED	0076
C377S	OEM
C377T	OEM
C377X	0076
C377Y	0076
C378(2S)	0155
C378-O	0155
C378-ORG	0155
C378-R	0155
C378-RED	0155
C378-Y	0155
C378-YEL	0155
C378A	0155
C378B	0155
C378C	0155
C378D	0155
C378E	OEM
C378E(TRANS)	0155
C378E-PD	OEM
C378F	0155
C378G	0155
C378GN	0155
C378H	0155
C378J	0155
C378K	0155
C378L	0155
C378M	OEM
C378M(TRANS)	0155
C378N	OEM
C378O	0155
C378OR	0155
C378P	OEM
C378PA	OEM
C378PB	OEM
C378PC	OEM
C378PD	OEM
C378R	0155
C378S	OEM
C378T	OEM
C378X	0155
C378Y	0155
C379(2S)	0284
C379A	0284
C379B	0284
C379C	0284
C379D	0284
C379E	0284
C379F	0284
C379G	0284
C379GN	0284
C379H	0284
C379J	0284
C379K	0284
C379L	0284
C379M	0284
C379OR	0284
C379R	0284
C379X	0284
C379Y	0284
C380	0284
C380-0(2S)	0284
C380-BRN	0284
C380-O(2S)	0284
C380-OR	0284
C380-ORG	0284
C380-R	0284
C380-RED	0284
C380-Y	0284
C380-YEL	0284
C380A	0192
C380A(SCR)	0192
C380A(TRANS)	0284
C380A-0	0284
C380A0	0284
C380A-O	0284
C380AO(2S)	0284
C380AR	0284
C380A-R(2S)	0284
C380ATV(2S)	0284
C380AX500	OEM
C380AX555	OEM
C380A-Y	0284
C380AY(2S)	0284
C380B	0192
C380B(TRANS)	0284
C380BPC	OEM
C380BX500	OEM
C380BX555	OEM
C380B-Y	0284
C380BY	0284
C380C	0159
C380C(TRANS)	0284
C380CX500	OEM
C380CX555	OEM
C380C-Y	0284
C380CY	0284
C380D	0159
C380D(SCR)	0159
C380D(TRANS)	0284
C380DX500	OEM
C380DX555	OEM
C380D-Y	0284
C380DY	0284
C380E	0159
C380E(TRANS)	0284
C380EX500	OEM
C380EX555	OEM
C380E-Y	0284
C380EY	0284
C380F	0284
C380F-Y	0284
C380FY	0284
C380G	0284
C380GN	0284
C380H	0284
C380J	0284
C380K	0284
C380L	0284
C380M	0159
C380M(TRANS)	0284
C380MX500	OEM
C380MX555	OEM
C380N	0096
C380NX500	OEM
C380NX555	OEM
C380O	0284
C380OR	0284
C380P	0096
C380PA	0096
C380PAX555	OEM
C380PB	0096
C380PBX555	OEM
C380PC	OEM
C380PX555	OEM
C380R(2S)	0284
C380RED	0284
C380S	0096
C380SX500	OEM
C380SX555	OEM
C380T	0096
C380T(TRANS)	0284
C380TX555	OEM
C380V	0284
C380X	0284
C380Y(2S)	0284
C380YEL	0284
C381(2S)	0113
C381-0(2S)	0113
C381-BN	0113
C381-BRN	0113
C381-O(2S)	0113
C381-OR	0113
C381-ORG	0113
C381-R(2S)	0113
C381-RED	0113
C381A	0113
C381B	0113
C381BN(2S)	0113
C381BN-1	0113
C381C	0113
C381D	0113
C381E	0113
C381F	0113
C381G	0113
C381GN	0113
C381H	0113
C381J	0113
C381K	0113
C381L	0113
C381M	0113
C381O	0113
C381OR	0113
C381R(2S)	0113
C381RED	0113
C381RL	0113
C381X	0113
C381Y	0113
C382(2S)	0184
C382-G	0184
C382-GR(2S)	0184
C382-GY	0184
C382-OR	0184
C382-R	0184
C382-V	0184
C382A	0184
C382B	0184
C382BK(2S)	0184
C382BK1	0184
C382BK2	0184
C382BL(2S)	0184
C382BN(2S)	0184
C382BR(2S)	0184
C382C	0184
C382D	0184
C382E	0184
C382F	0184
C382G(2S)	0184
C382GN	0184
C382GR	0184
C382GY	0184
C382H	0184
C382J	0184
C382K	0184
C382L	0184
C382M	0184
C382OR	0184
C382R(2S)	0184
C382V(2S)	0184
C382W	0184
C382X	0184
C382Y	0184
C383(2S)	0076
C383-OR	0076
C383A	0076
C383B	0076
C383C	0076
C383D	0076
C383E	0076
C383F	0076
C383G(2S)	0076
C383GN	0076
C383H	0076
C383J	0076
C383K	0076
C383L	0076
C383M	0076
C383OR	0076
C383R	0076
C383T(2S)	0076
C383TM	0076
C383W(2S)	0076
C383X	0076
C383Y(2S)	0076
C384(2S)	0127
C384(O)	0127
C384-0	0127
C384A	0454
C384A(TRANS)	0127
C384B	0454
C384B(TRANS)	0127
C384C	0454
C384C(TRANS)	0127
C384D	0454
C384D(TRANS)	0127
C384E	0454
C384E(TRANS)	0127
C384F	0127
C384G	0127
C384GN	0127
C384H	0127
C384J	0127
C384K	0127
C384L	0127
C384M	0454
C384M(TRANS)	0127
C384OR	0127
C384R	0127
C384X	0127
C384Y(2S)	0127
C385	0544
C385A	0454
C385A(SCR)	0454
C385A(TRANS)	0544
C385B	0454
C385B(TRANS)	0544
C385C	0454
C385C(TRANS)	0544
C385D	0454
C385D(TRANS)	0544
C385E	0454
C385E(TRANS)	0544
C385F	0544
C385G	0544
C385GN	0544
C385H	0544
C385J	0544
C385K	0544
C385L	0544
C385M	0454
C385M(TRANS)	0544
C385N	0584
C385OR	0544
C385R	0544
C385S	0584
C385X	0544
C385Y	0544
C386	0127
C386-0	0127
C386A	0127
C386AO	0127
C386B	0127
C386C	0127
C386D	0127
C386E	0127
C386F	0127
C386G	0127
C386GN	0127
C386H	0127
C386J	0127
C386K	0127
C386L	0127
C386M	0127
C386OR	0127
C386R	0127
C386X	0127
C386Y	0127
C387(2S)	0544
C387-G	0544
C387-OR	0544
C387A(2S)	0544
C387AG	0544
C387B	0544
C387C	0544
C387D	0544
C387E	0764
C387E(TRANS)	0544
C387F	0544
C387FA3	0544
C387G(2S)	0544
C387GN	0544
C387H	0544
C387J	0544
C387K	0544
C387L	0544
C387M	0764
C387M(TRANS)	0544
C387N	0478
C387OR	0544
C387P	0478
C387PA	0478
C387PB	0478
C387R	0544
C387S	0478
C387T	0478
C387X	0544
C387Y	0544
C388(2S)	0836
C388-A	0836
C388-O	0836
C388-OR	0836
C388A	0836
C388A(2S)	0836
C388A(JAPAN)	0836
C388A(KOREA)	0836
C388A-TM	0836
C388ATM	0836
C388ATMFA	0836
C388B	0836
C388C	0836
C388D	0836
C388E	0764
C388E(TRANS)	0836
C388F	0836
C388FA	0836
C388G	0836
C388GN	0836
C388H	0836
C388J	0836
C388K	0836
C388L	0836
C388M	0764
C388M(TRANS)	0836
C388N	0478
C388OR	0836
C388P	0478
C388PA	0478
C388PB	0478
C388R	0836
C388S	0478
C388T	0478
C388TM	0836
C388X	0836
C388Y	0836
C389(2S)	0007
C389-0	0007
C389-OR	0007
C389A	0007
C389AFP	0007
C389B	0007
C389BLB-O	0007
C389C	0007
C389D	0007
C389E	0007
C389F	0007
C389G	0007
C389GN	0007
C389H	0007
C389J	0007
C389K	0007
C389L	0007
C389LP	0007
C389M	0007
C389O	0007
C389OR	0007
C389P	0007
C389R(2S)	0007
C389X	0007
C389Y	0007
C390	0259
C390A	0259
C390AX500	OEM
C390AX550	OEM
C390B	2816
C390B(TRANS)	0259
C390BX500	OEM
C390BX550	OEM
C390C	2816
C390C(TRANS)	0259
C390CX500	OEM
C390CX550	OEM
C390D	2816
C390D(TRANS)	0259
C390DX500	OEM
C390DX550	OEM
C390E	2816
C390E(TRANS)	0259
C390EX500	OEM
C390EX550	OEM
C390EX555	OEM
C390F	0259
C390G	0259
C390GN	0259
C390H	0259
C390J	0259
C390K	0259
C390L	0259
C390M	1754
C390M(TRANS)	0259
C390MX500	OEM
C390MX550	OEM
C390MX555	OEM
C390N	1803
C390NX555	OEM
C390OR	0259
C390P	1803
C390PA	1803
C390PAX555	OEM
C390PB	1803
C390PBX555	OEM
C390PC	OEM
C390PX555	OEM
C390R	0259
C390S	1803
C390S555	OEM
C390SX555	OEM
C390T	1803
C390TX555	OEM
C390X	0259
C390Y	0259
C391	0008
C391A	0008
C391B	0008
C391C	0008
C391D	0008
C391E	0008
C391F	0008
C391G	0008
C391GN	0008
C391H	0008
C391J	0008
C391K	0008
C391L	0008
C391M	0008
C391OR	0008
C391PC	OEM
C391PD	OEM
C391PE	OEM
C391PM	OEM
C391PN	OEM
C391PS	OEM
C391R	0008
C391X	0008
C391Y	0008
C392(2S)	0259
C392A	OEM
C392A(TRANS)	0259
C392B	OEM
C392B(TRANS)	0259
C392C	OEM
C392C(TRANS)	0259
C392D	OEM
C392D(TRANS)	0259
C392E	OEM
C392E(TRANS)	0259
C392F(TRANS)	0259
C392G	0259
C392GN	0259
C392H	0259
C392J	0259
C392K	0259
C392L	0259
C392M	OEM
C392M(TRANS)	0259
C392OR	0259
C392R	0259
C392X	0259
C392Y	0259
C393	0079
C393A	OEM
C393B	OEM
C393C	0624
C393C(IC)	0624
C393D	OEM
C393E	OEM
C393M	OEM
C394(2S)	0155
C394-0(2S)	0155
C394-GR	0155

If replacement code is OEM, contact original manufacturer for replacement.

DEVICE TYPE	REPL CODE
C394-GRN	0155
C394-O(2S)	0155
C394-OR	0155
C394-ORG	0155
C394-R	0155
C394-RED	0155
C394-Y	0155
C394-YEL	0155
C394A	2049
C394A(TRANS)	0155
C394AP	0155
C394B	2049
C394B(TRANS)	0155
C394C	2049
C394C(TRANS)	0155
C394D	2049
C394D(TRANS)	0155
C394E	2049
C394E(TRANS)	0155
C394F	0155
C394G	0155
C394GN	0155
C394GR(2S)	0155
C394GRN	0155
C394H	0155
C394J	0155
C394K	0155
C394L	0155
C394M	2049
C394M(TRANS)	0155
C394O	0155
C394OR	0155
C394R(2S)	0155
C394RED	0155
C394S	OEM
C394W(2S)	0155
C394X	0155
C394Y(2S)	0155
C394YEL	0155
C395(2S)	0016
C395A	4774
C395A(SCR)	OEM
C395A(TRANS)	0016
C395A-O	0016
C395A-ORG	0016
C395A-R	0016
C395A-RED	0016
C395A-Y	0016
C395A-YEL	0016
C395B	OEM
C395B(TRANS)	0016
C395C	OEM
C395C(TRANS)	0016
C395D	OEM
C395D(TRANS)	0016
C395E	OEM
C395E(TRANS)	0016
C395F	0016
C395G	0016
C395GN	0016
C395H	0016
C395J	0016
C395K	0016
C395L	0016
C395M	OEM
C395M(TRANS)	0016
C395OR	0016
C395R(2S)	0016
C395S	OEM
C395X	0016
C395Y	0016
C396(2S)	0488
C396A	0488
C396B	0488
C396C	0488
C396D	0488
C396E	0488
C396F	0488
C396G	0488
C396GN	0488
C396GR	0488
C396H	0488
C396J	0488
C396K	0488
C396L	0488
C396M	0488
C396OR	0488
C396R	0488
C396X	0488
C396Y	0488
C397	0007
C397A	0007
C397B	0007
C397C	0007
C397D	0007
C397E	0764
C397E(TRANS)	0007
C397F	0007
C397G	0007
C397GN	0007
C397H	0007
C397J	0007
C397K	0007
C397L	0007
C397M	0764
C397M(TRANS)	0007
C397N	0478
C397OR	0007
C397P	0478
C397PA	0478
C397PB	0478
C397R	0007
C397S	0478
C397T	0478
C397X	0007
C397Y	0007
C398	0008
C398A	0008
C398B	0008
C398C	0008
C398D	0008
C398E	0764
C398E(TRANS)	0008
C398F	0008
C398FA1	0008
C398G	0008
C398GN	0008
C398H	0008
C398J	0008
C398K	0008
C398L	0008
C398M	0764
C398M(TRANS)	0008
C398N	0478
C398OR	0008
C398P	0478
C398PA	0478
C398PB	0478
C398R	0008
C398S	0478
C398T	0478
C398X	0008
C398Y	0008
C399(2S)	0008
C399A	0008
C399B	0008
C399C	0008
C399D	0008
C399E	0008
C399F	0008
C399FA1	0008
C399G	0008
C399GN	0008
C399H	0008
C399J	0008
C399K	0008
C399L	0008
C399M	0008
C399OR	0008
C399R	0008
C399X(2S)	0008
C399Y	0008
C400	0016
C400(2S)	0016
C400-O(2S)	0016
C400-GR(2S)	0016
C400-O	0016
C400-R(2S)	0016
C400-Y(2S)	0016
C400A	0016
C400B	0016
C400C	0016
C400D	0016
C400E	0016
C400F	0016
C400G	0016
C400GN	0016
C400H	0016
C400J	0016
C400K	0016
C400L	0016
C400M	0016
C400OR	0016
C400R	0016
C400X	0016
C400Y	0016
C401	0155
C401(2S)	0155
C401A	0155
C401B	0155
C401C	0155
C401D	0155
C401E	0155
C401F	0155
C401G	0155
C401GN	0155
C401H	0155
C401J	0155
C401K	0155
C401L	0155
C401M	0155
C401OR	0155
C401R	0155
C401X	0155
C401Y	0155
C402	0155
C402(2S)	0155
C402A(2S)	0155
C402B	0155
C402C	0155
C402D	0155
C402E	0155
C402F	0155
C402G	0155
C402GN	0155
C402H	0155
C402J	0155
C402K	0155
C402L	0155
C402M	0155
C402OR	0155
C402R	0155
C402X	0155
C402Y	0155
C403(2S)	0155
C403-OR	0155
C403A(2S)	0155
C403AL	0155
C403B	0155
C403C(2S)	0155
C403CG	0155
C403D	0155
C403E	0155
C403F	0155
C403G	0155
C403GN	0155
C403H	0155
C403J	0155
C403K	0155
C403L	0155
C403M	0155
C403OR	0155
C403R	0155
C403X	0155
C403Y	0155
C404(2S)	0155
C404A	0155
C404B	0155
C404C	0155
C404D	0155
C404E	0155
C404F	0155
C404G	0155
C404GN	0155
C404H	0155
C404J	0155
C404K	0155
C404L	0155
C404M	0155
C404OR	0155
C404R	0155
C404X	0155
C404Y	0155
C405(2S)	0016
C405A	0016
C405B	0016
C405C	0016
C405D	0016
C405E	0016
C405F	0016
C405G	0016
C405GN	0016
C405H	0016
C405J	0016
C405K	0016
C405L	0016
C405M	0016
C405OR	0016
C405R	0016
C405X	0016
C405Y	0016
C406(2S)	0016
C406A	0016
C406B	0016
C406C	0016
C406D	0016
C406E	0016
C406F	0016
C406G	0016
C406GN	0016
C406H	0016
C406J	0016
C406K	0016
C406L	0016
C406M	0016
C406OR	0016
C406R	0016
C406X	0016
C406Y	0016
C407	1955
C407(2S)	1955
C408	1955
C409(2S)	1955
C410	1955
C410(2S)	1955
C410A	1955
C411	1955
C411(2S)	1955
C412(2S)	0637
C413	0626
C413N	OEM
C414	0626
C415	0626
C416	0626
C420	0086
C420(2S)	0626
C423(2S)	0016
C423-O	0016
C423A	0016
C423B(2S)	0016
C423C(2S)	0016
C423D(2S)	0016
C423E(2S)	0016
C423F(2S)	0016
C423G	0016
C423GN	0016
C423H	0016
C423J	0016
C423K	0016
C423L	0016
C423M	0016
C423OR	0016
C423R	0016
C423X	0016
C423Y	0016
C424	0016
C424(2S)	0016
C424D(2S)	0016
C425	0086
C425(2S)	0016
C425A	0016
C425B(2S)	0016
C425C(2S)	0016
C425D(2S)	0016
C425E(2S)	0016
C425F(2S)	0016
C425G	0016
C425GN	0016
C425H	0016
C425K	0016
C425L	0016
C425M	0016
C425OR	0016
C425R	0016
C425X	0016
C425Y	0016
C426	0086
C426(2S)	0079
C426M	OEM
C427	0079
C428	0488
C428(2S)	0079
C429(2S)	0470
C429A	0470
C429B	0470
C429C	0470
C429D	0470
C429E	0470
C429F	0470
C429G	0470
C429GN	0470
C429H	0470
C429J(2S)	0470
C429K	0470
C429L	0470
C429M	0470
C429OR	0470
C429R	0470
C429X(2S)	0470
C429Y	0470
C430(2S)	0470
C430A	0470
C430AX500	OEM
C430AX550	OEM
C430B	0470
C430BX500	OEM
C430BX550	OEM
C430C	0470
C430CX500	OEM
C430CX550	OEM
C430D	0470
C430DX500	OEM
C430DX550	OEM
C430E	OEM
C430E(TRANS)	0470
C430EX500	OEM
C430EX555	OEM
C430F	0470
C430G	0470
C430GN	0470
C430H(2S)	0470
C430J	0470
C430K	0470
C430L	0470
C430M	OEM
C430M(TRANS)	0470
C430MX500	OEM
C430MX555	OEM
C430N	OEM
C430NX555	OEM
C430OR	0470
C430P	OEM
C430PA	OEM
C430PAX555	OEM
C430PB	OEM
C430PBX555	OEM
C430PC	OEM
C430PX555	OEM
C430R	0470
C430S	OEM
C430SX555	OEM
0430T	OEM
C430TX555	OEM
C430W(2S)	0470
C430X	0470
C430Y	0470
C431E1	OEM
C431E2	OEM
C431M1	OEM
C431M2	OEM
C431N1	OEM
C431N2	OEM
C431P1	OEM
C431P2	OEM
C431PA1	OEM
C431PA2	OEM
C431PB	OEM
C431PB1	OEM
C431PB2	OEM
C431PC	OEM
C431PC1	OEM
C431PC2	OEM
C431PD	OEM
C431PD1	OEM
C431PD2	OEM
C431PE	OEM
C431PE1	OEM
C431PE2	OEM
C431PM	OEM
C431PM1	OEM
C431PM2	OEM
C431PN	OEM
C431PN1	OEM
C431PN2	OEM
C431PS	OEM
C431PS1	OEM
C431PS2	OEM
C431S1	OEM
C431S2	OEM
C431T1	OEM
C431T2	OEM
C433	0079
C434	0236
C434A	OEM
C434B	OEM
C434C	OEM
C434D	OEM
C434E	OEM
C434M	OEM
C434S	OEM
C435A	OEM
C435B	OEM
C435C	OEM
C435D	OEM
C435E	OEM
C435M	OEM
C435S	OEM
C436E	OEM
C436M	OEM
C436N	OEM
C436P	OEM
C436PA	OEM
C436PB	OEM
C436S	OEM
C436T	OEM
C437	0626
C437E	OEM
C437M	OEM
C437N	OEM
C437P	OEM
C437PA	OEM
C437PB	OEM
C437S	OEM
C437T	OEM
C438	0693
C438E	OEM
C438M	OEM
C438N	OEM
C438P	OEM
C438PA	OEM
C438PB	OEM
C438S	OEM
C438T	OEM
C439	0018
C440(2S)	0488
C440E	4085
C440M	4085
C440N	1714
C440P	1714
C440PA	1714
C440PB	1714
C440PC	OEM
C440S	1714
C440T	1714
C441	0488
C441(2S)	0488
C441A	0488
C441B	0488
C441C	0488
C441D	0488
C441E	0488
C441F	0488
C441G	0488
C441GN	0488
C441H	0488
C441J	0488
C441K	0488
C441L	0488
C441M	0488
C441OR	0488
C441PC	OEM
C441PD	OEM
C441PE	OEM
C441PM	OEM
C441PN	OEM
C441PS	OEM
C441R	0488
C441X	0488
C441Y	0488
C442	0488
C442(2S)	0488
C442A	0488
C442B	0488
C442C	0488
C442D	0488
C442E	0488
C442F	0488
C442G	0488
C442GN	0488
C442H	0488
C442J	0488
C442K	0488
C442L	0488
C442M	0488
C442OR	0488
C442R	0488
C442X	0488
C442Y	0488
C443(2S)	0086
C443A	0086
C443B	0086
C443C	0086
C443D	0086
C443E	0086
C443F	0086
C443G	0086
C443GN	0086
C443H	0086
C443J	0086
C443K	0086
C443L	0086
C443M	0086
C443OR	0086
C443R	0086
C443X	0086
C443Y	0086
C444	0016
C444(2S)	0590
C444A	OEM
C444B	OEM
C444C	OEM
C444D	OEM
C444E	OEM
C444M	OEM
C444S	OEM
C445	0168
C445A	OEM
C445A(TRANS)	0168
C445B	OEM
C445B(TRANS)	0168
C445C	OEM
C445C(TRANS)	0168
C445D	OEM
C445D(TRANS)	0168
C445E	OEM
C445E(TRANS)	0168
C445F	0168
C445G	0168
C445GN	0168
C445H	0168
C445J	0168
C445K	0168
C445L	0168
C445M	OEM
C445M(TRANS)	0168
C445OR	0168
C445R	0168
C445S	OEM
C445X	0168
C445Y	0168
C446	5468
C447E	OEM
C447M	OEM
C447N	OEM
C447P	OEM
C447PA	OEM
C447PB	OEM
C447S	OEM
C447T	OEM
C448E	OEM
C448M	OEM
C448N	OEM
C448P	OEM
C448PA	OEM
C448PB	OEM
C448S	OEM
C448T	OEM
C449PE	OEM
C450	0016
C450E	OEM
C450E-1	OEM
C450E1	OEM
C450E-2	OEM
C450E2	OEM
C450M	OEM
C450M1	OEM
C450M2	OEM
C450N	OEM
C450N1	OEM
C450N2	OEM
C450P	OEM
C450P1	OEM
C450P2	OEM
C450PA	OEM
C450PA1	OEM
C450PA2	OEM
C450PB	OEM
C450PB1	OEM
C450PB2	OEM
C450PC	OEM
C450PC1	OEM
C450PC2	OEM
C450PD	OEM
C450PD1	OEM
C450PD2	OEM
C450S	OEM
C450S1	OEM
C450S2	OEM
C450T	OEM
C450T1	OEM
C450T2	OEM
C451E1	OEM
C451E2	OEM
C451M1	OEM
C451M2	OEM
C451N-1	OEM
C451N1	OEM
C451N-2	OEM
C451N2	OEM
C451P-1	OEM
C451P1	OEM
C451P-2	OEM
C451P2	OEM
C451PA-1	OEM
C451PA1	OEM
C451PA-2	OEM
C451PA2	OEM
C451PB	OEM
C451PB-1	OEM
C451PB1	OEM
C451PB-2	OEM
C451PB2	OEM
C451PC	OEM
C451PC-1	OEM
C451PC1	OEM
C451PC-2	OEM
C451PC2	OEM
C451PD	OEM
C451PD-1	OEM
C451PD1	OEM
C451PD-2	OEM
C451PD2	OEM
C451PE	OEM
C451PE-1	OEM
C451PE1	OEM
C451PE-2	OEM
C451PE2	OEM
C451PM	OEM
C451PM-1	OEM
C451PM1	OEM
C451PM-2	OEM
C451PM2	OEM
C451PN	OEM
C451PN-1	OEM
C451PN1	OEM
C451PN-2	OEM
C451PN2	OEM
C451PS	OEM
C451PS-1	OEM
C451PS1	OEM
C451PS-2	OEM
C451PS2	OEM
C451S-1	OEM
C451S1	OEM
C451S-2	OEM
C451S2	OEM
C451T-1	OEM
C451T1	OEM
C451T-2	OEM
C451T2	OEM
C454	0076
C454-3	0076
C454-5	0076
C454-C	0076
C454-OR	0076
C454A(2S)	0076
C454B	0076
C454B-6	0076
C454BL	0076
C454C	0076
C454C(JAPAN)	0076
C454D(2S)	0076
C454E	0076
C454F	0076
C454G	0076
C454GN	0076
C454H	0076
C454J	0076
C454K	0076
C454L(2S)	0076
C454LA(2S)	0076
C454M	0076
C454OR	0076
C454R	0076
C454X	0076
C454Y	0076
C455(2S)	0155
C455-OR	0155
C455A	0155
C455B	0155
C455C	0155
C455D	0155
C455E	0155
C455F	0155
C455G	0155
C455GN	0155
C455H	0155
C455J	0155
C455K	0155
C455L	0155
C455M	0155
C455OR	0155
C455R	0155

If replacement code is OEM, contact original manufacturer for replacement. 317

DEVICE TYPE	REPL CODE
C455X	0155
C455Y	0155
C456(2S)	0693
C456A(2S)	0693
C456B	0693
C456C	0693
C456D(2S)	0693
C456E	0693
C456F	0693
C456G	0693
C456GN	0693
C456H	0693
C456J	0693
C456K	0693
C456L	0693
C456M	0693
C456OR	0693
C456R	0693
C456X	0693
C456Y	0693
C457	0079
C457E	OEM
C457M	OEM
C457N	OEM
C457P	OEM
C457PA	OEM
C457PB	OEM
C457PC	OEM
C457PD	OEM
C457S	OEM
C457T	OEM
C458	0076
C458(JAPAN)	0076
C458-4	0076
C458-5	0076
C458-B	0076
C458-C	0076
C458-D	0076
C458-GR	0076
C458-O	0076
C458-OR	0076
C458-Y	0076
C458A(2S)	0076
C458AD(2S)	0076
C458AK	0076
C458B	0076
C458B(JAPAN)	0076
C458BC(2S)	0076
C458BD	0076
C458BL(2S)	0076
C458BM	0076
C458C	0076
C458C(JAPAN)	0076
C458CL	0076
C458CLG(2S)	0076
C458CM(2S)	0076
C458D	0076
C458D(2S)	0076
C458E	OEM
C458E(TRANS)	0076
C458F	0076
C458G(2S)	0076
C458GN	0076
C458H	0076
C458J	0076
C458K(2S)	0076
C458KB(2S)	0076
C458L(2S)	0076
C458L6	0076
C458LB(2S)	0076
C458LC	0076
C458LD	0076
C458LG	0076
C458LGA(2S)	0076
C458LGB	0076
C458LGBM(2S)	0076
C458LGC	0076
C458LGC-6	0076
C458LGD	0076
C458LGO(2S)	0076
C458LGR	0076
C458LGS(2S)	0076
C458M	5580
C458M(SCR)	OEM
C458M(TRANS)	0076
C458N	OEM
C458OR	0076
C458P	0284
C458P(SCR)	OEM
C458PA	OEM
C458PB	OEM
C458PC	OEM
C458PD	OEM
C458R	0076
C458RGS(2S)	0076
C458S	OEM
C458T	OEM
C458X	0076
C458Y	0076
C459(2S)	0284
C459A	0284
C459B(2S)	0284
C459C	0284
C459D(2S)	0284
C459E	0284
C459F	0284
C459G	0284
C459GN	0284
C459H	0284
C459J	0284
C459K	0284
C459L	0284
C459M	0284
C459OR	0284
C459R	0284
C459X	0284
C459Y	0284
C460	0151
C460(JAPAN)	0151
C460-5	0151
C460-B	0151
C460-C	0151
C460-OR	0151
C460A(2S)	0151
C460B	0151
C460BL	0151
C460C	0151
C460D(2S)	0151
C460E	0151
C460F	0151
C460G(2S)	0151
C460GB(2S)	0151
C460GN	0151
C460H(2S)	0151
C460J	0151
C460K(2S)	0151
C460L(2S)	0151
C460M	0151
C460OR	0151
C460R	0151
C460X	0151
C460Y	0151
C461	0151
C461-8F	0151
C461-A	0151
C461-B	0151
C461A	0151
C461AL	0151
C461B	0151
C461BF	0151
C461BK	0151
C461BL	0151
C461C	0151
C461E(2S)	0151
C461EP	0151
C461F	0151
C461L(2S)	0151
C462	0079
C463(2S)	0007
C463A	0007
C463B	0007
C463C	0007
C463D	0007
C463E	0007
C463F	0007
C463G	0007
C463GN	0007
C463H(2S)	0007
C463J	0007
C463K	0007
C463L	0007
C463M	0007
C463OR	0007
C463R	0007
C463X	0007
C463Y	0007
C464(2S)	0259
C464A	0259
C464B	0259
C464C(2S)	0259
C464D	0259
C464E	0259
C464F	0259
C464G	0259
C464GN	0259
C464H	0259
C464J	0259
C464K	0259
C464L	0259
C464M	0259
C464OR	0259
C464R	0259
C464X	0259
C464Y	0259
C465(2S)	0259
C465A	0259
C465B	0259
C465C	0259
C465D	0259
C465E	0259
C465F	0259
C465G	0259
C465GN	0259
C465H	0259
C465J	0259
C465K	0259
C465L	0259
C465M	0259
C465OR	0259
C465R	0259
C465X	0259
C465Y	0259
C466(2S)	0259
C466A	0259
C466B	0259
C466C	0259
C466D	0259
C466E	0259
C466F	0259
C466G	0259
C466GN	0259
C466H(2S)	0259
C466J	0259
C466K	0259
C466L	0259
C466M	0259
C466OR	0259
C466R	0259
C466X	0259
C466Y	0259
C467	0144
C468(2S)	0016
C468A(2S)	0016
C468B	0016
C468H	0016
C468LGR	0016
C469(2S)	0470
C469-OR	0470
C469A(2S)	0470
C469B	0470
C469C	0470
C469D	0470
C469E	0470
C469F(2S)	0470
C469G	0470
C469GN	0470
C469H	0470
C469J	0470
C469K(2S)	0470
C469L	0470
C469M	0470
C469OR	0470
C469Q(2S)	0470
C469R(2S)	0470
C469X	0470
C469Y	0470
C470(2S)	0233
C470-3	0233
C470-4	0233
C470-5	0233
C470-6	0233
C470A	0233
C470B	0233
C470C	0233
C470D	0233
C470E	0233
C470F	0233
C470G	0233
C470GN	0233
C470H	0233
C470J	0233
C470K	0233
C470L	0233
C470M	0233
C470OR	0233
C470R	0233
C470X	0233
C470Y	0233
C471	0018
C472	0224
C472A	0224
C472B	0224
C472C	0224
C472D	0224
C472E	0224
C472F	0224
C472G	0224
C472GN	0224
C472H	0224
C472J	0224
C472K	0224
C472L	0224
C472M	0224
C472OR	0224
C472R	0224
C472X	0224
C472Y(2S)	0224
C473	0016
C473AC	0016
C474	0079
C475(2S)	0470
C475A	0470
C475B	0470
C475C	0470
C475D	0470
C475E	0470
C475F	0470
C475G	0470
C475GN	0470
C475H	0470
C475J	0470
C475K(2S)	0470
C475L	0470
C475M	0470
C475OR	0470
C475R	0470
C475X	0470
C475Y	0470
C476(2S)	0470
C476A	0470
C476B	0470
C476C	0470
C476D	0470
C476E	OEM
C476E(TRANS)	0470
C476F	0470
C476G	0470
C476GN	0470
C476H	0470
C476J	0470
C476K	0470
C476L	0470
C476M	OEM
C476M(TRANS)	0470
C476N	OEM
C476OR	0470
C476P	OEM
C476PA	OEM
C476PB	OEM
C476R	0470
C476S	OEM
C476T	OEM
C476X	0470
C476Y	0470
C477(2S)	0007
C477A	0007
C477B	0007
C477C	0007
C477D	0007
C477E	OEM
C477E(TRANS)	0007
C477F	0007
C477G	0007
C477GN	0007
C477H	0007
C477J	0007
C477K	0007
C477L	0007
C477M	OEM
C477M(TRANS)	0007
C477N	OEM
C477OR	0007
C477P	OEM
C477PA	OEM
C477PB	OEM
C477PC	OEM
C477PD	OEM
C477R	0007
C477S	OEM
C477T	OEM
C477X	0007
C477Y	0007
C478(2S)	0016
C478-4(2S)	0016
C478-O	0016
C478A	0016
C478B	0016
C478C	0016
C478D(2S)	0016
C478E	OEM
C478E(TRANS)	0016
C478F	0016
C478G	0016
C478GN	0016
C478H	0016
C478J	0016
C478K	0016
C478L	0016
C478M	OEM
C478M(TRANS)	0016
C478N	OEM
C478OR	0016
C478P	OEM
C478PA	OEM
C478PB	OEM
C478PC	OEM
C478PD	OEM
C478R	0016
C478S	OEM
C478T	OEM
C478X	0016
C478Y	0016
C479(2S)	0086
C479A	0086
C479B	0086
C479C	0086
C479D	0086
C479E	0086
C479F	0086
C479G	0086
C479GN	0086
C479H	0086
C479J	0086
C479K	0086
C479L	0086
C479M	0086
C479OR	0086
C479R	0086
C479X	0086
C479Y	0086
C480	0320
C481(2S)	0693
C481-OR	0693
C481A	0693
C481B	0693
C481C	0693
C481D	0693
C481E	0693
C481F	0693
C481G	0693
C481GN	0693
C481H	0693
C481J	0693
C481K	0693
C481L	0693
C481M	0693
C481OR	0693
C481R	0693
C481X(2S)	0693
C481Y	0693
C482(2S)	1583
C482-0	1583
C482-GR(2S)	1583
C482-GRN	1583
C482-O(2S)	1583
C482-OR	1583
C482-ORG	1583
C482-Y(2S)	1583
C482-YEL	1583
C482A	1583
C482B	1583
C482C	1583
C482D	1583
C482E	1583
C482F	1583
C482G	1583
C482GN	1583
C482GR(2S)	1583
C482GRN	1583
C482GRY	1583
C482H	1583
C482J	1583
C482K	1583
C482L	1583
C482M	1583
C482OR	1583
C482R	1583
C482X(2S)	1583
C482Y(2S)	1583
C482YEL	1583
C483	1021
C484(2S)	1471
C484-BL	1471
C484-BLU	1471
C484-R	1471
C484-RED	1471
C484-Y	1471
C484-YEL	1471
C484A	1471
C484B	1471
C484BL(2S)	1471
C484C	1471
C484D	1471
C484E	1471
C484F	1471
C484G	1471
C484GN	1471
C484H	1471
C484J	1471
C484K	1471
C484L	1471
C484M	1471
C484OR	1471
C484R(2S)	1471
C484X	1471
C484Y(2S)	1471
C485(2S)	1471
C485-BL	1471
C485-BLU	1471
C485-OR	1471
C485-R	1471
C485-RED	1471
C485-Y	1471
C485-YEL	1471
C485A	1471
C485B	1471
C485BL(2S)	1471
C485C(2S)	1471
C485D	1471
C485E	1471
C485F	1471
C485G	1471
C485GN	1471
C485H	1471
C485J	1471
C485K	1471
C485L	1471
C485M	1471
C485OR	1471
C485R	1471
C485X	1471
C485Y(2S)	1471
C486(2S)	1471
C486-BL	1471
C486-BLU	1471
C486-R	1471
C486-RED	1471
C486-Y	1471
C486-YEL	1471
C486A	1471
C486B	1471
C486BL(2S)	1471
C486C	1471
C486D	1471
C486E	1471
C486F	1471
C486G	1471
C486GN	1471
C486H	1471
C486J	1471
C486K	1471
C486L	1471
C486M	1471
C486OR	1471
C486R	1471
C486X	1471
C486Y(2S)	1471
C487(2S)	0178
C487A	0178
C488(2S)	0178
C488H	0178
C489(2S)	0178
C489-BL	0178
C489-BLU	0178
C489-R	0178
C489-RED	0178
C489-Y	0178
C489-YEL	0178
C489A	0178
C489B	0178
C489C	0178
C489D	0178
C489E	0178
C489F	0178
C489G	0178
C489GN	0178
C489H	0178
C489J	0178
C489K	0178
C489L	0178
C489M	0178
C489OR	0178
C489R	0178
C489X	0178
C489Y	0178
C490(2S)	0178
C490-BL	0178
C490-BLU	0178
C490-R	0178
C490-RED	0178
C490-Y	0178
C490-YEL	0178
C491(2S)	0178
C491-BL	0178
C491-BLU	0178
C491-R	0178
C491-RED	0178
C491-Y	0178
C491-YEL	0178
C491A	0178
C491B	0178
C491BL(2S)	0178
C491C	0178
C491D	0178
C491E	0178
C491F	0178
C491G	0178
C491GN	0178
C491H	0178
C491J	0178
C491K	0178
C491L	0178
C491M	0178
C491OR	0178
C491R	0178
C491X	0178
C491Y(2S)	0178
C492(2S)	0177
C493(2S)	0861
C493-BL(2S)	0861
C493-R(2S)	0861
C493-Y(2S)	0861
C493A	0861
C493B	0861
C493C	0861
C493D	0861
C493E	0861
C493F	0861
C493G	0861
C493GN	0861
C493H	0861
C493J	0861
C493K	0861
C493L	0861
C493M	0861
C493OR	0861
C493R	0861
C493X	0861
C493Y	0861
C494(2S)	0615
C494-BL(2S)	0615
C494-R(2S)	0615
C494-Y(2S)	0615
C494A	0615
C494B	0615
C494BL(2S)	0615
C494C	0615
C494D	0615
C494E	0615
C494F	0615
C494G	0615
C494GN	0615
C494H	0615
C494J	0615
C494K	0615
C494L	0615
C494M	0615
C494OR	0615
C494R	0615
C494X	0615
C494Y	0615
C495(2S)	0781
C495-0	0781
C495-O(2S)	0781
C495-OR	0781
C495-ORG	0781
C495-R(2S)	0781
C495-RED	0781
C495-Y(2S)	0781
C495-YEL	0781
C495A	0781
C495B	0781
C495C	0781
C495D	0781
C495E	0781
C495F	0781
C495G	0781
C495GN	0781
C495H	0781
C495J	0781
C495K	0781
C495L	0781
C495M	0781
C495OR	0781
C495P	0781
C495R	0781
C495RED	0781
C495T(2S)	0781
C495T(CB)	1581
C495X	0781
C495Y(2S)	0781
C495YEL	0781
C496	0781
C496-0	0781
C496-O(2S)	0781
C496-OR	0781
C496-ORG	0781
C496-R(2S)	0781
C496-RED	0781
C496-Y(2S)	0781
C496-YEL	0781
C496A	0781
C496B	0781
C496C	0781
C496D	0781
C496E	0781
C496F	0781
C496G	0781
C496GN	0781
C496H	0781
C496J	0781
C496K	0781
C496L	0781
C496M	0781
C496OR	0781
C496R	0781
C496RED	0781
C496X	0781
C496Y(2S)	0781
C496YEL	0781
C497(2S)	0086
C497-0	0086
C497-O(2S)	0086
C497-OR	0086
C497-ORG	0086
C497-R(2S)	0086
C497-RED	0086
C497-Y(2S)	0086
C497-YEL	0086
C497A	0086
C497B	0086
C497C	0086
C497D	0086
C497E	0086
C497F	0086
C497G	0086
C497GN	0086
C497H	0086
C497J	0086
C497K	0086
C497L	0086
C497M	0086
C497OR	0086
C497R	0086
C497RED	0086
C497X	0086
C497Y	0086
C498(2S)	0086
C498-0	0086
C498-O(2S)	0086
C498-OR	0086
C498-ORG	0086
C498-R(2S)	0086
C498-RED	0086
C498-Y(2S)	0086
C498-YEL	0086
C498A	0086
C498B	0086
C498C	0086
C498D	0086
C498E	0086
C498F	0086
C498G	0086
C498GN	0086
C498H	0086
C498J	0086
C498K	0086
C498L	0086
C498M	0086
C498OR	0086
C498R	0086
C498RED	0086
C498X	0086

If replacement code is OEM, contact original manufacturer for replacement.

DEVICE TYPE	REPL CODE
C498Y	0086
C498YEL	0086
C499(2S)	2359
C499-OR	2359
C499-R	2359
C499-RED	2359
C499-RY(2S)	2359
C499-Y	2359
C499-YEL	2359
C499A	2359
C499B	2359
C499C	2359
C499D	2359
C499E	2359
C499F	2359
C499FA1	2359
C499G	2359
C499GN	2359
C499H	2359
C499J	2359
C499K	2359
C499L	2359
C499M	2359
C499OR	2359
C499R(2S)	2359
C499RED	2359
C499RY	2359
C499X	2359
C499Y(2S)	2359
C499YEL	2359
C500(2S)	0233
C500(N)	0233
C500(Y)	0233
C500A	0233
C500B	0233
C500C	0233
C500D	0233
C500E	0233
C500F	0233
C500G	0233
C500GN	0233
C500H	0233
C500J	0233
C500K	0233
C500L	0233
C500M	0233
C500OR	0233
C500R(2S)	0233
C500X	0233
C500Y(2S)	0233
C501	0086
C501-O	0086
C501-ORG	0086
C501-R	0086
C501-RED	0086
C501-Y	0086
C501-YEL	0086
C501A	OEM
C501A(TRANS)	0086
C501B	OEM
C501B(TRANS)	0086
C501C	OEM
C501C(TRANS)	0086
C501D	OEM
C501D(TRANS)	0086
C501E	OEM
C501E(TRANS)	0086
C501F	0086
C501G	0086
C501GN	0086
C501H	0086
C501J	0086
C501K	0086
C501L	OEM
C501L(2S)	0086
C501M	OEM
C501M(TRANS)	0086
C501N	OEM
C501O	0086
C501OR	0086
C501P	OEM
C501PA	OEM
C501PB	OEM
C501PC	OEM
C501PD	OEM
C501PE	OEM
C501PM	OEM
C501PN	OEM
C501PS	OEM
C501PT	OEM
C501R	0086
C501S	OEM
C501T	OEM
C501X	0086
C501Y	0086
C502	0693
C502(2S)	0693
C502A	0693
C502B	0693
C502C	0693
C502D	0693
C502E	0693
C502F	0693
C502G	0693
C502GN	0693
C502H	0693
C502J	0693
C502K	0693
C502L	OEM
C502L(TRANS)	0693
C502LA	OEM
C502M	0693
C502OR	0693
C502PE	OEM
C502PM	OEM
C502PN	OEM
C502PS	OEM
C502PT	OEM
C502R	0693
C502X	0693
C502Y	0693
C503(2S)	0086
C503-GR	0086
C503-O(2S)	0086
C503-Y(2S)	0086
C503A	0086
C503B	0086
C503C	0086
C503D	0086
C503E	0086
C503F	0086
C503G	0086
C503GN	0086
C503GR(2S)	0086
C503H	0086
C503J	0086
C503K	0086
C503L	0086
C503M	0086
C503OR	0086
C503R	0086
C503X	0086
C504(2S)	0086
C504-GR	0086
C504-O(2S)	0086
C504-Y(2S)	0086
C504A	0086
C504B	0086
C504C	0086
C504D	0086
C504E	0086
C504F	0086
C504G	0086
C504GN	0086
C504GR(2S)	0086
C504H	0086
C504J	0086
C504K	0086
C504L	0086
C504M	0086
C504OR	0086
C504R	0086
C504X	0086
C505(2S)	0233
C505-O(2S)	0233
C505-ORG	0233
C505-R(2S)	0233
C505-RED	0233
C505A	0233
C505B	0233
C505C	0233
C505D	0233
C505E	0233
C505F	0233
C505G	0233
C505GN	0233
C505H	0233
C505J	0233
C505K	0233
C505L	0233
C505M	0233
C505O	0233
C505OR	0233
C505R	0233
C505X	0233
C505Y	0233
C506(2S)	0233
C506-O(2S)	0233
C506-ORG	0233
C506-R(2S)	0233
C506-RED	0233
C506A	OEM
C506A(TRANS)	0233
C506B	OEM
C506B(TRANS)	0233
C506C	OEM
C506C(TRANS)	0233
C506D	OEM
C506D(TRANS)	0233
C506E	OEM
C506E(TRANS)	0233
C506F	0233
C506G	0233
C506GN	0233
C506H	0233
C506J	0233
C506K	0233
C506L	0233
C506M	OEM
C506M(TRANS)	0233
C506O	0233
C506OR	0233
C506R	0233
C506X	0233
C506Y	0233
C507(2S)	0233
C507-O	0233
C507-O(2S)	0233
C507-R(2S)	0233
C507-Y(2S)	0233
C507A	OEM
C507A(TRANS)	0233
C507B	OEM
C507B(TRANS)	0233
C507C	OEM
C507C(TRANS)	0233
C507D	OEM
C507D(TRANS)	0233
C507E	OEM
C507E(TRANS)	0233
C507F	0233
C507G	0233
C507GN	0233
C507H	0233
C507J	0233
C507K	0233
C507L	0233
C507M	OEM
C507M(TRANS)	0233
C507N	OEM
C507OR	0233
C507P	OEM
C507R	0233
C507S	OEM
C507T	OEM
C507X	0233
C507Y	0233
C508(2S)	0178
C508A	OEM
C508A(TRANS)	0178
C508B	OEM
C508B(TRANS)	0178
C508C	OEM
C508C(TRANS)	0178
C508D	OEM
C508D(TRANS)	0178
C508E	OEM
C508E(TRANS)	0178
C508F	0178
C508G	0178
C508GN	0178
C508M	OEM
C508N	OEM
C508OR	0178
C508P	OEM
C508PA	OEM
C508PB	OEM
C508S	OEM
C508T	OEM
C508X	0178
C508Y	0178
C509	0155
C509(O)	0155
C509-O	0155
C509-O	0155
C509-Y	0155
C509G(2S)	0155
C509G-O	0155
C509G-Y	0155
C509M	OEM
C509N	OEM
C509O	0155
C509P	OEM
C509PA	OEM
C509PB	OEM
C509S	OEM
C509T	OEM
C509Y(2S)	0155
C510	1471
C510-O	1471
C510-ORG	1471
C510-R	1471
C510-RED	1471
C510A	OEM
C510A(TRANS)	1471
C510B	OEM
C510B(TRANS)	1471
C510C	OEM
C510C(TRANS)	1471
C510D	OEM
C510D(TRANS)	1471
C510E	OEM
C510E(TRANS)	1471
C510F	1471
C510G	1471
C510GN	1471
C510H	1471
C510J	1471
C510K	1471
C510L	1471
C510M	OEM
C510M(TRANS)	1471
C510O	1471
C510OR	1471
C510R	1471
C510S	OEM
C510X	1471
C510Y	1471
C511	1471
C511-O	1471
C511-ORG	1471
C511-R	1471
C511-RED	1471
C511A	0442
C511A(TRANS)	1471
C511B	0934
C511B(TRANS)	1471
C511C	1213
C511C(TRANS)	1471
C511D	OEM
C511D(TRANS)	1471
C511E	1471
C511F	0442
C511F(TRANS)	1471
C511G	0442
C511G(TRANS)	1471
C511GN	1471
C511H	1213
C511H(TRANS)	1471
C511J	1471
C511K	1471
C511L	1471
C511M	1471
C511O	1471
C511OR	1471
C511R	1471
C511U	1386
C511X	1471
C511Y	1471
C512(2S)	1471
C512-O	1471
C512-O(2S)	1471
C512-ORG	1471
C512-R(2S)	1471
C512-RED	1471
C512A	1471
C512B	1471
C512C	1471
C512D	1471
C512E	1471
C512F	1471
C512G	1471
C512GN	1471
C512H	1471
C512J	1471
C512K	1471
C512L	1471
C512M	1471
C512O	1471
C512OR	1471
C512R	1471
C512X	1471
C512Y	1471
C513(2S)	1471
C513-O	1471
C513-O(2S)	1471
C513-ORG	1471
C513-R	1471
C513-RED	1471
C513A	1471
C513B	1471
C513C	1471
C513D	1471
C513E	1471
C513F	1471
C513G	1471
C513GN	1471
C513H	1471
C513J	1471
C513K	1471
C513L	1471
C513M	1471
C513O	1471
C513OR	1471
C513R(2S)	1471
C513X	1471
C513Y	1471
C514(2S)	0142
C514A	0142
C514B	0142
C514C	0142
C514D	0142
C514E	0142
C514F	0142
C514G	0142
C514GN	0142
C514H	0142
C514J	0142
C514K	0142
C514L	0142
C514M	0142
C514OR	0142
C514R	0142
C514X	0142
C514Y	0142
C515(2S)	0142
C515-OR	0142
C515A(2S)	0142
C515AM	0142
C515AX(2S)	0142
C515AY	0142
C515B	0142
C515BK	0142
C515C	0142
C515D	0142
C515E	0142
C515F	0142
C515G	0142
C515GN	0142
C515H	0142
C515J	0142
C515K	0142
C515L	0142
C515M	0142
C515OR	0142
C515R	0142
C515X	0142
C515Y	0142
C516(2S)	0086
C516A	0086
C516B	0086
C516C	0086
C516D	0086
C516E	0086
C516F	0086
C516G	0086
C516GN	0086
C516H	0086
C516J	0086
C516K	0086
C516L	0086
C516M	0086
C516OR	0086
C516R	0086
C516X	0086
C516Y	0086
C517(2S)	1401
C517-OR	1401
C517A	1401
C517B	1401
C517C(2S)	1401
C517D	1401
C517E	1401
C517F	1401
C517G	1401
C517GN	1401
C517H	1401
C517J	1401
C517K	1401
C517L	1401
C517M	1401
C517OR	1401
C517R	1401
C517S	1401
C517X	1401
C517Y	1401
C518	0168
C518A	0168
C519(2S)	0861
C519A(2S)	0861
C520	0861
C520A	0861
C520A(2S)	0861
C520B	OEM
C520C	OEM
C520D	OEM
C521(2S)	0861
C521A(2S)	0861
C522(2S)	2298
C522-O	5369
C522-O(2S)	2298
C522-ORG	2298
C522-R(2S)	2298
C522-RED	2298
C522O	2298
C522R	2298
C523(2S)	2298
C523-O	2298
C523-O(2S)	2298
C523-ORG	2298
C523-R(2S)	2298
C523-RED	2298
C523O	2298
C523R	2298
C524(2S)	3302
C524-O	2298
C524-O(2S)	3302
C524-ORG	2298
C524-R(2S)	2298
C524-RED	2298
C524O	2298
C524R	3302
C525(2S)	1401
C525-O	1401
C525-O(2S)	1401
C525-ORG	1401
C525-R(2S)	1401
C525-RED	1401
C525O	1401
C525R	1401
C526(2S)	0233
C526-O	0233
C526A(2S)	0233
C526B	0233
C526C	0233
C526D	0233
C526E	0233
C526F	0233
C526G	0233
C526GN	0233
C526H	0233
C526J	0233
C526K	0233
C526L	0233
C526M	0233
C526OR	0233
C526R	0233
C526X	0233
C526Y	0233
C527	0007
C528	0111
C529	0284
C529A	0284
C529B	0284
C529C	0284
C529D	0284
C529E	0284
C529F	0284
C529G	0284
C529GN	0284
C529H	0284
C529J	0284
C529K	0284
C529L	0284
C529M	0284
C529OR	0284
C529R	0284
C529X	0284
C529Y	0284
C530	0079
C530A	OEM
C530B	OEM
C530C	OEM
C530D	OEM
C530E	OEM
C530M	OEM
C531	0155
C532	0079
C532O	0079
C533	0079
C533A-5	OEM
C533A-6	OEM
C533A-G	OEM
C533A-M	OEM
C533A-X	OEM
C534	0079
C535	0127
C535-OR	0127
C535A	0127
C535ABC	0127
C535AL	0127
C535B	0127
C535B(JAPAN)	0127
C535C	0127
C535D	0127
C535E	0127
C535F	0127
C535G(2S)	0127
C535GN	0127
C535H	0127
C535J	0127
C535K	0127
C535L	0127
C535M	0127
C535OR	0127
C535R	0127
C535X	0127
C535Y	0127
C536	0532
C536(JAPAN)	0532
C536-D	0532
C536-E	0532
C536-F	0532
C536-G	0532
C536-OR	0532
C536A(2S)	0502
C536AF	0532
C536AG(2S)	0532
C536B(2S)	0532
C536C(2S)	0532
C536D(2S)	0532
C536DK(2S)	0532
C536E	0532
C536E(JAPAN)	0532
C536ED(2S)	0532
C536EH(2S)	0532
C536EJ(2S)	0532
C536EN(2S)	0532
C536EP	0532
C536ER(2S)	0532
C536ET(2S)	0532
C536EZ(2S)	0532
C536F	0532
C536F(JAPAN)	0532
C536F1(2S)	0532
C536F2(2S)	0532
C536FC	0532
C536FC(2S)	0532
C536FP(2S)	0532
C536FS(2S)	0532
C536FS6(2S)	0532
C536FZ(2S)	0532
C536G	0532
C536G(2S)	0532
C536G(JAPAN)	0532
C536G-1	0532
C536G1	0532
C536G2	0532
C536GF(2S)	0532
C536GJ	0532
C536GK(2S)	0532
C536GL	0532
C536GM	0532
C536GN	0532
C536GP	0532
C536GT(2S)	0532
C536GV(2S)	0532
C536GY(2S)	0532
C536GZ	0532
C536H(2S)	0532
C536J	0532
C536K	0532
C536K(JAPAN)	0532
C536KE	0532
C536KE(JAPAN)	0532
C536KF	0532
C536KF(JAPAN)	0532
C536KG	0532
C536KNP	0532
C536L	0532
C536M	0532
C536NP	0532
C536NPE	0532
C536NPF	0532
C536NPG	0532
C536OR	0532
C536R	0532
C536SP	0532
C536W(2S)	0532
C536X	0532
C536XL	0532
C536Y	0502
C536YF	0532
C537	0191
C537-C7	0191
C537-EV	0191
C537A	0111
C537ALC	0191
C537B	0191
C537BK	0191
C537C	0191
C537C7	0191
C537D(2S)	0191
C537D1	0191
C537D2(2S)	0191
C537E(2S)	0191
C537EF	0191
C537EH(2S)	0191
C537EJ(2S)	0191
C537EV	0191
C537F	0191
C537F1(2S)	0191
C537F2(2S)	0191
C537FC(2S)	0191
C537F-C7	0191
C537FC7	0191
C537FJ	0191
C537FK	0191
C537FV(2S)	0191
C537G(2S)	0191
C537G1(2S)	0191
C537G2	0191
C537GFL	0191
C537GI(2S)	0191
C537H(2S)	0191
C537HT(2S)	0191
C537WF	0191
C538	0079
C538-Q	0079
C538A(2S)	0079
C538A-P	0079
C538AQ(2S)	0079
C538A-R	0079
C538AR	0079
C538AS	0079
C538K	0079
C538P(2S)	0079
C538Q(2S)	0079
C538R	0079
C538S(2S)	0079
C538T(2S)	0079
C539(2S)	0016
C539R(2S)	0016
C539S(2S)	0016
C539T	0016
C540(2S)	0470
C540A	0470
C540B	0470
C540C	0470
C540D	0470
C540E	0470
C540F	0470
C540G	0470
C540GN	0470
C540H	0470
C540J	0470
C540K	0470
C540L	0470
C540M	0470
C540OR	0470
C540R	0470
C540X	0470
C540Y	0470
C541	0555
C542	0555
C543	0042
C543A	0042
C543B	0042
C543C	0042
C543D	0042
C543E	0042
C543F	0042
C543G	0042
C543GN	0042
C543H	0042
C543J	0042
C543K	0042
C543L	0042
C543M	0042
C543OR	0042
C543R	0042
C543X	0042
C543Y	0042

If replacement code is OEM, contact original manufacturer for replacement. 319

DEVICE TYPE	REPL CODE
C544(2S)	2195
C544A	2195
C544AG	2195
C544B	2195
C544C(2S)	2195
C544D(2S)	0127
C544E(2S)	2195
C544F	2195
C544G	2195
C544GN	2195
C544H	2195
C544J	2195
C544K	2195
C544L	2195
C544M	2195
C544OR	2195
C544R	2195
C544X	2195
C544Y	2195
C545(2S)	0127
C545A(2S)	0127
C545B(2S)	0127
C545C(2S)	0127
C545D(2S)	0127
C545E(2S)	0127
C546	0007
C546K	0007
C547	0111
C547C(EUROPE)	0079
C548	0079
C548(EUROPE)	0079
C548A(EUROPE)	0111
C548C	0079
C548C(EUROPE)	0079
C549C(EUROPE)	0111
C550	0555
C550A	0555
C551	0042
C552	0042
C553	0042
C554	0042
C554C	1469
C555	0488
C-555A	0627
C555A	0627
C556	0224
C557(EUROPE)	0037
C558	0037
C558(2S)	4841
C558(EUROPE)	0037
C558B(EUROPE)	0037
C558C(EUROPE)	0643
C559	0018
C559B(EUROPE)	0037
C560(2S)	0086
C560A	0086
C560B	0086
C560C	0086
C560D	0086
C560E	0086
C560F	0086
C560G	0086
C560GN	0086
C560H	0086
C560J	0086
C560K	0086
C560L	0086
C560M	0086
C560OR	0086
C560R	0086
C560X	0086
C560Y	0086
C561(2S)	1422
C561-OR	1422
C561A	1422
C561B	1422
C561C	1422
C561D	1422
C561E	1422
C561F	1422
C561G	1422
C561GN	1422
C561H	1422
C561J	1422
C561K	1422
C561L	1422
C561M	1422
C561OR	1422
C561R	1422
C561X	1422
C561Y	1422
C562(2S)	0216
C562(O)	0216
C562-OR	0216
C562A	0216
C562B	0216
C562C	0216
C562D	0216
C562E	0216
C562F	0216
C562G	0216
C562GN	0216
C562H	0216
C562J	0216
C562K	0216
C562L	0216
C562M	0216
C562O	0007
C562OR	0216
C562R	0216
C562X	0216
C562Y(2S)	0216
C563	0829
C563-F	0829
C563-G	0829
C563-OR	0829
C563A(2S)	0829
C563B	0829
C563C	0829
C563D	0829
C563E	0829
C563F	0829
C563G	0829
C563GN	0829
C563H	0829
C563J	0829
C563K	0829
C563L	0829
C563M	0829
C563OR	0829
C563R	0829
C563X	0829
C563Y	0829
C564(2S)	0016
C564A(2S)	0016
C564AP	0016
C564B	0016
C564C	0016
C564D	0016
C564E	0016
C564F	0016
C564G	0016
C564GN	0016
C564H	0016
C564J	0016
C564K	0016
C564L	0016
C564M	0016
C564OR	0016
C564P(2S)	0016
C564PL	0016
C564Q(2S)	0016
C564QC	0016
C564R(2S)	0016
C564S(2S)	0016
C564T(2S)	0016
C564X	0016
C564Y	0016
C565	0016
C566(2S)	0259
C566A	0259
C566B	0259
C566C	0259
C566D	0259
C566E	0259
C566F	0259
C566G	0259
C566GN	0259
C566H	0259
C566J	0259
C566K	0259
C566L	0259
C566M	0259
C566OR	0259
C566R	0259
C566X	0259
C566Y	0259
C567(2S)	0259
C567A	0259
C567B	0259
C567C	0259
C567D	0259
C567E	0259
C567F	0259
C567G	0259
C567GN	0259
C567H	0259
C567J	0259
C567K	0259
C567L	0259
C567M	0259
C567OR	0259
C567R	0259
C567X	0259
C567Y	0259
C568(2S)	0259
C568A	0259
C568B	0259
C568C	0259
C568D	0259
C568E	0259
C568F	0259
C568G	0259
C568GN	0259
C568H	0259
C568J	0259
C568K	0259
C568L	0259
C568M	0259
C568OR	0259
C568R	0259
C568X	0259
C568Y	0259
C569	0016
C570	0016
C571(2S)	2030
C572	3289
C573	3290
C575	0086
C575C2	2845
C576	0016
C576E	0016
C576F	0016
C576G	0016
C577	0016
C577H	2246
C578	0855
C579	0396
C580(2S)	0086
C580A	0086
C580B	0086
C580C	0086
C580D	0086
C580E	0086
C580F	0086
C580G	0086
C580GN	0086
C580H	0086
C580J	0086
C580K	0086
C580L	0086
C580M	0086
C580OR	0086
C580R	0086
C580T	0086
C580X	0086
C580Y	0086
C581	0007
C582(2S)	2634
C582-OR	2634
C582A(2S)	2634
C582B(2S)	2634
C582BC(2S)	2634
C582BX(2S)	2634
C582BY(2S)	2634
C582C(2S)	2634
C582D	2634
C582E	2634
C582EA	2634
C582EH	2634
C582F	2634
C582G	2634
C582GN	2634
C582H	2634
C582J	2634
C582K	2634
C582L	2634
C582M	2634
C582OR	2634
C582R	2634
C582X	2634
C582Y	2634
C583(2S)	0259
C584	0219
C585	0042
C586(2S)	0177
C587(2S)	0016
C587A(2S)	0016
C587B	0016
C587C	0016
C587D	0016
C587E	0016
C587F	0016
C587G	0016
C587GN	0016
C587H	0016
C587J	0016
C587K	0016
C587L	0016
C587M	0016
C587OR	0016
C587R	0016
C587X	0016
C587Y	0016
C588(2S)	0016
C588A	0016
C588B	0016
C588C	0016
C588D	0016
C588E	0016
C588F	0016
C588G	0016
C588GN	0016
C588H	0016
C588J	0016
C588K	0016
C588L	0016
C588M	0016
C588OR	0016
C588R	0016
C588X	0016
C588Y	0016
C589(2S)	0233
C589A	0233
C589B	0233
C589C	0233
C589D	0233
C589E	0233
C589F	0233
C589G	0233
C589GN	0233
C589H	0233
C589J	0233
C589K	0233
C589L	0233
C589M	0233
C589OR	0233
C589R	0233
C589X	0233
C589Y	0233
C590(2S)	0233
C590A	0233
C590B	0233
C590C	0233
C590D	0233
C590E	0233
C590F	0233
C590G	0233
C590GN	0233
C590H	0233
C590J	0233
C590K	0233
C590L	0233
C590M	0233
C590OR	0233
C590X	0233
C590Y(2S)	0233
C591	0168
C591A	0168
C591B	0168
C591C	0168
C591D	0168
C591E	0168
C591F	0168
C591G	0168
C591GN	0168
C591H	0168
C591J	0168
C591K	0168
C591L	0168
C591M	0168
C591OR	0168
C591R	0168
C591X	0168
C591Y	0168
C592	0555
C593(2S)	0016
C594(2S)	0016
C594-O	0016
C594-R	0016
C594-Y	0016
C594A	0016
C594B	0016
C594C	0016
C594D	0016
C594E	0016
C594F	0016
C594G	0016
C594GN	0016
C594H	0016
C594J	0016
C594K	0016
C594L	0016
C594M	0016
C594OR	0016
C594R	0016
C594X	0016
C594Y	0016
C595(2S)	0016
C595A	0016
C595B	0016
C595C	0016
C595D	0016
C595E	0016
C595F	0016
C595G	0016
C595GN	0016
C595H	0016
C595J	0016
C595K	0016
C595L	0016
C595M	0016
C595OR	0016
C595X	0016
C595Y	0016
C596(2S)	0016
C596(IC)	0851
C596A	0016
C596B	0016
C596C	0016
C596C(IC)	0851
C596D	0016
C596E	0016
C596F	0016
C596G	0016
C596GN	0016
C596H	0016
C596J	0016
C596K	0016
C596L	0016
C596M	0016
C596OR	0016
C596R	0016
C596X	0016
C596Y	0016
C597	0930
C598	0555
C599	0042
C600	0042
C600E	OEM
C600M	OEM
C600N	OEM
C600P	OEM
C600PA	OEM
C600PB	OEM
C600S	OEM
C600T	OEM
C601(2S)	0488
C601L	OEM
C601N	OEM
C601N(2S)	0488
C601P	OEM
C601PA	OEM
C601PB	OEM
C601PC	OEM
C601PD	OEM
C601PE	OEM
C601PM	OEM
C601PN	OEM
C601PS	OEM
C601PT	OEM
C601T	OEM
C602	0007
C602L	OEM
C602LA	OEM
C602LB	OEM
C602LC	OEM
C602LD	OEM
C602LE	OEM
C602LM	OEM
C602PM	OEM
C602PN	OEM
C602PS	OEM
C602PT	OEM
C603	0396
C604	0127
C605(2S)	0470
C605-B	0470
C605-OR	0470
C605A	0470
C605B	0470
C605C	0470
C605D	0470
C605E	0470
C605F	0470
C605G	0470
C605GN	0470
C605H	0470
C605J	0470
C605K(2S)	0470
C605L(2S)	0470
C605M(2S)	0470
C605OR	0470
C605Q(2S)	0470
C605R	0470
C605TW(2S)	0470
C605X	0470
C605Y	0470
C606(2S)	0470
C606-B	0470
C606A	0470
C606B	0470
C606C	0470
C606D	0470
C606E	0470
C606F	0470
C606G	0470
C606GN	0470
C606H	0470
C606J	0470
C606K	0470
C606L	0470
C606M	0470
C606N	0470
C606OR	0470
C606R	0470
C606X	0470
C606Y	0470
C607	0086
C608(2S)	1401
C608A	1401
C608AA	1401
C608B	1401
C608C	1401
C608D	1401
C608E(2S)	1401
C608F	1401
C608G	1401
C608GN	1401
C608H	1401
C608J	1401
C608K	1401
C608L	1401
C608M	1401
C608OR	1401
C608R	1401
C608T(2S)	1401
C608X	1401
C608Y	1401
C609(2S)	1401
C609-OR	1401
C609A	1401
C609B	1401
C609C	1401
C609D	1401
C609E	1401
C609F(2S)	1401
C609G	1401
C609GN	1401
C609H	1401
C609J	1401
C609K	1401
C609L	1401
C609M	OEM
C609M(TRANS)	1401
C609N	OEM
C609OR	1401
C609P	OEM
C609PA	OEM
C609PB	OEM
C609R	1401
C609S	OEM
C609T(2S)	1401
C609X	1401
C609Y	1401
C610	0037
C610(2S)	0086
C610A	0086
C610B	0086
C610C	0086
C610D	0086
C610E	0086
C610F	0086
C610G	0086
C610GN	0086
C610H	0086
C610J	0086
C610K	0086
C610L	0086
C610M	0086
C610OR	0086
C610R	0086
C610X	0086
C610Y	0086
C611	0259
C611(2S)	0259
C611A	0442
C611A(TRANS)	0259
C611B	0934
C611B(TRANS)	0259
C611C	OEM
C611C(TRANS)	0259
C611D	OEM
C611D(TRANS)	0259
C611E	0259
C611F	0442
C611F(TRANS)	0259
C611G	0934
C611G(TRANS)	0259
C611GN	0259
C611H	0259
C611J	0259
C611K	0259
C611L	0259
C611M	0259
C611OR	0259
C611R	0259
C611U	1386
C611X	0259
C611Y	0259
C612	0259
C612(2S)	0259
C612A	0259
C612B	0259
C612C	0259
C612D	0259
C612E	0259
C612F	0259
C612G	0259
C612GN	0259
C612H	0259
C612J	0259
C612K	0259
C612L	OEM
C612L(2S)	0259
C612M	0259
C612OR	0259
C612PE	OEM
C612PM	OEM
C612PN	OEM
C612PS	OEM
C612PT	OEM
C612R	0259
C612X	0259
C612Y	0259
C613	0144
C613(2S)	0144
C613A	0144
C613B	0144
C613C	0144
C613D	0144
C613E	0144
C613F	0144
C613G	0144
C613GN	0144
C613H	0144
C613J	0144
C613K	0144
C613L	OEM
C613L(TRANS)	0144
C613M	0144
C613OR	0144
C613PE	OEM
C613PM	OEM
C613PN	OEM
C613PS	OEM
C613PT	OEM
C613R	0144
C613X	0144
C613Y	0144
C614	0693
C614(2S)	0693
C614A	0693
C614B	0693
C614C	0693
C614D	0693
C614E(2S)	0693
C614F(2S)	0693
C614G(2S)	0693
C614GN	0693
C614H	0693
C614J	0693
C614K	0693
C614L	0693
C614M	0693
C614OR	0693
C614R	0693
C614X	0693
C614Y	0693
C615	0693
C615(2S)	0693
C615-OR	0693
C615A	0693
C615B(2S)	0693
C615C(2S)	0693
C615D(2S)	0693
C615E(2S)	0693
C615F	0693
C615G(2S)	0693
C615GN	0693
C615H	0693
C615J	0693
C615K	0693
C615L	0693
C615M	0693
C615OR	0693
C615R	0693
C615X	0693
C615Y	0693
C616	0626
C617	0626
C618	0007
C618A	0007
C619(2S)	0284
C619A	0284
C619B(2S)	0284
C619C(2S)	0284
C619D(2S)	0284
C619E	0284
C619F	0284
C619G	0284
C619GN	0284
C619H	0284
C619J	0284
C619K	0284
C619L	0284
C619M	0284
C619OR	0284
C619R	0284
C619X	0284
C619Y	0284
C620	0079
C620(2S)	0076
C620-D	0076
C620-E	0076
C620-OR	0076
C620A	0076
C620B	0076
C620C(2S)	0076
C620CD(2S)	0076
C620D(2S)	0076
C620DE(2S)	0076
C620E(2S)	0076
C620F	0076
C620G	0076
C620GN	0076
C620H	0076
C620J	0076
C620K	0076
C620L	0076
C620M	0076
C620OR	0076
C620R	0076
C620X	0076
C620Y	0076
C621	0284
C621(2S)	0284
C621A	0284
C621B	0284
C621C	0284
C621D	0284
C621E	0284
C621F	0284
C621G	0284
C621GN	0284
C621H	0284
C621J	0284
C621K	0284
C621L	0284
C621M	0284
C621OR	0284
C621R	0284
C621X	0284
C621Y	0284
C622	0016
C622(2S)	0016
C622A	0016
C622B	0016
C622C	0016
C622D	0016
C622E	0016
C622F	0016
C622G	0016

If replacement code is OEM, contact original manufacturer for replacement.

DEVICE TYPE	REPL CODE
C622GN	0016
C622H	0016
C622J	0016
C622K	0016
C622L	0016
C622M	0016
C622OR	0016
C622R	0016
C622X	0016
C622Y	0016
C623	OEM
C623(2S)	0016
C624	OEM
C624(2S)	0016
C625	OEM
C626	0016
C627(2S)	0233
C628(2S)	0488
C628E	0488
C628F	0488
C629(2S)	0224
C629-31	0224
C629-41	0224
C629A	0224
C629B	0224
C629C	0224
C629D	0224
C629E	0224
C629F	0224
C629G	0224
C629GN	0224
C629H	0224
C629J	0224
C629K	0224
C629L	0224
C629M	0224
C629OR	0224
C629R	0224
C629X	0224
C629Y	0224
C631	0284
C631(2S)	0284
C631A(2S)	0284
C631B	0284
C631C	0284
C631D	0284
C631E	0284
C631F	0284
C631G	0284
C631GN	0284
C631H	0284
C631J	0284
C631K	0284
C631L	0284
C631M	0284
C631OR	0284
C631R	0284
C631X	0284
C631Y	0284
C632	0284
C632(1)	2064
C632(2S)	2064
C632-OR	2064
C632A(2S)	2064
C632B	2064
C632C	2064
C632D	2064
C632E	2064
C632F	2064
C632G	2064
C632GN	2064
C632H	2064
C632J	2064
C632K	2064
C632L	2064
C632M	2064
C632OR	2064
C632R	2064
C632X	2064
C632Y	2064
C633	0284
C633(2S)	2064
C633-7(2S)	2064
C633-OR	2064
C633A(2S)	2064
C633B	2064
C633C	2064
C633D	2064
C633E	2064
C633F	2064
C633G(2S)	2064
C633GN	2064
C633H(2S)	2064
C633J	2064
C633K	2064
C633L	2064
C633M	2064
C633OR	2064
C633R	2064
C633X	2064
C633Y	2064
C634(2)	2064
C634(2S)	2064
C634-O	2064
C634-OR	2064
C634A(2S)	2064
C634AK	2064
C634AL	2064
C634AXL	2064

DEVICE TYPE	REPL CODE
C634B	2064
C634C	2064
C634D	2064
C634E	2064
C634F	2064
C634G	2064
C634GN	2064
C634H	2064
C634J	2064
C634K	2064
C634L	2064
C634M	2064
C634OR	2064
C634R	2064
C634SP	2064
C634X	2064
C634Y	2064
C635	0079
C635(EUROPE)	1376
C635A(2S)	0079
C636(2S)	0042
C636(EUROPE)	0472
C637	3289
C637(EUROPE)	0320
C638	3290
C638C	3290
C639	0016
C640	0470
C640(2S)	0470
C640A	0470
C640B(2S)	0470
C640C	0470
C640D	0470
C640E	0470
C640F	0470
C640G	0470
C640GN	0470
C640J	0470
C640K	0470
C640L	0470
C640M	0470
C640R	0470
C640X	0470
C641	0284
C641(2S)	0284
C641A	0284
C641B(2S)	0284
C641C	0284
C641D	0284
C641E	0284
C641F	0284
C641G	0284
C641GN	0284
C641H	0284
C641J	0284
C641K	0284
C641L	0284
C641M	0284
C641OR	0284
C641R	0284
C641X	0284
C641Y	0284
C642	0003
C642(2S)	0003
C642A(2S)	0003
C643	0223
C643(2S)	1142
C643-OR	1142
C643A(2S)	1142
C643B	1142
C643C	1142
C643D	1142
C643E	1142
C643F	1142
C643G	1142
C643GN	1142
C643H	1142
C643J	1142
C643K	1142
C643L	1142
C643M	1142
C643OR	1142
C643R	1142
C643X	1142
C643Y	1142
C644	0111
C644(2S)	0111
C644-OR	0111
C644A	0111
C644B	0111
C644C(2S)	0111
C644D	0111
C644E	0111
C644F	0111
C644F/494	0111
C644FH	0111
C644FHS	0111
C644FR(2S)	0111
C644FS(2S)	0111
C644G	0111
C644GN	0111
C644H(2S)	0111
C644J	0111
C644K	0111
C644L	0111
C644M	0111
C644OR	0111
C644P(2S)	0111
C644PJ(2S)	0111

DEVICE TYPE	REPL CODE
C644Q(2S)	0111
C644R	0111
C644S	0111
C644S/494	0111
C644ST	0111
C644T(2S)	0111
C644X	0111
C644Y	0111
C645(2S)	0669
C645-OR	0669
C645A(2S)	0669
C645B(2S)	0669
C645B-1	0669
C645C(2S)	0669
C645D	0669
C645E	0669
C645F	0669
C645G(2S)	0669
C645GN	0669
C645GR	0669
C645H	0669
C645J	0669
C645K	0669
C645L	0669
C645M	0669
C645N(2S)	0669
C645OR	0669
C645R	0669
C645V	0669
C645X	0669
C645Y	0669
C646(2S)	0615
C647(2S)	4316
C647Q(2S)	4316
C647R(2S)	4316
C648(2S)	0016
C648A	0016
C648B	0016
C648C	0016
C648D	0016
C648E	OEM
C648E(TRANS)	0016
C648F	0016
C648G	0016
C648H(2S)	0016
C648J	0016
C648K	0016
C648L	0016
C648M	OEM
C648M(TRANS)	0016
C648N	OEM
C648OR	0016
C648P	OEM
C648PA	OEM
C648PB	OEM
C648R	0016
C648S	OEM
C648T	OEM
C648X	0016
C648Y	0016
C649(2S)	0016
C649A	0016
C649B	0016
C649C	0016
C649D	0016
C649E	0016
C649F	0016
C649G	0016
C649GN	0016
C649H	0016
C649J	0016
C649K	0016
C649L	0016
C649M	0016
C649OR	0016
C649R	0016
C649X	0016
C649Y	0016
C650	0016
C650(2S)	0531
C650-OR	0531
C650-Y	0531
C650A	0531
C650B(2S)	0531
C650C	0531
C650D	0531
C650E	0531
C650F	0531
C650G	0531
C650GN	0531
C650H	0531
C650J	0531
C650K	0531
C650L	0531
C650M	0531
C650OR	0531
C650R	0531
C650X	0531
C650Y	0531
C651	0414
C651(2S)	0488
C652	0488
C652(2S)	0488
C653	0007
C653(2S)	0259
C654(2S)	0488
C654A	0488
C654B	0488
C654C	0488

DEVICE TYPE	REPL CODE
C654D	0488
C654E	0488
C654F	0488
C654G	0488
C654GN	0488
C654H	0488
C654J	0488
C654K	0488
C654L	0488
C654M	0488
C654OR	0488
C654R	0488
C654X	0488
C654Y	0488
C655	0079
C655(2S)	0016
C655A	0016
C655B	0016
C655C	0016
C655D	0016
C655E	0016
C655F	0016
C655G	0016
C655GN	0016
C655H	0016
C655J	0016
C655K	0016
C655L	0016
C655M	0016
C655OR	0016
C655R	0016
C655X	0016
C655Y	0016
C656(2S)	0259
C656A	0259
C656B	0259
C656C	0259
C656D	0259
C656E	0259
C656F	0259
C656G	0259
C656GN	0259
C656H	0259
C656J	0259
C656K	0259
C656L	0259
C656M	0259
C656OR	0259
C656R	0259
C656X	0259
C656Y	0259
C657(2S)	0127
C657A	0127
C657B	0127
C657C	0127
C657D	0127
C657E	0127
C657F	0127
C657G	0127
C657GN	0127
C657H	0127
C657J	0127
C657K	0127
C657L	0127
C657M	0127
C657OR	0127
C657R	0127
C657X	0127
C657Y	0127
C658(2S)	0127
C658A(2S)	0127
C658B	0127
C658C	0127
C658D	0127
C658E	0127
C658F	0127
C658G	0127
C658GN	0127
C658H	0127
C658J	0127
C658K	0127
C658L	0127
C658M	0127
C658OR	0127
C658R	0127
C658X	0127
C658Y	0127
C659(2S)	0127
C659A	0127
C659B	0127
C659C	0127
C659D	0127
C659E	0127
C659F	0127
C659G	0127
C659GN	0127
C659H	0127
C659J	0127
C659K	0127
C659L	0127
C659M	0127
C659OR	0127
C659R	0127
C659X	0127
C659Y	0127
C660	0047
C660(2S)	0007
C661	0047
C661(2S)	0007

DEVICE TYPE	REPL CODE
C661G	OEM
C662(2S)	0144
C662A	0144
C662B	0144
C662C	0144
C662D	0144
C662E	0144
C662F	0144
C662G	0144
C662GN	0144
C662H	0144
C662J	0144
C662K	0144
C662L	0144
C662M	0144
C662OR	0144
C662R	0144
C662X	0144
C662Y	0144
C663(2S)	0007
C663A	0007
C663B	0007
C663C	0007
C663D	0007
C663E	0007
C663F	0007
C663G	0007
C663GN	0007
C663H	0007
C663J	0007
C663K	0007
C663L	0007
C663M	0007
C663OR	0007
C663R	0007
C663X	0007
C663Y	0007
C664	0103
C664-OR	0103
C664A	0103
C664B(2S)	0103
C664C(2S)	0103
C664D	0103
C664E	0103
C664F	0103
C664L	0103
C664OR	0103
C664R	0103
C664Y	0103
C665	0861
C665(2S)	0861
C665H(2S)	0861
C665HA(2S)	0861
C665HB(2S)	0861
C666	OEM
C666(2S)	0177
C666C	0177
C667	OEM
C667(2S)	0007
C668(2S)	0127
C668-OR	0127
C668-SP	0127
C668A(2S)	0127
C668B(2S)	0127
C668B1(2S)	0127
C668BC2(2S)	0127
C668C(2S)	0127
C668C1(2S)	0127
C668C2	0127
C668CD(2S)	0127
C668D(2S)	0127
C668D0(2S)	0127
C668D1(2S)	0127
C668DE(2S)	0127
C668DO(2S)	0127
C668DV(2S)	0127
C668DX(2S)	0127
C668DZ(2S)	0127
C668E(2S)	0127
C668E1(2S)	0127
C668E2(2S)	0127
C668EP(2S)	0127
C668EV(2S)	0127
C668EX(2S)	0127
C668F(2S)	0127
C668G	0127
C668GN	0127
C668H	0127
C668K	0127
C668L	0127
C668M	0127
C668OR	0127
C668R	0127
C668SP	0127
C668X	0127
C668Y	0127
C669	0617
C669A	0617
C669AB	0617
C669C	0617
C669D	0617
C670-090ARC	OEM
C670-090ARCP	OEM
C670-090ARM	OEM
C670-090ARMP	OEM
C670-090ASC	OEM
C670-090ASCP	OEM
C670-090ASM	OEM
C670-090ASMP	OEM

DEVICE TYPE	REPL CODE
C670-090RC	OEM
C670-090RCP	OEM
C670-090RM	OEM
C670-090RMP	OEM
C670-090SC	OEM
C670-090SCP	OEM
C670-090SM	OEM
C670-090SMP	OEM
C670-180ARC	OEM
C670-180ARCP	OEM
C670-180ARM	OEM
C670-180ARMP	OEM
C670-180ASC	OEM
C670-180ASCP	OEM
C670-180ASM	OEM
C670-180ASMP	OEM
C670-180RC	OEM
C670-180RCP	OEM
C670-180RM	OEM
C670-180RMP	OEM
C670-180SC	OEM
C670-180SCP	OEM
C670-180SM	OEM
C670-180SMP	OEM
C673	0688
C673(2S)	0007
C673B	0007
C673C	0007
C673C(JAPAN)	0007
C673C2(2S)	0007
C673D(2S)	0007
C674	0127
C674(2S)	0127
C674(JAPAN)	0127
C674-B	0127
C674-F	0127
C674B(2S)	0127
C674C(2S)	0127
C674CK	0127
C674CL	0127
C674D(2S)	0127
C674E(2S)	0127
C674F(2S)	0127
C674G(2S)	0127
C675(2S)	0359
C676	0168
C677	0861
C678	0103
C679	1021
C679H	1021
C680	1021
C680(2S)	1496
C680A	1021
C680A(2S)	1496
C680B	1496
C680C	1496
C680G	1496
C680GN	1496
C680H	1496
C680J	1496
C680K	1496
C680L	1496
C680M	1496
C680R(2S)	1496
C680X	1496
C681	0359
C681(2S)	2420
C681(B)	2420
C681A	0359
C681A(2S)	2420
C681AYL	2420
C681L	2420
C681Y	2420
C681YL(2S)	2420
C682	0007
C682(2S)	0047
C682-OR	0047
C682A	0007
C682A(2S)	0047
C682B(2S)	0047
C682C	0047
C682D	0047
C682E	0047
C682F	0047
C682G	0047
C682GN	0047
C682H	0047
C682J	0047
C682K	0047
C682L	0047
C682M	0047
C682OR	0047
C682R	0047
C682X	0047
C682Y	0047
C683	0007
C683(2S)	0047
C683-0	0047
C683-OR	0047
C683A	0007
C683A(2S)	0047
C683B	0047
C683C	0047
C683D	0047
C683E	0047
C683F	0047
C683G	0047
C683GN	0047
C683H	0047

DEVICE TYPE	REPL CODE
C683J	0047
C683K	0047
C683L	0047
C683M	0047
C683OR	0047
C683P	0047
C683Q	0047
C683R	0047
C683S	0047
C683V(2S)	0047
C683X	0047
C683Y	0047
C684	0127
C684(2S)	0127
C684-OR	0127
C684A	0127
C684A(2S)	0127
C684B(2S)	0127
C684BK(2S)	0127
C684C	0127
C684D	0127
C684E	0127
C684F(2S)	0127
C684G	0127
C684GN	0127
C684H	0127
C684J	0127
C684K	0127
C684L	0127
C684M	0127
C684OR	0127
C684R	0127
C684TM	0127
C684X	0127
C684Y	0127
C685	0142
C685(2S)	0142
C685-0	0142
C685-O	0142
C685A	0142
C685A(2S)	0142
C685ABK	0142
C685AL	0142
C685B(2S)	0142
C685BK	0142
C685C	0142
C685D	0142
C685E	0142
C685F	0142
C685G	0142
C685GN	0142
C685H	0142
C685J	0142
C685K	0142
C685L	0142
C685M	0142
C685OR	0142
C685P(2S)	0142
C685R	0142
C685SY	0142
C685X	0142
C685Y(2S)	0142
C686(2S)	0233
C686A	0233
C686B	0233
C686C	0233
C686D	0233
C686E	0233
C686F	0233
C686G	0233
C686GN	0233
C686H	0233
C686J	0233
C686K	0233
C686L	0233
C686M	0233
C686OR	0233
C686R	0233
C686X	0233
C686Y	0233
C687(2S)	0177
C687A	0177
C687B	0177
C687C	0177
C687D	0177
C687E	0177
C687F	0177
C687G	0177
C687GN	0177
C687H	0177
C687J	0177
C687K	0177
C687L	0177
C687M	0177
C687OR	0177
C687R	0177
C687X	0177
C687Y	0177
C688(2S)	0224
C688-SP	0224
C688A	0224
C688B	0224
C688C	0224
C688D	0224
C688E	0224
C688F	0224
C688G	0224
C688GN	0224
C688H	0224

If replacement code is OEM, contact original manufacturer for replacement.

DEVICE TYPE	REPL CODE
C688J	0224
C688K	0224
C688L	0224
C688M	0224
C688OR	0224
C688R	0224
C688X	0224
C688Y	0224
C689(2S)	0016
C689A	0016
C689B	0016
C689C	0016
C689D	0016
C689E	0016
C689G	0016
C689GN	0016
C689H(2S)	0016
C689J	0016
C689K	0016
C689L	0016
C689M	0016
C689OR	0016
C689R	0016
C689X	0016
C689Y	0016
C690	3543
C690A	3543
C691	0555
C692	0555
C693	0547
C693-OR	0547
C693A	0547
C693B	0547
C693C	0547
C693D	0547
C693E	0547
C693EB(2S)	0547
C693ET(2S)	0547
C693F(2S)	0547
C693FC(2S)	0547
C693FL(2S)	0547
C693FP	0547
C693FU(2S)	0547
C693G	0547
C693GL(2S)	0547
C693GN	0547
C693GS(2S)	0547
C693GU(2S)	0547
C693GZ(2S)	0547
C693H(2S)	0547
C693J	0547
C693K	0547
C693L	0547
C693M	0547
C693NP	0547
C693OR	0547
C693R	0547
C693U	0547
C693X	0547
C693Y	0547
C694(2S)	0111
C694A	0111
C694B	0111
C694C	0111
C694D	0111
C694E(2S)	0111
C694F(2S)	0111
C694G(2S)	0111
C694GN	0111
C694H	0111
C694J	0111
C694K	0111
C694L	0111
C694M	0111
C694OR	0111
C694R	0111
C694X	0111
C694Y	0111
C694Z(2S)	0111
C695(2S)	0470
C696(2S)	0639
C696-4	0617
C696-OR	0617
C696A(2S)	0639
C696AA	0617
C696AB	0617
C696AD	0639
C696AE	0639
C696AF	0639
C696AG	0617
C696AH	0617
C696AI	0617
C696B(2S)	0617
C696BL	0617
C696C	0617
C696D(2S)	0639
C696E(2S)	0639
C696F(2S)	0639
C696G(2S)	0617
C696GN	0617
C696GU	0617
C696H(2S)	0639
C696I(2S)	0617
C696J	0617
C696K	0617
C696L	0617
C696M	0617
C696OR	0617
C696R	0617

DEVICE TYPE	REPL CODE
C696U	0617
C696X	0617
C696Y	0617
C697(2S)	1897
C697-OR	1897
C697A(2S)	1897
C697B	1897
C697C	1897
C697D(2S)	1897
C697E	1897
C697F(2S)	1897
C697G	1897
C697GN	1897
C697H	1897
C697J	1897
C697K	1897
C697L	1897
C697M	1897
C697OR	1897
C697R	1897
C697X	1897
C697Y	1897
C698	0626
C699	0590
C700	0590
C701(2S)	0018
C701A	0018
C701B	0018
C701C	0018
C701D	0018
C701E	0018
C701F	0018
C701G	0018
C701GN	0018
C701H	0018
C701J	0018
C701K	0018
C701L	OEM
C701L(TRANS)	0018
C701M	0018
C701OR	0018
C701PA	OEM
C701PB	OEM
C701PC	OEM
C701PCC701PD	OEM
C701PD	OEM
C701PE	OEM
C701PM	OEM
C701PN	OEM
C701PS	OEM
C701PT	OEM
C701R	0018
C701X	0018
C701Y	0018
C702(2S)	0018
C702A	0018
C702B	0018
C702C	0018
C702D	0018
C702E	0018
C702F	0018
C702G	0018
C702GN	0018
C702H	0018
C702J	0018
C702K	0018
C702L	OEM
C702L(TRANS)	0018
C702LA	OEM
C702LB	OEM
C702LC	OEM
C702LD	OEM
C702M	0018
C702OR	0018
C702R	0018
C702X	0018
C702Y	0018
C703	0042
C704	0042
C705(2S)	0127
C705A	0127
C705B(2S)	0127
C705C(2S)	0127
C705D(2S)	0127
C705E(2S)	0127
C705F(2S)	0127
C705G	0127
C705GN	0127
C705J	0127
C705K	0127
C705L	0127
C705M	0127
C705OR	0127
C705R	0127
C705TV(2S)	0127
C705TVV	0127
C705TW	0127
C705X	0127
C705Y	0127
C706	0007
C707(2S)	0259
C707A	0259
C707B	0259
C707C	0259
C707D	0259
C707E	0259
C707F	0259
C707G	0259
C707GN	0259

DEVICE TYPE	REPL CODE
C707H(2S)	0259
C707K	0259
C707L	0259
C707M	0259
C707OR	0259
C707R	0259
C707X	0259
C707Y	0259
C708(2S)	0086
C708-OR	0086
C708A(2S)	0086
C708AA(2S)	0086
C708AB(2S)	0086
C708AC(2S)	0086
C708AH(2S)	0086
C708B(2S)	0086
C708C(2S)	0086
C708D	0086
C708E	0086
C708F	0086
C708G	0086
C708GN	0086
C708H	0086
C708HA	0086
C708HB	0086
C708L	0086
C708M	0086
C708OR	0086
C708R	0086
C708X	0086
C708Y	0086
C709(2S)	0284
C709A	0284
C709B(2S)	0284
C709C(2S)	0284
C709CD(2S)	0284
C709D(2S)	0284
C709E	0284
C709F	0284
C709G	0284
C709GN	0284
C709H	0284
C709J	0284
C709L	0284
C709M	0284
C709OR	0284
C709X	0284
C709Y	0284
C710(2S)	0364
C710(C)	0079
C710(JAPAN)	0364
C710-0	0364
C710-3	0364
C710-5	0364
C710-13	0364
C710-14	0364
C710-D	0364
C710-E	0364
C710-OR	0364
C710AL	0364
C710B(2S)	0364
C710B2	0364
C710BC(2S)	0364
C710C(2S)	0364
C710D(2S)	0364
C710D(JAPAN)	0364
C710DB	0364
C710DE	0364
C710E(2S)	0364
C710F	0364
C710G	0364
C710GN	0364
C710H	0364
C710K	0364
C710L	0364
C710M	0364
C710OR	0364
C710R	0364
C710X	0364
C710XL	0364
C710Y	0364
C711(2S)	0376
C711-OR	0376
C711A(2S)	0376
C711A(JAPAN)	0376
C711AE	0376
C711A-E(2S)	0376
C711AE(JAPAN)	0376
C711A-F	0376
C711AF	0376
C711AG	0376
C711AN	0376
C711B	0376
C711C	0376
C711D(2S)	0376
C711E(2S)	0376
C711EF	0376
C711F(2S)	0376
C711G(2S)	2446
C711GN	0376
C711H	0376
C711J	0376
C711L	0376
C711M	0376
C711OR	0376
C711R	0376
C711X	0376
C711Y	0376
C712(2S)	0076

DEVICE TYPE	REPL CODE
C712A(2S)	0076
C712B	0076
C712BC	0076
C712C(2S)	0076
C712CD	0076
C712D(2S)	0076
C712DC	0076
C712E(2S)	0076
C712F	0076
C712G	0076
C712GN	0076
C712H	0076
C712J	0076
C712K	0076
C712L	OEM
C712L(TRANS)	0076
C712M	0076
C712OR	0076
C712PE	OEM
C712PM	OEM
C712PN	OEM
C712PS	OEM
C712PT	OEM
C712R	0076
C712W(2S)	0076
C712X	0076
C712Y	0076
C713(2S)	0284
C713A	0284
C713B	0284
C713C	0284
C713D	0284
C713E	0284
C713F	0284
C713G	0284
C713GN	0284
C713H	0284
C713J	0284
C713K	0284
C713L	OEM
C713L(TRANS)	0284
C713M	0284
C713MC	0284
C713MD	0284
C713ME	0284
C713OR	0284
C713PE	OEM
C713PM	OEM
C713PN	OEM
C713PS	OEM
C713PT	OEM
C713R	0284
C713W	0284
C713X	0284
C713Y	0284
C714	OEM
C714(2S)	0155
C714A	0155
C714B	0155
C714C	0155
C714D	0155
C714E	0155
C714F	0155
C714G	0155
C714GN	0155
C714H	0155
C714J	0155
C714K	0155
C714L	0155
C714M	0155
C714OR	0155
C714R	0155
C714X	0155
C714Y	0155
C715	0284
C715-OR	0284
C715A(2S)	0284
C715B(2S)	0284
C715C(2S)	0284
C715D(2S)	0284
C715E(2S)	0284
C715EJ(2S)	0284
C715EV(2S)	0284
C715F(2S)	0284
C715G	0284
C715GN	0284
C715H	0284
C715J	0284
C715K	0284
C715L	0284
C715M	0284
C715OR	0284
C715R	0284
C715X	0284
C715XL(2S)	0284
C715Y	0284
C716(2S)	0155
C716A	0155
C716B(2S)	0155
C716C(2S)	0155
C716D(2S)	0155
C716F(2S)	0155
C716G(2S)	0155
C716GN	0155
C716H	0155
C716J	0155
C716K	0155
C716L	0155
C716M	0155

DEVICE TYPE	REPL CODE
C716OR	0155
C716R	0155
C716X	0155
C716Y	0155
C717(2S)	0127
C717(JAPAN)	0127
C717-TM	0127
C717B(2S)	0127
C717BK(2S)	0127
C717BLK(2S)	0127
C717F	0127
C717G	0127
C717GN	0127
C717H	0127
C717K	0127
C717L	0127
C717M	0127
C717TM	0127
C717X	0127
C718	0079
C719	0155
C719Q	0155
C720	0007
C720(2S)	0007
C721	0079
C722	0127
C722(2S)	0127
C723	0127
C723BL	0127
C724	0155
C725(2S)	0155
C725-06	0155
C726	0079
C727(2S)	0710
C727A	0710
C727B	0710
C727C	0710
C727D	0710
C727E	0710
C727F	0710
C727G	0710
C727GN	0710
C727H	0710
C727J	0710
C727K	0710
C727L	0710
C727M	0710
C727R	0710
C727X	0710
C727Y	0710
C728(2S)	0710
C728A	0710
C728B	0710
C728D	0710
C728E	0710
C728F	0710
C728G	0710
C728GN	0710
C728H	0710
C728J	0710
C728K	0710
C728L	0710
C728M	0710
C728OR	0710
C728R	0710
C728X	0710
C728Y	0710
C729	0414
C730	2030
C731	0488
C731R(2S)	0488
C732(2S)	0111
C732-B	0111
C732-BL	0111
C732-BLU	0111
C732-G	0111
C732-GR	0111
C732-GRN	0111
C732-OR	0111
C732-V	0111
C732-V10	0111
C732-VIO	0111
C732A	0111
C732B	0111
C732BL(2S)	0111
C732BL-1	0111
C732BLU	0111
C732C	0111
C732D	0111
C732E	0111
C732F	0111
C732G	0111
C732GN	0111
C732GR(2S)	0111
C732GRB	0111
C732GRN	0111
C732H	0111
C732J	0111
C732L	0111
C732M	0111
C732OR	0111
C732R	0111
C732S(2S)	0111
C732V(2S)	0111
C732V10	0111
C732VIO	0111
C732X	0111
C732Y(2S)	0111
C733(2S)	0111

DEVICE TYPE	REPL CODE
C733-0(2S)	0111
C733-B	0111
C733-BL	0111
C733-BLU	0111
C733-G	0111
C733-GR	0111
C733-GRN	0111
C733-O(2S)	0111
C733-OR	0111
C733-ORG	0111
C733-Y	0111
C733-YEL	0111
C733A	OEM
C733B	0111
C733BL(2S)	0111
C733BLK	0111
C733BLU	0111
C733C	0111
C733D	0111
C733E	0111
C733ER	0111
C733F	0111
C733G	0111
C733GN	0111
C733GR(2S)	0111
C733GRN	0111
C733H	0111
C733J	0111
C733K	0111
C733L	0111
C733M	0111
C733O	0111
C733OR	0111
C733Q	0111
C733R(2S)	0111
C733S	0111
C733S-BL	0111
C733V(2S)	0111
C733X	0111
C733Y(2S)	0111
C733YEL	0111
C734	0076
C734-0(2S)	0076
C734-G	0076
C734-GR	0076
C734-GRN	0076
C734-O(2S)	0076
C734-OR	0076
C734-ORG	0076
C734-OY	0076
C734-R(2S)	0076
C734-RED	0076
C734-Y(2S)	0076
C734-YEL	0076
C734A	0076
C734B	0076
C734C	0076
C734D	0076
C734E	0076
C734F	0076
C734G	0076
C734GN	0076
C734GR(2S)	0076
C734GRN	0076
C734H	0076
C734J	0076
C734K	0076
C734L	0076
C734M	0076
C734OR	0076
C734R	0076
C734RED	0076
C734X	0076
C734Y(2S)	0076
C734YEL	0076
C735(2S)	0191
C735-0(2S)	0191
C735-GR	0191
C735-GRN	0191
C735-O(2S)	0191
C735-OR	0191
C735-ORG	0191
C735-ORN	0191
C735-OY	0191
C735-R(2S)	0191
C735-RED	0191
C735-Y	0191
C735-YEL	0191
C735A	0191
C735B(2S)	0191
C735C	0191
C735D	0191
C735E	0191
C735F(2S)	0191
C735FA3(2S)	0191
C735G	0191
C735GN	0191
C735GR(2S)	0191
C735GRN	0191
C735H(2S)	0191
C735J(2S)	0191
C735K(2S)	0191
C735L(2S)	0191
C735M	0191
C735O	0191
C735OR	0191
C735RED	0191
C735X	0191
C735Y(2S)	0191

DEVICE TYPE	REPL CODE
C735YEL	0191
C735YFA-5	0191
C736(2S)	0861
C736A	0861
C736B	0861
C736C	0861
C736D	0861
C736E	0861
C736F	0861
C736G	0861
C736GN	0861
C736H	0861
C736J	0861
C736K	0861
C736L	0861
C736M	0861
C736OR	0861
C736R	0861
C736X	0861
C736Y	0861
C737	0079
C737Y	0079
C738(2S)	0889
C738A	0889
C738B	0889
C738C(2S)	0889
C738D(2S)	0889
C738E	0889
C738F	0889
C738G	0889
C738GN	0889
C738H	0889
C738J	0889
C738K	0889
C738L	0889
C738M	0889
C738OR	0889
C738R	0889
C738X	0889
C738Y	0889
C739(2S)	0127
C739A	0127
C739B	0127
C739C(2S)	0127
C739D	0127
C739E	0127
C739F	0127
C739G	0127
C739GN	0127
C739H	0127
C739K	0127
C739L	0127
C739M	0127
C739OR	0127
C739R	0127
C739Y	0127
C740	0144
C740(2S)	0144
C740A	0144
C740B	0144
C740C	0144
C740D	0144
C740E	0144
C740F	0144
C740G	0144
C740GN	0144
C740H	0144
C740J	0144
C740K	0144
C740L	0144
C740M	0144
C740OR	0144
C740R	0144
C740X	0144
C740Y	0144
C741(2S)	0684
C741B	0684
C741C	0684
C741D	0684
C741E	0684
C741F	0684
C741GN	0684
C741H	0684
C741J	0684
C741K	0684
C741L	0684
C741M	0684
C741OR	0684
C741R	0684
C741X	0684
C741Y	0684
C742	0079
C742(2S)	0930
C743	0930
C743A(2S)	0930
C744	0086
C744(2S)	0086
C744A	0086
C745	0930
C746	0168
C746A(2S)	0168
C746B	0168
C746C	0168
C746D	0168
C746E	0168
C746F	0168
C746GN	0168
C746H	0168
C746J	0168

If replacement code is OEM, contact original manufacturer for replacement.

DEVICE TYPE	REPL CODE
C746K	0168
C746L	0168
C746M	0168
C746OR	0168
C746R	0168
C746X	0168
C746Y	0168
C748(2S)	0144
C748A	0144
C748C	0144
C748D	0144
C748E	0144
C748F	0144
C748G	0144
C748GN	0144
C748H	0144
C748J	0144
C748K	0144
C748L	0144
C748M	0144
C748OR	0144
C748R	0144
C748X	0144
C748Y	0144
C749	0930
C751	0111
C752	0546
C752(2S)	0546
C752-ORG-G	0546
C752-RED-G	0546
C752-YEL-G	0546
C752A	0546
C752B	0546
C752C	0546
C752D	0546
C752E	0546
C752F	0546
C752G(2S)	0546
C752GA	0546
C752GN	0546
C752G-O	0546
C752G-R	0546
C752G-TM-Y	0546
C752G-Y	0546
C752GY(JAPAN)	0546
C752H	0546
C752J	0546
C752K	0546
C752L	0546
C752M	0546
C752OR	0546
C752R	0546
C752X	0546
C752Y	0546
C753	0470
C754	0079
C755	0016
C756	0617
C756(4-4)	0617
C756(44)	0617
C756-1(2S)	0617
C756-2(2S)	0617
C756-2-4(2S)	0617
C756-2-5(2S)	0617
C756-3(2S)	0617
C756-4(2S)	0617
C756-OR	0617
C756A(2S)	0617
C756B	0617
C756C(2S)	0617
C756D(2S)	0617
C756E	0617
C756F	0617
C756G	0617
C756GN	0617
C756H	0617
C756J	0617
C756K	0617
C756L	0617
C756M	0617
C756OR	0617
C756R	0617
C756X	0617
C756Y	0617
C757	0470
C758	0074
C758OR	0074
C759	0538
C760	0079
C760(2S)	0103
C761(2S)	1146
C761A	1146
C761B	1146
C761C	1146
C761D	1146
C761E	1146
C761F	1146
C761G	1146
C761GN	1146
C761H	1146
C761J	1146
C761K	1146
C761L	1146
C761M	1146
C761OR	1146
C761P	1146
C761R	1146
C761X	1146
C761Y(2S)	1146
C761Z(2S)	1146
C762	0007
C762(2S)	1146
C762B	1146
C762C	1146
C762D	1146
C762E	1146
C762F	1146
C762G	1146
C762GN	1146
C762H	1146
C762J	1146
C762K	1146
C762L	1146
C762M	1146
C762R	1146
C762X	1146
C762Y	1146
C763(2S)	0127
C763(JAPAN)	0127
C763-C	0127
C763-OR	0127
C763A	0127
C763B(2S)	0127
C763C(2S)	0127
C763D(2S)	0127
C763E	0127
C763F	0127
C763G	0127
C763GN	0127
C763H	0127
C763J	0127
C763K	0127
C763L	0127
C763M	0127
C763OR	0127
C763X	0127
C763Y	0127
C764	0321
C764(2S)	0079
C765(2S)	0130
C765A	0130
C765B	0130
C765C	0130
C765D	0130
C765E	0130
C765F	0130
C765G	0130
C765GN	0130
C765H	0130
C765J	0130
C765K	0130
C765L	0130
C765M	0130
C765OR	0130
C765R	0130
C765X	0130
C765Y	0130
C766	0103
C767	0103
C768(2S)	0615
C768A	0615
C768B	0615
C768C	0615
C768D	0615
C768E	0615
C768F	0615
C768G	0615
C768GN	0615
C768H	0615
C768J	0615
C768K	0615
C768L	0615
C768M	0615
C768OR	0615
C768R	0615
C768X	0615
C768Y	0615
C769	0615
C770	0074
C771	0224
C771A	0224
C771B	0224
C771BX	0224
C771C	0224
C771D	0224
C771E	0224
C771F	0224
C771G	0224
C771GN	0224
C771H	0224
C771J	0224
C771K	0224
C771L	0224
C771M	0224
C771OR	0224
C771R	0224
C771X	0224
C771Y	0224
C772(2S)	1136
C772-OR	1136
C772A	1136
C772B	0224
C772B(2S)	1136
C772BG(2S)	1136
C772BH(2S)	1136
C772BV(2S)	1136
C772BX(2S)	1136
C772BY(2S)	1136
C772C	1136
C772C1(2S)	1136
C772C2(2S)	1136
C772CA	1136
C772CK(2S)	1136
C772CL(2S)	1136
C772CS(2S)	1136
C772CU(2S)	1136
C772CV(2S)	1136
C772CX(2S)	1136
C772D(2S)	1136
C772DJ(2S)	1136
C772DU(2S)	1136
C772DV(2S)	1136
C772DX(2S)	1136
C772DY(2S)	1136
C772E(2S)	1136
C772F(2S)	1136
C772G	1136
C772GN	1136
C772H	1136
C772J	1136
C772K(2S)	1136
C772KB(2S)	1136
C772KC(2S)	1136
C772KD(2S)	1136
C772KD1(2S)	1136
C772KD2(2S)	1136
C772L	1136
C772M	1136
C772OR	1136
C772R	1136
C772RB-D(2S)	1136
C772RD(2S)	1136
C772RS-D	1136
C772X	1136
C772Y	1136
C773(2S)	0783
C773A	0783
C773B	0783
C773C(2S)	0783
C773D(2S)	0783
C773E(2S)	0783
C773F	0783
C773G	0783
C773GN	0783
C773H	0783
C773J	0783
C773K	0783
C773L	0783
C773M	0783
C773OR	0783
C773R	0783
C773X	0783
C773Y	0783
C774(2S)	0693
C774B	0693
C774C	0693
C774D	0693
C774E	0693
C774F	0693
C774G	0693
C774GN	0693
C774H	0693
C774J	0693
C774K	0693
C774L	0693
C774M	0693
C774R	0693
C774X	0693
C774Y	0693
C775(2S)	0693
C775A	0693
C775B	0693
C775C	0693
C775D	0693
C775E	0693
C775F	0693
C775G	0693
C775GN	0693
C775H	0693
C775J	0693
C775K	0693
C775L	0693
C775M	0693
C775OR	0693
C775R	0693
C775X	0693
C775Y	0693
C776(2S)	1390
C776A	1390
C776B	1390
C776C	1390
C776D	1390
C776E	1390
C776F	1390
C776G	1390
C776GN	1390
C776H	1390
C776J	1390
C776K	1390
C776L	1390
C776M	1390
C776OR	1390
C776R	1390
C776X	1390
C776Y(2S)	1390
C777(2S)	1401
C777-OR	1401
C777A	1401
C777AP	1401
C777B	1401
C777C	1401
C777D	1401
C777E	1401
C777F	1401
C777G	1401
C777GN	1401
C777H	1401
C777J	1401
C777K	1401
C777L	1401
C777M	1401
C777OR	1401
C777R	1401
C777X	1401
C777Y	1401
C778(2S)	1401
C778A	1401
C778B(2S)	1401
C778C	1401
C778D	1401
C778E	1401
C778F	1401
C778G	1401
C778GN	1401
C778H	1401
C778J	1401
C778K	1401
C778L	1401
C778M	1401
C778OR	1401
C778R	1401
C778X	1401
C778Y	1401
C779(2S)	1021
C779-O	1021
C779-Q	1021
C779-R(2S)	1021
C779-Y(2S)	1021
C779O	1021
C780(2S)	0855
C780-O	0855
C780-ORG-G	0855
C780-R	0855
C780-RED-G	0855
C780-Y	0855
C780-YEL-G	0855
C780A	0855
C780AG(2S)	0855
C780AG-O(2S)	0855
C780AG-R(2S)	0855
C780AG-Y(2S)	0855
C780B	0855
C780C	0855
C780D	0855
C780E	0855
C780F	0855
C780G(2S)	0855
C780GA	0855
C780GN	0855
C780G-O	0855
C780G-R	0855
C780G-Y	0855
C780H	0855
C780J	0855
C780K	0855
C780L	0855
C780M	0855
C780O	0855
C780OR	0855
C780R	0855
C780X	0855
C780Y	0855
C781(2S)	0693
C781A	0693
C781AK	0693
C781B	0693
C781C	0693
C781D	0693
C781E	0693
C781F	0693
C781G	0693
C781H	0693
C781J	0693
C781K	0693
C781OR	0693
C781R	0693
C781X	0693
C781Y	0693
C782(2S)	1460
C782-OR	1460
C782A	1460
C782B	1460
C782C	1460
C782D	1460
C782E	1460
C782F	1460
C782G	1460
C782GN	1460
C782H	1460
C782J	1460
C782K	1460
C782L	OEM
C782L(TRANS)	1460
C782LA	OEM
C782LB	OEM
C782LC	OEM
C782LD	OEM
C782OR	1460
C782R	1460
C782X	1460
C782Y	1460
C783(2S)	1021
C783-O	1021
C783-R	1021
C783-Y	1021
C783CA	OEM
C783CB	OEM
C783CC	OEM
C783CD	OEM
C783CE	OEM
C783LB	OEM
C783LC	OEM
C783LD	OEM
C783LE	OEM
C783LM	OEM
C783LN	OEM
C783LP	OEM
C783LS	OEM
C783LT	OEM
C784(2S)	1136
C784-0(2S)	1136
C784-6	1136
C784-B	1136
C784-BN	1136
C784-BRN	1136
C784-O(2S)	1136
C784-OR	1136
C784-ORG	1136
C784-R	1136
C784-RED	1136
C784-Y	1136
C784A(2S)	1136
C784B	1136
C784BN(2S)	1136
C784BN-1	1136
C784BRN	1136
C784C	1136
C784D	1136
C784E	1136
C784F	1136
C784G	1136
C784GN	1136
C784H	1136
C784J	1136
C784K	1136
C784L	1136
C784M	1136
C784OR	1136
C784P	1136
C784Q	1136
C784R(2S)	1136
C784RA	1136
C784RED	1136
C784X	1136
C785(2S)	1136
C785-0	1136
C785-B	1136
C785-BN	1136
C785-BRN	1136
C785-O	1136
C785-ORG	1136
C785-R	1136
C785-RED	1136
C785-Y	1136
C785-YEL	1136
C785A	1136
C785B	1136
C785BL	1136
C785BN(2S)	1136
C785BR	1136
C785BRN	1136
C785C	1136
C785D(2S)	1136
C785E(2S)	1136
C785F	1136
C785G	1136
C785GN	1136
C785GR	1136
C785H	1136
C785JA	1136
C785K	1136
C785L	1136
C785M	1136
C785O	1136
C785R(2S)	1136
C785RA	1136
C785RED	1136
C785V	1136
C785X	1136
C785Y	1136
C785YEL	1136
C786(2S)	0216
C786A	0216
C786B	0216
C786C	0216
C786D	0216
C786E	0216
C786F	0216
C786G	0216
C786GN	0216
C786H	0216
C786J	0216
C786K	0216
C786L	0216
C786M	0216
C786OR	0216
C786R(2S)	0216
C786X	0216
C786Y	0216
C787(2S)	1146
C787A	1146
C787B	1146
C787C	1146
C787D	1146
C787E	1146
C787F	1146
C787G	1146
C787GN	1146
C787H	1146
C787K	1146
C787L	1146
C787M	1146
C787OR	1146
C787R	1146
C787X	1146
C787Y	1146
C788(2S)	0233
C788B	0233
C788C	0233
C788D	0233
C788E	0233
C788F	0233
C788G	0233
C788GN	0233
C788J	0233
C788K	0233
C788L	0233
C788M	0233
C788OR	0233
C788R	0233
C788X	0233
C788Y	0233
C789(2S)	0228
C789-0(2S)	0228
C789-O(2S)	0228
C789-R(2S)	0228
C789-Y(2S)	0228
C789A	0228
C789B	0228
C789C	0228
C789D	0228
C789E	0228
C789F	0228
C789G	0228
C789GN	0228
C789H	0228
C789J	0228
C789K	0228
C789L	0228
C789M	0228
C789OR	0228
C789R	0228
C789X	0228
C789Y	0228
C790	1488
C790-O	1488
C790-R	1488
C790-Y	1488
C790Y	1488
C791(2S)	1139
C791-OR	1139
C791A	1139
C791B	1139
C791C	1139
C791D	1139
C791E	1139
C791F	1139
C791FA1	1139
C791G	1139
C791GN	1139
C791H	1139
C791J	1139
C791K	1139
C791M	1139
C791OR	1139
C791R	1139
C791X	1139
C791Y	1139
C792	0220
C792FA-3	0220
C793(2S)	0103
C793-BL	0103
C793-BLU	0103
C793-R	0103
C793-RED	0103
C793-Y	0103
C793-YEL	0103
C793A	0103
C793B	0103
C793BL(2S)	0103
C793C	0103
C793E	0103
C793F	0103
C793G	0103
C793GN	0103
C793H	0103
C793J	0103
C793K	0103
C793L	0103
C793M	0103
C793OR	0103
C793R(2S)	0103
C793X	0103
C793Y(2S)	0103
C794	0103
C794A	0103
C794B	0103
C794C	0103
C794D	0103
C794E	0103
C794F	0103
C794G	0103
C794GN	0103
C794H	0103
C794J	0103
C794K	0103
C794L	0103
C794OR	0103
C794R(2S)	0103
C794RA	0103
C794X	0103
C794Y	0103
C795(2S)	0142
C795A(2S)	0142
C795B	0142
C795BN	0142
C795C	0142
C795D	0142
C795F	0142
C795G	0142
C795GN	0142
C795H	0142
C795J	0142
C795L	0142
C795M	0142
C795OR	0142
C795R	0142
C795X	0142
C795Y	0142
C796(2S)	0016
C796A	0016
C796B	0016
C796C	0016
C796D	0016
C796E	0016
C796F	0016
C796G	0016
C796GN	0016
C796H	0016
C796J	0016
C796K	0016
C796L	0016
C796M	0016
C796OR	0016
C796R	0016
C796X	0016
C796Y	0016
C797(2S)	0079
C797A	0079
C797B	0079
C797C	0079
C797D	0079
C797E	0079
C797F	0079
C797G	0079
C797GN	0079
C797H	0079
C797J	0079
C797K	0079
C797L	0079
C797M	0079
C797OR	0079
C797R	0079
C797X	0079
C797Y	0079
C798(2S)	0693
C798A	0693
C798B	0693
C798C	0693
C798D	0693
C798E	0693
C798G	0693
C798GN	0693
C798H	0693
C798J	0693
C798K	0693
C798L	0693
C798M	0693
C798OR	0693
C798R	0693
C798X	0693
C798Y	0693
C799(2S)	1401
C799-4	1401
C799A	1401
C799AP	1401
C799B	1401
C799C	1401
C799D	1401
C799E	1401
C799F	1401
C799G	1401
C799GN	1401
C799H	1401
C799J	1401
C799K(2S)	1401
C799L	1401
C799M	1401
C799OR	1401
C799R	1401
C799X	1401
C799Y	1401

If replacement code is OEM, contact original manufacturer for replacement. 323

DEVICE TYPE	REPL CODE
C800(2S)	0626
C800A	0626
C800B	0626
C800C	0626
C800D	0626
C800E	0626
C800F	0626
C800G	0626
C800GN	0626
C800H	0626
C800J	0626
C800K	0626
C800L	0626
C800M	0626
C800OR	0626
C800R	0626
C800X	0626
C800Y	0626
C801	0086
C802	0086
C803(2S)	0693
C803A	0693
C803B	0693
C803C	0693
C803D	0693
C803E	0693
C803F	0693
C803G	0693
C803H	0693
C803J	0693
C803K	0693
C803L	0693
C803M	0693
C803OR	0693
C803R	0693
C803X	0693
C803Y	0693
C804	0470
C804H	0470
C805(2S)	0711
C805A	0711
C805A1	0711
C805A2	0711
C805B	0711
C805C	0711
C805D	0711
C805E	0711
C805F	0711
C805G	0711
C805GN	0711
C805H	0711
C805J	0711
C805L	0711
C805OR	0711
C805R	0711
C805X	0711
C805Y	0711
C806(2S)	0359
C806A	0359
C806B	0359
C806C	0359
C806D	0359
C806E	0359
C806F	0359
C806G	0359
C806J	0359
C806L	0359
C806M	0359
C806OR	0359
C806R	0359
C806X	0359
C806Y	0359
C807(2S)	1955
C807A(2S)	1955
C807AK	1955
C808	2398
C809	0259
C810	0488
C811	0007
C812	0626
C812A	0626
C812B	0626
C812BST	OEM
C812C	0626
C812D	0626
C812E	0626
C812F	0626
C812G	0626
C812GN	0626
C812H	0626
C812J	0626
C812K	0626
C812L	0626
C812M	0626
C812OR	0626
C812R	0626
C812Y	0626
C814(2S)	0079
C814A	0079
C814B	0079
C814C	0079
C814D	0079
C814E	0079
C814F	0079
C814G	0079
C814GN	0079
C814H	0079
C814J	0079
C814K	0079
C814M	0079
C814OR	0079
C814R	0079
C814X	0079
C814Y	0079
C815(2S)	0155
C815-1	0155
C815-O	0079
C815A(2S)	0155
C815B(2S)	0155
C815BK	0155
C815C(2S)	0155
C815D	0155
C815E	0155
C815F(2S)	0155
C815G	0155
C815GN	0155
C815H	0155
C815J	0155
C815K(2S)	0155
C815L(2S)	0155
C815LJ	0155
C815M(2S)	0155
C815OR	0155
C815R	0155
C815S(2S)	0155
C815SA(2S)	0155
C815SC(2S)	0155
C815X	0155
C815Y	0155
C815Y(EBC)	1943
C815Y(KOREA)	0079
C816(2S)	0086
C816A	0086
C816B	0086
C816C	0086
C816D	0086
C816E	0086
C816F	0086
C816G	0086
C816GN	0086
C816H	0086
C816HL	0086
C816K(2S)	0086
C816L	0086
C816M	0086
C816OR	0086
C816R	0086
C816X	0086
C816Y	0086
C817	0259
C818(2S)	0168
C818A	0168
C818B	0168
C818C	0168
C818D	0168
C818E	0168
C818F	0168
C818G	0168
C818GN	0168
C818H	0168
C818J	0168
C818K	0168
C818L	0168
C818M	0168
C818OR	0168
C818R	0168
C818X	0168
C818Y	0168
C819	2675
C821(2S)	2030
C822(2S)	2030
C823	0414
C824	0414
C825	1021
C825A	1021
C825B	1021
C825C	1021
C825D	1021
C825E	1021
C825F	1021
C825G	1021
C825GN	1021
C825H	1021
C825J	1021
C825K	1021
C825L	1021
C825M	1021
C825OR	1021
C825R	1021
C825X	1021
C825Y	1021
C826(2S)	0086
C826A	0086
C826B	0086
C826C	0086
C826D	0086
C826E	0086
C826F	0086
C826G	0086
C826H	0086
C826J	0086
C826K	0086
C826L	0086
C826M	0086
C826OR	0086
C826R	0086
C826X	0086
C826Y	0086
C827(2S)	0086
C827A	0086
C827B	0086
C827C	0086
C827D	0086
C827E	0086
C827F	0086
C827G	0086
C827GN	0086
C827H	0086
C827J	0086
C827K	0086
C827M	0086
C827OR	0086
C827R	0086
C827X	0086
C827Y	0086
C828	1211
C828(N)	1211
C828-0	1211
C828-0(2S)	1211
C828-OR	1211
C828A(2S)	1211
C828A(JAPAN)	1211
C828AO	1211
C828AQ(2S)	1211
C828AR	1211
C828AR(2S)	1211
C828AS(2S)	1211
C828B	1211
C828C	1211
C828D	1211
C828E(2S)	1211
C828F(2S)	1211
C828G	1211
C828GN	1211
C828H(2S)	1211
C828HR	1211
C828K(2S)	1211
C828L	1211
C828LS(2S)	1211
C828M	1211
C828OR	1211
C828P(2S)	1211
C828PQ	1211
C828Q	1211
C828Q-6	1211
C828QRS(2S)	1211
C828R	1211
C828R(JAPAN)	1211
C828R/494	0111
C828R-1	1211
C828RA	1211
C828RH	1211
C828RS	1211
C828RST	1211
C828RT	1211
C828S(2S)	1211
C828S(JAPAN)	1211
C828T(2S)	1211
C828X	1211
C828Y(2S)	1211
C828YL	1211
C829	0151
C829-OR	0151
C829A(2S)	0151
C829AK	0151
C829B	0151
C829BC(2S)	0151
C829BJ	0151
C829BK	0151
C829C	0151
C829CL	0151
C829D(2S)	0151
C829E	0151
C829G	0151
C829GN	0151
C829H	0151
C829K	0151
C829L	0151
C829M	0151
C829OR	0151
C829R(2S)	0151
C829X(2S)	0151
C829Y(2S)	0151
C830(2S)	1139
C830A(2S)	1139
C830B(2S)	1139
C830C(2S)	1139
C830D	1139
C830E	1139
C830F	1139
C830G	1139
C830GN	1139
C830H	1139
C830J	1139
C830K	1139
C830L	1139
C830M	1139
C830OR	1139
C830R	1139
C830X	1139
C830Y	1139
C831	0042
C833	0424
C833BL(2S)	0424
C834L	0424
C835(2S)	0127
C836(2S)	0127
C836M	0127
C837(2S)	0224
C837A	0224
C837B	0224
C837C	0224
C837D	0224
C837E	0224
C837F(2S)	0224
C837G	0224
C837GN	0224
C837H(2S)	0224
C837J	0224
C837K(2S)	0224
C837KL	0224
C837L(2S)	0224
C837M	0224
C837OR	0224
C837R	0224
C837WF(2S)	0224
C837X	0224
C837Y	0224
C838	0191
C838-2	0191
C838-0	0191
C838A(2S)	0191
C838BL	0191
C838C(2S)	0191
C838E(2S)	0191
C838F(2S)	0191
C838H(2S)	0191
C838HF	0191
C838I	0191
C838J	0191
C838K(2S)	0191
C838L(2S)	0191
C838M(2S)	0191
C838R	0155
C839	0076
C839-E	0076
C839-F	0076
C839A(2S)	0076
C839B(2S)	0076
C839C(2S)	0076
C839D(2S)	0076
C839E(2S)	0076
C839F(2S)	0076
C839G	0076
C839GN	0076
C839H(2S)	0076
C839J(2S)	0076
C839J1	0076
C839JH	0076
C839K	0076
C839L(2S)	0076
C839M(2S)	0076
C839OR	0076
C839R	0076
C839X	0076
C839Y	0076
C840(2S)	2017
C840A(2S)	2017
C840AC(2S)	2017
C840B	2017
C840C	2017
C840D	2017
C840E	2017
C840F	2017
C840G	2017
C840GN	2017
C840H(2S)	2017
C840HP	2017
C840J	2017
C840K	2017
C840L	2017
C840M	2017
C840OR	2017
C840P	2017
C840Q	2017
C840R	2017
C840X	2017
C840Y	2017
C841	2030
C841H	2030
C844(2S)	0488
C844D	0488
C845	0488
C847(2S)	0016
C847A	0016
C847B	0016
C847C	0016
C847D	0016
C847E	0016
C847F	0016
C847G	0016
C847GN	0016
C847H	0016
C847J	0016
C847K	0016
C847L	0016
C847M	0016
C847OR	0016
C847R	0016
C847X	0016
C848(2S)	0016
C848A	0016
C848B	0016
C848C	0016
C848D	0016
C848E	0016
C848F	0016
C848G	0016
C848GN	0016
C848H	0016
C848J	0016
C848K	0016
C848L	0016
C848M	0016
C848OR	0016
C848R	0016
C848X	0016
C848Y	0016
C849(2S)	0016
C849A	0016
C849B	0016
C849C	0016
C849D	0016
C849E	0016
C849F	0016
C849G	0016
C849GN	0016
C849H	0016
C849J	0016
C849K	0016
C849L	0016
C849M	0016
C849OR	0016
C849R	0016
C849X	0016
C849Y	0016
C850(2S)	0016
C850A	0016
C850B	0016
C850C	0016
C850D	0016
C850E	0016
C850F	0016
C850G	0016
C850GN	0016
C850H	0016
C850J	0016
C850K	0016
C850L	0016
C850M	0016
C850OR	0016
C850R	0016
C850X	0016
C850Y	0016
C851(2S)	0130
C851A	0130
C851B	0130
C851C	0130
C851D	0130
C851E	0130
C851F	0130
C851G	0130
C851GN	0130
C851H	0130
C851K	0130
C851L	0130
C851M	0130
C851OR	0130
C851R	0130
C851X	0130
C851Y	0130
C852	0488
C852A	0488
C853(2S)	0218
C853-OR	0218
C853A(2S)	0218
C853B(2S)	0218
C853C(2S)	0218
C853D	0218
C853E	0218
C853F	0218
C853G	0218
C853GN	0218
C853H	0218
C853J	0218
C853K	0218
C853KLM(2S)	0218
C853L(2S)	0218
C853M	0218
C853OR	0218
C853R	0218
C853X	0218
C853Y	0218
C854	0414
C855	5824
C855(2S)	0414
C856(2S)	0725
C856-02(2S)	0725
C856-OR	0725
C856A	0725
C856B	0725
C856C(2S)	0725
C856D	0725
C856E	0725
C856F	0725
C856G	0725
C856GN	0725
C856J	0725
C856K	0725
C856L	0725
C856M	0725
C856OR	0725
C856R	0725
C856X	0725
C856Y	0725
C857(2S)	0233
C857H(2S)	0233
C857K	0233
C858(2S)	0111
C858A	0111
C858B	0111
C858C	0111
C858D	0111
C858E	0111
C858F(2S)	0111
C858FG(2S)	0111
C858G(2S)	0111
C858GA	0111
C858GN	0111
C858H	0111
C858J	0111
C858K	0111
C858L	0111
C858M	0111
C858OR	0111
C858R	0111
C858X	0111
C858Y	0111
C859(2S)	0111
C859A	0111
C859B	0111
C859D	0111
C859E(2S)	0111
C859F(2S)	0111
C859FG(2S)	0111
C859G(2S)	0111
C859GK(2S)	0111
C859GL	0111
C859GM	0111
C859GN	0111
C859H	0111
C859J	0111
C859K	0111
C859L	0111
C859M	0111
C859OR	0111
C859R	0111
C859X	0111
C859Y	0111
C860(2S)	0007
C860A	0007
C860B	0007
C860C(2S)	0007
C860D(2S)	0007
C860E(2S)	0007
C860F	0007
C860G	0007
C860GN	0007
C860H	0007
C860J	0007
C860K	0007
C860L	0007
C860M	0007
C860OR	0007
C860R	0007
C860X	0007
C860Y	0007
C861	0637
C862	0359
C863(2S)	0007
C863A	0007
C863B	0007
C863C	0007
C863D	0007
C863E	0007
C863F	0007
C863G	0007
C863GN	0007
C863H	0007
C863J	0007
C863K	0007
C863L	0007
C863M	0007
C863OR	0007
C863R	0007
C863X	0007
C863Y	0007
C864(2S)	0007
C865	0693
C866	5828
C866(2S)	0626
C866A	0626
C866B	0626
C866C	0626
C866D	0626
C866E	0626
C866F	0626
C866G	0626
C866GN	0626
C866H	0626
C866J	0626
C866K	0626
C866L	0626
C866M	0626
C866OR	0626
C866R	0626
C866X	0626
C866Y	0626
C867(2S)	1350
C867-0R	2200
C867-2	2200
C867-3	2200
C867-4	2200
C867-5	2200
C867-OR	2200
C867A	2200
C867B	2200
C867C	2200
C867D	2200
C867E	2200
C867F	2200
C867G	2200
C867GN	2200
C867H	2200
C867J	2200
C867K	2200
C867L	2200
C867M	2200
C867OR	2200
C867R	2200
C867X	2200
C867Y	2200
C868(2S)	0855
C868A	0855
C868B	0855
C868C	0855
C868D	0855
C868E	0855
C868F	0855
C868G	0855
C868GN	0855
C868H	0855
C868J	0855
C868K	0855
C868L	0855
C868M	0855
C868OR	0855
C868R	0855
C868X	0855
C868Y	0855
C869(2S)	0855
C869A	0855
C869B	0855
C869C	0855
C869D	0855
C869E	0855
C869F	0855
C869G	0855
C869GN	0855
C869J	0855
C869K	0855
C869L	0855
C869M	0855
C869OR	0855
C869R	0855
C869X	0855
C869Y	0855
C870(2S)	0076
C870A	0076
C870B	0076
C870C	0076
C870D	0076
C870E(2S)	0076
C870F(2S)	0076
C870FL	0076
C870G	0076
C870GN	0076
C870H	0076
C870J	0076
C870K	0076
C870L	0076
C870M	0076
C870OR	0076
C870R	0076
C870X	0076
C870Y	0076
C871(2S)	0151
C871-G	0151
C871A	0151
C871AM	0151
C871B	0151
C871C	0151
C871D(2S)	0151
C871E(2S)	0151
C871F(2S)	0151
C871G(2S)	0151
C871GN	0151
C871H	0151
C871J	0151
C871K	0151
C871L	0151
C871M	0151
C871OR	0151
C871R	0151
C871X	0151
C871Y	0151
C872	0414
C873	4389
C874	0018
C875(2S)	0086
C875-1(2S)	0086
C875-1C(2S)	0086
C875-1D(2S)	0086
C875-1E(2S)	0086
C875-1F(2S)	0086
C875-2(2S)	0086
C875-2C(2S)	0086
C875-2D(2S)	0086
C875-2E(2S)	0086
C875-2F(2S)	0086
C875-3(2S)	0086
C875-3C(2S)	0086
C875-3D(2S)	0086

324

If replacement code is OEM, contact original manufacturer for replacement.

DEVICE TYPE	REPL CODE
C875-3E(2S)	0086
C875-3F(2S)	0086
C875B	0086
C875C(2S)	0086
C875D(2S)	3392
C875DL	0086
C875E(2S)	3392
C875EL	0086
C875F(2S)	0086
C875G	0086
C875GN	0086
C875J	0086
C875K	0086
C875L	0086
C875M	0086
C875OR	0086
C875X	0086
C875Y	0086
C876(2S)	0086
C876-E	0086
C876-F	0086
C876A	0086
C876B	0086
C876C(2S)	0086
C876D(2S)	0086
C876E(2S)	0086
C876F(2S)	0086
C876G	0086
C876GN	0086
C876H	0086
C876J	0086
C876K	0086
C876L	0086
C876M	0086
C876OR	0086
C876R	0086
C876TV(2S)	0086
C876TVD(2S)	0086
C876TV-E	0086
C876TVE(2S)	0086
C876TVEF(2S)	0086
C876TV-F	0086
C876TVF	0086
C876X	0086
C876Y	0086
C877	0016
C878	0016
C879	0127
C880	0320
C880R	0320
C881(2S)	0218
C881A(2S)	0218
C881B(2S)	0218
C881C(2S)	0218
C881D(2S)	0218
C881E	0218
C881F	0218
C881G	0218
C881GN	0218
C881H	0218
C881K(2S)	0218
C881L(2S)	0218
C881M	0218
C881OR	0218
C881R	0218
C881X	0218
C881Y	0218
C882	0615
C883	0419
C884	0178
C885	0074
C885A	OEM
C886	0074
C887	0074
C888	0074
C889(2S)	0103
C890	3794
C891	2080
C892	0042
C893	2298
C894(2S)	0155
C894A	0155
C894B	0155
C894C	0155
C894D	0155
C894E	0155
C894F	0155
C894G	0155
C894GN	0155
C894H	0155
C894J	0155
C894K	0155
C894L	0155
C894M	0155
C894OR	0155
C894R	0155
C894X	0155
C894Y	0155
C895(2S)	0074
C895-2	0074
C895-3	0074
C895-4	0074
C895-5	0074
C896(2S)	0016
C896A	0016
C896B	0016
C896C	0016
C896D	0016
C896E	0016
C896F	0016
C896G	0016
C896GN	0016
C896J	0016
C896K	0016
C896L	0016
C896M	0016
C896OR	0016
C896R	0016
C896X	0016
C896Y	0016
C897(2S)	0177
C897A(2S)	0177
C897B(2S)	0177
C898(2S)	0177
C898A(2S)	0177
C898B(2S)	0177
C898D	0177
C898E	0177
C898F	0177
C898G	0177
C898GN	0177
C898H	0177
C898J	0177
C898K(2S)	0177
C898L	0177
C898M	0177
C898OR	0177
C898X	0177
C898Y	0177
C899	2386
C899A	2386
C899B	2386
C899C	2386
C899D	2386
C899E	2386
C899F	2386
C899G	2386
C899GN	2386
C899H	2386
C899J	2386
C899K(2S)	2386
C899L	2386
C899M	2386
C899OR	2386
C899R	2386
C899X	2386
C899Y	2386
C900(2S)	1212
C900-OR	1212
C900A(2S)	1212
C900AF	1212
C900B(2S)	1212
C900C(2S)	1212
C900D(2S)	1212
C900E(2S)	1212
C900F(2S)	1212
C900G	1212
C900J	1212
C900K	1212
C900L(2S)	1212
C900M(2S)	1212
C900OR	1212
C900R	1212
C900S	1212
C900SA	1212
C900SB	1212
C900SC	1212
C900SD	1212
C900U(2S)	1212
C900UE	1212
C900V	1212
C900VE	1212
C900X	1212
C900Y	1212
C901(2S)	0637
C901A(2S)	0637
C901B	0637
C901C	0637
C901D	0637
C901E	0637
C901F	0637
C901G	0637
C901GN	0637
C901H	0637
C901J	0637
C901K	0637
C901L	0637
C901M	0637
C901OR	0637
C901R	0637
C901X	0637
C901Y	0637
C902	0615
C903	0155
C904	0155
C905	0855
C906	0016
C906F	0016
C907(2S)	0016
C907A(2S)	0016
C907AC(2S)	0016
C907AD(2S)	0016
C907AH(2S)	0016
C907B	0016
C907C(2S)	0016
C907D(2S)	0016
C907E	0016
C907F	0016
C907G	0016
C907GN	0016
C907H(2S)	0016
C907HA(2S)	0016
C907J	0016
C907K	0016
C907L	0016
C907M	0016
C907OR	0016
C907R	0016
C907X	0016
C907Y	0016
C908	1344
C909	0555
C911	0555
C911A	0555
C912(2S)	0144
C912M	0144
C913(2S)	0855
C913A	0855
C913B	0855
C913C	0855
C913D	0855
C913E	0855
C913F	0855
C913G	0855
C913GN	0855
C913H	0855
C913J	0855
C913K	0855
C913L	0855
C913M	0855
C913OR	0855
C913R	0855
C913X	0855
C913Y	0855
C914	0016
C914A	0016
C915	0016
C915A	0016
C916	0042
C917(2S)	0007
C917A	0007
C917B	0007
C917C	0007
C917D	0007
C917E	0007
C917F	0007
C917G	0007
C917GN	0007
C917H	0007
C917J	0007
C917K(2S)	0007
C917L	0007
C917M	0007
C917OR	0007
C917R	0007
C917X	0007
C917Y	0007
C918(2S)	0224
C918A	0224
C918AL	0224
C918B	0224
C918C	0224
C918D	0224
C918E	0224
C918F	0224
C918G	0224
C918GN	0224
C918H	0224
C918J	0224
C918K	0224
C918L	0224
C918LF	0224
C918M	0224
C918OR	0224
C918R	0224
C918X	0224
C918XL	0224
C918Y	0224
C920(2S)	1204
C920-OQ	1204
C920-OR	1204
C920A	1204
C920B	1204
C920C	1204
C920CL	1204
C920D	1204
C920E(2S)	1204
C920F	1204
C920G	1204
C920GN	1204
C920H	1204
C920L	1204
C920M	1204
C920OR	1204
C920Q(2S)	1204
C920R(2S)	1204
C920X	1204
C920Y	1204
C921(2S)	2365
C921A	2365
C921B	2365
C921C	2365
C921C1(2S)	2365
C921CL	2365
C921D	2365
C921E	2365
C921F	2365
C921G	2365
C921GN	2365
C921H	2365
C921J	2365
C921K(2S)	2365
C921L(2S)	2365
C921M(2S)	2365
C921OR	2365
C921R	2365
C921W	2365
C921X	2365
C921Y	2365
C922(2S)	0931
C922A(2S)	0931
C922B(2S)	0931
C922C(2S)	0931
C922K(2S)	0931
C922L(2S)	0931
C922M(2S)	0931
C923(2S)	0547
C923A(2S)	0547
C923B(2S)	0547
C923C(2S)	0547
C923D(2S)	0547
C923E(2S)	0547
C923F(2S)	0547
C923G	0547
C923GN	0547
C923H	0547
C923K	0547
C923L	0547
C923M	0547
C923OR	0547
C923R	0547
C923X	0547
C923Y	0547
C924(2S)	0544
C924A	0544
C924B	0544
C924C	0544
C924D	0544
C924E(2S)	0544
C924F(2S)	0544
C924G	0544
C924GN	0544
C924H	0544
C924J	0544
C924K	0544
C924L	0544
C924M(2S)	0544
C924OR	0544
C924R	0544
C924X	0544
C924Y	0544
C925(2S)	0284
C925A	0284
C925B	0284
C925C	0284
C925D	0284
C925E	0284
C925F	0284
C925G	0284
C925GN	0284
C925H	0284
C925J	0284
C925K	0284
C925L	0284
C925M	0284
C925OR	0284
C925R	0284
C925X	0284
C925Y	0284
C926(2S)	0261
C926-OR	0261
C926A(2S)	0261
C926B	0261
C926C	0261
C926D	0261
C926E	0261
C926F	0261
C926G	0261
C926GN	0261
C926H	0261
C926J	0261
C926K	0261
C926L	0261
C926M	0261
C926OR	0261
C926R	0261
C926X	0261
C926Y	0261
C927(2S)	0007
C927A(2S)	0007
C927B(2S)	0007
C927C(2S)	0007
C927CJ(2S)	0007
C927CK	0007
C927CT	0007
C927CU(2S)	0007
C927CW(2S)	0007
C927D(2S)	0007
C927E(2S)	0007
C927F	0007
C927G	0007
C927GN	0007
C927H	0007
C927J	0007
C927K	0007
C927L	0007
C927M	0007
C927OR	0007
C927R	0007
C927X	0007
C927XL	0007
C927Y	0007
C927Z	0007
C928(2S)	0007
C928A	0007
C928B(2S)	0007
C928C(2S)	0007
C928D(2S)	0007
C928E(2S)	0007
C928F	0007
C928G	0007
C928GN	0007
C928H	0007
C928J	0007
C928K	0007
C928L	0007
C928M	0007
C928OR	0007
C928R	0007
C928X	0007
C928Y	0007
C929(2S)	1060
C929-0(2S)	1060
C929-O	1060
C929A	1060
C929B(2S)	1060
C929C(2S)	1060
C929C1(2S)	1060
C929D(2S)	1060
C929D1(2S)	1060
C929DE(2S)	1060
C929DP(2S)	1060
C929DU(2S)	1060
C929DV(2S)	1060
C929E(2S)	1489
C929ED(2S)	1060
C929EZ	1060
C929F(2S)	1060
C929FK(2S)	1060
C929G	1060
C929GN	1060
C929H	1060
C929J	1060
C929K	1060
C929L	1060
C929M	1060
C929NP	1060
C929OR	1060
C929R	1060
C929SP	1060
C929X	1060
C929Y	1060
C930(2S)	2195
C930-OR	2195
C930A	2195
C930B(2S)	2195
C930BK(2S)	2195
C930C(2S)	2195
C930C-IF	2195
C930CK(2S)	2195
C930CL(2S)	2195
C930CS(2S)	2195
C930D(2S)	2195
C930DB	2195
C930DC	2195
C930DE(2S)	2195
C930DK	2195
C930DS(2S)	2195
C930DT(2S)	2195
C930DT-2(2S)	2195
C930DX(2S)	2195
C930DZ(2S)	2195
C930E(2S)	2195
C930E(JAPAN)	2195
C930EP(2S)	2195
C930ET(2S)	2195
C930EV(2S)	2195
C930EX(2S)	2195
C930F(2S)	2195
C930G	2195
C930GN	2195
C930H	2195
C930J	2195
C930K	2195
C930L	2195
C930M	2195
C930NP	2195
C930OR	2195
C930R	2195
C930SP	2195
C930X	2195
C930Y	2195
C931(2S)	0219
C931C(2S)	0219
C931D(2S)	0219
C931E(2S)	0219
C932(2S)	0555
C932A	0555
C932B	0555
C932BK	0555
C932C	0555
C932D	0555
C932E(2S)	0555
C932F	0555
C932G	0555
C932GN	0555
C932H	0555
C932J	0555
C932K	0555
C932L	0555
C932M	0555
C932OR	0555
C932R	0555
C932X	0555
C932Y	0555
C933(2S)	0191
C933A	0191
C933B	0191
C933BB(2S)	0191
C933C(2S)	0191
C933D(2S)	0191
C933E(2S)	0191
C933F(2S)	0191
C933FB	0191
C933FP(2S)	0191
C933G(2S)	0191
C933GN	0191
C933H	0191
C933J	0191
C933K	0191
C933L	0191
C933M	0191
C933OR	0191
C933R	0191
C933X	0191
C933Y	0191
C934	0016
C934-O	0016
C934A	0016
C934B	0016
C934C(2S)	0016
C934D(2S)	0016
C934E(2S)	0016
C934F(2S)	0016
C934G(2S)	0016
C934GN	0016
C934H	0016
C934J	0016
C934K	0016
C934L	0016
C934M	0016
C934OR	0016
C934Q	0016
C934R	0016
C934X	0016
C934Y	0016
C935(2S)	0074
C935-OR	0074
C935A	0074
C935B	0074
C935C	0074
C935D	0074
C935E	0074
C935F	0074
C935G	0074
C935GN	0074
C935H	0074
C935J	0074
C935K	0074
C935M	0074
C935OR	0074
C935R	0074
C935X	0074
C935Y	0074
C936(2S)	0003
C936A	0003
C936B	0003
C936BK	0003
C936C	0003
C936D	0003
C936E	0003
C936F	0003
C936G	0003
C936GN	0003
C936H	0003
C936J	0003
C936K	0003
C936L	0003
C936M	0003
C936OR	0003
C936R	0003
C936X	0003
C936Y	0003
C937(2S)	0103
C937-01(2S)	0103
C937A(2S)	0103
C937B(2S)	0103
C937BK	0103
C937C	0103
C937D	0103
C937E	0103
C937F	0103
C937G	0103
C937GN	0103
C937H	0103
C937J	0103
C937K	0103
C937L	0103
C937M	0103
C937OR	0103
C937R	OEM
C937X	0103
C937Y	0103
C938(2S)	0155
C938-O	0155
C938-Y	1077
C938A(2S)	0155
C938B(2S)	0155
C938C(2S)	0155
C938D	0155
C938E	0155
C938F	0155
C938G	0155
C938GN	0155
C938H	0155
C938J	0155
C938K	0155
C938L	0155
C938M	0155
C938OR	0155
C938R	0155
C938X	0155
C938Y	0155
C939(2S)	0637
C939I	0637
C939L(2S)	0637
C940(2S)	0820
C940L(2S)	0820
C940M(2S)	0820
C940Q	0820
C941(2S)	0155
C941-04	0155
C941-0Y	0155
C941-O(2S)	0155
C941-OY	0155
C941-R(2S)	0155
C941-Y(2S)	0155
C941K	0155
C941O	0155
C941R(2S)	0155
C941TM	0155
C941TM-O	0155
C941Y	0155
C942	0016
C943(2S)	0016
C943A(2S)	0016
C943B(2S)	0016
C943C(2S)	0016
C943D	0016
C943E	0016
C943F	0016
C943G	0016
C943GN	0016
C943H	0016
C943J	0016
C943K	0016
C943L	0016
C943M	0016
C943OR	0016
C943R	0016
C943X	0016
C943Y	0016
C944(2S)	0076
C944S	0076
C945	0076
C945(JAPAN)	0076
C945-O	0076
C945-O(2S)	0076
C945-OR	0076
C945-YX	0076
C945A(2S)	0076
C945AK	0076
C945AP(2S)	0076
C945AQ(2S)	0076
C945AR	0076
C945B(2S)	0076
C945C(2S)	0076
C945D(2S)	0076
C945E(2S)	0076
C945F(2S)	0076
C945G(2S)	0076
C945GN	0076
C945H(2S)	0076
C945J	0076
C945K(2S)	0076
C945L(2S)	0076
C945LP	0076
C945LP(JAPAN)	0076
C945LQ	0076
C945M(2S)	0076
C945OR	0076
C945P	0076
C945P(2S)	0076
C945P(JAPAN)	0076
C945P1	0076
C945PJ	0076
C945PQ	0076
C945Q	0076
C945Q(2S)	0076
C945Q(JAPAN)	0076
C945QL(2S)	0076
C945QP(2S)	0076
C945R(2S)	0076
C945RA	0076
C945S(2S)	0076
C945T(2S)	0076
C945TK	0076
C945TP	0076
C945TQ(2S)	0076
C945X(2S)	0076
C945Y	0076
C945Y(KOREA)	0076
C947(2S)	0007

If replacement code is OEM, contact original manufacturer for replacement. 325

DEVICE TYPE	REPL CODE
C947A	0007
C947B	0007
C947C	0007
C947D	0007
C947E	0007
C947F	0007
C947G	0007
C947GN	0007
C947H	0007
C947J	0007
C947K	0007
C947L	0007
C947M	0007
C947OR	0007
C947R	0007
C947X	0007
C947Y	0007
C948(2S)	0216
C948A	0216
C948B	0216
C948D	0216
C948E	0216
C948F	0216
C948G	0216
C948GN	0216
C948H	0216
C948J	0216
C948K	0216
C948L	0216
C948M	0216
C948OR	0216
C948R	0216
C948X	0216
C948Y	0216
C949	0216
C950	0016
C951	0079
C952	0079
C953	0016
C954	0016
C955	0016
C956	0016
C957(2S)	0144
C957A	0144
C957AL	0144
C957B	0144
C957C	0144
C957D	0144
C957E	0144
C957F	0144
C957G	0144
C957GN	0144
C957H	0144
C957J	0144
C957K	0144
C957L	0144
C957M	0144
C957OR	0144
C957R	0144
C957X	0144
C957XL	0144
C957Y	0144
C959(2S)	0086
C959A(2S)	0086
C959B(2S)	0086
C959C(2S)	0086
C959D(2S)	0086
C959E	0086
C959F	0086
C959G	0086
C959GN	0086
C959H	0086
C959J	0086
C959K	0086
C959L	0086
C959M(2S)	0086
C959OR	0086
C959R	0086
C959S(2S)	0086
C959SA(2S)	0086
C959SB(2S)	0086
C959SC(2S)	0086
C959SD(2S)	0086
C959X	0086
C959Y	0086
C960	5522
C961	0615
C962	0615
C963	0016
C964	0016
C965	0016
C966(2S)	0016
C966A	0016
C966B	0016
C966C	0016
C966D	0016
C966E	0016
C966F	0016
C966G	0016
C966GN	0016
C966H	0016
C966J	0016
C966K	0016
C966L	0016
C966M	0016
C966OR	0016
C966R	0016
C966X	0016
C966Y	0016

DEVICE TYPE	REPL CODE
C967(2S)	0016
C967A	0016
C967B	0016
C967C	0016
C967D	0016
C967E	0016
C967F	0016
C967G	0016
C967GN	0016
C967H	0016
C967J	0016
C967K	0016
C967L	0016
C967M	0016
C967OR	0016
C967R	0016
C967X	0016
C967Y	0016
C968(2S)	2901
C968A	2901
C968B	2901
C968C	2901
C968D	2901
C968E	2901
C968F	2901
C968G	2901
C968GN	2901
C968H	2901
C968J	2901
C968K	2901
C968L	2901
C968M	2901
C968OR	2901
C968P(2S)	2901
C968R	2901
C968X	2901
C968Y	2901
C969	0016
C970	0016
C971(2S)	2924
C971A	2924
C971B	2924
C971BK	2924
C971C	2924
C971D	2924
C971E	2924
C971F	2924
C971G	2924
C971GN	2924
C971H	2924
C971J	2924
C971K	2924
C971L	2924
C971M	2924
C971OR	2924
C971R	2924
C971X	2924
C971Y	2924
C972(2S)	0086
C972A	0086
C972B	0086
C972C(2S)	0086
C972D(2S)	0086
C972E(2S)	0086
C972F	0086
C972G	0086
C972GN	0086
C972H	0086
C972J	0086
C972K	0086
C972L	0086
C972M	0086
C972OR	0086
C972R	0086
C972X	0086
C972Y	0086
C973	2080
C973A	2080
C975	1410
C975A	1410
C976	0086
C976TV	0086
C979	0016
C979-O	0016
C979-R	0016
C979-Y	0016
C979A	0016
C979A-O	0016
C979A-R	0016
C980	0284
C980AG	0284
C980AG-O	0284
C980AG-R	0284
C980G	0284
C980G-O	0284
C980G-R	0284
C980G-Y	0284
C981	0178
C982(2S)	0396
C983(2S)	0066
C983-O(2S)	0066
C983-O	0066
C983-R	0066
C983-Y(2S)	0066
C983FA-1	0066
C983FH-1	0066
C983O	0066
C983R(2S)	0066
C983S(2S)	0066

DEVICE TYPE	REPL CODE
C983Y(2S)	0066
C983YFA-1	0066
C984(2S)	0531
C984A(2S)	0531
C984B(2S)	0531
C984C(2S)	0531
C984D	0531
C984E	0531
C984F	0531
C984G	0531
C984GN	0531
C984H	0531
C984J	0531
C984L	0531
C984M	0531
C984OR	0531
C984R	0531
C984X	0531
C984Y	0531
C985	0111
C985A	0111
C987	0007
C987A	0007
C988	0007
C988A	0007
C988B	0007
C990	0042
C991(2S)	0488
C991A	0488
C991B	0488
C991C	0488
C991D	0488
C991E	0488
C991F	0488
C991G	0488
C991GN	0488
C991H	0488
C991J	0488
C991K	0488
C991L	0488
C991M	0488
C991OR	0488
C991R	0488
C991X	0488
C991Y	0488
C992(2S)	0488
C992A	0488
C992B	0488
C992C	0488
C992D	0488
C992E	0488
C992F	0488
C992G	0488
C992GN	0488
C992H	0488
C992J	0488
C992K	0488
C992L	0488
C992M	0488
C992OR	0488
C992R	0488
C992X	0488
C992Y	0488
C993(2S)	0016
C993D	0016
C993E	0016
C994	0079
C995(2S)	0168
C995A	0168
C995B	0168
C995C	0168
C995E	0168
C995F	0168
C995G	0168
C995GN	0168
C995H	0168
C995J	0168
C995K	0168
C995L	0168
C995M	0168
C995OR	0168
C995R	0168
C995X	0168
C995Y	0168
C996(2S)	3249
C997(2S)	0224
C997A	0224
C997B	0224
C997C	0224
C997D	0224
C997E	0224
C997F	0224
C997G	0224
C997GN	0224
C997H	0224
C997J	0224
C997K	0224
C997L	0224
C997M	0224
C997OR	0224
C997R	0224
C997X	0224
C997Y	0224
C998	3794
C999(2S)	0065
C999A	0065
C999B	0065
C999C	0065
C999D	0065

DEVICE TYPE	REPL CODE
C999E	0065
C999F	0065
C999G	0065
C999GN	0065
C999H	0065
C999J	0065
C999K	0065
C999L	0065
C999M	0065
C999OR	0065
C999R	0065
C999X	0065
C999Y	0065
C1000	0111
C1000(2S)	0111
C1000-BL(2S)	0111
C1000-GR(2S)	0111
C1000-Y(2S)	0111
C1000A	0111
C1000B	0111
C1000BL	0111
C1000C	0111
C1000D	0111
C1000E	0111
C1000F	0111
C1000G	0111
C1000G-BL	0111
C1000GBL	0111
C1000G-GR	0111
C1000GN	0111
C1000GR	0111
C1000H	0111
C1000J	0111
C1000K	0111
C1000L	0111
C1000M	0111
C1000OR	0111
C1000R	0111
C1000X	0111
C1000Y(2S)	0111
C1001	0414
C1001(2S)	2028
C1002	0111
C1003	0079
C1003A	OEM
C1004	0003
C1004(2S)	0003
C1004(TRANS)	0003
C1004A(2S)	0003
C1004A(TRANS)	0003
C1004B	0003
C1004C	0003
C1004D	0003
C1004E	0003
C1004F	0003
C1004G	0003
C1004GN	0003
C1004H	0003
C1004J	0003
C1004K	0003
C1004L	0003
C1004M	0003
C1004OR	0003
C1004R	0003
C1004X	0003
C1004Y	0003
C1005	0065
C1005(2S)	0065
C1005A	0065
C1005A(2S)	0065
C1005B	0065
C1005C	0065
C1005D	0065
C1005E	0065
C1005F	0065
C1005G	0065
C1005GN	0065
C1005H	0065
C1005J	0065
C1005K	0065
C1005L	0065
C1005M	0065
C1005OR	0065
C1005R	0065
C1005X	0065
C1005Y	0065
C1006(2S)	0111
C1006A	0111
C1006A(2S)	0111
C1006B(2S)	0111
C1006C(2S)	0111
C1007(2S)	0016
C1008(2S)	0086
C1008A	0086
C1008Y	OEM
C1008Y(KOREA)	0079
C1009	0224
C1009A	0224
C1009F1	0224
C1009F2	0224
C1009F3	0224
C1009F4	0224
C1009F5	0224
C1010	0111
C1010(TRANS)	0111
C1010A	0111
C1010A(TRANS)	0111
C1010B	0111
C1010B(TRANS)	0111

DEVICE TYPE	REPL CODE
C1010C(2S)	0111
C1010D	0111
C1010E	0111
C1010F	0111
C1010G	0111
C1010GN	0111
C1010H	0111
C1010J	0111
C1010K	0111
C1010L	0111
C1010M	0111
C1010OR	0111
C1010R	0111
C1010X	0111
C1010Y	0111
C1011	0693
C1012(2S)	0233
C1012A(2S)	0233
C1012B	0233
C1012C	0233
C1012D	0233
C1012E	0233
C1012F	0233
C1012G	0233
C1012GN	0233
C1012H	0233
C1012J	0233
C1012K	0233
C1012L	0233
C1012M	0233
C1012OR	0233
C1012R	0233
C1012X	0233
C1012Y	0233
C1013(2S)	2035
C1013-OR	2035
C1013A	2035
C1013B	2035
C1013C(2S)	2035
C1013D(2S)	2035
C1013E	2035
C1013F	2035
C1013G	2035
C1013GN	2035
C1013H	2035
C1013J	2035
C1013K	2035
C1013L	2035
C1013LJ	2035
C1013M	2035
C1013OR	2035
C1013PJ	2035
C1013R	2035
C1013X	2035
C1013Y	2035
C1014	2035
C1014(TRANS)	2035
C1014-1	2035
C1014-2	2035
C1014A	OEM
C1014A(TRANS)	2035
C1014B	2035
C1014B(TRANS)	2035
C1014BY	2035
C1014C(2S)	2035
C1014CD(2S)	2035
C1014D(2S)	2035
C1014D1(2S)	2035
C1014E	2035
C1014F	2035
C1014G	2035
C1014GA	2035
C1014GN	2035
C1014H	2035
C1014J	2035
C1014K	2035
C1014L	2035
C1014LG	2035
C1014LR	2035
C1014M	2035
C1014OR	2035
C1014R	2035
C1014W	2035
C1014X	2035
C1014Y	2035
C1015	OEM
C1015A	OEM
C1015B	OEM
C1016	OEM
C1016A	OEM
C1016B	OEM
C1017(2S)	2039
C1018(2S)	2039
C1018A	2039
C1018B(2S)	2039
C1018C	2039
C1018D	2039
C1018E	2039
C1018F	2039
C1018G	2039
C1018GN	2039
C1018H	2039
C1018J	2039
C1018K	2039
C1018L	2039
C1018M	2039
C1018R	2039
C1018X	2039
C1018Y	2039

DEVICE TYPE	REPL CODE
C1019	OEM
C1019A	OEM
C1019B	OEM
C1019C	0042
C1020	OEM
C1020A	OEM
C1020B	OEM
C1021	OEM
C1021A	OEM
C1021B	OEM
C1022	OEM
C1022A	OEM
C1022B	OEM
C1023	0127
C1023-O(2S)	0127
C1023-Y(2S)	0127
C1023A	0127
C1023B	0127
C1023C	0127
C1023D	0127
C1023E	0127
C1023F	0127
C1023G(2S)	0127
C1023GN	0127
C1023H	0127
C1023J	0127
C1023K	0127
C1023L	0127
C1023M	0127
C1023OR	0127
C1023R	0127
C1023X	0127
C1023Y	0127
C1024(2S)	0178
C1024-E	0178
C1024A	0178
C1024B(2S)	0178
C1024C(2S)	0178
C1024D(2S)	0178
C1024E(2S)	0178
C1024F(2S)	0178
C1024G	0178
C1024L	0178
C1024Y	0178
C1025	0178
C1025(TRANS)	0928
C1025A	OEM
C1025B	OEM
C1025CTV(2S)	0928
C1025D	0928
C1025E	0928
C1025J	0928
C1025MT	0928
C1026	0127
C1026(TRANS)	0127
C1026-O	0127
C1026-R	0127
C1026A	OEM
C1026A(TRANS)	0127
C1026B	OEM
C1026B(TRANS)	0127
C1026BL	0127
C1026C	0127
C1026D	0127
C1026E	0127
C1026F	0127
C1026G(2S)	0127
C1026GN	0127
C1026GR	0127
C1026H	0127
C1026J	0127
C1026K	0127
C1026L	0127
C1026M	0127
C1026OR	0127
C1026R	0127
C1026X	0127
C1026Y(2S)	0127
C1027(2S)	0637
C1029	OEM
C1029A	OEM
C1029B	OEM
C1030	0861
C1030(TRANS)	2048
C1030-OR	2048
C1030A	0861
C1030A(TRANS)	2048
C1030B	0861
C1030B(TRANS)	2048
C1030B2C	2048
C1030C(2S)	2048
C1030D(2S)	2048
C1030E	2048
C1030F	2048
C1030G	2048
C1030H	2048
C1030J	2048
C1030K	2048
C1030L	2048
C1030M	2048
C1030OR	2048
C1030P	0177
C1030R	2048
C1030X	2048
C1030Y	2048
C1031	1021
C1031(TRANS)	1021
C1031A	OEM
C1031B	OEM

DEVICE TYPE	REPL CODE
C1032	0127
C1032(TRANS)	0127
C1032A	OEM
C1032A(TRANS)	0127
C1032B	OEM
C1032B(TRANS)	0127
C1032BL	0127
C1032C	0127
C1032D	0127
C1032E	0127
C1032F	0127
C1032G(2S)	0127
C1032GN	0127
C1032H	0127
C1032J	0127
C1032K	0127
C1032L	0127
C1032M	0127
C1032OR	0127
C1032P	1035
C1032R	0127
C1032X	0127
C1032Y(2S)	0127
C1033(2S)	0710
C1033A(2S)	0710
C1033B	0710
C1033C	0710
C1033D	0710
C1033E	0710
C1033F	0710
C1033G	0710
C1033GN	0710
C1033H	0710
C1033J	0710
C1033K	0710
C1033L	0710
C1033OR	0710
C1033P	2086
C1033R	0710
C1033X	0710
C1033Y	0710
C1034(2S)	2053
C1034-3	2053
C1034-4	2053
C1034-5	2053
C1035	0007
C1035(TRANS)	0007
C1035A	OEM
C1035A(TRANS)	0007
C1035B	OEM
C1035B(TRANS)	0007
C1035C(2S)	0007
C1035D(2S)	0007
C1035E(2S)	0007
C1035F	0007
C1035GN	0007
C1035H	0007
C1035J	0007
C1035L	0007
C1035M	0007
C1035OR	0007
C1035P	1168
C1035R	0007
C1035X	0007
C1035Y	0007
C1036	0007
C1036(TRANS)	0007
C1036A	OEM
C1036A(TRANS)	0007
C1036B	OEM
C1036B(TRANS)	0007
C1036C	0007
C1036D	0007
C1036E	0007
C1036F	0007
C1036G	0007
C1036GN	0007
C1036H	0007
C1036J	0007
C1036K	0007
C1036L	0007
C1036M	0007
C1036OR	0007
C1036P	1820
C1036R	0007
C1036X	0007
C1036Y	0007
C1038P	OEM
C1039	OEM
C1039A	OEM
C1039B	OEM
C1039P	OEM
C1040	OEM
C1040A	OEM
C1040B	OEM
C1041	OEM
C1041A	OEM
C1041B	OEM
C1042	OEM
C1042(TRANS)	1581
C1042A	OEM
C1042B	OEM
C1043	2059
C1044(2S)	0007
C1044P	0033
C1045	0003
C1045(2S)	0003
C1045A	OEM
C1045B	0003

If replacement code is OEM, contact original manufacturer for replacement.

DEVICE TYPE	REPL CODE
C1045B(2S)	0003
C1045C(2S)	0003
C1045D(2S)	0003
C1045E(2S)	0003
C1045F	0003
C1045G	0003
C1045GN	0003
C1045H	0003
C1045J	0003
C1045K	0003
C1045L	0003
C1045M	0003
C1045OR	0003
C1045P	0081
C1045R(2S)	0003
C1045X	0003
C1045Y	0003
C1046	0065
C1046(2S)	0065
C1046-OR	0065
C1046A	OEM
C1046A(TRANS)	0065
C1046B	OEM
C1046B(TRANS)	0065
C1046C	0065
C1046D	0065
C1046E	0065
C1046F	0065
C1046G	0065
C1046GN	0065
C1046H	0065
C1046J	0065
C1046K	0065
C1046L	0065
C1046M	0065
C1046N	0065
C1046OR	0065
C1046P	0141
C1046P(HEP)	0141
C1046R	0065
C1046X	0065
C1046Y	0065
C1047(2S)	0113
C1047A	0113
C1047B(2S)	0113
C1047BC	0113
C1047BCD	0113
C1047C(2S)	0113
C1047D(2S)	0113
C1047E(2S)	0113
C1047F	0113
C1047G	0113
C1047GN	0113
C1047GR	0113
C1047H	0113
C1047J	0113
C1047K	0113
C1047L	0113
C1047M	0113
C1047R	0113
C1047X	0113
C1047Y	0113
C1048(2S)	0233
C1048B(2S)	0233
C1048C(2S)	0233
C1048D(2S)	0233
C1048DC	0233
C1048E(2S)	0233
C1048F(2S)	0233
C1049	OEM
C1049A	OEM
C1049B	OEM
C1050	0220
C1050C	0220
C1050D(2S)	0220
C1050E(2S)	0220
C1050F(2S)	0220
C1051(2S)	0177
C1051L	0177
C1052	0086
C1052P	0329
C1053	0086
C1053P	0354
C1054	0007
C1055	0424
C1055H(2S)	0424
C1055U	0424
C1056(2S)	0233
C1056A	0233
C1056B	0233
C1056C	0233
C1056D	0233
C1056E	0233
C1056F	0233
C1056G	0233
C1056GN	0233
C1056H	0233
C1056J	0233
C1056K	0233
C1056L	0233
C1056M	0233
C1056OR	0233
C1056R	0233
C1056X	0233
C1056Y	0233
C1057P	0461
C1058P	0461
C1059(2S)	0142
C1059A	0142
C1059B	0142
C1059C	0142
C1059D	0142
C1059E	0142
C1059F	0142
C1059G	0142
C1059GN	0142
C1059H	0142
C1059J	0142
C1059K	0142
C1059L	0142
C1059M	0142
C1059OR	0142
C1059R	0142
C1059X	0142
C1059Y	0142
C1060	0042
C1060(2S)	0042
C1060A	0042
C1060A(2S)	0042
C1060B	0042
C1060B(2S)	0042
C1060BL	0042
C1060BM(2S)	0042
C1060BY	0042
C1060C(2S)	0042
C1060D(2S)	0042
C1060E	0042
C1060F	0042
C1060G	0042
C1060GN	0042
C1060H	0042
C1060J	0042
C1060K	0042
C1060L	0042
C1060M	0042
C1060OR	0042
C1060R	0042
C1060X	0042
C1060Y	0042
C1061	0042
C1061(2S)	0042
C1061-C	0042
C1061A	0042
C1061A(TRANS)	0042
C1061B	0042
C1061B(TRANS)	0042
C1061BM	0042
C1061C(2S)	0042
C1061D(2S)	0042
C1061K	0042
C1061KA	0042
C1061KB	0042
C1061KC	0042
C1061SC	0042
C1061T(2S)	0042
C1061TB(2S)	0042
C1062	0187
C1062(TRANS)	0233
C1062A	OEM
C1062B	OEM
C1062P	0557
C1063	0018
C1064	0320
C1065	OEM
C1065A	OEM
C1065B	OEM
C1066	0144
C1066(TRANS)	0259
C1066A	OEM
C1066B	OEM
C1067	0007
C1068	0414
C1069	0086
C1069(TRANS)	0626
C1069A	OEM
C1069B	OEM
C1070(2S)	0007
C1070-1	0007
C1070-2	0007
C1070-B	0007
C1071(2S)	0016
C1072(2S)	0086
C1072A(2S)	0086
C1072B	0086
C1072C	0086
C1072D	0086
C1072E	0086
C1072F	0086
C1072G	0086
C1072GN	0086
C1072H	0086
C1072J	0086
C1072K	0086
C1072L	0086
C1072M	0086
C1072OR	0086
C1072R	0086
C1072X	0086
C1072Y	0086
C1074	2080
C1075	1410
C1076	2082
C1078	2085
C1079(2S)	0177
C1079-R	0177
C1079-Y	0177
C1080(2S)	0177
C1080-R	0177
C1080-Y	0177
C1080B	0177
C1080LB	0177
C1083	2030
C1084	0224
C1085	0178
C1086(2S)	0223
C1086A	0223
C1086B	0223
C1086C	0223
C1086D	0223
C1086E	0223
C1086F	0223
C1086G	0223
C1086GN	0223
C1086H	0223
C1086J	0223
C1086K	0223
C1086L	0223
C1086M(2S)	0223
C1086OR	0223
C1086R	0223
C1086X	0223
C1086Y	0223
C1088	0283
C1089	0283
C1089B	0283
C1089C	0283
C1089D	0283
C1090	0233
C1091A	0555
C1095-K	0219
C1096	0386
C1096-4Z-L	0386
C1096-4ZL	0386
C1096-O(KOREA)	0219
C1096-OR	0386
C1096A(2S)	0386
C1096B(2S)	0386
C1096C(2S)	0386
C1096D(2S)	0386
C1096E	0386
C1096F	0386
C1096G	0386
C1096GN	0386
C1096H	0386
C1096J	0386
C1096K(2S)	0386
C1096L(2S)	0386
C1096LM	0386
C1096M(2S)	0386
C1096N(2S)	0386
C1096OR	0386
C1096Q	0386
C1096R	0386
C1096X	0386
C1096Y	0386
C1098(2S)	0555
C1098(4)K	0555
C1098(4)L	0555
C1098-4K	0555
C1098-4L	0555
C1098-42M	0555
C1098A(2S)	0555
C1098B(2S)	0555
C1098C(2S)	0555
C1098D(2S)	0555
C1098L(2S)	0555
C1098M(2S)	0555
C1099	1138
C1099K	1138
C1100	0223
C1100(TRANS)	1142
C1100A	OEM
C1100A(TRANS)	1142
C1100B	OEM
C1100B(TRANS)	1142
C1100C	1142
C1100D	1142
C1100E	1142
C1100F	1142
C1100G	1142
C1100GN	1142
C1100H	1142
C1100J	1142
C1100K	1142
C1100L	1142
C1100M	1142
C1100OR	1142
C1100R	1142
C1100X	1142
C1100Y	1142
C1101	0003
C1101(TRANS)	0003
C1101A	0003
C1101A(TRANS)	0003
C1101A1	OEM
C1101A1DM	OEM
C1101A51	OEM
C1101ADM	OEM
C1101B	0003
C1101B(TRANS)	0003
C1101C(2S)	0003
C1101D(2S)	0003
C1101E(2S)	0003
C1101F(2S)	0003
C1101G	0003
C1101GN	0003
C1101H	0003
C1101J	0003
C1101K	0003
C1101L(2S)	0003
C1101M	0003
C1101OR	0003
C1101R	0003
C1101X	0003
C1101Y	0003
C1102	0142
C1102(TRANS)	0142
C1102A	0142
C1102A(TRANS)	0142
C1102B	0142
C1102B(TRANS)	0142
C1102C(2S)	0142
C1102K(2S)	0142
C1102L(2S)	0142
C1102M(2S)	0142
C1103(2S)	0233
C1103A(2S)	0233
C1103B(2S)	0233
C1103C(2S)	0233
C1103L(2S)	0233
C1104(2S)	1200
C1104A(2S)	1200
C1104B(2S)	1200
C1104C(2S)	1200
C1104L	1200
C1105	0142
C1105(2S)	0142
C1105A	0142
C1105A(TRANS)	0142
C1105B	0142
C1105B(TRANS)	0142
C1105C(2S)	0142
C1105D	0142
C1105E	0142
C1105F	0142
C1105G	0142
C1105GN	0142
C1105H	0142
C1105J	0142
C1105K(2S)	0142
C1105L(2S)	0142
C1105M(2S)	0142
C1105OR	0142
C1105R	0142
C1105X	0142
C1105Y	0142
C1106	0270
C1106(TRANS)	0220
C1106A	0270
C1106A(TRANS)	0220
C1106B	0270
C1106B(TRANS)	0220
C1106C(2S)	0220
C1106K(2S)	0220
C1106L(2S)	0220
C1106M(2S)	0220
C1106P	0220
C1106PQ	0220
C1106Q	0220
C1107	0236
C1107Q(2S)	0236
C1107YG	0236
C1108	0236
C1109	0236
C1109(TRANS)	0236
C1109A	OEM
C1109B	OEM
C1110	0236
C1111(2S)	0861
C1112	0861
C1113	0424
C1114(2S)	2112
C1115(2S)	0177
C1116(2S)	0538
C1116-0(2S)	0538
C1116-O	0538
C1116A	0538
C1117	0007
C1117A	0007
C1117B	0007
C1117C	0007
C1117D	0007
C1117E	0007
C1117F	0007
C1117G	0007
C1117GN	0007
C1117H	0007
C1117J	0007
C1117K	0007
C1117L	0007
C1117M	0007
C1117OR	0007
C1117R	0007
C1117X	0007
C1117Y	0007
C1122	1410
C1122A	1410
C1123(2S)	0079
C1123A	0079
C1123B	0079
C1123C	0079
C1123D	0079
C1123E	0079
C1123F	0079
C1123GN	0079
C1123H	0079
C1123J	0079
C1123K	0079
C1123L	0079
C1123M	0079
C1123OR	0079
C1123R	0079
C1123X	0079
C1123Y	0079
C1124(2S)	0264
C1124(13)	0264
C1124-OR	0264
C1124A	0264
C1124B	0264
C1124C	0264
C1124D	0264
C1124E	0264
C1124F	0264
C1124G	0264
C1124GN	0264
C1124H	0264
C1124J	0264
C1124K	0264
C1124L	0264
C1124M	0264
C1124OR	0264
C1124R	0264
C1124X	0264
C1124Y	0264
C1126(2S)	0224
C1126A	0224
C1126B	0224
C1126E	0224
C1126F	0224
C1126GN	0224
C1126J	0224
C1126K	0224
C1126L	0224
C1126M	0224
C1126OR	0224
C1126R	0224
C1126X	0224
C1126Y	0224
C1127(2S)	1062
C1127-1	1062
C1127-2	1062
C1127-0	1062
C1127-OR	1062
C1127A	1062
C1127B	1062
C1127C	1062
C1127D	1062
C1127E	1062
C1127F	1062
C1127G	1062
C1127GA	1062
C1127GN	1062
C1127H	1062
C1127J	1062
C1127JR	1062
C1127K	1062
C1127L	1062
C1127M	1062
C1127OR	1062
C1127R	1062
C1127X	1062
C1127Y	1062
C1128(2S)	0224
C1128-0	0224
C1128A	0224
C1128B	0224
C1128BL	0224
C1128C	0224
C1128D(2S)	0224
C1128G	0224
C1128H	0224
C1128M	0224
C1128R	0224
C1128S	0224
C1128Y	0224
C1129(2S)	0224
C1129-0	0224
C1129A	0224
C1129B	0224
C1129BL	0224
C1129C	0224
C1129G	0224
C1129M	0224
C1129R	0224
C1129Y	0224
C1130	0003
C1131	0637
C1132	0065
C1133	0065
C1133D	0065
C1140	1841
C1141	1841
C1141(TRANS)	1841
C1141A	OEM
C1141B	OEM
C1142	0359
C1143	0359
C1145	OEM
C1145A	OEM
C1145B	OEM
C1146	OEM
C1146A	OEM
C1146B	OEM
C1147	OEM
C1147A	OEM
C1147B	OEM
C1149	OEM
C1149A	OEM
C1149B	OEM
C1150	0086
C1150(TRANS)	0086
C1150A	OEM
C1150B	OEM
C1151	0003
C1151(TRANS)	0003
C1151A	0003
C1151A(TRANS)	0003
C1151B	OEM
C1152	0074
C1152(TRANS)	0074
C1152A	OEM
C1152B	OEM
C1152F(2S)	0074
C1152G(2S)	0074
C1153(2S)	1142
C1153A	1142
C1154(2S)	0223
C1155	0264
C1155(TRANS)	0264
C1155A	OEM
C1155B	OEM
C1156	0264
C1156(TRANS)	0264
C1156A	OEM
C1156A(TRANS)	0264
C1156B	OEM
C1156B(TRANS)	0264
C1156C	0264
C1156D	0264
C1156E	0264
C1156F	0264
C1156G	0264
C1156GN	0264
C1156H	1805
C1156H(TRANS)	0264
C1156K	0264
C1156L	0264
C1156M	0264
C1156OR	0264
C1156R	0264
C1156X	0264
C1156Y	0264
C1157(2S)	0264
C1157A	0264
C1157B	0264
C1157C	0264
C1157E	0264
C1157F	0264
C1157G	0264
C1157GN	0264
C1157H	0264
C1157J	0264
C1157K	0264
C1157L	0264
C1157M	0264
C1157OR	0264
C1157R	0264
C1157X	0264
C1157Y	0264
C1158(2S)	0470
C1159	0470
C1159(TRANS)	0007
C1159A	OEM
C1159B	OEM
C1160(2S)	0178
C1160-0	0178
C1160K(2S)	0178
C1160L(2S)	0178
C1161(2S)	0178
C1162(2S)	0558
C1162A(2S)	0558
C1162B(2S)	0558
C1162C(2S)	0558
C1162C(JAPAN)	0558
C1162CP(2S)	0558
C1162D(2S)	0558
C1162W	0558
C1162WBP(2S)	0558
C1162WT	0558
C1162WTB(2S)	0558
C1162WTC(2S)	0558
C1163	0275
C1164	0414
C1164-0	0414
C1164-R	0414
C1165	2030
C1165(TRANS)	0684
C1165A	OEM
C1165B	OEM
C1166	0155
C1166(TRANS)	0728
C1166-GR	0728
C1166-0	0728
C1166-R	0728
C1166-Y	0728
C1166A	OEM
C1166A(TRANS)	0728
C1166B	OEM
C1166B(TRANS)	0728
C1166C	0728
C1166E	0728
C1166F	0728
C1166G	0728
C1166GN	0728
C1166H	0728
C1166K	0728
C1166L	0728
C1166M	0728
C1166O(2S)	0728
C1166OR	0728
C1166U	0728
C1166Y(2S)	0728
C1167(2S)	0309
C1168(2S)	0142
C1168X(2S)	0142
C1169	6586
C1169(TRANS)	0626
C1169A	OEM
C1169B	OEM
C1170(2S)	1142
C1170-OR	1142
C1170A(2S)	1142
C1170B(2S)	1142
C1170BFA-2	1142
C1170C	1142
C1170D	1142
C1170E	1142
C1170F	1142
C1170FA-2	1142
C1170G	1142
C1170GN	1142
C1170H	1142
C1170J	1142
C1170K	1142
C1170L	1142
C1170M	1142
C1170OR	1142
C1170R	1142
C1170X	1142
C1170Y	1142
C1171(2S)	0065
C1172(2S)	0309
C1172A(2S)	0309
C1172B(2S)	0309
C1172C	0309
C1172D	0309
C1172E	0309
C1172F	0309
C1172G	0309
C1172GN	0309
C1172H	0309
C1172J	0309
C1172K	0309
C1172L	0309
C1172M	0309
C1172R	0309
C1172X	0309
C1172Y	0309
C1173(2S)	0042
C1173-0(2S)	0042
C1173-B	0042
C1173-C	0042
C1173-GR(2S)	0042
C1173-O(2S)	0042
C1173-R(2S)	0042
C1173-Y(2S)	0042
C1173A	0042
C1173B	0042
C1173GR	0042
C1173R(2S)	0042
C1173X(2S)	0042
C1173XO	0042
C1173XY	0042
C1173Y	0042
C1174(2S)	0309
C1174-OR	0309
C1174A	0309
C1174B	0309
C1174C	0309
C1174D	0309
C1174E	0309
C1174F	0309
C1174G	0309
C1174GN	0309
C1174H	0309
C1174J	0309
C1174K	0309
C1174L	0309
C1174M	0309
C1174OR	0309
C1174R	0309
C1174X	0309
C1174Y	0309
C1175(2S)	0191
C1175C(2S)	0191
C1175CTV	0191
C1175D(2S)	0191
C1175E(2S)	0191
C1175F(2S)	0191
C1176	2156
C1177	1189
C1178A	1966
C1180	0007
C1182	0007
C1182B(2S)	0007
C1182C(2S)	0007
C1182D(2S)	0007
C1184(2S)	0003
C1184A(2S)	0003
C1184B(2S)	0003
C1184C(2S)	0003
C1184D(2S)	0003
C1184E(2S)	0003

If replacement code is OEM, contact original manufacturer for replacement.

327

DEVICE TYPE	REPL CODE
C1185(2S)	0074
C1185A(2S)	0074
C1185B(2S)	0074
C1185C(2S)	0074
C1185K(2S)	0074
C1185L(2S)	0074
C1185M(2S)	0074
C1187(2S)	0224
C1187R(KOREA)	0224
C1188	0224
C1189	0224
C1189L	0224
C1190	1224
C1195(2S)	0103
C1195A	0103
C1195B	0103
C1195C	0103
C1195D	0103
C1195E	0103
C1195F	0103
C1195FA-1	0103
C1195FA-5	0103
C1195G	0103
C1195GN	0103
C1195GR	0103
C1195H	0103
C1195J	0103
C1195K	0103
C1195L	0103
C1195M	0103
C1195O	0103
C1195OR	0103
C1195R	0103
C1195X	0103
C1195Y	0103
C1199	0414
C1204(2S)	0155
C1204B(2S)	5897
C1204C(2S)	0155
C1204D(2S)	0155
C1205(2S)	2169
C1205A(2S)	2169
C1205B(2S)	2169
C1205C(2S)	2169
C1206	0086
C1206B	0086
C1209(2S)	0076
C1209C(2S)	0076
C1209D	0076
C1209E	0076
C1210(2S)	0945
C1210Y	0945
C1211(2S)	0155
C1212(2S)	0558
C1212A(2S)	0558
C1212AB(2S)	0558
C1212ABWT	0558
C1212AC(2S)	0558
C1212ACWT	0558
C1212B(2S)	0558
C1212C(2S)	0558
C1213	OEM
C1213(2S)	0191
C1213-OR	0191
C1213A	0191
C1213A(2S)	0191
C1213A(JAPAN)	0191
C1213AA(2S)	0191
C1213AB(2S)	0191
C1213AC	0191
C1213AC(2S)	0191
C1213AD(2S)	0191
C1213AK(2S)	0191
C1213AKB(2S)	0191
C1213AKC(2S)	0191
C1213AKD(2S)	0191
C1213B(2S)	0191
C1213BC(2S)	0191
C1213C	0191
C1213C(2S)	0191
C1213C(JAPAN)	0191
C1213CD(2S)	0191
C1213D(2S)	0191
C1213D-24	0191
C1213E	0191
C1213F	0191
C1213G	0191
C1213GN	0191
C1213H	0191
C1213J	0191
C1213K	0191
C1213L	0191
C1213M	0191
C1213OR	0191
C1213Q	0191
C1213X	0191
C1213Y	0191
C1214(2S)	0155
C1214A(2S)	0155
C1214B(2S)	0155
C1214C(2S)	0155
C1214D(2S)	0155
C1215(2S)	0127
C1215C	0127
C1215D	0127
C1215E	0127
C1215F	0127
C1215G	0127
C1215GN	0127
C1215H	0127
C1215J	0127
C1215K	0127
C1215L	0127
C1215M	0127
C1215OR	0127
C1215R	0127
C1215X	0127
C1215Y	0127
C1216	0224
C1217(2S)	0283
C1218(2S)	0086
C1219	0155
C1220	0155
C1220(TRANS)	0155
C1220-003	0155
C1220A	OEM
C1220A(TRANS)	0155
C1220AP	0155
C1220AQ	0155
C1220AR	0155
C1220B	OEM
C1220E(2S)	0155
C1220P	0155
C1220Q	0155
C1220R	0155
C1221	OEM
C1221A	OEM
C1221B	OEM
C1222	0111
C1222(TRANS)	2176
C1222A	0111
C1222A(TRANS)	2176
C1222B	0111
C1222B(TRANS)	2176
C1222C(2S)	2176
C1222D(2S)	2176
C1222E	2176
C1222H	2176
C1222U	2176
C1223	0414
C1224	0334
C1225	OEM
C1225A	OEM
C1225B	OEM
C1226	0219
C1226(TRANS)	0219
C1226-O(2S)	0219
C1226A	0219
C1226A(TRANS)	0219
C1226AC(2S)	0219
C1226ACF	0219
C1226AF	0219
C1226AP(2S)	0219
C1226AQ(2S)	0219
C1226AR	0219
C1226AR(2S)	0219
C1226ARL	0219
C1226B	0219
C1226B(TRANS)	0219
C1226BL	0219
C1226C(2S)	0219
C1226CF(2S)	0219
C1226D	0219
C1226E	0219
C1226F(2S)	0219
C1226G	0219
C1226H	0219
C1226L	0219
C1226OR	0219
C1226P(2S)	0219
C1226Q(2S)	0219
C1226R(2S)	0219
C1226RL	0219
C1226RLP	0219
C1226RLQ	0219
C1226RLR	0219
C1226Y	0219
C1227	0074
C1228	1955
C1228HA	OEM
C1229	1955
C1229(TRANS)	0168
C1229A	OEM
C1229B	OEM
C1229Q	0168
C1229R	0168
C1230	1955
C1231	0855
C1235	0142
C1235A	0142
C1235AL	0142
C1235AM	0142
C1235G	0142
C1236	0224
C1237(2S)	0930
C1237E(2S)	0930
C1239	1897
C1240	0224
C1241	1189
C1241A	1189
C1243(2S)	2005
C1243-24(2S)	2005
C1243C1(2S)	2005
C1243C2(2S)	2005
C1243D1(2S)	2005
C1243D2(2S)	2005
C1244(2S)	0079
C1246	0155
C1246A	0155
C1246R	0155
C1246S	0155
C1246T	0155
C1247	0155
C1247A	0155
C1247AF	0155
C1252	2194
C1252H2	2254
C1253	0414
C1253H2	1594
C1254	0007
C1256	2198
C1257	2156
C1258	1224
C1259	1963
C1260(2S)	0259
C1266	0086
C1267	2156
C1274	0016
C1275	0259
C1276	0111
C1277	0320
C1278(2S)	0855
C1278S(2S)	0855
C1279(2S)	0855
C1279S(2S)	0855
C1280(2S)	0396
C1280A(2S)	0396
C1280AS(2S)	0396
C1280S(2S)	0396
C1281	0079
C1282	0320
C1283	0079
C1285	0155
C1290	2214
C1292	0637
C1293	1060
C1293A	1060
C1293B(2S)	1060
C1293C	1060
C1293D	1060
C1295(2S)	1142
C1295-O	1142
C1295-O(2S)	1142
C1296	0065
C1298	1963
C1300	0065
C1303(2S)	1854
C1304(2S)	1496
C1306(2S)	0833
C1306A	0833
C1306I(2S)	0833
C1306K	0833
C1307(2S)	0830
C1307-1	0830
C1308(2S)	0309
C1308K(2S)	0309
C1308L	0309
C1308N	0309
C1309(2S)	0065
C1310	0284
C1311	0284
C1312(2S)	1212
C1312A	1212
C1312BC	1212
C1312C	1212
C1312D	1212
C1312E	1212
C1312F(2S)	1212
C1312G(2S)	1212
C1312GN	1212
C1312H(2S)	1212
C1312J	1212
C1312K	1212
C1312L	1212
C1312M	1212
C1312OR	1212
C1312R	1212
C1312X	1212
C1312Y(2S)	1212
C1313(2S)	0111
C1313B	0111
C1313Y(2S)	0111
C1314	1963
C1315	0233
C1316(2S)	2230
C1316-3	2230
C1317(2S)	0155
C1317-OR	0155
C1317-R	0155
C1317A	0155
C1317BC	0155
C1317C	0155
C1317E	0155
C1317G	0155
C1317GR	0155
C1317L	0155
C1317NC	0155
C1317OR	0155
C1317Q(2S)	0155
C1317R(2S)	0155
C1317S(2S)	0155
C1317T(2S)	0155
C1317V	0155
C1317Y	0155
C1318(2S)	0155
C1318B	0155
C1318C(2S)	0155
C1318E	0155
C1318F	0155
C1318G	0155
C1318GN	0155
C1318H	0155
C1318J	0155
C1318K	0155
C1318L	0155
C1318M	0155
C1318P	0155
C1318PR	0155
C1318Q(2S)	0155
C1318QP	0155
C1318QR	0155
C1318R(2S)	0155
C1318Y	0155
C1319	0007
C1319C	0007
C1320	0224
C1320A	0224
C1320B	0224
C1320C	0224
C1320D	0224
C1320E	0224
C1320F	0224
C1320G	0224
C1320GN	0224
C1320H	0224
C1320J	0224
C1320K	0224
C1320L	0224
C1320M	0224
C1320OR	0224
C1320R	0224
C1320X	0224
C1320Y	0224
C1321	0007
C1321Q2	0007
C1321Q3	0007
C1321Q4	0007
C1321Q5	0007
C1322	0177
C1324	0414
C1324C	0414
C1325(2S)	0885
C1325A(2S)	0885
C1325AK	0885
C1325AL	0885
C1326	0488
C1327(2S)	1212
C1327FS(2S)	1212
C1327R	1212
C1327S	1212
C1327T	1212
C1327TU	1212
C1327TV	1212
C1327U(2S)	1212
C1328(2S)	0111
C1328T(2S)	0111
C1328U(2S)	0111
C1330	0218
C1330(TRANS)	0218
C1330A	0218
C1330B	0218
C1330P	1797
C1331	2503
C1331(TRANS)	0007
C1331A	OEM
C1331B	OEM
C1332	2398
C1332A	OEM
C1332B	OEM
C1335	0155
C1335(TRANS)	1212
C1335-OR	1212
C1335A	0111
C1335A(TRANS)	1212
C1335B	0111
C1335B(TRANS)	1212
C1335C(2S)	1212
C1335D(2S)	1212
C1335E(2S)	1212
C1335F(2S)	1212
C1335G	1212
C1335GN	1212
C1335H	1212
C1335J	1212
C1335K	1212
C1335L	1212
C1335M	1212
C1335OR	1212
C1335R	1212
C1335X	1212
C1335Y	1212
C1336	OEM
C1336(TRANS)	0144
C1336A	OEM
C1336B	OEM
C1336JK	0144
C1337	1410
C1339	OEM
C1339A	OEM
C1339B	OEM
C1340	2156
C1342(2S)	0127
C1342-OR	0127
C1342A(2S)	0127
C1342B(2S)	0127
C1342C(2S)	0127
C1342D	0127
C1342E	0127
C1342F	0127
C1342G	0127
C1342GN	0127
C1342J	0127
C1342K	0127
C1342L	0127
C1342M	0127
C1342OR	0127
C1342R	0127
C1342X	0127
C1342Y	0127
C1343(2S)	0171
C1343-05	0171
C1343B(2S)	0171
C1343BL	0171
C1343D	0171
C1343E	0171
C1343F	0171
C1343G	0171
C1343GN	0171
C1343G-R	0171
C1343GR	0171
C1343H(2S)	0171
C1343J	0171
C1343K	0171
C1343L	0171
C1343M	0171
C1343O	0171
C1343OR	0171
C1343R	0171
C1343X	0171
C1343Y	0171
C1344(2S)	0547
C1344C(2S)	0547
C1344D(2S)	0547
C1344E(2S)	0547
C1344F(2S)	0547
C1345(2S)	0547
C1345C(2S)	0547
C1345D	0547
C1345E	0547
C1345F(2S)	0547
C1345KD	0547
C1345KE	0547
C1345KF	0547
C1346(2S)	0218
C1346R(2S)	0218
C1346S(2S)	0218
C1347(2S)	0218
C1347A	0218
C1347B	0218
C1347C	0218
C1347D	0218
C1347F	0218
C1347G	0218
C1347L	0218
C1347Q(2S)	0218
C1347R(2S)	0218
C1347RQ	0218
C1347X	0218
C1347Y	0218
C1348(2S)	0223
C1348-1	0223
C1348-2	0223
C1348-3	0223
C1349	0855
C1351	0626
C1352	0079
C1353	0626
C1353H2	1594
C1356C	OEM
C1356C2	0859
C1358(2S)	2040
C1358A	2040
C1358K(2S)	2040
C1358K1	2040
C1358K2	2040
C1358K3	2040
C1358L	2040
C1358M	2040
C1359(2S)	0151
C1359A(2S)	0151
C1359B(2S)	0151
C1359BC	0151
C1359C(2S)	0151
C1359Q	0151
C1360	1653
C1360(2S)	1653
C1360A	1653
C1361(2S)	0155
C1362(2S)	0155
C1362(47)	0155
C1363(2S)	0076
C1363CA	0678
C1364(2S)	0076
C1364-6	0076
C1364-8	0076
C1364-OR	0076
C1364A(2S)	0076
C1364B	0076
C1364C	0076
C1364D	0076
C1364E	0076
C1364H	0076
C1364K	0076
C1364L	0076
C1364M	0076
C1364OR	0076
C1364P	0284
C1364R	0076
C1364X	0076
C1364Y	0076
C1365	0414
C1366C2	2511
C1367(2S)	0003
C1367A(2S)	0003
C1368(2S)	1779
C1368B	1779
C1368C(2S)	1779
C1368D(2S)	1779
C1372	0155
C1372Y(2S)	0155
C1373	0111
C1373HA	2015
C1374	2257
C1374H	2257
C1375	0111
C1375H	0111
C1376	0079
C1376H	0079
C1377(2S)	0830
C1380	0016
C1380-BL	0016
C1380-GR	0016
C1380A	0016
C1380A-BL	0016
C1380A-GR	0016
C1381	1581
C1382(2S)	0558
C1382-0(2S)	0558
C1382-O	0558
C1382-Y	0558
C1383	0018
C1383-QR	0018
C1383NC	0018
C1383P(2S)	0018
C1383Q	0018
C1383Q(2S)	0018
C1383R(2S)	0018
C1383R/494	0590
C1383RS	0018
C1383S	0018
C1383S(2S)	0018
C1383X(2S)	0018
C1384	0018
C1384(2S)	0018
C1384-OR	0018
C1384A	0018
C1384B	0018
C1384C	0018
C1384D	0018
C1384E	0018
C1384F	0018
C1384G	0018
C1384GN	0018
C1384H	0018
C1384J	0018
C1384K	0018
C1384L	0018
C1384M	0018
C1384NC	0018
C1384OR	0018
C1384Q(2S)	0018
C1384R	0018
C1384R(2S)	0018
C1384R(JAPAN)	0018
C1384S	0018
C1384S(2S)	0018
C1384X	0018
C1384Y	0018
C1385	0016
C1385H	0016
C1386	0086
C1386H	0086
C1387	0414
C1388	0086
C1390	0592
C1390A	0127
C1390IW	0592
C1390JX	0592
C1390W(2S)	0592
C1390WH(2S)	0592
C1390WX(2S)	0592
C1390X(2S)	0592
C1390XK(2S)	0592
C1390YM(2S)	0592
C1391(2S)	0142
C1391VL(2S)	0142
C1393(2S)	0224
C1393CA	OEM
C1393K	0224
C1393L	0224
C1393M	0224
C1394(2S)	0224
C1395	0007
C1396(2S)	0007
C1398(2S)	0042
C1398P	0042
C1398Q(2S)	0042
C1399	0558
C1399E	0558
C1400	0525
C1402(2S)	0177
C1403	0538
C1403A	0538
C1406	2271
C1406B40C3700-2200	OEM
C1406HA	4009
C1406M	OEM
C1406Q	2271
C1407(2S)	2271
C1407B	2271
C1407Q	2271
C1407X	2271
C1409	0388
C1409A	0388
C1409AA	0388
C1409AB	0388
C1409AC	0388
C1409B	0388
C1409C	0388
C1410	0388
C1410A	0388
C1410AA	0388
C1410AB	0388
C1410AC	0388
C1410B	0388
C1410C	0388
C1411	0016
C1412	0855
C1412B80C3700-2200	OEM
C1412M	OEM
C1413(2S)	0065
C1413A(2S)	0065
C1413AH	0065
C1413B	0065
C1413C	0065
C1413D	0065
C1413E	0065
C1413F	0065
C1413G	0065
C1413GN	0065
C1413K	0065
C1413L	0065
C1413R	0065
C1413X	0065
C1413Y	0065
C1415	1077
C1415-05	1077
C1416(2S)	0016
C1416A	0016
C1417(2S)	0127
C1417C	0127
C1417D(1)	0127
C1417D(U)	0127
C1417F(2S)	0127
C1417V(2S)	0127
C1417VF	0127
C1417VW(2S)	0127
C1417W(2S)	0127
C1418(2S)	0042
C1419(2S)	2276
C1419-C	2276
C1419B(2S)	2276
C1419C(2S)	2276
C1424(2S)	0259
C1426	0626
C1427	0224
C1428	0111
C1429(2S)	0546
C1429-1(2S)	0546
C1429-2(2S)	0546
C1430	0617
C1431	1021
C1431-1	1021
C1431-2	1021
C1433	0637
C1434	1841
C1436	1841
C1437	0279
C1437-NC	0261
C1438	0079
C1439	0079
C1440	1841
C1441	1841
C1444	0419
C1445	0419
C1446(2S)	0638
C1446-O	0638
C1446LB(2S)	0638
C1446P	0638
C1446Q(2S)	0638
C1447	0638
C1447(JAPAN)	0638
C1447-0(2S)	0638
C1447-O	0638
C1447FA-2	0638
C1447GL	0638
C1447GL3	0638
C1448(2S)	1274
C1448A(2S)	1274
C1448C	1274
C1448LB	1274
C1449(2S)	0161
C1449CB	0161
C1449M	0161
C1450	1021
C1450S(2S)	1021
C1451	0710
C1452	0710
C1453	0111
C1454	0220
C1454-0	0220
C1454-O	0220
C1456	0142

If replacement code is OEM, contact original manufacturer for replacement.

DEVICE TYPE	REPL CODE
C1457	0855
C1463	0637
C1464	0626
C1466	0065
C1467	0065
C1468	1955
C1469	0359
C1469A	0359
C1470	OEM
C1470A	OEM
C1470B	OEM
C1471	OEM
C1471A	OEM
C1471B	OEM
C1472	6616
C1472(TRANS)	0396
C1472A	OEM
C1472B	OEM
C1472K(2S)	0396
C1472KA	0396
C1472KB	0396
C1473	0261
C1473-RNC	0261
C1473A	0261
C1473AH	0261
C1473AQ	0261
C1473AR	0261
C1473CN	0261
C1473NC	0261
C1473NE	0261
C1473P	0261
C1473Q	0261
C1473Q(JAPAN)	0261
C1473QNC	0261
C1473R	0261
C1473R(JAPAN)	0261
C1473RNC	0261
C1474(2S)	0018
C1474-3(2S)	0018
C1474-4(2S)	0018
C1474HA	5162
C1474J	0018
C1474S	0018
C1475	1967
C1475(13)	1967
C1475(TRANS)	1967
C1475-13	1967
C1475A	1967
C1475A(TRANS)	1967
C1475B	OEM
C1475D	1967
C1475H	1967
C1475K	1967
C1476	OEM
C1476A	OEM
C1476B	OEM
C1477(2S)	0359
C1478	0224
C1478A	0224
C1479	0414
C1480CA	3331
C1481CA	3830
C1485	0710
C1490	2156
C1490HA	4470
C1491	1189
C1493	0710
C1493NC	0710
C1493P4	0710
C1494	1963
C1500	OEM
C1501(2S)	0275
C1501P	0275
C1501Q(2S)	0275
C1501R(2S)	0275
C1502L	0168
C1504	2085
C1505(1)	0949
C1505(1)K	0949
C1505(1)L	0949
C1505(2S)	0949
C1505-1	0949
C1505I(2S)	0949
C1505K(2S)	0949
C1505L(2S)	0949
C1505LA(2S)	0949
C1506(2S)	0168
C1506K	0168
C1506L	0168
C1506M	0168
C1507	0949
C1507(2S)	0949
C1507-K	0949
C1507-0	0949
C1507-0(KOREA)	0168
C1507-Y	0949
C1507H	0949
C1507J	0949
C1507K(2S)	0949
C1507L(2S)	0949
C1507L(JAPAN)	0949
C1507M(2S)	0949
C1507Y	0949
C1509(2S)	0320
C1509-0	0320
C1509NC	0320
C15090	0320
C1509P	0320
C1509Q(2S)	0320

DEVICE TYPE	REPL CODE
C1509Y	0320
C1510	OEM
C1513	0414
C1513HA	3130
C1514	1077
C1514(2S)	1077
C1514(JAPAN)	1077
C1514-05	1077
C1514-14	1077
C1514-15	1077
C1514BK	1077
C1514BVC	1077
C1514CS-CVC	1077
C1514CVC	1077
C1514VC	1077
C1515	0710
C1515AX	0710
C1515C	0710
C1515K	0710
C1516	1935
C1516K	1935
C1516K-B	1935
C1516KC	1935
C1517	1698
C1517AK	1698
C1517AKB	1698
C1517AKC	1698
C1518	0018
C1518NC	0018
C1519	0168
C1520(1)K(JAPAN)	0168
C1520(2S)	0168
C1520-1	0168
C1520-O(KOREA)	0168
C1520C	0168
C1520I(2S)	0168
C1520K(2S)	0168
C1520K-1	0168
C1520L(2S)	0168
C1520L-1	0168
C1520M(2S)	0168
C1520M-1	0168
C1521	2343
C1521K(2S)	2343
C1521L(2S)	2343
C1522	1077
C1530CA	OEM
C1537(2S)	0111
C1537-0	0111
C1537B(2S)	0111
C1538(2S)	0111
C1538S(2S)	0111
C1538SA(2S)	0111
C1539	0079
C1540	0079
C1541	0155
C1542(2S)	0111
C1543	0224
C1544	0079
C1545	0396
C1546	0396
C1547(2S)	0007
C1550	0275
C1550-1	0275
C1552	2366
C1553	0007
C1553A	0007
C1555A	OEM
C1556	0693
C1565	0558
C1566(2S)	0275
C1566F	0275
C1567	0558
C1567A	0558
C1567R	0558
C1568	1779
C1568-R	1779
C1568R	1779
C1569	0638
C1569(2S)	0638
C1569(KOREA)	1077
C1569-0(2S)	0638
C1569-0	0638
C1569BK	0638
C1569FA-1	0638
C1569FA-3	0638
C1569FA-5	0638
C1569K	0638
C1569LB	0638
C1569LBO	0638
C1569LBR(2S)	0638
C1569LBY(2S)	0638
C15690	0638
C1569R(2S)	0638
C1569Y	0638
C1570	0111
C1570FL	0111
C1570GL	0111
C1570HL	0111
C1570LH	0111
C1571	0111
C1571G	0111
C1571H	0111
C1571L	0111
C1573(2S)	0261
C1573(TO126)	0261
C1573A	0261
C1573AR	0261
C1573BR	0261

DEVICE TYPE	REPL CODE
C1573P(2S)	0261
C1573P(TO126)	0261
C1573PQ	0261
C1573PQ(TO126)	0261
C1573Q	0261
C1573Q(TO126)	0261
C1573QNC	0261
C1573R	0261
C1574	0103
C1576	0359
C1577	0359
C1577A	0359
C1578	0359
C1579	0359
C1580	0359
C1581	2296
C1582	2296
C1583	2395
C1583F	2395
C1583G	2395
C1583H	2395
C1584	0538
C1585	2398
C1585F	2398
C1585H	2398
C1586	2398
C1588(2S)	0414
C1589	2039
C1596	0079
C1601	0224
C1605A	1966
C1606	0555
C1607	0326
C1608	0626
C1610	0615
C1617	2420
C1618	2421
C1618B	2421
C1619	0861
C1619A	0861
C1621	0144
C1621-0	0144
C1621B2	0144
C1621B3	0144
C1621B4	0144
C1622	0007
C1622A	0007
C1622D6	0007
C1622D7	0007
C1622D8	0007
C1622O	0007
C1622Y	0007
C1623	0719
C1623L3	0719
C1623L4	0719
C1623L5	0719
C1623L6	0719
C1623L7	0719
C1624	0236
C1624-0	0236
C1624-Y	0236
C1625	0236
C1625-0	0236
C1625-0	0236
C1625-Y	0236
C1625Y	0236
C1625YLBGH	0236
C1625YLBGL1	0236
C1626	0236
C1626-0	0236
C1626-Y	0236
C1626Y	0236
C1627	0728
C1627-0	0728
C1627-0(JAPAN)	0728
C1627-Y	0728
C1627-YFA	0728
C1627A	0728
C1627AK	1376
C1627A-Y	0728
C1627AY	0728
C1627AY(KOREA)	1376
C1627Y	0728
C1627Y(JAPAN)	0728
C1628	0264
C1628-0	0264
C1628-Y	0264
C1629	0130
C1629A	0130
C1629AO	0130
C1629AR	0130
C1629M	0130
C1629R	0130
C1630	0233
C1631	0018
C1632	0284
C1633(2S)	2437
C1634	2440
C1635	0086
C1636	2441
C1637	0111
C1638	0414
C1639(2S)	0016
C1641	0016
C1641Q	0016
C1641R	0016
C1647	0111
C1647Q	0111
C1647RY	0111

DEVICE TYPE	REPL CODE
C1648(2S)	0111
C1648E	0111
C1648EF	0111
C1648SH	0111
C1652	2452
C1653	0855
C1653N2	0855
C1653N3	0855
C1653N4	0855
C1654	0855
C1654N5	0855
C1654N6	0855
C1654N7	0855
C1663	0264
C1663H	0264
C1664	0625
C1664A	0625
C1664O	0625
C1664OR	0625
C1664Q	0625
C1664R	0625
C1665	0259
C1666	0359
C1667(2S)	0103
C1668	1966
C1669	0388
C1669-0	0388
C1669-R	0388
C1669-Y	0388
C1670(2S)	2463
C1670H	2463
C1670J	2463
C1670JA	2463
C1670JD	2463
C1670JW	2463
C1672	2465
C1674	1060
C1674(2S)	1060
C1674-0	0144
C1674AL	1060
C1674K	1060
C1674K(2S)	1060
C1674L	1060
C1674L(2S)	1060
C1674L(JAPAN)	1060
C1674M(2S)	1060
C1674R(KOREA)	0144
C1675(2S)	0076
C1675B	0076
C1675K(2S)	0076
C1675K(JAPAN)	0076
C1675L(2S)	0076
C1675M(2S)	0076
C1676	1963
C1678(2S)	2475
C1678E	2475
C1679(2S)	0830
C1680	OEM
C1680A	OEM
C1680B	OEM
C1681	0525
C1681(TRANS)	1746
C1681-BL	1746
C1681-GR	1746
C1681A	OEM
C1681A(TRANS)	1746
C1681B	0111
C1681B(TRANS)	1746
C1681B6	1746
C1681BL(2S)	1746
C1681C	1746
C1681F	1746
C1681G	1746
C1681GN	1746
C1681GR	1746
C1681H	1746
C1681J	1746
C1681K	1746
C1681L	1746
C1681M	1746
C1681O	1746
C1681OR	1746
C1681R	1746
C1681V	1746
C1682	0111
C1682(TRANS)	0111
C1682-BL	0111
C1682-GR	0111
C1682A	OEM
C1682B	OEM
C1682V	0111
C1683	0388
C1683-0	0388
C1683-Q	0388
C1683A	0388
C1683LA(2S)	0388
C1683P(2S)	0388
C1683Q	0388
C1683R(2S)	0388
C1684(2S)	0155
C1684BL	0155
C1684K	0155
C1684P	0155
C1684Q	0155
C1684R	0155
C1684S	0155
C1684T	0155
C1685	0284
C1685(TRANS)	0284

DEVICE TYPE	REPL CODE
C1685-0	0284
C1685-P	0284
C1685-Q	0284
C1685-R	0284
C1685A	OEM
C1685B	OEM
C1685C	0284
C1685CR	0284
C1685P(2S)	0284
C1685Q(2S)	0284
C1685Q(JAPAN)	0284
C1685QR	0284
C1685S(2S)	0284
C1685T	0284
C1686(2S)	0224
C1686B	0224
C1686V	0224
C1687(2S)	0224
C1688(2S)	0016
C1689	2485
C1706H	0710
C1707AH	0016
C1707AHB	0016
C1707H	0016
C1707HB	0016
C1707HC	0016
C1707HD	0016
C1708	0525
C1708A	0525
C1709	0079
C1717	0626
C1719	0855
C1720	0855
C1721	0018
C1722	1077
C1722BK	1077
C1722BKS	1077
C1722S	1077
C1723	1077
C1723-02	1077
C1723A	1077
C1724	0626
C1727	2503
C1728(2S)	1165
C1728-3(2S)	1165
C1728D(2S)	1165
C1728F	1165
C1728H	1165
C1729	2504
C1730	0127
C1730K	0127
C1730L	0127
C1734	0016
C1734H	0016
C1735	0284
C1739(2S)	0016
C1740	0151
C1740C	0151
C1740D	0151
C1740E(JAPAN)	0151
C1740L	0151
C1740P	0151
C1740Q	0151
C1740QH	0151
C1740QJ	0151
C1740QR	0151
C1740R	0151
C1740R(JAPAN)	0151
C1740RE	0151
C1740RH	0151
C1740RL	0151
C1740RM	0151
C1740RN(JAPAN)	0151
C1740RS	0151
C1740RZ	0151
C1740S	0151
C1740S(JAPAN)	0151
C1740SEJ	0151
C1740SRJ(JAPAN)	0151
C1740SRS	0151
C1740SSJ	0151
C1740SSK	0151
C1741	1505
C1746A	0079
C1747	2503
C1748	0187
C1749	1077
C1749XD	1077
C1752	0710
C1753	0710
C1755(2S)	1077
C1755C(2S)	1077
C1755D	1077
C1756(2S)	0638
C1756-0	0638
C1756C(2S)	0638
C1756D(2S)	0638
C1756D(JAPAN)	0638
C1756E	0638
C1756K(2S)	0638
C1756M	0638
C1757(2S)	1077
C1758	0283
C1760(2S)	1935
C1760-2	1935
C1760-3(2S)	1935
C1760H	1935
C1760K	1935
C1761	1935

DEVICE TYPE	REPL CODE
C1761KJ	1935
C1761LE	1935
C1761MC	1935
C1764	2523
C1765	0626
C1766	0376
C1766B	0376
C1768	2526
C1769	2528
C1770	0079
C1771	0016
C1773	2534
C1774	0079
C1775	0525
C1775A	0525
C1775AE	0525
C1775E	0525
C1775F	0525
C1776	0079
C1777	2534
C1778	0224
C1779	0224
C1780	0086
C1781	0016
C1781H	0016
C1781HA	0016
C1781HB	0016
C1781HC	0016
C1782	0861
C1783	0861
C1784	0538
C1785	2398
C1786	2398
C1787	1260
C1788	0155
C1788R	0155
C1789	0007
C1790	0259
C1790JD	0259
C1791	0142
C1800	OEM
C1800A	OEM
C1800B	OEM
C1801	0144
C1801(TRANS)	0259
C1801A	OEM
C1801B	OEM
C1802	0144
C1802(TRANS)	0224
C1802A	OEM
C1802B	OEM
C1807	0488
C1810	2575
C1810HU	2575
C1810J	2575
C1810JL	2575
C1811	0261
C1811-1	0261
C1811-2	0261
C1811KC	0261
C1812	OEM
C1813	0016
C1815	0076
C1815-0	0076
C1815-BL	0076
C1815-GR	0076
C1815-GRFA	0076
C1815-O	0076
C1815-O(JAPAN)	0076
C1815-O(KOREA)	0284
C1815-OFA	0076
C1815-Y	0076
C1815-YFA	0076
C1815BL	0076
C1815BL(KOREA)	0076
C1815FA	0076
C1815G	0076
C1815GR	0076
C1815GR(JAPAN)	0076
C1815GR(KOREA)	0076
C1815O	0076
C1815Y	0076
C1815Y(JAPAN)	0076
C1815Y(KOREA)	0076
C1816(2S)	2475
C1816H	2475
C1816HL	2475
C1817	0830
C1818	0177
C1819	0638
C1819M	0638
C1819ML	0638
C1819MR	0638
C1820	0233
C1826	0419
C1826(JAPAN)	0419
C1826-0	0419
C1826-O	0419
C1826-Y	0419
C1826D	0419
C1826G	0419
C1826O	0419
C1826P	0419
C1826Q	0419
C1826R	0419
C1826Y	0419
C1827	0236
C1828(2S)	2085
C1828B	2085

DEVICE TYPE	REPL CODE
C1828R	2085
C1829	2596
C1829C	2596
C1830	0538
C1831	0556
C1832	2602
C1833	0284
C1834	0284
C1836	0930
C1840	0111
C1840E	0111
C1840F	0111
C1840P	0111
C1841	0525
C1841E	0525
C1841F	0525
C1841P	0525
C1841U	0525
C1842	0111
C1842E	0111
C1843	0111
C1844	0111
C1845	0525
C1845E	0525
C1845Q	0525
C1845R	0525
C1845S	0525
C1846	0781
C1846-R	0781
C1846-S	0781
C1846B	0781
C1846P	0781
C1846Q	0781
C1846QRS	0781
C1846R	0781
C1846S	0781
C1847	0558
C1847-0	0558
C1847A	0558
C1847B	0558
C1847C	0558
C1847D	0558
C1847E	0558
C1847F	0558
C1847G	0558
C1847GN	0558
C1847LG	0558
C1847P	0558
C1847Q	0558
C1847R	0558
C1847V	0558
C1847VG	0558
C1847VQ	0558
C1847VR	0558
C1847X	0558
C1847Y	0558
C1848	0219
C1848P	0219
C1848Q	0219
C1848R	0219
C1848V	0219
C1849	0079
C1850	0079
C1851	0079
C1852	0079
C1853	1211
C1853B	1211
C1853C	1211
C1854	0284
C1854C	0284
C1854R	0284
C1854S	0284
C1855	0224
C1856	0224
C1856-02	0224
C1856M	0224
C1857	0079
C1859	0626
C1860	2626
C1861	2626
C1862	0187
C1864	0424
C1865	0723
C1866	0615
C1867	1955
C1868	1955
C1869	0615
C1870	2398
C1870CA-001	OEM
C1870CA-002	OEM
C1870CA-003	OEM
C1871A	1955
C1871CU	OEM
C1875	2636
C1875K	2636
C1875L	2636
C1875R	2636
C1881K	1203
C1885	0261
C1886	0259
C1887	0259
C1888	0626
C1890	0525
C1890A	0525
C1890AD	0525
C1890AD(JAPAN)	0525
C1890A-E	0525
C1890AE	0525
C1890AE(JAPAN)	0525

If replacement code is OEM, contact original manufacturer for replacement.

DEVICE TYPE	REPL CODE
C1890AF	0525
C1890D	0525
C1890E	0525
C1890F	0525
C1891	0223
C1892	2636
C1893	2643
C1893-O	2643
C1893FA-1	2643
C1894	0309
C1894K	0309
C1894N	0309
C1895	0309
C1896	0309
C1897	0086
C1898	0008
C1899	0008
C1900	0525
C1903	0558
C1904	0558
C1905	0949
C1905(1)	0949
C1905H	0949
C1905HLB	0949
C1906	0127
C1906(JAPAN)	0127
C1907	0127
C1908	2654
C1908E(2S)	2654
C1908H	2654
C1909(2S)	0930
C1909K	0930
C1909R	0930
C1913	0388
C1913A	0388
C1913AR	0388
C1914	0525
C1914A	0525
C1915	0525
C1919	0127
C1919C	0127
C1921	0261
C1921(JAPAN)	0261
C1921-03	0261
C1922	2643
C1923	2666
C1923-0	2666
C1923-O	2666
C1923A	2666
C1923BN	2666
C1923Y	2666
C1928	1967
C1929	0168
C1929LB	0168
C1929Q	0168
C1929R	0168
C1940	0079
C1941	1317
C1941-OY	1317
C1941K	1317
C1941L	1317
C1941M	1317
C1941M(JAPAN)	1317
C1942	2636
C1945	0830
C1946	OEM
C1946(TRANS)	2504
C1946A	OEM
C1946A(TRANS)	2504
C1946B	OEM
C1947	2677
C1949	OEM
C1949A	OEM
C1949B	OEM
C1951	1376
C1953	0558
C1954	0127
C1955	2677
C1956	0626
C1957(2S)	2684
C1957K	2684
C1959	0284
C1959-0	0284
C1959-O(KOREA)	0284
C1959-Y	0284
C1959-YFA	0284
C1959GR	0284
C1959Y	0284
C1959Y(JAPAN)	0284
C1959Y(KOREA)	0284
C1960	0284
C1962	0334
C1962-0	0334
C1963	1935
C1963-1	1935
C1963Y	1935
C1964(2S)	2475
C1964D	2475
C1965	2677
C1965A	2677
C1969	0830
C1969B	0830
C1969BH	0830
C1969H	0830
C1970	2693
C1971	2693
C1972	2694
C1973(2S)	0018
C1974(2S)	0830

DEVICE TYPE	REPL CODE
C1974C	0830
C1975(2S)	0930
C1976	2699
C1978	2693
C1980	1260
C1980S	1260
C1980T	1260
C1982	0264
C1983	2047
C1983-0	2047
C1983Q	2047
C1983R	2047
C1983Y	2047
C1984	1203
C1985	0419
C1985(JAPAN)	0419
C1986	0477
C1987	0424
C1989	0007
C1990	0127
C1990B	0127
C1991	0079
C1992	0016
C1993	0016
C1994	0016
C1995	0016
C1996	0016
C1997	0016
C1998	0079
C1999	0111
C2000	0155
C2000(2S)	0284
C2000L	0284
C2001	1505
C2001-L	1505
C2001A	0284
C2001F	1505
C2001G	1505
C2001I	1505
C2001K	1505
C2001K(JAPAN)	1505
C2001L	1505
C2001L1	1505
C2001M	1505
C2001P	OEM
C2001P(HEP)	2840
C2002	0945
C2002K	0945
C2002L	0945
C2002L(JAPAN)	0945
C2002M	0945
C2002P	OEM
C2003	0284
C2003K	0284
C2003P	OEM
C2004P	OEM
C2005P	3395
C2006G	OEM
C2007G	1354
C2008G	OEM
C2009	0224
C2009G	OEM
C2009G(HEP)	OEM
C2010G	OEM
C2011L	0224
C2012	2730
C2014	1376
C2017	1841
C2018	1841
C2020	0930
C2021	1132
C2021-Q	1132
C2021L	1132
C2021Q	1132
C2021Q(JAPAN)	1132
C2021R	1132
C2021R(JAPAN)	1132
C2021RJ	1132
C2021RL(JAPAN)	1132
C2021RM(JAPAN)	1132
C2021S	1132
C2021ST(JAPAN)	1132
C2021Y	1132
C2022	0949
C2023	2589
C2024	1581
C2025	0259
C2026	1795
C2026K	1795
C2027	0309
C2028	0884
C2028B	0884
C2028B20	0884
C2028D	0884
C2028L	0884
C2029	0930
C2029-1	0930
C2029-3	0930
C2029B	0930
C2029B10	0930
C2029C	0930
C2034	2742
C2035	0079
C2036	0558
C2037	2743
C2043	0830
C2053	0079
C2055	0079
C2056	2677

DEVICE TYPE	REPL CODE
C2057	0224
C2057-C	0224
C2057C	0224
C2057D	0224
C2057E	0224
C2057E1	0224
C2057F	0224
C2058S	0284
C2060	0018
C2060K	0018
C2060Q	0018
C2060Q(JAPAN)	0018
C2060R	0018
C2060R(JAPAN)	0018
C2061	0320
C2063	0577
C2063P	0577
C2067	1967
C2068	0638
C2068-GS-1	0638
C2068BKLB	0638
C2068FA-1	0638
C2068GS-1	0638
C2068I	0638
C2068LB	0638
C2068LBBK	0638
C2069	0016
C2070	0016
C2071	0275
C2073	1274
C2073(JAPAN)	1274
C2073(KOREA)	0388
C2073-4(JAPAN)	1274
C2073-B	1274
C2073-C	1274
C2073-LBGL2	1274
C2073-Z	1274
C2073A	1274
C2073AD	1274
C2073AD(JAPAN)	1274
C2073AE	1274
C2073B	1274
C2073BGS2	1274
C2073BGSC	1274
C2073C	1274
C2073D	1274
C2073E	1274
C2073FA-4	1274
C2073GL2	1274
C2073J	1274
C2073L	1274
C2073LB	1274
C2073LBGL	1274
C2073LBGL2	1274
C2073LBGS2	1274
C2073R	1274
C2073RD	1274
C2073RE	1274
C2073SO	1274
C2073T	1274
C2073Y	1274
C2074	1973
C2074C	1973
C2074Y	1973
C2075	2475
C2076	2787
C2076B	2787
C2076C	2787
C2076CB	2787
C2076CD	2787
C2076D	2787
C2078	2475
C2079	1581
C2079E	1581
C2080	0161
C2081	2794
C2085	0638
C2085P	0638
C2085Q	0638
C2086	2798
C2087	0079
C2088	1553
C2091	1581
C2092	0930
C2093	0830
C2094	2504
C2098	0830
C2099	2808
C2100	2296
C2101	3534
C2101(2S)	1189
C2101-1	OEM
C2101-2	OEM
C2101A	OEM
C2101A-2	OEM
C2101A-4	OEM
C2102	1224
C2102(2S)	1224
C2102-2	OEM
C2102A	4886
C2102A2	OEM
C2102A4	OEM
C2102A6	OEM
C2103	1963
C2103A	1963
C2107	0079
C2107G3	0079
C2109	0079
C2110	0086

DEVICE TYPE	REPL CODE
C2111	OEM
C2111(2S)	0016
C2111-1	OEM
C2111-2	OEM
C2112	OEM
C2112-2	OEM
C2115	2817
C2117	2677
C2118	2677
C2120	0860
C2120-0	0860
C2120-O	0860
C2120-Y	0860
C2120B125C3000-1800	OEM
C2120FA	0860
C2120M	OEM
C2120Y	0860
C2120Y(JAPAN)	0860
C2120Y(KOREA)	0860
C2120YFA	0860
C2121	0359
C2122	0359
C2122A	0359
C2123	0065
C2124	2820
C2125	2820
C2126	0178
C2127	0538
C2127A	0538
C2129	1967
C2130	1967
C2135	2833
C2137	1955
C2138	0168
C2139	1841
C2140	0074
C2140B250C3000-1800	OEM
C2140M	OEM
C2141	0264
C2141-10	0264
C2141KC	0264
C2141KD	0264
C2141LC	0264
C2141M	0264
C2141NE	0264
C2143	2817
C2145	0693
C2146	0930
C2151	1841
C2153	0079
C2166	2475
C2167	1274
C2167-Y	1274
C2167L	OEM
C2167L-70	OEM
C2167Y	1274
C2168	1274
C2168-O	1274
C2168-Y	1274
C2168Y	1274
C2178	0388
C2178Y	0388
C2180	1963
C2180B500C3000-1800	OEM
C2180M	OEM
C2181	2857
C2182	2485
C2184	0830
C2188	2041
C2189	0615
C2190	0065
C2191	0359
C2193	0710
C2194	0546
C2195	0830
C2196	0626
C2197	1963
C2198	0625
C2199	0615
C2200	0723
C2206	2208
C2206B	2208
C2206B40C3700-2200	OEM
C2206C	2208
C2206N	OEM
C2206Q	2208
C2206R	2208
C2207	0830
C2209	0161
C2209R	0161
C2210	0224
C2212	0144
C2212A	0144
C2212B080C3700-2200	OEM
C2212N	OEM
C2213	0144
C2215	0224
C2216	2874
C2220B125C3700-2200	OEM
C2220N	OEM
C2221	1973
C2222	1973
C2224	0334
C2224A	0334
C2228	1317
C2228A	1317
C2228C	1317
C2228D	1317
C2228D(JAPAN)	1317

DEVICE TYPE	REPL CODE
C2228E	1317
C2228E(JAPAN)	1317
C2228F	1317
C2228K	1317
C2228M	1317
C2228Y	1317
C2229	0066
C2229(KOREA)	0261
C2229-0	0066
C2229-O	0066
C2229-O(JAPAN)	0066
C2229-O(KOREA)	0261
C2229-Y	0066
C2229D	0066
C2229E	0066
C2229M	0066
C2229O	0066
C2229Y	0066
C2229Y(JAPAN)	0066
C2229Y(KOREA)	0261
C2230	0261
C2230-Y	0261
C2230A	0261
C2230A(JAPAN)	0261
C2230AG	0261
C2230A-GR	0261
C2230AGR	0261
C2230AGR(JAPAN)	0261
C2230A-Y	0261
C2230AY	0261
C2230AY(JAPAN)	0261
C2230AY(KOREA)	0261
C2230AYG	0261
C2230G	0261
C2230GR	0261
C2230Y	0261
C2231	0168
C2231A	0168
C2231Y	0168
C2233	1530
C2234	1963
C2235	1376
C2236	2882
C2236-0	2882
C2236-O(JAPAN)	2882
C2236-Y	2882
C2236AY(KOREA)	1559
C2236Q	2882
C2236Y	2882
C2236Y(JAPAN)	2882
C2237	2504
C2238	2883
C2240	2118
C2240GL	2118
C2240GR	2118
C2241	1077
C2242	1077
C2242BK	1077
C2242GL2	1077
C2242LB	1077
C2242LBGL2	1077
C2243	2885
C2244	0074
C2245	0074
C2246	0359
C2251-0	0261
C2256	2398
C2258	0275
C2259	2896
C2259C	2896
C2259G	2896
C2260	0177
C2261	0177
C2262	0177
C2263	0111
C2264	1967
C2267H	0187
C2271	0261
C2271C	0261
C2271D	0261
C2271D(JAPAN)	0261
C2271E	0261
C2271E(JAPAN)	0261
C2271M	0261
C2271M(JAPAN)	0261
C2271N	0261
C2271Z	0261
C2274	0155
C2274E(JAPAN)	0155
C2274K	0155
C2275	1274
C2275A	1274
C2276	2911
C2277	0079
C2278	0283
C2279	0334
C2281	1189
C2290	2918
C2291	2919
C2292	2900
C2293	2900
C2297	0419
C2298	0161
C2298A	0161
C2298B	0161
C2304	1841
C2306	4315
C2306(2S)	1841
C2307	1498

DEVICE TYPE	REPL CODE
C2308	0155
C2308B	0155
C2308G	OEM
C2309	0111
C2309D	0111
C2309E	0111
C2309F	0111
C2310	0284
C2310-0	0261
C2311	0161
C2312	0830
C2314	1581
C2314D	1581
C2315	0419
C2315CA	OEM
C2317	0388
C2320	0151
C2320(JAPAN)	0151
C2320L	0151
C2320LE(ECB)	0079
C2321	0615
C2322	0615
C2323	0615
C2324K	2942
C2329	2675
C2330-0	0261
C2330AY(JAPAN)	0261
C2330Y	0261
C2331	0388
C2331-0	1614
C2333	0261
C2334	2253
C2334K	2253
C2334L	2253
C2334L(JAPAN)	2253
C2335	0723
C2336	0388
C2336A	0388
C2336B	0388
C2337	0861
C2337A	0861
C2340N	OEM
C2344	1274
C2344D	1274
C2344E	1274
C2347	1581
C2348	0224
C2349	0127
C2350	0042
C2352	0224
C2354	0424
C2356	1841
C2359	0723
C2362	1218
C2362G	1218
C2362H	1218
C2362K	1218
C2362KF	1218
C2363	0079
C2365	0637
C2368	2978
C2369	2978
C2371	0275
C2371(1)	0275
C2371(1)L	0275
C2371(1)M	0275
C2371(8)L	0275
C2371K	0275
C2371L	0275
C2371M	0275
C2373	0723
C2373K	0723
C2373L	0723
C2373M	0723
C2375	0261
C2377	2208
C2377-C	2208
C2377C	2208
C2377D	2208
C2378	1376
C2382	1963
C2383	1553
C2383-0	1553
C2383-O	1553
C2383-O(JAPAN)	1553
C2383O	1553
C2383R	1553
C2383R(JAPAN)	1553
C2383Y	1553
C2384	0334
C2385	0111
C2388	1841
C2388A	1841
C2393D	0261
C2394D	0830
C2398	0177
C2401	2996
C2402	0538
C2406	0023
C2406M	0023
C2420	3012
C2425	0949
C2427	0723
C2428	0538
C2429	1841
C2429A	1841
C2430	0615
C2431	0615
C2432	0615

DEVICE TYPE	REPL CODE
C2433	2416
C2434	2416
C2435	1980
C2436	2602
C2441	0558
C2443-24	0546
C2456	0275
C2456(JAPAN)	0275
C2456LB	0275
C2456Z	0275
C2458	0076
C2458-O	0076
C2458BL	0076
C2458GR	0076
C2458Y	0076
C2458Y(JAPAN)	0076
C2459	1260
C2465	2978
C2467	2978
C2470	2978
C2471	0224
C2473	2824
C2481	0558
C2481(JAPAN)	0558
C2481-0	0558
C2481-O	0558
C2481R	0558
C2481Y	0558
C2482	0261
C2482(JAPAN)	0261
C2482(KOREA)	0066
C2482-1	0261
C2482-1(JAPAN)	0261
C2482BK	0261
C2482FA-1	0261
C2482FA1	0261
C2482K	0261
C2482V	0261
C2482Z	0261
C2483	0219
C2483-O	0219
C2483-Y	0219
C2483O	0219
C2483R	0219
C2483R(JAPAN)	0219
C2483Y	0219
C2483Y(JAPAN)	0219
C2484	3052
C2484P	3052
C2485	3052
C2486	3053
C2489	0538
C2491	1157
C2492	0538
C2493	0538
C2497	0558
C2497Q	0558
C2497R	0558
C2498	1795
C2499	2824
C2500	3064
C2500P	OEM
C2501	0723
C2501(JAPAN)	0723
C2501P	OEM
C2502	0723
C2502P	OEM
C2503P	OEM
C2504	0282
C2505	0723
C2506	0282
C2506(TRANS)	0723
C2506B40C1600-1100	OEM
C2507	1841
C2508	2857
C2512	0224
C2512B80C1600-1100	OEM
C2516	1157
C2516AK	1157
C2516AL	1157
C2516AM	1157
C2516K	1157
C2516L	1157
C2516M	1157
C2519	0127
C2520B125C1500-1000	OEM
C2522	0538
C2522A	0538
C2523	0538
C2525	2261
C2526	2261
C2527	1157
C2528	3083
C2530	3086
C2534	0723
C2536	1498
C2540	3090
C2540B250C1500-1000	OEM
C2542(JAPAN)	0723
C2545D	0111
C2545E	0111
C2545F	0111
C2548	1498
C2549	0224
C2550	0016
C2551	0261
C2551-0	0261
C2551-O(JAPAN)	0261

330

If replacement code is OEM, contact original manufacturer for replacement.

DEVICE TYPE	REPL CODE
C2551R	0261
C2552	0723
C2553	0723
C2555	2171
C2555Z	2171
C2556	0558
C2556A	0558
C2561	0127
C2562	3096
C2563	3053
C2564	2261
C2565	2261
C2568	0275
C2568(1)	0275
C2568(1)K	0275
C2568(1)KD(JAPAN)	0275
C2568(1)L	0275
C2568(1)LD	0275
C2568(1)M	0275
C2568K	0275
C2568KD	0275
C2568L	0275
C2568LD	0275
C2568LD(JAPAN)	0275
C2568LM	0275
C2568M	0275
C2570	2824
C2570A	2824
C2570AE	2824
C2575	0284
C2575L	0284
C2577	0194
C2578	0194
C2579	3053
C2580	3053
C2581	3053
C2582	0558
C2590	0558
C2591	0388
C2592	0388
C2602	0111
C2603	0513
C2603-E	0513
C2603-F	0513
C2603E	0513
C2603F	0513
C2606	0283
C2607	2398
C2608	2398
C2610	0261
C2610-05	0261
C2610-5	0261
C2610B	0261
C2610B(JAPAN)	0261
C2610BK	0261
C2610K	0261
C2611	0275
C2612	0168
C2613	0723
C2613(JAPAN)	0723
C2613K	0723
C2615A	0017
C2616	2900
C2617	2900
C2621	0275
C2621-C	0275
C2621-D	0275
C2621-E	0275
C2621-RA	0275
C2621-RAC	0275
C2621-RAD	0275
C2621-RAE	0275
C2621C	0275
C2621D	0275
C2621E	0275
C2621E(JAPAN)	0275
C2621RA	0275
C2626	1498
C2630	3090
C2631	0261
C2632	0261
C2633	1077
C2634-RS	0111
C2634NC	0111
C2634R	0111
C2634R(JAPAN)	0111
C2634RS	0111
C2634S	0111
C2634S(JAPAN)	0111
C2636	0127
C2637	1077
C2637L	1077
C2637R	1077
C2637RL	1077
C2646	0127
C2647	0224
C2647C	0224
C2653	0168
C2653(H)	0168
C2653C	0168
C2653CL	0168
C2653H	0168
C2653H(JAPAN)	0168
C2653HCL	0168
C2653HLB	0168
C2653L	0168
C2653LB	0168
C2655	0018
C2655-O	0018
C2655-Y	0018
C26550(JAPAN)	0018
C2655Y	0018
C2660	0388
C2665	3052
C2668	1136
C2669	0155
C2669-O(JAPAN)	0155
C2670	0155
C2671	2824
C2681	0194
C2687	0261
C2688	0275
C2688(2)	0275
C2688-K	0275
C2688-L	0275
C2688-M	0275
C2688-N	0275
C2688A	0275
C2688K	0275
C2688KA	0275
C2688KA(JAPAN)	0275
C2688L	0275
C2688LA	0275
C2688LA(JAPAN)	0275
C2688M	0275
C2688N	0275
C2690	0558
C2690A	0558
C2694	3165
C2703Y	1553
C2704	0558
C2705	1553
C2706	3053
C2708	4351
C2710	0155
C2710-O	0155
C2710-Y	0155
C2715M	0102
C2717	0309
C2717FA	0309
C2718	0018
C2719	0155
C2719(JAPAN)	0155
C2719K	0155
C2719L	0155
C2719L(JAPAN)	0155
C2720	3173
C2721	0018
C2724	0191
C2724-D	0191
C2724-E	0191
C2727	2817
C2729	2817
C2737	2824
C2738	3179
C2739	0723
C2740	3181
C2751L(JAPAN)	OEM
C2753	1498
C2773	3196
C2774	3196
C2780	1553
C2784	1260
C2785	0249
C2785(JAPAN)	0249
C2785E	0249
C2785F	0249
C2785F(JAPAN)	0249
C2785H	0249
C2785J	0249
C2785K	0249
C2786	0284
C2786L	0284
C2787	0127
C2790	2424
C2791	3199
C2792	3201
C2794	0558
C2794(JAPAN)	0558
C2809	2589
C28090	2589
C2809Q	2589
C2809V	2589
C2810	0723
C2815	0723
C2816	0723
C2818	0079
C2818H	0079
C2819	1841
C2819H	1841
C2820	1841
C2824	0558
C2826	2985
C2827	0723
C2829	1955
C2830	1841
C2831	2739
C2832	0168
C2832K	0168
C2832L	0168
C2837	0194
C2838	0044
C2839	0151
C2839-D	0151
C2839D	0151
C2839E	0151
C2840	0127
C2840D	0127
C2853D	1376
C2853E	1376
C2854D	1376
C2854E	1376
C2855D	1376
C2855E	1376
C2856E	1376
C2857	0261
C2860	1489
C2877	0161
C2878	3065
C2878A	3065
C2878A(JAPAN)	3065
C2878B	3065
C2878B(JAPAN)	3065
C2884	0127
C2898	0723
C2901	3243
C2901L	3243
C2902	1841
C2903	1841
C2909	0261
C2910	1553
C2911	0558
C2912	0558
C2913	0723
C2914	3236
C2914Z	3236
C2920	1331
C2921	3255
C2922	3196
C2923	0275
C2923RL	0275
C2928	3261
C2939	1498
C2939(JAPAN)	1498
C2958	1376
C2960	3270
C2960E	3270
C2960F	3270
C2960G	3270
C2964	2900
C2965	2900
C2971	1331
C2972	1331
C2976	3031
C2979	2085
C2981	3031
C2995	0525
C3000D	0284
C3000L	OEM
C3000P	0232
C3001	1532
C3001-0	1532
C3001-O	1532
C3001A	1532
C3001L	OEM
C3001M	1532
C3001P	0268
C3001T	1532
C3002B	OEM
C3002B-C	OEM
C3002P	0310
C3004L	OEM
C3004P	0357
C3007	3296
C3010	OEM
C3010A	OEM
C3010B	OEM
C3010L	OEM
C3010P	0507
C3015	OEM
C3015A	OEM
C3015B	OEM
C3016	OEM
C3016A	OEM
C3016B	OEM
C3017	0693
C3019	OEM
C3019A	OEM
C3019B	OEM
C3020	OEM
C3020A	OEM
C3020B	OEM
C3020L	OEM
C3020P	0692
C3021	OEM
C3021A	OEM
C3021B	OEM
C3022	OEM
C3022A	OEM
C3022B	OEM
C3025	OEM
C3025A	OEM
C3025B	OEM
C3026	OEM
C3026A	OEM
C3026B	OEM
C3029	OEM
C3029(TRANS)	2817
C3029A	OEM
C3029B	OEM
C3030	OEM
C3030A	OEM
C3030B	OEM
C3030L	OEM
C3030P	0867
C3031	OEM
C3031A	OEM
C3031B	OEM
C3032	OEM
C3032A	OEM
C3032B	OEM
C3035	OEM
C3035A	OEM
C3035B	OEM
C3036	OEM
C3036A	OEM
C3036B	OEM
C3038	2985
C3039	OEM
C3039(JAPAN)	0723
C3039A	OEM
C3039B	OEM
C3040	6697
C3040A	OEM
C3040B	OEM
C3040L	OEM
C3040P	1018
C3041	OEM
C3041A	OEM
C3041B	OEM
C3041L	OEM
C3041P	1032
C3042	6697
C3042A	OEM
C3042B	OEM
C3044	1331
C3044A	1331
C3045	OEM
C3045(TRANS)	1331
C3045A	OEM
C3045B	OEM
C3046	OEM
C3046(TRANS)	3304
C3046A	OEM
C3046B	OEM
C3049	OEM
C3049A	OEM
C3049B	OEM
C3050L	OEM
C3050P	0738
C3055	0723
C3056	0723
C3056A	0723
C3057	0723
C3059	OEM
C3059(TRANS)	0223
C3059A	OEM
C3059B	OEM
C3060	OEM
C3060(TRANS)	0223
C3060A	OEM
C3060B	OEM
C3061	OEM
C3061A	OEM
C3061B	OEM
C3062	OEM
C3062A	OEM
C3062B	OEM
C3063	0275
C3063RL	0275
C3065	OEM
C3065A	OEM
C3065B	OEM
C3066	OEM
C3066A	OEM
C3066B	OEM
C3073L	OEM
C3073P	1164
C3075L	OEM
C3075P	1423
C3076	3316
C3100	2296
C3100A	OEM
C3100B	OEM
C3101	OEM
C3101A	OEM
C3101ADM	OEM
C3101B	OEM
C3102	OEM
C3102A	OEM
C3102B	OEM
C3105	OEM
C3105A	OEM
C3105B	OEM
C3106	OEM
C3106A	OEM
C3106B	OEM
C3109	OEM
C3109A	OEM
C3109B	OEM
C3114T(JAPAN)	0155
C3116T	0558
C3140	OEM
C3140A	OEM
C3140B	OEM
C3141	0133
C3141A	OEM
C3141B	OEM
C3142	0080
C3143	0080
C3144	0604
C3145	OEM
C3145A	OEM
C3145B	OEM
C3146	OEM
C3146A	OEM
C3146B	OEM
C3149	3323
C3149A	OEM
C3149B	OEM
C3150	3323
C3150A	OEM
C3150B	OEM
C3151	3452
C3151A	OEM
C3151B	OEM
C3152	3452
C3152A	OEM
C3152B	OEM
C3155	0223
C3155A	OEM
C3155B	OEM
C3156	3351
C3156A	OEM
C3156B	OEM
C3157(JAPAN)	OEM
C3157L	3031
C3159	0723
C3159A	OEM
C3159B	OEM
C3165	OEM
C3165A	OEM
C3165B	OEM
C3166	OEM
C3166A	OEM
C3166B	OEM
C3174R	0723
C3174S	0723
C3175(JAPAN)	0723
C3180	3053
C3182	0194
C3187	3358
C3209	0261
C3209K	0261
C3209K(JAPAN)	0261
C3209L	0261
C3209L(JAPAN)	0261
C3209M	0261
C3212(JAPAN)	OEM
C3214	0065
C3220	3353
C3220A	OEM
C3220B	OEM
C3221	OEM
C3221A	OEM
C3221B	OEM
C3222	3354
C3222A	OEM
C3222B	OEM
C3225	OEM
C3225A	OEM
C3225B	OEM
C3226	OEM
C3226A	OEM
C3226B	OEM
C3237	3377
C3238	1077
C3258Y(JAPAN)	OEM
C3271N	0275
C3280	3401
C3293	0277
C3298B	OEM
C3299Y	0060
C3300	2351
C3303Y	OEM
C3306(JAPAN)	2171
C3310(JAPAN)	0723
C3311AR	2926
C3315C	OEM
C3330	2926
C3330A	OEM
C3330B	OEM
C3331	0018
C3331A	OEM
C3331B	OEM
C3331T	0018
C3332	OEM
C3332A	OEM
C3332B	OEM
C3334	0261
C3335	OEM
C3335A	OEM
C3335B	OEM
C3387	3437
C3413C	2926
C3450M	OEM
C3460	3326
C3467E	0261
C3470	2926
C3470A	OEM
C3470B	OEM
C3471	OEM
C3471A	OEM
C3471B	OEM
C3472	OEM
C3472A	OEM
C3472B	OEM
C3568(JAPAN)	OEM
C3619	0275
C3621	0558
C3681	OEM
C3681A	OEM
C3681B	OEM
C3682	OEM
C3682A	OEM
C3682B	OEM
C3708S	1376
C3720	0224
C3720A	0224
C3720B	0224
C3720C	0224
C3720D	0224
C3720F	0224
C3720G	0224
C3720GN	0224
C3720H	0224
C3720J	0224
C3720K	0224
C3720L	0224
C37200R	0224
C3720R	0224
C3720X	0224
C3720Y	0224
C3746	0060
C3746R	0060
C3747	0060
C3748	0060
C3748R	0060
C3789D	0275
C3789E	0275
C3795B(EUROPE)	OEM
C3800	OEM
C3800(TRANS)	0224
C3800A	OEM
C3800A(TRANS)	0224
C3800B	OEM
C3800B(TRANS)	0224
C3800C	0224
C3800D	0224
C3800E	0224
C3800F	0224
C3800G	0224
C3800GN	0224
C3800H	0224
C3800J	0224
C3800K	0224
C3800L	0224
C3800M	0224
C38000R	0224
C3800P	1199
C3800R	0224
C3800X	0224
C3800Y	0224
C3801L	OEM
C3801P	0828
C3802	OEM
C3802A	OEM
C3802B	OEM
C3802P	OEM
C3803P	OEM
C3804P	OEM
C3805P	OEM
C3806P	1369
C3807	OEM
C3831	OEM
C3832	2880
C3833	1498
C3854	0127
C3890	0723
C3902S	0558
C3940	0224
C3940A	0224
C3940B	0224
C3940C	0224
C3940D	0224
C3940E	0224
C3940F	0224
C3940G	0224
C3940GN	0224
C3940H	0224
C3940J	0224
C3940K	0224
C3940L	0224
C3940M	0224
C39400R	0224
C3940R	0224
C3940X	0224
C3940Y	0224
C3942	5479
C3987	3678
C4001P	OEM
C4002P	OEM
C4003P	OEM
C4004	3323
C4004P	OEM
C4005P	OEM
C4006P	OEM
C4007P	OEM
C4008P	OEM
C4009P	OEM
C4011	0466
C4012	OEM
C4012A	0018
C4012B	0018
C4012C	0018
C4012D	0018
C4012E	0018
C4012F	0018
C4012G	0018
C4012GN	0018
C4012H	0018
C4012J	0018
C4012L	0018
C4012M	0018
C4012X	0018
C4012Y	0018
C4013	OEM
C4014	3071
C4015	0057
C4016	0170
C4017	OEM
C4018	0052
C4019	OEM
C4020	0681
C4020P	OEM
C4021	OEM
C4021P	OEM
C4022	OEM
C4023	OEM
C4024	OEM
C4025	OEM
C4026	0436
C4027	OEM
C4028	OEM
C4029	OEM
C4030P	OEM
C4030S	OEM
C4031P	OEM
C4032P	OEM
C4033A	0224
C4033B	0224
C4033C	0224
C4033D	0224
C4033E	0224
C4033F	0224
C4033G	0224
C4033GN	0224
C4033H	0224
C4033J	0224
C4033K	0224
C4033L	0224
C4033M	0224
C40330R	0224
C4033P	OEM
C4033R	0224
C4033X	0224
C4033Y	0224
C4040	OEM
C4040P	OEM
C4041P	OEM
C4042P	OEM
C4050P	OEM
C4051P	OEM
C4052P	OEM
C4053P	OEM
C4054P	OEM
C4055P	OEM
C4056P	OEM
C4057L	OEM
C4057T	OEM
C4058P	OEM
C4059	1498
C4059P	0482
C4108	1498
C4116	0042
C4116A	0042
C4116B	0042
C4116C	0042
C4116D	0042
C4116E	0042
C4116F	0042
C4116G	0042
C4116GN	0042
C4116H	0042
C4116J	0042
C4116K	0042
C4116L	0042
C4116M	0042
C41160R	0042
C4116R	0042
C4116X	0042
C4116Y	0042
C4141-21816	OEM
C4159E	1157
C4169	1055
C4212(H)	OEM
C4212H	OEM
C4217E	0275
C4274	0723
C-4401	0133
C4404	OEM
C4418	2880
C4418Y	2880
C4423	2171
C4424M	3069
C4434A	OEM
C4547	OEM
C4558C	0356
C4570HA	OEM
C4590E	OEM
C4702	0031
C5001	OEM
C5002	OEM
C5003	OEM
C5004	OEM
C5005	0143
C5100	0168
C5100A	0168
C5100B	0168
C5100C	0168
C5100D	0168
C5100E	0168
C5100F	0168

If replacement code is OEM, contact original manufacturer for replacement. 331

DEVICE TYPE	REPL CODE
C5100G	0168
C5100GN	0168
C5100H	0168
C5100J	0168
C5100K	0168
C5100L	0168
C5100M	0168
C5100OR	0168
C5100R	0168
C5100Y	0168
C5110	0168
C5110A	0168
C5110B	0168
C5110C	0168
C5110D	0168
C5110E	0168
C5110F	0168
C5110G	0168
C5110GN	0168
C5110H	0168
C5110J	0168
C5110K	0168
C5110L	0168
C5110M	0168
C5110OR	0168
C5110R	0168
C5110X	0168
C5110Y	0168
C5116#	OEM
C5120	0555
C5130	0555
C5223A4M	OEM
C5335-5	OEM
C5335-6	OEM
C5335-G	OEM
C5335-M	OEM
C5335-X	OEM
C5370	0018
C5370A	0018
C5370B	0018
C5370C	0018
C5370D	0018
C5370E	0018
C5370F	0018
C5370G	0018
C5370GN	0018
C5370H	0018
C5370J	0018
C5370K	0018
C5370L	0018
C5370M	0018
C5370OR	0018
C5370R	0018
C5370X	0018
C5370Y	0018
C5430OR	0224
C6001	2089
C6003	0512
C6003P	OEM
C6004	OEM
C6007	0718
C6009P	1888
C6010	3731
C6010P	3915
C6011	1865
C6012	OEM
C6012A	OEM
C6013	2016
C6013A	OEM
C6014	1178
C6014A	3071
C6015	0057
C6015A	0057
C6016	1969
C6016A	OEM
C6016P	OEM
C6017	1674
C6017A	OEM
C6018	0052
C6018A	0052
C6019	0718
C6019A	OEM
C6020	0681
C6020A	0681
C6021	OEM
C6021A	OEM
C6022	OEM
C6022A	OEM
C6023	OEM
C6023A	OEM
C6024	OEM
C6024A	OEM
C6025	OEM
C6025A	OEM
C6026	OEM
C6026A	OEM
C6027	OEM
C6027A	OEM
C6028	OEM
C6028A	OEM
C6029	OEM
C6029A	OEM
C6030	OEM
C6030A	OEM
C6031	OEM
C6031A	OEM
C6032	OEM
C6032A	OEM
C6041	OEM

DEVICE TYPE	REPL CODE
C6041M	OEM
C6042	OEM
C6042M	OEM
C6043	OEM
C6043M	OEM
C6044	0672
C6044M	0672
C6045	OEM
C6045M	OEM
C6046	OEM
C6046M	OEM
C6047	OEM
C6047M	OEM
C6048	1266
C6048M	1266
C6049	OEM
C6049G	OEM
C6049M	OEM
C6049R	OEM
C6050	OEM
C6050G	0413
C6050M	OEM
C6051	OEM
C6051M	OEM
C6051P	OEM
C6052	0672
C6052G	OEM
C6052M	0406
C6052M(ZENER)	0672
C6052P	0308
C6052P(HEP)	0308
C6053G	OEM
C6053L	OEM
C6054G	OEM
C6054R	OEM
C6055L(HEP)	0687
C6056P	0696
C6056P(HEP)	0696
C6057P	0345
C6057P(HEP)	0345
C6059P	0780
C6059P(HEP)	0780
C6060P	0784
C6060P(HEP)	0784
C6061P	3189
C6062P	0659
C6062P(HEP)	0659
C6063P	0167
C6063P(HEP)	0167
C6065P	1929
C6065P(HEP)	1929
C6066P	1742
C6067G	0748
C6068P	0438
C6068P(HEP)	0438
C6070P	0348
C6070P(HEP)	0348
C6071P	0350
C6071P(HEP)	0350
C6072P	0746
C6072P(HEP)	0746
C6073P	2977
C6074P	0649
C6074P(HEP)	0649
C6075P	0850
C6076P	0391
C6076P(HEP)	0391
C6078R	OEM
C6079P	1797
C6080P	2264
C6080P(HEP)	2264
C6082P	0659
C6082P(HEP)	0659
C6083P	0167
C6083P(HEP)	0167
C6085P(HEP)	2438
C6087P	OEM
C6089	2147
C6089(HEP)	0748
C6091	1070
C6091G	1070
C6092G	OEM
C6093G	OEM
C6094P	OEM
C6095P	0438
C6096P	0514
C6096P(HEP)	0514
C6099P	3166
C6099T	OEM
C6100	0755
C6100A	0755
C6100P	0797
C6100P(HEP)	0797
C6101	0118
C6101A	0118
C6101P	1335
C6101P(HEP)	1335
C6102	0296
C6102A	0296
C6102P	0356
C6102P(HEP)	0356
C6103	0372
C6103A	0372
C6103P	1291
C6104	0036
C6104A	0036
C6104L	OEM
C6105	2224
C6105A	0274

DEVICE TYPE	REPL CODE
C6105P	OEM
C6106	0140
C6106A	0140
C6107	0041
C6107A	0041
C6107P	1290
C6108	0253
C6108A	0253
C6109	0466
C6109A	0466
C6110P	OEM
C6111P	0917
C6112	0062
C6112A	0062
C6112P	1187
C6113	0077
C6113A	0077
C6113P	0330
C6114	0165
C6114A	0165
C6114P	1311
C6115	0057
C6115A	0057
C6115P	OEM
C6116	0064
C6116A	0064
C6116P	2224
C6117	0181
C6117A	0181
C6117P	OEM
C6118	0052
C6118A	0052
C6118P	1275
C6119	0053
C6119A	0053
C6119P	OEM
C6120	0681
C6120P	2624
C6121	0440
C6121A	0440
C6121P	OEM
C6122	0371
C6122A	0371
C6122P	1827
C6123	0695
C6123A	0695
C6123P	3777
C6124	0700
C6124A	0700
C6124P	OEM
C6125	0489
C6125A	0489
C6125P	OEM
C6126	0450
C6126A	0450
C6126P	OEM
C6127	0195
C6127A	0195
C6127P	OEM
C6128	0166
C6128A	0166
C6128P	OEM
C6129	0010
C6129A	0010
C6129P	OEM
C6130	0032
C6130A	0032
C6130P	0967
C6131	0054
C6131A	0054
C6131P	0967
C6132	0068
C6132A	0068
C6132P	1288
C6133P	OEM
C6135P	OEM
C6136P	OEM
C6139P	OEM
C6140P	OEM
C6143P	OEM
C6144P	OEM
C6201	OEM
C6202	OEM
C6203	OEM
C6204	OEM
C6205	OEM
C6206	OEM
C6211	OEM
C6212	OEM
C6213	OEM
C6214	OEM
C6215	OEM
C6216	OEM
C6217	OEM
C6251	OEM
C6252	OEM
C6253	OEM
C6254	OEM
C6311	OEM
C6330	OEM
C6330A	OEM
C6331	OEM
C6331A	OEM
C6332	OEM
C6332A	OEM
C6391	1325
C6391A	1325
C6392	OEM
C6392A	OEM

DEVICE TYPE	REPL CODE
C6393	OEM
C6393A	OEM
C6394	OEM
C6394A	OEM
C6395	OEM
C6395A	OEM
C6396	OEM
C6396A	OEM
C6397	OEM
C6397A	OEM
C6398	OEM
C6399	OEM
C6644H(HEP)	0111
C6690	3350
C6691	3350
C6692	3350
C7076	0111
C7101	OEM
C7161AP	OEM
C7400P	0232
C7400P(HEP)	0232
C7401P	0268
C7401P(HEP)	0268
C7402P	0310
C7402P(HEP)	0310
C7403P	0331
C7404P	0357
C7405P	0381
C7406P	1197
C7407P	1329
C7408P	0462
C7408P(HEP)	0462
C7409P	0487
C7410P	0507
C7411P	0522
C7413P	1432
C7414P	2228
C7416P	1339
C7417P	1342
C7420P	0692
C7422P	OEM
C7423P	3429
C7425P	3438
C7426P	0798
C7426P(HEP)	0798
C7427P	0812
C7430P	0867
C7432P	0893
C7437P	3478
C7440P	1018
C7441AP	1032
C7445P	1074
C7446AP	1090
C7447AP	1100
C7448P	1117
C7450P	0738
C7451P	1160
C7453P	1177
C7454P	1193
C7460P	1265
C7470P	1394
C7472P	1417
C7473P	1164
C7473P(HEP)	1164
C7474P	1303
C7474P(HEP)	1303
C7475P	1423
C7476P	1150
C7476P(HEP)	1150
C7483P	0117
C7485P	0370
C7486P	1358
C7490AP	1199
C7490P(HEP)	1199
C7491AP	0974
C7492AP	0828
C7493AP	0564
C7495P	1477
C7496P	1705
C8000	OEM
C8000A	OEM
C8000B	OEM
C8000C	OEM
C8000D	OEM
C8001	OEM
C8001A	OEM
C8001B	OEM
C8001C	OEM
C8001D	OEM
C8002	OEM
C8002A	OEM
C8002B	OEM
C8002C	OEM
C8002D	OEM
C8008	OEM
C8008-1	OEM
C8020H	OEM
C8021H	OEM
C8022	OEM
C8031	OEM
C8035	OEM
C8035HL	OEM
C8035HL-1	OEM
C8035L	OEM
C8039	OEM
C8039-6	OEM
C8039H-8	OEM
C8039HL	OEM
C8041A	OEM

DEVICE TYPE	REPL CODE
C8048	OEM
C8048H	OEM
C8048H-1	OEM
C8048L	OEM
C8049	OEM
C8049H	OEM
C8051	OEM
C8080A	4467
C8080A-1	OEM
C8080A-2	OEM
C8085A	OEM
C8086	OEM
C8086-2	OEM
C8086-4	OEM
C8088	OEM
C8089	OEM
C8146	0018
C8155	OEM
C8155-2	OEM
C8156	OEM
C8156-2	OEM
C8185	OEM
C8185-2	OEM
C8202	OEM
C8205	OEM
C8212	1849
C8216	1852
C8218	OEM
C8219	OEM
C8224	1699
C8226	OEM
C8228	1858
C8231	OEM
C8232	OEM
C8237	OEM
C8237-2	OEM
C8238	OEM
C8243	OEM
C8251A	OEM
C8253	OEM
C8253-5	OEM
C8255A	OEM
C8255A-5	OEM
C8257	OEM
C8257-5	OEM
C8259A	OEM
C8259A-2	OEM
C8259A-8	OEM
C8271	OEM
C8271-6	OEM
C8271-8	OEM
C8272	OEM
C8273	OEM
C8273-4	OEM
C8273-8	OEM
C8275	OEM
C8279	OEM
C8279-5	OEM
C8282	OEM
C8283	OEM
C8284	OEM
C8286	OEM
C8287	OEM
C8288	OEM
C8289	OEM
C8290	0079
C8291	OEM
C8292	OEM
C8293	OEM
C8294	OEM
C8295	OEM
C8316A	OEM
C8355	OEM
C8355-2	OEM
C8641A	OEM
C8741A	OEM
C8748	OEM
C8748-6	OEM
C8749H	OEM
C8749H-8	OEM
C8751	OEM
C8755A	OEM
C8755A-2	OEM
C8783C	OEM
C8783CC	OEM
C9001	OEM
C9002	OEM
C9003	OEM
C9011E	0079
C9011F	0079
C9011H	0079
C9014A	0079
C9014A(KOREA)	0079
C9080	0126
C9081	0126
C9082	0037
C9083	0037
C9084	0037
C9085	0037
C9426	0224
C9634	0111
C10110	0015
C10159	0015
C10176	0015
C10215-2	0050
C10227	0004
C10230-3	0004
C10258	0050
C10260	0050

DEVICE TYPE	REPL CODE
C10261	0050
C10262	0050
C10279-1	0111
C10279-3	0016
C10291	0136
C10621	OEM
C11021	0004
C12712	0086
C12713	0710
C12714	0710
C12923	0086
C12924	0086
C12925	0079
C12926	0086
C13390	0079
C13391	0079
C13391A	0079
C13392	0086
C13393	0086
C13394	0086
C13398	0086
C13402	0710
C13404	0710
C13414	0710
C13415	0710
C13416	0710
C13417	0710
C13901	0016
C14256	0079
C14424	0710
C14425	0710
C19659	OEM
C21382	0015
C21383	0012
C21480	0143
C29120E	OEM
C29120M	OEM
C29120N	OEM
C29120P	OEM
C29120PA	OEM
C29120PB	OEM
C29120S	OEM
C29120T	OEM
C30012	OEM
C30013	OEM
C30099	OEM
C30116	OEM
C30116F	OEM
C30119	OEM
C30122	OEM
C30123	OEM
C30130	OEM
C30133	OEM
C30807	OEM
C30808	OEM
C30809	OEM
C30810	OEM
C30812	OEM
C30815	OEM
C30816	OEM
C30817	OEM
C30818E	OEM
C30822	OEM
C30831	OEM
C30843	OEM
C30844	OEM
C30845	OEM
C30846	OEM
C30847E	OEM
C30849	OEM
C30850	OEM
C30851	OEM
C30852	OEM
C30853	OEM
C30854	OEM
C30872	OEM
C30895	OEM
C30900E	OEM
C30902E	OEM
C30904E	OEM
C30905E	OEM
C30908E	OEM
C30910E	OEM
C30914E	OEM
C30916E	OEM
C30917E	OEM
C30919E	OEM
C30920E	OEM
C30921E	OEM
C30924E	OEM
C30925E	OEM
C30950E	OEM
C30950EL	OEM
C30950F	OEM
C30950FL	OEM
C30950G	OEM
C30950GL	OEM
C30954E	OEM
C30955E	OEM
C30956E	OEM
C30971E	OEM
C30971EL	OEM
C30979E	OEM
C31013	OEM
C32024S	OEM
C32816	OEM
C33725	0079
C36577	0126
C36578	0007

DEVICE TYPE	REPL CODE
C36579	0086
C36580	0016
C-36582	0321
C38085	OEM
C38121	OEM
C38122	OEM
C38123	OEM
C38124	OEM
C38129	OEM
C41010BA	OEM
C42010EB	OEM
C42010EC	OEM
C51909B	0037
C57401AF	OEM
C57401AJ	OEM
C57402AF	OEM
C57402F	OEM
C57402J	OEM
C67401AJ	OEM
C67401J	OEM
C67402AJ	OEM
C67402J	OEM
C68000E	OEM
C74107P	4151
C74109P	0962
C74121P	0175
C74123P	1149
C74125P	1174
C74126P	1184
C74132P	1261
C74141P	1367
C74145P	0614
C74147P	1442
C74148P	1455
C74150P	1484
C74151AP	1487
C74153P	1531
C74154P	1546
C74155P	1566
C74156P	1582
C74157P	1595
C74160AP	1621
C74162AP	1007
C74163AP	1656
C74164P	0729
C74165P	1675
C74166P	0231
C74170P	1711
C74173P	1755
C74174P	1759
C74175P	1776
C74176P	1784
C74177P	1792
C74180P	1818
C74181P	1831
C74182P	1845
C74184P	OEM
C74185AP	OEM
C74190P	1901
C74191P	1906
C74192P	1910
C74193P	1915
C74194P	OEM
C74195P	1932
C74196P	1939
C74197P	1945
C74198P	1953
C74199P	1960
C74251P	2283
C74259P	OEM
C74365P	1450
C74366P	1462
C74367P	1479
C74368P	1500
C75603-2	0617
C78010BB014	OEM
C78010BD031	OEM
C78020BA	OEM
C86002E	OEM
C86003E-RS	OEM
C86003E-TS	OEM
C86006E	OEM
C86007E	OEM
C86008E	OEM
C86009E	OEM
C86010E	OEM
C86011E	OEM
C86012E-RS	OEM
C86012E-TS	OEM
C86013E	OEM
C86014E	OEM
C86022E	OEM
C86023E	OEM
C86025E	OEM
C106009	OEM
C106509	OEM
C106516	OEM
C107009	OEM
C107016	OEM
C107509	OEM
C107516	OEM
C108016	OEM
C136009	OEM
C136509	OEM
C137009	OEM
C137509	OEM
C139000	0086
C139000A	0086
C206009	OEM

If replacement code is OEM, contact original manufacturer for replacement.

DEVICE TYPE	REPL CODE
C206509	OEM
C206516	OEM
C207009	OEM
C207016	OEM
C207509	OEM
C207516	OEM
C208016	OEM
C216509	OEM
C248507	0015
C251968-03	OEM
C254187	OEM
C523383	0079
C530041-1	0015
C642010ED	OEM
C1107832P6	1073
C1107832P7	0196
C1107832P9	0196
C2475078-3	0144
C2485076-3	0086
C2485077-2	0086
C2485078-1	0144
C2485079-1	0144
CA078G	OEM
CA080AE	OEM
CA080AS	OEM
CA080AT	OEM
CA080BE	OEM
CA080CS	OEM
CA080CT	OEM
CA080E	OEM
CA080S	OEM
CA080T	OEM
CA081AE	OEM
CA081AS	OEM
CA081AT	OEM
CA081BE	OEM
CA081CS	OEM
CA081CT	OEM
CA081E	OEM
CA081S	OEM
CA081T	OEM
CA082AE	OEM
CA082AS	OEM
CA082AT	OEM
CA082BE	OEM
CA082CS	OEM
CA082CT	OEM
CA082E	OEM
CA082S	OEM
CA082T	OEM
CA083AE	OEM
CA083BE	OEM
CA083E	OEM
CA-092	0012
CA0101AE	OEM
CA0101AG	OEM
CA0101AS	OEM
CA0101AS3	OEM
CA0101AS4	OEM
CA0101AT	OEM
CA0101AT3	OEM
CA0101AT4	OEM
CA0101E	OEM
CA0101S	OEM
CA0101T	OEM
CA0107E	OEM
CA0107G	OEM
CA0107S	OEM
CA0107S3W	OEM
CA0107T	OEM
CA0107T3W	OEM
CA0111E	OEM
CA0111G	OEM
CA0111S	OEM
CA0111T	OEM
CA0124E	OEM
CA0124G	OEM
CA0124GX	OEM
CA0139AE	OEM
CA0139AG	OEM
CA0139G	OEM
CA0139GX	OEM
CA0158AE	OEM
CA0158AG	OEM
CA0158AS	OEM
CA0158AT	OEM
CA0158E	OEM
CA0158G	OEM
CA0158S	OEM
CA0158T	OEM
CA0201AE	OEM
CA0201AG	OEM
CA0201AS	OEM
CA0201AT	OEM
CA0201G	OEM
CA0201S	OEM
CA0201T	OEM
CA0207E	OEM
CA0207G	OEM
CA0207S	OEM
CA0207T	OEM
CA0211E	OEM
CA0211G	OEM
CA0211S	OEM
CA0211T	OEM
CA0224E	OEM
CA0224G	OEM
CA0239AE	OEM
CA0239AG	OEM

DEVICE TYPE	REPL CODE
CA0239E	OEM
CA0239G	OEM
CA0239GX	OEM
CA0258AE	OEM
CA0258AG	OEM
CA0258AS	OEM
CA0258AT	OEM
CA0258E	OEM
CA0258G	OEM
CA0258S	OEM
CA0258T	OEM
CA0270AE	OEM
CA0270AW	OEM
CA0270BE	OEM
CA0270BW	OEM
CA0270CE	OEM
CA0270CW	OEM
CA0301AE	OEM
CA0301AEX	OEM
CA0301AG	OEM
CA0301AS	OEM
CA0301AT	OEM
CA0307E	OEM
CA0307EX	OEM
CA0307G	OEM
CA0307GX	OEM
CA0307S	OEM
CA0307T	OEM
CA0311E	OEM
CA0311G	OEM
CA0311GX	OEM
CA0311S	OEM
CA0311T	OEM
CA0324E	4191
CA0324EX	OEM
CA0324G	OEM
CA0324GX	OEM
CA0339AE	OEM
CA0339AG	OEM
CA0339E	OEM
CA0339EX	OEM
CA0339G	OEM
CA0339GX	OEM
CA0345	1686
CA0358AE	OEM
CA0358AG	OEM
CA0358AS	OEM
CA0358AT	OEM
CA0358E	OEM
CA0358EX	OEM
CA0358G	OEM
CA0358GX	OEM
CA0358S	OEM
CA0358T	OEM
CA0555CE	OEM
CA0555CEX	OEM
CA0555CS	OEM
CA0555CT	OEM
CA0555E	OEM
CA0555EX	OEM
CA0555G	OEM
CA0555S	OEM
CA0555T	OEM
CA0555T3W	OEM
CA0723CE	OEM
CA0723CEX	OEM
CA0723CT	OEM
CA0723CTX	OEM
CA0723E	OEM
CA0723EX	OEM
CA0723T	OEM
CA0723T3	OEM
CA0723T3W	OEM
CA0723T4	OEM
CA0741CE	OEM
CA0741CEX	OEM
CA0741CG	OEM
CA0741CGX	OEM
CA0741CS	OEM
CA0741CSX	OEM
CA0741CT	OEM
CA0741CTX	OEM
CA0741E	OEM
CA0741EX	OEM
CA0741G	OEM
CA0741GX	OEM
CA0741S	OEM
CA0741S3	OEM
CA0741SX	OEM
CA0741T	OEM
CA0741T1	OEM
CA0741T2	OEM
CA0741T3	OEM
CA0741T4	OEM
CA0741TX	OEM
CA0747CE	OEM
CA0747CG	OEM
CA0747CT	OEM
CA0747E	OEM
CA0747G	OEM
CA0747T	OEM
CA0747T1	OEM
CA0747T2	OEM
CA0747T3	OEM
CA0748CE	OEM
CA0748CEX	OEM
CA0748CG	OEM
CA0748CS	OEM
CA0748CT	OEM

DEVICE TYPE	REPL CODE
CA0748E	OEM
CA0748EX	OEM
CA0748S	OEM
CA0748S1	OEM
CA0748S2	OEM
CA0748S3	OEM
CA0748S4	OEM
CA0748T	OEM
CA0748T1	OEM
CA0748T2	OEM
CA0748T3	OEM
CA0748T4	OEM
CA0758E	OEM
CA0758Q	OEM
CA0810AQ	OEM
CA0810AQM	OEM
CA0810Q	OEM
CA0810QM	OEM
CA0920AE	OEM
CA0920AW	OEM
CA014803	OEM
CA060261-15	OEM
CA2D2	0004
CA-6C	OEM
CA-7C	OEM
CA-7S	OEM
CA-9	OEM
CA10	0015
CA-10X	OEM
CA-11	OEM
CA-12	OEM
CA-14	OEM
CA20	0015
CA50	0015
CA-90	0143
CA90	0133
CA100	0015
CA101AT	0093
CA101S	0935
CA101T	0093
CA102BA	0015
CA102DA	0015
CA102FA	0015
CA102HA	0015
CA102KA	1219
CA102MA	0015
CA102PA	0071
CA102RA	0071
CA102VA	0071
CA124E	0620
CA139AE	0176
CA139F	0176
CA139G	0176
CA150	0015
CA152AA	0071
CA152BA	0071
CA152CA	0071
CA152DA	0071
CA152EA	0071
CA152FA	0071
CA152GA	0071
CA152HA	0071
CA152KA	0071
CA152MA	0071
CA152PA	0071
CA152RA	0071
CA152TA	0071
CA152VA	0071
CA158AS	1667
CA158AT	1667
CA158S	1667
CA158T	1667
CA200	0015
CA201T	0093
CA211	1804
CA211AE	0659
CA211AQ	0659
CA211E	2093
CA211G	2093
CA224E	0620
CA224G	0620
CA239	0176
CA239A	0176
CA239AE	0176
CA239AG	0176
CA239E	0176
CA239G	0176
CA250	0015
CA258AG	5882
CA258AS	6180
CA258AT	6180
CA258S	1667
CA258T	1667
CA301AE	1290
CA301AG	1290
CA301AH	OEM
CA301AS	0093
CA301AT	0093
CA301E	1290
CA301G	1290
CA301T	0093
CA307	2267
CA307E	2267
CA307G	2267
CA307H	OEM
CA307S	1770
CA307T	1770
CA311	1804
CA311E	2093

DEVICE TYPE	REPL CODE
CA311G	2093
CA311S	1804
CA311T	1804
CA314E	2771
CA324E	0620
CA324G	0620
CA324H	OEM
CA339	0176
CA339A	0176
CA339AE	0176
CA339AG	0176
CA339E	0176
CA339G	0176
CA339H	OEM
CA358AS	1667
CA358AT	1667
CA358S	1667
CA358T	1667
CA386M	OEM
CA386N	OEM
CA386P	OEM
CA386PA	OEM
CA386PB	OEM
CA386PC	OEM
CA386PD	OEM
CA386S	OEM
CA386T	OEM
CA555CE	0967
CA555CG	0967
CA555CS	3592
CA555CT	3592
CA555E	0967
CA555G	0967
CA555S	3592
CA555T	3592
CA723	1183
CA723CE	0026
CA723CT	1183
CA723E	0026
CA723T	1183
CA741	0308
CA741C	0308
CA741CE	0308
CA741CG	0308
CA741CS	0308
CA741CT	0406
CA741E	0308
CA741G	0308
CA741S	1291
CA741T	0406
CA747CE	2342
CA747CF	2342
CA747CG	2342
CA747CH	OEM
CA747CT	2352
CA747E	2342
CA747F	2342
CA747G	2342
CA747T	2352
CA748CE	2433
CA748CG	2433
CA748CH	OEM
CA748CJ	2433
CA748CN	2433
CA748CS	OEM
CA748CT	2435
CA748E	2433
CA748G	2433
CA748J	2433
CA748N	2433
CA748S	4299
CA748T	2435
CA758E	1385
CA810Q	3866
CA820C	OEM
CA920	OEM
CA1020A	0015
CA1190	OEM
CA1190G	1162
CA1190GM	1162
CA1190GQ	1162
CA1190GQ/14	OEM
CA1190GQ/M	1162
CA1310	0514
CA1310AE	OEM
CA1310E	0514
CA1352	0391
CA1352E	0391
CA1365	0167
CA1391E	0842
CA1391G	OEM
CA1394E	2473
CA1394G	2473
CA1398E	0850
CA1458	0356
CA1458E	0356
CA1458EX	OEM
CA1458F	0356
CA1458G	0356
CA1458GX	OEM
CA1458S	0356
CA1458T	3108
CA1458TX	OEM
CA1524E	OEM
CA1524EX	OEM
CA1524G	OEM
CA1541D	OEM
CA1558E	0356
CA1558G	OEM

DEVICE TYPE	REPL CODE
CA1558S	3108
CA1558S3	OEM
CA1558SX	OEM
CA1558T	3108
CA1558T1	OEM
CA1558T2	OEM
CA1558T3	OEM
CA1558T4	OEM
CA1558TX	OEM
CA1724E	OEM
CA1724EX	OEM
CA1724G	OEM
CA1725E	OEM
CA1725EX	OEM
CA1725G	OEM
CA2002	1042
CA2002M	1042
CA2002V	1042
CA2004	1042
CA2004M	OEM
CA2020H	OEM
CA2065	0167
CA2111	0659
CA2111A	0659
CA2111AE	0659
CA2111AQ	0659
CA2136A	1434
CA2136AE	1434
CA2524E	OEM
CA2524EX	OEM
CA2524G	OEM
CA2800B	OEM
CA2800H	OEM
CA2810B	OEM
CA2810H	OEM
CA2812B	OEM
CA2812H	OEM
CA2813B	OEM
CA2813H	OEM
CA2818B	OEM
CA2818H	OEM
CA2820B	OEM
CA2820H	OEM
CA2830B	OEM
CA2830H	OEM
CA2832B	OEM
CA2832H	OEM
CA2840B	OEM
CA2842H	OEM
CA2850RB	OEM
CA2850RH	OEM
CA2870B	OEM
CA2870H	OEM
CA2875RB	OEM
CA2875RH	OEM
CA2876RB	OEM
CA2876RH	OEM
CA2904E	0765
CA2904G	OEM
CA3000	2662
CA3000T	2662
CA3001	2664
CA3001T	2664
CA3002	OEM
CA3004	OEM
CA3005	OEM
CA3006	OEM
CA3007	OEM
CA3008	OEM
CA3008A	OEM
CA3010	2515
CA3010A	2515
CA3010AT	2515
CA3010T	2515
CA3011	2593
CA3011T	2593
CA3012	2593
CA3012H	OEM
CA3012T	2593
CA3013	2600
CA3013S	2600
CA3013T	2600
CA3014	2600
CA3014S	2600
CA3014T	2600
CA3015	2515
CA3015A	2515
CA3015A1	OEM
CA3015A2	OEM
CA3015A3	OEM
CA3015A4	OEM
CA3015AT	2515
CA3015H	OEM
CA3015T	2515
CA3016	OEM
CA3016A	OEM
CA3017	0350
CA3018	1843
CA3018A	1843
CA3018A1	OEM
CA3018A2	OEM
CA3018A3	OEM
CA3018A4	OEM
CA3018AX	OEM
CA3018T	1843
CA3019	2673
CA3019T	2673
CA3020	2674
CA3020A	2674

DEVICE TYPE	REPL CODE
CA3020A1	OEM
CA3020A2	OEM
CA3020A3	OEM
CA3020A4	OEM
CA3020T	2674
CA3021	OEM
CA3021E	1327
CA3022	OEM
CA3023	OEM
CA3023H	OEM
CA3026	2676
CA3026H	OEM
CA3026T	2676
CA3027EH	OEM
CA3028	0817
CA3028A	0817
CA3028AF	0817
CA3028AH	OEM
CA3028AS	0817
CA3028AT	0817
CA3028B	0817
CA3028B1	OEM
CA3028B2	OEM
CA3028B3	OEM
CA3028B4	OEM
CA3028BF	0817
CA3028BS	0817
CA3028T	0817
CA3029	2680
CA3029A	2680
CA3029E	2680
CA3030	2680
CA3030A	2680
CA3030AE	2680
CA3030E	2680
CA3035	2681
CA3035H	OEM
CA3035T	2681
CA3035V	2681
CA3035V1	2681
CA3036	OEM
CA3037	2680
CA3037A	2680
CA3037AE	2680
CA3037E	2680
CA3038	2680
CA3038A	2680
CA3038AE	2680
CA3038E	2680
CA3039	2685
CA3039T	2685
CA3039X	OEM
CA3040	OEM
CA3041	2549
CA3041P	2549
CA3041T	2549
CA3042	0823
CA3042E	0823
CA3043	2688
CA3043T	2688
CA3044	2689
CA3044T	2689
CA3044V	2689
CA3044V1	2689
CA3044VI	OEM
CA3045	1686
CA3045E	1686
CA3045F	1686
CA3045F3	OEM
CA3045F3W	OEM
CA3045F4	OEM
CA3045FX	OEM
CA3045L	1686
CA3045X	OEM
CA3046	1686
CA3046E	1686
CA3046EX	OEM
CA3047E	3757
CA3048	2507
CA3048H	OEM
CA3049T	2676
CA3049T1	OEM
CA3049T2	OEM
CA3049T3	OEM
CA3049T4	OEM
CA3050	OEM
CA3051	OEM
CA3052	2507
CA3052E	2507
CA3053	0817
CA3053T	0817
CA3054	2696
CA3054E	2696
CA3054H	OEM
CA3054X	OEM
CA3056	0406
CA3056AE	2701
CA3058	2701
CA3058E	2701
CA3059	2701
CA3059E	2701
CA3059EX	OEM
CA3059H	OEM
CA3060	OEM
CA3060AD	OEM
CA3060BD	OEM
CA3060D	OEM
CA3060E	OEM
CA3060H	OEM

DEVICE TYPE	REPL CODE
CA3062	OEM
CA3064	0360
CA3064E	0797
CA3065	0167
CA3065,RCA	0167
CA3065D	0167
CA3065E	0167
CA3065F	0167
CA3065FC	0167
CA3065F.C.	0167
CA3065N	0167
CA3065PC	0167
CA3065RCA	0167
CA3066	2527
CA3066AE	2527
CA3066E	2527
CA3067	0324
CA3067AE	0324
CA3067E	0324
CA3068	2716
CA3070	0348
CA3070E	0348
CA3070G	0348
CA3071	0350
CA3071E	0350
CA3072	0661
CA3072E	0661
CA3075	1335
CA3075E	1335
CA3076	2720
CA3076T	2720
CA3078AE	1868
CA3078AH	OEM
CA3078AS	1885
CA3078AS3	OEM
CA3078AT	1885
CA3078AT1	OEM
CA3078AT2	OEM
CA3078AT3	OEM
CA3078AT4	OEM
CA3078E	1868
CA3078H	OEM
CA3078S	1885
CA3078T	1885
CA3079	2701
CA3079E	2701
CA3079EX	OEM
CA3080	2721
CA3080A	2721
CA3080A1	OEM
CA3080A2	OEM
CA3080A3	OEM
CA3080A4	OEM
CA3080AS	2021
CA3080ASX	OEM
CA3080AX	OEM
CA3080E	3784
CA3080EX	OEM
CA3080H	OEM
CA3080S	2721
CA3080SX	OEM
CA3080X	OEM
CA3081	2722
CA3081E	2722
CA3081EX	OEM
CA3081F	OEM
CA3081F3W	OEM
CA3081FX	OEM
CA3081N	OEM
CA3082	2723
CA3082F	OEM
CA3082F3W	OEM
CA3082N	OEM
CA3083	2724
CA3083EX	OEM
CA3083F	OEM
CA3083F3W	OEM
CA3084	OEM
CA3085	2317
CA3085A	6591
CA3085A1	OEM
CA3085A2	OEM
CA3085A3	OEM
CA3085A4	OEM
CA3085AE	2317
CA3085AS	OEM
CA3085AS3	OEM
CA3085B	OEM
CA3085B1	OEM
CA3085B2	OEM
CA3085B3	OEM
CA3085B4	OEM
CA3085BS	OEM
CA3085BS3	OEM
CA3085BT3	OEM
CA3085E	2317
CA3085H	OEM
CA3085S	OEM
CA3086	1686
CA3086E	1686
CA3086EX	OEM
CA3086F	OEM
CA-3088E	2242
CA3088E	2242
CA-3089E	2728
CA3089E	2728
CA3089F	2728
CA3089F3W	OEM
CA3089N	OEM

If replacement code is OEM, contact original manufacturer for replacement. 333

DEVICE TYPE	REPL CODE
CA3090	2728
CA3090AB	1832
CA3090AE	OEM
CA3090AQ	1832
CA3090E	1832
CA3090Q	1832
CA3091D	OEM
CA3091H	OEM
CA3093E	OEM
CA3094AE	OEM
CA3094AS	2993
CA3094AS3	OEM
CA3094AT	2993
CA3094AT1	OEM
CA3094AT2	OEM
CA3094AT3	OEM
CA3094AT4	OEM
CA3094BS	OEM
CA3094BT	OEM
CA3094E	OEM
CA3094EX	OEM
CA3094H	OEM
CA3094S	2993
CA3094T	2993
CA3094T1	OEM
CA3094T2	OEM
CA3094T3	OEM
CA3094T4	OEM
CA3095E	OEM
CA3096AE	3101
CA3096AEX	OEM
CA3096CE	3101
CA3096E	3101
CA3096EX	OEM
CA3097E	6423
CA3097EX	OEM
CA3098E	OEM
CA3098S	OEM
CA3098T	OEM
CA3099E	OEM
CA3099EX	OEM
CA3100E	OEM
CA3100H	OEM
CA3100S	3360
CA3100S3	OEM
CA3100SX	OEM
CA3100T	3360
CA3100T1	OEM
CA3100T2	OEM
CA3100T3	OEM
CA3100T4	OEM
CA3100TY	3360
CA3102E	OEM
CA3102H	OEM
CA3118AT	OEM
CA3118AT1	OEM
CA3118AT2	OEM
CA3118AT3	OEM
CA3118AT4	OEM
CA3118T	OEM
CA3120E	2438
CA3121	1327
CA3121E	1327
CA3121E-G	1327
CA3121EG	1327
CA3121G	1327
CA3123	1411
CA3123E	1411
CA3123Q	OEM
CA3125	1742
CA3125E	1742
CA3126	0516
CA3126E	OEM
CA3126EM	0516
CA3126EM1	0516
CA3126EMI	0516
CA3126FM1	0516
CA3126P	OEM
CA3126Q	0516
CA3127E	OEM
CA3127EX	OEM
CA3128E	OEM
CA3128Q	OEM
CA3130	2755
CA3130A	2755
CA3130AE	2755
CA3130AS	2755
CA3130AS3	OEM
CA3130AT	2755
CA3130AT1	OEM
CA3130AT2	OEM
CA3130AT3	OEM
CA3130AT4	OEM
CA3130B	2755
CA3130BS	OEM
CA3130BT	OEM
CA3130E	6633
CA3130EX	OEM
CA3130H	OEM
CA3130S	2755
CA3130S3	OEM
CA3130SX	OEM
CA3130T	2755
CA3130T1	OEM
CA3130T2	OEM
CA3130T3	OEM
CA3130T4	OEM
CA3130TX	OEM
CA3131EM	OEM

DEVICE TYPE	REPL CODE
CA3131PM	OEM
CA3132EM	OEM
CA3132PM	OEM
CA3134	2759
CA3134EM	2759
CA3134G	OEM
CA3134GM	4293
CA3134GQM	2759
CA3134P	OEM
CA3134PM	OEM
CA3134PQM	OEM
CA3134Q	2759
CA3134QM	2759
CA3135E	2480
CA3135G	2480
CA3136E	2481
CA3136G	2481
CA3137	2762
CA3137E	2762
CA3137EM	2762
CA3137EM1	2762
CA3137EMI	2762
CA3137Q	OEM
CA3138AG	OEM
CA3138G	OEM
CA3139	2038
CA3139E	2038
CA3139G	2038
CA3139GM1	2038
CA3139GMI	2038
CA3139GQ	2038
CA3139Q	2038
CA3140AE	4396
CA3140AEX	OEM
CA3140AS	4401
CA3140AS1	OEM
CA3140AS2	OEM
CA3140AS3	OEM
CA3140AS4	OEM
CA3140ASX	OEM
CA3140AT	4401
CA3140AT1	OEM
CA3140AT2	OEM
CA3140AT3	OEM
CA3140AT4	OEM
CA3140ATX	OEM
CA3140BS	OEM
CA3140BT	OEM
CA3140E	4396
CA3140EX	OEM
CA3140H	OEM
CA3140S	4401
CA3140S1	OEM
CA3140S2	OEM
CA3140S3	OEM
CA3140S4	OEM
CA3140SX	OEM
CA3140T	4401
CA3140T1	OEM
CA3140T2	OEM
CA3140T3	OEM
CA3140T4	OEM
CA3140TX	OEM
CA3141E	OEM
CA3142	2438
CA3142E	2438
CA3143	2771
CA3143E	2771
CA3143Q	2771
CA3144E	3780
CA3144G	3780
CA3144GQ	OEM
CA3144Q	3780
CA3145	2774
CA3145G	6641
CA3146AE	2478
CA3146E	2478
CA3151E	5788
CA3151G	3060
CA3151GM1	3060
CA3151GMI	3060
CA3152E	0391
CA3153G	3239
CA3153GM1	3239
CA3153GMI	3239
CA3154G	3675
CA3156	2785
CA3156E	2785
CA3156G	2785
CA3157G	3739
CA3158G	3674
CA3159	2790
CA3159G	2790
CA3160AE	4962
CA3160AS	4965
CA3160AS1	OEM
CA3160AS2	OEM
CA3160AS3	OEM
CA3160AS4	OEM
CA3160AT	4965
CA3160AT1	OEM
CA3160AT2	OEM
CA3160AT3	OEM
CA3160AT4	OEM
CA3160BS	OEM
CA3160BT	OEM
CA3160E	4962
CA3160EX	OEM
CA3160H	OEM

DEVICE TYPE	REPL CODE
CA3160S	4965
CA3160S1	OEM
CA3160S2	OEM
CA3160S3	OEM
CA3160S4	OEM
CA3160SX	OEM
CA3160T	4965
CA3160T1	OEM
CA3160T2	OEM
CA3160T3	OEM
CA3160T4	OEM
CA3160TX	OEM
CA3161E	4863
CA3161EX	OEM
CA3162E	0516
CA3162EX	OEM
CA3163G	3741
CA3164E	OEM
CA3165E	OEM
CA3165E1	OEM
CA3166E	5508
CA3168	2800
CA3168E	2800
CA3169M	OEM
CA3170	2803
CA3170E	2803
CA3170G	OEM
CA3172	2804
CA3172E	2804
CA3172G	2804
CA3177G	3933
CA3179G	OEM
CA3180Q	OEM
CA3183AE	OEM
CA3183AEX	OEM
CA3183E	OEM
CA3183EX	OEM
CA3189E	6024
CA3190G	OEM
CA3191E	3919
CA3192E	3735
CA3193AE	OEM
CA3193AEX	OEM
CA3193AS	OEM
CA3193ASX	OEM
CA3193AT	OEM
CA3193ATX	OEM
CA3193BE	OEM
CA3193BEX	OEM
CA3193BS	OEM
CA3193BSX	OEM
CA3193BT	OEM
CA3193BTX	OEM
CA3193E	OEM
CA3193EX	OEM
CA3193S	OEM
CA3193SX	OEM
CA3193T	OEM
CA3193TX	OEM
CA3194E	6660
CA3195	2815
CA3195E	2815
CA3199E	OEM
CA3207EE	OEM
CA3208EE	OEM
CA3208EH	OEM
CA3218E	1379
CA3221	1867
CA3221G	1867
CA3240AE	6003
CA3240AE1	1872
CA3240E	6003
CA3240E1	1872
CA3240EX	OEM
CA3240H	OEM
CA3260AE	6167
CA3260AS	6168
CA3260AT	6168
CA3260BS	OEM
CA3260BT	OEM
CA3260E	6167
CA3260EX	OEM
CA3260S	6168
CA3260SX	OEM
CA3260T	6168
CA3260TX	OEM
CA3280	OEM
CA3280AG	OEM
CA3280E	OEM
CA3280G	OEM
CA3289E	2728
CA3290AE	0624
CA3290AE1	OEM
CA3290AS	6430
CA3290AT	6430
CA3290BS	OEM
CA3290BT	OEM
CA3290E	0624
CA3290E1	OEM
CA3290EX	OEM
CA3290S	6430
CA3290T	6430
CA3300D	OEM
CA3300H	OEM
CA3308D	OEM
CA3401E	2232
CA3401H	OEM
CA3493AE	OEM
CA3493AS	OEM

DEVICE TYPE	REPL CODE
CA3493E	OEM
CA3493S	OEM
CA3524E	5140
CA3524G	OEM
CA3524H	OEM
CA3539	2680
CA3545	2685
CA3600E	OEM
CA3741CE	0308
CA3741E	0308
CA3748CT	0093
CA5470M	OEM
CA6078AH	OEM
CA6078AS	OEM
CA6078AT	OEM
CA6078T	OEM
CA6664	0015
CA6665	0015
CA6741CS	OEM
CA6741CT	OEM
CA6741S	OEM
CA6741T	OEM
CA6741T3	OEM
CA6741TX	OEM
CA7248	0015
CA7520	0534
CA8089F	OEM
CA8100M	OEM
CA8314	0015
CA19199	OEM
CA19200	OEM
CA30001	OEM
CA30002	OEM
CA30003	OEM
CA30004	OEM
CA30011	OEM
CA30012	OEM
CA30013	OEM
CA30014	OEM
CA30021	OEM
CA30022	OEM
CA30023	OEM
CA30024	OEM
CA30041	OEM
CA30042	OEM
CA30043	OEM
CA30044	OEM
CA30061	OEM
CA30062	OEM
CA30063	OEM
CA30064	OEM
CA30143	OEM
CA30144	OEM
CA30153	OEM
CA30191	OEM
CA30192	OEM
CA30193	OEM
CA30194	OEM
CA30261	OEM
CA30262	OEM
CA30263	OEM
CA30264	OEM
CA30391	OEM
CA30392	OEM
CA30393	OEM
CA30394	OEM
CA30451	OEM
CA30452	OEM
CA30453	OEM
CA30454	OEM
CA30581	OEM
CA30582	OEM
CA30583	OEM
CA30801	OEM
CA30803	OEM
CA30804	OEM
CA30853	OEM
CA30854	OEM
CA30900	1832
CA69001	OEM
CA69001A	OEM
CA69002	OEM
CA69002A	OEM
CA69003	OEM
CA69003A	OEM
CA69004	OEM
CA69004A	OEM
CAC5028A	0127
CAG13A	OEM
CAM601A	OEM
CAM604A	OEM
CARGENV1.0	OEM
CAT24C01A	OEM
CAT35C102HP	OEM
CAT35C102P	OEM
CAT35C202P	OEM
CAT59C11HP	OEM
CAT59C11P	OEM
CAT93C46AN	OEM
CAT93C46P	OEM
CAX15	OEM
CAX20	OEM
CAX25	OEM
CAX30	OEM
CAX1124AS	OEM
CAY10	OEM
CAY11	OEM
CAY12A	OEM
CAY12B	OEM

DEVICE TYPE	REPL CODE
CAY13	OEM
CAY14	OEM
CAY15	OEM
CAY16	OEM
CAY17	OEM
CB1A	OEM
CB1F4	0435
CB2Z-80	OEM
CB5	0015
CB5F	OEM
CB10	0015
CB10F	OEM
CB20	0015
CB20F	OEM
CB40	OEM
CB40F	OEM
CB50	0015
CB60	OEM
CB60F	OEM
CB80	OEM
CB80F	OEM
CB100	0087
CB100F	OEM
CB101	OEM
CB-103	0279
CB103	0136
CB104	0211
CB106	0143
CB150	0015
CB156	0050
CB157	0136
CB158	0136
CB161	0004
CB163	0143
CB200	0015
CB201	OEM
CB202	OEM
CB203	OEM
CB244	0050
CB246	0016
CB248	0004
CB249	0004
CB250	0015
CB254	0050
CB-393	0143
CB393	0143
CB5020	OEM
CB5021	OEM
CB5022	OEM
CB5023	OEM
CBA110	OEM
CBA111	OEM
CBA112	OEM
CBC800/204SCH	OEM
CBC800/204SCL	OEM
CBC800/204SIH	OEM
CBC800/204SIL	OEM
CBC800/204TCH	OEM
CBC800/204TCL	OEM
CBC800/204TIH	OEM
CBC800/204TIL	OEM
CBC800/208SCH	OEM
CBC800/208SCL	OEM
CBC800/208SIH	OEM
CBC800/208SIL	OEM
CBC800/208TCH	OEM
CBC800/208TCL	OEM
CBC800/208TIH	OEM
CBC800/208TIL	OEM
CBC800/216SCH	OEM
CBC800/216SCL	OEM
CBC800/216SIH	OEM
CBC800/216SIL	OEM
CBC800/216TCH	OEM
CBC800/216TCL	OEM
CBC800/216TIH	OEM
CBC800/216TIL	OEM
CC095509	OEM
CC4	OEM
CC4H	OEM
CC4V	OEM
CC-8	OEM
CC8	OEM
CC8V	OEM
CC-12	OEM
CC16	OEM
CC16V	OEM
CC80-C2	OEM
CC80-PP	OEM
CC80-PU	OEM
CC102BA	0015
CC102DA	0015
CC102FA	0015
CC102HA	0015
CC102KA	0015
CC102MA	0015
CC102PA	0071
CC102RA	0071
CC102VA	0071
CC152AA	0071
CC152BA	0071
CC152CA	0071
CC152DA	0071
CC152EA	0071
CC152FA	0071
CC152GA	0071
CC152HA	0071
CC152KA	0071
CC152MA	0071

DEVICE TYPE	REPL CODE
CC152PA	0071
CC152RA	0071
CC152TA	0071
CC152VA	0071
CC280	OEM
CC1168F	0016
CC1600	OEM
CC4012	OEM
CC4013	OEM
CC4015	OEM
CC4016	OEM
CC4018	OEM
CC4020	OEM
CC4022	OEM
CC4024	OEM
CC4027	OEM
CC4030	OEM
CC4033	OEM
CC7228G	OEM
CC59018F	0079
CC104816	OEM
CC105009	OEM
CC105016	OEM
CC105209	OEM
CC105216	OEM
CC105509	OEM
CC134816	OEM
CC135009	OEM
CC135016	OEM
CC135509	OEM
CC204816	OEM
CC205009	OEM
CC205216	OEM
CC205509	OEM
CC215509	OEM
CCB-1	OEM
CCC3500	OEM
CCD450ADC	OEM
CCD450DC	OEM
CCD3000	OEM
CCI-2001	OEM
CCI2001	OEM
CCI2002	OEM
CCI3001	OEM
CCJ5212	0079
CCS-1025	OEM
CCS-1025-1	OEM
CCS-1143	OEM
CCS1235G	0016
CCS2001H	0079
CCS2004B	0111
CCS2005B	0037
CCS-2006D	0079
CCS2006D	0144
CCS2008F015	0144
CCS4004	0016
CCS6168	0016
CCS6168F	0016
CCS6168G	0086
CCS6225F	0007
CCS6226G	0007
CCS6227F	0007
CCS6228F	0037
CCS6229H	0086
CCS7228	OEM
CCS9016D	0144
CCS9016E	0144
CCS9017	0007
CCS9017G925	0007
CCS9018E	0016
CCS9018F	0144
CCS9018H924	0007
CD-0000	0143
CD0000	0133
CD-0000N	0143
CD000	0143
CD005	0015
CD0014	0133
CD0014(MORSE)	0133
CD-0014N	0143
CD0014NA	0016
CD0014NG	0016
CD0015N	0016
CD-0021	0133
CD0021	0016
CD-0033	0631
CD0033	0631
CD0057	0133
CD-0071	0030
CD-05	0015
CD05	0015
CD-07	0469
CD07	0469
CD09	2938
CD1	OEM
CD-2	0015
CD2	0581
CD2A	4919
CD-2N	0015
CD-4	0015
CD5	OEM
CD12	OEM
CD-20	0133
CD21	OEM
CD22	OEM
CD23	OEM
CD24	OEM
CD26	OEM
CD27	OEM

DEVICE TYPE	REPL CODE
CD28	OEM
CD29	OEM
CD31	OEM
CD31-00001	OEM
CD31-00002	0188
CD31-00003	OEM
CD31-00004	OEM
CD31-00005	OEM
CD31-00006	0162
CD31-00007	0157
CD31-00008	0631
CD31-00009	OEM
CD31-00010	OEM
CD31-00011	3071
CD31-00012	0012
CD31-00013	OEM
CD31-00014	OEM
CD31-00015	0137
CD31-00016	OEM
CD31-00017	0002
CD31-00018	OEM
CD31-00019	OEM
CD31-00020	OEM
CD31-00021	OEM
CD31-00022	OEM
CD31-00023	0436
CD31-00024	OEM
CD31-00025	0039
CD31-10361	0436
CD31-10365	0002
CD31-12008	OEM
CD31-12009	OEM
CD31-12010	OEM
CD31-12011	OEM
CD31-12012	OEM
CD31-12013	OEM
CD31-12014	OEM
CD31-12015	0631
CD31-12016	OEM
CD31-12017	OEM
CD31-12018	3071
CD31-12019	0012
CD31-12020	OEM
CD31-12021	OEM
CD31-12022	0137
CD31-12023	OEM
CD31-12024	0002
CD31-12025	OEM
CD31-12026	OEM
CD31-12027	OEM
CD31-12028	OEM
CD31-12029	OEM
CD31-12030	0436
CD31-12031	OEM
CD31-12032	0039
CD31-12039	0012
CD32	OEM
CD32-12046	OEM
CD32-12047	OEM
CD32-12048	3071
CD32-12049	0012
CD32-12050	OEM
CD32-12051	OEM
CD32-12052	0137
CD32-12053	OEM
CD32-12054	0002
CD32-12055	OEM
CD32-12056	OEM
CD32-12057	OEM
CD32-12058	OEM
CD32-12059	OEM
CD32-12060	OEM
CD32-12061	OEM
CD32-12062	OEM
CD33	OEM
CD34	OEM
CD35	OEM
CD36	OEM
CD-37	0133
CD37	0133
CD-37A	0133
CD37A	0133
CD37A2	0015
CD38	6173
CD39	OEM
CD40A6AK	OEM
CD43	OEM
CD47	OEM
CD48	0157
CD51	OEM
CD56	OEM
CD61	OEM
CD62	0466
CD63	OEM
CD68	OEM
CD73/187/72	0564
CD73/187/73	5284
CD74AC00E	OEM
CD74HCT02E	4823
CD74HCT04E	3265
CD74HCT08E	3268
CD74HCT14E	3269
CD74HCT32E	3274
CD74HCT138E	6821
CD74HCT195E	5962
CD74HCT244E	5969
CD74HCT245E	4013
CD74HCT373E	5984
CD75	OEM

334

If replacement code is OEM, contact original manufacturer for replacement.

DEVICE TYPE	REPL CODE
CD82	OEM
CD88P105	OEM
CD91	0057
CD92	OEM
CD93	OEM
CD94	OEM
CD95	OEM
CD96	OEM
CD97	OEM
CD98	OEM
CD100	OEM
CD101	0143
CD200	OEM
CD201	OEM
CD202	OEM
CD203	OEM
CD400EBF	OEM
CD510BE	OEM
CD517BD	OEM
CD610	OEM
CD643	OEM
CD746A	OEM
CD747A	OEM
CD748A	OEM
CD749A	OEM
CD750A	OEM
CD751A	OEM
CD752A	OEM
CD753A	0466
CD754A	OEM
CD755A	OEM
CD756A	OEM
CD758A	OEM
CD759A	0052
CD821	0466
CD821A	0466
CD823	0466
CD823A	0466
CD825	0466
CD825A	0466
CD826	OEM
CD827	0466
CD827A	0466
CD828	OEM
CD829	0466
CD829A	0466
CD860	OEM
CD912	OEM
CD914	OEM
CD922	OEM
CD932	OEM
CD935	OEM
CD935A	OEM
CD936	OEM
CD936A	OEM
CD937	OEM
CD937A	OEM
CD942	OEM
CD952	OEM
CD962	OEM
CD962B	OEM
CD963B	0052
CD964B	OEM
CD965B	0681
CD966B	OEM
CD967B	OEM
CD968B	OEM
CD969B	OEM
CD970B	OEM
CD971B	OEM
CD972	OEM
CD972B	OEM
CD973B	OEM
CD974B	OEM
CD975B	OEM
CD976B	OEM
CD977B	OEM
CD978B	OEM
CD979B	OEM
CD980B	OEM
CD981B	OEM
CD982	OEM
CD982B	OEM
CD983B	OEM
CD984B	OEM
CD985B	OEM
CD986B	OEM
CD987B	OEM
CD988B	OEM
CD989B	OEM
CD990B	OEM
CD991B	OEM
CD992B	OEM
CD1111	0015
CD1112	0015
CD1113	0015
CD1114	0015
CD1115	0015
CD1116	0015
CD1117	0015
CD1121	0015
CD1122	0015
CD1123	0015
CD1124	0015
CD1125	0015
CD1126	0015
CD1127	0015
CD1141	0015
CD1142	0015
CD1143	0015
CD1147	0015
CD1148	0015
CD1149	0015
CD1151	0015
CD1224	0133
CD1324N	OEM
CD2147	OEM
CD2155NL	OEM
CD2156NL	OEM
CD2157NL	OEM
CD2300E	1812
CD2300E/830	1812
CD2301E	1848
CD2301E/861	1848
CD2302E	0141
CD2302E/846	0141
CD2303E	1833
CD2303E/849	1833
CD2304E	0081
CD2304E/845	0081
CD2305E	3365
CD2305E/848	3365
CD2306E	1035
CD2306E/832	1035
CD2307E	0033
CD2307E/844	0033
CD2308E	0557
CD2308E/862	0557
CD2309E	0337
CD2309E/863	0337
CD2310E	1820
CD2310E/836	1820
CD2311E/837	1824
CD2312E	1168
CD2314E	2086
CD2314E/833	2086
CD2315E	0354
CD2318E	0329
CD2434	OEM
CD2500E	OEM
CD2501E	OEM
CD2502E	OEM
CD2503E	OEM
CD2505	OEM
CD2545	2296
CD2810	OEM
CD2812	OEM
CD2813	OEM
CD3025	OEM
CD3034BFX	OEM
CD3080	2296
CD3122	0162
CD3123	OEM
CD3124	OEM
CD3125	OEM
CD3126	OEM
CD3127	OEM
CD3128	OEM
CD3129	OEM
CD3154	OEM
CD3155	OEM
CD3156	OEM
CD3168	OEM
CD3169	OEM
CD3171	0778
CD3172	OEM
CD3173	OEM
CD3174	0327
CD3285	OEM
CD3400	OEM
CD3401	OEM
CD3403	OEM
CD3449	OEM
CD3811	OEM
CD3872	OEM
CD4000AD	2013
CD4000AD3	OEM
CD4000AE	2013
CD4000AEX	OEM
CD4000AF	2013
CD4000AF3	OEM
CD4000AF3W	OEM
CD4000AFB	OEM
CD4000AFX	OEM
CD4000AK	OEM
CD4000AK3	OEM
CD4000AKB	OEM
CD4000AZ	2013
CD4000BD	2013
CD4000BD3	OEM
CD4000BE	2013
CD4000BEX	OEM
CD4000BF	2013
CD4000BF3	OEM
CD4000BF3W	OEM
CD4000BFX	OEM
CD4000BK	OEM
CD4000CJ	2013
CD4000CN	2013
CD4000MJ	2013
CD4000MW	2013
CD4000UBD	2013
CD4000UBD3	OEM
CD4000UBE	2013
CD4000UBEX	OEM
CD4000UBF	2013
CD4000UBF3W	OEM
CD4000UBFX	OEM
CD4000UBK	OEM
CD4001	0473
CD4001AD	0473
CD4001AD3	OEM
CD4001AE	0473
CD4001AEX	OEM
CD4001AF	0473
CD4001AF3	OEM
CD4001AF3W	OEM
CD4001AFB	OEM
CD4001AFX	OEM
CD4001AK	OEM
CD4001AK3	OEM
CD4001AKB	OEM
CD4001B	OEM
CD4001BCJ	0473
CD4001BCN	0473
CD4001BD	0473
CD4001BD3	OEM
CD4001BE	0473
CD4001BEX	OEM
CD4001BF	0473
CD4001BF3	OEM
CD4001BF3W	OEM
CD4001BFX	OEM
CD4001BK	OEM
CD4001BK3	OEM
CD4001BMJ	0473
CD4001BMW	0473
CD4001CJ	0473
CD4001CN	0473
CD4001MJ	0473
CD4001MW	0473
CD4001UBD	0473
CD4001UBD3	OEM
CD4001UBE	0473
CD4001UBEX	OEM
CD4001UBF	0473
CD4001UBF3	OEM
CD4001UBF3W	OEM
CD4001UBFX	OEM
CD4001UBK	OEM
CD4002	2044
CD4002AD	2044
CD4002AD3	OEM
CD4002AE	2044
CD4002AEX	OEM
CD4002AF	2044
CD4002AF3	OEM
CD4002AF3W	OEM
CD4002AFB	OEM
CD4002AFX	OEM
CD4002AK	OEM
CD4002AK3	OEM
CD4002AKB	OEM
CD4002BD	2044
CD4002BD3	OEM
CD4002BE	2044
CD4002BEX	OEM
CD4002BF	2044
CD4002BF3	OEM
CD4002BF3W	OEM
CD4002BFX	OEM
CD4002BK	OEM
CD4002BK3	OEM
CD4002CJ	2044
CD4002CN	2044
CD4002MJ	2044
CD4002MW	2044
CD4002UBD	2044
CD4002UBD3	OEM
CD4002UBE	2044
CD4002UBEX	OEM
CD4002UBF	2044
CD4002UBF3	OEM
CD4002UBF3W	OEM
CD4002UBFX	OEM
CD4002UBK	OEM
CD4004AE	OEM
CD4006	0641
CD4006AD	OEM
CD4006AD3	OEM
CD4006AE	0641
CD4006AEX	OEM
CD4006AF	OEM
CD4006AF3	OEM
CD4006AF3W	OEM
CD4006AFB	OEM
CD4006AFX	OEM
CD4006AH	OEM
CD4006AK	OEM
CD4006AK3	OEM
CD4006AKB	OEM
CD4006BD	OEM
CD4006BD3	OEM
CD4006BE	0641
CD4006BEX	OEM
CD4006BF	OEM
CD4006BF3	OEM
CD4006BF3W	OEM
CD4006BH	OEM
CD4006BK	OEM
CD4006BK3	OEM
CD4007AD	OEM
CD4007AD3	OEM
CD4007AE	2819
CD4007AEX	OEM
CD4007AF	2819
CD4007AF3	OEM
CD4007AF3W	OEM
CD4007AFB	OEM
CD4007AFX	OEM
CD4007AK3	OEM
CD4007AKB	OEM
CD4007C	OEM
CD4007CJ	2819
CD4007CN	2819
CD4007M	OEM
CD4007UBD	4897
CD4007UBE	2819
CD4007UBEX	OEM
CD4007UBF	4897
CD4007UBF3	OEM
CD4007UBF3W	OEM
CD4007UBFX	OEM
CD4007UBK	OEM
CD4007UBK3	OEM
CD4008AD	0982
CD4008AD3	OEM
CD4008AE	0982
CD4008AEX	OEM
CD4008AF	0982
CD4008AF3	OEM
CD4008AF3W	OEM
CD4008AFX	OEM
CD4008AK	OEM
CD4008AK3	OEM
CD4008B	0982
CD4008BCJ	0982
CD4008BCN	0982
CD4008BD	0982
CD4008BD3	OEM
CD4008BE	0982
CD4008BEX	OEM
CD4008BF	0982
CD4008BF3	OEM
CD4008BF3W	OEM
CD4008BJ	0982
CD4008BK	OEM
CD4008BK3	OEM
CD4008BMJ	0982
CD4008BMW	0982
CD4009AD	1988
CD4009AE	0001
CD4009AF	1988
CD4009AH	OEM
CD4009AK	OEM
CD4009AY	OEM
CD4009CJ	0001
CD4009CN	0001
CD4009MJ	3229
CD4009MW	OEM
CD4009UBD	1988
CD4009UBD3	OEM
CD4009UBE	1988
CD4009UBEX	OEM
CD4009UBF	1988
CD4009UBF3	OEM
CD4009UBF3W	OEM
CD4009UBFX	OEM
CD4009UBH	OEM
CD4009UBK	OEM
CD4009UBK3	OEM
CD4010AD	3222
CD4010AE	0394
CD4010AF	3222
CD4010AH	OEM
CD4010AK	OEM
CD4010AY	OEM
CD4010BD	3222
CD4010BD3	OEM
CD4010BE	0394
CD4010BEX	OEM
CD4010BF	3222
CD4010BF3	OEM
CD4010BF3W	OEM
CD4010BFX	OEM
CD4010BH	OEM
CD4010BK	OEM
CD4010BK3	OEM
CD4010CJ	0394
CD4010CN	0394
CD4010MJ	3222
CD4010MW	OEM
CD4011	0215
CD4011AD	0215
CD4011AD3	OEM
CD4011AE	0215
CD4011AEX	OEM
CD4011AF	0215
CD4011AF3	OEM
CD4011AF3W	OEM
CD4011AFB	OEM
CD4011AFX	OEM
CD4011AK	OEM
CD4011AK3	OEM
CD4011AKB	OEM
CD4011BCJ	0215
CD4011BCN	0215
CD4011BD	0215
CD4011BE	0215
CD4011BEX	OEM
CD4011BF	0215
CD4011BF3	OEM
CD4011BF3W	OEM
CD4011BFX	OEM
CD4011BK	OEM
CD4011BK3	OEM
CD4011BMJ	0215
CD4011BMW	0215
CD4011CJ	0215
CD4011CN	0215
CD4011MJ	0215
CD4011MW	0215
CD4011UBD	0215
CD4011UBD3	OEM
CD4011UBE	0215
CD4011UBEX	OEM
CD4011UBF	0215
CD4011UBF3	OEM
CD4011UBF3W	OEM
CD4011UBFX	OEM
CD4011UBK	OEM
CD4011UBK3	OEM
CD4012	0493
CD4012AD	0493
CD4012AD3	OEM
CD4012AE	0493
CD4012AEX	OEM
CD4012AF	0493
CD4012AF3	OEM
CD4012AF3W	OEM
CD4012AFB	OEM
CD4012AFX	OEM
CD4012AK	OEM
CD4012AK3	OEM
CD4012AKB	OEM
CD4012BD	0493
CD4012BD3	OEM
CD4012BE	0493
CD4012BEX	OEM
CD4012BF	0493
CD4012BF3	OEM
CD4012BF3W	OEM
CD4012BFX	OEM
CD4012BK	OEM
CD4012BK3	OEM
CD4012CJ	0493
CD4012CN	0493
CD4012MJ	0493
CD4012MW	0493
CD4012UBD	0493
CD4012UBD3	OEM
CD4012UBE	0493
CD4012UBEX	OEM
CD4012UBF	0493
CD4012UBF3	OEM
CD4012UBF3W	OEM
CD4012UBK	OEM
CD4013	0409
CD4013AD	0409
CD4013AD3	OEM
CD4013AE	0409
CD4013AEX	OEM
CD4013AF	0409
CD4013AF3	OEM
CD4013AF3W	OEM
CD4013AFB	OEM
CD4013AFX	OEM
CD4013AK	OEM
CD4013AK3	OEM
CD4013AKB	OEM
CD4013B	0409
CD4013BCJ	0409
CD4013BCN	0409
CD4013BD	0409
CD4013BD3	OEM
CD4013BE	0409
CD4013BEX	OEM
CD4013BF	0409
CD4013BF3	OEM
CD4013BF3W	OEM
CD4013BFX	OEM
CD4013BK	OEM
CD4013BK3	OEM
CD4013BMJ	0409
CD4013BMW	0409
CD4013BN	0409
CD4014AD	0854
CD4014AD3	OEM
CD4014AE	0854
CD4014AEX	OEM
CD4014AF	0854
CD4014AF3	OEM
CD4014AF3W	OEM
CD4014AFB	OEM
CD4014AFX	OEM
CD4014AH	OEM
CD4014AK	OEM
CD4014AK3	OEM
CD4014AKB	OEM
CD4014BD	0854
CD4014BD3	OEM
CD4014BE	0854
CD4014BEX	OEM
CD4014BF	0854
CD4014BF3	OEM
CD4014BF3W	OEM
CD4014BFX	OEM
CD4014BH	OEM
CD4014BK	OEM
CD4014BK3	OEM
CD4015	1008
CD4015AD	1008
CD4015AD3	OEM
CD4015AE	1008
CD4015AEX	OEM
CD4015AF	1008
CD4015AF3	OEM
CD4015AF3W	OEM
CD4015AFB	OEM
CD4015AFX	OEM
CD4015AH	OEM
CD4015AK	OEM
CD4015AK3	OEM
CD4015AKB	OEM
CD4015BD	1008
CD4015BD3	OEM
CD4015BE	1008
CD4015BEX	OEM
CD4015BF	1008
CD4015BFX	OEM
CD4015BH	OEM
CD4015BK	OEM
CD4015BK3	OEM
CD4016	1135
CD4016AD	1135
CD4016AD3	OEM
CD4016AE	1135
CD4016AEX	OEM
CD4016AF	1135
CD4016AF3	OEM
CD4016AF3W	OEM
CD4016AFX	OEM
CD4016AH	OEM
CD4016AK	OEM
CD4016AK3	OEM
CD4016AY	OEM
CD4016B	1135
CD4016BD	1135
CD4016BD3	OEM
CD4016BE	1135
CD4016BEX	OEM
CD4016BF	1135
CD4016BF3	OEM
CD4016BF3W	OEM
CD4016BFX	OEM
CD4016BH	OEM
CD4016BK	OEM
CD4016CJ	1135
CD4016CN	1135
CD4016MJ	1135
CD4017	0508
CD4017AD	0508
CD4017AD3	OEM
CD4017AE	0508
CD4017AEX	OEM
CD4017AF	0508
CD4017AF3	OEM
CD4017AF3W	OEM
CD4017AFB	OEM
CD4017AFX	OEM
CD4017AK	OEM
CD4017AK3	OEM
CD4017BCJ	0508
CD4017BCN	0508
CD4017BD	0508
CD4017BD3	OEM
CD4017BE	0508
CD4017BEX	OEM
CD4017BF	0508
CD4017BF3	OEM
CD4017BF3W	OEM
CD4017BFX	OEM
CD4017BK	OEM
CD4017BK3	OEM
CD4017BMJ	0508
CD4017BMW	0508
CD4018	1381
CD4018AD	1381
CD4018AD3	OEM
CD4018AE	1381
CD4018AEX	OEM
CD4018AF	1381
CD4018AFB	OEM
CD4018AFX	OEM
CD4018AK	OEM
CD4018AK3	OEM
CD4018AK8	OEM
CD4018AKB	OEM
CD4018BAF3W	OEM
CD4018BCJ	1381
CD4018BCN	1381
CD4018BD	1381
CD4018BD3	OEM
CD4018BE	1381
CD4018BEX	OEM
CD4018BF	1381
CD4018BF3W	OEM
CD4018BFX	OEM
CD4018BK	OEM
CD4018BK3	OEM
CD4018BMJ	1381
CD4018BMW	1381
CD4019	1517
CD4019AD	1517
CD4019AD3	OEM
CD4019AE	1517
CD4019AEX	OEM
CD4019AF	1517
CD4019AF3	OEM
CD4019AF3W	OEM
CD4019AFB	OEM
CD4019AFX	OEM
CD4019AH	OEM
CD4019AK	OEM
CD4019AK3	OEM
CD4019AKB	OEM
CD4019AY	OEM
CD4019BC	1517
CD4019BCJ	1517
CD4019BCN	1517
CD4019BD	1517
CD4019BD3	OEM
CD4019BE	1517
CD4019BEX	OEM
CD4019BF	1517
CD4019BF3	OEM
CD4019BF3W	OEM
CD4019BFX	OEM
CD4019BK	OEM
CD4019BK3	OEM
CD4019BM	OEM
CD4019BMJ	6103
CD4019BMW	OEM
CD4020	1651
CD4020AD	1651
CD4020AD3	OEM
CD4020AE	1651
CD4020AEX	OEM
CD4020AF	1651
CD4020AF3	OEM
CD4020AF3W	OEM
CD4020AFB	OEM
CD4020AFX	OEM
CD4020AK	OEM
CD4020AK3	OEM
CD4020AKB	OEM
CD4020BCJ	1651
CD4020BCN	1651
CD4020BD	1651
CD4020BD3	OEM
CD4020BE	1651
CD4020BEX	OEM
CD4020BF	1651
CD4020BF3	OEM
CD4020BF3W	OEM
CD4020BFX	OEM
CD4020BK3	OEM
CD4020BMJ	1651
CD4020BMW	1651
CD4021	1738
CD4021AD	1738
CD4021AD3	OEM
CD4021AE	1738
CD4021AEX	OEM
CD4021AF	1738
CD4021AF3	OEM
CD4021AF3W	OEM
CD4021AFB	OEM
CD4021AFX	OEM
CD4021AH	OEM
CD4021AK	OEM
CD4021AK3	OEM
CD4021AKB	OEM
CD4021AY	OEM
CD4021BD	1738
CD4021BD3	OEM
CD4021BE	1738
CD4021BEX	OEM
CD4021BF	1738
CD4021BF3	OEM
CD4021BF3W	OEM
CD4021BFX	OEM
CD4021BH	OEM
CD4021BK	OEM
CD4021BK3	OEM
CD4022	1247
CD4022AD	1247
CD4022AD3	OEM
CD4022AE	1247
CD4022AEX	OEM
CD4022AF	1247
CD4022AF3	OEM
CD4022AF3W	OEM
CD4022AFB	OEM
CD4022AFX	OEM
CD4022AK	OEM
CD4022AK3	OEM
CD4022AKB	OEM
CD4022BCJ	1247
CD4022BCN	1247
CD4022BD	1247
CD4022BD3	OEM
CD4022BE	1247
CD4022BEX	OEM
CD4022BF	1247
CD4022BF3	OEM
CD4022BF3W	OEM
CD4022BFX	OEM
CD4022BK	OEM
CD4022BMJ	1247
CD4022BMW	1247
CD4023	0515
CD4023AD	0515
CD4023AD3	OEM
CD4023AE	0515
CD4023AEX	OEM
CD4023AF	0515
CD4023AF3	OEM
CD4023AF3W	OEM
CD4023AFB	OEM
CD4023AFX	OEM
CD4023AK	OEM

If replacement code is OEM, contact original manufacturer for replacement. 335

DEVICE TYPE	REPL CODE
CD4023AK3	OEM
CD4023AKB	OEM
CD4023BCJ	0515
CD4023BCN	0515
CD4023BD	0515
CD4023BE	0515
CD4023BEX	OEM
CD4023BF	0515
CD4023BF3	OEM
CD4023BF3W	OEM
CD4023BFX	OEM
CD4023BK	OEM
CD4023BMJ	0515
CD4023BMW	0515
CD4023C	0515
CD4023CJ	0515
CD4023CN	0515
CD4023MJ	0515
CD4023MW	0515
CD4023UBD	0515
CD4023UBD3	OEM
CD4023UBE	0515
CD4023UBEX	OEM
CD4023UBF	0515
CD4023UBF3	OEM
CD4023UBF3W	OEM
CD4023UBFX	OEM
CD4023UBK	OEM
CD4024	1946
CD4024AD	1946
CD4024AD3	OEM
CD4024AE	1946
CD4024AEX	OEM
CD4024AF	1946
CD4024AF3	OEM
CD4024AF3W	OEM
CD4024AFB	OEM
CD4024AFX	OEM
CD4024AK	OEM
CD4024AK3	OEM
CD4024AKB	OEM
CD4024AT	OEM
CD4024BCJ	1946
CD4024BCN	1946
CD4024BD	1946
CD4024BD3	OEM
CD4024BE	1946
CD4024BEX	OEM
CD4024BF	1946
CD4024BF3W	OEM
CD4024BFX	OEM
CD4024BK	OEM
CD4024BK3	OEM
CD4024BMJ	1946
CD4024BMW	1946
CD4025	2061
CD4025AD	2061
CD4025AD3	OEM
CD4025AE	2061
CD4025AEX	OEM
CD4025AF	2061
CD4025AF3	OEM
CD4025AF3W	OEM
CD4025AFB	OEM
CD4025AFX	OEM
CD4025AK	OEM
CD4025AK3	OEM
CD4025AKB	OEM
CD4025BCJ	2061
CD4025BCN	2061
CD4025BD	2061
CD4025BE	2061
CD4025BEX	OEM
CD4025BF	2061
CD4025BF3	OEM
CD4025BF3W	OEM
CD4025BFX	OEM
CD4025BK	OEM
CD4025BK3	OEM
CD4025BMJ	2061
CD4025BMW	2061
CD4025CJ	2061
CD4025CN	2061
CD4025MJ	2061
CD4025MW	2061
CD4025UBD	2061
CD4025UBD3	OEM
CD4025UBE	2061
CD4025UBEX	OEM
CD4025UBF	2061
CD4025UBF3	OEM
CD4025UBF3W	OEM
CD4025UBFX	OEM
CD4025UBK	OEM
CD4026AD	2139
CD4026AD3	OEM
CD4026AE	2139
CD4026AEX	OEM
CD4026AF	2139
CD4026AF3	OEM
CD4026AF3W	OEM
CD4026AFX	OEM
CD4026AK	OEM
CD4026AK3	OEM
CD4026B3W	OEM
CD4026BD	2139
CD4026BE	2139
CD4026BEX	OEM
CD4026BF	2139
CD4026BF3	OEM
CD4026BFX	OEM
CD4026BH	OEM
CD4026BK	OEM
CD4027	1938
CD4027AD	1938
CD4027AD3	OEM
CD4027AE	1938
CD4027AEX	OEM
CD4027AF	1938
CD4027AF3	OEM
CD4027AF3W	OEM
CD4027AFB	OEM
CD4027AFX	OEM
CD4027AK	OEM
CD4027AK3	OEM
CD4027AKB	OEM
CD4027BCJ	1938
CD4027BCN	1938
CD4027BD	1938
CD4027BD3	OEM
CD4027BE	1938
CD4027BEX	OEM
CD4027BF	1938
CD4027BF3	OEM
CD4027BF3W	OEM
CD4027BFX	OEM
CD4027BK	OEM
CD4027BK3	OEM
CD4027BMJ	1938
CD4027BMW	1938
CD4028AD	2213
CD4028AD3	OEM
CD4028AE	2213
CD4028AEX	OEM
CD4028AF	2213
CD4028AF3	OEM
CD4028AF3W	OEM
CD4028AFX	OEM
CD4028AK	OEM
CD4028AK3	OEM
CD4028BCJ	2213
CD4028BCN	2213
CD4028BD	2213
CD4028BD3	OEM
CD4028BE	2213
CD4028BEX	OEM
CD4028BF	2213
CD4028BF3	OEM
CD4028BF3W	OEM
CD4028BFX	OEM
CD4028BK	OEM
CD4028BK3	OEM
CD4028BMJ	2213
CD4028BMW	2213
CD4028F	2213
CD4029AD	2218
CD4029AD3	OEM
CD4029AE	2218
CD4029AEX	OEM
CD4029AF	2218
CD4029AF3	OEM
CD4029AF3W	OEM
CD4029AFX	OEM
CD4029AK	OEM
CD4029AK3	OEM
CD4029BCJ	2218
CD4029BCN	2218
CD4029BD	2218
CD4029BD3	OEM
CD4029BE	2218
CD4029BEX	OEM
CD4029BF	2218
CD4029BF3	OEM
CD4029BF3W	OEM
CD4029BFX	OEM
CD4029BK	OEM
CD4029BMJ	2218
CD4029BMW	2218
CD4030	0495
CD4030AD	0495
CD4030AD3	OEM
CD4030AE	0495
CD4030AEX	OEM
CD4030AF	0495
CD4030AF3	OEM
CD4030AF3W	OEM
CD4030AFX	OEM
CD4030AK	OEM
CD4030AK3	OEM
CD4030BD	0495
CD4030BD3	OEM
CD4030BE	0495
CD4030BEX	OEM
CD4030BF	0495
CD4030BF3	OEM
CD4030BF3W	OEM
CD4030BFX	OEM
CD4030BK	OEM
CD4030BMW	0495
CD4030CJ	0495
CD4030CN	0495
CD4030MJ	0495
CD4030MW	0495
CD4031AD	2943
CD4031AD3	OEM
CD4031AE	2943
CD4031AEX	OEM
CD4031AF	2943
CD4031AF3	OEM
CD4031AF3W	OEM
CD4031AFX	OEM
CD4031AH	OEM
CD4031AK	OEM
CD4031AK3	OEM
CD4031AKB	OEM
CD4031BD	2943
CD4031BE	2943
CD4031BEX	OEM
CD4031BF	2943
CD4031BF3	OEM
CD4031BF3W	OEM
CD4031BFX	OEM
CD4031BH	OEM
CD4031BK	OEM
CD4031BK3	OEM
CD4032AD	2509
CD4032AE	2509
CD4032AEX	OEM
CD4032AF	2509
CD4032AK	OEM
CD4032BD	2509
CD4032BE	2509
CD4032BEX	OEM
CD4032BF	2509
CD4032BFX	OEM
CD4032BK	OEM
CD4033	2611
CD4033AD	2611
CD4033AD3	OEM
CD4033AE	2611
CD4033AEX	OEM
CD4033AF	2611
CD4033AF3	OEM
CD4033AF3W	OEM
CD4033AFX	OEM
CD4033AK	OEM
CD4033AK3	OEM
CD4033BD	2611
CD4033BE	2611
CD4033BEX	OEM
CD4033BF	2611
CD4033BF3	OEM
CD4033BF3W	OEM
CD4033BFX	OEM
CD4033BH	OEM
CD4033BK	OEM
CD4034AD	3570
CD4034AD3	OEM
CD4034AE	3570
CD4034AEX	OEM
CD4034AF	3570
CD4034AF3	OEM
CD4034AF3W	OEM
CD4034AH	OEM
CD4034AK	OEM
CD4034AK3	OEM
CD4034AY	3570
CD4034BD	3570
CD4034BE	3570
CD4034BEX	OEM
CD4034BF	3570
CD4034BF3	OEM
CD4034BF3W	OEM
CD4034BH	OEM
CD4034BK	OEM
CD4034BK3	OEM
CD4034FX	OEM
CD4035AD	2750
CD4035AD3	OEM
CD4035AE	2750
CD4035AEX	OEM
CD4035AF	2750
CD4035AF3	OEM
CD4035AF3W	OEM
CD4035AFX	OEM
CD4035AH	OEM
CD4035AK	OEM
CD4035AK3	OEM
CD4035AY	2750
CD4035BD	2750
CD4035BD3	OEM
CD4035BE	2750
CD4035BEX	OEM
CD4035BF	2750
CD4035BF3	OEM
CD4035BF3W	OEM
CD4035BFX	OEM
CD4035BH	OEM
CD4035BK	OEM
CD4035BK3	OEM
CD4036AD	OEM
CD4036AE	OEM
CD4036AEX	OEM
CD4036AF	OEM
CD4037AD	OEM
CD4037AE	OEM
CD4037AEX	OEM
CD4037AF	OEM
CD4037AFX	OEM
CD4037AK	OEM
CD4038AD	2953
CD4038AE	2953
CD4038AEX	OEM
CD4038AF	2953
CD4038AFX	OEM
CD4038BD	2953
CD4038BE	2953
CD4038BEX	OEM
CD4038BF	2953
CD4038BFX	OEM
CD4038BK	OEM
CD4038BK3	OEM
CD4039AD	OEM
CD4039AE	OEM
CD4039AEX	OEM
CD4039AK	OEM
CD4040	0056
CD4040AD	0056
CD4040AD3	OEM
CD4040AE	0056
CD4040AEX	OEM
CD4040AF	0056
CD4040AF3	OEM
CD4040AF3W	OEM
CD4040AFX	OEM
CD4040AK	OEM
CD4040AK3	OEM
CD4040BCJ	0056
CD4040BCN	0056
CD4040BD	0056
CD4040BD3	OEM
CD4040BE	0056
CD4040BEX	OEM
CD4040BF	0056
CD4040BF3	OEM
CD4040BF3W	OEM
CD4040BFX	OEM
CD4040BK	OEM
CD4040BK3	OEM
CD4040BMJ	0056
CD4040BMW	0056
CD4041AD	3145
CD4041AD3	OEM
CD4041AE	3145
CD4041AEX	OEM
CD4041AF	3145
CD4041AF3	OEM
CD4041AF3W	OEM
CD4041AFX	OEM
CD4041AH	OEM
CD4041AK	OEM
CD4041AK3	OEM
CD4041AY	3145
CD4041CJ	3145
CD4041CN	3145
CD4041MJ	3145
CD4041MW	OEM
CD4041UBD	3145
CD4041UBD3	OEM
CD4041UBE	3145
CD4041UBEX	OEM
CD4041UBF	3145
CD4041UBF3	OEM
CD4041UBF3W	OEM
CD4041UBFX	OEM
CD4041UBH	OEM
CD4041UBK	OEM
CD4041UBK3	OEM
CD4042	0121
CD4042AD	0121
CD4042AD3	OEM
CD4042AE	0121
CD4042AEX	OEM
CD4042AF	0121
CD4042AF3	OEM
CD4042AF3W	OEM
CD4042AFX	OEM
CD4042AK	OEM
CD4042AK3	OEM
CD4042BCJ	0121
CD4042BCN	0121
CD4042BD	0121
CD4042BD3	OEM
CD4042BE	0121
CD4042BEX	OEM
CD4042BF	0121
CD4042BF3	OEM
CD4042BF3W	OEM
CD4042BFX	OEM
CD4042BMJ	0121
CD4042BMW	0121
CD4043AD	1544
CD4043AD3	OEM
CD4043AE	1544
CD4043AEX	OEM
CD4043AF	1544
CD4043AF3	OEM
CD4043AF3W	OEM
CD4043AFX	OEM
CD4043AK	OEM
CD4043AK3	OEM
CD4043BD	1544
CD4043BD3	OEM
CD4043BE	1544
CD4043BEX	OEM
CD4043BF	1544
CD4043BF3	OEM
CD4043BF3W	OEM
CD4043BFX	OEM
CD4043BK	OEM
CD4043CJ	1544
CD4043CN	1544
CD4043MJ	1544
CD4043MW	1544
CD4044AD	2292
CD4044AD3	OEM
CD4044AE	2292
CD4044AEX	OEM
CD4044AF	2292
CD4044AF3	OEM
CD4044AF3W	OEM
CD4044AFX	OEM
CD4044AK	OEM
CD4044AK3	OEM
CD4044BD	2292
CD4044BD3	OEM
CD4044BE	2292
CD4044BEX	OEM
CD4044BF	2292
CD4044BF3	OEM
CD4044BF3W	OEM
CD4044BFX	OEM
CD4044BK	OEM
CD4044CJ	2292
CD4044CN	2292
CD4044MJ	2292
CD4044MW	2292
CD4045AD	OEM
CD4045AD3	OEM
CD4045AE	3408
CD4045AEX	OEM
CD4045AF	3408
CD4045AFX	OEM
CD4045AK	OEM
CD4045AK3	OEM
CD4045BD	3408
CD4045BE	3408
CD4045BEX	OEM
CD4045BF	3408
CD4045BFX	OEM
CD4045BH	OEM
CD4045BK	OEM
CD4046A	3394
CD4046AD	3394
CD4046AD3	OEM
CD4046AE	3779
CD4046AEX	OEM
CD4046AF	3394
CD4046AF3	OEM
CD4046AF3W	OEM
CD4046AFX	OEM
CD4046AK	OEM
CD4046AK3	OEM
CD4046BD	3394
CD4046BE	3394
CD4046BEX	OEM
CD4046BF	3394
CD4046BFX	OEM
CD4046BH	OEM
CD4046BK	OEM
CD4046BK3	OEM
CD4047AD	2315
CD4047AD3	OEM
CD4047AE	2315
CD4047AEX	OEM
CD4047AF	2315
CD4047AF3	OEM
CD4047AF3W	OEM
CD4047AFX	OEM
CD4047AK	OEM
CD4047AK3	OEM
CD4047BCJ	2315
CD4047BCN	2315
CD4047BD	2315
CD4047BD3	OEM
CD4047BE	2315
CD4047BEX	OEM
CD4047BF	2315
CD4047BF3	OEM
CD4047BF3W	OEM
CD4047BFX	OEM
CD4047BK	OEM
CD4047BK3	OEM
CD4047BMJ	2315
CD4047BMW	2315
CD4048AD	3422
CD4048AD3	OEM
CD4048AE	3423
CD4048AEX	OEM
CD4048AF	3423
CD4048AF3	OEM
CD4048AF3W	OEM
CD4048AFX	OEM
CD4048AK	OEM
CD4048AK3	OEM
CD4048BCJ	3423
CD4048BCN	3423
CD4048BD	3422
CD4048BD3	OEM
CD4048BE	3423
CD4048BEX	OEM
CD4048BF	3423
CD4048BF3	OEM
CD4048BF3W	OEM
CD4048BFX	OEM
CD4048BH	OEM
CD4048BK	OEM
CD4048BMJ	3423
CD4048BMW	OEM
CD4049AD	0001
CD4049AD3	OEM
CD4049AE	0001
CD4049AEX	OEM
CD4049AF	0001
CD4049AF3	OEM
CD4049AF3W	OEM
CD4049AFB	OEM
CD4049AFX	OEM
CD4049AH	OEM
CD4049AK	OEM
CD4049AK3	OEM
CD4049AKB	OEM
CD4049CJ	0001
CD4049CN	0001
CD4049MJ	0001
CD4049MW	OEM
CD4049UBD	0001
CD4049UBD3	OEM
CD4049UBE	0001
CD4049UBEX	OEM
CD4049UBF	0001
CD4049UBF3	OEM
CD4049UBF3W	OEM
CD4049UBFX	OEM
CD4049UBH	OEM
CD4049UBK	OEM
CD4049UBK3	OEM
CD4050	0394
CD4050AD	0394
CD4050AD3	OEM
CD4050AE	0394
CD4050AEX	OEM
CD4050AF	0394
CD4050AF3	OEM
CD4050AF3W	OEM
CD4050AFB	OEM
CD4050AFX	OEM
CD4050AH	OEM
CD4050AK	OEM
CD4050AK3	OEM
CD4050AKB	OEM
CD4050B	0394
CD4050BCJ	0394
CD4050BCN	0394
CD4050BD	0394
CD4050BD3	OEM
CD4050BE	0394
CD4050BEX	OEM
CD4050BF	0394
CD4050BF3	OEM
CD4050BF3W	OEM
CD4050BFX	OEM
CD4050BH	OEM
CD4050BK	OEM
CD4050BK3	OEM
CD4050BMJ	6211
CD4050BMW	OEM
CD4051	0362
CD4051AE	0362
CD4051B	0362
CD4051BCJ	0362
CD4051BCN	0362
CD4051BD	0362
CD4051BD3	OEM
CD4051BE	0362
CD4051BEX	OEM
CD4051BF	0362
CD4051BF3	OEM
CD4051BF3W	OEM
CD4051BFX	OEM
CD4051BH	OEM
CD4051BK	OEM
CD4051BK3	OEM
CD4051BMJ	0362
CD4051BMW	OEM
CD4052	0024
CD4052AE	0362
CD4052B	3418
CD4052BCJ	0024
CD4052BCN	0024
CD4052BD	0024
CD4052BD3	OEM
CD4052BE	0024
CD4052BEX	OEM
CD4052BF	0024
CD4052BF3	OEM
CD4052BF3W	OEM
CD4052BFX	OEM
CD4052BH	OEM
CD4052BK	OEM
CD4052BK3	OEM
CD4052BMJ	0024
CD4052BMW	OEM
CD4053BCJ	0034
CD4053BCN	0034
CD4053BD	0034
CD4053BD3	OEM
CD4053BE	0034
CD4053BEX	OEM
CD4053BF	0034
CD4053BF3	OEM
CD4053BF3W	OEM
CD4053BFX	OEM
CD4053BH	OEM
CD4053BK	OEM
CD4053BK3	OEM
CD4053BMJ	6490
CD4053BMW	OEM
CD4053BP	0034
CD4054BD	4450
CD4054BE	4450
CD4054BEX	OEM
CD4054BF	4450
CD4054BFX	OEM
CD4054BH	OEM
CD4054BK	OEM
CD4054BY	4450
CD4055	3272
CD4055AE	3272
CD4055BD	3272
CD4055BE	3272
CD4055BEX	OEM
CD4055BF	3272
CD4055BFX	OEM
CD4055BH	OEM
CD4055BK	OEM
CD4055BY	3272
CD4056BD	3661
CD4056BE	3661
CD4056BEX	OEM
CD4056BFX	OEM
CD4056BH	OEM
CD4056BK	OEM
CD4056BY	3661
CD4057AD	OEM
CD4057AD3	OEM
CD4057AK	OEM
CD4057AK3	OEM
CD4059	3276
CD4059AD	3276
CD4059AD3	OEM
CD4059AE	3276
CD4059AEX	OEM
CD4059AF	3276
CD4059AFX	OEM
CD4059AK	OEM
CD4059AK3	OEM
CD4060	0146
CD4060AD	0146
CD4060AD3	0146
CD4060AE	0146
CD4060AEX	OEM
CD4060AF	0146
CD4060AF3	OEM
CD4060AF3W	OEM
CD4060AFX	OEM
CD4060AK	OEM
CD4060AK3	OEM
CD4060BCJ	0146
CD4060BCN	0146
CD4060BD	0146
CD4060BD3	0146
CD4060BE	0146
CD4060BEX	OEM
CD4060BF	0146
CD4060BF3	OEM
CD4060BF3W	OEM
CD4060BFX	OEM
CD4060BH	0146
CD4060BK	OEM
CD4060BMJ	0146
CD4060BMW	0146
CD4061AD	OEM
CD4062AH	OEM
CD4062AK	OEM
CD4062AK3	OEM
CD4062AT	OEM
CD4063BD	3682
CD4063BD3	OEM
CD4063BE	0146
CD4063BEX	OEM
CD4063BF	3682
CD4063BF3	OEM
CD4063BF3W	OEM
CD4063BFX	OEM
CD4063BK	OEM
CD4063BK3	OEM
CD4065BF	OEM
CD4066	0101
CD4066AD	0101
CD4066AD3	OEM
CD4066AE	0101
CD4066AEX	OEM
CD4066AF	0101
CD4066AF3	OEM
CD4066AF3W	OEM
CD4066AFX	OEM
CD4066AH	OEM
CD4066AK	OEM
CD4066AK3	OEM
CD-4066B	0101
CD4066B	0101
CD4066BCJ	0101
CD4066BCN	0101
CD4066BD	0101
CD4066BD3	OEM
CD4066BE	0101
CD4066BEX	OEM
CD4066BEXV	OEM
CD4066BF	0101
CD4066BF3	OEM
CD4066BF3W	OEM
CD4066BFX	OEM
CD4066BH	OEM
CD4066BK	OEM
CD4066BK3	OEM
CD4066BMJ	0101
CD4066BMW	OEM
CD4067BD	3696
CD4067BD3	OEM
CD4067BE	3696
CD4067BEX	OEM
CD4067BF	3696

If replacement code is OEM, contact original manufacturer for replacement.

DEVICE TYPE	REPL CODE
CD4067BF3	OEM
CD4067BF3W	OEM
CD4067BFX	OEM
CD4067BH	OEM
CD4067BK	OEM
CD4068BD	2482
CD4068BD3	OEM
CD4068BE	2482
CD4068BEX	OEM
CD4068BF	2482
CD4068BF3	OEM
CD4068BF3W	OEM
CD4068BFX	OEM
CD4068BK	OEM
CD4068BK3	OEM
CD4069	3279
CD4069BE	0119
CD4069C	0119
CD4069CJ	0119
CD4069CM(SM)	OEM
CD4069CN	0119
CD4069M	0119
CD4069MJ	0119
CD4069MW	OEM
CD4069N	0119
CD4069UB	3279
CD4069UBD	0119
CD4069UBD3	OEM
CD4069UBE	0119
CD4069UBEX	OEM
CD4069UBF	0119
CD4069UBF3	OEM
CD4069UBF3W	OEM
CD4069UBFX	OEM
CD4069UBH	OEM
CD4069UBK	OEM
CD4069UBK3	OEM
CD4070	0495
CD4070BCJ	2494
CD4070BCN	2494
CD4070BD	2494
CD4070BD3	OEM
CD4070BE	2494
CD4070BEX	OEM
CD4070BF	2494
CD4070BF3	OEM
CD4070BF3W	OEM
CD4070BFB	OEM
CD4070BFX	OEM
CD4070BK	OEM
CD4070BK3	OEM
CD4070BMJ	2494
CD4070BMW	2494
CD4071BCJ	0129
CD4071BCN	0129
CD4071BD	0129
CD4071BD3	OEM
CD4071BE	0129
CD4071BEX	OEM
CD4071BF	0129
CD4071BF3	OEM
CD4071BF3W	OEM
CD4071BFB	OEM
CD4071BFX	OEM
CD4071BK	OEM
CD4071BK3	OEM
CD4071BMJ	0129
CD4071BMW	0129
CD4072BD	2502
CD4072BD3	OEM
CD4072BE	2502
CD4072BEX	OEM
CD4072BF	2502
CD4072BF3	OEM
CD4072BF3W	OEM
CD4072BFB	OEM
CD4072BFX	OEM
CD4072BK	OEM
CD4072BK3	OEM
CD4072BSO	OEM
CD4073BCJ	1528
CD4073BCN	1528
CD4073BD	1528
CD4073BD3	OEM
CD4073BE	1528
CD4073BEX	OEM
CD4073BF	1528
CD4073BF3	OEM
CD4073BF3W	OEM
CD4073BFB	OEM
CD4073BFX	OEM
CD4073BK	OEM
CD4073BK3	OEM
CD4073BMJ	1528
CD4073BMW	1528
CD4075BCJ	2518
CD4075BCN	2518
CD4075BD	2518
CD4075BD3	OEM
CD4075BE	2518
CD4075BEX	OEM
CD4075BF	2518
CD4075BF3	OEM
CD4075BF3W	OEM
CD4075BFB	OEM
CD4075BFX	OEM
CD4075BK	OEM
CD4075BK3	OEM
CD4075BMJ	2518

DEVICE TYPE	REPL CODE
CD4075BMN	2518
CD4075BMW	2518
CD4075BT	2518
CD4076BC	3455
CD4076BD	3455
CD4076BD3	OEM
CD4076BE	3455
CD4076BEX	OEM
CD4076BF	3455
CD4076BF3	OEM
CD4076BF3W	OEM
CD4076BFX	OEM
CD4076BH	OEM
CD4076BK	OEM
CD4076BK3	OEM
CD4076BM	3455
CD4077	3283
CD4077AK	OEM
CD4077BD	2536
CD4077BD3	OEM
CD4077BE	2536
CD4077BEX	OEM
CD4077BF	2536
CD4077BF3	OEM
CD4077BF3W	OEM
CD4077BFB	OEM
CD4077BFX	OEM
CD4077BK	OEM
CD4077BK3	OEM
CD4078BD	0915
CD4078BD3	OEM
CD4078BE	0915
CD4078BEX	OEM
CD4078BF	0915
CD4078BF3	OEM
CD4078BF3W	OEM
CD4078BFX	OEM
CD4078BK	OEM
CD4078BK3	OEM
CD4081	0621
CD4081B	3535
CD4081BCJ	0621
CD4081BCN	0621
CD4081BD	0621
CD4081BD3	OEM
CD4081BE	0621
CD4081BEX	OEM
CD4081BF	0621
CD4081BF3	OEM
CD4081BF3W	OEM
CD4081BFX	OEM
CD4081BK	OEM
CD4081BK3	OEM
CD4081BMJ	0621
CD4081BMW	0621
CD4082	0297
CD4082B	0297
CD4082BD	0297
CD4082BD3	OEM
CD4082BE	0297
CD4082BEX	OEM
CD4082BF	0297
CD4082BF3	OEM
CD4082BF3W	OEM
CD4082BFB	OEM
CD4082BFX	OEM
CD4082BK	OEM
CD4082BK3	OEM
CD4085BD	0300
CD4085BD3	OEM
CD4085BE	0300
CD4085BEX	OEM
CD4085BF	0300
CD4085BF3	OEM
CD4085BF3W	OEM
CD4085BFB	OEM
CD4085BFX	OEM
CD4085BK	OEM
CD4085BK3	OEM
CD4086BD	0530
CD4086BD3	OEM
CD4086BE	0530
CD4086BEX	OEM
CD4086BF	0530
CD4086BF3	OEM
CD4086BF3W	OEM
CD4086BFB	OEM
CD4086BFX	OEM
CD4086BK	OEM
CD4086BK3	OEM
CD4089BCJ	3778
CD4089BCN	3778
CD4089BD	3778
CD4089BD3	OEM
CD4089BE	3778
CD4089BEX	OEM
CD4089BF	3778
CD4089BF3	OEM
CD4089BF3W	OEM
CD4089BFX	OEM
CD4089BK	OEM
CD4089BK3	OEM
CD4089BMJ	3778
CD4089BMW	OEM
CD4093BCJ	2368
CD4093BCN	2368
CD4093BD	2368
CD4093BD3	OEM
CD4093BE	2368

DEVICE TYPE	REPL CODE
CD4093BEX	OEM
CD4093BF	2368
CD4093BF3	OEM
CD4093BF3W	OEM
CD4093BFX	OEM
CD4093BK	OEM
CD4093BK3	OEM
CD4093BMJ	2368
CD4093BMW	OEM
CD4094BD	1672
CD4094BD3	OEM
CD4094BE	1672
CD4094BEX	OEM
CD4094BF	1672
CD4094BF3	OEM
CD4094BF3W	OEM
CD4094BFX	OEM
CD4094BH	OEM
CD4094BK	OEM
CD4094BK3	OEM
CD4095BD	3796
CD4095BD3	OEM
CD4095BE	3796
CD4095BEX	OEM
CD4095BF	3796
CD4095BF3	OEM
CD4095BF3W	OEM
CD4095BFX	OEM
CD4095BK	OEM
CD4095BK3	OEM
CD4096BD	3798
CD4096BD3	OEM
CD4096BE	3798
CD4096BEX	OEM
CD4096BF	3798
CD4096BF3	OEM
CD4096BF3W	OEM
CD4096BFX	OEM
CD4096BK	OEM
CD4096BK3	OEM
CD4097BD	3802
CD4097BD3	OEM
CD4097BE	3802
CD4097BEX	OEM
CD4097BF	3802
CD4097BF3	OEM
CD4097BF3W	OEM
CD4097BFX	OEM
CD4097BH	OEM
CD4097BK	OEM
CD4097BK3	OEM
CD4098BD	3566
CD4098BD3	OEM
CD4098BE	3566
CD4098BEX	OEM
CD4098BF	3566
CD4098BF3	OEM
CD4098BF3W	OEM
CD4098BFX	OEM
CD4098BK	OEM
CD4098BK3	OEM
CD4099	3297
CD4099(ZENER)	OEM
CD4099BCJ	3297
CD4099BCN	3297
CD4099BD	3297
CD4099BD3	OEM
CD4099BE	3297
CD4099BEX	OEM
CD4099BF	3297
CD4099BF3	OEM
CD4099BF3W	OEM
CD4099BFX	OEM
CD4099BK	OEM
CD4099BK3	OEM
CD4099BMJ	3297
CD4099BMW	3297
CD4100	OEM
CD4101	OEM
CD4102	OEM
CD4103	0057
CD4104	OEM
CD4105	OEM
CD4106	0052
CD4107	OEM
CD4108	OEM
CD4109	0681
CD4110	OEM
CD4111	OEM
CD4112	OEM
CD4113	OEM
CD4114	OEM
CD4115	OEM
CD4116	0052
CD4117	0052
CD4118	0052
CD4119	OEM
CD4120	OEM
CD4121	0052
CD4122	0052
CD4123	OEM
CD4124	OEM
CD4125	OEM
CD4126	OEM
CD4127	OEM
CD4128	OEM
CD4129	OEM
CD4130	OEM
CD4131	OEM

DEVICE TYPE	REPL CODE
CD4132	OEM
CD4133	OEM
CD4134	OEM
CD4135	OEM
CD4148	OEM
CD4262	OEM
CD4370A	OEM
CD4371A	OEM
CD4372A	OEM
CD4502BD	1031
CD4502BD3	OEM
CD4502BE	1031
CD4502BEX	OEM
CD4502BF	1031
CD4502BF3	OEM
CD4502BF3W	OEM
CD4502BFX	OEM
CD4502BK	OEM
CD4502BK3	OEM
CD4503B	2042
CD4503BD	2042
CD4503BE	4367
CD4503BEX	OEM
CD4503BF	2042
CD4503BH	OEM
CD4508BD	OEM
CD4508BD3	OEM
CD4508BE	1800
CD4508BEX	OEM
CD4508BF	1800
CD4508BF3	OEM
CD4508BF3W	OEM
CD4508BFX	OEM
CD4508BK	OEM
CD4508BK3	OEM
CD4510BCJ	1952
CD4510BCN	1952
CD4510BD	1952
CD4510BE	1952
CD4510BEX	OEM
CD4510BF	1952
CD4510BF3	OEM
CD4510BF3W	OEM
CD4510BFX	OEM
CD4510BK	OEM
CD4510BMJ	1952
CD4510BMW	1952
CD4511BCJ	1535
CD4511BCN	1535
CD4511BD	1535
CD4511BD3	OEM
CD4511BE	1535
CD4511BEX	OEM
CD4511BF	1535
CD4511BF3	OEM
CD4511BF3W	OEM
CD4511BFX	OEM
CD4511BH	OEM
CD4511BK	OEM
CD4511BK3	OEM
CD4511BMJ	1660
CD4511BMW	OEM
CD4512BD	2108
CD4512BE	2108
CD4512BEX	OEM
CD4512BF	2108
CD4512BF3	OEM
CD4512BF3W	OEM
CD4512BFX	OEM
CD4512BH	OEM
CD4512BK	OEM
CD4514BC	1819
CD4514BD	1819
CD4514BD3	OEM
CD4514BE	1819
CD4514BEX	OEM
CD4514BF	1819
CD4514BF3	OEM
CD4514BF3W	OEM
CD4514BFX	OEM
CD4514BH	1819
CD4514BK	1819
CD4514BK3	OEM
CD4514BM	1819
CD4515BC	3555
CD4515BD	3555
CD4515BD3	OEM
CD4515BE	3555
CD4515BEX	OEM
CD4515BF	3555
CD4515BF3	OEM
CD4515BF3W	OEM
CD4515BFX	OEM
CD4515BH	3555
CD4515BK	3555
CD4515BK3	OEM
CD4515BM	3555
CD4516BCJ	2331
CD4516BCN	2331
CD4516BD	2331
CD4516BD3	OEM
CD4516BE	2331
CD4516BEX	OEM
CD4516BF	2331
CD4516BF3	OEM
CD4516BF3W	OEM
CD4516BFX	OEM
CD4516BK	OEM
CD4516BK3	OEM

DEVICE TYPE	REPL CODE
CD4516BMJ	2331
CD4516BMW	2331
CD4517BE	4220
CD4517BEX	OEM
CD4517BF	4220
CD4517BFX	OEM
CD4517BH	OEM
CD4518B	1037
CD4518BCJ	1037
CD4518BCN	1037
CD4518BD	1037
CD4518BD3	OEM
CD4518BE	1037
CD4518BEX	OEM
CD4518BF	1037
CD4518BF3	OEM
CD4518BF3W	OEM
CD4518BFX	OEM
CD4518BK	OEM
CD4518BK3	OEM
CD4518BMJ	1037
CD4518BMW	1037
CD4519BC	OEM
CD4519BCJ	OEM
CD4519BCN	OEM
CD4519BM	OEM
CD4519BMJ	OEM
CD4519BMW	OEM
CD4520B	2650
CD4520B3W	OEM
CD4520BCJ	2650
CD4520BCN	2650
CD4520BD	2650
CD4520BD3	OEM
CD4520BE	2650
CD4520BEX	2650
CD4520BF	2650
CD4520BF3	OEM
CD4520BFX	OEM
CD4520BK	OEM
CD4520BK3	OEM
CD4520BMJ	2650
CD4520BMW	2650
CD4521BE	4903
CD4522BC	2810
CD4522BE	2810
CD4522BM	2810
CD4526BC	3565
CD4526BCN	3565
CD4526BM	3565
CD4527BCJ	3116
CD4527BCN	3116
CD4527BD	3116
CD4527BD3	OEM
CD4527BE	3116
CD4527BEX	OEM
CD4527BF	3116
CD4527BF3	OEM
CD4527BF3W	OEM
CD4527BFX	OEM
CD4527BK	OEM
CD4527BK3	OEM
CD4527BMJ	3116
CD4527BMW	3116
CD4529BCN	4451
CD4532BD	1010
CD4532BD3	OEM
CD4532BE	1010
CD4532BEX	OEM
CD4532BF	1010
CD4532BF3	OEM
CD4532BF3W	OEM
CD4532BFX	OEM
CD4532BH	OEM
CD4532BK	OEM
CD4532BK3	OEM
CD4536BD	3659
CD4536BE	3659
CD4536BF	3659
CD4536BH	OEM
CD4538BCN	4238
CD4538BD	1057
CD4538BE	1057
CD4538BF	1057
CD4543BD	4932
CD4543BE	4932
CD4543BF	4932
CD4543BH	OEM
CD4555BD	2910
CD4555BD3	OEM
CD4555BE	2910
CD4555BEX	OEM
CD4555BF	2910
CD4555BF3	OEM
CD4555BF3W	OEM
CD4555BFX	OEM
CD4555BK	OEM
CD4555BK3	OEM
CD4556BD	3397
CD4556BD3	OEM
CD4556BE	3397
CD4556BEX	OEM
CD4556BF	3397
CD4556BF3	OEM
CD4556BF3W	OEM
CD4556BFX	OEM
CD4556BK	OEM
CD4556BK3	OEM
CD4565	OEM

DEVICE TYPE	REPL CODE
CD4565A	OEM
CD4566	3463
CD4566A	3463
CD4567	OEM
CD4567A	OEM
CD4568	OEM
CD4568A	OEM
CD4569	OEM
CD4569A	OEM
CD4570	OEM
CD4570A	OEM
CD4571	OEM
CD4571A	OEM
CD4572	3440
CD4572A	3440
CD4573	OEM
CD4573A	OEM
CD4574	OEM
CD4574A	OEM
CD4575	OEM
CD4575A	OEM
CD4576	OEM
CD4576A	OEM
CD4577	OEM
CD4577A	OEM
CD4578	OEM
CD4578A	OEM
CD4579	OEM
CD4579A	OEM
CD4580	OEM
CD4580A	OEM
CD4581	OEM
CD4581A	OEM
CD4582	OEM
CD4582A	OEM
CD4583	OEM
CD4583A	OEM
CD4584	OEM
CD4584A	OEM
CD4585BD	1365
CD4585BE	1365
CD4585BEX	OEM
CD4585BF	1365
CD4585BH	OEM
CD4614	OEM
CD4615	OEM
CD4616	OEM
CD4617	OEM
CD4618	OEM
CD4619	OEM
CD4620	OEM
CD4621	OEM
CD4622	OEM
CD4623	OEM
CD4624	OEM
CD4625	OEM
CD4626	OEM
CD4627	0466
CD4723BCJ	OEM
CD4723BCN	OEM
CD4723BMJ	OEM
CD4723BMW	OEM
CD4724BCJ	3432
CD4724BCN	3432
CD4724BD	3432
CD4724BE	3432
CD4724BEX	OEM
CD4724BF	3432
CD4724BFX	OEM
CD4724BH	OEM
CD4724BMJ	3432
CD4724BMW	OEM
CD4728	OEM
CD4728A	OEM
CD4729	OEM
CD4729A	OEM
CD4730	OEM
CD4730A	OEM
CD4731	OEM
CD4731A	OEM
CD4732	OEM
CD4732A	OEM
CD4733	OEM
CD4733A	OEM
CD4734	OEM
CD4734A	OEM
CD4735	0631
CD4735A	OEM
CD4736	OEM
CD4736A	OEM
CD4737	OEM
CD4737A	OEM
CD4738	OEM
CD4738A	OEM
CD4739	0012
CD4739A	OEM
CD4740	OEM
CD4740A	OEM
CD4741	OEM
CD4741A	OEM
CD4742	0137
CD4742A	OEM
CD4743	OEM
CD4743A	OEM
CD4744	0002
CD4744A	OEM
CD4745	OEM
CD4745A	OEM
CD4746	OEM

DEVICE TYPE	REPL CODE
CD4746A	OEM
CD4747	OEM
CD4747A	OEM
CD4748	OEM
CD4748A	OEM
CD4749	OEM
CD4749A	OEM
CD4750	OEM
CD4750A	OEM
CD4751	OEM
CD4751A	OEM
CD4752	OEM
CD4752A	OEM
CD4753	OEM
CD4753A	OEM
CD4754	OEM
CD4754A	OEM
CD4755	OEM
CD4755A	OEM
CD4756	OEM
CD4756A	OEM
CD4757	OEM
CD4757A	OEM
CD4758	OEM
CD4758A	OEM
CD4759	OEM
CD4759A	OEM
CD4760	OEM
CD4760A	OEM
CD4761	OEM
CD4761A	OEM
CD4762	OEM
CD4762A	OEM
CD4763	OEM
CD4763A	OEM
CD4764	OEM
CD4765	0057
CD4765A	0057
CD4766	0057
CD4766A	0057
CD4767	0057
CD4767A	0057
CD4768	0057
CD4768A	OEM
CD4770	0057
CD4770A	0057
CD4771	0057
CD4771A	0057
CD4772	0057
CD4772A	0057
CD4773	0057
CD4773A	0057
CD5221B	OEM
CD5222B	OEM
CD5223B	OEM
CD5224B	OEM
CD5225B	OEM
CD5226B	OEM
CD5227B	OEM
CD5228B	OEM
CD5229B	OEM
CD5230B	OEM
CD5231B	OEM
CD5232B	OEM
CD5233B	OEM
CD5234B	0466
CD5235B	0466
CD5236B	OEM
CD5237B	OEM
CD5238B	OEM
CD5239B	0057
CD5240B	OEM
CD5241B	OEM
CD5242B	0052
CD5243B	OEM
CD5244B	OEM
CD5245B	0681
CD5246B	OEM
CD5247B	OEM
CD5248B	OEM
CD5249B	OEM
CD5250B	OEM
CD5251B	OEM
CD5252B	OEM
CD5253B	OEM
CD5254B	OEM
CD5255B	OEM
CD5256B	OEM
CD5257B	OEM
CD5258B	OEM
CD5259B	OEM
CD5260B	OEM
CD5261B	OEM
CD5262B	OEM
CD5263B	OEM
CD5264B	OEM
CD5265B	OEM
CD5266B	OEM
CD5267B	OEM
CD5268B	OEM
CD5269B	OEM
CD5270B	OEM
CD5271B	OEM
CD5272B	OEM
CD5273A	OEM
CD5274A	OEM
CD5275A	OEM
CD5276A	OEM
CD5277B	OEM

If replacement code is OEM, contact original manufacturer for replacement.

DEVICE TYPE	REPL CODE	DEVICE TYPE	REPL CODE	DEVICE TYPE	REPL CODE	DEVICE TYPE	REPL CODE	DEVICE TYPE	REPL CODE	DEVICE TYPE	REPL CODE	DEVICE TYPE	REPL CODE
CD5278B	OEM	CD22006H	OEM	CD40109BF3W	OEM	CD40193BCN	1765	CD471440	OEM	CDLL1W110A	OEM	CDLL4157	OEM
CD5279B	OEM	CD22007V2H	OEM	CD40109BFX	OEM	CD40193BD	1765	CD471460	OEM	CDLL1W120	OEM	CDLL4453	OEM
CD5280B	OEM	CD22008V1H	OEM	CD40109BH	OEM	CD40193BE	1765	CD471490	OEM	CDLL1W120A	OEM	CDLL4460	OEM
CD5281B	OEM	CD22011E	OEM	CD40109BK	OEM	CD40193BEX	OEM	CD471540	OEM	CDLL1W130	OEM	CDLL4461	OEM
CD5328	1248	CD22012E	OEM	CD40110BD	4165	CD40193BF	1765	CD471560	OEM	CDLL1W130A	OEM	CDLL4462	OEM
CD5333B	OEM	CD22014E	OEM	CD40110BE	4165	CD40193BF3	OEM	CD471590	OEM	CDLL1W140	OEM	CDLL4463	OEM
CD5334B	OEM	CD22015E	OEM	CD40110BEX	OEM	CD40193BF3W	OEM	CD860011	1141	CDLL1W140A	OEM	CDLL4464	OEM
CD5335B	OEM	CD22018H	OEM	CD40110BF	4165	CD40193BFX	OEM	CD860037	0133	CDLL1W150	OEM	CDLL4465	OEM
CD5336B	OEM	CD22100D	OEM	CD40110BH	OEM	CD40193BK	OEM	CD3112018	0244	CDLL1W150A	OEM	CDLL4466	OEM
CD5337B	OEM	CD22100E	3013	CD40114BD	4234	CD40193BMJ	1765	CD3122055	0012	CDLL1W160	OEM	CDLL4467	OEM
CD5338B	OEM	CD22100EX	OEM	CD40114BE	4234	CD40193BMW	1765	CD3212055	0943	CDLL1W160A	OEM	CDLL4468	OEM
CD5339B	OEM	CD22100F	OEM	CD40114BEX	OEM	CD40194BD	1758	CDB-7605	OEM	CDLL1W170	OEM	CDLL4469	OEM
CD5340B	OEM	CD22101D	OEM	CD40114BF	4234	CD40194BE	1758	CDB-7606	OEM	CDLL1W170A	OEM	CDLL4470	OEM
CD5341B	0466	CD22101E	3019	CD40114BH	OEM	CD40194BEX	OEM	CDC00	OEM	CDLL1W180	OEM	CDLL4471	OEM
CD5342B	OEM	CD22101EX	OEM	CD40115D	OEM	CD40194BF	1758	CDC86X7-5	0016	CDLL1W180A	OEM	CDLL4472	OEM
CD5343B	OEM	CD22101F	OEM	CD40116D	3077	CD40194BFX	OEM	CDC430	0016	CDLL1W190	OEM	CDLL4473	OEM
CD5344B	OEM	CD22101FX	OEM	CD40116E	3077	CD40194BH	OEM	CDC496	0037	CDLL1W190A	OEM	CDLL4474	OEM
CD5345B	OEM	CD22102D	OEM	CD40117BD(A)	OEM	CD40194BK	OEM	CDC587	0086	CDLL1W200	OEM	CDLL4475	OEM
CD5346B	0057	CD22102E	3023	CD40117BE(A)	OEM	CD40208BD	5879	CDC731	0321	CDLL1W200A	OEM	CDLL4476	OEM
CD5347B	OEM	CD22102EX	OEM	CD40117BF(A)	OEM	CD40208BE	5879	CDC744	0233	CDLL200	OEM	CDLL4477	OEM
CD5348B	OEM	CD22102F	OEM	CD40147BD	5011	CD40208BF	5879	CDC745	0086	CDLL300	OEM	CDLL4478	OEM
CD5349B	0052	CD22102FX	OEM	CD40147BE	5011	CD40208BH	OEM	CDC746	0016	CDLL400	OEM	CDLL4479	OEM
CD5350B	OEM	CD22103D(A)	OEM	CD40147BF	5011	CD40208BK	OEM	CDC1201BC	0016	CDLL610	OEM	CDLL4480	OEM
CD5351B	OEM	CD22103H(A)	OEM	CD40147BH	OEM	CD40257BD	6260	CDC2010	0016	CDLL821	OEM	CDLL4481	OEM
CD5352B	OEM	CD22859D	OEM	CD40160BCJ	1349	CD40257BE	6260	CDC2010D	0016	CDLL821A	OEM	CDLL4482	OEM
CD5353B	OEM	CD22859E	5215	CD40160BCN	1349	CD40257BEX	OEM	CDC2510C-G	0016	CDLL822	OEM	CDLL4483	OEM
CD5354B	OEM	CD22859H	OEM	CD40160BD	1349	CD40257BF	6260	CDC4023A130	0016	CDLL823	OEM	CDLL4484	OEM
CD5355B	OEM	CD40061AD	1811	CD40160BDCD40160BE	OEM	CD40257BF3	OEM	CDC5000	0127	CDLL823A	OEM	CDLL4485	OEM
CD5356B	OEM	CD40061AE	1811	CD40160BE	1349	CD40257BF3W	OEM	CDC5000-1B	0144	CDLL824	OEM	CDLL4486	OEM
CD5357B	OEM	CD40061AH	OEM	CD40160BEX	OEM	CD40257BFX	OEM	CDC5008	0086	CDLL825	OEM	CDLL4487	OEM
CD5358B	OEM	CD40061D	OEM	CD40160BF	1349	CD40257BH	OEM	CDC5028A	0086	CDLL825A	OEM	CDLL4488	OEM
CD5359B	OEM	CD40061E	OEM	CD40160BF3	OEM	CD40257BK	OEM	CDC5038A	0144	CDLL826	OEM	CDLL4489	OEM
CD5360B	OEM	CD40100BD	3895	CD40160BF3W	OEM	CD-84857	0133	CDC5071A	0144	CDLL827	OEM	CDLL4490	OEM
CD5361B	OEM	CD40100BE	3895	CD40160BMJ	1349	CD86003	0133	CDC5075B	0144	CDLL827A	OEM	CDLL4491	OEM
CD5362B	OEM	CD40100BEX	OEM	CD40160BMW	1349	CD420140	4295	CDC-7609	OEM	CDLL829	OEM	CDLL4492	OEM
CD5363B	OEM	CD40100BF	3895	CD40161BCJ	1363	CD420160	2966	CDC-7609A	OEM	CDLL829A	OEM	CDLL4493	OEM
CD5364B	OEM	CD40100BF3	OEM	CD40161BCN	1363	CD420190	2966	CDC-7609B	OEM	CDLL935	OEM	CDLL4494	OEM
CD5365B	OEM	CD40100BF3W	OEM	CD40161BD	1363	CD420240	4295	CDC-7609C	OEM	CDLL935A	OEM	CDLL4495	OEM
CD5366B	OEM	CD40100BH	OEM	CD40161BE	1363	CD420260	2966	CDC-7609D	OEM	CDLL935B	OEM	CDLL4496	OEM
CD5367B	OEM	CD40100BK	OEM	CD40161BEX	OEM	CD420290	2966	CDC8000	0076	CDLL936	OEM	CDLL4565	OEM
CD5368B	OEM	CD40101BD	3960	CD40161BF	1363	CD420440	4295	CDC-8000-1	0079	CDLL936A	OEM	CDLL4565A	OEM
CD5369B	OEM	CD40101BE	3960	CD40161BF3	OEM	CD420460	2966	CDC8000-1	0086	CDLL936B	OEM	CDLL4566	OEM
CD5370B	OEM	CD40101BEX	OEM	CD40161BF3W	OEM	CD420490	2966	CDC8000-1B	0016	CDLL937	OEM	CDLL4566A	OEM
CD5371B	OEM	CD40101BF	3960	CD40161BFX	OEM	CD420640	4295	CDC8000-1C	0086	CDLL937A	OEM	CDLL4567	OEM
CD5372B	OEM	CD40101BF3	OEM	CD40161BMJ	1363	CD420660	2966	CDC8000-CM	0086	CDLL937B	OEM	CDLL4567A	OEM
CD5373B	OEM	CD40101BF3W	OEM	CD40161BMW	1363	CD420690	2966	CDC-8001	0016	CDLL938	OEM	CDLL4568	OEM
CD5374B	OEM	CD40101BK	OEM	CD40162BCJ	1378	CD420840	4295	CDC8001	0218	CDLL938A	OEM	CDLL4568A	OEM
CD5375B	OEM	CD40102BD	3998	CD40162BCN	1378	CD420860	2966	CDC8002	0018	CDLL938B	OEM	CDLL4569	OEM
CD5376B	OEM	CD40102BE	3998	CD40162BD	1378	CD420890	2966	CDC8002-1	0086	CDLL941	OEM	CDLL4569A	OEM
CD5377B	OEM	CD40102BEX	OEM	CD40162BE	1378	CD421040	4295	CDC8011B	0016	CDLL941A	OEM	CDLL4570	OEM
CD5378B	OEM	CD40102BF	3998	CD40162BEX	OEM	CD421060	2966	CDC8021	0016	CDLL941B	OEM	CDLL4570A	OEM
CD5379B	OEM	CD40102BF3	OEM	CD40162BF	1378	CD421090	2966	CDC8054	0016	CDLL942	OEM	CDLL4571	OEM
CD5380B	OEM	CD40102BF3W	OEM	CD40162BFX	OEM	CD421240	4295	CDC8201	0079	CDLL942A	OEM	CDLL4572	OEM
CD5381B	OEM	CD40102BFX	OEM	CD40162BMJ	1378	CD421260	2966	CDC8457	0133	CDLL942B	OEM	CDLL4572A	OEM
CD5382B	OEM	CD40102BK	OEM	CD40162BMW	1378	CD421290	2966	CDC-9000	0136	CDLL943	OEM	CDLL4573	OEM
CD5383B	OEM	CD40103BD	4029	CD40163BCJ	1397	CD421440	OEM	CDC9000-1	0037	CDLL943A	OEM	CDLL4573A	OEM
CD5384B	OEM	CD40103BE	4029	CD40163BCN	1397	CD421460	OEM	CDC-9000-1B	0126	CDLL943B	OEM	CDLL4574	OEM
CD5385B	OEM	CD40103BEX	OEM	CD40163BD	1397	CD421490	OEM	CDC9000-1B	0126	CDLL944	OEM	CDLL4574A	OEM
CD5386B	OEM	CD40103BF	4029	CD40163BE	1397	CD421540	OEM	CDC9000-1C	0786	CDLL944A	OEM	CDLL4575	OEM
CD5387B	OEM	CD40103BF3	OEM	CD40163BEX	OEM	CD421560	OEM	CDC9000-1D	0006	CDLL944B	OEM	CDLL4575A	OEM
CD5388B	OEM	CD40103BF3W	OEM	CD40163BF	1397	CD421590	OEM	CDC9002	0148	CDLL945	OEM	CDLL4576	OEM
CD5590	1189	CD40103BFX	OEM	CD40163BF3	OEM	CD430140	0647	CDC9002-1C	0086	CDLL945A	OEM	CDLL4576A	OEM
CD5645	0133	CD40103BK	OEM	CD40163BF3W	OEM	CD430160	2295	CDC9002-18	0086	CDLL945B	OEM	CDLL4577	OEM
CD5916	OEM	CD40104BD	4046	CD40163BFX	OEM	CD430190	2295	CDC-9002-IC	0150	CDLL2810	OEM	CDLL4577A	OEM
CD5944	OEM	CD40104BE	4046	CD40163BMJ	1397	CD430240	0647	CDC10000-1E	0037	CDLL3154	OEM	CDLL4578	OEM
CD5945	4012	CD40104BEX	OEM	CD40163BMW	1397	CD430260	2295	CDC12000	0079	CDLL3154A	OEM	CDLL4578A	OEM
CD6039	1063	CD40104BF	4046	CD40174BC	1542	CD430290	2295	CDC12000-1C	0016	CDLL3155	OEM	CDLL4579	OEM
CD6111	OEM	CD40104BF3	OEM	CD40174BD	1542	CD430440	0647	CDC12018C	0016	CDLL3155A	OEM	CDLL4579A	OEM
CD6112	OEM	CD40104BFX	OEM	CD40174BE	1542	CD430460	2295	CDC12030B	0127	CDLL3156	OEM	CDLL4580	OEM
CD7012	3521	CD40104BH	OEM	CD40174BEX	OEM	CD430490	2295	CDC12077F	0016	CDLL3156A	OEM	CDLL4580A	OEM
CD7186D	OEM	CD40104BK	OEM	CD40174BF	1542	CD430640	0647	CDC12108	0079	CDLL3157	OEM	CDLL4581	OEM
CD7211AME	OEM	CD40105BD	4060	CD40174BF3	OEM	CD430660	2295	CDC12112C	0144	CDLL3157A	OEM	CDLL4581A	OEM
CD7211E	OEM	CD40105BE	4060	CD40174BF3W	OEM	CD430690	2295	CDC12112D	0144	CDLL4099	OEM	CDLL4582	OEM
CD7211ME	OEM	CD40105BEX	OEM	CD40174BFX	OEM	CD430840	0647	CDC12112E	0144	CDLL4100	OEM	CDLL4582A	OEM
CD7216AC	OEM	CD40105BF	4060	CD40174BH	OEM	CD430860	2295	CDC12112F	0144	CDLL4101	OEM	CDLL4583	OEM
CD7216BC	OEM	CD40105BF3	OEM	CD40174BM	OEM	CD430890	2295	CDC13000	0079	CDLL4102	OEM	CDLL4583A	OEM
CD7216CC	OEM	CD40105BF3W	OEM	CD40175BC	1520	CD431040	0647	CDC-13000-1	0016	CDLL4103	OEM	CDLL4584	OEM
CD7216DC	OEM	CD40105BFX	OEM	CD40175BM	OEM	CD431060	2295	CDC13000-1	0079	CDLL4104	OEM	CDLL4584A	OEM
CD7217AC	OEM	CD40105BH	OEM	CD40181BD	5533	CD431090	2295	CDC13000-1B	0016	CDLL4105	OEM	CDLL4614	OEM
CD7217BC	OEM	CD40105BK	OEM	CD40181BE	5533	CD431240	0647	CDC13000-1C	0016	CDLL4106	OEM	CDLL4615	OEM
CD7217C	OEM	CD40106BCJ	3581	CD40181BEX	OEM	CD431260	2295	CDC13000-1D	0191	CDLL4107	OEM	CDLL4616	OEM
CD7217CC	OEM	CD40106BCN	3581	CD40181BF	5533	CD431290	2295	CDC13000-18	0016	CDLL4108	OEM	CDLL4617	OEM
CD7224AC	OEM	CD40106BD	3581	CD40181BF3	OEM	CD431440	OEM	CDC13000C	0079	CDLL4109	OEM	CDLL4618	OEM
CD7224C	OEM	CD40106BE	3581	CD40181BF3W	OEM	CD431460	OEM	CDC13016A	0016	CDLL4110	OEM	CDLL4619	OEM
CD7225AC	OEM	CD40106BEX	OEM	CD40181BFX	OEM	CD431490	OEM	CDC13019B	0079	CDLL4111	OEM	CDLL4620	OEM
CD7225C	OEM	CD40106BF	3581	CD40181BH	OEM	CD431540	OEM	CDC13500-1	0016	CDLL4112	OEM	CDLL4621	OEM
CD7226AC	OEM	CD40106BF3	OEM	CD40181BK	OEM	CD431560	OEM	CDC15018	0079	CDLL4113	OEM	CDLL4622	OEM
CD7226BC	OEM	CD40106BF3W	OEM	CD40182BD	4579	CD431590	OEM	CDC25100-6	0016	CDLL4114	OEM	CDLL4623	OEM
CD7227AC	OEM	CD40106BFX	OEM	CD40182BE	4579	CD470140	4494	CDC25100-G	0007	CDLL4115	OEM	CDLL4624	OEM
CD7227BC	OEM	CD40106BH	OEM	CD40182BEX	OEM	CD470160	2851	CDC60132	0079	CDLL4116	OEM	CDLL4625	OEM
CD7227C	OEM	CD40106BK	OEM	CD40182BF	4579	CD470190	2851	CDC90001B	0786	CDLL4117	OEM	CDLL4626	OEM
CD7227CC	OEM	CD40106BMJ	3581	CD40182BF3	OEM	CD470240	4494	CDC120700	0086	CDLL4118	OEM	CDLL4627	OEM
CD8000	0016	CD40106BMW	OEM	CD40182BF3W	OEM	CD470260	2851	CDC4306813	0016	CDLL4119	OEM	CDLL4678	OEM
CD-8457	0015	CD40107BD	4090	CD40182BK	OEM	CD470290	2851	CDCC6V2	OEM	CDLL4121	OEM	CDLL4679	OEM
CD8457	0133	CD40107BE	4090	CD40192BCJ	1753	CD470440	4494	CDG-00	0133	CDLL4122	OEM	CDLL4680	OEM
CD8547	0133	CD40107BEX	OEM	CD40192BCN	1753	CD470460	2851	CDG00	0133	CDLL4123	OEM	CDLL4681	OEM
CD12000	0016	CD40107BF	4090	CD40192BD	1753	CD470490	2851	CDG005	0015	CDLL4124	OEM	CDLL4682	OEM
CD13332	0015	CD40107BFX	OEM	CD40192BE	1753	CD470640	4494	CDG025	0133	CDLL4125	OEM	CDLL4683	OEM
CD13333	0604	CD40108BD	4119	CD40192BEX	OEM	CD470660	2851	CDG-21	0133	CDLL4126	OEM	CDLL4684	OEM
CD13334	0604	CD40108BE	4119	CD40192BF	1753	CD470690	2851	CDG21	0133	CDLL4127	OEM	CDLL4685	OEM
CD13335	0015	CD40108BEX	OEM	CD40192BF3	OEM	CD470840	4494	CDG-22	0133	CDLL4128	OEM	CDLL4686	OEM
CD13336	0604	CD40108BF	4119	CD40192BF3W	OEM	CD470860	2851	CDG22	0133	CDLL4129	OEM	CDLL4687	OEM
CD13337	0015	CD40108BH	OEM	CD40192BFX	OEM	CD470890	2851	CDG-24	0133	CDLL4130	OEM	CDLL4688	OEM
CD13338	0604	CD40108BK	OEM	CD40192BK	OEM	CD471040	4494	CDG24	0015	CDLL4131	OEM	CDLL4689	OEM
CD13339	0604	CD40109BD	4146	CD40192BMJ	1753	CD471060	2851	CDG24/3490	0133	CDLL4132	OEM	CDLL4690	OEM
CD22001H	OEM	CD40109BE	4146	CD40192BMW	1753	CD471090	2851	CDG27	0133	CDLL4133	OEM	CDLL4691	OEM
CD22003	OEM	CD40109BEX	OEM	CD40192CJ	1753	CD471240	4494	CDJ-00	0133	CDLL4134	OEM	CDLL4692	OEM
CD22003E	OEM	CD40109BF	4146	CD40192CN	1753	CD471260	2851	CDK-4	0015	CDLL4135	OEM	CDLL4693	OEM
CD22003R	OEM	CD40109BF3	OEM	CD40193BCJ	1765	CD471290	2851	CDLL1W110	OEM	CDLL4156	OEM	CDLL4694	OEM

If replacement code is OEM, contact original manufacturer for replacement.

DEVICE TYPE	REPL CODE	DEVICE TYPE	REPL CODE	DEVICE TYPE	REPL CODE	DEVICE TYPE	REPL CODE	DEVICE TYPE	REPL CODE	DEVICE TYPE	REPL CODE	DEVICE TYPE	REPL CODE
CDLL4695	OEM	CDLL4771A	OEM	CDLL5222B	OEM	CDLL5259	OEM	CDLL5519C	OEM	CDLL5541B	OEM	CDP18S629	OEM
CDLL4696	OEM	CDLL4772	OEM	CDLL5223	OEM	CDLL5259A	OEM	CDLL5519D	OEM	CDLL5541C	OEM	CDP18S640A1	OEM
CDLL4697	OEM	CDLL4772A	OEM	CDLL5223A	OEM	CDLL5259B	OEM	CDLL5520	OEM	CDLL5541D	OEM	CDP18S640V1	OEM
CDLL4698	OEM	CDLL4773	OEM	CDLL5223B	OEM	CDLL5260	OEM	CDLL5520A	OEM	CDLL5542	OEM	CDP18S641	OEM
CDLL4699	OEM	CDLL4773A	OEM	CDLL5224	OEM	CDLL5260A	OEM	CDLL5520B	OEM	CDLL5542A	OEM	CDP18S642	OEM
CDLL4700	OEM	CDLL4774	OEM	CDLL5224A	OEM	CDLL5260B	OEM	CDLL5520C	OEM	CDLL5542B	OEM	CDP18S643A	OEM
CDLL4701	OEM	CDLL4774A	OEM	CDLL5224B	OEM	CDLL5261	OEM	CDLL5520D	OEM	CDLL5542C	OEM	CDP18S644	OEM
CDLL4702	OEM	CDLL4775	OEM	CDLL5225	OEM	CDLL5261A	OEM	CDLL5521	OEM	CDLL5542D	OEM	CDP18S646	OEM
CDLL4703	OEM	CDLL4775A	OEM	CDLL5225A	OEM	CDLL5261B	OEM	CDLL5521A	OEM	CDLL5543	OEM	CDP18S647	OEM
CDLL4704	OEM	CDLL4776	OEM	CDLL5225B	OEM	CDLL5262	OEM	CDLL5521B	OEM	CDLL5543A	OEM	CDP18S648	OEM
CDLL4705	OEM	CDLL4776A	OEM	CDLL5226	OEM	CDLL5262A	OEM	CDLL5521C	OEM	CDLL5543B	OEM	CDP18S651	OEM
CDLL4706	OEM	CDLL4777	OEM	CDLL5226A	OEM	CDLL5262B	OEM	CDLL5521D	OEM	CDLL5543C	OEM	CDP18S652	OEM
CDLL4707	OEM	CDLL4777A	OEM	CDLL5226B	OEM	CDLL5263	OEM	CDLL5522	OEM	CDLL5543D	OEM	CDP18S653V1	OEM
CDLL4708	OEM	CDLL4778	OEM	CDLL5227	OEM	CDLL5263A	OEM	CDLL5522A	OEM	CDLL5544	OEM	CDP18S653V2	OEM
CDLL4709	OEM	CDLL4778A	OEM	CDLL5227A	OEM	CDLL5263B	OEM	CDLL5522B	OEM	CDLL5544A	OEM	CDP18S654	OEM
CDLL4710	OEM	CDLL4779	OEM	CDLL5227B	OEM	CDLL5264	OEM	CDLL5522C	OEM	CDLL5544B	OEM	CDP18S657	OEM
CDLL4711	OEM	CDLL4779A	OEM	CDLL5228	OEM	CDLL5264A	OEM	CDLL5522D	OEM	CDLL5544C	OEM	CDP18S658	OEM
CDLL4712	OEM	CDLL4780	OEM	CDLL5228A	OEM	CDLL5264B	OEM	CDLL5523	OEM	CDLL5544D	OEM	CDP18S660	OEM
CDLL4713	OEM	CDLL4780A	OEM	CDLL5228B	OEM	CDLL5265	OEM	CDLL5523A	OEM	CDLL5545	OEM	CDP18S661B	OEM
CDLL4714	OEM	CDLL4781	OEM	CDLL5229	OEM	CDLL5265A	OEM	CDLL5523B	OEM	CDLL5545A	OEM	CDP18S661V3	OEM
CDLL4715	OEM	CDLL4781A	OEM	CDLL5229A	OEM	CDLL5265B	OEM	CDLL5523C	OEM	CDLL5545B	OEM	CDP18S662	OEM
CDLL4716	OEM	CDLL4782	OEM	CDLL5229B	OEM	CDLL5266	OEM	CDLL5523D	OEM	CDLL5545C	OEM	CDP18S670	OEM
CDLL4717	OEM	CDLL4782A	OEM	CDLL5230	OEM	CDLL5266A	OEM	CDLL5524	OEM	CDLL5545D	OEM	CDP18S675	OEM
CDLL4728	OEM	CDLL4783	OEM	CDLL5230A	OEM	CDLL5266B	OEM	CDLL5524A	OEM	CDLL5546	OEM	CDP18S676	OEM
CDLL4728A	OEM	CDLL4783A	OEM	CDLL5230B	OEM	CDLL5267	OEM	CDLL5524B	OEM	CDLL5546A	OEM	CDP18S691	OEM
CDLL4729	OEM	CDLL4784	OEM	CDLL5231	OEM	CDLL5267A	OEM	CDLL5524C	OEM	CDLL5546B	OEM	CDP18U42CD	OEM
CDLL4729A	OEM	CDLL4784A	OEM	CDLL5231A	OEM	CDLL5267B	OEM	CDLL5524D	OEM	CDLL5546C	OEM	CDP1801CR	OEM
CDLL4730	OEM	CDLL4829	OEM	CDLL5231B	OEM	CDLL5268	OEM	CDLL5525	OEM	CDLL5546D	OEM	CDP1801CU	OEM
CDLL4730A	OEM	CDLL4830	OEM	CDLL5232	OEM	CDLL5268A	OEM	CDLL5525A	OEM	CDLL5711	OEM	CDP1801R	OEM
CDLL4731	OEM	CDLL4896	OEM	CDLL5232A	OEM	CDLL5268B	OEM	CDLL5525B	OEM	CDLL5712	OEM	CDP1801U	OEM
CDLL4731A	OEM	CDLL4896A	OEM	CDLL5232B	OEM	CDLL5269	OEM	CDLL5525C	OEM	CDLL5817	OEM	CDP1802ACD	3193
CDLL4732	OEM	CDLL4897	OEM	CDLL5233	OEM	CDLL5269A	OEM	CDLL5525D	OEM	CDLL5818	OEM	CDP1802ACE	3193
CDLL4732A	OEM	CDLL4897A	OEM	CDLL5233A	OEM	CDLL5269B	OEM	CDLL5526	OEM	CDLL5819	OEM	CDP1802AD	3193
CDLL4733	OEM	CDLL4898	OEM	CDLL5233B	OEM	CDLL5270	OEM	CDLL5526A	OEM	CDLL6309	OEM	CDP1802AE	3193
CDLL4733A	OEM	CDLL4898A	OEM	CDLL5234	OEM	CDLL5270A	OEM	CDLL5526B	OEM	CDLL6310	OEM	CDP1802BCD	3193
CDLL4734	OEM	CDLL4899	OEM	CDLL5234A	OEM	CDLL5270B	OEM	CDLL5526C	OEM	CDLL6311	OEM	CDP1802BCE	3193
CDLL4734A	OEM	CDLL4899A	OEM	CDLL5234B	OEM	CDLL5271	OEM	CDLL5526D	OEM	CDLL6312	OEM	CDP1802CD	3193
CDLL4735	OEM	CDLL4900	OEM	CDLL5235	OEM	CDLL5271A	OEM	CDLL5527	OEM	CDLL6313	OEM	CDP1802CD3	OEM
CDLL4735A	OEM	CDLL4900A	OEM	CDLL5235A	OEM	CDLL5271B	OEM	CDLL5527A	OEM	CDLL6314	OEM	CDP1802CE	3193
CDLL4736	OEM	CDLL4901	OEM	CDLL5235B	OEM	CDLL5272	OEM	CDLL5527B	OEM	CDLL6315	OEM	CDP1802D	3193
CDLL4736A	OEM	CDLL4901A	OEM	CDLL5236	OEM	CDLL5272A	OEM	CDLL5527C	OEM	CDLL6316	OEM	CDP1802D3	OEM
CDLL4737	OEM	CDLL4902	OEM	CDLL5236A	OEM	CDLL5272B	OEM	CDLL5527D	OEM	CDLL6317	OEM	CDP1802E	3193
CDLL4737A	OEM	CDLL4902A	OEM	CDLL5236B	OEM	CDLL5273	OEM	CDLL5528	OEM	CDLL6318	OEM	CDP1804ACD	OEM
CDLL4738	OEM	CDLL4903	OEM	CDLL5237	OEM	CDLL5273A	OEM	CDLL5528A	OEM	CDLL6319	OEM	CDP1804CE	OEM
CDLL4738A	OEM	CDLL4903A	OEM	CDLL5237A	OEM	CDLL5273B	OEM	CDLL5528B	OEM	CDLL6320	OEM	CDP1804D	OEM
CDLL4739	OEM	CDLL4904	OEM	CDLL5237B	OEM	CDLL5274	OEM	CDLL5528C	OEM	CDLL6321	OEM	CDP1804E	OEM
CDLL4739A	OEM	CDLL4904A	OEM	CDLL5238	OEM	CDLL5274A	OEM	CDLL5528D	OEM	CDLL6322	OEM	CDP1805CD	3322
CDLL4740	OEM	CDLL4905	OEM	CDLL5238A	OEM	CDLL5274B	OEM	CDLL5529	OEM	CDLL6323	OEM	CDP1805CE	3322
CDLL4740A	OEM	CDLL4905A	OEM	CDLL5238B	OEM	CDLL5275	OEM	CDLL5529A	OEM	CDLL6324	OEM	CDP1805D	3322
CDLL4741	OEM	CDLL4906	OEM	CDLL5239	OEM	CDLL5275A	OEM	CDLL5529B	OEM	CDLL6325	OEM	CDP1805E	3322
CDLL4741A	OEM	CDLL4906A	OEM	CDLL5239A	OEM	CDLL5275B	OEM	CDLL5529C	OEM	CDLL6326	OEM	CDP1821CD	OEM
CDLL4742	OEM	CDLL4907	OEM	CDLL5239B	OEM	CDLL5276	OEM	CDLL5529D	OEM	CDLL6327	OEM	CDP1821CD3	OEM
CDLL4742A	OEM	CDLL4907A	OEM	CDLL5240	OEM	CDLL5276A	OEM	CDLL5530	OEM	CDLL6328	OEM	CDP1821CE	OEM
CDLL4743	OEM	CDLL4908	OEM	CDLL5240A	OEM	CDLL5276B	OEM	CDLL5530A	OEM	CDLL6329	OEM	CDP1821CH	OEM
CDLL4743A	OEM	CDLL4908A	OEM	CDLL5240B	OEM	CDLL5277	OEM	CDLL5530B	OEM	CDLL6330	OEM	CDP1821D	OEM
CDLL4744	OEM	CDLL4909	OEM	CDLL5241	OEM	CDLL5277A	OEM	CDLL5530C	OEM	CDLL6331	OEM	CDP1821E	OEM
CDLL4744A	OEM	CDLL4909A	OEM	CDLL5241A	OEM	CDLL5277B	OEM	CDLL5530D	OEM	CDLL6332	OEM	CDP1822CD	3981
CDLL4745	OEM	CDLL4910	OEM	CDLL5241B	OEM	CDLL5278	OEM	CDLL5531	OEM	CDLL6333	OEM	CDP1822CD3	OEM
CDLL4745A	OEM	CDLL4910A	OEM	CDLL5242	OEM	CDLL5278A	OEM	CDLL5531A	OEM	CDLL6334	OEM	CDP1822CE	3981
CDLL4746	OEM	CDLL4911	OEM	CDLL5242A	OEM	CDLL5278B	OEM	CDLL5531B	OEM	CDLL6335	OEM	CDP1822CH	OEM
CDLL4746A	OEM	CDLL4911A	OEM	CDLL5242B	OEM	CDLL5279	OEM	CDLL5531C	OEM	CDLL6336	OEM	CDP1822D	3981
CDLL4747	OEM	CDLL4912	OEM	CDLL5243	OEM	CDLL5279A	OEM	CDLL5531D	OEM	CDLL6337	OEM	CDP1822E	3981
CDLL4747A	OEM	CDLL4912A	OEM	CDLL5243A	OEM	CDLL5279B	OEM	CDLL5532	OEM	CDLL6338	OEM	CDP1823CD	4021
CDLL4748	OEM	CDLL4913	OEM	CDLL5243B	OEM	CDLL5280	OEM	CDLL5532A	OEM	CDLL6339	OEM	CDP1823CD3	OEM
CDLL4748A	OEM	CDLL4913A	OEM	CDLL5244	OEM	CDLL5280A	OEM	CDLL5532B	OEM	CDLL6340	OEM	CDP1823CE	4021
CDLL4749	OEM	CDLL4914	OEM	CDLL5244A	OEM	CDLL5280B	OEM	CDLL5532C	OEM	CDLL6341	OEM	CDP1823CH	OEM
CDLL4749A	OEM	CDLL4914A	OEM	CDLL5244B	OEM	CDLL5281	OEM	CDLL5532D	OEM	CDLL6342	OEM	CDP1823D	4021
CDLL4750	OEM	CDLL4915	OEM	CDLL5245	OEM	CDLL5281A	OEM	CDLL5533	OEM	CDLL6343	OEM	CDP1823E	4021
CDLL4750A	OEM	CDLL4915A	OEM	CDLL5245A	OEM	CDLL5281B	OEM	CDLL5533A	OEM	CDLL6344	OEM	CDP1824CD	4041
CDLL4751	OEM	CDLL4916	OEM	CDLL5245B	OEM	CDLL5283	OEM	CDLL5533B	OEM	CDLL6345	OEM	CDP1824CD3	OEM
CDLL4752	OEM	CDLL4916A	OEM	CDLL5246	OEM	CDLL5284	OEM	CDLL5533C	OEM	CDLL6346	OEM	CDP1824CE	4041
CDLL4752A	OEM	CDLL4917	OEM	CDLL5246A	OEM	CDLL5285	OEM	CDLL5533D	OEM	CDLL6347	OEM	CDP1824CH	OEM
CDLL4753	OEM	CDLL4917A	OEM	CDLL5246B	OEM	CDLL5286	OEM	CDLL5534	OEM	CDLL6348	OEM	CDP1824D	4041
CDLL4753A	OEM	CDLL4918	OEM	CDLL5247	OEM	CDLL5287	OEM	CDLL5534A	OEM	CDLL6349	OEM	CDP1824D3	OEM
CDLL4754	OEM	CDLL4918A	OEM	CDLL5247A	OEM	CDLL5288	OEM	CDLL5534B	OEM	CDLL6350	OEM	CDP1824E	4041
CDLL4754A	OEM	CDLL4919	OEM	CDLL5247B	OEM	CDLL5289	OEM	CDLL5534C	OEM	CDLL6351	OEM	CDP1825CD	OEM
CDLL4755	OEM	CDLL4919A	OEM	CDLL5248	OEM	CDLL5290	OEM	CDLL5534D	OEM	CDLL6352	OEM	CDP1825CE	OEM
CDLL4755A	OEM	CDLL4920	OEM	CDLL5248A	OEM	CDLL5291	OEM	CDLL5535	OEM	CDLL6353	OEM	CDP1825CH	OEM
CDLL4756	OEM	CDLL4920A	OEM	CDLL5248B	OEM	CDLL5292	OEM	CDLL5535A	OEM	CDLL6354	OEM	CDP1825D	OEM
CDLL4756A	OEM	CDLL4921	OEM	CDLL5249	OEM	CDLL5293	OEM	CDLL5535B	OEM	CDLL6355	OEM	CDP1825E	OEM
CDLL4757	OEM	CDLL4921A	OEM	CDLL5249A	OEM	CDLL5294	OEM	CDLL5535C	OEM	CDLL6485	OEM	CDP1831CD	OEM
CDLL4757A	OEM	CDLL4922	OEM	CDLL5249B	OEM	CDLL5295	OEM	CDLL5535D	OEM	CDLL6486	OEM	CDP1831CE	OEM
CDLL4758	OEM	CDLL4922A	OEM	CDLL5250	OEM	CDLL5296	OEM	CDLL5536	OEM	CDLL6487	OEM	CDP1831CH	OEM
CDLL4758A	OEM	CDLL4923	OEM	CDLL5250A	OEM	CDLL5297	OEM	CDLL5536A	OEM	CDLL6488	OEM	CDP1831D	OEM
CDLL4759	OEM	CDLL4923A	OEM	CDLL5250B	OEM	CDLL5298	OEM	CDLL5536B	OEM	CDLL6490	OEM	CDP1831E	OEM
CDLL4759A	OEM	CDLL4924	OEM	CDLL5251	OEM	CDLL5299	OEM	CDLL5536C	OEM	CDLL6491	OEM	CDP1832CD	OEM
CDLL4760	OEM	CDLL4924A	OEM	CDLL5251A	OEM	CDLL5500	OEM	CDLL5536D	OEM	CDLLL4571A	OEM	CDP1832CE	OEM
CDLL4760A	OEM	CDLL4925	OEM	CDLL5251B	OEM	CDLL5501	OEM	CDLL5537	OEM	CDP18S030	OEM	CDP1832CH	OEM
CDLL4761	OEM	CDLL4925A	OEM	CDLL5252	OEM	CDLL5502	OEM	CDLL5537A	OEM	CDP18S205V1	OEM	CDP1832D	OEM
CDLL4761A	OEM	CDLL4926	OEM	CDLL5252A	OEM	CDLL5503	OEM	CDLL5537B	OEM	CDP18S508	OEM	CDP1832E	OEM
CDLL4762	OEM	CDLL4926A	OEM	CDLL5252B	OEM	CDLL5504	OEM	CDLL5537C	OEM	CDP18S510	OEM	CDP1833CD	OEM
CDLL4762A	OEM	CDLL4927	OEM	CDLL5253	OEM	CDLL5505	OEM	CDLL5537D	OEM	CDP18S601	OEM	CDP1833CE	OEM
CDLL4763	OEM	CDLL4927A	OEM	CDLL5253A	OEM	CDLL5506	OEM	CDLL5538	OEM	CDP18S602	OEM	CDP1833CH	OEM
CDLL4763A	OEM	CDLL4928	OEM	CDLL5253B	OEM	CDLL5507	OEM	CDLL5538A	OEM	CDP18S603	OEM	CDP1833D	OEM
CDLL4764	OEM	CDLL4928A	OEM	CDLL5254	OEM	CDLL5508	OEM	CDLL5538B	OEM	CDP18S604B	OEM	CDP1833E	OEM
CDLL4764A	OEM	CDLL4929	OEM	CDLL5254A	OEM	CDLL5509	OEM	CDLL5538C	OEM	CDP18S605	OEM	CDP1834CD	OEM
CDLL4765	OEM	CDLL4929A	OEM	CDLL5254B	OEM	CDLL5510	OEM	CDLL5538D	OEM	CDP18S606	OEM	CDP1834CE	OEM
CDLL4765A	OEM	CDLL4930	OEM	CDLL5255	OEM	CDLL5511	OEM	CDLL5539	OEM	CDP18S607	OEM	CDP1834CH	OEM
CDLL4766	OEM	CDLL4930A	OEM	CDLL5255A	OEM	CDLL5512	OEM	CDLL5539A	OEM	CDP18S608	OEM	CDP1834D	OEM
CDLL4766A	OEM	CDLL4931	OEM	CDLL5255B	OEM	CDLL5513	OEM	CDLL5539B	OEM	CDP18S609	OEM	CDP1834E	OEM
CDLL4767	OEM	CDLL4931A	OEM	CDLL5256	OEM	CDLL5514	OEM	CDLL5539C	OEM	CDP18S610	OEM	CDP1851CD	4587
CDLL4767A	OEM	CDLL4932	OEM	CDLL5256A	OEM	CDLL5518	OEM	CDLL5539D	OEM	CDP18S620	OEM	CDP1851CE	4587
CDLL4768	OEM	CDLL4932A	OEM	CDLL5256B	OEM	CDLL5518A	OEM	CDLL5540	OEM	CDP18S621	OEM	CDP1851D	4587
CDLL4768A	OEM	CDLL5179	OEM	CDLL5257	OEM	CDLL5518B	OEM	CDLL5540A	OEM	CDP18S621V1	OEM	CDP1851E	4587
CDLL4769	OEM	CDLL5221	OEM	CDLL5257A	OEM	CDLL5518C	OEM	CDLL5540B	OEM	CDP18S622	OEM	CDP1852CD	4661
CDLL4769A	OEM	CDLL5221A	OEM	CDLL5257B	OEM	CDLL5518D	OEM	CDLL5540C	OEM	CDP18S623A	OEM	CDP1852CD3	OEM
CDLL4770	OEM	CDLL5221B	OEM	CDLL5258	OEM	CDLL5519	OEM	CDLL5540D	OEM	CDP18S625	OEM	CDP1852CE	4661
CDLL4770A	OEM	CDLL5222	OEM	CDLL5258A	OEM	CDLL5519A	OEM	CDLL5541	OEM	CDP18S626	OEM	CDP1852D	4661
CDLL4771	OEM	CDLL5222A	OEM	CDLL5258B	OEM	CDLL5519B	OEM	CDLL5541A	OEM	CDP18S627	OEM	CDP1852D3	OEM

If replacement code is OEM, contact original manufacturer for replacement.

DEVICE TYPE	REPL CODE
CDP1852E	4661
CDP1852H	OEM
CDP1853CD	4732
CDP1853CD3	OEM
CDP1853CE	4732
CDP1853D	4732
CDP1853D3	OEM
CDP1853E	4732
CDP1854ACD	4361
CDP1854ACD3	OEM
CDP1854ACE	4361
CDP1854AD	4361
CDP1854AD3	OEM
CDP1854AE	4361
CDP1855CD	4793
CDP1855CE	4793
CDP1855CEX	OEM
CDP1855D	4793
CDP1855DX	OEM
CDP1855E	4793
CDP1855EX	OEM
CDP1856CD	OEM
CDP1856CD3	OEM
CDP1856CDX	OEM
CDP1856CE	OEM
CDP1856CEX	OEM
CDP1856D	OEM
CDP1856D3	OEM
CDP1856DX	OEM
CDP1856E	OEM
CDP1856EX	OEM
CDP1857CD	OEM
CDP1857CD3	OEM
CDP1857CDX	OEM
CDP1857CE	OEM
CDP1857CEX	OEM
CDP1857D	OEM
CDP1857D3	OEM
CDP1857DX	OEM
CDP1857E	OEM
CDP1857EX	OEM
CDP1858CD	OEM
CDP1858CD3	OEM
CDP1858CDX	OEM
CDP1858CE	OEM
CDP1858CEX	OEM
CDP1858D	OEM
CDP1858D3	OEM
CDP1858DX	OEM
CDP1858E	OEM
CDP1858EX	OEM
CDP1859CD	OEM
CDP1859CD3	OEM
CDP1859CDX	OEM
CDP1859CE	OEM
CDP1859CEX	OEM
CDP1859D	OEM
CDP1859D3	OEM
CDP1859DX	OEM
CDP1859E	OEM
CDP1859EX	OEM
CDP1861CD	4921
CDP1861CE	4921
CDP1862CD	4931
CDP1862CE	4931
CDP1863CD	OEM
CDP1863CE	OEM
CDP1863CEX	OEM
CDP1863D	OEM
CDP1863E	OEM
CDP1864CD	4963
CDP1864CE	4963
CDP1866CD	4997
CDP1866CE	4997
CDP1866D	4997
CDP1866E	4997
CDP1867CD	OEM
CDP1867CE	OEM
CDP1867D	OEM
CDP1867E	OEM
CDP1868CD	OEM
CDP1868CE	OEM
CDP1868D	OEM
CDP1868E	OEM
CDP1869CD	5053
CDP1869CE	5053
CDP1869D	5053
CDP1869E	5053
CDP1870CD	OEM
CDP1870CE	OEM
CDP1870D	OEM
CDP1870E	OEM
CDP1871CD	5138
CDP1871CE	5138
CDP1871D	5138
CDP1871E	5138
CDP1872CD	5173
CDP1872CE	5173
CDP1873CD	5194
CDP1873CE	5194
CDP1873CEX	OEM
CDP1874CD	5213
CDP1874CE	5213
CDP1875CD	5221
CDP1875CE	5221
CDP1876CD	5234
CDP1876CDX	OEM
CDP1876CE	5234
CDP1876CEX	OEM
CDP1876D	5234
CDP1876DX	OEM
CDP1876E	5234
CDP1876EX	OEM
CDP1877CD	5246
CDP1877CE	5246
CDP1877E	5246
CDP1888E	OEM
CDP6402CD	OEM
CDP6402CE	5523
CDP6402D	OEM
CDP6402E	OEM
CDPR512CD	OEM
CDPR512D	OEM
CDPR522CD	OEM
CDPR522D	OEM
CDQ1004	0233
CDQ1011	0855
CDQ1012	0855
CDQ1014	0855
CDQ1018	0079
CDQ1021	0079
CDQ1024	0079
CDQ1037	0855
CDQ1044	0855
CDQ1045	0855
CDQ10001	0016
CDQ10002	0016
CDQ10003	0016
CDQ10004	0016
CDQ10005	0016
CDQ10006	0016
CDQ10007	0016
CDQ10008	0016
CDQ10009	0016
CDQ10010	0016
CDQ10011	0086
CDQ10012	0086
CDQ10013	0233
CDQ10014	0086
CDQ10015	0233
CDQ10016	0016
CDQ10017	0016
CDQ10018	0016
CDQ10019	0016
CDQ10020	0016
CDQ10021	0016
CDQ10022	0016
CDQ10023	0016
CDQ10024	0016
CDQ10025	0016
CDQ10026	0016
CDQ10027	0016
CDQ10028	0016
CDQ10032	0016
CDQ10033	0086
CDQ10034	0233
CDQ10035	0198
CDQ10036	0198
CDQ10037	0233
CDQ10044	0590
CDQ10045	0233
CDQ10046	0233
CDQ10047	0233
CDQ10048	0086
CDQ10049	0233
CDQ10051	0086
CDQ10052	0086
CDQ10053	0086
CDQ10054	OEM
CDQ10055	OEM
CDQ10056	OEM
CDQ10057	0086
CDQ10058	0086
CDR-2	0015
CDR-4	0015
CDR125AL	OEM
CDR125AP	OEM
CDS-16B	0015
CDT1309	0160
CDT1310	0160
CDT1311	0160
CDT1312	0969
CDT1313	0969
CDT1315	0969
CDT1319	0160
CDT1320	0160
CDT1321	0160
CDT1322	0969
CDT1349	0160
CDT1349A	0160
CDT1350	0160
CDT1350A	0160
CDT4012	OEM
CDT4013	OEM
CDT4014	OEM
CDT4015	OEM
CDT4016	OEM
CDX34D	OEM
CDX1250M	OEM
CDZ-9V	0012
CDZ-318-75	0644
CDZ318-75	0361
CDZ-C9V	0012
CE0360/7839	0004
CE0361/7839	0004
CE0362/7839	0004
CE0363/7839	0164
CE0378/7839	0030
CE0398/7839	0015
CE0398-7839	0535
CE0495/7839	0143
CE03607839	0211
CE37	0133
CE401	0015
CE402	0015
CE403	0015
CE404	0015
CE405	0015
CE406	0015
CE407	0071
CE408	0071
CE409	0071
CE410	0071
CE501	0015
CE502	0015
CE503	0015
CE504	0015
CE505	0015
CE506	0015
CE507	0071
CE508	0071
CE509	0071
CE510	0071
CE4001B	0079
CE4001C	0079
CE4002D	0126
CE4003D	0086
CE4003E	0079
CE4004C	0079
CE4005C	0037
CE4008B	0224
CE4008C	0224
CE4008D	0224
CE4008E	0224
CE4010D	0144
CE4010E	0144
CE4012D	0037
CE4012UBFX	OEM
CE4013E	0079
CE41009-00F	OEM
CE213811	0004
CEC6050	0015
CEM3310	OEM
CEM3320	OEM
CEM3330	OEM
CEM3335	OEM
CEM3340	OEM
CEM3345	OEM
CEM3350	OEM
CEM3360	OEM
CEN530	OEM
CEN544	OEM
CEN558	OEM
CER6B	0015
CER67	0015
CER67A	0015
CER67B	0015
CER67C	0015
CER67F	1325
CER68	0015
CER68A	0015
CER68B	0015
CER68C	0015
CER-69	0015
CER69	0015
CER69A	0015
CER69B	0015
CER69C	0015
CER70	0015
CER70A	0015
CER70B	0015
CER70C	0015
CER-71	0015
CER71	0015
CER71A	0015
CER71B	0015
CER71C	0015
CER-71CA	0015
CER71F	OEM
CER72	0071
CER72A	0071
CER72B	0071
CER72C	0071
CER72D	0071
CER72F	0071
CER73	0071
CER73A	0071
CER73B	0071
CER73C	0071
CER73D	0071
CER73F	0071
CER500	0015
CER500A	0015
CER500B	0015
CER500C	0015
CER500F	OEM
CER670	0015
CER670A	0015
CER670B	0015
CER670C	0015
CER680	0015
CER680A	0015
CER680B	0015
CER680C	0015
CER690	0015
CER690A	0015
CER690B	0015
CER690C	0015
CER700	0015
CER700A	0015
CER700B	0015
CER700C	0015
CER710	0015
CER710A	0015
CER710B	0015
CER710C	0015
CER720	0071
CER720A	0071
CER720B	0071
CER720C	0071
CER730	0071
CER730A	0071
CER730B	0071
CER730C	0071
CER1200F	OEM
CF-092	0012
CF-07005	0733
CF3	0549
CF4-28	OEM
CF10	OEM
CF15	OEM
CF20	OEM
CF24	OEM
CF25	OEM
CF30	OEM
CF35	OEM
CF40	OEM
CF45	OEM
CF50	OEM
CF102BA	OEM
CF102DA	0015
CF102FA	OEM
CF102HA	OEM
CF102KA	OEM
CF102MA	OEM
CF102PA	0071
CF102RA	0071
CF102VA	0087
CF152AA	0071
CF152BA	0071
CF152DA	0071
CF152FA	0071
CF152HA	0071
CF152KA	0071
CF152MA	0071
CF152PA	0071
CF152RA	0071
CF152VA	0087
CF-1295H	0086
CF2386	4150
CF37212N	OEM
CF61872N	OEM
CF77316AFT	OEM
CFA6.8D	0062
CFA6.8D5	0062
CFA6.8D10	0062
CFA7.5D	0077
CFA7.5D5	0077
CFA7.5D10	0077
CFA8.2D	0165
CFA8.2D5	0165
CFA8.2D10	0165
CFA9.1D	0057
CFA9.1D5	0057
CFA9.1D10	0057
CFA10D	0064
CFA10D5	0064
CFA10D10	0064
CFA11D	0181
CFA11D5	0181
CFA11D10	0181
CFA12D	0052
CFA12D5	0052
CFA12D10	0052
CFA13D	0053
CFA13D5	0053
CFA13D10	0053
CFA14D	0873
CFA14D5	0873
CFA14D10	0873
CFA15D	0681
CFA15D5	0681
CFA15D10	0681
CFA16D	0440
CFA16D5	0440
CFA16D10	0440
CFA17D	0210
CFA17D5	0210
CFA17D10	0210
CFA18D	0371
CFA18D5	0371
CFA18D10	0371
CFA19D	0666
CFA19D5	0666
CFA19D10	0666
CFA20D	0695
CFA20D5	0695
CFA20D10	0695
CFA22D	0700
CFA22D5	0700
CFA22D10	0700
CFA24D	0489
CFA24D5	0489
CFA24D10	0489
CFA25D	0709
CFA25D5	0709
CFA25D10	0709
CFA27D	0450
CFA27D5	0450
CFA27D10	0709
CFA28D	0257
CFA28D5	0257
CFA28D10	0257
CFA30D	0195
CFA30D5	0195
CFA30D10	0195
CFA33D	0166
CFA33D5	0166
CFA33D10	0166
CFB6.8D	0062
CFB6.8D5	0062
CFB6.8D10	0062
CFB7.5D	OEM
CFB7.5D5	0077
CFB7.5D10	0077
CFB8.2D	0165
CFB8.2D5	0165
CFB8.2D10	0165
CFB9.1D	0057
CFB9.1D5	0057
CFB9.1D10	0057
CFB10D	0064
CFB10D5	0064
CFB10D10	0064
CFB11D	0181
CFB11D5	0181
CFB11D10	0181
CFB12D	0052
CFB12D5	0052
CFB12D10	0052
CFB13D	0053
CFB13D5	0053
CFB13D10	0053
CFB14D	0873
CFB14D5	0873
CFB14D10	0873
CFB15D	0681
CFB15D5	0681
CFB15D10	0681
CFB16D	0440
CFB16D5	0440
CFB16D10	0440
CFB17D	0210
CFB17D5	0210
CFB17D10	0210
CFB18D	0371
CFB18D5	0371
CFB18D10	0371
CFB19D	0666
CFB19D5	0666
CFB19D10	0666
CFB20D	0695
CFB20D5	0695
CFB20D10	0695
CFB22D	0700
CFB22D5	0700
CFB22D10	0700
CFB24D	0489
CFB24D5	0489
CFB24D10	0489
CFB25D	0709
CFB25D5	0709
CFB25D10	0709
CFB27D	0450
CFB27D5	0450
CFB27D10	0450
CFB30D	0195
CFB30D5	0195
CFB30D10	0195
CFB33D	0166
CFB33D5	0166
CFB33D10	0166
CFC4/500	OEM
CFC6.8D	0062
CFC6.8D5	0062
CFC6.8D10	0062
CFC7.5D	0077
CFC7.5D5	0077
CFC7.5D10	0077
CFC8.2D	0165
CFC8.2D5	0165
CFC8.2D10	0165
CFC9.1D	0057
CFC9.1D5	0057
CFC9.1D10	0057
CFC10D	0064
CFC10D5	0064
CFC10D10	0064
CFC11D	0181
CFC11D5	0181
CFC11D10	0181
CFC12D	0052
CFC12D5	0052
CFC12D10	0052
CFC13D	0053
CFC13D5	0053
CFC13D10	0053
CFC14D	0873
CFC14D5	0873
CFC14D10	0873
CFC15D	0681
CFC15D5	0681
CFC15D10	0681
CFC16D	0440
CFC16D5	0440
CFC16D10	0440
CFC17D	0210
CFC17D5	0210
CFC17D10	0210
CFC18D	0371
CFC18D5	0371
CFC18D10	0371
CFC19D	0666
CFC19D5	0666
CFC19D10	0666
CFC20D	0695
CFC20D5	0695
CFC20D10	0695
CFC22D	0700
CFC22D5	0700
CFC22D10	0700
CFC24D	0489
CFC24D5	0489
CFC24D10	0489
CFC25D	0709
CFC25D5	0709
CFC25D10	0709
CFC27D	0450
CFC27D5	0450
CFC27D10	0450
CFC30D	0195
CFC30D5	0195
CFC30D10	0195
CFC33D	0166
CFC33D5	0166
CFC33D10	0166
CFCD/400	OEM
CFD8201CP	OEM
CFL-5	OEM
CFM13026	OEM
CFR-10	0769
CFR10	OEM
CFR15	OEM
CFR20	OEM
CFR25	OEM
CFR30	OEM
CFR35	OEM
CFR40	OEM
CFR45	OEM
CFR50	OEM
CFR5185A	OEM
CFR5186A	OEM
CFR5187A	OEM
CFR5188A	OEM
CFY11	OEM
CFY12	OEM
CFY20	OEM
CFZ12D	OEM
CFZ12D5	OEM
CFZ12D10	OEM
CG030A	OEM
CG030B	OEM
CG040A	OEM
CG040C	OEM
CG040D	OEM
CG040E	OEM
CG-1	OEM
CG1	0016
CG1(DIO)	0102
CG1(DIODE)	0102
CG-1/DG-1	OEM
CG1/DG1	OEM
CG1-540	OEM
CG2	0102
CG2(DIO)	0102
CG-2/DG-2	OEM
CG2/DG2	OEM
CG3	OEM
CG3(DIO)	OEM
CG-3/DG-3	OEM
CG3/DG3	OEM
CG3.22.2FW	OEM
CG3.22.12FB	OEM
CG11G1	OEM
CG12-E	0143
CG12E	0143
C-G59A	OEM
CG60H	OEM
CG61H	0143
CG62H	0143
CG63H	0143
CG64H	0143
CG65H	0143
CG66H	0143
CG70H	OEM
CG71H	OEM
CG72H	OEM
CG74H	0143
CG80H	OEM
CG81H	OEM
CG82H	OEM
CG83H	OEM
CG84H	OEM
CG85H	OEM
CG86H	0143
CG90H	OEM
CG91AH	OEM
CG92AH	OEM
CG94H	OEM
CG125	OEM
CG125A	OEM
CG125B	OEM
CG125C	OEM
CG125D	OEM
CG127	OEM
CG127A	OEM
CG127B	OEM
C-G189A	OEM
CG512	OEM
CG4000	OEM
CG4100	OEM
CG4103	OEM
CG4200	OEM
CG5500A	OEM
CG5600A	OEM
CG5700A	OEM
CG5705	OEM
CG24015A	0033
CG80286-6C	OEM
CG80286-10	OEM
CGB-540	OEM
CGB204001-14	OEM
CGB204002-02	OEM
CGB374008-01	OEM
CGB374202-01	OEM
CGB374203-02	OEM
CGB374205-01	OEM
CGB394208-01	OEM
CGB408001-16	OEM
CGB408002-03	OEM
CGB445005-01	OEM
CGB596402-06	OEM
CGB596402-07	OEM
CGB596403-10	OEM
CGB596403-11	OEM
CGB596405-09	OEM
CGB596405-10	OEM
CGB596408-02	OEM
CGB596410-03	OEM
CGB647101-09	OEM
CGB647103-08	OEM
CGB647105-04	OEM
CGB717701-04	OEM
CGB717702-03	OEM
CGB717704-01	OEM
CGB798405-01	OEM
CGC081201-07	OEM
CGC101201-03	OEM
CGC121301-02	OEM
CGD125L	OEM
CGD462	0143
CGD591	0143
CGD685	0143
CGD1029	0143
C-GE9A	OEM
C-GE21	OEM
CGE-50	0050
CGE-51	0050
CGE-52	0004
CGE-53	0164
CGE-54	2839
CGE-60	0008
CGE-61	0326
CGE-62	0111
CGE-64	0396
CGE-66	0042
CGE-68	0142
CGE-69	0919
CGE-500	0133
CGJ-1	0102
CGS-540	OEM
CGY11A	OEM
CGY11B	OEM
CGY12A	OEM
CGY12B	OEM
CGY13A	OEM
CGY13B	OEM
CGY14A	OEM
CGY14B	OEM
CH10	OEM
CH16.8	OEM
CH16.8A	OEM
CH17.5	OEM
CH17.5A	OEM
CH18.2	OEM
CH18.2A	OEM
CH19.1	OEM
CH19.1A	OEM
CH20	OEM
CH30	OEM
CH40	OEM
CH50	OEM
CH109A2	OEM
CH109AZ2	OEM
CH109B2	OEM
CH109C2	OEM
CH109D2	OEM
CH109E2	OEM
CH109F2	OEM
CH109Z2	OEM
CH110	OEM
CH110A	OEM
CH111	OEM
CH111A	OEM
CH112	OEM
CH112A	OEM
CH113	OEM
CH113A	OEM
CH115	OEM
CH115A	OEM
CH116	OEM
CH116A	OEM
CH118	OEM

If replacement code is OEM, contact original manufacturer for replacement.

DEVICE TYPE	REPL CODE
CH118A	OEM
CH119A	OEM
CH119AZ	OEM
CH119B	OEM
CH119C	OEM
CH119D	0015
CH119E	OEM
CH119F	OEM
CH119Z	OEM
CH120	OEM
CH120A	OEM
CH122	OEM
CH122A	OEM
CH124	OEM
CH124A	OEM
CH127	OEM
CH127A	OEM
CH130	OEM
CH130A	OEM
CH133	OEM
CH133A	OEM
CH302BA	OEM
CH302BD	OEM
CH302FA	OEM
CH302HA	OEM
CH302KA	OEM
CH302MA	0087
CH302PA	0087
CH302RA	0087
CH746	OEM
CH746/25	OEM
CH747	OEM
CH747/25	OEM
CH748	OEM
CH748/25	OEM
CH749	OEM
CH749/25	OEM
CH750	OEM
CH750/25	OEM
CH751	OEM
CH751/25	OEM
CH752	OEM
CH752/25	OEM
CH753	0466
CH753/25	OEM
CH754	OEM
CH754/25	OEM
CH755	OEM
CH755/25	OEM
CH756	OEM
CH756/25	OEM
CH757	0057
CH757/25	OEM
CH758	OEM
CH758/25	OEM
CH759	0052
CH759/25	OEM
CH821	0466
CH823	0466
CH825	0466
CH827	0466
CH829	0466
CH962	OEM
CH962/25	OEM
CH963	0052
CH963/25	OEM
CH964	OEM
CH964/25	OEM
CH965	0681
CH965/25	OEM
CH966	OEM
CH966/25	OEM
CH967	OEM
CH967/25	OEM
CH968	OEM
CH968/25	OEM
CH969	OEM
CH969/25	OEM
CH970	OEM
CH970/25	OEM
CH971	OEM
CH971/25	OEM
CH972	OEM
CH972/25	OEM
CH973	OEM
CH973/25	OEM
CH974	OEM
CH974/25	OEM
CH975	OEM
CH975/25	OEM
CH976	OEM
CH976/25	OEM
CH977	OEM
CH977/25	OEM
CH978	OEM
CH978/25	OEM
CH979	OEM
CH979/25	OEM
CH980	OEM
CH980/25	OEM
CH981	OEM
CH981/25	OEM
CH982	OEM
CH982/25	OEM
CH983	OEM
CH983/25	OEM
CH984	OEM
CH984/25	OEM
CH985	OEM
CH985/25	OEM
CH986	OEM
CH986/25	OEM
CH987	OEM
CH987/25	OEM
CH988	OEM
CH988/25	OEM
CH989	OEM
CH989/25	OEM
CH990	OEM
CH990/25	OEM
CH991	OEM
CH991/25	OEM
CH992	OEM
CH992/25	OEM
CH1213	OEM
CH1214	OEM
CH1215	OEM
CH1216	OEM
CH1253	OEM
CH1267A	OEM
CH1290	OEM
CH1295	OEM
CH1296	OEM
CH1511	OEM
CH1513	OEM
CH1514	OEM
CH1515	OEM
CH1516	OEM
CH1517	OEM
CH1518	OEM
CH1611	OEM
CH1612	OEM
CH1613	OEM
CH1614	OEM
CH1615	OEM
CH1616	OEM
CH1621	OEM
CH1622	OEM
CH1623	OEM
CH1624	OEM
CH1625	OEM
CH1820(A)	OEM
CH3065	0167
CH4099	OEM
CH4099/25	OEM
CH4100	OEM
CH4100/25	OEM
CH4101	OEM
CH4101/25	OEM
CH4102	OEM
CH4102/25	OEM
CH4103	0057
CH4103/25	OEM
CH4104	OEM
CH4104/25	OEM
CH4105	OEM
CH4105/25	OEM
CH4106	0052
CH4107	OEM
CH4108	0873
CH4109	0681
CH4110	OEM
CH4111	OEM
CH4112	OEM
CH4113	0943
CH4114	OEM
CH4115	OEM
CH4116	OEM
CH4117	1596
CH4118	OEM
CH4119	0257
CH4120	OEM
CH4121	OEM
CH4122	OEM
CH4123	OEM
CH4124	OEM
CH4125	OEM
CH4126	OEM
CH4127	OEM
CH4128	OEM
CH4129	OEM
CH4130	OEM
CH4131	OEM
CH4132	OEM
CH4133	2997
CH4134	OEM
CH4135	OEM
CH4370	OEM
CH4371	OEM
CH4372	OEM
CH4565A	OEM
CH4566A	OEM
CH4567A	OEM
CH4568A	OEM
CH4569A	OEM
CH4570A	OEM
CH4571A	OEM
CH4572A	OEM
CH4573A	OEM
CH4574A	OEM
CH4575A	OEM
CH4576A	OEM
CH4577A	OEM
CH4578A	OEM
CH4579A	OEM
CH4580A	OEM
CH4581A	OEM
CH4582A	OEM
CH4583A	OEM
CH4584A	OEM
CH4614	OEM
CH4614/25	OEM
CH4615	OEM
CH4615/25	OEM
CH4616	OEM
CH4616/25	OEM
CH4617	OEM
CH4617/25	OEM
CH4618	OEM
CH4618/25	OEM
CH4619	OEM
CH4619/25	OEM
CH4620	OEM
CH4620/25	OEM
CH4621	OEM
CH4621/25	OEM
CH4622	OEM
CH4622/25	OEM
CH4623	OEM
CH4623/25	OEM
CH4624	OEM
CH4624/25	OEM
CH4625	OEM
CH4626	OEM
CH4626/25	OEM
CH4627	0466
CH4627/25	OEM
CH4728	0289
CH4728/25	OEM
CH4729	OEM
CH4729/25	OEM
CH4730	0451
CH4730/25	OEM
CH4731	0528
CH4731/25	OEM
CH4732	OEM
CH4732/25	OEM
CH4733	OEM
CH4733/25	OEM
CH4734	5688
CH4734/25	OEM
CH4735	0631
CH4735/25	OEM
CH4736	OEM
CH4736/25	OEM
CH4737	OEM
CH4737/25	OEM
CH4738	OEM
CH4738/25	OEM
CH4739	0012
CH4739/25	OEM
CH4740	OEM
CH4740/25	OEM
CH4741	OEM
CH4741/25	OEM
CH4742	0137
CH4742/25	OEM
CH4743	OEM
CH4743/25	OEM
CH4744	0002
CH4744/25	OEM
CH4745	OEM
CH4745/25	OEM
CH4746	OEM
CH4746/25	OEM
CH4747	OEM
CH4747/25	OEM
CH4748	OEM
CH4748/25	OEM
CH4749	OEM
CH4749/25	OEM
CH4750	OEM
CH4750/25	OEM
CH4751	OEM
CH4751/25	OEM
CH4752	OEM
CH4752/25	OEM
CH4753	OEM
CH4753/25	OEM
CH4754	OEM
CH4754/25	OEM
CH4755	OEM
CH4755/25	OEM
CH4756	OEM
CH4756/25	OEM
CH4757	OEM
CH4757/25	OEM
CH4758	OEM
CH4758/25	OEM
CH4759	OEM
CH4759/25	OEM
CH4760	OEM
CH4760/25	OEM
CH4761	1181
CH4761/25	OEM
CH4762	OEM
CH4762/25	OEM
CH4763	1301
CH4763/25	OEM
CH4764	0098
CH4764/25	OEM
CH5221	OEM
CH5221/25	OEM
CH5222	OEM
CH5222/25	OEM
CH5223	OEM
CH5223/25	OEM
CH5224	OEM
CH5224/25	OEM
CH5225	OEM
CH5225/25	OEM
CH5226	OEM
CH5226/25	OEM
CH5227	OEM
CH5227/25	OEM
CH5228	OEM
CH5228/25	OEM
CH5229	OEM
CH5229/25	OEM
CH5230	OEM
CH5230/25	OEM
CH5231	OEM
CH5231/25	OEM
CH5232	OEM
CH5232/25	OEM
CH5233	0091
CH5233/25	OEM
CH5234	0466
CH5234/25	OEM
CH5235	OEM
CH5235/25	OEM
CH5236	OEM
CH5236/25	OEM
CH5237	OEM
CH5237/25	OEM
CH5238	OEM
CH5238/25	OEM
CH5239	0057
CH5239/25	OEM
CH5240	OEM
CH5240/25	OEM
CH5241	OEM
CH5241/25	OEM
CH5242	0052
CH5242/25	OEM
CH5243	OEM
CH5243/25	OEM
CH5244	OEM
CH5244/25	OEM
CH5245	0681
CH5245/25	OEM
CH5246	OEM
CH5246/25	OEM
CH5247	1639
CH5247/25	OEM
CH5248	OEM
CH5248/25	OEM
CH5249	OEM
CH5249/25	OEM
CH5250	OEM
CH5250/25	OEM
CH5251	OEM
CH5251/25	OEM
CH5252	OEM
CH5252/25	OEM
CH5253	OEM
CH5253/25	OEM
CH5254	OEM
CH5254/25	OEM
CH5255	OEM
CH5255/25	OEM
CH5256	OEM
CH5256/25	OEM
CH5257	OEM
CH5257/25	OEM
CH5258	OEM
CH5258/25	OEM
CH5259	OEM
CH5259/25	OEM
CH5260	OEM
CH5260/25	OEM
CH5261	OEM
CH5261/25	OEM
CH5262	OEM
CH5262/25	OEM
CH5263	OEM
CH5263/25	OEM
CH5264	1148
CH5264/25	OEM
CH5265	OEM
CH5265/25	OEM
CH5266	OEM
CH5266/25	OEM
CH5267	OEM
CH5267/25	OEM
CH5268	OEM
CH5268/25	OEM
CH5269	OEM
CH5269/25	OEM
CH5270	OEM
CH5270/25	OEM
CH5271	OEM
CH5271/25	OEM
CH5272	OEM
CH5272/25	OEM
CH5273	OEM
CH5273/25	OEM
CH5274	OEM
CH5274/25	OEM
CH5275	0245
CH5275/25	OEM
CH5276	OEM
CH5276/25	OEM
CH5277	OEM
CH5277/25	OEM
CH5278	0871
CH5278/25	OEM
CH5279	OEM
CH5279/25	OEM
CH5280	OEM
CH5280/25	OEM
CH5281	OEM
CH5281/25	OEM
CHA4Z3.6	0188
CHA4Z5.1	0162
CHA4Z5.6	0157
CHAZ6.2	0631
CHAZ6.2A	0631
CHAZ7.5	OEM
CHAZ7.5A	OEM
CHAZ62.A	0631
CHMZ3.6	0188
CHMZ5.1	0162
CHMZ5.6	0157
CHS70ANE11P	OEM
CHS70BGE11P	OEM
CHS70GE11PF	OEM
CHS74GS21PF	OEM
CHV1070A	OEM
CHV1080A	OEM
CHV1090A	OEM
CHV1570A	OEM
CHV1580A	OEM
CHV1590A	OEM
CHV2030-01	OEM
CHV2060A	OEM
CHV2080A	OEM
CHV2090A	OEM
CHZ10	0170
CHZ10A	0170
CHZ210A	0170
CI1	OEM
CI2	OEM
CI3	OEM
CI4	OEM
CI5	OEM
CI-1002	0817
CI-1003	1335
CI-1004	0649
CI1103	OEM
CI1103-2	OEM
CI1123	OEM
CI2711	0016
CI2712	0016
CI2713	0016
CI2714	0016
CI2923	0016
CI2924	0016
CI2925	0016
CI2926	0016
CI3390	0016
CI3391	0016
CI3391A	0016
CI3392	0016
CI3393	0016
CI3394	0016
CI3395	0016
CI3396	0016
CI3397	0016
CI3398	0016
CI3402	0016
CI3403	0016
CI3404	0016
CI3405	0016
CI3414	0079
CI3415	0016
CI3416	0016
CI3417	0016
CI3704	0086
CI3705	0086
CI3706	0086
CI3900	0016
CI3900A	0016
CI3901	0016
CI4256	0016
CI4424	0016
CI4425	0016
CI6800-2	OEM
CI-6800-2/16	OEM
CI-6800-2/32	OEM
CI-6800-2/48	OEM
CI-6800-2/64	OEM
CI8080	OEM
CI8086	OEM
CI68002	OEM
CI-68002A	OEM
CI68002A	OEM
CIJ70645	0123
CIL194	0224
CIL194A	0224
CIL194B	0224
CIL195	0224
CIL195C	OEM
CIL195D	OEM
CIL250	OEM
CIL251	OEM
CIL252	OEM
CIL253	OEM
CIL254	OEM
CIL255	OEM
CIL256	OEM
CIL257	OEM
CIL350	OEM
CIL351	OEM
CIL352	OEM
CIL353	OEM
CIL354	OEM
CIL355	OEM
CIL356	OEM
CIL357	OEM
CIL358	OEM
CIL359	OEM
CIL360	OEM
CIL361	OEM
CIL362	OEM
CIL363	OEM
CIL364	OEM
CIL365	OEM
CIL366	OEM
CIL367	OEM
CIL368	OEM
CIL369	OEM
CIL500/022	OEM
CIL500/024	OEM
CIL500/027	OEM
CIL500/030	OEM
CIL500/033	OEM
CIL500/039	OEM
CIL500/043	OEM
CIL500/047	OEM
CIL500/056	OEM
CIL500/062	OEM
CIL500/068	OEM
CIL500/075	OEM
CIL500/082	OEM
CIL500/091	OEM
CIL500/100	OEM
CIL500/110	OEM
CIL500/120	OEM
CIL500/130	OEM
CIL500/140	OEM
CIL500/150	OEM
CIL500/160	OEM
CIL500/180	OEM
CIL500/200	OEM
CIL500/220	OEM
CIL500/240	OEM
CIL500/270	OEM
CIL500/300	OEM
CIL500/330	OEM
CIL500/360	OEM
CIL500/390	OEM
CIL500/430	OEM
CIL500/470	OEM
CIL500/510	OEM
CIL500/560	OEM
CIL500/620	OEM
CIL500/680	OEM
CIL511	0144
CIL512	0144
CIL513	0144
CIL521	0144
CIL522	0144
CIL523	0144
CIL-531	0079
CIL531	0144
CIL-532	0079
CIL532	0144
CIL533	0144
CIL1300	OEM
CIL1301	OEM
CIL1302	OEM
CIL1303	OEM
CIL1304	OEM
CIL1305	OEM
CINCH	OEM
CI-PCM	OEM
CI-S100/16	OEM
CI-S100/32	OEM
CI-S100/48	OEM
CI-S100/64	OEM
CJ5201	0016
CJ5202	0016
CJ5203	0016
CJ5204	0004
CJ5205	OEM
CJ-5206	0016
CJ5206	0079
CJ5206A	0590
CJ-5207	0016
CJ5207	0079
CJ-5208	0016
CJ-5209	0126
CJ5209	0126
CJ-5210	0086
CJ5210	0086
CJ-5211	0079
CJ5211	0016
CJ-5212	0079
CJ5212	0016
CJ5213	0086
CJ5214	0086
CJ5215	0086
CJCA001	OEM
CJCA002	OEM
CJCA007	OEM
CJCA008	OEM
CJSE001	OEM
CJSE002	OEM
CJSE003	OEM
CJSE004	OEM
CJSE005	OEM
CJSE006	OEM
CJSE009	OEM
CJSE010	OEM
CJSE011	OEM
CJSE012	OEM
CJSE013	OEM
CJSE014	OEM
CJSE017	OEM
CJSE018	OEM
CJSE019	OEM
CJSE020	OEM
CJSE021	OEM
CJSE022	OEM
CJSE033	OEM
CJSE034	OEM
CJSE035	OEM
CJSE036	OEM
CJSE037	OEM
CJSE038	OEM
CJSE039	OEM
CJSE040	OEM
CJSE041	OEM
CJSE042	OEM
CJSE043	OEM
CJSE044	OEM
CJSE045	OEM
CJSE046	OEM
CJSE047	OEM
CJSE048	OEM
CJSE049	OEM
CJSE050	OEM
CJSE052	OEM
CJSE053	OEM
CJSE057	OEM
CJSE058	OEM
CJSE059	OEM
CJSE061	OEM
CJSE062	OEM
CJSE063	OEM
CJSE064	OEM
CJSE065	OEM
CJSE066	OEM
CJSE067	3359
CJSE068	OEM
CJSE069	OEM
CJSE070	OEM
CJSE071	1905
CJSE072	OEM
CK	OEM
CK4	0136
CK4A	0136
CK13	0004
CK13A	0004
CK14	0279
CK14A	0279
CK16	0279
CK16A	0279
CK17	0279
CK17A	0279
CK22	0004
CK22A	0004
CK22B	0004
CK22C	0004
CK25	0279
CK25A	0279
CK26	0279
CK26A	0279
CK27	0279
CK27A	0279
CK28	0136
CK28A	0136
CK64	0004
CK64A	0004
CK64B	0004
CK64C	0004
CK65	0004
CK65A	0004
CK65B	0004
CK65C	0004
CK66	0004
CK66A	0004
CK66B	0004
CK66C	0004
CK67	0004
CK67A	0004
CK67B	0004
CK67C	0004
CK83	0050
CK131	0911
CK-134A	3662
CK261	0595
CK262	0595
CK273	OEM
CK277	OEM
CK302BA	OEM
CK302DA	OEM
CK302FA	OEM
CK302HA	OEM
CK302KA	OEM
CK302MA	2621
CK302PA	2621
CK302RA	2621
CK398	0855
CK419	0016
CK420	0016
CK421	0016
CK422	0016
CK474	0016
CK475	0016
CK476	0016
CK477	0016

If replacement code is OEM, contact original manufacturer for replacement.

DEVICE TYPE	REPL CODE
CK661	0279
CK662	0279
CK705	0143
CK-706	0143
CK706	0143
CK706-P	0143
CK706A	0143
CK706P	0143
CK710	0911
CK715	0143
CK721	0211
CK722	0211
CK725	0211
CK727	0211
CK731	0911
CK751	0211
CK754	0211
CK759	0279
CK759A	0279
CK760	0279
CK760A	0279
CK761	0279
CK762	0136
CK766	0136
CK766A	0136
CK768	0279
CK776	0279
CK776A	0279
CK790	0211
CK791	0211
CK793	0211
CK794	0211
CK798	OEM
CK799	OEM
CK800	OEM
CK863	OEM
CK863B	OEM
CK870	0211
CK871	0211
CK872	0211
CK875	0211
CK878	0211
CK879	0211
CK882	0211
CK888	0211
CK891	0004
CK892	0004
CK942	0037
CK1101	OEM
CK1101P	OEM
CK1102	OEM
CK1102P	OEM
CK1103	OEM
CK1103P	OEM
CK1104	OEM
CK1104P	OEM
CK1105	OEM
CK1106	OEM
CK1108	OEM
CK1111	OEM
CK1111P	OEM
CK1112	OEM
CK1112P	OEM
CK1113	OEM
CK1113P	OEM
CK1114	OEM
CK1115	OEM
CK1116	OEM
CK1117	OEM
CK1121	OEM
CK1121W	OEM
CK1122	OEM
CK1122B	OEM
CK1122W	OEM
CK1123	OEM
CK1124	OEM
CK1201	OEM
CK1202	OEM
CK1203	OEM
CK1204	OEM
CK1205	OEM
CK1206	OEM
CK1207	OEM
CK1208	OEM
CK1209	OEM
CK1210	OEM
CK1211	OEM
CK1212	OEM
CK1213	OEM
CK1214	OEM
CK1216	OEM
CK1217	OEM
CK1218	OEM
CK1219	OEM
CK1220	OEM
CK1221	OEM
CK1222	OEM
CK1223	OEM
CK1224	OEM
CK1225	OEM
CK1226	OEM
CK1227	OEM
CK1228	OEM
CK1230	OEM
CK1231	OEM
CK1232	OEM
CK1233	OEM
CK1234	OEM
CK1241	OEM

DEVICE TYPE	REPL CODE
CK1242	OEM
CK1243	OEM
CK1244	OEM
CK1245	OEM
CK1246	OEM
CK1247	OEM
CK1248	OEM
CK1249	OEM
CK1250	OEM
CK1251	OEM
CK1252	OEM
CK1253	OEM
CK1254	OEM
CK1255	OEM
CK1256	OEM
CK1257	OEM
CK1258	OEM
CK1260	OEM
CK1261	OEM
CK1262	OEM
CK1263	OEM
CK1264	OEM
CK1265	OEM
CK1266	OEM
CK1267	OEM
CK1268	OEM
CK1271	OEM
CK1273	OEM
CK1274	OEM
CK1275	OEM
CK1276	OEM
CK1277	OEM
CK1278	OEM
CK1279	OEM
CK1280	OEM
CK1281	OEM
CK1282	OEM
CK1283	OEM
CK1284	OEM
CK1285	OEM
CK1286	OEM
CK1287	OEM
CK1288	OEM
CK1289	OEM
CK1290	OEM
CK1291	OEM
CK1292	OEM
CK1293	OEM
CK2000	OEM
CK2000B	OEM
CK2002	OEM
CK2003	OEM
CK2008P	OEM
CK2013	OEM
CK2015	OEM
CK2018	OEM
CK2019	OEM
CK2024	OEM
CK2025P	OEM
CK2028	OEM
CK2028A	OEM
CK2028B	OEM
CK2029	OEM
CK2030	OEM
CK2032	OEM
CK2033	OEM
CK2034	OEM
CK2035	OEM
CK2037	OEM
CK2038	OEM
CK2039	OEM
CK2040	OEM
CK2041	OEM
CK2042	OEM
CK2043	OEM
CK2046	OEM
CK2051	OEM
CK2052	OEM
CK2053	OEM
CK2060	OEM
CK2065	OEM
CK2066	OEM
CK2067	OEM
CK2070	OEM
CK2071	OEM
CK2072	OEM
CK2078	OEM
CK2080	OEM
CK2086	OEM
CK2095	OEM
CK2101	OEM
CK2102	OEM
CK2103	OEM
CK2104	OEM
CK2105	OEM
CK2106	OEM
CK2112	OEM
CK2114	OEM
CK2117	OEM
CK2118	OEM
CK2124	OEM
CK2125	OEM
CK2127	OEM
CK2129	OEM
CK2132	OEM
CK2137	OEM
CK2139	OEM
CK2140	OEM
CK2141	OEM

DEVICE TYPE	REPL CODE
CK2142	OEM
CK2143	OEM
CK2145	OEM
CK2146	OEM
CK2147	OEM
CK2148	OEM
CK2149	OEM
CK2150	OEM
CK2151	OEM
CK2153	OEM
CK2154	OEM
CK2155	OEM
CK2157	OEM
CK2160	OEM
CK2161	OEM
CK2162	OEM
CK2170	OEM
CK2171	OEM
CK2172	OEM
CK2173	OEM
CK2177	OEM
CK2178	OEM
CK2190P	OEM
CK2195	OEM
CK-3300	OEM
CK3300	OEM
CL05	0015
CL010	0015
CL025	0015
CL1	0015
CL1.5	0015
CL-2	OEM
CL2	0015
CL-2(F)	OEM
CL3	0015
CL3P7L	OEM
CL4	0015
CL5	0015
CL5M2	OEM
CL5M2L	OEM
CL5M3	OEM
CL5M4	OEM
CL5M4L	OEM
CL5M5	OEM
CL5M5L	OEM
CL5M7	OEM
CL5M9M	OEM
CL5P4	OEM
CL5P4L	OEM
CL5P5	OEM
CL5P5L	OEM
CL5P5M	OEM
CL5P9M	OEM
CL6	0015
CL7	0015
CL7P4	OEM
CL7P4L	OEM
CL7P5	OEM
CL7P5H-ID	OEM
CL7P5HL	OEM
CL7P5L	OEM
CL7P7HL	OEM
CL7P7HM	OEM
CL7P9L	OEM
CL8	0015
CL9P4L	OEM
CL9P5	OEM
CL9P5HL	OEM
CL9P5L	OEM
CL9P7HL	OEM
CL9P7HLL	OEM
CL9P9L	OEM
CL9P9LL	OEM
CL10	OEM
CL12	0311
CL13	0311
CL14	OEM
CL15	0536
CL16	OEM
CL17	OEM
CL18	OEM
CL19	OEM
CL20	OEM
CL25	OEM
CL30	OEM
CL35	OEM
CL40	OEM
CL45	OEM
CL50	OEM
CL100	0586
CL110	0586
CL111	OEM
CL112	OEM
CL113	OEM
CL114	OEM
CL116(P)	OEM
CL116P	6245
CL120	0311
CL155D	OEM
CL166(D)	OEM
CL166(P)	OEM
CL166C	0016
CL166C,D	0079
CL166D	0016
CL252D57JU	OEM
CL254A17JVW	OEM
CL254D16EU	OEM
CL602	OEM
CL603	OEM

DEVICE TYPE	REPL CODE
CL603A	OEM
CL603AL	OEM
CL604	OEM
CL604L	OEM
CL604M	OEM
CL605	OEM
CL605L	OEM
CL607	OEM
CL607L	OEM
CL702	OEM
CL702/2	OEM
CL702L	OEM
CL702L2	OEM
CL703	OEM
CL703/2	OEM
CL703A	OEM
CL703L	OEM
CL703L2	OEM
CL703M	OEM
CL704	OEM
CL704/2	OEM
CL704L	OEM
CL704L2	OEM
CL704M	OEM
CL705	OEM
CL705/2	OEM
CL705HL	OEM
CL705HL2	OEM
CL705L	OEM
CL705M	OEM
CL707	OEM
CL707H	OEM
CL707HL	OEM
CL707HM	OEM
CL707L	OEM
CL707M	OEM
CL709L	OEM
CL902	OEM
CL902L	OEM
CL902N	OEM
CL903	OEM
CL903A	OEM
CL903AN	OEM
CL903L	OEM
CL903N	OEM
CL904	OEM
CL904L	OEM
CL904N	OEM
CL905	OEM
CL905H	OEM
CL905HL	OEM
CL905HLL	OEM
CL905HN	OEM
CL905L	OEM
CL905N	OEM
CL907	OEM
CL907H	OEM
CL907HL	OEM
CL907HN	OEM
CL907L	OEM
CL907N	OEM
CL909L	OEM
CL1020	OEM
CL1200	OEM
CL1210	OEM
CL1220	OEM
CL1230	OEM
CL1305	OEM
CL1325	OEM
CL1355	OEM
CL1375	OEM
CL1395	OEM
CL1506	0272
CL1506B	OEM
CL1510	0311
CL1511	0311
CL1520	OEM
CL1800	OEM
CL1800M	OEM
CL1800W	OEM
CL1810	OEM
CL1810M	OEM
CL1810W	OEM
CL1811	OEM
CL1811M	OEM
CL1811W	OEM
CL1820	OEM
CL1820M	OEM
CL1820W	OEM
CL1821	OEM
CL1821M	OEM
CL1821W	OEM
CL1830	OEM
CL1830M	OEM
CL1830W	OEM
CL1831	OEM
CL1831M	OEM
CL1831W	OEM
CL1835	OEM
CL1835M	OEM
CL1835W	OEM
CL1836	OEM
CL1836M	OEM
CL1836W	OEM
CL1840	OEM
CL1840M	OEM
CL1840W	OEM
CL1841	OEM
CL1841M	OEM

DEVICE TYPE	REPL CODE
CL1841W	OEM
CL1850	OEM
CL1850M	OEM
CL1850W	OEM
CL1851	OEM
CL1851M	OEM
CL1851W	OEM
CL1860	OEM
CL1860M	OEM
CL1860W	OEM
CL1861	OEM
CL1861M	OEM
CL1861W	OEM
CL1870	OEM
CL1870M	OEM
CL1870W	OEM
CL1871	OEM
CL1871M	OEM
CL1871W	OEM
CL2210	OEM
CL2220	OEM
CL3201	OEM
CL3310	OEM
CL3320	OEM
CL4710	OEM
CL4720	OEM
CL6810	OEM
CL7500	OEM
CL7520	OEM
CL8630	OEM
CL8630S	OEM
CL8633	OEM
CL8633S	OEM
CL8640R	OEM
CL8640T	OEM
CL8690	OEM
CLA7	OEM
CLA7AA	OEM
CLA7D	OEM
CLA7DA	OEM
CLA60	OEM
CLA65AA	OEM
CLA90	OEM
CLA90AA	OEM
CLA3130-150-806	OEM
CLA3130-173-001	OEM
CLA3130-176-001	OEM
CLA3130-184-802	OEM
CLA3131-01	OEM
CLA3131-02	OEM
CLA3131-03	OEM
CLA3132-01	OEM
CLA3132-02	OEM
CLA3132-03	OEM
CLA3133-01	OEM
CLA3133-02	OEM
CLA3133-03	OEM
CLA3134-01	OEM
CLA3134-02	OEM
CLA3135-01	OEM
CLA3135-02	OEM
CLA3150-150-806	OEM
CLA3150-173-001	OEM
CLA3150-176-001	OEM
CLA3150-184-802	OEM
CLC064	OEM
CLD31	OEM
CLD41	OEM
CLD42	OEM
CLD56	OEM
CLD71	OEM
CLEAK-02101	OEM
CLEAK-02200	0319
CLEAK-02201	1404
CLEAK-02300	0319
CLEAK-02301	1404
CLEAK-02601	3082
CLEAK-02701	1203
CLEAK-02701(2SD560)	OEM
CLEAK-05401	1203
CLEAK-05501	OEM
CLEAK-05703	OEM
CLEAK-05704	OEM
CLEAK-05705	OEM
CLEAK-05707	OEM
CLEAK-05708	OEM
CLEAK-05709	OEM
CLEAK-05710	2672
CLEAK-05903	2672
CLEAK-06002	2672
CLEAK-06102	0806
CLEAK-06201	0806
CLEAK-09801	OEM
CLEAK-11904	1628
CLEAK-12004	0806
CLEAK-14201	1628
CLEAK-14401	1628
CLED-1	OEM
CLED-1F	OEM
CLED-5	OEM
CLED400	OEM
CLI5	0311
CLI-6	0311
CLI-7	0311
CLI-8	0311
CLI-11	1047
CLI-12	1047
CLI-13	OEM
CLI-14	1047

DEVICE TYPE	REPL CODE
CLI25	5327
CLI-506	0311
CLI-800	1407
CLI-810	1407
CLI-811	1407
CLI-820	1407
CLI-821	1407
CLI-830	1407
CLI-831	1407
CLI-835	1407
CLI-836	1407
CLI-840	2612
CLI-841	2612
CLI-851	2612
CLI-860	2612
CLI-861	2612
CLI-870	2612
CLI-871	2612
CLK-24	OEM
CLK-24C	OEM
CLM05	0015
CLM1	0015
CLM1.5	OEM
CLM2	OEM
CLM3	OEM
CLM4	OEM
CLM5	OEM
CLM5H10A	OEM
CLM6	OEM
CLM7	OEM
CLM7H16A	OEM
CLM8	OEM
CLM50	OEM
CLM51	OEM
CLM60	OEM
CLM61	OEM
CLM3000	OEM
CLM3006A	OEM
CLM3012A	OEM
CLM3120A	OEM
CLM3500	OEM
CLM4006A	OEM
CLM4012A	OEM
CLM4120A	OEM
CLM6000	OEM
CLM6200	OEM
CLM6500	OEM
CLM8000	OEM
CLM8200-2	OEM
CLM8500	OEM
CLM8500/2	OEM
CLM8500HV	OEM
CLM8600	OEM
CLM9000	OEM
CLR5	OEM
CLR10	OEM
CLR15	OEM
CLR20	OEM
CLR25	OEM
CLR30	OEM
CLR35	OEM
CLR40	OEM
CLR45	OEM
CLR50	OEM
CLR2049	OEM
CLR2050	2297
CLR2060	3508
CLR2090	OEM
CLR2170	OEM
CLR2180	3508
CLR2191	OEM
CLR3180	OEM
CLR4180	OEM
CLR5101	OEM
CLR5101-2	OEM
CLT2010	OEM
CLT2020	OEM
CLT2030	OEM
CLT2064	OEM
CLT2065	OEM
CLT2130	2297
CLT2140	2297
CLT2150	3825
CLT2160	2297
CLT2164	OEM
CLT2165	OEM
CLT3020	OEM
CLT3030	OEM
CLT3160	OEM
CLT3170	OEM
CLT4020	OEM
CLT4030	OEM
CLT4140	OEM
CLT4150	OEM
CLT4160	OEM
CLT4170	OEM
CLT5160	OEM
CLT5170	OEM
CLVA43A	OEM
CLVA47A	OEM
CLVA51A	OEM
CLVA56A	OEM
CLVA62A	0466
CLVA68A	OEM
CLVA75A	OEM
CLVA82A	OEM
CLVA91A	0057
CLVA100A	OEM
CLZ80-4/2	OEM

DEVICE TYPE	REPL CODE
CLZ80-4/8	OEM
CLZ80-16/2	OEM
CLZ80-16/8	OEM
CM	0196
CM05	OEM
CM0770	0086
CM0SMM74C00N	2100
CM4-20	OEM
CM4-21	OEM
CM4-22	OEM
CM4-23	OEM
CM4-24	OEM
CM4-25	OEM
CM4-43	OEM
CM4-43A	OEM
CM4-43B	OEM
CM4-73A	OEM
CM4-80B	OEM
CM4-81B	OEM
CM4-82B	OEM
CM4-83	3153
CM4-83-1	3153
CM4-83-2	3153
CM4-83-3	3153
CM4-84B	1348
CM4-84B-0	1348
CM4-84B-1	1348
CM4-84B-2	OEM
CM4-85B	OEM
CM4-86B	OEM
CM4-244A	OEM
CM4-244B	OEM
CM4-264	OEM
CM4-282B	OEM
CM4-282B-2	OEM
CM4-283B	OEM
CM4-284B	1951
CM4-284B-2	1951
CM4-344A	0835
CM4-344B	OEM
CM4-382B	OEM
CM4-382B-2	OEM
CM4-383B	OEM
CM4-384B	1767
CM4-384B-2	1767
CM4-444A	3067
CM4-444B	OEM
CM4-482B	OEM
CM4-482B-2	OEM
CM4-483B	OEM
CM4-484B	3245
CM4-484B-2	3245
CM4-544A	3095
CM4-544B	OEM
CM4-564	OEM
CM4-582B	OEM
CM4-582B-2	OEM
CM4-583B	OEM
CM4-584B	3128
CM4-584B-2	3128
CM5-5	OEM
CM5-11	OEM
CM5-12	OEM
CM5-21	OEM
CM5-22	OEM
CM5-23	OEM
CM5-27	OEM
CM5-29	OEM
CM5-31	OEM
CM5-32	OEM
CM10-12A	2082
CM-12	0124
CM20-12	OEM
CM20-12A	2825
CM25-12	3545
CM25-28	OEM
CM25-28A	OEM
CM30-12	6447
CM30-12A	2841
CM40-12	2841
CM45-12	OEM
CM45-12A	2841
CM45-28	OEM
CM50	OEM
CM60/12	OEM
CM60/15	OEM
CM60-12	OEM
CM60-12A	3547
CM80-28	OEM
CM100/12	OEM
CM100/15	OEM
CM106	OEM
CM107	OEM
CM108	OEM
CM109	OEM
CM110	OEM
CM200/12	OEM
CM200/15	OEM
CM300/12	OEM
CM300/15	OEM
CM301AN	1290
CM500/5	OEM
CM600	OEM
CM601	OEM
CM602	1147
CM603	1147
CM640	OEM
CM641	OEM
CM642	1147

342

If replacement code is OEM, contact original manufacturer for replacement.

DEVICE TYPE	REPL CODE
CM643	6630
CM644	OEM
CM645	OEM
CM646	1147
CM647	5264
CM697	OEM
CM800	OEM
CM856	OEM
CM860	OEM
CM1000/5	OEM
CM1310C	OEM
CM1310P	OEM
CM1600-1C	OEM
CM1600-1P	OEM
CM1600-2C	OEM
CM1600-2P	OEM
CM1600-3C	OEM
CM1600-3P	OEM
CM1600C	OEM
CM1600P	OEM
CM2000/5	OEM
CM2550	0160
CM3200-2C	OEM
CM3200-2D	OEM
CM3200-2P	OEM
CM3200-3C	OEM
CM3200-3D	OEM
CM3200-3P	OEM
CM3200-C	OEM
CM3200-D	OEM
CM3200-P	OEM
CM3200C	OEM
CM3200P	OEM
CM3900	2232
CM4000	2013
CM4000AD	2013
CM4000AE	2013
CM4001	0473
CM4001AD	0473
CM4001AE	0473
CM4002	2044
CM4002AD	2044
CM4002AE	2044
CM4004AD	OEM
CM4004AE	OEM
CM4006AD	0641
CM4006AE	0641
CM4006AF	OEM
CM4007	2819
CM4007AD	2819
CM4007AE	2819
CM4008AD	0982
CM4008AE	0982
CM4009	1988
CM4009AD	1988
CM4009AE	0001
CM4010AD	3222
CM4010AE	0394
CM4011	0215
CM4011AD	0215
CM4011AE	0215
CM4012	0493
CM4012AD	0493
CM4012AE	0493
CM4013	0409
CM4013AD	0409
CM4013AE	0409
CM4014AD	0854
CM4014AE	0854
CM4014AF	OEM
CM4015	1008
CM4015AD	1008
CM4015AE	1008
CM4015AF	OEM
CM4016	1135
CM4016AD	1135
CM4016AE	1135
CM4017	0508
CM4017AD	0508
CM4017AE	0508
CM4018AD	1381
CM4018AE	1381
CM4019	1517
CM4019AD	1517
CM4019AE	1517
CM4020	1651
CM4020AD	1651
CM4020AE	1651
CM4021	1738
CM4021AD	1738
CM4021AE	1738
CM4021AF	OEM
CM4022AD	1247
CM4022AE	1247
CM4023	0515
CM4023AD	0515
CM4023AE	0515
CM4024	1946
CM4024AD	1946
CM4024AE	1946
CM4025	2061
CM4025AD	2061
CM4025AE	2061
CM4026AD	2139
CM4026AE	2139
CM4027	1938
CM4027AD	1938
CM4027AE	1938
CM4028AD	2213

DEVICE TYPE	REPL CODE
CM4028AE	2213
CM4029AD	2218
CM4029AE	2218
CM4030	0495
CM4030AD	0495
CM4030AE	0495
CM4032AD	2509
CM4032AE	2509
CM4033AD	2611
CM4033AE	2611
CM4035AD	2750
CM4035AE	2750
CM4035AF	OEM
CM4037AD	OEM
CM4037AE	OEM
CM4038AD	2953
CM4038AE	2953
CM4040	0056
CM4040AD	0056
CM4040AE	0056
CM4041AD	3145
CM4041AE	3145
CM4042	0121
CM4042AD	0121
CM4042AE	0121
CM4043AD	1544
CM4043AE	1544
CM4044AD	2292
CM4044AE	2292
CM4047AD	2315
CM4047AE	2315
CM4047AF	2315
CM4048AD	3422
CM4048AE	3423
CM4049	0001
CM4049AD	0001
CM4049AE	0001
CM4050	0394
CM4050AD	0394
CM4050AE	0394
CM4051	0362
CM4052	0024
CM4066AD	0101
CM4066AE	0101
CM4066AF	OEM
CM4066AH	OEM
CM4069B	0119
CM4081	0621
CM4102AD	OEM
CM4102AE	OEM
CM4102D	OEM
CM4102E	OEM
CM4116AD	0518
CM4116AE	0518
CM4500	OEM
CM4501	OEM
CM4503	OEM
CM4518	1037
CM4520	2650
CM5770-512	OEM
CM6400-3C	OEM
CM6400-3P	OEM
CM6400A3C	OEM
CM6400A3P	OEM
CM6400A-C	OEM
CM6400A-P	OEM
CM6400C	OEM
CM6400P	OEM
CM7163	0079
CM8470	0015
CM8640E	0211
CMB-7601	OEM
CMB-7601A	OEM
CMB-7602	OEM
CMB-7602A	OEM
CMC68/04	OEM
CMC68/15	OEM
CMC68/15B	OEM
CMC68/15C	OEM
CMC68/15G	3956
CMC1530A	OEM
CMC1535A	OEM
CMC1540A	OEM
CMC2510A	OEM
CMC2512A	OEM
CMC2515A	OEM
CMC2530A	OEM
CMC2535A	OEM
CMC2540A	2602
CMC4010A	OEM
CMC4012A	OEM
CMC4015A	OEM
CMC4030A	OEM
CMC4035A	OEM
CMC4040A	2602
CMC7010A	3956
CMC7012A	3956
CMC7015A	3956
CME30-12	OEM
CME50-12	OEM
CME70-12	OEM
CMEM-8K	OEM
CMEM-16K	OEM
CMEM-32K	OEM
CMK-29EHB	OEM
CM0770	0079
CMP01BJ	OEM
CMP01BY	OEM
CMP01BZ	OEM

DEVICE TYPE	REPL CODE
CMP01CJ	OEM
CMP01CP	OEM
CMP01CY	OEM
CMP01CZ	OEM
CMP01EJ	OEM
CMP01EP	OEM
CMP01EY	OEM
CMP01EZ	OEM
CMP01GR	OEM
CMP01J	OEM
CMP01N	OEM
CMP01Y	OEM
CMP01Z	OEM
CMP02BJ	OEM
CMP02BY	OEM
CMP02BZ	OEM
CMP02CJ	OEM
CMP02CP	OEM
CMP02CY	OEM
CMP02CZ	OEM
CMP02EJ	OEM
CMP02EP	OEM
CMP02EY	OEM
CMP02EZ	OEM
CMP02GR	OEM
CMP02J	OEM
CMP02N	OEM
CMP02Y	OEM
CMP02Z	OEM
CMP04BY	OEM
CMP04FP	OEM
CMP04FY	OEM
CMP05AJ(M)	OEM
CMP05AZ(M)	OEM
CMP05BJ(M)	OEM
CMP05BZ(M)	OEM
CMP05EJ(A)	OEM
CMP05EP	OEM
CMP05EZ(M)	OEM
CMP05FJ(A)	OEM
CMP05FP	OEM
CMP05FZ(M)	OEM
CMP81CY	OEM
CMP81EY	OEM
CMP82CJ	OEM
CMP82CY	OEM
CMP82EJ	OEM
CMP82EY	OEM
CMP1115	OEM
CMX740	OEM
CN2484	0086
CN5310	2599
CN5310(K)	2599
CN5310(L)	2599
CN5310(M)	2599
CN5310K	2599
CN5310L	2599
CN5310M	2599
CN5311	2599
CN5311CL	2599
CN5311K	2599
CN5311KL	2599
CN5311LM	2599
CN5411	5004
CN5510	3997
CN5520	3564
CN32536N	OEM
CND101A	OEM
CND1001A	OEM
CND1002A	OEM
CND2001A	OEM
CND2002A	OEM
CND3001A	OEM
CND3002A	OEM
CND4001A	OEM
CND6001A	OEM
CND6002A	OEM
CND6003A	OEM
CND6004A	OEM
CND6005A	OEM
CND6006A	OEM
CND6007A	OEM
CND6008A	OEM
CND6009A	OEM
CND6010A	OEM
CND6011A	OEM
CND6012A	OEM
CNM5A	OEM
CNM5B	OEM
CNM5C	OEM
CNM5D	OEM
CNM5E	OEM
CNM5EN	OEM
CNM10A	OEM
CNM10B	OEM
CNM10C	OEM
CNM10D	OEM
CNM10E	OEM
CNM10EN	OEM
CNM20A	OEM
CNM20B	OEM
CNM20C	OEM
CNM20D	OEM
CNM20E	OEM
CNM20EN	OEM
CNM50A	OEM
CNM50B	OEM
CNM50C	OEM
CNM50D	OEM

DEVICE TYPE	REPL CODE
CNM50E	OEM
CNM50EN	OEM
CNM100A	OEM
CNM100B	OEM
CNM100C	OEM
CNM100D	OEM
CNM100E	OEM
CNM100EN	OEM
CNM1000A	OEM
CNR21	OEM
CNX21	OEM
CNX21T	OEM
CNX35	0311
CNX35U	0311
CNX36	0311
CNX38	OEM
CNX48	OEM
CNY6	OEM
CNY17-1	OEM
CNY17-2	OEM
CNY17-3	OEM
CNY17-4	OEM
CNY17-I	OEM
CNY17-II	OEM
CNY17-III	OEM
CNY17-IV	OEM
CNY17I	OEM
CNY17II	OEM
CNY17III	OEM
CNY17IV	OEM
CNY18-1	OEM
CNY18-2	OEM
CNY18-3	OEM
CNY18-4	OEM
CNY18III	OEM
CNY18IV	OEM
CNY21	OEM
CNY28	2612
CNY29	2612
CNY30	OEM
CNY31	2616
CNY32	2617
CNY33	OEM
CNY34	OEM
CNY35	OEM
CNY36	2616
CNY37	1407
CNY42	OEM
CNY43	OEM
CNY47	OEM
CNY47A	OEM
CNY48	1047
CNY50	OEM
CNY50-1	OEM
CNY51	OEM
CNY52	OEM
CNY53	OEM
CNY57	OEM
CNY57A	OEM
CNY62	OEM
CNY63	OEM
CNY64	OEM
CNY65	OEM
CNY65B	OEM
CNY70	OEM
C009	OEM
C02L55A57V	OEM
C06C	0015
C010	OEM
C020A	OEM
C020B	OEM
C040A	OEM
C040B	OEM
C049	0015
C080	OEM
C0231	OEM
C0231-1	OEM
C0231-3	OEM
C0231-4	OEM
C0231H	OEM
C0231H1	OEM
C0231H3	OEM
C0231H4	OEM
C0231HV	OEM
C0231HV1	OEM
C0231HV3	OEM
C0231HV4	OEM
C0231HVY	OEM
C0231HY	OEM
C0231T	OEM
C0231T1	OEM
C0231T3	OEM
C0231T4	OEM
C0231TV	OEM
C0231TV1	OEM
C0231TV3	OEM
C0231TV4	OEM
C0231TVY	OEM
C0231TY	OEM
C0231V	OEM
C0231V1	OEM
C0231V3	OEM
C0231V4	OEM
C0231VH	OEM
C0231VY	OEM
C0231Y	OEM
C0232	OEM
C0232-3	OEM
C0232-5	OEM

DEVICE TYPE	REPL CODE
C0232T	OEM
C0232T3	OEM
C0232T5	OEM
C0232TV	OEM
C0232TV3	OEM
C0232TV5	OEM
C0232V	OEM
C0232V3	OEM
C0232V5	OEM
C0233	OEM
C0233-1	OEM
C0233-2	OEM
C0233-3	OEM
C0233-4	OEM
C0233-5	OEM
C0233-6	OEM
C0233FU1	OEM
C0233FU2	OEM
C0233FU3	OEM
C0233FU4	OEM
C0233FU5	OEM
C0233FU6	OEM
C0233FUT	OEM
C0233FUT1	OEM
C0233FUT2	OEM
C0233FUT3	OEM
C0233FUT4	OEM
C0233FUT5	OEM
C0233FUT6	OEM
C0233FUTV	OEM
C0233FUTV1	OEM
C0233FUTV2	OEM
C0233FUTV3	OEM
C0233FUTV4	OEM
C0233FUTV5	OEM
C0233FUTV6	OEM
C0233FUV	OEM
C0233FUV1	OEM
C0233FUV2	OEM
C0233FUV3	OEM
C0233FUV4	OEM
C0233FUV5	OEM
C0233FUV6	OEM
C0233FW	OEM
C0233FW1	OEM
C0233FW2	OEM
C0233FW3	OEM
C0233FW4	OEM
C0233FW5	OEM
C0233FW6	OEM
C0233FWT	OEM
C0233FWT1	OEM
C0233FWT2	OEM
C0233FWT3	OEM
C0233FWT4	OEM
C0233FWT5	OEM
C0233FWT6	OEM
C0233FWTV	OEM
C0233FWTV1	OEM
C0233FWTV2	OEM
C0233FWTV3	OEM
C0233FWTV4	OEM
C0233FWTV5	OEM
C0233FWTV6	OEM
C0233FWV	OEM
C0233FWV1	OEM
C0233FWV2	OEM
C0233FWV3	OEM
C0233FWV4	OEM
C0233FWV5	OEM
C0233FWV6	OEM
C0233FX	OEM
C0233FX1	OEM
C0233FX2	OEM
C0233FXTV	OEM
C0233FXTV1	OEM
C0233FXTV2	OEM
C0233FXTV3	OEM
C0233FXTV4	OEM
C0233FXTV5	OEM
C0233FXTV6	OEM
C0233FXV	OEM
C0233FXV1	OEM
C0233FXV2	OEM
C0233FXV3	OEM
C0233FXV4	OEM
C0233FXV5	OEM
C0233FXV6	OEM
C0233H	OEM
C0233H1	OEM
C0233H2	OEM
C0233H3	OEM
C0233H4	OEM
C0233H5	OEM
C0233H6	OEM
C0233HR	OEM
C0233HR1	OEM
C0233HR2	OEM
C0233HR3	OEM
C0233HR4	OEM
C0233HR5	OEM
C0233HR6	OEM
C0233HRV	OEM
C0233HRV1	OEM
C0233HRV2	OEM
C0233HRV3	OEM
C0233HRV4	OEM
C0233HRV5	OEM
C0233HRV6	OEM

DEVICE TYPE	REPL CODE
C0233HTV	OEM
C0233HTV1	OEM
C0233HTV2	OEM
C0233HTV3	OEM
C0233HTV4	OEM
C0233HTV5	OEM
C0233HTV6	OEM
C0233ME	OEM
C0233ME1	OEM
C0233ME2	OEM
C0233ME3	OEM
C0233MEHA	OEM
C0233MEHA1	OEM
C0233MEHAV	OEM
C0233MEHAV1	OEM
C0233MEHB1	OEM
C0233MEHBV	OEM
C0233MEHBV1	OEM
C0233MEHV	OEM
C0233MET	OEM
C0233MET1	OEM
C0233MET2	OEM
C0233MET3	OEM
C0233METV	OEM
C0233METV1	OEM
C0233METV2	OEM
C0233METV3	OEM
C0233MEV	OEM
C0233MEV1	OEM
C0233MEV2	OEM
C0233MEV3	OEM
C0233T	OEM
C0233T1	OEM
C0233T2	OEM
C0233T3	OEM
C0233T4	OEM
C0233T5	OEM
C0233T6	OEM
C0233TV	OEM
C0233TV1	OEM
C0233TV2	OEM
C0233TV3	OEM
C0233TV4	OEM
C0233TV5	OEM
C0233TV6	OEM
C0233U	OEM
C0233U1	OEM
C0233U2	OEM
C0233U3	OEM
C0233U4	OEM
C0233U5	OEM
C0233U6	OEM
C0233UT	OEM
C0233UT1	OEM
C0233UT2	OEM
C0233UT3	OEM
C0233UT4	OEM
C0233UT5	OEM
C0233UT6	OEM
C0233UTV	OEM
C0233UTV1	OEM
C0233UTV2	OEM
C0233UTV3	OEM
C0233UTV4	OEM
C0233UTV5	OEM
C0233UTV6	OEM
C0233V1	OEM
C0233V2	OEM
C0233V3	OEM
C0233V4	OEM
C0233V5	OEM
C0233V6	OEM
C0233VFW	OEM
C0233VFWR	OEM
C0233VH	OEM
C0233VHR	OEM
C0233VR	OEM
C0233VW	OEM
C0233VWR	OEM
C0233W	OEM
C0233W1	OEM
C0233W2	OEM
C0233W3	OEM
C0233W4	OEM
C0233W5	OEM
C0233W6	OEM
C0233WT	OEM
C0233WT1	OEM
C0233WT2	OEM
C0233WT3	OEM
C0233WT4	OEM
C0233WT5	OEM
C0233WT6	OEM
C0233WTV	OEM
C0233WTV1	OEM
C0233WTV2	OEM
C0233WTV3	OEM
C0233WTV4	OEM
C0233WTV5	OEM
C0233WTV6	OEM
C0233X	OEM
C0233X1	OEM
C0233X2	OEM
C0233X3	OEM
C0233X4	OEM
C0233X5	OEM
C0233X6	OEM
C0233XT	OEM
C0233XT1	OEM

DEVICE TYPE	REPL CODE
C0233XT2	OEM
C0233XT3	OEM
C0233XT4	OEM
C0233XT5	OEM
C0233XT6	OEM
C0233XTV	OEM
C0233XTV1	OEM
C0233XTV2	OEM
C0233XTV3	OEM
C0233XTV4	OEM
C0233XTV5	OEM
C0233XTV6	OEM
C0234-3	OEM
C0234A	OEM
C0234A3	OEM
C0234AV	OEM
C0234AV3	OEM
C0234B	OEM
C0234B3	OEM
C0234BV	OEM
C0234BV3	OEM
C0235	OEM
C0235-3	OEM
C0235T	OEM
C0235T3	OEM
C0235T5	OEM
C0235TV	OEM
C0235TV3	OEM
C0235TV5	OEM
C0235V	OEM
C0235V3	OEM
C0235V5	OEM
C0236	OEM
C0236-1	OEM
C0236-3	OEM
C0236-4	OEM
C0236T	OEM
C0236T1	OEM
C0236T3	OEM
C0236T4	OEM
C0236TV	OEM
C0236TV1	OEM
C0236TV3	OEM
C0236TV4	OEM
C0236TVY	OEM
C0236TY	OEM
C0236V	OEM
C0236V1	OEM
C0236V3	OEM
C0236V4	OEM
C0236VY	OEM
C0236Y	OEM
C0238A	OEM
C0238A2	OEM
C0238A3	OEM
C0238AV	OEM
C0238AV2	OEM
C0238AV3	OEM
C0238B	OEM
C0238B2	OEM
C0238B3	OEM
C0238BV	OEM
C0238BV2	OEM
C0238BV3	OEM
C0238T2	OEM
C0238T3	OEM
C0238TV	OEM
C0238TV2	OEM
C0238TV3	OEM
C0239A2	OEM
C0239A3	OEM
C0239AV	OEM
C0239AV2	OEM
C0239AV3	OEM
C0239B	OEM
C0239B2	OEM
C0239B3	OEM
C0239BV	OEM
C0239BV2	OEM
C0239BV3	OEM
C0251A27	OEM
C0251A27U	OEM
C0251A27V	OEM
C0251A27VU	OEM
C0251A27VW	OEM
C0251A27VX	OEM
C0251A27W	OEM
C0251A27X	OEM
C0251A57	OEM
C0251A57U	OEM
C0251A57V	OEM
C0251A57VU	OEM
C0251A57VW	OEM
C0251A57VX	OEM
C0251A57W	OEM
C0251A57X	OEM
C0251B16	OEM
C0251B16U	OEM
C0251B16V	OEM
C0251B16VU	OEM
C0251B16VW	OEM
C0251B16VX	OEM
C0251B16W	OEM
C0251B16X	OEM
C0251C36	OEM
C0251C36U	OEM
C0251C36V	OEM
C0251C36VU	OEM
C0251C36VW	OEM

If replacement code is OEM, contact original manufacturer for replacement. 343

DEVICE TYPE	REPL CODE
CO251C36VX	OEM
CO251C36W	OEM
CO251C36X	OEM
CO251D56	OEM
CO251D56U	OEM
CO251D56V	OEM
CO251D56VU	OEM
CO251D56VW	OEM
CO251D56VX	OEM
CO251D56W	OEM
CO251D56X	OEM
CO251E15	OEM
CO251E15U	OEM
CO251E15V	OEM
CO251E15VU	OEM
CO251E15VW	OEM
CO251E15VX	OEM
CO251E15W	OEM
CO251E15X	OEM
CO251F25	OEM
CO251F25U	OEM
CO251F25V	OEM
CO251F25VU	OEM
CO251F25VW	OEM
CO251F25VX	OEM
CO251F25W	OEM
CO251F25X	OEM
CO252A17	OEM
CO252A17IVW	OEM
CO252A17IVX	OEM
CO252A17IW	OEM
CO252A17IX	OEM
CO252A17J	OEM
CO252A17JU	OEM
CO252A17JV	OEM
CO252A17JVW	OEM
CO252A17JVX	OEM
CO252A17JW	OEM
CO252A17JX	OEM
CO252A17JXU	OEM
CO252A17K	OEM
CO252A17KU	OEM
CO252A17KV	OEM
CO252A17KVU	OEM
CO252A17U	OEM
CO252A17V	OEM
CO252A17VU	OEM
CO252A17VW	OEM
CO252A17VX	OEM
CO252A17W	OEM
CO252A17X	OEM
CO252A58	OEM
CO252A58J	OEM
CO252A58JU	OEM
CO252A58JV	OEM
CO252A58JVU	OEM
CO252A58JVW	OEM
CO252A58JVX	OEM
CO252A58JW	OEM
CO252A58JX	OEM
CO252A58K	OEM
CO252A58KU	OEM
CO252A58KV	OEM
CO252A58KVU	OEM
CO252A58KVW	OEM
CO252A58KVX	OEM
CO252A58KW	OEM
CO252A58KX	OEM
CO252A58U	OEM
CO252A58V	OEM
CO252A58VU	OEM
CO252A58VW	OEM
CO252A58VX	OEM
CO252A58W	OEM
CO252A58X	OEM
CO252B17	OEM
CO252B17J	OEM
CO252B17JU	OEM
CO252B17JV	OEM
CO252B17JVU	OEM
CO252B17JVW	OEM
CO252B17JVX	OEM
CO252B17JW	OEM
CO252B17JX	OEM
CO252B17K	OEM
CO252B17KU	OEM
CO252B17KV	OEM
CO252B17KVU	OEM
CO252B17KVW	OEM
CO252B17KVX	OEM
CO252B17KW	OEM
CO252B17KX	OEM
CO252B17U	OEM
CO252B17V	OEM
CO252B17VU	OEM
CO252B17VW	OEM
CO252B17VX	OEM
CO252B17W	OEM
CO252B17X	OEM
CO252B27	OEM
CO252B27J	OEM
CO252B27JU	OEM
CO252B27JV	OEM
CO252B27JVU	OEM
CO252B27JVW	OEM
CO252B27JVX	OEM
CO252B27JW	OEM
CO252B27JX	OEM
CO252B27K	OEM
CO252B27KU	OEM
CO252B27KV	OEM
CO252B27KVU	OEM
CO252B27KVW	OEM
CO252B27KVX	OEM
CO252B27KW	OEM
CO252B27KX	OEM
CO252B27U	OEM
CO252B27V	OEM
CO252B27VU	OEM
CO252B27VW	OEM
CO252B27VX	OEM
CO252B27W	OEM
CO252B27X	OEM
CO252B57	OEM
CO252B57J	OEM
CO252B57JU	OEM
CO252B57JV	OEM
CO252B57JVU	OEM
CO252B57JVW	OEM
CO252B57JVX	OEM
CO252B57JW	OEM
CO252B57JX	OEM
CO252B57K	OEM
CO252B57KU	OEM
CO252B57KV	OEM
CO252B57KVU	OEM
CO252B57KVW	OEM
CO252B57KVX	OEM
CO252B57KW	OEM
CO252B57KX	OEM
CO252B57U	OEM
CO252B57V	OEM
CO252B57VU	OEM
CO252B57VW	OEM
CO252B57VX	OEM
CO252B57W	OEM
CO252B57X	OEM
CO252C16	OEM
CO252C16J	OEM
CO252C16JU	OEM
CO252C16JV	OEM
CO252C16JVU	OEM
CO252C16JVW	OEM
CO252C16JVX	OEM
CO252C16JW	OEM
CO252C16JX	OEM
CO252C16K	OEM
CO252C16KU	OEM
CO252C16KV	OEM
CO252C16KVU	OEM
CO252C16KVW	OEM
CO252C16KVX	OEM
CO252C16KW	OEM
CO252C16KX	OEM
CO252C16U	OEM
CO252C16V	OEM
CO252C16VU	OEM
CO252C16VW	OEM
CO252C16VX	OEM
CO252C16W	OEM
CO252C16X	OEM
CO252C37	OEM
CO252C37J	OEM
CO252C37JU	OEM
CO252C37JV	OEM
CO252C37JVU	OEM
CO252C37JVW	OEM
CO252C37JVX	OEM
CO252C37JW	OEM
CO252C37JX	OEM
CO252C37K	OEM
CO252C37KU	OEM
CO252C37KV	OEM
CO252C37KVU	OEM
CO252C37KVW	OEM
CO252C37KVX	OEM
CO252C37KW	OEM
CO252C37KX	OEM
CO252C37U	OEM
CO252C37V	OEM
CO252C37VU	OEM
CO252C37VW	OEM
CO252C37VX	OEM
CO252C37W	OEM
CO252C37X	OEM
CO252C57	OEM
CO252C57J	OEM
CO252C57JU	OEM
CO252C57JV	OEM
CO252C57JVU	OEM
CO252C57JVW	OEM
CO252C57JVX	OEM
CO252C57JW	OEM
CO252C57JX	OEM
CO252C57K	OEM
CO252C57KU	OEM
CO252C57KV	OEM
CO252C57KVU	OEM
CO252C57KVW	OEM
CO252C57KVX	OEM
CO252C57KW	OEM
CO252C57KX	OEM
CO252C57U	OEM
CO252C57V	OEM
CO252C57VU	OEM
CO252C57VW	OEM
CO252C57VX	OEM
CO252C57W	OEM
CO252C57X	OEM
CO252D16	OEM
CO252D16J	OEM
CO252D16JU	OEM
CO252D16JV	OEM
CO252D16JVU	OEM
CO252D16JVW	OEM
CO252D16JX	OEM
CO252D16K	OEM
CO252D16KU	OEM
CO252D16KV	OEM
CO252D16KVU	OEM
CO252D16KVW	OEM
CO252D16KVX	OEM
CO252D16KW	OEM
CO252D16KX	OEM
CO252D16U	OEM
CO252D16V	OEM
CO252D16VU	OEM
CO252D16VW	OEM
CO252D16VX	OEM
CO252D16W	OEM
CO252D16X	OEM
CO252D57	OEM
CO252D57J	OEM
CO252D57JV	OEM
CO252D57JVU	OEM
CO252D57JVW	OEM
CO252D57JVX	OEM
CO252D57JW	OEM
CO252D57JX	OEM
CO252D57K	OEM
CO252D57KU	OEM
CO252D57KV	OEM
CO252D57KVU	OEM
CO252D57KVW	OEM
CO252D57KVX	OEM
CO252D57KW	OEM
CO252D57KX	OEM
CO252D57U	OEM
CO252D57V	OEM
CO252D57VU	OEM
CO252D57VW	OEM
CO252D57VX	OEM
CO252D57W	OEM
CO252D57X	OEM
CO252E16	OEM
CO252E16J	OEM
CO252E16JU	OEM
CO252E16JV	OEM
CO252E16JVU	OEM
CO252E16JVX	OEM
CO252E16JW	OEM
CO252E16JX	OEM
CO252E16K	OEM
CO252E16KU	OEM
CO252E16KV	OEM
CO252E16KVU	OEM
CO252E16KVW	OEM
CO252E16KVX	OEM
CO252E16KW	OEM
CO252E16KX	OEM
CO252E16U	OEM
CO252E16UVW	OEM
CO252E16V	OEM
CO252E16VU	OEM
CO252E16VW	OEM
CO252E16VX	OEM
CO252E16W	OEM
CO252E16X	OEM
CO252E26	OEM
CO252E26J	OEM
CO252E26JU	OEM
CO252E26JV	OEM
CO252E26JVU	OEM
CO252E26JVW	OEM
CO252E26JVX	OEM
CO252E26JW	OEM
CO252E26JX	OEM
CO252E26K	OEM
CO252E26KU	OEM
CO252E26KV	OEM
CO252E26KVU	OEM
CO252E26KVW	OEM
CO252E26KVX	OEM
CO252E26KW	OEM
CO252E26KX	OEM
CO252E26U	OEM
CO252E26V	OEM
CO252E26VU	OEM
CO252E26VW	OEM
CO252E26VX	OEM
CO252E26W	OEM
CO252E26X	OEM
CO252E56	OEM
CO252E56J	OEM
CO252E56JU	OEM
CO252E56JV	OEM
CO252E56JVU	OEM
CO252E56JVW	OEM
CO252E56JVX	OEM
CO252E56JW	OEM
CO252E56JX	OEM
CO252E56K	OEM
CO252E56KU	OEM
CO252E56KV	OEM
CO252E56KVU	OEM
CO252E56KVW	OEM
CO252E56KVX	OEM
CO252E56KW	OEM
CO252E56KX	OEM
CO252E56V	OEM
CO252E56VU	OEM
CO252E56VW	OEM
CO252E56VX	OEM
CO252E56W	OEM
CO252E56X	OEM
CO252F16	OEM
CO252F16J	OEM
CO252F16JU	OEM
CO252F16JVU	OEM
CO252F16JVW	OEM
CO252F16JVX	OEM
CO252F16JW	OEM
CO252F16JX	OEM
CO252F16K	OEM
CO252F16KU	OEM
CO252F16KV	OEM
CO252F16KVU	OEM
CO252F16KVW	OEM
CO252F16KVX	OEM
CO252F16KW	OEM
CO252F16KX	OEM
CO252F16U	OEM
CO252F16V	OEM
CO252F16VU	OEM
CO252F16VW	OEM
CO252F16VX	OEM
CO252F16W	OEM
CO252F16X	OEM
CO252F26	OEM
CO252F26J	OEM
CO252F26JU	OEM
CO252F26JV	OEM
CO252F26JVU	OEM
CO252F26JVW	OEM
CO252F26JVX	OEM
CO252F26JW	OEM
CO252F26JX	OEM
CO252F26K	OEM
CO252F26KU	OEM
CO252F26KV	OEM
CO252F26KVU	OEM
CO252F26KVW	OEM
CO252F26KVX	OEM
CO252F26KW	OEM
CO252F26KX	OEM
CO252F26U	OEM
CO252F26V	OEM
CO252F26VU	OEM
CO252F26VW	OEM
CO252F26VX	OEM
CO252F26W	OEM
CO252F26X	OEM
CO252F56	OEM
CO252F56J	OEM
CO252F56JU	OEM
CO252F56JV	OEM
CO252F56JVU	OEM
CO252F56JVW	OEM
CO252F56JVX	OEM
CO252F56JW	OEM
CO252F56JX	OEM
CO252F56K	OEM
CO252F56KU	OEM
CO252F56KV	OEM
CO252F56KVU	OEM
CO252F56KVW	OEM
CO252F56KVX	OEM
CO252F56KW	OEM
CO252F56KX	OEM
CO252F56U	OEM
CO252F56V	OEM
CO252F56VU	OEM
CO252F56VW	OEM
CO252F56VX	OEM
CO252F56W	OEM
CO252F56X	OEM
CO252V16JVX	OEM
CO252V16UW	OEM
CO254A17	OEM
CO254A17E	OEM
CO254A17EU	OEM
CO254A17EV	OEM
CO254A17EVU	OEM
CO254A17EVW	OEM
CO254A17EVX	OEM
CO254A17EW	OEM
CO254A17EX	OEM
CO254A17J	OEM
CO254A17JU	OEM
CO254A17JV	OEM
CO254A17JVU	OEM
CO254A17JVX	OEM
CO254A17JW	OEM
CO254A17JX	OEM
CO254A17K	OEM
CO254A17KU	OEM
CO254A17KV	OEM
CO254A17KVU	OEM
CO254A17KVW	OEM
CO254A17KVX	OEM
CO254A17KW	OEM
CO254A17KX	OEM
CO254A17M	OEM
CO254A17MU	OEM
CO254A17MV	OEM
CO254A17MVU	OEM
CO254A17MVW	OEM
CO254A17MVX	OEM
CO254A17MW	OEM
CO254A17MX	OEM
CO254A17U	OEM
CO254A17V	OEM
CO254A17VU	OEM
CO254A17VW	OEM
CO254A17VX	OEM
CO254A17W	OEM
CO254A17X	OEM
CO254A57	OEM
CO254A57E	OEM
CO254A57EU	OEM
CO254A57EV	OEM
CO254A57EVU	OEM
CO254A57EVW	OEM
CO254A57EVX	OEM
CO254A57EW	OEM
CO254A57EX	OEM
CO254A57J	OEM
CO254A57JU	OEM
CO254A57JV	OEM
CO254A57JVU	OEM
CO254A57JVW	OEM
CO254A57JVX	OEM
CO254A57JW	OEM
CO254A57JX	OEM
CO254A57K	OEM
CO254A57KU	OEM
CO254A57KV	OEM
CO254A57KVU	OEM
CO254A57KVW	OEM
CO254A57KVX	OEM
CO254A57KW	OEM
CO254A57KX	OEM
CO254A57M	OEM
CO254A57MU	OEM
CO254A57MV	OEM
CO254A57MVU	OEM
CO254A57MVW	OEM
CO254A57MVX	OEM
CO254A57MW	OEM
CO254A57MX	OEM
CO254A57U	OEM
CO254A57V	OEM
CO254A57VU	OEM
CO254A57VW	OEM
CO254A57VX	OEM
CO254A57W	OEM
CO254A57X	OEM
CO254B16	OEM
CO254B16E	OEM
CO254B16EU	OEM
CO254B16EV	OEM
CO254B16EVU	OEM
CO254B16EVW	OEM
CO254B16EVX	OEM
CO254B16EW	OEM
CO254B16EX	OEM
CO254B16J	OEM
CO254B16JU	OEM
CO254B16JV	OEM
CO254B16JVU	OEM
CO254B16JVW	OEM
CO254B16JVX	OEM
CO254B16JW	OEM
CO254B16JX	OEM
CO254B16K	OEM
CO254B16KU	OEM
CO254B16KV	OEM
CO254B16KVU	OEM
CO254B16KVW	OEM
CO254B16KVX	OEM
CO254B16KW	OEM
CO254B16KX	OEM
CO254B16M	OEM
CO254B16MU	OEM
CO254B16MV	OEM
CO254B16MVU	OEM
CO254B16MVW	OEM
CO254B16MVX	OEM
CO254B16MW	OEM
CO254B16MX	OEM
CO254B16U	OEM
CO254B16V	OEM
CO254B16VU	OEM
CO254B16VW	OEM
CO254B16VX	OEM
CO254B16W	OEM
CO254B16X	OEM
CO254B27	OEM
CO254B27E	OEM
CO254B27EU	OEM
CO254B27EV	OEM
CO254B27EVU	OEM
CO254B27EVW	OEM
CO254B27EVX	OEM
CO254B27EW	OEM
CO254B27EX	OEM
CO254B27J	OEM
CO254B27JU	OEM
CO254B27JV	OEM
CO254B27JVU	OEM
CO254B27JVW	OEM
CO254B27JVX	OEM
CO254B27JW	OEM
CO254B27JX	OEM
CO254B27K	OEM
CO254B27KU	OEM
CO254B27KV	OEM
CO254B27KVU	OEM
CO254B27KVW	OEM
CO254B27KVX	OEM
CO254B27KW	OEM
CO254B27KX	OEM
CO254B27M	OEM
CO254B27MU	OEM
CO254B27MV	OEM
CO254B27MVU	OEM
CO254B27MVW	OEM
CO254B27MVX	OEM
CO254B27MW	OEM
CO254B27MX	OEM
CO254B27U	OEM
CO254B27V	OEM
CO254B27VU	OEM
CO254B27VW	OEM
CO254B27VX	OEM
CO254B27W	OEM
CO254B27X	OEM
CO254B57	OEM
CO254B57E	OEM
CO254B57EU	OEM
CO254B57EV	OEM
CO254B57EVU	OEM
CO254B57EVW	OEM
CO254B57EVX	OEM
CO254B57EW	OEM
CO254B57EX	OEM
CO254B57J	OEM
CO254B57JU	OEM
CO254B57JV	OEM
CO254B57JVU	OEM
CO254B57JVW	OEM
CO254B57JVX	OEM
CO254B57JW	OEM
CO254B57JX	OEM
CO254B57K	OEM
CO254B57KU	OEM
CO254B57KV	OEM
CO254B57KVU	OEM
CO254B57KVW	OEM
CO254B57KVX	OEM
CO254B57KW	OEM
CO254B57KX	OEM
CO254B57M	OEM
CO254B57MU	OEM
CO254B57MV	OEM
CO254B57MVU	OEM
CO254B57MVW	OEM
CO254B57MVX	OEM
CO254B57MW	OEM
CO254B57MX	OEM
CO254B57U	OEM
CO254B57V	OEM
CO254B57VU	OEM
CO254B57VW	OEM
CO254B57VX	OEM
CO254B57W	OEM
CO254B57X	OEM
CO254C16	OEM
CO254C16E	OEM
CO254C16EU	OEM
CO254C16EV	OEM
CO254C16EVU	OEM
CO254C16EVW	OEM
CO254C16EVX	OEM
CO254C16EW	OEM
CO254C16EX	OEM
CO254C16J	OEM
CO254C16JU	OEM
CO254C16JV	OEM
CO254C16JVU	OEM
CO254C16JVW	OEM
CO254C16JVX	OEM
CO254C16JW	OEM
CO254C16JX	OEM
CO254C16K	OEM
CO254C16KU	OEM
CO254C16KV	OEM
CO254C16KVU	OEM
CO254C16KVW	OEM
CO254C16KVX	OEM
CO254C16KW	OEM
CO254C16KX	OEM
CO254C16M	OEM
CO254C16MU	OEM
CO254C16MV	OEM
CO254C16MVU	OEM
CO254C16MVW	OEM
CO254C16MVX	OEM
CO254C16MW	OEM
CO254C16MX	OEM
CO254C16U	OEM
CO254C16V	OEM
CO254C16VU	OEM
CO254C16VW	OEM
CO254C16VX	OEM
CO254C16W	OEM
CO254C16X	OEM
CO254C36	OEM
CO254C36E	OEM
CO254C36EU	OEM
CO254C36EV	OEM
CO254C36EVU	OEM
CO254C36EVW	OEM
CO254C36EVX	OEM
CO254C36EW	OEM
CO254C36EX	OEM
CO254C36J	OEM
CO254C36JU	OEM
CO254C36JV	OEM
CO254C36JVU	OEM
CO254C36JVW	OEM
CO254C36JVX	OEM
CO254C36JW	OEM
CO254C36JX	OEM
CO254C36K	OEM
CO254C36KU	OEM
CO254C36KV	OEM
CO254C36KVU	OEM
CO254C36KVW	OEM
CO254C36KVX	OEM
CO254C36KW	OEM
CO254C36KX	OEM
CO254C36M	OEM
CO254C36MU	OEM
CO254C36MV	OEM
CO254C36MVU	OEM
CO254C36MVW	OEM
CO254C36MVX	OEM
CO254C36MW	OEM
CO254C36MX	OEM
CO254C36U	OEM
CO254C36V	OEM
CO254C36VU	OEM
CO254C36VW	OEM
CO254C36VX	OEM
CO254C36W	OEM
CO254C36X	OEM
CO254C37	OEM
CO254C37E	OEM
CO254C37EU	OEM
CO254C37EV	OEM
CO254C37EVU	OEM
CO254C37EVW	OEM
CO254C37EVX	OEM
CO254C37EW	OEM
CO254C37EX	OEM
CO254C37J	OEM
CO254C37JU	OEM
CO254C37JV	OEM
CO254C37JVU	OEM
CO254C37JVW	OEM
CO254C37JVX	OEM
CO254C37JW	OEM
CO254C37JX	OEM
CO254C37K	OEM
CO254C37KU	OEM
CO254C37KV	OEM
CO254C37KVU	OEM
CO254C37KVW	OEM
CO254C37KVX	OEM
CO254C37KW	OEM
CO254C37KX	OEM
CO254C37M	OEM
CO254C37MU	OEM
CO254C37MV	OEM
CO254C37MVU	OEM
CO254C37MVW	OEM
CO254C37MVX	OEM
CO254C37MW	OEM
CO254C37MX	OEM
CO254C37U	OEM
CO254C37V	OEM
CO254C37VU	OEM
CO254C37VW	OEM
CO254C37VX	OEM
CO254C37W	OEM
CO254C37X	OEM
CO254C56JX	OEM
CO254D16	OEM
CO254D16E	OEM
CO254D16EV	OEM
CO254D16EVU	OEM
CO254D16EVW	OEM
CO254D16EVX	OEM
CO254D16EW	OEM
CO254D16EX	OEM
CO254D16J	OEM
CO254D16JU	OEM
CO254D16JV	OEM
CO254D16JVU	OEM
CO254D16JVW	OEM
CO254D16JVX	OEM
CO254D16JW	OEM
CO254D16JX	OEM
CO254D16K	OEM
CO254D16KU	OEM
CO254D16KV	OEM
CO254D16KVU	OEM
CO254D16KVW	OEM
CO254D16KVX	OEM
CO254D16KW	OEM
CO254D16KX	OEM
CO254D16M	OEM
CO254D16MU	OEM
CO254D16MV	OEM
CO254D16MVU	OEM
CO254D16MVW	OEM
CO254D16MVX	OEM
CO254D16MW	OEM
CO254D16MX	OEM
CO254D16U	OEM

If replacement code is OEM, contact original manufacturer for replacement.

DEVICE TYPE	REPL CODE
C0254D16V	OEM
C0254D16VU	OEM
C0254D16VW	OEM
C0254D16VX	OEM
C0254D16W	OEM
C0254D16X	OEM
C0254D56	OEM
C0254D56E	OEM
C0254D56EU	OEM
C0254D56EV	OEM
C0254D56EVU	OEM
C0254D56EVW	OEM
C0254D56EVX	OEM
C0254D56EW	OEM
C0254D56EX	OEM
C0254D56J	OEM
C0254D56JU	OEM
C0254D56JV	OEM
C0254D56JVU	OEM
C0254D56JVW	OEM
C0254D56JVX	OEM
C0254D56JW	OEM
C0254D56JX	OEM
C0254D56K	OEM
C0254D56KU	OEM
C0254D56KV	OEM
C0254D56KVU	OEM
C0254D56KVW	OEM
C0254D56KVX	OEM
C0254D56KW	OEM
C0254D56KX	OEM
C0254D56M	OEM
C0254D56MU	OEM
C0254D56MV	OEM
C0254D56MVU	OEM
C0254D56MVW	OEM
C0254D56MVX	OEM
C0254D56MW	OEM
C0254D56MX	OEM
C0254D56U	OEM
C0254D56V	OEM
C0254D56VU	OEM
C0254D56VW	OEM
C0254D56VX	OEM
C0254D56X	OEM
C0254D57	OEM
C0254D57E	OEM
C0254D57EU	OEM
C0254D57EV	OEM
C0254D57EVU	OEM
C0254D57EVW	OEM
C0254D57EVX	OEM
C0254D57EW	OEM
C0254D57EX	OEM
C0254D57J	OEM
C0254D57JU	OEM
C0254D57JV	OEM
C0254D57JVU	OEM
C0254D57JVW	OEM
C0254D57JVX	OEM
C0254D57JW	OEM
C0254D57JX	OEM
C0254D57K	OEM
C0254D57KU	OEM
C0254D57KV	OEM
C0254D57KVU	OEM
C0254D57KVW	OEM
C0254D57KVX	OEM
C0254D57KW	OEM
C0254D57KX	OEM
C0254D57M	OEM
C0254D57MU	OEM
C0254D57MV	OEM
C0254D57MVU	OEM
C0254D57MVW	OEM
C0254D57MVX	OEM
C0254D57MW	OEM
C0254D57MX	OEM
C0254D57U	OEM
C0254D57V	OEM
C0254D57VU	OEM
C0254D57VW	OEM
C0254D57W	OEM
C0254D57X	OEM
C0254E16	OEM
C0254E16E	OEM
C0254E16EU	OEM
C0254E16EV	OEM
C0254E16EVU	OEM
C0254E16EVW	OEM
C0254E16EVX	OEM
C0254E16EW	OEM
C0254E16EX	OEM
C0254E16J	OEM
C0254E16JU	OEM
C0254E16JV	OEM
C0254E16JVU	OEM
C0254E16JVW	OEM
C0254E16JVX	OEM
C0254E16JW	OEM
C0254E16JX	OEM
C0254E16K	OEM
C0254E16KU	OEM
C0254E16KV	OEM
C0254E16KVU	OEM
C0254E16KVW	OEM
C0254E16KVX	OEM
C0254E16KW	OEM
C0254E16KX	OEM
C0254E16M	OEM
C0254E16MU	OEM
C0254E16MV	OEM
C0254E16MVU	OEM
C0254E16MVW	OEM
C0254E16MVX	OEM
C0254E16MW	OEM
C0254E16MX	OEM
C0254E16U	OEM
C0254E16V	OEM
C0254E16VU	OEM
C0254E16VW	OEM
C0254E16VX	OEM
C0254E16W	OEM
C0254E16X	OEM
C0254E26	OEM
C0254E26E	OEM
C0254E26EU	OEM
C0254E26EV	OEM
C0254E26EVU	OEM
C0254E26EVW	OEM
C0254E26EVX	OEM
C0254E26EW	OEM
C0254E26EX	OEM
C0254E26J	OEM
C0254E26JU	OEM
C0254E26JV	OEM
C0254E26JVU	OEM
C0254E26JVW	OEM
C0254E26JVX	OEM
C0254E26JW	OEM
C0254E26JX	OEM
C0254E26K	OEM
C0254E26KU	OEM
C0254E26KV	OEM
C0254E26KVU	OEM
C0254E26KVW	OEM
C0254E26KVX	OEM
C0254E26KW	OEM
C0254E26KX	OEM
C0254E26M	OEM
C0254E26MU	OEM
C0254E26MV	OEM
C0254E26MVU	OEM
C0254E26MVW	OEM
C0254E26MVX	OEM
C0254E26MW	OEM
C0254E26MX	OEM
C0254E26U	OEM
C0254E26V	OEM
C0254E26VU	OEM
C0254E26VW	OEM
C0254E26VX	OEM
C0254E26W	OEM
C0254E26X	OEM
C0254E56	OEM
C0254E56E	OEM
C0254E56EU	OEM
C0254E56EV	OEM
C0254E56EVU	OEM
C0254E56EVW	OEM
C0254E56EVX	OEM
C0254E56EW	OEM
C0254E56EX	OEM
C0254E56J	OEM
C0254E56JU	OEM
C0254E56JV	OEM
C0254E56JVU	OEM
C0254E56JVW	OEM
C0254E56JVX	OEM
C0254E56JW	OEM
C0254E56K	OEM
C0254E56KU	OEM
C0254E56KV	OEM
C0254E56KVU	OEM
C0254E56KVW	OEM
C0254E56KVX	OEM
C0254E56KW	OEM
C0254E56KX	OEM
C0254E56M	OEM
C0254E56MU	OEM
C0254E56MV	OEM
C0254E56MVU	OEM
C0254E56MVW	OEM
C0254E56MVX	OEM
C0254E56MW	OEM
C0254E56MX	OEM
C0254E56U	OEM
C0254E56V	OEM
C0254E56VU	OEM
C0254E56VW	OEM
C0254E56VX	OEM
C0254E56W	OEM
C0254E56X	OEM
C0254F16E	OEM
C0254F16EU	OEM
C0254F16EV	OEM
C0254F16EVU	OEM
C0254F16EVW	OEM
C0254F16EVX	OEM
C0254F16EW	OEM
C0254F16EX	OEM
C0254F16J	OEM
C0254F16JU	OEM
C0254F16JV	OEM
C0254F16JVU	OEM
C0254F16JVW	OEM
C0254F16JVX	OEM
C0254F16JW	OEM
C0254F16JX	OEM
C0254F16K	OEM
C0254F16KU	OEM
C0254F16KV	OEM
C0254F16KVU	OEM
C0254F16KVW	OEM
C0254F16KVX	OEM
C0254F16KW	OEM
C0254F16KX	OEM
C0254F16M	OEM
C0254F16MU	OEM
C0254F16MV	OEM
C0254F16MVU	OEM
C0254F16MVW	OEM
C0254F16MVX	OEM
C0254F16MW	OEM
C0254F16MX	OEM
C0254F16U	OEM
C0254F16V	OEM
C0254F16VU	OEM
C0254F16VW	OEM
C0254F16VX	OEM
C0254F16W	OEM
C0254F16X	OEM
C0254F26	OEM
C0254F26E	OEM
C0254F26EU	OEM
C0254F26EV	OEM
C0254F26EVU	OEM
C0254F26EVW	OEM
C0254F26EVX	OEM
C0254F26EW	OEM
C0254F26EX	OEM
C0254F26J	OEM
C0254F26JU	OEM
C0254F26JV	OEM
C0254F26JVU	OEM
C0254F26JVW	OEM
C0254F26JVX	OEM
C0254F26JW	OEM
C0254F26JX	OEM
C0254F26K	OEM
C0254F26KU	OEM
C0254F26KV	OEM
C0254F26KVU	OEM
C0254F26KVW	OEM
C0254F26KW	OEM
C0254F26KX	OEM
C0254F26M	OEM
C0254F26MU	OEM
C0254F26MV	OEM
C0254F26MVU	OEM
C0254F26MVW	OEM
C0254F26MVX	OEM
C0254F26MW	OEM
C0254F26MX	OEM
C0254F26U	OEM
C0254F26V	OEM
C0254F26VU	OEM
C0254F26VW	OEM
C0254F26VX	OEM
C0254F26W	OEM
C0254F26X	OEM
C0254F56	OEM
C0254F56E	OEM
C0254F56EU	OEM
C0254F56EV	OEM
C0254F56EVU	OEM
C0254F56EVX	OEM
C0254F56EW	OEM
C0254F56EX	OEM
C0254F56J	OEM
C0254F56JU	OEM
C0254F56JV	OEM
C0254F56JVU	OEM
C0254F56JVW	OEM
C0254F56JVX	OEM
C0254F56JW	OEM
C0254F56JX	OEM
C0254F56K	OEM
C0254F56KU	OEM
C0254F56KV	OEM
C0254F56KVU	OEM
C0254F56KVW	OEM
C0254F56KVX	OEM
C0254F56KW	OEM
C0254F56KX	OEM
C0254F56M	OEM
C0254F56MU	OEM
C0254F56MV	OEM
C0254F56MVU	OEM
C0254F56MVW	OEM
C0254F56MVX	OEM
C0254F56MW	OEM
C0254F56MX	OEM
C0254F56U	OEM
C0254F56V	OEM
C0254F56VU	OEM
C0254F56VW	OEM
C0254F56VX	OEM
C0254F56W	OEM
C0254F56X	OEM
C0255A17	OEM
C0255A17M	OEM
C0255A17MP	OEM
C0255A17MU	OEM
C0255A17MV	OEM
C0255A17MVP	OEM
C0255A17MVU	OEM
C0255A17MVX	OEM
C0255A17MX	OEM
C0255A17P	OEM
C0255A17U	OEM
C0255A17V	OEM
C0255A17VP	OEM
C0255A17VU	OEM
C0255A17VX	OEM
C0255A17X	OEM
C0255A57	OEM
C0255A57M	OEM
C0255A57MP	OEM
C0255A57MU	OEM
C0255A57MV	OEM
C0255A57MVP	OEM
C0255A57MVU	OEM
C0255A57MVX	OEM
C0255A57MX	OEM
C0255A57P	OEM
C0255A57U	OEM
C0255A57V	OEM
C0255A57VP	OEM
C0255A57VU	OEM
C0255A57VX	OEM
C0255B16	OEM
C0255B16M	OEM
C0255B16MP	OEM
C0255B16MU	OEM
C0255B16MV	OEM
C0255B16MVP	OEM
C0255B16MVU	OEM
C0255B16MVX	OEM
C0255B16MX	OEM
C0255B16P	OEM
C0255B16U	OEM
C0255B16V	OEM
C0255B16VP	OEM
C0255B16VU	OEM
C0255B16VX	OEM
C0255B16X	OEM
C0255B27	OEM
C0255B27M	OEM
C0255B27MP	OEM
C0255B27MU	OEM
C0255B27MV	OEM
C0255B27MVP	OEM
C0255B27MVU	OEM
C0255B27MVX	OEM
C0255B27MX	OEM
C0255B27P	OEM
C0255B27U	OEM
C0255B27V	OEM
C0255B27VP	OEM
C0255B27VU	OEM
C0255B27VX	OEM
C0255B27X	OEM
C0255B57	OEM
C0255B57M	OEM
C0255B57MP	OEM
C0255B57MU	OEM
C0255B57MV	OEM
C0255B57MVP	OEM
C0255B57MVU	OEM
C0255B57MVX	OEM
C0255B57MX	OEM
C0255B57P	OEM
C0255B57U	OEM
C0255B57V	OEM
C0255B57VP	OEM
C0255B57VU	OEM
C0255B57VX	OEM
C0255B57X	OEM
C0255C16	OEM
C0255C16M	OEM
C0255C16MP	OEM
C0255C16MU	OEM
C0255C16MV	OEM
C0255C16MVP	OEM
C0255C16MVU	OEM
C0255C16MVX	OEM
C0255C16MX	OEM
C0255C16P	OEM
C0255C16U	OEM
C0255C16V	OEM
C0255C16VP	OEM
C0255C16VU	OEM
C0255C16VX	OEM
C0255C16X	OEM
C0255C36	OEM
C0255C36M	OEM
C0255C36MP	OEM
C0255C36MU	OEM
C0255C36MV	OEM
C0255C36MVP	OEM
C0255C36MVU	OEM
C0255C36MVX	OEM
C0255C36MX	OEM
C0255C36P	OEM
C0255C36U	OEM
C0255C36V	OEM
C0255C36VP	OEM
C0255C36VU	OEM
C0255C36VX	OEM
C0255C36X	OEM
C0255C37	OEM
C0255C37M	OEM
C0255C37MP	OEM
C0255C37MU	OEM
C0255C37MV	OEM
C0255C37MVP	OEM
C0255C37MVU	OEM
C0255C37MVX	OEM
C0255C37MX	OEM
C0255C37P	OEM
C0255C37U	OEM
C0255C37V	OEM
C0255C37VP	OEM
C0255C37VU	OEM
C0255C37VX	OEM
C0255C37X	OEM
C0255D16	OEM
C0255D16M	OEM
C0255D16MP	OEM
C0255D16MU	OEM
C0255D16MV	OEM
C0255D16MVP	OEM
C0255D16MVU	OEM
C0255D16MVX	OEM
C0255D16MX	OEM
C0255D16P	OEM
C0255D16U	OEM
C0255D16V	OEM
C0255D16VP	OEM
C0255D16VU	OEM
C0255D16VX	OEM
C0255D16X	OEM
C0255D56	OEM
C0255D56M	OEM
C0255D56MP	OEM
C0255D56MU	OEM
C0255D56MV	OEM
C0255D56MVP	OEM
C0255D56MVU	OEM
C0255D56MVX	OEM
C0255D56MX	OEM
C0255D56P	OEM
C0255D56U	OEM
C0255D56V	OEM
C0255D56VP	OEM
C0255D56VU	OEM
C0255D56VX	OEM
C0255D56X	OEM
C0255D57	OEM
C0255D57M	OEM
C0255D57MP	OEM
C0255D57MU	OEM
C0255D57MV	OEM
C0255D57MVP	OEM
C0255D57MVU	OEM
C0255D57MVX	OEM
C0255D57MX	OEM
C0255D57P	OEM
C0255D57U	OEM
C0255D57V	OEM
C0255D57VP	OEM
C0255D57VU	OEM
C0255D57VX	OEM
C0255D57X	OEM
C0255E16	OEM
C0255E16M	OEM
C0255E16MP	OEM
C0255E16MU	OEM
C0255E16MV	OEM
C0255E16MVP	OEM
C0255E16MVU	OEM
C0255E16MVX	OEM
C0255E16MX	OEM
C0255E16P	OEM
C0255E16U	OEM
C0255E16V	OEM
C0255E16VP	OEM
C0255E16VU	OEM
C0255E16VX	OEM
C0255E16X	OEM
C0255E26	OEM
C0255E26M	OEM
C0255E26MP	OEM
C0255E26MU	OEM
C0255E26MV	OEM
C0255E26MVP	OEM
C0255E26MVU	OEM
C0255E26MVX	OEM
C0255E26MX	OEM
C0255E26P	OEM
C0255E26U	OEM
C0255E26V	OEM
C0255E26VP	OEM
C0255E26VU	OEM
C0255E26VX	OEM
C0255E26X	OEM
C0255E56	OEM
C0255E56MP	OEM
C0255E56MU	OEM
C0255E56MV	OEM
C0255E56MVP	OEM
C0255E56MVU	OEM
C0255E56MVX	OEM
C0255E56MX	OEM
C0255E56P	OEM
C0255E56U	OEM
C0255E56V	OEM
C0255E56VP	OEM
C0255E56VU	OEM
C0255E56VX	OEM
C0255E56X	OEM
C0255F16	OEM
C0255F16M	OEM
C0255F16MP	OEM
C0255F16MU	OEM
C0255F16MV	OEM
C0255F16MVP	OEM
C0255F16MVU	OEM
C0255F16MVX	OEM
C0255F16MX	OEM
C0255F16P	OEM
C0255F16U	OEM
C0255F16V	OEM
C0255F16VP	OEM
C0255F16VU	OEM
C0255F16VX	OEM
C0255F16X	OEM
C0255F26	OEM
C0255F26M	OEM
C0255F26MP	OEM
C0255F26MU	OEM
C0255F26MV	OEM
C0255F26MVP	OEM
C0255F26MVU	OEM
C0255F26MVX	OEM
C0255F26MX	OEM
C0255F26P	OEM
C0255F26U	OEM
C0255F26V	OEM
C0255F26VP	OEM
C0255F26VU	OEM
C0255F26VX	OEM
C0255F26X	OEM
C0255F56	OEM
C0255F56M	OEM
C0255F56MP	OEM
C0255F56MU	OEM
C0255F56MV	OEM
C0255F56MVP	OEM
C0255F56MVU	OEM
C0255F56MVX	OEM
C0255F56MX	OEM
C0255F56P	OEM
C0255F56U	OEM
C0255F56V	OEM
C0255F56VP	OEM
C0255F56VU	OEM
C0255F56VX	OEM
C0255F56X	OEM
C0271VA	OEM
C0271VB	OEM
C0273V	OEM
C0274V	OEM
C0275HA	OEM
C0275HB	OEM
C0275VA	OEM
C0275VB	OEM
C0281	OEM
C0281-1	OEM
C0281-2	OEM
C0281-3	OEM
C0281-4	OEM
C0281-5	OEM
C0281-6	OEM
C0281T	OEM
C0281T1	OEM
C0281T2	OEM
C0281T3	OEM
C0281T4	OEM
C0281T5	OEM
C0281T6	OEM
C0281Y	OEM
C0281Y1	OEM
C0281Y2	OEM
C0281Y3	OEM
C0281Y4	OEM
C0281Y5	OEM
C0281Y6	OEM
C0282	OEM
C0282-1	OEM
C0282-2	OEM
C0282-3	OEM
C0282-4	OEM
C0282-5	OEM
C0282-6	OEM
C0282T	OEM
C0282T1	OEM
C0282T2	OEM
C0282T3	OEM
C0282T4	OEM
C0282T5	OEM
C0282T6	OEM
C0284U	OEM
C0284U1	OEM
C0284U2	OEM
C0284U3	OEM
C0284U4	OEM
C0284U5	OEM
C0284U6	OEM
C0284UT	OEM
C0284UT1	OEM
C0284UT2	OEM
C0284UT3	OEM
C0284UT4	OEM
C0284UT5	OEM
C0284UT6	OEM
C0284UTV	OEM
C0284UTV1	OEM
C0284UTV2	OEM
C0284UTV3	OEM
C0284UTV4	OEM
C0284UTV5	OEM
C0284UTV6	OEM
C0284UV	OEM
C0284UV1	OEM
C0284UV2	OEM
C0284UV3	OEM
C0284UV4	OEM
C0284UV5	OEM
C0284UV6	OEM
C0284W	OEM
C0284W1	OEM
C0284W2	OEM
C0284W3	OEM
C0284W4	OEM
C0284W5	OEM
C0284W6	OEM
C0284WT	OEM
C0284WT1	OEM
C0284WT2	OEM
C0284WT3	OEM
C0284WT4	OEM
C0284WT5	OEM
C0284WT6	OEM
C0284WTV	OEM
C0284WTV1	OEM
C0284WTV2	OEM
C0284WTV3	OEM
C0284WTV4	OEM
C0284WTV5	OEM
C0284WTV6	OEM
C0284WV1	OEM
C0284WV2	OEM
C0284WV3	OEM
C0284WV4	OEM
C0284WV5	OEM
C0284WV6	OEM
C0284X	OEM
C0284X1	OEM
C0284X2	OEM
C0284X3	OEM
C0284X4	OEM
C0284X5	OEM
C0284X6	OEM
C0284XT	OEM
C0284XT1	OEM
C0284XT2	OEM
C0284XT3	OEM
C0284XT4	OEM
C0284XT5	OEM
C0284XT6	OEM
C0284XTV	OEM
C0284XTV1	OEM
C0284XTV2	OEM
C0284XTV3	OEM
C0284XTV4	OEM
C0284XTV5	OEM
C0284XTV6	OEM
C0284XY	OEM
C0284XY1	OEM
C0284XY2	OEM
C0284XY3	OEM
C0284XY4	OEM
C0284XY5	OEM
C0284XY6	OEM
C0410V	0071
C0510	0071
C0536	OEM
C0536-1	OEM
C0536-3	OEM
C0536T	OEM
C0536T1	OEM
C0536T3	OEM
C0536TV1	OEM
C0536TV3	OEM
C0536V	OEM
C0536V1	OEM
C0536V3	OEM
C0633A3	OEM
C0633AV	OEM
C0633B	OEM
C0633B3	OEM
C0633BV	OEM
C0633BV3	OEM
C0636A	OEM
C0636A1	OEM
C0636A3	OEM
C0636A5	OEM
C0636AV	OEM
C0636AV1	OEM
C0636AV3	OEM
C0636AV5	OEM
C0636B	OEM
C0636B1	OEM
C0636B3	OEM
C0636B5	OEM
C0636BV	OEM
C0636BV1	OEM
C0636BV3	OEM
C0636BV5	OEM
C01433-09	0518
C02138V3	OEM
C02555E56M	OEM
C0-10174-02	1686
C0-10444-22	OEM
C0-10444D-03	OEM
C0-10745-03	3041
C0-10750-03	1962
C0-10816	0394
C010816-XX	0394
C012294-22	OEM
C012294B-01	OEM
C012296D-01	OEM

If replacement code is OEM, contact original manufacturer for replacement.

345

DEVICE TYPE	REPL CODE
CO12296D-22	OEM
CO12399B	OEM
CO12499B-01	OEM
CO14313	0453
CO14336	0362
CO14341	1652
CO14344	0422
CO14345	1646
CO-14348	0619
CO14377	3036
CO14599B-01	OEM
CO14795	OEM
CO14805-01	OEM
CO14805-22	OEM
CO14806-12	3036
CO19156-05	OEM
CO25912-38	OEM
CO25913-38	OEM
CO25914-38	OEM
CO25915-38	OEM
CO26028	OEM
CO26034-01	OEM
CO26035-01	OEM
COC13000-1C	0590
COC13000-IC	0626
COD1-6045	0015
COD1-6046	0015
COD1-6047	0015
COD1-6048	0015
COD1531	0015
COD1532	0015
COD1533	0015
COD1534	0015
COD1535	0015
COD1536	0015
COD1537	0071
COD1538	0071
COD1551	0015
COD1552	0015
COD1553	0015
COD1554	0015
COD1555	0015
COD1556	0015
COD1575	0015
COD1611	0015
COD1612	0015
COD1613	0015
COD1614	0015
COD1615	0015
COD1616	0015
COD1617	0071
COD1618	0071
COD11556	0015
COD15524	0015
COD15534	0015
COD15544	0015
COD15564	0015
COD16047	0015
CODI531	0015
CODI532	0015
CODI533	0015
CODI534	0015
CODI535	0015
CODI536	0015
CODI537	0071
CODI538	0071
CODI551	0015
CODI552	0015
CODI553	0015
CODI554	0015
CODI555	0015
CODI556	0015
CODI617	0071
CODI1531	0015
CODI5314	OEM
CODI5324	OEM
CODI5334	OEM
CODI5344	OEM
CODI5354	OEM
CODI5364	2621
CODI5514	OEM
CODI5524	OEM
CODI5534	OEM
CODI5544	OEM
CODI5554	OEM
CODI5564	OEM
CODI6041	OEM
CODI6042	OEM
CODI6043	OEM
CODI6044	OEM
CODI6045	0015
CODI6046	OEM
CODI6047	0015
CODI6048	OEM
CODI6049	OEM
CODI6050	OEM
CODI6051	OEM
CODI6052	OEM
CODI11556	0015
CODI15524	0015
CODI15534	0015
CODI15544	0015
CODI15564	0015
COM1553A	OEM
COM1671	OEM
COM1863	OEM
COM2017	OEM
COM2017H	OEM
COM2502	OEM

DEVICE TYPE	REPL CODE
COM2502/H	OEM
COM2601	OEM
COM2651	OEM
COM2661-1	OEM
COM2661-2	OEM
COM2661-3	OEM
COM5016	OEM
COM5016T	OEM
COM5025	OEM
COM5026	OEM
COM5026T	OEM
COM5036	OEM
COM5036T	OEM
COM5046	OEM
COM5046T	OEM
COM8004	OEM
COM8017	OEM
COM8018	OEM
COM8046	OEM
COM8046T	OEM
COM8116	OEM
COM8116T	OEM
COM8126	OEM
COM8126T	OEM
COM8136	OEM
COM8136T	OEM
COM8146	OEM
COM8146T	OEM
COM8251A	OEM
COM8502	OEM
COM9004	OEM
COM9026	OEM
COP302D	OEM
COP302J	OEM
COP302MD	OEM
COP302MJ	OEM
COP302MN	OEM
COP302N	OEM
COP304D	OEM
COP304J	OEM
COP304LD	OEM
COP304LJ	OEM
COP304LN	OEM
COP304N	OEM
COP310CD	OEM
COP310CJ	OEM
COP310CN	OEM
COP310LD	OEM
COP310LJ	OEM
COP310LN	OEM
COP311CD	OEM
COP311CJ	OEM
COP311CN	OEM
COP311LD	OEM
COP311LJ	OEM
COP311LN	OEM
COP320CD	OEM
COP320CJ	OEM
COP320CN	OEM
COP320D	OEM
COP320J	OEM
COP320LD	OEM
COP320LJ	OEM
COP320LN	OEM
COP320N	OEM
COP321CD	OEM
COP321CJ	OEM
COP321CN	OEM
COP321D	OEM
COP321J	OEM
COP321LD	OEM
COP321LJ	OEM
COP321LN	OEM
COP321N	OEM
COP322D	OEM
COP322J	OEM
COP322LD	OEM
COP322LJ	OEM
COP322LN	OEM
COP322N	OEM
COP340D	OEM
COP340J	OEM
COP340N	OEM
COP341D	OEM
COP341J	OEM
COP341N	OEM
COP342D	OEM
COP342J	OEM
COP342N	OEM
COP344CD	OEM
COP344CJ	OEM
COP344CN	OEM
COP344LD	OEM
COP344LJ	OEM
COP344LN	OEM
COP345CD	OEM
COP345CJ	OEM
COP345CN	OEM
COP345LD	OEM
COP345LJ	OEM
COP345LN	OEM
COP364D	OEM
COP364J	OEM
COP364N	OEM
COP365D	OEM
COP365J	OEM
COP365N	OEM
COP384D	OEM
COP384J	OEM

DEVICE TYPE	REPL CODE
COP384N	OEM
COP385D	OEM
COP385J	OEM
COP385N	OEM
COP401LD	OEM
COP401LJ	OEM
COP401LN	OEM
COP402D	OEM
COP402J	OEM
COP402MD	OEM
COP402MJ	OEM
COP402MN	OEM
COP402N	OEM
COP404D	OEM
COP404J	OEM
COP404LD	OEM
COP404LJ	OEM
COP404LN	OEM
COP404N	OEM
COP410CD	OEM
COP410CJ	OEM
COP410CN	OEM
COP410LD	OEM
COP410LJ	OEM
COP410LN	OEM
COP411CD	OEM
COP411CJ	OEM
COP411CN	OEM
COP411LD	OEM
COP411LJ	OEM
COP411LN	OEM
COP420CD	OEM
COP420CJ	OEM
COP420CN	OEM
COP420D	OEM
COP420J	OEM
COP420LD	OEM
COP420LJ	OEM
COP420LN	OEM
COP420N	OEM
COP420RD	OEM
COP420RJ	OEM
COP420RN	OEM
COP421CD	OEM
COP421CJ	OEM
COP421CN	OEM
COP421D	OEM
COP421J	OEM
COP421LD	OEM
COP421LJ	OEM
COP421LN	OEM
COP421N	OEM
COP422D	OEM
COP422J	OEM
COP422LD	OEM
COP422LJ	OEM
COP422LN	OEM
COP422N	OEM
COP440D	OEM
COP440J	OEM
COP440N	OEM
COP440RD	OEM
COP440RJ	OEM
COP440RN	OEM
COP441D	OEM
COP441J	OEM
COP441N	OEM
COP442D	OEM
COP442J	OEM
COP442N	OEM
COP444CD	OEM
COP444CJ	OEM
COP444CN	OEM
COP444LJ	OEM
COP444LN	OEM
COP444LRD	OEM
COP444LRJ	OEM
COP444LRN	OEM
COP4440D	OEM
COP445CD	OEM
COP445CJ	OEM
COP445LD	OEM
COP445LJ	OEM
COP445LN	OEM
COP464D	OEM
COP464J	OEM
COP464N	OEM
COP465D	OEM
COP465J	OEM
COP465N	OEM
COP472D	OEM
COP472N	OEM
COP472N-3	OEM
COP484D	OEM
COP484J	OEM
COP484N	OEM
COP485D	OEM
COP485J	OEM
COP485N	OEM
COP2304D	OEM
COP2304J	OEM
COP2304N	OEM
COP2340D	OEM
COP2340N	OEM
COP2341D	OEM
COP2341J	OEM
COP2341N	OEM
COP2342D	OEM
COP2342J	OEM

DEVICE TYPE	REPL CODE
COP2342N	OEM
COP2404D	OEM
COP2404J	OEM
COP2404N	OEM
COP2440D	OEM
COP2440J	OEM
COP2440N	OEM
COP2440RD	OEM
COP2440RJ	OEM
COP2440RN	OEM
COP2441D	OEM
COP2441N	OEM
COP2442D	OEM
COP2442J	OEM
COP2442N	OEM
CP1	OEM
CP1A	OEM
CP2	OEM
CP2A	OEM
CP10-12	OEM
CP22	OEM
CP82C55A	OEM
CP82C59A	OEM
CP98	OEM
CP100	OEM
CP101	OEM
CP102	0071
CP102BA	0015
CP102DA	0015
CP102FA	0015
CP102HA	0015
CP102KA	0015
CP102MA	0015
CP102PA	0071
CP102RA	0071
CP102VA	0071
CP103	0071
CP104	OEM
CP110	OEM
CP115	OEM
CP119	OEM
CP121	OEM
CP123	OEM
CP124	OEM
CP126	OEM
CP127	OEM
CP128	OEM
CP129	OEM
CP130	OEM
CP131	OEM
CP132	OEM
CP133	OEM
CP134	OEM
CP135	OEM
CP136	OEM
CP137	OEM
CP138	OEM
CP139	OEM
CP140	OEM
CP141	OEM
CP142	OEM
CP143	OEM
CP144	OEM
CP145	OEM
CP146	OEM
CP147	OEM
CP148	OEM
CP149	OEM
CP150	OEM
CP151	OEM
CP152	OEM
CP152AA	0071
CP152BA	0071
CP152CA	0071
CP152DA	0071
CP152EA	0071
CP152FA	0071
CP152GA	0071
CP152HA	0071
CP152KA	0071
CP152MA	0071
CP152PA	0071
CP152RA	0071
CP152TA	0071
CP152VA	0071
CP153	OEM
CP154	OEM
CP155	OEM
CP156	OEM
CP157	OEM
CP158	OEM
CP398	OEM
CP400	0103
CP401	0103
CP402	OEM
CP403	0855
CP404	0103
CP405	0103
CP406	0103
CP407	0103
CP408	0103
CP409	0086
CP430	OEM
CP431	OEM
CP432	OEM
CP433	OEM
CP600	OEM
CP601	OEM
CP602	OEM

DEVICE TYPE	REPL CODE
CP640	OEM
CP643	OEM
CP650	OEM
CP651	OEM
CP652	OEM
CP653	OEM
CP664	OEM
CP665	OEM
CP666	OEM
CP701	0236
CP702	0236
CP703	0855
CP704	0236
CP800	0164
CP801	0164
CP802	0164
CP803	0164
CP1005	OEM
CP1007GL	OEM
CP1009GLR	OEM
CP1600	OEM
CP-1610	OEM
CP-1610K	OEM
CP2006A	OEM
CP2009	OEM
CP2009A	OEM
CP2010	OEM
CP2010A	OEM
CP2011	OEM
CP2011A	OEM
CP2012	OEM
CP2012A	OEM
CP2013	1161
CP2013A	1161
CP2015	OEM
CP2015A	OEM
CP2016	OEM
CP2016A	OEM
CP2018	1756
CP2018A	1756
CP2020	1921
CP2020A	1921
CP2022	OEM
CP2022A	OEM
CP2024	OEM
CP2024A	OEM
CP2025GR	OEM
CP2027	1941
CP2027A	1941
CP2030	OEM
CP2030A	OEM
CP2032	OEM
CP2033	OEM
CP2033A	OEM
CP2036	OEM
CP2036A	OEM
CP2039	OEM
CP2039A	OEM
CP2043	OEM
CP2043A	OEM
CP2047	OEM
CP2047A	OEM
CP2051	1961
CP2051A	1961
CP2056	OEM
CP2056A	OEM
CP2062	OEM
CP2062A	OEM
CP2068	1976
CP2068A	1976
CP2075	OEM
CP2075A	OEM
CP2082	OEM
CP2082A	OEM
CP2091	OEM
CP2091A	OEM
CP2100	OEM
CP2100A	OEM
CP2110	OEM
CP2110A	OEM
CP2120	OEM
CP2130	OEM
CP2130A	OEM
CP2140	OEM
CP2143	OEM
CP2150	OEM
CP2150A	OEM
CP2160	OEM
CP2160A	OEM
CP2170	OEM
CP2170A	OEM
CP2180	OEM
CP2180A	OEM
CP2200	1398
CP2200A	1398
CP2220	OEM
CP2220A	OEM
CP2250	OEM
CP2250A	OEM
CP2275	OEM
CP2275A	OEM
CP3009	OEM
CP3009A	OEM
CP3010	OEM
CP3010A	OEM
CP3011	OEM
CP3011A	OEM
CP3012	OEM
CP3012A	OEM

DEVICE TYPE	REPL CODE
CP3013	OEM
CP3013A	OEM
CP3015	OEM
CP3015A	OEM
CP3016	OEM
CP3016A	OEM
CP3018	OEM
CP3018A	OEM
CP3020	OEM
CP3020A	OEM
CP3022	OEM
CP3022A	OEM
CP3024	OEM
CP3024A	OEM
CP3027	OEM
CP3027A	OEM
CP3030	OEM
CP3030A	OEM
CP3033	OEM
CP3033A	OEM
CP3036	OEM
CP3036A	OEM
CP3039	OEM
CP3039A	OEM
CP3043	OEM
CP3043A	OEM
CP3047	OEM
CP3047A	OEM
CP3051	OEM
CP3051A	OEM
CP3056	OEM
CP3056A	OEM
CP3062	OEM
CP3062A	OEM
CP3068	OEM
CP3068A	OEM
CP3075	OEM
CP3075A	OEM
CP3082	OEM
CP3082A	OEM
CP3091	OEM
CP3091A	OEM
CP3100	OEM
CP3100A	OEM
CP3110	OEM
CP3110A	OEM
CP3120	OEM
CP3120A	OEM
CP3120E	2438
CP3130	OEM
CP3130A	OEM
CP3140	OEM
CP3150	OEM
CP3150A	OEM
CP3160	OEM
CP3160A	OEM
CP3170	OEM
CP3170A	OEM
CP3180	OEM
CP3180A	OEM
CP3200	OEM
CP3200A	OEM
CP3220	OEM
CP3220A	OEM
CP3250	OEM
CP3250A	OEM
CP3275	OEM
CP3275A	OEM
CP5011C	OEM
CP3212055	0012
CPS1002	OEM
CPS1113	OEM
CPS1540B	2602
CPS1545B	2602
CPS1550B	2602
CPS2510B	2602
CPS2512B	2602
CPS2515B	2602
CPS2540B	2602
CPS2545B	2602
CPS2550B	2602
CPS4010B	2602
CPS4012B	2602
CPS4015B	2602
CPS4040B	2602
CPS4045B	2602
CPS4050B	2602
CPS7010B	3956
CPS7012B	3956
CPS7015B	3956
CPS15553-101	1035
CPS-16676-1	2067
CPT12035	OEM
CPT12040	OEM
CPT12045	OEM
CPT12050	OEM
CPT20120	OEM
CPT20125	OEM
CPT30035	OEM
CPT30040	OEM
CPT30045	OEM
CPT30050	OEM
CPU/6800	OEM
CPU001	OEM
CPU-001-010	OEM
CPU-001-030	OEM
CPU-001-210	OEM
CPU-001-230	OEM
CPU012	OEM

DEVICE TYPE	REPL CODE
CPU-012-310	OEM
CPU-012-311	OEM
CPU019	OEM
CPU-019-210	OEM
CPU-019-211	OEM
CPU-019-212	OEM
CPU-019-310	OEM
CPU-019-311	OEM
CPU-019-312	OEM
CPU-800	OEM
CPU-6805	OEM
CPU7811G	OEM
CPU7811HG	OEM
CPX5058H-540Q	OEM
CPZ-48000	OEM
CQ1	0004
CQ4-32	OEM
CQ209S	OEM
CQ216X	OEM
CQ216Y	OEM
CQ327	OEM
CQ327R	OEM
CQ330	OEM
CQ330R	OEM
CQ331	OEM
CQ331R	OEM
CQ332	OEM
CQ332R	OEM
CQ427	OEM
CQ427R	OEM
CQ430	OEM
CQ430R	OEM
CQ431	OEM
CQ431R	OEM
CQ432	OEM
CQ432R	OEM
CQ30148A	OEM
CQB56-2	OEM
CQEAK-00801	OEM
CQEAK-00805	OEM
CQEAK-01011	OEM
CQEAK-01103	0806
CQEAK-03001	OEM
CQEAK-03202	OEM
CQL10	OEM
CQL10A	OEM
CQL10B	OEM
CQT10	OEM
CQT940A	0160
CQT940B	0160
CQT940BA	0160
CQT1075	0160
CQT1076	0160
CQT1077	0160
CQT1110	0160
CQT1110A	0160
CQT1111	0160
CQT1111A	0160
CQT1112	0160
CQV10-3	OEM
CQV10-4	OEM
CQV11-4	OEM
CQV11-5	OEM
CQV11-6	OEM
CQV13-4	OEM
CQV13-5	OEM
CQV13-6	OEM
CQV14-3	OEM
CQV14-4	OEM
CQV14-5	OEM
CQV14-6	OEM
CQV15-3	OEM
CQV15-4	OEM
CQV15-6	OEM
CQV16-2	OEM
CQV16-3	OEM
CQV16-4	OEM
CQV18-2	OEM
CQV18-3	OEM
CQV18-4	OEM
CQV19-2	OEM
CQV19-3	OEM
CQV19-4	OEM
CQV20-3	OEM
CQV20-4	OEM
CQV21-4	OEM
CQV21-5	OEM
CQV21-6	OEM
CQV23-4	OEM
CQV23-5	OEM
CQV23-6	OEM
CQV24-3	OEM
CQV24-4	OEM
CQV24-5	OEM
CQV24-6	OEM
CQV25-3	OEM
CQV25-4	OEM
CQV25-5	OEM
CQV25-6	OEM
CQV26-2	OEM
CQV26-3	OEM
CQV26-4	OEM
CQV28-2	OEM
CQV28-3	OEM
CQV28-4	OEM
CQV29-2	OEM
CQV29-3	OEM
CQV29-4	OEM
CQV30A	OEM

If replacement code is OEM, contact original manufacturer for replacement.

DEVICE TYPE	REPL CODE
CQV30B	OEM
CQV30C	OEM
CQV31D	OEM
CQV31E	OEM
CQV33D	OEM
CQV33E	OEM
CQV35D	OEM
CQV36-3	OEM
CQV36-4	OEM
CQV36-5	OEM
CQV38-3	OEM
CQV38-4	OEM
CQV38-5	OEM
CQV39-3	OEM
CQV39-4	OEM
CQV39-5	OEM
CQV41-3	OEM
CQV41-4	OEM
CQV41-5	OEM
CQV43-3	OEM
CQV43-4	OEM
CQV43-5	OEM
CQV45-3	OEM
CQV45-4	OEM
CQV45-5	OEM
CQV51F	OEM
CQV51G	OEM
CQV51H	OEM
CQV51J	OEM
CQV53F	OEM
CQV53G	OEM
CQV53H	OEM
CQV53J	OEM
CQV55G	OEM
CQV55H	OEM
CQV55J	OEM
CQV55K	OEM
CQV56-3	OEM
CQV56-4	OEM
CQV58-2	OEM
CQV58-3	OEM
CQV58-4	OEM
CQV59-2	OEM
CQV59-4	OEM
CQV60	OEM
CQV61	OEM
CQV62	OEM
CQW10	OEM
CQW11	OEM
CQW12	OEM
CQW13	OEM
CQW14	OEM
CQW24	OEM
CQW32	OEM
CQW51	OEM
CQW54	OEM
CQX10	3153
CQX10-I	OEM
CQX10-II	OEM
CQX10-III	OEM
CQX10-IV	OEM
CQX10I	OEM
CQX10II	OEM
CQX10III	OEM
CQX10IV	OEM
CQX11	1767
CQX11-I	OEM
CQX11-II	OEM
CQX11-III	OEM
CQX11-IV	OEM
CQX11I	OEM
CQX11II	OEM
CQX11III	OEM
CQX11IV	OEM
CQX12	3128
CQX12-I	OEM
CQX12-II	OEM
CQX12-III	OEM
CQX12-IV	OEM
CQX12I	OEM
CQX12II	OEM
CQX12III	OEM
CQX12IV	OEM
CQX13	OEM
CQX13-1	OEM
CQX13-2	OEM
CQX13I	OEM
CQX13II	OEM
CQX14	OEM
CQX15	OEM
CQX16	OEM
CQX17	OEM
CQX18	OEM
CQX19	OEM
CQX21	3965
CQX23-1	OEM
CQX23-2	OEM
CQX23I	OEM
CQX23II	OEM
CQX24	OEM
CQX24B	OEM
CQX25N	OEM
CQX26N	OEM
CQX27N	OEM
CQX28	OEM
CQX29	OEM
CQX30	OEM
CQX31	OEM
CQX32	OEM

DEVICE TYPE	REPL CODE
CQX33-1	OEM
CQX33-2	OEM
CQX33I	OEM
CQX33II	OEM
CQX35	OEM
CQX36	OEM
CQX37	OEM
CQX41NA	OEM
CQX41NB	OEM
CQX42NA	OEM
CQX42NB	OEM
CQX43N	OEM
CQX46	OEM
CQX47	OEM
CQX51	OEM
CQX51-1	OEM
CQX51-2	OEM
CQX51-3	OEM
CQX54	OEM
CQX55	OEM
CQX56	OEM
CQX57	OEM
CQX58	OEM
CQX60	OEM
CQX61	OEM
CQX62	OEM
CQX63	OEM
CQX64	OEM
CQX65	OEM
CQX66	OEM
CQX67	OEM
CQX68	OEM
CQX74	OEM
CQX75	OEM
CQX76	OEM
CQX77	OEM
CQX78	OEM
CQY10	OEM
CQY11A	OEM
CQY11B	OEM
CQY11C	OEM
CQY11D	OEM
CQY12A	OEM
CQY12B	OEM
CQY13	OEM
CQY13B	OEM
CQY14	OEM
CQY15	OEM
CQY17IV	OEM
CQY17V	OEM
CQY24B	6443
CQY24B-I	OEM
CQY24B-II	OEM
CQY24B-IV	OEM
CQY27	OEM
CQY31	OEM
CQY32	OEM
CQY33NE	OEM
CQY33NF	OEM
CQY34NE	OEM
CQY34NF	OEM
CQY35NE	OEM
CQY35NR	OEM
CQY36N	OEM
CQY37N	OEM
CQY40	OEM
CQY41N	OEM
CQY49B	OEM
CQY49C	OEM
CQY50	OEM
CQY52	OEM
CQY54	2990
CQY54-I	OEM
CQY54-II	OEM
CQY54-III	OEM
CQY58A	OEM
CQY58A-1	OEM
CQY58A-2	OEM
CQY58A-I	OEM
CQY58A-II	OEM
CQY65	2990
CQY72L	1767
CQY73N	OEM
CQY74	OEM
CQY75N	OEM
CQY77I	OEM
CQY77II	OEM
CQY77III	OEM
CQY78I	OEM
CQY78II	OEM
CQY78III	OEM
CQY80	0311
CQY80N	0536
CQY85NA	OEM
CQY85NB	OEM
CQY86NA	OEM
CQY86NB	OEM
CQY87NQ	OEM
CQY89A	OEM
CQY89A-1	OEM
CQY89A1	OEM
CQY89A-2	OEM
CQY94	1767
CQY94-I	OEM
CQY94-II	OEM
CQY94-III	OEM
CQY94-IV	OEM
CQY95	OEM
CQY95-I	OEM

DEVICE TYPE	REPL CODE
CQY95-II	OEM
CQY95-III	OEM
CQY96	OEM
CQY96-I	OEM
CQY96-II	OEM
CQY96-III	OEM
CQY96-IV	OEM
CQY97	3095
CQY97-I	OEM
CQY97-II	OEM
CQY97-III	OEM
CQY98	OEM
CQY99	0511
CR	OEM
CR/E	0015
CR0000	0143
CR005-01A	OEM
CR005-01B	OEM
CR005-01C	OEM
CR005-01D	OEM
CR005-01E	OEM
CR005-05A	OEM
CR005-05B	OEM
CR005-05C	OEM
CR005-05D	OEM
CR005-05E	OEM
CR005-10A	OEM
CR005-10B	OEM
CR005-10C	OEM
CR005-10D	OEM
CR005-10E	OEM
CR005-50A	OEM
CR005-50B	OEM
CR005-50C	OEM
CR005-50D	OEM
CR005-50E	OEM
CR02A1	OEM
CR02A2	OEM
CR02A4	OEM
CR02A6	OEM
CR02A8	OEM
CR02AM	0340
CR02AM-1	0340
CR02AM1	0340
CR02AM2	OEM
CR02AM-4	0058
CR02AM4	0058
CR02AM6	OEM
CR02AM-8	0403
CR02AM8	OEM
CR02AM10	OEM
CR02AN4	0058
CR03A-1	OEM
CR03AM1	OEM
CR03AM2	OEM
CR03AM4	OEM
CR03AM6	OEM
CR03AM8	OEM
CR03AM10	OEM
CR03AM12	OEM
CR05	OEM
CR022	OEM
CR024	OEM
CR027	OEM
CR030	OEM
CR033	OEM
CR039	OEM
CR043	OEM
CR047	OEM
CR056	OEM
CR062	OEM
CR068	OEM
CR075	OEM
CR082	OEM
CR091	OEM
CR0121A	0998
CR0121B	0998
CR0121D	1028
CR0121M	1140
CR0122A	2078
CR0122B	0500
CR0122C	OEM
CR0122D	0705
CR0122E	OEM
CR0122F	OEM
CR0122M	0857
CR0122N	OEM
CR0137-14	OEM
CR1-021C	OEM
CR1-051C	0179
CR1-051CA	0174
CR1-051CB	0179
CR1-101C	0179
CR1-101CA	3801
CR1-101CB	0340
CR1-151C	OEM
CR1-201C	0179
CR1-201CA	3575
CR1-201CB	0058
CR1-251C	OEM
CR1-301C	0342
CR1-301CA	0342
CR1-301CB	0403
CR1-401C	0342
CR1-401CA	0342
CR1-401CB	OEM
CR1T01HY1	OEM
CR1T01HY2	OEM
CR1T01HY3	OEM

DEVICE TYPE	REPL CODE
CR1T02HY1	OEM
CR1T02HY2	OEM
CR1T02HY3	OEM
CR1T03HY1	OEM
CR1T03HY2	OEM
CR1T03HY3	OEM
CR1T04HY1	OEM
CR1T04HY2	OEM
CR1T04HY3	OEM
CR1T05HY1	OEM
CR1T05HY2	OEM
CR1T05HY3	OEM
CR1T06HY1	OEM
CR1T06HY2	OEM
CR1T06HY3	OEM
CR1TX5HY1	OEM
CR1TX5HY2	OEM
CR1TX5HY3	OEM
CR2-160	OEM
CR2AM1	1250
CR2AM2	0442
CR2AM4	0934
CR2AM6	0095
CR2AM-8	0095
CR2AM8	0095
CR2AM10	1234
CR2AM12	1234
CR2T01HY	OEM
CR2T01HY1	OEM
CR2T02HY	OEM
CR2T02HY1	OEM
CR2T03HY	OEM
CR2T03HY1	OEM
CR2T04HY	OEM
CR2T04HY1	OEM
CR2T05HY	OEM
CR2T05HY1	OEM
CR2T06HY	OEM
CR2T06HY1	OEM
CR2TX5HY	OEM
CR2TX5HY1	OEM
CR3-080	OEM
CR3-100	OEM
CR3AM1	1250
CR3AM2	0442
CR3AM4	0934
CR3AM6	0095
CR3AM-8	OEM
CR3AM8	0095
CR3AMZ	0095
CR3AMZ-8	0095
CR3AMZ8	0095
CR3CM	0095
CR3CM-1	1250
CR3CM-2	0442
CR3CM-4	0934
CR3CM-6	0095
CR3CM-8	0095
CR3CM8	0095
CR3CM-8-208	0095
CR3CM10	1234
CR3CM12	1234
CR-3D	OEM
CR3DZ2	OEM
CR3DZ4	OEM
CR3DZ6	OEM
CR3DZ8	OEM
CR3E1	OEM
CR3E2	OEM
CR3E4	OEM
CR3E-6	OEM
CR3E6	OEM
CR3E8	OEM
CR3E10	OEM
CR3E12	OEM
CR3EM1	OEM
CR3EM2	OEM
CR3EM4	OEM
CR3EM6	OEM
CR3EM8	OEM
CR3JM6	OEM
CR3JM8	OEM
CR4-051A	OEM
CR4-051B	OEM
CR4-051C	OEM
CR4-101A	OEM
CR4-101B	OEM
CR4-101C	OEM
CR4-201A	OEM
CR4-201B	OEM
CR4-201C	OEM
CR4-301A	OEM
CR4-301B	OEM
CR4-301C	OEM
CR4-401A	OEM
CR4-401B	OEM
CR4-401C	OEM
CR4-501A	OEM
CR4-501B	OEM
CR4-501C	OEM
CR4-601A	OEM
CR4-601B	OEM
CR4-601C	OEM
CR4-701A	OEM
CR4-701B	OEM
CR4-701C	OEM
CR4-801A	OEM
CR4-801B	OEM
CR4-801C	OEM

DEVICE TYPE	REPL CODE
CR4-901A	OEM
CR4-901B	OEM
CR4-901C	OEM
CR4-1001A	OEM
CR4-1001B	OEM
CR4-1001C	OEM
CR4U01FY	5965
CR4U01FY1	OEM
CR4U02FY	5973
CR4U02FY1	OEM
CR4U03FY	5988
CR4U03FY1	OEM
CR4U04FY	5988
CR4U04FY1	OEM
CR4U05FY	6008
CR4U05FY1	OEM
CR4U06FY	6008
CR4U06FY1	OEM
CR4U08FY	OEM
CR4U08FY1	OEM
CR4U10FY	OEM
CR4U10FY1	OEM
CR4UX5FY	6965
CR4UX5FY1	OEM
CR4.021A	OEM
CR4.051A	OEM
CR4.071A	OEM
CR4.101A	OEM
CR4.151A	OEM
CR4.201A	OEM
CR4.251A	OEM
CR4.301A	OEM
CR5-021B	OEM
CR5-051B	OEM
CR5-052AB	OEM
CR5-052BB	OEM
CR5-052CB	OEM
CR5-052DB	OEM
CR5-052EB	OEM
CR5-052GB	OEM
CR5-071B	OEM
CR5-101B	OEM
CR5-102AB	OEM
CR5-102B	OEM
CR5-102BB	OEM
CR5-102CCB	OEM
CR5-102DB	OEM
CR5-102EB	OEM
CR5-102GB	OEM
CR5-201B	OEM
CR5-202AB	OEM
CR5-202B	OEM
CR5-202BB	OEM
CR5-202CB	OEM
CR5-202DB	OEM
CR5-202EB	OEM
CR5-202GB	OEM
CR5-301B	OEM
CR5-302AB	OEM
CR5-302B	OEM
CR5-302BB	OEM
CR5-302CB	OEM
CR5-302DB	OEM
CR5-302EB	OEM
CR5-302GB	OEM
CR5-401B	OEM
CR5-402AB	OEM
CR5-402B	OEM
CR5-402BB	OEM
CR5-402CB	OEM
CR5-402DB	OEM
CR5-402EB	OEM
CR5-402GB	OEM
CR5-501B	OEM
CR5-502AB	OEM
CR5-502B	OEM
CR5-502BB	OEM
CR5-502CB	OEM
CR5-502DB	OEM
CR5-502EB	OEM
CR5-502GB	OEM
CR5-601B	OEM
CR5-602AB	OEM
CR5-602B	OEM
CR5-602BB	OEM
CR5-602CB	OEM
CR5-602DB	OEM
CR5-602EB	OEM
CR5-602GB	OEM
CR5-701B	OEM
CR5-801B	OEM
CR5-1029B	OEM
CR5-2029B	OEM
CR5-3029B	OEM
CR5-4029B	OEM
CR5-5029B	OEM
CR5-6029B	OEM
CR5AS-8	OEM
CR5AS8	OEM
CR5B-6	1478
CR5B-8	1478
CR5B-10	0682
CR5B-12	0682
CR6-051B	OEM
CR6-051BA	OEM
CR6-051C	OEM
CR6-051CA	OEM
CR6-052AB	OEM
CR6-052BB	OEM

DEVICE TYPE	REPL CODE
CR6-052CB	OEM
CR6-101B	OEM
CR6-101BA	OEM
CR6-101C	OEM
CR6-101CA	OEM
CR6-201B	OEM
CR6-201BA	OEM
CR6-201C	OEM
CR6-201CA	OEM
CR6-301B	OEM
CR6-301BA	OEM
CR6-301C	OEM
CR6-301CA	OEM
CR6-401B	OEM
CR6-401BA	OEM
CR6-401C	OEM
CR6-401CA	OEM
CR6-403RB	OEM
CR6-403RBA	OEM
CR6-501B	OEM
CR6-501BA	OEM
CR6-501C	OEM
CR6-501CA	OEM
CR6-503RB	OEM
CR6-503RBA	OEM
CR6-601B	OEM
CR6-601BA	OEM
CR6-601C	OEM
CR6-601CA	OEM
CR6-603RB	OEM
CR6-603RBA	OEM
CR6-703RB	OEM
CR6-703RBA	OEM
CR6-803B	OEM
CR6-803RB	OEM
CR6-803RBA	OEM
CR6-903B	OEM
CR6-903RB	OEM
CR6-903RBA	OEM
CR6-903RC	OEM
CR6-903RCA	OEM
CR6-1003B	OEM
CR6-1003RB	OEM
CR6-1003RBA	OEM
CR6-1003RC	OEM
CR6-1003RCA	OEM
CR6-1103RBA	OEM
CR6-1103RC	OEM
CR6-1103RCA	OEM
CR6-1203B	OEM
CR6-1203RB	OEM
CR6-1203RBA	OEM
CR6-1203RC	OEM
CR6-1203RCA	OEM
CR6-1303RB	OEM
CR6-1303RBA	OEM
CR6-1303RC	OEM
CR6-1303RCA	OEM
CR6-1403RB	OEM
CR6-1403RBA	OEM
CR6-1403RC	OEM
CR6-1403RCA	OEM
CR6-1503RB	OEM
CR6-1503RBA	OEM
CR6-1503RC	OEM
CR6-1503RCA	OEM
CR6AM-2	2078
CR6AM-4	0500
CR6AM-6	0705
CR6AM-8	0705
CR6AM8	OEM
CR6AM10	OEM
CR6AM12	OEM
CR7K103A3	OEM
CR7K103A4	OEM
CR7K103A5	OEM
CR7K103A35	OEM
CR7K103A45	OEM
CR7K203A3	OEM
CR7K203A4	OEM
CR7K203A5	OEM
CR7K203A35	OEM
CR7K203A45	OEM
CR7K303A3	OEM
CR7K303A4	OEM
CR7K303A5	OEM
CR7K303A35	OEM
CR7K303A45	OEM
CR7K403A3	OEM
CR7K403A4	OEM
CR7K403A5	OEM
CR7K403A35	OEM
CR7K403A45	OEM
CR7K503A3	OEM
CR7K503A4	OEM
CR7K503A5	OEM
CR7K503A35	OEM
CR7K503A45	OEM
CR7K603A3	OEM
CR7K603A4	OEM
CR7K603A5	OEM
CR7K603A35	OEM
CR7K603A45	OEM
CR7K703A3	OEM
CR7K703A4	OEM
CR7K703A5	OEM
CR7K703A35	OEM
CR7K703A45	OEM
CR7K803A3	OEM

DEVICE TYPE	REPL CODE
CR7K803A4	OEM
CR7K803A5	OEM
CR7K803A35	OEM
CR7K803A45	OEM
CR7K903A3	OEM
CR7K903A4	OEM
CR7K903A5	OEM
CR7K903A35	OEM
CR7K903A45	OEM
CR7K1003A3	OEM
CR7K1003A4	OEM
CR7K1003A5	OEM
CR7K1003A35	OEM
CR7K1003A45	OEM
CR7K1103A3	OEM
CR7K1103A4	OEM
CR7K1103A5	OEM
CR7K1103A35	OEM
CR7K1103A45	OEM
CR7K1203A3	OEM
CR7K1203A4	OEM
CR7K1203A5	OEM
CR7K1203A35	OEM
CR7K1203A45	OEM
CR7K1303A3	OEM
CR7K1303A4	OEM
CR7K1303A5	OEM
CR7K1303A35	OEM
CR7K1303A45	OEM
CR7K1403A3	OEM
CR7K1403A4	OEM
CR7K1403A5	OEM
CR7K1403A35	OEM
CR7K1403A45	OEM
CR7K1503A3	OEM
CR7K1503A4	OEM
CR7K1503A5	OEM
CR7K1503A35	OEM
CR7K1503A45	OEM
CR7K1603A4	OEM
CR7K1603A5	OEM
CR7K1603A35	OEM
CR7K1603A45	OEM
CR7K1703A4	OEM
CR7K1703A5	OEM
CR7K1703A45	OEM
CR7K1803A4	OEM
CR7K1803A5	OEM
CR7K1803A45	OEM
CR7K1903A5	OEM
CR7K1903A45	OEM
CR7K2003A5	OEM
CR7K2003A45	OEM
CR7K2103A5	OEM
CR7K2103A45	OEM
CR7K2203A5	OEM
CR7K2203A45	OEM
CR7K2303A5	OEM
CR8-051A	OEM
CR8-051B	OEM
CR8-051C	OEM
CR8-101A	OEM
CR8-101B	OEM
CR8-101C	OEM
CR8-102CC	OEM
CR8-201A	OEM
CR8-201B	OEM
CR8-201C	OEM
CR8-202BC	OEM
CR8-301A	OEM
CR8-301B	OEM
CR8-301C	OEM
CR8-302GC	OEM
CR8-401A	OEM
CR8-401B	OEM
CR8-401C	OEM
CR8-501A	OEM
CR8-501B	OEM
CR8-501C	OEM
CR8-601A	OEM
CR8-601B	OEM
CR8-601C	OEM
CR8-701A	OEM
CR8-701B	OEM
CR8-701C	OEM
CR8-801A	OEM
CR8-801B	OEM
CR8-801C	OEM
CR8-901A	OEM
CR8-901B	OEM
CR8-901C	OEM
CR8-1001A	OEM
CR8-1001B	OEM
CR8-1001C	OEM
CR8AM8	OEM
CR8U01FY	OEM
CR8U02FY	OEM
CR8U02FY1	OEM
CR8U03FY	OEM
CR8U03FY1	OEM
CR8U04FY	OEM
CR8U04FY1	OEM
CR8U05FY	OEM
CR8U05FY1	OEM
CR8U06FY	OEM
CR8U06FY1	OEM
CR8U08FY	OEM
CR8U08FY1	OEM
CR8U10FY	OEM

If replacement code is OEM, contact original manufacturer for replacement.

347

DEVICE TYPE	REPL CODE
CR8U10FY1	OEM
CR8UX5FY	OEM
CR8UX5FY1	OEM
CR8.021A	OEM
CR8.051A	OEM
CR8.071A	OEM
CR8.101A	OEM
CR8.151A	OEM
CR8.201A	OEM
CR8.251A	OEM
CR8.301A	OEM
CR9K403A2	OEM
CR9K403A25	OEM
CR9K503A2	OEM
CR9K503A25	OEM
CR9K603A2	OEM
CR9K603A25	OEM
CR9K703A2	OEM
CR9K703A25	OEM
CR9K803A2	OEM
CR9K803A25	OEM
CR9K903A25	OEM
CR9K1003A25	OEM
CR9K1103A25	OEM
CR9K1203A25	OEM
CR9K1303A25	OEM
CR9K1403A25	OEM
CR9K1503A25	OEM
CR10	OEM
CR10-051B	OEM
CR10-052AB	OEM
CR10-052BB	OEM
CR10-052CB	OEM
CR10-052DB	OEM
CR10-052EB	OEM
CR10-052GB	OEM
CR10-101B	OEM
CR10-102AB	OEM
CR10-102B	OEM
CR10-102BB	OEM
CR10-102CB	OEM
CR10-102DB	OEM
CR10-102EB	OEM
CR10-102GB	OEM
CR10-201B	OEM
CR10-202AB	OEM
CR10-202B	OEM
CR10-202BB	OEM
CR10-202CB	OEM
CR10-202DB	OEM
CR10-202EB	OEM
CR10-202GB	OEM
CR10-301B	OEM
CR10-302AB	OEM
CR10-302B	OEM
CR10-302BB	OEM
CR10-302CB	OEM
CR10-302DB	OEM
CR10-302EB	OEM
CR10-302GB	OEM
CR10-401B	OEM
CR10-402AB	OEM
CR10-402B	OEM
CR10-402BB	OEM
CR10-402CB	OEM
CR10-402DB	OEM
CR10-402EB	OEM
CR10-402GB	OEM
CR10-501B	OEM
CR10-502AB	OEM
CR10-502B	OEM
CR10-502BB	OEM
CR10-502CB	OEM
CR10-502DB	OEM
CR10-502EB	OEM
CR10-502GB	OEM
CR10-601B	OEM
CR10-602AB	OEM
CR10-602B	OEM
CR10-602BB	OEM
CR10-602CB	OEM
CR10-602DB	OEM
CR10-602EB	OEM
CR10-701B	OEM
CR10-1001B	OEM
CR10-1029B	OEM
CR10-2029B	OEM
CR10-3029B	OEM
CR10-4029B	OEM
CR10-5029B	OEM
CR10-6029B	OEM
CR10A	OEM
CR10B	OEM
CR10B-1	2430
CR10B-2	2430
CR10B2	OEM
CR10B-4	0430
CR10B4	OEM
CR10B-6	1478
CR10B6	OEM
CR10B-8	1478
CR10B8	OEM
CR10B-10	0682
CR10B10	OEM
CR10B-12	0682
CR10B12	OEM
CR10B16	OEM
CR10C	OEM
CR10C2	0562
CR10C4	0757
CR10C6	0735
CR10C8	0735
CR10C10	0759
CR10C12	0759
CR10C16	0761
CR10CY2	OEM
CR10CY4	OEM
CR10CY6	OEM
CR10CY8	OEM
CR10CY10	OEM
CR10CY12	OEM
CR10D	OEM
CR10E	OEM
CR10EY2	OEM
CR10EY4	OEM
CR10EY6	OEM
CR10EY10	OEM
CR10EY12	OEM
CR10F	OEM
CR10G	OEM
CR10H	OEM
CR12-051B	0464
CR12-051BA	0464
CR12-051C	OEM
CR12-051CA	OEM
CR12-052AB	OEM
CR12-052BB	OEM
CR12-052CB	OEM
CR12-101B	0464
CR12-101BA	0464
CR12-101C	OEM
CR12-101CA	OEM
CR12-201B	0464
CR12-201BA	0464
CR12-201C	OEM
CR12-201CA	OEM
CR12-301B	0717
CR12-301BA	0717
CR12-301C	OEM
CR12-301CA	OEM
CR12-401B	0717
CR12-401BA	0717
CR12-401C	OEM
CR12-401CA	OEM
CR12-403RB	OEM
CR12-403RBA	OEM
CR12-501B	0720
CR12-501BA	0720
CR12-501C	OEM
CR12-501CA	OEM
CR12-503RB	OEM
CR12-503RBA	OEM
CR12-601B	0720
CR12-601BA	0720
CR12-601C	OEM
CR12-601CA	OEM
CR12-603RB	OEM
CR12-603RBA	OEM
CR12-703RB	OEM
CR12-703RBA	OEM
CR12-803B	OEM
CR12-803RB	OEM
CR12-803RBA	OEM
CR12-903B	OEM
CR12-903RB	0674
CR12-903RBA	0674
CR12-903RC	OEM
CR12-903RCA	OEM
CR12-1003B	OEM
CR12-1003RB	0674
CR12-1003RBA	0674
CR12-1003RC	OEM
CR12-1003RCA	OEM
CR12-1103B	OEM
CR12-1103RB	0674
CR12-1103RBA	0674
CR12-1103RC	OEM
CR12-1103RCA	OEM
CR12-1203B	OEM
CR12-1203RB	0674
CR12-1203RBA	0674
CR12-1203RC	OEM
CR12-1203RCA	OEM
CR12-1303RB	OEM
CR12-1303RBA	OEM
CR12-1303RC	0674
CR12-1303RCA	0674
CR12-1403RB	OEM
CR12-1403RBA	OEM
CR12-1403RC	OEM
CR12-1403RCA	OEM
CR12-1503RB	OEM
CR12-1503RBA	OEM
CR12-1503RC	OEM
CR12-1503RCA	OEM
CR12A-6	2623
CR12A-8	2623
CR12A-10	0747
CR12A-12	0759
CR12A-14	0761
CR12A-16	0761
CR12J02JY1	OEM
CR12M01JY	OEM
CR12M01JY1	OEM
CR12M02JY	OEM
CR12M02JY1	OEM
CR12M03JY	OEM
CR12M03JY1	OEM
CR12M04JY	OEM
CR12M04JY1	OEM
CR12M05JY	OEM
CR12M05JY1	OEM
CR12M06JY	OEM
CR12M06JY1	OEM
CR12M08JY	OEM
CR12M08JY1	OEM
CR12M10JY	OEM
CR12M10JY1	OEM
CR12M11JY	OEM
CR12M11JY1	OEM
CR12M12JY	OEM
CR12M12JY1	OEM
CR12M13JY	OEM
CR12M13JY1	OEM
CR12M14JY	OEM
CR12M14JY1	OEM
CR12MX5JY1	OEM
CR12U01JY	OEM
CR12U01JY1	OEM
CR12U02JY	OEM
CR12U03JY	OEM
CR12U03JY1	OEM
CR12U04JY	OEM
CR12U04JY1	OEM
CR12U05JY	OEM
CR12U05JY1	OEM
CR12U06JY	OEM
CR12U06JY1	OEM
CR12U08JY	OEM
CR12U08JY1	OEM
CR12U10JY	OEM
CR12U10JY1	OEM
CR12U11JY	OEM
CR12U11JY1	OEM
CR12U12JY	OEM
CR12U12JY1	OEM
CR12U13JY	OEM
CR12U13JY1	OEM
CR12U14JY	OEM
CR12U14JY1	OEM
CR12UX5JY	OEM
CR12UX5JY1	OEM
CR16-051B	OEM
CR16-052AB	OEM
CR16-052BB	OEM
CR16-052CB	OEM
CR16-052DB	OEM
CR16-052EB	OEM
CR16-052GB	OEM
CR16-101B	OEM
CR16-102AB	OEM
CR16-102B	OEM
CR16-102BB	OEM
CR16-102CB	OEM
CR16-102DB	OEM
CR16-102EB	OEM
CR16-102GB	OEM
CR16-201B	OEM
CR16-202AB	OEM
CR16-202B	OEM
CR16-202BB	OEM
CR16-202CB	OEM
CR16-202DB	OEM
CR16-202EB	OEM
CR16-202GB	OEM
CR16-301B	OEM
CR16-302AB	OEM
CR16-302B	OEM
CR16-302BB	OEM
CR16-302CB	OEM
CR16-302DB	OEM
CR16-302EB	OEM
CR16-302GB	OEM
CR16-401B	OEM
CR16-402AB	OEM
CR16-402B	OEM
CR16-402BB	OEM
CR16-402CB	OEM
CR16-402DB	OEM
CR16-402EB	OEM
CR16-402GB	OEM
CR16-501B	OEM
CR16-502AB	OEM
CR16-502B	OEM
CR16-502BB	OEM
CR16-502CB	OEM
CR16-502DB	OEM
CR16-502EB	OEM
CR16-502GB	OEM
CR16-601B	OEM
CR16-602AB	OEM
CR16-602B	OEM
CR16-602BB	OEM
CR16-602CB	OEM
CR16-602DB	OEM
CR16-602EB	OEM
CR16-602GB	OEM
CR16-701B	OEM
CR16-801B	OEM
CR16-1029B	OEM
CR16-2029B	OEM
CR16-3029B	OEM
CR16-4029B	OEM
CR16-5029B	OEM
CR16-6029B	OEM
CR16A	OEM
CR16C	OEM
CR16D	OEM
CR16E	OEM
CR16F	OEM
CR16G	OEM
CR16H	OEM
CR18-051B	0464
CR18-051BA	0464
CR18-051C	OEM
CR18-051CA	OEM
CR18-052AB	OEM
CR18-052BB	OEM
CR18-052CB	OEM
CR18-101B	0464
CR18-101BA	OEM
CR18-101C	OEM
CR18-101CA	OEM
CR18-101RA	0464
CR18-201B	0464
CR18-201BA	0464
CR18-201C	OEM
CR18-201CA	OEM
CR18-301B	0717
CR18-301BA	0717
CR18-301C	OEM
CR18-301CA	OEM
CR18-303RCA	OEM
CR18-401B	0717
CR18-401BA	0717
CR18-401C	OEM
CR18-401CA	OEM
CR18-402AB	OEM
CR18-403RB	OEM
CR18-403RBA	OEM
CR18-501B	0720
CR18-501BA	0720
CR18-501C	OEM
CR18-501CA	OEM
CR18-503RB	OEM
CR18-503RBA	OEM
CR18-601B	0720
CR18-601BA	0720
CR18-601C	OEM
CR18-601CA	OEM
CR18-603RB	OEM
CR18-603RBA	OEM
CR18-703RB	OEM
CR18-703RBA	OEM
CR18-803B	OEM
CR18-803RB	OEM
CR18-803RBA	OEM
CR18-903B	OEM
CR18-903RB	0674
CR18-903RBA	0674
CR18-903RBAC	OEM
CR18-903RBC	OEM
CR18-903RC	OEM
CR18-903RCA	OEM
CR18-903RCAC	OEM
CR18-903RCC	OEM
CR18-1003B	OEM
CR18-1003RB	0674
CR18-1003RBA	0674
CR18-1003RBAC	OEM
CR18-1003RBC	OEM
CR18-1003RC	OEM
CR18-1003RCA	OEM
CR18-1003RCAC	OEM
CR18-1003RCC	OEM
CR18-1103RB	0674
CR18-1103RBA	0674
CR18-1103RBAC	OEM
CR18-1103RBC	OEM
CR18-1103RC	OEM
CR18-1103RCA	OEM
CR18-1103RCAC	OEM
CR18-1103RCC	OEM
CR18-1203B	OEM
CR18-1203RB	0674
CR18-1203RBA	0674
CR18-1203RBAC	OEM
CR18-1203RBC	OEM
CR18-1203RC	OEM
CR18-1203RCA	OEM
CR18-1203RCAC	OEM
CR18-1203RCC	OEM
CR18-1303RB	0674
CR18-1303RBA	0674
CR18-1303RBAC	OEM
CR18-1303RBC	OEM
CR18-1303RC	OEM
CR18-1303RCAC	OEM
CR18-1303RCC	OEM
CR18-1403RB	OEM
CR18-1403RBA	OEM
CR18-1403RBAC	OEM
CR18-1403RBC	OEM
CR18-1403RC	OEM
CR18-1403RCA	OEM
CR18-1403RCAC	OEM
CR18-1403RCC	OEM
CR18-1503RB	OEM
CR18-1503RBA	OEM
CR18-1503RBAC	OEM
CR18-1503RBC	OEM
CR18-1503RC	OEM
CR18-1503RCA	OEM
CR18-1503RCAC	OEM
CR18-1503RCC	OEM
CR20-051B	OEM
CR20-051BA	OEM
CR20-051C	OEM
CR20-051CA	OEM
CR20-101B	OEM
CR20-101BA	OEM
CR20-101C	OEM
CR20-101CA	OEM
CR20-201B	OEM
CR20-201BA	OEM
CR20-201C	OEM
CR20-201CA	OEM
CR20-301B	OEM
CR20-301BA	OEM
CR20-301C	OEM
CR20-301CA	OEM
CR20-401B	OEM
CR20-401BA	OEM
CR20-401C	OEM
CR20-401CA	OEM
CR20-501B	OEM
CR20-501BA	OEM
CR20-501C	OEM
CR20-501CA	OEM
CR20-601B	OEM
CR20-601BA	OEM
CR20-601C	OEM
CR20-601CA	OEM
CR20-903RB	OEM
CR20-903RBA	OEM
CR20-903RBAC	OEM
CR20-903RBC	OEM
CR20-903RC	OEM
CR20-903RCA	OEM
CR20-903RCAC	OEM
CR20-903RCC	OEM
CR20-1003RB	OEM
CR20-1003RBA	OEM
CR20-1003RBAC	OEM
CR20-1003RBC	OEM
CR20-1003RC	OEM
CR20-1003RCA	OEM
CR20-1003RCAC	OEM
CR20-1003RCC	OEM
CR20-1103RB	OEM
CR20-1103RBA	OEM
CR20-1103RBAC	OEM
CR20-1103RBC	OEM
CR20-1103RC	OEM
CR20-1103RCA	OEM
CR20-1103RCAC	OEM
CR20-1103RCC	OEM
CR20-1203RB	OEM
CR20-1203RBA	OEM
CR20-1203RBAC	OEM
CR20-1203RBC	OEM
CR20-1203RC	OEM
CR20-1203RCA	OEM
CR20-1203RCAC	OEM
CR20-1203RCC	OEM
CR20-1303RB	OEM
CR20-1303RBA	OEM
CR20-1303RBAC	OEM
CR20-1303RBC	OEM
CR20-1303RC	OEM
CR20-1303RCA	OEM
CR20-1303RCAC	OEM
CR20-1303RCC	OEM
CR20-1403RB	OEM
CR20-1403RBA	OEM
CR20-1403RBAC	OEM
CR20-1403RBC	OEM
CR20-1403RC	OEM
CR20-1403RCA	OEM
CR20-1403RCAC	OEM
CR20-1403RCC	OEM
CR20-1503RB	OEM
CR20-1503RBA	OEM
CR20-1503RBAC	OEM
CR20-1503RBC	OEM
CR20-1503RC	OEM
CR20-1503RCA	OEM
CR20-1503RCAC	OEM
CR20-1503RCC	OEM
CR20A-1	2497
CR20A-2	0226
CR20A2	OEM
CR20A-4	1640
CR20A4	OEM
CR20A-6	2623
CR20A6	OEM
CR20A-8	2623
CR20A8	OEM
CR20A-10	0747
CR20A10	OEM
CR20A-12	0720
CR20A12	OEM
CR20A-14	0745
CR20A-16	0745
CR20A16	OEM
CR20A20	OEM
CR20AY-2	0799
CR20AY-4	0799
CR20AY-6	0799
CR20AY-8	0799
CR20AY-10	0799
CR20AY-12	0799
CR20EY2	OEM
CR20EY4	OEM
CR20EY6	OEM
CR20EY8	OEM
CR20EY10	OEM
CR20EY12	OEM
CR20EY16	OEM
CR20F2	OEM
CR20F4	OEM
CR20F6	OEM
CR20F8	OEM
CR20F10	OEM
CR20F12	OEM
CR20F16	OEM
CR20F20	OEM
CR20F24	OEM
CR20M01JY	OEM
CR20M01JY1	OEM
CR20M02JY	OEM
CR20M02JY1	OEM
CR20M03JY	OEM
CR20M03JY1	OEM
CR20M04JY	OEM
CR20M04JY1	OEM
CR20M05JY	OEM
CR20M05JY1	OEM
CR20M06JY	OEM
CR20M06JY1	OEM
CR20M08JY	OEM
CR20M08JY1	OEM
CR20M10JY	OEM
CR20M10JY1	OEM
CR20M11JY	OEM
CR20M11JY1	OEM
CR20M12JY	OEM
CR20M12JY1	OEM
CR20M13JY	OEM
CR20M13JY1	OEM
CR20M14JY	OEM
CR20M14JY1	OEM
CR20MX5JY	OEM
CR20MX5JY1	OEM
CR20U01JY	OEM
CR20U01JY1	OEM
CR20U02JY	OEM
CR20U02JY1	OEM
CR20U03JY	OEM
CR20U03JY1	OEM
CR20U04JY	OEM
CR20U04JY1	OEM
CR20U05JY	OEM
CR20U05JY1	OEM
CR20U06JY	OEM
CR20U06JY1	OEM
CR20U08JY	OEM
CR20U08JY1	OEM
CR20U10JY	OEM
CR20U10JY1	OEM
CR20U11JY	OEM
CR20U11JY1	OEM
CR20U12JY	OEM
CR20U12JY1	OEM
CR20U13JY	OEM
CR20U13JY1	OEM
CR20U14JY	OEM
CR20U14JY1	OEM
CR20UX5JY	OEM
CR20UX5JY1	OEM
CR24-051B	OEM
CR24-051BC	OEM
CR24-051C	OEM
CR24-051CC	OEM
CR24-052AB	OEM
CR24-052BB	OEM
CR24-052CB	OEM
CR24-101B	OEM
CR24-101BC	OEM
CR24-101C	OEM
CR24-101CC	OEM
CR24-201B	OEM
CR24-201BC	OEM
CR24-201C	OEM
CR24-201CC	OEM
CR24-301B	OEM
CR24-301BC	OEM
CR24-301C	OEM
CR24-301CC	OEM
CR24-401B	OEM
CR24-401BC	OEM
CR24-401C	OEM
CR24-401CC	OEM
CR24-403RB	OEM
CR24-403RBA	OEM
CR24-501B	OEM
CR24-501BC	OEM
CR24-501C	OEM
CR24-501CC	OEM
CR24-503RB	OEM
CR24-503RBA	OEM
CR24-601B	OEM
CR24-601BC	OEM
CR24-601C	OEM
CR24-601CC	OEM
CR24-603RB	OEM
CR24-603RBA	OEM
CR24-703RB	OEM
CR24-703RBA	OEM
CR24-803B	OEM
CR24-803RB	OEM
CR24-803RBA	OEM
CR24-903B	OEM
CR24-903RB	OEM
CR24-903RBA	OEM
CR24-903RBAC	OEM
CR24-903RBC	OEM
CR24-903RC	OEM
CR24-903RCA	OEM
CR24-903RCAC	OEM
CR24-903RCC	OEM
CR24-1003B	OEM
CR24-1003RB	OEM
CR24-1003RBA	OEM
CR24-1003RBAC	OEM
CR24-1003RBC	OEM
CR24-1003RC	OEM
CR24-1003RCA	OEM
CR24-1003RCAC	OEM
CR24-1003RCC	OEM
CR24-1103RB	OEM
CR24-1103RBA	OEM
CR24-1103RBAC	OEM
CR24-1103RBC	OEM
CR24-1103RC	OEM
CR24-1103RCA	OEM
CR24-1103RCAC	OEM
CR24-1103RCC	OEM
CR24-1203B	OEM
CR24-1203RB	OEM
CR24-1203RBA	OEM
CR24-1203RBAC	OEM
CR24-1203RBC	OEM
CR24-1203RC	OEM
CR24-1203RCA	OEM
CR24-1203RCAC	OEM
CR24-1203RCC	OEM
CR24-1303RB	OEM
CR24-1303RBA	OEM
CR24-1303RBAC	OEM
CR24-1303RBC	OEM
CR24-1303RC	OEM
CR24-1303RCA	OEM
CR24-1303RCAC	OEM
CR24-1303RCC	OEM
CR24-1403RB	OEM
CR24-1403RBA	OEM
CR24-1403RBAC	OEM
CR24-1403RBC	OEM
CR24-1403RC	OEM
CR24-1403RCA	OEM
CR24-1403RCAC	OEM
CR24-1403RCC	OEM
CR24-1503RB	OEM
CR24-1503RBA	OEM
CR24-1503RBAC	OEM
CR24-1503RBC	OEM
CR24-1503RC	OEM
CR24-1503RCA	OEM
CR24-1503RCAC	OEM
CR24-1503RCC	OEM
CR24M01JY	OEM
CR24M01JY1	OEM
CR24M02JY	OEM
CR24M02JY1	OEM
CR24M03JY	OEM
CR24M03JY1	OEM
CR24M04JY	OEM
CR24M04JY1	OEM
CR24M05JY	OEM
CR24M05JY1	OEM
CR24M06JY	OEM
CR24M06JY1	OEM
CR24M08JY	OEM
CR24M08JY1	OEM
CR24M10JY	OEM
CR24M10JY1	OEM
CR24M11JY	OEM
CR24M11JY1	OEM
CR24M12JY	OEM
CR24M12JY1	OEM
CR24M13JY	OEM
CR24M13JY1	OEM
CR24M14JY	OEM
CR24M14JY1	OEM
CR24MX5JY	OEM
CR24MX5JY1	OEM
CR24U01JY	OEM
CR24U01JY1	OEM
CR24U02JY	OEM
CR24U02JY1	OEM
CR24U03JY	OEM
CR24U03JY1	OEM
CR24U04JY	OEM
CR24U04JY1	OEM
CR24U05JY	OEM
CR24U05JY1	OEM
CR24U06JY	OEM
CR24U06JY1	OEM
CR24U08JY	OEM
CR24U08JY1	OEM
CR24U10JY	OEM
CR24U10JY1	OEM
CR24U11JY	OEM
CR24U11JY1	OEM
CR24U12JY	OEM
CR24U12JY1	OEM
CR24U13JY	OEM
CR24U13JY1	OEM
CR24U14JY	OEM
CR24U14JY1	OEM
CR24UX5JY	OEM
CR24UX5JY1	OEM

If replacement code is OEM, contact original manufacturer for replacement.

DEVICE TYPE	REPL CODE
CR25-051B	OEM
CR25-101B	OEM
CR25-201B	OEM
CR25-301B	OEM
CR25-401B	OEM
CR25-501B	OEM
CR25-601B	OEM
CR25-701B	OEM
CR25-801B	OEM
CR27-051B	OEM
CR27-051BA	OEM
CR27-051C	OEM
CR27-051CA	OEM
CR27-101B	OEM
CR27-101BA	OEM
CR27-101C	OEM
CR27-101CA	OEM
CR27-201B	OEM
CR27-201BA	OEM
CR27-201C	OEM
CR27-201CA	OEM
CR27-301B	OEM
CR27-301BA	OEM
CR27-301C	OEM
CR27-301CA	OEM
CR27-401B	OEM
CR27-401BA	OEM
CR27-401C	OEM
CR27-401CA	OEM
CR27-501B	OEM
CR27-501BA	OEM
CR27-501C	OEM
CR27-501CA	OEM
CR27-601B	OEM
CR27-601BA	OEM
CR27-601C	OEM
CR27-601CA	OEM
CR27-903RB	OEM
CR27-903RBA	OEM
CR27-903RC	OEM
CR27-903RCA	OEM
CR27-1003RB	OEM
CR27-1003RBA	OEM
CR27-1003RC	OEM
CR27-1003RCA	OEM
CR27-1103RB	OEM
CR27-1103RBA	OEM
CR27-1103RC	OEM
CR27-1103RCA	OEM
CR27-1203RB	OEM
CR27-1203RBA	OEM
CR27-1203RC	OEM
CR27-1203RCA	OEM
CR27-1303RB	OEM
CR27-1303RBA	OEM
CR27-1303RC	OEM
CR27-1303RCA	OEM
CR27-1403RB	OEM
CR27-1403RBA	OEM
CR27-1403RC	OEM
CR27-1403RCA	OEM
CR27-1503RB	OEM
CR27-1503RBA	OEM
CR27-1503RC	OEM
CR27-1503RCA	OEM
CR28-051B	OEM
CR28-051BA	OEM
CR28-051C	OEM
CR28-051CA	OEM
CR28-101B	OEM
CR28-101BA	OEM
CR28-101C	OEM
CR28-101CA	OEM
CR28-201B	OEM
CR28-201BA	OEM
CR28-201C	OEM
CR28-201CA	OEM
CR28-301B	OEM
CR28-301BA	OEM
CR28-301C	OEM
CR28-301CA	OEM
CR28-401B	OEM
CR28-401BA	OEM
CR28-401C	OEM
CR28-401CA	OEM
CR28-501B	OEM
CR28-501BA	OEM
CR28-501C	OEM
CR28-501CA	OEM
CR28-601B	OEM
CR28-601BA	OEM
CR28-601C	OEM
CR28-601CA	OEM
CR28-903RB	OEM
CR28-903RBA	OEM
CR28-903RC	OEM
CR28-903RCA	OEM
CR28-1003RB	OEM
CR28-1003RBA	OEM
CR28-1003RC	OEM
CR28-1003RCA	OEM
CR28-1103RB	OEM
CR28-1103RBA	OEM
CR28-1103RC	OEM
CR28-1103RCA	OEM
CR28-1203RB	OEM
CR28-1203RBA	OEM
CR28-1203RC	OEM
CR28-1203RCA	OEM

DEVICE TYPE	REPL CODE
CR28-1303RB	OEM
CR28-1303RBA	OEM
CR28-1303RC	OEM
CR28-1303RCA	OEM
CR28-1403RB	OEM
CR28-1403RBA	OEM
CR28-1403RC	OEM
CR28-1403RCA	OEM
CR28-1503RB	OEM
CR28-1503RBA	OEM
CR28-1503RC	OEM
CR28-1503RCA	OEM
CR30-01	OEM
CR30-02	OEM
CR30-04	OEM
CR30-06	OEM
CR30-08	OEM
CR30-053A	OEM
CR30-10	OEM
CR30-103A	OEM
CR30-103AA	OEM
CR30-104A	OEM
CR30-104LA	OEM
CR30-203A	OEM
CR30-203AA	OEM
CR30-204A	OEM
CR30-204LA	OEM
CR30-303A	OEM
CR30-303AA	OEM
CR30-304A	OEM
CR30-304LA	OEM
CR30-403A	OEM
CR30-403AA	OEM
CR30-404A	OEM
CR30-503A	OEM
CR30-503AA	OEM
CR30-504A	OEM
CR30-504LA	OEM
CR30-603A	OEM
CR30-603AA	OEM
CR30-604A	OEM
CR30-604LA	OEM
CR30-703A	OEM
CR30-703AA	OEM
CR30-704LA	OEM
CR30-803A	OEM
CR30-803AA	OEM
CR30-804LA	OEM
CR30-903A	OEM
CR30-903AA	OEM
CR30-904LA	OEM
CR30-1003A	OEM
CR30-1003AA	OEM
CR30-1004LA	OEM
CR30-1103A	OEM
CR30-1103AA	OEM
CR30-1104LA	OEM
CR30-1203A	OEM
CR30-1203AA	OEM
CR30-1204LA	OEM
CR30-1303A	OEM
CR30-1303AA	OEM
CR30-1403A	OEM
CR30-1403AA	OEM
CR31-103A	0463
CR31-104LA	OEM
CR31-203A	0733
CR31-204LA	OEM
CR31-303A	0463
CR31-304LA	OEM
CR31-403A	0463
CR31-403AA	OEM
CR31-404LA	OEM
CR31-503A	0463
CR31-503AA	0463
CR31-504LA	OEM
CR31-603A	0463
CR31-603AA	0463
CR31-604LA	OEM
CR31-703A	0463
CR31-703AA	0463
CR31-704LA	OEM
CR31-803A	0463
CR31-803AA	0463
CR31-804LA	OEM
CR31-903A	0463
CR31-903AA	0463
CR31-904LA	OEM
CR31-1003A	0463
CR31-1003AA	0463
CR31-1004LA	OEM
CR31-1103A	0463
CR31-1103AA	0463
CR31-1104LA	OEM
CR31-1203A	0463
CR31-1203AA	0463
CR31-1204LA	OEM
CR31-1303A	0463
CR31-1303AA	0463
CR32M01JY	OEM
CR32M01JY1	OEM
CR32M02JY	OEM
CR32M02JY1	OEM
CR32M03JY	OEM
CR32M03JY1	OEM
CR32M04JY	OEM
CR32M04JY1	OEM
CR32M05JY	OEM
CR32M05JY1	OEM

DEVICE TYPE	REPL CODE
CR32M06JY	OEM
CR32M06JY1	OEM
CR32M08JY	OEM
CR32M08JY1	OEM
CR32M10JY	OEM
CR32M10JY1	OEM
CR32M11JY	OEM
CR32M11JY1	OEM
CR32M12JY	OEM
CR32M12JY1	OEM
CR32M13JY	OEM
CR32M13JY1	OEM
CR32M14JY	OEM
CR32M14JY1	OEM
CR32MX5JY	OEM
CR32MX5JY1	OEM
CR32U01JY	OEM
CR32U01JY1	OEM
CR32U02JY	OEM
CR32U02JY1	OEM
CR32U03JY	OEM
CR32U03JY1	OEM
CR32U04JY	OEM
CR32U04JY1	OEM
CR32U05JY	OEM
CR32U05JY1	OEM
CR32U06JY	OEM
CR32U06JY1	OEM
CR32U08JY	OEM
CR32U08JY1	OEM
CR32U10JY	OEM
CR32U10JY1	OEM
CR32U11JY	OEM
CR32U11JY1	OEM
CR32U12JY	OEM
CR32U12JY1	OEM
CR32U13JY	OEM
CR32U13JY1	OEM
CR32U14JY	OEM
CR32U14JY1	OEM
CR32UX5JY	OEM
CR32UX5JY1	OEM
CR33J03JY1	OEM
CR33M01JY	OEM
CR33M01JY1	OEM
CR33M02JY	OEM
CR33M02JY1	OEM
CR33M03JY	OEM
CR33M03JY1	OEM
CR33M04JY	OEM
CR33M04JY1	OEM
CR33M05JY	OEM
CR33M05JY1	OEM
CR33M06JY	OEM
CR33M06JY1	OEM
CR33M08JY	OEM
CR33M08JY1	OEM
CR33M10JY	OEM
CR33M10JY1	OEM
CR33M11JY	OEM
CR33M11JY1	OEM
CR33M12JY	OEM
CR33M12JY1	OEM
CR33M13JY	OEM
CR33M13JY1	OEM
CR33M14JY	OEM
CR33M14JY1	OEM
CR33MX5JY	OEM
CR33MX5JY1	OEM
CR33U01JY	OEM
CR33U01JY1	OEM
CR33U02JY	OEM
CR33U02JY1	OEM
CR33U03JY	OEM
CR33U04JY	OEM
CR33U04JY1	OEM
CR33U05JY	OEM
CR33U05JY1	OEM
CR33U06JY	OEM
CR33U06JY1	OEM
CR33U08JY	OEM
CR33U08JY1	OEM
CR33U10JY	OEM
CR33U10JY1	OEM
CR33U11JY	OEM
CR33U11JY1	OEM
CR33U12JY	OEM
CR33U12JY1	OEM
CR33U13JY	OEM
CR33U13JY1	OEM
CR33U14JY	OEM
CR33U14JY1	OEM
CR33UX5JY	OEM
CR33UX5JY1	OEM
CR40A4	OEM
CR40A6	OEM
CR40A8	OEM
CR40A10	OEM
CR40A12	OEM
CR40A16	OEM
CR40A20	OEM
CR45U01JY	OEM
CR45U01JY1	OEM
CR45U02JY	OEM
CR45U02JY1	OEM
CR45U03JY	OEM
CR45U03JY1	OEM
CR45U04JY	OEM
CR45U04JY1	OEM

DEVICE TYPE	REPL CODE
CR45U05JY	OEM
CR45U05JY1	OEM
CR45U06JY	OEM
CR45U06JY1	OEM
CR45U08JY	OEM
CR45U08JY1	OEM
CR45U10JY	OEM
CR45U10JY1	OEM
CR45U11JY	OEM
CR45U11JY1	OEM
CR45U12JY	OEM
CR45U12JY1	OEM
CR45U13JY	OEM
CR45U13JY1	OEM
CR45U14JY	OEM
CR45U14JY1	OEM
CR45UX5JY	OEM
CR45UX5JY1	OEM
CR46U01JY	OEM
CR46U01JY1	OEM
CR46U02JY	OEM
CR46U02JY1	OEM
CR46U03JY	OEM
CR46U03JY1	OEM
CR46U04JY	OEM
CR46U04JY1	OEM
CR46U05JY	OEM
CR46U05JY1	OEM
CR46U06JY	OEM
CR46U06JY1	OEM
CR46UX5JY	OEM
CR46UX5JY1	OEM
CR50	OEM
CR50-01	OEM
CR50-02	OEM
CR50-04	OEM
CR50-06	OEM
CR50-08	OEM
CR50-053A	OEM
CR50-10	OEM
CR50-104A	OEM
CR50-204A	OEM
CR50-304A	OEM
CR50-404A	OEM
CR50-504A	OEM
CR50-604A	OEM
CR50-1004AA	OEM
CR50-1104AA	OEM
CR50-1204AA	OEM
CR51-103A	0463
CR51-203A	0463
CR51-303A	0463
CR51-503A	0463
CR51-503AA	0463
CR51-603A	0463
CR51-603AA	0463
CR51-703A	0463
CR51-703AA	0463
CR51-803A	0463
CR51-803AA	0463
CR51-804AA	OEM
CR51-804BA	OEM
CR51-804CA	OEM
CR51-903A	0463
CR51-903AA	0463
CR51-904AA	OEM
CR51-904BA	OEM
CR51-904CA	OEM
CR51-1003A	0463
CR51-1003AA	0463
CR51-1004AA	OEM
CR51-1103A	0463
CR51-1103AA	0463
CR51-1104AA	OEM
CR51-1203A	0463
CR51-1203AA	0463
CR51-1204AA	OEM
CR51-1303A	0463
CR51-1303AA	0463
CR51J06JY	OEM
CR51M01JY	OEM
CR51M01JY1	OEM
CR51M02JY	OEM
CR51M02JY1	OEM
CR51M03JY	OEM
CR51M03JY1	OEM
CR51M04JY	OEM
CR51M04JY1	OEM
CR51M05JY	OEM
CR51M05JY1	OEM
CR51M06JY1	OEM
CR51M08JY	OEM
CR51M08JY1	OEM
CR51M10JY	OEM
CR51M10JY1	OEM
CR51M11JY	OEM
CR51M11JY1	OEM
CR51M12JY	OEM
CR51M12JY1	OEM
CR51M13JY	OEM
CR51M13JY1	OEM
CR51M14JY	OEM
CR51M14JY1	OEM
CR51MX5JY	OEM
CR51MX5JY1	OEM
CR51U01JY	OEM
CR51U01JY1	OEM
CR51U02JY	OEM
CR51U02JY1	OEM

DEVICE TYPE	REPL CODE
CR51U03JY	OEM
CR51U03JY1	OEM
CR51U04JY	OEM
CR51U04JY1	OEM
CR51U05JY	OEM
CR51U05JY1	OEM
CR51U06JY	OEM
CR51U06JY1	OEM
CR51U08JY	OEM
CR51U08JY1	OEM
CR51U10JY	OEM
CR51U10JY1	OEM
CR51U11JY	OEM
CR51U11JY1	OEM
CR51U12JY	OEM
CR51U12JY1	OEM
CR51U13JY	OEM
CR51U13JY1	OEM
CR51U14JY	OEM
CR51U14JY1	OEM
CR51UX5JY	OEM
CR51UX5JY1	OEM
CR70-051A	0463
CR70-051AA	0463
CR70-051C	0463
CR70-051CA	0463
CR70-101A	0463
CR70-101AA	0463
CR70-101C	0463
CR70-101CA	0463
CR70-201A	0463
CR70-201AA	0463
CR70-201C	0463
CR70-201CA	0463
CR70-301A	0463
CR70-301AA	0463
CR70-301C	0463
CR70-301CA	0463
CR70-401A	0463
CR70-401AA	0463
CR70-401C	0463
CR70-401CA	0463
CR70-501A	0463
CR70-501AA	0463
CR70-501C	0463
CR70-501CA	0463
CR70-601A	0463
CR70-601AA	0463
CR70-601C	0463
CR70-601CA	0463
CR70-701A	0463
CR70-701AA	0463
CR70-701C	0463
CR70-701CA	0463
CR70-801A	0463
CR70-801AA	0463
CR70-801C	0463
CR70-801CA	0463
CR70-901A	0463
CR70-901AA	0463
CR70-901C	0463
CR70-901CA	0463
CR70-1001A	0463
CR70-1001AA	0463
CR70-1001C	0463
CR70-1001CA	0463
CR70-1101A	0463
CR70-1101AA	0463
CR70-1101C	0463
CR70-1101CA	0463
CR70-1201A	0463
CR70-1201AA	0463
CR70-1201C	0463
CR70-1201CA	0463
CR70-1301A	0463
CR70-1301AA	0463
CR70-1301C	0463
CR70-1301CA	0463
CR70B2	OEM
CR70B4	OEM
CR70B6	OEM
CR70B8	OEM
CR70B10	OEM
CR70B12	OEM
CR70B14	OEM
CR70B16	OEM
CR70C4	0603
CR70C6	0605
CR70C8	0605
CR70C10	0605
CR70C12	0605
CR70C14	OEM
CR70C16	0463
CR70C20	0463
CR70C24	0463
CR70CX4	OEM
CR70CX6	OEM
CR70CX8	OEM
CR70CX10	OEM
CR70CX12	OEM
CR70CX16	OEM
CR70CX20	OEM
CR70CY4	OEM
CR70CY6	OEM
CR70CY8	OEM
CR70CY10	OEM
CR70CY12	OEM
CR70CY16	OEM
CR71M01JY	OEM

DEVICE TYPE	REPL CODE
CR71M01JY1	OEM
CR71M02JY	OEM
CR71M02JY1	OEM
CR71M03JY	OEM
CR71M03JY1	OEM
CR71M04JY	OEM
CR71M04JY1	OEM
CR71M05JY	OEM
CR71M05JY1	OEM
CR71M06JY	OEM
CR71M06JY1	OEM
CR71M08JY	OEM
CR71M08JY1	OEM
CR71M10JY	OEM
CR71M10JY1	OEM
CR71M11JY	OEM
CR71M11JY1	OEM
CR71M12JY	OEM
CR71M12JY1	OEM
CR71M13JY	OEM
CR71M13JY1	OEM
CR71M14JY	OEM
CR71M14JY1	OEM
CR71MX5JY	OEM
CR71MX5JY1	OEM
CR71U01JY	OEM
CR71U01JY1	OEM
CR71U02JY	OEM
CR71U02JY1	OEM
CR71U03JY	OEM
CR71U03JY1	OEM
CR71U04JY	OEM
CR71U04JY1	OEM
CR71U05JY	OEM
CR71U05JY1	OEM
CR71U06JY	OEM
CR71U06JY1	OEM
CR71U08JY	OEM
CR71U08JY1	OEM
CR71U10JY	OEM
CR71U10JY1	OEM
CR71U11JY	OEM
CR71U12JY	OEM
CR71U12JY1	OEM
CR71U13JY	OEM
CR71U13JY1	OEM
CR71U14JY	OEM
CR71U14JY1	OEM
CR71UX5JY	OEM
CR71UX5JY1	OEM
CR80.021	OEM
CR80.051	OEM
CR80.071	OEM
CR80.101	OEM
CR80.151	OEM
CR80.201	OEM
CR80.251	OEM
CR80.301	OEM
CR81F01JY	OEM
CR81F02JY	OEM
CR81F03JY	OEM
CR81F04JY	OEM
CR81F05JY	OEM
CR81F06JY	OEM
CR81F08JY	OEM
CR81F10JY	OEM
CR81F11JY	OEM
CR81F12JY	OEM
CR81F13JY	OEM
CR81FX5JY	OEM
CR81M01JY	OEM
CR81M02JY	OEM
CR81M02JY1	OEM
CR81M03JY	OEM
CR81M04JY	OEM
CR81M05JY	OEM
CR81M06JY	OEM
CR81M08JY	OEM
CR81M10JY	OEM
CR81M11JY	OEM
CR81M12JY	OEM
CR81M13JY	OEM
CR81M14JY	OEM
CR81MX5JY	OEM
CR81MX5JY1	OEM
CR81U01JY	OEM
CR81U02JY	OEM
CR81U03JY	OEM
CR81U04JY	OEM
CR81U05JY	OEM
CR81U06JY	OEM
CR81U08JY	OEM
CR81U10JY	OEM
CR81U11JY	OEM
CR81U12JY	OEM
CR81U13JY	OEM
CR81U14JY	OEM
CR81UX5JY	OEM
CR100	OEM
CR100-01	OEM
CR100-02	OEM
CR100-04	OEM
CR100-06	OEM
CR100-08	OEM
CR100-10	OEM
CR100AL4	OEM
CR100AL6	OEM
CR100AL8	OEM
CR100AL10	OEM

DEVICE TYPE	REPL CODE
CR100AL12	OEM
CR100AL16	OEM
CR100AL20	OEM
CR100AL24	OEM
CR100AX4	OEM
CR100AX6	OEM
CR100AX8	OEM
CR100AX10	OEM
CR100AX12	OEM
CR100AX16	OEM
CR100AX20	OEM
CR100AY4	OEM
CR100AY6	OEM
CR100AY8	OEM
CR100AY10	OEM
CR100AY12	OEM
CR100AY16	OEM
CR100CX24	OEM
CR100CX28	OEM
CR100CX30	OEM
CR100CX32	OEM
CR100CX34	OEM
CR100CX36	OEM
CR100DX24	OEM
CR100DX28	OEM
CR100DX32	OEM
CR100DX34	OEM
CR100DX36	OEM
CR100.021	OEM
CR100.051	OEM
CR100.071	OEM
CR100.101	OEM
CR100.151	OEM
CR100.201	OEM
CR100.251	OEM
CR100.301	OEM
CR101F01JY	OEM
CR101F02JY	OEM
CR101F03JY	OEM
CR101F04JY	OEM
CR101F05JY	OEM
CR101F06JY	OEM
CR101F08JY	OEM
CR101F10JY	OEM
CR101F11JY	OEM
CR101F12JY	OEM
CR101F13JY	OEM
CR101F14JY	OEM
CR101FX5JY	OEM
CR101M01JY	OEM
CR101M02JY	OEM
CR101M03JY	OEM
CR101M04JY	OEM
CR101M05JY	OEM
CR101M06JY	OEM
CR101M08JY	OEM
CR101M10JY	OEM
CR101M11JY	OEM
CR101M12JY	OEM
CR101M13JY	OEM
CR101M14JY	OEM
CR101MX5JY	OEM
CR101U01JY	OEM
CR101U02JY	OEM
CR101U03JY	OEM
CR101U04JY	OEM
CR101U05JY	OEM
CR101U06JY	OEM
CR101U08JY	OEM
CR101U10JY	OEM
CR101U11JY	OEM
CR101U12JY	OEM
CR101U13JY	OEM
CR101U14JY	OEM
CR101UX5JY	OEM
CR103	0769
CR103A	0895
CR103B	0058
CR103C	0403
CR103D	0403
CR103E	1673
CR103M	1673
CR103N	OEM
CR103S	OEM
CR103Y	1129
CR103YY	0340
CR104	1293
CR105A	2396
CR105B	2396
CR105C	6235
CR105D	6235
CR105E	6095
CR105M	6095
CR110	OEM
CR111F01JY	OEM
CR111F02JY	OEM
CR111F03JY	OEM
CR111F04JY	OEM
CR111F05JY	OEM
CR111F06JY	OEM
CR111F08JY	OEM
CR111F10JY	OEM
CR111F11JY	OEM
CR111F12JY	OEM
CR111F13JY	OEM
CR111F14JY	OEM
CR111FX5JY	OEM
CR111M01JY	OEM
CR111M02JY	OEM

If replacement code is OEM, contact original manufacturer for replacement.

DEVICE TYPE	REPL CODE
CR111M03JY	OEM
CR111M04JY	OEM
CR111M05JY	OEM
CR111M06JY	OEM
CR111M08JY	OEM
CR111M10JY	OEM
CR111M11JY	OEM
CR111M12JY	OEM
CR111M13JY	OEM
CR111M14JY	OEM
CR111MX5JY	OEM
CR111U01JY	OEM
CR111U02JY	OEM
CR111U03JY	OEM
CR111U04JY	OEM
CR111U05JY	OEM
CR111U06JY	OEM
CR111U08JY	OEM
CR111U10JY	OEM
CR111U11JY	OEM
CR111U12JY	OEM
CR111U13JY	OEM
CR111U14JY	OEM
CR111UX5JY	OEM
CR120	OEM
CR121A	OEM
CR121B	OEM
CR121D	OEM
CR121F01JY	OEM
CR121F02JY	OEM
CR121F03JY	OEM
CR121F04JY	OEM
CR121F05JY	OEM
CR121F06JY	OEM
CR121F08JY	OEM
CR121F10JY	OEM
CR121F11JY	OEM
CR121F12JY	OEM
CR121F13JY	OEM
CR121F14JY	OEM
CR121FX5JY	OEM
CR121M	OEM
CR121M01JY	OEM
CR121M01JY1	OEM
CR121M02JY	OEM
CR121M03JY	OEM
CR121M03JY1	OEM
CR121M04JY	OEM
CR121M04JY1	OEM
CR121M05JY	OEM
CR121M05JY1	OEM
CR121M06JY	OEM
CR121M06JY1	OEM
CR121M08JY	OEM
CR121M08JY1	OEM
CR121M10JY	OEM
CR121M10JY1	OEM
CR121M11JY	OEM
CR121M12JY	OEM
CR121M13JY	OEM
CR121M14JY	OEM
CR121MX5JY	OEM
CR121MX5JY1	OEM
CR121N	OEM
CR121U01JY	OEM
CR121U02JY	OEM
CR121U03JY	OEM
CR121U04JY	OEM
CR121U05JY	OEM
CR121U06JY	OEM
CR121U08JY	OEM
CR121U10JY	OEM
CR121U11JY	OEM
CR121U12JY	OEM
CR121U13JY	OEM
CR121U14JY	OEM
CR121UX5JY	OEM
CR130	OEM
CR135F01JY	OEM
CR135F02JY	OEM
CR135F03JY	OEM
CR135F04JY	OEM
CR135F05JY	OEM
CR135F06JY	OEM
CR135F08JY	OEM
CR135F10JY	OEM
CR135FX5JY	OEM
CR135U01JY	OEM
CR135U01JY2	OEM
CR135U02JY	OEM
CR135U02JY2	OEM
CR135U03JY	OEM
CR135U03JY2	OEM
CR135U04JY	OEM
CR135U04JY2	OEM
CR135U05JY	OEM
CR135U05JY2	OEM
CR135U06JY	OEM
CR135U06JY2	OEM
CR135U08JY	OEM
CR135U10JY	OEM
CR135U10JY2	OEM
CR135U11JY	OEM
CR135U11JY2	OEM
CR135U12JY	OEM
CR135U12JY2	OEM
CR135U13JY	OEM
CR135U13JY2	OEM
CR135U14JY	OEM

DEVICE TYPE	REPL CODE
CR135U14JY2	OEM
CR135UX5JY	OEM
CR135UX5JY2	OEM
CR140	OEM
CR140F01JY	OEM
CR140F02JY	OEM
CR140F03JY	OEM
CR140F04JY	OEM
CR140F05JY	OEM
CR140F06JY	OEM
CR140F08JY	OEM
CR140F10JY	OEM
CR140F11JY	OEM
CR140F12JY	OEM
CR140F13JY	OEM
CR140F14JY	OEM
CR140FX5JY	OEM
CR140U01JY	OEM
CR140U01JY2	OEM
CR140U02JY	OEM
CR140U02JY2	OEM
CR140U03JY	OEM
CR140U03JY2	OEM
CR140U04JY	OEM
CR140U04JY2	OEM
CR140U05JY	OEM
CR140U05JY2	OEM
CR140U06JY	OEM
CR140U06JY2	OEM
CR140U08JY	OEM
CR140U08JY2	OEM
CR140U10JY	OEM
CR140U11JY	OEM
CR140U11JY2	OEM
CR140U12JY	OEM
CR140U12JY2	OEM
CR140U13JY	OEM
CR140U13JY2	OEM
CR140U14JY	OEM
CR140U14JY2	OEM
CR140UX5JY	OEM
CR140UX5JY2	OEM
CR150	OEM
CR150-051A	OEM
CR150-052A3	OEM
CR150-052A4	OEM
CR150-052A5	OEM
CR150-052A6	OEM
CR150-101A	OEM
CR150-102A3	OEM
CR150-102A4	OEM
CR150-102A5	OEM
CR150-102A6	OEM
CR150-102B	OEM
CR150-201A	OEM
CR150-202A3	OEM
CR150-202A4	OEM
CR150-202A5	OEM
CR150-202A6	OEM
CR150-202B	OEM
CR150-301A	OEM
CR150-302A3	OEM
CR150-302A4	OEM
CR150-302A5	OEM
CR150-302A6	OEM
CR150-302B	OEM
CR150-401A	OEM
CR150-402A3	OEM
CR150-402A4	OEM
CR150-402A5	OEM
CR150-402A6	OEM
CR150-402B	OEM
CR150-501A	OEM
CR150-502A3	OEM
CR150-502A4	OEM
CR150-502A5	OEM
CR150-502A6	OEM
CR150-502B	OEM
CR150-601A	OEM
CR150-601A3	OEM
CR150-602A3	OEM
CR150-602A4	OEM
CR150-602A5	OEM
CR150-602A6	OEM
CR150-602B	OEM
CR150-701A	OEM
CR150-701A3	OEM
CR150-702A3	OEM
CR150-702A4	OEM
CR150-702A5	OEM
CR150-702A6	OEM
CR150-702B	OEM
CR150-801A	OEM
CR150-801A3	OEM
CR150-802A3	OEM
CR150-802A4	OEM
CR150-802A5	OEM
CR150-802A6	OEM
CR150-802B	OEM
CR150-901A	OEM
CR150-902B	OEM
CR150-1001A	OEM
CR150-1001A3	OEM
CR150-1002B	OEM
CR150-1101A	OEM
CR150-1101A3	OEM
CR150-1102B	OEM
CR150-1201A3	OEM
CR150-1202B	OEM

DEVICE TYPE	REPL CODE
CR150-1301A3	OEM
CR150B2	OEM
CR150B4	OEM
CR150B6	OEM
CR150B8	OEM
CR150B10	OEM
CR150B12	OEM
CR150B16	OEM
CR150B20	OEM
CR150B24	OEM
CR150BX2	OEM
CR150BX4	OEM
CR150BX6	OEM
CR150BX8	OEM
CR150BX10	OEM
CR150BX12	OEM
CR150BX14	OEM
CR150BX16	OEM
CR150BX18	OEM
CR150BX20	OEM
CR150BY2	OEM
CR150BY4	OEM
CR150BY6	OEM
CR150BY8	OEM
CR150BY10	OEM
CR150BY12	OEM
CR150DM4	OEM
CR150DM6	OEM
CR150DM8	OEM
CR150DM10	OEM
CR150DM12	OEM
CR150DM16	OEM
CR150DM20	OEM
CR150DM24	OEM
CR150DM28	OEM
CR150DM32	OEM
CR150DM36	OEM
CR150DX4	OEM
CR150DX6	OEM
CR150DX8	OEM
CR150DX10	OEM
CR150DX12	OEM
CR150DX16	OEM
CR150DX20	OEM
CR150DY4	OEM
CR150DY6	OEM
CR150DY8	OEM
CR150DY10	OEM
CR150DY12	OEM
CR150F2	OEM
CR150F4	1889
CR150F6	1889
CR150F8	1889
CR150F10	1889
CR150F12	1889
CR150F16	0733
CR150F20	0733
CR150F24	OEM
CR150F28	OEM
CR150F32	OEM
CR150F36	OEM
CR151-103A	OEM
CR151-203A	OEM
CR151-303A	OEM
CR151-403A	OEM
CR151-503A	OEM
CR151-603A	OEM
CR151-703A	OEM
CR151-803A	OEM
CR151-903A	OEM
CR151-1003A	OEM
CR151-1103A	OEM
CR151-1203A	OEM
CR151-1303A	OEM
CR152-103A	OEM
CR152-203A	OEM
CR152-303A	OEM
CR152-403A	OEM
CR152-503A	OEM
CR152-603A	OEM
CR152-703A	OEM
CR152-803A	OEM
CR152-903A	OEM
CR152-1003A	OEM
CR152-1103A	OEM
CR152-1203A	OEM
CR152-1303A	OEM
CR152-1403A	OEM
CR152-1503A	OEM
CR153-103A	OEM
CR153-203A	OEM
CR153-303A	OEM
CR153-403A	OEM
CR153-503A	OEM
CR153-603A	OEM
CR153-703A	OEM
CR153-803A	OEM
CR153-903A	OEM
CR153-1003A	OEM
CR153-1103A	OEM
CR153-1203A	OEM
CR153-1303A	OEM
CR153-1403A	OEM
CR153-1503A	OEM
CR155-604NA	OEM
CR155-704NA	OEM
CR155-804NA	OEM
CR155-904NA	OEM
CR155-1004NA	OEM

DEVICE TYPE	REPL CODE
CR159-901A3	OEM
CR160	OEM
CR180	OEM
CR200	OEM
CR203A	0895
CR203B	0058
CR203C	0403
CR203D	0403
CR203E	1673
CR203M	1673
CR203N	OEM
CR203S	OEM
CR203Y	1129
CR203YY	0340
CR220	OEM
CR240	OEM
CR250AX2	OEM
CR250AX4	OEM
CR250AX6	OEM
CR250AX8	OEM
CR250AX10	OEM
CR250AX16	OEM
CR250AX20	OEM
CR250AXAX12	OEM
CR250AY2	OEM
CR250AY4	OEM
CR250AY6	OEM
CR250AY8	OEM
CR250AY10	OEM
CR250AY12	OEM
CR250B2	OEM
CR250B6	OEM
CR250B8	OEM
CR250B10	OEM
CR250B12	OEM
CR250B14	OEM
CR250B16	OEM
CR250B18	OEM
CR250B20	OEM
CR250B24	OEM
CR250DP4	OEM
CR250DP6	OEM
CR250DP8	OEM
CR250F2	OEM
CR250F4	OEM
CR250F6	OEM
CR250F8	OEM
CR250F10	OEM
CR250F12	OEM
CR250F16	OEM
CR250F20	OEM
CR250F24	OEM
CR250F28	OEM
CR250F32	OEM
CR250F36	OEM
CR250GX2	OEM
CR250GX4	OEM
CR250GX6	OEM
CR250GX8	OEM
CR250GX10	OEM
CR250GX12	OEM
CR250GX16	OEM
CR250GX20	OEM
CR250GY2	OEM
CR250GY4	OEM
CR250GY6	OEM
CR250GY8	OEM
CR250GY10	OEM
CR250GY12	OEM
CR250J2	OEM
CR250J4	1889
CR250J6	1889
CR250J8	1889
CR250J10	1889
CR250J12	1889
CR250J16	0733
CR250J20	0733
CR250J24	0733
CR250J28	OEM
CR250J32	OEM
CR250J36	OEM
CR250JX2	OEM
CR250JX4	OEM
CR250JX6	OEM
CR250JX8	OEM
CR250JX10	OEM
CR250JX12	OEM
CR250JX16	OEM
CR250JX20	OEM
CR250JY2	OEM
CR250JY4	OEM
CR250JY6	OEM
CR250JY8	OEM
CR250JY10	OEM
CR250JY12	OEM
CR250JY16	OEM
CR252-103A	OEM
CR252-203A	OEM
CR252-303A	OEM
CR252-403A	OEM
CR252-503A	OEM
CR252-603A	OEM
CR252-703A	OEM
CR252-803A	OEM
CR252-903A	OEM
CR252-1003A	OEM
CR252-1103A	OEM
CR252-1203A	OEM
CR252-1303A	OEM

DEVICE TYPE	REPL CODE
CR252-1403A	OEM
CR252-1503A	OEM
CR253-103A	OEM
CR253-203A	OEM
CR253-303A	OEM
CR253-403A	OEM
CR253-503A	OEM
CR253-603A	OEM
CR253-605A	OEM
CR253-703A	OEM
CR253-705A	OEM
CR253-803A	OEM
CR253-805A	OEM
CR253-903A	OEM
CR253-905A	OEM
CR253-1003A	OEM
CR253-1005A	OEM
CR253-1103A	OEM
CR253-1105A	OEM
CR253-1203A	OEM
CR253-1205A	OEM
CR253-1303A	OEM
CR253-1305A	OEM
CR253-1403A	OEM
CR253-1503A	OEM
CR270	OEM
CR300	OEM
CR300A2	OEM
CR300A4	OEM
CR300A6	OEM
CR300A8	OEM
CR300A10	OEM
CR300A12	OEM
CR300A14	OEM
CR300A16	OEM
CR300A18	OEM
CR300A20	OEM
CR300A24	OEM
CR300A28	OEM
CR300A32	OEM
CR300A36	OEM
CR300AW2	OEM
CR300AW4	OEM
CR300AW6	OEM
CR300AW8	OEM
CR300AW10	OEM
CR300AW12	OEM
CR300AW16	OEM
CR300AW20	OEM
CR300AW24	OEM
CR300AX2	OEM
CR300AX4	OEM
CR300AX6	OEM
CR300AX8	OEM
CR300AX10	OEM
CR300AX12	OEM
CR300AX16	OEM
CR300AX20	OEM
CR300AY2	OEM
CR300AY4	OEM
CR300AY6	OEM
CR300AY8	OEM
CR300AY10	OEM
CR300AY12	OEM
CR300F2	OEM
CR300F4	OEM
CR300F6	OEM
CR300F8	OEM
CR300F10	OEM
CR300F12	OEM
CR300F16	OEM
CR300F20	OEM
CR300F24	OEM
CR300F28	OEM
CR300F32	OEM
CR300F36	OEM
CR300FX40	OEM
CR300FX50	OEM
CR303-404LA	OEM
CR303A	OEM
CR303B	OEM
CR303C	OEM
CR303D	OEM
CR303E	OEM
CR303M	OEM
CR303N	OEM
CR303S	OEM
CR303Y	OEM
CR303YY	OEM
CR330	OEM
CR350A20	OEM
CR350A24	OEM
CR350A28	OEM
CR350A32	OEM
CR350A36	OEM
CR353	0133
CR360	OEM
CR390	OEM
CR400EL4	OEM
CR400EL6	OEM
CR400EL8	OEM
CR400EL10	OEM
CR400EL12	OEM
CR400EL16	OEM
CR400EL20	OEM
CR400EL24	OEM
CR400EX4	OEM
CR400EX6	OEM
CR400EX8	OEM

DEVICE TYPE	REPL CODE
CR400EX10	OEM
CR400EX12	OEM
CR400EX16	OEM
CR400EX20	OEM
CR400EX24	OEM
CR400EY4	OEM
CR400EY6	OEM
CR400EY8	OEM
CR400EY10	OEM
CR400EY12	OEM
CR400EY16	OEM
CR400FM28	OEM
CR400FM32	OEM
CR400FM36	OEM
CR430	OEM
CR470	OEM
CR530	OEM
CR604SC0101	OEM
CR604SC0202	OEM
CR604SC0303	OEM
CR604SC0404	OEM
CR604SC0505	OEM
CR604SC0606	OEM
CR604SC0707	OEM
CR604SC0808	OEM
CR604SC0909	OEM
CR604SC1010	OEM
CR604SC1111	OEM
CR604SC1212	OEM
CR604SC1313	OEM
CR604SC1414	OEM
CR604SC1415	OEM
CR605SC0101	OEM
CR605SC0202	OEM
CR605SC0303	OEM
CR605SC0404	OEM
CR605SC0505	OEM
CR605SC0606	OEM
CR605SC0707	OEM
CR605SC0808	OEM
CR605SC0909	OEM
CR605SC1010	OEM
CR605SC1111	OEM
CR605SC1212	OEM
CR605SC1313	OEM
CR605SC1414	OEM
CR605SC1515	OEM
CR606SC0101	OEM
CR606SC0202	OEM
CR606SC0303	OEM
CR606SC0404	OEM
CR606SC0505	OEM
CR606SC0606	OEM
CR606SC0707	OEM
CR606SC0808	OEM
CR606SC0909	OEM
CR606SC1010	OEM
CR606SC1111	OEM
CR606SC1212	OEM
CR606SC1313	OEM
CR606SC1414	OEM
CR607SC0101	OEM
CR607SC0202	OEM
CR607SC0303	OEM
CR607SC0404	OEM
CR607SC0505	OEM
CR607SC0606	OEM
CR607SC0707	OEM
CR607SC0808	OEM
CR607SC0909	OEM
CR607SC1010	OEM
CR607SC1111	OEM
CR607SC1212	OEM
CR607SC1313	OEM
CR607SC1414	OEM
CR607SC1515	OEM
CR608SA0101	OEM
CR608SA0202	OEM
CR608SA0303	OEM
CR608SA0404	OEM
CR608SA0505	OEM
CR608SA0606	OEM
CR608SA0707	OEM
CR608SA0808	OEM
CR608SA0909	OEM
CR608SA1010	OEM
CR608SA1111	OEM
CR608SA1212	OEM
CR608SA1313	OEM
CR608SA1414	OEM
CR608SA1515	OEM
CR608SC0101	OEM
CR608SC0202	OEM
CR608SC0303	OEM
CR608SC0404	OEM
CR608SC0505	OEM
CR608SC0606	OEM
CR608SC0707	OEM
CR608SC0808	OEM
CR608SC0909	OEM
CR608SC1010	OEM
CR608SC1111	OEM
CR608SC1212	OEM
CR608SC1313	OEM
CR608SC1414	OEM
CR608SC1515	OEM
CR702SC0101	OEM
CR702SC0202	OEM
CR702SC0303	OEM

DEVICE TYPE	REPL CODE
CR702SC0404	OEM
CR702SC0505	OEM
CR702SC0606	OEM
CR702SC0707	OEM
CR702SC0808	OEM
CR702SC0909	OEM
CR702SC1010	OEM
CR702SC1111	OEM
CR702SC1212	OEM
CR702SC1313	OEM
CR702SC1414	OEM
CR702SC1515	OEM
CR703SC0101	OEM
CR703SC0202	OEM
CR703SC0303	OEM
CR703SC0404	OEM
CR703SC0505	OEM
CR703SC0606	OEM
CR703SC0707	OEM
CR703SC0808	OEM
CR703SC0909	OEM
CR703SC1010	OEM
CR703SC1111	OEM
CR703SC1212	OEM
CR703SC1313	OEM
CR703SC1414	OEM
CR703SC1515	OEM
CR703SW0101	OEM
CR703SW0202	OEM
CR703SW0303	OEM
CR703SW0404	OEM
CR703SW0505	OEM
CR703SW0606	OEM
CR703SW0707	OEM
CR703SW0808	OEM
CR703SW0909	OEM
CR703SW1010	OEM
CR703SW1111	OEM
CR703SW1212	OEM
CR703SW1313	OEM
CR703SW1414	OEM
CR703SW1515	OEM
CR704SC0101	OEM
CR704SC0202	OEM
CR704SC0303	OEM
CR704SC0404	OEM
CR704SC0505	OEM
CR704SC0606	OEM
CR704SC0707	OEM
CR704SC0808	OEM
CR704SC0909	OEM
CR704SC1010	OEM
CR704SC1111	OEM
CR704SC1212	OEM
CR704SC1313	OEM
CR704SC1414	OEM
CR704SC1515	OEM
CR704SC1616	OEM
CR705SC0101	OEM
CR705SC0202	OEM
CR705SC0303	OEM
CR705SC0404	OEM
CR705SC0505	OEM
CR705SC0606	OEM
CR705SC0707	OEM
CR705SC0808	OEM
CR705SC0909	OEM
CR705SC1010	OEM
CR705SC1111	OEM
CR705SC1212	OEM
CR705SC1313	OEM
CR705SC1414	OEM
CR705SC1515	OEM
CR705SC1616	OEM
CR705SC1717	OEM
CR705SC1818	OEM
CR705SW0101	OEM
CR705SW0202	OEM
CR705SW0303	OEM
CR705SW0404	OEM
CR705SW0505	OEM
CR705SW0606	OEM
CR705SW0707	OEM
CR705SW0808	OEM
CR705SW1010	OEM
CR705SW1111	OEM
CR705SW1212	OEM
CR705SW1313	OEM
CR705SW1414	OEM
CR705SW1515	OEM
CR705SW1616	OEM
CR705SW1717	OEM
CR705SW1818	OEM
CR705XW0909	OEM
CR706SC0101	OEM
CR706SC0202	OEM
CR706SC0303	OEM
CR706SC0404	OEM
CR706SC0505	OEM
CR706SC0606	OEM
CR706SC0707	OEM
CR706SC0808	OEM
CR706SC0909	OEM
CR706SC1010	OEM
CR706SC1111	OEM
CR706SC1212	OEM
CR706SC1313	OEM
CR706SC1414	OEM
CR706SC1515	OEM

If replacement code is OEM, contact original manufacturer for replacement.

DEVICE TYPE	REPL CODE
CR706SC1616	OEM
CR706SC1717	OEM
CR706SC1818	OEM
CR706SC1919	OEM
CR706SC2020	OEM
CR707SC0101	OEM
CR707SC0202	OEM
CR707SC0303	OEM
CR707SC0404	OEM
CR707SC0505	OEM
CR707SC0606	OEM
CR707SC0707	OEM
CR707SC0808	OEM
CR707SC0909	OEM
CR707SC1010	OEM
CR707SC1111	OEM
CR707SC1212	OEM
CR707SC1313	OEM
CR707SC1414	OEM
CR707SC1515	OEM
CR707SC1616	OEM
CR707SC1717	OEM
CR707SC1818	OEM
CR707SC1919	OEM
CR707SC2020	OEM
CR707SC2121	OEM
CR707SC2222	OEM
CR707SC2323	OEM
CR707SW0101	OEM
CR707SW0202	OEM
CR707SW0303	OEM
CR707SW0404	OEM
CR707SW0505	OEM
CR707SW0606	OEM
CR707SW0707	OEM
CR707SW0808	OEM
CR707SW0909	OEM
CR707SW1010	OEM
CR707SW1111	OEM
CR707SW1212	OEM
CR707SW1313	OEM
CR707SW1414	OEM
CR707SW1515	OEM
CR707SW1616	OEM
CR707SW1717	OEM
CR707SW1818	OEM
CR707SW1919	OEM
CR707SW2020	OEM
CR707SW2121	OEM
CR707SW2222	OEM
CR707SW2323	OEM
CR801	0015
CR804SC0101	OEM
CR804SC0202	OEM
CR804SC0303	OEM
CR804SC0404	OEM
CR804SC0505	OEM
CR804SC0606	OEM
CR804SC0707	OEM
CR804SC0808	OEM
CR804SC0909	OEM
CR804SC1010	OEM
CR804SC1111	OEM
CR804SC1212	OEM
CR804SC1313	OEM
CR804SC1414	OEM
CR804SC1515	OEM
CR804SC1616	OEM
CR804SW0101	OEM
CR804SW0202	OEM
CR804SW0303	OEM
CR804SW0404	OEM
CR804SW0505	OEM
CR804SW0606	OEM
CR804SW0707	OEM
CR804SW0808	OEM
CR804SW0909	OEM
CR804SW1010	OEM
CR804SW1111	OEM
CR804SW1212	OEM
CR804SW1313	OEM
CR804SW1414	OEM
CR804SW1515	OEM
CR804SW1616	OEM
CR807SB0101	OEM
CR807SB0202	OEM
CR807SB0303	OEM
CR807SB0404	OEM
CR807SB0505	OEM
CR807SB0606	OEM
CR807SB0707	OEM
CR807SB0808	OEM
CR807SB0909	OEM
CR807SB1010	OEM
CR807SB1111	OEM
CR807SB1212	OEM
CR807SB1313	OEM
CR807SB1414	OEM
CR807SB1515	OEM
CR807SB1616	OEM
CR807SB1717	OEM
CR807SB1818	OEM
CR807SB1919	OEM
CR807SB2020	OEM
CR807SB2121	OEM
CR807SB2222	OEM
CR807SB2323	OEM
CR807SB2424	OEM
CR807SB2525	OEM

DEVICE TYPE	REPL CODE
CR807SC0101	OEM
CR807SC0202	OEM
CR807SC0303	OEM
CR807SC0404	OEM
CR807SC0505	OEM
CR807SC0606	OEM
CR807SC0707	OEM
CR807SC0808	OEM
CR807SC0909	OEM
CR807SC1010	OEM
CR807SC1111	OEM
CR807SC1212	OEM
CR807SC1313	OEM
CR807SC1414	OEM
CR807SC1515	OEM
CR807SC1616	OEM
CR807SC1717	OEM
CR807SC1818	OEM
CR807SC1919	OEM
CR807SC2020	OEM
CR807SC2121	OEM
CR807SC2222	OEM
CR807SC2323	OEM
CR807SC2424	OEM
CR807SC2525	OEM
CR807SW0101	OEM
CR807SW0202	OEM
CR807SW0303	OEM
CR807SW0404	OEM
CR807SW0505	OEM
CR807SW0606	OEM
CR807SW0707	OEM
CR807SW0808	OEM
CR807SW0909	OEM
CR807SW1010	OEM
CR807SW1111	OEM
CR807SW1212	OEM
CR807SW1313	OEM
CR807SW1414	OEM
CR807SW1515	OEM
CR807SW1616	OEM
CR807SW1717	OEM
CR807SW1818	OEM
CR807SW1919	OEM
CR807SW2020	OEM
CR807SW2121	OEM
CR807SW2222	OEM
CR807SW2323	OEM
CR807SW2424	OEM
CR807SW2525	OEM
CR951	0087
CR952	0087
CR953	0087
CR954	0087
CR955	0087
CR956	0137
CR1034	0015
CR1035	0015
CR1040	OEM
CR1141	OEM
CR1142	OEM
CR1143	OEM
CR1144	OEM
CR1145	OEM
CR1146	OEM
CR1157	0720
CR4120	OEM
CR5000	0290
CR18903RB	OEM
CR32077-1	1024
CR32077R	1024
CR181003RB	OEM
CR181103RB	OEM
CR181203RB	OEM
CR181303RB	OEM
CR181403RB	OEM
CRAM/RAM108	OEM
CRAM-108-230	OEM
CRAM-108-250	OEM
CRAM-108-290	OEM
CRC150AY8	OEM
CRD821	0466
CRD823	0466
CRD825	0466
CRD827	0466
CRD829	0466
CRD921	0466
CRD923	0466
CRD925	0466
CRD927	0466
CRD929	OEM
CRE0004D	OEM
CRE3	OEM
CRG20	OEM
CRG40	OEM
CRG60	OEM
CRG100	OEM
CRG150	OEM
CRG200	OEM
CRHG3	OEM
CRHG4	OEM
CRHG5	OEM
CRHG6	OEM
CRHG7	OEM
CRHG8	OEM
CRHG9	OEM
CRHG10	OEM
CRL-216	OEM
CRO2AM	OEM

DEVICE TYPE	REPL CODE
CRR0240	OEM
CRR0360	OEM
CRR0560	OEM
CRR0800	OEM
CRR1250	OEM
CRR1950	OEM
CRR2900	OEM
CRR4300	OEM
CRS1/35AF	OEM
CRS1-05AF	OEM
CRS1-10AF	OEM
CRS1-20AF	OEM
CRS1-30AF	OEM
CRS1-40AF	OEM
CRS1-50AF	OEM
CRS3/35AF	OEM
CRS3/50	OEM
CRS3/60	OEM
CRS3-05AF	OEM
CRS3-10AF	OEM
CRS3-20AF	OEM
CRS3-30AF	OEM
CRS3-40AF	OEM
CRS3-50AF	OEM
CRS20	OEM
CRS25/05AF	OEM
CRS25/10AF	OEM
CRS25/20AF	OEM
CRS25/30AF	OEM
CRS25/35AF	OEM
CRS25/40AF	OEM
CRS25/50	OEM
CRS25/60	OEM
CRS25-05AF	OEM
CRS25-20AF	OEM
CRS40	OEM
CRS60	OEM
CRS70-05AF	OEM
CRS70-10AF	OEM
CRS70-20AF	OEM
CRS70-30AF	OEM
CRS70-35AF	OEM
CRS70-50	OEM
CRS100	OEM
CRS150	OEM
CRS200	OEM
CRS449-16IY1	OEM
CRS2020	OEM
CRT15	OEM
CRT20	OEM
CRT25	OEM
CRT30	OEM
CRT1544	0160
CRT1545	0160
CRT1552	0160
CRT1553	0160
CRT1592	OEM
CRT1602	0160
CRT3602A	0160
CRT5027	OEM
CRT5037	OEM
CRT5047	OEM
CRT5057	OEM
CRT7004A	OEM
CRT7004B	OEM
CRT7004C	OEM
CRT8002A	OEM
CRT8002B	OEM
CRT8002C	OEM
CRT8021	OEM
CRT8021-003	OEM
CRT9006-83	OEM
CRT9006-135	OEM
CRT9007	OEM
CRT9021	OEM
CRT9212	OEM
CRT96364A	OEM
CRT96364B	OEM
CS-0040	OEM
CS08	OEM
CS0.6-02G02	OEM
CS0.6-04G02	OEM
CS0.6-08D02	OEM
CS0.6-08G02	OEM
CS0.6-10D02	OEM
CS0.6-10G02	OEM
CS0.6-12	OEM
CS0.8-02D02	OEM
CS0.8-04D02	OEM
CS0.8-06D02	OEM
CS0.8-07D02	OEM
CS1-02	OEM
CS1-04	OEM
CS1-06	OEM
CS1-08	OEM
CS1-08G03	OEM
CS1-10G03	OEM
CS1-12G03	OEM
CS1.2-02D02	OEM
CS1.2-04D02	OEM
CS1.2-05D02	OEM
CS1.2-06D02	OEM
CS1.2-07D02	OEM
CS2.5-04Z02	OEM
CS2.5-06Z02	OEM
CS3-02	2084
CS3-02D02	OEM
CS3-02G01	OEM
CS3-04	0705

DEVICE TYPE	REPL CODE
CS3-04D02	OEM
CS3-05G01	OEM
CS3-06	0857
CS3-06D02	OEM
CS3-06G01	OEM
CS3-07D02	OEM
CS3-07G01	OEM
CS3B	OEM
CS3BR	OEM
CS3.5-02D02	OEM
CS3.5-02G02	OEM
CS3.5-04D02	OEM
CS3.5-04G02	OEM
CS3.5-05D02	OEM
CS3.5-05G02	OEM
CS3.5-06D02	OEM
CS3.5-06G02	OEM
CS3.5-07D02	OEM
CS4-100	OEM
CS4-200	OEM
CS4-350	OEM
CS4-450	OEM
CS4B	OEM
CS4.9-02	OEM
CS4.9-04	0735
CS4.9-06	0799
CS5-02+	0464
CS5-02D02	OEM
CS5-02G02	OEM
CS5-02G03	OEM
CS5-04+	0717
CS5-04D02	OEM
CS5-04G01	OEM
CS5-04G02	OEM
CS5-06+	0720
CS5-06D02	OEM
CS5-06G02	OEM
CS5-06G03	OEM
CS5-08+	2025
CS5-08D02	OEM
CS5-10+	2025
CS5-10D02	OEM
CS5-12+	2025
CS5-12D02	OEM
CS5-100	OEM
CS5-200	OEM
CS5-400	OEM
CS5-500	OEM
CS5-600	OEM
CS5-800	OEM
CS5-1000	OEM
CS5B	OEM
CS6-02D01	OEM
CS6-04D01	OEM
CS6-06D01	OEM
CS6-07D01	OEM
CS6-08D01	OEM
CS7	OEM
CS7A	OEM
CS8-02	0740
CS8-02D02	OEM
CS8-02D03	OEM
CS8-02G02	OEM
CS8-02G03	OEM
CS8-02N	2430
CS8-04	0735
CS8-04D02	OEM
CS8-04D03	OEM
CS8-04G02	OEM
CS8-04G03	OEM
CS8-04I03	OEM
CS8-05N	2430
CS8-06	0759
CS8-06D02	OEM
CS8-06D03	OEM
CS8-06G02	OEM
CS8-06I03	OEM
CS8-08D02	OEM
CS8-08D03	OEM
CS8-08I02	OEM
CS8-08I03	OEM
CS8-10D02	OEM
CS8-10D03	OEM
CS8-10I02	OEM
CS8-10I03	OEM
CS8-12D02	OEM
CS8-12D03	OEM
CS8-14I02	OEM
CS8-14I03	OEM
CS8-100	OEM
CS8-200	OEM
CS8-400	OEM
CS8-500	OEM
CS8-600	OEM
CS8-800	OEM
CS8-1000	OEM
CS9B	OEM
CS9BR	OEM
CS10	OEM
CS10-02G02	OEM
CS10-02M	1641
CS10-04G02	OEM
CS10-05M	1641
CS10-05N	2430
CS10-06G02	OEM
CS10-07G02	OEM
CS10-08G02	OEM
CS10-1M	1641
CS10-1N	2430

DEVICE TYPE	REPL CODE
CS10-2M	1641
CS10-2N	0430
CS10-3M	1574
CS10-3N	1478
CS10-4M	1574
CS10-4N	1478
CS10-6M	1655
CS10-6N	0682
CS10-100	OEM
CS10-200	OEM
CS10-400	OEM
CS10A	OEM
CS10B	OEM
CS10BR	OEM
CS11B	OEM
CS11C	0174
CS11D	0179
CS11E	OEM
CS11G	0179
CS11H	0179
CS11J	OEM
CS11K	0342
CS11L	OEM
CS11M	0342
CS11N	OEM
CS12B	OEM
CS12BR	OEM
CS12C	OEM
CS12D	OEM
CS12E	OEM
CS12G	OEM
CS12J	OEM
CS12L	OEM
CS12M	OEM
CS12N	OEM
CS13-02	0464
CS13-02+	0464
CS13-02G02	OEM
CS13-04	2623
CS13-04+	0717
CS13-04G02	OEM
CS13-04G03	OEM
CS13-06	0720
CS13-06+	0720
CS13-06G02	OEM
CS13-06G03	OEM
CS13-08+	2025
CS13-08G02	OEM
CS13-08G03	OEM
CS13-10+	2025
CS13-10G02	OEM
CS13-10G03	OEM
CS13-12+	2025
CS13-12G02	OEM
CS13-12G03	OEM
CS14	OEM
CS15	OEM
CS15-02G02	OEM
CS15-04G02	OEM
CS15-06G02	OEM
CS15-07G02	OEM
CS15-08G02	OEM
CS15-100	OEM
CS15-100A	OEM
CS15-200	OEM
CS15-200A	OEM
CS15-400	OEM
CS15-400A	OEM
CS15-500	OEM
CS15-500A	OEM
CS15-600	OEM
CS15-600A	OEM
CS15-700	OEM
CS15-700A	OEM
CS15,9-04+	0717
CS15,9-06+	0720
CS15,9-08+	2025
CS15,9-10+	2025
CS15.9-02	OEM
CS15.9-04	0735
CS15.9-04GP2	OEM
CS15.9-04GP3	OEM
CS15.9-05	OEM
CS15.9-06GP2	OEM
CS15.9-06GP3	OEM
CS15.9-08GP2	OEM
CS15.9-08GP3	OEM
CS15.9-08GU2	OEM
CS15.9-08GU3	OEM
CS15.9-10GP2	OEM
CS15.9-10GP3	OEM
CS15.9-10GU2	OEM
CS15.9-10GU3	OEM
CS15.906	0799
CS16-02+	0464
CS16-02D01	OEM
CS16-02D02	OEM
CS16-02D03	OEM
CS16-02G01	OEM
CS16-02G02	OEM
CS16-02G03	OEM
CS16-04+	0717
CS16-04D01	OEM
CS16-04D02	OEM
CS16-04D03	OEM
CS16-04G01	OEM
CS16-04G02	OEM
CS16-04G03	OEM
CS16-06	0720

DEVICE TYPE	REPL CODE
CS16-06+	0720
CS16-06D01	OEM
CS16-06D02	OEM
CS16-06D03	OEM
CS16-06G01	OEM
CS16-06G02	OEM
CS16-06G03	OEM
CS16-08	0745
CS16-08+	2025
CS16-08D01	OEM
CS16-08D02	OEM
CS16-08D03	OEM
CS16-08I01	OEM
CS16-08I02	OEM
CS16-08I03	OEM
CS16-10	4771
CS16-10+	2025
CS16-10D01	OEM
CS16-10D02	OEM
CS16-10D03	OEM
CS16-10I01	OEM
CS16-10I02	OEM
CS16-10I03	OEM
CS16-12	OEM
CS16-12+	2025
CS16-12D01	OEM
CS16-12D03	OEM
CS16-12I01	OEM
CS16-12I02	OEM
CS16-12I03	OEM
CS16-14I01	OEM
CS16-14I02	OEM
CS16-14I03	OEM
CS16-16I01	OEM
CS16-16I02	OEM
CS16-16I03	OEM
CS16-100	OEM
CS16-200	OEM
CS16-400	OEM
CS16-500	OEM
CS16-600	OEM
CS16-800	OEM
CS16-1000	OEM
CS-16E	0015
CS16E	0015
CS18	OEM
CS20-02R	3275
CS20-05M	3287
CS20-05N	2174
CS20-05R	2174
CS20-1M	1640
CS20-1N	0562
CS20-1R	0562
CS20-1.5R	3227
CS20-2M	1641
CS20-2N	0757
CS20-2R	0757
CS20-2.5R	3237
CS20-3R	3240
CS20-4M	OEM
CS20-4N	0735
CS20-4R	0735
CS20-5R	3260
CS20-6M	1655
CS20-6N	0759
CS20-6R	0759
CS21B	OEM
CS21C	OEM
CS21D	OEM
CS21E	OEM
CS21G	OEM
CS21J	OEM
CS21K	OEM
CS21L	OEM
CS21M	OEM
CS21N	OEM
CS21P	OEM
CS21Q	OEM
CS21R	OEM
CS22-04	OEM
CS22-06	OEM
CS22-08	OEM
CS22-10	OEM
CS22-11	OEM
CS22-12	OEM
CS22-13	OEM
CS22-400	OEM
CS22-500	OEM
CS22-600	OEM
CS22-700	OEM
CS22-800	OEM
CS22-900	OEM
CS22-1000	OEM
CS22-1100	OEM
CS22-1200	OEM
CS22-1300	OEM
CS22B	OEM
CS22C	OEM
CS22D	OEM
CS22E	OEM
CS22G	OEM
CS22J	OEM
CS22K	OEM
CS22L	OEM
CS22M	OEM
CS22N	OEM
CS22P	OEM
CS22Q	OEM
CS22R	OEM

DEVICE TYPE	REPL CODE
CS23	OEM
CS23-02D03	OEM
CS23-02G03	1694
CS23-02G01	OEM
CS23-02G02	OEM
CS23-02G03	OEM
CS23-04D03	OEM
CS23-04G01	OEM
CS23-04G02	OEM
CS23-04G03	OEM
CS23-06D03	OEM
CS23-06G01	OEM
CS23-06G02	OEM
CS23-06G03	OEM
CS23-08D03	OEM
CS23-08I01	OEM
CS23-08I02	OEM
CS23-08I03	OEM
CS23-10D03	OEM
CS23-10I01	OEM
CS23-10I02	OEM
CS23-10I03	OEM
CS23-12D03	OEM
CS23-12I01	OEM
CS23-12I02	OEM
CS23-12I03	OEM
CS23-14I01	OEM
CS23-14I02	OEM
CS23-14I03	OEM
CS23-16I01	OEM
CS23-16I02	OEM
CS23-16I03	OEM
CS24	OEM
CS25-02M	2497
CS25-02N	3275
CS25-02R	3275
CS25-05M	OEM
CS25-05N	2174
CS25-05R	2174
CS25-1M	1640
CS25-1N	0562
CS25-1R	0562
CS25-2M	1641
CS25-2N	0757
CS25-2R	0757
CS25-3R	3240
CS25-4M	OEM
CS25-4R	0735
CS25-6M	1655
CS25-6N	0759
CS25-6R	0759
CS25-7R	2848
CS25-8N	0761
CS25-8R	0761
CS28	OEM
CS30-100	OEM
CS30-100BX	OEM
CS30-100BY	OEM
CS30-100CX	OEM
CS30-100CY	OEM
CS30-200	OEM
CS30-200BX	OEM
CS30-200BY	OEM
CS30-200CX	OEM
CS30-200CY	OEM
CS30-300BX	OEM
CS30-300BY	OEM
CS30-300CX	OEM
CS30-300CY	OEM
CS30-400	OEM
CS30-400BX	OEM
CS30-400BY	OEM
CS30-400CX	OEM
CS30-400CY	OEM
CS30-500	OEM
CS30-500BX	OEM
CS30-500BY	OEM
CS30-500CX	OEM
CS30-500CY	OEM
CS30-600	OEM
CS30-600BX	OEM
CS30-600BY	OEM
CS30-600CX	OEM
CS30-600CY	OEM
CS30-700BX	OEM
CS30-700BY	OEM
CS30-700CX	OEM
CS30-700CY	OEM
CS31B	OEM
CS31C	OEM
CS31D	OEM
CS31E	OEM
CS31G	OEM
CS31J	OEM
CS31K	OEM
CS31L	OEM
CS31M	OEM
CS31N	OEM
CS31P	OEM
CS31Q	OEM
CS31R	OEM
CS32B	OEM
CS32C	OEM
CS32D	OEM
CS32E	OEM
CS32G	OEM
CS32J	OEM
CS32K	OEM
CS32L	OEM

If replacement code is OEM, contact original manufacturer for replacement.

351

DEVICE TYPE	REPL CODE
CS32M	OEM
CS32N	OEM
CS32P	OEM
CS32Q	OEM
CS32R	OEM
CS33-02+	3970
CS33-04+	3970
CS33-06+	3970
CS33-08+	3970
CS33-10+	0674
CS33-12+	0674
CS35-02M	1640
CS35-02N	3246
CS35-02R	3246
CS35-04G03	OEM
CS35-05M	1640
CS35-05N	0726
CS35-05R	0726
CS35-06G03	OEM
CS35-08G03	OEM
CS35-1M	1640
CS35-1N	0707
CS35-1R	0707
CS35-1.5R	0464
CS35-2M	1640
CS35-2N	0464
CS35-2R	0464
CS35-2.5R	0716
CS35-4M	2623
CS35-4N	0717
CS35-4R	0717
CS35-6M	2625
CS35-6N	0720
CS35-6R	0720
CS35-10G03	OEM
CS35-12G03	OEM
CS38	OEM
CS38-08GU2	OEM
CS38-08GV2	OEM
CS38-12GV2	OEM
CS39-02	OEM
CS39-11	OEM
CS39C	OEM
CS40-600	OEM
CS40-800	OEM
CS40-1000	OEM
CS40-1100	OEM
CS40-1200	OEM
CS40-1300	OEM
CS40-1400	OEM
CS40-1500	OEM
CS41B	OEM
CS41C	OEM
CS41D	OEM
CS41E	OEM
CS41G	OEM
CS41J	OEM
CS41K	OEM
CS41L	OEM
CS41M	OEM
CS41N	OEM
CS41P	OEM
CS41Q	OEM
CS41R	OEM
CS42-06+	0463
CS42-08+	0463
CS42-10+	0463
CS42-12+	0463
CS42-12I02	OEM
CS42-14I02	OEM
CS42-16I02	OEM
CS42-600	OEM
CS42-800	OEM
CS42-1000	OEM
CS42-1200	OEM
CS42-1400	OEM
CS42-1600	OEM
CS48	OEM
CS50-06+	0463
CS50-06G01	OEM
CS50-06G02	OEM
CS50-06H01	OEM
CS50-06H02	OEM
CS50-08+	0463
CS50-08G01	OEM
CS50-08H02	OEM
CS50-08H01	OEM
CS50-08I01	OEM
CS50-08I02	OEM
CS50-10+	0463
CS50-10H01	OEM
CS50-10H02	OEM
CS50-10I01	OEM
CS50-10I02	OEM
CS50-11G01	OEM
CS50-11G02	OEM
CS50-11H01	OEM
CS50-11H02	OEM
CS50-11I01	OEM
CS50-11I02	OEM
CS50-12+	0463
CS50-12H01	OEM
CS50-12H02	OEM
CS50-12I01	OEM
CS50-12I02	OEM
CS50-13G01	OEM
CS50-13G02	OEM
CS50-13H01	OEM
CS50-13H02	OEM
CS50-13I01	OEM
CS50-13I02	OEM
CS50-14H01	OEM
CS50-14H02	OEM
CS50-14I01	OEM
CS50-14I02	OEM
CS50-15G01	OEM
CS50-15G02	OEM
CS50-15H01	OEM
CS50-15H02	OEM
CS50-15I01	OEM
CS50-15I02	OEM
CS50-16I01	OEM
CS50-16I02	OEM
CS50-17G01	OEM
CS50-17I01	OEM
CS50-17I02	OEM
CS54-06G01	OEM
CS54-06G04	OEM
CS54-08I01	OEM
CS54-08I04	OEM
CS54-10I01	OEM
CS54-10I04	OEM
CS54-12I01	OEM
CS54-12I04	OEM
CS54-14I01	OEM
CS54-14I04	OEM
CS54-16I01	OEM
CS60	0201
CS65-600	OEM
CS65-800	OEM
CS65-1000	OEM
CS65-1100	OEM
CS65-1200	OEM
CS65-1300	OEM
CS65-1400	OEM
CS65-1500	OEM
CS70-06G01	OEM
CS70-06G02	OEM
CS70-06H01	OEM
CS70-06H02	OEM
CS70-08H01	OEM
CS70-08H02	OEM
CS70-08I01	OEM
CS70-08I02	OEM
CS70-10H01	OEM
CS70-10H02	OEM
CS70-10I01	OEM
CS70-10I02	OEM
CS70-11G01	OEM
CS70-11G02	OEM
CS70-11H01	OEM
CS70-11H02	OEM
CS70-11I01	OEM
CS70-11I02	OEM
CS70-12H01	OEM
CS70-12H02	OEM
CS70-12I01	OEM
CS70-12I02	OEM
CS70-13G01	OEM
CS70-13G02	OEM
CS70-13H01	OEM
CS70-13H02	OEM
CS70-13I01	OEM
CS70-13I02	OEM
CS70-14H01	OEM
CS70-14H02	OEM
CS70-14I01	OEM
CS70-14I02	OEM
CS70-15G01	OEM
CS70-15G02	OEM
CS70-15H01	OEM
CS70-15H02	OEM
CS70-15I01	OEM
CS70-15I02	OEM
CS70-16H01	OEM
CS70-16H02	OEM
CS70-16I01	OEM
CS70-16I02	OEM
CS70-17G01	OEM
CS70-17G02	OEM
CS70-17I01	OEM
CS70-17I02	OEM
CS70-18I01	OEM
CS70-18I02	OEM
CS72-1	OEM
CS72-1M	OEM
CS72-2	OEM
CS72-2M	OEM
CS72-3	OEM
CS72-3M	OEM
CS72-4	OEM
CS72-4M	OEM
CS72-5	OEM
CS72-5M	OEM
CS72-6	OEM
CS72-6M	OEM
CS72-7	OEM
CS72-7M	OEM
CS72-8	OEM
CS72-8M	OEM
CS78-06GU2	OEM
CS78-06GU3	OEM
CS78-06GV2	OEM
CS78-06GV3	OEM
CS78-06H03	OEM
CS78-08GU2	OEM
CS78-08GU3	OEM
CS78-08GV2	OEM
CS78-08H02	OEM
CS78-08H03	OEM
CS78-10GU2	OEM
CS78-10GU3	OEM
CS78-10GV2	OEM
CS78-10GV3	OEM
CS78-10H02	OEM
CS78-10H03	OEM
CS78-12GU2	OEM
CS78-12GU3	OEM
CS78-12GV2	OEM
CS78-12GV3	OEM
CS78-12H02	OEM
CS78-12H03	OEM
CS78-13H02	OEM
CS78-13H03	OEM
CS79-02	OEM
CS79-04	OEM
CS79-06H02	OEM
CS79-06H03	OEM
CS79-08GW2	OEM
CS79-08GW3	OEM
CS79-08H02	OEM
CS79-08H03	OEM
CS79-10GW2	OEM
CS79-10GW3	OEM
CS79-10H02	OEM
CS79-10H03	OEM
CS79-11	OEM
CS79-12GV2	OEM
CS79-12GV3	OEM
CS79-12GW2	OEM
CS79-12GW3	OEM
CS79-12GX2	OEM
CS79-12GX3	OEM
CS79-12H02	OEM
CS79-12H03	OEM
CS79-13GX3	OEM
CS79-13H02	OEM
CS79-13H03	OEM
CS80-06I02	OEM
CS80-08I02	OEM
CS80-10I02	OEM
CS80-11I02	OEM
CS80-12I02	OEM
CS80-15I02	OEM
CS80-16I02	OEM
CS80-17I02	OEM
CS80-18I02	OEM
CS80I02	OEM
CS100	OEM
CS100-36I02	OEM
CS101-40I02	OEM
CS-102	OEM
CS-102-1	OEM
CS102-1	OEM
CS110-06G01	OEM
CS110-06G02	OEM
CS110-08I01	OEM
CS110-08I02	OEM
CS110-10I01	OEM
CS110-10I02	OEM
CS110-12I01	OEM
CS110-12I02	OEM
CS110-14I01	OEM
CS110-14I02	OEM
CS110-16I01	OEM
CS110-16I02	OEM
CS110-18G01	OEM
CS110-18G02	OEM
CS110-18I01	OEM
CS110-18I02	OEM
CS120	0201
CS-122	OEM
CS122	OEM
CS122A	OEM
CS122AM	OEM
CS122B	OEM
CS122BM	OEM
CS122C	OEM
CS122CM	OEM
CS122D	OEM
CS122DM	OEM
CS122E	OEM
CS122EM	OEM
CS122M	OEM
CS122MM	OEM
CS122N	OEM
CS122NM	OEM
CS122S	OEM
CS122SM	OEM
CS124E3	OEM
CS124F3	OEM
CS-127	OEM
CS127	OEM
CS-129	OEM
CS129	OEM
CS-130	OEM
CS130	OEM
CS130-11I02	OEM
CS130-12I02	OEM
CS130-13G02	OEM
CS130-13I02	OEM
CS130-14I02	OEM
CS130-16I02	OEM
CS130-17G02	OEM
CS130-17I02	OEM
CS130-18I02	OEM
CS130-600	OEM
CS130-800	OEM
CS130-1000	OEM
CS130-1100	OEM
CS130-1200	OEM
CS130-1300	OEM
CS130-1400	OEM
CS130-1600	OEM
CS130-1800	OEM
CS-131	OEM
CS131A	1017
CS131A+	1017
CS131AZ	1017
CS131AZ+	1017
CS131B	1017
CS131B+	1017
CS131C	1017
CS131C+	1017
CS131D	1219
CS131D(STUD)	1017
CS131D+	1030
CS131E	1030
CS131F	1030
CS131F+	1030
CS131Z	1017
CS131Z+	1017
CS-132	OEM
CS149-04	OEM
CS149-06G02	OEM
CS149-06I02	OEM
CS149-08G02	OEM
CS149-08I02	OEM
CS149-10G02	OEM
CS149-10I02	OEM
CS149-11	OEM
CS149-12G02	OEM
CS149-12I02	OEM
CS149-13G02	OEM
CS149-13I02	OEM
CS160-12I02	OEM
CS160-14I02	OEM
CS160-16I02	OEM
CS166	OEM
CS179	OEM
CS-180	OEM
CS180	0374
CS186-04G01	OEM
CS186-06G01	OEM
CS186-08I01	OEM
CS186-12I01	OEM
CS186-14I01	OEM
CS186-16I01	OEM
CS188	OEM
CS189	OEM
CS189-02G05	OEM
CS189-04G05	OEM
CS189-07	OEM
CS189-11	OEM
CS190-08I01	OEM
CS190-08I04	OEM
CS190-12I01	OEM
CS190-12I04	OEM
CS190-14I01	OEM
CS190-14I04	OEM
CS195-600	OEM
CS195-800	OEM
CS195-1000	OEM
CS195-1100	OEM
CS195-1200	OEM
CS195-1300	OEM
CS195-1400	OEM
CS195-1500	OEM
CS195-1600	OEM
CS210-04G01	OEM
CS210-04G04	OEM
CS210-04I01	OEM
CS210-04I04	OEM
CS210-06G01	OEM
CS210-06G04	OEM
CS210-06I01	OEM
CS210-06I04	OEM
CS210-08G01	OEM
CS210-08G04	OEM
CS210-08I01	OEM
CS210-08I04	OEM
CS210-10G01	OEM
CS210-10G04	OEM
CS210-10I01	OEM
CS210-10I04	OEM
CS210-12G01	OEM
CS210-12G04	OEM
CS210-12I01	OEM
CS210-12I04	OEM
CS220-08I02	OEM
CS220-5	OEM
CS220-5M	OEM
CS220-7	OEM
CS220-7M	OEM
CS220-9	OEM
CS220-9M	OEM
CS220-12I02	OEM
CS220-14I02	OEM
CS220-16I02	OEM
CS221-5	OEM
CS221-5M	OEM
CS221-7	OEM
CS221-7M	OEM
CS221-9	OEM
CS221-9M	OEM
CS226-04G01	OEM
CS226-06G01	OEM
CS226-08I01	OEM
CS226-12I01	OEM
CS226-14I01	OEM
CS226-16I01	OEM
CS239-02G03	OEM
CS239-02I03	OEM
CS239-04G03	OEM
CS239-04I03	OEM
CS239-06G03	OEM
CS239-06I03	OEM
CS250-08I01	OEM
CS250-1	OEM
CS250-10G01	OEM
CS250-10I01	OEM
CS250-12I01	OEM
CS250-14I01	OEM
CS250-15I01	OEM
CS250-16I01	OEM
CS-258	OEM
CS-258A	OEM
CS-263	OEM
CS295-08I01	OEM
CS295-08I04	OEM
CS295-12I01	OEM
CS295-12I04	OEM
CS295-14I01	OEM
CS295-14I04	OEM
CS295-16I01	OEM
CS295-16I04	OEM
CS299DC	OEM
CS299DI	OEM
CS300-06G03	OEM
CS300-06HW2	OEM
CS300-06I03	OEM
CS300-08I03	OEM
CS300-10I01	OEM
CS300-11G03	OEM
CS300-11I03	OEM
CS300-12I03	OEM
CS300-13G03	OEM
CS300-13I03	OEM
CS300-16I03	OEM
CS300-17G03	OEM
CS300-17I03	OEM
CS302BA	OEM
CS302DA	OEM
CS302FA	OEM
CS302HA	OEM
CS302KA	OEM
CS302MA	2621
CS302PA	2621
CS302RA	2621
CS311-27I01	OEM
CS311-30I01	OEM
CS311-32I01	OEM
CS330-04G01	OEM
CS330-04G04	OEM
CS330-04I01	OEM
CS330-04I04	OEM
CS330-06G01	OEM
CS330-06G04	OEM
CS330-06I01	OEM
CS330-06I04	OEM
CS330-08G01	OEM
CS330-08G04	OEM
CS330-08I01	OEM
CS330-08I04	OEM
CS330-10G01	OEM
CS330-10G04	OEM
CS330-10I01	OEM
CS330-10I04	OEM
CS330-12G01	OEM
CS330-12G04	OEM
CS330-12I01	OEM
CS330-12I04	OEM
CS349-06	OEM
CS349-07	OEM
CS349-08	OEM
CS349-10	OEM
CS349-11	OEM
CS349-12	OEM
CS349-13	OEM
CS351-18I01	OEM
CS351-20I01	OEM
CS351-23I01	OEM
CS351-25I01	OEM
CS351-27I01	OEM
CS360	0016
CS369-10I01	OEM
CS370-04G01	OEM
CS370-04G04	OEM
CS370-04I01	OEM
CS370-04I04	OEM
CS370-06G01	OEM
CS370-06G04	OEM
CS370-06I01	OEM
CS370-06I04	OEM
CS399-07	OEM
CS399-08HW2	OEM
CS399-11	OEM
CS399-12I01	OEM
CS399-13I01	OEM
CS400-04G02	OEM
CS400-04H02	OEM
CS400-04I02	OEM
CS400-06G02	OEM
CS400-06H02	OEM
CS400-06I01	OEM
CS400-06I02	OEM
CS400-08G02	OEM
CS400-08H02	OEM
CS400-08I01	OEM
CS400-08I02	OEM
CS400-10H02	OEM
CS400-10I01	OEM
CS400-10I02	OEM
CS400-11G02	OEM
CS400-11H02	OEM
CS400-11I01	OEM
CS400-11I02	OEM
CS400-12H02	OEM
CS400-12I01	OEM
CS400-12I02	OEM
CS400-13G02	OEM
CS400-13H02	OEM
CS400-13I01	OEM
CS400-13I02	OEM
CS400-14H02	OEM
CS400-14I01	OEM
CS400-14I02	OEM
CS400-15H02	OEM
CS400-15I01	OEM
CS400-15I02	OEM
CS400-16H02	OEM
CS400-16I01	OEM
CS400-16I02	OEM
CS-401	OEM
CS401-18H02	OEM
CS401-18I01	OEM
CS401-20H02	OEM
CS401-20I01	OEM
CS401-21H02	OEM
CS401-21I01	OEM
CS401-22G02	OEM
CS401-22H02	OEM
CS401-22I01	OEM
CS401-22I02	OEM
CS401-23H02	OEM
CS401-23I01	OEM
CS401-24H02	OEM
CS401-24I01	OEM
CS401-25H02	OEM
CS401-25I01	OEM
CS-402	OEM
CS411-18I01	OEM
CS411-20I01	OEM
CS411-23I01	OEM
CS411-25I01	OEM
CS415-02G01	OEM
CS415-03G01	OEM
CS415-05G01	OEM
CS-450	OEM
CS-460	OEM
CS460	OEM
CS-460B	0016
CS-461	OEM
CS-461B	0144
CS-462	OEM
CS-463	OEM
CS-464	OEM
CS-480	OEM
CS480	OEM
CS-481	OEM
CS481	OEM
CS-482	OEM
CS482	OEM
CS-483	OEM
CS483	OEM
CS-484	OEM
CS484	OEM
CS-486	OEM
CS486	OEM
CS-487	OEM
CS487	OEM
CS-488	OEM
CS488	OEM
CS-489	OEM
CS489	OEM
CS500-08	OEM
CS500-08I04	OEM
CS500-10	OEM
CS500-10I04	OEM
CS500-12	OEM
CS500-12I04	OEM
CS500-14	OEM
CS500-14I04	OEM
CS500-15	OEM
CS500-15I04	OEM
CS500-16	OEM
CS500-16I04	OEM
CS550-08I01	OEM
CS550-10I01	OEM
CS550-12I01	OEM
CS550-13G01	OEM
CS550-13I01	OEM
CS550-14I01	OEM
CS550-15I01	OEM
CS550-16I01	OEM
CS-560	OEM
CS560	OEM
CS-580	OEM
CS580	OEM
CS601-18I01	OEM
CS601-20I01	OEM
CS601-22I01	OEM
CS601-24I01	OEM
CS601-25I01	OEM
CS661-27I01	OEM
CS661-30I01	OEM
CS661-32I01	OEM
CS661-35I01	OEM
CS696	0016
CS697	0016
CS706	0016
CS718	0016
CS718A	0016
CS720A	0016
CS901	OEM
CS-901ZHF	0037
CS901ZHF	0037
CS902	OEM
CS903	OEM
CS904	OEM
CS905	OEM
CS918	0144
CS925M	0016
CS929	0007
CS930	0007
CS956	0086
CS1000-12I01	OEM
CS1000-14I01	OEM
CS1000-16I01	OEM
CS1000-17I01	OEM
CS1001-20I01	OEM
CS1001-22I01	OEM
CS1001-24I01	OEM
CS1001-25I01	OEM
CS1014	0144
CS1014D	0144
CS1014E	0144
CS1014F	0144
CS1014G	0007
CS1014H	0007
CS1018	0144
CS1021-32I01	OEM
CS1021-38I01	OEM
CS1021-40I01	OEM
CS1068	0079
CS1120C	0007
CS-1120C1	0079
CS-1120C2	0079
CS1120D	0007
CS-1120D1	0079
CS1120E	0007
CS1120F	0007
CS-1120H	0079
CS1120H	0007
CS-1120I	0079
CS1120I	0079
CS1121G	0037
CS-1124G	OEM
CS1124G	0150
CS1129E	0086
CS1166	0016
CS1166D	0079
CS1166D-G	0079
CS1166E	0016
CS1166F	0079
CS1166G	0016
CS1166H	0016
CS1166H/F	0016
CS1168E	0144
CS1168F	0016
CS1168G	0079
CS1168H	0016
CS1170F	0037
CS1221F	0037
CS1225D	0144
CS1225E	0144
CS1225F	0144
CS1225H	0086
CS1226	0144
CS1226E	0144
CS1226F	0144
CS1226G	0144
CS1226H	0144
CS1226N	0079
CS1227	0144
CS1227D	0144
CS1227E	0144
CS1227F	0144
CS1227G	0144
CS1228	0037
CS1228E	0037
CS1229	0016
CS1229A	0016
CS1229B	0016
CS1229C	0016
CS1229D	0016
CS1229E	0016
CS1229F	0016
CS1229G	0016
CS1229H	0016
CS1229K	0086
CS1229N	0086
CS1235C	0016
CS1235E	0144
CS-1235F	0016
CS1235G	0076
CS1236D	0016
CS1236H	0016
CS1237	0126
CS1238	0144
CS-1238F	0079
CS1238F	0016
CS1238G	0144

352

If replacement code is OEM, contact original manufacturer for replacement.

DEVICE TYPE	REPL CODE
CS1238H	0144
CS1238I	0144
CS-1238P	0079
CS1238P	0016
CS1243E	0144
CS1243H	0144
CS1244H	0144
CS1244J	0144
CS-1244X	0079
CS1244X	0144
CS1245F	0016
CS1245G	0016
CS1245H	0016
CS1245I	0079
CS1245T	0016
CS1248	0086
CS1248I	0086
CS1248T	0086
CS1250E	0016
CS1250F	0086
CS1251E	0037
CS1251F	0037
CS1252B	0144
CS1252C	0144
CS1255H	0086
CS1255HF	0786
CS1255M	0590
CS1256H	0126
CS1256HG	0590
CS1256MC	0378
CS1257	0016
CS-1258	0079
CS1258	0016
CS-1259	0079
CS1259	0016
CS1283A	0016
CS1284B	0007
CS1284F	0007
CS1284G	0007
CS1284H	0007
CS1286	0079
CS1288	0016
CS1289	0016
CS1293	0144
CS1294E	0037
CS-1294F	0150
CS1294H	0037
CS1295E	0016
CS1295G	0016
CS1295H	0086
CS1300-04G01	OEM
CS1300-08I01	OEM
CS1300-12I01	OEM
CS1300-14I01	OEM
CS1300-16I01	OEM
CS1300-18I01	OEM
CS1303	0037
CS-1305	0079
CS1305	0086
CS1308	0037
CS1312G	0126
CS-1330	0079
CS1330	0007
CS1330A	0144
CS1330B	0144
CS1330C	0144
CS1330D	0079
CS1340D	0144
CS1340E	0144
CS1340F	0144
CS1340G	0144
CS1340H	0144
CS1340I	0016
CS1344	0016
CS1345	0016
CS1347	0233
CS1348	0016
CS1349	0016
CS1350	0144
CS1351	0144
CS-1352	0590
CS1352	0086
CS1353	0016
CS1354	0037
CS-1359	0079
CS1359	0144
CS1360	0144
CS-1361E	0079
CS1361E	0144
CS-1361F	0079
CS1361F	0144
CS-1361G	0079
CS1361G	0016
CS1362	0016
CS1363	0016
CS1368	0016
CS1368A	0016
CS1368B	0016
CS1368C	0016
CS1368D	0016
CS1369	0126
CS1369D	0150
CS1370	0016
CS1371	0016
CS-1372	0086
CS1372	0016
CS1383	0016
CS-1386E	0016
CS-1386H	0079
CS1386H	0144
CS1420	0016
CS1453E	0016
CS1453F	0086
CS1453G	0086
CS1460E	0007
CS1460H	0007
CS1461J	0007
CS1461X	0007
CS1462F	0007
CS1462I	0086
CS1463A	0016
CS1464H	0086
CS1465H	0126
CS1502A	OEM
CS1502B	OEM
CS1504	OEM
CS1508G	0144
CS1509E	0144
CS1509F	0144
CS1518E	0144
CS1555	0144
CS1585	0016
CS1585E/F	0016
CS1585G	0016
CS1585H	0127
CS1589E	0007
CS1589F	0007
CS1589S	0007
CS1591LE	0086
CS1594E	0007
CS1596E	0007
CS1609F	0086
CS1613	0086
CS1661	0144
CS1664	0086
CS1665	0016
CS1702C	0079
CS1711	0086
CS1758	0004
CS1759	0208
CS1834	0144
CS1893	0086
CS1909B	0018
CS1910B	0527
CS1990	0086
CS2000	OEM
CS2001	0016
CS2001H	0079
CS2004	0016
CS-2004C	0144
CS2004C	0079
CS2004D	0016
CS2005	0150
CS-2005B	0037
CS2005B	0150
CS-2005C	0037
CS2006	0016
CS2006G	0144
CS-2007G	0144
CS2007G	0079
CS-2007H	0144
CS2007H	0079
CS2008	0144
CS-2008F	0144
CS-2008G	0144
CS2008G	0144
CS-2008H	0144
CS2008H	0144
CS2008H552	0144
CS2023	0590
CS-2082	OEM
CS2082	0786
CS-2083	0079
CS-2142	0786
CS2142	0786
CS-2143	0590
CS2218	0016
CS2219	0016
CS2221	0016
CS2222	0016
CS2368	OEM
CS2369	0016
CS2481	0016
CS2483	0855
CS2484	0086
CS2639	OEM
CS2640	OEM
CS2641	OEM
CS2642	OEM
CS2643	OEM
CS2644	OEM
CS2657	OEM
CS2711	0016
CS2712	0016
CS2713	0016
CS2714	0016
CS2715	0007
CS2716	0007
CS2907D8	OEM
CS2917	2302
CS2917-1D14	OEM
CS2917D8	OEM
CS2922	0016
CS2923	0016
CS2924	0016
CS2925	0016
CS2941	0037
CS-3001B	0144
CS3001B	0079
CS-3024	0396
CS3390	0016
CS3391	0016
CS3391A	0016
CS3392	0016
CS3393	0016
CS3394	0016
CS3395	0016
CS3396	0016
CS3397	0016
CS3398	0016
CS3402	0016
CS3403	0016
CS3404	0016
CS3405	0016
CS3414	0016
CS3415	0016
CS3416	0016
CS3417	0016
CS3605	0016
CS3606	0016
CS3607	0016
CS3662	0007
CS3663	0007
CS3702	0037
CS3703	0037
CS3704	0086
CS3705	0086
CS3706	0086
CS3707	0007
CS3708	0007
CS3709	0007
CS3710	0007
CS3711	0007
CS3842A	OEM
CS3843	0016
CS3844	0016
CS3845	0016
CS3854A	0016
CS3859	0016
CS3860	0016
CS3906	0037
CS4001	0488
CS4003	0016
CS4004D	OEM
CS4005	0086
CS4006	0086
CS4007	0016
CS4012	0016
CS4013	0037
CS4021	0016
CS4060	0016
CS4061	0016
CS4062	0016
CS4193	0016
CS4194	0016
CS5995	0627
CS-6168F	0079
CS6168F	0016
CS-6168G	0016
CS6168G	0086
CS-6168H	0016
CS6168H	0079
CS-6225E	0127
CS6225E	0079
CS-6225F	0079
CS6225F	0144
CS-6225G	0016
CS6225G	0079
CS6226F	0144
CS-6227E	0079
CS6227E	0144
CS-6227F	0079
CS6227F	0144
CS-6227G	0144
CS6227G	0079
CS6228F	0037
CS-6228G	0126
CS6228G	0378
CS6229F	0016
CS6395	OEM
CS6395M	OEM
CS6396	OEM
CS6396M	OEM
CS6397	OEM
CS6397M	OEM
CS6398	OEM
CS6398M	OEM
CS6399	OEM
CS6399M	OEM
CS6401	OEM
CS6401M	OEM
CS6402	OEM
CS6402M	OEM
CS6403	OEM
CS6403M	OEM
CS6404	OEM
CS6404M	OEM
CS6405	OEM
CS6405M	OEM
CS6505	OEM
CS6505M	OEM
CS6506	OEM
CS6506M	OEM
CS6507	OEM
CS6507M	OEM
CS6508	OEM
CS6508M	OEM
CS6509	OEM
CS6509M	OEM
CS7228E	OEM
CS7228G	0126
CS7229F	0086
CS7229G	0016
CS8050	0320
CS9001	0144
CS9010	0079
CS-9011	0016
CS9011	0016
CS9011(C)	0016
CS9011(E)(F)	0079
CS9011(EF)	0079
CS9011(F)	0016
CS9011(GH)	0079
CS9011(I)	0016
CS9011D	0016
CS9011E	0016
CS-9011F	0079
CS9011F	0016
CS-9011G	0016
CS9011G	0016
CS9011H	0016
CS9011I	0016
CS9011N	0079
CS9012	0006
CS9012E	0037
CS9012E-F	0037
CS9012F	0037
CS9012FG	0037
CS9012G	0037
CS9012H	0037
CS9012HE	0037
CS-9012HF	0037
CS9012HF	0037
CS9012HG	0037
CS-9012HH	0126
CS9012HH	0037
CS9012I	0037
CS-9013	0079
CS9013	0016
CS9013(HG)	0161
CS9013B	0016
CS9013E	0016
CS9013E-F	0086
CS9013F	0016
CS9013G	0016
CS9013H	0016
CS-9013HE	0079
CS9013HE	0016
CS9013HF	0016
CS-9013HG	0086
CS9013HG	0016
CS-9013HH	0150
CS9013HH	0016
CS-9014	0007
CS9014	0016
CS9014(C)	0079
CS9014A	0016
CS9014B	0016
CS9014B-C	0079
CS9014C	0016
CS9014C/3490	0016
CS9014D	0037
CS9014G	0079
CS9015	0037
CS9015A	OEM
CS9015B	0037
CS9015C	0037
CS9015C2	0037
CS9015D	0037
CS-9016	0224
CS9016	0224
CS9016(G)	0079
CS-9016D	0224
CS9016D	0224
CS9016E	0224
CS9016EF	0224
CS9016F	0224
CS9016F(TRUETONE)	0079
CS9016F(WESTGHSE)	0079
CS9016FG	0224
CS9016G	0224
CS9016H	0224
CS9017	0007
CS9017F	0007
CS9017G	0007
CS9017H	0007
CS9018	0144
CS-9018D	0079
CS9018D	0144
CS9018E	0144
CS9018EF	0144
CS9018F	0144
CS9018FG	0144
CS9018G	0144
CS9019	0079
CS9021G-I	0144
CS9022LE	0086
CS9101B	0016
CS9102	0037
CS9102B	0126
CS9103B	0086
CS9103C	0086
CS9104	0111
CS9123C1	0150
CS9124-C2	0144
CS9124B1	0144
CS9124BI	OEM
CS9125-B1	0144
CS-9125B	0016
CS9125B	0016
CS9126	0016
CS9128	0150
CS9128-B2	0037
CS9128C1	0037
CS9129	0037
CS9129(B)	0150
CS9129-B1	0150
CS9129B1	0037
CS9129B2	0037
CS9417	0590
CS9600-4	0016
CS9600-5	0016
CS-12941	0079
CS13401	0016
CS20014	OEM
CS23122	OEM
CS29008	OEM
CS29009	OEM
CS29010	OEM
CS29011	OEM
CS29012	OEM
CS29013	OEM
CS-90111	0079
CS90111	0016
CS90144	0911
CSA7200B150-806	OEM
CSA7200B173-001	OEM
CSA7200B176-001	OEM
CSA7200B184-802	OEM
CSA7205	OEM
CSA7205A	OEM
CSA7205B	OEM
CSA7205C	OEM
CSB05	0241
CSB1	0241
CSB2	0241
CSB4	4501
CSB6	3503
CSB8	3503
CSB10	3503
CSB151	OEM
CSB152	OEM
CSB154	OEM
CSB156	OEM
CSB158	OEM
CSB251	OEM
CSB252	OEM
CSB254	OEM
CSB256	OEM
CSB258	OEM
CSB351	OEM
CSB352	OEM
CSB354	OEM
CSB356	OEM
CSB358	4501
CSB640J	OEM
CSB1505	OEM
CSB1510	OEM
CSB2505	OEM
CSB2510	OEM
CSB3505	OEM
CSB3510	OEM
CSB7000B150-802	OEM
CSB7000B173-001	OEM
CSB7000B176-001	OEM
CSB7000B184-802	OEM
CSB7002-01	OEM
CSB7002-02	OEM
CSB7002-03	OEM
CSB7002-04	OEM
CSB7002-05	OEM
CSB7002-06	OEM
CSB7002-07	OEM
CSB7003-01	OEM
CSB7003-02	OEM
CSB7003-03	OEM
CSB7003-04	OEM
CSB7100B150-802	OEM
CSB7100B173-001	OEM
CSB7100B176-001	OEM
CSB7100B184-802	OEM
CSB7201-01	OEM
CSB7201-02	OEM
CSB7201-03	OEM
CSB7401-01	OEM
CSB7401-02	OEM
CSB7401-03	OEM
CSB7500-150-802	OEM
CSB7500-173-001	OEM
CSB7500-176-001	OEM
CSB7500-184-802	OEM
CSBC941	OEM
CSC12	OEM
CSD2310	OEM
CSD2312	OEM
CSD2313	OEM
CSD2314	OEM
CSD2315	0124
CSD2316	OEM
CSD2317	OEM
CSD2325	OEM
CSD2359	0124
CSF02AM2	OEM
CSF02AM4	OEM
CSF02AM8	OEM
CSF0.7-04FT1	OEM
CSF7.9-04GT2	OEM
CSF7.9-04GT3	OEM
CSF7.9-06GT2	OEM
CSF7.9-06GT3	OEM
CSF7.9-08GT2	OEM
CSF7.9-08GT3	OEM
CSF11-02ER1	OEM
CSF11-04ER1	OEM
CSF11-04ET1	OEM
CSF11-06EP1	OEM
CSF11-08EP1	OEM
CSF11-08ET1	OEM
CSF34-08GW3	OEM
CSF34-10GW3	OEM
CSF34-12GW3	OEM
CSF37-02GS3	OEM
CSF37-02GU3	OEM
CSF37-04GS3	OEM
CSF37-04GU3	OEM
CSF315-02HP1	OEM
CSF315-02HS1	OEM
CSF315-02IP1	OEM
CSF315-02IS1	OEM
CSF315-03HP1	OEM
CSF315-03HS1	OEM
CSF315-03IP1	OEM
CSF315-03IS1	OEM
CSF315-04HP1	OEM
CSF315-04HS1	OEM
CSF315-04IP1	OEM
CSF315-04IS1	OEM
CSF315-05HP1	OEM
CSF315-05HS1	OEM
CSF315-05IP1	OEM
CSF315-05IS1	OEM
CSF367-06HV1	OEM
CSF367-08HU1	OEM
CSF367-08HV1	OEM
CSF367-10HU1	OEM
CSF367-10HV1	OEM
CSF369-11HX1	OEM
CSF369-11IV1	OEM
CSF369-12HZ1	OEM
CSF369-12IV1	OEM
CSF369-12IW1	OEM
CSF369-13HX1	OEM
CSF369-13IV1	OEM
CSF369-13IW1	OEM
CSF369-14IV1	OEM
CSF375-02HP1	OEM
CSF375-02HU1	OEM
CSF375-02IP1	OEM
CSF375-02IU1	OEM
CSF375-03HP1	OEM
CSF375-03HU1	OEM
CSF375-03IP1	OEM
CSF375-03IU1	OEM
CSF375-04HP1	OEM
CSF375-04HU1	OEM
CSF375-04IP1	OEM
CSF375-04IU1	OEM
CSF375-05HP1	OEM
CSF375-05HU1	OEM
CSF375-05IP1	OEM
CSF375-05IU1	OEM
CSF399-11IW1	OEM
CSF399-12HV1	OEM
CSF399-12IW1	OEM
CSF399-12IX1	OEM
CSF399-13HV1	OEM
CSF399-13IW1	OEM
CSF399-13IX1	OEM
CSF495-02HP1	OEM
CSF495-02HU1	OEM
CSF495-02IP1	OEM
CSF495-02IU1	OEM
CSF495-03HP1	OEM
CSF495-03HU1	OEM
CSF495-03IP1	OEM
CSF495-03IU1	OEM
CSF495-04HP1	OEM
CSF495-04HU1	OEM
CSF495-04IP1	OEM
CSF495-04IU1	OEM
CSF495-05HP1	OEM
CSF495-05HU1	OEM
CSF495-05IP1	OEM
CSF495-05IU1	OEM
CSF499-11IW1	OEM
CSF499-11IX1	OEM
CSF499-12IW1	OEM
CSF499-12IX1	OEM
CSF499-13IW1	OEM
CSF499-13IX1	OEM
CSF547-08IU1	OEM
CSF547-08IV1	OEM
CSF547-08IW1	OEM
CSF547-09IU1	OEM
CSF547-09IV1	OEM
CSF547-09IW1	OEM
CSF547-10IU1	OEM
CSF547-10IV1	OEM
CSF547-10IW1	OEM
CSF548-11IV1	OEM
CSF548-11IW1	OEM
CSF548-11IX1	OEM
CSF548-12IV1	OEM
CSF548-12IW1	OEM
CSF548-12IX1	OEM
CSF548-13IV1	OEM
CSF548-13IW1	OEM
CSF548-13IX1	OEM
CSF549-14IV1	OEM
CSF549-14IW1	OEM
CSF549-14IX1	OEM
CSF549-15IW1	OEM
CSF549-15IX1	OEM
CSF549-15IY1	OEM
CSF549-16IW1	OEM
CSF549-16IX1	OEM
CSF549-16IY1	OEM
CSF551-18IX1	OEM
CSF551-18IY1	OEM
CSF551-18IZ1	OEM
CSF551-20IX1	OEM
CSF551-20IY1	OEM
CSF551-20IZ1	OEM
CSF595-02HP1	OEM
CSF595-02HU1	OEM
CSF595-04HP1	OEM
CSF595-05HP1	OEM
CSI-06G03	OEM
CSKB40C800	OEM
CSKB40C1200	OEM
CSKB80C800	OEM
CSKB80C1200	OEM
CSKB250C800	OEM
CSKB250C1200	OEM
CSKB500C800	OEM
CSKB500C1200	OEM
CSL300	OEM
CSL311	OEM
CSL311L	OEM
CSM2B2	OEM
CSM3B1	0442
CSM3B2	0934
CSM7301-01	OEM
CSM7301-02	OEM
CSM7301-03	OEM
CSM7301-04	OEM
CSM7301-05	OEM
CSM7301-06	OEM
CSO68-8	0030
CSP4.7	OEM
CSP7	OEM
CSP14	OEM
CSP16.5	OEM
CSP28	OEM
CSR301	OEM
CSR447-08IU1	OEM
CSR447-08IW1	OEM
CSR447-09IU1	OEM
CSR447-09IW1	OEM
CSR447-10IU1	OEM
CSR447-10IW1	OEM
CSR448-11IV1	OEM
CSR448-11IX1	OEM
CSR448-12IV1	OEM
CSR448-12IX1	OEM
CSR448-13IV1	OEM
CSR448-13IX1	OEM
CSR449-14IW1	OEM
CSR449-14IY1	OEM
CSR449-15IW1	OEM
CSR449-15IY1	OEM
CSR449-16IW1	OEM
CSR451-18IX1	OEM
CSR451-18IZ1	OEM
CSR451-20IX1	OEM
CSR451-20IZ1	OEM
CSR5700	OEM
CSR5701	OEM
CSR5702	OEM
CSR5705	OEM
CSSD2003	OEM
CST30	OEM
CST1739	0085
CST1740	0085
CST1741	0085
CST1742	0085
CST1743	0160
CST1744	0160
CST1745	0160
CST1746	0160
CT-06C	0239
CT08	OEM
CT11-1A	2367
CT11-2A	2378
CT11-4A	1403
CT12-1A	2367
CT12-2A	2378
CT12-4A	1403
CT15-4	OEM
CT15-4M	OEM
CT15-5	OEM
CT15-5M	OEM
CT15-6	OEM
CT15-6M	OEM
CT15-7	OEM
CT15-7M	OEM
CT15-8	OEM
CT15-8M	OEM
CT15-9	OEM
CT15-9M	OEM
CT15-10	OEM
CT15-10M	OEM

If replacement code is OEM, contact original manufacturer for replacement.

353

DEVICE TYPE	REPL CODE
CT15A4	OEM
CT15A4M	OEM
CT15A5	OEM
CT15A5M	OEM
CT15A6	OEM
CT15A6M	OEM
CT15A7	OEM
CT15A7M	OEM
CT15A8	OEM
CT15A8M	OEM
CT15A9	OEM
CT15A9M	OEM
CT15A10	OEM
CT15A10M	OEM
CT16X7	0907
CT16XT	0196
CT18	OEM
CT21	0133
CT22	1325
CT23	0080
CT24	0604
CT26	0133
CT27	1325
CT28	0080
CT29	0604
CT30-1A	2336
CT30-2A	2337
CT30-4A	2340
CT31	0133
CT31-1A	2367
CT31-2A	2378
CT31-4A	1403
CT32	1325
CT32-05N	0154
CT32-1A	2367
CT32-1N	0154
CT32-2A	2378
CT32-2N	0154
CT32-4A	1403
CT32-4N	0147
CT32-6A	2371
CT32-6N	0278
CT33	0604
CT33-1A	2336
CT33-2A	2337
CT33-4A	2340
CT34	0604
CT36	0133
CT37	0604
CT38	0080
CT39	0604
CT40	0124
CT41	0124
CT42	0124
CT43	0124
CT44	0124
CT45	0124
CT46	0124
CT47	0124
CT48	OEM
CT48(DIODE)	0124
CT49	0124
CT50	0124
CT51	0124
CT51-403A	0463
CT52	0124
CT53	0124
CT54	0124
CT55	0124
CT56	0124
CT57	0124
CT58	0124
CT59	0124
CT62-05N	0154
CT62-1N	0154
CT62-2N	0154
CT62-4N	0147
CT62-5N	0278
CT62-6N	0278
CT70	0124
CT71	0124
CT72	0124
CT73	0124
CT74	0124
CT75	0124
CT76	0124
CT77	0124
CT78	0124
CT79	0124
CT82-2N	0154
CT82-4N	0147
CT82-6N	0278
CT100	0015
CT102-05N	0154
CT102-1N	0154
CT102-2N	0154
CT102-4N	0147
CT102-5N	4465
CT152-05N	0154
CT152-1N	0154
CT152-2N	0154
CT152-4N	0147
CT152-5N	4465
CT156	0133
CT157	0080
CT158	0604
CT159	0604
CT161	0133
CT162	0133
CT163	0604
CT164	0604
CT182	1325
CT183	0080
CT184	0604
CT185	0604
CT186	0790
CT200	0015
CT220-3	OEM
CT220-5	OEM
CT220-7	OEM
CT220-9	OEM
CT221-3	OEM
CT221-5	OEM
CT221-7	OEM
CT221-9	OEM
CT223-4	OEM
CT223-4M	OEM
CT223-5	OEM
CT223-5M	OEM
CT223-6	OEM
CT223-6M	OEM
CT223-7	OEM
CT223-7M	OEM
CT223-8	OEM
CT223-8M	OEM
CT223-9	OEM
CT223-9M	OEM
CT223-10	OEM
CT223-10M	OEM
CT223A4	OEM
CT223A5	OEM
CT223A5M	OEM
CT223A6	OEM
CT223A6M	OEM
CT223A7	OEM
CT223A7M	OEM
CT223A8	OEM
CT223A8M	OEM
CT223A9	OEM
CT223A9M	OEM
CT223A10	OEM
CT223A10M	OEM
CT256	0133
CT257	0080
CT258	0604
CT259	0604
CT282	0133
CT283	0080
CT284	0604
CT285	0604
CT286	0790
CT300	0015
CT302-2N	2004
CT302-4N	2006
CT302-6N	2007
CT401-2N	2004
CT401-4N	2006
CT401-6N	2007
CT402-2N	2004
CT461	0143
CT600	0015
CT760	OEM
CT762	OEM
CT764	OEM
CT767	OEM
CT768	OEM
CT769	OEM
CT770	OEM
CT1009	0004
CT1012	0127
CT1013	0127
CT1017	0164
CT1018	0007
CT1019	0007
CT1020	0007
CT1021	0007
CT1022	0211
CT1023	0211
CT1024	0211
CT1122	0160
CT1124	0160
CT1124A	0160
CT1124B	0160
CT1300	0144
CT1454	OEM
CT1460	OEM
CT1462	OEM
CT1464	OEM
CT1500	0144
CT-2002	0143
CT2002	0143
CT-2005	0143
CT2005	0123
CT2006	0030
CT2007	0143
CT2008	0123
CT2010	OEM
CT2012	OEM
CT-2017	0030
CT2017	OEM
CT2200	OEM
CT-3003	0015
CT3003	0015
CT-3005	0015
CT3005(RATIO-DET.)	0123
CT-4002	OEM
CT5603	OEM
CT5604	OEM
CT5606	OEM
CT5611	OEM
CT5650	OEM
CT5651	OEM
CT5652	OEM
CT6342	OEM
CT6342A	OEM
CT6343	OEM
CT6343A	OEM
CT6344	OEM
CT6344A	OEM
CT6345	OEM
CT6345A	OEM
CT6346	OEM
CT6346A	OEM
CT6347	OEM
CT6347A	OEM
CT6348	OEM
CT6348A	OEM
CT6349	OEM
CT6349A	OEM
CTB-23	1227
CTB-23L	1227
CTB-24	1227
CTB-24L	1227
CTB-33	2219
CTB-33M	2219
CTB-33S	2219
CTB-34	1931
CTB-34H	2219
CTB-34S	2219
CTC120A	OEM
CTD1322	OEM
CTG-11R	1716
CTG-11S	1227
CTG12	1024
CTG-12R	1716
CTG-12S	1227
CTG-14R	OEM
CTG-14S	0966
CTG-21R	1716
CTG-21S	1227
CTG-22R	1716
CTG-22S	1227
CTG-23R	OEM
CTG-23S	0966
CTG-24R	OEM
CTG-24S	0966
CTG-31R	OEM
CTG-31S	2219
CTG-32R	OEM
CTG-32S	2219
CTG-33R	OEM
CTG-33S	4409
CTG-34R	OEM
CTG-34S	4409
CTL-2S	1227
CTL-11S	1227
CTL-12S	1227
CTL-21S	1227
CTL-22S	1227
CTL-31S	2219
CTL-32S	2219
CTM-20	OEM
CTM20	OEM
CTM20B	OEM
CTM-20R	1716
CTM20R	OEM
CTM-20S	1227
CTM20S	OEM
CTM-21	OEM
CTM21	OEM
CTM-21R	1716
CTM21R	OEM
CTM-21S	1227
CTM21S	OEM
CTM-22	OEM
CTM22	OEM
CTM-22R	1716
CTM22R	OEM
CTM-22S	1227
CTM22S	OEM
CTM-22U	OEM
CTM-24	OEM
CTM24	OEM
CTM-24R	OEM
CTM24R	OEM
CTM-24S	OEM
CTM24S	OEM
CTM-24U	OEM
CTM-26	OEM
CTM26	OEM
CTM-26R	OEM
CTM26R	OEM
CTM-26S	OEM
CTM26S	OEM
CTM-30R	OEM
CTM-30S	2219
CTM-31R	OEM
CTM-31S	2219
CTM-32R	OEM
CTM-32S	2219
CTM-34R	OEM
CTM-34S	OEM
CTN50	0071
CTN61	OEM
CTN62	OEM
CTN64	OEM
CTN66	OEM
CTN68	OEM
CTN100	0071
CTN151	OEM
CTN152	OEM
CTN154	OEM
CTN156	OEM
CTN158	OEM
CTN200	0015
CTN251	OEM
CTN252	OEM
CTN254	OEM
CTN256	OEM
CTN258	OEM
CTN300	0071
CTN351	OEM
CTN352	OEM
CTN354	OEM
CTN356	OEM
CTN358	OEM
CTN400	0071
CTN500	0071
CTN600	0071
CTN605	OEM
CTN610	OEM
CTN800	0071
CTN1000	0071
CTN1505	OEM
CTN1510	OEM
CTN2505	OEM
CTN2510	OEM
CTN3505	OEM
CTN3510	OEM
CTNRB151	OEM
CTNRB152	OEM
CTNRB153	OEM
CTNRB154	OEM
CTNRB155	OEM
CTNRB156	OEM
CTNRB157	OEM
CTP50	0071
CTP61	OEM
CTP62	OEM
CTP64	OEM
CTP66	OEM
CTP68	OEM
CTP100	0071
CTP128	OEM
CTP151	OEM
CTP152	OEM
CTP154	OEM
CTP156	OEM
CTP158	OEM
CTP200	0071
CTP251	OEM
CTP252	OEM
CTP254	OEM
CTP256	OEM
CTP258	OEM
CTP300	0071
CTP351	OEM
CTP352	OEM
CTP354	OEM
CTP356	OEM
CTP358	OEM
CTP400	0071
CTP-461	0143
CTP461	3284
CTP500	0071
CTP573	0143
CTP600	0071
CTP605	OEM
CTP610	OEM
CTP800	0071
CTP1000	0071
CTP1002	OEM
CTP1003	OEM
CTP1004	OEM
CTP1005	OEM
CTP1006	OEM
CTP1032	0004
CTP1033	0004
CTP1034	0004
CTP1035	0004
CTP1036	0004
CTP1102	OEM
CTP1104	0085
CTP1106	0085
CTP1108	0085
CTP1109	0085
CTP1111	0160
CTP1117	0085
CTP1119	0085
CTP1124	0160
CTP1127	OEM
CTP1133	0160
CTP1135	0160
CTP1136	0160
CTP1137	0160
CTP1265	0160
CTP1266	0160
CTP1296	0160
CTP1297	0160
CTP1303	OEM
CTP1306	0160
CTP1307	0160
CTP1314	OEM
CTP1320	OEM
CTP1330	OEM
CTP1340	OEM
CTP1350	OEM
CTP1360	OEM
CTP1390	OEM
CTP1400	OEM
CTP1410	OEM
CTP1500	0160
CTP1503	0160
CTP1504	0160
CTP1506	OEM
CTP1507	OEM
CTP1508	0160
CTP1509	0435
CTP1510	OEM
CTP1511	0160
CTP1512	0435
CTP1513	0160
CTP1514	0160
CTP1530	OEM
CTP1544	0599
CTP1545	0599
CTP1550	0160
CTP1551	0160
CTP1552	0599
CTP1553	0599
CTP1728	0160
CTP1729	0160
CTP1730	0160
CTP1731	0160
CTP1732	0160
CTP1733	0160
CTP1735	0160
CTP1736	0160
CTP1739	0160
CTP1740	0085
CTP-2001-1001	0004
CTP-2001-1002	0004
CTP-2001-1003	0004
CTP-2001-1004	0004
CTP-2001-1007	0016
CTP-2001-1008	0016
CTP-2001-1009	0004
CTP-2001-1010	0143
CTP-2001-1011	0015
CTP-2001-1012	0015
CTP-2006-1001	0004
CTP-2006-1002	0004
CTP-2006-1003	0004
CTP-2006-1004	0143
CTP2076-1001	0004
CTP2076-1002	0004
CTP2076-1003	0004
CTP2076-1004	0004
CTP2076-1005	0004
CTP2076-1006	0004
CTP2076-1007	0004
CTP2076-1008	0004
CTP2076-1009	0004
CTP2076-1010	0004
CTP2076-1011	0004
CTP2076-1012	0004
CTP2505	OEM
CTP2510	OEM
CTP3500	0160
CTP3503	0160
CTP3504	0160
CTP3505	OEM
CTP3508	0160
CTP3510	OEM
CTP3544	0599
CTP3545	0599
CTP3550	OEM
CTP3551	OEM
CTP3552	0599
CTP3553	0599
CTPRB151	OEM
CTPRB152	OEM
CTPRB153	OEM
CTPRB154	OEM
CTPRB155	OEM
CTPRB156	OEM
CTPRB157	OEM
CTS0002H/B	OEM
CTS0032	OEM
CTS0033	OEM
CTS0034CB	OEM
CTS-3FU	OEM
CTS11	OEM
CTS101A	OEM
CTS101AH/B	OEM
CTS108A	OEM
CTS108AH/B	OEM
CTS111H/B	OEM
CTS256AL2	OEM
CTS861	OEM
CTS861H/B	OEM
CTU-1S	1227
CTU-2R	4890
CTU-2S	OEM
CTU-3FU	OEM
CTU3FU	OEM
CTU-11R	1716
CTU-11S	1227
CTU-12R	1716
CTU-12S	1227
CTU12S	1227
CTU-14R	OEM
CTU-14S	OEM
CTU-16R	OEM
CTU-16S	OEM
CTU-20	OEM
CTU20	OEM
CTU-20R	1716
CTU20R	1089
CTU-20S	1227
CTU20S	1227
CTU-21	OEM
CTU21	OEM
CTU-21R	1716
CTU21R	1716
CTU-21S	1227
CTU21S	1227
CTU-22	OEM
CTU22	OEM
CTU-22R	1716
CTU22R	1716
CTU-22S	1227
CTU22S	1227
CTU-22U	OEM
CTU-24	OEM
CTU24	OEM
CTU-24R	OEM
CTU24R	OEM
CTU-24S	OEM
CTU24S	OEM
CTU-25	OEM
CTU-26	OEM
CTU26	OEM
CTU-26R	OEM
CTU26R	OEM
CTU-26S	OEM
CTU26S	OEM
CTU-30R	OEM
CTU-30S	2219
CTU-31R	OEM
CTU-31S	2219
CTU-32R	OEM
CTU-32S	2219
CTU-32U	OEM
CTU-34R	OEM
CTU-34S	OEM
CTU-36R	OEM
CTU-36S	OEM
CTU-G3DR	OEM
CTUG26R	OEM
CTUS1R	OEM
CTUS1R6	OEM
CTU-S16R	OEM
CTUS16R	OEM
CTV	1024
CTZ3.0	0118
CTZ3.0A	0118
CTZ3.3	0296
CTZ3.3A	0296
CTZ3.6	0372
CTZ3.6A	0372
CTZ3.9	0036
CTZ3.9A	0036
CTZ4.3	0274
CTZ4.3A	0274
CTZ4.7	0140
CTZ4.7A	0140
CTZ5.1	0041
CTZ5.1A	0041
CTZ5.6	0253
CTZ5.6A	0253
CTZ6.2	0466
CTZ6.2A	0466
CTZ6.8	0062
CTZ6.8A	0062
CTZ7.5	0077
CTZ7.5A	0077
CTZ8.2	0165
CTZ8.2A	0165
CTZ9.1	0057
CTZ9.1A	0057
CTZ10	0064
CTZ10A	0064
CTZ11	0181
CTZ11A	0181
CTZ12	0052
CTZ12A	0052
CTZ13	0053
CTZ13A	0053
CTZ15	0681
CTZ15A	0681
CTZ16	0440
CTZ16A	0440
CTZ18	0371
CTZ18A	0371
CTZ20	0695
CTZ20A	0695
CTZ22	0700
CTZ22A	0700
CTZ24	0489
CTZ24A	0489
CTZ27	0450
CTZ27A	0450
CTZ30	0195
CTZ30A	0195
CTZ33	0166
CTZ33A	0166
CTZ36	0010
CTZ36A	0010
CTZ39	0032
CTZ39A	0032
CTZ43	0054
CTZ43A	0054
CTZ47	0068
CTZ47A	0068
CTZC6.8	2120
CTZC6.8A	2120
CTZC6.8B	2120
CTZC6.8C	OEM
CTZC6.8D	2120
CTZC6.8E	OEM
CTZC7.5	OEM
CTZC7.5A	0475
CTZC7.5B	0475
CTZC7.5C	OEM
CTZC7.5D	0475
CTZC7.5E	OEM
CTZC8.2	OEM
CTZC8.2A	0499
CTZC8.2B	0499
CTZC8.2C	OEM
CTZC8.2D	0499
CTZC8.2E	OEM
CTZC9.1	OEM
CTZC9.1A	0679
CTZC9.1B	0679
CTZC9.1C	OEM
CTZC9.1D	0679
CTZC9.1E	OEM
CTZC10	OEM
CTZC10A	0225
CTZC10B	0225
CTZC10C	OEM
CTZC10D	0225
CTZC10E	OEM
CTZC11	OEM
CTZC11A	0230
CTZC11B	0230
CTZC11C	OEM
CTZC11D	0230
CTZC11E	OEM
CTZC12	OEM
CTZC12A	0234
CTZC12B	0234
CTZC12C	OEM
CTZC12D	0234
CTZC12E	OEM
CTZC13	1161
CTZC13A	1161
CTZC13B	1161
CTZC13C	OEM
CTZC13D	1161
CTZC13E	OEM
CTZC14	OEM
CTZC14A	1387
CTZC14B	1387
CTZC14C	OEM
CTZC14D	1387
CTZC14E	OEM
CTZC15	OEM
CTZC15A	0247
CTZC15B	0247
CTZC15C	OEM
CTZC15D	0247
CTZC15E	OEM
CTZC17	OEM
CTZC17A	1170
CTZC17B	1170
CTZC17C	OEM
CTZC17D	1170
CTZC17E	OEM
CTZC18	1756
CTZC18A	1756
CTZC18B	1756
CTZC18C	OEM
CTZC18D	1756
CTZC18E	OEM
CTZC19	OEM
CTZC19A	2379
CTZC19B	2379
CTZC19C	OEM
CTZC19D	2379
CTZC19E	OEM
CTZC20	1921
CTZC20A	1921
CTZC20B	1921
CTZC20C	OEM
CTZC20D	1921
CTZC20E	OEM
CTZC22	OEM
CTZC22A	0269
CTZC22B	0269
CTZC22C	OEM
CTZC22D	0269
CTZC22E	OEM
CTZC24	OEM
CTZC24A	0273
CTZC24B	0273
CTZC24C	OEM
CTZC24D	0273
CTZC24E	OEM
CTZC25	OEM
CTZC25A	2383
CTZC25B	2383
CTZC25C	OEM
CTZC25D	2383
CTZC25E	OEM
CTZC27	1941
CTZC27A	1941
CTZC27B	1941
CTZC27C	OEM
CTZC27D	1941
CTZC27E	OEM

If replacement code is OEM, contact original manufacturer for replacement.

DEVICE TYPE	REPL CODE
CTZC30	OEM
CTZC30A	0305
CTZC30B	0305
CTZC30C	OEM
CTZC30D	0305
CTZC30E	OEM
CTZC33	OEM
CTZC33A	0314
CTZC33B	0314
CTZC33C	OEM
CTZC33D	0314
CTZC33E	OEM
CTZC36	OEM
CTZC36A	0316
CTZC36B	0316
CTZC36C	OEM
CTZC36D	0316
CTZC36E	OEM
CTZC39	OEM
CTZC39A	0322
CTZC39B	0322
CTZC39C	OEM
CTZC39D	0322
CTZC39E	OEM
CTZC43	OEM
CTZC43A	0333
CTZC43B	0333
CTZC43C	OEM
CTZC43D	0333
CTZC43E	OEM
CTZC45	OEM
CTZC45A	0343
CTZC45B	0343
CTZC45C	OEM
CTZC45D	OEM
CTZC45E	OEM
CTZC47	OEM
CTZC47A	0343
CTZC47B	0343
CTZC47C	OEM
CTZC47D	0343
CTZC47E	OEM
CTZC50	OEM
CTZC50A	0027
CTZC50B	0027
CTZC50C	OEM
CTZC50D	OEM
CTZC50E	OEM
CTZC51	1961
CTZC51A	1961
CTZC51B	0027
CTZC51C	OEM
CTZC51D	0027
CTZC51E	OEM
CTZC52	OEM
CTZC52A	0027
CTZC52B	0027
CTZC52C	OEM
CTZC52D	OEM
CTZC52E	OEM
CTZC56	OEM
CTZC56A	0266
CTZC56B	0266
CTZC56C	OEM
CTZC56D	0266
CTZC56E	OEM
CTZC62	OEM
CTZC62A	0382
CTZC62B	0382
CTZC62C	OEM
CTZC62D	0382
CTZC62E	OEM
CTZC68	1976
CTZC68A	1976
CTZC68B	1976
CTZC68C	OEM
CTZC68D	1976
CTZC68E	OEM
CTZC75	OEM
CTZC75A	0421
CTZC75B	0421
CTZC75C	OEM
CTZC75D	0421
CTZC75E	OEM
CTZC82	OEM
CTZC82A	0439
CTZC82B	0439
CTZC82C	OEM
CTZC82D	0439
CTZC82E	OEM
CTZC91	OEM
CTZC91A	0238
CTZC91B	0238
CTZC91C	OEM
CTZC91D	0238
CTZC91E	OEM
CTZC100	OEM
CTZC100A	1172
CTZC100B	1172
CTZC100C	OEM
CTZC100D	OEM
CTZC100E	OEM
CTZC105	OEM
CTZC105A	1182
CTZC105B	1182
CTZC105C	OEM
CTZC105D	OEM
CTZC105E	OEM
CTZC110	OEM

DEVICE TYPE	REPL CODE
CTZC110A	1182
CTZC110B	1182
CTZC110C	OEM
CTZC110D	OEM
CTZC110E	OEM
CTZC120	OEM
CTZC120A	1198
CTZC120B	1198
CTZC120C	OEM
CTZC120D	1198
CTZC120E	OEM
CTZC130	OEM
CTZC130A	1209
CTZC130B	1209
CTZC130C	OEM
CTZC130D	OEM
CTZC130E	OEM
CTZC140	OEM
CTZC140A	1870
CTZC140B	1870
CTZC140C	OEM
CTZC140D	1870
CTZC140E	OEM
CTZC150	OEM
CTZC150A	0642
CTZC150B	0642
CTZC150C	OEM
CTZC150D	0642
CTZC150E	OEM
CTZC160	OEM
CTZC160A	1246
CTZC160B	1246
CTZC160C	OEM
CTZC160D	1246
CTZC160E	OEM
CTZC180	OEM
CTZC180A	1269
CTZC180B	1269
CTZC180C	OEM
CTZC180D	1269
CTZC180E	OEM
CTZC200	1398
CTZC200A	1398
CTZC200B	1398
CTZC200C	OEM
CTZC200D	1398
CTZC200E	OEM
CU-12E	0934
CU1496A	OEM
CV-2	OEM
CV7	OEM
CV8	OEM
CV9	OEM
CV12E	0095
CV71	OEM
CV291	OEM
CV425	0143
CV442	0143
CV448	0143
CV830	OEM
CV831	OEM
CV832	0623
CV833	OEM
CV834	0030
CV835	OEM
CV836	OEM
CV837	OEM
CV838	OEM
CV839	OEM
CV840	OEM
CV1006	OEM
CV1006A	OEM
CV1006B	OEM
CV1006C	OEM
CV1006D	OEM
CV1008	OEM
CV1008A	OEM
CV1008B	OEM
CV1008C	OEM
CV1008D	OEM
CV1010	OEM
CV1010A	OEM
CV1010B	OEM
CV1010C	OEM
CV1010D	OEM
CV1012	OEM
CV1012A	OEM
CV1012B	OEM
CV1012C	OEM
CV1012D	OEM
CV1014	OEM
CV1014A	OEM
CV1014B	OEM
CV1014C	OEM
CV1014D	OEM
CV1016	OEM
CV1016A	OEM
CV1016B	OEM
CV1016C	OEM
CV1016D	OEM
CV1106	OEM
CV1106A	OEM
CV1106B	OEM
CV1106C	OEM
CV1106D	OEM
CV1108	OEM
CV1108A	OEM
CV1108B	OEM
CV1108C	OEM

DEVICE TYPE	REPL CODE
CV1108D	OEM
CV1110	OEM
CV1110A	OEM
CV1110B	OEM
CV1110C	OEM
CV1110D	OEM
CV1112	OEM
CV1112A	OEM
CV1112B	OEM
CV1112C	OEM
CV1112D	OEM
CV1114	OEM
CV1114A	OEM
CV1114B	OEM
CV1114C	OEM
CV1114D	OEM
CV1116	OEM
CV1116A	OEM
CV1116B	OEM
CV1116C	OEM
CV1116D	OEM
CV1620	0549
CV1622	OEM
CV1624	0005
CV1626	0715
CV1628	OEM
CV1630	OEM
CV1632	OEM
CV1634	0623
CV1636	OEM
CV1638	0030
CV1640	OEM
CV1642	OEM
CV1644	OEM
CV1646	OEM
CV1648	OEM
CV1650	OEM
CV1652	OEM
CV1654	OEM
CV1656	OEM
CV1658	OEM
CV1660	OEM
CV1662	OEM
CV1664	OEM
CV1666	OEM
CV1844	OEM
CV1858B	OEM
CV1858D	OEM
CV1860B	OEM
CV1860D	OEM
CV1862B	OEM
CV1862D	OEM
CV1863B	OEM
CV1863D	OEM
CV1864B	OEM
CV1864D	OEM
CV1865B	OEM
CV1865D	OEM
CV1866	OEM
CV1866B	OEM
CV1866D	OEM
CV1868B	OEM
CV1868D	OEM
CV1870B	OEM
CV1870D	OEM
CV1871B	OEM
CV1871D	OEM
CV1872B	OEM
CV1872D	OEM
CV1873B	OEM
CV1873D	OEM
CV2116	OEM
CV2154	OEM
CV2155	OEM
CV2226	OEM
CV2228	OEM
CV2346	OEM
CV2355	OEM
CV2356	OEM
CV2357	OEM
CV3676	OEM
CV5007	0549
CV5008	OEM
CV5010	0005
CV5012	0715
CV5015	OEM
CV5018	OEM
CV5020	OEM
CV5022	0623
CV5027	OEM
CV5033	0030
CV5039	OEM
CV5047	OEM
CV5056	OEM
CV5068	OEM
CV5082	OEM
CV5100	OEM
CV5123	OEM
CV6002	OEM
CV6071	OEM
CV6072	OEM
CV6199	OEM
CV6234	OEM
CV7108	OEM
CV7109	OEM
CV7180	OEM
CV7181	OEM
CV7182	OEM
CV7183	OEM

DEVICE TYPE	REPL CODE
CV7377	OEM
CV7378	OEM
CV7636	OEM
CV7728	OEM
CV7729	OEM
CV7739	OEM
CV7771	OEM
CV7772	OEM
CV8163	OEM
CV8164	OEM
CV9424	OEM
CV10758	OEM
CVA1115A	OEM
CVA1115B	OEM
CVA1115C	OEM
CVA1116A	OEM
CVA1116B	OEM
CVA1116C	OEM
CVA1116D	OEM
CVA1116E	OEM
CVA1116F	OEM
CVA1116G	OEM
CVA1130A	OEM
CVA1130B	OEM
CVA1130C	OEM
CVA1145B	OEM
CVA1145D	OEM
CVA1145E	OEM
CVB1015A	OEM
CVB1015B	OEM
CVB1015C	OEM
CVB1030A	OEM
CVB1030B	OEM
CVB1030C	OEM
CVB1045B	OEM
CVB1045D	OEM
CVB1045E	OEM
CVH2090-17	OEM
CVH2030-02	OEM
CVH2030-03	OEM
CVH2030-04	OEM
CVH2030-05	OEM
CVH2030-07	OEM
CVH2030-08	OEM
CVH2030-09	OEM
CVH2030-10	OEM
CVH2030-11	OEM
CVH2030-13	OEM
CVH2030-14	OEM
CVH2030-15	OEM
CVH2030-16	OEM
CVH2030-17	OEM
CVH2030-19	OEM
CVH2030-20	OEM
CVH2030-21	OEM
CVH2030-22	OEM
CVH2030-23	OEM
CVH2030-25	OEM
CVH2030-26	OEM
CVH2030-27	OEM
CVH2030A	OEM
CVH2030B	OEM
CVH2030C	OEM
CVH2030D	OEM
CVH2030G	OEM
CVH2030H	OEM
CVH2030J	OEM
CVH2045-01	OEM
CVH2045-02	OEM
CVH2045-03	OEM
CVH2045-04	OEM
CVH2045-05	OEM
CVH2045-07	OEM
CVH2045-08	OEM
CVH2045-09	OEM
CVH2045-10	OEM
CVH2045-11	OEM
CVH2045-13	OEM
CVH2045-14	OEM
CVH2045-15	OEM
CVH2045-16	OEM
CVH2045-17	OEM
CVH2045-19	OEM
CVH2045A	OEM
CVH2045B	OEM
CVH2045C	OEM
CVH2045D	OEM
CVH2045E	OEM
CVH2045F	OEM
CVH2045G	OEM
CVH2045H	OEM
CVH2045J	OEM
CVH2060-03	OEM
CVH2060-04	OEM
CVH2060-05	OEM
CVH2060-07	OEM
CVH2060-08	OEM
CVH2060-09	OEM
CVH2060-10	OEM
CVH2060-11	OEM
CVH2060-13	OEM
CVH2060-14	OEM
CVH2060-15	OEM
CVH2060-16	OEM
CVH2060-17	OEM
CVH2060-19	OEM
CVH2060-20	OEM
CVH2060-21	OEM
CVH2060-22	OEM

DEVICE TYPE	REPL CODE
CVH2060-23	OEM
CVH2060-25	OEM
CVH2060-26	OEM
CVH2060-27	OEM
CVH2060B	OEM
CVH2060C	OEM
CVH2060D	OEM
CVH2060E	OEM
CVH2060F	OEM
CVH2060G	OEM
CVH2060H	OEM
CVH2060J	OEM
CVH2060K	OEM
CVH2060L	OEM
CVH2060M	OEM
CVH2090-03	OEM
CVH2090-04	OEM
CVH2090-05	OEM
CVH2090-07	OEM
CVH2090-08	OEM
CVH2090-09	OEM
CVH2090-10	OEM
CVH2090-11	OEM
CVH2090-13	OEM
CVH2090-14	OEM
CVH2090-15	OEM
CVH2090-16	OEM
CVH2090-17	OEM
CVH2090-19	OEM
CVH2090-20	OEM
CVH2090-21	OEM
CVH2090B	OEM
CVH2090C	OEM
CVH2090D	OEM
CVH2090E	OEM
CVH2090F	OEM
CVH2090G	OEM
CVH2090J	OEM
CVH2090K	OEM
CVH2090L	OEM
CVH2090M	OEM
CVH3030E	OEM
CVJ70653	0030
CWW-010	OEM
CX002	OEM
CX003	OEM
CX-0031	0019
CX-0033	0143
CX-0035	0015
CX-0036	0143
CX0036	0143
CX-0037	0015
CX0037	0015
CX-0039	0015
CX0039	0015
CX-0040	0015
CX0040	0015
CX-0041	0030
CX0041	0143
CX-0042	0143
CX0042	0123
CX-0045	0143
CX0045	0143
CX-0047	0143
CX0047	0015
CX-0048	0015
CX0048	0015
CX-0049	0526
CX0049	0015
CX-0051	0644
CX0051	0170
CX-0052	0137
CX0052	0137
CX-0054	0015
CX0054	0535
CX-0055	0133
CX-016A	OEM
CX-016B	OEM
CX-025D	OEM
CX-031	OEM
CX-031-10	OEM
CX-031-20	OEM
CX-031-30	OEM
CX032B	OEM
CX064	3876
CX-064-2	3876
CX065	3877
CX065B	3877
CX-075	4588
CX-075B	4588
CX075B	4588
CX-080	OEM
CX085B	OEM
CX089	1624
CX089D	1624
CX-093	0167
CX093D	0167
CX095	3891
CX095A	3891
CX-095C	3891
CX095C	3891
CX-095D	3891
CX095D	3891
CX-095E	3891
CX095E	3891
CX-099	OEM
CX-0411	OEM
CX-0412	OEM
CX-0432	OEM

DEVICE TYPE	REPL CODE
CX-0441	OEM
CX-0451	OEM
CX-0461	OEM
CX-0462	OEM
CX088535	OEM
CX088535-119S	OEM
CX-100	OEM
CX100B	4360
CX-100D	4360
CX100D	4360
CX-101B	OEM
CX101G	OEM
CX103D	OEM
CX-104A	OEM
CX-104B-1	OEM
CX-130	3904
CX130	3904
CX-131A	4197
CX131A	4197
CX-133A	3652
CX133A	3652
CX-134A	3662
CX134A	3662
CX-135	3907
CX135	3907
CX135A	OEM
CX136	3909
CX-136A	3909
CX136A	3909
CX-137A	4230
CX137A	4230
CX-138	3911
CX138	3911
CX-138A	3911
CX138A	OEM
CX-139A	4178
CX139A	4178
CX-141	3913
CX141	3913
CX-141A	OEM
CX141A	3913
CX-143	3916
CX143	3916
CX-143A	3916
CX143A	3916
CX-145	3918
CX145	3918
CX-150	OEM
CX150	OEM
CX-150B	OEM
CX150B	OEM
CX157	3927
CX158	3928
CX161	OEM
CX162	3931
CX170	3935
CX172	3939
CX173	3941
CX177	3943
CX-177B	3943
CX177B	3943
CX-177C	OEM
CX181	3947
CX183	OEM
CX-186	OEM
CX186	OEM
CX-187	OEM
CX187	OEM
CX-187A	OEM
CX187A	OEM
CX-188	OEM
CX188	OEM
CX-194A	OEM
CX-194A-2	OEM
CX-194B-0	OEM
CX-196	OEM
CX196	OEM
CX196A	OEM
CX-501	OEM
CX501	OEM
CX-504	OEM
CX504	OEM
CX-520-102N	OEM
CX520-102N	OEM
CX520-108N	OEM
CX520-111N	OEM
CX522-030	OEM
CX524-216N	OEM
CX-525-1374K	OEM
CX525-1374K	OEM
CX526-017	OEM
CX526-025	OEM
CX530-507N	OEM
CX555	0762
CX-555A	0762
CX555A	0762
CX-556	2599
CX556	2599
CX556A	2599
CX-556B	3522
CX556B	0485
CX-557	2888
CX557	2601
CX-557A	2601
CX557A	2601
CX-557B	6053
CX557B	2888
CX-557S	2601
CX557S	2888

DEVICE TYPE	REPL CODE
CX701	OEM
CX701A	OEM
CX702	OEM
CX702A	OEM
CX703	OEM
CX703A	OEM
CX703B	OEM
CX704	OEM
CX726A	OEM
CX-728	OEM
CX754	OEM
CX-759-220-04	OEM
CX-760B	OEM
CX-760E	OEM
CX-761A	OEM
CX-766	OEM
CX-775A	OEM
CX775A	OEM
CX-779	OEM
CX-786	OEM
CX-789	OEM
CX789	OEM
CX-804	OEM
CX804	OEM
CX807	OEM
CX-810	OEM
CX-811	OEM
CX-813	OEM
CX-814	OEM
CX-815	OEM
CX-816	OEM
CX822	OEM
CX-825	OEM
CX830A	OEM
CX-832	OEM
CX-841	OEM
CX-841A	OEM
CX841A	OEM
CX842B	3891
CX-843	4102
CX843	4102
CX-843A	4102
CX843A	4102
CX843B	OEM
CX847	OEM
CX-848	4103
CX848	4103
CX855	OEM
CX855A	OEM
CX855B	OEM
CX-864	OEM
CX-865	OEM
CX-866	OEM
CX-867	OEM
CX-868	OEM
CX-869	OEM
CX-870A	OEM
CX-874	OEM
CX874	OEM
CX-875A	OEM
CX875A	OEM
CX877	OEM
CX-882	OEM
CX-883	OEM
CX883	OEM
CX885	OEM
CX-885A	OEM
CX885A	OEM
CX885B	OEM
CX-892	OEM
CX-894	OEM
CX894	OEM
CX901	OEM
CX904	OEM
CX906	OEM
CX908	OEM
CX918	OEM
CX954	OEM
CX956	OEM
CX958	OEM
CX-1000	4360
CX1124AS	OEM
CX2016A	OEM
CX5034H-0805	OEM
CX-7600	OEM
CX-7905A	OEM
CX-7932	OEM
CX7932	OEM
CX7933	OEM
CX7934	OEM
CX7935	OEM
CX-7944	OEM
CX7947	OEM
CX7948	OEM
CX-7958	OEM
CX7958	OEM
CX7959	OEM
CX7977	OEM
CX7978	OEM
CX-9000	1024
CX9000	1024
CX-9001	0015
CX9001	0015
CX-10026	OEM
CX10026	OEM
CX10032A	OEM
CX-20008	OEM
CX20013	OEM
CX20013A	OEM

If replacement code is OEM, contact original manufacturer for replacement.

355

DEVICE TYPE	REPL CODE	DEVICE TYPE	REPL CODE	DEVICE TYPE	REPL CODE	DEVICE TYPE	REPL CODE	DEVICE TYPE	REPL CODE	DEVICE TYPE	REPL CODE	DEVICE TYPE	REPL CODE
CX20014	OEM	CXA1314P	OEM	CXL157	0275	CXL1025	1179	CXL5101	0255	CXL5221	0459	CXL5508	3213
CX20014A	OEM	CXA1315P	OEM	CXL158	0164	CXL1027	2849	CXL5102	0871	CXL5222	0483	CXL5511	3651
CX20017	OEM	CXA1334S	OEM	CXL159	0079	CXL1062	0399	CXL5103	0363	CXL5223	0504	CXL5512	3349
CX20029	OEM	CXA1373Q	OEM	CXL160	0050	CXL1063	2562	CXL5104	2831	CXL5224	0519	CXL5513	3579
CX-20061	OEM	CXA-1387	OEM	CXL161	0007	CXL1090	2834	CXL5105	0417	CXL5225	0537	CXL5514	0717
CX20061	OEM	CXA1387S	OEM	CXL162	0074	CXL1139	3880	CXL5111	0777	CXL5226	0063	CXL5515	1574
CX20073	OEM	CXA1414P	OEM	CXL163	0637	CXL1501M	OEM	CXL5112	0791	CXL5227	0397	CXL5516	1655
CX20082	OEM	CXA1465AS	OEM	CXL164	0003	CXL5000	1266	CXL5113	0801	CXL5228	0593	CXL5517	1640
CX20082-0	OEM	CXA1526P	OEM	CXL165	0065	CXL5001	2847	CXL5114	0815	CXL5229	0611	CXL5518	2623
CX20083	OEM	CXA1534S	OEM	CXL166	0276	CXL5002	0755	CXL5115	0827	CXL5230	0629	CXL5519	2625
CX20085	OEM	CXA1594L	OEM	CXL167	0287	CXL5003	0672	CXL5116	0437	CXL5231	0645	CXL5520	0717
CX20100	OEM	CXA4559	OEM	CXL168	0293	CXL5004	0118	CXL5117	0870	CXL5232	0663	CXL5521	0717
CX20106	OEM	CXA20112	OEM	CXL169	0299	CXL5005	0289	CXL5118	3099	CXL5240	0809	CXL5522	0717
CX20106A	OEM	CXA20125	OEM	CXL170	0250	CXL5005P	OEM	CXL5119	0185	CXL5241	0821	CXL5523	0717
CX20108	OEM	CXB0026AMR	OEM	CXL171	0283	CXL5006	0188	CXL5120	0205	CXL5242	0840	CXL5524	1478
CX20109	OEM	CXD1017Q	OEM	CXL172	0396	CXL5007	0451	CXL5121	0475	CXL5243	0862	CXL5525	0717
CX20111	OEM	CXD1068A	OEM	CXL173BP	0290	CXL5008	0528	CXL5122	0499	CXL5244	0879	CXL5526	0717
CX20111-T6	OEM	CXD1095Q	OEM	CXL175	0178	CXL5009	0446	CXL5123	3285	CXL5245	0891	CXL5527	0717
CX-20112	OEM	CXD1120P	OEM	CXL176	0841	CXL5010	0162	CXL5124	0679	CXL5246	0908	CXL5528	3260
CX20112	2843	CXD1120P1	OEM	CXL177	0133	CXL5011	0157	CXL5125	0225	CXL5247	0920	CXL5529	0759
CX20114	OEM	CXD1125Q	OEM	CXL178MP	0133	CXL5012	0091	CXL5126	0230	CXL5248	0938	CXL5530	2848
CX20115A	OEM	CXD1130Q	OEM	CXL179	0599	CXL5013	0631	CXL5127	0234	CXL5249	0952	CXL5531	0761
CX20125	OEM	CXD1130QZ	OEM	CXL180	1671	CXL5014	0025	CXL5128	0237	CXL5250	0972	CXL5540	0717
CX20129	OEM	CXD1135QZ	OEM	CXL181	0130	CXL5015	0644	CXL5129	1387	CXL5251	0988	CXL5541	0717
CX20133	OEM	CXD1157Q	OEM	CXL182	0556	CXL5016	0244	CXL5130	0251	CXL5252	1003	CXL5542	0717
CX20139	OEM	CXD1158M	OEM	CXL183	1190	CXL5017	0318	CXL5131	0251	CXL5253	1013	CXL5543	0464
CX20157	OEM	CXD1159Q-T3	OEM	CXL184	0161	CXL5018	0012	CXL5132	1170	CXL5254	0883	CXL5544	0717
CX20159	OEM	CXD1161M3	OEM	CXL185	0455	CXL5019	0170	CXL5133	0256	CXL5255	1043	CXL5545	0717
CX20174	OEM	CXD1161P-2	OEM	CXL186	0555	CXL5020	0313	CXL5134	2379	CXL5256	1052	CXL5546	0773
CX20180	OEM	CXD1162P	OEM	CXL187	1257	CXL5021	0137	CXL5135	0262	CXL5257	0926	CXL5547	0720
CX20183	OEM	CXD1204R-T3	OEM	CXL188	0264	CXL5022	0053	CXL5136	0269	CXL5258	1072	CXL5640	2367
CX20183F	OEM	CXD1220AQ	OEM	CXL189	0378	CXL5023	0873	CXL5137	0273	CXL5259	1088	CXL5641	2378
CX20185	OEM	CXD2500Q	OEM	CXL190	0264	CXL5024	0002	CXL5138	2383	CXL5260	1098	CXL5642	1403
CX20187	OEM	CXD2550P	OEM	CXL191	0334	CXL5025	0440	CXL5139	0291	CXL5261	1115	CXL5643	2371
CX-20192	OEM	CXD2551P	OEM	CXL192	0590	CXL5026	0210	CXL5140	1169	CXL5262	1127	CXL5650	2336
CX20192	OEM	CXK1001P	OEM	CXL193	0786	CXL5027	0490	CXL5141	0305	CXL5263	1144	CXL5651	2337
CX-20193	OEM	CXK1004L	OEM	CXL194	0855	CXL5028	0666	CXL5142	0314	CXL5264	1156	CXL5652	2340
CX20193	OEM	CXK1005P	OEM	CXL195	0693	CXL5029	0526	CXL5143	0316	CXL5265	1166	CXL5661	0400
CX22011	OEM	CXK1006L	OEM	CXL196	0419	CXL5030	0560	CXL5144	0322	CXL5266	1176	CXL5662	2340
CX23035	OEM	CXK1011	OEM	CXL197	0848	CXL5031	0398	CXL5145	0333	CXL5267	1191	CXL5663	0418
CX23040	OEM	CXK1011P	OEM	CXL198	0168	CXL5032	0709	CXL5146	0343	CXL5268	1201	CXL5664	0418
CX23041-01	OEM	CXK5816M-10L	OEM	CXL199	0111	CXL5033	0436	CXL5147	0027	CXL5269	1214	CXL5665	0418
CX23041-09	OEM	CXK5816M-15L	OEM	CXL210	2039	CXL5034	0257	CXL5148	0266	CXL5270	1223	CXL5666	0418
CX23042-10	OEM	CXK5816PN-12L	OEM	CXL211	1357	CXL5035	0721	CXL5149	2829	CXL5271	1237	CXL5667	0418
CX201291	OEM	CXK5816PN-15L	OEM	CXL218	0899	CXL5036	0039	CXL5150	0382	CXL5272	1256	CXL5673	0154
CX-520102N	OEM	CXK5864AP-70L	OEM	CXL219	1671	CXL5037	0010	CXL5151	0401	CXL5273	1263	CXL5675	0147
CX520102N	OEM	CXK5864BSP-10L	OEM	CXL220	0843	CXL5038	0346	CXL5152	0421	CXL5274	1280	CXL5676	4465
CX-520108N	OEM	CXK5864M-15L	OEM	CXL221	0843	CXL5039	0925	CXL5153	0439	CXL5275	1289	CXL5677	0278
CX520108N	OEM	CXL011	OEM	CXL222	0212	CXL5040	0993	CXL5154	2999	CXL5276	1297	CXL5680	3117
CX-520111N	OEM	CXL100	0279	CXL223	0103	CXL5041	0497	CXL5155	0238	CXL5277	1312	CXL5681	3118
CX522030	OEM	CXL101	0038	CXL224	0626	CXL5042	0863	CXL5156	1172	CXL5278	1321	CXL5682	3119
CX564171	OEM	CXL102	0211	CXL225	3249	CXL5043	1148	CXL5157	1182	CXL5279	1330	CXL5683	3121
CXA153AS	OEM	CXL102A	0136	CXL226	1004	CXL5044	0778	CXL5158	1198	CXL5280	1343	CXL5684	3122
CXA495D	0126	CXL103	0038	CXL226MP	1004	CXL5045	1258	CXL5159	1209	CXL5281	1355	CXL5686	3124
CXA1011M	4444	CXL104	0085	CXL228	1698	CXL5046	1181	CXL5160	1870	CXL5282	1374	CXL5693	2004
CXA1011P	3054	CXL104MP	3004	CXL238	0309	CXL5047	0327	CXL5161	0642	CXL5283	1391	CXL5695	2006
CXA1013	OEM	CXL105	0435	CXL309K	1911	CXL5048	2997	CXL5162	1246	CXL5284	1402	CXL5697	2007
CXA1013A	OEM	CXL106	0150	CXL370	3759	CXL5049	1301	CXL5163	2091	CXL5285	1413	CXL5800	0087
CXA1013AS	OEM	CXL107	0127	CXL501	0128	CXL5050	0098	CXL5164	1269	CXL5286	1427	CXL5801	0087
CXA1013S	OEM	CXL108	0144	CXL502	0201	CXL5051	0149	CXL5165	2210	CXL5287	1435	CXL5802	0087
CXA1019S	OEM	CXL109	0143	CXL503	0286	CXL5052	0186	CXL5166	0600	CXL5290	1475	CXL5803	0087
CXA1072R-T3	OEM	CXL110	0143	CXL504	0374	CXL5053	0213	CXL5172	4167	CXL5291	1497	CXL5804	0087
CXA1081	OEM	CXL112	0911	CXL505	0752	CXL5054	0245	CXL5173	2381	CXL5292	1513	CXL5805	0087
CXA1081M	OEM	CXL113	0196	CXL506	0102	CXL5055	0028	CXL5174	2024	CXL5293	1523	CXL5806	0087
CXA1081Q	OEM	CXL114	0479	CXL507	0102	CXL5056	0255	CXL5175	2385	CXL5294	1539	CXL5808	0087
CXA1081S	OEM	CXL115	1073	CXL508	1296	CXL5057	0871	CXL5176	1429	CXL5295	1558	CXL5809	0087
CXA1082AQ	OEM	CXL116	0015	CXL509	2072	CXL5058	0363	CXL5177	2391	CXL5296	1577	CXL5830	0097
CXA1082AS	OEM	CXL117	0015	CXL510	2073	CXL5059	2831	CXL5178	1436	CXL5400	1129	CXL5831	0927
CXA1082BQ	OEM	CXL118	0769	CXL511	1440	CXL5060	0417	CXL5179	2399	CXL5401	0340	CXL5832	0097
CXA1082BS	OEM	CXL119	1293	CXL512	2074	CXL5061	2975	CXL5180	2206	CXL5402	0895	CXL5833	5420
CXA1082Q	OEM	CXL120	0469	CXL513	1313	CXL5062	OEM	CXL5181	1449	CXL5403	2326	CXL5834	0097
CXA1100P	OEM	CXL121	0160	CXL514	3604	CXL5063	1302	CXL5182	0221	CXL5404	0058	CXL5835	0941
CXA1101	OEM	CXL121MP	0160	CXL516	OEM	CXL5064	2981	CXL5183	1481	CXL5452	0934	CXL5836	0800
CXA1101P	OEM	CXL123	1478	CXL518	1780	CXL5065	1703	CXL5184	2406	CXL5453	0934	CXL5837	4443
CXA1102P	OEM	CXL123A	0079	CXL519	0124	CXL5066	0289	CXL5185	1608	CXL5454	0934	CXL5839	1006
CXA1110BS	OEM	CXL124	0142	CXL703A	0627	CXL5067	0451	CXL5186	0505	CXL5455	0934	CXL5840	2065
CXA1111P	OEM	CXL125	0087	CXL704	2600	CXL5068	0446	CXL5187	0686	CXL5456	1213	CXL5841	5467
CXA1114	OEM	CXL126	0136	CXL705A	0748	CXL5069	0446	CXL5188	0864	CXL5457	0095	CXL5842	2070
CXA1114P	OEM	CXL127	0969	CXL706	0574	CXL5070	0298	CXL5189	1014	CXL5461	2084	CXL5843	1067
CXA1115BP	OEM	CXL128	0086	CXL708	0659	CXL5071	0025	CXL5190	1145	CXL5462	2078	CXL5846	2077
CXA1124	OEM	CXL129	0126	CXL709	0673	CXL5072	0244	CXL5191	1264	CXL5463	0500	CXL5847	1130
CXA1124A	OEM	CXL130	0103	CXL710	0823	CXL5073	1075	CXL5192	1392	CXL5465	0705	CXL5848	0607
CXA1124AS	OEM	CXL130MP	1506	CXL711	2689	CXL5074	0313	CXL5193	1524	CXL5470	1478	CXL5849	1180
CXA1124BS	OEM	CXL131	0222	CXL713	0661	CXL5075	0416	CXL5194	1071	CXL5471	1478	CXL5850	0097
CXA1124S	OEM	CXL131MP	0222	CXL714	0348	CXL5076	1639	CXL5195	1701	CXL5472	1478	CXL5851	0979
CXA1127M	OEM	CXL132	0321	CXL715	0350	CXL5077	0490	CXL5196	1707	CXL5473	1478	CXL5852	0097
CXA1134AS	OEM	CXL133	0321	CXL718	0649	CXL5078	0943	CXL5197	1712	CXL5474	1478	CXL5853	0904
CXA1163	OEM	CXL134	0188	CXL722	0696	CXL5079	0526	CXL5198	1725	CXL5475	3626	CXL5854	0097
CXA1182	OEM	CXL135	0162	CXL725	0687	CXL5080	0560	CXL5199	1737	CXL5476	3405	CXL5855	0984
CXA1182Q-Z	OEM	CXL137	0631	CXL726	2593	CXL5081	0398	CXL5200	1750	CXL5480	3385	CXL5856	0097
CXA1182QZ	OEM	CXL138	0644	CXL727	2507	CXL5082	1596	CXL5201	2431	CXL5481	1095	CXL5857	0987
CXA1198A	OEM	CXL139	0012	CXL728	2527	CXL5083	1664	CXL5202	1761	CXL5482	2471	CXL5858	0800
CXA1200BQ	OEM	CXL140	0170	CXL729	0324	CXL5084	0721	CXL5203	1777	CXL5483	0240	CXL5859	0991
CXA1201Q	OEM	CXL141	0313	CXL730	2716	CXL5085	0346	CXL5204	1785	CXL5484	2635	CXL5860	0200
CXA1202R	OEM	CXL142	0137	CXL731	2438	CXL5086	0346	CXL5205	1793	CXL5485	0671	CXL5861	0995
CXA1204Q	OEM	CXL143	0361	CXL734	1748	CXL5087	0925	CXL5206	1185	CXL5486	2782	CXL5862	0204
CXA1228	OEM	CXL144	0100	CXL738	0850	CXL5088	0993	CXL5207	1810	CXL5487	0332	CXL5863	0510
CXA1228S	OEM	CXL145	0002	CXL747	1797	CXL5089	0497	CXL5208	0022	CXL5491	0717	CXL5866	0206
CXA1238S	OEM	CXL146	0436	CXL749	0391	CXL5090	0863	CXL5209	0070	CXL5492	0717	CXL5867	1002
CXA1240	OEM	CXL147	0039	CXL760	2089	CXL5091	1148	CXL5210	0132	CXL5494	0717	CXL5868	0583
CXA1264AS	OEM	CXL148	1823	CXL780	0360	CXL5092	1258	CXL5211	0172	CXL5496	0682	CXL5869	0942
CXA1264S	OEM	CXL149	0778	CXL781	2720	CXL5093	1181	CXL5212	0207	CXL5500	0717	CXL5870	0097
CXA1271Q	OEM	CXL150	0327	CXL783	0797	CXL5094	2997	CXL5213	0227	CXL5501	0717	CXL5871	0529
CXA1272Q-Z	OEM	CXL151	0149	CXL786	2688	CXL5095	1301	CXL5214	0263	CXL5502	0717	CXL5872	0097
CXA1279S	OEM	CXL152	0042	CXL787	2242	CXL5096	0098	CXL5215	0306	CXL5503	0717	CXL5873	0743
CXA1291	OEM	CXL153	0919	CXL788	2728	CXL5097	0186	CXL5216	0325	CXL5504	0740	CXL5874	0097
CXA1291P	OEM	CXL154	0233	CXL790	0345	CXL5098	0028	CXL5217	0352	CXL5505	0717	CXL5875	0760
CXA1313	OEM	CXL155	2736	CXL949	2530	CXL5099	0245	CXL5218	0377	CXL5506	0717	CXL5876	0800
CXA1313S	OEM	CXL156	0087	CXL1024	1581	CXL5100	0028	CXL5220	0433	CXL5507	0717	CXL5877	0772

If replacement code is OEM, contact original manufacturer for replacement.

DEVICE TYPE	REPL CODE
CXL5878	0800
CXL5879	0533
CXL5880	0116
CXL5881	0796
CXL5882	0122
CXL5883	0810
CXL5886	0131
CXL5887	0540
CXL5890	0145
CXL5891	0545
CXL5940	0800
CXL5941	1992
CXL5942	0800
CXL5943	3234
CXL5944	0800
CXL5945	1567
CXL5946	0800
CXL5947	3244
CXL5948	0800
CXL5949	3251
CXL5950	5489
CXL5951	3256
CXL5952	1576
CXL5953	3263
CXL5980	3160
CXL5981	1620
CXL5982	2873
CXL5986	1116
CXL5987	1099
CXL5988	1118
CXL5989	1103
CXL5990	0800
CXL5991	0258
CXL5992	1186
CXL5993	1634
CXL5994	0315
CXL5995	0267
CXL5998	1124
CXL5999	1111
CXL6002	0045
CXL6003	0280
CXL6020	3716
CXL6021	2640
CXL6022	2629
CXL6023	2670
CXL6026	2633
CXL6027	2741
CXL6030	2639
CXL6031	2828
CXL6034	1995
CXL6035	2879
CXL6038	2652
CXL6039	2946
CXL6040	2657
CXL6041	3022
CXL6042	3846
CXL6043	3088
CXL6044	2631
CXL6045	3178
CXL6050	1551
CXL6051	2165
CXL6054	2813
CXL6055	2168
CXL6058	4244
CXL6059	3556
CXL6060	2823
CXL6061	2177
CXL6064	2844
CXL6065	2183
CXL6068	2806
CXL6069	2202
CXL6072	2454
CXL6073	2324
CXL6400	1659
CXL6401	2123
CXL6402	0312
CXL6406	3603
CXL6407	3298
CXL6408	2137
CXL6409	1167
CXLM1	OEM
CXO-043B	OEM
CXP5016-201	OEM
CXP5024H-003	OEM
CXP5034H-080	OEM
CXP5034H080S	OEM
CXP5048H159S	OEM
CXP5058-051	OEM
CXP5058-088	OEM
CXP5058-133Q	OEM
CXP5058-178Q	OEM
CXP5058H-081Q	OEM
CXP5058H-087Q	OEM
CXP5058H-088	OEM
CXP5058H-114Q	OEM
CXP5068H	OEM
CXP5068H-028S	OEM
CXP5068H-055S	OEM
CXP5068H-057S	OEM
CXP5068H-SV2764	OEM
CXP5086	OEM
CXP5086H	OEM
CXP5086H-004S	OEM
CXP5086H015	OEM
CXP50116	OEM
CXP50116-101Q	OEM
CXP50116-XXX	OEM
CXP50584-540Q	OEM
CXP80116-0900	OEM
CXP80116-615Q	OEM
CXP80424	OEM
CXP80424-065S	OEM
CXQ88501-216	OEM
CXQ88535	OEM
CXQ88535-111	OEM
CXQ88535-111S	OEM
CXQ88535-119	OEM
CXQ-88535-119S	OEM
CXQ88535-119S	OEM
CXQ88551-1300	OEM
CXY10	OEM
CXY11	OEM
CXY11A	OEM
CXY11B	OEM
CXY11C	OEM
CXY11C09	OEM
CXY11C10	OEM
CXY11C11	OEM
CXY11D	OEM
CXY11E	OEM
CXY12	OEM
CXY13D	OEM
CXY13E	OEM
CXY13E09	OEM
CXY13E10	OEM
CXY13E11	OEM
CXY13F	OEM
CXY14A	OEM
CXY14B	OEM
CXY14C	OEM
CXY14D	OEM
CXY14E	OEM
CXY14F	OEM
CXY15A	OEM
CXY15B	OEM
CXY15C	OEM
CXY15D	OEM
CXY15E	OEM
CXY15F	OEM
CXY16A	OEM
CXY16B	OEM
CXY16C	OEM
CXY16D	OEM
CXY16E	OEM
CXY16F	OEM
CXY17A	OEM
CXY17B	OEM
CXY17C	OEM
CXY17D	OEM
CXY17E	OEM
CXY17F	OEM
CXY18A	OEM
CXY18B	OEM
CXY18C	OEM
CXY18D	OEM
CXY18E	OEM
CXY18F	OEM
CXY19	OEM
CXY19A	OEM
CXY19B	OEM
CXY20	OEM
CXY21	OEM
CXY22A	OEM
CXY22B	OEM
CXY23A	OEM
CXY23B	OEM
CXY23C	OEM
CXY23D	OEM
CXY24A	OEM
CXY24B	OEM
CY1	1024
CY2	4391
CY3F	OEM
CY4F	OEM
CY5	OEM
CY5F	OEM
CY6F	OEM
CY7	OEM
CY7F	OEM
CY10	OEM
CY20	OEM
CY40	0015
CY50	0015
CY80	0087
CY100	0071
CY501H	OEM
CY751H	OEM
CY2456	OEM
CY2457	OEM
CYAD471	OEM
CYDAC429	OEM
CYDAC430	OEM
CYN21EXI	OEM
CYN64	OEM
CYN65	OEM
CYN65EXI	OEM
CYN66	OEM
CYN71	OEM
CYN75A	OEM
CYN75B	OEM
CYN75C	OEM
CYT1549	OEM
CYT1550	OEM
CYT1551	OEM
CYT1552	OEM
CYT1553	OEM
CYT1554	OEM
CYT1555	OEM
CYT1556	OEM
CYT1557	OEM
CYT1558	OEM
CYT1559	OEM
CYT1560	OEM
CZ072	0077
CZ078	0644
CZ-092	0012
CZ092	0012
CZ-094	0012
CZ094	0012
CZ3.3	0289
CZ3.6	0188
CZ3.9	0451
CZ4.3	0528
CZ4.7	0446
CZ5	OEM
CZ5.1	0162
CZ5.6	0157
CZ6	OEM
CZ6.2	0631
CZ6.8	0025
CZ6.8A	0025
CZ6.8B	0025
CZ6.8C	OEM
CZ6.8D	0025
CZ7.5	0644
CZ7.5A	0644
CZ7.5B	0644
CZ7.5C	0644
CZ7.5D	0644
CZ8	OEM
CZ8.2	0244
CZ8.2A	0244
CZ8.2B	0244
CZ8.2C	3071
CZ8.2D	0244
CZ9	OEM
CZ9.1	0012
CZ9.1A	0012
CZ9.1B	0012
CZ9.1C	0057
CZ9.1D	OEM
CZ10	0170
CZ10A	0170
CZ10B	0170
CZ10C	OEM
CZ10D	0170
CZ11	0313
CZ11A	0313
CZ11B	0313
CZ11C	OEM
CZ11D	0313
CZ12	0137
CZ12A	0137
CZ12B	0137
CZ12C	0137
CZ12D	0137
CZ13	0361
CZ13A	0361
CZ13B	0361
CZ13C	OEM
CZ13D	0361
CZ14	0100
CZ14A	0100
CZ14B	0100
CZ14C	OEM
CZ14D	0100
CZ15	0002
CZ15A	0002
CZ15B	0002
CZ15C	0002
CZ15D	0002
CZ16	0416
CZ16A	0416
CZ16B	0416
CZ16C	OEM
CZ16D	0416
CZ17	1639
CZ17A	1639
CZ17B	1639
CZ17C	OEM
CZ17D	1639
CZ18	0490
CZ18A	0490
CZ18B	0490
CZ18C	OEM
CZ18D	0490
CZ19	0943
CZ19A	0943
CZ19B	0943
CZ19C	OEM
CZ19D	0943
CZ20	0526
CZ20A	0526
CZ20B	0526
CZ20D	0526
CZ22	0560
CZ22A	0560
CZ22B	0560
CZ22C	OEM
CZ22D	0560
CZ24	0398
CZ24A	0398
CZ24B	0398
CZ24C	OEM
CZ24D	0398
CZ25	1596
CZ25A	1596
CZ25B	1596
CZ25C	1596
CZ25D	1596
CZ27	0436
CZ27A	0436
CZ27B	0436
CZ27C	OEM
CZ27D	0436
CZ30	0721
CZ30A	0721
CZ30B	0721
CZ30C	OEM
CZ30D	0721
CZ33	0039
CZ33A	0039
CZ33B	0039
CZ33C	OEM
CZ33D	0039
CZ36	0814
CZ36A	0346
CZ36B	0814
CZ36C	0814
CZ36D	0814
CZ39	0346
CZ39A	0346
CZ39B	0346
CZ39C	0346
CZ39D	0346
CZ43	0925
CZ43A	0925
CZ43B	0925
CZ43C	0925
CZ43D	0925
CZ47	0993
CZ47A	0993
CZ47B	0993
CZ47C	0993
CZ47D	0993
CZ50	0497
CZ50A	0497
CZ50B	0497
CZ50C	OEM
CZ50D	OEM
CZ51	0497
CZ51A	0497
CZ51B	0497
CZ51C	0497
CZ51D	0497
CZ52	0497
CZ52A	0497
CZ52B	OEM
CZ52C	OEM
CZ52D	OEM
CZ56	0863
CZ56A	0863
CZ56B	0863
CZ56C	0863
CZ56D	0863
CZ62	0778
CZ62A	0778
CZ62B	0778
CZ62C	0778
CZ62D	0778
CZ68	2144
CZ68A	2144
CZ68B	2144
CZ68C	2144
CZ68D	2144
CZ75	1181
CZ75A	1181
CZ75B	1181
CZ75C	1181
CZ75D	1181
CZ82	0327
CZ82A	0327
CZ82B	0327
CZ82C	0327
CZ82D	0327
CZ91	1301
CZ91A	1301
CZ91B	1301
CZ91C	1301
CZ91D	1301
CZ100	0098
CZ100A	0098
CZ100B	0098
CZ100D	0098
CZ105	0149
CZ105A	0149
CZ105B	0149
CZ105C	OEM
CZ105D	OEM
CZ110	0149
CZ110A	0149
CZ110B	0149
CZ110C	0149
CZ110D	0149
CZ120	0186
CZ120A	0186
CZ120B	0186
CZ120C	0186
CZ120D	0186
CZ130	0213
CZ130A	0213
CZ130B	0213
CZ130C	0213
CZ130D	0213
CZ140	0245
CZ140A	0245
CZ140B	0245
CZ140C	0245
CZ140D	0245
CZ150	0028
CZ150A	0028
CZ150B	0028
CZ150C	0028
CZ150D	0028
CZ160	0255
CZ160A	0255
CZ160B	0255
CZ160C	0255
CZ160D	0255
CZ175	0363
CZ175A	0363
CZ175B	0363
CZ175C	OEM
CZ175D	OEM
CZ180	0363
CZ180A	0363
CZ180B	0363
CZ180C	0363
CZ180D	0363
CZ200	0417
CZ200A	0417
CZ200B	0417
CZ200C	0417
CZ200D	0417
CZ220	OEM
CZ220A	OEM
CZ220B	OEM
CZ220C	OEM
CZ220D	OEM
CZ255	1596
CZ821	0466
CZ821A	0466
CZ822	0466
CZ823	0466
CZ823A	0466
CZ824	0466
CZ825	0466
CZ825A	0466
CZ827	0466
CZ827A	0466
CZ829	0466
CZ829A	0466
CZ935	0057
CZ935A	0057
CZ935B	0057
CZ936	0057
CZ936A	0057
CZ936B	0057
CZ937	0057
CZ937A	0057
CZ937B	0057
CZ938	0057
CZ938A	0057
CZ938B	0057
CZ939	0057
CZ939A	0057
CZ939B	0057
CZ4097	1172
CZ4097A	1172
CZ4098	0642
CZ4098A	0642
CZ4565	0466
CZ4565A	0466
CZ4566	0466
CZ4566A	0466
CZ4567	0466
CZ4567A	0466
CZ4568	0466
CZ4568A	0466
CZ4569	0466
CZ4569A	0466
CZ4570	0466
CZ4570A	0466
CZ4571	0466
CZ4571A	0466
CZ4572	0466
CZ4572A	0466
CZ4573	0466
CZ4573A	0466
CZ4574	0466
CZ4574A	0466
CZ4881	0526
CZ4881A	0262
CZ4883	0234
CZ4883A	0234
CZ5063	0205
CZ5063A	0205
CZ5064	0475
CZ5064A	0475
CZ5065	0499
CZ5065A	0499
CZ5066	0679
CZ5066A	0679
CZ5067	0225
CZ5067A	0225
CZ5068	0230
CZ5068A	0230
CZ5069	0237
CZ5069A	0237
CZ5070	1387
CZ5070A	1387
CZ5071	0247
CZ5071A	0247
CZ5072	0251
CZ5072A	0251
CZ5073	0256
CZ5073A	0256
CZ5074	0269
CZ5074A	0269
CZ5075	0273
CZ5075A	0273
CZ5076	0291
CZ5076A	0291
CZ5077	0305
CZ5077A	0305
CZ5078	0314
CZ5078A	0314
CZ5079	0316
CZ5079A	0316
CZ5080	0322
CZ5080A	0322
CZ5081	0322
CZ5081A	0322
CZ5082	0333
CZ5082A	0333
CZ5083	0343
CZ5083A	0343
CZ5084	0343
CZ5084A	0343
CZ5085	0027
CZ5085A	0027
CZ5086	0027
CZ5086A	0027
CZ5087	0266
CZ5087A	0266
CZ5088	2829
CZ5088A	2829
CZ5089	0382
CZ5089A	0382
CZ5090	0401
CZ5090A	0401
CZ5091	0401
CZ5091A	0401
CZ5092	0421
CZ5092A	0421
CZ5093	0439
CZ5093A	0439
CZ5094	0439
CZ5094A	0439
CZ5095	0238
CZ5095A	0238
CZ5096	1182
CZ5096A	1182
CZ5097	1198
CZ5097A	1198
CZ5098	1209
CZ5098A	1209
CZ5099	1870
CZ5099A	1870
CZ5100	1246
CZ5100A	1246
CZ5101	2091
CZ5101A	2091
CZ5102	1269
CZ5102A	1269
CZ5103	2210
CZ5103A	2210
CZ5104	0600
CZ5104A	0600
CZA6D5	OEM
CZA6.8D	0062
CZA6.8D5	0062
CZA6.8D10	0062
CZA7.5D	0077
CZA7.5D5	0077
CZA7.5D10	0077
CZA8.2D	0165
CZA8.2D5	0165
CZA8.2D10	0165
CZA9.1D	0057
CZA9.1D5	0057
CZA9.1D10	0057
CZA10D	0064
CZA10D5	0064
CZA10D10	0064
CZA11D	0181
CZA11D5	0181
CZA11D10	0181
CZA12D	0052
CZA12D5	0052
CZA12D10	0052
CZA13D	0053
CZA13D5	0053
CZA13D10	0053
CZA14D	0873
CZA14D5	0873
CZA14D10	0873
CZA15D	0681
CZA15D5	0681
CZA15D10	0681
CZA16D	0440
CZA16D5	0440
CZA16D10	0440
CZA17D	0210
CZA17D5	0210
CZA17D10	0210
CZA18D	0371
CZA18D5	0371
CZA18D10	0371
CZA19D	0666
CZA19D5	0666
CZA19D10	0666
CZA20D	0695
CZA20D5	0695
CZA20D10	0695
CZA22D	0700
CZA22D5	0700
CZA22D10	0700
CZA24D	0489
CZA24D5	0489
CZA24D10	0489
CZA25D	0709
CZA25D5	0709
CZA25D10	0709
CZA27D	0450
CZA27D5	0450
CZA27D10	0450
CZA28D	0257
CZA28D5	0257
CZA28D10	0257
CZA30D	0195
CZA30D5	0195
CZA30D10	0195
CZA33D	0166
CZA33D5	0166
CZA33D10	0166
CZA36D	0010
CZA36D5	0010
CZA36D10	0010
CZA39D	0032
CZA39D5	0032
CZA39D10	0032
CZA43D	0054
CZA43D5	0054
CZA43D10	0054
CZA47D	0068
CZA47D5	0068
CZA47D10	0068
CZA51D	0092
CZA51D5	0092
CZA51D10	0092
CZA56D	0125
CZA56D5	0125
CZA56D10	0125
CZA60D	2301
CZA60D5	2301
CZA60D10	2301
CZA62D	0152
CZA62D5	0152
CZA62D10	0152
CZA68D	0173
CZA68D5	0173
CZA68D10	0173
CZA75D	0094
CZA75D5	0094
CZA75D10	0094
CZA82D	0049
CZA82D5	0049
CZA82D10	0049
CZA87D	0104
CZA87D5	0104
CZA87D10	0104
CZA91D	0156
CZA91D5	0156
CZA91D10	0156
CZA100D	0189
CZA100D5	0189
CZA100D10	0189
CZA105D	0099
CZA105D5	0099
CZA105D10	0099
CZA110D	0099
CZA110D5	0099
CZA110D10	0099
CZA120D	0089
CZA120D5	0089
CZA120D10	0089
CZA130D	0285
CZA130D5	0285
CZA130D10	0285
CZA140D	0252
CZA140D5	0252
CZA140D10	0252
CZA150D	0336
CZA150D5	0336
CZA150D10	0336
CZA160D	0366
CZA160D5	0366
CZA160D10	0366
CZA175D	0420
CZA175D5	0420
CZA175D10	0420
CZA180D	0420
CZA180D5	0420
CZA180D10	0420
CZA200D	1464
CZA200D5	1464
CZA200D10	1464
CZAJ102	0015
CZB6.8D	0062
CZB6.8D5	0062
CZB6.8D10	0062
CZB7.5D	0077
CZB7.5D5	0077
CZB7.5D10	0077
CZB8.2D	0165
CZB8.2D5	0165
CZB8.2D10	0165
CZB8.2DD5	OEM
CZB9.1D	0057
CZB9.1D5	0057
CZB9.1D10	0057
CZB10D	0064

If replacement code is OEM, contact original manufacturer for replacement.

357

DEVICE TYPE	REPL CODE
CZB10D5	0064
CZB10D10	0064
CZB11D	0181
CZB11D5	0181
CZB11D10	0181
CZB12D	0052
CZB12D5	0052
CZB12D10	0052
CZB13D	0053
CZB13D5	0053
CZB13D10	0053
CZB14D	0873
CZB14D5	0873
CZB14D10	0873
CZB15D	0681
CZB15D5	0681
CZB15D10	0681
CZB16D	0440
CZB16D5	0440
CZB16D10	0440
CZB17D	0210
CZB17D5	0210
CZB17D10	0210
CZB18D	0371
CZB18D5	0371
CZB18D10	0371
CZB19D	0666
CZB19D5	0666
CZB19D10	0666
CZB20D	0695
CZB20D5	0695
CZB20D10	0695
CZB22D	0700
CZB22D5	0700
CZB22D10	0700
CZB24D	0489
CZB24D5	0489
CZB24D10	0489
CZB25D	0709
CZB25D5	0709
CZB25D10	0709
CZB30D	0195
CZB30D5	0195
CZB30D10	0195
CZB33D	0166
CZB33D5	0166
CZB33D10	0166
CZB36D	0010
CZB36D5	0010
CZB36D10	0010
CZB39D	0032
CZB39D5	0032
CZB39D10	0032
CZB43D	0054
CZB43D5	0054
CZB43D10	0054
CZB47D	0068
CZB47D5	0068
CZB47D10	0068
CZB51D	0092
CZB51D5	0092
CZB51D10	0092
CZB56D	0125
CZB56D5	0125
CZB56D10	0125
CZB62D	0152
CZB62D5	0152
CZB62D10	0152
CZB68D	0173
CZB68D5	0173
CZB68D10	0173
CZB75D	0094
CZB75D5	0094
CZB75D10	0094
CZB82D	0049
CZB82D5	0049
CZB82D10	0049
CZB91D	0156
CZB91D5	0156
CZB91D10	0156
CZB100D	0189
CZB100D5	0189
CZB100D10	0189
CZB105D	0099
CZB105D5	0099
CZB105D10	0099
CZB110D	0099
CZB110D5	0099
CZB110D10	0099
CZB120D	0089
CZB120D5	0089
CZB120D10	0089
CZB130D	0285
CZB130D5	0285
CZB130D10	0285
CZB140D	0252
CZB140D5	0252
CZB140D10	0252
CZB150D	0336
CZB150D5	0336
CZB150D10	0336
CZB160D	0366
CZB160D5	0366
CZB160D10	0366
CZB175D	0420
CZB175D5	0420
CZB175D10	0420
CZB180D	0420
CZB180D5	0420
CZB180D10	0420
CZB200D	1464
CZB200D5	1464
CZB200D10	1464
CZC6.8D	0062
CZC6.8D5	0062
CZC6.8D10	0062
CZC7.5D	0077
CZC7.5D5	0077
CZC7.5D10	0077
CZC8.2D	0165
CZC8.2D5	0165
CZC8.2D10	0165
CZC9.1D	0057
CZC9.1D5	0057
CZC9.1D10	0057
CZC10D	0064
CZC10D5	0064
CZC10D10	0064
CZC11D	0181
CZC11D5	0181
CZC11D10	0181
CZC12D	0052
CZC12D5	0052
CZC12D10	0052
CZC13D	0053
CZC13D5	0053
CZC13D10	0053
CZC14D	0873
CZC14D5	0873
CZC14D10	0873
CZC15D	0681
CZC15D5	0681
CZC15D10	0681
CZC16D	0440
CZC16D5	0440
CZC16D10	0440
CZC17D	0210
CZC17D5	0210
CZC17D10	0210
CZC19D	0666
CZC19D5	0666
CZC19D10	0666
CZC20D	0695
CZC20D5	0695
CZC20D10	0695
CZC22D	0700
CZC22D5	0700
CZC22D10	0700
CZC24D	0489
CZC24D5	0489
CZC24D10	0489
CZC25D	0709
CZC25D5	0709
CZC25D10	0709
CZC27D	0450
CZC27D5	0450
CZC27D10	0450
CZC30D	0195
CZC30D5	0195
CZC30D10	0195
CZC33D	0166
CZC33D5	0166
CZC33D10	0166
CZC36D	0010
CZC36D5	0010
CZC36D10	0010
CZC39D	0032
CZC39D5	0032
CZC39D10	0032
CZC43D	0054
CZC43D5	0054
CZC43D10	0054
CZC47D	0068
CZC47D5	0068
CZC47D10	0068
CZC51D	0092
CZC51D5	0092
CZC51D10	0092
CZC56D	0125
CZC56D5	0125
CZC56D10	0125
CZC62D	0152
CZC62D5	0152
CZC62D10	0152
CZC68D	0173
CZC68D5	0173
CZC68D10	0173
CZC75D	0094
CZC75D5	0094
CZC75D10	0094
CZC82D	0049
CZC82D5	0049
CZC82D10	0049
CZC91D	0156
CZC91D5	0156
CZC91D10	0156
CZC100D	0189
CZC100D5	0189
CZC100D10	0189
CZC105D	0099
CZC105D5	0099
CZC105D10	0099
CZC110D	0099
CZC110D5	0099
CZC110D10	0099
CZC120D	0089
CZC120D5	0089
CZC120D10	0089
CZC130D	0285
CZC130D5	0285
CZC130D10	0285
CZC140D	0252
CZC140D5	0252
CZC140D10	0252
CZC150D	0336
CZC150D5	0336
CZC150D10	0336
CZC160D	0366
CZC160D5	0366
CZC160D10	0366
CZC175D	0420
CZC175D5	0420
CZC175D10	0420
CZC180D	0420
CZC180D5	0420
CZC180D10	0420
CZC200D	1464
CZC200D5	1464
CZC200D10	1464
CZD010	0170
CZD010-5	0170
CZD011	0181
CZD011-5	0181
CZD012	0052
CZD012-5	0052
CZD013	0053
CZD013-5	0053
CZD014	0100
CZD014-5	0100
CZD015	0681
CZD015-5	0681
CZD016	0440
CZD016-5	0440
CZD018	0371
CZD018-5	OEM
CZD020	0695
CZD020-5	0695
CZD022	0700
CZD022-5	0700
CZD024	0489
CZD024-5	0489
CZD6.8D	0062
CZD6.8D5	0062
CZD6.8D10	0062
CZD7.5D	0077
CZD7.5D5	0077
CZD7.5D10	0077
CZD8.2D	0165
CZD8.2D5	0165
CZD8.2D10	0165
CZD9.1D	0057
CZD9.1D5	0057
CZD9.1D10	0057
CZD10D	0064
CZD10D5	0064
CZD10D10	0064
CZD11D	0181
CZD11D5	0181
CZD11D10	0181
CZD12D	0052
CZD12D5	0052
CZD12D10	0052
CZD13D	0053
CZD13D5	0053
CZD13D10	0053
CZD14D	0873
CZD14D5	0873
CZD14D10	0873
CZD15D	0681
CZD15D5	0681
CZD15D10	0681
CZD16D	0440
CZD16D5	0440
CZD16D10	0440
CZD17D	0210
CZD17D5	0210
CZD17D10	0210
CZD18D	0371
CZD18D5	0371
CZD18D10	0371
CZD19D	0666
CZD19D5	0666
CZD19D10	0666
CZD20D	0695
CZD20D5	0695
CZD20D10	0695
CZD22D	0700
CZD22D5	0700
CZD22D10	0700
CZD24D	0489
CZD24D5	0489
CZD24D10	0489
CZD25D	0709
CZD25D5	0709
CZD25D10	0709
CZD27D	0450
CZD27D5	0450
CZD27D10	0450
CZD28D	0257
CZD28D5	0257
CZD28D10	0257
CZD30D	0195
CZD30D5	0195
CZD30D10	0195
CZD33D	0166
CZD33D5	0166
CZD33D10	0166
CZD36D	0010
CZD36D5	0010
CZD36D10	0010
CZD39D	0032
CZD39D5	0032
CZD39D10	0032
CZD43D	0054
CZD43D5	0054
CZD43D10	0054
CZD47D	0068
CZD47D5	0068
CZD47D10	0068
CZD51D	0092
CZD51D5	0092
CZD51D10	0092
CZD56D	0125
CZD56D5	0125
CZD56D10	0125
CZD60D	2301
CZD60D5	2301
CZD60D10	2301
CZD62D	0152
CZD62D5	0152
CZD62D10	0152
CZD68D	0173
CZD68D5	0173
CZD68D10	0173
CZD75D	0094
CZD75D5	0094
CZD75D10	0094
CZD82D	0049
CZD82D5	0049
CZD82D10	0049
CZD87D	0104
CZD87D5	0104
CZD87D10	0104
CZD91D	0156
CZD91D5	0156
CZD91D10	0156
CZD100D	0189
CZD100D5	0189
CZD100D10	0189
CZD105D	0099
CZD105D5	0099
CZD105D10	0099
CZD110D	0099
CZD110D5	0099
CZD110D10	0099
CZD120D	0089
CZD120D5	0089
CZD120D10	0089
CZD130D	0285
CZD130D5	0285
CZD130D10	0285
CZD140D	0252
CZD140D5	0252
CZD140D10	0252
CZD150D	0336
CZD150D5	0336
CZD150D10	0336
CZD160D	0366
CZD160D5	0366
CZD160D10	0366
CZD175D	0420
CZD175D5	0420
CZD175D10	0420
CZD180D	0420
CZD180D5	0420
CZD180D10	0420
CZD200D	1464
CZD200D5	1464
CZD200D10	1464
CZE6.8D	0062
CZE6.8D5	0062
CZE6.8D10	0062
CZE7.5D	0077
CZE7.5D5	0077
CZE7.5D10	0077
CZE8.2D	0165
CZE8.2D5	0165
CZE8.2D10	0165
CZE9.1D	0057
CZE9.1D5	0057
CZE9.1D10	0057
CZE10D	0064
CZE10D5	0064
CZE10D10	0064
CZE11D	0181
CZE11D5	0181
CZE11D10	0181
CZE12D	0052
CZE12D5	0052
CZE12D10	0052
CZE13D	0053
CZE13D5	0053
CZE13D10	0053
CZE14D	0873
CZE14D5	0873
CZE14D10	0873
CZE15D	0681
CZE15D5	0681
CZE15D10	0681
CZE16D	0440
CZE16D5	0440
CZE16D10	0440
CZE17D	0210
CZE17D5	0210
CZE17D10	0210
CZE18	0371
CZE18D5	0371
CZE18D10	0371
CZE19D	0666
CZE19D5	0666
CZE19D10	0666
CZE20D	0695
CZE20D5	0695
CZE20D10	0695
CZE22D	0700
CZE22D5	0700
CZE22D10	0700
CZE24D	0489
CZE24D5	0489
CZE24D10	0489
CZE25D	0709
CZE25D5	0709
CZE25D10	0709
CZE27D	0450
CZE27D5	0450
CZE27D10	0450
CZE30D	0195
CZE30D5	0195
CZE30D10	0195
CZE33D	0166
CZE33D5	0166
CZE33D10	0166
CZE36D	0010
CZE36D5	0010
CZE36D10	0010
CZE39D	0032
CZE39D5	0032
CZE39D10	0032
CZE43D	0054
CZE43D5	0054
CZE43D10	0054
CZE47D	0068
CZE47D5	0068
CZE47D10	0068
CZE51D	0092
CZE51D5	0092
CZE51D10	0092
CZE56D	0125
CZE56D5	0125
CZE56D10	0125
CZE62D	0152
CZE62D5	0152
CZE62D10	0152
CZE68D	0173
CZE68D5	0173
CZE68D10	0173
CZE75D	0094
CZE75D5	0094
CZE75D10	0094
CZE82D	0049
CZE82D5	0049
CZE82D10	0049
CZE91D	0156
CZE91D5	0156
CZE91D10	0156
CZE100D	0189
CZE100D5	0189
CZE100D10	0189
CZE105D	0099
CZE105D5	0099
CZE105D10	0099
CZE110D	0099
CZE110D5	0099
CZE110D10	0099
CZE120D	0089
CZE120D5	0089
CZE120D10	0089
CZE130D	0285
CZE130D5	0285
CZE130D10	0285
CZE140D	0252
CZE140D5	0252
CZE140D10	0252
CZE150D	0336
CZE150D5	0336
CZE150D10	0336
CZE160D	0366
CZE160D5	0366
CZE160D10	0366
CZE175D	0420
CZE175D5	0420
CZE175D10	0420
CZE180D	0420
CZE180D5	0420
CZE180D10	0420
CZE200D	1464
CZE200D5	1464
CZE200D10	1464
CZF1.8D	OEM
CZF1.8D5	OEM
CZF1.8D10	OEM
CZF2.0D	OEM
CZF2.0D5	OEM
CZF2.0D10	OEM
CZF2.2D	OEM
CZF2.2D5	OEM
CZF2.2D10	OEM
CZF2.4D	1266
CZF2.4D5	1266
CZF2.4D10	1266
CZF2.7D	0755
CZF2.7D5	0755
CZF2.7D10	0755
CZF3.0D	0118
CZF3.0D5	0118
CZF3.0D10	0118
CZF3.3D	0296
CZF3.3D5	0296
CZF3.3D10	0296
CZF3.6D	0372
CZF3.6D5	0372
CZF3.6D10	0372
CZF3.9D	0036
CZF3.9D5	0036
CZF3.9D10	0036
CZF4.3D	0274
CZF4.3D5	0274
CZF4.3D10	0274
CZF4.7D	0140
CZF4.7D5	0140
CZF4.7D10	0140
CZF5.1D	0041
CZF5.1D5	0041
CZF5.1D10	0041
CZF5.6D	0253
CZF5.6D5	0253
CZF5.6D10	0253
CZF6.2D	0466
CZF6.2D5	0466
CZF6.2D10	0466
CZF6.8D	0062
CZF6.8D5	0062
CZF6.8D10	0062
CZF7.5D	0077
CZF7.5D5	0077
CZF7.5D10	0077
CZF8.2D	0165
CZF8.2D5	0165
CZF8.2D10	0165
CZF9.1D	0057
CZF9.1D5	0057
CZF9.1D10	0057
CZF10D	0064
CZF10D5	0064
CZF10D10	0064
CZF12D	0052
CZF12D5	0052
CZF12D10	0052
CZG2.4D	1266
CZG2.4D5	1266
CZG2.4D10	1266
CZG2.7D	0755
CZG2.7D5	0755
CZG2.7D10	0755
CZG3.0D	0118
CZG3.0D5	0118
CZG3.0D10	0118
CZG3.3D	0296
CZG3.3D5	0296
CZG3.3D10	0296
CZG3.6D	0372
CZG3.6D5	0372
CZG3.6D10	0372
CZG3.9D	0036
CZG3.9D5	0036
CZG3.9D10	0036
CZG4.3D	0274
CZG4.3D5	0274
CZG4.3D10	0274
CZG4.7D	0140
CZG4.7D5	0140
CZG4.7D10	0140
CZG5.1D	0041
CZG5.1D5	0041
CZG5.1D10	0041
CZG5.6D	0253
CZG5.6D5	0253
CZG5.6D10	0253
CZG6.2D	0466
CZG6.2D5	0466
CZG6.2D10	0466
CZG6.8D	0062
CZG6.8D5	0062
CZG6.8D10	0062
CZG7.5D	0077
CZG7.5D5	0077
CZG7.5D10	0077
CZG8.2D	0165
CZG8.2D5	0165
CZG8.2D10	0165
CZG9.1D	0057
CZG9.1D5	0057
CZG9.1D10	0057
CZG10D	0064
CZG10D5	0064
CZG10D10	0064
CZG12D	0052
CZG12D5	0052
CZG12D10	0052
D	OEM
D/7A	OEM
D002	OEM
D004	0015
D006	0127
D008	0004
D009	0224
D-00169C	0143
D-00184R	0133
D-00204R	0143
D-00269C	0143
D-00284R	0143
D-00369C	0644
D-00384R	0015
D-00469C	0631
D-00484R	0143
D-00569C	0012
D-00669C	0143
D01-100	0015
D02S	0005
D02Z6-2W	0466
D02Z62W	0466
D-05	0015
D05	0015
D05G	0023
D010	0123
D018	0004
D019	0136
D020	0628
D021	0628
D030	0004
D031	0004
D031(CHAN.MASTER)	0079
D038	0164
D043	0004
D048	0016
D053	0016
D058	0144
D059	0004
D063	0136
D069	0016
D072	0224
D073	0136
D078	0628
D079	0050
D080	0160
D081	0160
D082	1665
D083	0208
D084	0233
D085	0208
D086	0050
D087	0007
D088	0144
D093	0019
D0123WX	2340
D0201YR	3298
D-0501	OEM
D0515L	3785
D0520L	3785
D0535J	OEM
D0535W	OEM
D0550J	OEM
D0555W	OEM
D0565J	OEM
D0570W	OEM
D0J020A90	0123
D0J020A900	0123
D0.2S10	OEM
D0.22/80X41	OEM
D0.22/100X11	OEM
D0.22/125X31	OEM
D0.22/150X31	OEM
D0.24S10	OEM
D0.25S8	OEM
D0.42S5	OEM
D1/2-12	OEM
D1-7E	OEM
D1-8	0012
D1-12B	OEM
D1-12E	OEM
D1-26	0015
D1-52S	0015
D1-S2RB	OEM
D1A	0244
D1AT015550	0133
D1B	0196
D1C	0196
D1CA	OEM
D1CA20R	0015
D1D	0071
D1E	0015
D1F	0102
D1G	0012
D1H	0015
D1I0A243A0	0124
D1J	0015
D1J70542	0143
D1J70543	0143
D1J70544	0015
D1J70545	0133
D1JA	OEM
D1JA20	OEM
D1K	0071
D1K20	0023
D1K20H	1082
D1K40	0023
D1K58	OEM
D1L	0015
D1M	0157
D1M(TRANS)	OEM
D1N20R	OEM
D1N4002	0080
D1NL20	1082
D1NS4	OEM
D1NS6	OEM
D1NS6-TA2	OEM
D1R5GZ61	0071
D1R5GZ61FA	0071
D1R20	0182
D1R20Z	0604
D1R38	0016
D1R40Z	0790
D1R60	0182

If replacement code is OEM, contact original manufacturer for replacement.

DEVICE TYPE	REPL CODE
D1R80	0182
D1R100	0182
D1R150	0182
D1S	0361
D1S34	0143
D1S1553	0133
D1S1554	0133
D1S1555	0133
D1S1887FA	0015
D-1S2473	0133
D1S2775-1	0494
D-1SS133	0133
D1T	0100
D1TH61	0071
D1U	0244
D1V0001320	0124
D1V20	0023
D1V40	0182
D1V60	0182
D1VT001310	0124
D1VT001320	0124
D1VT024720	0133
D1W	0436
D1Y	0127
D1Z	0002
D1ZBLU	0002
D1ZRED	0100
D1ZVIO	0361
D1ZYEL	0002
D1.5/200	OEM
D1.5/400	OEM
D1.5/600	OEM
D1.5/800	OEM
D1.5/1000	OEM
D1.5-400	OEM
D1.5-600	OEM
D1.5-800	OEM
D1.5-1000	OEM
D-2	0143
D2-1	0015
D2-12B	OEM
D2-12E	OEM
D2B000R2M0	3829
D2B000RH10	0023
D2B000RU20	0023
D2B000RU30	0282
D2B000SR2M	3829
D2B00EU01A	0023
D2B00RU1P0	0023
D2BF00RU20	0023
D2BF0RU4A0	0102
D2BFMI15MR	1089
D2BFMI15MS	1791
D2BH00EU2Z	0023
D2BHRM11C0	0071
D2BJ00RU4Z	0031
D2BT0EU01A	0023
D2E	0039
D2F	OEM
D2G	0789
D2G-1	0789
D2G-2	0789
D2G-3	0137
D2G-4	0137
D2H	0015
D2J	0015
D2L0040070	0023
D2L0TVR06G	0015
D2LFRGP30G	0017
D2LT040070	0023
D2M	0201
D2M5001	OEM
D2M5002	OEM
D2M5003	OEM
D2N	0286
D2R31	0143
D2R38	0016
D2S4MF	OEM
D2S100	0031
D2S200	0031
D2S400	0031
D2S800	0102
D2SBA	OEM
D2SBA40	0293
D2T918	0259
D2T2904	0037
D2T2904A	0037
D2T2905	0037
D2T2905A	0037
D2U	0143
D2Y	0752
D2Z	0012
D2Z-2	0436
D3-200	0031
D3-400	0031
D3-600	0031
D3-800	0087
D3-1300	OEM
D3A	0914
D3F	0012
D3G	5236
D3H	0631
D3N	0789
D3R	0015
D3R38	0015
D3R39	0015
D3S3M	0031
D3S4M	0031
D3S800	OEM

DEVICE TYPE	REPL CODE
D3S1000	OEM
D3S1200	OEM
D3SB10	0724
D3SB20	OEM
D3SB60	0732
D3SB1057	OEM
D3SBA10	6206
D3SBA20	OEM
D3SBA40	1039
D3SBA60	1039
D3SBA60-4103	1039
D3U	0015
D3V	0015
D3W	0137
D3Y	0631
D3Z	0015
D4	0196
D4-2	0030
D4-28G	OEM
D4BB10	OEM
D4BB20	OEM
D4BB40	OEM
D4C28	0086
D4C29	0086
D4C30	0086
D4C31	0086
D4D20	0086
D4D21	0086
D4D22	0007
D4D24	0198
D4D25	0198
D4D26	0198
D4G	0201
D4H	0039
D4J	0039
D4L	0071
D4M	0015
D4N	0789
D4P	0100
D4R	0143
D4R26	0015
D4SB60L	OEM
D4SB60L-F	OEM
D4.5-400	OEM
D4.5-700	OEM
D4.5-1100	OEM
D4.5-1400	OEM
D5	0479
D5B	0002
D5D	OEM
D5E29	OEM
D5E35	OEM
D5E36	OEM
D5E-37	2123
D5E37	2123
D5E-43	1167
D5E43	1167
D5E-44	2123
D5E44	2123
D5E-45	1167
D5E45	1167
D5F840	OEM
D5F860	OEM
D5FB10	OEM
D5FB10F	OEM
D5FB20	OEM
D5FB40	OEM
D5FB60	OEM
D5G	0023
D5H	0023
D5J37	1659
D5J-43	1659
D5J43	1659
D5J-44	1659
D5J44	1659
D5J45	1659
D5K1	OEM
D5K2	OEM
D5KC20	1227
D5KC20H	1227
D5KC20R	1716
D5KC20RH	1716
D5KC40	0966
D5KC40H	OEM
D5KC40R	OEM
D5KD20	OEM
D5KD20H	OEM
D5KD40	OEM
D5LC20	1227
D5LCA20	1227
D5R35	0015
D5R39	0015
D5S3M	OEM
D5S4M	OEM
D5SB10	1034
D5SB20	1034
D5SB20F	OEM
D5SB40	1039
D5SB60	1039
D5SBA10	1034
D5SC4MR	OEM
D5V	0133
D5W	0631
D5Z	OEM
D6	1073
D6/400	OEM
D6/400A	OEM
D6/800	OEM
D6/800A	OEM

DEVICE TYPE	REPL CODE
D6/1200	OEM
D6/1200A	OEM
D6/1400	OEM
D6/1400A	OEM
D6/1600	OEM
D6/1600A	OEM
D6-700	OEM
D6-1100	OEM
D6C	1313
D6HZ	0015
D6K20	1137
D6K20H	1119
D6K20R	OEM
D6K20RH	OEM
D6K40	1137
D6K40R	OEM
D6M	0244
D6U	0560
D6.2	0631
D7	1073
D7A30	0086
D7A31	0086
D7A32	0086
D7B2	1955
D7C1	OEM
D7C2	OEM
D7C3	OEM
D7D1	OEM
D7D2	OEM
D7D3	OEM
D7D13	OEM
D7E	0133
D7E1	OEM
D7E2	OEM
D7E3	OEM
D7F1	OEM
D7F2	OEM
D7F3	OEM
D7F4	OEM
D7G1	OEM
D7G2	OEM
D7G3	OEM
D7L	1639
D7M	0030
D7N	0030
D7S	0244
D7ST4010(A)	OEM
D7ST4013(A)	OEM
D7ST4015(A)	OEM
D7ST4510(A)	OEM
D7ST4513(A)	OEM
D7ST5010(A)	OEM
D7Z	0133
D8-400B	OEM
D8-400C	OEM
D8-700B	OEM
D8-700C	OEM
D8-800B	OEM
D8-800C	OEM
D8-1100B	OEM
D8-1100C	OEM
D8-1200B	OEM
D8-1200C	OEM
D8-1400B	OEM
D8-1400C	OEM
D8-1600B	OEM
D8-1600C	OEM
D8G	0102
D8HZ	0071
D8L	0102
D8LCA20	1227
D8M	0102
D8N	OEM
D8P	0361
D8U	1075
D9B	0019
D9C	OEM
D9D	0019
D9E	0143
D9F	OEM
D9G	0644
D9I	0019
D9K	0019
D9L	0143
D9M	1075
D9SZ	0143
D9V	0019
D10B551-2,3	OEM
D10B553-2,3	OEM
D10B555-2,3	OEM
D10B556-2,-3	OEM
D10B1051	0127
D10B1055	0127
D10C573-2,-3	OEM
D10G1051	0127
D10G1052	0127
D10H551-2,-3	OEM
D10H553-2,-3	OEM
D10N400B	OEM
D10N400C	OEM
D10N800B	OEM
D10N800C	OEM
D10N1200B	OEM
D10N1200C	OEM
D10N1400B	OEM
D10N1400C	OEM
D10N1600B	OEM
D10N1600C	OEM
D10P	OEM

DEVICE TYPE	REPL CODE
D10S6CM	OEM
D10SC3M	1015
D10SC3MR	OEM
D10SC4M	1015
D10SC4MR	OEM
D10VD60Z	OEM
D11	0208
D11A	0208
D11B	0208
D11B551-2,-3	OEM
D11B551-2,3	OEM
D11B552-2,3	OEM
D11B555-2,-3	OEM
D11B556-2,-3	OEM
D11B560-2,3	OEM
D11B1052	OEM
D11B1055	OEM
D11C	0208
D11C1B1	0086
D11C1F1	0079
D11C2D1B20	0079
D11C3B1	0086
D11C3F1	0590
D11C5B1	0086
D11C5F1	0079
D11C7B1	0086
D11C7F1	OEM
D11C10B1	0086
D11C10F1	0142
D11C11B1	0086
D11C11F1	0142
D11C201B20	0142
D11C203B20	0142
D11C205B20	0142
D11C207B20	0142
D11C210B20	0142
D11C211B20	0142
D11C551-2,-3	OEM
D11C553-2,-3	OEM
D11C557-2,-3	OEM
D11C702	OEM
D11C704	OEM
D11C710	OEM
D11C1051	OEM
D11C1053	OEM
D11C1057	OEM
D11C1536	0626
D11D	0208
D11E	0208
D11E404	OEM
D11E405	OEM
D11E406	OEM
D11E407	OEM
D11F	0208
D11G	0208
D11GN	0208
D11H	0208
D11J	0208
D11K	0208
D11L	0208
D11M	0208
D110R	0208
D11R	0208
D11X	0208
D11Y	0208
D12	0074
D12-03	OEM
D12-05	OEM
D12-10A	OEM
D12-15A	OEM
D12-20	OEM
D12-28G	OEM
D12-30	OEM
D12-35	OEM
D12-50	OEM
D12A	0074
D12A8	OEM
D12B	0074
D12C	0074
D12E	0074
D12E026	OEM
D12E109	OEM
D12E126	OEM
D12F	0074
D12G	0074
D12GN	0074
D12H	0074
D12J	0074
D12K	0074
D12L	0074
D12M	0074
D120R	0074
D12R	0074
D12X	0074
D12X010	OEM
D12X011	OEM
D12X012	OEM
D12X013	OEM
D12X014	OEM
D12X015	OEM
D12X043	0855
D12X047	1471
D12X070	OEM
D12X084A	OEM
D12Y	0074
D13	0435
D13H1	OEM
D13H2	OEM
D13K1	0312

DEVICE TYPE	REPL CODE
D13K2	OEM
D13K3	OEM
D13T1	0312
D13T2	0312
D13T3	0312
D13T4	0312
D13TDS442X	0124
D13TGMA010	0124
D14	0150
D14T000880	OEM
D14U001660	OEM
D15(2S)	0130
D15-03	OEM
D15-05	OEM
D15-10A	OEM
D15-15A	OEM
D15-20	OEM
D15-30	OEM
D15-35	OEM
D15-50	OEM
D15-100/5	OEM
D15-100/12	OEM
D15-100/24	OEM
D15-100/28	OEM
D15A	0015
D15A(TRANS)	0130
D15B	0130
D15C	0015
D15C(TRANS)	0130
D15D	0130
D15E	0130
D15F	0130
D15G	0130
D15GN	0130
D15H	0130
D15J	0130
D15K	0130
D15L	0130
D15M	0130
D150R	0130
D15R	0130
D15T015850	0124
D15X	0130
D15Y	0130
D16(2S)	0130
D16A	0130
D16B	0130
D16C	0130
D16D	0130
D16E	0130
D16E7	0016
D16E9	0016
D16EC18	0016
D16F	0130
D16G	0130
D16G6	0127
D16GN	0130
D16H	0130
D16J	0130
D16K	0130
D16K1	0127
D16K2	0127
D16K3	0127
D16K4	0127
D16L	0130
D16M	0130
D160R	0130
D16P1	0396
D16P2	0396
D16P3	OEM
D16P4	0396
D16PC2	OEM
D16R	0130
D16U3	0196
D16U4	0196
D16X	0130
D16Y	0130
D17	0130
D17A	0130
D17C	0130
D17D	0130
D17E	0130
D17F	0130
D17GN	0130
D17H	0130
D17J	0130
D17K	0130
D17L	0130
D17M	0130
D17R	0130
D17S800C	OEM
D17S1000C	OEM
D17S1200C	OEM
D17SR800C	OEM
D17SR1000C	OEM
D17SR1200C	OEM
D17T001320	0124
D17T024720	0133
D17U001310	0124
D17X	0130
D17Y	0130
D18	0015
D18(TRANS)	0861
D18A12	0161
D19	0208
D19A	0208
D19B	0208
D19C	0208
D19E	0208

DEVICE TYPE	REPL CODE
D19F	0208
D19G	0208
D19GN	0208
D19H	0208
D19J	0208
D19K	0208
D19M	0208
D19Y	0208
D20	0595
D20(2S)	0208
D20A	0208
D20B	0208
D20C	0208
D20D	0208
D20E	0208
D20F	0208
D20G	0208
D20GN	0208
D20H	0208
D20J	0208
D20K	0208
D20L	0208
D20M	0208
D200R	0208
D20R	0208
D20VT60	OEM
D20X	0208
D20Y	0208
D21(2S)	0208
D21A	0208
D21B	0208
D21C	0208
D21D	0208
D21E	0208
D21F	0208
D21G	0208
D21GN	0208
D21H	0208
D21J	0208
D21K	0208
D21L	0208
D21M	0208
D210R	0208
D21R	0208
D21S1000C	OEM
D21S1200C	OEM
D21S1400C	OEM
D21X	0208
D21Y	0208
D22	0208
D22A	0208
D22B	0208
D22C	0208
D22D	0208
D22E	0208
D22F	0208
D22G	0208
D22GN	0208
D22H	0208
D22J	0208
D22K	0208
D22L	0208
D22M	0208
D22N	0087
D220R	0208
D22R	0208
D22X	0208
D22Y	0208
D23(2S)	0208
D23A	0208
D23B	0208
D23C	0208
D23C2000G	OEM
D23D	0208
D23E	0208
D23F	0208
D23F130TAL	0015
D23FDFA05G	0023
D23FDFC10E	0023
D23FDFH10G	0023
D23FFH10TG	0023
D23G	0208
D23GDSF10T	1881
D23GN	0208
D23H	0208
D23HDSA12T	0071
D23J	0208
D23K	0208
D23L	0208
D23M	0208
D230R	0208
D23R	0208
D23TDF05G	0023
D23TDFD05G	0023
D23TDSA12T	0087
D23TDSF10B	0080
D23TDSF10T	0015
D23TFD05TG	0023
D23TFH10TG	0023
D23X	0208
D23Y	0208
D24	0142
D24(TRANS)	0142
D24/400B	OEM
D24/400C	OEM
D24/800B	OEM
D24/800C	OEM
D24/1200B	OEM
D24/1200C	OEM

DEVICE TYPE	REPL CODE
D24/1400B	OEM
D24/1400C	OEM
D24/1600B	OEM
D24/1600C	OEM
D24/1800B	OEM
D24/1800C	OEM
D24A	0142
D24A3391	0111
D24A3391A	0111
D24A3392	0111
D24A3393	0111
D24A3394	0144
D24A3900	0111
D24A3900A	0111
D24B(2S)	0142
D24C(2S)	0142
D24CK(2S)	0142
D24D(2S)	0142
D24DR	0142
D24E(2S)	0142
D24F(2S)	0142
D24F00V09G	0023
D24G	0142
D24GN	0142
D24H	0142
D24J	0142
D24K(2S)	OEM
D24KC(2S)	0142
D24KD(2S)	0142
D24KE(2S)	0142
D24L	0142
D24M	0142
D24N400B	OEM
D24N400C	OEM
D24N400U	OEM
D24N800B	OEM
D24N800C	OEM
D24N800U	OEM
D24N1200B	OEM
D24N1200C	OEM
D24N1200U	OEM
D24N1400B	OEM
D24N1400C	OEM
D24N1400U	OEM
D24N1600B	OEM
D24N1600C	OEM
D24N1600U	OEM
D24NR400B	OEM
D24NR400C	OEM
D24NR400U	OEM
D24NR800B	OEM
D24NR800C	OEM
D24NR800U	OEM
D24NR1200B	OEM
D24NR1200C	OEM
D24NR1200U	OEM
D24NR1400B	OEM
D24NR1400C	OEM
D24NR1400U	OEM
D24NR1600B	OEM
D24NR1600C	OEM
D24NR1600U	OEM
D240R	0142
D24R	0142
D24X	0142
D24Y(2S)	0142
D24YC	0142
D24YD(2S)	0142
D24YE(2S)	0142
D24YF(2S)	0142
D24YK(2S)	0142
D24YKC	0142
D24YL	0142
D24YLC(2S)	0142
D24YLD(2S)	0142
D24YLE	0142
D24YLF	0142
D24YM	0142
D24YMC	0142
D24YME	0142
D25	0208
D25-02C	2219
D25A	0208
D25B	0208
D25C	0208
D25C(TRANS)	0208
D25D	0208
D25E	0208
D25G	0208
D25GN	0208
D25H	0208
D25J	0208
D25K	0208
D25L	0208
D25M	0208
D250R	0208
D25R	0208
D25T5566B0	0015
D25X	0208
D25Y	0208
D26	0861
D26A(2S)	0861
D26B(2S)	0861
D26B1	0127
D26B2	0127
D26C(2S)	0861
D26C1	0127
D26C2	0127
D26C3	0127

If replacement code is OEM, contact original manufacturer for replacement.

359

DEVICE TYPE	REPL CODE
D26C4	0111
D26C5	0111
D26D	0861
D26E	0861
D26E-1	0111
D26E1	OEM
D26E-2	0144
D26E2	0127
D26E-3	0144
D26E3	OEM
D26E-4	0007
D26E4	OEM
D26E-5	0111
D26E5	OEM
D26E-6	0144
D26E6	OEM
D26E-7	0111
D26E7	OEM
D26F	0861
D26G	0861
D26G-1	0007
D26G1	0127
D26GN	0861
D26H	0861
D26J	0861
D26K	0861
D26L	0861
D26M	0861
D26OR	0861
D26P1	OEM
D26P2	OEM
D26P3	OEM
D26R	0861
D26X	0861
D26Y	0861
D27	0208
D27C1	0042
D27C2	0042
D27C3	0042
D27C4	0042
D27C256D-20	OEM
D27C512D-15	OEM
D27C5120-15	OEM
D27D1	1257
D27D2	1257
D27D3	1257
D27D4	1257
D28	0015
D28(TRANS)	0042
D28-08	0102
D28A	0042
D28A05	0546
D28A0P04Q0	1015
D28A1	0042
D28A2	0042
D28A3	0042
D28A4	0042
D28A5	0042
D28A5KQ600	OEM
D28A6	0042
D28A7	0042
D28A9	0042
D28A10	0042
D28A12	0042
D28A13	0042
D28B	0042
D28B1	OEM
D28C	0042
D28C1	OEM
D28C2	OEM
D28C3	OEM
D28C4	OEM
D28C5	OEM
D28C7	OEM
D28C8	OEM
D28D	0042
D28D(2S)	0042
D28D07	0590
D28D1	0042
D28D2	0042
D28D3	0042
D28D4	0042
D28D5	0042
D28D7	0042
D28D8	0555
D28D10	0042
D28E	0042
D28E(2S)	0042
D28F	0042
D28F00BB4C	0023
D28F00BB40	0023
D28F00SR2M	3829
D28F30DF20	0087
D28F300F60	0031
D28FMI15MS	0372
D28G	0042
D28G10E100	0071
D28GN	0042
D28H	0042
D28H20E100	0071
D28HRM11C0	0071
D28J	0042
D28K	0042
D28L	0042
D28L30DF20	0031
D28M	0042
D28OR	0042
D28R	0042
D28T011E10	0015

DEVICE TYPE	REPL CODE
D28T011E20	0015
D28T011ES1	0015
D28T0ELS40	0023
D28T10E100	0071
D28T10ELS6	0023
D28X	0042
D28Y	0042
D29	0042
D29-04HZ	OEM
D29-08	1208
D29A	0042
D29A4	0037
D29A5	0037
D29A6	0037
D29A7	0855
D29A8	0855
D29A9	0037
D29A10	0855
D29A11	0855
D29B	0042
D29E	0042
D29E01	0527
D29E01J1	0786
D29E02	0527
D29E02J1	0527
D29E04	0527
D29E04J1	0527
D29E05	0527
D29E05J1	0527
D29E06	0527
D29E06J1	0527
D29E08	0786
D29E08J1	0786
D29E09	0786
D29E09J1	0786
D29E1	0037
D29E1-J1	0786
D29E1J1	0786
D29E2	0037
D29E2-J1	0786
D29E2J1	0786
D29E4	0037
D29E4-J1	0786
D29E4J1	0786
D29E5	0037
D29E5-J1	0786
D29E5J1	0786
D29E6	0037
D29E6-J1	0786
D29E6J1	0786
D29E7	0037
D29E7J1	0786
D29E8	0037
D29E8J1	0786
D29E9	0786
D29E9-J1	0786
D29E9J1	0786
D29E10	0786
D29E10-J1	0786
D29E10J1	0786
D29F	0042
D29F1	0688
D29F2	0688
D29F3	0688
D29F4	0688
D29F5	0037
D29F6	0037
D29F7	0037
D29GN	0042
D29J	0042
D29K	0042
D29L	0042
D29M	0042
D29OR	0042
D29R	0042
D29X	0042
D29Y	0042
D30	0208
D30(2S)	0208
D30-0(2S)	0208
D30-0R	0208
D30-N(2S)	0208
D30-0	0208
D30-OR	0208
D30A	0208
D30A1	0037
D30A2	0037
D30A3	0037
D30A4	0037
D30A5	0037
D30B	0208
D30C	0208
D30D	0208
D30E	0208
D30F	0208
D30G	0208
D30GN	0208
D30H	0208
D30J	0208
D30K	0208
D30L	0208
D30M	0208
D30N	0208
D30OR	0208
D30P	0208
D30R	0208
D30S3	OEM
D30S4	OEM
D30S1000C	OEM

DEVICE TYPE	REPL CODE
D30S1200C	OEM
D30S1400C	OEM
D30VT60	OEM
D30X	0208
D30Y	0208
D31	0208
D31-02C	OEM
D31B	0208
D31B(2S)	0208
D31C	0208
D31D(2S)	0208
D31E	0208
D31F	0208
D31G	0208
D31GN	0208
D31H	0208
D31J	0208
D31K	0208
D31L	0208
D31M	0208
D31OR	0208
D31R	0208
D31X	0208
D31Y	0208
D32	0208
D32A	0208
D32B	0208
D32C	0208
D32D	0208
D32E	0208
D32F	0208
D32G	0208
D32GN	0208
D32H	0208
D32H1	0320
D32H2	0320
D32H4	0320
D32H5	0320
D32H7	0710
D32H8	0710
D32H9	0710
D32J	0208
D32K	0208
D32K1	0079
D32K2	0079
D32L	0208
D32L1	OEM
D32L2	OEM
D32L3	OEM
D32L4	OEM
D32L5	OEM
D32L6	OEM
D32M	0208
D32OR	0208
D32P1	0111
D32P2	0111
D32P3	0111
D32P4	0111
D32R	0208
D32S1	0396
D32S2	0396
D32S3	0396
D32S4	0396
D32S5	0264
D32S6	1203
D32S7	1203
D32S8	0264
D32S9	0264
D32S10	1203
D32W7	0710
D32W12	0079
D32X	0208
D32Y	0208
D33	OEM
D33(2S)	0007
D33A	0007
D33B	0007
D33C(2S)	0007
D33D	0007
D33D1	OEM
D33D2	OEM
D33D3	OEM
D33D4	OEM
D33D5	OEM
D33D6	OEM
D33D21	0320
D33D21-J1	0218
D33D21J1	0218
D33D22	0320
D33D22-J1	0218
D33D22J1	0218
D33D22J2	0018
D33D24	0320
D33D24-J1	0590
D33D24J1	0590
D33D25	0320
D33D25-J1	0218
D33D25J1	0218
D33D26	0320
D33D26-J1	0218
D33D26J1	0218
D33D27	0320
D33D27J1	0218
D33D28	0016
D33D28J1	0590
D33D29	0320
D33D29-J1	0218
D33D29J1	0218
D33D30	0320

DEVICE TYPE	REPL CODE
D33D30-J1	0218
D33D30J1	0218
D33E	0007
D33E01J1	0527
D33E02J1	0527
D33F	0007
D33G	0007
D33GN	0007
D33H	0007
D33J	0007
D33K	0007
D33K1	2763
D33K2	OEM
D33K3	OEM
D33L	0007
D33OR	0007
D33P2	OEM
D33X	0007
D33Y	0007
D34	0208
D34/400B	OEM
D34/400C	OEM
D34/800B	OEM
D34/800C	OEM
D34/1200B	OEM
D34/1200C	OEM
D34/1400B	OEM
D34/1400C	OEM
D34/1600B	OEM
D34/1600C	OEM
D34/1800B	OEM
D34/1800C	OEM
D34A	0208
D34B	0208
D34C	0208
D34C1	OEM
D34C2	OEM
D34C3	OEM
D34C4	OEM
D34C5	OEM
D34C6	OEM
D34D	0208
D34E	0208
D34F	0208
D34G	0208
D34GN	0208
D34H	0208
D34J	0208
D34J1	0037
D34J2	0037
D34J4	0037
D34J5	0037
D34K	0208
D34L	0208
D34M	0208
D34N400B	OEM
D34N400C	OEM
D34N400U	OEM
D34N800B	OEM
D34N800C	OEM
D34N800U	OEM
D34N1200B	OEM
D34N1200C	OEM
D34N1200U	OEM
D34N1400B	OEM
D34N1400C	OEM
D34N1400U	OEM
D34N1600B	OEM
D34N1600C	OEM
D34N1600U	OEM
D34NR400B	OEM
D34NR400C	OEM
D34NR400U	OEM
D34NR800B	OEM
D34NR800C	OEM
D34NR800U	OEM
D34NR1200B	OEM
D34NR1200C	OEM
D34NR1200U	OEM
D34NR1400B	OEM
D34NR1400C	OEM
D34NR1400U	OEM
D34NR1600B	OEM
D34NR1600C	OEM
D34NR1600U	OEM
D34OR	0208
D34R	0208
D34X	0208
D34Y	0208
D35(2S)	0208
D36	0208
D36A	0208
D36B	0208
D36C	0208
D36D	0208
D36E	0208
D36F	0208
D36G	0208
D36GN	0208
D36H	0208
D36J	0208
D36K	0208
D36L	0208
D36M	0208
D36OR	0208
D36R	0208
D36X	0208
D36Y	0208
D37(2S)	0208

DEVICE TYPE	REPL CODE
D37A(2S)	0208
D37B(2S)	0208
D37C(2S)	0208
D37D	0208
D37E	0208
D37F	0208
D37G	0208
D37GN	0208
D37H	0208
D37K	0208
D37L	0208
D37M	0208
D37OR	0208
D37R	0208
D37X	0208
D37Y	0208
D38	0208
D38A	0208
D38B	0208
D38C	0208
D38D	0208
D38E	0208
D38F	0208
D38G	0208
D38GN	0208
D38H	0208
D38H1	0079
D38H1-3	OEM
D38H1-6	0079
D38H2	0079
D38H3	0079
D38H4	0855
D38H4-6	0855
D38H5	0855
D38H6	0855
D38H7	0855
D38H8	0855
D38H9	0855
D38J	0208
D38K	0208
D38L	0208
D38L1	2770
D38L1-3	OEM
D38L1-6	OEM
D38L2	2770
D38L3	2770
D38L4	2770
D38L4-6	OEM
D38L5	2770
D38L6	2770
D38M	0208
D38OR	0208
D38R	0208
D38S1	0079
D38S1-4	OEM
D38S1-10	OEM
D38S2	OEM
D38S3	OEM
D38S4	OEM
D38S5	0079
D38S6	OEM
D38S7	OEM
D38S8	0079
D38S8-10	OEM
D38S9	0079
D38S10	OEM
D38V1	0710
D38V2	0710
D38V3	0710
D38W5-11	OEM
D38W7	0855
D38W8	0855
D38W8-10	OEM
D38W9	OEM
D38W10	OEM
D38W12	0855
D38W13	OEM
D38W13-14	OEM
D38W14	OEM
D38X	0208
D38Y	0208
D38Y1-3	0079
D39C1	OEM
D39C1-3	OEM
D39C1-6	OEM
D39C2	OEM
D39C3	OEM
D39C4	OEM
D39C4-6	OEM
D39C5	OEM
D39C6	OEM
D39J1	0037
D39J1-3	OEM
D39J1-6	0079
D39J2	0037
D39J3	0037
D39J4	0037
D39J4-6	OEM
D39J5	0037
D39J6	0037
D39J7	0472
D39J8	0472
D39J9	0472
D40C1	2243
D40C2	3490
D40C3	3491
D40C4	2243
D40C5	3490
D40C6	OEM

DEVICE TYPE	REPL CODE
D40C7	2243
D40C8	3490
D40D	OEM
D40D1	0561
D40D1F	1973
D40D2	0561
D40D3	0561
D40D4	0561
D40D4F	1973
D40D5	0561
D40D7	0561
D40D8	0561
D40D10	0561
D40D11	0561
D40D13	0561
D40D14	0561
D40E1	0555
D40E5	1680
D40E7	0555
D40H	OEM
D40HL	OEM
D40K1	3492
D40K2	3492
D40K3	3492
D40K4	3492
D40N1	0283
D40N1F	0283
D40N2	0283
D40N2F	0283
D40N3	0283
D40N3F	0283
D40N4	0283
D40N4F	0283
D40N5	0283
D40P1	0334
D40P3	0283
D40P5	0283
D40V1	0283
D40V2	0283
D40V3	0283
D40V4	0283
D40V5	OEM
D40V6	OEM
D41	0130
D41A	0130
D41B	0130
D41C	0130
D41D	0130
D41D1	1357
D41D2	1357
D41D4	1357
D41D5	1357
D41D7	1357
D41D8	1357
D41D10	1357
D41D11	1357
D41D13	1357
D41D14	1357
D41E	0130
D41E1	1165
D41E5	1165
D41E7	1165
D41F	0130
D41G	0130
D41GN	0130
D41H	0130
D41J	0130
D41K	0130
D41K1	3493
D41K2	3493
D41K3	3493
D41K4	3493
D41L	0130
D41M	0130
D41OR	0130
D41R	0130
D41X	0130
D41Y	0130
D42-400	OEM
D42-700	OEM
D42-1100	OEM
D42-1400	OEM
D42C1	0555
D42C2	0555
D42C3	0555
D42C4	0555
D42C5	0555
D42C6	0555
D42C7	0555
D42C8	0555
D42C9	0555
D42C10	0419
D42C11	0419
D42C12	0419
D42D1	1203
D42D2	OEM
D42D3	OEM
D42D4	OEM
D42D5	OEM
D42D6	OEM
D42R1	0168
D42R2	0168
D42R3	0168
D42R4	0168
D42T1	OEM
D42T2	OEM
D42T3	OEM
D42T4	OEM
D42T5	OEM

DEVICE TYPE	REPL CODE
D42T6	OEM
D42T7	OEM
D42T8	OEM
D43	0208
D43A(2S)	0208
D43B	0208
D43C	0208
D43C1	1257
D43C2	1257
D43C3	1257
D43C4	1257
D43C4#	1257
D43C5	1257
D43C6	1257
D43C7	0919
D43C8	1257
D43C9	1257
D43C10	0848
D43C11	0848
D43C12	0848
D43D	0208
D43D1	0597
D43D2	OEM
D43D3	OEM
D43D4	OEM
D43D5	OEM
D43D6	OEM
D43E	0208
D43F	0208
D43G	0208
D43GN	0208
D43H	0208
D43J	0208
D43K	0208
D43L	0208
D43M	0208
D43OR	0208
D43R	0208
D43X	0208
D43Y	0208
D44	0208
D44A	0208
D44A10#	0060
D44B	0208
D44C	0208
D44C1	0060
D44C2	0060
D44C3	0060
D44C4	0236
D44C5	0060
D44C6	0060
D44C7	0060
D44C8	0060
D44C9	0060
D44C10	0060
D44C11	0060
D44C12	0060
D44C88	0555
D44D	0208
D44D1	1203
D44D2	1203
D44D3	1203
D44D4	1203
D44D5	1203
D44D6	1203
D44E	0208
D44E1	2220
D44E2	2220
D44E3	2220
D44F	0208
D44G	0208
D44GN	0208
D44H	0208
D44H1	0556
D44H2	0556
D44H4	0556
D44H5	0556
D44H7	0060
D44H8	0556
D44H10	0060
D44H11	0060
D44J	0208
D44K	0208
D44L	0208
D44M	0208
D44M1	0060
D44M2	0060
D44M4	0060
D44M5	0060
D44M7	0060
D44M8	0060
D44M10	0060
D44M11	0060
D44Q1	2985
D44Q2	2985
D44Q3	2985
D44Q5#	2985
D44R	0208
D44R1	0168
D44R2	0168
D44R3	0168
D44R4	0168
D44R5	0168
D44R6	0168
D44R7	2985
D44R8	0168
D44T1	2985
D44T2	2985
D44T3	2985

If replacement code is OEM, contact original manufacturer for replacement.

DEVICE TYPE	REPL CODE
D44T4	3414
D44T5	2985
D44T6	2985
D44T7	2985
D44T8	2985
D44TA	OEM
D44TD3	0723
D44TD4	0723
D44TD5	0723
D44TE3	0723
D44TE4	0723
D44TE5	0723
D44VH1	0477
D44VH4	0477
D44VH7	0477
D44VH10	0477
D44VM1	0060
D44VM4	0060
D44VM7	0060
D44VM10	0060
D44X	0208
D44Y	0208
D45	0074
D45C	0015
D45C1	1298
D45C2	1298
D45C3	1298
D45C4	0676
D45C5	1298
D45C6	1298
D45C7	1298
D45C8	1298
D45C9	1298
D45C10	1298
D45C11	1298
D45C12	1298
D45CZ	0015
D45D1	0597
D45D2	0597
D45D3	0597
D45D4	0597
D45D5	0597
D45D6	0597
D45E1	2222
D45E2	2222
D45E3	2222
D45H1	1190
D45H2	1190
D45H4	1190
D45H-5	4357
D45H5	1190
D45H7	1298
D45H8	1359
D45H9	1359
D45H10	1190
D45H11	1298
D45H12	1298
D45HN	0676
D45M1	1298
D45M2	1298
D45M4	1298
D45M5	1298
D45M7	1298
D45M8	1298
D45M9	1298
D45M10	1298
D45M11	1298
D45M12	1298
D45VH1	1359
D45VH4	1359
D45VH7	1359
D45VH10	1359
D45VM1	1298
D45VM4	1298
D45VM7	1298
D45VM10	1298
D46	0074
D47	0615
D47C7	2243
D48	0015
D48(TRANS)	0042
D49(2S)	0042
D49A	0042
D49B	0042
D49C	0042
D49D	0042
D49E	0042
D49F	0042
D49G	0042
D49GN	0042
D49J	0042
D49K	0042
D49L	0042
D49M	0042
D49OR	0042
D49R	0042
D49X	0042
D49Y	0042
D50	1325
D50(TRANS)	0861
D50A	0861
D50B	0861
D50C	0861
D50D	0861
D50E	0861
D50F	0861
D50G	0861
D50GN	0861
D50H	0861

DEVICE TYPE	REPL CODE
D50J	0861
D50K	0861
D50L	0861
D50M	0861
D50OR	0861
D50R	0861
D50X	0861
D50Y	0861
D51	0861
D51A	0861
D51B	0861
D51C	0861
D51D	0861
D51E	0861
D51F	0861
D51G	0861
D51GN	0861
D51H	0861
D51J	0861
D51K	0861
D51L	0861
D51M	0861
D51OR	0861
D51R	0861
D51X	0861
D51Y	0861
D52	0103
D53(2S)	0130
D53A	0130
D53B	0130
D53C	0130
D53E	0130
D53F	0130
D53G	0130
D53GN	0130
D53H	0130
D53J	0130
D53K	0130
D53L	0130
D53M	0130
D53OR	0130
D53R	0130
D53X	0130
D53Y	0130
D54	0130
D55	0130
D55A(2S)	0130
D56(2S)	4397
D56A	2200
D56B	2200
D56C	2200
D56D	2200
D56E	2200
D56F	2200
D56G	2200
D56GN	2200
D56H	2200
D56J	2200
D56K	2200
D56L	2200
D56M	2200
D56OR	2200
D56R	2200
D56W1	0309
D56W2	0065
D56X	2200
D56Y	2200
D57(2S)	0178
D58(2S)	0178
D59(2S)	0074
D60(2S)	0074
D60/400B	OEM
D60/800B	OEM
D60/1200B	OEM
D60/1400B	OEM
D60/1600B	OEM
D60-700	OEM
D60-1100	OEM
D60H	OEM
D60HL	OEM
D60N400B	OEM
D60N400C	OEM
D60N400U	OEM
D60N800B	OEM
D60N800C	OEM
D60N800U	OEM
D60N1200B	OEM
D60N1200C	OEM
D60N1200U	OEM
D60N1400B	OEM
D60N1400C	OEM
D60N1400U	OEM
D60N1600B	OEM
D60N1600C	OEM
D60N1600U	OEM
D60NR400B	OEM
D60NR400C	OEM
D60NR400U	OEM
D60NR800B	OEM
D60NR800C	OEM
D60NR800U	OEM
D60NR1200B	OEM
D60NR1200C	OEM
D60NR1200U	OEM
D60NR1400B	OEM
D60NR1400C	OEM
D60NR1400U	OEM
D60NR1600B	OEM
D60NR1600C	OEM

DEVICE TYPE	REPL CODE
D60NR1600U	OEM
D60T257510	OEM
D60T259010	OEM
D60T307510	OEM
D60T309010	OEM
D60T357510	OEM
D60T404010	OEM
D60T405010	OEM
D60T406010	OEM
D60T454010	OEM
D60T455010	OEM
D60T504010	OEM
D60T703005	OEM
D60T704005	OEM
D60T753005	OEM
D60T754005	OEM
D60T803005	OEM
D60T804005	OEM
D61(2S)	0208
D61A	0208
D61B	0208
D61C	0208
D61D	0208
D61E	0208
D61F	0208
D61G	0208
D61GN	0208
D61H	0208
D61J	0208
D61K	0208
D61L	0208
D61M	0208
D61OR	0208
D61R	0208
D61X	0208
D61Y	0208
D62(2S)	0208
D62A	0208
D62B	0208
D62C	0208
D62D	0208
D62E	0208
D62G	0208
D62GN	0208
D62H	0208
D62J	0208
D62K	0208
D62L	0208
D62M	0208
D62R	0208
D62T257510	OEM
D62T259010	OEM
D62T307510	OEM
D62T309010	OEM
D62T357510	OEM
D62T404010	OEM
D62T405010	OEM
D62T406010	OEM
D62T454010	OEM
D62T455010	OEM
D62T504010	OEM
D62X	0208
D62Y	0208
D63	0208
D63A	0208
D63B	0208
D63C	0208
D63E	0208
D63F	0208
D63G	0208
D63GN	0208
D63H	0208
D63J	0208
D63K	0208
D63L	0208
D63M	0208
D63OR	0208
D63R	0208
D63X	0208
D63Y	0208
D64	0208
D64A	0208
D64B	0208
D64C	0208
D64D	0208
D64E	0208
D64F	0208
D64G	0208
D64GN	0208
D64H	0208
D64J	0208
D64K	0208
D64M	0208
D64OR	0208
D64R	0208
D64TS3	OEM
D64TS5	OEM
D64VE3	1955
D64VE4	1955
D64VE5	1955
D64VP3	1955
D64VP4	1955
D64VP5	1841
D64VS3	1841
D64VS4	1841
D64VS5	1955
D64X	0208
D64Y	0208
D65	0208

DEVICE TYPE	REPL CODE
D65-1(2S)	0208
D65A	0208
D65B	0208
D65C	0015
D65C(TRANS)	0208
D65D	0208
D65E	0208
D65F	0208
D65G	0208
D65GN	0208
D65H	0208
D65J	0208
D65K	0208
D65L	0208
D65M	0208
D65OR	0208
D65R	0208
D65X	0208
D65Y	0208
D66	0208
D66A	0208
D66B	0208
D66C	0208
D66D	0208
D66DV5	OEM
D66DV6	OEM
D66DV7	OEM
D66E	0208
D66EV5	OEM
D66EV6	OEM
D66EV7	OEM
D66F	0208
D66G	0208
D66GN	0208
D66GV6	OEM
D66H	0208
D66J	0208
D66K	0208
D66L	0208
D66M	0208
D66OR	0208
D66R	0208
D66X	0208
D66Y	0208
D67(2S)	0177
D67B(2S)	0177
D67C(2S)	0177
D67D(2S)	0177
D67DE5	OEM
D67DE6	OEM
D67DE7	OEM
D67E(2S)	0177
D68	0103
D68(TRANS)	0130
D68A	0130
D68B(2S)	0130
D68C(2S)	0130
D68D(2S)	0130
D68E(2S)	0130
D68F	0130
D68G	0130
D68GN	0130
D68H	0130
D68J	0130
D68L	0130
D68M	0130
D68OR	0130
D68R	0130
D68X	0130
D68Y	0130
D69(2S)	6001
D70(2S)	0130
D70A	0130
D70B	0130
D70C	0130
D70D	0130
D70E	0130
D70F	0130
D70G	0130
D70GN	0130
D70H	0130
D70J	0130
D70K	0130
D70L	0130
D70M	0130
D70OR	0130
D70R	0130
D70X	0130
D70Y	0130
D71(2S)	0178
D72	0208
D72-2C(2S)	0208
D72-3C(2S)	0208
D72-4C(2S)	0208
D72-6	0208
D72-OR	0208
D72A(2S)	0208
D72B(2S)	0208
D72C(2S)	0208
D72D	0208
D72E	0208
D72EJ	0208
D72F	0208
D72G	0208
D72GA	0208
D72H	0208
D72J	0208
D72K	0208
D72L	0208

DEVICE TYPE	REPL CODE
D72M	0208
D72OR	0208
D72P	0208
D72R	0208
D72RE(2S)	0208
D72X	0208
D72Y	0208
D73(2S)	0861
D73Y	OEM
D73Y(KOREA)	1157
D74(2S)	0284
D75(2S)	0208
D75A(2S)	0208
D75AH(2S)	0208
D75B(2S)	0208
D75C(2S)	0208
D75D	0208
D75E	0208
D75F	0208
D75G	0208
D75GN	0208
D75H(2S)	0208
D75J	0208
D75K	0208
D75L	0208
D75M	0208
D75N400B	OEM
D75N400C	OEM
D75N400U	OEM
D75N800B	OEM
D75N800C	OEM
D75N800U	OEM
D75N1200B	OEM
D75N1200C	OEM
D75N1200U	OEM
D75N1400B	OEM
D75N1400C	OEM
D75N1400U	OEM
D75N1600B	OEM
D75N1600C	OEM
D75N1600U	OEM
D75NR400B	OEM
D75NR400C	OEM
D75NR400U	OEM
D75NR800B	OEM
D75NR800C	OEM
D75NR800U	OEM
D75NR1200B	OEM
D75NR1200C	OEM
D75NR1200U	OEM
D75NR1400B	OEM
D75NR1400C	OEM
D75NR1400U	OEM
D75NR1600B	OEM
D75NR1600C	OEM
D75NR1600U	OEM
D75OR	0208
D76FI3T	OEM
D77(2S)	0208
D77-A	0208
D77A(2S)	0208
D77AH(2S)	0208
D77B(2S)	0208
D77C(2S)	0208
D77D(2S)	0208
D77E	0208
D77F	0208
D77G	0208
D77GN	0208
D77H(2S)	0208
D77J	0208
D77L	0208
D77M	0208
D77OR	0208
D77P(2S)	0208
D77R	0208
D77X	0208
D77Y	0208
D78(2S)	2980
D78A(2S)	2980
D79(2S)	6667
D80(2S)	0130
D80A	0130
D80B	0130
D80C	0130
D80C39	OEM
D80C49	OEM
D80D	0130
D80E	0130
D80F	0130
D80G	0130
D80GN	0130
D80H	0130
D80H(2S)	0130
D80H(DIODE)	OEM
D80HL	OEM
D80J	0130
D80K	0130
D80L	0130
D80OR	0130
D80R	0130
D80X	0130
D80Y	0130
D81(2S)	0861
D81A	0861
D81B	0861
D81C	0861
D81E	0861
D81F	0861

DEVICE TYPE	REPL CODE
D81G	0861
D81GN	0861
D81H	0861
D81J	0861
D81K	0861
D81L	0861
D81M	0861
D81OR	0861
D81R	0861
D81X	0861
D81Y	0861
D82(2S)	0861
D82-OR	0861
D82A(2S)	0861
D82B	0861
D82C	0861
D82C288-8	OEM
D82D	0861
D82E	0861
D82F	0861
D82G	0861
D82GN	0861
D82H	0861
D82J	0861
D82K	0861
D82L	0861
D82M	0861
D82OR	0861
D82R	0861
D82X	0861
D82Y	0861
D83(2S)	0861
D83-004	OEM
D84(2S)	0861
D85C	0071
D85GR	0723
D88	0861
D88(TRANS)	0861
D88A(2S)	0861
D88OY	0861
D90(2S)	0042
D90A	0042
D90B	0042
D90C	0042
D90D	0042
D90E	0042
D90F	0042
D90G	0042
D90GN	0042
D90H	0042
D90J	0042
D90K	0042
D90L	0042
D90M	0042
D90OR	0042
D90X	0042
D90Y	0042
D91(2S)	0042
D91A	0042
D91B	0042
D91E	0042
D91F(2S)	0042
D91G	0042
D91GN	0042
D91H	0042
D91J	0042
D91L	0042
D91M	0042
D91OR	0042
D91R	0042
D91X	0042
D91Y	0042
D92(2S)	0178
D92D(2S)	0178
D92F13R6B0	0372
D92T03R9B2	0036
D92T05R1B2	0041
D92T05R6B2	0253
D92T06R2B2	0466
D92T06R2B3	0466
D92T06R8B2	0062
D92T09R1B2	0057
D92T0110B2	0181
D92T0110B3	0181
D92T0120B2	0999
D92T0150B1	0873
D92T0200B2	0666
D92T0270B2	0450
D92T0270B3	0436
D92T0300B4	0195
D92T0360B0	0010
D92UA3600B	0010
D93	0074
D93T03R30Y	OEM
D93T04R30Y	0528
D93T04R70X	0140
D93T05R10X	0041
D93T05R10Y	0041
D93T05R60Y	0253
D93T05R100	0041
D93T06R20Y	0466
D93T06R20Z	0292
D93T06R80Y	0062
D93T06R200	0466
D93T07R50Z	0077
D93T08R20X	0165
D93T09R10Y	OEM
D93T01000X	OEM
D93T01100Y	0181

DEVICE TYPE	REPL CODE
D93T01200Y	0052
D93T01300X	0053
D93T01300Y	0053
D93T01800Y	0371
D93T02000X	0695
D93T02700Y	0450
D93T03000Y	0195
D94(2S)	0388
D94TA5R1B2	0041
D94TA5R6J2	0877
D94TA6R2B2	OEM
D94TA6R8J2	0062
D94TA9R1J2	OEM
D94TA110J3	0181
D94TA120B2	0999
D94TA120J2	0999
D94TA120J3	0999
D94TA130J2	OEM
D94UA6R2J2	0292
D96(2S)	0208
D96A	0208
D96B	0208
D96C	0208
D96D	0208
D96E	0208
D96F	0208
D96G	0208
D96GN	0208
D96H	0208
D96J	0208
D96K	0208
D96L	0208
D96OR	0208
D96R	0208
D96X	0208
D96Y	0208
D97U05R10B	0041
D97U05R60B	0253
D97U05R108	0041
D97U06R20B	0466
D97U06R80B	0466
D97U01100B	0181
D97U01200B	0999
D100	0015
D100(TRANS)	0208
D100-400	OEM
D100-700	OEM
D100-1100	OEM
D100-1400	OEM
D100-1800	OEM
D100A(2S)	0208
D100B	0208
D100C	0208
D100D	0208
D100E	0208
D100F	0208
D100G	0208
D100GN	0208
D100H	OEM
D100H(2S)	0208
D100J	0208
D100K	0208
D100L	0208
D100M	0208
D100OR	0208
D100R	0208
D100X	0208
D100Y	0208
D101	0595
D101AK	0595
D101B	0004
D102	0178
D102-0	0178
D102-O(2S)	0178
D102-R(2S)	0178
D102-Y(2S)	0178
D102A	0178
D102B	0178
D102BS	OEM
D102BS-1	OEM
D102BSM	OEM
D102BSM-1	OEM
D102BSMZS	OEM
D102BSMZS-1	OEM
D102BSQ	OEM
D102BSQ-1	OEM
D102BSQZS	OEM
D102BSQZS-1	OEM
D102BST	OEM
D102BST-1	OEM
D102BSTZS	OEM
D102BSTZS-1	OEM
D102BSZS	OEM
D102BSZS-1	OEM
D102C	0178
D102D	0178
D102E	0178
D102F	0178
D102G	0178
D102GN	0178
D102H	0178
D102J	0178
D102K	0178
D102L	0178
D102M	0178
D102OR	0178
D102R	0178
D102X	0178
D102Y	0178

If replacement code is OEM, contact original manufacturer for replacement.

361

DEVICE TYPE	REPL CODE
D103	0178
D103-0	0178
D103-O(2S)	0178
D103-R(2S)	0178
D103-Y(2S)	0178
D104	0208
D104A	0208
D104B	0208
D104BS	OEM
D104BS-1	OEM
D104BSM	OEM
D104BSM-1	OEM
D104BSMZS	OEM
D104BSMZS-1	OEM
D104BSQ	OEM
D104BSQ-1	OEM
D104BSQZS	OEM
D104BSQZS-1	OEM
D104BST	OEM
D104BST-1	OEM
D104BSTZS	OEM
D104BSTZS-1	OEM
D104BSZS	OEM
D104BSZS-1	OEM
D104C	0208
D104D	0208
D104E	0208
D104F	0208
D104G	0208
D104GN	0208
D104H	0208
D104K	0208
D104L	0208
D104M	0208
D104OR	0208
D104R	0208
D104X	0208
D104Y	0208
D105	0208
D105A	0208
D105B	0208
D105C	0071
D105C(TRANS)	0208
D105D	OEM
D105D(2S)	0208
D105DS	OEM
D105DS-1	OEM
D105DSM	OEM
D105DSM-1	OEM
D105DSMZS	OEM
D105DSMZS-1	OEM
D105DSQ	OEM
D105DSQ-1	OEM
D105DSQZS	OEM
D105DSQZS-1	OEM
D105DST	OEM
D105DST-1	OEM
D105DSTZS	OEM
D105DSTZS-1	OEM
D105DSZS	OEM
D105DSZS-1	OEM
D105E	0208
D105F	0208
D105G	0208
D105GN	0208
D105H	0208
D105J	0208
D105K	0208
D105L	0208
D105M	0208
D105OR	0208
D105R	0208
D105X	0208
D105Y	0208
D107	0103
D107E	OEM
D108	0071
D108(TRANS)	0103
D110	0177
D110-0	0177
D110-O(2S)	0177
D110-ORG	0177
D110-R(2S)	0177
D110-RED	0177
D110-Y(2S)	0177
D110-YEL	0177
D110A243A0	0124
D110A243AC	0124
D110DS	OEM
D110DS-1	OEM
D110DSM	OEM
D110DSM-1	OEM
D110DSMZS	OEM
D110DSMZS-1	OEM
D110DSQ	OEM
D110DSQ-1	OEM
D110DSQZS	OEM
D110DSQZS-1	OEM
D110DST	OEM
D110DST-1	OEM
D110DSTZS	OEM
D110DSTZS-1	OEM
D110DSZS	OEM
D110DSZS-1	OEM
D111	0177
D111-0	0177
D111-O(2S)	0177
D111-ORG	0177
D111-R(2S)	0177

DEVICE TYPE	REPL CODE
D111-RED	0177
D111-Y(2S)	0177
D111-YEL	0177
D111R	0177
D112BS	OEM
D112BS-1	OEM
D112BSM	OEM
D112BSM-1	OEM
D112BSMZS	OEM
D112BSMZS-1	OEM
D112BSQ	OEM
D112BSQ-1	OEM
D112BSQZS	OEM
D112BSQZS-1	OEM
D112BST	OEM
D112BST-1	OEM
D112BSTZS	OEM
D112BSTZS-1	OEM
D112BSZS	OEM
D112BSZS-1	OEM
D113(2S)	0130
D113-0	0130
D113-O(2S)	0130
D113-ORG	0130
D113-R(2S)	0130
D113-RED	0130
D113-Y(2S)	0130
D113-YEL	0130
D113A	0916
D113R	0130
D114(2S)	0130
D114-0	0130
D114-O(2S)	0130
D114-ORG	0130
D114-R(2S)	0130
D114-RED	0130
D114-Y(2S)	0130
D114-YEL	0130
D114R	0130
D116	0103
D117	0615
D117C	0615
D118	0177
D118-B	0177
D118-BL	0177
D118-BLU	0177
D118-R	0177
D118-RED	0177
D118-Y	0177
D118-YEL	0177
D118A	0177
D118BL(2S)	0177
D118C	0177
D118D	0177
D118R(2S)	0177
D118Y(2S)	0177
D119	0177
D119-BL	0177
D119-BLU	0177
D119-R	0177
D119-RED	0177
D119-Y	0177
D119-YEL	0177
D119A	0177
D119B	0177
D119BL(2S)	0177
D119C	0177
D119D	0177
D119R(2S)	0177
D119Y(2S)	0177
D120(2S)	1471
D120/400B	OEM
D120/800B	OEM
D120/1200B	OEM
D120/1400B	OEM
D120/1600B	OEM
D120/1800B	OEM
D120-700	OEM
D120-1100	OEM
D120D	1471
D120E	1471
D120F	1471
D120G	1471
D120GN	1471
D120H(2S)	1471
D120J	1471
D120K	1471
D120L	1471
D120M	1471
D120OR	1471
D120R	1471
D120S800B	OEM
D120S1000B	OEM
D120S1200B	OEM
D120S1400B	OEM
D120SR800B	OEM
D120X	1471
D120Y	1471
D121(2S)	1471
D121C	1471
D121D	1471
D121E	1471
D121F	1471
D121G	1471
D121GN	1471
D121H(2S)	1471
D121J	1471
D121K	1471
D121L	1471

DEVICE TYPE	REPL CODE
D121M	1471
D121N400B	OEM
D121N400V	OEM
D121N800B	OEM
D121N800V	OEM
D121N1200B	OEM
D121N1200V	OEM
D121N1400B	OEM
D121N1400V	OEM
D121N1800B	OEM
D121N1800V	OEM
D121NR400B	OEM
D121NR400V	OEM
D121NR800B	OEM
D121NR800V	OEM
D121NR1200B	OEM
D121NR1200V	OEM
D121NR1400B	OEM
D121NR1400V	OEM
D121NR1800B	OEM
D121NR1800V	OEM
D121OR	1471
D121R	1471
D121X	1471
D121Y	1471
D122	0042
D123	0236
D123AL	OEM
D123AP	OEM
D123BP	OEM
D123CDD	OEM
D123CFD	OEM
D123IDD	OEM
D124	0861
D124(RECT.)	0015
D124A(2S)	0861
D124AH(2S)	0861
D124B	0861
D124C	0861
D124E	0861
D124F	0861
D124G	0861
D124GN	0861
D124H	0861
D124J	0861
D124K	0861
D124L	0861
D124M	0861
D124OR	0861
D124R	0861
D124X	0861
D124Y	0861
D125	0861
D125A(2S)	0861
D125AH(2S)	0861
D125AP	OEM
D125B	0861
D125BP	OEM
D125C	OEM
D125C(TRANS)	0861
D125CDD	OEM
D125CFD	OEM
D125E	0861
D125F	0861
D125G	0861
D125GN	0861
D125H	0861
D125IDD	OEM
D125IFD	OEM
D125J	0861
D125K	0861
D125L	0861
D125M	0861
D125MDD	OEM
D125MFD	OEM
D125OR	0861
D125R	0861
D125X	0861
D125Y	0861
D126	0861
D126H(2S)	0861
D126HA(2S)	0861
D126HB(2S)	0861
D127	0208
D127A(2S)	0208
D127B	0208
D127C	0208
D127D	0208
D127E	0208
D127F	0208
D127G	0208
D127GN	0208
D127H	0208
D127J	0208
D127K	0208
D127L	0208
D127M	0208
D127OR	0208
D127R	0208
D127X	0208
D127Y	0208
D128	0208
D128A(2S)	0208
D128B	0208
D128C	0208
D128D	0208
D128E	0208
D128F	0208
D128G	0208

DEVICE TYPE	REPL CODE
D128GN	0208
D128H	0208
D128J	0208
D128K	0208
D128L	0208
D128M	0208
D128OR	0208
D128R	0208
D128X	0208
D128Y	0208
D129	0178
D129-BL(2S)	0178
D129-BLU	0178
D129-R(2S)	0178
D129-RED	0178
D129-Y(2S)	0178
D129-YEL	0178
D129AL	OEM
D129AP	OEM
D129BP	OEM
D129IDD	OEM
D129IFD	OEM
D129MDD	OEM
D129MFD	OEM
D130	1139
D130-BL	1139
D130-BLU	1139
D130-R(2S)	1139
D130-RED	1139
D130-Y(2S)	1139
D130-YEL	1139
D130A	1139
D130B	1139
D130BL(2S)	1139
D130C	1139
D130D	1139
D130DS442X	0124
D130E	1139
D130F	1139
D130G	1139
D130GMA010	0124
D130GN	1139
D130H	1139
D130J	1139
D130K	1139
D130OR	1139
D130R	1139
D130X	1139
D130Y	1139
D131	0615
D132	0130
D133	0079
D133(CHAN.MASTER)	0144
D134	0018
D134A	0018
D134C	0018
D134D	0018
D134F	0018
D134G	0018
D134GN	0018
D134H	0018
D134J	0018
D134K	0018
D134L	0018
D134M	0018
D134OR	0018
D134R	0018
D134X	0018
D134Y	0018
D135	0004
D136	0142
D136D	0142
D136E	0142
D136F	0142
D136G	0142
D136GN	0142
D136J	0142
D136K	0142
D136L	0142
D136M	0142
D136OR	0142
D136R	0142
D136X	0142
D136Y	0142
D137	0142
D137A	0142
D137B	0142
D137C	0142
D137D	0142
D137F	0142
D137G	0142
D137H	0142
D137J	0142
D137K	0142
D137L	0142
D137M	0142
D137OR	0142
D137R	0142
D137X	0142
D137Y	0142
D138	0168
D139	0168
D139AA	OEM
D139AL	OEM
D139BA	OEM
D139BP	OEM
D139CJ	OEM
D141	0016
D141(2S)	0042

DEVICE TYPE	REPL CODE
D141(CHAN.MASTER)	0144
D141A	0042
D141B	0042
D141C	0042
D141E	0042
D141F	0042
D141G	0042
D141GN	0042
D141H	0042
D141H01(2S)	0042
D141J	0042
D141K	0042
D141L	0042
D141M	0042
D141OR	0042
D141R	0042
D141X	0042
D141Y	0042
D142(2S)	0178
D142A	0178
D142B	0178
D142C	0178
D142D	0178
D142E	0178
D142F	0178
D142G	0178
D142GN	0178
D142H	0178
D142J	0178
D142K	0178
D142L	0178
D142M(2S)	0178
D142OR	0178
D142R	0178
D142X	0178
D142Y	0178
D143(2S)	0178
D144(2S)	0178
D144S	0015
D145(2S)	0178
D146(2S)	0042
D146A	0042
D146B	0042
D146C	0042
D146D	0042
D146E	0042
D146F	0042
D146G	0042
D146GN	0042
D146H	0042
D146J	0042
D146K	0042
D146L	0042
D146OR	0042
D146R	0042
D146UK(2S)	0042
D146VK	0042
D146X	0042
D146Y	0042
D147(2S)	0042
D147A	0042
D147B	0042
D147C	0042
D147D	0042
D147E	0042
D147F	0042
D147GN	0042
D147H	0042
D147J	0042
D147K	0042
D147L	0042
D147M	0042
D147OR	0042
D147R	0042
D147X	0042
D147Y	0042
D148	0042
D149	0086
D150(2S)	0178
D150/2800B	OEM
D150/3200B	OEM
D150/3600B	OEM
D150A	0178
D150B	0178
D150C	0178
D150E	0178
D150F	0178
D150G	0178
D150GN	0178
D150H	OEM
D150H(2S)	0178
D150J	0178
D150K	0178
D150L	0178
D150M	0178
D150OR	0178
D150R	0178
D150R3200B	OEM
D150R3600B	OEM
D150X	0178
D150Y	0178
D151(2S)	0615
D151A	0615
D151B	0615
D151C	0615
D151E	0615
D151F	0615
D151G	0615
D151GN	0615

DEVICE TYPE	REPL CODE
D151H	0615
D151J	0615
D151K	0615
D151L	0615
D151M	0615
D151OR	0615
D151R	0615
D151Y	0615
D152(2S)	0388
D152(CHAN.MASTER)	0693
D152A	0388
D152B	0388
D152C	0388
D152D	0388
D152E	0388
D152F	0388
D152G	0388
D152GN	0388
D152H	0388
D152J	0388
D152K	0388
D152L	0388
D152M	0388
D152OR	0388
D152R	0388
D152X	0388
D152Y	0388
D154(2S)	0236
D154A	0236
D154B	0236
D154C	0236
D154E	0236
D154F	0236
D154G	0236
D154GN	0236
D154H	0236
D154J	0236
D154K	0236
D154L	0236
D154M	0236
D154R	0236
D154X	0236
D154Y	0236
D155	0178
D155-H	0178
D155-K	0178
D155H(2S)	0178
D155K(2S)	0178
D155L(2S)	0178
D156	0142
D156B	0142
D156C	0142
D156D	0142
D156E	0142
D156F	0142
D156G	0142
D156GN	0142
D156H	0142
D156K	0142
D156L	0142
D156M	0142
D156OR	0142
D156R	0142
D156X	0142
D156Y	0142
D157(2S)	0142
D157A	0142
D157B(2S)	0142
D157C	0142
D157D	0142
D157G	0142
D157GN	0142
D157H	0142
D157J	0142
D157K	0142
D157L	0142
D157OR	0142
D157R	0142
D157X	0142
D157Y	0142
D158(2S)	1021
D158A	1021
D158B	1021
D158C	1021
D158D	1021
D158E	1021
D158F	1021
D158GN	1021
D158H	1021
D158J	1021
D158K	1021
D158L	1021
D158M	1021
D158OR	1021
D158R	1021
D158X	1021
D158Y	1021
D159(2S)	1021
D159A	1021
D159B	1021
D159C	1021
D159D	1021
D159E	1021
D159F	1021
D159G	1021
D159GN	1021
D159H	1021
D159J	1021
D159K	1021

DEVICE TYPE	REPL CODE
D159L	1021
D159M	1021
D159OR	1021
D159R	1021
D159X	1021
D159Y	1021
D160(2S)	0626
D161(2S)	0615
D161A	0615
D161B	0615
D161C	0615
D161D	0615
D161E	0615
D161F	0615
D161G	0615
D161GN	0615
D161H	0615
D161J	0615
D161K	0615
D161L	0615
D161M	0615
D161OR	0615
D161R	0615
D161X	0615
D161Y	0615
D162(2S)	0208
D162A	0208
D162B	0208
D162C	0208
D162D	0208
D162E	0208
D162F	0208
D162G	0208
D162GN	0208
D162H	0208
D162J	0208
D162K	0208
D162L	0208
D162M	0208
D162OR	0208
D162R	0208
D162X	0208
D162Y	0208
D163(2S)	0103
D163A	0103
D163B	0103
D163C	0103
D163D	0103
D163E	0103
D163F	0103
D163G	0103
D163GN	0103
D163H	0103
D163J	0103
D163K	0103
D163L	0103
D163M	0103
D163OR	0103
D163R	0103
D163X	0103
D163Y	0103
D164(2S)	0103
D164A	0103
D164B	0103
D164C	0103
D164D	0103
D164E	0103
D164F	0103
D164G	0103
D164GN	0103
D164H	0103
D164J	0103
D164K	0103
D164L	0103
D164M	0103
D164OR	0103
D164R	0103
D164X	0103
D164Y	0103
D165	1955
D166(2S)	1955
D167(2S)	0208
D167A	0208
D167B	0208
D167C	0208
D167E	0208
D167F	0208
D167G	0208
D167GN	0208
D167H	0208
D167J	0208
D167K	0208
D167L	0208
D167M	0208
D167OR	0208
D167R	0208
D167X	0208
D167Y	0208
D168	3339
D169AK	OEM
D169AP	OEM
D169CJ	OEM
D169CK	OEM
D170(2S)	0208
D170/2800T	OEM
D170A(2S)	0208
D170AA(2S)	0208
D170AB(2S)	0208
D170AC(2S)	0208

362 If replacement code is OEM, contact original manufacturer for replacement.

DEVICE TYPE	REPL CODE
D170B(2S)	0208
D170BC(2S)	0208
D170C(2S)	0208
D171	0637
D172	0103
D172(IR)	0102
D172-F	0102
D172A	0103
D172B	0103
D172C	0103
D172D	0103
D172E	0103
D172F	0103
D172G	0103
D172GN	0103
D172H	0103
D172J	0103
D172K	0103
D172L	0103
D172M	0103
D172OR	0103
D172R	0103
D172X	0103
D172Y	0103
D173	0130
D173A	0130
D173B	0130
D173C	0130
D173D	0130
D173E	0130
D173F	0130
D173G	0130
D173GN	0130
D173H	0130
D173J	0130
D173K	0130
D173M	0130
D173OR	0130
D173X	0130
D173Y	0130
D174	0103
D174A	0103
D174B	0103
D174C	0103
D174D	0103
D174E	0103
D174F	0103
D174G	0103
D174GN	0103
D174H	0103
D174J	0103
D174K	0103
D174L	0103
D174M	0103
D174R	0103
D174X	0103
D174Y	0103
D175(2S)	0103
D175A	0103
D175B	0103
D175C	0103
D175D	0103
D175E	0103
D175F	0103
D175G	0103
D175GN	0103
D175H	0103
D175J	0103
D175K	0103
D175L	0103
D175M	0103
D175OR	0103
D175R	0103
D175X	0103
D175Y	0103
D176	0012
D176(TRANS)	0130
D176A	0130
D176B	0130
D176C	0130
D176D	0130
D176E	0130
D176F	0130
D176G	0130
D176GN	0130
D176H	0130
D176J	0130
D176K	0130
D176L	0130
D176M	0130
D176OR	0130
D176X	0130
D176Y	0130
D177(2S)	0615
D178(2S)	0208
D178A(2S)	0208
D178B	0208
D178C	0208
D178D	0208
D178E	0208
D178F	0208
D178G	0208
D178GN	0208
D178H	0208
D178J	0208
D178K	0208
D178L	0208
D178M	0208
D178Q(2S)	0208

DEVICE TYPE	REPL CODE
D178T(2S)	0208
D178X	0208
D178Y	0208
D180	0861
D180(2S)	2766
D180A(2S)	2766
D180B(2S)	2766
D180C(2S)	2766
D180D(2S)	2766
D180F	2766
D180G	2766
D180GN	2766
D180H	2766
D180J	2766
D180K	2766
D180L	2766
D180M(2S)	2766
D180OR	2766
D180R	2766
D180X	2766
D180Y	2766
D181(2S)	1955
D181A	1955
D182(2S)	0086
D182A	0086
D182B	0086
D182C	0086
D182D	0086
D182E	0086
D182F	0086
D182G	0086
D182GN	0086
D182H	0086
D182J	0086
D182K	0086
D182L	0086
D182OR	0086
D182R	0086
D182X	0086
D182Y	0086
D183(2S)	0086
D183B	0086
D183E	0086
D183GN	0086
D183K	0086
D183L	0086
D183OR	0086
D183R	0086
D184(2S)	0042
D184A	0042
D184B	0042
D184C	0042
D184D	0042
D184E	0042
D184F	0042
D184H	0042
D184J	0042
D184K	0042
D184L	0042
D184M	0042
D184OR	0042
D184Y	0042
D185	0042
D186(2S)	0208
D186A(2S)	0208
D186B(2S)	0208
D186C	0208
D186D	0208
D186E	0208
D186F	0208
D186G	0208
D186GN	0208
D186H	0208
D186J	0208
D186K	0208
D186L	0208
D186M	0208
D186OR	0208
D186R	0208
D186X	0208
D186Y	0208
D187	0208
D187-OR	0208
D187A(2S)	0208
D187B	0208
D187C	0208
D187D	0208
D187E	0208
D187F	0208
D187G	0208
D187GN	0208
D187H	0208
D187J	0208
D187K	0208
D187L	0208
D187M	0208
D187OR	0208
D187R(2S)	0208
D187X	0208
D187Y(2S)	0208
D188	2534
D188A(2S)	2534
D188B(2S)	2534
D188C(2S)	2534
D188D	2534
D188E	2534
D188F	2534
D188G	2534
D188GN	2534

DEVICE TYPE	REPL CODE
D188H	2534
D188J	2534
D188L	2534
D188M	2534
D188OR	2534
D188R	2534
D188X	2534
D188Y	2534
D189(2S)	0177
D189A(2S)	0177
D189B	0177
D189C	0177
D189D	0177
D189E	0177
D189F	0177
D189G	0177
D189GN	0177
D189H	0177
D189J	0177
D189K	0177
D189L	0177
D189M	0177
D189OR	0177
D189R	0177
D189X	0177
D189Y	0177
D190	0142
D190B	0142
D190C	0142
D190D	0142
D190E	0142
D190F	0142
D190GN	0142
D190H	0142
D190J	0142
D190K	0142
D190L	0142
D190M	0142
D190OR	0142
D190R	0142
D190X	0142
D190Y	0142
D191	0208
D192(2S)	0208
D193	0208
D194(2S)	0208
D195	0208
D195A(2S)	0208
D195B	0208
D195C	0208
D195D	0208
D195E	0208
D195F	0208
D195G	0208
D195GN	0208
D195H	0208
D195J	0208
D195K	0208
D195L	0208
D195M	0208
D195OR	0208
D195R	0208
D195X	0208
D195Y	0208
D198(2S)	0042
D198A	0042
D198AP	0042
D198AQ	0042
D198AR	0042
D198B	0042
D198C	0042
D198D	0042
D198F	0042
D198G	0042
D198H(2S)	0042
D198HQ(2S)	0042
D198HR(2S)	0042
D198J	0042
D198K	0042
D198OR	0042
D198P(2S)	0042
D198Q(2S)	0042
D198R(2S)	0042
D198S(2S)	0042
D198V(2S)	0042
D198X	0042
D198Y	0042
D199(2S)	0003
D200	0223
D200(2S)	0223
D200(IR)	0133
D200-OR	0223
D200A(2S)	0223
D200B	0223
D200C	0223
D200D	0223
D200E	0223
D200F	0223
D200G	0223
D200GN	0223
D200H	0223
D200H(TRANS)	0223
D200HL	OEM
D200J	0223
D200K	0223
D200L	0223
D200M	0223
D200MP	0133
D200MP(IR)	0133

DEVICE TYPE	REPL CODE
D200OR	0223
D200X	0223
D200Y	0223
D201(0)	0861
D201(2S)	0861
D201-0	0861
D201A	0861
D201B	0861
D201C	0861
D201F	0861
D201G	0861
D201GN	0861
D201H	0861
D201J	0861
D201K	0861
D201L	0861
D201M(2S)	0861
D201MO	0861
D201MY	0861
D201Q	0861
D201X	0861
D201Y(2S)	0861
D202(2S)	0861
D203(2S)	0861
D204(2S)	0086
D204A	0086
D204B	0086
D204BL	0086
D204BS	OEM
D204BS-1	OEM
D204BSM	OEM
D204BSM-1	OEM
D204BSMZS	OEM
D204BSMZS-1	OEM
D204BSQ	OEM
D204BSQ-1	OEM
D204BSQZS	OEM
D204BSQZS-1	OEM
D204BST	OEM
D204BST-1	OEM
D204BSTZS	OEM
D204BSTZS-1	OEM
D204BSZS	OEM
D204BSZS-1	OEM
D204C	0086
D204D	0086
D204E	0086
D204F	0086
D204G	0086
D204GA	0086
D204GN	0086
D204H	0086
D204J	0086
D204K	0086
D204L(2S)	0086
D204M	0086
D204R	0086
D204Y	0086
D205(2S)	0086
D205A	0086
D205B	0086
D205C	0086
D205D	0086
D205E	0086
D205F	0086
D205G	0086
D205GN	0086
D205H	0086
D205J	0086
D205L	0086
D205M	0086
D205OR	0086
D205R	0086
D205X	0086
D205Y	0086
D206	0133
D206(2S)	0538
D206A	0538
D207	0074
D207(2S)	0103
D207(DIODE)	OEM
D207A	0103
D208	0538
D208(2S)	0615
D208(DIODE)	OEM
D208A	0615
D209	OEM
D210	OEM
D211	0103
D211(2S)	0103
D211(DIODE)	OEM
D211-OR	0103
D211A	0103
D211B	0103
D211C	0103
D211D	0103
D211E	0103
D211F	0103
D211G	0103
D211GN	0103
D211H	0103
D211J	0103
D211K	0103
D211L	0103
D211M	0103
D211OR	0103
D211R	0103
D211X	0103
D211Y	0103

DEVICE TYPE	REPL CODE
D212(2S)	0103
D212A	0103
D212B	0103
D212BS	OEM
D212BS-1	OEM
D212BSM	OEM
D212BSM-1	OEM
D212BSMZS	OEM
D212BSMZS-1	OEM
D212BSQ	OEM
D212BSQ-1	OEM
D212BSQZS	OEM
D212BSQZS-1	OEM
D212BST	OEM
D212BST-1	OEM
D212BSTZS	OEM
D212BSTZS-1	OEM
D212BSZS	OEM
D212BSZS-1	OEM
D212C	0103
D212D	0103
D212E	0103
D212F	0103
D212G	0103
D212GN	0103
D212H	0103
D212J	0103
D212K	0103
D212L	0103
D212M	0103
D212OR	0103
D212R	0103
D212X	0103
D212Y	0103
D213(2S)	0177
D214	0177
D215(2S)	0086
D216	0086
D217(2S)	0861
D218(2S)	0861
D219(2S)	0086
D219A	0086
D219A(2S)	0086
D219A(DIODE)	OEM
D219B	0086
D219C	0086
D219D	0086
D219E	0086
D219F	0086
D219G	0086
D219GN	0086
D219H	0086
D219J	0086
D219K	0086
D219L	0086
D219M	0086
D219OR	0086
D219R	0086
D219X	0086
D219Y	0086
D220	0023
D220(TRANS)	0086
D220-1M	1208
D220-1N	1208
D220A	0086
D220A(2S)	0086
D220A(DIODE)	OEM
D220B	0086
D220B(2S)	0086
D220B(DIODE)	OEM
D220C	0086
D220D	0086
D220E	0086
D220F	0086
D220G	0086
D220GN	0086
D220H	0086
D220J	0086
D220K	0086
D220L	0086
D220M(2S)	0086
D220OR	0086
D220R	0086
D220X	0086
D220Y	0086
D221(2S)	0086
D221F	0086
D222	1471
D222A	1471
D222B	1471
D222C	1471
D222D	1471
D222E	1471
D222F	1471
D222G	1471
D222GN	1471
D222H	1471
D222J	1471
D222K	1471
D222L	1471
D222M	1471
D222OR	1471
D222R	1471
D222X	1471
D222Y	1471
D223(2S)	1471
D223A	1471
D223B	1471
D223B(2S)	1471

DEVICE TYPE	REPL CODE
D223B(DIODE)	OEM
D223C	1471
D223D	1471
D223E	1471
D223F	1471
D223G	1471
D223GN	1471
D223H	1471
D223J	1471
D223K	1471
D223L	1471
D223M	1471
D223OR	1471
D223R	1471
D223X	1471
D223Y	1471
D224	1471
D226(2S)	0178
D226-0(2S)	0178
D226-0	0178
D226A(2S)	0178
D226A(0)	0178
D226AO	0178
D226AP(2S)	0178
D226B	0178
D226B(2S)	0178
D226B(DIODE)	0015
D226BP(2S)	0178
D226C	0178
D226D	0015
D226E	0178
D226F	0178
D226G	0015
D226G(2S)	0178
D226GN	0178
D226H	0178
D226J	0178
D226K	0178
D226L	0178
D226M	0178
D226OR	0178
D226P(2S)	0178
D226Q(2S)	0178
D226R	0178
D226V	0015
D226X	0178
D226Y	0178
D227	1409
D227-175	1409
D227-OR	1409
D227A(2S)	1409
D227B(2S)	1409
D227C(2S)	1409
D227D(2S)	1409
D227E(2S)	1409
D227G	1409
D227GN	1409
D227H	1409
D227J	1409
D227K	1409
D227L(2S)	1409
D227LF	1409
D227M	1409
D227OR	1409
D227R(2S)	1409
D227V	1409
D227X	1409
D227Y	1409
D228(2S)	0155
D228F	0155
D228G	0155
D228GN	0155
D228H	0155
D228J	0155
D228K	0155
D228L	0155
D228M	0155
D228OR	0155
D228R	0155
D228X	0155
D228Y	0155
D229D	OEM
D229E	OEM
D229G	0223
D229G(DIODE)	OEM
D229V	4023
D230DFA05G	0023
D230HI	0102
D231	0130
D231DFC15L	0102
D232(2S)	0130
D232A	0130
D234(2S)	0228
D234-0(2S)	0228
D234-O(2S)	0228
D234-ORG	0228
D234-R(2S)	0228
D234-RED	0228
D234-Y(2S)	0228
D234-YEL	0228
D234A	0228
D234B	0228
D234C	0228
D234D	0228
D234E	0228
D234F	0228
D234G	0228
D234GA	0228
D234GN	0228

DEVICE TYPE	REPL CODE
D234G-O	0228
D234G-R	0228
D234GR	0228
D234G-Y	0228
D234H	0228
D234J	0228
D234K	0228
D234L	0228
D234M	0228
D234N	0228
D234O	0228
D234OR	0228
D234R	0228
D234X	0228
D234Y	0228
D235(2S)	0228
D235-0(2S)	0228
D235-O(2S)	0228
D235-OR	0228
D235-ORG	0228
D235-R(2S)	0228
D235-RED	0228
D235-Y(2S)	0228
D235-YEL	0228
D235A	0228
D235B	0228
D235C	0228
D235D(2S)	0228
D235E	0228
D235F	0228
D235G(2S)	0228
D235GN	0228
D235G-O	0228
D235G-R	0228
D235G-Y	0228
D235H	0228
D235J	0228
D235L	0228
D235LBY	0228
D235M	0228
D235O	0228
D235OR	0228
D235R(2S)	0228
D235RED	0228
D235RY	0228
D235X	0228
D235Y(2S)	0228
D236	4036
D236(RECT.)	0276
D236A	4036
D236B	4036
D236C	4036
D236D	4036
D236E	4036
D236F	4036
D236G	4036
D236GN	4036
D236H	4036
D236J	4036
D236K	4036
D236L	4036
D236M	4036
D236R	4036
D236X	4036
D236Y	4036
D237	0178
D238(2S)	0178
D238F(2S)	0178
D240/200B	OEM
D240/400B	OEM
D240/600B	OEM
D240/700B	OEM
D240-100	OEM
D240-300	OEM
D240-500	OEM
D240R200B	OEM
D240R200B#	1017
D240R400B	OEM
D240R400B#	1030
D240R600B	OEM
D240R600B#	1030
D240R700B	OEM
D240R700B#	1040
D240S800B	OEM
D240S1000B	OEM
D240S1200B	OEM
D240S1400B	OEM
D241	0042
D242	OEM
D242(2S)	0419
D242A	OEM
D242B	OEM
D242YLC	0419
D243	5855
D243(2S)	0236
D243A	OEM
D243B	OEM
D244	0236
D245	OEM
D245A	OEM
D245B	OEM
D246	0223
D246(2S)	0223
D246(DIODE)	OEM
D246A	OEM
D246A(2S)	0223
D246B	OEM
D246B(2S)	0223
D246C	0223

If replacement code is OEM, contact original manufacturer for replacement.

DEVICE TYPE	REPL CODE
D246D	0223
D246E	0223
D246F	0223
D246G	0223
D246GN	0223
D246H	0223
D246J	0223
D246K	0223
D246L	0223
D246M	0223
D246OR	0223
D246R	0223
D246X	0223
D246Y	0223
D247	OEM
D247(2S)	0615
D247B	OEM
D247K	0615
D248B	OEM
D249	0130
D250	0130
D250/400E	OEM
D250/800E	OEM
D250/1200E	OEM
D250/1400E	OEM
D250/1600E	OEM
D250/1800E	OEM
D250-700	OEM
D250-1100	OEM
D250H	OEM
D250HL	OEM
D250R400E	OEM
D250R800E	OEM
D250R1200E	OEM
D250R1400E	OEM
D250R1600E	OEM
D250R1800E	OEM
D250S1000E	OEM
D250S1200E	OEM
D250S1400E	OEM
D250S1600E	OEM
D251	1021
D251N800B	OEM
D251N800E	OEM
D251N800V	OEM
D251N1200B	OEM
D251N1200E	OEM
D251N1200V	OEM
D251N1400B	OEM
D251N1400E	OEM
D251N1400V	OEM
D251NR800B	OEM
D251NR800V	OEM
D251NR1200B	OEM
D251NR1200E	OEM
D251NR1200V	OEM
D251NR1400B	OEM
D251NR1400E	OEM
D251NR1800B	OEM
D251NR1800E	OEM
D251NR1800V	OEM
D254(2S)	0178
D255(2S)	0178
D255N200B	OEM
D255N200V	OEM
D255N400B	OEM
D255N400V	OEM
D255N600B	OEM
D255N600V	OEM
D255N700B	OEM
D255N700V	OEM
D255N800B	OEM
D255N800V	OEM
D255NR200B	OEM
D255NR200V	OEM
D255NR400B	OEM
D255NR400V	OEM
D255NR600B	OEM
D255NR600V	OEM
D255NR700B	OEM
D255NR700V	OEM
D255NR800B	OEM
D255NR800V	OEM
D256	0042
D257(2S)	0419
D258	0236
D258S800T	OEM
D258S1000T	OEM
D258S1200T	OEM
D258S1400T	OEM
D258S1600T	OEM
D259	0236
D260	0615
D261(2S)	0218
D261-0	0218
D261-0	0218
D261A(2S)	0218
D261B(2S)	0218
D261C(2S)	0218
D261D(2S)	0218
D261E(2S)	0218
D261F(2S)	0218
D261G	0218
D261GN	0218
D261H	0218
D261J	0218
D261K	0218
D261L(2S)	0218
D261M	0218
D261OR	0218
D261P(2S)	0218
D261Q	0218
D261R(2S)	0218
D261S	0218
D261U	0218
D261V(2S)	0218
D261W(2S)	0218
D261X	0218
D261Y	0218
D262	0359
D265	0359
D266	0359
D269/2800	OEM
D269/3200	OEM
D269/3600	OEM
D270/3200T	OEM
D270/3600T	OEM
D272	0359
D273	0359
D274	0359
D280-400	OEM
D280-700	OEM
D280-1100	OEM
D280-1400	OEM
D280-1800	OEM
D280F5KF20	1119
D283(2S)	0074
D284(2S)	0424
D285(2S)	0074
D286	0538
D287(2S)	0538
D287A	0538
D287B	0538
D287C	0538
D288(2S)	0419
D288A(2S)	0419
D288B(2S)	0419
D288C(2S)	0419
D288K	0419
D288L(2S)	0419
D289(2S)	0419
D289A(2S)	0419
D289B(2S)	0419
D289C(2S)	0419
D290(2S)	0178
D291(2S)	4036
D291-0	4036
D291B	4036
D291BL	4036
D291C	4036
D291D	4036
D291E	4036
D291F	4036
D291G	4036
D291GA	4036
D291GN	4036
D291H	4036
D291J	4036
D291K	4036
D291L	4036
D291M	4036
D291OR	4036
D291R	4036
D291X	4036
D291Y	4036
D292	0042
D292(CHAN.MASTER)	0127
D292-0	0042
D292A	0042
D292B	0042
D292BL	0042
D292C	0042
D292D	0042
D292E	0042
D292F	0042
D292G	0042
D292GA	0042
D292GN	0042
D292H	0042
D292J	0042
D292K	0042
D292L	0042
D292M	0042
D292OR	0042
D292R	0042
D292X	0042
D292Y	0042
D293	0359
D294(2S)	0359
D297(2S)	0178
D299(2S)	0223
D299A	0223
D299B	0223
D299C	0223
D299E	0223
D299F	0223
D299G	0223
D299GN	0223
D299H	0223
D299J	0223
D299K	0223
D299M	0223
D299OR	0223
D299R	0223
D299X	0223
D299Y	0223
D300	0223
D300(2S)	0223
D300-700	OEM
D300-1100	OEM
D300A	0223
D300B(2S)	0223
D300C	0223
D300D	0223
D300G	0223
D300H	0223
D300J	0223
D300N400E	OEM
D300N800E	OEM
D300N1200E	OEM
D300N1400E	OEM
D300N1600E	OEM
D300N1800E	OEM
D300R400E	OEM
D300R800E	OEM
D300R1200E	OEM
D300R1400E	OEM
D300R1600E	OEM
D300R1800E	OEM
D301	3956
D302	OEM
D303	OEM
D304	OEM
D305	OEM
D310	1841
D311	1841
D312(2S)	0003
D312A	0003
D312B	0003
D312C	0003
D312D	0003
D312E	0003
D312F	0003
D312G	0003
D312GN	0003
D312H	0003
D312J	0003
D312K	0003
D312L	0003
D312M	0003
D312X	0003
D312Y	0003
D313	0042
D313(JAPAN)	0042
D313A	0042
D313B	0042
D313C(2S)	0042
D313D(2S)	0042
D313DE	0042
D313E	0042
D313F(2S)	0042
D313G	0042
D313GN	0042
D313H	0042
D313L	0042
D313M	0042
D313N	0042
D313R	0042
D313Y	0042
D314	0042
D314A	0042
D314B	0042
D314C	0042
D314D	0042
D314E	0042
D314GN	0042
D314H	0042
D314L	0042
D314M	0042
D314N	0042
D314R	0042
D314Y	0042
D315(2S)	4186
D315C	4186
D315D	4186
D315E	4186
D316	0177
D316-1	0177
D316-2	0177
D317(2S)	0419
D317A(2S)	0419
D317AF	0419
D317AP	0419
D317F(2S)	0419
D317P(2S)	0419
D318(2S)	0419
D318-0	0419
D318A(2S)	0419
D318B	0419
D318P	0419
D318Q	0419
D319(2S)	0538
D320(2S)	0074
D320(DIODE)	0290
D320(IR)	0290
D320F	0290
D321(2S)	0359
D322(2S)	0177
D322A(2S)	0177
D322B(2S)	0177
D322C(2S)	0177
D323(2S)	0177
D323A(2S)	0177
D323B(2S)	0177
D323C(2S)	0177
D324(2S)	0142
D324E	0142
D325(2S)	0555
D325-1	0555
D325-OR	0555
D325A	0555
D325B	0555
D325C(2S)	0555
D325D(2S)	0555
D325E(2S)	0555
D325F(2S)	0555
D325G	0555
D325GN	0555
D325H	0555
D325J	0555
D325K	0555
D325L	0555
D325M	0555
D325OR	0555
D325R	OEM
D325X	0555
D325Y	0555
D326	0142
D326A	0142
D326B	0142
D326C	0142
D326D	0142
D326E	0142
D326L	0142
D326M	0142
D326OR	0142
D326X	0142
D326Y	0142
D327(2S)	0284
D327-V	0284
D327A(2S)	0284
D327B(2S)	0284
D327C(2S)	0284
D327D(2S)	0284
D327E(2S)	0284
D327F(2S)	0284
D327L	0284
D327OR	0284
D327R	0284
D328(2S)	0086
D328S(2S)	0086
D329	0187
D330	1597
D330D(2S)	1597
D330E	1597
D331	0042
D332	0861
D334(2S)	0177
D334A(2S)	0177
D334R(2S)	0177
D335	0130
D336(2S)	0320
D338	0130
D339	0177
D339-1	0177
D339-2	0177
D340	0177
D340-1	0177
D340-2	0177
D341(2S)	0103
D341H(2S)	0103
D342(2S)	0419
D343(2S)	0228
D343A	0228
D343B	0228
D343C	0228
D343D	0228
D343H	0228
D343J	0228
D343K	0228
D344	0419
D345	0419
D346	0419
D347	0419
D348	0309
D349	0396
D350	2040
D350A	2040
D350Q(2S)	2040
D350T	2040
D351(2S)	0359
D352	0208
D352D(2S)	0208
D352H	0208
D353(2S)	0220
D354	0623
D355(2S)	0018
D355C(2S)	0018
D355D	0018
D356	0236
D356C	0236
D356D	0236
D356E	0236
D357	0236
D357C	0236
D357D	0236
D357E	0236
D358	0236
D358C	0236
D358D	0236
D358E	0236
D358N400T	OEM
D358N800T	OEM
D358N1200T	OEM
D358N1400T	OEM
D358N1600T	OEM
D358N1800T	OEM
D359(2S)	1597
D359C(2S)	1597
D359C2(2S)	1597
D359D(2S)	1597
D359D1(2S)	1597
D359D2(2S)	1597
D360(2S)	0042
D360D(2S)	0042
D360E(2S)	0042
D361	0042
D361C	0042
D361D	0042
D362	1157
D365	0042
D365A	0042
D365B	0042
D365H(2S)	0042
D365P	0042
D366	0042
D366A	0042
D367(2S)	0208
D367A(2S)	0208
D367B(2S)	0208
D367C(2S)	0208
D367E(2S)	0208
D367F(2S)	0208
D367H	0208
D367J	0208
D367K	0208
D367L	0208
D367M	0208
D367OR	0208
D367R	0208
D367X	0208
D367Y	0208
D368(2S)	0309
D369	1152
D369(2S)	0538
D369-0	0538
D369-0	0538
D369C	0538
D369Y	0538
D370	0177
D371	0861
D371-0	0861
D371-R	0861
D371-Y	0861
D375	0615
D376	1955
D376A	1955
D377	1955
D378	0626
D379(2S)	0177
D380(2S)	0309
D380A	0309
D381	0236
D381K	0236
D381L	0236
D381M	0236
D382(2S)	0236
D383(2S)	0359
D384	3336
D385	1203
D386	0388
D386A(2S)	0388
D386A-D	0388
D386AD	0388
D386A-E	0388
D386AE	0388
D386E	0388
D386Y(2S)	0388
D387	0388
D387A	0388
D387AC	0388
D387AD	0388
D387AE	0388
D387AF(2S)	0388
D387AS	0388
D387D	0388
D387E	0388
D387S	0388
D388	0861
D389(2S)	0042
D389-0	0042
D389-0(2S)	0042
D389A(2S)	0042
D389AF	0042
D389AF0	0042
D389AFO	0042
D389AFP(2S)	0042
D389AO	0042
D389AP	0042
D389AQ	0042
D389BLB	0042
D389BLB-0	0042
D389BLB-P	0042
D389BP	0042
D389L	0042
D389LB(2S)	0042
D389LBP	0042
D389LP	0042
D389P	0042
D389Q	0042
D389R	0042
D390	0042
D390A	0042
D390P	0042
D390Q	0042
D392	0284
D393	0359
D394	0309
D395	0359
D396	0359
D400	0018
D400(2S)	2882
D400-1400	OEM
D400E	2882
D400E(2S)	2882
D400F(2S)	2882
D400N1600E	OEM
D400N1800E	OEM
D400N2000E	OEM
D400N2200E	OEM
D400N2400E	OEM
D400N2600E	OEM
D400N2800E	OEM
D400P1(2S)	2882
D400P2	2882
D400R1600E	OEM
D400R1800E	OEM
D400R2000E	OEM
D400R2200E	OEM
D400R2400E	OEM
D400R2600E	OEM
D400R2800E	OEM
D401	1274
D401-3800	OEM
D401-4200	OEM
D401-4600	OEM
D401-0	1274
D401-Y	1274
D401A	1274
D401A(JAPAN)	1274
D401A-K	1274
D401AK	1274
D401AK(JAPAN)	1274
D401A-L	1274
D401AL	1274
D401AL(JAPAN)	1274
D401AM	1274
D401E	1274
D401EK	1274
D401H	1274
D401I	1274
D401IJ	1274
D401K	1274
D401L	1274
D401LA	1274
D401M	1274
D401N3600E	OEM
D401N3800E	OEM
D401N4000E	OEM
D401N4400E	OEM
D401N4800E	OEM
D401R	1274
D401R3600E	OEM
D401R4000E	OEM
D401R4400E	OEM
D401R4800E	OEM
D401Y	0388
D401Y(JAPAN)	1274
D402	0388
D402A	0388
D402AK	0388
D402AL	0388
D402AM	0388
D402K	0388
D402L	0388
D402M	0388
D404	0419
D404G	0419
D405	OEM
D405(2S)	1203
D405NR2000	OEM
D405NR2200	OEM
D405NR2400	OEM
D405NR2600	OEM
D405NR2800	OEM
D408BS	OEM
D408BS-1	OEM
D408BSM	OEM
D408BSM-1	OEM
D408BSMZS	OEM
D408BSMZS-1	OEM
D408BSQ	OEM
D408BSQ-1	OEM
D408BSQZS	OEM
D408BSQZS-1	OEM
D408BST	OEM
D408BST-1	OEM
D408BSTZS	OEM
D408BSTZS-1	OEM
D408BSZS	OEM
D408BSZS-1	OEM
D409	1203
D411	2422
D413	0233
D414	0558
D414Q	0558
D415	0558
D415P	0558
D415Q	0558
D415R	0558
D415Y	0558
D416	0518
D416(TRANS)	0309
D417	0861
D418(2S)	0065
D419	1203
D422	0424
D423	0424
D424(2S)	0538
D425(2S)	0177
D425-0	0177
D425-R	0177
D425O	0177
D426	0177
D426-0	0177
D426-R	0177
D427	0177
D427-0	0177
D427-R	0177
D428	0861
D428-0	0861
D428-R	0861
D428N800	OEM
D428N1200	OEM
D428N1400	OEM
D428N1800	OEM
D429	0359
D430	0615
D431	0615
D431(IR)	0023
D431-F	0102
D431S2400T	OEM
D431S2800T	OEM
D431S3200T	OEM
D431S3600T	OEM
D432	0615
D432C1	1257
D437	0359
D437W	0359
D438	0191
D438/200T	OEM
D438/400T	OEM
D438/600T	OEM
D438/700T	OEM
D438/800T	OEM
D438E	0191
D439	0558
D439E	0558
D448N400	OEM
D448N600	OEM
D448N700	OEM
D448N800	OEM
D450-700	OEM
D450-1100	OEM
D450N400E	OEM
D450N800E	OEM
D450N1200E	OEM
D450N1400E	OEM
D450R400E	OEM
D450R800E	OEM
D450R1200E	OEM
D450R1400E	OEM
D452N400	OEM
D452N800	OEM
D452N1200	OEM
D452N1400	OEM
D452N1800	OEM
D452NR400	OEM
D452NR800	OEM
D452NR1200	OEM
D452NR1400	OEM
D452NR1800	OEM
D458(2S)	0359
D458C	0359
D459	2220
D460	1203
D461	0637
D463	2411
D464	2422
D467	0945
D467-C	0945
D467B	0945
D467C	0945
D467C(JAPAN)	0945
D468	0018
D468A	0018
D468AC	0018
D468B(2S)	0018
D468C(2S)	0018
D468D	0018
D468E	0018
D468F	0018
D468G	0018
D468GN	0018
D468H	0018
D468L	0018
D468LN	0018
D468Y	0018
D469	0177
D470	1740
D470-B	1740
D470A	1740
D470B	1740
D471	0018
D471(2S)	0018
D471(JAPAN)	0018
D471-L	0018
D471A	0018
D471B	0018
D471C	0018
D471D	0018
D471E	0018
D471G	0018

If replacement code is OEM, contact original manufacturer for replacement.

DEVICE TYPE	REPL CODE
D471GN	0018
D471K	0018
D471L(2S)	0018
D471M	0018
D471N	0018
D471OR	0018
D471R	0018
D471X	0018
D471Y	0018
D473H	0018
D474K	0007
D475	0042
D475A	0042
D476	0419
D476A	0419
D476AKB	0419
D476AKC	0419
D476B	0419
D476C	0419
D476D	0419
D476G	0419
D476KB	0419
D476KC	0419
D476O	0419
D476YL	0419
D477	0042
D478	0388
D478-C	0388
D478A-01	0388
D478B	0388
D478BS	0388
D478C	0388
D478CS	0388
D478D	0388
D478Y	0388
D478YL	0388
D479	0161
D480	0161
D480-1600	OEM
D480-1800	OEM
D480-2000	OEM
D480-2200	OEM
D480-2400	OEM
D480-2600	OEM
D480-2800	OEM
D481	0161
D482	0275
D483	0275
D484	0168
D485	0161
D486	0161
D487	0161
D488	0161
D489	0161
D490	0161
D491	0556
D492	0103
D493	0556
D494	0556
D495	0556
D495S2000	OEM
D495S2200T	OEM
D495S2400T	OEM
D495S2600T	OEM
D496	3487
D497	3487
D498	3487
D499	0556
D500	0015
D500(TRANS)	0556
D501	0556
D502	2411
D503	2411
D504	2422
D505	2422
D506	2422
D510DS	OEM
D510DS-1	OEM
D510DSM	OEM
D510DSM-1	OEM
D510DSMZS	OEM
D510DSMZS-1	OEM
D510DSQ	OEM
D510DSQ-1	OEM
D510DSQZS	OEM
D510DST	OEM
D510DST-1	OEM
D510DSTZS	OEM
D510DSTZS-1	OEM
D510DSZS	OEM
D510DSZS-1	OEM
D513	0042
D517	0309
D518	0178
D519	0424
D520	0130
D520DS	OEM
D520DS-1	OEM
D520DSM	OEM
D520DSM-1	OEM
D520DSMZS	OEM
D520DSMZS-1	OEM
D520DSQ	OEM
D520DSQ-1	OEM
D520DSQZS	OEM
D520DSQZS-1	OEM
D520DST	OEM
D520DST-1	OEM
D520DSTZS	OEM

DEVICE TYPE	REPL CODE
D520DSTZS-1	OEM
D520DSZS	OEM
D520DSZS-1	OEM
D522	0103
D523	2411
D524	1384
D525	4183
D525-O	4183
D525-Y	4183
D525R	4183
D525Y	4183
D526	2969
D526-O	2969
D528/400	OEM
D528/800	OEM
D528/1200	OEM
D528/1400	OEM
D528N1600T	OEM
D528N1800T	OEM
D528N2000T	OEM
D528N2200T	OEM
D528N2400T	OEM
D528N2600T	OEM
D528N2800T	OEM
D531	0419
D532	5604
D533	0359
D535	2398
D536	1955
D537	1955
D538	1841
D538A	1841
D539	0359
D539A	0359
D544	0419
D545	0018
D545E	0018
D545F	0018
D545G	0018
D546	2085
D546K	2085
D549	0553
D552	2398
D553	4800
D553-O(JAPAN)	4800
D553Y	4800
D554	1021
D554C-118	OEM
D554C-188	OEM
D555	0861
D556	0538
D557	0538
D560	1203
D562(2S)	0830
D562A	0830
D562B	0830
D562C	0830
D562D	0830
D562E	0830
D562K	0830
D562L	0830
D562OR	0830
D562R	0830
D562X	0830
D562Y	0830
D564	4182
D570	0419
D571	1967
D571K	1967
D571K(JAPAN)	1967
D571L	1967
D572	0359
D573	0359
D575	4841
D575L	4841
D576	0233
D577	0065
D579	0178
D580	0742
D581	0177
D581A	0177
D582	4857
D582A	4857
D586	2911
D586A	2911
D586R	2911
D587	2911
D587A	2911
D588	2911
D588A	2911
D589	0065
D590	0086
D591	0111
D591R	0111
D592	0284
D592ANC	0284
D592NC	0284
D592R	0284
D593	0168
D597	0861
D598	0861
D598N400T	OEM
D598N800T	OEM
D598N1200T	OEM
D598N1400T	OEM
D599	0111
D600	0558
D600K	0558
D603	0155

DEVICE TYPE	REPL CODE
D604	0074
D605	0359
D606	0359
D608	0388
D608A	0388
D611	0424
D612	1779
D612E	1779
D612K	1779
D613	0060
D613P	0060
D617	2422
D619	1935
D620	0161
D620D12200	0120
D621	2820
D621EB	OEM
D621EC	OEM
D621ED	OEM
D621EE	OEM
D621EF	OEM
D621EG	OEM
D622	0424
D624	0233
D625	5622
D627	2636
D628EB	OEM
D628EC	OEM
D628ED	OEM
D628EE	OEM
D628EF	OEM
D628EG	OEM
D628H	2422
D629/3600	OEM
D629/4000	OEM
D629/4400	OEM
D629/4800	OEM
D629H	2422
D630	0130
D631	2416
D631N3600T	OEM
D631N4000T	OEM
D631N4400T	OEM
D631N4800T	OEM
D632	0270
D632P	0270
D632Q	0270
D632R	0270
D633	1203
D634	1203
D635	1203
D636	0577
D636-0	0577
D636-O	0577
D636-Q	0577
D636-Q(JAPAN)	0577
D636-R	0577
D636-R(JAPAN)	0577
D636-S	0577
D636P	0577
D636Q	0577
D636R	0577
D636S	0577
D636T	0577
D637	0577
D637-O	0577
D637-P	0577
D637-Q	0577
D637-Q(JAPAN)	0577
D637-QR	0577
D637-R	0577
D637-R(JAPAN)	0577
D637-S	0577
D637C	0577
D637CR	0577
D637O	0577
D637P	0577
D637PQR	0577
D637Q	0577
D637Q(JAPAN)	0577
D637QR	0577
D637R	0577
D637S	0577
D637T	0577
D638	0667
D638-R	0667
D638P	0667
D638Q	0667
D638R	0667
D638S	0667
D639	0667
D639P	0667
D639Q	0667
D639R	0667
D639S	0667
D639T	0667
D640	0359
D641	1841
D647A	1376
D649	0065
D649Q	0065
D654	0086
D655D	1967
D655D(JAPAN)	0016
D655E	1967
D655F	1967
D656	0178
D657	0074
D660	0626

DEVICE TYPE	REPL CODE
D661	0577
D661-R(JAPAN)	0577
D661S	0577
D661T	0577
D662	0710
D663	0359
D664	1203
D665	0538
D666	1376
D666A	1376
D666AB	1376
D666AC	1376
D666B	1376
D666C	1376
D666D	1376
D667	1376
D667A	1376
D667AB	1376
D667AC	1376
D667B	1376
D667C	1376
D667D	1376
D668AB	0558
D668AC	0558
D668B	0558
D668D	0558
D668N2000	OEM
D668N2200	OEM
D668N2400	OEM
D668N2600	OEM
D668N2800	OEM
D669	0558
D669AB	0558
D669AC	0558
D669B	0558
D669C	0558
D669D	0558
D670H	1384
D671	0155
D673	0861
D674	0861
D675	0538
D676	0538
D677	0074
D683	1841
D683A	1841
D683S	1841
D685	1841
D686	1203
D687	1203
D688	1471
D689	0055
D691	1203
D692	2411
D692M	2411
D692Q	2411
D693	0074
D704	0060
D704D	0060
D704E	0060
D705	0359
D706	0074
D707	0359
D711BS	OEM
D711BS-1	OEM
D711BSM	OEM
D711BSM-1	OEM
D711BSMZS	OEM
D711BSMZS-1	OEM
D711BSQ	OEM
D711BSQ-1	OEM
D711BSQZS	OEM
D711BSQZS-1	OEM
D711BST	OEM
D711BST-1	OEM
D711BSTZS	OEM
D711BSTZS-1	OEM
D716	3052
D717	3052
D718	0194
D720D(2S)	0208
D720E(2S)	0208
D720PJ	0208
D721	1203
D722	5641
D723	0236
D724	0388
D725	0065
D725-06	0065
D726	0236
D727	3557
D729H	3483
D730H	1384
D732	0861
D732K	0861
D733	0538
D733K	0538
D733U	0538
D734	1505
D734E	1505
D734F	1505
D734G	1505
D735	2261
D735-O	2261
D736	2261
D738	2261
D743	1274
D743A	1274
D743R	1274

DEVICE TYPE	REPL CODE
D745	2261
D745A	2261
D745B	2261
D748	3197
D748A	3197
D748A-01	3197
D748A-01A	3197
D748B	3197
D749	0359
D749P	0359
D750	0538
D751	0194
D753	0538
D754	0320
D755	0525
D755D	0525
D755E	0525
D755F	0525
D756	0525
D756A	0525
D756AF	0525
D756D	0525
D756E	0525
D757	0168
D757C	0168
D757D	0168
D758	1077
D758C	1077
D758D	1077
D761	0388
D761D	0388
D761E	0388
D761V	0388
D761VL	0388
D761VR	0388
D761VRD	0388
D761VRE	0388
D762	0690
D762-O(JAPAN)	0690
D762P	0690
D762P(JAPAN)	0690
D762Q	0690
D763	1376
D764	0223
D765	0223
D765AC	OEM
D766	2085
D766D	2085
D766P	2085
D766Q	2085
D766R	2085
D767R	0155
D768(JAPAN)	1948
D768K	1948
D772	0388
D772B	0388
D772BLB	0388
D773	0018
D773K	0018
D773K(JAPAN)	0018
D773L	0018
D773U	0018
D774	2019
D774-4	2019
D774-K	2019
D774K	2019
D774K(JAPAN)	2019
D774U2	2019
D776	2526
D777	0270
D777-1	0270
D777FA-1	0270
D777FA-5	0270
D777FA5	0270
D778	0284
D778Q	0284
D778R	0284
D780C-1	3441
D781	0558
D783	0309
D784	2820
D785	2820
D787B	0710
D787C	0710
D787D	0710
D787E	0710
D788	0018
D788B	0018
D788C	0018
D788D	0018
D788E	0018
D789	2539
D789B	2539
D789C	2539
D789C(JAPAN)	2539
D789D	2539
D789D(JAPAN)	2539
D789E	2539
D789E(JAPAN)	2539
D789M	2539
D789P	2539
D790B	1376
D790C	1376
D792	0309
D792S	0309
D792T	0309
D793	0558
D793Q	0558
D794	0161

DEVICE TYPE	REPL CODE
D794(2)	0161
D794A	0161
D794AD	0161
D794AQ	0161
D794AQ(JAPAN)	0161
D794D	0161
D794P	0161
D794Q	0161
D794R	0161
D795	0830
D795A	0830
D795AQ	0830
D795P	0830
D795Q	0830
D797	2416
D798N400	OEM
D798N800	OEM
D798N1200	OEM
D798N1400	OEM
D798N1800	OEM
D800	0071
D801	1841
D802	3031
D803	2422
D803Q	2422
D804	0042
D804H	0042
D804HLB	0042
D804HP	0042
D807	1485
D807M	1485
D809	0558
D810	4376
D811	5650
D812	1157
D812BS	OEM
D812BS-1	OEM
D812BSM-1	OEM
D812BSMZS	OEM
D812BSMZS-1	OEM
D812BSQ	OEM
D812BSQZS	OEM
D812BSQZS-1	OEM
D812BSTZS	OEM
D812BSTZS-1	OEM
D812BSZS	OEM
D812BSZS-1	OEM
D814A	0077
D814B	0318
D814D	0053
D814G	0181
D814V	0064
D815A	OEM
D815B	OEM
D815D	OEM
D815E	OEM
D815G	OEM
D815SZ	OEM
D815V	OEM
D816A	OEM
D816B	OEM
D816BS	OEM
D816BS-1	OEM
D816BSM	OEM
D816BSM-1	OEM
D816BSMZS	OEM
D816BSMZS-1	OEM
D816BSQ	OEM
D816BSQ-1	OEM
D816BSQZS	OEM
D816BSQZS-1	OEM
D816BST	OEM
D816BST-1	OEM
D816BSTZS	OEM
D816BSTZS-1	OEM
D816BSZS	OEM
D816BSZS-1	OEM
D816D	OEM
D816G	OEM
D816V	OEM
D817A	OEM
D817B	OEM
D817G	OEM
D817V	OEM
D818	2636
D818(IR)	0290
D819	2643
D820	2040
D820-1(JAPAN)	2040
D821	0309
D822	5309
D822P	5309
D822Q	5309
D823	1157
D829	OEM
D835	5212
D836	1203
D836A	1203
D836Q	1203
D836R	1203
D837	1203
D837A	1203
D837AB	1203
D837AD	1203
D837AQ	1203
D837AR	1203
D837B	1203
D837LB	1203
D837O	1203

DEVICE TYPE	REPL CODE
D837P	1203
D837Q	1203
D837R	1203
D838	2820
D838B	2820
D841	2985
D843	0060
D844	0194
D844E	0194
D845	2261
D845O	2261
D849	0065
D850	2643
D855	1157
D855A	1157
D855B	1157
D856	0060
D856A	0060
D856B	0060
D856L	0060
D856LB	0060
D856M	0060
D856MLB	0060
D856O	0060
D856P	0060
D856Q	0060
D856R	0060
D857	0060
D857A	0060
D857B	0060
D858	5354
D858(IC)	2238
D858A	5354
D858B	5354
D859	0168
D859A	0168
D859B	0168
D860	0168
D860A	0168
D860B	0168
D863	1376
D864K	1948
D866	3096
D866A	3096
D866B	3096
D866D	3096
D866P	3096
D866Q	3096
D866R	3096
D867	0177
D868	0055
D869	0055
D869-L	0055
D869B	0055
D869FA	0055
D869L	0055
D870	0055
D870A	0055
D870FA	0055
D870Z	0055
D871	0055
D871Z	0055
D873	4704
D876	0388
D877	0178
D878	0103
D880	0456
D880-O	0456
D880-Y	0456
D880GR	0456
D880Y	0456
D880Y(JAPAN)	0456
D880Y(KOREA)	0456
D882	0161
D882P	0161
D882Q	0161
D882R	0161
D884	0723
D886	0060
D886A	0060
D886F	0060
D886P	0060
D886Q	0060
D889	0111
D889Q	0111
D889R	0111
D889T	0111
D890	0525
D892	2770
D892A	2770
D892AR	2770
D893	0396
D893A	0396
D894	0553
D895	3053
D896	3053
D897A	0055
D898	0055
D898-B13	0055
D898A	0055
D898B	0055
D900A	0055
D900B	0055
D900B-06	0055
D900D	0055
D903	0055
D904	0055
D904P	0055
D904P(JAPAN)	OEM

If replacement code is OEM, contact original manufacturer for replacement.

365

DEVICE TYPE	REPL CODE
D906	0055
D907	3052
D917	0723
D918	0477
D919	0155
D920	0074
D920B	0074
D929	2526
D933H	5321
D940W01120	0137
D946	0553
D946A	0553
D950	2643
D950Q	2643
D951	0055
D952	0223
D953	0223
D957A	0055
D957A-03	0055
D958	0525
D958R	0525
D958S	0525
D958T	0525
D958U	0525
D959LB	1157
D959Q	1157
D960	0236
D960Q(JAPAN)	5522
D961	1157
D969	0667
D973	0009
D973A	0009
D973AR	1376
D973Q	0009
D973R	0009
D973S	0009
D974	1376
D975	0911
D975(TRANS)	0558
D975C	0558
D976	0911
D976(TRANS)	0723
D978	5212
D985	3658
D985-L	3658
D985K	3658
D985L	3658
D985M	3658
D985T	3658
D986	2942
D986(1)KA(JAPAN)	2942
D986(JAPAN)	2942
D986K	2942
D986L(JAPAN)	2942
D987	0723
D991K	5212
D992M	3316
D993	0055
D993A	0055
D994	0055
D995	2820
D997	2398
D1000	0071
D1000A60	OEM
D1010	0111
D1010S	0111
D1011	0525
D1012	0284
D1012F	0284
D1012G1	0284
D1016	0055
D1017	2589
D1018	2589
D1020	0018
D1020H	0018
D1021	0018
D1022	1203
D1024	1203
D1025	2085
D1032	3052
D1032A	3052
D1035	1157
D1036	2261
D1039	3509
D1040	0538
D1041	3510
D1044	0134
D1044A	0134
D1046	0194
D1047	0194
D1051	0018
D1051Q	0018
D1051R	0018
D1052	2058
D1052A	2058
D1052AFA	2058
D1052FA	2058
D1055	0009
D1055Q	0009
D1055R	0009
D1059	2187
D1060(JAPAN)	0060
D1060K	0060
D1061	0060
D1062	1955
D1063	3052
D1064	3052
D1064(JAPAN)	3052
D1069	0723

DEVICE TYPE	REPL CODE
D1076	3316
D1076L	3316
D1078B	3316
D1079C	3316
D1079LB	3316
D1079LC	3316
D1080C	3316
D1080LC	3316
D1081B	3316
D1081C	3316
D1081LB	3316
D1081LC	3316
D1083	3316
D1083L	3316
D1085K	5212
D1092	3474
D1092FA	3474
D1093	2965
D1094	3544
D1098-42M	0555
D1101	0321
D1102	0321
D1103	0065
D1110	0130
D1110A	0130
D1115K	5212
D1126K	1948
D1127K	1948
D1130	0130
D1130K	0130
D1131B	0236
D1131C	0236
D1131D	0236
D1132B	0236
D1132C	0236
D1132D	0236
D1133B	0236
D1133C	0236
D1133D	0236
D1135(JAPAN)	0236
D1135-5(JAPAN)	0236
D1135C(JAPAN)	0236
D1136	0388
D1138	0388
D1138-C	0388
D1138-D	0388
D1138-O	0388
D1138-Y	0388
D1138C	0388
D1138C(JAPAN)	0388
D1138Y	0388
D1139B	0388
D1140	0130
D1142	1533
D1148	3053
D1153	0396
D1161-1	OEM
D1161-2	OEM
D1161-4	OEM
D1161-5	OEM
D1161-6	OEM
D1161-7	OEM
D1161-8	OEM
D1161-9	OEM
D1161-10	OEM
D1161-11	OEM
D1161-12	OEM
D1161C1	OEM
D1161C2	OEM
D1161C3	OEM
D1161C4	OEM
D1161C5	OEM
D1161C6	OEM
D1161C7	OEM
D1161C8	OEM
D1161C9	OEM
D1161C10	OEM
D1161C11	OEM
D1161C12	OEM
D1162K	5212
D1162L	5212
D1162M	5212
D1164K	3195
D1164L	3195
D1164M	3195
D1171	0055
D1172S	0015
D1173	0055
D1175	3574
D1177	0321
D1177C	0558
D1178	0321
D1178C	0558
D1179	0558
D1180	3577
D1181	0321
D1182	OEM
D1183	0309
D1184	0309
D1184T41	OEM
D1184T42	OEM
D1184T43	OEM
D1184T44	OEM
D1184T46	OEM
D1184T47	OEM
D1184T48	OEM
D1184T49	OEM
D1184T51	OEM

DEVICE TYPE	REPL CODE
D1184T52	OEM
D1184T53	OEM
D1184T54	OEM
D1185	0309
D1186	0309
D1187	3248
D1190(JAPAN)	5360
D1193	3582
D1195	1203
D1197	1563
D1201	3009
D1201(2S)	1841
D1202	1841
D1203	3009
D1203(2S)	3009
D1206Q	0667
D1206R	0667
D1207S	3882
D1207T(JAPAN)	3882
D1208	2411
D1208FA	2411
D1218	2350
D1226	2452
D1226Q	2452
D1246T	1492
D1264P	0388
D1265	1154
D1265-LB	1154
D1265-O	1154
D1265-O(JAPAN)	1154
D1265-OP	1154
D1265-P	1154
D1265B	1154
D1265L	1154
D1265LB	1154
D1265O	1154
D1265OP	1154
D1265P	1154
D1265P(JAPAN)	1154
D1266AQ	0060
D1266P	0060
D1266P(JAPAN)	0060
D1266Q	0060
D1271BP	1157
D1273	0922
D1273P	0922
D1273Q	0922
D1274B	3950
D1276-AP	1203
D1276-LB	1203
D1276A	1203
D1276AP	1203
D1276B	1203
D1276LB	1203
D1276P	1203
D1277B	1203
D1277B(JAPAN)	1203
D1283	0208
D1294	2961
D1294FA	2961
D1301	0321
D1301(2S)	0055
D1302	0321
D1303	0321
D1308K(JAPAN)	3107
D1308L(JAPAN)	3107
D1314	1498
D1318	0086
D1344E	0055
D1347	0018
D1353	3646
D1354	3647
D1355	3648
D1356	3649
D1376	3658
D1376K	3658
D1390	2739
D1392(JAPAN)	2350
D1395	2350
D1396	1533
D1397	1533
D1397B	1533
D1398	1533
D1398S	1533
D1398S-CA	1533
D1406	3096
D1406-Y	3096
D1406GR	3096
D1406Y	3096
D1406Y(JAPAN)	3096
D1420	0321
D1421	0321
D1422	OEM
D1423AS	2926
D1426	1533
D1426(JAPAN)	1533
D1427	1533
D1427-LB	1533
D1428	1533
D1438	3658
D1439	1533
D1439(JAPAN)	1533
D1439P	1533
D1439Q	1533
D1439RL	1533
D1441	1533
D1445	0015
D1453	1533
D1455	1533

DEVICE TYPE	REPL CODE
D1459	3683
D1459Q	3683
D1459R	3683
D1491L(JAPAN)	1055
D1497	3326
D1511C-072	OEM
D1511C-073	OEM
D1511C-074	OEM
D1554	1533
D1555	0551
D1555-LB	0551
D1556	1533
D1556-LB	1533
D1579K	OEM
D1585K	0236
D1593L	OEM
D1593M	OEM
D1617	OEM
D1626	2801
D1627	3753
D1637	1055
D1637Y	1055
D1645	OEM
D1647	0277
D1649	1533
D1650	1533
D1651	0551
D1652	1533
D1666	0144
D1709ACT-128	OEM
D1709ACT-746	OEM
D1709C	OEM
D1709C-011	OEM
D1709C-515	OEM
D1709C-520	OEM
D1709C521	OEM
D1709C-538	OEM
D1709CT	OEM
D1709CT-113	OEM
D1709CT-118	OEM
D1709CT-121	OEM
D1709CT-713	OEM
D1709CT-715	OEM
D1709CT715	OEM
D1711CU517	OEM
D1720B	OEM
D1720C	OEM
D1722B	OEM
D1722C	OEM
D1724B	OEM
D1724BS	OEM
D1724BS-1	OEM
D1724BSM	OEM
D1724BSM-1	OEM
D1724BSMZS	OEM
D1724BSMZS-1	OEM
D1724BSQ	OEM
D1724BSQ-1	OEM
D1724BSQZS	OEM
D1724BSQZS-1	OEM
D1724BST	OEM
D1724BST-1	OEM
D1724BSTZS	OEM
D1724BSTZS-1	OEM
D1724BSZS	OEM
D1724BSZS-1	OEM
D1724C	OEM
D1726	0715
D1726B	OEM
D1726C	OEM
D1728	1533
D1728B	OEM
D1728C	OEM
D1730	1533
D1730B	OEM
D1730C	OEM
D1732	OEM
D1732B	OEM
D1732C	OEM
D1734	0623
D1734B	OEM
D1734C	OEM
D1736	OEM
D1736B	OEM
D1736C	OEM
D1738	0030
D1738B	OEM
D1738C	OEM
D1740	OEM
D1740B	OEM
D1740C	OEM
D1742	OEM
D1742B	OEM
D1742C	OEM
D1744	OEM
D1744B	OEM
D1744C	OEM
D1746	OEM
D1746B	OEM
D1746C	OEM
D1748	OEM
D1748B	OEM
D1748C	OEM
D1750	OEM
D1750B	OEM
D1750C	OEM
D1783L(JAPAN)	2350
D1785	OEM
D1788	3107

DEVICE TYPE	REPL CODE
D1800/2000	OEM
D1800/2200	OEM
D1800/2600	OEM
D1800/3000	OEM
D1800N2400	OEM
D1800N2400T	OEM
D1800N2800	OEM
D1800N2800T	OEM
D1800N3200	OEM
D1800N3200T	OEM
D1800N3600	OEM
D1809N2400	OEM
D1809N2800	OEM
D1809N3200	OEM
D1809N3600	OEM
D1832	0042
D1833	0042
D1833F	0042
D1843	3821
D1843L	3821
D1846	2116
D1847	OEM
D1876	2116
D1877	2116
D1878	2116
D1879	2116
D1880	0388
D1881	OEM
D1888	1948
D1894	0065
D1900	OEM
D1910	1533
D1911	1533
D1913-O	0042
D1913R	0042
D1929	1055
D1929Q	1055
D1941	3326
D1943G	OEM
D1959-02	3454
D1978	OEM
D2010	OEM
D2010P	OEM
D2012	1157
D2015L	3785
D2020L	3785
D2035J	OEM
D2035W	OEM
D2046	OEM
D2050J	OEM
D2055W	OEM
D2065J	OEM
D2070W	OEM
D2101S	1208
D2102S	1208
D2103S	1208
D2103SF	1208
D2112A	OEM
D2112A-2	OEM
D2112A-4	OEM
D2114	2037
D2114-2	2037
D2114A4	2037
D2114A5	2037
D2114AL1	OEM
D2114AL2	OEM
D2114AL3	2037
D2114AL4	2037
D2114L	2037
D2114L2	2037
D2114L3	2037
D2115A	OEM
D2115A-2	OEM
D2115AL	OEM
D2115AL-2	OEM
D2115H2	OEM
D2115H3	OEM
D2115H4	OEM
D2125A	OEM
D2125A-2	OEM
D2125AL	OEM
D2125AL-2	OEM
D2125H1	OEM
D2125H2	OEM
D2125H3	OEM
D2125H4	OEM
D2141-2	OEM
D2141-3	OEM
D2141-4	OEM
D2141-5	OEM
D2141L-3	OEM
D2141L-4	OEM
D2141L-5	OEM
D2142	OEM
D2142-2	OEM
D2142-3	OEM
D2142L	OEM
D2142L3	OEM
D2144-3	OEM
D2147	OEM
D2147-3	OEM
D2147H	OEM
D2147H1	OEM
D2147H2	OEM
D2147H3	OEM
D2147HL	OEM
D2147L	OEM
D2148	OEM
D2148-3	OEM

DEVICE TYPE	REPL CODE
D2148H	OEM
D2148H3	OEM
D2148HL	OEM
D2148HL3	OEM
D2148L	OEM
D2148L-3	OEM
D2149H	OEM
D2149H2	OEM
D2149H3	OEM
D2149HL	OEM
D2149HL3	OEM
D2187A-25	OEM
D2200N2000	OEM
D2200N2200	OEM
D2200N2400	OEM
D2200N2600	OEM
D2200N2800	OEM
D2201A	1208
D2201B	1208
D2201D	1208
D2201F	1208
D2201M	1208
D2201N	1208
D2209N2000	OEM
D2209N2200	OEM
D2209N2400	OEM
D2209N2600	OEM
D2209N2800	OEM
D2223BS	OEM
D2223BS-1	OEM
D2223BSM	OEM
D2223BSM-1	OEM
D2223BSMZS	OEM
D2223BSMZS-1	OEM
D2223BSQ	OEM
D2223BSQ-1	OEM
D2223BSQZS	OEM
D2223BSQZS-1	OEM
D2223BST	OEM
D2223BST-1	OEM
D2223BSTZS	OEM
D2223BSTZS-1	OEM
D2223BSZS	OEM
D2223BSZS-1	OEM
D2228N200	OEM
D2228N400	OEM
D2228N600	OEM
D2228N800	OEM
D2340	0042
D2350	0042
D2364C	OEM
D2600EF	0015
D2600F	1208
D2600M	1208
D2601DF	1208
D2601E	1208
D2601EF	1208
D2601M	1208
D2716D	2263
D2716D-Q1P-4	2263
D2716D-Q1X-0	2263
D2732A	2672
D2732D	2672
D2764	0806
D2764A-2	0806
D2764D	0806
D2801C	OEM
D2803C	OEM
D2812C	OEM
D2814C	OEM
D2816C	OEM
D3202Y	2137
D3205	OEM
D3207A	OEM
D3207A-1	OEM
D3222	OEM
D3232	OEM
D3242	OEM
D3245	OEM
D3313J	OEM
D3313K	OEM
D3404	OEM
D3436	0015
D3508	OEM
D3530	OEM
D3628A	2881
D3628A-1	2881
D3858-10	OEM
D4001-1400	OEM
D4001-1600	OEM
D4001-1800	OEM
D4001-2000	OEM
D4001-2200	OEM
D4002BC	2044
D4003	OEM
D4004	OEM
D4011BC	0215
D4012BC	0493
D4013BC	0409
D4015L	3785
D4016C-3	OEM
D4016CX-15	1887
D4017BC	0508
D4020L	3785
D4027BC	1938
D4030BC	0495
D4035J	OEM
D4035W	OEM
D4040	OEM

DEVICE TYPE	REPL CODE
D4040BC	0056
D4049UBC	0001
D4050J	OEM
D4052BC	0024
D4053BC	0034
D4053G	OEM
D4055W	OEM
D4065J	OEM
D4066BC	0101
D4066SIP	OEM
D4069C	0119
D4069UBC	0119
D4070W	OEM
D4074	OEM
D4074A	OEM
D4075	OEM
D4075A	OEM
D4075B	OEM
D4075C	OEM
D4075D	OEM
D4075E	OEM
D4075F	OEM
D4075G	OEM
D4075H	OEM
D4081	0621
D4081A	OEM
D4081BC	0621
D4082	OEM
D4082A	OEM
D4082B	OEM
D4082D	OEM
D4084	OEM
D4084A	OEM
D4084B	OEM
D4089	OEM
D4092	OEM
D4121	OEM
D4127	OEM
D4128	OEM
D4136	OEM
D4136A	OEM
D4136B	OEM
D4140	OEM
D4140A	OEM
D4140B	OEM
D4140C	OEM
D4140D	OEM
D4140E	OEM
D4141	OEM
D4141A	OEM
D4141B	OEM
D4141C	OEM
D4141D	OEM
D4141E	OEM
D4148C	OEM
D4148E	OEM
D4151	OEM
D4151A	OEM
D4155	OEM
D4160	OEM
D4160BC	1349
D4164C-2	2341
D4164C-3	2341
D4164C-15	2341
D4168	OEM
D4168A	OEM
D4168B	OEM
D4168C	OEM
D4168C-15	OEM
D4168C-20	OEM
D4168D	OEM
D4175	OEM
D4175A	OEM
D4180	OEM
D4180C	OEM
D4180E	OEM
D4181C	OEM
D4181D	OEM
D4181E	OEM
D4186C	OEM
D4186D	OEM
D4186E	OEM
D4186F	OEM
D4187C	OEM
D4187D	OEM
D4187E	OEM
D4188B	OEM
D4188C	OEM
D4188D	OEM
D4188E	OEM
D4188F	OEM
D4189B	OEM
D4189C	OEM
D4189D	OEM
D4189E	OEM
D4189F	OEM
D4194	OEM
D4194A	OEM
D4195	OEM
D4195A	OEM
D4196	OEM
D4196A	OEM
D4200	OEM
D4200-1	OEM
D4200-2	OEM
D4200-3	OEM
D4200A-E	OEM
D4200F	OEM
D4200G	OEM

If replacement code is OEM, contact original manufacturer for replacement.

DEVICE TYPE	REPL CODE
D4200H	OEM
D4200J-L	OEM
D4201	OEM
D4201-1	OEM
D4201-2	OEM
D4201-3	OEM
D4201A-E	OEM
D4201F	OEM
D4201G	OEM
D4201H	OEM
D4201J	OEM
D4201K	OEM
D4202	OEM
D4202-1	OEM
D4202-2	OEM
D4202-3	OEM
D4202A-E	OEM
D4202F	OEM
D4202G	OEM
D4202H	OEM
D4203	OEM
D4203-1	OEM
D4203-2	OEM
D4203-3	OEM
D4203A-E	OEM
D4203F	OEM
D4203G	OEM
D4204	OEM
D4204-1	OEM
D4204-2	OEM
D4204-3	OEM
D4204A-E	OEM
D4205	OEM
D4205-1	OEM
D4205-2	OEM
D4205-3	OEM
D4205A	OEM
D4205B	OEM
D4206	OEM
D4206-1	OEM
D4206-2	OEM
D4206-3	OEM
D4206A	OEM
D4207	OEM
D4207-1	OEM
D4207-2	OEM
D4207-3	OEM
D4210	OEM
D4210-1	OEM
D4210-2	OEM
D4210-3	OEM
D4210A-E	OEM
D4210F	OEM
D4210G	OEM
D4210H	OEM
D4210J-L	OEM
D4211	OEM
D4211-1	OEM
D4211-2	OEM
D4211-3	OEM
D4211A-E	OEM
D4211F	OEM
D4211G	OEM
D4211H	OEM
D4211J	OEM
D4211K	OEM
D4212	OEM
D4212-1	OEM
D4212-2	OEM
D4212-3	OEM
D4212A-E	OEM
D4212F	OEM
D4212G	OEM
D4212H	OEM
D4213	OEM
D4213-1	OEM
D4213-2	OEM
D4213-3	OEM
D4213A-E	OEM
D4213F	OEM
D4213G	OEM
D4214	OEM
D4214-1	OEM
D4214-2	OEM
D4214-3	OEM
D4214A-E	OEM
D4215	OEM
D4215-1	OEM
D4215-2	OEM
D4215-3	OEM
D4215A	OEM
D4215B	OEM
D4216	OEM
D4216-1	OEM
D4216-2	OEM
D4216-3	OEM
D4216A	OEM
D4217-1	OEM
D4217-2	OEM
D4217-3	OEM
D4220	OEM
D4220-1	OEM
D4220-2	OEM
D4220-3	OEM
D4220A-E	OEM
D4220F	OEM
D4220G	OEM
D4220H	OEM
D4220J	OEM
D4220K	OEM
D4221	OEM
D4221-1	OEM
D4221-2	OEM
D4221-3	OEM
D4221A-E	OEM
D4221F	OEM
D4221G	OEM
D4221H	OEM
D4221J	OEM
D4222	OEM
D4222-1	OEM
D4222-2	OEM
D4222-3	OEM
D4222A-E	OEM
D4222F	OEM
D4222G	OEM
D4223	OEM
D4223-1	OEM
D4223-2	OEM
D4223-3	OEM
D4223A-E	OEM
D4223F	OEM
D4224	OEM
D4224-1	OEM
D4224-2	OEM
D4224-3	OEM
D4224A-D	OEM
D4225	OEM
D4225-1	OEM
D4225-2	OEM
D4225-3	OEM
D4225A	OEM
D4226	OEM
D4226-1	OEM
D4226-2	OEM
D4226-3	OEM
D4227	OEM
D4227-1	OEM
D4227-2	OEM
D4227-3	OEM
D4230	OEM
D4230-1	OEM
D4230-2	OEM
D4230-3	OEM
D4230A-E	OEM
D4230F	OEM
D4230G	OEM
D4230H	OEM
D4230J	OEM
D4231	OEM
D4231-1	OEM
D4231-2	OEM
D4231-3	OEM
D4231A-E	OEM
D4231F	OEM
D4231G	OEM
D4231H	OEM
D4232	OEM
D4232-1	OEM
D4232-2	OEM
D4232-3	OEM
D4232A-E	OEM
D4232F	OEM
D4233	OEM
D4233-1	OEM
D4233-2	OEM
D4233-3	OEM
D4233A-D	OEM
D4234	OEM
D4234-1	OEM
D4234-2	OEM
D4234-3	OEM
D4234A	OEM
D4234B	OEM
D4235	OEM
D4235-1	OEM
D4235-2	OEM
D4235-3	OEM
D4236-1	OEM
D4236-2	OEM
D4236-3	OEM
D4237-1	OEM
D4237-2	OEM
D4237-3	OEM
D4240	OEM
D4240-1	OEM
D4240-2	OEM
D4240-3	OEM
D4240A-E	OEM
D4240F	OEM
D4240G	OEM
D4240H	OEM
D4240J	OEM
D4241	OEM
D4241-1	OEM
D4241-2	OEM
D4241-3	OEM
D4241A-E	OEM
D4241F	OEM
D4241G	OEM
D4241H	OEM
D4242	OEM
D4242-1	OEM
D4242-2	OEM
D4242-3	OEM
D4242A-E	OEM
D4242F	OEM
D4243	OEM
D4243-1	OEM
D4243-2	OEM
D4243-3	OEM
D4243A-D	OEM
D4244	OEM
D4244-1	OEM
D4244-2	OEM
D4244-3	OEM
D4244A	OEM
D4244B	OEM
D4245	OEM
D4245-1	OEM
D4245-2	OEM
D4245-3	OEM
D4246-1	OEM
D4246-2	OEM
D4246-3	OEM
D4247-1	OEM
D4247-2	OEM
D4247-3	OEM
D4250	0177
D4250-1	OEM
D4250-2	OEM
D4250-3	OEM
D4250A-E	OEM
D4250F	OEM
D4251	OEM
D4251-1	OEM
D4251-2	OEM
D4251-3	OEM
D4251A-E	OEM
D4252	OEM
D4252-1	OEM
D4252-2	OEM
D4252-3	OEM
D4252A-D	OEM
D4253	OEM
D4253-1	OEM
D4253-2	OEM
D4253-3	OEM
D4253A-C	OEM
D4254	OEM
D4254-1	OEM
D4254-2	OEM
D4254-3	OEM
D4254A	OEM
D4255-1	OEM
D4255-2	OEM
D4255-3	OEM
D4256-2	OEM
D4256-3	OEM
D4257-2	OEM
D4257-3	OEM
D4260	OEM
D4260-1	OEM
D4260-2	OEM
D4260-3	OEM
D4260A	OEM
D4260B	OEM
D4260C	OEM
D4261	OEM
D4261-1	OEM
D4261-2	OEM
D4261-3	OEM
D4261A	OEM
D4261B	OEM
D4262	OEM
D4262-1	OEM
D4262-2	OEM
D4262-3	OEM
D4262A	OEM
D4263	OEM
D4263-1	OEM
D4263-2	OEM
D4263-3	OEM
D4263A	OEM
D4264	OEM
D4264-1	OEM
D4264-2	OEM
D4264-3	OEM
D4265-1	OEM
D4265-2	OEM
D4265-3	OEM
D4266-3	OEM
D4267-3	OEM
D4270	OEM
D4270-1	OEM
D4270-2	OEM
D4270-3	OEM
D4271	OEM
D4271-1	OEM
D4271-2	OEM
D4271-3	OEM
D4272-1	OEM
D4272-2	OEM
D4272-3	OEM
D4274-2	OEM
D4274-3	OEM
D4275-2	OEM
D4275-3	OEM
D4276-3	OEM
D4277-3	OEM
D4300	OEM
D4300A	OEM
D4300B-E	OEM
D4300F	OEM
D4300G	OEM
D4300H	OEM
D4300J	OEM
D4300K	OEM
D4301	OEM
D4301A	OEM
D4301B-E	OEM
D4301F	OEM
D4301G	OEM
D4301H	OEM
D4301J	OEM
D4301K	OEM
D4302	OEM
D4302A	OEM
D4302B-E	OEM
D4302F	OEM
D4302G	OEM
D4302H	OEM
D4302J	OEM
D4302K	OEM
D4303	OEM
D4303A	OEM
D4303B-E	OEM
D4303F	OEM
D4303G	OEM
D4303H	OEM
D4303J	OEM
D4303K	OEM
D4310	OEM
D4310A	OEM
D4310B-E	OEM
D4310F	OEM
D4310G	OEM
D4310H	OEM
D4310J	OEM
D4310K	OEM
D4311	OEM
D4311A	OEM
D4311B-E	OEM
D4311F	OEM
D4311G	OEM
D4311H	OEM
D4311J	OEM
D4311K	OEM
D4312	OEM
D4312A	OEM
D4312B-E	OEM
D4312F	OEM
D4312G	OEM
D4312H	OEM
D4312J	OEM
D4312K	OEM
D4313	OEM
D4313A	OEM
D4313B-E	OEM
D4313F	OEM
D4313G	OEM
D4313H	OEM
D4313J	OEM
D4313K	OEM
D4320	OEM
D4320A	OEM
D4320B-E	OEM
D4320F	OEM
D4320G	OEM
D4320H	OEM
D4320J	OEM
D4321	OEM
D4321A	OEM
D4321B-E	OEM
D4321F	OEM
D4321G	OEM
D4321H	OEM
D4321J	OEM
D4322	OEM
D4322A	OEM
D4322B-E	OEM
D4322F	OEM
D4322G	OEM
D4322H	OEM
D4322J	OEM
D4323	OEM
D4323A	OEM
D4323B-E	OEM
D4323F	OEM
D4323G	OEM
D4323H	OEM
D4323J	OEM
D4330	OEM
D4330A	OEM
D4330B-E	OEM
D4330F	OEM
D4330G	OEM
D4330H	OEM
D4330J	OEM
D4331	OEM
D4331A	OEM
D4331B-E	OEM
D4331F	OEM
D4331G	OEM
D4331H	OEM
D4331J	OEM
D4332	OEM
D4332A	OEM
D4332B-E	OEM
D4332F	OEM
D4332G	OEM
D4332H	OEM
D4332J	OEM
D4333	OEM
D4333A	OEM
D4333B-E	OEM
D4333F	OEM
D4333G	OEM
D4333H	OEM
D4333J	OEM
D4340	OEM
D4340A	OEM
D4340B-E	OEM
D4340F	OEM
D4341	OEM
D4341A	OEM
D4341B-E	OEM
D4341F	OEM
D4342	OEM
D4342A	OEM
D4342B-E	OEM
D4342F	OEM
D4343	OEM
D4343A	OEM
D4343B-E	OEM
D4343F	OEM
D4350	OEM
D4350A	OEM
D4350B-D	OEM
D4351	OEM
D4351A	OEM
D4351B-D	OEM
D4352	OEM
D4352A	OEM
D4352B-D	OEM
D4353	OEM
D4353A	OEM
D4353B-D	OEM
D4360	OEM
D4360A	OEM
D4361	OEM
D4361A	OEM
D4362	OEM
D4362A	OEM
D4363	OEM
D4363A	OEM
D4364C-15L	OEM
D4364C-20L	OEM
D4400	OEM
D4400A	OEM
D4400BE	OEM
D4400F	OEM
D4400G	OEM
D4400H	OEM
D4400J	OEM
D4400K	OEM
D4400N200	OEM
D4400N400	OEM
D4400N600	OEM
D4400N800	OEM
D4401	OEM
D4401A	OEM
D4401B-E	OEM
D4401F	OEM
D4401G	OEM
D4401H	OEM
D4401J	OEM
D4401K	OEM
D4402	OEM
D4402A-E	OEM
D4402F	OEM
D4402G	OEM
D4402H	OEM
D4402J	OEM
D4402K	OEM
D4403	OEM
D4403A-E	OEM
D4403F	OEM
D4403G	OEM
D4403H	OEM
D4403J	OEM
D4403K	OEM
D4409N200	OEM
D4409N400	OEM
D4409N600	OEM
D4409N800	OEM
D4410	OEM
D4410A	OEM
D4410B-E	OEM
D4410F	OEM
D4410G	OEM
D4410H	OEM
D4410J	OEM
D4410K	OEM
D4411	OEM
D4411A	OEM
D4411B-E	OEM
D4411F	OEM
D4411G	OEM
D4411H	OEM
D4411J	OEM
D4411K	OEM
D4412	OEM
D4412A-E	OEM
D4412F	OEM
D4412G	OEM
D4412H	OEM
D4412J	OEM
D4412K	OEM
D4413	OEM
D4413A-E	OEM
D4413F	OEM
D4413G	OEM
D4413H	OEM
D4420	OEM
D4420A	OEM
D4420B-E	OEM
D4420F	OEM
D4420G	OEM
D4420H	OEM
D4420J	OEM
D4421A	OEM
D4421B-E	OEM
D4421F	OEM
D4421G	OEM
D4421H	OEM
D4421J	OEM
D4422	OEM
D4422A-E	OEM
D4422F	OEM
D4422G	OEM
D4422H	OEM
D4422J	OEM
D4423	OEM
D4423A-E	OEM
D4423F	OEM
D4423G	OEM
D4423H	OEM
D4423J	OEM
D4430	OEM
D4430A	OEM
D4430B-E	OEM
D4430F	OEM
D4430G	OEM
D4430H	OEM
D4430J	OEM
D4431	OEM
D4431A	OEM
D4431A-B	OEM
D4431F	OEM
D4431G	OEM
D4431H	OEM
D4431J	OEM
D4432	OEM
D4432A-E	OEM
D4432F	OEM
D4432G	OEM
D4432H	OEM
D4432J	OEM
D4433	OEM
D4433A-E	OEM
D4433F	OEM
D4433G	OEM
D4433H	OEM
D4433J	OEM
D4440	OEM
D4440A	OEM
D4440B-E	OEM
D4440F	OEM
D4441	OEM
D4441A	OEM
D4441B-E	OEM
D4441F	OEM
D4442	OEM
D4442A-E	OEM
D4442F	OEM
D4443	OEM
D4443A-E	OEM
D4443F	OEM
D4450	OEM
D4450A	OEM
D4450B-D	OEM
D4451	OEM
D4451A	OEM
D4451B-D	OEM
D4452	OEM
D4452A-D	OEM
D4453	OEM
D4453A-D	OEM
D4460	OEM
D4460A	OEM
D4462	OEM
D4462A	OEM
D4463	OEM
D4463A	OEM
D4500X	OEM
D4500Y	OEM
D4500Z	OEM
D4501X	OEM
D4501Y	OEM
D4501Z	OEM
D4502X	OEM
D4502Y	OEM
D4502Z	OEM
D4503X	OEM
D4503Y	OEM
D4503Z	OEM
D4504X	OEM
D4504Y	OEM
D4504Z	OEM
D4505X	OEM
D4505Y	OEM
D4505Z	OEM
D4506X	OEM
D4506Y	OEM
D4506Z	OEM
D4510X	OEM
D4510Y	OEM
D4510Z	OEM
D4511X	OEM
D4511Y	OEM
D4511Z	OEM
D4512X	OEM
D4512Y	OEM
D4512Z	OEM
D4513X	OEM
D4513Y	OEM
D4513Z	OEM
D4514X	OEM
D4514Y	OEM
D4514Z	OEM
D4515X	OEM
D4515Y	OEM
D4515Z	OEM
D4516X	OEM
D4516Y	OEM
D4516Z	OEM
D4520Y	OEM
D4520Z	OEM
D4521X	OEM
D4521Y	OEM
D4521Z	OEM
D4522X	OEM
D4522Y	OEM
D4522Z	OEM
D4523X	OEM
D4523Y	OEM
D4523Z	OEM
D4524X	OEM
D4524Y	OEM
D4524Z	OEM
D4525X	OEM
D4525Y	OEM
D4525Z	OEM
D4526X	OEM
D4526Y	OEM
D4526Z	OEM
D4530X	OEM
D4530Y	OEM
D4530Z	OEM
D4531X	OEM
D4531Y	OEM
D4531Z	OEM
D4532X	OEM
D4532Y	OEM
D4532Z	OEM
D4533X	OEM
D4533Y	OEM
D4533Z	OEM
D4534X	OEM
D4534Y	OEM
D4534Z	OEM
D4535X	OEM
D4535Y	OEM
D4535Z	OEM
D4536X	OEM
D4536Y	OEM
D4536Z	OEM
D4540X	OEM
D4540Y	OEM
D4540Z	OEM
D4541X	OEM
D4541Y	OEM
D4541Z	OEM
D4542X	OEM
D4542Y	OEM
D4542Z	OEM
D4543X	OEM
D4543Y	OEM
D4543Z	OEM
D4544X	OEM
D4544Y	OEM
D4544Z	OEM
D4545X	OEM
D4545Y	OEM
D4545Z	OEM
D4546X	OEM
D4546Y	OEM
D4546Z	OEM
D4550X	OEM
D4550Y	OEM
D4550Z	OEM
D4551X	OEM
D4551Y	OEM
D4551Z	OEM
D4552X	OEM
D4552Y	OEM
D4552Z	OEM
D4553X	OEM
D4553Y	OEM
D4553Z	OEM
D4554X	OEM
D4554Y	OEM
D4554Z	OEM
D4555X	OEM
D4555Y	OEM
D4555Z	OEM
D4556X	OEM
D4556Y	OEM
D4556Z	OEM
D4560X	OEM
D4560Y	OEM
D4560Z	OEM
D4561X	OEM
D4561Y	OEM
D4561Z	OEM
D4562X	OEM
D4562Y	OEM
D4562Z	OEM
D4563X	OEM
D4563Y	OEM
D4563Z	OEM
D4564X	OEM

If replacement code is OEM, contact original manufacturer for replacement.

367

DEVICE TYPE	REPL CODE
D4564Y	OEM
D4564Z	OEM
D4565X	OEM
D4565Y	OEM
D4565Z	OEM
D4566X	OEM
D4566Y	OEM
D4566Z	OEM
D4570X	OEM
D4570Y	OEM
D4570Z	OEM
D4571X	OEM
D4571Y	OEM
D4571Z	OEM
D4572X	OEM
D4572Y	OEM
D4572Z	OEM
D4573X	OEM
D4573Y	OEM
D4573Z	OEM
D4574X	OEM
D4574Y	OEM
D4574Z	OEM
D4575X	OEM
D4575Y	OEM
D4575Z	OEM
D4576X	OEM
D4576Y	OEM
D4576Z	OEM
D4600	OEM
D4600-1	OEM
D4600-2	OEM
D4600-3	OEM
D4600A-E	OEM
D4600FH	OEM
D4600J-L	OEM
D4600N	OEM
D4600P	OEM
D4601	OEM
D4601-1	OEM
D4601-2	OEM
D4601-3	OEM
D4601A-E	OEM
D4601F-H	OEM
D4601J-L	OEM
D4602	OEM
D4602-1	OEM
D4602-2	OEM
D4602-3	OEM
D4602A-E	OEM
D4602F	OEM
D4602G	OEM
D4602H	OEM
D4603	OEM
D4603-1	OEM
D4603-2	OEM
D4603-3	OEM
D4603A-E	OEM
D4603F	OEM
D4603G	OEM
D4604	OEM
D4604-1	OEM
D4604-2	OEM
D4604-3	OEM
D4604A-E	OEM
D4605	OEM
D4605-1	OEM
D4605-2	OEM
D4605-3	OEM
D4605A	OEM
D4605B	OEM
D4606	OEM
D4606-1	OEM
D4606-2	OEM
D4606-3	OEM
D4606A	OEM
D4607	OEM
D4607-1	OEM
D4607-2	OEM
D4607-3	OEM
D4610	OEM
D4610-1	OEM
D4610-2	OEM
D4610-3	OEM
D4610A-E	OEM
D4610F	OEM
D4610G	OEM
D4610H	OEM
D4610J-L	OEM
D4611	OEM
D4611-1	OEM
D4611-2	OEM
D4611-3	OEM
D4611A-E	OEM
D4611F-H	OEM
D4611J	OEM
D4611K	OEM
D4612	OEM
D4612-1	OEM
D4612-2	OEM
D4612-3	OEM
D4612A-E	OEM
D4612F	OEM
D4612G	OEM
D4612H	OEM
D4613	OEM
D4613-1	OEM
D4613-2	OEM
D4613-3	OEM
D4613A-E	OEM
D4613F	OEM
D4613G	OEM
D4614	OEM
D4614-1	OEM
D4614-2	OEM
D4614-3	OEM
D4614A-E	OEM
D4615	OEM
D4615-1	OEM
D4615-2	OEM
D4615-3	OEM
D4615A	OEM
D4615B	OEM
D4616	OEM
D4616-1	OEM
D4616-2	OEM
D4616-3	OEM
D4616A	OEM
D4617	OEM
D4617-1	OEM
D4617-2	OEM
D4617-3	OEM
D4620	OEM
D4620-1	OEM
D4620-2	OEM
D4620-3	OEM
D4620A-E	OEM
D4620F-H	OEM
D4620J-L	OEM
D4620X	OEM
D4621	OEM
D4621-1	OEM
D4621-2	OEM
D4621-3	OEM
D4621A-E	OEM
D4621F-H	OEM
D4621J	OEM
D4622	OEM
D4622-1	OEM
D4622-2	OEM
D4622-3	OEM
D4622A-E	OEM
D4622F	OEM
D4622G	OEM
D4623	OEM
D4623-1	OEM
D4623-2	OEM
D4623-3	OEM
D4623A-E	OEM
D4623F	OEM
D4624	OEM
D4624-1	OEM
D4624-2	OEM
D4624-3	OEM
D4624A-D	OEM
D4625	OEM
D4625-1	OEM
D4625-2	OEM
D4625-3	OEM
D4625A	OEM
D4626	OEM
D4626-1	OEM
D4626-2	OEM
D4626-3	OEM
D4627	OEM
D4627-1	OEM
D4627-2	OEM
D4627-3	OEM
D4630	OEM
D4630-1	OEM
D4630-2	OEM
D4630-3	OEM
D4630A-E	OEM
D4630F-H	OEM
D4630J	OEM
D4630K	OEM
D4631	OEM
D4631-2	OEM
D4631-3	OEM
D4631A-E	OEM
D4631F-H	OEM
D4632	OEM
D4632-1	OEM
D4632-2	OEM
D4632-3	OEM
D4632A-E	OEM
D4632AMR	OEM
D4632F	OEM
D4633	OEM
D4633-1	OEM
D4633-2	OEM
D4633-3	OEM
D4633A-D	OEM
D4634	OEM
D4634-1	OEM
D4634-2	OEM
D4634-3	OEM
D4634A	OEM
D4634B	OEM
D4635	OEM
D4635-1	OEM
D4635-2	OEM
D4635-3	OEM
D4636-1	OEM
D4636-2	OEM
D4636-3	OEM
D4637-1	OEM
D4637-2	OEM
D4637-3	OEM
D4640	OEM
D4640-1	OEM
D4640-2	OEM
D4640-3	OEM
D4640A-E	OEM
D4640F	OEM
D4640G	OEM
D4640H	OEM
D4640J	OEM
D4641	OEM
D4641-1	OEM
D4641-2	OEM
D4641-3	OEM
D4641A-E	OEM
D4641F-H	OEM
D4642	OEM
D4642-1	OEM
D4642-2	OEM
D4642-3	OEM
D4642A-E	OEM
D4642F	OEM
D4643	OEM
D4643-2	OEM
D4643-3	OEM
D4643A-D	OEM
D4644	OEM
D4644-1	OEM
D4644-2	OEM
D4644-3	OEM
D4644A	OEM
D4644B	OEM
D4645	OEM
D4645-1	OEM
D4645-2	OEM
D4645-3	OEM
D4646-1	OEM
D4646-2	OEM
D4646-3	OEM
D4647-1	OEM
D4647-2	OEM
D4647-3	OEM
D4650	OEM
D4650-1	OEM
D4650-2	OEM
D4650-3	OEM
D4650A-E	OEM
D4650F	OEM
D4651	OEM
D4651-1	OEM
D4651-2	OEM
D4651-3	OEM
D4651A-E	OEM
D4652	OEM
D4652-1	OEM
D4652-2	OEM
D4652-3	OEM
D4652A-D	OEM
D4653	OEM
D4653-1	OEM
D4653-2	OEM
D4653-3	OEM
D4653A-C	OEM
D4654	OEM
D4654-1	OEM
D4654-2	OEM
D4654-3	OEM
D4654A	OEM
D4655-1	OEM
D4655-2	OEM
D4655-3	OEM
D4656-2	OEM
D4656-3	OEM
D4657-2	OEM
D4657-3	OEM
D4660	OEM
D4660-1	OEM
D4660-2	OEM
D4660-3	OEM
D4660A-C	OEM
D4661	OEM
D4661-1	OEM
D4661-2	OEM
D4661-3	OEM
D4661A	OEM
D4661B	OEM
D4662	OEM
D4662-1	OEM
D4662-2	OEM
D4662-3	OEM
D4662A	OEM
D4663	OEM
D4663-1	OEM
D4663-2	OEM
D4663-3	OEM
D4663A	OEM
D4664	OEM
D4664-1	OEM
D4664-2	OEM
D4664-3	OEM
D4665-2	OEM
D4665-3	OEM
D4666-3	OEM
D4667-3	OEM
D4670	OEM
D4670-1	OEM
D4670-2	OEM
D4670-3	OEM
D4670A	OEM
D4671	OEM
D4671-1	OEM
D4671-2	OEM
D4671-3	OEM
D4672	OEM
D4672-1	OEM
D4672-2	OEM
D4672-3	OEM
D4674-1	OEM
D4674-2	OEM
D4674-3	OEM
D4675-2	OEM
D4675-3	OEM
D4676-3	OEM
D4677-3	OEM
D4710	OEM
D4710A	OEM
D4710B-E	OEM
D4710F	OEM
D4710G	OEM
D4710H	OEM
D4710J	OEM
D4710K	OEM
D4711	OEM
D4711A	OEM
D4711B-E	OEM
D4711F	OEM
D4711G	OEM
D4711H	OEM
D4711J	OEM
D4711K	OEM
D4712	OEM
D4712A	OEM
D4712B-E	OEM
D4712F	OEM
D4712G	OEM
D4712H	OEM
D4712J	OEM
D4712K	OEM
D4713	OEM
D4713A	OEM
D4713B-E	OEM
D4713F	OEM
D4713G	OEM
D4713H	OEM
D4713J	OEM
D4713K	OEM
D4720	OEM
D4720A	OEM
D4720B-E	OEM
D4720F	OEM
D4720G	OEM
D4720H	OEM
D4720J	OEM
D4721	OEM
D4721A	OEM
D4721B-E	OEM
D4721F	OEM
D4721G	OEM
D4721H	OEM
D4721J	OEM
D4722	OEM
D4722A	OEM
D4722B-E	OEM
D4722F	OEM
D4722G	OEM
D4722H	OEM
D4722J	OEM
D4723	OEM
D4723A	OEM
D4723B-E	OEM
D4723F	OEM
D4723G	OEM
D4723H	OEM
D4723J	OEM
D4730	OEM
D4730A	OEM
D4730B-E	OEM
D4730F	OEM
D4730G	OEM
D4730H	OEM
D4730J	OEM
D4731	OEM
D4731A	OEM
D4731B-E	OEM
D4731F	OEM
D4731G	OEM
D4731H	OEM
D4731J	OEM
D4732	OEM
D4732A	OEM
D4732B-E	OEM
D4732F	OEM
D4732G	OEM
D4732H	OEM
D4732J	OEM
D4733	OEM
D4733A	OEM
D4733B-E	OEM
D4733F	OEM
D4733G	OEM
D4733H	OEM
D4733J	OEM
D4740	OEM
D4740A	OEM
D4740B-E	OEM
D4740F	OEM
D4741	OEM
D4741A	OEM
D4741B-E	OEM
D4741F	OEM
D4742	OEM
D4742A	OEM
D4742B-E	OEM
D4742F	OEM
D4743	OEM
D4743A	OEM
D4743B-E	OEM
D4743F	OEM
D4750	OEM
D4750A	OEM
D4750B-D	OEM
D4751	OEM
D4751A	OEM
D4751B-D	OEM
D4752	OEM
D4752A	OEM
D4752B-D	OEM
D4753	OEM
D4753A	OEM
D4753B-D	OEM
D4760	OEM
D4760A	OEM
D4761	OEM
D4761A	OEM
D4762	OEM
D4762A	OEM
D4763	OEM
D4763A	OEM
D4767	2243
D4770	OEM
D4771	OEM
D4772	OEM
D4773	OEM
D4782	OEM
D4782A	OEM
D4801	OEM
D4801-1	OEM
D4801-2	OEM
D4801-3	OEM
D4801A-E	OEM
D4801F	OEM
D4801G	OEM
D4801H	OEM
D4801J	OEM
D4801K	OEM
D4802	OEM
D4802-1	OEM
D4802-2	OEM
D4802-3	OEM
D4802A-E	OEM
D4802F-H	OEM
D4803	OEM
D4803-1	OEM
D4803-2	OEM
D4803-3	OEM
D4803A-E	OEM
D4803F	OEM
D4803G	OEM
D4804	OEM
D4804-1	OEM
D4804-2	OEM
D4804-3	OEM
D4804A-E	OEM
D4805	OEM
D4805-1	OEM
D4805-2	OEM
D4805-3	OEM
D4805A	OEM
D4805B	OEM
D4806	OEM
D4806-1	OEM
D4806-2	OEM
D4806-3	OEM
D4806A	OEM
D4807	OEM
D4807-1	OEM
D4807-2	OEM
D4807-3	OEM
D4811	OEM
D4811-1	OEM
D4811-2	OEM
D4811-3	OEM
D4811A-3	OEM
D4811A-E	OEM
D4811F-H	OEM
D4811F-J	OEM
D4811F-K	OEM
D4812	OEM
D4812-1	OEM
D4812-2	OEM
D4812-3	OEM
D4812A-E	OEM
D4812F-H	OEM
D4813	OEM
D4813-1	OEM
D4813-2	OEM
D4813-3	OEM
D4813A-3	OEM
D4813F	OEM
D4813G	OEM
D4814	OEM
D4814-1	OEM
D4814-2	OEM
D4814-3	OEM
D4814A-E	OEM
D4815	OEM
D4815-1	OEM
D4815-2	OEM
D4815-3	OEM
D4815A	OEM
D4815B	OEM
D4816	OEM
D4816-1	OEM
D4816-2	OEM
D4816-3	OEM
D4816A	OEM
D4817	OEM
D4817-1	OEM
D4817-2	OEM
D4817-3	OEM
D4821	OEM
D4821-1	OEM
D4821-2	OEM
D4821-3	OEM
D4821A-E	OEM
D4821F-H	OEM
D4821F-J	OEM
D4822	OEM
D4822-1	OEM
D4822-2	OEM
D4822-3	OEM
D4822A-E	OEM
D4822F	OEM
D4822G	OEM
D4823	OEM
D4823-1	OEM
D4823-2	OEM
D4823-3	OEM
D4823A-E	OEM
D4823F	OEM
D4824	OEM
D4824-1	OEM
D4824-2	OEM
D4824-3	OEM
D4824A-D	OEM
D4825	OEM
D4825-1	OEM
D4825-2	OEM
D4825-3	OEM
D4825A	OEM
D4826	OEM
D4826-1	OEM
D4826-2	OEM
D4826-3	OEM
D4827	OEM
D4827-1	OEM
D4827-2	OEM
D4827-3	OEM
D4831	OEM
D4831-1	OEM
D4831-2	OEM
D4831-3	OEM
D4831A-E	OEM
D4831F-H	OEM
D4832	OEM
D4832-1	OEM
D4832-2	OEM
D4832-3	OEM
D4832A-E	OEM
D4832F	OEM
D4833	OEM
D4833-1	OEM
D4833-2	OEM
D4833-3	OEM
D4833A-D	OEM
D4834	OEM
D4834-1	OEM
D4834-2	OEM
D4834-3	OEM
D4834A	OEM
D4834B	OEM
D4835	OEM
D4835-1	OEM
D4835-2	OEM
D4835-3	OEM
D4836-1	OEM
D4836-2	OEM
D4836-3	OEM
D4837-1	OEM
D4837-2	OEM
D4837-3	OEM
D4841	OEM
D4841-1	OEM
D4841-2	OEM
D4841-3	OEM
D4841A-E	OEM
D4841F-H	OEM
D4842	OEM
D4842-1	OEM
D4842-2	OEM
D4842-3	OEM
D4842A-E	OEM
D4842F	OEM
D4843	OEM
D4843-1	OEM
D4843-2	OEM
D4843-3	OEM
D4843A-D	OEM
D4844	OEM
D4844-1	OEM
D4844-2	OEM
D4844-3	OEM
D4844A	OEM
D4844B	OEM
D4845	OEM
D4845-1	OEM
D4845-2	OEM
D4845-3	OEM
D4846-1	OEM
D4846-2	OEM
D4846-3	OEM
D4847-1	OEM
D4847-2	OEM
D4847-3	OEM
D4851	OEM
D4851-1	OEM
D4851-2	OEM
D4851-3	OEM
D4851A-E	OEM
D4852	OEM
D4852-1	OEM
D4852-2	OEM
D4852-3	OEM
D4852A-D	OEM
D4853	OEM
D4853-1	OEM
D4853-2	OEM
D4853-3	OEM
D4853A-C	OEM
D4854	OEM
D4854-1	OEM
D4854-2	OEM
D4854-3	OEM
D4854A	OEM
D4855-1	OEM
D4855-2	OEM
D4855-3	OEM
D4856-2	OEM
D4856-3	OEM
D4857-2	OEM
D4857-3	OEM
D4861	OEM
D4861-1	OEM
D4861-2	OEM
D4861-3	OEM
D4861A	OEM
D4861B	OEM
D4862	OEM
D4862-1	OEM
D4862-2	OEM
D4862-3	OEM
D4862A	OEM
D4863	OEM
D4863-1	OEM
D4863-2	OEM
D4863-3	OEM
D4863A	OEM
D4864	OEM
D4864-1	OEM
D4864-2	OEM
D4864-3	OEM
D4865-1	OEM
D4865-2	OEM
D4865-3	OEM
D4866-3	OEM
D4867-3	OEM
D4871	OEM
D4871-1	OEM
D4871-2	OEM
D4871-3	OEM
D4872	OEM
D4872-1	OEM
D4872-2	OEM
D4872-3	OEM
D4873-1	OEM
D4873-2	OEM
D4873-3	OEM
D4874-1	OEM
D4874-2	OEM
D4874-3	OEM
D4875-2	OEM
D4875-3	OEM
D4876-3	OEM
D4877-3	OEM
D4912	OEM
D4912A	OEM
D4912B	OEM
D4920F	OEM
D4920G	OEM
D4920H	OEM
D4920J	OEM
D4926A	OEM
D4927	OEM
D4938	OEM
D4938A	OEM
D4939	OEM
D4940	OEM
D4941	OEM
D4942	OEM
D4957	OEM
D4957A	OEM
D4957B	OEM
D4957H	OEM
D4957J-L	OEM
D4957J-N	OEM
D4961	OEM
D4961A	OEM
D4961B	OEM
D4961C	OEM
D4962	OEM
D4962B	OEM
D4962C	OEM
D4963	OEM
D4963A	OEM
D4963B	OEM
D4963C	OEM

368

If replacement code is OEM, contact original manufacturer for replacement.

DEVICE TYPE	REPL CODE
D4964	OEM
D4964A	OEM
D4964B	OEM
D4964C	OEM
D4965	OEM
D4965A	OEM
D4965B	OEM
D4965C	OEM
D4966	OEM
D4966A	OEM
D4966B	OEM
D4966C	OEM
D4971	OEM
D4971A	OEM
D4971B	OEM
D4971C	OEM
D4972	OEM
D4972A	OEM
D4972B	OEM
D4972C	OEM
D4973	OEM
D4973A	OEM
D4973B	OEM
D4973C	OEM
D4974	OEM
D4974A	OEM
D4974B	OEM
D4974C	OEM
D4975	OEM
D4975A	OEM
D4975B	OEM
D4975C	OEM
D4976	OEM
D4976A	OEM
D4976B	OEM
D4976C	OEM
D5002-06	OEM
D5002-12	OEM
D5002-18	OEM
D5002-24	OEM
D5002-30	OEM
D5002-36	OEM
D5002-42	OEM
D5002-48	OEM
D5005-06	OEM
D5005-12	OEM
D5005-18	OEM
D5006-06	OEM
D5006-12	OEM
D5006-18	OEM
D5006-24	OEM
D5006-30	OEM
D5006-36	OEM
D5007-06	OEM
D5007-12	OEM
D5007-18	OEM
D5008-06	OEM
D5008-12	OEM
D5008-18	OEM
D5008-24	OEM
D5008-30	OEM
D5009-06	OEM
D5009-12	OEM
D5018-06	OEM
D5020	OEM
D5020A	OEM
D5020B	OEM
D5020C	OEM
D5020D	OEM
D5021	OEM
D5021A	OEM
D5021B	OEM
D5021C	OEM
D5021D	OEM
D5022	OEM
D5022A	OEM
D5022B	OEM
D5022C	OEM
D5022D	OEM
D5023	OEM
D5023A	OEM
D5023B	OEM
D5023C	OEM
D5023D	OEM
D5024	OEM
D5024A	OEM
D5024B	OEM
D5025	OEM
D5025A	OEM
D5025B	OEM
D5025C	OEM
D5026	OEM
D5026A	OEM
D5026B	OEM
D5030A	OEM
D5030B	OEM
D5030C	OEM
D5030D	OEM
D5031A	OEM
D5031B	OEM
D5031C	OEM
D5031D	OEM
D5036A	OEM
D5046	OEM
D5046A	OEM
D5046B	OEM
D5046C	OEM
D5047	OEM
D5047A	OEM
D5047B	OEM
D5047C	OEM
D5047D	OEM
D5047E	OEM
D5047F	OEM
D5047G	OEM
D5047H	OEM
D5061	OEM
D5061A	OEM
D5061B	OEM
D5061C	OEM
D5062	OEM
D5062A	OEM
D5062B	OEM
D5062C	OEM
D5063	OEM
D5063A	OEM
D5063B	OEM
D5063C	OEM
D5064	OEM
D5064A	OEM
D5064B	OEM
D5064C	OEM
D5065	OEM
D5065A	OEM
D5065B	OEM
D5065C	OEM
D5066	OEM
D5066A	OEM
D5066B	OEM
D5066C	OEM
D5071	OEM
D5071A	OEM
D5071B	OEM
D5071C	OEM
D5072	OEM
D5072A	OEM
D5072B	OEM
D5072C	OEM
D5073	OEM
D5073A	OEM
D5073B	OEM
D5073C	OEM
D5074	OEM
D5074A	OEM
D5074B	OEM
D5074C	OEM
D5075	OEM
D5075A	OEM
D5075B	OEM
D5075C	OEM
D5076	OEM
D5076A	OEM
D5076B	OEM
D5076C	OEM
D5082B	OEM
D5082C	OEM
D5082D	OEM
D5082E	OEM
D5082F	OEM
D5090	OEM
D5090A	OEM
D5091AM	OEM
D5091M	OEM
D5092AM	OEM
D5092BM	OEM
D5092M	OEM
D5104-10	OEM
D5104-15	OEM
D5104-20	OEM
D5109-2	OEM
D5109-4	OEM
D5109-6	OEM
D5109-8	OEM
D5146	OEM
D5146A	OEM
D5146B	OEM
D5146C	OEM
D5146D	OEM
D5146E	OEM
D5146F	OEM
D5146G	OEM
D5146H	OEM
D5147	OEM
D5147A	OEM
D5147B	OEM
D5147C	OEM
D5147D	OEM
D5147E	OEM
D5147F	OEM
D5147G	OEM
D5147H	OEM
D5151	OEM
D5151A	OEM
D5151B	OEM
D5167	OEM
D5221CM	OEM
D5221EM	OEM
D5221FM	OEM
D5221GM	OEM
D5223CM	OEM
D5223EM	OEM
D5223F	OEM
D5223FM	OEM
D5223G	OEM
D5233	OEM
D5235	OEM
D5235-1	OEM
D5236	OEM
D5244	OEM
D5244-06	OEM
D5244-12	OEM
D5244-18	OEM
D5244-24	OEM
D5244-30	OEM
D5244-36	OEM
D5244-42	OEM
D5244A	OEM
D5244B	OEM
D5244C	OEM
D5244D	OEM
D5244E	OEM
D5244F	OEM
D5244G	OEM
D5245-06	OEM
D5245-12	OEM
D5245-18	OEM
D5245-24	OEM
D5245-30	OEM
D5245-36	OEM
D5245A	OEM
D5245B	OEM
D5245C	OEM
D5245D	OEM
D5245E	OEM
D5245F	OEM
D5246-06	OEM
D5246-12	OEM
D5246-18	OEM
D5246-24	OEM
D5246-30	OEM
D5246A	OEM
D5246B	OEM
D5246C	OEM
D5246D	OEM
D5246E	OEM
D5252	OEM
D5253B	OEM
D5253BM	OEM
D5253C	OEM
D5253CM	OEM
D5253D	OEM
D5253DM	OEM
D5253E	OEM
D5253EM	OEM
D5254-06	OEM
D5254-12	OEM
D5254-18	OEM
D5254A	OEM
D5254A-D	OEM
D5254B	OEM
D5254C	OEM
D5255-06	OEM
D5255-12	OEM
D5255-18	OEM
D5255A	OEM
D5255B	OEM
D5255C	OEM
D5256-06	OEM
D5256-12	OEM
D5256A	OEM
D5256B	OEM
D5258	OEM
D5264	OEM
D5264A	OEM
D5264B	OEM
D5265	OEM
D5265A	OEM
D5277D	0015
D5278B	OEM
D5278BM	OEM
D5278C	OEM
D5278CM	OEM
D5278D	OEM
D5278DM	OEM
D5278E	OEM
D5278EM	OEM
D5282C	OEM
D5282D	OEM
D5282E	OEM
D5282F	OEM
D5282FM	OEM
D5282FMR	OEM
D5282G	OEM
D5282GM	OEM
D5282GMR	OEM
D5298	OEM
D5320	OEM
D5320A	OEM
D5320B	OEM
D5321	OEM
D5321A	OEM
D5321B	OEM
D5322	OEM
D5322A	OEM
D5322B	OEM
D5323	OEM
D5323A	OEM
D5323B	OEM
D5326	OEM
D5326A	OEM
D5326AM	OEM
D5326AMR	OEM
D5326B	OEM
D5326BM	OEM
D5326BMR	OEM
D5326M	OEM
D5326MR	OEM
D5337	OEM
D5337-00	OEM
D5337-06	OEM
D5337-12	OEM
D5337A	OEM
D5337B	OEM
D5338	OEM
D5339	OEM
D5340-5	OEM
D5340-6	OEM
D5340-G	OEM
D5340-M	OEM
D5340-X	OEM
D5345-5	OEM
D5345-6	OEM
D5345-G	OEM
D5345-M	OEM
D5345-X	OEM
D5347	OEM
D5347A	OEM
D5347B	OEM
D5353B	OEM
D5353BM	OEM
D5353BMR	OEM
D5353C	OEM
D5353CM	OEM
D5353CMR	OEM
D5353D	OEM
D5353DM	OEM
D5353DMR	OEM
D5353E	OEM
D5353EM	OEM
D5353EMR	OEM
D5353F	OEM
D5353FM	OEM
D5353MR	OEM
D5357	OEM
D5357A	OEM
D5357B	OEM
D5360	OEM
D5360-5	OEM
D5360-6	OEM
D5360-G	OEM
D5360-M	OEM
D5360-X	OEM
D5360A	OEM
D5361	OEM
D5361A	OEM
D5362	OEM
D5362A	OEM
D5363	OEM
D5363A	OEM
D5364	OEM
D5364A	OEM
D5365	OEM
D5365A	OEM
D5371	OEM
D5371A	OEM
D5371B	OEM
D5371C	OEM
D5371D	OEM
D5391C	OEM
D5392	OEM
D5392A	OEM
D5392AM	OEM
D5392AMR	OEM
D5392B	OEM
D5392BM	OEM
D5392BMR	OEM
D5392M	OEM
D5392MR	OEM
D5400	OEM
D5400-1	OEM
D5400-2	OEM
D5400-3	OEM
D5400A-E	OEM
D5400F-H	OEM
D5400J-L	OEM
D5401	OEM
D5401-1	OEM
D5401-2	OEM
D5401-3	OEM
D5401A-E	OEM
D5401F-H	OEM
D5401F-J	OEM
D5401F-K	OEM
D5402	OEM
D5402-1	OEM
D5402-2	OEM
D5402-3	OEM
D5402A-E	OEM
D5402F-H	OEM
D5403	2949
D5403-1	OEM
D5403-2	OEM
D5403-3	OEM
D5403A-E	OEM
D5403F	OEM
D5403G	OEM
D5404	2950
D5404-1	OEM
D5404-2	OEM
D5404-3	OEM
D5404A-E	OEM
D5405	OEM
D5405-1	OEM
D5405-2	OEM
D5405-3	OEM
D5405A	OEM
D5405B	OEM
D5410	2951
D5410-1	OEM
D5410-2	OEM
D5410-3	OEM
D5410A-E	OEM
D5410F-H	OEM
D5410J-L	OEM
D5411	OEM
D5411-1	OEM
D5411-2	OEM
D5411-3	OEM
D5411A-E	OEM
D5411F-H	OEM
D5411F-J	OEM
D5411F-K	OEM
D5412	OEM
D5412-1	OEM
D5412-2	OEM
D5412-3	OEM
D5412A-E	OEM
D5412F-H	OEM
D5413	OEM
D5413-1	OEM
D5413-2	OEM
D5413-3	OEM
D5413A-E	OEM
D5413F	OEM
D5413G	OEM
D5414	OEM
D5414-1	OEM
D5414-2	OEM
D5414-3	OEM
D5414A-E	OEM
D5415	OEM
D5415-1	OEM
D5415-2	OEM
D5415-3	OEM
D5415A	OEM
D5415B	OEM
D5420	OEM
D5420-1	OEM
D5420-2	OEM
D5420-3	OEM
D5420A-E	OEM
D5420F-H	OEM
D5420F-J	OEM
D5420F-K	OEM
D5421	OEM
D5421-1	OEM
D5421-2	OEM
D5421-3	OEM
D5421A-E	OEM
D5421F-H	OEM
D5421F-J	OEM
D5422	OEM
D5422-1	OEM
D5422-2	OEM
D5422-3	OEM
D5422A-E	OEM
D5422F	OEM
D5422G	OEM
D5423	OEM
D5423-1	OEM
D5423-2	OEM
D5423-3	OEM
D5423A-E	OEM
D5423F	OEM
D5424	OEM
D5424-1	OEM
D5424-2	OEM
D5424-3	OEM
D5424A-D	OEM
D5425	OEM
D5425-1	OEM
D5425-2	OEM
D5425-3	OEM
D5425A	OEM
D5430	OEM
D5430-1	OEM
D5430-2	OEM
D5430-3	OEM
D5430A-E	OEM
D5430F-H	OEM
D5430F-J	OEM
D5431	OEM
D5431-2	OEM
D5431-3	OEM
D5431A-E	OEM
D5431F-H	OEM
D5432	OEM
D5432-1	OEM
D5432-2	OEM
D5432-3	OEM
D5432A-E	OEM
D5432F	OEM
D5433	OEM
D5433-1	OEM
D5433-2	OEM
D5433-3	OEM
D5433A-D	OEM
D5434	OEM
D5434-1	OEM
D5434-2	OEM
D5434-3	OEM
D5434A	OEM
D5434B	OEM
D5435	OEM
D5435-1	OEM
D5435-2	OEM
D5435-3	OEM
D5440	OEM
D5440-1	OEM
D5440-2	OEM
D5440-3	OEM
D5440A-E	OEM
D5440F-H	OEM
D5440F-J	OEM
D5441	OEM
D5441-1	OEM
D5441-2	OEM
D5441-3	OEM
D5441A-E	OEM
D5441F-H	OEM
D5442	OEM
D5442-1	OEM
D5442-2	OEM
D5442-3	OEM
D5442A-F	OEM
D5442F	OEM
D5443	OEM
D5443-1	OEM
D5443-2	OEM
D5443-3	OEM
D5443A-D	OEM
D5444	OEM
D5444-1	OEM
D5444-2	OEM
D5444-3	OEM
D5444-48	OEM
D5444A	OEM
D5444B	OEM
D5450	OEM
D5450-1	OEM
D5450-2	OEM
D5450-3	OEM
D5450A-E	OEM
D5450F	OEM
D5451	OEM
D5451-1	OEM
D5451-2	OEM
D5451-3	OEM
D5451A-E	OEM
D5452	OEM
D5452-1	OEM
D5452-2	OEM
D5452-3	OEM
D5452A-D	OEM
D5453	OEM
D5453-1	OEM
D5453-2	OEM
D5453-3	OEM
D5453A-C	OEM
D5459BSQ	OEM
D5459BSQ-1	OEM
D5459BSQZS	OEM
D5459BSQZS-1	OEM
D5459BST	OEM
D5459BST-1	OEM
D5459BSTZS	OEM
D5459BSTZS-1	OEM
D5459BSZS	OEM
D5459BSZS-1	OEM
D5495BS	OEM
D5495BS-1	OEM
D5495BSM	OEM
D5495BSM-1	OEM
D5495BSMZS	OEM
D5495BSMZS-1	OEM
D5503	OEM
D5503A	OEM
D5503B	OEM
D5503C	OEM
D5506A	OEM
D5506B	OEM
D5506C	OEM
D5507	OEM
D5507A	OEM
D5507B	OEM
D5507C	OEM
D5509	OEM
D5509A	OEM
D5509B	OEM
D5509C	OEM
D5509D	OEM
D5520	OEM
D5520A	OEM
D5520B	OEM
D5521	OEM
D5521A	OEM
D5521B	OEM
D5522	OEM
D5522A	OEM
D5522B	OEM
D5523	OEM
D5523A	OEM
D5523B	OEM
D5540	OEM
D5560	OEM
D5560A	OEM
D5560B	OEM
D5561	OEM
D5561A	OEM
D5561B	OEM
D5562	OEM
D5562A	OEM
D5562B	OEM
D5563	OEM
D5563A	OEM
D5563B	OEM
D5564	OEM
D5564A	OEM
D5564B	OEM
D5565	OEM
D5565A	OEM
D5565B	OEM
D5570	OEM
D5570A	OEM
D5570B	OEM
D5571	OEM
D5571A	OEM
D5571B	OEM
D5572	OEM
D5572A	OEM
D5572B	OEM
D5573	OEM
D5573A	OEM
D5573B	OEM
D5574	OEM
D5574A	OEM
D5574B	OEM
D5575	OEM
D5575A	OEM
D5575B	OEM
D5600	OEM
D5600A	OEM
D5610	OEM
D5611	OEM
D5612	OEM
D5615H	OEM
D5616H	OEM
D5621G	OEM
D5621H	OEM
D5623G	OEM
D5623H	OEM
D5632	OEM
D5632A	OEM
D5632AM	OEM
D5632M	OEM
D5632MR	OEM
D5634	OEM
D5638	OEM
D5650A	OEM
D5650B	OEM
D5650C	OEM
D5650D	OEM
D5650E	OEM
D5668A	OEM
D5668B	OEM
D5668C	OEM
D5668D	OEM
D5668E	OEM
D5669A	OEM
D5669B	OEM
D5669C	OEM
D5669D	OEM
D5669E	OEM
D5690B	OEM
D5720	OEM
D5720A	OEM
D5720B	OEM
D5721	OEM
D5722	OEM
D5723	OEM
D5723A	OEM
D5723B	OEM
D5733	OEM
D5754	OEM
D5754A	OEM
D5760A	OEM
D5760B	OEM
D5760C	OEM
D5760D	OEM
D5761A	OEM
D5761B	OEM
D5761C	OEM
D5761D	OEM
D5762A	OEM
D5762B	OEM
D5762C	OEM
D5762D	OEM
D5763A	OEM
D5763B	OEM
D5763C	OEM
D5763D	OEM
D5807A	OEM
D5807B	OEM
D5807C	OEM
D5807D	OEM
D5807E	OEM
D5817	OEM
D5817A	OEM
D5818	OEM
D5818A	OEM
D5820	OEM
D5820A	OEM
D5820B	OEM
D5820C	OEM
D5821	OEM
D5821A	OEM
D5821B	OEM
D5821C	OEM
D5822	OEM
D5822A	OEM
D5822B	OEM
D5822C	OEM
D5823	OEM

If replacement code is OEM, contact original manufacturer for replacement.

DEVICE TYPE	REPL CODE
D5823A	OEM
D5823B	OEM
D5823C	OEM
D5824	OEM
D5824A	OEM
D5824B	OEM
D5824C	OEM
D5825A	OEM
D5825B	OEM
D5825C	OEM
D5826	OEM
D5826A	OEM
D5826B	OEM
D5826C	OEM
D5827	OEM
D5827A	OEM
D5828	OEM
D5828A	OEM
D5829	OEM
D5829A	OEM
D5840	OEM
D5840A	OEM
D5840B	OEM
D5840C	OEM
D5840E	OEM
D5841	OEM
D5841A	OEM
D5842	OEM
D5842A	OEM
D5843	OEM
D5843A	OEM
D5844	OEM
D5844A	OEM
D5845	OEM
D5845A	OEM
D5846	OEM
D5846A	OEM
D5847	OEM
D5847A	OEM
D5848	OEM
D5848A	OEM
D5855	OEM
D5880C	OEM
D5890A	OEM
D5890B	OEM
D5890C	OEM
D5890D	OEM
D5890E	OEM
D5905A	OEM
D5905B	OEM
D5905C	OEM
D5905D	OEM
D5910	OEM
D5910A	OEM
D5910B	OEM
D5910C	OEM
D5940	OEM
D5940A	OEM
D5940B	OEM
D5940C	OEM
D5940D	OEM
D5940E	OEM
D5940F	OEM
D5940G	OEM
D5940H	OEM
D5940J	OEM
D5950	OEM
D5950A	OEM
D5950B	OEM
D5950C	OEM
D5950D	OEM
D5950E	OEM
D5950F	OEM
D5950G	OEM
D5950H	OEM
D5950J	OEM
D5964A	OEM
D5964B	OEM
D5964C	OEM
D5964D	OEM
D5964E	OEM
D5968	OEM
D5968A	OEM
D5968B	OEM
D5968C	OEM
D5968D	OEM
D5968E	OEM
D5968F	OEM
D5982A	OEM
D5982B	OEM
D5982C	OEM
D5982D	OEM
D5982E	OEM
D5994A	OEM
D5994B	OEM
D5994C	OEM
D5994D	OEM
D5994E	OEM
D6015L	3785
D6020L	3785
D6035J	OEM
D6035W	OEM
D6050J	OEM
D6055W	OEM
D6065J	OEM
D6070W	OEM
D6104C	OEM
D6104C001	OEM
D6105C	OEM

DEVICE TYPE	REPL CODE
D6105C(UPD6105C)	OEM
D6105C02	OEM
D6117C	OEM
D6121G001	OEM
D6124CA-612	OEM
D6125A-712	OEM
D6140C001	OEM
D6145C	OEM
D6145C-001	OEM
D6325C	1869
D6326C	OEM
D6330	OEM
D6330A	OEM
D6330B	OEM
D6330C	OEM
D6330D	OEM
D6331	OEM
D6331A	OEM
D6331B	OEM
D6331C	OEM
D6331D	OEM
D6332	OEM
D6332A	OEM
D6332B	OEM
D6332C	OEM
D6332D	OEM
D6333	OEM
D6333A	OEM
D6333B	OEM
D6333C	OEM
D6333D	OEM
D6334	OEM
D6334A	OEM
D6334B	OEM
D6334C	OEM
D6334D	OEM
D6335	OEM
D6335A	OEM
D6335B	OEM
D6335C	OEM
D6335D	OEM
D6336	OEM
D6336A	OEM
D6336B	OEM
D6336C	OEM
D6336D	OEM
D6337	OEM
D6337A	OEM
D6337B	OEM
D6337C	OEM
D6337D	OEM
D6338	OEM
D6338A	OEM
D6338B	OEM
D6338C	OEM
D6338D	OEM
D6462	0133
D6599	OEM
D6623	0015
D6623A	0015
D6624	0015
D6624A	0015
D6625	0015
D6625A	0015
D6645	OEM
D6701	OEM
D6718	OEM
D6719	OEM
D6721	OEM
D6722	OEM
D6726	0133
D6743	OEM
D6900	OEM
D6901	OEM
D6901G	OEM
D6902	OEM
D6903	OEM
D6904	OEM
D6905	OEM
D6906	OEM
D6907	OEM
D6908	OEM
D6909	OEM
D6910	OEM
D6911	OEM
D7132	OEM
D7201C	OEM
D7220D-1	OEM
D7486J	1358
D7503G-186	OEM
D7507CU-246	OEM
D7516AGF558	OEM
D7519HG-555	OEM
D7537AC-026	OEM
D7585BS	OEM
D7585BS-1	OEM
D7585BSM	OEM
D7585BSM-1	OEM
D7585BSMZS	OEM
D7585BSMZS-1	OEM
D7585BSQ	OEM
D7585BSQ-1	OEM
D7585BSQZS	OEM
D7585BSQZS-1	OEM
D7585BST	OEM
D7585BST-1	OEM
D7585BSTZS	OEM
D7585BSTZS-1	OEM
D7585BSZS	OEM

DEVICE TYPE	REPL CODE
D7585BSZS-1	OEM
D7800G	OEM
D7801G-176	OEM
D7810HCW	OEM
D7810HG	OEM
D7811G	OEM
D8015L	OEM
D8020H	OEM
D8020L	OEM
D8021	OEM
D8021H	OEM
D8022	OEM
D8031	OEM
D8035	OEM
D8035HL	OEM
D8035HL-1	OEM
D8035J	OEM
D8035L	OEM
D8035W	OEM
D8039	OEM
D8039-6	OEM
D8039H-8	OEM
D8039HL	OEM
D8039LC	OEM
D8041A	OEM
D8041AC	OEM
D8048	OEM
D8048H-1	OEM
D8048HC	OEM
D8048HC545	OEM
D8048L	OEM
D8049	OEM
D8049H	OEM
D8049HC	OEM
D8049HC-029	OEM
D8050J	OEM
D8051	OEM
D8055W	OEM
D8065J	OEM
D8070W	OEM
D8080A	OEM
D8080A-1	OEM
D8080A-2	OEM
D8085A	OEM
D8085AC	OEM
D8085AC-2	OEM
D8085AH-2	OEM
D8086	OEM
D8086-2	OEM
D8086-4	OEM
D8088	OEM
D8088-2	OEM
D8088D	OEM
D8089	OEM
D8155	OEM
D8155-2	OEM
D8155C	OEM
D8155H	OEM
D8156	OEM
D8156-2	OEM
D8185	OEM
D8185-2	OEM
D8202	OEM
D8205	OEM
D8212	OEM
D8216	OEM
D8218	OEM
D8219	OEM
D8224	OEM
D8226	OEM
D8228	OEM
D8231	OEM
D8232	OEM
D8237	OEM
D8237-2	OEM
D8237A-5	OEM
D8237AC-5	OEM
D8237AS	OEM
D8238	OEM
D8243	OEM
D8251A	OEM
D8251AC	OEM
D8251AFC	OEM
D8253	OEM
D8253-5	OEM
D8253C-2	OEM
D8253C-5	OEM
D8253C5	OEM
D8255A	OEM
D8255A-5	0051
D8255AC-2	0051
D8255AC-5	0051
D8257	OEM
D8257-5	OEM
D8259A	OEM
D8259A-2	OEM
D8259A-8	OEM
D8259AC	OEM
D8259AC-2	OEM
D8271-6	OEM
D8271-8	OEM
D8272	OEM
D8273	OEM
D8273-	OEM
D8273-8	OEM
D8275	OEM
D8279	OEM
D8279-5	OEM
D8282	OEM

DEVICE TYPE	REPL CODE
D8283	OEM
D8284	OEM
D8284A	OEM
D8286	OEM
D8287	OEM
D8288	OEM
D8289	OEM
D8291	OEM
D8292	OEM
D8293	OEM
D8295	OEM
D8355	OEM
D8355-2	OEM
D8410	0143
D8596BS	OEM
D8596BS-1	OEM
D8596BSM	OEM
D8596BSM-1	OEM
D8596BSMZS	OEM
D8596BSMZS-1	OEM
D8596BSQ	OEM
D8596BSQ-1	OEM
D8596BSQZS	OEM
D8596BSQZS-1	OEM
D8596BST	OEM
D8596BST-1	OEM
D8596BSTZS	OEM
D8596BSTZS-1	OEM
D8596BSZS	OEM
D8596BSZS-1	OEM
D8641A	OEM
D8741A	OEM
D8742	OEM
D8748	OEM
D8748-6	OEM
D8748HD	OEM
D8749H	OEM
D8749H-8	OEM
D8749HC	OEM
D8751	OEM
D8755A	OEM
D8755A-2	OEM
D9011	OEM
D9011A	OEM
D9011B	OEM
D9011C	OEM
D9011D	OEM
D9011E	OEM
D9012	OEM
D9012A	OEM
D9012B	OEM
D9012C	OEM
D9012D	OEM
D9012E	OEM
D9013	OEM
D9013A	OEM
D9013B	OEM
D9013C	OEM
D9013D	OEM
D9013E	OEM
D9014	OEM
D9014A	OEM
D9014B	OEM
D9014C	OEM
D9014D	OEM
D9014E	OEM
D9634	0111
D10167	0015
D10168	0015
D10611DM	OEM
D20000BB40	0102
D21489	0015
D22400C#	0315
D22800C#	0045
D23128EC	OEM
D24000V09G	0023
D27128	1628
D27128A	1628
D27128A-3	1628
D27128A20	1628
D27128D	1628
D27128D-2	OEM
D27128D-482US	OEM
D27256	OEM
D27256-1	OEM
D27256-2	OEM
D27256-25	OEM
D27256-XX	OEM
D27256AD-2	OEM
D27256D	OEM
D27256J-2	OEM
D27512	OEM
D27512J	OEM
D27512J-1	OEM
D27512J-2	OEM
D28000BB40	0023
D28010ELS6	0023
D33400C#	0315
D33800C#	0045
D41256C	OEM
D41256C-12	OEM
D41256C-15	OEM
D41264C-12	OEM
D41264C-15	OEM
D41416C-15	OEM
D41464C-15	OEM
D42272AGF	OEM
D42832C-12L	OEM
D42832C-15L	OEM

DEVICE TYPE	REPL CODE
D60400C#	2786
D60800C#	2818
D65006CW015	OEM
D65006CW-LC	OEM
D65006CW-LC2	OEM
D65006CW-LCII	OEM
D65006CW-NL	OEM
D65013GF216	OEM
D65022GF116	OEM
D71054GB	OEM
D75104G-576	OEM
D75104GF-752	OEM
D75108GF-720	OEM
D75116CW-091	OEM
D75208CW-058	OEM
D75208CW-069	OEM
D75208CW-287	OEM
D75216ACW095	OEM
D75216AGF558	OEM
D75216AGF568	OEM
D75216AGF609	OEM
D75516GF-019	OEM
D75516GF-025	OEM
D75516GF-045	OEM
D82284-6	OEM
D82288-6	OEM
D82871	OEM
D92004R7B0	0140
D92004R7B1	0140
D92005R1B0	0041
D92007R5B0	0077
D92007R5B1	0077
D92013R6B0	0372
D93004R70X	0140
D93004R70Z	0041
D93005R10X	0041
D93005R600	0253
D93006R80Y	0062
D93007R50Y	0077
D93019R11B	0012
D97006R20B	0466
D101167	0015
D118441-JH00	OEM
D118441-LE00	OEM
D118441-LH00	OEM
D118442-JH00	OEM
D118442-LE00	OEM
D118442-LH00	OEM
D118443-JH00	OEM
D118443-LE00	OEM
D118443-LH00	OEM
D118444-JH00	OEM
D118444-LE00	OEM
D118444-LH00	OEM
D118445-JH00	OEM
D118445-LE00	OEM
D118445-LH00	OEM
D118446-JH00	OEM
D118446-LE00	OEM
D118446-LH00	OEM
D118447-JH00	OEM
D118447-LE00	OEM
D118447-LH00	OEM
D118448-JH00	OEM
D118448-LE00	OEM
D118448-LH00	OEM
D118449-JH00	OEM
D118449-LE00	OEM
D118449-LH00	OEM
D118450-JH00	OEM
D118450-LE00	OEM
D118450-LH00	OEM
D118451-JH00	OEM
D118451-LE00	OEM
D118451-LH00	OEM
D118452-JH00	OEM
D118452-LE00	OEM
D118452-LH00	OEM
D118453-JH00	OEM
D118453-LE00	OEM
D118453-LH00	OEM
D118454-JH00	OEM
D118454-LE00	OEM
D118454-LH00	OEM
D118455-JH00	OEM
D118455-LE00	OEM
D118455-LH00	OEM
D120400C#	1975
D120800C#	0652
D150400C#	1975
D150800C#	0652
D230130TAL	0015
D240200B#	1017
D240400B#	1030
D240600B#	1030
D240700B#	1040
D280010D10	0015
D280010D40	0071
D481111	OEM
D484242-2	OEM
D756012	OEM
D919695	3384
D919698	3808
D919699	3781
D919700	3669
D6400023GB	1914
D9200110B0	0181
D9200110B2	0181
D9200110B3	0181

DEVICE TYPE	REPL CODE
D9200120B1	0052
D9200180B0	0371
D9200300B4	0195
D34002410-001	1063
D34013890-002	1896
D92015600B	0863
D93001000Y	0064
D93001100Y	0181
D93001200X	0052
D93001200Y	0999
D93001300Y	0053
D93001300Z	0053
D93001600Y	0440
D93002700X	0450
D93002700Y	0450
D93003000Y	0195
D93011201B	0137
D93011801B	0490
D93012701C	1664
D93013001B	0721
D170001310	0124
D920011082	0181
D930013000	0053
DA000	0015
DA001	0015
DA002	0015
DA058	0071
DA0601	OEM
DA0602	OEM
DA0D	OEM
DA1Z-8	OEM
DA1.5/200	0087
DA1.5/400	0087
DA1.5/600	0087
DA1.5/800	0087
DA1.5/1000	0087
DA3	OEM
DA3/200	0087
DA3/400	0087
DA3/600	0087
DA3/800	0087
DA3/1000	0087
DA3F3	0432
DA-3N	OEM
DA-3P	OEM
DA4	OEM
DA4/600	OEM
DA4/800	OEM
DA-4N	OEM
DA4N	OEM
DA-4P	OEM
DA4P	OEM
DA6/400	OEM
DA6/800	OEM
DA6/1200	OEM
DA6/1400	OEM
DA6/1600	OEM
DA6-1100	OEM
DA6-1400	OEM
DA6-1600	OEM
DA-6NC	OEM
DA-6PC	OEM
DA-8N	OEM
DA8N	OEM
DA-8P	OEM
DA8P	OEM
DA90	0143
DA90M	OEM
DA101	0124
DA101A	0124
DA101B	0124
DA101G	OEM
DA101GR	OEM
DA101N	OEM
DA102	0124
DA102A	0124
DA102B	0124
DA103	OEM
DA106	OEM
DA106K	OEM
DA203	1083
DA-203X	1083
DA203X	OEM
DA-203Y	1083
DA203Y	OEM
DA204	OEM
DA204K	OEM
DA-204X	1083
DA204X	OEM
DA-204Y	1083
DA204Y	OEM
DA205	0133
DA210S	OEM
DA402	OEM
DA711	OEM
DA716	OEM
DA776	OEM
DA777	OEM
DA778	OEM
DA1000	0080
DA1001	0015
DA1002	0015
DA1006	0015
DA1058	0071
DA1200CN	OEM
DA1201CN	OEM
DA1202CN	OEM
DA1203CN	OEM
DA1600	OEM

DEVICE TYPE	REPL CODE
DA1701	0102
DA1702	0102
DA1703	0914
DA1704	0914
DA2000	OEM
DA2010	OEM
DA2020	OEM
DA2068	0071
DA2080	OEM
DA2100	OEM
DA2100V1	OEM
DA2110	OEM
DA2110V1	OEM
DA2120	OEM
DA2120V1	OEM
DA2500	OEM
DAAY001002	0123
DAAY002001	0015
DAAY003002	0133
DAAY004001	0133
DAAY010092	0012
DAAY032001	OEM
DAC01AY	OEM
DAC01BY	OEM
DAC01CY	OEM
DAC01DY	OEM
DAC01FY	OEM
DAC01G	OEM
DAC01GR	OEM
DAC01HY	OEM
DAC01N	OEM
DAC01Y	OEM
DAC02ACX	OEM
DAC02BCX	OEM
DAC02CCX	OEM
DAC02DDX	OEM
DAC02GR	OEM
DAC02N	OEM
DAC03ADX1	OEM
DAC03BDX1	OEM
DAC03CDX1	OEM
DAC03DDX1	OEM
DAC04BCX	OEM
DAC04CCX	OEM
DAC04DDX	OEM
DAC04G	OEM
DAC04GR	OEM
DAC04GT	OEM
DAC04N	OEM
DAC04NT	OEM
DAC05AX	OEM
DAC05BX	OEM
DAC05CX	OEM
DAC05EX	OEM
DAC05FX	OEM
DAC05GX	OEM
DAC06BX	OEM
DAC06CX	OEM
DAC06EX	OEM
DAC06FX	OEM
DAC06GX	OEM
DAC-08ADM	OEM
DAC-08ADM/883B	OEM
DAC08AF	OEM
DAC-08AQ	OEM
DAC08AQ	OEM
DAC-08BC	OEM
DAC-08BM	OEM
DAC-08CDC	OEM
DAC-08CDM	OEM
DAC08CF	OEM
DAC08CN	OEM
DAC-08CP	OEM
DAC08CP	OEM
DAC-08CQ	OEM
DAC08CQ	OEM
DAC-08DM	OEM
DAC-08DM/883B	OEM
DAC08ED	OEM
DAC-08EDC	OEM
DAC-08EDM	OEM
DAC08EN	OEM
DAC-08EP	OEM
DAC08EP	OEM
DAC-08EQ	OEM
DAC08EY	OEM
DAC08F	OEM
DAC08G	OEM
DAC08GR	OEM
DAC08GT	OEM
DAC-08HDC	OEM
DAC-08HDM	OEM
DAC08HF	OEM
DAC08HN	OEM
DAC-08HP	OEM
DAC08HP	OEM
DAC-08HQ	OEM
DAC08HQ	OEM
DAC08N	OEM
DAC08NT	OEM
DAC08Q	OEM
DAC0800LAJ	OEM
DAC0800LCJ	OEM
DAC0800LCN	OEM
DAC0800LD	OEM
DAC0800LJ	OEM
DAC0801LCJ	OEM
DAC0801LCN	OEM
DAC0802LCJ	OEM

If replacement code is OEM, contact original manufacturer for replacement.

DEVICE TYPE	REPL CODE
DAC0802LCN	OEM
DAC0802LD	OEM
DAC0806LCJ	OEM
DAC0806LCN	5217
DAC0807LCJ	OEM
DAC0807LCN	5217
DAC0808LCJ	OEM
DAC0808LCN	OEM
DAC0808LD	OEM
DAC0808LJ	OEM
DAC0830LCD	OEM
DAC0830LCN	OEM
DAC0830LD	OEM
DAC0831LCD	OEM
DAC0831LCN	OEM
DAC0831LD	OEM
DAC0832LCD	OEM
DAC0832LCN	OEM
DAC0832LD	OEM
DAC02701-102	OEM
DAC02701-103	OEM
DAC02701-112(M)	OEM
DAC02701-113(M)	OEM
DAC02701-202	OEM
DAC02701-203	OEM
DAC02701-212(M)	OEM
DAC02701-213(M)	OEM
DAC1	OEM
DAC2	OEM
DAC3	OEM
DAC-10BDM	OEM
DAC-10BDM/883B	OEM
DAC10BX	OEM
DAC-10CDM	OEM
DAC-10CDM/883B	OEM
DAC10CX	OEM
DAC-10FDC	OEM
DAC10FX	OEM
DAC10G	OEM
DAC-10GDC	OEM
DAC10GX	OEM
DAC10HT	OEM
DAC10HT-1	OEM
DAC10N	OEM
DAC11	OEM
DAC12	OEM
DAC12AV	OEM
DAC12BV	OEM
DAC12EV	OEM
DAC12FV	OEM
DAC12GV	OEM
DAC20CP	OEM
DAC20CQ	OEM
DAC20EP	OEM
DAC20EQ	OEM
DAC20G	OEM
DAC20N	OEM
DAC76CX	OEM
DAC76DX	OEM
DAC76EX	OEM
DAC76G	OEM
DAC76N	OEM
DAC76X	OEM
DAC86CX	OEM
DAC86EX	OEM
DAC87CX	OEM
DAC87EX	OEM
DAC88CX	OEM
DAC88EX	OEM
DAC89CX	OEM
DAC89EX	OEM
DAC90BG	OEM
DAC90BGQ(M)	OEM
DAC90SG	OEM
DAC90SGQ(M)	OEM
DAC100AAQ7	OEM
DAC100AAQ8	OEM
DAC100ABQ7	OEM
DAC100ABQ8	OEM
DAC100ACQ3	OEM
DAC100ACQ4	OEM
DAC100ACQ5	OEM
DAC100ACQ6	OEM
DAC100ACQ7	OEM
DAC100ACQ8	OEM
DAC100BBQ5	OEM
DAC100BBQ6	OEM
DAC100BBQ7	OEM
DAC100BBQ8	OEM
DAC100BCQ3	OEM
DAC100BCQ4	OEM
DAC100BCQ5	OEM
DAC100BCQ6	OEM
DAC100BCQ7	OEM
DAC100BCQ8	OEM
DAC100CCQ3	OEM
DAC100CCQ4	OEM
DAC100CCQ5	OEM
DAC100CCQ6	OEM
DAC100CCQ7	OEM
DAC100CCQ8	OEM
DAC100DDQ3	OEM
DAC100DDQ4	OEM
DAC100DDQ7	OEM
DAC100DDQ8	OEM
DAC101EQ	OEM
DAC101FQ	OEM
DAC101GQ	OEM
DAC206AY	OEM
DAC206BY	OEM
DAC206EY	OEM
DAC206FY	OEM
DAC206G	OEM
DAC206N	OEM
DAC208AX	OEM
DAC208BX	OEM
DAC208EX	OEM
DAC208FX	OEM
DAC210ASX	OEM
DAC210AX	OEM
DAC210BSX	OEM
DAC210BX	OEM
DAC210ESX	OEM
DAC210EX	OEM
DAC210FSX	OEM
DAC210FX	OEM
DAC210G	OEM
DAC210GR	OEM
DAC210GX	OEM
DAC210N	OEM
DAC230/E-6	OEM
DAC-230-200	OEM
DAC-230-300	OEM
DAC331B-14-1	OEM
DAC331B-14-2	OEM
DAC331C-14-1	OEM
DAC331C-14-2	OEM
DAC562C	OEM
DAC562M	OEM
DAC-681C	OEM
DAC-681M	OEM
DAC685V-BC	OEM
DAC685V-BR	OEM
DAC685V-DC	OEM
DAC685V-DR	OEM
DAC687I-BM	OEM
DAC687I-DM	OEM
DAC736K	OEM
DAC800CBI-I	OEM
DAC800CBI-V	OEM
DAC808A	OEM
DAC808AX	OEM
DAC808BX	OEM
DAC808EX	OEM
DAC808FX	OEM
DAC808G	OEM
DAC808GR	OEM
DAC808GX	OEM
DAC808N	OEM
DAC850CBI-I	OEM
DAC850CBI-V	OEM
DAC851CBI-I	OEM
DAC851CBI-V	OEM
DAC888AX	OEM
DAC888BX	OEM
DAC888EX	OEM
DAC888FX	OEM
DAC888G	OEM
DAC888N	OEM
DAC1000LCD	OEM
DAC1000LCN	OEM
DAC1000LD	OEM
DAC1001LCD	OEM
DAC1001LCN	OEM
DAC1001LD	OEM
DAC1002LCD	OEM
DAC1002LCN	OEM
DAC1002LD	OEM
DAC1003LCD	OEM
DAC1003LCN	OEM
DAC1003LD	OEM
DAC1004LCD	OEM
DAC1004LCN	OEM
DAC1004LD	OEM
DAC1005LCD	OEM
DAC1005LCN	OEM
DAC1005LD	OEM
DAC1006LCD	OEM
DAC1006LCN	OEM
DAC1006LD	OEM
DAC1007LCD	OEM
DAC1007LCN	OEM
DAC1007LD	OEM
DAC1008LCD	OEM
DAC1008LCN	OEM
DAC1008LD	OEM
DAC1010LD	OEM
DAC1020LCD	OEM
DAC1021LCD	OEM
DAC1021LD	OEM
DAC1022LCD	OEM
DAC1022LD	OEM
DAC1200HCD	OEM
DAC1200HD	OEM
DAC1201HCD	OEM
DAC1201HD	OEM
DAC1202HCD	OEM
DAC1202HD	OEM
DAC1203HCD	OEM
DAC1203HD	OEM
DAC1208LCD	OEM
DAC1209LCD	OEM
DAC1210LCD	OEM
DAC1218LD	OEM
DAC1219LD	OEM
DAC1220LCD	OEM
DAC1220LD	OEM
DAC1221LCD	OEM
DAC1221LD	OEM
DAC1222LCD	OEM
DAC1222LD	OEM
DAC1230LCD	OEM
DAC1231LCD	OEM
DAC1232LCD	OEM
DAC1280A	OEM
DAC1280ACD	OEM
DAC1280HCD	OEM
DAC1285ACD	OEM
DAC1285AD	OEM
DAC1285HCD	OEM
DAC1285HD	OEM
DAC1286HCD	OEM
DAC1286HD	OEM
DAC1287HCD	OEM
DAC1408A6P	OEM
DAC1408A6Q	OEM
DAC1408A7P	OEM
DAC1408A7Q	OEM
DAC1408A8P	OEM
DAC1408A8Q	OEM
DAC1408AG	OEM
DAC1408G	OEM
DAC1508ABQ	OEM
DAC-4565DDC	OEM
DAC-4565JDC	OEM
DAC-4565SDM	OEM
DAC-4565SDM/883B	OEM
DAC-4881B	OEM
DAC-4881B/883B	OEM
DAC-4881D	OEM
DAC-4881F	OEM
DAC-6012ADC	OEM
DAC-6012ADM	OEM
DAC-6012DC	OEM
DAC-6012DM/883B	OEM
DAC6851-BC	OEM
DAC6851-BR	OEM
DAC6851-DC	OEM
DAC6851-DR	OEM
DAC7520C	OEM
DAC7520M	OEM
DAC7520R	OEM
DAC7521C	OEM
DAC7521M	OEM
DAC7521R	OEM
DAC7523C	OEM
DAC7523M	OEM
DAC7523R	OEM
DAC7533C	OEM
DAC7533M	OEM
DAC7533R	OEM
DAC7541C	OEM
DAC7541M	OEM
DAC7541R	OEM
DAC-HA10BC	OEM
DAC-HA10BC1	OEM
DAC-HA10BM	OEM
DAC-HA10BM1	OEM
DAC-HA10BR	OEM
DAC-HA10BR1	OEM
DAC-HA12BC	OEM
DAC-HA12BC1	OEM
DAC-HA12BM	OEM
DAC-HA12BM1	OEM
DAC-HA12BR	OEM
DAC-HA12BR1	OEM
DAC-HA12DC	OEM
DAC-HA12DC1	OEM
DAC-HA12DM	OEM
DAC-HA12DM1	OEM
DAC-HA12DR	OEM
DAC-HA12DR1	OEM
DAC-HA14BC	OEM
DAC-HA14BC1	OEM
DAC-HA14BM	OEM
DAC-HA14BM1	OEM
DAC-HA14BR	OEM
DAC-HA14BR1	OEM
DAC-IC8BC	OEM
DAC-IC8BM	OEM
DAC-IC10B	OEM
DAC-IC10BC	OEM
DAC-IC10BM	OEM
DAC-UP8BC	OEM
DAC-UP8BM	OEM
DAD02G	OEM
DAG1A05	0031
DAG1A1	0031
DAG1A2	0031
DAG1A3	0031
DAG1A4	0031
DAJ201	0689
DAN-4	OEM
DAN-4A	OEM
DAN-4B	OEM
DAN-10	OEM
DAN-110	OEM
DAN-201	OEM
DAN201	3460
DAN201K	OEM
DAN201V	3460
DAN201VA	3460
DAN201W	0196
DAN201X	3460
DAN202	0901
DAN202K	0901
DAN202K-N	OEM
DAN202KVA	0901
DAN202VA	0901
DAN202VAK	OEM
DAN205	OEM
DAN206	OEM
DAN207-100	4640
DAN207-200	4640
DAN207-400	4640
DAN-208	OEM
DAN208	OEM
DAN208-100	1791
DAN208-200	0199
DAN209	3163
DAN209S	3163
DAN211	1791
DAN217	OEM
DAN217-T147	OEM
DAN235K	OEM
DAN401	OEM
DAN401VA	OEM
DAN403	OEM
DAN404	OEM
DAN601	OEM
DAN601VA	OEM
DAN801	OEM
DAN801VA	OEM
DAN802	OEM
DAN802VA	OEM
DANZ00600	0143
DANZ006000	0019
DANZ0060000	0143
DAP-4	0392
DAP-4A	0392
DAP-4B	0392
DAP-10	0392
DAP-110	0392
DAP201	2189
DAP201N	3840
DAP201VA	0689
DAP202	0897
DAP202K	0897
DAP202K-T96	OEM
DAP202KVA	OEM
DAP202VA	OEM
DAP202VAK	OEM
DAP204K	OEM
DAP207-100	4701
DAP207-200	4701
DAP207-400	4701
DAP208	OEM
DAP208-100	1089
DAP208-200	1009
DAP209	3840
DAP209S	3840
DAP211	1089
DAP401	OEM
DAP401VA	OEM
DAP404	OEM
DAP601	3098
DAP601VA	OEM
DAP801	OEM
DAP801VA	OEM
DAP802	OEM
DAP802VA	OEM
DAR01G	OEM
DAR01GR	OEM
DAR01N	OEM
DAS-250A	OEM
DAS-250B	OEM
DAS400	OEM
DAS-952R	OEM
DASZ158800	0133
DAT1	OEM
DAT1A	0136
DAT2	0136
DB/65	OEM
DB08	OEM
DB1A	6232
DB1B	OEM
DB1D	6232
DB1F	6232
DB1M	3503
DB1N	3503
DB1P	3503
DB3	5289
DB4	5290
DB6	5291
DB7T2MR150	OEM
DB16	OEM
DB101	0241
DB101G	0241
DB102	0241
DB102G	0241
DB103	0241
DB103G	0241
DB104	4501
DB104BSXXXX	OEM
DB104G	4501
DB105	1864
DB105DXXXX	OEM
DB105G	1864
DB106	3503
DB106G	3503
DB107	3503
DB107G	3503
DB110DSXXXX	OEM
DB112BSXXXX	OEM
DB202	0015
DB204	0790
DB204BSXXXX	OEM
DB206	0015
DB208	0072
DB210	0071
DB212	0102
DB212BSXXXX	OEM
DB510DSXXXX	OEM
DB600T	OEM
DB600W	OEM
DB601T	OEM
DB601W	OEM
DB602T	OEM
DB602W	OEM
DB604T	OEM
DB604W	OEM
DB606T	OEM
DB606W	OEM
DB608T	OEM
DB608W	OEM
DB610T	OEM
DB610W	OEM
DB711BSXXXX	OEM
DB776	OEM
DB777	OEM
DB778	OEM
DB800T	OEM
DB800W	OEM
DB801T	OEM
DB801W	OEM
DB802T	OEM
DB802W	OEM
DB804T	OEM
DB804W	OEM
DB806T	OEM
DB806W	OEM
DB808T	OEM
DB808W	OEM
DB810T	OEM
DB810W	OEM
DB812BSXXXX	OEM
DB816BSXXXX	OEM
DB826	OEM
DB1200T	OEM
DB1200W	OEM
DB1201T	OEM
DB1201W	OEM
DB1202T	OEM
DB1202W	OEM
DB1204T	OEM
DB1204W	OEM
DB1206T	OEM
DB1206W	OEM
DB1208T	OEM
DB1208W	OEM
DB1210T	OEM
DB1210W	OEM
DB1500T	OEM
DB1500W	OEM
DB1501T	OEM
DB1501W	OEM
DB1502T	OEM
DB1502W	OEM
DB1504T	OEM
DB1504W	OEM
DB1506T	OEM
DB1506W	OEM
DB1508T	OEM
DB1508W	OEM
DB1510T	OEM
DB1510W	OEM
DB1724BSXXXX	OEM
DB2500T	OEM
DB2500W	OEM
DB2501T	OEM
DB2501W	OEM
DB2502T	OEM
DB2502W	OEM
DB2504T	OEM
DB2504W	OEM
DB2506T	OEM
DB2506W	OEM
DB2508T	OEM
DB2508W	OEM
DB2510T	OEM
DB2510W	OEM
DB3500T	OEM
DB3500W	OEM
DB3501T	OEM
DB3501W	OEM
DB3502T	OEM
DB3502W	OEM
DB3504T	OEM
DB3504W	OEM
DB3506T	OEM
DB3506W	OEM
DB3508T	OEM
DB3508W	OEM
DB3510T	OEM
DB3510W	OEM
DB5459BSXXXX	OEM
DB8596BSXXXX	OEM
DBA10B	0276
DBA10C	0287
DBA10E	0293
DBA10G	0299
DBA20B	0319
DBA20C	1404
DBA20CK15	OEM
DBA20E	0468
DBA30B	0319
DBA30C	1404
DBA30CK12	OEM
DBA30E	0468
DBA30G	0441
DBA40B	0319
DBA40C	1404
DBA40E	0468
DBA60B	1404
DBA60C	0468
DBA60E	0468
DBA100B	0319
DBA100C	1404
DBA100E	0468
DBA408BSXXXX	OEM
DBAZ073304	0527
DBB10	OEM
DBB10B	1864
DBB10C	1864
DBB10E	1864
DBB10G	1864
DBBY001003	0617
DBBY003001	0219
DBBY003002	0219
DBBY005001	0930
DBBY407004	0419
DBC1	OEM
DBC2	OEM
DBC3	OEM
DBC4	OEM
DBC5	OEM
DBC6	OEM
DBC7	OEM
DBC8	OEM
DBC9	OEM
DBCZ037300	0111
DBCZ039404	0224
DBCZ073304	0111
DBCZ073503	0155
DBCZ073504	0191
DBCZ083905	0076
DBCZ083906	0016
DBCZ094504	0111
DBCZ0373000	1293
DBCZ101800	2039
DBCZ136406	0016
DBCZ176003	1935
DBCZ373000	0111
DBF60B	1034
DBL45-12	OEM
DBL60-12	OEM
DBL567	OEM
DBX72L	OEM
DBX158L	OEM
DBX158M	OEM
DBX167L	OEM
DBX167M	OEM
DBX184LS	OEM
DBX184MX	OEM
DBX185L	OEM
DBX185M	OEM
DBXAN6291	3403
DC	1791
DC3B24	OEM
DC3B28	OEM
DC3B29	OEM
DC5R4	OEM
DC5U4	OEM
DC5V4	OEM
DC5Y3	OEM
DC5Z3	OEM
DC5Z4	OEM
DC6AX5	OEM
DC6X4	OEM
DC7	OEM
DC7A	OEM
DC7B	OEM
DC7C	OEM
DC7D	OEM
DC-9	0004
DC-10	0004
DC10.5	OEM
DC-12	0164
DC-13	0143
DC14V	OEM
DC25Z6	OEM
DC28V	OEM
DC42V	OEM
DC56V	OEM
DC80	OEM
DC95A2	OEM
DC101	OEM
DC102	OEM
DC104	OEM
DC106	OEM
DC108	OEM
DC110	OEM
DC165A2	OEM
DC169A2	OEM
DC169A2A	OEM
DC205A2	OEM
DC209A2	OEM
DC209B2	OEM
DC209B2A	OEM
DC250R	OEM
DC269A2	OEM
DC300.5	OEM
DC301	OEM
DC302	OEM
DC304	OEM
DC306	OEM
DC308	OEM
DC310	OEM
DC326A2	OEM
DC329A2	OEM
DC371A	OEM
DC405A2	OEM
DC406A2	OEM
DC442	OEM
DC575	OEM
DC576	OEM
DC600.5	OEM
DC601	OEM
DC602	OEM
DC604	OEM
DC606	OEM
DC608	OEM
DC610	OEM
DC610A2	OEM
DC673	OEM
DC806A2	OEM
DC809B2	OEM
DC866	OEM
DC872	OEM
DC1015A2	OEM
DC1016	OEM
DC1017	OEM
DC1018	OEM
DC1019	OEM
DC1020	OEM
DC1020A	OEM
DC1022	OEM
DC1028A	OEM
DC1100-01	OEM
DC1100-03	OEM
DC1100-05	OEM
DC1100-10	OEM
DC1100-20	OEM
DC1151	OEM
DC1152	OEM
DC1181G	OEM
DC1181H	OEM
DC1181J	OEM
DC1186F	OEM
DC1186G	OEM
DC1201A	OEM
DC1201B	OEM
DC1201C	OEM
DC1201D	OEM
DC1201E	OEM
DC1201F	OEM
DC1202A	OEM
DC1202B	OEM
DC1202C	OEM
DC1202E	OEM
DC1203A	OEM
DC1203B	OEM
DC1203C	OEM
DC1203D	OEM
DC1203E	OEM
DC1204A	OEM
DC1204B	OEM
DC1204C	OEM
DC1204D	OEM
DC1204E	OEM
DC1205A	OEM
DC1205B	OEM
DC1205C	OEM
DC1205D	OEM
DC1222A	OEM
DC1222B	OEM
DC1222C	OEM
DC1222D	OEM
DC1222E	OEM
DC1231A	OEM
DC1231B	OEM
DC1231C	OEM
DC1231D	OEM
DC1231E	OEM
DC1232A	OEM
DC1232B	OEM
DC1232C	OEM
DC1232D	OEM
DC1232E	OEM
DC1233A	OEM
DC1233B	OEM
DC1233C	OEM
DC1233D	OEM
DC1233E	OEM
DC1234A	OEM
DC1234B	OEM
DC1234C	OEM
DC1234D	OEM
DC1234E	OEM
DC1251F	OEM
DC1251G	OEM
DC1251H	OEM
DC1251J	OEM
DC1252F	OEM
DC1252G	OEM
DC1252H	OEM
DC1253F	OEM
DC1253G	OEM
DC1253H	OEM
DC1254E	OEM
DC1254F	OEM
DC1254G	OEM
DC1255F	OEM

If replacement code is OEM, contact original manufacturer for replacement. 371

DEVICE TYPE	REPL CODE
DC1255G	OEM
DC1255H	OEM
DC1256F	OEM
DC1256G	OEM
DC1272F	OEM
DC1272G	OEM
DC1272H	OEM
DC1281F	OEM
DC1281G	OEM
DC1281H	OEM
DC1281J	OEM
DC1282F	OEM
DC1282G	OEM
DC1282H	OEM
DC1283F	OEM
DC1283G	OEM
DC1283H	OEM
DC1284E	OEM
DC1284F	OEM
DC1284G	OEM
DC1301	OEM
DC1301A	OEM
DC1301C	OEM
DC1302	OEM
DC1302C	OEM
DC1303	OEM
DC1304	OEM
DC1304/3	OEM
DC1304C	OEM
DC1306	OEM
DC1307	OEM
DC1308	OEM
DC1309	OEM
DC1311	OEM
DC1312	OEM
DC1313	OEM
DC1314	OEM
DC1316	OEM
DC1320	OEM
DC1321	OEM
DC1322	OEM
DC1323	OEM
DC1324	OEM
DC1325	OEM
DC1332	OEM
DC1333	OEM
DC1333C	OEM
DC1334	OEM
DC1335	OEM
DC1336	OEM
DC1340	OEM
DC1346	OEM
DC1501	OEM
DC1501/1	OEM
DC1501E	OEM
DC1501F	OEM
DC1501G	OEM
DC1502	OEM
DC1502E	OEM
DC1502F	OEM
DC1502G	OEM
DC1503	OEM
DC1504	OEM
DC1504E	OEM
DC1504F	OEM
DC1504G	OEM
DC1505	OEM
DC1505F	OEM
DC1505G	OEM
DC1505H	OEM
DC1506	OEM
DC1506E	OEM
DC1506F	OEM
DC1506G	OEM
DC1507	OEM
DC1507F	OEM
DC1507G	OEM
DC1507H	OEM
DC1508F	OEM
DC1508G	OEM
DC1508H	OEM
DC1509	OEM
DC1510	OEM
DC1511F	OEM
DC1511G	OEM
DC1511H	OEM
DC1512	OEM
DC1512/1	OEM
DC1513	OEM
DC1514	OEM
DC1515	OEM
DC1516	OEM
DC1517	OEM
DC1518	OEM
DC1519	OEM
DC1520	OEM
DC1521	OEM
DC1523	OEM
DC1526	OEM
DC1527	OEM
DC1528	OEM
DC1529	OEM
DC1533E	OEM
DC1533F	OEM
DC1533G	OEM
DC1534E	OEM
DC1534F	OEM
DC1534G	OEM
DC1535	OEM
DC1536F	OEM
DC1536G	OEM
DC1539/1	OEM
DC1542	OEM
DC1544/1	OEM
DC1544/3	OEM
DC1544/5	OEM
DC1544/7	OEM
DC1544/8	OEM
DC1546	OEM
DC1547	OEM
DC1551	OEM
DC1553	OEM
DC1554	OEM
DC1557	OEM
DC1558	OEM
DC1560	OEM
DC1570E	OEM
DC1570F	OEM
DC1570G	OEM
DC1571E	OEM
DC1571F	OEM
DC1571G	OEM
DC1572E	OEM
DC1572F	OEM
DC1572G	OEM
DC1573E	OEM
DC1573F	OEM
DC1573G	OEM
DC1574E	OEM
DC1574F	OEM
DC1574G	OEM
DC1575E	OEM
DC1575F	OEM
DC1575G	OEM
DC1576E	OEM
DC1576F	OEM
DC1576G	OEM
DC1577E	OEM
DC1577F	OEM
DC1577G	OEM
DC1578E	OEM
DC1578F	OEM
DC1578G	OEM
DC1579E	OEM
DC1585	OEM
DC1590/1	OEM
DC1590/2	OEM
DC1590/3	OEM
DC1591	OEM
DC1593	OEM
DC1595	OEM
DC1596	OEM
DC1597	OEM
DC1612B2	OEM
DC1612B2A	OEM
DC1612C2	OEM
DC1612C2A	OEM
DC1612D2	OEM
DC2010	OEM
DC2011	OEM
DC2011A	OEM
DC2011AR	OEM
DC2011B	OEM
DC2011BR	OEM
DC2011C	OEM
DC2011CR	OEM
DC2011D	OEM
DC2011DR	OEM
DC2011G	OEM
DC2011GR	OEM
DC2012	OEM
DC2013	OEM
DC2013A	OEM
DC2013AR	OEM
DC2013B	OEM
DC2013BR	OEM
DC2013C	OEM
DC2013CR	OEM
DC2013D	OEM
DC2013DR	OEM
DC2013G	OEM
DC2013GR	OEM
DC2014	OEM
DC2014A	OEM
DC2014B	OEM
DC2014C	OEM
DC2015	OEM
DC2015B2	OEM
DC2016	OEM
DC2017	OEM
DC2018	OEM
DC2020	OEM
DC2023	OEM
DC2101A	OEM
DC2101B	OEM
DC2101C	OEM
DC2101G	OEM
DC2103A	OEM
DC2103B	OEM
DC2103C	OEM
DC2103G	OEM
DC2104A	OEM
DC2104B	OEM
DC2104C	OEM
DC2104F	OEM
DC2104G	OEM
DC2110A	OEM
DC2110B	OEM
DC2110C	OEM
DC2110G	OEM
DC2118B	OEM
DC2118C	OEM
DC2118G	OEM
DC2130A	OEM
DC2130G	OEM
DC2133A	OEM
DC2133G	OEM
DC2135A	OEM
DC2135G	OEM
DC2140A	OEM
DC2140G	OEM
DC2171H	OEM
DC2172H	OEM
DC2403A	OEM
DC2410A	OEM
DC2412A	OEM
DC2418A	OEM
DC2418A1	OEM
DC2419A	OEM
DC2419A1	OEM
DC2443A	OEM
DC2460A	OEM
DC2510A	OEM
DC2510B	OEM
DC2510C	OEM
DC2510D	OEM
DC2510G	OEM
DC2512A	OEM
DC2512B	OEM
DC2512C	OEM
DC2512D	OEM
DC2512G	OEM
DC2518A	OEM
DC2518B	OEM
DC2518C	OEM
DC2518D	OEM
DC2518G	OEM
DC2519A	OEM
DC2519B	OEM
DC2519C	OEM
DC2519D	OEM
DC2519G	OEM
DC2521A	OEM
DC2521B	OEM
DC2521C	OEM
DC2521D	OEM
DC2521G	OEM
DC2552A	OEM
DC2552B	OEM
DC2552C	OEM
DC2552D	OEM
DC2552G	OEM
DC2610A	OEM
DC2611	OEM
DC2612A	OEM
DC2613	OEM
DC2614	OEM
DC2615	OEM
DC2616	OEM
DC2618A	OEM
DC2619A	OEM
DC2624D	OEM
DC2652A	OEM
DC2801A	OEM
DC2802G	OEM
DC2825E	OEM
DC2840E	OEM
DC2841E	OEM
DC2842E	OEM
DC2843E	OEM
DC2844E	OEM
DC2845E	OEM
DC2846E	OEM
DC2847E	OEM
DC2848E	OEM
DC2849E	OEM
DC2850E	OEM
DC2870C	OEM
DC2906A	OEM
DC2907A	OEM
DC3010	OEM
DC3011	OEM
DC3012	OEM
DC3012S	OEM
DC3013	OEM
DC3015	OEM
DC3016	OEM
DC3018	OEM
DC3021	OEM
DC3022	OEM
DC3024	OEM
DC3439	OEM
DC3440	OEM
DC4021A00	OEM
DC4021A01	OEM
DC4021A02	OEM
DC4021B00	OEM
DC4021B01	OEM
DC4021B02	OEM
DC4021C00	OEM
DC4021C01	OEM
DC4021C02	OEM
DC4021D00	OEM
DC4021D01	OEM
DC4021D02	OEM
DC4021E00	OEM
DC4021E01	OEM
DC4021E02	OEM
DC4021F00	OEM
DC4021F01	OEM
DC4021F02	OEM
DC4021H00	OEM
DC4021H01	OEM
DC4021H02	OEM
DC4021J00	OEM
DC4021J01	OEM
DC4021J02	OEM
DC4021K00	OEM
DC4021K01	OEM
DC4021K02	OEM
DC4021L00	OEM
DC4021L01	OEM
DC4021L02	OEM
DC4021M00	OEM
DC4021M01	OEM
DC4021M02	OEM
DC4021N00	OEM
DC4021N01	OEM
DC4021N02	OEM
DC4021P00	OEM
DC4021P01	OEM
DC4021P02	OEM
DC4022A00	OEM
DC4022A01	OEM
DC4022A02	OEM
DC4022B00	OEM
DC4022B01	OEM
DC4022B02	OEM
DC4022C00	OEM
DC4022C01	OEM
DC4022C02	OEM
DC4022D00	OEM
DC4022D01	OEM
DC4022D02	OEM
DC4022E00	OEM
DC4022E01	OEM
DC4022E02	OEM
DC4022F00	OEM
DC4022F01	OEM
DC4022F02	OEM
DC4022G00	OEM
DC4022G01	OEM
DC4022G02	OEM
DC4022H00	OEM
DC4022H01	OEM
DC4022H02	OEM
DC4022J00	OEM
DC4022J01	OEM
DC4022J02	OEM
DC4022K00	OEM
DC4022K01	OEM
DC4022K02	OEM
DC4022L00	OEM
DC4022L01	OEM
DC4022L02	OEM
DC4023A00	OEM
DC4023A01	OEM
DC4023A02	OEM
DC4023B00	OEM
DC4023B01	OEM
DC4023B02	OEM
DC4023C00	OEM
DC4023C01	OEM
DC4023C02	OEM
DC4023D00	OEM
DC4023D01	OEM
DC4023D02	OEM
DC4023E00	OEM
DC4023E01	OEM
DC4023E02	OEM
DC4023F00	OEM
DC4023F01	OEM
DC4023F02	OEM
DC4023G00	OEM
DC4023G01	OEM
DC4023G02	OEM
DC4023H00	OEM
DC4023H01	OEM
DC4023H02	OEM
DC4023J00	OEM
DC4023J01	OEM
DC4023J02	OEM
DC4031A00	OEM
DC4031A01	OEM
DC4031A02	OEM
DC4031B00	OEM
DC4031B01	OEM
DC4031B02	OEM
DC4031C00	OEM
DC4031C01	OEM
DC4031C02	OEM
DC4031D00	OEM
DC4031D01	OEM
DC4031D02	OEM
DC4031E00	OEM
DC4031E01	OEM
DC4031E02	OEM
DC4031F00	OEM
DC4031F01	OEM
DC4031F02	OEM
DC4031G00	OEM
DC4031G01	OEM
DC4031G02	OEM
DC4031H00	OEM
DC4031H01	OEM
DC4031H02	OEM
DC4031J00	OEM
DC4031J01	OEM
DC4031J02	OEM
DC4031K00	OEM
DC4031K01	OEM
DC4031K02	OEM
DC4031L00	OEM
DC4031L01	OEM
DC4031L02	OEM
DC4031M00	OEM
DC4031M01	OEM
DC4031M02	OEM
DC4032A00	OEM
DC4032A01	OEM
DC4032A02	OEM
DC4032B00	OEM
DC4032B01	OEM
DC4032B02	OEM
DC4032C00	OEM
DC4032C01	OEM
DC4032C02	OEM
DC4032D00	OEM
DC4032D01	OEM
DC4032D02	OEM
DC4032E00	OEM
DC4032E01	OEM
DC4032E02	OEM
DC4032F00	OEM
DC4032F01	OEM
DC4032F02	OEM
DC4032G00	OEM
DC4032G01	OEM
DC4032G02	OEM
DC4032H00	OEM
DC4032H01	OEM
DC4032H02	OEM
DC4032J00	OEM
DC4032J01	OEM
DC4032J02	OEM
DC4032K00	OEM
DC4032K01	OEM
DC4032K02	OEM
DC4032L00	OEM
DC4032L01	OEM
DC4032L02	OEM
DC4033A00	OEM
DC4033A01	OEM
DC4033A02	OEM
DC4033B00	OEM
DC4033B01	OEM
DC4033B02	OEM
DC4033C00	OEM
DC4033C01	OEM
DC4033C02	OEM
DC4033D00	OEM
DC4033D01	OEM
DC4033D02	OEM
DC4033E00	OEM
DC4033E01	OEM
DC4033E02	OEM
DC4033F00	OEM
DC4033F01	OEM
DC4033F02	OEM
DC4033G00	OEM
DC4033G01	OEM
DC4033G02	OEM
DC4033H00	OEM
DC4033H01	OEM
DC4033H02	OEM
DC4033J00	OEM
DC4033J01	OEM
DC4033J02	OEM
DC4034A00	OEM
DC4034A01	OEM
DC4034A02	OEM
DC4034B00	OEM
DC4034B01	OEM
DC4034B02	OEM
DC4034C00	OEM
DC4034C01	OEM
DC4034C02	OEM
DC4034D00	OEM
DC4034D01	OEM
DC4034D02	OEM
DC4034E00	OEM
DC4034E01	OEM
DC4034E02	OEM
DC4041A00	OEM
DC4041A01	OEM
DC4041A02	OEM
DC4041B00	OEM
DC4041B01	OEM
DC4041B02	OEM
DC4041C00	OEM
DC4041C01	OEM
DC4041C02	OEM
DC4041D00	OEM
DC4041D01	OEM
DC4041D02	OEM
DC4041E00	OEM
DC4041E01	OEM
DC4041E02	OEM
DC4041F00	OEM
DC4041F01	OEM
DC4041F02	OEM
DC4041G00	OEM
DC4041G01	OEM
DC4041G02	OEM
DC4041H00	OEM
DC4041H01	OEM
DC4041H02	OEM
DC4041J00	OEM
DC4041J01	OEM
DC4041J02	OEM
DC4041K00	OEM
DC4041K01	OEM
DC4041K02	OEM
DC4041L00	OEM
DC4041L01	OEM
DC4041L02	OEM
DC4042A00	OEM
DC4042A01	OEM
DC4042A02	OEM
DC4042B00	OEM
DC4042B01	OEM
DC4042B02	OEM
DC4042C00	OEM
DC4042C01	OEM
DC4042C02	OEM
DC4042D00	OEM
DC4042D01	OEM
DC4042D02	OEM
DC4042E00	OEM
DC4042E01	OEM
DC4042E02	OEM
DC4042F00	OEM
DC4042F01	OEM
DC4042F02	OEM
DC4042G00	OEM
DC4042G01	OEM
DC4042G02	OEM
DC4042H00	OEM
DC4042H01	OEM
DC4042H02	OEM
DC4042J00	OEM
DC4042J01	OEM
DC4042J02	OEM
DC4042K00	OEM
DC4042K01	OEM
DC4042K02	OEM
DC4042L00	OEM
DC4042L01	OEM
DC4042L02	OEM
DC4043A00	OEM
DC4043A01	OEM
DC4043A02	OEM
DC4043B00	OEM
DC4043B01	OEM
DC4043B02	OEM
DC4043C00	OEM
DC4043C01	OEM
DC4043C02	OEM
DC4043D00	OEM
DC4043D01	OEM
DC4043D02	OEM
DC4043E00	OEM
DC4043E01	OEM
DC4043E02	OEM
DC4043F00	OEM
DC4043F01	OEM
DC4043F02	OEM
DC4043G00	OEM
DC4043G01	OEM
DC4043G02	OEM
DC4043H00	OEM
DC4043H01	OEM
DC4043H02	OEM
DC4043J00	OEM
DC4043J01	OEM
DC4043J02	OEM
DC4044A00	OEM
DC4044A01	OEM
DC4044A02	OEM
DC4044B00	OEM
DC4044B01	OEM
DC4044B02	OEM
DC4044C00	OEM
DC4044C01	OEM
DC4044C02	OEM
DC4044D00	OEM
DC4044D01	OEM
DC4044D02	OEM
DC4045A00	OEM
DC4045A01	OEM
DC4045A02	OEM
DC4045B00	OEM
DC4045B01	OEM
DC4045B02	OEM
DC4051A00	OEM
DC4051A01	OEM
DC4051A02	OEM
DC4051B00	OEM
DC4051B01	OEM
DC4051B02	OEM
DC4051C00	OEM
DC4051C01	OEM
DC4051C02	OEM
DC4051D00	OEM
DC4051D01	OEM
DC4051D02	OEM
DC4051E00	OEM
DC4051E01	OEM
DC4051E02	OEM
DC4051F00	OEM
DC4051F01	OEM
DC4051F02	OEM
DC4051G00	OEM
DC4051G01	OEM
DC4051G02	OEM
DC4051H00	OEM
DC4051H01	OEM
DC4051H02	OEM
DC4051J00	OEM
DC4051J01	OEM
DC4051J02	OEM
DC4051K00	OEM
DC4051K01	OEM
DC4051K02	OEM
DC4051L00	OEM
DC4051L01	OEM
DC4051L02	OEM
DC4052A00	OEM
DC4052A01	OEM
DC4052A02	OEM
DC4052B00	OEM
DC4052B01	OEM
DC4052B02	OEM
DC4052C00	OEM
DC4052C01	OEM
DC4052C02	OEM
DC4052D00	OEM
DC4052D01	OEM
DC4052D02	OEM
DC4052E00	OEM
DC4052E01	OEM
DC4052E02	OEM
DC4052F00	OEM
DC4052F01	OEM
DC4052F02	OEM
DC4052G00	OEM
DC4052G01	OEM
DC4052G02	OEM
DC4052H00	OEM
DC4052H01	OEM
DC4052H02	OEM
DC4052J00	OEM
DC4052J01	OEM
DC4052J02	OEM
DC4053A00	OEM
DC4053A01	OEM
DC4053A02	OEM
DC4053B00	OEM
DC4053B01	OEM
DC4053B02	OEM
DC4053C00	OEM
DC4053C01	OEM
DC4053C02	OEM
DC4053D00	OEM
DC4053D01	OEM
DC4053D02	OEM
DC4053E00	OEM
DC4053E01	OEM
DC4053E02	OEM
DC4053F00	OEM
DC4053F01	OEM
DC4053F02	OEM
DC4054A00	OEM
DC4054A01	OEM
DC4054A02	OEM
DC4054B00	OEM
DC4054B01	OEM
DC4054B02	OEM
DC4054C00	OEM
DC4054C01	OEM
DC4054C02	OEM
DC4054D00	OEM
DC4054D01	OEM
DC4054D02	OEM
DC4061A00	OEM
DC4061A01	OEM
DC4061A02	OEM
DC4061B00	OEM
DC4061B01	OEM
DC4061B02	OEM
DC4061C00	OEM
DC4061C01	OEM
DC4061C02	OEM
DC4061D00	OEM
DC4061D01	OEM
DC4061D02	OEM
DC4061E00	OEM
DC4061E01	OEM
DC4061E02	OEM
DC4061F00	OEM
DC4061F01	OEM
DC4061F02	OEM
DC4061G00	OEM
DC4061G01	OEM
DC4061G02	OEM
DC4061H00	OEM
DC4061H01	OEM
DC4061H02	OEM
DC4061J00	OEM
DC4061J01	OEM
DC4061J02	OEM
DC4062A00	OEM
DC4062A01	OEM
DC4062A02	OEM
DC4062B00	OEM
DC4062B01	OEM
DC4062B02	OEM
DC4062C00	OEM
DC4062C01	OEM
DC4062C02	OEM
DC4062D00	OEM
DC4062D01	OEM
DC4062D02	OEM

If replacement code is OEM, contact original manufacturer for replacement.

DEVICE TYPE	REPL CODE
DC4062E00	OEM
DC4062E01	OEM
DC4062E02	OEM
DC4062F00	OEM
DC4062F01	OEM
DC4062F02	OEM
DC4063A00	OEM
DC4063A01	OEM
DC4063A02	OEM
DC4063B00	OEM
DC4063B01	OEM
DC4063B02	OEM
DC4063C00	OEM
DC4063C01	OEM
DC4063C02	OEM
DC4063D00	OEM
DC4063D01	OEM
DC4063D02	OEM
DC4063E00	OEM
DC4063E01	OEM
DC4063E02	OEM
DC4064A00	OEM
DC4064A01	OEM
DC4064A02	OEM
DC4064B00	OEM
DC4064B01	OEM
DC4064B02	OEM
DC4064C00	OEM
DC4064C01	OEM
DC4064C02	OEM
DC4121A01	OEM
DC4121A02	OEM
DC4121B01	OEM
DC4121B02	OEM
DC4121C01	OEM
DC4121C02	OEM
DC4121D01	OEM
DC4121D02	OEM
DC4121E01	OEM
DC4121E02	OEM
DC4121F01	OEM
DC4121F02	OEM
DC4121G01	OEM
DC4121G02	OEM
DC4121H01	OEM
DC4121H02	OEM
DC4121J01	OEM
DC4121J02	OEM
DC4121K01	OEM
DC4121K02	OEM
DC4121L01	OEM
DC4121L02	OEM
DC4121M01	OEM
DC4121M02	OEM
DC4121N01	OEM
DC4121N02	OEM
DC4121P01	OEM
DC4121P02	OEM
DC4122A01	OEM
DC4122A02	OEM
DC4122B01	OEM
DC4122B02	OEM
DC4122C01	OEM
DC4122C02	OEM
DC4122D01	OEM
DC4122D02	OEM
DC4122E01	OEM
DC4122E02	OEM
DC4122F01	OEM
DC4122F02	OEM
DC4122G01	OEM
DC4122G02	OEM
DC4122H01	OEM
DC4122H02	OEM
DC4122J01	OEM
DC4122J02	OEM
DC4122K01	OEM
DC4122K02	OEM
DC4122L01	OEM
DC4122L02	OEM
DC4122M01	OEM
DC4122M02	OEM
DC4131A01	OEM
DC4131A02	OEM
DC4131B01	OEM
DC4131B02	OEM
DC4131C01	OEM
DC4131C02	OEM
DC4131D01	OEM
DC4131D02	OEM
DC4131E01	OEM
DC4131E02	OEM
DC4131F01	OEM
DC4131F02	OEM
DC4131G01	OEM
DC4131G02	OEM
DC4131H01	OEM
DC4131H02	OEM
DC4131J01	OEM
DC4131J02	OEM
DC4131K01	OEM
DC4131K02	OEM
DC4131L01	OEM
DC4131L02	OEM
DC4131M01	OEM
DC4131M02	OEM
DC4132A01	OEM
DC4132A02	OEM
DC4132B01	OEM

DEVICE TYPE	REPL CODE
DC4132B02	OEM
DC4132C01	OEM
DC4132C02	OEM
DC4132D01	OEM
DC4132D02	OEM
DC4132E01	OEM
DC4132E02	OEM
DC4132F01	OEM
DC4132F02	OEM
DC4132G01	OEM
DC4132G02	OEM
DC4132H01	OEM
DC4132H02	OEM
DC4132J01	OEM
DC4132J02	OEM
DC4132K01	OEM
DC4132K02	OEM
DC4132L01	OEM
DC4132L02	OEM
DC4132M01	OEM
DC4132M02	OEM
DC4141A01	OEM
DC4141A02	OEM
DC4141B01	OEM
DC4141B02	OEM
DC4141C01	OEM
DC4141C02	OEM
DC4141D01	OEM
DC4141D02	OEM
DC4141E01	OEM
DC4141E02	OEM
DC4141F01	OEM
DC4141F02	OEM
DC4141G01	OEM
DC4141G02	OEM
DC4141H01	OEM
DC4141H02	OEM
DC4141J01	OEM
DC4141J02	OEM
DC4141K01	OEM
DC4141K02	OEM
DC4141L01	OEM
DC4141L02	OEM
DC4141M01	OEM
DC4141M02	OEM
DC4142A01	OEM
DC4142A02	OEM
DC4142B01	OEM
DC4142B02	OEM
DC4142C01	OEM
DC4142C02	OEM
DC4142D01	OEM
DC4142D02	OEM
DC4142E01	OEM
DC4142E02	OEM
DC4142F01	OEM
DC4142F02	OEM
DC4142G01	OEM
DC4142G02	OEM
DC4142H01	OEM
DC4142H02	OEM
DC4142J01	OEM
DC4142J02	OEM
DC4142K01	OEM
DC4142K02	OEM
DC4142L01	OEM
DC4142L02	OEM
DC4151A01	OEM
DC4151A02	OEM
DC4151B01	OEM
DC4151B02	OEM
DC4151C01	OEM
DC4151C02	OEM
DC4151D01	OEM
DC4151D02	OEM
DC4151E01	OEM
DC4151E02	OEM
DC4151F01	OEM
DC4151F02	OEM
DC4151G01	OEM
DC4151G02	OEM
DC4151H01	OEM
DC4151H02	OEM
DC4151J01	OEM
DC4151J02	OEM
DC4151K01	OEM
DC4151K02	OEM
DC4151L01	OEM
DC4151L02	OEM
DC4152A01	OEM
DC4152A02	OEM
DC4152B01	OEM
DC4152B02	OEM
DC4152C01	OEM
DC4152C02	OEM
DC4152D01	OEM
DC4152D02	OEM
DC4152E01	OEM
DC4152E02	OEM
DC4152F01	OEM
DC4152F02	OEM
DC4152G01	OEM
DC4152G02	OEM
DC4152H01	OEM
DC4152H02	OEM
DC4152J01	OEM
DC4152J02	OEM
DC4161A01	OEM
DC4161A02	OEM

DEVICE TYPE	REPL CODE
DC4161B01	OEM
DC4161B02	OEM
DC4161C01	OEM
DC4161C02	OEM
DC4161D01	OEM
DC4161D02	OEM
DC4161E01	OEM
DC4161E02	OEM
DC4161F01	OEM
DC4161F02	OEM
DC4161G01	OEM
DC4161G02	OEM
DC4161H01	OEM
DC4161H02	OEM
DC4161J01	OEM
DC4161J02	OEM
DC4162A01	OEM
DC4162A02	OEM
DC4162B01	OEM
DC4162B02	OEM
DC4162C01	OEM
DC4162C02	OEM
DC4162D01	OEM
DC4162D02	OEM
DC4162E01	OEM
DC4162E02	OEM
DC4162F01	OEM
DC4162F02	OEM
DC4201	OEM
DC4202	OEM
DC4210	OEM
DC4210B	3878
DC4211	OEM
DC4211B	OEM
DC4212	OEM
DC4212B	OEM
DC4213	OEM
DC4213B	OEM
DC4214	OEM
DC4214B	OEM
DC4215	OEM
DC4215B	OEM
DC4216	OEM
DC4216B	OEM
DC4217	OEM
DC4217B	OEM
DC4218B	OEM
DC4220	OEM
DC4221	OEM
DC4222	OEM
DC4223	OEM
DC4224	OEM
DC4224B	OEM
DC4225	OEM
DC4225B	OEM
DC4226	OEM
DC4226B	OEM
DC4227B	OEM
DC4228B	OEM
DC4229D	OEM
DC4229F	OEM
DC4230	OEM
DC4231	OEM
DC4232	OEM
DC4232B	OEM
DC4233	OEM
DC4233B	OEM
DC4234	OEM
DC4234B	OEM
DC4235	OEM
DC4240	OEM
DC4241	OEM
DC4242	OEM
DC4243	OEM
DC4243C	OEM
DC4244	OEM
DC4244C	OEM
DC4245	OEM
DC4253	OEM
DC4254	OEM
DC4255	OEM
DC4255B	OEM
DC4256	OEM
DC4256B	OEM
DC4257	OEM
DC4257B	OEM
DC4265B	OEM
DC4266B	OEM
DC4267B	OEM
DC4285B	OEM
DC4286B	OEM
DC4287B	OEM
DC4298	OEM
DC4299	OEM
DC4301A	OEM
DC4301B	OEM
DC4301C	OEM
DC4302A	OEM
DC4302B	OEM
DC4303A	OEM
DC4303B	OEM
DC4304A	OEM
DC4304B	OEM
DC4305A	OEM
DC4305B	OEM
DC4352	OEM
DC4371A	OEM
DC4371B	OEM
DC4372A	OEM

DEVICE TYPE	REPL CODE
DC4372B	OEM
DC4373A	OEM
DC4373B	OEM
DC4374A	OEM
DC4374B	OEM
DC4375A	OEM
DC4375B	OEM
DC5021	OEM
DC5022	OEM
DC5023	OEM
DC5108	OEM
DC5125	OEM
DC5141	OEM
DC5142	OEM
DC5143	OEM
DC5404	OEM
DC5405	OEM
DC5412	OEM
DC5414	OEM
DC5415	OEM
DC5416	OEM
DC5423	OEM
DC5424	OEM
DC5425	OEM
DC5441	OEM
DC5442	OEM
DC5443	OEM
DC5445	OEM
DC5623	OEM
DC5631	OEM
DC5632	OEM
DC5651	OEM
DC5652	OEM
DC5653	OEM
DC8008	OEM
DC8020	OEM
DC8457	0133
DC16055A	OEM
DC20026A2	OEM
DC40026B2	OEM
DC40046A	OEM
DC40066A	OEM
DC40125A	OEM
DC80025B	OEM
DCA010	0897
DCA010W5-TA	OEM
DCA015	4830
DCA015A4-TA	OEM
DCA25B	0199
DCA25C	0199
DCA25E	0199
DCB010	5181
DCB010W6-TA	OEM
DCB015	0901
DCB015-TB	OEM
DCB015A6-TA	OEM
DCB015TA	OEM
DCB015TB	0901
DCB25B	1009
DCB25C	1009
DCB25E	1009
DCB100	OEM
DCB100F	OEM
DCB101	OEM
DCB101F	OEM
DCB102	OEM
DCB102F	OEM
DCB104	OEM
DCB104F	OEM
DCB106	OEM
DCB106F	OEM
DCB108	OEM
DCB110	OEM
DCBFTS3FU0	OEM
DCC010	OEM
DCC010W7-TA	OEM
DCC016	OEM
DCC025	OEM
DCC050GACC	OEM
DCC050GBCA	OEM
DCC050RACC	OEM
DCC050RBCA	OEM
DCC050RBCC	OEM
DCC050YACC	OEM
DCC050YBCA	OEM
DCC0501RACC	OEM
DCC0501RBCA	OEM
DCC100GCA	OEM
DCC100GCC	OEM
DCC100GH.E.CC	OEM
DCC100YCA	OEM
DCC100YCC	OEM
DCC100YH.E.CC	OEM
DCC1001RCA	OEM
DCC1001RCC	OEM
DCC1001RH.E.CC	OEM
DCC1630	OEM
DCC10018	OEM
DCC10018AG	OEM
DCC10018AIR	OEM
DCC10018AR	OEM
DCC10018AY	OEM
DCC10018LG	OEM
DCC10018LIR	OEM
DCC10018LR	OEM
DCC10018LY	OEM
DCC10030	OEM
DCD015	2189
DCE015	0689

DEVICE TYPE	REPL CODE
DCE5/15/150	OEM
DCE12/15/150	OEM
DCE24/15/150	OEM
DCE28/15/150	OEM
DCERB12-01	0023
DCESAC82-004	1015
DCI5/15/60	OEM
DCI12/15/60	OEM
DCI28/15/60	OEM
DCI177	OEM
DCI178	OEM
DCP102	OEM
DCR5-5	OEM
DCR5-5-5	OEM
DCR5-12	OEM
DCR5-12-12	OEM
DCR5-15	OEM
DCR5-15-15	OEM
DCR12-5	OEM
DCR12-12	OEM
DCR12-12-12	OEM
DCR12-15	OEM
DCR12-15-15	OEM
DCR403ST0101	OEM
DCR403ST0102	OEM
DCR403ST0202	OEM
DCR403ST0203	OEM
DCR403ST0303	OEM
DCR403ST0304	OEM
DCR403ST0404	OEM
DCR403ST0405	OEM
DCR403ST0505	OEM
DCR403ST0506	OEM
DCR403ST0606	OEM
DCR403ST0607	OEM
DCR403ST0707	OEM
DCR403ST0709	OEM
DCR405ST0101	OEM
DCR405ST0102	OEM
DCR405ST0202	OEM
DCR405ST0203	OEM
DCR405ST0303	OEM
DCR405ST0304	OEM
DCR405ST0404	OEM
DCR405ST0405	OEM
DCR405ST0505	OEM
DCR405ST0506	OEM
DCR405ST0606	OEM
DCR405ST0607	OEM
DCR405ST0707	OEM
DCR405ST0709	OEM
DCR405ST0808	OEM
DCR405ST0810	OEM
DCR405ST0909	OEM
DCR405ST1010	OEM
DCR405ST1012	OEM
DCR405ST1111	OEM
DCR405ST1113	OEM
DCR405ST1212	OEM
DCR405ST1215	OEM
DCR405ST1313	OEM
DCR405ST1316	OEM
DCR424ST0101T	OEM
DCR424ST0101V	OEM
DCR424ST0101W	OEM
DCR424ST0101X	OEM
DCR424ST0101Z	OEM
DCR424ST0202T	OEM
DCR424ST0202V	OEM
DCR424ST0202W	OEM
DCR424ST0202X	OEM
DCR424ST0202Z	OEM
DCR424ST0303T	OEM
DCR424ST0303V	OEM
DCR424ST0303W	OEM
DCR424ST0303X	OEM
DCR424ST0303Z	OEM
DCR424ST0404T	OEM
DCR424ST0404V	OEM
DCR424ST0404W	OEM
DCR424ST0404X	OEM
DCR424ST0404Z	OEM
DCR424ST0505T	OEM
DCR424ST0505V	OEM
DCR424ST0505X	OEM
DCR424ST0505Z	OEM
DCR424ST0606	OEM
DCR424ST0606T	OEM
DCR424ST0606V	OEM
DCR424ST0606W	OEM
DCR424ST0606X	OEM
DCR424ST0606Z	OEM
DCR425ST0101A	OEM
DCR425ST0101B	OEM
DCR425ST0101M	OEM
DCR425ST0101N	OEM
DCR425ST0101P	OEM
DCR425ST0101R	OEM
DCR425ST0101S	OEM
DCR425ST0101T	OEM
DCR425ST0101W	OEM
DCR425ST0101X	OEM
DCR425ST0101Z	OEM
DCR425ST0202A	OEM
DCR425ST0202B	OEM
DCR425ST0202L	OEM
DCR425ST0202M	OEM
DCR425ST0202N	OEM
DCR425ST0202P	OEM

DEVICE TYPE	REPL CODE
DCR425ST0202R	OEM
DCR425ST0202T	OEM
DCR425ST0202W	OEM
DCR425ST0202Z	OEM
DCR425ST0303A	OEM
DCR425ST0303B	OEM
DCR425ST0303L	OEM
DCR425ST0303M	OEM
DCR425ST0303N	OEM
DCR425ST0303P	OEM
DCR425ST0303R	OEM
DCR425ST0303S	OEM
DCR425ST0303T	OEM
DCR425ST0303V	OEM
DCR425ST0303W	OEM
DCR425ST0303X	OEM
DCR425ST0303Z	OEM
DCR425ST0404A	OEM
DCR425ST0404L	OEM
DCR425ST0404M	OEM
DCR425ST0404N	OEM
DCR425ST0404P	OEM
DCR425ST0404R	OEM
DCR425ST0404S	OEM
DCR425ST0404V	OEM
DCR425ST0404W	OEM
DCR425ST0404X	OEM
DCR425ST0404Z	OEM
DCR425ST0505A	OEM
DCR425ST0505B	OEM
DCR425ST0505L	OEM
DCR425ST0505M	OEM
DCR425ST0505N	OEM
DCR425ST0505P	OEM
DCR425ST0505R	OEM
DCR425ST0505S	OEM
DCR425ST0505V	OEM
DCR425ST0505W	OEM
DCR425ST0505X	OEM
DCR425ST0505Z	OEM
DCR425ST0606A	OEM
DCR425ST0606B	OEM
DCR425ST0606L	OEM
DCR425ST0606M	OEM
DCR425ST0606N	OEM
DCR425ST0606P	OEM
DCR425ST0606R	OEM
DCR425ST0606S	OEM
DCR425ST0606V	OEM
DCR425ST0606W	OEM
DCR425ST0606X	OEM
DCR425ST0606Z	OEM
DCR485ST0101Z	OEM
DCR503ST0202	OEM
DCR504ST0101	OEM
DCR504ST0202	OEM
DCR504ST0303	OEM
DCR504ST0404	OEM
DCR504ST0505	OEM
DCR504ST0606	OEM
DCR504ST0707	OEM
DCR504ST0808	OEM
DCR504ST0909	OEM
DCR504ST1010	OEM
DCR504ST1111	OEM
DCR504ST1212	OEM
DCR504ST1313	OEM
DCR504ST1414	OEM
DCR504ST1515	OEM
DCR508ST0101	OEM
DCR508ST0911	OEM
DCR525SM0101M	OEM
DCR525SM0101N	OEM
DCR525SM0101P	OEM
DCR525SM0101R	OEM
DCR525SM0101S	OEM
DCR525SM0101T	OEM
DCR525SM0101V	OEM
DCR525SM0101W	OEM
DCR525SM0101X	OEM
DCR525SM0101Z	OEM
DCR525SM0202M	OEM
DCR525SM0202N	OEM
DCR525SM0202P	OEM
DCR525SM0202R	OEM
DCR525SM0202S	OEM
DCR525SM0202T	OEM
DCR525SM0202V	OEM
DCR525SM0202W	OEM
DCR525SM0202X	OEM
DCR525SM0202Z	OEM
DCR525SM0303M	OEM
DCR525SM0303N	OEM
DCR525SM0303P	OEM
DCR525SM0303R	OEM
DCR525SM0303S	OEM
DCR525SM0303T	OEM
DCR525SM0303V	OEM
DCR525SM0303W	OEM
DCR525SM0303Z	OEM
DCR525SM0404M	OEM
DCR525SM0404N	OEM
DCR525SM0404P	OEM
DCR525SM0404R	OEM
DCR525SM0404S	OEM
DCR525SM0404T	OEM
DCR525SM0404V	OEM
DCR525SM0404W	OEM
DCR525SM0404X	OEM

DEVICE TYPE	REPL CODE
DCR525SM0404Z	OEM
DCR525SM0505M	OEM
DCR525SM0505N	OEM
DCR525SM0505P	OEM
DCR525SM0505R	OEM
DCR525SM0505S	OEM
DCR525SM0505T	OEM
DCR525SM0505V	OEM
DCR525SM0505W	OEM
DCR525SM0505X	OEM
DCR525SM0505Z	OEM
DCR525SM0606M	OEM
DCR525SM0606N	OEM
DCR525SM0606P	OEM
DCR525SM0606R	OEM
DCR525SM0606S	OEM
DCR525SM0606T	OEM
DCR525SM0606V	OEM
DCR525SM0606W	OEM
DCR525SM0606X	OEM
DCR525SM0606Z	OEM
DCR604SE0101	OEM
DCR604SE0202	OEM
DCR604SE0303	OEM
DCR604SE0404	OEM
DCR604SE0505	OEM
DCR604SE0606	OEM
DCR604SE0707	OEM
DCR604SE0808	OEM
DCR604SE0909	OEM
DCR604SE1010	OEM
DCR604SE1111	OEM
DCR604SE1212	OEM
DCR604SE1313	OEM
DCR604SE1414	OEM
DCR604SK0101	OEM
DCR604SK0202	OEM
DCR604SK0303	OEM
DCR604SK0404	OEM
DCR604SK0505	OEM
DCR604SK0606	OEM
DCR604SK0707	OEM
DCR604SK0808	OEM
DCR604SK0909	OEM
DCR604SK1010	OEM
DCR604SK1111	OEM
DCR604SK1212	OEM
DCR604SK1313	OEM
DCR604SM0101	OEM
DCR604SM0202	OEM
DCR604SM0303	OEM
DCR604SM0404	OEM
DCR604SM0505	OEM
DCR604SM0606	OEM
DCR604SM0707	OEM
DCR604SM0808	OEM
DCR604SM0909	OEM
DCR604SM1010	OEM
DCR604SM1111	OEM
DCR604SM1212	OEM
DCR604SM1313	OEM
DCR604SM1414	OEM
DCR604SM1515	OEM
DCR605SK0101	OEM
DCR605SK0202	OEM
DCR605SK0303	OEM
DCR605SK0404	OEM
DCR605SK0505	OEM
DCR605SK0606	OEM
DCR605SK0707	OEM
DCR605SK0808	OEM
DCR605SK0909	OEM
DCR605SK1010	OEM
DCR605SK1111	OEM
DCR605SK1212	OEM
DCR605SK1313	OEM
DCR605SM0101	OEM
DCR605SM0202	OEM
DCR605SM0303	OEM
DCR605SM0404	OEM
DCR605SM0505	OEM
DCR605SM0606	OEM
DCR605SM0707	OEM
DCR605SM0808	OEM
DCR605SM0909	OEM
DCR605SM1010	OEM
DCR605SM1111	OEM
DCR605SM1212	OEM
DCR605SM1313	OEM
DCR605SM1414	OEM
DCR605SM1515	OEM
DCR703SL0101	OEM
DCR703SL0202	OEM
DCR703SL0303	OEM
DCR703SL0404	OEM
DCR703SL0505	OEM
DCR703SL0606	OEM
DCR703SL0707	OEM
DCR703SL0808	OEM
DCR703SL0909	OEM
DCR703SL1010	OEM
DCR703SL1111	OEM
DCR703SL1212	OEM
DCR703SL1313	OEM
DCR703SL1414	OEM
DCR703SL1515	OEM
DCR703SM0101	OEM
DCR703SM0202	OEM
DCR703SM0203	OEM

If replacement code is OEM, contact original manufacturer for replacement. 373

DEVICE TYPE	REPL CODE
DCR703SM0303	OEM
DCR703SM0404	OEM
DCR703SM0505	OEM
DCR703SM0606	OEM
DCR703SM0707	OEM
DCR703SM0808	OEM
DCR703SM0909	OEM
DCR703SM1010	OEM
DCR703SM1111	OEM
DCR703SM1212	OEM
DCR703SM1313	OEM
DCR703SM1414	OEM
DCR703SM1515	OEM
DCR704SL0101	OEM
DCR704SL0202	OEM
DCR704SL0303	OEM
DCR704SL0404	OEM
DCR704SL0505	OEM
DCR704SL0606	OEM
DCR704SL0707	OEM
DCR704SL0808	OEM
DCR704SL0909	OEM
DCR704SL1010	OEM
DCR704SL1111	OEM
DCR704SL1212	OEM
DCR704SL1313	OEM
DCR704SL1414	OEM
DCR704SL1515	OEM
DCR704SL1616	OEM
DCR704SM0101	OEM
DCR704SM0202	OEM
DCR704SM0303	OEM
DCR704SM0404	OEM
DCR704SM0505	OEM
DCR704SM0606	OEM
DCR704SM0707	OEM
DCR704SM0808	OEM
DCR704SM0909	OEM
DCR704SM1010	OEM
DCR704SM1111	OEM
DCR704SM1212	OEM
DCR704SM1313	OEM
DCR704SM1414	OEM
DCR704SM1515	OEM
DCR704SM1616	OEM
DCR705SM0101	OEM
DCR705SM0202	OEM
DCR705SM0303	OEM
DCR705SM0404	OEM
DCR705SM0505	OEM
DCR705SM0606	OEM
DCR705SM0707	OEM
DCR705SM0808	OEM
DCR705SM0909	OEM
DCR705SM1010	OEM
DCR705SM1111	OEM
DCR705SM1212	OEM
DCR705SM1313	OEM
DCR705SM1414	OEM
DCR705SM1515	OEM
DCR705SM1616	OEM
DCR705SM1717	OEM
DCR705SM1818	OEM
DCR706SL0202	OEM
DCR706SL0303	OEM
DCR706SL0404	OEM
DCR706SL0505	OEM
DCR706SL0606	OEM
DCR706SL0707	OEM
DCR706SL0808	OEM
DCR706SL0909	OEM
DCR706SL1010	OEM
DCR706SL1111	OEM
DCR706SL1212	OEM
DCR706SL1313	OEM
DCR706SL1414	OEM
DCR706SL1515	OEM
DCR706SL1616	OEM
DCR706SL1717	OEM
DCR706SM0101	OEM
DCR706SM0202	OEM
DCR706SM0303	OEM
DCR706SM0404	OEM
DCR706SM0505	OEM
DCR706SM0606	OEM
DCR706SM0707	OEM
DCR706SM0808	OEM
DCR706SM0909	OEM
DCR706SM1010	OEM
DCR706SM1111	OEM
DCR706SM1212	OEM
DCR706SM1313	OEM
DCR706SM1414	OEM
DCR706SM1515	OEM
DCR706SM1616	OEM
DCR706SM1717	OEM
DCR706SM1818	OEM
DCR706SM1919	OEM
DCR706SM2020	OEM
DCR707SL0101	OEM
DCR707SL0202	OEM
DCR707SL0303	OEM
DCR707SL0404	OEM
DCR707SL0505	OEM
DCR707SL0606	OEM
DCR707SL0707	OEM
DCR707SL0808	OEM
DCR707SL0909	OEM
DCR707SL1010	OEM

DEVICE TYPE	REPL CODE
DCR707SL1111	OEM
DCR707SL1212	OEM
DCR707SL1313	OEM
DCR707SL1414	OEM
DCR707SL1515	OEM
DCR707SL1616	OEM
DCR707SL1717	OEM
DCR707SL1818	OEM
DCR707SL1919	OEM
DCR707SL2020	OEM
DCR707SL2121	OEM
DCR707SL2222	OEM
DCR707SL2323	OEM
DCR707SM0101	OEM
DCR707SM0202	OEM
DCR707SM0303	OEM
DCR707SM0404	OEM
DCR707SM0505	OEM
DCR707SM0606	OEM
DCR707SM0707	OEM
DCR707SM0808	OEM
DCR707SM0909	OEM
DCR707SM1010	OEM
DCR707SM1111	OEM
DCR707SM1212	OEM
DCR707SM1313	OEM
DCR707SM1414	OEM
DCR707SM1417	OEM
DCR707SM1515	OEM
DCR707SM1616	OEM
DCR707SM1717	OEM
DCR707SM1818	OEM
DCR707SM1919	OEM
DCR707SM2020	OEM
DCR707SM2121	OEM
DCR707SM2222	OEM
DCR707SM2323	OEM
DCR707SM2424	OEM
DCR707SM2525	OEM
DCR802SM0101	OEM
DCR802SM0202	OEM
DCR802SM0303	OEM
DCR802SM0404	OEM
DCR802SM0505	OEM
DCR802SM0606	OEM
DCR803SM0101	OEM
DCR803SM0202	OEM
DCR803SM0303	OEM
DCR803SM0404	OEM
DCR803SM0505	OEM
DCR803SM0606	OEM
DCR803SM0707	OEM
DCR803SM0808	OEM
DCR803SM0909	OEM
DCR803SM1010	OEM
DCR803SM1111	OEM
DCR803SM1212	OEM
DCR803SM1313	OEM
DCR803SM1414	OEM
DCR803SM1515	OEM
DCR803SM1616	OEM
DCR803SM1717	OEM
DCR803WM1818	OEM
DCR804SM0101	OEM
DCR804SM0102	OEM
DCR804SM0203	OEM
DCR804SM0303	OEM
DCR804SM0404	OEM
DCR804SM0505	OEM
DCR804SM0606	OEM
DCR804SM0707	OEM
DCR804SM0808	OEM
DCR804SM0909	OEM
DCR804SM1010	OEM
DCR804SM1111	OEM
DCR804SM1212	OEM
DCR804SM1313	OEM
DCR804SM1515	OEM
DCR804SM1616	OEM
DCR806SM1515	OEM
DCR806SM1616	OEM
DCR806SM1717	OEM
DCR806SM1818	OEM
DCR806SM1919	OEM
DCR806SM2020	OEM
DCR806SM2121	OEM
DCR806SM2222	OEM
DCR806SM2323	OEM
DCR806SM2424	OEM
DCR806SM2525	OEM
DCR806SM2626	OEM
DCR806SM2727	OEM
DCR806SM2828	OEM
DCR806SM2929	OEM
DCR806SM3030	OEM
DCR807SM0101	OEM
DCR807SM0202	OEM
DCR807SM0303	OEM
DCR807SM0404	OEM
DCR807SM0505	OEM
DCR807SM0606	OEM
DCR807SM0707	OEM
DCR807SM0808	OEM
DCR807SM0909	OEM
DCR807SM1010	OEM
DCR807SM1111	OEM
DCR807SM1212	OEM
DCR807SM1313	OEM
DCR807SM1414	OEM

DEVICE TYPE	REPL CODE
DCR807SM1515	OEM
DCR807SM1616	OEM
DCR807SM1717	OEM
DCR807SM1818	OEM
DCR807SM1919	OEM
DCR807SM2020	OEM
DCR807SM2121	OEM
DCR807SM2222	OEM
DCR807SM2323	OEM
DCR807SM2424	OEM
DCR807SM2525	OEM
DCR807SM2626	OEM
DCR818SM2525	OEM
DCR818SM2626	OEM
DCR818SM2727	OEM
DCR818SM2828	OEM
DCR818SM2929	OEM
DCR818SM3030	OEM
DCR818SM3131	OEM
DCR818SM3232	OEM
DCR818SM3333	OEM
DCR818SM3434	OEM
DCR818SM3535	OEM
DCR818SM3636	OEM
DCR818SM3737	OEM
DCR818SM3838	OEM
DCR818SM3939	OEM
DCR818SM4040	OEM
DCR854SM0101	OEM
DCR854SM0202	OEM
DCR854SM0303	OEM
DCR854SM0404	OEM
DCR854SM0505	OEM
DCR854SM0606	OEM
DCR854SM0707	OEM
DCR854SM0808	OEM
DCR854SM0909	OEM
DCR854SM1010	OEM
DCR854SM1111	OEM
DCR854SM1212	OEM
DCR854SM1313	OEM
DCR857SM0101	OEM
DCR857SM0202	OEM
DCR857SM0303	OEM
DCR857SM0404	OEM
DCR857SM0505	OEM
DCR857SM0606	OEM
DCR857SM0707	OEM
DCR857SM0808	OEM
DCR857SM0909	OEM
DCR857SM1010	OEM
DCR857SM1111	OEM
DCR857SM1212	OEM
DCR860SM0101	OEM
DCR860SM0202	OEM
DCR860SM0303	OEM
DCR860SM0404	OEM
DCR860SM0505	OEM
DCR860SM0606	OEM
DCR860SM0707	OEM
DCR860SM0808	OEM
DCR860SM0909	OEM
DCR860SM1010	OEM
DCR860SM1111	OEM
DCR860SM1212	OEM
DCR860SM1313	OEM
DCR880SM0101	OEM
DCR880SM0202	OEM
DCR880SM0303	OEM
DCR880SM0404	OEM
DCR880SM0505	OEM
DCR880SM0606	OEM
DCR880SM0707	OEM
DCR880SM0808	OEM
DCR880SM0909	OEM
DCR880SM1010	OEM
DCR880SM1111	OEM
DCR880SM1212	OEM
DCR880SM1313	OEM
DCR880SM1414	OEM
DCR880SM1515	OEM
DCR880SM1616	OEM
DCR880SM1717	OEM
DCR880SM1818	OEM
DCR880SM1919	OEM
DCR880SM2020	OEM
DCR884SM0101	OEM
DCR884SM0202	OEM
DCR884SM0303	OEM
DCR884SM0404	OEM
DCR884SM0505	OEM
DCR884SM0606	OEM
DCR884SM0707	OEM
DCR884SM0808	OEM
DCR884SM0909	OEM
DCR884SM1010	OEM
DCR884SM1111	OEM
DCR884SM1212	OEM
DCR884SM1313	OEM
DCR884SM1414	OEM
DCR884SM1515	OEM
DCR887SM0101	OEM
DCR887SM0202	OEM
DCR887SM0303	OEM
DCR887SM0404	OEM
DCR887SM0505	OEM
DCR887SM0606	OEM
DCR887SM0707	OEM
DCR887SM0808	OEM

DEVICE TYPE	REPL CODE
DCR887SM0909	OEM
DCR887SM1010	OEM
DCR887SM1111	OEM
DCR887SM1212	OEM
DCR887SM1313	OEM
DCR1003SN0101	OEM
DCR1003SN0202	OEM
DCR1003SN0303	OEM
DCR1003SN0404	OEM
DCR1003SN0505	OEM
DCR1003SN0606	OEM
DCR1003SN0707	OEM
DCR1003SN0808	OEM
DCR1003SN0909	OEM
DCR1003SN1010	OEM
DCR1003SN1111	OEM
DCR1003SN1212	OEM
DCR1003SN1313	OEM
DCR1003SN1414	OEM
DCR1003SN1515	OEM
DCR1003SN1616	OEM
DCR1003SN1717	OEM
DCR1003SN1818	OEM
DCR1004SM0101	OEM
DCR1004SM0202	OEM
DCR1004SM0303	OEM
DCR1004SM0404	OEM
DCR1004SM0505	OEM
DCR1004SM0606	OEM
DCR1004SM0707	OEM
DCR1004SM0808	OEM
DCR1004SM0909	OEM
DCR1004SM1010	OEM
DCR1004SM1111	OEM
DCR1004SM1212	OEM
DCR1004SM1313	OEM
DCR1004SM1414	OEM
DCR1004SM1515	OEM
DCR1004SN0101	OEM
DCR1004SN0202	OEM
DCR1004SN0303	OEM
DCR1004SN0404	OEM
DCR1004SN0505	OEM
DCR1004SN0606	OEM
DCR1004SN0707	OEM
DCR1004SN0808	OEM
DCR1004SN0909	OEM
DCR1004SN1010	OEM
DCR1004SN1111	OEM
DCR1004SN1212	OEM
DCR1004SN1313	OEM
DCR1004SN1414	OEM
DCR1004SN1515	OEM
DCR1004SN1616	OEM
DCR1004SN1717	OEM
DCR1004SN1818	OEM
DCR1006SN1515	OEM
DCR1006SN1616	OEM
DCR1006SN1717	OEM
DCR1006SN1818	OEM
DCR1006SN1919	OEM
DCR1006SN2020	OEM
DCR1006SN2121	OEM
DCR1006SN2222	OEM
DCR1006SN2323	OEM
DCR1006SN2424	OEM
DCR1006SN2525	OEM
DCR1006SN2626	OEM
DCR1006SN2727	OEM
DCR1006SN2828	OEM
DCR1006SN2929	OEM
DCR1006SN3030	OEM
DCR1007SN0101	OEM
DCR1007SN0202	OEM
DCR1007SN0303	OEM
DCR1007SN0404	OEM
DCR1007SN0505	OEM
DCR1007SN0606	OEM
DCR1007SN0707	OEM
DCR1007SN0808	OEM
DCR1007SN0909	OEM
DCR1007SN1010	OEM
DCR1007SN1111	OEM
DCR1007SN1212	OEM
DCR1007SN1313	OEM
DCR1007SN1414	OEM
DCR1007SN1515	OEM
DCR1007SN1616	OEM
DCR1007SN1717	OEM
DCR1007SN1818	OEM
DCR1007SN1919	OEM
DCR1007SN2020	OEM
DCR1007SN2121	OEM
DCR1007SN2222	OEM
DCR1007SN2323	OEM
DCR1007SN2424	OEM
DCR1007SN2525	OEM
DCR1007SN2626	OEM
DCR1007SN2727	OEM
DCR1007SN2828	OEM
DCR1007SN2929	OEM
DCR1007SN3030	OEM
DCR1018SN3131	OEM
DCR1018SN4141	OEM
DCR1018SN4242	OEM
DCR1018SN4343	OEM
DCR1018SN4444	OEM
DCR1018SN4545	OEM
DCR1054SD0606N	OEM

DEVICE TYPE	REPL CODE
DCR1054SD0606P	OEM
DCR1054SD0606R	OEM
DCR1054SD0606S	OEM
DCR1054SD0707N	OEM
DCR1054SD0707P	OEM
DCR1054SD0707R	OEM
DCR1054SD0707S	OEM
DCR1054SD0808N	OEM
DCR1054SD0808P	OEM
DCR1054SD0808R	OEM
DCR1054SD0808S	OEM
DCR1054SD0909N	OEM
DCR1054SD0909P	OEM
DCR1054SD0909R	OEM
DCR1054SD0909S	OEM
DCR1054SD1010N	OEM
DCR1054SD1010P	OEM
DCR1054SD1010R	OEM
DCR1054SD1010S	OEM
DCR1054SD1111N	OEM
DCR1054SD1111P	OEM
DCR1054SD1111R	OEM
DCR1054SD1111S	OEM
DCR1054SD1212N	OEM
DCR1054SD1212P	OEM
DCR1054SD1212R	OEM
DCR1054SD1212S	OEM
DCR1054SD1313N	OEM
DCR1054SD1313P	OEM
DCR1054SD1313R	OEM
DCR1054SD1313S	OEM
DCR1054SD1414N	OEM
DCR1054SD1414P	OEM
DCR1054SD1414R	OEM
DCR1054SD1414S	OEM
DCR1054SD1415N	OEM
DCR1054SD1415P	OEM
DCR1054SD1415R	OEM
DCR1054SD1415S	OEM
DCR1278SD2424	OEM
DCR1278SD2525	OEM
DCR1278SD2626	OEM
DCR1278SD2727	OEM
DCR1278SD2828	OEM
DCR1278SD2929	OEM
DCR1278SD3030	OEM
DCR1278SD3131	OEM
DCR1278SD3232	OEM
DCR1278SD3333	OEM
DCR1278SD3535	OEM
DCR1278SD3636	OEM
DCR1278SD3737	OEM
DCR1284SD2121	OEM
DCR1284SD2222	OEM
DCR1284SD2323	OEM
DCR1284SD2424	OEM
DCR1284SD2525	OEM
DCR1284SD2626	OEM
DCR1284SD2727	OEM
DCR1284SD2828	OEM
DCR1284SD2929	OEM
DCR1284SD3030	OEM
DCR1284SD3131	OEM
DCR1284SD3232	OEM
DCR1284SD3333	OEM
DCR1284SD3434	OEM
DCR1284SD3535	OEM
DCR1284SD3636	OEM
DCR1284SD3737	OEM
DCR1476SU2424	OEM
DCR1476SU2525	OEM
DCR1476SU2626	OEM
DCR1476SU2727	OEM
DCR1476SU2828	OEM
DCR1476SU2929	OEM
DCR1476SU3030	OEM
DCR1476SU3131	OEM
DCR1476SU3232	OEM
DCR1476SU3333	OEM
DCR1476SU3434	OEM
DCR1476SU3535	OEM
DCR1476SU3636	OEM
DCR1476SU3737	OEM
DCR1476SU3838	OEM
DCR1476SU3939	OEM
DCR1478SU3131	OEM
DCR1478SU3232	OEM
DCR1478SU3333	OEM
DCR1478SU3434	OEM
DCR1478SU3535	OEM
DCR1478SU3737	OEM
DCR1478SU3838	OEM
DCR1478SU3939	OEM
DCR1478SU4040	OEM
DCR1478SU4141	OEM
DCR1478SU4242	OEM
DCR1478SU4343	OEM
DCS025	OEM
DCS026-014	OEM
DCS026-014-25	OEM
DCS050	OEM
DCS86/16	OEM
DCU5-5	OEM
DCU5-12-12	OEM
DCU5-15-15	OEM
DCU12-5	OEM
DCU12-12-12	OEM
DCU12-15-15	OEM
DCV1	OEM

DEVICE TYPE	REPL CODE
DCV3	OEM
DCV6	0087
DCV12	OEM
DCV15	OEM
DCW12/5/3000	OEM
DCW12/5/4000	OEM
DCW12/12/1700	OEM
DCW12/15/1500	OEM
DCW14/15/1500	OEM
DCW24/5/3000	OEM
DCW24/5/4000	OEM
DCW24/12/1700	OEM
DCW48/5/3000	OEM
DCW48/5/4000	OEM
DCW48/12/1700	OEM
DCW48/15/1500	OEM
DD-000	0015
DD000	1325
DD-003	0015
DD003	0015
DD-006	0015
DD006	0015
DD-007	0015
DD007	0015
DD04	0196
DD04(IR)	0196
DD05	0479
DD05(IR)	0479
DD06	1073
DD06(IR)	1073
DD07(IR)	1073
DD07K	OEM
DD08K	OEM
DD09K	OEM
DD056	0015
DD058	0071
DD0.22/80X41	OEM
DD1S954	0133
DD3RLFB01L	OEM
DD10	OEM
DD10A	0369
DD10F-100	OEM
DD10K	OEM
DD11K	OEM
DD12J	OEM
DD13K	OEM
DD15	OEM
DD15K	OEM
DD20	OEM
DD20A	OEM
DD21S100	OEM
DD21S800	OEM
DD21S1200	OEM
DD22S800	OEM
DD22S1000	OEM
DD22S1200	OEM
DD22S1400	OEM
DD25	OEM
DD25F-20	2240
DD25F-40	2240
DD25F-60	2240
DD25F-80	2240
DD25F-100	OEM
DD25F-120	OEM
DD25F-140	OEM
DD25F-160	OEM
DD30	OEM
DD30A	OEM
DD31N400	1787
DD31N800	1787
DD31N1200	1787
DD31N1400	OEM
DD31S800	OEM
DD31S1000	OEM
DD31S1200	OEM
DD31S1400	OEM
DD35	OEM
DD40	OEM
DD40A	OEM
DD40F-20	2240
DD40F-40	2240
DD40F-60	2240
DD40F-80	2240
DD40F-100	OEM
DD40F-120	OEM
DD40F-140	OEM
DD40F-160	OEM
DD45S800	OEM
DD45S1000	OEM
DD45S1200	OEM
DD53S1000	OEM
DD53S1200	OEM
DD53S1400	OEM
DD55F-100	OEM
DD55FF-20	OEM
DD55FF-40	OEM
DD55FF-60	OEM
DD55FF-80	OEM
DD55FF-120	OEM
DD55FF-140	OEM
DD55FF-160	OEM
DD61N400K	OEM
DD61N800K	OEM
DD61N1200K	OEM
DD61N1400K	OEM
DD61N1600K	OEM
DD61S1000	OEM
DD61S1200	OEM
DD61S1400	OEM

DEVICE TYPE	REPL CODE
DD62S400	OEM
DD62S600	OEM
DD62S800	OEM
DD62S1000	OEM
DD65N400	2178
DD65N800	2178
DD65N1200	2178
DD65N1400	OEM
DD65N1600	OEM
DD68S1000	OEM
DD68S1200	OEM
DD68S1400	OEM
DD70F-20	2178
DD70F-40	2178
DD70F-60	2178
DD70F-80	2178
DD70F-100	OEM
DD70F-120	OEM
DD70F-140	OEM
DD70F-160	OEM
DD76N400K	OEM
DD76N800K	OEM
DD76N1200K	OEM
DD76N1400K	OEM
DD76N1600K	OEM
DD81S1000	OEM
DD81S1200	OEM
DD81S1400	OEM
DD82S400	OEM
DD82S600	OEM
DD82S800	OEM
DD85N400	2178
DD85N800	2178
DD85N1200	2178
DD85N1400	OEM
DD85N1600	OEM
DD85S800	OEM
DD85S1000	OEM
DD85S1200	OEM
DD85S1400	OEM
DD86N400K	OEM
DD86N800K	OEM
DD86N1200K	OEM
DD86N1400K	OEM
DD86N1600K	OEM
DD86N1800K	OEM
DD90F-20	6309
DD90F-40	6309
DD90F-60	6309
DD90F-80	6309
DD90F-100	OEM
DD90F-120	OEM
DD90F-140	OEM
DD90F-160	OEM
DD106N400K	OEM
DD106N800K	OEM
DD106N1200K	OEM
DD106N1400K	OEM
DD106N1600K	OEM
DD106N1800K	OEM
DD110F-20	OEM
DD110F-40	OEM
DD110F-60	OEM
DD110F-80	OEM
DD110F-120	OEM
DD110F-140	OEM
DD110F-160	OEM
DD130F-20	OEM
DD130F-40	OEM
DD130F-60	OEM
DD130F-80	OEM
DD130F-100	OEM
DD130F-120	OEM
DD130F-140	OEM
DD130F-160	OEM
DD151N400K	OEM
DD151N800K	OEM
DD151N1200K	OEM
DD151N1400K	OEM
DD151N1600K	OEM
DD151N1800K	OEM
DD160F-20	OEM
DD160F-40	OEM
DD160F-60	OEM
DD160F-80	OEM
DD160F-100	OEM
DD160F-120	OEM
DD160F-140	OEM
DD160F-160	OEM
DD175C	0015
DD176C	0015
DD177C	0015
DD236	0015
DD250N2000K	OEM
DD250N2200K	OEM
DD250N2400K	OEM
DD250N2500K	OEM
DD260N400K	OEM
DD260N800K	OEM
DD260N1200K	OEM
DD260N1400K	OEM
DD260N1600K	OEM
DD260N1800K	OEM
DD261N2000K	OEM
DD261N2200K	OEM
DD261N2400K	OEM
DD261N2500K	OEM
DD266	0015
DD268	0071

If replacement code is OEM, contact original manufacturer for replacement.

DEVICE TYPE	REPL CODE
DD700	OEM
DD710	OEM
DD711	OEM
DD713	OEM
DD716	OEM
DD810A(A)	OEM
DD811A(A)	OEM
DD813A(A)	OEM
DD816A(A)	OEM
DD1000	1325
DD1001	0015
DD1003	0015
DD1006	0015
DD1056	0015
DD1057	0015
DD1058	0071
DD1712A	OEM
DD2066	0015
DD2068	0071
DD2320	0015
DD2321	0015
DD2326	OEM
DD2327	0087
DD2520	OEM
DD2520A	OEM
DD2573	OEM
DD2573A	OEM
DD3020	OEM
DD3026	OEM
DD3076	OEM
DD3078	0087
DD3520	OEM
DD3520A	OEM
DD3573	OEM
DD3573A	OEM
DD3750	OEM
DD3751	OEM
DD3752	OEM
DD3753	OEM
DD3754	OEM
DD3755	OEM
DD3756	OEM
DD4020	OEM
DD4026	OEM
DD4066	OEM
DD4067	OEM
DD4068	OEM
DD4520	OEM
DD4521	OEM
DD4523	OEM
DD4526	OEM
DD5620H	OEM
DD5620S	OEM
DD5620V	OEM
DD5621H	OEM
DD5621S	OEM
DD5621V	OEM
DD5623H	OEM
DD5623S	OEM
DD5623V	OEM
DD5626H	OEM
DD5626S	OEM
DD5626V	OEM
DD6120H	OEM
DD6120S	OEM
DD6120V	OEM
DD6121H	OEM
DD6121S	OEM
DD6121V	OEM
DD6123H	OEM
DD6123S	OEM
DD6123V	OEM
DD6126H	OEM
DD6126S	OEM
DD6126V	OEM
DD6202	OEM
DD6205	OEM
DD6210	OEM
DD6220	OEM
DD6230	OEM
DD6240	OEM
DD6520(A)	OEM
DD6521(A)	OEM
DD6523(A)	OEM
DD6526(A)	OEM
DD6620(A)	OEM
DD6621(A)	OEM
DD6623(A)	OEM
DD6626(A)	OEM
DD6720(A)	OEM
DD6721(A)	OEM
DD6723(A)	OEM
DD6726(A)	OEM
DD6727(A)	OEM
DD6802	OEM
DD6805	OEM
DD6810	OEM
DD6820	OEM
DD6830	OEM
DD6840	OEM
DD7120	OEM
DD7121	OEM
DD7123	OEM
DD7126	OEM
DD7211AC	OEM
DD7211AMC	OEM
DD7211C	OEM
DD7211MC	OEM
DD7212AC	OEM
DD7212AMC	OEM
DD7212C	OEM
DD7212MC	OEM
DD7218BAC	OEM
DD7218BBC	OEM
DD7218BCC	OEM
DD7218BDC	OEM
DD7218EC	OEM
DD75516GF-045	OEM
DD232323	OEM
DD10000019	OEM
DD10000020	OEM
DD20000016	OEM
DD20000028	OEM
DD20000041	OEM
DD20000077	OEM
DD20000107	OEM
DD20000181	OEM
DD40000460	OEM
DD40000563	OEM
DD40000605	OEM
DD40000617	OEM
DD40001002	OEM
DD40001026	OEM
DD50000020	OEM
DDAC-10-1	OEM
DDAC-10-3	OEM
DDAC-11-1	OEM
DDAC-11-3	OEM
DDAC-12-1	OEM
DDAC-12-3	OEM
DDAY001001	0019
DDAY001010	0019
DDAY001022	0019
DDAY002001	0023
DDAY002002	0015
DDAY003001	OEM
DDAY004001	0133
DDAY006002	0030
DDAY007001	5024
DDAY008001	0466
DDAY008003	0244
DDAY008020	0062
DDAY009001	0157
DDAY009003	0416
DDAY009007	0416
DDAY09001	OEM
DDAY010002	0012
DDAY010005	0012
DDAY010007	0077
DDAY042001	0015
DDAY047001	0133
DDAY047005	0133
DDAY-048001	0124
DDAY048001	0133
DDAY048007	0124
DDAY048008	0124
DDAY048012	0133
DDAY048013	0124
DDAY048014	0133
DDAY067001	0715
DDAY069001	0133
DDAY090001	0163
DDAY101001	0019
DDAY103001	0015
DDAY108001	0644
DDAY126001	0057
DDAY1003001	OEM
DDB-4009	OEM
DDB-4037	OEM
DDB-4503	OEM
DDB-4504	OEM
DDB-4517	OEM
DDB-4517A	OEM
DDB5098	OEM
DDB-6224	OEM
DDB6224	OEM
DDB-6672	OEM
DDB-6672A	OEM
DDB-6673	OEM
DDB6673Y	OEM
DDB6783	OEM
DDBY002001	0023
DDBY003001	0006
DDBY003002	0006
DDBY003003	0006
DDBY004001	0006
DDBY007002	0148
DDBY008001	0688
DDBY104002	0527
DDBY209003	0364
DDBY216002	0224
DDBY219001	1136
DDBY222002	0076
DDBY224001	0076
DDBY224003	0076
DDBY224004	0076
DDBY224006	0076
DDBY227001	0219
DDBY227004	0386
DDBY228001	0042
DDBY230001	0833
DDBY231002	0830
DDBY233001	0076
DDBY246001	0781
DDBY256001	0884
DDBY257001	0930
DDBY259001	0076
DDBY259002	0076
DDBY261002	2195
DDBY262001	1211
DDBY269001	0127
DDBY270001	2787
DDBY272001	0018
DDBY273001	0076
DDBY277002	0151
DDBY278001	2276
DDBY278002	2276
DDBY283001	0127
DDBY287001	0127
DDBY288001	1581
DDBY289001	0930
DDBY295002	1060
DDBY299001	0076
DDBY301001	0155
DDBY307003	0830
DDBY407001	0042
DDBY407004	0419
DDBY410001	0945
DDBY410002	0945
DDBY4233001	0111
DDC-4561	OEM
DDC-4561A	OEM
DDC-4561B	OEM
DDC-4561C	OEM
DDC-4561D	OEM
DDC-4562	OEM
DDC-4562A	OEM
DDC-4562B	OEM
DDC-4562C	OEM
DDC-4562D	OEM
DDC-4563	OEM
DDC-4563A	OEM
DDC-4563B	OEM
DDC-4563C	OEM
DDC-4563D	OEM
DDC-4564	OEM
DDC-4564A	OEM
DDC-4564B	OEM
DDC-4564C	OEM
DDC-4564D	OEM
DDC-4565	OEM
DDC-4565A	OEM
DDC-4565B	OEM
DDC-4565C	OEM
DDC-4565D	OEM
DDC6757	OEM
DDC6757A	OEM
DDC6757B	OEM
DDC6757C	OEM
DDC6757D	OEM
DDCY001002	0683
DDCY002002	0321
DDCY006001	0321
DDCY007002	0148
DDCY103001	0843
DDCY104001	0410
DDCY104002	0212
DDCY104003	0410
DDE-201	0015
DDE6889	OEM
DDE6890	OEM
DDEY001001	0413
DDEY002001	0817
DDEY004001	0905
DDEY007001	OEM
DDEY015001	1007
DDEY017001	1369
DDEY019001	0011
DDEY020001	3751
DDEY026001	1290
DDEY027001	1152
DDEY028001	1187
DDEY029001	1199
DDEY030001	0232
DDEY031001	OEM
DDEY032001	1369
DDEY033001	OEM
DDEY037001	3754
DDEY042001	1288
DDEY046001	1288
DDEY055001	2238
DDEY058001	0215
DDEY061001	1805
DDEY064001	2246
DDEY070001	OEM
DDEY082001	4405
DDEY084001	0215
DDEY087001	2290
DDEY088001	1288
DDEY089001	0215
DDEY091001	1805
DDEY093001	1288
DDEY097001	4145
DDEY101001	OEM
DDEY109001	1532
DDEY123001	2512
DDEY130001	3980
DDEY131001	4567
DDEY132001	6808
DDEY133001	4564
DDEY146001	4571
DDEY147001	2312
DDEY148001	OEM
DDEY149001	0751
DDEY155001	OEM
DDEY157001	4227
DDEY171001	4227
DDEY172001	4399
DDEY173001	OEM
DDEY179001	0701
DDEY196001	OEM
DDEY1089001	OEM
DDF4021001	0120
DDF4091001	1805
DDFY007001	0139
DDFY017001	0312
DDFY020001	0139
DDFY021001	0120
DDFY021001#	0339
DDFY055001	2238
DDFY091001	1805
DDMV-1	0143
DDMV-2	0143
DDT12	OEM
DDV325	OEM
DE	OEM
DE-087	2290
DE2A	0124
DE3	0124
DE7RA5R10B	OEM
DE7RA5R60B	OEM
DE7RA6R80B	OEM
DE7RA8R20A	OEM
DE14	0015
DE14A	0015
DE16	0015
DE16A	0015
DE100	OEM
DE101	OEM
DE102	OEM
DE103	OEM
DE104	0124
DE105	OEM
DE106	OEM
DE110	0124
DE111	0124
DE112	0124
DE113	0124
DE114	0124
DE115	0124
DE125	OEM
DE-201	0015
DE201	0015
DE210	OEM
DE220	OEM
DE232	OEM
DE240	OEM
DE420A	OEM
DE432A	OEM
DE1000	OEM
DE1714A	OEM
DE1716A	OEM
DE1717A	OEM
DE1718A	OEM
DE1719A	OEM
DE1720A	OEM
DE1722A	OEM
DE1724A	OEM
DE1726A	OEM
DE3101/2	OEM
DE3101/5	OEM
DEC5651	OEM
DEEY004001	0905
DEP1712A	OEM
DEP1714A	OEM
DEP1716A	OEM
DEP1717A	OEM
DEP1718A	OEM
DEP1719A	OEM
DEP1720A	OEM
DEP1722A	OEM
DEP1724A	OEM
DEP1726A	OEM
DER1	0071
DER2	OEM
DER3	OEM
DER4	OEM
DER5	OEM
DER6	OEM
DER7	OEM
DER8	OEM
DER9	OEM
DER10	OEM
DER11	OEM
DER12	OEM
DER13	OEM
DER14	OEM
DER15	OEM
DERB26-20	0344
DESFH205	OEM
DF005	0241
DF005M	0241
DF005S	OEM
DF01	0241
DF01M	0241
DF01S	OEM
DF02	0241
DF02M	0241
DF02S	OEM
DF04	4501
DF04M	4501
DF04S	OEM
DF06	1864
DF06M	1864
DF06S	OEM
DF08	3503
DF08M	3503
DF08S	OEM
DF1H	0102
DF-2	0103
DF2	0715
DF10	3503
DF10M	3503
DF10S	OEM
DF15	OEM
DF20	OEM
DF25	OEM
DF30	OEM
DF35	OEM
DF40	OEM
DF64D	0071
DF100	OEM
DF252-02	OEM
DF252-04	OEM
DF252-06	OEM
DF252-08	OEM
DF252-10	OEM
DF252-12	OEM
DF252-14	OEM
DF320	6473
DF320ADJ	OEM
DF320ADK	OEM
DF320DJ	OEM
DF320DK	OEM
DF320DP	OEM
DF321	OEM
DF321DP	OEM
DF322	OEM
DF322DJ	OEM
DF322DK	OEM
DF322DP	OEM
DF323DJ	OEM
DF323DP	OEM
DF328DJ	OEM
DF331/332	OEM
DF412CJ	OEM
DF451-01	OEM
DF451-02	OEM
DF451-04	OEM
DF451-06	OEM
DF451-08	OEM
DF451-10	OEM
DF451-12	OEM
DF451-14	OEM
DF452-02	OEM
DF452-04	OEM
DF452-06	OEM
DF452-08	OEM
DF452-10	OEM
DF452-12	OEM
DF452-14	OEM
DF452-15	OEM
DF652-02	OEM
DF652-04	OEM
DF652-06	OEM
DF652-08	OEM
DF652-10	OEM
DF652-12	OEM
DF652-14	OEM
DF652-16	OEM
DF652-18	OEM
DF652-20	OEM
DF652-22	OEM
DF652-24	OEM
DF652-25	OEM
DF752-02	OEM
DF752-04	OEM
DF752-06	OEM
DF752-08	OEM
DF752-11	OEM
DF752-12	OEM
DF752-14	OEM
DF752-16	OEM
DF752-18	OEM
DF752-20	OEM
DFA01C	0133
DFA01G	0023
DFA01J	0017
DFA01L	0017
DFA01R	0017
DFA03L	OEM
DFA03R	OEM
DFA05B	0023
DFA05C	0023
DFA05E	0023
DFA05G	0023
DFA05G-KB4	0023
DFA05G-KBG	0023
DFA1A1	1082
DFA1A2	0023
DFA1A4	0023
DFA1A4-T3	0023
DFA1A4-Y	0023
DFA1A4-Z	0023
DFB03R	0344
DFB03T	0344
DFB03W	0344
DFB05B	0023
DFB05C	0023
DFB05E	0023
DFB05G	0023
DFC05J	0017
DFC05L	0017
DFC05N	0017
DFC05R	0017
DFC10E	0023
DFC10E-KB4	0023
DFC10G	0023
DFC15L	0102
DFC15L-KC5	0102
DFD05	OEM
DFD05B	0015
DFD05C	0015
DFD05E	0015
DFD05G	0023
DFD05T	0023
DFD05TE-BT	OEM
DFD05TG	0023
DFD05TG-BT	0023
DFEQA02-05C	0041
DFEQA02-06	0091
DFEQA02-06A	0253
DFEQA02-06C	0091
DFEQA02-06CDE	0091
DFEQA02-06D	0466
DFEQA02-08A	0077
DFEQA02-08D	0077
DFEQA02-09D	0057
DFEQA02-10B	0064
DFEQA02-10C	0064
DFEQA02-12B	0053
DFEQA02-16A	0440
DFEQA02-23A	0489
DFEQA02-30C	0166
DFEQA02-35B	0010
DFERA81-004	0023
DFERB12-01	0023
DFERB12-02	0023
DFERC04-02	0071
DFERC04-02F	0559
DFF20B10	OEM
DFF20B12	OEM
DFF50B10	OEM
DFF50B12	OEM
DFG1A2	0604
DFG1A4	0790
DFG1A6	0015
DFG1A8	0072
DFG2A2	0087
DFG2A4	0087
DFG2A6	0087
DFG2A8	0087
DFH10B	0015
DFH10C	0015
DFH10E	0015
DFH10G	0015
DFH10G-KB4	0023
DFH10GKB4	0023
DFH10J	0071
DFH10TG	0023
DFH10TG-AT1	0023
DFH10TG-KB4	0023
DFM1A2	0023
DFM1A4	0023
DFM1SA4	0023
DFNA3-50	OEM
DFNA3-100	OEM
DFP027	OEM
DFP068	OEM
DFP140	OEM
DFP180	OEM
DFP240	OEM
DFS80A8	OEM
DFS80A8R	OEM
DFS80A10	OEM
DFS80A10R	OEM
DFS80A13	OEM
DFS80A13R	OEM
DFS80A15	OEM
DFS80A15R	OEM
DFS250A8	OEM
DFS250A10	OEM
DFS250A13	OEM
DFS250A15	OEM
DFS250AR8	OEM
DFS250AR10	OEM
DFS250AR13	OEM
DFS250AR15	OEM
DG1	0102
DG1-005	0023
DG1K	0071
DG1M	0015
DG1MR	0015
DG-1N	0102
DG1N	0102
DG1N60	0019
DG1NK	OEM
DG-1NR	0102
DG1NR	0182
DG1PR	0015
DG1S34	0143
DG1S188	0143
DG1S188-FM	2217
DG2	0102
DG2-006	0023
DG3	OEM
DG11	OEM
DG-13	0918
DG13	5317
DG13TV	5317
DG-14	0969
DG14	5317
DG20ABK	OEM
DG100J	OEM
DG100K	OEM
DG100M	OEM
DG106AAR	OEM
DG111CDD	OEM
DG111CFD	OEM
DG111IDD	OEM
DG111IFD	OEM
DG111MDD	OEM
DG111MFD	OEM
DG112CDD	OEM
DG112CFD	OEM
DG112IDD	OEM
DG112IFD	OEM
DG112MDD	OEM
DG112MFD	OEM
DG116CDD	OEM
DG116CFD	OEM
DG116IDD	OEM
DG116IFD	OEM
DG116MDD	OEM
DG116MFD	OEM
DG118CDD	OEM
DG118CFD	OEM
DG118IDD	OEM
DG118IFD	OEM
DG118MDD	OEM
DG118MFD	OEM
DG120CDD	OEM
DG120CFD	OEM
DG120IDD	OEM
DG120IFD	OEM
DG120MDD	OEM
DG120MFD	OEM
DG121CDD	OEM
DG121CFD	OEM
DG121IDD	OEM
DG121IFD	OEM
DG121MDD	OEM
DG121MFD	OEM
DG123AL	OEM
DG123AP	OEM
DG123BP	OEM
DG123CDD	OEM
DG123CFD	OEM
DG123IDD	OEM
DG123IFD	OEM
DG123MDD	OEM
DG123MFD	OEM
DG125AL	OEM
DG125AP	OEM
DG125BP	OEM
DG125CDD	OEM
DG125CFD	OEM
DG125IDD	OEM
DG125IFD	OEM
DG125MDD	OEM
DG125MFD	OEM
DG126ADD	OEM
DG126AFD	OEM
DG126AL	OEM
DG126AP	OEM
DG126BDD	OEM
DG126BFD	OEM
DG126BP	OEM
DG129ADD	OEM
DG129AFD	OEM
DG129AL	OEM
DG129AP	OEM
DG129BDD	OEM
DG129BFD	OEM
DG129BP	OEM
DG-130	OEM
DG130	5317
DG133ADD	OEM
DG133AFD	OEM
DG133AL	OEM
DG133AP	OEM
DG133BDD	OEM
DG133BFD	OEM
DG133BP	OEM
DG134ADD	OEM
DG134AFD	OEM
DG134AL	OEM
DG134AP	OEM
DG134BDD	OEM
DG134BFD	OEM
DG134BP	OEM
DG139ADD	OEM
DG139AFD	OEM
DG139AL	OEM
DG139AP	OEM
DG139BDD	OEM
DG139BFD	OEM
DG139BP	OEM
DG140ADD	OEM
DG140AFD	OEM
DG140AL	OEM
DG140BDD	OEM
DG140BFD	OEM
DG141ADD	OEM
DG141AFD	OEM
DG141AL	OEM
DG141AP	OEM
DG141BDD	OEM
DG141BFD	OEM
DG141BP	OEM
DG142ADD	OEM
DG142AFD	OEM
DG142AL	OEM

If replacement code is OEM, contact original manufacturer for replacement.

375

DEVICE TYPE	REPL CODE
DG142AP	OEM
DG142BDD	OEM
DG142BFD	OEM
DG142BP	OEM
DG143ADD	OEM
DG143AFD	OEM
DG143AL	OEM
DG143AP	OEM
DG143BDD	OEM
DG143BFD	OEM
DG143BP	OEM
DG144ADD	OEM
DG144AFD	OEM
DG144AL	OEM
DG144AP	OEM
DG144BDD	OEM
DG144BFD	OEM
DG144BP	OEM
DG145ADD	OEM
DG145AFD	OEM
DG145AL	OEM
DG145BDD	OEM
DG145BFD	OEM
DG146ADD	OEM
DG146AFD	OEM
DG146AL	OEM
DG146AP	OEM
DG146BDD	OEM
DG146BFD	OEM
DG146BP	OEM
DG151ADD	OEM
DG151AFD	OEM
DG151AL	OEM
DG151AP	OEM
DG151BDD	OEM
DG151BFD	OEM
DG151BP	OEM
DG152ADD	OEM
DG152AFD	OEM
DG152AL	OEM
DG152AP	OEM
DG152BDD	OEM
DG152BFD	OEM
DG152BP	OEM
DG153ADD	OEM
DG153AFD	OEM
DG153AL	OEM
DG153BDD	OEM
DG153BFD	OEM
DG154ADD	OEM
DG154AFD	OEM
DG154AL	OEM
DG154AP	OEM
DG154BDD	OEM
DG154BFD	OEM
DG154BP	OEM
DG161ADD	OEM
DG161AFD	OEM
DG161AL	OEM
DG161AP	OEM
DG161BDD	OEM
DG161BFD	OEM
DG161BP	OEM
DG162ADD	OEM
DG162AFD	OEM
DG162AL	OEM
DG162AP	OEM
DG162BDD	OEM
DG162BFD	OEM
DG162BP	OEM
DG163ADD	OEM
DG163AFD	OEM
DG163AL	OEM
DG163BDD	OEM
DG163BFD	OEM
DG164ADD	OEM
DG164AFD	OEM
DG164AL	OEM
DG164AP	OEM
DG164BDD	OEM
DG164BFD	OEM
DG164BP	OEM
DG172AL	OEM
DG172AP	OEM
DG172BP	OEM
DG172CJ	OEM
DG180AA	OEM
DG180AL	OEM
DG180AP	OEM
DG180APDD	OEM
DG180APDE	OEM
DG180APJD	OEM
DG180BA	OEM
DG180BL	OEM
DG180BP	OEM
DG180BPDD	OEM
DG180BPJD	OEM
DG181AA	OEM
DG181AL	OEM
DG181AP	OEM
DG181APDD	OEM
DG181APJD	OEM
DG181BA	OEM
DG181BL	OEM
DG181BP	OEM
DG181BPDD	OEM
DG181BPJD	OEM
DG182AA	OEM
DG182AL	OEM

DEVICE TYPE	REPL CODE
DG182AP	OEM
DG182APDD	OEM
DG182APJD	OEM
DG182BA	OEM
DG182BL	OEM
DG182BP	OEM
DG182BPDD	OEM
DG182BPDE	OEM
DG182BPJD	OEM
DG182BPJE	OEM
DG183AL	OEM
DG183AP	OEM
DG183APDE	OEM
DG183APJE	OEM
DG183BL	OEM
DG183BP	OEM
DG184AL	OEM
DG184AP	OEM
DG184APDE	OEM
DG184APJE	OEM
DG184BL	OEM
DG184BP	OEM
DG185AL	OEM
DG185AP	OEM
DG185APDE	OEM
DG185APJE	OEM
DG185BL	OEM
DG185BP	OEM
DG185BPDE	OEM
DG185BPJE	OEM
DG186AA	OEM
DG186AL	OEM
DG186AP	OEM
DG186APDD	OEM
DG186APJD	OEM
DG186BA	OEM
DG186BL	OEM
DG186BP	OEM
DG186BPDD	OEM
DG186BPJD	OEM
DG187AL	OEM
DG187AP	OEM
DG187APDD	OEM
DG187APJD	OEM
DG187BA	OEM
DG187BL	OEM
DG187BP	OEM
DG187BPDD	OEM
DG187BPJD	OEM
DG188AA	OEM
DG188AL	OEM
DG188AP	OEM
DG188APDD	OEM
DG188APJD	OEM
DG188BA	OEM
DG188BL	OEM
DG188BP	OEM
DG188BPDD	OEM
DG188BPJD	OEM
DG189AL	OEM
DG189AP	OEM
DG189APDE	OEM
DG189APJE	OEM
DG189BL	OEM
DG189BP	OEM
DG189BPDE	OEM
DG189BPJE	OEM
DG190AL	OEM
DG190AP	OEM
DG190APDE	OEM
DG190APJE	OEM
DG190BL	OEM
DG190BP	OEM
DG190BPDE	OEM
DG190BPJE	OEM
DG191AL	OEM
DG191AP	OEM
DG191APDE	OEM
DG191APJE	OEM
DG191BL	OEM
DG191BP	OEM
DG191BPDE	OEM
DG191BPJE	OEM
DG200AA	OEM
DG200AAA	OEM
DG200AAK	OEM
DG200ABA	OEM
DG200ABK	OEM
DG200ACJ	OEM
DG200ACK	OEM
DG200AK	OEM
DG200AL	OEM
DG200AP	OEM
DG200BA	OEM
DG200BK	OEM
DG200BL	OEM
DG200BP	OEM
DG200CJ	OEM
DG201AAK	OEM
DG201ABK	OEM
DG201ACJ	OEM
DG201ACK	OEM
DG201AK	OEM
DG201CJ	OEM
DG202AK(A)	OEM
DG202BK(A)	OEM
DG202CJ(A)	OEM
DG202CK(A)	OEM
DG211CJ	OEM

DEVICE TYPE	REPL CODE
DG212CJ(A)	OEM
DG243AK(A)	OEM
DG243CJ(A)	OEM
DG243CK(A)	OEM
DG281AA	OEM
DG281AP	OEM
DG281BA	OEM
DG281BP	OEM
DG284AP	OEM
DG284BP	OEM
DG287AA	OEM
DG287AP	OEM
DG287BA	OEM
DG287BP	OEM
DG290AP	OEM
DG290BP	OEM
DG300AA	OEM
DG300AAA	OEM
DG300AAK	OEM
DG300AAL	OEM
DG300ABK	OEM
DG300ACJ	OEM
DG300ACK	OEM
DG300AP	OEM
DG300BA	OEM
DG300BP	OEM
DG300CJ	OEM
DG301AA	OEM
DG301AAA	OEM
DG301AAK	OEM
DG301ABA	OEM
DG301ABK	OEM
DG301ACJ	OEM
DG301ACK	OEM
DG301AP	OEM
DG301BA	OEM
DG301BP	OEM
DG301CJ	OEM
DG302AAK	OEM
DG302AAL	OEM
DG302ACJ	OEM
DG302ACK	OEM
DG302AP	OEM
DG302BP	OEM
DG302CJ	OEM
DG303AAK	OEM
DG303AAL	OEM
DG303ABK	OEM
DG303ACJ	OEM
DG303ACK	OEM
DG303AP	OEM
DG303BP	OEM
DG303CJ	OEM
DG304AA	OEM
DG304AAK	OEM
DG304AAL	OEM
DG304ABA	OEM
DG304ABK	OEM
DG304ACJ	OEM
DG304ACK	OEM
DG304AP	OEM
DG304BA	OEM
DG304BP	OEM
DG304CJ	OEM
DG305AA	OEM
DG305AAA	OEM
DG305AAK	OEM
DG305AAL	OEM
DG305ABA	OEM
DG305ABK	OEM
DG305ACJ	OEM
DG305ACK	OEM
DG305AP	OEM
DG305BA	OEM
DG305BP	OEM
DG305CJ	OEM
DG306AAK	OEM
DG306AAL	OEM
DG306ABK	OEM
DG306ACJ	OEM
DG306ACK	OEM
DG306AP	OEM
DG306BP	OEM
DG306CJ	OEM
DG307AAK	OEM
DG307AAL	OEM
DG307ABK	OEM
DG307ACJ	OEM
DG307ACK	OEM
DG307AP	OEM
DG307BP	OEM
DG307CJ	OEM
DG308CJ	OEM
DG309CJ	OEM
DG381AA	OEM
DG381AAA	OEM
DG381AAK	OEM
DG381ABA	OEM
DG381ABK	OEM
DG381ACJ	OEM
DG381ACK	OEM
DG381AP	OEM
DG381BA	OEM
DG381BP	OEM
DG381CJ	OEM
DG384AAK	OEM
DG384ABK	OEM
DG384ACJ	OEM
DG384ACK	OEM

DEVICE TYPE	REPL CODE
DG384AP	OEM
DG384BP	OEM
DG384CJ	OEM
DG387AA	OEM
DG387AAA	OEM
DG387AAK	OEM
DG387ABA	OEM
DG387ABK	OEM
DG387ACJ	OEM
DG387ACK	OEM
DG387AP	OEM
DG387BA	OEM
DG387BP	OEM
DG387CJ	OEM
DG390AAK	OEM
DG390ABK	OEM
DG390ACJ	OEM
DG390ACK	OEM
DG390AP	OEM
DG390BP	OEM
DG390CJ	OEM
DG501AP	OEM
DG501BP	OEM
DG501CJ	OEM
DG503AP	OEM
DG503BP	OEM
DG506ABR	OEM
DG506ACJ	OEM
DG506AR	OEM
DG506BR	OEM
DG506CJ	OEM
DG507AAR	OEM
DG507ABR	OEM
DG507ACJ	OEM
DG507AR	OEM
DG507BR	OEM
DG507CJ	OEM
DG508AAK	OEM
DG508ABK	OEM
DG508ACJ	OEM
DG508ACK	OEM
DG508AL	OEM
DG508AP	OEM
DG508BP	OEM
DG508CJ	OEM
DG509AAK	OEM
DG509ABK	OEM
DG509ACJ	OEM
DG509ACK	OEM
DG509AL	OEM
DG509AP	OEM
DG509BP	OEM
DG509CJ	OEM
DG515ADICE	OEM
DG515AP	OEM
DG515BP	OEM
DG515CJ	OEM
DG516ADICE	OEM
DG516AR	OEM
DG516BR	OEM
DG516CJ	OEM
DG528AK	OEM
DG528BK(A)	OEM
DG528CJ(A)	OEM
DG529AK(A)	OEM
DG529BK(A)	OEM
DG529CJ(A)	OEM
DG5040AK(A)	OEM
DG5040AL(A)	OEM
DG5040CJ(A)	OEM
DG5040CK(A)	OEM
DG5041AA(A)	OEM
DG5041AK(A)	OEM
DG5041AL(A)	OEM
DG5041CJ(A)	OEM
DG5041CK(A)	OEM
DG5042AA(A)	OEM
DG5042AK(A)	OEM
DG5042AL(A)	OEM
DG5042CJ(A)	OEM
DG5042CK(A)	OEM
DG5043AK(A)	OEM
DG5043AL(A)	OEM
DG5043CJ(A)	OEM
DG5043CK(A)	OEM
DG5044AA(A)	OEM
DG5044AK(A)	OEM
DG5044AL(A)	OEM
DG5044CK(A)	OEM
DG5045AK(A)	OEM
DG5045AL(A)	OEM
DG5045CJ(A)	OEM
DG5045CK(A)	OEM
DGA5	0133
DGA187AA	OEM
DGA5768	OEM
DGA5768A	OEM
DGA5768B	OEM
DGA5768C	OEM
DGA5768D	OEM
DGA6036	OEM
DGA6036A	OEM
DGA6036B	OEM
DGA6238	OEM
DGA6238A	OEM
DGA6238B	OEM
DGB6126	OEM
DGB6126A	OEM
DGB6200	OEM

DEVICE TYPE	REPL CODE
DGB6200A	OEM
DGB6201	OEM
DGB6201A	OEM
DGB6202	OEM
DGB6202A	OEM
DGB6203	OEM
DGB6203A	OEM
DGB6204	OEM
DGB6204A	OEM
DGB8081	OEM
DGB8091	OEM
DGB8094	OEM
DGB8095	OEM
DGB8121	OEM
DGB8122	OEM
DGB8123	OEM
DGB8125	OEM
DGB8131	OEM
DGB8132	OEM
DGB8133	OEM
DGB8134	OEM
DGB8135	OEM
DGB8141	OEM
DGB8144	OEM
DGB8145	OEM
DGB8154	OEM
DGB8155	OEM
DGB8156	OEM
DGB8181	OEM
DGB8191	OEM
DGB8194	OEM
DGB8195	OEM
DGB8211	OEM
DGB8212	OEM
DGB8213	OEM
DGB8214	OEM
DGB8215	OEM
DGB8216	OEM
DGB8221	OEM
DGB8222	OEM
DGB8223	OEM
DGB8224	OEM
DGB8225	OEM
DGB8231	OEM
DGB8232	OEM
DGB8233	OEM
DGB8234	OEM
DGB8235	OEM
DGB8241	OEM
DGB8244	OEM
DGB8245	OEM
DGB8254	OEM
DGB8255	OEM
DGB8256	OEM
DGB8281	OEM
DGB8291	OEM
DGB8294	OEM
DGB8295	OEM
DGB8311	OEM
DGB8312	OEM
DGB8313	OEM
DGB8314	OEM
DGB8315	OEM
DGB8321	OEM
DGB8322	OEM
DGB8323	OEM
DGB8324	OEM
DGB8325	OEM
DGB8332	OEM
DGB8333	OEM
DGB8334	OEM
DGB8335	OEM
DGB8344	OEM
DGB8345	OEM
DGB8354	OEM
DGB8355	OEM
DGB8356	OEM
DGB8411	OEM
DGB8412	OEM
DGB8413	OEM
DGB8414	OEM
DGB8415	OEM
DGB8421	OEM
DGB8422	OEM
DGB8423	OEM
DGB8424	OEM
DGB8425	OEM
DGB8431	OEM
DGB8432	OEM
DGB8433	OEM
DGB8434	OEM
DGB8435	OEM
DGB8444	OEM
DGB8445	OEM
DGB8454	OEM
DGB8455	OEM
DGB8456	OEM
DGB8511	OEM
DGB8512	OEM
DGB8513	OEM
DGB8515	OEM
DGB8521	OEM
DGB8522	OEM
DGB8523	OEM
DGB8524	OEM
DGB8525	OEM
DGB8531	OEM
DGB8532	OEM
DGB8533	OEM

DEVICE TYPE	REPL CODE
DGB8534	OEM
DGB8535	OEM
DGB8544	OEM
DGB8545	OEM
DGB8554	OEM
DGB8555	OEM
DGB8556	OEM
DGB8612	OEM
DGB8613	OEM
DGB8615	OEM
DGB8622	OEM
DGB8623	OEM
DGB8624	OEM
DGB8625	OEM
DGB8632	OEM
DGB8633	OEM
DGB8634	OEM
DGB8635	OEM
DGB8712	OEM
DGB8713	OEM
DGB8714	OEM
DGB8715	OEM
DGB8722	OEM
DGB8724	OEM
DGB8725	OEM
DGB8732	OEM
DGB8733	OEM
DGB8734	OEM
DGB8735	OEM
DGB8812	OEM
DGB8813	OEM
DGB8822	OEM
DGB8823	OEM
DGB8912	OEM
DGB8913	OEM
DGB8922	OEM
DGB8923	OEM
DGB9211	OEM
DGB9212	OEM
DGB9213	OEM
DGB9214	OEM
DGB9215	OEM
DGB9221	OEM
DGB9222	OEM
DGB9223	OEM
DGB9224	OEM
DGB9225	OEM
DGB9234	OEM
DGB9235	OEM
DGB9244	OEM
DGB9245	OEM
DGB9246	OEM
DGB9311	OEM
DGB9312	OEM
DGB9313	OEM
DGB9314	OEM
DGB9315	OEM
DGB9321	OEM
DGB9322	OEM
DGB9323	OEM
DGB9324	OEM
DGB9325	OEM
DGB9334	OEM
DGB9335	OEM
DGB9344	OEM
DGB9346	OEM
DGB9411	OEM
DGB9412	OEM
DGB9413	OEM
DGB9414	OEM
DGB9415	OEM
DGB9421	OEM
DGB9422	OEM
DGB9423	OEM
DGB9424	OEM
DGB9425	OEM
DGB9434	OEM
DGB9435	OEM
DGDS135D	0023
DGDS135E	0023
DGDS442	0133
DGDS442X	0124
DGDSB15C	0071
DGDSF10C	0023
DGGMA01	0124
DGGMA01-L	0133
DGGZA3.9-X	0036
DGGZA3.9X	0036
DGGZA4.3-Y	0274
DGGZA4.3Y	0274
DGGZA5.1-X	0041
DGGZA5.1-Y	0582
DGGZA5.1-Z	0041
DGGZA5.1X	0041
DGGZA5.1Y	0041
DGGZA5.6-Y	0253
DGGZA6.2	0466
DGGZA6.2-X	0466
DGGZA6.2-XYZ	0091
DGGZA6.2-Y	0466
DGGZA6.2X	0466
DGGZA7.5-Y	0077
DGGZA8.2-Y	0165
DGGZA9.1-Z	0057
DGGZA9.1Z	0057
DGGZA10-T	0064
DGGZA10-Y	0064
DGGZA10-Z	0064
DGGZA10Y	0064

DEVICE TYPE	REPL CODE
DGGZA13-X	0053
DGGZA13X	0053
DGGZA16-Y	0440
DGGZA22-Z	0700
DGGZA24-Y	0489
DGGZA27-Y	0450
DGGZA30	0195
DGGZA30-Y	0195
DGGZA36-Y	0010
DGGZA36Y	0010
DGGZA39-Y	0032
DGGZM6.2-B2	0466
DGGZM6.8-B2	OEM
DGGZM7.5-B2	0077
DGGZM8.2-B2	0165
DGGZM9.1-B2	0057
DGGZM20-B2	0695
DGGZM24-B2	0489
DGIN	0102
DGL5630	1319
DGM	0244
D-GM-2	0143
DGM-2	0143
DGM-3	0143
DGM3	0143
DGM111AL	OEM
DGM111AP	OEM
DGM111BP	OEM
DGM122AL	OEM
DGM122AP	OEM
DGM122BP	OEM
DGM181BA	OEM
DGM181BJ	OEM
DGM181BK	OEM
DGM181BL	OEM
DGM182AA	OEM
DGM182AJ	OEM
DGM182AK	OEM
DGM182AL	OEM
DGM182BA	OEM
DGM182BJ	OEM
DGM182BK	OEM
DGM184BJ	OEM
DGM184BK	OEM
DGM184BL	OEM
DGM185AJ	OEM
DGM185AL	OEM
DGM185BJ	OEM
DGM185BK	OEM
DGM185BL	OEM
DGM187BA	OEM
DGM187BJ	OEM
DGM188AA	OEM
DGM188AJ	OEM
DGM188AK	OEM
DGM188AL	OEM
DGM188BA	OEM
DGM188BK	OEM
DGM188BL	OEM
DGM190BJ	OEM
DGM190BK	OEM
DGM190BL	OEM
DGM191AJ	OEM
DGM191AK	OEM
DGM191AL	OEM
DGM191BJ	OEM
DGM191BK	OEM
DGM191BL	OEM
DGMS181BA	OEM
DGMS181BK	OEM
DGMS181BL	OEM
DGMS182AA	OEM
DGMS182AJ	OEM
DGMS182AK	OEM
DGMS182AL	OEM
DGMS182BA	OEM
DGMS182BJ	OEM
DGMS182BK	OEM
DGMS182BL	OEM
DGMS184BJ	OEM
DGMS184BK	OEM
DGMS184BL	OEM
DGMS185AJ	OEM
DGMS185AK	OEM
DGMS185AL	OEM
DGMS185BJ	OEM
DGMS185BK	OEM
DGMS185BL	OEM
DGMS187BA	OEM
DGMS187BJ	OEM
DGMS187BK	OEM
DGMS187BL	OEM
DGMS188AA	OEM
DGMS188AJ	OEM
DGMS188AK	OEM
DGMS188AL	OEM
DGMS188BA	OEM
DGMS188BJ	OEM
DGMS188BK	OEM
DGMS188BL	OEM
DGMS191BJ	OEM
DGMS191BK	OEM
DGS4B10	0319
DH0006CH	OEM
DH0006CN	OEM
DH0006H	OEM
DH0008CH	OEM
DH0008CN	OEM
DH0008H	OEM

376

If replacement code is OEM, contact original manufacturer for replacement.

DEVICE TYPE	REPL CODE
DH-001	0015
DH-002	0015
DH0011AH	OEM
DH0011CH	OEM
DH0011CN	OEM
DH0011H	OEM
DH0016CN	OEM
DH0017CN	OEM
DH0018CN	OEM
DH0028CH	OEM
DH0028CN	OEM
DH0034CD	OEM
DH0034CH	OEM
DH0034D	OEM
DH0034H	OEM
DH0069	OEM
DH1S2076	0133
DH1S2076A	0124
DH4R2	0015
DH4R4	OEM
DH4R6	OEM
DH14	0015
DH14A	0015
DH16	0015
DH16A	0015
DH3467CD	OEM
DH3467CN	OEM
DH3468CD	OEM
DH3468CN	OEM
DH3724CD	OEM
DH3724CN	OEM
DH3725CD	OEM
DH3725CN	OEM
DHA16	OEM
DHA20	OEM
DHA6520	OEM
DHA6520A	OEM
DHA6520B	OEM
DHA6520C	OEM
DHA6520D	OEM
DHA6522	OEM
DHA6522A	OEM
DHA6522B	OEM
DHA6522C	OEM
DHA6522D	OEM
DHA6523	OEM
DHA6523A	OEM
DHA6523B	OEM
DHA6523C	OEM
DHA6523D	OEM
DHA6524	OEM
DHA6524A	OEM
DHA6524B	OEM
DHA6524C	OEM
DHA6524D	OEM
DHA6525	OEM
DHA6525A	OEM
DHA6525B	OEM
DHA6525C	OEM
DHA6525D	OEM
DHB08	OEM
DHB10	OEM
DHB12	OEM
DHB14	OEM
DHB16	OEM
DHB18	OEM
DHD800	0133
DHD805	0133
DHD806	0133
DHD8001	0133
DHG3A120	OEM
DHG3B140	OEM
DHG3C160	OEM
DHG3D200	OEM
DHG3F250	OEM
DHG3G80	OEM
DHHZT33	3417
DHR21	OEM
DI-1	0143
DI-2	0143
DI-5	0755
DI-7	0015
DI7	0015
DI-8	0057
DI-8(COURIER)	0012
DI-8(DIODE)	0143
DI-20	0124
DI-42S	0015
DI42S	0015
DI-46	0015
DI46	0015
DI-52S	0015
DI52S	0015
DI-55	0015
DI-56	0015
DI56	0015
DI-71	0015
DI-72S	0015
DI72S	0015
DI-172S	0015
DI210	OEM
DI220	OEM
DI230	OEM
DI232	OEM
DI240	OEM
DI242	OEM
DI300	OEM
DI302	OEM
DI445	OEM

DEVICE TYPE	REPL CODE
DI446	OEM
DI500B	OEM
DI502B	OEM
DI503B	OEM
DI504B	OEM
DI505B	OEM
DI507B	OEM
DI508B	OEM
DI509B	OEM
DI510B	OEM
DI512B	OEM
DI513B	OEM
DI514B	OEM
DI603A	OEM
DI604A	OEM
DI605A	OEM
DI-645	0015
DI645	0015
DI-646	0015
DI646	0015
DI-647	0015
DI-648	0015
DI-649	0015
DI-650	0071
DI650	0071
DI-705	0015
DI803A	OEM
DI804A	OEM
DI805A	OEM
DI914-1B	OEM
DI914-1Q	OEM
DI914-1QM	OEM
DI914-2B	OEM
DI914-2Q	OEM
DI914-2QM	OEM
DI914-3B	OEM
DI914-3Q	OEM
DI914-3QM	OEM
DI-1649	0015
DI1649	0015
DI5117/5120	OEM
DI5118/5121	OEM
DI5119/5122	OEM
DI5119-1	OEM
DI5140	OEM
DI5180	OEM
DI5240	OEM
DI5280	OEM
DI-8020(A)	OEM
DIA	0244
DIAM01Z	0015
DIB	0196
DIB005	OEM
DIB01	OEM
DIB02	OEM
DIB04	OEM
DIB06	OEM
DIB08	OEM
DIB10	OEM
DIC	0196
DICA1	OEM
DICR1	0071
DICR2	OEM
DICR3	OEM
DICR4	OEM
DICR5	OEM
DICR6	OEM
DICR7	OEM
DICR8	OEM
DICR9	OEM
DICR10	OEM
DICR11	OEM
DICR12	OEM
DICR13	OEM
DICR14	OEM
DICR15	OEM
DID	0071
DIDS442X	0124
DIDS448-FA1	0124
DIE	0015
DII-203-200	OEM
DII-203-201	OEM
DII-203-300	OEM
DII-203-301	OEM
DIJ	0015
DIJ61224	0143
DIJ70485	0030
DIJ70486	0133
DIJ70488	0015
DIJ70542	0143
DIJ70543	0123
DIJ70544	0015
DIJ70545	0133
DIJ70644	0123
DIJ70645	0143
DIJ70646	0143
DIJ70695	0015
DIJ71273	0133
DIJ71711	0133
DIJ71776	0143
DIJ71777	0030
DIJ71778	0123
DIJ71779	0392
DIJ71895-1	1141
DIJ71958	0015
DIJ71959	0015
DIJ71960	0133
DIJ71961	0752
DIJ72163	0102

DEVICE TYPE	REPL CODE
DIJ72164	0133
DIJ72165	0012
DIJ72166	0143
DIJ72167	0102
DIJ72168	0015
DIJ72169	0098
DIJ72170	0102
DIJ72171	0102
DIJ72172	1075
DIJ72174	0102
DIJ72290	0102
DIJ72291	0102
DIJ72292	0087
DIJ72293	0631
DIJ72294	0143
DIJ72653	OEM
DIJ72702	0549
DIK	0071
DIK40	OEM
DIL	0015
DIM	0157
DINS4	OEM
DIO11	OEM
DIO-204-200	OEM
DIO-204-300	OEM
DIP630	OEM
DIP630PM	OEM
DIP631L	OEM
DIP631R	OEM
DIP632	OEM
DIP640	OEM
DIP640PM	OEM
DIP641L	OEM
DIP641R	OEM
DIP642	OEM
DIP650	OEM
DIP650PM	OEM
DIP651L	OEM
DIP651R	OEM
DIP652	OEM
DIP850	OEM
DIP850PM	OEM
DIP851L	OEM
DIP851R	OEM
DIP852	OEM
DIP1050	OEM
DIP1050A	OEM
DIP1050PM-1	OEM
DIP1051L	OEM
DIP1051R	OEM
DIP1052	OEM
DIPLINK-1A	OEM
DIPLINK-1B	OEM
DIR100	OEM
DIR170	OEM
DIS-1S	0015
DIS1S	0015
DIS990-060	OEM
DIV100HP	OEM
DIV100JP	OEM
DIV100KP	OEM
DJ74S472J	OEM
DK19	0143
DK20	0143
DK21	0143
DK48	OEM
DK130FA	OEM
DK130FB	OEM
DK130FX	OEM
DK130FY	OEM
DK150FA	OEM
DK150FB	OEM
DK150FX	OEM
DK150FY	OEM
DK170FA	OEM
DK170FB	OEM
DK170FX	OEM
DK170FY	OEM
DK750	OEM
DK751	OEM
DK752	OEM
DK753	OEM
DK754	OEM
DK755	OEM
DK756	OEM
DK757	OEM
DK758	OEM
DK1002FA	OEM
DK1002FQ	OEM
DK1002FW	OEM
DK1002FX	OEM
DK1002FZ	OEM
DK1004FA	OEM
DK1004FW	OEM
DK1004FX	OEM
DK1004FZ	OEM
DK1006FA	OEM
DK1006FQ	OEM
DK1006FW	OEM
DK1006FX	OEM
DK1006FZ	OEM
DK1008FA	OEM
DK1008FW	OEM
DK1008FX	OEM
DK1008FZ	OEM
DK1010FA	OEM
DK1010FW	OEM
DK1010FX	OEM
DK1010FZ	OEM

DEVICE TYPE	REPL CODE
DK1012FA	OEM
DK1012FX	OEM
DK1012FZ	OEM
DK1014FZ	OEM
DK1102FA	OEM
DK1102FQ	OEM
DK1102FW	OEM
DK1102FX	OEM
DK1102FZ	OEM
DK1104FA	OEM
DK1104FQ	OEM
DK1104FW	OEM
DK1104FX	OEM
DK1104FZ	OEM
DK1106FA	OEM
DK1106FB	OEM
DK1106FQ	OEM
DK1106FW	OEM
DK1106FX	OEM
DK1106FZ	OEM
DK1108FA	OEM
DK1108FW	OEM
DK1108FX	OEM
DK1108FZ	OEM
DK1110FA	OEM
DK1110FX	OEM
DK1110FZ	OEM
DK1112FZ	OEM
DK1301FA	OEM
DK1301FQ	OEM
DK1302FA	OEM
DK1302FQ	OEM
DK1302FW	OEM
DK1302FX	OEM
DK1302FZ	OEM
DK1304FA	OEM
DK1304FQ	OEM
DK1304FW	OEM
DK1304FX	OEM
DK1304FZ	OEM
DK1306FA	OEM
DK1306FQ	OEM
DK1306FW	OEM
DK1306FX	OEM
DK1306FZ	OEM
DK1308FA	OEM
DK1308FW	OEM
DK1308FX	OEM
DK1308FZ	OEM
DK1310FA	OEM
DK1310FX	OEM
DK1310FZ	OEM
DK1312FZ	OEM
DK1408FX	OEM
DK2401FW	OEM
DK2401FX	OEM
DK2401FY	OEM
DK2401FZ	OEM
DK2402FA	OEM
DK2402FB	OEM
DK2402FQ	OEM
DK2402FW	OEM
DK2402FX	OEM
DK2402FY	OEM
DK2402FZ	OEM
DK2404FA	OEM
DK2404FB	OEM
DK2404FQ	OEM
DK2404FW	OEM
DK2404FX	OEM
DK2404FY	OEM
DK2404FZ	OEM
DK2406FA	OEM
DK2406FB	OEM
DK2406FQ	OEM
DK2406FW	OEM
DK2406FX	OEM
DK2406FY	OEM
DK2408FA	OEM
DK2408FB	OEM
DK2408FW	OEM
DK2408FX	OEM
DK2408FY	OEM
DK2408FZ	OEM
DK2410FA	OEM
DK2410FB	OEM
DK2410FX	OEM
DK2410FY	OEM
DK2412FB	OEM
DK2502FA	OEM
DK2502FB	OEM
DK2502FQ	OEM
DK2502FW	OEM
DK2502FX	OEM
DK2502FY	OEM
DK2504FA	OEM
DK2504FB	OEM
DK2504FQ	OEM
DK2504FW	OEM
DK2504FX	OEM
DK2504FY	OEM
DK2506FA	OEM
DK2506FB	OEM
DK2506FQ	OEM
DK2506FW	OEM
DK2506FX	OEM
DK2506FY	OEM
DK2508FA	OEM
DK2508FB	OEM

DEVICE TYPE	REPL CODE
DK2508FW	OEM
DK2508FX	OEM
DK2508FY	OEM
DK2510FA	OEM
DK2510FB	OEM
DK2510FX	OEM
DK2510FY	OEM
DK2512FB	OEM
DK2702FA	OEM
DK2702FQ	OEM
DK2702FX	OEM
DK2702FZ	OEM
DK2704FA	OEM
DK2704FQ	OEM
DK2704FX	OEM
DK2704FZ	OEM
DK2706FA	OEM
DK2706FQ	OEM
DK2706FW	OEM
DK2706FX	OEM
DK2706FY	OEM
DK2706FZ	OEM
DK2708FA	OEM
DK2708FB	OEM
DK2708FX	OEM
DK2708FY	OEM
DK2708FZ	OEM
DK2710FB	OEM
DK2710FZ	OEM
DK7510	OEM
DK7512	OEM
DK7515	OEM
DKDS1555	0133
DKEK-04	1732
DKLR114E	1605
DKLR124E	OEM
DKV6510	OEM
DKV6510A	OEM
DKV6510B	OEM
DKV6515	OEM
DKV6515A	OEM
DKV6515B	OEM
DKV6516	OEM
DKV6516A	OEM
DKV6516B	OEM
DKV6517	OEM
DKV6517A	OEM
DKV6517B	OEM
DKV6518	OEM
DKV6518A	OEM
DKV6518B	OEM
DKV6520	OEM
DKV6520A	OEM
DKV6520B	OEM
DKV6520C	OEM
DKV6520D	OEM
DKV6522	OEM
DKV6522A	OEM
DKV6522B	OEM
DKV6522C	OEM
DKV6522D	OEM
DKV6523	OEM
DKV6523A	OEM
DKV6523B	OEM
DKV6523C	OEM
DKV6523D	OEM
DKV6524	OEM
DKV6524A	OEM
DKV6524B	OEM
DKV6524C	OEM
DKV6524D	OEM
DKV6525	OEM
DKV6525A	OEM
DKV6525B	OEM
DKV6525C	OEM
DKV6525D	OEM
DKV6526	OEM
DKV6526A	OEM
DKV6526B	OEM
DKV6526C	OEM
DKV6526D	OEM
DKV6527	OEM
DKV6527A	OEM
DKV6527B	OEM
DKV6527C	OEM
DKV6527D	OEM
DKV6533	OEM
DKV6533A	0005
DKV6533B	OEM
DKV6533C	OEM
DKV6533D	OEM
DKV6533E	OEM
DKV6533F	OEM
DKV6534	OEM
DKV6534A	OEM
DKV6534B	OEM
DKV6534C	OEM
DKV6534D	OEM
DKV6534E	OEM
DKV6534F	OEM
DKV6550A	OEM
DKV6550B	OEM
DKV6550C	OEM
DKV6550D	OEM
DKV6550E	OEM
DL1CL3	OEM
DL1CL3G	OEM
DL1F	OEM
DL1FG	OEM

DEVICE TYPE	REPL CODE
DL1KL	OEM
DL1KLG	OEM
DL1L	OEM
DL-1L3	OEM
DL-1LGN	OEM
DL-1LRN	OEM
DL1ML	OEM
DL-11S2	OEM
DL11S2	OEM
DL11S2G	OEM
DL-11S2R1	OEM
DL11S2R1	OEM
DL11S2RS	OEM
DL-25G	OEM
DL25G	OEM
DL-25R	OEM
DL25R	OEM
DL57	OEM
DL59	OEM
DL201	OEM
DL202	OEM
DL203	OEM
DL204	OEM
DL330M	OEM
DL340M	OEM
DL401	OEM
DL402	OEM
DL403	OEM
DL404	OEM
DL416	OEM
DL430M	OEM
DL440M	OEM
DL601	OEM
DL602	OEM
DL603	OEM
DL604	OEM
DL801	OEM
DL802	OEM
DL803	OEM
DL804	OEM
DL-1152R1	OEM
DL1414	OEM
DL1416	OEM
DL2416	OEM
DL3400	OEM
DL3401	OEM
DL3403	OEM
DL3405	OEM
DL3406	OEM
DL3416	OEM
DL3416H	OEM
DL3422	OEM
DL3531	OEM
DL4509	OEM
DL4530	OEM
DL4770	OEM
DL5735	OEM
DL7750	OEM
DL7751	OEM
DL7756	OEM
DL7760	OEM
DLA5544	OEM
DLA5544A	OEM
DLA5544B	OEM
DLA5544C	OEM
DLA5544D	OEM
DLA5544E	OEM
DLA5544F	OEM
DLA6929	OEM
DLA6929A	OEM
DLA6929B	OEM
DLD271	0511
DLG7670	OEM
DLG7671	OEM
DLG7673	OEM
DLG7676	OEM
DL-IIS2R1	OEM
DL-ILR	OEM
DL03900	OEM
DL03901	OEM
DL03903	OEM
DL03905	OEM
DL03906	OEM
DL04770	OEM
DL07610	OEM
DL07611	OEM
DL07613	OEM
DL07614	OEM
DL07616	OEM
DL07650	OEM
DL07651	OEM
DL07653	OEM
DL07656	OEM
DLP238	OEM
DLS1585	OEM
DLS1586	OEM
DLV11E	OEM
DLV11F	OEM
DLV11J	OEM
DLV11KA	OEM
DLXAAEL0196	OEM
DLY7660	OEM
DLY7661	OEM
DLY7663	OEM
DLY7666	OEM
DM01B	OEM
DM02B	OEM
DM03B	OEM
DM05A	OEM

DEVICE TYPE	REPL CODE
DM06A	OEM
DM0700	OEM
DM0A90A-M	0019
DM-2	OEM
DM-3	OEM
DM3-7E	OEM
DM-4	OEM
DM4	OEM
DM-7	OEM
DM7S65N	OEM
DM-8	OEM
DM-9	1748
DM-10	OEM
DM10	OEM
DM10-28B1	OEM
DM-11	0673
DM11	0673
DM-11A	0673
DM-12	OEM
DM-14	0649
DM14	0649
DM-19	3376
DM-20	1411
DM20-28B1	OEM
DM-22	OEM
DM22	OEM
DM-24	1929
DM24	1929
DM-25	OEM
DM2503W	OEM
DM-26	2264
DM28	OEM
DM-29	OEM
DM-30	2264
DM-31	0673
DM31	0673
DM-32	1411
DM32	1411
DM-33	1187
DM-35	3388
DM-36	0514
DM36	OEM
DM-37	3389
DM-39	OEM
DM-40	0356
DM40-12BA	OEM
DM40-28BY	OEM
DM-41	1434
DM41X40B	OEM
DM41X40C	OEM
DM-43	OEM
DM-44	1385
DM44	1385
DM-45	OEM
DM-46	OEM
DM-47	OEM
DM-48	OEM
DM-50	3391
DM-51	2728
DM-54	1929
DM54	1929
DM54H00J	OEM
DM54H01J	OEM
DM54H08J	OEM
DM54H10J	OEM
DM54H11J	OEM
DM54H20J	OEM
DM54H21J	OEM
DM54H30J	OEM
DM54H40J	OEM
DM54H50J	OEM
DM54H62J	OEM
DM54H74J	OEM
DM54L002	OEM
DM54L00J	OEM
DM54L02J	OEM
DM54L02W	OEM
DM54L03J	OEM
DM54L10W	OEM
DM54L20J	OEM
DM54L20W	OEM
DM54L30J	OEM
DM54L42AJ	OEM
DM54L42AW	OEM
DM54L51J	OEM
DM54L54J	OEM
DM54L54W	OEM
DM54L55J	OEM
DM54L55W	OEM
DM54L71J	OEM
DM54L71W	OEM
DM54L72J	OEM
DM54L72W	OEM
DM54L73J	OEM
DM54L73W	OEM
DM54L74J	OEM
DM54L74W	OEM
DM54L75AJ	OEM
DM54L75AW	OEM
DM54L78J	OEM
DM54L78W	OEM
DM54L85J	OEM
DM54L85W	OEM
DM54L86J	OEM
DM54L86W	OEM
DM54L89AJ	OEM
DM54L89AW	OEM
DM54L90J	OEM
DM54L90W	OEM

If replacement code is OEM, contact original manufacturer for replacement.

377

DEVICE TYPE	REPL CODE
DM54L91J	OEM
DM54L91W	OEM
DM54L93J	OEM
DM54L93W	OEM
DM54L95J	OEM
DM54L95W	OEM
DM54L98J	OEM
DM54L98W	OEM
DM54L154AF	OEM
DM54L154AJ	OEM
DM54L164AJ	OEM
DM54L164AW	OEM
DM54L165AJ	OEM
DM54L165AW	OEM
DM54L192J	OEM
DM54L192W	OEM
DM54L193J	OEM
DM54L193W	OEM
DM54LS13J	OEM
DM54LS13N	OEM
DM54LS13W	OEM
DM54LS14J	OEM
DM54LS14N	OEM
DM54LS14W	OEM
DM54LS77W	OEM
DM54LS83AJ	OEM
DM54LS83AW	OEM
DM54LS85J	OEM
DM54LS85W	OEM
DM54LS90J	OEM
DM54LS90W	OEM
DM54LS92J	OEM
DM54LS92W	OEM
DM54LS93J	OEM
DM54LS93W	OEM
DM54LS125AJ	OEM
DM54LS125AN	OEM
DM54LS125AW	OEM
DM54LS126AJ	OEM
DM54LS126AW	OEM
DM54LS132J	OEM
DM54LS132N	OEM
DM54LS132W	OEM
DM54LS154F	OEM
DM54LS154J	OEM
DM54LS155J	OEM
DM54LS155W	OEM
DM54LS156J	OEM
DM54LS156W	OEM
DM54LS160AJ	OEM
DM54LS160AW	OEM
DM54LS161AJ	OEM
DM54LS161AW	OEM
DM54LS162AJ	OEM
DM54LS162AW	OEM
DM54LS163AJ	OEM
DM54LS163AW	OEM
DM54LS164J	OEM
DM54LS164W	OEM
DM54LS165J	OEM
DM54LS165W	OEM
DM54LS166J	OEM
DM54LS166W	OEM
DM54LS170J	OEM
DM54LS170W	OEM
DM54LS173J	OEM
DM54LS173W	OEM
DM54LS174J	OEM
DM54LS174W	OEM
DM54LS175J	OEM
DM54LS175W	OEM
DM54LS190J	OEM
DM54LS190W	OEM
DM54LS191J	OEM
DM54LS191W	OEM
DM54LS192J	OEM
DM54LS192W	OEM
DM54LS193J	OEM
DM54LS193W	OEM
DM54LS194AJ	OEM
DM54LS194AW	OEM
DM54LS195AJ	OEM
DM54LS195AW	OEM
DM54LS196J	OEM
DM54LS196W	OEM
DM54LS197J	OEM
DM54LS197W	OEM
DM54LS240J	OEM
DM54LS241J	OEM
DM54LS242J	OEM
DM54LS243J	OEM
DM54LS244J	OEM
DM54LS245J	OEM
DM54LS245N	OEM
DM54LS251J	OEM
DM54LS251W	OEM
DM54LS253J	OEM
DM54LS253W	OEM
DM54LS255BJ	OEM
DM54LS255BW	OEM
DM54LS257BJ	OEM
DM54LS257BW	OEM
DM54LS259J	OEM
DM54LS259W	OEM
DM54LS283J	OEM
DM54LS283W	OEM
DM54LS290J	OEM
DM54LS290W	OEM
DM54LS293J	OEM

DEVICE TYPE	REPL CODE
DM54LS293W	OEM
DM54LS352J	OEM
DM54LS352N	OEM
DM54LS352W	OEM
DM54LS353J	OEM
DM54LS353N	OEM
DM54LS353W	OEM
DM54LS365AJ	OEM
DM54LS365AN	OEM
DM54LS365AW	OEM
DM54LS366AJ	OEM
DM54LS366AN	OEM
DM54LS366AW	OEM
DM54LS367AJ	OEM
DM54LS367AN	OEM
DM54LS367AW	OEM
DM54LS368AJ	OEM
DM54LS368AN	OEM
DM54LS368AW	OEM
DM54LS373J	OEM
DM54LS373W	OEM
DM54LS374J	OEM
DM54LS374W	OEM
DM54LS390J	OEM
DM54LS390W	OEM
DM54LS393J	OEM
DM54LS393W	OEM
DM54LS670J	OEM
DM54LS670N	OEM
DM54LS670W	OEM
DM54LS952	OEM
DM54LS962	OEM
DM54S160J	OEM
DM54S160W	OEM
DM54S162J	OEM
DM54S162W	OEM
DM54S163J	OEM
DM54S163W	OEM
DM54S174J	OEM
DM54S174W	OEM
DM54S175J	OEM
DM54S175W	OEM
DM54S181J	OEM
DM54S182J	OEM
DM54S188J	OEM
DM54S194J	OEM
DM54S194W	OEM
DM54S195J	OEM
DM54S195W	OEM
DM54S196J	OEM
DM54S196W	OEM
DM54S197J	OEM
DM54S197W	OEM
DM54S240J	OEM
DM54S241J	OEM
DM54S242J	OEM
DM54S243J	OEM
DM54S244J	OEM
DM54S251J	OEM
DM54S251W	OEM
DM54S253J	OEM
DM54S253W	OEM
DM54S257J	OEM
DM54S257W	OEM
DM54S258J	OEM
DM54S258W	OEM
DM54S280J	OEM
DM54S280W	OEM
DM54S283J	OEM
DM54S283W	OEM
DM54S287J	OEM
DM54S288J	OEM
DM54S299J	OEM
DM54S373J	OEM
DM54S373W	OEM
DM54S381J	OEM
DM54S387J	OEM
DM54S472AJ	OEM
DM54S472J	OEM
DM54S473AJ	OEM
DM54S473J	OEM
DM54S474AJ	OEM
DM54S474J	OEM
DM54S475AJ	OEM
DM54S475J	OEM
DM54S570J	OEM
DM54S571J	OEM
DM54S572J	OEM
DM54S573AJ	OEM
DM54S573J	OEM
DM54S940J	OEM
DM54S941J	OEM
DM-56	OEM
DM-59	3398
DM64X64A	OEM
DM64X64B	OEM
DM-65	0839
DM-68	OEM
DM-70	OEM
DM-71	OEM
DM71L22J	OEM
DM71L22W	OEM
DM71L23J	OEM
DM71L23W	OEM
DM-72	OEM
DM-73	OEM
DM-74	OEM
DM74ALS	OEM
DM74ALS00N	2392

DEVICE TYPE	REPL CODE
DM74ALS02N	OEM
DM74ALS04AN	OEM
DM74ALS08N	OEM
DM74ALS10N	OEM
DM74ALS27N	OEM
DM74ALS32N	2646
DM74ALS74AN	OEM
DM74ALS138N	5655
DM74ALS175N	OEM
DM74ALS244N	OEM
DM74ALS245AN	OEM
DM74ALS573N	OEM
DM74H00J	0677
DM74H00N	0677
DM74H01J	5241
DM74H01N	5241
DM74H04J	1896
DM74H04N	1896
DM74H05	3221
DM74H05J	3221
DM74H05L	3221
DM74H05N	3221
DM74H08J	5258
DM74H08N	5258
DM74H10J	0680
DM74H10N	0680
DM74H11J	2382
DM74H11N	2382
DM74H20J	3670
DM74H20N	3670
DM74H21J	4772
DM74H21N	4772
DM74H22J	4516
DM74H22N	4516
DM74H30J	5284
DM74H30N	5284
DM74H40J	0554
DM74H40N	0554
DM74H50J	1781
DM74H50N	1781
DM74H51J	1933
DM74H51N	1933
DM74H52J	2009
DM74H52N	2009
DM74H53J	2090
DM74H53N	2090
DM74H54J	2158
DM74H54N	2158
DM74H55J	3129
DM74H55N	3129
DM74H60J	5312
DM74H60N	5312
DM74H61J	2638
DM74H61N	2638
DM74H62J	2705
DM74H62N	2705
DM74H71J	3233
DM74H71N	3233
DM74H72J	3281
DM74H72N	3281
DM74H73J	2444
DM74H73N	2444
DM74H74J	2472
DM74H74N	2472
DM74H76J	5208
DM74H76N	5208
DM74H78J	5320
DM74H78N	5320
DM74L00N	OEM
DM74L02N	OEM
DM74L03N	OEM
DM74L04	OEM
DM74L10N	OEM
DM74L20N	OEM
DM74L30N	OEM
DM74L42AN	OEM
DM74L51N	OEM
DM74L54N	OEM
DM74L55N	OEM
DM74L71N	OEM
DM74L72N	OEM
DM74L73N	OEM
DM74L74N	OEM
DM74L78N	OEM
DM74L85N	OEM
DM74L85W	OEM
DM74L86N	OEM
DM74L89AN	OEM
DM74L90N	OEM
DM74L91N	OEM
DM74L91W	OEM
DM74L93F	0651
DM74L93J	0651
DM74L93N	0651
DM74L95N	OEM
DM74L98N	OEM
DM74L123N	OEM
DM74L154AN	OEM
DM74L164AN	OEM
DM74L165AN	OEM
DM74L192N	OEM
DM74L193N	OEM
DM74LS00N	1519
DM74LS01N	1537
DM74LS02N	1550
DM74LS03N	1569
DM74LS04M	OEM
DM74LS04N	1585
DM74LS05N	1598

DEVICE TYPE	REPL CODE
DM74LS08N	1623
DM74LS09N	1632
DM74LS10N	1652
DM74LS11N	1657
DM74LS12N	1669
DM74LS13J	1678
DM74LS13N	1678
DM74LS13W	1678
DM74LS14J	1688
DM74LS14N	1688
DM74LS14W	1688
DM74LS20N	0035
DM74LS26N	1372
DM74LS27N	0183
DM74LS32N	0088
DM74LS38N	1828
DM74LS40N	0135
DM74LS42N	1830
DM74LS47N	1834
DM74LS48N	1838
DM74LS51	1027
DM74LS51N	1027
DM74LS55N	0452
DM74LS74AN	0243
DM74LS75N	1859
DM74LS83AN	2204
DM74LS85N	0426
DM74LS86N	0288
DM74LS92N	1876
DM74LS93N	1877
DM74LS109AN	1895
DM74LS112AN	2115
DM74LS123N	6897
DM74LS125AN	0075
DM74LS126AJ	2850
DM74LS126AN	2850
DM74LS126AW	2850
DM74LS132J	1615
DM74LS132N	1615
DM74LS132W	1615
DM74LS138N	0422
DM74LS139N	0153
DM74LS151	5044
DM74LS151N	1636
DM74LS153N	0953
DM74LS154N	4956
DM74LS155N	0209
DM74LS156N	1644
DM74LS157N	5690
DM74LS158N	OEM
DM74LS160AN	0831
DM74LS161AN	0852
DM74LS161N	5074
DM74LS162AN	0874
DM74LS163AN	0887
DM74LS163N	0887
DM74LS164N	4274
DM74LS165N	4289
DM74LS166N	4301
DM74LS170N	2605
DM74LS173N	5125
DM74LS174M	OEM
DM74LS174N	0260
DM74LS175N	1662
DM74LS190N	1676
DM74LS191N	1677
DM74LS191NB	OEM
DM74LS192N	1679
DM74LS193N	1682
DM74LS194AN	1294
DM74LS195AN	1305
DM74LS196	2807
DM74LS196N	2807
DM74LS197N	2450
DM74LS221N	6957
DM74LS240N	0447
DM74LS240WM	OEM
DM74LS241N	1715
DM74LS242N	1717
DM74LS243N	0900
DM74LS244N	0453
DM74LS244WM	OEM
DM74LS245N	0458
DM74LS247N	1721
DM74LS251N	1726
DM74LS253N	1728
DM74LS257BN	1733
DM74LS258BN	1735
DM74LS259N	3175
DM74LS279N	3259
DM74LS283N	1768
DM74LS290N	4352
DM74LS293N	0082
DM74LS352J	0768
DM74LS352N	0756
DM74LS352W	0756
DM74LS353J	0768
DM74LS353N	0768
DM74LS353W	0768
DM74LS365AJ	0937
DM74LS365AN	0937
DM74LS365AW	0937
DM74LS366AJ	0950
DM74LS366AN	0950
DM74LS366AW	0950
DM74LS367AJ	0971
DM74LS367AN	0971
DM74LS367AW	0971
DM74LS367N	0971

DEVICE TYPE	REPL CODE
DM74LS368AJ	0985
DM74LS368AN	0985
DM74LS368AW	0985
DM74LS373N	0704
DM74LS374N	0708
DM74LS390N	1278
DM74LS393N	0813
DM74LS670J	1122
DM74LS670N	1122
DM74LS670W	1122
DM74LS952	OEM
DM74LS962	OEM
DM74S00J	0699
DM74S00N	0699
DM74S03J	2203
DM74S03N	2203
DM74S04J	2248
DM74S04N	2248
DM74S05J	2305
DM74S05N	2305
DM74S08N	OEM
DM74S10J	2426
DM74S10N	2426
DM74S11J	2428
DM74S11N	2428
DM74S15N	2432
DM74S20J	1011
DM74S20N	1011
DM74S22J	2442
DM74S22N	2442
DM74S40N	2456
DM74S51N	4241
DM74S64N	2476
DM74S65N	2477
DM74S74N	2483
DM74S86N	2489
DM74S112N	1607
DM74S113N	1613
DM74S114N	1619
DM74S133N	OEM
DM74S135N	OEM
DM74S138N	OEM
DM74S139N	OEM
DM74S140N	1875
DM74S151N	1944
DM74S153N	2138
DM74S157N	1685
DM74S158N	OEM
DM74S160N	OEM
DM74S161N	OEM
DM74S162N	OEM
DM74S163N	0887
DM74S174N	2119
DM74S175N	2128
DM74S181N	2151
DM74S182N	2152
DM74S188J	3139
DM74S188N	3139
DM74S194N	1920
DM74S195N	OEM
DM74S196N	OEM
DM74S197N	OEM
DM74S240J	OEM
DM74S240N	OEM
DM74S241J	OEM
DM74S241N	OEM
DM74S242N	OEM
DM74S243N	OEM
DM74S244N	OEM
DM74S251N	2184
DM74S253N	OEM
DM74S257N	OEM
DM74S258N	2191
DM74S280N	2205
DM74S283N	OEM
DM74S287J	2209
DM74S287N	2209
DM74S288J	2161
DM74S288N	2161
DM74S299N	OEM
DM74S373N	2249
DM74S374N	2251
DM74S381N	OEM
DM74S387J	1907
DM74S387N	1907
DM74S472AJ	2304
DM74S472AN	2304
DM74S472N	2304
DM74S473AJ	3257
DM74S473AN	3257
DM74S473J	3257
DM74S473N	3257
DM74S474AJ	2306
DM74S474AN	2306
DM74S474J	2306
DM74S474N	2306
DM74S475AJ	2308
DM74S475AN	2308
DM74S475J	2308
DM74S475N	2308
DM74S570J	2372
DM74S570N	2372
DM74S571J	2373
DM74S571N	2373
DM74S572AJ	2374
DM74S572AN	2374
DM74S572J	2374
DM74S572N	2374
DM74S573AJ	2376

DEVICE TYPE	REPL CODE
DM74S573AN	2376
DM74S573J	2376
DM74S573N	2376
DM74S940J	OEM
DM74S940N	OEM
DM74S941N	OEM
DM-75	OEM
DM75L11D	OEM
DM75L11F	OEM
DM75L11J	OEM
DM75L11N	OEM
DM75L11W	OEM
DM75L12F	OEM
DM75L12J	OEM
DM75L12N	OEM
DM75L12W	OEM
DM75L51J	OEM
DM75L51W	OEM
DM75L52F	OEM
DM75L52J	OEM
DM75L52N	OEM
DM75L52W	OEM
DM75L54F	OEM
DM75L54J	OEM
DM75L54N	OEM
DM75L54W	OEM
DM75L60J	OEM
DM75L60W	OEM
DM75L63J	OEM
DM75L63W	OEM
DM-76	OEM
DM76L13J	OEM
DM76L13W	OEM
DM76L24J	OEM
DM76L24N	OEM
DM76L75F	OEM
DM76L75J	OEM
DM76L75N	OEM
DM76L75W	OEM
DM76L76F	OEM
DM76L76J	OEM
DM76L76N	OEM
DM76L76W	OEM
DM76L90J	OEM
DM76L90W	OEM
DM76L93F	OEM
DM76L93J	OEM
DM76L93N	OEM
DM76L97J	OEM
DM76L97W	OEM
DM76L99J	OEM
DM76L99W	OEM
DM76LS52	OEM
DM76LS62	OEM
DM76S64J	OEM
DM76S128J	OEM
DM-77	0119
DM77S180J	OEM
DM77S181J	OEM
DM77S184J	OEM
DM77S185J	OEM
DM77S188J	OEM
DM77S190J	OEM
DM77S191J	OEM
DM77S288J	OEM
DM-78	OEM
DM-79	OEM
DM-80	OEM
DM80L06N	OEM
DM80X80C	OEM
DM-81	OEM
DM81L22N	OEM
DM81L23N	OEM
DM-82	OEM
DM-83	OEM
DM-84	3398
DM-85	3409
DM85L11D	OEM
DM85L11F	OEM
DM85L11N	OEM
DM85L12F	OEM
DM85L12J	OEM
DM85L12N	OEM
DM85L51N	OEM
DM85L52F	OEM
DM85L52J	OEM
DM85L52N	OEM
DM85L54F	OEM
DM85L54J	OEM
DM85L54N	OEM
DM85L60N	OEM
DM85L63N	OEM
DM85S68D	OEM
DM85S68N	OEM
DM-86	1135
DM86L13N	OEM
DM86L24J	OEM
DM86L75F	OEM
DM86L75J	OEM
DM86L75N	OEM
DM86L76F	OEM
DM86L76J	OEM
DM86L76N	OEM
DM86L90N	OEM
DM86L93F	OEM
DM86L93J	OEM
DM86L93N	OEM
DM86L97N	OEM
DM86L99N	OEM

DEVICE TYPE	REPL CODE
DM86LS52	OEM
DM86LS62	OEM
DM86S64J	OEM
DM86S128J	OEM
DM86S128N	OEM
DM-87	0176
DM87	0176
DM87S180J	OEM
DM87S180N	OEM
DM87S181J	OEM
DM87S181N	OEM
DM87S184J	OEM
DM87S184N	OEM
DM87S185J	3137
DM87S185N	3137
DM87S188J	OEM
DM87S188N	OEM
DM87S190J	OEM
DM87S190N	OEM
DM87S191J	OEM
DM87S191N	OEM
DM87S288J	OEM
DM87S288N	OEM
DM-88	2242
DM88	2242
DM-89	OEM
DM-90	2755
DM90	2755
DM-91	1187
DM91	1187
DM-92	1187
DM-94	0619
DM-96	OEM
DM-97	OEM
DM-98	3398
DM101A	OEM
DM102BSXXXX	OEM
DM-103	0621
DM-104	1288
DM104BSXXXX	OEM
DM105DXXXX	OEM
DM-106	0083
DM106	0083
DM106A	OEM
DM-107	2294
DM-108	OEM
DM-110	4220
DM110DSXXXX	OEM
DM112BSXXXX	OEM
DM128X24A	OEM
DM128X128C	OEM
DM150P	OEM
DM204BSXXXX	OEM
DM208FS	OEM
DM208FS-1	OEM
DM208FSM	OEM
DM208FSM-1	OEM
DM208FSMZS	OEM
DM208FSMZS-1	OEM
DM208FSQ	OEM
DM208FSQ-1	OEM
DM208FSQZS	OEM
DM208FSQZS-1	OEM
DM208FST	OEM
DM208FST-1	OEM
DM208FSTZS	OEM
DM208FSTZS-1	OEM
DM212BSXXXX	OEM
DM218BS	OEM
DM218BS-1	OEM
DM218BSM	OEM
DM218BSM-1	OEM
DM218BSMZS	OEM
DM218BSMZS-1	OEM
DM218BSQ	OEM
DM218BSQZS	OEM
DM218BSQZS-2	OEM
DM218BST	OEM
DM218BST-1	OEM
DM218BSTZS	OEM
DM218BSTZS-1	OEM
DM218BSZS	OEM
DM218BSZS-1	OEM
DM250	OEM
DM256X64A	OEM
DM256X256B	OEM
DM258X26B	OEM
DM350	OEM
DM400B	OEM
DM408BSXXXX	OEM
DM450	OEM
DM510DSXXXX	OEM
DM520DSXXXX	OEM
DM550	OEM
DM650	OEM
DM711BSXXXX	OEM
DM750	OEM
DM812BSXXXX	OEM
DM816BSXXXX	OEM
DM852N	OEM
DM930N	1812
DM932N	1035
DM933N	2086
DM935N	1168
DM936N	1820
DM937N	1824
DM944N	0033
DM945N	0081
DM946N	0141

378

If replacement code is OEM, contact original manufacturer for replacement.

DEVICE TYPE	REPL CODE
DM948N	3365
DM949N	1833
DM950	OEM
DM958N	0461
DM961N	1848
DM962N	0557
DM963N	0337
DM1724BSXXXX	OEM
DM1800N	OEM
DM1801N	OEM
DM1883A	OEM
DM1883B	OEM
DM2223BSXXXX	OEM
DM2502CJ	OEM
DM2502CN	OEM
DM2502CW	OEM
DM2502J	OEM
DM2502W	OEM
DM2503CJ	OEM
DM2503CN	OEM
DM2503CW	OEM
DM2503J	OEM
DM2504CF	OEM
DM2504CN	OEM
DM2504F	OEM
DM2504J	OEM
DM3000	OEM
DM3001	OEM
DM3510	OEM
DM3520	OEM
DM3530	OEM
DM3540	OEM
DM5400J	OEM
DM5400W	OEM
DM5401J	OEM
DM5401W	OEM
DM5402J	OEM
DM5402W	OEM
DM5403J	OEM
DM5408J	OEM
DM5408W	OEM
DM5409J	OEM
DM5409W	OEM
DM5410J	OEM
DM5410W	OEM
DM5411J	OEM
DM5413J	OEM
DM5413N	OEM
DM5413W	OEM
DM5414J	OEM
DM5414N	OEM
DM5414W	OEM
DM5416J	OEM
DM5416W	OEM
DM5417J	OEM
DM5417W	OEM
DM5420J	OEM
DM5420W	OEM
DM5423J	OEM
DM5423W	OEM
DM5425J	OEM
DM5425W	OEM
DM5427J	OEM
DM5427W	OEM
DM5430J	OEM
DM5430W	OEM
DM5432J	OEM
DM5432W	OEM
DM5437J	OEM
DM5437W	OEM
DM5438J	OEM
DM5438W	OEM
DM5440J	OEM
DM5440W	OEM
DM5441AJ	OEM
DM5441AW	OEM
DM5442J	OEM
DM5442W	OEM
DM5445J	OEM
DM5445W	OEM
DM5446AJ	OEM
DM5446AN	OEM
DM5446AW	OEM
DM5447AJ	OEM
DM5447AN	OEM
DM5447AW	OEM
DM5448J	OEM
DM5448N	OEM
DM5448W	OEM
DM5450J	OEM
DM5450W	OEM
DM5451J	OEM
DM5451W	OEM
DM5453J	OEM
DM5453W	OEM
DM5454J	OEM
DM5454W	OEM
DM5459BSXXXX	OEM
DM5460J	OEM
DM5460W	OEM
DM5470J	OEM
DM5470W	OEM
DM5472J	OEM
DM5472W	OEM
DM5473J	OEM
DM5473W	OEM
DM5474J	OEM
DM5474W	OEM
DM5475J	OEM

DEVICE TYPE	REPL CODE
DM5475W	OEM
DM5476J	OEM
DM5476W	OEM
DM5483J	OEM
DM5483W	OEM
DM5485J	OEM
DM5485W	OEM
DM5486J	OEM
DM5486W	OEM
DM5489BJ	OEM
DM5489BN	OEM
DM5490AJ	OEM
DM5490J	OEM
DM5490W	OEM
DM5492AJ	OEM
DM5492AW	OEM
DM5492J	OEM
DM5492W	OEM
DM5493AJ	OEM
DM5493AW	OEM
DM5493J	OEM
DM5493W	OEM
DM5495J	OEM
DM5495W	OEM
DM5496J	OEM
DM5496W	OEM
DM6003	OEM
DM6004	OEM
DM6009	OEM
DM6010	OEM
DM6015	OEM
DM6016	OEM
DM6020	OEM
DM6021	OEM
DM6022	OEM
DM6030	OEM
DM6040	OEM
DM6050	OEM
DM7091J	OEM
DM7091N	OEM
DM7091W	OEM
DM7092J	OEM
DM7092N	OEM
DM7092W	OEM
DM7121J	OEM
DM7121W	OEM
DM7123J	OEM
DM7123W	OEM
DM7130D	OEM
DM7130F	OEM
DM7130J	OEM
DM7131J	OEM
DM7131N	OEM
DM7131W	OEM
DM7136J	OEM
DM7136W	OEM
DM7145J	OEM
DM7160D	OEM
DM7160J	OEM
DM7160W	OEM
DM7200J	OEM
DM7200N	OEM
DM7200W	OEM
DM7214J	OEM
DM7214W	OEM
DM7219F	OEM
DM7219J	OEM
DM7220J	OEM
DM7220N	OEM
DM7220W	OEM
DM7280J	OEM
DM7280W	OEM
DM7281J	OEM
DM7281W	OEM
DM7373N	1164
DM7400	0232
DM7400J	0232
DM7400N	0232
DM7401J	0268
DM7401N	0268
DM7402J	0310
DM7402N	0310
DM7403J	0331
DM7403N	0331
DM7404N	0357
DM7405N	0381
DM7406N	1197
DM7407	5932
DM7407N	1329
DM7408J	0462
DM7408N	0462
DM7409J	0487
DM7409N	0487
DM7410J	0507
DM7410N	0507
DM7411J	0522
DM7411N	0522
DM7413J	1432
DM7413N	1432
DM7413W	OEM
DM7414J	2228
DM7414N	2228
DM7414W	OEM
DM74150	1484
DM7416N	1339
DM7417N	1342
DM7420J	0692
DM7420N	0692
DM7423J	3429

DEVICE TYPE	REPL CODE
DM7423N	3429
DM7423W	3429
DM7425J	3438
DM7425N	3438
DM7425W	3438
DM7426N	0798
DM7427J	0812
DM7427N	0812
DM7427W	0812
DM7430J	0867
DM7430N	0867
DM7432J	0893
DM7432N	0893
DM7437J	3478
DM7437N	3478
DM7437W	3478
DM7438J	0990
DM7438N	0990
DM7438W	0990
DM7440J	1018
DM7440N	1018
DM7441AJ	1032
DM7441AN	1032
DM7441N	1032
DM7442J	1046
DM7442N	1046
DM7445J	1074
DM7445N	1074
DM7445W	1074
DM7446AJ	1090
DM7446AN	1090
DM7446AW	OEM
DM7447AJ	1100
DM7447AN	1100
DM7447AW	OEM
DM7447N	1100
DM7448J	1117
DM7448N	1117
DM7448W	1117
DM7450J	0738
DM7450N	0738
DM7451J	1160
DM7451N	1160
DM7453J	1177
DM7453N	1177
DM7454J	1193
DM7454N	1193
DM7460J	1265
DM7460N	1265
DM7470J	1394
DM7470N	1394
DM7472J	1417
DM7472N	1417
DM7473	5937
DM7473J	1164
DM7473N	1164
DM7474J	1303
DM7474M	1303
DM7474N	1303
DM7475J	1423
DM7475N	1423
DM7476J	1150
DM7476N	1150
DM7483J	3092
DM7483N	0117
DM7485N	1423
DM7486J	1358
DM7486N	1358
DM7488N	4817
DM7489N	5358
DM7490	1199
DM7490AN	1199
DM7490J	1199
DM7490N	1199
DM7491AN	0974
DM7492AN	0828
DM7492J	0828
DM7492N	0828
DM7493AN	0564
DM7493J	0564
DM7493N	0564
DM7495N	1477
DM7496J	1705
DM7496N	1705
DM7496W	OEM
DM7497J	2912
DM7511J	OEM
DM7511N	OEM
DM7511W	OEM
DM7512J	OEM
DM7512N	OEM
DM7512W	OEM
DM7542J	OEM
DM7542W	OEM
DM7544J	OEM
DM7544W	OEM
DM7546J	OEM
DM7546W	OEM
DM7551J	OEM
DM7551W	OEM
DM7552J	OEM
DM7552W	OEM
DM7553J	OEM
DM7553W	OEM
DM7554J	OEM
DM7554W	OEM
DM7555J	OEM
DM7555N	OEM
DM7555W	OEM

DEVICE TYPE	REPL CODE
DM7556J	OEM
DM7556N	OEM
DM7556W	OEM
DM7560J	OEM
DM7560W	OEM
DM7563J	OEM
DM7563W	OEM
DM7570J	OEM
DM7570W	OEM
DM7585BSXXXX	OEM
DM7590J	OEM
DM7590W	OEM
DM7599J	OEM
DM7599N	OEM
DM7613J	OEM
DM7613W	OEM
DM7819J	OEM
DM7819N	OEM
DM7819W	OEM
DM7853J	OEM
DM7853W	OEM
DM7875AD	OEM
DM7875AJ	OEM
DM7875AW	OEM
DM7875BD	OEM
DM7875BJ	OEM
DM7875BW	OEM
DM8091J	OEM
DM8091N	OEM
DM8091W	OEM
DM8092J	OEM
DM8092N	OEM
DM8092W	OEM
DM8121N	2283
DM8123N	5801
DM8130D	OEM
DM8130F	OEM
DM8130N	OEM
DM8131J	OEM
DM8131N	OEM
DM8136N	OEM
DM8160	OEM
DM8160J	OEM
DM8160N	OEM
DM8160W	OEM
DM8200J	OEM
DM8200N	OEM
DM8214N	6636
DM8219N	5930
DM8220J	OEM
DM8220N	OEM
DM8280J	1784
DM8280N	1784
DM8280W	OEM
DM8281J	1792
DM8281N	1792
DM8281W	OEM
DM8300N	OEM
DM8301J	2182
DM8301N	2182
DM8301W	OEM
DM8310N	OEM
DM8316N	5820
DM8318N	4082
DM8334J	OEM
DM8334N	OEM
DM8334W	OEM
DM8511J	OEM
DM8511N	OEM
DM8511W	OEM
DM8512W	OEM
DM8542N	5838
DM8544N	OEM
DM8546N	6846
DM8551N	1915
DM8552J	OEM
DM8552W	OEM
DM8553J	OEM
DM8553N	6270
DM8553W	OEM
DM8554J	OEM
DM8554N	6271
DM8554W	OEM
DM8555N	6272
DM8556N	5840
DM8560	1910
DM8560J	1910
DM8560N	1910
DM8563J	1915
DM8563N	1915
DM8570N	0729
DM8590N	1675
DM8596BSXXXX	OEM
DM8601J	2252
DM8601N	2252
DM8601W	OEM
DM8602J	OEM
DM8602N	2270
DM8602W	OEM
DM8613N	5953
DM8678J	OEM
DM8678N	OEM
DM8810N	0798
DM8811N	OEM
DM8819J	OEM
DM8819N	OEM
DM8819W	OEM
DM8853J	OEM
DM8853N	1730

DEVICE TYPE	REPL CODE
DM8853W	OEM
DM8875AJ	OEM
DM8875AN	OEM
DM8875BJ	OEM
DM8875BN	OEM
DM8890N	2032
DM8898N	OEM
DM8899N	OEM
DM9002CJ	OEM
DM9002CN	OEM
DM9003CJ	OEM
DM9003CN	OEM
DM9004CJ	OEM
DM9004CN	OEM
DM9005CJ	OEM
DM9005CN	OEM
DM9006CJ	OEM
DM9006CN	OEM
DM9008CJ	OEM
DM9008CN	OEM
DM9009CJ	OEM
DM9009CN	OEM
DM9012CJ	OEM
DM9012CN	OEM
DM9016CJ	OEM
DM9016CN	OEM
DM9093N	0354
DM9094N	1622
DM9097N	1472
DM9099N	0329
DM9300J	OEM
DM9300W	OEM
DM9301J	2182
DM9301N	2182
DM9301W	OEM
DM9310J	OEM
DM9310W	OEM
DM9316J	OEM
DM9316W	OEM
DM9318J	4082
DM9334J	OEM
DM9334W	OEM
DM9601J	2252
DM9601N	2252
DM9601W	OEM
DM9602J	OEM
DM9602N	OEM
DM9602W	OEM
DM10101J	OEM
DM10102J	OEM
DM10105J	OEM
DM10106J	OEM
DM10107J	OEM
DM10109J	OEM
DM10110J	OEM
DM10111J	OEM
DM10112J	OEM
DM10117J	OEM
DM10118J	OEM
DM10119J	OEM
DM10121J	OEM
DM10348-03	OEM
DM10348-04	OEM
DM10414J	OEM
DM10414N	OEM
DM10415AJ	OEM
DM10415AN	OEM
DM10415J	OEM
DM10415N	OEM
DM10470A	OEM
DM10470J	OEM
DM10470L	OEM
DM54107J	OEM
DM54121J	OEM
DM54121W	OEM
DM54125J	OEM
DM54125N	OEM
DM54125W	OEM
DM54126J	OEM
DM54126W	OEM
DM54132J	OEM
DM54132N	OEM
DM54132W	OEM
DM54141J	OEM
DM54141W	OEM
DM54147J	OEM
DM54147W	OEM
DM54148J	OEM
DM54148W	OEM
DM54155J	OEM
DM54155W	OEM
DM54156J	OEM
DM54156W	OEM
DM54160AJ	OEM
DM54160AW	OEM
DM54161AJ	OEM
DM54161AW	OEM
DM54162AJ	OEM
DM54162AW	OEM
DM54163AJ	OEM
DM54163AW	OEM
DM54164J	OEM
DM54164W	OEM
DM54165J	OEM
DM54165W	OEM
DM54166J	OEM
DM54166W	OEM
DM54170N	OEM
DM54173J	OEM

DEVICE TYPE	REPL CODE
DM54173W	OEM
DM54174J	OEM
DM54174W	OEM
DM54175J	OEM
DM54175W	OEM
DM54182J	OEM
DM54184J	OEM
DM54184W	OEM
DM54185AJ	OEM
DM54185AW	OEM
DM54191J	OEM
DM54191W	OEM
DM54192W	OEM
DM54193J	OEM
DM54193W	OEM
DM54194J	OEM
DM54194W	OEM
DM54195J	OEM
DM54195W	OEM
DM54196J	OEM
DM54197J	OEM
DM54198J	OEM
DM54198W	OEM
DM54199J	OEM
DM54199W	OEM
DM54251J	OEM
DM54251W	OEM
DM54259J	OEM
DM54259W	OEM
DM54365J	OEM
DM54365N	OEM
DM54365W	OEM
DM54366J	OEM
DM54366N	OEM
DM54366W	OEM
DM54367J	OEM
DM54367N	OEM
DM54367W	OEM
DM54368J	OEM
DM54368N	OEM
DM54368W	OEM
DM74107J	0936
DM74107N	0936
DM74121J	0175
DM74121N	0175
DM74123	1149
DM74123N	1149
DM74125J	1174
DM74125N	1174
DM74125W	OEM
DM74126N	1184
DM74132J	1261
DM74132N	1261
DM74132W	OEM
DM74141J	1367
DM74141N	1367
DM74141W	OEM
DM74145	0614
DM74145N	0614
DM74145W	OEM
DM74147J	1442
DM74147N	1442
DM74147W	OEM
DM74148G	OEM
DM74148GM	OEM
DM74148GMR	OEM
DM74148J	OEM
DM74148N	OEM
DM74148W	OEM
DM74150	1484
DM74150N	1484
DM74151	1487
DM74151N	1487
DM74153	1531
DM74153N	1531
DM74154	1546
DM74154F	OEM
DM74154J	1546
DM74154N	1546
DM74155N	1566
DM74156N	1582
DM74157N	1595
DM74160AN	1621
DM74160N	1621
DM74161AN	1635
DM74161N	1635
DM74162	1007
DM74162AN	1007
DM74162N	1007
DM74163AN	1656
DM74163N	1656
DM74164N	0729
DM74165N	1675
DM74166N	0231
DM74170N	1711
DM74173N	1755
DM74174	1759
DM74174N	1759
DM74175N	1776
DM74176J	1784
DM74176N	1784
DM74176W	OEM
DM74177J	1792
DM74177N	1792
DM74177W	OEM
DM74180J	1818
DM74180N	1818
DM74180W	OEM
DM74181J	1831

DEVICE TYPE	REPL CODE
DM74181N	1831
DM74182N	1845
DM74184N	OEM
DM74185AN	1857
DM74190	1901
DM74190J	1901
DM74190N	1901
DM74190W	OEM
DM74191J	1906
DM74191N	1906
DM74191W	OEM
DM74192J	1910
DM74192N	1910
DM74193	1915
DM74193J	1915
DM74193N	1915
DM74194N	OEM
DM74195N	1932
DM74196N	1939
DM74197N	1945
DM74198N	1953
DM74199N	1960
DM74251N	2283
DM74259N	OEM
DM74365J	1450
DM74365N	1450
DM74365W	OEM
DM74366J	1462
DM74366N	1462
DM74366W	OEM
DM74367J	1479
DM74367N	1479
DM74367W	OEM
DM74368J	1500
DM74368N	1500
DM74368W	OEM
DMA6497	OEM
DMA6497A	OEM
DMA6497AM	OEM
DMA6497AMR	OEM
DMA6497B	OEM
DMA6497BM	OEM
DMA6497BMR	OEM
DMA6497C	OEM
DMA6497CM	OEM
DMA6497CMR	OEM
DMA6497M	OEM
DMA6497MR	OEM
DMA6498AM	OEM
DMA6498AMR	OEM
DMA6498CM	OEM
DMA6498CMR	OEM
DMA6499	OEM
DMA6499A	OEM
DMA6499AMR	OEM
DMA6499B	OEM
DMA6499BM	OEM
DMA6499BMR	OEM
DMA6499MR	OEM
DMB5-12	OEM
DMB15-12	OEM
DMB20-12	OEM
DMB30-12	OEM
DMB-4500	OEM
DMB-4500A	OEM
DMB-4501	OEM
DMB-4501A	OEM
DMB6411	OEM
DMB6411A	OEM
DMB6411B	OEM
DMB6411C	OEM
DMB-6780	OEM
DMB-6780A	OEM
DMB-6781	OEM
DMB-6781A	OEM
DMB-6782	OEM
DMB-6782A	OEM
DMD5600	OEM
DMD5600A	OEM
DMD5817	OEM
DMD5817A	OEM
DMD5818	OEM
DMD5818A	OEM
DMD5819	OEM
DMD5827	OEM
DMD5827A	OEM
DMD5828	OEM
DMD5828A	OEM
DMD5835	OEM
DMD5841	OEM
DMD5841A	OEM
DMD5842	OEM
DMD5845	OEM
DMD5845A	OEM
DMD5846	OEM
DMD-6022	OEM
DMD6022	OEM
DMD-6022A	OEM
DMD6022A	OEM
DMD-6023	OEM
DMD6023	OEM
DMD-6023A	OEM
DMD6023A	OEM
DMD-6288	OEM
DMD-6288A	OEM
DMD-6298	OEM
DMD-6298A	OEM
DMD-6395	OEM
DMD-6395A	OEM

If replacement code is OEM, contact original manufacturer for replacement.

379

DEVICE TYPE	REPL CODE
DMD6459	OEM
DMD6459A	OEM
DMD-6460	OEM
DMD-6460A	OEM
DMD-6829	OEM
DMD-6829A	OEM
DMD-6884	OEM
DMD-6884A	OEM
DMD-6885	OEM
DMD-6885A	OEM
DMD-6886	OEM
DMD-6886A	OEM
DME6L	OEM
DME7	OEM
DME25	OEM
DME30L	OEM
DME50	OEM
DME120L	OEM
DME150	OEM
DME250	OEM
DME300	OEM
DME375	OEM
DME600	OEM
DME800	OEM
DME6507	OEM
DME6561	OEM
DME6562	OEM
DME6563	OEM
DME6957	OEM
DMF-4000	OEM
DMF4000	OEM
DMF-4011	OEM
DMF-4011A	OEM
DMF-4012	OEM
DMF-4012A	OEM
DMF-4035	OEM
DMF-4035A	OEM
DMF-4040	OEM
DMF-4040A	OEM
DMF-4052	OEM
DMF-4052A	OEM
DMF-4059	OEM
DMF-4059A	OEM
DMF4788	OEM
DMF4788A	OEM
DMF4792	OEM
DMF-5079	OEM
DMF-5079A	OEM
DMF-5080	OEM
DMF-5080A	OEM
DMF6034	OEM
DMF6034A	OEM
DMF6034B	OEM
DMF6035	OEM
DMF6035A	OEM
DMF6035B	OEM
DMF6037	OEM
DMF6037A	OEM
DMF6037B	OEM
DMF6106	OEM
DMF6106A	OEM
DMF6106AM	OEM
DMF6106B	OEM
DMF6106CM	OEM
DMF6106M	OEM
DMF6107	OEM
DMF6107A	OEM
DMF6107AM	OEM
DMF6107B	OEM
DMF6107BM	OEM
DMF6107CM	OEM
DMF6107M	OEM
DMF6130	OEM
DMF6130A	OEM
DMF6131	OEM
DMF6131A	OEM
DMF6131B	OEM
DMF6132	OEM
DMF6132A	OEM
DMF6132B	OEM
DMF-6426	OEM
DMF-6426A	OEM
DMG-6412	OEM
DMG6412	OEM
DMG-6412A	OEM
DMG-6413	OEM
DMG6413	OEM
DMG-6413A	OEM
DMG-6414	OEM
DMG6414	OEM
DMG-6414A	OEM
DMG-6415	OEM
DMJ-4007	OEM
DMJ-4014	OEM
DMJ-4015	OEM
DMJ-4502	OEM
DMJ4759	OEM
DMJ4771	OEM
DMJ4798	OEM
DMJ-5034	OEM
DMJ6564	OEM
DMJ-6665	OEM
DMJ-6666	OEM
DMJ-6668	OEM
DMJ-6669	OEM
DMJ-6670	OEM
DMJ-6777	OEM
DMJ-6778	OEM
DMJ-6784	OEM

DEVICE TYPE	REPL CODE
DMJ-6785	OEM
DMJ-6786	OEM
DMJ-6788	OEM
DMJ-6789	OEM
DMJ-6990	OEM
DMK4791	OEM
DMK-5068	OEM
DMK-5068A	OEM
DMM102BSXXXX	OEM
DMM104BSXXXX	OEM
DMM105DXXXX	OEM
DMM110DSXXXX	OEM
DMM112BSXXXX	OEM
DMM204BSXXXX	OEM
DMM208FSXXXX	OEM
DMM212BSXXXX	OEM
DMM218BSXXXX	OEM
DMM408BSXXXX	OEM
DMM510DSXXXX	OEM
DMM520DSXXXX	OEM
DMM711BSXXXX	OEM
DMM812BSXXXX	OEM
DMM816BSXXXX	OEM
DMM1724BSXXXX	OEM
DMM5459BSXXXX	OEM
DMM7585BSXXXX	OEM
DMM8596BSXXXX	OEM
DMMA700	0335
DMMA4043-H	0274
DMMA4051-H	0041
DMMA4051-M	0582
DMMA4075-M	0077
DMMA4082-M	0165
DMMA4091-M	0057
DMMA4100-M	0064
DMMA4200-M	0695
DMMA4270-M	0436
DM0A90A-M	0143
DMP4025DB	OEM
DMPAL10H8JM	OEM
DMPAL10H8NC	OEM
DMPAL10L8JM	OEM
DMPAL10L8NC	OEM
DMPAL12H6JM	OEM
DMPAL12H6NC	OEM
DMPAL12L6JM	OEM
DMPAL12L6NC	OEM
DMPAL14H4JM	OEM
DMPAL14H4NC	OEM
DMPAL14L4JM	OEM
DMPAL14L4NC	OEM
DMPAL16A4JM	OEM
DMPAL16A4NC	OEM
DMPAL16C1JM	OEM
DMPAL16C1NC	OEM
DMPAL16H2JM	OEM
DMPAL16H2NC	OEM
DMPAL16L2JM	OEM
DMPAL16L2NC	OEM
DMPAL16L8JM	OEM
DMPAL16R4JM	OEM
DMPAL16R6JM	OEM
DMPAL16R6NC	OEM
DMPAL16R8JM	OEM
DMPAL16R8NC	OEM
DMPAL16X4JM	OEM
DMPAL16X4NC	OEM
DMX88EQ	OEM
DMX88FQ	OEM
DN0700A	OEM
DN0701	OEM
DN0702	OEM
DN74LS00	OEM
DN74LS02	1550
DN74LS04	OEM
DN74LS05	OEM
DN74LS08	1623
DN74LS09	1632
DN74LS14P	1688
DN74LS32	0088
DN74LS74	OEM
DN74LS125P	0075
DN74LS132	1615
DN74LS138	OEM
DN74LS156	1644
DN74LS174P	0260
DN74LS240P	0447
DN74LS244	0453
DN74LS245P	0458
DN74LS373	0704
DN262-02	OEM
DN262-04	OEM
DN262-06	OEM
DN262-08	OEM
DN262-10	OEM
DN262-12	OEM
DN262-14	OEM
DN262-16	OEM
DN262-18	OEM
DN262-20	OEM
DN462-02	OEM
DN462-04	OEM
DN462-06	OEM
DN462-08	OEM
DN462-10	OEM
DN462-12	OEM
DN462-14	OEM
DN462-16	OEM
DN462-18	OEM

DEVICE TYPE	REPL CODE
DN462-20	OEM
DN662-02	OEM
DN662-04	OEM
DN662-06	OEM
DN662-08	OEM
DN662-10	OEM
DN662-12	OEM
DN662-14	OEM
DN662-16	OEM
DN662-18	OEM
DN662-20	OEM
DN662-22	OEM
DN662-24	OEM
DN662-25	OEM
DN681L	OEM
DN761-20	OEM
DN761-22	OEM
DN761-24	OEM
DN761-26	OEM
DN761-28	OEM
DN761-30	OEM
DN761-32	OEM
DN761-34	OEM
DN762-02	OEM
DN762-04	OEM
DN762-06	OEM
DN762-08	OEM
DN762-10	OEM
DN762-12	OEM
DN762-14	OEM
DN762-16	OEM
DN762-18	OEM
DN762-20	OEM
DN811	4091
DN819	4095
DN834	OEM
DN835	OEM
DN837	OEM
DN838	4099
DN839	OEM
DN850	4105
DN851	OEM
DN852	1589
DN852P	1589
DN918	OEM
DN961-02	OEM
DN961-04	OEM
DN961-06	OEM
DN961-08	OEM
DN961-10	OEM
DN961-12	OEM
DN961-14	OEM
DN961-16	OEM
DN961-18	OEM
DN961-20	OEM
DN961-22	OEM
DN961-24	OEM
DN961-25	OEM
DN1000	OEM
DN1000A	OEM
DN1001	OEM
DN1002	OEM
DN1005AM	OEM
DN1005BM	OEM
DN1005CM	OEM
DN-1006-2	OEM
DN1946	0141
DN2000	OEM
DN2001	OEM
DN2002	OEM
DN2175	OEM
DN2219A	OEM
DN2222A	OEM
DN2484	OEM
DN3000	OEM
DN3000A	OEM
DN3001	OEM
DN3002	OEM
DN3066A	OEM
DN3067A	OEM
DN3068A	OEM
DN3069A	OEM
DN3070A	OEM
DN3071A	OEM
DN3365A	OEM
DN3366A	OEM
DN3367A	OEM
DN3368A	OEM
DN3369A	OEM
DN3370A	OEM
DN3436A	OEM
DN3437A	OEM
DN3438A	OEM
DN3439	OEM
DN3458A	OEM
DN3459A	OEM
DN3460A	OEM
DN5000	OEM
DN5001	OEM
DN5002	OEM
DN5564	OEM
DN5565	OEM
DN5566	OEM
DN5567	OEM
DN6338-A	0484
DN6368	OEM
DN6811	4671
DN6835	OEM
DN6837	OEM

DEVICE TYPE	REPL CODE
DN6838	0484
DN6838A	0484
DN6839	OEM
DN6851	OEM
DN6851H1	2535
DN6851HI	2535
DN7432	OEM
DN8000	OEM
DN8001	OEM
DN8002	OEM
DN9000	OEM
DNA5856	OEM
DND800	0133
DNMPC574J	1319
DNN03602D9	OEM
DNN03604D9	OEM
DNN03606D9	OEM
DNN03608D9	OEM
DNN03610D9	OEM
DNN03612D9	OEM
DNN03614D9	OEM
DNN03616D9	OEM
DNN03618D9	OEM
DNN03620D9	OEM
DNN05002D13	OEM
DNN05004D13	OEM
DNN05006D13	OEM
DNN05008D13	OEM
DNN05010D13	OEM
DNN05012D13	OEM
DNN05014D13	OEM
DNN05016D13	OEM
DNN05018D13	OEM
DNN05020D13	OEM
DNN07802D20	OEM
DNN07804D20	OEM
DNN07806D20	OEM
DNN07808D20	OEM
DNN07810D20	OEM
DNN07812D20	OEM
DNN07814D20	OEM
DNN07816D20	OEM
DNN07818D20	OEM
DNN07820D20	OEM
DNN07822D20	OEM
DNN07824D20	OEM
DNN07826D20	OEM
DNN07828D20	OEM
DNN07830D20	OEM
DNN07832D20	OEM
DNN07834D20	OEM
DNN08502D20	OEM
DNN08504D20	OEM
DNN08506D20	OEM
DNN08508D20	OEM
DNN08510D20	OEM
DNN08512D20	OEM
DNN08514D20	OEM
DNN08516D20	OEM
DNN08518D20	OEM
DNN08520D20	OEM
DNRD3.9E-B1	0036
DNRD5.1E-B3	0041
DNRD5.6E-B2	0253
DNRD6.2E	0466
DNRD6.2E-B1-B3	0466
DNRD6.2E-B2	0466
DNRD6.2E-B3	0466
DNRD6.2L	0466
DNRD7.5E	0077
DNRD7.5E-B3	0077
DNRD8.2E-B3	0165
DNRD10E-B1	0064
DNRD10E-B3	0064
DNRD10F-B1	0064
DNRD11E-B1	0181
DNRD13E-B2	0053
DNRD16E-B3	0440
DNRD24E-B2	0489
DNRD27E-B4	0436
DNRD33E-B1	0166
DNRD39E-B1	0032
DNRD39E-C2	0032
DNUPC574J	1319
DNX1	OEM
DNX1A	OEM
DNX2	OEM
DNX2A	OEM
DNX3	OEM
DNX4	3104
DNX4A	3104
DNX5	OEM
DNX5A	OEM
DNX6	OEM
DNX6A	OEM
DNX7	OEM
DNX7A	OEM
DNX8	OEM
DNX8A	OEM
DNX9	OEM
DNX9A	OEM
DNX31	OEM
D0-7	0289
D019	0211
D031	0079
D038	0211
D043	0211
D048	OEM
D063	0050

DEVICE TYPE	REPL CODE
D078	0211
D079	0050
D080	0085
D081	0160
D083	0038
D085	0038
D086	0050
D087	0127
D088	0127
D0104BSXXXX	OEM
D0105DXXXX	OEM
D0110DSXXXX	OEM
D0112BSXXXX	OEM
D0204BSXXXX	OEM
D0208FSXXXX	OEM
D0212BSXXXX	OEM
D0218BSXXXX	OEM
D0408BSXXXX	OEM
D0510DSXXXX	OEM
D0520DSXXXX	OEM
D0711BSXXXX	OEM
D0812BSXXXX	OEM
D0816BSXXXX	OEM
D01724BSXXXX	OEM
D05459BSXXXX	OEM
D07585BSXXXX	OEM
D08596BSXXXX	OEM
DOD-202-200	OEM
DOD-202-201	OEM
DOD-202-300	OEM
DOD-202-301	OEM
DOF4021001	0120
DOM102BSXXXX	OEM
DOM104BSXXXX	OEM
DOM105DXXXX	OEM
DOM110DSXXXX	OEM
DOM112BSXXXX	OEM
DOM204BSXXXX	OEM
DOM208FSXXXX	OEM
DOM212BSXXXX	OEM
DOM218BSXXXX	OEM
DOM408BSXXXX	OEM
DOM510DSXXXX	OEM
DOM520DSXXXX	OEM
DOM711BSXXXX	OEM
DOM812BSXXXX	OEM
DOM816BSXXXX	OEM
DOM1724BSXXXX	OEM
DOM5495BSXXXX	OEM
DOM7585BSXXXX	OEM
DOM8596BSXXXX	OEM
DOS118B	OEM
DOS118B-1	OEM
DOS118BM	OEM
DOS118BM-1	OEM
DOS118BMZS	OEM
DOS118BMZS-1	OEM
DOS118BQ	OEM
DOS118BQ-1	OEM
DOS118BQZS	OEM
DOS118BQZS-1	OEM
DOS118BT	OEM
DOS118BT-1	OEM
DOS118BTZS	OEM
DOS118BTZS-1	OEM
DOS118BZS	OEM
DOS118BZS-1	OEM
DOUBLER	OEM
DOZ105DXXXX	OEM
DP0300	OEM
DP0301	OEM
DP0302	OEM
DP0700	OEM
DP0701	OEM
DP0702	OEM
DP2	OEM
DP3	OEM
DP4	OEM
DP13B00-2	0276
DP13B01-2	0276
DP13B02-2	0287
DP13B04-2	0293
DP100	0071
DP146	OEM
DP147	OEM
DP1000	OEM
DP1000A	OEM
DP1001	OEM
DP1002	OEM
DP1003	OEM
DP1004	OEM
DP1005	OEM
DP1005A000	OEM
DP1005A003	OEM
DP1005AM	OEM
DP1005B000	OEM
DP1005B003	OEM
DP1005BM	OEM
DP1005C000	OEM
DP1005C003	OEM
DP1005CM	OEM
DP1006	OEM
DP1007	OEM
DP1008	OEM
DP1009	OEM
DP1010	OEM
DP1501	OEM
DP1502	OEM
DP1503	OEM

DEVICE TYPE	REPL CODE
DP1504	OEM
DP1505	OEM
DP1506	OEM
DP2000	OEM
DP2001	OEM
DP2002	OEM
DP2605	OEM
DP2907A	OEM
DP3000	OEM
DP3000A	OEM
DP3001	OEM
DP3002	OEM
DP5000	OEM
DP5001	OEM
DP5002	OEM
DP7303J	OEM
DP7304BJ	OEM
DP7307J	OEM
DP7308J	OEM
DP7310J	OEM
DP7311J	OEM
DP8000	OEM
DP8001	OEM
DP8002	OEM
DP8216	1852
DP8216J	1852
DP8216M	OEM
DP8216MJ	OEM
DP8216N	1852
DP8226	OEM
DP8226J	OEM
DP8226M	OEM
DP8226MJ	OEM
DP8226N	OEM
DP8303J	OEM
DP8303N	OEM
DP8304BJ	OEM
DP8304BN	OEM
DP8307J	OEM
DP8307N	OEM
DP8308J	OEM
DP8308N	OEM
DP8310J	OEM
DP8310N	OEM
DP8311J	OEM
DP8311N	OEM
DP8340J	OEM
DP8340N	OEM
DP8341J	OEM
DP8341N	OEM
DP8342J	OEM
DP8342N	OEM
DP8343N	OEM
DP8350N	OEM
DP8352N	OEM
DP8353N	OEM
DP8408	OEM
DP8409	OEM
DPA68/1M	OEM
DPB101-00S	OEM
DPB102-00S	OEM
DPB103-00S	OEM
DPB104-00S	OEM
DPB105-00S	OEM
DPH302	2604
DPT121	OEM
DPT122	OEM
DPT123	OEM
DPT124	OEM
DPT200	OEM
DPT2600	OEM
DPZ15-30R	OEM
DPZ15-33R	OEM
DPZ15-36R	OEM
DPZ15-45R	OEM
DPZ15-47R	OEM
DPZ15-50R	OEM
DQA05	OEM
DQA08	OEM
DQA0115V	OEM
DQA10	OEM
DQA12	OEM
DQA15	OEM
DQA20	OEM
DQA25	OEM
DQA30	OEM
DQA50	OEM
DQB05	OEM
DQB08	OEM
DQB10	OEM
DQB12	OEM
DQB15	OEM
DQB20	OEM
DQB25	OEM
DQB30	OEM
DQB50	OEM
DQN1006	OEM
DR1	0015
DR1PR	0015
DR2	4176
DR3	0015
DR4	0015
DR5	0015
DR50	0080
DR100	0015
DR120GB2	OEM
DR128	0143
DR150	OEM
DR200	0015

DEVICE TYPE	REPL CODE
DR202	0015
DR204	0790
DR206	0015
DR207	0143
DR208	0072
DR209	0133
DR210	0071
DR211	OEM
DR212	0102
DR213	0143
DR272	OEM
DR283	0143
DR291	0143
DR292	OEM
DR295	0143
DR300	0015
DR301	0133
DR302	0143
DR303	0143
DR304	OEM
DR305	OEM
DR306	0143
DR307	0143
DR308	0143
DR309	0143
DR310	OEM
DR311	OEM
DR312	OEM
DR313	0143
DR314	0143
DR315	OEM
DR316	OEM
DR317	0143
DR318	0143
DR319	0143
DR321	OEM
DR322	OEM
DR323	0143
DR324	0143
DR325	OEM
DR326	0143
DR327	0133
DR328	0143
DR329	0143
DR330	0143
DR336	0143
DR337	0143
DR338	0143
DR351	0143
DR352	0143
DR362	OEM
DR365	0143
DR366	0143
DR379	OEM
DR385	0143
DR389	0143
DR400	0015
DR401	0143
DR402	OEM
DR403	OEM
DR404	OEM
DR407	OEM
DR408	OEM
DR412-12-10	OEM
DR418	0143
DR419	OEM
DR422	OEM
DR426	0143
DR427	0015
DR434	0143
DR435	1325
DR437	OEM
DR449	0143
DR450	0071
DR459	OEM
DR463	0143
DR464	0143
DR481	OEM
DR482	0143
DR498	OEM
DR500	0015
DR521	0023
DR562	OEM
DR600	0023
DR-630	OEM
DR-630EW	OEM
DR-630NS	OEM
DR-640	OEM
DR-640EW	OEM
DR-640NS	OEM
DR650	OEM
DR650EW	OEM
DR650NS	OEM
DR661	OEM
DR664	0124
DR667	OEM
DR668	0080
DR669	0015
DR670	0790
DR671	0015
DR672	OEM
DR673	OEM
DR674	OEM
DR675	OEM
DR677	0124
DR688	OEM
DR694	0023
DR695	0015
DR698	0015

If replacement code is OEM, contact original manufacturer for replacement.

DEVICE TYPE	REPL CODE
DR699	0790
DR700	0071
DR800	0071
DR826	0790
DR827	OEM
DR833	0023
DR848	0015
DR852	0124
DR863	0015
DR900	0071
DR999	OEM
DR1000	0071
DR1100	0015
DR1200	0978
DR5101	0015
DR5102	0015
DR-104532	1403
DRA01B	0895
DRA01C	0058
DRA01E	0403
DRA03A	0340
DRA03B	0895
DRA03C	0058
DRA03D	0403
DRA03E	0403
DRA03F	1673
DRA2A	1250
DRA2B	0442
DRA2C	0934
DRA2E	0095
DRA2F	OEM
DRA2G	OEM
DRA3B	OEM
DRA3C	OEM
DRA3E	OEM
DRA3F	OEM
DRA3GB	OEM
DRA5B	2078
DRA5C	0500
DRA5E	0705
DRA5G	0857
DRA8B	1673
DRA8C	1673
DRA8E	0179
DRA8G	0946
DRA40	5659
DRA402	OEM
DRA404	OEM
DRA406	OEM
DRA408	OEM
DRA410	OEM
DRB2B	OEM
DRB2C	OEM
DRB2E	OEM
DRB3B	0442
DRB3C	0934
DRB3E	0095
DRB100-02R	OEM
DRB100-04R	OEM
DRB100-06R	OEM
DRB100-08R	OEM
DRB100-10R	OEM
DRB100-12R	OEM
DRBT100-02R	OEM
DRBT100-04R	OEM
DRBT100-06R	OEM
DRBT100-08R	OEM
DRBT100-10R	OEM
DRBT100-12R	OEM
DRC2E	OEM
DRC3E	0705
DRN02702D9	OEM
DRN02704D9	OEM
DRN02706D9	OEM
DRN02708D9	OEM
DRN02710D9	OEM
DRN02712D9	OEM
DRN02714D9	OEM
DRN03902D13	OEM
DRN03904D13	OEM
DRN03906D13	OEM
DRN03908D13	OEM
DRN03910D13	OEM
DRN03912D13	OEM
DRN03914D13	OEM
DRN03915D13	OEM
DRN05502D17	OEM
DRN05504D17	OEM
DRN05506D17	OEM
DRN05508D17	OEM
DRN05510D17	OEM
DRN05512D17	OEM
DRN05514D17	OEM
DRN05516D17	OEM
DRN05518D17	OEM
DRN05520D17	OEM
DRN05522D17	OEM
DRN05524D17	OEM
DRN05525D17	OEM
DRN07002D20	OEM
DRN07004D20	OEM
DRN07006D20	OEM
DRN07008D20	OEM
DRN07010D20	OEM
DRN07012D20	OEM
DRN07014D20	OEM
DRN07016D20	OEM
DRN07018D20	OEM
DRN07020D20	OEM

DEVICE TYPE	REPL CODE
DRS1	0015
DRS2	0087
DRS5E	0705
DRS101	0015
DRS102	0015
DRS104	0015
DRS106	0015
DRS107	0071
DRS108	0071
DRS110	0071
DRS112	OEM
DRS114	OEM
DRS114C	OEM
DRS114D	OEM
DRS163	1017
DRS164	1030
DRS165	1030
DRS166	1030
DRS167	4223
DRS168	4223
DRS169	4223
DRS185R	OEM
DRS203	1017
DRS204	1030
DRS205	1030
DRS206	1030
DRS207	4223
DRS208	4223
DRS209	4223
DRS243	1017
DRS244	1030
DRS245	1030
DRS246	1030
DRS247	4223
DRS248	4223
DRS249	4223
DRS250	3872
DRS251	3872
DRS252	3872
DRS253	OEM
DRS254	OEM
DRS1851	OEM
DRS1852	OEM
DRS1852R	OEM
DRS1853	OEM
DRS1853R	OEM
DRS1854	OEM
DRS1854R	OEM
DRS1855	OEM
DRS1855R	OEM
DRV11	OEM
DRV11B	OEM
DRX10	OEM
DRZ4300R	OEM
DS(I)35-02A#	2786
DS(I)35-04A#	2786
DS(I)35-07A#	2818
DS0025CH	OEM
DS0025CN	OEM
DS0025CN8	OEM
DS0025H	OEM
DS0026CG	OEM
DS0026CH	OEM
DS0026CJ	OEM
DS0026CJ-8	OEM
DS0026CJ8	OEM
DS0026CN	OEM
DS0026CN8	OEM
DS0026F	OEM
DS0026G	OEM
DS0026H	OEM
DS0026J	OEM
DS0026J-8	OEM
DS0026J8	OEM
DS0026W	OEM
DS0056CG	OEM
DS0056CH	OEM
DS0056CJ	OEM
DS0056CJ-8	OEM
DS0056CJ8	OEM
DS0056CN	OEM
DS0056CN8	OEM
DS0056G	OEM
DS0056H	OEM
DS0056J	OEM
DS0056J-8	OEM
DS0056J8	OEM
DS-0065	0015
DS0065	0015
DS0.5-200A	OEM
DS0.5-400A	OEM
DS0.5-600A	OEM
DS0.5-800A	OEM
DS0.5-1000A	OEM
DS0.5A	OEM
DS0.5A1	OEM
DS0.5A2	OEM
DS0.5A3	OEM
DS0.5A4	OEM
DS0.9-04A	OEM
DS0.9-08A	OEM
DS0.9-12A	OEM
DS0.9-14A	OEM
DS0.9-16A	OEM
DS0.9-18A	OEM
DS-1	0208
DS1	0015
DS-1(DELCO)	0208
DS1-200B	OEM

DEVICE TYPE	REPL CODE
DS1-400B	2621
DS1-600B	OEM
DS1-800B	OEM
DS1-1000B	OEM
DS1A	OEM
DS1B	0016
DS1B1	2621
DS1B2	2621
DS1B3	OEM
DS1B4	OEM
DS-1K	0071
DS1K	0023
DS1K7	0015
DS-1M	0015
DS1M	0023
DS-1N	0222
DS1N	OEM
DS-1P	0015
DS1P	0015
DS-1U	0914
DS1U	OEM
DS1.2-04A	OEM
DS1.2-08A	OEM
DS1.2-12A	OEM
DS1.2-14A	OEM
DS1.2-16A	OEM
DS1.2-18A	OEM
DS1.2A6	OEM
DS1.2A9	OEM
DS1.2A12	OEM
DS1.2A15	OEM
DS-1.5-2	0087
DS1.8-18A	OEM
DS2	0595
DS2(LEAD)	OEM
DS2(LED)	OEM
DS2-04A	OEM
DS2-08A	OEM
DS2-12A	OEM
DS2-14A	OEM
DS2-16A	OEM
DS2-18A	OEM
DS2B6	2621
DS2B9	2621
DS2B12	OEM
DS2B15	OEM
DS2CDL-25	OEM
DS2DL-1LGN	OEM
DS2K	0015
DS2L	OEM
DS-2M	0102
DS2M	0023
DS-2N	0087
DS2N	0023
DS2N22	0015
DS2P	0535
DS3	0004
DS3-200A	OEM
DS3-400A	OEM
DS3-600A	OEM
DS3-800A	OEM
DS3-1000A	OEM
DS3A	OEM
DS3A1	OEM
DS3A2	OEM
DS3A3	OEM
DS3A4	OEM
DS4	0595
DS5	0595
DS5-200B	OEM
DS5-400B	OEM
DS5-600B	OEM
DS5-800B	OEM
DS5-1000B	OEM
DS5A	OEM
DS5B1	OEM
DS5B2	OEM
DS5B3	OEM
DS5B4	OEM
DS5BN	0319
DS5BN-L	0015
DS6	0595
DS6-08F	OEM
DS6-12F	OEM
DS6-14F	OEM
DS6-16F	OEM
DS6-18A	OEM
DS6A6	OEM
DS6A9	OEM
DS6A12	OEM
DS6A15	OEM
DS7	0595
DS-8	0004
DS8	0595
DS8T26AJ	4022
DS8T26AN	4022
DS8T28J	0576
DS8T28MJ	0576
DS8T28N	0576
DS9	0595
DS9-04F	OEM
DS9-08F	OEM
DS9-12F	OEM
DS9-14F	OEM
DS9-16F	OEM
DS9-18A	OEM
DS9B6	OEM
DS9B9	OEM
DS9B12	OEM

DEVICE TYPE	REPL CODE
DS9B15	OEM
DS-10	0015
DS10-200C	OEM
DS10-400C	OEM
DS10-600C	OEM
DS10-800C	OEM
DS10-1000C	OEM
DS10C	OEM
DS10C1	OEM
DS10C2	OEM
DS10C3	OEM
DS10C4	OEM
DS10S1	OEM
DS10S2	OEM
DS10S3	OEM
DS11	0595
DS12	0595
DS-13	0071
DS13	0004
DS-13(COURIER)	0015
DS-13A(SANYO)	0015
DS-13B(SANYO)	0015
DS13C	0865
DS13E	0847
DS-14	0004
DS14	0136
DS-14(DIODE)	0015
DS-14(SANYO)	0914
DS14C	0865
DS14E	0847
DS15A	0071
DS15B	0072
DS15C	0023
DS15E	0023
DS15F	OEM
DS15G	0017
DS16	0004
DS-16(SEARS-DIODE)	0015
DS-16A	0015
DS16A	0015
DS-16A(SANYO)	0071
DS-16B	0015
DS16B	0015
DS-16B(SANYO)	0015
DS-16B(SYLVANIA)	0015
DS16C	0015
DS-16C(SANYO)	0015
DS-16D	0015
DS16D	0023
DS-16D(SANYO)	0015
DS-16E	0015
DS16E	0015
DS-16E(SANYO)	0015
DS16N	0015
DS16NA	0071
DS16NB	0015
DS16NC	0015
DS-16ND	0015
DS16ND	0023
DS-16NE	0015
DS16NE	0015
DS-16NY	0015
DS-16YA	0015
DS-17	0196
DS17	0023
DS17(ADMIRAL)	0015
DS-17(SANYO)	0015
DS17-02A	OEM
DS17-04A	OEM
DS17-06A	OEM
DS17-08A	OEM
DS-17-6A	0015
DS17-12A	OEM
DS17-14A	OEM
DS17-16A	OEM
DS17-18A	OEM
DS17N	0015
DS17S2	OEM
DS17S3	OEM
DS17S6	OEM
DS-18	0015
DS18	0023
DS-18(DELCO)	0150
DS-18(GE)	0015
DS-18(SANYO)	0015
DS18(SEARS)	0015
DS18N	0015
DS-19	0004
DS19	0604
DS-19(RECTIFIER)	0015
DS-19(SANYO)	0015
DS19C	OEM
DS19E	OEM
DS19G	OEM
DS19J	OEM
DS20-200C	OEM
DS20-400C	OEM
DS20-600C	OEM
DS20-800	OEM
DS20-800C	OEM
DS20-1000C	OEM
DS20B	OEM
DS20C	OEM
DS20C1	OEM
DS20C2	OEM
DS20C3	OEM
DS20C4	OEM
DS20E	OEM
DS20G	OEM

DEVICE TYPE	REPL CODE
DS20J	OEM
DS20S1	OEM
DS20S2	OEM
DS20S3	OEM
DS21	0279
DS-22	0279
DS22	0279
DS22-04A	0258
DS22-08A	OEM
DS22-12A	OEM
DS22-14A	OEM
DS22-16A	OEM
DS22-18A	OEM
DS22C6	OEM
DS22C9	OEM
DS22C12	OEM
DS22C15	OEM
DS23	0279
DS-24	0136
DS24	0136
DS-25	0136
DS25	0136
DS-26	0164
DS26	0004
DS26LS31CJ	OEM
DS26LS31CN	OEM
DS26LS31MJ	OEM
DS26LS32CJ	OEM
DS26LS32CN	OEM
DS26LS32MJ	OEM
DS26LS33CJ	OEM
DS26LS33CN	OEM
DS26LS33MJ	OEM
DS26S10J	OEM
DS26S10MJ	OEM
DS26S10N	OEM
DS26S11J	OEM
DS26S11MJ	OEM
DS26S11N	OEM
DS-27	0143
DS27	0143
DS-28(DELCO)	0279
DS29	0004
DS-31	0025
DS31	0133
DS31(DELCO)	0143
DS-32	0143
DS32	0143
DS-33	0143
DS33	0143
DS33(DELCO)	0143
DS-34	0050
DS34	0050
DS-35	0050
DS35	0050
DS35-02A	2741
DS35-04A	2879
DS35-08A	OEM
DS35-12A	OEM
DS35-14A	OEM
DS35-16A	OEM
DS35-18A	OEM
DS35S2	OEM
DS35S3	OEM
DS35S6	OEM
DS-36	0050
DS36	0136
DS-37	0050
DS37	0050
DS-38	0133
DS38	0136
DS38(DELCO)	0050
DS38(SANYO)	0015
DS-39	0143
DS39	0123
DS40Q-04F	OEM
DS-41	0050
DS41	0050
DS-42	0050
DS42	0050
DS42-04#	2786
DS42-04A	OEM
DS42-07#	2818
DS42-08A	OEM
DS42-12A	OEM
DS42-14A	OEM
DS42-16A	OEM
DS42-18A	OEM
DS42C6	OEM
DS42C9	OEM
DS42C12	OEM
DS42C15	OEM
DS-43	0012
DS43	0012
DS-44	0079
DS44	0016
DS-45	0079
DS45	0016
DS45-200C	OEM
DS45-400	OEM
DS45-400C	OEM
DS45-600	OEM
DS45-600C	OEM
DS45-800	OEM
DS45-800C	OEM
DS45-1000C	OEM
DS45B	OEM
DS45C1	OEM
DS45C2	OEM

DEVICE TYPE	REPL CODE
DS45C3	OEM
DS45C4	OEM
DS-46	0079
DS46	0016
DS-47	0016
DS47	0016
DS48	0012
DS-49	0244
DS50	0157
DS-51	0050
DS51	0136
DS-52	0050
DS52	0136
DS-53	0211
DS53	0279
DS-55	0030
DS55	0030
DS-56	0050
DS56	0050
DS58(SANYO)	0015
DS-60	0396
DS-62	0050
DS62	0050
DS-63	0050
DS63	0050
DS-64	0050
DS64	0050
DS-65	0050
DS65	0050
DS-66	0016
DS66	0016
DS-66W	0079
DS-67	0016
DS67	0016
DS-67W	0079
DS67W	0016
DS-68	0150
DS68	0150
DS-70	2220
DS-71	0127
DS71	0127
DS-72	0127
DS72	0127
DS-73	0127
DS73	0127
DS-74	0127
DS74	0127
DS-75	0079
DS75	0127
DS75-02B	OEM
DS75-04B	OEM
DS75-06B	OEM
DS75-08B	OEM
DS75-12B	OEM
DS75-14B	OEM
DS75-16B	OEM
DS-76	0016
DS76	0016
DS-77	0079
DS77	0016
DS-78	0007
DS78	0007
DS78C20J	OEM
DS78C120J	OEM
DS78L12J	OEM
DS78LS120J	OEM
DS-79	0015
DS79	0015
DS-79(DELCO)	0015
DS-80	0015
DS80	0015
DS80-04A	1337
DS80-08A	OEM
DS80-12A	OEM
DS80-14A	OEM
DS80-16A	OEM
DS80-18A	OEM
DS-81	0224
DS81	0007
DS-82	0037
DS82	0037
DS-83	0037
DS83	0037
DS-85	0007
DS85	0007
DS-86	0126
DS86	0150
DS-87	0902
DS-88	0321
DS88	0321
DS88C20J	OEM
DS88C20N	OEM
DS88C120J	OEM
DS88C120N	OEM
DS88L12J	OEM
DS88L12N	OEM
DS88LS120J	OEM
DS88LS120N	OEM
DS89	0229
DS90SM19	OEM
DS-94	0155
DS96	0150
DS-97	0133
DS97	0133
DS97(DELCO)	0133
DS99	0012
DS-102	0212
DS-103	0030
DS104	0133

DEVICE TYPE	REPL CODE
DS-105	0212
DS-106	0212
DS-107	0162
DS-108	0137
DS-110	0100
DS110-04A	OEM
DS110-08A	OEM
DS110-12A	OEM
DS110-14A	OEM
DS110-16A	OEM
DS110-18A	OEM
DS110C6	OEM
DS110C9	OEM
DS110C12	OEM
DS110C15	OEM
DS111	4972
DS-113	0124
DS-113A	0102
DS113A	OEM
DS-113B	0102
DS113B	5214
DS113C	OEM
DS-114	0030
DS114	0030
DS-117	0133
DS117	0133
DS118	OEM
DS118A	0242
DS118B	0535
DS118C	0959
DS118D	0811
DS118E	0916
DS-130	0015
DS130A	0072
DS-130B	0015
DS130B	0015
DS-130C	0015
DS130C	0015
DS130D	0015
DS-130E	0015
DS130E	0015
DS130NA	0071
DS130NB	0015
DS130NC	0015
DS130ND	0015
DS130N-E	OEM
DS130NE	0015
DS130T	0071
DS130TA	0071
DS-130TA-L	0015
DS130TA-L	0015
DS130TAL-FB2	0015
DS-130TA-S	0015
DS130TB	0071
DS130TC	0071
DS130TD	0071
DS130TE	0071
DS-130YB	0015
DS130YC	0015
DS130YE	0015
DS-131	0015
DS131	0023
DS-131A	0015
DS131A	0015
DS-131B	0015
DS131B	0015
DS132	1089
DS132A	0015
DS-132B	0015
DS132B	0015
DS133	OEM
DS133A	0015
DS133B	0102
DS135	0023
DS135AT	OEM
DS135B	OEM
DS135C	0023
DS135C-AT	0023
DS135D	0023
DS135D-FA3	0023
DS135D-KB1	OEM
DS135D-KB3	OEM
DS135E	0023
DS135F	0023
DS-149	0244
DS149	0244
DS150	0071
DS150A	0071
DS150B	0071
DS150C	0071
DS151	OEM
DS152	OEM
DS-159	0025
DS159	0631
DS160(G.E.)	0015
DS-170	OEM
DS170-18L	OEM
DS170-20L	OEM
DS170-25L	OEM
DS175-02L	OEM
DS175-04L	OEM
DS175-06L	OEM
DS175-08L	OEM
DS175-10L	OEM
DS175-12L	OEM
DS175-14L	OEM
DS175-16L	OEM
DS183AA	3160
DS183BA	2873

If replacement code is OEM, contact original manufacturer for replacement.

DEVICE TYPE	REPL CODE	DEVICE TYPE	REPL CODE	DEVICE TYPE	REPL CODE	DEVICE TYPE	REPL CODE	DEVICE TYPE	REPL CODE	DEVICE TYPE	REPL CODE	DEVICE TYPE	REPL CODE
DS183CA	1116	DS353FA	1118	DS-509	0103	DS1101SM03	OEM	DS1652J	OEM	DS3245J	OEM	DS7812J	OEM
DS183DA	1116	DS353GA	0800	DS509	0103	DS1101SM04	OEM	DS1653J	OEM	DS3245N	OEM	DS7819J	OEM
DS183EA	1118	DS353HA	0800	DS-512	0086	DS1101SM05	OEM	DS1671H	OEM	DS3486J	OEM	DS7819W	OEM
DS183FA	1118	DS353KA	1186	DS512	0086	DS1101SM06	OEM	DS1671J	OEM	DS3486N	OEM	DS7820AF	OEM
DS183GA	0800	DS353MA	0315	DS-513	0042	DS1101SM07	OEM	DS1671J-8	OEM	DS3487J	OEM	DS7820AJ	OEM
DS183HA	0800	DS353PA	1124	DS513	0042	DS1101SM08	OEM	DS1674J	OEM	DS3487N	OEM	DS7820AN	OEM
DS183KA	1186	DS353RA	1124	DS-514	0103	DS1101SM09	OEM	DS1675J	OEM	DS3587J	OEM	DS7820AW	OEM
DS183MA	0315	DS353TA	0045	DS514	0103	DS1101SM10	OEM	DS1677D	OEM	DS3603J	OEM	DS7820F	OEM
DS183PA	1124	DS353VA	0045	DS-515	0160	DS1101SM11	OEM	DS1678J	OEM	DS3603N	OEM	DS7820J	OEM
DS183RA	1124	DS390-04	OEM	DS515	0160	DS1101SM12	OEM	DS1679J	OEM	DS3604J	OEM	DS7820N	OEM
DS183TA	0045	DS390-04J	OEM	DS-519	0103	DS1104SM01	OEM	DS1686H	OEM	DS3604N	OEM	DS7830F	OEM
DS183VA	0045	DS390-06J	OEM	DS519	0103	DS1104SM02	OEM	DS1686J	OEM	DS3611H	OEM	DS7830J	OEM
DS184	OEM	DS390-08J	OEM	DS-520	0160	DS1104SM03	OEM	DS1686J-8	OEM	DS3611J-8	OEM	DS7830N	OEM
DS185D	OEM	DS400	OEM	DS520	0160	DS1104SM04	OEM	DS1687H	OEM	DS3611N	OEM	DS7831	OEM
DS185E	OEM	DS400-07F	OEM	DS525	0435	DS1104SM05	OEM	DS1687J	OEM	DS3612H	OEM	DS7831J	OEM
DS185F	OEM	DS400-11F	OEM	DS570	0435	DS1104SM06	OEM	DS1687J-8	OEM	DS3612J-8	OEM	DS7832	OEM
DS-189	0313	DS400-14F	OEM	DS677	OEM	DS1104SM07	OEM	DS1691J	OEM	DS3612N	OEM	DS7832J	OEM
DS189	0313	DS400-17F	OEM	DS-781	0127	DS1104SM08	OEM	DS1692J	OEM	DS3613H	OEM	DS7833J	OEM
DS-190	2060	DS400-20F	OEM	DS804SE07	OEM	DS1104SM09	OEM	DS2004SN10	OEM	DS3613J-8	OEM	DS7834J	OEM
DS190	OEM	DS400-23F	OEM	DS804SE08	OEM	DS1104SM10	OEM	DS2004SN11	OEM	DS3613N	OEM	DS7835J	OEM
DS200	OEM	DS401	OEM	DS804SE09	OEM	DS1104SM11	OEM	DS2004SN12	OEM	DS3614H	OEM	DS7836J	OEM
DS201	OEM	DS402	OEM	DS804SE10	OEM	DS1104SM12	OEM	DS2004SN13	OEM	DS3614J-8	OEM	DS7837J	OEM
DS202	OEM	DS402-ST01	OEM	DS804SE11	OEM	DS1104SM13	OEM	DS2004SN14	OEM	DS3614N	OEM	DS7838J	OEM
DS203AA	3160	DS402-ST02	OEM	DS804SE12	OEM	DS1104SM14	OEM	DS2004SN15	OEM	DS3617N	OEM	DS7839J	OEM
DS203BA	2873	DS402-ST04	OEM	DS804SE13	OEM	DS1104SM15	OEM	DS2004SN16	OEM	DS3628J	OEM	DS7856J	OEM
DS203CA	1116	DS402-ST05	OEM	DS804SE14	OEM	DS1104SM16	OEM	DS2004SN17	OEM	DS3628N	OEM	DS7858J	OEM
DS203DA	1116	DS402-ST06	OEM	DS804SE15	OEM	DS1104SM17	OEM	DS2004SN18	OEM	DS3630J	OEM	DS7880J	OEM
DS203EA	1118	DS402ST01	OEM	DS804SE16	OEM	DS1104SM18	OEM	DS2004SN19	OEM	DS3630N	OEM	DS7889J	OEM
DS203FA	1118	DS402ST02	OEM	DS804SE17	OEM	DS1104SM19	OEM	DS2004SN20	OEM	DS3631H	OEM	DS7897AJ	OEM
DS203GA	0800	DS402ST03	OEM	DS804SE18	OEM	DS1104SM20	OEM	DS2004SN21	OEM	DS3631J-8	OEM	DS8626N	OEM
DS203HA	0800	DS402ST04	OEM	DS804SE19	OEM	DS1104SM21	OEM	DS2004SN22	OEM	DS3631N	OEM	DS8629N	OEM
DS203KA	1186	DS402ST05	OEM	DS804SE20	OEM	DS1104SM22	OEM	DS2004SN23	OEM	DS3632H	OEM	DS8640J	OEM
DS203MA	0315	DS402ST06	OEM	DS804SE21	OEM	DS1104SM23	OEM	DS2004SN24	OEM	DS3632J-8	OEM	DS8640N	OEM
DS203PA	1124	DS402ST07	OEM	DS820A	OEM	DS1104SM24	OEM	DS2007SN24	OEM	DS3632N	OEM	DS8641J	OEM
DS203RA	1124	DS402ST08	OEM	DS904SL18	OEM	DS1104SM25	OEM	DS2007SN25	OEM	DS3633H	OEM	DS8641N	OEM
DS203TA	0045	DS402ST09	OEM	DS904SL10	OEM	DS1104SM26	OEM	DS2007SN26	OEM	DS3633J	OEM	DS8647N	OEM
DS203VA	1620	DS402ST10	OEM	DS904SL11	OEM	DS1104SM27	OEM	DS2007SN29	OEM	DS3633J-8	OEM	DS8648N	OEM
DS230A	0102	DS402ST11	OEM	DS904SL12	OEM	DS1104SM28	OEM	DS2007SN30	OEM	DS3633N	OEM	DS8654N	OEM
DS230B	0023	DS402ST12	OEM	DS904SL13	OEM	DS1104SM29	OEM	DS2007SN31	OEM	DS3634H	OEM	DS8656N	OEM
DS230C	0017	DS403AA	3160	DS904SL14	OEM	DS1107SM24	OEM	DS2007SN32	OEM	DS3634N	OEM	DS8664N	OEM
DS230D	0017	DS403BA	2873	DS904SL15	OEM	DS1107SM25	OEM	DS2007SN33	OEM	DS3642H	OEM	DS8665N	OEM
DS240-02A	OEM	DS403CA	1116	DS904SL16	OEM	DS1107SM26	OEM	DS2007SN34	OEM	DS3642J-8	OEM	DS8666N	OEM
DS240-02A#	1017	DS403DA	1116	DS904SL17	OEM	DS1107SM27	OEM	DS2007SN35	OEM	DS3644J	OEM	DS8667N	OEM
DS240-04A	OEM	DS403EA	1118	DS904SL19	OEM	DS1107SM28	OEM	DS2007SN36	OEM	DS3644N	OEM	DS8668	OEM
DS240-04A#	1030	DS403FA	1118	DS904SL20	OEM	DS1107SM29	OEM	DS2007SN37	OEM	DS3645J	OEM	DS8669N	OEM
DS240-06A	OEM	DS403GA	0800	DS904SL21	OEM	DS1107SM30	OEM	DS2007SN38	OEM	DS3647D	OEM	DS8692N	OEM
DS240-06A#	1030	DS403HA	0800	DS904SL22	OEM	DS1107SM31	OEM	DS2007SN39	OEM	DS3647N	OEM	DS8800H	OEM
DS240-07A	OEM	DS403KA	1186	DS904SL23	OEM	DS1107SM32	OEM	DS2007SN40	OEM	DS3648N	OEM	DS8810J	OEM
DS240-07A#	1040	DS403MA	0315	DS904SL24	OEM	DS1107SM33	OEM	DS2007SN2728	OEM	DS3649J	OEM	DS8810N	OEM
DS250-04F	OEM	DS403PA	1124	DS904SL25	OEM	DS1107SM34	OEM	DS2009SN30	OEM	DS3649N	OEM	DS8811J	OEM
DS250-04L	OEM	DS403RA	1124	DS904SL26	OEM	DS1107SM35	OEM	DS2009SN31	OEM	DS3650J	OEM	DS8811N	OEM
DS250-07F	OEM	DS403TA	0045	DS904SL27	OEM	DS1107SM36	OEM	DS2009SN32	OEM	DS3650N	OEM	DS8812J	OEM
DS250-07L	OEM	DS403VA	0045	DS904SL28	OEM	DS1109SM30	OEM	DS2009SN33	OEM	DS3651J	OEM	DS8812N	OEM
DS250-11F	OEM	DS-410	0133	DS904SL29	OEM	DS1109SM31	OEM	DS2009SN34	OEM	DS3651N	OEM	DS8819J	OEM
DS250-11L	OEM	DS410	0133	DS904SM10	OEM	DS1109SM32	OEM	DS2009SN35	OEM	DS3652J	OEM	DS8819N	OEM
DS250-14F	OEM	DS-410(AMPEX)	0133	DS904SM11	OEM	DS1109SM33	OEM	DS2009SN36	OEM	DS3652N	OEM	DS8820AF	OEM
DS250-14L	OEM	DS410(COURIER)	0133	DS904SM12	OEM	DS1109SM34	OEM	DS2009SN37	OEM	DS3653J	OEM	DS8820AJ	OEM
DS250-17F	OEM	DS410(EMERSON)	0133	DS904SM13	OEM	DS1109SM35	OEM	DS2009SN38	OEM	DS3653N	OEM	DS8820AN	OEM
DS250-17L	OEM	DS410(FANON)	0133	DS904SM14	OEM	DS1109SM36	OEM	DS2009SN39	OEM	DS3654N	OEM	DS8820F	OEM
DS250-20F	OEM	DS410(G.E.)	0143	DS904SM15	OEM	DS1109SM37	OEM	DS2009SN40	OEM	DS3662N	OEM	DS8820J	OEM
DS250-20L	OEM	DS-410(MOTOROLA)	0016	DS904SM16	OEM	DS1109SM38	OEM	DS2009SN41	OEM	DS3671H	OEM	DS8820N	OEM
DS250-23F	OEM	DS410(OLYMPIC)	0133	DS904SM17	OEM	DS1109SM39	OEM	DS2009SN42	OEM	DS3671J	OEM	DS8822N	OEM
DS250-23L	OEM	DS410(WESTINGHOUSE)	0133	DS904SM18	OEM	DS1109SM40	OEM	DS2009SN43	OEM	DS3671J-8	OEM	DS8830	OEM
DS253AA	3160	DS410R	0133	DS904SM19	OEM	DS1109SM41	OEM	DS2009SN44	OEM	DS3671N	OEM	DS8830F	OEM
DS253BA	2873	DS410R(G.E.)	0143	DS904SM20	OEM	DS1109SM42	OEM	DS2012SM42	OEM	DS3674J	OEM	DS8830J	OEM
DS253CA	1116	DS412SE40	OEM	DS904SM21	OEM	DS1109SM43	OEM	DS2012SM43	OEM	DS3674N	OEM	DS8830N	OEM
DS253DA	1116	DS412SE41	OEM	DS904SM22	OEM	DS1109SM44	OEM	DS2012SM44	OEM	DS3675J	OEM	DS8831	OEM
DS253EA	1118	DS412SE42	OEM	DS904SM23	OEM	DS1112SM47-18	OEM	DS2012SM45	OEM	DS3675N	OEM	DS8831J	OEM
DS253FA	1118	DS412SE43	OEM	DS904SM24	OEM	DS1112SM48-18	OEM	DS2012SM46	OEM	DS3677D	OEM	DS8831N	OEM
DS253GA	0800	DS412SE44	OEM	DS904SM25	OEM	DS1112SM49-18	OEM	DS2012SM47	OEM	DS3677N	OEM	DS8832	OEM
DS253HA	0800	DS422S2	OEM	DS904SM26	OEM	DS1112SM50-18	OEM	DS2012SM48	OEM	DS3678J	OEM	DS8832J	OEM
DS253KA	1186	DS-430	0015	DS904SM27	OEM	DS1112SM51-18	OEM	DS2012SM49	OEM	DS3678N	OEM	DS8832N	OEM
DS253MA	0315	DS430	0015	DS904SM28	OEM	DS1112SM52-18	OEM	DS2012SM50	OEM	DS3679J	OEM	DS8833J	OEM
DS253PA	1124	DS430(VARISTOR)	0139	DS904SM29	OEM	DS1112SM53-18	OEM	DS2012SM51	OEM	DS3679N	OEM	DS8833N	OEM
DS253RA	1124	DS430-04J	OEM	DS912SM25	OEM	DS1112SM54-18	OEM	DS2012SM52	OEM	DS3680J	OEM	DS8834J	OEM
DS253TA	0045	DS430-06J	OEM	DS912SM26	OEM	DS1112SM55-18	OEM	DS2012SM53	OEM	DS3680N	OEM	DS8834N	OEM
DS253VA	0045	DS430-08J	OEM	DS912SM27	OEM	DS1112SM56-18	OEM	DS2012SM54	OEM	DS3686H	OEM	DS8835J	OEM
DS290-08J	OEM	DS430-10J	OEM	DS912SM28	OEM	DS1488J	0503	DS2012SM55	OEM	DS3686J	OEM	DS8835N	OEM
DS290-12J	OEM	DS430-12J	OEM	DS912SM29	OEM	DS1488N	0503	DS2012SM56	OEM	DS3686J-8	OEM	DS8836J	OEM
DS290-14J	OEM	DS430-14J	OEM	DS912SM30	OEM	DS1489AJ	0506	DS2016	OEM	DS3686N	OEM	DS8836N	OEM
DS290-16J	OEM	DS430-16J	OEM	DS912SM31	OEM	DS1489AN	0506	DS2020	OEM	DS3687H	OEM	DS8837J	OEM
DS300	OEM	DS441	0124	DS912SM32	OEM	DS1489J	0506	DS2030	OEM	DS3687J	OEM	DS8837N	OEM
DS301	OEM	DS-442	0133	DS912SM33	OEM	DS1489N	0506	DS2040	OEM	DS3687J-8	OEM	DS8838	OEM
DS302	OEM	DS442	0133	DS912SM34	OEM	DS1603J	OEM	DS2050	OEM	DS3687N	OEM	DS8838J	OEM
DS303AA	3160	DS442AT	OEM	DS912SM35	OEM	DS1611H	OEM	DS2060	OEM	DS3691J	OEM	DS8838N	OEM
DS303BA	2873	DS442BT	OEM	DS912SM36	OEM	DS1611J-8	OEM	DS2070	OEM	DS3691N	OEM	DS8839J	OEM
DS303CA	1116	DS442FM	0133	DS912SM37	OEM	DS1612H	OEM	DS2080	OEM	DS3692J	OEM	DS8839N	OEM
DS303DA	1116	DS442S2	0133	DS912SM38	OEM	DS1612J-8	OEM	DS2106SU20	OEM	DS3692N	OEM	DS8856J	OEM
DS303EA	1118	DS442VB5	OEM	DS912SM39	OEM	DS1613H	OEM	DS2106SU21	OEM	DS4001	OEM	DS8856N	OEM
DS303FA	1118	DS442VG1	OEM	DS912SM40	OEM	DS1613J-8	OEM	DS2106SU22	OEM	DS4003	0023	DS8857J	OEM
DS303GA	0800	DS442X	0124	DS912SM41	OEM	DS1614H	OEM	DS2106SU23	OEM	DS4148	0133	DS8858J	OEM
DS303HA	0800	DS442X-BT	0124	DS912SM42	OEM	DS1614J-8	OEM	DS2106SU24	OEM	DS4510	OEM	DS8858N	OEM
DS303KA	1186	DS443	0133	DS912SM43	OEM	DS1628J	OEM	DS2106SU25	OEM	DS4520	OEM	DS8859AJ	OEM
DS303MA	0315	DS446	0124	DS912SM44	OEM	DS1630J	OEM	DS2106SU26	OEM	DS4530	OEM	DS8859AN	OEM
DS303PA	1124	DS448	0133	DS912SM45	OEM	DS1631H	OEM	DS2106SU27	OEM	DS4540	OEM	DS8861N	OEM
DS303RA	1124	DS448-FA1	0124	DS912SM46	OEM	DS1631J-8	OEM	DS2106SU28	OEM	DS4550	OEM	DS8863N	OEM
DS303TA	0045	DS448FA1	0124	DS912SM47	OEM	DS1632H	OEM	DS2106SU29	OEM	DS4560	OEM	DS8867N	OEM
DS303VA	0045	DS452	0023	DS912SM48	OEM	DS1632J-8	OEM	DS2106SU30	OEM	DS4570	OEM	DS8869AJ	OEM
DS315N	OEM	DS454	0023	DS912SM49	OEM	DS1633H	OEM	DS2106SU31	OEM	DS4638J	OEM	DS8869AN	OEM
DS316N	OEM	DS456	OEM	DS912SM50	OEM	DS1633J-8	OEM	DS2106SU32	OEM	DS4645N	OEM	DS8870	1691
DS330A	0023	DS500	OEM	DS912SM51	OEM	DS1634H	OEM	DS2106SU33	OEM	DS5295G	0023	DS8870J	1687
DS330B	0023	DS-501	0435	DS912SM52	OEM	DS1634J-8	OEM	DS2106SU34	OEM	DS5295J	0023	DS8870N	1691
DS330C	0017	DS501	0435	DS912SM53	OEM	DS1644J	OEM	DS2106SU35	OEM	DS5534J	OEM	DS8871N	OEM
DS330D	0017	DS502	0435	DS912SM54	OEM	DS1645J	OEM	DS2106SU36	OEM	DS5538J	OEM	DS8872N	OEM
DS353AA	3160	DS-503	0085	DS912SM55	OEM	DS1647D	OEM	DS2657	OEM	DS7640J	OEM	DS8873N	OEM
DS353BA	2873	DS503	0085	DS912SM56	OEM	DS1648J	OEM	DS3010	OEM	DS7641J	OEM	DS8874N	OEM
DS353CA	1116	DS504	0435	DS923SM47	OEM	DS1649J	OEM	DS3020	OEM	DS7800H	OEM	DS8877N	OEM
DS353DA	1116	DS505	0435	DS1101SM01	OEM	DS1650J	OEM	DS3030	OEM	DS7810J	OEM	DS8880F	1782
DS353EA	1118	DS506	0435	DS1101SM02	OEM	DS1651J	OEM	DS3040	OEM	DS7811J	OEM	DS8880J	1782

382 If replacement code is OEM, contact original manufacturer for replacement.

DEVICE TYPE	REPL CODE
DS8880N	1782
DS8881N	OEM
DS8884AN	OEM
DS8885J	OEM
DS8885N	OEM
DS8887J	OEM
DS8887N	OEM
DS8889J	1866
DS8889N	1866
DS8891J	OEM
DS8891N	OEM
DS8897AJ	OEM
DS8897AN	OEM
DS8906	OEM
DS8907	OEM
DS8908	OEM
DS8963N	OEM
DS8973N	OEM
DS8975N	OEM
DS8980N	OEM
DS8981J	OEM
DS8981N	OEM
DS16149J	OEM
DS16177D	OEM
DS16179J	OEM
DS36147D	OEM
DS36147N	OEM
DS36149J	OEM
DS36149N	OEM
DS36177D	OEM
DS36177N	OEM
DS36179J	OEM
DS36179N	OEM
DS54552J-8	OEM
DS54553J-8	OEM
DS54554J-8	OEM
DS55107J	OEM
DS55108J	OEM
DS55109J	OEM
DS55113J	OEM
DS55114J	OEM
DS55115J	OEM
DS55121J	OEM
DS55122J	OEM
DS55325J	OEM
DS55451H	OEM
DS55451J-8	OEM
DS55452H	OEM
DS55452J-8	OEM
DS55453H	OEM
DS55453J-8	OEM
DS55454H	OEM
DS55454J-8	OEM
DS55461H	OEM
DS55461J-8	OEM
DS55462H	OEM
DS55462J-8	OEM
DS55463H	OEM
DS55463J-8	OEM
DS55464H	OEM
DS55464J-8	OEM
DS55493J	OEM
DS55494J	OEM
DS74592J	OEM
DS75107J	OEM
DS75107N	OEM
DS75108J	OEM
DS75108N	OEM
DS75113J	OEM
DS75113N	OEM
DS75114J	OEM
DS75114N	OEM
DS75115J	OEM
DS75115N	OEM
DS75121J	OEM
DS75121N	OEM
DS75122J	OEM
DS75122N	OEM
DS75123J	OEM
DS75123N	OEM
DS75124J	OEM
DS75124N	OEM
DS75125J	OEM
DS75125N	OEM
DS75127J	OEM
DS75127N	OEM
DS75128J	OEM
DS75128N	OEM
DS75129J	OEM
DS75129N	OEM
DS75150J	OEM
DS75150J-8	OEM
DS75150N	OEM
DS75154J	OEM
DS75154N	OEM
DS75207J	OEM
DS75207N	OEM
DS75208J	OEM
DS75208N	OEM
DS75325J	OEM
DS75325N	OEM
DS75361J-8	OEM
DS75361N	OEM
DS75362J-8	OEM
DS75362N	OEM
DS75364J-8	OEM
DS75365J	OEM
DS75365N	OEM
DS75450J	OEM
DS75450N	1222
DS75451H	OEM
DS75451J-8	OEM
DS75451M	OEM
DS75451N	1235
DS75452H	OEM
DS75452J-8	OEM
DS75452M	OEM
DS75452N	1253
DS75453H	OEM
DS75453J-8	OEM
DS75453M	OEM
DS75453N	1262
DS75454H	OEM
DS75454J-8	OEM
DS75454N	1279
DS75461H	OEM
DS75461J-8	OEM
DS75461N	OEM
DS75462H	OEM
DS75462J-8	OEM
DS75462N	OEM
DS75463H	OEM
DS75463J-8	OEM
DS75463N	OEM
DS75464H	OEM
DS75464J-8	OEM
DS75464N	OEM
DS75491J	OEM
DS75491N	1718
DS75492J	OEM
DS75492N	1729
DS75493J	OEM
DS75493N	4933
DS75494J	OEM
DS75494N	4934
DSA010	0124
DSA015	0124
DSA0.5A1100	OEM
DSA0.5A1400	OEM
DSA0.5A1700	OEM
DSA0.9-12A	OEM
DSA0.9-14A	OEM
DSA0.9-16A	OEM
DSA0.9-18A	OEM
DSA1A1	0080
DSA1A2	0604
DSA1A4	0790
DSA1A1100	OEM
DSA1A1400	OEM
DSA1A1700	OEM
DSA1C1	0023
DSA1.2-12A	OEM
DSA1.2-14A	OEM
DSA1.2-16A	OEM
DSA1.2-18A	OEM
DSA1.8-18A	OEM
DSA2-12A	OEM
DSA2-14A	OEM
DSA2-16A	OEM
DSA2-18A	OEM
DSA3A1	OEM
DSA3A1100	OEM
DSA3A1400	OEM
DSA3A1700	OEM
DSA5B1100	OEM
DSA5B1400	OEM
DSA5B1700	OEM
DSA6-12F	OEM
DSA6-14F	OEM
DSA6-16F	OEM
DSA6-18A	OEM
DSA9-12F	OEM
DSA9-14F	OEM
DSA9-16F	OEM
DSA9-18A	OEM
DSA10C1100	OEM
DSA10C1400	OEM
DSA10C1700	OEM
DSA10G	0071
DSA10J	0071
DSA10L	0071
DSA12B	0087
DSA12C	0087
DSA12E	0087
DSA12EQ	0087
DSA12G	0087
DSA12J	0087
DSA12L	0087
DSA12T	0071
DSA12TL	0087
DSA12TL-AT1	0087
DSA12TL-FB2	0071
DSA17-12A	OEM
DSA17-14A	OEM
DSA17-16A	OEM
DSA17-18A	OEM
DSA17B	0071
DSA17C	0559
DSA17E	0071
DSA17KC-5	OEM
DSA20B	0102
DSA20C	0102
DSA20E	0102
DSA20G	0102
DSA20J	0102
DSA22-12A	OEM
DSA22-14A	OEM
DSA22-16A	OEM
DSA22-18A	OEM
DSA26B	0087
DSA26C	0087
DSA26E	0087
DSA35-12A	OEM
DSA35-14A	OEM
DSA35-16A	OEM
DSA35-18A	OEM
DSA-40SN110	OEM
DSA42-12A	OEM
DSA42-14A	OEM
DSA42-16A	OEM
DSA42-18A	OEM
DSA-64SN110	OEM
DSA75-12B	OEM
DSA75-14B	OEM
DSA75-16B	OEM
DSA80-12A	OEM
DSA80-14A	OEM
DSA80-16A	OEM
DSA80-18A	OEM
DSA110-12A	OEM
DSA110-14A	OEM
DSA110-16A	OEM
DSA110-18A	OEM
DSA150	0133
DSA175-11B	OEM
DSA175-14B	OEM
DSA200B1100	OEM
DSA200B1400	OEM
DSA200B1700	OEM
DSA250-11F	OEM
DSA250-11L	OEM
DSA250-14F	OEM
DSA250-14L	OEM
DSA250-17F	OEM
DSA250-17L	OEM
DSA250-20F	OEM
DSA250-20L	OEM
DSA250-23F	OEM
DSA250-23L	OEM
DSA251-54F	OEM
DSA301LS-C	OEM
DSA304-11A	OEM
DSA304-14A	OEM
DSA304-17A	OEM
DSA304-20A	OEM
DSA304-23A	OEM
DSA400-11F	OEM
DSA400-11KC	OEM
DSA400-11NC	OEM
DSA400-14F	OEM
DSA400-14KC	OEM
DSA400-14NC	OEM
DSA400-17F	OEM
DSA400-17KC	OEM
DSA400-17NC	OEM
DSA400-20F	OEM
DSA400-20KC	OEM
DSA400-20NC	OEM
DSA400-23F	OEM
DSA400-23KC	OEM
DSA400-23NC	OEM
DSA401-26GE	OEM
DSA401-26LE	OEM
DSA401-29GE	OEM
DSA401-29LE	OEM
DSA401-32GE	OEM
DSA401-32LE	OEM
DSA401-38GG	OEM
DSA401-38LG	OEM
DSA401-44GG	OEM
DSA401-44LG	OEM
DSA401-50GG	OEM
DSA401-50LG	OEM
DSA401-54F	OEM
DSA403-38GG	OEM
DSA403-38L1G	OEM
DSA403-44GG	OEM
DSA403-44L1G	OEM
DSA403-50GG	OEM
DSA403-50L1G	OEM
DSA405-38AG	OEM
DSA405-44AG	OEM
DSA405-50AG	OEM
DSA503-23GE	OEM
DSA503-23L1E	OEM
DSA503-26GE	OEM
DSA503-26L1E	OEM
DSA503-29G	OEM
DSA503-29GE	OEM
DSA503-29L1E	OEM
DSA503-32GE	OEM
DSA503-32L1E	OEM
DSA603-11GC	OEM
DSA603-11L1C	OEM
DSA603-14GC	OEM
DSA603-14L1C	OEM
DSA603-17GC	OEM
DSA603-17L1C	OEM
DSA603-20GC	OEM
DSA603-20L1C	OEM
DSA605-23AE	OEM
DSA605-26AE	OEM
DSA605-29AE	OEM
DSA605-32AE	OEM
DSA607-38A	OEM
DSA705-11A	OEM
DSA705-11AC	OEM
DSA705-14A	OEM
DSA705-14AC	OEM
DSA705-17A	OEM
DSA705-17AC	OEM
DSA705-20A	OEM
DSA705-20AC	OEM
DSA705-23B	OEM
DSA707-23A	OEM
DSA707-26A	OEM
DSA707-29A	OEM
DSA707-32A	OEM
DSA807-11A	OEM
DSA807-14A	OEM
DSA807-17A	OEM
DSA807-20A	OEM
DSA908-38AG	OEM
DSA908-44AG	OEM
DSA908-50AG	OEM
DSA1208-23AE	OEM
DSA1208-26AE	OEM
DSA1208-29AE	OEM
DSA1208-32AE	OEM
DSA1508-11AC	OEM
DSA1508-14AC	OEM
DSA1508-17AC	OEM
DSA1508-20AC	OEM
DSA1508-23A	OEM
DSA6920	OEM
DSA6920A	OEM
DSA6920B	OEM
DSA6920C	OEM
DSA6921	OEM
DSA6921A	OEM
DSA6922	OEM
DSA6922A	OEM
DSA6922B	OEM
DSA6922C	OEM
DSA6923	OEM
DSA6923A	OEM
DSA6923B	OEM
DSA6923C	OEM
DSA-6925	OEM
DSA6925	OEM
DSA-6925A	OEM
DSA6925A	OEM
DSA-6925B	OEM
DSA6925B	OEM
DSA-6925C	OEM
DSA6925C	OEM
DSA6926	OEM
DSA6926A	OEM
DSA6927	OEM
DSA6927A	OEM
DSA6927B	OEM
DSA6927C	OEM
DSA-6928	OEM
DSA6928	OEM
DSA-6928A	OEM
DSA6928A	OEM
DSA-6928B	OEM
DSA6928B	OEM
DSA-6928C	OEM
DSA6928C	OEM
DSAI17-16A	OEM
DSAI17-18A	OEM
DSAI35-18A	OEM
DSAI75-11B	OEM
DSAI75-14B	OEM
DSAI75-16A	OEM
DSAI80-16A	OEM
DSAI80-18A	OEM
DSAI110-16A	OEM
DSAI110-18A	OEM
DSAI250-11F	OEM
DSAI250-11L	OEM
DSAI250-14F	OEM
DSAI250-14L	OEM
DSAI250-17F	OEM
DSAI250-17G	OEM
DSAI250-17L	OEM
DSAI250-17M	OEM
DSAI250-20F	OEM
DSAI250-20G	OEM
DSAI250-20L0L	OEM
DSAI250-20M	OEM
DSAI250-23F	OEM
DSAI250-23G	OEM
DSAI250-23L	OEM
DSAI250-23M	OEM
DSAS05-0	OEM
DSAS05-2	OEM
DSAS05-4	OEM
DSAS05-6	OEM
DSAS07-0	OEM
DSAS07-2	OEM
DSAS07-4	OEM
DSAS07-6	OEM
DSAS09-0	OEM
DSAS09-2	OEM
DSAS09-4	OEM
DSAS09-6	OEM
DSAS5U	OEM
DSAS6U	OEM
DSAS7U	OEM
DSAS8U	OEM
DSAS9U	OEM
DSAS10U	OEM
DSAS11-0	OEM
DSAS11-2	OEM
DSAS11-4	OEM
DSAS11-6	OEM
DSAS11U	OEM
DSAS12U	OEM
DSAS13-0	OEM
DSAS13-2	OEM
DSAS13-4	OEM
DSAS13-6	OEM
DSAS13U	OEM
DSAS14U	OEM
DSAS15-0	OEM
DSAS15-1	OEM
DSAS15-2	OEM
DSAS15-3	OEM
DSAS15-4	OEM
DSAS15-5	OEM
DSAS15-6	OEM
DSAS15-7	OEM
DSAS15-8	OEM
DSAS15-9	OEM
DSAS15U	OEM
DSAS16U	OEM
DSAS17-0	OEM
DSAS17-4	OEM
DSAS19-0	OEM
DSAS19-4	OEM
DSAS21-0	OEM
DSAS21-4	OEM
DSAS23-0	OEM
DSAS23-4	OEM
DSAS25-0	OEM
DSAS25-4	OEM
DSAS27-0	OEM
DSAS27-4	OEM
DSAS29-0	OEM
DSAS29-4	OEM
DSAS31-0	OEM
DSAS31-4	OEM
DSB010	0124
DSB015	0124
DSB015A2-TA	OEM
DSB15B	0102
DSB15C	0071
DSB15E	0102
DSB15G	0102
DSB15TC	OEM
DSB6477A	OEM
DSB6477B	OEM
DSB6477C	OEM
DSB6477D	OEM
DSB6477E	OEM
DSB6478A	OEM
DSB6478B	OEM
DSB6478C	OEM
DSB6478D	OEM
DSB6478E	OEM
DSB6479A	OEM
DSB6479B	OEM
DSB6479C	OEM
DSB6479D	OEM
DSB6479E	OEM
DSB6480A	OEM
DSB6480B	OEM
DSB6480C	OEM
DSB6480D	OEM
DSB6480E	OEM
DSB6481A	OEM
DSB6481B	OEM
DSB6481C	OEM
DSB6481D	OEM
DSB6481E	OEM
DSB6482A	OEM
DSB6482B	OEM
DSB6482C	OEM
DSB6482D	OEM
DSB6482E	OEM
DSB6483A	OEM
DSB6483B	OEM
DSB6483C	OEM
DSB6483D	OEM
DSB6483E	OEM
DSB6484A	OEM
DSB6484B	OEM
DSB6484C	OEM
DSB6484D	OEM
DSB6484E	OEM
DSB6485A	OEM
DSB6485B	OEM
DSB6485C	OEM
DSB6485D	OEM
DSB6485E	OEM
DSB6486A	OEM
DSB6486B	OEM
DSB6486C	OEM
DSB6486D	OEM
DSB6486E	OEM
DSB6487A	OEM
DSB6487B	OEM
DSB6487C	OEM
DSB6487D	OEM
DSB6487E	OEM
DSB6488A	OEM
DSB6488B	OEM
DSB6488C	OEM
DSB6488D	OEM
DSB6488E	OEM
DSB6489A	OEM
DSB6489B	OEM
DSB6489C	OEM
DSB6489D	OEM
DSB6489E	OEM
DSB6490A	OEM
DSB6490B	OEM
DSB6490C	OEM
DSB6490D	OEM
DSB6490E	OEM
DSB6491A	OEM
DSB6491B	OEM
DSB6491C	OEM
DSB6491D	OEM
DSB6491E	OEM
DSB6492A	OEM
DSB6492B	OEM
DSB6492C	OEM
DSB6492D	OEM
DSB6492E	OEM
DSBC941	OEM
DSBN-1	0015
DSC010	0124
DSC30TC-KD2	OEM
DSC5012A115-60	OEM
DSC5012A115-60M	OEM
DSC5012B26-400	OEM
DSC5012B26-400M	OEM
DSC5012B115-60	OEM
DSC5012B115-60M	OEM
DSC5012B115-400	OEM
DSC5012B115-400M	OEM
DSC5012C115-60M	OEM
DSC5112A115-400M	OEM
DSD010	0124
DSD0.8-02B	0031
DSD0.9-02A	OEM
DSD1.2-01A	OEM
DSD1.2-06A	OEM
DSD2-01A	OEM
DSD2-02A	OEM
DSD2-04A	OEM
DSD2-06A	OEM
DSD2-08A	OEM
DSD2-10A	OEM
DSD12-02A	OEM
DSD12-04A	OEM
DSD12-06A	OEM
DSD12-08A	OEM
DSD12-12A	OEM
DSD12-14A	OEM
DSD12-16A	OEM
DSD17-01A	OEM
DSD17-01B	OEM
DSD17-02A	OEM
DSD17-02B	OEM
DSD17-04A	OEM
DSD17-04B	OEM
DSD17-06B	OEM
DSD17-07A	OEM
DSD17-08B	OEM
DSD17-015B	OEM
DSD17-11A	OEM
DSD17-12B	OEM
DSD17-14A	OEM
DSD17-14B	OEM
DSD17-16B	OEM
DSD35-01A	OEM
DSD35-02A	OEM
DSD35-04A	OEM
DSD35-06A	OEM
DSD35-07A	OEM
DSD35-08A	OEM
DSD35-12A	OEM
DSD35-14A	OEM
DSD35-16A	OEM
DSD84	0906
DSD110-12A	OEM
DSD110-14A	OEM
DSD110-16A	OEM
DSD113-01B	OEM
DSD113-015B	OEM
DSD120-01B	OEM
DSD120-015B	OEM
DSD136-01B	OEM
DSD136-015B	OEM
DSD304-06A	OEM
DSD304-06C	OEM
DSD304-08A	OEM
DSD304-08C	OEM
DSD304-10A	OEM
DSD304-10C	OEM
DSD304-11A	OEM
DSD304-11C	OEM
DSD304-12A	OEM
DSD304-12C	OEM
DSD304-14A	OEM
DSD304-16A	OEM
DSD605-11A	OEM
DSD605-14A	OEM
DSD605-16A	OEM
DSD605-18A	OEM
DSD605-20A	OEM
DSD625-25A	OEM
DSD625-25D	OEM
DSD625-30A	OEM
DSD635-22A	OEM
DSD635-22D	OEM
DSD635-25A	OEM
DSD1028-25A	OEM
DSD1028-25D	OEM
DSD1028-30A	OEM
DSD1038-22A	OEM
DSD1038-22D	OEM
DSD8649V3FY	OEM
DSD8744	OEM
DSD8923	OEM
DSDI7-01B	OEM
DSDI7-015B	OEM
DSDI13-01B	OEM
DSDI13-015B	OEM
DSDI17-16B	OEM
DSDI20-01B	OEM
DSDI20-015B	OEM
DSDI35-16A	OEM
DSDI36-01B	OEM
DSDI36-015B	OEM
DSF10	OEM
DSF10A	1325
DSF10B	0023
DSF-10B-BT	0080
DSF10BT	OEM
DSF10C	0023
DSF10CBT	OEM
DSF10C-KB1	OEM
DSF10E	0023
DSF10G	0015
DSF10TB	0015
DSF10TB-BT-A	0015
DSF10TB-KB1	1881
DSF10TC	OEM
DSF402ST01	OEM
DSF402ST02	OEM
DSF402ST03	OEM
DSF402ST04	OEM
DSF402ST05	OEM
DSF402ST06	OEM
DSF402ST07	OEM
DSF402ST08	OEM
DSF402ST09	OEM
DSF402ST10	OEM
DSF402ST11	OEM
DSF402ST12	OEM
DSF502ST06	OEM
DSF502ST07	OEM
DSF502ST08	OEM
DSF502ST09	OEM
DSF502ST10	OEM
DSF502ST11	OEM
DSF502ST12	OEM
DSF805SE01	OEM
DSF805SE02	OEM
DSF805SE03	OEM
DSF805SE04	OEM
DSF805SE05	OEM
DSF805SE06	OEM
DSF805SE07	OEM
DSF805SE08	OEM
DSF805SE09	OEM
DSF805SE10	OEM
DSF805SE11	OEM
DSF805SE12	OEM
DSF808SE06	OEM
DSF808SE07	OEM
DSF808SE08	OEM
DSF808SE09	OEM
DSF808SE10	OEM
DSF808SE11	OEM
DSF808SE12	OEM
DSF912SM01	OEM
DSF912SM02	OEM
DSF912SM03	OEM
DSF912SM04	OEM
DSF912SM05	OEM
DSF912SM06	OEM
DSF912SM07	OEM
DSF912SM08	OEM
DSF912SM09	OEM
DSF912SM10	OEM
DSF912SM11	OEM
DSF912SM12	OEM
DSF912SM13	OEM
DSF912SM14	OEM
DSF912SM15	OEM
DSF912SM16	OEM
DSF912SM17	OEM
DSF912SM18	OEM
DSF912SM19	OEM
DSF912SM20	OEM
DSF912SM21	OEM
DSF912SM22	OEM
DSF912SM23	OEM
DSF912SM24	OEM
DSF912SM25	OEM
DSF912SM26	OEM
DSF1108SM01	OEM
DSF1108SM02	OEM
DSF1108SM03	OEM
DSF1108SM04	OEM
DSF1108SM05	OEM
DSF1108SM06	OEM
DSF1108SM07	OEM
DSF1108SM08	OEM
DSF1108SM09	OEM
DSF1108SM10	OEM
DSF1108SM11	OEM
DSF1108SM12	OEM
DSF1112SG09	OEM
DSF1112SG10	OEM
DSF1112SG11	OEM
DSF1112SG12	OEM

If replacement code is OEM, contact original manufacturer for replacement.

383

DEVICE TYPE	REPL CODE
DSF1112SG13	OEM
DSF1112SG14	OEM
DSF1112SG15	OEM
DSF1112SG16	OEM
DSF1112SG17	OEM
DSF1112SG18	OEM
DSF1112SG19	OEM
DSF1112SG20	OEM
DSF1112SG21	OEM
DSF1112SG22	OEM
DSF1112SG23	OEM
DSF1112SG24	OEM
DSF1112SG25	OEM
DSF1112SM20	OEM
DSF1112SM21	OEM
DSF1112SM22	OEM
DSF1112SM23	OEM
DSF1112SM24	OEM
DSF1112SM25	OEM
DSF1114SM21	OEM
DSF1114SM22	OEM
DSF1114SM23	OEM
DSF1114SM24	OEM
DSF1114SM25	OEM
DSF1114SM26	OEM
DSF1114SM27	OEM
DSF1114SM28	OEM
DSF1114SM29	OEM
DSF1114SM30	OEM
DSF1114SM31	OEM
DSF1114SM32	OEM
DSF1114SM33	OEM
DSF1114SM34	OEM
DSF1114SM35	OEM
DSF1114SM36	OEM
DSF2013SD13	OEM
DSF2013SD14	OEM
DSF2013SD15	OEM
DSF2013SD16	OEM
DSF2013SD17	OEM
DSF2013SD18	OEM
DSF2013SD19	OEM
DSF2013SD20	OEM
DSF2013SD21	OEM
DSF2013SD22	OEM
DSF2013SD23	OEM
DSF2013SD24	OEM
DSF2013SD25	OEM
DSF2013SD26	OEM
DSF2030SD21	OEM
DSF2030SD22	OEM
DSF2030SD23	OEM
DSF2030SD25	OEM
DSF2030SD26	OEM
DSF2030SD27	OEM
DSF2030SD28	OEM
DSF2030SD29	OEM
DSF2030SD30	OEM
DSF2030SD31	OEM
DSF2030SD32	OEM
DSF2030SD33	OEM
DSF2030SD34	OEM
DSF2030SD35	OEM
DSF2030SD36	OEM
DSF2030SDD24	OEM
DSG6358A	OEM
DSG6358B	OEM
DSG6358C	OEM
DSG6358D	OEM
DSG6358E	OEM
DSG6470A	OEM
DSG6470B	OEM
DSG6470C	OEM
DSG6470D	OEM
DSG6470E	OEM
DSG6474A	OEM
DSG6474B	OEM
DSG6474C	OEM
DSG6474D	OEM
DSG6474E	OEM
DSH4785-10	OEM
DSH4785-40	OEM
DSH4787-10	OEM
DSH4787-15	OEM
DSH4787-20	OEM
DSH4787-30	OEM
DSH4787-40	OEM
DSH6172	OEM
DSH6173	OEM
DSH6174	OEM
DSI17-16A	OEM
DSI17-18A	OEM
DSI35-16A	OEM
DSI35-18A	OEM
DSI75-16A	OEM
DSI80-16A	OEM
DSI80-18A	OEM
DSI110-16A	OEM
DSI110-18A	OEM
DSI250-04F	OEM
DSI250-04L	OEM
DSI250-07F	OEM
DSI250-07L	OEM
DSI250-11F	OEM
DSI250-11L	OEM
DSI250-14F	OEM
DSI250-14L	OEM
DSI250-17F	OEM
DSI250-17G	OEM
DSI250-17L	OEM
DSI250-17M	OEM
DSI250-20F	OEM
DSI250-20G	OEM
DSI250-20L	OEM
DSI250-20M	OEM
DSI250-23F	OEM
DSI250-23G	OEM
DSI250-23L	OEM
DSI250-23M	OEM
DS-IM	0015
DS-IN	0208
DSJ6110	OEM
DSJ6111	OEM
DSJ6112	OEM
DSJ6811A	OEM
DSJ6811B	OEM
DSJ6812A	OEM
DSK10B	OEM
DSK10C	OEM
DSK10C-BT	OEM
DSM1A1	1082
DSM1D1	OEM
DSM30A4	OEM
DSM30A6	OEM
DSM4380A	OEM
DSM4380B	OEM
DSM4380C	OEM
DSM4380D	OEM
DSM4380E	OEM
DSM4381A	OEM
DSM4381B	OEM
DSM4381C	OEM
DSM4381D	OEM
DSM4381E	OEM
DSN6560-50	OEM
DSN6566-50	OEM
DSP2500A20	OEM
DSP2500A25	OEM
DSP2500A30	OEM
DSR51	OEM
DSR54	OEM
DSR55	OEM
DSR56	OEM
DSR3050	1082
DSR3051	1082
DSR3100	1082
DSR3101	1082
DSR3150	OEM
DSR3151	1082
DSR3200	OEM
DSR3201	1082
DSR3400X	OEM
DSR3500X	OEM
DSR3600X	OEM
DSR3700X	OEM
DSR3800X	OEM
DSR5050	OEM
DSR5051	OEM
DSR5052	OEM
DSR5100	OEM
DSR5101	OEM
DSR5102	OEM
DSR5150	OEM
DSR5151	OEM
DSR5200	OEM
DSR5201	OEM
DSR5202	OEM
DSR5400X	OEM
DSR5500X	OEM
DSR5600X	OEM
DSR5700X	OEM
DSR5800X	OEM
DSR31000X	OEM
DSR34000X	OEM
DSR35000X	OEM
DSR36000X	OEM
DSR37000X	OEM
DSR38000X	OEM
DSR51000X	OEM
DSR54000X	OEM
DSR55000X	OEM
DSR56000X	OEM
DSR57000X	OEM
DSR58000X	OEM
DSS100A8	OEM
DSS100A8R	OEM
DSS100A10	OEM
DSS100A10R	OEM
DSS100A13	OEM
DSS100A13R	OEM
DSS100A15	OEM
DSS100A15R	OEM
DSS300A8	OEM
DSS300A8R	OEM
DSS300A10	OEM
DSS300A10R	OEM
DSS300A13	OEM
DSS300A13R	OEM
DSS300A15	OEM
DSS300A15R	OEM
DSS953	0133
DSS16685	0143
DST1	OEM
DSZ412SE40	OEM
DSZ412SE41	OEM
DSZ412SE42	OEM
DSZ412SE43	OEM
DSZ412SE44	OEM
DSZ3006	OEM
DSZ3007	OEM
DSZ3008	3071
DSZ3009	0057
DSZ3010	OEM
DSZ3011	OEM
DSZ3012	0052
DSZ3013	OEM
DSZ3014	OEM
DSZ3015	OEM
DSZ3016	OEM
DSZ3018	OEM
DSZ3020	OEM
DSZ3022	OEM
DSZ3024	OEM
DSZ3027	OEM
DSZ3030	OEM
DSZ3033	OEM
DSZ3036	OEM
DSZ3040	OEM
DSZ3045	OEM
DSZ3050	OEM
DSZ3056	OEM
DSZ3060	1148
DSZ3062	OEM
DSZ3070	OEM
DSZ3075	OEM
DSZ3080	OEM
DSZ3090	OEM
DSZ3100	OEM
DSZ4110	1172
DSZ4210	1172
DSZ4706	0205
DSZ4707	0475
DSZ4708	0499
DSZ4709	0679
DSZ4710	0225
DSZ4712	0234
DSZ4713	0237
DSZ4715	0247
DSZ4716	0251
DSZ4718	0256
DSZ4720	0262
DSZ4722	0269
DSZ4724	0273
DSZ4727	0291
DSZ4730	0305
DSZ4733	0314
DSZ4736	0010
DSZ4739	0316
DSZ4743	0333
DSZ4747	0343
DSZ4751	0027
DSZ4756	0266
DSZ4762	0382
DSZ4768	0401
DSZ4775	0421
DSZ4782	0439
DSZ4791	0238
DSZ4806	0205
DSZ4807	0475
DSZ4808	0499
DSZ4809	0679
DSZ4810	0225
DSZ4812	0234
DSZ4813	0237
DSZ4815	0247
DSZ4816	0256
DSZ4818	0256
DSZ4820	0262
DSZ4822	0269
DSZ4824	0273
DSZ4827	0291
DSZ4830	0305
DSZ4833	0314
DSZ4836	0316
DSZ4839	0322
DSZ4843	0333
DSZ4847	0343
DSZ4851	0027
DSZ4856	0266
DSZ4862	0382
DSZ4868	0401
DSZ4875	0421
DSZ4882	0439
DSZ4891	0238
DSZ5110	1172
DSZ5210	1172
DSZ5706	0205
DSZ5707	0475
DSZ5708	0499
DSZ5709	0679
DSZ5710	0225
DSZ5712	0234
DSZ5713	0237
DSZ5714	1387
DSZ5715	0247
DSZ5716	0251
DSZ5718	0256
DSZ5720	0262
DSZ5722	0269
DSZ5724	0273
DSZ5727	0291
DSZ5730	0305
DSZ5733	0314
DSZ5736	0316
DSZ5740	0322
DSZ5745	0343
DSZ5750	0027
DSZ5756	0266
DSZ5760	2829
DSZ5766	0401
DSZ5770	0401
DSZ5775	0421
DSZ5780	0439
DSZ5790	0238
DSZ5806	0205
DSZ5807	0475
DSZ5808	0499
DSZ5809	0679
DSZ5810	0225
DSZ5812	0234
DSZ5813	0237
DSZ5814	1387
DSZ5815	0247
DSZ5816	0251
DSZ5818	0256
DSZ5820	0262
DSZ5822	0269
DSZ5824	0273
DSZ5827	0291
DSZ5830	0305
DSZ5833	0314
DSZ5836	0316
DSZ5840	0322
DSZ5845	0343
DSZ5850	0027
DSZ5856	0266
DSZ5860	2829
DSZ5870	0401
DSZ5875	0421
DSZ5880	0439
DSZ5890	0238
DT2C14	OEM
DT2C15	OEM
DT10E	OEM
DT10F	OEM
DT25	OEM
DT41	0160
DT57C01	OEM
DT57C01DI	OEM
DT57C01SE	OEM
DT57C02	OEM
DT57C03	OEM
DT80	0435
DT88C	OEM
DT88E	OEM
DT88F	OEM
DT88G	OEM
DT100	0435
DT104BSXXXX	OEM
DT105DXXXX	OEM
DT110	OEM
DT110DSXXXX	OEM
DT112BSXXXX	OEM
DT161	0016
DT180FA	OEM
DT183AA	1620
DT183BA	0254
DT183CA	1099
DT183DA	1099
DT183EA	1103
DT183FA	1103
DT183GA	0258
DT183HA	0258
DT183KA	1634
DT183MA	0267
DT183PA	1111
DT183RA	1111
DT183TA	0280
DT183VA	0280
DT203AA	1620
DT203BA	0254
DT203CA	1099
DT203DA	1099
DT203EA	1103
DT203FA	1103
DT203GA	0258
DT203HA	0258
DT203KA	1634
DT203MA	0267
DT203PA	1111
DT203RA	1111
DT203TA	0280
DT203VA	0280
DT204BSXXXX	OEM
DT210FA	OEM
DT210FB	OEM
DT210FQFQ	OEM
DT210FW	OEM
DT210FX	OEM
DT210FY	OEM
DT212	OEM
DT212BSXXXX	OEM
DT214	OEM
DT215	OEM
DT220FA	OEM
DT220FB	OEM
DT220FQ	OEM
DT220FW	OEM
DT220FX	OEM
DT220FY	OEM
DT230A	0133
DT230B	0015
DT230C	OEM
DT230C#	OEM
DT230F	0133
DT230FA	OEM
DT230FB	OEM
DT230FQ	OEM
DT230FX	OEM
DT230FY	OEM
DT230G	0133
DT230H	0102
DT230H1	0015
DT230HI	OEM
DT230HI#	OEM
DT240FA	OEM
DT240FB	OEM
DT240FQ	OEM
DT240FW	OEM
DT240FX	OEM
DT240FY	OEM
DT250FA	OEM
DT250FB	OEM
DT250FW	OEM
DT250FX	OEM
DT250FY	OEM
DT253AA	1620
DT253BA	0254
DT253CA	1099
DT253DA	1099
DT253EA	1103
DT253FA	1103
DT253GA	0258
DT253HA	0258
DT253KA	1634
DT253MA	0267
DT253PA	1111
DT253RA	1111
DT253TA	0280
DT253VA	0280
DT260FA	OEM
DT260FB	OEM
DT260FQ	OEM
DT260FW	OEM
DT260FX	OEM
DT260FY	OEM
DT270FA	OEM
DT270FB	OEM
DT270FW	OEM
DT270FX	OEM
DT270FY	OEM
DT280FB	OEM
DT280FW	OEM
DT280FX	OEM
DT280FY	OEM
DT300	OEM
DT300A	OEM
DT301	OEM
DT302	OEM
DT303	OEM
DT303AA	1620
DT303BA	0254
DT303CA	1099
DT303DA	1099
DT303EA	1103
DT303FA	1103
DT303GA	0258
DT303HA	0258
DT303KA	1634
DT303MA	0267
DT303PA	1111
DT303RA	1111
DT303TA	0280
DT303VA	0280
DT304	OEM
DT305	OEM
DT306	OEM
DT306-300	OEM
DT307	OEM
DT307-300	OEM
DT308	OEM
DT308-300	OEM
DT309	OEM
DT309-300	OEM
DT310	OEM
DT310-300	OEM
DT310FA	OEM
DT310FB	OEM
DT310FQ	OEM
DT310FW	OEM
DT310FX	OEM
DT310FY	OEM
DT311	OEM
DT311-300	OEM
DT312	OEM
DT312-300	OEM
DT313	OEM
DT313-300	OEM
DT314	OEM
DT314-300	OEM
DT315	OEM
DT315-300	OEM
DT316	OEM
DT320FA	OEM
DT320FB	OEM
DT320FQ	OEM
DT320FW	OEM
DT320FX	OEM
DT320FY	OEM
DT330FA	OEM
DT330FB	OEM
DT330FX	OEM
DT330FY	OEM
DT340FA	OEM
DT340FB	OEM
DT340FQ	OEM
DT340FW	OEM
DT340FX	OEM
DT340FY	OEM
DT350FA	OEM
DT350FB	OEM
DT350FX	OEM
DT350FY	OEM
DT353AA	1620
DT353BA	0254
DT353CA	1099
DT353DA	1099
DT353EA	1103
DT353FA	1103
DT353GA	0258
DT353HA	0258
DT353KA	1634
DT353MA	0267
DT353PA	1111
DT353RA	1111
DT353TA	0280
DT353VA	0280
DT360FA	OEM
DT360FB	OEM
DT360FQ	OEM
DT360FW	OEM
DT360FX	OEM
DT360FY	OEM
DT380FA	OEM
DT380FB	OEM
DT380FW	OEM
DT380FX	OEM
DT380FY	OEM
DT390FA	OEM
DT390FB	OEM
DT390FX	OEM
DT390FY	OEM
DT401	0085
DT403AA	1620
DT403BA	0254
DT403CA	1099
DT403DA	1099
DT403EA	1103
DT403FA	1103
DT403GA	0258
DT403HA	0258
DT403KA	1634
DT403MA	0267
DT403PA	1111
DT403RA	1111
DT403TA	0280
DT403VA	0280
DT408BSXXXX	OEM
DT510DSXXXX	OEM
DT520DSXXXX	OEM
DT600	OEM
DT600A	OEM
DT601	OEM
DT602	OEM
DT603	OEM
DT604	OEM
DT605	OEM
DT606	OEM
DT606-300	OEM
DT607	OEM
DT607-300	OEM
DT608	OEM
DT608-300	OEM
DT609	OEM
DT609-300	OEM
DT610	OEM
DT610-300	OEM
DT611	OEM
DT611-300	OEM
DT612	OEM
DT612-300	OEM
DT613	OEM
DT613-300	OEM
DT614	OEM
DT614-300	OEM
DT615	OEM
DT615-300	OEM
DT616	OEM
DT711BSXXXX	OEM
DT812	0284
DT816BSXXXX	OEM
DT820	OEM
DT825	OEM
DT830	OEM
DT835	OEM
DT900	OEM
DT900A	OEM
DT901	OEM
DT902	OEM
DT903	OEM
DT904	OEM
DT905	OEM
DT906	OEM
DT906-300	OEM
DT907	OEM
DT907-300	OEM
DT908	OEM
DT908-300	OEM
DT909	OEM
DT909-300	OEM
DT910	OEM
DT910-300	OEM
DT911	OEM
DT911-300	OEM
DT912	OEM
DT912-300	OEM
DT913	OEM
DT913-300	OEM
DT914	OEM
DT914-300	OEM
DT915	OEM
DT915-300	OEM
DT916	OEM
DT1003	0233
DT1040	0160
DT1110	0086
DT1111	0086
DT1112	0086
DT1120	0086
DT1121	0086
DT1122	0086
DT1311	0086
DT1321	0086
DT1510	0086
DT1511	0086
DT1512	0086
DT1520	0086
DT1521	0086
DT1522	0086
DT1602	0233
DT1603	0233
DT1610	0198
DT1612	0233
DT1613	0233
DT1621	0086
DT1711D114	OEM
DT1711D116	OEM
DT1711D132	OEM
DT1711DI	OEM
DT1711DIC	OEM
DT1711DIDMA	OEM
DT1711DIPG	OEM
DT1711SE	OEM
DT1711SE14	OEM
DT1711SE32	OEM
DT1711SE64	OEM
DT1711SEC	OEM
DT1711SEDMA	OEM
DT1711SEPG	OEM
DT1712DI	OEM
DT1712DI14	OEM
DT1712DI16	OEM
DT1712DI32	OEM
DT1712DIC	OEM
DT1712DIDMA	OEM
DT1712DIPG	OEM
DT1712SE	OEM
DT1712SE14	OEM
DT1712SE32	OEM
DT1712SE64	OEM
DT1712SEC	OEM
DT1712SEDMA	OEM
DT1712SEPG	OEM
DT1715	OEM
DT1715DMA	OEM
DT1715R	OEM
DT1719	OEM
DT1719DMA	OEM
DT1719PG	OEM
DT1719R	OEM
DT1722	OEM
DT1723	OEM
DT1724BSXXXX	OEM
DT1735	OEM
DT1738	OEM
DT1739	OEM
DT1741	OEM
DT1742	OEM
DT1744	OEM
DT1748	OEM
DT1751	OEM
DT1755	OEM
DT1759	OEM
DT1761	OEM
DT1762	OEM
DT1764	OEM
DT1765	OEM
DT1768	OEM
DT1769	OEM
DT1781	OEM
DT1782	OEM
DT1784	OEM
DT1785	OEM
DT1788	OEM
DT1789	OEM
DT1841	OEM
DT1842	OEM
DT1843	OEM
DT2009	OEM
DT2010	OEM
DT2100FA	OEM
DT2100FB	OEM
DT2100FX	OEM
DT2100FY	OEM
DT2120FB	OEM
DT2722	OEM
DT2724	OEM
DT2725	OEM
DT2726	OEM
DT2727	OEM
DT2762	OEM
DT2764	OEM
DT2765	OEM

384 If replacement code is OEM, contact original manufacturer for replacement.

DEVICE TYPE	REPL CODE
DT2766	OEM
DT2767	OEM
DT2768	OEM
DT2769	OEM
DT2771	OEM
DT2781	OEM
DT2782	OEM
DT2784	OEM
DT2785	OEM
DT3100FA	OEM
DT3100FB	OEM
DT3100FX	OEM
DT3100FY	OEM
DT3120FB	OEM
DT3301	0178
DT3302	0178
DT3752	OEM
DT3754	OEM
DT3755	OEM
DT3762	OEM
DT3772D15710-0M	OEM
DT3772D15710-0V	OEM
DT3772D15710-4M	OEM
DT3772D15710-4V	OEM
DT3772D15710-8M	OEM
DT3772D15710-8V	OEM
DT3772D15712-0M	OEM
DT3772D15712-0V	OEM
DT3772D15712-4M	OEM
DT3772D15712-4V	OEM
DT3772D15712-8M	OEM
DT3772D15712-8V	OEM
DT3772D15714-0M	OEM
DT3772D15714-0V	OEM
DT3772D15714-4M	OEM
DT3772D15714-4V	OEM
DT3772D15714-8M	OEM
DT3772D15714-8V	OEM
DT3772D15716-0M	OEM
DT3772D15716-0V	OEM
DT3772D15716-4M	OEM
DT3772D15716-4V	OEM
DT3772D15716-8M	OEM
DT3772D15716-8V	OEM
DT3772SE5710-0M	OEM
DT3772SE5710-0V	OEM
DT3772SE5710-4M	OEM
DT3772SE5710-4V	OEM
DT3772SE5710-8M	OEM
DT3772SE5710-8V	OEM
DT3772SE5712-0M	OEM
DT3772SE5712-0V	OEM
DT3772SE5712-4M	OEM
DT3772SE5712-4V	OEM
DT3772SE5712-8M	OEM
DT3772SE5712-8V	OEM
DT3772SE5714-0M	OEM
DT3772SE5714-0V	OEM
DT3772SE5714-4M	OEM
DT3772SE5714-4V	OEM
DT3772SE5714-8M	OEM
DT3772SE5714-8V	OEM
DT3772SE5716-0M	OEM
DT3772SE5716-0V	OEM
DT3772SE5716-4M	OEM
DT3772SE5716-4V	OEM
DT3772SE5716-8M	OEM
DT3772SE5716-8V	OEM
DT3774D15710-0M	OEM
DT3774D15710-0V	OEM
DT3774D15710-4M	OEM
DT3774D15710-4V	OEM
DT3774D15710-8M	OEM
DT3774D15710-8V	OEM
DT3774D15712-0M	OEM
DT3774D15712-0V	OEM
DT3774D15712-4M	OEM
DT3774D15712-4V	OEM
DT3774D15712-8V	OEM
DT3774D15714-0M	OEM
DT3774D15714-0V	OEM
DT3774D15714-4M	OEM
DT3774D15714-4V	OEM
DT3774D15714-8M	OEM
DT3774D15714-8V	OEM
DT3774D15716-0M	OEM
DT3774D15716-0V	OEM
DT3774D15716-4M	OEM
DT3774D15716-4V	OEM
DT3774D15716-8M	OEM
DT3774D15716-8V	OEM
DT3774SE5710-0M	OEM
DT3774SE5710-0V	OEM
DT3774SE5710-4M	OEM
DT3774SE5710-4V	OEM
DT3774SE5710-8M	OEM
DT3774SE5710-8V	OEM
DT3774SE5712-0M	OEM
DT3774SE5712-0V	OEM
DT3774SE5712-4M	OEM
DT3774SE5712-4V	OEM
DT3774SE5712-8M	OEM
DT3774SE5712-8V	OEM
DT3774SE5714-0M	OEM
DT3774SE5714-0V	OEM
DT3774SE5714-4M	OEM
DT3774SE5714-4V	OEM
DT3774SE5714-8M	OEM
DT3774SE5714-8V	OEM

DEVICE TYPE	REPL CODE
DT3774SE5716-0M	OEM
DT3774SE5716-0V	OEM
DT3774SE5716-4M	OEM
DT3774SE5716-4V	OEM
DT3774SE5716-8M	OEM
DT3774SE5716-8V	OEM
DT4011	0103
DT4110	0103
DT4111	0103
DT4112	0130
DT4120	0103
DT4121	0103
DT4303	0359
DT4304	0359
DT4305	0359
DT4306	0359
DT4335	OEM
DT4336	OEM
DT4500	OEM
DT4500A	OEM
DT4501	OEM
DT4502	OEM
DT4503	OEM
DT4504	OEM
DT4505	OEM
DT4506	OEM
DT4506-300	OEM
DT4507-300	OEM
DT4508	OEM
DT4508-300	OEM
DT4509	OEM
DT4509-300	OEM
DT4510	OEM
DT4510-300	OEM
DT4511	OEM
DT4511-300	OEM
DT4512	OEM
DT4512-300	OEM
DT4513	OEM
DT4513-300	OEM
DT4514	OEM
DT4514-300	OEM
DT4515	OEM
DT4515-300	OEM
DT4516	OEM
DT5335	OEM
DT5336	OEM
DT5459BSXXXX	OEM
DT5701	OEM
DT5702	OEM
DT5703	OEM
DT5710	OEM
DT5710A	OEM
DT5714	OEM
DT5716	OEM
DT5720	OEM
DT5750	OEM
DT6103	OEM
DT6104	OEM
DT6110	0160
DT6812	OEM
DT7585BSXXXX	OEM
DT8596BSXXXX	OEM
DT15060	OEM
DT15150	OEM
DT171514	OEM
DT171514R4	OEM
DTA05B	4381
DTA05C	4381
DTA05E	4382
DTA2B	2284
DTA2C	2284
DTA2E	2284
DTA3C	2284
DTA3E	2284
DTA3F	OEM
DTA3G	OEM
DTA8C	0588
DTA8E	0571
DTA8F	0589
DTA8G	0589
DTA10C	0588
DTA10E	0571
DTA10F	0589
DTA10G	0589
DTA12C	0767
DTA12E	0739
DTA12F	0612
DTA12G	0612
DTA16C	0767
DTA16E	0739
DTA16F	0612
DTA16G	0612
DTA113ZS	OEM
DTA114	OEM
DTA114A	4109
DTA114EA	4109
DTA114EF	6442
DTA114EK	1881
DTA114EKT97	OEM
DTA114ES	4109
DTA114F	OEM
DTA114K	1881
DTA114S	4109
DTA114STP	4109
DTA114T	OEM
DTA114TF	OEM
DTA114TK	OEM
DTA114Y	OEM

DEVICE TYPE	REPL CODE
DTA114YK	OEM
DTA114YS	OEM
DTA123YS	OEM
DTA124	4768
DTA124(N)	1026
DTA124A	1026
DTA124EA	1026
DTA124EF	6526
DTA124EFT	OEM
DTA124EK	0698
DTA124EKTP	0698
DTA124EL	OEM
DTA124ES	1026
DTA124ES-T	1026
DTA124ESZ	1026
DTA124EU	OEM
DTA124EV	OEM
DTA124F	1026
DTA124FS	OEM
DTA124K	0698
DTA124K(15)	0698
DTA124L	OEM
DTA124N	1026
DTA124S	1026
DTA124TA	OEM
DTA124TF	OEM
DTA124TK	OEM
DTA124TKT97	OEM
DTA124TL	OEM
DTA124TS	OEM
DTA124TU	OEM
DTA124TV	OEM
DTA124X	OEM
DTA124XA	OEM
DTA124XF	OEM
DTA124XK	OEM
DTA124XL	OEM
DTA124XS	OEM
DTA124XU	OEM
DTA124XV	OEM
DTA143	OEM
DTA143A	OEM
DTA143E	OEM
DTA143EA	OEM
DTA143EK	OEM
DTA143ES	OEM
DTA143ESA	OEM
DTA143X	OEM
DTA143XF	OEM
DTA143XK	OEM
DTA143XS	OEM
DTA143XSZ	OEM
DTA144	4067
DTA144(N)	4067
DTA144A	4067
DTA144E	OEM
DTA144EA	4067
DTA144EF	6674
DTA144EK	3241
DTA144EK-16	OEM
DTA144ES	4067
DTA144ES-T	OEM
DTA144F	5486
DTA144KK(16)	OEM
DTA144N	5486
DTA144S	4067
DTA144STP	4067
DTA144TKT97	OEM
DTA144TL	OEM
DTA144TS	4067
DTA144TSTP	4067
DTA144W	OEM
DTA144WS	OEM
DTA1011	0160
DTA6001	OEM
DTA6001A	OEM
DTA6002	OEM
DTA6002A	OEM
DTA6003	OEM
DTA6003A	OEM
DTA6004	OEM
DTA6004A	OEM
DTA6005	OEM
DTA6005A	OEM
DTA6007	OEM
DTA6007A	OEM
DTA6008	OEM
DTA6008A	OEM
DTA6009	OEM
DTA6009A	OEM
DTA6010	OEM
DTA6010A	OEM
DTA6011	OEM
DTA6011A	OEM
DTA6013	OEM
DTA6013A	OEM
DTA6014	OEM
DTA6014A	OEM
DTA6015	OEM
DTA6015A	OEM
DTA6016	OEM
DTA6016A	OEM
DTA6017	OEM
DTA6017A	OEM
DTA6019	OEM
DTA6019A	OEM
DTA6027	OEM
DTA6027A	OEM
DTA6028	OEM

DEVICE TYPE	REPL CODE
DTA6028A	OEM
DTA6029	OEM
DTA6029A	OEM
DTA6030	OEM
DTA6030A	OEM
DTB10C	0550
DTB10E	0550
DTB10F	0550
DTB10G	0550
DTB12C	OEM
DTB12E	OEM
DTB12F	OEM
DTB12G	OEM
DTB16C	0902
DTB16E	0902
DTB16F	0902
DTB16G	0902
DTB5724	OEM
DTB5725	OEM
DTC16C	0902
DTC16E	0902
DTC16F	0902
DTC16G	0902
DTC-114	0826
DTC114	0826
DTC114A	0826
DTC114E	0826
DTC114EA	0826
DTC114EF	0826
DTC114EK	3442
DTC114EKT96	OEM
DTC114ES	0826
DTC114ESB	2088
DTC114ESC	2088
DTC114ESE	0826
DTC114ESN	0826
DTC114E-S-T	0826
DTC114ES-T	0826
DTC114ESZ	0826
DTC114F	OEM
DTC114FS	OEM
DTC114N	OEM
DTC114S	0826
DTC114TK	OEM
DTC114TKT97	OEM
DTC114Y	OEM
DTC114YK	OEM
DTC114YS	0826
DTC114YSK	OEM
DTC114YSR	OEM
DTC124	5207
DTC124(N)	0881
DTC124A	0881
DTC124EA	0881
DTC124EF	5581
DTC124EFM	OEM
DTC124EFT	OEM
DTC124EK	5584
DTC124EKTP	3442
DTC124EL	OEM
DTC124ES	0881
DTC124ES-DCTP	0881
DTC124ES-T	0881
DTC124EST	0881
DTC124ESZ	0881
DTC124EU	OEM
DTC124EV	OEM
DTC124F	0881
DTC124K	0975
DTC124K(25)	0975
DTC124L	OEM
DTC124N	0881
DTC124S	0881
DTC124TA	OEM
DTC124TF	OEM
DTC124TK	OEM
DTC124TL	OEM
DTC124TS	OEM
DTC124TU	OEM
DTC124TV	OEM
DTC124X	OEM
DTC124XA	OEM
DTC124XF	OEM
DTC124XK	OEM
DTC124XL	OEM
DTC124XS	OEM
DTC124XU	OEM
DTC124XV	OEM
DTC143	OEM
DTC143A	OEM
DTC143E	OEM
DTC143EA	OEM
DTC143EF	OEM
DTC143EK	OEM
DTC143ES	OEM
DTC143T	OEM
DTC143TA	OEM
DTC143TS	OEM
DTC143X	OEM
DTC143XS	OEM
DTC143XSZ	OEM
DTC143Z	OEM
DTC144	0892
DTC144A	0892
DTC144E	0892
DTC144EA	0892
DTC144EF	5310
DTC144EK	3439
DTC144EL-TL2	OEM

DEVICE TYPE	REPL CODE
DTC144E-S	5310
DTC144ES	0892
DTC144ESD	0892
DTC144ES-DCTP	0892
DTC144ES-T	OEM
DTC144ES-TP	0892
DTC144ESTP	0892
DTC144ESZ	0892
DTC144F	0892
DTC144K	3439
DTC144K(26)	OEM
DTC144K-26	OEM
DTC144N	0892
DTC144N-DCTP	OEM
DTC144S	0892
DTC144SD	0892
DTC144TK	OEM
DTC144W	OEM
DTC144WF	OEM
DTC144WK	OEM
DTC314TA	OEM
DTC314TS	OEM
DTC363EK	OEM
DTC363ES	OEM
DTC363TK	OEM
DTC363TS	OEM
DTC2400	0599
D-TEX-8	1843
DTG-110	0085
DTG110	0160
DTG110A	0599
DTG110B	0599
DTG400M	0599
DTG-600	0599
DTG600	0599
DTG-601	0599
DTG601	0599
DTG-602	0599
DTG602	0599
DTG-603	0599
DTG603	0599
DTG-603M	0599
DTG603M	0599
DTG1000	0599
DTG-1010	0969
DTG1010	0969
DTG1011	0160
DTG1040	0160
DTG1110	0969
DTG1110B	OEM
DTG1200	0599
DTG1210A	OEM
DTG-2000	0599
DTG2000	0599
DTG2000A	0599
DTG2000H	0599
DTG-2100	0599
DTG2100	0599
DTG2100A	0599
DTG2200	0599
DTG2400	0599
DTH2411	OEM
DTH2412	OEM
DTH2413	OEM
DTH2511	OEM
DTH2512	OEM
DTH2513	OEM
DTH2611	OEM
DTH2612	OEM
DTH2613	OEM
DTH2711	OEM
DTH2712	OEM
DTH2713	OEM
DTH2811	OEM
DTH2812	OEM
DTH2813	OEM
DTH3011	OEM
DTH3011A	OEM
DTH3012	OEM
DTH3012A	OEM
DTH3014	OEM
DTH3111	OEM
DTH3111A	OEM
DTH3112	OEM
DTH3112A	OEM
DTH3113	OEM
DTH3113A	OEM
DTH3114	OEM
DTH3211	OEM
DTH3211A	OEM
DTH3212	OEM
DTH3212A	OEM
DTH3214	OEM
DTH3311	OEM
DTH3311A	OEM
DTH3312	OEM
DTH3312A	OEM
DTH3314	OEM
DTH3411	OEM
DTH3411A	OEM
DTH3412	OEM
DTH3412A	OEM
DTH3414	OEM
DTH3511	OEM
DTH3511A	OEM
DTH3512	OEM
DTH3512A	OEM
DTH3514	OEM
DTH3611	OEM

DEVICE TYPE	REPL CODE
DTH3611A	OEM
DTH3612	OEM
DTH3612A	OEM
DTH3614	OEM
DTH3711	OEM
DTH3711A	OEM
DTH3712	OEM
DTH3712A	OEM
DTH3714	OEM
DTH3811	OEM
DTH3811A	OEM
DTH3812	OEM
DTH3812A	OEM
DTH3813	OEM
DTH3813A	OEM
DTH3814	OEM
DTML9093	0354
DTML9099	0329
DTML9930	1812
DTML9932	1035
DTML9933	2086
DTML9935	1168
DTML9936	1820
DTML9944	0033
DTML9945	0081
DTML9946	0141
DTML9948	3365
DTML9949	1833
DTML9961	1848
DTML9962	0557
DTML9963	0337
DTN1006	OEM
DTN9000	OEM
DTN9000T	OEM
DTN9001	OEM
DTN9001T	OEM
DTS013	0003
DTS-0710	0074
DTS0710	0074
DTS-0713	0003
DTS0713	0003
DTS06506	OEM
DTS-103	0538
DTS103	0538
DTS-104	0538
DTS104	0538
DTS-105	0538
DTS105	0538
DTS-106	0538
DTS106	0538
DTS-107	0538
DTS107	0431
DTS108	0538
DTS-310	0359
DTS310	0359
DTS-311	0359
DTS311	0359
DTS400	OEM
DTS-401	0074
DTS401	0074
DTS-402	0074
DTS402	0359
DTS-403	0065
DTS403	0359
DTS-409	0065
DTS409	2398
DTS-410	0074
DTS410	0103
DTS-411	0074
DTS411	0270
DTS-413	0074
DTS413	0309
DTS-423	1955
DTS423	0309
DTS-423M	3009
DTS423M	0359
DTS-424	0359
DTS424	0359
DTS-425	0359
DTS425	0359
DTS-430	4511
DTS430	1955
DTS-431	0065
DTS431	0359
DTS-431M	0065
DTS431M	0359
DTS-515	3009
DTS515	0074
DTS-516	3009
DTS516	3009
DTS-517	3009
DTS517	3009
DTS-518	3009
DTS518	3009
DTS-519	3009
DTS519	1955
DTS520	OEM
DTS520MX	OEM
DTS-701	0003
DTS701	0003
DTS-702	0065
DTS702	0065
DTS-704	0003
DTS704	0065
DTS-708	0065
DTS-709	0065
DTS-710	0065
DTS-712	0065
DTS-714	0065

DEVICE TYPE	REPL CODE
DTS720	OEM
DTS-723	0065
DTS-801	0223
DTS801	0223
DTS-802	0065
DTS802	0065
DTS-804	0003
DTS804	0309
DTS812MX	OEM
DTS2000	OEM
DTS2001	OEM
DTS2002	OEM
DTS2003	OEM
DTS3704	0065
DTS3704A	0065
DTS3704B	0065
DTS3705	0074
DTS3705A	0074
DTS3705B	0074
DTS4010	OEM
DTS4025	OEM
DTS4026	OEM
DTS4039	OEM
DTS4041	OEM
DTS4059	OEM
DTS4061	OEM
DTS4062	2602
DTS4066	2602
DTS4067	2602
DTS4072	2602
DTS4074	2602
DTS4075	2602
DTZ6V8A	OEM
DTZ6V8P	OEM
DTZ7V5	OEM
DTZ7V5A	OEM
DTZ7V5P	OEM
DTZ8V2	OEM
DTZ8V2A	OEM
DTZ8V2P	OEM
DTZ9V1	OEM
DTZ9V1A	OEM
DTZ9V1P	OEM
DTZ10	OEM
DTZ10A	OEM
DTZ10P	OEM
DTZ11	OEM
DTZ11A	OEM
DTZ11P	OEM
DTZ12	OEM
DTZ12A	OEM
DTZ12P	OEM
DTZ13	1161
DTZ13A	1161
DTZ13P	OEM
DTZ15	OEM
DTZ15A	OEM
DTZ15P	OEM
DTZ16	OEM
DTZ16A	OEM
DTZ16P	OEM
DTZ18	1756
DTZ18A	1756
DTZ18P	OEM
DTZ20	1921
DTZ20A	1921
DTZ20P	OEM
DTZ22	OEM
DTZ22A	OEM
DTZ22P	OEM
DTZ24	OEM
DTZ24A	OEM
DTZ24P	OEM
DTZ27	1941
DTZ27A	1941
DTZ27P	OEM
DTZ30	OEM
DTZ30A	OEM
DTZ30P	OEM
DTZ33	OEM
DTZ33A	OEM
DTZ33P	OEM
DTZ36	OEM
DTZ36A	OEM
DTZ36P	OEM
DTZ39	OEM
DTZ39A	OEM
DTZ39P	OEM
DTZ43	OEM
DTZ43A	OEM
DTZ43P	OEM
DTZ47	OEM
DTZ47A	OEM
DTZ47P	OEM
DTZ51	1961
DTZ51A	1961
DTZ51P	OEM
DTZ56	OEM
DTZ56A	OEM
DTZ56P	OEM
DTZ62	OEM
DTZ62A	OEM
DTZ62P	OEM
DTZ68	1976
DTZ68A	1976
DTZ68P	OEM
DTZ75	OEM
DTZ75A	OEM
DTZ75P	OEM

If replacement code is OEM, contact original manufacturer for replacement.

385

DEVICE TYPE	REPL CODE	DEVICE TYPE	REPL CODE	DEVICE TYPE	REPL CODE	DEVICE TYPE	REPL CODE	DEVICE TYPE	REPL CODE	DEVICE TYPE	REPL CODE	DEVICE TYPE	REPL CODE
DTZ82	OEM	DV28120U	OEM	DVE4550B	OEM	DVE4558-05	OEM	DVE6953D	OEM	DVH6634F	OEM	DVH6693E	OEM
DTZ82A	OEM	DV28120V	OEM	DVE4550C	OEM	DVE4558-06	OEM	DVE6953E	OEM	DVH6634G	OEM	DVH6693F	OEM
DTZ82P	OEM	DV28120X	OEM	DVE4550D	OEM	DVE4558-07	OEM	DVE6953F	OEM	DVH6634H	OEM	DVH6693G	OEM
DTZ91	OEM	DVA4580A	OEM	DVE4550E	OEM	DVE4558-08	OEM	DVE6953G	OEM	DVH6634J	OEM	DVH6693H	OEM
DTZ91A	OEM	DVA4580B	OEM	DVE4550F	OEM	DVE4558-11	OEM	DVE6953H	OEM	DVH6641A	OEM	DVH6693J	OEM
DTZ91P	OEM	DVA4580C	OEM	DVE4550G	OEM	DVE4558-12	OEM	DVE6953J	OEM	DVH6641B	OEM	DVH6693K	OEM
DTZ100	OEM	DVA4580D	OEM	DVE4550H	OEM	DVE4558-13	OEM	DVE6953K	OEM	DVH6641C	OEM	DVH6693L	OEM
DTZ100A	OEM	DVA4580E	OEM	DVE4551A	OEM	DVE4558-14	OEM	DVE6954A	OEM	DVH6641D	OEM	DVH6693M	OEM
DTZ100P	OEM	DVA4580F	OEM	DVE4551B	OEM	DVE4558-15	OEM	DVE6954B	OEM	DVH6641E	OEM	DVH6694B	OEM
DTZ110	OEM	DVA6180	OEM	DVE4551C	OEM	DVE4558-16	OEM	DVE6954C	OEM	DVH6641F	OEM	DVH6694C	OEM
DTZ110A	OEM	DVA6181	OEM	DVE4551D	OEM	DVE4558-17	OEM	DVE6954D	OEM	DVH6641G	OEM	DVH6694D	OEM
DTZ110P	OEM	DVA6181A	OEM	DVE4551E	OEM	DVE4558-21	OEM	DVE6954E	OEM	DVH6641H	OEM	DVH6694E	OEM
DTZ120	OEM	DVA6181B	OEM	DVE4551F	OEM	DVE4558-22	OEM	DVE6954F	OEM	DVH6641J	OEM	DVH6694F	OEM
DTZ120A	OEM	DVA6182	OEM	DVE4551G	OEM	DVE4558-23	OEM	DVE6954G	OEM	DVH6642A	OEM	DVH6694G	OEM
DTZ120P	OEM	DVA6182A	OEM	DVE4551H	OEM	DVE4558-24	OEM	DVE6954H	OEM	DVH6642B	OEM	DVH6694H	OEM
DTZ130	OEM	DVA6182B	OEM	DVE4552A	OEM	DVE4558-25	OEM	DVE6954J	OEM	DVH6642C	OEM	DVH6694J	OEM
DTZ130A	OEM	DVA6183	OEM	DVE4552B	OEM	DVE4558-26	OEM	DVE6954K	OEM	DVH6642D	OEM	DVH6694K	OEM
DTZ130P	OEM	DVA6183A	OEM	DVE4552C	OEM	DVE4558-31	OEM	DVE6955A	OEM	DVH6642E	OEM	DVH6694L	OEM
DTZ150	OEM	DVA6183B	OEM	DVE4552D	OEM	DVE4558-32	OEM	DVE6955C	OEM	DVH6642F	OEM	DVH6694M	OEM
DTZ150A	OEM	DVA6184	OEM	DVE4552E	OEM	DVE4558-33	OEM	DVE6955D	OEM	DVH6642G	OEM	DVH6730-01	OEM
DTZ150P	OEM	DVA6184A	OEM	DVE4552F	OEM	DVE4558-34	OEM	DVE6955E	OEM	DVH6642H	OEM	DVH6730-02	OEM
DTZ160	OEM	DVA6185	OEM	DVE4552G	OEM	DVE4558-35	OEM	DVE6955F	OEM	DVH6642J	OEM	DVH6730-03	OEM
DTZ160A	OEM	DVA6185A	OEM	DVE4552H	OEM	DVE4558-41	OEM	DVE6955G	OEM	DVH6643A	OEM	DVH6730-04	OEM
DTZ160P	OEM	DVA6185B	OEM	DVE4555A	OEM	DVE4558-42	OEM	DVE6955H	OEM	DVH6643B	OEM	DVH6730-05	OEM
DTZ170	OEM	DVA6186	OEM	DVE4555B	OEM	DVE4558-43	OEM	DVE6955J	OEM	DVH6643C	OEM	DVH6730-07	OEM
DTZ170A	OEM	DVA6186A	OEM	DVE4555C	OEM	DVE4558-44	OEM	DVE6955K	OEM	DVH6643D	OEM	DVH6730-08	OEM
DTZ170P	OEM	DVA6186B	OEM	DVE4555D	OEM	DVE4558-51	OEM	DVE6956A	OEM	DVH6643E	OEM	DVH6730-09	OEM
DTZ180	OEM	DVA6187	OEM	DVE4555E	OEM	DVE4558-52	OEM	DVE6956B	OEM	DVH6643F	OEM	DVH6730-10	OEM
DTZ180A	OEM	DVA6187A	OEM	DVE4555F	OEM	DVE4558-53	OEM	DVE6956C	OEM	DVH6643G	OEM	DVH6730-11	OEM
DTZ180P	OEM	DVA6187B	OEM	DVE4555G	OEM	DVE4558-61	OEM	DVE6956D	OEM	DVH6643H	OEM	DVH6730-13	OEM
DTZ200	1398	DVA6188	OEM	DVE4555H	OEM	DVE4558-62	OEM	DVE6956E	OEM	DVH6643J	OEM	DVH6730-14	OEM
DTZ200A	1398	DVA6188A	OEM	DVE4556-01	OEM	DVE4558-71	OEM	DVE6956F	OEM	DVH6644A	OEM	DVH6730-15	OEM
DTZ200P	OEM	DVA6188B	OEM	DVE4556-02	OEM	DVE4560-00	OEM	DVE6956G	OEM	DVH6644B	OEM	DVH6730-16	OEM
DTZ220	OEM	DVA6735A	OEM	DVE4556-03	OEM	DVE4560-06	OEM	DVE6956H	OEM	DVH6644C	OEM	DVH6730-17	OEM
DTZ220A	OEM	DVA6735B	OEM	DVE4556-04	OEM	DVE4560-12	OEM	DVE6956J	OEM	DVH6644D	OEM	DVH6730-19	OEM
DTZ220P	OEM	DVA6735C	OEM	DVE4556-05	OEM	DVE4560-18	OEM	DVE6956K	OEM	DVH6644E	OEM	DVH6730-20	OEM
DTZ250A	OEM	DVA6735D	OEM	DVE4556-06	OEM	DVE4560-24	OEM	DVF4559-01	OEM	DVH6644F	OEM	DVH6730-21	OEM
DTZ250P	OEM	DVA6736A	OEM	DVE4556-07	OEM	DVE4576A	OEM	DVF4559-02	OEM	DVH6644G	OEM	DVH6730-22	OEM
DTZ280A	OEM	DVA6736B	OEM	DVE4556-08	OEM	DVE4576B	OEM	DVF4559-03	OEM	DVH6644H	OEM	DVH6730-23	OEM
DTZ280P	OEM	DVA6736C	OEM	DVE4556-11	OEM	DVE4576C	OEM	DVF4559-04	OEM	DVH6644J	OEM	DVH6730-25	OEM
DTZ300A	OEM	DVA6736D	OEM	DVE4556-12	OEM	DVE4576D	OEM	DVF4559-11	OEM	DVH6661B	OEM	DVH6730-26	OEM
DTZ300P	OEM	DVA6737A	OEM	DVE4556-13	OEM	DVE4576E	OEM	DVF4559-12	OEM	DVH6661C	OEM	DVH6730-27	OEM
DTZ320A	OEM	DVA6737B	OEM	DVE4556-14	OEM	DVE4576F	OEM	DVF4559-21	OEM	DVH6661D	OEM	DVH6731-01	OEM
DTZ320P	OEM	DVA6737C	OEM	DVE4556-15	OEM	DVE4576G	OEM	DVF4559-22	OEM	DVH6661E	OEM	DVH6731-02	OEM
DTZ350A	OEM	DVA6737D	OEM	DVE4556-16	OEM	DVE4576H	OEM	DVF4559-23	OEM	DVH6661F	OEM	DVH6731-03	OEM
DTZ350P	OEM	DVA6737E	OEM	DVE4556-17	OEM	DVE4588-01	OEM	DVF4559-24	OEM	DVH6661G	OEM	DVH6731-04	OEM
DTZ400A	OEM	DVA6738A	OEM	DVE4556-21	OEM	DVE4588-02	OEM	DVF4559-31	OEM	DVH6661H	OEM	DVH6731-05	OEM
DTZ400P	OEM	DVA6738B	OEM	DVE4556-22	OEM	DVE4588-03	OEM	DVF4559-32	OEM	DVH6661J	OEM	DVH6731-07	OEM
DTZ440A	OEM	DVA6738C	OEM	DVE4556-23	OEM	DVE4588-11	OEM	DVF4559-41	OEM	DVH6661K	OEM	DVH6731-08	OEM
DTZ440P	OEM	DVA6738D	OEM	DVE4556-24	OEM	DVE4588-12	OEM	DVF4559-42	OEM	DVH6661L	OEM	DVH6731-09	OEM
DU1	0050	DVA6738E	OEM	DVE4556-25	OEM	DVE4588-13	OEM	DVF4559-43	OEM	DVH6661M	OEM	DVH6731-10	OEM
DU2	0050	DVA6738F	OEM	DVE4556-26	OEM	DVE5003-04	OEM	DVH6150	OEM	DVH6662B	OEM	DVH6731-11	OEM
DU3	0004	DVA6738G	OEM	DVE4556-31	OEM	DVE5033-01	OEM	DVH6150A	OEM	DVH6662C	OEM	DVH6731-13	OEM
DU4	0164	DVA6738H	OEM	DVE4556-32	OEM	DVE5033-02	OEM	DVH6150B	OEM	DVH6662D	OEM	DVH6731-14	OEM
DU5	0004	DVA6739A	OEM	DVE4556-33	OEM	DVE5033-03	OEM	DVH6150C	OEM	DVH6662E	OEM	DVH6731-15	OEM
DU6	0085	DVA6739B	OEM	DVE4556-34	OEM	DVE5033-05	OEM	DVH6150D	OEM	DVH6662F	OEM	DVH6731-16	OEM
DU7	0435	DVA6739C	OEM	DVE4556-35	OEM	DVE5033-06	OEM	DVH6151	OEM	DVH6662G	OEM	DVH6731-17	OEM
DU12	0050	DVA6739D	OEM	DVE4556-41	OEM	DVE5033-07	OEM	DVH6151A	OEM	DVH6662H	OEM	DVH6731-19	OEM
DU47	0435	DVA6739E	OEM	DVE4556-42	OEM	DVE5033-08	OEM	DVH6151B	OEM	DVH6662J	OEM	DVH6731-20	OEM
DU400	0015	DVA6739F	OEM	DVE4556-43	OEM	DVE5033-09	OEM	DVH6151C	OEM	DVH6662K	OEM	DVH6731-21	OEM
DU600	0015	DVB6100A	OEM	DVE4556-44	OEM	DVE5033-10	OEM	DVH6151D	OEM	DVH6662L	OEM	DVH6731-22	OEM
DU800	0071	DVB6100B	OEM	DVE4556-51	OEM	DVE5033-11	OEM	DVH6151E	OEM	DVH6662M	OEM	DVH6731-23	OEM
DU1000	0071	DVB6100C	OEM	DVE4556-52	OEM	DVE5033-12	OEM	DVH6151F	OEM	DVH6663B	OEM	DVH6731-25	OEM
DU4339	OEM	DVB6101A	OEM	DVE4556-53	OEM	DVE5033-13	OEM	DVH6151G	OEM	DVH6663C	OEM	DVH6731-26	OEM
DU4340	3350	DVB6101B	OEM	DVE4556-61	OEM	DVE5033-14	OEM	DVH6152	OEM	DVH6663D	OEM	DVH6731-27	OEM
DUNTH0002CE00	OEM	DVB6101C	OEM	DVE4556-62	OEM	DVE6347	OEM	DVH6152A	OEM	DVH6663E	OEM	DVH6732-01	OEM
DUNTH0017DE00	OEM	DVB6101D	OEM	DVE4556-71	OEM	DVE6347A	OEM	DVH6152B	OEM	DVH6663F	OEM	DVH6732-02	OEM
DUNTH0032DE00	OEM	DVB6101E	OEM	DVE4557-01	OEM	DVE6347B	OEM	DVH6152C	OEM	DVH6663G	OEM	DVH6732-03	OEM
DUV11	OEM	DVB6102A	OEM	DVE4557-02	OEM	DVE6347C	OEM	DVH6160	OEM	DVH6663H	OEM	DVH6732-04	OEM
DV13C	0865	DVB6102B	OEM	DVE4557-03	OEM	DVE6347D	OEM	DVH6160A	OEM	DVH6663J	OEM	DVH6732-05	OEM
DV13E	0847	DVB6102C	OEM	DVE4557-04	OEM	DVE6347E	OEM	DVH6161	OEM	DVH6663K	OEM	DVH6732-07	OEM
DV14C	0865	DVB6102D	OEM	DVE4557-05	OEM	DVE6347F	OEM	DVH6161A	OEM	DVH6663L	OEM	DVH6732-08	OEM
DV14E	0847	DVB6103A	OEM	DVE4557-06	OEM	DVE6347G	OEM	DVH6161B	OEM	DVH6663M	OEM	DVH6732-09	OEM
DV45	OEM	DVB6103B	OEM	DVE4557-07	OEM	DVE6347H	OEM	DVH6161C	OEM	DVH6664B	OEM	DVH6732-10	OEM
DV1006	OEM	DVB6103C	OEM	DVE4557-08	OEM	DVE6722A	OEM	DVH6162	OEM	DVH6664C	OEM	DVH6732-11	OEM
DV1007	OEM	DVB6103D	OEM	DVE4557-11	OEM	DVE6722B	OEM	DVH6162A	OEM	DVH6664D	OEM	DVH6732-13	OEM
DV1110	OEM	DVB6104A	OEM	DVE4557-12	OEM	DVE6722C	OEM	DVH6162B	OEM	DVH6664E	OEM	DVH6732-14	OEM
DV1111	OEM	DVB6104B	OEM	DVE4557-13	OEM	DVE6722D	OEM	DVH6631A	OEM	DVH6664F	OEM	DVH6732-15	OEM
DV1112	OEM	DVB6104C	OEM	DVE4557-14	OEM	DVE6722E	OEM	DVH6631B	OEM	DVH6664G	OEM	DVH6732-16	OEM
DV1202S	OEM	DVB6104D	OEM	DVE4557-15	OEM	DVE6722F	OEM	DVH6631C	OEM	DVH6664H	OEM	DVH6732-17	OEM
DV1202W	OEM	DVB6850A	OEM	DVE4557-16	OEM	DVE6810A	OEM	DVH6631D	OEM	DVH6664J	OEM	DVH6732-19	OEM
DV1205S	OEM	DVB6850B	OEM	DVE4557-17	OEM	DVE6810B	OEM	DVH6631E	OEM	DVH6664K	OEM	DVH6732-20	OEM
DV1205W	OEM	DVB6850C	OEM	DVE4557-21	OEM	DVE6810C	OEM	DVH6631F	OEM	DVH6664L	OEM	DVH6732-21	OEM
DV1210S	OEM	DVB6851A	OEM	DVE4557-22	OEM	DVE6810D	OEM	DVH6631G	OEM	DVH6664M	OEM	DVH6732-22	OEM
DV1210W	OEM	DVB6851B	OEM	DVE4557-23	OEM	DVE6810E	OEM	DVH6631H	OEM	DVH6691B	OEM	DVH6732-23	OEM
DV1220S	OEM	DVB6851C	OEM	DVE4557-24	OEM	DVE6810F	OEM	DVH6631J	OEM	DVH6691C	OEM	DVH6732-25	OEM
DV1220W	OEM	DVB6852A	OEM	DVE4557-25	OEM	DVE6951A	OEM	DVH6632A	OEM	DVH6691D	OEM	DVH6732-26	OEM
DV1230T	OEM	DVB6852B	OEM	DVE4557-26	OEM	DVE6951B	OEM	DVH6632B	OEM	DVH6691E	OEM	DVH6732-27	OEM
DV1230W	OEM	DVB6852C	OEM	DVE4557-31	OEM	DVE6951C	OEM	DVH6632C	OEM	DVH6691F	OEM	DVH6733-01	OEM
DV1240T	OEM	DVB6860A	OEM	DVE4557-32	OEM	DVE6951D	OEM	DVH6632D	OEM	DVH6691G	OEM	DVH6733-02	OEM
DV1240W	OEM	DVB6860B	OEM	DVE4557-33	OEM	DVE6951E	OEM	DVH6632E	OEM	DVH6691H	OEM	DVH6733-03	OEM
DV2209	0030	DVB6860C	OEM	DVE4557-34	OEM	DVE6951F	OEM	DVH6632F	OEM	DVH6691J	OEM	DVH6733-04	OEM
DV2805S	OEM	DVB6861A	OEM	DVE4557-35	OEM	DVE6951G	OEM	DVH6632G	OEM	DVH6691K	OEM	DVH6733-05	OEM
DV2810S	OEM	DVB6861B	OEM	DVE4557-41	OEM	DVE6951H	OEM	DVH6632H	OEM	DVH6691L	OEM	DVH6733-07	OEM
DV2810X	OEM	DVB6861C	OEM	DVE4557-42	OEM	DVE6951J	OEM	DVH6632J	OEM	DVH6691M	OEM	DVH6733-08	OEM
DV2820S	OEM	DVB6862A	OEM	DVE4557-43	OEM	DVE6951K	OEM	DVH6633A	OEM	DVH6692B	OEM	DVH6733-09	OEM
DV2820V	OEM	DVB6862B	OEM	DVE4557-44	OEM	DVE6952A	OEM	DVH6633B	OEM	DVH6692C	OEM	DVH6733-10	OEM
DV2820W	OEM	DVB6870A	OEM	DVE4557-51	OEM	DVE6952B	OEM	DVH6633C	OEM	DVH6692D	OEM	DVH6733-11	OEM
DV2820X	OEM	DVB6870B	OEM	DVE4557-52	OEM	DVE6952C	OEM	DVH6633D	OEM	DVH6692E	OEM	DVH6733-13	OEM
DV2840V	OEM	DVB6870C	OEM	DVE4557-53	OEM	DVE6952D	OEM	DVH6633E	OEM	DVH6692F	OEM	DVH6733-14	OEM
DV2880T	OEM	DVB6871A	OEM	DVE4557-61	OEM	DVE6952E	OEM	DVH6633F	OEM	DVH6692G	OEM	DVH6733-15	OEM
DV2880U	OEM	DVB6871B	OEM	DVE4557-62	OEM	DVE6952F	OEM	DVH6633G	OEM	DVH6692H	OEM	DVH6733-16	OEM
DV2880V	OEM	DVB6871C	OEM	DVE4557-71	OEM	DVE6952G	OEM	DVH6633H	OEM	DVH6692J	OEM	DVH6733-17	OEM
DV2880W	OEM	DVB6872A	OEM	DVE4557G	OEM	DVE6952H	OEM	DVH6633J	OEM	DVH6692K	OEM	DVH6733-19	OEM
DV2880X	OEM	DVB6872B	OEM	DVE4557H	OEM	DVE6952J	OEM	DVH6634A	OEM	DVH6692L	OEM	DVH6733-20	OEM
DV3805W	OEM	DVD5001	OEM	DVE4558-01	OEM	DVE6952K	OEM	DVH6634B	OEM	DVH6692M	OEM	DVH6733-21	OEM
DV3810W	OEM	DVD5001A	OEM	DVE4558-02	OEM	DVE6953A	OEM	DVH6634C	OEM	DVH6693B	OEM	DVH6733-22	OEM
DV3840X	OEM	DVE955B	OEM	DVE4558-03	OEM	DVE6953B	OEM	DVH6634D	OEM	DVH6693C	OEM	DVH6733-23	OEM
DV28120T	OEM	DVE4550A	OEM	DVE4558-04	OEM	DVE6953C	OEM	DVH6634E	OEM	DVH6693D	OEM	DVH6733-25	OEM

386 If replacement code is OEM, contact original manufacturer for replacement.

DEVICE TYPE	REPL CODE
DVH6733-26	OEM
DVH6733-27	OEM
DVH6734-01	OEM
DVH6734-02	OEM
DVH6734-03	OEM
DVH6734-04	OEM
DVH6734-05	OEM
DVH6734-07	OEM
DVH6734-08	OEM
DVH6734-09	OEM
DVH6734-10	OEM
DVH6734-11	OEM
DVH6734-13	OEM
DVH6734-14	OEM
DVH6734-15	OEM
DVH6734-16	OEM
DVH6734-17	OEM
DVH6734-19	OEM
DVH6734-20	OEM
DVH6734-21	OEM
DVH6734-22	OEM
DVH6734-23	OEM
DVH6734-25	OEM
DVH6734-26	OEM
DVH6734-27	OEM
DVH6740-01	OEM
DVH6740-02	OEM
DVH6740-03	OEM
DVH6740-04	OEM
DVH6740-05	OEM
DVH6740-07	OEM
DVH6740-08	OEM
DVH6740-09	OEM
DVH6740-10	OEM
DVH6740-11	OEM
DVH6740-13	OEM
DVH6740-14	OEM
DVH6740-15	OEM
DVH6740-16	OEM
DVH6740-17	OEM
DVH6740-19	OEM
DVH6741-01	OEM
DVH6741-02	OEM
DVH6741-03	OEM
DVH6741-04	OEM
DVH6741-05	OEM
DVH6741-07	OEM
DVH6741-08	OEM
DVH6741-09	OEM
DVH6741-10	OEM
DVH6741-11	OEM
DVH6741-13	OEM
DVH6741-14	OEM
DVH6741-15	OEM
DVH6741-16	OEM
DVH6741-17	OEM
DVH6741-19	OEM
DVH6742-01	OEM
DVH6742-02	OEM
DVH6742-03	OEM
DVH6742-04	OEM
DVH6742-05	OEM
DVH6742-07	OEM
DVH6742-08	OEM
DVH6742-09	OEM
DVH6742-10	OEM
DVH6742-11	OEM
DVH6742-13	OEM
DVH6742-14	OEM
DVH6742-15	OEM
DVH6742-16	OEM
DVH6742-17	OEM
DVH6742-19	OEM
DVH6743-01	OEM
DVH6743-02	OEM
DVH6743-03	OEM
DVH6743-04	OEM
DVH6743-05	OEM
DVH6743-07	OEM
DVH6743-08	OEM
DVH6743-09	OEM
DVH6743-10	OEM
DVH6743-11	OEM
DVH6743-13	OEM
DVH6743-14	OEM
DVH6743-15	OEM
DVH6743-16	OEM
DVH6743-17	OEM
DVH6743-19	OEM
DVH6744-01	OEM
DVH6744-02	OEM
DVH6744-03	OEM
DVH6744-04	OEM
DVH6744-05	OEM
DVH6744-07	OEM
DVH6744-08	OEM
DVH6744-09	OEM
DVH6744-10	OEM
DVH6744-11	OEM
DVH6744-13	OEM
DVH6744-14	OEM
DVH6744-15	OEM
DVH6744-16	OEM
DVH6744-17	OEM
DVH6744-19	OEM
DVH6760-03	OEM
DVH6760-04	OEM
DVH6760-05	OEM
DVH6760-07	OEM

DEVICE TYPE	REPL CODE
DVH6760-08	OEM
DVH6760-09	OEM
DVH6760-10	OEM
DVH6760-11	OEM
DVH6760-13	OEM
DVH6760-14	OEM
DVH6760-15	OEM
DVH6760-16	OEM
DVH6760-17	OEM
DVH6760-19	OEM
DVH6760-20	OEM
DVH6760-21	OEM
DVH6760-22	OEM
DVH6760-23	OEM
DVH6760-25	OEM
DVH6760-26	OEM
DVH6760-27	OEM
DVH6761-03	OEM
DVH6761-04	OEM
DVH6761-05	OEM
DVH6761-07	OEM
DVH6761-08	OEM
DVH6761-09	OEM
DVH6761-10	OEM
DVH6761-11	OEM
DVH6761-13	OEM
DVH6761-14	OEM
DVH6761-15	OEM
DVH6761-16	OEM
DVH6761-17	OEM
DVH6761-19	OEM
DVH6761-20	OEM
DVH6761-21	OEM
DVH6761-22	OEM
DVH6761-23	OEM
DVH6761-25	OEM
DVH6761-26	OEM
DVH6761-27	OEM
DVH6761B	OEM
DVH6761C	OEM
DVH6761D	OEM
DVH6761E	OEM
DVH6761F	OEM
DVH6761G	OEM
DVH6761H	OEM
DVH6761J	OEM
DVH6761K	OEM
DVH6761L	OEM
DVH6761M	OEM
DVH6762-03	OEM
DVH6762-04	OEM
DVH6762-05	OEM
DVH6762-07	OEM
DVH6762-08	OEM
DVH6762-09	OEM
DVH6762-10	OEM
DVH6762-11	OEM
DVH6762-13	OEM
DVH6762-14	OEM
DVH6762-15	OEM
DVH6762-16	OEM
DVH6762-17	OEM
DVH6762-19	OEM
DVH6762-20	OEM
DVH6762-21	OEM
DVH6762-22	OEM
DVH6762-23	OEM
DVH6762-25	OEM
DVH6762-26	OEM
DVH6762-27	OEM
DVH6762B	OEM
DVH6762C	OEM
DVH6762D	OEM
DVH6762E	OEM
DVH6762F	OEM
DVH6762G	OEM
DVH6762H	OEM
DVH6762J	OEM
DVH6762K	OEM
DVH6762L	OEM
DVH6762M	OEM
DVH6763-03	OEM
DVH6763-04	OEM
DVH6763-05	OEM
DVH6763-07	OEM
DVH6763-08	OEM
DVH6763-09	OEM
DVH6763-10	OEM
DVH6763-11	OEM
DVH6763-13	OEM
DVH6763-14	OEM
DVH6763-15	OEM
DVH6763-16	OEM
DVH6763-17	OEM
DVH6763-19	OEM
DVH6763-20	OEM
DVH6763-21	OEM
DVH6763-22	OEM
DVH6763-23	OEM
DVH6763-25	OEM
DVH6763-26	OEM
DVH6763-27	OEM
DVH6763B	OEM
DVH6763C	OEM
DVH6763D	OEM
DVH6763E	OEM
DVH6763F	OEM
DVH6763G	OEM
DVH6763H	OEM

DEVICE TYPE	REPL CODE
DVH6763J	OEM
DVH6763K	OEM
DVH6763L	OEM
DVH6763M	OEM
DVH6764-03	OEM
DVH6764-04	OEM
DVH6764-05	OEM
DVH6764-07	OEM
DVH6764-08	OEM
DVH6764-09	OEM
DVH6764-10	OEM
DVH6764-11	OEM
DVH6764-13	OEM
DVH6764-14	OEM
DVH6764-15	OEM
DVH6764-16	OEM
DVH6764-17	OEM
DVH6764-19	OEM
DVH6764-20	OEM
DVH6764-21	OEM
DVH6764-22	OEM
DVH6764-23	OEM
DVH6764-25	OEM
DVH6764-26	OEM
DVH6764-27	OEM
DVH6764B	OEM
DVH6764C	OEM
DVH6764D	OEM
DVH6764E	OEM
DVH6764F	OEM
DVH6764G	OEM
DVH6764H	OEM
DVH6764J	OEM
DVH6764K	OEM
DVH6764L	OEM
DVH6764M	OEM
DVH6790-03	OEM
DVH6790-04	OEM
DVH6790-05	OEM
DVH6790-07	OEM
DVH6790-08	OEM
DVH6790-09	OEM
DVH6790-10	OEM
DVH6790-11	OEM
DVH6790-13	OEM
DVH6790-14	OEM
DVH6790-15	OEM
DVH6790-16	OEM
DVH6790-17	OEM
DVH6790-19	OEM
DVH6790-20	OEM
DVH6790-21	OEM
DVH6791-03	OEM
DVH6791-04	OEM
DVH6791-05	OEM
DVH6791-07	OEM
DVH6791-08	OEM
DVH6791-09	OEM
DVH6791-10	OEM
DVH6791-11	OEM
DVH6791-13	OEM
DVH6791-14	OEM
DVH6791-15	OEM
DVH6791-16	OEM
DVH6791-17	OEM
DVH6791-19	OEM
DVH6791-20	OEM
DVH6791-21	OEM
DVH6792-03	OEM
DVH6792-04	OEM
DVH6792-05	OEM
DVH6792-07	OEM
DVH6792-08	OEM
DVH6792-09	OEM
DVH6792-10	OEM
DVH6792-11	OEM
DVH6792-13	OEM
DVH6792-14	OEM
DVH6792-15	OEM
DVH6792-16	OEM
DVH6792-17	OEM
DVH6792-19	OEM
DVH6792-20	OEM
DVH6792-21	OEM
DVH6793-03	OEM
DVH6793-04	OEM
DVH6793-05	OEM
DVH6793-07	OEM
DVH6793-08	OEM
DVH6793-09	OEM
DVH6793-10	OEM
DVH6793-11	OEM
DVH6793-13	OEM
DVH6793-14	OEM
DVH6793-15	OEM
DVH6793-16	OEM
DVH6793-17	OEM
DVH6793-19	OEM
DVH6793-20	OEM
DVH6793-21	OEM
DVH6794-04	OEM
DVH6794-05	OEM
DVH6794-07	OEM
DVH6794-08	OEM
DVH6794-09	OEM
DVH6794-10	OEM
DVH6794-11	OEM
DVH6794-13	OEM
DVH6794-14	OEM

DEVICE TYPE	REPL CODE
DVH6794-15	OEM
DVH6794-16	OEM
DVH6794-17	OEM
DVH6794-19	OEM
DVH6794-20	OEM
DVH6794-21	OEM
DVV004	0030
DW144	OEM
DWA010	OEM
DWMA154WA	2189
DWMA154WK	0689
DWP-300A	OEM
DWP400	OEM
DX-0007	0023
DX-0022	0124
DX0022	0124
DX0033TA	0133
DX0038CE	0023
DX0045GE	0124
DX0049GE	OEM
DX0053GE	0124
DX0055CE	0015
DX-0061	0162
DX-0079	0133
DX-0080	0133
DX-0081	0133
DX0085TA	0023
DX0086CE	0023
DX0086TA	0023
DX-0087	0012
DX-0099	0015
DX0101CE	0023
DX0105TA	0023
DX0110CE	0790
DX0113TA	2496
DX0115CE	0023
DX0117TA	0023
DX0123CE	0023
DX0124TA	0071
DX0125CE	0023
DX-0126	0549
DX0126CE	0023
DX0128CE	0087
DX0130CE	0023
DX0131CE	0023
DX0132CE	6198
DX0135TA	0023
DX0142CE	0124
DX-0143	0031
DX-0147	OEM
DX-0150	0139
DX0152CE	0468
DX0153CE	0023
DX-0154	OEM
DX0154CE	0023
DX0155CE	1082
DX-0156	0123
DX-0159	0253
DX0159CE	0023
DX0159DE	0023
DX-0161	0019
DX0161CE	0023
DX-0162	0123
DX-0164	0755
DX0164CE	0344
DX0179CE	0124
DX0181CE	0031
DX0200CE	1864
DX0202CE	0023
DX0203CE	0031
DX0204CE	1083
DX0206	0080
DX0208CE	1864
DX0220CE	0604
DX0226CE	0023
DX0229CE	0102
DX0234CE	0031
DX-0235	0700
DX0235CE	0023
DX0236CE	0133
DX0237CE	0124
DX-0241	0143
DX0247CE	0282
DX0248CE	0023
DX-0253	0019
DX-0255	0133
DX-0259	0133
DX-0270	0133
DX-0273	0133
DX-0287	0133
DX-0289	OEM
DX-0299	0133
DX-0301	0005
DX-0307	0030
DX-0313	0139
DX-0314	0139
DX-0316	0139
DX-0349	0015
DX-0365	0139
DX0382CE	OEM
DX-0398	0041
DX-0402	0057
DX-0403	0999
DX-0405	0053
DX-0408	0466
DX-0445	0080
DX-0475	0015
DX0475	0015
DX-0516	0120

DEVICE TYPE	REPL CODE
DX-0529	0188
DX-0530	0466
DX-0543	0133
DX-0576	0143
DX-0587	0023
DX-0611	0123
DX-0650	1914
DX-0685	0133
DX-0697	0120
DX-0713	0100
DX-0721	0023
DX-0723	0549
DX-0725	0143
DX-0726	0319
DX-0727	0253
DX-0728	0057
DX-0729	0165
DX-0735	0253
DX-0749	0715
DX-0750	0139
DX-0752	0139
DX-0856	0213
DX-0862	0181
DX-0872	0139
DX-0983	0062
DX-0987	0162
DX-0999	0140
DX57	OEM
DX58	OEM
DX206	OEM
DX260	OEM
DX267	OEM
DX276	OEM
DX285	OEM
DX286	OEM
DX290	OEM
DX332	OEM
DX342	OEM
DX343	OEM
DX368	OEM
DX373	OEM
DX423	OEM
DX450	OEM
DX453	OEM
DX453B	OEM
DX481	OEM
DX482	OEM
DX520	0015
DX1007	0030
DX-1034	0170
DX-1039	0015
DX1039	0015
DX-1043	0062
DX-1044	0077
DX-1080	0030
DX1080	0623
DX-1082	0102
DX-1126	0253
DX-1131	0030
DX-1132	0253
DX-1139	0133
DX-1147	4262
DX-1161	0023
DX-1162	1864
DX-1163	0137
DX-1165	0095
DX1193	0041
DX1194	0091
DX-1195	0039
DX-1196	0005
DX1196	0005
DX-1221	OEM
DX-1222	0062
DX-1228	0274
DX-1229	0559
DX-1256	0392
DX-1258	0296
DX-1325	0143
DX-1346	0057
DX-1392	0005
DX-1430	0023
DX-1535	0873
DX-1662	0071
DX-1663	0064
DX-1691	0644
DX-1692	0106
DX-1753	0062
DX-1772	0372
DX-1773	0023
DX-1829	0165
DX-1834	0057
DX-1912	0023
DX-1968	OEM
DX-1969	OEM
DX-1991	0064
DX-1993	0041
DX-2060	0062
DX-2061	0165
DX-2137	1864
DX-2149	0253
DX-2150	0181
DX-2230	0133
DX-2231	0041
DX-2232	0604
DX-2236	OEM
DX-2253	0631
DX-2257	0282
DX-2272	0124
DX-2273	0023

DEVICE TYPE	REPL CODE
DX-2274	0023
DX-2275	0023
DX-2276	0790
DX-2277	0023
DX-2278	0560
DX-2279	0695
DX-2280	0049
DX-2281	0095
DX-2285	OEM
DX-2306	0052
DX2321	0087
DX2322	0143
DX2323	0036
DX2327	0133
DX-2443	0023
DX-2446	0031
DX-2447	0124
DX-2451	0137
DX-2510	OEM
DX-2511	OEM
DX-2517	0064
DX-2555	0165
DX-2556	0023
DX-2558	OEM
DX-2617	0023
DX-3975	0150
DX6873	0143
DXA08A818	OEM
DXA020401	OEM
DXA020402	OEM
DXA020403	OEM
DXA020404	OEM
DXA020405	OEM
DXA020406	OEM
DXA020407	OEM
DXA020408	OEM
DXA020409	OEM
DXA020410	OEM
DXA020411	OEM
DXA020412	OEM
DXA020413	OEM
DXA020414	OEM
DXA020415	OEM
DXA020416	OEM
DXA020417	OEM
DXA020418	OEM
DXA020419	OEM
DXA020420	OEM
DXA020601	OEM
DXA020602	OEM
DXA020603	OEM
DXA020604	OEM
DXA020605	OEM
DXA020606	OEM
DXA020607	OEM
DXA020608	OEM
DXA020609	OEM
DXA020610	OEM
DXA020611	OEM
DXA020612	OEM
DXA020613	OEM
DXA020614	OEM
DXA020615	OEM
DXA020801	OEM
DXA020802	OEM
DXA020803	OEM
DXA020804	OEM
DXA020805	OEM
DXA020806	OEM
DXA020807	OEM
DXA020808	OEM
DXA020809	OEM
DXA020810	OEM
DXA020811	OEM
DXA020812	OEM
DXA020813	OEM
DXA020814	OEM
DXA020815	OEM
DXA040802	OEM
DXA040803	OEM
DXA040804	OEM
DXA040805	OEM
DXA040806	OEM
DXA040807	OEM
DXA040808	OEM
DXA040809	OEM
DXA040810	OEM
DXA040811	OEM
DXA040812	OEM
DXA040813	OEM
DXA040814	OEM
DXA040815	OEM
DXA040816	OEM
DXA040817	OEM
DXA040818	OEM
DXA040819	OEM
DXA040820	OEM
DXA040821	OEM
DXA040822	OEM
DXA040823	OEM
DXA040824	OEM
DXA051001	OEM
DXA051002	OEM
DXA051003	OEM
DXA051004	OEM
DXA051005	OEM
DXA051006	OEM
DXA051007	OEM
DXA051008	OEM

DEVICE TYPE	REPL CODE
DXA051009	OEM
DXA051010	OEM
DXA051011	OEM
DXA051012	OEM
DXA061801	OEM
DXA061802	OEM
DXA061803	OEM
DXA061804	OEM
DXA061805	OEM
DXA061806	OEM
DXA061807	OEM
DXA061808	OEM
DXA061809	OEM
DXA061810	OEM
DXA061811	OEM
DXA061812	OEM
DXA061813	OEM
DXA061814	OEM
DXA061815	OEM
DXA081201	OEM
DXA081202	OEM
DXA081203	OEM
DXA081204	OEM
DXA081205	OEM
DXA081206	OEM
DXA081207	OEM
DXA081208	OEM
DXA081209	OEM
DXA081210	OEM
DXA081211	OEM
DXA081212	OEM
DXA081801	OEM
DXA081802	OEM
DXA081803	OEM
DXA081804	OEM
DXA081805	OEM
DXA081806	OEM
DXA081807	OEM
DXA081808	OEM
DXA081809	OEM
DXA081810	OEM
DXA081811	OEM
DXA081812	OEM
DXA081813	OEM
DXA081814	OEM
DXA081815	OEM
DXA081816	OEM
DXA081817	OEM
DXA081819	OEM
DXA081820	OEM
DXA3115-01	OEM
DXA3115-02	OEM
DXA3115-03	OEM
DXA3157-01	OEM
DXA3157-02	OEM
DXA3157-03	OEM
DXL2501A	OEM
DXL2501A-P70	OEM
DXL2502A	OEM
DXL2502A-P70	OEM
DXL2503A	OEM
DXL2503A-CR	OEM
DXL2503A-CRES	OEM
DXL3501A	OEM
DXL3501A-P100F	OEM
DXL3503A	OEM
DXL3503A-CR	OEM
DXL3503A-CRES	OEM
DXL3504A	OEM
DXL3504A-CR	OEM
DXL3504A-CRES	OEM
DXL3615A	OEM
DXL3615A-P100F	OEM
DXL3630A	OEM
DXL3630A-P100F	OEM
DY1SS131	0124
DY1SS133	0133
DYC124XS	OEM
DYDA203	1083
DYDAN201VA	3460
DYDAP201VA	0689
DYLTZ-G15	OEM
DYLTZ-R15	OEM
DYMTZ5.1-B	0582
DYMTZ5.1-C	0041
DYMTZ6.2-C	0466
DYMTZ6.8-C	OEM
DYMTZ7.5-C	0077
DYMTZ7.5C	0077
DYMTZ8.2-C	0165
DYMTZ9.1-C	0057
DYMTZ10-C	0064
DYMTZ20-D	0695
DYMTZ24-C	0489
DYSLR-34UR3F	OEM
DYSLR-34UR5F	OEM
DYSLR-40MC3F	OEM
DYSLR-40UR3F	OEM
DYSLR-40UR5F	OEM
DYSLR-54UR	OEM
DYSLR-54UR-H	OEM
DYSLR-55MC	OEM
DYSLR-55MC-H	OEM
DZ-081	0244
DZ0820	0244
DZ5.1B	OEM
DZ5.6B	OEM
DZ5.6BH	OEM
DZ6.8B	OEM

If replacement code is OEM, contact original manufacturer for replacement.

387

DEVICE TYPE	REPL CODE
DZ6.8BM	OEM
DZ9A4	0037
DZ9A5	OEM
DZ10A	0170
DZ10B	0189
DZ10BM	OEM
DZ-12	0137
DZ12	0361
DZ-12A	0137
DZ12A	0052
DZ12B	0089
DZ13BM	OEM
DZ-15A	0002
DZ15A	0681
DZ15B	0336
DZ15BH	OEM
DZ15BM	OEM
DZ16BM	OEM
DZ18A	0371
DZ18B	0420
DZ22A	0700
DZ27A	0436
DZ33A	0039
DZ39A	0032
DZ47A	0068
DZ56A	0125
DZ68A	0173
DZ82A	0327
DZ120	OEM
DZ120A	0999
DZ800	OEM
DZ805	OEM
DZ806	OEM
DZ78103C	OEM
DZB6.2	0631
DZB6.8	0025
DZB6.8C	0025
DZB7.5	0644
DZB7.5C	0644
DZB8.2	0244
DZB8.2C	0244
DZB9.1	0012
DZB9.1C	0012
DZB10	0170
DZB10C	0170
DZB11	0313
DZB11C	0313
DZB12	0137
DZB12C	0137
DZB13	0361
DZB13C	0361
DZB15	0002
DZB15C	0002
DZB16	0416
DZB16C	0416
DZB18	0490
DZB18C	0490
DZB20	0526
DZB20C	0526
DZB22	0560
DZB22C	0560
DZB24	0398
DZB24C	0398
DZB27	0436
DZB27C	0436
DZB30	0721
DZC30	0721
DZC50	0497
DZJ.6BM	OEM
DZSLP-138C-51	OEM
DZSLP-982A-50	OEM
DZV11B	OEM
E	OEM
E0011	0030
E0018	0143
E01A05	OEM
E01A05KA	OEM
E01A05KB	OEM
E01A05LC	OEM
E05	OEM
E05A01LA	OEM
E05A02	OEM
E05A02LA	OEM
E05A03	OEM
E05A03BA	OEM
E05A03CA	OEM
E05A03EA	OEM
E05A09BA	OEM
E05A09KA0123	OEM
E05A10AA	OEM
E05A15HA	OEM
E05A16GA	OEM
E05A29YA	OEM
E05A30	OEM
E05A30YA	OEM
E09-306112	0133
E-044A	0004
E044A	0211
E-065	0136
E-066	0136
E066	0211
E-067	0136
E067	0211
E-068	0136
E068	0211
E-070	0004
E070	0050
E-075L	0015
E075L	0015
E0100AD	0895
E0100FD	0340
E0100YD	1129
E0102AA	0895
E0102AB	0895
E0102AD	0895
E0102FA	0340
E0102FB	0340
E0102FD	0340
E0102YA	1129
E0102YB	1129
E0102YD	1129
E0105	0211
E0350-002	OEM
E0350-003	OEM
E0704-W	0015
E-0704W	0015
E0704W	0535
E0771-3	0012
E0771-6	0100
E0771-7	0137
E0788-C	0015
E0788C	0015
E01011BA	OEM
E02041HA	OEM
E03090-002	0287
E03155-001	0015
E03155-002	0015
E03155-091	OEM
E03450-00	OEM
E05020AA	OEM
E05203BA	OEM
E1	0015
E1A	0127
E1A3	1325
E1B	1722
E1B3	OEM
E1B5	OEM
E1B6	OEM
E1B7	OEM
E1B8	OEM
E1B9	OEM
E1C3	OEM
E1CM-0060	1044
E1D3	OEM
E1E3	OEM
E1F3	OEM
E1G3	OEM
E1H3	1627
E1K3	1627
E1M3	0071
E1N3	0071
E1P	OEM
E2	0015
E2A3	OEM
E2B3	OEM
E2C3	OEM
E2D3	OEM
E2E3	OEM
E2F3	OEM
E2G3	OEM
E2H3	1627
E2K3	2621
E2M3	2621
E2N3	2621
E-2SC536AG-SP	0532
E-2SC536E-NP	0532
E-2SC930D-NP	2195
E-2SC930E-NP	2195
E-2SC1923-O	2666
E-2SD734G	1505
E3	0015
E3A3	OEM
E3B3	OEM
E3C3	OEM
E3D3	OEM
E3E3	OEM
E3F3	OEM
E3G3	OEM
E3H3	1627
E3K3	1627
E3M3	OEM
E3N3	OEM
E4	0164
E4A3	OEM
E4B3	OEM
E4C	OEM
E4C3	OEM
E4D3	OEM
E4E3	OEM
E4F3	OEM
E4G3	OEM
E4H3	1627
E4HZ	OEM
E4K	OEM
E4K3	1627
E4M3	OEM
E4N3	OEM
E5	0015
E5A3	OEM
E5B3	OEM
E5C3	OEM
E5D3	OEM
E5E3	OEM
E5F3	OEM
E5G3	OEM
E5H3	1627
E5K3	1627
E5M3	OEM
E5N3	OEM
E5T20A12.4	0234
E5T20A14.6	0247
E5T20A16.8	1170
E5T20A18.5	2379
E5T20A21	0269
E5T20A23	0273
E5T20A27	0291
E5T20A30	0305
E5T20A33	0314
E5T20A37	0316
E5T20A43	0333
E5T20A47	0343
E5T20A51	0027
E5T20A56	0266
E5T20A62	0382
E5T20A68	0401
E5T20A75	0421
E5T20A82	0439
E5T20A87	2999
E5T20A91	0238
E5T20A100	1172
E5T20A105	1182
E5T20A110	1182
E5T20A120	1198
E5T20A130	1209
E5T20A140	1870
E5T20A150	0642
E5T20A175	1269
E5T20A200	0600
E5T50A12.4	0234
E5T50A14.6	0247
E5T50A16.8	1170
E5T50A18.5	2379
E5T50A21	0269
E5T50A23	0273
E5T50A27	0291
E5T50A30	0305
E5T50A33	0314
E5T50A37	0316
E5T50A43	0333
E5T50A47	0343
E5T50A51	0027
E5T50A56	0266
E5T50A62	0382
E5T50A68	0401
E5T50A75	0421
E5T50A82	0439
E5T50A87	2999
E5T50A91	0238
E5T50A100	1172
E5T50A105	1182
E5T50A110	1182
E5T50A120	1198
E5T50A130	1209
E5T50A140	1870
E5T50A150	0642
E5T50A175	1269
E5T50A200	0600
E6	0015
E6A3	OEM
E6B3	OEM
E6C3	OEM
E6D3	OEM
E6E3	OEM
E6F3	OEM
E6G3	OEM
E6H3	1627
E6HZS	OEM
E6K3	1627
E6M3	OEM
E6N3	OEM
E7	OEM
E7A3	OEM
E7B3	OEM
E7C3	OEM
E7D3	OEM
E7E3	6019
E7F3	OEM
E7G3	OEM
E7H3	1627
E7K3	1627
E7M3	OEM
E7N3	OEM
E8	0071
E8HZ	OEM
E9	0071
E10	0071
E10DS1	OEM
E10DS2	OEM
E10DS4	OEM
E10FS1	OEM
E10FS2	OEM
E10HZ	OEM
E10QS03	OEM
E10QS04	OEM
E10QS05	OEM
E10QS06	OEM
E10QS09	OEM
E10QS10	OEM
E11	OEM
E11FS1	OEM
E11FS2	OEM
E11FS3	OEM
E11FS4	OEM
E12	OEM
E13-000-03	0016
E13-000-04	0016
E13-001-02	0037
E13-001-03	0037
E13-001-04	0037
E13-002-03	0016
E13-003-00	0016
E13-003-01	0016
E13-004-00	0326
E13-005-02	0016
E13-006-02	0037
E13-007-00	0283
E13-008-00	0074
E13-009-00	0065
E13-0-1-01	0752
E13-010-00	0334
E13-011-00	0334
E13-012-00	0556
E13-013-03	0469
E13-013-04	0469
E13-017-01	0133
E13-020-00	0015
E13-021-01	0752
E13-021-03	0469
E13-20-00	0015
E14C350	0015
E20C30	0143
E21	0015
E25C5	0015
E30C60	0143
E30Hs	OEM
E39ED	OEM
E-41	0015
E41	0015
E49A-B380-340-30	OEM
E49A-B500-450-30	OEM
E49B30-25-30	OEM
E49B60-52-30	OEM
E49B125-110-30	OEM
E49B250-225-30	OEM
E49B380-340-30	OEM
E49B500-450-30	OEM
E50A-DB380-500-40	OEM
E50A-DB500-670-40	OEM
E50DB30-38-40	OEM
E50DB60-78-40	OEM
E50DB125-165-40	OEM
E50DB250-330-40	OEM
E50DB380-500-40	OEM
E50DB500-670-40	OEM
E50HR	OEM
E50HS	OEM
E61	OEM
E-80	OEM
E81	OEM
E84	0170
E100	4150
E100HR	OEM
E100HS	OEM
E-101	OEM
E101	2922
E-101L	OEM
E-102	5121
E102	2922
E102(ELCOM)	0015
E103	0321
E105	0136
E106(ELCOM)	0015
E108	0071
E108(ELCOM)	0071
E109	OEM
E110	OEM
E111	1147
E112	3102
E113	1147
E114	3102
E125C200	0015
E132	0004
E135	0015
E143	0015
E146	0015
E150HR	OEM
E150L	0015
E151A	0464
E151B	0464
E151C	0464
E151D	0464
E151E	0717
E151F	0717
E151H	0717
E151K	0720
E151M	0720
E151P	0674
E151S	0674
E151V	0674
E-158	0211
E158	0004
E161A	0464
E161B	0464
E161C	0464
E161D	0464
E161E	0717
E174	OEM
E175	OEM
E176	OEM
E177	OEM
E181	0004
E181A	0004
E181B	0004
E181C	0004
E181D	0004
E-185B121712	0086
E185B121712	0275
E201	3350
E-202	OEM
E202	0087
E202(ELCOM)	0087
E203	3350
E210	0079
E211	1382
E212	0079
E213	0037
E214B	0211
E230	3350
E231	3350
E232	1147
E241	0004
E241A	0004
E241A(SCR)	0464
E241B	0004
E241B(SCR)	0464
E241C	0464
E241D	0464
E241E	0717
E241F	0717
E241H	0717
E241K	0720
E241M	0720
E241P	0674
E241S	0674
E241V	0674
E241Z	0674
E241ZB	0674
E241ZD	0674
E262	0137
E270	OEM
E271	OEM
E-272	OEM
E295ZZ01	0143
E300	0321
E300(ELCOM)	0916
E300D2	OEM
E300D7	OEM
E300F2	OEM
E300F7	OEM
E300L	0015
E-301	OEM
E301D2	OEM
E301D7	OEM
E301F2	OEM
E301F7	OEM
E302(ELCOM)	0242
E302D2	OEM
E302D7	OEM
E302F2	OEM
E302F7	OEM
E303D2	OEM
E303D7	OEM
E303F2	OEM
E303F7	OEM
E304	3350
E304(ELCOM)	0535
E304D2	OEM
E304D7	OEM
E304F2	OEM
E304F7	OEM
E305	3350
E305D2	OEM
E305D7	OEM
E305F2	OEM
E305F7	OEM
E306(ELCOM)	0959
E306D2	OEM
E306D7	OEM
E306F2	OEM
E306F7	OEM
E308	0811
E308(ELCOM)	0811
E309	OEM
E310	OEM
E311	OEM
E312	OEM
E-352	OEM
E413	OEM
E415	OEM
E-452	OEM
E-452-2	OEM
E500	OEM
E500L	0015
E-501	OEM
E501	OEM
E502	OEM
E503	OEM
E504	OEM
E505	OEM
E506	OEM
E507	OEM
E-562	OEM
E602	OEM
E603	OEM
E605	OEM
E607	OEM
E610	OEM
E650L	0015
E656	0133
E660	0196
E700	OEM
E-701	OEM
E701	OEM
E702	OEM
E703	OEM
E705	OEM
E707	OEM
E710	OEM
E715	OEM
E722	OEM
E744B	OEM
E750(ELCOM)	0015
E752(ELCOM)	0015
E756(ELCOM)	0015
E758(ELCOM)	0071
E760(ELCOM)	0071
E814-0	OEM
E814-1	OEM
E814-2	OEM
E814-3	OEM
E814-4	OEM
E814-6	OEM
E814-8	OEM
E815-0	OEM
E815-1	OEM
E815-2	OEM
E815-3	OEM
E815-4	OEM
E815-6	OEM
E815-8	OEM
E842	0144
E843	0144
E844	0144
E1000	OEM
E1010	0015
E1011	0015
E1018N	0015
E1020	OEM
E1020F	OEM
E1031RT	0143
E1031RXT	0143
E1042	0287
E1100	OEM
E1121R	0133
E1124	0015
E1138R	0133
E1143RD	0087
E1145R	0102
E1145RED	0102
E1145RJH	0102
E1146J	0015
E1146R	0015
E1153RB	0015
E1156RD	0015
E1157RNA	0015
E1158ZA	0298
E1174R	1293
E1176	0196
E1176R	1141
E1184	OEM
E1200	OEM
E1221R	0133
E1229R	0133
E1237RF	0023
E1256R	0133
E1266R	0344
E1270R	0023
E1286R	0133
E1293Z	0010
E1294Z	0010
E1300	OEM
E1303Z	0091
E1304R	0071
E1308R	0023
E1314R	6451
E1315R	0087
E1322Z	0466
E1324R	0133
E1332R	0124
E1336R	0344
E1339R	0023
E1340R	0344
E1410	0015
E1411	0015
E1412	0015
E1412R	0023
E1413	0015
E1413R	0023
E1415	0015
E1428R	0023
E1436ZB	6924
E1440	0015
E1442R	0023
E1466Z	0166
E1490R	0282
E1500	OEM
E1500-1	OEM
E1500F	OEM
E1510	OEM
E1510F	OEM
E1512L	5082
E1516R	0023
E1518R	0023
E1520	OEM
E1520F	OEM
E1533R	0023
E1534R	0023
E1577P	OEM
E1598R	0133
E1600	OEM
E1614L	OEM
E1616R	0282
E1618R	0023
E1634ZXU	0466
E1639Z	0057
E1645Z	0137
E1650Z	0181
E1660Z	0041
E1670Z	0372
E1672Z	0166
E1686ZXU	OEM
E1704R	0559
E1705R	0344
E1712A	OEM
E1714A	OEM
E1716A	OEM
E1717A	OEM
E1717R	0559
E1718A	OEM
E1719A	OEM
E1720A	OEM
E1720R	0071
E1722A	OEM
E1724A	OEM
E1725RM	0282
E1726A	OEM
E1750Z	0298
E1756ZB	0057
E1756ZC	0057
E1775R	0133
E1779R	0282
E1786R	0023
E1789R	0023
E1791R	0023
E1794R	0023
E1810ZA	0195
E1810ZB	0195
E1821ZA	0062
E1821ZB	0062
E1821ZC	0062
E1821ZD	0077
E1823Z	0077
E1823ZA	0077
E1823ZB	0077
E1828ZA	0053
E1828ZB	0999
E1829R	0559
E1852	0137
E1860Z	OEM
E2000	OEM
E2004	OEM
E2070	2982
E2106B40C5000-3300	OEM
E2112B80C5000-3300	OEM
E2220B125C5000-3300	OEM
E2240B250C5000-3300	OEM
E2412	0279
E2427	0595
E-2428	5389
E2428	0595
E-2429	5389
E2429	0595
E2430	0016
E2431	0016
E2434	0144
E-2435	5390
E2435	0144
E-2436	2514
E2436	0016
E2438	0050
E2439	0050
E2440	0050
E2441	0086
E2444	0016
E2445	0164
E2447	0208
E2448	0004
E2449	0086
E2450	0050
E2451	0136
E2452	0016
E2453	0004
E2454	0016
E2455	0016
E2456	OEM
E2457	OEM
E2459	0016
E2460	0142
E2461	0016
E-2462	0050
E2462	0050
E2464	2839
E2465	0004
E2466	0208
E2467	0004
E2474	0050
E2475	0050
E2476	0004
E2477	0050
E2478	0050
E2479	0050
E2480	0004
E2481	0004
E2482	0004
E2484	0123
E2486	0631
E2495	2507
E2496	0042
E2497	0016
E2498	0126
E2499	0016
E2500	OEM
E2502	OEM

If replacement code is OEM, contact original manufacturer for replacement.

DEVICE TYPE	REPL CODE
E2506B40C5000-3300	OEM
E2506N	OEM
E2512B80C5000-3300	OEM
E2512N	OEM
E2525	OEM
E2620B125C5000-3300	OEM
E2620N	OEM
E2640B250C5000-3300	OEM
E2640N	OEM
E3006	0015
E3274A	OEM
E3274B	OEM
E3389	OEM
E3469	OEM
E3509A	OEM
E3509A-H	OEM
E3509H	OEM
E3509L	OEM
E3513	OEM
E3513H	OEM
E3513L	OEM
E3514	OEM
E3518	OEM
E3521	OEM
E3521H	OEM
E3521L	OEM
E3522	OEM
E3523	OEM
E3524	OEM
E3526	OEM
E3753	OEM
E3774	OEM
E3776	OEM
E3803	OEM
E3806B40C5000-3300	OEM
E3812B80C5000-3300	OEM
E3820B125C5000-3300	OEM
E3824	OEM
E3824A	OEM
E3825	OEM
E3832	OEM
E3840B250C5000-3300	OEM
E3902	OEM
E4676B	0015
E5100	OEM
E5102	OEM
E5103	OEM
E5104	OEM
E5106	OEM
E5108	OEM
E7441	0015
E7460	OEM
E7462	OEM
E7464	OEM
E7466	OEM
E7468	OEM
E8327B	OEM
E8343	OEM
E9625	0224
E10116	0015
E10157	0015
E10171	0015
E10172	0015
E10416A	OEM
E11401	OEM
E17336	2855
E21135	0123
E21430	0143
E21431	0631
E23036	0924
E24100	0015
E24101	0087
E24103	0016
E24104	0004
E24105	0208
E24106	0004
E24107	0222
E25056	0924
E570022-01	0178
EA000-13000	0215
EA000-17200	1688
EA000-22600	0704
EA000-36400	OEM
EA000-44600	0051
EA000-75500	OEM
EA000-95300	OEM
EA0002	0050
EA0007	0050
EA0009	0004
EA001-02200	0051
EA001-02700	1887
EA001-02703	1887
EA001-06300	OEM
EA001-06700	OEM
EA001-07100	OEM
EA001-07200	OEM
EA001-08700	OEM
EA001-21400	OEM
EA005	0015
EA006-41400	OEM
EA006-41500	OEM
EA0013	0144
EA0015	0015
EA0016	0015
EA0031	0015
EA0053	0050
EA0081	0086
EA0083	OEM
EA0085	OEM

DEVICE TYPE	REPL CODE
EA0086	0126
EA0087	0126
EA0088	0150
EA0090	0086
EA0091	0144
EA0092	0016
EA0093	0144
EA0094	0144
EA0095	0144
EA01-07R	0002
EA010	0015
EA020	0015
EA030	0015
EA040	0015
EA050	0015
EA060	0015
EA080	0071
EA0X12	3687
EA1-380	0161
EA1SY11	0050
EA15X1	0016
EA15X2	0004
EA15X3	0004
EA15X4	0004
EA15X5	0050
EA15X6	0435
EA15X7	0004
EA15X8	0004
EA15X9	0016
EA15X10	0160
EA15X11	0050
EA15X11CL	0050
EA15X12	0160
EA15X13	0050
EA15X14	1009
EA15X15	0160
EA15X15CL	0160
EA15X18	0016
EA15X18CL	0155
EA15X19	0004
EA15X19CL	0004
EA15X19P	0004
EA15X20	0016
EA15X22	0016
EA15X23	0004
EA15X24	0016
EA15X25	0004
EA15X26	0160
EA15X27	0050
EA15X28	0004
EA15X29	0050
EA15X30	0050
EA15X31	0016
EA15X33	0160
EA15X35	0160
EA15X36	0004
EA15X37	0016
EA15X38	0160
EA15X40	0050
EA15X41	0050
EA15X43	0050
EA15X44	0016
EA15X44P	0144
EA15X45	0016
EA15X45CL	0144
EA15X45P	0144
EA15X48	0144
EA15X49	0144
EA15X50	0144
EA15X51	0144
EA15X52	0016
EA15X53	0160
EA15X54	0144
EA15X55	0144
EA15X55P	0144
EA15X56	0016
EA15X56CL	0042
EA15X57	0086
EA15X58	0016
EA15X59	0016
EA15X60	0079
EA15X63	0016
EA15X63CL	0155
EA15X66	0050
EA15X67	0004
EA15X67CL	0004
EA15X68	0016
EA15X69	0150
EA15X70	0150
EA15X71	0150
EA15X72	0016
EA15X73	0016
EA15X75	0016
EA15X75CL	0155
EA15X76	0016
EA15X76CL	0155
EA15X77	0016
EA15X77CL	0155
EA15X83	0016
EA15X84	0016
EA15X84CL	0155
EA15X85	0016
EA15X85CL	0155
EA15X86	0016
EA15X88	0160
EA15X90	0079
EA15X91	0016
EA15X94	0144
EA15X94CL	0144

DEVICE TYPE	REPL CODE
EA15X94P	0144
EA15X96	0016
EA15X101	0016
EA15X102	0086
EA15X103	0016
EA15X103CL	0155
EA15X111	0016
EA15X112	0016
EA15X113	0144
EA15X121	0178
EA15X121CL	0178
EA15X122	0124
EA15X123	0130
EA15X124	1671
EA15X126	0446
EA15X130	0224
EA15X130A	0144
EA15X131	0144
EA15X131A	0144
EA15X132	0144
EA15X132L	0144
EA15X133	0136
EA15X133P	0050
EA15X134	0127
EA15X134L	0144
EA15X135	0127
EA15X135L	0144
EA15X136	0016
EA15X137	0076
EA15X139	0222
EA15X140	0136
EA15X141	0136
EA15X142	0016
EA15X143	0016
EA15X144	0086
EA15X152	0111
EA15X153	0016
EA15X154	0222
EA15X157	0076
EA15X160	0555
EA15X161	0111
EA15X162	0016
EA15X163	0016
EA15X164	0004
EA15X165	0321
EA15X167	0016
EA15X168	0086
EA15X169	0321
EA15X171	0133
EA15X172	0133
EA15X173	0160
EA15X180	0076
EA15X185	0006
EA15X189	0592
EA15X190	0151
EA15X192	1202
EA15X193	3126
EA15X194	0006
EA15X203	0004
EA15X207	0004
EA15X212	0004
EA15X213	0111
EA15X233	0006
EA15X237	0016
EA15X238	0321
EA15X239	0127
EA15X240	0592
EA15X241	1212
EA15X242	0148
EA15X243	0455
EA15X244	1779
EA15X245	0111
EA15X246	1471
EA15X247	0396
EA15X248	0555
EA15X249	0155
EA15X250	0018
EA15X251	0151
EA15X256	0155
EA15X257	0164
EA15X258	0111
EA15X259	0111
EA15X264	0111
EA15X266	0396
EA15X267	0155
EA15X268	0527
EA15X269	0558
EA15X270	0520
EA15X272	0016
EA15X273	0786
EA15X274	0590
EA15X288	0111
EA15X325	1211
EA15X326	1056
EA15X327	0042
EA15X328	0919
EA15X329	3490
EA15X330	0016
EA15X331	0016
EA15X332	2243
EA15X333	0042
EA15X334	0919
EA15X335	0076
EA15X336	0127
EA15X349	0590
EA15X350	0076
EA15X351	1136
EA15X352	1212
EA15X353	0376

DEVICE TYPE	REPL CODE
EA15X354	0376
EA15X355	0111
EA15X356	1854
EA15X359	2882
EA15X360	0191
EA15X361	0111
EA15X362	1581
EA15X363	0930
EA15X364	0364
EA15X365	0364
EA15X367	0364
EA15X370	0016
EA15X371	0079
EA15X372	2684
EA15X373	0155
EA15X374	0076
EA15X376	1060
EA15X378	0155
EA15X379	0224
EA15X380	1935
EA15X381	0833
EA15X383	0781
EA15X385	0006
EA15X386	1212
EA15X393	0127
EA15X394	3126
EA15X395	0006
EA15X396	0527
EA15X397	0018
EA15X400	1270
EA15X401	1270
EA15X402	0212
EA15X404	0076
EA15X405	0212
EA15X408	0728
EA15X412	1390
EA15X413	2798
EA15X414	0930
EA15X415	0544
EA15X421	0006
EA15X437	0224
EA15X441	0284
EA15X446	3017
EA15X456	0018
EA15X461	1060
EA15X483	0224
EA15X488	1505
EA15X524	0111
EA15X525	0042
EA15X534	5817
EA15X625	1376
EA15X945	0076
EA15X947	5055
EA15X1014	0079
EA15X1015	OEM
EA15X1061	OEM
EA15X1117	0079
EA15X1150	OEM
EA15X1422	0127
EA15X1710	0042
EA15X2015	0144
EA15X2024	0127
EA15X2025	0127
EA15X2110	0079
EA15X2112	0079
EA15X2522	0018
EA15X3118	0919
EA15X4064	0127
EA15X4152	0144
EA15X4335	0284
EA15X4531	0590
EA15X4532	0016
EA15X4631	0338
EA15X4662	OEM
EA15X4810	0284
EA15X4812	0284
EA15X5939	0079
EA15X6840	0004
EA15X7112	0016
EA15X7113	0144
EA15X7114	0144
EA15X7115	0016
EA15X7117	0127
EA15X7118	0016
EA15X7119	0016
EA15X7120	0016
EA15X7121	0042
EA15X7125	0127
EA15X7136	0224
EA15X7137	0037
EA15X7140	0144
EA15X7141	0127
EA15X7173	0008
EA15X7174	0008
EA15X7175	0016
EA15X7176	0016
EA15X7177	0144
EA15X7178	0008
EA15X7179	0008
EA15X7215	0127
EA15X7228	0144
EA15X7231	0127
EA15X7232	0016
EA15X7233	0224
EA15X7234	0224
EA15X7235	0224
EA15X7236	0224
EA15X7242	0224
EA15X7243	0144

DEVICE TYPE	REPL CODE
EA15X7244	0224
EA15X7245	0111
EA15X7262	0079
EA15X7263	0127
EA15X7264	0127
EA15X7514	0016
EA15X7517	0016
EA15X7519	0590
EA15X7583	0111
EA15X7586	0016
EA15X7587	0144
EA15X7588	0079
EA15X7589	0079
EA15X7590	0016
EA15X7592	0527
EA15X7635	0086
EA15X7638	0016
EA15X7639	0527
EA15X7643	0016
EA15X7722	0144
EA15X7732	0037
EA15X7737	0037
EA15X8118	0919
EA15X8119	0042
EA15X8122	0378
EA15X8124	0042
EA15X8126	0486
EA15X8130	0919
EA15X8180	OEM
EA15X8442	0004
EA15X8443	0208
EA15X8444	0004
EA15X8502	0016
EA15X8511	0016
EA15X8514	0018
EA15X8515	0016
EA-15X8517	0086
EA15X8517	0018
EA15X8518	0079
EA15X8519	0079
EA15X8520	0079
EA15X8521	0320
EA15X8522	0431
EA15X8523	0079
EA15X8524	0431
EA15X8525	0079
EA15X8529	0016
EA15X8576	0079
EA15X8589	0144
EA15X8601	0079
EA15X8602	0079
EA15X8605	0455
EA15X8608	0144
EA15X8609	0144
EA15X8610	0144
EA16X1	0143
EA16X2	0015
EA16X4	0789
EA16X5	0143
EA16X6	0789
EA16X8	0015
EA16X9	0143
EA16X11	0143
EA16X13	0015
EA16X16	0789
EA16X19	0030
EA16X20	0133
EA16X21	0015
EA16X22	0143
EA16X27	0143
EA16X28	0030
EA16X29	0137
EA16X30	0015
EA16X31	0030
EA16X33	0015
EA16X34	0015
EA16X35	0574
EA16X38	0398
EA16X39	0133
EA16X48	0143
EA16X49	0133
EA16X54	0080
EA16X55	0015
EA16X59	0133
EA16X60	0133
EA16X61	0133
EA16X62	0012
EA16X68	0139
EA16X69	0139
EA16X71	0015
EA16X73	0120
EA16X75	0133
EA16X77	0137
EA16X80	0631
EA16X81	0361
EA16X82	0012
EA16X84	0133
EA16X88	0644
EA16X89	0036
EA16X91	0124
EA16X92	0023
EA16X94	0133
EA16X95	0124
EA16X97	0143
EA16X101	0133
EA16X105	0133
EA16X106	0030
EA16X107	0139
EA16X110	0133

DEVICE TYPE	REPL CODE
EA16X116	0120
EA16X117	0623
EA16X118	0157
EA16X122	0133
EA16X123	0298
EA16X124	0002
EA16X125	0644
EA16X126	0041
EA16X127	0030
EA16X134	0133
EA16X135	0124
EA16X136	0041
EA16X140	0143
EA16X144	0140
EA16X146	0133
EA16X147	0623
EA16X148	0143
EA16X149	0535
EA16X150	0064
EA16X152	0133
EA16X154	0253
EA16X157	0170
EA16X162	0137
EA16X166	0549
EA16X171	0133
EA16X177	0030
EA16X192	0005
EA16X193	1266
EA16X203	1767
EA16X402	1075
EA16X421	0466
EA16X422	OEM
EA16X424	0064
EA16X426	0165
EA16X427	0005
EA16X438	0165
EA16X441	0143
EA16X442	0133
EA16X443	0313
EA16X445	0064
EA16X446	0133
EA16X447	0253
EA16X451	0005
EA16X455	0064
EA16X456	OEM
EA16X462	0140
EA16X463	0005
EA16X464	0015
EA16X474	0681
EA16X475	0253
EA16X476	0106
EA16X477	0133
EA16X483	0062
EA16X494	OEM
EA16X504	0123
EA16X505	0064
EA16X506	0080
EA16X939	0124
EA16X1049	5627
EA16X4532	0079
EA33C8390	2052
EA33X8333	4588
EA33X8341	OEM
EA33X8348	OEM
EA33X8351	2849
EA33X8352	2487
EA33X8356	2546
EA33X8363	2590
EA33X8364	1601
EA33X8367	0574
EA33X8368	4486
EA33X8369	OEM
EA33X8371	4463
EA33X8372	1469
EA33X8373	1832
EA33X8374	2550
EA33X8375	0514
EA33X8382	OEM
EA33X8383	4588
EA33X8384	3286
EA33X8385	1164
EA33X8386	1164
EA33X8388	1704
EA33X8389	1044
EA33X8392	1532
EA33X8393	OEM
EA33X8394	1532
EA33X8395	3980
EA33X8396	1044
EA33X8399	0141
EA33X8450	2279
EA33X8455	OEM
EA33X8456	OEM
EA33X8465	2702
EA33X8467	OEM
EA33X8468	0967
EA33X8469	0026
EA33X8470	OEM
EA33X8471	OEM
EA33X8475	OEM
EA33X8476	OEM
EA33X8477	OEM
EA33X8478	OEM
EA33X8479	0308
EA33X8487	OEM
EA33X8488	OEM
EA33X8489	OEM
EA33X8492	OEM
EA33X8493	OEM

DEVICE TYPE	REPL CODE
EA33X8497	5240
EA33X8500	0905
EA33X8501	3515
EA33X8506	1899
EA33X8508	3980
EA33X8509	1532
EA33X8511	0514
EA33X8520	OEM
EA33X8521	4746
EA33X8522	5247
EA33X8523	2801
EA33X8524	3753
EA33X8532	5103
EA33X8535	0701
EA33X8536	OEM
EA33X8537	5103
EA33X8543	OEM
EA33X8544	OEM
EA33X8545	0751
EA33X8548	3034
EA33X8559	0358
EA33X8562	OEM
EA33X8564	5103
EA33X8569	5113
EA33X8570	OEM
EA33X8571	OEM
EA33X8572	2288
EA33X8583	5260
EA33X8584	2702
EA33X8585	0428
EA33X8593	OEM
EA33X8600	2702
EA33X8601	OEM
EA33X8605	1519
EA33X8607	1251
EA33X8609	OEM
EA33X8626	OEM
EA33X8642	OEM
EA33X8675	OEM
EA33X8705	1251
EA33X8706	2572
EA33X8707	4645
EA33X8717	3764
EA33X8956	OEM
EA33X9054	OEM
EA33X9213	OEM
EA41X556	4548
EA50X12	3687
EA57X1	0015
EA57X3	0015
EA57X4	0080
EA57X8	0015
EA57X10	0015
EA57X11	0015
EA57X14	0023
EA75X1	0015
EA85X8476	OEM
EA93X8542	OEM
EA100	0071
EA330E	OEM
EA330M	OEM
EA330N	OEM
EA330P	OEM
EA330PB	OEM
EA330PD	OEM
EA330PE	OEM
EA390A	OEM
EA390B	OEM
EA390D	OEM
EA390M	OEM
EA390N	OEM
EA390P	OEM
EA390PB	OEM
EA390PD	OEM
EA390PM	OEM
EA397A	OEM
EA397B	OEM
EA397D	OEM
EA397M	OEM
EA397N	OEM
EA397P	OEM
EA397PB	OEM
EA397PD	OEM
EA397PM	OEM
EA398A	OEM
EA398B	OEM
EA398D	OEM
EA398M	OEM
EA398N	OEM
EA398P	OEM
EA398PB	OEM
EA398PD	OEM
EA398PM	OEM
EA403	0392
EA430E	OEM
EA430M	OEM
EA430N	OEM
EA430P	OEM
EA430PB	OEM
EA430PD	OEM
EA430PM	OEM
EA437A	OEM
EA437B	OEM
EA437D	OEM
EA437M	OEM
EA437N	OEM
EA437P	OEM
EA437PB	OEM
EA437PD	OEM

If replacement code is OEM, contact original manufacturer for replacement.

389

DEVICE TYPE	REPL CODE
EA437PM	OEM
EA540L	OEM
EA540LA	OEM
EA540LB	OEM
EA540LC	OEM
EA540LD	OEM
EA596N	OEM
EA596P	OEM
EA596PA	OEM
EA596PB	OEM
EA596PC	OEM
EA596PD	OEM
EA596T	OEM
EA640L	OEM
EA640LQ	OEM
EA640P	OEM
EA640PB	OEM
EA640PD	OEM
EA640PM	OEM
EA640PN	OEM
EA641L	OEM
EA641LA	OEM
EA641LB	OEM
EA641LC	OEM
EA641LD	OEM
EA641LE	OEM
EA641LM	OEM
EA696L	OEM
EA696PE	OEM
EA696PM	OEM
EA696PN	OEM
EA696PS	OEM
EA696PT	OEM
EA740L	OEM
EA740PD	OEM
EA740PE	OEM
EA740PM	OEM
EA740PN	OEM
EA1072	0015
EA1080	0016
EA1081	0004
EA1082	0160
EA1085	OEM
EA1123	0143
EA1128	0016
EA1129	0016
EA1135	0016
EA1145	0016
EA1318	0137
EA1337	0050
EA1338	0050
EA1339	0050
EA1340	0050
EA1341	0160
EA1342	0050
EA1343	0144
EA1344	0016
EA1345	0016
EA1346	0004
EA1385	0030
EA1405	0133
EA1406	0016
EA1407	0016
EA1408	0016
EA1448	0015
EA1451	0016
EA1452	0016
EA1499	0016
EA1549	0086
EA1562	0144
EA1563	0144
EA1564	0016
EA1578	0016
EA1581	0016
EA1628	0016
EA1629	0016
EA1630	0016
EA1638	0016
EA1661	0133
EA1672	0015
EA1684	0086
EA1695	0016
EA1696	0016
EA1697	0016
EA1698	0086
EA1700	0160
EA1703	0016
EA1716	0016
EA1718	0016
EA1733	0144
EA1735	0016
EA1740	0103
EA1760	3679
EA1778	0079
EA1793	0144
EA1872	0016
EA1873	0086
EA2114L-15PC	OEM
EA2114L-20PC	OEM
EA2114L-25PC	OEM
EA2114L-30PC	OEM
EA2114LPC	OEM
EA2131	0127
EA2132	0127
EA2133	0136
EA2134	0004
EA2135	0004
EA2136	0164
EA2137	0123

DEVICE TYPE	REPL CODE
EA2138	0030
EA2140	0015
EA2176	0004
EA2271	0016
EA2429	0111
EA2488	0555
EA2489	0016
EA2490	0016
EA2491	0136
EA2493	0151
EA2494	0151
EA2495	0151
EA2496	0127
EA2497	0136
EA2498	0136
EA2499	0015
EA2500	0137
EA2501	0015
EA2502	0143
EA2503	0030
EA2600	0144
EA2601	0144
EA2602	0144
EA2603	0144
EA2604	0144
EA2605	0144
EA2606	0123
EA2607	0133
EA2608	0157
EA2738	0111
EA2739	0016
EA2740	0532
EA2741	0015
EA2770	0016
EA2770(N)	0079
EA2771	0111
EA2812	0127
EA3127	0143
EA3149	0016
EA3211	0111
EA3278	0321
EA3280	OEM
EA3281	OEM
EA3282	0574
EA3406	0144
EA3447	0133
EA3674	0555
EA3713	1136
EA3714	0006
EA3715	0919
EA3716	0042
EA3717	0005
EA3718	0143
EA3719	0137
EA3763	0111
EA3827	0015
EA3866	0012
EA3989	0015
EA3990	0218
EA4025	1212
EA4055	0555
EA4085	0555
EA4104L	OEM
EA4104P	OEM
EA4104PA	OEM
EA4104PB	OEM
EA4104PD	OEM
EA4104PE	OEM
EA4104PM	OEM
EA4104PN	OEM
EA4112	0016
EA4156N	OEM
EA4156P	OEM
EA4156PA	OEM
EA4156PB	OEM
EA4156PD	OEM
EA4156PE	OEM
EA4157L	OEM
EA4157LB	OEM
EA4157LD	OEM
EA4157LM	OEM
EA4157PN	OEM
EA4157PS	OEM
EA4158L	OEM
EA4158LB	OEM
EA4158LD	OEM
EA4158LM	OEM
EA4158LN	OEM
EA4158LP	OEM
EA4158PN	OEM
EA4158PS	OEM
EA5316	OEM
EA5711	0015
EA-6801	OEM
EA6801	1226
EA7316A-1	2279
EA-7316B	2279
EA7316B	2279
EA7316D	OEM
EA7317B	2279
EA7317C	OEM
EA7317D	OEM
EA8308A-5DC	OEM
EA8308A-5PC	OEM
EA8308AC	OEM
EA8308ADC	OEM
EA8308AL	OEM
EA8308AP	OEM
EA8308APC	OEM

DEVICE TYPE	REPL CODE
EA8316ADC	OEM
EA8316ADM	OEM
EA8316E-5DC	OEM
EA8316E-5PC	OEM
EA8316EDC	OEM
EA8316EDL	OEM
EA8316EPC	OEM
EA8332A1DC	OEM
EA8332A1PC	OEM
EA8332ADC	OEM
EA8332APC	OEM
EA8332B1DC	OEM
EA8332B1PC	OEM
EA8332BDC	OEM
EA8332BPC	OEM
EA8364DC	OEM
EA8364PC	OEM
EAA00-02700	0781
EAA00-11300	1203
EAA00-12800	1203
EAA00-13400	0076
EAA00-13900	2253
EAA00-16800	1203
EAA00-17400	1203
EAA00-17500	0076
EAA00-19700	OEM
EAA00-19800	OEM
EAA00-19900	OEM
EAB00-04000	0520
EAB00-06500	0597
EAB00-06600	0148
EAB00-07100	0148
EAB00-08300	0676
EAB00-08600	0597
EAB00-08900	0429
EAB00-09500	1338
EAB00-09900	0429
EAB00-Q6600	0148
EAC00-00400	0133
EAC00-00600	0023
EAC00-05400	0023
EAC00-09300	3460
EAC00-09500	3559
EAC00-10000	OEM
EAC00-13100	0015
EAC00-13200	OEM
EACT0-00300	0124
EACT0-00400	0133
EACT0-08100	2520
EAD00-08200	0052
EAD00-08400	0053
EAD00-08700	0436
EAD00-09200	0466
EAD00-10100	0140
EAD00-10400	0140
EAD00-15000	0062
EAD00-15100	0002
EAD00-16700	0631
EAD00-17200	0993
EAD00-20200	0466
EAD00-20700	0314
EAD00-20800	0814
EAD00-21700	0170
EAD00-25300	0436
EADT0-16700	0631
EADT0-25300	0436
EAE00-12600	1404
EAE00-14700	1034
EAF00-01600	0272
EAI-380	0161
E-AN7110E	5136
EAO00-36400	OEM
EAO00-39500	OEM
EAO00-75500	OEM
EAO00-95300	OEM
EAO01-00600	1887
EAO01-21400	OEM
EAO01-23300	OEM
EAO06-30000	OEM
EAO06-30100	OEM
EAO06-56300	OEM
EAO06-64300	OEM
EAQ00-02000	0357
EAQ00-05000	1253
EAQ00-07500	1197
EAQ00-07514	1197
EAQ00-09600	OEM
EAQ00-09800	OEM
EAQ00-1200	1585
EAQ00-11100	0967
EAQ00-11300	3478
EAQ00-12100	1519
EAQ00-12200	1585
EAQ00-12300	1623
EAQ00-12400	1652
EAQ00-12700	0243
EAQ00-12900	0973
EAQ00-12914	0973
EAQ00-13000	0209
EAQ00-13100	0260
EAQ00-15200	1329
EAQ00-17200	1688
EAQ00-17600	0088
EAQ00-18700	0422
EAQ00-19000	0937
EAQ00-19300	0708
EAQ00-19400	0453
EAQ00-20300	0887
EAQ00-21500	0153

DEVICE TYPE	REPL CODE
EAQ00-22100	0458
EAQ00-22600	0704
EAQ00-22614	0704
EAQ00-22900	0209
EAQ00-23600	1733
EAQ00-24000	1821
EAQ00-24700	1644
EAQ00-30000	0503
EAQ00-30200	0506
EAQ00-30300	1125
EAQ00-75500	OEM
EAS00-00700	0619
EAS00-05800	0176
EAS00-06100	0356
EAS00-09000	0308
EAS00-09700	1827
EAS00-12014	OEM
EAS00-12800	OEM
EAS00-12900	0624
EAS00-13500	0330
EAS00-16800	OEM
EAS00-17800	OEM
EAT00-04200	OEM
EAT00-04300	OEM
EAT00-04500	OEM
EAT00-08900	OEM
EAT00-09000	OEM
EAT00-09100	1586
EAW00-00700	0321
EAX5X249	0155
EAY00-01100	OEM
EAY00-01300	OEM
EAY00-02600	OEM
EB0001	0004
EB0003	0004
EB1(ELCOM)	0276
EB2(ELCOM)	0293
EB3(ELCOM)	0276
EB4(ELCOM)	0287
EB6(ELCOM)	0293
EB7(ELCOM)	0299
EB9(ELCOM)	0276
EB10(ELCOM)	0287
EB11(ELCOM)	0293
EB12(ELCOM)	0299
EB13(ELCOM)	0250
EB383	OEM
EBR11-01	4176
EBR3432S	OEM
EBR5504S	OEM
EC080	0087
EC-0677	OEM
EC-0678	OEM
EC-0726	OEM
EC-0751	OEM
EC-0776	OEM
EC-0777	OEM
EC-0856	OEM
EC-0877	OEM
EC-0884	OEM
EC-0885	OEM
EC-0973	OEM
EC60L	0201
EC68A21P	OEM
EC72L	0201
EC100	0071
EC103A	0895
EC103B	0058
EC103C	OEM
EC103D	0403
EC103Y	1129
EC106A1	0442
EC106A2	0442
EC106B1	0934
EC106B2	0934
EC106D1	0095
EC106D2	0095
EC106F1	1250
EC106F2	1250
EC106M1	5626
EC106M2	3575
EC106Y1	1386
EC106Y2	1386
EC107A1	3801
EC107A2	3801
EC107B1	3575
EC107B2	3575
EC107D1	0095
EC107D2	0095
EC107F1	0174
EC107F2	0174
EC107M1	OEM
EC107M2	0174
EC107Y1	4384
EC107Y2	4384
EC120	OEM
EC350E	OEM
EC350M	OEM
EC350N	OEM
EC350P	OEM
EC350PA	OEM
EC350PB	OEM
EC350PD	OEM
EC350PM	OEM
EC354A	OEM
EC354B	OEM
EC354C	OEM
EC354D	OEM
EC354E	OEM

DEVICE TYPE	REPL CODE
EC354M	OEM
EC355A	OEM
EC355B	OEM
EC355C	OEM
EC355D	OEM
EC355E	OEM
EC355M	OEM
EC358E	OEM
EC358M	OEM
EC358N	OEM
EC358P	OEM
EC358PB	OEM
EC364A	OEM
EC364B	OEM
EC364C	OEM
EC364D	OEM
EC364E	OEM
EC364M	OEM
EC364N	OEM
EC365A	OEM
EC365B	OEM
EC365C	OEM
EC365D	OEM
EC365E	OEM
EC365M	OEM
EC365N	OEM
EC376E	OEM
EC376M	OEM
EC376N	OEM
EC376P	OEM
EC376PB	OEM
EC376PD	OEM
EC377E	OEM
EC377M	OEM
EC377N	OEM
EC377P	OEM
EC377PB	OEM
EC377PD	OEM
EC378E	OEM
EC378M	OEM
EC378N	OEM
EC378P	OEM
EC378PB	OEM
EC378PD	OEM
EC380A	OEM
EC380AX500	OEM
EC380AX555	OEM
EC380B	OEM
EC380BX500	OEM
EC380BX555	OEM
EC380CX500	OEM
EC380CX555	OEM
EC380D	OEM
EC380DX500	OEM
EC380DX555	OEM
EC380M	OEM
EC380MX500	OEM
EC380MX555	OEM
EC380N	OEM
EC380NX500	OEM
EC380NX555	OEM
EC380P	OEM
EC380PB	OEM
EC380PBX500	OEM
EC380PBX555	OEM
EC380PD	OEM
EC380PM	OEM
EC380PX500	OEM
EC380PX555	OEM
EC384A	OEM
EC384B	OEM
EC384C	OEM
EC384D	OEM
EC384E	OEM
EC384M	OEM
EC384N	OEM
EC384S	OEM
EC385A	OEM
EC385C	OEM
EC385D	OEM
EC385E	OEM
EC385M	OEM
EC385N	OEM
EC385S	OEM
EC387E	OEM
EC387M	OEM
EC387N	OEM
EC387P	OEM
EC387PB	OEM
EC388E	OEM
EC388M	OEM
EC388N	OEM
EC388P	OEM
EC388PB	OEM
EC390AX500	OEM
EC390AX550	OEM
EC390AX555	OEM
EC390BX500	OEM
EC390BX550	OEM
EC390CX500	OEM
EC390CX550	OEM
EC390DX500	OEM
EC390DX550	OEM
EC390DX555	OEM
EC390EX550	OEM
EC390MX500	OEM
EC390MX555	OEM
EC390NX500	OEM
EC390NX555	OEM

DEVICE TYPE	REPL CODE
EC390PBX555	OEM
EC390PX555	OEM
EC391L	OEM
EC391P	OEM
EC391PB	OEM
EC391PD	OEM
EC391PM	OEM
EC391PN	OEM
EC392A	OEM
EC392B	OEM
EC392C	OEM
EC392D	OEM
EC392E	OEM
EC392M	OEM
EC393A	OEM
EC393B	OEM
EC393C	OEM
EC393D	OEM
EC393E	OEM
EC393M	OEM
EC394A	OEM
EC394B	OEM
EC394C	OEM
EC394D	OEM
EC394E	OEM
EC394M	OEM
EC395A	OEM
EC395B	OEM
EC395C	OEM
EC395D	OEM
EC395E	OEM
EC395M	OEM
EC397E	OEM
EC397M	OEM
EC397N	OEM
EC397P	OEM
EC397PB	OEM
EC398E	OEM
EC398M	OEM
EC398N	OEM
EC398P	OEM
EC398PB	OEM
EC401	0015
EC402	0015
EC430AX500	OEM
EC430AX550	OEM
EC430AX555	OEM
EC430BX500	OEM
EC430BX550	OEM
EC430BX555	OEM
EC430CX500	OEM
EC430CX550	OEM
EC430DX500	OEM
EC430DX550	OEM
EC430DX555	OEM
EC430EX550	OEM
EC430MX500	OEM
EC430MX555	OEM
EC430NX500	OEM
EC430NX555	OEM
EC430PBX555	OEM
EC430PX555	OEM
EC431L	OEM
EC431P	OEM
EC431PB	OEM
EC431PD	OEM
EC431PM	OEM
EC431PN	OEM
EC434A	OEM
EC434B	OEM
EC434C	OEM
EC434D	OEM
EC434E	OEM
EC434M	OEM
EC434S	OEM
EC435A	OEM
EC435B	OEM
EC435C	OEM
EC435D	OEM
EC435E	OEM
EC435M	OEM
EC435S	OEM
EC436E	OEM
EC436M	OEM
EC436N	OEM
EC436P	OEM
EC436PB	OEM
EC437E	OEM
EC437M	OEM
EC437N	OEM
EC437P	OEM
EC437PB	OEM
EC438E	OEM
EC438M	OEM
EC438N	OEM
EC438P	OEM
EC438PB	OEM
EC441L	OEM
EC441P	OEM
EC441PB	OEM
EC441PD	OEM
EC441PM	OEM
EC441PN	OEM
EC444A	OEM
EC444B	OEM
EC444C	OEM
EC444D	OEM
EC444E	OEM
EC444M	OEM

DEVICE TYPE	REPL CODE
EC444S	OEM
EC445A	OEM
EC445B	OEM
EC445C	OEM
EC445D	OEM
EC445E	OEM
EC445M	OEM
EC445S	OEM
EC447E	OEM
EC447M	OEM
EC447N	OEM
EC447P	OEM
EC447PB	OEM
EC448E	OEM
EC448M	OEM
EC448N	OEM
EC448P	OEM
EC448PB	OEM
EC449PE	OEM
EC449PM	OEM
EC449PN	OEM
EC449PS	OEM
EC450E	OEM
EC450M	OEM
EC450N	OEM
EC450P	OEM
EC450PA	OEM
EC450PB	OEM
EC450PD	OEM
EC451E1	OEM
EC451M1	OEM
EC451N1	OEM
EC451PB1	OEM
EC451PD1	OEM
EC451PM1	OEM
EC451PN1	OEM
EC457E	OEM
EC457M	OEM
EC457N	OEM
EC457P	OEM
EC457PB	OEM
EC457PD	OEM
EC458E	OEM
EC458M	OEM
EC458N	OEM
EC458P	OEM
EC458PB	OEM
EC458PD	OEM
EC476E	OEM
EC476M	OEM
EC476N	OEM
EC476P	OEM
EC476PB	OEM
EC476PD	OEM
EC477E	OEM
EC477M	OEM
EC477N	OEM
EC477P	OEM
EC477PB	OEM
EC477PD	OEM
EC478E	OEM
EC478M	OEM
EC478N	OEM
EC478P	OEM
EC478PB	OEM
EC478PD	OEM
EC590BX555	OEM
EC601L	OEM
EC601P	OEM
EC601PB	OEM
EC601PD	OEM
EC601PM	OEM
EC601PN	OEM
EC602L	OEM
EC602LB	OEM
EC602LD	OEM
EC602LM	OEM
EC602PN	OEM
EC612L	OEM
EC612PE	OEM
EC612PM	OEM
EC612PN	OEM
EC612PS	OEM
EC612PT	OEM
EC613L	OEM
EC613PE	OEM
EC613PM	OEM
EC613PN	OEM
EC613PS	OEM
EC613PT	OEM
EC648E	OEM
EC648M	OEM
EC648N	OEM
EC648P	OEM
EC648PB	OEM
EC702L	OEM
EC702LB	OEM
EC702LD	OEM
EC702LM	OEM
EC702PN	OEM
EC712L	OEM
EC712PA	OEM
EC712PB	OEM
EC712PD	OEM
EC712PN	OEM
EC713L	OEM
EC713PA	OEM
EC713PB	OEM
EC713PD	OEM

If replacement code is OEM, contact original manufacturer for replacement.

DEVICE TYPE	REPL CODE
EC713PM	OEM
EC713PN	OEM
EC-829	OEM
EC-877	OEM
EC-877-JPN	OEM
EC-884	OEM
EC-885	OEM
EC-936	OEM
EC961	0861
EC-973	OEM
EC973	OEM
EC4101-1M	OEM
EC4101-1N	OEM
EC4101-1P	OEM
EC4101-1PB	OEM
EC4105-1A	OEM
EC4105-1B	OEM
EC4105-1C	OEM
EC4105-1D	OEM
EC4105-1E	OEM
EC4131-1M	OEM
EC4131-1N	OEM
EC4131-PB	OEM
EC4135-1A	OEM
EC4135-1B	OEM
EC4135-1C	OEM
EC4135-1D	OEM
EC4135-1E	OEM
EC4158L	OEM
EC4158LB	OEM
EC4158LD	OEM
EC4158LM	OEM
EC4158LN	OEM
EC4158LR	OEM
EC4158PN	OEM
EC-A041	OEM
EC-A042	OEM
EC-A043	OEM
EC-A051	OEM
EC-A056	OEM
EC-A063	1586
EC-A078	OEM
EC-A104	OEM
EC-A104J	OEM
EC-A137	OEM
ECC-01262	1035
ECC-01263	0081
ECC-01264	0141
ECC-01265	0557
ECC-01266	2067
ECC-01267	1812
ECCG5220AK	OEM
ECG1V010	1681
ECG1V014	1997
ECG1V015	1304
ECG1V017	2309
ECG1V020	2763
ECG1V025	4297
ECG1V030	5638
ECG1V035	2907
ECG1V040	4199
ECG1V050	4395
ECG1V060	4158
ECG1V075	4834
ECG1V095	5066
ECG1V115	4072
ECG1V130	1364
ECG1V150	0246
ECG1V250	1322
ECG1V275	1648
ECG1V300	4394
ECG2V010	1684
ECG2V014	1998
ECG2V015	1309
ECG2V017	2310
ECG2V020	2769
ECG2V025	3044
ECG2V030	3046
ECG2V035	2913
ECG2V040	3049
ECG2V050	3056
ECG2V060	3061
ECG2V075	3075
ECG2V095	3087
ECG2V115	3094
ECG2V130	0832
ECG2V150	1982
ECG2V250	1324
ECG2V275	1650
ECG2V300	2023
ECG2V420	3226
ECG2V480	1093
ECG10	2824
ECG11	1492
ECG12	3954
ECG13	0014
ECG14	4971
ECG15	2208
ECG16	0577
ECG17	2464
ECG18	2452
ECG19	0355
ECG20	0009
ECG21	4043
ECG22	3563
ECG23	1795
ECG24	3882
ECG25	4468
ECG26	1260

DEVICE TYPE	REPL CODE
ECG27	4037
ECG28	3955
ECG29	4280
ECG30	4279
ECG31	1553
ECG32	1514
ECG33	0044
ECG34	3585
ECG35	4966
ECG36	0194
ECG36MP	5294
ECG37	3082
ECG37MCP	4398
ECG38	0787
ECG39	4402
ECG40	2896
ECG41	4967
ECG42	2395
ECG43	4968
ECG44	2919
ECG45	4969
ECG46	2770
ECG47	2833
ECG48	3749
ECG49	0818
ECG50	3294
ECG51	2985
ECG52	4976
ECG53	3009
ECG54	1157
ECG54MP	5502
ECG55	0713
ECG55MCP	3740
ECG56	2058
ECG57	0625
ECG58	3196
ECG59	3601
ECG60	3656
ECG60MP	5587
ECG61	4081
ECG61MCP	2000
ECG61MP	5599
ECG62	2820
ECG63	2817
ECG64	2978
ECG65	1332
ECG66	4970
ECG67	1456
ECG68	3561
ECG68MCP	4778
ECG69	2293
ECG70	3449
ECG71	3470
ECG72	0933
ECG73	2637
ECG74	2846
ECG74C00	2100
ECG74C02	2102
ECG74C04	2930
ECG74C08	2106
ECG74C10	2107
ECG74C14	3002
ECG74C20	2110
ECG74C30	3100
ECG74C32	3105
ECG74C42	2130
ECG74C48	2135
ECG74C73	2148
ECG74C74	2149
ECG74C76	2150
ECG74C85	2157
ECG74C90	2160
ECG74C93	2163
ECG74C95	3367
ECG74C107	3782
ECG74C151	3944
ECG74C154	3957
ECG74C157	3972
ECG74C161	3984
ECG74C164	3999
ECG74C173	4026
ECG74C174	4030
ECG74C175	4034
ECG74C192	4056
ECG74C193	4059
ECG74C221	3018
ECG74C240	2928
ECG74C244	4166
ECG74C373	4388
ECG74C374	4392
ECG74C901	4527
ECG74C902	4528
ECG74C903	4529
ECG74C904	4530
ECG74C922	5496
ECG74C923	5498
ECG74C925	4540
ECG74H00	0677
ECG74H01	5241
ECG74H04	1896
ECG74H05	3221
ECG74H08	5258
ECG74H10	0680
ECG74H11	2382
ECG74H20	3670
ECG74H21	4772
ECG74H22	4516
ECG74H30	5284
ECG74H40	0554

DEVICE TYPE	REPL CODE
ECG74H50	1781
ECG74H51	1933
ECG74H52	2009
ECG74H53	2090
ECG74H54	2158
ECG74H55	3129
ECG74H60	5312
ECG74H61	2638
ECG74H62	2705
ECG74H71	3233
ECG74H72	3281
ECG74H73	2444
ECG74H74	2472
ECG74H76	5208
ECG74H78	5320
ECG74H86	5680
ECG74H87	2557
ECG74H101	5424
ECG74H102	5426
ECG74H103	2941
ECG74H106	5159
ECG74H108	0180
ECG74H183	4329
ECG74HC00	6468
ECG74HC02	1443
ECG74HC04	1446
ECG74HC08	4225
ECG74HC10	6789
ECG74HC11	5432
ECG74HC14	6493
ECG74HC32	6516
ECG74HC86	5438
ECG74HC109	6484
ECG74HC123	6754
ECG74HC125	6755
ECG74HC126	6756
ECG74HC132	6757
ECG74HC138	6758
ECG74HC139	6759
ECG74HC151	6760
ECG74HC153	6761
ECG74HC154	6762
ECG74HC161	5315
ECG74HC163	6763
ECG74HC164	6764
ECG74HC165	6765
ECG74HC173	6766
ECG74HC174	6767
ECG74HC175	6768
ECG74HC240	1968
ECG74HC244	6771
ECG74HC257	6772
ECG74HC259	6773
ECG74HC273	6774
ECG74HC299	6777
ECG74HC373	6781
ECG74HC374	6782
ECG74HC377	6783
ECG74HC390	6784
ECG74HC393	6785
ECG74HC573	6794
ECG74HC574	6795
ECG74HC4020	5512
ECG74HC4040	5514
ECG74HC4053	5516
ECG74HC4060	5518
ECG74HC4067	5519
ECG74HC40105	5918
ECG74HCT00	3264
ECG74HCT04	3265
ECG74HCT08	3268
ECG74HCT14	3269
ECG74HCT32	3274
ECG74HCT138	5957
ECG74HCT161	5961
ECG74HCT163	5963
ECG74HCT174	5967
ECG74HCT240	5972
ECG74HCT244	5969
ECG74HCT273	5974
ECG74HCT373	5984
ECG74HCT374	5992
ECG74HCT573	6009
ECG74HCT574	6010
ECG74L93	0651
ECG74LS00	1519
ECG74LS01	1537
ECG74LS02	1550
ECG74LS03	1569
ECG74LS04	1585
ECG74LS05	1598
ECG74LS08	1623
ECG74LS09	1632
ECG74LS10	1652
ECG74LS11	1657
ECG74LS12	1669
ECG74LS13	1678
ECG74LS14	1688
ECG74LS15	1697
ECG74LS20	0035
ECG74LS21	1752
ECG74LS22	1764
ECG74LS26	1372
ECG74LS27	0183
ECG74LS28	0467
ECG74LS30	0822
ECG74LS32	0088
ECG74LS33	1821
ECG74LS37	1719

DEVICE TYPE	REPL CODE
ECG74LS38	1828
ECG74LS40	0135
ECG74LS42	1830
ECG74LS47	1834
ECG74LS48	1838
ECG74LS49	1839
ECG74LS51	1027
ECG74LS54	1846
ECG74LS55	0452
ECG74LS73	1856
ECG74LS74A	0243
ECG74LS75	1859
ECG74LS76A	2166
ECG74LS77	1861
ECG74LS78	1862
ECG74LS83A	2204
ECG74LS85	0426
ECG74LS86	0288
ECG74LS90	1871
ECG74LS91	1874
ECG74LS92	1876
ECG74LS93	1877
ECG74LS95	2887
ECG74LS95B	0766
ECG74LS107	1592
ECG74LS109A	1895
ECG74LS112A	6979
ECG74LS113	2241
ECG74LS114	2286
ECG74LS122	1610
ECG74LS123	0973
ECG74LS125A	0075
ECG74LS126	2850
ECG74LS132	1615
ECG74LS133	3366
ECG74LS136	1618
ECG74LS138	0422
ECG74LS139	0153
ECG74LS145	1554
ECG74LS147	4330
ECG74LS148	3856
ECG74LS151	1636
ECG74LS153	0953
ECG74LS155	0209
ECG74LS156	1644
ECG74LS157	1153
ECG74LS158	1646
ECG74LS160A	0831
ECG74LS161A	0852
ECG74LS162A	0874
ECG74LS163A	0887
ECG74LS164	4274
ECG74LS164A	OEM
ECG74LS165	4289
ECG74LS166	4301
ECG74LS168A	0961
ECG74LS169A	0980
ECG74LS170	2605
ECG74LS173	5125
ECG74LS174	0260
ECG74LS175	1662
ECG74LS181	1668
ECG74LS190	1676
ECG74LS191	1677
ECG74LS192	1679
ECG74LS193	1682
ECG74LS194A	1294
ECG74LS195A	1305
ECG74LS196	2807
ECG74LS197	2450
ECG74LS221	1230
ECG74LS240	0447
ECG74LS241	1715
ECG74LS242	1717
ECG74LS243	0900
ECG74LS244	0453
ECG74LS245	0458
ECG74LS246A	OEM
ECG74LS247	1721
ECG74LS248	1723
ECG74LS249	1724
ECG74LS251	1726
ECG74LS253	1728
ECG74LS257	1733
ECG74LS258	1735
ECG74LS259	3175
ECG74LS260	5859
ECG74LS266	0587
ECG74LS273	0888
ECG74LS279	3259
ECG74LS280	1762
ECG74LS283	5861
ECG74LS290	4352
ECG74LS293	0082
ECG74LS295A	2212
ECG74LS298	3337
ECG74LS299	4353
ECG74LS348	0660
ECG74LS352	0756
ECG74LS353	0768
ECG74LS363	5869
ECG74LS364	5870
ECG74LS365A	0937
ECG74LS366A	0950
ECG74LS367	0971
ECG74LS368	0985
ECG74LS373	0704
ECG74LS374	0708
ECG74LS377	1112

DEVICE TYPE	REPL CODE
ECG74LS378	1125
ECG74LS379	1143
ECG74LS386	1221
ECG74LS390	1278
ECG74LS393	0813
ECG74LS395A	1320
ECG74LS398	1373
ECG74LS399	1388
ECG74LS490	2199
ECG74LS540	2519
ECG74LS541	2525
ECG74LS624	3112
ECG74LS625	3120
ECG74LS626	3125
ECG74LS627	3133
ECG74LS629	3146
ECG74LS640	0664
ECG74LS641	0685
ECG74LS642	0714
ECG74LS643	2045
ECG74LS645	0770
ECG74LS670	1122
ECG74S00	0699
ECG74S02	2223
ECG74S03	2203
ECG74S04	2248
ECG74S05	2305
ECG74S08	2547
ECG74S09	2642
ECG74S10	2426
ECG74S11	2428
ECG74S15	2432
ECG74S20	1011
ECG74S22	2442
ECG74S30	3681
ECG74S40	2456
ECG74S51	4241
ECG74S64	2476
ECG74S65	2477
ECG74S74	2483
ECG74S86	2489
ECG74S112	1607
ECG74S113	1613
ECG74S114	1619
ECG74S124	2113
ECG74S133	1808
ECG74S134	1816
ECG74S138	2125
ECG74S140	1875
ECG74S151	1944
ECG74S153	2138
ECG74S157	1685
ECG74S158	2141
ECG74S174	2119
ECG74S175	2128
ECG74S181	2151
ECG74S188	3139
ECG74S194	1920
ECG74S251	2184
ECG74S258	2191
ECG74S287	2209
ECG74S288	2161
ECG74S387	1907
ECG74S454	3137
ECG74S472	2304
ECG74S473	3257
ECG74S474	2306
ECG74S475	2308
ECG74S478	2881
ECG74S479	2835
ECG74S570	2372
ECG74S571	2373
ECG74S572	2374
ECG74S573	2376
ECG75	2936
ECG76	2059
ECG76MP	5819
ECG77	2194
ECG78	4972
ECG79	3747
ECG80	2575
ECG80C95	3148
ECG80C96	3150
ECG80C97	3151
ECG81	2034
ECG82	2449
ECG83	4930
ECG84	4974
ECG85	0284
ECG86	2526
ECG87	0861
ECG87MP	5896
ECG88	3459
ECG88MCP	4420
ECG88MP	5903
ECG89	0055
ECG90	0525
ECG91	0643
ECG92	2261
ECG93	3537
ECG93L08	2114
ECG93L16	2660
ECG93MCP	3271
ECG94	0270
ECG95	4187
ECG96	3969
ECG96L02	1459
ECG96LS02	2906
ECG96S02	4228

DEVICE TYPE	REPL CODE
ECG97	1980
ECG98	2602
ECG99	3956
ECG100	0279
ECG101	0595
ECG102	0211
ECG102A	0004
ECG103	0038
ECG103A	0208
ECG104	0085
ECG104MP	3004
ECG105	0435
ECG106	0150
ECG107	0127
ECG108	0144
ECG109	0143
ECG110	1106
ECG110A	1106
ECG110MP	0123
ECG111	0911
ECG112	0911
ECG113	0196
ECG113A	0196
ECG114	0479
ECG115	1073
ECG116	0015
ECG116(4)	OEM
ECG117	0229
ECG117A	4549
ECG118	0769
ECG119	1293
ECG120	0469
ECG121	0160
ECG121MP	0265
ECG122	0240
ECG123	0198
ECG123A	0016
ECG123AP	0079
ECG124	0142
ECG125	0071
ECG125(2)	OEM
ECG126	0136
ECG126A	0628
ECG127	0969
ECG128	0086
ECG128P	4945
ECG129	0126
ECG129MCP	4100
ECG129P	1587
ECG130	0103
ECG130MP	1506
ECG131	0222
ECG131MP	0816
ECG132	3667
ECG133	3443
ECG134	0188
ECG134A	0188
ECG135	0162
ECG135A	0162
ECG136	0157
ECG136A	0157
ECG137	0631
ECG137A	0631
ECG138	0644
ECG138A	0644
ECG139	0012
ECG139A	0012
ECG140	0170
ECG140A	0170
ECG141	0789
ECG141A	0789
ECG142	0137
ECG142A	0137
ECG143	0361
ECG143A	0361
ECG144	0100
ECG144A	0100
ECG145	0002
ECG145A	0002
ECG146	0436
ECG146A	0436
ECG147	0039
ECG147A	0039
ECG148	1823
ECG148A	1823
ECG149	0778
ECG149A	0778
ECG150	0327
ECG150A	0327
ECG151	0149
ECG151A	0149
ECG152	0042
ECG152MP	4998
ECG153	0919
ECG153MCP	4156
ECG154	0233
ECG155	2736
ECG156	0087
ECG157	0275
ECG158	0164
ECG159	0037
ECG159MCP	1371
ECG160	0050
ECG161	0007
ECG162	0074
ECG163	0637
ECG163A	0637
ECG164	0003
ECG165	0065

DEVICE TYPE	REPL CODE
ECG166	0276
ECG167	0287
ECG168	0293
ECG169	0299
ECG170	0250
ECG171	0283
ECG172	0396
ECG172A	0396
ECG173BP	0290
ECG174	0918
ECG175	0178
ECG176	0841
ECG177	0133
ECG178MP	0907
ECG179	0599
ECG179MP	5439
ECG180	1671
ECG180MCP	3093
ECG181	0130
ECG181MP	5377
ECG182	0556
ECG183	1190
ECG184	0161
ECG184MP	5494
ECG185	0455
ECG185MCP	4525
ECG186	0555
ECG186A	0219
ECG187	1257
ECG187A	1045
ECG188	0546
ECG189	0378
ECG190	0264
ECG191	0334
ECG192	0590
ECG192-1	0218
ECG192A	0218
ECG193	0786
ECG193-1	1233
ECG193A	1233
ECG194	0855
ECG195	0693
ECG195A	0693
ECG196	0419
ECG197	0848
ECG198	0168
ECG199	0111
ECG210	0561
ECG211	1357
ECG213	0432
ECG214	3700
ECG215	3702
ECG216	1518
ECG217	3704
ECG218	0899
ECG219	0486
ECG219MCP	5401
ECG220	0843
ECG221	0349
ECG222	0212
ECG223	0103
ECG224	0626
ECG225	3249
ECG226	1004
ECG226MP	1851
ECG227	3708
ECG228	1698
ECG228A	1698
ECG229	0224
ECG230	0239
ECG231	0061
ECG232	3477
ECG233	0326
ECG234	0688
ECG235	0930
ECG236	0830
ECG237	1401
ECG238	0309
ECG239	2320
ECG240	3712
ECG241	2969
ECG242	3136
ECG243	2411
ECG244	2262
ECG245	3339
ECG246	3340
ECG247	2422
ECG248	2415
ECG249	1384
ECG250	2429
ECG251	3483
ECG252	3484
ECG253	0553
ECG254	2869
ECG255	3718
ECG256	3719
ECG257	3343
ECG258	3486
ECG259	3487
ECG260	3488
ECG261	1203
ECG262	0597
ECG263	2220
ECG264	2222
ECG265	2243
ECG266	3490
ECG267	3491
ECG268	3492
ECG269	3493

If replacement code is OEM, contact original manufacturer for replacement. 391

DEVICE TYPE	REPL CODE
ECG270	0134
ECG271	0073
ECG272	3495
ECG273	3496
ECG274	3336
ECG275	3497
ECG276	1642
ECG277	2200
ECG278	0414
ECG279	2321
ECG279A	2321
ECG280	0177
ECG280MP	2127
ECG281	2002
ECG281MCP	5669
ECG282	0617
ECG283	0359
ECG284	0538
ECG284MP	2355
ECG285	1588
ECG285MCP	6002
ECG286	1021
ECG287	0710
ECG288	0338
ECG289	0155
ECG289A	0155
ECG289AMP	1215
ECG289MP	2740
ECG290	0006
ECG290A	0006
ECG290AMCP	3644
ECG291	0236
ECG292	0676
ECG292MCP	3224
ECG293	0018
ECG293MP	3020
ECG294	0527
ECG295	1581
ECG296	2186
ECG297	0320
ECG297MP	3217
ECG298	0431
ECG299	2039
ECG300	2035
ECG300MP	3342
ECG302	1165
ECG306	1935
ECG307	1421
ECG308	1702
ECG308P	4534
ECG309K	1911
ECG310	2313
ECG310P	4526
ECG311	0488
ECG312	0321
ECG313	0470
ECG314	1814
ECG315	1967
ECG316	0259
ECG317	2918
ECG318	2296
ECG319	0008
ECG319P	0008
ECG320	1963
ECG320F	2857
ECG321	1740
ECG322	1973
ECG323	0886
ECG324	1471
ECG325	1189
ECG326	2959
ECG327	2465
ECG328	0615
ECG329	2675
ECG330	3517
ECG330W	5867
ECG331	0477
ECG331MP	4121
ECG332	1359
ECG332MCP	3892
ECG333	2808
ECG334	3519
ECG335	3521
ECG336	3523
ECG337	3524
ECG338	3525
ECG338F	5110
ECG339	3526
ECG340	2699
ECG341	3528
ECG342	2693
ECG343	2694
ECG344	2504
ECG345	3012
ECG346	2030
ECG347	3532
ECG348	3534
ECG349	2156
ECG350	1224
ECG350F	5209
ECG351	1966
ECG352	3165
ECG353	3536
ECG354	3538
ECG355	3539
ECG356	3540
ECG357	3542
ECG358	1024
ECG358A	4391

DEVICE TYPE	REPL CODE
ECG358B	4947
ECG358C	5406
ECG359	3543
ECG360	2485
ECG361	2028
ECG362	3516
ECG363	2080
ECG364	1410
ECG365	2082
ECG366	3545
ECG367	2841
ECG368	3547
ECG369	2085
ECG370	3759
ECG370A	3759
ECG371	OEM
ECG372	OEM
ECG373	0558
ECG374	0520
ECG375	0388
ECG376	1077
ECG377	0060
ECG378	1298
ECG379	0723
ECG380	2911
ECG380MP	2708
ECG381	3527
ECG382	1376
ECG383	0472
ECG384	0424
ECG385	1955
ECG386	1841
ECG387	2416
ECG387MP	3158
ECG388	2398
ECG389	0223
ECG390	3052
ECG391	0853
ECG392	3557
ECG393	3558
ECG394	2589
ECG395	3562
ECG396	0187
ECG397	0434
ECG398	1638
ECG399	0261
ECG425A	OEM
ECG425B	OEM
ECG425C	OEM
ECG425D	OEM
ECG425E	OEM
ECG425F	OEM
ECG425G	OEM
ECG425H	OEM
ECG425J	OEM
ECG425K	OEM
ECG425L	OEM
ECG435K28	OEM
ECG435K30	OEM
ECG435K42	OEM
ECG435K64	OEM
ECG451	1382
ECG452	2861
ECG453	3043
ECG454	2439
ECG455	0367
ECG456	3577
ECG457	2922
ECG458	1747
ECG459	3104
ECG460	1133
ECG461	2917
ECG462	3583
ECG463	3787
ECG464	0838
ECG465	0977
ECG466	1147
ECG467	3102
ECG468	3790
ECG469	3791
ECG470	3586
ECG471	2523
ECG472	3387
ECG473	3293
ECG474	3587
ECG475	3289
ECG476	3290
ECG477	3090
ECG478	3591
ECG479	1344
ECG480	3593
ECG481	3595
ECG482	3596
ECG483	3597
ECG484	3598
ECG485	3599
ECG486	0684
ECG487	3794
ECG488	2677
ECG489	2436
ECG500	0190
ECG500A	0190
ECG501	0128
ECG501A	0128
ECG501B	0128
ECG502	0201
ECG503	0286
ECG504	0374
ECG505	0752

DEVICE TYPE	REPL CODE
ECG506	0102
ECG507	0914
ECG508	1296
ECG508/R-3A3	1296
ECG509	2072
ECG509/R-3AT2	2072
ECG510	2073
ECG510/R-3DB3	2073
ECG511	1440
ECG511/R-2AV2	1440
ECG512	2074
ECG512/R-6DW4	2074
ECG513	1313
ECG514	3604
ECG514/R-3DS3	3604
ECG515	1208
ECG516	3803
ECG517	0405
ECG518	1780
ECG519	0124
ECG520	2956
ECG521	3805
ECG522	1493
ECG523	1061
ECG523/3306	1061
ECG524	3607
ECG524V13	0824
ECG524V15	3381
ECG524V25	1326
ECG524V27	4780
ECG524V30	4785
ECG524V42	3806
ECG524V48	0776
ECG525	0344
ECG526	1696
ECG526A	1696
ECG527	3807
ECG527A	5625
ECG528	2097
ECG529	2524
ECG530	3610
ECG531	2777
ECG532	0405
ECG533	1700
ECG534	2954
ECG535	2957
ECG536	1986
ECG536A	1986
ECG537	1188
ECG538	2956
ECG539	1048
ECG540	3810
ECG541	3613
ECG542	3614
ECG543	3811
ECG544	3615
ECG545	3812
ECG546	3616
ECG547	3813
ECG548	3617
ECG549	3814
ECG550	3815
ECG551	0182
ECG552	0023
ECG553	0163
ECG554	3814
ECG555	2496
ECG556	3621
ECG557	3622
ECG558	0017
ECG559	3818
ECG560	3324
ECG561	3819
ECG562	3822
ECG563	3824
ECG564	3826
ECG565	3624
ECG568	2647
ECG568A	6052
ECG570	3829
ECG576	1356
ECG577	3833
ECG578	3834
ECG579	3559
ECG580	0031
ECG581	1137
ECG582	3835
ECG583	3837
ECG584	0335
ECG585	0730
ECG586	2520
ECG587	1082
ECG588	0541
ECG590	3163
ECG591	3840
ECG592	3841
ECG593	3703
ECG594	3842
ECG595	0901
ECG596	0897
ECG597	1119
ECG598	1654
ECG599	3507
ECG600	1914
ECG601	0139
ECG604	3638
ECG605	0120
ECG605A	0339
ECG606	3639

DEVICE TYPE	REPL CODE
ECG607	3407
ECG610	0549
ECG611	0005
ECG612	0715
ECG613	0623
ECG614	0030
ECG615	3417
ECG615A	1319
ECG616	1023
ECG617	3642
ECG618	3643
ECG700	3674
ECG701	3675
ECG702	2774
ECG703	0627
ECG703A	5849
ECG704	2600
ECG705	2147
ECG705A	2147
ECG706	2549
ECG707	0748
ECG708	0659
ECG709	0673
ECG710	0823
ECG711	2689
ECG712	0167
ECG713	0661
ECG714	0348
ECG715	0350
ECG716	3677
ECG717	3679
ECG718	0649
ECG719	1929
ECG720	0438
ECG721	2264
ECG722	0696
ECG723	1335
ECG724	0817
ECG725	0687
ECG726	2593
ECG727	2507
ECG728	2527
ECG729	0324
ECG730	2716
ECG731	2438
ECG732	2535
ECG733	2535
ECG734	1748
ECG735	2979
ECG736	1748
ECG737	1434
ECG738	0850
ECG739	0746
ECG740	0375
ECG740A	0375
ECG741	3689
ECG742	3690
ECG743	1385
ECG744	1411
ECG745	2902
ECG746	0780
ECG747	1797
ECG748	0784
ECG748A	0784
ECG749	0391
ECG750	3189
ECG752	0512
ECG753	3731
ECG754	0718
ECG755	2016
ECG756	1178
ECG757	1178
ECG758	3875
ECG759	1661
ECG760	2089
ECG761	1865
ECG762	OEM
ECG763	2266
ECG764	3879
ECG765	3879
ECG766	1888
ECG766A	1888
ECG767	0618
ECG768	3884
ECG769	OEM
ECG770	2878
ECG771	OEM
ECG772	1969
ECG772A	1969
ECG773	1674
ECG774	OEM
ECG775	3886
ECG776	3887
ECG777	OEM
ECG778	0356
ECG778A	0356
ECG778S	1689
ECG778SM	5433
ECG779	0368
ECG779-1	0368
ECG779A	0368
ECG780	0360
ECG781	2720
ECG782	0373
ECG783	0797
ECG784	2674
ECG785	2681
ECG786	2688
ECG787	2242

DEVICE TYPE	REPL CODE
ECG788	2728
ECG789	1832
ECG790	0345
ECG791	1327
ECG792	2153
ECG793	2032
ECG794	3346
ECG795	3166
ECG796	1969
ECG797	0516
ECG798	1742
ECG799	1601
ECG800	2947
ECG801	0514
ECG802	3715
ECG803	3717
ECG804	2535
ECG805	3376
ECG806	3388
ECG807	3720
ECG808	2584
ECG809	2663
ECG810	2460
ECG810A	2460
ECG811	OEM
ECG812	3724
ECG813	3898
ECG814	2977
ECG814A	2977
ECG815	0842
ECG816	1070
ECG817	1902
ECG818	2480
ECG819	1867
ECG820	2790
ECG821	2804
ECG822	2785
ECG823	3034
ECG824	3050
ECG825	3070
ECG826	3905
ECG828	3057
ECG829	1888
ECG830	1318
ECG831	3908
ECG832	3733
ECG832SM	5943
ECG833	1534
ECG834	0176
ECG834SM	2715
ECG835	3363
ECG836	2473
ECG837	3914
ECG838	3915
ECG839	3917
ECG840	2131
ECG841	3735
ECG842	3919
ECG843	2481
ECG844	3920
ECG845	3921
ECG846	1508
ECG847	3922
ECG848	3924
ECG849	3739
ECG850	3926
ECG851	3741
ECG852	2011
ECG853	3742
ECG854	3929
ECG855	0808
ECG856	3744
ECG857M	3627
ECG857SM	6209
ECG858M	3695
ECG858SM	4044
ECG859	3357
ECG859SM	4073
ECG860	3746
ECG861	3932
ECG862	3027
ECG863	3933
ECG864	0301
ECG865	3934
ECG866	3937
ECG867	3938
ECG868	3940
ECG869	2866
ECG870	2154
ECG871	3360
ECG872	3942
ECG873	2095
ECG874	3945
ECG875	1096
ECG876	3033
ECG877	3948
ECG878	1415
ECG879	3280
ECG880	3951
ECG887M	3152
ECG888M	3885
ECG889M	3288
ECG900	2662
ECG901	2664
ECG902	2721
ECG903	2515
ECG904	1843
ECG905	2673
ECG906	2676

DEVICE TYPE	REPL CODE
ECG907	2685
ECG908	2680
ECG909	1291
ECG909D	1695
ECG910	1786
ECG910D	1789
ECG911	1879
ECG911D	1886
ECG912	1686
ECG913	3757
ECG914	2701
ECG915	1545
ECG916	2722
ECG917	2696
ECG918	2540
ECG918M	2545
ECG918SM	2543
ECG919	2552
ECG919D	2548
ECG920	3967
ECG921	3641
ECG922	1804
ECG922M	2093
ECG922SM	4106
ECG923	1183
ECG923D	0026
ECG924	2207
ECG924M	2495
ECG925	2863
ECG926	3748
ECG927	1113
ECG927D	1110
ECG927SM	4209
ECG928	1667
ECG928M	0765
ECG928S	3202
ECG928SM	2854
ECG929	2724
ECG930	2755
ECG931	1905
ECG932	2836
ECG933	3359
ECG934	3761
ECG935	2710
ECG936	3762
ECG937	3576
ECG937M	5901
ECG938	0890
ECG938M	2231
ECG939	3766
ECG940	1908
ECG941	0406
ECG941D	1964
ECG941M	0308
ECG941S	6365
ECG941SM	1965
ECG942	3000
ECG943	3767
ECG943M	0624
ECG943SM	3089
ECG944	3768
ECG944M	3400
ECG945	3976
ECG946	3618
ECG947	2352
ECG947D	2342
ECG948	2796
ECG948SM	2789
ECG949	2530
ECG950	1817
ECG951	3361
ECG952	3769
ECG953	3771
ECG954	3772
ECG955M	0967
ECG955MC	0580
ECG955S	3899
ECG955SM	2744
ECG956	2541
ECG957	2709
ECG958	2244
ECG959	3774
ECG960	0619
ECG961	1275
ECG962	0917
ECG963	2624
ECG964	1187
ECG965	2764
ECG966	0330
ECG967	1827
ECG968	1311
ECG969	3777
ECG970	2811
ECG971	3531
ECG972	2224
ECG973	0413
ECG973D	3751
ECG974	0011
ECG975	1290
ECG975SM	2339
ECG976	2267
ECG977	1288
ECG978	3254
ECG978C	2842
ECG978SM	2583
ECG979	3986
ECG980	3779
ECG981	0083
ECG982	2803

DEVICE TYPE	REPL CODE
ECG983	3391
ECG984	3239
ECG985	3780
ECG986	3060
ECG987	0620
ECG987SM	3172
ECG988	2285
ECG989	3347
ECG990	1482
ECG991	3550
ECG992	2232
ECG993	3783
ECG994	3773
ECG994M	3775
ECG995	2302
ECG995M	4471
ECG996	3784
ECG997	2995
ECG998	3996
ECG999	OEM
ECG999M	5204
ECG999SM	5200
ECG1000	1226
ECG1001	4363
ECG1002	0383
ECG1003	0574
ECG1004	0872
ECG1005	2546
ECG1006	1206
ECG1008	2991
ECG1009	0837
ECG1010	0858
ECG1011	0876
ECG1012	0021
ECG1013	0138
ECG1014	0351
ECG1015	2388
ECG1016	2390
ECG1017	2423
ECG1018	2457
ECG1019	2487
ECG1020	OEM
ECG1021	2142
ECG1022	4476
ECG1023	4477
ECG1024	3506
ECG1025	1179
ECG1026	2445
ECG1027	2849
ECG1028	4479
ECG1029	2247
ECG1030	4481
ECG1031	4482
ECG1032	4483
ECG1033	4484
ECG1034	2862
ECG1035	4485
ECG1036	4486
ECG1037	4031
ECG1038	4338
ECG1039	1611
ECG1040	4489
ECG1041	4490
ECG1042	4491
ECG1043	4320
ECG1045	2377
ECG1046	0523
ECG1047	2855
ECG1048	0668
ECG1049	0648
ECG1050	2864
ECG1051	3736
ECG1052	0428
ECG1053	2551
ECG1054	2554
ECG1055	2556
ECG1056	1826
ECG1057	2555
ECG1058	2111
ECG1059	3966
ECG1060	2559
ECG1061	2560
ECG1062	0399
ECG1063	2562
ECG1064	2563
ECG1065	2564
ECG1066	2565
ECG1067	2566
ECG1068	2567
ECG1069	2576
ECG1070	4014
ECG1071	2580
ECG1072	2568
ECG1073	2573
ECG1074	2569
ECG1075	0465
ECG1075A	0465
ECG1076	0940
ECG1077	0924
ECG1078	3318
ECG1079	4495
ECG1080	0849
ECG1081	1152
ECG1081A	1152
ECG1082	2246
ECG1083	2827
ECG1084	2859
ECG1085	2607
ECG1086	2860

If replacement code is OEM, contact original manufacturer for replacement.

DEVICE TYPE	REPL CODE
ECG1087	1012
ECG1088	5576
ECG1089	0633
ECG1090	2834
ECG1091	0958
ECG1092	2300
ECG1093	4498
ECG1094	0043
ECG1095	4406
ECG1096	1624
ECG1097	3232
ECG1098	3901
ECG1099	4196
ECG1100	0905
ECG1101	2610
ECG1102	2608
ECG1103	1983
ECG1104	2046
ECG1105	4502
ECG1106	2606
ECG1107	3625
ECG1108	1383
ECG1109	2615
ECG1110	2289
ECG1111	2453
ECG1112	2462
ECG1113	2145
ECG1114	4506
ECG1115	1239
ECG1115A	3866
ECG1116	4084
ECG1117	3946
ECG1118	1909
ECG1119	4509
ECG1120	2020
ECG1121	0385
ECG1122	0602
ECG1123	3973
ECG1124	4463
ECG1125	3968
ECG1126	4513
ECG1127	4348
ECG1128	3859
ECG1130	1316
ECG1131	4514
ECG1132	4515
ECG1133	2216
ECG1134	2921
ECG1135	2051
ECG1136	3106
ECG1137	2571
ECG1139	3880
ECG1140	2845
ECG1141	3788
ECG1142	1469
ECG1148	2837
ECG1149	4517
ECG1150	4518
ECG1151	4990
ECG1152	2484
ECG1153	3332
ECG1154	4520
ECG1155	1044
ECG1156	2988
ECG1158	0875
ECG1159	0878
ECG1160	3650
ECG1161	2914
ECG1162	3977
ECG1162A	OEM
ECG1163	2581
ECG1164	3238
ECG1165	2746
ECG1166	2754
ECG1167	1704
ECG1168	2579
ECG1169	4331
ECG1170	2512
ECG1171	0093
ECG1172	1369
ECG1173	3242
ECG1174	2038
ECG1175	2759
ECG1176	2762
ECG1177	2771
ECG1178	3660
ECG1179	2550
ECG1180	2590
ECG1181	2570
ECG1182	3993
ECG1183	4133
ECG1184	4532
ECG1185	1470
ECG1186	0846
ECG1187	0851
ECG1188	2594
ECG1189	4325
ECG1190	4535
ECG1191	4025
ECG1192	1532
ECG1193	3286
ECG1194	1805
ECG1195	4145
ECG1196	1049
ECG1197	4539
ECG1198	2238
ECG1199	3754
ECG1200	4174
ECG1201	4541
ECG1202	2364
ECG1203	2290
ECG1204	4405
ECG1205	2903
ECG1206	4542
ECG1207	4619
ECG1208	4543
ECG1209	4544
ECG1210	2609
ECG1211	2179
ECG1212	4545
ECG1213	4546
ECG1214	0646
ECG1215	2510
ECG1216	0910
ECG1217	0412
ECG1218	1561
ECG1219	1602
ECG1220	5591
ECG1221	4550
ECG1222	5592
ECG1223	1516
ECG1224	4024
ECG1225	2645
ECG1226	0701
ECG1227	0616
ECG1228	3161
ECG1229	4551
ECG1230	2644
ECG1231	1162
ECG1231A	1051
ECG1232	1042
ECG1233	4160
ECG1234	2008
ECG1235	4552
ECG1236	2268
ECG1237	3606
ECG1238	3961
ECG1239	3231
ECG1240	4006
ECG1241	2614
ECG1242	1501
ECG1243	4553
ECG1244	2737
ECG1245	0898
ECG1246	4554
ECG1247	4555
ECG1248	1251
ECG1249	3980
ECG1250	4010
ECG1251	4556
ECG1252	4557
ECG1253	4558
ECG1254	3763
ECG1255	2592
ECG1256	4559
ECG1257	4560
ECG1258	4561
ECG1259	5517
ECG1260	4563
ECG1261	1120
ECG1262	4564
ECG1263	2932
ECG1264	4001
ECG1265	4002
ECG1266	4004
ECG1267	4007
ECG1268	4008
ECG1269	4017
ECG1270	5463
ECG1271	4567
ECG1272	3515
ECG1273	4568
ECG1274	5600
ECG1275	5601
ECG1276	3723
ECG1277	3398
ECG1278	4571
ECG1279	5602
ECG1280	5603
ECG1281	4572
ECG1282	4573
ECG1283	4575
ECG1284	4576
ECG1285	0749
ECG1286	0751
ECG1287	4578
ECG1288	4493
ECG1289	4580
ECG1290	4027
ECG1291	4582
ECG1292	3416
ECG1293	4584
ECG1294	3949
ECG1295	5003
ECG1296	0067
ECG1297	4319
ECG1298	4591
ECG1299	5004
ECG1300	3877
ECG1301	4588
ECG1302	3935
ECG1303	4589
ECG1304	3939
ECG1305	3941
ECG1306	3943
ECG1307	3947
ECG1308	3891
ECG1309	4590
ECG1310	3931
ECG1311	3876
ECG1312	3927
ECG1313	3928
ECG1314	5450
ECG1315	5609
ECG1316	5610
ECG1317	5611
ECG1318	2281
ECG1319	1114
ECG1320	4592
ECG1321	4593
ECG1322	4594
ECG1323	4595
ECG1324	4596
ECG1325	4597
ECG1326	4599
ECG1327	4600
ECG1328	4601
ECG1329	4602
ECG1330	4603
ECG1331	4604
ECG1332	5616
ECG1333	4606
ECG1334	4607
ECG1335	4608
ECG1336	4609
ECG1337	4610
ECG1338	1428
ECG1339	4612
ECG1340	4613
ECG1341	4614
ECG1342	4615
ECG1343	4617
ECG1344	4618
ECG1345	1892
ECG1346	4620
ECG1347	4621
ECG1348	4622
ECG1349	4623
ECG1350	4624
ECG1351	4625
ECG1352	4626
ECG1353	5617
ECG1354	4627
ECG1355	4629
ECG1356	5008
ECG1357	5009
ECG1358	4088
ECG1359	5010
ECG1360	5619
ECG1361	4632
ECG1362	5013
ECG1363	4633
ECG1364	4634
ECG1365	4635
ECG1366	4636
ECG1367	4637
ECG1368	4638
ECG1369	4639
ECG1370	4641
ECG1371	4642
ECG1372	4643
ECG1373	3860
ECG1374	3665
ECG1375	2767
ECG1376	3666
ECG1377	3299
ECG1378	4644
ECG1379	4645
ECG1380	4646
ECG1381	4647
ECG1382	1940
ECG1383	4648
ECG1384	4649
ECG1385	4651
ECG1386	3209
ECG1387	4302
ECG1388	4653
ECG1389	4654
ECG1390	5015
ECG1391	4655
ECG1392	4656
ECG1393	4658
ECG1394	4659
ECG1395	4035
ECG1396	0491
ECG1397	5016
ECG1398	5018
ECG1399	5019
ECG1400	1572
ECG1401	3317
ECG1402	3809
ECG1403	3325
ECG1404	4662
ECG1405	4663
ECG1406	3997
ECG1407	4664
ECG1408	4665
ECG1409	0678
ECG1409C	5958
ECG1410	2599
ECG1411	0762
ECG1412	4666
ECG1413	0069
ECG1414	4669
ECG1415	4416
ECG1416	0485
ECG1417	2601
ECG1418	4102
ECG1419	4670
ECG1420	0548
ECG1421	4671
ECG1422	1575
ECG1423	4227
ECG1424	4399
ECG1425	4677
ECG1426	0670
ECG1427	4678
ECG1428	1570
ECG1429	4679
ECG1430	0912
ECG1431	4680
ECG1432	5026
ECG1433	4681
ECG1434	0866
ECG1435	4682
ECG1436	4355
ECG1437	4469
ECG1438	4683
ECG1439	3074
ECG1440	3692
ECG1441	4684
ECG1442	4685
ECG1443	5029
ECG1444	4005
ECG1445	1016
ECG1446	4000
ECG1447	4687
ECG1448	3989
ECG1449	4689
ECG1450	3985
ECG1451	4690
ECG1452	4692
ECG1453	2492
ECG1454	3216
ECG1455	4694
ECG1456	5640
ECG1457	4695
ECG1458	4696
ECG1459	2508
ECG1460	4697
ECG1461	2686
ECG1462	4698
ECG1463	3167
ECG1464	4699
ECG1465	0358
ECG1466	2052
ECG1467	4676
ECG1468	3923
ECG1469	4700
ECG1470	3198
ECG1471	1192
ECG1472	4703
ECG1473	4705
ECG1474	4707
ECG1475	4708
ECG1476	4710
ECG1477	4711
ECG1478	4712
ECG1479	1437
ECG1480	4480
ECG1481	4714
ECG1482	4715
ECG1483	0859
ECG1484	4716
ECG1485	5564
ECG1486	3671
ECG1487	3982
ECG1488	2237
ECG1489	4719
ECG1490	4721
ECG1491	4723
ECG1492	4724
ECG1493	4725
ECG1494	4726
ECG1495	4727
ECG1496	4071
ECG1497	4728
ECG1498	4729
ECG1499	4730
ECG1500	4731
ECG1501	4733
ECG1502	4735
ECG1503	4736
ECG1504	4737
ECG1505	4739
ECG1506	5615
ECG1507	4740
ECG1508	3039
ECG1509	3040
ECG1510	0804
ECG1511	4741
ECG1512	4216
ECG1513	4742
ECG1514	4743
ECG1515	4746
ECG1516	4747
ECG1517	4750
ECG1518	4751
ECG1519	4752
ECG1520	1617
ECG1521	3888
ECG1522	2511
ECG1523	4754
ECG1525	2669
ECG1526	4757
ECG1527	4758
ECG1528	2312
ECG1529	2884
ECG1530	4760
ECG1531	4762
ECG1532	2043
ECG1533	4763
ECG1534	4765
ECG1535	5065
ECG1536	4766
ECG1537	4767
ECG1538	0328
ECG1539	1580
ECG1540	4285
ECG1541	2668
ECG1542	4243
ECG1543	4769
ECG1544	4770
ECG1545	0906
ECG1546	3462
ECG1547	0658
ECG1548	3461
ECG1549	3042
ECG1550	1420
ECG1551	3698
ECG1552	2888
ECG1553	3476
ECG1554	5067
ECG1555	5647
ECG1556	5068
ECG1557	3764
ECG1558	2094
ECG1559	5069
ECG1560	1308
ECG1561	5070
ECG1562	5071
ECG1563	2898
ECG1564	5651
ECG1565	3028
ECG1566	4521
ECG1567	3668
ECG1568	5077
ECG1569	0107
ECG1570	4899
ECG1571	5080
ECG1572	4047
ECG1573	1666
ECG1574	3865
ECG1575	2170
ECG1576	3726
ECG1577	5083
ECG1578	3389
ECG1579	5085
ECG1580	0347
ECG1581	4050
ECG1582	3916
ECG1583	5662
ECG1584	3918
ECG1585	5088
ECG1586	3913
ECG1587	5663
ECG1588	4178
ECG1589	0445
ECG1590	3911
ECG1591	5089
ECG1592	4230
ECG1593	5090
ECG1594	3909
ECG1595	5548
ECG1596	3907
ECG1597	5091
ECG1598	3662
ECG1599	3652
ECG1600	5093
ECG1601	4197
ECG1602	5095
ECG1603	3904
ECG1604	0460
ECG1605	4360
ECG1606	5096
ECG1607	5097
ECG1608	0657
ECG1609	2513
ECG1610	3055
ECG1611	5099
ECG1612	2760
ECG1613	5100
ECG1614	5665
ECG1615	4773
ECG1616	2868
ECG1617	5666
ECG1618	3045
ECG1619	2772
ECG1620	5101
ECG1621	5102
ECG1622	4981
ECG1623	5667
ECG1624	5103
ECG1625	3707
ECG1626	4756
ECG1627	2781
ECG1628	2062
ECG1629	3713
ECG1630	0754
ECG1631	5105
ECG1632	5106
ECG1633	4210
ECG1634	2572
ECG1635	5107
ECG1636	2983
ECG1637	5108
ECG1638	5670
ECG1639	4214
ECG1640	5671
ECG1641	5109
ECG1644	5672
ECG1645	5673
ECG1646	5674
ECG1647	4288
ECG1648	5111
ECG1649	5112
ECG1650	2109
ECG1651	4441
ECG1652	5675
ECG1653	5676
ECG1654	5113
ECG1655	2815
ECG1656	1433
ECG1657	4339
ECG1658	2641
ECG1659	5114
ECG1660	2632
ECG1661	4284
ECG1662	5115
ECG1663	5116
ECG1664	5117
ECG1665	4103
ECG1666	5118
ECG1667	2370
ECG1668	3728
ECG1669	3250
ECG1670	4473
ECG1671	3640
ECG1672	5120
ECG1673	1977
ECG1674	0970
ECG1675	3329
ECG1676	2031
ECG1677	4923
ECG1678	4959
ECG1679	2409
ECG1680	3098
ECG1681	5122
ECG1682	5123
ECG1683	3800
ECG1684	4840
ECG1685	3223
ECG1686	5679
ECG1687	2288
ECG1688	5126
ECG1689	0694
ECG1690	5127
ECG1691	5128
ECG1692	5129
ECG1693	5130
ECG1700	5132
ECG1701	5133
ECG1702	5134
ECG1703	3686
ECG1704	5136
ECG1705	0484
ECG1706	5681
ECG1707	3301
ECG1708	4313
ECG1709	5137
ECG1710	2055
ECG1711	2531
ECG1712	2056
ECG1713	2057
ECG1714M	2661
ECG1714S	2015
ECG1715	2014
ECG1716	3776
ECG1717	5139
ECG1718	4194
ECG1719	2092
ECG1720	5140
ECG1721	2802
ECG1722	2814
ECG1723	2812
ECG1724	4713
ECG1725	2104
ECG1726	5141
ECG1727	3701
ECG1728	0534
ECG1729	1813
ECG1730	5143
ECG1731	5144
ECG1732	1562
ECG1733	2358
ECG1734	5145
ECG1735	2369
ECG1736	3327
ECG1737	1586
ECG1738	2852
ECG1739	1379
ECG1740	4083
ECG1741	4569
ECG1742	1631
ECG1743	3410
ECG1744	3403
ECG1745	5146
ECG1746	5124
ECG1747	4281
ECG1748	3314
ECG1749	5148
ECG1750	5149
ECG1751	2180
ECG1752	3481
ECG1753	5150
ECG1754	2164
ECG1755	1086
ECG1756	5689
ECG1757	5151
ECG1758	4706
ECG1759	2079
ECG1760	0944
ECG1761	5153
ECG1762	5155
ECG1763	5692
ECG1764	5156
ECG1765	5693
ECG1766	5694
ECG1767	4964
ECG1768	4533
ECG1769	4537
ECG1770	4585
ECG1771	0387
ECG1772	4286
ECG1773	0727
ECG1774	5157
ECG1775	4074
ECG1776	3897
ECG1777	2348
ECG1778	3857
ECG1779	3848
ECG1780	1521
ECG1781	1022
ECG1782	4066
ECG1783	4131
ECG1784	5698
ECG1785	5699
ECG1786	3352
ECG1787	3130
ECG1788	4314
ECG1789	4349
ECG1790	3206
ECG1791	5162
ECG1792	4009
ECG1793	0578
ECG1794	2254
ECG1795	1594
ECG1796	5163
ECG1797	2929
ECG1798	3068
ECG1799	2998
ECG1800	3331
ECG1801	3830
ECG1802	5702
ECG1803	3132
ECG1804	1245
ECG1805	4306
ECG1806	5703
ECG1807	5228
ECG1808	5165
ECG1809	5166
ECG1810	3869
ECG1811	5167
ECG1812	5168
ECG1813	5169
ECG1814	5170
ECG1815	2490
ECG1816	5172
ECG1817	5174
ECG1818	5175
ECG1819	5176
ECG1820	5177
ECG1821	5705
ECG1822	2389
ECG1823	2402
ECG1824	3306
ECG1825	3321
ECG1826	4312
ECG1827	3765
ECG1828	4838
ECG1829	5178
ECG1830	5179
ECG1831	5180
ECG1832	5706
ECG1833	5707
ECG1834	4054
ECG1835	4246
ECG1836	4310
ECG1837	4309
ECG1838	0457
ECG1839	3896
ECG1840	3530
ECG1841	3273
ECG1842	3680
ECG1843	4955
ECG1844	3220
ECG1845	0552
ECG1846	3309
ECG1847	2099
ECG1848	2893
ECG1849	5182
ECG1850	3127
ECG1851	5708
ECG1852	3453
ECG1853	5709
ECG1854D	5983
ECG1854M	5960
ECG1855	2330
ECG1856	0481
ECG1857	5711
ECG1858	5712
ECG1859	3054
ECG1860	2843

If replacement code is OEM, contact original manufacturer for replacement.

DEVICE TYPE	REPL CODE
ECG1861	3871
ECG1862	3727
ECG1863	4032
ECG1864	1473
ECG1865	5713
ECG1866	5714
ECG1867	1159
ECG1868	4795
ECG1869	5715
ECG1869SM	4055
ECG1870	3448
ECG1871	5183
ECG1872	2403
ECG1873	4417
ECG1874	5184
ECG1875	5185
ECG1876	5186
ECG1877	1474
ECG1878	5716
ECG1879	1430
ECG1880	2287
ECG1881	2397
ECG1882	4080
ECG1883	2318
ECG1884	2401
ECG1885	2738
ECG1886	4782
ECG1887	5717
ECG1888	5718
ECG1889	5719
ECG1890	5292
ECG1891	1927
ECG1892	3051
ECG1893	2172
ECG1894	3310
ECG1895	2273
ECG1896	3894
ECG1897	3900
ECG1898	5720
ECG1899	5721
ECG1900	5187
ECG1901	5188
ECG1902	1775
ECG1903	1825
ECG1905	4952
ECG1906	4427
ECG1907	4799
ECG1908	4430
ECG1909	1710
ECG1910	4794
ECG1911	2697
ECG1912	2239
ECG1913	1993
ECG1914	3906
ECG1915	5193
ECG1916	1989
ECG1917	4429
ECG1918	2443
ECG1919	5195
ECG1920	3605
ECG1923	5196
ECG1924	3828
ECG1925	3529
ECG1926	5197
ECG1927	5198
ECG1928	2451
ECG1930	2155
ECG1932	2779
ECG1934	5199
ECG1934X	2517
ECG1936	4264
ECG1938	5202
ECG1940	5203
ECG1941	5723
ECG1942	5724
ECG2000	5211
ECG2001	3684
ECG2002	4155
ECG2003	4846
ECG2004	4045
ECG2011	0839
ECG2012	1001
ECG2013	1126
ECG2014	1252
ECG2015	4848
ECG2016	4849
ECG2017	4850
ECG2018	4852
ECG2019	4853
ECG2020	4854
ECG2021	3839
ECG2022	3864
ECG2023	2723
ECG2024	2800
ECG2025	4856
ECG2026	4019
ECG2027	1691
ECG2028	1782
ECG2029	4860
ECG2030	1866
ECG2031	4862
ECG2032	4863
ECG2040	4290
ECG2041	5728
ECG2042	4519
ECG2043	4691
ECG2045	5730
ECG2046	5731
ECG2047	5216
ECG2049	0501
ECG2050	4864
ECG2051	4865
ECG2052	5732
ECG2053	3743
ECG2054	4867
ECG2055	0482
ECG2056	5217
ECG2057	5733
ECG2060	2279
ECG2061	2702
ECG2062	3925
ECG2063	5734
ECG2064	5735
ECG2065	5736
ECG2070	4868
ECG2071	4869
ECG2072	4870
ECG2073	4872
ECG2074	4456
ECG2075	4874
ECG2076	4875
ECG2077	4876
ECG2078	4878
ECG2079	0963
ECG2080	4879
ECG2081	4880
ECG2082	4881
ECG2083	4882
ECG2084	4075
ECG2085	4781
ECG2086	5218
ECG2087	4883
ECG2088	5219
ECG2090	5738
ECG2102	4886
ECG2104	4887
ECG2107	4815
ECG2114	2037
ECG2117	0518
ECG2128	1887
ECG2147	1683
ECG2164	2341
ECG2200	5727
ECG2201	5749
ECG2202	3546
ECG2203	5743
ECG2204	5750
ECG2205	5751
ECG2206	5752
ECG2207	5753
ECG2300	3326
ECG2301	3437
ECG2302	1533
ECG2303	2739
ECG2304	2351
ECG2305	3401
ECG2306	3628
ECG2307	2973
ECG2308	2171
ECG2309	2757
ECG2310	4376
ECG2311	1498
ECG2312	2880
ECG2313	3504
ECG2314	5244
ECG2315	1503
ECG2316	5245
ECG2317	4269
ECG2318	5248
ECG2319	3354
ECG2320	2976
ECG2321	0539
ECG2322	0281
ECG2323	5251
ECG2324	3454
ECG2325	3323
ECG2326	3107
ECG2327	3187
ECG2328	3402
ECG2329	5252
ECG2330	3474
ECG2331	2116
ECG2332	0277
ECG2333	4510
ECG2334	2350
ECG2335	2961
ECG2336	3678
ECG2337	3426
ECG2338	1055
ECG2339	3424
ECG2340	5253
ECG2341	3838
ECG2342	3836
ECG2343	1948
ECG2344	1957
ECG2345	4015
ECG2346	4016
ECG2348	3499
ECG2349	2412
ECG2350	2404
ECG2351	5255
ECG2352	5256
ECG2354	5761
ECG2355	0826
ECG2356	4109
ECG2357	2307
ECG2358	3114
ECG2359	0892
ECG2360	4067
ECG2361	2926
ECG2362	0013
ECG2380	1457
ECG2381	5263
ECG2382	3059
ECG2383	2256
ECG2384	5764
ECG2385	5661
ECG2386	1658
ECG2387	5005
ECG2388	2162
ECG2390	5264
ECG2392	5266
ECG2400	5765
ECG2401	4410
ECG2402	2891
ECG2403	4419
ECG2404	5267
ECG2405	5268
ECG2406	1722
ECG2407	1741
ECG2408	0719
ECG2409	1731
ECG2410	2316
ECG2411	5357
ECG2412	3345
ECG2413	5271
ECG2414	3442
ECG2415	1881
ECG2416	0975
ECG2417	0698
ECG2418	3439
ECG2419	3241
ECG2426	5272
ECG2427	5273
ECG2428	0662
ECG2429	3600
ECG2430	3433
ECG2431	5274
ECG2532	5007
ECG2708	4351
ECG2716	2263
ECG2732	2672
ECG2764	0806
ECG2800	1835
ECG2909	OEM
ECG3000	1970
ECG3001	1978
ECG3002	1974
ECG3003	1972
ECG3004	5020
ECG3005	5021
ECG3006	5022
ECG3007	2990
ECG3008	3067
ECG3009	5023
ECG3010	0835
ECG3011	3095
ECG3012	5024
ECG3012A	3134
ECG3013	5025
ECG3013A	3140
ECG3014	3420
ECG3015	3421
ECG3016	3693
ECG3017	0511
ECG3018	1605
ECG3019	5027
ECG3020	1348
ECG3021	3128
ECG3022	1951
ECG3023	3245
ECG3024	1767
ECG3025	3153
ECG3026	2181
ECG3027	4120
ECG3028	0586
ECG3029	3203
ECG3029A	3203
ECG3030	3965
ECG3031	5030
ECG3032	2297
ECG3033	2604
ECG3034	3825
ECG3035	3156
ECG3035A	3156
ECG3036	3508
ECG3037	5031
ECG3038	5032
ECG3039	5033
ECG3040	0536
ECG3041	0311
ECG3042	0272
ECG3043	4358
ECG3044	4845
ECG3045	2096
ECG3046	2221
ECG3047	4961
ECG3048	4975
ECG3049	5034
ECG3050	4900
ECG3051	4901
ECG3052	4783
ECG3053	5035
ECG3054	5036
ECG3055	5037
ECG3056	4786
ECG3057	4127
ECG3058	5038
ECG3059	5039
ECG3060	5040
ECG3061	4902
ECG3062	5042
ECG3063	5043
ECG3064	5045
ECG3065	4784
ECG3068	5046
ECG3069	5047
ECG3070	5048
ECG3071	5049
ECG3074	4262
ECG3075	4267
ECG3076	4266
ECG3077	4268
ECG3078	2192
ECG3079	2185
ECG3080	2362
ECG3081	3333
ECG3082	5050
ECG3083	1101
ECG3084	1047
ECG3085	5323
ECG3086	1393
ECG3087	5325
ECG3088	5326
ECG3089	5327
ECG3090	5328
ECG3091	0235
ECG3092	1281
ECG3093	5329
ECG3094	5568
ECG3095	5330
ECG3096	5331
ECG3097	5332
ECG3098	0112
ECG3099	2678
ECG3100	1407
ECG3101	2612
ECG3102	2616
ECG3103	5335
ECG3104	5556
ECG3105	4791
ECG3111	5336
ECG3112	5337
ECG3113	5338
ECG3114	5060
ECG3115	5062
ECG3116	5063
ECG3117	5064
ECG3120	2083
ECG3121	3930
ECG3130	5341
ECG3131	4928
ECG3150	5073
ECG3151	5075
ECG3152	5076
ECG3153	5078
ECG3154	5119
ECG3155	5079
ECG3156	4369
ECG3157	2036
ECG3158	4948
ECG3160	5082
ECG3161	1069
ECG3162	5084
ECG3163	4686
ECG3164	3450
ECG3165	5086
ECG3166	3990
ECG3167	1123
ECG3168	5087
ECG3169	5346
ECG3170	5347
ECG3171	4973
ECG3172	5853
ECG3173	1959
ECG3174	5339
ECG3180	5349
ECG3181	5350
ECG3182	5351
ECG3200	5854
ECG3201	2682
ECG3202	2726
ECG3470	2732
ECG3539	2618
ECG3880	3441
ECG3881	1893
ECG3882	5242
ECG4000	2013
ECG4001	0473
ECG4001B	0473
ECG4002	2044
ECG4002B	2044
ECG4006B	0641
ECG4007	2819
ECG4007B	2819
ECG4008B	0982
ECG4011	0215
ECG4011B	0215
ECG4012	0493
ECG4012B	0493
ECG4013	0409
ECG4013B	0409
ECG4014	0854
ECG4014B	0854
ECG4015	1008
ECG4015B	1008
ECG4016	1135
ECG4016B	1135
ECG4017	0508
ECG4017B	0508
ECG4018B	1381
ECG4019	1517
ECG4019B	1517
ECG4020	1651
ECG4020B	1651
ECG4021	1738
ECG4021B	1738
ECG4022B	1247
ECG4023	0515
ECG4023B	0515
ECG4024	1946
ECG4024B	1946
ECG4025	2061
ECG4025B	2061
ECG4026B	2139
ECG4027	1938
ECG4027B	1938
ECG4028	2213
ECG4028B	2213
ECG4029	2218
ECG4029B	2218
ECG4030	0495
ECG4030B	0495
ECG4031B	2943
ECG4032B	2509
ECG4033B	2611
ECG4034B	3570
ECG4035B	2750
ECG4038B	2953
ECG4040	0056
ECG4040B	0056
ECG4041	3145
ECG4042	0121
ECG4042B	0121
ECG4043B	1544
ECG4044B	2292
ECG4045B	3408
ECG4046B	3394
ECG4047B	2315
ECG4048B	3423
ECG4049	0001
ECG4049B	0001
ECG4050	0394
ECG4050B	0394
ECG4051	0362
ECG4051B	0362
ECG4052	0024
ECG4052B	0024
ECG4053B	0034
ECG4055	3272
ECG4055B	3272
ECG4056B	3661
ECG4060B	0146
ECG4063B	3682
ECG4066B	0101
ECG4067B	3696
ECG4068	2482
ECG4068B	2482
ECG4069	0119
ECG4070B	2494
ECG4071	0129
ECG4071B	0129
ECG4072B	2502
ECG4073B	1528
ECG4075B	2518
ECG4076B	3455
ECG4077	2536
ECG4077B	2536
ECG4078	0915
ECG4078B	0915
ECG4081	0621
ECG4081B	0621
ECG4082B	0297
ECG4085	0300
ECG4085B	0300
ECG4086	0530
ECG4086B	0530
ECG4089B	3778
ECG4093B	2368
ECG4094B	1672
ECG4095B	3796
ECG4096B	3798
ECG4097B	3802
ECG4098B	3566
ECG4099	3297
ECG4099B	3297
ECG4256	1463
ECG4501	3758
ECG4502	1031
ECG4502B	1031
ECG4506	5941
ECG4506B	3721
ECG4508B	1800
ECG4510B	1952
ECG4511B	1535
ECG4512	2108
ECG4512B	2108
ECG4513B	4889
ECG4514B	1819
ECG4515B	3555
ECG4516B	2331
ECG4517B	4220
ECG4518	1037
ECG4518B	1037
ECG4520	2650
ECG4520B	2650
ECG4521B	4903
ECG4522	2810
ECG4522B	2810
ECG4526B	3565
ECG4527	3116
ECG4527B	3116
ECG4528B	3168
ECG4529B	4451
ECG4531B	3292
ECG4532B	1010
ECG4536B	3659
ECG4538B	1057
ECG4539	3611
ECG4539B	3611
ECG4541B	4929
ECG4543B	4932
ECG4547B	4943
ECG4551B	4950
ECG4553B	4951
ECG4555	2910
ECG4555B	2910
ECG4556	3397
ECG4556B	3397
ECG4558B	4960
ECG4562B	1029
ECG4566B	3463
ECG4568B	3573
ECG4569B	4408
ECG4582B	4579
ECG4583B	1286
ECG4585B	1365
ECG4597B	4048
ECG4598B	4237
ECG4900	2380
ECG4901	5979
ECG4902	3085
ECG4903	2120
ECG4918	3143
ECG4919	1161
ECG4926	3162
ECG4927	1756
ECG4928	3171
ECG4929	1921
ECG4934	1904
ECG4935	1941
ECG4950	0563
ECG4951	1961
ECG4958	0825
ECG4959	1976
ECG4988	1395
ECG4989	1398
ECG5000	1266
ECG5000A	1266
ECG5001	2847
ECG5001A	2847
ECG5002	0755
ECG5002A	0755
ECG5003	0672
ECG5003A	0672
ECG5004	0118
ECG5004A	0118
ECG5005	0296
ECG5005A	0296
ECG5006	0372
ECG5006A	0372
ECG5007	0036
ECG5007A	0036
ECG5008	0274
ECG5008A	0274
ECG5009	0140
ECG5009A	0140
ECG5010	0041
ECG5010A	0041
ECG5010T1	0582
ECG5011	0253
ECG5011A	0253
ECG5011T1	0877
ECG5012	0091
ECG5012A	0091
ECG5013	0466
ECG5013A	0466
ECG5013T1	0292
ECG5014	0062
ECG5014A	0062
ECG5015	0077
ECG5015A	0077
ECG5016	0165
ECG5016A	0165
ECG5017	0318
ECG5017A	0318
ECG5018	0057
ECG5018A	0057
ECG5019	0064
ECG5019A	0064
ECG5019T1	0248
ECG5020	0181
ECG5020A	0181
ECG5021	0052
ECG5021A	0052
ECG5021T1	0999
ECG5022	0053
ECG5022A	0053
ECG5023	0873
ECG5023A	0873
ECG5024	0681
ECG5024A	0681
ECG5025	0440
ECG5025A	0440
ECG5026	0210
ECG5026A	0210
ECG5027	0371
ECG5027A	0371
ECG5028	0666
ECG5028A	0666
ECG5029	0695
ECG5029A	0695
ECG5030	0700
ECG5030A	0700
ECG5031	0489
ECG5031A	0489
ECG5032	0709
ECG5032A	0709
ECG5033	0450
ECG5033A	0450
ECG5034	0257
ECG5034A	0257
ECG5034C	OEM
ECG5035	0195
ECG5035A	0195
ECG5036	0166
ECG5036A	0166
ECG5037	0010
ECG5037A	0010
ECG5038	0032
ECG5038A	0032
ECG5039	0054
ECG5039A	0054
ECG5040	0068
ECG5040A	0068
ECG5041	0092
ECG5041A	0092
ECG5042	0125
ECG5042A	0125
ECG5043	2301
ECG5043A	2301
ECG5044	0152
ECG5044A	0152
ECG5045	0173
ECG5045A	0173
ECG5046	0094
ECG5046A	0094
ECG5047	0049
ECG5047A	0049
ECG5048	0104
ECG5048A	0104
ECG5049	0156
ECG5049A	0156
ECG5050	0189
ECG5050A	0189
ECG5051	0099
ECG5051A	0099
ECG5052	0089
ECG5052A	0089
ECG5053	0285
ECG5053A	0285
ECG5054	0252
ECG5054A	0252
ECG5055	0336
ECG5055A	0336
ECG5056	0366
ECG5056A	0366
ECG5057	0390
ECG5057A	0390
ECG5058	0420
ECG5058A	0420
ECG5059	0448
ECG5059A	0448
ECG5060	1464
ECG5060A	1464
ECG5061	2975
ECG5061A	2975
ECG5063	1302
ECG5063A	1302
ECG5064	2981
ECG5064A	2981
ECG5065	1703
ECG5065A	1703
ECG5066	0289
ECG5066A	0289
ECG5067	0451
ECG5067A	0451
ECG5068	0528
ECG5068A	0528
ECG5069	0446
ECG5069A	0446
ECG5070	0298
ECG5070A	0298
ECG5071	0025
ECG5071A	0025
ECG5072	0244
ECG5072A	0244
ECG5073	1075
ECG5073A	1075
ECG5074	0313
ECG5074A	0313
ECG5075	0416
ECG5075A	0416
ECG5076	1639
ECG5076A	1639
ECG5077	0490
ECG5077A	0490
ECG5078	0943
ECG5078A	0943
ECG5079	0526
ECG5079A	0526
ECG5080	0560
ECG5080A	0560

If replacement code is OEM, contact original manufacturer for replacement.

DEVICE TYPE	REPL CODE
ECG5081	0398
ECG5081A	0398
ECG5082	1596
ECG5082A	1596
ECG5083	1664
ECG5083A	1664
ECG5084	0721
ECG5084A	0721
ECG5085	0814
ECG5085A	0814
ECG5086	0346
ECG5086A	0346
ECG5087	0925
ECG5087A	0925
ECG5088	0993
ECG5088A	0993
ECG5089	0497
ECG5089A	0497
ECG5090	0863
ECG5090A	0863
ECG5091	1148
ECG5091A	1148
ECG5092	1258
ECG5092A	1258
ECG5093	1181
ECG5093A	1181
ECG5093T	OEM
ECG5094	2997
ECG5094A	2997
ECG5095	1301
ECG5095A	1301
ECG5096	0098
ECG5096A	0098
ECG5097	0186
ECG5097A	0186
ECG5098	0213
ECG5098A	0213
ECG5099	0245
ECG5099A	0245
ECG5100	0028
ECG5100A	0028
ECG5101	0255
ECG5101A	0255
ECG5102	0871
ECG5102A	0871
ECG5103	0363
ECG5103A	0363
ECG5104	2831
ECG5104A	2831
ECG5105	0417
ECG5105A	0417
ECG5107T2	3889
ECG5111	0777
ECG5111A	0777
ECG5112	0791
ECG5112A	0791
ECG5113	0801
ECG5113A	0801
ECG5114	0815
ECG5114A	0815
ECG5115	0827
ECG5115A	0827
ECG5116	0437
ECG5116A	0437
ECG5117	0870
ECG5117A	0870
ECG5118	3099
ECG5118A	3099
ECG5119	0185
ECG5119A	0185
ECG5120	0205
ECG5120A	0205
ECG5121	0475
ECG5121A	0475
ECG5122	0499
ECG5122A	0499
ECG5123	3285
ECG5123A	3285
ECG5124	0679
ECG5124A	0679
ECG5125	0225
ECG5125A	0225
ECG5126	0230
ECG5126A	0230
ECG5127	0234
ECG5127A	0234
ECG5128	0237
ECG5128A	0237
ECG5129	1387
ECG5129A	1387
ECG5130	0247
ECG5130A	0247
ECG5131	0251
ECG5131A	0251
ECG5132	1170
ECG5132A	1170
ECG5133	0256
ECG5133A	0256
ECG5134	2379
ECG5134A	2379
ECG5135	0262
ECG5135A	0262
ECG5136	0269
ECG5136A	0269
ECG5137	0273
ECG5137A	0273
ECG5138	2383
ECG5138A	2383
ECG5139	0291
ECG5139A	0291
ECG5140	1169
ECG5140A	1169
ECG5141	0305
ECG5141A	0305
ECG5142	0314
ECG5142A	0314
ECG5143	0316
ECG5143A	0316
ECG5144	0322
ECG5144A	0322
ECG5145	0333
ECG5145A	0333
ECG5146	0343
ECG5146A	0343
ECG5147	0027
ECG5147A	0027
ECG5148	0266
ECG5148A	0266
ECG5149	2829
ECG5149A	2829
ECG5150	0382
ECG5150A	0382
ECG5151	0401
ECG5151A	0401
ECG5152	0421
ECG5152A	0421
ECG5153	0439
ECG5153A	0439
ECG5154	2999
ECG5154A	2999
ECG5155	0238
ECG5155A	0238
ECG5156	1172
ECG5156A	1172
ECG5157	1182
ECG5157A	1182
ECG5158	1198
ECG5158A	1198
ECG5159	1209
ECG5159A	1209
ECG5160	1870
ECG5160A	1870
ECG5161	0642
ECG5161A	0642
ECG5162	1246
ECG5162A	1246
ECG5163	2091
ECG5163A	2091
ECG5164	1269
ECG5164A	1269
ECG5165	2210
ECG5165A	2210
ECG5166	0600
ECG5166A	0600
ECG5172	4167
ECG5172A	4167
ECG5172AK	1000
ECG5172K	1000
ECG5173	2381
ECG5173A	2381
ECG5173AK	1370
ECG5173K	1370
ECG5174	2024
ECG5174A	2024
ECG5174AK	0542
ECG5174K	0542
ECG5175	2385
ECG5175A	2385
ECG5175AK	2387
ECG5175K	2387
ECG5176	1429
ECG5176A	1429
ECG5176AK	2101
ECG5176K	2101
ECG5177	2391
ECG5177A	2391
ECG5177AK	2394
ECG5177K	2394
ECG5178	1436
ECG5178A	1436
ECG5178AK	1890
ECG5178K	1890
ECG5179	2399
ECG5179A	2399
ECG5179AK	2400
ECG5179K	2400
ECG5180	2206
ECG5180A	2206
ECG5180AK	0691
ECG5180K	0691
ECG5181	1449
ECG5181A	1449
ECG5181AK	1591
ECG5181K	1591
ECG5182	0221
ECG5182A	0221
ECG5182AK	1606
ECG5182K	1606
ECG5183	1481
ECG5183A	1481
ECG5183AK	1612
ECG5183K	1612
ECG5184	2406
ECG5184A	2406
ECG5184AK	2408
ECG5184K	2408
ECG5185	1608
ECG5185A	1608
ECG5185AK	0622
ECG5185K	0622
ECG5186	0505
ECG5186A	0505
ECG5186AK	0986
ECG5186K	0986
ECG5187	0686
ECG5187A	0686
ECG5187AK	0989
ECG5187K	0989
ECG5188	0864
ECG5188A	0864
ECG5188AK	1254
ECG5188K	1254
ECG5189	1014
ECG5189A	1014
ECG5189AK	1240
ECG5189K	1240
ECG5190	1145
ECG5190A	1145
ECG5190AK	1626
ECG5190K	1626
ECG5191	1264
ECG5191A	1264
ECG5191AK	1629
ECG5191K	1629
ECG5192	1392
ECG5192A	1392
ECG5192AK	1693
ECG5192K	1693
ECG5193	1524
ECG5193A	1524
ECG5193AK	1630
ECG5193K	1630
ECG5194	1071
ECG5194A	1071
ECG5194AK	1706
ECG5194K	1706
ECG5195	1701
ECG5195A	1701
ECG5195AK	1709
ECG5195K	1709
ECG5196	1707
ECG5196A	1707
ECG5196AK	1720
ECG5196K	1720
ECG5197	1712
ECG5197A	1712
ECG5197AK	0722
ECG5197K	0722
ECG5198	1725
ECG5198A	1725
ECG5198AK	1745
ECG5198K	1745
ECG5199	1737
ECG5199A	1737
ECG5199AK	1757
ECG5199K	1757
ECG5200	1750
ECG5200A	1750
ECG5200AK	1771
ECG5200K	1771
ECG5201	2431
ECG5201A	2431
ECG5201AK	2434
ECG5201K	2434
ECG5202	1761
ECG5202A	1761
ECG5202AK	1783
ECG5202K	1783
ECG5203	1777
ECG5203A	1777
ECG5203AK	1788
ECG5203K	1788
ECG5204	1785
ECG5204A	1785
ECG5204AK	1798
ECG5204K	1798
ECG5205	1793
ECG5205A	1793
ECG5205AK	1806
ECG5205K	1806
ECG5206	1185
ECG5206A	1185
ECG5206AK	1815
ECG5206K	1815
ECG5207	1810
ECG5207A	1810
ECG5207AK	1829
ECG5207K	1829
ECG5208	0022
ECG5208A	0022
ECG5208AK	1842
ECG5208K	1842
ECG5209	0070
ECG5209A	0070
ECG5209AK	1850
ECG5209K	1850
ECG5210	0132
ECG5210A	0132
ECG5210AK	1855
ECG5210K	1855
ECG5211	0172
ECG5211A	0172
ECG5211AK	1863
ECG5211K	1863
ECG5212	0207
ECG5212A	0207
ECG5212AK	1873
ECG5212K	1873
ECG5213	0227
ECG5213A	0227
ECG5213AK	2455
ECG5213K	2455
ECG5214	0263
ECG5214A	0263
ECG5214AK	1884
ECG5214K	1884
ECG5215	0306
ECG5215A	0306
ECG5215AK	1891
ECG5215K	1891
ECG5216	0325
ECG5216A	0325
ECG5216AK	0731
ECG5216K	0731
ECG5217	0352
ECG5217A	0352
ECG5217AK	1898
ECG5217K	1898
ECG5218	0377
ECG5218A	0377
ECG5218AK	2459
ECG5218K	2459
ECG5219	0408
ECG5219A	0408
ECG5219AK	1903
ECG5219K	1903
ECG5220	0433
ECG5220A	0433
ECG5220AK	1155
ECG5220K	1155
ECG5221	0459
ECG5221A	0459
ECG5221AK	1913
ECG5221K	1913
ECG5222	0483
ECG5222A	0483
ECG5222AK	1922
ECG5222K	1922
ECG5223	0504
ECG5223A	0504
ECG5223AK	1930
ECG5223K	1930
ECG5224	0519
ECG5224A	0519
ECG5224AK	1936
ECG5224K	1936
ECG5225	0537
ECG5225A	0537
ECG5225AK	1942
ECG5225K	1942
ECG5226	0063
ECG5226A	0063
ECG5226AK	1950
ECG5226K	1950
ECG5227	0397
ECG5227A	0397
ECG5227AK	0353
ECG5227K	0353
ECG5228	0593
ECG5228A	0593
ECG5228AK	2479
ECG5228K	2479
ECG5229	0611
ECG5229A	0611
ECG5229AK	0665
ECG5229K	0665
ECG5230	0629
ECG5230A	0629
ECG5230AK	0771
ECG5230K	0771
ECG5231	0645
ECG5231A	0645
ECG5231AK	2486
ECG5231K	2486
ECG5232	0663
ECG5232A	0663
ECG5232AK	1065
ECG5232K	1065
ECG5240	0809
ECG5240A	0809
ECG5240AK	2695
ECG5240K	2695
ECG5241	0821
ECG5241A	0821
ECG5241AK	2698
ECG5241K	2698
ECG5242	0840
ECG5242A	0840
ECG5242AK	2700
ECG5242K	2700
ECG5243	0862
ECG5243A	0862
ECG5243AK	2703
ECG5243K	2703
ECG5244	0879
ECG5244A	0879
ECG5244AK	2706
ECG5244K	2706
ECG5245	0891
ECG5245A	0891
ECG5245AK	2707
ECG5245K	2707
ECG5246	0908
ECG5246A	0908
ECG5246AK	2711
ECG5246K	2711
ECG5247	0920
ECG5247A	0920
ECG5247AK	2713
ECG5247K	2713
ECG5248	0938
ECG5248A	0938
ECG5248AK	2717
ECG5248K	2717
ECG5249	0952
ECG5249A	0952
ECG5249AK	1216
ECG5249K	1216
ECG5250	0972
ECG5250A	0972
ECG5250AK	2719
ECG5250K	2719
ECG5251	0988
ECG5251A	0988
ECG5251AK	1228
ECG5251K	1228
ECG5252	1003
ECG5252A	1003
ECG5252AK	1243
ECG5252K	1243
ECG5253	1013
ECG5253A	1013
ECG5253AK	1259
ECG5253K	1259
ECG5254	0883
ECG5254A	0883
ECG5254AK	1267
ECG5254K	1267
ECG5255	1043
ECG5255A	1043
ECG5255AK	1283
ECG5255K	1283
ECG5256	1052
ECG5256A	1052
ECG5256AK	2725
ECG5256K	2725
ECG5257	0926
ECG5257A	0926
ECG5257AK	1292
ECG5257K	1292
ECG5258	1072
ECG5258A	1072
ECG5258AK	1300
ECG5258K	1300
ECG5259	1088
ECG5259A	1088
ECG5259AK	2729
ECG5259K	2729
ECG5260	1098
ECG5260A	1098
ECG5260AK	1314
ECG5260K	1314
ECG5261	1115
ECG5261A	1115
ECG5261AK	2731
ECG5261K	2731
ECG5262	1127
ECG5262A	1127
ECG5262AK	1323
ECG5262K	1323
ECG5263	1144
ECG5263A	1144
ECG5263AK	1334
ECG5263K	1334
ECG5264	1156
ECG5264A	1156
ECG5264AK	1346
ECG5264K	1346
ECG5265	1166
ECG5265A	1166
ECG5265AK	2733
ECG5265K	2733
ECG5266	1176
ECG5266A	1176
ECG5266AK	1361
ECG5266K	1361
ECG5267	1191
ECG5267A	1191
ECG5267AK	2735
ECG5267K	2735
ECG5268	1201
ECG5268A	1201
ECG5268AK	1377
ECG5268K	1377
ECG5269	1214
ECG5269A	1214
ECG5269AK	1396
ECG5269K	1396
ECG5270	1223
ECG5270A	1223
ECG5270AK	1405
ECG5270K	1405
ECG5271	1237
ECG5271A	1237
ECG5271AK	1419
ECG5271K	1419
ECG5272	1256
ECG5272A	1256
ECG5272AK	1431
ECG5272K	1431
ECG5273	1263
ECG5273A	1263
ECG5273AK	2745
ECG5273K	2745
ECG5274	1280
ECG5274A	1280
ECG5274AK	1438
ECG5274K	1438
ECG5275	1289
ECG5275A	1289
ECG5275AK	2749
ECG5275K	2749
ECG5276	1297
ECG5276A	1297
ECG5276AK	1452
ECG5276K	1452
ECG5277	1312
ECG5277A	1312
ECG5277AK	2752
ECG5277K	2752
ECG5278	1321
ECG5278A	1321
ECG5278AK	1465
ECG5278K	1465
ECG5279	1330
ECG5279A	1330
ECG5279AK	2756
ECG5279K	2756
ECG5280	1343
ECG5280A	1343
ECG5280AK	0608
ECG5280K	0608
ECG5281	1355
ECG5281A	1355
ECG5281AK	1502
ECG5281K	1502
ECG5282	1374
ECG5282A	1374
ECG5282AK	1515
ECG5282K	1515
ECG5283	1391
ECG5283A	1391
ECG5283AK	1529
ECG5283K	1529
ECG5284	1402
ECG5284A	1402
ECG5284AK	1541
ECG5284K	1541
ECG5285	1413
ECG5285A	1413
ECG5285AK	1565
ECG5285K	1565
ECG5286	1427
ECG5286A	1427
ECG5286AK	2775
ECG5286K	2775
ECG5287	1435
ECG5287A	1435
ECG5287AK	2776
ECG5287K	2776
ECG5288	1448
ECG5288A	1448
ECG5288AK	1499
ECG5288K	1499
ECG5289	1461
ECG5289A	1461
ECG5289AK	2778
ECG5289K	2778
ECG5290	1475
ECG5290A	1475
ECG5290AK	2780
ECG5290K	2780
ECG5291	1497
ECG5291A	1497
ECG5291AK	2783
ECG5291K	2783
ECG5292	1513
ECG5292A	1513
ECG5292AK	2788
ECG5292K	2788
ECG5293	1523
ECG5293A	1523
ECG5293AK	2791
ECG5293K	2791
ECG5294	1539
ECG5294A	1539
ECG5294AK	2793
ECG5294K	2793
ECG5295	1558
ECG5295A	1558
ECG5295AK	2795
ECG5295K	2795
ECG5296	1577
ECG5296A	1577
ECG5296AK	2797
ECG5296K	2797
ECG5304	0106
ECG5305	1999
ECG5306	2384
ECG5307	0782
ECG5309	0724
ECG5310	0732
ECG5311	0737
ECG5312	0319
ECG5313	1404
ECG5314	0468
ECG5315	0441
ECG5316	1412
ECG5317	2425
ECG5318	2994
ECG5319	3006
ECG5320	3021
ECG5322	2347
ECG5324	2353
ECG5326	2354
ECG5327	2356
ECG5328	2357
ECG5329	1036
ECG5330	1039
ECG5331	1041
ECG5332	1864
ECG5334	3503
ECG5335	5629
ECG5338	5631
ECG5340	1633
ECG5342	1663
ECG5344	1579
ECG5346	5633
ECG5348	5634
ECG5351	4272
ECG5360	0799
ECG5368	0650
ECG5369	0020
ECG5371	0521
ECG5372	0108
ECG5374	0423
ECG5375	1860
ECG5377	1690
ECG5378	0341
ECG5380	0454
ECG5381	0584
ECG5386	0764
ECG5387	0478
ECG5400	1129
ECG5401	0340
ECG5402	0895
ECG5403	2326
ECG5404	0058
ECG5405	0403
ECG5406	1673
ECG5408	0179
ECG5409	0342
ECG5410	3315
ECG5411	4384
ECG5412	0174
ECG5413	3801
ECG5414	3575
ECG5415	3291
ECG5416	1494
ECG5417	0998
ECG5418	1028
ECG5419	1140
ECG5421	6030
ECG5422	3253
ECG5423	1912
ECG5424	1981
ECG5425	5429
ECG5426	1038
ECG5427	5643
ECG5428	5644
ECG5429	5373
ECG5431	3252
ECG5432	6032
ECG5433	6033
ECG5434	2255
ECG5437	0712
ECG5438	0304
ECG5440	3852
ECG5442	4508
ECG5444	2255
ECG5446	3368
ECG5448	3370
ECG5452	1386
ECG5453	1250
ECG5454	0442
ECG5455	0934
ECG5456	1213
ECG5457	0095
ECG5458	1234
ECG5460	4496
ECG5461	2084
ECG5462	2078
ECG5463	0500
ECG5465	0705
ECG5466	0857
ECG5468	0323
ECG5470	1102
ECG5471	2904
ECG5472	0957
ECG5473	2905
ECG5474	2908
ECG5475	3626
ECG5476	3405
ECG5480	3385
ECG5481	1095
ECG5482	2471
ECG5483	0240
ECG5484	2635
ECG5485	0671
ECG5486	2782
ECG5487	0332
ECG5491	2430
ECG5492	0430
ECG5494	1478
ECG5496	0682
ECG5500	3073
ECG5501	2497
ECG5502	0736
ECG5503	3076
ECG5504	0740
ECG5505	3080
ECG5506	2889
ECG5507	0742

If replacement code is OEM, contact original manufacturer for replacement.

DEVICE TYPE	REPL CODE
ECG5508	3213
ECG5509	0747
ECG5511	3651
ECG5512	3349
ECG5513	3579
ECG5514	1641
ECG5515	1574
ECG5516	1655
ECG5517	1640
ECG5518	2623
ECG5519	2625
ECG5520	3275
ECG5521	2174
ECG5522	0562
ECG5523	3227
ECG5524	0757
ECG5525	3237
ECG5526	3240
ECG5527	0735
ECG5528	3260
ECG5529	0759
ECG5530	2848
ECG5531	0761
ECG5534	0226
ECG5534A	1526
ECG5536	4989
ECG5538	5836
ECG5539	4988
ECG5540	3246
ECG5541	0726
ECG5542	0707
ECG5543	0464
ECG5544	0716
ECG5545	0717
ECG5546	0773
ECG5547	0720
ECG5548	0745
ECG5550	2499
ECG5552	0393
ECG5554	0606
ECG5556	0946
ECG5558	1504
ECG5562	1837
ECG5564	1844
ECG5566	3185
ECG5567	1694
ECG5568	3970
ECG5569	0674
ECG5570	0603
ECG5572	0605
ECG5574	0463
ECG5575	0636
ECG5577	0217
ECG5579	0653
ECG5580	1076
ECG5582	1078
ECG5584	1094
ECG5587	1889
ECG5589	0733
ECG5590	0192
ECG5591	0159
ECG5592	0096
ECG5594	2816
ECG5595	1754
ECG5596	1803
ECG5598	4085
ECG5599	1714
ECG5600	4341
ECG5601	1744
ECG5602	4343
ECG5603	3458
ECG5604	4058
ECG5605	0480
ECG5606	4345
ECG5607	4346
ECG5608	0567
ECG5609	0929
ECG5610	0059
ECG5611	5452
ECG5612	5453
ECG5613	0948
ECG5614	4366
ECG5615	0951
ECG5616	0954
ECG5617	0955
ECG5618	0960
ECG5620	3549
ECG5621	5454
ECG5622	1081
ECG5623	1085
ECG5624	0407
ECG5625	1087
ECG5626	0411
ECG5627	1091
ECG5628	1092
ECG5629	2284
ECG5631	0573
ECG5632	0566
ECG5633	0588
ECG5634	0569
ECG5635	0571
ECG5636	0572
ECG5637	0589
ECG5638	5226
ECG5640	2367
ECG5641	2378
ECG5642	1403
ECG5643	2371
ECG5645	0550

DEVICE TYPE	REPL CODE
ECG5646	1447
ECG5649	5456
ECG5650	2336
ECG5651	2337
ECG5652	2340
ECG5653	5457
ECG5655	4381
ECG5656	4382
ECG5657	4404
ECG5660	0395
ECG5661	0400
ECG5662	0404
ECG5663	0418
ECG5664	0418
ECG5665	0418
ECG5666	0418
ECG5667	0418
ECG5667A	0418
ECG5668A	6018
ECG5669A	3425
ECG5671	2188
ECG5672	5461
ECG5673	0154
ECG5675	0147
ECG5676	4465
ECG5677	0278
ECG5679	0902
ECG5680	3117
ECG5681	3118
ECG5682	3119
ECG5683	3121
ECG5684	3122
ECG5685	3123
ECG5686	3124
ECG5687	4038
ECG5688	1058
ECG5689	1307
ECG5690	1880
ECG5693	2004
ECG5695	2006
ECG5697	2007
ECG5699	0788
ECG5700	1425
ECG5701	1670
ECG5702	2278
ECG5703	2282
ECG5704	5700
ECG5705	5701
ECG5710	0647
ECG5711	4295
ECG5712	4494
ECG5720	2295
ECG5721	2966
ECG5722	2851
ECG5800	0110
ECG5801	0947
ECG5802	0242
ECG5803	1736
ECG5804	0535
ECG5805	1760
ECG5806	0959
ECG5808	0811
ECG5809	0916
ECG5812	1272
ECG5814	1277
ECG5815	1282
ECG5817	1285
ECG5818	1557
ECG5819	1538
ECG5820	2140
ECG5821	3110
ECG5822	0706
ECG5823	2939
ECG5826	3475
ECG5827	4924
ECG5828	3498
ECG5829	5477
ECG5830	0703
ECG5831	0927
ECG5832	4077
ECG5833	5420
ECG5834	0575
ECG5835	0941
ECG5836	2049
ECG5837	4443
ECG5838	0994
ECG5839	1006
ECG5840	2065
ECG5841	5467
ECG5842	2070
ECG5843	1067
ECG5846	2077
ECG5847	1130
ECG5848	0607
ECG5849	1180
ECG5850	0964
ECG5851	0979
ECG5852	3688
ECG5853	0904
ECG5854	0983
ECG5855	0984
ECG5856	3697
ECG5857	0987
ECG5858	0197
ECG5859	0991
ECG5860	0200
ECG5861	0995
ECG5862	0204
ECG5863	0510

DEVICE TYPE	REPL CODE
ECG5866	0206
ECG5867	1002
ECG5868	0583
ECG5869	0942
ECG5870	0084
ECG5871	0529
ECG5872	0090
ECG5873	0743
ECG5874	0097
ECG5875	0760
ECG5876	0105
ECG5877	0772
ECG5878	0109
ECG5879	0533
ECG5880	0116
ECG5881	0796
ECG5882	0122
ECG5883	0810
ECG5886	0131
ECG5887	0540
ECG5890	0145
ECG5891	0545
ECG5892	5417
ECG5893	1229
ECG5894	5482
ECG5895	1231
ECG5896	2872
ECG5897	1232
ECG5898	5483
ECG5899	1236
ECG5900	3705
ECG5901	2349
ECG5902	3711
ECG5903	1244
ECG5904	1104
ECG5905	2360
ECG5908	3722
ECG5909	1255
ECG5910	2982
ECG5911	0444
ECG5912	1590
ECG5913	4917
ECG5914	5189
ECG5915	5394
ECG5916	0865
ECG5917	1625
ECG5918	5190
ECG5919	5398
ECG5920	0847
ECG5921	1242
ECG5922	5192
ECG5923	5399
ECG5924	1599
ECG5925	1196
ECG5928	1600
ECG5929	2124
ECG5932	1604
ECG5933	2236
ECG5940	1991
ECG5941	1992
ECG5942	1241
ECG5943	3234
ECG5944	1241
ECG5945	1567
ECG5946	5487
ECG5947	3244
ECG5948	1571
ECG5949	3251
ECG5950	5489
ECG5951	3256
ECG5952	1576
ECG5953	3263
ECG5962	4938
ECG5963	2537
ECG5966	2591
ECG5967	2544
ECG5980	3160
ECG5981	1620
ECG5982	2873
ECG5983	0254
ECG5986	1116
ECG5987	1099
ECG5988	1118
ECG5989	1103
ECG5990	0800
ECG5991	0258
ECG5992	1186
ECG5993	1634
ECG5994	0315
ECG5995	0267
ECG5998	1124
ECG5999	1111
ECG6002	0045
ECG6003	0280
ECG6006	1522
ECG6007	1512
ECG6008	0029
ECG6009	1836
ECG6010	0596
ECG6011	1840
ECG6013	3785
ECG6020	3716
ECG6021	2640
ECG6022	2629
ECG6023	2670
ECG6026	2633
ECG6027	2741
ECG6030	2639
ECG6031	2828

DEVICE TYPE	REPL CODE
ECG6034	1995
ECG6035	2879
ECG6038	2652
ECG6039	2946
ECG6040	2657
ECG6041	3022
ECG6042	3846
ECG6043	3088
ECG6044	2631
ECG6045	3178
ECG6048	4242
ECG6049	3725
ECG6050	1551
ECG6051	2165
ECG6054	2813
ECG6055	2168
ECG6058	4244
ECG6059	3556
ECG6060	2823
ECG6061	2177
ECG6064	2844
ECG6065	2183
ECG6068	2806
ECG6069	2202
ECG6072	2454
ECG6073	2324
ECG6074	2751
ECG6075	1734
ECG6076	2786
ECG6077	1772
ECG6078	2818
ECG6079	1807
ECG6084	0610
ECG6085	1015
ECG6087	2493
ECG6090	1931
ECG6094	1536
ECG6102	4957
ECG6103	2299
ECG6104	0744
ECG6105	2765
ECG6106	4222
ECG6107	4221
ECG6110	1217
ECG6112	1195
ECG6113	2146
ECG6115	0474
ECG6116	4835
ECG6118	2126
ECG6154	0594
ECG6155	1337
ECG6156	1975
ECG6157	1894
ECG6158	0652
ECG6159	0193
ECG6162	3277
ECG6163	0202
ECG6200	3631
ECG6202	3634
ECG6204	3635
ECG6206	2809
ECG6208	4125
ECG6210	4134
ECG6220	1787
ECG6230	2178
ECG6240	1227
ECG6241	5684
ECG6244	1716
ECG6246	2219
ECG6247	5856
ECG6354	1017
ECG6355	0496
ECG6356	1030
ECG6357	1766
ECG6358	1040
ECG6359	1778
ECG6362	2805
ECG6363	3138
ECG6400	1659
ECG6400A	1659
ECG6400B	4304
ECG6401	2123
ECG6402	0312
ECG6403	4169
ECG6404	3373
ECG6405	4335
ECG6406	4505
ECG6407	3298
ECG6408	5776
ECG6409	1167
ECG6410	1882
ECG6411	5290
ECG6412	5537
ECG6415	5539
ECG6416	5540
ECG6417	5542
ECG6418	5543
ECG6419	5544
ECG6502	3036
ECG6507	3041
ECG6508	3164
ECG6532	1962
ECG6664	4251
ECG6800	0384
ECG6802	0389
ECG6809	5829
ECG6809E	2105
ECG6810	2075
ECG6820	OEM

DEVICE TYPE	REPL CODE
ECG6821	0443
ECG6850	0509
ECG6860	2667
ECG6875	4118
ECG6880	4437
ECG6885	4566
ECG6886	4570
ECG6887	4577
ECG6888	4586
ECG6889	0576
ECG7000	6020
ECG7001	5639
ECG7002	6111
ECG7003	4177
ECG7004	5891
ECG7005	4866
ECG7006	6021
ECG7007	4452
ECG7008	0517
ECG7009	3645
ECG7010	3473
ECG7011	6022
ECG7012	3344
ECG7013	4470
ECG7014	6023
ECG7015	3590
ECG7016	6024
ECG7017	6025
ECG7018	3015
ECG7019	4843
ECG7020	6026
ECG7021	6112
ECG7022	6113
ECG7023	6115
ECG7024	6116
ECG7025	6117
ECG7026	6118
ECG7027	6119
ECG7028	6120
ECG7029	6121
ECG7030	6122
ECG7031	6123
ECG7032	6124
ECG7033	6125
ECG7034	6126
ECG7035	6127
ECG7036	6128
ECG7037	6129
ECG7038	6130
ECG7039	6131
ECG7040	6132
ECG7041	6133
ECG7042	6134
ECG7043	6135
ECG7044	6136
ECG7045	6137
ECG7046	6138
ECG7047	6139
ECG7048	6140
ECG7049	6141
ECG7050	6142
ECG7051	6143
ECG7052	6145
ECG7053	6146
ECG7054	6147
ECG7055	6148
ECG7056	6149
ECG7057	6150
ECG7058	6151
ECG7059	6152
ECG7060	6153
ECG7061	6154
ECG7062	6155
ECG7063	6156
ECG7064	6157
ECG7065	6158
ECG7066	6159
ECG7067	6160
ECG7068	6161
ECG7069	6162
ECG7070	6163
ECG7071	6164
ECG7072	6165
ECG7073	5500
ECG7074	6166
ECG7214	5858
ECG7400	0232
ECG7401	0268
ECG7402	0310
ECG7403	0331
ECG7404	0357
ECG7405	0381
ECG7406	1197
ECG7407	1329
ECG7408	0462
ECG7409	0487
ECG7410	0507
ECG7411	0522
ECG7412	2227
ECG7413	1432
ECG7414	2228
ECG7416	1339
ECG7417	1342
ECG7420	0692
ECG7421	1347
ECG7422	4523
ECG7423	3429
ECG7425	3438
ECG7426	0798

DEVICE TYPE	REPL CODE
ECG7427	0812
ECG7428	4117
ECG7430	0867
ECG7432	0893
ECG7433	4130
ECG7437	3478
ECG7438	0990
ECG7439	5722
ECG7440	1018
ECG7441	1032
ECG7442	1046
ECG7443	1054
ECG7444	1066
ECG7445	1074
ECG7446	1090
ECG7447	1100
ECG7448	1117
ECG7450	0738
ECG7451	1160
ECG7453	1177
ECG7454	1193
ECG7460	1265
ECG7470	1394
ECG7472	1417
ECG7473	1164
ECG7474	1303
ECG7475	1423
ECG7476	1150
ECG7480	1527
ECG7481	3092
ECG7482	1564
ECG7483	0117
ECG7485	0370
ECG7486	1358
ECG7488A	4817
ECG7489	5358
ECG7490	1199
ECG7491	0974
ECG7492	0828
ECG7493A	0564
ECG7494	1692
ECG7495	1477
ECG7496	1705
ECG7497	2912
ECG8063	2909
ECG8070	2915
ECG8076	2916
ECG8080A	4467
ECG8081	2920
ECG8085	2923
ECG8090	2927
ECG8092	6236
ECG8096	2933
ECG8098	2363
ECG8103	2935
ECG8108	2940
ECG8115	2944
ECG8118	2945
ECG8123	5801
ECG8125	2948
ECG8139	2962
ECG8149	2970
ECG8167	3005
ECG8181	3007
ECG8212	1849
ECG8213	2972
ECG8214	5927
ECG8216	1852
ECG8219	5930
ECG8223	5814
ECG8224	1699
ECG8226	2984
ECG8228	1858
ECG8233	2063
ECG8234	2069
ECG8235	2076
ECG8242	2992
ECG8250	2173
ECG8255	0051
ECG8266	2260
ECG8301	2182
ECG8308	1064
ECG8309	5430
ECG8314	2468
ECG8316	5820
ECG8318	4082
ECG8321	5821
ECG8328	5822
ECG8345M	OEM
ECG8368	5825
ECG8370	5826
ECG8374	5827
ECG8520	5837
ECG8542	5838
ECG8546	5839
ECG8552	6268
ECG8553	6270
ECG8554	6271
ECG8555	6272
ECG8556	5840
ECG8613	5953
ECG8853	1730
ECG9093	0354
ECG9094	1622
ECG9097	1472
ECG9099	0329
ECG9109	1340
ECG9110	2871
ECG9111	2931

DEVICE TYPE	REPL CODE
ECG9112	1918
ECG9135	1609
ECG9157	1424
ECG9158	0461
ECG9200	4095
ECG9221	OEM
ECG9285	OEM
ECG9301	6311
ECG9302	6312
ECG9303	6313
ECG9304	6314
ECG9306	6315
ECG9307	6316
ECG9311	6318
ECG9312	6319
ECG9321	6322
ECG9322	6323
ECG9323	6324
ECG9324	6325
ECG9325	6326
ECG9326	6327
ECG9331	6328
ECG9332	6329
ECG9333	6330
ECG9334	6331
ECG9335	6332
ECG9342	6333
ECG9343	6334
ECG9347	6336
ECG9361	6338
ECG9362	6339
ECG9363	6340
ECG9367	6342
ECG9368	6343
ECG9370	1284
ECG9371	1406
ECG9372	1547
ECG9375	6344
ECG9380	6345
ECG9381	6346
ECG9382	6347
ECG9383	4940
ECG9390	6348
ECG9391	6349
ECG9392	6350
ECG9393	6351
ECG9394	6352
ECG9400	6353
ECG9401	4105
ECG9402	4099
ECG9403	1589
ECG9600	6320
ECG9601	2252
ECG9602	2270
ECG9615	5220
ECG9660	0613
ECG9661	2574
ECG9662	2542
ECG9663	2964
ECG9664	3003
ECG9665	3025
ECG9666	4079
ECG9667	3037
ECG9668	2417
ECG9669	2986
ECG9670	2334
ECG9671	4086
ECG9672	0078
ECG9673	0795
ECG9674	4098
ECG9675	4101
ECG9676	4107
ECG9677	4108
ECG9678	4110
ECG9679	4112
ECG9680	4115
ECG9681	3016
ECG9682	3010
ECG9683	4122
ECG9684	4124
ECG9685	4128
ECG9686	4132
ECG9688	4136
ECG9689	4137
ECG9690	4140
ECG9691	4143
ECG9696	4157
ECG9800	0844
ECG9801	0868
ECG9802	0882
ECG9803	0894
ECG9804	0913
ECG9805	0923
ECG9806	0939
ECG9807	0956
ECG9808	0976
ECG9809	0992
ECG9810	1005
ECG9811	1019
ECG9812	1033
ECG9813	4458
ECG9814	4461
ECG9900	3384
ECG9903	3808
ECG9904	3781
ECG9905	3669
ECG9906	4170
ECG9907	4172
ECG9908	3793

If replacement code is OEM, contact original manufacturer for replacement.

DEVICE TYPE	REPL CODE
ECG9909	3797
ECG9910	1248
ECG9911	1354
ECG9912	3843
ECG9913	3847
ECG9914	1063
ECG9915	3845
ECG9917	OEM
ECG9921	3303
ECG9923	OEM
ECG9924	2840
ECG9926	3868
ECG9927	4154
ECG9930	1812
ECG9931	3032
ECG9932	1035
ECG9933	2086
ECG9935	1168
ECG9936	1820
ECG9937	1824
ECG9941	2598
ECG9944	0033
ECG9945	0081
ECG9946	0141
ECG9948	3365
ECG9949	1833
ECG9950	2595
ECG9951	2067
ECG9961	1848
ECG9962	0557
ECG9963	0337
ECG9974	1799
ECG9976	3393
ECG9982	6413
ECG9989	3395
ECG9990	6416
ECG15005	5989
ECG15006	5259
ECG15007	4912
ECG15008	4548
ECG15009	5575
ECG15019	1796
ECG15020	3858
ECG15021	5990
ECG15022	5991
ECG15023	5993
ECG40085	3415
ECG40085B	3415
ECG40097	4367
ECG40097B	4367
ECG40098	0427
ECG40098B	0427
ECG40100B	3895
ECG40106B	3581
ECG40160	1349
ECG40160B	1349
ECG40161	1363
ECG40161B	1363
ECG40162	1378
ECG40162B	1378
ECG40163	1397
ECG40163B	1397
ECG40174	1542
ECG40174B	1542
ECG40175B	1520
ECG40182B	4579
ECG40192	1753
ECG40192B	1753
ECG40193	1765
ECG40193B	1765
ECG40194	1758
ECG40194B	1758
ECG40195	1773
ECG40195B	1773
ECG56004	0767
ECG56006	0739
ECG56008	0612
ECG56010	0869
ECG56014	6185
ECG56015	5227
ECG56016	5230
ECG56017	1649
ECG56018	1956
ECG56019	6000
ECG56020	5511
ECG56022	3169
ECG56024	3177
ECG56026	3192
ECG56028	6013
ECG56030	5745
ECG56031	3663
ECG56033	6012
ECG65101	4524
ECG74107	0936
ECG74109	0962
ECG74110	0981
ECG74111	0996
ECG74121	0175
ECG74122	1131
ECG74123	1149
ECG74125	1174
ECG74126	1184
ECG74128	1210
ECG74132	1261
ECG74136	1306
ECG74141	1367
ECG74142	1380
ECG74143	1399
ECG74144	1408
ECG74145	0614
ECG74147	1442
ECG74150	1484
ECG74151	1487
ECG74152	1509
ECG74153	1531
ECG74154	1546
ECG74155	1566
ECG74156	1582
ECG74157	1595
ECG74158	4372
ECG74160	1621
ECG74161	1635
ECG74162	1007
ECG74163	1656
ECG74164	0729
ECG74165	1675
ECG74166	0231
ECG74170	1711
ECG74173	1755
ECG74174	1759
ECG74175	1776
ECG74176	1784
ECG74177	1792
ECG74178	1802
ECG74179	1809
ECG74180	1818
ECG74181	1831
ECG74182	1845
ECG74190	1901
ECG74191	1906
ECG74192	1910
ECG74193	1915
ECG74195	1932
ECG74196	1939
ECG74197	1945
ECG74198	1953
ECG74199	1960
ECG74221	2129
ECG74249	2274
ECG74251	2283
ECG74290	2588
ECG74293	2620
ECG74365	1450
ECG74366	1462
ECG74367	1479
ECG74368	1500
ECG74390	3210
ECG74393	3225
ECG74490	3619
ECG75188	0503
ECG75189	0506
ECG75450B	1222
ECG75451B	1235
ECG75452B	1253
ECG75453B	1262
ECG75454B	1279
ECG75491B	1718
ECG75492B	1729
ECG75493	4933
ECG75494	4934
ECG75497	5726
ECG75498	4936
ECG-HIDIV-1	2949
ECG-HIDIV-2	2950
ECG-HIDIV-3	2952
ECG-HIDIV-4	2951
ECG-HIDIV-12	5265
ECN2511SPV	OEM
ECR0510	0071
ECR405ST0911	OEM
ECR-600-2	0015
ECR600-2	0015
ECXB0061	OEM
ECX-B0063	OEM
ECX-B0085B	OEM
ECX-B0085C	OEM
ECXB0087	OEM
ECX-B0095	OEM
ECXB0095	OEM
ECXB1026	OEM
ECXB1027	OEM
ECXB1028	OEM
ECXB1028B	OEM
ECX-B1040	OEM
ECXB1050C	OEM
ECXB1060	OEM
ED0011	0057
ED0012	0057
ED0031	0282
ED0032	0133
ED0036	0091
ED0039	0681
ED0056	0282
ED0059	0133
ED0067	0480
ED0084A	0253
ED0084B	0253
ED0084C	0091
ED0084D	0466
ED01	OEM
ED01-06	OEM
ED03	OEM
ED05	OEM
ED0109E	0466
ED0111	0118
ED0114XT	0901
ED0116XT	0901
ED0120	0023
ED0147	0672
ED0152	OEM
ED0173	0071
ED0202	OEM
ED0214F	0466
ED0226A	0873
ED0278	0023
ED0328	0062
ED0353	0023
ED0366	0023
ED0372	0031
ED2(ELCOM)	0911
ED3(ELCOM)	0911
ED-3TV	OEM
ED-3TV1	0079
ED-4	0015
ED4	0015
ED4(ELCOM)	0143
ED-5	0015
ED5	0015
ED-6	0015
ED6	0015
ED6(ELCOM)	0143
ED-6C3	OEM
ED6C3	OEM
ED-6C3R	OEM
ED6.2EB	0631
ED7	0015
ED7(ELCOM)	0911
ED-7TV	OEM
ED-7TV1	0201
ED8(ELCOM)	0087
ED-8H1	OEM
ED8H1	OEM
ED-8N1	OEM
ED8N1	OEM
ED-9	OEM
ED9	0143
ED9(ELCOM)	0143
ED10(ELCOM)	0123
ED10L	0102
ED-11	OEM
ED11	6304
ED11(ELCOM)	0123
ED11EB	0181
ED12(ELCOM)	0143
ED-13TV1	0286
ED-15	OEM
ED15	OEM
ED-15TV1	0286
ED-15TV3	0286
ED-16H1	0374
ED16H1	OEM
ED-16N1	OEM
ED16N1	OEM
ED20	OEM
ED-22TV1	OEM
ED24(ELCOM)	0290
ED-24H1	OEM
ED24H1	OEM
ED29(ELCOM)	0087
ED31(ELCOM)	0133
ED32(ELCOM)	0133
ED33(ELCOM)	0918
ED-45TV1	OEM
ED46	0143
ED50	OEM
ED50-01	OEM
ED50-02	OEM
ED50-03	OEM
ED51	0050
ED52	0279
ED53	0279
ED54B	0279
ED55	0004
ED56	0004
ED57	0004
ED-60	0143
ED60	0143
ED-75X1	OEM
ED75X1	OEM
ED95	OEM
ED-100X1	OEM
ED100X1	OEM
ED101R	OEM
ED101RG	OEM
ED102G	OEM
ED102GKB	OEM
ED102R	OEM
ED102RKB	OEM
ED102RKW	OEM
ED103G	OEM
ED103GK	OEM
ED103R	OEM
ED103RK	OEM
ED104R	OEM
ED104RK	OEM
ED105G	OEM
ED105GK	OEM
ED105R	OEM
ED105RK	OEM
ED106R	OEM
ED106RK	OEM
ED107G	OEM
ED107GK	OEM
ED107R	OEM
ED107RK	OEM
ED108G	OEM
ED108GKB	OEM
ED108GKW	OEM
ED108R	OEM
ED108RKB	OEM
ED108RKW	OEM
ED109R	OEM
ED109RKB	OEM
ED109RKW	OEM
ED110R	OEM
ED113G	OEM
ED113R	OEM
ED113Y	OEM
ED114G	OEM
ED114R	OEM
ED114Y	OEM
ED115G	OEM
ED115R	OEM
ED116R	OEM
ED120L	0201
ED120R	OEM
ED121G	OEM
ED121R	OEM
ED122G	OEM
ED122R	OEM
ED123G	OEM
ED123R	OEM
ED123Y	OEM
ED124G	OEM
ED124R	OEM
ED124Y	OEM
ED-125X1	OEM
ED125X1	OEM
ED-150X1	OEM
ED150X1	OEM
ED150Z	0016
ED202G	OEM
ED202R	OEM
ED209G	OEM
ED209R	OEM
ED209Y	OEM
ED216G	OEM
ED216R	OEM
ED216Y	OEM
ED220G	OEM
ED220R	OEM
ED220Y	OEM
ED226A	OEM
ED226G	OEM
ED226R	OEM
ED226Y	OEM
ED322	OEM
ED402	OEM
ED553G	OEM
ED553R	OEM
ED553Y	OEM
ED592K	0224
ED592M	0144
ED700A	OEM
ED700G	OEM
ED700H	OEM
ED7000	OEM
ED700P	OEM
ED700R	OEM
ED700Y	OEM
ED703A	OEM
ED703G	OEM
ED703H	OEM
ED7030	OEM
ED703P	OEM
ED703R	OEM
ED703Y	OEM
ED704A	OEM
ED704G	OEM
ED704H	OEM
ED7040	OEM
ED704P	OEM
ED704R	OEM
ED704Y	OEM
ED706A	OEM
ED706G	OEM
ED706H	OEM
ED7060	OEM
ED706P	OEM
ED706R	OEM
ED706Y	OEM
ED708H	OEM
ED710A	OEM
ED710G	OEM
ED710H	OEM
ED7100	OEM
ED710P	OEM
ED710R	OEM
ED710Y	OEM
ED713A	OEM
ED713G	OEM
ED713J	OEM
ED7130	OEM
ED713P	OEM
ED713R	OEM
ED713Y	OEM
ED714A	OEM
ED714G	OEM
ED714H	OEM
ED7140	OEM
ED714P	OEM
ED714R	OEM
ED714Y	OEM
ED716A	OEM
ED716G	OEM
ED716H	OEM
ED7160	OEM
ED716P	OEM
ED716R	OEM
ED716Y	OEM
ED718H	OEM
ED720A	OEM
ED720G	OEM
ED720H	OEM
ED7200	OEM
ED720P	OEM
ED720R	OEM
ED720Y	OEM
ED723A	OEM
ED723G	OEM
ED723H	OEM
ED7230	OEM
ED723P	OEM
ED723R	OEM
ED723Y	OEM
ED724A	OEM
ED724G	OEM
ED724H	OEM
ED7240	OEM
ED724P	OEM
ED724R	OEM
ED724Y	OEM
ED726A	OEM
ED726G	OEM
ED726H	OEM
ED7260	OEM
ED726P	OEM
ED726R	OEM
ED726Y	OEM
ED728H	OEM
ED740A	OEM
ED740G	OEM
ED740H	OEM
ED7400	OEM
ED740P	OEM
ED740R	OEM
ED740Y	OEM
ED743A	OEM
ED743G	OEM
ED743H	OEM
ED7430	OEM
ED743P	OEM
ED743R	OEM
ED743Y	OEM
ED744A	OEM
ED744G	OEM
ED744H	OEM
ED7440	OEM
ED744P	OEM
ED744R	OEM
ED744Y	OEM
ED746A	OEM
ED746G	OEM
ED746H	OEM
ED7460	OEM
ED746P	OEM
ED746R	OEM
ED746Y	OEM
ED748H	OEM
ED750A	OEM
ED750G	OEM
ED750H	OEM
ED7500	OEM
ED750P	OEM
ED750R	OEM
ED750Y	OEM
ED753A	OEM
ED753G	OEM
ED753H	OEM
ED7530	OEM
ED753P	OEM
ED753R	OEM
ED753Y	OEM
ED754A	OEM
ED754G	OEM
ED754H	OEM
ED7540	OEM
ED754P	OEM
ED754R	OEM
ED754Y	OEM
ED756A	OEM
ED756G	OEM
ED756H	OEM
ED7560	OEM
ED756P	OEM
ED756R	OEM
ED756Y	OEM
ED758H	OEM
ED1052	OEM
ED1104K	OEM
ED-1402	0016
ED1402	1943
ED1402A	0016
ED1402A/09-30506	0079
ED1402A/09-305066	0016
ED1402B	0016
ED1402C	0076
ED1402D	0079
ED1402E	0076
ED1502	2195
ED1502A	0224
ED1502B	0079
ED-1502C	0224
ED1502C	0127
ED1502D	0079
ED1502E	0127
ED1502F	0224
ED1502P	0224
ED1502R	0326
ED-1602	OEM
ED1602(C)	0037
ED1602A	2245
ED1602B	2245
ED1602C	0037
ED1602D	0037
ED1602E	0037
ED1702(L)	OEM
ED1702K	0079
ED1702L	0016
ED1702L/09-30506	0079
ED1702L/09-305068	0016
ED1702M	0076
ED1702N	0018
ED1704L	0079
ED1802-0	0037
ED1802-O	0150
ED1802C	0527
ED1802K	OEM
ED1802L	0338
ED1802M	0037
ED1802N	0527
ED1802N,M	0150
ED1804	0015
ED1892	0015
ED2106	0015
ED2107	0015
ED2108	0015
ED2109	0015
ED2110	0015
ED2200	OEM
ED2842	0015
ED2843	0015
ED2844	0015
ED2845	0015
ED2846	0015
ED2847	0071
ED2848	0071
ED2849	0071
ED2910	0071
ED2911	0071
ED2912	0071
ED2913	0071
ED2914	0015
ED2915	0015
ED2916	0015
ED2917	0015
ED2918	0015
ED2919	0015
ED2920	0015
ED2921	0015
ED2922	0071
ED2923	0071
ED2924	0071
ED3000	0015
ED3000A	0015
ED3000B	0015
ED3001	0015
ED3001A	0015
ED3001B	0015
ED3002	0015
ED3002A	0015
ED3002B	0015
ED3003	0015
ED3003A	0015
ED3003B	0015
ED3003S	0015
ED3004	0015
ED3004A	0015
ED3004B	0015
ED3005	0023
ED3005A	0015
ED3005B	0015
ED3006	0015
ED3006A	0015
ED3006B	0015
ED3007	0071
ED3007A	0071
ED3007B	0071
ED3008	0071
ED3008A	0071
ED3008B	0071
ED3009	0071
ED3009A	0071
ED3009B	0071
ED3010	0071
ED3010A	0071
ED3010B	0071
ED5053	OEM
ED5053G	OEM
ED5053R	OEM
ED5053Y	OEM
ED5290	OEM
ED8307	OEM
ED8308	OEM
ED8309	OEM
ED8310	OEM
ED8311	OEM
ED8312	OEM
ED219464	0143
ED224548	0015
ED224550	0015
ED269464	OEM
ED302379	0133
ED329128	0015
ED329130	0015
ED491130	1075
ED494583	0015
ED498150	0943
ED511097	0015
ED511918	0398
ED514721	0133
ED515790	0133
ED516420	0133
ED520762	OEM
ED536062	0133
ED560913	0133
ED703876	0124
ED703883	0210
ED703904	0023
EDF1A	1864
EDF1AM	OEM
EDF1B	1864
EDF1BM	OEM
EDF1C	1864
EDF1CM	OEM
EDF1D	1864
EDF1DM	OEM
EDF703882	0053
EDG-0001	0143
EDG-0003	0019
EDG-0006	0123
EDG-0014	0133
EDG-1	0143
EDG-3	0019
EDH2-30	OEM
EDH4-75	OEM
EDH4-100	OEM
EDH4-125	OEM
EDH4-150	OEM
EDH12	OEM
EDH18	OEM
EDH36	OEM
EDH36-1	OEM
EDH36-2	OEM
EDH36-3	OEM
EDJ-363	0015
EDMF-15B	0286
EDMF-25B	0374
EDMF25B	0374
EDS-0001	0133
EDS-0002	0023
EDS-0004	0023
EDS-0014	0133
EDS-0017	0015
EDS-0024	0023
EDS-0038	0139
EDS-0042	0030
EDS-1	0133
EDS-4	0023
EDS-11	0015
E-DS17	0023
EDS-17	0015
E-DS18	0023
EDS-31	0030
E-DS135D	0023
E-DS442	0133
E-DS442-VG1	0133
E-DS442VG1	0133
E-DS442YG1	0133
EDZ-0045	0057
EDZ-2	0644
EDZ-11	0416
EDZ-14	0244
EDZ-19	0091
EDZ-20	0025
EDZ-23	0012
EDZ-24	0244
EE5A-3.3	0289
EE5A-3.6	0188
EE5A-3.9	0451
EE5A-4.3	0528
EE5A-4.7	0446
EE5A-5.1	0162
EE5A-5.6	0157
EE5A-6.2	0631
EE5A-6.8	0025
EE5A-7.5	0644
EE5A-8.2	0244
EE5A-9.1	0012
EE5A-10	0170
EE5A-11	0313
EE5A-12G	0137
EE5A-14	0100
EE5A-15	0002
EE5A-20G	0526
EE5A-22	0560
EE5A-24	0398
EE5A-26	0436
EE5A-27	0436
EE5A-29	0721
EE5A-33G	0039
EE5A-36	0814
EE5A-39	0346
EE5A-43	0925
EE5A-47	0993
EE5A-51	0497
EE5A-55	1823
EE5A-56	0863
EE5A-62A	0778
EE5A-68	1258
EE5A-82P	0327
EE5A-91	1301
EE5A-110A	0149

If replacement code is OEM, contact original manufacturer for replacement.

397

DEVICE TYPE	REPL CODE
EE5A-115	0789
EE5A-120	0186
EE5A-129	0361
EE5A-130	0213
EE5A-140	0245
EE5A-150	0028
EE5A-160	0255
EE5A-162	0416
EE5A-170	0871
EE5A-177	0490
EE5A-180	0363
EE5A-190	2831
EE5A-200	0417
EE5A-200G	0417
EE301	0259
EECG-1234	0155
EER600-2	0229
EE-SJ3	OEM
EE-SJ5	OEM
EE-SX315	OEM
EE-TP109	OEM
EF1(ELCOM)	0321
EF2(ELCOM)	0321
EF3	0321
EF4(ELCOM)	0212
EF5(ELCOM)	0212
EF68A00C	OEM
EF68A00CV	OEM
EF68A00P	OEM
EF68A00PV	OEM
EF68A10C	OEM
EF68A10CP	OEM
EF68A10CV	OEM
EF68A10P	OEM
EF68A21C	OEM
EF68A21CV	OEM
EF68A21PV	OEM
EF68A50C	OEM
EF68A50CP	OEM
EF68A50CV	OEM
EF68A50P	OEM
EF68A50PV	OEM
EF68A52C	OEM
EF68A52CV	OEM
EF68A52P	OEM
EF68A52PV	OEM
EF68B00C	OEM
EF68B00P	OEM
EF68B10C	OEM
EF68B10P	OEM
EF68B21C	OEM
EF68B21P	OEM
EF68B50C	OEM
EF68B50P	OEM
EF68B52C	OEM
EF68B52P	OEM
EF75CN1	OEM
EF75CN3	OEM
EF75M1	OEM
EF75M3	OEM
EF75N6	OEM
EF75N12	OEM
EF100	0071
EF125CN1	OEM
EF125CN3	OEM
EF125M1	OEM
EF125M3	OEM
EF125N6	OEM
EF125N12	OEM
EF150	OEM
EF175CN1	OEM
EF175CN3	OEM
EF175M1	OEM
EF175M3	OEM
EF175N6	OEM
EF175N12	OEM
EF200	0344
EF4116BC-15	OEM
EF4116BC-20	OEM
EF4116BC-25	OEM
EF4116BC-30	OEM
EF4116BJ-15	OEM
EF4116BJ-25	OEM
EF4116BJ-30	OEM
EF6800C	OEM
EF6800CMB	OEM
EF6800CV	OEM
EF6800P	OEM
EF6800PV	OEM
EF6802C	OEM
EF6802P	OEM
EF6805P2C	OEM
EF6805P2J	OEM
EF6805P2P	OEM
EF6810C	2075
EF6810CMB	OEM
EF6810CP	OEM
EF6810CV	OEM
EF6810P	2075
EF6821C	OEM
EF6821CMB	OEM
EF6821CV	OEM
EF6821P	OEM
EF6821PV	OEM
EF6850C	OEM
EF6850CMB	OEM
EF6850CP	OEM
EF6850CV	OEM
EF6850P	OEM

DEVICE TYPE	REPL CODE
EF6850PV	OEM
EF6852C	OEM
EF6852CMB	OEM
EF6852CV	OEM
EF6852P	OEM
EF6852PV	OEM
EF9364AC	OEM
EF9364AP	OEM
EF9364BC	OEM
EF9364BP	OEM
EF68000	OEM
EFD13A	OEM
EFD13B	OEM
EFD13C	OEM
EFD13D	OEM
EFD13E	OEM
EFD13F	OEM
EFD13G	OEM
EFE13A	OEM
EFE13B	OEM
EFE13C	OEM
EFE13D	OEM
EFE13E	OEM
EFE13F	OEM
EFE13G	OEM
EFE14A	OEM
EFE14B	OEM
EFE14C	OEM
EFE14D	OEM
EFE14E	OEM
EFE14F	OEM
EFE14G	OEM
EFE15A	OEM
EFE15B	OEM
EFE15C	OEM
EFE15D	OEM
EFE15E	OEM
EFE15F	OEM
EFE15G	OEM
EFF13A	OEM
EFF13B	OEM
EFF13C	OEM
EFF13D	OEM
EFF13E	OEM
EFF13F	OEM
EFF13G	OEM
EFF14A	OEM
EFF14B	OEM
EFF14C	OEM
EFF14D	OEM
EFF14E	OEM
EFF14F	OEM
EFF14G	OEM
EFF15A	OEM
EFF15B	OEM
EFF15C	OEM
EFF15D	OEM
EFF15E	OEM
EFF15F	OEM
EFF15G	OEM
EFG13A	OEM
EFG13B	OEM
EFG13C	OEM
EFG13D	OEM
EFG13E	OEM
EFG13F	OEM
EFG13G	OEM
EFG14A	OEM
EFG14B	OEM
EFG14C	OEM
EFG14D	OEM
EFG14E	OEM
EFG14F	OEM
EFG14G	OEM
EFG15A	OEM
EFG15B	OEM
EFG15C	OEM
EFG15D	OEM
EFG15E	OEM
EFG15F	OEM
EFG15G	OEM
EFM-VE10	OEM
EFR1A	OEM
EFR1B	OEM
EFR1C	OEM
EFR1D	OEM
EFR3A	OEM
EFR3B	OEM
EFR3C	OEM
EFR3D	OEM
EFR5A	OEM
EFR5B	OEM
EFR5C	OEM
EFR5D	OEM
EFR8A	OEM
EFR8B	OEM
EFR8C	OEM
EFR8D	OEM
EFS-16S1	OEM
EFS-32D1/D2	OEM
EFS-32U2	OEM
EFS-ADC1	OEM
EFS-DAC1	OEM
EFS-MPU2	OEM
EFS-MPU9	OEM
EFS-P8IO	OEM
EFS-P160	OEM
EFS-P161	OEM
EFS-PTIM	OEM

DEVICE TYPE	REPL CODE
EFS-VIE1	OEM
EFS-VIG1	OEM
EFT-P064	OEM
EG-01	OEM
EG01	0790
EG01A	0015
EG01C	0017
EG01Y	1082
EG01Z	1082
EG1	0790
EG1A	0015
EG1Y	1082
EG100	0015
EG100H	0015
EG200	OEM
EG250	OEM
EG300	OEM
EGL27A	OEM
EGL27B	OEM
EGL27C	OEM
EGL27D	OEM
EGL27F	OEM
EGL27G	OEM
EGL41A	OEM
EGL41B	OEM
EGL41C	OEM
EGL41D	OEM
EGL41F	OEM
EGL41G	OEM
EGP10A	0494
EGP10B	0494
EGP10C	0494
EGP10D	0494
EGP10F	0494
EGP10G	0494
EGP20A	0031
EGP20B	0031
EGP20C	0031
EGP20D	0031
EGP20F	0031
EGP20G	0031
EGP30A	0031
EGP30B	0031
EGP30C	0031
EGP30D	0031
EGP30F	0031
EGP30G	0031
EGP30GL	OEM
EGP30GL-6072	OEM
EGP50A	1352
EGP50B	1352
EGP50C	1352
EGP50D	1352
EGP50F	1352
EGP50G	1352
E-GZA5R1Z	0041
EH1	0023
EH-1A	0023
EH1A	0023
EH1Y1	OEM
EH-1Z	0023
EH1Z	0023
EH-1ZV	0023
EH2C11	0015
EH2C11/7+12/1	0015
EH250	OEM
EH300	OEM
EH350	OEM
EH400	OEM
E-HA12413	3764
EHD-AP4023S	OEM
EHD-HA6475	OEM
EHF4047B	OEM
EHF40163B	OEM
EHM312A12	OEM
EHM315S02	OEM
EHM-822A29	OEM
EHM-J12E94	OEM
EHM-K046W66(K)	OEM
EHM-K320E69	0674
EHM-K320F69	OEM
EHM-K720A72FB	OEM
EHM-K720A73FB	OEM
EHMK722P	OEM
EHM-K724F13S	OEM
EHMK3342W92K	OEM
EHM-VCR0019	OEM
EHT1500B	OEM
EHT1700B	OEM
EHT1750B	OEM
EI1001	OEM
EI299700	3436
EI307200	4719
EI703843	2237
EI703907	4216
EICM-0060	1044
EICM-14	1983
EICM-19	2594
EIP	OEM
EJ350	OEM
EJ400	OEM
EJ450	OEM
EJ500	OEM
EJA17-25	0374
EK-03	0730
EK03	0730
EK03W	OEM
EK-04	1732
EK04	0730

DEVICE TYPE	REPL CODE
EK04LF	0730
EK06W	OEM
EK13	0494
EK14	0494
EK14-F5	4235
EK136	0004
EK159	0279
EK450	OEM
EK500	OEM
EK600	OEM
EKB32-02	OEM
EL0018	OEM
EL0069	OEM
EL-1	OEM
EL1	OEM
EL1-Z	1082
EL1CL3	OEM
EL1F	OEM
EL1K3	OEM
EL1KL2	OEM
EL1KL3	OEM
EL1L1	OEM
EL-1L2	OEM
EL1L2	OEM
EL-1L3	3300
EL1ML2	OEM
EL1Z	1082
EL1Z-V1	0023
EL2	OEM
EL7L	OEM
EL23F	OEM
EL45F	OEM
EL74A	OEM
EL74HCT244	OEM
EL74HCT374	OEM
EL75	0224
EL119	OEM
EL131	0321
EL214	0086
EL222	OEM
EL231	0127
EL232	0016
EL238	0016
EL264	0126
EL270	OEM
EL271	OEM
EL401	0396
EL403	0076
EL434	0127
EL453	OEM
EL603	OEM
EL613	5595
EL627	0127
EL642	0079
EL645	OEM
EL-724	0398
EL850	OEM
E-LA1492	OEM
E-LA4192	2370
E-LB1423	OEM
ELI	OEM
ELIZ-V1	0124
ELM100	0279
ELM102	0211
ELM102A	0004
ELM103A	0208
ELM104	0085
ELM104MP	3004
ELM105	0435
ELM106	0150
ELM107	0127
ELM108	0144
ELM109	0143
ELM110MP	0123
ELM112	0911
ELM113	0196
ELM114	0479
ELM116	0015
ELM117	0015
ELM118	0769
ELM120	0469
ELM121	0160
ELM121MP	0265
ELM123	0198
ELM123A	0016
ELM124	0142
ELM125	0071
ELM127	0969
ELM128	0086
ELM129	0126
ELM130	0103
ELM130MP	1506
ELM131	0222
ELM135	0162
ELM136	0157
ELM137	0631
ELM138	0644
ELM139	0012
ELM140	0170
ELM142	0137
ELM144	0100
ELM152	0042
ELM153	0848
ELM154	0233
ELM156	0087
ELM157	0275
ELM158	0164
ELM159	0037
ELM160	0050

DEVICE TYPE	REPL CODE
ELM161	0007
ELM162	0074
ELM163	0637
ELM164	0003
ELM165	0065
ELM166	0276
ELM167	0287
ELM168	0106
ELM169	0782
ELM170	0782
ELM171	0283
ELM172A	0396
ELM175	0178
ELM177	0133
ELM180	1671
ELM181	0130
ELM182	0556
ELM183	1190
ELM184	0161
ELM185	0455
ELM186	0219
ELM187	1045
ELM188	0546
ELM189	0378
ELM190	0334
ELM191	0334
ELM192	0218
ELM193	0786
ELM194	0855
ELM195A	0693
ELM196	0419
ELM197	0848
ELM198	0168
ELM199	0111
ELM210	0561
ELM211	1357
ELM218	0899
ELM219	0486
ELM221	0349
ELM222	0212
ELM224	0626
ELM229	0224
ELM234	0688
ELM235	0930
ELM236	0830
ELM237	1401
ELM241	0556
ELM242	1190
ELM243	2411
ELM263	2220
ELM281	2002
ELM287	0710
ELM288	0338
ELM500A	0190
ELM502	0201
ELM503	0286
ELM504	0752
ELM505	0752
ELM506	0102
ELM513	1313
ELM519	0124
ELM5400	0895
ELM5404	0058
ELM5800	0959
ELM5804	0959
ELM5809	0087
ELM5830	0964
ELM5831	0810
ELM5842	0204
ELM5843	0810
ELM5850	0964
ELM5851	0810
ELM5862	0122
ELM5863	0810
ELM6408	2137
ELP3.3	0289
ELP3.6	0188
ELP3.9	0451
ELP4.3	0528
ELP4.7	0446
ELP5.6	0157
ELP6.2	0631
ELP6.8	0025
ELP7.5	0644
ELP8.2	0244
ELP9.1	0012
ELP10	0170
ELP11	0313
ELP12G	0137
ELP14	0002
ELP15	0002
ELP20G	0526
ELP22	0560
ELP24	0398
ELP26	0436
ELP27	0436
ELP29	0721
ELP33G	0039
ELP36	0814
ELP39G	0346
ELP43	0925
ELP47	0993
ELP51	0497
ELP55	1823
ELP56	0863
ELP62C	0778
ELP68	1258
ELP82B	0327
ELP91	1301

DEVICE TYPE	REPL CODE
ELP110	0149
ELP115G	0789
ELP120	0186
ELP129	0361
ELP130	0213
ELP140	0245
ELP150	0028
ELP160	0255
ELP170	0871
ELP178	0490
ELP180	0363
ELP190	2831
ELP200	0417
ELP200G	0417
EL-SKL	OEM
EL-SKLT	OEM
EM01	0015
EM01A	0072
EM01Z	0133
EM01ZW	0015
EM02B	4344
EM02BM	0071
EM02BMV	0071
EM02BMV0	0071
EM-1	0015
EM1	0015
EM1A	0072
EM1B	0071
EM1C	0017
EM1J2	0015
EM1Y	0604
EM-1Z	0604
EM1Z	0023
EM1Z1	0015
EM-1ZS	0604
EM1ZV	0604
EM2	0071
EM2A	0071
EM2B	0071
EM51	OEM
EM401	0015
EM402	0015
EM403	0015
EM404	0015
EM405	0015
EM406	0015
EM407	0071
EM408	0071
EM409	0071
EM410	0071
EM500	0015
EM501	0015
EM502	0015
EM503	0015
EM504	0015
EM505	0015
EM506	0015
EM507	0071
EM508	0071
EM509	0071
EM510	0071
EM513	0344
EM600	OEM
EM1021	0015
EM1095	OEM
EM1114	OEM
EM1114A	OEM
EM1114B	OEM
EM1114C	OEM
EM1137L	OEM
EM1138	OEM
EM1138M	OEM
EM1149	OEM
EM-1171	0015
EM1188	OEM
EM1502	OEM
EM1507	OEM
EM1508	OEM
EMI04700	OEM
EMK3342W98K	OEM
EMM-VCR0019	OEM
EMRL01-06	OEM
EMRL01-08	OEM
EMS-72272	0124
EN10	0079
EN30	0079
EN40	0079
EN697	0016
EN706	0016
EN708	0016
EN718A	0144
EN722	0037
EN744	0016
EN870	0086
EN871	0855
EN914	0016
EN915	0079
EN916	0144
EN918	0144
EN930	0016
EN956	0016
EN1132	0037
EN1364	1162
EN1364/1231	1162
EN1613	0086
EN1711	0086
EN2219	0016
EN2222	0016
EN2369	OEM

DEVICE TYPE	REPL CODE
EN2369A	0016
EN2484	0111
EN2894	0037
EN2894A	0037
EN2905	0126
EN2907	0037
EN3009	0016
EN3011	0016
EN3013	0016
EN3014	0016
EN3250	0037
EN3502	0126
EN3504	0037
EN3903	0076
EN3904	0016
EN3905	0037
EN3906	0006
EN3962	0037
EN11235	1420
EN11238	3250
EN11301	1162
EN11401	3317
EN11414	3325
EN11436	2109
EN11438	3060
EO-44A	0211
EO44A	0004
EO65	0279
EO66	0279
EO67	0279
EO68	0279
EO70	0136
EO105	0279
EO704	0015
EOT521XXX	OEM
EOT522XXX	OEM
EP01C	0541
EP6X10	0133
EP6X11	0102
EP14X226	OEM
EP14X326	OEM
EP15X0045	OEM
EP15X0217	OEM
EP15X1	0079
EP15X2	0079
EP15X3	0111
EP15X4	0126
EP15X5	0086
EP15X6	0155
EP15X6(PNP)	2464
EP15X7	0016
EP15X8	0079
EP15X9	0079
EP15X10	0058
EP15X11	0419
EP15X12	0309
EP15X13	0786
EP15X14	0419
EP15X15	0919
EP15X16	0142
EP15X17	0037
EP15X18	0233
EP15X19	0388
EP15X20	0326
EP15X21	0786
EP15X22	0042
EP15X23	0919
EP15X24	1357
EP15X25	0561
EP15X26	0037
EP15X27	0283
EP15X28	0065
EP15X29	0130
EP15X30	0419
EP15X31	0095
EP15X32	0558
EP15X33	0086
EP15X34	1021
EP15X35	0142
EP15X36	0212
EP15X37	0127
EP15X38	0127
EP15X39	0079
EP15X40	0212
EP15X41	0224
EP15X42	0224
EP15X43	0419
EP15X44	0848
EP15X45	0065
EP15X48	0203
EP15X50	0168
EP15X51	0786
EP15X52	0006
EP15X53	0037
EP15X54	0326
EP15X55	0144
EP15X57	0006
EP15X58	0210
EP15X60	0037
EP15X61	0283
EP15X64	0212
EP15X68	0042
EP15X83	0079
EP15X85	0079
EP15X86	0079
EP15X87	0079
EP15X88	0079
EP15X89	0079
EP15X90	0037

398

If replacement code is OEM, contact original manufacturer for replacement.

DEVICE TYPE	REPL CODE
EP15X90(IC)	0619
EP15X91	0264
EP15X92	0076
EP15X93	0191
EP15X94	3644
EP15X94(PNP)	OEM
EP15X95	3308
EP15X96	0386
EP15X97	0042
EP15X98	0224
EP15X99	0127
EP15X101	0191
EP15X102	0419
EP15X104	3881
EP15X105	0388
EP15X106	0058
EP15X107	0037
EP15X108	2596
EP15X109	2770
EP15X110	0076
EP15X123	0388
EP15X124	3308
EP15X125	0127
EP15X126	0006
EP15X128	0006
EP15X141	0224
EP15X142	0236
EP15X143	0079
EP15X217	1981
EP15X218	0055
EP15X221	0818
EP15X222	3294
EP15X223	4511
EP15X224	5436
EP15X225	0006
EP15X226	0079
EP15X227	OEM
EP15X228	0818
EP15X231	OEM
EP15X232	OEM
EP15X233	OEM
EP15X244	OEM
EP15X288	0818
EP15X400	OEM
EP16X1	1141
EP16X2	0269
EP16X3	0019
EP16X4	0133
EP16X5	0002
EP16X6	0196
EP16X7	0086
EP16X8	0030
EP16X10	0102
EP16X11	0102
EP16X12	0644
EP16X13	0015
EP16X14	OEM
EP16X15	0133
EP16X16	0398
EP16X17	0028
EP16X18	OEM
EP16X19	0181
EP16X20	0133
EP16X21	0123
EP16X22	0133
EP16X23	0133
EP16X24	0017
EP16X25	0162
EP16X27	0124
EP16X29	0289
EP16X30	0062
EP16X32	0721
EP16X33	OEM
EP16X34	2496
EP16X36	0137
EP16X42	0911
EP16X49	0124
EP16X50	0124
EP16X51	0133
EP16X52	0681
EP16X53	0123
EP16X54	1319
EP16X58	0210
EP16X59	0124
EP16X61	0466
EP16X66	0124
EP16X68	0002
EP16X69	0181
EP16X70	0077
EP16X71	0023
EP16X73	0446
EP16X74	0528
EP16X135	OEM
EP16X145	0023
EP16X147	0133
EP16X148	0814
EP16X149	0023
EP16X152	0041
EP16X153	0466
EP16X154	0023
EP16X155	0064
EP16X156	0436
EP16X157	1404
EP16X158	OEM
EP16X161	OEM
EP16X165	OEM
EP16X166	OEM
EP16X167	0140
EP16X217	OEM

DEVICE TYPE	REPL CODE
EP20	0338
EP21G	OEM
EP21R	OEM
EP21Y	OEM
EP25	0037
EP35	0786
EP36X12	0644
EP41X1	OEM
EP41X14	OEM
EP41X68	OEM
EP41X70	OEM
EP57X1	0023
EP57X2	0752
EP57X3	1313
EP57X4	0023
EP57X5	0017
EP57X7	OEM
EP57X9	0102
EP57X10	0023
EP57X11	1137
EP57X12	0015
EP57X54	0015
EP57X156	OEM
EP62G	OEM
EP62R	OEM
EP62X41	1493
EP62X57	3815
EP62X61	1493
EP62X76	6290
EP62X84	6291
EP62X167	OEM
EP62Y	OEM
EP64G	OEM
EP64R	OEM
EP64Y	OEM
EP84X0035	OEM
EP84X0222	OEM
EP84X1	0846
EP84X2	0167
EP84X3	0661
EP84X4	0797
EP84X5	0797
EP84X6	0167
EP84X7	2527
EP84X8	0391
EP84X9	0661
EP84X10	0846
EP84X11	0692
EP84X12	0850
EP84X13	0232
EP84X14	OEM
EP84X15	OEM
EP84X16	OEM
EP84X17	OEM
EP84X18	0564
EP84X19	1149
EP84X20	2232
EP84X25	3865
EP84X30	1135
EP84X32	OEM
EP84X34	0069
EP84X35	1049
EP84X36	3690
EP84X37	0842
EP84X50	OEM
EP84X59	OEM
EP84X60	4469
EP84X62	5088
EP84X63	5548
EP84X64	OEM
EP84X65	OEM
EP84X66	OEM
EP84X67	5091
EP84X69	0356
EP84X71	2632
EP84X72	4320
EP84X73	0167
EP84X74	0872
EP84X76	OEM
EP84X77	OEM
EP84X78	1617
EP84X80	0912
EP84X81	1162
EP84X82	2011
EP84X100	5089
EP84X101	OEM
EP84X102	OEM
EP84X103	OEM
EP84X104	OEM
EP84X105	OEM
EP84X106	OEM
EP84X107	OEM
EP84X108	OEM
EP84X109	3666
EP84X119	0620
EP84X143	OEM
EP84X154	0859
EP84X213	0859
EP84X214	2109
EP84X215	1192
EP84X216	2868
EP84X217	0330
EP84X220	OEM
EP84X221	2109
EP84X222	OEM
EP84X224	OEM
EP84X226	OEM
EP84X227	5412
EP84X228	OEM

DEVICE TYPE	REPL CODE
EP84X229	3726
EP84X230	OEM
EP84X232	OEM
EP84X233	OEM
EP84X234	OEM
EP84X235	OEM
EP84X236	OEM
EP84X237	OEM
EP84X238	OEM
EP84X239	OEM
EP84X240	3581
EP84X241	3168
EP84X242	0508
EP84X243	OEM
EP84X244	OEM
EP84X245	OEM
EP84X246	OEM
EP84X250	4417
EP84X251	OEM
EP84X252	OEM
EP84X253	OEM
EP84X255	OEM
EP84X256	OEM
EP84X257	OEM
EP84X258	OEM
EP84X261	OEM
EP84X288	OEM
EP-100	0042
EP100	1357
EP-101A	0149
EP101A	0561
EP120	OEM
EP121	OEM
EP122	OEM
EP123	OEM
EP162	0416
EP200	0015
EP-276	0419
EP276	0419
EP400	0015
EP-421	0919
EP-422	0042
EP600	0015
EP-637	0264
EP-797	0042
EP800	0071
EP-801	0042
EP-802	0919
EP-943	0919
EP-944	0042
EP-976	0378
EP1000	0071
EP1014A	OEM
EP1014B	OEM
EP1014D	OEM
EP1014E	OEM
EP1014H	OEM
EP1016A	OEM
EP1016B	OEM
EP1016D	OEM
EP1016E	OEM
EP1016H	OEM
EP1017A	OEM
EP1017B	OEM
EP1017D	OEM
EP1017E	OEM
EP1017H	OEM
EP1018A	OEM
EP1018B	OEM
EP1018D	OEM
EP1018E	OEM
EP1018H	OEM
EP1019A	OEM
EP1019B	OEM
EP1019D	OEM
EP1019E	OEM
EP1019H	OEM
EP1020A	OEM
EP1020B	OEM
EP1020D	OEM
EP1020E	OEM
EP1020H	OEM
EP1022A	OEM
EP1022B	OEM
EP1022D	OEM
EP1022E	OEM
EP1022H	OEM
EP1024A	OEM
EP1024B	OEM
EP1024D	OEM
EP1024E	OEM
EP1024H	OEM
EP1026A	OEM
EP1026B	OEM
EP1026D	OEM
EP1026E	OEM
EP1026H	OEM
EP1028A	OEM
EP1028B	OEM
EP1028D	OEM
EP1028E	OEM
EP1028H	OEM
EP1030A	OEM
EP1030B	OEM
EP1030D	OEM
EP1030E	OEM
EP1030H	OEM
EP1032A	OEM

DEVICE TYPE	REPL CODE
EP1032B	OEM
EP1032D	OEM
EP1032E	OEM
EP1032H	OEM
EP1034A	OEM
EP1034B	OEM
EP1034D	OEM
EP1034E	OEM
EP1034H	OEM
EP1036A	OEM
EP1036B	OEM
EP1036D	OEM
EP1036E	OEM
EP1036H	OEM
EP1038A	OEM
EP1038B	OEM
EP1038D	OEM
EP1038E	OEM
EP1038H	OEM
EP1259	0015
EP1259-2	0015
EP-1428-2H	0015
EP1428-2H	0015
EP1712A	OEM
EP1714A	OEM
EP1716A	OEM
EP1717A	OEM
EP1718A	OEM
EP1719A	OEM
EP1720A	OEM
EP1722A	OEM
EP1724A	OEM
EP1726A	OEM
EP1736A	OEM
EP-2798	0196
EP2798	0133
EP-3053	0042
EP-3149	0535
EP3149	0015
EP-3572	0196
EP-5219-1	1073
EP-5619-2/7628	0015
EP-5641-1	0286
EP-5641H-2	0374
EP5641H-2	0374
EP5641H2	0374
EPB22-15	0102
EPG20G	0031
EPG30GL-6072	OEM
EPM60/12	OEM
EPM60/15	OEM
EPM100/12	OEM
EPM100/15	OEM
EPM200/12	OEM
EPM200/15	OEM
EPM300/12	OEM
EPM300/15	OEM
EPR9	0012
EPROM-32	OEM
EPROM-64	OEM
EPROM306/E-6	OEM
EPROM332/E-6	OEM
EPROM-332-200	OEM
EPROM-332-300	OEM
EPW29	OEM
EPX2	0079
EPX15X17	0037
EPX59	0124
EPX68	0002
EQ01-07RE	0025
EQ-09R	0012
EQ1	2922
EQA01-01	0012
EQA01-05	0041
EQA01-05R	0140
EQA01-05S	0041
EQA01-05T	0041
EQA01-06	0091
EQA01-06D	OEM
EQA01-06R	0253
EQA01-06S	0091
EQA01-06S13	0091
EQA01-06SB	0091
EQA01-06SC	0091
EQA01-06SD	0298
EQA01-06T	0466
EQA01-07	0062
EQA01-07R	0062
EQA01-07R2	3428
EQA01-07RE	0025
EQA01-07S	0062
EQA01-08	0077
EQA01-08A	0077
EQA01-08D	OEM
EQA01-08R	0077
EQA01-08RG	OEM
EQA01-08S	0165
EQA01-08SF	OEM
EQA01-09	0318
EQA01-09(R)	0012
EQA01-09C	0057
EQA01-09R	0318
EQA01-09S	0057
EQA01-09S1	0057
EQA01-067	0631
EQA01-072	0644
EQA01-6S	0091
EQA01-10	0064
EQA01-10B	OEM

DEVICE TYPE	REPL CODE
EQA01-10R	0532
EQA01-10R2	6094
EQA01-10S	0064
EQA01-11	0181
EQA01-11R	0313
EQA01-11S	0181
EQA01-11SB	OEM
EQA01-11SE	0313
EQA01-11SV	0181
EQA01-11Z	5094
EQA01-12	0052
EQA01-12M	OEM
EQA01-12R	0999
EQA01-12R1A	OEM
EQA01-12S	0052
EQA01-12S1	0052
EQA01-12Z	0137
EQA01-13	0053
EQA01-13R	0053
EQA01-13R2	OEM
EQA01-14	0873
EQA01-14R	0873
EQA01-14RD	0100
EQA01-15	0681
EQA01-15R	0681
EQA01-15RL	0681
EQA01-15RLV	0681
EQA01-16	0440
EQA01-16R	0440
EQA01-17	0210
EQA01-17R	0210
EQA01-18	0371
EQA01-18A	0371
EQA01-18R	0371
EQA01-19	0666
EQA01-19R	0666
EQA01-20	0695
EQA01-20R	0695
EQA01-20RB	0526
EQA01-21	0700
EQA01-21R	0700
EQA01-22	0700
EQA01-22R	0700
EQA01-23AC	OEM
EQA01-24	0489
EQA01-24R	0489
EQA01-24RR	0398
EQA01-25	0709
EQA01-25R	0709
EQA01-26	0450
EQA01-26R	0450
EQA01-28	0257
EQA01-28R	0257
EQA01-28R2	0257
EQA01-30	0195
EQA01-30R	0195
EQA01-32	0195
EQA01-32R	0195
EQA01-33	0166
EQA01-33F	0166
EQA01-33R	0166
EQA01-33RF	0166
EQA01-35	0010
EQA01-35R	0010
EQA01-35RC	0010
EQA01-115	0313
EQA01-Z4RA	0721
EQA02-03M	OEM
EQA02-05	0041
EQA02-05(C)	0041
EQA02-05(D)	0041
EQA02-05-A	0041
EQA02-05-B	0041
EQA02-05-D	0041
EQA02-05A	0140
EQA02-05AB	0140
EQA02-05B	0140
EQA02-05C	0041
EQA02-05CD	0041
EQA02-05CDB	0041
EQA02-05D	0041
EQA02-05E	0041
EQA02-05EF	0041
EQA02-05F	0041
EQA02-05M1	0041
EQA02-06	0091
EQA02-06(A)	0253
EQA02-06(B)	0253
EQA02-06(C)	0091
EQA02-06(CDE)	0091
EQA02-06(D)	0091
EQA02-06-A	0253
EQA02-06-B	0253
EQA02-06A	0253
EQA02-06AB	0253
EQA02-06B	0253
EQA02-06C	0091
EQA02-06CD	0091
EQA-02-06D	0091
EQA02-06D	0466
EQA02-06D-TAPG	0091
EQA02-06E	0466
EQA02-06EF	0466
EQA02-06F	0466
EQA02-06M2	OEM
EQA02-06M4	OEM
EQA02-06M6	0091
EQA02-06S	0091
EQA02-07	0062

DEVICE TYPE	REPL CODE
EQA02-07A	0062
EQA02-07AB	0062
EQA02-07ABD	0062
EQA02-07B	0062
EQA02-07C	0062
EQA02-07CD	0062
EQA02-07CDA	0077
EQA02-07D	0077
EQA02-07M6	0062
EQA02-07Z	OEM
EQA02-08	0165
EQA02-08(D)	0077
EQA02-08A	0077
EQA02-08AB	0077
EQA02-08B	0077
EQA02-08C	0165
EQA02-08CD	0165
EQA02-08D	0077
EQA02-08M3	0077
EQA02-08S	OEM
EQA02-08S3	0165
EQA02-09	0057
EQA02-09(C)	0057
EQA02-09(D)	0057
EQA02-09-C0	0057
EQA02-09-CD	0057
EQA02-09A	0057
EQA02-09AB	0318
EQA02-09AV	0057
EQA02-09B	0057
EQA02-09B(1%)	OEM
EQA02-09C	0057
EQA02-09CD	0057
EQA02-09D	0057
EQA02-10	0064
EQA02-10(A)	0064
EQA02-10(B)	0064
EQA02-10(C)	0064
EQA02-10-A	0064
EQA02-10-B	0064
EQA02-10-C	0064
EQA02-10-CD	0064
EQA02-10-D	0064
EQA02-10A	0064
EQA02-10AB	0064
EQA02-10B	0064
EQA02-10C	0064
EQA02-10CD	0064
EQA02-10CDA	0064
EQA02-10D	0064
EQA02-11	0181
EQA02-11A	0181
EQA02-11AB	0181
EQA02-11B	0052
EQA02-11C	0052
EQA02-11CD	0052
EQA02-11CDB	0052
EQA02-11D	0181
EQA02-11N4N	OEM
EQA02-11Z	OEM
EQA02-12	0052
EQA02-12A	0053
EQA02-12AB	0053
EQA02-12B	0053
EQA02-12M	OEM
EQA02-12M1	0052
EQA02-12Z	OEM
EQA02-13	0053
EQA02-13-A	0053
EQA02-13-B	0053
EQA02-13A	0053
EQA02-13AB	0053
EQA02-13B	6594
EQA02-13M2	OEM
EQA02-14	0873
EQA02-14-A	0873
EQA02-14-AB	0681
EQA02-14-B	0873
EQA02-14A	0873
EQA02-14AB	0873
EQA02-14B	0873
EQA02-15	0681
EQA02-15A	0681
EQA02-15AB	0681
EQA02-15M	0681
EQA02-16	0440
EQA02-16A	0440
EQA02-16AB	0440
EQA02-16B	1220
EQA02-17	0210
EQA02-17AB	0210
EQA02-17B	4764
EQA02-17M2	OEM
EQA02-18	0371
EQA02-18A	0371
EQA02-18AB	0666
EQA02-18B	5158
EQA02-20	0695
EQA02-20AB	0695
EQA02-20B	0695
EQA02-21	0700
EQA02-21AB	0700
EQA02-22	0700
EQA02-22AB	0700
EQA02-23	0489
EQA02-23(A)	0489
EQA02-23AC	OEM
EQA02-23ACA	0489
EQA02-25	0709

DEVICE TYPE	REPL CODE
EQA02-25AC	0709
EQA02-25C	0709
EQA02-28	0257
EQA02-28AC	0257
EQA02-28B	OEM
EQA02-28C	0257
EQA02-30	0195
EQA02-30A	0195
EQA02-30AC	0195
EQA02-30B	0195
EQA02-30C	0166
EQA02-32	0166
EQA02-32AC	0166
EQA02-32B	0166
EQA02-33	0166
EQA02-33A	0166
EQA02-33AC	0166
EQA02-33B	0166
EQA02-35	0010
EQA02-35B	0010
EQA02-35R3	0010
EQA03-05A	OEM
EQA03-05B	0041
EQA03-05C	OEM
EQA03-05D	OEM
EQA03-05E	OEM
EQA03-05F	OEM
EQA03-06A	OEM
EQA03-06B	OEM
EQA03-06C	0091
EQA03-06D	OEM
EQA03-06E	OEM
EQA03-06F	OEM
EQA03-07A	OEM
EQA03-07B	OEM
EQA03-07C	OEM
EQA03-07D	OEM
EQA03-08A	OEM
EQA03-08B	OEM
EQA03-08C	OEM
EQA03-08D	OEM
EQA03-09A	0318
EQA03-09B	OEM
EQA03-09C	OEM
EQA03-09D	OEM
EQA03-10A	OEM
EQA03-10B	OEM
EQA03-10C	OEM
EQA03-10D	OEM
EQA03-11A	0181
EQA03-11B	OEM
EQA03-11C	OEM
EQA03-11D	OEM
EQA03-12A	OEM
EQA03-12B	OEM
EQA03-13A	OEM
EQA03-13B	OEM
EQA03-14A	OEM
EQA03-14B	OEM
EQA03-15A	OEM
EQA03-15B	OEM
EQA03-16A	0440
EQA03-16B	OEM
EQA03-17A	OEM
EQA03-17B	OEM
EQA03-18A	OEM
EQA03-18B	OEM
EQA03-20A	OEM
EQA03-20B	OEM
EQA03-21A	OEM
EQA03-21B	OEM
EQA03-22A	OEM
EQA03-22B	OEM
EQA03-23A	OEM
EQA03-23B	OEM
EQA03-23C	OEM
EQA03-25A	OEM
EQA03-25B	OEM
EQA03-25C	OEM
EQA03-28A	OEM
EQA03-28B	OEM
EQA03-28C	OEM
EQA03-30A	OEM
EQA03-30B	OEM
EQA03-30C	OEM
EQA03-32A	OEM
EQA03-32B	OEM
EQA03-32C	OEM
EQA03-33A	OEM
EQA03-33B	OEM
EQA03-33C	OEM
EQA03-35A	OEM
EQA03-35B	OEM
EQA03-35C	OEM
EQA09R	0012
EQA010ST	0157
EQA0105T	0157
EQA0106R	0253
EQA0106T	0466
EQA0107	0062
EQA0108	0077
EQA0108R	0077
EQA-0109S	0012
EQA0111	0181
EQA0116	0440
EQA0205	0041
EQA0205A	0041
EQA0205B	0041
EQA0206	0091

If replacement code is OEM, contact original manufacturer for replacement.

399

DEVICE TYPE	REPL CODE
EQA0206C	0466
EQA0207	0062
EQA0207D	0077
EQA0209CD	0057
EQA0210(B)	0064
EQA0210A	0064
EQA0210B	0064
EQA0210C	0064
EQA0210D	0064
EQA0212AB	0052
EQA0213	0053
EQA0213A	0053
EQA0213B	0053
EQA0214	0873
EQA0214A	0873
EQA0214B	0873
EQA0220	0695
EQA0305B	0041
EQA0305C	OEM
EQA0306C	0091
EQA0308AB	4775
EQA0309A	0318
EQA0311A	0181
EQA0313AB	4877
EQA0313B	0466
EQA0313BV3	4877
EQA0313BV5	4877
EQA0333A	OEM
EQA-9	0012
EQA107R	0025
EQA107RE	0025
EQA120R	0526
EQA01-06	OEM
EQA01-06R	OEM
EQA01-24RR	OEM
EQAQ1-35RC	0316
EQA.9	0012
EQB0-06V	0298
EQB01	0137
EQB01-05	0162
EQB01-05SA	0162
EQB01-05TV	OEM
EQB01-06	0298
EQB01-06V	0298
EQB01-06Y	0298
EQB01-07	0644
EQB01-07S	OEM
EQB01-08	0244
EQB01-08S1	0244
EQB01-09	1075
EQB01-09B	1075
EQB01-011Z	0313
EQB01-095	OEM
EQB01-1R50	OEM
EQB01-2R25	OEM
EQB01-3R00	1703
EQB01-3R75	OEM
EQB01-4R50	OEM
EQB01-10	0170
EQB01-11	0313
EQB01-11Q	0313
EQB01-11Q(ZD)	0313
EQB01-11QV	0313
EQB01-11Z	0313
EQB01-12	0137
EQB01-12A	0137
EQB01-12B	0137
EQB01-12BV	0137
EQB01-12M	0137
EQB01-12R	0137
EQB01-12Z	0137
EQB01-13	0361
EQB01-14	0100
EQB01-15	0002
EQB01-15Z	0002
EQB01-15ZB	0002
EQB01-16	0416
EQB01-17	1639
EQB01-18	0490
EQB01-19	0943
EQB01-20	0526
EQB01-21	0560
EQB01-22	0560
EQB01-24	0398
EQB01-24RR	0398
EQB01-25	1596
EQB01-26	0436
EQB01-28	1664
EQB01-30	0721
EQB01-32	0039
EQB01-33	0039
EQB01-35	0814
EQB01-35E	OEM
EQB01-50	0497
EQB01-90S	0012
EQB01-100	0098
EQB01-112	3874
EQB01-150	0028
EQB-0108	0244
EQB11-50	0092
EQB35E	OEM
EQBO1-06V	OEM
EQBO1-07	OEM
EQBO1-10	0170
EQC01-10	0087
EQC04-02	0071
EQD01-09	0012
EQF-0004	3672
EQF-0009	3672
EQF-3	0321
EQF-4	0683
EQG01-12A	0137
EQG-6	0160
EQG-8	0160
EQG-9	0004
EQG-12A	0137
EQG-15	0004
EQG-20	0279
EQH-1	0208
EQH-20	0595
EQR-0016	0006
EQR-0038	0006
EQR-1	0150
EQS-0018	0151
EQS-0061	0076
EQS-0100	0076
EQS-0102	1212
EQS-0159	0830
EQS-0160	0833
EQS-0165	0155
EQS-0184	1935
EQS-0192	0191
EQS-0195	0364
EQS-0196	0364
EQS-0198	0224
EQS-5	0151
EQS-9	0191
EQS-10	0111
EQS-11	0111
EQS-18	0151
EQS-19	0470
EQS-20	0470
EQS-21	0144
EQS-22	0155
EQS-56	4144
EQS-57	0693
EQS-60	1401
EQS-61	0076
EQS-62	0079
EQS-64	0079
EQS-66	0555
EQS-67	0555
EQS-78	1212
EQS-86	1897
EQS-89	0386
EQS-100	0076
EQS131	0076
EQS-139	2195
EQS-141	0830
EQZ02-06D	6109
ER0082	OEM
ER1	0023
ER2	0023
ER2-06	OEM
ER4	0023
ER5(ELCOM)	0469
ER6	2505
ER7(ELCOM)	0190
ER8	OEM
ER10(ELCOM)	5417
ER10R(ELCOM)	1229
ER11	0015
ER11(ELCOM)	5482
ER11R(ELCOM)	1231
ER12	0015
ER12(ELCOM)	2872
ER12R(ELCOM)	1232
ER13(ELCOM)	1236
ER13R(ELCOM)	1236
ER14(ELCOM)	3705
ER14R(ELCOM)	2349
ER15(ELCOM)	3711
ER15R(ELCOM)	1244
ER15X4	0050
ER15X5	0050
ER15X6	0050
ER15X7	0004
ER15X8	0016
ER15X9	0004
ER15X10	0160
ER15X11	0050
ER15X12	0050
ER15X13	0050
ER15X14	0050
ER15X15	0050
ER15X16	0050
ER15X17	0004
ER15X18	0016
ER15X19	0050
ER15X20	0050
ER15X21	0050
ER15X22	0004
ER15X23	0004
ER15X24	0136
ER15X25	0136
ER15X26	0279
ER16(ELCOM)	1104
ER17(ELCOM)	3722
ER17R(ELCOM)	1255
ER18(ELCOM)	2982
ER18R(ELCOM)	0444
ER20(ELCOM)	3160
ER20R(ELCOM)	1620
ER21	0015
ER21(ELCOM)	1116
ER21R(ELCOM)	0254
ER22	0015
ER22(ELCOM)	1116
ER22R(ELCOM)	1099
ER23(ELCOM)	1118
ER23R(ELCOM)	1103
ER24(ELCOM)	0800
ER24R(ELCOM)	0258
ER25(ELCOM)	1186
ER25R(ELCOM)	0267
ER26(ELCOM)	0315
ER26R(ELCOM)	0267
ER27(ELCOM)	1124
ER28(ELCOM)	0045
ER28R(ELCOM)	0280
ER31	0015
ER32(ELCOM)	0190
ER41	0015
ER42	0015
ER51	0015
ER57X2	0015
ER57X3	0015
ER57X4	0015
ER61	0015
ER62	0015
ER81	0071
ER101	0015
ER102	0229
ER102D	0015
ER103D	0015
ER103E	0015
ER104D	0015
ER105D	0015
ER106D	0015
ER107D	0071
ER108D	0071
ER181	0015
ER182	0015
ER183	0015
ER184	0015
ER185	0015
ER186	0071
ER187	0071
ER201	0015
ER-300	4240
ER301	0015
ER308	0071
ER310	0071
ER312	OEM
ER381	0015
ER401	0015
ER402	0015
ER403	0015
ER404	0015
ER405	0015
ER406	0071
ER407	0071
ER410	0015
ER442	0344
ER443	0344
ER444	0344
ER501	0015
ER510	0015
ER601	0015
ER801	0071
ER881-004	OEM
ER1001	0071
ER1075	OEM
ER1400	1835
ER2000	0031
ER2001	0031
ER2002	0031
ER2003	0031
ER2004	0031
ER2005	1208
ER2006	OEM
ER2051	OEM
ER2051HR	OEM
ER2051IR	OEM
ER2055	OEM
ER2055HR	OEM
ER2055IR	OEM
ER2810HR	OEM
ER2810IR	OEM
ER3400	OEM
ER3400HR	OEM
ER3400I	OEM
ER3400IR	OEM
ER5304(A)	OEM
ER5716	OEM
ER5716HR(A)	OEM
ER5816(A)	OEM
ER5816HR(A)	OEM
ER5816IR(A)	OEM
ER5901(A)	OEM
ER5901HR(A)	OEM
ER5901IR(A)	OEM
ER5916(A)	OEM
ER5916HR(A)	OEM
ER5916IR(A)	OEM
ER59256	OEM
ERA01-35RC	0361
ERA0106R	0253
ERA15-01	0023
ERA15-01AVRB	OEM
ERA15-01V3	0023
ERA15-01V5	OEM
ERA15-02	0023
ERA15-02A	OEM
ERA15-02V3	0015
ERA15-02VH	OEM
ERA15-02VH-T	0023
ERA15-02Y	OEM
ERA15-04	0023
ERA15-06	0023
ERA15-08	0017
ERA15-10	0017
ERA18-02	0023
ERA18-04	0023
ERA21-02	0604
ERA21-04	0790
ERA21-06	0015
ERA22-02	0604
ERA22-04	0790
ERA22-04V	0790
ERA22-04V3	0790
ERA22-06	0015
ERA22-08	0072
ERA22-10	0017
ERA32-01	1082
ERA34-10	OEM
ERA38-04	0015
ERA38-05	0015
ERA48-02	0023
ERA48-04	0023
ERA81-004	0023
ERA81-004G	0730
ERA81-005	OEM
ERA82-004	0494
ERA82-005	OEM
ERA83-006	OEM
ERA84-009	0023
ERA91-02	1082
ERA1501	0023
ERA1501-01V3	0023
ERA1502	5551
ERA1804	0023
ERA2202	0023
ERA2204	0023
ERA2206	0271
ERA4804	OEM
ERA81004	0730
ERA81004G	0730
ERB01-01	0015
ERB01-05	0162
ERB01-07	0025
ERB01-10	0071
ERB02-10	0102
ERB02-12	0102
ERB06-13	0017
ERB06-15	0017
ERB06-15V	0017
ERB-06B	0015
ERB-07RE	0025
ERB0615V	0017
ERB2P-04	0023
ERB6.2B2	OEM
ERB-6.2EB2	0466
ERB11-01	0015
ERB-12-01	0080
ERB12-01	0023
ERB-12-01G	0015
ERB12-01G	0015
ERB-12-01R	0023
ERB-12-01RK	0604
ERB12-01RK	0023
ERB12-01U4	0023
ERB12-01V	0080
ERB-12-02	0124
ERB12-02	0023
ERB-12-02R	0015
ERB12-02RK	0023
ERB12-02S	OEM
ERB12-02V	0015
ERB12-04	0071
ERB12-04RK	0023
ERB12-06	0071
ERB12-10	0071
ERB12-11	0015
ERB15	4176
ERB16-08	0102
ERB16-12	0102
ERB21-10	0102
ERB21-12	0102
ERB21-15	0102
ERB22-10	0102
ERB22-12	0102
ERB22-15	0015
ERB24-02B	0102
ERB24-02D	0023
ERB24-04	0023
ERB24-04A	0023
ERB24-04B	0023
ERB-24-04C	0023
ERB24-04C	0023
ERB24-04CV	0023
ERB24-04D	0023
ERB24-06	0023
ERB24-06A	0015
ERB24-06B	0023
ERB24-06B-D	OEM
ERB24-06C	0023
ERB24-06D	0102
ERB26-15	0344
ERB26-20	0344
ERB26-20L	0344
ERB26-20M	0344
ERB26-20MV	0344
ERB28-02	0023
ERB28-04	0023
ERB28-04B	0023
ERB28-04C	0023
ERB-28-04D	0023
ERB28-04D	0023
ERB28-04DV	0071
ERB28-06	2505
ERB28-06D	0023
ERB28-06DV	0023
ERB29-02	0023
ERB29-04	0023
ERB30-13	0102
ERB30-15	0182
ERB32-01	0541
ERB32-01L3	0541
ERB35-02	0604
ERB38-05	OEM
ERB41-04	OEM
ERB42-04	OEM
ERB43	0023
ERB43-02	0023
ERB43-04	0023
ERB43-04G	0023
ERB43-04V	0023
ERB43-08	0017
ERB44-02	0023
ERB44-04	0023
ERB44-04V	0023
ERB44-06	0023
ERB44-08	0017
ERB44-6	0023
ERB44-10	0071
ERB44-D6E	OEM
ERB47-02	0604
ERB-81	2520
ERB81	0071
ERB81-004	2520
ERB83-004	0031
ERB84-009	0031
ERB91-02	1082
ERB93-02	0541
ERB1201	6467
ERB1201U4	0015
ERB1202	0071
ERB2404C	0023
ERB4302	0023
ERB4304	0023
ERB4304G	0023
ERB4304V	0023
ERB4404V	0023
ERB4702	0604
ERB5104	OEM
ERB81004	2520
ERC-01-005	OEM
ERC-01-02	0071
ERC01-02	0559
ERC01-02E	OEM
ERC01-02F	0071
ERC01-02FL	0031
ERC01-02FL12	0071
ERC01-02L	0559
ERC01-02L-12	0071
ERC01-02L12	0071
ERC01-04	0071
ERC01-04F	0087
ERC01-06	0559
ERC01-06C	OEM
ERC01-06E	OEM
ERC-01-10	0087
ERC03-01	0865
ERC03-03	0847
ERC04-02	0071
ERC04-02E3	0071
ERC04-02F	0559
ERC04-02L	OEM
ERC04-04	0559
ERC04-04C	0071
ERC04-04F	0071
ERC04-06	0559
ERC04-10	0071
ERC05-06	0559
ERC05-08	0071
ERC05-08V	0071
ERC05-10	0071
ERC05-10B	OEM
ERC06-13	0102
ERC06-15	0017
ERC06-15L	0017
ERC06-15S	0344
ERC0102L	0071
ERC0402	0071
ERC0402E3	0071
ERC0508	0071
ERC0508V	0071
ERC0510	0071
ERC0510V	0071
ERC0615	0344
ERC10ZK241U	OEM
ERC12-08	0071
ERC13-08	0071
ERC16-06	0023
ERC16-10	0087
ERC16-12	3211
ERC20-02	1137
ERC20-04	1137
ERC20-06	1654
ERC20-08	OEM
ERC20M-04	1171
ERC24-04	0023
ERC24-06	0023
ERC24-06S	0023
ERC25-04	0282
ERC25-06	0282
ERC25-06M	OEM
ERC25-06S	0023
ERC26-13	0102
ERC-26-13L	0344
ERC26-13L	0344
ERC26-15	0182
ERC-26-15S	0102
ERC26-15S	0158
ERC26-15T	0102
ERC26-131	0102
ERC27-13	0102
ERC27-15	0182
ERC29-02	OEM
ERC29-04	OEM
ERC30-01	0541
ERC33-02	1082
ERC35-02	0031
ERC38-04	1352
ERC38-05	1362
ERC38-06	3833
ERC44-04	0023
ERC46-02	0031
ERC46-04	0031
ERC47-02	0031
ERC47-04	0031
ERC48-02	OEM
ERC62-004	OEM
ERC80-004	OEM
ERC81-004	0031
ERC84-009	3559
ERC88-009	OEM
ERC90-02	5980
ERC91-02	0541
ERC510	0071
ERC1208	0071
ERC1308	0071
ERC2902	OEM
ERC4702	0031
ERC81004	0087
ERCC4-06	0071
ERD02-06	OEM
ERD03-02	0559
ERD03-02J	OEM
ERD03-04	0535
ERD07-13	0182
ERD07-15	0182
ERD07-15L	0102
ERD08M-15	OEM
ERD0715	0182
ERD18-08S	OEM
ERD24-005	1590
ERD24-01	0865
ERD24-02	0865
ERD24-04	3110
ERD24-06	2939
ERD27-10	0545
ERD28-04	0031
ERD28-04S	0031
ERD28-06	0031
ERD28-08	0102
ERD28-08S	0102
ERD29-02	0031
ERD29-02H3	0031
ERD29-04	0031
ERD29-04H2	0559
ERD29-06	0031
ERD29-08J	1208
ERD32-01	0541
ERD32-01L22	OEM
ERD33-02	0541
ERD47-02	0031
ERD51-01	0097
ERD51-03	0109
ERD51-06	0122
ERD51-09	0145
ERD51-12	OEM
ERD74-005	1590
ERD74-01	0865
ERD74-02	0865
ERD74-04	2140
ERD74-06	0706
ERD75-005	4910
ERD75-01	4910
ERD75-02	4910
ERD77-10	OEM
ERD80-004	OEM
ERD81-004	0610
ERD81B004	OEM
ERD100	0015
ERD200	0015
ERD300	0015
ERD400	0015
ERD500	0015
ERD600	0015
ERD700	0071
ERD800	0071
ERD900	0071
ERD1000	0071
ERD2902H3	0031
ERD2904	0023
ERE24-005	1590
ERE24-01	0865
ERE24-02	0865
ERE24-04	1836
ERE24-06	1840
ERE51-01	2872
ERE51-03	1104
ERE51-06	2982
ERE51-09	6875
ERE51-12	OEM
ERE74-005	1590
ERE74-01	0865
ERE74-02	0865
ERE74-04	0847
ERE74-06	0596
ERE75-005	1522
ERE75-01	1522
ERE75-02	1522
ERE81-004	1536
ERE81B004	OEM
ERG24-005	1512
ERG24-01	1512
ERG24-02	1512
ERG24-04	1836
ERG27-10	OEM
ERG51-01	1522
ERG51-03	0029
ERG51-06	0315
ERG51-09	0045
ERG51-12	OEM
ERG74-005	1522
ERG74-01	1522
ERG74-02	1522
ERG74-04	0029
ERG75-005	1522
ERG75-01	1522
ERG75-02	1522
ERG77-10	OEM
ERG81-004	1536
ERG81A-004	1536
ERN04-20	OEM
ERN26-08	OEM
ERP04-25	OEM
ERP04-30	OEM
ERP15-16	OEM
ERPF5B0M050F	OEM
ERPF5B0M050K	OEM
ERPF5B0M080F	OEM
ERP-F5B0M080H	OEM
ERPF5B0M080K	OEM
ERPW5B0M030D	OEM
ERPW5B0M050D	OEM
ERPZ4B0M080B	OEM
ERPZ5B0M080A	OEM
ERR03-25	OEM
ERR03-30	OEM
ERS37	OEM
ERS100	0086
ERS120	0187
ERS123AP	OEM
ERS128	OEM
ERS140	0187
ERS152	OEM
ERS156	OEM
ERS160	0187
ERS180	0187
ERS200	0187
ERS210	OEM
ERS225	0187
ERS229	OEM
ERS230	OEM
ERS234	OEM
ERS244	OEM
ERS246	OEM
ERS250	0187
ERS261	OEM
ERS275	0187
ERS301	0187
ERS325	0187
ERS350	0187
ERS375	0187
ERS385	OEM
ERS401	0187
ERS425	0187
ERS450	0187
ERS475	0168
ERS519	OEM
ERS552	OEM
ERS856	OEM
ERS960	OEM
ERS961	OEM
ERS962	OEM
ERS966	OEM
ERS967	OEM
ERS972	OEM
ERTD2ZFL351S	OEM
ERTD2ZFL601S	OEM
ERTD2ZGL351S	OEM
ERV-02F2150	0015
ERZ08A3K11	0139
ERZ-08A3K101	0139
ERZ08A3M	OEM
ERZ08D3J301	OEM
ERZ08D3K101	OEM
ERZ-08D3K121	0186
ERZ1SA32S251	OEM
ERZ15A32S251	0139
ERZ15D3K471	0139
ERZ-B14DK510Z	OEM
ERZ-C03DK220	1997
ERZC03DK220	1997
ERZC03DK220S	1997
ERZ-C07DK101	4158
ERZ-C07DK121	4834
ERZ-C07DK201	1364
ERZ-C07DK241	0246

If replacement code is OEM, contact original manufacturer for replacement.

DEVICE TYPE	REPL CODE
ERZ-C07DK391	1322
ERZ-C07DK431	1648
ERZ-C07DK471	4394
ERZ-C10DK241	1982
ERZC10DK241U	1982
ERZC10ZK241U	1982
ERZC10ZK24166	OEM
ERZ-C14DK101	3061
ERZ-C14DK102	OEM
ERZ-C14DK151	3087
ERZ-C14DK182	OEM
ERZ-C14DK201	0832
ERZ-C14DK201U	0832
ERZ-C14DK241	1982
ERZ-C14DK330	2769
ERZ-C14DK390	3044
ERZ-C14DK391	1324
ERZ-C14DK431	1650
ERZ-C14DK470	3046
ERZ-C14DK560	2913
ERZ-C14DK680	3049
ERZ-C14DK681	3226
ERZ-C14DK751	OEM
ERZ-C14DK781	1093
ERZ-C14DK820	3056
ERZ-C14DK821	OEM
ERZ-C14DK911	OEM
ERZ-C20DK102	OEM
ERZ-C20DK182	OEM
ERZ-C20DK201	0824
ERZ-C20DK201U	0824
ERZ-C20DK241	3381
ERZ-C20DK391	1326
ERZ-C20DK431	4780
ERZ-C20DK681	3806
ERZ-C20DK751	OEM
ERZ-C20DK781	0776
ERZ-C20DK821	OEM
ERZ-C20DK911	OEM
ERZC100K241	1982
ERZC100K241U	1982
ERZ-M10DK220	OEM
ES01	0182
ES01A	0182
ES01F	0182
ES01V	0182
ES01Z	0182
ES-1	0023
ES1	0023
ES1(ELCOM)	0050
ES-1A	0182
ES1A	0023
ES-1C	OEM
ES1F	0017
ES1F-V1	0017
ES1KX122	0224
ES-1V	0023
ES1V	0023
ES1Z	0023
ES2(ELCOM)	0004
ES3	0136
ES3(ELCOM)	0004
ES4(ELCOM)	0164
ES5	0595
ES5(ELCOM)	0208
ES6(ELCOM)	0208
ES7	0085
ES7(ELCOM)	0222
ES8(ELCOM)	0050
ES9	0085
ES9(ELCOM)	0085
ES10	0435
ES10(ELCOM)	0435
ES11	0127
ES11(ELCOM)	0050
ES13	0085
ES13(ELCOM)	0085
ES14	0136
ES14(ELCOM)	0050
ES15	0127
ES15(ELCOM)	0050
ES15X1	0016
ES15X2	0144
ES15X3	0144
ES15X4	0004
ES15X6	0144
ES15X7	0016
ES15X8	0004
ES15X9	0037
ES15X10	0144
ES15X11	0016
ES15X12	0042
ES15X14	0016
ES15X16	0016
ES15X17	0160
ES15X18	0144
ES15X19	0144
ES15X20	0016
ES15X21	OEM
ES15X22	0326
ES15X23	0016
ES15X24	0016
ES15X29	OEM
ES15X30	0144
ES15X31	0004
ES15X32	0004
ES15X33	OEM
ES15X35	OEM
ES15X36	OEM
ES15X37	0016
ES15X38	OEM
ES15X39	OEM
ES15X40	OEM
ES15X41	OEM
ES15X42	0016
ES15X43	0160
ES15X44	OEM
ES15X45	0085
ES15X46	OEM
ES15X48	0208
ES15X49	0004
ES15X50	0004
ES15X51	0085
ES15X52	0969
ES15X53	0004
ES15X54	0969
ES15X55	0004
ES15X56	0007
ES15X57	0007
ES15X58	0016
ES15X59	0233
ES15X60	0144
ES15X61	0136
ES15X62	0016
ES15X63	0004
ES15X64	0016
ES15X65	0007
ES15X66	0127
ES15X67	0284
ES15X68	0016
ES15X69	0233
ES15X70	0016
ES15X71	0208
ES15X72	0208
ES15X73	0136
ES15X74	0208
ES15X75	0164
ES15X76	0016
ES15X77	1665
ES15X78	0085
ES15X79	0007
ES15X80	0127
ES15X81	0127
ES15X82	0127
ES15X83	0016
ES15X84	0016
ES15X85	0016
ES15X86	0042
ES15X87	0007
ES15X88	0007
ES15X89	0233
ES15X90	0203
ES15X91	1698
ES15X92	0321
ES15X93	0086
ES15X94	0065
ES15X95	0142
ES15X96	0007
ES15X97	2195
ES15X98	0178
ES15X99	1004
ES15X100	0004
ES15X101	0037
ES15X102	0127
ES15X103	OEM
ES15X104	0007
ES15X105	0007
ES15X106	0326
ES15X107	0037
ES15X119	0007
ES15X120	0127
ES15X121	0127
ES15X122	0007
ES15X123	0007
ES15X125	0388
ES15X126	0637
ES15X127	0326
ES15X128	0037
ES15X502SB77C	0004
ES15X532SB155A	0004
ES15X552SA15V	0004
ES15X612SA351B	0136
ES16(ELCOM)	0103
ES16X2	0143
ES16X3	0143
ES16X4	0133
ES16X5	0143
ES16X6	0143
ES16X7	0143
ES16X8	0137
ES16X9	0015
ES16X10	0229
ES16X11	OEM
ES16X12	0143
ES16X13	0015
ES16X14	0143
ES16X15	0918
ES-16X16	0102
ES16X16	0102
ES16X17	OEM
ES16X20	0102
ES16X21	0123
ES16X24	0133
ES16X25	0015
ES16X26	OEM
ES16X27	0124
ES16X28	0102
ES16X29	0560
ES16X30	0133
ES16X31	0102
ES16X32	0133
ES16X33	0087
ES16X38	0015
ES16X40	0133
ES16X41	0526
ES16X61	OEM
ES16X70	0123
ES16X103	0143
ES17(ELCOM)	0004
ES18	0160
ES18(ELCOM)	0085
ES19	0004
ES19(ELCOM)	0050
ES20(ELCOM)	0016
ES21	0435
ES21(ELCOM)	0160
ES22	0161
ES22(ELCOM)	0086
ES23	0004
ES23(ELCOM)	0050
ES24(ELCOM)	0142
ES25	0279
ES25(ELCOM)	0050
ES26	0279
ES26(ELCOM)	0004
ES27(ELCOM)	0599
ES28(ELCOM)	2736
ES29	0222
ES29(ELCOM)	0222
ES30(ELCOM)	2839
ES31(ELCOM)	0103
ES32(ELCOM)	0233
ES33(ELCOM)	0074
ES34(ELCOM)	0037
ES35(ELCOM)	1506
ES36(ELCOM)	0178
ES36X103	0143
ES37(ELCOM)	0164
ES38	0161
ES38(ELCOM)	0208
ES39(ELCOM)	0275
ES41	0136
ES41(ELCOM)	0050
ES42(ELCOM)	0969
ES43(ELCOM)	0130
ES44(ELCOM)	0178
ES45(ELCOM)	0178
ES46	0198
ES46(ELCOM)	0016
ES47(ELCOM)	1659
ES47X1	0015
ES47X4	0015
ES49(ELCOM)	0899
ES50	0222
ES50(ELCOM)	0222
ES51	0015
ES51(ELCOM)	0126
ES51X65	0086
ES53(ELCOM)	0016
ES54(ELCOM)	0007
ES55(ELCOM)	0074
ES56(ELCOM)	0086
ES57(ELCOM)	0086
ES57X1	0015
ES57X2	0015
ES57X4	0015
ES57X5	0015
ES57X6	0196
ES57X7	0644
ES57X8	0102
ES57X9	0102
ES57X11	0752
ES57X12	0133
ES57X13	0286
ES57X14	0287
ES57X20	0286
ES57X21	0286
ES57X22	OEM
ES57X23	OEM
ES57X35	OEM
ES57X39	OEM
ES58	0161
ES59(ELCOM)	0599
ES61(ELCOM)	1004
ES62(ELCOM)	0086
ES63	0222
ES63(ELCOM)	0841
ES65(ELCOM)	0037
ES66(ELCOM)	0556
ES68	0455
ES69(ELCOM)	0103
ES70	0710
ES71(ELCOM)	0074
ES73(ELCOM)	0007
ES75(ELCOM)	0396
ES75X1	0167
ES76(ELCOM)	0283
ES80(ELCOM)	0042
ES81	0378
ES81(ELCOM)	0919
ES82	0161
ES82(ELCOM)	0546
ES83	0455
ES83(ELCOM)	0378
ES84	0637
ES84(ELCOM)	0637
ES84X1	2991
ES84X2	2457
ES84X3	0167
ES84X6	0167
ES85(ELCOM)	0016
ES86(ELCOM)	0007
ES88	0161
ES89	0283
ES89(ELCOM)	0283
ES90	0486
ES91(ELCOM)	0841
ES92	3343
ES93	3486
ES94	3249
ES95	0065
ES95(ELCOM)	0065
ES96(ELCOM)	0334
ES97	0855
ES105	0553
ES106	2869
ES108	2411
ES109	2262
ES481A	OEM
ES481B	OEM
ES481C	OEM
ES481D	OEM
ES481E	OEM
ES481F	OEM
ES482A	OEM
ES482B	OEM
ES482C	OEM
ES482D	OEM
ES482E	OEM
ES482F	OEM
ES483A	OEM
ES483B	OEM
ES483C	OEM
ES483D	OEM
ES483E	OEM
ES483F	OEM
ES484A	OEM
ES484B	OEM
ES484C	OEM
ES484D	OEM
ES484E	OEM
ES484F	OEM
ES485A	OEM
ES485B	OEM
ES485C	OEM
ES485D	OEM
ES485E	OEM
ES485F	OEM
ES501	0435
ES501(ELCOM)	0435
ES503	0160
ES503(ELCOM)	0085
ES581A	OEM
ES581B	OEM
ES581C	OEM
ES581D	OEM
ES581E	OEM
ES581F	OEM
ES582A	OEM
ES582B	OEM
ES582C	OEM
ES582D	OEM
ES582E	OEM
ES582F	OEM
ES583A	OEM
ES583B	OEM
ES583C	OEM
ES583D	OEM
ES583E	OEM
ES583F	OEM
ES584A	OEM
ES584B	OEM
ES584C	OEM
ES584D	OEM
ES584E	OEM
ES584F	OEM
ES585A	OEM
ES585B	OEM
ES585C	OEM
ES585D	OEM
ES585E	OEM
ES585F	OEM
ES1010	OEM
ES1015	OEM
ES1025	OEM
ES1035	OEM
ES1050	OEM
ES1063	OEM
ES1075	OEM
ES1513	0286
ES1627	0133
ES2010	OEM
ES2015	OEM
ES2025	OEM
ES2035	OEM
ES2050	OEM
ES2063	OEM
ES2075	OEM
ES3010	OEM
ES3015	OEM
ES3025	OEM
ES3035	OEM
ES3050	OEM
ES3063	OEM
ES3075	OEM
ES3110	0136
ES3111	0136
ES3112	0136
ES3113	0136
ES3114	0136
ES3115	0136
ES3116	0136
ES3120	0004
ES3121	0004
ES3122	0004
ES3123	0004
ES3124	0004
ES3125	0004
ES3126	0004
ES3266	0144
ES3501	OEM
ES3511	OEM
ES4010	OEM
ES4015	OEM
ES4025	OEM
ES4050	OEM
ES4063	OEM
ES4075	OEM
ES10100	OEM
ES10110	0222
ES10125	OEM
ES10155	OEM
ES10186	0127
ES10187	0151
ES10188	0151
ES10189	0143
ES10190	0030
ES10222	1211
ES10223	1211
ES10224	0143
ES10225	0143
ES10231	0111
ES10232	0079
ES10233	0015
ES10234	0137
ES15046	0127
ES15047	0127
ES15048	0079
ES15049	0111
ES15050	0016
ES15051	1257
ES15052	0111
ES15054	0143
ES15055	0030
ES15056	0015
ES15057	0133
ES15102	0127
ES15226	0086
ES15227	0555
ES20100	OEM
ES20125	OEM
ES20155	OEM
ES30100	OEM
ESA-06	0293
ESA06	0293
ESA10-98	0015
ESA10-99	0015
ESA-10C	0015
ESA-10N	0015
ESA213	0136
ESA233	0136
ESAB03-01	OEM
ESAB03-02	OEM
ESAB03-04	OEM
ESAB33-02CS	1227
ESAB82-004	2493
ESAB85-009	1227
ESAB92-02	1227
ESAB92M-02	1015
ESAC02-C	OEM
ESAC02-N	OEM
ESAC06-06	0441
ESAC25-02C	1227
ESAC25-02D	OEM
ESAC25-02N	1716
ESAC25-04C	OEM
ESAC25-04D	OEM
ESAC25-04N	OEM
ESAC25C/N02	OEM
ESAC25C/N04	OEM
ESAC31-01C	1227
ESAC31-01D	OEM
ESAC31-01N	1716
ESAC31-02C	1227
ESAC31-02D	OEM
ESAC31-02N	1716
ESAC33-02C	1227
ESAC33-02CS	1227
ESAC33-02D	OEM
ESAC33-02N	1716
ESAC75-005	6392
ESAC75-01	2809
ESAC75-02	2809
ESAC81-004	0579
ESAC82-004	1015
ESAC83-004	1931
ESAC85-009	1227
ESAC87-009	2219
ESAC92-02	1227
ESAC93-02	2219
ESAC2504C	OEM
ESAD25-02C	2219
ESAD25-02D	OEM
ESAD25-02N	OEM
ESAD25-04C	4409
ESAD25-04D	OEM
ESAD25-04N	OEM
ESAD25-06	OEM
ESAD31-02C	OEM
ESAD33-02C	2329
ESAD33-02CS	2219
ESAD33-02D	OEM
ESAD33-02N	OEM
ESAD75-005	2211
ESAD75-01	2809
ESAD75-02	2809
ESAD81-004	0579
ESAD81-004A	OEM
ESAD82-004	OEM
ESAD85-009	2219
ESAD92-02	2219
ESAE31-06T	OEM
ESAE31-08T	OEM
ESAG31-06T	OEM
ESAG31-08T	OEM
ESAG32-06T	OEM
ESAG32-08T	OEM
ESAG73-03C	OEM
ESAG73-03D	OEM
ESAG73-03N	OEM
ESAG73-06C	OEM
ESAG73-06D	OEM
ESAG73-06N	OEM
ESAG84-004	OEM
ESAH73-03C	OEM
ESAH73-03D	OEM
ESAH73-03N	OEM
ESAH73-06C	OEM
ESAH73-06D	OEM
ESAH73-06N	OEM
ESBB01-1R50	OEM
ESBB01-2R25	OEM
ESBB01-3R00	1703
ESBB01-3R75	OEM
ESBB01-4R50	OEM
ESBC604	OEM
ESBC604H	OEM
ESBC614G	OEM
ESCA25-02C	OEM
ESCA83-004	OEM
ESDA-5	OEM
ESDA5	OEM
ESDA5H	OEM
ESDA5J	OEM
ESDA5K	OEM
ESDA-8	OEM
ESDA8	OEM
ESDA-10	OEM
ESDA10	OEM
ESDA-12	OEM
ESDA12	OEM
ESDA-15	OEM
ESDA15	OEM
ESDA-20	OEM
ESDA20	OEM
ESDA-25	OEM
ESDA25	OEM
ESDA-30	OEM
ESDA30	OEM
ESDA-50	OEM
ESDA50	OEM
ESI-LA1111P	0383
ESI-MSM5807	OEM
ESI-UPC30C	0648
ESI-UPC1020H	3650
ESJA03-13	OEM
ESJA17-16	OEM
ESJA17-20	OEM
ESJA17-25	OEM
ESJA18-16	OEM
ESJA18-20	OEM
ESJA18-25	OEM
ESJA18-30	OEM
ESJA19-30	0286
ESJA25-04	OEM
ESJA25-06	OEM
ESJA25-08	OEM
ESJA25-10	OEM
ESJA25-12	OEM
ESJA25-12S	OEM
ESJA25-16	OEM
ESJA25-20	OEM
ESJA31-16	OEM
ESJA31-20	0374
ESJA31-24	OEM
ESJA34-06	OEM
ESJA35-10	OEM
ESJA35-12	OEM
ESJA37-16	OEM
ESJA37-20	OEM
ESJA37-24	OEM
ESJA52-10	OEM
ESJA52-12	OEM
ESJA52-14	OEM
ESJA53-16	OEM
ESJA53-18	OEM
ESJA53-20	OEM
ESJA54-06	OEM
ESJA54-08	OEM
ESJA56-20	OEM
ESJA56-24	OEM
ESJA57-04	OEM
ESK-1	0015
ESK1	0015
ESK1/02	0015
ESK1/06	0015
ESK1/10	OEM
ESK1/12	OEM
ESK100/08	OEM
ESK100/10	OEM
ESK100/12	OEM
ESK100/14	OEM
ESK100/16	OEM
ESKA1/10	OEM
ESKA1/12	OEM
ESKE40C500	0015
ESKE125C500	0071
ESM16	1841
ESM22-100	OEM
ESM22-100N	OEM
ESM22-200	OEM
ESM22-200N	OEM
ESM22-300	OEM
ESM22-300N	OEM
ESM22-400	OEM
ESM22-400N	OEM
ESM22-500	OEM
ESM22-500N	OEM
ESM22-600	OEM
ESM22-600N	OEM
ESM23-100	OEM
ESM23-100N	OEM
ESM23-200	OEM
ESM23-200N	OEM
ESM23-300	OEM
ESM23-300N	OEM
ESM23-400	OEM
ESM23-400N	OEM
ESM23-500	OEM
ESM23-500N	OEM
ESM23-600	OEM
ESM23-600N	OEM
ESM25	OEM
ESM25A	OEM
ESM100	OEM
ESM113	2411
ESM114	2411
ESM117	3339
ESM118	3339
ESM1350P	OEM
ESM181-200R	OEM
ESM181-300R	OEM
ESM181-400R	OEM
ESM181-500R	OEM
ESM181-600R	OEM
ESM193-400	OEM
ESM193-600	OEM
ESM193-800	OEM
ESM193-900	OEM
ESM193-1000	OEM
ESM194-600	OEM
ESM194-800	OEM
ESM194-1000	OEM
ESM194-1200	OEM
ESM213	OEM
ESM214	OEM
ESM217	OEM
ESM218	OEM
ESM222R	OEM
ESM227	OEM
ESM227N	OEM
ESM231	OEM
ESM243-50	OEM
ESM243-100	OEM
ESM243-200	OEM
ESM243-300	OEM
ESM243-300R	OEM
ESM243-400	OEM
ESM244-50	OEM
ESM244-100	OEM
ESM244-200	OEM
ESM244-300	OEM
ESM244-400	OEM
ESM244-500	OEM
ESM244-600	OEM
ESM244-800	OEM
ESM244-1000	OEM
ESM245-50	OEM
ESM245-200	OEM
ESM245-400	OEM
ESM245-600	OEM
ESM245-800	OEM
ESM245-1000	OEM
ESM245-1000R	OEM
ESM255-50	OEM
ESM255-100	OEM
ESM255-200	OEM
ESM255-300	OEM
ESM255-400	OEM
ESM269	OEM
ESM282	OEM
ESM282A	OEM
ESM283	OEM
ESM310	OEM
ESM381	OEM
ESM382	OEM
ESM383	OEM
ESM432	OEM
ESM432C	OEM
ESM532C	OEM
ESM579	OEM
ESM582	0133
ESM622	OEM

If replacement code is OEM, contact original manufacturer for replacement.

401

DEVICE TYPE	REPL CODE
ESM623	OEM
ESM632C	OEM
ESM635	OEM
ESM636	OEM
ESM637	OEM
ESM638	OEM
ESM639	OEM
ESM640	OEM
ESM642	OEM
ESM643	OEM
ESM691	OEM
ESM692	OEM
ESM693	OEM
ESM700	OEM
ESM707	OEM
ESM732C	OEM
ESM737	OEM
ESM738	OEM
ESM765-100	OEM
ESM765-200	OEM
ESM765-400	OEM
ESM765-600	OEM
ESM765-800	OEM
ESM837	OEM
ESM855	OEM
ESM856	OEM
ESM870	OEM
ESM871	OEM
ESM900	OEM
ESM910	OEM
ESM990-200	OEM
ESM990-300	OEM
ESM990-400	OEM
ESM1000	OEM
ESM1406	OEM
ESM1410	OEM
ESM1503	OEM
ESM1600B	OEM
ESM1602	OEM
ESM2060	OEM
ESM3045AV	OEM
ESM3045DV	OEM
ESM4014	OEM
ESM4015	OEM
ESM4016	OEM
ESM4017	OEM
ESM4045AV	OEM
ESM4045DV	OEM
ESM4091	OEM
ESM4092	OEM
ESM4093	OEM
ESM4116-200	OEM
ESM4116-400	OEM
ESM4116-500	OEM
ESM4116-600	OEM
ESM4120-600	OEM
ESM4120-800	OEM
ESM4120-900	OEM
ESM4120-1000	OEM
ESM4391	OEM
ESM4392	OEM
ESM4393	OEM
ESM4446	OEM
ESM4448	OEM
ESM5045DV	OEM
ESM6045AV	OEM
ESM6045DV	OEM
ESP43	OEM
ESP550	OEM
ESP5100	OEM
ESP5200	OEM
ESP5300	OEM
ESP5400	OEM
ESP5500	OEM
ESP5600	OEM
ESP5800	OEM
ESP51000	OEM
ESPA02-30A	OEM
ESPA03	OEM
ESPA03-40	OEM
ESPA05-30	3807
ESPA11-40	1313
ESPA91	2647
ESPA94	2647
ESZ5.1	0041
ESZ5.6	0253
ESZ6.2	0466
ESZ6.8	0062
ESZ7.5	0077
ESZ8.2	0165
ESZ9.1	0057
ESZ10	0064
ESZ11	0181
ESZ12	0052
ET1	0050
ET1X1	OEM
ET2	0050
ET3	0211
ET4	0211
ET5	0211
ET6	0085
ET7	0435
ET8	0595
ET9	0595
ET10	0038
ET11	0038
ET12	0136
ET15X1	0004
ET15X2	0127

DEVICE TYPE	REPL CODE
ET15X3	0144
ET15X4	0160
ET15X5	0969
ET15X7	0144
ET15X8	0233
ET15X9	0127
ET15X10	0155
ET15X11	0155
ET15X12	0086
ET15X13	0016
ET15X14	0016
ET15X15	0016
ET15X16	0016
ET15X17	0599
ET15X18	0144
ET15X19	0155
ET15X20	0155
ET15X21	0144
ET15X23	0079
ET15X24	0016
ET15X25	0004
ET15X26	0969
ET15X27	0079
ET15X29	0050
ET15X30	0127
ET15X31	0004
ET15X32	0279
ET15X33	0037
ET15X34	0233
ET15X35	OEM
ET15X36	0086
ET15X37	0016
ET15X38	0126
ET15X39	0126
ET15X40	0969
ET15X41	0016
ET15X42	0016
ET15X43	0160
ET15X44	OEM
ET15X45	0016
ET15X54	0079
ET16X1	0143
ET16X6	0911
ET16X7	0196
ET16X10	0196
ET16X11	0196
ET16X13	0911
ET16X14	0911
ET16X15	0137
ET16X16	0229
ET16X16X	0229
ET16X17	0157
ET16X19	0143
ET16X20	0143
ET16X21	0143
ET16X22	OEM
ET16X23	OEM
ET30X85	OEM
ET30X87	OEM
ET41X27	4391
ET41X37	0143
ET41X47	4391
ET47X27	4391
ET51X3	0016
ET51X25	0015
ET52X25	0015
ET55-25	0015
ET55X25	0015
ET55X29	0015
ET57X25	0015
ET57X26	0469
ET57X29	0015
ET57X30	0015
ET57X31	1293
ET57X32	0769
ET57X33	0015
ET57X34	OEM
ET57X35	0015
ET57X36	OEM
ET57X37	OEM
ET57X38	0015
ET57X39	0102
ET57X40	0102
ET57X41	1293
ET57X44	OEM
ET58X32	0769
ET161X1	OEM
ET192	OEM
ET-192-01	OEM
ET200	0015
ET400	0015
ET401	OEM
ET402	OEM
ET403	2757
ET409	OEM
ET410	OEM
ET411	OEM
ET413	OEM
ET423	OEM
ET424	OEM
ET425	OEM
ET430	OEM
ET431	OEM
ET515	OEM
ET516	OEM
ET517	OEM
ET518	OEM
ET519	OEM
ET600	0015

DEVICE TYPE	REPL CODE
ET670	0841
ET701	OEM
ET708	OEM
ET709	OEM
ET710	OEM
ET721	OEM
ET801	OEM
ET1002	OEM
ET1004	OEM
ET1006	OEM
ET1008	OEM
ET1511	0004
ET2002	OEM
ET2004	OEM
ET2006	OEM
ET2008	OEM
ET3002	OEM
ET3004	OEM
ET3006	OEM
ET3008	OEM
ET4002	OEM
ET4004	OEM
ET4006	OEM
ET4008	OEM
ET4039	OEM
ET4040	OEM
ET4041	OEM
ET4045	OEM
ET4050	OEM
ET4055	OEM
ET4059	OEM
ET4060	OEM
ET4061	OEM
ET4065	OEM
ET5000	OEM
ET5001	OEM
ET5002	OEM
ET5004	OEM
ET5006	OEM
ET5008	OEM
ET5060	OEM
ET5061	OEM
ET5062	OEM
ET5063	2602
ET5064	OEM
ET5065	OEM
ET5066	OEM
ET5251	1980
ET5252	1980
ET5253	1980
ET6000	OEM
ET6001	OEM
ET6002	OEM
ET6060	OEM
ET6061	OEM
ET6062	OEM
ET6251	OEM
ET6252	OEM
ET6253	OEM
ET6542	OEM
ET6543	OEM
ET6544	OEM
ET6545	OEM
ET6546	OEM
ET6547	OEM
ET10015	OEM
ET10016	OEM
ET10020	OEM
ET10021	OEM
ET35035	0688
ET234854	0155
ET238894	0016
ET307195	2118
ET329218	0155
ET338894	1471
ET350335	0688
ET368021	0016
ET379462	0111
ET398711	0111
ET398777	0111
ET412626	0016
ET453611	0219
ET491051	0321
ET495371	0555
ET517263	0111
ET517375	0930
ET539122	0527
ET703844	0076
ET703854	0076
ET703865	0688
ET703867	3052
ET703872	0194
ET703873	0853
ET703874	0728
ET703875	0688
ET703878	0431
ET703879	3082
ET703881	0066
ET703887	5233
ET703894	0456
ET704334	0127
E-TA7328AP	4734
E-TA7335P	4336
E-TA7343P	4339
E-TA7343PS	4339
ETD-1N60	0019
ETD1S2788	0124
ETD-10D1	0015
ETD-10D2	0015

DEVICE TYPE	REPL CODE
ETD-5046	0143
ETDCDG21	0133
ETD-HZ7C	0077
ETD-RD9.1FB	0012
ETD-RD75	0077
ETD-SD46	0143
ETD-SG9150	0133
ETD-V06C	0015
ETI-13	5640
ETI-21	0383
ETI-22	0514
ETI-23	1044
ETP2008	0233
ETP3114	0233
ETP3923	0233
ETP5092	0187
ETP5095	0168
ETS-003	0103
ETS-068	0016
ETS-069	0126
ETS-070	0086
ETS-071	0126
ETTB-2SB176	0004
ETTB-2SB176A	0004
ETTB-2SB176B	0004
ETTB-2SB176R	0004
ETTB-75LB	0004
ETTB-367B	0222
ETTC-2SC490	0178
ETTC-458LG	0016
ETTC-930D	2195
ETTC-945	0076
ETTC-CD8000	0016
ETTC-CD12000	0016
ETTC-CD13000	0016
ETT-CDC-12000	0016
ETTD-235	0228
ETX18	0155
EU01	0023
EU01A	0023
EU01Z	0023
EU02	0182
EU02A	0023
EU02Z	0023
EU-1	0023
EU1	0023
EU-1A	0023
EU1A	0023
EU-1AV	0023
EU-1V	0023
EU1V	5890
EU-1Z	0023
EU1Z	0023
EU1ZV1	0023
EU-2	0023
EU2	0023
EU2A	0023
EU-2V	0023
EU2V	0023
EU2YX	0023
EU2YXV1	0023
EU2Z	0023
EU2ZV	0023
EU15X1	0144
EU15X2	0144
EU15X3	0144
EU15X4	0911
EU15X5	OEM
EU15X6	0144
EU15X27	0086
EU15X34	0086
EU16X1	0143
EU16X2	0143
EU16X3	OEM
EU16X4	0911
EU16X5	OEM
EU16X7	0015
EU16X8	0479
EU16X11	0133
EU16X14	0911
EU16X19	0123
EU16X20	0015
EU16X27	4116
EU16X40	OEM
EU30X87	0030
EU57X30	0015
EU57X31	1293
EU57X32	0769
EU57X38	0469
EU57X40	0015
EU-Z	0023
EUZ	0023
EV0004	OEM
EV12R	OEM
EV15	0002
EV16X20	0102
EVD-3	0133
EVM511	0015
EVM711	OEM
EVMEH2AC11/1	OEM
EVMEH2C12/1	OEM
EVR1	OEM
EVR1A	OEM
EVR1B	OEM
EVR4	0157
EVR4A	0157
EVR4B	0157
EVR5	0631
EVR5A	0631

DEVICE TYPE	REPL CODE
EVR5B	0631
EVR6	0298
EVR6A	0298
EVR6B	0298
EVR7	0025
EVR7A	0025
EVR7B	0025
EVR8	0244
EVR8A	0244
EVR8B	0244
EVR9	0012
EVR9A	0012
EVR9B	0012
EVR10	0170
EVR10A	0170
EVR10B	0170
EVR11	0789
EVR11A	0789
EVR11B	0789
EVR12	0137
EVR12A	0137
EVR12B	0137
EVR13	0361
EVR13A	0053
EVR13B	0361
EVR14	0100
EVR14A	0100
EVR14B	0100
EVR15	0002
EVR15A	0002
EVR15B	0002
EVR16	0416
EVR16A	0416
EVR16B	0416
EVR17	1639
EVR17A	1639
EVR17B	1639
EVR18	0490
EVR18A	0490
EVR18B	0490
EVR19	0943
EVR19A	0943
EVR19B	0943
EVR20	0526
EVR20A	0526
EVR20B	0526
EVR21	0560
EVR21A	0560
EVR21B	0560
EVR22	0560
EVR22A	0560
EVR22B	0560
EVR23	0398
EVR23A	0398
EVR23B	0398
EVR24	0398
EVR24A	0398
EVR24B	0398
EVR25	1596
EVR25A	1596
EVR25B	1596
EVR26	0436
EVR26A	0436
EVR26B	0436
EVR27	0436
EVR27A	0436
EVR27B	0436
EVR28	1664
EVR28A	1664
EVR28B	1664
EVR30	0721
EVR30A	0721
EVR30B	0721
EVR32	0039
EVR32A	0039
EVR32B	0039
EVR36	0814
EVR36A	0814
EVR36B	0814
EVR39	0346
EVR39A	0346
EVR39B	0346
EVR43	0346
EVR43A	0346
EVR43B	0346
EVR47	0993
EVR47A	0993
EVR47B	0993
EVR50	0497
EVR50A	0497
EVR50B	0497
EVR56	1823
EVR56A	1823
EVR56B	1823
EVR60	1148
EVR60A	1148
EVR60B	1148
EVR68	2144
EVR68A	2144
EVR68B	2144
EVR75	1181
EVR75A	1181
EVR75B	1181
EVR82	0327
EVR82A	0327
EVR82B	0327
EVR91	1301
EVR91A	1301
EVR91B	1301

DEVICE TYPE	REPL CODE
EVR100	0098
EVR100A	0098
EVR100B	0098
EVR110	0149
EVR110A	0149
EVR110B	0149
EVR150	0028
EVR150A	0028
EVR150B	0028
EVS-K112C	0196
EW02-05A	OEM
EW10X76	4912
EW10X103	5989
EW14X18	0120
EW14X232	1982
EW14X258	OEM
EW14X486	1982
EW15R	OEM
EW15X0399	OEM
EW15X6	0155
EW15X19	0127
EW15X20	1376
EW15X21	0076
EW15X22	0006
EW15X23	1505
EW15X24	0723
EW15X25	0076
EW15X26	0919
EW15X27	0006
EW15X28	OEM
EW15X29	0037
EW15X30	0076
EW15X31	0558
EW15X32	0076
EW15X33	0558
EW15X42	0076
EW15X44	0203
EW15X51	0261
EW15X55	0037
EW15X57	0079
EW15X58	0037
EW15X59	0919
EW15X63	0079
EW15X64	0168
EW15X66	0076
EW15X67	0055
EW15X70	0155
EW15X71	0558
EW15X78	0113
EW15X106	0396
EW15X108	0922
EW15X110	0076
EW15X130	1132
EW15X135	2464
EW15X139	0161
EW15X144	0819
EW15X148	1338
EW15X151	0472
EW15X152	4282
EW15X154	2208
EW15X156	0881
EW15X158	0577
EW15X159	0165
EW15X160	0667
EW15X165	0018
EW15X168	0819
EW15X171	0577
EW15X172	0577
EW15X178	0819
EW15X183	0577
EW15X187	2208
EW15X188	1967
EW15X190	0355
EW15X199	0667
EW15X204	0009
EW15X206	0577
EW15X215	0819
EW15X219	0667
EW15X223	0006
EW15X224	2195
EW15X225	0042
EW15X226	1505
EW15X231	0127
EW15X232	2882
EW15X233	0527
EW15X234	0191
EW15X235	3096
EW15X236	0148
EW15X237	0919
EW15X238	0558
EW15X240	0148
EW15X241	0419
EW15X242	0066
EW15X243	2874
EW15X244	3017
EW15X254	0076
EW15X258	0643
EW15X260	0819
EW15X262	0060
EW15X267	0881
EW15X268	0014
EW15X269	1026
EW15X272	6187
EW15X276	2464
EW15X278	0060
EW15X279	0819
EW15X285	4282
EW15X286	0667
EW15X287	5367

DEVICE TYPE	REPL CODE
EW15X291	5353
EW15X292	0640
EW15X310	0168
EW15X315	0577
EW15X316	0577
EW15X317	0667
EW15X320	0060
EW15X322	0527
EW15X327	0261
EW15X328	0690
EW15X329	0819
EW15X330	2643
EW15X341	0643
EW15X342	1132
EW15X343	2041
EW15X344	0723
EW15X345	0723
EW15X346	0006
EW15X359	0261
EW15X360	0577
EW15X363	0018
EW15X366	4109
EW15X367	4067
EW15X368	0826
EW15X369	0892
EW15X370	4109
EW15X372	0826
EW15X373	0892
EW15X374	0819
EW15X375	0819
EW15X376	0455
EW15X377	1298
EW15X378	2985
EW15X379	0009
EW15X380	OEM
EW15X383	0006
EW15X386	OEM
EW15X406	0060
EW15X413	1154
EW15X415	1154
EW15X421	1026
EW15X427	OEM
EW15X428	1132
EW15X433	0009
EW15X450	0076
EW15X457	0819
EW15X467	3104
EW15X487	3282
EW15X520	0388
EW15X521	0836
EW15X522	0284
EW15X523	0066
EW15X524	1533
EW15X525	0881
EW15X526	4109
EW15X529	0892
EW15X531	OEM
EW15X549	0111
EW15X550	OEM
EW15X564	1298
EW15X566	1505
EW15X567	0723
EW15X568	0127
EW15X570	4569
EW15X571	0261
EW15X572	0006
EW15X573	0261
EW15X574	0860
EW15X575	2351
EW15X576	0191
EW15X577	0513
EW15X578	0006
EW15X579	1533
EW15X580	1274
EW15X581	0155
EW15X582	0191
EW15X583	0155
EW15X584	2882
EW15X585	0513
EW15X588	0007
EW15X589	1317
EW15X590	1779
EW15X591	1203
EW15X592	0275
EW15X593	3574
EW15X594	0750
EW15X595	0261
EW15X596	0018
EW15X597	0284
EW15X598	0111
EW15X619	0690
EW15X620	0261
EW15X628	0261
EW15X629	2768
EW15X634	0275
EW15X635	1533
EW16X9	0133
EW16X10	0124
EW16X11	0023
EW16X12	0023
EW16X13	0466
EW16X14	0140
EW16X15	0133
EW16X17	0030
EW16X19	0139
EW16X21	0077
EW16X22	0015
EW16X26	1404
EW16X36	0023

If replacement code is OEM, contact original manufacturer for replacement.

DEVICE TYPE	REPL CODE
EW16X39	0466
EW16X59	0023
EW16X76	3460
EW16X82	0755
EW16X92	0730
EW16X93	2520
EW16X97	0253
EW16X98	0023
EW16X102	0124
EW16X105	0015
EW16X106	0133
EW16X109	0133
EW16X110	0124
EW16X111	0124
EW16X114	0077
EW16X116	0181
EW16X118	0695
EW16X121	0023
EW16X124	0631
EW16X135	0015
EW16X159	0165
EW16X160	0873
EW16X165	0120
EW16X167	0140
EW16X169	0023
EW16X171	0296
EW16X175	0023
EW16X176	0339
EW16X189	0019
EW16X190	0672
EW16X193	0124
EW16X194	0143
EW16X196	0023
EW16X197	0036
EW16X200	0023
EW16X201	OEM
EW16X202	0071
EW16X204	0253
EW16X205	0057
EW16X206	0440
EW16X207	0700
EW16X209	5402
EW16X218	2217
EW16X221	0023
EW16X223	0041
EW16X224	0253
EW16X226	0124
EW16X227	0124
EW16X231	0689
EW16X232	2189
EW16X234	0466
EW16X235	1997
EW16X237	0053
EW16X238	0450
EW16X242	0181
EW16X243	0053
EW16X245	0560
EW16X248	0041
EW16X249	0999
EW16X251	0062
EW16X253	0371
EW16X254	0195
EW16X255	0140
EW16X256	1404
EW16X257	0124
EW16X258	0490
EW16X259	0244
EW16X260	0165
EW16X261	0077
EW16X262	OEM
EW16X264	0165
EW16X265	0450
EW16X266	0195
EW16X270	0071
EW16X292	0124
EW16X296	0140
EW16X297	0721
EW16X298	0062
EW16X300	0053
EW16X301	0681
EW16X302	0077
EW16X303	0133
EW16X304	0120
EW16X305	0133
EW16X306	0015
EW16X307	0025
EW16X308	0023
EW16X309	0023
EW16X310	0181
EW16X311	0019
EW16X312	0023
EW16X313	0071
EW16X314	1083
EW16X321	0182
EW16X323	0031
EW16X324	0446
EW16X325	0124
EW16X326	0023
EW16X327	0339
EW16X328	0062
EW16X329	0064
EW16X330	0053
EW16X331	0053
EW16X332	0635
EW16X334	0293
EW16X336	0124
EW16X337	0023
EW16X338	0071
EW16X343	0140
EW16X352	0023
EW16X354	0023
EW16X358	0019
EW16X363	0023
EW16X365	1083
EW16X366	0253
EW16X367	0062
EW16X368	0873
EW16X370	0052
EW16X371	0689
EW16X372	0440
EW16X373	1227
EW16X374	0057
EW16X375	0064
EW16X376	0057
EW16X377	0468
EW16X378	0077
EW16X381	3417
EW16X391	0466
EW16X395	0057
EW16X397	0057
EW16X405	0999
EW16X407	0181
EW16X408	0031
EW16X409	0041
EW16X415	0053
EW16X437	0339
EW16X478	0392
EW16X480	OEM
EW16X481	OEM
EW16X482	0124
EW16X483	4333
EW16X484	0023
EW16X485	0023
EW16X486	0790
EW16X487	0137
EW16X488	0559
EW16X489	2219
EW16X490	0124
EW16X491	0700
EW16X492	0541
EW16X494	1864
EW16X501	0077
EW16X518	OEM
EW16X526	0124
EW16X527	0005
EW16X529	0017
EW16X530	0023
EW16X531	0031
EW16X532	0036
EW16X533	0041
EW16X534	OEM
EW16X535	0052
EW16X536	0057
EW16X537	0062
EW16X538	0064
EW16X539	OEM
EW16X540	0072
EW16X541	0023
EW16X542	0015
EW16X543	0091
EW16X544	0100
EW16X545	0106
EW16X546	0112
EW16X547	0118
EW16X548	0124
EW16X549	0071
EW16X550	0133
EW16X551	0140
EW16X552	0023
EW16X553	0064
EW16X554	0023
EW16X555	0158
EW16X556	0091
EW16X557	0165
EW16X558	0166
EW16X559	0023
EW16X560	0023
EW16X561	0002
EW16X562	0181
EW16X563	0071
EW16X564	0041
EW16X565	OEM
EW16X566	0195
EW16X567	0052
EW16X572	OEM
EW16X583	0124
EW16X584	0241
EW16X585	0248
EW16X586	0062
EW16X587	0077
EW16X588	0257
EW16X589	0158
EW16X590	0091
EW16X594	0274
EW16X595	0282
EW16X596	0053
EW16X597	0292
EW16X598	0298
EW16X599	0057
EW16X600	0023
EW16X601	0071
EW16X603	OEM
EW16X605	0023
EW16X606	0091
EW16X607	0318
EW16X608	0181
EW16X609	OEM
EW16X610	0017
EW16X611	0041
EW16X612	0023
EW16X613	OEM
EW16X614	0335
EW16X615	0057
EW16X616	0339
EW16X617	OEM
EW16X618	0124
EW16X619	0077
EW16X620	0023
EW16X622	0071
EW16X630	OEM
EW16X651	0436
EW16X652	0077
EW16X656	0450
EW16X657	0166
EW16X658	0071
EW16X712	0017
EW20	OEM
EW41X7	OEM
EW41X29	2083
EW41X59	2604
EW41X97	1767
EW41X98	1951
EW41X129	OEM
EW41X146	OEM
EW41X159	OEM
EW41X184	1767
EW41X216	OEM
EW41X224	OEM
EW41X257	OEM
EW41X258	1767
EW41X259	OEM
EW41X397	2678
EW41X530	OEM
EW41X561	OEM
EW41X595	OEM
EW41X609	OEM
EW41X619	0241
EW41X620	OEM
EW41X650	OEM
EW41X652	OEM
EW41X685	OEM
EW41X723	OEM
EW41X724	OEM
EW51	OEM
EW53/1	OEM
EW53/2	OEM
EW57X1	0080
EW57X2	0023
EW58/1	OEM
EW58/2	OEM
EW59	OEM
EW69	OEM
EW84X0425	5141
EW84X0594	OEM
EW84X0622	OEM
EW84X0783	OEM
EW84X0898	OEM
EW84X12	1319
EW84X13	OEM
EW84X14	0598
EW84X15	4339
EW84X16	OEM
EW84X17	OEM
EW84X18	4746
EW84X30	0508
EW84X60	2015
EW84X114	0167
EW84X115	2511
EW84X156	0176
EW84X172	2042
EW84X192	0356
EW84X196	0624
EW84X217	2008
EW84X224	3202
EW84X230	OEM
EW84X232	0765
EW84X233	0765
EW84X239	0694
EW84X252	0754
EW84X254	OEM
EW84X255	6171
EW84X267	4074
EW84X268	0167
EW84X269	1580
EW84X270	0485
EW84X271	OEM
EW84X272	1835
EW84X273	1319
EW84X296	2062
EW84X310	1192
EW84X312	2056
EW84X313	OEM
EW84X314	2531
EW84X315	5126
EW84X317	5168
EW84X318	OEM
EW84X319	4838
EW84X320	5167
EW84X322	5178
EW84X323	3130
EW84X324	OEM
EW84X326	OEM
EW84X327	3848
EW84X329	6175
EW84X352	3130
EW84X355	5707
EW84X365	OEM
EW84X370	1813
EW84X372	0176
EW84X375	2057
EW84X376	OEM
EW84X377	5143
EW84X378	OEM
EW84X379	OEM
EW84X380	OEM
EW84X381	5166
EW84X382	OEM
EW84X383	OEM
EW84X384	OEM
EW84X385	2014
EW84X386	OEM
EW84X387	OEM
EW84X388	OEM
EW84X389	1059
EW84X390	OEM
EW84X391	OEM
EW84X394	4416
EW84X416	1934
EW84X422	3698
EW84X423	5116
EW84X424	5003
EW84X425	5141
EW84X426	0970
EW84X427	3462
EW84X431	1319
EW84X439	OEM
EW84X440	4306
EW84X441	6182
EW84X442	5165
EW84X443	5166
EW84X444	3869
EW84X445	5169
EW84X446	5170
EW84X447	OEM
EW84X448	0112
EW84X451	3848
EW84X452	4281
EW84X453	0619
EW84X464	1938
EW84X470	0024
EW84X473	OEM
EW84X474	OEM
EW84X475	OEM
EW84X476	OEM
EW84X477	OEM
EW84X478	OEM
EW84X479	2055
EW84X480	3403
EW84X481	0694
EW84X482	OEM
EW84X483	0356
EW84X484	6184
EW84X485	OEM
EW84X486	2513
EW84X487	2051
EW84X488	0356
EW84X489	OEM
EW84X490	3776
EW84X491	OEM
EW84X492	OEM
EW84X493	OEM
EW84X494	OEM
EW84X495	OEM
EW84X496	0101
EW84X497	OEM
EW84X498	4312
EW84X499	2884
EW84X502	OEM
EW84X503	OEM
EW84X504	OEM
EW84X505	OEM
EW84X506	OEM
EW84X526	1311
EW84X536	5165
EW84X537	OEM
EW84X538	OEM
EW84X539	OEM
EW84X589	5703
EW84X594	OEM
EW84X595	4417
EW84X596	OEM
EW84X598	OEM
EW84X624	3130
EW84X635	OEM
EW84X738	5136
EW84X744	5228
EW84X747	0330
EW84X756	0119
EW84X761	4306
EW84X762	OEM
EW84X763	4054
EW84X764	OEM
EW84X765	OEM
EW84X766	1059
EW84X767	3869
EW84X768	OEM
EW84X769	OEM
EW84X770	4078
EW84X771	5232
EW84X772	OEM
EW84X774	4306
EW84X776	OEM
EW84X777	OEM
EW84X782	2109
EW84X783	4083
EW84X784	2104
EW84X785	0308
EW84X786	OEM
EW84X787	OEM
EW84X788	0356
EW84X789	OEM
EW84X790	OEM
EW84X791	OEM
EW84X792	6144
EW84X793	0412
EW84X794	3479
EW84X795	OEM
EW84X796	OEM
EW84X797	OEM
EW84X798	OEM
EW84X799	OEM
EW84X801	OEM
EW84X802	OEM
EW84X803	OEM
EW84X804	OEM
EW84X805	OEM
EW84X806	OEM
EW84X807	OEM
EW84X808	OEM
EW84X810	4309
EW84X811	OEM
EW84X812	OEM
EW84X813	OEM
EW84X822	OEM
EW84X863	0409
EW84X864	OEM
EW84X865	0356
EW84X866	OEM
EW84X868	OEM
EW84X875	OEM
EW84X888	2641
EW84X894	3680
EW84X895	4955
EW84X897	4284
EW84X898	OEM
EW84X899	0906
EW84X900	0658
EW84X901	0167
EW84X902	0835
EW84X903	OEM
EW84X904	OEM
EW84X905	1022
EW84X906	0534
EW84X907	OEM
EW84X908	OEM
EW84X909	3897
EW84X910	1977
EW84X911	3765
EW84X912	5823
EW84X913	5116
EW84X914	3800
EW84X915	OEM
EW84X920	4202
EW84X976	1521
EW84X977	6023
EW84X978	3860
EW84X979	0331
EW84X980	OEM
EW84X981	OEM
EW84X1002	OEM
EW84X1004	OEM
EW84X1006	OEM
EW84X1007	1569
EW84X1008	4349
EW84X1009	3701
EW84X1010	2348
EW84X1072	OEM
EW84Z316	5170
EW162	0144
EW163	0127
EW164	0127
EW165	0127
EW165V	0016
EW166	0143
EW167	0143
EW168	0123
EW169	0087
EW169B	0015
EW181	0016
EW182	0016
EW183	0919
EW183B	0178
EW212	0007
EW721	OEM
EW722	OEM
EW723	OEM
EWA127	OEM
EWC108	OEM
EWQ202	0037
EX0010GE	0253
EX0011GE	0681
EX0019TA	0053
EX0020CE	OEM
EX0020GE	0041
EX0021TA	0181
EX0023GE	0170
EX0024CE	0466
EX0038CE	0137
EX0041TA	0062
EX0042TA	0140
EX0044CE	0064
EX0045TA	0877
EX0046TA	0077
EX0047CE	0999
EX0047TA	0064
EX0048CE	0466
EX0051CE22.5V	0700
EX0061CE	0137
EX0065CE	0440
EX0074CE	0642
EX0084CE	1181
EX0085CE	0062
EX0088CE	0062
EX0089CE	0165
EX0091CE	0700
EX0092CE	0372
EX0092CE3.9V	0036
EX0101CE	0755
EX0102CE	OEM
EX0103CE	0253
EX0106CE	0049
EX0111-XS	OEM
EX0112CE	0371
EX0113CE15V	0440
EX0114CE9.1V	0057
EX0116CE	OEM
EX0116GE	0062
EX0130CE	0695
EX0131CE	0041
EX0136CE	0814
EX0137CE	0041
EX0137TA	0140
EX0138CE	0062
EX0140CE	0062
EX0146-XS	OEM
EX0147CE	0077
EX0152CE	0213
EX0155CE	0041
EX0161CE	0077
EX0161CEZZ	0077
EX0163CE	0156
EX0166CE	0681
EX0192CE	0631
EX0193CE	0181
EX0200CE	0052
EX0216-XS	OEM
EX0217CE	0873
EX0219CE	0166
EX0221-XS	OEM
EX0222-XS	OEM
EX0225-XS	OEM
EX0375GEZZ	0877
EX0443CE	0036
EX0444CE	0372
EX0598CE	OEM
EX0D43TA5.6V	0253
EX15X25	0004
EX15X336	0127
EX16X10	0133
EX16X27	0133
EX33X8392	1532
EX39	2147
EX39-X	2147
EX42	2803
EX42-X	0348
EX42X	0348
EX46-X	0661
EX48	0167
EX48-X	0350
EX62-X	0345
EX76-X	0015
EX85B-X	0769
EX89/211-X	0143
EX142-X	0133
EX215-X	1313
EX499-X	0079
EX500-X	0079
EX524-X	3052
EX695-X	0079
EX699-X	0150
EX743-X	0233
EX744-X	0086
EX746-X	0037
EX748-X	0079
EX831-X	0637
EX868-X	0283
EX888-X	0079
EX911-X	0275
EX4035	0696
EX4053	0696
EX795427C	OEM
EXB341	OEM
EXB341-0A	OEM
EXB341-0A	OEM
EXC	OEM
EXD019TA	0053
EXDA415	OEM
EXDA420	OEM
EXDA435	OEM
EXDA435C	OEM
EXDA635	OEM
EXO-512	OEM
EXO-2480	OEM
EXPANDOPROM	OEM
EXPANDORAM	OEM
EXPANDORAMII	OEM
EXT954-20C	2092
EXT954-25C	3476
EXT95247C	3476
EXT95423C	3461
EXT95425C	OEM
EXT95427C	3476
EXV420DIR5JB	0143
EYV320D010JB	0139
EYV320D1R2J3	0139
EYV320DIR2J2	OEM
EYV320DIR213	0139
EYV-420D1R5JA	0015
EYV420D1R5JB	0143
EYV420DIR5JB	0143
EYV3200010IB	OEM
EYZP-307-900	0759
EYZP623	0037
EYZP632	0079
EYZP791	0079
EYZP808	0688
EZ01	0023
EZ01Z	0023
EZ055	OEM
EZ056	OEM
EZ057	OEM
EZ058	OEM
EZ059	OEM
EZ060	OEM
EZ062	OEM
EZ063	OEM
EZ065	OEM
EZ066	OEM
EZ068	OEM
EZ069	OEM
EZ070	OEM
EZ072	OEM
EZ074	OEM
EZ075	OEM
EZ077	OEM
EZ079	OEM
EZ081	OEM
EZ083	OEM
EZ085	OEM
EZ087	OEM
EZ091	0057
EZ093	OEM
EZ095	OEM
EZ097	OEM
EZ099	OEM
EZ3-7(ELCOM)	0205
EZ3-12(ELCOM)	0234
EZ3-15(ELCOM)	0247
EZ3-20(ELCOM)	0262
EZ3A	OEM
EZ4(ELCOM)	0451
EZ5(ELCOM)	0446
EZ5R6(ELCOM)	0157
EZ6(ELCOM)	0025
EZ6A	OEM
EZ7(ELCOM)	0644
EZ8A	3071
EZ9(ELCOM)	0012
EZ10(ELCOM)	0170
EZ10-7(ELCOM)	1449
EZ10-8(ELCOM)	1481
EZ10-10(ELCOM)	0505
EZ10-12(ELCOM)	0864
EZ10-24(ELCOM)	1725
EZ10-28(ELCOM)	2431
EZ10A	OEM
EZ10B	OEM
EZ12(ELCOM)	0137
EZ12A	0137
EZ12B	OEM
EZ15(ELCOM)	0002
EZ15A	0002
EZ15B	OEM
EZ18(ELCOM)	0490
EZ18A	OEM
EZ18B	OEM
EZ19G	OEM
EZ19R	OEM
EZ19Y	OEM
EZ20G	OEM
EZ20R	OEM
EZ20Y	OEM
EZ22(ELCOM)	0560
EZ22A	OEM
EZ27A	OEM
EZ33(ELCOM)	0039
EZ33A	OEM
EZ39(ELCOM)	0346
EZ47(ELCOM)	0993
EZ47A	OEM
EZ56(ELCOM)	0863
EZ56A	OEM
EZ68(ELCOM)	2144
EZ68A	OEM
EZ82(ELCOM)	0327
EZ82A	OEM
EZ100	OEM
EZ101	OEM
EZ104	OEM
EZ106	OEM
EZ109	OEM
EZ111	OEM
EZ114	OEM
EZ117	OEM
EZ119	OEM
EZ122	OEM
EZ125	OEM
EZ127	OEM
EZ129	OEM
EZ132	OEM
EZ135	OEM
EZ138	OEM

DEVICE TYPE	REPL CODE
EZ141	OEM
EZ144	OEM
EZ148	OEM
EZ150	0002
EZ152	OEM
EZ156	OEM
EZ161	OEM
EZ167	OEM
EZ173	OEM
EZ179	OEM
EZ186	OEM
EZ193	OEM
EZ200	OEM
EZ207	OEM
EZ214	OEM
EZ221	OEM
EZ228	OEM
EZ235	OEM
EZ242	OEM
EZ249	OEM
EZ250	OEM
EZ259	OEM
EZ269	OEM
EZ279	OEM
EZ289	OEM
EZ299	OEM
EZ300	OEM
EZ309	OEM
EZ319	OEM
EZ329	OEM
EZ339	OEM
EZ350	OEM
EZ361	OEM
EZ372	OEM
EZ400	OEM
EZRC07DK201	OEM
EZT308	1843
E.S57X9	0102
F0010	2861
F0015	0321
F0021	0321
F0-02-200D	OEM
F0-02-400D	OEM
F0-02ED	OEM
F0-04ED	OEM
F0-30EDP	OEM
F-05	0015
F05	0015
F031	0133
F046	0133
F060	0133
F084	0133
F0111	OEM
F0810BH	0712
F0810DH	0712
F0810MH	0304
F0810NH	0323
F0R1B	0895
F0R3G	0403
F0R3G6.J	0403
F1	0079
F1(DIODE)	0023
F1-02	0023
F1-04	0023
F1-06	0023
F1-08	0023
F1A3	OEM
F1B3	OEM
F1B5	OEM
F1B6	OEM
F1B7	OEM
F1B8	OEM
F1B9	OEM
F1C3	OEM
F1D3	OEM
F1E3	OEM
F1F3	OEM
F1G3	OEM
F1H3	6051
F1K3	6051
F1M3	OEM
F1N3	OEM
F1V	OEM
F2	0015
F2A3	OEM
F2B3	OEM
F2C3	OEM
F2D	0934
F2D3	OEM
F2E3	OEM
F2F3	OEM
F2G3	OEM
F2H3	6051
F2K3	6051
F2M3	OEM
F2N3	OEM
F3	0015
F3A3	OEM
F3B3	OEM
F3C3	OEM
F3D3	OEM
F3E3	OEM
F3F3	OEM
F3G3	OEM
F3H3	OEM
F3K3	OEM
F3M3	OEM
F3N3	OEM
F3P3	OEM

DEVICE TYPE	REPL CODE
F3R3	OEM
F3S3	OEM
F4	0015
F4-005	0687
F4A3	OEM
F4B3	OEM
F4C3	OEM
F4D3	OEM
F4E3	OEM
F4F3	OEM
F4G3	OEM
F4H3	OEM
F4K3	OEM
F4M3	OEM
F4N3	OEM
F4P3	OEM
F4R3	OEM
F4S3	OEM
F5	0015
F5A3	OEM
F5B3	OEM
F5C3	OEM
F5D1	OEM
F5D2	OEM
F5D3	OEM
F5E1	OEM
F5E2	OEM
F5E3	OEM
F5F1	3203
F5F3	OEM
F5G3	6076
F5H3	OEM
F5K3	OEM
F5KF20	1119
F5KQ60	OEM
F5M3	OEM
F5N3	OEM
F5P3	OEM
F5R3	OEM
F5S3	OEM
F6	0015
F6A3	OEM
F6B3	OEM
F6C3	OEM
F6D3	OEM
F6E3	OEM
F6F3	OEM
F6G3	OEM
F6H3	OEM
F6K3	OEM
F6M3	OEM
F6N3	OEM
F6P3	OEM
F6R3	OEM
F6S3	OEM
F7A3	OEM
F7B3	OEM
F7C3	OEM
F7D3	OEM
F7E3	OEM
F7F3	OEM
F7G3	OEM
F7H3	OEM
F7K3	OEM
F7M3	OEM
F7N3	OEM
F7P3	OEM
F7R3	OEM
F7S3	OEM
F8	0071
F10	0071
F10P04Q	1015
F11	2320
F11C01FC	OEM
F11C05DC	OEM
F11C05DM	OEM
F11C06DC	OEM
F11C24DC	OEM
F11C24DM	OEM
F11C58DC	OEM
F11C70DC	OEM
F11C70DM	OEM
F11C83DC	OEM
F11C90DC	OEM
F11C90DM	OEM
F11C91DC	OEM
F11C91DM	OEM
F11Q	2320
F12	OEM
F12(DIODE)	0031
F14	0015
F14-C	0015
F-14A	0015
F14A	0015
F14A-P	0015
F14AP	0015
F14B	0023
F14BP	0015
F-14C	0015
F14C	0023
F14CP	0015
F14D	0071
F14DP	0023
F14E	0071
F14F	0071
F14H	0071
F14J	0071
F15	5259
F15X	OEM

DEVICE TYPE	REPL CODE
F16H1	0466
F16K2DC	OEM
F16K3DC	0518
F16K4DC	0518
F16K5DC	0518
F20	0160
F20-1001	0144
F20-1002	0144
F20-1003	0144
F20-1004	0144
F20-1005	0144
F20-1006	0004
F20-1007	0004
F20-1008	0004
F20-1009	0004
F20-1010	0143
F20-1012	0143
F20-1013	0143
F20-1014	0143
F20-1015	0015
F20-1016	0015
F21	2621
F22	0736
F24E-001	0030
F24T-011-013	0144
F24T-011-015	0224
F24T-016-024	0127
F24T-029	OEM
F24T-029-001	0016
F25	0742
F30	2497
F32	0562
F34	0757
F36	3240
F38	OEM
F38C70DC	OEM
F38C70DL	OEM
F38C70DM	OEM
F38C70PC	OEM
F38C70PM	OEM
F38E70DC	OEM
F38E70DL	OEM
F38E70DM	OEM
F38E70PC	OEM
F38E70PL	OEM
F38E70PM	OEM
F38L72DC	OEM
F38L72DL	OEM
F38L72DM	OEM
F38L72PC	OEM
F38L72PL	OEM
F38L72PM	OEM
F38T56DC	OEM
F38T56DL	OEM
F38T56DM	OEM
F38T56PC	OEM
F38T56PL	OEM
F38T56PM	OEM
F38Z	OEM
F40A	0726
F40H	OEM
F41	OEM
F41Z	OEM
F42	OEM
F42Z	OEM
F50A	OEM
F60A	OEM
F61	2621
F61Z	2621
F62	2621
F62Z	2621
F-67-E	0085
F67E	0160
F68A10CS	OEM
F68A10P	OEM
F68A10S	OEM
F68A21CP	OEM
F68A21CS	OEM
F68A21P	OEM
F68A21S	OEM
F68A40CP	OEM
F68A40CS	OEM
F68A40P	OEM
F68A40S	OEM
F68A44P	OEM
F68A45ACP	OEM
F68A45ACS	OEM
F68A45AP	OEM
F68A45AS	OEM
F68A45CP	OEM
F68A45CS	OEM
F68A45P	OEM
F68A45S	OEM
F68A50P	OEM
F68A50S	OEM
F68A52CP	OEM
F68A52CS	OEM
F68A52P	OEM
F68A52S	OEM
F68A54CP	OEM
F68A54CS	OEM
F68A54P	OEM
F68A54S	OEM
F68A488CP	OEM
F68A488CS	OEM
F68A488P	OEM
F68A488S	OEM
F68B21P	OEM
F68B21S	OEM

DEVICE TYPE	REPL CODE
F68B40P	OEM
F68B40S	OEM
F68B44P	OEM
F68B45AP	OEM
F68B45AS	OEM
F68B45P	OEM
F68B45S	OEM
F68B50P	OEM
F68B50S	OEM
F68B52P	OEM
F68B52S	OEM
F68B54P	OEM
F68B54S	OEM
F68B488P	OEM
F68B488S	OEM
F-74LS04PC	1585
F-74LS86PC	0288
F74LS174PC	OEM
F-74LS390PC	1278
F74S138	2125
F-74S138PC	2125
F75F	OEM
F78L05AC	1288
F78L05AV	1288
F78L05AWC	1288
F78L06	2285
F78L06AC	2826
F78L06C	2285
F78L062AC	2826
F78L62AC	2285
F78L62AWC	2826
F78L62WV	2285
F80H	OEM
F81	0742
F81Z	2621
F82	0742
F82Z	0087
F96N	0144
F100	OEM
F100H	OEM
F101	0087
F102	0087
F102Z	OEM
F103	OEM
F103P	0150
F104	0065
F105	0065
F106	0065
F107	OEM
F108	OEM
F109	OEM
F110	OEM
F111	OEM
F112	OEM
F112C1	OEM
F113	OEM
F113A	0023
F113B	0023
F113D	0023
F113E	0023
F113F	0182
F114	0023
F114B	0102
F114D	0102
F114E	0023
F114F	0102
F115	0103
F116	0103
F117	0065
F117A	0065
F118	0065
F118A	0065
F119	0065
F119A	0065
F120	0065
F120A	0065
F121	OEM
F121-546	0079
F121-603	0150
F121-60216	0150
F121-433804	0016
F121A	OEM
F122	OEM
F122A	OEM
F123	OEM
F123A	OEM
F124	OEM
F124A	OEM
F136	0143
F150H	OEM
F150HL	OEM
F200	OEM
F200H	OEM
F200HL	OEM
F204	0378
F209	0037
F211	0720
F211A	0720
F215-1001	0144
F215-1002	0144
F215-1003	0144
F215-1004	0144
F215-1005	0144
F215-1006	0004
F215-1007	0004
F215-1008	0004
F215-1009	0004
F215-1010	0143
F215-1012	0143

DEVICE TYPE	REPL CODE
F215-1013	0143
F215-1014	0143
F215-1016	0015
F215-1017	0015
F222	0016
F230GG0A	OEM
F230HH0A	OEM
F248A	1814
F250H	OEM
F250HL	OEM
F266	2635
F266A	2905
F267	0671
F267A	2908
F268	0671
F268A	2908
F274	0350
F300HL	OEM
F-302-1	0079
F302-1	0016
F302-2	0016
F-302-1532	0079
F302-1532	0016
F-302-2532	0079
F302-2532	0016
F306-001	0016
F306-022	0016
F324	0802
F324(EUROPE)	0802
F336GD	4928
F336HD	3965
F366	0016
F400	OEM
F422	0261
F422(EUROPE)	0261
F422P	0261
F423	OEM
F450	OEM
F495	OEM
F501	0007
F501(ZENITH)	0007
F501-16	0007
F502	0007
F502(ZENITH)	0007
F523	0007
F531	0016
F549-1	0037
F572-1	0016
F587	0016
F600	OEM
F610	0030
F625-1	0086
F-677	0100
F699	0037
F757PC	0696
F767PC	0696
F927-11G	OEM
F927-21G	OEM
F927-31G	OEM
F927-41G	OEM
F927-51G	OEM
F927-61G	OEM
F927-71G	OEM
F1005	OEM
F1016DC	OEM
F1016DM	OEM
F1016FM	OEM
F1022	OEM
F1025	OEM
F1030	OEM
F1031	OEM
F1032	OEM
F1032B	OEM
F1032L	OEM
F1032U	OEM
F1032Z	OEM
F1033	OEM
F1034	OEM
F1035	2959
F1036	1133
F1037	OEM
F1038	OEM
F1039	OEM
F1040	OEM
F1041	OEM
F1042	OEM
F1043	OEM
F1044	OEM
F1050	OEM
F1054	OEM
F1055	OEM
F1056	OEM
F1088	0463
F1089	OEM
F1090	OEM
F1091	OEM
F1092	OEM
F1093	1094
F1094	0957
F1095	2908
F1096	3405
F1103	1078
F1119	OEM
F1120	OEM
F1121	OEM
F1123	2647
F1127	OEM
F1128	OEM
F1168A	0239

DEVICE TYPE	REPL CODE
F1203M	OEM
F1212M	OEM
F1220M	OEM
F1227L	OEM
F1228L	OEM
F1322	OEM
F1462	0321
F1463	0321
F1612BH	0393
F1612DH	0606
F1612MH	0946
F1612NH	1504
F1802H	OEM
F1802R	OEM
F2004	2439
F2005(HEP)	0843
F2006	OEM
F2007A(HEP)	0212
F2008	OEM
F2009	OEM
F2016AP12	OEM
F2040	OEM
F2041	0786
F2042	OEM
F2043	OEM
F2055	OEM
F2084	OEM
F2085	OEM
F2098	OEM
F2099	OEM
F2101	OEM
F2104	OEM
F2106	OEM
F2107	OEM
F2114-2DC	OEM
F2114-2PC	OEM
F2114-3DC	OEM
F2114-3PC	OEM
F2114DC	OEM
F2114L2DC	OEM
F2114L2PC	OEM
F2114L3DC	OEM
F2114L3PC	OEM
F2114LDC	OEM
F2114LPC	OEM
F2114PC	OEM
F2120	OEM
F2124	OEM
F2125	OEM
F2128	OEM
F2129	OEM
F2130	OEM
F2131	OEM
F2137	OEM
F2147	OEM
F2153	OEM
F2154	OEM
F2161	OEM
F2169	OEM
F2180	OEM
F2184	OEM
F2191	OEM
F2194	OEM
F2195	OEM
F2196	OEM
F2197	OEM
F2427	0144
F2443	0016
F2448	0016
F2450	0144
F2480	0211
F2547	OEM
F2548	OEM
F2552	OEM
F2576	OEM
F2577	OEM
F2578	OEM
F2584	0016
F2633	0144
F2634	0144
F2636	0144
F2708-1DC	OEM
F2708DC	OEM
F2708DL	OEM
F2708DM	OEM
F2716DC	OEM
F2901ADC	OEM
F2901ADM	OEM
F2901APC	OEM
F2909	OEM
F2910	OEM
F2911	OEM
F2912	OEM
F2914	OEM
F2917/8315	OEM
F2919	OEM
F2920	OEM
F2922	OEM
F2923	OEM
F2924	OEM
F2932	OEM
F2933/DOD034	OEM
F2934	OEM
F2945	OEM
F2946	OEM
F2947	OEM
F2948	OEM
F3003	OEM
F3004	OEM

DEVICE TYPE	REPL CODE
F3012	OEM
F3519	0016
F3530	0144
F3532	0016
F3532-30P	OEM
F3532-30S	OEM
F3532-35P	OEM
F3532-35S	OEM
F3532-45P	OEM
F3532-45S	OEM
F3533-30P	OEM
F3533-30S	OEM
F3533-35P	OEM
F3533-35S	OEM
F3533-45P	OEM
F3533-45S	OEM
F3535	0007
F3549	0126
F3559	0037
F3560	0086
F3561	0086
F3564-25(A)	OEM
F3564-35(A)	OEM
F3565	0086
F3565-25(A)	OEM
F3565-35(A)	OEM
F3566-25(A)	OEM
F3566-35(A)	OEM
F3568-25(A)	OEM
F3568-35(A)	OEM
F3569	0016
F3569-25(A)	OEM
F3569-35(A)	OEM
F3570	0037
F3570-25(A)	OEM
F3570-35(A)	OEM
F3571	0016
F3574	0007
F3589	0086
F3590	0037
F3597	0037
F3846CP	OEM
F3846CS	OEM
F3846DM	OEM
F3846P	OEM
F3846S	OEM
F3850DC	OEM
F3850DL	OEM
F3850DM	OEM
F3851DC	OEM
F3851DL	OEM
F3851DM	OEM
F3851PC	OEM
F3851PL	OEM
F3851PM	OEM
F3854DC	OEM
F3854DL	OEM
F3854DM	OEM
F3854PC	OEM
F3854PL	OEM
F3856DC	OEM
F3856DL	OEM
F3856DM	OEM
F3856PC	OEM
F3856PL	OEM
F3856PM	OEM
F3861DC	OEM
F3861DL	OEM
F3861DM	OEM
F3861PC	OEM
F3861PL	OEM
F3861PM	OEM
F3870DC	OEM
F3870DL	OEM
F3870DM	OEM
F3870PC	OEM
F3870PL	OEM
F3870PM	OEM
F3871DC	OEM
F3871DL	OEM
F3871DM	OEM
F3871PC	OEM
F3871PL	OEM
F3871PM	OEM
F3872DC	OEM
F3872DL	OEM
F3872DM	OEM
F3872PC	OEM
F3872PL	OEM
F3872PM	OEM
F3876DC	OEM
F3876DL	OEM
F3876DM	OEM
F3876PC	OEM
F3876PL	OEM
F3876PM	OEM
F4001	0473
F4002	2044
F4007	2819
F4011	0215
F4011P	OEM
F4011PC	0215
F4012	0493
F4013	0409
F4015	1008
F4016	1135
F4017	0508
F4017D	OEM
F4019	1517

If replacement code is OEM, contact original manufacturer for replacement.

DEVICE TYPE	REPL CODE
F4020	1651
F4021	1738
F4023	0515
F4024	1946
F4024B	1946
F4025	2061
F4025B	2061
F4026B	2139
F4027	1938
F4029	2218
F4029E	OEM
F4029PC	2218
F4030	0495
F4032B	2509
F4040	0056
F4042	0121
F4049	0001
F4049PC	0001
F4050	0394
F4051	0362
F4052	0024
F4074	OEM
F4075	2518
F4076	3455
F4077BPC	2536
F4081	0621
F4084	OEM
F4123A	OEM
F4129	OEM
F4146	OEM
F4150	OEM
F4156	OEM
F4171A	OEM
F4185	OEM
F4186	OEM
F4187F	OEM
F4511	1535
F4511PC	1535
F4512BPC	4153
F4518	1037
F4528B	3168
F4706	0144
F4709	0086
F4846-1	2530
F5380-1	OEM
F5380-5	OEM
F5380-6	OEM
F5380-G	OEM
F5380-M	OEM
F5380-X	OEM
F-5404DM	OEM
F5404DM	0357
F6446P	OEM
F6810CP	2075
F6810CS	2075
F6810DM	2075
F6810P	2075
F6810S	2075
F6820P	OEM
F6820S	OEM
F6821CP	0443
F6821DM	0443
F6821P	0443
F6821S	0443
F6840CP	OEM
F6840CS	OEM
F6840DL	OEM
F6840DM	OEM
F6840P	OEM
F6840S	OEM
F6844P	OEM
F6845ACP	OEM
F6845ACS	OEM
F6845AP	OEM
F6845AS	OEM
F6845CS	OEM
F6845P	OEM
F6845S	OEM
F6846S	OEM
F6847P	OEM
F6847S	OEM
F6850CP	0509
F6850CS	0509
F6850DL	0509
F6850DM	0509
F6850P	0509
F6850S	0509
F6852CP	OEM
F6852CS	OEM
F6852DLQB	OEM
F6852DMQB	OEM
F6852P	OEM
F6852S	OEM
F6854CP	OEM
F6854CS	OEM
F6854DL	OEM
F6854DM	OEM
F6854P	OEM
F6854S	OEM
F6856CP	OEM
F6856CS	OEM
F6856DM	OEM
F6856P	OEM
F6856S	OEM
F7316	0079
F-7402PC	0310
F7403PC	OEM
F-7404PC	0357
F-7417PC	1342

DEVICE TYPE	REPL CODE
F7417PC	1342
F7430PC	0867
F7473PC	OEM
F7474PC	1303
F7476PC	1150
F8114	0735
F9014D	0155
F9316PC	1635
F9423DC	OEM
F9423PC	OEM
F9443	OEM
F9444	OEM
F9445-16DC	OEM
F9445-16DM	OEM
F9445-16DMQB	OEM
F9445-20DC	OEM
F9445-20DM	OEM
F9445-20DMQB	OEM
F9445-24DC	OEM
F9445-24DM	OEM
F9445-24DMQB	OEM
F9446	OEM
F9447	OEM
F9448	OEM
F9449DC	OEM
F9449DM	OEM
F9470DC	OEM
F9470DL	OEM
F9470DM	OEM
F9600	0016
F9623	0016
F9623(G.E.)	0144
F9623F	0079
F9625	0144
F10000DC	OEM
F10000DM	OEM
F10000FC	OEM
F10000FM	OEM
F10010DC	OEM
F10010DM	OEM
F10010FM	OEM
F10100DC	OEM
F10101DC	OEM
F10103DC	OEM
F10104DC	OEM
F10105DC	OEM
F10106DC	OEM
F10107DC	OEM
F10109DC	OEM
F10110DC	OEM
F10111DC	OEM
F10113DC	OEM
F10117DC	OEM
F10118DC	OEM
F10119DC	OEM
F10121DC	OEM
F10124	0015
F10130DC	OEM
F10131DC	OEM
F10133DC	OEM
F10135DC	OEM
F10136DC	OEM
F10137DC	OEM
F10141DC	OEM
F10141FC	OEM
F10145ADC	OEM
F10145AFC	OEM
F10148	0015
F10153DC	OEM
F10160DC	OEM
F10166DC	OEM
F10168DC	OEM
F10170DC	OEM
F10175DC	OEM
F10176DC	OEM
F10176FC	OEM
F10176PC	OEM
F10179DC	OEM
F10180	0015
F10180DC	OEM
F10181DC	OEM
F10186DC	OEM
F10186FC	OEM
F10186PC	OEM
F10210DC	OEM
F10211DC	OEM
F10231DC	OEM
F10405DC	OEM
F10405FC	OEM
F10410DC	OEM
F10410FC	OEM
F10410PC	OEM
F10414DC	OEM
F10414FC	OEM
F10415ADC	OEM
F10415AFC	OEM
F10415DC	OEM
F10415FC	OEM
F10416DC	OEM
F10416FC	OEM
F10422DC	OEM
F10422FC	OEM
F10470DC	OEM
F10500DM	OEM
F10501DM	OEM
F10501FM	OEM
F10502DM	OEM
F10502FM	OEM
F10503DM	OEM

DEVICE TYPE	REPL CODE
F10503FM	OEM
F10504DM	OEM
F10504FM	OEM
F10505DM	OEM
F10505FM	OEM
F10506DM	OEM
F10506FM	OEM
F10507DM	OEM
F10507FM	OEM
F10509DM	OEM
F10509FM	OEM
F10510DM	OEM
F10510FM	OEM
F10511DM	OEM
F10511FM	OEM
F10513DM	OEM
F10513FM	OEM
F10517DM	OEM
F10517FM	OEM
F10518DM	OEM
F10518FM	OEM
F10519DM	OEM
F10519FM	OEM
F10521DM	OEM
F10521FM	OEM
F10530DM	OEM
F10530FM	OEM
F10531DM	OEM
F10531FM	OEM
F10533DM	OEM
F10533FM	OEM
F10535DM	OEM
F10535FM	OEM
F10536DM	OEM
F10536FM	OEM
F10537DM	OEM
F10537FM	OEM
F10541DM	OEM
F10541FM	OEM
F10545ADM	OEM
F10545AFM	OEM
F10553DM	OEM
F10553FM	OEM
F10560DM	OEM
F10560FM	OEM
F10566DM	OEM
F10566FM	OEM
F10568DM	OEM
F10568FM	OEM
F10570DM	OEM
F10570FM	OEM
F10575DM	OEM
F10575FM	OEM
F10576DM	OEM
F10576FM	OEM
F10579DM	OEM
F10579FM	OEM
F10580DM	OEM
F10580FM	OEM
F10581DM	OEM
F10581FM	OEM
F10586DM	OEM
F10586FM	OEM
F10610DM	OEM
F10610FM	OEM
F10611FM	OEM
F10631DM	OEM
F10631FM	OEM
F-10896	6031
F-12227	0023
F-12737	0042
F12737	2498
F-13316	0042
F-13317	0236
F-14168	0133
F-14201	OEM
F-14753	2498
F-14959	0133
F-15023	0133
F-15024	0133
F-15684	2987
F15810	0144
F15835	0144
F15840	0016
F15840-1	0016
F15841	0144
F16032	OEM
F16081	OEM
F16105	OEM
F-16147	0133
F16201	OEM
F16202	OEM
F16203	OEM
F16413	OEM
F16456	OEM
F16488	OEM
F20303	0143
F21490	0037
F27002	0015
F-28309	OEM
F-28908	OEM
F-28909	OEM
F-28910	OEM
F-28911	OEM
F-28912	OEM
F-28936	OEM
F35316-25P	OEM
F35316-25S	OEM
F35316-30P	OEM

DEVICE TYPE	REPL CODE
F35316-30S	OEM
F50116	0007
F68316-35P	OEM
F68316-35S	OEM
F68316-45P	OEM
F68316-45S	OEM
F68332-30P	OEM
F68332-30S	OEM
F68332-35P	OEM
F68332-45P	OEM
F68332-45S	OEM
F68488CP	OEM
F68488CS	OEM
F68488DL	OEM
F68488DM	OEM
F68488P	OEM
F68488S	OEM
F69916	0086
F73216	0050
F-74390PC	OEM
F75116	0016
F78105AV	1288
F95000DC	OEM
F95002DC	OEM
F95003DC	OEM
F95004DC	OEM
F95010DC	OEM
F95016DC	OEM
F95029DC	OEM
F95101DC	OEM
F95102DC	OEM
F95103DC	OEM
F95105DC	OEM
F95106DC	OEM
F95107DC	OEM
F95109DC	OEM
F95110DC	OEM
F95111DC	OEM
F95130DC	OEM
F95231DC	OEM
F100101DC	OEM
F100101FC	OEM
F100102DC	OEM
F100102FC	OEM
F100107DC	OEM
F100107FC	OEM
F100112DC	OEM
F100112FC	OEM
F100113DC	OEM
F100113FC	OEM
F100114DC	OEM
F100114FC	OEM
F100117DC	OEM
F100117FC	OEM
F100118DC	OEM
F100118FC	OEM
F100125DC	OEM
F100125FC	OEM
F100130DC	OEM
F100130FC	OEM
F100131DC	OEM
F100131FC	OEM
F100141DC	OEM
F100141FC	OEM
F100142DC	OEM
F100142FC	OEM
F100145DC	OEM
F100145FC	OEM
F100150DC	OEM
F100150FC	OEM
F100151DC	OEM
F100151FC	OEM
F100155DC	OEM
F100155FC	OEM
F100156DC	OEM
F100156FC	OEM
F100160DC	OEM
F100160FC	OEM
F100163DC	OEM
F100163FC	OEM
F100164DC	OEM
F100164FC	OEM
F100165DC	OEM
F100165FC	OEM
F100166DC	OEM
F100166FC	OEM
F100170DC	OEM
F100170FC	OEM
F100171DC	OEM
F100171FC	OEM
F100179DC	OEM
F100179FC	OEM
F100180DC	OEM
F100180FC	OEM
F100181DC	OEM
F100181FC	OEM
F100182DC	OEM
F100182FC	OEM
F100183DC	OEM
F100183FC	OEM
F100194DC	OEM
F100194FC	OEM
F100220	OEM
F100414DC	OEM
F100414FC	OEM
F100415DC	OEM
F100415FC	OEM
F100416DC	OEM
F100416FC	OEM

DEVICE TYPE	REPL CODE
F100422DC	OEM
F100422FC	OEM
F100470DC	OEM
F100470FC	OEM
F814997G8503	OEM
F303030000	OEM
F304059000	OEM
F315056000	OEM
F315060000	OEM
F317055000	OEM
FA002	OEM
FA-1	0143
FA1A4M-L33	OEM
FA1A4P	OEM
FA1L3Z	OEM
FA1L4M-L31	OEM
FA-2	0030
FA-3	OEM
FA-4	0071
FA4	0015
FA6	0015
FA-7	OEM
FA8	0071
FA111	0133
FA2000	OEM
FA2001	OEM
FA2001T	OEM
FA2002	OEM
FA2002T	OEM
FA2003	OEM
FA2004	OEM
FA2005	OEM
FA2006	OEM
FA2007	OEM
FA2008	OEM
FA2009	OEM
FA2010	OEM
FA2011	OEM
FA2310	OEM
FA2310E	0133
FA2310U	0133
FA2320	OEM
FA2320E	0133
FA2320U	0133
FA2330	OEM
FA2330E	0133
FA2330U	0133
FA-2711	OEM
FA4000	OEM
FA4001	OEM
FA4002	OEM
FA4003	OEM
FA4004	OEM
FA4005	OEM
FA4006	OEM
FA4007	OEM
FA4008	OEM
FA4009	OEM
FA4010	OEM
FA4011	OEM
FA4071A	OEM
FA4075	OEM
FA4310	OEM
FA4320	OEM
FA4330	OEM
FA6001	OEM
FA6001D	0627
FA6001T	OEM
FA6004	OEM
FA6005	OEM
FA6005T	OEM
FA6007	OEM
FA6007M	OEM
FA6007N	OEM
FA6007T	OEM
FA6008(M)	OEM
FA-6008D	OEM
FA-6008T	4490
FA6008T	6424
FA6013	OEM
FA6013D	OEM
FA6016	OEM
FA6017	OEM
FA6018	OEM
FA6018(D)	OEM
FA-6018(M)	OEM
FA6019	OEM
FA-6019(M)	OEM
FA8001	OEM
FA8002	OEM
FA8003	OEM
FA8004	OEM
FA8005	0789
FA8006	0789
FA8007	0789
FA8008	0789
FA8009	0002
FA8010	0002
FA8011	0002
FA8012	0002
FA100252	OEM
FA100443	OEM
FA5353121	OEM
FAA237D	OEM
FAG013D	OEM
FAN3132R	OEM
FAN3132T	OEM
FAN4050D	OEM
FAN4050R	OEM

DEVICE TYPE	REPL CODE
FAN4050T	OEM
FAN4071D	OEM
FAN4071R	OEM
FAN4071T	OEM
FAN4137R	OEM
FAN4137T	OEM
FAN5132D	OEM
FAN5132R	OEM
FAN5132T	OEM
FAN6102D	OEM
FAN6102R	OEM
FAN6102T	OEM
FAN6133R	OEM
FAN31861R	OEM
FAN31861T	OEM
FAN40551D	OEM
FAN40551R	OEM
FAN40551T	OEM
FAN41041D	OEM
FAN41041R	OEM
FAN41041T	OEM
FAN41052D	OEM
FAN41052R	OEM
FAN41052T	OEM
FAN41851D	OEM
FAN41851R	OEM
FAN41851T	OEM
FAN41860R	OEM
FAN41860T	OEM
FAN60584D	OEM
FAN60584R	OEM
FAN60584T	OEM
FAN60585D	OEM
FAN60585R	OEM
FAN60585T	OEM
FAN61821D	OEM
FAN61821R	OEM
FAN61821T	OEM
FAN605831D	OEM
FAN605831R	OEM
FAN605831T	OEM
FAR-3HS	OEM
FAR-4HS	OEM
FAS16061R	OEM
FAT-3HS	OEM
FAT-4HS	OEM
FB30G	0031
FB100D4	OEM
FB100D-6	OEM
FB100D-8	OEM
FB100D-12	OEM
FB100D-16	OEM
FB100D-20	OEM
FB100D-24	OEM
FB150D-4	OEM
FB150D-6	OEM
FB150D-8	OEM
FB150D-12	OEM
FB150D-16	OEM
FB150D-20	OEM
FB150D-24	OEM
FB-200	0293
FB200	0293
FB-274	OEM
FB274	2377
FB300D-4	OEM
FB300D-6	OEM
FB300D-8	OEM
FB300D-12	OEM
FB300D-16	OEM
FB300D-20	OEM
FB300D-24	OEM
FB401	0050
FB402	0050
FB403	0050
FB420	0004
FB421	0004
FB440	0050
FB1001	2347
FB1001L	0319
FB1002	0319
FB1002L	1404
FB1003	OEM
FB1004	2353
FB1004L	0468
FB1006	2354
FB1006L	0441
FB1043	0143
FB2500	2347
FB2501	2347
FB2502	2347
FB2504	2347
FB2506	2354
FB3500	1633
FB3501	1633
FB3502	1633
FB3504	2897
FB3506	2897
FB6853	0016
FB8056	5995
FB8550	6035
FBC404M3L	OEM
FBM31DB	OEM
FBM43DA	OEM
FBN5175D	OEM
FBN5185R	OEM
FBN5185T	OEM
FBP-00-024	0720
FBS3425F	3123

DEVICE TYPE	REPL CODE
FBS3515F	0278
FBS3525F	3124
FBS3610F	0418
FBTX070	0086
FC10D	OEM
FC10E	OEM
FC11D	OEM
FC11E	OEM
FC12D	OEM
FC12E	OEM
FC13D	OEM
FC13E	OEM
FC14D	OEM
FC14E	OEM
FC31A	OEM
FC31B	OEM
FC33B	OEM
FC34B	OEM
FC42	OEM
FC44	OEM
FC51	OEM
FC51A	OEM
FC51H	OEM
FC51M	OEM
FC-52	0030
FC52	0030
FC52A	OEM
FC-52M	0030
FC52M	0030
FC53	OEM
FC53A	OEM
FC53M	OEM
FC54	OEM
FC54A	OEM
FC54M	OEM
FC55	0005
FC56	1023
FC57	1023
FC62	OEM
FC63	OEM
FC64M	OEM
FC65M	OEM
FC66M	OEM
FC74LS90	1871
FC74LS93	1877
FC74LS196N	2807
FC81	0005
FC82	0549
FC91	0133
FC210R	OEM
FC210S	OEM
FC225R	OEM
FC225S	OEM
FC240R	OEM
FC240S	OEM
FC5006	0144
FC100240	OEM
FC100347	OEM
FC100348	OEM
FC100350	OEM
FC100535	OEM
FC100541	OEM
FC100542	OEM
FC100611	OEM
FC100628	OEM
FCB61C65L-70P	OEM
FCD0003PC	0133
FCD0014NCS	0133
FCD0070ANC	0030
FCD0070PC	0030
FCD0074	0030
FCD810	0536
FCD810C	0311
FCD810D	0311
FCD811	0311
FCD820	0536
FCD820A	0536
FCD820B	0536
FCD820C	0311
FCD820D	0311
FCD825	0311
FCD825A	0311
FCD825C	0311
FCD825D	0311
FCD830	0536
FCD830C	0311
FCD830D	0311
FCD831C	0311
FCD831D	0311
FCD836C	0311
FCD836D	0311
FCD850	1047
FCD850C	1047
FCD855	1101
FCD855C	1101
FCD860	1047
FCD860C	1047
FCD865	1047
FCD865C	1047
FCD880	1393
FCD885	1393
FCH101	OEM
FCH111	OEM
FCH121	OEM
FCH131	OEM
FCH141	OEM
FCH151	OEM
FCH161	OEM
FCH171	OEM

If replacement code is OEM, contact original manufacturer for replacement. 405

DEVICE TYPE	REPL CODE
FCH181	OEM
FCH191	OEM
FCH221	OEM
FCH231	OEM
FCH301	OEM
FCJ101	OEM
FCJ111	OEM
FCJ121	OEM
FCJ131	OEM
FCJ141	OEM
FCJ191	OEM
FCJ201	OEM
FCJ211	OEM
FCJ221	OEM
FCK111	OEM
FCN16062R	OEM
FCR8U01HA	OEM
FCR8U01HC	OEM
FCR8U01HD	OEM
FCR8U02HA	OEM
FCR8U02HC	OEM
FCR8U02HD	OEM
FCR8U03HA	OEM
FCR8U03HC	OEM
FCR8U03HD	OEM
FCR8U04HA	OEM
FCR8U04HC	OEM
FCR8U04HD	OEM
FCR8U05HA	OEM
FCR8U05HC	OEM
FCR8U05HD	OEM
FCR8U06HA	OEM
FCR8U06HC	OEM
FCR8U06HD	OEM
FCR9U01JC	OEM
FCR9U01JD	OEM
FCR9U01JG	OEM
FCR9U02JC	OEM
FCR9U02JD	OEM
FCR9U02JG	OEM
FCR9U03JC	OEM
FCR9U03JD	OEM
FCR9U03JG	OEM
FCR9U04JC	OEM
FCR9U04JD	OEM
FCR9U04JG	OEM
FCR9U05JC	OEM
FCR9U05JD	OEM
FCR9U05JG	OEM
FCR9U06JC	OEM
FCR9U06JD	OEM
FCR9U06JG	OEM
FCR9U07JA	OEM
FCR9U07JC	OEM
FCR9U08JA	OEM
FCR9U08JC	OEM
FCR9U09JA	OEM
FCR9U09JC	OEM
FCR9U10JA	OEM
FCR9U10JC	OEM
FCR9U11JA	OEM
FCR9U11JC	OEM
FCR9U12JA	OEM
FCR9U12JC	OEM
FCR12U01JC	OEM
FCR12U01JD	OEM
FCR12U01JG	OEM
FCR12U02JC	OEM
FCR12U02JD	OEM
FCR12U02JG	OEM
FCR12U03JC	OEM
FCR12U03JD	OEM
FCR12U03JG	OEM
FCR12U04JC	OEM
FCR12U04JD	OEM
FCR12U04JG	OEM
FCR12U05JC	OEM
FCR12U05JD	OEM
FCR12U05JG	OEM
FCR12U06JC	OEM
FCR12U06JD	OEM
FCR12U06JG	OEM
FCR12U07JA	OEM
FCR12U07JC	OEM
FCR12U08JA	OEM
FCR12U08JC	OEM
FCR12U09JA	OEM
FCR12U09JC	OEM
FCR12U10JA	OEM
FCR12U10JC	OEM
FCR12U11JA	OEM
FCR12U11JC	OEM
FCR12U12JA	OEM
FCR12U12JC	OEM
FCR20U01JC	OEM
FCR20U01JD	OEM
FCR20U01JG	OEM
FCR20U02JC	OEM
FCR20U02JD	OEM
FCR20U02JG	OEM
FCR20U03JC	OEM
FCR20U03JD	OEM
FCR20U03JG	OEM
FCR20U04JC	OEM
FCR20U04JD	OEM
FCR20U04JG	OEM
FCR20U05JC	OEM
FCR20U05JD	OEM
FCR20U05JG	OEM

DEVICE TYPE	REPL CODE
FCR20U06JC	OEM
FCR20U06JD	OEM
FCR20U06JG	OEM
FCR20U07JA	OEM
FCR20U07JC	OEM
FCR20U08JA	OEM
FCR20U08JC	OEM
FCR20U09JA	OEM
FCR20U09JC	OEM
FCR20U10JA	OEM
FCR20U10JC	OEM
FCR20U11JA	OEM
FCR20U11JC	OEM
FCR20U12JA	OEM
FCR20U12JC	OEM
FCR24U01JC	OEM
FCR24U01JD	OEM
FCR24U01JG	OEM
FCR24U02JC	OEM
FCR24U02JD	OEM
FCR24U02JG	OEM
FCR24U03JC	OEM
FCR24U03JD	OEM
FCR24U03JG	OEM
FCR24U04JC	OEM
FCR24U04JD	OEM
FCR24U04JG	OEM
FCR24U05JC	OEM
FCR24U05JD	OEM
FCR24U05JG	OEM
FCR24U06JC	OEM
FCR24U06JD	OEM
FCR24U06JG	OEM
FCR24U07JA	OEM
FCR24U07JC	OEM
FCR24U08JA	OEM
FCR24U08JC	OEM
FCR24U09JA	OEM
FCR24U09JC	OEM
FCR24U10JA	OEM
FCR24U10JC	OEM
FCR24U11JA	OEM
FCR24U11JC	OEM
FCR24U12JA	OEM
FCR24U12JC	OEM
FCR31U01JB	OEM
FCR31U01JC	OEM
FCR31U01JD	OEM
FCR31U02JB	OEM
FCR31U02JC	OEM
FCR31U02JD	OEM
FCR31U03JB	OEM
FCR31U03JC	OEM
FCR31U03JD	OEM
FCR31U04JB	OEM
FCR31U04JC	OEM
FCR31U04JD	OEM
FCR31U05JB	OEM
FCR31U05JC	OEM
FCR31U05JD	OEM
FCR31U06JB	OEM
FCR31U06JC	OEM
FCR31U06JD	OEM
FCR31U07JA	OEM
FCR31U07JB	OEM
FCR31U08JA	OEM
FCR31U08JB	OEM
FCR31U09JA	OEM
FCR31U09JB	OEM
FCR31U10JA	OEM
FCR31U10JB	OEM
FCR31U11JA	OEM
FCR31U11JB	OEM
FCR43U01JA	OEM
FCR43U01JB	OEM
FCR43U01JM	OEM
FCR43U02JA	OEM
FCR43U02JB	OEM
FCR43U02JM	OEM
FCR43U03JA	OEM
FCR43U03JB	OEM
FCR43U03JM	OEM
FCR43U04JA	OEM
FCR43U04JB	OEM
FCR43U04JM	OEM
FCR43U05JA	OEM
FCR43U05JB	OEM
FCR43U06JA	OEM
FCR43U06JB	OEM
FCR43U06JM	OEM
FCR43U07JA	OEM
FCR43U07JB	OEM
FCR43U07JM	OEM
FCR43U08JA	OEM
FCR43U08JB	OEM
FCR43U08JM	OEM
FCR43U09J,	OEM
FCR43U09JA	OEM
FCR43U09JB	OEM
FCR43U10JA	OEM
FCR43U10JB	OEM
FCR43U10JM	OEM
FCR43U11JA	OEM
FCR43U11JB	OEM
FCR43U11JM	OEM
FCR43U12JA	OEM
FCR43U12JB	OEM
FCR44U01JC	OEM
FCR44U01UD	OEM

DEVICE TYPE	REPL CODE
FCR44U02JC	OEM
FCR44U02JD	OEM
FCR44U03JC	OEM
FCR44U03JD	OEM
FCR44U04JC	OEM
FCR44U04JD	OEM
FCR44U05JC	OEM
FCR44U05JD	OEM
FCR44U06JC	OEM
FCR44U06JD	OEM
FCR50U01JC	OEM
FCR70U05JD	OEM
FCR80U03JB	OEM
FCR80U03JC	OEM
FCR80U03JD	OEM
FCR80U04JC	OEM
FCR80U04JD	OEM
FCR80U05JC	OEM
FCR80U05JD	OEM
FCR80U06JC	OEM
FCR80U06JD	OEM
FCR80U07JB	OEM
FCR80U08JB	OEM
FCR80U09JB	OEM
FCR80U10JB	OEM
FCR80U11JB	OEM
FCR100U09JB	OEM
FCS916F	0224
FCS1168E	0144
FCS1168E641	0144
FCS1168F813	0016
FCS1168G	0016
FCS1168G704	0016
FCS1170F	0037
FCS1225E	0144
FCS1227E	0144
FCS1227E814	0144
FCS1227F	0144
FCS1227F743	0144
FCS1227G	0144
FCS1227G810	0144
FCS1229	0086
FCS1229F	0016
FCS1229G	0016
FCS1795D	0126
FCS8013HG	OEM
FCS8050C	0155
FCS8550	0006
FCS8550C	0006
FCS9011E	0079
FCS9011F	0079
FCS9011G	0284
FCS9011H	0079
FCS9012	0037
FCS-9012F	0037
FCS-9012G	0037
FCS9012G	0037
FCS9012H	0037
FCS9012HE	0037
FCS9012HG	0037
FCS9012HH	0150
FCS9013	0284
FCS-9013F	0079
FCS9013F	0079
FCS9013F,G	0016
FCS9013FG	0016
FCS-9013G	0079
FCS9013G	0284
FCS9013H	0284
FCS9013HG	0079
FCS9013HH	0079
FCS9014	0079
FCS9014(B)	0079
FCS9014B	0079
FCS9014C	0111
FCS9014D	0144
FCS9015B	0037
FCS-9015C	0150
FCS9015C	2461
FCS9015D	0037
FCS9016	0127
FCS9016D	0127
FCS9016E	0127
FCS-9016F	0364
FCS9016F	0079
FCS-9016G	0079
FCS9016G	0127
FCS9016H	0144
FCS9018	0144
FCS9018D	0144
FCS9018E	0144
FCS-9018F	0016
FCS9018F	0144
FCS9018G	0144
FCS9018H	0144
FCS9066	0144
FCT1035	OEM
FCT1135	OEM
FCY101	OEM
FD3	0015
FD6	0015
FD8	OEM
FD13	OEM
FD13A	OEM
FD13B	OEM
FD13C	OEM
FD13D	OEM
FD13E	OEM
FD13F	OEM

DEVICE TYPE	REPL CODE
FD13G	OEM
FD23	OEM
FD43	OEM
FD63	0087
FD80A4	OEM
FD80A6	OEM
FD80A8	OEM
FD80A10	OEM
FD83	2621
FD100	0124
FD103	0087
FD111	0133
FD150B4	OEM
FD150B6	OEM
FD150B8FD150B10	OEM
FD160L	0286
FD200	0133
FD200B-2	OEM
FD200B2	OEM
FD200B-4	OEM
FD200B4	OEM
FD200B-8	OEM
FD200B8	OEM
FD200B-16	OEM
FD200B16	OEM
FD200E-2	OEM
FD200E2	OEM
FD200E-4	OEM
FD200E4	OEM
FD200E-8	OEM
FD200E8	OEM
FD200E-16	OEM
FD200E16	OEM
FD222	0133
FD250A12	OEM
FD250A16	OEM
FD250A-20	OEM
FD250A-24	OEM
FD250A-28	OEM
FD250A30	OEM
FD250A-32	OEM
FD250A-36	OEM
FD250A-40	OEM
FD250B-12	OEM
FD250B-16	OEM
FD250B-20	OEM
FD250DM28	OEM
FD250DM32	OEM
FD250DM36	OEM
FD250DM40	OEM
FD300	0604
FD333	0133
FD400	0604
FD400DL12	OEM
FD400DL20	OEM
FD400DL24	OEM
FD500C32	OEM
FD500C36	OEM
FD500C-40	OEM
FD500C40	OEM
FD500C-50	OEM
FD500C50	OEM
FD500C-56	OEM
FD500C56	OEM
FD500C-60	OEM
FD500C60	OEM
FD500D10	OEM
FD500D12	OEM
FD500D16	OEM
FD500D20	OEM
FD500E12	OEM
FD500E-16	OEM
FD500E16	OEM
FD500E-20	OEM
FD500E20	OEM
FD500E-24	OEM
FD500E24	OEM
FD500E-28	OEM
FD500E28	OEM
FD500E30	OEM
FD500E-32	OEM
FD500E32	OEM
FD500E-36	OEM
FD500E36	OEM
FD500E-40	OEM
FD500E40	OEM
FD500E-50	OEM
FD500E50	OEM
FD500E-60	OEM
FD500E60	OEM
FD500E70	OEM
FD500E80	OEM
FD500EV-70	OEM
FD500EV70	OEM
FD500EV-80	OEM
FD500EV80	OEM
FD500d24	OEM
FD600	0124
FD600-1	OEM
FD600-2	OEM
FD600-3	OEM
FD600-4	OEM
FD600-5	OEM
FD600-6	OEM
FD600-7	OEM
FD600-8	OEM
FD600-9	OEM
FD600-10	OEM
FD600-12	OEM

DEVICE TYPE	REPL CODE
FD600-14	OEM
FD600-16	OEM
FD600-18	OEM
FD600-20	OEM
FD600-22	OEM
FD600-24	OEM
FD600-26	OEM
FD600-28	OEM
FD600-30	OEM
FD700	4953
FD750-2	OEM
FD750-4	OEM
FD750-6	OEM
FD750-12	OEM
FD750-16	OEM
FD750-20	OEM
FD750-24	OEM
FD777	0124
FD900-1	OEM
FD900-2	OEM
FD900-3	OEM
FD900-4	OEM
FD900-5	OEM
FD900-6	OEM
FD900-7	OEM
FD900-8	OEM
FD900-9	OEM
FD900-10	OEM
FD900-12	OEM
FD900-14	OEM
FD900-16	OEM
FD900-18	OEM
FD900-20	OEM
FD1000-2	OEM
FD1000-4	OEM
FD1000-6	OEM
FD1000-12	OEM
FD1000-16	OEM
FD1000-20	OEM
FD1000-24	OEM
FD1000A12	OEM
FD1000A-16	OEM
FD1000A16	OEM
FD1000A-20	OEM
FD1000A20	OEM
FD1000A-24	OEM
FD1000A24	OEM
FD1000A-28	OEM
FD1000A28	OEM
FD1000A-32	OEM
FD1000A32	OEM
FD1000A-36	OEM
FD1000A36	OEM
FD1000A-40	OEM
FD1000A40	OEM
FD1000A-50	OEM
FD1000A50	OEM
FD1000A-56	OEM
FD1000A56	OEM
FD1000A70	OEM
FD1000A80	OEM
FD1000D16	OEM
FD1000D20	OEM
FD1000D24	OEM
FD1000D28	OEM
FD1000D32	OEM
FD1000D36	OEM
FD1000D40	OEM
FD1000D50	OEM
FD1000D56	OEM
FD-1029-4	0037
FD-1029-4&	0037
FD-1029-EE	0211
FD-1029-JE	0122
FD-1073-BF	0232
FD-1073-BG	0310
FD-1073-BH	0331
FD-1073-BJ	0357
FD-1073-BM	0462
FD-1073-BN	0507
FD-1073-BR	0692
FD-1073-BS	0867
FD-1073-BU	1018
FD-1073-BW	1160
FD-1073-CA	1358
FD1389	OEM
FD1559	0535
FD1599	0015
FD1600A-16	OEM
FD1600A16	OEM
FD1600A-20	OEM
FD1600A20	OEM
FD1600A-24	OEM
FD1600A24	OEM
FD1600A-28	OEM
FD1600A28	OEM
FD1600A-32	OEM
FD1600A32	OEM
FD1600A-36	OEM
FD1600A36	OEM
FD1600A-40	OEM
FD1600A40	OEM
FD1600A-50	OEM
FD1600A50	OEM
FD1600BP-2	OEM
FD1600BP2	OEM
FD1600BP-4	OEM
FD1600BP4	OEM
FD1600BP-6	OEM

DEVICE TYPE	REPL CODE
FD1600BP6	OEM
FD1600BP-8	OEM
FD1600BP8	OEM
FD1600BP-10	OEM
FD1600BP10	OEM
FD1708	0133
FD1761A-02	OEM
FD1761B-02	OEM
FD1763A-02	OEM
FD1765A-02	OEM
FD1765B-02	OEM
FD1767A-02	OEM
FD1767B-02	OEM
FD1771-B01	OEM
FD1771A01	OEM
FD1771B01	OEM
FD1791A02	OEM
FD1791B02	OEM
FD1792A02	OEM
FD1792B02	OEM
FD1793A02	OEM
FD1793B-02	OEM
FD1793B02	OEM
FD1794A02	OEM
FD1794B02	OEM
FD1795A02	OEM
FD1795B02	OEM
FD1797A02	OEM
FD1797B02	OEM
FD1843	0133
FD1873B-02	OEM
FD1980	0143
FD2055	OEM
FD2389	OEM
FD3389	0015
FD3405	0914
FD3500AH-16	OEM
FD3500AH-20	OEM
FD3500AH-24	OEM
FD3500AH-28	OEM
FD3500AH-32	OEM
FD3500AH-36	OEM
FD3500AH-40	OEM
FD3500AH-50	OEM
FD3500AH56	OEM
FD6389	OEM
FD6451	0133
FD6489	0133
FD6666	OEM
FD17718-01	OEM
FDA548	OEM
FDA555	OEM
FDC11	OEM
FDC91C36	OEM
FDC765AC	OEM
FDC1761-02	OEM
FDC1763-02	OEM
FDC1765-02	OEM
FDC1767-02	OEM
FDC1791-02	OEM
FDC1792-02	OEM
FDC1793-02	OEM
FDC1794-02	OEM
FDC1795-02	OEM
FDC1797-02	OEM
FDC3070	OEM
FDC3400	OEM
FDC3400-1	OEM
FDC3600	OEM
FDC4376	OEM
FDC4558	OEM
FDC9216	OEM
FDC9216B	OEM
FDC9229	OEM
FDC9229B	OEM
FDD-1N	OEM
FDD-2N	OEM
FDD-3N	OEM
FDD-4N	OEM
FDG559	OEM
FDH-9	0133
FDH300	0604
FDH333	0604
FDH400	0015
FDH-444	0124
FDH444	0124
FDH600	0102
FDH666	0133
FDH694	0133
FDH900	0133
FDH999	0124
FDH1000	1325
FDH6072	OEM
FDH6229	0133
FDM1006	0133
FDM1007	0133
FDN400	0604
FDN444	0604
FDN600	0133
FDN666	0133
FDR-2L	OEM
FDR-5AL	OEM
FDR-5L	OEM
FDR116Z	OEM
FDR126Z1	OEM
FDR131Z2	OEM
FDR300	OEM
FDR600	OEM
FDR700	OEM

DEVICE TYPE	REPL CODE
FDT-2L	OEM
FDT-5L	OEM
FDU6603	OEM
FDZ10A	OEM
FDZ10B	OEM
FDZ12A	OEM
FDZ12B	OEM
FDZ15A	OEM
FDZ15B	OEM
FDZ18A	OEM
FDZ18B	OEM
FDZ22A	OEM
FDZ27A	OEM
FDZ33A	OEM
FDZ39A	OEM
FDZ47A	OEM
FDZ56A	OEM
FDZ68A	OEM
FDZ82A	OEM
FE00202ATF	OEM
FE040EABR	OEM
FE071AAB	OEM
FE0101	OEM
FE0101ATF	OEM
FE0101ATFB	OEM
FE0101ATFG	OEM
FE0101ATFQ	OEM
FE0101ATFR	OEM
FE0101ATG	OEM
FE0101ATGG	OEM
FE0101ATGO	OEM
FE0101ATGR	OEM
FE0101ATH	OEM
FE0101ATHB	OEM
FE0101ATHG	OEM
FE0101ATHR	OEM
FE0101ATI	OEM
FE0101ATIB	OEM
FE0101ATIG	OEM
FE0101ATIQ	OEM
FE0101ATIR	OEM
FE0101ATJ	OEM
FE0101ATJB	OEM
FE0101ATJG	OEM
FE0101ATJQ	OEM
FE0101ATJR	OEM
FE0101TFB	OEM
FE0101TFG	OEM
FE0101TFQ	OEM
FE0101TFR	OEM
FE0101TG	OEM
FE0101TGB	OEM
FE0101TGG	OEM
FE0101TGQ	OEM
FE0101TGR	OEM
FE0101TH	OEM
FE0101THB	OEM
FE0101THG	OEM
FE0101THR	OEM
FE0101TI	OEM
FE0101TIB	OEM
FE0101TIG	OEM
FE0101TIQ	OEM
FE0101TIR	OEM
FE0101TJ	OEM
FE0101TJB	OEM
FE0101TJG	OEM
FE0101TJQ	OEM
FE0101TJR	OEM
FE0201	OEM
FE0201A	OEM
FE0201AA	OEM
FE0201AAB	OEM
FE0201AAG	OEM
FE0201AAQ	OEM
FE0201AAR	OEM
FE0201AB	OEM
FE0201ABB	OEM
FE0201ABG	OEM
FE0201ABQ	OEM
FE0201ABR	OEM
FE0201AC	OEM
FE0201ACB	OEM
FE0201ACG	OEM
FE0201ACR	OEM
FE0201AD	OEM
FE0201ADB	OEM
FE0201ADG	OEM
FE0201ADQ	OEM
FE0201ADR	OEM
FE0201AE	OEM
FE0201AEG	OEM
FE0201AEQ	OEM
FE0201AER	OEM
FE0201AG	OEM
FE0201AQ	OEM
FE0201AR	OEM
FE0201ATF	OEM
FE0201ATFB	OEM
FE0201ATFG	OEM
FE0201ATFQ	OEM
FE0201ATFR	OEM
FE0201ATG	OEM
FE0201ATGB	OEM
FE0201ATGG	OEM
FE0201ATGQ	OEM
FE0201ATGR	OEM
FE0201ATH	OEM
FE0201ATHB	OEM

If replacement code is OEM, contact original manufacturer for replacement.

DEVICE TYPE	REPL CODE
FE0201ATHG	OEM
FE0201ATHR	OEM
FE0201ATI	OEM
FE0201ATIB	OEM
FE0201ATIG	OEM
FE0201ATIQ	OEM
FE0201ATIR	OEM
FE0201ATJ	OEM
FE0201ATJB	OEM
FE0201ATJG	OEM
FE0201ATJQ	OEM
FE0201ATJR	OEM
FE0201B	OEM
FE0201BB	OEM
FE0201BG	OEM
FE0201BQ	OEM
FE0201BR	OEM
FE0201C	OEM
FE0201CB	OEM
FE0201CG	OEM
FE0201CR	OEM
FE0201D	OEM
FE0201DB	OEM
FE0201DG	OEM
FE0201DQ	OEM
FE0201DR	OEM
FE0201E	OEM
FE0201EB	OEM
FE0201EG	OEM
FE0201EQ	OEM
FE0201ER	OEM
FE0201TF	OEM
FE0201TFB	OEM
FE0201TFG	OEM
FE0201TFQ	OEM
FE0201TFR	OEM
FE0201TG	OEM
FE0201TGB	OEM
FE0201TGG	OEM
FE0201TGQ	OEM
FE0201TGR	OEM
FE0201TH	OEM
FE0201THB	OEM
FE0201THG	OEM
FE0201THR	OEM
FE0201TI	OEM
FE0201TIB	OEM
FE0201TIG	OEM
FE0201TIQ	OEM
FE0201TIR	OEM
FE0201TJ	OEM
FE0201TJB	OEM
FE0201TJG	OEM
FE0201TJQ	OEM
FE0201TJR	OEM
FE0202	OEM
FE0202A	OEM
FE0202AA	OEM
FE0202AAB	OEM
FE0202AAG	OEM
FE0202AAQ	OEM
FE0202AAR	OEM
FE0202AB	OEM
FE0202ABB	OEM
FE0202ABG	OEM
FE0202ABQ	OEM
FE0202ABR	OEM
FE0202AC	OEM
FE0202ACB	OEM
FE0202ACG	OEM
FE0202AD	OEM
FE0202ADB	OEM
FE0202ADG	OEM
FE0202ADQ	OEM
FE0202ADR	OEM
FE0202AE	OEM
FE0202AEB	OEM
FE0202AEQ	OEM
FE0202AER	OEM
FE0202AG	OEM
FE0202AQ	OEM
FE0202AR	OEM
FE0202ATFB	OEM
FE0202ATFG	OEM
FE0202ATFQ	OEM
FE0202ATFR	OEM
FE0202ATG	OEM
FE0202ATGB	OEM
FE0202ATGG	OEM
FE0202ATGQ	OEM
FE0202ATGR	OEM
FE0202ATH	OEM
FE0202ATHB	OEM
FE0202ATHG	OEM
FE0202ATI	OEM
FE0202ATIB	OEM
FE0202ATIG	OEM
FE0202ATIQ	OEM
FE0202ATIR	OEM
FE0202ATJ	OEM
FE0202ATJB	OEM
FE0202ATJG	OEM
FE0202ATJQ	OEM
FE0202ATJR	OEM
FE0202B	OEM
FE0202BB	OEM
FE0202BG	OEM
FE0202BQ	OEM
FE0202BR	OEM
FE0202C	OEM
FE0202CB	OEM
FE0202CG	OEM
FE0202CR	OEM
FE0202D	OEM
FE0202DB	OEM
FE0202DG	OEM
FE0202DQ	OEM
FE0202DR	OEM
FE0202E	OEM
FE0202EB	OEM
FE0202EG	OEM
FE0202EQ	OEM
FE0202ER	OEM
FE0202TFB	OEM
FE0202TFG	OEM
FE0202TFQ	OEM
FE0202TFR	OEM
FE0202TGB	OEM
FE0202TGG	OEM
FE0202TGQ	OEM
FE0202TGR	OEM
FE0202THB	OEM
FE0202THG	OEM
FE0202THR	OEM
FE0202TIB	OEM
FE0202TIG	OEM
FE0202TIQ	OEM
FE0202TIR	OEM
FE0202TJB	OEM
FE0202TJG	OEM
FE0202TJQ	OEM
FE0202TJR	OEM
FE0203	OEM
FE0203A	OEM
FE0203AA	OEM
FE0203AAB	OEM
FE0203AAG	OEM
FE0203AAQ	OEM
FE0203AAR	OEM
FE0203AB	OEM
FE0203ABB	OEM
FE0203ABG	OEM
FE0203ABQ	OEM
FE0203ABR	OEM
FE0203AC	OEM
FE0203ACB	OEM
FE0203ACR	OEM
FE0203AD	OEM
FE0203ADB	OEM
FE0203ADG	OEM
FE0203ADQ	OEM
FE0203ADR	OEM
FE0203AE	OEM
FE0203AEB	OEM
FE0203AEG	OEM
FE0203AEQ	OEM
FE0203AER	OEM
FE0203AG	OEM
FE0203AQ	OEM
FE0203AR	OEM
FE0203ATF	OEM
FE0203ATFB	OEM
FE0203ATFG	OEM
FE0203ATFQ	OEM
FE0203ATFR	OEM
FE0203ATGB	OEM
FE0203ATGG	OEM
FE0203ATGQ	OEM
FE0203ATGR	OEM
FE0203ATH	OEM
FE0203ATHB	OEM
FE0203ATHG	OEM
FE0203ATHR	OEM
FE0203ATI	OEM
FE0203ATIB	OEM
FE0203ATIG	OEM
FE0203ATIQ	OEM
FE0203ATIR	OEM
FE0203ATJB	OEM
FE0203ATJG	OEM
FE0203ATJQ	OEM
FE0203ATJR	OEM
FE0203B	OEM
FE0203BB	OEM
FE0203BG	OEM
FE0203BQ	OEM
FE0203BR	OEM
FE0203C	OEM
FE0203CB	OEM
FE0203CG	OEM
FE0203CR	OEM
FE0203D	OEM
FE0203DG	OEM
FE0203DQ	OEM
FE0203DR	OEM
FE0203E	OEM
FE0203EB	OEM
FE0203EG	OEM
FE0203EQ	OEM
FE0203ER	OEM
FE0203TF	OEM
FE0203TFB	OEM
FE0203TFQ	OEM
FE0203TFR	OEM
FE0203TG	OEM
FE0203TGB	OEM
FE0203TGG	OEM
FE0203TGQ	OEM
FE0203TGR	OEM
FE0203TH	OEM
FE0203THB	OEM
FE0203THG	OEM
FE0203THR	OEM
FE0203TI	OEM
FE0203TIB	OEM
FE0203TIG	OEM
FE0203TIQ	OEM
FE0203TIR	OEM
FE0203TJ	OEM
FE0203TJB	OEM
FE0203TJQ	OEM
FE0203TJR	OEM
FE0204A	OEM
FE0204B	OEM
FE0204C	OEM
FE0204D	OEM
FE0204E	OEM
FE0204F	OEM
FE0204G	OEM
FE0204H	OEM
FE0204I	OEM
FE0204J	OEM
FE0205	OEM
FE0205A	OEM
FE0205B	OEM
FE0205C	OEM
FE0205D	OEM
FE0205E	OEM
FE0205F	OEM
FE0205G	OEM
FE0205H	OEM
FE0205I	OEM
FE0205J	OEM
FE0206	OEM
FE0206A	OEM
FE0206AA	OEM
FE0206AAB	OEM
FE0206AAG	OEM
FE0206AAQ	OEM
FE0206AAR	OEM
FE0206AB	OEM
FE0206ABB	OEM
FE0206ABG	OEM
FE0206ABQ	OEM
FE0206ABR	OEM
FE0206AC	OEM
FE0206ACB	OEM
FE0206ACG	OEM
FE0206ACR	OEM
FE0206AD	OEM
FE0206ADB	OEM
FE0206ADG	OEM
FE0206ADQ	OEM
FE0206ADR	OEM
FE0206AE	OEM
FE0206AEB	OEM
FE0206AEG	OEM
FE0206AEQ	OEM
FE0206AER	OEM
FE0206AG	OEM
FE0206AQ	OEM
FE0206AR	OEM
FE0206ATF	OEM
FE0206ATFB	OEM
FE0206ATFG	OEM
FE0206ATFQ	OEM
FE0206ATFR	OEM
FE0206ATG	OEM
FE0206ATGB	OEM
FE0206ATGG	OEM
FE0206ATGQ	OEM
FE0206ATGR	OEM
FE0206ATH	OEM
FE0206ATHB	OEM
FE0206ATHG	OEM
FE0206ATHR	OEM
FE0206ATI	OEM
FE0206ATIB	OEM
FE0206ATIG	OEM
FE0206ATIQ	OEM
FE0206ATIR	OEM
FE0206ATJ	OEM
FE0206ATJB	OEM
FE0206ATJG	OEM
FE0206ATJQ	OEM
FE0206ATJR	OEM
FE0206B	OEM
FE0206BB	OEM
FE0206BG	OEM
FE0206BQ	OEM
FE0206BR	OEM
FE0206C	OEM
FE0206CB	OEM
FE0206CG	OEM
FE0206CR	OEM
FE0206D	OEM
FE0206DB	OEM
FE0206DG	OEM
FE0206DQ	OEM
FE0206DR	OEM
FE0206E	OEM
FE0206EB	OEM
FE0206EG	OEM
FE0206EQ	OEM
FE0206ER	OEM
FE0206TF	OEM
FE0206TFB	OEM
FE0206TFG	OEM
FE0206TFQ	OEM
FE0206TFR	OEM
FE0206TG	OEM
FE0206TGB	OEM
FE0206TGG	OEM
FE0206TGQ	OEM
FE0206TGR	OEM
FE0206TH	OEM
FE0206THB	OEM
FE0206THG	OEM
FE0206THR	OEM
FE0206TI	OEM
FE0206TIB	OEM
FE0206TIG	OEM
FE0206TIQ	OEM
FE0206TIR	OEM
FE0206TJ	OEM
FE0206TJG	OEM
FE0206TJQ	OEM
FE0206TJR	OEM
FE0208	OEM
FE0208A	OEM
FE0208AA	OEM
FE0208AAB	OEM
FE0208AAG	OEM
FE0208AAR	OEM
FE0208AB	OEM
FE0208ABB	OEM
FE0208ABG	OEM
FE0208ABR	OEM
FE0208AC	OEM
FE0208ACB	OEM
FE0208ACG	OEM
FE0208ACR	OEM
FE0208AD	OEM
FE0208ADB	OEM
FE0208ADG	OEM
FE0208ADR	OEM
FE0208AE	OEM
FE0208AEB	OEM
FE0208AEG	OEM
FE0208AER	OEM
FE0208AG	OEM
FE0208AQ	OEM
FE0208AR	OEM
FE0208ATF	OEM
FE0208ATFB	OEM
FE0208ATFG	OEM
FE0208ATFR	OEM
FE0208ATG	OEM
FE0208ATGB	OEM
FE0208ATGG	OEM
FE0208ATGR	OEM
FE0208ATH	OEM
FE0208ATHB	OEM
FE0208ATHG	OEM
FE0208ATHR	OEM
FE0208ATI	OEM
FE0208ATIB	OEM
FE0208ATIG	OEM
FE0208ATIR	OEM
FE0208ATJ	OEM
FE0208ATJB	OEM
FE0208ATJG	OEM
FE0208B	OEM
FE0208BB	OEM
FE0208BG	OEM
FE0208BQ	OEM
FE0208BR	OEM
FE0208C	OEM
FE0208CB	OEM
FE0208CG	OEM
FE0208CR	OEM
FE0208D	OEM
FE0208DB	OEM
FE0208DG	OEM
FE0208DQ	OEM
FE0208DR	OEM
FE0208E	OEM
FE0208EB	OEM
FE0208EG	OEM
FE0208EQ	OEM
FE0208ER	OEM
FE0208TF	OEM
FE0208TFB	OEM
FE0208TFG	OEM
FE0208TFQ	OEM
FE0208TFR	OEM
FE0208TG	OEM
FE0208TGB	OEM
FE0208TGG	OEM
FE0208TGQ	OEM
FE0208TGR	OEM
FE0208TH	OEM
FE0208THB	OEM
FE0208THG	OEM
FE0208THR	OEM
FE0208TI	OEM
FE0208TIB	OEM
FE0208TIG	OEM
FE0208TIQ	OEM
FE0208TIR	OEM
FE0208TJ	OEM
FE0208TJB	OEM
FE0208TJG	OEM
FE0208TJQ	OEM
FE0208TJR	OEM
FE0220ACR	OEM
FE0401	OEM
FE0401A	OEM
FE0401AA	OEM
FE0401AAB	OEM
FE0401AAG	OEM
FE0401AAR	OEM
FE0401AB	OEM
FE0401ABB	OEM
FE0401ABG	OEM
FE0401ABQ	OEM
FE0401ABR	OEM
FE0401AC	OEM
FE0401ACB	OEM
FE0401ACG	OEM
FE0401ACR	OEM
FE0401AD	OEM
FE0401ADB	OEM
FE0401ADG	OEM
FE0401ADQ	OEM
FE0401ADR	OEM
FE0401AE	OEM
FE0401AEB	OEM
FE0401AEG	OEM
FE0401AEQ	OEM
FE0401AER	OEM
FE0401AG	OEM
FE0401AQ	OEM
FE0401AR	OEM
FE0401ATF	OEM
FE0401ATFB	OEM
FE0401ATFG	OEM
FE0401ATFQ	OEM
FE0401ATFR	OEM
FE0401ATG	OEM
FE0401ATGB	OEM
FE0401ATGG	OEM
FE0401ATGQ	OEM
FE0401ATGR	OEM
FE0401ATH	OEM
FE0401ATHB	OEM
FE0401ATHG	OEM
FE0401ATHR	OEM
FE0401ATI	OEM
FE0401ATIG	OEM
FE0401ATIQ	OEM
FE0401ATIR	OEM
FE0401ATJ	OEM
FE0401ATJG	OEM
FE0401ATJQ	OEM
FE0401ATJR	OEM
FE0401B	OEM
FE0401BB	OEM
FE0401BG	OEM
FE0401BQ	OEM
FE0401BR	OEM
FE0401C	OEM
FE0401CB	OEM
FE0401CG	OEM
FE0401CR	OEM
FE0401D	OEM
FE0401DB	OEM
FE0401DG	OEM
FE0401DQ	OEM
FE0401DR	OEM
FE0401E	OEM
FE0401EB	OEM
FE0401EG	OEM
FE0401EQ	OEM
FE0401ER	OEM
FE0401TF	OEM
FE0401TFB	OEM
FE0401TFG	OEM
FE0401TFQ	OEM
FE0401TFR	OEM
FE0401TG	OEM
FE0401TGB	OEM
FE0401TGG	OEM
FE0401TGQ	OEM
FE0401TGR	OEM
FE0401TH	OEM
FE0401THB	OEM
FE0401THG	OEM
FE0401THR	OEM
FE0401TI	OEM
FE0401TIB	OEM
FE0401TIG	OEM
FE0401TIQ	OEM
FE0401TIR	OEM
FE0401TJ	OEM
FE0401TJB	OEM
FE0401TJG	OEM
FE0401TJQ	OEM
FE0401TJR	OEM
FE0402	OEM
FE0402A	OEM
FE0402AA	OEM
FE0402AAB	OEM
FE0402AAG	OEM
FE0402AAQ	OEM
FE0402AAR	OEM
FE0402AB	OEM
FE0402ABB	OEM
FE0402ABG	OEM
FE0402ABQ	OEM
FE0402ABR	OEM
FE0402AC	OEM
FE0402ACB	OEM
FE0402ACG	OEM
FE0402ACR	OEM
FE0402AD	OEM
FE0402ADB	OEM
FE0402ADG	OEM
FE0402ADQ	OEM
FE0402ADR	OEM
FE0402AE	OEM
FE0402AEB	OEM
FE0402AEG	OEM
FE0402AEQ	OEM
FE0402AER	OEM
FE0402AG	OEM
FE0402AQ	OEM
FE0402AR	OEM
FE0402ATF	OEM
FE0402ATFB	OEM
FE0402ATFG	OEM
FE0402ATFQ	OEM
FE0402ATFR	OEM
FE0402ATG	OEM
FE0402ATGB	OEM
FE0402ATGG	OEM
FE0402ATGQ	OEM
FE0402ATGR	OEM
FE0402ATH	OEM
FE0402ATHB	OEM
FE0402ATHG	OEM
FE0402ATHR	OEM
FE0402ATI	OEM
FE0402ATIB	OEM
FE0402ATIG	OEM
FE0402ATIQ	OEM
FE0402ATIR	OEM
FE0402ATJ	OEM
FE0402ATJB	OEM
FE0402ATJG	OEM
FE0402ATJR	OEM
FE0402B	OEM
FE0402BB	OEM
FE0402BG	OEM
FE0402BQ	OEM
FE0402BR	OEM
FE0402C	OEM
FE0402CB	OEM
FE0402CG	OEM
FE0402CR	OEM
FE0402D	OEM
FE0402DB	OEM
FE0402DG	OEM
FE0402DQ	OEM
FE0402DR	OEM
FE0402E	OEM
FE0402EB	OEM
FE0402EG	OEM
FE0402EQ	OEM
FE0402ER	OEM
FE0402TF	OEM
FE0402TFB	OEM
FE0402TFG	OEM
FE0402TFQ	OEM
FE0402TFR	OEM
FE0402TG	OEM
FE0402TGB	OEM
FE0402TGG	OEM
FE0402TGQ	OEM
FE0402TGR	OEM
FE0402TH	OEM
FE0402THB	OEM
FE0402THG	OEM
FE0402THR	OEM
FE0402TI	OEM
FE0402TIB	OEM
FE0402TIG	OEM
FE0402TIQ	OEM
FE0402TIR	OEM
FE0402TJ	OEM
FE0402TJB	OEM
FE0402TJG	OEM
FE0402TJQ	OEM
FE0402TJR	OEM
FE0403	OEM
FE0403A	OEM
FE0403AA	OEM
FE0403AAB	OEM
FE0403AAG	OEM
FE0403AAQ	OEM
FE0403AAR	OEM
FE0403AB	OEM
FE0403ABB	OEM
FE0403ABG	OEM
FE0403ABQ	OEM
FE0403AC	OEM
FE0403ACB	OEM
FE0403ACG	OEM
FE0403ACR	OEM
FE0403AD	OEM
FE0403ADB	OEM
FE0403ADG	OEM
FE0403ADQ	OEM
FE0403AE	OEM
FE0403AEB	OEM
FE0403AEG	OEM
FE0403AEQ	OEM
FE0403AER	OEM
FE0403AG	OEM
FE0403AQ	OEM
FE0403AR	OEM
FE0403ATF	OEM
FE0403ATFB	OEM
FE0403ATFG	OEM
FE0403ATFQ	OEM
FE0403ATFR	OEM
FE0403ATG	OEM
FE0403ATGB	OEM
FE0403ATGG	OEM
FE0403ATGQ	OEM
FE0403ATGR	OEM
FE0403ATH	OEM
FE0403ATHB	OEM
FE0403ATHG	OEM
FE0403ATHR	OEM
FE0403ATI	OEM
FE0403ATIB	OEM
FE0403ATIG	OEM
FE0403ATIQ	OEM
FE0403ATIR	OEM
FE0403ATJ	OEM
FE0403ATJB	OEM
FE0403ATJG	OEM
FE0403ATJQ	OEM
FE0403ATJR	OEM
FE0403BB	OEM
FE0403BG	OEM
FE0403BQ	OEM
FE0403BR	OEM
FE0403C	OEM
FE0403CB	OEM
FE0403CG	OEM
FE0403CR	OEM
FE0403D	OEM
FE0403DB	OEM
FE0403DG	OEM
FE0403DQ	OEM
FE0403DR	OEM
FE0403E	OEM
FE0403EB	OEM
FE0403EG	OEM
FE0403EQ	OEM
FE0403ER	OEM
FE0403TF	OEM
FE0403TFB	OEM
FE0403TFG	OEM
FE0403TFQ	OEM
FE0403TFR	OEM
FE0403TG	OEM
FE0403TGB	OEM
FE0403TGG	OEM
FE0403TGQ	OEM
FE0403TGR	OEM
FE0403TH	OEM
FE0403THB	OEM
FE0403THG	OEM
FE0403THR	OEM
FE0403TI	OEM
FE0403TIB	OEM
FE0403TIG	OEM
FE0403TIQ	OEM
FE0403TIR	OEM
FE0403TJ	OEM
FE0403TJB	OEM
FE0403TJQ	OEM
FE0403TJR	OEM
FE0404AB	OEM
FE0404F	OEM
FE0404G	OEM
FE0404H	OEM
FE0404I	OEM
FE0404J	OEM
FE0404TF	OEM
FE0404TFB	OEM
FE0404TFG	OEM
FE0404TFQ	OEM
FE0404TFR	OEM
FE0404TG	OEM
FE0404TGB	OEM
FE0404TGG	OEM
FE0404TGQ	OEM
FE0404TGR	OEM
FE0404TH	OEM
FE0404THB	OEM
FE0404THG	OEM
FE0404THR	OEM
FE0404TI	OEM
FE0404TIB	OEM
FE0404TIG	OEM
FE0404TIQ	OEM
FE0404TIR	OEM
FE0404TJ	OEM
FE0404TJB	OEM
FE0404TJG	OEM
FE0404TJQ	OEM
FE0404TJR	OEM
FE0405	OEM
FE0405A	OEM
FE0405AA	OEM
FE0405AAB	OEM
FE0405AAG	OEM
FE0405AAQ	OEM
FE0405AAR	OEM
FE0405ABB	OEM
FE0405ABG	OEM
FE0405ABQ	OEM
FE0405ABR	OEM
FE0405AC	OEM
FE0405ACB	OEM
FE0405ACG	OEM
FE0405ACR	OEM
FE0405AD	OEM
FE0405ADB	OEM

If replacement code is OEM, contact original manufacturer for replacement.

407

DEVICE TYPE	REPL CODE
FE0405ADG	OEM
FE0405ADQ	OEM
FE0405ADR	OEM
FE0405AE	OEM
FE0405AEB	OEM
FE0405AEG	OEM
FE0405AEQ	OEM
FE0405AER	OEM
FE0405AG	OEM
FE0405AQ	OEM
FE0405AR	OEM
FE0405ATF	OEM
FE0405ATFB	OEM
FE0405ATFG	OEM
FE0405ATFQ	OEM
FE0405ATFR	OEM
FE0405ATG	OEM
FE0405ATGB	OEM
FE0405ATGG	OEM
FE0405ATGQ	OEM
FE0405ATGR	OEM
FE0405ATH	OEM
FE0405ATHB	OEM
FE0405ATHG	OEM
FE0405ATHR	OEM
FE0405ATI	OEM
FE0405ATIB	OEM
FE0405ATIG	OEM
FE0405ATIQ	OEM
FE0405ATIR	OEM
FE0405ATJ	OEM
FE0405ATJB	OEM
FE0405ATJG	OEM
FE0405ATJQ	OEM
FE0405ATJR	OEM
FE0405B	OEM
FE0405BB	OEM
FE0405BG	OEM
FE0405BQ	OEM
FE0405BR	OEM
FE0405C	OEM
FE0405CB	OEM
FE0405CG	OEM
FE0405CR	OEM
FE0405DB	OEM
FE0405DG	OEM
FE0405DQ	OEM
FE0405DR	OEM
FE0405E	OEM
FE0405EB	OEM
FE0405EG	OEM
FE0405EQ	OEM
FE0405ER	OEM
FE0405TF	OEM
FE0405TFB	OEM
FE0405TFG	OEM
FE0405TFQ	OEM
FE0405TFR	OEM
FE0405TG	OEM
FE0405TGB	OEM
FE0405TGG	OEM
FE0405TGQ	OEM
FE0405TGR	OEM
FE0405TH	OEM
FE0405THB	OEM
FE0405THG	OEM
FE0405THR	OEM
FE0405TI	OEM
FE0405TIB	OEM
FE0405TIG	OEM
FE0405TIQ	OEM
FE0405TIR	OEM
FE0405TJ	OEM
FE0405TJB	OEM
FE0405TJG	OEM
FE0405TJQ	OEM
FE0405TJR	OEM
FE0501	OEM
FE0501A	OEM
FE0501AA	OEM
FE0501AAB	OEM
FE0501AAG	OEM
FE0501AAQ	OEM
FE0501AAR	OEM
FE0501AB	OEM
FE0501ABB	OEM
FE0501ABG	OEM
FE0501ABQ	OEM
FE0501ABR	OEM
FE0501AC	OEM
FE0501ACB	OEM
FE0501ACG	OEM
FE0501ACR	OEM
FE0501AD	OEM
FE0501ADB	OEM
FE0501ADG	OEM
FE0501ADQ	OEM
FE0501ADR	OEM
FE0501AE	OEM
FE0501AEB	OEM
FE0501AEG	OEM
FE0501AEQ	OEM
FE0501AER	OEM
FE0501AG	OEM
FE0501AQ	OEM
FE0501AR	OEM
FE0501ATF	OEM
FE0501ATFB	OEM
FE0501ATFG	OEM
FE0501ATFQ	OEM
FE0501ATFR	OEM
FE0501ATG	OEM
FE0501ATGB	OEM
FE0501ATGQ	OEM
FE0501ATGR	OEM
FE0501ATH	OEM
FE0501ATHB	OEM
FE0501ATHG	OEM
FE0501ATHR	OEM
FE0501ATI	OEM
FE0501ATIB	OEM
FE0501ATIG	OEM
FE0501ATIQ	OEM
FE0501ATIR	OEM
FE0501ATJ	OEM
FE0501ATJB	OEM
FE0501ATJG	OEM
FE0501ATJQ	OEM
FE0501ATJR	OEM
FE0501B	OEM
FE0501BB	OEM
FE0501BG	OEM
FE0501BQ	OEM
FE0501BR	OEM
FE0501C	OEM
FE0501CB	OEM
FE0501CG	OEM
FE0501D	OEM
FE0501DB	OEM
FE0501DG	OEM
FE0501DQ	OEM
FE0501DR	OEM
FE0501E	OEM
FE0501EB	OEM
FE0501EG	OEM
FE0501EQ	OEM
FE0501ER	OEM
FE0501TFB	OEM
FE0501TFG	OEM
FE0501TFQ	OEM
FE0501TFR	OEM
FE0501TG	OEM
FE0501TGB	OEM
FE0501TGG	OEM
FE0501TGQ	OEM
FE0501TGR	OEM
FE0501TH	OEM
FE0501THB	OEM
FE0501THG	OEM
FE0501THR	OEM
FE0501TI	OEM
FE0501TIB	OEM
FE0501TIG	OEM
FE0501TIQ	OEM
FE0501TIR	OEM
FE0501TJ	OEM
FE0501TJB	OEM
FE0501TJG	OEM
FE0501TJQ	OEM
FE0501TJR	OEM
FE0502	OEM
FE0502A	OEM
FE0502AA	OEM
FE0502AAB	OEM
FE0502AAG	OEM
FE0502AAQ	OEM
FE0502AAR	OEM
FE0502AB	OEM
FE0502ABB	OEM
FE0502ABG	OEM
FE0502ABQ	OEM
FE0502ABR	OEM
FE0502AC	OEM
FE0502ACB	OEM
FE0502ACG	OEM
FE0502ACR	OEM
FE0502AD	OEM
FE0502ADB	OEM
FE0502ADG	OEM
FE0502ADQ	OEM
FE0502ADR	OEM
FE0502AE	OEM
FE0502AEB	OEM
FE0502AEG	OEM
FE0502AEQ	OEM
FE0502AER	OEM
FE0502AG	OEM
FE0502AQ	OEM
FE0502AR	OEM
FE0502ATF	OEM
FE0502ATFB	OEM
FE0502ATFG	OEM
FE0502ATFQ	OEM
FE0502ATFR	OEM
FE0502ATG	OEM
FE0502ATGB	OEM
FE0502ATGG	OEM
FE0502ATGQ	OEM
FE0502ATGR	OEM
FE0502ATH	OEM
FE0502ATHB	OEM
FE0502ATHG	OEM
FE0502ATHR	OEM
FE0502ATI	OEM
FE0502ATIB	OEM
FE0502ATIG	OEM
FE0502ATIQ	OEM
FE0502ATIR	OEM
FE0502ATJ	OEM
FE0502ATJB	OEM
FE0502ATJG	OEM
FE0502ATJQ	OEM
FE0502ATJR	OEM
FE0502B	OEM
FE0502BB	OEM
FE0502BG	OEM
FE0502BQ	OEM
FE0502BR	OEM
FE0502C	OEM
FE0502CB	OEM
FE0502CG	OEM
FE0502CR	OEM
FE0502D	OEM
FE0502DB	OEM
FE0502DG	OEM
FE0502DQ	OEM
FE0502DR	OEM
FE0502E	OEM
FE0502EB	OEM
FE0502EG	OEM
FE0502EQ	OEM
FE0502ER	OEM
FE0502TF	OEM
FE0502TFB	OEM
FE0502TFG	OEM
FE0502TFQ	OEM
FE0502TFR	OEM
FE0502TG	OEM
FE0502TGB	OEM
FE0502TGG	OEM
FE0502TGQ	OEM
FE0502TGR	OEM
FE0502TH	OEM
FE0502THB	OEM
FE0502THG	OEM
FE0502THR	OEM
FE0502TI	OEM
FE0502TIB	OEM
FE0502TIG	OEM
FE0502TIQ	OEM
FE0502TIR	OEM
FE0502TJ	OEM
FE0502TJB	OEM
FE0502TJG	OEM
FE0502TJQ	OEM
FE0502TJR	OEM
FE0505CR	OEM
FE0601	OEM
FE0601A	OEM
FE0601AA	OEM
FE0601AAB	OEM
FE0601AAG	OEM
FE0601AAQ	OEM
FE0601AAR	OEM
FE0601AB	OEM
FE0601ABB	OEM
FE0601ABG	OEM
FE0601ABQ	OEM
FE0601ABR	OEM
FE0601AC	OEM
FE0601ACB	OEM
FE0601ACG	OEM
FE0601ACR	OEM
FE0601AD	OEM
FE0601ADB	OEM
FE0601ADG	OEM
FE0601ADQ	OEM
FE0601ADR	OEM
FE0601AE	OEM
FE0601AEG	OEM
FE0601AEQ	OEM
FE0601AER	OEM
FE0601AQ	OEM
FE0601AR	OEM
FE0601ATF	OEM
FE0601ATFB	OEM
FE0601ATFG	OEM
FE0601ATFQ	OEM
FE0601ATFR	OEM
FE0601ATG	OEM
FE0601ATGB	OEM
FE0601ATGG	OEM
FE0601ATGQ	OEM
FE0601ATGR	OEM
FE0601ATH	OEM
FE0601ATHB	OEM
FE0601ATHG	OEM
FE0601ATHR	OEM
FE0601ATI	OEM
FE0601ATIB	OEM
FE0601ATIG	OEM
FE0601ATIQ	OEM
FE0601ATIR	OEM
FE0601ATJ	OEM
FE0601ATJB	OEM
FE0601ATJG	OEM
FE0601ATJR	OEM
FE0601B	OEM
FE0601BB	OEM
FE0601BG	OEM
FE0601BQ	OEM
FE0601BR	OEM
FE0601C	OEM
FE0601CB	OEM
FE0601CG	OEM
FE0601CR	OEM
FE0601D	OEM
FE0601DB	OEM
FE0601DG	OEM
FE0601DQ	OEM
FE0601DR	OEM
FE0601E	OEM
FE0601EB	OEM
FE0601EG	OEM
FE0601EQ	OEM
FE0601ER	OEM
FE0601TF	OEM
FE0601TFB	OEM
FE0601TFG	OEM
FE0601TFQ	OEM
FE0601TFR	OEM
FE0601TG	OEM
FE0601TGB	OEM
FE0601TGG	OEM
FE0601TGQ	OEM
FE0601TGR	OEM
FE0601TH	OEM
FE0601THB	OEM
FE0601THG	OEM
FE0601THR	OEM
FE0601TI	OEM
FE0601TIB	OEM
FE0601TIG	OEM
FE0601TIQ	OEM
FE0601TIR	OEM
FE0601TJ	OEM
FE0601TJB	OEM
FE0601TJG	OEM
FE0601TJQ	OEM
FE0601TJR	OEM
FE0602F	OEM
FE0602G	OEM
FE0602H	OEM
FE0602I	OEM
FE0602J	OEM
FE0602TF	OEM
FE0602TFB	OEM
FE0602TFG	OEM
FE0602TFR	OEM
FE0602TG	OEM
FE0602TGB	OEM
FE0602TGG	OEM
FE0602TGR	OEM
FE0602TH	OEM
FE0602THB	OEM
FE0602THG	OEM
FE0602THR	OEM
FE0602TI	OEM
FE0602TIB	OEM
FE0602TIF	OEM
FE0602TIG	OEM
FE0602TJ	OEM
FE0602TJB	OEM
FE0602TJG	OEM
FE0602TJR	OEM
FE0701	OEM
FE0701A	OEM
FE0701AA	OEM
FE0701AAG	OEM
FE0701AAQ	OEM
FE0701AAR	OEM
FE0701AB	OEM
FE0701ABB	OEM
FE0701ABG	OEM
FE0701ABQ	OEM
FE0701ABR	OEM
FE0701AC	OEM
FE0701ACB	OEM
FE0701ACG	OEM
FE0701ACR	OEM
FE0701AD	OEM
FE0701ADB	OEM
FE0701ADG	OEM
FE0701ADQ	OEM
FE0701ADR	OEM
FE0701AE	OEM
FE0701AEB	OEM
FE0701AEG	OEM
FE0701AEQ	OEM
FE0701AER	OEM
FE0701AG	OEM
FE0701AQ	OEM
FE0701AR	OEM
FE0701ATF	OEM
FE0701ATFB	OEM
FE0701ATFG	OEM
FE0701ATFQ	OEM
FE0701ATFR	OEM
FE0701ATG	OEM
FE0701ATGB	OEM
FE0701ATGG	OEM
FE0701ATGQ	OEM
FE0701ATH	OEM
FE0701ATHB	OEM
FE0701ATHG	OEM
FE0701ATHR	OEM
FE0701ATI	OEM
FE0701ATIB	OEM
FE0701ATIG	OEM
FE0701ATIQ	OEM
FE0701ATIR	OEM
FE0701ATJ	OEM
FE0701ATJB	OEM
FE0701ATJG	OEM
FE0701ATJQ	OEM
FE0701ATJR	OEM
FE0701B	OEM
FE0701BB	OEM
FE0701BG	OEM
FE0701BQ	OEM
FE0701BR	OEM
FE0701C	OEM
FE0701CB	OEM
FE0701CG	OEM
FE0701CR	OEM
FE0701D	OEM
FE0701DB	OEM
FE0701DG	OEM
FE0701DQ	OEM
FE0701DR	OEM
FE0701E	OEM
FE0701EB	OEM
FE0701EG	OEM
FE0701EQ	OEM
FE0701ER	OEM
FE0701TF	OEM
FE0701TFB	OEM
FE0701TFG	OEM
FE0701TFQ	OEM
FE0701TFR	OEM
FE0701TG	OEM
FE0701TGB	OEM
FE0701TGG	OEM
FE0701TGQ	OEM
FE0701TGR	OEM
FE0701TH	OEM
FE0701THB	OEM
FE0701THG	OEM
FE0701THR	OEM
FE0701TI	OEM
FE0701TIB	OEM
FE0701TIG	OEM
FE0701TIQ	OEM
FE0701TIR	OEM
FE0701TJ	OEM
FE0701TJG	OEM
FE0701TJQ	OEM
FE0701TJR	OEM
FE0801	OEM
FE0801A	OEM
FE0801AA	OEM
FE0801AAB	OEM
FE0801AAG	OEM
FE0801AAQ	OEM
FE0801AAR	OEM
FE0801AB	OEM
FE0801ABB	OEM
FE0801ABG	OEM
FE0801ABQ	OEM
FE0801ABR	OEM
FE0801AC	OEM
FE0801ACB	OEM
FE0801ACG	OEM
FE0801ACR	OEM
FE0801AD	OEM
FE0801ADB	OEM
FE0801ADG	OEM
FE0801ADR	OEM
FE0801AE	OEM
FE0801AEB	OEM
FE0801AEG	OEM
FE0801AEQ	OEM
FE0801AER	OEM
FE0801AG	OEM
FE0801AR	OEM
FE0801ATF	OEM
FE0801ATFB	OEM
FE0801ATFG	OEM
FE0801ATFQ	OEM
FE0801ATFR	OEM
FE0801ATG	OEM
FE0801ATGB	OEM
FE0801ATGG	OEM
FE0801ATGQ	OEM
FE0801ATGR	OEM
FE0801ATH	OEM
FE0801ATHB	OEM
FE0801ATHG	OEM
FE0801ATHR	OEM
FE0801ATIB	OEM
FE0801ATIG	OEM
FE0801ATIQ	OEM
FE0801ATIR	OEM
FE0801ATJ	OEM
FE0801ATJB	OEM
FE0801ATJG	OEM
FE0801ATJQ	OEM
FE0801ATJR	OEM
FE0801B	OEM
FE0801BB	OEM
FE0801BG	OEM
FE0801BQ	OEM
FE0801C	OEM
FE0801CB	OEM
FE0801CG	OEM
FE0801CR	OEM
FE0801D	OEM
FE0801DB	OEM
FE0801DG	OEM
FE0801DQ	OEM
FE0801DR	OEM
FE0801E	OEM
FE0801EB	OEM
FE0801EG	OEM
FE0801EQ	OEM
FE0801ER	OEM
FE0801TF	OEM
FE0801TFB	OEM
FE0801TFG	OEM
FE0801TFQ	OEM
FE0801TFR	OEM
FE0801TG	OEM
FE0801TGB	OEM
FE0801TGG	OEM
FE0801TGQ	OEM
FE0801TGR	OEM
FE0801TH	OEM
FE0801THB	OEM
FE0801THG	OEM
FE0801THR	OEM
FE0801TI	OEM
FE0801TIB	OEM
FE0801TIG	OEM
FE0801TIR	OEM
FE0801TJ	OEM
FE0801TJG	OEM
FE0801TJQ	OEM
FE0801TJR	OEM
FE0801TKQ	OEM
FE0802	OEM
FE0802A	OEM
FE0802AA	OEM
FE0802AAB	OEM
FE0802AAG	OEM
FE0802AAQ	OEM
FE0802AAR	OEM
FE0802AB	OEM
FE0802ABB	OEM
FE0802ABG	OEM
FE0802ABR	OEM
FE0802AC	OEM
FE0802ACB	OEM
FE0802ACG	OEM
FE0802ACR	OEM
FE0802AD	OEM
FE0802ADB	OEM
FE0802ADG	OEM
FE0802ADQ	OEM
FE0802ADR	OEM
FE0802AE	OEM
FE0802AEB	OEM
FE0802AEG	OEM
FE0802AEQ	OEM
FE0802AER	OEM
FE0802AG	OEM
FE0802ATF	OEM
FE0802ATFB	OEM
FE0802ATFG	OEM
FE0802ATFQ	OEM
FE0802ATFR	OEM
FE0802ATG	OEM
FE0802ATGB	OEM
FE0802ATGG	OEM
FE0802ATGQ	OEM
FE0802ATGR	OEM
FE0802ATH	OEM
FE0802ATHB	OEM
FE0802ATHG	OEM
FE0802ATHR	OEM
FE0802ATI	OEM
FE0802ATIB	OEM
FE0802ATIG	OEM
FE0802ATIQ	OEM
FE0802ATIR	OEM
FE0802ATJ	OEM
FE0802ATJB	OEM
FE0802ATJG	OEM
FE0802ATJQ	OEM
FE0802ATJR	OEM
FE0802B	OEM
FE0802BB	OEM
FE0802BG	OEM
FE0802C	OEM
FE0802CB	OEM
FE0802D	OEM
FE0802DB	OEM
FE0802DG	OEM
FE0802E	OEM
FE0802EB	OEM
FE0802EG	OEM
FE0802TF	OEM
FE0802TFB	OEM
FE0802TFG	OEM
FE0802TG	OEM
FE0802TGB	OEM
FE0802TGG	OEM
FE0802TH	OEM
FE0802THB	OEM
FE0802THG	OEM
FE0802THR	OEM
FE0802TI	OEM
FE0802TIB	OEM
FE0802TIR	OEM
FE0802TJ	OEM
FE0802TJB	OEM
FE0802TJR	OEM
FE0803	OEM
FE0803ATF	OEM
FE0803ATFB	OEM
FE0803ATFG	OEM
FE0803ATFR	OEM
FE0803ATG	OEM
FE0803ATGB	OEM
FE0803ATGG	OEM
FE0803ATGQ	OEM
FE0803ATGR	OEM
FE0803ATH	OEM
FE0803ATHB	OEM
FE0803ATHG	OEM
FE0803ATHR	OEM
FE0803ATI	OEM
FE0803ATIB	OEM
FE0803ATIG	OEM
FE0803ATIQ	OEM
FE0803ATIR	OEM
FE0803ATJ	OEM
FE0803ATJB	OEM
FE0803ATJG	OEM
FE0803ATJQ	OEM
FE0803ATJR	OEM
FE0803TF	OEM
FE0803TFB	OEM
FE0803TFG	OEM
FE0803TFQ	OEM
FE0803TFR	OEM
FE0803TG	OEM
FE0803TGB	OEM
FE0803TGG	OEM
FE0803TGQ	OEM
FE0803TGR	OEM
FE0803TH	OEM
FE0803THB	OEM
FE0803THG	OEM
FE0803THR	OEM
FE0803TI	OEM
FE0803TIB	OEM
FE0803TIF	OEM
FE0803TIG	OEM
FE0803TIQ	OEM
FE0803TJ	OEM
FE0803TJB	OEM
FE0803TJG	OEM
FE0803TJQ	OEM
FE0803TJR	OEM
FE0804A	OEM
FE0804B	OEM
FE0804C	OEM
FE0804D	OEM
FE0804E	OEM
FE0804F	OEM
FE0804G	OEM
FE0804H	OEM
FE0804I	OEM
FE0804J	OEM
FE0820ABQ	OEM
FE1A	0494
FE1B	0494
FE1C	0494
FE1D	0494
FE2A	0031
FE2B	0031
FE2C	0031
FE2D	0031
FE3A	0031
FE3B	0031
FE3C	0031
FE3D	0031
FE5A	1352
FE5B	1352
FE5C	1352
FE5D	1352
FE6A	OEM
FE6B	OEM
FE6C	OEM
FE6D	OEM
FE8A	1119
FE8B	1119
FE8C	1119
FE8D	1119
FE8F	1654
FE8G	1654
FE13A	OEM
FE13B	OEM
FE13C	OEM
FE13D	OEM
FE13E	OEM
FE13F	OEM
FE13G	OEM
FE14A	OEM
FE14B	OEM
FE14C	OEM
FE14D	OEM
FE14E	OEM
FE14F	OEM
FE14G	OEM
FE15A	OEM
FE15B	OEM
FE15C	OEM
FE15D	OEM
FE15E	OEM
FE15F	OEM
FE15G	OEM
FE16A	0903
FE16B	0903
FE16C	0903
FE16D	0903
FE16F	OEM
FE16G	OEM
FE30A	OEM
FE30B	OEM
FE30C	OEM
FE30D	OEM
FE30F	OEM

If replacement code is OEM, contact original manufacturer for replacement.

DEVICE TYPE	REPL CODE
FE30G	OEM
FE-100	0321
FE100	0321
FE-100(IR)	0321
FE100(IR)	0321
FE-100A	0321
FE100A	0321
FE-102	0321
FE102	0321
FE-102A	0321
FE102A	0321
FE103	OEM
FE104	OEM
FE-104A	0321
FE104A	0321
FE200	OEM
FE202	OEM
FE204	OEM
FE250	OEM
FE252	OEM
FE254	OEM
FE300	OEM
FE302	OEM
FE304	OEM
FE350	OEM
FE352	OEM
FE354	OEM
FE-400	0321
FE400	0321
FE400A	OEM
FE-402	0299
FE402	0321
FE-402A	0321
FE402A	0321
FE-404A	0321
FE404A	0321
FE1001	OEM
FE1001A	OEM
FE1001B	OEM
FE1001C	OEM
FE1001D	OEM
FE1001E	OEM
FE1001F	OEM
FE1001G	OEM
FE1001H	OEM
FE1001I	OEM
FE1001J	OEM
FE1202A	OEM
FE1202B	OEM
FE1202C	OEM
FE1202D	OEM
FE1202E	OEM
FE1202F	OEM
FE1202G	OEM
FE1202H	OEM
FE1202I	OEM
FE1202J	OEM
FE1600	OEM
FE1901	OEM
FE1901A	OEM
FE1901AA	OEM
FE1901AAB	OEM
FE1901AAG	OEM
FE1901AAQ	OEM
FE1901AAR	OEM
FE1901AB	OEM
FE1901ABB	OEM
FE1901ABG	OEM
FE1901ABQ	OEM
FE1901ABR	OEM
FE1901AC	OEM
FE1901ACB	OEM
FE1901ACG	OEM
FE1901ACR	OEM
FE1901AD	OEM
FE1901ADB	OEM
FE1901ADG	OEM
FE1901ADQ	OEM
FE1901ADR	OEM
FE1901AE	OEM
FE1901AEB	OEM
FE1901AEG	OEM
FE1901AEQ	OEM
FE1901AG	OEM
FE1901AQ	OEM
FE1901AR	OEM
FE1901B	OEM
FE1901BB	OEM
FE1901BG	OEM
FE1901BQ	OEM
FE1901BR	OEM
FE1901C	OEM
FE1901CB	OEM
FE1901CG	OEM
FE1901CR	OEM
FE1901D	OEM
FE1901DB	OEM
FE1901DG	OEM
FE1901DQ	OEM
FE1901DR	OEM
FE1901E	OEM
FE1901EB	OEM
FE1901EG	OEM
FE1901EQ	OEM
FE1901ER	OEM
FE2201	OEM
FE2201ATF	OEM
FE2201ATFB	OEM
FE2201ATFG	OEM
FE2201ATFQ	OEM
FE2201ATFR	OEM
FE2201ATG	OEM
FE2201ATGB	OEM
FE2201ATGG	OEM
FE2201ATGQ	OEM
FE2201ATGR	OEM
FE2201ATHB	OEM
FE2201ATHG	OEM
FE2201ATHR	OEM
FE2201ATI	OEM
FE2201ATIB	OEM
FE2201ATIG	OEM
FE2201ATIQ	OEM
FE2201ATIR	OEM
FE2201ATJ	OEM
FE2201ATJB	OEM
FE2201ATJG	OEM
FE2201ATJQ	OEM
FE2201ATJR	OEM
FE2201TF	OEM
FE2201TFB	OEM
FE2201TFG	OEM
FE2201TFQ	OEM
FE2201TFR	OEM
FE2201TG	OEM
FE2201TGB	OEM
FE2201TGG	OEM
FE2201TGQ	OEM
FE2201TGR	OEM
FE2201TH	OEM
FE2201THB	OEM
FE2201THG	OEM
FE2201THR	OEM
FE2201TI	OEM
FE2201TIB	OEM
FE2201TIG	OEM
FE2201TIQ	OEM
FE2201TIR	OEM
FE2201TJ	OEM
FE2201TJB	OEM
FE2201TJG	OEM
FE2201TJQ	OEM
FE2201TJR	OEM
FE3000A	OEM
FE3010A	OEM
FE3020	OEM
FE3030	OEM
FE4302	2922
FE4303	3219
FE4304	3219
FE5245	0321
FE5246	3219
FE5247	3219
FE5457	3219
FE5458	3219
FE5459	3219
FE5484	3219
FE5485	3219
FE5486	3219
FE13301	OEM
FED070JA	OEM
FED070JA1	OEM
FED071W	OEM
FED080JA	OEM
FED080JA1	OEM
FED080JA2	OEM
FED080JH	OEM
FED080JL	OEM
FED081SA	OEM
FED081SH	OEM
FED081W	OEM
FED0202C	OEM
FED0202D	OEM
FED0203C	OEM
FED0203D	OEM
FED0206C	OEM
FED0206D	OEM
FED0401C	OEM
FED0401D	OEM
FED0501C	OEM
FED0501D	OEM
FED0601C	OEM
FED0601D	OEM
FED0701C	OEM
FED0701D	OEM
FED-1D	OEM
FED-2D	OEM
FED-3D	OEM
FED-4D	OEM
FED16AT	OEM
FED16BT	OEM
FED16CT	OEM
FED16DT	OEM
FED16FT	OEM
FED16GT	OEM
FED16HT	OEM
FED16JT	OEM
FED30AM	OEM
FED30AP	OEM
FED30BM	OEM
FED30BP	OEM
FED30CM	OEM
FED30CP	OEM
FED30DM	OEM
FED30DP	OEM
FED30FM	OEM
FED30FP	OEM
FED30GM	OEM
FED30GP	OEM
FED30HM	OEM
FED30HP	OEM
FED30JP	OEM
FED110JA	OEM
FED130JA	OEM
FED131S	OEM
FED131X	OEM
FED150JA	OEM
FELA400	OEM
FEN16AT	1716
FEN16BT	1716
FEN16CT	1716
FEN16DT	1716
FEN16FT	OEM
FEN16GT	OEM
FEN16HT	OEM
FEN16JT	OEM
FEN30AM	OEM
FEN30AP	OEM
FEN30BM	OEM
FEN30BP	OEM
FEN30CM	OEM
FEN30CP	OEM
FEN30DM	OEM
FEN30DP	OEM
FEN30FM	OEM
FEN30FP	OEM
FEN30GM	OEM
FEN30GP	OEM
FEN30HM	OEM
FEN30HP	OEM
FEN30JP	OEM
FEO654A	OEM
FEO654B	OEM
FEO654C	OEM
FEP5DT	1227
FEP16AT	1227
FEP16BT	1227
FEP16CT	1227
FEP16DT	1227
FEP16FT	5684
FEP16GT	5684
FEP16HT	5684
FEP16JT	5684
FEP30AM	OEM
FEP30AP	2219
FEP30BM	OEM
FEP30BP	2219
FEP30CM	OEM
FEP30CP	2219
FEP30DM	OEM
FEP30DP	2219
FEP30FM	OEM
FEP30FP	4409
FEP30GM	OEM
FEP30GP	4409
FEP30HM	OEM
FEP30HP	4409
FEP30JM	OEM
FEP30JP	4409
FER8AT	OEM
FER8BT	OEM
FER8CT	OEM
FER8DT	OEM
FER8FT	OEM
FER8GT	OEM
FER8HT	OEM
FER8JT	OEM
FER16AT	OEM
FER16BT	OEM
FER16CT	OEM
FER16DT	OEM
FER16FT	OEM
FER16GT	OEM
FER16HT	OEM
FER16JT	OEM
FES8AT	1137
FES8BT	1137
FES8CT	1137
FES8DT	1137
FES8FT	1137
FES8GT	1137
FES8HT	1654
FES8JT	1654
FES16AT	1654
FES16BT	1654
FES16CT	1654
FES16DT	1654
FES16FT	OEM
FES16GT	OEM
FES16HT	OEM
FES16JT	OEM
FF05	OEM
FF023900	6576
FF10	OEM
FF13A	OEM
FF13B	OEM
FF13C	OEM
FF13D	OEM
FF13E	OEM
FF13F	OEM
FF13G	OEM
FF14A	OEM
FF14B	OEM
FF14C	OEM
FF14D	OEM
FF14E	OEM
FF14F	OEM
FF14G	OEM
FF15	OEM
FF15A	OEM
FF15B	OEM
FF15C	OEM
FF15D	OEM
FF15E	OEM
FF15F	OEM
FF15G	OEM
FF102	OEM
FF108	OEM
FF274	0350
FF400	0321
FF409	OEM
FF411	OEM
FF412	OEM
FF413	OEM
FF600	OEM
FF617	OEM
FF626	OEM
FF627	OEM
FFC-4030	0718
FFD-1	OEM
FFD11	OEM
FFD12	OEM
FFD21	OEM
FFD22	OEM
FFD41	OEM
FFD51	OEM
FFD71	OEM
FFD81	OEM
FFZB9	OEM
FG-01	OEM
FG-2N	0071
FG2N	5214
FG-2N/10D-4	0102
FG-2N2	0102
FG-2NA	0015
FG2NA	OEM
FG2PC	0102
FG13A	OEM
FG13B	OEM
FG13C	OEM
FG13D	OEM
FG13E	OEM
FG13F	OEM
FG13G	OEM
FG14A	OEM
FG14B	OEM
FG14C	OEM
FG14D	OEM
FG14E	OEM
FG14F	OEM
FG14G	OEM
FG15A	OEM
FG15B	OEM
FG15C	OEM
FG15DFG15E	OEM
FG15F	OEM
FG15G	OEM
FG24SC1	OEM
FG24SD1GLR	OEM
FG24SD1GRY	OEM
FG24SG1	OEM
FG28SB1	OEM
FG28SB1GR	OEM
FG28SD1	OEM
FG28SJ1	OEM
FG28SL1	OEM
FG34	OEM
FG35	OEM
FG36	OEM
FG36A2	OEM
FG37	OEM
FG38C2	OEM
FG46A5	OEM
FG46C5	OEM
FG47A2	OEM
FG48A2	OEM
FG48B2	OEM
FG48C2	OEM
FG48D6	OEM
FG48E1	OEM
FG48E1A	OEM
FG48K6	OEM
FG48P2	OEM
FG48SA1	OEM
FG48SD1BGLR	OEM
FG48SD1BGRY	OEM
FG48SD1GR	OEM
FG48W2	OEM
FG48X2	OEM
FG48Y2A	OEM
FG58E2	OEM
FG58GW	OEM
FG78A1	OEM
FG78C2	OEM
FG79B6	OEM
FG79C6	OEM
FG80SB1GLR	OEM
FG80SB1GRY	OEM
FG80SB6	OEM
FG85A1	OEM
FG85C1	OEM
FG85D2	OEM
FG85E2	OEM
FG94B1	OEM
FG94C1	OEM
FG94G	OEM
FG95A1	OEM
FG95B1	OEM
FG95F6	OEM
FG95H6	OEM
FG95J6	OEM
FG95K2	OEM
FG95M1	OEM
FG97C6	OEM
FG97D6	OEM
FG97L6	OEM
FG99A2	OEM
FG99C1	OEM
FG99D1	OEM
FG99E1	OEM
FG100SA1	OEM
FG100SB1	OEM
FG101E4S1	OEM
FG101SB	OEM
FG105E1	OEM
FG106A2	OEM
FG108A1	OEM
FG108A1A	OEM
FG108M1	OEM
FG115A6	OEM
FG115C1	OEM
FG115E7	OEM
FG115F7	OEM
FG116A6	OEM
FG116B7	OEM
FG116C6	OEM
FG116D6	OEM
FG117C6	OEM
FG117C7	OEM
FG117D6	OEM
FG118A1	OEM
FG118E7	OEM
FG119A1	OEM
FG119B7	OEM
FG120S1	OEM
FG124B2	OEM
FG125A2	OEM
FG126A2	OEM
FG134A2	OEM
FG135B5	OEM
FG135C1	OEM
FG135E7	OEM
FG135F	OEM
FG135G	OEM
FG136C6	OEM
FG137A1	OEM
FG137C6	OEM
FG137D6	OEM
FG137E7	OEM
FG137F6	OEM
FG138A1	OEM
FG138B7	OEM
FG138G7	OEM
FG139A1	OEM
FG139A3	OEM
FG139D1	OEM
FG139E1	OEM
FG139E7	OEM
FG139F7	OEM
FG139N7	OEM
FG144B2	OEM
FG146A6	OEM
FG157C1	OEM
FG157C7	OEM
FG157D7	OEM
FG159A2	OEM
FG159B7	OEM
FG165A	OEM
FG166A2	OEM
FG169B2	OEM
FG169RA2	OEM
FG179A2	OEM
FG202SA2	OEM
FG206A2	OEM
FG209A2	OEM
FG209M3	OEM
FG210B9	OEM
FG213B9	OEM
FG213C10	OEM
FG213D10	OEM
FG326A2	OEM
FG326B2	OEM
FG326B2A	OEM
FG405A2	OEM
FG410E2	OEM
FG410F1	OEM
FG412D1	OEM
FG413D1	OEM
FG415C1	OEM
FG415E6	OEM
FG425A1	OEM
FG510A1	OEM
FG510B1	OEM
FG511E6	OEM
FG512A1	OEM
FG512F1	OEM
FG514A1	OEM
FG515B6	OEM
FG515B7	OEM
FG515F1	OEM
FG516B1	OEM
FG518B1	OEM
FG520A1	OEM
FG610A1	OEM
FG612A1	OEM
FG614A1	OEM
FG619B1	OEM
FG620A1	OEM
FG620F1	OEM
FG710B1	OEM
FG710C1	OEM
FG713ES1	OEM
FG715B1	OEM
FG715BRS1	OEM
FG715D1	OEM
FG715G2	OEM
FG816A	OEM
FG912E1	OEM
FG913B1	OEM
FG913ES1	OEM
FG914RB	OEM
FG914RB1	OEM
FG915R1	OEM
FG1115RC1	OEM
FG1210RA1	OEM
FG1211RA1	OEM
FG1213A1	OEM
FG1213RB5	OEM
FG1213RE1	OEM
FG1213RF1	OEM
FG1215RB6	OEM
FG1712A2	OEM
FGG1001	OEM
FGM03-2	0190
FGM03-4	0190
FGT3055	OEM
FH100	0911
FH340M	0750
FH1100	0911
FH1109	OEM
FH1200	OEM
FH70401E	2549
FH2000571-4	4032
FHB5	OEM
FHB6	OEM
FHB7	OEM
FHB8	OEM
FHB9	OEM
FHE5	OEM
FHE6	OEM
FHE7	OEM
FHE8	OEM
FHE9	OEM
FHV1B	OEM
FHV1C	OEM
FHV1D	OEM
FHV1E	OEM
FHV2C	OEM
FHV2D	OEM
FHV2E	OEM
FHV2F	OEM
FHV2G	OEM
FHV2H	OEM
FHV3G	OEM
FHV3H	OEM
FHV3M	OEM
FHV4R	OEM
FHV4V	OEM
FHV4W	OEM
FHV4X	OEM
FHV4Y	OEM
FI	OEM
FI0049	OEM
FI-06	OEM
FI100	0838
FI1023	0127
FIB5	OEM
FIB6	OEM
FIB7	OEM
FIB8	OEM
FIB9	OEM
FID151W	OEM
FID080MA	OEM
FID080ML	OEM
FID081W	OEM
FIL-2SD	OEM
FIL-3C	OEM
FIL-3V	OEM
FIL-5C	OEM
FIL-5V	OEM
FIL-20C	OEM
FIL-20V	OEM
FIL-24D	OEM
FIL-29D	OEM
FIL-100C	OEM
FIL-100V	OEM
FIL-C4D	OEM
FIL-C10D	OEM
FIP4B8	OEM
FIP4B15S	OEM
FIP4C9	OEM
FIP4C9B	OEM
FIP4E8S	OEM
FIP4F8S	OEM
FIP4ST41	OEM
FIP5B13S	OEM
FIP5B15	OEM
FIP5D8	OEM
FIP5D10	OEM
FIP5D15S	OEM
FIP5F8S	OEM
FIP5H15	OEM
FIP5LT32	OEM
FIP5LT36ZY1	OEM
FIP5LT61ZK	OEM
FIP6A8S	OEM
FIP6A13	OEM
FIP6C8	OEM
FIP6CM7	OEM
FIP6E6	OEM
FIP6F13	OEM
FIP7BM10	OEM
FIP7BM10A	OEM
FIP7BT13ZRK	OEM
FIP7BT25ZYK	OEM
FIP7CM8	OEM
FIP7D8	OEM
FIP7EM11	OEM
FIP7GM7	OEM
FIP7GM10	OEM
FIP8A5	OEM
FIP8A5R	OEM
FIP8BT30ZK	OEM
FIP8MT05ZYK	OEM
FIP9AM10	OEM
FIP9B7	OEM
FIP9B8	OEM
FIP9BM10	OEM
FIP9C5	OEM
FIP9D5	OEM
FIP9HM7	OEM
FIP9J5	OEM
FIP9J5A	OEM
FIP9MT19ZK	OEM
FIP10A20	OEM
FIP10AM10	OEM
FIP10BT16ZK	OEM
FIP10KM7	OEM
FIP11B8A	OEM
FIP11B10	OEM
FIP11BT23GK	OEM
FIP11BT33ZK	OEM
FIP11CM6	OEM
FIP11DM6	OEM
FIP11HM6	OEM
FIP11YM6	OEM
FIP12KM7	OEM
FIP13B13	OEM
FIP13C10	OEM
FIP13C10A	OEM
FIP14DM8	OEM
FIP16A5R	OEM
FIP16B6X	OEM
FIP16B11X	OEM
FIP18A14R	OEM
FIP18BT12Z	OEM
FIP20B9X	OEM
FIP20C9X	OEM
FIP24A15YS	OEM
FIP24A17YS	OEM
FIP24BW16YS	OEM
FIP40A5X	OEM
FIP60B30T	OEM
FIP100D	0535
FIP101B8A6	OEM
FIP307	OEM
FIP325	OEM
FIP574	OEM
FIPBC8S	OEM
FIP-PEL1009	OEM
FIT5609C	OEM
FJ001A	OEM
FJ001B	OEM
FJ002B	OEM
FJ04A2-28	OEM
FJ04A2-28GG	OEM
FJ0204-12AA	OEM
FJ0230-12	OEM
FJ0230-12FF	OEM
FJ0240-12GG	OEM
FJ0402-12	OEM
FJ0402-12FF	OEM
FJ0402-28FF	OEM
FJ0402E	OEM
FJ0403-28	OEM
FJ0403-28RR	OEM
FJ0406-28	OEM
FJ0406-28FF	OEM
FJ0406-28RR	OEM
FJ0408-12	OEM
FJ0408-12FF	OEM
FJ0410-28	OEM
FJ0410-28FF	OEM
FJ0410-28RR	OEM
FJ0415-12	OEM
FJ0415-12FF	OEM
FJ0425-28	OEM
FJ0425-28FF	OEM
FJ0425-28RR	OEM
FJ0430-12	OEM
FJ0430-12GG	OEM
FJ0480-28	OEM
FJ0480-28GG	OEM
FJ0801-12	OEM
FJ0801-12LL	OEM
FJ0804-12	OEM
FJ0804-12LL	OEM
FJ0807B12LL	OEM
FJ0812-12	OEM
FJ0812-12LL	OEM
FJ0820B12LL	OEM
FJ20P5E18	OEM
FJ101E	OEM

If replacement code is OEM, contact original manufacturer for replacement. 409

DEVICE TYPE	REPL CODE
FJ101M	OEM
FJ101R	OEM
FJ201E	OEM
FJ201F	OEM
FJ201M	OEM
FJ201R	OEM
FJ202E	OEM
FJ202F	OEM
FJ203E	OEM
FJ203F	OEM
FJ401E	OEM
FJ401F	OEM
FJ401J	OEM
FJ402F	OEM
FJ402J	OEM
FJ450E	OEM
FJ451E	OEM
FJ451J	OEM
FJ451LE	OEM
FJ451X	OEM
FJ901E	OEM
FJ901F	OEM
FJ901M	OEM
FJ901R	OEM
FJ902E	OEM
FJ902F	OEM
FJ902M	OEM
FJ902R	OEM
FJ951E	OEM
FJ952E	OEM
FJ954DD	OEM
FJ954E	OEM
FJ2301B-24	OEM
FJ2301B24BB	OEM
FJ2302B-24	OEM
FJ2302B24BB	OEM
FJ2304B-24	OEM
FJ2304B24BB	OEM
FJ2306B-24	OEM
FJ2306B24BB	OEM
FJ7201BB	OEM
FJ7201CC	OEM
FJ9203BB	OEM
FJ9203CC	OEM
FJ9203DD	OEM
FJ9208BB	OEM
FJ9208CC	OEM
FJ9208DD	OEM
FJ9215BB	OEM
FJ9215CC	OEM
FJ9215DD	OEM
FJ9225BB	OEM
FJ9225CC	OEM
FJ9225DD	OEM
FJ9235BB	OEM
FJ9235CC	OEM
FJ70351E	OEM
FJA705716	OEM
FJH101	0867
FJH101-7430	0867
FJH111	0692
FJH111-7420	0692
FJH121	0507
FJH121-7410	0507
FJH131	0232
FJH131-7400	0232
FJH141	1018
FJH141-7440	1018
FJH151	0738
FJH151-7450	0738
FJH161	1160
FJH161-7451	1160
FJH171	1177
FJH171-7453	1177
FJH181	1193
FJH181-7454	1193
FJH191	1527
FJH201	1564
FJH211	0117
FJH221	0310
FJH221-7402	0310
FJH231	0268
FJH231-7401	0268
FJH241	0357
FJH251	0381
FJH261	1046
FJH261-7442	1046
FJH291	0331
FJH291-7403	0331
FJH301	0798
FJH301-7426	0798
FJH311	0268
FJH311-7401	0268
FJH311-7401S1	OEM
FJH321	0381
FJJ101	1394
FJJ111	1417
FJJ111-7472	1417
FJJ121	1164
FJJ121-7473	1164
FJJ131	1303
FJJ131-7474	1303
FJJ141	1199
FJJ141-7490	1199
FJJ152	0828
FJJ181	1423
FJJ181-7475	1423
FJJ191	1150
FJJ191-7476	1150

DEVICE TYPE	REPL CODE
FJJ211	0564
FJJ211-7493	0564
FJJ251-7492	0828
FJJ261	0936
FJJ261-74107	0936
FJK101	0175
FJK101-74121	0175
FJL101	1032
FJT1100	0133
FJT1101	0914
FJT1118	0914
FJT1134	0914
FJY101	1265
FJY101-7460	1265
FK914	0144
FK918	0144
FK2369A	0144
FK2484	0144
FK2894	0150
FK3014	0144
FK3299	0144
FK3300	0144
FK3484	0079
FK3494	0079
FK3502	0855
FK3503	0855
FK3962	OEM
FK3964	OEM
FL1S1	OEM
FL1S2	OEM
FL1S5	OEM
FL1S10	OEM
FL1S15	OEM
FL1S20	OEM
FL1S25	OEM
FL2S1	OEM
FL2S2	OEM
FL2S5	OEM
FL2S10	OEM
FL2S15	OEM
FL2S20	OEM
FL2S25	OEM
FL3S1	OEM
FL3S2	OEM
FL3S5	OEM
FL3S10	OEM
FL3S15	OEM
FL3S20	OEM
FL3S25	OEM
FL101	OEM
FL274	0167
FLC02WF	OEM
FLC08	OEM
FLC08ME	OEM
FLC053WG	OEM
FLC081WF	OEM
FLC081X	OEM
FLC081XP	OEM
FLC091WF	OEM
FLC15	OEM
FLC15ME	OEM
FLC30	OEM
FLC30ME	OEM
FLC103WG	OEM
FLC151MF	OEM
FLC151WF	OEM
FLC151X	OEM
FLC161WF	OEM
FLC181XP	OEM
FLC253MH-6	OEM
FLC253MH-8	OEM
FLC301MG-4	OEM
FLC301MG6	OEM
FLC301MG-8	OEM
FLC301MG8	OEM
FLC311MG-4	OEM
FLD073WB	OEM
FLD080WA	OEM
FLD081WA	OEM
FLD083JA	OEM
FLD083WB	OEM
FLD130WA	OEM
FLD131WA	OEM
FLD133JA	OEM
FLD133WA	OEM
FLH101	0232
FLH111	0507
FLH121	0692
FLH131	0867
FLH141	1018
FLH151	0738
FLH161	1160
FLH171	1177
FLH181	1193
FLH191	0310
FLH201	0268
FLH211	0357
FLH221	1527
FLH231	1564
FLH241	0117
FLH271	0381
FLH281	1046
FLH291	0331
FLH291U	0798
FLH341	1358
FLH351	1432
FLH361	1054
FLH371	1066

DEVICE TYPE	REPL CODE
FLH381	0462
FLH391	0487
FLH401	1831
FLH411	1845
FLH421	1818
FLH431	0370
FLH441	2557
FLH451	4329
FLH481	1197
FLH481T	1339
FLH491	1329
FLH491T	1342
FLH501	2227
FLH511	3429
FLH521	3438
FLH531	3478
FLH541	0990
FLH551	1117
FLH581	0522
FLH601	1261
FLH611	4523
FLH621	0812
FLH631	0893
FLJ101	1394
FLJ111	1417
FLJ121	1164
FLJ131	1150
FLJ141	1303
FLJ151	1423
FLJ161	1199
FLJ171	0828
FLJ181	0564
FLJ191	1477
FLJ201	1901
FLJ211	1906
FLJ221	0974
FLJ231	1692
FLJ241	1910
FLJ251	1915
FLJ261	1705
FLJ271	0936
FLJ311	1953
FLJ321	1960
FLJ331	2912
FLJ381	1939
FLJ391	1945
FLJ401	1621
FLJ411	1635
FLJ421	1007
FLJ431	1656
FLJ441	0729
FLJ451	1675
FLJ461	0231
FLJ531	1759
FLJ541	1776
FLJ561	1932
FLK012WF	OEM
FLK012XP	OEM
FLK022WG	OEM
FLK022XP	OEM
FLK022XV	OEM
FLK052WG	OEM
FLK052XV	OEM
FLK101	0175
FLK102MH-14	OEM
FLK102XV	OEM
FLK111	1131
FLK121	1149
FLK202MH-14	OEM
FLK202XV	OEM
FLL10ME	OEM
FLL17ME	OEM
FLL35ME	OEM
FLL50MK	OEM
FLL100MK	OEM
FLL101	1367
FLL111	1074
FLL111T	0614
FLL121	1090
FLL121T	1100
FLL121U	1090
FLL121V	1100
FLM0910-2	OEM
FLM0910-4C	OEM
FLM1011-2	OEM
FLM1011-4C	OEM
FLM1112-4C	OEM
FLM1213-4C	OEM
FLM1414-2	OEM
FLM1414-4C	OEM
FLM3742-3	OEM
FLM3742-4B	OEM
FLM3742-5	OEM
FLM3742-6	OEM
FLM3742-8B	OEM
FLM4450-3	OEM
FLM4450-4B	OEM
FLM4450-5	OEM
FLM4450-6	OEM
FLM4450-8B	OEM
FLM5359-8B	OEM
FLM5964-3	OEM
FLM5964-3B	OEM
FLM5964-4C	OEM
FLM5964-5	OEM
FLM5964-5IM	OEM
FLM5964-8C	OEM
FLM6472-3B	OEM
FLM6472-4C	OEM

DEVICE TYPE	REPL CODE
FLM6472-5	OEM
FLM6472-8C	OEM
FLM7177-3BN	OEM
FLM7177-4C	OEM
FLM7177-5	OEM
FLM7177-8C	OEM
FLM7785-4	OEM
FLM7785-4C	OEM
FLM7785-8C	OEM
FLQ101	5358
FLQ111	3092
FLQ131	1711
FLR014XP	OEM
FLR024XP	OEM
FLR024XV	OEM
FLR054XV	OEM
FLS02W	OEM
FLS09	OEM
FLS09ME	OEM
FLS16	OEM
FLS16ME	OEM
FLS31	OEM
FLS31ME	OEM
FLS50	OEM
FLS50ME	OEM
FLT-U2	OEM
FLV100	OEM
FLV101	OEM
FLV104A	OEM
FLV110	OEM
FLV111	OEM
FLV117	1348
FLV140	OEM
FLV150	1348
FLV-160	OEM
FLV160	OEM
FLV310	OEM
FLV311	OEM
FLV340	OEM
FLV350	OEM
FLV360	OEM
FLV410	OEM
FLV411	OEM
FLV440	OEM
FLV450	3128
FLV460	OEM
FLV510	OEM
FLV511	OEM
FLV540	OEM
FLV550	OEM
FLV551	OEM
FLV560	OEM
FLX03MB	OEM
FLX06MB	OEM
FLX12MB	OEM
FLX30MB	OEM
FLX102MH-12	OEM
FLX202MH-12	OEM
FLZ80	OEM
FM009M	0196
FM1J2	0015
FM2A	OEM
FM50	OEM
FM75	OEM
FM100	OEM
FM150	OEM
FM200	OEM
FM201	OEM
FM211N	0015
FM250	OEM
FM708	0144
FM709	0144
FM720A	0144
FM870	0144
FM871	0144
FM910	0144
FM911	0144
FM914	0144
FM1100	OEM
FM1100A	OEM
FM1101	OEM
FM1101A	OEM
FM1102	OEM
FM1102A	OEM
FM1103	OEM
FM1103A	OEM
FM1104	OEM
FM1104A	OEM
FM1105	OEM
FM1105A	OEM
FM1106	OEM
FM1106A	OEM
FM1107	OEM
FM1107A	OEM
FM1108	OEM
FM1108A	OEM
FM1109	OEM
FM1109A	OEM
FM1110	OEM
FM1110A	OEM
FM1111	OEM
FM1111A	OEM
FM1200	OEM
FM1201	OEM
FM1202	OEM
FM1203	OEM
FM1204	OEM
FM1205	OEM
FM1206	OEM

DEVICE TYPE	REPL CODE
FM1207	OEM
FM1208	OEM
FM1209	OEM
FM1210	OEM
FM1211	OEM
FM1613	0144
FM1711	0144
FM1893	0233
FM2242	0016
FM2368	0144
FM2369	0144
FM2846	0144
FM2894	0150
FM3014	0144
FM3954	OEM
FM3954A	OEM
FM3955	OEM
FM3955A	OEM
FM3956	OEM
FM3957	OEM
FM3958	3176
FMC2	OEM
FMG1	OEM
FMG2	OEM
FMG2(G2)	OEM
FMG4T98	OEM
FMGG26	OEM
FMG-G26S	1654
FMG-G36S	OEM
FML12S	5815
FMLG12	OEM
FML-G12S	1119
FMLG12S	1119
FML-G12S(F)	1119
FML-G12SF	OEM
FML-G16S	1171
FMMD109	OEM
FMMD914	OEM
FMMD3102	OEM
FMMT2222	OEM
FMMT2222A	OEM
FMMT2369	OEM
FMMT2907	OEM
FMMT3903	OEM
FMMT3904	OEM
FMMT3905	OEM
FMMT3906	OEM
FMMTA05	OEM
FMMTA06	OEM
FMMTA12	OEM
FMMTA13	OEM
FMMTA14	OEM
FMMTA20	OEM
FMMTA55	OEM
FMMTA56	OEM
FMP-G12S	OEM
FMPS-A20	0079
FMPSA20	0079
FMS-3FU	OEM
FMU-11SLF-F	5815
FMU32S	OEM
FMU-115LF-F	OEM
FMW1	OEM
FN1L4M-M31	OEM
FN-51-1A	0079
FN651	OEM
FN651(0)	OEM
FN651-B	OEM
FN651-O	OEM
FN651-R	OEM
FN651-Y	OEM
FN1024	OEM
FN1034	OEM
FN2907	0037
FN4117	OEM
FN4117A	OEM
FN4118A	OEM
FN4119	OEM
FN4119A	OEM
FN4392	OEM
FN4393	OEM
FNA12	OEM
FND100	OEM
FND350	OEM
FND357	OEM
FND358	OEM
FND360	OEM
FND367	OEM
FND368	OEM
FND500	2185
FND501	OEM
FND507	2192
FND508	OEM
FND530	OEM
FND531	OEM
FND537	OEM
FND538	OEM
FND540	OEM
FND541	OEM
FND547	OEM
FND548	OEM
FND550	OEM
FND551	OEM
FND557	OEM
FND560	OEM
FND561	OEM
FND567	OEM
FND568	OEM
FND800	OEM

DEVICE TYPE	REPL CODE
FND807	2362
FO5	0015
FOD-12	OEM
FOD100	OEM
FOE-7	OEM
FOE-16	OEM
FOP40A5AX	OEM
FOR1A411E	0895
FOR1B	0895
FOR2D	1129
FOR2G	OEM
FOR-2G41	OEM
FOR2G41	OEM
FOR3G	0403
FOR36	OEM
FORIB	OEM
FOS100	0111
FOS101	0111
FOS104	0079
FP50BG2	OEM
FP54ALS16L8J	OEM
FP54ALS16L8N	OEM
FP54ALS16R4J	OEM
FP54ALS16R4N	OEM
FP54ALS16R6J	OEM
FP54ALS16R6N	OEM
FP54ALS16R8J	OEM
FP54ALS16R8N	OEM
FP54AS839JT	OEM
FP54AS839NT	OEM
FP54AS840JT	OEM
FP54AS840NT	OEM
FP54LS333JT	OEM
FP54LS333NT	OEM
FP54LS335JT	OEM
FP54LS335NT	OEM
FP74ALS16L8J	OEM
FP74ALS16L8N	OEM
FP74ALS16R4J	OEM
FP74ALS16R4N	OEM
FP74ALS16R6J	OEM
FP74ALS16R6N	OEM
FP74ALS16R8J	OEM
FP74ALS16R8N	OEM
FP74AS839JT	OEM
FP74AS839NT	OEM
FP74AS840JT	OEM
FP74AS840NT	OEM
FP74LS333JT	OEM
FP74LS333NT	OEM
FP74LS335JT	OEM
FP74LS335NT	OEM
FP4339	OEM
FP4340	OEM
FP50801	0127
FP100002S	OEM
FP100110S	OEM
FP100111S	OEM
FP100112S	OEM
FP100113S	OEM
FPA100	OEM
FPA102	OEM
FPA103	OEM
FPA104	OEM
FPA105	OEM
FPA106	OEM
FPA107	OEM
FPA108	OEM
FPA720	OEM
FPB-A	OEM
FPD080CA	OEM
FPD080MA	OEM
FPD081MA	OEM
FPD140M3	OEM
FPD150C	OEM
FPD150M	OEM
FPD150M3	OEM
FPE104	OEM
FPE700	OEM
FPLAS93459PC	OEM
FPM100	OEM
FPM200	OEM
FPN100	OEM
FPN2907	0037
FPN3563	0144
FPO100	OEM
FPQ2222	0539
FPQ2907	0281
FPQ3467	OEM
FPQ3468	OEM
FPQ3724	OEM
FPQ3725	OEM
FPR40-1001	0016
FPR40-1003	0144
FPR40-1004	0004
FPR40-1005	0004
FPR40-1006	0143
FPR50-1001	0016
FPR50-1002	0016
FPR50-1003	0144
FPR50-1004	0144
FPR50-1005	0004
FPR50-1006	0004
FPT100	OEM
FPT100A	OEM
FPT100B	OEM
FPT101	OEM
FPT110	OEM
FPT110A	OEM

DEVICE TYPE	REPL CODE
FPT120	OEM
FPT120A	OEM
FPT120B	OEM
FPT130	OEM
FPT130A	OEM
FPT130B	OEM
FPT220	OEM
FPT320	OEM
FPT330	OEM
FPT500	2297
FPT510	2297
FPT510A	2297
FPT540A	OEM
FPT550	OEM
FPT700	OEM
FPT720	OEM
FPZ5V6	OEM
FPZ6V2	0631
FPZ6V8	OEM
FPZ7V5	OEM
FPZ8V2	0244
FPZ9V1	0012
FPZ10	OEM
FPZ11	OEM
FPZ12	0137
FQ3467	OEM
FQ3468	OEM
FQ3724	OEM
FQ3725	OEM
FQB01-35	0814
FQL0008A	OEM
FQL0008B	OEM
FR061	0023
FR062	0023
FR063	0023
FR064	0023
FR065	0023
FR066	0017
FR067	0017
FR0401AAQ	OEM
FR-1	0015
FR1	0015
FR1-54A	0015
FR1D	0133
FR-1H	0015
FR1H	0015
FR-1H(M)	0015
FR-1HM	0015
FR-1M	0015
FR1M	0015
FR1MB	0015
FR-1MD	0015
FR1MD	5307
FR-1N	0015
FR-1P	0015
FR1P	0023
FR-1U	0015
FR1U	0015
FR-2	0015
FR2	0023
FR2-005	0102
FR2-02	0023
FR2-02(DIO)	0015
FR2-02(RECT)	0102
FR2-02C	0015
FR2-04	0102
FR2-06	0023
FR2-08	0102
FR2-020	0015
FR2-0Z	0015
FR2-10	0102
FR-2M	0015
FR2M	0015
FR2P	4176
FR2PC	0535
FR2U	OEM
FR7	OEM
FR-10	0102
FR10	0015
FR15	OEM
FR20	OEM
FR25	OEM
FR30	OEM
FR40	OEM
FR101	0023
FR101G	1082
FR102	0023
FR102G	1082
FR103	0023
FR103G	1082
FR104	0023
FR104G	0271
FR105	0023
FR105G	0023
FR106	0017
FR106G	0017
FR107	0017
FR107G	0017
FR150AX10	OEM
FR150DX12	OEM
FR150DX16	OEM
FR150DX20	OEM
FR150DX24	OEM
FR150DY4	OEM
FR150DY6	OEM
FR150DY8	OEM
FR150DY10	OEM
FR150DY12	OEM
FR150DY16	OEM

If replacement code is OEM, contact original manufacturer for replacement.

DEVICE TYPE	REPL CODE
FR151	2068
FR151G	OEM
FR152	2068
FR152G	OEM
FR153	0023
FR153G	OEM
FR154	3147
FR154G	OEM
FR155	0031
FR155G	OEM
FR155P	0023
FR156	0102
FR156G	OEM
FR157	0102
FR157G	OEM
FR201	2068
FR201G	OEM
FR-202	0015
FR202	2068
FR202C	OEM
FR202G	OEM
FR203	2068
FR203G	OEM
FR204	6451
FR204G	OEM
FR205	0031
FR205G	OEM
FR206	0102
FR206G	OEM
FR207	0102
FR207G	OEM
FR251	0031
FR252	0031
FR253	0031
FR254	0031
FR255	0031
FR256	1917
FR257	1917
FR300AX10	OEM
FR300DX12	OEM
FR300DX16	OEM
FR300DX20	OEM
FR300DX24	OEM
FR300DY4	OEM
FR300DY6	OEM
FR300DY8	OEM
FR300DY10	OEM
FR300DY12	OEM
FR300DY16	OEM
FR301	2068
FR301G	OEM
FR302	2068
FR302G	4042
FR303	2068
FR303G	OEM
FR304	6451
FR304G	OEM
FR305	6451
FR305G	OEM
FR306	3159
FR306G	OEM
FR307	3159
FR307G	OEM
FR401	OEM
FR500AW12	OEM
FR500AW16	OEM
FR500AW20	OEM
FR500AW24	OEM
FR500AX12	OEM
FR500AX16	OEM
FR500AX20	OEM
FR500AX24	OEM
FR500AX26	OEM
FR500AY4	OEM
FR500AY6	OEM
FR500AY8	OEM
FR500AY10	OEM
FR500AY12	OEM
FR500AY16	OEM
FR500AY20	OEM
FR500AY24	OEM
FR501	1352
FR600AW40	OEM
FR600AW50	OEM
FR600AX40	OEM
FR600AX50	OEM
FR601	OEM
FR602	OEM
FR603	OEM
FR604	OEM
FR605	OEM
FR606	OEM
FR607	OEM
FR801	1137
FR801R	OEM
FR802	1137
FR802R	OEM
FR803	1137
FR803R	OEM
FR804	1137
FR804R	OEM
FR805	1654
FR805R	OEM
FR806	OEM
FR806R	OEM
FR807	OEM
FR807R	OEM
FR1000BW50	OEM
FR1000BX50	OEM

DEVICE TYPE	REPL CODE
FR1001	OEM
FR-1033	0769
FR1033	0769
FR1502E10	OEM
FR1502E11	OEM
FR1502F10	OEM
FR1502F11	OEM
FR2001	OEM
FR3001	2259
FR4001	OEM
FRA81-004	OEM
FRB12-01RK	0604
FRB24-06B	OEM
FRB80-004	OEM
FRB81-004	OEM
FRC26-13L	0102
FRH-101	0015
FRP1610	3507
FRR7	OEM
FRR10	OEM
FRR15	OEM
FRR20	OEM
FRR25	OEM
FRR30	OEM
FRR40	OEM
FRR80-3	OEM
FR-U	0015
FS	OEM
FS1-2AA	OEM
FS1-2CA	OEM
FS1-4AA	OEM
FS1-4CA	OEM
FS1-6AA	OEM
FS1-6CA	OEM
FS1-8AA	OEM
FS1-10AA	OEM
FS1-12AA	OEM
FS19	0143
FS21	OEM
FS23	OEM
FS24	OEM
FS32B	OEM
FS36	OEM
FS125	OEM
FS340M	0750
FS503PA	0652
FS503RA	0652
FS503VA	0652
FS703PA	0652
FS703RA	0652
FS703VA	0652
FS-1133	0079
FS1168E641	0079
FS1168F813	0079
FS1221	0016
FS1308	0127
FS1331	0086
FS1682	0007
FS1974	0016
FS1978	0693
FS2003-1	0103
FS2042	0590
FS2043	0079
FS-2299	0150
FS2299	0050
FS3266	0144
FS3683	0144
FS7805	4273
FS-7812	0330
FS7812	0330
FS24226	0037
FS24954	0037
FS26382	0150
FS27233	0086
FS27604	0079
FS32669	0127
FS35529	0144
FS326690	0144
FSA1169	1073
FSA1177	0196
FSA1178	0196
FSA1202	1073
FSA1410M	OEM
FSA1411M	OEM
FSA2002M	OEM
FSA2003M	OEM
FSA2500M	OEM
FSA2501M	OEM
FSA2501P	OEM
FSA2502M	OEM
FSA2503M	OEM
FSA2503P	OEM
FSA2504M	OEM
FSA2509M	OEM
FSA2509P	OEM
FSA2510M	OEM
FSA2510P	OEM
FSA2563M	OEM
FSA2563P	OEM
FSA2564M	OEM
FSA2564P	OEM
FSA2565M	OEM
FSA2565P	OEM
FSA2566M	OEM
FSA2566P	OEM
FSA2610M	OEM
FSA2619M	OEM
FSA2619P	OEM
FSA2620P	OEM

DEVICE TYPE	REPL CODE
FSA2621M	OEM
FSA2702M	OEM
FSA2703M	OEM
FSA2704M	OEM
FSA2705M	OEM
FSA2719M	OEM
FSA2719P	OEM
FSA2720M	OEM
FSA2720P	OEM
FSA2721M	OEM
FSC05FA	OEM
FSC10LF	OEM
FSC10X	OEM
FSC11LF	OEM
FSC9015D	0037
FSE1001	0144
FSE3001	0144
FSE5002	0144
FSN6-2AA	OEM
FSN6-2CA	OEM
FSN6-4AA	OEM
FSN6-4CA	OEM
FSN6-6AA	OEM
FSN6-6CA	OEM
FSN6-8AA	OEM
FSN6-8CA	OEM
FSN6-10AA	OEM
FSN6-10CA	OEM
FSP-1	0144
FSP1	0127
FSP2	OEM
FSP5	OEM
FSP22	OEM
FSP-42	0144
FSP42	OEM
FSP-42-1	0144
FSP42-1	0144
FSP55	OEM
FSP-164	0144
FSP164	0144
FSP-165	0144
FSP165	0144
FSP-166	0144
FSP166	0144
FSP-166-1	0144
FSP166-1	0144
FSP-215	0144
FSP215	OEM
FSP220	OEM
FSP-242-1	0144
FSP242-1	0144
FSP-270-1	0144
FSP270-1	OEM
FSP-288-1	0015
FSP288-1	4176
FSP-289-1	0144
FSP289-1	OEM
FSP400	OEM
FSP598	OEM
FSS226A	OEM
FSS226B	OEM
FSS226C	OEM
FSS226D	OEM
FST2	0015
FST3	0015
FSX01WF	OEM
FSX11X	OEM
FSX51W	OEM
FSX51WF	OEM
FSX51X	OEM
FSX52W	OEM
FSX52WF	OEM
FSX52X	OEM
FSX53W	OEM
FSX53WF	OEM
FSX53X	OEM
FSY07	OEM
FT001	0086
FT002	0086
FT003	0086
FT004	0086
FT004A	0086
FT005	0016
FT006	0016
FT008	0016
FT008A	0016
FT0019H	0086
FT0019M	0037
FT012	OEM
FT020	OEM
FT023	0016
FT024	0016
FT025	0016
FT026	0016
FT027	0086
FT044	OEM
FT052	0037
FT053	0016
FT-0601	0212
FT0601	OEM
FT-1	0015
FT1	0133
FT-1M	0102
FT1M	0102
FT-1N	0015
FT1N	0015
FT-1P	0102
FT1P	0102
FT-10	0015

DEVICE TYPE	REPL CODE
FT10	0071
FT14A	0015
FT19H	0037
FT19M	0037
FT30A1C	OEM
FT30A1D	OEM
FT30A1N	OEM
FT30A2C	OEM
FT30A2D	OEM
FT30A2N	OEM
FT30AAC	OEM
FT30AAD	OEM
FT30AAN	OEM
FT34C	0233
FT34D	0233
FT34G	0321
FT34Y	0321
FT40	0079
FT45	0007
FT47	0388
FT48	0168
FT49	0168
FT50	0168
FT57	OEM
FT100B14	OEM
FT100BX14	OEM
FT100BY14	OEM
FT100DM4	OEM
FT100DM6	OEM
FT100DM8	OEM
FT100DM10	OEM
FT100DM12	OEM
FT100DM16	OEM
FT100DM20	OEM
FT100DM24	OEM
FT100DM28	OEM
FT100DM32	OEM
FT100DM36	OEM
FT100DX4	OEM
FT100DX6	OEM
FT100DX8	OEM
FT100DX10	OEM
FT100DX12	OEM
FT100DX16	OEM
FT100DX20	OEM
FT100DY4	OEM
FT100DY6	OEM
FT100DY8	OEM
FT100DY10	OEM
FT100DY12	OEM
FT100DY16	OEM
FT101BX2	OEM
FT101BX4	OEM
FT101BX6	OEM
FT107A	0396
FT107B	0111
FT118	0007
FT150B2	OEM
FT150B4	OEM
FT150B8	OEM
FT150B12	OEM
FT150B16	OEM
FT150B20	OEM
FT150B24	OEM
FT150B28	OEM
FT150B32	OEM
FT150BX2	OEM
FT150BY2	OEM
FT150D68	OEM
FT150DX4	OEM
FT150DX6	OEM
FT150DX8	OEM
FT150DX10	OEM
FT150DX12	OEM
FT150DX16	OEM
FT150DX20	OEM
FT150DY4	OEM
FT150DY6	OEM
FT150DY10	OEM
FT150DY12	OEM
FT150DY16	OEM
FT150EM16	OEM
FT150EM20	OEM
FT150EM24	OEM
FT150EM28	OEM
FT150EM32	OEM
FT150EM36	OEM
FT150EX16	OEM
FT150EX20	OEM
FT150EX24	OEM
FT150EX28	OEM
FT150EX32	OEM
FT150EX36	OEM
FT151BX2	OEM
FT151BX4	OEM
FT151BX6	OEM
FT250BX2	OEM
FT250BY2	OEM
FT250DM4	OEM
FT250DM6	OEM
FT250DM8	OEM
FT250DM10	OEM
FT250DM12	OEM
FT250DM16	OEM
FT250DM20	OEM
FT250DM24	OEM
FT250DM28	OEM
FT250DM32	OEM
FT250DM36	OEM

DEVICE TYPE	REPL CODE
FT250DX4	OEM
FT250DX6	OEM
FT250DX8	OEM
FT250DX10	OEM
FT250DX12	OEM
FT250DX16	OEM
FT250DX20	OEM
FT250DY4	OEM
FT250DY6	OEM
FT250DY8	OEM
FT250DY10	OEM
FT250DY12	OEM
FT250DY16	OEM
FT251BX2	OEM
FT251BX4	OEM
FT251BX6	OEM
FT251BX8	OEM
FT251BY4	OEM
FT251BY6	OEM
FT251BY8	OEM
FT300	0142
FT300A2	OEM
FT300A4	OEM
FT300A6	OEM
FT300A8	OEM
FT300A10	OEM
FT300A12	OEM
FT300A16	OEM
FT300A20	OEM
FT300A24	OEM
FT300A28	OEM
FT300A32	OEM
FT300A36	OEM
FT300A40	OEM
FT300A50	OEM
FT300AH40	OEM
FT300AH50	OEM
FT300C2	OEM
FT300C4	OEM
FT300C6	OEM
FT300C8	OEM
FT300C10	OEM
FT300C12	OEM
FT300DL4	OEM
FT300DL6	OEM
FT300DL8	OEM
FT300DL10	OEM
FT300DL12	OEM
FT300DL16	OEM
FT300DL20	OEM
FT300DL24	OEM
FT300DM28	OEM
FT300DM32	OEM
FT300DM36	OEM
FT300DX4	OEM
FT300DX6	OEM
FT300DX8	OEM
FT300DX10	OEM
FT300DX12	OEM
FT300DX16	OEM
FT300DX20	OEM
FT300DX42	OEM
FT300DY4	OEM
FT300DY6	OEM
FT300DY8	OEM
FT300DY10	OEM
FT300DY12	OEM
FT300DY16	OEM
FT300EM16	OEM
FT300EM20	OEM
FT300EM24	OEM
FT300EM28	OEM
FT300EM32	OEM
FT300EM36	OEM
FT300EX16	OEM
FT300EX20	OEM
FT300EX24	OEM
FT300EX28	OEM
FT300EX32	OEM
FT300EX36	OEM
FT301AX2	OEM
FT301AX4	OEM
FT301AX6	OEM
FT317	OEM
FT317A	OEM
FT317B	5445
FT340	0555
FT359	OEM
FT401	0637
FT402	0065
FT410	0103
FT411	0270
FT413	0074
FT417	OEM
FT417A	OEM
FT417B	5574
FT423	0074
FT427	1973
FT430	1980
FT431	0637
FT500-32	OEM
FT500-36	OEM
FT500-40	OEM
FT500-50	OEM
FT500-60	OEM
FT500A16	OEM
FT500A20	OEM
FT500A24	OEM
FT500A28	OEM

DEVICE TYPE	REPL CODE
FT500A32	OEM
FT500A36	OEM
FT500A40	OEM
FT500A50	OEM
FT500A60	OEM
FT500A80	OEM
FT500AH60	OEM
FT500AH70	OEM
FT500AH80	OEM
FT500AL4	OEM
FT500AL6	OEM
FT500AL8	OEM
FT500AL10	OEM
FT500AL12	OEM
FT500AL16	OEM
FT500AL20	OEM
FT500AL24	OEM
FT500AL28	OEM
FT500AM16	OEM
FT500AM20	OEM
FT500AM24	OEM
FT500AM28	OEM
FT500AM32	OEM
FT500AM36	OEM
FT500AM40	OEM
FT500AM50	OEM
FT500AW12	OEM
FT500AW16	OEM
FT500AW20	OEM
FT500AW24	OEM
FT500AW26	OEM
FT500AX8	OEM
FT500AX10	OEM
FT500AX12	OEM
FT500AX16	OEM
FT500AX20	OEM
FT500AY2	OEM
FT500AY4	OEM
FT500AY6	OEM
FT500AY8	OEM
FT500AY10	OEM
FT500AY12	OEM
FT500AY14	OEM
FT500AY16	OEM
FT500BX20	OEM
FT500BX24	OEM
FT500BX26	OEM
FT500BY20	OEM
FT500BY24	OEM
FT500BY26	OEM
FT500C8	OEM
FT500C10	OEM
FT500C12	OEM
FT500C16	OEM
FT500C20	OEM
FT500C24	OEM
FT500C28	OEM
FT500DL4	OEM
FT500DL6	OEM
FT500DL8	OEM
FT500DL10	OEM
FT500DL12	OEM
FT500DL16	OEM
FT500DL20	OEM
FT500DL24	OEM
FT500DL28	OEM
FT500DX16	OEM
FT500DX20	OEM
FT500DX24	OEM
FT500DY16	OEM
FT500DY20	OEM
FT500DY24	OEM
FT500EX20	OEM
FT500EX24	OEM
FT500EY20	OEM
FT500EY24	OEM
FT500GZ16	OEM
FT500GZ20	OEM
FT500GZ24	OEM
FT520	1077
FT527	0930
FT600A6	OEM
FT600A8	OEM
FT600A10	OEM
FT600A12	OEM
FT701	OEM
FT704	0838
FT709	0144
FT800C4	OEM
FT800C6	OEM
FT800C8	OEM
FT800C10	OEM
FT800C12	OEM
FT800C16	OEM
FT800C20	OEM
FT800C24	OEM
FT800DL4	OEM
FT800DL6	OEM
FT800DL8	OEM
FT800DL10	OEM
FT800DL12	OEM
FT800DL16	OEM
FT800DL20	OEM
FT800DL24	OEM
FT1000A16	OEM
FT1000A20	OEM
FT1000A24	OEM
FT1000A28	OEM
FT1000A32	OEM

DEVICE TYPE	REPL CODE
FT1000A36	OEM
FT1000A40	OEM
FT1000A50	OEM
FT1000B80	OEM
FT1000BV60	OEM
FT1000BV70	OEM
FT1000BV80	OEM
FT1000CM16	OEM
FT1000CM20	OEM
FT1000CM24	OEM
FT1000CM28	OEM
FT1000CM32	OEM
FT1000CM36	OEM
FT1000CX16	OEM
FT1000CX20	OEM
FT1000CX24	OEM
FT1000CX28	OEM
FT1000CX32	OEM
FT1000CX36	OEM
FT1200A2	OEM
FT1200A4	OEM
FT1200A6	OEM
FT1200A8	OEM
FT1200A10	OEM
FT1200A12	OEM
FT1210	OEM
FT1315	0144
FT1324B	0144
FT1324C	0144
FT1341	0037
FT1500AL4	OEM
FT1500AL6	OEM
FT1500AL8	OEM
FT1500AL12	OEM
FT1500AL16	OEM
FT1500AL20	OEM
FT1500AL24	OEM
FT1500DL4	OEM
FT1500DL6	OEM
FT1500DL8	OEM
FT1500DL12	OEM
FT1500DL16	OEM
FT1500DL20	OEM
FT1500DL24	OEM
FT1500DV60	OEM
FT1500DV70	OEM
FT1500DV80	OEM
FT1500EX16	OEM
FT1500EX20	OEM
FT1500EX24	OEM
FT1500EY16	OEM
FT1500EY20	OEM
FT1500EY24	OEM
FT1607R	OEM
FT1608R	OEM
FT1702	0150
FT1717AR	OEM
FT1746	0037
FT1869	OEM
FT1870	OEM
FT1871	OEM
FT1872	OEM
FT1873	OEM
FT1874	OEM
FT1881	OEM
FT1882	OEM
FT1883	OEM
FT1884	OEM
FT1885	OEM
FT2009	OEM
FT2010	OEM
FT2011	OEM
FT2012	OEM
FT2013	OEM
FT2014	OEM
FT2483	OEM
FT2484	OEM
FT2500BH16	OEM
FT2500BH20	OEM
FT2500BH24	OEM
FT2500BH28	OEM
FT2500BH32	OEM
FT2500BH36	OEM
FT2500BH40	OEM
FT2500BH50	OEM
FT2500BH56	OEM
FT2955	1359
FT2974	OEM
FT2978	OEM
FT3001C	OEM
FT3001D	OEM
FT3001N	OEM
FT3002C	OEM
FT3002D	OEM
FT3002N	OEM
FT3003D	OEM
FT3003N	OEM
FT3055	0477
FT3567	0079
FT3568	0079
FT3569	0079
FT3638	0037
FT3641	0233
FT3642	0018
FT3643	0016
FT3644	0786
FT3645	0527
FT3820	OEM
FT3838	OEM

If replacement code is OEM, contact original manufacturer for replacement. 411

DEVICE TYPE	REPL CODE	DEVICE TYPE	REPL CODE	DEVICE TYPE	REPL CODE	DEVICE TYPE	REPL CODE	DEVICE TYPE	REPL CODE	DEVICE TYPE	REPL CODE	DEVICE TYPE	REPL CODE
FT3909	OEM	FV1014C	OEM	FZ6.2T10	0631	FZJ165	OEM	G05-010-A	0016	G05704	OEM	G4H3	0652
FT4017	OEM	FV1014D	OEM	FZ6.5T10	0631	FZK101	OEM	G05-011-A	0016	G05704B	OEM	G4HZ	OEM
FT4018	OEM	FV1016	OEM	FZ10A	0170	FZK105	OEM	G05-012-G	0111	G05704C	OEM	G4J	0959
FT4019	OEM	FV1016A	OEM	FZ10B	0098	FZL101	OEM	G05-015-D	0016	G05705	0042	G4K	0959
FT4020	OEM	FV1016B	OEM	FZ12A	0137	FZL105	OEM	G05-015C	0016	G08005L	3017	G4K3	1975
FT4021	OEM	FV1016C	OEM	FZ12B	0186	FZL111	4940	G05-034-D	0016	G09007	1983	G4M	0916
FT4022	OEM	FV1016D	OEM	FZ12T5	0137	FZL121	OEM	G05-035-D	0016	G09009	1206	G4M3	0652
FT4023	OEM	FV-1043	0549	FZ12T10	0137	FZL121S	OEM	G05-035-D,E	0111	G09015	0574	G4N1	0074
FT4024	OEM	FV1043	0549	FZ14T5	0100	FZL125	OEM	G05-035-E	0111	G030010-1R	OEM	G4N3	0652
FT4025	OEM	FV2369A	0144	FZ14T10	0100	FZL125X	OEM	G05-035D	0111	G030010-2R	OEM	G4.3T5	0528
FT4354	0037	FV2484	0144	FZ15A	0002	FZL131	OEM	G05-035E	0016	G030010-3R	OEM	G4.3T10	0528
FT4355	0037	FV2747C	0279	FZ15T5	0002	FZL131S	OEM	G05-036-B	0079	G030012-1R	OEM	G4.3T20	0528
FT4356	OEM	FV2894	0150	FZ15T10	0002	FZL135	OEM	G05-036-C	1211	G030012-2R	OEM	G4.7T5	0446
FT5040	0037	FV3014	0144	FZ18A	0490	FZL135S	OEM	G05-036-C,D,E	0016	G030012-3R	OEM	G4.7T10	0446
FT5041	0037	FV3299	0144	FZ22A	0560	FZL141	OEM	G05-036-D	1211	G030015-1R	OEM	G4.7T20	0446
FT5315	OEM	FV3300	0144	FZ27A	0436	FZL141S	OEM	G05-036-E	1211	G030015-2R	OEM	G5	0015
FT5320	OEM	FV3502	0855	FZ27T5	0436	FZL145	OEM	G05-036B	0284	G030015-3R	OEM	G5A	OEM
FT5321	OEM	FV3503	0855	FZ27T10	0436	FZL145S	OEM	G05-036C	0284	G030018-1R	OEM	G5A3	0594
FT5701	OEM	FV3962	OEM	FZ33A	0039	FZY101	OEM	G05-036D	0016	G030018-3R	OEM	G5B	OEM
FT5701AM	OEM	FV3964	OEM	FZ39A	0346	FZY105	OEM	G05-036E	0016	G030022-1R	OEM	G5B3	0594
FT5702	OEM	FW50	0276	FZ47A	0993	G00001B	OEM	G05-037-A	0224	G030022-2R	OEM	G5C	0143
FT5702M	OEM	FW100	0015	FZ56A	0863	G00004A	0143	G05-037-B	0151	G030022-3R	OEM	G5C3	0594
FT5709	OEM	FW200	0287	FZ68A	2144	G00005B	OEM	G05-037-D	0151	G030027-1R	OEM	G5D	OEM
FT5709M	OEM	FW300	0293	FZ82A	0327	G00008A	0019	G05-037B	0016	G030027-2R	OEM	G5D3	0594
FT5712M	0539	FW400	0015	FZ101	0079	G0000.5B	OEM	G05-050-C	0127	G030027-3R	OEM	G5E3	0594
FT5713M	0539	FW500	0015	FZ309B	4171	G0001	0136	G05-055-C	0155	G060007-1R	OEM	G5F	0143
FT5714M	0281	FW600	0015	FZ901	0162	G0003	0050	G05-055-D	0155	G060007-2R	OEM	G5F3	0594
FT5722R	OEM	FW600A	0015	FZ1215	0137	G0004	0164	G05-055-E	0155	G060010-1R	OEM	G5G3	0594
FT5723M	OEM	FW800	0250	FZA-1D	OEM	G0005	0164	G05-059	OEM	G060010-2R	OEM	G5H1	OEM
FT5726DR	OEM	FW1000	0250	FZA-2D	OEM	G0006	0211	G05-063-R	1136	G060010-3R	OEM	G5H3	1975
FT5727BR	OEM	FWB3001	0287	FZD6V8	2120	G0007	0004	G05-064-A	0079	G060012-1R	OEM	G5K	0143
FT5727DR	OEM	FWB3002	0287	FZD8V2	OEM	G0009	0004	G05-065-A	1060	G060012-2R	OEM	G5K3	1975
FT5728BR	OEM	FWB3003	0293	FZD10	OEM	G00010B	OEM	G05-066A	0076	G060012-3R	OEM	G5M3	0652
FT5742M	OEM	FWB3004	0293	FZD12	OEM	G00020B	OEM	G05-406-C	0455	G060015-1R	OEM	G5N3	0652
FT5743M	OEM	FWB3005	0299	FZD15	OEM	G00050B	OEM	G05-413A	0155	G060015-2R	OEM	G5R	OEM
FT5748M	OEM	FWB3006	0299	FZD18	1756	G00-003-A	0019	G05-413B	0155	G060015-3R	OEM	G5U	OEM
FT5751M	OEM	FWL50	0276	FZD22	OEM	G00-004-A	0143	G05-413C	0155	G060018-1R	OEM	G5.1T5	0162
FT5753M	OEM	FWL100	0015	FZD27	1941	G00-008-A	0143	G05-413D	0155	G060018-2R	OEM	G5.1T10	0162
FT5754M	OEM	FWL200	0015	FZD33	OEM	G00-009-A	0143	G05-415	OEM	G060018-3R	OEM	G5.1T20	0162
FT5764M	OEM	FWL300	0015	FZD39	OEM	G00-012-A	0133	G05-415-B	0018	G060022-1R	OEM	G5.6T5	0157
FT5828DR	OEM	FWL400	0293	FZD47	OEM	G00-012A	0133	G05-416-C	1779	G060022-2R	OEM	G5.6T10	0157
FT6200	OEM	FWL500	0299	FZD56	OEM	G00-013-8	0143	G05-705	OEM	G060022-3R	OEM	G5.6T20	0157
FT7207A	OEM	FWL600	0299	FZD62	OEM	G00-014-A	0133	G05-706-D	0532	G060027-1R	OEM	G6	0015
FT7207B	OEM	FWL700	0250	FZD68	1976	G00-073-8	OEM	G05-706-E	0532	G060027-2R	OEM	G6A	OEM
FTD3440	0334	FWL800	0250	FZD82	OEM	G00-502-A	0015	G06-711-B	0555	G060027-3R	OEM	G6A3	OEM
FTIM	0102	FWL1000	0250	FZD100	OEM	G00-502A	0015	G06-714C	0219	G0Q-535-B	0015	G6B	OEM
FT0654A	OEM	FWLA50	0276	FZD120	OEM	G00-534-A	0015	G06-717-B	0161	G1	0015	G6B3	OEM
FT0654B	OEM	FWLA100	0276	FZD150	OEM	G00-535-B	0023	G06-717-B(10)	0561	G1A	3855	G6C	OEM
FT0654C	OEM	FWLA200	0287	FZD180	OEM	G00-535A	0015	G06-717-B,C,D	0561	G1B	0023	G6D	OEM
FT0654D	OEM	FWLA300	0293	FZH101	OEM	G00-536-A	0015	G06-717-C	0161	G1D	3855	G6D3	OEM
FT0654E	OEM	FWLA400	0293	FZH101A	OEM	G00-536A	0015	G06-717-D	0161	G1G	3855	G6E3	OEM
FTR129	0224	FWLA500	0299	FZH105A	OEM	G00-543-A	0015	G08-005L	0321	G1HA	0143	G6F	OEM
FTR1003A	OEM	FWLA600	0299	FZH111	OEM	G00-551-A	0015	G08-007-B	1270	G1J	0229	G6F3	OEM
FU1K	0102	FWLA700	0250	FZH111A	OEM	G00-803-A	0133	G08D	0087	G1K	2613	G6G3	OEM
FU-1M	0102	FWLA800	0250	FZH115B	OEM	G001A0A	OEM	G09-006-A	2247	G1M	2613	G6H3	OEM
FU1M	0102	FWLA1000	0250	FZH121	OEM	G001A0B	OEM	G09-006-B	2247	G1RG3K	1208	G6HZ	0122
FU-1MA	0023	FWLC50	0287	FZH125	OEM	G001A0C	OEM	G09-006-C	2247	G2	1219	G6K3	OEM
FU-1N	0023	FWLC100	0287	FZH131	OEM	G001A0D	OEM	G09-007-A	1983	G2A	0015	G6M3	OEM
FU1N	0102	FWLC200	0287	FZH135	OEM	G0011	0595	G09-007-B	1983	G2B	0087	G6N3	OEM
FU-1NA	0023	FWLC300	0293	FZH141	OEM	G00100B	OEM	G09-008-B	1012	G2D	0023	G6P3	OEM
FU1NA	0023	FWLC400	0293	FZH145	OEM	G00200B	OEM	G09-008-C	1012	G2DG1	0071	G6R3	OEM
FU1P	0102	FWLC500	0732	FZH151	OEM	G00500A	OEM	G09-008-D	1012	G2G	0087	G6S3	OEM
FU1U	0015	FWLC600	0299	FZH155	OEM	G00500B	OEM	G09-008-E	1012	G2J	0087	G6U	OEM
FU2	OEM	FWLC700	OEM	FZH161	OEM	G00500C	OEM	G09-009-A	1206	G2K	0087	G6.2T5	0631
FU5D-703E	OEM	FWLC800	0250	FZH165	OEM	G00500D	OEM	G09-009-C	OEM	G2M	0087	G6.2T10	0631
FU5F7715393	1545	FWLC1000	0250	FZH165B	OEM	G00502A	0023	G09-010-A	2247	G2SC1175-D	OEM	G6.2T20	0631
FU6A7709393	1695	FWLD50	0319	FZH171	OEM	G00515A	0198	G09-011-A	4338	G3	0015	G6.8T5	0025
FU-1043	0549	FWLD100	0319	FZH175	OEM	G00535	0015	G09-012-A	4338	G3A	0110	G6.8T10	0025
FU-IM	0023	FWLD200	1404	FZH181	OEM	G00535B	4176	G09-012-B	4338	G3A3	0594	G6.8T20	0025
FUIU	0015	FWLD300	OEM	FZH185	OEM	G01	0015	G09-012-C	4338	G3B	0947	G7	0911
FUL914-28	1063	FWLD400	0468	FZH191	OEM	G01-012-F	0170	G09-013-A	2111	G3B3	0594	G7A	0911
FUL923	OEM	FWLD500	OEM	FZH195	OEM	G01-036-G	0057	G09-013-A(1)	2111	G3C3	0594	G7D	0143
FUN14LH026	0438	FWLD600	0441	FZH201	OEM	G01-036-H	0012	G09-015-B	0574	G3D	0947	G7E	0143
FV5D770339	0627	FWLD700	OEM	FZH205	OEM	G01-036A	0631	G09-017-A	2632	G3D3	0594	G7F	0143
FV-11	0139	FWLD800	1412	FZH211	OEM	G01-037-A	0137	G09-017-B	2632	G3E3	0594	G7G	0143
FV21	0644	FWLD1000	OEM	FZH211S	OEM	G01-083-A	0133	G09-017-C	2632	G3F3	0594	G7SE211	0486
FV-22	0631	FX0003CE	OEM	FZH215B	OEM	G01-209-B	0133	G09-017-D	2632	G3G	0535	G7.5T5	0644
FV-23	0143	FX0007CE	1158	FZH231	OEM	G01-209B	0133	G09-018-A	2728	G3G3	0594	G7.5T10	0644
FV23	0143	FX0011CE	1158	FZH235	OEM	G01-217-A	0139	G09-028-A	0514	G3H3	1975	G7.5T20	0644
FV-24	0298	FX0014CE	1281	FZH241	OEM	G01-401-A	0030	G09-029-B	0428	G3J	0811	G8	0071
FV24	0133	FX41	OEM	FZH245	OEM	G01-406-A	0623	G09-029-C	1983	G3K	0811	G8HZ	OEM
FV123	OEM	FX45	OEM	FZH245B	OEM	G01-407-A	0030	G09-029-D	1983	G3K3	1975	G8.2T5	0244
FV214	0120	FX47	OEM	FZH251	OEM	G01-603-A	OEM	G09-029B	1983	G3M	0916	G8.2T10	0244
FV310G	OEM	FX274	0348	FZH255B	OEM	G01-803-A	0133	G09-034-A	0514	G3M3	0652	G8.2T20	0244
FV914	0144	FX709	0127	FZH261	OEM	G01-803A	0133	G09-502-A	OEM	G3N3	0652	G9.1T5	0012
FV918	0144	FX914	0224	FZH265B	OEM	G01A	0911	G09-505-A	OEM	G3.0T5	1703	G9.1T10	0012
FV1006	OEM	FX918	0224	FZH271	OEM	G02	0015	G09-508-A	OEM	G3.0T10	1703	G9.1T20	0012
FV1006A	OEM	FX2368	0079	FZH275	OEM	G02A	0911	G0500.5B	OEM	G3.0T20	1703	G10	0071
FV1006B	OEM	FX2369A	0224	FZH281	OEM	G03-007	OEM	G01036	0012	G3.3T5	0289	G10HZ	OEM
FV1006C	OEM	FX2483	0855	FZH285B	OEM	G03-007C	0161	G01209	0133	G3.3T10	0289	G10T5	0170
FV1006D	OEM	FX2894	0037	FZH291	OEM	G03-014	OEM	G01211	0015	G3.3T20	0289	G10T10	0170
FV1008	OEM	FX3013	0224	FZH295B	OEM	G03-017-B	0006	G01401A	0715	G3.6T5	0188	G10T20	0170
FV1008A	OEM	FX3014	0224	FZH301	OEM	G03-404-B	0126	G01803	0133	G3.6T10	0188	G11	0004
FV1008B	OEM	FX3299	0018	FZH305	OEM	G03-404-C	0126	G03001B-2R	OEM	G3.6T20	1703	G11T5	0313
FV1008C	OEM	FX3300	0079	FZJ101	OEM	G03-406-C	0455	G03007	0037	G3.9T5	0451	G11T10	0313
FV1008D	OEM	FX3502	0855	FZJ105	OEM	G03-406-C(5)	1357	G03014	0527	G3.9T10	0451	G11T20	0313
FV1010	OEM	FX3724	0018	FZJ111	OEM	G03-407-Y	0006	G05001B	OEM	G3.9T20	0451	G12	0004
FV1010A	OEM	FX3962	0786	FZJ115	OEM	G03-703C	0676	G05005B	OEM	G4	0015	G12T5	0137
FV1010B	OEM	FX3964	0688	FZJ121	OEM	G04-041B	0127	G05010B	OEM	G4A	0087	G12T10	0137
FV1010C	OEM	FX4046	0079	FZJ125	OEM	G04-701-A	0160	G05015	0198	G4A3	0594	G12T20	0137
FV1010D	OEM	FX4960	0590	FZJ131	OEM	G04-704-A	0222	G05015D	0198	G4B	0947	G13	0050
FV1012	OEM	FZ-2	OEM	FZJ135	OEM	G04-711-E	0164	G05015E	0198	G4B3	0594	G13T5	0361
FV1012A	OEM	FZ3.6T5	0188	FZJ141	OEM	G04-711-F	0164	G05020B	OEM	G4C3	0594	G13T10	0361
FV1012B	OEM	FZ3.6T10	0188	FZJ141A	OEM	G04-711-F,E,G,H	0164	G05035	0016	G4D	0242	G13T20	0361
FV1012C	OEM	FZ-4	OEM	FZJ145A	OEM	G04-711-G	0164	G05036	0016	G4D3	0594	G14	0004
FV1012D	OEM	FZ5.1T5	0162	FZJ151	OEM	G04-711-H	0164	G05041A	OEM	G4E3	0594	G15R4	OEM
FV1014	OEM	FZ5.1T10	0162	FZJ151A	OEM	G05-003-A	0326	G05050B	OEM	G4F3	0594	G15T5	0137
FV1014A	OEM	FZ5.6T5	0157	FZJ155A	OEM	G05-003-B	0151	G05059	0016	G4G	0535	G15T10	0002
FV1014B	OEM	FZ5.6T10	0157	FZJ161	OEM	G05-004A	0144	G05415	0018	G4G3	0594	G15T20	0002

If replacement code is OEM, contact original manufacturer for replacement.

DEVICE TYPE	REPL CODE
G16	0038
G16T5	0416
G16T10	0416
G16T20	0416
G17	0038
G18	0038
G18T5	0490
G18T10	0490
G18T20	0490
G19	0160
G20T5	0526
G20T10	0526
G20T20	0526
G22T5	0560
G22T10	0560
G22T20	0560
G24T5	0398
G24T10	0398
G24T20	0398
G25X01G	OEM
G25X02G	OEM
G25X15G	OEM
G27T5	0436
G27T10	0436
G27T20	0436
G30R4	OEM
G30T5	0721
G30T10	0721
G30T20	0721
G50X01D	OEM
G50X02D	OEM
G50X15D	OEM
G60R4	OEM
G65HZ	OEM
G65SC02C-3	OEM
G65SC02C-4	OEM
G65SC02CI-3	OEM
G65SC02CI-4	OEM
G65SC02CM-2	OEM
G65SC02CM-3	OEM
G65SC02CM-4	OEM
G65SC02D-3	OEM
G65SC02D-4	OEM
G65SC02DI-3	OEM
G65SC02DI-4	OEM
G65SC02DM-2	OEM
G65SC02DM-3	OEM
G65SC02DM-4	OEM
G65SC02E-3	OEM
G65SC02E-4	OEM
G65SC02EI-3	OEM
G65SC02EI-4	OEM
G65SC02EM-2	OEM
G65SC02EM-3	OEM
G65SC02EM-4	OEM
G65SC02P-3	OEM
G65SC02P-4	OEM
G65SC02PI-3	OEM
G65SC02PI-4	OEM
G65SC02PM-3	OEM
G65SC02X-3	OEM
G65SC02X-4	OEM
G65SC02XI-4	OEM
G65SC02XM-2	OEM
G65SC02XM-3	OEM
G65SC02XM-4	OEM
G65SC03C-1	OEM
G65SC03C-2	OEM
G65SC03C-3	OEM
G65SC03C-4	OEM
G65SC03CI-2	OEM
G65SC03CI-3	OEM
G65SC03CI-4	OEM
G65SC03CM-1	OEM
G65SC03CM-2	OEM
G65SC03CM-3	OEM
G65SC03CM-4	OEM
G65SC03D-1	OEM
G65SC03D-2	OEM
G65SC03D-3	OEM
G65SC03D-4	OEM
G65SC03DI-1	OEM
G65SC03DI-2	OEM
G65SC03DI-3	OEM
G65SC03DI-4	OEM
G65SC03DM-1	OEM
G65SC03DM-2	OEM
G65SC03DM-3	OEM
G65SC03DM-4	OEM
G65SC03E-1	OEM
G65SC03E-3	OEM
G65SC03E-4	OEM
G65SC03EI-1	OEM
G65SC03EI-2	OEM
G65SC03EI-3	OEM
G65SC03EI-4	OEM
G65SC03EM-1	OEM
G65SC03EM-2	OEM
G65SC03EM-3	OEM
G65SC03EM-4	OEM
G65SC03P-1	OEM
G65SC03P-2	OEM
G65SC03P-3	OEM
G65SC03P-4	OEM
G65SC03PI-1	OEM
G65SC03PI-2	OEM
G65SC03PI-3	OEM
G65SC03PI-4	OEM
G65SC03PM-1	OEM
G65SC03PM-2	OEM
G65SC03PM-3	OEM
G65SC03PM-4	OEM
G65SC03X-1	OEM
G65SC03X-2	OEM
G65SC03X-3	OEM
G65SC03X-4	OEM
G65SC03XI-1	OEM
G65SC03XI-2	OEM
G65SC03XI-3	OEM
G65SC03XI-4	OEM
G65SC03XM-1	OEM
G65SC03XM-2	OEM
G65SC03XM-3	OEM
G65SC03XM-4	OEM
G65SC04C04	OEM
G65SC04C-3	OEM
G65SC04CI-2	OEM
G65SC04CI-3	OEM
G65SC04CI-4	OEM
G65SC04CM-2	OEM
G65SC04CM-3	OEM
G65SC04CM-4	OEM
G65SC04D-3	OEM
G65SC04D-4	OEM
G65SC04DI-2	OEM
G65SC04DI-3	OEM
G65SC04DI-4	OEM
G65SC04DM-2	OEM
G65SC04DM-3	OEM
G65SC04DM-4	OEM
G65SC04E-3	OEM
G65SC04E-4	OEM
G65SC04EI-2	OEM
G65SC04EI-3	OEM
G65SC04EI-4	OEM
G65SC04EM-2	OEM
G65SC04EM-3	OEM
G65SC04EM-4	OEM
G65SC04P-3	OEM
G65SC04P-4	OEM
G65SC04PI-2	OEM
G65SC04PI-3	OEM
G65SC04PI-4	OEM
G65SC04PM-2	OEM
G65SC04PM-3	OEM
G65SC04PM-4	OEM
G65SC04X-3	OEM
G65SC04X-4	OEM
G65SC04XI-2	OEM
G65SC04XI-3	OEM
G65SC04XI-4	OEM
G65SC04XM-2	OEM
G65SC04XM-3	OEM
G65SC04XM-4	OEM
G65SC05C-1	OEM
G65SC05C-2	OEM
G65SC05C-3	OEM
G65SC05C-4	OEM
G65SC05CI-1	OEM
G65SC05CI-2	OEM
G65SC05CI-3	OEM
G65SC05CI-4	OEM
G65SC05CM-1	OEM
G65SC05CM-2	OEM
G65SC05CM-3	OEM
G65SC05CM-4	OEM
G65SC05D-1	OEM
G65SC05D-2	OEM
G65SC05D-3	OEM
G65SC05D-4	OEM
G65SC05DI-1	OEM
G65SC05DI-2	OEM
G65SC05DI-3	OEM
G65SC05DI-4	OEM
G65SC05DM-1	OEM
G65SC05DM-2	OEM
G65SC05DM-3	OEM
G65SC05DM-4	OEM
G65SC05E-1	OEM
G65SC05E-2	OEM
G65SC05E-3	OEM
G65SC05E-4	OEM
G65SC05EI-1	OEM
G65SC05EI-2	OEM
G65SC05EI-3	OEM
G65SC05EI-4	OEM
G65SC05EM-1	OEM
G65SC05EM-2	OEM
G65SC05EM-3	OEM
G65SC05EM-4	OEM
G65SC05P-1	OEM
G65SC05P-2	OEM
G65SC05P-3	OEM
G65SC05P-4	OEM
G65SC05PI-1	OEM
G65SC05PI-2	OEM
G65SC05PI-3	OEM
G65SC05PI-4	OEM
G65SC05PM-1	OEM
G65SC05PM-2	OEM
G65SC05PM-3	OEM
G65SC05PM-4	OEM
G65SC05X-1	OEM
G65SC05X-2	OEM
G65SC05X-4	OEM
G65SC05XI-1	OEM
G65SC05XI-2	OEM
G65SC05XI-3	OEM
G65SC05XM-1	OEM
G65SC05XM-2	OEM
G65SC05XM-3	OEM
G65SC06C-2	OEM
G65SC06C-3	OEM
G65SC06C-4	OEM
G65SC06CI-1	OEM
G65SC06CI-2	OEM
G65SC06CI-3	OEM
G65SC06CI-4	OEM
G65SC06CM-1	OEM
G65SC06CM-2	OEM
G65SC06CM-3	OEM
G65SC06CM-4	OEM
G65SC06D-1	OEM
G65SC06D-2	OEM
G65SC06D-3	OEM
G65SC06D-4	OEM
G65SC06DI-1	OEM
G65SC06DI-2	OEM
G65SC06DI-3	OEM
G65SC06DI-4	OEM
G65SC06DM-1	OEM
G65SC06DM-2	OEM
G65SC06DM-3	OEM
G65SC06DM-4	OEM
G65SC06E-1	OEM
G65SC06E-2	OEM
G65SC06E-3	OEM
G65SC06E-4	OEM
G65SC06EI-1	OEM
G65SC06EI-2	OEM
G65SC06EI-3	OEM
G65SC06EI-4	OEM
G65SC06EM-1	OEM
G65SC06EM-2	OEM
G65SC06EM-3	OEM
G65SC06EM-4	OEM
G65SC06P-2	OEM
G65SC06P-3	OEM
G65SC06P-4	OEM
G65SC06PI-1	OEM
G65SC06PI-2	OEM
G65SC06PI-3	OEM
G65SC06PI-4	OEM
G65SC06PM-1	OEM
G65SC06PM-2	OEM
G65SC06PM-3	OEM
G65SC06PM-4	OEM
G65SC06X-1	OEM
G65SC06X-2	OEM
G65SC06X-3	OEM
G65SC06X-4	OEM
G65SC06XI-1	OEM
G65SC06XI-2	OEM
G65SC06XI-3	OEM
G65SC06XI-4	OEM
G65SC06XM-1	OEM
G65SC06XM-2	OEM
G65SC06XM-3	OEM
G65SC06XM-4	OEM
G65SC07C-1	OEM
G65SC07C-2	OEM
G65SC07C-3	OEM
G65SC07CI-1	OEM
G65SC07CI-2	OEM
G65SC07CI-3	OEM
G65SC07CM-1	OEM
G65SC07CM-2	OEM
G65SC07D-1	OEM
G65SC07D-2	OEM
G65SC07D-3	OEM
G65SC07DI-1	OEM
G65SC07DI-2	OEM
G65SC07DI-3	OEM
G65SC07DM-1	OEM
G65SC07DM-2	OEM
G65SC07E-1	OEM
G65SC07E-2	OEM
G65SC07E-3	OEM
G65SC07EI-1	OEM
G65SC07EI-2	OEM
G65SC07EI-3	OEM
G65SC07EM-1	OEM
G65SC07EM-2	OEM
G65SC07P-1	OEM
G65SC07P-2	OEM
G65SC07P-3	OEM
G65SC07PI-1	OEM
G65SC07PI-2	OEM
G65SC07PI-3	OEM
G65SC07PM-1	OEM
G65SC07X-1	OEM
G65SC07X-2	OEM
G65SC07X-3	OEM
G65SC07XI-1	OEM
G65SC07XI-2	OEM
G65SC07XI-3	OEM
G65SC07XM-1	OEM
G65SC07XM-2	OEM
G65SC12C-1	OEM
G65SC12C-2	OEM
G65SC12C-3	OEM
G65SC12C-4	OEM
G65SC12CI-1	OEM
G65SC12CI-2	OEM
G65SC12CI-3	OEM
G65SC12CI-4	OEM
G65SC12CM-1	OEM
G65SC12CM-2	OEM
G65SC12CM-3	OEM
G65SC12CM-4	OEM
G65SC12D-1	OEM
G65SC12D-2	OEM
G65SC12D-3	OEM
G65SC12D-4	OEM
G65SC12DI-1	OEM
G65SC12DI-2	OEM
G65SC12DI-4	OEM
G65SC12DM-1	OEM
G65SC12DM-2	OEM
G65SC12DM-3	OEM
G65SC12DM-4	OEM
G65SC12E-1	OEM
G65SC12E-2	OEM
G65SC12E-3	OEM
G65SC12E-4	OEM
G65SC12EI-1	OEM
G65SC12EI-2	OEM
G65SC12EI-3	OEM
G65SC12EI-4	OEM
G65SC12EM-1	OEM
G65SC12EM-2	OEM
G65SC12EM-3	OEM
G65SC12EM-4	OEM
G65SC12P-1	OEM
G65SC12P-2	OEM
G65SC12P-3	OEM
G65SC12P-4	OEM
G65SC12PI-1	OEM
G65SC12PI-2	OEM
G65SC12PI-3	OEM
G65SC12PI-4	OEM
G65SC12PM-1	OEM
G65SC12PM-2	OEM
G65SC12PM-3	OEM
G65SC12PM-4	OEM
G65SC12X-1	OEM
G65SC12X-2	OEM
G65SC12X-3	OEM
G65SC12X-4	OEM
G65SC12XI-1	OEM
G65SC12XI-2	OEM
G65SC12XI-3	OEM
G65SC12XI-4	OEM
G65SC12XM-1	OEM
G65SC12XM-2	OEM
G65SC12XM-3	OEM
G65SC12XM-4	OEM
G65SC13C-1	OEM
G65SC13C-2	OEM
G65SC13C-3	OEM
G65SC13C-4	OEM
G65SC13CI-1	OEM
G65SC13CI-2	OEM
G65SC13CI-4	OEM
G65SC13CM-1	OEM
G65SC13CM-2	OEM
G65SC13CM-3	OEM
G65SC13CM-4	OEM
G65SC13D-1	OEM
G65SC13D-2	OEM
G65SC13D-3	OEM
G65SC13D-4	OEM
G65SC13DI-1	OEM
G65SC13DI-2	OEM
G65SC13DI-3	OEM
G65SC13DI-4	OEM
G65SC13DM-1	OEM
G65SC13DM-2	OEM
G65SC13DM-3	OEM
G65SC13DM-4	OEM
G65SC13E-1	OEM
G65SC13E-2	OEM
G65SC13E-3	OEM
G65SC13E-4	OEM
G65SC13EI-1	OEM
G65SC13EI-2	OEM
G65SC13EI-3	OEM
G65SC13EI-4	OEM
G65SC13EM-1	OEM
G65SC13EM-2	OEM
G65SC13EM-3	OEM
G65SC13EM-4	OEM
G65SC13P-1	OEM
G65SC13P-2	OEM
G65SC13P-3	OEM
G65SC13PI-1	OEM
G65SC13PI-2	OEM
G65SC13PI-3	OEM
G65SC13PI-4	OEM
G65SC13PM-1	OEM
G65SC13PM-2	OEM
G65SC13PM-3	OEM
G65SC13PM-4	OEM
G65SC13X-1	OEM
G65SC13X-2	OEM
G65SC13X-3	OEM
G65SC13X-4	OEM
G65SC13XI-1	OEM
G65SC13XI-2	OEM
G65SC13XI-3	OEM
G65SC13XI-4	OEM
G65SC13XM-1	OEM
G65SC13XM-2	OEM
G65SC13XM-3	OEM
G65SC13XM-4	OEM
G65SC14C-1	OEM
G65SC14C-2	OEM
G65SC14C-3	OEM
G65SC14C-4	OEM
G65SC14CI-1	OEM
G65SC14CI-2	OEM
G65SC14CI-3	OEM
G65SC14CI-4	OEM
G65SC14CM-1	OEM
G65SC14CM-2	OEM
G65SC14CM-3	OEM
G65SC14CM-4	OEM
G65SC14D-1	OEM
G65SC14D-2	OEM
G65SC14D-3	OEM
G65SC14D-4	OEM
G65SC14DI-1	OEM
G65SC14DI-2	OEM
G65SC14DI-3	OEM
G65SC14DI-4	OEM
G65SC14DM-1	OEM
G65SC14DM-2	OEM
G65SC14DM-3	OEM
G65SC14DM-4	OEM
G65SC14E-1	OEM
G65SC14E-2	OEM
G65SC14E-3	OEM
G65SC14E-4	OEM
G65SC14EI-1	OEM
G65SC14EI-2	OEM
G65SC14EI-3	OEM
G65SC14EI-4	OEM
G65SC14EM-1	OEM
G65SC14EM-2	OEM
G65SC14EM-3	OEM
G65SC14EM-4	OEM
G65SC14P-1	OEM
G65SC14P-2	OEM
G65SC14P-3	OEM
G65SC14P-4	OEM
G65SC14PI-1	OEM
G65SC14PI-2	OEM
G65SC14PI-3	OEM
G65SC14PI-4	OEM
G65SC14PM-1	OEM
G65SC14PM-2	OEM
G65SC14PM-3	OEM
G65SC14PM-4	OEM
G65SC14X-1	OEM
G65SC14X-2	OEM
G65SC14X-3	OEM
G65SC14XI-1	OEM
G65SC14XI-2	OEM
G65SC14XI-3	OEM
G65SC14XI-4	OEM
G65SC14XM-1	OEM
G65SC14XM-2	OEM
G65SC14XM-3	OEM
G65SC14XM-4	OEM
G65SC15C-1	OEM
G65SC15C-2	OEM
G65SC15C-3	OEM
G65SC15C-4	OEM
G65SC15CI-1	OEM
G65SC15CI-2	OEM
G65SC15CI-3	OEM
G65SC15CI-4	OEM
G65SC15CM-1	OEM
G65SC15CM-2	OEM
G65SC15CM-3	OEM
G65SC15CM-4	OEM
G65SC15D-1	OEM
G65SC15D-2	OEM
G65SC15D-3	OEM
G65SC15D-4	OEM
G65SC15DI-1	OEM
G65SC15DI-2	OEM
G65SC15DI-3	OEM
G65SC15DI-4	OEM
G65SC15DM-1	OEM
G65SC15DM-2	OEM
G65SC15DM-3	OEM
G65SC15DM-4	OEM
G65SC15E-1	OEM
G65SC15E-2	OEM
G65SC15E-3	OEM
G65SC15E-4	OEM
G65SC15EI-1	OEM
G65SC15EI-2	OEM
G65SC15EI-3	OEM
G65SC15EI-4	OEM
G65SC15EM-1	OEM
G65SC15EM-2	OEM
G65SC15EM-3	OEM
G65SC15EM-4	OEM
G65SC15P-1	OEM
G65SC15P-2	OEM
G65SC15P-3	OEM
G65SC15P-4	OEM
G65SC15PI-1	OEM
G65SC15PI-2	OEM
G65SC15PI-3	OEM
G65SC15PI-4	OEM
G65SC15PM-1	OEM
G65SC15PM-2	OEM
G65SC15PM-3	OEM
G65SC15PM-4	OEM
G65SC15X-1	OEM
G65SC15X-2	OEM
G65SC15X-3	OEM
G65SC15X-4	OEM
G65SC15XI-1	OEM
G65SC15XI-2	OEM
G65SC15XI-3	OEM
G65SC15XI-4	OEM
G65SC15XM-1	OEM
G65SC15XM-2	OEM
G65SC15XM-3	OEM
G65SC15XM-4	OEM
G65SC22P-2	OEM
G65SC102C-1	OEM
G65SC102C-2	OEM
G65SC102C-3	OEM
G65SC102C-4	OEM
G65SC102CI-1	OEM
G65SC102CI-2	OEM
G65SC102CI-3	OEM
G65SC102CI-4	OEM
G65SC102CM-1	OEM
G65SC102CM-2	OEM
G65SC102CM-3	OEM
G65SC102CM-4	OEM
G65SC102D-1	OEM
G65SC102D-2	OEM
G65SC102D-3	OEM
G65SC102D-4	OEM
G65SC102DI-1	OEM
G65SC102DI-2	OEM
G65SC102DI-3	OEM
G65SC102DI-4	OEM
G65SC102DM-1	OEM
G65SC102DM-2	OEM
G65SC102DM-3	OEM
G65SC102DM-4	OEM
G65SC102E-1	OEM
G65SC102E-2	OEM
G65SC102E-3	OEM
G65SC102E-4	OEM
G65SC102EI-1	OEM
G65SC102EI-2	OEM
G65SC102EI-3	OEM
G65SC102EI-4	OEM
G65SC102EM-2	OEM
G65SC102EM-3	OEM
G65SC102EM-4	OEM
G65SC102P-1	OEM
G65SC102P-2	OEM
G65SC102P-3	OEM
G65SC102P-4	OEM
G65SC102PI-1	OEM
G65SC102PI-2	OEM
G65SC102PI-3	OEM
G65SC102PI-4	OEM
G65SC102PM-1	OEM
G65SC102PM-2	OEM
G65SC102PM-3	OEM
G65SC102PM-4	OEM
G65SC102X-1	OEM
G65SC102X-2	OEM
G65SC102X-3	OEM
G65SC102X-4	OEM
G65SC102XI-1	OEM
G65SC102XI-2	OEM
G65SC102XI-3	OEM
G65SC102XI-4	OEM
G65SC102XM-1	OEM
G65SC102XM-2	OEM
G65SC102XM-3	OEM
G65SC102XM-4	OEM
G65SC103C-1	OEM
G65SC103C-2	OEM
G65SC103C-3	OEM
G65SC103C-4	OEM
G65SC103CI-1	OEM
G65SC103CI-2	OEM
G65SC103CI-3	OEM
G65SC103CI-4	OEM
G65SC103CM-1	OEM
G65SC103CM-2	OEM
G65SC103CM-3	OEM
G65SC103CM-4	OEM
G65SC103D-1	OEM
G65SC103D-2	OEM
G65SC103D-3	OEM
G65SC103D-4	OEM
G65SC103DI-1	OEM
G65SC103DI-2	OEM
G65SC103DI-3	OEM
G65SC103DI-4	OEM
G65SC103DM-1	OEM
G65SC103DM-2	OEM
G65SC103DM-3	OEM
G65SC103DM-4	OEM
G65SC103E-1	OEM
G65SC103E-2	OEM
G65SC103E-3	OEM
G65SC103E-4	OEM
G65SC103EI-1	OEM
G65SC103EI-2	OEM
G65SC103EI-3	OEM
G65SC103EI-4	OEM
G65SC103EM-1	OEM
G65SC103EM-2	OEM
G65SC103EM-3	OEM
G65SC103P-1	OEM
G65SC103P-2	OEM
G65SC103P-3	OEM
G65SC103PI-1	OEM
G65SC103PI-2	OEM
G65SC103PI-3	OEM
G65SC103PI-4	OEM
G65SC103PM-1	OEM
G65SC103PM-2	OEM
G65SC103PM-3	OEM
G65SC103PM-4	OEM
G65SC103X-1	OEM
G65SC103X-2	OEM
G65SC103X-3	OEM
G65SC103XI-1	OEM
G65SC103XI-2	OEM
G65SC103XI-3	OEM
G65SC103XI-4	OEM
G65SC103XM-1	OEM
G65SC103XM-2	OEM
G65SC103XM-3	OEM
G65SC103XM-4	OEM
G65SC104C-1	OEM
G65SC104C-3	OEM
G65SC104C-4	OEM
G65SC104CI-1	OEM
G65SC104CI-2	OEM
G65SC104CI-3	OEM
G65SC104CM-1	OEM
G65SC104CM-2	OEM
G65SC104CM-3	OEM
G65SC104CM-4	OEM
G65SC104D-1	OEM
G65SC104D-2	OEM
G65SC104D-3	OEM
G65SC104D-4	OEM
G65SC104DI-1	OEM
G65SC104DI-2	OEM
G65SC104DI-3	OEM
G65SC104DM-1	OEM
G65SC104DM-2	OEM
G65SC104DM-3	OEM
G65SC104DM-4	OEM
G65SC104E-1	OEM
G65SC104E-2	OEM
G65SC104E-3	OEM
G65SC104E-4	OEM
G65SC104EI-1	OEM
G65SC104EI-2	OEM
G65SC104EI-3	OEM
G65SC104EM-1	OEM
G65SC104EM-2	OEM
G65SC104EM-3	OEM
G65SC104EM-4	OEM
G65SC104P-1	OEM
G65SC104P-2	OEM
G65SC104P-3	OEM
G65SC104P-4	OEM
G65SC104PI-1	OEM
G65SC104PI-2	OEM
G65SC104PI-3	OEM
G65SC104PM-1	OEM
G65SC104PM-2	OEM
G65SC104PM-4	OEM
G65SC104X-1	OEM
G65SC104X-2	OEM
G65SC104X-3	OEM
G65SC104XI-1	OEM
G65SC104XI-2	OEM
G65SC104XI-3	OEM
G65SC104XM-1	OEM
G65SC104XM-2	OEM
G65SC104XM-3	OEM
G65SC104XM-4	OEM
G65SC105C-1	OEM
G65SC105C-2	OEM
G65SC105C-3	OEM
G65SC105C-4	OEM
G65SC105CI-1	OEM
G65SC105CI-2	OEM
G65SC105CI-3	OEM
G65SC105CI-4	OEM
G65SC105CM-1	OEM
G65SC105CM-2	OEM
G65SC105CM-3	OEM
G65SC105CM-4	OEM
G65SC105D-1	OEM
G65SC105D-2	OEM
G65SC105D-3	OEM
G65SC105D-4	OEM
G65SC105DI-1	OEM
G65SC105DI-2	OEM
G65SC105DI-3	OEM
G65SC105DI-4	OEM
G65SC105DM-1	OEM
G65SC105DM-2	OEM
G65SC105DM-3	OEM
G65SC105DM-4	OEM
G65SC105E-1	OEM
G65SC105E-2	OEM
G65SC105E-3	OEM
G65SC105E-4	OEM
G65SC105EI-1	OEM
G65SC105EI-2	OEM
G65SC105EI-3	OEM
G65SC105EI-4	OEM
G65SC105EM-1	OEM
G65SC105EM-2	OEM
G65SC105EM-4	OEM
G65SC105P-1	OEM
G65SC105P-2	OEM
G65SC105P-3	OEM
G65SC105P-4	OEM
G65SC105PI-1	OEM

If replacement code is OEM, contact original manufacturer for replacement.

DEVICE TYPE	REPL CODE
G65SC105PI-2	OEM
G65SC105PI-3	OEM
G65SC105PI-4	OEM
G65SC105PM-1	OEM
G65SC105PM-2	OEM
G65SC105PM-3	OEM
G65SC105PM-4	OEM
G65SC105X-1	OEM
G65SC105X-2	OEM
G65SC105X-3	OEM
G65SC105X-4	OEM
G65SC105XI-1	OEM
G65SC105XI-2	OEM
G65SC105XI-3	OEM
G65SC105XI-4	OEM
G65SC105XM-1	OEM
G65SC105XM-2	OEM
G65SC105XM-3	OEM
G65SC105XM-4	OEM
G65SC106C-1	OEM
G65SC106C-2	OEM
G65SC106C-3	OEM
G65SC106C-4	OEM
G65SC106CI-1	OEM
G65SC106CI-2	OEM
G65SC106CI-3	OEM
G65SC106CI-4	OEM
G65SC106CM-1	OEM
G65SC106CM-2	OEM
G65SC106CM-3	OEM
G65SC106CM-4	OEM
G65SC106D-1	OEM
G65SC106D-2	OEM
G65SC106D-3	OEM
G65SC106D-4	OEM
G65SC106DI-1	OEM
G65SC106DI-2	OEM
G65SC106DI-3	OEM
G65SC106DI-4	OEM
G65SC106DM-1	OEM
G65SC106DM-2	OEM
G65SC106DM-3	OEM
G65SC106DM-4	OEM
G65SC106E-1	OEM
G65SC106E-2	OEM
G65SC106E-3	OEM
G65SC106E-4	OEM
G65SC106EI-1	OEM
G65SC106EI-2	OEM
G65SC106EI-3	OEM
G65SC106EI-4	OEM
G65SC106EM-1	OEM
G65SC106EM-2	OEM
G65SC106EM-3	OEM
G65SC106EM-4	OEM
G65SC106P-1	OEM
G65SC106P-2	OEM
G65SC106P-3	OEM
G65SC106P-4	OEM
G65SC106PI-1	OEM
G65SC106PI-2	OEM
G65SC106PI-3	OEM
G65SC106PI-4	OEM
G65SC106PM-1	OEM
G65SC106PM-2	OEM
G65SC106PM-3	OEM
G65SC106PM-4	OEM
G65SC106X-1	OEM
G65SC106X-2	OEM
G65SC106X-3	OEM
G65SC106X-4	OEM
G65SC106XI-1	OEM
G65SC106XI-2	OEM
G65SC106XI-3	OEM
G65SC106XI-4	OEM
G65SC106XM-1	OEM
G65SC106XM-2	OEM
G65SC106XM-3	OEM
G65SC106XM-4	OEM
G65SC107C-1	OEM
G65SC107C-2	OEM
G65SC107C-3	OEM
G65SC107C-4	OEM
G65SC107CI-1	OEM
G65SC107CI-2	OEM
G65SC107CI-3	OEM
G65SC107CI-4	OEM
G65SC107CM-1	OEM
G65SC107CM-2	OEM
G65SC107CM-3	OEM
G65SC107CM-4	OEM
G65SC107D-1	OEM
G65SC107D-2	OEM
G65SC107D-3	OEM
G65SC107D-4	OEM
G65SC107DI-1	OEM
G65SC107DI-2	OEM
G65SC107DI-3	OEM
G65SC107DI-4	OEM
G65SC107DM-1	OEM
G65SC107DM-2	OEM
G65SC107DM-3	OEM
G65SC107DM-4	OEM
G65SC107E-1	OEM
G65SC107E-2	OEM
G65SC107E-3	OEM
G65SC107E-4	OEM
G65SC107EI-1	OEM
G65SC107EI-2	OEM

DEVICE TYPE	REPL CODE
G65SC107EI-3	OEM
G65SC107EI-4	OEM
G65SC107EM-1	OEM
G65SC107EM-2	OEM
G65SC107EM-3	OEM
G65SC107EM-4	OEM
G65SC107P-1	OEM
G65SC107P-2	OEM
G65SC107P-3	OEM
G65SC107P-4	OEM
G65SC107PI-1	OEM
G65SC107PI-2	OEM
G65SC107PI-3	OEM
G65SC107PI-4	OEM
G65SC107PM-1	OEM
G65SC107PM-2	OEM
G65SC107PM-3	OEM
G65SC107PM-4	OEM
G65SC107X-1	OEM
G65SC107X-2	OEM
G65SC107X-4	OEM
G65SC107XI-1	OEM
G65SC107XI-2	OEM
G65SC107XI-3	OEM
G65SC107XI-4	OEM
G65SC107XM-1	OEM
G65SC107XM-2	OEM
G65SC107XM-3	OEM
G65SC107XM-4	OEM
G65SC112C-1	OEM
G65SC112C-2	OEM
G65SC112C-3	OEM
G65SC112C-4	OEM
G65SC112CI-1	OEM
G65SC112CI-2	OEM
G65SC112CI-3	OEM
G65SC112CI-4	OEM
G65SC112CM-1	OEM
G65SC112CM-2	OEM
G65SC112CM-3	OEM
G65SC112CM-4	OEM
G65SC112D-1	OEM
G65SC112D-2	OEM
G65SC112D-3	OEM
G65SC112D-4	OEM
G65SC112DI-1	OEM
G65SC112DI-3	OEM
G65SC112DI-4	OEM
G65SC112DM-1	OEM
G65SC112DM-2	OEM
G65SC112DM-3	OEM
G65SC112DM-4	OEM
G65SC112E-1	OEM
G65SC112E-2	OEM
G65SC112E-3	OEM
G65SC112E-4	OEM
G65SC112EI-1	OEM
G65SC112EI-2	OEM
G65SC112EI-3	OEM
G65SC112EI-4	OEM
G65SC112EM-1	OEM
G65SC112EM-2	OEM
G65SC112EM-3	OEM
G65SC112EM-4	OEM
G65SC112P-1	OEM
G65SC112P-2	OEM
G65SC112P-3	OEM
G65SC112P-4	OEM
G65SC112PI-1	OEM
G65SC112PI-2	OEM
G65SC112PI-3	OEM
G65SC112PM-1	OEM
G65SC112PM-2	OEM
G65SC112PM-3	OEM
G65SC112PM-4	OEM
G65SC112X-1	OEM
G65SC112X-2	OEM
G65SC112X-3	OEM
G65SC112X-4	OEM
G65SC112XI-1	OEM
G65SC112XI-2	OEM
G65SC112XI-3	OEM
G65SC112XI-4	OEM
G65SC112XM-1	OEM
G65SC112XM-2	OEM
G65SC112XM-3	OEM
G65SC112XM-4	OEM
G65SC115C-1	OEM
G65SC115C-2	OEM
G65SC115C-3	OEM
G65SC115C-4	OEM
G65SC115CI-1	OEM
G65SC115CI-2	OEM
G65SC115CI-3	OEM
G65SC115CI-4	OEM
G65SC115CM-1	OEM
G65SC115CM-2	OEM
G65SC115CM-3	OEM
G65SC115CM-4	OEM
G65SC115D-2	OEM
G65SC115D-3	OEM
G65SC115D-4	OEM
G65SC115DI-1	OEM
G65SC115DI-2	OEM
G65SC115DI-3	OEM
G65SC115DI-4	OEM
G65SC115DM-1	OEM
G65SC115DM-2	OEM
G65SC115DM-3	OEM

DEVICE TYPE	REPL CODE
G65SC115DM-4	OEM
G65SC115E-1	OEM
G65SC115E-2	OEM
G65SC115E-3	OEM
G65SC115E-4	OEM
G65SC115EI-1	OEM
G65SC115EI-2	OEM
G65SC115EI-3	OEM
G65SC115EI-4	OEM
G65SC115EM-1	OEM
G65SC115EM-2	OEM
G65SC115EM-3	OEM
G65SC115EM-4	OEM
G65SC115P-1	OEM
G65SC115P-2	OEM
G65SC115P-3	OEM
G65SC115P-4	OEM
G65SC115PI-1	OEM
G65SC115PI-2	OEM
G65SC115PI-3	OEM
G65SC115PI-4	OEM
G65SC115PM-1	OEM
G65SC115PM-2	OEM
G65SC115PM-3	OEM
G65SC115PM-4	OEM
G65SC115X-1	OEM
G65SC115X-2	OEM
G65SC115X-3	OEM
G65SC115X-4	OEM
G65SC115XI-1	OEM
G65SC115XI-2	OEM
G65SC115XI-3	OEM
G65SC115XI-4	OEM
G65SC115XM-1	OEM
G65SC115XM-2	OEM
G65SC115XM-3	OEM
G65SC115XM-4	OEM
G65SC140PM-3	OEM
G65SC150EM-3	OEM
G65SC1103EM-4	OEM
G65SCP7PM-2	OEM
G65XC05X-3	OEM
G74SC137D	OEM
G74SC137P	OEM
G74SC138D	OEM
G74SC138P	OEM
G74SC139D	OEM
G74SC139P	OEM
G74SC240D	OEM
G74SC240P	OEM
G74SC241D	OEM
G74SC241P	OEM
G74SC244D	OEM
G74SC244P	OEM
G74SC245D	OEM
G74SC245P	OEM
G74SC373D	OEM
G74SC373P	OEM
G74SC374D	OEM
G74SC374P	OEM
G85HZ	OEM
G95G	0023
G100A	0015
G100B	0015
G100D	0015
G100G	0015
G100J	0015
G100K	0071
G100M	0071
G105	OEM
G105A	OEM
G105B	OEM
G105HZ	OEM
G106A1SD	OEM
G106A1SH	OEM
G106A2SD	OEM
G106A2SG	OEM
G106A2SH	OEM
G106A12G	OEM
G106B1SD	OEM
G106B1SG	OEM
G106B1SH	OEM
G106B2SD	OEM
G106B2SG	OEM
G106B2SH	OEM
G106C1SD	OEM
G106C1SG	OEM
G106C1SH	OEM
G106C2SD	OEM
G106C2SG	OEM
G106C2SH	OEM
G106D1SD	OEM
G106D1SG	OEM
G106D1SH	OEM
G106D2SD	OEM
G106D2SG	OEM
G106D2SH	OEM
G106E1SD	OEM
G106E1SG	OEM
G106E1SH	OEM
G106E2SD	OEM
G106E2SG	OEM
G106E2SH	OEM
G106F1SD	OEM
G106F1SG	OEM
G106F1SH	OEM
G106F2SD	OEM
G106F2SG	OEM
G106F2SH	OEM

DEVICE TYPE	REPL CODE
G106M1SD	OEM
G106M1SG	OEM
G106M1SH	OEM
G106M2SD	OEM
G106M2SG	OEM
G106M2SH	OEM
G110	0435
G110A	0005
G110B	OEM
G112A	OEM
G115	OEM
G115A	OEM
G115AP	OEM
G115B	OEM
G115BP	OEM
G115CDE	OEM
G115CFE	OEM
G115IDE	OEM
G115IFE	OEM
G115MDE	OEM
G115MFE	OEM
G116AL	OEM
G116AP	OEM
G116CDD	OEM
G116CFD	OEM
G116IDD	OEM
G116IFD	OEM
G116MDD	OEM
G116MFD	OEM
G117AL	OEM
G117CDD	OEM
G117CFD	OEM
G117IDD	OEM
G117IFD	OEM
G117MDD	OEM
G117MFD	OEM
G118AL	OEM
G118AP	OEM
G118CDD	OEM
G118CFD	OEM
G118IDD	OEM
G118IFD	OEM
G118MDD	OEM
G118MFD	OEM
G119AL	OEM
G119CDD	OEM
G119CFD	OEM
G119IDD	OEM
G119IFD	OEM
G119MDD	OEM
G119MFD	OEM
G122	0623
G122AL	OEM
G122B	OEM
G123AL	OEM
G123AP	OEM
G123BP	OEM
G123CDD	OEM
G123CFD	OEM
G123IDD	OEM
G123IFD	OEM
G123MDD	OEM
G123MFD	OEM
G125IFD	OEM
G125MFD	OEM
G126IFD	OEM
G126MFD	OEM
G127IFD	OEM
G127MFD	OEM
G128IFD	OEM
G128MFD	OEM
G129	OEM
G129IFD	OEM
G129MFD	OEM
G130	0015
G130IFD	OEM
G130MFD	OEM
G131IFD	OEM
G131MFD	OEM
G132IFD	OEM
G132MFD	OEM
G133	0030
G133A	0030
G133B	OEM
G147	OEM
G147A	OEM
G147B	OEM
G154	0143
G155	0143
G156	0143
G157	0143
G158	0143
G159	0143
G168	OEM
G168A	OEM
G168B	OEM
G182AG	0911
G198	0143
G199	0143
G200	0143
G206	0549
G206A	0549
G206B	OEM
G210	0005
G210A	0005
G210B	OEM
G215	OEM
G215A	OEM
G215B	OEM

DEVICE TYPE	REPL CODE
G222	0015
G222A	0623
G222B	OEM
G233	0030
G233A	0030
G233B	OEM
G247	OEM
G247A	OEM
G247B	OEM
G268	OEM
G268A	OEM
G268B	OEM
G296	0015
G297	0143
G306	0549
G306A	0549
G306B	OEM
G310	0005
G310A	0005
G310B	OEM
G315	OEM
G315A	OEM
G315B	OEM
G322	0623
G322A	0623
G322B	OEM
G333	0030
G333A	0030
G333B	OEM
G347	OEM
G347A	OEM
G347B	OEM
G406	0549
G406A	0549
G406B	OEM
G409	0143
G410	0005
G410A	0005
G410B	OEM
G415	OEM
G415A	OEM
G415B	OEM
G422	0623
G422A	0623
G422B	OEM
G433	0030
G433A	0030
G433B	OEM
G498	0143
G506	0964
G506A	0549
G506B	OEM
G510	0005
G510A	0005
G510B	OEM
G511A	OEM
G511B	OEM
G511C	OEM
G511D	OEM
G511F	OEM
G511U	OEM
G515	OEM
G515A	OEM
G515B	OEM
G522A	0623
G522B	OEM
G522C	OEM
G580	0143
G603A	OEM
G603B	OEM
G603C	OEM
G604A	OEM
G604B	OEM
G604C	OEM
G605A	OEM
G605B	OEM
G605C	OEM
G610A	0005
G610B	OEM
G610C	OEM
G611A	OEM
G611B	OEM
G611C	OEM
G611D	OEM
G611F	OEM
G611U	OEM
G615A	OEM
G615B	OEM
G615C	OEM
G618	0599
G657	0015
G659	0015
G700	0015
G701	0015
G702	0015
G702A	OEM
G702B	OEM
G702C	OEM
G704	0143
G766	0143
G788	0143
G789	0143
G790	0143
G814	0143
G815	0143
G816	0143
G820	0143
G821	0143
G822	0143

DEVICE TYPE	REPL CODE
G823	0143
G824	0143
G825	0143
G844	0143
G845	0143
G846	0143
G847	0143
G868	0143
G869	0143
G900	OEM
G1006	0983
G-1010	0143
G1010	0143
G1010A	0133
G1106	0583
G1110	0145
G1149	0015
G1179	0015
G1200	OEM
G1206	OEM
G1210	OEM
G1210-3	OEM
G1220-3	OEM
G1230-3	OEM
G1242	0015
G1288	0143
G1330IFD	OEM
G1330MFD	OEM
G1340IFD	OEM
G1340MFD	OEM
G1350IFD	OEM
G1350MFD	OEM
G1360IFD	OEM
G1360MFD	OEM
G1501	0604
G1506	OEM
G1810-3	OEM
G1820-3	OEM
G1830-3	OEM
G1850	0031
G1851	0031
G1852	0031
G1854	0031
G1856	0031
G2006	0983
G2010	0097
G3006	0197
G3010	0109
G3010-3	OEM
G3020-3	OEM
G3030-3	OEM
G4006	0197
G4010	0109
G4090	0239
G4104CI	OEM
G4104CM	OEM
G4320P	OEM
G4325CM	OEM
G4325P	OEM
G4326CM	OEM
G4326P	OEM
G5006	0204
G5010	0122
G5010-3	OEM
G5019	0196
G5020-3	OEM
G5030-3	OEM
G5080PI(A)	OEM
G5087DI(A)	OEM
G5087P(A)	OEM
G5089DI(A)	OEM
G5089P(A)	OEM
G5316D3	OEM
G5316P3	OEM
G5364D-3	OEM
G5364D-4	OEM
G5364P-3	OEM
G5364P-4	OEM
G5365D-3	OEM
G5365D-4	OEM
G5365P-3	OEM
G5365P-4	OEM
G5815	OEM
G5927	OEM
G6000	2691
G6002	3955
G6003	0085
G6004	0435
G6005	0160
G6006	0435
G6007	0969
G6008	0969
G6009	0599
G6010	4898
G6011	1414
G6012	3267
G6013	0160
G6014	0599
G6015	0599
G6017	0969
G6018	0599
G8006	0206
G8010	0540
G8860DI	OEM
G8860DI(A)	OEM
G8860P	OEM
G8860P(A)	OEM
G8860PI	OEM
G8860PI(A)	OEM

DEVICE TYPE	REPL CODE
G8862P	OEM
G8862PI	OEM
G8863DI	OEM
G8863PI	OEM
G8865DI	OEM
G8865PI	OEM
G8912DI(A)	OEM
G9423	0224
G9600	0016
G9600(G.E.)	0016
G9623	0016
G9625	0224
G9696	0016
G10001D	OEM
G10002D	OEM
G10015D	OEM
G10119	0015
G13403	OEM
G13638	0037
G15001D	OEM
G15002D	OEM
G15015D	OEM
G16506	0595
G18337	OEM
G18341	OEM
G18403	OEM
G18410	OEM
G18415	OEM
G18419	OEM
G20001G	OEM
G20002G	OEM
G20015G	OEM
G25001D	OEM
G25002D	OEM
G25015D	OEM
G30001G	OEM
G30002G	OEM
G30015G	OEM
G40001G	OEM
G40002G	OEM
G40015G	OEM
G50001D	OEM
G50002D	OEM
G50015D	OEM
G59019	0196
G59122	0196
G59815	OEM
G101079	0595
G390503S1	1545
G612994	3808
G65010042	OEM
G65020054	OEM
GA1	OEM
GA2	OEM
GA100	OEM
GA101	OEM
GA102	OEM
GA200	OEM
GA200A	OEM
GA201	OEM
GA201A	OEM
GA300	OEM
GA300A	OEM
GA301	OEM
GA301A	OEM
GA500	0200
GA504A	OEM
GA504B	OEM
GA504V	OEM
GA4558	OEM
GA5087PI(A)	OEM
GA5319	OEM
GA52609	OEM
GA-52829	0136
GA52829	0279
GA52830	OEM
GA52837	OEM
GA52996	OEM
GA53080	OEM
GA53104	OEM
GA-53149	0136
GA53149	0279
GA53194	OEM
GA53213	OEM
GA53233	OEM
GA-53242	0136
GA53242	0279
GA53270	0595
GAD2000	OEM
GAD2001	OEM
GAD2002	OEM
GAD2003	OEM
GAD3000	OEM
GAD3001	OEM
GAD3002	OEM
GAD3003	OEM
GAL10	OEM
GAL11	OEM
GAL12	OEM
GA02D-3	OEM
GA05D-D	OEM
GA010C-D	OEM
GA010C-H	OEM
GA010D-D	OEM
GA010D-H	OEM
GA010E-D	OEM
GA010E-H	OEM
GA010F-D	OEM
GA010F-H	OEM

If replacement code is OEM, contact original manufacturer for replacement.

Original Device Types

GAO10G-D—GC5511K

DEVICE TYPE	REPL CODE	DEVICE TYPE	REPL CODE	DEVICE TYPE	REPL CODE	DEVICE TYPE	REPL CODE	DEVICE TYPE	REPL CODE	DEVICE TYPE	REPL CODE	DEVICE TYPE	REPL CODE
GA010G-D	OEM	GBS3310F	0411	GC1182	0050	GC1513A	OEM	GC1706B	OEM	GC1761A	OEM	GC4050	OEM
GA010G-H	OEM	GBS3315F	0147	GC1183	0004	GC1513B	OEM	GC1706C	OEM	GC1761B	OEM	GC4051	OEM
GA010I-D	OEM	GBS3325F	3122	GC1184	0004	GC1513D	OEM	GC1706D	OEM	GC1761C	OEM	GC4052	OEM
GA010I-H	OEM	GBS3410F	0321	GC1185	0208	GC1513E	OEM	GC1706E	OEM	GC1762	OEM	GC4053	OEM
GA020C-D	OEM	GBS3415F	0147	GC1186	0004	GC1513H	OEM	GC1706H	OEM	GC1762A	OEM	GC4054	OEM
GA020C-H	OEM	GBX10422AD	OEM	GC1187	0004	GC1514A	OEM	GC1707	OEM	GC1762B	OEM	GC4057	0160
GA020D-D	OEM	GC31	0279	GC1200	OEM	GC1514B	OEM	GC1707A	OEM	GC1762C	OEM	GC4062	0160
GA020D-H	OEM	GC32	0279	GC1201	OEM	GC1514D	OEM	GC1707B	OEM	GC1763	0005	GC4087	0160
GA020E-D	OEM	GC33	0279	GC1202	OEM	GC1514E	OEM	GC1707C	OEM	GC1763A	OEM	GC4094	0222
GA020E-H	OEM	GC34	0279	GC1203	OEM	GC1514H	OEM	GC1707D	OEM	GC1763B	OEM	GC4097	0160
GA020F-D	OEM	GC35	0279	GC1204	OEM	GC1573	0050	GC1707E	OEM	GC1763C	OEM	GC4100	OEM
GA020F-H	OEM	GC60	0279	GC1205	OEM	GC1600	OEM	GC1707H	OEM	GC1764	0715	GC4101	OEM
GA020G-D	OEM	GC61	0279	GC1206	OEM	GC1600A	OEM	GC1708	OEM	GC1764A	OEM	GC4102	OEM
GA020G-H	OEM	GC148	0208	GC1207	OEM	GC1600B	OEM	GC1708A	OEM	GC1764B	OEM	GC4103	OEM
GA020I-D	OEM	GC150RE	OEM	GC1208	OEM	GC1600D	OEM	GC1708B	OEM	GC1764C	OEM	GC4111	0160
GA020I-H	OEM	GC181	0279	GC1209	OEM	GC1600E	OEM	GC1708C	OEM	GC1765	OEM	GC4144	0004
GA050C-D	OEM	GC182	0279	GC1210	OEM	GC1600H	OEM	GC1708D	OEM	GC1765A	OEM	GC4156	0160
GA050C-H	OEM	GC250	0004	GC1247	OEM	GC1601	OEM	GC1708E	OEM	GC1765B	OEM	GC4162	OEM
GA050D-D	OEM	GC282	0050	GC1257	0004	GC1601A	OEM	GC1708H	OEM	GC1765C	OEM	GC4182	OEM
GA050D-H	OEM	GC283	0050	GC1300	OEM	GC1601B	OEM	GC1709	OEM	GC1766	OEM	GC4210	OEM
GA050E-D	OEM	GC284	0050	GC1301	OEM	GC1601D	OEM	GC1709A	OEM	GC1766A	OEM	GC4211	OEM
GA050E-H	OEM	GC285	0208	GC1302	0279	GC1601E	OEM	GC1709B	OEM	GC1766B	OEM	GC4212	OEM
GA050F-D	OEM	GC286	0208	GC1303	OEM	GC1601H	OEM	GC1709C	OEM	GC1766C	OEM	GC4213	0841
GA050F-H	OEM	GC343	0004	GC1304	OEM	GC1602	OEM	GC1709D	OEM	GC1767	0623	GC4214	OEM
GA050G-D	OEM	GC360	0279	GC1305	OEM	GC1602A	OEM	GC1709E	OEM	GC1767A	OEM	GC4215	OEM
GA050G-H	OEM	GC387	0050	GC1306	OEM	GC1602B	OEM	GC1709H	OEM	GC1767B	OEM	GC4220	OEM
GA050I-D	OEM	GC388	0050	GC1307	OEM	GC1602D	OEM	GC1710	OEM	GC1767C	OEM	GC4221	OEM
GA050I-H	OEM	GC389	0050	GC1308	OEM	GC1602E	OEM	GC1710A	OEM	GC1768	OEM	GC4222	OEM
GA0100C-D	OEM	GC408	0004	GC1309	OEM	GC1602H	OEM	GC1710B	OEM	GC1768A	OEM	GC4223	OEM
GA0100C-H	OEM	GC452	0595	GC1310	OEM	GC1603	OEM	GC1710C	OEM	GC1768B	OEM	GC4224	OEM
GA0100D-D	OEM	GC453	0595	GC1422	0004	GC1603A	OEM	GC1710D	OEM	GC1768C	OEM	GC4225	OEM
GA0100D-H	OEM	GC454	0595	GC1423	0208	GC1603B	OEM	GC1710E	OEM	GC1769	OEM	GC4251	0160
GA0100E-D	OEM	GC460	0050	GC1500	OEM	GC1603D	OEM	GC1710H	OEM	GC1769A	OEM	GC4267-2	0160
GA0100E-H	OEM	GC461	0050	GC1500A	OEM	GC1603E	OEM	GC1711	OEM	GC1769B	OEM	GC4271	OEM
GA0100F-D	OEM	GC462	0050	GC1500B	OEM	GC1603H	OEM	GC1711A	OEM	GC1769C	OEM	GC4272	OEM
GA0100F-H	OEM	GC463	0208	GC1500D	OEM	GC1604	OEM	GC1711B	OEM	GC1770	OEM	GC4273	OEM
GA0100G-D	OEM	GC464	0004	GC1500E	OEM	GC1604A	OEM	GC1711C	OEM	GC1770A	OEM	GC4274	OEM
GA0100G-H	OEM	GC465	0208	GC1500H	OEM	GC1604B	OEM	GC1711D	OEM	GC1770B	OEM	GC4275	OEM
GA0100I-D	OEM	GC466	0004	GC1501	OEM	GC1604D	OEM	GC1711E	OEM	GC1770C	OEM	GC4310	OEM
GA0100I-H	OEM	GC467	0208	GC1501A	OEM	GC1604E	OEM	GC1711H	OEM	GC1800	OEM	GC4311	OEM
GA0200C-D	OEM	GC520	0004	GC1501B	OEM	GC1604H	OEM	GC1712	OEM	GC1801	OEM	GC4312	OEM
GA0200C-H	OEM	GC521	0004	GC1501D	OEM	GC1605	OEM	GC1712A	OEM	GC1802	OEM	GC4313	OEM
GA0200D-D	OEM	GC532	0279	GC1501E	OEM	GC1605A	OEM	GC1712B	OEM	GC1803	OEM	GC4314	OEM
GA0200D-H	OEM	GC551	0004	GC1501H	OEM	GC1605B	OEM	GC1712C	OEM	GC1804	OEM	GC4315	OEM
GA0200E-D	OEM	GC552	0004	GC1502	OEM	GC1605D	OEM	GC1712D	OEM	GC1805	OEM	GC4320	OEM
GA0200E-H	OEM	GC578	0004	GC1502A	OEM	GC1605E	OEM	GC1712E	OEM	GC1806	OEM	GC4321	OEM
GA0200F-D	OEM	GC579	0004	GC1502B	OEM	GC1605H	OEM	GC1712H	OEM	GC1807	OEM	GC4322	OEM
GA0200F-H	OEM	GC580	0004	GC1502D	OEM	GC1606	OEM	GC1713	OEM	GC1808	OEM	GC4323	OEM
GA0200G-D	OEM	GC581	0004	GC1502E	OEM	GC1606A	OEM	GC1713A	OEM	GC1809	OEM	GC4324	OEM
GA0200G-H	OEM	GC588	0004	GC1502H	OEM	GC1606B	OEM	GC1713B	OEM	GC1810	OEM	GC4325	OEM
GA0200I-D	OEM	GC608	0208	GC1503	OEM	GC1606D	OEM	GC1713C	OEM	GC1811	OEM	GC4371	OEM
GA0200I-E	OEM	GC609	0208	GC1503A	OEM	GC1606E	OEM	GC1713D	OEM	GC1812	OEM	GC4372	OEM
GA0200I-H	OEM	GC630	0050	GC1503B	OEM	GC1606H	OEM	GC1713E	OEM	GC1813	OEM	GC4373	OEM
GAP01AX	OEM	GC630A	0050	GC1503D	OEM	GC1607	OEM	GC1713H	OEM	GC1814	OEM	GC4374	OEM
GAP01BX	OEM	GC631	0050	GC1503E	OEM	GC1607A	OEM	GC1714	OEM	GC1815	OEM	GC4375	OEM
GAP01EP	OEM	GC639	0004	GC1503H	OEM	GC1607B	OEM	GC1714A	OEM	GC1816	OEM	GC4410	OEM
GAP01EX	OEM	GC640	0004	GC1504	OEM	GC1607D	OEM	GC1714B	OEM	GC2510	OEM	GC4411	OEM
GAP01FP	OEM	GC641	0160	GC1504A	OEM	GC1607E	OEM	GC1714C	OEM	GC2511	OEM	GC4412	OEM
GAP01FX	OEM	GC655A	OEM	GC1504B	OEM	GC1607H	OEM	GC1714D	OEM	GC2512	OEM	GC4413	OEM
GAP01N	OEM	GC666	OEM	GC1504D	OEM	GC1608	OEM	GC1714E	OEM	GC2513	OEM	GC4430	OEM
GARE	0631	GC680	0004	GC1504H	OEM	GC1608A	OEM	GC1714H	OEM	GC2514	OEM	GC4431	OEM
GAU401	OEM	GC681	0004	GC1505	OEM	GC1608B	OEM	GC1715	OEM	GC2515	OEM	GC4432	OEM
GB08D	0604	GC682	0004	GC1505A	OEM	GC1608D	OEM	GC1715A	OEM	GC2516	OEM	GC4433	OEM
GB-1	0143	GC691	0160	GC1505B	OEM	GC1608E	OEM	GC1715B	OEM	GC2520	OEM	GC4490	OEM
GB1	0133	GC692	0160	GC1505D	OEM	GC1608H	OEM	GC1715C	OEM	GC2521	OEM	GC4491	OEM
GB107	OEM	GC733B	0211	GC1505E	OEM	GC1609	OEM	GC1715D	OEM	GC2522	OEM	GC4492	OEM
GB110	OEM	GC783	0198	GC1505H	OEM	GC1609A	OEM	GC1715E	OEM	GC2523	OEM	GC4493	OEM
GB120	OEM	GC784	0198	GC1506	OEM	GC1609B	OEM	GC1715H	OEM	GC2524	OEM	GC4510	OEM
GB200	OEM	GC816	OEM	GC1506A	OEM	GC1609D	OEM	GC1716	OEM	GC2525	OEM	GC4511	OEM
GB200A	OEM	GC817	OEM	GC1506B	OEM	GC1609E	OEM	GC1716A	OEM	GC2526	OEM	GC4512	OEM
GB201	OEM	GC818	OEM	GC1506D	OEM	GC1609H	OEM	GC1716B	OEM	GC2530	OEM	GC4513	OEM
GB201A	OEM	GC841	OEM	GC1506E	OEM	GC1610	OEM	GC1716C	OEM	GC2531	OEM	GC4530	OEM
GB207	OEM	GC856	0004	GC1506H	OEM	GC1611	OEM	GC1716D	OEM	GC2532	OEM	GC4531	OEM
GB210	OEM	GC864	0004	GC1507	OEM	GC1612	OEM	GC1716E	OEM	GC2533	OEM	GC4532	OEM
GB220	OEM	GC927	OEM	GC1507A	OEM	GC1613	OEM	GC1716H	OEM	GC2534	OEM	GC4533	OEM
GB300	OEM	GC928	OEM	GC1507B	OEM	GC1615-1	0086	GC1717	OEM	GC2535	OEM	GC4590	OEM
GB300A	OEM	GC929	OEM	GC1507D	OEM	GC1700	OEM	GC1717A	OEM	GC2536	OEM	GC4591	OEM
GB301	OEM	GC968	OEM	GC1507E	OEM	GC1700A	OEM	GC1717B	OEM	GC2540	OEM	GC4592	OEM
GB301A	OEM	GC971	OEM	GC1507H	OEM	GC1701	OEM	GC1717C	OEM	GC2541	OEM	GC4593	OEM
GB307	OEM	GC1000	OEM	GC1508	OEM	GC1702	OEM	GC1717D	OEM	GC2542	OEM	GC4710	OEM
GB310	OEM	GC1003	0050	GC1508A	OEM	GC1702A	OEM	GC1717E	OEM	GC2543	OEM	GC4711	OEM
GB320	OEM	GC1004	0050	GC1508B	OEM	GC1702B	OEM	GC1717H	OEM	GC2544	OEM	GC4712	OEM
GB407	OEM	GC1005	0050	GC1508D	OEM	GC1702C	OEM	GC1718	OEM	GC2545	OEM	GC4720	OEM
GB410	OEM	GC1006	0050	GC1508E	OEM	GC1702D	OEM	GC1719	OEM	GC2546	OEM	GC4721	OEM
GB420	OEM	GC1007	0050	GC1508H	OEM	GC1702E	OEM	GC1720	OEM	GC3202	OEM	GC4722	OEM
GB507	OEM	GC1034	0595	GC1509	OEM	GC1702H	OEM	GC1754	OEM	GC3203	OEM	GC5000	0004
GB510	OEM	GC1035	0595	GC1509A	OEM	GC1703	OEM	GC1754B	OEM	GC3204	OEM	GC5010	0211
GB520	OEM	GC1036	0595	GC1509B	OEM	GC1703A	OEM	GC1754C	OEM	GC3205	OEM	GC5012	0143
GBD100A	OEM	GC1081	0136	GC1509D	OEM	GC1703B	OEM	GC1755	OEM	GC3206	OEM	GC5411	OEM
GBD250A	OEM	GC1092	0050	GC1509E	OEM	GC1703C	OEM	GC1755B	OEM	GC3207	OEM	GC5412	OEM
GBDX25A	OEM	GC1093	OEM	GC1509H	OEM	GC1703D	OEM	GC1755C	OEM	GC3208	OEM	GC5413	OEM
GBDX50A	OEM	GC1093X3	0050	GC1510	OEM	GC1703E	OEM	GC1756	OEM	GC3209	OEM	GC5414	OEM
GBG1000	5022	GC1097	0004	GC1510A	OEM	GC1703H	OEM	GC1756B	OEM	GC3302	OEM	GC5421	OEM
GBI1	OEM	GC1101	0004	GC1510B	OEM	GC1704	OEM	GC1756C	OEM	GC3303	OEM	GC5422	OEM
GBS176D	OEM	GC1134	0004	GC1510D	OEM	GC1704A	OEM	GC1757	OEM	GC3304	OEM	GC5423	OEM
GBS210E	OEM	GC1136	0004	GC1510E	OEM	GC1704B	OEM	GC1757B	OEM	GC3304A	OEM	GC5424	OEM
GBS216	OEM	GC1137	0208	GC1510H	OEM	GC1704C	OEM	GC1757C	OEM	GC3305	OEM	GC5431	OEM
GBS266E	0407	GC1142	0050	GC1511	OEM	GC1704D	OEM	GC1758	OEM	GC3306	OEM	GC5432	OEM
GBS276D	OEM	GC1143	0004	GC1511A	OEM	GC1704E	OEM	GC1758B	OEM	GC3307	OEM	GC5441	OEM
GBS410E	OEM	GC1144	0016	GC1511B	OEM	GC1704H	OEM	GC1758C	OEM	GC3307A	OEM	GC5511A	OEM
GBS416	OEM	GC1145	0004	GC1511D	OEM	GC1705	OEM	GC1759	OEM	GC3308	OEM	GC5511B	OEM
GBS466E	0411	GC1146	0050	GC1511E	OEM	GC1705A	OEM	GC1759A	OEM	GC4020	0160	GC5511C	OEM
GBS476D	OEM	GC1148	0050	GC1511H	OEM	GC1705B	OEM	GC1759B	OEM	GC4021	OEM	GC5511D	OEM
GBS3110F	0404	GC1149	0050	GC1512	OEM	GC1705C	OEM	GC1759C	OEM	GC4022	0279	GC5511E	OEM
GBS3115F	0154	GC1150	0004	GC1512A	OEM	GC1705D	OEM	GC1760	OEM	GC4023	OEM	GC5511F	OEM
GBS3125F	3119	GC1155	0050	GC1512B	OEM	GC1705E	OEM	GC1760A	OEM	GC4025	OEM	GC5511G	OEM
GBS3210F	0407	GC1159	0279	GC1512D	OEM	GC1705H	OEM	GC1760B	OEM	GC4025X	OEM	GC5511H	OEM
GBS3215F	0154	GC1163	OEM	GC1512H	OEM	GC1706	OEM	GC1760C	OEM	GC4032	OEM	GC5511J	OEM
GBS3225F	3121	GC1164	OEM	GC1513	OEM	GC1706A	OEM	GC1761	0549	GC4045	0160	GC5511K	OEM

If replacement code is OEM, contact original manufacturer for replacement.

415

DEVICE TYPE	REPL CODE
GC5511L	OEM
GC5511M	OEM
GC5512A	OEM
GC5512B	OEM
GC5512C	OEM
GC5512D	OEM
GC5512E	OEM
GC5512F	OEM
GC5512G	OEM
GC5512H	OEM
GC5512J	OEM
GC5512K	OEM
GC5512L	OEM
GC5512M	OEM
GC5513A	OEM
GC5513B	OEM
GC5513C	OEM
GC5513D	OEM
GC5513E	OEM
GC5513F	OEM
GC5513G	OEM
GC5513H	OEM
GC5513J	OEM
GC5513K	OEM
GC5513L	OEM
GC5513M	OEM
GC5514A	OEM
GC5514B	OEM
GC5514C	OEM
GC5514D	OEM
GC5514E	OEM
GC5514F	OEM
GC5514G	OEM
GC5514J	OEM
GC5514K	OEM
GC5514L	OEM
GC5514M	OEM
GC5515A	OEM
GC5515B	OEM
GC5515C	OEM
GC5515D	OEM
GC5515E	OEM
GC5515F	OEM
GC5515G	OEM
GC5515H	OEM
GC5515J	OEM
GC5515K	OEM
GC5515L	OEM
GC5516A	OEM
GC5516B	OEM
GC5516C	OEM
GC5516D	OEM
GC5516E	OEM
GC5516F	OEM
GC5516G	OEM
GC5516H	OEM
GC5516J	OEM
GC5516K	OEM
GC5517A	OEM
GC5517B	OEM
GC5517C	OEM
GC5517D	OEM
GC5517E	OEM
GC5517F	OEM
GC5517G	OEM
GC5517H	OEM
GC5517J	OEM
GC5518A	OEM
GC5518B	OEM
GC5518C	OEM
GC5518D	OEM
GC5518E	OEM
GC5518F	OEM
GC5518G	OEM
GC5518H	OEM
GC5519A	OEM
GC5519B	OEM
GC5519C	OEM
GC5519D	OEM
GC5519E	OEM
GC5519F	OEM
GC5519G	OEM
GC5531C	OEM
GC5531D	OEM
GC5531E	OEM
GC5531F	OEM
GC5531G	OEM
GC5532C	OEM
GC5532D	OEM
GC5532E	OEM
GC5532F	OEM
GC5532G	OEM
GC5533C	OEM
GC5533D	OEM
GC5533E	OEM
GC5533F	OEM
GC5533G	OEM
GC5534C	OEM
GC5534D	OEM
GC5534E	OEM
GC5534F	OEM
GC5534G	OEM
GC5535C	OEM
GC5535D	OEM
GC5535E	OEM
GC5535F	OEM
GC5535G	OEM
GC5536C	OEM
GC5536D	OEM

DEVICE TYPE	REPL CODE
GC5536E	OEM
GC5536F	OEM
GC5536G	OEM
GC5537C	OEM
GC5537D	OEM
GC5537E	OEM
GC5537F	OEM
GC5538C	OEM
GC5538D	OEM
GC5538E	OEM
GC5539C	OEM
GC5539D	OEM
GC5601A	OEM
GC5601B	OEM
GC5601C	OEM
GC5601D	OEM
GC5601E	OEM
GC5601F	OEM
GC5601G	OEM
GC5601H	OEM
GC5602A	OEM
GC5602B	OEM
GC5602C	OEM
GC5602D	OEM
GC5602E	OEM
GC5602F	OEM
GC5602G	OEM
GC5602H	OEM
GC5605A	OEM
GC5605B	OEM
GC5605C	OEM
GC5605D	OEM
GC5605E	OEM
GC5605F	OEM
GC5605G	OEM
GC5605H	OEM
GC5607A	OEM
GC5607B	OEM
GC5607C	OEM
GC5607D	OEM
GC5607E	OEM
GC5607F	OEM
GC5607G	OEM
GC5610A	OEM
GC5610B	OEM
GC5610C	OEM
GC5610D	OEM
GC5610E	OEM
GC5610F	OEM
GC5610G	OEM
GC5615A	OEM
GC5615B	OEM
GC5615C	OEM
GC5615D	OEM
GC5615E	OEM
GC5615F	OEM
GC5620A	OEM
GC5620B	OEM
GC5620C	OEM
GC5620D	OEM
GC5620E	OEM
GC5620F	OEM
GC5625A	OEM
GC5625B	OEM
GC5625C	OEM
GC5625D	OEM
GC5625E	OEM
GC5630A	OEM
GC5630B	OEM
GC5630C	OEM
GC5630D	OEM
GC5630E	OEM
GC5640A	OEM
GC5640B	OEM
GC5640C	OEM
GC5640D	OEM
GC5640E	OEM
GC5650A	OEM
GC5650B	OEM
GC5650C	OEM
GC5650D	OEM
GC5730A	OEM
GC5730B	OEM
GC5730C	OEM
GC5730D	OEM
GC5730E	OEM
GC5740A	OEM
GC5740B	OEM
GC5740C	OEM
GC5740D	OEM
GC5740E	OEM
GC5750A	OEM
GC5750B	OEM
GC5750C	OEM
GC5750D	OEM
GC5830A	OEM
GC5830B	OEM
GC5830C	OEM
GC5830D	OEM
GC5830E	OEM
GC5840A	OEM
GC5840B	OEM
GC5840C	OEM
GC5840D	OEM
GC5840E	OEM
GC5850A	OEM
GC5850B	OEM
GC5850C	OEM
GC5850D	OEM

DEVICE TYPE	REPL CODE
GC5901	OEM
GC5902	OEM
GC5903	OEM
GC5904	OEM
GC51101	OEM
GC51102	OEM
GC51103	OEM
GC51104	OEM
GC51105	OEM
GC51106	OEM
GC51107	OEM
GC51108	OEM
GC51109	OEM
GC51110	OEM
GC51111	OEM
GC51112	OEM
GC51113	OEM
GC51301	OEM
GC51302	OEM
GC51303	OEM
GC51304	OEM
GC51305	OEM
GC51306	OEM
GC51307	OEM
GC51308	OEM
GC51309	OEM
GC51310	OEM
GC51311	OEM
GC51312	OEM
GC51313	OEM
GC51401	OEM
GC51402	OEM
GC51403	OEM
GC51404	OEM
GC51405	OEM
GC51406	OEM
GC51407	OEM
GC51408	OEM
GC51409	OEM
GC51410	OEM
GC51411	OEM
GC51412	OEM
GC51413	OEM
GC51601	OEM
GC51602	OEM
GC51603	OEM
GC51604	OEM
GC51605	OEM
GC51606	OEM
GC51607	OEM
GC51608	OEM
GC51609	OEM
GC51610	OEM
GC51611	OEM
GC51612	OEM
GC55010A	OEM
GC55010B	OEM
GC55010C	OEM
GC55010D	OEM
GC55010E	OEM
GC55010F	OEM
GC55015A	OEM
GC55015B	OEM
GC55015C	OEM
GC55015D	OEM
GC55015E	OEM
GC55015F	OEM
GC55020A	OEM
GC55020B	OEM
GC55020C	OEM
GC55020D	OEM
GC55020E	OEM
GC55020F	OEM
GC55025A	OEM
GC55025B	OEM
GC55025C	OEM
GC55025D	OEM
GC55025E	OEM
GC55025F	OEM
GC55030A	OEM
GC55030B	OEM
GC55030C	OEM
GC55030D	OEM
GC55030E	OEM
GC55030F	OEM
GC55035A	OEM
GC55035B	OEM
GC55035C	OEM
GC55035D	OEM
GCC830	OEM
GCC830A	OEM
GCC830B	OEM
GC0201	OEM
GC0205	OEM
GC0501	OEM
GC0505	OEM
GC01001	OEM
GC01005	OEM
GC02001	OEM
GC02005	OEM
GC03001	OEM
GC03005	OEM
GC04001	OEM
GC04005	OEM
GC05001	OEM
GC05005	OEM
GCS10	OEM
GCS20	OEM
GCS30	OEM

DEVICE TYPE	REPL CODE
GCS40	OEM
GD1E	0143
GD1P	0143
GD1Q	0143
GD2E	0143
GD3E	OEM
GD4E	0143
GD5E	0143
GD6E	0143
GD8E	0143
GD10	0143
GD11E	0143
GD12	0015
GD12E	0143
GD13E	0143
GD-25	0143
GD25	0143
GD-26	0143
GD-29	0143
GD-30	0143
GD72E/3	0143
GD72E/4	0143
GD72E/5	0143
GD72E3	0143
GD72E4	0143
GD72E5	0143
GD73E/3	0143
GD73E/4	0143
GD73E/5	0143
GD73E3	0143
GD73E4	0143
GD73E5	0143
GD74E/3	0143
GD74E/4	0143
GD74E/5	0143
GD74E3	0143
GD74E4	0143
GD74E5	0143
GD74LS00	1519
GD74LS04	1585
GD74LS06	OEM
GD74LS07	OEM
GD74LS21	1752
GD74LS32	0088
GD74LS74A	0243
GD74LS125A	0075
GD74LS138	0422
GD74LS157	1153
GD74LS158	1646
GD74LS175	1662
GD74LS240	0447
GD74LS244	0453
GD74LS245	0458
GD74LS373	0704
GD74S04	2248
GD74S08	2547
GD74S74	2483
GD107A	0019
GD308A	OEM
GD308AA	OEM
GD308B	OEM
GD308C	OEM
GD308D	OEM
GD308E	OEM
GD311A	OEM
GD311AA	OEM
GD311B	OEM
GD311C	OEM
GD311D	OEM
GD311E	OEM
GD314A	OEM
GD314AA	OEM
GD314B	OEM
GD314C	OEM
GD314D	OEM
GD314E	OEM
GD318A	OEM
GD318AA	OEM
GD318B	OEM
GD318C	OEM
GD318D	OEM
GD400	0143
GD401	0143
GD402	0143
GD402A	OEM
GD403	0019
GD404	0019
GD405	0019
GD406	0143
GD407	0143
GD408	0143
GD408A	OEM
GD408B	OEM
GD408C	OEM
GD408D	OEM
GD408E	OEM
GD409	0143
GD410	OEM
GD411	0143
GD411A	OEM
GD411B	OEM
GD411C	OEM
GD411D	OEM
GD411E	OEM
GD507A	OEM
GD508A	OEM
GD508AA	OEM
GD508B	OEM
GD508C	OEM

DEVICE TYPE	REPL CODE
GD508D	OEM
GD508E	OEM
GD-510	0133
GD510	0143
GD511A	OEM
GD511AA	OEM
GD511B	OEM
GD511C	OEM
GD511D	OEM
GD511E	OEM
GD514A	OEM
GD514AA	OEM
GD514B	OEM
GD514C	OEM
GD514D	OEM
GD514E	OEM
GD518A	OEM
GD518AA	OEM
GD518B	OEM
GD518C	OEM
GD518D	OEM
GD663	0143
GD731	OEM
GD732	OEM
GD733	OEM
GD741	OEM
GD742	OEM
GD743	OEM
GD744	OEM
GD800-1	OEM
GD800-2	OEM
GD800-3	OEM
GD800-4	OEM
GD800-5	OEM
GD800-6	OEM
GD800-7	OEM
GD800-8	OEM
GD800-9	OEM
GD800-10	OEM
GD800-12	OEM
GD800-14	OEM
GD800-16	OEM
GD800-18	OEM
GD800-20	OEM
GD800-22	OEM
GD800-24	OEM
GD800-26	OEM
GD800-28	OEM
GD800-30	OEM
GD1001	0143
GD1250-2	OEM
GD1250-4	OEM
GD1250-6	OEM
GD1250-12	OEM
GD1250-16	OEM
GD1250-20	OEM
GD1250-24	OEM
GD1400-1	OEM
GD1400-2	OEM
GD1400-3	OEM
GD1400-4	OEM
GD1400-5	OEM
GD1400-6	OEM
GD1400-7	OEM
GD1400-8	OEM
GD1400-9	OEM
GD1400-10	OEM
GD1400-12	OEM
GD1400-14	OEM
GD1400-16	OEM
GD1400-18	OEM
GD1400-20	OEM
GD3638	0133
GD4011B	OEM
GD4052B	0024
GD4066	0101
GD4066B	0101
GD4066BD	0101
GD4066BP	0101
GD4207GD	OEM
GD7815	OEM
GD7818	OEM
GD75188	0503
GD75189A	0506
GE-1	0279
GE1C-166	2862
GE-1N506	0015
GE-1N5061	0023
GE1.14CX511	OEM
GE-2	0211
GE-3	0160
GE-4	0435
GE-5	0595
GE5ZD-3.3	0777
GE5ZD-3.6	0791
GE5ZD-3.9	0801
GE5ZD-4.3	0815
GE5ZD-4.7	0827
GE5ZD-5.0	0437
GE5ZD-5.1	0437
GE5ZD-5.6	0870
GE5ZD-5.8	6080
GE5ZD-6.0	3099
GE5ZD-6.2	0185
GE5ZD-6.6	0205
GE5ZD-6.8	0205
GE5ZD-7.5	0475
GE5ZD-8.0	0499
GE5ZD-8.1	0499

DEVICE TYPE	REPL CODE
GE5ZD-8.2	0499
GE5ZD-8.7	3285
GE5ZD-9.1	0679
GE5ZD-10	0225
GE5ZD-11	0230
GE5ZD-12	0234
GE5ZD-13	0237
GE5ZD-14	1387
GE5ZD-15	0247
GE5ZD-16	0251
GE5ZD-17	1170
GE5ZD-18	0256
GE5ZD-19	2379
GE5ZD-20	0262
GE5ZD-21	0269
GE5ZD-22	0269
GE5ZD-24	0273
GE5ZD-25	2383
GE5ZD-27	0291
GE5ZD-28	1169
GE5ZD-30	0305
GE5ZD-33	0314
GE-6	0595
GE-6GC1	0196
GE-6GD1	0196
GE-6GX1	1073
GE6.2	0631
GE6.2A	0631
GE6.2B	0631
GE-7	0595
GE-8	0595
GE-9	0050
GE-9A	0050
GE-10	0079
GE-10A	0111
GE-11	0127
GE-12	0142
GE-13MP	3004
GE-14	0103
GE-15MP	1506
GE-16	0085
GE-17	0931
GE-18	0086
GE-19	0103
GE-20	0016
GE-21	0150
GE-21A	0126
GE-22	0037
GE-23	0178
GE-24MP	0178
GE-25	0969
GE-26	0919
GE-27	0283
GE-28	0555
GE-29	1257
GE-30	0222
GE-31MP	0816
GE-32	0168
GE-33	0556
GE-34	1190
GE-35	0074
GE-36	0359
GE-37	0003
GE-38	0065
GE-39	0007
GE-40	0233
GE-41	4391
GE-42	1024
GE42-7	0015
GE-43	2736
GE-44	0222
GE-45	4182
GE-46	1401
GE-47	0018
GE-47MP	3020
GE-48	0527
GE-49	1004
GE-50	0050
GE-51	0050
GE-52	0136
GE-53	0164
GE-54	2839
GE-55	0556
GE-56	1190
GE-57	0161
GE-58	0455
GE-59	0208
GE-60	2195
GE-61	0224
GE-62	0111
GE-63	0218
GE-63A	0590
GE-64	0396
GE-65	0688
GE-66	0042
GE-66A	0042
GE-67	1233
GE-67A	0786
GE-69	1298
GE-69A	0919
GE-72	0074
GE-73	0637
GE-74	1671
GE-75	0130
GE-76	0599
GE-77	0177
GE-80	0841
GE-81	0016
GE-82	0037

DEVICE TYPE	REPL CODE
GE-83	0546
GE-84	0378
GE-85	0111
GE-86	0127
GE-88	1376
GE-89	0472
GE-90	0030
GE-91	0488
GE-92	1740
GE-117	0465
GE-121	0160
GE-121MP	0265
GE-123	0198
GE-123AP	0079
GE-129	0127
GE129	0127
GE-130	0015
GE-131MP	0816
GE-163A	0637
GE-166	0276
GE-167	0287
GE-168	0293
GE-169	0299
GE-178MP	0907
GE-195A	0693
GE-205	2600
GE-208	0050
GE-210	0284
GE-211	0364
GE-212	0151
GE-213	0076
GE-214	0259
GE-215	0930
GE-216	0830
GE-217	0264
GE-218	0378
GE-219	5913
GE-220	0855
GE-221	2714
GE-222	0710
GE-223	0338
GE-224	0334
GE-225	3712
GE-226	0546
GE-227	4141
GE-228	0434
GE-229	0187
GE-230	5914
GE-231	5915
GE-232	0830
GE-233	5916
GE-234	0899
GE-235	0233
GE-236	2039
GE-237	0065
GE-238	2820
GE-239	0599
GE-240	0040
GE-241	0419
GE-242	OEM
GE-243	0086
GE-244	0126
GE-245	0050
GE-246	0178
GE-247	0219
GE-248	1045
GE-249	0334
GE-250	0848
GE-251	0168
GE-252	0561
GE-253	1357
GE-254	0432
GE-255	3052
GE-256	3249
GE-257	1698
GE-258	3477
GE-259	0309
GE-260	1740
GE-261	0414
GE-262	0177
GE-262MP	2127
GE-263	2002
GE-264	0617
GE-265	0538
GE-265MP	2355
GE-265P	0538
GE-266	1588
GE-267	1021
GE-268	0155
GE-268MP	1215
GE-269	0006
GE-270	1581
GE-271	0320
GE-271MP	3217
GE-272	0431
GE-273	2035
GE-273MP	3342
GE-274	1421
GE-275	1165
GE-276	1935
GE-277	0488
GE-278	0470
GE-279	1967
GE-280	0259
GE-281	2918
GE-282	2296
GE-283	0008
GE-284	1963
GE-285	5913

416 If replacement code is OEM, contact original manufacturer for replacement.

DEVICE TYPE	REPL CODE
GE-286	3532
GE-287	1224
GE-288	1963
GE-289A	0155
GE-291	OEM
GE-292	OEM
GE-293	OEM
GE-294	3387
GE-295	1224
GE-296	1963
GE-297	2030
GE-298	1963
GE-299	0414
GE-300	0133
GE-301	1698
GE-302	0236
GE-303	0676
GE-304	3343
GE-305	0290
GE-309K	1911
GE-312	0321
GE-314	1814
GE-320	0169
GE-321	OEM
GE-322	0930
GE-323	0886
GE-324	OEM
GE-325	0168
GE-326	2243
GE-327	0224
GE-328	0615
GE-329	0930
GE-330	2959
GE-331	1581
GE-332	0830
GE-333	5921
GE-334	0527
GE-335	OEM
GE-336	1581
GE-337	1973
GE-338	OEM
GE-339	5922
GE-340	OEM
GE-341	2969
GE-342	3136
GE-343	2411
GE-344	2262
GE-345	1203
GE-346	0178
GE-347	0843
GE-348	3336
GE-349	2220
GE-350	2422
GE-351	3339
GE-352	3340
GE-353	0597
GE-354	2808
GE-355	3483
GE-356	3486
GE-357	3496
GE-358	2415
GE-359	3484
GE-360	0553
GE-361	3487
GE-362	0134
GE-363	2465
GE-367	2841
GE-368	3493
GE-375	0388
GE-380	2911
GE-381	3527
GE-389	0223
GE-414	0133
GE-504	0015
GE-504A	0015
GE-505	0071
GE-509	2613
GE-509A	0071
GE-510	0071
GE-511	0102
GE-512	0087
GE-513	1313
GE-514	0124
GE-515	1208
GE-516	1493
GE-517	1493
GE-518	0190
GE-519	0405
GE-520	0128
GE-521	1696
GE-522	1986
GE-522A	1986
GE-523	1493
GE-524	2777
GE-525	0405
GE-526	1700
GE-527	0190
GE-528	1061
GE-529	2524
GE-530	0344
GE-531	0071
GE-532	1282
GE-533	0344
GE-534	2954
GE-535	2957
GE-536	1188
GE-537	2956
GE-538	1048
GE-539	3805

DEVICE TYPE	REPL CODE
GE-540	3610
GE-548	3617
GE-550	5938
GE-551	0182
GE-601	0139
GE-663	0590
GE-700	0239
GE-701	2313
GE-702	1702
GE-703	5946
GE-704	0061
GE-705	1642
GE-706	2549
GE-720	3506
GE-721	2849
GE-722	1179
GE-723	2834
GE-724	4479
GE-725	4545
GE-726	4990
GE-727	OEM
GE-730	2716
GE-750	3607
GE-761	1865
GE-792	2153
GE-793	2032
GE-794	3346
GE-812	3724
GE-818	2480
GE-822	2785
GE-961	1275
GE-962	0917
GE-972	2224
GE-973	0413
GE-984	3239
GE-1005	2546
GE-1021	2142
GE-1038	4338
GE-1110	2289
GE-1127	4348
GE-1162	3977
GE-1164	3238
GE-1169	4331
GE-1175	2759
GE-1178	3660
GE-1179	2550
GE-1183	4133
GE-1192	1532
GE-1193	3286
GE-1194	1805
GE-1196	1049
GE-1198	2238
GE-1211	2179
GE-1218	1561
GE-1219	1602
GE-1228	3161
GE-1231	1162
GE-1232	1042
GE-1239	3231
GE-1257	4560
GE-1258	4561
GE-1259	5517
GE-1260	4563
GE-3229	0042
GE-3265	0016
GE3265	0079
GE-3638	0143
GE3638	0143
GE-4000	2013
GE-4001	0473
GE-4002	2044
GE-4007	2819
GE-4009	1988
GE-4011	0215
GE-4012	0493
GE-4013	0409
GE-4015	1008
GE-4016	1135
GE-4017	0508
GE-4019	1517
GE-4020	1651
GE-4021	1738
GE-4023	0515
GE-4024	1946
GE-4025	2061
GE-4027	1938
GE-4030	0495
GE-4040	0056
GE-4042	0121
GE-4049	0001
GE-4050	0394
GE-4051	0362
GE-4052	0024
GE-4055	3272
GE-4081	0621
GE-4300A1	2970
GE-4415A	2972
GE-4518	1037
GE-5004	0994
GE-5005	1006
GE-5008	2070
GE-5009	1067
GE-5012	0607
GE-5013	1180
GE-5016	0983
GE-5017	0984
GE-5020	0197
GE-5021	0991
GE-5024	0204

DEVICE TYPE	REPL CODE
GE-5025	0510
GE-5028	0583
GE-5029	0942
GE-5032	0097
GE-5033	0760
GE-5036	0109
GE-5037	0533
GE-5040	0122
GE-5041	0810
GE-5044	0145
GE-5045	0545
GE-5048	1241
GE-5056	1576
GE-5057	3263
GE-5060	2602
GE5060	2602
GE-5061	2602
GE5061	2602
GE-5062	1841
GE5062	2602
GE-5062A	OEM
GE-5063A	1302
GE-5064	2872
GE-5065	1232
GE-5068	3705
GE-5069	2349
GE-5072	1104
GE-5073	2360
GE-5076	2982
GE-5077	0444
GE-5096	1116
GE-5097	1099
GE-5100	0800
GE-5101	0258
GE-5104	0315
GE-5105	0267
GE-5108	0045
GE-5109	0280
GE-5128	2813
GE-5129	2168
GE-5132	2823
GE-5133	2177
GE-5136	2844
GE-5137	2183
GE-5140	2454
GE-5141	2324
GE-5142	3088
GE-5151A	0401
GE-5155A	0238
GE-5190A	1145
GE-5304	0106
GE-5312	0319
GE-5314	0468
GE-5322	2347
GE-5400	1129
GE-5401	0340
GE-5402	0895
GE-5404	0058
GE-5414	3575
GE-5415	3291
GE-5442	4508
GE-5444	2255
GE-5448	3370
GE-5453	1250
GE-5455	0934
GE-5457	0095
GE-5463	0500
GE-5512	3349
GE-5642	1403
GE-5801	0947
GE6060	2602
GE6061	2602
GE6062	2602
GE6063	0133
GE6251	1980
GE6252	2602
GE6253	2602
GE-6366	0015
GE6366	0015
GE-6400A	1659
GE-6401	2123
GE-6402	0312
GE-7400	0232
GE-7402	0310
GE-7404	0357
GE-7406	1197
GE7406	OEM
GE-7408	0462
GE-7410	0507
GE-7413	1432
GE-7416	1339
GE-7417	1342
GE-7420	0692
GE-7427	0812
GE-7430	0867
GE-7432	0893
GE-7441	1032
GE-7447	1100
GE-7448	1117
GE-7451	1160
GE-7473	1164
GE-7474	1303
GE-7475	1423
GE-7476	1150
GE-7485	0370
GE-7486	1358
GE-7490	1199
GE-7492	0828
GE10000	2602

DEVICE TYPE	REPL CODE
GE10001	2602
GE10002	2602
GE10003	2602
GE10006	2602
GE10007	2602
GE10020	OEM
GE10021	OEM
GE10022	3956
GE10023	2602
GE-74123	1149
GE-74145	0614
GE-74150	1484
GE-74154	1546
GE-74192	1910
GE-74193	1915
GE-74196	1939
GEA6.2(E)B2	0466
GEA15A	1272
GEA-107	OEM
GEA-109	OEM
GEA-110	OEM
GEA-114	OEM
GEA114B	0031
GEA-121	3294
GEAU-1-40A	OEM
GEAU-1-60A	OEM
GEAU-1-520A	OEM
GEAU-1-520AS	OEM
GEAU-1-40742	OEM
GEAU-1-40742HS	OEM
GEAU-1-44782	OEM
GEAU-1-44782HS	OEM
GEAU-2-40A	OEM
GEAU-2-60A	OEM
GEAU-2-520A	OEM
GEAU-2-520AS	OEM
GEAU-2-40742	OEM
GEAU-2-40742HS	OEM
GEAU-2-44782	OEM
GEAU-2-44782HS	OEM
GEAU-5-40A	OEM
GEAU-5-60A	OEM
GEAU-5-520A	OEM
GEAU-5-520AS	OEM
GEAU-5-40742	OEM
GEAU-5-40742HS	OEM
GEAU-5-44782	OEM
GEAU-5-44782HS	OEM
GEB100	0319
GEB101	0319
GEB102	1404
GEB104	0468
GEB106	0441
GEB108	1412
GEBR-206	1404
GEBR-425	2353
GEBR-600	0299
GEBR-1000	0250
GECD-1-9145-1	OEM
GECD-1-9145-2HS	OEM
GECD-2-9145-1	OEM
GECD-2-9145-2HS	OEM
GECD-5-9145-1	OEM
GECD-5-9145-2HS	OEM
GE-CR1	0769
GECR-1	0769
GE-CR2	1293
GECR-2	1293
GE-CR3	0469
GECR-3	0469
GECR-4	0201
GECR-5	0286
GECR-6	0374
GECR-7	0752
GECU-1-9145-1	OEM
GECU-1-9145-2HS	OEM
GECU-2-9145-1	OEM
GECU-2-9145-2HS	OEM
GECU-5-9145-1	OEM
GECU-5-9145-2HS	OEM
GED05B850	2217
GEDO5B850	0143
GE-FET-1	3017
GE-FET-2	0321
GE-FET-3	0843
GE-FET-4	0212
GE-FET-5	0212
GE-FET-6	0349
GEFR-4	2951
GE-FR8	2949
GEFR-8	2949
GE-FR9	2950
GEFR-9	2950
GEFR-10	2952
GEFR-12	5265
GEHG-1-9145-1	OEM
GEHG-1-9145-2HS	OEM
GEHG-2-9145-1	OEM
GEHG-2-9145-2HS	OEM
GEHG-5-9145-1	OEM
GEHG-5-9145-2HS	OEM
GE-IC2	0167
GEIC-2	0167
GEIC-3	2147
GEIC-4	0348
GEIC-5	0661
GE-IC6	0350
GEIC-6	0350
GE-IC7	0438

DEVICE TYPE	REPL CODE
GEIC-7	0438
GE-IC8	0649
GEIC-8	0649
GEIC-9	0696
GEIC-10	0659
GE-IC11	0673
GEIC-11	0673
GEIC-12	0627
GEIC-13	2438
GEIC-14	2264
GEIC-15	1335
GEIC-16	1434
GEIC-17	1748
GEIC-18	0345
GEIC-19	0687
GEIC-20	0360
GEIC-21	0797
GEIC-22	2527
GEIC-23	0324
GEIC-24	1411
GEIC-25	2530
GEIC-26	0784
GEIC-27	2535
GEIC-28	1929
GEIC-29	0850
GEIC-30	0746
GEIC-31	0375
GEIC-32	1385
GEIC-33	2538
GEIC-34	1601
GEIC-35	0514
GEIC-36	0872
GEIC-37	0858
GEIC-38	1206
GEIC-39	0385
GEIC-40	0602
GEIC-41	0849
GEIC-42	2546
GEIC-43	2549
GEIC43	OEM
GEIC-44	2551
GEIC-45	2554
GEIC-46	2555
GEIC-47	2556
GEIC-48	1826
GEIC-49	2111
GEIC-50	2559
GEIC-51	2560
GEIC-52	2561
GEIC-53	2562
GEIC-54	2563
GEIC-55	2564
GEIC-56	2565
GEIC-57	2566
GEIC-58	2567
GEIC-59	2568
GEIC-60	2569
GEIC-61	2570
GEIC-62	2571
GEIC-63	2573
GEIC-64	2576
GEIC-65	2578
GEIC-66	2579
GEIC-67	2580
GEIC-68	2581
GEIC-69	2582
GEIC-70	0616
GEIC-71	0875
GEIC-72	0878
GEIC-73	0043
GEIC-74	2510
GEIC-75	2550
GEIC-76	0412
GEIC-77	0837
GEIC-79	0876
GEIC-80	2590
GEIC-81	2593
GEIC-82	2594
GEIC-83	2593
GEIC-84	2600
GEIC-86	0817
GEIC-87	1383
GEIC-88	2560
GEIC-89	0823
GEIC-90	2606
GEIC-91	2046
GEIC-92	0905
GEIC-93	2608
GEIC-94	1983
GEIC-95	2610
GEIC-96	0872
GEIC-97	0391
GEIC-98	0849
GEIC-99	2615
GEIC-100	OEM
GEIC-101	4502
GEIC-102	4476
GEIC-103	1012
GEIC-104	2607
GEIC-105	3859
GEIC-106	2921
GEIC-107	2216
GEIC-109	4514
GEIC-110	4515
GEIC-111	1316
GEIC-112	6085
GEIC-113	4553
GEIC-114	2268
GEIC-115	0784

DEVICE TYPE	REPL CODE
GEIC-116	2855
GEIC-117	0465
GEIC-118	0523
GEIC-119	4463
GEIC-120	0633
GEIC-121	0648
GEIC-122	0668
GEIC-123	2864
GEIC-124	0924
GEIC-125	0940
GEIC-126	0958
GEIC-127	2859
GEIC-128	1469
GEIC-130	2300
GEIC-131	3736
GEIC-132	4495
GEIC-133	2864
GEIC-135	0428
GEIC-136	3318
GEIC-137	4532
GEIC-138	2845
GEIC-139	1470
GEIC-140	2246
GEIC-142	2860
GEIC-143	2560
GEIC-147	0167
GEIC-148	0167
GEIC-149	0872
GEIC-150	4546
GEIC-153	4551
GEIC-154	3606
GEIC-155	0514
GEIC-156	0602
GEIC-157	0043
GEIC-158	0385
GEIC-159	1611
GEIC-160	4490
GEIC-161	4489
GEIC-162	2247
GEIC-163	4481
GEIC-164	4483
GEIC-165	4484
GEIC-166	2862
GEIC-167	4485
GEIC-168	4486
GEIC-169	4320
GEIC-170	4031
GEIC-171	2632
GEIC-172	1686
GEIC-173	0093
GEIC-175	0846
GEIC-176	0851
GEIC-178	2903
GEIC-179	1044
GEIC-180	2664
GEIC-181	2008
GEIC-182	3332
GEIC-183	0784
GEIC-184	0399
GEIC-185	1291
GEIC-190	0619
GEIC-191	1187
GEIC191	1187
GEIC-193	1303
GEIC-194	0268
GEIC-196	3650
GEIC-197	1152
GEIC197	2886
GEIC-199	1369
GEIC-201	4498
GEIC-202	4550
GEIC-203	2644
GEIC-204	2645
GEIC-205	2600
GEIC-207	2689
GEIC-208	3677
GEIC-209	3679
GEIC-210	2507
GEIC-211	OEM
GEIC-212	2979
GEIC-213	3690
GEIC-214	1385
GEIC-215	1411
GEIC-216	2902
GEIC-217	0780
GEIC-218	1797
GEIC-219	3189
GEIC-220	0356
GEIC-221	0368
GEIC-222	0360
GEIC-223	2720
GEIC-224	0373
GEIC-225	0797
GEIC-226	2681
GEIC-227	2688
GEIC-228	2242
GEIC-229	2728
GEIC-230	0345
GEIC-231	1327
GEIC-232	3166
GEIC-233	0516
GEIC-234	1742
GEIC-235	3715
GEIC-236	2674
GEIC-237	3717
GEIC-238	3376
GEIC-239	3388
GEIC-240	3720
GEIC-241	2460

DEVICE TYPE	REPL CODE
GEIC-242	3724
GEIC-243	2977
GEIC-244	0842
GEIC-245	2662
GEIC-246	2676
GEIC-247	2685
GEIC-248	2680
GEIC-249	1291
GEIC-250	1695
GEIC-251	1786
GEIC-252	1789
GEIC-253	1879
GEIC-254	1886
GEIC-255	3757
GEIC-256	2701
GEIC-257	2722
GEIC-258	2696
GEIC-259	1183
GEIC-260	0026
GEIC-261	2863
GEIC-262	1908
GEIC-263	0406
GEIC-264	1964
GEIC-265	0308
GEIC-266	3618
GEIC-267	2352
GEIC-268	2352
GEIC-269	0967
GEIC-271	2991
GEIC-272	4477
GEIC-273	4482
GEIC-274	4338
GEIC-275	2827
GEIC-276	3625
GEIC-277	4506
GEIC-278	1239
GEIC-279	4084
GEIC-280	3946
GEIC-281	3973
GEIC-282	6373
GEIC-284	3106
GEIC-285	4517
GEIC-286	4518
GEIC-287	4520
GEIC-288	2515
GEIC-289	1843
GEIC-290	2673
GEIC-291	1501
GEIC-292	1251
GEIC-293	2932
GEIC-294	OEM
GEIC-295	1516
GEIC-296	4024
GEIC-297	OEM
GEIC-298	4005
GEIC-299	3985
GEIC-300	2914
GEIC-301	3238
GEIC-302	3242
GEIC-303	3993
GEIC-304	1290
GEIC-310	OEM
GEIC-311	3901
GEIC-312	1624
GEIC-313	4513
GEIC-314	2051
GEIC-315	2746
GEIC-316	2754
GEIC-317	1704
GEIC-318	2051
GEIC-319	2289
GEIC-320	3977
GEIC-321	3238
GEIC-322	4331
GEIC-323	3660
GEIC-324	2550
GEIC-325	4133
GEIC-326	1532
GEIC-327	1805
GEIC-328	1049
GEIC-329	2179
GEIC-330	1561
GEIC-331	1602
GEIC-332	3161
GEIC-333	1162
GEIC-334	1042
GEIC-335	3231
GEIC-336	4563
GEL211AL1	0659
GEL211F1	0659
GEL2111	0659
GEL2111AL1	0659
GEL2111F1	0659
GEL2113	0673
GEL2113AL1	0673
GEL2113F1	0673
GEL2114	0661
GEL3072F1	0345
GEM1	OEM
GEM2	OEM
GEM3	OEM
GEM4	OEM
GEM8	OEM
GEM9	OEM
GE-M100	0050
GEMR-1	0097
GEMR-2	0865
GEMR-3	0717
GEMR-4	1478

If replacement code is OEM, contact original manufacturer for replacement. 417

DEVICE TYPE	REPL CODE
GEMR-5	1386
GEMR-6	1680
GEN11760	0918
GEPS2001	0536
GER4001	0071
GER4002	0071
GER4003	0071
GER4004	0071
GER4005	0071
GER4006	0071
GER4007	0071
GER-A	0004
GER-A-D	0050
GES92	0076
GES93	0037
GES97	0079
GES98	0855
GES929	0079
GES930	0079
GES2221	0079
GES2221A	0079
GES2222	0079
GES2222A	0079
GES2483	0079
GES2646	2123
GES2647	1167
GES2904	0037
GES2905	0037
GES2905A	2245
GES2906	0037
GES2907	0037
GES2923	0079
GES2924	0079
GES2925	0079
GES2926	0079
GES3053	0079
GES3390	OEM
GES3391	OEM
GES3391A	OEM
GES3392	0079
GES3393	0079
GES3395	0079
GES3396	0079
GES3397	0079
GES3414	0079
GES3415	0079
GES3416	0079
GES3417	0079
GES3565	0079
GES3566	0079
GES3567	0855
GES3568	0855
GES3569	0855
GES4121	0037
GES4122	0037
GES4248	0037
GES5305	0396
GES5306	0396
GES5306A	0396
GES5307	0396
GES5308	0396
GES5308A	6815
GES5368	0079
GES5369	0079
GES5370	0079
GES5371	0079
GES5372	0037
GES5373	0037
GES5374	0037
GES5375	0037
GES5447	0037
GES5448	0037
GES5449	0016
GES5450	0016
GES5451	0079
GES5810	0320
GES5811	0037
GES5812	0320
GES5813	0037
GES5814	0079
GES5815	0037
GES5816	0079
GES5817	0037
GES5818	0079
GES5819	0037
GES5820	0320
GES5821	0037
GES5822	0079
GES5823	0037
GES5824	0079
GES5825	0079
GES5826	0079
GES5827	0079
GES5827A	0079
GES5828	0111
GES5828A	0111
GES6000	0079
GES6001	0037
GES6002	0079
GES6003	0037
GES6004	0079
GES6005	0037
GES6006	0079
GES6007	0037
GES6010	0086
GES6011	0037
GES6012	0086
GES6013	0037
GES6014	0086

DEVICE TYPE	REPL CODE
GES6015	0037
GES6016	0086
GES6017	0037
GES6218	0710
GES6219	0710
GES6220	0710
GES6221	0855
GES6222	0079
GES6224	0079
GES6426	3749
GES6427	3749
GES6560	0079
GES6561	0079
GES6562	OEM
GES6563	0037
GES60002#	0079
GESS-2AV2	1440
GESS-3A3	1296
GESS-3AT2	2072
GESS-3DB3	2073
GESS-6DW4	2074
GET0-50P	0164
GET3	OEM
GET4	OEM
GET5	OEM
GET6	OEM
GET7	OEM
GET8	OEM
GET9	OEM
GET15	OEM
GET102	OEM
GET-103	0211
GET103	0004
GET104	OEM
GET105	OEM
GET106	OEM
GET110	OEM
GET111	OEM
GET-113	0211
GET113	0004
GET-113A	0211
GET113A	0004
GET-114	0211
GET114	0004
GET115	OEM
GET116	OEM
GET120	OEM
GET535	0164
GET536	0164
GET538	0164
GET571	OEM
GET-572	0160
GET572	0160
GET573	OEM
GET574	OEM
GET581	0160
GET582	0160
GET583	0160
GET584	0160
GET585	OEM
GET586	OEM
GET671	0050
GET-672	0050
GET672	0050
GET-672A	0050
GET672A	0050
GET-673	0050
GET673	0050
GET691	0050
GET-692	0050
GET692	0050
GET693	0050
GET706	0016
GET708	0016
GET870	OEM
GET871	0136
GET872	0136
GET873	0136
GET-873A	0050
GET873A	0136
GET874	0136
GET875	0136
GET880	0279
GET881	0279
GET882	0279
GET-883	0050
GET883	0136
GET884	0004
GET885	0136
GET887	0279
GET888	0279
GET889	0279
GET890	0279
GET891	0279
GET892	0279
GET895	0279
GET896	0279
GET897	0279
GET898	0211
GET914	0016
GET929	0086
GET930	0086
GET931	0050
GET2221	0016
GET2221A	0079
GET2222	0016
GET2222A	0079
GET2369	0016
GET2483	0111

DEVICE TYPE	REPL CODE
GET2904	0150
GET2905	0150
GET2906	0527
GET2907	0527
GET3013	0016
GET3014	0016
GET3562	0111
GET3563	0224
GET3638	0037
GET3638A	0037
GET3646	0016
GET3903	0079
GET3904	0079
GET3905	0150
GET3906	0150
GET4870	2123
GET4871	1167
GET5116	0050
GET5117	0050
GET5305	0396
GET5306	0396
GET5306A	OEM
GET5307	0396
GET5308	0396
GET5308A	0396
GET5457	OEM
GET5458	OEM
GET5459	OEM
GET-FET-6	0349
GET0-50P	0164
GEVR-100	1288
GEVR-101	0619
GEVR-102	0619
GEVR-104	1275
GEVR-105	1275
GEVR-106	0083
GEVR-107	1187
GEVR-108	1187
GEVR-109	1817
GEVR-110	0330
GEVR-111	0330
GEVR-112	1825
GEVR-113	1827
GEVR-114	1827
GEVR-115	1183
GEVR-116	1183
GE-X1	0240
GE-X3	2174
GE-X4	0464
GE-X5	1250
GE-X8	0038
GEX8	0038
GE-X9	0004
GE-X10	2123
GE-X11	0244
GE-X12	0154
GE-X13	2137
GE-X16	0671
GE-X16A1938	0016
GE-X17	0312
GE-X18	0555
GE-X36	0015
GEX36	0015
GE-X66	0143
GEX66	0015
GEX541	OEM
GEX542	OEM
GEXM66	OEM
GE-Z83	0470
GEZD-3.3	0289
GEZD-3.6	0188
GEZD-3.9	0451
GEZD-4.3	0528
GEZD-4.7	0446
GEZD-5.0	0162
GEZD-5.1	0162
GEZD-5.6	0157
GEZD-5.8	3099
GEZD-6.0	0298
GEZD-6.2	0631
GEZD-6.6	0025
GEZD-6.8	0025
GEZD-7.5	0644
GEZD-8.0	0244
GEZD-8.1	0244
GEZD-8.2	0244
GEZD-8.7	1075
GEZD-9.1	0012
GEZD-10	0170
GEZD-10-4	0170
GEZD-10.4	0064
GEZD-11	0313
GEZD-11.5	0789
GEZD-12	0137
GEZD-13	0361
GEZD-14	0100
GEZD-15	0002
GEZD-16	0416
GEZD-17	1639
GEZD-18	0490
GEZD-19	0943
GEZD-20	0526
GEZD-22	0560
GEZD-24	0398
GEZD-25	1596
GEZD-27	0436
GEZD-28	1664
GEZD-30	0721
GEZD-33	0039

DEVICE TYPE	REPL CODE
GEZD-35	0814
GEZD-36	0814
GEZD-39	0346
GEZD-43	0925
GEZD-47	0993
GEZD-51	0497
GEZD-55	1823
GEZD-56	0863
GEZD-60	1148
GEZD-62	0778
GEZD-68	1258
GEZD-75	1181
GEZD-82	0327
GEZD-87	2997
GEZD-91	1301
GEZD-100	0098
GEZD-110	0149
GEZD-120	0186
GEZD-130	0213
GEZD-140	0245
GEZD-150	0028
GEZD-160	0255
GEZD-170	0871
GEZD-180	0363
GEZD-190	2831
GEZD-200	0417
GEZJ252A	0015
GEZJ252B	0015
GEZN-1-9145-1	OEM
GEZN-2-9145-1	OEM
GEZN-3-9145-1	OEM
GEZN-5-9145-1	OEM
GF021A2	OEM
GF0D1A1	OEM
GF20	0211
GF21	0211
GF32	0211
GF45017	OEM
GFA03L	0017
GFA03R	0017
GFB30B	0031
GFB30C	0031
GFB30E	0031
GFB-30G	4861
GFB30G	0023
GFB30G-FD1	0031
GFB7496D	OEM
GFD10B	0023
GFD10C	0023
GFD10E	0023
GFD10G	0023
GFE10	0017
GFE10R	0182
GFE10RGET0-50P	OEM
GFH6001	OEM
GFH6002	OEM
GFH6003	OEM
GFOD1A1	OEM
GFOD1B1	OEM
GFOD1B2	OEM
GFOE1A1	OEM
GFOE1A2	OEM
GFT20	OEM
GFT20/15	0004
GFT20/30	0004
GFT20/60	OEM
GFT20R	0004
GFT21	OEM
GFT21/15	0004
GFT21/30	0004
GFT21/60	OEM
GFT21R	0004
GFT22	OEM
GFT22/15	0164
GFT22/30	0164
GFT22/60	OEM
GFT22R	0164
GFT25	OEM
GFT25/15	0004
GFT25/30	0004
GFT25/60	OEM
GFT25R	0004
GFT26	OEM
GFT30	OEM
GFT31	0004
GFT31/15	0164
GFT31/30	0004
GFT31/60	OEM
GFT32	0004
GFT32/15	OEM
GFT32/30	OEM
GFT32/60	OEM
GFT34	0004
GFT34/15	OEM
GFT34/30	OEM
GFT34/60	OEM
GFT41	OEM
GFT42A	OEM
GFT42B	OEM
GFT43	OEM
GFT43A	OEM
GFT43B	OEM
GFT44	0050
GFT44/15E	OEM
GFT44/30	OEM
GFT45	0050
GFT45/30	OEM
GFT2006	OEM
GFT2006/30	OEM

DEVICE TYPE	REPL CODE
GFT2006/60	OEM
GFT2006/90	OEM
GFT3008/20	OEM
GFT3008/40	0211
GFT3008/60	OEM
GFT3008/80	OEM
GFT3408/20	OEM
GFT3408/40	OEM
GFT3408/60	OEM
GFT3408/80	OEM
GFT4012	OEM
GFT4012/30	OEM
GFT4012/60	OEM
GFT4308/40	OEM
GFT4308/60	OEM
GFT4308/80	OEM
GFT4412/30	OEM
GFT4412/60	OEM
GFT4608/40	OEM
GFT4608/60	OEM
GFT4608/80	OEM
GFT8024	OEM
GH1D	OEM
GH-1E	0102
GH-1F	0182
GH1F	0344
GH2-021	OEM
GH-3E	0182
GH-3F	0102
GH3F	0158
GH3FLF	0158
GHC801	OEM
GHC801A	OEM
GHC801B	OEM
GHV-02SSN	OEM
GHV06BSS	OEM
GHV-06SSN	OEM
GHV-2	OEM
GHV2	OEM
GHV-3	OEM
GHV3	OEM
GHV-4	OEM
GHV4	OEM
GHV-5	OEM
GHV5	OEM
GHV-6	OEM
GHV-7	OEM
GHV7	OEM
GHV-8	OEM
GHV8	OEM
GHV-9	OEM
GHV-10	OEM
GHV-10SL	OEM
GHV-10SS	0201
GHV-10SSN	OEM
GHV-11	OEM
GHV-12	OEM
GHV-12SL	OEM
GHV-12SS	0201
GHV-12SSN	OEM
GHV-13	OEM
GHV-14	OEM
GHV-14SL	OEM
GHV-14SS	0286
GHV-14SSN	OEM
GHV-15	OEM
GHV-16	OEM
GHV-16SL	OEM
GHV-16SSN	OEM
GHV-18SS	0374
GHV-18SSN	OEM
GHV-20SL	OEM
GHV-24SL	OEM
GI08B	0015
GI1	0279
GI-1N4385	0015
GI2	0211
GI3	0136
GI4	0211
GI5	0595
GI6	0595
GI7	0595
GI8	0038
GI9	0435
GI10	0016
GI82AG	OEM
GI-100-1	0015
GI103A	OEM
GI103B	OEM
GI103G	OEM
GI103V	OEM
GI212-152-04	0441
GI254	0023
GI263	OEM
GI298-03	0023
GI-300B	0015
GI-300D	0015
GI304A	OEM
GI304B	OEM
GI305A	OEM
GI305B	OEM
GI307A	OEM
GI308A	OEM
GI308B	OEM
GI308D	OEM
GI308E	OEM
GI308G	OEM
GI308I	OEM
GI308K	OEM

DEVICE TYPE	REPL CODE
GI308SZ	OEM
GI308V	OEM
GI323-04	0023
GI339-04	0102
GI356-03	1227
GI401A	OEM
GI401B	OEM
GI402D	OEM
GI403A	OEM
GI411	0015
GI415B	0023
GI419-0	0015
GI419B	0015
GI420	0015
GI428B	0015
GI437B	0031
GI500	0110
GI501	0947
GI502	0242
GI504	0535
GI506	0959
GI508	0811
GI510	0916
GI750	1272
GI751	1272
GI752	1277
GI754	1277
GI756	1282
GI758	1285
GI810	0023
GI811	0023
GI812	0023
GI814	0023
GI816	0023
GI817	0017
GI818	0102
GI820	1352
GI821	1352
GI822	1352
GI824	1356
GI826	1362
GI828	1362
GI850	0031
GI851	0031
GI852	0031
GI854	0031
GI856	0031
GI910	0031
GI911	0031
GI912	0031
GI914	0031
GI916	0031
GI917	1483
GI918	OEM
GI1001	0494
GI1002	0494
GI1003	0494
GI1004	0494
GI1101	0031
GI1102	0031
GI1103	0031
GI1104	0031
GI1301	OEM
GI1302	OEM
GI1303	OEM
GI1304	OEM
GI1401	1137
GI1401R	OEM
GI1402	1137
GI1402R	OEM
GI1403	1137
GI1403R	OEM
GI1404	1137
GI1404R	OEM
GI2401	1227
GI2401R	1716
GI2402	1227
GI2402R	1716
GI2403	1227
GI2403R	1716
GI2404	1227
GI2404R	1716
GI2500	OEM
GI2501	OEM
GI2502	OEM
GI2504	OEM
GI2506	OEM
GI2508	OEM
GI2510	OEM
GI2601	OEM
GI2601R	OEM
GI2602	OEM
GI2602R	OEM
GI2603	OEM
GI2603R	OEM
GI2604	OEM
GI2604R	OEM
GI2605	OEM
GI2605R	OEM
GI2606	OEM
GI2606R	OEM
GI-2711	0079
GI2711	0016
GI-2712	0079
GI2712	0016
GI-2713	0855
GI2713	0079
GI-2714	0079
GI2714	0016

DEVICE TYPE	REPL CODE
GI-2715	0007
GI2715	0016
GI-2716	0007
GI2716	0016
GI-2921	0007
GI2921	0016
GI-2922	0007
GI2922	0016
GI-2923	0007
GI2923	0016
GI-2924	0111
GI2924	0016
GI-2925	0111
GI2925	OEM
GI-2926	0008
GI2926	OEM
GI3002	0015
GI-3008	0015
GI-3391	0111
GI-3391A	0111
GI-3392	0111
GI3392	OEM
GI-3393	0111
GI-3394	0111
GI-3395	0111
GI-3396	0111
GI-3397	0111
GI-3398	0111
GI-3402	0855
GI-3403	0079
GI-3404	0855
GI-3405	0079
GI-3414	0855
GI-3415	0079
GI-3416	0079
GI-3417	0079
GI-3566	0855
GI-3605	0007
GI-3606	0007
GI-3607	0007
GI-3638	0855
GI3638	0037
GI-3638A	0855
GI3638A	0037
GI-3641	0079
GI3641	0016
GI-3642	0079
GI-3643	0079
GI3643	0016
GI-3644	0527
GI3644	0037
GI-3702	0855
GI3702	0037
GI-3703	0855
GI3703	0037
GI-3704	0079
GI3704	0016
GI-3705	0079
GI3705	0016
GI-3706	0079
GI3706	0016
GI-3707	0111
GI3707	0016
GI-3708	0111
GI3708	0016
GI-3709	0111
GI3709	0016
GI-3710	0111
GI3710	0016
GI-3711	0111
GI3711	0016
GI-3721	0111
GI-3793	0855
GI3793	0007
GI-3794	0855
GI3794	OEM
GI-3900	0111
GI-3900A	0111
GI3992-17	0015
GI5823	OEM
GI5824	OEM
GI5825	OEM
GI6506	0595
GI8301	OEM
GI12605	OEM
GI12605R	OEM
GI12606	OEM
GI12606R	OEM
GI405919-4	OEM
GIB2500	5652
GIB2501	5652
GIB2502	5653
GIB2504	5654
GIB2506	5656
GIB2508	5658
GIB2510	5660
GIB3500	5790
GIB3501	5790
GIB3502	5790
GIB3504	5791
GIB3506	5791
GIB3508	5793
GIB3510	5793
GID	0015
GIFE16A	1227
GIFE16D	OEM
GI-P100-D	0015
GIP100-D	0087
GIP100D	0015

418

If replacement code is OEM, contact original manufacturer for replacement.

DEVICE TYPE	REPL CODE
GIRG3K	1208
GI-TVC3	0469
GJ3M	OEM
GJ4M	0015
GJ5M	OEM
GJ6M	OEM
GL1HD51	OEM
GL1HD101	OEM
GL1HY102	OEM
GL-1N4385	0015
GL1PR101	OEM
GL1PR102	OEM
GL1PR111	OEM
GL2AR1	OEM
GL2HY1	OEM
GL2PG1	OEM
GL2PR1	OEM
GL2PR6	OEM
GL2PR9	OEM
GL3AR1	OEM
GL3AR2	OEM
GL3AR3	OEM
GL3D403	OEM
GL3D405	OEM
GL3HD1	OEM
GL3HD5	OEM
GL3HY1	OEM
GL3HY2	OEM
GL3HY3	OEM
GL3HY8	OEM
GL3N403	OEM
GL3N405	OEM
GL3N407	OEM
GL3NG1	OEM
GL3NG5	OEM
GL3P01	OEM
GL3P403	OEM
GL3P405	OEM
GL3P407	OEM
GL3P503	OEM
GL3PG1	OEM
GL3PG2	OEM
GL3PG3	OEM
GL3PG5	OEM
GL3PR1	OEM
GL3PR2	OEM
GL3PR3	OEM
GL-3PR7	OEM
GL3PR8	OEM
GL4AR2	OEM
GL4HY2	OEM
GL4NG2	OEM
GL4PG2	OEM
GL4PR2	OEM
GL4R04A	OEM
GL4R06A	OEM
GL4R10A	OEM
GL5AR1	3153
GL5AR2	1951
GL-5HD5	OEM
GL5HD5	OEM
GL5HD10	OEM
GL5HD21	OEM
GL-5HD23	OEM
GL5HY1	OEM
GL5HY2	OEM
GL5HY5	OEM
GL5HY8	OEM
GL5HY41	OEM
GL-5IID23	OEM
GL5ND5	OEM
GL5NG6	5282
GL5NG10	OEM
GL5NP5	OEM
GL5PG1	OEM
GL5PG2	OEM
GL-5PG5	OEM
GL5PG5	OEM
GL5PG22	OEM
GL5PR002	OEM
GL5PR1	OEM
GL-5PR2	OEM
GL5PR2	OEM
GL5PR5	OEM
GL5PR6	1951
GL6D201	OEM
GL6N201	OEM
GL6N202	OEM
GL6N402	OEM
GL6P201	4267
GL6P202	OEM
GL6P401	OEM
GL6R201	OEM
GL6R202	OEM
GL7D212	OEM
GL7N201	OEM
GL-7N202	OEM
GL8D04	OEM
GL8D06	OEM
GL8D303D	OEM
GL8G03	OEM
GL8G04	OEM
GL8N03D	OEM
GL8N04	OEM
GL8N06	OEM
GL8P03	OEM
GL8P03D	OEM
GL8P04	OEM
GL8PR22	OEM
GL8R03	OEM
GL8R03D	OEM
GL8R06	OEM
GL8R10	OEM
GL9HD2	OEM
GL9HD4	5346
GL9HD6	OEM
GL9HD9	OEM
GL9HD10	OEM
GL9HD22	OEM
GL9HD23	OEM
GL9HD24	OEM
GL9HP2	OEM
GL9HY2	OEM
GL9HY4	4973
GL9HY6	OEM
GL9HY9	OEM
GL9HY10	OEM
GL9HY22	OEM
GL9HY23	OEM
GL9HY24	OEM
GL9N06	OEM
GL9N06A	OEM
GL9ND2	OEM
GL9ND24	OEM
GL9NG2	OEM
GL9NG4	OEM
GL9NG5	OEM
GL9NG9	OEM
GL9NG10	OEM
GL9NG22	OEM
GL9NG23	OEM
GL9NG24	OEM
GL9NP2	OEM
GL9NP24	OEM
GL9PG2	OEM
GL9PG3	OEM
GL9PG4	5347
GL9PG9	OEM
GL9PG12	OEM
GL9PG24	OEM
GL9PG34	OEM
GL9PR2	OEM
GL9PR3	OEM
GL9PR4	5346
GL9PR5	OEM
GL9PR6	OEM
GL9PR9	OEM
GL9PR10	OEM
GL9PR12	OEM
GL9PR19	OEM
GL9PR22	OEM
GL9PR23	OEM
GL-9PR24	OEM
GL9PR24	OEM
GL9PR34	OEM
GL19G102	OEM
GL27A	OEM
GL27B	OEM
GL27D	OEM
GL27G	OEM
GL27J	OEM
GL27K	OEM
GL27M	OEM
GL31AR	2990
GL-32AR	2990
GL-40-RG	OEM
GL41A	OEM
GL41B	OEM
GL41D	OEM
GL41G	OEM
GL41J	OEM
GL41K	OEM
GL41M	OEM
GL50G	OEM
GL-52B	OEM
GL56	1972
GL68	OEM
GL105G11	OEM
GL105H5	OEM
GL105H11	OEM
GL105M5	OEM
GL105M11	OEM
GL105N5	OEM
GL105N11	OEM
GL105R5	OEM
GL105R11	OEM
GL105R53	OEM
GL106H5	OEM
GL106M5	OEM
GL106N5	OEM
GL-106NS	OEM
GL106R5	OEM
GL106R50	OEM
GL107G12	OEM
GL107H12	OEM
GL107N12	OEM
GL107R12	OEM
GL107S12	OEM
GL112G9	OEM
GL112G13	OEM
GL112H9	OEM
GL112H13	OEM
GL112M2	OEM
GL112M9	OEM
GL112M13	OEM
GL112N9	OEM
GL112N13	OEM
GL112R3	OEM
GL112R9	OEM
GL112R13	OEM
GL112S9	OEM
GL112S13	OEM
GL112T9	OEM
GL112T13	OEM
GL211	0835
GL324	OEM
GL348	OEM
GL350	OEM
GL358	0765
GL393	OEM
GL410	OEM
GL430	OEM
GL-450	2678
GL450	2678
GL-450V	2678
GL450V	OEM
GL451	2678
GL452S	OEM
GL504	OEM
GL513F	OEM
GL514	OEM
GL520	OEM
GL-521	OEM
GL-526	OEM
GL528	3300
GL552	OEM
GL-750S	OEM
GL-751RS	OEM
GL-950S	OEM
GL-951RS	OEM
GL-1001	OEM
GL-1002	OEM
GL-1003	OEM
GL1010	0491
GL1050S	OEM
GL1051RS	OEM
GL1130	0727
GL3101A	2104
GL3101A/B	OEM
GL3101B	2104
GL3120	0534
GL-3201	0167
GL3201	0167
GL3301	2109
GL3301B	2109
GL3320	0552
GL3401	OEM
GL3711	OEM
GL3812	OEM
GL3820	OEM
GL4484	OEM
GL4558	3406
GL4850	1767
GL4950	1767
GL7445	OEM
GL7805	0619
GL7805A	OEM
GL7806	4317
GL7809	OEM
GL7812	0330
GL7815	1311
GLA28	OEM
GLA28A	OEM
GLA28B	OEM
GLA31	OEM
GLA31A	OEM
GLA31B	OEM
GLA35	OEM
GLA35A	OEM
GLA35B	OEM
GLA39	0188
GLA39A	0188
GLA39B	0451
GLA43	0528
GLA43A	0528
GLA43B	0528
GLA47	0162
GLA47A	0162
GLA47B	0446
GLA51	0162
GLA51A	0162
GLA51B	0162
GLA56	0157
GLA56A	0157
GLA56B	0157
GLA62	0631
GLA62A	0631
GLA62B	0631
GLA68	0025
GLA68A	0025
GLA68B	0025
GLA75	0644
GLA75A	0644
GLA75B	0644
GLA82	0244
GLA82A	0244
GLA82B	0244
GLA91	0012
GLA91A	0012
GLA91B	0012
GLA100	0170
GLA100A	0170
GLA100B	0170
GLE102	OEM
GLE502	OEM
GLE703	OEM
GLPHY4	4973
GLT12	OEM
GLT24	OEM
GLT47	OEM
GLT120	OEM
GM0290	0050
GM0375	0050
GM0376	0050
GM0377	0050
GM0378	0293
GM0380	0144
GM0384	OEM
GM-1	0087
GM-1A	0087
GM-1B	0071
GM-1C	0071
GM1J2	0071
GM-1Z	0087
GM-3	0087
GM3	0087
GM-3A	0087
GM-3B	0087
GM3B	0559
GM-3C	0916
GM3DM	OEM
GM-3Y	0087
GM3Y	0023
GM-3Z	0087
GM3Z	0087
GM30A	3631
GM30B	3631
GM30D	3631
GM30G	3634
GM30J	3635
GM30K	OEM
GM290	0050
GM290A	0050
GM308	0007
GM320MP-5.2	1275
GM378	0050
GM378A	0050
GM-380	OEM
GM380	0136
GM384	OEM
GM428	0160
GM656A	0050
GM760	0037
GM-770	0127
GM770	0127
GM770GM0375	OEM
GM875	0050
GM876	0050
GM877	0050
GM878	0050
GM878A	0050
GM878AB	0050
GM878B	0050
GM3043	OEM
GM3742-01	OEM
GM3742-02	OEM
GMA-01	0124
GMA01	0124
GMA01-01-BT	0124
GMA01-4-BT	OEM
GMA01-8T	OEM
GMA01-AT	OEM
GMA-01-BT	0124
GMA01-BT	0124
GMA01-FY1	OEM
GMA01-L	0133
GMA01L	0133
GMA-10-BT	0124
GMB01	0124
GMB01B	0124
GMB01BT	0124
GMB01L	0124
GMD1	OEM
GMD2	OEM
GMD5	OEM
GME040-1	0037
GME0404	0150
GME0404-1	0150
GME0404-2	0150
GME404-1	0150
GME1001	0016
GME1002	0016
GME2001	0016
GME2002	0016
GME3001	0144
GME3002	0144
GME4001	0016
GME4002	0016
GME4003	0016
GME6001	0127
GME6002	0127
GME6003	0016
GME9001	0144
GME9002	0144
GME9021	0144
GME9022	0144
GMO290	0050
GMO375	0050
GMO376	0050
GMO377	0050
GMO378	0050
GMO-380	0079
GMO380	0007
GMP-5	OEM
GMP5	OEM
GMP-5A	OEM
GMP5A	OEM
GMP-5B	OEM
GMP5B	OEM
GN13G	1281
GN1036E	OEM
GN-1039E-006	OEM
GN2050	OEM
GN3002U	OEM
GN3100E	OEM
GN3210	OEM
GN3500	OEM
GN3600	OEM
G01-803A	0162
G03-007C	0555
G03-404-B	0126
G03PR5	OEM
G04-041B	0079
G04-701-A	0085
G04-703-A	0841
G04-704-A	0222
G04-711-E	0164
G04-711-F	0164
G04-711-G	0164
G04-711-H	0164
G05-003-A	0079
G05-003-B	0079
G05-004A	0127
G05-010-A	0016
G05-011-A	0016
G05-015-C	0079
G05-015-D	0086
G05-034-D	0086
G05-035-D	0111
G05-035-D,E	0111
G05-035-E	0111
G05-036-C,D,E	0079
G05-036B	0079
G05-036C	0079
G05-036D	0086
G05-036E	0079
G05-037B	0079
G05-050-C	0079
G05-055-D	0086
G05-413A	0086
G06-714C	0555
G06-717-B	0555
G08-005L	0321
GO0-004-A	0143
GO0-008-A	0143
GO0-009-A	0143
GO0-012-A	0162
GO0-013-8	0143
GO0-014-A	0162
GO0-535-B	0535
GO0-536A	0535
GO0-543-A	0535
GP05A	0015
GP08B	0015
GP-08D	0087
GP08D	0087
GP08DPKG3	OEM
GP08DPKG23	0087
GP08G	0959
GP1	0015
GP1A52HR	OEM
GP1A521	OEM
GP1F31T	OEM
GP1L01	OEM
GP1L01F	OEM
GP1L02	OEM
GP1S01F	OEM
GP1S02	OEM
GP1S03	OEM
GP1S04	OEM
GP1S53	OEM
GP1U50X	OEM
GP1U52	OEM
GP1U521H	OEM
GP1U521Y	OEM
GP1U561	OEM
GP1U721Q	OEM
GP1U721Y	OEM
GP-2	OEM
GP2	OEM
GP2-015	OEM
GP2-345	0133
GP2-354	0133
GP2L01	OEM
GP2L01F	OEM
GP2L02	OEM
GP2S01	OEM
GP2S01F	OEM
GP2S02	5556
GP2S04A	OEM
GP2S04B	OEM
GP2S09-B	OEM
GP2S09-C	OEM
GP3A21	OEM
GP-6-019	OEM
GP6C10	OEM
GP6C20	OEM
GP6C30	OEM
GP10	OEM
GP10A	1325
GP10B	0080
GP10C	0015
GP10D	0023
GP10G	0790
GP10G5020	OEM
GP10J	0015
GP10K	0072
GP10M	0071
GP10N	0344
GP10Q	0344
GP10T	0344
GP10V	0344
GP10W	0344
GP10Y	0344
GP15	0087
GP15A	0071
GP15B	0015
GP15B(L)	0071
GP15BL	0071
GP15D	0015
GP15G	0071
GP15J	0071
GP15J-16	0071
GP15K	0071
GP15M	0071
GP16	OEM
GP20A	0071
GP20B	0071
GP20D	0071
GP20G	0023
GP20J	0071
GP20K	0071
GP20M	0071
GP25A	0110
GP-25B	0015
GP25B	0947
GP25D	0242
GP25G	0535
GP25J	0959
GP25K	0811
GP25M	0916
GP30A	0110
GP-30B	0947
GP30B	0947
GP-30D	0916
GP30D	0242
GP30G	0535
GP30J	0959
GP30JG	0959
GP30K	0811
GP30M	0916
GP80A	1137
GP80B	1137
GP80D	1137
GP80G	1137
GP80J	1654
GP80K	OEM
GP80M	OEM
GP106	0071
GP130	OEM
GP139	0004
GP139A	0004
GP139B	0004
GP150	OEM
GP175	OEM
GP199	OEM
GP204	4344
GP230	0015
GP250	0015
GP252	0087
GP-300	0242
GP330	0124
GP340	0124
GP350	OEM
GP360	OEM
GP411	OEM
GP411F	OEM
GP415	OEM
GP450	OEM
GP450F	OEM
GP500	OEM
GP1432	0160
GP1448	OEM
GP1462	OEM
GP1493	0160
GP1494	0160
GP1600	OEM
GP1622	0435
GP1882	0160
GP2354	0143
GP2364	0143
GP-6019	OEM
GP6019	OEM
GPA1100	OEM
GPC215	OEM
GPC215A	OEM
GPD020	OEM
GPD040	OEM
GPD050	OEM
GPD060	OEM
GPD070	OEM
GPD1	OEM
GPD5	OEM
GPD201	OEM
GPD202	OEM
GPD251	OEM
GPD252	OEM
GPD401	OEM
GPD402	OEM
GPD403	OEM
GPD404	OEM
GPD411	OEM
GPD420	OEM
GPD426	OEM
GPD430	OEM
GPD440	OEM
GPD461	OEM
GPD462	OEM
GPD463	OEM
GPD464	OEM
GPD470	OEM
GPD520	OEM
GPD540	OEM
GPD550	OEM
GPD620	OEM
GPD620C	OEM
GPD620P	OEM
GPD630C	OEM
GPD630P	OEM
GPD640C	OEM
GPD640P	OEM
GPD660C	OEM
GPD660P	OEM
GPD670C	OEM
GPD670P	OEM
GPD720P	OEM
GPD726	OEM
GPD730P	OEM
GPD740P	OEM
GPD760P	OEM
GPD770P	OEM
GPD886	OEM
GPD1001	OEM
GPD1002	OEM
GPD1003	OEM
GPD1061	OEM
GPD1062	OEM
GPD1063	OEM
GPIB11V-2	OEM
GPIU5	OEM
GPL4A	OEM
GPL1001	OEM
GPM1NA	0143
GPM1NB	0143
GPM1NC	0143
GPM2NA	0143
GPM2NB	0143
GPP1A	OEM
GPP1B	OEM
GPP1D	OEM
GPP1G	OEM
GPP1J	OEM
GPP1K	OEM
GPP1M	OEM
GPP5A	OEM
GPP5B	OEM
GPP5D	OEM
GPP5G	OEM
GPP5J	OEM
GPP5K	OEM
GPP10A	0182
GPP10B	0182
GPP10D	0182
GPP10G	0182
GPP10J	0182
GPP10K	0182
GPP10M	0182
GPP15A	0102
GPP15B	0102
GPP15D	0102
GPP15G	0102
GPP15J	0102
GPP15K	0102
GPP15M	0102
GPP30A	0031
GPP30B	0031
GPP30D	0031
GPP30G	0031
GPP30J	0031
GPP30K	1208
GPP30M	1917
GPP60A	OEM
GPP60B	OEM
GPP60D	OEM
GPP60G	OEM
GPP60J	OEM
GPP60K	OEM
GPP60M	OEM
GPR-1	OEM
GPS203	OEM
GPT	OEM
GPT-16	0160
GPT16	0085
GQ5Y	OEM
GR10-602GB	OEM
GR16	0071
GR17	OEM
GR18	OEM
GR19	OEM
GR20	OEM
GR21	OEM
GR22	0087
GR23	0087
GR24	0087
GR606	0706
GR612	0706
GR727	OEM
GR806	OEM
GR812	OEM
GRE5036	OEM
GRE5036-ZB	OEM
GRE7159	OEM
GRE7189	OEM

If replacement code is OEM, contact original manufacturer for replacement.

419

Original Device Types

DEVICE TYPE	REPL CODE	DEVICE TYPE	REPL CODE	DEVICE TYPE	REPL CODE	DEVICE TYPE	REPL CODE	DEVICE TYPE	REPL CODE	DEVICE TYPE	REPL CODE	DEVICE TYPE	REPL CODE
GREA4	OEM	GS2017-H	1077	GS9022I	0338	GSR5	OEM	GT34S	0279	GT-759R	0211	GU-1A	0023
GREA7	OEM	GS2017G	1077	GS9022J	0338	GSR6	OEM	GT-35	2704	GT759R	0004	GU1A100SB	OEM
GREA7A	OEM	GS2017H	0261	GS9022P	0338	GSR7	OEM	GT35	0208	GT-760	0004	GU-1B	0102
GREA10B	OEM	GS2020-1	OEM	GS9022Q	0338	GSR8	OEM	GT36	0767	GT760	0279	GU-1C	0102
GREA14	OEM	GS2020-2	OEM	GS9023	0079	GSR9	OEM	GT38	OEM	GT760R	0211	GU-1E	0102
GREA14A	OEM	GS2023-G	OEM	GS9023(H)	0079	GSR10	OEM	GT40	0004	GT760R	0004	GU-1F	0182
GREA19B	OEM	GS2052(G)	3706	GS9023-1	0079	GSR11	OEM	GT41	0004	GT-761	0004	GU-1Z	0023
GREA29A	OEM	GS2052(H)	0919	GS9023-G	0079	GSR12	OEM	GT42	0004	GT761	0279	GU-3	0023
GREA35	OEM	GS2052D	0919	GS9023-H	0079	GSR13	OEM	GT43	0004	GT-761R	0211	GU3	0023
GREA38B	OEM	GS2052G	0919	GS9023-I	0079	GSR14	OEM	GT44	0004	GT761R	0279	GU-3A	0023
GREA70	OEM	GS2052H	0919	GS9023G	0079	GSR15	OEM	GT45	0004	GT-762	0004	GU3A	0102
GREA72A	OEM	GS2053-G	0919	GS9023H	0079	GSRU15030	OEM	GT46	0004	GT762	0279	GU3B	0102
GREA95B	OEM	GS2053-I	0713	GS9023I	0079	GSRU15035	OEM	GT47	0004	GT-762R	0211	GU-3C	0023
GREA145A	OEM	GS2053H	3706	GS9023J	0079	GSRU15040	OEM	GT48	OEM	GT762R	0279	GU3C	0023
GREA190B	OEM	GS2053H	3706	GS9023K	0016	GSRU20030	OEM	GT56	0612	GT-763	0004	GU-3SY	0031
GRU-2A	0102	GS3020-1	OEM	GS9024	0284	GSRU20035	OEM	GT58	OEM	GT763	0004	GU3SY	OEM
GRU2A	0102	GS3020-2	OEM	GS9024(J)	0284	GSRU20040	OEM	GT-66	0136	GT-764	0279	GU-3SZ	0242
GS2C117	OEM	GS3020-3	OEM	GS9024(K)	0284	GSTU4030	1331	GT66	0136	GT764	0279	GU3SZ	0242
GS6.2	OEM	GS3020-4	OEM	GS9024-I	0284	GSTU4035	1331	GT68	OEM	GT766	0279	GU-3Z	0023
GS6.2A	OEM	GS3030-1	OEM	GS9024J	0284	GSTU4040	1331	GT74	0211	GT766A	0279	GV-3SY	0031
GS13	OEM	GS3030-2	OEM	GS9024K	0284	GSTU6030	1331	GT75	0211	GT792	0595	GV5760	0133
GS23	OEM	GS3030-3	OEM	GS9025(J)	0079	GSTU6035	1331	GT81	0211	GT792R	OEM	GV6063	0016
GS43	OEM	GS3040-1	OEM	GS9025H	0079	GSTU6040	1331	GT-81H	0279	GT811	OEM	GW1	OEM
GS63	OEM	GS3040-2	OEM	GS9025I	0079	GSTU8035	4315	GT81H	0279	GT812	OEM	GW2	OEM
GS73E/3	0143	GS3040-3	OEM	GS9025J	0079	GSTU8040	4315	GT-81HS	0279	GT832	0279	GW3	OEM
GS83	OEM	GS3040-4	OEM	GS9025J-1	0284	GSTU10030	4315	GT81HS	0004	GT-903	0038	GW5	OEM
GS100	OEM	GS4021-1	OEM	GS9027	2319	GSTU10035	4315	GT81R	0004	GT903	0208	GW10	OEM
GS100L	OEM	GS4021-2	OEM	GS9027(G)	0261	GSTU10040	4315	GT82	0211	GT904	0595	GW11	OEM
GS101A	OEM	GS4021-3	OEM	GS9027(H)	0261	GSTU15018	4315	GT-83	0279	GT-905	0038	GXB10100	OEM
GS102	OEM	GS4021-4	OEM	GS9027G	0261	GSTU15020	4315	GT83	0279	GT905	0595	GXB10100D	OEM
GS103	OEM	GS4123-1	OEM	GS9027H	0261	GSTU30018	OEM	GT-87	0279	GT905R	0595	GXB10100P	OEM
GS120	OEM	GS4123-2	OEM	GS9032H	0338	GSTU30020	OEM	GT87	0279	GT906AM	OEM	GXB10101	OEM
GS135	OEM	GS4123-3	OEM	GS9032I	0338	GSV101	OEM	GT-88	0279	GT-947	0038	GXB10101D	OEM
GS150	OEM	GS4123-4	OEM	GS9032J	0338	GSV102	OEM	GT88	0279	GT947	0595	GXB10101P	OEM
GS160	OEM	GS5040-1	OEM	GS9033	0079	GSV103	OEM	GT100	0279	GT948	0595	GXB10102	OEM
GS161	OEM	GS5040-2	OEM	GS9033(I)	0079	GSZ2.7	0755	GT-109	0211	GT948R	0038	GXB10102D	OEM
GS162	OEM	GS5040-3	OEM	GS9033(J)	0079	GSZ2.7A	0755	GT109	0004	GT949	0038	GXB10102P	OEM
GS163	OEM	GS5628	0369	GS9033H	0710	GSZ3.0	0118	GT109R	0004	GT949R	0595	GXB10103	OEM
GS164	0369	GS7812	OEM	GS9033I	0710	GSZ3.0A	0118	GT115	OEM	GT1079	0595	GXB10104	OEM
GS165	OEM	GS8008-09	OEM	GS9033J	0710	GSZ3.3	0296	GT115A	OEM	GT-1200	0595	GXB10104P	OEM
GS170	OEM	GS8008-09A	OEM	GS9038H	OEM	GSZ3.3A	0296	GT115D	OEM	GT1200	0595	GXB10105	OEM
GS172	OEM	GS8008-09B	OEM	GS9038I	OEM	GSZ3.6	0372	GT115G	OEM	GT1201	0595	GXB10105D	OEM
GS300	OEM	GS8038-06A	OEM	GS9038J	OEM	GSZ3.6A	0372	GT115V	OEM	GT1202	0595	GXB10105P	OEM
GS301	OEM	GS8108-01A	OEM	GS578030	OEM	GSZ3.9	0036	GT122	0211	GT1223	0004	GXB10106	OEM
GS302	OEM	GS8908-01A	OEM	GSA15B	0071	GSZ3.9A	0036	GT122A	OEM	GT1604	0279	GXB10106D	OEM
GS370	OEM	GS8908-02A	OEM	GSA15C	0071	GSZ4.3	0274	GT122B	OEM	GT1605	0279	GXB10106P	OEM
GS372	OEM	GS8908-02B	OEM	GSA15E	0071	GSZ4.3A	0274	GT122G	OEM	GT1606	0279	GXB10107	OEM
GS400L	OEM	GS8908-02C	OEM	GSA15G	0071	GSZ4.7	0140	GT122V	OEM	GT1607	0279	GXB10107D	OEM
GS401L	OEM	GS8908-02D	OEM	GSA30B	0087	GSZ4.7A	0140	GT123	0211	GT1608	0595	GXB10108	OEM
GS402L	OEM	GS8908-04D	OEM	GSA30C	0087	GSZ5.1	0041	GT124A	OEM	GT1609	0595	GXB10109	OEM
GS403L	OEM	GS8908-041A	OEM	GSA30E	0087	GSZ5.1A	0041	GT124B	OEM	GT1624	OEM	GXB10109D	OEM
GS404L	OEM	GS9011(I)	0079	GSA30G	0087	GSZ5.6	0253	GT124V	OEM	GT1644	0037	GXB10110	OEM
GS405L	OEM	GS9011(J)	0079	GSA30J	0087	GSZ5.6A	0253	GT125A	OEM	GT1658	0208	GXB10110P	OEM
GS420L	OEM	GS9011-F	0079	GSB1A	OEM	GSZ6.2	0466	GT125B	OEM	GT1665	0004	GXB10111	OEM
GS450L	OEM	GS9011-G	0079	GSB1B	OEM	GSZ6.2A	0466	GT125D	OEM	GT2693	0211	GXB10111D	OEM
GS463L	OEM	GS9011-H	0079	GSB1C	OEM	GSZ6.8	0062	GT125E	OEM	GT2694	0279	GXB10111P	OEM
GS468L	OEM	GS9011-I	0079	GSB2	OEM	GSZ6.8A	0062	GT125G	OEM	GT2695	0211	GXB10112	OEM
GS469L	OEM	GS9011F	0079	GSB3A	OEM	GSZ7.5	0077	GT125I	OEM	GT2696	0211	GXB10113	OEM
GS600L	OEM	GS9011G	1943	GSB3B	OEM	GSZ7.5A	0077	GT125K	OEM	GT2765	0595	GXB10113D	OEM
GS601	OEM	GS9011H	0079	GSB3C	OEM	GSZ8.2	0165	GT125L	OEM	GT2766	0595	GXB10113P	OEM
GS611	OEM	GS9011I	0079	GSB10B	0071	GSZ8.2A	0165	GT125SZ	OEM	GT2767	0595	GXB10117	OEM
GS614	OEM	GS9011J	0079	GSB10C	0071	GSZ9.1	0057	GT125V	OEM	GT2768	0208	GXB10117D	OEM
GS660	OEM	GS9012-G	0037	GSB10E	0071	GSZ9.1A	0057	GT132	0004	GT2883	0211	GXB10117P	OEM
GS1020-1	OEM	GS9012-H	0037	GSB10G	0023	GSZ10	0064	GT-153	0279	GT2884	0595	GXB10118	OEM
GS1020-2	OEM	GS9012-I	0037	GSB10J	0071	GSZ10A	0064	GT153	0279	GT2885	0211	GXB10118D	OEM
GS1020-3	OEM	GS9012H	0037	GSB10L	0071	GSZ11	0181	GT167	0595	GT2886	0595	GXB10118P	OEM
GS1020-4	OEM	GS9012I	0037	GSB100	OEM	GSZ11A	0181	GT200	OEM	GT2887	0211	GXB10119	OEM
GS1030-1	OEM	GS9012J	0037	GSB10142	OEM	GSZ12	0052	GT-210H	0279	GT2888	0595	GXB10119D	OEM
GS1030-2	OEM	GS9012N	OEM	GSB10231D	OEM	GSZ12A	0052	GT210H	0279	GT2906	0595	GXB10119P	OEM
GS1030-3	OEM	GS9014	0079	GSB10231P	OEM	GSZ13	0053	GT215	OEM	GT3150	0595	GXB10121	OEM
GS1140-1	OEM	GS9014-G	0168	GSBX011	OEM	GSZ13A	0053	GT222	0211	GT5116	0136	GXB10121D	OEM
GS1140-2	OEM	GS9014-H	0079	GSC2052G	0919	GSZ15	0681	GT229	0595	GT5117	0136	GXB10123D	OEM
GS1140-3	OEM	GS9014-I	0079	GSC2052H	0919	GSZ15A	0681	GT-269	0211	GT5148	0136	GXB10123P	OEM
GS2012	0042	GS9014-J	0079	GSDB10008	OEM	GSZ16	0440	GT269	0279	GT5149	0136	GXB10124	OEM
GS2012(G)	0042	GS9014-K	0079	GSDS50018	OEM	GSZ16A	0440	GT315	OEM	GT5151	0136	GXB10124P	OEM
GS2012(H)	0042	GS9014H	0284	GSDS50020	OEM	GSZ18	0371	GT322M4	OEM	GT5153	0279	GXB10125P	OEM
GS2012G	0042	GS9014I	0079	GSDU7530	3354	GSZ18A	0371	GT322M5	OEM	GT8000	2602	GXB10129P	OEM
GS2012H	0042	GS9014J	0079	GSDU7535	3354	GT06	0588	GT322M6	OEM	GT8001	2602	GXB10130	OEM
GS2013	2498	GS9014K	0079	GSDU7540	3354	GT08	OEM	GT322M7	OEM	GT8002	2602	GXB10130D	OEM
GS2013(G)	0042	GS9015-H	0037	GSH047B	OEM	GT015	OEM	GT328A	0050	GT8003	1980	GXB10130P	OEM
GS2013(H)	0042	GS9015-I	0037	GSH051A/AN3231K	OEM	GT-1	OEM	GT328B	0050	GT8004	1980	GXB10131	OEM
GS2013-G	0042	GS9015-J	0037	GSH3007B	OEM	GT2	0050	GT336	0208	GT8005	1980	GXB10131D	OEM
GS2013-H	0042	GS9015H	0037	GSH3009	OEM	GT3	0050	GT346A	0050	GT8100	2415	GXB10131P	OEM
GS2013-I	0042	GS9015I	0037	GSH3013	OEM	GT11	0279	GT346B	0050	GT8101	2415	GXB10133	OEM
GS2013-O	0042	GS9015J	0037	GSH3015	OEM	GT13	0279	GT364	0038	GT8102	2415	GXB10135	OEM
GS2013-Y	0042	GS9018-G	0079	GSH6026B	OEM	GT-14	0279	GT365	0038	GT8103	2415	GXB10136	OEM
GS2013G	0456	GS9018-H	0079	GSH6234	OEM	GT14	0004	GT366	0038	GTA1	OEM	GXB10136D	OEM
GS2013H	0456	GS9018-I	0079	GSH6235	OEM	GT-14H	0279	GT402D	OEM	GTA2	OEM	GXB10136P	OEM
GS2014	0168	GS9018F	0016	GSH6235C	OEM	GT14H	0004	GT402E	OEM	GTA3	OEM	GXB10137	OEM
GS2014(G)	0168	GS9018G	0079	GSH7323A	OEM	GT15T5	0002	GT402I	OEM	GTE1	0279	GXB10139	OEM
GS2014-G	0168	GS9019	6057	GSH8701	OEM	GT16	0767	GT402SZ	OEM	GTE-2	0211	GXB10140	OEM
GS2014-H	0168	GS9019-G	0710	GSH8702	OEM	GT18	0004	GT404D	OEM	GTE2	0279	GXB10140D	OEM
GS2014-I	0168	GS9019-H	0284	GSH8703	OEM	GT-20	0279	GT404E	OEM	GTJ33141	0136	GXB10140P	OEM
GS2014G	0168	GS9019-I	0284	GSH8705	OEM	GT20	0211	GT404I	OEM	GTJ33229	0136	GXB10141	OEM
GS2014H	0168	GS9019-J	0284	GSH9025	0079	GT-20H	0279	GT404SZ	OEM	GTJ33230	0136	GXB10141D	OEM
GS2014I	0168	GS9019G	2001	GS-I9011	0079	GT20H	0004	GT406A	OEM	GTJ33231	0004	GXB10141P	OEM
GS2015	2133	GS9019H	0076	GSM51	1325	GT20R	0004	GT415	OEM	GTJ33232	0004	GXB10142D	OEM
GS2015(D)	0388	GS9019I	0710	GSM52	1325	GT24H	0050	GT515	OEM	GTJ33350	0911	GXB10142P	OEM
GS2015(E)	0388	GS9022	0037	GSM53	0015	GT26	0767	GT600	OEM	GTL1	OEM	GXB10144	OEM
GS2015D	0388	GS9022(G)	0338	GSM54	0015	GT28	OEM	GT705A	OEM	GTL3	OEM	GXB10144F	OEM
GS2015E	0388	GS9022(H)	0338	GSM56	OEM	GT31	0004	GT705B	OEM	GTSMPA	OEM	GXB10145	OEM
GS2015H	0388	GS9022-G	0284	GSM57	OEM	GT32	0004	GT705D	OEM	GTSMPB	OEM	GXB10145E	OEM
GS2016(H)	0388	GS9022-H	0284	GSM482	0015	GT33	0004	GT705G	OEM	GTSMPC	OEM	GXB10148	OEM
GS2016-H	0388	GS9022F	0037	GSM483	0015	GT34	0211	GT705V	OEM	GTSMPD	OEM		
GS2016H	0388	GS9022G	0338	GSM914	OEM	GT-34HV	0136	GT751	0004	GTSMPE	OEM		
GS2017	1077	GS9022H	0338	GSR1	0071	GT34HV	0004	GT758	0211	GTV	0279		
GS2017(G)	1077			GSR2	OEM	GT-34S	0211	GT-759	0279	GTX-2001	0160		
GS2017(H)	1077			GSR3	OEM			GT759	0211	GTX2001	0160		
GS2017-G	1077			GSR4	OEM					GU-1	0023		

If replacement code is OEM, contact original manufacturer for replacement.

DEVICE TYPE	REPL CODE
GXB10148D	OEM
GXB10148P	OEM
GXB10149	OEM
GXB10149D	OEM
GXB10149F	OEM
GXB10155	OEM
GXB10155F	OEM
GXB10155N	OEM
GXB10160	OEM
GXB10160D	OEM
GXB10160P	OEM
GXB10161	OEM
GXB10161P	OEM
GXB10162	OEM
GXB10162P	OEM
GXB10165	OEM
GXB10170	OEM
GXB10171P	OEM
GXB10172	OEM
GXB10172D	OEM
GXB10175	OEM
GXB10175D	OEM
GXB10175P	OEM
GXB10176	OEM
GXB10176D	OEM
GXB10176P	OEM
GXB10179	OEM
GXB10179D	OEM
GXB10179P	OEM
GXB10180	OEM
GXB10180D	OEM
GXB10180P	OEM
GXB10181	OEM
GXB10181D	OEM
GXB10181P	OEM
GXB10191P	OEM
GXB10210	OEM
GXB10210D	OEM
GXB10210P	OEM
GXB10211	OEM
GXB10211D	OEM
GXB10211P	OEM
GXB10231	OEM
GXB10405	OEM
GXB10405D	OEM
GXB10415	OEM
GXB10415A	OEM
GXB10415AD	OEM
GXB10415AE	OEM
GXB10415ALD	OEM
GXB10415BD	OEM
GXB10415BLD	OEM
GXB10415D	OEM
GXB10415E	OEM
GXB10415LD	OEM
GXB10422AD	OEM
GXB10422AF	OEM
GXB10422BD	OEM
GXB10422D	OEM
GXB100415	OEM
GXB100422AF	OEM
GXB100473	OEM
GXI3.3G	0289
GXI3.6	0188
GXI3.9	0451
GXI4.3	0528
GXI4.7	0446
GXI5.1	0162
GXI5.6	0157
GXI6.2	0631
GXI6.8	0025
GXI7.5	0644
GXI8.2	0244
GXI9.1	0012
GXI10	0170
GXI11	0313
GXI12G	0137
GXI14	0100
GXI15	0002
GXI20G	0526
GXI22	0560
GXI24	0398
GXI26	0436
GXI27	0436
GXI29	0721
GXI33G	0039
GXI36	0814
GXI39	0346
GXI43	0925
GXI47	0993
GXI51	0497
GXI55	1823
GXI56	0863
GXI62L	0778
GXI68	1258
GXI82	0327
GXI91	1301
GXI111	0149
GXI115	0789
GXI120	0186
GXI128	0361
GXI130	0497
GXI140	0245
GXI150G	0028
GXI160	0255
GXI161	0416
GXI170	0871
GXI178	0490
GXI180	0363

DEVICE TYPE	REPL CODE
GXI190	2831
GXI200	0417
GXI200G	0417
GYMTZ9.1-C	0057
GYW76	0023
GZ1-3.3G	0289
GZ1-3.6	0289
GZ1-3.9	0451
GZ1-4.3	0528
GZ1-4.7	0446
GZ1-5.1	0162
GZ1-5.6	0157
GZ1-6.2	0631
GZ1-6.8	0025
GZ1-7.5	0644
GZ1-8.2	0244
GZ1-9.1	0012
GZ1-10	0170
GZ1-11	0313
GZ1-12G	0137
GZ1-14	0100
GZ1-15	0002
GZ1-20G	0526
GZ1-22	0560
GZ1-24	0398
GZ1-26	0436
GZ1-27	0436
GZ1-29	0721
GZ1-33G	0039
GZ1-36	0814
GZ1-39	0346
GZ1-43	0925
GZ1-47	0993
GZ1-51	0497
GZ1-55	1823
GZ1-56	0863
GZ1-62P	0778
GZ1-68	1258
GZ1-91	1301
GZ1-110A	0149
GZ1-115G	0789
GZ1-120	0186
GZ1-127	0361
GZ1-130G	0213
GZ1-140	0245
GZ1-150G	0028
GZ1-160	0255
GZ1-161	0416
GZ1-170	0871
GZ1-178	0490
GZ1-180	0363
GZ1-190	2831
GZ1-200	0417
GZ1-200G	0417
GZ5.1	2391
GZ6A	OEM
GZ6.2	0631
GZ8A	OEM
GZ9.1	1608
GZ10A	OEM
GZ10B	OEM
GZ12A	OEM
GZ12B	OEM
GZ15A	OEM
GZ15B	OEM
GZ18A	OEM
GZ18B	OEM
GZ22A	OEM
GZ27	0436
GZ27A	OEM
GZ33A	5997
GZ39A	OEM
GZ47A	OEM
GZ56A	OEM
GZ68A	OEM
GZ82A	OEM
GZA056U	0253
GZA2.0	0371
GZA2.0X	OEM
GZA2.2	OEM
GZA2.2X	OEM
GZA2.2Z	OEM
GZA2.4	1266
GZA2.4X	OEM
GZA2.4Z	1266
GZA2.7	0755
GZA2.7X	0755
GZA2.7Y	OEM
GZA2.7Z	OEM
GZA3.0	0118
GZA3.0Y	OEM
GZA3.0Z	OEM
GZA3.3	0296
GZA3.3-Y-BT	OEM
GZA3.3X	0296
GZA3.3Y	OEM
GZA3.3Z	OEM
GZA3.6	0372
GZA3.6A1	OEM
GZA3.6X	OEM
GZA3.6Z	OEM
GZA3.9	0036
GZA3.9(Y)	0036
GZA3.9-X	0036
GZA3.9X	0036
GZA3.9Y	OEM
GZA3.9Z	OEM
GZA4.3	0274
GZA4.3(Y)	0274

DEVICE TYPE	REPL CODE
GZA4.3-Y	0274
GZA4.3-Y-BT	0528
GZA4.3Y	0274
GZA4.3Z	OEM
GZA4.7	0140
GZA4.7-X-BT	0140
GZA4.7X	0140
GZA4.7Y	0140
GZA4.7Z	0041
GZA5.1	0253
GZA5.1(X)	0041
GZA5.1(Y)	0041
GZA5.1(Z)	0041
GZA5.1-BT	0041
GZA5.1-X-BT	0041
GZA5.1-Y	0582
GZA5.1-Y-BT	0041
GZA5.1-Y-BT-T	0041
GZA5.1L	0041
GZA5.1U	5816
GZA5.1X	0041
GZA5.1Y	0041
GZA5.1Y-AT	OEM
GZA5.1Z	5816
GZA5.6	0253
GZA5.6-Y	0253
GZA5.6-Y-BT	0253
GZA5.6L	0877
GZA5.6U	5348
GZA5.6X	OEM
GZA5.6Y	0253
GZA5.6Z	OEM
GZA6.2	0466
GZA6.2(X)	0466
GZA6.2(XYZ)	0091
GZA6.2(Y)	0466
GZA6.2-BT	0466
GZA6.2-X	0466
GZA6.2-Y	0466
GZA6.2-Y-BT	0466
GZA6.2-Z-BT	0292
GZA6.2BT	0466
GZA6.2L	0091
GZA6.2U	0466
GZA6.2X	OEM
GZA6.2Y	0466
GZA6.2Y-BT	0466
GZA6.2Z	0292
GZA6.2Z-AT	OEM
GZA6.8	0062
GZA6.8-Y	0062
GZA6.8-Y-BT	0062
GZA6.8L	3335
GZA6.8X	OEM
GZA6.8Y	0062
GZA6.8Z	0062
GZA7.5	0077
GZA7.5(Y)	0077
GZA7.5-Y	0077
GZA7.5-Z-BT	0077
GZA7.5V	0077
GZA7.5X	6220
GZA7.5Y	0077
GZA7.5Z	0077
GZA8.2	0165
GZA8.2(Y)	0165
GZA8.2-X-BT	0165
GZA8.2-Y	0165
GZA8.2X	OEM
GZA8.2Y	4245
GZA8.2Z	OEM
GZA9.1	0057
GZA9.1-Y-BT	OEM
GZA9.1-Z	0057
GZA9.1E	0057
GZA9.1L	6405
GZA9.1X	OEM
GZA9.1Y	OEM
GZA9.1Z	0057
GZA10	0064
GZA10(Y)	0064
GZA10-(Y)	0064
GZA10-X-BT	OEM
GZA10-Y	0064
GZA10-Z	0064
GZA10L	1249
GZA10X	OEM
GZA10Y	0064
GZA10Z	1249
GZA11	0181
GZA11-Y-BT	0181
GZA11BT	0181
GZA11X	OEM
GZA11Y	0181
GZA11YBT	0181
GZA11Z	0181
GZA12	0052
GZA12-Y-BT	0999
GZA12BT	0052
GZA12X	0052
GZA12Y	0999
GZA12YBT	0052
GZA12Z	OEM
GZA13	0053
GZA13(X)	0053
GZA13-A-BT	0053
GZA13-X-BT	0053
GZA13-Y	0053
GZA13-Y-BT	0053

DEVICE TYPE	REPL CODE
GZA13U	0053
GZA13X	0053
GZA13Y	0053
GZA13Z	0053
GZA15	0681
GZA15U	1097
GZA15Y	OEM
GZA15Z	OEM
GZA16	0440
GZA16-Y	0440
GZA16Y	0440
GZA16Z	OEM
GZA18	0371
GZA18-Y-BT	0371
GZA18U	4764
GZA18X	OEM
GZA18Y	0371
GZA18Y-BT	0371
GZA18Z	OEM
GZA20	0695
GZA20-X-BT	0695
GZA20X	0695
GZA20Y	OEM
GZA22	0700
GZA22(Z)	0700
GZA24	0489
GZA24-Y	0489
GZA24Z	OEM
GZA27	0450
GZA-27-0Z	0450
GZA27-Y	0450
GZA27-Y-BT	0450
GZA27BT	0450
GZA-27X	0450
GZA27X	0450
GZA27Y	0450
GZA27YBT	0450
GZA27Z	OEM
GZA30	0195
GZA30-Y	0195
GZA30-Y-BT	0195
GZA30BT	0195
GZA30Y	0195
GZA30Z	OEM
GZA33	0166
GZA33X	OEM
GZA33Y	0166
GZA36	0010
GZA36(Y)	0010
GZA36-Y	0010
GZA36Y	0010
GZA39	0032
GZA39-Y	0032
GZA43	0054
GZA43X	OEM
GZA47	0068
GZA51	0092
GZB2.0	OEM
GZB2.2	OEM
GZB2.4	OEM
GZB2.7	1302
GZB3.0	1703
GZB3.3	0289
GZB3.6	0188
GZB3.6B	0372
GZB3.9	0451
GZB4.3	0528
GZB4.7	0446
GZB5.1	0162
GZB5.6	0157
GZB6.2	0631
GZB6.8	0025
GZB7.5	0644
GZB7.5C	0644
GZB8.2	0244
GZB9.1	0012
GZB9.1B	0012
GZB9.1C	0012
GZB10	0170
GZB10C	0170
GZB11	0313
GZB11C	0313
GZB12	0137
GZB12B	0137
GZB12C	0137
GZB13	0361
GZB13C	0361
GZB15	0002
GZB15C	0002
GZB16	0416
GZB16C	0416
GZB18	0490
GZB18B	0490
GZB18C	0490
GZB20	0526
GZB20C	0526
GZB22	0560
GZB22C	0560
GZB24	0398
GZB24C	0398
GZB27	1664
GZB27C	1664
GZB30	0721
GZB30B	0721
GZB30C	0721
GZB33	0039
GZB36	0814
GZF1100D	OEM
GZF1100P	OEM

DEVICE TYPE	REPL CODE
GZF1106D	OEM
GZF1106P	OEM
GZF1201P	OEM
GZF1202P	OEM
GZF1400D	OEM
GZF1400P	OEM
GZM5.6	0253
GZM6.2	0466
GZM6.2(B2)	0466
GZM6.2B2	OEM
GZM6.8	0062
GZM6.8-B2	OEM
GZM6.8B2	OEM
GZM7.5	0077
GZM7.5(B2)	0077
GZM7.5-B2	0077
GZM7.5B2	OEM
GZM7.5C	OEM
GZM8.2	0165
GZM8.2(B2)	0165
GZM9.1	0057
GZM9.1(B2)	0057
GZM9.1B2	OEM
GZM10	0064
GZM11	0181
GZM12	0052
GZM13	0053
GZM15	0681
GZM16	0440
GZM18	0371
GZM20	0695
GZM20(B2)	0695
GZM20-B2	0695
GZM20B2	OEM
GZM22	0700
GZM24	0489
GZM24(B2)	0489
GZM24-B2	0489
GZS2.0	OEM
GZS2.0X-BT	OEM
GZS2.2	OEM
GZS2.2X	OEM
GZS2.2Z	OEM
GZS2.4	1266
GZS2.7	0755
GZS3.0	0118
GZS3.3	0296
GZS3.6	0372
GZS3.9	0036
GZS4.3	0274
GZS4.3Z	0274
GZS4.7	0140
GZS5.1	0140
GZS5.1Y	6677
GZS5.6	0253
GZS5.6Y	OEM
GZS5.6Z	OEM
GZS6.2	0466
GZS6.2X	OEM
GZS6.2Y	OEM
GZS6.2Z	OEM
GZS6.8	0062
GZS6.8Y	0062
GZS7.5	0077
GZS7.5Z	OEM
GZS8.2	0165
GZS8.2Y	OEM
GZS9.1	0057
GZS9.1BT	OEM
GZS9.1X	OEM
GZS9.1Y	0057
GZS9.1Z	OEM
GZS10	0064
GZS10X	OEM
GZS10Y	OEM
GZS11	0181
GZS11Y	OEM
GZS12	0052
GZS12Y	OEM
GZS13	0053
GZS15	0681
GZS16	0440
GZS18	0371
GZS20	0695
GZS20Z	OEM
GZS22	0700
GZS24	0489
GZS24Z	0489
GZS27	0450
GZS27R	OEM
GZS27R-BT	OEM
GZS30	0195
GZS30R	OEM
GZS30Y-BT	OEM
GZS33	0166
GZS36	0010
GZS39	0032
GZS39X	OEM
GZS39Y	OEM
GZS39Z	OEM
H*22A	0700
H*51A	0092
H(P-Z0424	0436
H0004	OEM
H0005	OEM
H01G	OEM
H01J	OEM
H01L	OEM
H01M	OEM

DEVICE TYPE	REPL CODE
H03CF	OEM
H03DA	OEM
H03EA	OEM
H07	OEM
H078	1293
H087	0143
H089	0137
H091	0143
H0R3D	OEM
H1V	0144
H1Z	0023
H2P15	0050
H2SE303	OEM
H3A	OEM
H3D42	OEM
H3MLR	OEM
H5A3	1017
H5B2N3	OEM
H5B3	1017
H5C3	1017
H5D3	1017
H5E3	1017
H5F3	1017
H5G3	1017
H5H3	1030
H5K3	1030
H5M3	1040
H5N3	1040
H6A3	OEM
H6B3	OEM
H6C3	OEM
H6D3	OEM
H6E3	OEM
H6F3	OEM
H6G3	OEM
H6H3	OEM
H6K3	OEM
H6M3	OEM
H6N3	OEM
H6P3	OEM
H6R3	OEM
H6S3	OEM
H8D1133	OEM
H8D1134	OEM
H8D1147	OEM
H8D1177	OEM
H8D1193	OEM
H10	0004
H11A1	0311
H11A2	0272
H11A3	0272
H11A4	0311
H11A5	0311
H11A10	OEM
H11A520	0311
H11A550	0311
H11A5100	0311
H11AA1	5327
H11AA2	5327
H11AA3	OEM
H11AA4	OEM
H11AV1	OEM
H11AV1A	OEM
H11AV2	OEM
H11AV3	OEM
H11AX	2096
H11B1	1047
H11B2	1047
H11B3	1047
H11B255	1101
H11B256	OEM
H11BX522	1047
H11C1	2221
H11C2	2221
H11C3	2221
H11C4	2221
H11C5	2221
H11C6	2221
H11D1	5326
H11D2	5326
H11D3	5326
H11D4	5326
H11F1	5323
H11F2	5323
H11F3	5323
H11G1	OEM
H11G2	OEM
H11G3	OEM
H11J1	4961
H11J2	4961
H11J3	4961
H11J4	4961
H11J5	4961
H11L1	5328
H11L2	5328
H12	0435
H12A	0435
H15B	OEM
H15D	OEM
H15M	OEM
H15N	OEM
H18CPU	OEM
H21A1	1407
H21A2	1407
H21A3	1407
H21A4	1407
H21A5	1407
H21A6	1407
H21B1	2612

DEVICE TYPE	REPL CODE
H21B2	2612
H21B3	2612
H21B4	2612
H21B5	2612
H21B6	2612
H22A1	2616
H22A2	2616
H22A3	2616
H22A4	2616
H22A5	2616
H22A6	2616
H22B1	5335
H22B2	5335
H22B3	5335
H22B4	5335
H22B5	5335
H22B6	5335
H23A1	OEM
H23B1	OEM
H24A1	3333
H24A2	3333
H24B1	5050
H24B2	5050
H36A2U57	OEM
H36A2U57D	OEM
H50	0015
H62SC01-1	OEM
H62SC03-1	OEM
H62SC06-1	OEM
H62SC09-1	OEM
H62SC12-1	OEM
H62SC15-1	OEM
H62SC18-1	OEM
H68AN01-1	OEM
H68AT01-1	OEM
H68CC01-1	OEM
H68CC02-1	OEM
H68CM08-1	OEM
H68DB03-1	OEM
H68DM48-1	OEM
H68DN01-1	OEM
H68DT01-1	OEM
H68DX01-1	OEM
H68FD01-1(A)	OEM
H68FD03-1	OEM
H68FD04-1(A)	OEM
H68MV01-1	OEM
H68OCC01-1	OEM
H68ODM12	OEM
H68OMN01	OEM
H68PM32-1	OEM
H68PR03-1	OEM
H68PW03-1	OEM
H68SB02-1	OEM
H68SB03-1	OEM
H68SM16-1	OEM
H68XM68-1	OEM
H69DB01-1	OEM
H69SB01-1	OEM
H70	OEM
H74A1	OEM
H74C1	OEM
H74C2	OEM
H74SC137C(A)	OEM
H74SC137D(A)	OEM
H74SC137P(A)	OEM
H74SC138C(A)	OEM
H74SC138D(A)	OEM
H74SC138P(A)	OEM
H74SC139C(A)	OEM
H74SC139D(A)	OEM
H74SC139P(A)	OEM
H74SC237C(A)	OEM
H74SC237D(A)	OEM
H74SC237P(A)	OEM
H74SC238C(A)	OEM
H74SC238D(A)	OEM
H74SC238P(A)	OEM
H74SC239C(A)	OEM
H74SC239D(A)	OEM
H74SC239P(A)	OEM
H74SC240C(MA)	OEM
H74SC240D(MA)	OEM
H74SC240P(MA)	OEM
H74SC241C(MA)	OEM
H74SC241D(MA)	OEM
H74SC241P(MA)	OEM
H74SC242C(MA)	OEM
H74SC242D(MA)	OEM
H74SC242P(MA)	OEM
H74SC243C(MA)	OEM
H74SC243D(MA)	OEM
H74SC243P(MA)	OEM
H74SC244C(MA)	OEM
H74SC244D(MA)	OEM
H74SC244P(MA)	OEM
H74SC245C(MA)	OEM
H74SC245D(MA)	OEM
H74SC245P(MA)	OEM
H74SC540C(MA)	OEM
H74SC540D(MA)	OEM
H74SC540P(MA)	OEM
H74SC541C(MA)	OEM
H74SC541D(MA)	OEM
H74SC541P(MA)	OEM
H89/1	0769
H100	0015
H101	0196
H102	0016

DEVICE TYPE	REPL CODE
H102D1	0078
H102D2	0078
H102D6	0078
H103A	0160
H103D1	4086
H103D2	4086
H103D6	4086
H103SH	2367
H104	0079
H104D1	0613
H104D2	0613
H104D6	0613
H105D1	0795
H105D2	0795
H105D6	0795
H109	0087
H109D1	OEM
H109D6	OEM
H110D1	OEM
H110D2	OEM
H110D6	OEM
H111D1	OEM
H111D2	OEM
H111D6	OEM
H112D1	3016
H112D6	3016
H113SH	2367
H114B	OEM
H114D	OEM
H114M	OEM
H115B	OEM
H115C	OEM
H115D	OEM
H115D1	4110
H115D6	4110
H117D1	OEM
H117D6	OEM
H118D1	4115
H118D6	4115
H119D1	4108
H119D6	4108
H121	OEM
H122D1	2417
H122D2	2417
H122D6	2417
H123SH	2378
H124D1	2574
H124D2	2574
H124D6	2574
H142	0124
H156D1	OEM
H156D2	OEM
H156D6	OEM
H157D1	OEM
H157D2	OEM
H157D6	OEM
H158D1	OEM
H158D2	OEM
H158D6	OEM
H159D1	OEM
H160D1	OEM
H165D1	OEM
H166D1	OEM
H167D1	OEM
H168D1	OEM
H200	0015
H200E	OEM
H200EA	OEM
H200EB	OEM
H202B1	0078
H203B1	0078
H204B1	0613
H205B1	0795
H209B1	OEM
H210B1	OEM
H211B1	OEM
H215	2716
H218-10	OEM
H221	0797
H222B1	2417
H224B1	2574
H227B1	OEM
H254B4	0015
H254E4	0015
H256B1	OEM
H257B1	OEM
H258B1	OEM
H284D4	0023
H300	0015
H-300B	OEM
H312K4	OEM
H315F4	0015
H315M2	0015
H315Y6	OEM
H316	0143
H326B4	0023
H386-9	0752
H386C-5	OEM
H400	0015
H410	0914
H431	1313
H438	OEM
H439	OEM
H440	OEM
H441	OEM
H442	0144
H443	OEM
H445	1313
H463	OEM
H466	OEM
H467	OEM
H468	OEM
H475	0015
H-484	1313
H484	1313
H484-1	1313
H485-62	0374
H486W	0374
H500	0015
H501	0196
H505W	0286
H521	0201
H521-35	0286
H521-55	0286
H540	OEM
H541	OEM
H542	OEM
H580B1A	OEM
H580B1B	OEM
H585	0015
H590B1A	OEM
H590B1B	OEM
H598	0286
H598-10	0286
H600	0015
H614	0143
H615	0196
H616	0015
H617	0015
H618	0015
H619	0015
H620	0015
H621	0071
H622	0769
H623	0133
H624	0143
H625	0015
H626	0015
H629B1	OEM
H632B1	OEM
H635B1	OEM
H635F1	OEM
H680BS01(A)	OEM
H680FD01(A)	OEM
H680SB01	OEM
H680TR01(A)	OEM
H701	OEM
H702	OEM
H703	OEM
H770B1	OEM
H771B1	OEM
H772B1	OEM
H773B1	OEM
H781	0015
H783	0015
H800	0071
H815	0102
H816	0374
H850	OEM
H-881	0071
H881	0015
H889	0133
H890	0914
H891	0015
H909	6215
H931	0016
H932	0233
H933	0016
H934	0016
H1000	0071
H1017A	0535
H1144-1	OEM
H1152	OEM
H1153	1313
H-1567	0079
H1567	0016
H1701-9	0201
H1701-10	0201
H1701-11	0201
H1701-12	0201
H1701-15	OEM
H1703-13	0286
H1703-14	0286
H1703-15	0286
H1703-16	0374
H1802	5771
H1809	OEM
H2535-5	OEM
H2535-6	OEM
H2621	OEM
H2622	OEM
H4439A06	OEM
H5535-5	OEM
H5535-6	OEM
H5535-G	OEM
H5535-M	OEM
H5535-X	OEM
H5540-5	OEM
H5540-6	OEM
H5540-G	OEM
H5540-M	OEM
H5540-X	OEM
H5545-5	OEM
H5545-6	OEM
H5545-G	OEM
H5545-M	OEM
H5545-X	OEM
H5560-G	OEM
H5560-M	OEM
H5560-X	OEM
H6010	OEM
H6010C	OEM
H6020	OEM
H7126-3	0015
H7618	0546
H8287	0143
H8287-4	0143
H8513A	0143
H8513D	0143
H9275-A	OEM
H9423	0016
H9623	0016
H9625	0144
H9696	0016
H10174	0015
H20052	0015
H61220-C	OEM
H70420M	OEM
H120029A	OEM
H801193	OEM
H21100015	OEM
H21100016	OEM
H21100018	OEM
H21400014	0133
H21400015	0124
H21400018	0023
H21400026	0133
H21500029	0091
H21500086	0118
H23100024	0148
H23100045	0688
H23100051	0338
H23200019	0527
H25300013	OEM
H26200009	3104
H28900001	OEM
H31100125	OEM
H31100127	1008
H31100128	0621
H31100129	0001
H31100130	2483
HA00052	0279
HA00053	0279
HA-0054	0150
HA-00102	0136
HA-00354	0050
HA-00495	0037
HA-00496	0455
HA00562	0006
HA-00564	0688
HA-00610	0006
HA-00634	0676
HA-00636	2010
HA-00643	1233
HA-00699	0676
HA-00733	0006
HA-1	0102
HA1-2600-2	OEM
HA1-2602-2	OEM
HA1-2605-5	OEM
HA1-2620-2	OEM
HA1-2622-2	OEM
HA1-2625-5	OEM
HA1-4741-2	OEM
HA1-4741-5	2796
HA1-4741-8	OEM
HA1-4741-B	OEM
HA2-2500-2	OEM
HA2-2502-2	OEM
HA2-2505-5	OEM
HA2-2510-2	OEM
HA2-2512-2	OEM
HA2-2515-5	OEM
HA2-2520-2	OEM
HA2-2522-2	OEM
HA2-2525-5	OEM
HA2-2600-2	OEM
HA2-2602-2	OEM
HA2-2605-5	OEM
HA2-2620-2	OEM
HA2-2622-2	OEM
HA2-2625-5	OEM
HA3-4741-5	2796
HA3-4741-5DB	OEM
HA6A1	OEM
HA9-2500-2	OEM
HA9-2502-2	OEM
HA9-2505-5	OEM
HA9-2510-2	OEM
HA9-2512-2	OEM
HA9-2515-5	OEM
HA9-2520-2	OEM
HA9-2522-2	OEM
HA9-2525-5	OEM
HA9-2600-2	OEM
HA9-2602-2	OEM
HA9-2605-5	OEM
HA9-2620-2	OEM
HA9-2622-2	OEM
HA9-2625-5	OEM
HA10	OEM
HA-11A	0181
HA-11B	0181
HA-11C	0181
HA-12	0279
HA12	0050
HA-15	0136
HA15	0279
HA20	OEM
HA25	OEM
HA30	0050
HA40	OEM
HA-49	0628
HA49	0279
HA50	0015
HA-52	0136
HA52	0136
HA-53	0628
HA53	0136
HA54	0004
HA56	0004
HA60K	OEM
HA60P	OEM
HA70	0050
HA75	OEM
HA100	0015
HA-101	0136
HA102	0136
HA103	0136
HA104	0136
HA120EL	OEM
HA120KL	OEM
HA120TL	OEM
HA178M05	0619
HA178M05P	0619
HA178M06P	0917
HA178M07P	OEM
HA178M08	1187
HA178M08P	1187
HA178M059A	OEM
HA178M12P	0330
HA178M15P	1311
HA178M18P	2244
HA178M20P	OEM
HA178M24P	2224
HA180EN	OEM
HA180KN	OEM
HA180LN	OEM
HA180LO	OEM
HA180TN	OEM
HA200	0015
HA-201	0211
HA201	0136
HA202	0279
HA-234	0050
HA234	0050
HA-234B	0050
HA235	0136
HA-235A	0050
HA235A	0050
HA-235C	0050
HA240	0050
HA240E0	OEM
HA240L0	OEM
HA250T0	OEM
HA266	0050
HA267	0050
HA-268	0050
HA268	0050
HA-269	0136
HA269	0050
HA300	0015
HA300EP	OEM
HA300LP	OEM
HA300TP	OEM
HA321J	0050
HA-330	0211
HA330	0136
HA342	0136
HA-350	0136
HA350	0050
HA-350A	0136
HA-353	0136
HA353	0050
HA-353C	0136
HA-354	0136
HA354	0050
HA-354B	0136
HA400	0015
HA471	0136
HA500	0015
HA-505	1257
HA505	0919
HA525	0050
HA600	0015
HA800	0071
HA1000	0071
HA1040	0050
HA1075R	OEM
HA1077R	OEM
HA1105R	OEM
HA1106R	OEM
HA1107R	OEM
HA1108	2560
HA1108-0M	OEM
HA1108R	OEM
HA1108.IF	OEM
HA1108.0M	OEM
HA1111SW	0438
HA1112	4325
HA1113	4535
HA1115	0438
HA1115(W)	0438
HA1115W	0438
HA1117	0602
HA1118	0043
HA1119	0385
HA1124	0167
HA1124D	0167
HA1124DS	0167
HA1124S	0167
HA1124Z	0167
HA1125	0167
HA1125D	0167
HA1125S	0167
HA1126	0872
HA1126AW	0872
HA1126D	0872
HA1126DW	0872
HA-1128	OEM
HA1128	0167
HA1128E	0167
HA1133	2716
HA1137	2728
HA1137(W)	2728
HA1137P	2728
HA1137W	2728
HA1138	4726
HA1139A	4331
HA1141	0167
HA1141G	OEM
HA11410	OEM
HA1141R	OEM
HA1141Y	OEM
HA1142	OEM
HA1142A	OEM
HA1142G	OEM
HA11420	OEM
HA1142R	OEM
HA1142Y	OEM
HA1143G	OEM
HA11430	OEM
HA1143R	OEM
HA1143Y	OEM
HA1144	4546
HA1144G	OEM
HA11440	OEM
HA1144R	OEM
HA1144Y	OEM
HA1146	0872
HA1147	OEM
HA1148	4551
HA1150	0514
HA1151	3606
HA1152	0849
HA1154	0167
HA1155	OEM
HA1156	0514
HA1156(W)	0514
HA1156-6C	0514
HA1156-612	OEM
HA1156H	0514
HA1156W	0514
HA1156WP	0514
HA1157	0602
HA1157P	OEM
HA1158	0043
HA1158-0	0043
HA1159	0385
HA1162Z	OEM
HA1166	OEM
HA1166A	OEM
HA1166X	OEM
HA1166Y	OEM
HA1166Z	OEM
HA1167	OEM
HA1174ANT	OEM
HA1177	1049
HA1178	OEM
HA1179	OEM
HA1180	OEM
HA1181G	OEM
HA11810	OEM
HA1181R	OEM
HA1181Y	OEM
HA1182G	OEM
HA11820	OEM
HA1182R	OEM
HA1182Y	OEM
HA1183G	OEM
HA11830	OEM
HA1183R	OEM
HA1183Y	OEM
HA1184G	OEM
HA11840	OEM
HA1184R	OEM
HA1184Y	OEM
HA1196	4716
HA1197	6231
HA1197W	0646
HA1199	4027
HA1199P	6527
HA-1201	OEM
HA1201	1611
HA-1202	4490
HA1202	4490
HA1203	4491
HA1211	4489
HA1215A	OEM
HA1215B	OEM
HA1215C	OEM
HA1216A	OEM
HA1216B	OEM
HA1216C	OEM
HA1217A	OEM
HA1217B	OEM
HA1217C	OEM
HA1218A	OEM
HA1218B	OEM
HA1218C	OEM
HA1219A	OEM
HA1219B	OEM
HA1219C	OEM
HA1220A	0549
HA1220B	OEM
HA1220C	OEM
HA1222A	OEM
HA1222B	OEM
HA1222C	OEM
HA1224A	0005
HA1224B	OEM
HA1224C	OEM
HA1226A	0715
HA1226B	OEM
HA1226C	OEM
HA1228A	OEM
HA1228B	OEM
HA1228C	OEM
HA1230A	OEM
HA1230B	OEM
HA1230C	OEM
HA1234A	0623
HA1234B	OEM
HA1234C	OEM
HA1236A	OEM
HA1236B	OEM
HA1236C	OEM
HA1238A	0030
HA1238B	OEM
HA1238C	OEM
HA1301	2515
HA1304	0406
HA-1306	OEM
HA1306	2247
HA-1306P	2247
HA1306P	2247
HA1306PU	2247
HA1306W	2247
HA1306WU	2247
HA1308	4481
HA-1310	OEM
HA1310	4482
HA-1311	OEM
HA1311	4483
HA1311W	4483
HA1312	4484
HA1313	2862
HA1316	4486
HA1318PU	4338
HA1318PU-1	4338
HA1318PU-2	4338
HA1318PU-3	4338
HA1319	4320
HA1322	4031
HA1322C	4031
HA1325	3961
HA1338	4481
HA-1339	5497
HA1339	4331
HA1339A	4331
HA1342	3231
HA1342A	3231
HA1348	OEM
HA1350	0004
HA1353	0849
HA1360	0004
HA1364	1162
HA1366	4563
HA1366R	1120
HA1366W	4563
HA1366WR	1120
HA1374	6246
HA1374A	6246
HA1377	5018
HA1377A	5018
HA1385	OEM
HA1388	5019
HA1389R	4658
HA1392	5096
HA1393	5095
HA1394	OEM
HA1396	OEM
HA1397	OEM
HA1403	OEM
HA1406	2632
HA1406-2	2632
HA1406-3	2632
HA1406-4	2632
HA1452	4480
HA1452W	4480
HA1702A	OEM
HA1702B	OEM
HA1702D	OEM
HA1702E	OEM
HA1702H	OEM
HA1703A	OEM
HA1703B	OEM
HA1703D	OEM
HA1703E	OEM
HA1703H	OEM
HA1704A	OEM
HA1704B	OEM
HA1704D	OEM
HA1704E	OEM
HA1704H	OEM
HA1705A	OEM
HA1705B	OEM
HA1705D	OEM
HA1705E	OEM
HA1705H	OEM
HA1706A	OEM
HA1706B	OEM
HA1706D	OEM
HA1706E	OEM
HA1706H	OEM
HA1707A	OEM
HA1707B	OEM
HA1707D	OEM
HA1707E	OEM
HA1707H	OEM
HA1708A	OEM
HA1708B	OEM
HA1708D	OEM
HA1708E	OEM
HA1708G	OEM
HA1708H	OEM
HA1709A	OEM
HA1709B	OEM
HA1709D	OEM
HA1709E	OEM
HA1709H	OEM
HA1710A	OEM
HA1710B	OEM
HA1710D	OEM
HA1710H	OEM
HA1711A	OEM
HA1711B	OEM
HA1711D	OEM
HA1711E	OEM
HA1711H	OEM
HA1712A	OEM
HA1712B	OEM
HA1712D	OEM
HA1712E	OEM
HA1712H	OEM
HA1713A	OEM
HA1713B	OEM
HA1713D	OEM
HA1713E	OEM
HA1713H	OEM
HA1714A	OEM
HA1714B	OEM
HA1714D	OEM
HA1714E	OEM
HA1714H	OEM
HA1715A	OEM
HA1715B	OEM
HA1715D	OEM
HA1715E	OEM
HA1715H	OEM
HA1716A	OEM
HA1716B	OEM
HA1716D	OEM
HA1716E	OEM
HA1716H	OEM
HA1717A	OEM
HA1717D	OEM
HA1717E	OEM
HA1717H	OEM
HA1807	OEM
HA1812GS	OEM
HA1812PS	OEM
HA1813PS	OEM
HA1822A	OEM
HA1822B	OEM
HA1822C	OEM
HA1824A	OEM
HA1824B	OEM
HA1824C	OEM
HA1826A	OEM
HA1826B	OEM
HA1826C	OEM
HA1836A	OEM
HA1836B	OEM
HA1836C	OEM
HA1838A	OEM
HA1838B	OEM
HA1838C	OEM
HA1844A	OEM
HA1844B	OEM
HA1844C	OEM
HA1848A	OEM
HA1848B	OEM
HA1848C	OEM
HA1850A	OEM
HA1850B	OEM
HA1850C	OEM
HA1915A	OEM
HA1915B	OEM
HA1915C	OEM
HA1916A	OEM
HA1916B	OEM
HA1916C	OEM
HA1917A	OEM
HA1917B	OEM
HA1917C	OEM
HA1918A	OEM
HA1918B	OEM
HA1918C	OEM
HA1919A	OEM
HA1919B	OEM
HA1919C	OEM

If replacement code is OEM, contact original manufacturer for replacement.

DEVICE TYPE	REPL CODE
HA1920A	0549
HA1920B	OEM
HA1920C	OEM
HA1922A	OEM
HA1922B	OEM
HA1922C	OEM
HA1924A	0005
HA1924B	OEM
HA1924C	OEM
HA1926A	0715
HA1926B	OEM
HA1926C	OEM
HA1928A	OEM
HA1928B	OEM
HA1928C	OEM
HA1930A	OEM
HA1930B	OEM
HA1930C	OEM
HA1934A	0623
HA1934B	OEM
HA1934C	OEM
HA1936A	OEM
HA1936B	OEM
HA1936C	OEM
HA1938A	0030
HA1938B	OEM
HA1938C	OEM
HA1940A	OEM
HA1940B	OEM
HA1940C	OEM
HA1942A	OEM
HA1942B	OEM
HA1942C	OEM
HA1944A	OEM
HA1944B	OEM
HA1944C	OEM
HA1946A	OEM
HA1946B	OEM
HA1946C	OEM
HA1948A	OEM
HA1948B	OEM
HA1948C	OEM
HA1950A	OEM
HA1950B	OEM
HA1950C	OEM
HA2000	OEM
HA2001	0321
HA2010	0321
HA2020	OEM
HA2132R	OEM
HA2133R	OEM
HA2134R	OEM
HA2137R	OEM
HA21420	OEM
HA2142R	OEM
HA21430	OEM
HA2143R	OEM
HA21440	OEM
HA2144R	OEM
HA21470	OEM
HA2147R	OEM
HA2190	0050
HA2356	0050
HA2400	OEM
HA2404	OEM
HA2405	OEM
HA2420	OEM
HA2425	OEM
HA2500	OEM
HA2502	OEM
HA2505	OEM
HA2507	OEM
HA2510	OEM
HA2512	OEM
HA2515	OEM
HA2517	OEM
HA2520	OEM
HA2522	OEM
HA2525	OEM
HA2526	OEM
HA2527	OEM
HA2539-2	OEM
HA2539-5	OEM
HA2539-8	OEM
HA2540-2(A)	OEM
HA2540-5(A)	OEM
HA2540-B	OEM
HA2600	OEM
HA2602	OEM
HA2605	OEM
HA2607	OEM
HA2620	OEM
HA2622	OEM
HA2625	OEM
HA2627	OEM
HA2630	OEM
HA2635	OEM
HA2640	OEM
HA2645	OEM
HA2655	OEM
HA2720	OEM
HA2740-2(A)	OEM
HA2740-5(A)	OEM
HA3210	0050
HA3480	0050
HA3670	0050
HA4071	OEM
HA4400	0050
HA4602-2	OEM

DEVICE TYPE	REPL CODE
HA4605-5	OEM
HA4622-2	OEM
HA4625-5	OEM
HA4741-2	OEM
HA4741-5	2796
HA4900-2	OEM
HA4900-8	OEM
HA4905-5	OEM
HA4920-2	OEM
HA4925-5	OEM
HA4950-2	OEM
HA4950-5	OEM
HA4950-8	OEM
HA5001	0595
HA5002	0595
HA5003	0595
HA5005	0595
HA5009	0595
HA5010	0208
HA5011	0595
HA5012	0595
HA5014	0595
HA5016	0595
HA5020	0595
HA5021	0595
HA5022	0595
HA5023	0595
HA5024	0595
HA5025	0595
HA5026	0595
HA5062-2	OEM
HA5062-5	3695
HA5062A5	OEM
HA5062B5	OEM
HA5064-2	OEM
HA5064-5(A)	OEM
HA5064A5(A)	OEM
HA5064B5(A)	OEM
HA5082-2	OEM
HA5082-5	OEM
HA5082A5	OEM
HA5082B5	OEM
HA5084-2	OEM
HA5084-5	3357
HA5084-8	OEM
HA5084A5	OEM
HA5084B5	OEM
HA5100-2	OEM
HA5100-5	OEM
HA5105-5	OEM
HA5110-2	OEM
HA5110-5	OEM
HA5115-5	OEM
HA5130-2	OEM
HA5130-5	OEM
HA5130-8	OEM
HA5135-2	OEM
HA5135-5	OEM
HA5135-8	OEM
HA5160-2	OEM
HA5160-5	OEM
HA5160-8	OEM
HA5162-5	OEM
HA5170-2(A)	OEM
HA5170-5(A)	OEM
HA5170-8(A)	OEM
HA5190-2	OEM
HA5190-8	OEM
HA5195-5	OEM
HA5905-6	OEM
HA7206	0855
HA7207	0855
HA7501	0037
HA7502	0037
HA7506	0037
HA7507	0037
HA7510	0037
HA7520	0786
HA7521	0786
HA7522	0786
HA7523	0786
HA7524	0786
HA7526	0786
HA7527	0786
HA7528	0786
HA7530	0126
HA7531	0126
HA7532	0527
HA7533	0037
HA7534	0037
HA7535	0338
HA7536	0037
HA7537	0037
HA7538	0037
HA7539	0338
HA7540	0338
HA7541	0338
HA7542	0338
HA7543	0037
HA7597	0037
HA7598	0037
HA7599	0037
HA7630	0126
HA7631	0126
HA7632	0126
HA7633	0037
HA7723	0126
HA7725	0126
HA7730	0786

DEVICE TYPE	REPL CODE
HA7731	0126
HA7732	0786
HA7733	0126
HA7734	0786
HA7735	0786
HA7736	0786
HA7737	0786
HA7804	0037
HA7806	0037
HA7807	OEM
HA7808	0037
HA7809	OEM
HA7810	0037
HA7815	0037
HA8832	OEM
HA9048	0855
HA9049	0855
HA9054	0855
HA9055	0855
HA9056	0855
HA9057	0855
HA9058	0855
HA9059	0855
HA9078	0855
HA9079	0855
HA9500	0126
HA9501	0126
HA9502	0126
HA9531	0855
HA9531A	0855
HA9532	0855
HA9532A	0855
HA9532B	0037
HA11103	0167
HA11107	0167
HA11112	4325
HA11113	4535
HA11115W	0438
HA11120-1	OEM
HA11123	OEM
HA11211	3671
HA11215A	4700
HA11218	OEM
HA11219	4769
HA11220	4663
HA11221	4724
HA11222	OEM
HA11223W	4715
HA11225	2237
HA11226	5211
HA11227	3028
HA11228	4546
HA11229	2170
HA11230	OEM
HA11231	3674
HA11235	1420
HA11238	3250
HA11238N	3250
HA11244	4770
HA11247	0067
HA11251	4721
HA11251A	4700
HA11252A	OEM
HA-11401	OEM
HA11401	3317
HA11408A	OEM
HA11409	5090
HA11410	OEM
HA11412	4705
HA11412A	4705
HA11413	3764
HA11413A	OEM
HA11414	3325
HA11417	5093
HA11418	OEM
HA11423	1192
HA11431	0445
HA11431NT	0445
HA11433	OEM
HA11434	4705
HA11436	2109
HA11436A	2109
HA11440	2104
HA11440A	2104
HA11441	6463
HA11442	OEM
HA11445	OEM
HA11446	2109
HA11480	2109
HA11480A	2109
HA11508	OEM
HA11510NT	4452
HA11511CNT	OEM
HA11511CNT-01	OEM
HA11511NT	OEM
HA11513	OEM
HA11516C4	3606
HA11516E1	3606
HA11516F1	OEM
HA11516J	3606
HA11518	OEM
HA11525MP	OEM
HA11525NT	OEM
HA11528NT	OEM
HA11529	OEM
HA11529NT	OEM
HA11532MP	OEM
HA11532NT	OEM
HA11539NT	OEM

DEVICE TYPE	REPL CODE
HA11541	OEM
HA11541NT	OEM
HA11559NT	OEM
HA11561	OEM
HA11566	OEM
HA11566NT	OEM
HA11569FS	OEM
HA11569W	OEM
HA11574	OEM
HA11574FS	OEM
HA11580	1049
HA11701	5088
HA11702	5662
HA11703	5548
HA11704	OEM
HA11705	OEM
HA11706	5091
HA11710	OEM
HA11711	5089
HA11712	OEM
HA11712A	OEM
HA11713	OEM
HA11714	5093
HA11715	5067
HA11716	OEM
HA11718	OEM
HA11719	OEM
HA11720	OEM
HA11721	OEM
HA11722	OEM
HA11724	OEM
HA11725	OEM
HA11726	OEM
HA11727	OEM
HA11732	OEM
HA-11741	OEM
HA11741	OEM
HA11741NT	OEM
HA-11744	OEM
HA11744	OEM
HA-11745	OEM
HA11745	OEM
HA11747	6502
HA11747-A	5681
HA11747A	5681
HA11747ANT	5681
HA11747BNT	2469
HA11749	5679
HA11752	OEM
HA11753NT	OEM
HA11757ANT	OEM
HA11757NT	OEM
HA11758NT	OEM
HA11787	OEM
HA11788	OEM
HA11793	OEM
HA11793ANT	OEM
HA11793NT	OEM
HA11797	OEM
HA11797NT	OEM
HA11803	OEM
HA11811NT2	OEM
HA11816NT	OEM
HA11825NT	OEM
HA11837	OEM
HA11837NT	OEM
HA11839NT	OEM
HA11845NT	OEM
HA11847NT	OEM
HA11853ANT	OEM
HA11853BNT	OEM
HA11853NT	OEM
HA11856A	OEM
HA11856ANT	OEM
HA11870NT	OEM
HA11876MP	OEM
HA11876NT	OEM
HA11887	OEM
HA11887V	OEM
HA11888	OEM
HA11888V	OEM
HA12002	5107
HA12002-W	5107
HA12003	0701
HA12005	OEM
HA12006	OEM
HA12009	OEM
HA12010	OEM
HA12013	0358
HA12016	OEM
HA12017	OEM
HA12018	OEM
HA12019	OEM
HA12024	OEM
HA12025	OEM
HA12026	1251
HA12028	OEM
HA12038	OEM
HA12044	OEM
HA12045	5707
HA12046	OEM
HA12047	OEM
HA12048FP	OEM
HA12058	OEM
HA12058NT	OEM
HA12072ANT	OEM
HA12072NT	OEM
HA12084BNT	OEM
HA12085NT	OEM

DEVICE TYPE	REPL CODE
HA12088NT	OEM
HA12116NT	OEM
HA12117NT	OEM
HA12118NT	OEM
HA12134	OEM
HA12136	OEM
HA12138NT	OEM
HA12150NT	OEM
HA12411	5085
HA12412	5069
HA12413	3764
HA12413-03	3764
HA12417	OEM
HA12418	OEM
HA12430	OEM
HA13006	OEM
HA13007	OEM
HA13115	OEM
HA13402	OEM
HA13403	2172
HA13403V	OEM
HA13407	OEM
HA13407A	OEM
HA13408	OEM
HA13412	OEM
HA13421	4866
HA13421A	4866
HA13430	OEM
HA13430A	OEM
HA13434	OEM
HA13434MP	OEM
HA13434NT	OEM
HA13435	OEM
HA13455	OEM
HA14066B	OEM
HA16613AP	OEM
HA16631P	2732
HA16642MP	OEM
HA17008G	OEM
HA17008P	OEM
HA17012GB	OEM
HA17012GC	OEM
HA17080GS	OEM
HA17080GSA	OEM
HA17080PS	OEM
HA17080PSA	OEM
HA17082GS	OEM
HA17082GSA	OEM
HA17082PS	OEM
HA17082PSA	OEM
HA17083G	OEM
HA17083GA	OEM
HA17083P	OEM
HA17083PA	OEM
HA17084G	OEM
HA17084P	OEM
HA17084PA	OEM
HA17093PS	OEM
HA17094PS	0765
HA17301G	2232
HA17301P	2232
HA17339	0176
HA17358	0765
HA17393	0624
HA17408P	5217
HA17431P	OEM
HA17458GS	0356
HA17458PS	0356
HA17524G	OEM
HA17524P	6195
HA17555	0967
HA17555PS	0967
HA17558	0356
HA17715G	OEM
HA17723G	0026
HA17733G	OEM
HA17741	0308
HA17741G	0308
HA17741GS	0308
HA17741PS	0308
HA17747G	2342
HA17747P	2342
HA17805	0619
HA17805H	0619
HA17805P	0619
HA17806P	0917
HA17807P	OEM
HA17808P	1187
HA17812	6110
HA17812P	0330
HA17812W	OEM
HA17815P	1311
HA17818P	2244
HA17824P	2224
HA17901G	0176
HA17901P	6099
HA17902G	0620
HA17902P	0620
HA17903GS	2294
HA17903PS	2294
HA17904	0765
HA17904GS	OEM
HA17904PS	0765
HA18031	OEM
HA19211NT	OEM
HA19216	OEM
HA19216MP	OEM
HA19507MP	OEM
HA19508	OEM

DEVICE TYPE	REPL CODE
HA19508AMP	OEM
HA19508MP	OEM
HA19510	OEM
HA44015	OEM
HA114323	1192
HA118002	OEM
HA118002FP	OEM
HA118003MP	OEM
HA118003NT	OEM
HA118014NT	OEM
HA118018NT	OEM
HA118031	OEM
HA118039NT	OEM
HA118041NT	OEM
HA118053NT	OEM
HA118059	OEM
HA118088NT	OEM
HA118104	OEM
HA118105NT	OEM
HA118108NT	OEM
HA118114NT	OEM
HA118115	OEM
HA118120	OEM
HA118121FP	OEM
HAB005	0087
HAB010	OEM
HAB020	OEM
HAB060	OEM
HAB080	OEM
HAB100	OEM
HAB1500	OEM
HAB1501	OEM
HAB1502	OEM
HAD1000A	OEM
HAF0385	OEM
HAG20011	OEM
HAG20019	OEM
HAG20021	OEM
HAG20029	OEM
HAL10H8CF	OEM
HAL10H8CJ	OEM
HAL10H8CN	OEM
HAL10H8MF	OEM
HAL10H8MJ	OEM
HAL10H8MN	OEM
HAL10L8CF	OEM
HAL10L8CJ	OEM
HAL10L8CN	OEM
HAL10L8MF	OEM
HAL10L8MJ	OEM
HAL10L8MN	OEM
HAL12H6CF	OEM
HAL12H6CJ	OEM
HAL12H6CN	OEM
HAL12H6MF	OEM
HAL12H6MJ	OEM
HAL12H6MN	OEM
HAL12L6CF	OEM
HAL12L6CJ	OEM
HAL12L6CN	OEM
HAL12L6MF	OEM
HAL12L6MJ	OEM
HAL12L6MN	OEM
HAL12L10CF	OEM
HAL12L10CJ	OEM
HAL12L10CN	OEM
HAL12L10MF	OEM
HAL12L10MJ	OEM
HAL12L10MN	OEM
HAL14H4CF	OEM
HAL14H4CJ	OEM
HAL14H4CN	OEM
HAL14H4MF	OEM
HAL14H4MJ	OEM
HAL14H4MN	OEM
HAL14L4CF	OEM
HAL14L4CJ	OEM
HAL14L4CN	OEM
HAL14L4MF	OEM
HAL14L4MJ	OEM
HAL14L4MN	OEM
HAL14L8CF	OEM
HAL14L8CJ	OEM
HAL14L8CN	OEM
HAL14L8CNS	OEM
HAL14L8MF	OEM
HAL14L8MJ	OEM
HAL14L8MN	OEM
HAL16A4CF	OEM
HAL16A4CJ	OEM
HAL16A4CN	OEM
HAL16A4MF	OEM
HAL16A4MJ	OEM
HAL16A4MN	OEM
HAL16C1CF	OEM
HAL16C1CJ	OEM
HAL16C1CN	OEM
HAL16C1MF	OEM
HAL16C1MJ	OEM
HAL16C1MN	OEM
HAL16H2CF	OEM
HAL16H2CJ	OEM
HAL16H2CN	OEM
HAL16H2MF	OEM
HAL16H2MJ	OEM
HAL16H2MN	OEM
HAL16L2CF	OEM
HAL16L2CJ	OEM
HAL16L2CN	OEM

DEVICE TYPE	REPL CODE
HAL16L2MF	OEM
HAL16L2MJ	OEM
HAL16L2MN	OEM
HAL16L6CF	OEM
HAL16L6CJ	OEM
HAL16L6CN	OEM
HAL16L6MF	OEM
HAL16L6MJ	OEM
HAL16L6MN	OEM
HAL16L8ACN	OEM
HAL16L8CF	OEM
HAL16L8CJ	OEM
HAL16L8CN	OEM
HAL16L8MF	OEM
HAL16L8MJ	OEM
HAL16L8MN	OEM
HAL16LBACN	OEM
HAL16R4CF	OEM
HAL16R4CJ	OEM
HAL16R4CN	OEM
HAL16R4MF	OEM
HAL16R4MJ	OEM
HAL16R4MN	OEM
HAL16R6CF	OEM
HAL16R6CJ	OEM
HAL16R6CN	OEM
HAL16R6MF	OEM
HAL16R6MJ	OEM
HAL16R6MN	OEM
HAL16R8CF	OEM
HAL16R8CJ	OEM
HAL16R8CN	OEM
HAL16R8MF	OEM
HAL16R8MJ	OEM
HAL16R8MN	OEM
HAL16X4CF	OEM
HAL16X4CJ	OEM
HAL16X4CN	OEM
HAL16X4MF	OEM
HAL16X4MJ	OEM
HAL16X4MN	OEM
HAL18L4CF	OEM
HAL18L4CJ	OEM
HAL18L4CN	OEM
HAL18L4MF	OEM
HAL18L4MJ	OEM
HAL18L4MN	OEM
HAL20C1CF	OEM
HAL20C1CJ	OEM
HAL20C1CN	OEM
HAL20C1MJ	OEM
HAL20L2CF	OEM
HAL20L2CJ	OEM
HAL20L2CN	OEM
HAL20L2MF	OEM
HAL20L2MJ	OEM
HAL20L2MN	OEM
HAL20L10CF	OEM
HAL20L10CJ	OEM
HAL20L10CN	OEM
HAL20L10MF	OEM
HAL20L10MJ	OEM
HAL20L10MN	OEM
HAL20X4CF	OEM
HAL20X4CJ	OEM
HAL20X4CN	OEM
HAL20X4CNS	OEM
HAL20X4MF	OEM
HAL20X4MJ	OEM
HAL20X4MN	OEM
HAL20X8CF	OEM
HAL20X8CJ	OEM
HAL20X8CN	OEM
HAL20X8MF	OEM
HAL20X8MJ	OEM
HAL20X8MN	OEM
HAL20X10CF	OEM
HAL20X10CJ	OEM
HAL20X10CN	OEM
HAL20X10MF	OEM
HAL20X10MJ	OEM
HAL20X10MN	OEM
HAM-1	0004
HAR10	0015
HAR15	0015
HAR20	0015
HB-00054	0004
HB-00056	0004
HB-00156	0004
HB-00171	0004
HB-00172	0004
HB-00173	0004
HB-00175	0004
HB-00176	0004
HB-00178	0004
HB-00186	0004
HB-00187	0004
HB-00303	0211
HB-00324	0164
HB-00370	0211
HB-00405	0164
HB-00564	0527
HB1	OEM
HB2	0015
HB3	1325
HB-7B	0025
HB-12B	0361
HB12B	0137
HB-32	0136

If replacement code is OEM, contact original manufacturer for replacement.

DEVICE TYPE	REPL CODE
HB32	0004
HB-33	0136
HB33	0004
HB50	0071
HB-54	0004
HB54	0004
HB55	0004
HB-56	0004
HB56	0004
HB-75	0004
HB75	0004
HB-75B	0211
HB75B	0004
HB75C	0004
HB-77	0004
HB77	0004
HB77B	0004
HB-77C	0211
HB77C	0004
HB-85	0004
HB100	OEM
HB-156	0211
HB156	0004
HB156C	0004
HB171	0004
HB-172	0004
HB172	0004
HB-173	0004
HB-175	0004
HB175	0004
HB176	0004
HB178	0004
HB-186	0136
HB186	0004
HB-187	0136
HB187	0004
HB200	OEM
HB-233	OEM
HB233(A)	OEM
HB263	0004
HB270	0004
HB300	OEM
HB324	0164
HB332	OEM
HB333	OEM
HB352	OEM
HB353	OEM
HB356	OEM
HB-365	0164
HB365	0164
HB367	0222
HB400	OEM
HB-415	0211
HB415	0164
HB422	0136
HB-459	0211
HB459	0004
HB-461	0136
HB461	0841
HB-475	0164
HB475	0164
HB500	OEM
HB600	0087
HB800	0087
HB1000	0087
HB4059AD	OEM
HB-18005	OEM
HB18005	OEM
HB-18007	OEM
HBC4000AD	2013
HBC4000AF	2013
HBC4000AK	2013
HBC4001AD	0473
HBC4001AF	0473
HBC4001AK	0473
HBC4002AD	2044
HBC4002AF	2044
HBC4002AK	2044
HBC4006AD	OEM
HBC4006AF	OEM
HBC4006AK	OEM
HBC4008AD	0982
HBC4008AF	0982
HBC4008AK	0982
HBC4011AD	0215
HBC4011AF	0215
HBC4011AK	0215
HBC4012AD	0493
HBC4012AF	0493
HBC4012AK	0493
HBC4013AD	0409
HBC4013AF	0409
HBC4013AK	0409
HBC4014AD	OEM
HBC4014AF	OEM
HBC4014AK	OEM
HBC4015AD	OEM
HBC4015AF	OEM
HBC4015AK	OEM
HBC4017AD	0508
HBC4017AF	0508
HBC4017AK	0508
HBC4018AD	1381
HBC4018AF	1381
HBC4018AK	1381
HBC4020AD	1651
HBC4020AF	1651
HBC4020AK	1651
HBC4021AD	OEM

DEVICE TYPE	REPL CODE
HBC4021AF	OEM
HBC4021AK	OEM
HBC4022AD	1247
HBC4022AE	1247
HBC4022AF	1247
HBC4022AK	1247
HBC4023AD	0515
HBC4023AF	0515
HBC4023AK	0515
HBC4024AD	1946
HBC4024AF	1946
HBC4024AK	1946
HBC4025AD	2061
HBC4025AF	2061
HBC4025AK	2061
HBC4026AD	OEM
HBC4026AF	OEM
HBC4026AK	OEM
HBC4027AD	1938
HBC4027AF	1938
HBC4027AK	1938
HBC4028AD	2213
HBC4028AF	2213
HBC4028AK	2213
HBC4029AD	2218
HBC4029AF	2218
HBC4029AK	2218
HBC4030AD	0495
HBC4030AF	0495
HBC4030AK	0495
HBC4031AD	OEM
HBC4031AF	OEM
HBC4031AK	OEM
HBC4032AD	OEM
HBC4032AF	OEM
HBC4032AK	OEM
HBC4033AD	OEM
HBC4033AF	OEM
HBC4033AK	OEM
HBC4034AD	OEM
HBC4034AK	OEM
HBC4035AD	OEM
HBC4035AF	OEM
HBC4035AK	OEM
HBC4036AD	OEM
HBC4036AK	OEM
HBC4037AD	OEM
HBC4037AF	OEM
HBC4037AK	OEM
HBC4038AF	OEM
HBC4038AK	OEM
HBC4039AD	OEM
HBC4039AK	OEM
HBC4040AD	0056
HBC4040AF	0056
HBC4040AK	0056
HBC4042AD	0121
HBC4042AF	0121
HBC4042AK	0121
HBC4043AD	1544
HBC4043AF	1544
HBC4043AK	1544
HBC4044AD	2292
HBC4044AF	2292
HBC4044AK	2292
HBC4045AD	OEM
HBC4045AF	OEM
HBC4045AK	OEM
HBC4047AD	2315
HBC4047AK	2315
HBC4048AD	OEM
HBC4048AF	OEM
HBC4048AK	OEM
HBC4054AF	OEM
HBC4054AK	OEM
HBC4055AD	3272
HBC4055AF	3272
HBC4055AK	3272
HBC4056AD	OEM
HBC4056AF	OEM
HBC4056AK	OEM
HBC4057AD	OEM
HBC4059AK	OEM
HBC4060AD	0146
HBC4060AF	0146
HBC4060AK	0146
HBC4062AK	OEM
HBF4000AE	2013
HBF4000AF	2013
HBF4001	0473
HBF4001A	0473
HBF4001AE	0473
HBF4001AF	0473
HBF4002	2044
HBF4002A	2044
HBF4002AE	2044
HBF4002AF	2044
HBF4006AE	0641
HBF4006AF	0641
HBF4007	2819
HBF4008AE	0982
HBF4008AF	0982
HBF4009	1988
HBF4009A	0001
HBF4011	0215
HBF4011A	0215
HBF4011AE	0215
HBF4011AF	0215
HBF4012	0493

DEVICE TYPE	REPL CODE
HBF4012A	0493
HBF4012AE	0493
HBF4012AF	0493
HBF4013	0409
HBF4013A	0409
HBF4013AE	0409
HBF4013AF	0409
HBF4014A	0854
HBF4014AE	0854
HBF4014AF	OEM
HBF4015A	1008
HBF4015AE	OEM
HBF4015AF	OEM
HBF4016	1135
HBF4016A	1135
HBF4017	0508
HBF4017A	0508
HBF4017AE	0508
HBF4017AF	0508
HBF4018AE	1381
HBF4018AF	1381
HBF4019A	1517
HBF4020	1651
HBF4020A	1651
HBF4020AE	1651
HBF4020AF	1651
HBF4021	1738
HBF4021A	1738
HBF4021AE	OEM
HBF4021AF	OEM
HBF4022AE	1247
HBF4022AF	1247
HBF4023	0515
HBF4023A	0515
HBF4023AE	0515
HBF4023AF	0515
HBF4024	1946
HBF4024A	1946
HBF4024AE	1946
HBF4024AF	1946
HBF4025	2061
HBF4025A	2061
HBF4025AE	2061
HBF4025AF	2061
HBF4026AE	OEM
HBF4026AF	OEM
HBF4027	1938
HBF4027A	1938
HBF4027AE	1938
HBF4027AF	1938
HBF4028A	2213
HBF4028AE	2213
HBF4028AF	2213
HBF4029A	2218
HBF4029AE	2218
HBF4029AF	2218
HBF4030A	0495
HBF4030AE	0495
HBF4030AF	0495
HBF4031AE	OEM
HBF4031AF	OEM
HBF4032AE	2509
HBF4032AF	2509
HBF4033AE	2611
HBF4033AF	2611
HBF4034AD	OEM
HBF4034AE	3570
HBF4035AE	OEM
HBF4035AF	OEM
HBF4036AD	OEM
HBF4036AE	OEM
HBF4037AE	OEM
HBF4037AF	OEM
HBF4038AE	2953
HBF4038AF	2953
HBF4039AD	OEM
HBF4039AE	OEM
HBF4040A	0056
HBF4040AE	0056
HBF4040AF	0056
HBF4042A	0121
HBF4042AE	0121
HBF4042AF	0121
HBF4043AE	1544
HBF4043AF	1544
HBF4044AE	2292
HBF4044AF	2292
HBF4045AE	OEM
HBF4045AF	OEM
HBF4047AE	2315
HBF4048AE	3422
HBF4048AF	3422
HBF4049A	0001
HBF4050A	0394
HBF4051A	0362
HBF4052A	0024
HBF4054AE	OEM
HBF4054AF	OEM
HBF4055AE	3272
HBF4055AF	3272
HBF4056AE	OEM
HBF4056AF	OEM
HBF4057AD	OEM
HBF4059AD	OEM
HBF4059AE	OEM
HBF4060AE	0146
HBF4060AF	0146
HBF4062AE	OEM
HBG20011	OEM

DEVICE TYPE	REPL CODE
HBG20019	OEM
HBG20021	OEM
HBG20029	OEM
HC-00184	0470
HC-00227	0016
HC-00268	0086
HC-00372	0224
HC-00373	0111
HC-00380	0127
HC-00394	0155
HC-00458	0079
HC-00460	0079
HC-00461	0151
HC-00481	0222
HC-00496	0161
HC-00509	0079
HC-00535	0224
HC-00536	0111
HC-00537	0079
HC-00644	0086
HC-00668	0144
HC-00693	0079
HC-00711	0111
HC-00730	0595
HC-00732	0111
HC-00735	0079
HC-00772	0144
HC-00784	1136
HC-00828	1211
HC-00829	0127
HC-00838	0079
HC00838	0079
HC-00839	0076
HC-00871	0079
HC-00900	1212
HC-00920	0127
HC-00921	0079
HC-00923	0547
HC-00924	0079
HC-00929	0224
HC-00930	0127
HC00930	0224
HC-00945	0076
HC-01000	0111
HC-01047	0127
HC-01060	0555
HC-01096	0386
HC-01098	0555
HC-01209	0086
HC-01226	0219
HC-01317	0086
HC-01318	0155
HC-01327	1212
HC-01335	0111
HC-01359	0127
HC-01390	0592
HC-01417	0127
HC-01820	0079
HC-01830	0144
HC-2	0344
HC2	5254
HC5	OEM
HC8	OEM
HC10	OEM
HC12	OEM
HC14	OEM
HC15	OEM
HC-30	0015
HC30	0087
HC-39	0015
HC39	0087
HC50	0087
HC-56	0079
HC67	0015
HC67F	0071
HC-68	0015
HC68	0015
HC68F	OEM
HC69	0015
HC69F	OEM
HC70	OEM
HC70F	OEM
HC71	0015
HC71F	2621
HC72	0071
HC72F	0087
HC73	0071
HC73F	0087
HC80	0015
HC100	OEM
HC200	OEM
HC206	0144
HC300	OEM
HC300F	OEM
HC371	0079
HC372	0079
HC-373	0079
HC373	0079
HC380	0127
HC381	0127
HC394	0127
HC400	OEM
HC454	0127
HC458	0079
HC460	0127
HC461	0127
HC-495	0555
HC495	0042
HC500	0015

DEVICE TYPE	REPL CODE
HC500F	OEM
HC502C	OEM
HC503C	OEM
HC515	0142
HC-521	OEM
HC521	OEM
HC-535	0079
HC535	0127
HC535A	0127
HC535B	0127
HC-537	0111
HC537	0127
HC539	0079
HC545	0127
HC-561	0079
HC561	0079
HC600	0087
HC645	0144
HC-668	0007
HC668	0144
HC670	0015
HC680	0015
HC700	0015
HC710	0015
HC720	0071
HC730	0071
HC-772	0079
HC772	0144
HC784	0127
HC800	0087
HC829	0144
HC-1000	0111
HC1000	OEM
HC1200	OEM
HC1200F	OEM
HC1240-1	OEM
HC2000H	OEM
HC2000H3	OEM
HC2000H4	OEM
HC2500	OEM
HC6809E	OEM
HC7001	OEM
HC7002	OEM
HC7004	OEM
HC7005	OEM
HC7006	OEM
HC7007	OEM
HC7008	OEM
HC7060	OEM
HC7082	OEM
HC7083	OEM
HC7084	0030
HC7085	OEM
HC7086	OEM
HC7087	OEM
HC7088	OEM
HC7089	OEM
HC7090	OEM
HC7095	OEM
HC7096	OEM
HC7097	OEM
HC7098	OEM
HC7127	OEM
HC10125	OEM
HC-50102	0895
HC100603	2487
HC1000109	0627
HC1000111-0	0627
HC1000114-0	2593
HC1000117-0	0649
HC1000217	0406
HC1000217-0	1964
HC1000403	2546
HC1000405	OEM
HC1000417	1601
HC1000503	2487
HC1000505	2607
HC1000603	4254
HC1000703	2849
HC1001001	4320
HC1001103	OEM
HC1001203	OEM
HC1001703	OEM
HC10001090	0627
HC10001200	2512
HC10002050	0905
HC10002170	0406
HC10003060	OEM
HC10004010	0514
HC10004110	0232
HC10006170	0514
HC10008060	3763
HC10019210	2614
HC10022010	2008
HC10023010	3231
HC10034050	2008
HC10036010	3764
HC10044030	1940
HCC4000BD	2013
HCC4000BF	2013
HCC4000BK	2013
HCC4001BD	0473
HCC4001BF	0473
HCC4001BK	0473
HCC4002BD	2044
HCC4002BF	2044
HCC4002BK	2044
HCC4006BD	OEM
HCC4006BF	0641

DEVICE TYPE	REPL CODE
HCC4006BK	OEM
HCC4008BD	0982
HCC4008BF	0982
HCC4008BK	0982
HCC4011BD	0215
HCC4011BF	0215
HCC4011BK	0215
HCC4012BD	0493
HCC4012BF	0493
HCC4012BK	0493
HCC4013BD	0409
HCC4013BF	0409
HCC4013BK	0409
HCC4014BD	OEM
HCC4014BF	3180
HCC4014BK	OEM
HCC4015BD	OEM
HCC4015BF	6176
HCC4015BK	OEM
HCC4016BD	OEM
HCC4016BF	1135
HCC4016BK	OEM
HCC4017BD	0508
HCC4017BF	0508
HCC4017BK	0508
HCC4018BD	1381
HCC4018BF	1381
HCC4018BK	1381
HCC4019BD	OEM
HCC4019BF	1517
HCC4019BK	OEM
HCC4020BD	1651
HCC4020BF	1651
HCC4020BK	1651
HCC4021BD	OEM
HCC4021BF	1738
HCC4021BK	OEM
HCC4022BD	1247
HCC4022BE	1247
HCC4022BF	1247
HCC4022BK	1247
HCC4023BD	0515
HCC4023BF	0515
HCC4023BK	0515
HCC4024BD	1946
HCC4024BF	1946
HCC4024BK	1946
HCC4025BD	2061
HCC4025BF	2061
HCC4025BK	2061
HCC4026BD	OEM
HCC4026BF	2139
HCC4026BK	OEM
HCC4027BD	1938
HCC4027BF	1938
HCC4027BK	1938
HCC4028BD	2213
HCC4028BF	2213
HCC4028BK	2213
HCC4029BD	2218
HCC4029BF	2218
HCC4029BK	2218
HCC4030BD	OEM
HCC4030BF	0495
HCC4030BK	OEM
HCC4031BD	OEM
HCC4031BF	2943
HCC4031BK	OEM
HCC4032BD	OEM
HCC4032BF	2509
HCC4032BK	OEM
HCC4033BD	OEM
HCC4033BF	2611
HCC4033BK	OEM
HCC4034BD	OEM
HCC4035BD	OEM
HCC4035BF	2750
HCC4035BK	OEM
HCC4038BD	OEM
HCC4038BF	2953
HCC4038BK	OEM
HCC4040BD	0056
HCC4040BF	0056
HCC4040BK	0056
HCC4042BD	0121
HCC4042BF	0121
HCC4042BK	0121
HCC4043BD	1544
HCC4043BF	1544
HCC4043BK	1544
HCC4044BD	2292
HCC4044BF	2292
HCC4044BK	2292
HCC4045BD	OEM
HCC4045BF	3408
HCC4045BK	OEM
HCC4047BD	OEM
HCC4047BF	2315
HCC4047BK	OEM
HCC4048BD	OEM
HCC4048BF	3423
HCC4048BK	OEM
HCC4049BD	OEM
HCC4049BF	OEM
HCC4049BK	OEM
HCC4050BD	OEM
HCC4050BK	OEM
HCC4051BD	OEM
HCC4051BF	0362

DEVICE TYPE	REPL CODE
HCC4051BK	OEM
HCC4052BD	OEM
HCC4052BF	0024
HCC4052BK	OEM
HCC4053BD	OEM
HCC4053BF	0034
HCC4053BK	OEM
HCC4054BD	OEM
HCC4054BF	4450
HCC4054BK	OEM
HCC4055BD	OEM
HCC4055BF	3272
HCC4055BK	OEM
HCC4056BD	3661
HCC4056BF	3661
HCC4056BK	3661
HCC4060BD	0146
HCC4060BF	0146
HCC4060BK	0146
HCC4063BD	3682
HCC4063BF	3682
HCC4063BK	3682
HCC4066BD	OEM
HCC4066BF	0101
HCC4066BK	OEM
HCC4068BD	2482
HCC4068BF	2482
HCC4068BK	2482
HCC4070BD	2494
HCC4070BF	2494
HCC4070BK	2494
HCC4071BD	0129
HCC4071BF	0129
HCC4071BK	0129
HCC4072BD	2502
HCC4072BF	2502
HCC4072BK	2502
HCC4073BD	1528
HCC4073BF	1528
HCC4073BK	1528
HCC4075BD	2518
HCC4075BF	2518
HCC4075BK	2518
HCC4076BD	OEM
HCC4076BF	3455
HCC4076BK	OEM
HCC4077BD	2536
HCC4077BF	2536
HCC4077BK	2536
HCC4078BD	0915
HCC4078BF	0915
HCC4078BK	0915
HCC4081BD	0621
HCC4081BF	0621
HCC4081BK	0621
HCC4082BD	0297
HCC4082BF	0297
HCC4082BK	0297
HCC4085BD	0300
HCC4085BF	0300
HCC4085BK	0300
HCC4086BD	0530
HCC4086BF	0530
HCC4086BK	0530
HCC4089BD	OEM
HCC4089BF	3778
HCC4089BK	OEM
HCC4094BD	OEM
HCC4094BF	1672
HCC4094BK	OEM
HCC4095BD	OEM
HCC4095BF	3796
HCC4095BK	OEM
HCC4096BD	OEM
HCC4096BF	3798
HCC4096BK	OEM
HCC4098BD	3566
HCC4098BF	3566
HCC4098BK	3566
HCC4099BD	3297
HCC4099BF	3297
HCC4099BK	3297
HCC4508BD	OEM
HCC4508BK	OEM
HCC4510BD	1952
HCC4510BE	1952
HCC4510BF	1952
HCC4510BK	1952
HCC4511BD	1535
HCC4511BF	1535
HCC4511BK	1535
HCC4514BD	1819
HCC4515BD	3555
HCC4516BD	2331
HCC4516BF	2331
HCC4516BK	2331
HCC4518BD	1037
HCC4518BF	1037
HCC4518BK	1037
HCC4520BD	2650
HCC4520BF	2650
HCC4520BK	2650
HCC4527BD	3116
HCC4527BF	3116
HCC4527BK	3116
HCC4532BD	OEM
HCC4532BF	1010
HCC4532BK	OEM
HCC4555BD	2910

If replacement code is OEM, contact original manufacturer for replacement.

DEVICE TYPE	REPL CODE
HCC4555BF	2910
HCC4555BK	2910
HCC4556BD	3397
HCC4556BF	3397
HCC4556BK	3397
HCC40100BD	3895
HCC40100BF	3895
HCC40100BK	OEM
HCC40101BD	OEM
HCC40101BF	OEM
HCC40101BK	OEM
HCC40102BD	3998
HCC40102BF	3998
HCC40102BK	OEM
HCC40103BD	4029
HCC40103BF	4029
HCC40103BK	OEM
HCC40105BD	OEM
HCC40105BF	OEM
HCC40105BK	OEM
HCC40106BD	OEM
HCC40106BF	3581
HCC40106BK	OEM
HCC40109BD	OEM
HCC40109BF	OEM
HCC40109BK	OEM
HCC40160BD	1349
HCC40160BF	1349
HCC40160BK	1349
HCC40161BD	1363
HCC40161BF	1363
HCC40161BK	1363
HCC40162BD	OEM
HCC40162BF	1378
HCC40162BK	1378
HCC40163BD	1397
HCC40163BF	1397
HCC40163BK	1397
HCC40174BD	1542
HCC40174BF	1542
HCC40174BK	1542
HCC40182BD	OEM
HCC40182BF	4579
HCC40182BK	OEM
HCCA100	OEM
HCF0088	OEM
HCF4000BE	2013
HCF4000BF	2013
HCF4001BE	0473
HCF4001BF	0473
HCF4002BE	2044
HCF4002BF	2044
HCF4006BE	0641
HCF4006BF	0641
HCF4007UBE	4897
HCF4008BE	0982
HCF4008BF	0982
HCF4011BE	0215
HCF4011BF	0215
HCF4012BE	0493
HCF4012BF	0493
HCF4013BE	0409
HCF4013BF	0409
HCF4014BE	0854
HCF4014BF	0854
HCF4015BE	1008
HCF4015BF	1008
HCF4016BE	1135
HCF4016BF	1135
HCF4017BE	0508
HCF4017BF	0508
HCF4018BE	1381
HCF4018BF	1381
HCF4019BE	1517
HCF4019BF	1517
HCF4020BE	1651
HCF4020BF	1651
HCF4021BE	1738
HCF4021BF	1738
HCF4022BE	1247
HCF4022BF	1247
HCF4023BE	0515
HCF4023BF	0515
HCF4024BE	1946
HCF4024BF	1946
HCF4025BE	2061
HCF4025BF	2061
HCF4026BE	2139
HCF4026BF	2139
HCF4027BE	1938
HCF4027BF	1938
HCF4028BE	2213
HCF4028BF	2213
HCF4029BE	2218
HCF4029BF	2218
HCF4030BE	0495
HCF4030BF	0495
HCF4031BE	2943
HCF4031BF	2943
HCF4032BE	2509
HCF4032BF	2509
HCF4033BE	2611
HCF4033BF	2611
HCF4034BD	OEM
HCF4034BE	3570
HCF4035BE	2750
HCF4035BF	2750
HCF4038BF	2953
HCF4040BE	0056

DEVICE TYPE	REPL CODE
HCF4040BF	0056
HCF4042BE	0121
HCF4042BF	0121
HCF4043BE	1544
HCF4043BF	1544
HCF4044BE	2292
HCF4044BF	2292
HCF4045BE	3408
HCF4045BF	3408
HCF4047BE	2315
HCF4047BF	2315
HCF4048BE	3423
HCF4048BF	3423
HCF4049BE	0001
HCF4049BF	0001
HCF4050BE	0394
HCF4050BF	0394
HCF4051BE	0362
HCF4051BF	0362
HCF4052BE	0024
HCF4052BF	0024
HCF4053BE	0034
HCF4053BF	0034
HCF4054BE	4450
HCF4054BF	4450
HCF4055BE	3272
HCF4055BF	3272
HCF4056BE	3661
HCF4056BF	3661
HCF4058BE	OEM
HCF4060BE	0146
HCF4060BF	0146
HCF4063BE	3682
HCF4063BF	3682
HCF4066BE	0101
HCF4066BF	0101
HCF4068BE	2482
HCF4068BF	2482
HCF4070BE	2494
HCF4070BF	2494
HCF4071BE	0129
HCF4071BF	0129
HCF4072BE	2502
HCF4072BF	2502
HCF4073BE	1528
HCF4073BF	1528
HCF4075BE	2518
HCF4075BF	2518
HCF4076BE	3455
HCF4076BF	3455
HCF4077BE	2536
HCF4077BF	2536
HCF4078BE	0915
HCF4078BF	0915
HCF4081BE	0621
HCF4081BF	0621
HCF4082BE	0297
HCF4082BF	0297
HCF4085BE	0300
HCF4085BF	0300
HCF4086BE	0530
HCF4086BF	0530
HCF4086BK	0530
HCF4089BE	3778
HCF4089BF	3778
HCF4094BE	1672
HCF4094BF	1672
HCF4095BE	3796
HCF4095BF	3796
HCF4096BE	3798
HCF4096BF	3798
HCF4098BE	3566
HCF4098BF	3566
HCF4099BE	3297
HCF4099BF	3297
HCF4502BE	1031
HCF4508BD	OEM
HCF4510BE	1952
HCF4510BF	1952
HCF4511BE	1535
HCF4511BF	1535
HCF4514BD	1819
HCF4514BE	1819
HCF4515BD	3555
HCF4515BE	3555
HCF4516BE	2331
HCF4516BF	2331
HCF4518BE	1037
HCF4518BF	1037
HCF4520BE	2650
HCF4520BF	2650
HCF4527BE	3116
HCF4527BF	3116
HCF4532BE	1010
HCF4532BF	1010
HCF4555BE	2910
HCF4555BF	2910
HCF4556BE	3397
HCF4556BF	3397
HCF10160BE	OEM
HCF40100BE	3895
HCF40100BF	3895
HCF40101BE	OEM
HCF40101BF	3960
HCF40102BE	OEM
HCF40102BF	3998
HCF40103BE	OEM
HCF40103BF	4029
HCF40105BE	OEM

DEVICE TYPE	REPL CODE
HCF40105BF	4060
HCF40106BE	3581
HCF40106BF	3581
HCF40109BE	OEM
HCF40109BF	4146
HCF40160BE	1349
HCF40160BF	1349
HCF40161BE	1363
HCF40161BF	1363
HCF40162BE	1378
HCF40162BF	1378
HCF40163BE	1397
HCF40163BF	1397
HCF40174BE	1542
HCF40174BF	1542
HCF40182BE	4579
HCF40182BF	4579
HCMP1802ACD	OEM
HCMP1802ACL	OEM
HCMP1802ACP	OEM
HCMP1802ACY	OEM
HCMP1802AD	OEM
HCMP1802AL	OEM
HCMP1802AP	OEM
HCMP1802AY	OEM
HCMP1822CD	OEM
HCMP1822CP	OEM
HCMP1823CD	OEM
HCMP1823CH	OEM
HCMP1823CP	OEM
HCMP1824CD	OEM
HCMP1824CP	OEM
HCMP1824D	OEM
HCMP1824P	OEM
HCMP1831CD	OEM
HCMP1831CP	OEM
HCMP1831D	OEM
HCMP1831P	OEM
HCMP1832CD	OEM
HCMP1832CP	OEM
HCMP1832D	OEM
HCMP1832P	OEM
HCMP1833CD	OEM
HCMP1833CP	OEM
HCMP1833D	OEM
HCMP1833P	OEM
HCMP1834CD	OEM
HCMP1834CP	OEM
HCMP1834D	OEM
HCMP1834P	OEM
HCMP1835CD	OEM
HCMP1835CP	OEM
HCMP1835D	OEM
HCMP1835P	OEM
HCMP1836CD	OEM
HCMP1836CP	OEM
HCMP1836D	OEM
HCMP1836P	OEM
HCMP1852CD	OEM
HCMP1852CP	OEM
HCMP1852CY	OEM
HCMP1852D	OEM
HCMP1852P	OEM
HCMP1852Y	OEM
HCMP1853CD	OEM
HCMP1853CP	OEM
HCMP1853D	OEM
HCMP1853P	OEM
HCMP1854CD	OEM
HCMP1854CP	OEM
HCMP1854D	OEM
HCMP1854P	OEM
HCMP1856CD	OEM
HCMP1856CP	OEM
HCMP1856D	OEM
HCMP1856P	OEM
HCMP1857CD	OEM
HCMP1857CP	OEM
HCMP1857D	OEM
HCMP1857P	OEM
HCMP1858CD	OEM
HCMP1858CP	OEM
HCMP1858D	OEM
HCMP1858P	OEM
HCMP1859CD	OEM
HCMP1859CP	OEM
HCMP1859D	OEM
HCMP1859P	OEM
HCPL-2502	OEM
HCPL-2530	OEM
HCPL2530	5330
HCPL-2531	OEM
HCPL-2601	OEM
HCPL-2602	OEM
HCPL-2630	5568
HCPL2630	5568
HCPL-2631	OEM
HCPL-2730	OEM
HCPL-2731	OEM
HCPL-3700	OEM
HCPL-4562	OEM
HCPL-4661	OEM
HCR5-100	OEM
HCR5-200	OEM
HCR5-300	OEM
HCR5-400	OEM
HCR30P	OEM
HCR50N	OEM
HCR50P	OEM

DEVICE TYPE	REPL CODE
HCR100N	OEM
HCR100P	OEM
HCR150N	OEM
HCR150P	OEM
HCR200N	OEM
HCR200P	OEM
HCR300P	OEM
HCR400P	OEM
HCR1020	OEM
HCR1025	OEM
HCR1030	OEM
HCR1040	OEM
HCR1050	OEM
HCR1070	OEM
HCR1100	OEM
HCR4038BE	OEM
HCT373	5984
HCU04	OEM
HCV	0015
HD0000206	0139
HD-00072	0208
HD-00227	0016
HD-00261	0218
HD-00471	0018
HD-1	0015
HD1-74C00	2100
HD1-74C02	2102
HD1-74C08	2106
HD1-74C10	2107
HD1-74C20	2110
HD1-74C42	2130
HD1-74C48	2135
HD1-74C73	2148
HD1-74C74	2149
HD1-74C76	2150
HD1-74C85	2157
HD1-74C90	2160
HD1-74C93	2163
HD1-74C154	3957
HD1-74C161	3984
HD1-74C192	4056
HD1-74C193	4059
HD1-74C221	0349
HD1-6495-2	OEM
HD1-6495-9	OEM
HD1-6495A-2	OEM
HD1-6495A-9	OEM
HD1-15530-2	OEM
HD1-15530-9	OEM
HD1-15531-2	OEM
HD1-15531-9	OEM
HD3	OEM
HD3-4702-2	OEM
HD3-4702-9	OEM
HD4-4702-2	OEM
HD4-4702-9	OEM
HD4-6440-2	OEM
HD4-6440-9	OEM
HD4-15530-2	OEM
HD4-15530-9	OEM
HD4-15531-2	OEM
HD4-15531-9	OEM
HD9-54C20	OEM
HD9-54C93	OEM
HD9-74C00	2100
HD9-74C02	2102
HD9-74C08	2106
HD9-74C10	2107
HD9-74C20	2110
HD9-74C42	2130
HD9-74C48	2135
HD9-74C73	2148
HD9-74C74	2149
HD9-74C76	2150
HD9-74C85	2157
HD9-74C90	2160
HD9-74C93	2163
HD9-74C154	3957
HD9-74C161	3984
HD9-74C192	4056
HD9-74C193	4059
HD9-74C221	3018
HD9-15530-2	OEM
HD9-15530-9	OEM
HD10	2085
HD10-001-01	0143
HD20-003-01	0015
HD61J228P	OEM
HD63A03Y	OEM
HD63A03YF	OEM
HD63A03YP	OEM
HD63B03X	OEM
HD63B03XP	OEM
HD63B03YP	OEM
HD68A00	OEM
HD68A09	OEM
HD68A09EP	2105
HD68A21	OEM
HD68A21P	OEM
HD68A44C	OEM
HD68A44P	OEM
HD68A45SP	OEM
HD68A50	OEM
HD68A52	OEM
HD68B00	OEM
HD68B09	OEM
HD68B21	OEM
HD68B21P	OEM
HD68B40	OEM

DEVICE TYPE	REPL CODE
HD68B40P	OEM
HD68B45P	OEM
HD74ALS00	OEM
HD74ALS01	OEM
HD74ALS03	OEM
HD74ALS04	OEM
HD74ALS04P	OEM
HD74ALS05	OEM
HD74ALS08	OEM
HD74ALS09	OEM
HD74ALS20	OEM
HD74ALS21	OEM
HD74ALS22	OEM
HD74ALS74	OEM
HD74ALS109	OEM
HD74ALS112	OEM
HD74ALS112P	OEM
HD74ALS113	OEM
HD74ALS113P	OEM
HD74ALS114	OEM
HD74ALS114P	OEM
HD74ALS175	OEM
HD74ALS175P	OEM
HD74HC00P	OEM
HD74HC04P	OEM
HD74HC10	OEM
HD74HC74P	1552
HD74HC374FP	OEM
HD74LS00	1519
HD74LS00P	1519
HD74LS01	1537
HD74LS01P	1537
HD74LS02	1550
HD74LS02P	1550
HD74LS03	1569
HD74LS03P	1569
HD74LS04	1585
HD74LS04P	1585
HD74LS05	1598
HD74LS05P	1598
HD74LS07P	OEM
HD74LS08	1623
HD74LS08P	1623
HD74LS09	1632
HD74LS09P	1632
HD74LS10	1652
HD74LS10P	1652
HD74LS11	1657
HD74LS11P	1657
HD74LS12	1669
HD74LS12P	1669
HD74LS13	1678
HD74LS13P	1678
HD74LS14	1688
HD74LS14P	1688
HD74LS15	1697
HD74LS15P	1697
HD74LS20	0035
HD74LS20P	0035
HD74LS21	1752
HD74LS21P	1752
HD74LS22	1764
HD74LS22P	1764
HD74LS26	1372
HD74LS26P	1372
HD74LS27	0183
HD74LS27P	0183
HD74LS30	0822
HD74LS30P	0822
HD74LS32	0088
HD74LS32P	0088
HD74LS37	1719
HD74LS37P	1719
HD74LS38	1828
HD74LS38P	1828
HD74LS40	0135
HD74LS40P	0135
HD74LS42	1830
HD74LS42P	1830
HD74LS47	1834
HD74LS47P	1834
HD74LS48	1838
HD74LS48P	1838
HD74LS49	1839
HD74LS49P	1839
HD74LS51	1027
HD74LS51P	1027
HD74LS54	1846
HD74LS54P	1846
HD74LS55	0452
HD74LS55P	0452
HD74LS73	1856
HD74LS73P	1856
HD74LS74	0243
HD74LS74A	0243
HD74LS74AP	0243
HD74LS75	1859
HD74LS75P	1859
HD74LS76	2166
HD74LS76P	2166
HD74LS77	1861
HD74LS77P	1861
HD74LS78	1862
HD74LS78P	1862
HD74LS83A	2204
HD74LS83AP	2204
HD74LS85	0426
HD74LS85P	0426
HD74LS86	0288

DEVICE TYPE	REPL CODE
HD74LS86P	0288
HD74LS90	1871
HD74LS90P	1871
HD74LS91	1874
HD74LS91P	1874
HD74LS92	1876
HD74LS92P	1876
HD74LS93	1877
HD74LS93P	1877
HD74LS95B	0766
HD74LS95BP	0766
HD74LS96	OEM
HD74LS96P	OEM
HD74LS107	1592
HD74LS107P	1592
HD74LS109A	1895
HD74LS109AP	1895
HD74LS109P	4885
HD74LS112	2115
HD74LS112A	OEM
HD74LS112P	2115
HD74LS113	2241
HD74LS113P	2241
HD74LS114	2286
HD74LS114P	2286
HD74LS122	1610
HD74LS122P	1610
HD74LS123	0973
HD74LS123P	0973
HD74LS125	OEM
HD74LS125AP	0075
HD74LS132P	OEM
HD74LS136	1618
HD74LS136P	1618
HD74LS138	0422
HD74LS138P	0422
HD74LS139	0153
HD74LS139P	0153
HD74LS145	1554
HD74LS145P	1554
HD74LS148	3856
HD74LS148P	3856
HD74LS151	1636
HD74LS151P	1636
HD74LS152	OEM
HD74LS152P	OEM
HD74LS153	0953
HD74LS153P	0953
HD74LS154	4956
HD74LS154P	4956
HD74LS155	0209
HD74LS155P	0209
HD74LS156	1644
HD74LS156P	1644
HD74LS157	1153
HD74LS157P	1153
HD74LS158	1646
HD74LS158P	1646
HD74LS160	0831
HD74LS161	0852
HD74LS161P	0852
HD74LS162	0874
HD74LS162P	0874
HD74LS163	0887
HD74LS163P	0887
HD74LS164	4274
HD74LS164P	4274
HD74LS166	4301
HD74LS166P	4301
HD74LS174	0260
HD74LS174P	0260
HD74LS175	1662
HD74LS175P	1662
HD74LS181	1668
HD74LS181P	1668
HD74LS190	1676
HD74LS190P	1676
HD74LS191	1677
HD74LS191P	1677
HD74LS192	1679
HD74LS192P	1679
HD74LS193	1682
HD74LS193P	1682
HD74LS194A	1294
HD74LS194AP	1294
HD74LS195A	1305
HD74LS195AP	1305
HD74LS221	1230
HD74LS221P	1230
HD74LS240	0447
HD74LS240P	0447
HD74LS241	1715
HD74LS241P	1715
HD74LS244	0453
HD74LS244P	0453
HD74LS245WP	0458
HD74LS247	1721
HD74LS247P	1721
HD74LS248	1723
HD74LS248P	1723
HD74LS249	1724
HD74LS249P	1724
HD74LS251	1726
HD74LS251P	1726
HD74LS253	1728
HD74LS253P	1728
HD74LS257	1733
HD74LS257P	1733
HD74LS258	1735

DEVICE TYPE	REPL CODE
HD74LS258P	1735
HD74LS259	3175
HD74LS259P	3175
HD74LS266	0587
HD74LS266P	0587
HD74LS273P	0888
HD74LS279	3259
HD74LS279P	3259
HD74LS280	1762
HD74LS280P	1762
HD74LS283	1768
HD74LS283P	1768
HD74LS290	4352
HD74LS290P	4352
HD74LS293	0082
HD74LS293P	0082
HD74LS295B	2212
HD74LS295BP	2212
HD74LS298	3337
HD74LS298P	3337
HD74LS299	4353
HD74LS299P	4353
HD74LS365AP	0937
HD74LS367AP	0971
HD74LS373P	0704
HD74LS374P	0708
HD74LS375	OEM
HD74LS375P	OEM
HD74LS386	1221
HD74LS386P	1221
HD74LS390	1278
HD74LS390P	1278
HD74LS393	0813
HD74LS393P	0813
HD74LS490	2199
HD74LS490P	2199
HD74LS610P	OEM
HD74LS668	OEM
HD74LS668P	OEM
HD74LS669	OEM
HD74LS669P	OEM
HD74LSS76P	2166
HD74S00	0699
HD74S00P	0699
HD74S03	2203
HD74S03P	2203
HD74S04	2248
HD74S04P	2248
HD74S05	2305
HD74S05N	OEM
HD74S05P	2305
HD74S10	2426
HD74S10P	2426
HD74S11	2428
HD74S11P	2428
HD74S11S	2428
HD74S15	2432
HD74S15P	2432
HD74S20	1011
HD74S20P	1011
HD74S22	2442
HD74S22P	2442
HD74S40	2456
HD74S40P	2456
HD74S64	2476
HD74S64P	2476
HD74S65	2477
HD74S65P	2477
HD74S74	2483
HD74S74P	2483
HD74S86	2489
HD74S86P	2489
HD74S112	1607
HD74S112P	1607
HD74S113	1613
HD74S113P	1613
HD74S114	1619
HD74S114P	1619
HD74S133	1808
HD74S133P	1808
HD74S134	1816
HD74S134P	1816
HD74S140	1875
HD74S140P	1875
HD74S151	1944
HD74S151P	1944
HD74S174	2119
HD74S174P	2119
HD74S175P	2128
HD74S181	2151
HD74S181P	2151
HD74S251	2184
HD74S251P	2184
HD74S280P	OEM
HD-187	0595
HD224E	OEM
HD237	OEM
HD268T26	OEM
HD268T26P	OEM
HD405P	OEM
HD408B05	OEM
HD468B21	OEM
HD468B21P	OEM
HD740LP	0268
HD1062	OEM
HD1075G	OEM
HD10750	OEM
HD1075R	OEM
HD1075Y	OEM

If replacement code is OEM, contact original manufacturer for replacement.

425

DEVICE TYPE	REPL CODE	DEVICE TYPE	REPL CODE	DEVICE TYPE	REPL CODE	DEVICE TYPE	REPL CODE	DEVICE TYPE	REPL CODE	DEVICE TYPE	REPL CODE	DEVICE TYPE	REPL CODE
HD1076G	OEM	HD2100-2	OEM	HD2528P	0331	HD5002	OEM	HD7474P	1303	HD14053BP	0034	HD38800B28(AUP)	OEM
HD1076O	OEM	HD2100-3	OEM	HD2529	1417	HD5003	OEM	HD7475	1423	HD14066B	0101	HD38800B32	OEM
HD1076R	OEM	HD2100-4	OEM	HD2529P	1417	HD5004	OEM	HD7475P	1423	HD14066BCP	0101	HD38800R04	OEM
HD1076Y	OEM	HD2100-5	OEM	HD2530	0936	HD6101-2	OEM	HD7485	0370	HD14066BP	0101	HD38800R05	OEM
HD1077G	OEM	HD2100-6	OEM	HD2530P	0936	HD6101-9	OEM	HD7485P	0370	HD14068B	2482	HD38805A22	OEM
HD1077O	OEM	HD2100-7	OEM	HD2531	1074	HD6101C-9	OEM	HD7486	1358	HD14069UB	0119	HD38805SA44	OEM
HD1077R	OEM	HD2100-8	OEM	HD2531P	1074	HD6147	0015	HD7486P	1358	HD14070B	2494	HD38820-L39	OEM
HD1077Y	OEM	HD2100-9	OEM	HD2532	1100	HD6301V1E01P	OEM	HD7490A	1199	HD14071B	0129	HD38820L26	OEM
HD1078G	OEM	HD2100-10	OEM	HD2532P	1100	HD6301Y0PC06	OEM	HD7490AP	1199	HD14072B	2502	HD38820L35	OEM
HD1078O	OEM	HD2100-12	OEM	HD2533	1692	HD6303YP	OEM	HD7492A	0828	HD14073B	1528	HD38820L38	OEM
HD1078R	OEM	HD2100-14	OEM	HD2533P	1692	HD6305Y0A05P	OEM	HD7492AP	0828	HD14075B	2518	HD38820L39	OEM
HD1078Y	OEM	HD2100-16	OEM	HD2534	1477	HD6305Y0A08P	OEM	HD7493A	0564	HD14076B	3455	HD38820L44	OEM
HD1105G	OEM	HD2100-18	OEM	HD2534P	1477	HD6305Y0C28P	OEM	HD7493AD	0564	HD14077B	2536	HD38820L47	OEM
HD1105O	OEM	HD2100-20	OEM	HD2535	0117	HD6305Y1FC24	OEM	HD7493AP	0564	HD14078B	0915	HD38825L06	OEM
HD1105R	OEM	HD2135A	OEM	HD2535P	0117	HD6305Y2F	OEM	HD7493P	0564	HD14081B	0621	HD38825L11	OEM
HD1105Y	OEM	HD2145G	OEM	HD2536	1046	HD6305YOA04P	OEM	HD7496	1705	HD14081BP	0621	HD38870L46	OEM
HD1106G	OEM	HD2145R	OEM	HD2536P	1046	HD6305YOA06P	OEM	HD7496P	1705	HD14082B	0297	HD38941	OEM
HD1106O	OEM	HD2201	1035	HD2537	1054	HD6305YOC28P	OEM	HD7601P	OEM	HD14093B	2368	HD38980A	2702
HD1106R	OEM	HD2201P	1035	HD2537P	1054	HD6305YOC29P	OEM	HD10101	OEM	HD14101G	OEM	HD38980C	2702
HD1106Y	OEM	HD2202	2086	HD2538P	1066	HD6305YOC53P	OEM	HD10102	OEM	HD14101R	OEM	HD38986	OEM
HD1107G	OEM	HD2202P	2086	HD2539	1394	HD6402C9	OEM	HD10104	OEM	HD14160B	OEM	HD38991	2279
HD1107O	OEM	HD2203	0141	HD2539P	1394	HD6800	OEM	HD10105	OEM	HD14161B	OEM	HD38991A	2702
HD1107R	OEM	HD2203P	0141	HD2540	1711	HD6802	OEM	HD10106	OEM	HD14162B	OEM	HD38992	OEM
HD1107Y	OEM	HD2204	1812	HD2540P	1711	HD6803-1	OEM	HD10107	OEM	HD14163B	OEM	HD38993	4308
HD1108G	OEM	HD2204P	1812	HD2541	1910	HD6803P-1	OEM	HD10109	OEM	HD14174B	1542	HD38993A	4308
HD1108O	OEM	HD2205	0081	HD2541P	1910	HD6805S1P-A05	OEM	HD10110	OEM	HD14175B	1520	HD38998A	OEM
HD1108R	OEM	HD2205P	0081	HD2542	1915	HD6805S1PA22	OEM	HD10111	OEM	HD14194B	1758	HD42851	3763
HD1108Y	OEM	HD2206	1820	HD2542P	1915	HD6805V1B20P	OEM	HD10116	OEM	HD14443B	OEM	HD42851A2	3763
HD1111G	OEM	HD2206P	1820	HD2543	0175	HD6805V1N06P	OEM	HD10117	OEM	HD14447B	OEM	HD42853	4558
HD1111O	OEM	HD2207	0557	HD2543P	0175	HD6805V1N13P	OEM	HD10118	OEM	HD14501UB	3758	HD42856	OEM
HD1111R	OEM	HD2207P	0557	HD2544	0990	HD6805V1P	OEM	HD10119	OEM	HD14502B	1031	HD43019A	OEM
HD1111Y	OEM	HD2208	1168	HD2544P	0990	HD6805W	OEM	HD10121	OEM	HD14503B	2042	HD44007A	OEM
HD1112G	OEM	HD2208P	1168	HD2545	1432	HD6805WOP	OEM	HD10124	OEM	HD14503P	2042	HD44015	OEM
HD1112O	OEM	HD2209	0033	HD2545P	1432	HD6805X2P	OEM	HD10130	OEM	HD14505B	OEM	HD44040	OEM
HD1112R	OEM	HD2209P	0033	HD2546	1705	HD6809	5829	HD10131	OEM	HD14506B	3721	HD44042	OEM
HD1112Y	OEM	HD2210	0329	HD2546P	1705	HD6809EP	2105	HD10132	OEM	HD14508B	1800	HD44053	OEM
HD1113G	OEM	HD2210P	0329	HD2547	1831	HD6821	OEM	HD10133	OEM	HD14510B	1952	HD44100	OEM
HD1113O	OEM	HD2211	0354	HD2547P	1831	HD6821P	0443	HD10134	OEM	HD14511B	1535	HD44753	OEM
HD1113R	OEM	HD2211P	0354	HD2548	1484	HD6843SC	OEM	HD10136	OEM	HD14511BP	1660	HD44801	OEM
HD1113Y	OEM	HD2213	1424	HD2548P	1484	HD6843SP	OEM	HD10145	OEM	HD14512B	2108	HD44801A05	OEM
HD1115G	OEM	HD2213&	1424	HD2549	1487	HD6844C	OEM	HD10147	OEM	HD14512BP	4153	HD44801SB82	OEM
HD1115O	OEM	HD2214	0461	HD2549P	1487	HD6844P	OEM	HD10148	OEM	HD14514B	1819	HD44820A17	OEM
HD1115R	OEM	HD2214P	0461	HD2550	0462	HD6845C	OEM	HD10160	OEM	HD14515B	1819	HD44820A48	OEM
HD1115Y	OEM	HD2215	0557	HD2550P	0462	HD6845P	OEM	HD10161	OEM	HD14516B	2331	HD44820B02	OEM
HD1131G	OEM	HD2215P	0557	HD2551	0487	HD6845SP	OEM	HD10162	OEM	HD14517B	4220	HD44820B24	OEM
HD1131O	OEM	HD2216	1824	HD2551P	0487	HD6850	OEM	HD10164	OEM	HD14518B	1037	HD44820B36	OEM
HD1131R	OEM	HD2216P	1824	HD2552	3478	HD6852	OEM	HD10165	OEM	HD14519B	OEM	HD44860A92	OEM
HD1131Y	OEM	HD2500-1	OEM	HD2552P	3478	HD6865	0015	HD10174	OEM	HD14520B	2650	HD44860B23	OEM
HD1132G	OEM	HD2500-2	OEM	HD2555	0614	HD7400	0232	HD10175	OEM	HD14520BP	5768	HD44860B39	OEM
HD1132O	OEM	HD2500-3	OEM	HD2555P	0614	HD7400P	0232	HD10179	OEM	HD14521B	OEM	HD46505RP-2	OEM
HD1132R	OEM	HD2500-4	OEM	HD2558	1367	HD7401P	0268	HD10180	OEM	HD14522B	OEM	HD46505SP	OEM
HD1132Y	OEM	HD2500-5	OEM	HD2558P	1367	HD7402	0310	HD10181	OEM	HD14524B	OEM	HD46505SP-1	OEM
HD1133G	OEM	HD2500-6	OEM	HD2560	0798	HD7402P	0310	HD10209	OEM	HD14526B	3565	HD46508P	OEM
HD1133O	OEM	HD2500-7	OEM	HD2560P	0798	HD7403	0331	HD10210	OEM	HD14527B	3116	HD46508P-1	OEM
HD1133R	OEM	HD2500-8	OEM	HD2561	1149	HD7403P	0331	HD10211	OEM	HD14530B	OEM	HD46508PA-1	OEM
HD1133Y	OEM	HD2500-9	OEM	HD2561P	1149	HD7404	0357	HD10230	OEM	HD14531B	OEM	HD46818P	OEM
HD1134G	OEM	HD2500-10	OEM	HD2562	1845	HD7404P	0357	HD10231	OEM	HD14532B	1010	HD46846	OEM
HD1134O	OEM	HD2500-12	OEM	HD2562P	1845	HD7405	0381	HD10551	OEM	HD14534B	OEM	HD46846P	OEM
HD1134R	OEM	HD2500-16	OEM	HD2563	4329	HD7405P	0381	HD14000UB	2013	HD14536B	3659	HD48801B85	OEM
HD1134Y	OEM	HD2500-20	OEM	HD2563P	4329	HD7406	1197	HD14001B	0473	HD14537B	OEM	HD49403NT	OEM
HD1310	OEM	HD2501	1018	HD2564	1531	HD7406N	1197	HD14001BP	3214	HD14538B	1057	HD49409FS	OEM
HD1310A	OEM	HD2501P	1018	HD2564P	1531	HD7406P	1197	HD14002B	2044	HD14538BP	1057	HD49412FS	OEM
HD1320	OEM	HD2502	1265	HD2572	1939	HD7407	1329	HD14006B	0641	HD14539B	OEM	HD49416FS	OEM
HD1320A	OEM	HD2502P	1265	HD2572P	1939	HD7407P	1329	HD14007UB	2819	HD14541B	4929	HD49704	OEM
HD1330	OEM	HD2503	0232	HD2573	1945	HD7410	0507	HD14008B	0982	HD14543B	4932	HD49705	OEM
HD1330A	OEM	HD2503P	0232	HD2573P	1945	HD7410P	0507	HD14011B	0215	HD14549B	OEM	HD49707	OEM
HD1500-1	OEM	HD2504	0692	HD2580	1546	HD7412	2227	HD14011BP	0215	HD14552B	OEM	HD49714ANT	OEM
HD1500-2	OEM	HD2504P	0692	HD2580P	1546	HD7412P	2227	HD14012B	0493	HD14553B	OEM	HD49721A	OEM
HD1500-3	OEM	HD2505	1160	HD2912	OEM	HD7414	2228	HD14013B	0409	HD14554B	OEM	HD49721NT	OEM
HD1500-4	OEM	HD2505P	1160	HD2916	OEM	HD7414P	2228	HD14013BP	6207	HD14555B	2910	HD49723ANT	OEM
HD1500-5	OEM	HD2506	0738	HD2923	OEM	HD7416	1339	HD14014B	0854	HD14556B	3397	HD49723NT	OEM
HD1500-6	OEM	HD2506P	0738	HD3000-1	OEM	HD7416P	1339	HD14015B	1008	HD14557B	OEM	HD49741	OEM
HD1500-7	OEM	HD2507	0507	HD3000-2	OEM	HD7417	1342	HD14016B	1135	HD14558B	4960	HD49741NT	OEM
HD1500-8	OEM	HD2507P	0507	HD3000-3	OEM	HD7417P	1342	HD14016BP	4087	HD14559B	OEM	HD49747N	OEM
HD1500-9	OEM	HD2508	0867	HD3000-4	OEM	HD7420	0692	HD14017	OEM	HD14560B	6101	HD49747NT	OEM
HD1500-10	OEM	HD2508P	0867	HD3000-5	OEM	HD7420P	0692	HD14017B	0508	HD14562B	OEM	HD61905	OEM
HD1500-12	OEM	HD2509	0268	HD3000-6	OEM	HD7426	0798	HD14018B	1381	HD14568B	3573	HD62990	OEM
HD1500-14	OEM	HD2509P	0268	HD3863	OEM	HD7426P	0798	HD14020B	1651	HD14569B	3573	HD62991	OEM
HD1500-16	OEM	HD2510	1303	HD4000	2013	HD7427	0812	HD14020BP	6637	HD14572UB	3440	HD68000P8	OEM
HD1500-18	OEM	HD2510P	1303	HD4001	0473	HD7427P	0812	HD14021B	1738	HD14580B	OEM	HD74107	0936
HD1500-20	OEM	HD2511	0310	HD4001BP	OEM	HD7430	0867	HD14022B	1247	HD14581B	OEM	HD74107P	0936
HD1500-22	OEM	HD2511P	0310	HD4002	2044	HD7430P	0867	HD14023B	0515	HD14582B	OEM	HD74121	0175
HD1500-24	OEM	HD2512	1177	HD4007	2819	HD7432	0893	HD14024B	1946	HD14584BP	3581	HD74121P	0175
HD1500-26	OEM	HD2512P	1177	HD4009	1988	HD7432P	0893	HD14025B	2061	HD14681BP	OEM	HD74123P	1149
HD1500-28	OEM	HD2513	1564	HD4011	0215	HD7438P	0990	HD14027B	1938	HD-20008	0102	HD74125	1174
HD1500-30	OEM	HD2513P	1564	HD4012	0493	HD7440	1018	HD14028B	2213	HD36990	OEM	HD74125P	1174
HD1705	OEM	HD2514	1193	HD4013	0409	HD7440P	1018	HD14028BP	4123	HD37980	OEM	HD74126	1184
HD1705A	OEM	HD2514P	1193	HD4015	1008	HD7442A	1046	HD14032B	2509	HD38480A	OEM	HD74126P	1184
HD1706	OEM	HD2515	1164	HD4016	1135	HD7442AP	1046	HD14034B	3570	HD38570A91	OEM	HD74132	1261
HD1707	OEM	HD2515P	1164	HD4017	0508	HD7443A	1054	HD14035B	2750	HD38630A26	OEM	HD74132P	1261
HD1810	OEM	HD2516	1150	HD4019	1517	HD7443AP	1054	HD14038B	2953	HD38700A01	OEM	HD74150	1484
HD1811	OEM	HD2516P	1150	HD4020	1651	HD7444A	1066	HD14040B	0056	HD38701A06	OEM	HD74150P	1484
HD1812	OEM	HD2517	1423	HD4021	1738	HD7444AP	1066	HD14040BP	6770	HD38702A23	OEM	HD74151A	1487
HD1840	OEM	HD2517P	1423	HD4023	0515	HD7450	0738	HD14042B	0121	HD38702A25	OEM	HD74151AP	1487
HD1841	OEM	HD2519	1199	HD4024	1946	HD7450P	0738	HD14042BP	0121	HD38750-B05	OEM	HD74153P	4370
HD1842	OEM	HD2519P	1199	HD4025	2061	HD7451	1160	HD14042P	0121	HD38750A51	OEM	HD74155	1566
HD1870	OEM	HD2520	0564	HD4027	1938	HD7451P	1160	HD14043B	1544	HD38750A53	OEM	HD74155P	1566
HD1871	OEM	HD2520P	0564	HD4030	0495	HD7453	1177	HD14044B	2292	HD38750A78	OEM	HD74156	1582
HD1872	OEM	HD2521	0828	HD4040	0056	HD7453P	1177	HD14044BP	2292	HD38750A79	OEM	HD74156P	1582
HD2000	0015	HD2521P	0828	HD4049	0001	HD7454	1193	HD14046BP	6804	HD38750A85	OEM	HD74159P	OEM
HD2000-2	OEM	HD2522	0357	HD4050	0394	HD7454P	1193	HD14049UB	0001	HD38750A89	OEM	HD74160	1621
HD2000-4	OEM	HD2522P	0357	HD4101	OEM	HD7460	1265	HD14050B	0394	HD38750A91	OEM	HD74160P	1621
HD2000-6	OEM	HD2523	0381	HD4102	OEM	HD7460P	1265	HD14050BP	0394	HD38757A10	OEM	HD74161	1635
HD2000-12	OEM	HD2523P	0381	HD4285	OEM	HD7471P	1342	HD14051B	0362	HD38800A50	OEM	HD74161P	1635
HD2000-16	OEM	HD2524	0974	HD4518	1037	HD7472	1417	HD14051BP	0362	HD38800A57	OEM	HD74162	1007
HD2000-20	OEM	HD2524P	0974	HD4702-2	OEM	HD7472P	1417	HD14052	OEM	HD38800B11	OEM	HD74162P	1007
HD2000-24	OEM	HD2526	1358	HD4702-9	OEM	HD7473AP	1164	HD14052B	0024	HD38800B11(BUP)	OEM	HD74163	1656
HD2000-301	0015	HD2526P	1358	HD5000	OEM	HD7473P	1164	HD14052BP	0024	HD38800B27	OEM	HD74163P	1656
HD2100-1	OEM	HD2528	0331	HD5001	OEM	HD7474	1303	HD14053B	0034	HD38800B28	OEM	HD74164	0729

If replacement code is OEM, contact original manufacturer for replacement.

DEVICE TYPE	REPL CODE
HD74164P	0729
HD74166	0231
HD74166P	0231
HD74174	1759
HD74174P	1759
HD74175	1776
HD74175P	1776
HD74177P	1792
HD74180	1818
HD74180P	1818
HD74190	1901
HD74190P	1901
HD74191	1906
HD74191P	1906
HD74194	1920
HD74194P	1920
HD74198	1953
HD74198P	1953
HD74199	1960
HD74199P	1960
HD75107A	OEM
HD75107AP	OEM
HD75108A	OEM
HD75108AP	OEM
HD75109	OEM
HD75109P	OEM
HD75110	OEM
HD75110P	OEM
HD75154	OEM
HD75154P	OEM
HD75188	0503
HD75188P	0503
HD75189	0506
HD75189P	0506
HD75450A	1222
HD75451A	1235
HD75451AP	1235
HD75452	1253
HD75452P	1253
HD75453	1262
HD75453P	1262
HD75454	1279
HD75454P	1279
HD100101	OEM
HD100101F	OEM
HD100102	OEM
HD100102F	OEM
HD100107	OEM
HD100107F	OEM
HD100112	OEM
HD100112F	OEM
HD100114(A)	OEM
HD100117	OEM
HD100117F	OEM
HD100118	OEM
HD100118F	OEM
HD100122	OEM
HD100122F	OEM
HD100123	OEM
HD100123F	OEM
HD100124(A)	OEM
HD100124F(A)	OEM
HD100125(A)	OEM
HD100125F(A)	OEM
HD100130	OEM
HD100130F	OEM
HD100131	OEM
HD100131F	OEM
HD100136	OEM
HD100136F	OEM
HD100141	OEM
HD100141F	OEM
HD100142	OEM
HD100142F	OEM
HD100145	OEM
HD100145F	OEM
HD100150F	OEM
HD100151	OEM
HD100151F	OEM
HD100155	OEM
HD100155F	OEM
HD100156	OEM
HD100156F	OEM
HD100158	OEM
HD100158F	OEM
HD100160	OEM
HD100160F	OEM
HD100163	OEM
HD100163F	OEM
HD100164	OEM
HD100164F	OEM
HD100165	OEM
HD100165F	OEM
HD100166	OEM
HD100166F	OEM
HD100170	OEM
HD100170F	OEM
HD100171	OEM
HD100171F	OEM
HD100179	OEM
HD100179F	OEM
HD100180	OEM
HD100180F	OEM
HD100181	OEM
HD100181F	OEM
HD146818P	OEM
HD200207	0015
HD200301	0015
HD252538	1066

DEVICE TYPE	REPL CODE
HD300101-0	OEM
HD404302SA02	OEM
HD404708H-A35	OEM
HD404708H-A51	OEM
HD404709A01S	OEM
HD404709S	OEM
HD440071	OEM
HD440072	OEM
HD614042-XXXX(1283M)	OEM
HD614042F	OEM
HD614042FB93	OEM
HD614042FF41	OEM
HD614042FG43	OEM
HD614042FG66	OEM
HD614042FG74	OEM
HD614042FG86	OEM
HD614042FH48	OEM
HD614042FH55	OEM
HD614042FH60	OEM
HD614042SC23	OEM
HD614042SC67	OEM
HD614042SD76	OEM
HD614042SD97	OEM
HD614042SE15	OEM
HD614042SE25	OEM
HD614042SE43	OEM
HD614042SE46	OEM
HD614042SE47	OEM
HD614042SE57	OEM
HD614042SE60	OEM
HD614042SE94	OEM
HD614042SF07	OEM
HD614042SF11	OEM
HD614042SF44	OEM
HD614042SF45	OEM
HD614042SG25	OEM
HD614042SG47	OEM
HD614042SG69	OEM
HD614042SH58	OEM
HD614042SH75	OEM
HD614042SH89	OEM
HD614042SJ57	OEM
HD614043SA09	OEM
HD614043XXXX	OEM
HD614045SE85	OEM
HD614080-SA02	OEM
HD614080-SA05	OEM
HD614080-SA19	OEM
HD614080SA97	OEM
HD614080SB05	OEM
HD614080SB70	OEM
HD614085S	OEM
HD614085SA06	OEM
HD614085SA14	OEM
HD614085SA39	OEM
HD614085SA64	OEM
HD614088SB42	OEM
HD614088SC56	OEM
HD614088SC58	OEM
HD614120PA22	OEM
HD614128SA61	OEM
HD-1000101	0143
HD1000101	0143
HD1000101-0	0143
HD1000105	0123
HD1000105-0	0123
HD1000107	0143
HD1000107-0	0143
HD1000301	0143
HD1000302	0143
HD1000303	0143
HD1000303-0	0143
HD1000309	0644
HD1000320	0123
HD-2000106	0133
HD2000106	0133
HD-2000108	0102
HD2000108	0087
HD2000110	0229
HD2000110-0	0015
HD2000206	0133
HD2000301	0015
HD2000301-0	0015
HD2000305	0015
HD2000307	0015
HD-2000308	0015
HD2000308	0015
HD2000413	0015
HD2000501	0023
HD2000510	0015
HD2000610	0015
HD2000703	0015
HD2000710	0196
HD2000803	0015
HD2000903	0015
HD2001005	0133
HD2001105	0133
HD2001310	0015
HD3000101-0	0137
HD3000109-0	0313
HD3000113	0313
HD3000201-0	0721
HD3000213	0010
HD-3000301	0015
HD3000309	0644
HD3000309-0	0644
HD3000401	0012
HD-3000409	0644

DEVICE TYPE	REPL CODE
HD3000409	0244
HD3001009	0313
HD3001009-0	0181
HD3001109	0002
HD3001109-0	0100
HD3001809	0313
HD3002109	0100
HD3002409	0052
HD3003109	0244
HD3003309	0041
HD4000109	0143
HD4000909	0030
HD4074709A01S	OEM
HD4074709HCF001	OEM
HD4074709S	OEM
HD10001010	0143
HD10001050	0019
HD10002020	0143
HD20001100	0015
HD20001210	0133
HD20003010	0015
HD20005100	0087
HD20007030	0015
HD20011050	0133
HD20023100	0015
HD30001090	0181
HD30001200	0170
HD30010090	0313
HD30011090	0100
HD30017090	0012
HD30019090	0644
HD30023090	0062
HD30042090	0157
HD40001060	0030
HD40009090	0030
HD300223090	OEM
HDA412	OEM
HDA420	OEM
HDA496	OEM
HDAS-8	OEM
HDAS-16	OEM
HDK8610	OEM
HDS1395	OEM
HDS9001	OEM
HDS9009	OEM
HDS9010	0392
HDSP-0760	OEM
HDSP-0761	OEM
HDSP-0762	OEM
HDSP-0763	OEM
HDSP-0770	OEM
HDSP-0771	OEM
HDSP-0772	OEM
HDSP-0860	OEM
HDSP-0863	OEM
HDSP-0960	OEM
HDSP-0961	OEM
HDSP-0962	OEM
HDSP-0963	OEM
HDSP-2000	OEM
HDSP-2001	OEM
HDSP2002	OEM
HDSP-2010	OEM
HDSP2300	OEM
HDSP2301	OEM
HDSP2302	OEM
HDSP-2416	OEM
HDSP-2424	OEM
HDSP-2432	OEM
HDSP-2440	OEM
HDSP-2470	OEM
HDSP-2471	OEM
HDSP-2472	OEM
HDSP2490	OEM
HDSP2491	OEM
HDSP2492	OEM
HDSP-3400	OEM
HDSP-3401	OEM
HDSP-3403	OEM
HDSP-3405	OEM
HDSP-3406	OEM
HDSP-3530	5042
HDSP-3531	5035
HDSP-3533	OEM
HDSP-3536	OEM
HDSP-3730	OEM
HDSP-3731	OEM
HDSP-3733	OEM
HDSP-3736	OEM
HDSP-3900	OEM
HDSP-3901	OEM
HDSP-3903	OEM
HDSP-3905	OEM
HDSP-3906	OEM
HDSP-4030	OEM
HDSP-4031	5037
HDSP-4033	OEM
HDSP-4036	OEM
HDSP-4130	OEM
HDSP-4131	OEM
HDSP-4133	OEM
HDSP-4136	OEM
HDSP-4200	OEM
HDSP-4201	OEM
HDSP-4203	OEM
HDSP-4205	OEM
HDSP-4206	OEM
HDSP-6300	OEM
HDSP-6504	OEM

DEVICE TYPE	REPL CODE
HDSP6504	OEM
HDSP-6508	OEM
HDSP6508	OEM
HDSP-8716	OEM
HDSP-8724	OEM
HDSP-8732	OEM
HDSP-8740	OEM
HDU0014	OEM
H-DX0038CE	0023
H-DX0046CE	0124
H-DX0086TA	0023
H-DX0105TA	0023
H-DX0181CE	0031
H-DX0248CE	0023
HE-0A90	0143
HE-1N34	0143
HE-1N34A	0143
HE-1N60	0019
HE-1N60P	0143
HE-1S188	0143
HE-1S426	0143
HE-1S446	0143
HE-1S555	0623
HE-56-56	0124
HE-56-58	0466
HE-56-73	0133
HE-56-93	0133
HE-56-655	6816
HE-57-27	0015
HE-57-42	0087
HE-57-64	0071
HE-57-65	0080
HE-57-614	0811
HE212	OEM
HE212E	OEM
HE215	OEM
HE215E	OEM
HE224	OEM
HE-234-264	0023
HE-234-266	0137
HE-234-267	0023
HE-234-271	0164
HE-234-272	0164
HE-234-273	0283
HE-234-274	0016
HE-234-275	0079
HE-234-276	2985
HE-234-290	0079
HE-234-299	0124
HE-234-353	0023
HE-234-521	0102
HE-234-522	0079
HE-234-523	0079
HE-234-526	0023
HE237E	OEM
HE252	OEM
HE252E	OEM
HE381	OEM
HE381E	OEM
HE383	OEM
HE383E	OEM
HE384	OEM
HE384E	OEM
HE-417-195	0275
HE-417-282	0538
HE-417-811	0076
HE-417-821	0079
HE-417-822	0037
HE-417-823	0312
HE-417-834	0334
HE-417-864	0086
HE-417-865	0037
HE-417-874	0006
HE-417-875	0076
HE-417-923	0309
HE-417-924	0676
HE-417-926	0546
HE-417-932	0556
HE-417-937	0079
HE-433-110	OEM
HE-442-4	2681
HE-442-21	0356
HE-442-22	0308
HE-442-24	2155
HE-442-25	2207
HE-442-30	1911
HE-442-39	1290
HE-442-48	OEM
HE-442-50	OEM
HE-442-54	0619
HE-442-60	2224
HE-442-63	1311
HE-442-66	2231
HE-442-71	2232
HE-442-73	OEM
HE-442-74	0368
HE-442-75	2093
HE-442-99	1135
HE-442-602	0620
HE-442-604	3684
HE-442-613	3777
HE-442-615	0687
HE-442-622	OEM
HE-442-623	2755
HE-442-624	OEM
HE-442-627	1288
HE-442-630	1275
HE-442-635	3915
HE-442-636	4716

DEVICE TYPE	REPL CODE
HE-442-640	2721
HE-442-644	1817
HE-442-647	3394
HE-442-648	2495
HE-442-650	OEM
HE-442-651	2836
HE-442-654	3347
HE-442-655	OEM
HE-442-659	3864
HE-442-663	0330
HE-442-664	1827
HE-442-665	4429
HE-442-672	4045
HE-442-673	4715
HE-442-674	0330
HE-442-675	1827
HE-442-676	OEM
HE-442-677	4646
HE-442-682	3839
HE-442-686	0375
HE-442-687	OEM
HE-442-688	3733
HE-442-691	1187
HE-442-693	OEM
HE-442-702	1905
HE-442-703	OEM
HE-442-715	2755
HE-443-3	0867
HE-443-4	1417
HE-443-5	1164
HE-443-6	1303
HE-443-7	1199
HE-443-9	OEM
HE-443-10	OEM
HE-443-12	0507
HE-443-13	1423
HE-443-15	0738
HE-443-16	1150
HE-443-17	1367
HE-443-21	OEM
HE-443-22	0175
HE-443-23	1131
HE-443-25	1487
HE-443-26	0699
HE-443-34	0828
HE-443-36	1100
HE-443-44	1432
HE-443-45	0462
HE-443-46	0310
HE-443-53	1046
HE-443-54	0331
HE-443-66	1910
HE-443-68	0680
HE-443-70	2941
HE-443-72	1342
HE-443-73	1339
HE-443-74	1253
HE-443-77	0990
HE-443-87	0614
HE-443-89	0487
HE-443-90	1149
HE-443-460	OEM
HE-443-603	0215
HE-443-604	2819
HE-443-606	1938
HE-443-607	0409
HE-443-612	1915
HE-443-622	1442
HE-443-623	1546
HE-443-625	1261
HE-443-626	OEM
HE-443-628	1939
HE-443-629	1199
HE-443-640	0564
HE-443-642	0381
HE-443-680	1477
HE-443-683	OEM
HE-443-695	0473
HE-443-696	OEM
HE-443-703	0473
HE-443-704	2044
HE-443-706	0129
HE-443-707	3555
HE-443-708	2331
HE-443-709	2163
HE-443-711	1721
HE-443-712	2061
HE-443-713	2213
HE-443-717	1184
HE-443-718	1305
HE-443-719	0587
HE-443-720	3151
HE-443-721	OEM
HE-443-722	2252
HE-443-727	1459
HE-443-728	1519
HE-443-729	1678
HE-443-730	0243
HE-443-731	4352
HE-443-732	0822
HE-443-733	0082
HE-443-737	1037
HE-443-738	3397
HE-443-745	1569
HE-443-751	0621
HE-443-752	1662
HE-443-753	OEM
HE-443-754	0447
HE-443-755	1585

DEVICE TYPE	REPL CODE
HE-443-757	0852
HE-443-762	4467
HE-443-764	2037
HE-443-769	4274
HE-443-777	3566
HE-443-778	2368
HE-443-779	1550
HE-443-780	1623
HE-443-781	1859
HE-443-782	0209
HE-443-783	1247
HE-443-784	0495
HE-443-785	3018
HE-443-791	0453
HE-443-792	1615
HE-443-794	0503
HE-443-795	0506
HE-443-797	1652
HE-443-798	0035
HE-443-799	1153
HE-443-800	0183
HE-443-801	2807
HE-443-802	1733
HE-443-804	3175
HE-443-805	0888
HE-443-807	1830
HE-443-811	0075
HE-443-813	1871
HE-443-814	OEM
HE-443-815	1682
HE-443-816	1632
HE-443-817	1679
HE-443-818	1598
HE-443-819	OEM
HE-443-822	0153
HE-443-824	1715
HE-443-827	0384
HE-443-828	1856
HE-443-829	2166
HE-443-836	1542
HE-443-837	0704
HE-443-838	1877
HE-443-839	0900
HE-443-840	4118
HE-443-841	1108
HE-443-842	OEM
HE-443-843	0443
HE-443-854	3259
HE-443-855	1768
HE-443-856	OEM
HE-443-857	0971
HE-443-858	2228
HE-443-860	OEM
HE-443-863	0708
HE-443-864	1657
HE-443-867	0704
HE-443-871	1819
HE-443-872	1688
HE-443-874	OEM
HE-443-875	0088
HE-443-877	0422
HE-443-879	0260
HE-443-881	3441
HE-443-884	1717
HE-443-885	0458
HE-443-886	0493
HE-443-887	0515
HE-443-888	3721
HE-443-889	1554
HE-443-891	0288
HE-443-892	4301
HE-443-896	2223
HE-443-897	2248
HE-443-898	0775
HE-443-899	2477
HE-443-900	2483
HE-443-901	2121
HE-443-904	0518
HE-443-906	OEM
HE-443-909	0516
HE-443-912	3856
HE-443-913	OEM
HE-443-915	2489
HE-443-916	3566
HE-443-919	2850
HE-443-920	0426
HE-443-921	1278
HE-443-927	3276
HE-443-928	0982
HE-443-929	0508
HE-443-930	2315
HE-443-934	0887
HE-443-935	2138
HE-443-942	0973
HE-443-944	OEM
HE-443-958	0146
HE-443-967	1197
HE-443-970	2341
HE-443-973	0813
HE-443-983	2128
HE-443-985	2128
HE-443-991	0394
HE-443-998	OEM
HE-443-999	3112
HE-443-1001	1762
HE-443-1009	OEM
HE-443-1011	OEM
HE-443-1012	OEM
HE-443-1020	1329

DEVICE TYPE	REPL CODE
HE-443-1021	0051
HE-443-1024	0985
HE-443-1031	OEM
HE-443-1034	1828
HE-443-1036	1644
HE-443-1037	1733
HE-443-1040	2906
HE-443-1045	OEM
HE-443-1047	OEM
HE-443-1051	OEM
HE-443-1053	2119
HE-443-1058	2525
HE-443-1066	OEM
HE-443-1070	OEM
HE-443-1072	OEM
HE-443-1073	OEM
HE-443-1078	OEM
HE-443-1080	OEM
HE-443-1082	OEM
HE-443-1084	OEM
HE-443-1097	OEM
HE-443-1098	OEM
HE-443-1112	2270
HE-443-1119	OEM
HE-443-1165	OEM
HE-443-1166	OEM
HE-443-1167	OEM
HE-443-1168	OEM
HE-443-1169	OEM
HE-443-1170	OEM
HE-443-1172	OEM
HE-443-1173	1122
HE-443-1174	OEM
HE-443-1178	OEM
HE-443-1198	OEM
HE-443-1228	OEM
HE-443-1229	OEM
HE-443-1230	OEM
HE-443-1231	OEM
HE-443-1232	OEM
HE-443-1254	OEM
HE-444-224	OEM
HE-444-225	OEM
HE-444-226	OEM
HE-444-227	OEM
HE-444-228	2209
HE-444-229-4	1628
HE-444-230-1	OEM
HE-444-230-2	OEM
HE-444-231	OEM
HE-444-232	OEM
HE-444-234	OEM
HE-444-235	OEM
HE-444-238	OEM
HE-444-238-1	OEM
HE-444-241	OEM
HE-444-260-4	1628
HE-444-274	OEM
HE-444-287	OEM
HE-444-292	OEM
HE-444-314	OEM
HE-444-320	OEM
HE500	OEM
HE581	OEM
HE581E	OEM
HE583	OEM
HE583E	OEM
HE584	OEM
HE584E	OEM
HE-1024	0143
HE8006	OEM
HE8101	OEM
HE-10001	0143
HE-10002	0019
HE-10003	0143
HE-10024	0143
HE-10025	2217
HE-10027	0143
HE-10030	0133
HE-10044	0123
HE-15188	0143
HE-15426	0143
HE-15446	0143
HE-20011	0015
HE-20049	0644
HE98241A	OEM
HE98245	OEM
HE-CD0000	0143
HEDS-1000	OEM
HEDS-3000	OEM
HEF0175P	OEM
HEF4000	OEM
HEF4000B	2013
HEF4000BD	2013
HEF4000BP	2013
HEF4000BT	OEM
HEF4000P	2013
HEF4001	OEM
HEF4001BD	0473
HEF4001BP	0473
HEF4001BT	OEM
HEF4001P	0473
HEF4001U	OEM
HEF4001UBD	OEM
HEF4001UBP	OEM
HEF4001UBT	OEM
HEF4002	OEM
HEF4002BD	2044
HEF4002BP	2044

If replacement code is OEM, contact original manufacturer for replacement.

DEVICE TYPE	REPL CODE
HEF4002BT	OEM
HEF4002P	2044
HEF4006B	0641
HEF4006BD	0641
HEF4006BP	0641
HEF4006BT	OEM
HEF4006P	0641
HEF4008	OEM
HEF4008B	0982
HEF4008BD	0982
HEF4008BP	0982
HEF4008BT	OEM
HEF4008P	0982
HEF4011	OEM
HEF4011BD	0215
HEF4011BP	0215
HEF4011BT	OEM
HEF4011P	0215
HEF4011U	OEM
HEF4011UBD	OEM
HEF4011UBP	OEM
HEF4011UBT	OEM
HEF4012	0493
HEF4012BD	0493
HEF4012BP	0493
HEF4012BT	OEM
HEF4012P	0493
HEF4013	OEM
HEF4013BD	0409
HEF4013BP	0409
HEF4013BT	OEM
HEF4013P	0409
HEF4014B	0854
HEF4014BD	0854
HEF4014BP	0854
HEF4014BT	OEM
HEF4014P	0854
HEF4015B	1008
HEF4015BD	1819
HEF4015BP	1819
HEF4015BT	OEM
HEF4015P	1008
HEF4016BD	1135
HEF4016BP	1135
HEF4016BT	OEM
HEF4017	OEM
HEF4017BD	0508
HEF4017BP	0508
HEF4017BT	OEM
HEF4017P	0508
HEF4018	OEM
HEF4018BD	1381
HEF4018BP	1381
HEF4018BT	OEM
HEF4018P	1381
HEF4019BD	1517
HEF4019BP	1517
HEF4019BT	OEM
HEF4020	OEM
HEF4020BD	1651
HEF4020BP	1651
HEF4020BT	OEM
HEF4020P	1651
HEF4021B	1738
HEF4021BD	1738
HEF4021BP	1738
HEF4021BT	OEM
HEF4021P	1738
HEF4022	OEM
HEF4022BD	1247
HEF4022BP	1247
HEF4022BT	OEM
HEF4022P	1247
HEF4023	OEM
HEF4023BD	0515
HEF4023BP	0515
HEF4023BT	OEM
HEF4023P	0515
HEF4024	OEM
HEF4024BD	1946
HEF4024BP	1946
HEF4024BT	OEM
HEF4024P	1946
HEF4025	OEM
HEF4025BD	2061
HEF4025BP	2061
HEF4025BT	OEM
HEF4025P	2061
HEF4027	OEM
HEF4027BD	1938
HEF4027BP	1938
HEF4027BT	OEM
HEF4027P	1938
HEF4028	OEM
HEF4028B	2213
HEF4028BD	2213
HEF4028BP	2213
HEF4028BT	OEM
HEF4028P	2213
HEF4029	OEM
HEF4029B	2218
HEF4029BD	2218
HEF4029BP	2218
HEF4029BT	OEM
HEF4029P	2218
HEF4030	OEM
HEF4030BD	0495
HEF4030BP	0495
HEF4030BT	OEM
HEF4030P	0495
HEF4031B	2943
HEF4031BD	2943
HEF4031BP	2943
HEF4031BT	OEM
HEF4031P	2943
HEF4032P	OEM
HEF4035B	2750
HEF4035BD	2750
HEF4035BP	2750
HEF4035BT	OEM
HEF4035P	2750
HEF4040	OEM
HEF4040BD	0056
HEF4040BP	0056
HEF4040BT	OEM
HEF4040P	0056
HEF4041BD	3145
HEF4041BP	3145
HEF4041BT	OEM
HEF4042	OEM
HEF4042BD	0121
HEF4042BP	0121
HEF4042BT	OEM
HEF4042P	0121
HEF4043	OEM
HEF4043BD	1544
HEF4043BP	1544
HEF4043BT	OEM
HEF4043P	1544
HEF4044	OEM
HEF4044B	2292
HEF4044BD	2292
HEF4044BP	2292
HEF4044BT	OEM
HEF4044P	2292
HEF4047	OEM
HEF4047B	2315
HEF4047BD	2315
HEF4047BP	2315
HEF4047BT	OEM
HEF4049BD	0001
HEF4049BP	0001
HEF4049BT	OEM
HEF4049P	5379
HEF4050BD	0394
HEF4050BP	0394
HEF4050BT	OEM
HEF4050P	OEM
HEF4051BD	0362
HEF4051BP	0362
HEF4051BT	OEM
HEF4052BD	0024
HEF4052BP	0024
HEF4052BT	OEM
HEF4053BD	0034
HEF4053BP	0034
HEF4053BT	OEM
HEF4059BD	OEM
HEF4059BP	OEM
HEF4060BD	OEM
HEF4060BP	OEM
HEF4060BT	OEM
HEF4066BD	0101
HEF4066BP	0101
HEF4066BT	OEM
HEF4067BD	4215
HEF4067BP	4215
HEF4068	OEM
HEF4068BD	2482
HEF4068BP	2482
HEF4068BT	OEM
HEF4068P	2482
HEF4069P	0119
HEF4069UBD	0119
HEF4069UBP	0119
HEF4069UBT	OEM
HEF4070	OEM
HEF4070BD	2494
HEF4070BP	2494
HEF4070BT	OEM
HEF4070P	2494
HEF4071	OEM
HEF4071BD	0129
HEF4071BP	0129
HEF4071BT	OEM
HEF4071P	0129
HEF4072	OEM
HEF4072BD	2502
HEF4072BP	2502
HEF4072BT	OEM
HEF4072P	2502
HEF4073	OEM
HEF4073B	1528
HEF4073BD	1528
HEF4073BP	1528
HEF4073BT	OEM
HEF4073P	1528
HEF4075	OEM
HEF4075B	2518
HEF4075BD	2518
HEF4075BP	2518
HEF4075BT	OEM
HEF4076B	3455
HEF4076BD	3455
HEF4076BP	3455
HEF4076BT	OEM
HEF4076P	3455
HEF4077	OEM
HEF4077B	2536
HEF4077BD	2536
HEF4077BP	2536
HEF4077BT	OEM
HEF4077P	2536
HEF4078	OEM
HEF4078BD	0915
HEF4078BP	0915
HEF4078BT	OEM
HEF4078P	0915
HEF4081	OEM
HEF4081BD	0621
HEF4081BP	0621
HEF4081BT	OEM
HEF4081P	0621
HEF4082	OEM
HEF4082BD	0297
HEF4082BP	0297
HEF4082BT	OEM
HEF4082P	0297
HEF4085	OEM
HEF4085BD	0300
HEF4085BP	0300
HEF4085BT	OEM
HEF4085P	0300
HEF4086	OEM
HEF4086B	0530
HEF4086BD	0530
HEF4086BP	0530
HEF4086BT	OEM
HEF4086P	0530
HEF4093BD	2368
HEF4093BP	2368
HEF4093BT	OEM
HEF4094BD	OEM
HEF4094BP	OEM
HEF4094BT	OEM
HEF4104BD	OEM
HEF4104BP	OEM
HEF4502BD	1031
HEF4502BP	1031
HEF4502BT	OEM
HEF4505BD	OEM
HEF4505BP	OEM
HEF4508	OEM
HEF4508BD	1800
HEF4508BP	1800
HEF4510	OEM
HEF4510B	1952
HEF4510BD	1952
HEF4510BP	1952
HEF4511B	1535
HEF4511BD	1535
HEF4511BP	1535
HEF4511BT	OEM
HEF4512BD	2108
HEF4512BP	2108
HEF4512BT	OEM
HEF4514BD	3555
HEF4514BP	1819
HEF4515BD	3555
HEF4515BP	3555
HEF4516	OEM
HEF4516B	2331
HEF4516BD	2331
HEF4516BP	2331
HEF4516BT	OEM
HEF4517BD	OEM
HEF4517BP	OEM
HEF4518	OEM
HEF4518BD	1037
HEF4518BP	1037
HEF4518BT	OEM
HEF4518P	1037
HEF4519BD	OEM
HEF4519BP	OEM
HEF4519BT	OEM
HEF4520	OEM
HEF4520BD	2650
HEF4520BP	2650
HEF4520BT	OEM
HEF4520P	2650
HEF4521	OEM
HEF4521BD	OEM
HEF4521BP	OEM
HEF4521BT	OEM
HEF4522	OEM
HEF4522BD	2810
HEF4522BP	2810
HEF4522BT	OEM
HEF4526	OEM
HEF4526BD	OEM
HEF4526BT	OEM
HEF4527BD	OEM
HEF4527BP	OEM
HEF4528	OEM
HEF4528B	3168
HEF4528BD	3168
HEF4528BP	3168
HEF4528BT	OEM
HEF4531	OEM
HEF4531B	3292
HEF4531BD	3292
HEF4531BP	3292
HEF4531BT	OEM
HEF4532BD	OEM
HEF4532BP	OEM
HEF4534	OEM
HEF4534BD	OEM
HEF4534BP	OEM
HEF4538BD	OEM
HEF4538BP	1057
HEF4538BT	OEM
HEF4539BD	3611
HEF4539BP	3611
HEF4539BT	OEM
HEF4541BD	OEM
HEF4541BP	OEM
HEF4541BT	OEM
HEF4543BD	OEM
HEF4543BP	OEM
HEF4543BT	OEM
HEF4555BD	2910
HEF4555BP	2910
HEF4556BD	3397
HEF4556BP	3397
HEF4557BD	OEM
HEF4557BP	OEM
HEF4557BT	OEM
HEF4585	OEM
HEF4585BD	1365
HEF4585BP	1365
HEF4585BT	OEM
HEF4720	OEM
HEF4720B	OEM
HEF4720BD	OEM
HEF4720BP	OEM
HEF4720P	OEM
HEF4720VD	OEM
HEF4720VP	OEM
HEF4721B	OEM
HEF4721P	OEM
HEF4724	OEM
HEF4724BD	OEM
HEF4724BP	OEM
HEF4724BT	OEM
HEF4731BD	OEM
HEF4731BP	OEM
HEF4731VD	OEM
HEF4731VP	OEM
HEF4736B	OEM
HEF4736P	OEM
HEF4737	OEM
HEF4737BD	OEM
HEF4737BP	OEM
HEF4737VD	OEM
HEF4737VP	OEM
HEF4738V	OEM
HEF4738VE	OEM
HEF4738VP	OEM
HEF4739V	OEM
HEF4752VD	OEM
HEF4752VP	OEM
HEF4753BD	OEM
HEF4753BP	OEM
HEF4754VD	OEM
HEF4754VP	OEM
HEF40097BD	4367
HEF40097BP	4367
HEF40097BT	OEM
HEF40097P	OEM
HEF40098BD	0427
HEF40098BN	0427
HEF40098BP	0427
HEF40098BT	OEM
HEF40098P	0427
HEF40106BD	OEM
HEF40106BP	OEM
HEF40106BT	OEM
HEF40160	OEM
HEF40160B	1349
HEF40160BD	1349
HEF40160BP	1349
HEF40160BT	OEM
HEF40161	OEM
HEF40161B	1363
HEF40161BD	1363
HEF40161BP	1363
HEF40161BT	OEM
HEF40162	OEM
HEF40162B	1378
HEF40162BD	1378
HEF40162BP	1378
HEF40162BT	OEM
HEF40163	OEM
HEF40163B	1397
HEF40163BD	1397
HEF40163BP	1397
HEF40163BT	OEM
HEF40174B	1542
HEF40174BD	1542
HEF40174BP	1542
HEF40174BT	OEM
HEF40174P	1542
HEF40175B	1520
HEF40175BD	1520
HEF40175BP	1520
HEF40175BT	OEM
HEF40192	OEM
HEF40192BD	1753
HEF40192BP	1753
HEF40192BT	OEM
HEF40192P	1753
HEF40193	OEM
HEF40193BD	1765
HEF40193BP	1765
HEF40193BT	OEM
HEF40193P	1765
HEF40194B	1758
HEF40194BD	1758
HEF40194BP	1758
HEF40194BT	OEM
HEF40194P	1758
HEF40195B	1773
HEF40195BD	1773
HEF40195BP	1773
HEF40195BT	OEM
HEF40195P	OEM
HEF40240B	OEM
HEF40244B	OEM
HE-M8489	0133
HEMT-3300	OEM
HEMT-6000	OEM
HEP-0700	0911
HEP1	0136
HEP1-RT	0136
HEP-2	0050
HEP2	0279
HEP2-RT	0279
HEP3	0050
HEP3-RT	0050
HEP50	0079
HEP50-RT	0079
HEP51	0126
HEP51-RT	0126
HEP52	0037
HEP52-RT	0037
HEP53	0079
HEP53-RT	0079
HEP54	0079
HEP54-RT	0079
HEP55	2528
HEP55-RT	0191
HEP56	0144
HEP56-RT	0144
HEP57	0037
HEP57-RT	0037
HEP75	0590
HEP75-RT	0590
HEP76	0786
HEP76-RT	0786
HEP101	0170
HEP102	0188
HEP103	0631
HEP104	0012
HEP105	0137
HEP134	0143
HEP135	0143
HEP151	1991
HEP152	0865
HEP153	1241
HEP154	0015
HEP155	0080
HEP156	0604
HEP157	0015
HEP158	0015
HEP159	0071
HEP160	0071
HEP161	0110
HEP162	0242
HEP165	0196
HEP166	1073
HEP170	0071
HEP175	0276
HEP176	0287
HEP177	0293
HEP178	0299
HEP200	0085
HEP200-RT	0085
HEP201	0435
HEP230	0085
HEP230-RT	0085
HEP230X2	0142
HEP231	0435
HEP231-RT	0435
HEP232	0160
HEP232-RT	0160
HEP233	0435
HEP233-RT	0435
HEP234	0969
HEP234-RT	0969
HEP235	0969
HEP236	0599
HEP-237	0432
HEP237	0432
HEP237-RT	0432
HEP238	1414
HEP238-RT	0076
HEP239	3267
HEP239-RT	3267
HEP240	0142
HEP240-RT	0142
HEP241	0178
HEP241-RT	0178
HEP242	0126
HEP242-RT	0126
HEP243	0086
HEP243-RT	0086
HEP244	0275
HEP244-RT	0275
HEP245	0161
HEP245-RT	0161
HEP-246	0455
HEP246	0455
HEP246-RT	0676
HEP247	0538
HEP247-RT	0538
HEP-248	1671
HEP248	0486
HEP248-RT	0486
HEP250	0211
HEP250-RT	0211
HEP251	0004
HEP251-RT	0004
HEP252	0211
HEP252-RT	0211
HEP253	0164
HEP253-RT	0164
HEP254	0208
HEP254-RT	0208
HEP280	0004
HEP281	0004
HEP300	1102
HEP302	0957
HEP304	2497
HEP305-RT	OEM
HEP306	0740
HEP307-RT	OEM
HEP310	1167
HEP310-RT	1167
HEP311	3298
HEP312	0007
HEP320	1129
HEP340	0588
HEP570	OEM
HEP572	3393
HEP573	3395
HEP580	0320
HEP581	1354
HEP582	OEM
HEP583	OEM
HEP584	1063
HEP590	1070
HEP591	2600
HEP592	OEM
HEP593	OEM
HEP-594	0649
HEP594	0649
HEP-595	0438
HEP595	0438
HEP600	OEM
HEP601	2591
HEP602	0162
HEP603	0157
HEP604	0789
HEP605	0361
HEP606	0100
HEP607	0002
HEP608	0436
HEP609	0039
HEP610	1823
HEP610-RT	0863
HEP611	0778
HEP612	0327
HEP613	0149
HEP620	1574
HEP621	1574
HEP622	3368
HEP623	0160
HEP623-RT	0160
HEP624	0085
HEP624-RT	0085
HEP-625	0599
HEP625	0969
HEP625-RT	0969
HEP-626	0599
HEP626	0085
HEP626-RT	0085
HEP627	0599
HEP627-RT	0599
HEP628	0085
HEP628-RT	0085
HEP629	0211
HEP629-RT	0211
HEP630	0164
HEP630-RT	0164
HEP631	0211
HEP631-RT	0211
HEP632	0004
HEP632-RT	0004
HEP633	0211
HEP633-RT	0211
HEP634	0004
HEP634-RT	0004
HEP635	0136
HEP635-RT	0136
HEP636	0136
HEP636-RT	0136
HEP637	0050
HEP638	0136
HEP638-RT	0136
HEP639	0136
HEP639-RT	0136
HEP640	0136
HEP640-RT	0136
HEP641	0595
HEP641-RT	0595
HEP642	0222
HEP643	0222
HEP643X2	0222
HEP644	0969
HEP644-RT	0969
HEP700	0455
HEP700-RT	0455
HEP701	0161
HEP701-RT	0161
HEP702	0899
HEP702-RT	0899
HEP703	0178
HEP703-RT	0178
HEP703X2	0178
HEP704	0103
HEP704-RT	0103
HEP704X2	1506
HEP-705	1671
HEP705	0103
HEP705-RT	0136
HEP706	0233
HEP706-RT	0233
HEP-707	0074
HEP707	0074
HEP707-RT	0074
HEP708	0037
HEP708-RT	0037
HEP709	1136
HEP709-RT	1136
HEP710	0126
HEP710-RT	0126
HEP711	0086
HEP712	0488
HEP712-RT	0488
HEP713	0233
HEP713-RT	0233
HEP-714	0168
HEP714	0264
HEP714-RT	0264
HEP715	0527
HEP715-RT	0527
HEP716	0037
HEP716-RT	0037
HEP717	0037
HEP717-RT	0037
HEP718	0144
HEP718-RT	0144
HEP719	0224
HEP719-RT	0224
HEP720	0224
HEP720-RT	0224
HEP721	0127
HEP721-RT	0127
HEP722	0144
HEP722-RT	0144
HEP723	0016
HEP723-RT	0016
HEP724	0016
HEP724-RT	0016
HEP725	0079
HEP725-RT	0079
HEP726	0111
HEP726-RT	0111
HEP727	0144
HEP727-RT	0144
HEP728	0016
HEP728-RT	0016
HEP729	0016
HEP729-RT	0016
HEP730	0111
HEP730-RT	0111
HEP731	0127
HEP731-RT	0127
HEP732	0127
HEP732-RT	0127
HEP733	0127
HEP733-RT	0127
HEP734	0127
HEP734-RT	0127
HEP735	0079
HEP735-RT	0079
HEP736	0079
HEP736-RT	0079
HEP737	0111
HEP737-RT	0111
HEP738	0079
HEP738-RT	0079
HEP739	0037
HEP739-RT	0037
HEP-740	0359
HEP740	0637
HEP740-RT	0637
HEP801	0321
HEP801-RT	0321
HEP802	0321
HEP802-RT	0321
HEP803	0321
HEP803-RT	0321
HEP3806P	1369
HEP6005	0160
HEP6060P	0784
HEP6061P	3189
HEPC0900P	2542
HEPC0901P	2964
HEPC0902P	2417
HEPC0903P	2986
HEPC0904P	2334
HEPC0905P	2574
HEPC0906P	3003
HEPC0907P	3010
HEPC0908P	3016
HEPC0909P	0078
HEPC0910P	3025
HEPC0911P	3037
HEPC0912P	2964
HEPC74LS00P	1519
HEPC74LS02P	1550

If replacement code is OEM, contact original manufacturer for replacement.

DEVICE TYPE	REPL CODE	DEVICE TYPE	REPL CODE	DEVICE TYPE	REPL CODE	DEVICE TYPE	REPL CODE	DEVICE TYPE	REPL CODE	DEVICE TYPE	REPL CODE	DEVICE TYPE	REPL CODE
HEPC74LS03P	1569	HEPC3805P	OEM	HEPC6083P	2377	HEPC7450P	0738	HEPG0008	0136	HEPR0136	0122	HEPR1221	2255
HEPC74LS04P	1585	HEPC3806P	1369	HEP-C6085P	2438	HEPC7451P	1160	HEP-G0009	0136	HEPR0136R	0810	HEPR1222	3368
HEPC74LS05P	1598	HEPC3807P	2270	HEPC6085P	2438	HEPC7453P	1177	HEPG0009	0136	HEP-R0137	0145	HEPR1223	3370
HEPC74LS08P	1623	HEPC4000P	2013	HEPC6087P	OEM	HEPC7454P	1193	HEP-G0010	0136	HEPR0137	0131	HEPR1241	1478
HEPC74LS10P	1652	HEPC4001P	0473	HEP-C6089	2147	HEPC7460P	1265	HEPG0010	0136	HEPR0137R	0540	HEPR1242	1478
HEPC74LS11P	1657	HEPC4002P	2044	HEPC6089	0748	HEPC7470P	1394	HEP-G0011	0595	HEP-R0138	0145	HEPR1243	1478
HEPC74LS13P	1678	HEPC4003P	2061	HEPC6090	2535	HEPC7472P	1417	HEPG0011	0595	HEPR0138	0145	HEPR1244	1478
HEPC74LS14P	1688	HEPC4004P	2494	HEPC6091	1070	HEPC7473P	1164	HEPG630	0211	HEPR0138R	0545	HEPR1245	1478
HEPC74LS20P	0035	HEPC4005P	2819	HEPC6091G	1070	HEPC7474P	1303	HEPG631	0164	HEPR0160	0800	HEPR1246	2782
HEPC74LS27P	0183	HEPC4006P	3440	HEPC6092G	OEM	HEPC7475P	1423	HEP-G6000	0085	HEPR0160R	1992	HEPR1247	0332
HEPC74LS30P	0822	HEPC4007P	2819	HEPC6093G	OEM	HEPC7476P	1150	HEPG6000	0085	HEPR0161	0800	HEPR1300	0717
HEPC74LS32P	0088	HEPC4008P	2292	HEP-C6094P	0649	HEPC7483P	0117	HEPG6000P/G	0085	HEPR0161R	3234	HEPR1301	0717
HEPC74LS42P	1830	HEPC4009P	1988	HEPC6094P	0649	HEPC7485P	0370	HEPG6001	0599	HEPR0162	0800	HEPR1302	0717
HEPC74LS51P	1027	HEPC4020P	1651	HEP-C6095P	0438	HEPC7486P	1358	HEPG6001-RT	0599	HEPR0162R	1567	HEPR1304	0717
HEPC74LS54P	1846	HEPC4021P	1738	HEPC6095P	0438	HEPC7490AP	1199	HEPG6001P/G	0599	HEPR0164	0800	HEPR1306	0717
HEPC74LS55P	0452	HEPC4030P	0495	HEP-C6096P	0514	HEPC7490P	1199	HEPG6002	0432	HEPR0164R	3251	HEPR1307	0717
HEPC74LS74P	0243	HEPC4031P	1952	HEPC6096P	0514	HEPC7491AP	0974	HEP-G6003	0085	HEPR0166	1576	HEPR1471	0717
HEPC74LS86P	0288	HEPC4032P	2810	HEP-C6099P	3166	HEPC7492AP	0828	HEPG6003	0085	HEPR0166R	3263	HEPR1472	0717
HEPC74LS90P	1871	HEPC4033P	1037	HEPC6099P	3166	HEPC7492P	0828	HEPG6003P/G	0085	HEPR0170	0071	HEPR1473	0717
HEPC74LS93P	1877	HEPC4040P	0056	HEP-C6100P	0797	HEPC7493AP	0564	HEP-G6004	0435	HEPR0180	0087	HEPR1475	0717
HEPC74LS109P	1895	HEPC4041P	1535	HEPC6100P	0797	HEPC7495P	1477	HEPG6004	0435	HEPR0220	2591	HEPR1701	0418
HEPC74LS136P	1618	HEPC4042P	0121	HEP-C6101P	1335	HEPC7496P	1705	HEPG6005	0160	HEPR0220R	2544	HEPR1702	0418
HEPC74LS138P	0422	HEPC4050P	0394	HEPC6101P	1335	HEPC74107P	0936	HEPG6005P/G	0085	HEPR0222	2591	HEPR1703	4381
HEPC74LS151P	1636	HEPC4051P	0362	HEP-C6102P	0356	HEPC74109P	0962	HEP-G6006	0432	HEPR0222R	OEM	HEPR1711	0588
HEPC74LS153P	0953	HEPC4052P	0024	HEPC6102P	0356	HEPC74121P	0175	HEPG6006	0432	HEP-R0250	1116	HEPR1712	0588
HEPC74LS155P	0209	HEPC4053P	3394	HEP-C6103P	1291	HEPC74123P	1149	HEP-G6007	0969	HEPR0250	0800	HEPR1713	0588
HEPC74LS157P	1153	HEPC4054P	1819	HEPC6103P	1291	HEPC74125P	1174	HEPG6007	0969	HEPR0250R	0545	HEPR1715	0480
HEPC74LS158P	1646	HEPC4055P	3272	HEPC6104L	1183	HEPC74126P	1184	HEPG6007P/G	0969	HEP-R0251	1116	HEPR1721	1081
HEPC74LS170P	2605	HEPC4056P	OEM	HEPC6105P	2224	HEPC74132P	1261	HEPG6008	0969	HEPR0251	0800	HEPR1722	1085
HEPC74LS174P	0260	HEPC4057L	OEM	HEPC6107P	1290	HEPC74141P	1367	HEPG6008P/G	0969	HEPR0251R	1229	HEPR1723	0407
HEPC74LS175P	1662	HEPC4057T	OEM	HEPC6110P	0619	HEPC74145P	0614	HEP-G6009	0599	HEP-R0253	1116	HEPR1725	0411
HEPC74LS181P	1668	HEPC4058P	3659	HEPC6111P	0917	HEPC74147P	1442	HEPG6009	0599	HEPR0253	0800	HEPR1750	0400
HEPC74LS190P	1676	HEPC4059P	0482	HEPC6112P	1187	HEPC74148P	1455	HEPG6009P/G	0599	HEPR0253R	1099	HEPR1751	0407
HEPC74LS191P	1677	HEPC6001	0627	HEPC6113P	0330	HEPC74150P	1484	HEP-G6010	0432	HEP-R0254	0800	HEPR1752	0411
HEPC74LS192P	1679	HEPC6003	0512	HEPC6114P	1311	HEPC74151AP	1487	HEPG6010	0432	HEPR0254	0800	HEPR1781	3118
HEPC74LS193P	1682	HEPC6003P	0512	HEPC6115P	2244	HEPC74153P	1531	HEP-G6011	0841	HEPR0254R	1103	HEPR1782	3119
HEPC74LS196P	2807	HEPC6004	OEM	HEPC6116P	2224	HEPC74154P	1546	HEPG6011	0841	HEP-R0255	0800	HEPR1783	3121
HEPC74LS197P	2450	HEPC6007	0718	HEPC6117P	OEM	HEPC74155P	1566	HEPG6012	3267	HEPR0255	0800	HEPR1785	3123
HEPC74LS251P	1726	HEPC6009	1888	HEPC6118P	1275	HEPC74156P	1582	HEPG6013	0085	HEPR0255R	0258	HEPR2001	4169
HEPC74LS253P	1728	HEPC6009P	1888	HEPC6119P	OEM	HEPC74157P	1595	HEPG6013P/G	0085	HEP-R0256	0315	HEP-R2002	3298
HEPC74LS257P	1733	HEPC6010	3731	HEPC6120P	2624	HEPC74160AP	1621	HEP-G6014	0599	HEPR0256	1186	HEPR2002	3298
HEPC74LS258P	1735	HEPC6010P	3731	HEPC6121P	2764	HEPC74161AP	1635	HEPG6014	0599	HEPR0256R	1634	HEP-R2021	3373
HEPC74LS259P	3175	HEPC6011	1865	HEPC6122P	1827	HEPC74162AP	1007	HEPG6014P/G	0599	HEP-R0257	0315	HEPR2021	3373
HEPC74LS279P	3259	HEPC6013	2016	HEPC6123P	3777	HEPC74163AP	1656	HEP-G6015	0599	HEPR0257	0315	HEPR2500	0549
HEPC74LS298P	3337	HEPC6014	1178	HEPC6124P	3774	HEPC74164P	0729	HEPG6015	0599	HEPR0257R	0267	HEPR2501	0005
HEPC74LS367P	0971	HEPC6015	0618	HEPC6125P	3531	HEPC74165P	1675	HEPG6015P/G	0599	HEPR0500	0730	HEPR2502	0715
HEPC74LS368P	0985	HEPC6016	1969	HEPC6126P	1601	HEPC74166P	0231	HEPG6016	0222	HEPR0505	OEM	HEPR2503	0030
HEPC74LS670P	1122	HEPC6016C	1969	HEPC6127P	3715	HEPC74170P	1711	HEPG6017	0969	HEPR0510	OEM	HEPR2504	OEM
HEPC1030P	1812	HEPC6016P	3917	HEPC6128P	3717	HEPC74173P	1755	HEPG6017P/G	0969	HEPR0515	OEM	HEPR2505	OEM
HEPC1032P	1035	HEPC6017	1674	HEPC6129P	2796	HEPC74174P	1759	HEP-G6018	0599	HEPR0520	1536	HEPR3001	0769
HEPC1033P	2086	HEPC6019	0718	HEPC6130P	0967	HEPC74175P	1776	HEPG6018	0599	HEPR0600	0102	HEPR3010	0102
HEPC1035P	1168	HEPC6049G	OEM	HEPC6131P	0967	HEPC74176P	1784	HEPG6018P/G	0599	HEPR0602	0102	HEPR3012	0344
HEPC1036P	1820	HEPC6049R	3618	HEP-C6132P	1288	HEPC74177P	1792	HEPP0001	2297	HEP-R0604	0087	HEPR3100	1313
HEPC1038P	OEM	HEPC6050G	0413	HEPC6132P	1288	HEPC74180P	1818	HEPP0002	OEM	HEPR0604	0102	HEPR3201	1493
HEPC1039P	OEM	HEPC6051L	OEM	HEP-C6133P	1817	HEPC74181P	1831	HEPP0003	0007	HEP-R0606	0102	HEPR3203	0190
HEPC1044P	0033	HEPC6051P	OEM	HEPC6133P	1817	HEPC74182P	1845	HEP-P0160	1991	HEPR0606	0102	HEPR4012	0344
HEPC1045P	0081	HEPC6052G	0406	HEPC6134P	3361	HEPC74184P	OEM	HEPP1001	3156	HEP-R0700	0911	HEPR9001	0196
HEPC1046P	0141	HEPC6052P	0308	HEPC6135P	4430	HEPC74185AP	OEM	HEPP2000	OEM	HEPR0700	0911	HEPR9002	1073
HEPC1052P	0329	HEPC6053G	OEM	HEPC6136P	1275	HEPC74190P	1901	HEPP2001	OEM	HEPR0801	0276	HEPR9003	0479
HEPC1053P	0354	HEPC6053L	OEM	HEP-C6137P	1825	HEPC74191P	1906	HEPP2002	OEM	HEPR0802	0276	HEP-R9134	2217
HEPC1056P	0141	HEPC6054G	OEM	HEPC6137P	1825	HEPC74192P	1910	HEPP2005	1348	HEPR0803	0287	HEPR9134	0143
HEPC1057P	1424	HEPC6054R	OEM	HEPC6138P	4952	HEPC74193P	1915	HEPP5000	0536	HEPR0804	0293	HEPR9134A	0143
HEPC1058P	0461	HEP-C6055L	0687	HEPC6139P	1710	HEPC74194P	OEM	HEPP5001	1047	HEPR0805	0299	HEP-R9135	2217
HEPC1062P	0557	HEPC6055L	0687	HEPC6140P	OEM	HEPC74195P	1932	HEPP5002	4961	HEPR0841	0276	HEPR9135	0143
HEPC2001P	2840	HEPC6056P	0696	HEPC6142P	1288	HEPC74196P	1939	HEPR0050	0015	HEPR0842	0276	HEPR9136	0143
HEPC2002P	OEM	HEP-C6057P	0345	HEPC6143P	OEM	HEPC74197P	1945	HEPR0051	0015	HEPR0843	0287	HEPR9137	0124
HEPC2003P	OEM	HEPC6057P	0661	HEPC6144P	0083	HEPC74198P	1953	HEPR0052	0015	HEPR0845	0293	HEP-R0138	0145
HEPC2004P	3393	HEPC6058P	0350	HEPC6800P	0384	HEPC74199P	1960	HEPR0053	0015	HEPR0846	0299	HEP-S0001	0855
HEPC2005P	3395	HEP-C6059P	0780	HEPC6802P	0389	HEPC74251P	2283	HEPR0054	0015	HEPR0851	0276	HEPS0001	0855
HEPC2006G	1063	HEPC6059P	0780	HEPC6810P	2075	HEPC74259P	OEM	HEPR0055	0071	HEPR0852	0276	HEPS0001-RT	0855
HEPC2007G	1354	HEP-C6060P	0784	HEPC6821P	0443	HEPC74365P	1450	HEPR0056	0071	HEPR0853	0287	HEP-S0002	0590
HEPC2008G	OEM	HEPC6060P	1206	HEPC6850P	0509	HEPC74366P	1462	HEPR0070	0947	HEPR0855	0293	HEPS0002	0079
HEPC2009G	OEM	HEP-C6061P	3189	HEPC6860P	2667	HEPC74367P	1479	HEPR0071	0242	HEPR0856	0299	HEPS0002-RT	0079
HEPC2010G	1063	HEPC6061P	3189	HEPC7161AP	OEM	HEPC74368P	1500	HEPR0072	0535	HEPR0861	2347	HEP-S0003	0590
HEPC2012G	1063	HEP-C6062P	0659	HEPC7400P	0232	HEPD0002	4786	HEPR0074	0959	HEPR0862	2347	HEPS0003	0590
HEPC2500P	OEM	HEPC6062P	0659	HEPC7401P	0268	HEPD0012	5039	HEPR0076	0811	HEPR0863	2347	HEPS0003-RT	0590
HEPC2501P	OEM	HEP-C6063P	0167	HEPC7402P	0310	HEPD0101	4901	HEPR0078	0916	HEPR0865	0468	HEPS0004	0079
HEPC2502P	2840	HEPC6063P	2377	HEPC7403P	0331	HEPD1002	OEM	HEPR0080	0087	HEPR0866	2354	HEPS0004-RT	0079
HEPC2503P	OEM	HEP-C6065P	1929	HEPC7404P	0357	HEPD1201	4267	HEPR0081	0087	HEPR0875	2353	HEP-S0005	0855
HEPC3000L	0232	HEPC6065P	1929	HEPC7405P	0381	HEPF0010	3667	HEPR0082	0087	HEPR0876	2353	HEPS0005	0855
HEPC3000P	0232	HEP-C6066P	1742	HEPC7406P	1197	HEP-F0015	0321	HEPR0084	0087	HEPR0877	2353	HEP-S0006	0688
HEPC3001L	0268	HEPC6066P	1742	HEPC7407P	1329	HEPF0015	0321	HEPR0086	0087	HEPR0878	2353	HEPS0006	0688
HEPC3001P	0268	HEPC6067G	0748	HEPC7408P	0462	HEP-F0021	0321	HEPR0090	0087	HEPR0879	1579	HEPS0006-RT	0688
HEPC3002P	0310	HEPC6067P	2147	HEPC7409P	0487	HEPF0021	0321	HEPR0091	0087	HEPR0880	2347	HEPS0007	0855
HEPC3004L	0357	HEP-C6068P	0438	HEPC7410P	0507	HEPF1035	2959	HEPR0092	0087	HEPR0881	2347	HEPS0007-RT	0855
HEPC3004P	0357	HEPC6068P	0696	HEPC7411P	0522	HEPF1036	0321	HEPR0094	0087	HEPR0882	2347	HEPS0008	0224
HEPC3010L	0507	HEP-C6069G	0360	HEPC7413P	1432	HEPF2004	0212	HEPR0096	0087	HEPR0883	2353	HEPS0009	1489
HEPC3010P	0507	HEPC6069G	0360	HEPC7414P	2228	HEP-F2005	0843	HEPR0097	0087	HEPR0884	2354	HEPS0010	0224
HEPC3020L	0692	HEP-C6070P	0348	HEPC7416P	1339	HEPF2005	0843	HEPR0098	0087	HEPR0890	1633	HEPS0011	0079
HEPC3020P	0692	HEPC6070P	0348	HEPC7417P	1342	HEPF2007	0212	HEPR0100	1272	HEPR0891	1633	HEPS0012	0126
HEPC3030L	0867	HEP-C6071P	0350	HEPC7420P	0692	HEPF2007A	0212	HEPR0101	1272	HEPR0892	1633	HEPS0013	0150
HEPC3030P	0867	HEPC6071P	0350	HEPC7422P	4523	HEP-G0001	0136	HEPR0102	1272	HEPR0894	1663	HEPS0014	0590
HEPC3040L	1018	HEP-C6072P	0746	HEPC7423P	3429	HEPG0001	0136	HEPR0104	1277	HEPR0896	1663	HEPS0015	0079
HEPC3040P	1018	HEPC6072P	1742	HEPC7425P	3438	HEP-G0002	0050	HEPR0106	1282	HEPR1001	1129	HEP-S0016	0127
HEPC3041L	1032	HEPC6073P	0696	HEPC7426P	0798	HEPG0002	0050	HEP-R0130	0097	HEPR1002	0340	HEPS0016	0144
HEPC3050L	0738	HEP-C6074P	0649	HEPC7427P	0812	HEP-G0003	0050	HEPR0130	0097	HEPR1003	0895	HEPS0017	0224
HEPC3050P	0738	HEPC6074P	0649	HEPC7430P	0867	HEPG0003	0050	HEPR0130-RT	2872	HEPR1004	2326	HEPS0019	0150
HEPC3073L	1164	HEP-C6075P	0850	HEPC7432P	0893	HEP-G0004	0164	HEPR0130R	0529	HEPR1005	0058	HEPS0020	0144
HEPC3073P	1164	HEPC6075P	0850	HEPC7437P	3478	HEPG0004	0279	HEP-R0131	0097	HEPR1101	5373	HEP-S0021	0016
HEPC3075L	1423	HEP-C6076P	0391	HEPC7438P	0990	HEP-G0005	0164	HEPR0131	0097	HEPR1102	5373	HEPS0021	0144
HEPC3075P	1423	HEPC6076P	0391	HEPC7440P	1018	HEPG0005	0279	HEPR0131-RT	2872	HEPR1103	5373	HEPS0022	0079
HEPC3401L	1032	HEPC6078R	OEM	HEPC7441AP	1032	HEPG0005P/G	0279	HEPR0131R	0743	HEPR1202	1574	HEP-S0023	0111
HEPC3800L	1199	HEP-C6079P	1797	HEPC7441P	1032	HEP-G0006	0164	HEP-R0132	0097	HEPR1205	1574	HEPS0023	0111
HEPC3800P	1199	HEPC6079P	1469	HEPC7442P	1046	HEPG0006	0279	HEPR0132	0097	HEPR1215	1386	HEP-S0024	0111
HEPC3801L	0828	HEP-C6080P	2264	HEPC7445P	1074	HEPG0006P/G	0279	HEPR0132R	0760	HEPR1216	0442	HEPS0024	0111
HEPC3801P	0828	HEPC6080P	2264	HEPC7446AP	1090	HEP-G0007	0164	HEP-R0134	0109	HEPR1217	0442	HEPS0025	0079
HEPC3802P	OEM	HEP-C6082P	0659	HEPC7447AP	1100	HEPG0007	0279	HEPR0134	0109	HEPR1218	0934	HEP-S0026	0037
HEPC3803P	2252	HEPC6082P	0673	HEPC7447P	1100	HEPG0007P/G	0279	HEPR0134R	0533	HEPR1219	3291	HEPS0026	0037
HEPC3804P	1135	HEP-C6083P	0167	HEPC7448P	1117	HEP-G0008	0136	HEP-R0136	0122	HEPR1220	4508	HEPS0027	0710

If replacement code is OEM, contact original manufacturer for replacement. 429

DEVICE TYPE	REPL CODE
HEPS0028	0338
HEPS0029	0338
HEP-S0030	0016
HEPS0030	0079
HEP-S0031	0688
HEPS0031	0688
HEP-S0032	0037
HEPS0032	0037
HEP-S0033	0224
HEPS0033	0224
HEPS0034	0016
HEPS0035	0079
HEPS0036	0079
HEPS0037	0037
HEPS0038	0079
HEPS0039	0259
HEPS0040	0079
HEP-S3001	1401
HEPS-3001	4182
HEPS3001	0626
HEPS3002	0626
HEPS3003	0126
HEPS3004	0626
HEPS3005	3532
HEPS3006	1963
HEPS3007	1963
HEPS3008	0488
HEPS3009	1963
HEPS3010	0626
HEPS3011	0693
HEP-S3012	0126
HEPS3012	0126
HEPS3013	0488
HEPS3014	0488
HEP-S3019	0264
HEPS3019	0264
HEPS3020	0626
HEP-S3021	0334
HEPS3021	0334
HEP-S3022	0334
HEPS3022	0334
HEPS3022-RT	0334
HEP-S3023	0561
HEPS3023	0561
HEPS3023-RT	0561
HEP-S3024	0561
HEPS3024	0561
HEP-S3025	0561
HEPS3025	0561
HEPS3025-RT	0561
HEP-S3026	0546
HEPS3026	0546
HEPS3026-RT	0546
HEP-S3027	1357
HEPS3027	1357
HEPS3027-RT	1357
HEP-S3028	1357
HEPS3028	1357
HEP-S3029	1357
HEPS3029	1357
HEPS3029-RT	1357
HEP-S3030	0378
HEPS3030	0378
HEPS3030-RT	0378
HEP-S3031	0378
HEPS3031	0378
HEPS3031-RT	0378
HEP-S3032	0378
HEPS3032	0378
HEP-S3033	0233
HEPS3033	0233
HEP-S3034	0233
HEPS3034	0233
HEP-S3035	0233
HEPS3035	0233
HEPS3036	2296
HEPS3037	2918
HEPS3038	0414
HEPS3039	1224
HEPS3040	1963
HEPS3041	1963
HEPS3042	2675
HEPS3043	1973
HEPS3044	1581
HEPS3045	0555
HEPS3046	3165
HEPS3047	0561
HEPS3048	0334
HEPS3049	0334
HEPS3050	1357
HEPS3051	0334
HEPS3052	2808
HEPS3053	3521
HEPS3054	0848
HEPS3055	0848
HEPS3060	0419
HEPS3061	0419
HEPS3062	0930
HEP-S5000	0161
HEPS5000	0161
HEP-S5001	0556
HEPS5001	0556
HEPS5001-RT	0556
HEP-S5002	1190
HEPS5002	1190
HEPS5002-RT	1190
HEP-S5003	0161
HEPS5003	0161
HEPS5003-RT	0161

DEVICE TYPE	REPL CODE
HEP-S5004	0556
HEPS5004	0556
HEP-S5005	1190
HEPS5005	1190
HEP-S5006	0455
HEPS5006	0455
HEP-S5007	0455
HEPS5007	0455
HEPS5007-RT	0455
HEP-S5008	1190
HEPS5008	1190
HEPS5008-RT	1190
HEP-S5009	1190
HEPS5009	1190
HEPS5009-RT	1190
HEP-S5010	1190
HEPS5010	1190
HEPS5010-RT	1190
HEP-S5011	0142
HEPS5011	0142
HEP-S5012	0178
HEPS5012	0178
HEP-S5013	0126
HEPS5013	0126
HEP-S5014	0086
HEPS5014	0626
HEP-S5015	0275
HEPS5015	0275
HEP-S5018	0899
HEPS5018	0899
HEP-S5019	0178
HEPS5019	0178
HEP-S5020	0074
HEPS5020	0637
HEPS5021	0065
HEPS5022	0527
HEP-S5023	0126
HEPS5023	0126
HEP-S5024	0233
HEPS5024	0233
HEP-S5025	0233
HEPS5025	0233
HEP-S5026	0233
HEPS5026	0086
HEPS5027	0161
HEPS5028	1421
HEP-S7000	0130
HEPS7000	0130
HEP-S7001	1671
HEPS7001	1671
HEP-S7002	0103
HEPS7002	0103
HEP-S7003	1671
HEPS7003	0486
HEP-S7004	0103
HEPS7004	0130
HEPS7005	0065
HEPS7006	0309
HEPS7007	1671
HEPS7008	0130
HEPS9001	0312
HEPS9002	2123
HEPS9002UNIJ	2123
HEP-S9100	0396
HEPS9100	0396
HEPS9101	0553
HEPS9102	3343
HEPS9103	3495
HEP-S9120	3477
HEPS9120	3477
HEPS9121	2869
HEPS9122	2222
HEPS9123	3496
HEPS9140	2411
HEPS9141	2262
HEPS9142	3483
HEPS9143	3484
HEPS9144	2262
HEPS9145	2411
HEPS9146	3339
HEPS9147	2415
HEPS9148	2422
HEPS9149	2415
HEPS9150	1203
HEPS9151	OEM
HEPS9152	3486
HEPS9153	OEM
HEPTO-36	OEM
HEP-Z0206	0289
HEPZ0206	0188
HEPZ0206A	0296
HEP-Z0208	0451
HEPZ0208	0188
HEPZ0208A	0036
HEP-Z0210	0446
HEPZ0210	0446
HEPZ0210A	0140
HEP-Z0211	0162
HEPZ0211	0162
HEPZ0211A	0041
HEP-Z0212	0157
HEPZ0212	0157
HEPZ0212A	0253
HEP-Z0214	0631
HEPZ0214	0631
HEPZ0214A	0466
HEP-Z0215	0025
HEPZ0215	0025
HEPZ0215A	0062

DEVICE TYPE	REPL CODE
HEP-Z0216	0644
HEPZ0216	0644
HEPZ0216A	0077
HEP-Z0217	0244
HEPZ0217	0244
HEPZ0217A	0165
HEP-Z0219	0012
HEPZ0219	0012
HEPZ0219A	0057
HEP-Z0220	0170
HEPZ0220	0170
HEPZ0220A	0064
HEP-Z0222	0137
HEPZ0222	0137
HEPZ0222A	0052
HEP-Z0225	0002
HEPZ0225	0002
HEPZ0225A	0681
HEP-Z0228	0490
HEPZ0228	0490
HEPZ0228A	0371
HEP-Z0230	0526
HEPZ0230	0526
HEPZ0230A	0695
HEP-Z0231	0560
HEPZ0231	0560
HEPZ0231A	0700
HEP-Z0234	0436
HEPZ0234	0436
HEPZ0234A	0450
HEP-Z0254	0213
HEPZ0254	0285
HEPZ0254A	0285
HEP-Z0255	0245
HEPZ0255	0028
HEPZ0255A	0752
HEP-Z0401	0289
HEPZ0401	0188
HEP-Z0402	0188
HEPZ0402	0188
HEP-Z0403	0451
HEPZ0403	0188
HEP-Z0405	0446
HEPZ0405	0446
HEP-Z0406	0162
HEPZ0406	0162
HEP-Z0407	0157
HEPZ0407	0157
HEP-Z0408	0631
HEPZ0408	0631
HEP-Z0409	0025
HEPZ0409	0025
HEP-Z0410	0644
HEPZ0410	0644
HEP-Z0411	0244
HEPZ0411	0244
HEPZ0412	0012
HEPZ0413	0170
HEPZ0414	0313
HEPZ0415	0137
HEPZ0416	0137
HEP-Z0417	0100
HEPZ0417	0002
HEP-Z0418	0002
HEPZ0418	0002
HEP-Z0419	0416
HEPZ0419	0002
HEP-Z0420	0490
HEPZ0420	0490
HEP-Z0421	0526
HEPZ0421	0526
HEP-Z0422	0560
HEPZ0422	0560
HEP-Z0423	0398
HEPZ0423	0398
HEP-Z0424	0436
HEPZ0424	0436
HEP-Z0425	1664
HEPZ0425	1664
HEP-Z0426	0039
HEPZ0426	0039
HEP-Z0427	0814
HEPZ0427	0039
HEP-Z0428	0346
HEPZ0428	0346
HEP-Z0430	0993
HEPZ0430	0993
HEP-Z0432	0863
HEPZ0432	0993
HEP-Z0433	0778
HEPZ0433	0778
HEP-Z0436	0327
HEPZ0436	0327
HEP-Z0438	0098
HEPZ0438	0098
HEP-Z0439	0149
HEPZ0439	0149
HEP-Z0440	0186
HEPZ0440	0186
HEP-Z0442	0028
HEPZ0442	0028
HEP-Z0444	0363
HEPZ0444	0363
HEP-Z0445	0417
HEPZ0445	0417
HEPZ1409	0446
HEPZ2500	0777
HEPZ2502	0801
HEPZ2504	0827

DEVICE TYPE	REPL CODE
HEPZ2506	0870
HEPZ2508	0185
HEP-Z2510	0475
HEPZ2510	0475
HEP-Z2513	0679
HEPZ2513	0679
HEP-Z2514	0225
HEPZ2514	0225
HEP-Z2516	0234
HEPZ2516	0234
HEP-Z2519	0247
HEPZ2519	0251
HEP-Z2522	0256
HEPZ2522	0256
HEP-Z2525	0269
HEPZ2525	0269
HEP-Z2526	0273
HEPZ2526	0273
HEP-Z2528	0291
HEPZ2528	0291
HEP-Z2530	0305
HEPZ2530	0305
HEP-Z2531	0314
HEPZ2531	0314
HEPZ2537	0266
HEPZ2542	0439
HEPZ2545	1172
HEPZ2547	1198
HEPZ2548	1209
HEPZ2551	0028
HEPZ3500	0542
HEPZ3500R	0313
HEPZ3502	2101
HEPZ3502R	1429
HEPZ3504	1890
HEPZ3504R	1436
HEPZ3505	0691
HEPZ3507	1606
HEPZ3511	1608
HEPZ3512	0505
HEPZ3512R	0986
HEP-Z3514	0864
HEPZ3514	0864
HEPZ3514R	1254
HEP-Z3516	1264
HEPZ3516	1264
HEPZ3516R	1629
HEPZ3518	1071
HEPZ3518R	1706
HEPZ3520	1712
HEPZ3520R	0722
HEPZ3522	1750
HEPZ3522R	1771
HEPZ3524	1777
HEPZ3524R	1788
HEPZ3530	0207
HEPZ3530R	1873
HEPZ3534	0352
HEPZ3534R	1898
HEPZ3536	0433
HEPZ3536R	1155
HEPZ4026	OEM
HER101	0541
HER102	0541
HER103	0541
HER104	OEM
HER105	OEM
HER106	OEM
HER107	OEM
HER151	0541
HER152	0541
HER153	0541
HER154	1352
HER155	1352
HER156	OEM
HER157	OEM
HER301	4042
HER302	4042
HER303	4042
HER304	1352
HER305	1352
HER306	1362
HER307	1362
HER601	OEM
HER602	OEM
HER603	OEM
HER604	OEM
HER605	OEM
HER801	1119
HER802	1119
HER803	1119
HER804	1654
HER805	1654
HER1601	0903
HER1602	0903
HER1603	0903
HER1604	0966
HER1605	0966
HER3001	2259
HER3002	2259
HER3003	2259
HER3004	4409
HER3005	4409
HER-R0257	0315
HERR3201	1493
HERR3203	0190
HER-R0257	0315
HES8011B	OEM
HES8018	OEM

DEVICE TYPE	REPL CODE
HES8039A	OEM
HES8042	OEM
HES8042B	OEM
HES8045	OEM
HES8045A	OEM
HES-8053	OEM
HES8053	OEM
HES8102	OEM
HES8109	OEM
HES8110	OEM
HES8120	OEM
HES8121	OEM
HES8121B	OEM
HES8121C	OEM
HES8601B	OEM
HE-SD1	0015
HESD-1	0102
H-EX0019GE	0681
H-EX0021TA	0181
H-EX0047CE	0052
H-EX0049CE	0041
H-EX0061CE	0137
H-EX0089CE	0165
H-EX0091CE	0700
H-EX0247CE	0631
HEX3000	OEM
HF-0SW05	0015
HF0W05	0015
HF-1	0102
HF1	0102
HF-1A	0023
HF1A	0102
HF-1B	0102
HF1B	0102
HF-1C	0102
HF1C	0102
HF-1S85	0715
HF-1S334	0012
HF-1S339	0012
HF-1S553	0755
HF-1Z	0102
HF1Z	0102
HF2	0079
HF3	0079
HF3H	0050
HF3M	0050
HF4	0079
HF4A	OEM
HF4B	OEM
HF4C	OEM
HF5	0079
HF6	0079
HF6H	0050
HF6M	0050
HF7	0079
HF8	0079
HF9	0086
HF10	0126
HF11	0555
HF12	1257
HF12H	0050
HF12M	0050
HF12N	0050
HF15	0555
HF15-04D03	OEM
HF16	1257
HF17	0111
HF19	0160
HF-19D	0599
HF20	0160
HF20H	0050
HF20M	0050
HF-35	0050
HF35	0136
HF40	0855
HF43	0283
HF-47	0150
HF47	0688
HF50	0079
HF50H	0050
HF50M	0050
HF51	1257
HF57	0042
HF58	0919
HF100	OEM
HF200	OEM
HF-10024	0143
HF-20002	0030
HF-20004	0012
HF-20005	0030
HF-20007	0755
HF-20008	0143
HF-20011	0012
HF-20014	0133
HF-20032	0015
HF20032	0133
HF-20033	0025
HF-20034	0133
HF-20035	0030
HF-20040	0030
HF-20041	0137
HF-20042	0015
HF-20046	0030
HF-20047	0015
HF-20048	0133
HF-20050	0015
HF-20052	0015
HF-20060	0133
HF20060	0133

DEVICE TYPE	REPL CODE
HF-20061	0133
HF-20062	0549
HF-20063	0124
HF-20064	0133
HF-20065	0012
HF-20066	0120
HF20066	0015
HF-20067	0015
HF-20071	0071
HF-20072	0005
HF-20075	OEM
HF-20080	0715
HF-20083	0015
HF-20084	0015
HF-20088	0143
HF-20094	0715
HF-20095	0133
HF-20105	0139
HF-20116	0030
HF-20123	0133
HF-20124	0133
HF200191A	0321
HF200191A/	0321
HF200191A-0	0321
HF200191A0	0321
HF200191A0	0321
HF200191B-0	0321
HF200191B0	0321
HF200191B0	0321
HF200301B	0321
HF200301B0	0321
HF200301B0	0321
HF200301C-0	0321
HF200301C-0	0321
HF200301E	0212
HF200411B	1202
HF200411C0	1202
HF309301E	0111
HF2000411B	0321
HFB7	OEM
HFBR-0010	OEM
HFBR-1001	OEM
HFBR-1002	OEM
HFBR-2001	OEM
HFBR-3099	OEM
HF-DS410	0133
HFET-1001	OEM
HFET1101	OEM
HFET1102	OEM
HFET-2001	OEM
HFET2201	OEM
HFET2202	OEM
HFET-2204	OEM
HFET5001	OEM
HF-MV2	0139
HFR5	OEM
HFR10	OEM
HFR15	OEM
HFR20	OEM
HFS-04	5877
HFS23	OEM
HFSA3	0102
HF-SD1	0023
HFSD-1	0102
HFSD1	0102
HF-SD1/BB-4	0102
HF-SD-1A	0015
HFSD-1A	0102
HFSD1A	0015
HFSD-1B	0102
HFSD1B	0015
HF-SD-1C	0015
HFSD-1C	0102
HFSD1C	6297
HF-SD-1Z	0102
HFSD-1Z	0102
HFSD1Z	0102
HFSD12	0087
HFSD-14	0102
HFSD18	OEM
HFSG005	0015
HG61H20B24F	OEM
HG62B40B41F	OEM
HG1001	OEM
HG1002	OEM
HG1003	OEM
HG1004	OEM
HG1005	OEM
HG1006	OEM
HG1007	OEM
HG1008	OEM
HG1009	OEM
HG1010	OEM
HG1011	OEM
HG1012	OEM
HG1090	0143
HG5001	0143
HG5002	0143
HG5003	0143
HG5004	0143
HG5005	0143
HG5006	0143
HG5007	0143
HG5008	0143
HG5009	0143
HG5020	0143
HG5078	0143
HG5079	0143
HG5085	0143

DEVICE TYPE	REPL CODE
HG5088	0143
HG5808	0143
HG100101	OEM
HGCDTE-1-40A	OEM
HGCDTE-1-40AS	OEM
HGCDTE-1-60A	OEM
HGCDTE-1-60AS	OEM
HGCDTE-1-520A	OEM
HGCDTE-1-520AS	OEM
HGCDTE-1-40742	OEM
HGCDTE-1-44782	OEM
HGCDTE-2-520A	OEM
HGCDTE-2-520AS	OEM
HGCDTE-2-40742	OEM
HGCDTE-2-44782	OEM
HGCDTE-5-40A	OEM
HGCDTE-5-40AS	OEM
HGCDTE-5-52-AS	OEM
HGCDTE-5-60A	OEM
HGCDTE-5-60AS	OEM
HGCDTE-5-520A	OEM
HGCDTE-5-40742	OEM
HGCDTE-5-44782	OEM
HGR1	0015
HGR2	0015
HGR3	0015
HGR4	0015
HGR-5	0015
HGR5	1325
HG-R10	0015
HGR-10	0015
HGR10	0080
HGR-20	0015
HGR20	0133
HGR-30	0015
HGR30	0133
HGR-40	0015
HGR40	0790
HGR-60	0015
HGR60	0015
HH1157	OEM
HH7372	OEM
HI0-524-6	OEM
HI03SC	2336
HI03SD	2336
HI03SG	2336
HI03SH	2336
HI03SS	2336
HI1-200-2	OEM
HI1-200-4	OEM
HI1-200-5	OEM
HI1-201-1	OEM
HI1-201-2	OEM
HI1-201-4	OEM
HI1-201-5	OEM
HI1-300-2	OEM
HI1-300-5	OEM
HI1-300-8	OEM
HI1-301-2	OEM
HI1-301-5	OEM
HI1-301-8	OEM
HI1-302-2	OEM
HI1-302-5	OEM
HI1-302-8	OEM
HI1-303-2	OEM
HI1-303-5	OEM
HI1-303-8	OEM
HI1-304-2	OEM
HI1-304-5	OEM
HI1-304-8	OEM
HI1-305-2	OEM
HI1-305-5	OEM
HI1-305-8	OEM
HI1-306-2	OEM
HI1-306-5	OEM
HI1-306-8	OEM
HI1-307-2	OEM
HI1-307-8	OEM
HI1-381-2(A)	OEM
HI1-381-5(A)	OEM
HI1-381-8(A)	OEM
HI1-384-2(A)	OEM
HI1-384-5(A)	OEM
HI1-384-8(A)	OEM
HI1-387-2(A)	OEM
HI1-387-5(A)	OEM
HI1-387-8(A)	OEM
HI1-390-2(A)	OEM
HI1-390-5(A)	OEM
HI1-390-8(A)	OEM
HI1-506-2	OEM
HI1-506-5	OEM
HI1-506A-2	OEM
HI1-506A-5	OEM
HI1-507-2	OEM
HI1-507-5	OEM
HI1-507A-2	OEM
HI1-507A-5	OEM
HI1-508A-2	OEM
HI1-508A-5	OEM
HI1-509A-2	OEM
HI1-509A-5	OEM
HI1-524-2	OEM
HI1-524-5	OEM
HI1-524-8	OEM
HI1-539-2	OEM
HI1-539-4	OEM
HI1-539-5	OEM
HI1-539-8	OEM

430 If replacement code is OEM, contact original manufacturer for replacement.

DEVICE TYPE	REPL CODE	DEVICE TYPE	REPL CODE	DEVICE TYPE	REPL CODE	DEVICE TYPE	REPL CODE	DEVICE TYPE	REPL CODE	DEVICE TYPE	REPL CODE	DEVICE TYPE	REPL CODE
HI1-562-2	OEM	HIT5609C	0018	HL55723	2138	HLP30RGB	OEM	HM1-6501-2	OEM	HM1-76321-8	OEM	HM4-6512-2	OEM
HI1-562-4	OEM	HIT9011	OEM	HL55763	0462	HLP30RGC	OEM	HM1-6501-5	OEM	HM1-76641-2	OEM	HM4-6513-5	OEM
HI1-562-5	OEM	HIT9014N	OEM	HL55764	1531	HLP30RGD	OEM	HM1-6503-5	OEM	HM1-76641-5	OEM	HM4-6514-2	OEM
HI1-562-8	OEM	HIT9014N-C	0079	HL55861	1484	HLP30RLA	OEM	HM1-6504-2	OEM	HM1-76641-8	OEM	HM4-6514-5	OEM
HI1-562A2	OEM	HIT9015N	OEM	HL55862	0357	HLP30RLB	OEM	HM1-6504-5	OEM	HM-2	0139	HM4-6514B2	OEM
HI1-562A4	OEM	H-IX0065CE	1420	HL56320	2426	HLP30RLC	OEM	HM1-6504B2	OEM	HM3-6322-2	OEM	HM4-6516-2	OEM
HI1-562A5	OEM	HJ-00191	OEM	HL56420	0232	HLP30RLD	OEM	HM1-6505-2	OEM	HM3-6501-2	OEM	HM4-6516-9	OEM
HI1-562A8	OEM	HJ15	0004	HL56421	0357	HLP30TA	OEM	HM1-6505-5	OEM	HM3-6501-5	OEM	HM4-6518-2	OEM
HI1-1800A2	OEM	HJ15D	0050	HL56422	0692	HLP30TB	OEM	HM1-6508-2	OEM	HM3-6503-5	OEM	HM4-6518-5	OEM
HI1-1800A5	OEM	HJ17	0004	HL56423	0867	HLP30TC	OEM	HM1-6508-5	3164	HM3-6504-2	OEM	HM4-6518B2	OEM
HI1-1818A-2	OEM	HJ17D	0004	HL56424	0990	HLP30TD	OEM	HM1-6512-2	OEM	HM3-6504-5	OEM	HM4-6561-2	OEM
HI1-1818A-5	OEM	HJ22	0004	HL56425	1303	HLP30WRA	OEM	HM1-6513-5	OEM	HM3-6504B2	OEM	HM4-6561-5	OEM
HI1-1828A-2	OEM	HJ22D	0004	HL56426	0370	HLP30WRB	OEM	HM1-6514-2	OEM	HM3-6505-2	OEM	HM4-6561B2	OEM
HI1-1828A-5	OEM	HJ23	0004	HL56427	1477	HLP30WRC	OEM	HM1-6514-5	OEM	HM3-6505-5	OEM	HM5-6564-2	OEM
HI1-1840-2	OEM	HJ23D	0004	HL56429	1910	HLP30WRD	OEM	HM1-6514B2	OEM	HM3-6508-2	OEM	HM5-6564-5	OEM
HI1-5040-2	OEM	HJ32	0050	HL56430	1915	HLP30WTA	OEM	HM1-6516-2	OEM	HM3-6508-5	3164	HM6.8	0062
HI1-5040-5	OEM	HJ34	0050	HL56431	5159	HLP30WTB	OEM	HM1-6516-9	OEM	HM3-6512-2	OEM	HM6.8A	0062
HI1-5047-2	OEM	HJ34A	0050	HL56842	0117	HLP30WTC	OEM	HM1-6518-2	OEM	HM3-6513-5	OEM	HM6.8B	0062
HI1-5047-5	OEM	HJ35	0085	HL56899	0507	HLP30WTD	OEM	HM1-6518-5	OEM	HM3-6514-2	OEM	HM7.5	0077
HI1-5047A-2	OEM	HJ37	0050	HLC9694-01-2210	OEM	HLP40RA	OEM	HM1-6518B2	OEM	HM3-6514-5	OEM	HM7.5A	0077
HI1-5047A-5	OEM	HJ41	0279	HLCD0437	OEM	HLP40RB	OEM	HM1-6551-2	OEM	HM3-6514B2	OEM	HM7.5B	0077
HI1-5048-2	OEM	HJ43	0004	HLCD0437(A)	OEM	HLP40RC	OEM	HM1-6551-5	OEM	HM3-6516-2	OEM	HM8.2	0165
HI1-5048-5	OEM	HJ50	0004	HLCD0438	OEM	HLP40RD	OEM	HM1-6551B2	OEM	HM3-6516-9	OEM	HM8.2A	0165
HI1-5049-2	OEM	HJ51	0004	HLCD0438A(A)	OEM	HLP40RGA	OEM	HM1-6561-2	OEM	HM3-6518-2	OEM	HM8.2B	0165
HI1-5049-5	OEM	HJ54	0004	HLCD0488	OEM	HLP40RGB	OEM	HM1-6561-5	OEM	HM3-6518-5	OEM	HM9-0168-8	OEM
HI1-5050-2	OEM	HJ55	0050	HLCD0515D	OEM	HLP40RGC	OEM	HM1-6561B2	OEM	HM3-6518B2	OEM	HM9-6501-2	OEM
HI1-5050-5	OEM	HJ56	0050	HLCD0515P	OEM	HLP40RGD	OEM	HM1-6562-2	OEM	HM3-6551-2	OEM	HM9-6501-5	OEM
HI1-5051-2	OEM	HJ57	0050	HLCD0538A	OEM	HLP40RLA	OEM	HM1-6562-5	OEM	HM3-6551-5	OEM	HM9-6503-5	OEM
HI1-5051-5	OEM	HJ60	0004	HLCD0538A(A)	OEM	HLP40RLB	OEM	HM1-6562B2	OEM	HM3-6551B2	OEM	HM9-6504-2	OEM
HI1-5607-2(A)	OEM	HJ60A	0050	HLCD0539A	OEM	HLP40RLC	OEM	HM1-6611-2	OEM	HM3-6561-2	OEM	HM9-6504-5	OEM
HI1-5607-5(A)	OEM	HJ60C	0050	HLCD0539A(A)	OEM	HLP40RLD	OEM	HM1-6611-5	OEM	HM3-6561-5	OEM	HM9-6504B2	OEM
HI1-5607-8(A)	OEM	HJ62	0004	HLCD0540	OEM	HLP40TB	OEM	HM1-7602-2	OEM	HM3-6561B2	OEM	HM9-6505-2	OEM
HI1-5608-2(A)	OEM	HJ70	0050	HLCD0540(A)	OEM	HLP40TC	OEM	HM1-7602-5	3139	HM3-6562-2	OEM	HM9-6505-5	OEM
HI1-5608-5(A)	OEM	HJ71	0164	HLCD0541	OEM	HLP40TD	OEM	HM1-7603-2	OEM	HM3-6562-5	OEM	HM9-6508-2	OEM
HI1-5608-8(A)	OEM	HJ72	0164	HLCD0542	OEM	HLP40WRA	OEM	HM1-7603-5	2161	HM3-6562B2	OEM	HM9-6508-5	OEM
HI1-5609-2(A)	OEM	HJ73	0164	HLCD0548	OEM	HLP40WRB	OEM	HM1-7608-2	OEM	HM3-7602-2	OEM	HM9-6513-5	OEM
HI1-5609-5(A)	OEM	HJ74	0164	HLCD0550D	OEM	HLP40WRC	OEM	HM1-7608-5	OEM	HM3-7602-5	3139	HM9-6514-2	OEM
HI1-5609-8(A)	OEM	HJ75	0050	HLCD0550P	OEM	HLP40WRD	OEM	HM1-7610-2	OEM	HM3-7603-2	OEM	HM9-6514-5	OEM
HI1-5610-2	OEM	HJ226	0164	HLCD0551D	OEM	HLP40WTB	OEM	HM1-7610-5	1907	HM3-7603-5	2161	HM9-6514B2	OEM
HI1-5610-5	OEM	HJ228	0164	HLCD0551P	OEM	HLP40WTC	OEM	HM1-7610A2	OEM	HM3-7608-2	OEM	HM9-6518-2	OEM
HI1-5610-8	OEM	HJ230	0164	HLCD0607	OEM	HLP40WTD	OEM	HM1-7610A5	OEM	HM3-7608-5	OEM	HM9-6518-5	OEM
HI1-5612-2	OEM	HJ315	0164	HLCD07211-1P	OEM	HLP50RB	OEM	HM1-7611-2	OEM	HM3-7610-2	OEM	HM9-6518B2	OEM
HI1-5612-5	OEM	HJ606	0004	HLCD07211-2P	OEM	HLP50RC	OEM	HM1-7611-5	2209	HM3-7610-5	1907	HM9-6551-2	OEM
HI1-5612-8	OEM	HJX2	0004	HLCD07211-3P	OEM	HLP50RD	OEM	HM1-7611A2	OEM	HM3-7610A2	OEM	HM9-6551-5	OEM
HI2-300-2	OEM	HK-00049	0321	HLCD07211-4P	OEM	HLP50RGB	OEM	HM1-7611A5	OEM	HM3-7610A5	1907	HM9-6551B2	OEM
HI2-301-2	OEM	HK-00330	0321	HLCD7211	OEM	HLP50RGC	OEM	HM1-7616-2	OEM	HM3-7611-2	OEM	HM9-6561-2	OEM
HI2-304-2	OEM	HK103A	OEM	HLMP-0300	OEM	HLP50RGD	OEM	HM1-7616-5	OEM	HM3-7611-5	2209	HM9-6561-5	OEM
HI2-305-2	OEM	HK103K	OEM	HLMP-0301	OEM	HLP50RLB	OEM	HM1-7620-2	OEM	HM3-7611A2	OEM	HM9-6561B2	OEM
HI2-381-2(A)	OEM	HK203A	OEM	HLMP-0400	OEM	HLP50RLC	OEM	HM1-7620-5	2372	HM3-7611A5	2209	HM9-6562-2	OEM
HI2-381-8(A)	OEM	HK203K	OEM	HLMP-0401	OEM	HLP50RLD	OEM	HM1-7620A2	OEM	HM3-7620-2	OEM	HM9-6562-5	OEM
HI2-387-2(A)	OEM	HK403A	OEM	HLMP-0500	OEM	HLP50TB	OEM	HM1-7620A5	OEM	HM3-7620-5	2372	HM9-6562B2	OEM
HI2-387-5(A)	OEM	HK403K	OEM	HLMP-0501	OEM	HLP50TC	OEM	HM1-7621-2	OEM	HM3-7620A2	OEM	HM9-6611-2	OEM
HI2-387-8(A)	OEM	HK603A	OEM	HLMP301	OEM	HLP50TD	OEM	HM1-7621-5	2373	HM3-7620A5	2372	HM9-6611-5	OEM
HI3-300-5	OEM	HK603K	OEM	HLMP401	OEM	HLP50WRB	OEM	HM1-7621A2	OEM	HM3-7621-2	OEM	HM9-7602-2	OEM
HI3-301-5	OEM	HK803A	OEM	HLMP504	OEM	HLP50WRC	OEM	HM1-7621A5	OEM	HM3-7621-5	2373	HM9-7602-5	OEM
HI3-302-5	OEM	HK803K	OEM	HLMP-1300	OEM	HLP50WRD	OEM	HM1-7640-2	2308	HM3-7621A2	OEM	HM9-7603-2	OEM
HI3-303-5	OEM	HK1000	OEM	HLMP-1301	OEM	HLP50WTB	OEM	HM1-7640-5	6916	HM3-7621A5	2373	HM9-7603-5	OEM
HI3-304-5	OEM	HK1001	OEM	HLMP-1302	OEM	HLP50WTC	OEM	HM1-7640A2	OEM	HM3-7640-2	OEM	HM9-7608-2	OEM
HI3-305-5	OEM	HK1003A	OEM	HLMP-1400	OEM	HLP50WTD	OEM	HM1-7640A5	OEM	HM3-7640-5	2308	HM9-7608-5	OEM
HI3-306-5	OEM	HK1003K	OEM	HLMP-1401	OEM	HLP60RB	OEM	HM1-7641-2	OEM	HM3-7640A2	OEM	HM9-7610-2	OEM
HI3-307-5	OEM	HK1203A	OEM	HLMP-1402	OEM	HLP60RC	OEM	HM1-7641-5	2306	HM3-7640A5	2308	HM9-7610-5	OEM
HI3-381-5(A)	OEM	HK1203K	OEM	HLMP-1500	OEM	HLP60RD	OEM	HM1-7641A2	OEM	HM3-7641-2	OEM	HM9-7610A2	OEM
HI3-384-5(A)	OEM	HKT-158	0079	HLMP-1501	OEM	HLP60RGB	OEM	HM1-7641A5	OEM	HM3-7641-5	2306	HM9-7610A5	OEM
HI3-387-5(A)	OEM	HKT-161	0079	HLMP-1502	OEM	HLP60RGC	OEM	HM1-7642-2	OEM	HM3-7641A2	OEM	HM9-7611-2	OEM
HI3-390-5(A)	OEM	HKZ101	OEM	HLMP-2300	OEM	HLP60RGD	OEM	HM1-7642-5	2374	HM3-7641A5	2306	HM9-7611-5	OEM
HI13SC	2336	HKZ101S	OEM	HLMP-2350	OEM	HLP60RLB	OEM	HM1-7642A-2	OEM	HM3-7642-2	OEM	HM9-7611A2	OEM
HI13SD	2336	HL-00005	OEM	HLMP-2400	OEM	HLP60RLC	OEM	HM1-7642A-5	2374	HM3-7642-5	2374	HM9-7611A5	OEM
HI13SG	2336	HL103A	2872	HLMP-2450	OEM	HLP60RLD	OEM	HM1-7642P-2	OEM	HM3-7642A-2	OEM	HM9-7616-2	OEM
HI13SH	2367	HL103K	2275	HLMP-2500	OEM	HLP60TB	OEM	HM1-7642P-5	OEM	HM3-7642P-2	OEM	HM9-7616-5	OEM
HI13SS	2336	HL203A	2872	HLMP-2550	OEM	HLP60TC	OEM	HM1-7643-2	OEM	HM3-7642P-5	OEM	HM9-7620-2	OEM
HI23SC	2337	HL203K	2275	HLMP-2600	OEM	HLP60TD	OEM	HM1-7643-5	2376	HM3-7643-2	OEM	HM9-7620-5	OEM
HI23SD	2337	HL403A	1104	HLMP-2620	OEM	HLP60WRB	OEM	HM1-7643A-2	OEM	HM3-7643-5	2376	HM9-7620A2	OEM
HI23SG	2337	HL403K	0471	HLMP-2635	OEM	HLP60WRD	OEM	HM1-7643A-5	2376	HM3-7643A-2	OEM	HM9-7620A5	OEM
HI23SH	2378	HL603A	1104	HLMP-2655	OEM	HLP60WTB	OEM	HM1-7643P-2	OEM	HM3-7643A-5	2376	HM9-7621-2	OEM
HI23SS	2337	HL603K	0471	HLMP-2670	OEM	HLP60WTC	OEM	HM1-7643P-5	OEM	HM3-7643P-2	OEM	HM9-7621-5	OEM
HI33SD	2340	HL803A	2982	HLMP-2685	OEM	HLP60WTD	OEM	HM1-7648-2	OEM	HM3-7643P-5	OEM	HM9-7621A2	OEM
HI33SG	2340	HL803K	0444	HLMP-2700	OEM	HLP1400	OEM	HM1-7648-5	3257	HM3-7643Q-5	OEM	HM9-7621A5	OEM
HI33SH	1403	HL1003A	2982	HLMP-2720	OEM	HLP1500	OEM	HM1-7649-2	OEM	HM3-7648-2	OEM	HM9-7640-2	OEM
HI33SS	2340	HL1003K	0444	HLMP-2735	OEM	HLP1600	OEM	HM1-7649-5	2304	HM3-7648-5	3257	HM9-7640-5	OEM
HI43SC	2340	HL1203A	OEM	HLMP-2755	OEM	HLP2400	OEM	HM1-7680-2	OEM	HM3-7649-2	OEM	HM9-7640A2	OEM
HI43SD	2340	HL1203K	OEM	HLMP-2770	OEM	HLP2500	OEM	HM1-7680-5	2835	HM3-7649-5	2304	HM9-7640A5	OEM
HI43SG	2340	HL1403A	OEM	HLMP-2785	OEM	HLP2600	OEM	HM1-7680A5	OEM	HM3-7680-2	OEM	HM9-7641-2	OEM
HI43SH	1403	HL1403K	OEM	HLMP-2800	OEM	HLP3400	OEM	HM1-7680P2	OEM	HM3-7680-5	2835	HM9-7641-5	OEM
HI43SS	2340	HL7801E	OEM	HLMP-2835	OEM	HLP3500	OEM	HM1-7680P5	OEM	HM3-7680A5	OEM	HM9-7641A2	OEM
HI53SC	OEM	HL7801G	OEM	HLMP-2855	OEM	HLP3600	OEM	HM1-7680R2	OEM	HM3-7680P2	OEM	HM9-7641A5	OEM
HI53SD	OEM	HL18998	0232	HLMP-2870	OEM	HLP5400	OEM	HM1-7680R5	OEM	HM3-7680P5	OEM	HM9-7642-2	OEM
HI53SG	OEM	HL18999	1303	HLMP-2885	OEM	HLP5420	OEM	HM1-7681-2	OEM	HM3-7680R2	OEM	HM9-7642-5	OEM
HI53SH	2371	HL19000	0357	HLMP-3105	OEM	HLP5500	OEM	HM1-7681-5	2881	HM3-7680R5	OEM	HM9-7642A-2	OEM
HI53SS	OEM	HL19001	0507	HLMP-3112	OEM	HLP5600	OEM	HM1-7681A5	OEM	HM3-7681-2	OEM	HM9-7642A-5	OEM
HI63SD	OEM	HL19002	1164	HLMP-3600	OEM	HLS1-25	OEM	HM1-7681P2	OEM	HM3-7681-5	2881	HM9-7642P-2	OEM
HI63SG	OEM	HL19003	0692	HLMP-3650	OEM	HLS1-50	OEM	HM1-7681P5	OEM	HM3-7681A5	OEM	HM9-7642P-5	OEM
HI63SH	2371	HL19004	0310	HLMP-3680	OEM	HLS1-100	OEM	HM1-7681R2	OEM	HM3-7681P2	OEM	HM9-7643-2	OEM
HI63SS	OEM	HL19005	0331	HLMP-6203	OEM	HLS1-150	OEM	HM1-7681R5	OEM	HM3-7681P5	OEM	HM9-7643-5	OEM
HI516-5(A)	OEM	HL19006	0564	HLMP-6204	OEM	HLS1-200	OEM	HM1-7684-2	OEM	HM3-7681R2	OEM	HM9-7643A-2	OEM
HI516-8(A)	OEM	HL19008	0175	HLMP-6205	OEM	HLS1-300	OEM	HM1-7684P2	OEM	HM3-7681R5	OEM	HM9-7643A-5	OEM
HI518-5(A)	OEM	HL19009	1046	HLMP-6600	OEM	HLS2-25	OEM	HM1-7684P5	OEM	HM3-7684-2	OEM	HM9-7643P-2	OEM
HI518-8(A)	OEM	HL19010	1150	HLMP-6620	OEM	HLS2-50	OEM	HM1-7685-2	OEM	HM3-7684-5	OEM	HM9-7643P-5	OEM
HIB005	6945	HL19011	1018	HLP0TA	OEM	HLS2-100	OEM	HM1-7685-5	3137	HM3-7684P2	OEM	HM9-7648-2	OEM
HIB010	OEM	HL19012	1423	HLP0WTA	OEM	HLS2-150	OEM	HM1-7685P2	OEM	HM3-7684P5	OEM	HM9-7648-5	OEM
HIDIV-1	2949	HL19013	0867	HLP20RA	OEM	HLS2-200	OEM	HM1-7685P5	OEM	HM3-7685-2	OEM	HM9-7649-2	OEM
HIDIV-2	2950	HL19014	1358	HLP20RGA	OEM	HLS2-300	OEM	HM1-76160-2	OEM	HM3-7685-5	3137	HM9-7649-5	OEM
HIDIV-3	2952	HL19015	1199	HLP20RLA	OEM	HLS25	OEM	HM1-76160-5	OEM	HM3-7685P2	OEM	HM9-7680-2	OEM
HIFI	0015	HL53424	1812	HLP20TA	OEM	HLSS-0533D	OEM	HM1-76161-2	OEM	HM3-7685P5	OEM	HM9-7680-5	OEM
HILA7016//	OEM	HL53426	1168	HLP20WRA	OEM	HLSS-0533H	OEM	HM1-76161-5	OEM	HM4-6503-5	OEM	HM9-7680A5	OEM
HI053SC	OEM	HL53428	0033	HLP20WTA	OEM	HM-00049	0279	HM1-76165-2	OEM	HM4-6504-2	OEM	HM9-7680P2	OEM
HI053SD	OEM	HL53429	0141	HLP30RA	OEM	HM01301	OEM	HM1-76165-5	OEM	HM4-6504-5	OEM	HM9-7680P5	OEM
HI053SG	OEM	HL55660	0522	HLP30RC	OEM	HM-08014	0004	HM1-76165-8	OEM	HM4-6504B2	OEM	HM9-7680R2	OEM
HI053SH	OEM	HL-55661	0699	HLP30RD	OEM	HM1-768-5	OEM	HM1-76321-2	OEM	HM4-6505-2	OEM	HM9-7680R5	OEM
HIT5609A	OEM	HL55663	2125	HLP30RGA	OEM	HM1-6322-2	OEM	HM1-76321-5	OEM	HM4-6505-5	OEM	HM9-7681-2	OEM

If replacement code is OEM, contact original manufacturer for replacement.

DEVICE TYPE	REPL CODE
HM9-7681-5	OEM
HM9-7681A5	OEM
HM9-7681P2	OEM
HM9-7681P5	OEM
HM9-7681R2	OEM
HM9-7681R5	OEM
HM9-7684-2	OEM
HM9-7684-5	OEM
HM9-7684P2	OEM
HM9-7684P5	OEM
HM9-7685-2	OEM
HM9-7685-5	OEM
HM9-7685P2	OEM
HM9-7685P5	OEM
HM9-76160-2	OEM
HM9-76160-5	OEM
HM9-76161-2	OEM
HM9-76161-5	OEM
HM9.1	0057
HM9.1A	0057
HM9.1B	0012
HM10	0064
HM10A	0064
HM10B	0170
HM11	0181
HM11A	0181
HM11A1A	OEM
HM11B	0181
HM12	0052
HM12A	0052
HM12B	0052
HM13	0053
HM13A	0053
HM13B	0053
HM15	0681
HM15A	0681
HM15B	0681
HM16	0440
HM16A	0440
HM16B	0440
HM18	0371
HM18A	0371
HM18B	0371
HM20	0695
HM20A	0695
HM20B	0695
HM22	0700
HM22A	0560
HM22B	0700
HM24	0489
HM24A	0489
HM24B	0489
HM27	0450
HM27A	0450
HM27B	0436
HM30	0195
HM30A	0195
HM30B	0195
HM33	0166
HM33A	0166
HM33B	0166
HM36	0010
HM36A	0010
HM36B	0010
HM39	0032
HM39A	0032
HM39B	0032
HM43	0054
HM43A	0054
HM43B	0054
HM47	0068
HM47A	0068
HM47B	0068
HM51	0092
HM51A	0497
HM51B	0092
HM56	0125
HM56A	0125
HM56B	0125
HM62	0152
HM62A	0152
HM62B	0152
HM68	0173
HM68A	0173
HM68B	0173
HM75	0094
HM75A	0094
HM75B	0094
HM82	0049
HM82A	0049
HM82B	0049
HM91	0156
HM91A	0156
HM91B	0156
HM100	0189
HM100A	0189
HM100B	0189
HM110	0099
HM110A	0099
HM110B	0099
HM120	0089
HM120A	0089
HM120B	0089
HM130	0285
HM130A	0285
HM130B	0285
HM150	0336
HM150A	0336
HM150B	0336
HM160	0366
HM160A	0366
HM160B	0366
HM180	0420
HM180A	0420
HM180B	0420
HM200	1464
HM200A	1464
HM200B	1464
HM331	OEM
HM383B01	0190
HM468A10	OEM
HM468A10P	OEM
HM2110	OEM
HM2110-1	OEM
HM2112	OEM
HM2112-1	OEM
HM2504	OEM
HM2504-1	OEM
HM2510	OEM
HM2510-1	OEM
HM2510-2	OEM
HM2511	OEM
HM2511-1	OEM
HM4315P	OEM
HM4334-3	OEM
HM4334-4	OEM
HM4334P-3	OEM
HM4334P3L	OEM
HM4334P-4	OEM
HM4334P4L	OEM
HM4716A-1	OEM
HM4716A-2	OEM
HM4716A-3	OEM
HM4716A-4	OEM
HM4716AP-1	OEM
HM4716AP-2	OEM
HM4716AP-3	OEM
HM4716AP-4	OEM
HM4816A3	OEM
HM4816A3E	OEM
HM4816A4	OEM
HM4816A7	OEM
HM4816AP3	OEM
HM4816AP3E	OEM
HM4816AP4	OEM
HM4816AP7	OEM
HM4864-2	4426
HM4864-3	2341
HM4864A12	OEM
HM4864A15	OEM
HM4864A20	OEM
HM4864AP12	OEM
HM4864AP15	OEM
HM4864AP20	OEM
HM4864I2	OEM
HM4864I3	OEM
HM4864K2	OEM
HM4864K3	OEM
HM4864P-2	2341
HM4864P2	OEM
HM4864P-3	OEM
HM4864P3	OEM
HM6116	1887
HM6116-2	OEM
HM6116-3	1887
HM6116-4	1887
HM6116FP2	OEM
HM6116FP-3	OEM
HM6116FP3	1887
HM6116FP-4	OEM
HM6116FP4	1887
HM6116FP-200	OEM
HM6116L2	OEM
HM6116L3	OEM
HM6116L4	OEM
HM6116LFP2	OEM
HM6116LFP-3	OEM
HM6116LFP3	OEM
HM6116LFP4(A)	OEM
HM6116LI2	OEM
HM6116LI3	OEM
HM6116LI4	OEM
HM6116LP-2	OEM
HM6116LP-3	OEM
HM6116LP-4	1887
HM6116P	OEM
HM6116P-2	OEM
HM6116P-3	1887
HM6116P-4	6041
HM6116P4	1887
HM6116PI2	OEM
HM6116PI3	OEM
HM6116PI4	OEM
HM6117FP3	OEM
HM6117FP4	OEM
HM6117LFP3(A)	OEM
HM6117LFP4(A)	OEM
HM6117LP3	OEM
HM6117LP4	OEM
HM6117P3	OEM
HM6147	OEM
HM6147-3	OEM
HM6147H35	OEM
HM6147H45(A)	OEM
HM6147HLP35	OEM
HM6147HLP45	OEM
HM6147HP35	OEM
HM6147HP45	OEM
HM6147LP	OEM
HM6147LP-3	OEM
HM6147P	OEM
HM6147P-3	OEM
HM6148	OEM
HM6148-6	OEM
HM6148LP	OEM
HM6148LP-6	OEM
HM6148P	OEM
HM6148P-6	OEM
HM6167	OEM
HM6167-6	OEM
HM6167-8	OEM
HM6167LP	OEM
HM6167LP6	OEM
HM6167LP8	OEM
HM6167P	OEM
HM6167P6	OEM
HM6167P8	OEM
HM6264	OEM
HM6264-150	OEM
HM6264ALP-10	OEM
HM6264ALP-15	OEM
HM6264ALSP	OEM
HM6264ALSP-12	OEM
HM6264ALSP-15	OEM
HM6264LP-15	OEM
HM6264P	OEM
HM6264P-15	OEM
HM6264P-100NS	OEM
HM6264P-150	OEM
HM6322A2	OEM
HM6501B2	OEM
HM6504B2	OEM
HM6504B9	OEM
HM6511-2	OEM
HM6533-2	OEM
HM6543-2	OEM
HM6611A2	OEM
HM6641-5	OEM
HM6661-2	OEM
HM6661-5	OEM
HM6661A2	OEM
HM7091	OEM
HM-7101	OEM
HM7101HD	OEM
HM7603	OEM
HM9101	OEM
HM9102	OEM
HM9105	OEM
HM9306	OEM
HM10414	OEM
HM10414-1	OEM
HM10422	OEM
HM10422-6(A)	OEM
HM10470	OEM
HM10470-1	OEM
HM10474	OEM
HM10474-1	OEM
HM10480	OEM
HM16100-2	OEM
HM16100-5	OEM
HM16100A2	OEM
HM16100A5	OEM
HM16100C2	OEM
HM16100C5	OEM
HM46810	OEM
HM46810P	OEM
HM50256-15	1463
HM50256-20	1463
HM50256P-12	1463
HM50256P-15	1463
HM50256P-20	1463
HM50464P-12	OEM
HM50464P-15	OEM
HM53051P-45	OEM
HM53461	OEM
HM53461P-12B	OEM
HM53461ZP-12	OEM
HM65256	OEM
HM65256BLP	OEM
HM65256BLP-12	OEM
HM65256BLP-120NS	OEM
HM65256BLSP	OEM
HM65256BLSP-12	OEM
HM65256BP	OEM
HM65256BSP	OEM
HM100415	OEM
HM100422	OEM
HM100422F	OEM
HM100470	OEM
HM100470-1	OEM
HM100474	OEM
HM100474-1	OEM
HM100474F	OEM
HM472114-3	4113
HM472114-4	4113
HM472114A-1	OEM
HM472114A-2	OEM
HM472114AP-1	OEM
HM472114AP-2	OEM
HM472114P-3	2037
HM472114P-4	4113
HMB917	OEM
HMCS42	OEM
HMCS42C	OEM
HMCS43	OEM
HMCS43C	OEM
HMCS44A	OEM
HMCS44C	OEM
HMCS45A	OEM
HMCS45C	OEM
HMG251	0124
HMG252	0318
HMG625	0124
HMG625A	0124
HMG626	OEM
HMG626A	OEM
HMG627	OEM
HMG659	OEM
HMG662	OEM
HMG662A	OEM
HMG663	OEM
HMG663A	OEM
HMG789	0124
HMG790	0124
HMG791	0124
HMG792	0124
HMG793	OEM
HMG794	OEM
HMG795	OEM
HMG796	OEM
HMG810	OEM
HMG811	0124
HMG812	0124
HMG813	0124
HMG814	OEM
HMG815	OEM
HMG818	OEM
HMG837A	OEM
HMG840	OEM
HMG844	OEM
HMG891	OEM
HMG897	OEM
HMG898	OEM
HMG899	OEM
HMG900	OEM
HMG901	OEM
HMG903	0124
HMG903A	0124
HMG904	0124
HMG904A	0124
HMG905	0124
HMG905A	0124
HMG906	0124
HMG906A	0124
HMG907	0124
HMG907A	0124
HMG908	0124
HMG908A	OEM
HMG914	OEM
HMG914A	OEM
HMG914B	OEM
HMG915	OEM
HMG916	OEM
HMG916A	OEM
HMG916B	OEM
HMG925	OEM
HMG926	OEM
HMG927	OEM
HMG929	OEM
HMG930	OEM
HMG948	OEM
HMG993	0124
HMG3062	OEM
HMG3063	OEM
HMG3064	OEM
HMG3065	OEM
HMG3066	OEM
HMG3067	0124
HMG3068	0124
HMG3069	OEM
HMG3123	0124
HMG3124	0124
HMG3206	OEM
HMG3207	OEM
HMG3257	OEM
HMG3258	OEM
HMG3567	OEM
HMG3593	0124
HMG3594	OEM
HMG3596	0124
HMG3598	OEM
HMG3600	OEM
HMG3601	OEM
HMG3602	OEM
HMG3603	OEM
HMG3604	OEM
HMG3605	OEM
HMG3606	OEM
HMG3607	OEM
HMG3608	OEM
HMG3609	OEM
HMG3669	OEM
HMG3722	OEM
HMG3731	OEM
HMG3872	OEM
HMG3873	OEM
HMG3954	OEM
HMG3956	OEM
HMG4009	OEM
HMG4043	OEM
HMG4086	OEM
HMG4092	OEM
HMG4147	0124
HMG4148	OEM
HMG4149	OEM
HMG4150	OEM
HMG4151	OEM
HMG4152	OEM
HMG4153	OEM
HMG4154	OEM
HMG4305	OEM
HMG4308	OEM
HMG4313	OEM
HMG4314	OEM
HMG4317	OEM
HMG4319	OEM
HMG4322	OEM
HMG4373	OEM
HMG4375	OEM
HMG9001	OEM
HMG9002	OEM
HMG9003	OEM
HMG9004	OEM
HMG9005	OEM
HMG9006	OEM
HMG9007	OEM
HMG9008	OEM
HMG9009	OEM
HMG9010	0124
HMMP1802ACD	OEM
HMMP1802ACL	OEM
HMMP1802ACY	OEM
HMMP1802AD	OEM
HMMP1802AL	OEM
HMMP1802AY	OEM
HN-00002	0015
HN-00003	0143
HN-00005	0052
HN-00008	0015
HN-00012	0057
HN-00018	0023
HN-00024	0057
HN-00025	0700
HN-00032	0015
HN-00033	0030
HN-00045	0030
HN-00052	0030
HN-00053	0139
HN-00061	0170
HN-0047	0133
HN100	0538
HN101	OEM
HN102	OEM
HN103	OEM
HN104	OEM
HN106	OEM
HN107	OEM
HN108	OEM
HN109	OEM
HN110	OEM
HN111	OEM
HN112	OEM
HN113	OEM
HN2756G25	OEM
HN25044	2374
HN25045	4275
HN25084	OEM
HN25084S	OEM
HN25085	3137
HN25085S	3137
HN25088	2835
HN25088S	2835
HN25089	2881
HN25089S	2881
HN25168S	OEM
HN25169S	OEM
HN27256G	OEM
HN27256G-25	OEM
HN27256G-XX	OEM
HN43128	OEM
HN43128P	OEM
HN48016P	OEM
HN48364P	OEM
HN61256	OEM
HN61256P	OEM
HN61364P	OEM
HN462532	5007
HN462532G	5007
HN462532G2	5007
HN462716G	2263
HN462716G1	OEM
HN462716GI	OEM
HN462732	2672
HN462732G	2672
HN462732G2	OEM
HN482764G	0806
HN482764G(A)	OEM
HN482764G-3	0806
HN482764G3(A)	OEM
HN482764G4	OEM
HN613128P	OEM
HN4827128G-25	1628
HN4827232AG	OEM
HND1	OEM
HNVM3004	OEM
HNVM3008D	OEM
HNVM3008H	OEM
HNVM3008P	OEM
HNVM3108D	OEM
HNVM3108H	OEM
HNVM3108P	OEM
HNVM3704D	OEM
HNVM3704H	OEM
HNVM3704P	OEM
HNVM3708	OEM
H070	0769
H091	0143
H099	0469
H0300	0969
HOR3D	OEM
HOR3D4-L	OEM
HOS050	OEM
HOS050A	OEM
HOS050C	OEM
HP-3FR2	OEM
HP3FR2	OEM
HP3K	OEM
HP3ML	OEM
HP3MLRII	OEM
HP-5A	0015
HP-5FR2	OEM
HP-5FR3	OEM
HP5FR3	OEM
HP6	OEM
HP8	OEM
HP10	OEM
HP74LS240P	0447
HP80	0143
HP100	OEM
HP101	OEM
HP102	OEM
HP104	OEM
HP105	OEM
HP106	OEM
HP107	OEM
HP108	OEM
HP109	OEM
HP110	OEM
HP111	OEM
HP205	0015
HP3209	OEM
HP4510	1281
HP4562	OEM
HP5082-0001	OEM
HP5082-0008	OEM
HP5082-0009	OEM
HP5082-0012	OEM
HP5082-0013	OEM
HP5082-0015	OEM
HP5082-0017	OEM
HP5082-0018	OEM
HP5082-0020	OEM
HP5082-0021	OEM
HP5082-0023	OEM
HP5082-0024	OEM
HP5082-0025	OEM
HP5082-0029	OEM
HP5082-0030	OEM
HP5082-0031	OEM
HP5082-0032	OEM
HP5082-0034	OEM
HP5082-0039	OEM
HP5082-0047	OEM
HP5082-0049	OEM
HP5082-0057	OEM
HP5082-0058	OEM
HP5082-0087	OEM
HP5082-0090	OEM
HP5082-0094	OEM
HP5082-0097	OEM
HP5082-0103	0124
HP5082-0112	OEM
HP5082-0113	OEM
HP5082-0114	OEM
HP5082-0132	0124
HP5082-0133	0124
HP5082-0134	0124
HP5082-0151	OEM
HP5082-0152	OEM
HP5082-0153	OEM
HP5082-0154	OEM
HP5082-0180	OEM
HP5082-0181	OEM
HP5082-0182	OEM
HP5082-0240	OEM
HP5082-0241	OEM
HP5082-0242	OEM
HP5082-0243	OEM
HP5082-0251	OEM
HP5082-0252	OEM
HP5082-0253	OEM
HP5082-0254	OEM
HP5082-0299	OEM
HP5082-0300	OEM
HP5082-0305	OEM
HP5082-0306	OEM
HP5082-0307	OEM
HP5082-0308	OEM
HP5082-0309	OEM
HP5082-0310	OEM
HP5082-0320	OEM
HP5082-0321	OEM
HP5082-0335	OEM
HP5082-0340	OEM
HP5082-0360	OEM
HP5082-0364	OEM
HP5082-0365	OEM
HP5082-0370	OEM
HP5082-0375	OEM
HP5082-0386	OEM
HP5082-0437	OEM
HP5082-0438	OEM
HP5082-0439	OEM
HP5082-0800	OEM
HP5082-0803	OEM
HP5082-0805	OEM
HP5082-0810	OEM
HP5082-0815	OEM
HP5082-0820	OEM
HP5082-0821	OEM
HP5082-0825	OEM
HP5082-0830	OEM
HP5082-0833	OEM
HP5082-0835	OEM
HP5082-0840	OEM
HP5082-0885	OEM
HP5082-1001	OEM
HP5082-1002	OEM
HP5082-1006	OEM
HP5082-2080	OEM
HP5082-2200	OEM
HP5082-2201	OEM
HP5082-2202	OEM
HP5082-2203	OEM
HP5082-2207	OEM
HP5082-2208	OEM
HP5082-2209	OEM
HP5082-2210	OEM
HP5082-2213	OEM
HP5082-2214	OEM
HP5082-2215	OEM
HP5082-2221	OEM
HP5082-2223	OEM
HP5082-2225	OEM
HP5082-2351	OEM
HP5082-2353	OEM
HP5082-2354	OEM
HP5082-2366	OEM
HP5082-2374	OEM
HP5082-2500	OEM
HP5082-2511	OEM
HP5082-2521	OEM
HP5082-2523	OEM
HP5082-2524	OEM
HP5082-2544	OEM
HP5082-2551	OEM
HP5082-2552	OEM
HP5082-2553	OEM
HP5082-2554	OEM
HP5082-2555	OEM
HP5082-2563	OEM
HP5082-2564	OEM
HP5082-2566	OEM
HP5082-2577	OEM
HP5082-2579	OEM
HP5082-2602	OEM
HP5082-2707	OEM
HP5082-2740	OEM
HP5082-2752	OEM
HP5082-2758	OEM
HP5082-2759	OEM
HP5082-2800	0133
HP5082-2827	OEM
HP5082-2833	OEM
HP5082-3001	0133
HP5082-3006	OEM
HP5082-3007	OEM
HP5082-3008	OEM
HP5082-3009	OEM
HP5082-3051	OEM
HP5082-3052	OEM
HP5082-3080	0133
HP5082-4104	OEM
HP5082-4107	OEM
HP5082-4120	OEM
HP5082-4201	OEM
HP5082-4303	OEM
HP5082-4309	OEM
HP5082-4310	OEM
HP5082-4320	OEM
HP5082-4351	OEM
HP5082-4400	OEM
HP5082-4405	OEM
HP5082-4417	OEM
HP33001A	OEM
HP33002A	OEM
HP33101A	OEM
HP33102A	OEM
HP33201A	OEM
HP33202A	OEM
HP35860A	0016
HP35867B	OEM
HP35867E	OEM
HPA4202	OEM
HPF4519	OEM
HPS1610	OEM
HPS1611	OEM
HPS1612	OEM
HPS1640	OEM
HPS1641	OEM
HPS1642	OEM
HPS1670	OEM
HPS1671	OEM
HPS1672	OEM
HR	OEM
HR-05A	0015
HR-1	0004
HR1	0050
HR-1S85	0030
HR-2	0004
HR2	0050
HR-2A	0004
HR2A	0211

If replacement code is OEM, contact original manufacturer for replacement.

DEVICE TYPE	REPL CODE
HR-2A(PENNCREST)	0015
HR2.3	OEM
HR2.8	OEM
HR-3	0004
HR3	0211
HR-3FR	OEM
HR3N0187	OEM
HR3N0200	OEM
HR3.8	OEM
HR-4	0004
HR4	0211
HR-4A	0004
HR4A	0279
HR4.4	OEM
HR-5	0164
HR5	0279
HR-5A	0015
HR5A	0023
HR5A8E	0015
HR-5AX2	0015
HR-5B	0015
HR5B	0015
HR5.4	OEM
HR-6	0004
HR6	0211
HR6.5	OEM
HR-7	0004
HR7	0050
HR-7A	0004
HR7A	0211
HR-8	0004
HR8	0211
HR-8A	0004
HR8A	0279
HR-9	0004
HR9	0211
HR-9A	0004
HR9A	0279
HR9.0	OEM
HR10	0015
HR-11	0016
HR11	0015
HR-11A	0016
HR11A	0079
HR-11B	0016
HR11B	0079
HR-12	0086
HR-13	0016
HR13	0015
HR-13A	0016
HR13A	0079
HR-14	0111
HR14	0079
HR-14A	0016
HR14A	0079
HR-15	0111
HR15	0136
HR-15A	0016
HR15A	0079
HR-16	0016
HR16	0079
HR-16A	0016
HR16A	0079
HR-17	0016
HR17	0079
HR-17A	0016
HR17A	0079
HR-18	0016
HR18	0079
HR-18A	0016
HR18A	0079
HR-19	0016
HR19	0079
HR-19A	0016
HR19A	0079
HR-19E	0599
HR-20	0050
HR20	0050
HR-20A	0050
HR20A	0050
HR-21	0050
HR21	0050
HR-21A	0050
HR21A	0050
HR-22	0050
HR22	0050
HR-22A	0050
HR22A	0050
HR-22B	0050
HR22B	0050
HR-24	0050
HR24	0050
HR-24A	0050
HR24A	0050
HR-25	0050
HR25	0050
HR-25A	0050
HR25A	0050
HR-26	0050
HR26	0050
HR-26A	0050
HR26A	0050
HR-27	0050
HR27	0050
HR-27A	0050
HR27A	0050
HR28	0086
HR29	0086
HR-30	0136

DEVICE TYPE	REPL CODE
HR30	0164
HR-32	0079
HR32	0079
HR-36	0079
HR36	0079
HR-37	0016
HR37	0079
HR-38	0079
HR38	0590
HR-39	0004
HR39	0127
HR-40	0050
HR40	0050
HR41	0050
HR42	0050
HR-43	0050
HR43	0050
HR44	0050
HR-45	0050
HR45	0050
HR46	0050
HR-47	0111
HR47	0111
HR-48	0079
HR48	0079
HR50	0050
HR-51	0050
HR51	0050
HR52	0050
HR53	0004
HR-58	0127
HR58	0144
HR-59	0127
HR59	0144
HR-60	0079
HR60	0144
HR-61	0211
HR61	0004
HR62	0079
HR63	0079
HR64	0079
HR65	0079
HR66	0079
HR-67	0590
HR67	0590
HR-68	0419
HR-69	0555
HR69	0042
HR-70	1257
HR70	0919
HR-71	0037
HR71	0037
HR72	0786
HR-73	0561
HR-74	1357
HR76	0127
HR77	0224
HR78	0224
HR79	0127
HR80	0127
HR81	0086
HR82	0590
HR83	0590
HR-84	0150
HR84	0150
HR85	0561
HR86	1357
HR87	0224
HR101	0085
HR-101A	0160
HR101A	0160
HR102	0160
HR102C	0160
HR103	0160
HR103A	0160
HR105	0160
HR105A	0160
HR105B	0160
HR-106	0142
HR106	0142
HR107	0142
HR-107(PHILCO)	0178
HR107H	0178
HR-200	0242
HR200	1596
HR400	6114
HR600	0087
HR761	OEM
HR762	OEM
HR763	OEM
HR764	OEM
HR771	OEM
HR772	OEM
HR773	OEM
HR774	OEM
HR800	0559
HR878A	OEM
HR878B	OEM
HR879A	OEM
HR879B	OEM
HR881A	OEM
HR881B	OEM
HR932	OEM
HR952	OEM
HR952F	OEM
HR953	OEM
HR953F	OEM
HR954	OEM
HR954F	OEM

DEVICE TYPE	REPL CODE
HR961F	OEM
HR982	OEM
HR982F-1	OEM
HR982F-2	OEM
HR1000	0087
HR1301	OEM
HR1301F	OEM
HR1870B	OEM
HR1871B	OEM
HR1872B	OEM
HR1874B	OEM
HR3027	OEM
HR3028	OEM
HR3029	OEM
HR3030	OEM
HR3031	OEM
HR3032	OEM
HR40836	0050
HR40837	0050
HR43835	0050
HR43838	0050
HR45838	0050
HR45910	0050
HR45913	0050
HR104961C	1257
HR448636	0050
HRD100	OEM
HRD100F	OEM
HRD101	OEM
HRD102	OEM
HRD200	OEM
HRD200F	OEM
HRE16	OEM
HRE16A	OEM
HRE18.5	OEM
HRE18.5A	OEM
HRE25.5	OEM
HRE25.5A	OEM
HRE28	OEM
HRE28A	OEM
HRE32	OEM
HRE32A	OEM
HRE34.5	OEM
HRE34.5A	OEM
HRE41.5	OEM
HRE41.5A	OEM
HRE48	OEM
HRE48A	OEM
HRE50.5	OEM
HRE50.5A	OEM
HRE53.5	OEM
HRE53.5A	OEM
HRE56.5	OEM
HRE56.5A	OEM
HRE60	OEM
HRE60A	OEM
HRE62.5	OEM
HRE62.5A	OEM
HRE64	OEM
HRE64A	OEM
HRE66.5	OEM
HRE66.5A	OEM
HRE69	OEM
HRE69A	OEM
HRE73.5	OEM
HRE73.5A	OEM
HRE76	OEM
HRE76A	OEM
HRE80	OEM
HRE80A	OEM
HRE82.5	OEM
HRE82.5A	OEM
HRE89	OEM
HRE89A	OEM
HRE96	OEM
HRE96A	OEM
HRP22	0023
HRP32	0023
HRW34	1227
HRW36	1227
HS04	OEM
HS04S	OEM
HS07	6700
HS08	0998
HS034	OEM
HS034S	OEM
HS1	OEM
HS1/7	0769
HS1/9	0769
HS-1B	0374
HS2	OEM
HS3	OEM
HS3/1	OEM
HS5	0004
HS6	OEM
HS6/1	0201
HS7/1	0769
HS7/17M	0769
HS7/17N	0769
HS8	0769
HS8/1	0769
HS8-1	0769
HS-9/1	0769
HS9/1	0769
HS9/17M	0752
HS9/17N	0752
HS10	OEM
HS10/1	0286
HS11	OEM

DEVICE TYPE	REPL CODE
HS12	0390
HS13	OEM
HS14	OEM
HS14S	OEM
HS-15	0211
HS15	0211
HS15/1	0752
HS15/1A(SONY)	0201
HS15/1B	0201
HS-15/1C	0286
HS15/1C	0286
HS-15/12	0201
HS15/16	0286
HS15-1C	0286
HS17	6700
HS17D	0004
HS18	0998
HS-20	0752
HS20	0201
HS-20/1	0201
HS20/1	0752
HS20/1A5	0286
HS20/1B	0752
HS20/1C	0752
HS20/1D	OEM
HS20/16	0286
HS20-1	0752
HS20-1A	0752
HS20-1BS	0752
HS20-1C	0201
HS20-12	0286
HS20-16S	0286
HS20M	0286
HS-22D	0211
HS22D	0136
HS23D	0211
HS24	OEM
HS24S	OEM
HS25	0374
HS25/1	0374
HS25/1B	0374
HS25/1C	0752
HS25/12S	0286
HS25-1B	0015
HS27	6700
HS28	0998
HS29D	0136
HS30	0374
HS-30/1B	0374
HS30/1B	5262
HS30/1BS	OEM
HS30/1C	0752
HS30-1B	0374
HS30-1C	0752
HS30-16	0374
HS34	OEM
HS35S	OEM
HS37	6709
HS38	1028
HS40	OEM
HS40A	OEM
HS41A	OEM
HS42A	OEM
HS43A	OEM
HS44	OEM
HS44S	OEM
HS47	6709
HS48	1028
HS50	OEM
HS52	OEM
HS53	OEM
HS54	OEM
HS54S	OEM
HS57	6710
HS58	1140
HS60	OEM
HS64	OEM
HS64S	OEM
HS67	6710
HS68	1140
HS75	OEM
HS102	0004
HS133	0911
HS151B	0201
HS170	0211
HS290	0211
HS811	0769
HS816	0590
HS891	OEM
HS902A	0911
HS903	OEM
HS1001	0015
HS1002	0015
HS1003	0015
HS1004	0133
HS1005	0133
HS1006	0133
HS1007	0015
HS1008	0015
HS1009	0015
HS1010	0015
HS1011	0015
HS1012	0015
HS1020	0015
HS-1168	0016
HS-1225	0144
HS-1226	0144
HS-1227	0144
HS-1229	0016

DEVICE TYPE	REPL CODE
HS1395	OEM
HS1516	0201
HS2013-I	OEM
HS2027	0755
HS2030	0118
HS2033	0296
HS2036	0188
HS2038	0188
HS2039	0188
HS2047	0162
HS2051	0162
HS2056	0157
HS2062	0466
HS2068	0062
HS2075	0077
HS2082	0165
HS2091	0057
HS2100	0170
HS2110	0181
HS2120	0052
HS2135	0873
HS2150	0681
HS2165	0416
HS2180	0371
HS2200	0695
HS2220	0700
HS2240	0489
HS2270	0436
HS2300	0195
HS2330	0039
HS3043	OEM
HS3103	0015
HS3104	0015
HS3105	0133
HS3106	OEM
HS3108	0071
HS3110	0071
HS5305	OEM
HS5306	OEM
HS5306A	OEM
HS5307	OEM
HS5308	OEM
HS5308A	OEM
HS5810	0590
HS5811	0786
HS5812	0590
HS5813	0786
HS5814	0590
HS5815	0786
HS5816	0590
HS5817	0786
HS5818	0590
HS5819	0786
HS5820	0590
HS5821	0786
HS5822	0590
HS5823	0786
HS7027	0755
HS7030	0118
HS7033	0296
HS7036	0188
HS7039	0188
HS7043	0274
HS7047	0140
HS7051	0162
HS7056	0157
HS7062	0466
HS7068	0062
HS7075	0077
HS7082	0165
HS7091	0057
HS7100	0170
HS7110	0181
HS7120	0052
HS7135	0873
HS7150	0681
HS7165	0210
HS7180	0371
HS7200	0695
HS7220	0700
HS7240	0489
HS7270	0436
HS7300	0195
HS7330	0039
HS8014	OEM
HS8407	0065
HS9001	OEM
HS9009	OEM
HS9010	0124
HS9096	OEM
HS9501	OEM
HS9502	0124
HS9503	0124
HS9504	OEM
HS9505	0124
HS9506	0124
HS9508	0124
HS9509	0124
HS-40014	0079
HS-40016	0079
HS-40017	0127
HS-40019	0144
HS40019	OEM
HS-40020	0144
HS40021	0007
HS40022	0007
HS40023	0007
HS40024	0007
HS40025	0007

DEVICE TYPE	REPL CODE
HS40026	0086
HS-40027	0037
HS-40030	0111
HS-40031	0037
HS40032	0126
HS-40035	0037
HS-40037	0016
HS-40039	0079
HS-40040	0037
HS-40044	0016
HS-40045	0144
HS-40046	0016
HS-40047	0144
HS-40049	0144
HS40049	0144
HS-40050	0037
HS-40053	2461
HS-40054	0079
HS-40055	0144
HS-40057	0006
HS52005	OEM
HS950707	OEM
HSA1015	0148
HSC015	OEM
HSC-1	0087
HSC1	0071
HSC2	OEM
HSC3	OEM
HSC4	OEM
HSC5	OEM
HSC6	OEM
HSC7	OEM
HSC8	OEM
HSC9	OEM
HSC10	OEM
HSC11	OEM
HSC12	OEM
HSC15	OEM
HSC18	OEM
HSC20	OEM
HSC25	OEM
HSC1815	0076
HSC3921	OEM
HSC3954	OEM
HSC4391	OEM
HSC4392	OEM
HSC4393	OEM
HSC4416	OEM
HSC4416A	OEM
HSC5163	OEM
HSC5457	OEM
HSC5457A	OEM
HSC5458	OEM
HSC5458A	OEM
HSC5459	OEM
HSC5459A	OEM
HSC5484	OEM
HSC5485	OEM
HSC5486	OEM
HSC5638	OEM
HSC5639	OEM
HSC5640	OEM
HSCH-1001	0080
HSFD-1	0071
HSFD1	0102
HSFD-1A	0015
HSFD-1A(SONY-58	0102
HSFD-1Z	0015
HSFD-1Z(SONY-BLANKIN	0139
HSFD-1Z(SONY-STANDBY	0015
HSG5140	OEM
HSG5420	OEM
HSK23	OEM
HSK83	OEM
HSK110	OEM
HSK120	OEM
HSK121	OEM
HSK122	OEM
HSK140/14	OEM
HSK141/10	OEM
HSK142/07	OEM
HSK143/45	OEM
HSK144/37	OEM
HSK145/27	OEM
HSK146/20	OEM
HSK147/14	OEM
HSK148/10	OEM
HSK149/20	OEM
HSK150/14	OEM
HSK152/10	OEM
HSK227	OEM
HSK277	OEM
HSK816	OEM
HSK866A	OEM
HSK869B	OEM
HSK872A	OEM
HSK8008	OEM
HSKE5200	OEM
HSKE11000	OEM
HSM2692	OEM
HSM2693	OEM
HSM2694	OEM
HSM2835	0897
HSM2836	4830
HSM2837	0901
HSM2838	4830
HSM2838C	OEM

DEVICE TYPE	REPL CODE
HSP1001	0133
HSP1007	0133
HSP1010	0133
HSP1011	0133
HSP1013	0133
HSP1020	0604
HSR276	OEM
HSR276S	OEM
HSSH3D4	OEM
HST1050	0074
HST1051	0637
HST1052	0637
HST1053	0637
HST1054	0637
HST1055	0074
HST1056	0637
HST1057	0637
HST1058	0637
HST1059	0637
HST1060	0074
HST1061	0637
HST1062	0637
HST1063	0637
HST1064	0637
HST4451	0283
HST4452	0283
HST4453	0283
HST4454	0283
HST4483	0626
HST5001	0111
HST5002	0283
HST5003	0283
HST5004	0283
HST5005	0283
HST5006	0283
HST5007	0283
HST5008	0283
HST5009	0283
HST5010	0283
HST5051	0283
HST5052	0283
HST5053	0283
HST5054	0283
HST5055	0283
HST5056	0283
HST5501	0626
HST5502	0283
HST5503	0283
HST5504	0283
HST5505	0283
HST5506	0626
HST5507	0283
HST5508	0283
HST5509	0283
HST5510	0283
HST5511	0626
HST5551	0283
HST5552	0283
HST5553	0283
HST5554	0283
HST5555	0283
HST5556	0283
HST5906	0830
HST7401	0626
HST7402	0283
HST7403	0283
HST7411	0626
HST7412	0283
HST7413	0283
HST7414	0626
HST7415	0283
HST7416	0283
HST7417	0626
HST7418	0168
HST7419	0168
HST7901	0168
HST7902	0168
HST7903	0168
HST7904	0168
HST7905	0168
HST7907	0168
HST7908	0168
HST7909	0168
HST7910	0168
HST9001	0626
HST9002	0283
HST9003	0283
HST9004	0626
HST9005	0283
HST9006	0283
HST9007	0626
HST9008	0283
HST9009	0283
HST9010	0626
HST-9201	0103
HST-9205	0103
HST-9206	0103
HST-9210	0103
HSZ12EB3	0999
HT	OEM
HT040519C	2839
HT040519C(2SB405)	0164
HT040519C(2SD72)	0208
HT0405190C	2839
HT1-050	OEM
HT1-050A	OEM
HT1-050B	OEM
HT1-050C	OEM
HT1-050T	OEM

If replacement code is OEM, contact original manufacturer for replacement.

DEVICE TYPE	REPL CODE	DEVICE TYPE	REPL CODE	DEVICE TYPE	REPL CODE	DEVICE TYPE	REPL CODE	DEVICE TYPE	REPL CODE	DEVICE TYPE	REPL CODE	DEVICE TYPE	REPL CODE
HT2-050	OEM	HT4457	OEM	HT5317	OEM	HT104951B-0	0037	HT304580A	0016	HT309451L0	0076	HTS4916	OEM
HT2-050A	OEM	HT4468	OEM	HT5318	OEM	HT104951C	0037	HT304580B	0016	HT309451R0	0076	HTS4966	OEM
HT2-050B	OEM	HT4495	OEM	HT5404	OEM	HT104971A	0126	HT304580C0	0016	HT309452A0	0076	HTS4966B	OEM
HT2-050C	OEM	HT4497	OEM	HT5408	OEM	HT104971A-0	0126	HT304580C0	0079	HT309680B	0086	HTS5637	OEM
HT2-050T	OEM	HT4501	OEM	HT5417A	OEM	HT104971A0	0126	HT304580K	0016	HT309714A-0	0086	HTS5706	OEM
HT3-050	OEM	HT4503A	OEM	HT5422A	OEM	HT104971A-0	0126	HT304580Y0	0016	HT309714A-0	2924	HTS5706C	OEM
HT3-050A	OEM	HT4504	OEM	HT5424	OEM	HT104971A0	0126	HT304580Y0	0079	HT309841B0	0086	HTS5726	OEM
HT3-050B	OEM	HT4504A	OEM	HT5424C	OEM	HT105611	0037	HT304580Z	0016	HT309841B0	0086	HTS5776B	OEM
HT3-050C	OEM	HT4504A-5B2	OEM	HT5425	OEM	HT105611A	0037	HT304581	0016	HT309842A-0	0016	HTS7115	OEM
HT3-050T	OEM	HT4505	OEM	HT5425A	OEM	HT105611B	0037	HT304581A	0016	HT309842A-0	0086	HTS7115T	OEM
HT4-050	OEM	HT4506	OEM	HT5426	OEM	HT105611B0	0037	HT304581B	0016	HT310001F	0111	HTV80	OEM
HT4-050A	OEM	HT4506A	OEM	HT5426A	OEM	HT105611B0	0037	HT304581B-0	0016	HT310002A	0111	HTV90	OEM
HT4-050B	OEM	HT4506AS	OEM	HT5428	OEM	HT105611C	0037	HT304581B-0	0079	HT311621B	0042	HTV100	OEM
HT4-050C	OEM	HT4511	OEM	HT5434B	OEM	HT105612B	0006	HT304581C	0016	HT312131C0	0191	HTV300	OEM
HT4-050T	OEM	HT4515	OEM	HT5438	OEM	HT105621B-0	0037	HT304601B0	0151	HT313171R	0155	HTV350	OEM
HT5-050	OEM	HT4516	OEM	HT5465A	OEM	HT105621B0	0037	HT304601B0	0079	HT313172A	0155	HTV400	OEM
HT5-050A	OEM	HT4532A	OEM	HT5467A	OEM	HT105621B-0	0150	HT304601C0	0144	HT313181C	0086	HTV450	OEM
HT5-050B	OEM	HT4541	OEM	HT5469B	OEM	HT105621B0	0037	HT304601C0	0079	HT313271T	1212	HTZ11BL	0181
HT5-050C	OEM	HT4609	OEM	HT5478E	OEM	HT105641C	0688	HT304611B	0144	HT313272B	0111	HV0000102	0004
HT5-050T	OEM	HT4611	OEM	HT5490B	OEM	HT105641D	0688	HT304861	0086	HT313591C0	0151	HV0000105	0139
HT6-100	OEM	HT4611A	OEM	HT5493	OEM	HT105641H	0203	HT304861A	0086	HT313592B	0151	HV0000105-0	0015
HT6-100A	OEM	HT4612A	OEM	HT5498S	OEM	HT105642B	0688	HT304861B	0016	HT313681B0	1779	HV0000202	0143
HT6-100B	OEM	HT4613A	OEM	HT5505	OEM	HT105642C0	0203	HT304911	0178	HT313831X	0018	HV0000206	0120
HT6-100C	OEM	HT4614A	OEM	HT5506B	OEM	HT106731B	0037	HT304911A	0178	HT313832C	0018	HV0000212	OEM
HT6-100T	OEM	HT4615A	OEM	HT5511	OEM	HT106731B0	0148	HT304911B	0178	HT313841R	0018	HV0000302	0127
HT7-100	OEM	HT4615B	OEM	HT5513	OEM	HT107211T	0688	HT304941X	0103	HT314071Q	2271	HV0000405	0164
HT7-100A	OEM	HT4616A	OEM	HT5516	OEM	HT107331Q0	0006	HT304961C-0	0555	HT316751M0	0076	HV0000405-0	0136
HT7-100B	OEM	HT4616B	OEM	HT5516B	OEM	HT200540	0004	HT304961C-0	0555	HT318291D0	0016	HV0000705	0015
HT7-100C	OEM	HT4620A	OEM	HT5520	OEM	HT200540A	0004	HT304971A	0086	HT31909100	0076	HV00001050	0133
HT7-100T	OEM	HT4620C	OEM	HT5520B	OEM	HT200541	0004	HT304971A0	0086	HT31957100	2684	HV00001060	0139
HT8-100	OEM	HT4629	OEM	HT5523	OEM	HT200541A	0004	HT304971A0	0086	HT340519C	0038	HV-03SS	OEM
HT8-100A	OEM	HT4635	OEM	HT5523D	OEM	HT200541B	0004	HT304971B	0086	HT400721	0208	HV-05	0290
HT8-100B	OEM	HT4635A	OEM	HT5523E	OEM	HT200541B-0	0004	HT305351B0	0127	HT400721A	0208	HV05	OEM
HT8-100C	OEM	HT4636	OEM	HT5523F	OEM	HT200541C	0050	HT305351C0	0144	HT400721B	0208	HV-06SS	OEM
HT8-100T	OEM	HT4637C	OEM	HT5523G	OEM	HT200561	0004	HT305351C0	0079	HT400721C	0208	HV-08	OEM
HT25	OEM	HT4648	OEM	HT5525B	OEM	HT200561A	0004	HT305361E	0532	HT400721D	0208	HV-08SS	OEM
HT25A	OEM	HT4651A	OEM	HT5535A	OEM	HT200561B	0004	HT305361G	0532	HT400721E	0208	HV2.5-10	OEM
HT33-02	OEM	HT4652	OEM	HT5535B	OEM	HT200561C	0004	HT305371E	0016	HT400723	0208	HV2.5-10F	OEM
HT90A	OEM	HT4653	OEM	HT5535C	OEM	HT200561C-0	0004	HT305642B	0688	HT400723A	0208	HV2.5-12	OEM
HT91A	OEM	HT4673	OEM	HT5539C	OEM	HT200751B	0004	HT306441	0079	HT400723B	0208	HV2.5-12F	OEM
HT92A	OEM	HT4677D	OEM	HT5545	OEM	HT200770B	0004	HT306441A	0111	HT400770B	0208	HV2.5-15	OEM
HT93A	OEM	HT4705C	OEM	HT5550	OEM	HT200771	0004	HT306441A0	0086	HT401191	0103	HV2.5-15F	OEM
HT94A	OEM	HT4706	OEM	HT5563A	OEM	HT200771A	0004	HT306441A0	0086	HT401191A	0103	HV2.5-18	OEM
HT95A	OEM	HT4706A	OEM	HT5566A	OEM	HT200771B	0004	HT306441B	0016	HT401191B	0103	HV2.5-18F	OEM
HT96A	OEM	HT4712B	OEM	HT5580-8F	OEM	HT200771C	0004	HT306441B-0	0016	HT401193A0	0177	HV5	OEM
HT100	0037	HT4712C	OEM	HT5588	OEM	HT201721A	0004	HT306441B0	0016	HT401301B0	0178	HV5-5	1780
HT101	0037	HT4714	OEM	HT5648D-8K01	OEM	HT201721D	0004	HT306441B-0	0086	HT401301B0	0178	HV5-5F	1780
HT102	0155	HT4723	OEM	HT5654-9B24	OEM	HT201725A	0004	HT306441B0	0086	HT402352B	0042	HV5-7	1780
HT103	0155	HT4724	OEM	HT5681F	OEM	HT201752A	OEM	HT306441C	0016	HT403131E0	0042	HV5-7F	1780
HT321B-0	OEM	HT4724A	OEM	HT5684B	OEM	HT201782A	0004	HT306441C-0	0016	HT403131E0	0419	HV5-10	1780
HT400	0016	HT4724B	OEM	HT5687C	OEM	HT201861A	0004	HT306441C-0	0086	HT403132A0	0042	HV5-10F	1780
HT401	0016	HT4734B	OEM	HT5688E	OEM	HT201871L	0004	HT306442A	0111	HT403151E	4186	HV5-12	OEM
HT559	OEM	HT4736	OEM	HT5718A	OEM	HT203243A	1056	HT306442B	0111	HT403152A	4186	HV5-12F	OEM
HT1067A	OEM	HT4753A	OEM	HT5751B-0A27	OEM	HT203701	0004	HT306451	0144	HT403152B	0178	HV5-15	OEM
HT1077	OEM	HT4763	OEM	HT5751B-9J24	OEM	HT203701A	0004	HT306451A	0127	HT403523A	0208	HV5-15F	OEM
HT4204	OEM	HT4763-6D	OEM	HT5755A	OEM	HT203701B	0004	HT306451B	0144	HT404001E	0590	HV5-20	OEM
HT4205	OEM	HT4763-7A	OEM	HT6202	OEM	HT204051	0164	HT306451H	0079	HT600011F	0037	HV5-20F	OEM
HT4206	OEM	HT4765	OEM	HT6210B	OEM	HT204051B	0164	HT306681C	0127	HT600011H	0037	HV5-25	OEM
HT4214	OEM	HT4765A	OEM	HT6213A	OEM	HT204051C	0164	HT306962A-0	0144	HT70011100	3136	HV5-25F	OEM
HT4214-1L	OEM	HT4765B	OEM	HT6217A	OEM	HT204051D	0164	HT306962A-0	0079	HT800011F	0016	HV5-30	OEM
HT4215	OEM	HT4765C	OEM	HT6502A	OEM	HT204051E	0164	HT307321A	0016	HT800011G	0016	HV5-30F	OEM
HT4215-1L	OEM	HT4773	OEM	HT6506B	OEM	HT204053	0164	HT307321B-0	0016	HT800011H	0016	HV5-40	OEM
HT4216-1L	OEM	HT4784A	OEM	HT6506C	OEM	HT204053A	0164	HT307321B-0	0079	HT800011K	0016	HV5-40F	OEM
HT4226	OEM	HT4785	OEM	HT6507B	OEM	HT204053B	0164	HT307322A	0111	HT800012F	0086	HV8	3614
HT4233	OEM	HT4785B	OEM	HT6508A	OEM	HT204071D	0160	HT307331B	0016	HT800191H	0086	HV10	3614
HT-4234	OEM	HT4785D	OEM	HT6508B	OEM	HT204736	0222	HT307331C	0111	HT1001510	0004	HV10-5	1780
HT4234	OEM	HT4793F	OEM	HT7109B	OEM	HT303620B	0016	HT307331C0	0079	HT2000771C	0004	HV10-5F	1780
HT4235	OEM	HT4795	OEM	HT7120-8D13	OEM	HT303711A	0191	HT307331C0	0111	HT2040710A	0160	HV10-7	1780
HT4235A	OEM	HT4795A	OEM	HT7127B	OEM	HT303711A-0	0144	HT307341	0086	HT2046710	0222	HV10-7F	1780
HT4235B	OEM	HT4806B	OEM	HT7188	OEM	HT303711A0	0079	HT307341A	0086	HT3036201	0079	HV10-10	1780
HT4236	OEM	HT4814C	OEM	HT7222B	OEM	HT303711A-0	0079	HT307341B	0079	HT3036210	0016	HV10-10F	1780
HT4245	OEM	HT4815C	OEM	HT7222C	OEM	HT303711A0	0079	HT307341C-0	0079	HT3037010	0144	HV10-12	OEM
HT4245A	OEM	HT4816B	OEM	HT9001P	OEM	HT303711B	0191	HT307341C-0	0086	HT3037201	0144	HV10-12F	OEM
HT4245B	OEM	HT4822	OEM	HT10234UB	0050	HT303711B-0	0079	HT307342B	0086	HT3037201A	0144	HV10-15	OEM
HT4245C	OEM	HT4832	OEM	HT20436A	0222	HT303711B0	0079	HT307342C	0076	HT3037201B	0144	HV10-15F	OEM
HT4255	OEM	HT4832C	OEM	HT20451A	0164	HT303711B-0	0079	HT307720B	0127	HT3037210	0016	HV10-20	OEM
HT4256A	OEM	HT4842C	OEM	HT30491C	0086	HT303711B0	0079	HT307721C	0127	HT3037210-0	0016	HV10-20F	OEM
HT4264	OEM	HT4843B	OEM	HT30494	0103	HT303711C	0127	HT307721D	0127	HT3037210-0	0079	HV10-25	OEM
HT4265B	OEM	HT4871	OEM	HT30494X	0103	HT303720A	0144	HT307902B	1488	HT3037310	0127	HV10-25F	OEM
HT4265C	OEM	HT4885	OEM	HT31041C0	0113	HT303721-0	0016	HT308013-B	1211	HT3038013-B	0127	HV10-30	OEM
HT4273	OEM	HT4885S	OEM	HT36441B	0111	HT303721D	0016	HT308281B0	1211	HT3073310	0079	HV10-30F	OEM
HT4275	OEM	HT4886	OEM	HT38281D	0079	HT303730	0016	HT308281C	0079	HT3082810	0086	HV10-40	OEM
HT4285	OEM	HT4895	OEM	HT-49356	OEM	HT303730A	0016	HT308281D	1211	HT6000210	0037	HV10-40F	OEM
HT4364	OEM	HT4904	OEM	HT55706C	OEM	HT303801	0127	HT308281G	1211	HT7000310	0899	HV10E1	OEM
HT4401	OEM	HT4944A	OEM	HT101011X	0136	HT303801A	0127	HT308281H	1211	HT7000410-0	OEM	HV10P1	OEM
HT4403	OEM	HT4946D	OEM	HT101021A	0136	HT303801A0	0127	HT308281O	0079	HT7000410-0	0126	HV12	0004
HT4404	OEM	HT4964	OEM	HT102341	0050	HT303801A0	0079	HT308282A	0079	HT8000101	0233	HV14	3614
HT4407	OEM	HT4971D	OEM	HT102341A	0050	HT303801B	0127	HT308282A-0	0079	HT8000710	0015	HV-15	0143
HT4412	OEM	HT4974C	OEM	HT102341B	0050	HT303801B-0	0127	HT308282A-0	0079	HT8001210	0086	HV15	0143
HT4413	OEM	HT5111A	OEM	HT102341C	0050	HT303801B0	0127	HT308282B	0111	HT8001310	0086	HV-15(RECT)	0344
HT4414	OEM	HT5125	OEM	HT102351	0050	HT303801B-0	0079	HT308291A	0016	HT8001610	0007	HV15E1	OEM
HT4415A	OEM	HT5126	OEM	HT102351A	0050	HT303801B0	0079	HT308291A-0	0127	HT8001710	0007	HV-15F	OEM
HT4421A	OEM	HT5163	OEM	HT103501	0050	HT303801C	0127	HT308291A-0	0016	HT8001810	0016	HV15P1	OEM
HT4422	OEM	HT5164A	OEM	HT103501A	0136	HT303801C0	0127	HT308291B	0016	HT9000310	0103	HV16	0004
HT4425	OEM	HT5165	OEM	HT103531C	0136	HT303801C0	0079	HT308291B-0	0016	HT9000410-0	0103	HV17	0004
HT4429	OEM	HT5166	OEM	HT103541B	0136	HT30387100	0544	HT308291B0	0151	HT9000410-0	0103	HV17B	0004
HT4437	OEM	HT5181	OEM	HT104861	0086	HT303941	0144	HT308291B-0	0079	HT30373100	0016	HV17C	OEM
HT4437-5A	OEM	HT5197A	OEM	HT104861A	0086	HT303941A	0144	HT308291B0	0151	HT30387100	0544	HV18	OEM
HT4438	OEM	HT5198	OEM	HT104861B	0086	HT303941B	0144	HT308291C	0151	HT30733100	0111	HV19	0004
HT4438A	OEM	HT5201	OEM	HT104941B-0	0037	HT304508K	0079	HT308291D0	0151	HT30945120	0079	HV-20	0344
HT4440	OEM	HT5202	OEM	HT104941B-0	0037	HT304531	0016	HT308301B0	0042	HT31909100	0076	HV20E1	OEM
HT4442	OEM	HT5221A	OEM	HT104941C-0	0037	HT304531A	0016	HT308301B0	0178	HT31957100	2684	HV20E2	OEM
HT4443	OEM	HT5239	OEM	HT104941C0	0037	HT304531B	0016	HT309002A0	1212	HT32362280	1218	HV-20F	OEM
HT4444	OEM	HT5263	OEM	HT104941C-0	0688	HT304531C	0016	HT309291C	1060	HT70003100	OEM	HV20G	OEM
HT4444A	OEM	HT5271E	OEM	HT104941C0	0150	HT304540A0	0144	HT309291E	0127	HT90003100	OEM	HV20P1	OEM
HT4445	OEM	HT5280E	OEM	HT104942A	0688	HT304540A0	0079	HT309301C	2195	HTK0022	OEM	HV20P2	OEM
HT4446	OEM	HT5291C	OEM	HT104951A-0	0037	HT304540B0	0016	HT309301D	2195	HTK0054	3104	HV-21	0344
HT4448	OEM	HT5292	OEM	HT104951A-0	0150	HT304540B0	0079	HT309301E	0111	HTK0062	0321	HV-21F	OEM
HT4453	OEM	HT5293	OEM	HT104951B	0037	HT304580	0016	HT309301F	0111	HTS1068C	OEM	HV-23	0139

434

If replacement code is OEM, contact original manufacturer for replacement.

DEVICE TYPE	REPL CODE
HV23	0139
HV-23(ELGIN)	1914
HV23-G	0139
HV-23BL	0143
HV23F	0139
HV-23G	0139
HV23G	0139
HV-23G(BL)	0133
HV23G(WT)	1914
HV-23GB	0139
HV23GB	0139
HV-23GBL	1914
HV23GBL	1914
HV23GW	0139
HV23GWT	1914
HV23GY	0139
HV-23GYL	0139
HV-25	0133
HV25	0016
HV-25(DIODE)	0133
HV25(HITACHI)	0133
HV-25(RCA)	0133
HV25-5	1780
HV25-5F	1780
HV25-7	1780
HV25-7F	1780
HV25-10	1780
HV25-10F	1780
HV25-12	OEM
HV25-12F	OEM
HV25-15	OEM
HV25-15F	OEM
HV25-20	OEM
HV25-20F	OEM
HV25-25	OEM
HV25-25F	OEM
HV25-30	OEM
HV25-30F	OEM
HV25-40	OEM
HV25-40F	OEM
HV25E2	OEM
HV25P2	OEM
HV-26	0015
HV26	1914
HV-26G	0015
HV26G	OEM
HV-27	0133
HV-30	OEM
HV30E2	OEM
HV30E3	OEM
HV-30F	OEM
HV30G	OEM
HV30P2	OEM
HV30P3	OEM
HV-40	OEM
HV40E3	OEM
HV40E4	OEM
HV-40F	OEM
HV40G	OEM
HV40P3	OEM
HV40P4	OEM
HV40TN	OEM
HV-46	0120
HV46	0120
HV46G	0120
HV-46GR	0015
HV460	0120
HV46R	0120
HV-50	OEM
HV50E4	OEM
HV50E6	OEM
HV-50F	OEM
HV50G	OEM
HV50ML	OEM
HV-60	OEM
HV60E6	OEM
HV-60F	OEM
HV60G	OEM
HV60TN	OEM
HV70	OEM
HV70E6	OEM
HV70G	OEM
HV70ML	OEM
HV75	OEM
HV-80	0139
HV80	0139
HV80E	OEM
HV80E6	OEM
HV80G	OEM
HV90E	OEM
HV90G	OEM
HV-100	0015
HV100	OEM
HV100E	OEM
HV100G	OEM
HV106	OEM
HV106F	OEM
HV108	OEM
HV108F	OEM
HV110	OEM
HV110F	OEM
HV112	OEM
HV112F	OEM
HV115	OEM
HV115F	OEM
HV120E	OEM
HV140E	OEM
HV160E	OEM
HV180E	OEM
HV200E	OEM
HV206	OEM
HV206F	OEM
HV208	OEM
HV208F	OEM
HV210	OEM
HV210F	OEM
HV212	OEM
HV212F	OEM
HV215	OEM
HV215F	OEM
HV236WT	OEM
HV-801	0143
HV9601	0030
HVB2	OEM
HVB4	OEM
HVB6	OEM
HVB10	OEM
HVB20	OEM
HVB30	OEM
HVB40	OEM
HVB50	OEM
HVC2	OEM
HVC4	OEM
HVC6	OEM
HVC10	OEM
HVC-15	0344
HVC-15F	OEM
HVC-20	0344
HVC-20F	OEM
HVC-25	OEM
HVC-25F	OEM
HVC-30	OEM
HVC-30F	OEM
HVC-40	OEM
HVC-40F	OEM
HVC-50	OEM
HVC-50F	OEM
HVC-60	OEM
HVC-60F	OEM
HVC-V87	OEM
HVD-1	2949
HVD-2	2950
HVD2	OEM
HVD-3	2952
HVD-4	2951
HVD4	OEM
HVD6	OEM
HVD10	OEM
HVD-12	5265
HVD20	OEM
HVD30	OEM
HVD40	OEM
HVD50	OEM
HVE2	OEM
HVE4	OEM
HVE6	OEM
HVK89	OEM
HVK1109-866	OEM
HVK1110-872	OEM
HVM16	OEM
HVM89	OEM
HVM1600	0190
HVMRA	0769
HVP5	3613
HVP8	3613
HVP10	3613
HVP12	3617
HVP14	OEM
HVP15	OEM
HVP16	OEM
HVPR10-12	3617
HVR-1X-01A	OEM
HVR-3B	6644
HVR-3H	OEM
HVR-3H2	OEM
HVR5	OEM
HVR-5A	6644
HVT-5	OEM
HVT-15SS	0201
HVT-20SS	0286
HVT-22	0286
HVT-22DA	0201
HVT22SS	OEM
HVT-25SS	0374
HVT30	OEM
HVT-30S	0374
HVT-30SS	0374
HVT200	0233
HVT400	1061
HVT401	OEM
HVT600	OEM
HVT800	OEM
HVT900	OEM
HVT1000	OEM
HVT-DF18	OEM
HVT-DF25	OEM
HVTR60	OEM
HVU359TRF	OEM
HW6.8	0025
HW6.8A	0025
HW6.8B	0025
HW7.5	0644
HW7.5A	0644
HW7.5B	0644
HW8.2	0244
HW8.2A	0244
HW8.2B	0244
HW9.1	0012
HW9.1A	0012
HW9.1B	0012
HW9.81B	0012
HW10	0170
HW10A	0170
HW10B	0170
HW11	0313
HW11A	0313
HW11B	0789
HW12	0137
HW12A	0137
HW12B	0137
HW13	0361
HW13A	0361
HW13B	0361
HW15	0002
HW15A	0002
HW15B	0002
HW16	0416
HW16A	0416
HW16B	0416
HW18	0490
HW18A	0490
HW18B	0490
HW20	0526
HW20A	0526
HW20B	0526
HW22	0560
HW22A	0560
HW22B	0560
HW24	0398
HW24A	0398
HW24B	0398
HW27	0436
HW27A	0436
HW27B	0436
HW30	0721
HW30A	0721
HW30B	0721
HW33	0039
HW33A	0039
HW33B	0039
HW36	0814
HW36A	0814
HW36B	0814
HW39	0346
HW39A	0346
HW39B	0346
HW43	0925
HW43A	0925
HW43A3A	OEM
HW43B	0925
HW47	0993
HW47A	0993
HW47B	0993
HW51	0497
HW51A	0497
HW51B	0497
HW56	0863
HW56A	0863
HW56B	1823
HW62	0778
HW62A	0778
HW62B	0778
HW68	1258
HW68A	1258
HW68B	2144
HW75	1181
HW75A	1181
HW75B	1181
HW82	0327
HW82A	0327
HW82B	0327
HW91	1301
HW91A	1301
HW91B	1301
HW100	0098
HW100A	0098
HW100B	0398
HW110	0149
HW110A	0149
HW110B	0149
HW120	0186
HW120A	0186
HW120B	0186
HW130	0213
HW130A	0213
HW130B	0213
HW150	0028
HW150A	0028
HW150B	0028
HW160	0255
HW160A	0255
HW160B	0255
HW180	0363
HW180A	0363
HW180B	0363
HW200	0417
HW200A	0417
HW200B	0417
HW2061	OEM
HW2063	OEM
HW2063A	OEM
HW9062	OEM
HW9362	OEM
HW9364	OEM
HX20G	OEM
HX30G	OEM
HX40G	OEM
HX50G	OEM
HX50ML	OEM
HX60G	OEM
HX70G	OEM
HX70ML	OEM
HX80E	OEM
HX80G	OEM
HX90E	OEM
HX90G	OEM
HX100E	OEM
HX100G	OEM
HX120E	OEM
HX140E	OEM
HX160E	OEM
HX180E	OEM
HX200E	OEM
HX50001	0144
HX50002	0016
HX50003	0127
HX-50063	0079
HX-50072	0079
HX-50091	0224
HX-50092	0079
HX-50094	0037
HX-50097	0079
HX-50102	0895
HX-50103	0590
HX-50104	0786
HX-50105	0037
HX-50106	2039
HX-50107	0079
HX-50108	0086
HX-50109	0431
HX-50110	0127
HX-50112	0037
HX-50113	0079
HX-50128	0037
HX-50161	0079
HX-50172	0016
HX-50176	0037
HX-50180	0396
HX-50181	0079
HY5C2	0582
HY93C46	OEM
HY-101	OEM
HY-101SHINEI	OEM
HY6589	OEM
HY6590	OEM
HY3045801C	0016
HYB4116-P2	0518
HYB4116-P3	0518
HYB4164-P2	2341
HZ2	OEM
HZ2(H)	OEM
HZ2ALL	4256
HZ2B	OEM
HZ2B1	OEM
HZ2BLL	OEM
HZ2C	1268
HZ2C1	1266
HZ2C2	1268
HZ2CLL	1266
HZ2LL	OEM
HZ2.0P	OEM
HZ2.2P	OEM
HZ2.4P	OEM
HZ2.7E	0755
HZ2.7P	1302
HZ3	0118
HZ3(H)	0118
HZ-3A	OEM
HZ3A	OEM
HZ3A07	0118
HZ3A2	5833
HZ-3A3	OEM
HZ3A3	6824
HZ3ALL	0672
HZ3B	0118
HZ3B2	0118
HZ3B3	6824
HZ3BLL	0118
HZ3C	OEM
HZ3C1	0296
HZ3C-2	0296
HZ3C2	0296
HZ3C2-01	0296
HZ3C3	0296
HZ3D	OEM
HZ3H	0296
HZ3LL	0118
HZ3.0E	0118
HZ3.0P	1703
HZ3.3E	0296
HZ3.3P	0188
HZ3.6	0372
HZ3.6CP	0372
HZ3.6CPTA	0372
HZ3.6E	0372
HZ3.6P	0188
HZ3.9E	0036
HZ3.9P	0451
HZ4	0036
HZ-4(A)	0372
HZ-4(A)1	0372
HZ4(A1)	0372
HZ-4(A1)1	0372
HZ4(A1)1	0372
HZ4(H)	0036
HZ4A	OEM
HZ4A04	0036
HZ-4A1	0372
HZ4A-1	0372
HZ4A1	0372
HZ-4A2	0372
HZ4A-2	0372
HZ4A2	0372
HZ4A3	5904
HZ-4B	0036
HZ4B	0274
HZ4B-1	0036
HZ4B1	0036
HZ4B1S3	OEM
HZ-4B2	0036
HZ4B-2	0036
HZ4B2	0036
HZ4B3	0036
HZ4BC	OEM
HZ4C	0274
HZ4C1	0274
HZ4C2	0274
HZ4C3	5142
HZ4C11	OEM
HZ4CLL	OEM
HZ4CZ	OEM
HZ4H	0451
HZ4H4	0372
HZ4HB	0036
HZ4HC	0274
HZ4LL	0036
HZ4.3E	0274
HZ4.3P	0528
HZ4.7CPTA	OEM
HZ4.7E	0140
HZ4.7P	0446
HZ-5	0162
HZ5	0140
HZ5(C)1	0582
HZ5(C)3	0582
HZ5(H)	0140
HZ5A	OEM
HZ5A1	5142
HZ5A2	OEM
HZ5ALL	OEM
HZ-5B	0140
HZ5B	0140
HZ5B-1	0140
HZ5B1	5986
HZ5B-1-05	0140
HZ5B-2	0140
HZ5B2	0140
HZ5B3	0041
HZ-5C	0582
HZ5C	0041
HZ-5C1	0041
HZ5C-1	0041
HZ5C1	0248
HZ5C1TD	0041
HZ5C-2	0041
HZ5C2	0041
HZ-5C3	0582
HZ5C-3	0582
HZ5C3	0582
HZ5CLL	0582
HZ5LL	0140
HZ5.0C2	0582
HZ5.1E	0041
HZ5.1P	0162
HZ5.6E	0253
HZ5.6P	0157
HZ6	0091
HZ-6(A)	0877
HZ6(A)1	0877
HZ6(B)	0091
HZ6(B)1	0877
HZ6(B)2	0157
HZ6(B)3	0091
HZ6(B2)	0157
HZ6(C)	OEM
HZ6(C)-1	0091
HZ6(C)1	0091
HZ6(C)3	0292
HZ-6(C3)	0466
HZ6(H)	0091
HZ6(H)L	0091
HZ-6A	0877
HZ6A	0582
HZ6A-1	0877
HZ6A1	0877
HZ6A1L	0582
HZ6A1V	0041
HZ-6A2	0253
HZ6A2	0041
HZ6A2L	OEM
HZ6A-3	0877
HZ6A3	5348
HZ6A19	0091
HZ-6B	0253
HZ6B	0253
HZ-6B1	0877
HZ6B1	0253
HZ-6B2	0877
HZ6B2	0157
HZ6B2/TA	0877
HZ6B2L	OEM
HZ-6B3	0091
HZ6B3	0091
HZ6B3L	0091
HZ6B20	0091
HZ-6C	0091
HZ6C	0466
HZ-6C-1	0091
HZ-6C1	0091
HZ6C-1	0091
HZ6C1	0091
HZ6C2	0466
HZ6C2L	0466
HZ-6C-3	0466
HZ-6C3	0292
HZ6C3	0466
HZ6C21	0292
HZ6CV	0091
HZ6L	0091
HZ-6L-B2	0091
HZ6L-B2	0091
HZ6LB2	5348
HZ6V	0091
HZ-6Z	0091
HZ6.2E	0466
HZ6.2P	0631
HZ6.2PB	0631
HZ6.3	0631
HZ6.8E	0062
HZ6.8P	0025
HZ-7	0062
HZ7	0062
HZ7(A)	0062
HZ-7(B)	0062
HZ7(B)	0062
HZ7(B)1	0062
HZ7(B)2	0062
HZ7(B)3	0062
HZ7(C)	0077
HZ7(C)1	0077
HZ7(C)3	0077
HZ7(H)	0062
HZ7(H)L	0062
HZ-7A	0062
HZ7A	0062
HZ-7A(B)	0644
HZ7A-1	0062
HZ7A1	0466
HZ7A2	OEM
HZ7A2L	OEM
HZ7A-3	0062
HZ7A3	0062
HZ7A33	0025
HZ-7AGR	0025
HZ-7B	0025
HZ7B	0062
HZ7B-1	0062
HZ7B1	3335
HZ-7B2	0062
HZ7B2	0062
HZ7B2L	OEM
HZ7B2LV1	0062
HZ-7B3	0062
HZ7B3	OEM
HZ7B3L	OEM
HZ-7C	0062
HZ7C	0077
HZ-7C-1	0077
HZ-7C1	0077
HZ7C1	0077
HZ7C2	6220
HZ7C2L	OEM
HZ7C3	0077
HZ-7GR	0062
HZ7H	0644
HZ7L	0062
HZ7LB2	OEM
HZ-7NB	0062
HZ7.5E	0077
HZ7.5P	0644
HZ8.2E	0165
HZ8.2P	0244
HZ-9	0012
HZ9	0057
HZ9(A)1	0165
HZ9(A)3	0165
HZ9(C)	0057
HZ9(C)1	0057
HZ9(C)3	0057
HZ9(H)	0318
HZ9(H)L	0318
HZ9-C1	0057
HZ-9A	0318
HZ9A	0318
HZ-9A1	0165
HZ9A-1	0165
HZ9A1	0165
HZ-9A2	0165
HZ9A-2	0165
HZ9A2	0165
HZ9A3	0165
HZ9A26	OEM
HZ9AL	OEM
HZ-9B	0012
HZ9B	1075
HZ9B1	6895
HZ9B-2	0057
HZ9B2	6895
HZ9B-3	0057
HZ9B3	0318
HZ9B24	0057
HZ9BZ	0318
HZ-9C	0057
HZ9C	OEM
HZ-9C1	0057
HZ9C1	0057
HZ9C-2	0057
HZ9C2	0057
HZ-9C3	0057
HZ9C-3	0057
HZ9C3	6405
HZ-9C-GR	OEM
HZ9H	0012
HZ9L	0057
HZ9.1	0057
HZ9.1B1	0012
HZ9.1E	0057
HZ9.1P	0012
HZ9.1PB	0012
HZ10E	0064
HZ10P	0170
HZ-11	0313
HZ11	0181
HZ-11(A)	0313
HZ11(A)	0248
HZ11(A1)	0064
HZ-11(B)	0313
HZ11(B)	0248
HZ11(B)2	0181
HZ-11(C)	0313
HZ11(C)	0248
HZ-11(C)-T2	0248
HZ-11(C)T2	0181
HZ-11(C)TZ	0181
HZ11(H)	0181
HZ11(H)L	0181
HZ-11A	0248
HZ11A	0064
HZ11A/B	OEM
HZ11A/B/C	OEM
HZ-11A-1	0181
HZ-11A1	0181
HZ11A1	0064
HZ11A2	1249
HZ11A-3	0248
HZ11A3	1249
HZ-11ABC	0181
HZ-11B	0248
HZ11B	0181
HZ-11B1	0064
HZ11B1	0064
HZ11B1V	0064
HZ-11B2	0181
HZ11B-2	0181
HZ11B2	1249
HZ11B-2L	0181
HZ11B2L	0181
HZ11B-2LTA	0181
HZ-11B-3	OEM
HZ-11C	0248
HZ11C	0181
HZ11C1L	OEM
HZ11C2	0181
HZ-11C2L	0181
HZ11C2L	0181
HZ11C-3	0181
HZ11C25	0052
HZ11E	0181
HZ11H	0313
HZ11L	0181
HZ-11LC2	0181
HZ11LC2	0181
HZ11P	0313
HZ-12	0137
HZ12	0053
HZ-12(A)	0052
HZ12(A)	0052
HZ12(A)1	0999
HZ12(A)2	0999
HZ-12(B)	0052
HZ12(B)	0052
HZ-12(B)1	0999
HZ12(B)1	0999
HZ12(B)2	0053
HZ-12(C)	0052
HZ12(C)	0052
HZ-12(C1)	0052
HZ12(C1)	0052
HZ-12(C2)	0999
HZ12(C2)	0999
HZ-12(C3)	0999
HZ12(C3)	0999
HZ12(H)	0053
HZ12(H)L	0053
HZ12-3	0053
HZ12-C	0052
HZ-12A	0052
HZ12A	0052
HZ12A1	1368
HZ12A2	0999
HZ-12A3	0052
HZ12A-3	0052
HZ12A3	0999
HZ-12ABC	0052
HZ-12B	0053
HZ12B	0053
HZ-12B1	0999
HZ12B-1	0053
HZ12B1	0999
HZ-12B2	0052
HZ12B-2	0053
HZ12B2	0053
HZ12B2L	OEM

If replacement code is OEM, contact original manufacturer for replacement.

DEVICE TYPE	REPL CODE
HZ12B-3	0053
HZ12B3	1389
HZ12B14	0999
HZ12B14(TP)	0999
HZ12BL2	OEM
HZ-12C	0052
HZ12C	0052
HZ12C1	1389
HZ-12C3	0999
HZ12C-3	0873
HZ12C3	0999
HZ12E	0052
HZ12H	0361
HZ12L	0052
HZ12P	0137
HZ12PB	0999
HZ13E	0053
HZ13P	0100
HZ-15	0681
HZ15	0681
HZ15(H)	0681
HZ15(H)L	0681
HZ15-1	0873
HZ15-2	1097
HZ15-3	0681
HZ15E	0681
HZ15H	0002
HZ15L	0681
HZ15P	0002
HZ15PB	0002
HZ16	0440
HZ16(H)	0440
HZ16(H)L	0440
HZ16-2	1220
HZ16-3	0210
HZ16E	0440
HZ16H	0416
HZ16L	0440
HZ16P	0416
HZ18	0371
HZ18(H)	0371
HZ18(H)L	0371
HZ18-09	0371
HZ18-1	0210
HZ18-2	0371
HZ18-3	0371
HZ18-3L	OEM
HZ18E	0371
HZ18L	0371
HZ18P	0490
HZ20	0695
HZ20(H)	0695
HZ20(H)L	0695
HZ20-04	0695
HZ20-04(AU)	0695
HZ20-1L	0695
HZ20-2	0695
HZ20-3	0695
HZ20-3L	0695
HZ20-3T2	0695
HZ20-3TS	0695
HZ20-BL	OEM
HZ20E	0695
HZ20L	0695
HZ-20L1	OEM
HZ20P	0526
HZ20TE	0695
HZ-20VC	0526
HZ22	0700
HZ22(H)	0700
HZ22(H)L	0700
HZ22-01	4855
HZ22-01T2	0700
HZ22-04	0700
HZ22-1	0700
HZ22-2	0700
HZ22-2L	0700
HZ22-3	0700
HZ22-3L	OEM
HZ22E	0700
HZ22H	0560
HZ22L	0700
HZ22L-3	0700
HZ22L3	0700
HZ22P	0560
HZ24	0489
HZ24(H)	0489
HZ24(H)L	0489
HZ24-1L	0489
HZ24-2	0489
HZ-24-2L	0489
HZ24-2L	0489
HZ24-12	0489
HZ24BP	OEM
HZ24E	0489
HZ24H	0398
HZ24L	0489
HZ24L-2	0489
HZ24L2	2448
HZ24P	0398
HZ27	0450
HZ27(H)	0450
HZ27(H)L	0450
HZ-27-1	0709
HZ27-1	2229
HZ27-2	0450
HZ-27BP	0450
HZ27BP	0450
HZ27E	0450

DEVICE TYPE	REPL CODE
HZ27H	0436
HZ27L	0450
HZ27P	0436
HZ30	0195
HZ30(H)	0195
HZ30(H)L	0195
HZ30-1	0195
HZ30-1L	0195
HZ30-1T	OEM
HZ30-2	2419
HZ30-2L	0195
HZ30E	0195
HZ30H	0721
HZ30L	0195
HZ30P	0721
HZ30PB	0721
HZ33	0166
HZ33(H)	0166
HZ33(H)L	0166
HZ33-2	2659
HZ33-2L	0166
HZ33-3L	OEM
HZ33E	0166
HZ33H	0039
HZ33L	0166
HZ33P	0039
HZ33S1	0166
HZ-35	0010
HZ35	0010
HZ35-TP	0010
HZ35TP	2876
HZ-36	0010
HZ36	0010
HZ36(H)	0010
HZ36(H)L	0010
HZ36-1	0010
HZ36-2	2876
HZ36-3	2876
HZ36E	0010
HZ36H	0814
HZ36L	0010
HZ36P	0814
HZ39E	0032
HZ43	0274
HZ47	OEM
HZ55C1	OEM
HZ56	OEM
HZ68	OEM
HZ82	OEM
HZ100	OEM
HZ120	OEM
HZ150	OEM
HZ242L	0489
HZ272	0450
HZ303B	0118
HZ304B	0036
HZ310B	0064
HZ312A	0052
HZ361	OEM
HZ414-B3	0100
HZ502	0041
HZ603	OEM
HZ2201TZ	0560
HZ5226	0289
HZ5227	0188
HZ5228	0451
HZ5229	0528
HZ5230	0446
HZ53461ZP-12	OEM
HZD7.5	OEM
HZEH	0289
HZK2	OEM
HZK3	OEM
HZK4	OEM
HZK5	OEM
HZK6	OEM
HZK6L	OEM
HZK7	OEM
HZK7L	OEM
HZK9	OEM
HZK9L	OEM
HZK11	OEM
HZK11L	OEM
HZK12	OEM
HZK12L	OEM
HZK15	OEM
HZK15L	OEM
HZK16	OEM
HZK16L	OEM
HZK18	OEM
HZK18L	OEM
HZK20	OEM
HZK20L	OEM
HZK22	OEM
HZK22L	OEM
HZK24	OEM
HZK24L	OEM
HZK27	OEM
HZK27L	OEM
HZK30	OEM
HZK30L	OEM
HZK33	OEM
HZK33L	OEM
HZK36	OEM
HZK36L	OEM
HZL004	OEM
HZM3A	OEM
HZM3B	OEM
HZM3C	OEM

DEVICE TYPE	REPL CODE
HZM4A	OEM
HZM4B	OEM
HZM4C	OEM
HZM5A	OEM
HZM5B	OEM
HZM5C	OEM
HZM6A	OEM
HZM6B	OEM
HZM6C	OEM
HZM7A	OEM
HZM7B	OEM
HZM7C	OEM
HZM9A	OEM
HZM9B	OEM
HZM9C	OEM
HZM11A	OEM
HZM11B	OEM
HZM11C	OEM
HZM12A	OEM
HZM12B	OEM
HZM12C	OEM
HZM15	OEM
HZM16	OEM
HZM18	OEM
HZM20	OEM
HZM22	OEM
HZM24	OEM
HZM27	OEM
HZM30	OEM
HZM33	OEM
HZM36	OEM
HZS2-B	1266
HZS2B	1266
HZS2B1	OEM
HZS2B1TA	OEM
HZS2B2	OEM
HZS2BLL	OEM
HZS2BT	OEM
HZS2C2	OEM
HZS2.0N	OEM
HZS2.2N	OEM
HZS2.4N	1266
HZS2.7E	0755
HZS2.7N	0755
HZS3A2	OEM
HZS3B1	OEM
HZS3B2	OEM
HZS3C1	OEM
HZS3.0E	0118
HZS3.0N	0118
HZS3.0NB2	6583
HZS3.3E	0296
HZS3.3N	0296
HZS3.6E	0372
HZS3.6EB1	0372
HZS3.6EB1-TD	0372
HZS3.6N	0372
HZS3.9E	0036
HZS3.9N	0036
HZS3.0NB2	OEM
HZS4A1	OEM
HZS4A2	OEM
HZS4B1	OEM
HZS4B2	OEM
HZS4BLL	OEM
HZS4C	OEM
HZS4R3EB1	OEM
HZS4R7EB2	OEM
HZS4.3E	0274
HZS4.3EB1	OEM
HZS4.3EB2	OEM
HZS4.3N	0274
HZS4.7E	0140
HZS4.7EB1	OEM
HZS4.7EB2	OEM
HZS4.7MB2-1TJ	OEM
HZS4.7N	0140
HZS4.7NB2-1TJ	0140
HZS4.7NBZ-ITJ	OEM
HZS5A2	OEM
HZS5A3	OEM
HZS5B1	OEM
HZS5B2	OEM
HZS5B2TA	OEM
HZS-5C1	OEM
HZS5C1	OEM
HZS5C-2	0582
HZS5C2T	OEM
HZS5C3	OEM
HZS5R1EB2-T	0041
HZS5R6JB2-TE	0877
HZS5.1B3	0041
HZS5.1E	0041
HZS5.1EB	0041
HZS5.1EB1	OEM
HZS5.1EB2	0041
HZS5.1JB2	0582
HZS5.1N	0041
HZS5.1NB1	OEM
HZS5.1NB2	5816
HZS5.6	OEM
HZS5.6B	OEM
HZS5.6E	0253
HZS5.6EB1	0877
HZS5.6EB2	0253
HZS5.6J	0253
HZS5.6JB2	OEM
HZS5.6N	0253
HZS6A-1L	0582

DEVICE TYPE	REPL CODE
HZS6A1L	0877
HZS6AL	OEM
HZS6B1	OEM
HZS6B1L	OEM
HZS6B2	2974
HZS6B2/TA	0877
HZS6B2L	OEM
HZS6B3	OEM
HZS6B3L	OEM
HZS6C	0292
HZS6C1	OEM
HZS6C1L	OEM
HZS6C1LTA	OEM
HZS6C-2	0292
HZS6C2	OEM
HZS6C2L	OEM
HZS6C3	OEM
HZS6C3L	OEM
HZS6LB1	OEM
HZS6R2EB2-T	OEM
HZS6R2JB2-T	0292
HZS6R8JB1	OEM
HZS6R8JB2-TE	0062
HZS6.2E	0466
HZS6.2J	0466
HZS6.2JB2	0292
HZS6.2N	0466
HZS6.2NB2	OEM
HZS6.8E	0062
HZS6.8EB2	OEM
HZS6.8J	0062
HZS6.8JB1	OEM
HZS6.8JB2	OEM
HZS6.8N	0062
HZS7-A1	OEM
HZS7A-1	OEM
HZS7A1	OEM
HZS-7A2	OEM
HZS7B1	OEM
HZS7B1L	OEM
HZS7B2	OEM
HZS7B2L	OEM
HZS7B3L	OEM
HZS7C1	OEM
HZS7C-3	OEM
HZS7C3	OEM
HZS7.5E	0077
HZS7.5EB1	OEM
HZS7.5EB2	OEM
HZS7.5J	0077
HZS7.5N	0077
HZS8.2E	0165
HZS8.2J	0165
HZS8.2N	0165
HZS8.2NB2	OEM
HZS9-C3	OEM
HZS9A	OEM
HZS9A1L	OEM
HZS9A-2	0165
HZS9A2	OEM
HZS9A3	OEM
HZS9AL	OEM
HZS9B-3	0318
HZS9B3	OEM
HZS9C1	OEM
HZS9C1L	OEM
HZS9C2	OEM
HZS9C2TA	OEM
HZS9C3	OEM
HZS9C3L	OEM
HZS9R1EB3	OEM
HZS9R1JB2-TE	OEM
HZS9.1E	0057
HZS9.1EB2	OEM
HZS9.1EB3	OEM
HZS9.1F	OEM
HZS9.1J	0057
HZS9.1JB1	OEM
HZS9.1JB3	OEM
HZS9.1N	0057
HZS10E	0064
HZS10EB1	0248
HZS10J	0064
HZS10N	0064
HZS11A2	OEM
HZS11A2L	OEM
HZS11A3	OEM
HZS11B1	OEM
HZS11B2	OEM
HZS11B3	OEM
HZS11B3L	OEM
HZS11C1L	OEM
HZS11C2L	OEM
HZS11E	0181
HZS11J	0181
HZS11JB3	OEM
HZS11JB3-TE	0181
HZS11N	0181
HZS12	OEM
HZS12-C3T	0873
HZS12A2L	OEM
HZS-12B	OEM
HZS12B	OEM
HZS12B1L	OEM
HZS12B2	2405
HZS12B2L	0999
HZS12B2TA	0053
HZS12B3	OEM
HZS12BL	OEM

DEVICE TYPE	REPL CODE
HZS12C1	OEM
HZS12C1L	OEM
HZS12C1TA	OEM
HZS12C2L	OEM
HZS12C2LTA	OEM
HZS12C-3	0873
HZS12C3	2414
HZS12C3T	OEM
HZS12E	0052
HZS12EB2	0999
HZS12EB2-T	0999
HZS12EB3	0999
HZS12J	0052
HZS12JB2	0999
HZS12JB2-TE	0999
HZS12JB3	0999
HZS12JB3-T	0999
HZS12L	0999
HZS12L(B2)	0999
HZS12LC1	OEM
HZS12LC2	OEM
HZS12N	0052
HZS13E	0053
HZS13J	0053
HZS13JB2-TE	OEM
HZS13N	0053
HZS15-3	2250
HZS15-3L-TB	OEM
HZS15-3TD	0681
HZS15E	0681
HZS15J	0681
HZS15N	0681
HZS15NB2	OEM
HZS16E	0440
HZS16J	0440
HZS16N	0440
HZS18E	0371
HZS18J	0371
HZS18N	0371
HZS20-1	OEM
HZS20-1L	OEM
HZS20-2	0695
HZS20-2TD	0695
HZS20E	0695
HZS20J	0695
HZS20N	0695
HZS22-1L	OEM
HZS22-3L	0700
HZS22E	0700
HZS22J	0700
HZS22L1	OEM
HZS22N	0700
HZS24-1L	0489
HZS24-2L	OEM
HZS24-3	OEM
HZS24E	0489
HZS24J	0489
HZS24N	0489
HZS24NB2	OEM
HZS24NB3	OEM
HZS27	OEM
HZS27-2L	0450
HZS27-3L	0709
HZS27E	0450
HZS27L3	0709
HZS27N	0450
HZS30	0195
HZS30-1	0195
HZS30-2	OEM
HZS30-2L	OEM
HZS30-3L	OEM
HZS30E	0195
HZS30N	0195
HZS30T	OEM
HZS33-1	OEM
HZS33-2	OEM
HZS33-2L	OEM
HZS33E	0166
HZS33L2	OEM
HZS33N	0166
HZS36-1	OEM
HZS36-1L	0010
HZS36-2L	0010
HZS36-L2	0010
HZS36E	0010
HZS36JB2-TE	0010
HZS36L1	0010
HZS36L2	0010
HZS36N	0010
HZS39E	0032
HZS39N	0032
HZS331L	OEM
HZS682	OEM
HZT5	OEM
HZT6C2	OEM
HZT7A1	OEM
HZT7A2	OEM
HZT7A3	OEM
HZT7B1	OEM
HZT7B2	OEM
HZT7B3	OEM
HZT7C1	OEM
HZT7C2	OEM
HZT9	OEM
HZT22	OEM
HZT31	OEM
HZT-33	3417
HZT33	3417
HZT33-01	3417

DEVICE TYPE	REPL CODE
HZT33-02	1319
HZT33-02-TE	1319
HZT33-02T	1319
HZT33-04	1319
HZT33-04T	1319
HZT33-05	3417
HZT33-10	1319
HZT33-12	3417
HZT33S1	1319
HZT-3301	3417
HsK151/10	OEM
I	OEM
I00DF01120	2843
I00DF10110	3054
I00DF11240	OEM
I00SE01250	OEM
I01B98M090	1775
I01S058360	1521
I01SD57530	3713
I02A98L050	1288
I02A978120	0330
I02DB13820	2868
I02DC13710	2599
I02DE14020	0578
I02DF148C	3830
I02DF1480C	3331
I02DF1481C	3830
I02DF12350	OEM
I02DF13970	OEM
I02DF18700	OEM
I02I90574J	1319
I02S010310	0898
I02SD13780	2031
I02SD14980	4964
I02SF12520	2254
I02SF12530	1594
I02SP12410	OEM
I02SP12770	4756
I03A98M050	0619
I03A98M060	0917
I03A98M090	1775
I03A98M120	0330
I03B98M050	0619
I03B98M060	0917
I03B98M090	1775
I03B98M120	1883
I03B97812V	OEM
I03D040660	0101
I03D063240	0620
I03D072200	2998
I03D078200	OEM
I03D079100	2641
I03D079130	4309
I03D079400	0678
I03D37323A	OEM
I03D373170	4213
I03DA7530N	3765
I03DD78000	0328
I03DE75200	0534
I03DE76520	OEM
I03DE79550	OEM
I03DG73200	OEM
I03S06358T	OEM
I03S063580	3202
I03S063930	6874
I03S064580	2884
I03S070160	1022
I03S072220	OEM
I03S073080	3448
I03S073560	OEM
I03S073580	OEM
I03S079100	2641
I03S973100	OEM
I03SD78350	2330
I03SD78380	OEM
I03SP41400	0358
I03SP44450	3301
I04D317870	OEM
I04D380140	OEM
I04TE25110	OEM
I05D076300	3726
I05D386040	OEM
I05DA7607A	0906
I05DB7680	OEM
I05DB76780	OEM
I05DC7676A	OEM
I05DC8608A	OEM
I05DC86080	OEM
I05DC86200	OEM
I05DE7777P	3206
I05DE8601B	OEM
I05DE8725N	OEM
I05DE76440	0658
I05DE76810	4899
I05DE77780	OEM
I05DE86540	OEM
I05DE86550	OEM
I05DE86770	3206
I05DE87820	OEM
I05S925080	2180
I05SP72220	4571
I05SP73680	OEM
I06DA365SP	3590
I06DE20250	OEM
I06S51954A	OEM
I07D003240	OEM
I07D069930	0624
I07D767AS0	OEM
I07DG7212S	OEM

DEVICE TYPE	REPL CODE
I07S06239N	OEM
I07S010358	OEM
I07S062470	OEM
I07S077550	OEM
I07T67751L	OEM
I08D369643	OEM
I01901280L	4078
I01901280M	3479
I02190574J	1319
I02990574J	1319
I031956310	1319
I039956300	1319
I079907070	OEM
I2AU3A0010	OEM
I2B4900410	3310
I2B4901100	OEM
I2B4910410	2273
I2LSI50030	OEM
I2MH92012A	OEM
I3PS035	0226
I3PS135	0226
I3PS235	0226
I3PS335	0226
I3PS435	0226
I3PS535	0226
I3PS635	0226
I3PT030	0902
I3PT040	0902
I3PT130	0902
I3PT140	0902
I3PT230	0902
I3PT240	0902
I3PT330	0902
I3PT340	0902
I3PT430	0902
I3PT440	0902
I3PT530	0902
I3PT540	0902
I3PT630	0902
I3PT640	0902
I4DDS82500	OEM
I4GD400780	OEM
I4QDL80860	OEM
I4QDL82590	OEM
I4SDZ765A0	OEM
I5PD14053B	0034
I5PD468180	OEM
I6PDC14880	0503
I6PDC14890	0506
I6UD91C360	OEM
I8WP400390	OEM
I8WP400400	OEM
I8WP400410	OEM
I23S953320	2287
I23S953420	OEM
I23S954220	OEM
I27D09001A	OEM
I31D012250	OEM
I41D41256C	1463
I42D400420	OEM
I42D412640	OEM
I42DD82370	OEM
I42DD82530	OEM
I43D030060	OEM
I43D030080	OEM
I51D08031B	OEM
I51DT80020	OEM
I52D001130	OEM
I52D003930	0624
I52D040530	0034
I52D061430	OEM
I52DE61040	OEM
I52DT1011A	4444
I53D040010	0473
I53D0HC050	OEM
I53D3664NA	OEM
I53D890600	OEM
I53D890660	OEM
I53DHC1740	OEM
I54D50010C	OEM
I55D04052B	0024
I55D04066B	0101
I55D04538B	1057
I55D06015C	OEM
I55D040010	0473
I55D060070	OEM
I55D083820	OEM
I55D090200	OEM
I55D0H0000	OEM
I55D0HC020	1443
I55D4HC040	1446
I55D4HC140	3817
I55DHC123P	3851
I55DHC2400	4163
I55DHCU04D	4522
I56D004550	OEM
I56D086300	OEM
I56DT7002A	OEM
I61D4LS140	1688
I61DLS1250	0075
I61DLS1740	0260
I61DLS2400	0447
I61DLS2440	0453
I61DLS2450	0458
I61DLS3730	0704
I64D7406P0	1197
I83F030110	OEM
I97D49005A	OEM
I97D49008B	OEM

If replacement code is OEM, contact original manufacturer for replacement.

DEVICE TYPE	REPL CODE
I431D	OEM
I538	0015
I818	0062
I964(6	0133
I2764	0806
I2764-2	0806
I6289	0571
I8085	OEM
I8085A	OEM
I8085AH-2	OEM
I8155H-2	OEM
I8251-A	OEM
I8251A	OEM
I8255	0051
I9623	0144
I9631	0086
I10008-01	OEM
I27128	1628
I98763-3	0097
I98936-2	0147
I473688-1	0058
I5450015B	OEM
IA5D400431	OEM
IA5D400441	OEM
IAM-1	OEM
IAM-3	OEM
IAM1048	OEM
IAPST523E	OEM
IAZ33	OEM
IB	0286
IB198	0455
IC00000172	OEM
IC00001267	OEM
IC00001292	OEM
IC00001450	OEM
IC00001759	OEM
IC00001760	OEM
IC00001802	OEM
IC00001814	OEM
IC00001838	OEM
IC-00028	OEM
IC2(ECS)	1843
IC-2(RCA)	0823
IC2DF13930	OEM
IC3	3679
IC3(PHILCO)	3679
IC-4	2560
IC-5	0373
IC5	0627
IC-5(ELCOM)	0627
IC-5(PHILCO)	0373
IC-6	2689
IC6	2689
IC-6(PHILCO)	2689
IC-7	0627
IC7	0627
IC-8	0784
IC8	0784
IC-8B	2600
IC8B	0784
IC-8B#	0784
IC-8T26	4437
IC-8T28	0576
IC-8T95	4566
IC-12	0659
IC12	0748
IC-12(PHILCO)	0348
IC-13	0350
IC13	3679
IC-13(PHILCO)	0350
IC-14	0746
IC14	0746
IC-14(PHILCO)	0746
IC-15	0167
IC15	0167
IC-15(PHILCO)	0167
IC-16	0360
IC-16(PHILCO)	0360
IC-17	0780
IC17	0649
IC-17(ELCOM)	0649
IC-17(PHILCO)	0780
IC-18	0438
IC18	0438
IC-18(PHILCO)	1797
IC-19	0774
IC19	0748
IC-19#	2147
IC-19(PHILCO)	0368
IC-20	0026
IC-20(PHILCO)	0026
IC21	0373
IC-21(ELCOM)	0512
IC21(ELCOM)	0512
IC-23	0375
IC23	0375
IC-23(PHILCO)	0375
IC23(PHILCO)	0375
IC-25	2147
IC-25(ELCOM)	0748
IC25(ELCOM)	0748
IC-26	0784
IC26	2377
IC-26(ELCOM)	0784
IC-27(PHILCO)	0368
IC-28	0391
IC29(ELCOM)	1843
IC30(ELCOM)	1812
IC31(ELCOM)	1820

DEVICE TYPE	REPL CODE
IC-32	0368
IC32(ELCOM)	0141
IC33(ELCOM)	0354
IC-34	0780
IC34(ELCOM)	0557
IC35(ELCOM)	1545
IC41(ELCOM)	2515
IC-55(ELCOM)	2840
IC-56(ELCOM)	3384
IC-58(ELCOM)	1248
IC-59(ELCOM)	1354
IC-61(ELCOM)	1063
IC-62(ELCOM)	1063
IC-63(ELCOM)	OEM
IC-65(ELCOM)	3395
IC-68B21	OEM
IC-68B50	OEM
IC-71(ELCOM)	0867
IC-74(ELCOM)	0268
IC-74L03	1569
IC-74LS02	1550
IC-74LS04	1585
IC-74LS12	1669
IC-74LS20	0035
IC-74LS75	1859
IC-74LS86	0288
IC-74LS138	0422
IC-74LS139	0153
IC-74LS157	1153
IC-74LS163	0887
IC-74LS165	4289
IC-74LS193	1682
IC-74LS390	1278
IC-74S138	2125
IC-75(ELCOM)	0738
IC-79(ELCOM)	1477
IC-80(ELCOM)	0232
IC-81(ELCOM)	0564
IC-82(ELCOM)	0310
IC-83(ELCOM)	0331
IC-84(ELCOM)	0357
IC-85(ELCOM)	0381
IC-86(ELCOM)	0507
IC-87(ELCOM)	0692
IC-88(ELCOM)	1018
IC-90(ELCOM)	1046
IC-91	0627
IC91	0627
IC-91(ELCOM)	1160
IC-92(ELCOM)	1177
IC-93(ELCOM)	1193
IC-94(ELCOM)	1417
IC-95(ELCOM)	1164
IC-96(ELCOM)	1423
IC-97(ELCOM)	1303
IC-98(ELCOM)	1199
IC-99(ELCOM)	1150
IC-100(ELCOM)	0828
IC101(COLUMBIA)	0396
IC-101(ELCOM)	1100
IC-101-004	3901
IC-102(ELCOM)	0462
IC-103(ELCOM)	1432
IC-104(ELCOM)	1197
IC-105(ELCOM)	1339
IC-106(ELCOM)	0175
IC-112	0849
IC112	0849
IC126	4502
IC132	2569
IC136	3736
IC142	2864
IC146	0872
IC-201(ELCOM)	0696
IC-211(ELCOM)	2515
IC-213(ELCOM)	3915
IC213(ELCOM)	3915
IC-217(ELCOM)	1674
IC217(ELOCM)	1674
IC-220(ELCOM)	2542
IC-221(ELCOM)	3025
IC-222(ELCOM)	4079
IC-223(ELCOM)	3037
IC-224(ELCOM)	0078
IC-225(ELCOM)	2964
IC229(ELCOM)	0081
IC-234(ELCOM)	0329
IC-237(ELCOM)	0956
IC-243(ELCOM)	1888
IC-244(ELCOM)	0618
IC-276(ELCOM)	0033
IC-279(ELCOM)	3365
IC-280(ELCOM)	1035
IC-281(ELCOM)	2086
IC-282(ELCOM)	OEM
IC-285	0718
IC285	0718
IC-285(ELCOM)	0718
IC285(ELCOM)	0718
IC-286(ELCOM)	1865
IC286(ELCOM)	1865
IC-288(ELCOM)	0368
IC288(ELCOM)	0368
IC-290(ELCOM)	2016
IC290(ELCOM)	2016
IC-298(ELCOM)	2089
IC298(ELCOM)	2089
IC311(ELCOM)	2716
IC-312	2803

DEVICE TYPE	REPL CODE
IC320(ELCOM)	1832
IC-409(ELCOM)	2964
IC-410(ELCOM)	2417
IC-412(ELCOM)	2334
IC-413(ELCOM)	2574
IC-414(ELCOM)	3003
IC-415(ELCOM)	3010
IC-419(ELCOM)	1424
IC-420(ELCOM)	0461
IC-423(ELCOM)	OEM
IC-432(ELCOM)	OEM
IC-433(ELCOM)	1178
IC-435(ELCOM)	2016
IC-441(ELCOM)	2986
IC-442(ELCOM)	2016
IC-443(ELCOM)	1178
IC-444(ELCOM)	3875
IC-445(ELCOM)	1661
IC-446(ELCOM)	2266
IC-447(ELCOM)	3879
IC-448(ELCOM)	3879
IC-449(ELCOM)	3884
IC-450(ELCOM)	2878
IC-451(ELCOM)	1969
IC-453(ELCOM)	3887
IC-455(ELCOM)	0354
IC500	0627
IC-500(ELCOM)	1564
IC500(IR)	0627
IC501	2600
IC501(ELCOM)	2089
IC-502	2147
IC502	2147
IC-503	2147
IC503	0748
IC503(IR)	0748
IC-504	0659
IC504	0659
IC-505	0673
IC505	0673
IC505(IR)	0673
IC506	0823
IC-507	0167
IC507	0167
IC507(IR)	0167
IC-508	0661
IC508	0661
IC-508(ELCOM)	0465
IC508(IR)	0661
IC-509	0348
IC509	0348
IC509(IR)	0348
IC-510	0350
IC510	0350
IC510(IR)	0350
IC-511	0649
IC511	0649
IC512	0438
IC-512(ELCOM)	1611
IC512(IR)	0438
IC-513	0696
IC513	0696
IC-517(ELCOM)	4491
IC-520(ELCOM)	0967
IC-524(ELCOM)	0375
IC-526(ELCOM)	3759
IC-547(ELCOM)	0138
IC-548(ELCOM)	2388
IC-549(ELCOM)	0021
IC-550(ELCOM)	2484
IC-551(ELCOM)	2457
IC-555	0967
IC-603(ELCOM)	2535
IC-605(ELCOM)	0375
IC703E	OEM
IC724	2840
IC-903	0748
IC903	0748
IC904	OEM
IC908	OEM
IC908-PC	OEM
IC918	OEM
IC-1489	0506
IC-2114-L3	2037
IC-3130	2755
IC4001BP	0473
IC5026BP	OEM
IC-6205A	OEM
IC-6502	3036
IC-6850	0509
IC-7157	OEM
IC-7400	0232
IC-7402	0310
IC-7403	0331
IC-7404	0357
IC-7408	0462
IC-7408N	0462
IC-7410	0507
IC-7417	1342
IC-7420	0692
IC7420	0692
IC-7430	0867
IC-7438	0990
IC-7474	1303
IC-7475	1423
IC7475	1423
IC-7476	1150
IC-7492	0828
IC9012F	OEM

DEVICE TYPE	REPL CODE
IC25681	2957
IC-74123	1149
IC-74148	1455
IC-74151	1487
IC-74165	1675
IC-74174	1759
IC-74175	1776
IC-74390	3210
IC743024	OEM
IC743038	0693
IC743039	0693
IC743040	0224
IC743041	0224
IC743042	0016
IC743043	0006
IC743044	0155
IC743045	0930
IC743046	0321
IC743047	0012
IC743048	0015
IC743049	0124
IC743050	0143
IC743051	0133
IC3002271D	0261
IC30022710	0261
IC-BASIC1	OEM
IC-BASIC2	OEM
IC-BASIC3	OEM
IC-BASIC4	OEM
ICBASIC4	OEM
ICC6401	OEM
ICC6402	OEM
ICC6403	OEM
ICC6404	OEM
ICC6405	OEM
ICC6406	OEM
ICC6407	OEM
IC-CARCEN	OEM
IC-CARGEN	OEM
ICF-1	0627
ICF-201	OEM
ICF-202	OEM
ICF-203	OEM
IC-L2114-550	2037
ICL7106CM44	OEM
ICL7106CPL	4865
ICL7106RCPL	OEM
ICL7107CDL	5293
ICL7107CJL	OEM
ICL7107CM44	OEM
ICL7107CPL	4864
ICL7107RCPL	OEM
ICL7116CM44	OEM
ICL7116CPL	5734
ICL7116RCPL	OEM
ICL7117CPL	OEM
ICL7117RCPL	OEM
ICL7126CDL	OEM
ICL7126CJL	OEM
ICL7126CPL	0501
ICL7126RCPL	5842
ICL7129CM44	OEM
ICL7129CPL	3183
ICL7129RCPL	OEM
ICL7660	OEM
ICL8038	0301
ICM7555CBA	2744
ICM7555IPA	0580
ICM7555ITV	OEM
ICM7555MTV	OEM
ICM7556IPD	OEM
ICM7556MJD	OEM
ICP50	OEM
ICP75516-063	OEM
ICP-F10	5989
ICP-F15	5259
ICP-F20	4912
ICP-F25	4548
ICP-F38	5575
ICP-F50	OEM
ICP-F75	OEM
ICP-N5	1796
ICP-N10	3858
ICP-N15	5990
ICP-N20	5991
ICP-N25	5993
ICP-N38	OEM
ICP-N50	OEM
ICP-N75	OEM
ICR1001	2068
ICR1002	2068
ICR1003	2068
ICR1004	OEM
ICR1005	0023
ICR1006	0017
ICR1007	0017
ICR1501	2068
ICR1502	2068
ICR1503	2068
ICR1504	OEM
ICR1505	0031
ICR1506	0102
ICR1507	0102
ICR3001	OEM
ICR3002	OEM
ICR3003	OEM
ICR3004	OEM
ICR3005	0031
ICR3006	1917

DEVICE TYPE	REPL CODE
ICR3007	1917
ICR6001	OEM
ICR6002	OEM
ICR6003	OEM
ICR6004	OEM
ICR6005	OEM
ICR6006	OEM
ICR6007	OEM
IC-SYN600	OEM
IC-SYNMON	OEM
ICT-5	OEM
ICT-8	OEM
ICT-10	OEM
ICT-12	OEM
ICT-15	OEM
ICT-18	OEM
ICT-22	OEM
ICT-36	OEM
ICT-45	OEM
ICTE-5	OEM
ICTE5	OEM
ICTE-5C	5362
ICTE5C	OEM
ICTE5S	OEM
ICTE5SC	OEM
ICTE-8	OEM
ICTE8	OEM
ICTE-8C	OEM
ICTE8C	OEM
ICTE-10	OEM
ICTE-10C	OEM
ICTE-12	OEM
ICTE12	OEM
ICTE-12C	OEM
ICTE12C	OEM
ICTE-15	OEM
ICTE15	OEM
ICTE-15C	OEM
ICTE15C	OEM
ICTE-18	OEM
ICTE18	OEM
ICTE-18C	OEM
ICTE18C	OEM
ICTE19	OEM
ICTE19C	OEM
ICTE-22	OEM
ICTE22	OEM
ICTE-22C	OEM
ICTE22C	OEM
ICTE-36	OEM
ICTE36	OEM
ICTE-36C	OEM
ICTE36C	OEM
ICTE-45	OEM
ICTE45	OEM
ICTE-45C	OEM
ICTE45C	OEM
ID20-0308	0381
ID100	1129
ID101	0340
ID102	0895
ID103	0058
ID104	0058
ID105	0403
ID106	0403
ID200	1129
ID201	0340
ID202	OEM
ID203	0058
ID300	0403
ID301	OEM
ID600	OEM
ID601	OEM
ID602	OEM
ID603	OEM
ID604	OEM
ID605	OEM
ID606	OEM
ID2732A-3	2672
ID8088	OEM
ID8284A	OEM
ID8288	OEM
ID27128A-3	1628
IDAZ472	0036
IDAZ472A	0036
IDAZ824	0466
IDAZ824A	0466
IDAZ824B	0466
IDAZ3397	0036
IDAZ3397A	0036
IDAZ3397B	0036
IDAZ3397C	OEM
IDAZ3398	0140
IDAZ3398A	0140
IDAZ3398B	0140
IDAZ3398C	OEM
IDAZ3399	0041
IDAZ3399A	0041
IDAZ3399B	0162
IDAZ3399C	OEM
IDAZ3403	0052
IDAZ3403A	0052
IDAZ3403B	0052
IDAZ3403C	0052
IDAZ3404	0681
IDAZ3404A	0681
IDAZ3404B	0681
IDH0742	0101
IDH0802	0034

DEVICE TYPE	REPL CODE
IDUPC7912H	1827
IE12Z5	0137
IE460B	0224
IE535A	OEM
IE535B	OEM
IE-850	0208
IE850	0079
IF-65	0004
IF65	0211
IF6008T	OEM
IFE-450	OEM
IFEWC108	OEM
IFF-450A	OEM
IFSANYO-002	OEM
IFSANYO002	OEM
IFSANYO002(SANYO002)	OEM
IFSANYO-003	OEM
IFSANYO003	OEM
IFSANYO-004	OEM
IFSANYO004	OEM
IFSI-3122P	4264
IG-100	0435
IG-15630	OEM
IGD-2	OEM
IGL78M05	0619
IGL78M06	0917
IGLA3150	2508
IGLA6324	0620
IGLA6458DF	0356
IGLA7030	OEM
IGLA7031	OEM
IGLA7032	OEM
IGLA7033	OEM
IGLA7042	OEM
IGLA7224	4202
IGLA7905	OEM
IGLB1214	OEM
IGLB1240	OEM
IGLB1290	3839
IGLB1620	OEM
IGLB1645	OEM
IGLB1649	5157
IGLC4011	0215
IGLC4011B	0215
IGLC4013B	0409
IGLC4069UB	0119
IGLC4081B	0328
IGLC6502B-633	OEM
IGLC7900	OEM
IGLM6402H-158	OEM
IGLM6402H-238	OEM
IGLM6402H-329	OEM
IGLM6405H-215	OEM
IGLM6405H-330	OEM
IGLM6416E-159	OEM
IGLM6416E-209	OEM
IGLM6416E-217	OEM
IGLM6416E-239	OEM
IGLM6417E-302	OEM
IGLM8854-1912	OEM
IGSPT6402L04	OEM
IGSPT640203	OEM
IGSTK5321SL	OEM
IGSTK5322	2281
IGSTK5322H	OEM
IGSTK5327SL	OEM
IGSTK5346	OEM
IGSTK5352	OEM
IGSTK5431	2358
IGSTK5431SL	2358
IGSTK5431ST	2358
IGSTK5461ST	OEM
IGSTK6962	3314
IGSTK6972	3321
IGT8D20	OEM
IGT8D21	OEM
IGT8E20	OEM
IGT8E21	OEM
IHHA1174ANT	OEM
IHHA11711	5089
IHHA11713	OEM
IHHA11714	5093
IHHA11715	5067
IHHA11722	OEM
IHHA11724	OEM
IHHA11725	OEM
IHHA11726	OEM
IHHA-11741	OEM
IHHA11741	OEM
IHHA-11744	OEM
IHHA11744	OEM
IHHA-11745	OEM
IHHA11745	OEM
IHHA11747ANT	5681
IHHA11749	5679
IHHA11847NT	OEM
IHHD38701A06	OEM
IHHD44801A05	OEM
IHTS4966	OEM
I-HY-101	OEM
IISPI1050-01	OEM
IISPR1050-01	OEM
IISPT2300L01	OEM
IISPT2370H07	OEM
IISPT3240L05	OEM
IITL431CLP	OEM
IITMS1024	OEM
IITMS1025N2LC	OEM
IJ4B41	OEM

DEVICE TYPE	REPL CODE
IJNJM4558DM	0356
IKSANYO002	OEM
IL081ACDP	OEM
IL1	0311
IL5	0272
IL12	0311
IL15	0311
IL16	0311
IL74	0311
ILA30	1047
ILA55	1101
ILA7621	0387
ILCA2-30	1047
ILD1020	0021
ILH0096	1173
ILH0111	1192
ILL0052	0358
ILM0292	2155
ILM340T12	0330
ILMC14013B	0409
ILMC14081B	0621
ILT0014	1012
IM15/1B	OEM
IM4004	0790
IMAN262	2932
IMC1358P	0167
IMDN6838	0484
IMI1	OEM
IMMN1280-M	OEM
IMS171	OEM
IMS2620P-15	OEM
IMSG171S-35	OEM
IMT1	OEM
IMZ1	OEM
IN60-1	0143
IN962B	0313
IN967B	OEM
IN2054-68	1017
IN3161-74	1017
IN4002	OEM
IN4051	1030
IN4066BP	0101
IN4532	OEM
IN4587-96	0594
IN5936B	OEM
IN6264	OEM
IN6265	OEM
IN6266	OEM
IN8250N-B	OEM
INC61684	0914
INF	OEM
INJ33348	0196
INJ33349	0143
INJ60034	0143
INJ60284	0143
INJ61224	0123
INJ61225	0631
INJ61227	0015
INJ61433	0133
INJ61434	0015
INJ61435	0196
INJ61675	0143
INJ61677	0133
INJ61725	0133
INJ61726	0015
INJ70972	0196
INJ70973	0143
INJ70980	0143
INMOSS348A	OEM
INMPC1363C	0678
INMPC1363CA	1934
INMPC1373H	2015
INMPC1373HA	2015
INMPC1513HA	3130
INMPD552C	OEM
INMPD4011BC	0215
INMPD4013BC	0409
INMPD4066BC	0101
INMPD4081C	0328
INMPD4093BC	2368
INMPD7519G-530	OEM
INMPD14027BC	1938
INS82LS05N	5889
INS8039N-11	OEM
INS8246N	OEM
INS8250AN	OEM
INS8250AV	OEM
INS8250BN	OEM
INS8250N	OEM
INS8250N-B	OEM
INUPC1373H	2015
INUPD4011BC	0215
INUPD4013BC	0409
INUPD4066BC	0101
INUPD4081C	0328
INUPD4093BC	2368
INUPD7519G-53	OEM
INV5000SNE	OEM
IOB1680	OEM
IP	OEM
IP20-0001	0364
IP20-0002	0364
IP20-0005	1897
IP20-0006	0076
IP20-0007	0042
IP20-006	0224
IP20-0010	3126
IP20-0012	0683
IP20-0015	0123

If replacement code is OEM, contact original manufacturer for replacement.

437

DEVICE TYPE	REPL CODE
IP20-0016	0123
IP20-0017	0143
IP20-0018	0002
IP20-0019	0012
IP20-0020	0143
IP20-0021	0133
IP20-0022	0023
IP20-0023	0139
IP20-0025	0790
IP20-0027	0025
IP20-0028	2766
IP20-0029	0364
IP20-0032	0076
IP20-0034	5318
IP20-0035	0683
IP20-0036	0228
IP20-0037	1136
IP20-0038	0155
IP20-0039	0076
IP20-0040	0191
IP20-0041	0191
IP20-0046	0006
IP20-0048	1390
IP20-0054	0023
IP20-0055	0139
IP20-0060	0019
IP20-0061	0133
IP20-0076	0208
IP20-0078	3017
IP20-0083	0042
IP20-0086	0162
IP20-0103	2684
IP20-0110	0127
IP20-0120	0080
IP20-0122	0076
IP20-0123	2039
IP20-0131	2039
IP20-0132	1581
IP20-0135	2475
IP20-0145	0133
IP20-0151	0030
IP20-0154	0830
IP20-0155	0833
IP20-0156	0161
IP20-0157	0410
IP20-0159	0006
IP20-0160	0208
IP20-0161	1044
IP20-0164	0559
IP20-0165	0155
IP20-0166	0030
IP20-0167	0015
IP20-0172	2035
IP20-0174	0627
IP20-0179	0151
IP20-0184	0133
IP20-0185	0715
IP20-0186	0025
IP20-0191	0076
IP20-0192	0148
IP20-0203	0298
IP20-0204	0005
IP20-0205	0232
IP20-0206	1303
IP20-0207	0564
IP20-0208	4516
IP20-0209	1635
IP20-0210	0011
IP20-0211	0527
IP20-0212	4186
IP20-0213	0006
IP20-0214	0155
IP20-0216	0124
IP20-0217	0688
IP20-0218	1025
IP20-0219	OEM
IP20-0220	2285
IP20-0230	0558
IP20-0231	0191
IP20-0233	0313
IP20-0234	OEM
IP20-0244	0139
IP20-0253	2285
IP20-0266	OEM
IP20-0281	4006
IP20-0282	0133
IP20-0283	0143
IP20-0284	0466
IP20-0305	1270
IP20-0308	0381
IP20-0310	0268
IP20-0315	0564
IP20-0316	1303
IP20-0317	1120
IP20-0318	OEM
IP20-0319	OEM
IP20-0323	0042
IP20-0331	2475
IP20-0429	1532
IP20-0431	OEM
IP20-0447	2279
IP20-0448	0558
IP20-0519	OEM
IP20-2010	0011
IP28-0006	OEM
IP28-0016	OEM
IP28-0017	OEM
IP100	1129
IP101	0340

DEVICE TYPE	REPL CODE
IP102	0895
IP103	2326
IP104	0058
IP105	0403
IP106	0403
IP117	OEM
IP117A	OEM
IP117AHV	OEM
IP117HV	OEM
IP120-5	OEM
IP120-12	OEM
IP120-15	OEM
IP120A-5	OEM
IP120A-12	OEM
IP120A-15	OEM
IP123-5	OEM
IP123-12	OEM
IP123-15	OEM
IP123A-5	OEM
IP123A-12	OEM
IP123A-15	OEM
IP137	OEM
IP137A	OEM
IP137AHV	OEM
IP137HV	OEM
IP138	OEM
IP138A	OEM
IP140-5	OEM
IP140-12	OEM
IP140-15	OEM
IP140A-5	OEM
IP140A-12	OEM
IP140A-15	OEM
IP150	OEM
IP150A	OEM
IP217	OEM
IP217A	OEM
IP217AHV	OEM
IP217HV	OEM
IP220-5	OEM
IP220-12	OEM
IP220-15	OEM
IP220A-5	OEM
IP220A-12	OEM
IP220A-15	OEM
IP223-5	OEM
IP223-12	OEM
IP223-15	OEM
IP223A-5	OEM
IP223A-12	OEM
IP223A-15	OEM
IP237	OEM
IP237A	OEM
IP237AHV	OEM
IP237HV	OEM
IP238	OEM
IP238A	OEM
IP240-5	OEM
IP240-12	OEM
IP240-15	OEM
IP240A-5	OEM
IP240A-12	OEM
IP240A-15	OEM
IP250	OEM
IP250A	OEM
IP293	OEM
IP293D	OEM
IP293DA	OEM
IP293E	OEM
IP317	2697
IP317A	OEM
IP317AHV	OEM
IP317HV	OEM
IP320-5	OEM
IP320-12	OEM
IP320-15	OEM
IP320A-5	OEM
IP320A-12	OEM
IP320A-15	OEM
IP323-5	OEM
IP323-12	OEM
IP323-15	OEM
IP323A-5	OEM
IP323A-12	OEM
IP323A-15	OEM
IP337	OEM
IP337A	OEM
IP337AHV	OEM
IP337HV	OEM
IP338	OEM
IP338A	OEM
IP340-5	1911
IP340-12	3906
IP340-15	OEM
IP340A-5	OEM
IP340A-12	OEM
IP340A-15	OEM
IP350	OEM
IP350A	OEM
IP494A	OEM
IP494AC	OEM
IP1524	OEM
IP1524B	OEM
IP1525A	OEM
IP1526	OEM
IP1526A	OEM
IP1527A	OEM
IP1543	OEM
IP1544	OEM

DEVICE TYPE	REPL CODE
IP1842	OEM
IP1843	OEM
IP2064	OEM
IP2065	OEM
IP2066	OEM
IP2067	OEM
IP2068	OEM
IP2069	OEM
IP2070	OEM
IP2071	OEM
IP2074	OEM
IP2075	OEM
IP2076	OEM
IP2077	OEM
IP2524	OEM
IP2524B	OEM
IP2525A	OEM
IP2526	OEM
IP2526A	OEM
IP2527A	OEM
IP2543	OEM
IP2544	OEM
IP2842	OEM
IP2843	OEM
IP3524	OEM
IP3524B	OEM
IP3525A	OEM
IP3526	OEM
IP3526A	OEM
IP3527A	OEM
IP3543	OEM
IP3544	OEM
IP3842	OEM
IP3843	OEM
IP5560	OEM
IP5560C	OEM
IP5561	OEM
IP5561C	OEM
IP7805	0619
IP7805A	0619
IP7812	0330
IP7812A	OEM
IP7815	1311
IP7815A	OEM
IP7905	1275
IP7905A	OEM
IP7912	1827
IP7912A	OEM
IP7915	3777
IP7915A	OEM
IP8051	OEM
IP8085AH	OEM
IP8085AH-2	OEM
IP8088	OEM
IP8251A	OEM
IP8255A-5	0051
IP8259A	OEM
IP33063	OEM
IP34060	OEM
IP34063	OEM
IP35060	OEM
IP35063	OEM
IPL32	OEM
IPSV01DEAN	OEM
IPSV7031AN	OEM
IPSV7031BN	OEM
IPSV7031CN	OEM
IPSV7032AN	OEM
IPSV7032CN	OEM
IPSV7033AN	OEM
IPSV7034DN	OEM
IPX	OEM
IR1F	0102
IR2A	0015
IR2C07	OEM
IR2C32	OEM
IR2E	0015
IR2E01	OEM
IR2E02	OEM
IR2E16	OEM
IR2E27A	OEM
IR2E31	OEM
IR2E31A	OEM
IR2P02	OEM
IR2P02T	OEM
(IR)2SA495	0006
(IR)2SA564A	0203
(IR)2SB186	0004
(IR)2SB187	0004
(IR)2SB367A	0222
(IR)2SB405	0164
(IR)2SB474	1004
(IR)2SB481	0222
(IR)2SC281B	0531
(IR)2SC372	0076
(IR)2SC373	0076
(IR)2SC380A0	0284
(IR)2SC403A	0155
(IR)2SC454B	0076
(IR)2SC458B	0076
(IR)2SC460B	0151
(IR)2SC535B	0127
(IR)2SC536	0532
(IR)2SC537B	0191
(IR)2SC538A	0079
(IR)2SC633A	2064
(IR)2SC634A	2064
(IR)2SC644	0111
(IR)2SC682A	0047

DEVICE TYPE	REPL CODE
(IR)2SC710	0364
(IR)2SC717	0127
(IR)2SC772	1136
(IR)2SC828A	1211
(IR)2SC829B	0151
(IR)2SC838	0191
(IR)2SC945	0076
IR3C02A	OEM
IR3M02A	OEM
IR3N05	6629
IR3N06	6890
IR3N34	OEM
IR3T24	OEM
IR4N09A	OEM
IR5A	0340
IR5B	0058
IR5C	0403
IR5D	OEM
IR5F	1129
IR5G	OEM
IR5GZ61	0071
IR5H	OEM
IR5JA	0143
IR5LC10P04Q	1015
IR5U	OEM
IR6A	0179
IR6B	0179
IR6C	0342
IR6D	0342
IR6F	OEM
IR6G	OEM
IR6H	OEM
IR6U	OEM
IR10E6J	0015
IR10E6X	0015
IR20	0015
IR20HB5	1590
IR20HB20	0865
IR20HB40	0847
IR30A	6952
IR30A2	0464
IR30B	0740
IR30B2	0464
IR30C	0717
IR30C2	0720
IR30D	0735
IR30D2	0720
IR30DF	0087
IR30E	0747
IR30E2	0720
IR30F	2497
IR30F2	0464
IR30M2	0720
IR30U	2497
IR30U2	0464
IR31A	6955
IR31B	6955
IR31C	6956
IR31D	6956
IR31D8	OEM
IR31E	OEM
IR31F	6955
IR31U	6955
IR32A	1640
IR32B	OEM
IR32C	1574
IR32D	OEM
IR32E	1655
IR32F	OEM
IR32U	2497
IR33A	OEM
IR33B	OEM
IR33C	OEM
IR33D	OEM
IR33E	OEM
IR33F	OEM
IR33U	OEM
IR106A1	0442
IR106A1-C	0442
IR106A2	0442
IR106A3	0442
IR106A4	0442
IR106A41	0442
IR106B1	0934
IR106B1-C	0934
IR106B2	0934
IR106B3	0934
IR106B4	0934
IR106B41	0934
IR106C1	1213
IR106C1-C	1213
IR106C2	1213
IR106C3	1213
IR106C4	1213
IR106C41	1213
IR106D1	0095
IR106D2	0095
IR106D3	0095
IR106D4	0095
IR106D41	0095
IR106F1	1250
IR106F2	1250
IR106F3	1250
IR106F4	1250
IR106F41	1250
IR106Q1	1386
IR106Q2	1386
IR106Q3	1386
IR106Q4	1386

DEVICE TYPE	REPL CODE
IR106Q41	1386
IR106Y1	1386
IR106Y1-C	1386
IR106Y2	1386
IR106Y3	1386
IR106Y4	1386
IR106Y41	OEM
IR122A	2078
IR122A-C	2078
IR122B	0500
IR122B-C	0500
IR122C	0705
IR122C-C	0705
IR122D	0705
IR122D-C	0705
IR122F	2084
IR122F-C	2084
IR122M4	OEM
IR122M5	OEM
IR122M6	OEM
IR140A	0799
IR140B	0799
IR140C	0799
IR140D	0799
IR140F	0799
IR141A	0799
IR141B	0799
IR141C	0799
IR141D	0799
IR141F	0799
IR401	1955
IR402	0359
IR403	0359
IR409	0074
IR410	0270
IR411	0270
IR413	0065
IR423	0074
IR424	3029
IR425	3029
IR515	0359
IR516	0359
IR517	0359
IR518	0359
IR519	0359
IR640	3339
IR641	3339
IR642	0134
IR645	3340
IR646	3340
IR647	0073
IR660	OEM
IR663	OEM
IR665	OEM
IR682	2174
IR683	0562
IR684	3227
IR685	0757
IR685#	0464
IR686	3237
IR687	3240
IR688	0735
IR689	3260
IR690	0759
IR692	0761
IR701	OEM
IR708	OEM
IR709	OEM
IR710	OEM
IR721	OEM
IR801	0223
IR802	OEM
IR806	OEM
IR900	2262
IR901	2262
IR1000	2411
IR1001	2411
IR1010	OEM
IR1020	OEM
IR1600	1102
IR1601	2904
IR1602	0957
IR1603	2905
IR1604	2908
IR1771	1095
IR1772	2471
IR1774	0240
IR1776	2635
IR1777	0671
IR1778	2782
IR1843A	2497
IR1844A	0736
IR1846A	0740
IR1848A	2889
IR1849A	0742
IR1850A	3213
IR2160	1659
IR2432	OEM
IR2434	OEM
IR3702	OEM
IR3771	OEM
IR3772	OEM
IR3773	OEM
IR4039	2602
IR4040	2602
IR4041	2602
IR4045	2602
IR4050	2602
IR4055	2602

DEVICE TYPE	REPL CODE
IR4059	2602
IR4060	2602
IR4061	2602
IR4065	2602
IR4502	OEM
IR5000	2602
IR5001	3340
IR5002	6579
IR5060	2602
IR5061	2602
IR5062	2602
IR5063	OEM
IR5064	OEM
IR5065	OEM
IR5066	OEM
IR5251	OEM
IR5252	OEM
IR5253	6298
IR6000	2602
IR6001	2602
IR6002	2602
IR6060	2602
IR6061	2602
IR6062	2602
IR6251	1980
IR6252	2602
IR6253	2602
IR6302	OEM
IR6542	OEM
IR6543	OEM
IR6544	OEM
IR6545	OEM
IR6546	OEM
IR6547	1841
IR6582	OEM
IR6583	OEM
IR9358	2894
IR9393	0624
IR9431	OEM
IR13006	OEM
IR13007	OEM
IR13066	OEM
IR94558	OEM
IRC-5	2255
IRC5	1250
IRC10	0442
IRC20	0934
IRD-54	2704
IRD54	2704
IRD54-C	2704
IR-D431	0102
IR-D818	0290
IRD3899	1522
IRD3900	1522
IRD3901	1522
IRD3902	0029
IRD3903	0029
IRD3909	1522
IRD3910	1522
IRD3911	1522
IRD3912	0029
IRD3913	0029
IRE-150	OEM
IRE-151	OEM
IRE-160	OEM
IRE-160FA	OEM
IRE-160FB	OEM
IRE161	OEM
IRE165	OEM
IRE170	OEM
IRF120	OEM
IRF121	OEM
IRF122	OEM
IRF123	OEM
IRF130	OEM
IRF131	OEM
IRF132	OEM
IRF133	OEM
IRF140	OEM
IRF141	OEM
IRF142	OEM
IRF143	OEM
IRF150	OEM
IRF151	OEM
IRF152	OEM
IRF153	OEM
IRF153R	OEM
IRF220	5549
IRF221	5549
IRF222	5549
IRF223	5549
IRF230	OEM
IRF231	OEM
IRF232	OEM
IRF233	OEM
IRF233R	OEM
IRF240	OEM
IRF241	OEM
IRF242	OEM
IRF243	OEM
IRF250	OEM
IRF251	OEM
IRF252	OEM
IRF253	OEM
IRF253R	OEM
IRF320	1658
IRF321	1658
IRF322	1658
IRF323	1658

DEVICE TYPE	REPL CODE
IRF330	OEM
IRF331	OEM
IRF332	OEM
IRF333	OEM
IRF340	OEM
IRF341	OEM
IRF342	OEM
IRF343	OEM
IRF350	OEM
IRF351	OEM
IRF352	OEM
IRF352R	OEM
IRF353	OEM
IRF353R	OEM
IRF420	OEM
IRF421	OEM
IRF422	OEM
IRF423	OEM
IRF430	OEM
IRF431	OEM
IRF432	OEM
IRF433	OEM
IRF440	OEM
IRF441	OEM
IRF442	OEM
IRF443	OEM
IRF450	OEM
IRF451	OEM
IRF452	OEM
IRF452R	OEM
IRF453	OEM
IRF453R	OEM
IRF510	3059
IRF511	2325
IRF512	3059
IRF513	2325
IRF513R	OEM
IRF520	3059
IRF521	3059
IRF521R	OEM
IRF522	3059
IRF522R	OEM
IRF523	2325
IRF523R	OEM
IRF530	4970
IRF531	4970
IRF532	4970
IRF533	4970
IRF540	OEM
IRF541	OEM
IRF542	OEM
IRF543	OEM
IRF610	1456
IRF611	1456
IRF612	1456
IRF613	1456
IRF620	5618
IRF621	2162
IRF622	1456
IRF623	2162
IRF630	5618
IRF631	2162
IRF632	1456
IRF633	5621
IRF640	OEM
IRF641	OEM
IRF642	5623
IRF643	OEM
IRF643R	OEM
IRF710	1456
IRF711	1456
IRF712	1456
IRF713	1456
IRF713R	OEM
IRF720	1456
IRF721	1456
IRF722	1456
IRF723	1456
IRF730	OEM
IRF731	OEM
IRF732	1456
IRF733	1456
IRF740	OEM
IRF741	OEM
IRF742	OEM
IRF743	OEM
IRF820	5649
IRF821	5649
IRF821R	OEM
IRF822	1457
IRF823	1457
IRF823R	OEM
IRF830	OEM
IRF831	1456
IRF832	OEM
IRF833	5657
IRF840	5661
IRF840I	5661
IRF841	5661
IRF842	1643
IRF843	1643
IRF9130	OEM
IRF9131	2256
IRF9132	OEM
IRF9133	2256
IRF9140	OEM
IRF9141	OEM
IRF9142	OEM
IRF9143	OEM

If replacement code is OEM, contact original manufacturer for replacement.

DEVICE TYPE	REPL CODE
IRF9230	OEM
IRF9231	OEM
IRF9232	OEM
IRF9233	OEM
IRF9241	OEM
IRF9242	OEM
IRF9243	OEM
IRF9340	OEM
IRF9510	6188
IRF9511	6188
IRF9512	6188
IRF9513	6188
IRF9520	2256
IRF9521	2256
IRF9522	2256
IRF9523	2256
IRF9530	2256
IRF9531	2256
IRF9532	2256
IRF9533	2256
IRF9540	OEM
IRF9541	OEM
IRF9542	OEM
IRF9543	OEM
IRF9610	OEM
IRF9611	6188
IRF9612	OEM
IRF9613	6188
IRF9620	OEM
IRF9621	6188
IRF9622	OEM
IRF9623	6188
IRF9630	OEM
IRF9631	OEM
IRF9632	OEM
IRF9633	6188
IRF9640	OEM
IRF9641	OEM
IRF9642	OEM
IRF9643	OEM
IRFBC40	OEM
IRFD1Z0	OEM
IRFD1Z3	OEM
IRFD110	OEM
IRFD111	OEM
IRFD112	OEM
IRFD113	OEM
IRFD120	OEM
IRFD123	OEM
IRFD210	OEM
IRFD213	OEM
IRFD220	OEM
IRFD321R	OEM
IRFD322R	OEM
IRFD323R	OEM
IRFD9110	OEM
IRFD9113	OEM
IRFD9120	OEM
IRFD9121	OEM
IRFD9122	OEM
IRFD9123	OEM
IRFD9210	OEM
IRFD9213	OEM
IRFE100	0321
IRFF110	OEM
IRFF110R	OEM
IRFF111	OEM
IRFF112	OEM
IRFF113	OEM
IRFF113R	OEM
IRFF120	OEM
IRFF121	OEM
IRFF122	OEM
IRFF123	OEM
IRFF123R	OEM
IRFF130	OEM
IRFF131	OEM
IRFF132	OEM
IRFF133	OEM
IRFF210	OEM
IRFF211	OEM
IRFF212	OEM
IRFF213	OEM
IRFF213R	OEM
IRFF220	OEM
IRFF221	OEM
IRFF222	OEM
IRFF223	OEM
IRFF223R	OEM
IRFF230	OEM
IRFF231	OEM
IRFF232	OEM
IRFF233	OEM
IRFF310	OEM
IRFF311	OEM
IRFF312	OEM
IRFF313	OEM
IRFF320	OEM
IRFF321	OEM
IRFF322	OEM
IRFF323	OEM
IRFF330	OEM
IRFF331	OEM
IRFF332	OEM
IRFF333	OEM
IRFF423R	OEM
IRFF430	OEM
IRFF431	OEM
IRFF432	OEM
IRFF433	OEM
IRFP353R	OEM
IRFP448	OEM
IRFP453R	OEM
IRFS1Z0	OEM
IRFS1Z3	OEM
IRFU121	OEM
IRFZ20	OEM
IRFZ22	OEM
IRFZ30	OEM
IRFZ32	OEM
IRFZ40	OEM
IRFZ42	OEM
IRIF	0102
IRKD71-12	1787
IRKD101-14	2178
IRKH26-04	2233
IRKH26-06	2233
IRKH26-08	2233
IRKH26-10	2233
IRKH26-12	2233
IRKH26-14	OEM
IRKH26-16	OEM
IRKH26-18	OEM
IRKH41-04	2233
IRKH41-06	2233
IRKH41-08	2233
IRKH41-10	2233
IRKH41-12	2233
IRKH41-14	OEM
IRKH41-16	OEM
IRKH41-18	OEM
IRKH56-04	2233
IRKH56-06	2233
IRKH56-08	2233
IRKH56-10	2233
IRKH56-12	2233
IRKH56-14	OEM
IRKH56-16	OEM
IRKH56-18	OEM
IRKH57-12	4295
IRKH71-04	2226
IRKH71-06	2226
IRKH71-08	2226
IRKH71-10	2226
IRKH71-12	2226
IRKH71-14	OEM
IRKH71-16	OEM
IRKH71-18	OEM
IRKH91-04	2226
IRKH91-06	2226
IRKH91-08	2226
IRKH91-10	2226
IRKH91-12	2226
IRKH91-14	OEM
IRKH91-16	OEM
IRKH91-18	OEM
IRKH92-12	2966
IRKH132-14D20	OEM
IRKH132-16D25	OEM
IRKH162-14D20	OEM
IRKH162-16D25	OEM
IRKH180-14D20	OEM
IRKH180-16D25	OEM
IRKH210-14D20	OEM
IRKH210-16D20	OEM
IRKH250-14D20	OEM
IRKH250-16D25	OEM
IRKK26-04	OEM
IRKK26-06	OEM
IRKK26-08	OEM
IRKK26-10	OEM
IRKK26-12	OEM
IRKK26-14	OEM
IRKK26-16	OEM
IRKK26-18	OEM
IRKK41-04	OEM
IRKK41-06	OEM
IRKK41-08	OEM
IRKK41-10	OEM
IRKK41-12	OEM
IRKK41-14	OEM
IRKK41-16	OEM
IRKK41-18	OEM
IRKK56-04	OEM
IRKK56-06	OEM
IRKK56-08	OEM
IRKK56-10	OEM
IRKK56-12	OEM
IRKK56-14	OEM
IRKK56-16	OEM
IRKK56-18	OEM
IRKK71-04	OEM
IRKK71-06	OEM
IRKK71-08	OEM
IRKK71-10	OEM
IRKK71-12	OEM
IRKK71-14	OEM
IRKK71-16	OEM
IRKK71-18	OEM
IRKK91-04	OEM
IRKK91-06	OEM
IRKK91-08	OEM
IRKK91-10	OEM
IRKK91-12	OEM
IRKK91-14	OEM
IRKK91-16	OEM
IRKK91-18	OEM
IRKL57-12	4494
IRKL92-12	2851
IRKL132-14D20	OEM
IRKL132-16D25	OEM
IRKL162-14D20	OEM
IRKL162-16D25	OEM
IRKL180-14D20	OEM
IRKL180-16D25	OEM
IRKL210-14D20	OEM
IRKL210-16D20	OEM
IRKL250-14D20	OEM
IRKL250-16D25	OEM
IRKN26-04	OEM
IRKN26-06	OEM
IRKN26-08	OEM
IRKN26-10	OEM
IRKN26-12	OEM
IRKN26-14	OEM
IRKN26-16	OEM
IRKN26-18	OEM
IRKN41-04	OEM
IRKN41-06	OEM
IRKN41-08	OEM
IRKN41-10	OEM
IRKN41-12	OEM
IRKN41-14	OEM
IRKN41-16	OEM
IRKN41-18	OEM
IRKN56-04	OEM
IRKN56-06	OEM
IRKN56-08	OEM
IRKN56-10	OEM
IRKN56-12	OEM
IRKN56-14	OEM
IRKN56-16	OEM
IRKN56-18	OEM
IRKN71-04	OEM
IRKN71-06	OEM
IRKN71-08	OEM
IRKN71-10	OEM
IRKN71-12	OEM
IRKN71-14	OEM
IRKN71-16	OEM
IRKN71-18	OEM
IRKN91-04	OEM
IRKN91-06	OEM
IRKN91-08	OEM
IRKN91-10	OEM
IRKN91-12	OEM
IRKN91-14	OEM
IRKN91-16	OEM
IRKN91-18	OEM
IRKT26-04	1937
IRKT26-06	OEM
IRKT26-08	1937
IRKT26-10	1937
IRKT26-12	1937
IRKT26-14	OEM
IRKT26-16	OEM
IRKT26-18	OEM
IRKT41-04	1937
IRKT41-06	1937
IRKT41-08	1937
IRKT41-10	1937
IRKT41-12	1937
IRKT41-14	OEM
IRKT41-16	OEM
IRKT41-18	OEM
IRKT56-04	1937
IRKT56-06	1937
IRKT56-08	1937
IRKT56-10	1937
IRKT56-12	1937
IRKT56-14	OEM
IRKT56-16	OEM
IRKT56-18	OEM
IRKT57-12	0647
IRKT71-04	1928
IRKT71-06	1928
IRKT71-08	1928
IRKT71-10	1928
IRKT71-12	1928
IRKT71-14	OEM
IRKT71-16	OEM
IRKT71-18	OEM
IRKT91-04	1928
IRKT91-06	1928
IRKT91-08	1928
IRKT91-10	1928
IRKT91-12	1928
IRKT91-14	OEM
IRKT91-16	OEM
IRKT91-18	OEM
IRKT92-12	2295
IRKU26-04	OEM
IRKU26-06	OEM
IRKU26-08	OEM
IRKU26-10	OEM
IRKU26-12	OEM
IRKU26-14	OEM
IRKU26-16	OEM
IRKU26-18	OEM
IRKU41-04	OEM
IRKU41-06	OEM
IRKU41-08	OEM
IRKU41-10	OEM
IRKU41-12	OEM
IRKU41-14	OEM
IRKU41-16	OEM
IRKU41-18	OEM
IRKU56-04	OEM
IRKU56-06	OEM
IRKU56-08	OEM
IRKU56-10	OEM
IRKU56-12	OEM
IRKU56-14	OEM
IRKU56-16	OEM
IRKU56-18	OEM
IRKU71-04	OEM
IRKU71-06	OEM
IRKU71-08	OEM
IRKU71-10	OEM
IRKU71-12	OEM
IRKU71-14	OEM
IRKU71-16	OEM
IRKU71-18	OEM
IRKU91-04	OEM
IRKU91-06	OEM
IRKU91-08	OEM
IRKU91-10	OEM
IRKU91-12	OEM
IRKU91-14	OEM
IRKU91-16	OEM
IRKU91-18	OEM
IRKV26-04	OEM
IRKV26-06	OEM
IRKV26-08	OEM
IRKV26-10	OEM
IRKV26-12	OEM
IRKV26-14	OEM
IRKV26-16	OEM
IRKV26-18	OEM
IRKV41-04	OEM
IRKV41-06	OEM
IRKV41-08	OEM
IRKV41-10	OEM
IRKV41-12	OEM
IRKV41-14	OEM
IRKV41-16	OEM
IRKV41-18	OEM
IRKV56-04	OEM
IRKV56-06	OEM
IRKV56-08	OEM
IRKV56-10	OEM
IRKV56-12	OEM
IRKV56-14	OEM
IRKV56-16	OEM
IRKV56-18	OEM
IRKV71-04	OEM
IRKV71-06	OEM
IRKV71-08	OEM
IRKV71-10	OEM
IRKV71-12	OEM
IRKV71-14	OEM
IRKV71-16	OEM
IRKV71-18	OEM
IRKV91-04	OEM
IRKV91-06	OEM
IRKV91-08	OEM
IRKV91-10	OEM
IRKV91-12	OEM
IRKV91-14	OEM
IRKV91-16	OEM
IRKV91-18	OEM
IRL60	OEM
IRSANY0002	OEM
IRSANY0-002	OEM
IRSANYO002	OEM
IRSANY0-003	OEM
IRSANY0003	OEM
IRSANY0-004	OEM
IRSANY0004	OEM
IRSANY0-012	OEM
IRT26-06	1937
IRT82	0407
IRTR01	0085
IRTR02	0085
IRTR03	0435
IRTR04	0211
IRTR05	0279
IRTR06	0050
IRTR07	0050
IRTR08	0595
IRTR09	0038
IRTR10	0595
IRTR11	0279
IRTR12	0050
IRTR14	0164
IRTR16	0160
IRTR16X2	0142
IRTR17	0050
IRTR18	0050
IRTR19	0150
IRTR20	0037
IRTR21	0018
IRTR22	0079
IRTR23	0142
IRTR24	0079
IRTR25	0693
IRTR26	0103
IRTR27	0969
IRTR28	0150
IRTR30	0150
IRTR31	0006
IRTR32	0275
IRTR36MP	0130
IRTR37	0787
IRTR-50	0222
IRTR50	0222
IRTR50X2	0816
IRTR-51	0111
IRTR51	0111
IRTR-52	0786
IRTR52	0037
IR-TR53	0086
IRTR-53	0590
IRTR53	0086
IRTR-54	0150
IRTR54	0527
IRTR-55	0555
IRTR55	0555
IRTR-56	1257
IRTR56	1257
IRTR-57	0178
IRTR57	0419
IRTR-58	1021
IRTR58	0899
IRTR-59	0103
IRTR59	0103
IRTR-60	0283
IRTR60	0283
IRTR-61	0103
IRTR61	0103
IRTR61X2	1506
IRTR-62	0079
IRTR62	0016
IRTR-63	0930
IRTR63	0016
IRTR-64	0555
IRTR64	0693
IRTR-65	0693
IRTR65	0693
IRTR-66	0617
IRTR-67	0637
IRTR67	0637
IRTR-68	0003
IRTR68	0003
IRTR-69	0396
IRTR69	0396
IRTR-70	0224
IRTR70	0007
IRTR-71	0007
IRTR71	0007
IRTR-72	0546
IRTR72	0546
IRTR-73	0378
IRTR73	0378
IRTR-74	0264
IRTR74	0264
IRTR-75	0334
IRTR75	0334
IRTR-76	0042
IRTR76	0042
IRTR-77	0919
IRTR77	0919
IRTR-78	0233
IRTR78	0233
IRTR-79	0283
IRTR79	0283
IRTR-80	0144
IRTR80	0144
IRTR81	1021
IRTR82	0841
IRTR-83	0144
IRTR83	0144
IRTR84	0164
IRTR-85	0164
IRTR85	0004
IRTR-86	0855
IRTR86	0198
IRTR-87	0626
IRTR87	0086
IRTR-88	0378
IRTR88	0126
IRTR91	2736
IRTR92	0419
IRTR93	0065
IRTR94MP	1851
IRTR-95	0007
IRTR95	0144
IRTRFE100	0321
IRW106A1	0442
IRW106C1	1213
IRW106Y1	1386
IRW122A	2078
IRW122B	0500
IRW122F	2084
IRWC470-1300	OEM
IRZ1300	0542
IRZ1302	2101
IRZ1304	1890
IRZ1306	1591
IRZ1308	1612
IRZ1310	0986
IS002	OEM
IS003	OEM
IS08	0998
IS010	2499
IS015	OEM
IS020	6982
IS01209	0139
IS18	0998
IS28	4384
IS38	1028
IS48	0705
IS58	1140
IS68	1140
IS86	0030
IS110	0023
IS115	OEM
IS120	0114
IS-136	OEM
IS188AM	OEM
IS188FM	OEM
IS210	0393
IS215	OEM
IS220	0393
IS310	0606
IS315	OEM
IS320	0606
IS352M	0030
IS410	0606
IS415	OEM
IS420	0606
IS426	OEM
IS-446D	1141
IS510	0946
IS515	OEM
IS520	0946
IS553	OEM
IS554	OEM
IS610	0946
IS615	OEM
IS620	0946
IS1209	0139
IS1210	0139
IS1211	0139
IS-1212	0162
IS1212	0133
IS2095	OEM
ISB473	0222
ISB-3101-01	OEM
ISB-3101-02	OEM
ISB3600	OEM
ISB-3812-01	OEM
ISB-3812-02	OEM
ISB-3812-03	OEM
ISB-3812-04	OEM
ISBF1	0004
ISC71	OEM
ISC72	OEM
ISC82	OEM
ISC92	OEM
ISC302A	OEM
ISC302B	OEM
ISC302C	OEM
ISC302D	OEM
ISC302E	OEM
ISC302F	OEM
ISC363	OEM
ISC363A	OEM
ISC363B	OEM
ISC363C	OEM
ISC363D	OEM
ISC363E	OEM
ISC386	OEM
ISC386A	OEM
ISD-162	0038
ISD162	0038
ISO100AP(A)	OEM
ISO100BP(A)	OEM
ISO100CP(A)	OEM
ISO162	0595
ISPS035	OEM
ISPS135	OEM
ISPS235	OEM
ISPS335	OEM
ISPS435	OEM
ISPS535	OEM
ISPS635	OEM
ISPT030	3169
ISPT040	3169
ISPT130	3169
ISPT140	3169
ISPT230	3169
ISPT240	3169
ISPT330	3177
ISPT340	3177
ISPT430	3177
ISPT440	3177
ISPT530	3192
ISPT540	3192
ISPT630	3192
ISPT640	3192
ISS54	OEM
ISS106	OEM
ISS119	OEM
ISS120	0124
ISS122	0023
ISS-8053ALR	OEM
ISSRM2114C3	2037
ISSRM211403	2037
ISV87	4321
ISV97	OEM
ISV121	0133
IT06	0550
IT08	0550
IT08A	0550
IT08B	OEM
IT08HA	0550
IT08HX	0550
IT010	0550
IT010A	0550
IT010B	OEM
IT010HA	0550
IT010HX	0550
IT015	0767
IT015A	OEM
IT015B	OEM
IT015HA	OEM
IT015HX	OEM
IT4B42	1864
IT10D4K	0015
IT16	0550
IT18	0550
IT18A	0550
IT18B	OEM
IT18HA	0550
IT18HX	0550
IT22	0143
IT22A	0143
IT22AM	0143
IT22B	0143
IT23	0143
IT23A	0143
IT23G	0143
IT23S	0143
IT25	OEM
IT25-4	OEM
IT26	0550
IT28	0550
IT28HA	0550
IT28HX	0550
IT32	OEM
IT33	OEM
IT36	0550
IT38	0571
IT38B	OEM
IT38HA	0550
IT38HX	0550
IT40	0133
IT46	0550
IT48	0571
IT48A	0550
IT48B	OEM
IT48HA	0550
IT48HX	0550
IT56	0550
IT58	0550
IT58A	0550
IT58B	OEM
IT58HA	0550
IT58HX	0550
IT66	0550
IT68	0550
IT68A	0550
IT68B	OEM
IT68HA	0550
IT68HX	0550
IT100	OEM
IT101	OEM
IT108	0321
IT110	0550
IT110A	0550
IT110B	OEM
IT110HA	0550
IT115	0767
IT115A	OEM
IT115B	OEM
IT115HA	OEM
IT115HX	OEM
IT120	0079
IT120A	OEM
IT121	0079
IT122	0111
IT124	0396
IT125	OEM
IT126	OEM
IT127	OEM
IT128	OEM
IT129	OEM
IT130	OEM
IT130A	OEM
IT131	OEM
IT132	OEM
IT136	OEM
IT137	OEM
IT138	OEM
IT139	OEM
IT205A	0050
IT210	0550
IT210A	0550
IT210B	OEM
IT210HA	0550
IT210HX	0550
IT215	0767
IT215A	OEM
IT215B	OEM
IT215HA	OEM
IT215HX	OEM
IT243	0162
IT261	0143
IT262	0143
IT263	0143
IT310	0550
IT310A	0550
IT310B	OEM
IT310HA	0550
IT310HX	0550
IT315	0739
IT315A	OEM
IT315B	OEM
IT315HA	OEM
IT315HX	OEM
IT410	0550
IT410A	0550

If replacement code is OEM, contact original manufacturer for replacement.

439

DEVICE TYPE	REPL CODE
IT410B	OEM
IT410HA	0550
IT410HX	0550
IT415	0739
IT415B	OEM
IT415HA	OEM
IT415HX	OEM
IT500	OEM
IT501	OEM
IT502	OEM
IT503	1219
IT510	0550
IT510A	0550
IT510B	OEM
IT510HA	0550
IT510HX	0550
IT515	2033
IT515A	OEM
IT515B	OEM
IT515HA	OEM
IT515HX	OEM
IT610	0550
IT610A	0550
IT610B	OEM
IT610HA	0550
IT610HX	0550
IT615	0612
IT615A	OEM
IT615B	OEM
IT615HA	OEM
IT615HX	OEM
IT918	0007
IT918A	0111
IT929	0007
IT930	0007
IT1700	OEM
IT1750	OEM
IT2218	0079
IT2219	0079
IT2221	0079
IT2222	0079
IT2483	0855
IT2484	OEM
IT2604	0855
IT2605	0855
IT2904	0855
IT2905	0855
IT2906	0855
IT2907	0855
IT5911	OEM
IT5912	OEM
ITA7176AP	0167
ITA7607AP	0906
ITA7608CP5	2043
ITA7609P-2	4071
ITA7609P2	4071
ITC103-1	1129
ITC103-2	0340
ITC103-3	0895
ITC103-4	0058
ITC103-5	0403
ITC103-6	0403
ITC918A	0111
ITE4091	OEM
ITE4092	OEM
ITE4093	OEM
ITE4391	3102
ITE4392	OEM
ITE4393	OEM
ITE4416	0321
ITH61	0071
ITR3T24	OEM
ITS5817	0110
ITS5818	0110
ITS5823	1272
ITS5824	1272
ITS5825	1272
ITT10HX	OEM
ITT33	0124
ITT44	0124
ITT73	0229
ITT73N	0124
ITT74H00N	0677
ITT74H01N	5241
ITT74H04N	1896
ITT74H05N	3221
ITT74H10N	0680
ITT74H11N	2382
ITT74H20N	3670
ITT74H21N	4772
ITT74H30N	5284
ITT74H40N	0554
ITT74H50N	1781
ITT74H51N	1933
ITT74H53N	2090
ITT74H54N	2158
ITT74H60N	5312
ITT74H72N	3281
ITT74H73N	2444
ITT74H74N	2472
ITT74H76N	5208
ITT102	0143
ITT142	0133
ITT181-1	0133
ITT200	0124
ITT210	0030
ITT-243	OEM
ITT301	0143
ITT-310	0030
ITT310	0623
ITT310G	0030
ITT-310S	0030
ITT310S	0030
ITT310Y	0030
ITT350	0015
ITT-401	0030
ITT401	OEM
ITT-410	0715
ITT410	0030
ITT410B	OEM
ITT410S	OEM
ITT410ST	0030
ITT413	0133
ITT417	0137
ITT600	0124
ITT601	0124
ITT718	0143
ITT895	0079
ITT920	0124
ITT921	0133
ITT922	0182
ITT923	0182
ITT930-5	1812
ITT930N	1812
ITT932-5	1035
ITT932N	1035
ITT933-5	2086
ITT933N	2086
ITT935-5	1168
ITT935N	1168
ITT936-5	1820
ITT936N	1820
ITT937-5	1824
ITT937N	1824
ITT941-5	2598
ITT941N	2598
ITT944-5	0033
ITT944N	0033
ITT945-5	0081
ITT945N	0081
ITT946-5	0141
ITT946N	0141
ITT948-5	3365
ITT948N	3365
ITT949-5	1833
ITT949N	1833
ITT951-5	2067
ITT951N	2067
ITT961-5	1848
ITT961N	1848
ITT962-5	0557
ITT962N	0557
ITT963-5	0337
ITT963N	0337
ITT973	0037
ITT975	0079
ITT1330	1797
ITT1352	0391
ITT1800-5	0844
ITT1800N	0844
ITT1801N	0868
ITT1806-5	0939
ITT1806N	0939
ITT1807-5	0939
ITT1807N	0956
ITT1808-5	0976
ITT1808N	0976
ITT1809-5	0992
ITT1809N	0992
ITT1810-5	1005
ITT1810N	1005
ITT1811-5	1019
ITT1811N	1019
ITT2001	0133
ITT2002	0133
ITT2003	2505
ITT2018	OEM
ITT2147-55D	OEM
ITT2147-55J	OEM
ITT2147-55N	OEM
ITT2147-70D	OEM
ITT2147-70J	OEM
ITT2147-70LD	OEM
ITT2147-70LJ	OEM
ITT2147-70LN	OEM
ITT2147-70N	OEM
ITT2147-90D	OEM
ITT2147-90J	OEM
ITT2147-90N	OEM
ITT2147H-55D	OEM
ITT2147H-55J	OEM
ITT2147H-55N	OEM
ITT2167-45D	OEM
ITT2167-45N	OEM
ITT2167-55D	OEM
ITT2167-55N	OEM
ITT2167-70D	OEM
ITT2167-70N	OEM
ITT2168-45D	OEM
ITT2168-45N	OEM
ITT2168-55D	OEM
ITT2168-55N	OEM
ITT2168-70D	OEM
ITT2168-70N	OEM
ITT3001	0133
ITT3002	0604
ITT3003	0133
ITT3064	0797
ITT3065	0167
ITT-3105	0030
ITT3105	OEM
ITT4000G	1325
ITT4027-2	OEM
ITT4027-2D	OEM
ITT4027-2N	OEM
ITT4027-3	OEM
ITT4027-3D	OEM
ITT4027-3N	OEM
ITT4027-4	OEM
ITT4027-4D	OEM
ITT4027-4N	OEM
ITT4027-6	OEM
ITT4027-6D	OEM
ITT4027-6N	OEM
ITT4116-2D	OEM
ITT4116-2N	OEM
ITT4116-3	0518
ITT4116-3D	OEM
ITT4116-3N	OEM
ITT4116-4	0518
ITT4116-4D	OEM
ITT4116-4N	OEM
ITT4164-15	OEM
ITT4164-20	OEM
ITT5059	0080
ITT5060	0604
ITT5061	0790
ITT5062	0015
ITT5101S	OEM
ITT5116-2	OEM
ITT5401	OEM
ITT7163	OEM
ITT7164	OEM
ITT7215	0133
ITT7400N	0232
ITT7401N	0268
ITT7402N	0310
ITT7403N	0331
ITT7404N	0357
ITT7405N	0381
ITT7406N	1197
ITT7407N	1329
ITT7408N	0462
ITT7409N	0487
ITT7410N	0507
ITT7411N	0522
ITT7412N	2227
ITT7413N	1432
ITT7416N	1339
ITT7417N	1342
ITT7420N	0692
ITT7421N	1347
ITT7425N	3438
ITT7426N	0798
ITT7428N	4117
ITT7430N	0867
ITT7432N	0893
ITT7433N	4130
ITT7437N	3478
ITT7438N	0990
ITT7440N	1018
ITT7442N	1046
ITT7443N	1054
ITT7444N	1066
ITT7445N	1074
ITT7446AN	1090
ITT7447AN	1100
ITT7448N	1117
ITT7450N	0738
ITT7451N	1160
ITT7453N	1177
ITT7454N	1193
ITT7460N	1265
ITT7470N	1394
ITT7472N	1417
ITT7473N	1164
ITT7475N	1423
ITT7476N	1150
ITT7480N	1527
ITT7482N	1564
ITT7483N	0117
ITT7486N	1358
ITT7490N	1199
ITT7491AN	0974
ITT7492N	0828
ITT7493N	0564
ITT7494N	1692
ITT7495AN	1477
ITT7496N	1705
ITT9093-5	0354
ITT9093N	0354
ITT9094-5	1622
ITT9094N	1622
ITT9097-5	1472
ITT9097N	1472
ITT9099-5	0329
ITT9099N	0329
ITT9900JL	OEM
ITT9900JL-40	OEM
ITT74107N	0936
ITT74109N	0962
ITT74121N	0175
ITT74122N	1131
ITT74123N	1149
ITT74141N	1367
ITT74145N	0614
ITT74150N	1484
ITT74151N	1487
ITT74152N	1509
ITT74153N	1531
ITT74154N	1546
ITT74155N	1566
ITT74156N	1582
ITT74160N	1621
ITT74161N	1635
ITT74162N	1007
ITT74163N	1656
ITT74164N	0729
ITT74165N	1675
ITT74174N	1759
ITT74175N	1776
ITT74180N	1818
ITT74181N	1831
ITT74182N	1845
ITT74190N	1901
ITT74192N	1910
ITT74193N	1915
ITT74195N	1932
ITT330419	0790
ITT412142	0133
ITTA75902P	0823
ITTC4027B	1938
ITTC4030BP	0495
ITTC4049BP	0001
ITTC4052BP	0024
ITTC5012BP	2042
ITTC5066BP	OEM
ITTD62504P	OEM
ITTMS1025N2LC	OEM
IULM1131CN	OEM
IUPC1363C	0678
IUPD1937C	2079
IUPD1986C	4706
IVM-1	OEM
IVM1	OEM
IVM-3	OEM
IVN5000AND	OEM
IVN5000ANE	OEM
IVN5000ANF	OEM
IVN5000ANH	OEM
IVN5000BND	OEM
IVN5000BNE	OEM
IVN5000BNF	OEM
IVN5000SND	OEM
IVN5000SNE	OEM
IVN5000SNF	OEM
IVN5000SNH	OEM
IVN5000TND	OEM
IVN5000TNE	OEM
IVN5000TNF	OEM
IVN5000TNG	OEM
IVN5000TNH	OEM
IVN5001AND	OEM
IVN5001ANE	OEM
IVN5001ANF	OEM
IVN5001ANH	OEM
IVN5001BND	OEM
IVN5001BNE	OEM
IVN5001BNF	OEM
IVN5001SND	OEM
IVN5001SNE	OEM
IVN5001SNF	OEM
IVN5001SNH	OEM
IVN5001TND	OEM
IVN5001TNE	OEM
IVN5001TNF	OEM
IVN5001TNG	OEM
IVN5001TNH	OEM
IVN5200HND	OEM
IVN5200HNE	OEM
IVN5200HNF	OEM
IVN5200HNH	OEM
IVN5200KND	OEM
IVN5200KNE	OEM
IVN5200KNF	OEM
IVN5200KNH	OEM
IVN5200TND	OEM
IVN5200TNE	OEM
IVN5200TNF	OEM
IVN5200TNH	OEM
IVN5201CND	OEM
IVN5201CNE	4970
IVN5201CNF	OEM
IVN5201CNH	3059
IVN5201HND	OEM
IVN5201HNE	OEM
IVN5201HNF	OEM
IVN5201HNH	OEM
IVN5201KND	OEM
IVN5201KNE	OEM
IVN5201KNF	OEM
IVN5201KNH	OEM
IVN5201TND	OEM
IVN5201TNE	OEM
IVN5201TNF	OEM
IVN5201TNH	OEM
IVN6000CNS	1456
IVN6000CNT	1457
IVN6000CNU	1457
IVN6000KNR	OEM
IVN6000KNS	OEM
IVN6000KNT	OEM
IVN6000KNU	OEM
IVN6000TNS	OEM
IVN6000TNT	OEM
IVN6000TNU	OEM
IVN6100TNS	OEM
IVN6100TNT	OEM
IVN6100TNU	OEM
IVN6200CNE	4970
IVN6200CNF	4970
IVN6200CNH	4970
IVN6200CNM	OEM
IVN6200CNP	OEM
IVN6200CNS	1456
IVN6200CNT	OEM
IVN6200CNU	OEM
IVN6200CNW	OEM
IVN6200CNX	OEM
IVN6200KNE	OEM
IVN6200KNF	OEM
IVN6200KNH	OEM
IVN6200KNM	OEM
IVN6200KNP	OEM
IVN6200KNS	1658
IVN6200KNT	OEM
IVN6200KNU	OEM
IVN6200KNW	OEM
IVN6200KNX	OEM
IVN6300ANE	OEM
IVN6300ANF	OEM
IVN6300ANH	OEM
IVN6300ANM	OEM
IVN6300ANP	OEM
IVN6300ANS	OEM
IVN6300ANT	OEM
IVN6300ANU	OEM
IVN6300SNE	OEM
IVN6300SNF	OEM
IVN6300SNH	OEM
IVN6300SNM	OEM
IVN6300SNP	OEM
IVN6300SNS	OEM
IVN6300SNT	OEM
IVN6300SNU	OEM
IVN6660	OEM
IVN6661	OEM
IW	OEM
IW01-08J	0244
IWM5-1454L	OEM
IWM51454L	OEM
IX0027CE	OEM
IX0037CE	1319
IX0043CE	0167
IX0054CE	2845
IX0058GE	OEM
IX0069CE	0473
IX0084TA	OEM
IX0085TA	0598
IX0086TA	4339
IX0088TA	OEM
IX047GE	OEM
IX0137CE	2180
IX0137CE2SA562T(Q)	OEM
IX0144CE	OEM
IX0178CE	1580
IX0199CE	2079
IX0212CE	3640
IX0212CEZZ	3640
IX0213CE	2868
IX0213CEZZ	OEM
IX0214CE	3726
IX0225CE	3299
IX0232CE	1835
IX0233CEZZ	OEM
IX0238CE	2031
IX0238CEZZ	OEM
IX0243CE	0167
IX0248CE	OEM
IX0252CE	0069
IX0252CEZZ	0069
IX0260CE	2641
IX0275CE	4047
IX0280CE	OEM
IX0308C	OEM
IX0308CE	OEM
IX0314CE	OEM
IX0325C	5598
IX0325CE	OEM
IX0359CE	OEM
IX0359CEZZ	OEM
IX0406GE	OEM
IX0416CE	4009
IX0424CE	OEM
IX0430GE	OEM
IX0487CE	2254
IX0488CE	0412
IX0499CE	1594
IX0508GE	OEM
IX0539CE	OEM
IX0580CE	OEM
IX0581CE	OEM
IX0600CE	3206
IX0614CE	OEM
IX0633CE	4271
IX0634CE	OEM
IX0638CE	0619
IX0669CE	OEM
IX0692CE	OEM
IX0735CE	OEM
IX0800CE	OEM
IX0820CE	OEM
IX0943CE	OEM
IX0948CE	4066
IX0950CE	OEM
IX103AF	OEM
IX1030CE	OEM
IX1031AF	OEM
IX1077CE	OEM
IX1132CE	OEM
IX1190CE	3473
IX1231CE	OEM
IX1247CE	OEM
IX1525AF	OEM
IX1712CE	OEM
IX1890CE	OEM
IX1891CE	OEM
IX5004CE	OEM
IXD2201A	OEM
IXD2210	OEM
IXD2212D	OEM
IXMSL9371RS	OEM
IXMSL9372RS	OEM
IXMSL9373RS	OEM
IXMSL9378RS	5238
IXXEEA00020	OEM
IXXEEA00030	OEM
IYBA5102AALC	2094
IYBA5112LS	OEM
IYBA5115	OEM
IYBA6109U	OEM
IYBA6304A	2409
IYBA6305	OEM
IYBA6334	OEM
IZ0008CE	OEM
IZ0027CE	OEM
IZ0073CE	OEM
IZA169DR	OEM
IZZ0008	OEM
J005	2347
J01	5301
J02	5301
J04	5303
J-05	0015
J05	0102
J05G	0087
J06	5305
J-1	0015
J1	0102
J1G	0087
J-2	0015
J2	0102
J2-4570	0015
J2G	0087
J-4	0015
J4	0102
J4-1000	0232
J4-1002	0310
J4-1004	0357
J4-1010	0507
J4-1047	1100
J4-1075	1423
J4-1076	1150
J4-1090	1199
J4-1092	0828
J4-1121	0175
J4-1203	0375
J4-1215	0308
J4-1555	0967
J4-1600	0198
J4-1601	0071
J4-1602	0535
J4-1605	0287
J4-1610	0124
J4-1615	0162
J4-1619	0298
J4-1620	0012
J4-1622	0137
J4-1625	0211
J4-1626	0155
J4-1628	0016
J4-1630	0016
J4-1632	0037
J4-1634	0396
J4-1636	0326
J4-1638	0085
J4-1640	0103
J4-1642	0538
J4-1644	0111
J4-1645	0037
J4-1648	0126
J4-1649	0086
J4-1650	0037
J4-1651	0855
J4-1654	0419
J4-1655	0848
J4-1664	1351
J4-1665	1359
J4-1668	3340
J4-1669	3339
J4-1672	1671
J4-1673	0130
J4-1700	1882
J4-1710	3350
J4-1711	0321
J4-1713	0212
J4-1725	0934
J4-1730	0588
J4-1730(DIAC)	2704
J4-1730(TRIAC)	0588
J4A3	1017
J4B3	1017
J4C3	1017
J4D3	1017
J4E3	1017
J4EB	1017
J4F3	1017
J4G	0087
J4G3	1017
J4H3	1030
J4K3	1030
J4M3	1040
J4N3	1040
J5A3	1017
J5B3	1017
J5C3	1017
J5CB	1017
J5D3	1017
J5E3	1017
J5EB	1017
J5F3	1017
J5G3	1017
J5H3	1030
J5K3	1030
J5M3	1040
J5N3	1040
J5P3	OEM
J5R3	OEM
J5S3	OEM
J-6	0015
J6	0102
J6G	0087
J-8	0071
J8	0102
J8G	0087
J-10	0071
J10	0102
J10G	0087
J11J	OEM
J11L	OEM
J11X	OEM
J20	OEM
J39B	0005
J39C	0030
J100	0015
J101	OEM
J102	2256
J103	OEM
J105	0065
J105-18	OEM
J105GR	OEM
J106	OEM
J106-18	OEM
J107	0127
J107-18	OEM
J108	0144
J108-18	OEM
J109	OEM
J109-18	OEM
J110	OEM
J110-18	OEM
J111	3790
J111-18	5541
J112	0321
J112-18	OEM
J113	3791
J113-18	5830
J114	OEM
J139A	0016
J147	OEM
J174	OEM
J174-18	OEM
J175	OEM
J175-18	OEM
J176	OEM
J176-18	OEM
J177	OEM
J177-18	OEM
J187	0144
J200	OEM
J201	1747
J201-18	OEM
J202	1747
J202-18	OEM
J203	OEM
J203-18	OEM
J204	OEM
J204-18	OEM
J210	OEM
J211	OEM
J212	OEM
J230	OEM
J230-18	OEM
J231	OEM
J232	OEM
J232-18	OEM
J241	0123
J242	0143
J243	0143
J245X	OEM
J270	2436
J270-18	6400
J271	OEM
J300	OEM
J304	0321
J305	OEM
J308	0321
J309	0321
J310	OEM
J400	0142
J401	OEM
J402	OEM
J403	OEM

If replacement code is OEM, contact original manufacturer for replacement.

DEVICE TYPE	REPL CODE
J404	OEM
J405	OEM
J406	OEM
J410CN	OEM
J412CN	OEM
J422CN	OEM
J460	OEM
J461	OEM
J462	OEM
J463	OEM
J464	OEM
J465	OEM
J466	OEM
J503	OEM
J504	OEM
J505	OEM
J506	OEM
J507	OEM
J508	OEM
J509	OEM
J510	OEM
J511	OEM
J527-0A	OEM
J527-0C	OEM
J527-0D	OEM
J527-1A	OEM
J527-1C	OEM
J527-1D	OEM
J527-2A	OEM
J527-2C	OEM
J527-2D	OEM
J527-3A	OEM
J527-3C	OEM
J527-3D	OEM
J527-4A	OEM
J527-4C	OEM
J527-4D	OEM
J527-5A	OEM
J527-5C	OEM
J527-5D	OEM
J527-6A	OEM
J527-6C	OEM
J527-6D	OEM
J527-7A	OEM
J527-7C	OEM
J527-7D	OEM
J527-8A	OEM
J527-8C	OEM
J527-8D	OEM
J527-9A	OEM
J527-9C	OEM
J527-9D	OEM
J527-10A	OEM
J527-10C	OEM
J527-10D	OEM
J581	0855
J582	0855
J583	0855
J584	0855
J585	0855
J586	0855
J587	0855
J588	0855
J589	0855
J594	0855
J595	0855
J596	0855
J600	OEM
J623	0007
J624	0007
J625	0855
J626	0007
J627	0007
J628	0855
J629	0007
J630	0007
J631	0855
J650-1	OEM
J650-2	OEM
J650-3	OEM
J650-4	OEM
J650-5	OEM
J650-6	OEM
J650-7	OEM
J650-8	OEM
J650-9	OEM
J650-10	OEM
J650-11	OEM
J650-12	OEM
J650-13	OEM
J650-14	OEM
J650-15	OEM
J685	0019
J961B(G.E.)	0016
J1000-7400	0232
J1000-7402	0310
J1000-7404	0357
J1000-7410	0507
J1000-7447	1100
J1000-7476	1150
J1000-7490	1199
J1000-7492	0828
J1000-74121	0175
J1000-NE555	0967
J2441	0143
J4091	OEM
J4092	OEM
J4093	OEM
J4220	OEM

DEVICE TYPE	REPL CODE
J4221	OEM
J4222	OEM
J4223	OEM
J4224	OEM
J4302	OEM
J4303	OEM
J4304	OEM
J4338	OEM
J4339	OEM
J4391	OEM
J4392	OEM
J4393	OEM
J4416	OEM
J4856	OEM
J4857	OEM
J4858	OEM
J4859	OEM
J4860	OEM
J4861	OEM
J5062	0050
J5063	0004
J5064	0004
J6014	OEM
J6014A	OEM
J6015	OEM
J6015A	OEM
J9400	5440
J9680	0037
J9697	0037
J20104	OEM
J20104A	OEM
J20437	0015
J20438	0137
J24186	0157
J24262	0298
J24366	0222
J24458	0016
J24561	0127
J24562	0127
J24563	0127
J24564	0079
J24565	0079
J24566	0142
J24567	0123
J24569	0030
J24570	0015
J24596	0144
J24620	0050
J24621	0050
J24622	0050
J24623	0050
J24624	0016
J24625	0016
J24626	0004
J24628	0123
J24630	0015
J24631	0631
J24632	0012
J24635	0144
J24636	0144
J24637	0144
J24639	0004
J24640	0037
J24641	0016
J24642	0178
J24643	0123
J24645	0015
J24647	0015
J24658	0076
J24701	0127
J24752	0016
J24753	0016
J24754	1647
J24755	0133
J24756	0015
J24812	0111
J24813	0144
J24814	0144
J24817	0079
J24820	0123
J24832	0006
J24833	0004
J24834	0004
J24838	0143
J24840	0030
J24842	0151
J24843	0151
J24844	0284
J24845	0191
J24846	0076
J24852	0144
J24855	0079
J24858	0030
J24863	0144
J24868	0208
J24869	0004
J24870	0004
J24871	0015
J24872	0170
J24874	0079
J24875	0111
J24877	0023
J24878	0111
J24903	0127
J24904	0144
J24905	0144
J24906	0079
J24907	0079
J24908	0126

DEVICE TYPE	REPL CODE
J24909	0079
J24910	0030
J24911	0143
J24912	0133
J24913	0143
J24914	0143
J24915	0144
J24916	0079
J24919	0229
J24920	0015
J24921	0144
J24923	0144
J24932	0111
J24933	0144
J24934	0004
J24935	0015
J24939	0015
J24940	0015
J24950	0030
J34155	OEM
J41625	0211
J41642	0103
J41645	0037
J41700	1659
J101183	0015
J241015	4100
J241054	0079
J241099	0079
J241100	0015
J241101	OEM
J241102	0015
J241104	OEM
J241105	0030
J241111	2839
J241111(2SB370)	0004
J241111(2SD170)	0208
J241142	0015
J241164	0004
J241177	0127
J241178	0164
J241179	0631
J241181	0030
J241182	0133
J241183	0102
J241184	0030
J241185	0208
J241186	0157
J241188	0127
J241189	0127
J241190	0004
J241212	0229
J241219	0391
J241221	0633
J241222	0167
J241236	0061
J241239	0030
J241241	0042
J241245	0143
J241250	0161
J241251	0079
J241252	0419
J241253	0037
J241255	0086
J241256	0086
J241257	OEM
J241258	0899
J241259	0037
J241260	0015
J241270	0784
J241275	2990
J310159	0004
J310224	0004
J310249	0016
J310250	0016
J310251	0050
J310252	0004
J320020	0015
J320041	0143
JA101	0006
JA101(P)	0006
JA101(Q)	0006
JA101-R	OEM
JA101P	0006
JA101PQR	6666
JA101Q	0006
JA101R	OEM
JA1050	0037
JA1050G	0037
JA1050W	0037
JA1200	0079
JA1350	0079
JA1350A	0079
JA1350B	0111
JA1350W	0111
JA1350Y	0111
JA-1555	0967
JA1600G	0079
JA7010	0191
JA7072	0161
JA-H	0079
JA-KCDP	0087
JA-L	0079
JAM702C	0015
JAN1N1184	OEM
JAN1N1184R	OEM
JAN1N1186	OEM
JAN1N1186R	OEM
JAN1N1188	OEM
JAN1N1188R	OEM

DEVICE TYPE	REPL CODE
JAN1N1190	OEM
JAN1N1190R	OEM
JAN1N1614	OEM
JAN1N1615	OEM
JAN1N1616	OEM
JAN1N3289	OEM
JAN1N3291	OEM
JAN1N3293	OEM
JAN1N3294	OEM
JAN1N3295	OEM
JAN1N3713	OEM
JAN1N3715	OEM
JAN1N3719	OEM
JAN1N3721	OEM
JAN1N3766	OEM
JAN1N3766R	OEM
JAN1N3768	OEM
JAN1N3768R	OEM
JAN1N3890	OEM
JAN1N3890R	OEM
JAN1N3891	OEM
JAN1N3891R	OEM
JAN1N3893	OEM
JAN1N3893R	OEM
JAN1N3909	OEM
JAN1N3909R	OEM
JAN1N3910	OEM
JAN1N3910R	OEM
JAN1N3911	OEM
JAN1N3911R	OEM
JAN1N3912	OEM
JAN1N3912R	OEM
JAN1N3913	OEM
JAN1N3913R	OEM
JAN1N4148-1	OEM
JAN1N4150	OEM
JAN1N4153	OEM
JAN1N4454	OEM
JAN1N4459	OEM
JAN1N4531	OEM
JAN1N4532	OEM
JAN2N489A	OEM
JAN2N490A	OEM
JAN2N491A	OEM
JAN2N492A	OEM
JAN2N493A	OEM
JAN2N494A	OEM
JAN2N1021	OEM
JAN2N1559A	0160
JAN2N2323	OEM
JAN2N2323A	OEM
JAN2N2324	OEM
JAN2N2324A	OEM
JAN2N2326	OEM
JAN2N2326A	OEM
JAN2N2328	OEM
JAN2N2328A	OEM
JAN2N2329	OEM
JANDOD001	OEM
JANDOD002	OEM
JANDOD003	OEM
JANDOD004	OEM
JANDOD005	OEM
JANDOD007	OEM
JANDOD008	OEM
JANDOD009	OEM
JANDOD010	OEM
JANDOD011	OEM
JANDOD012	OEM
JANDOD013	OEM
JANDOD015	OEM
JANDOD016	OEM
JANDOD017	OEM
JANDOD019	OEM
JANDOD020	OEM
JANDOD021	OEM
JANDOD022	OEM
JANDOD023	OEM
JANDOD024	OEM
JANDOD025	OEM
JANDOD028	OEM
JANDOD029	OEM
JANDOD030	OEM
JANDOD031	OEM
JANDOD032	OEM
JANDOD033	OEM
JANDOD034	OEM
JANDOD035	OEM
JANDOD036	OEM
JANDOD037	OEM
JANDOD039	OEM
JANDOD0141	OEM
JANTX1N4150	OEM
JANTX1N4153	OEM
JANTX1N4454	OEM
JANTX1N4532	OEM
JANTX2N489A	OEM
JANTX2N490A	OEM
JANTX2N491A	OEM
JANTX2N492A	OEM
JANTX2N493A	OEM
JANTX2N494A	OEM
JANTX2N2323	OEM
JANTX2N2324	OEM
JANTX2N2326	OEM
JANTX2N2328	OEM
JANTX2N2329	OEM
JANTX1184/R	OEM
JB-00030	0015

DEVICE TYPE	REPL CODE
JB00030	0535
JB-00036	0229
JB00036	0276
JB-7B3B1	0299
JB6101C-058	OEM
JB8253P-5	OEM
JB8255AP-5	0051
JB8259AP	OEM
JB-BB1A	0015
JBM5W1793-02P	OEM
JC	OEM
JC-00012	0015
JC-00014	0015
JC-00017	0102
JC-00025	0015
JC-00028	0015
JC-00032	0015
JC00032	0535
JC-00033	0015
JC-00035	0015
JC-00037	0015
JC-00042	0023
JC-00044	0015
JC-00045	0015
JC-00047	0023
JC-00049	0023
JC00049	0015
JC00050	0015
JC-00051	0015
JC-00055	0080
JC-00059	0087
JC-10D1	0015
JC74HC151ND	OEM
JC100	0435
JC501	0076
JC501(P)	0284
JC501(Q)	0284
JC501-0	0284
JC501P	0076
JC501PQ	0076
JC501Q	0076
JC501R	0076
JC-DS16E	0015
JC-KS05	0015
JCMBL8088	OEM
JCMBL8288	OEM
JCN1	0015
JCN2	0015
JCN3	0015
JCN4	0015
JCN5	0015
JCN6	0015
JCN7	0071
JC-SD-1X	0015
JC-SD-1Z	0015
JC-SD1Z	0015
JC-SG005	0015
JC-V03C	0015
JCV1	OEM
JCV-2	0015
JCV2	0015
JCV-3	0015
JCV3	0015
JCV4	OEM
JCV5	OEM
JCV6	OEM
JCV7	0071
JCV10	OEM
JD-00040	0015
JD180L	0374
JD200L	0374
JD2300-1	OEM
JD2300-2	OEM
JD2300-4	OEM
JD2300-6	OEM
JD2300-8	OEM
JD2300-10	OEM
JD2300-12	OEM
JD2300-14	OEM
JD2300-16	OEM
JD2300-18	OEM
JD2300-20	OEM
JD2300-22	OEM
JD2300-24	OEM
JD2300-26	OEM
JD2300-28	OEM
JD2300-30	OEM
JD2300-32	OEM
JD2300-34	OEM
JD2300-36	OEM
JD2300-38	OEM
JD2300-40	OEM
JD2300-42	OEM
JD2300-44	OEM
JD3000-1	OEM
JD3000-2	OEM
JD3000-4	OEM
JD3000-6	OEM
JD3000-8	OEM
JD3000-10	OEM
JD3000-12	OEM
JD3000-14	OEM
JD3000-16	OEM
JD3000-18	OEM
JD3000-20	OEM
JD3000-22	OEM
JD3000-24	OEM
JD3000-26	OEM
JD3000-28	OEM

DEVICE TYPE	REPL CODE
JD3000-30	OEM
JD4000-1	OEM
JD4000-2	OEM
JD4000-3	OEM
JD4000-4	OEM
JD4000-5	OEM
JD4000-6	OEM
JD4000-7	OEM
JD4000-8	OEM
JD4000-9	OEM
JD4000-10	OEM
JD4000-11	OEM
JD4000-12	OEM
JD4000-13	OEM
JD4000-14	OEM
JD4000-15	OEM
JD4000-16	OEM
JD4000-17	OEM
JD4000-18	OEM
JD4000-19	OEM
JD4000-20	OEM
JD4000-21	OEM
JD4000-22	OEM
JD4000-23	OEM
JD4000-24	OEM
JD4000-25	OEM
JD4500-1	OEM
JD4500-2	OEM
JD4500-3	OEM
JD4500-4	OEM
JD4500-5	OEM
JD4500-6	OEM
JD4500-7	OEM
JD4500-8	OEM
JD4500-9	OEM
JD4500-10	OEM
JD4500-11	OEM
JD4500-12	OEM
JD5000-1	OEM
JD5000-2	OEM
JD5000-3	OEM
JD5000-4	OEM
JD5000-5	OEM
JD5000-6	OEM
JD6000-1	OEM
JD6000-2	OEM
JD6000-3	OEM
JD6000-4	OEM
JD6000-5	OEM
JD6000-6	OEM
JD6101C054	OEM
JD-8049HC-029	OEM
JD-8088D	OEM
JD8251AC	OEM
JD8288D	OEM
JD-BB1A	0015
JD-SD1D	0015
JDSD1D	0015
JD-SD1Z	0015
JE90NF	0079
JE108	0161
JE181	0161
JE210	0848
JE1033B	0321
JE4011	OEM
JE7001	2293
JE8050	4945
JE8050C	OEM
JE8550	1587
JE8550B	0527
JE8550C	0527
JE8550D	OEM
JE9011	4389
JE9011B	0111
JE9011C	0111
JE9011D	0079
JE9011E	0079
JE9011F	0079
JE9011G	0016
JE9011H	0079
JE9011I	0079
JE9012D	0037
JE9012E	0037
JE9012F	0037
JE9012G	0037
JE9012H	0037
JE9013	0079
JE9013D	0079
JE9013E	0079
JE9013F	0079
JE9013G	0079
JE9013H	0079
JE9014	0079
JE9014A	0079
JE9014B	0710
JE9014C	4811
JE9014D	0111
JE9015	0037
JE9015A	0037
JE9015B	0527
JE9015C	0037
JE9016	0144
JE9016D	0144
JE9016E	0144
JE9016F	0144
JE9016G	0144
JE9016H	0144
JE9016I	0144
JE9018D	0144

DEVICE TYPE	REPL CODE
JE9018E	0144
JE9018F	0144
JE9018G	0144
JE9018H	0144
JE9018I	0144
JE9042	0710
JE9042B	0710
JE9042C	0710
JE9100	OEM
JE9100A	0079
JE9101	OEM
JE9112	4945
JE9112A	OEM
JE9112B	0037
JE9112C	0037
JE9112D	OEM
JE9113A	OEM
JE9113B	OEM
JE9113C	0079
JE9113D	OEM
JEM1	0435
JEM2	0435
JEM3	0435
JEM4	0435
JEM5	0435
JF20	OEM
JF20D	OEM
JF23B	OEM
JF71	OEM
JF72	OEM
JF232	OEM
JF421L	OEM
JF444L	OEM
JF447L	OEM
JF-1033	0321
JF1033	0321
JF1033B	0321
JF1033G	0321
JF1033S	0321
JGLC651483005	OEM
JH2101	OEM
JH2102	OEM
JH2103	OEM
JH2104	OEM
JH2105	OEM
JH2106	OEM
JJ80	0769
JJ650	0769
JK10B	OEM
JK11B	OEM
JK30A	OEM
JK60A	OEM
JKV8	OEM
JKV8F	OEM
JKV10	OEM
JKV10F	OEM
JKV12	OEM
JKV12F	OEM
JL-40A	0133
JL40A	0133
JL41A	0015
JL41AM	0015
JM40	0133
JM401	0133
JNHD46505SP-1	OEM
JNJ61673	0321
JO2015A	OEM
JP2-22D	OEM
JP8-02B	OEM
JP9-2.5	OEM
JP9-2.5C	OEM
JP9-2.5D	OEM
JP9-2.5E	OEM
JP9-2.5F	OEM
JP9-2.5H	OEM
JP9-2.5L	OEM
JP9-7D	OEM
JP9-7L	OEM
JP9-7T	OEM
JP9-15B	OEM
JP9-15D	OEM
JP9-18	OEM
JP9-22B	OEM
JP9-22L	OEM
JP9-50A	OEM
JP40	0085
JP5062	0050
JP5063	0004
JP5064	0004
JP575005	0123
JP575995	0123
JR05	0136
JR5	0004
JR10	0050
JR15	0004
JR30	0050
JR30X	0050
JR40	0085
JR100	0050
JR200	0050
JRC386D	6450
JRC733	OEM
JRC8686	OEM
JS2737AS	OEM
JS8804AS	OEM
JSP6009	3136
JSP7001	0224
JSP7001B	0079
JSP7005	0144

If replacement code is OEM, contact original manufacturer for replacement. 441

DEVICE TYPE	REPL CODE
JSP7006	0144
JSP7010	OEM
JT-1601-40	0016
JT-1601-41	0911
JT-E1014	0143
JT-E1024D	0015
JT-E1031	0143
JT-E1064	0015
JT-E1095	0769
JU0001	OEM
JU0002	OEM
JU0010	OEM
JU0011	OEM
JU0012	OEM
JU0013	OEM
JU0014	OEM
JU0015	OEM
JU0016	OEM
JU0017	OEM
JU0018	OEM
JU0019	OEM
JU0020	OEM
JU0021	OEM
JU0023	OEM
JU0025	OEM
JU0027	OEM
JU0028	OEM
JU0029	OEM
JU0045	OEM
JU0046	OEM
JU0053	OEM
JU0056	OEM
JU0063	OEM
JU0069	OEM
JU0070	OEM
JU0077	OEM
JU0080	OEM
JU0081	OEM
JU0083	OEM
JU0089	OEM
JU0097	OEM
JU0104	OEM
JU0108	OEM
JU0109	OEM
JU0110	OEM
JU0123	OEM
JU0125	OEM
JU0126	OEM
JU0128	OEM
JU0132	OEM
JU0133	OEM
JU0135	OEM
JU0163	OEM
JU0173	OEM
JU0178	OEM
JU0180	OEM
JU0191	OEM
JU0192	OEM
JU0193	OEM
JU0199	OEM
JU0200	OEM
JU0210	OEM
JU0211	OEM
JU0212	OEM
JU0214	OEM
JU0219	OEM
JU0223	OEM
JU0229	OEM
JU0239	OEM
JU0240	OEM
JU0241	OEM
JU0266	OEM
JU0267	OEM
JU0280	OEM
JU0285	OEM
JU0286	OEM
JU0303	OEM
JU0309	OEM
JU0318	OEM
JU0323	OEM
JU0332	OEM
JU0348	OEM
JUD286	OEM
JUD318	OEM
JUD164	OEM
JZ5.6	0157
JZ5.6A	0157
JZ5.6B	0157
JZ5.6C	OEM
JZ5.6D	OEM
JZ6.2	0631
JZ6.2A	0631
JZ6.2B	0631
JZ6.2C	0631
JZ6.2D	0631
JZ6.8	0025
JZ6.8A	0025
JZ6.8B	0025
JZ6.8C	OEM
JZ6.8D	OEM
JZ7.5	0644
JZ7.5A	0644
JZ7.5B	0644
JZ7.5C	OEM
JZ7.5D	OEM
JZ8.2	0244
JZ8.2A	0244
JZ8.2B	0244
JZ8.2C	3071
JZ8.2D	3071
JZ9.1	0012
JZ9.1A	0012
JZ9.1B	0012
JZ9.1C	0012
JZ9.1D	OEM
JZ10	0170
JZ10A	0170
JZ10B	0170
JZ10C	OEM
JZ10D	OEM
JZ11	0313
JZ11A	0313
JZ11B	0313
JZ11C	OEM
JZ11D	OEM
JZ12	0137
JZ12A	0137
JZ12B	0137
JZ12C	0137
JZ12D	OEM
JZ13	0361
JZ13A	0361
JZ13B	0361
JZ13C	OEM
JZ13D	OEM
JZ14	0100
JZ14A	0100
JZ14B	0100
JZ14C	OEM
JZ14D	OEM
JZ15	0002
JZ15A	0002
JZ15B	0002
JZ15C	0002
JZ15D	OEM
JZ16	0416
JZ16A	0416
JZ16B	0416
JZ16C	OEM
JZ16D	OEM
JZ17	1639
JZ17A	1639
JZ17B	1639
JZ17C	OEM
JZ17D	OEM
JZ18	0490
JZ18A	0490
JZ18B	0490
JZ18C	OEM
JZ18D	OEM
JZ19	0943
JZ19A	0943
JZ19B	0943
JZ19C	OEM
JZ19D	OEM
JZ20	0526
JZ20A	0526
JZ20B	0526
JZ20C	OEM
JZ20D	OEM
JZ22	0560
JZ22A	0560
JZ22B	0560
JZ22C	OEM
JZ22D	OEM
JZ24	0398
JZ24A	0398
JZ24B	0398
JZ24C	OEM
JZ24D	OEM
JZ25	1596
JZ25A	1596
JZ25B	1596
JZ25C	OEM
JZ25D	OEM
JZ27	0436
JZ27A	0436
JZ27B	0436
JZ27C	OEM
JZ27D	OEM
JZ30	0721
JZ30A	0721
JZ30B	0721
JZ30C	OEM
JZ30D	OEM
JZ33	0039
JZ33A	0039
JZ33B	0039
JZ33C	OEM
JZ33D	OEM
JZ36	0814
JZ36A	0814
JZ36B	0814
JZ36C	OEM
JZ36D	OEM
JZ39	0346
JZ39A	0346
JZ39B	0346
JZ39C	OEM
JZ39D	OEM
JZ43	0925
JZ43A	0925
JZ43B	0925
JZ43C	OEM
JZ43D	OEM
JZ45	0993
JZ45A	0993
JZ45B	0993
JZ45C	OEM
JZ45D	OEM
JZ47	0993
JZ47A	0993
JZ47B	0993
JZ47C	OEM
JZ50	0497
JZ50A	0497
JZ50B	0497
JZ50C	OEM
JZ50D	OEM
JZ51	0497
JZ51A	0497
JZ51B	0497
JZ51C	OEM
JZ51D	OEM
JZ52	0497
JZ52A	0497
JZ52B	0497
JZ52C	OEM
JZ52D	OEM
JZ56	0863
JZ56A	0863
JZ56B	0863
JZ56C	OEM
JZ56D	OEM
JZ62	0778
JZ62A	0778
JZ62B	0778
JZ62C	OEM
JZ62D	OEM
JZ68	2144
JZ68A	2144
JZ68B	2144
JZ68C	OEM
JZ68D	OEM
JZ75	1181
JZ75A	1181
JZ75B	1181
JZ75C	OEM
JZ75D	OEM
JZ82	0327
JZ82A	0327
JZ82B	0327
JZ82C	OEM
JZ82D	OEM
JZ91	1301
JZ91A	1301
JZ91B	1301
JZ91C	OEM
JZ91D	OEM
JZ100	0098
JZ100A	0098
JZ100B	0098
JZ100C	OEM
JZ100D	OEM
JZ105	0149
JZ105A	0149
JZ105B	0149
JZ105C	OEM
JZ105D	OEM
JZ110	0149
JZ110A	0149
JZ110B	0149
JZ110C	OEM
JZ110D	OEM
JZ120	0186
JZ120A	0186
JZ120B	0186
JZ120C	OEM
JZ120D	OEM
JZ130	0213
JZ130A	0213
JZ130B	0213
JZ130C	OEM
JZ130D	OEM
JZ140	0245
JZ140A	0245
JZ140B	0245
JZ140C	OEM
JZ140D	OEM
JZ150	0028
JZ150A	0028
JZ150B	0028
JZ150C	OEM
JZ150D	OEM
JZ160	0255
JZ160A	0255
JZ160B	0255
JZ160C	OEM
JZ160D	OEM
JZ175	0363
JZ175A	0363
JZ175B	0363
JZ175C	OEM
JZ175D	OEM
JZ180	0363
JZ180A	0363
JZ180B	0363
JZ180C	OEM
JZ180D	OEM
JZ200A	0417
JZ200B	0417
JZ200C	OEM
JZ200D	OEM
JZ220	OEM
JZ220A	OEM
JZ220B	OEM
JZ220C	OEM
K-005	OEM
K-01	OEM
K-02	OEM
K-04	OEM
K-06	OEM
K0201E	1288
K04774	0085
K1	OEM
K1A5	0015
K1B5	0015
K1C5	0015
K1D5	0015
K1E5	0015
K1F5	0015
K1G5	0015
K1H5	0015
K1K5	0071
K1M5	0071
K1N5	OEM
K1N4748A518	OEM
K1V5	5539
K1V6	5540
K1V10	5542
K1V11	5543
K1V12	5544
K1.3G22/1A	0293
K1.3G22-1A	0276
K1.3G22A	0015
K2	OEM
K2A5	0015
K2B5	0015
K2C5	0015
K2CDP22/1B	0782
K2CDP221B	0276
K2D5	0015
K2DP12	0015
K2E5	0015
K2F5	0015
K2G	0015
K2G5	0015
K2H5	0071
K2K5	0071
K2M5	0071
K2N5	OEM
K3	0143
K3A	OEM
K3A5	OEM
K3AST47	0911
K3B5	0015
K3C5	0015
K3D5	0015
K3E	0911
K3E5	OEM
K3F	OEM
K3F5	0015
K3G5	0015
K3H5	0071
K3K5	0071
K3M5	0071
K3N5	OEM
K4-500	0164
K4-501	0208
K4-505	0037
K4-506	0016
K4-507	0198
K4-510	0144
K4-520	0085
K4-521	0085
K4-525	0103
K4-550	0143
K4-555	0015
K4-557	0015
K4-584	0934
K4-586(DIAC)	2704
K4-586(TRIAC)	0588
K4-590	0308
K4-598	0375
K4-632	3350
K4-634	0321
K4A5	0015
K4B5	0015
K4C5	0015
K4D5	0015
K4E5	0015
K4F5	0015
K4G5	0015
K4H5	0071
K4K5	0071
K4M5	0071
K4N5	OEM
K5	OEM
K5A5	0015
K5B5	0015
K5C5	0015
K5D5	0015
K5E5	0015
K5F5	0015
K5G5	0015
K5H5	0071
K5K5	0071
K5M5	0071
K5N5	OEM
K6	0143
K6A5	0087
K6B5	0087
K6C5	OEM
K6D5	OEM
K6E5	OEM
K6F5	OEM
K6G5	0087
K6H5	0087
K6K5	2621
K6M5	2621
K6N5	OEM
K7A5	0087
K7B5	0087
K7C5	0087
K7D5	OEM
K7E5	OEM
K7F5	OEM
K7G5	0087
K7H5	0087
K7K5	0087
K7M5	0087
K7N5	OEM
K8A5	0087
K8B5	0087
K8D5	OEM
K8E5	OEM
K8F5	OEM
K8G5	0087
K8H5	0087
K8K5	0087
K8M5	0087
K8N5	OEM
K11	0321
K12	0321
K12-0(1-GATE)	0321
K13	0321
K14-0066-1	0164
K14-0066-4	0279
K14-0066-6	0224
K14-0066-12	0079
K14-0066-13	0086
K15	3350
K15-GR(1-GATE)	0321
K15-0(1-GATE)	0321
K16HA	0321
K17(2S)	0321
K17-0	0321
K17-0(1-GATE)	0321
K17-OR	0321
K17A	0321
K17B	0321
K17BL	0321
K17GR	0321
K17O	0321
K17R	0321
K17Y	0321
K19	0683
K19-14	0683
K19-BL	0683
K19-GR	0683
K19-Y	0683
K19A	0683
K19B	0683
K19BB	0683
K19BL	0683
K19FET	0683
K19GB	0683
K19GE	0683
K19GR(2S)	0683
K19H	0683
K19K	0683
K19V	0683
K19Y(2S)	0683
K20	2439
K22Y	0321
K23	3672
K23A(2S)	3672
K23A8	3672
K23A9	3672
K23A-540	3672
K23A540	3672
K23G	3672
K24	0321
K24(1-GATE)	0321
K24C	0321
K24C(1-GATE)	0321
K24D	0321
K24D(1-GATE)	0321
K24DR	0321
K24DR(1-GATE)	0321
K24E	0321
K24E(1-GATE)	0321
K24F	0321
K24F(1-GATE)	0321
K24G	0321
K24G(1-GATE)	0321
K25	0321
K25A	OEM
K25B	OEM
K25C	0321
K25D	0321
K25E	0321
K25ET	0321
K25F	0321
K25G	0321
K26	OEM
K27	OEM
K27A	OEM
K29	OEM
K29M	OEM
K30	3017
K30-0	3017
K30-0(1-GATE)	0321
K30-Y	3017
K30A	3017
K30A-1	3017
K30A-GR	3017
K30AGR	3017
K30AGR(JAPAN)	3017
K30A-0	3017
K30AO	3017
K30AO(JAPAN)	3017
K30A-R	3017
K30ATM-0	3017
K30A-Y	3017
K30AY	3017
K30AY(JAPAN)	3017
K30D	3017
K30GR	3017
K30M	OEM
K30O	3017
K30R	3017
K30Y(2S)	3017
K31	3672
K31C(2S)	0321
K32	0321
K32A(2-GATE)	0349
K32B	0321
K32B(2-GATE)	0349
K32C(2-GATE)	0349
K32D(2-GATE)	0349
K33	1270
K33D	1270
K33E(2S)	1270
K33F(2S)	1270
K33H	1270
K33M	OEM
K34	0321
K34(2S)	3126
K34A	3126
K34B	3126
K34C(2S)	3126
K34D(2S)	3126
K34E(2S)	3126
K34M	OEM
K35	0321
K35(1-GATE)	0321
K35-0	0321
K35-0(1-GATE)	0321
K35-1	0321
K35-1(1-GATE)	0321
K35-2	0321
K35-2(1-GATE)	0321
K35A	0321
K35A(1-GATE)	0321
K35BL	0321
K35BL(1-GATE)	0321
K35C	0321
K35C(1-GATE)	0321
K35G(1-GATE)	0349
K35GN	0321
K35GN(1-GATE)	0321
K35M	OEM
K35R	0321
K35R(1-GATE)	0321
K35Y	0321
K35Y(1-GATE)	0321
K37	0321
K37H	0321
K39	0212
K39(2-GATE)	0212
K39A	0212
K39B	0212
K39P	0212
K39P(2-GATE)	0212
K39Q	0212
K39Q(2-GATE)	0349
K39R(2-GATE)	0349
K39R(2GATE)	0349
K40	3320
K40(2-GATE)	0349
K40-3	3320
K40A	3320
K40A(2-GATE)	0349
K40B	3320
K40B(2-GATE)	0349
K40C	3320
K40C(2-GATE)	0349
K40C(JAPAN)	3320
K40D	3320
K40D(2-GATE)	0349
K40M(2-GATE)	0349
K41	1202
K41C	1202
K41D	1202
K41E	1202
K41E1	1202
K41F	1202
K42	0321
K42(2S)	0321
K42-CM1	0321
K42-CMI	0321
K43	1747
K43-3	1747
K43-4	1747
K43-OR	1747
K43A	1747
K43B	1747
K43C	1747
K43D	1747
K43E	1747
K43F	1747
K43GN	1747
K43H	1747
K43J	1747
K43K	1747
K43L	1747
K43M	1747
K43OR	1747
K43R	1747
K43S	1747
K43X	1747
K43Y	1747
K44	0321
K44C	0321
K44D	0321
K45	0843
K45(2-GATE)	0212
K45B	0843
K45B(09)(2-GATE)	0212
K45B(2-GATE)	0843
K46B15	OEM
K46B30	OEM
K46B60	OEM
K46B100	OEM
K46B150	OEM
K46B200	OEM
K46HZ	OEM
K47(2S)	2922
K48	3219
K49(2S)	1270
K49E2	1270
K49F(2S)	1270
K49H(2S)	1270
K49H1	1270
K49H2	1270
K49I(2S)	1270
K49M	1270
K52	0143
K54	1270
K54B	1270
K54C	1270
K55	0321
K55C	0321
K55CD	0321
K55D	0321
K55DE	0321
K55R	0321
K57-130751	OEM
K57-569745	OEM
K60	0143
K61	1202
K61GR	1202
K61Y	1202
K66	3104
K66HZ	OEM
K68	3308
K68-L	3308
K68-M	3308
K68A	3308
K68AL	3308
K68A-M	3308
K68AM	3308
K68L	3308
K68M	3308
K68Q	3308
K72	2917
K81	OEM
K81(JAPAN)	OEM
K83	0321
K84	3104
K86HZ	OEM
K87HB	3104
K87HD	3104
K104	0321
K104H	0321
K105	1747
K105(JAPAN)	1747
K105E	1747
K105F	1747
K106	0321
K107	0321
K107-1	0321
K107-2	0321
K107-4	0321
K108	OEM
K112	0196
K-112C	0196
K112C	0196
K112D	0479
K113	1147
K115J510-1	0196
K115J510-1,2	0196
K115J510-2	0196
K115J511-2	0143
K117	3104
K117-BL	3104
K117A	3104
K117BL	3104
K117GR	3104
K117J460-1	0196
K117J460-2	0196
K117Y	3104
K118	1747
K118-O	1747
K118-R	1747
K118I	0126
K118J966-1	0479
K118J966-2	1073
K118J966-3	1073
K118J966-4	1073
K118J9663	1073
K118R	1747

If replacement code is OEM, contact original manufacturer for replacement.

DEVICE TYPE	REPL CODE
K119	0321
K120	1382
K121	1747
K121-2	1747
K-122	0196
K122	0196
K122-J176-1	0769
K122-J176-2	0769
K122-J177P1	1293
K-122C	0196
K122C	0196
K122D	0479
K122J176-1	0769
K122J176-2	0769
K122J177-P1	1293
K136S(JAPAN)	OEM
K141	1147
K141A	1147
K144IE6	OEM
K147D	OEM
K152	0321
K152-3	0321
K152LA	0321
K155AG1	OEM
K155ID3	OEM
K155IE1	OEM
K155IE2	OEM
K155IE4	OEM
K155IE7	OEM
K155IE8	OEM
K155IE9	OEM
K155IM1	OEM
K155IM2	OEM
K155IM3	OEM
K155IP3	OEM
K155IR13	OEM
K155KP5	OEM
K155KP7	OEM
K155LA1	OEM
K155LA2	OEM
K155LA3	OEM
K155LA6	OEM
K155LA7	OEM
K155LA8	OEM
K155LA11	OEM
K155LA12	OEM
K155LD1	OEM
K155LD3	OEM
K155LE1	OEM
K155LE2	OEM
K155LE3	OEM
K155LE6	OEM
K155LI1	OEM
K155LI5	OEM
K155LL1	OEM
K155LN1	OEM
K155LN2	OEM
K155LN3	OEM
K155LN4	OEM
K155LP7	OEM
K155LR1	OEM
K155LR3	OEM
K155LR4	OEM
K155PR6	OEM
K155PR7	OEM
K155RE3	OEM
K155RE21	OEM
K155RE22	OEM
K155RE23	OEM
K155RE24	OEM
K155RP1	OEM
K155RU1	OEM
K155RU2	OEM
K155RU5	OEM
K155TM2	OEM
K155TM5	OEM
K155TM7	OEM
K155TV1	OEM
K161	3577
K168D	0321
K168F	0321
K170	0321
K175LE10	OEM
K176ID1	OEM
K176IE1	OEM
K176IE2	OEM
K176IE3	OEM
K176IE4	OEM
K176IE5	OEM
K176IE8	OEM
K176IR2	OEM
K176IR3	OEM
K176IR10	OEM
K176LA7	OEM
K176LA8	OEM
K176LA9	OEM
K176LE5	OEM
K176LE6	OEM
K176LI1	OEM
K176LP1	OEM
K176LP2	OEM
K176LP4	OEM
K176LP11	OEM
K176LP12	OEM
K176LS1	OEM
K176RM1	OEM
K176RU2	OEM
K176TM2	OEM
K176TV1	OEM

DEVICE TYPE	REPL CODE
K191	3219
K192	0321
K194	0321
K195H	1382
K196R	3219
K197	0321
K197YC	0321
K197YD	0321
K197YE	0321
K200	1219
K212	1382
K212AE	1382
K212E	1382
K218	OEM
K249-1608722	OEM
K301R(JAPAN)	OEM
K304	0321
K308	OEM
K314	OEM
K314A	OEM
K315	OEM
K316	OEM
K316A	OEM
K319	1456
K335	OEM
K347A	OEM
K351	OEM
K352	OEM
K359	OEM
K370	OEM
K370W	OEM
K371	OEM
K371W	OEM
K372	OEM
K372W	OEM
K376L	OEM
K377L	OEM
K381	1747
K381-E	1747
K383	4970
K384	OEM
K385	OEM
K386	OEM
K386W	OEM
K387	OEM
K387L	OEM
K391	1324
K391A	OEM
K408	OEM
K408A	OEM
K408B	OEM
K415	OEM
K417-68	0136
K510Z	OEM
K540	OEM
K656	OEM
K678-3M180100RC	OEM
K678-4M180/5	OEM
K700-1	OEM
K728	OEM
K728T	OEM
K743A	OEM
K743B	OEM
K744	OEM
K745	OEM
K746	OEM
K765	OEM
K766	OEM
K767	OEM
K768	OEM
K769	OEM
K770	OEM
K771	OEM
K774	OEM
K805	OEM
K806	OEM
K824	OEM
K882	0143
K901	OEM
K902	OEM
K903	OEM
K904	OEM
K905	OEM
K917	OEM
K918	OEM
K920	OEM
K928	OEM
K1001	OEM
K1002	OEM
K1003	OEM
K1004	OEM
K1004(CXK1004L)	OEM
K1005	OEM
K1005(SM)	OEM
K1011	OEM
K1011(IC)	OEM
K1038	OEM
K1039	OEM
K1040	OEM
K1140	OEM
K1201	OEM
K1202	OEM
K1240	OEM
K1440	OEM
K1501	OEM
K1502	OEM
K1504	0838
K1507B	OEM
K1615	0196

DEVICE TYPE	REPL CODE
K1615AC	0196
K1616	0479
K1616AC	0479
K1617	1073
K1617AC	1073
K2001	0127
K2040	OEM
K2070	0144
K2071	0144
K2072	0007
K2073	0007
K2101	0414
K2101A	0414
K2102	0414
K2102A	0414
K2103	0414
K2103A	0414
K2104	0414
K2104A	0414
K2105	0414
K2105A	0414
K2106	0414
K2106A	0414
K2107	0414
K2107A	0414
K2108	0414
K2108A	0414
K2109	0144
K2109A	0259
K2110	0144
K2110A	0259
K2111	0144
K2111A	0259
K2112	0144
K2112A	0259
K2113	0144
K2113A	0259
K2114	0144
K2114A	0259
K2115	0007
K2115A	0259
K2116	0144
K2116A	0259
K2117	0144
K2117A	0259
K2118	0144
K2118A	0259
K2119	0127
K2119A	0259
K2120	0127
K2120A	0259
K2121	0127
K2121A	0259
K2122	0127
K2122A	0259
K2123	0127
K2123A	0259
K2124	0127
K2124A	0259
K2125	0127
K2125A	0259
K2126	0127
K2126A	0259
K2127	0127
K2127A	0259
K2501	0127
K2502	0127
K2503	0127
K2507	0414
K2509	0127
K2523	0414
K2524	0414
K2525	0259
K2601	0414
K2601A	0414
K2601C	0127
K2602	0414
K2602A	0414
K2602C	0127
K2603	0414
K2603A	0414
K2603C	0127
K2604	0127
K2604A	0259
K2604C	0127
K2607	0414
K2607A	0414
K2608	0414
K2608A	0414
K2609	0414
K2609A	0414
K2610	0414
K2610A	0414
K2611	0414
K2611A	0414
K2612	0414
K2612A	0414
K2613	0414
K2613A	0414
K2614	0414
K2614A	0414
K2615	0127
K2615A	0259
K2616	0127
K2616A	0259
K2857C	0007
K2857P	0007
K3004	OEM
K3005	OEM

DEVICE TYPE	REPL CODE
K3006	OEM
K3007	OEM
K3010P	4961
K3020P	4975
K3040	OEM
K3069	OEM
K3073	OEM
K3076	OEM
K3077	OEM
K3078-6975	OEM
K3079	OEM
K3080	OEM
K3081	OEM
K3091	OEM
K3094	OEM
K3097	OEM
K3098	OEM
K3111	OEM
K3118	OEM
K3217H	OEM
K3270	OEM
K3271	OEM
K3276H	OEM
K3282	OEM
K3283	OEM
K3284	OEM
K3286	OEM
K3287	OEM
K3342W92K	OEM
K3382	OEM
K3383	OEM
K3384	OEM
K3683C	0007
K3683P	0007
K3880C	0007
K3880P	0144
K4002	0127
K4040	OEM
K4540	OEM
K4560	1313
K4586	0588
K4590	OEM
K4634	0321
K5001	0144
K5002	0144
K5003	0144
K5010	OEM
K5011	OEM
K5012	0326
K5020	OEM
K5040	OEM
K5100	OEM
K5150	OEM
K5151	OEM
K5200	OEM
K5250	OEM
K5256	OEM
K5258	OEM
K5500	OEM
K5502	OEM
K5503C	0259
K5504	OEM
K5550	OEM
K5552	OEM
K5554	OEM
K5560-5	OEM
K5560-6	OEM
K6001N	0855
K6002	0855
K6002N	0855
K6003	0855
K6009	0855
K6012	0855
K6022	0855
K6040	OEM
K6100	OEM
K6150	OEM
K6200	OEM
K6202	OEM
K6203	OEM
K6250	OEM
K6251	OEM
K6252	OEM
K6253	OEM
K6500	OEM
K6502	OEM
K6550	OEM
K6552	OEM
K7100	OEM
K7150	OEM
K7200	OEM
K7250	OEM
K8010	OEM
K8013P	OEM
K8020	OEM
K8030	OEM
K8031P	OEM
K8040	OEM
K-8073	OEM
K8100	OEM
K8101	OEM
K8102	OEM
K8103	OEM
K8105	OEM
K8110	OEM
K8111	OEM
K8112	OEM
K8113	OEM
K8114	OEM

DEVICE TYPE	REPL CODE
K8120	OEM
K8121	OEM
K8130	OEM
K8138E	OEM
K8139E	1225
K8140	OEM
K8141	OEM
K8150	OEM
K8151	OEM
K8152	OEM
K8153	OEM
K8154	OEM
K8155	OEM
K8160	OEM
K8161	OEM
K8162	OEM
K8163	OEM
K8164	OEM
K8165	OEM
K8170	OEM
K8171	OEM
K8180	OEM
K8181	OEM
K8190	OEM
K8191	OEM
K8324	OEM
K8700	OEM
K8701	OEM
K8702	OEM
K8703	OEM
K8710	OEM
K8711	OEM
K8712	OEM
K8713	OEM
K8713-16	OEM
K8720	OEM
K8730	OEM
K8740	OEM
K8900	OEM
K8920	OEM
K8940	OEM
K8941	OEM
K8950	OEM
K9000	OEM
K9001	OEM
K9002	OEM
K9010	OEM
K9011	OEM
K9012	OEM
K9014	OEM
K9015	OEM
K9020	OEM
K9021	OEM
K9022	OEM
K9682	0037
K18046	0940
K26044	0958
K26174	2860
K53342W98K	OEM
K75508-1	0050
K76026	4558
K1038345-22A	0196
K1038345-22C	1073
K1038345-22E	0479
K8532799	0015
K8533058-1	0015
K8533137	0196
K8534992P1	0196
K8534992P2	0196
KA1Z25	0086
KA33V	1319
KA431CD	5200
KA507A	OEM
KA507V	OEM
KA509A	OEM
KA509B	OEM
KA509V	OEM
KA510A	OEM
KA510B	OEM
KA510D	OEM
KA510E	OEM
KA510G	OEM
KA510V	OEM
KA513A	OEM
KA513B	OEM
KA562-Y	0006
KA562Y	0006
KA602A	OEM
KA602B	OEM
KA602D	OEM
KA602G	OEM
KA602V	OEM
KA651	OEM
KA701A	OEM
KA1002R	OEM
KA1002RF	OEM
KA1003RF	OEM
KA1004R	OEM
KA1004RF	OEM
KA1006R	OEM
KA1006RF	OEM
KA1008R	OEM
KA1008RF	OEM
KA1010R	OEM
KA1010RF	OEM
KA1015-0	0006
KA1330	OEM
KA1390	OEM
KA1450	OEM

DEVICE TYPE	REPL CODE
KA1510	OEM
KA1570	OEM
KA1630	OEM
KA1690	OEM
KA1750	OEM
KA2101	0167
KA2107	OEM
KA2131	0970
KA2153	0658
KA2155	0552
KA2181	2015
KA2192	OEM
KA2201	6289
KA2201N	OEM
KA2221	OEM
KA2224	2572
KA2247	OEM
KA2249	OEM
KA2261	1251
KA2281	OEM
KA2284	OEM
KA2911	0906
KA2914A	4047
KA2915	OEM
KA2918	OEM
KA2919	0534
KA4559	0321
KA7809C	OEM
KA7812	0330
KA7812C	OEM
KA8301	OEM
KA22062	OEM
KAP1151	OEM
KAP1152	OEM
KAQ6502	2976
KB9CVV	0016
KB102	0133
KB-162	0139
KB162	0133
KB-162C5	0139
KB-162C5A	0139
KB-162C5B	OEM
KB162N	0139
KB162W	0139
KB-165	0139
KB165	0139
KB167	1914
KB-169	0139
KB169	0139
KB-182	0015
KB202	0287
KB209	OEM
KB-262	0120
KB262	0120
KB-262C4	OEM
KB-262M	OEM
KB-265	0139
KB265	0139
KB265A	0133
KB-265C4	OEM
KB-269	0120
KB269	0139
KB296	3200
KB-362	OEM
KB-362M	OEM
KB-365	0139
KB365	OEM
KB-369	OEM
KB369	OEM
KB-462	OEM
KB462F	3407
KB-465	OEM
KB-469	OEM
KB3600-PRO	OEM
KB4400	OEM
KB4409	0514
KB4419	OEM
KB4420B	OEM
KB4424	OEM
KB4431	OEM
KB4432	OEM
KB4433	OEM
KB4436	OEM
KB4437	OEM
KB4438	OEM
KB4441	OEM
KB4446	OEM
KB4448	OEM
KB4454	OEM
KB8339	0016
KB8416	0079
KBCTD15-005	OEM
KBCTD15-02	OEM
KBCTD15-04	OEM
KBCTD15-06	OEM
KBCTD15-08	OEM
KBCTD15-10	OEM
KBCTP15-005	OEM
KBCTP15-02	OEM
KBCTP15-04	OEM
KBCTP15-06	OEM
KBCTP15-08	OEM
KBCTP15-10	OEM
KBF005	4745
KBF-02	0724
KBF02	4745
KBF04	4749
KBF06	4749
KBF08	4753

DEVICE TYPE	REPL CODE
KBF10	4753
KBH2502	2347
KBH2504	2353
KBH2506	2354
KBL005	0724
KBL01	0724
KBL-02	OEM
KBL02	2994
KBL04	0732
KBL05	OEM
KBL06	3006
KBL08	0737
KBL10	3021
KBP-005	0276
KBP005	0276
KBP01	0276
KBP-02	OEM
KBP02	0287
KBP04	0293
KBP06	0299
KBP08	0250
KBP-10	0250
KBP10	0250
KBPC005	0319
KBPC02	1404
KBPC02A	OEM
KBPC04	0468
KBPC04A	OEM
KBPC06	0441
KBPC06A	OEM
KBPC08	1412
KBPC08A	OEM
KBPC10	2425
KBPC10-005	5386
KBPC10-01	2347
KBPC10-02	2347
KBPC10-04	2353
KBPC10-06	2354
KBPC10-08	2356
KBPC10-10	2357
KBPC12-005	2347
KBPC12-02	2347
KBPC12-04	2353
KBPC12-06	2354
KBPC12-08	2356
KBPC12-10	2357
KBPC15-005	2347
KBPC15-02	2347
KBPC15-04	2353
KBPC15-06	2354
KBPC15-08	2356
KBPC15-10	2357
KBPC25-005	2347
KBPC25-02	2347
KBPC25-04	2353
KBPC25-06	2354
KBPC25-08	2356
KBPC25-10	2357
KBPC35-005	1633
KBPC35-02	1633
KBPC35-04	1663
KBPC35-06	1663
KBPC35-08	1579
KBPC35-10	1579
KBPC101	0319
KBPC102	1404
KBPC102A	OEM
KBPC104	0468
KBPC104A	OEM
KBPC106	0441
KBPC106A	OEM
KBPC108	1412
KBPC108A	OEM
KBPC110	2425
KBPC601	0319
KBPC602	1404
KBPC604	0468
KBPC606	0441
KBPC608	1412
KBPC610	2425
KBPC-801	0319
KBPC801	0319
KBPC802	1404
KBPC802T	2347
KBPC804	0468
KBPC804T	2353
KBPC806	0441
KBPC806T	2354
KBPC808	1412
KBPC808T	2356
KBPC810	2425
KBPC810T	2357
KBPC1005	0319
KBPC1201	2347
KBPC1202	2347
KBPC1204	2353
KBPC1206	2354
KBPC1208	2356
KBPC1210	2357
KBPC1501	2347
KBPC1502	2347
KBPC1504	2353
KBPC1506	2354
KBPC1508	2356
KBPC1510	2357
KBPC2501	2347
KBPC2502	2347
KBPC2502W	OEM
KBPC2504	2353

If replacement code is OEM, contact original manufacturer for replacement.

443

DEVICE TYPE	REPL CODE
KBPC2506	2354
KBPC2508	2356
KBPC2510	2357
KBPC3501	1633
KBPC3502	1633
KBPC3504	1663
KBPC3506	1663
KBPC3508	1579
KBPC3510	1579
KBPC6005	0319
KBPC8005	0319
KBPC8005T	2347
KBPC12005	2347
KBPC15005	2347
KBPC25005	2347
KBPC35005	1633
KBPS-005	1325
KBPS-02	OEM
KBPS-04	OEM
KBPS-06	OEM
KBPS-08	OEM
KBPS-10	OEM
KBU4A	1036
KBU4B	1036
KBU4D	1036
KBU4G	1039
KBU4J	1039
KBU4K	5059
KBU4M	5059
KBU6A	1036
KBU6B	1036
KBU6D	1036
KBU6G	1039
KBU6J	1039
KBU6K	1041
KBU6M	1041
KBU8A	OEM
KBU8B	OEM
KBU8D	OEM
KBU8G	OEM
KBU8J	OEM
KBU8K	OEM
KBU8M	OEM
KC0-8CP	0015
KC0-8CP11/1+12/1	0015
KC06E11/8	0015
KC08C11/8	0015
KC08C11/10	0015
KC08C21/5	0015
KC08C22/19	0015
KC08C215	0015
KC08C221	0015
KC08C1110	0015
KC08C2219	0276
KC0911/8	0015
KC06911	0015
KC0.8C22/1	0276
KC0.8CP	0015
KC0.8CP11	0015
KC0.8CP11/1	0015
KC0.8CP11/1+121Y	0015
KC0.8CP12/1	0015
KC1.3C	0015
KC1.3C3X11/1	0015
KC1.3C22/1	0015
KC1.3G	0015
KC1.3G12/1X2	0015
KC1.3G22/1A	0015
KC2AP22/1B	0276
KC2AP221B	0276
KC2AP22116	0782
KC2BP22/1B	0015
KC2D22/1	0276
KC2D22/1A	0782
KC2D221	0015
KC2DP	0015
KC2DP11/1	0015
KC2DP12/1	0015
KC2DP12/1N	0015
KC2DP12/2	0015
KC2DP22/1	0015
KC2DP22/1B	0276
KC2DP22/1C	0782
KC2DP22/16	0782
KC2DP121N	0015
KC2DP122	0015
KC2DP221	0015
KC2DP221B	0015
KC2DP221C	0276
KC2G	0133
KC2G11/1	0015
KC2G11/1+12/1	0015
KC2G11/1&12/1	0015
KC2G12/1	0015
KC13C221	0015
KC112A	0196
KC383C	4560
KC388A	0284
KC580C	OEM
KC580C1	1049
KC581C	4561
KC582C	4556
KC583C	4560
KC850C1	0043
KC1322/1	0015
KC1815-GR	0284
KC1815-Y	0284
KC1815Y	0284
KC1959-O	0284
KCD-80P11/1+12/1	0102
KCDP12-1	0087
KC06E11/8	0535
KC08C11/8	0535
KC08C21/5	0535
KC08C22/19	0535
KC0-8CP11/1-12/1	0015
KC0911/8	0535
KC0.8C22/1	0782
KC0.8CP11	0015
KC0.8CP11/1+12/1	0015
KCS1674R	OEM
KD11HA	OEM
KD11HF	OEM
KD27	0143
KD102A	OEM
KD102B	OEM
KD103A	0133
KD103B	0133
KD104A	OEM
KD202A	OEM
KD202B	OEM
KD202D	OEM
KD202E	OEM
KD202G	OEM
KD202I	OEM
KD202K	OEM
KD202L	OEM
KD202M	OEM
KD202N	OEM
KD202R	OEM
KD202S	OEM
KD202SZ	OEM
KD202V	OEM
KD204A	OEM
KD204B	OEM
KD204V	OEM
KD205A	OEM
KD205B	OEM
KD205D	OEM
KD205E	OEM
KD205G	OEM
KD205V	OEM
KD206A	OEM
KD206B	OEM
KD206V	OEM
KD208A	OEM
KD209A	OEM
KD209B	OEM
KD209V	OEM
KD229D	OEM
KD229E	OEM
KD300A	0133
KD407A	OEM
KD409A	OEM
KD503A	OEM
KD503B	OEM
KD514A	OEM
KD518A	OEM
KD519A	OEM
KD520A	OEM
KD521A	OEM
KD521V	OEM
KD522A	OEM
KD522B	OEM
KD1925P	OEM
KD1926P	OEM
KD2101	0004
KD2102	0016
KD2103	0015
KD2104	0015
KD2114	1843
KD2118	0086
KD2119	0144
KD2120	0126
KD2121	0841
KD2124	0038
KD2130	0212
KD2131	6267
KD2501	0170
KD2503	0631
KD2504	0012
KD2505	0137
KD2541	0414
KD4002	0414
KD4025	0414
KD5000	0144
KD5051	OEM
KD5052	OEM
KD5053	OEM
KD5054	OEM
KD5055	OEM
KD6000-1	OEM
KD6000-2	OEM
KD6000-3	OEM
KD6000-4	OEM
KD6000-5	OEM
KD6000-6	OEM
KD6311	0523
KDA4002	OEM
KDC-80P11/1912/1	0102
KDD-0013	0143
KDD0015	0057
KDD0032	0080
KDD0041	0133
KDF11-AA	OEM
KDF11-HK	OEM
KDF11-LK	OEM
KDS288Y	OEM
KDS362	0388
KDS362N	0723
KDS1553	0133
KDS1554	0133
KDS1555	0133
KDS1555-T	0133
KDS2236	OEM
KDT-16	OEM
KE-262	0015
KE3586	OEM
KE3684	2922
KE3685	2922
KE3687	2922
KE3970	3102
KE3971	OEM
KE3972	OEM
KE4091	3102
KE4092	OEM
KE4093	OEM
KE4220	2922
KE4221	OEM
KE4222	OEM
KE4223	3219
KE4224	3219
KE4391	3102
KE4392	OEM
KE4393	OEM
KE4416	0321
KE4856	3102
KE4857	OEM
KE4858	OEM
KE4859	3102
KE4860	OEM
KE4861	OEM
KE5103	2922
KE5104	3219
KE5105	0321
KE5460	OEM
KEY-C00CV	OEM
KEY-C00SV	OEM
KEY-C00SV-F	OEM
KF-104	OEM
KF104	OEM
KF3509	0488
KFLD20	OEM
KFLD20A	OEM
KFLD30	OEM
KFLD30A	OEM
KFLD40	OEM
KFLD40A	OEM
KFLD50	OEM
KFLD50A	OEM
KFLD60	OEM
KFLD60A	OEM
KG100D	OEM
KG100F	OEM
KG100G	OEM
KG100H	OEM
KGB0430SX	OEM
KGB0431SX	OEM
KGB0440SX	OEM
KGB0521SX	OEM
KGB0522SX	OEM
KGB0523SX	OEM
KGB0524SX	OEM
KGB0611SX	OEM
KGB0612SX	OEM
KGB0613SX	OEM
KGB0614SX	OEM
KGB0711SX	OEM
KGB0712SX	OEM
KGB0713SX	OEM
KGB0714SX	OEM
KGD1420SX	OEM
KGD1421SX	OEM
KGD1422SX	OEM
KGD1423SX	OEM
KGD1424SX	OEM
KGD1430SX	OEM
KGD1431SX	OEM
KGD1440SX	OEM
KGD1521SX	OEM
KGD1522SX	OEM
KGD1523SX	OEM
KGD1524SX	OEM
KGD1611SX	OEM
KGD1612SX	OEM
KGD1613SX	OEM
KGD1614SX	OEM
KGD1711SX	OEM
KGD1712SX	OEM
KGD1714SX	OEM
KGE41007	0015
KGE41013	4498
KGE41054	0376
KGE41055	0151
KGE41061	2035
KGE41414	0018
KGE41959	0143
KGE46109	0133
KGE46146	0076
KGE46338	0076
KGE46441	1012
KGE46442	1532
KGE46465	0133
KGS1000	0004
KGS1001	0164
KGS1002	OEM
KGS1003	OEM
KGS1004	OEM
KGS1005	OEM
KH3207	OEM
KH5015	OEM
KH5196	OEM
KH5197	OEM
KH5198	OEM
KH5199	OEM
KHA109	OEM
KHA125	OEM
KHA136	OEM
KHP3	OEM
KHP4	OEM
KHP5	OEM
KHP6	OEM
KHP7	OEM
KHP8	OEM
KHP9	OEM
KHP10	OEM
KHP15	OEM
KHP20	OEM
KHP25	OEM
KHP30	OEM
KHP35	OEM
KHP40	OEM
KHP45	OEM
KHP50	OEM
KIA78L005AP	5345
KIA574P(ZENER)	OEM
KIA4558P	OEM
KIA7033	OEM
KIA7033P	OEM
KIA7042	OEM
KIA7042P	OEM
KIA7137P	OEM
KIA7205	OEM
KIA7205AP	1044
KIA7205P	1044
KIA7310P	1532
KIA7313AP	0358
KIA7313AP(B/C)	OEM
KIA7343P	OEM
KIA7358P	OEM
KIA7366P	OEM
KIA7373AP	0358
KIA7630	3726
KIA7630P	3726
KIA7640AP	3680
KIA7668BP	OEM
KIA7812P	0330
KIA65393S	OEM
KIA75558P	OEM
KIA75902P	OEM
KIA78005AP	OEM
KIA78006P	OEM
KIA78012AP	3445
KIA78012AP(KEC)	0330
KIA78012P	OEM
KIU12AM	OEM
KIU12BM	OEM
KJ6001	OEM
KJ6007N	OEM
KJA733C-G-T	OEM
KJA733C-L-T	OEM
KL5	OEM
KL10	OEM
KL15	OEM
KL20	OEM
KL25	OEM
KL30	OEM
KL35	OEM
KL40	OEM
KL45	OEM
KL50	OEM
KL101A	OEM
KL101B	OEM
KL101V	OEM
KL105A	OEM
KL105B	OEM
KL105V	OEM
KLG114	OEM
KLG124E	OEM
KLG205E	OEM
KLG206E	OEM
KLG-208E	OEM
KLH704	0079
KLH1422	0079
KLH4567	0015
KLH4577	0015
KLH4746	0037
KLH4747	3495
KLH4763	0133
KLH4781	0848
KLH4792	0127
KLH4793	0696
KLH5489	0649
KLK1422	OEM
KLN1068	OEM
KLR5	OEM
KLR10	OEM
KLR15	OEM
KLR20	OEM
KLR25	OEM
KLR114	OEM
KLR114E	1605
KLR114F	1605
KLR124E	OEM
KLR162E	OEM
KLR205E	OEM
KLR206E	OEM
KLR208E	OEM
KLR226E	OEM
KLR226ERD	OEM
KLY124E	OEM
KM41C464P-10	OEM
KM155KP5	OEM
KM155KP7	OEM
KM858C	2238
KM858C/11	OEM
KM904	OEM
KM905	OEM
KM917E	0079
KM917F	0076
KM917G	0079
KM918	OEM
KM918E	0144
KM918F	0144
KM934	OEM
KM935	OEM
KM3502P	OEM
KM4164-15	2341
KM4164A-15	OEM
KM5624	4558
KM6264BL-10L	OEM
KM7245BP	OEM
KM7245P	OEM
KM41256-12	OEM
KM41256-15	OEM
KM41256AP-12	5635
KM41256AP-15	1463
KN2	0196
KN1201	OEM
KN1201A	OEM
KN1203	OEM
KN1204	OEM
KN1301	OEM
KN1401	OEM
KN2203	OEM
KN2207	OEM
KN2209	OEM
KN2222	0079
KN2907	0037
KNL8251LA	OEM
K020-01	OEM
K020-02	OEM
K020-03	OEM
K025-51	OEM
K025-52	OEM
K025-53	OEM
K025-181	OEM
K04774	0085
K0S25201-1	0143
K0S25201-2	0143
K0S25211-2	0025
K0S25221-1	0030
K0S25642-10	0136
K0S25642-20	0136
K0S25642-40	0136
K0S25643-10	0136
K0S25643-15	0136
K0S25651-20	0004
K0S25657-53	0004
K0S25661-20	0085
K0S25671-20	0216
K0S25671-21	0216
K0S25671-23	0216
KP20-01	OEM
KP20-02	OEM
KP20-03	OEM
KP202D	OEM
KP202E	OEM
KP302A	OEM
KP302B	OEM
KP302G	OEM
KP302V	OEM
KP303A	OEM
KP303B	OEM
KP303D	OEM
KP303E	OEM
KP303G	OEM
KP303I	OEM
KP303SZ	OEM
KP303V	OEM
KP307A	OEM
KP307B	OEM
KP307D	OEM
KP307E	OEM
KP307G	OEM
KP307SZ	OEM
KP307V	OEM
KP308A	OEM
KP308B	OEM
KP308D	OEM
KP308G	OEM
KP308V	OEM
KP312A	OEM
KP312B	OEM
KP313A	OEM
KP313B	OEM
KP313V	OEM
KP314A	OEM
KP350A	OEM
KP350B	OEM
KP350V	OEM
KP901A	OEM
KP901B	OEM
KP902A	OEM
KP902B	OEM
KP902V	OEM
KP903A	OEM
KP903B	OEM
KP903V	OEM
KP904A	OEM
KPB02	0287
KPB04	0293
KPB08	0250
KPB10	0250
KPC107	OEM
KPC107A	OEM
KPC107B	OEM
KPC107C	OEM
KPC107D	OEM
KPC112	OEM
KPC112A	OEM
KPC112B	OEM
KPC112C	OEM
KPC112D	OEM
KPC113	OEM
KPC113A	OEM
KPC113B	OEM
KPC113C	OEM
KPC113D	OEM
KPC114	OEM
KPC114A	OEM
KPC114B	OEM
KPC114C	OEM
KPC114D	OEM
KPC115	OEM
KPC115A	OEM
KPC115B	OEM
KPC115C	OEM
KPC115D	OEM
KPC116	OEM
KPC116A	OEM
KPC116B	OEM
KPC116C	OEM
KPC116D	OEM
KPC117	OEM
KPC117A	OEM
KPC117B	OEM
KPC117C	OEM
KPC117D	OEM
KPC122	OEM
KPC122A	OEM
KPC122B	OEM
KPC122C	OEM
KPC122D	OEM
KPC123	OEM
KPC123A	OEM
KPC123B	OEM
KPC123C	OEM
KPC123D	OEM
KPC124	OEM
KPC124A	OEM
KPC124B	OEM
KPC124C	OEM
KPC124D	OEM
KPC125	OEM
KPC125A	OEM
KPC125B	OEM
KPC125C	OEM
KPC125D	OEM
KPC126	OEM
KPC126A	OEM
KPC126B	OEM
KPC126C	OEM
KPC126D	OEM
KPC127	OEM
KPC127A	OEM
KPC127B	OEM
KPC127C	OEM
KPC127D	OEM
KPC128	OEM
KPC128A	OEM
KPC128B	OEM
KPC128C	OEM
KPC128D	OEM
KPC129	OEM
KPC129A	OEM
KPC129B	OEM
KPC129C	OEM
KPC129D	OEM
KPC130	OEM
KPC130A	OEM
KPC130B	OEM
KPC130C	OEM
KPC130D	OEM
KPC132	OEM
KPC132A	OEM
KPC132B	OEM
KPC132C	OEM
KPC132D	OEM
KPC133	OEM
KPC133A	OEM
KPC133B	OEM
KPC133C	OEM
KPC133D	OEM
KPC134	OEM
KPC134A	OEM
KPC134B	OEM
KPC134C	OEM
KPC134D	OEM
KPC135	OEM
KPC135A	OEM
KPC135B	OEM
KPC135C	OEM
KPC135D	OEM
KPC136	OEM
KPC136A	OEM
KPC136B	OEM
KPC136C	OEM
KPC136D	OEM
KPC137	OEM
KPC137A	OEM
KPC137B	OEM
KPC137C	OEM
KPC137D	OEM
KPC138	OEM
KPC138A	OEM
KPC138B	OEM
KPC138C	OEM
KPC138D	OEM
KPC139	OEM
KPC139A	OEM
KPC139B	OEM
KPC139C	OEM
KPC139D	OEM
KPC140	OEM
KPC140A	OEM
KPC140B	OEM
KPC140C	OEM
KPC140D	OEM
KPC141	OEM
KPC141A	OEM
KPC141B	OEM
KPC141C	OEM
KPC141D	OEM
KPD1404	0270
KPD2502M	OEM
KPG107	OEM
KPG107A	OEM
KPG107B	OEM
KPG110	OEM
KPG110A	OEM
KPG110B	OEM
KPG115	OEM
KPG115A	OEM
KPG115B	OEM
KPG122	OEM
KPG122A	OEM
KPG122B	OEM
KPG133	OEM
KPG133A	OEM
KPG133B	OEM
KPG139	OEM
KPG139A	OEM
KPG139B	OEM
KPG147	OEM
KPG147A	OEM
KPG147B	OEM
KPG207	OEM
KPG207A	OEM
KPG207B	OEM
KPG210	OEM
KPG210A	OEM
KPG210B	OEM
KPG215	OEM
KPG215A	OEM
KPG215B	OEM
KPG222	OEM
KPG222A	OEM
KPG222B	OEM
KPG233	OEM
KPG233A	OEM
KPG233B	OEM
KPG239	OEM
KPG239A	OEM
KPG239B	OEM
KPG247	OEM
KPG247A	OEM
KPG247B	OEM
KPG307	OEM
KPG307A	OEM
KPG307B	OEM
KPG310	OEM
KPG310A	OEM
KPG310B	OEM
KPG315	OEM
KPG315A	OEM
KPG315B	OEM
KPG322	OEM
KPG322A	OEM
KPG322B	OEM
KPG333	OEM
KPG333A	OEM
KPG333B	OEM
KPG339	OEM
KPG339A	OEM
KPG339B	OEM
KPG6682	0016
KPS202A	OEM
KPS202B	OEM
KPS202G	OEM
KPS202V	OEM
KQ20-01	OEM
KQ20-02	OEM
KQ20-03	OEM
KR50	OEM
KR51	OEM
KR52	OEM
KR53	OEM
KR54	OEM
KR55	OEM
KR56	OEM
KR57	OEM
KR58	OEM

444

If replacement code is OEM, contact original manufacturer for replacement.

DEVICE TYPE	REPL CODE	DEVICE TYPE	REPL CODE	DEVICE TYPE	REPL CODE	DEVICE TYPE	REPL CODE	DEVICE TYPE	REPL CODE	DEVICE TYPE	REPL CODE	DEVICE TYPE	REPL CODE
KR59	OEM	KR-Q0001	0004	KS123GA	0109	KS2062B	0631	KSC539-Y	OEM	KSC2330-0	0261	KT102AA	0927
KR60	OEM	KR-Q0002	0004	KS123HA	0109	KS2091A	0012	KSC581C	OEM	KSC2330-Y	0261	KT102BA	0941
KR123AA	OEM	KR-Q0004	0004	KS123KA	0122	KS2091B	0012	KSC582C	OEM	KSC23300	0261	KT102CA	0941
KR123BA	OEM	KR-Q0005	0143	KS123MA	0122	KS2100A	0170	KSC815	0079	KSC2330Y	0261	KT102DA	0941
KR123CA	OEM	KR-Q1010	0004	KS123PA	0131	KS2100B	0170	KSC815(O)	0079	KSC2331	1614	KT102EA	0994
KR123DA	OEM	KR-Q1011	0004	KS123RA	0131	KS2120A	0137	KSC815(Y)	0079	KSC2331-0	1614	KT102FA	1006
KR123EA	OEM	KR-Q1012	0004	KS123TA	0145	KS2120B	0137	KSC815-0	0076	KSC2331-0Y	0018	KT102GA	1006
KR123FA	OEM	KR-Q1013	0016	KS123VA	0145	KS2150A	0002	KSC815-O	0079	KSC2331-Y	1614	KT102HA	1006
KR123GA	OEM	KS-05	0015	KS150A	0002	KS2150B	0002	KSC815-OY	0079	KSC23310	1614	KT102KA	1067
KR123HA	OEM	KS05	0015	KS150B	0002	KS3060	OEM	KSC815-Y	0079	KSC2331Y	1614	KT102MA	1067
KR123KA	OEM	KS030A	1703	KS162AA	0703	KS-3302	OEM	KSC815D	0079	KSC2340	0261	KT102PA	1130
KR123MA	OEM	KS033A	0289	KS162BA	0575	KS3302	OEM	KSC815D-O	0079	KSC2785	2926	KT102RA	1130
KR123PA	OEM	KS033B	0296	KS162CA	0575	KS4060	OEM	KSC815Y	0079	KSD73	1157	KT102TA	1180
KR123RA	OEM	KS036A	0188	KS162DA	0575	KS5060	OEM	KSC838	0079	KSD73(O)	1157	KT102VA	1180
KR123TA	OEM	KS039A	0451	KS162EA	0994	KS5302	OEM	KSC838(O)	0155	KSD73-0	1157	KT123AA	0529
KR123VA	OEM	KS039B	0036	KS162FA	0994	KS5410	OEM	KSC838-0	0155	KSD73-0	1157	KT123BA	0760
KR-162	0124	KS043A	0528	KS162GA	0994	KS5803B	OEM	KSC838-O	0155	KSD73-Y	1157	KT123CA	0760
KR162AA	OEM	KS047A	0446	KS162HA	0994	KS6060	OEM	KSC838A-O	OEM	KSD73Y	1157	KT123DA	0760
KR162BA	OEM	KS047B	0140	KS162KA	2070	KS8060	OEM	KSC838CY	OEM	KSD227(Y)	0079	KT123EA	0533
KR162CA	OEM	KS051A	0162	KS162MA	2070	KS10969-L5	1339	KSC853(Y)	0079	KSD227-0	0284	KT123FA	0533
KR162DA	OEM	KS056A	0157	KS162PA	2077	KS20967-L1	0232	KSC945	0079	KSD261	0079	KT123GA	0533
KR162EA	OEM	KS056B	0157	KS162RA	2077	KS20967-L2	0357	KSC945(G)	0284	KSD261(O)	0590	KT123HA	0533
KR162FA	OEM	KS062A	0631	KS162TA	0607	KS20967-L3	1358	KSC945(O)	0079	KSD261(Y)	0590	KT123KA	0810
KR162GA	OEM	KS9-20B	OEM	KS162VA	0607	KS20969-L2	0117	KSC945(Y)	0079	KSD261-0	0590	KT123MA	0810
KR162HA	OEM	KS9-20D	OEM	KS196A	OEM	KS20969-L3	0828	KSC945-G	0079	KSD261-0	0079	KT123PA	0540
KR162KA	OEM	KS9-20G	OEM	KS196B	OEM	KS20969-L4	1477	KSC945-O	0079	KSD261-0Y	0590	KT123RA	0540
KR162MA	OEM	KS30A	0188	KS196G	OEM	KS21282-L1	0462	KSC945-OY	0079	KSD261-Y	0590	KT123TA	0545
KR162PA	OEM	KS30AF	0188	KS302AA	0703	KS21282-L2	3438	KSC945-Y	0079	KSD261Y	0590	KT123VA	0545
KR162RA	OEM	KS30B	0188	KS302BA	0575	KS21282-L3	0893	KSC945C	OEM	KSD288	2969	KT162AA	0927
KR162TA	OEM	KS30BF	0188	KS302CA	0575	KS51900-11	OEM	KSC945C-G	OEM	KSD361N	0388	KT162BA	0941
KR162VA	OEM	KS31A	0188	KS302DA	0575	KSA495Y	0037	KSC945C-K	OEM	KSD362	1157	KT162CA	0941
KR252AA	OEM	KS31AF	OEM	KS302EA	0994	KSA539	0037	KSC945G	0076	KSD362(R)	0388	KT162DA	0941
KR252BA	OEM	KS32A	0188	KS302FA	0994	KSA539-0	0148	KSC945Y	0076	KSD362-C	1157	KT162EA	0994
KR252CA	OEM	KS32AF	0188	KS302GA	0994	KSA539-O	0037	KSC1008	0079	KSD362-N	0388	KT162FA	1006
KR252DA	OEM	KS32B	0188	KS302HA	0994	KSA539-Y	0037	KSC1008(Y)	0079	KSD362-NR	0388	KT162GA	1006
KR252EA	OEM	KS32BF	0188	KS302KA	2070	KSA539Y	0037	KSC1008-0	0079	KSD362-R	0388	KT162HA	1006
KR252FA	OEM	KS33A	OEM	KS302MA	2070	KSA542-0	0006	KSC1008-O	5041	KSD362-Y	1157	KT162KA	1067
KR252GA	OEM	KS33AF	OEM	KS302PA	2077	KSA542-O	0037	KSC1008-Y	0079	KSD362C	1157	KT162MA	1067
KR252HA	OEM	KS34A	0162	KS302RA	2077	KSA542Y	0006	KSC1008C	0079	KSD362C(Y)	1157	KT162PA	1130
KR252KA	OEM	KS34AF	0162	KS302TA	0607	KSA562	0006	KSC1008Y	0079	KSD362C-Y	1157	KT162RA	1130
KR252MA	OEM	KS34B	0162	KS302VA	0607	KSA562-O	0006	KSC1096	0219	KSD362N	1157	KT162TA	1180
KR252PA	OEM	KS34BF	0162	KS433A	OEM	KSA562TM	0037	KSC1096(O)	0219	KSD362R	1157	KT162VA	1180
KR252RA	OEM	KS35A	0162	KS439A	OEM	KSA562TM-O	0006	KSC1096-0	0236	KSD362Y	1157	KT208A	OEM
KR252TA	OEM	KS35A2	OEM	KS471A	OEM	KSA614	0676	KSC1096-O	0219	KSD363	0723	KT208B	OEM
KR252VA	OEM	KS35AF	0162	KS502AA	0964	KSA614(Y)	0676	KSC1096-Y	0219	KSD401	0388	KT208D	OEM
KR302AA	OEM	KS36A	0157	KS502BA	0983	KSA614-O	5931	KSC1096Y	0236	KSD401(O)	0388	KT208E	OEM
KR302BA	OEM	KS36AF	0157	KS502CA	0983	KSA614-Y	0676	KSC1187	0224	KSD401(Y)	0388	KT208G	OEM
KR302CA	OEM	KS36B	0157	KS502DA	0983	KSA614Y	0676	KSC1187(O)	0224	KSD401-7	0388	KT208I	OEM
KR302DA	OEM	KS36BF	0157	KS502EA	0197	KSA634	1045	KSC1187(R)	0224	KSD401-O	0388	KT208K	OEM
KR302EA	OEM	KS37A	0466	KS502FA	0197	KSA634(O)	1045	KSC1187-0	0224	KSD401-Y	0388	KT208L	OEM
KR302FA	OEM	KS37AF	0466	KS502GA	0197	KSA634(Y)	1045	KSC1187-O	0224	KSD401A	0388	KT208M	OEM
KR302GA	OEM	KS38A	OEM	KS502HA	0197	KSA634-0	0676	KSC1187-R	0224	KSD401Y	0388	KT208S	OEM
KR302HA	OEM	KS38AF	OEM	KS502KA	0204	KSA634-O	1045	KSC1187C	0224	KSD415-0	0261	KT208V	OEM
KR302KA	OEM	KS38B	OEM	KS502MA	0204	KSA634-Y	1045	KSC1187O	0224	KSD415-O	0710	KT218	0079
KR302MA	OEM	KS38BF	OEM	KS502PA	0206	KSA634Y	0676	KSC1187R	0224	KSD415-Y	0710	KT218F	0855
KR302PA	OEM	KS39A	OEM	KS502RA	0206	KSA639-0	OEM	KSC1189R	0079	KSD415D	0710	KT302A	OEM
KR302RA	OEM	KS39AF	OEM	KS502TA	0583	KSA642	0037	KSC1394	2293	KSD415O	0710	KT302AA	0927
KR302TA	OEM	KS40A	OEM	KS502VA	0583	KSA642-0	0006	KSC1395	0144	KSD415R	0261	KT302B	OEM
KR302VA	OEM	KS40AF	OEM	KS512A	0137	KSA642-O	0037	KSC1507	0168	KSD415Y	0261	KT302BA	0941
KR502AA	OEM	KS40B	OEM	KS515A	0002	KSA642-Y	0037	KSC1507(O)	0168	KSD471-Y	0320	KT302CA	0941
KR502BA	OEM	KS40BF	OEM	KS560	OEM	KSA6420	0638	KSC1507-0	0638	KSD471Y	0018	KT302DA	0941
KR502CA	OEM	KS41A	0057	KS602AA	0964	KSA643	0037	KSC-1507-O	0168	KSD807M	1485	KT302EA	0994
KR502DA	OEM	KS41AF	0057	KS602BA	0983	KSA643(O)	0037	KSC1507-O	0168	KSD1051	0103	KT302FA	1006
KR502EA	OEM	KS42A	0170	KS602CA	0983	KSA643(Y)	0037	KSC-1507-Y	0168	KSD1052	0177	KT302G	OEM
KR502FA	OEM	KS42AF	0170	KS602DA	0983	KSA643-0	0527	KSC1507-Y	0168	KSD1053	0177	KT302GA	1006
KR502GA	OEM	KS42B	0170	KS602EA	0197	KSA643-O	0037	KSC1507A0	0168	KSD1054	0177	KT302HA	1006
KR502HA	OEM	KS42BF	0170	KS602FA	0197	KSA643-OY	0786	KSC1507A-O	0168	KSD1055	0103	KT302KA	1067
KR502KA	OEM	KS43A	OEM	KS602GA	0197	KSA643-Y	0037	KSC1507AO	0168	KSD1056	0103	KT302MA	1067
KR502MA	OEM	KS43AF	OEM	KS602HA	0197	KSA6430	1233	KSC1507A-Y	0638	KSD1057	0177	KT302PA	1130
KR502PA	OEM	KS44A	0052	KS602KA	0204	KSA643Y	0527	KSC1507AY	0168	KSD1058	0177	KT302RA	1130
KR502RA	OEM	KS44AF	0052	KS602MA	0204	KSA653	0786	KSC1507K	0638	KSD2101	0178	KT302TA	1180
KR502TA	OEM	KS44B	0052	KS602PA	0206	KSA708	0037	KSC1507L	0168	KSD2102	0178	KT302V	OEM
KR502VA	OEM	KS44BF	0052	KS602RA	0206	KSA708(O)	0037	KSC15070	0338	KSD2103	0178	KT302VA	1180
KR602AA	OEM	KS45AF	OEM	KS602TA	0583	KSA708(Y)	0037	KSC1507Y	0638	KSD2201	0177	KT326A	OEM
KR602BA	OEM	KS46	0002	KS602VA	0583	KSA708-O	1587	KSC1509-O	OEM	KSD2202	0177	KT326B	OEM
KR602CA	OEM	KS46AF	0681	KS751AA	0703	KSA708-Y	1587	KSC1520	0168	KSD2203	0130	KT339B	OEM
KR602DA	OEM	KS46BF	0681	KS751BA	0575	KSA708D	OEM	KSC1520(O)	0168	KSD3055	0130	KT339D	OEM
KR602EA	OEM	KS47AF	OEM	KS751CA	0575	KSA708Y	0037	KSC1520(Y)	0168	KSD3771	0130	KT339G	OEM
KR602FA	OEM	KS48AF	OEM	KS751DA	0575	KSA733	0037	KSC1520-O	0168	KSD3772	0130	KT339V	OEM
KR602GA	OEM	KS48BF	OEM	KS751EA	0994	KSA733(O)	0037	KSC1520-R	0168	KSD3773	0359	KT345A	OEM
KR602HA	OEM	KS74HCTLS245	OEM	KS751FA	0994	KSA733(Y)	0037	KSC1520Y	0638	KSD4150	0710	KT345B	OEM
KR602KA	OEM	KS77	OEM	KS751GA	0994	KSA733-0	0006	KSC1674	0144	KSD4154	0710	KT345V	OEM
KR602MA	OEM	KS77B	OEM	KS751HA	0994	KSA733-O	0037	KSC1674(O)	0224	KSD9701	0538	KT375A	OEM
KR602PA	OEM	KS78	OEM	KS751KA	2070	KSA733-Y	0037	KSC1674(R)	0144	KSD9701A	0538	KT375B	OEM
KR602RA	OEM	KS79B	OEM	KS751MA	2070	KSA733C-G-T	OEM	KSC1674-0	0144	KSD9702	0538	KT502AA	0979
KR602TA	OEM	KS100A	0170	KS751PA	2077	KSA733C-L-T	OEM	KSC1674-O	0144	KSD9702A	0538	KT502BA	0984
KR602VA	OEM	KS100B	0170	KS751RA	2077	KSA733Y	0006	KSC16740	0224	KSD9703	0538	KT502CA	0984
KR866	OEM	KS102AA	0703	KS751TA	0607	KSA735-O	0037	KSC1674R	0144	KSD9703A	0538	KT502DA	0984
KR867	OEM	KS102BA	0575	KS751VA	0607	KSA928AY	OEM	KSC1675	0079	KSD9704	0538	KT502EA	0991
KR2376	OEM	KS102CA	0575	KS1060	OEM	KSA931	1587	KSC1675-0	0836	KSD9705	0538	KT502FA	0991
KR-2376-XX	OEM	KS102DA	0575	KS1160	OEM	KSA931-O	OEM	KSC1675-O	0079	KSD9706	0538	KT502GA	0991
KR2376-XX	OEM	KS102EA	0994	KS1260	OEM	KSA931Y	OEM	KSC1675-Y	0079	KSD9707	0538	KT502HA	0991
KR3600	OEM	KS102FA	0994	KS1460	OEM	KSA940	1900	KSC1675R	0284	KSDT7601	OEM	KT502KA	0510
KR-3600-PRO	OEM	KS102GA	0994	KS2033A	0289	KSA950Y	OEM	KSC1675Y	0079	KSKE12C500	0071	KT502MA	0510
KR3600-PRO	OEM	KS102HA	0994	KS2033B	0296	KSA1015	0006	KSC1684	OEM	KSKE40C200	0015	KT502PA	1002
KR-3600-ST	OEM	KS102KA	2070	KS2036A	0188	KSA1015Y	0006	KSC1815-Y	OEM	KSKE40C500	0015	KT502RA	1002
KR-3600-STD	OEM	KS102MA	2070	KS2036B	0372	KSA1175	0013	KSC1815Y	1943	KSKE125C200	0071	KT502TA	0942
KR-3600-XX	OEM	KS102PA	2077	KS2039A	0451	KSA6643-O	1233	KSC2073	1274	KSP1171	0615	KT502VA	0942
KR3600PRO	OEM	KS102RA	2077	KS2039B	0188	KSA7339	OEM	KSC2120Y	0155	KSP1172	0615	KT600	0018
KR3600ST	OEM	KS102TA	0607	KS2043A	0528	KSB546	1638	KSC2230-O	0261	KSP1173	0615	KT600F	0018
KR3600STD	OEM	KS102VA	0607	KS2043B	0274	KSB546-O	1900	KSC2310	0261	KSP1174	0615	KT600G	0168
KR6003	0435	KS120A	0137	KS2047A	0446	KSB546Y	OEM	KSC2310-O	0261	KSP1175	0615	KT600T	0018
KR8417	0079	KS120B	0137	KS2047B	0162	KSB564(Y)	0527	KSC2310-OY	0261	KSP1176	0615	KT602AA	0979
KRA1080	OEM	KS123AA	0084	KS2051A	0162	KSB564-Y	0527	KSC2310-Y	0261	KSR1001	OEM	KT602BA	0984
KRA1081	OEM	KS123BA	0097	KS2051B	0162	KSB564A	0527	KSC2310Y	0261	KSR1004	0892	KT602CA	0984
KRC105M	OEM	KS123CA	0097	KS2056A	0157	KSB564A-Y	0431	KSC2328	3882	KSR2001	OEM	KT602DA	0984
KRC111M	OEM	KS123DA	0097	KS2056B	0157	KSB564Y	0527	KSC2328A-Y	3882	KSR2004	4067	KT602EA	0991
KRC1205	OEM	KS123EA	0109	KS2060	OEM	KSC105G	OEM	KSC2328AY	3882	KSS240A	OEM	KT602FA	0991
KRC1211	OEM	KS123FA	0109	KS2062A	0631	KSC184(O)	0079	KSC2330	0261	KSS9808	OEM	KT602GA	0991

If replacement code is OEM, contact original manufacturer for replacement.

DEVICE TYPE	REPL CODE
KT602HA	0991
KT602KA	0510
KT602MA	0510
KT602PA	1002
KT602RA	1002
KT602TA	0942
KT602VA	0942
KT751AA	0927
KT751BA	0941
KT751CA	0941
KT751DA	0941
KT751EA	0994
KT751FA	1006
KT751GA	1006
KT751HA	1006
KT751KA	1067
KT751MA	1067
KT751PA	1130
KT751RA	1130
KT751TA	1180
KT751VA	1180
KT1017	0160
KT1815-GR	0284
KT8740	OEM
KTA473	0919
KTA473-O	0919
KTA473A	OEM
KTA473Y	OEM
KTA562	0006
KTA562(Y)	0006
KTA562-O	0006
KTA562-TM	0006
KTA562-Y	0006
KTA562A	0006
KTA5620	0006
KTA562TM	0006
KTA562TM-O	0006
KTA562TM-O(TA)	0006
KTA562TM-O-TA	OEM
KTA562TM-Y	0006
KTA562TMY	0006
KTA562TM-Y(TA)	0006
KTA562TM-Y-O	0006
KTA562Y	0006
KTA733	0037
KTA817	4028
KTA817-Y	OEM
KTA817A	OEM
KTA-940	1638
KTA940	1900
KTA949-O	1514
KTA950	5817
KTA950-O	0006
KTA950-Y	0527
KTA950-Y(TA)	0527
KTA950Y	0006
KTA965-Y	1514
KTA965Y	1514
KTA966-Y	0527
KTA966A	OEM
KTA966AY	0527
KTA966Y	OEM
KTA968-Y	1638
KTA968A-Y	1638
KTA968Y	1638
KTA1013-O	1514
KTA1015	0148
KTA1015(O)	0006
KTA1015(Y)	0006
KTA1015-O	3079
KTA1015-G	0006
KTA1015-GR	0148
KTA1015-O	0006
KTA1015-Y	0148
KTA1015-Y(TA)	0148
KTA1015A	0006
KTA1015GR	0148
KTA1015O	0006
KTA1015Y	0148
KTA1162(SG)	OEM
KTA1266-TP-Y	4440
KTA1266Y	4440
KTA1267GR	OEM
KTA1270-TA-Y	0006
KTA1270-TP-Y	0006
KTA1270Y	0006
KTA1271-TP-Y	0472
KTA1271Y	0472
KTA4558P	OEM
KTA7805	OEM
KTA7812	OEM
KTB595	0713
KTB595-O	OEM
KTB595-O	0713
KTB595Y	0713
KTB596-O	3706
KTB834	6046
KTB834-O	6046
KTB834-Y	6046
KTB834Y	0848
KTB988-O	OEM
KTC0141(TM-O)	OEM
KTC200-Y	0016
KTC200Y	0016
KTC380-O	0284
KTC380TM-O	0144
KTC382	0224
KTC388	0284
KTC388A	0836
KTC388A(TA)	0284
KTC388A-TM	0284
KTC388ATM	0284
KTC388ATMFA	0284
KTC388AY	OEM
KTC732TM-BL	0502
KTC1001	OEM
KTC1096-O	0219
KTC1173	0042
KTC1173-O	0042
KTC1173Y	OEM
KTC1627	1376
KTC1627-O	1376
KTC1627-Y	1376
KTC1627A	1376
KTC1627A-Y	1376
KTC1627AY	1376
KTC1627A-Y(TA)	1376
KTC1627AY(TA)	1376
KTC1627Y	1376
KTC1815	0076
KTC1815(Y)	0284
KTC1815-BL	0284
KTC1815-D	0284
KTC1815-G	0006
KTC1815-GR	0284
KTC1815-GRFA-1	0284
KTC1815-O	0284
KTC1815-O(TA)	0284
KTC1815-O-TA	OEM
KTC1815-TP-Y	0076
KTC1815-Y	0284
KTC1815-Y(TA)	0284
KTC-1815BL	0284
KTC1815BL	0076
KTC1815D	0284
KTC1815G	OEM
KTC1815GR	0076
KTC1815O	0284
KTC-1815Y	0284
KTC1815Y	0076
KTC1923	OEM
KTC1923(O)	0224
KTC1923-O	0224
KTC1923Y	OEM
KTC1959	0379
KTC1959-O	0284
KTC1959-Y	0284
KTC1959Y	0284
KTC2068	0638
KTC2068(FA-1)	0638
KTC2068-1	0638
KTC2068-FA1	OEM
KTC2068FA-1	0638
KTC2068I	0638
KTC2073	0388
KTC2073FA-2	0388
KTC2120	0860
KTC2120(Y)	0155
KTC2120-O	0155
KTC2120-Y	0155
KTC2120-Y(TA)	0860
KTC2120-Y(TR)	0155
KTC2120Y	0860
KTC2229	0261
KTC-2229-O	0261
KTC2229-O	0261
KTC2229-Y	0261
KTC2229-Y(TA)	0261
KTC2229D	0261
KTC-2229K	0261
KTC2229O	0261
KTC2229Y	0261
KTC2230	0261
KTC2230(GR)	OEM
KTC2230-GR	0261
KTC2230-TP	OEM
KTC2230-Y	0261
KTC2230A	0261
KTC2230A(Y)	0261
KTC2230A-GR	0261
KTC2230AGR	0261
KTC2230A-Y	0261
KTC2230AY	0261
KTC2230GR	0261
KTC2230TP	0261
KTC2230Y	0261
KTC2233	0388
KTC2233FA-1	0388
KTC2235-Y	6093
KTC2235Y	1553
KTC2236A	OEM
KTC2236AY	1559
KTC2236Y	OEM
KTC2238A	0388
KTC2238A-Y	0388
KTC2240	OEM
KTC2240BL	OEM
KTC2240GR	OEM
KTC2310-O	0261
KTC2330-O	OEM
KTC2383-Y	1553
KTC2383Y	1553
KTC2482	0066
KTC2482(TA)	0261
KTC2482FA-1	0261
KTC2482K	0261
KTC2482TA	2319
KTC2482Y	0066
KTC2712(LG)	OEM
KTC3197	1084
KTC3197-AT	1084
KTC3197-TP	1084
KTC3197TP	1084
KTC3198-TA-Y	0284
KTC3198-TP-Y	0284
KTC3198Y	0284
KTC3199GR	OEM
KTC3202-TP-Y	0379
KTC3203-TP-Y	1376
KTC3203-Y	OEM
KTC3203Y	1376
KTC3206-Y	0261
KTC3227-TP	0320
KTC3227-Y	0320
KTC3227Y	OEM
KTC9011	OEM
KTC9011A-G	OEM
KTC9013A	0079
KTC9013A(H)	0079
KTC9013A(I)	0079
KTC9014(C)	0079
KTC9014A	0079
KTC9014A(C)	0079
KTC9014A(D)	0079
KTC9014A-B	OEM
KTC9014A-C	OEM
KTC9014AC	0079
KTC9014C	0079
KTC9015(C)	0037
KTC9015A	0037
KTC9015A(B)	0037
KTC9015A-B	OEM
KTC9016A-G	OEM
KTC9016A-H	OEM
KTC9018F	OEM
KTC9018G	OEM
KTD19TM(GR)	OEM
KTD525-O	OEM
KTD718	OEM
KTD880	0042
KTD880(GR)	0042
KTD880(Y)	0042
KTD880-O	0456
KTD880-Y	0042
KTD880GR	OEM
KTD880Y	0456
KTD1351-O	OEM
KTD1351-Y	0402
KTD1351Y	0402
KTD1406	OEM
KTD1406Y	0060
KTD1414	OEM
KTD1554	1533
KTD1555	0551
KTD1651	1533
KTD2058Y	OEM
KTD7180	OEM
KTD8800	0042
KTK19(GR)	OEM
KTK117A	OEM
KTK161YR	OEM
KTR0710C	0364
KTR0815C	0155
KTR0839C	0076
KTR0945C	6551
KTR1017	2039
KTR1096C	0386
KTR1687C	0224
KTTA1015O	0006
KU6HZ	OEM
KU902	OEM
KU904	OEM
KU906	OEM
KU908	OEM
KU910	OEM
KU912	OEM
KU914	OEM
KU1302	OEM
KU1304	OEM
KU1306	OEM
KU1308	OEM
KU1310	OEM
KU1312	OEM
KU1314	OEM
KV0714-2	OEM
KV-1	0004
KV1	0004
KV-2	0211
KV2	0004
KV-3	6953
KV3	OEM
KV-4	0004
KV4	0004
KV-4D	0211
KV-5	OEM
KV5	OEM
KV-14	0279
KV107	OEM
KV107A	OEM
KV107B	OEM
KV107C	OEM
KV107D	OEM
KV123	OEM
KV123A	OEM
KV123B	OEM
KV123C	OEM
KV123D	OEM
KV124	OEM
KV124A	OEM
KV124B	OEM
KV124C	OEM
KV124D	OEM
KV127	OEM
KV128	OEM
KV132	OEM
KV133	OEM
KV134	OEM
KV135	OEM
KV136	OEM
KV137	OEM
KV138	OEM
KV139	OEM
KV156	OEM
KV157	OEM
KV158	OEM
KV159	OEM
KV160	OEM
KV161	OEM
KV169	OEM
KV171	OEM
KV172	OEM
KV173	OEM
KV1225	OEM
KV1226	OEM
KV1230Z	OEM
KV1234Z	OEM
KV1235	OEM
KV1235Z	OEM
KV1235Z3	OEM
KV1235Z3-1	OEM
KV1235Z3-2	OEM
KV1235Z3-3	OEM
KV1235Z3-4	OEM
KV1235Z3-5	OEM
KV1235Z3-A	OEM
KV1235Z3-B	OEM
KV1235Z3-C	OEM
KV1235Z3-D	OEM
KV1235Z3-E	OEM
KV1235Z5-A	OEM
KV1235Z5-B	OEM
KV1235Z5-C	OEM
KV1235Z5-D	OEM
KV1235Z5-E	OEM
KV1236	3643
KV1236Z	OEM
KV1250	OEM
KV1250M	OEM
KV1260	OEM
KV1260M	OEM
KV1260Z	OEM
KV1310	OEM
KV1310-6	OEM
KV1310A	OEM
KV1310A-3	OEM
KV1320	OEM
KV1330A-2	OEM
KV1340A-3	OEM
KV2003	OEM
KV2160	OEM
KV2203	OEM
KV2303	OEM
KV2403	OEM
KV2503	OEM
KV2603	OEM
KV2703	OEM
KV5139	OEM
KV5140	OEM
KV5141	OEM
KV5142	OEM
KV5143	OEM
KV13120A-3	OEM
KVR10	0170
KVTKDS288Y	OEM
KVTKSA928AY	OEM
KX-1	0133
KX-1005	OEM
KY5DPF	6976
KY1011	OEM
KY4042	OEM
KY4043	OEM
KY4099	OEM
KY8607	OEM
KYA1015Y	OEM
KZ5DPF	OEM
KZ6	0025
KZ6A	0025
KZ6ZA	0025
KZ-8A	0244
KZ62A	0466
KZ91A	0057
KZ1075	0077
KZ1075-M	0077
KZ1075M	OEM
KZL083	OEM
L05-E	0071
L-0650	OEM
L-0651	OEM
L-0662	OEM
L1/1H	OEM
L1/2H	0133
L1/3H	0133
L1/4H	OEM
L1/5H	OEM
L1/6H	OEM
L1/8H	OEM
L1/10H	OEM
L1/15H	OEM
L1/20H	OEM
L1A0091	OEM
L1H1	OEM
L1V	OEM
L3	OEM
L3/1H	OEM
L3/2H	0015
L3/3H	OEM
L3/4H	OEM
L3/5H	OEM
L3/6H	OEM
L3/8H	OEM
L3/10H	OEM
L3/15H	OEM
L3/20H	OEM
L4	0111
L5	0111
L6	0719
L6/1H	OEM
L6/2H	0015
L6/3H	OEM
L6/4H	OEM
L6/5H	OEM
L6/6H	OEM
L6/8H	OEM
L6/10H	OEM
L6/15H	OEM
L6/20H	OEM
L6-SAM	0719
L6A	OEM
L6B	OEM
L6C	OEM
L6D	OEM
L6F	OEM
L6U	OEM
L6X12	OEM
L7	0111
L7A	OEM
L7B	OEM
L7C	OEM
L7D	OEM
L7F	OEM
L7U	OEM
L7X12	OEM
L8/1H	OEM
L8/2H	0015
L8/3H	OEM
L8/4H	OEM
L8/5H	OEM
L8/6H	OEM
L8/8H	OEM
L8/10H	OEM
L8/15H	OEM
L8/20H	OEM
L8H6.2	OEM
L14B	OEM
L14B1	OEM
L14B2	OEM
L14B3	OEM
L14B4	OEM
L14F1	3508
L14F2	3508
L14G1	3825
L14G2	2297
L14G3	2297
L14H1	3825
L14H2	3825
L14H3	3825
L14H4	3825
L14T1	OEM
L14T2	OEM
L14T3	OEM
L14T4	OEM
L14T5	OEM
L15C1	OEM
L15C2	OEM
L15D1	OEM
L15D2	OEM
L20	OEM
L32H	0015
L33-SAM	3442
L34	OEM
L62H	0015
L78LR05C	OEM
L78LR05D	OEM
L78LR05D-MA	OEM
L78M05	0619
L78M05-A	0619
L78M05-LU	0619
L78M05-RA	0619
L78M05ABV	0619
L78M05C-V	0619
L78M05CV	0619
L78M05N000	OEM
L78M06	0917
L78M06SA	0917
L78M09	1775
L78M09-RA	1775
L78M09-SA	1775
L78M09SA	1775
L78M12	0330
L78M12-LU	0330
L78M12-RA	0330
L78M12-SA	1883
L78M12CV	0330
L78M12RL	0330
L78MR05	OEM
L78MR05-FA	OEM
L78MR06-FA	OEM
L78N05	1288
L78N06	5572
L78N06-SE	0917
L78N12	0330
L78N12-RA	0330
L79M05	OEM
L79M05N000	OEM
L82H	0071
L120	0201
L123CB	0026
L150LA2	OEM
L180	0374
L241	OEM
L272	5983
L272B	5983
L272M	5960
L272MB	5960
L274	2377
L292	6021
L292V	6021
L293B	5148
L295	5149
L296	5122
L296P	OEM
L296V	5122
L298	OEM
L298N	OEM
L347N	OEM
L-417-29BLK	0160
L-417-29GRN	0160
L-417-29WHT	0160
L-417-60	0160
L563G	OEM
L780S05-FA	OEM
L842	0144
L1010	OEM
L1010A	OEM
L1010B	OEM
L1014	OEM
L1014A	OEM
L1014B	OEM
L1015	OEM
L1015A	OEM
L1015B	OEM
L1016	OEM
L1016A	OEM
L1016B	OEM
L1019	OEM
L1019A	OEM
L1019B	OEM
L1020	OEM
L1020A	OEM
L1020B	OEM
L1021	OEM
L1021A	OEM
L1021B	OEM
L1022	OEM
L1022A	OEM
L1022B	OEM
L1025	OEM
L1025A	OEM
L1025B	OEM
L1026	OEM
L1026A	OEM
L1026B	OEM
L1029	OEM
L1029A	OEM
L1029B	OEM
L1030	OEM
L1030A	OEM
L1030B	OEM
L1031	OEM
L1031A	OEM
L1031B	OEM
L1032	OEM
L1032A	OEM
L1032B	OEM
L1035	OEM
L1035A	OEM
L1035B	OEM
L1036	OEM
L1036A	OEM
L1036B	OEM
L1039	OEM
L1039A	OEM
L1039B	OEM
L1040	OEM
L1040A	OEM
L1040B	OEM
L1041	OEM
L1041A	OEM
L1041B	OEM
L1042	OEM
L1042A	OEM
L1042B	OEM
L1045	OEM
L1045A	OEM
L1045B	OEM
L1046	OEM
L1046A	OEM
L1046B	OEM
L1049	OEM
L1049A	OEM
L1049B	OEM
L1060	OEM
L1060A	OEM
L1060B	OEM
L1061	OEM
L1061A	OEM
L1061B	OEM
L1062	OEM
L1062A	OEM
L1062B	OEM
L1065	OEM
L1065A	OEM
L1065B	OEM
L1066	OEM
L1066A	OEM
L1066B	OEM
L1069	OEM
L1069A	OEM
L1069B	OEM
L1100	OEM
L1100A	OEM
L1100B	OEM
L1101	OEM
L1101A	OEM
L1101B	OEM
L1102	OEM
L1102A	OEM
L1102B	OEM
L1105	OEM
L1105A	OEM
L1105B	OEM
L1106	OEM
L1106A	OEM
L1106B	OEM
L1141	OEM
L1141A	OEM
L1141B	OEM
L1145	OEM
L1145A	OEM
L1145B	OEM
L1146	OEM
L1146A	OEM
L1146B	OEM
L1147	OEM
L1147A	OEM
L1147B	OEM
L1149	OEM
L1149A	OEM
L1149B	OEM
L1150	OEM
L1150A	OEM
L1150B	OEM
L1151	OEM
L1151A	OEM
L1151B	OEM
L1152	OEM
L1152A	OEM
L1152B	OEM
L1155	OEM
L1155A	OEM
L1155B	OEM
L1156	OEM
L1156A	OEM
L1156B	OEM
L1165	OEM
L1165A	OEM
L1165B	OEM
L1166	OEM
L1166A	OEM
L1166B	OEM
L1169	OEM
L1169A	OEM
L1169B	OEM
L1220	OEM
L1220A	OEM
L1220B	OEM
L1221	OEM
L1221A	OEM
L1221B	OEM
L1222	OEM
L1222A	OEM
L1222B	OEM
L1225	OEM
L1225A	OEM
L1225B	OEM
L-1481	OEM
L-1540	OEM
L-1541	OEM
L1946	OEM
L1946A	OEM
L1946B	OEM
L1949	OEM
L1949A	OEM
L1949B	OEM
L2114-550	2037
L2732	OEM
L3010	OEM
L3010A	OEM
L3010B	OEM
L3015	OEM
L3015A	OEM
L3015B	OEM
L3016	OEM
L3016A	OEM
L3016B	OEM
L3019	OEM
L3019A	OEM
L3019B	OEM
L3020	OEM
L3020A	OEM
L3020B	OEM
L3021	OEM
L3021A	OEM

If replacement code is OEM, contact original manufacturer for replacement.

DEVICE TYPE	REPL CODE	DEVICE TYPE	REPL CODE	DEVICE TYPE	REPL CODE	DEVICE TYPE	REPL CODE	DEVICE TYPE	REPL CODE	DEVICE TYPE	REPL CODE	DEVICE TYPE	REPL CODE
L3021B	OEM	L3165	OEM	L4231J-L	OEM	L4706	OEM	L4852F	OEM	L4953G	OEM	L8202E	OEM
L3022	OEM	L3165A	OEM	L4232	OEM	L4707	OEM	L4852G	OEM	L4953H	OEM	L8203A	OEM
L3022A	OEM	L3165B	OEM	L4232A-E	OEM	L4708	OEM	L4852H	OEM	L4954	OEM	L8203B	OEM
L3022B	OEM	L3166	OEM	L4232F	OEM	L4709	OEM	L4853	OEM	L4954A-E	OEM	L8203C	OEM
L3025	OEM	L3166A	OEM	L4232G	OEM	L4710	OEM	L4853A-E	OEM	L4955	OEM	L8204	OEM
L3025A	OEM	L3166B	OEM	L4232H	OEM	L4711	OEM	L4853F	OEM	L4955A-D	OEM	L8204A	OEM
L3025B	OEM	L3220	OEM	L4232J	OEM	L4712	OEM	L4853G	OEM	L4956	OEM	L8204B	OEM
L3026	OEM	L3220A	OEM	L4232K	OEM	L4713	OEM	L4853H	OEM	L4956A-D	OEM	L8204C	OEM
L3026A	OEM	L3220B	OEM	L4233	OEM	L4714	OEM	L4854	OEM	L4957	OEM	L8205	OEM
L3026B	OEM	L3221	OEM	L4233A-E	OEM	L4715	OEM	L4854A-E	OEM	L4957A-B	OEM	L8205A	OEM
L3029	OEM	L3221A	OEM	L4233F	OEM	L4716	OEM	L4854F	OEM	L4966	OEM	L8205B	OEM
L3029A	OEM	L3221B	OEM	L4233G	OEM	L4717	OEM	L4854G	OEM	L4966A	OEM	L8206	OEM
L3029B	OEM	L3222	OEM	L4233H	OEM	L4718	OEM	L4855	OEM	L4966B	OEM	L8206A	OEM
L3030	OEM	L3222A	OEM	L4233J	OEM	L4719	OEM	L4855A-D	OEM	L4966C	OEM	L8206B	OEM
L3030A	OEM	L3222B	OEM	L4234	OEM	L4720	OEM	L4856	OEM	L4967	OEM	L8206C	OEM
L3030B	OEM	L3225A	OEM	L4234A-E	OEM	L4721	OEM	L4856A	OEM	L4967A	OEM	L8206D	OEM
L3031	OEM	L3225B	OEM	L4234F	OEM	L4722	OEM	L4856B	OEM	L4967B	OEM	L8206E	OEM
L3031A	OEM	L4000KS	2340	L4234G	OEM	L4750	OEM	L4856C	OEM	L4970	OEM	L8207	OEM
L3031B	OEM	L4066B	OEM	L4234H	OEM	L4751	OEM	L4866	OEM	L4971	OEM	L8207A	OEM
L3032	OEM	L4120	OEM	L4235	OEM	L4752	OEM	L4866A-C	OEM	L4972	OEM	L8207B	OEM
L3032A	OEM	L4122	OEM	L4235A-E	OEM	L4753	OEM	L4867	OEM	L4973	OEM	L8207C	OEM
L3032B	OEM	L4130	OEM	L4235F	OEM	L4754	OEM	L4867A	OEM	L4974	OEM	L8207D	OEM
L3035	OEM	L4131	OEM	L4242	OEM	L4755	OEM	L4867B	OEM	L4975	OEM	L8207E	OEM
L3035A	OEM	L4132	OEM	L4242A-E	OEM	L4756	OEM	L4877	OEM	L4976	OEM	L8208	OEM
L3035B	OEM	L4134	OEM	L4242F	OEM	L4757	OEM	L4877A	OEM	L4977	OEM	L8208A	OEM
L3036	OEM	L4135	OEM	L4242G	OEM	L4758	OEM	L4877B	OEM	L4978	OEM	L8208B	OEM
L3036A	OEM	L4136	OEM	L4242H	OEM	L4759	OEM	L4921	OEM	L4980	OEM	L8208C	OEM
L3036B	OEM	L4138	OEM	L4242J	OEM	L4765	OEM	L4921A-E	OEM	L4981	OEM	L8209	OEM
L3039	OEM	L4139	OEM	L4243	OEM	L4766	OEM	L4921F	OEM	L4982	OEM	L8209A	OEM
L3039A	OEM	L4140	OEM	L4243A-E	OEM	L4767	OEM	L4921G	OEM	L4983	OEM	L8209B	OEM
L3039B	OEM	L4141	OEM	L4243F	OEM	L4768	OEM	L4921H	OEM	L4984	OEM	L8209C	OEM
L3040	OEM	L4142	OEM	L4243G	OEM	L4769	OEM	L4921J-L	OEM	L4985	OEM	L8210	OEM
L3040A	OEM	L4143	OEM	L4243H	OEM	L4770	OEM	L4921M	OEM	L4986	OEM	L8210A	OEM
L3040B	OEM	L4144	OEM	L4244	OEM	L4771	OEM	L4922	OEM	L4987	OEM	L8210B	OEM
L3041	OEM	L4145	OEM	L4244A-E	OEM	L4772	OEM	L4922A-E	OEM	L4988	OEM	L8210C	OEM
L3041A	OEM	L4146	OEM	L4244F	OEM	L4773	OEM	L4922F	OEM	L5005	OEM	L8211	OEM
L3041B	OEM	L4147	OEM	L4245	OEM	L4774	OEM	L4922G	OEM	L5021	0004	L8211A	OEM
L3042	OEM	L4150	OEM	L4245A-E	OEM	L4775	OEM	L4922J-L	OEM	L5022	0004	L8211B	OEM
L3042A	OEM	L4153	OEM	L4252	OEM	L4776	OEM	L4923	OEM	L5022A	0004	L8211C	OEM
L3042B	OEM	L4154	OEM	L4252A-E	OEM	L4818B	OEM	L4923A-E	OEM	L5025	0004	L8211D	OEM
L3045	OEM	L4154A	OEM	L4252F	OEM	L4821	OEM	L4923F	OEM	L5025A	0004	L8211E	OEM
L3045A	OEM	L4154B	OEM	L4252G	OEM	L4821A-E	OEM	L4923G	OEM	L5108	0050	L8212	OEM
L3045B	OEM	L4155	OEM	L4252H	OEM	L4821F	OEM	L4923H	OEM	L5121	0050	L8212A	OEM
L3046	OEM	L4155A	OEM	L4253	OEM	L4821G	OEM	L4923J-L	OEM	L5122	0050	L8212B	OEM
L3046A	OEM	L4155B	OEM	L4253A-E	OEM	L4821H	OEM	L4924	OEM	L5181	0050	L8212C	OEM
L3046B	OEM	L4156	OEM	L4253F	OEM	L4822	OEM	L4924A-E	OEM	L5431	OEM	L8213	OEM
L3049	OEM	L4156A	OEM	L4254	OEM	L4822A-E	OEM	L4924F	OEM	L5630	1319	L8213A	OEM
L3049A	OEM	L4156B	OEM	L4254A-E	OEM	L4822F	OEM	L4924G	OEM	L5631	1319	L8213B	OEM
L3049B	OEM	L4157	OEM	L4255	OEM	L4822G	OEM	L4924H	OEM	L5631-AA	1319	L8214	OEM
L3059	OEM	L4157A	OEM	L4255A-D	OEM	L4822H	OEM	L4924J	OEM	L6210	OEM	L8214A	OEM
L3059A	OEM	L4157B	OEM	L4356	OEM	L4822J	OEM	L4924K	OEM	L6506	OEM	L8214B	OEM
L3059B	OEM	L4160	OEM	L4356A	OEM	L4822K	OEM	L4931	OEM	L7801A	OEM	L8215	OEM
L3060	OEM	L4164	OEM	L4356B	OEM	L4823	OEM	L4931A-K	OEM	L7805ACCV	OEM	L8215A	OEM
L3060A	OEM	L4164A	OEM	L4357	OEM	L4823A-E	OEM	L4931F	OEM	L7805ACV	OEM	L8215B	OEM
L3060B	OEM	L4164B	OEM	L4357A	OEM	L4823F	OEM	L4931G	OEM	L7806	1333	L8216	OEM
L3061A	OEM	L4165	OEM	L4358	OEM	L4823G	OEM	L4931H	OEM	L7808CY	1187	L8216A	OEM
L3061B	OEM	L4165A	OEM	L4366	OEM	L4823H	OEM	L4931J-L	OEM	L7809	1336	L8216B	OEM
L3062	OEM	L4165B	OEM	L4366A	OEM	L4823J	OEM	L4932	OEM	L7812	1341	L8313A	OEM
L3062A	OEM	L4166	OEM	L4366B	OEM	L4824	OEM	L4932A-E	OEM	L7812CV	0330	L8313B	OEM
L3062B	OEM	L4166A	OEM	L4367	OEM	L4824A-E	OEM	L4932F	OEM	L7812V-SA	OEM	L8314A	OEM
L3065	OEM	L4166B	OEM	L4367A	OEM	L4824F	OEM	L4932G	OEM	L7815CV	1311	L8314B	OEM
L3065A	OEM	L4167	OEM	L4368	OEM	L4824G	OEM	L4932H	OEM	L7815V	OEM	L8315A	OEM
L3065B	OEM	L4167A	OEM	L4377	OEM	L4824H	OEM	L4932J	OEM	L7818CT	3605	L8315B	OEM
L3066	OEM	L4167B	OEM	L4377A	OEM	L4831	OEM	L4932K	OEM	L7824CT	3828	L8316A	OEM
L3066A	OEM	L4170	OEM	L4412	OEM	L4831A-E	OEM	L4933	OEM	L7912CV	6512	L8316B	OEM
L3066B	OEM	L4171	OEM	L4413	OEM	L4831F	OEM	L4933A-E	OEM	L7918CT	5196	L8317A	OEM
L3100	OEM	L4172	OEM	L4414	OEM	L4831G	OEM	L4933G	OEM	L7924CT	3529	L8317B	OEM
L3100A	OEM	L4173	OEM	L4503	OEM	L4831H	OEM	L4933H	OEM	L8156	OEM	L8323A	OEM
L3100B	OEM	L4174	OEM	L4505	OEM	L4831J-L	OEM	L4933J	OEM	L8156A-D	OEM	L8323B	OEM
L3101	OEM	L4175	OEM	L4506	OEM	L4832	OEM	L4933K	OEM	L8157	OEM	L8324A	OEM
L3101A	OEM	L4178	OEM	L4507	OEM	L4832A-E	OEM	L4934	OEM	L8157A-C	OEM	L8324B	OEM
L3101B	OEM	L4181	OEM	L4510	OEM	L4832F	OEM	L4934A-E	OEM	L8158	OEM	L8325B	OEM
L3102	OEM	L4181A	OEM	L4520	OEM	L4832G	OEM	L4934F	OEM	L8158A	OEM	L8326A	OEM
L3102A	OEM	L4185	OEM	L4530	OEM	L4832H	OEM	L4934G	OEM	L8158B	OEM	L8326B	OEM
L3102B	OEM	L4185A	OEM	L4540	OEM	L4832J	OEM	L4934H	OEM	L8166	OEM	L8327A	OEM
L3105	OEM	L4185B	OEM	L4650	OEM	L4832K	OEM	L4935	OEM	L8166A-D	OEM	L8327B	OEM
L3105A	OEM	L4190	OEM	L4650A	OEM	L4833	OEM	L4935A-E	OEM	L8167	OEM	L8333A	OEM
L3105B	OEM	L4190A	OEM	L4651	OEM	L4833A-E	OEM	L4935F	OEM	L8167A	OEM	L8333B	OEM
L3106	OEM	L4190B	OEM	L4651A	OEM	L4833F	OEM	L4942	OEM	L8167B	OEM	L8334A	OEM
L3106A	OEM	L4190C	OEM	L4652	OEM	L4833G	OEM	L4942A-E	OEM	L8168	OEM	L8334B	OEM
L3106B	OEM	L4221	OEM	L4652A	OEM	L4833H	OEM	L4942F	OEM	L8168A	OEM	L8335A	OEM
L3140	OEM	L4221A-E	OEM	L4653	OEM	L4833J	OEM	L4942G	OEM	L8168B	OEM	L8335B	OEM
L3140A	OEM	L4221F	OEM	L4653A	OEM	L4834	OEM	L4942H	OEM	L8176	OEM	L8336A	OEM
L3140B	OEM	L4221G	OEM	L4654	OEM	L4834A-E	OEM	L4942J	OEM	L8176A	OEM	L8336B	OEM
L3141A	OEM	L4221H	OEM	L4654A	OEM	L4834F	OEM	L4943	OEM	L8176B	OEM	L8337A	OEM
L3141B	OEM	L4221J-L	OEM	L4655	OEM	L4834G	OEM	L4943A-E	OEM	L8176C	OEM	L8337B	OEM
L3145	OEM	L4222	OEM	L4655A	OEM	L4834H	OEM	L4943F	OEM	L8177	OEM	L8343A	OEM
L3145A	OEM	L4222A-E	OEM	L4656	OEM	L4835	OEM	L4943G	OEM	L8177A	OEM	L8343B	OEM
L3145B	OEM	L4222F	OEM	L4656A	OEM	L4835A-E	OEM	L4943H	OEM	L8177B	OEM	L8344A	OEM
L3146	OEM	L4222G	OEM	L4660	OEM	L4835F	OEM	L4944	OEM	L8178	OEM	L8344B	OEM
L3146A	OEM	L4222H	OEM	L4660A	OEM	L4842	OEM	L4944A-E	OEM	L8178A	OEM	L8345	OEM
L3146B	OEM	L4222J	OEM	L4661	OEM	L4842A-E	OEM	L4944F	OEM	L8187	OEM	L8345A	OEM
L3149	OEM	L4222K	OEM	L4661A	OEM	L4842F	OEM	L4945	OEM	L8187A	OEM	L8345B	OEM
L3149A	OEM	L4223	OEM	L4662	OEM	L4842G	OEM	L4945A-E	OEM	L8187B	OEM	L8346A	OEM
L3149B	OEM	L4223A-E	OEM	L4662A	OEM	L4842H	OEM	L4946	OEM	L8188	OEM	L8346B	OEM
L3150	OEM	L4223F	OEM	L4663	OEM	L4842J	OEM	L4946A-D	OEM	L8188A	OEM	L8347A	OEM
L3150A	OEM	L4223G	OEM	L4663A	OEM	L4843	OEM	L4947	OEM	L8200	OEM	L8347B	OEM
L3150B	OEM	L4223H	OEM	L4664	OEM	L4843A-E	OEM	L4947A	OEM	L8200A	OEM	L8350	OEM
L3151	OEM	L4223J	OEM	L4664A	OEM	L4843F	OEM	L4947B	OEM	L8200B	OEM	L8351	OEM
L3151A	OEM	L4224	OEM	L4665	OEM	L4843G	OEM	L4947C	OEM	L8200C	OEM	L8352	OEM
L3152	OEM	L4224A-E	OEM	L4665A	OEM	L4843H	OEM	L4952	OEM	L8201	OEM	L8353	OEM
L3152A	OEM	L4224F	OEM	L4666	OEM	L4844	OEM	L4952A-E	OEM	L8201A	OEM	L8354	OEM
L3152B	OEM	L4224G	OEM	L4666A	OEM	L4844F	OEM	L4952F	OEM	L8201B	OEM	L8355	OEM
L3155	OEM	L4224H	OEM	L4700	OEM	L4844G	OEM	L4952G	OEM	L8201C	OEM	L8356	OEM
L3155A	OEM	L4231	OEM	L4701	OEM	L4845	OEM	L4952H	OEM	L8202	OEM	L8370	OEM
L3155B	OEM	L4231A-E	OEM	L4702	OEM	L4845A-E	OEM	L4953	OEM	L8202A	OEM	L8380	OEM
L3156	OEM	L4231F	OEM	L4703	OEM	L4852	OEM	L4953A-E	OEM	L8202B	OEM	L8413A	OEM
L3156A	OEM	L4231G	OEM	L4704	OEM	L4852A-E	OEM	L4953F	OEM	L8202C	OEM	L8413B	OEM
L3156B	OEM	L4231H	OEM	L4705	OEM							L8202D	OEM	L8414A	OEM

If replacement code is OEM, contact original manufacturer for replacement.

DEVICE TYPE	REPL CODE
L8414B	OEM
L8415A	OEM
L8415B	OEM
L8416A	OEM
L8416B	OEM
L8417A	OEM
L8417B	OEM
L8423A	OEM
L8423B	OEM
L8424A	OEM
L8424B	OEM
L8425A	OEM
L8425B	OEM
L8426A	OEM
L8426B	OEM
L8427A	OEM
L8427B	OEM
L8433A	OEM
L8433B	OEM
L8434A	OEM
L8434B	OEM
L8435A	OEM
L8435B	OEM
L8436A	OEM
L8436B	OEM
L8437A	OEM
L8437B	OEM
L8443A	OEM
L8443B	OEM
L8444A	OEM
L8444B	OEM
L8445A	OEM
L8445B	OEM
L8446A	OEM
L8446B	OEM
L8447A	OEM
L8447B	OEM
L8503	OEM
L8504	OEM
L8505	OEM
L8512	OEM
L8513	OEM
L8514	OEM
L8551	OEM
L8552	OEM
L8553	OEM
L8554	OEM
L8555	OEM
L8563	OEM
L8564	OEM
L8565	OEM
L8566	OEM
L8567	OEM
L8621	OEM
L8621A	OEM
L8621B-E	OEM
L8621F-H	OEM
L8621J-L	OEM
L8621M	OEM
L8622	OEM
L8622A	OEM
L8622B-E	OEM
L8622F-H	OEM
L8622J2J	OEM
L8622K	OEM
L8631	OEM
L8631A	OEM
L8631B-E	OEM
L8631F-H	OEM
L8631J-L	OEM
L8632	OEM
L8632A	OEM
L8632B-E	OEM
L8632F-H	OEM
L8632J	OEM
L8632K	OEM
L8633	OEM
L8633A	OEM
L8633B-E	OEM
L8633F-H	OEM
L8633J	OEM
L8642	OEM
L8642A	OEM
L8642B-E	OEM
L8642F-H	OEM
L8642J	OEM
L8643	OEM
L8643A	OEM
L8643B-E	OEM
L8643F-H	OEM
L8644	OEM
L8644A	OEM
L8644B-E	OEM
L8644F	OEM
L8644G	OEM
L8645	OEM
L8645A	OEM
L8645B-E	OEM
L8653	OEM
L8653A	OEM
L8653B-3	OEM
L8653F	OEM
L8653G	OEM
L8654	OEM
L8654A	OEM
L8654B-E	OEM
L8654F	OEM
L8655	OEM
L8655A	OEM
L8655B-E	OEM
L8656	OEM
L8656A	OEM
L8656B-D	OEM
L8666	OEM
L8666A	OEM
L8666B-D	OEM
L8667	OEM
L8667A	OEM
L8667B	OEM
L8667C	OEM
L8668	OEM
L8668A	OEM
L8676	OEM
L8676A	OEM
L8676B	OEM
L8676C	OEM
L8677	OEM
L8677A	OEM
L8677B	OEM
L8678	OEM
L8678A	OEM
L8687	OEM
L8687A	OEM
L8687B	OEM
L8700	OEM
L8700A	OEM
L8701	OEM
L8701A	OEM
L8702	OEM
L8702A	OEM
L8703	OEM
L8703A	OEM
L8704	OEM
L8704A	OEM
L8850	OEM
L8851	OEM
L8852	OEM
L8853	OEM
L8860	OEM
L8861	OEM
L8862	OEM
L8870	OEM
L8871	OEM
L8872	OEM
L8900	OEM
L8901	OEM
L8902	OEM
L8903	OEM
L8904	OEM
L8905	OEM
L8906	OEM
L8910	OEM
L8911	OEM
L8912	OEM
L8913	OEM
L8914	OEM
L8915	OEM
L8916	OEM
L314141	OEM
L-612099	0462
L-612106	3438
L-612107	0893
L-612150	1531
L-612158	1339
L-612161	0729
L2091241-2	0050
L2091241-3	0050
LA60	0201
LA-71	4783
LA-72	4902
LA-73	4784
LA-74	4786
LA80	0201
LA111	OEM
LA174B	OEM
LA300	0015
LA-301MB	OEM
LA-301MC	OEM
LA-301ML	OEM
LA-301MM	OEM
LA-3010B	OEM
LA-3010C	OEM
LA-3010L	OEM
LA-3010M	OEM
LA-301VB	OEM
LA-301VC	OEM
LA-301VL	OEM
LA-301VM	OEM
LA-301YB	OEM
LA-301YC	OEM
LA-301YL	OEM
LA-301YM	OEM
LA350	0412
LA361	OEM
LA600	0015
LA703	OEM
LA703E	0627
LA733(P)	OEM
LA780Z	OEM
LA800	0015
LA1014	OEM
LA1017	OEM
LA1024	OEM
LA1027	OEM
LA1034	OEM
LA1038	OEM
LA1041	0138
LA1110	0351
LA1111	0383
LA1111P	0383
LA1135	OEM
LA1140	0460
LA1140B	OEM
LA1150	OEM
LA1150N	OEM
LA1152N	1437
LA1175	OEM
LA1177	OEM
LA1180	OEM
LA1185	OEM
LA1186N	OEM
LA1200	0574
LA-1201	0574
LA1201	0574
LA1201(B)	0574
LA1201(C)	0574
LA1201-22	OEM
LA1201B	0574
LA1201C	0574
LA1201C-W	0574
LA1201L	OEM
LA-1201T	0574
LA1201T	0574
LA1201W	0574
LA1210	0598
LA1210L	0598
LA1221	OEM
LA1222	0616
LA1230	0632
LA1231	0634
LA1231N	0634
LA1235	OEM
LA1240	0646
LA1245	0657
LA1260	OEM
LA1260S	OEM
LA1261	OEM
LA1265	OEM
LA1265S	OEM
LA1265T	OEM
LA1266	OEM
LA1267	OEM
LA1320A	3216
LA1342	0823
LA1352	0846
LA1353	0849
LA1354	0851
LA1357	0859
LA1357A	OEM
LA1357AB	0859
LA1357B	0859
LA1357N	0859
LA1357NA	OEM
LA1357NB	0859
LA1357R	3369
LA1363	0167
LA1363W	0167
LA1364	0872
LA1364N	0872
LA1365	0167
LA1365N	0167
LA1365V	OEM
LA1366	0875
LA1366N	0875
LA1367	0878
LA1368	0850
LA1368BP	4379
LA1368CW	4380
LA1369	0880
LA1373	0043
LA1374	0385
LA1375	0602
LA1376	0602
LA1385	0898
LA1390	0910
LA1390B	0910
LA1390C	0910
LA1425	0965
LA1460	1016
LA1461	1020
LA1503	OEM
LA1805	OEM
LA1810	OEM
LA1810SSK	OEM
LA1851N	OEM
LA2010	OEM
LA2015	OEM
LA2026	OEM
LA2037	OEM
LA2110	OEM
LA2400	OEM
LA2600S	3074
LA2730	OEM
LA2746	OEM
LA2770	OEM
LA2800	OEM
LA3018	1843
LA3086N	1686
LA3115	2492
LA3148	2507
LA3150	2508
LA3155	2510
LA3160	2512
LA3161	2516
LA3166N	0875
LA3190	0910
LA3201	2550
LA3210	2052
LA3210ALC	2052
LA3220	2572
LA3225T	OEM
LA3226T	OEM
LA3245	OEM
LA3246	OEM
LA-3300	2546
LA3300	2546
LA-3301	1206
LA3301	1206
LA3310	2644
LA3311	2645
LA3320	OEM
LA3350	0412
LA3350A	0412
LA3361	1251
LA3361A	1251
LA3365	OEM
LA3370	2686
LA3375	OEM
LA3376P	OEM
LA3390	OEM
LA3400	OEM
LA3400N	OEM
LA3401	OEM
LA-3410	5036
LA3410	OEM
LA-3420	5043
LA-3430	OEM
LA3430	OEM
LA3430P	OEM
LA-3440	5039
LA3600	OEM
LA3605	OEM
LA-3610	5035
LA-3620	5042
LA-3630	OEM
LA-3640	5038
LA-3810	5037
LA-3820	5045
LA-3830	OEM
LA-3840	5040
LA-3910	OEM
LA-3920	OEM
LA-3930	OEM
LA-3940	OEM
LA4000	OEM
LA4030	OEM
LA4030-7	2991
LA4030P	0837
LA4031P	0858
LA4032P	0876
LA4100	2590
LA4100DN	OEM
LA4101	2590
LA4102	3161
LA4102KN	OEM
LA4108R	OEM
LA4112	3167
LA4125	1940
LA4125T	1940
LA4126	1940
LA4126T	1949
LA4140	0358
LA4140-1	OEM
LA4145	OEM
LA4160	OEM
LA4170	3191
LA4180	OEM
LA4182	3194
LA4183	3194
LA4190	2370
LA4190T	OEM
LA4192	2370
LA4192S	2370
LA4201	3198
LA4220	2179
LA4230	3209
LA4250	3209
LA4260	3223
LA4261	3223
LA4261T	2890
LA4265	OEM
LA4270	3068
LA4275	OEM
LA4280	OEM
LA4280-TV	OEM
LA4282	OEM
LA4400	3286
LA4400FR	3286
LA4400Y	2179
LA4420	2179
LA4440	3299
LA4440-R	3299
LA4440R	3299
LA4445	3301
LA4460N	OEM
LA4465	OEM
LA4500	OEM
LA4505	3329
LA4507	OEM
LA4512B	OEM
LA4555	OEM
LA4570	OEM
LA4597	OEM
LA5003LP	OEM
LA5005	OEM
LA5100	OEM
LA5110N	OEM
LA5112	1437
LA5112N	1437
LA5112N-B	OEM
LA5112N-G	1437
LA5112R	OEM
LA5115N	1437
LA5192P	OEM
LA5511	OEM
LA5512	OEM
LA5515	OEM
LA5522	OEM
LA5523	OEM
LA5535N	OEM
LA5536N	OEM
LA5601	OEM
LA5666	OEM
LA5667	OEM
LA6324	0620
LA6324N	OEM
LA6339	0176
LA6358	0765
LA6358S	3202
LA6358T	OEM
LA6393D	6568
LA6393S	OEM
LA6458	OEM
LA6458D	0356
LA6458DF	0356
LA6458DS	OEM
LA6458M	OEM
LA6458S	2884
LA6458SS	OEM
LA-6460	OEM
LA6462D	OEM
LA6462S	OEM
LA-6480	OEM
LA6500	OEM
LA6510	OEM
LA6510L	OEM
LA6515	OEM
LA6520	4057
LA6532M	OEM
LA-6660	OEM
LA-6680	OEM
LA-6760	2192
LA-6780	2185
LA-6860	OEM
LA-6880	OEM
LA-6960	OEM
LA-6980	OEM
LA7000	OEM
LA7000S	OEM
LA7003	OEM
LA7003S	OEM
LA7005	OEM
LA7005S	OEM
LA7007	OEM
LA7007S	OEM
LA7009	OEM
LA7009S	OEM
LA7011	OEM
LA7013	OEM
LA7016	1022
LA7016//-1	1022
LA7017	OEM
LA7018	OEM
LA7019	OEM
LA7031	OEM
LA7032	OEM
LA7033	OEM
LA7034	OEM
LA7040	2094
LA7042	OEM
LA7051	OEM
LA7053	OEM
LA7054	OEM
LA7054Z	OEM
LA7055	OEM
LA7058	OEM
LA7058R	OEM
LA7060	OEM
LA7070	OEM
LA7071	OEM
LA7090	OEM
LA7095	OEM
LA7096	OEM
LA7110	OEM
LA7113	OEM
LA7116	OEM
LA7117	OEM
LA7122	OEM
LA7122S	OEM
LA7124	OEM
LA7210	OEM
LA7212	OEM
LA7213	OEM
LA7220	2998
LA7221	OEM
LA7222	4201
LA7224	4202
LA7225	OEM
LA7227	OEM
LA7237	OEM
LA7270M	OEM
LA7280MA	OEM
LA7293M	OEM
LA7295	OEM
LA7296-PK	OEM
LA7297	OEM
LA7300	OEM
LA7301M	OEM
LA7305	OEM
LA7305A	OEM
LA7305N	OEM
LA7306	OEM
LA7306N	OEM
LA7309	OEM
LA7309N	OEM
LA7315	OEM
LA7316A	OEM
LA7317	4213
LA7318	OEM
LA7320	OEM
LA7320M	OEM
LA7321	OEM
LA7321M	OEM
LA7322	OEM
LA7323	OEM
LA7323A	OEM
LA7325	OEM
LA7505	OEM
LA7507	4243
LA7510	OEM
LA7520	0534
LA7521	OEM
LA7522	OEM
LA7525	OEM
LA-7530	3765
LA7530	3765
LA7530N	3765
LA7531	OEM
LA7545	OEM
LA7550	OEM
LA7555	OEM
LA7600N	OEM
LA7601	1977
LA7601G	1977
LA-7601W	1977
LA7601W	1977
LA7610	OEM
LA7620	0552
LA7621	0387
LA7625	0481
LA7626	0457
LA7628	OEM
LA7629	0517
LA7650	OEM
LA7650K	4032
LA7650K-N	OEM
LA7650KN	4032
LA7651N	OEM
LA7651P	OEM
LA7652	OEM
LA7655	4032
LA7655N	4032
LA7655N(SMC)	OEM
LA7670	4261
LA7671	OEM
LA7673	OEM
LA7690	4111
LA7696	OEM
LA7751	OEM
LA7760	3331
LA7761	3830
LA7765	OEM
LA7800	0328
LA7800R	0328
LA7802	1580
LA7806	4285
LA7808	OEM
LA7809	OEM
LA7810	OEM
LA7811	4286
LA7820	OEM
LA7822	OEM
LA7823	4288
LA7830	0727
LA7831	2929
LA7835	2330
LA7835-TV	2330
LA7835K	2330
LA7836	OEM
LA7836)TV	OEM
LA7836-TV	OEM
LA7837	OEM
LA7838	4291
LA7900	OEM
LA7905	OEM
LA7910	2641
LA7911	OEM
LA7912	4307
LA7913	4309
LA7915	4310
LA7916	4311
LA7920	4313
LA7925	OEM
LA7926	OEM
LA7930	OEM
LA7934	OEM
LA7935	OEM
LA7938	OEM
LA7940	0678
LA7950	OEM
LA7951	OEM
LA7952	OEM
LA7953	OEM
LA7954	OEM
LA7955	OEM
LA7956	OEM
LA7957	OEM
LA7970	OEM
LA7990	OEM
LA9000	OEM
LA9000N	OEM
LA9010	OEM
LA9100	OEM
LA9200N	OEM
LA9200NM	OEM
LA13301	1206
LAA300	0015
LAA600	0015
LAA800	0015
LAB1363	0167
LAC010	OEM
LAD010	4509
LAD-011	2020
LAD011	2020
LAG570	OEM
LAG600	OEM
LAG624	OEM
LAP-011	1226
LAP011	1226
LAP-012	4363
LAS723	1183
LAS723B	1183
LAS1505	1911
LASER128ROM	OEM
LB120	OEM
LB-156	OEM
LB156	OEM
LB160	0374
LB-202MB	OEM
LB-202ML	OEM
LB-2020B	OEM
LB-2020L	OEM
LB-202VL	OEM
LB-202VR	OEM
LB-202YB	OEM
LB-202YL	OEM
LB-203MB	OEM
LB-203ML	OEM
LB-2030B	OEM
LB-2030L	OEM
LB-203VB	OEM
LB-203VL	OEM
LB230	OEM
LB-402MA	OEM
LB-402MK	OEM
LB-4020A	OEM
LB-4020K	OEM
LB-402VA	OEM
LB-402VK	OEM
LB402YL1	OEM
LB602-MA	OEM
LB-602MA	OEM
LB602MA-2	OEM
LB602MA2	OEM
LB-602MA2Z	OEM
LB-603MA	OEM
LB-603VA	OEM
LB1021	OEM
LB1200	OEM
LB1205	OEM
LB1214	OEM
LB1240	OEM
LB1259	OEM
LB1274	4876
LB1274K	4876
LB1274KF	OEM
LB1274KFT	OEM
LB1275	4875
LB1275K	OEM
LB1287	4075
LB1287K	OEM
LB1288	5191
LB1290	3839
LB1331	5068
LB1332	5068
LB1403	5070
LB1403N	OEM
LB1405	4746
LB1408	OEM
LB1409	4742
LB1412	OEM
LB1413N	OEM
LB1415	OEM
LB1416	4216
LB1419	OEM
LB1423	OEM
LB1423N	OEM
LB1433N	OEM
LB1500	OEM
LB1501	OEM
LB1515	OEM
LB1550	OEM
LB1551	OEM
LB-1620	OEM
LB1620	OEM
LB1624D	OEM
LB1624H	OEM
LB1630	OEM
LB1631MTP	OEM
LB1639	OEM
LB1641	OEM
LB1642	OEM
LB1645	OEM

If replacement code is OEM, contact original manufacturer for replacement.

DEVICE TYPE	REPL CODE
LB1645N	OEM
LB1646	OEM
LB1649	5157
LB1684H	OEM
LB1731	OEM
LB-2000	0141
LB2000	0141
LB2001	0557
LB2002	1812
LB2003	1035
LB2004	0033
LB2005	2086
LB2006	1820
LB2007	1168
LB2030	0081
LB2031	0354
LB2032	0329
LB2100	1833
LB2101	0337
LB2102	1848
LB2106	1824
LB2130	3365
LB2131	1622
LB2132	1472
LB3000	0232
LB3001	0507
LB3001(FANON)	2390
LB3002	0692
LB3003	0867
LB3004	0738
LB3005	1265
LB3006	0357
LB3008	0310
LB3009	1018
LB3060	1527
LB3150	1199
LB3175	0974
LB3500	OEM
LB-6410	OEM
LB-6430	OEM
LB-6440	OEM
LB-6610	OEM
LB-6630	OEM
LB-6640	OEM
LB-6650	OEM
LB-6710	4262
LB-6730	4266
LB-6740	4267
LB-6750	4268
LB-6810	OEM
LB-6830	OEM
LB-6840	OEM
LB-6850	OEM
LB-6910	OEM
LB-6930	OEM
LB-6940	OEM
LB-6950	OEM
LB8555S	OEM
LBA-01Z1	0276
LBA-02	0287
LBA-02Z1	0276
LBA-04	0293
LBA-04Z1	0293
LBA-06	0299
LBA-08	0250
LBA-10	0250
LBC547B	OEM
LBC547C	OEM
LC0.09M11/15	1293
LC0.09M1115	0015
LC6.5A	OEM
LC7.0A	OEM
LC7.5A	OEM
LC8.0A	OEM
LC8.5A	OEM
LC9.0A	OEM
LC10A	OEM
LC11A	OEM
LC12A	OEM
LC13A	OEM
LC14A	OEM
LC15	OEM
LC16	OEM
LC17	OEM
LC18	OEM
LC20	OEM
LC22	OEM
LC24	OEM
LC26	OEM
LC28	OEM
LC30	OEM
LC33	OEM
LC36	OEM
LC40	OEM
LC43	OEM
LC45	OEM
LC48	OEM
LC51	OEM
LC54	OEM
LC58	OEM
LC60	OEM
LC64	OEM
LC70	OEM
LC74HC02M	OEM
LC74HC05	OEM
LC74HC138	OEM
LC74HC174	OEM
LC74HCU04	OEM
LC75	OEM
LC80	OEM
LC90	OEM
LC100	OEM
LC110	OEM
LC120	OEM
LC130	OEM
LC150	OEM
LC160	OEM
LC170	OEM
LC180	OEM
LC-204MB	OEM
LC-204MD	OEM
LC-204ML	OEM
LC-204MN	OEM
LC-2040B	OEM
LC-2040D	OEM
LC-2040N	OEM
LC-204PL	OEM
LC-204RB	OEM
LC-204RD	OEM
LC-204RL	OEM
LC-204RN	OEM
LC-289(ELCOM)	1742
LC654H4069	OEM
LC945(P)	OEM
LC3019	OEM
LC3019A	OEM
LC3019B	OEM
LC3029	OEM
LC3029A	OEM
LC3029B	OEM
LC3039	OEM
LC3039A	OEM
LC3039B	OEM
LC3049	OEM
LC3049A	OEM
LC3049B	OEM
LC3059	OEM
LC3059A	OEM
LC3059B	OEM
LC3149	OEM
LC3149A	OEM
LC3149B	OEM
LC3514A	OEM
LC3514AD	OEM
LC3514D	OEM
LC3517A-15	OEM
LC3517AM-15	OEM
LC3517AS-15	OEM
LC3517BM-15	OEM
LC3517BML15T	OEM
LC3517BS	OEM
LC3517BS-15	OEM
LC3664N-10	OEM
LC3664N-12	OEM
LC4001B	0473
LC4001BP	0473
LC4011	0215
LC4011B	0215
LC4013B	0409
LC4013BM	OEM
LC4016B	4087
LC4066B	0101
LC4066BH	OEM
LC4069UB	0119
LC4071B	0129
LC4075B	6259
LC4081B	0328
LC4966	OEM
LC4969	OEM
LC6502B-633	OEM
LC6510C773	OEM
LC6512A3377	OEM
LC6512A3997	OEM
LC6512D797	OEM
LC6514B-729	OEM
LC6514B-3357	OEM
LC6521H-3257	OEM
LC6521H-3351	OEM
LC6521H-3755	OEM
LC6522C-3433	OEM
LC6523H304	OEM
LC6523H-3043	OEM
LC6526CPA	OEM
LC6527C-3570	OEM
LC6528C-3175	OEM
LC6528C-3421	OEM
LC6528C-3664	OEM
LC6538D-3753	OEM
LC6538D-3830	OEM
LC6538D-3992	OEM
LC6543H	OEM
LC6543H-3313	OEM
LC6543H-3384	OEM
LC6543H-3390	OEM
LC6543H-4016	OEM
LC6554H-3683	OEM
LC6554H3683	OEM
LC6554H-3906	OEM
LC6554H-4069	OEM
LC6554H4069	OEM
LC6554H-4082	OEM
LC6558D-3253	OEM
LC6568H-3350	OEM
LC6568H-3379	OEM
LC6658C	OEM
LC6658C-3395	OEM
LC7110	2346
LC7113	OEM
LC7120	4766
LC7130	OEM
LC7131	4708
LC7135	OEM
LC7136	OEM
LC7137	OEM
LC7150	OEM
LC7180	OEM
LC7181	OEM
LC7191	OEM
LC7217	OEM
LC7218	OEM
LC7220	OEM
LC7250	OEM
LC7265	OEM
LC7351	OEM
LC7360	OEM
LC7363	OEM
LC7385	OEM
LC7401	OEM
LC7410	OEM
LC7411-05	OEM
LC7411-08	OEM
LC7411-8011	OEM
LC7412	OEM
LC7412-8015	OEM
LC7413	OEM
LC7413C-8022	OEM
LC7414	OEM
LC7415	OEM
LC7416-8065	OEM
LC7416-8071	OEM
LC7416-8083	OEM
LC7418-8067	OEM
LC7418-8073	OEM
LC7418-8081	OEM
LC7418-8086	OEM
LC7419	OEM
LC7419-8090	OEM
LC7431	OEM
LC7431M	OEM
LC7432	OEM
LC7432M	OEM
LC7440	OEM
LC7440E	OEM
LC7450	OEM
LC7458A-02	OEM
LC7460	OEM
LC7461-8101	OEM
LC7461M	OEM
LC7461M-8100	OEM
LC7462M	OEM
LC7463M	OEM
LC7464M	OEM
LC7465M	OEM
LC7480	OEM
LC7512	OEM
LC7522	OEM
LC7533	OEM
LC7550	OEM
LC7566	OEM
LC7570	OEM
LC7580	OEM
LC7582	OEM
LC7582B	OEM
LC7583	OEM
LC7640	OEM
LC7800	OEM
LC7816	OEM
LC7818	OEM
LC7821	OEM
LC7860J	OEM
LC7860N	OEM
LC7863A	OEM
LC7880	OEM
LC7880M	OEM
LC7881-B	OEM
LC7881-C	OEM
LC7881B	OEM
LC7881C	OEM
LC7900	OEM
LC8991	OEM
LC35188ML	OEM
LC66508B-3721	OEM
LC66508B-3762	OEM
LC66508B-4142	OEM
LC66508B-4197	OEM
LC75280	OEM
LC89060	OEM
LC89060M	OEM
LC89066	OEM
LC89066M	OEM
LC89080	OEM
LC89086	OEM
LC864024A	OEM
LC864024A-5413	OEM
LC651483005	OEM
LCC-2	OEM
LCC-3	OEM
LCC-4	OEM
LCC-5	OEM
LCC-6	OEM
LCC-7	OEM
LCC-8	OEM
LCC-9	OEM
LCC-10	OEM
LCC-11	OEM
LCC-12	OEM
LCC-13	OEM
LCC-14	OEM
LCC-15	OEM
LCC-16	OEM
LCC-FS	OEM
LCD15M	OEM
LCD915-51	OEM
LCD9898	OEM
LCE6.5A	OEM
LCE7.0A	OEM
LCE7.5A	OEM
LCE8.0A	OEM
LCE8.5A	OEM
LCE9.0A	OEM
LCE10A	OEM
LCE11A	3143
LCE12A	OEM
LCE13A	OEM
LCE14A	OEM
LCE15A	3162
LCE16A	OEM
LCE17A	3171
LCE18A	OEM
LCE20A	OEM
LCE22A	1904
LCE24A	OEM
LCE26A	OEM
LCE28A	OEM
LCE30A	OEM
LCE33A	OEM
LCE36A	OEM
LCE40A	OEM
LCE43A	0563
LCE45A	OEM
LCE48A	OEM
LCE51A	OEM
LCE54A	OEM
LCE58A	0825
LCE60A	OEM
LCE64A	OEM
LCE70A	OEM
LCE75A	OEM
LCE80A	OEM
LCE90A	OEM
LCE100A	OEM
LCE110A	OEM
LCE120A	OEM
LCE130A	OEM
LCE150A	OEM
LCE160A	OEM
LCE170A	1395
LC0.09M11/15	1293
LCS1008P	0167
LC.09M	0015
LC.09M11/15	0015
LD	OEM
LD-001DU	OEM
LD-001MG	OEM
LD-001VR	OEM
LD-001YY	OEM
LD-002GB	OEM
LD-002RB	OEM
LD-002UB	OEM
LD-002YB	OEM
LD-003GB	OEM
LD-003RB	OEM
LD-003UB	OEM
LD-003YB	OEM
LD34R	0124
LD37A	OEM
LD-64R	OEM
LD100	OEM
LD101	OEM
LD-101DU	OEM
LD-101MG	OEM
LD-101VR	OEM
LD-101YY	OEM
LD102	OEM
LD128	0911
LD-201DU	OEM
LD-201MC	OEM
LD-201MG	OEM
LD-201VR	OEM
LD-201YY	OEM
LD271	0511
LD271H	OEM
LD271E7317	OEM
LD274	OEM
LD300	2390
LD-701DU	OEM
LD-701MG	OEM
LD-701VR	OEM
LD-701YY	OEM
LD-702DU	OEM
LD-702MG	OEM
LD-702VR	OEM
LD-702YY	OEM
LD-706DU	OEM
LD-706MG	OEM
LD-706VR	OEM
LD-706YY	OEM
LD1020	0021
LD1020A	0021
LD1041	0138
LD-1110	0351
LD1110	0351
LD3000	2388
LD3001	2390
LD3001W	2390
LD-3001X	OEM
LD3001X	2390
LD3040	2423
LD3061	2445
LD3080	2457
LD3110	2484
LD3110A	2484
LD3120	2487
LD3141	OEM
LD-3150	2142
LD3150	2142
LD-3150C	OEM
LD3150C	2142
LD315009-308025	OEM
LDA400	0079
LDA400MP	0079
LDA401	0079
LDA401MP	0079
LDA402	0079
LDA404	0086
LDA405	0086
LDA406	0086
LDA408	0086
LDA410	0111
LDA412	0414
LDA420	0396
LDA450	0126
LDA451	0527
LDA452	0150
LDA453	0527
LDA454	0688
LDA455	0688
LDD10	OEM
LDD50	OEM
LDF603	3577
LDF604	3577
LDF605	4150
LDF691	OEM
LDF692	OEM
LDF693	OEM
LDR05	OEM
LDR07	OEM
LDS200	0086
LDS201	0086
LDS202	0150
LDS203	0150
LDS206	0079
LDS207	0111
LDS208	0396
LDS210	0079
LDS257	0688
LDZ70/6A2	0466
LDZ70/9A1	0057
LE93CS56B1	OEM
LE2668E	OEM
LED55B	0586
LED55BF	0586
LED55C	0586
LED55CF	0586
LED56	0586
LED56F	0586
LED-15005	1063
LED21085	1248
LED21092	2067
LEDU-1	OEM
LEDU-4	OEM
LEDU-9	OEM
LEDU-12	OEM
LEDV3	OEM
LF155AH	OEM
LF155H	OEM
LF155J	OEM
LF156AH	OEM
LF156H	OEM
LF156J	OEM
LF157AH	OEM
LF157H	OEM
LF157J	OEM
LF255H	OEM
LF255J	OEM
LF255N	OEM
LF256H	OEM
LF256J	OEM
LF256N	OEM
LF257H	OEM
LF257J	OEM
LF257N	OEM
LF347	3357
LF347BN	OEM
LF347N	3357
LF351N	6446
LF353	3695
LF353N	3695
LF355	3627
LF355AH	5880
LF355BH	OEM
LF355BJ	OEM
LF355BN	5881
LF355H	3576
LF355J	5901
LF355N	5901
LF356	5901
LF356AH	5880
LF356BH	OEM
LF356BJ	OEM
LF356BN	5881
LF356H	3576
LF356J	5901
LF356N	5901
LF357AH	5880
LF357BH	OEM
LF357BJ	OEM
LF357BN	5881
LF357H	3576
LF357J	5901
LF357N	5901
LF11201D	OEM
LF11202D	OEM
LF11331D	OEM
LF11332D	OEM
LF11333D	OEM
LF13201D	OEM
LF13201M	OEM
LF13201N	OEM
LF13202D	OEM
LF13202M	OEM
LF13202N	OEM
LF13331D	OEM
LF13331M	OEM
LF13331N	3932
LF13332D	OEM
LF13332M	OEM
LF13332N	OEM
LF13333D	OEM
LF13333M	OEM
LF13333N	OEM
LFB01	OEM
LFB-01L	OEM
LFB01L	OEM
LFM5	OEM
LFRC-27-15	0023
LG1353G	OEM
LG1354G	OEM
LG1454G	OEM
LH0115A	OEM
LH5060	OEM
LH5060B	OEM
LH5116-15	OEM
LH5116N	OEM
LH5116N-15	OEM
LH21256-12	1463
LH534187	OEM
LHV1B	0344
LHV1C	0344
LHV2D	0344
LHV2E	OEM
LHV2F	OEM
LHV3G	OEM
LHV3H	OEM
LHV3K	OEM
LHV4M	OEM
LHV4Q	OEM
LHV4R	OEM
LHV5T	OEM
LHV5V	OEM
LI201	OEM
LI210G1	OEM
LI2108	OEM
LID6.8	OEM
LID6.8A	OEM
LID7.5	OEM
LID7.5A	OEM
LID8.2	OEM
LID8.2A	OEM
LID9.1	OEM
LID9.1A	OEM
LID10	OEM
LID10A	OEM
LID11	OEM
LID11A	OEM
LID12	OEM
LID12A	OEM
LID13	OEM
LID13A	OEM
LID15	OEM
LID15A	OEM
LID16	OEM
LID16A	OEM
LID18	OEM
LID18A	OEM
LID20	OEM
LID20A	OEM
LID22	OEM
LID22A	OEM
LID24	OEM
LID24A	OEM
LID27	OEM
LID27A	OEM
LID30	OEM
LID30A	OEM
LID33	OEM
LID33A	OEM
LID929	0111
LID930	0111
LJ-152	0037
LJ152	0037
LJ152(0)	0037
LJ152(0)	0150
LJ152G	0037
LK1352P	0391
LKA4020	OEM
LKB52P	0391
LL-2	0015
LL2	0015
LL4821J-L	OEM
LM-035MG-A	OEM
LM-035MG-B	OEM
LM-035VR-A	OEM
LM-035VR-B	OEM
LM-035YY-A	OEM
LM-035YY-B	OEM
LM7-28	OEM
LM11	OEM
LM11CH	OEM
LM11CJ	OEM
LM11CJ-8	OEM
LM11CLH	OEM
LM11CLI	OEM
LM11CLI-8	OEM
LM11CLJ	OEM
LM11CLJ-8	OEM
LM11CLN	OEM
LM11CLN-14	OEM
LM11CN	OEM
LM11CN-14	OEM
LM11H	OEM
LM11J	OEM
LM11J-8	OEM
LM31GCPHLM-U	OEM
LM55SCN	3254
LM59NV	OEM
LM78CN	OEM
LM78L05	5538
LM78L05A	1288
LM78L05ACH	1288
LM78L05ACI	1288
LM78L05ACZ	1288
LM78L08ACH	0083
LM78L08ACZ	0083
LM78L08CH	0083
LM78L12	1817
LM78L12ACZ	1817
LM78MR05-FA	OEM
LM101A	OEM
LM101ADE	OEM
LM101ADE/883B	OEM
LM101AGC	OEM
LM101AH	0093
LM101AH/883B	OEM
LM101AJ	OEM
LM101H	0093
LM107	OEM
LM108AF	OEM
LM108AH	OEM
LM108AJ	OEM
LM108AJ-8	OEM
LM108AN	OEM
LM108F	OEM
LM108H	OEM
LM108J	OEM
LM108J-8	OEM
LM108N	OEM
LM111	OEM
LM111H	0415
LM111J-8	OEM
LM112H	OEM
LM117H	OEM
LM117K	OEM
LM117LH	OEM
LM117MR	OEM
LM123AK	OEM
LM123K	0655
LM124	0656
LM124A	0656
LM124J	OEM
LM124J/883B	OEM
LM1310N	0514
LM137H	OEM
LM137K	OEM
LM137MR	OEM
LM139	OEM
LM139AJ	OEM
LM139AJ/883B	OEM
LM139J	OEM
LM139J/883B	OEM
LM140K-5.0	0655
LM140K-6.0	OEM
LM140K-8.0	OEM
LM140K-12	1916
LM140K-15	1919
LM140K-18	OEM
LM140K-24	OEM
LM148	OEM
LM148J	OEM
LM148J/883B	OEM
LM150K	OEM
LM158	OEM
LM158A	OEM
LM158AJ	OEM
LM158H	OEM
LM158J	OEM
LM193	OEM
LM193A	OEM
LM193AH	OEM
LM193H	OEM
LM201A	OEM
LM201ADE	OEM
LM201AH	0093
LM201AJ	OEM
LM201AN	1290
LM201AND	OEM
LM201H	0093
LM207H	1770
LM207N	0308
LM208AD	OEM
LM208AF	OEM
LM208AH	OEM
LM208AJ	OEM

If replacement code is OEM, contact original manufacturer for replacement.

DEVICE TYPE	REPL CODE
LM208AJ-8	OEM
LM208AN	OEM
LM208F	OEM
LM208H	OEM
LM208J	OEM
LM208J-8	OEM
LM208N	OEM
LM209H	OEM
LM209K	1790
LM211	OEM
LM211H	1804
LM211J-8	OEM
LM212H	OEM
LM217H	OEM
LM217MR	OEM
LM218	OEM
LM223AK	OEM
LM223K	1905
LM224	0656
LM224A	0656
LM224AD	0620
LM224AF	0620
LM224AJ	0620
LM224AN	0620
LM224D	0620
LM224J	0620
LM224N	0620
LM237H	OEM
LM237K	OEM
LM237MR	OEM
LM238K	OEM
LM239	0176
LM239A	0176
LM239AA	OEM
LM239AF	OEM
LM239AJ	0176
LM239AN	0176
LM239F	OEM
LM239J	0176
LM239N	0176
LM246J	OEM
LM246N	OEM
LM248	OEM
LM248J	OEM
LM248N	OEM
LM249J	OEM
LM250K	OEM
LM258	OEM
LM258A	OEM
LM258AH	1667
LM258AJ	5882
LM258AN	1667
LM258AT	1667
LM258D	OEM
LM258FE	OEM
LM258H	1667
LM258J	OEM
LM258JG	0765
LM258N	0765
LM258P	0765
LM258T	1667
LM260H	OEM
LM260N14	OEM
LM261H	OEM
LM261J	OEM
LM275D	OEM
LM292H	OEM
LM292J	OEM
LM293	OEM
LM293A	OEM
LM293AFE	OEM
LM293AH	OEM
LM293AN	OEM
LM293AT	OEM
LM293FE	OEM
LM293H	OEM
LM293JG	OEM
LM293N	OEM
LM293P	OEM
LM293T	OEM
LM299AH	OEM
LM299AH-20	OEM
LM299H	OEM
LM301A	OEM
LM301AD	2339
LM301ADE	1290
LM301AF	OEM
LM301AFE	OEM
LM301AH	0093
LM301AJ	OEM
LM301AJD	OEM
LM301AJDS	OEM
LM301AJG	OEM
LM301AJS	OEM
LM301AN	1290
LM301AN-14	OEM
LM301AND	OEM
LM301ANDS	OEM
LM301ANS	OEM
LM301AP	1290
LM301AT	1290
LM301AU	OEM
LM301AV	1290
LM301F	OEM
LM302H	2207
LM304F	OEM
LM304H	OEM
LM304J	OEM
LM304N	OEM
LM305AH	OEM
LM305AJG	OEM
LM305AP	2155
LM305H	2451
LM305JG	OEM
LM305P	OEM
LM305T	2451
LM306	OEM
LM306H	OEM
LM306J	OEM
LM306JG	OEM
LM306N	OEM
LM306P	OEM
LM306U	OEM
LM307	OEM
LM307DE	2267
LM307F	2267
LM307H	2466
LM307J	2267
LM307J14	OEM
LM307JG	OEM
LM307N	2267
LM307P	2267
LM307T	1770
LM307U	OEM
LM307V	OEM
LM308AD	OEM
LM308AF	OEM
LM308AH	0890
LM308AH-1	OEM
LM308AH-2	OEM
LM308AJ	OEM
LM308AJ-8	0890
LM308AJ8	OEM
LM308AJ-8D	OEM
LM308AJ-8DS	OEM
LM308AJ-8S	OEM
LM308AN	2231
LM308AND	OEM
LM308ANDS	OEM
LM308ANS	OEM
LM308AT	0890
LM308D	2231
LM308DE	OEM
LM308F	OEM
LM308H	0890
LM308J	OEM
LM308J-8	2231
LM308J8	OEM
LM308J-8D	OEM
LM308J-8DS	OEM
LM308J-8S	OEM
LM308N	2231
LM308ND	OEM
LM308NDS	OEM
LM308NS	OEM
LM308T	0890
LM309DA	1911
LM309DB	OEM
LM309H	OEM
LM309K	1911
LM310D	OEM
LM310H	2207
LM310J	OEM
LM310J8	OEM
LM310N	2495
LM311	1804
LM311D	2093
LM311DE	OEM
LM311F	2093
LM311H	1804
LM311J	OEM
LM311J-8	OEM
LM311J8	OEM
LM311J-8D	OEM
LM311J-8DS	OEM
LM311J-8S	OEM
LM311JG	6292
LM311N	2093
LM311N-14	OEM
LM311N14	OEM
LM311ND	OEM
LM311NDS	2093
LM311NS	OEM
LM311P	2093
LM311T	1804
LM311U	OEM
LM311V	OEM
LM312H	OEM
LM313H	OEM
LM316AH	OEM
LM316H	OEM
LM317	2697
LM317H	OEM
LM317HVH	OEM
LM317HVK	OEM
LM317K	1183
LM317KA	OEM
LM317KC	2541
LM317LH	OEM
LM317LZ	5187
LM317MP	OEM
LM317MR	OEM
LM317MT	OEM
LM317T	2541
LM318	2543
LM318DE	OEM
LM318H	2540
LM318J	OEM
LM318J-8	2545
LM318JG	2545
LM318M	2543
LM318N	2545
LM318P	2545
LM318U	OEM
LM319F	2548
LM319H	2552
LM319J	2548
LM319K	2552
LM319N	2548
LM320H5.0	OEM
LM320H12	OEM
LM320H15	OEM
LM320K5.0	1993
LM320K12	5193
LM320K15	5195
LM320KC5.0	OEM
LM320KC12	OEM
LM320KC15	OEM
LM320L-12	1825
LM320LZ5.0	OEM
LM320LZ-12	1825
LM320LZ12	1825
LM320LZ15	4952
LM320MLP5.0	OEM
LM320MLP5.0TB	OEM
LM320MLP12	OEM
LM320MLP12TB	OEM
LM320MLP15	OEM
LM320MLP15TB	OEM
LM320MP5.0	OEM
LM320MP5.0TB	OEM
LM320MP-5.2	1275
LM320MP-12	1827
LM320MP12	OEM
LM320MP12TB	OEM
LM320MP15	OEM
LM320MP15TB	OEM
LM320MP-24	3531
LM320T-5.0	1275
LM320T5.0	1275
LM320T-5.2	1275
LM320T-6.0	2624
LM320T6.0	2624
LM320T8.0	1187
LM320T-12	1827
LM320T12	1827
LM320T-15	3777
LM320T15	3777
LM320T-24	3531
LM320T24	3531
LM321H	OEM
LM322H	OEM
LM322N	OEM
LM323AK	OEM
LM323AT	OEM
LM323K	1905
LM323T	OEM
LM324	0620
LM324A	0620
LM324AD	0620
LM324AF	0620
LM324AJ	0620
LM324AN	0620
LM324D	0620
LM324F	0656
LM324J	0620
LM324JD	OEM
LM324JDS	OEM
LM324JS	OEM
LM324M	OEM
LM324N	0620
LM324ND	OEM
LM324NDS	OEM
LM324NS	OEM
LM325AN	OEM
LM325H	OEM
LM325N	OEM
LM326H	OEM
LM329AH	OEM
LM329BH	OEM
LM329BZ	OEM
LM329CH	OEM
LM329CZ	OEM
LM329DH	OEM
LM329DZ	OEM
LM329N	OEM
LM330T5.0	OEM
LM331AH	OEM
LM331AN	OEM
LM331H	OEM
LM331N	OEM
LM334H	OEM
LM334Z	OEM
LM335AH	OEM
LM335AZ	OEM
LM335H	OEM
LM335Z	OEM
LM336BH	OEM
LM336BZ	OEM
LM336H	OEM
LM336Z	OEM
LM337	OEM
LM337H	OEM
LM337HVH	OEM
LM337HVK	OEM
LM337K	2697
LM337LZ	5188
LM337MP	OEM
LM337MR	OEM
LM337MT	6566
LM337T	2709
LM338K	2710
LM339	0176
LM339A	0176
LM339AA	OEM
LM339AF	OEM
LM339AJ	0176
LM339AM	OEM
LM339AN	0176
LM339D	2715
LM339DP	0176
LM339F	OEM
LM339J	0176
LM339JD	OEM
LM339JDS	OEM
LM339JS	OEM
LM339M	OEM
LM339M(SM)	OEM
LM339N	0176
LM339ND	OEM
LM339NDS	OEM
LM339NS	OEM
LM340	1801
LM340-5	1911
LM340-5DA	1911
LM340-5KC	0619
LM340-5U	0619
LM340-6	OEM
LM340-6DA	OEM
LM340-6KC	0917
LM340-6U	0917
LM340-8	OEM
LM340-8DA	OEM
LM340-8KC	1187
LM340-8U	1187
LM340-10	OEM
LM340-10KC	OEM
LM340-12	3906
LM340-12DA	3828
LM340-12KC	0330
LM340-12U	0330
LM340-15	OEM
LM340-15DA	1989
LM340-15KC	OEM
LM340-15U	1311
LM340-18	OEM
LM340-18DA	OEM
LM340-18KC	2244
LM340-18U	2244
LM340-24	OEM
LM340-24DA	OEM
LM340-24KC	2224
LM340-24U	2224
LM340AK5.0	1790
LM340AK12	3906
LM340AK15	1989
LM340AT5.0	0619
LM340AT12	1341
LM340AT15	4276
LM340CT	OEM
LM340CT0.2	OEM
LM340K-5.0	0655
LM340K5.0	1911
LM340K-6.0	OEM
LM340K-8.0	OEM
LM340K-12	3906
LM340K12	1987
LM340K-15	1989
LM340K15	1989
LM340K-18	3605
LM340K-24	3828
LM340KC5.0	1790
LM340KC12	3906
LM340KC15	1989
LM340T	0619
LM340T-5	0619
LM340T5	0619
LM340T-5.0	0619
LM340T5.0	0619
LM340T-5.0R	0619
LM340T-6	0917
LM340T-6.0	0917
LM340T6.0	0917
LM340T-6.0R	0917
LM340T-8.0	1187
LM340T8.0	1187
LM340T-12	0330
LM340T12	0330
LM340T-12R	0330
LM340T-15	1311
LM340T15	1311
LM340T-15R	1311
LM340T-18	2244
LM340T-24	2224
LM340T24	2224
LM340T-24R	2224
LM340TS	OEM
LM340U5	0619
LM340U6	0917
LM340U8	1187
LM340U12	0330
LM340U15	1311
LM340U24	2224
LM341-5	0619
LM341-6	0917
LM341-12	0330
LM341-15	1311
LM341-24	2224
LM341P5	OEM
LM341P-5.0	0619
LM341P5.0	0619
LM341P5.0TB	OEM
LM341P-6.0	0917
LM341P-8.0	1187
LM341P8.0	1187
LM341P-12	0330
LM341P12	0330
LM341P12TB	OEM
LM341P-15	1311
LM341P15	1311
LM341P15TB	OEM
LM341P-24	2224
LM342P-5	OEM
LM342P5.0	5908
LM342P12	0330
LM342P15	1311
LM343H	OEM
LM343J	OEM
LM343N	OEM
LM344H	OEM
LM345K5.0	OEM
LM345K5.2	OEM
LM346J	OEM
LM346N	OEM
LM348	2796
LM348AJ	OEM
LM348AN	OEM
LM348D	2789
LM348J	2796
LM348N	2796
LM349	OEM
LM349J	OEM
LM349N	OEM
LM350K	2811
LM350T	OEM
LM350T12	OEM
LM358	0765
LM358A	OEM
LM358AH	1667
LM358AJ	OEM
LM358AN	0765
LM358AT	0765
LM358D	2854
LM358FE	OEM
LM358H	1667
LM358J	0765
LM358JD	OEM
LM358JDS	OEM
LM358JG	0765
LM358JS	OEM
LM358L	1667
LM358M	2854
LM358N	0765
LM358NB	1667
LM358ND	OEM
LM358NDS	OEM
LM358NS	OEM
LM358P	0765
LM358PS	OEM
LM358S	2865
LM358T	1667
LM359J	2866
LM359N	2866
LM360H	OEM
LM360N	OEM
LM360N14	OEM
LM361H	OEM
LM361J	OEM
LM361N	OEM
LM363AD	OEM
LM363AH10	OEM
LM363AH100	OEM
LM363AH500	OEM
LM363D	OEM
LM363H10	OEM
LM363H100	OEM
LM363H500	OEM
LM370	3759
LM373N	2947
LM375D	OEM
LM375N	2947
LM376JG	OEM
LM376N	2155
LM376P	OEM
LM377	6602
LM377-N	1482
LM377KC	2709
LM-377N	2535
LM377N	1482
LM377N10	2535
LM378N	2989
LM379S	OEM
LM380	0375
LM380N	0375
LM381A	3000
LM381AA	OEM
LM381AN	3000
LM381N	3000
LM382A	OEM
LM382N	OEM
LM383	1042
LM383AT	1042
LM383T	1042
LM384N	3027
LM386	3034
LM386(SM)	OEM
LM386A	3034
LM386F	OEM
LM386LM	3034
LM386N	3034
LM386N-1	3034
LM386N-2	OEM
LM386N-3	3034
LM386N-4	OEM
LM387	3050
LM387AN	3050
LM387N	3050
LM387V	OEM
LM388N	3057
LM388N-1	3057
LM388N-2	OEM
LM388N-3	OEM
LM388NE1	OEM
LM388NE2	OEM
LM388NE3	OEM
LM389N	OEM
LM390AH	0786
LM390AI	0786
LM390AJ	0786
LM390N	3070
LM391N	3081
LM391N-60	3081
LM391N-80	3081
LM392H	OEM
LM392J	OEM
LM392N	OEM
LM393	OEM
LM393A	OEM
LM393AFE	OEM
LM393AH	OEM
LM393AJ	OEM
LM393AN	OEM
LM393AT	OEM
LM393FE	OEM
LM393H	OEM
LM393J	OEM
LM393JG	6970
LM393M	3089
LM393N	0624
LM393NB	0624
LM393P	0624
LM393T	OEM
LM396K	OEM
LM399AH	0590
LM399AH-50	OEM
LM399AI	0590
LM399AJ	0590
LM399H	OEM
LM529CH	OEM
LM529CN	OEM
LM555	0967
LM555C	0967
LM555CH	3592
LM555CJ	0967
LM555CN	0967
LM555CN#1	0967
LM555CN#2	0967
LM555H	3592
LM555J	OEM
LM556CJ	OEM
LM556CN	3254
LM556D	2583
LM556J	OEM
LM556M	2583
LM565CN	3347
LM566CH	3773
LM566CN	3775
LM566H	3773
LM566N	3775
LM567CM	5943
LM640SG-2031	OEM
LM703	0627
LM703E	0627
LM703L	0627
LM703LH	0627
LM-703LN	0627
LM703LN	0627
LM709AH	OEM
LM709C	4175
LM709CH	1291
LM709CN	1695
LM709H	OEM
LM710CH	1786
LM710CN	1789
LM710H	OEM
LM710N	OEM
LM711CH	1879
LM711CN	1886
LM711H	4181
LM723CG	1183
LM723CH	1183
LM723CJ	OEM
LM723CN	0026
LM723H	1183
LM723J	OEM
LM723N	4205
LM725AH	OEM
LM725CH	2863
LM725CN	OEM
LM725H	OEM
LM733	OEM
LM733CH	1113
LM733CN	1110
LM733H	OEM
LM741	0308
LM741AH	0406
LM741AJ14	OEM
LM741C	0406
LM741CH	0406
LM741CJ	0308
LM741CJ-14	OEM
LM741CJ14	OEM
LM741CM	1965
LM741CN	0308
LM741EH	0406
LM741EN	0308
LM741H883	OEM
LM741J14	OEM
LM741N	0308
LM746	0661
LM746H	0748
LM746N	0345
LM747AH	2352
LM747AJ	2342
LM747CH	2352
LM747CJ	2342
LM747CN	2342
LM747EH	2352
LM747EJ	2342
LM747EN	OEM
LM747H	2352
LM747H883	OEM
LM747J	2342
LM748CH	0093
LM748CJ	OEM
LM748CN	3861
LM748CN7	6097
LM748H	2435
LM748J	OEM
LM748N	2433
LM758N	OEM
LM760CH	OEM
LM760CN	OEM
LM832(A)	OEM
LM833	OEM
LM833M	OEM
LM833M63	OEM
LM833N	OEM
LM856C	OEM
LM1011	OEM
LM1011A	OEM
LM1011AN	6797
LM1011N	4846
LM1014AN	OEM
LM1014N	OEM
LM1019N	OEM
LM1030	OEM
LM1035	OEM
LM1037	OEM
LM1038	OEM
LM1090E	0079
LM1090F	0079
LM1090G	0079
LM1110A	0144
LM1110B	0127
LM1111A	OEM
LM1111B	OEM
LM1111C	OEM
LM1111CN	OEM
LM1112B	OEM
LM1112C	OEM
LM1112CN	OEM
LM1117	0111
LM1117(A)	OEM
LM1117(B)	OEM
LM1117C	0111
LM1117D	0079
LM1120B	0127
LM1120C	0127
LM1121A	OEM
LM1121B	OEM
LM1121C	OEM
LM1123H	0144
LM-1129	0079
LM-1130	0079
LM1131	OEM
LM1131A	OEM
LM1131B	OEM
LM1131C	OEM
LM-1132	0079
LM-1133	0079
LM1133	0326
LM1138	0224
LM1138E/F	0224
LM1138G/F	0224
LM1138G/H	0144
LM1138H/I	0224
LM-1147	0079
LM-1148	0079
LM-1149	0037
LM-1150	0037
LM-1151	0037
LM-1153	0037
LM-1154	0283
LM-1155	0079
LM-1156	0334
LM-1157	0556
LM-1158	0015
LM-1159	0133
LM1159	0133
LM-1160	0015
LM1160	0015
LM1274	OEM

If replacement code is OEM, contact original manufacturer for replacement.

DEVICE TYPE	REPL CODE
LM1304	0649
LM1304N	0649
LM1305	0438
LM1305M	0438
LM1305N	0438
LM1305N01	0438
LM1307	0696
LM1307A	0696
LM1307E	0696
LM-1307N	0696
LM1307N	0696
LM1307N01	0696
LM1307P	0696
LM1307PQ	0696
LM1307W	0696
LM1310	0514
LM-1310N	0514
LM1310N	0514
LM1310N01	0514
LM1329	0516
LM1351#	0784
LM1351N	0784
LM1391N	0842
LM1403	0079
LM1404	0037
LM1408J-6	OEM
LM1408J-7	OEM
LM1408J-8	OEM
LM1408N-6	4252
LM1408N-7	4252
LM1408N-8	OEM
LM1414J	OEM
LM1414N	OEM
LM1415-6	0016
LM1415-7	0016
LM1415J	OEM
LM1458	0356
LM1458AN	OEM
LM1458C	2457
LM1458H	3108
LM1458J	OEM
LM1458M	0356
LM1458N	0356
LM1496	0413
LM1496H	0413
LM1496J	3751
LM1496N	3751
LM1501H	0086
LM1502H	0126
LM1508D-8	OEM
LM1508J-8	OEM
LM1540	0079
LM1540(B)	OEM
LM1540C	0111
LM1558AH	OEM
LM1558AJ	OEM
LM1558H	3108
LM1558J	OEM
LM1566F	0079
LM1596H	0413
LM1614D	0079
LM1614M	0079
LM1795	0037
LM1796	0261
LM1800	1385
LM1800A	1385
LM1800N	1385
LM1801	OEM
LM1812A	OEM
LM1815N	OEM
LM1818	0079
LM1818N	4472
LM1819N	4473
LM1820	1411
LM1820A	1411
LM1820N	1411
LM1821S	4488
LM1823	1415
LM1823N	1415
LM1828N	OEM
LM1829	0516
LM1830N	OEM
LM1834	0030
LM1837(A)	OEM
LM1841	1434
LM1845M	2438
LM1848N	OEM
LM1850	OEM
LM-1862	0015
LM1862	0015
LM1865(A)	OEM
LM1866(A)	OEM
LM1868N	OEM
LM1870	1473
LM1877	1482
LM1877N	1482
LM1877N-1	OEM
LM1877N-2	OEM
LM1877N-3	1482
LM1877N-4	OEM
LM1877N-5	OEM
LM1877N-6	OEM
LM1877N-7	OEM
LM1877N-8	OEM
LM1877N-9	4069
LM1877N-10	1482
LM1880F	OEM
LM1889	1508
LM1889N	1508

DEVICE TYPE	REPL CODE
LM1894N	OEM
LM1895	OEM
LM1896N	4803
LM1897	OEM
LM1900J	OEM
LM1932	0102
LM1946H	0413
LM1965(A)	OEM
LM1996H	OEM
LM2000N	OEM
LM2001N	OEM
LM2002AT	OEM
LM2002T	OEM
LM2020	0150
LM-2111	0659
LM2111	0659
LM2111A	0659
LM2111M	0659
LM-2111N	0659
LM2111N	0659
LM2111N01	0659
LM2113N01	0673
LM2152	0079
LM-2589	0037
LM2682	0079
LM2701	0264
LM2808N	OEM
LM2877P	OEM
LM2895	OEM
LM2896	2288
LM2896P1	2288
LM2896P2	OEM
LM2900	2232
LM2900J	OEM
LM2900N	2232
LM2901	0176
LM2901D	2715
LM2901F	OEM
LM2901J	0176
LM2901N	0176
LM2901NDS	OEM
LM2901NS	OEM
LM2902	0620
LM2902D	3172
LM2902J	0620
LM2902N	0620
LM2903	2294
LM2903D	OEM
LM2903FE	OEM
LM2903H	OEM
LM2903JG	OEM
LM2903M	OEM
LM2903N	2294
LM2903P	OEM
LM2903T	OEM
LM2904	OEM
LM2904D	OEM
LM2904H	OEM
LM2904J	0765
LM2904JG	0765
LM2904L	1667
LM2904M	6087
LM2904N	0765
LM2904P	0765
LM2905N	OEM
LM2907N	OEM
LM2907N-8	OEM
LM2907N8	OEM
LM2908J	OEM
LM2908N	OEM
LM2917	2302
LM2917-8	2302
LM2917J	2302
LM2917M	OEM
LM2917N	2302
LM2917N-8	4471
LM2917N8	4471
LM2924J	OEM
LM2924N	OEM
LM2931AT5.0	OEM
LM2931AZ5.0	OEM
LM2931T	OEM
LM2931T5.0	OEM
LM2931Z5.0	OEM
LM2936Z-5	OEM
LM2936Z-5.0	OEM
LM2940CT	OEM
LM2940CT-5.0	OEM
LM2940T5	OEM
LM2940T5M	OEM
LM3028AH	0817
LM3028BH	0817
LM3045D	1686
LM3045J	1686
LM3045N	1686
LM3046N	6203
LM3053H	0817
LM3064M	0360
LM3064N	0797
LM3064N-01	0797
LM3064N01	OEM
LM3065	0167
LM3065N	0167
LM3065N01	0167
LM3067N	0324
LM3070A	0348
LM3070N	0348
LM3070N01	0348
LM3071A	0350

DEVICE TYPE	REPL CODE
LM3071N	0350
LM3071N01	0350
LM3072	0661
LM3072N	0661
LM3075N01	1335
LM3075N01A	1335
LM3080AN	3784
LM3080N	6237
LM3086	OEM
LM3086N	1686
LM3086W	1686
LM3089N	2728
LM3105	0438
LM3189N	6303
LM3216	OEM
LM3231	OEM
LM3301N	2232
LM3302	0176
LM3302J	0176
LM3302N	0176
LM3401N	6538
LM3429-50	OEM
LM3524J	OEM
LM3524N	5140
LM3820N	6833
LM3862M	3034
LM3900	2232
LM3900J	OEM
LM3900N	2232
LM3905N	OEM
LM3909	3033
LM3909N	3033
LM3911N	OEM
LM3914	3039
LM3914D	OEM
LM3914N	3039
LM3915	3040
LM3916	3042
LM3999Z	OEM
LM4250	OEM
LM4250C	OEM
LM4250CH	3768
LM4250CJ	OEM
LM4250CN	3400
LM4250F	OEM
LM4250H	OEM
LM4250J	OEM
LM4500AN	OEM
LM5047	OEM
LM6402A	OEM
LM6402A-022	OEM
LM6402A022	OEM
LM6402A-095	OEM
LM6402A095	OEM
LM6402A127	OEM
LM6402A-220	OEM
LM6402A220	OEM
LM6402A-221	OEM
LM6402A221	OEM
LM6402G-582	OEM
LM6402G-1844	OEM
LM6402G-1957	OEM
LM6402G-1999	OEM
LM6402H-158	OEM
LM6402H-238	OEM
LM6402H-274	OEM
LM6402H-329	OEM
LM6402H-344	OEM
LM6402H-350	OEM
LM6402H-562	OEM
LM6402H1871	OEM
LM6405G031	OEM
LM6405H-215	OEM
LM6405H-330	OEM
LM6405H-SA069	OEM
LM6405H-SB173	OEM
LM6413-1830(TN2001A)	OEM
LM6413E	OEM
LM6413E-342	OEM
LM6413E-554	OEM
LM6413E-563	OEM
LM6413E-1807	OEM
LM6413E-1968	OEM
LM6413E-1969	OEM
LM6413E-2068	OEM
LM6413E-2069	OEM
LM6413E-2088	OEM
LM6413E-2099	OEM
LM6413E-2129	OEM
LM6413E-2130	OEM
LM6416E	OEM
LM6416E-159	OEM
LM6416E-202	OEM
LM6416E-209	OEM
LM6416E-217	OEM
LM6416E-239	OEM
LM6416E-351	OEM
LM6416E-363	OEM
LM6416E-410	OEM
LM6416E-557	OEM
LM6416E-1917	OEM
LM6416E-1942	OEM
LM6416E-2084	OEM
LM6416E-2085	OEM
LM6417E-302	OEM
LM6417E-1838	OEM
LM7000	OEM
LM7001	OEM
LM7805CT	1801

DEVICE TYPE	REPL CODE
LM7808A-8	0083
LM7812	0330
LM7812CT	5885
LM7905CT	1275
LM7912CT	1827
LM8000	0590
LM8050I/J	0079
LM8071	OEM
LM-8360	OEM
LM8360	2279
LM8361	2279
LM8361D	2279
LM8361DH	2702
LM8362	OEM
LM8363	1238
LM8363D	1238
LM8363DH	OEM
LM8363H	1238
LM8364	OEM
LM8365	OEM
LM8368	OEM
LM8372	OEM
LM8460	OEM
LM8471	OEM
LM8521	OEM
LM8523	OEM
LM8560	3925
LM8560B	OEM
LM8561	OEM
LM8562	OEM
LM8569	OEM
LM8854-576	OEM
LM8854-1851	OEM
LM8854-1912	OEM
LM8942	OEM
LM8972	OEM
LM9016F	0127
LM9018F	1943
LM9018G/F	0079
LM11123H	OEM
LM11700AJ	OEM
LM13080N	OEM
LM13080P	OEM
LM13600	OEM
LM13600A	OEM
LM13600AD	OEM
LM13600AN	OEM
LM13600D	OEM
LM13600M	OEM
LM13600N	2154
LM13700AN	OEM
LM13700J	OEM
LM13700N	OEM
LM24102	OEM
LM39000A30	OEM
LM40101	OEM
LMA-595	OEM
LMC555CM	2744
LMC-1992	OEM
LMC1992	OEM
LMC1992N	OEM
LMH8	OEM
LMP15	0002
LMP15-20	0002
LMP15A	0002
LMQ5	OEM
LMS15	OEM
LMS20	OEM
LMS25	OEM
LMS30	OEM
LMS40	OEM
LMS50	OEM
LMS60	OEM
LMS80	OEM
LMS100	OEM
LMS120	OEM
LMS150	OEM
LMS180	OEM
LMS8560	OEM
LMZ3.3	0777
LMZ3.3-20	6084
LMZ3.3A	0777
LMZ3.6	0791
LMZ3.6-20	0791
LMZ3.6A	0791
LMZ3.9	0801
LMZ3.9-20	0801
LMZ3.9A	0801
LMZ4.3	0815
LMZ4.3-20	0815
LMZ4.3A	0815
LMZ4.7	0827
LMZ4.7-20	0827
LMZ4.7A	0827
LMZ5.1	0437
LMZ5.1-20	0437
LMZ5.1A	0437
LMZ5.6	0437
LMZ5.6-20	0870
LMZ5.6A	0870
LMZ6.2	0185
LMZ6.2-20	0185
LMZ6.2A	0185
LMZ6.8	0205
LMZ6.8A	0205
LMZ7.5	0475
LMZ7.5A	0475
LMZ8.2	0499
LMZ8.2A	0499

DEVICE TYPE	REPL CODE
LMZ9.1	0679
LMZ9.1A	0679
LMZ10	0225
LMZ10A	0225
LMZ11	0230
LMZ11A	0230
LMZ12	0234
LMZ12A	0234
LMZ13	0237
LMZ13A	0237
LMZ14	1387
LMZ14A	1387
LMZ15	0247
LMZ15A	0247
LMZ16	0251
LMZ16A	0251
LMZ18	0256
LMZ18A	0256
LMZ20	0262
LMZ20A	0262
LMZ22	0269
LMZ22A	0269
LMZ24	0273
LMZ24A	0273
LMZ27	0291
LMZ27A	0291
LMZ30	0305
LMZ30A	0305
LMZ33	0314
LMZ33A	0314
LMZ36	0316
LMZ36A	0316
LMZ39	0322
LMZ39A	0322
LMZ43	0333
LMZ43A	0333
LMZ47	0343
LMZ47A	0343
LMZ51	0027
LMZ51A	0027
LMZ56	0266
LMZ56A	0266
LMZ62	0205
LMZ62A	0382
LMZ68	0401
LMZ68A	0401
LMZ75	0421
LMZ75A	0421
LMZ82	0439
LMZ82A	0439
LMZ91	0238
LMZ91A	0238
LMZ100	1172
LMZ100A	1172
LMZ110	1182
LMZ110-20	1182
LMZ110A	1182
LMZ120	1198
LMZ120-20	1198
LMZ120A	1198
LMZ130	1209
LMZ130-20	1209
LMZ130A	1209
LMZ150	0642
LMZ150-20	0642
LMZ150A	0642
LMZ160	1246
LMZ160-20	1246
LMZ160A	1246
LMZ180	1269
LMZ180-20	1269
LMZ180A	1269
LMZ200	0600
LMZ200-20	0600
LMZ200A	0600
LN0312CP3	OEM
LN0312P3	OEM
LN02202P	4369
LN02302P	2036
LN02402P	4948
LN03202P	4369
LN03302P	2036
LN03402P	4948
LN04202P	4369
LN04302P	2036
LN04402P	4948
LN05101P1	OEM
LN05101P2	OEM
LN05103P	OEM
LN05201P	OEM
LN05202P	4369
LN05203P	OEM
LN05301P	OEM
LN05302P	2036
LN05401P	OEM
LN05402P	4948
LN06202P	4369
LN06302P	2036
LN06402P	4948
LN07202P	4369
LN07302P	2036
LN07402P	4948
LN014210P	OEM
LN018315P	OEM
LN033417P	OEM
LN041395P1	OEM
LN051219P2	OEM
LN061219P2	OEM
LN072163P	OEM

DEVICE TYPE	REPL CODE
LN072198P	OEM
LN072198P4	OEM
LN072203P	OEM
LN078328P	OEM
LN12	OEM
LN15BP	OEM
LN15WP	OEM
LN15WP.F	OEM
LN16BP	OEM
LN16WP.F	OEM
LN21CALULFKT	OEM
LN21CP.H	OEM
LN21CP.HL	OEM
LN21GCPHLM	OEM
LN21RCPH	1951
LN21RCPHL	1951
LN21RCPHLM	OEM
LN21RCPHLM-V	OEM
LN21RCPHLMV	1951
LN21RCPHV	1951
LN21RCP.H	OEM
LN21RCP.HL	OEM
LN21RPH	OEM
LN21RPH-(C2)	OEM
LN21RPH-(CF1)	OEM
LN21RPH-(TA)	OEM
LN21RPH-C	OEM
LN21RPHL	1951
LN21RPHLM	OEM
LN21RPSLLS	OEM
LN21RP.H	OEM
LN21RP.HL	OEM
LN21WP.H	OEM
LN21WP.HL	OEM
LN23SCP	OEM
LN23SRP	OEM
LN23SWP	OEM
LN25CP	OEM
LN25RCP	OEM
LN25RP	OEM
LN25WP	OEM
LN26RP	OEM
LN28RCP	OEM
LN-28RP	2990
LN28RP	5466
LN28WP	OEM
LN28WPVT	OEM
LN29RCP	OEM
LN29RP	OEM
LN29RPP	OEM
LN31GCPH(U)	1767
LN31GCPH(U)-(C)	1767
LN31GCPHILMU	1767
LN31GCPHL	1767
LN31GCPHLM	1767
LN31GCPHLM(U)	1767
LN31GCPHLM-U	1767
LN31GCPHLMU	1767
LN31GCPHL-U	1767
LN31GCPHLU	1767
LN31GCPILMU	1767
LN31GCP-UH	1767
LN31GCP-UHL	1767
LN31GCPUHL	1767
LN31GCP.H	1767
LN31GCP.HL	1767
LN31GCUPHL-U	1767
LN31GPHL	1767
LN31GP.H	1767
LN31GP.HL	1767
LN33SGP	OEM
LN33SGP-H	OEM
LN35BP	OEM
LN35GCP	OEM
LN35GP	OEM
LN36BP	OEM
LN38GCP	OEM
LN38GCPH	OEM
LN38GP	OEM
LN38GP(C)	OEM
LN38GPL	0835
LN39GCP	OEM
LN39GP	OEM
LN40GCP	OEM
LN41TPHL	OEM
LN41YCPH	3128
LN41YCPHL	OEM
LN41YCPHLM	OEM
LN41YCP.H	OEM
LN41YCP.HL	OEM
LN41YPHL	OEM
LN41YP.H	OEM
LN41YP.HL	OEM
LN43SYP	OEM
LN45YCP	OEM
LN45YP	OEM
LN46YP	OEM
LN48YCPH	OEM
LN48YP	OEM
LN49YP	OEM
LN51F	OEM
LN51L	OEM
LN52	OEM
LN55	OEM
LN57	OEM
LN58	OEM
LN59	2678
LN59NV	2678
LN59SAN	OEM

DEVICE TYPE	REPL CODE
LN62S	OEM
LN65	OEM
LN66	5605
LN66-S	OEM
LN66C	5605
LN66NC	OEM
LN66S	5605
LN66SNC	OEM
LN70	OEM
LN71	OEM
LN81CPH	OEM
LN81CPHL	OEM
LN81CP.H	OEM
LN81CP.HL	OEM
LN81RCPH	OEM
LN81RCPH-(C)	OEM
LN81RCPHL	OEM
LN81RCPSL	OEM
LN81RCP.H	OEM
LN81RCP.HL	OEM
LN81RP.H	OEM
LN81RP.HL	OEM
LN85	OEM
LN85RCP	OEM
LN88RCPH	OEM
LN210RP	OEM
LN210WP	OEM
LN211RP	OEM
LN211WP	OEM
LN212RP	5853
LN213RP	OEM
LN216RP-LS	OEM
LN217RP	4369
LN217RPH	OEM
LN219RP	OEM
LN220RP	OEM
LN220RP-LS	OEM
LN221RP	OEM
LN222RP	OEM
LN222RPH	OEM
LN224	OEM
LN224RP	OEM
LN224RPH	OEM
LN226RP	OEM
LN227RP	OEM
LN228RP	OEM
LN229RP	OEM
LN229RPH	OEM
LN230RA	OEM
LN230RP	OEM
LN233RP	OEM
LN235RPH	OEM
LN238RPH	OEM
LN242RP	OEM
LN242RPH	OEM
LN248RP-LS	OEM
LN249RP	OEM
LN250RP	OEM
LN260RCPP	OEM
LN310GP	OEM
LN311GP	OEM
LN311GPHL	OEM
LN312GP	1959
LN313GP	2036
LN316GP-LS	OEM
LN317GPH	OEM
LN319GP	OEM
LN320GP	OEM
LN320GP-LS	OEM
LN320GPLS	OEM
LN321GP	OEM
LN322GP	OEM
LN322GPH	OEM
LN324GP	OEM
LN324GP2	OEM
LN324GP3	OEM
LN324GPH	OEM
LN326GP	OEM
LN327GP	OEM
LN328GP	OEM
LN329GP	OEM
LN329GPH	OEM
LN333GP	OEM
LN335GPH	OEM
LN338GPH	OEM
LN340GCP	OEM
LN342RPH	OEM
LN348GP-LS	OEM
LN410YP	OEM
LN411YP	OEM
LN412YP	5339
LN413YP	OEM
LN416YP-LS	OEM
LN417YP	4948
LN417YPH	OEM
LN419YP	OEM
LN420YP	OEM
LN420YP(U)MS	OEM
LN421YP	OEM
LN422YP	OEM
LN422YPH	OEM
LN424YP	OEM
LN424YPH	OEM
LN426YP	OEM
LN427YP	OEM
LN428YP	OEM
LN429YP	OEM
LN429YPH	OEM
LN433YP	OEM

If replacement code is OEM, contact original manufacturer for replacement.

451

DEVICE TYPE	REPL CODE
LN435YPH	OEM
LN438YPH	OEM
LN440YCP	OEM
LN442RPH	OEM
LN442YP	OEM
LN448YP-LS	OEM
LN512GA	OEM
LN513GK	OEM
LN513GK-S	OEM
LN5130A	OEM
LN5130K	OEM
LN5130K-S	OEM
LN513RA	OEM
LN513RK	OEM
LN513RK-S	OEM
LN513YA	OEM
LN513YK	OEM
LN513YK-S	OEM
LN514GA	OEM
LN514GK	OEM
LN5140A	OEM
LN5140K	OEM
LN514RA	5046
LN514RK	OEM
LN514YA	OEM
LN514YK	OEM
LN516GA	OEM
LN516GK	OEM
LN5160A	OEM
LN5160K	OEM
LN516RA	OEM
LN516RK	OEM
LN516YA	OEM
LN516YK	OEM
LN524GA	OEM
LN524GAS	OEM
LN524GK	OEM
LN524RA	4262
LN524RAL1	OEM
LN524RAS	OEM
LN524RK	OEM
LN524YA	OEM
LN524YK	OEM
LN526GA	OEM
LN526GADP	OEM
LN526GA-L	OEM
LN526GK	OEM
LN526MI	4262
LN526RA	4262
LN526RK	4267
LN526YA	OEM
LN526YK	OEM
LN543GA	OEM
LN543GAH	OEM
LN543GK	OEM
LN543GKH	OEM
LN543RA	OEM
LN543RAH	OEM
LN543RK	OEM
LN543RKH	OEM
LN543YA	OEM
LN543YAH	OEM
LN543YK	OEM
LN543YKH	OEM
LN655	OEM
LN831RP	OEM
LN840RCP	OEM
LN846RP-LS	OEM
LN1304N01	0649
LN1310	0514
LN1328A	OEM
LN2064B	4781
LN5240A	OEM
LN5240K	OEM
LN5260A	OEM
LN5260K	OEM
LN5430A	OEM
LN5430A.H	OEM
LN5430K	OEM
LN5430K.H	OEM
LN10204P	OEM
LN108399P	OEM
LN142154P	OEM
LN261478PH	OEM
LNA0410	OEM
LNA328	OEM
LNA328B	OEM
LNA331	OEM
LNA331A	OEM
LNA331B	OEM
LNA335	OEM
LNA335A	OEM
LNA335B	OEM
LNA339	OEM
LNA339A	0036
LNA339B	OEM
LNA343	0274
LNA343A	0274
LNA343B	OEM
LNA347	0140
LNA347A	0140
LNA347B	OEM
LNA351	OEM
LNA351A	0437
LNA351B	OEM
LNA356	OEM
LNA356A	0157
LNA356B	OEM
LNA362	0631

DEVICE TYPE	REPL CODE
LNA362A	0631
LNA362B	OEM
LNA368	OEM
LNA368A	0025
LNA368B	OEM
LNA375	OEM
LNA375A	0644
LNA375B	OEM
LNA382	3071
LNA382A	0244
LNA382B	3071
LNA391	0012
LNA391A	0012
LNA391B	OEM
LNA1100	OEM
LNA3100	OEM
LNA3100A	0170
LNA3100B	OEM
LO100BV	OEM
LO100DV	OEM
LO100MV	OEM
LO3001	OEM
LOG100JP	OEM
LP/HP2100	OEM
LP1H	0015
LP1S	OEM
LP1SU	OEM
LP2H	0015
LP2S	OEM
LP2SU	OEM
LP3H	0015
LP4H	0015
LP100	0124
LP101	OEM
LP102	OEM
LP271	OEM
LP1014A	OEM
LP1014B	OEM
LP1014D	OEM
LP1014E	OEM
LP1014H	OEM
LP1016A	OEM
LP1016B	OEM
LP1016D	OEM
LP1016E	OEM
LP1016H	OEM
LP1017A	OEM
LP1017B	OEM
LP1017D	OEM
LP1017E	OEM
LP1017H	OEM
LP1018A	OEM
LP1018B	OEM
LP1018D	OEM
LP1018E	OEM
LP1018H	OEM
LP1019B	OEM
LP1019E	OEM
LP1019H	OEM
LP1020A	OEM
LP1020B	OEM
LP1020D	OEM
LP1020E	OEM
LP1020H	OEM
LP1022A	OEM
LP1022B	OEM
LP1022D	OEM
LP1022E	OEM
LP1022H	OEM
LP1024A	OEM
LP1024B	OEM
LP1024D	OEM
LP1024E	OEM
LP1024H	OEM
LP1026A	OEM
LP1026B	OEM
LP1026D	OEM
LP1026E	OEM
LP1026H	OEM
LP1028A	OEM
LP1028B	OEM
LP1028D	OEM
LP1028E	OEM
LP1028H	OEM
LP1030A	OEM
LP1030B	OEM
LP1030D	OEM
LP1030E	OEM
LP1030H	OEM
LP1032A	OEM
LP1032B	OEM
LP1032D	OEM
LP1032E	OEM
LP1032H	OEM
LP1034A	OEM
LP1034B	OEM
LP1034D	OEM
LP1034E	OEM
LP1034H	OEM
LP1036A	OEM
LP1036B	OEM
LP1036D	OEM
LP1036E	OEM
LP1036H	OEM
LP1038A	OEM
LP1038B	OEM
LP1038D	OEM
LP1038E	OEM
LP1038H	OEM

DEVICE TYPE	REPL CODE
LP1057R	OEM
LP1919A	OEM
LP9510I	OEM
LP9510J	OEM
LPA1H	1219
LPA2H	OEM
LPA3H	OEM
LPCL11	OEM
LPI11	OEM
LPM3.3	0289
LPM3.3-20	0289
LPM3.3A	0289
LPM3.6	0188
LPM3.6-20	0188
LPM3.6A	0188
LPM3.9	0451
LPM3.9-20	0451
LPM3.9A	0451
LPM4.3	0528
LPM4.3-20	0528
LPM4.3A	0528
LPM4.7	0162
LPM4.7-20	0446
LPM4.7A	0162
LPM5.1	0162
LPM5.1-20	0162
LPM5.1A	0162
LPM5.6	0157
LPM5.6-20	0157
LPM5.6A	0157
LPM6.2	0631
LPM6.2-20	0631
LPM6.2A	0631
LPM6.8	0025
LPM6.8-20	0025
LPM6.8A	0025
LPM7.5	0644
LPM7.5-20	0644
LPM7.5A	0644
LPM8.2	0244
LPM8.2-20	0244
LPM8.2A	0244
LPM9.1	0012
LPM9.1-20	0012
LPM9.1A	0012
LPM10	0170
LPM10-20	0170
LPM10A	0170
LPM11	0789
LPM11-20	0313
LPM11A	0313
LPM12	0137
LPM12-20	0137
LPM12A	0137
LPM13	0361
LPM13-20	0361
LPM13A	0361
LPM15	0002
LPM15-20	0002
LPM15A	0002
LPM16	0416
LPM16-20	0416
LPM16A	0416
LPM18	0490
LPM18-20	0490
LPM18A	0490
LPM20	0526
LPM20-20	0526
LPM20A	0526
LPM22	0560
LPM22-20	0560
LPM22A	0560
LPM24	0398
LPM24-20	0398
LPM24A	0398
LPM27	0436
LPM27-20	0436
LPM27A	0436
LPM30	0721
LPM30-20	0721
LPM30A	0721
LPM33	0039
LPM33-20	0039
LPM33A	0039
LPM36	0814
LPM36-20	0814
LPM36A	0814
LPM39	0346
LPM39-20	0346
LPM39A	0346
LPM43	0925
LPM43-20	0925
LPM43A	0925
LPM47	0993
LPM47-20	0993
LPM47A	0993
LPM51	0497
LPM51-20	0497
LPM51A	0497
LPM56	1823
LPM56-20	0863
LPM56A	0863
LPM62	0778
LPM62-20	0778
LPM62A	0778
LPM68	1258
LPM68-20	2144
LPM68A	1258
LPM75	1181

DEVICE TYPE	REPL CODE
LPM75-20	1181
LPM75A	1181
LPM82	0327
LPM82-20	0327
LPM82A	0327
LPM91	1301
LPM91-20	1301
LPM91A	1301
LPM100	0098
LPM100-20	OEM
LPM100A	0098
LPM110	0149
LPM110-20	0149
LPM110A	0149
LPM120	0186
LPM120-20	0186
LPM120A	0186
LPM130	0213
LPM130-20	0213
LPM130A	0213
LPM150	0028
LPM150-20	0028
LPM150A	0028
LPM160	0255
LPM160-20	0255
LPM160A	0255
LPM180	0363
LPM180-20	0363
LPM180A	0363
LPM200	0417
LPM200-20	0417
LPM200A	0417
LPM-596	OEM
LPT100	OEM
LPT100A	OEM
LPT100B	OEM
LPT110	OEM
LPT110A	OEM
LPT110B	OEM
LPZT8.2	0244
LPZT10	0170
LPZT12	0137
LPZT15	0002
LPZT18	0490
LPZT22	0560
LPZT27	0436
LPZT33	0039
LQV4M1957	OEM
LR5GZ61	0071
LR33H	0296
LR36H	OEM
LR39CH	0188
LR43CH	0274
LR47CH	0162
LR50	6945
LR51CH	0162
LR51D	0041
LR51E	0041
LR56CH	0162
LR56D	0253
LR56E	0253
LR62CH	0466
LR62D	0466
LR62E	0466
LR68CH	0062
LR68D	0062
LR68E	0062
LR75CH	0077
LR75D	0077
LR75E	0077
LR82CH	0165
LR82D	0165
LR82E	0165
LR91CH	0057
LR91D	0057
LR91E	0057
LR100CH	0064
LR100D	0064
LR100E	0064
LR110CH	0181
LR110D	0181
LR110E	0181
LR120CH	0052
LR120D	0140
LR120E	0052
LR130CH	0053
LR130D	0053
LR130E	0053
LR150CH	0681
LR150D	0681
LR150E	0681
LR160CH	0440
LR160D	0440
LR160E	0440
LR180CH	0371
LR180D	0371
LR180E	0371
LR200CH	0695
LR200D	0695
LR200E	0695
LR220D	0700
LR220E	0700
LR240D	0489
LR240E	0489
LR270D	0450
LR270E	0450
LR300D	0195
LR300E	0195
LR301R	OEM

DEVICE TYPE	REPL CODE
LR330D	0166
LR330E	0166
LR360D	0010
LR360E	0010
LR390D	0032
LR390E	0032
LR505P	OEM
LR1351G	OEM
LR1352G	OEM
LR1361E	OEM
LR1362E	OEM
LR1363E	OEM
LR1364E	OEM
LR1371R	OEM
LR1372R	OEM
LR1373R	OEM
LR1374R	OEM
LR1381Y	OEM
LR1382Y	OEM
LR1383Y	OEM
LR1384Y	OEM
LR1451G	OEM
LR1455G	OEM
LR1461E	OEM
LR1464E	OEM
LR1465E	OEM
LR1471R	OEM
LR1474R	OEM
LR1475R	OEM
LR1481Y	OEM
LR1484Y	OEM
LR1485Y	OEM
LR1704R	OEM
LR1705R	OEM
LR1706R	OEM
LR1707R	OEM
LR1717R	OEM
LR1720R	OEM
LR1723R	OEM
LR1737R	OEM
LR1738R	OEM
LR1739R	OEM
LR1740R	OEM
LR1743R	OEM
LR1800	OEM
LR1801	OEM
LR1804	OEM
LR1805	OEM
LR2601A	OEM
LR2665E	OEM
LR2666E	OEM
LR2671R	OEM
LR2673P	OEM
LR2674R	OEM
LR2675R	OEM
LR2676R	OEM
LR2678R	OEM
LR2703	OEM
LR3419	OEM
LR3714	OEM
LR3714M	OEM
LR3784R	OEM
LR3785R	OEM
LR4089	OEM
LR4803	OEM
LR4806	OEM
LR4806B	OEM
LR4806R	OEM
LR4816B	OEM
LR6504R	OEM
LR6508R	OEM
LR7164R	OEM
LR8321	OEM
LR8322	OEM
LR8330	OEM
LR37631	OEM
LR37632	OEM
LR40992	2734
LR40993	6233
LR48066T	OEM
LRQ849	0079
LRR-50	0015
LRR50	0015
LRR-100	0015
LRR100	0015
LRR-200	0015
LRR200	0015
LRR-300	0015
LRR300	0015
LRR-400	0015
LRR400	0015
LRR-500	0015
LRR500	0015
LS00	1519
LS-0095-AR-213	0111
LS02	1550
LS02(SM)	OEM
LS05	1598
LS05(MIN)	OEM
LS05FP(MIN)	OEM
LS05FP(SM)	OEM
LS06	OEM
LS045T	OEM
LS-0142	1434
LS14	1688
LS14D	OEM
LS15	1697
LS16-1	OEM
LS20	0035

DEVICE TYPE	REPL CODE
LS25	OEM
LS32	0088
LS32N	0088
LS40	0135
LS50	OEM
LS51N	1027
LS52	0085
LS60	OEM
LS74	0243
LS80	OEM
LS86	0288
LS100	OEM
LS101AT	OEM
LS101T	OEM
LS107T	OEM
LS120	OEM
LS125	0075
LS126AD	OEM
LS139	0153
LS141AT	OEM
LS141CB	OEM
LS141CM	OEM
LS141CT	OEM
LS141T	OEM
LS148AT	OEM
LS148CB	OEM
LS148CM	OEM
LS148CT	OEM
LS148T	OEM
LS155	0209
LS157N	1153
LS166	0231
LS174	0260
LS201AT	OEM
LS201B	OEM
LS201M	OEM
LS201T	OEM
LS204AT	OEM
LS204CB	OEM
LS204CM	OEM
LS204CT	OEM
LS204M	OEM
LS204T	OEM
LS207T	OEM
LS240	0447
LS240M	OEM
LS244	0453
LS245	0458
LS245(SM)	OEM
LS285A	OEM
LS301AB	OEM
LS301AM	OEM
LS301AT	0093
LS307B	2267
LS307M	OEM
LS307T	OEM
LS342	OEM
LS373	0704
LS374	0708
LS400	OEM
LS500	OEM
LS505P	OEM
LS600	OEM
LS602	OEM
LS610	OEM
LS656	OEM
LS656B	OEM
LS703L	0627
LS709AT	OEM
LS709CB	OEM
LS709CT	OEM
LS709T	OEM
LS776CB	OEM
LS776CM	OEM
LS776CT	OEM
LS776T	OEM
LS953	OEM
LS3705	0079
LS5484	0321
LS5485	0321
LS7030	OEM
LS7031	OEM
LS7040	OEM
LS7056	OEM
LS7060	OEM
LS7061	OEM
LS7062	OEM
LS7100	OEM
LS7110	OEM
LS7210	OEM
LS7220	OEM
LS7225	OEM
LS7231	OEM
LS7232	OEM
LS7233	OEM
LS7234	OEM
LS7235	OEM
LS7236	OEM
LS7240	OEM
LS7270	OEM
LS7709	OEM
LS7717	OEM
LS7718	OEM
LS7721	OEM
LS7722	OEM
LS7723	OEM
LS7724	OEM
LS7726	OEM
LS7727	OEM

DEVICE TYPE	REPL CODE
LS7728	OEM
LS7729	OEM
LS7730	OEM
LS7738	OEM
LS7739	OEM
LS7746	OEM
LS7747	OEM
LS7748	OEM
LS7749	OEM
LS7750	OEM
LS7751	OEM
LS7754	OEM
LS8045M	OEM
LSA13	OEM
LSA17	OEM
LSC5D	OEM
LSC14	OEM
LSC30D	OEM
LSC1008	0167
LSC1008P	0167
LSC89919B	OEM
LSC89921B	OEM
LSI-11	OEM
LSM88441Y	OEM
LSM88492Y	OEM
LST153S	OEM
LST154R	OEM
LST515AR10	OEM
LST700	OEM
LST700L	OEM
LST710	OEM
LST710L	OEM
LST711	OEM
LST711L	OEM
LST712	OEM
LST712L	OEM
LST713	OEM
LST713L	OEM
LST722	OEM
LST722L	OEM
LST733	OEM
LST733L	OEM
LST1052	OEM
LST1056	OEM
LST3300S	OEM
LST4053	OEM
LST4053F	OEM
LST4054-1	OEM
LST4153	OEM
LST4153F	OEM
LST4153S	OEM
LST4154	OEM
LST4154S	OEM
LST4253	OEM
LST4253F	OEM
LST4254	OEM
LST4353	OEM
LST4354	OEM
LST4753	OEM
LST4754	OEM
LST5053	OEM
LST5053R	OEM
LST5053R5	OEM
LST5053R10	OEM
LST5054-1	OEM
LST5054-1R5	OEM
LST5054-1R10	OEM
LST5054R	OEM
LST5152	OEM
LST5152R	OEM
LST5152R5	OEM
LST5152R10	OEM
LST5152S	OEM
LST5153	OEM
LST5153R	OEM
LST5153R5	OEM
LST5153R10	OEM
LST5154	OEM
LST5154R5	OEM
LST5154S	OEM
LST5252	OEM
LST5252R	OEM
LST5252R5	OEM
LST5252R10	OEM
LST5253	1767
LST5253R	OEM
LST5253R5	OEM
LST5253R10	OEM
LST5254	OEM
LST5254R	OEM
LST5254R5	OEM
LST5352	OEM
LST5352R	OEM
LST5352R5	OEM
LST5352R10	OEM
LST5353	3128
LST5353R	OEM
LST5353R5	OEM
LST5353R10	OEM
LST5354	OEM
LST5354R	OEM
LST5354R5	OEM
LST5354R10	OEM
LST5752	OEM
LST5752R	OEM
LST5752R5	OEM
LST5752R10	OEM
LST5753	1951
LST5753R	OEM

452

If replacement code is OEM, contact original manufacturer for replacement.

DEVICE TYPE	REPL CODE
LST5753R5	OEM
LST5753R10	OEM
LST5754	OEM
LST5754R	OEM
LST5754R5	OEM
LST5754R10	OEM
LST525410	OEM
LSX900	OEM
LT0028	OEM
LT0038	OEM
LT0047	OEM
LT-1E21A	OEM
LT-1H11A	OEM
LT3P8D	OEM
LT51	OEM
LT55	OEM
LT67T-24	OEM
LT101AR	OEM
LT101R	OEM
LT106RC	OEM
LT111AR	OEM
LT111R	OEM
LT116RC	OEM
LT131AG	OEM
LT131G	OEM
LT136GC	OEM
LT151AY	OEM
LT151Y	OEM
LT156YC	OEM
LT181Y	OEM
LT191AE	OEM
LT191E	OEM
LT196EC	OEM
LT201CRD	OEM
LT201R	OEM
LT201RD	OEM
LT202CRT	OEM
LT202RT	OEM
LT203	OEM
LT203R	OEM
LT203RD	OEM
LT204RT	OEM
LT205CWD	OEM
LT205RW	OEM
LT206CWC	OEM
LT206RC	OEM
LT207RW	OEM
LT208RC	OEM
LT209R	OEM
LT209RD	OEM
LT-211	OEM
LT211CRD	OEM
LT211R	OEM
LT211RD	OEM
LT212CRT	OEM
LT212RT	OEM
LT213R	OEM
LT213RD	OEM
LT214RT	OEM
LT215CWD	OEM
LT215RW	OEM
LT216CWC	OEM
LT216RC	OEM
LT217RW	OEM
LT218RC	OEM
LT219R	OEM
LT219RD	OEM
LT221CRD	OEM
LT221R	OEM
LT221RD	OEM
LT222CRT	OEM
LT222RT	OEM
LT223R	OEM
LT223RD	OEM
LT224RT	OEM
LT229R	OEM
LT229RD	OEM
LT231CGD	OEM
LT231G	OEM
LT231GD	OEM
LT232CGT	OEM
LT232GT	OEM
LT233G	OEM
LT233GD	OEM
LT234CWD	OEM
LT234GT	OEM
LT235GW	OEM
LT236CWC	OEM
LT236GC	OEM
LT237GW	OEM
LT238GC	OEM
LT239G	OEM
LT239GD	OEM
LT251CYD	OEM
LT251Y	OEM
LT251YD	OEM
LT252CYT	OEM
LT252YT	OEM
LT253Y	OEM
LT253YD	OEM
LT254YT	OEM
LT255CWD	OEM
LT255YW	OEM
LT256CWC	OEM
LT256YC	OEM
LT257YW	OEM
LT258YC	OEM
LT259Y	OEM
LT259YD	OEM
LT271A	OEM
LT271AD	OEM
LT272AT	OEM
LT273A	OEM
LT273AD	OEM
LT274AT	OEM
LT291CED	OEM
LT291E	OEM
LT291ED	OEM
LT292CET	OEM
LT292ET	OEM
LT293E	OEM
LT293ED	OEM
LT294ET	OEM
LT295CWD	OEM
LT295EW	OEM
LT296CWD	OEM
LT296EC	OEM
LT297EW	OEM
LT298EC	OEM
LT299E	OEM
LT299ED	OEM
LT301E	OEM
LT301G	OEM
LT301P	OEM
LT301R	OEM
LT301Y	OEM
LT302A	OEM
LT302E	OEM
LT302G	OEM
LT302P	OEM
LT302R	OEM
LT302Y	OEM
LT303A	OEM
LT303E	OEM
LT303G	OEM
LT303P	OEM
LT303R	OEM
LT303Y	OEM
LT304E	OEM
LT304G	OEM
LT304P	OEM
LT304R	OEM
LT304Y	OEM
LT305E	OEM
LT305G	OEM
LT305HR	OEM
LT305P	OEM
LT305R	OEM
LT305Y	OEM
LT311G	OEM
LT311HR	OEM
LT311R	OEM
LT311Y	OEM
LT312E	OEM
LT312G	OEM
LT312HR	OEM
LT312R	OEM
LT312Y	OEM
LT313G	OEM
LT313HR	OEM
LT313R	OEM
LT313Y	OEM
LT314E	OEM
LT314G	OEM
LT314R	OEM
LT314Y	OEM
LT315E	OEM
LT315G	OEM
LT315R	OEM
LT315Y	OEM
LT316G	OEM
LT316R	OEM
LT317G	OEM
LT317R	OEM
LT318G	OEM
LT318R	OEM
LT319G	OEM
LT319R	OEM
LT322G	OEM
LT322P	OEM
LT322RA	OEM
LT323G	OEM
LT323P	OEM
LT323R	OEM
LT323RA	OEM
LT332R	OEM
LT334	OEM
LT373	OEM
LT374	OEM
LT381	OEM
LT382	OEM
LT502P	OEM
LT502R	OEM
LT503P	OEM
LT503R	OEM
LT504P	OEM
LT504R	OEM
LT505P	OEM
LT505R	OEM
LT506E	OEM
LT506G	OEM
LT506P	OEM
LT506R	OEM
LT506Y	OEM
LT507E	OEM
LT507G	OEM
LT507P	OEM
LT507R	OEM
LT507Y	OEM
LT508E	OEM
LT508G	OEM
LT508P	OEM
LT508R	OEM
LT508Y	OEM
LT509E	OEM
LT509G	OEM
LT509P	OEM
LT509R	OEM
LT509Y	OEM
LT512	OEM
LT512R	OEM
LT513	OEM
LT513R	OEM
LT514	OEM
LT514R	OEM
LT515	OEM
LT515R	OEM
LT516	OEM
LT516R	OEM
LT517	OEM
LT517R	OEM
LT518	OEM
LT518R	OEM
LT519	OEM
LT519R	OEM
LT522R	OEM
LT522RA	OEM
LT523E	OEM
LT523G	OEM
LT523GA	OEM
LT523R	OEM
LT523RA	OEM
LT523Y	OEM
LT524E	OEM
LT524G	OEM
LT524GA	OEM
LT524R	OEM
LT524RA	OEM
LT524Y	OEM
LT527E	OEM
LT527G	OEM
LT527Ga	OEM
LT-527R	OEM
LT527R	OEM
LT527RA	OEM
LT527Y	OEM
LT528E	OEM
LT528G	OEM
LT528GA	OEM
LT528R	OEM
LT528RA	OEM
LT532G	OEM
LT532R	OEM
LT533G	OEM
LT533R	OEM
LT534	OEM
LT542HR	OEM
LT542R	OEM
LT543HR	OEM
LT543R	OEM
LT544HR	OEM
LT544R	OEM
LT545HR	OEM
LT545R	OEM
LT546E	OEM
LT546G	OEM
LT546P	OEM
LT546R	OEM
LT546Y	OEM
LT547E	OEM
LT547G	OEM
LT547P	OEM
LT547R	OEM
LT547Y	OEM
LT548E	OEM
LT548G	OEM
LT548P	OEM
LT548R	OEM
LT548Y	OEM
LT549E	OEM
LT549G	OEM
LT549P	OEM
LT549R	OEM
LT549Y	OEM
LT581	OEM
LT582	OEM
LT583	OEM
LT584	OEM
LT612A	OEM
LT612AP	OEM
LT612D	OEM
LT612DG	OEM
LT612DP	OEM
LT617A	OEM
LT617A-12	OEM
LT617AG	OEM
LT617AG-12	OEM
LT617AP	OEM
LT617AP-12	OEM
LT617D	OEM
LT617D-12	OEM
LT617DG	OEM
LT617DG-12	OEM
LT617DP	OEM
LT617DP-12	OEM
LT621AG	OEM
LT622A	OEM
LT622AG	OEM
LT622AP	OEM
LT622D	OEM
LT622DP	OEM
LT627A	OEM
LT627A-12	OEM
LT627AG	OEM
LT627AG-12	OEM
LT627AP	OEM
LT627AP-12	OEM
LT627D	OEM
LT627D-12	OEM
LT627DG	OEM
LT627DG-12	OEM
LT627DP	OEM
LT627DP-12	OEM
LT633DG	OEM
LT637A	OEM
LT637A-12	OEM
LT637A-24	OEM
LT637AG	OEM
LT637AG-12	OEM
LT637AG-24	OEM
LT637AP	OEM
LT637AP-12	OEM
LT637AP-24	OEM
LT637D	OEM
LT637D-12	OEM
LT637DG	OEM
LT637DG-12	OEM
LT637DP	OEM
LT637DP-12	OEM
LT647A	OEM
LT647A-12	OEM
LT647AG	OEM
LT647AG-12	OEM
LT647AP	OEM
LT647AP-12	OEM
LT647D	OEM
LT647D-12	OEM
LT647DG	OEM
LT647DG-12	OEM
LT647DP	OEM
LT647DP-12	OEM
LT656-12	OEM
LT656-24	OEM
LT656G-12	OEM
LT656G-24	OEM
LT656PG-12	OEM
LT656PG-24	OEM
LT656T	OEM
LT656T-12	OEM
LT656T-24	OEM
LT656TG	OEM
LT656TG-12	OEM
LT656TG-24	OEM
LT656TP	OEM
LT656TPG-12	OEM
LT656TPG-24	OEM
LT667-12	OEM
LT667-24	OEM
LT667A	OEM
LT667A-12	OEM
LT667A-24	OEM
LT667AG	OEM
LT667AG-12	OEM
LT667AG-24	OEM
LT667AP	OEM
LT667AP-12	OEM
LT667AP-24	OEM
LT667D	OEM
LT667D-12	OEM
LT667DG	OEM
LT667DG-12	OEM
LT667DP	OEM
LT667DP-12	OEM
LT667G-12	OEM
LT667G-24	OEM
LT667N	OEM
LT667N-12	OEM
LT667N-24	OEM
LT667NG	OEM
LT667NP	OEM
LT667PG-12	OEM
LT667PG-24	OEM
LT668-12	OEM
LT668-24	OEM
LT668G-24	OEM
LT668PG-12	OEM
LT668PG-24	OEM
LT676-12	OEM
LT676-24	OEM
LT676G-12	OEM
LT676G-24	OEM
LT676PG-12	OEM
LT676PG-24	OEM
LT676T	OEM
LT676T-12	OEM
LT676TG	OEM
LT676TP	OEM
LT677	OEM
LT677-12	OEM
LT677-24	OEM
LT677A-12	OEM
LT677A-24	OEM
LT677AG	OEM
LT677AG-12	OEM
LT677AG-24	OEM
LT677AP	OEM
LT677AP-12	OEM
LT677AP-24	OEM
LT677D	OEM
LT677D-12	OEM
LT677DG-12	OEM
LT677DP	OEM
LT677DP-12	OEM
LT677G-12	OEM
LT677G-24	OEM
LT677N	OEM
LT677N-12	OEM
LT677N-24	OEM
LT677NG	OEM
LT677NP	OEM
LT677PG-12	OEM
LT677PG-24	OEM
LT678-12	OEM
LT678-24	OEM
LT678G-12	OEM
LT678G-24	OEM
LT678PG-12	OEM
LT678PG-24	OEM
LT687A	OEM
LT687A-12	OEM
LT687A-24	OEM
LT687AG	OEM
LT687AP	OEM
LT687B	OEM
LT687B-12	OEM
LT687B-24	OEM
LT687BG	OEM
LT687BG-12	OEM
LT687BG-24	OEM
LT687BP	OEM
LT687BP-12	OEM
LT687BP-24	OEM
LT687D	OEM
LT687D-12	OEM
LT687DG	OEM
LT687DG-12	OEM
LT687DP	OEM
LT687DP-12	OEM
LT696A	OEM
LT696AG	OEM
LT696APG	OEM
LT697-12	OEM
LT697-24	OEM
LT697A	OEM
LT697A-12	OEM
LT697A-24	OEM
LT697AG	OEM
LT697AP	OEM
LT697B	OEM
LT697B-12	OEM
LT697B-24	OEM
LT697BG	OEM
LT697BG-12	OEM
LT697BG-24	OEM
LT697BP	OEM
LT697BP-12	OEM
LT697BP-24	OEM
LT697D	OEM
LT697D-12	OEM
LT697DG	OEM
LT697DG-12	OEM
LT697DP	OEM
LT697DP-12	OEM
LT697G-12	OEM
LT697G-24	OEM
LT697PG-12	OEM
LT697PG-24	OEM
LT698-12	OEM
LT698-24	OEM
LT698G-12	OEM
LT698G-24	OEM
LT698PG-12	OEM
LT698PG-24	OEM
LT699-12	OEM
LT699-24	OEM
LT699G-12	OEM
LT699G-24	OEM
LT699PG-12	OEM
LT699PG-24	OEM
LT707A	OEM
LT707AK	OEM
LT707AS	OEM
LT707B	OEM
LT707BK	OEM
LT707C	OEM
LT707CK	OEM
LT707CS	OEM
LT707D	OEM
LT707DK	OEM
LT707DS	OEM
LT707GA	OEM
LT707GAK	OEM
LT707GAS	OEM
LT707GB	OEM
LT707GBK	OEM
LT707GBS	OEM
LT707GC	OEM
LT707GCK	OEM
LT707GCS	OEM
LT707GD	OEM
LT707GDK	OEM
LT707GDS	OEM
LT734	OEM
LT737	OEM
LT737-12	OEM
LT737-24	OEM
LT737A	OEM
LT737AP	OEM
LT737AP-12	OEM
LT737G	OEM
LT737G-12	OEM
LT737G-24	OEM
LT737P	OEM
LT737P-12	OEM
LT737P-24	OEM
LT755	OEM
LT755-12	OEM
LT755-24	OEM
LT755G	OEM
LT755G-12	OEM
LT755G-24	OEM
LT755P	OEM
LT755P-12	OEM
LT755P-24	OEM
LT756	OEM
LT765R	OEM
LT767A	OEM
LT767A-12	OEM
LT767AP	OEM
LT767AP-12	OEM
LT781	OEM
LT782	OEM
LT783	OEM
LT784	OEM
LT797	OEM
LT797-12	OEM
LT797-24	OEM
LT797A-12	OEM
LT797AP	OEM
LT797AP-12	OEM
LT797G	OEM
LT797G-12	OEM
LT797G-24	OEM
LT797P	OEM
LT797P-12	OEM
LT797P-24	OEM
LT816AK	OEM
LT816BK	OEM
LT816CK	OEM
LT816DK	OEM
LT829	OEM
LT831	OEM
LT832	OEM
LT834	OEM
LT917A	OEM
LT917A-12	OEM
LT917AG	OEM
LT917AG-12	OEM
LT917AR	OEM
LT917AR-12	OEM
LT927A	OEM
LT927A-12	OEM
LT927AG	OEM
LT927AG-12	OEM
LT927AR	OEM
LT927AR-12	OEM
LT937A	OEM
LT937A-12	OEM
LT937AG	OEM
LT937AG-12	OEM
LT937AR	OEM
LT937AR-12	OEM
LT955	OEM
LT955-12	OEM
LT955-24	OEM
LT955A	OEM
LT955A-12	OEM
LT955AG	OEM
LT955AG-12	OEM
LT955AR	OEM
LT955AR-12	OEM
LT955G	OEM
LT955G-12	OEM
LT955G-24	OEM
LT975	OEM
LT975-12	OEM
LT975-24	OEM
LT975A	OEM
LT975A-12	OEM
LT975AG	OEM
LT975AG-12	OEM
LT975AR	OEM
LT975AR-12	OEM
LT975G	OEM
LT975G-12	OEM
LT975G-24	OEM
LT997A	OEM
LT997A-12	OEM
LT997AG	OEM
LT997AG-12	OEM
LT997AR	OEM
LT997AR-12	OEM
LT1000	OEM
LT1001A	OEM
LT1014	OEM
LT1016(E)	0079
LT1016D	0144
LT1016E	0144
LT1016H	0224
LT1016I	0144
LT1016I,H	0079
LT1016T	OEM
LT1016T,H	0079
LT1017	OEM
LT1024	OEM
LT1034	OEM
LT1038	OEM
LT1057E	OEM
LT1057G	OEM
LT1057HR	OEM
LT1057P	OEM
LT1057R	OEM
LT1057Y	OEM
LT1201	OEM
LT1202	OEM
LT1203	OEM
LT1203R	OEM
LT1211	OEM
LT1212	OEM
LT1213	OEM
LT1213R	OEM
LT1214	OEM
LT1221	OEM
LT1222	OEM
LT1223	OEM
LT1224	OEM
LT1231	OEM
LT1232	OEM
LT1233	OEM
LT1233G	OEM
LT1234	OEM
LT1251	OEM
LT1252	OEM
LT1253	OEM
LT1253Y	OEM
LT1254	OEM
LT1291	OEM
LT1292	OEM
LT1293	OEM
LT1293E	OEM
LT1294	OEM
LT1466	OEM
LT1478	OEM
LT1488	OEM
LT1498	OEM
LT1588A	OEM
LT1604	OEM
LT1720E	OEM
LT1720G	OEM
LT1720P	OEM
LT1720R	OEM
LT1720Y	OEM
LT1723E	OEM
LT1723G	OEM
LT1723P	OEM
LT1723R	OEM
LT1723Y	OEM
LT1740E	OEM
LT1740G	OEM
LT1740P	OEM
LT1740R	OEM
LT1740Y	OEM
LT1743E	OEM
LT1743G	OEM
LT1743P	OEM
LT1743R	OEM
LT1743Y	OEM
LT1784E	OEM
LT1784P	OEM
LT1784R	OEM
LT1785E	OEM
LT1785P	OEM
LT1785R	OEM
LT1800E	OEM
LT1800G	OEM
LT1800HR	OEM
LT1800P	OEM
LT1800R	OEM
LT1800Y	OEM
LT1801E	OEM
LT1801G	OEM
LT1801HR	OEM
LT1801P	OEM
LT1801R	OEM
LT1801Y	OEM
LT1802E	OEM
LT1802G	OEM
LT1802HR	OEM
LT1802P	OEM
LT1802R	OEM
LT1802Y	OEM
LT1803E	OEM
LT1803G	OEM
LT1803HR	OEM
LT1803P	OEM
LT1803R	OEM
LT1803Y	OEM
LT1804AR	OEM
LT1804E	OEM
LT1804G	OEM
LT1804HR	OEM
LT1804P	OEM
LT1804R	OEM
LT1804Y	OEM
LT1805AR	OEM
LT1805E	OEM
LT1805G	OEM
LT1805HR	OEM
LT1805P	OEM
LT1805R	OEM
LT1805Y	OEM
LT1806E	OEM
LT1806G	OEM

DEVICE TYPE	REPL CODE
LT1806HR	OEM
LT1806P	OEM
LT1806R	OEM
LT1806Y	OEM
LT1807G	OEM
LT1807HR	OEM
LT1807P	OEM
LT1807R	OEM
LT1807Y	OEM
LT1808E	OEM
LT1808G	OEM
LT1808HR	OEM
LT1808P	OEM
LT1808R	OEM
LT1808Y	OEM
LT1809E	OEM
LT1809G	OEM
LT1809HR	OEM
LT1809P	OEM
LT1809Y	OEM
LT1810AP	OEM
LT1810E	OEM
LT1810G	OEM
LT1810HR	OEM
LT1810P	OEM
LT1810R	OEM
LT1810Y	OEM
LT1811AP	OEM
LT1811E	OEM
LT1811G	OEM
LT1811HR	OEM
LT1811P	OEM
LT1811R	OEM
LT1811Y	OEM
LT1812E	OEM
LT1812G	OEM
LT1812HR	OEM
LT1812P	OEM
LT1812R	OEM
LT1812Y	OEM
LT1813E	OEM
LT1813G	OEM
LT1813HR	OEM
LT1813P	OEM
LT1813R	OEM
LT1813Y	OEM
LT1814E	OEM
LT1814G	OEM
LT1814HR	OEM
LT1814P	OEM
LT1814R	OEM
LT1814Y	OEM
LT1815E	OEM
LT1815G	OEM
LT1815HR	OEM
LT1815P	OEM
LT1815R	OEM
LT1815Y	OEM
LT1816E	OEM
LT1816G	OEM
LT1816HR	OEM
LT1816P	OEM
LT1816R	OEM
LT1816Y	OEM
LT1817E	OEM
LT1817G	OEM
LT1817HR	OEM
LT1817P	OEM
LT1817R	OEM
LT1817Y	OEM
LT1818E	OEM
LT1818G	OEM
LT1818HR	OEM
LT1818P	OEM
LT1818R	OEM
LT1819E	OEM
LT1819G	OEM
LT1819HR	OEM
LT1819P	OEM
LT1819R	OEM
LT1819Y	OEM
LT1820AR	OEM
LT1820E	OEM
LT1820G	OEM
LT1820HR	OEM
LT1820P	OEM
LT1820R	OEM
LT1820Y	OEM
LT1821AR	OEM
LT1821E	OEM
LT1821G	OEM
LT1821HR	OEM
LT1821P	OEM
LT1821R	OEM
LT1821Y	OEM
LT1824AP	OEM
LT1824E	OEM
LT1824G	OEM
LT1824HR	OEM
LT1824P	OEM
LT1824R	OEM
LT1824Y	OEM
LT1825AP	OEM
LT1825E	OEM
LT1825G	OEM
LT1825HR	OEM
LT1825P	OEM
LT1825R	OEM
LT1825Y	OEM
LT2001	OEM
LT2001AR	OEM
LT2001R	OEM
LT2015	OEM
LT2037	OEM
LT2203R	OEM
LT2211AR	OEM
LT2211R	OEM
LT2213R	OEM
LT2231AG	OEM
LT2231G	OEM
LT2233G	OEM
LT2251AY	OEM
LT2251Y	OEM
LT2253Y	OEM
LT2291AE	OEM
LT2291E	OEM
LT2293E	OEM
LT3005	OEM
LT3014	OEM
LT3046	OEM
LT3156	OEM
LT3156G	OEM
LT3167	OEM
LT3201R	OEM
LT3202R	OEM
LT3203R	OEM
LT3204R	OEM
LT3207R	OEM
LT3208R	OEM
LT3209R	OEM
LT-3211B	OEM
LT3211R	OEM
LT3212R	OEM
LT3213R	OEM
LT3214R	OEM
LT3215R	OEM
LT3216R	OEM
LT3217R	OEM
LT3218R	OEM
LT3219R	OEM
LT3223R	OEM
LT3226R	OEM
LT3229R	OEM
LT3231G	OEM
LT3232G	OEM
LT3233G	OEM
LT3234G	OEM
LT3235G	OEM
LT3236G	OEM
LT3237G	OEM
LT3238G	OEM
LT3239G	OEM
LT3251Y	OEM
LT3252Y	OEM
LT3253Y	OEM
LT3254Y	OEM
LT3255Y	OEM
LT3256Y	OEM
LT3257Y	OEM
LT3258Y	OEM
LT3259Y	OEM
LT3291E	OEM
LT3292E	OEM
LT3293E	OEM
LT3294E	OEM
LT3295E	OEM
LT3296E	OEM
LT3297E	OEM
LT3298E	OEM
LT3299E	OEM
LT3382	OEM
LT3400E	OEM
LT3400G	OEM
LT3400P	OEM
LT3400R	OEM
LT3400Y	OEM
LT3401AP	OEM
LT3401E	OEM
LT3401G	OEM
LT3401HAR	OEM
LT3401P	OEM
LT3401R	OEM
LT3401Y	OEM
LT3403AP	OEM
LT3403E	OEM
LT3403G	OEM
LT3403HAr	OEM
LT3403P	OEM
LT3403R	OEM
LT3403Y	OEM
LT3405E	OEM
LT3405G	OEM
LT3405P	OEM
LT3405R	OEM
LT3405Y	OEM
LT3406AP	OEM
LT3406E	OEM
LT3406G	OEM
LT3406HAR	OEM
LT3406P	OEM
LT3406R	OEM
LT3406Y	OEM
LT3700	OEM
LT3746	OEM
LT3772	OEM
LT3784E	OEM
LT3784P	OEM
LT3784R	OEM
LT3785	OEM
LT3785E	OEM
LT3785P	OEM
LT3785R	OEM
LT3867	OEM
LT3867-12	OEM
LT3867-24	OEM
LT3867G	OEM
LT3867G-12	OEM
LT3867G-24	OEM
LT3877	OEM
LT3877-12	OEM
LT3877-24	OEM
LT3877G	OEM
LT3877G-12	OEM
LT3877G-24	OEM
LT3881	OEM
LT3882	OEM
LT4201R	OEM
LT4201RD	OEM
LT4202RT	OEM
LT4203B	OEM
LT4203P	OEM
LT4203R	OEM
LT4203RD	OEM
LT4204RT	OEM
LT4205RW	OEM
LT4206RC	OEM
LT4207RW	OEM
LT4208RC	OEM
LT4211R	OEM
LT4211RD	OEM
LT4211RT	OEM
LT4213R	OEM
LT4213RD	OEM
LT4214RT	OEM
LT4215RW	OEM
LT4216RC	OEM
LT4217RW	OEM
LT4218RC	OEM
LT4221R	OEM
LT4221RD	OEM
LT4222RT	OEM
LT4223B	OEM
LT4223P	OEM
LT4223R	OEM
LT4223RD	OEM
LT4224RT	OEM
LT4231G	OEM
LT4231GD	OEM
LT4232GT	OEM
LT4233B	OEM
LT4233G	OEM
LT4233P	OEM
LT-4234G	OEM
LT4234GT	OEM
LT4235GW	OEM
LT4236GC	OEM
LT4237GW	OEM
LT4238GC	OEM
LT4251Y	OEM
LT4252YT	OEM
LT4253B	OEM
LT4253P	OEM
LT4253Y	OEM
LT4254YT	OEM
LT4255YW	OEM
LT4256YC	OEM
LT4257YW	OEM
LT4258YC	OEM
LT4271A	OEM
LT4272AT	OEM
LT4273A	OEM
LT4274AT	OEM
LT4291E	OEM
LT4292ET	OEM
LT4293E	OEM
LT4294ET	OEM
LT4295EW	OEM
LT4296EC	OEM
LT4297EW	OEM
LT4298EC	OEM
LT4400	OEM
LT4446	OEM
LT4485	OEM
LT4700	OEM
LT4746	OEM
LT4772	OEM
LT4785	OEM
LT5020	OEM
LT5022	0599
LT5025	0599
LT5028	0599
LT5031	0599
LT5034	0599
LT5038	OEM
LT5039	OEM
LT5042	OEM
LT5045	OEM
LT5048	OEM
LT5051	OEM
LT5054	0599
LT5057	0599
LT5060	0599
LT5063	0599
LT5066	0599
LT5069	0599
LT5072	0160
LT5075	0160
LT5077B	OEM
LT5077C	OEM
LT5078	0160
LT5081	OEM
LT5084	OEM
LT5087	OEM
LT5090	0160
LT5093	0160
LT5096	OEM
LT5099	0160
LT5102	0160
LT5105	OEM
LT5108	0160
LT5111	0160
LT5114	OEM
LT5117	OEM
LT5120	OEM
LT5123	OEM
LT5140	OEM
LT5157	OEM
LT5158	OEM
LT5159	OEM
LT5160	OEM
LT5161	OEM
LT5162	OEM
LT5164	OEM
LT5165	OEM
LT5177B	OEM
LT5201	OEM
LT5201RD	OEM
LT5202	OEM
LT5202RT	OEM
LT5203LR	OEM
LT5203R	OEM
LT5204LRT	OEM
LT5204RT	OEM
LT5209	OEM
LT5210	OEM
LT5211RD	OEM
LT5212RT	OEM
LT5213R	OEM
LT5214RT	OEM
LT5221RD	OEM
LT5222RT	OEM
LT5223R	OEM
LT5231GD	OEM
LT5233G	OEM
LT5234GT	OEM
LT5251YD	OEM
LT5252YT	OEM
LT5253Y	OEM
LT5254YT	OEM
LT5277B	OEM
LT5291ED	OEM
LT5292ET	OEM
LT5293E	OEM
LT5294ET	OEM
LT5377B	OEM
LT5382	OEM
LT5388	OEM
LT5415	OEM
LT5491	OEM
LT5515	OEM
LT5777B	OEM
LT5881	OEM
LT5882	OEM
LT5917	OEM
LT5918	OEM
LT5921	OEM
LT5922	OEM
LT6203R	OEM
LT6223R	OEM
LT6233G	OEM
LT6253Y	OEM
LT6293E	OEM
LT6510	OEM
LT6530	OEM
LT6540	OEM
LT6550	OEM
LT6610	OEM
LT6630	OEM
LT6640	OEM
LT6650	OEM
LT6710	OEM
LT6730	OEM
LT6740	OEM
LT-6740R	OEM
LT6750	OEM
LT6810	OEM
LT6830	OEM
LT6840	OEM
LT6850	OEM
LT7120	OEM
LT7201R	OEM
LT7211R	OEM
LT7231G	OEM
LT7231PG	OEM
LT7251Y	OEM
LT7291E	OEM
LT7382	OEM
LT7650R	OEM
LT7653R	OEM
LT7656R	OEM
LT7660Y	OEM
LT7661Y	OEM
LT7663Y	OEM
LT7666Y	OEM
LT7670G	OEM
LT7671G	OEM
LT7673G	OEM
LT7676G	OEM
LT7680E	OEM
LT7681E	OEM
LT7683E	OEM
LT7686E	OEM
LT7750R	OEM
LT7751R	OEM
LT7756R	OEM
LT7760R	OEM
LT7881	OEM
LT7882	OEM
LT8211	OEM
LT8212	OEM
LT8213	OEM
LT8214	OEM
LT8215	OEM
LT8231	OEM
LT8232	OEM
LT8233	OEM
LT8234	OEM
LT8235	OEM
LT8251	OEM
LT8252	OEM
LT8253	OEM
LT8254	OEM
LT8255	OEM
LT8291	OEM
LT8292	OEM
LT8293	OEM
LT8294	OEM
LT8295	OEM
LT8500R1	OEM
LT9213R	OEM
LT9223A	OEM
LT9230D	OEM
LT9233G	OEM
LT9233PG	OEM
LT9253Y	OEM
LT9293E	OEM
LT9320H	OEM
LT9323H	OEM
LT10203-1	OEM
LT10203-2	OEM
LT10207	OEM
LT10208	OEM
LT10223	OEM
LT10223B1	OEM
LT10223B2	OEM
LT10223C2	OEM
LT10233	OEM
LT10233B1	OEM
LT10233B2	OEM
LT10233C1	OEM
LT10233C2	OEM
LT10253	OEM
LT10253B1	OEM
LT10253B2	OEM
LT10253C1	OEM
LT10253C2	OEM
LT13202	OEM
LT13204	OEM
LT13211	OEM
LT13212	OEM
LT13213	OEM
LT13214	OEM
LT13223	OEM
LT13231	OEM
LT13232	OEM
LT13233	OEM
LT13234	OEM
LT13251	OEM
LT13252	OEM
LT13253	OEM
LT13254	OEM
LT13291	OEM
LT13293	OEM
LT13294	OEM
LT52124	OEM
LT53124	OEM
LT57124	OEM
LT57173	OEM
LTA320	OEM
LTA709	OEM
LTA709C	OEM
LTA741	OEM
LTA741C	OEM
LTA747	OEM
LTA747C	OEM
LTC3211A	OEM
LTC53173	5351
LTD482	OEM
LTE1016	0224
LTE1016(G.E.)	0144
LTG312A	OEM
LTG313A	OEM
LTG314A	OEM
LTG315A	OEM
LTG320	OEM
LTG321	OEM
LTG324	OEM
LTG325	OEM
LTG326	OEM
LTG327	OEM
LTG352	OEM
LTG353	OEM
LTG370	OEM
LTG371	OEM
LTG2110	OEM
LTG2120	OEM
LTG4115	OEM
LTG4125	OEM
LTG8101	OEM
LTH1016	0224
LTH1016(G.E.)	0144
LTK817	4837
LTL-2234GT	OEM
LTL3211A	OEM
LTL9213A	5346
LTL9233A	5347
LTL9253A	4973
LTL42135F	OEM
LTL42735F	OEM
LTL54173	5350
LTL57173	5349
LTR306	OEM
LTR307	OEM
LTR308	OEM
LTR309	OEM
LTR312	OEM
LTR313	OEM
LTR314	OEM
LTR315	OEM
LTR320	OEM
LTR321	OEM
LTR322	OEM
LTR323	OEM
LTR324	OEM
LTR325	OEM
LTR326	OEM
LTR327	OEM
LTR352	OEM
LTR353	OEM
LTR370	OEM
LTR371	OEM
LTR-546E	OEM
LTR2110	OEM
LTR2120	OEM
LTR4115	OEM
LTR4125	OEM
LTR4224	OEM
LTR8101	OEM
LTV817B	OEM
LTZ-G15	OEM
LTZ-MG15	OEM
LTZ-MR15	OEM
LTZ-MR15-T77	OEM
LTZ-MU15	OEM
LTZ-R15	OEM
LTZ-U15	OEM
LU2N544	0136
LU547P	OEM
L-UPD8155C	OEM
LV1140	OEM
LV1200	OEM
LV4100	OEM
LVA43A	0274
LVA43B	OEM
LVA43C	OEM
LVA47A	0140
LVA47B	OEM
LVA47C	OEM
LVA51A	0041
LVA51B	OEM
LVA51C	OEM
LVA56A	0253
LVA56B	OEM
LVA56C	OEM
LVA62A	0466
LVA62B	OEM
LVA62C	OEM
LVA68A	0062
LVA68B	OEM
LVA68C	OEM
LVA75A	0077
LVA75B	OEM
LVA75C	OEM
LVA82A	0165
LVA82B	3071
LVA82C	OEM
LVA91A	0057
LVA91B	OEM
LVA91C	OEM
LVA100A	0346
LVA100B	OEM
LVA100C	OEM
LVA150	0041
LVA150A	OEM
LVA150B	OEM
LVA150C	OEM
LVA153	OEM
LVA153A	OEM
LVA153B	OEM
LVA153C	OEM
LVA156	0253
LVA156A	0157
LVA156B	OEM
LVA156C	OEM
LVA159	OEM
LVA159A	OEM
LVA159B	OEM
LVA159C	OEM
LVA162	0466
LVA162A	1328
LVA162B	OEM
LVA162C	OEM
LVA165	OEM
LVA165A	OEM
LVA165B	OEM
LVA165C	OEM
LVA168	0062
LVA168A	OEM
LVA168B	OEM
LVA168C	OEM
LVA171	OEM
LVA171A	OEM
LVA171B	OEM
LVA171C	OEM
LVA174	OEM
LVA174A	OEM
LVA174C	OEM
LVA177	OEM
LVA177A	OEM
LVA177B	OEM
LVA177C	OEM
LVA180	0244
LVA180A	OEM
LVA180B	OEM
LVA180C	OEM
LVA183	OEM
LVA183A	OEM
LVA183B	OEM
LVA183C	OEM
LVA186	OEM
LVA186A	OEM
LVA186B	OEM
LVA186C	OEM
LVA189	OEM
LVA189A	OEM
LVA189B	OEM
LVA189C	OEM
LVA192	OEM
LVA192A	OEM
LVA192B	OEM
LVA192C	OEM
LVA195	OEM
LVA195A	OEM
LVA195B	OEM
LVA195C	OEM
LVA198	OEM
LVA198A	OEM
LVA198B	OEM
LVA198C	OEM
LVA343A	0274
LVA343B	OEM
LVA343C	OEM
LVA347A	0140
LVA347B	OEM
LVA347C	OEM
LVA351A	0162
LVA351B	OEM
LVA351C	OEM
LVA356A	0157
LVA356B	OEM
LVA356C	OEM
LVA362A	0631
LVA362B	OEM
LVA362C	OEM
LVA368A	0025
LVA368B	OEM
LVA368C	OEM
LVA375A	0644
LVA375B	OEM
LVA375C	OEM
LVA382A	0244
LVA382B	3071
LVA382C	OEM
LVA391A	0012
LVA391B	OEM
LVA391C	OEM
LVA450	0041
LVA450A	OEM
LVA450B	OEM
LVA450C	OEM
LVA453A	OEM
LVA453B	OEM
LVA453C	OEM
LVA456A	0157
LVA456B	OEM
LVA456C	OEM
LVA459A	OEM
LVA459B	OEM
LVA459C	OEM
LVA462A	1328
LVA462B	OEM
LVA462C	OEM
LVA465A	OEM
LVA465B	OEM
LVA465C	OEM
LVA468A	3428
LVA468B	OEM
LVA468C	OEM
LVA471A	OEM
LVA471B	OEM
LVA471C	OEM
LVA474A	OEM
LVA474B	OEM
LVA474C	OEM
LVA477A	OEM
LVA477B	OEM
LVA477C	OEM
LVA480A	OEM
LVA480B	OEM
LVA480C	OEM
LVA483A	OEM
LVA483B	OEM
LVA483C	OEM

If replacement code is OEM, contact original manufacturer for replacement.

DEVICE TYPE	REPL CODE
LVA486A	OEM
LVA486B	OEM
LVA486C	OEM
LVA489A	OEM
LVA489B	OEM
LVA489C	OEM
LVA492A	OEM
LVA492B	OEM
LVA492C	OEM
LVA495A	OEM
LVA495B	OEM
LVA495C	OEM
LVA498A	OEM
LVA498B	OEM
LVA498C	OEM
LVA513	OEM
LVA513A	OEM
LVA519S2	OEM
LVA521	OEM
LVA521S	OEM
LVA522A	OEM
LVA522S	OEM
LVA522S-2	OEM
LVA522SA-2	OEM
LVA523A	OEM
LVA523S	OEM
LVA1043A	0528
LVA1043B	OEM
LVA1043C	OEM
LVA1047A	0446
LVA1047B	OEM
LVA1047C	OEM
LVA1051A	0162
LVA1051B	OEM
LVA1051C	OEM
LVA1056A	0157
LVA1056B	OEM
LVA1056C	OEM
LVA1062A	0631
LVA1062B	OEM
LVA1062C	OEM
LVA1068A	0025
LVA1068B	OEM
LVA1068C	OEM
LVA1075A	0644
LVA1075B	OEM
LVA1075C	OEM
LVA1082A	0244
LVA1082B	OEM
LVA1082C	OEM
LVA1091A	0012
LVA1091B	OEM
LVA1091C	OEM
LVA3100A	0346
LVA3100B	OEM
LVA3100C	OEM
LVA10100A	0346
LVA10100B	OEM
LVA10100C	OEM
LWK-1A	OEM
LWK-2	OEM
LWK-3	OEM
LX738	OEM
LY30	OEM
LY50	OEM
LY61	OEM
LY70	OEM
LY100	OEM
LZ4.7	0162
LZ5.6	0157
LZ6.8	OEM
LZ10	0170
LZZ1-3.3	0289
LZZ1-3.6	0188
LZZ1-3.9	0451
LZZ1-4.3	0528
LZZ1-4.7	0446
LZZ1-5.1	0162
LZZ1-5.6	0157
LZZ1-6.2	0631
LZZ1-6.8	0025
LZZ1-7.5	0644
LZZ1-8.2	0244
LZZ1-9.1	0012
LZZ1-10	0170
LZZ1-11	0313
LZZ1-12	0137
LZZ1-14	0100
LZZ1-15	0002
LZZ1-20	0526
LZZ1-22	0560
LZZ1-24	0398
LZZ1-26	0436
LZZ1-27	0436
LZZ1-29	0721
LZZ1-33G	0039
LZZ1-36	0814
LZZ1-39	0346
LZZ1-43	0925
LZZ1-47	0993
LZZ1-51	0497
LZZ1-55	1823
LZZ1-56	0863
LZZ1-62	0778
LZZ1-68	1258
LZZ1-82	0327
LZZ1-91	1301
LZZ1-110B	0149
LZZ1-115G	0789
LZZ1-120	0186
LZZ1-128	0361
LZZ1-130	0213
LZZ1-140	0245
LZZ1-150	0028
LZZ1-160	0255
LZZ1-161	0416
LZZ1-170	0871
LZZ1-180	0363
LZZ1-190	2831
LZZ1-200	0417
LZZ1-200G	0417
M005T1	OEM
M006B1	OEM
M006D1	OEM
M009T1	OEM
M-0027	0015
M0027	0015
M012	0144
M024	0144
M054B1	OEM
M055B1	OEM
M083B1	4519
M086B1	4691
M087B1	OEM
M089B1	OEM
M089D1	OEM
M089F1	OEM
M0810	OEM
M0816	OEM
M0818	OEM
M0870	OEM
M02010GA	OEM
M02010GA-J245X	OEM
M02010GA-J319X	OEM
M02011GA	OEM
M02011GA-J301X	OEM
M06075B200Z	OEM
M050430-582SP	OEM
M050430-583SP	OEM
M0C604A	OEM
M0C1000	0536
M0TMJE371	0455
M0TMJE521	0161
M0Z	0015
M1	OEM
M1-152	0071
M1-301	0133
M1A1	0071
M1A5	0071
M1A9	0071
M1B1	0071
M1B5	0071
M1B9	0071
M1BF	OEM
M1C1	0071
M1C5	0071
M1C9	0071
M1D	OEM
M1D1	0071
M1D5	0071
M1D9	0071
M1E1	0071
M1E5	0071
M1E9	0071
M1F1	0071
M1F5	0071
M1F9	0071
M1G1	0071
M1G5	0071
M1G9	0071
M1H	0015
M1H1	0071
M1H5	0071
M1H9	0071
M1K1	0071
M1K5	0071
M1K9	0071
M1M1	0071
M1M5	0071
M1M9	0071
M1S-12795B	0103
M1X	0086
M1Z	0023
M1Z30	OEM
M1Z43	OEM
M-2	0196
M2	OEM
M2-100	OEM
M2-100R	OEM
M2-200	OEM
M2-200R	OEM
M2-400	OEM
M2-400R	OEM
M2-600	OEM
M2-600R	OEM
M2-800	OEM
M2-800R	OEM
M2-1000	OEM
M2-1000R	OEM
M2-1200	OEM
M2-1200R	OEM
M2A1	0071
M2A5	0071
M2A9	0071
M2B	0071
M2B1	0071
M2B5	0071
M2B9	0071
M2C1	0071
M2C5	0071
M2C9	0071
M2D1	0071
M2D5	0071
M2D9	0071
M2E1	0071
M2E5	0071
M2E9	0071
M2F1	0071
M2F5	0071
M2F9	0071
M2G1	0071
M2G5	0071
M2G9	0071
M2GH1	0071
M2H1	2621
M2H5	0071
M2H9	0071
M2K1	0071
M2K5	0071
M2K9	0071
M2M1	0071
M2M5	0071
M2M9	0071
M2N168A	0595
M2.5A	0087
M-3	OEM
M3	OEM
M3A1	0071
M3A5	0071
M3A9	0071
M3B1	0071
M3B5	0071
M3B9	0071
M3C1	0071
M3C5	0071
M3C9	0071
M3D1	0071
M3D5	0071
M3D9	0071
M3E1	0071
M3E5	0071
M3E9	0071
M3F1	0071
M3F5	0071
M3F9	0071
M3G	0480
M3G1	0071
M3G5	0071
M3G9	0071
M3H1	0071
M3H5	0071
M3H9	2621
M3K1	0071
M3K5	0071
M3K9	0071
M3M1	0071
M3M5	0071
M3M9	0071
M3025BM	OEM
M3Z6.8	0205
M3Z6.8A	0205
M3Z7.5	0475
M3Z7.5A	0475
M3Z8.2	0499
M3Z8.2A	0499
M3Z9.1	0679
M3Z9.1A	0679
M3Z10	0225
M3Z10A	0225
M3Z11	0237
M3Z11A	0230
M3Z12	0234
M3Z12A	0234
M3Z13	0237
M3Z13A	0237
M3Z15	0247
M3Z15A	0247
M3Z16	0251
M3Z16A	0251
M3Z18	0256
M3Z18A	0256
M3Z20	0262
M3Z20A	0262
M3Z22	0269
M3Z22A	0269
M3Z24	0273
M3Z24A	0273
M3Z27	0291
M3Z27A	0291
M3Z30	0305
M3Z30A	0305
M3Z33	0314
M3Z33A	0314
M3Z36	0316
M3Z36A	0316
M3Z39	0322
M3Z39A	0322
M3Z43	0333
M3Z43A	0333
M3Z47	0343
M3Z47A	0343
M3Z51	0027
M3Z51A	0027
M3Z56	0266
M3Z56A	0266
M3Z62	0382
M3Z62A	0382
M3Z68	0401
M3Z68A	0401
M3Z75	0421
M3Z75A	0421
M3Z82	0439
M3Z82A	0439
M3Z91	0238
M3Z91A	0238
M3Z100	1172
M3Z100A	1172
M3Z110	1182
M3Z110A	1182
M3Z120	1198
M3Z120A	1198
M3Z130	1209
M3Z130A	1209
M3Z150	0642
M3Z150A	0642
M3Z160	1246
M3Z160A	1246
M3Z180	1269
M3Z180A	1269
M3Z200	0600
M3Z200A	0600
M4	0855
M4A1	0087
M4A5	0087
M4A9	0087
M4B1	0087
M4B5	0087
M4B9	0087
M4B-31	0071
M4B31	0015
M4B31-13	0015
M4B-31-22	0319
M4B32	0319
M4B41	5402
M4B41-13	0087
M4B41-S	OEM
M4C1	0087
M4C5	0087
M4C9	0087
M4C-31	0071
M4C-31-32	0071
M4D1	0087
M4D5	0087
M4D9	0087
M4E1	0087
M4E9	0087
M4F1	0087
M4F5	0087
M4F9	0087
M4G1	0087
M4G5	0087
M4G9	0087
M4H1	0087
M4H5	0087
M4H9	0087
M4HZ	0015
M4K1	0087
M4K5	0087
M4K9	0087
M4L20-3	OEM
M4L20-8	OEM
M4L20-28	OEM
M4L20A	OEM
M4L20M3	OEM
M4L20M8	OEM
M4L20M28	OEM
M4L30-3	OEM
M4L30-8	OEM
M4L30-28	OEM
M4L30A	OEM
M4L30M3	OEM
M4L30M8	OEM
M4L30M28	OEM
M4L40-3	OEM
M4L40-8	OEM
M4L40-28	OEM
M4L40A	OEM
M4L40M3	OEM
M4L40M8	OEM
M4L40M28	OEM
M4L50-3	OEM
M4L50-8	OEM
M4L50-28	OEM
M4L50A	OEM
M4L50M3	OEM
M4L50M8	OEM
M4L50M28	OEM
M4L2052	OEM
M4L2053	OEM
M4L2054	OEM
M4M1	0087
M4M5	0087
M4M9	0087
M4Z3.3	0188
M4Z3.3-20	0296
M4Z3.3A	0188
M4Z3.6	0372
M4Z3.6A	0372
M4Z3.9	0188
M4Z3.9-20	0036
M4Z3.9A	0188
M4Z4.3	0274
M4Z4.3-20	0274
M4Z4.3A	0274
M4Z4.7	0162
M4Z4.7-20	0162
M4Z4.7A	0162
M4Z5.1	0162
M4Z5.1-20	0162
M4Z5.1A	0162
M4Z5.6	0157
M4Z5.6-20	0157
M4Z5.6A	0157
M4Z6.2	0466
M4Z6.2-20	0631
M4Z6.2A	0631
M4Z6.8	0062
M4Z6.8-20	0062
M4Z6.8A	0152
M4Z7.5	0077
M4Z7.5-20	0077
M4Z7.5A	0077
M4Z8.2	0165
M4Z8.2-20	0165
M4Z8.2A	0165
M4Z9.1	0057
M4Z9.1-20	0057
M4Z9.1A	0057
M4Z10	0170
M4Z10-20	0170
M4Z10A	0170
M4Z11	0181
M4Z11-20	0181
M4Z11A	0181
M4Z12	0052
M4Z12-20	0052
M4Z12A	0052
M4Z13	0053
M4Z13-20	0053
M4Z13A	0053
M4Z15	0681
M4Z15-20	0681
M4Z15A	0681
M4Z16	0440
M4Z16-20	0440
M4Z16A	0440
M4Z18	0371
M4Z18-20	0371
M4Z18A	0371
M4Z20	0695
M4Z20-20	0695
M4Z20A	0695
M4Z22	0700
M4Z22-20	0700
M4Z22A	0700
M4Z24	OEM
M4Z24-20	0489
M4Z24A	0489
M4Z27	0436
M4Z27-20	0436
M4Z27A	0436
M4Z30	1075
M4Z30-20	0195
M4Z30A	0195
M4Z33	0039
M4Z33-20	0166
M4Z33A	0166
M4Z36	0010
M4Z36-20	0010
M4Z36A	0010
M4Z39	0032
M4Z39-20	0032
M4Z39A	0032
M4Z43	0054
M4Z43-20	0054
M4Z43A	0054
M4Z47	0068
M4Z47-20	0068
M4Z47A	0068
M4Z51	0092
M4Z51-20	0092
M4Z51A	0092
M4Z56	0125
M4Z56-20	0125
M4Z56A	0125
M4Z62	0778
M4Z62-20	0152
M4Z62A	0778
M4Z68	0173
M4Z68-20	0173
M4Z68A	0173
M4Z75	0094
M4Z75-20	0094
M4Z75A	0094
M4Z82	0327
M4Z82-20	0049
M4Z82A	0049
M4Z91	0156
M4Z91-20	0156
M4Z91A	0156
M4Z100	0189
M4Z100-20	0189
M4Z100A	0189
M4Z110	0149
M4Z110-20	6843
M4Z110A	0099
M4Z120	0089
M4Z120-20	0089
M4Z120A	0089
M4Z130	0285
M4Z130-20	0285
M4Z130A	0285
M4Z150	0336
M4Z150-20	0336
M4Z150A	0336
M4Z160	0366
M4Z160-20	0366
M4Z160A	0366
M4Z180	0420
M4Z180-20	0420
M4Z180A	0420
M4Z200	1464
M4Z200-20	1464
M4Z200A	1464
M5	0855
M5-1454L	OEM
M5A	0359
M5A5	OEM
M5B	0359
M5B5	OEM
M5C	0359
M5C5	OEM
M5D	0359
M5D5	OEM
M5E5	OEM
M5F5	OEM
M5F78M09L	OEM
M5F78M12L	OEM
M5F7805	0619
M5F7805L	OEM
M5F7806	OEM
M5F7807	OEM
M5F7808	OEM
M5F7809	OEM
M5F7812	OEM
M5F7812L	OEM
M5F7907	OEM
M5F7909	OEM
M5F7924	OEM
M5G5	OEM
M5G1400P	1835
M5H5	OEM
M5K5	OEM
M5K4116P-2	OEM
M5K4116P-3	OEM
M5K4116S-2	OEM
M5K4164-15	OEM
M5K4164ANP	OEM
M5K4164ANP-12	2341
M5K4164ANP-15	2341
M5K4164AP	OEM
M5K4164NP12	OEM
M5K4164NP15	OEM
M5K4164NP20	OEM
M5K4164NS15	OEM
M5K4164NS20	OEM
M5K4164P12	OEM
M5K4164P15	OEM
M5K4164P20	OEM
M5K4164S-15	4251
M5K4164S-20	4251
M5K41165-3	OEM
M5L2101AP-4	OEM
M5L2102AP-4	OEM
M5L2102AS-4	OEM
M5L2111AP-4	OEM
M5L2112AP-4	OEM
M5L2114LP	OEM
M5L2114LP-2	OEM
M5L2114LP-3	2037
M5L2114LS-2	OEM
M5L2114LS-3	OEM
M5L2716K	2263
M5L2732K	2672
M5L2732K-6	2672
M5L2764K	0806
M5L2764K-2	0806
M5L2764K2	OEM
M5L2764K3	OEM
M5L2764K-FA552	0806
M5L5101LP-1	OEM
M5L8039P-11	OEM
M5L8049-124P-6	OEM
M5L8049-565P	OEM
M5L8049-570P	OEM
M5L8088S-2	OEM
M5L8155P	OEM
M5L8216P	1852
M5L8226P	OEM
M5L8243P	OEM
M5L8251AP	OEM
M5L8251AP-5	OEM
M5L8253P-5	OEM
M5L8255AP-5	0051
M5L8259AP	OEM
M5L8279P	OEM
M5L8279P-5	OEM
M5L27128K	1628
M5L27128K-2	OEM
M5L27256K	OEM
M5L27256K-2	OEM
M5L27256K-X	OEM
M5L27512K-17	OEM
M5M4C264	OEM
M5M4C264L-12	OEM
M5M4C500AL	OEM
M5M4C500L	OEM
M5M4C500L-10	OEM
M5M5	OEM
M5M8N10	OEM
M5M2167S55	OEM
M5M2167S70	OEM
M5M2364-169P	OEM
M5M4164ANP	OEM
M5M4256P	OEM
M5M4257P-15	OEM
M5M4416P	OEM
M5M4416P-15	OEM
M5M4464AP	OEM
M5M4464P	OEM
M5M5116P	OEM
M5M5116P15	OEM
M5M5117P	OEM
M5M5117P12	OEM
M5M5117P15	OEM
M5M5118P	OEM
M5M5118P12	OEM
M5M5118P15	OEM
M5M5165P-10	OEM
M5M5165P-15	OEM
M5M5165P-70	OEM
M5M5165P70	OEM
M5M5178P-55	OEM
M5N5	OEM
M5P5	OEM
M5R4558P	3406
M5T4044P-20	OEM
M5T4044P-30	OEM
M5T4044P-45	OEM
M5T4044S-30	OEM
M5T4044S-45	OEM
M5T40445-20	OEM
M5W1793-02P	OEM
M5Z6.8	0205
M5Z6.8A	0205
M5Z7.5	0475
M5Z7.5A	0475
M5Z8.2	0499
M5Z8.2A	0499
M5Z9.1	0679
M5Z9.1A	0679
M5Z10	0225
M5Z10A	0225
M5Z11	0230
M5Z11A	0230
M5Z12	0234
M5Z12A	0234
M5Z13	0237
M5Z13A	0237
M5Z15	0247
M5Z15A	0247
M5Z16	0251
M5Z16A	0251
M5Z18	0256
M5Z18A	0256
M5Z20	0262
M5Z20A	0262
M5Z22	0269
M5Z22A	0269
M5Z24	0273
M5Z24A	0273
M5Z27	0291
M5Z27A	0291
M5Z33	0314
M5Z33A	0314
M5Z36	0316
M5Z36A	0316
M5Z39	0322
M5Z39A	0322
M5Z43	0333
M5Z43A	0333
M5Z47	0343
M5Z47A	0343
M5Z51	0027
M5Z51A	0027
M5Z56	0266
M5Z56A	0266
M5Z62	0382
M5Z62A	0382
M5Z68	0401
M5Z68A	0401
M5Z75	0421
M5Z75A	0421
M5Z82	0439
M5Z82A	0439
M5Z91	0238
M5Z91A	0238
M5Z100	1172
M5Z100A	1172
M5Z110	1182
M5Z120	1198
M5Z120A	1198
M5Z130	1209
M5Z130A	1209
M5Z150	0642
M5Z150A	0642
M5Z160	1246
M5Z160A	1246
M5Z180	1269
M5Z180A	1269
M5Z200	0600
M5Z200A	0600
M5.6Z	0253
M6	0855
M6-100	OEM
M6-100R	OEM
M6-200	OEM
M6-200R	OEM
M6-400	OEM
M6-400R	OEM
M6-600	OEM
M6-600R	OEM
M6-800	OEM

If replacement code is OEM, contact original manufacturer for replacement.

DEVICE TYPE	REPL CODE
M6-800R	OEM
M6-1000	OEM
M6-1000R	OEM
M6-1200	OEM
M6-1200R	OEM
M6-SAM	1731
M6HZ	0015
M6M80011AL	OEM
M6M80011AP	OEM
M6M80011L	OEM
M6M80011P	OEM
M6M80021L	OEM
M6M80021P	OEM
M6.2Z	0466
M6.8	0030
M6.8Z	0062
M7	0688
M7A5	OEM
M7B5	OEM
M7C5	OEM
M7D5	OEM
M7E5	OEM
M7F5	OEM
M7G5	OEM
M7H5	OEM
M7K5	OEM
M7M5	OEM
M7N5	OEM
M7P5	OEM
M7.5Z	0077
M8HZ	0071
M8T28B	OEM
M8.2Z	0165
M9Z	0057
M10A	0615
M10A10KA	OEM
M10A10LA	OEM
M10A17EA	OEM
M10B	0615
M10D	0074
M10HZ	OEM
M10Z	0170
M11Z	0181
M12	0015
M12A02RA	OEM
M12H	OEM
M12Z	0137
M13Z	0053
M14	0015
M14H	OEM
M15H	OEM
M15HZ	OEM
M15K	OEM
M15Z	0681
M16-100	OEM
M16-100R	OEM
M16-200	OEM
M16-200R	OEM
M16-400	OEM
M16-400R	OEM
M16-600	OEM
M16-600R	OEM
M16-800	OEM
M16-800R	OEM
M16-1000	OEM
M16-1000R	OEM
M16-1200	OEM
M16-1200R	OEM
M16Z	0440
M18TB7	OEM
M18Z	0371
M20	OEM
M20H	OEM
M20HZ	OEM
M20K	OEM
M20Z	0695
M21C	0058
M21C/Q	0058
M21C/R	0058
M21C5	0058
M21CA	0403
M21C-K	OEM
M21CQ	0058
M21C-R	0058
M21CR	0058
M21CY	0058
M21F	OEM
M22	0015
M22P2	OEM
M22P3	OEM
M22P4	OEM
M22Z	0700
M23C	0934
M23CA	0934
M23P-X504	OEM
M23P-X509	OEM
M23P-X516	OEM
M24	0079
M24A	0079
M24B	0079
M24P-X502	OEM
M24Z	0489
M25	0079
M25-100	OEM
M25-100R	OEM
M25-103A	OEM
M25-200	OEM
M25-200R	OEM
M25-203A	OEM
M25-400	OEM
M25-400R	OEM
M25-403A	OEM
M25-600	OEM
M25-600R	OEM
M25-603A	OEM
M25-800	OEM
M25-800R	OEM
M25-803A	OEM
M25-1000	OEM
M25-1000R	OEM
M25-1200	OEM
M25-1200R	OEM
M25A	0079
M25A2	0079
M25A10PA	OEM
M25B	0079
M25B2	0079
M25Hz	OEM
M26	0133
M26P-X504	OEM
M26P-X505	OEM
M26P-X516	OEM
M26P-X517	OEM
M26P-X531	OEM
M26P-X558	OEM
M26P-X560	OEM
M26W0	0139
M26WA	0120
M26X256	OEM
M27Z	0436
M28P-X507	OEM
M28P-X508	OEM
M30	OEM
M30G	OEM
M30HZ	OEM
M30K	OEM
M30Z	0195
M-31	0102
M32P-X503	OEM
M32P-X506	OEM
M32P-X508	OEM
M32P-X509	OEM
M-33	OEM
M33Z	0166
M34A	0143
M40	OEM
M40K	OEM
M41-100	OEM
M41-101A	OEM
M41-200	OEM
M41-201A	OEM
M41-400	OEM
M41-401A	OEM
M41-600	OEM
M41-601A	OEM
M41-800	OEM
M41-801A	OEM
M41-1000	OEM
M41-1200	OEM
M42	0015
M46F	OEM
M47F	OEM
M50A	OEM
M50K	OEM
M51	0143
M54	0079
M54A	0079
M54B	0079
M54BLK	0079
M54BLU	0079
M54BRN	0079
M54C	0102
M54D	0079
M54E	0079
M54GRN	0079
M54ORN	0079
M54RED	0079
M54WHT	0079
M54YEL	0079
M60	0143
M60A	OEM
M60H	OEM
M60K	OEM
M62	0015
M63P-X503	OEM
M65-031	OEM
M65-032	OEM
M65-045	OEM
M65A	0037
M65B	0037
M65C	0037
M65D	0037
M65E	0037
M65F	0037
M67	0015
M67A	0015
M67B	0015
M67C	0015
M67P-X504	OEM
M68	0015
M68A	0015
M68B	0015
M68BSA1	OEM
M68BSA2	OEM
M68BSA4	OEM
M68C	0015
M68D1M2A	OEM
M68KVAM	OEM
M68KVM01A1	OEM
M68KVM01A2	OEM
M68KVM02-1	OEM
M68KVM02-3	OEM
M68KVM11-1	OEM
M68KVM11-2	OEM
M68KVM21(A)	OEM
M68KVM40(A)	OEM
M68KVM80-1	OEM
M68KVM80-2	OEM
M68KVM80-4	OEM
M68KVMCC1	OEM
M68KVMPM1	OEM
M68KVMPS1	OEM
M68KWW	OEM
M68MM01	OEM
M68MM01A	OEM
M68MM01A1	OEM
M68MM01A2	OEM
M68MM01B	OEM
M68MM01B1A	OEM
M68MM01D	OEM
M68MM02	OEM
M68MM03	OEM
M68MM03-1	OEM
M68MM03-2	OEM
M68MM04	OEM
M68MM04A	OEM
M68MM05A	OEM
M68MM05B	OEM
M68MM05C	OEM
M68MM06	OEM
M68MM07	OEM
M68MM09	OEM
M68MM10A	OEM
M68MM10B	OEM
M68MM10C	OEM
M68MM13A	OEM
M68MM13B	OEM
M68MM13C	OEM
M68MM13D	OEM
M68MM14	OEM
M68MM14A	OEM
M68MM15A	OEM
M68MM15A1	OEM
M68MM16-1	OEM
M68MM16-2	OEM
M68MM16-3	OEM
M68MM17	OEM
M68MM18(A)	OEM
M68MM19	OEM
M68MM19A	OEM
M68MM19SB	OEM
M68MM22	OEM
M68MMFLC1	OEM
M68RWIN1-1(A)	OEM
M68RWIN1-2(A)	OEM
M69	0015
M69A	0015
M69B	0015
M69C	0015
M70	0015
M70-101A	OEM
M70-101K	OEM
M70-201A	OEM
M70-201K	OEM
M70-401A	OEM
M70-401K	OEM
M70-601A	OEM
M70-601K	OEM
M70-801A	OEM
M70-801K	OEM
M70A	0015
M70B	0015
M70C	0015
M71	0015
M71-100	OEM
M71-100R	OEM
M71-101A	OEM
M71-200	OEM
M71-200R	OEM
M71-201A	OEM
M71-400	OEM
M71-400R	OEM
M71-401A	OEM
M71-600	OEM
M71-600R	OEM
M71-601A	OEM
M71-800	OEM
M71-800R	OEM
M71-801A	OEM
M71-1000	OEM
M71-1000R	OEM
M71-1200	OEM
M71-1200R	OEM
M71A	0015
M71B	0015
M71C	0015
M72	0071
M72A	0071
M72B	0071
M72C	0071
M72D	0087
M73	0071
M73A	0071
M73B	0071
M73C	0071
M73P1	OEM
M73P-X502	OEM
M74ALS00AP	OEM
M74ALS02P	OEM
M74ALS04P	OEM
M74ALS27P	OEM
M74ALS32P	OEM
M74ALS109P	OEM
M74ALS244P	OEM
M74ALS573P	OEM
M74H002	OEM
M74HC02P	OEM
M74HC08P	OEM
M74HC14P	OEM
M74HC74P	OEM
M74HC138P	OEM
M74HC251P	OEM
M74HC374P	OEM
M74HC4053B1	OEM
M74LS00	2392
M74LS00P	1519
M74LS02P	1550
M74LS03P	1569
M74LS04	6039
M74LS04P	1585
M74LS05	6040
M74LS05P	1598
M74LS06P	OEM
M74LS08	6042
M74LS08P	1623
M74LS09P	1632
M74LS10P	1652
M74LS11P	1657
M74LS12P	1669
M74LS13P	1678
M74LS14	OEM
M74LS14P	1688
M74LS15P	1697
M74LS20P	0035
M74LS21P	1752
M74LS22P	1764
M74LS27P	0183
M74LS30P	0822
M74LS32P	0088
M74LS37P	1719
M74LS38P	1828
M74LS40P	0135
M74LS42P	1830
M74LS47P	1834
M74LS48P	1838
M74LS51P	1027
M74LS73AP	1856
M74LS73P	1856
M74LS74	6049
M74LS74AP	0243
M74LS74P	0243
M74LS75P	1859
M74LS76AP	2166
M74LS83AP	2204
M74LS83P	2204
M74LS85P	0426
M74LS86BP	0288
M74LS86P	0288
M74LS90P	1871
M74LS91P	1874
M74LS92P	1876
M74LS93P	1877
M74LS95BP	0766
M74LS96P	OEM
M74LS107AP	1592
M74LS107P	1592
M74LS109AP	1895
M74LS109P	1895
M74LS112AP	2115
M74LS113AP	2241
M74LS114AP	2286
M74LS122P	1610
M74LS123P	0973
M74LS125AP	0075
M74LS126AP	2850
M74LS132P	1615
M74LS133P	3366
M74LS136P	1618
M74LS138BP	0422
M74LS138P	0422
M74LS139	OEM
M74LS139P	0153
M74LS145P	1554
M74LS148P	3856
M74LS151P	1636
M74LS153P	0953
M74LS155P	0209
M74LS156P	1644
M74LS157P	1153
M74LS158P	1646
M74LS160AP	0831
M74LS161AP	0852
M74LS161P	0852
M74LS162AP	0874
M74LS163AP	0887
M74LS163P	0887
M74LS164P	4274
M74LS165P	4289
M74LS166AP	4301
M74LS166P	4301
M74LS170P	2605
M74LS173AP	5125
M74LS174P	0260
M74LS175P	1662
M74LS183P	OEM
M74LS190P	1676
M74LS191P	1677
M74LS192P	1679
M74LS193P	1682
M74LS194AP	1294
M74LS195AP	1305
M74LS196P	2807
M74LS197P	2450
M74LS221P	1230
M74LS240P	0447
M74LS241P	1715
M74LS242P	1717
M74LS243P	0900
M74LS244P	0453
M74LS245P	0458
M74LS247P	1721
M74LS248P	1723
M74LS251P	1726
M74LS253P	1728
M74LS256P	OEM
M74LS257AP	1733
M74LS258AP	1735
M74LS259P	3175
M74LS266P	0587
M74LS273P	0888
M74LS279P	3259
M74LS280P	1762
M74LS283P	1768
M74LS290P	4352
M74LS293P	0082
M74LS295AP	2212
M74LS295BP	2212
M74LS298P	3337
M74LS299P	4353
M74LS323P	OEM
M74LS352P	0756
M74LS353P	0768
M74LS365AP	0937
M74LS366AP	0950
M74LS367AP	0971
M74LS368AP	0985
M74LS373P	0704
M74LS374P	0708
M74LS375P	OEM
M74LS377P	1112
M74LS386P	1221
M74LS390P	1278
M74LS393P	0813
M74LS395AP	1320
M74LS395P	1320
M74LS490P	2199
M74LS620P	OEM
M74LS640-1P	0664
M74LS641-1P	0685
M74LS642-1P	0714
M74LS643-1P	2045
M74LS644-1P	OEM
M74LS645-1P	0770
M74LS668P	OEM
M74LS669P	OEM
M74LS670P	1122
M75	2872
M76	0050
M77	0050
M78	0050
M78A	0050
M78B	0050
M78BLK	0050
M78C	0050
M78D	0050
M78E	0050
M78GRN	0050
M78L12CP	OEM
M78RED	0050
M78YEL	0050
M79H048	OEM
M80	OEM
M80C51-45	OEM
M80C51F-49	OEM
M80C51F-520	OEM
M80C154	OEM
M80C154-1	OEM
M80C154V-1	OEM
M80K	OEM
M81	OEM
M82	0071
M82P-X500	OEM
M83C154-228	OEM
M84	0085
M84B	0160
M89	OEM
M91	0127
M91A	0079
M91A01	0015
M91A02	0015
M91A03	0015
M91A06	0071
M91B	0079
M91BGRN	0079
M91C	0079
M91CM624	0079
M91D	0079
M91E	0079
M91F	0079
M91FM624	0079
M95	0143
M100	0321
M100-101A	OEM
M100-101K	OEM
M100-201A	OEM
M100-201K	OEM
M100-401A	OEM
M100-401K	OEM
M100-601A	OEM
M100-601K	OEM
M100-801A	OEM
M100-801K	OEM
M100A	1325
M100B	0080
M100D	0604
M100G	0790
M100J	0015
M100K	0072
M100M	0071
M101	3583
M101B2R	OEM
M101B4R	OEM
M101B6R	OEM
M101T2R	OEM
M101T4R	OEM
M101T6R	OEM
M102	0071
M106B1	OEM
M108	0004
M116	6614
M116A	OEM
M119	OEM
M120DB1	OEM
M120DF1	OEM
M120K	OEM
M124J779-1	0015
M128	OEM
M128J422	2937
M128J422-1	0469
M128J753	0469
M128J753-1	0469
M132	6617
M135	0644
M140-1	0127
M140-3	0079
M142A-B1	OEM
M142A-D1	OEM
M142B1	OEM
M142D1	OEM
M147B1	OEM
M150	0015
M150-1	0133
M150K	OEM
M151-100	OEM
M151-100R	OEM
M151-200	OEM
M151-200R	OEM
M151-400	OEM
M151-400R	OEM
M151-600	OEM
M151-600R	OEM
M151-800	OEM
M151-800R	OEM
M151-1000	OEM
M151-1000R	OEM
M151-1200	OEM
M151-1200R	OEM
M-152R	0071
M159A	OEM
M163	OEM
M164	OEM
M172A	0015
M190	OEM
M190B	OEM
M193	OEM
M193AB1	OEM
M193B1	OEM
M200K	OEM
M203	OEM
M204	OEM
M-204B	0015
M204B	0015
M206	OEM
M207	OEM
M250D1	OEM
M252B1AA	OEM
M252B1AD	OEM
M252D1AA	OEM
M253B1AA	OEM
M253B1AC	OEM
M253D1AA	OEM
M254B1AD	OEM
M254B1AM	OEM
M255B1AB	OEM
M258B1	OEM
M259B1	OEM
M300K	OEM
M304	OEM
M304/4050	2016
M310	OEM
M311	OEM
M351	0050
M366-1	0065
M380	0375
M404	OEM
M405	OEM
M423N	OEM
M-433	0396
M433	0396
M440	OEM
M441	OEM
M484	0079
M500	0015
M500A	0015
M500B	0015
M500C	0015
M501	0160
M502	OEM
M503A	OEM
M503DA	OEM
M504A	OEM
M505	OEM
M509	OEM
M510	OEM
M511	OEM
M511A	OEM
M513B	OEM
M517	OEM
M5190P	0850
M521	OEM
M523	OEM
M529	OEM
M530	0086
M530J	OEM
M530K	OEM
M530L	OEM
M537A	OEM
M538A	OEM
M539	OEM
M540J	OEM
M540K	OEM
M546	0007
M549	OEM
M554	OEM
M565	OEM
M566	OEM
M569	OEM
M570	OEM
M573	OEM
M574	OEM
M575	OEM
M575B	OEM
M577B	OEM
M578B	OEM
M579	OEM
M586	OEM
M595B	OEM
M596	OEM
M597	OEM
M598B	OEM
M604	0276
M604HT	0015
M605	OEM
M608	OEM
M612	0007
M613	0007
M614	0007
M644	0037
M652/PIC	0150
M652P1C	0126
M652PIC	0126
M670	0015
M670A	0015
M670B	0015
M670C	0015
M671	0079
M680	0015
M680A	0015
M680B	0015
M680C	0015
M690	0015
M690A	0015
M690B	0015
M690C	0015
M700	0015
M700A	0015
M700B	0015
M700C	0015
M701B	0015
M702	0071
M702B	0071
M702B1	OEM
M702C	0015
M702D1	OEM
M702D2	OEM
M706B1	OEM
M710	0015
M710A	0015
M710B	0015
M710C	0015
M714B1	OEM
M714D1	OEM
M720	0071
M720A	0071
M720B	0071
M720C	0071
M726	3493
M730	0071
M730A	0071
M730B	0071
M730B1	OEM
M730C	0071
M730D1	OEM
M731B1	OEM
M731D1	OEM
M738	OEM
M738B1	OEM
M740	6651
M740B1	OEM
M741	OEM
M741B1	OEM
M747	OEM
M747B1	OEM

If replacement code is OEM, contact original manufacturer for replacement.

DEVICE TYPE	REPL CODE	DEVICE TYPE	REPL CODE	DEVICE TYPE	REPL CODE	DEVICE TYPE	REPL CODE	DEVICE TYPE	REPL CODE	DEVICE TYPE	REPL CODE	DEVICE TYPE	REPL CODE
M750B1	OEM	M1041B	OEM	M1330	OEM	M2147-F1	OEM	M3101A	OEM	M4027P-3B1	OEM	M4553BRN	0004
M750D1	OEM	M1042	OEM	M1330A	OEM	M2163	3163	M3101B	OEM	M4027P-3D1	OEM	M4553GRN	0004
M751B1	OEM	M1042A	OEM	M1330B	OEM	M2167	3163	M3102	OEM	M4027P-3F1	OEM	M4553ORN	0004
M751D1	OEM	M1042B	OEM	M1331	OEM	M2169	3163	M3102A	OEM	M4027P-4B1	OEM	M4553PUR	0435
M752B1	OEM	M1045	OEM	M1331A	OEM	M2207	0025	M3102B	OEM	M4027P-4D1	OEM	M4553RED	0004
M752D1	OEM	M1045A	OEM	M1331B	OEM	M2316E-D1	OEM	M3105	OEM	M4027P-4F1	OEM	M4553YEL	0004
M754B1	OEM	M1045B	OEM	M1332	OEM	M2332B1	OEM	M3105A	OEM	M4030BP	OEM	M4562	0164
M754D1	OEM	M1046	OEM	M1332A	OEM	M2332D1	OEM	M3105B	OEM	M4040BP	0056	M4563	0004
M758	0157	M1046A	OEM	M1332B	OEM	M2333/250	OEM	M3106	OEM	M4042BP	0121	M4564	0004
M773	0079	M1046B	OEM	M1335	OEM	M2333B1	OEM	M3106A	OEM	M4043BP	1544	M4565	0004
M773RED	0079	M1049	OEM	M1335A	OEM	M2333D1	OEM	M3106B	OEM	M4049BP	4278	M4567	0211
M774	0079	M1049A	OEM	M1335B	OEM	M2400	OEM	M3109	OEM	M4050BP	0394	M4570	0085
M774ORN	0079	M1049B	OEM	M1336	OEM	M2497	0015	M3109A	OEM	M4051BP	0362	M4573	0004
M775	0079	M1060	OEM	M1336A	OEM	M2513DP	0735	M3109B	OEM	M4052BP	0024	M4582	0160
M775BRN	0079	M1060A0A	OEM	M1336B	OEM	M2513MP	0759	M3150	OEM	M4053BP	0034	M4582BRN	0160
M776	0079	M1060B	OEM	M1337	OEM	M2513NP	0761	M3150A	OEM	M4066BP	0101	M4583	0160
M776GRN	0079	M1061	OEM	M1339	OEM	M2513PP	OEM	M3150B	OEM	M4069UBP	0119	M4583RED	0160
M779	0016	M1061A	OEM	M1339A	OEM	M2532F1	OEM	M3151	OEM	M4071BP	0129	M4584	0160
M779BLU	0079	M1061B	OEM	M1339B	OEM	M2537-1F1	OEM	M3151A	OEM	M4081BP	0621	M4584BP	OEM
M780	0016	M1062	OEM	M1341	OEM	M2716	2263	M3151B	OEM	M4116P-2B1	OEM	M4584GRN	0160
M780WHT	0079	M1062A	OEM	M1347	OEM	M2716-1F1	OEM	M3152	OEM	M4116P-2D1	OEM	M4586	0136
M783	0079	M1062B	OEM	M1348	OEM	M2716F1	2263	M3152A	OEM	M4116P-2F1	OEM	M4589	0136
M783RED	0079	M1065	OEM	M1350	OEM	M2716M	2263	M3152B	OEM	M4116P-3B1	OEM	M4590	0037
M784	0079	M1065A	OEM	M1353	OEM	M2732-2F1	OEM	M3155	OEM	M4116P-3D1	OEM	M4594	0079
M784ORN	0079	M1065B	OEM	M1354	OEM	M2732AF1	2672	M3155A	OEM	M4116P-3F1	OEM	M4595	0004
M785	0079	M1066	OEM	M1355	OEM	M2764A-20	OEM	M3155B	OEM	M4116P-4B1	OEM	M4596	0211
M785YEL	0079	M1066A	OEM	M1358P	0391	M2797-02/L2376-01	OEM	M3156	OEM	M4116P-4D1	OEM	M4597	0211
M786	0016	M1066B	OEM	M1359	OEM	M2816	OEM	M3156A	OEM	M4116P-4F1	OEM	M4597GRN	0211
M787	0016	M1069	OEM	M1369	OEM	M3013DP	0717	M3156B	OEM	M4313	0004	M4597RED	0211
M787BLU	0079	M1069A	OEM	M1373	OEM	M3013MP	0720	M3159	OEM	M4315	0004	M4603	0136
M791	0079	M1069B	OEM	M1379	OEM	M3013NP	0745	M3159A	OEM	M4327	0211	M4604	0136
M813A	0139	M1100	OEM	M1400	OEM	M3013PP	OEM	M3159B	OEM	M4331	0160	M4605	0136
M818	0079	M1100A	OEM	M1400-1	0127	M3016	0015	M3220	OEM	M4363	0136	M4605RED	0136
M818WHT	0079	M1101	OEM	M1406	OEM	M3020	OEM	M3220A	OEM	M4363BLU	0136	M4606	0160
M819	0233	M1101A	OEM	M1407	OEM	M3020A	OEM	M3220B	OEM	M4363GRN	0136	M4607	0211
M822	0079	M1102	2808	M1470	OEM	M3020B	OEM	M3221	OEM	M4363ORN	0136	M4608	0160
M822A	0079	M1102A	OEM	M1470A	OEM	M3021	OEM	M3221A	OEM	M4363WHT	0136	M4619	0085
M822A-BLU	0079	M1102B	OEM	M1470B	OEM	M3021A	OEM	M3221B	OEM	M4364	0136	M4619RED	0160
M822B	0079	M1105	OEM	M1471	OEM	M3021B	OEM	M3222	OEM	M4365	0136	M4620	0085
M823	0079	M1105A	OEM	M1471A	OEM	M3022	OEM	M3222A	OEM	M4366	0136	M4620GRN	0160
M823B	0079	M1105B	OEM	M1471B	OEM	M3022A	OEM	M3222B	OEM	M4367	0136	M4621	0136
M823WHT	0079	M1106	OEM	M1472	OEM	M3022B	OEM	M3225	OEM	M4368	0136	M4622	0435
M827	0079	M1106A	OEM	M1472A	OEM	M3025	OEM	M3225A	OEM	M4388	0136	M4623	0969
M827BRN	0079	M1106B	OEM	M1472B	OEM	M3025A	OEM	M3225B	OEM	M4389	0279	M4624	0079
M828	0126	M1109	OEM	M1475	OEM	M3025B	OEM	M3226	OEM	M4398	0004	M4627	0211
M828GRN	0079	M1109A	OEM	M1475A	OEM	M3026	OEM	M3226A	OEM	M4439	0050	M4628A	OEM
M829A	0037	M1109B	OEM	M1475B	OEM	M3026A	OEM	M3226B	OEM	M4442	0037	M4630	0079
M829B	0037	M1150	OEM	M1476	OEM	M3026B	OEM	M3230A	OEM	M4450	0164	M4632	0136
M829C	0037	M1150A	OEM	M1476A	OEM	M3029	OEM	M3330	OEM	M4454	0136	M4634	OEM
M829D	0037	M1150B	OEM	M1476B	OEM	M3029A	OEM	M3330A	OEM	M4456	0136	M4640	0599
M829E	0037	M1151	3553	M1506	OEM	M3029B	OEM	M3330B	OEM	M4457	0136	M4640P	0599
M829F	0037	M1151A	OEM	M1507	OEM	M3030	OEM	M3331	OEM	M4459	0969	M4648	0233
M833	0037	M1151B	OEM	M1680	OEM	M3030A	OEM	M3331A	OEM	M4462	0004	M4649	0085
M841	OEM	M1152	OEM	M1680A	OEM	M3030B	OEM	M3331B	OEM	M4463	0085	M4652	0969
M844	0161	M1152A	3553	M1680B	OEM	M3031	OEM	M3332	OEM	M4464	0079	M4653	0012
M847	0079	M1152B	OEM	M1681	OEM	M3031A	OEM	M3332A	OEM	M4465	0079	M4659	0100
M847BLK	0079	M1155	OEM	M1681A	OEM	M3031B	OEM	M3332B	OEM	M4466	0004	M4663	0039
M895	OEM	M1155A	OEM	M1681B	OEM	M3032	OEM	M3335	OEM	M4466ORN	0164	M4689	0086
M912	0275	M1155B	OEM	M1682	OEM	M3032A	OEM	M3335A	OEM	M4468	0004	M4697	0050
M924	0079	M1156	OEM	M1682A	OEM	M3032B	OEM	M3335B	OEM	M4468BRN	0164	M4699	0327
M954-644	OEM	M1156A	OEM	M1682B	OEM	M3035	OEM	M3451M8-561SP	OEM	M4469	0004	M4700	0595
M1000B	OEM	M1156B	OEM	M1685	OEM	M3035A	OEM	M3470	OEM	M4469RED	0164	M4701	0599
M1001B	OEM	M1159	OEM	M1685A	OEM	M3035B	OEM	M3470A	OEM	M4470	0004	M4702	0599
M1020	OEM	M1159A	OEM	M1685B	OEM	M3036	OEM	M3470B	OEM	M4470ORN	0164	M4704	0327
M1020A	OEM	M1159B	OEM	M1713DP	0735	M3036A	OEM	M3471	OEM	M4471	0004	M4705	0079
M1020B	OEM	M1200	OEM	M1713MP	0759	M3036B	OEM	M3471A	OEM	M4471YEL	0164	M4706	0079
M1021	OEM	M1220	OEM	M1713NP	0761	M3039	OEM	M3471B	OEM	M4472	0004	M4709	0144
M1021A	OEM	M1220A	OEM	M1713PP	OEM	M3039A	OEM	M3472	OEM	M4472GRN	0164	M4709RED/RED	0144
M1021B	OEM	M1220B	OEM	M1751	OEM	M3039B	OEM	M3472A	OEM	M4473	0164	M4714	0079
M1022	OEM	M1221	OEM	M1800	OEM	M3040	OEM	M3472B	OEM	M4474	0004	M4715	0103
M1022A	OEM	M1221A	OEM	M1800A	OEM	M3040A	OEM	M3519	0079	M4474YEL	0164	M4719	OEM
M1022B	OEM	M1221B	OEM	M1800B	OEM	M3040B	OEM	M3567-2	0161	M4475	0004	M-4721	0079
M1024B5	OEM	M1222	OEM	M1801	OEM	M3041	OEM	M3636	OEM	M4475GRN	0164	M-4722	OEM
M1025	OEM	M1222A	OEM	M1801A	OEM	M3041A	OEM	M3681	OEM	M4476	0004	M4722	0160
M1025A	OEM	M1222B	OEM	M1801B	OEM	M3041B	OEM	M3681A	OEM	M4476BLU	0164	M4722BLU	0160
M1025B	OEM	M1223	OEM	M1802	OEM	M3042	OEM	M3681B	OEM	M4477	0004	M4722GRN	0160
M1025B5	OEM	M1224	OEM	M1802A	OEM	M3042A	OEM	M3682	OEM	M4477PUR	0164	M4722ORN	0240
M1025B5BA	OEM	M1225	OEM	M1802B	OEM	M3042B	OEM	M3682A	OEM	M4478	0126	M4722PUR	0160
M1025B5BB	OEM	M1225A	OEM	M2002	0817	M3045	OEM	M3682B	OEM	M4484	0050	M4722RED	0160
M1025B5C5	OEM	M1225B	OEM	M2003	1686	M3045A	OEM	M3764-15RS	2341	M4485	0050	M4722YEL	0160
M1025B5CA	OEM	M1226	OEM	M2009	1969	M3045B	OEM	M3764-20RS	2341	M4486	0050	M4727	0085
M1026	OEM	M1226A	OEM	M2012ALB1-2	OEM	M3046	OEM	M3764A-15	OEM	M4501	0136	M4728	0149
M1026A	OEM	M1226B	OEM	M2016	1686	M3046A	OEM	M3800	OEM	M4504	0050	M4730	0160
M1026B	OEM	M1227	OEM	M2032	2722	M3046B	OEM	M3800A	OEM	M4505E	OEM	M4732	0079
M1029	OEM	M1229	OEM	M2102AB1	OEM	M3049	OEM	M3800B	OEM	M4506	0050	M-4733	OEM
M1029A	OEM	M1229A	OEM	M2102AB1-2	OEM	M3049A	OEM	M3802	OEM	M4507	0050	M4733	0144
M1029B	OEM	M1229B	OEM	M2102AB1-4	OEM	M3049B	OEM	M3802A	OEM	M4508B	1800	M4734	0079
M1030	OEM	M1230	OEM	M2102AB1-6	OEM	M3059	OEM	M3802B	OEM	M4509	0136	M4736	0015
M1030A	OEM	M1233	OEM	M2102AD1	OEM	M3059A	OEM	M3864B-21	OEM	M4510	0164	M4737	0079
M1030B	OEM	M1243	OEM	M2102AD1-2	OEM	M3059B	OEM	M4001	OEM	M4510BP	1952	M4739	0079
M1031	OEM	M1300	OEM	M2102AD1-4	OEM	M3060	OEM	M4001BP	0473	M4512BP	2108	M4745	0037
M1031A	OEM	M1302	OEM	M2102AD1-6	OEM	M3060A	OEM	M4002BP	2044	M4514BP	1819	M4746	0127
M1031B	OEM	M1304	OEM	M2102AF1	OEM	M3060B	OEM	M4011	OEM	M4515BP	3555	M4756	0007
M1032	OEM	M1305	OEM	M2102AF1-2	OEM	M3061	OEM	M4011BP	0215	M4516BP	2331	M4757	0127
M1032A	OEM	M1306	OEM	M2102AF1-4	OEM	M3061A	OEM	M4011UBP	OEM	M4518BP	1037	M4765	0079
M1032B	OEM	M1308	OEM	M2102AF1-6	OEM	M3061B	OEM	M4012BP	0493	M4520BP	2650	M4766	0160
M1035	OEM	M1310	OEM	M2102ALB1	OEM	M3062	OEM	M4013DP	OEM	M4524	0050	M4767	0160
M1035A	OEM	M1311	OEM	M2102ALB1-4	OEM	M3062A	OEM	M4013MP	OEM	M4525	0037	M4768	0079
M1035B	OEM	M1312	OEM	M2102ALD1	OEM	M3062B	OEM	M4013NP	OEM	M4526	0050	M4789	0079
M1036	OEM	M1313	OEM	M2102ALD1-2	OEM	M3065	OEM	M4013PP	OEM	M4528BP	3168	M4815	0037
M1036B	OEM	M1315	OEM	M2102ALD1-4	OEM	M3065A	OEM	M4015B	1008	M4537	OEM	M4815D	0037
M1039	OEM	M1316	OEM	M2102ALF1	OEM	M3065B	OEM	M4016BP	1135	M4539BP	3611	M4816	0012
M1039A	OEM	M1320	OEM	M2102ALF1-2	OEM	M3066	OEM	M4020BP	1651	M4543	OEM	M4818	OEM
M1039B	OEM	M1321	OEM	M2102ALF1-4	OEM	M3066A	OEM	M4023BP	0515	M4545	0136	M4819	0233
M1040	OEM	M1323	OEM	M-2115	OEM	M3066B	OEM	M4024BP	1946	M4545BLU	0136	M4820	0144
M1040A	OEM	M1325	OEM	M2128-20	1887	M3100	OEM	M4025BP	2061	M4545WHT	0136	M4821	0079
M1040B	OEM	M1326	OEM	M2147-3B1	OEM	M3100A	OEM	M4027P-2B1	OEM	M4552	0100	M4825	0127
M1041	OEM	M1327	OEM	M2147-3F1	OEM	M3100B	OEM	M4027P-2D1	OEM	M4553	0004	M4826	0144
M1041A	OEM	M1328	OEM	M2147-B1	OEM	M3101	OEM	M4027P-2F1	OEM	M4553BLU	0004	M4826F	OEM

If replacement code is OEM, contact original manufacturer for replacement. 457

DEVICE TYPE	REPL CODE
M4834	0079
M4837	0144
M4838	0233
M4839	0233
M4840	0079
M4840A	0127
M4840E	0004
M4841	0079
M4842	0079
M4842A	0079
M4842C	0079
M4843	0233
M4844	0079
M4845	0144
M4847	OEM
M4850	0789
M4851	0789
M4852	0079
M4853	0233
M4854	0079
M4855	0144
M4857	0144
M4858	0039
M4860	0050
M4872	0142
M4882	0103
M4885	0142
M4887A	0085
M4888	0160
M4888A	0160
M4888B	0160
M4898	0079
M4900	0074
M4901	0637
M4906	0079
M4910	0150
M4917	0196
M4918	0086
M4919	0086
M4920	0142
M4926	0079
M4927	0233
M4933	0079
M4936	0178
M4937	0079
M4941	0079
M4952	0079
M4953	0079
M4967	OEM
M4970	0079
M4995	0637
M4998	0275
M5005	OEM
M5005A	OEM
M5016	OEM
M5019	OEM
M5021	OEM
M5023	OEM
M5024	OEM
M5025	OEM
M5028	OEM
M5031	OEM
M5032	OEM
M5033	OEM
M5034A	OEM
M5035	OEM
M5042S	OEM
M5048	OEM
M5051	OEM
M5052	OEM
M5053	OEM
M5054	OEM
M5055	OEM
M5057	OEM
M5059	OEM
M5060	OEM
M5061	OEM
M5062	OEM
M5063-2J70B	OEM
M5064H	OEM
M5065	OEM
M5067H	OEM
M5075	OEM
M5076	OEM
M5077	OEM
M5079A	OEM
M5080	OEM
M5081	OEM
M5083A	OEM
M5084	OEM
M5085	OEM
M5086	OEM
M5087	OEM
M5089	OEM
M5091A	OEM
M5094	OEM
M5097	OEM
M5100	OEM
M5101	4406
M5101-245	OEM
M5101P	4406
M5105	OEM
M5106	3232
M5106P	3232
M5108	4196
M5108-9170	4196
M5108P	4196
M5109	2696
M5109P	6224

DEVICE TYPE	REPL CODE
M5111	OEM
M5112	3901
M5112Y	3901
M5113	2600
M5113P	OEM
M5113T	2600
M5114B	OEM
M5115	2289
M5115P	2289
M5115P-9085	2289
M5115PA	2289
M5115PR	2289
M5115PRA	2988
M5115R	OEM
M5115RP	2988
M5117A	OEM
M5117B	OEM
M5117C	OEM
M5117D	OEM
M5117E	OEM
M5117F	OEM
M5117G	OEM
M5117H	OEM
M5117L	4588
M5118L	6048
M5120L	OEM
M5123	OEM
M5124	3901
M5125	OEM
M5125X	OEM
M5126A	OEM
M5127	OEM
M5128-20	OEM
M5128-20(SM)	OEM
M5130P	OEM
M5131P	1624
M5132P	OEM
M5133	OEM
M5134	1624
M5134-8266	1624
M5134P	1624
M5135	4562
M5135P	0872
M5136	OEM
M5137	OEM
M5138P	OEM
M5142	OEM
M-5142P	OEM
M5142P	OEM
M5143	0167
M5143P	0167
M5144BP	0167
M5144P	0167
M5146P	3891
M5149	OEM
M5151RE	OEM
M5152L	2512
M5153L	0514
M5153P	0514
M5154	OEM
M5155	OEM
M5155L	OEM
M5155P	4513
M5156	OEM
M5157A	OEM
M5157B	OEM
M5157C	OEM
M5157D	OEM
M5162	OEM
M5163	OEM
M5165LL	OEM
M5167	OEM
M5168	OEM
M5169	1797
M5169P	1797
M5170	OEM
M5172L	OEM
M5174P	OEM
M5176P	1797
M5182	OEM
M5183	0391
M5183P	0391
M5185AP	0762
M5185P	0762
M5186AP	0912
M5186AP(RED)	OEM
M5186BP	0912
M5186P	0912
M5186P/AP	OEM
M5187	OEM
M5187P	OEM
M5190P	0850
M5191	OEM
M5191P	2864
M5192P	4133
M5193	OEM
M5193P	4319
M5194AP	OEM
M5194L	OEM
M5194P	OEM
M5195	4591
M5195P	4591
M5196A	OEM
M5196B	OEM
M5196F	OEM
M5196P	OEM
M5197	OEM
M5198	OEM
M5199	OEM

DEVICE TYPE	REPL CODE
M5201FP	OEM
M5201L	OEM
M5201P	OEM
M5204P	OEM
M5210P	OEM
M5212L	OEM
M5213L	OEM
M5214L	OEM
M5215L	OEM
M5218AL	OEM
M5218L	1689
M5218P	3406
M5218PF	OEM
M5220L	OEM
M5220P	OEM
M5221P	OEM
M5222L	OEM
M5223L	OEM
M5223P	3406
M5224P	0620
M5226P	OEM
M5227P	OEM
M5228P	OEM
M5229P	OEM
M5230L	OEM
M5231	OEM
M5231L	OEM
M5231TL	OEM
M5233P	0624
M5236L	5715
M5236ML	4055
M5237L	OEM
M5238L	OEM
M5238PF	OEM
M5239L	OEM
M5248P	OEM
M5251L	OEM
M5256	OEM
M5258	OEM
M5278L-05	1288
M5278L05	1288
M5278L10	OEM
M5278L-56	OEM
M5278L56	OEM
M5285	0004
M5290P	OEM
M5294P	OEM
M5299A	OEM
M5304	1265
M5304P	1265
M5310	0867
M5310P	0867
M5311	OEM
M5323BP	0990
M5323P	1054
M5340	OEM
M5340P	OEM
M5352	0738
M5352P	0738
M5362	1046
M5362P	1046
M5372	1417
M5372P	1417
M5373	OEM
M5374	1303
M5374P	1303
M5375	1394
M5375P	1394
M5395	1477
M5395P	1477
M5468L-D	OEM
M5508K	OEM
M5701	OEM
M5709	OEM
M5730	OEM
M5730A	OEM
M5735-5	OEM
M5735-6	OEM
M5735-G	OEM
M5735-M	OEM
M5735-X	OEM
M5740-5	OEM
M5740-6	OEM
M5740-G	OEM
M5740-M	OEM
M5740-X	OEM
M5745-5	OEM
M5745-6	OEM
M5745-G	OEM
M5745-M	OEM
M5745-X	OEM
M5930	1812
M5930P	1812
M5932	1035
M5932P	1035
M5933	2086
M5933P	2086
M5935	1168
M5935P	1168
M5936	1820
M5936P	1820
M5937	1824
M5937P	1824
M5944	0033
M5944P	0033
M5945	0081
M5945P	0081
M5946	0141
M5946P	0141

DEVICE TYPE	REPL CODE
M5948	3365
M5948P	3365
M5949	1833
M5949P	1833
M5951	OEM
M5953	0354
M5953P	0354
M5955P	1472
M5956	1622
M5956P	1622
M5961	1848
M5961P	1848
M5962	0557
M5962P	0557
M5963	0337
M5963P	0337
M6400A	OEM
M6840	0279
M6931	0424
M6964-2	OEM
M6964-3	OEM
M6984	OEM
M6990	OEM
M6990-7203V1	OEM
M7002	0233
M7003	0016
M7006	0079
M7014	0198
M7015	0016
M7032H	OEM
M7033	0016
M7366	OEM
M7611AP	0069
M7641	1164
M7644BP	0658
M7800B	OEM
M7880	OEM
M7895	OEM
M8000H	OEM
M-8008	OEM
M8014	0030
M-8016(A)	OEM
M8051-178	OEM
M8062A	0004
M8062B	0004
M8062C	0004
M8073B	0004
M8073C	0279
M8082B1	OEM
M8100	OEM
M8105	0016
M8106	OEM
M8108	OEM
M8108A	OEM
M8108B	OEM
M8116	0136
M8120	0595
M-8124	0911
M8124	0050
M8128	OEM
M8221	0079
M8222	0015
M8303	0723
M8317B	0374
M8320	1780
M-8371-10000	OEM
M8394-100	OEM
M8399	0015
M8411	OEM
M8444	OEM
M8482	0911
M8482A	OEM
M8482C	6572
M8482F	0911
M8482FA-4	0911
M8484	OEM
M8486	OEM
M8487	OEM
M8489	0124
M8489-A	0143
M-8489A	0133
M8489A	0124
M8500	OEM
M8504	OEM
M8511	0030
M8513	0139
M8513(LAFAYETTE)	0133
M8513-0	0124
M8513-O	0139
M-8513A	0133
M8513A	0139
M8513A(O)	1914
M8513A0	0139
M8513A-4	OEM
M8513A-C	OEM
M8513A-O	0139
M8513AO	1914
M8513A-R	0139
M-8513R	0019
M8513R	0139
M8515	0012
M8550	OEM
M8555	0124
M8569	0907
M8604	0004
M8604A	0004
M8628	OEM
M8640	0164
M8640A	0164

DEVICE TYPE	REPL CODE
M8640E	0136
M8640E(C-M)	0133
M8640E(DIO)	0133
M8640E(TRANSISTOR)	0164
M8640E(XSTR)	0211
M-8641A	0164
M8652	OEM
M8700	OEM
M8714	OEM
M8724LM	OEM
M8830	OEM
M9002	0164
M9010	0007
M9010A	OEM
M9032	0016
M9063	OEM
M9090	0969
M9092	0038
M9093	0038
M9095	0016
M9134	0555
M9138	0086
M9142	0160
M9148	0211
M9159	0016
M9170	0198
M9184	0086
M9197	0111
M9198	0004
M-9202-15KV	OEM
M9206	1219
M9209	0086
M9213-100	OEM
M9213-200	OEM
M9213-450	OEM
M9216	OEM
M9220	OEM
M9225	0178
M9228	0086
M9235	0015
M9237	0160
M-9242-10KV	OEM
M9244	0103
M9248	0079
M9249	0004
M9255	0160
M9256	2123
M9257A	OEM
M9257B	OEM
M9257C	OEM
M9257D	OEM
M9259	0103
M9263	0160
M9264	1659
M9266	0007
M9274	0178
M9278	0103
M9301	0178
M9302	0103
M9305	OEM
M9306	1814
M9306B1	OEM
M9308	0126
M9312	0015
M9314	0015
M9317	0015
M9319	0015
M9321	0103
M9328	0037
M9329	0111
M9330	OEM
M9338	0111
M9342	0160
M9344	1671
M9348	0919
M9359	1671
M9380	0086
M9389	0155
M9393	0178
M9400	0126
M9408	0074
M9436	0160
M9450	0007
M9481	0007
M9482	0144
M9491	0198
M9514	0037
M9519	0086
M9525	0016
M9526	0037
M9527	0037
M9531	0037
M9532	0016
M9556	0161
M9561	0086
M9570	0016
M9571	0037
M9582	0455
M9715	0130
M9731	OEM
M9732	OEM
M9736	OEM
M9737	5480
M9741	3545
M9742	OEM
M9746	OEM
M9747	OEM
M12050CA	OEM
M12051CA	OEM

DEVICE TYPE	REPL CODE
M14818A	OEM
M16010C	0133
M16911	OEM
M22100B1	OEM
M22100D1	OEM
M23163B1	OEM
M27256F1	OEM
M31001	0016
M33611	0253
M34300-221SP	OEM
M34300-223SP	OEM
M34300-227SP	OEM
M34302M8-511	OEM
M34302M8-511SP	OEM
M34302M8-512SP	OEM
M34302M8-514SP	OEM
M34350N6-522SP	OEM
M34350N6-524SP	OEM
M34350N6-527SP	OEM
M34350N6-528SP	OEM
M34350N6-561SP	OEM
M34350N6-562SP	OEM
M34350N6-566SP	OEM
M34350N6-567SP	OEM
M36000-5B1	OEM
M36000-5D1	OEM
M37100	OEM
M37100M8	OEM
M37100M8-110SP	OEM
M37100M8-115SP	OEM
M37100M8-222SP	OEM
M37100M8-521SP	OEM
M37100M8-711SP	OEM
M37100M8-717SP	OEM
M37100M8-919SP	OEM
M37100M8-8155P	OEM
M37100M8-B16SP	OEM
M37100M8-C16SP	OEM
M37100M8-C17SP	OEM
M37101M4-521SP	OEM
M37101M4-522SP	OEM
M37200M6-A16SP	OEM
M37204M8	OEM
M37204M8-652SP	OEM
M37211M2-520SP	OEM
M37250M6-561SP	OEM
M38128A-43	OEM
M40175BP	1520
M40308B	OEM
M41032A	0071
M41223-2	0015
M41256-15	OEM
M41256A	OEM
M41464-10	OEM
M41464-12	OEM
M41464-15	OEM
M50110AP	OEM
M50110BP	OEM
M50110CP	OEM
M50110P	OEM
M50111AP	OEM
M50111BP	OEM
M50111CP	OEM
M50111P	OEM
M50112P	OEM
M50115AP	OEM
M50115BP	OEM
M50115CP	OEM
M50115P	OEM
M50116AP	OEM
M50116BP	OEM
M50116CP	OEM
M50116P	OEM
M50117AP	OEM
M50117BP	OEM
M50117CP	OEM
M50117P	OEM
M50119P	OEM
M50143-003P	OEM
M50143-007P	OEM
M50143-007SP	OEM
M50161-020SP	OEM
M50161-059SP	OEM
M50161-151SP	OEM
M50161-152SP	OEM
M50161-154SP	OEM
M50161-251	OEM
M50161-251SP	OEM
M50161-452SP	OEM
M50161-453SP	OEM
M50161-454SP	OEM
M50161-459SP	OEM
M50161-542SP	OEM
M50163-55SP	OEM
M50199P	OEM
M50422P	OEM
M50430-582SP	OEM
M50430-583SP	OEM
M50433B-501S	OEM
M50433B-502SP	OEM
M50434-122-SP	OEM
M50436-594SP	OEM
M50439-513SP	OEM
M50439-517SP	OEM
M50439-519SP	OEM
M50439-614SP	OEM
M50439-711SP	OEM
M50439-919FP	OEM
M50441-540SP	OEM

DEVICE TYPE	REPL CODE
M50441-561BSP	OEM
M50441-561SP	OEM
M50442-505SP	OEM
M50442-506SP	OEM
M50442-508SP	OEM
M50442-522SP	OEM
M50442-525SP	OEM
M50442-526SP	OEM
M50442-562SP	OEM
M50442-563SP	OEM
M50442-564SP	OEM
M50442-577SP	OEM
M50442-620SP	OEM
M50442-622SP	OEM
M50442-623SP	OEM
M50442-624SP	OEM
M50442-625SP	OEM
M50442-626SP	OEM
M50442-671SP	OEM
M50442-674SP	OEM
M50445-010SP	OEM
M50450-001P	OEM
M50450-007P	OEM
M50450-031P	OEM
M50452-003	OEM
M50452-019P	OEM
M50452A-003P	OEM
M50452A-006P	OEM
M50453-015P	OEM
M50454-054SP	OEM
M50455-001SP	OEM
M50455-003SP	OEM
M50455-007SP	OEM
M50459-001SP	OEM
M50460-044P	OEM
M50460-055P	OEM
M50461-56FB	OEM
M50467-033FP	OEM
M50541FP	OEM
M50542-003	OEM
M50554-001SP	OEM
M50554-003SP	OEM
M50560-001P	OEM
M50560-125P	OEM
M50560-145	OEM
M50560-145P	OEM
M50560-155P	OEM
M50560-198P	OEM
M50561-021P	OEM
M50574BSP	OEM
M50720-408SP	OEM
M50725-116SP	OEM
M50725-151SP	OEM
M50725-648SP	OEM
M50730-601SP	OEM
M50731-608SP	OEM
M50731-611SP	OEM
M50734SP	OEM
M50734SP-10	OEM
M50742-404SP	OEM
M50742-653SP	OEM
M50743FP	OEM
M50746-145SP	OEM
M50746-412SP	OEM
M50747-408SP	OEM
M50747-458SP	OEM
M50747-A71	OEM
M50752-101SP	OEM
M50752-620SP	OEM
M50752-622SP	OEM
M50752-626SP	OEM
M50752-635SP	OEM
M50754-115SP	OEM
M50754-360SP	OEM
M50754-363SP	OEM
M50754-644SP	OEM
M50754-673SP	OEM
M50754-679SP	OEM
M50754-680SP	OEM
M50754-688SP	OEM
M50754-689SP	OEM
M50757-301SP	OEM
M50757-311SP	OEM
M50757-610SP	OEM
M50757-621SP	OEM
M50757-640SP	OEM
M50757-660SP	OEM
M50757-671SP	OEM
M50757-690SP	OEM
M50757-691SP	OEM
M50757-692SP	OEM
M50760-670P	OEM
M50761-258P	OEM
M50761-417P	OEM
M50761-418P	OEM
M50761-420P	OEM
M50761-439P	OEM
M50761-668P	OEM
M50763-610SP	OEM
M50765-441SP	OEM
M50769-330P	OEM
M50925-302SP	OEM
M50930-410FP	OEM
M50930-432FP	OEM
M50930-921SP	OEM
M50940-123SP	OEM
M50940-440SP	OEM
M50940-441SP	OEM
M50941-404SP	OEM

If replacement code is OEM, contact original manufacturer for replacement.

DEVICE TYPE	REPL CODE
M50941-413SP	OEM
M50942-261FP	OEM
M50950-621SP	OEM
M50950-623SP	OEM
M50950-626SP	OEM
M50950-661SP	OEM
M50954-325SP	OEM
M50954-644SP	OEM
M50954-662SP	OEM
M50954-666SP	OEM
M50954-668SP	OEM
M50954-683SP	OEM
M50955-233SP	OEM
M50955-237SP	OEM
M50955-669SP	OEM
M50955-701SP	OEM
M50955-941SP	OEM
M50955-943SP	OEM
M50957-191SP	OEM
M50957-192SP	OEM
M50957-197SP	OEM
M50957-657SP	OEM
M50958-302SP	OEM
M50964-212SP	OEM
M51003L	OEM
M51014L	OEM
M51017AP	OEM
M51018AP	OEM
M51029P	OEM
M51104L	OEM
M51124	3901
M51131L	OEM
M51132L	OEM
M51132L-600	OEM
M51140AP	OEM
M51146P	OEM
M51164L	OEM
M51171L	4588
M51172P	4355
M51173AP	OEM
M51177L	OEM
M51182	4676
M51182L	4676
M51201L	OEM
M51202	1899
M51202L	1899
M51203L	OEM
M51204	0866
M51204L	0866
M51205L	OEM
M51206L	OEM
M51207L	6496
M51231P	OEM
M51232L	OEM
M51232L-600	OEM
M51232P	OEM
M51233P	OEM
M51240P	OEM
M51242P	5892
M51247	3242
M51247P	3242
M51251P	OEM
M51271SP	OEM
M51301P	OEM
M51307BSP	3309
M51308SP	OEM
M51320P	OEM
M51321P	OEM
M51326P	OEM
M51329P	OEM
M51340P	OEM
M51342P	OEM
M51345AP	OEM
M51346AP	OEM
M51354AP	1433
M51354APMN1217A	OEM
M51354APO	1433
M51354P	1433
M51355P	5676
M51356	5742
M51356P	5742
M51358P	0906
M51363	OEM
M51363P	OEM
M51364P	OEM
M51365-SP	OEM
M51365P	6647
M51365SP	3590
M51366P	2535
M51366SP	2099
M51375P	4102
M51376BSP	6023
M51376BZT	OEM
M51376SP	4271
M51378L	OEM
M51380P	OEM
M51381P	OEM
M51382P	OEM
M51383P	OEM
M51386L	4040
M51389P	4469
M51392P	OEM
M51401K	OEM
M51401P	OEM
M51408SP	OEM
M51411SP	OEM
M51414BSP	OEM
M51414SP	OEM
M51454L	OEM
M51460P	OEM
M51475G-3B	OEM
M51483P	OEM
M51485L	OEM
M51489L	OEM
M51494L	OEM
M51496P	OEM
M51501L	OEM
M51502L	1899
M51503L	OEM
M51513L	4559
M51513LB	4559
M51515L	4582
M51516L	4632
M51517L	4634
M51518L	5013
M51521L	2512
M51522AL	OEM
M51522L	OEM
M51523AL	OEM
M51523L	OEM
M51542AP	OEM
M51544AL	6803
M51544L	4750
M51564P	OEM
M51565P	OEM
M51567P	OEM
M51654AP	OEM
M51654P	OEM
M51660L	OEM
M51709T	1291
M51796P	OEM
M51802L	OEM
M51802P	OEM
M51841P	0967
M51843P	OEM
M51845L	OEM
M51846L	OEM
M51847P	OEM
M51848L	3899
M51848P	0967
M51849L	OEM
M51901P	OEM
M51903L	0804
M51904L	OEM
M51910P	OEM
M51953A	OEM
M51953AL	OEM
M51953B	OEM
M51953BL	OEM
M51954AL	OEM
M51955AL	OEM
M51957AL	OEM
M51970L	OEM
M51971L	OEM
M51976FP	OEM
M52005P	OEM
M52025SP	OEM
M52029FP	OEM
M52030ASP	OEM
M52030SP	OEM
M52041SP	OEM
M52054FP	OEM
M52055FP	OEM
M52055P	OEM
M52303ASP	OEM
M52303SP	OEM
M52470AP	OEM
M52470P	OEM
M52472P	OEM
M52678P	OEM
M52679FP	OEM
M52679P	OEM
M52682FP	OEM
M52684AFP	OEM
M52686AP	OEM
M52686FP	OEM
M52686P	OEM
M52687L	OEM
M52690SP	OEM
M52691FP	OEM
M52692SP	OEM
M52800FP	OEM
M52803P	OEM
M52812FP	OEM
M53200	0232
M53200P	0232
M53201	0268
M53201P	0268
M53202	0310
M53202P	0310
M53203	0331
M53203P	0331
M53204	0357
M53204P	0357
M53205	0381
M53205P	0381
M53206	6427
M53206P	1197
M53207P	1329
M53208P	0462
M53209P	0487
M53210	0507
M53210P	0507
M53213P	1432
M53214P	2228
M53216P	1339
M53217P	1342
M53220	0692
M53220P	0692
M53225P	3438
M53227P	0812
M53230	0867
M53230P	0867
M53232	OEM
M53237P	3478
M53238P	0990
M53240	1018
M53240P	1018
M53241	1032
M53241P	1032
M53242	1046
M53242P	1046
M53243	1054
M53243P	1054
M53244	1066
M53244P	1066
M53245P	1074
M53247	1100
M53247P	1100
M53248	1117
M53248A	1117
M53248P	1117
M53250	0738
M53250P	0738
M53253	1177
M53253P	1177
M53260	1265
M53260P	1265
M53270	1394
M53270P	1394
M53272	1417
M53272P	1417
M53273	1164
M53273P	1164
M53274	1303
M53274P	1303
M53275	1423
M53275P	1423
M53276	1150
M53276P	1150
M53280	1527
M53280P	1527
M53283	0117
M53283P	0117
M53284P	OEM
M53285P	0370
M53286	1358
M53286P	1358
M53289P	5358
M53290	1199
M53290P	1199
M53291	0974
M53291P	0974
M53292	0828
M53292P	0828
M53293	0564
M53293P	0564
M53295	1477
M53295P	1477
M53296	1705
M53296P	1705
M53307	0936
M53307P	0936
M53321	0175
M53321P	0175
M53322P	1131
M53323P	1149
M53325P	1174
M53326P	1184
M53332P	1261
M53335P	OEM
M53345P	0614
M53350P	1484
M53351	1487
M53351P	1487
M53353P	1531
M53354P	1546
M53355P	1566
M53356P	1582
M53357P	OEM
M53358P	OEM
M53360P	1621
M53361P	1635
M53362P	1007
M53363P	1656
M53364P	0729
M53365P	1675
M53366P	0231
M53370P	1711
M53374P	1759
M53375P	1776
M53380	1818
M53380P	1818
M53381P	1831
M53382P	1845
M53385P	OEM
M53390P	1901
M53391P	1906
M53392	1910
M53392P	1910
M53393	1915
M53393P	1915
M53398P	1953
M53399P	1960
M53478P	OEM
M54401AP	OEM
M54402P	OEM
M54405P	OEM
M54406P	OEM
M54408P	OEM
M54410	OEM
M54454P	OEM
M54455L	OEM
M54456L	OEM
M54459L	5146
M54462	OEM
M54470	OEM
M54471	OEM
M54472	OEM
M54477	OEM
M54477L	OEM
M54502P	OEM
M54503P	OEM
M54504P	OEM
M54512L	OEM
M54513P	OEM
M54514AP	OEM
M54514P	OEM
M54515P	OEM
M54516P	4075
M54517P	0963
M54519P	0963
M54521P	4878
M54522P	4853
M54523P	1126
M54524P	0839
M54525P	1001
M54526P	1252
M54527P	4876
M54528P	4875
M54529P	4874
M54530P	4456
M54531P	4456
M54532P	OEM
M54533P	4872
M54534P	4870
M54535P	4869
M54536P	4868
M54537P	OEM
M54538P	OEM
M54539P	OEM
M54542L	OEM
M54543AL	OEM
M54543L	2062
M54543L-B	2062
M54543LB	2062
M54544AL	OEM
M54545L	OEM
M54548L	1927
M54549AL	OEM
M54549L	3051
M54549LA	OEM
M54560P	OEM
M54561P	OEM
M54562P	OEM
M54563P	OEM
M54564P	OEM
M54565P	OEM
M54566P	OEM
M54567P	OEM
M54568P	OEM
M54569P	OEM
M54571P	OEM
M54576FP	OEM
M54577FP	OEM
M54577P	OEM
M54578P	OEM
M54580	OEM
M54580P	OEM
M54600P	OEM
M54601P	OEM
M54602P	OEM
M54603P	OEM
M54604P	OEM
M54605P	OEM
M54610P	OEM
M54641L	OEM
M54644BL	OEM
M54644L	OEM
M54645AL	OEM
M54646P	OEM
M54648AL-B	OEM
M54648L-8	OEM
M54648L-B	OEM
M54648L-C	OEM
M54648L-D	OEM
M54649L	OEM
M54654P	OEM
M54700K	OEM
M54700P	OEM
M54700S	OEM
M54730K	OEM
M54730P	OEM
M54730P-2	OEM
M54730S	OEM
M54740AP	OEM
M54740AS	OEM
M54741AP	OEM
M54741AS	OEM
M54802P	OEM
M54817P	OEM
M54818L	OEM
M54819L	OEM
M54832P	OEM
M54872L	OEM
M54873P	OEM
M54874P	OEM
M54876-141P	OEM
M54899	OEM
M54899P	OEM
M54940P	OEM
M54955P	OEM
M54955P-A	OEM
M56529AP	OEM
M56529P	OEM
M58321	OEM
M58333-XXXP	OEM
M58334-XXXP	OEM
M58371	OEM
M58412P	OEM
M58413P	OEM
M58418P	4050
M58434P	OEM
M58435P	OEM
M58436-001P	OEM
M58437-001P	OEM
M58472P	1164
M58473P	OEM
M58476-141P	OEM
M58478P	4050
M58479P	OEM
M58480P	OEM
M58481P	OEM
M58482P	OEM
M58483P	OEM
M58484P	OEM
M58485P	2852
M58487P	OEM
M58609-04P	OEM
M58609-04S	OEM
M58609-09P	OEM
M58609-09S	OEM
M58630P	OEM
M58653P	OEM
M58657P	OEM
M58658	OEM
M58658P	OEM
M58659P	OEM
M58725P	1887
M58725P-15	OEM
M58725S-15	OEM
M58731-001S	OEM
M58735-064P	OEM
M58735-065P	OEM
M58735XXXP	OEM
M58741P	OEM
M58839-606P	OEM
M58839-608P	OEM
M58839-608SP	OEM
M58839-609P	OEM
M58839-622SP	OEM
M58839-623P	OEM
M58839-642P	OEM
M58839-660P	OEM
M58839-670P	OEM
M58872P	OEM
M58981P30	OEM
M58981P45	OEM
M58981S-45	OEM
M60002A	OEM
M60002A-0107	OEM
M60002A-0107SP	OEM
M60025-1001SP	OEM
M60032-1006FP	OEM
M60201	OEM
M60306	OEM
M60307	OEM
M61048	OEM
M61203L	OEM
M62359P	OEM
M64100BA	OEM
M64100BB086	OEM
M64100KB	OEM
M64104CA	OEM
M64200CA	OEM
M66310P	OEM
M66320P	OEM
M67154SL	OEM
M73003	OEM
M75205-1	0084
M75205-2	0529
M75516-2	0050
M75516-2P	0050
M75516-2R	0050
M-75517-1	0211
M75517-1	0004
M75517-2	0004
M75537-2	0841
M-75543-1	0178
M75543-1	0042
M75545-1	0007
M75547-1	0144
M75547-2	0144
M75561-7	0004
M75561-8	0126
M75561-10RK	0843
M75561-17	0126
M75561-23	0349
M75561-23RN	0349
M81461B-12RS-PSZ	OEM
M100412	0015
M100449	1024
M105064	0469
M105330	1024
M106379	0015
M109474	0196
M112826	0015
M138841-180	OEM
M138841-180J	OEM
M442256AJ-10	OEM
M449192	OEM
M450072	OEM
M467857	OEM
M468487-8545H	OEM
M501121P	OEM
M502030SP	OEM
M506868	OEM
M509040	OEM
M514940	OEM
M755162-P	0050
M755162-R	0050
M840176P	OEM
M840176P-SH	OEM
M881464-12	OEM
M8534992	0196
M8534992-2	0196
M50439517S	OEM
M50560198P	OEM
M69907209V1	OEM
MA00017	OEM
MA00087CP	OEM
MA00088CP	OEM
MA00287	OEM
MA00318CP	OEM
MA00357CP	OEM
MA00357MD	OEM
MA0401	0126
MA0402	0126
MA0404	0037
MA0404-1	0150
MA0404-2	0150
MA0411	0150
MA0412	0527
MA0413	0150
MA0414	0037
MA03080	OEM
MA1	0050
MA1Z	0015
MA2	0015
MA3.0EB	0118
MA4B300	OEM
MA4C11	OEM
MA4C100	OEM
MA4C100B	OEM
MA4C100C	OEM
MA4C102	OEM
MA4C102B	OEM
MA4C102C	OEM
MA4C103	OEM
MA4C103B	OEM
MA4C103C	OEM
MA4C104	OEM
MA4C104B	OEM
MA4C104C	OEM
MA4C105	OEM
MA4C105B	OEM
MA4C105C	OEM
MA4C106	OEM
MA4C106B	OEM
MA4C106C	OEM
MA4C107	OEM
MA4C107B	OEM
MA4C107C	OEM
MA4C108	OEM
MA4C108B	OEM
MA4C108C	OEM
MA4C109	OEM
MA4C109B	OEM
MA4C109C	OEM
MA4C110	OEM
MA4C110B	OEM
MA4C110C	OEM
MA4C111	OEM
MA4C111B	OEM
MA4C111C	OEM
MA4C112	OEM
MA4C112B	OEM
MA4C112C	OEM
MA4C113	OEM
MA4C113B	OEM
MA4C113C	OEM
MA4C114B	OEM
MA4C114C	OEM
MA4C157	OEM
MA4C157B	OEM
MA4C157C	OEM
MA4C158	OEM
MA4C158B	OEM
MA4C158C	OEM
MA4C250D	OEM
MA4C250H	OEM
MA4C251D	OEM
MA4C251H	OEM
MA4C252D	OEM
MA4C252H	OEM
MA4C253D	OEM
MA4C253H	OEM
MA4C254D	OEM
MA4C254H	OEM
MA4C255D	OEM
MA4C255H	OEM
MA4C256D	OEM
MA4C256H	OEM
MA4C257D	OEM
MA4C257H	OEM
MA4C258D	OEM
MA4C258H	OEM
MA4C260D	OEM
MA4C260H	OEM
MA4C261D	OEM
MA4C261H	OEM
MA4C262D	OEM
MA4C262H	OEM
MA4C263D	OEM
MA4C263H	OEM
MA4C264H	OEM
MA4C265D	OEM
MA4C265H	OEM
MA4C266D	OEM
MA4C266H	OEM
MA4C267D	OEM
MA4C267H	OEM
MA4C268D	OEM
MA4C268H	OEM
MA4C270D	OEM
MA4C270H	OEM
MA4C271D	OEM
MA4C271H	OEM
MA4C272D	OEM
MA4C272H	OEM
MA4C273D	OEM
MA4C273H	OEM
MA4C274D	OEM
MA4C274H	OEM
MA4C275D	OEM
MA4C275H	OEM
MA4C276D	OEM
MA4C276H	OEM
MA4C277D7D	OEM
MA4C277H	OEM
MA4C278D	OEM
MA4C278H	OEM
MA4C400	OEM
MA4C400A	OEM
MA4C400B	OEM
MA4C400C	OEM
MA4C400D	OEM
MA4C400D1	OEM
MA4C400D2	OEM
MA4C401	OEM
MA4C401A	OEM
MA4C401B	OEM
MA4C401C	OEM
MA4C401D	OEM
MA4C401D1	OEM
MA4C401D2	OEM
MA4C402	OEM
MA4C402A	OEM
MA4C402B	OEM
MA4C402C	OEM
MA4C402D	OEM
MA4C402D1	OEM
MA4C402D2	OEM
MA4C403	OEM
MA4C403A	OEM
MA4C403B	OEM
MA4C403C	OEM
MA4C403D	OEM
MA4C403D1	OEM
MA4C403D2	OEM
MA4C404	OEM
MA4C404A	OEM
MA4C404B	OEM
MA4C404C	OEM
MA4C404D	OEM
MA4C404D1	OEM
MA4C404D2	OEM
MA4C405	OEM
MA4C405A	OEM
MA4C405B	OEM
MA4C405C	OEM
MA4C405D	OEM
MA4C405D1	OEM
MA4C405D2	OEM
MA4C550	OEM
MA4C550B	OEM
MA4C550C	OEM
MA4C551	OEM
MA4C551B	OEM
MA4C551C	OEM
MA4C552	OEM
MA4C552B	OEM
MA4C552C	OEM
MA4C553	OEM
MA4C553B	OEM
MA4C553C	OEM
MA4C554	OEM
MA4C554B	OEM
MA4C554C	OEM
MA4C555	OEM
MA4C555B	OEM
MA4C555C	OEM
MA4C556	OEM
MA4C556B	OEM
MA4C556C	OEM
MA4C557	OEM
MA4C557B	OEM
MA4C557C	OEM
MA4C558	OEM
MA4C558B	OEM
MA4C558C	OEM
MA4C559	OEM
MA4C559B	OEM

If replacement code is OEM, contact original manufacturer for replacement.

459

DEVICE TYPE	REPL CODE
MA4C559C	OEM
MA4C560	OEM
MA4C560B	OEM
MA4C560C	OEM
MA4C561	OEM
MA4C561B	OEM
MA4C561C	OEM
MA4C562B	OEM
MA4C562C	OEM
MA4C563B	OEM
MA4C563C	OEM
MA4C700D	OEM
MA4C700H	OEM
MA4C701D	OEM
MA4C701H	OEM
MA4C702D	OEM
MA4C702H	OEM
MA4C703D	OEM
MA4C703H	OEM
MA4C704D	OEM
MA4C704H	OEM
MA4C705D	OEM
MA4C705H	OEM
MA4C710D	OEM
MA4C710H	OEM
MA4C711D	OEM
MA4C711H	OEM
MA4C712D	OEM
MA4C712H	OEM
MA4C713D	OEM
MA4C713H	OEM
MA4C714D	OEM
MA4C714H	OEM
MA4C715D	OEM
MA4C715H	OEM
MA4C720D	OEM
MA4C720H	OEM
MA4C721D	OEM
MA4C721H	OEM
MA4C722D	OEM
MA4C722H	OEM
MA4C723D	OEM
MA4C723H	OEM
MA4C724D	OEM
MA4C724H	OEM
MA4C725D	OEM
MA4C725H	OEM
MA4C850	OEM
MA4C850A	OEM
MA4C850B	OEM
MA4C850C	OEM
MA4C850D	OEM
MA4C850D1	OEM
MA4C850D2	OEM
MA4C851	OEM
MA4C851A	OEM
MA4C851B	OEM
MA4C851C	OEM
MA4C851D	OEM
MA4C851D1	OEM
MA4C851D2	OEM
MA4C852	OEM
MA4C852A	OEM
MA4C852B	OEM
MA4C852C	OEM
MA4C852D	OEM
MA4C852D1	OEM
MA4C852D2	OEM
MA4C853	OEM
MA4C853A	OEM
MA4C853B	OEM
MA4C853C	OEM
MA4C853D	OEM
MA4C853D1	OEM
MA4C853D2	OEM
MA4E003	OEM
MA4E004	OEM
MA4E005	OEM
MA4E180	OEM
MA4E181	OEM
MA4E182	OEM
MA4E183	OEM
MA4E184	OEM
MA4E185	OEM
MA4E186	OEM
MA4E187	OEM
MA4E188	OEM
MA4E189	OEM
MA4E190	OEM
MA4E191	OEM
MA4E200	OEM
MA4E201	OEM
MA4E202	OEM
MA4E203	OEM
MA4E204	OEM
MA4E205	OEM
MA4E206	OEM
MA4E207	OEM
MA4E208	OEM
MA4P101	OEM
MA4P102	OEM
MA4P103-30	OEM
MA4P202-30	OEM
MA4P203-30	OEM
MA4P303-30	OEM
MA4P404-30	OEM
MA4P504-30	OEM
MA4P505-30	OEM
MA4P506-30	OEM
MA4P604-30	OEM
MA4P606-30	OEM
MA4P607	OEM
MA4P608	OEM
MA4P709	OEM
MA4c264D	OEM
MA5	OEM
MA6Y	OEM
MA8	0143
MA-10	0396
MA10	0396
MA11	OEM
MA13	OEM
MA15	OEM
MA17	OEM
MA18	OEM
MA20	OEM
MA21	0143
MA23	3638
MA23(B)	0143
MA23A	3638
MA-23B	3638
MA23B	3638
MA25	6951
MA25A	3638
MA25B	OEM
MA-26	0139
MA26	0139
MA-26-1	0139
MA26-2	0139
MA26A	0139
MA26G	0139
MA26T	0120
MA26T-A	0120
MA26TA	0120
MA26TB	OEM
MA26TO	0120
MA26TO-A	0120
MA26TOA	0120
MA26TOA-B	0120
MA26TO-B	0120
MA26W	0120
MA26W0	0120
MA26W0-B	0120
MA26W0B	0120
MA26WA	0139
MA26W-B	0120
MA26WB	0120
MA26WD	0120
MA26WO	0120
MA26WO-A	0120
MA26WO-B	0120
MA26WOB	0120
MA26Y	OEM
MA27	0339
MA27-A	0120
MA27-B	0120
MA27-C	0120
MA27A	6407
MA27B	0120
MA27Q-A	0120
MA27QA	OEM
MA27Q-B	0120
MA27T	0339
MA27T-A	0339
MA27TA	0339
MA27T-ATA	0339
MA27T-B	0339
MA27TB	0339
MA27TBTA	0339
MA27W	0120
MA27W-A	0120
MA27WA	0339
MA27WATA	0339
MA27WATP	0120
MA27W-B	0120
MA27WB	0339
MA27WBTA	0339
MA28	OEM
MA28-A	OEM
MA28-B	OEM
MA28T-A	OEM
MA28T-B	OEM
MA28W-A	OEM
MA29-A	OEM
MA29-B	OEM
MA29T-A	OEM
MA29TA	OEM
MA29T-B	OEM
MA29TB	0339
MA29W-A	OEM
MA29W-B	OEM
MA29WB	OEM
MA29WBA	OEM
MA29W-BTA	OEM
MA30	OEM
MA30S	OEM
MA32	OEM
MA40	OEM
MA41	OEM
MA47	0143
MA48	OEM
MA49	OEM
MA50	0015
MA51A	0143
MA53	2496
MA56	0133
MA56T	OEM
MA57	0124
MA60	2621
MA61	2704
MA62	5776
MA72	2496
MA73	2496
MA74HC4053F	OEM
MA77	OEM
MA80	2621
MA90	0143
MA100	0279
MA101	0015
MA102	0015
MA102A	OEM
MA102B	OEM
MA102C	OEM
MA102E	OEM
MA102F	OEM
MA102G	OEM
MA102H	OEM
MA102I	OEM
MA102J	OEM
MA103	0015
MA106	OEM
MA-110	0299
MA110	OEM
MA111	0023
MA1110	OEM
MA112	0211
MA113	0211
MA114	0211
MA115	0211
MA116	0211
MA117	0211
MA120	OEM
MA121	OEM
MA150	0133
MA150DD	0133
MA150FV	0124
MA150LF	0124
MA150TA	0124
MA150TA5	0133
MA150TP	0133
MA150TR	OEM
MA150WK	0124
MA151A	0124
MA151A(MA)	OEM
MA151K	3703
MA151K(MH)	3703
MA151KPSK	OEM
MA151K-TW	0124
MA151K-W	OEM
MA151WA	0897
MA151WA(MN)	0897
MA151WK	0901
MA151WK(MT)	OEM
MA151WKPSK	5387
MA152A	OEM
MA152K	3703
MA152WA	0897
MA152WA-TX	OEM
MA152WK	0901
MA152WK(MU)	0901
MA152WKTA	OEM
MA152WK-TW	0901
MA152WKTX	0901
MA153	0133
MA153(MC)	0133
MA153A	OEM
MA153TW	OEM
MA154	0689
MA154WA	2189
MA154WE	OEM
MA154WK	0689
MA155WA	2189
MA155WK	3163
MA156	1083
MA157	OEM
MA157A	OEM
MA158	3841
MA159	0124
MA159A	OEM
MA160	OEM
MA160A	OEM
MA160MID	OEM
MA-161	0124
MA161	0133
MA161C	0124
MA161TA	0124
MA161TA5	0124
MA161TP	0124
MA162	0124
MA162A	0124
MA162LF	0124
MA162TA5	0124
MA162TP	0124
MA165	0124
MA165-T2	0124
MA165-Y	0124
MA165SAN	OEM
MA165TA	0124
MA165TA5	0124
MA165TA5-VT	0124
MA165.SAN	0124
MA166	0124
MA166(C)	0124
MA166C	0124
MA167	0124
MA167A	0124
MA167TA	OEM
MA170	0124
MA171	0124
MA171TA5	0124
MA175WA	2189
MA175WK	0689
MA176WA	2189
MA176WK	0689
MA178	0124
MA179	0124
MA180	OEM
MA181	0023
MA182	0023
MA183	0023
MA184	0023
MA185	0023
MA186	0023
MA188	1082
MA190	0124
MA190WK	OEM
MA194	OEM
MA195	0124
MA195-5(TA5)	OEM
MA199	OEM
MA203	0023
MA203A	0017
MA206	0004
MA207CP	OEM
MA208	OEM
MA209	1272
MA211	0015
MA211S	1285
MA212	OEM
MA212A	OEM
MA212B	OEM
MA212C	OEM
MA212D	OEM
MA214	OEM
MA214B	OEM
MA214C	OEM
MA214D	OEM
MA215	0015
MA215A	1285
MA217	OEM
MA217A	OEM
MA217B	OEM
MA217C	OEM
MA218	OEM
MA219G	OEM
MA221	OEM
MA221A	OEM
MA221B	OEM
MA221C	OEM
MA221D	OEM
MA222	OEM
MA223	OEM
MA231	OEM
MA231A	OEM
MA231B	OEM
MA232	OEM
MA232A	OEM
MA232B	OEM
MA233	OEM
MA238	0279
MA239	OEM
MA239A	OEM
MA239B	OEM
MA240	0004
MA240A	OEM
MA240B	OEM
MA240C	OEM
MA241	OEM
MA242	0015
MA242BC	0087
MA242C	0015
MA242CR	OEM
MA242R	OEM
MA242RC	0087
MA245	OEM
MA246	OEM
MA246A	OEM
MA249	OEM
MA250	OEM
MA251	OEM
MA252	OEM
MA253	OEM
MA257	OEM
MA257T	OEM
MA258	OEM
MA259	OEM
MA260	0339
MA261	OEM
MA262	OEM
MA263	OEM
MA264	OEM
MA265	OEM
MA266	OEM
MA270	OEM
MA271	OEM
MA272	OEM
MA273	OEM
MA274	OEM
MA277	OEM
MA277-A	OEM
MA278	OEM
MA279	OEM
MA281	OEM
MA285	OEM
MA286	0279
MA287	0279
MA288	0279
MA291	OEM
MA293	OEM
MA294	OEM
MA300CD	OEM
MA301	0715
MA302	0623
MA303	0030
MA308CD	OEM
MA311	0030
MA319	6408
MA320	0715
MA320B	0715
MA320B2	0715
MA320G1	0715
MA320G1NR	0715
MA320GIVR	OEM
MA321	OEM
MA322	OEM
MA322-PM	OEM
MA323	OEM
MA324	1023
MA325	1023
MA325B	1023
MA325G	1023
MA326	OEM
MA327	OEM
MA328	OEM
MA329	OEM
MA330	0005
MA332	0623
MA332A	OEM
MA332B	OEM
MA332C	OEM
MA332CP	OEM
MA333CP	OEM
MA334	OEM
MA335	OEM
MA336CP	OEM
MA337	OEM
MA339CP	OEM
MA340	0549
MA341	OEM
MA342	OEM
MA342-B	OEM
MA342-M	OEM
MA342CP	OEM
MA345	6410
MA345B	OEM
MA350	0023
MA351	0023
MA356	5901
MA370	OEM
MA393	0004
MA393A	0004
MA393B	0004
MA393C	0004
MA393E	0004
MA393G	0004
MA393R	0004
MA400	OEM
MA401	OEM
MA404A1	OEM
MA404B1	OEM
MA404C1	OEM
MA404D1	OEM
MA404E1	OEM
MA404F1	OEM
MA404G1	OEM
MA408A	OEM
MA408B	OEM
MA412	OEM
MA414	OEM
MA417	OEM
MA418	OEM
MA418A	OEM
MA418B	OEM
MA419	OEM
MA419A	OEM
MA421A	OEM
MA421B	OEM
MA423A	OEM
MA425	OEM
MA428	OEM
MA432	OEM
MA433	0911
MA433D2	OEM
MA435	OEM
MA437	OEM
MA439	OEM
MA441	OEM
MA443	OEM
MA443A	OEM
MA443B	OEM
MA444	OEM
MA444A	OEM
MA444B	OEM
MA444C	OEM
MA444D	OEM
MA445	OEM
MA445A	OEM
MA445B	OEM
MA449B	OEM
MA449C	OEM
MA449D	OEM
MA449E	OEM
MA449F	OEM
MA450A	OEM
MA450B	OEM
MA450C	OEM
MA450D	OEM
MA450E	OEM
MA450F	OEM
MA450G	OEM
MA450H	OEM
MA451A	OEM
MA451B	OEM
MA451C	OEM
MA451D	OEM
MA451E	OEM
MA451F	OEM
MA452	OEM
MA452A	OEM
MA452B	OEM
MA458B	OEM
MA458C	OEM
MA458D	OEM
MA458E	OEM
MA458F	OEM
MA459B	OEM
MA459C	OEM
MA459D	OEM
MA459F	OEM
MA460A	OEM
MA460B	OEM
MA460C	OEM
MA460D	OEM
MA460E	OEM
MA460F	OEM
MA460G	OEM
MA460H	OEM
MA461	OEM
MA461A	OEM
MA461B	OEM
MA490	OEM
MA490A	OEM
MA490B	OEM
MA490C	OEM
MA490D	OEM
MA490E	OEM
MA490F	OEM
MA490G	OEM
MA490H	OEM
MA491	OEM
MA491A	OEM
MA491B	OEM
MA491C	OEM
MA491D	OEM
MA491E	OEM
MA491F	OEM
MA491G	OEM
MA491H	OEM
MA492C	OEM
MA492D	OEM
MA492E	OEM
MA492F	OEM
MA492G	OEM
MA493B	OEM
MA493C	OEM
MA494	OEM
MA494A	OEM
MA494B	OEM
MA494C	OEM
MA494D	OEM
MA500CP	OEM
MA522	OEM
MA522VT	OEM
MA550	OEM
MA551	3703
MA553	OEM
MA615	1780
MA619	0201
MA622	0286
MA625	0286
MA630	0374
MA649	1227
MA650	1227
MA651	2219
MA653	0966
MA654	0966
MA655	4409
MA661	2219
MA669	1227
MA670	1227
MA671	2219
MA673	0966
MA674	0966
MA675	4409
MA700	0335
MA700A	0335
MA700ATA	OEM
MA701	OEM
MA701A	OEM
MA702	OEM
MA704	OEM
MA704A	OEM
MA709AMJ	OEM
MA709AMJG	OEM
MA709CJ	OEM
MA709CJG	OEM
MA709CN	OEM
MA709CP	OEM
MA709MJ	OEM
MA709MP	OEM
MA710	OEM
MA711	OEM
MA711CJ	OEM
MA711CN	OEM
MA711MJ	OEM
MA715	1780
MA720	0715
MA721TW	OEM
MA723CJ	OEM
MA723CN	OEM
MA723MJ	OEM
MA723MN	OEM
MA723TA	OEM
MA725	0286
MA730	0286
MA733CJ	OEM
MA733CN	OEM
MA733MN	OEM
MA741	0308
MA741CJ	OEM
MA741CJG	OEM
MA741CN	OEM
MA741CP	OEM
MA741MJ	OEM
MA741MJG	OEM
MA741MP	OEM
MA747-1CJ	OEM
MA747-1CN	OEM
MA747-1MJ	OEM
MA747CJ	OEM
MA747CN	OEM
MA747MJ	OEM
MA748CJ	OEM
MA748CJG	OEM
MA748CL	OEM
MA748CN	OEM
MA748CP	OEM
MA748MJ	OEM
MA748MJG	OEM
MA748MP	OEM
MA767	0696
MA767PC	0696
MA790	0143
MA815	0004
MA840	OEM
MA856	0124
MA856TV	0124
MA858	0124
MA859	0124
MA860	OEM
MA862	OEM
MA881	0004
MA882	0004
MA883	0004
MA884	0004
MA885	0004
MA886	0004
MA887	0004
MA888	0004
MA889	0004
MA890	0004
MA891	0004
MA892	0004
MA893	0004
MA894	0211
MA895	0211
MA896	0211
MA897	0211
MA898	0211
MA899	0211
MA-900	0143
MA900	0211
MA901	0279
MA902	0004
MA903	0004
MA904	0004
MA909	0004
MA910	0004
MA1024	1266
MA1027	0755
MA1028L	0672
MA1030	0118
MA1030H	OEM
MA1030M	0118
MA1033	0296
MA1033L	0296
MA1036	0372
MA1036H	OEM
MA1039	0036
MA1039L	0036
MA1043	0054
MA1043H	0274
MA1043M	0274
MA1047	0446
MA1047A	0140
MA1047H	0140
MA1047L	OEM
MA1047M	0140
MA1051	0041
MA1051H	0041
MA1051HTV	0041
MA1051L	0041
MA1051M	0582
MA1051TP	0041
MA1056	0157
MA1056H	0157
MA1056M	0157
MA1062	0466
MA1062H	0466
MA1062LF	0466
MA1062LM	0466
MA1062M	0466
MA1068	0062

460 If replacement code is OEM, contact original manufacturer for replacement.

DEVICE TYPE	REPL CODE
MA1068H	0062
MA1068L	0062
MA1068T	0062
MA1075	0077
MA1075M	0077
MA1075TA	0077
MA1082	0244
MA1082L	0165
MA1082M	0165
MA1091	0057
MA1091-M	0057
MA1091M	0057
MA1100	0064
MA1100H	0064
MA1100M	0248
MA1110	0181
MA1110(DIODE)	0023
MA1110M	0181
MA1110TA	0181
MA1114	5094
MA1120	0999
MA1120-L	0052
MA1120A	0052
MA1120L	0052
MA1120M	0052
MA1125	0167
MA1128	0167
MA1130	0053
MA1130H	0053
MA1130LF	0053
MA1130M	0053
MA1130MH	0053
MA1140	OEM
MA1140-M	0873
MA1150	0681
MA1150A	0681
MA1150M	OEM
MA1150TA	0681
MA1160	0440
MA1180	0371
MA1180M	OEM
MA1190	5158
MA1200	0695
MA1220	0700
MA1240	0489
MA1270	0450
MA1270H	0450
MA1300	0053
MA1300M	0195
MA1306W	2247
MA1318	0004
MA1330	0166
MA1330M	0195
MA1360	0010
MA1360H	5557
MA1360M	OEM
MA1390H	OEM
MA1420(M)	OEM
MA1501TP	0041
MA1545	OEM
MA1700	0211
MA1701	0080
MA1701(DIODE)	0102
MA1702	0164
MA1702(DIODE)	0133
MA1703	0211
MA1703(DIODE)	0133
MA1704	0211
MA1704(DIODE)	0124
MA1705	0211
MA1706	0211
MA1707	0211
MA1708	0211
MA2043	0528
MA2051	0162
MA2056	0157
MA2062	0631
MA2068	0025
MA2075	0644
MA2082	0244
MA2091	0012
MA2100	0170
MA2100B	0170
MA2110	0313
MA2110BLF	OEM
MA2120	0137
MA2130	0361
MA2150	0002
MA2160	0416
MA2160B	0416
MA2169	OEM
MA2180	0490
MA2180A	OEM
MA2180B	OEM
MA2200	0526
MA2220	0560
MA2240	0398
MA2270	0436
MA2300	0195
MA2330	0039
MA2360	0814
MA2390	0346
MA2430	0925
MA2470	0993
MA2510	0497
MA2560	0863
MA2801	OEM
MA2802	OEM
MA2803	OEM

DEVICE TYPE	REPL CODE
MA2804	OEM
MA2805	OEM
MA2807	OEM
MA2808	OEM
MA2810	OEM
MA2811	OEM
MA2812	OEM
MA2813	OEM
MA2820	OEM
MA2822	OEM
MA2823	OEM
MA2824	OEM
MA3024	OEM
MA3027	OEM
MA3030	OEM
MA3033	OEM
MA3036	OEM
MA3039	OEM
MA3043	OEM
MA3047	OEM
MA3047-L	OEM
MA3047H	OEM
MA3047L	OEM
MA3047M	OEM
MA3051	OEM
MA3051-H	OEM
MA3051H	OEM
MA3051L	OEM
MA3056	OEM
MA3056L	OEM
MA3056M	OEM
MA3062	0466
MA3062-M	OEM
MA3062L	0466
MA3062M	OEM
MA3062TW	OEM
MA3065	0167
MA3068	OEM
MA3068H	OEM
MA3068L	OEM
MA3068M	OEM
MA3075	OEM
MA3075L	OEM
MA3075M	OEM
MA3082	OEM
MA3082L	OEM
MA3082M	OEM
MA3091	0057
MA3091L	0057
MA3091M	OEM
MA3100	OEM
MA3100(M)	OEM
MA3100L	OEM
MA3100M	OEM
MA3110	OEM
MA3110L	OEM
MA3120	OEM
MA3120L	0052
MA3130	OEM
MA3130L	OEM
MA3150	0681
MA3150L	0681
MA3160	OEM
MA3160L	OEM
MA3180	OEM
MA3180L	OEM
MA3200	OEM
MA3200L	OEM
MA3220	OEM
MA3220L	OEM
MA3227	OEM
MA3228	OEM
MA3229	OEM
MA3230	OEM
MA3231	OEM
MA3232	OEM
MA3233	OEM
MA3234	OEM
MA3240	OEM
MA3240L	OEM
MA3240M	OEM
MA3270	OEM
MA3300	OEM
MA3330	OEM
MA3360	OEM
MA4011B	OEM
MA4011C	OEM
MA4011D	OEM
MA4019B	OEM
MA4019C	OEM
MA4019D	OEM
MA4019E	OEM
MA4019F	OEM
MA4019G	OEM
MA4024	1266
MA4027	0755
MA4027M	5081
MA4027MTA	5081
MA4030	0118
MA4030(M)	OEM
MA4030(M)-Y	OEM
MA4030-M	0118
MA4030M	0118
MA4030MTA	OEM
MA4033	0296
MA4033L	OEM
MA4033MTA	OEM
MA4034	OEM
MA4035	OEM

DEVICE TYPE	REPL CODE
MA4036	0372
MA4036-M	0372
MA4036L	OEM
MA4036M	0372
MA4037	OEM
MA4038	OEM
MA4039	0036
MA4039H	OEM
MA4039HTA	OEM
MA4041A	OEM
MA4041B	OEM
MA4041C	OEM
MA4041D	OEM
MA4041E	OEM
MA4041F	OEM
MA4041G	OEM
MA4042	OEM
MA4042A	OEM
MA4042A1	OEM
MA4042A2	OEM
MA4042B	OEM
MA4042B1	OEM
MA4042C	OEM
MA4042D	OEM
MA4042D1	OEM
MA4042E	OEM
MA4042E1	OEM
MA4042F	OEM
MA4042F1	OEM
MA4042G	OEM
MA4042G1	OEM
MA4043	0274
MA4043(H)	0274
MA4043(M)	OEM
MA4043(M)-Y	OEM
MA4043-H	0274
MA4043H	5142
MA4043M	0274
MA4044A	OEM
MA4044A1	OEM
MA4044A2	OEM
MA4044B	OEM
MA4044B1	OEM
MA4044B2	OEM
MA4044C	OEM
MA4044C1	OEM
MA4044D	OEM
MA4044D1	OEM
MA4044E	OEM
MA4044E1	OEM
MA4044F	OEM
MA4044F1	OEM
MA4044G	OEM
MA4044G1	OEM
MA4045A	OEM
MA4045A1	OEM
MA4045A2	OEM
MA4045B	OEM
MA4045B1	OEM
MA4045B2	OEM
MA4045C	OEM
MA4045C1	OEM
MA4045D	OEM
MA4045D1	OEM
MA4045E	OEM
MA4045E1	OEM
MA4045F	OEM
MA4045F1	OEM
MA4045G	OEM
MA4046A	OEM
MA4046A1	OEM
MA4046B	OEM
MA4046B1	OEM
MA4046C	OEM
MA4046C1	OEM
MA4046D	OEM
MA4046D1	OEM
MA4046E	OEM
MA4046E1	OEM
MA4046F	OEM
MA4046F1	OEM
MA4046G	OEM
MA4047	0140
MA4047(H)	0140
MA4047(H)-Y	0140
MA4047(M)	0140
MA4047(M)-Y	0140
MA4047-H	0140
MA4047A	OEM
MA4047A1	OEM
MA4047B	OEM
MA4047B1	OEM
MA4047C	OEM
MA4047C1	OEM
MA4047D	OEM
MA4047D1	OEM
MA4047E	OEM
MA4047E1	OEM
MA4047F	OEM
MA4047F1	OEM
MA4047G	OEM
MA4047G1	OEM
MA4047H	0140
MA4047L	0140
MA4047M	0140
MA4047MTA	0140
MA4048A	OEM
MA4048A1	OEM
MA4048B	OEM

DEVICE TYPE	REPL CODE
MA4048B1	OEM
MA4048C	OEM
MA4048C1	OEM
MA4048D	OEM
MA4048D1	OEM
MA4048E	OEM
MA4048E1	OEM
MA4048F	OEM
MA4048G	OEM
MA4051	0041
MA4051(H)	0041
MA4051(H)-Y	0041
MA4051(L)	OEM
MA4051(L)-Y	OEM
MA4051(M)	0041
MA4051(M)-T2	OEM
MA4051-M	0582
MA4051A	OEM
MA4051A1	OEM
MA4051A2	OEM
MA4051AA	OEM
MA4051AA1	OEM
MA4051B	OEM
MA4051B1	OEM
MA4051C	OEM
MA4051C1	OEM
MA4051D	OEM
MA4051D1	OEM
MA4051E	OEM
MA4051E1	OEM
MA4051F	OEM
MA4051F1	OEM
MA4051G	OEM
MA4051G1	OEM
MA4051H	0041
MA4051L	OEM
MA4051LM	0041
MA4051M	0041
MA4051MTA	0041
MA4051N-M	0582
MA4052A	OEM
MA4052A1	OEM
MA4052A2	OEM
MA4052AA	OEM
MA4052AA1	OEM
MA4052B	OEM
MA4052B1	OEM
MA4052C	OEM
MA4052C1	OEM
MA4052D	OEM
MA4052D1	OEM
MA4052E	OEM
MA4052E1	OEM
MA4052F	OEM
MA4052F1	OEM
MA4052G	OEM
MA4052G1	OEM
MA4054A	OEM
MA4054A1	OEM
MA4054A2	OEM
MA4054AA	OEM
MA4054AA1	OEM
MA4054AA2	OEM
MA4054B	OEM
MA4054B1	OEM
MA4054B2	OEM
MA4054C	OEM
MA4054C1	OEM
MA4054D	OEM
MA4054D1	OEM
MA4054E	OEM
MA4054E1	OEM
MA4054F	OEM
MA4054F1	OEM
MA4054G	OEM
MA4054G1	OEM
MA4055A	OEM
MA4055A1	OEM
MA4055A2	OEM
MA4055AA	OEM
MA4055AA1	OEM
MA4055AA2	OEM
MA4055B	OEM
MA4055B1	OEM
MA4055B2	OEM
MA4055C	OEM
MA4055C1	OEM
MA4055D	OEM
MA4055D1	OEM
MA4055E	OEM
MA4055E1	OEM
MA4055F	OEM
MA4055F1	OEM
MA4055G	OEM
MA4056	0253
MA4056(M)	0253
MA4056(M)-T2	0253
MA4056(M)-Y	0253
MA4056-M	0253
MA4056A	OEM
MA4056B	OEM
MA4056B1	OEM
MA4056C	OEM
MA4056C1	OEM
MA4056D	OEM
MA4056D1	OEM
MA4056E	OEM
MA4056E1	OEM
MA4056F	OEM

DEVICE TYPE	REPL CODE
MA4056F1	OEM
MA4056G	OEM
MA4056H	0253
MA4056MTA	OEM
MA4057A	OEM
MA4057A1	OEM
MA4057B	OEM
MA4057B1	OEM
MA4057C	OEM
MA4057C1	OEM
MA4057D	OEM
MA4057D1	OEM
MA4057E	OEM
MA4057E1	OEM
MA4057F	OEM
MA4057F1	OEM
MA4057G	OEM
MA4057G1	OEM
MA4058A	OEM
MA4058A1	OEM
MA4058B	OEM
MA4058B1	OEM
MA4058C	OEM
MA4058C1	OEM
MA4058D	OEM
MA4058D1	OEM
MA4058E	OEM
MA4058E1	OEM
MA4058F	OEM
MA4058F1	OEM
MA4058G	OEM
MA4060A	OEM
MA4060AA	OEM
MA4060B	OEM
MA4060C	OEM
MA4060D	OEM
MA4061A	OEM
MA4061AA	OEM
MA4061B	OEM
MA4061C	OEM
MA4061D	OEM
MA4062	0466
MA4062(H)	0466
MA4062(H)-T2	0466
MA4062(L)	0999
MA4062(M)	0999
MA4062(M)-T2	0466
MA4062(M)-Y	0999
MA4062-L	0466
MA4062A	OEM
MA4062B	OEM
MA4062C	OEM
MA4062D	OEM
MA4062H	0466
MA4062HTA	0466
MA4062L	0091
MA4062LTA	OEM
MA4062M	0466
MA4062MTA	OEM
MA4062N-H	OEM
MA4063	OEM
MA4064	OEM
MA4065	OEM
MA4068	0062
MA4068(L)	0062
MA4068(L)-T2	0062
MA4068(L)-Y	0062
MA4068(M)	0062
MA4068(M)-T2	0062
MA4068(M)-Y	0062
MA4068(N)	0062
MA4068(N)C1-T2	0062
MA4068(N)C1-Y	0062
MA4068(N)V1	0062
MA4068(N)V1-Y	0062
MA4068-M	0062
MA4068-MM	0062
MA4068H	0062
MA4068L	0062
MA4068M	0062
MA4071B	OEM
MA4072B	OEM
MA4075	0077
MA4075(M)	0077
MA4075-H	0077
MA4075-M	0077
MA4075H	0077
MA4075L	0077
MA4075M	0077
MA4082	0165
MA4082(M)	OEM
MA4082(M)-Y	OEM
MA4082-H	0165
MA4082-L	4245
MA4082-M	0165
MA4082L	OEM
MA4082M	0165
MA4082MTA	OEM
MA4083	OEM
MA4084	OEM
MA4085	OEM
MA4086	OEM
MA4091	0057
MA4091(M)	0057
MA4091(M)-T2	0057
MA4091(M)-Y	0057
MA4091-L	0057
MA4091-M	0057
MA4091L	0057

DEVICE TYPE	REPL CODE
MA4091M	0057
MA4091N-H	OEM
MA4091N-L	0057
MA4091N-M	0057
MA4098AA	OEM
MA4099D	OEM
MA4100	0064
MA4100(M)	0064
MA4100(M)-T2	0064
MA4100(M)-Y	0064
MA4100-H	0064
MA4100-M	0064
MA4100H	0064
MA4100M	0064
MA4100MTA	OEM
MA4100N	0064
MA4101	0016
MA4102	0016
MA4103	0016
MA4104	0016
MA4110	0181
MA4110(M)	OEM
MA4110(M)-Y	OEM
MA4110-L	0181
MA4110-M	0181
MA4110L	OEM
MA4110MTA	OEM
MA4110TA	0181
MA4116	OEM
MA4120	0052
MA4120(M)	0052
MA4120(M)-T2	0052
MA4120(M)-Y	0052
MA4120-H	0052
MA4120H	0053
MA4120L	OEM
MA4120M	0999
MA4120MTA	0999
MA4123	OEM
MA4123A	OEM
MA4123B	OEM
MA4124	OEM
MA4124A	OEM
MA4125	OEM
MA4125A	OEM
MA4126	OEM
MA4126A	OEM
MA4127	OEM
MA4127A	OEM
MA4128	OEM
MA4129	OEM
MA4130	0053
MA4130(H)	0999
MA4130(H)-T2	0999
MA4130(H)-Y	0999
MA4130(L)	0053
MA4130(L)-Y	0053
MA4130A	OEM
MA4130H	0053
MA4130L	0053
MA4130M	0053
MA4131	OEM
MA4131A	OEM
MA4133	OEM
MA4135	OEM
MA4136	OEM
MA4136A	OEM
MA4137	OEM
MA4139	OEM
MA4140-H	0873
MA4142	OEM
MA4142A	OEM
MA4146	OEM
MA4147	OEM
MA4148	OEM
MA4150	0681
MA4150(L)	0681
MA4150(L)-T2	0681
MA4150(L)-Y	0681
MA4150(M)	0681
MA4150(M)-T2	OEM
MA4150(M)-Y	0681
MA4150-M	0681
MA4150M	0681
MA4150MTA	OEM
MA4160	0440
MA4160-M	0440
MA4160M	0440
MA4160N-M	0440
MA4171	OEM
MA4172	OEM
MA4173	OEM
MA4174	OEM
MA4180	0371
MA4180-H	4764
MA4180M	0371
MA4180MTA	OEM
MA4200	0695
MA4200(M)	OEM
MA4200(M)-Y	OEM
MA4200-M	0695
MA4200H	OEM
MA4200M	OEM
MA4220	0700
MA4220-T	OEM
MA4220H	0700
MA4220M	OEM
MA4220T	OEM
MA4230	0392

DEVICE TYPE	REPL CODE
MA4240	0489
MA4240-M	0543
MA4240H	OEM
MA4245	OEM
MA4251	OEM
MA4253	OEM
MA4254	OEM
MA4255	OEM
MA4256	OEM
MA4257	OEM
MA4259	OEM
MA4260	OEM
MA4261	OEM
MA4263	OEM
MA4264	OEM
MA4265	OEM
MA4266	OEM
MA4267	OEM
MA4268	OEM
MA4270	0450
MA4270(M)	0436
MA4270(M)-Y	0450
MA4270-H	0450
MA4270M	0450
MA4273B	OEM
MA4273C	OEM
MA4273D	OEM
MA4273E	OEM
MA4273F	OEM
MA4273G	OEM
MA4280	OEM
MA4281	OEM
MA4282	OEM
MA4283	OEM
MA4284	OEM
MA4285	OEM
MA4286	OEM
MA4287	OEM
MA4288	OEM
MA4289	OEM
MA4290	OEM
MA4291	OEM
MA4292	OEM
MA4296	OEM
MA4297	OEM
MA4298	OEM
MA4300	0195
MA4300H	OEM
MA4300M	0195
MA4300MTA	OEM
MA4321A	OEM
MA4321A1	OEM
MA4321AA	OEM
MA4321AA1	OEM
MA4321B	OEM
MA4321B1	OEM
MA4321C	OEM
MA4321C1	OEM
MA4321D	OEM
MA4321D1	OEM
MA4321E	OEM
MA4321E1	OEM
MA4321F	OEM
MA4321G	OEM
MA4322A	OEM
MA4322A1	OEM
MA4322AA	OEM
MA4322AA1	OEM
MA4322B	OEM
MA4322B1	OEM
MA4322C	OEM
MA4322C1	OEM
MA4322D	OEM
MA4322D1	OEM
MA4322E	OEM
MA4322E1	OEM
MA4322F	OEM
MA4322G	OEM
MA4324A	OEM
MA4324A1	OEM
MA4324B	OEM
MA4324B1	OEM
MA4324C	OEM
MA4324C1	OEM
MA4324D	OEM
MA4324D1	OEM
MA4324E	OEM
MA4324E1	OEM
MA4324F	OEM
MA4324F1	OEM
MA4324G	OEM
MA4325A	OEM
MA4325A1	OEM
MA4325AA	OEM
MA4325AA1	OEM
MA4325B	OEM
MA4325B1	OEM
MA4325C	OEM
MA4325C1	OEM
MA4325D	OEM
MA4325D1	OEM
MA4325E	OEM
MA4325E1	OEM
MA4325F	OEM
MA4325F1	OEM
MA4325G	OEM
MA4326A	OEM
MA4326A1	OEM
MA4326AA	OEM

If replacement code is OEM, contact original manufacturer for replacement. 461

DEVICE TYPE	REPL CODE
MA4326AA1	OEM
MA4326B	OEM
MA4326B1	OEM
MA4326C	OEM
MA4326C1	OEM
MA4326D	OEM
MA4326D1	OEM
MA4326E	OEM
MA4326E1	OEM
MA4326F	OEM
MA4326F1	OEM
MA4326G	OEM
MA4327A	OEM
MA4327A1	OEM
MA4327B	OEM
MA4327B1	OEM
MA4327C	OEM
MA4327C1	OEM
MA4327D	OEM
MA4327D1	OEM
MA4327E	OEM
MA4327E1	OEM
MA4328A	OEM
MA4328A1	OEM
MA4328B	OEM
MA4328B1	OEM
MA4328C	OEM
MA4328C1	OEM
MA4328D	OEM
MA4328D1	OEM
MA4330	0166
MA4330(L)	0166
MA4330(L)-Y	0166
MA4330(M)	0166
MA4330(M)-T2	0166
MA4330(M)-Y	0166
MA4330H	OEM
MA4330L	OEM
MA4330M	OEM
MA4331A	OEM
MA4331B	OEM
MA4331C	OEM
MA4331D	OEM
MA4331E	OEM
MA4331F	OEM
MA4331G	OEM
MA4332A	OEM
MA4332B	OEM
MA4332C	OEM
MA4332D	OEM
MA4332E	OEM
MA4332F	OEM
MA4332G	OEM
MA4333A	OEM
MA4333B	OEM
MA4333C	OEM
MA4333D	OEM
MA4333E	OEM
MA4333F	OEM
MA4333G	OEM
MA4334A	OEM
MA4334A1	OEM
MA4334A2	OEM
MA4334B	OEM
MA4334B1	OEM
MA4334B2	OEM
MA4334C	OEM
MA4334C1	OEM
MA4334C2	OEM
MA4334D	OEM
MA4334D1	OEM
MA4334E	OEM
MA4334E1	OEM
MA4334G	OEM
MA4335A	OEM
MA4335A1	OEM
MA4335A2	OEM
MA4335AA	OEM
MA4335AA1	OEM
MA4335AA2	OEM
MA4335B	OEM
MA4335B1	OEM
MA4335B2	OEM
MA4335D	OEM
MA4335D1	OEM
MA4335D2	OEM
MA4335E	OEM
MA4335E1	OEM
MA4335F	OEM
MA4335G	OEM
MA4336A	OEM
MA4336A1	OEM
MA4336A2	OEM
MA4336AA	OEM
MA4336AA1	OEM
MA4336AA2	OEM
MA4336B	OEM
MA4336B1	OEM
MA4336B2	OEM
MA4336C	OEM
MA4336C1	OEM
MA4336C2	OEM
MA4336D	OEM
MA4336D1	OEM
MA4336D2	OEM
MA4336E	OEM
MA4336E1	OEM
MA4336F	OEM
MA4336G	OEM
MA4337A	OEM
MA4337A1	OEM
MA4337B	OEM
MA4337B1	OEM
MA4337C	OEM
MA4337C1	OEM
MA4337D	OEM
MA4337D1	OEM
MA4337E	OEM
MA4337E1	OEM
MA4337F	OEM
MA4337F1	OEM
MA4337G	OEM
MA4338A	OEM
MA4338A1	OEM
MA4338B	OEM
MA4338B1	OEM
MA4338C	OEM
MA4338C1	OEM
MA4338D	OEM
MA4338D1	OEM
MA4338E	OEM
MA4338E1	OEM
MA4338F	OEM
MA4341A	OEM
MA4341A1	OEM
MA4341A2	OEM
MA4341AA	OEM
MA4341AA1	OEM
MA4341AA2	OEM
MA4341B	OEM
MA4341B1	OEM
MA4341B2	OEM
MA4341C	OEM
MA4341C1	OEM
MA4341C2	OEM
MA4341D	OEM
MA4341D1	OEM
MA4341D2	OEM
MA4341E	OEM
MA4341E1	OEM
MA4341F	OEM
MA4341F1	OEM
MA4341G	OEM
MA4341G1	OEM
MA4342A	OEM
MA4342A1	OEM
MA4342A2	OEM
MA4342AA	OEM
MA4342AA1	OEM
MA4342AA2	OEM
MA4342B	OEM
MA4342B1	OEM
MA4342B2	OEM
MA4342C	OEM
MA4342C1	OEM
MA4342C2	OEM
MA4342D	OEM
MA4342D1	OEM
MA4342D2	OEM
MA4342E	OEM
MA4342E1	OEM
MA4342F	OEM
MA4342F1	OEM
MA4342G	OEM
MA4342G1	OEM
MA4343A	OEM
MA4343A1	OEM
MA4343A2	OEM
MA4343AA	OEM
MA4343AA1	OEM
MA4343AA2	OEM
MA4343B	OEM
MA4343B1	OEM
MA4343B2	OEM
MA4343C	OEM
MA4343C1	OEM
MA4343C2	OEM
MA4343D	OEM
MA4343D1	OEM
MA4343D2	OEM
MA4343E	OEM
MA4343E1	OEM
MA4343F	OEM
MA4343F1	OEM
MA4343G	OEM
MA4344A	OEM
MA4344A1	OEM
MA4344A2	OEM
MA4344B	OEM
MA4344B1	OEM
MA4344B2	OEM
MA4344C	OEM
MA4344C1	OEM
MA4344C2	OEM
MA4344D	OEM
MA4344D1	OEM
MA4344D2	OEM
MA4344E	OEM
MA4344E1	OEM
MA4344E2	OEM
MA4344F	OEM
MA4344F1	OEM
MA4344G	OEM
MA4344G1	OEM
MA4345A	OEM
MA4345A1	OEM
MA4345A2	OEM
MA4345AA	OEM
MA4345AA1	OEM
MA4345AA2	OEM
MA4345B	OEM
MA4345B1	OEM
MA4345B2	OEM
MA4345C	OEM
MA4345C1	OEM
MA4345C2	OEM
MA4345D	OEM
MA4345D1	OEM
MA4345D2	OEM
MA4345E	OEM
MA4345E1	OEM
MA4345F	OEM
MA4345F1	OEM
MA4345G	OEM
MA4346A	OEM
MA4346A1	OEM
MA4346A2	OEM
MA4346AA	OEM
MA4346AA1	OEM
MA4346AA2	OEM
MA4346B	OEM
MA4346B1	OEM
MA4346B2	OEM
MA4346C	OEM
MA4346C1	OEM
MA4346C2	OEM
MA4346D	OEM
MA4346D1	OEM
MA4346D2	OEM
MA4346E	OEM
MA4346E1	OEM
MA4346F	OEM
MA4346F1	OEM
MA4346G	OEM
MA4347A	OEM
MA4347A1	OEM
MA4347B	OEM
MA4347B1	OEM
MA4347C	OEM
MA4347C1	OEM
MA4347D	OEM
MA4347D1	OEM
MA4347E	OEM
MA4347E1	OEM
MA4347F	OEM
MA4347G	OEM
MA4348A	OEM
MA4348A1	OEM
MA4348B	OEM
MA4348B1	OEM
MA4348C	OEM
MA4348C1	OEM
MA4348D	OEM
MA4348D1	OEM
MA4348E	OEM
MA4348E1	OEM
MA4348F	OEM
MA4351A	OEM
MA4351A1	OEM
MA4351A2	OEM
MA4351AA	OEM
MA4351AA1	OEM
MA4351AA2	OEM
MA4351B	OEM
MA4351B1	OEM
MA4351B2	OEM
MA4351C	OEM
MA4351C1	OEM
MA4351C2	OEM
MA4351D	OEM
MA4351D1	OEM
MA4351D2	OEM
MA4351E	OEM
MA4351E1	OEM
MA4351F	OEM
MA4351F1	OEM
MA4351G	OEM
MA4351G1	OEM
MA4352A	OEM
MA4352A1	OEM
MA4352A2	OEM
MA4352AA	OEM
MA4352AA1	OEM
MA4352AA2	OEM
MA4352B	OEM
MA4352B1	OEM
MA4352B2	OEM
MA4352C	OEM
MA4352C1	OEM
MA4352C2	OEM
MA4352D	OEM
MA4352D1	OEM
MA4352D2	OEM
MA4352E	OEM
MA4352E1	OEM
MA4352F	OEM
MA4352F1	OEM
MA4352G	OEM
MA4352G1	OEM
MA4353A	OEM
MA4353A1	OEM
MA4353A2	OEM
MA4353AA	OEM
MA4353AA1	OEM
MA4353AA2	OEM
MA4353B	OEM
MA4353B1	OEM
MA4353B2	OEM
MA4353C	OEM
MA4353C1	OEM
MA4353C2	OEM
MA4353D	OEM
MA4353D1	OEM
MA4353D2	OEM
MA4353E	OEM
MA4353E1	OEM
MA4353F	OEM
MA4353F1	OEM
MA4353G	OEM
MA4354A	OEM
MA4354A1	OEM
MA4354A2	OEM
MA4354B	OEM
MA4354B1	OEM
MA4354B2	OEM
MA4354C	OEM
MA4354C1	OEM
MA4354C2	OEM
MA4354D	OEM
MA4354D1	OEM
MA4354D2	OEM
MA4354E	OEM
MA4354E1	OEM
MA4354E2	OEM
MA4354F	OEM
MA4354F1	OEM
MA4354G	OEM
MA4354G1	OEM
MA4355A	OEM
MA4355A1	OEM
MA4355A2	OEM
MA4355AA	OEM
MA4355AA1	OEM
MA4355AA2	OEM
MA4355B	OEM
MA4355B1	OEM
MA4355B2	OEM
MA4355C	OEM
MA4355C1	OEM
MA4355C2	OEM
MA4355D	OEM
MA4355D1	OEM
MA4355D2	OEM
MA4355E	OEM
MA4355E1	OEM
MA4355F	OEM
MA4355F1	OEM
MA4355G	OEM
MA4356AA	OEM
MA4356AA1	OEM
MA4356AA2	OEM
MA4356B	OEM
MA4356B1	OEM
MA4356B2	OEM
MA4356C	OEM
MA4356C1	OEM
MA4356C2	OEM
MA4356D	OEM
MA4356D1	OEM
MA4356D2	OEM
MA4356E	OEM
MA4356E1	OEM
MA4356F	OEM
MA4356F1	OEM
MA4356G	OEM
MA4357A	OEM
MA4357A1	OEM
MA4357B	OEM
MA4357B1	OEM
MA4357C	OEM
MA4357C1	OEM
MA4357D	OEM
MA4357D1	OEM
MA4357E	OEM
MA4357E1	OEM
MA4357F	OEM
MA4357F1	OEM
MA4357G	OEM
MA4358A	OEM
MA4358A1	OEM
MA4358B	OEM
MA4358B1	OEM
MA4358C	OEM
MA4358C1	OEM
MA4358D	OEM
MA4358D1	OEM
MA4358E	OEM
MA4358E1	OEM
MA4358F	OEM
MA4360	0010
MA4360H	OEM
MA4360M	OEM
MA4361	OEM
MA4362	OEM
MA4372C	OEM
MA4373C	OEM
MA4374C	OEM
MA4375C	OEM
MA4375E	OEM
MA4380	OEM
MA4381	OEM
MA4382	OEM
MA4383	OEM
MA4384	OEM
MA4385	OEM
MA4386	OEM
MA4387	OEM
MA4388	5570
MA4400	OEM
MA4400A	OEM
MA4404	0211
MA4404A	0211
MA4472	OEM
MA4473	OEM
MA4497A	OEM
MA4497B	OEM
MA4497C	OEM
MA4501	0041
MA4534	OEM
MA4535	OEM
MA4536	OEM
MA4537	OEM
MA4538	OEM
MA4539	OEM
MA4540	OEM
MA4541	OEM
MA4542	OEM
MA4544	OEM
MA4546	OEM
MA4547	OEM
MA4551	OEM
MA4552	OEM
MA4553	OEM
MA4554	OEM
MA4555	OEM
MA4556	OEM
MA4557	OEM
MA4562	OEM
MA4570A	OEM
MA4570A1	OEM
MA4570B	OEM
MA4570B1	OEM
MA4570C	OEM
MA4570C1	OEM
MA4570D	OEM
MA4570D1	OEM
MA4570E	OEM
MA4570E1	OEM
MA4571A	OEM
MA4571A1	OEM
MA4571A2	OEM
MA4571B	OEM
MA4571B1	OEM
MA4571B2	OEM
MA4571C	OEM
MA4571C1	OEM
MA4571C2	OEM
MA4571D	OEM
MA4571D1	OEM
MA4571D2	OEM
MA4571E	OEM
MA4571E1	OEM
MA4571E2	OEM
MA4572A	OEM
MA4572A1	OEM
MA4572B	OEM
MA4572B1	OEM
MA4573A	OEM
MA4573A1	OEM
MA4573A2	OEM
MA4573B	OEM
MA4573B1	OEM
MA4573B2	OEM
MA4583A	OEM
MA4583B	OEM
MA4583C	OEM
MA4604A	OEM
MA4604A1	OEM
MA4604B	OEM
MA4604C	OEM
MA4605A	OEM
MA4605B	OEM
MA4605C	OEM
MA4606A	OEM
MA4606A1	OEM
MA4606A2	OEM
MA4606B	OEM
MA4606C	OEM
MA4607A	OEM
MA4607A1	OEM
MA4607A2	OEM
MA4607B	OEM
MA4607C	OEM
MA4608A	OEM
MA4608B	OEM
MA4608C	OEM
MA4609A	OEM
MA4609B	OEM
MA4609C	OEM
MA4610	OEM
MA4610A	OEM
MA4613	OEM
MA4614	OEM
MA4615	OEM
MA4616	OEM
MA4617	OEM
MA4618	OEM
MA4619	OEM
MA4619A	OEM
MA4623	OEM
MA4623A	OEM
MA4624	OEM
MA4624A	OEM
MA4625	OEM
MA4625A	OEM
MA4631A	OEM
MA4631A1	OEM
MA4631A2	OEM
MA4633A	OEM
MA4633A1	OEM
MA4644A-E	OEM
MA4645B-E	OEM
MA4646C-E	OEM
MA4651A	OEM
MA4651B	OEM
MA4651C	OEM
MA4652A	OEM
MA4652B	OEM
MA4652C	OEM
MA4653A	OEM
MA4653B	OEM
MA4653C	OEM
MA4654A	OEM
MA4654A1	OEM
MA4654B	OEM
MA4654C	OEM
MA4655	OEM
MA4663A2	OEM
MA4670	0160
MA4684	OEM
MA4685	OEM
MA4686	OEM
MA4687	OEM
MA4688	OEM
MA4701B	OEM
MA4701B1	OEM
MA4701C	OEM
MA4701C1	OEM
MA4701D	OEM
MA4701D1	OEM
MA4701E	OEM
MA4701E1	OEM
MA4701F	OEM
MA4701F1	OEM
MA4701G	OEM
MA4701G1	OEM
MA4701H	OEM
MA4701H1	OEM
MA4701I	OEM
MA4701I1	OEM
MA4702A	OEM
MA4702A1	OEM
MA4702B	OEM
MA4702B1	OEM
MA4702C	OEM
MA4702C1	OEM
MA4702D	OEM
MA4702D1	OEM
MA4702E	OEM
MA4702E1	OEM
MA4702F	OEM
MA4702F1	OEM
MA4702G	OEM
MA4702G1	OEM
MA4703B	OEM
MA4703C	OEM
MA4703D	OEM
MA4703E	OEM
MA4703F	OEM
MA4703G	OEM
MA4704B	OEM
MA4704C	OEM
MA4704D	OEM
MA4704E	OEM
MA4704F	OEM
MA4704G	OEM
MA4732A	OEM
MA4732B	OEM
MA4732C	OEM
MA4733A	OEM
MA4733B	OEM
MA4733C	OEM
MA4748	OEM
MA4749	OEM
MA4750	OEM
MA4751	OEM
MA4752	OEM
MA4753	OEM
MA4754	OEM
MA4755	OEM
MA4756	OEM
MA4760A	OEM
MA4760AA	OEM
MA4760B	OEM
MA4760C	OEM
MA4760D	OEM
MA4761A	OEM
MA4761AA	OEM
MA4761B	OEM
MA4761C	OEM
MA4761D	OEM
MA4762	OEM
MA4763	OEM
MA4764	OEM
MA4765	OEM
MA4811	OEM
MA4811A	OEM
MA4811B	OEM
MA4811C	OEM
MA4811D	OEM
MA4812	OEM
MA4812A	OEM
MA4812B	OEM
MA4812C	OEM
MA4813	OEM
MA4813A	OEM
MA4813B	OEM
MA4814	OEM
MA4814A	OEM
MA4814B	OEM
MA4815	OEM
MA4815A	OEM
MA4825B1	OEM
MA4825B2	OEM
MA4825C1	OEM
MA4825C2	OEM
MA4825D1	OEM
MA4825D2	OEM
MA4825E1	OEM
MA4825E2	OEM
MA4826B1	OEM
MA4826B2	OEM
MA4826C1	OEM
MA4826C2	OEM
MA4826D1	OEM
MA4826D2	OEM
MA4850	OEM
MA4851	OEM
MA4852	OEM
MA4853	OEM
MA4854	OEM
MA4855	OEM
MA4856	OEM
MA4861C	OEM
MA4861D	OEM
MA4861E	OEM
MA4861F	OEM
MA4861G	OEM
MA4861H	OEM
MA4882	OEM
MA4883	OEM
MA4942H	OEM
MA4944H	OEM
MA4946J	OEM
MA4948J	OEM
MA4950A	OEM
MA4950B	OEM
MA4951A	OEM
MA4951B	OEM
MA4952B	OEM
MA4952C	OEM
MA4953B	OEM
MA4953C	OEM
MA4954B	OEM
MA4954C	OEM
MA4954D	OEM
MA4955C	OEM
MA4955D	OEM
MA4955E	OEM
MA4956C	OEM
MA4956D	OEM
MA4956E	OEM
MA4956F	OEM
MA4957D	OEM
MA4957E	OEM
MA4957F	OEM
MA4958E	OEM
MA4958F	OEM
MA4960A	OEM
MA4960B	OEM
MA4961A	OEM
MA4961B	OEM
MA4962B	OEM
MA4962C	OEM
MA4963B	OEM
MA4963C	OEM
MA4964B	OEM
MA4964C	OEM
MA4964D	OEM
MA4965B	OEM
MA4965C	OEM
MA4965D	OEM
MA4965E	OEM
MA4966C	OEM
MA4966D	OEM
MA4966E	OEM
MA4966F	OEM
MA4967D	OEM
MA4967E	OEM
MA4967F	OEM
MA4967G	OEM
MA4968E	OEM
MA4968F	OEM
MA4968G	OEM
MA4969E	OEM
MA4969F	OEM
MA4969G	OEM
MA4980	OEM
MA4984	OEM
MA4985	OEM
MA4986	OEM
MA4987	OEM
MA4988	OEM
MA4989	OEM
MA4990	OEM
MA4992	OEM
MA4998	OEM
MA5047	OEM
MA5051	OEM
MA5056	OEM
MA5062	OEM
MA5068	OEM
MA5075	OEM

462

If replacement code is OEM, contact original manufacturer for replacement.

DEVICE TYPE	REPL CODE
MA5082	OEM
MA5091	OEM
MA5100	OEM
MA5110	OEM
MA5113	2593
MA5120	OEM
MA5130	OEM
MA5150	OEM
MA5160	OEM
MA5180	OEM
MA5186AP	0912
MA5200	OEM
MA5220	OEM
MA5240	OEM
MA5292C	OEM
MA6001	0016
MA6002	0016
MA6003	0016
MA6082	OEM
MA6101	0086
MA6102	0016
MA-6301	OEM
MA6301	2020
MA6301T	2020
MA7300	4155
MA7700A-0004	OEM
MA7700A-0005	OEM
MA7700K-0001	OEM
MA7700K-0002	OEM
MA7700K-0003	OEM
MA7705	OEM
MA7707H	OEM
MA7707J	OEM
MA7707J-0003	OEM
MA7707J-0012	OEM
MA7707J-0013	OEM
MA7707N-0006	OEM
MA7707N-0008	OEM
MA7707N-0009	OEM
MA7707N-0012	OEM
MA7707N-0013	OEM
MA7707N-0014	OEM
MA7707N-0015	OEM
MA7708	OEM
MA7709A-0001	OEM
MA7709A-0003	OEM
MA7709A-0005	OEM
MA7709A-0007	OEM
MA7709A-0009	OEM
MA7709A-0011	OEM
MA7709A-0012	OEM
MA7709A-0013	OEM
MA7709A-0014	OEM
MA7709A-0015	OEM
MA7709U-0012	OEM
MA7709U-0013	OEM
MA7709U-0014	OEM
MA7709U-0015	OEM
MA7710	OEM
MA7715A-000003	OEM
MA7715A-0001	OEM
MA7715A-0002	OEM
MA7715A-0004	OEM
MA7715A-0005	OEM
MA7715A-0006	OEM
MA7715A-0007	OEM
MA7715A-0008	OEM
MA7715A-0009	OEM
MA7715A-0012	OEM
MA7715A-0013	OEM
MA7715U-0012	OEM
MA7715U-0013	OEM
MA7717J-0009	OEM
MA7717N-0001	OEM
MA7717N-0002	OEM
MA7717N-0003	OEM
MA7717N-0004	OEM
MA7717N-0005	OEM
MA7717N-0006	OEM
MA7717N-0007	OEM
MA7717N-0008	OEM
MA7717N-0012	OEM
MA7717N-0013	OEM
MA7742J-0001	OEM
MA7742N-0005	OEM
MA7742N-0007	OEM
MA7742N-0009	OEM
MA7742N-0011	OEM
MA7742N-0012	OEM
MA7744A-0001	OEM
MA7744A-0003	OEM
MA7744A-0005	OEM
MA7744A-0007	OEM
MA7744A-0009	OEM
MA7744A-0012	OEM
MA7757J-0012	OEM
MA7757J-0013	OEM
MA7805	0619
MA7805UC	OEM
MA7807	OEM
MA7809	OEM
MA7811	OEM
MA7816	OEM
MA7817	OEM
MA8001	0086
MA8002	0086
MA8003	0320
MA8047M	OEM
MA8051-M	OEM

DEVICE TYPE	REPL CODE
MA8051M	OEM
MA8334	OEM
MA8342-0001	OEM
MA8342-0002	OEM
MA8342-0003	OEM
MA8342-0004	OEM
MA8342-0005	OEM
MA8342-0006	OEM
MA8342-0007	OEM
MA8342-0008	OEM
MA8342-0009	OEM
MA8342-0010	OEM
MA8342-0011	OEM
MA8343-0001	OEM
MA8343-0005	OEM
MA8343-0006	OEM
MA8343-0050	OEM
MA8343-0051	OEM
MA8343-0052	OEM
MA8343-0053	OEM
MA8343-0054	OEM
MA8343-0055	OEM
MA8345-0001	OEM
MA8345-0002	OEM
MA8345-0003	OEM
MA8345-0056	OEM
MA8345-0057	OEM
MA8345-0058	OEM
MA8345-0059	OEM
MA9001	0488
MA9002	0488
MA9003	0488
MA11238N	OEM
MA13080	OEM
MA34022	OEM
MA40000	OEM
MA40001	OEM
MA40002	OEM
MA40003	OEM
MA40006	OEM
MA40007	OEM
MA40008	OEM
MA40009	OEM
MA40012	OEM
MA40013	OEM
MA40014	OEM
MA40015	OEM
MA40024	OEM
MA40025	OEM
MA40026	OEM
MA40027	OEM
MA40028	OEM
MA40029	OEM
MA40033	OEM
MA40034	OEM
MA40035	OEM
MA40040	OEM
MA40041	OEM
MA40042	OEM
MA40043	OEM
MA40051D	OEM
MA40051E	OEM
MA40051F	OEM
MA40051G	OEM
MA40051H	OEM
MA40052	OEM
MA40053	OEM
MA40054	OEM
MA40061	OEM
MA40062	OEM
MA40071-1	OEM
MA40071D	OEM
MA40071E	OEM
MA40071F	OEM
MA40071G	OEM
MA40071H	OEM
MA40071I	OEM
MA40072	OEM
MA40073	OEM
MA40074	OEM
MA40075	OEM
MA40081	OEM
MA40082	OEM
MA40100	OEM
MA40101	OEM
MA40102	OEM
MA40103	OEM
MA40104	OEM
MA40105	OEM
MA40106	OEM
MA40107	OEM
MA40110	OEM
MA40111	OEM
MA40115	OEM
MA40116	OEM
MA40120	OEM
MA40121	OEM
MA40122	OEM
MA40123	OEM
MA40124	OEM
MA40126	OEM
MA40127	OEM
MA40128	OEM
MA40140	OEM
MA40150	OEM
MA40151	OEM
MA40152	OEM
MA40153	OEM
MA40154	OEM

DEVICE TYPE	REPL CODE
MA40155	OEM
MA40156	OEM
MA40157	OEM
MA40160	OEM
MA40161	OEM
MA40162	OEM
MA40163	OEM
MA40165	OEM
MA40166	OEM
MA40167	OEM
MA40168	OEM
MA40170	OEM
MA40171	OEM
MA40172	OEM
MA40173	OEM
MA40174	OEM
MA40175	OEM
MA40176	OEM
MA40177	OEM
MA40178	OEM
MA40182	OEM
MA40183	OEM
MA40184	OEM
MA40190	OEM
MA40191	OEM
MA40192	OEM
MA40193	OEM
MA40194	OEM
MA40195	OEM
MA40201	OEM
MA40202	OEM
MA40203	OEM
MA40204	OEM
MA40205	OEM
MA40206	OEM
MA40207	OEM
MA40208	OEM
MA40215	OEM
MA40216	OEM
MA40220	OEM
MA40221	OEM
MA40222	OEM
MA40227	OEM
MA40228	OEM
MA40230	OEM
MA40231	OEM
MA40232	OEM
MA40233	OEM
MA40234	OEM
MA40235	OEM
MA40236	OEM
MA40237	OEM
MA40240	OEM
MA40241	OEM
MA40242	OEM
MA40243	OEM
MA40244	OEM
MA40245	OEM
MA40246	OEM
MA40248	OEM
MA40249	OEM
MA40251	OEM
MA40252	OEM
MA40253	OEM
MA40254	OEM
MA40255	OEM
MA40256	OEM
MA40257	OEM
MA40258	OEM
MA40265	OEM
MA40266	OEM
MA40267	OEM
MA40268	OEM
MA40270	OEM
MA40271	OEM
MA40272	OEM
MA40273	OEM
MA40274	OEM
MA40291	OEM
MA40292	OEM
MA40293	OEM
MA40294	OEM
MA40295	OEM
MA40296	OEM
MA40410	OEM
MA40412	OEM
MA40417	OEM
MA40423	OEM
MA40426	OEM
MA40427	OEM
MA40428	OEM
MA40430	OEM
MA40431	OEM
MA40432	OEM
MA40433	OEM
MA40434	OEM
MA40435	OEM
MA40436	OEM
MA40439	OEM
MA40440	OEM
MA40441	OEM
MA40442	OEM
MA40443	OEM
MA40444	OEM
MA40445	OEM
MA40446	OEM
MA40447	OEM
MA40449	OEM
MA40480	OEM

DEVICE TYPE	REPL CODE
MA40490	OEM
MA40491	OEM
MA40492	OEM
MA40493-226	OEM
MA40494-227	OEM
MA40495-228	OEM
MA40496-227	OEM
MA40497-227	OEM
MA40499	OEM
MA40543	OEM
MA40995	OEM
MA40996	OEM
MA40997	OEM
MA40998	OEM
MA40999	OEM
MA41201C	OEM
MA41201D	OEM
MA41201E	OEM
MA41201F	OEM
MA41201G	OEM
MA41202C	OEM
MA41202D	OEM
MA41202E	OEM
MA41202F	OEM
MA41202G	OEM
MA41205	OEM
MA41206	OEM
MA41207	OEM
MA41220C	OEM
MA41220E	OEM
MA41220F	OEM
MA41220G	OEM
MA41221D	OEM
MA41221E	OEM
MA41221F	OEM
MA41222	OEM
MA41223	OEM
MA41224	OEM
MA41225	OEM
MA41500	OEM
MA41501	OEM
MA41502	OEM
MA41503	OEM
MA41504	OEM
MA41505	OEM
MA41506	OEM
MA41507	OEM
MA41508	OEM
MA41509	OEM
MA41510	OEM
MA41511	OEM
MA41512	OEM
MA41513	OEM
MA41514	OEM
MA41515	OEM
MA41516	OEM
MA41801	OEM
MA41802	OEM
MA41803	OEM
MA41804	OEM
MA41805	OEM
MA41806	OEM
MA41807	OEM
MA41808	OEM
MA41809	OEM
MA41810	OEM
MA41811	OEM
MA41812	OEM
MA41813	OEM
MA41814	OEM
MA41816	OEM
MA41817	OEM
MA41819	OEM
MA41820	OEM
MA42001-509	OEM
MA42002-509	OEM
MA42003-509	OEM
MA42004-509	OEM
MA42005-509	OEM
MA42006-510	OEM
MA42008-511	OEM
MA42009-509	OEM
MA42010-509	OEM
MA42010-510	OEM
MA42011-510	OEM
MA42012-510	OEM
MA42014-509	OEM
MA42015-510	OEM
MA42016-510	OEM
MA42020-509	OEM
MA42021-509	OEM
MA42022-509	OEM
MA42023-509	OEM
MA42024-509	OEM
MA42025-509	OEM
MA42026-509	OEM
MA42027-509	OEM
MA42028-509	OEM
MA42051-509	OEM
MA42051-510	OEM
MA42051-511	OEM
MA42052-509	OEM
MA42052-510	OEM
MA42052-511	OEM
MA42055-510	OEM
MA42055-511	OEM
MA42056-510	OEM
MA42056-511	OEM
MA42057-510	OEM

DEVICE TYPE	REPL CODE
MA42057-511	OEM
MA42060	OEM
MA42061	OEM
MA42062	OEM
MA42063	OEM
MA42100-509	OEM
MA42100-510	OEM
MA42100-511	OEM
MA42100-512	OEM
MA42110-509	OEM
MA42110-510	OEM
MA42110-511	OEM
MA42110-512	OEM
MA42111-509	OEM
MA42111-510	OEM
MA42111-511	OEM
MA42112-509	OEM
MA42112-510	OEM
MA42112-511	OEM
MA42113-509	OEM
MA42113-510	OEM
MA42113-511	OEM
MA42120-508	OEM
MA42121-508	OEM
MA42122-509	OEM
MA42123-509	OEM
MA42141-509	OEM
MA42141-510	OEM
MA42141-511	OEM
MA42142-509	OEM
MA42142-510	OEM
MA42142-511	OEM
MA42143-509	OEM
MA42143-510	OEM
MA42143-511	OEM
MA42151-511	OEM
MA42161-511	OEM
MA42162-511	OEM
MA42181-510	OEM
MA42191-510	OEM
MA43000	OEM
MA43001	OEM
MA43002	OEM
MA43003	OEM
MA43004	OEM
MA43005	OEM
MA43007	OEM
MA43030	OEM
MA43031	OEM
MA43032	OEM
MA43033	OEM
MA43034	OEM
MA43035	OEM
MA43036	OEM
MA43037	OEM
MA43543	OEM
MA43556A	OEM
MA43556A1	OEM
MA43556A2	OEM
MA43592	OEM
MA44010	OEM
MA44020	OEM
MA44030	OEM
MA44040	OEM
MA44050	OEM
MA44051	OEM
MA44052	OEM
MA44053	OEM
MA44058	OEM
MA44060	OEM
MA44061	OEM
MA44070	OEM
MA44071	OEM
MA44100	OEM
MA44110	OEM
MA44120	OEM
MA44130	OEM
MA44140	OEM
MA44150	OEM
MA44200	OEM
MA44210	OEM
MA44220	OEM
MA44230	OEM
MA44240	OEM
MA44250	OEM
MA44300	OEM
MA44310	OEM
MA44320	OEM
MA44900A	OEM
MA44900B	OEM
MA44900C	OEM
MA44900D	OEM
MA44900E	OEM
MA44900F	OEM
MA44901A	OEM
MA44901B	OEM
MA44901C	OEM
MA44901D	OEM
MA44901E	OEM
MA44901F	OEM
MA44902A	OEM
MA44902B	OEM
MA44902C	OEM
MA44902D	OEM
MA44902E	OEM
MA44902F	OEM
MA44903A	OEM
MA44903B	OEM
MA44903C	OEM

DEVICE TYPE	REPL CODE
MA44903D	OEM
MA44903E	OEM
MA44903F	OEM
MA44904A	OEM
MA44904B	OEM
MA44904C	OEM
MA44904D	OEM
MA44904E	OEM
MA44904F	OEM
MA44905A	OEM
MA44905B	OEM
MA44905C	OEM
MA44905D	OEM
MA44905E	OEM
MA44905F	OEM
MA44906A	OEM
MA44906B	OEM
MA44906C	OEM
MA44906D	OEM
MA44906E	OEM
MA44906F	OEM
MA44907A	OEM
MA44907B	OEM
MA44907C	OEM
MA44907D	OEM
MA44907E	OEM
MA44907F	OEM
MA44908A	OEM
MA44909A	OEM
MA44910A	OEM
MA44911A	OEM
MA45000	OEM
MA45001	OEM
MA45002	OEM
MA45003	OEM
MA45004	OEM
MA45005	OEM
MA45006	OEM
MA45007	OEM
MA45008	OEM
MA45009	OEM
MA45010	OEM
MA45011	OEM
MA45012	OEM
MA45013	OEM
MA45014	OEM
MA45015	OEM
MA45054	OEM
MA45055	OEM
MA45056	OEM
MA45062	OEM
MA45063	OEM
MA45064	OEM
MA45065	OEM
MA45066	OEM
MA45067	OEM
MA45068	OEM
MA45070	OEM
MA45071	0715
MA45072	OEM
MA45073	OEM
MA45074	OEM
MA45075	OEM
MA45101	OEM
MA45102	OEM
MA45103	OEM
MA45104	OEM
MA45105	OEM
MA45106	OEM
MA45107	OEM
MA45108	OEM
MA45109	OEM
MA45110	OEM
MA45111	0549
MA45112	0005
MA45113	OEM
MA45114	0623
MA45115	0030
MA45116	OEM
MA45121	OEM
MA45122	OEM
MA45123	OEM
MA45124	OEM
MA45125	OEM
MA45126	OEM
MA45127	OEM
MA45128	OEM
MA45129	OEM
MA45130	OEM
MA45131	0549
MA45132	0005
MA45133	OEM
MA45134	0623
MA45135	OEM
MA45136	OEM
MA45141	OEM
MA45142	OEM
MA45143	OEM
MA45144	OEM
MA45145	OEM
MA45146	OEM
MA45147	OEM
MA45148	OEM
MA45149	OEM
MA45150	OEM
MA45151	0715
MA45152	OEM
MA45153	OEM
MA45154	OEM

DEVICE TYPE	REPL CODE
MA45156	OEM
MA45157	OEM
MA45158	0549
MA45159	OEM
MA45160	0005
MA45161	0715
MA45162	OEM
MA45164	OEM
MA45165	OEM
MA45166	OEM
MA45167	OEM
MA45168	0549
MA45169	OEM
MA45170	OEM
MA45171	0715
MA45172	OEM
MA45225	OEM
MA45226	OEM
MA45226C	OEM
MA45227	OEM
MA45227C	OEM
MA45228	OEM
MA45228C	OEM
MA45229	OEM
MA45229C	OEM
MA45230	OEM
MA45230C	OEM
MA45231	OEM
MA45231C	OEM
MA45232	OEM
MA45232C	OEM
MA45233	OEM
MA45233C	OEM
MA45234	OEM
MA45234C	OEM
MA45235	OEM
MA45235C	OEM
MA45236	OEM
MA45236C	OEM
MA45237	OEM
MA45237C	OEM
MA45238	OEM
MA45238C	OEM
MA45239C	OEM
MA45240C	OEM
MA45241C	OEM
MA45242C	OEM
MA45245	OEM
MA45246	OEM
MA45246C	OEM
MA45247	OEM
MA45247C	OEM
MA45248	OEM
MA45248C	OEM
MA45249	OEM
MA45249C	OEM
MA45250	OEM
MA45250C	OEM
MA45251	OEM
MA45251C	OEM
MA45252	OEM
MA45252C	OEM
MA45253	OEM
MA45253C	OEM
MA45254	OEM
MA45254C	OEM
MA45255	OEM
MA45255C	OEM
MA45256	OEM
MA45256C	OEM
MA45257	OEM
MA45257C	OEM
MA45258	OEM
MA45258C	OEM
MA45259	OEM
MA45259C	OEM
MA45260	OEM
MA45260C	OEM
MA45261	OEM
MA45261C	OEM
MA45262	OEM
MA45262C	OEM
MA45263	OEM
MA45263C	OEM
MA45264	OEM
MA45264C	OEM
MA45265	OEM
MA45265C	OEM
MA45266	OEM
MA45266C	OEM
MA45267	OEM
MA45267C	OEM
MA45268	OEM
MA45268C	OEM
MA45269	OEM
MA45269C	OEM
MA45270	OEM
MA45270C	OEM
MA45271	OEM
MA45271C	OEM
MA45272	OEM
MA45272C	OEM
MA45273	OEM
MA45274	OEM
MA45275	OEM
MA45276	OEM
MA45277	OEM
MA45278	OEM
MA45279	OEM

If replacement code is OEM, contact original manufacturer for replacement.

463

DEVICE TYPE	REPL CODE
MA45280	OEM
MA45290	OEM
MA45290C	OEM
MA45291	OEM
MA45291C	OEM
MA45292	OEM
MA45293	OEM
MA45293C	OEM
MA45294	OEM
MA45294C	OEM
MA45295	OEM
MA45295C	OEM
MA45296	OEM
MA45296C	OEM
MA45297	OEM
MA45297C	OEM
MA45298	OEM
MA45298C	OEM
MA45299	OEM
MA45299C	OEM
MA45330	OEM
MA45331	OEM
MA45332	OEM
MA45333	OEM
MA45334	OEM
MA45335	OEM
MA45336	OEM
MA45337	OEM
MA45338	OEM
MA45339	OEM
MA45340	OEM
MA45341	OEM
MA45342	OEM
MA45343	OEM
MA45345	OEM
MA45346	OEM
MA45347	OEM
MA45348	OEM
MA45349	OEM
MA45350	OEM
MA45351	OEM
MA45352	OEM
MA45353	OEM
MA45354	OEM
MA45355	OEM
MA45356	OEM
MA45357	OEM
MA45358	OEM
MA45360	OEM
MA45361	OEM
MA45362	OEM
MA45363	OEM
MA45364	OEM
MA45365	OEM
MA45366	OEM
MA45367	OEM
MA45368	OEM
MA45369	OEM
MA45370	OEM
MA45371	OEM
MA45372	OEM
MA46021	OEM
MA46022	OEM
MA46023	OEM
MA46024	OEM
MA46025	OEM
MA46026	OEM
MA46027	OEM
MA46028	OEM
MA46029	OEM
MA46030	OEM
MA46031	OEM
MA46032	OEM
MA46033	OEM
MA46034	OEM
MA46035	OEM
MA46520A	OEM
MA46520B	OEM
MA46520C	OEM
MA46520D	OEM
MA46522A	OEM
MA46522B	OEM
MA46522C	OEM
MA46522D	OEM
MA46523A	OEM
MA46523B	OEM
MA46523C	OEM
MA46523D	OEM
MA46524A	OEM
MA46524B	OEM
MA46524C	OEM
MA46524D	OEM
MA46525A	OEM
MA46525B	OEM
MA46525C	OEM
MA46525D	OEM
MA46533A	OEM
MA46533B	OEM
MA46533C	OEM
MA46533D	OEM
MA46533E	OEM
MA46533F	OEM
MA46534A	OEM
MA46534B	OEM
MA46534C	OEM
MA46534D	OEM
MA46534E	OEM
MA46534F	OEM
MA46540C	OEM

DEVICE TYPE	REPL CODE
MA46540D	OEM
MA46540E	OEM
MA46540F	OEM
MA46541C	OEM
MA46541D	OEM
MA46541E	OEM
MA46541F	OEM
MA46542C	OEM
MA46542D	OEM
MA46542E	OEM
MA46543B	OEM
MA46543C	OEM
MA46543D	OEM
MA46543E	OEM
MA46544B	OEM
MA46544C	OEM
MA46544D	OEM
MA46545B	OEM
MA46545C	OEM
MA46545D	OEM
MA46546A	OEM
MA46546B	OEM
MA46546C	OEM
MA46547A	OEM
MA46547B	OEM
MA46547C	OEM
MA46550C	OEM
MA46550D	OEM
MA46550E	OEM
MA46550F	OEM
MA46551C	OEM
MA46551D	OEM
MA46551E	OEM
MA46551F	OEM
MA46552C	OEM
MA46556A	OEM
MA46556B	OEM
MA46556C	OEM
MA46557A	OEM
MA46557B	OEM
MA46557C	OEM
MA46560C	OEM
MA46560D	OEM
MA46560E	OEM
MA46560F	OEM
MA46561C	OEM
MA46561D	OEM
MA46561E	OEM
MA46561F	OEM
MA46562C	OEM
MA46562D	OEM
MA46562E	OEM
MA46563B	OEM
MA46563C	OEM
MA46563D	OEM
MA46563E	OEM
MA46564B	OEM
MA46564C	OEM
MA46564D	OEM
MA46565B	OEM
MA46565C	OEM
MA46565D	OEM
MA46566A	OEM
MA46566B	OEM
MA46566C	OEM
MA46567A	OEM
MA46567B	OEM
MA46567C	OEM
MA46570C	OEM
MA46570D	OEM
MA46570E	OEM
MA46570F	OEM
MA46571C	OEM
MA46571D	OEM
MA46571E	OEM
MA46571F	OEM
MA46572C	OEM
MA46572D	OEM
MA46572E	OEM
MA46573B	OEM
MA46573C	OEM
MA46573D	OEM
MA46573E	OEM
MA46574B	OEM
MA46574C	OEM
MA46574D	OEM
MA46575B	OEM
MA46575C	OEM
MA46575D	OEM
MA46576A	OEM
MA46576B	OEM
MA46576C	OEM
MA46577A	OEM
MA46577B	OEM
MA46577C	OEM
MA46600D	OEM
MA46600E	OEM
MA46600F	OEM
MA46600G	OEM
MA46600H	OEM
MA46600J	OEM
MA46601D	OEM
MA46601E	OEM
MA46601F	OEM
MA46601G	OEM
MA46602D	OEM
MA46602E	OEM
MA46602F	OEM
MA46603D	OEM

DEVICE TYPE	REPL CODE
MA46603E	OEM
MA46604D	OEM
MA46610D	OEM
MA46610E	OEM
MA46610F	OEM
MA46610G	OEM
MA46610H	OEM
MA46611D	OEM
MA46611E	OEM
MA46611F	OEM
MA46611G	OEM
MA46612D	OEM
MA46612E	OEM
MA46612F	OEM
MA46613D	OEM
MA46613E	OEM
MA46614D	OEM
MA46620D	OEM
MA46620E	OEM
MA46620F	OEM
MA46620G	OEM
MA46621D	OEM
MA46621E	OEM
MA46621F	OEM
MA46622D	OEM
MA46622E	OEM
MA46623D	OEM
MA46623E	OEM
MA46624D	OEM
MA47000	OEM
MA47001	OEM
MA47002	OEM
MA47003	OEM
MA47004	OEM
MA47005	OEM
MA47006	OEM
MA47007	OEM
MA47008	OEM
MA47009	OEM
MA47010	OEM
MA47011	OEM
MA47012	OEM
MA47013	OEM
MA47014	OEM
MA47015	OEM
MA47016	OEM
MA47017	OEM
MA47018	OEM
MA47019	OEM
MA47020	OEM
MA47021	OEM
MA47022	OEM
MA47023	OEM
MA47024	OEM
MA47025	OEM
MA47026	OEM
MA47027	OEM
MA47028	OEM
MA47029	OEM
MA47030	OEM
MA47031	OEM
MA47032	OEM
MA47033	OEM
MA47034	OEM
MA47035	OEM
MA47036	OEM
MA47037	OEM
MA47038	OEM
MA47039	OEM
MA47040	OEM
MA47041	OEM
MA47042	OEM
MA47043	OEM
MA47044	OEM
MA47045	OEM
MA47046	OEM
MA47047	OEM
MA47051	OEM
MA47052	OEM
MA47053	OEM
MA47054	OEM
MA47057	OEM
MA47068	OEM
MA47070	OEM
MA47075	OEM
MA47076	OEM
MA47077	OEM
MA47078	OEM
MA47079	OEM
MA47080	OEM
MA47081	OEM
MA47082	OEM
MA47083	OEM
MA47084	OEM
MA47085	OEM
MA47086	OEM
MA47088	OEM
MA47089	OEM
MA47090	OEM
MA47091	OEM
MA47100	OEM
MA47101	OEM
MA47102	OEM
MA47103	OEM
MA47104	OEM
MA47105	OEM
MA47106	OEM
MA47107	OEM
MA47108	OEM

DEVICE TYPE	REPL CODE
MA47109	OEM
MA47110	OEM
MA47111	OEM
MA47120	OEM
MA47121	OEM
MA47122	OEM
MA47123	OEM
MA47126	OEM
MA47127	OEM
MA47128	OEM
MA47129	OEM
MA47130	OEM
MA47160	OEM
MA47161	OEM
MA47162	OEM
MA47200	OEM
MA47201	OEM
MA47202	OEM
MA47203	OEM
MA47204	OEM
MA47205	OEM
MA47206	OEM
MA47207	OEM
MA47208	OEM
MA47220	OEM
MA47221	OEM
MA47222	OEM
MA47223	OEM
MA47266	OEM
MA47301	OEM
MA47302	OEM
MA47400	OEM
MA47401	OEM
MA47402	OEM
MA47403	OEM
MA47404	OEM
MA47405	OEM
MA47406	OEM
MA47407	OEM
MA47408	OEM
MA47409	OEM
MA47410	OEM
MA47411	OEM
MA47412	OEM
MA47413	OEM
MA47414	OEM
MA47416	OEM
MA47418	OEM
MA47419	OEM
MA47420	OEM
MA47421	OEM
MA47422	OEM
MA47423	OEM
MA47424	OEM
MA47425	OEM
MA47426	OEM
MA47427	OEM
MA47600	OEM
MA47865	OEM
MA47867	OEM
MA47868	OEM
MA47869	OEM
MA47870	OEM
MA47876	OEM
MA47878	OEM
MA47879	OEM
MA47880	OEM
MA47881	OEM
MA47883	OEM
MA47890-131	OEM
MA47890-150	OEM
MA47891-109	OEM
MA47891-131	OEM
MA47891-150	OEM
MA47892-109	OEM
MA47892-131	OEM
MA47892-150	OEM
MA47893-30	OEM
MA47893-109	OEM
MA47893-131	OEM
MA47894-30	OEM
MA47894-109	OEM
MA47894-131	OEM
MA47895-30	OEM
MA47895-54	OEM
MA47895-109	OEM
MA47895-131	OEM
MA47896-30	OEM
MA47896-54	OEM
MA47896-131	OEM
MA47897-30	OEM
MA47897-54	OEM
MA47897-131	OEM
MA47898-30	OEM
MA47898-54	OEM
MA47898-131	OEM
MA47899-30	OEM
MA47899-54	OEM
MA47899-131	OEM
MA48501A	OEM
MA48501B-F	OEM
MA48501G	OEM
MA48501H-K	OEM
MA48502A	OEM
MA48502B-F	OEM
MA48502G	OEM
MA48502H-K	OEM
MA48503A	OEM
MA48503B-F	OEM

DEVICE TYPE	REPL CODE
MA48503G	OEM
MA48503H	OEM
MA48503I	OEM
MA48504A	OEM
MA48504B-F	OEM
MA48504G	OEM
MA48504H	OEM
MA48505A	OEM
MA48505B-F	OEM
MA48505G	OEM
MA48506A	OEM
MA48506B-F	OEM
MA48507A	OEM
MA48507B-F	OEM
MA48508A	OEM
MA48508B-E	OEM
MA48509A	OEM
MA48509B-E	OEM
MA48510A	OEM
MA48510B-E	OEM
MA48511A	OEM
MA48511B-E	OEM
MA48701A	OEM
MA48701B-F	OEM
MA48701G	OEM
MA48701H-K	OEM
MA48702A	OEM
MA48702B-F	OEM
MA48702G	OEM
MA48702H-K	OEM
MA48703A	OEM
MA48703B-F	OEM
MA48703G	OEM
MA48703H-K	OEM
MA48704A	OEM
MA48704B-F	OEM
MA48704G	OEM
MA48704H-J	OEM
MA48705A	OEM
MA48705B-F	OEM
MA48705G	OEM
MA48705H	OEM
MA48705I	OEM
MA48706A	OEM
MA48706AB-F	OEM
MA48707A	OEM
MA48707B-F	OEM
MA48708A	OEM
MA48708B-E	OEM
MA48709A	OEM
MA48709B-E	OEM
MA48710A	OEM
MA48710B-E	OEM
MA48711A	OEM
MA48711B-E	OEM
MA49104	OEM
MA49105	OEM
MA49107	OEM
MA49109	OEM
MA49110	OEM
MA49117-118	OEM
MA49121	OEM
MA49122	OEM
MA49123	OEM
MA49124	OEM
MA49126-118	OEM
MA49126-138	OEM
MA49128-138	OEM
MA49135	OEM
MA49136	OEM
MA49137	OEM
MA49138	OEM
MA49139	OEM
MA49140-118	OEM
MA49145	OEM
MA49146	OEM
MA49147	OEM
MA49151	OEM
MA49152	OEM
MA49153	OEM
MA49154	OEM
MA49156	OEM
MA49157	OEM
MA49158	OEM
MA49159	OEM
MA49161	OEM
MA49162	OEM
MA49163	OEM
MA49164	OEM
MA49166	OEM
MA49167	OEM
MA49168	OEM
MA49169	OEM
MA49170	OEM
MA49171	OEM
MA49172	OEM
MA49172-138	OEM
MA49173	OEM
MA49173-138	OEM
MA49177-138	OEM
MA49178-118	OEM
MA49179-118	OEM
MA49179-138	OEM
MA49180-118	OEM
MA49180-138	OEM
MA49181-138	OEM
MA49182-138	OEM
MA49183	OEM
MA49184	OEM

DEVICE TYPE	REPL CODE
MA49185	OEM
MA49186	OEM
MA49187	OEM
MA49188	OEM
MA49189	OEM
MA49190	OEM
MA49191	OEM
MA49192	OEM
MA49193	OEM
MA49195	OEM
MA49260	OEM
MA49265	OEM
MA49508	OEM
MA49618	OEM
MA49628	OEM
MA51355P	OEM
MA60391CP	OEM
MA-80391CP	OEM
MA4914848	OEM
MAB8021	OEM
MAB8421P-F016	OEM
MAB8421PF016	OEM
MAB8421PF047	OEM
MAB8421P-F065	OEM
MAB8441P	OEM
MAB8441P/T158	OEM
MAB8441P-T012	OEM
MAB8441P-T018	OEM
MAB8441P-T023	OEM
MAB8441P-T042	OEM
MAB8441P-T050	OEM
MAB8441P-T065	OEM
MAB8441P-T082	OEM
MAB8441P-T105	OEM
MAB8441P-T107	OEM
MAB8441P-T120	OEM
MAB-8461P-W077	OEM
MAB8461P-W077	OEM
MAB8461P-W086	OEM
MAC2-1	0395
MAC2-2	0400
MAC2-3	0404
MAC2-4	0407
MAC2-5	0411
MAC2-6	0411
MAC2-8	0418
MAC5-1	0395
MAC5-2	0400
MAC5-3	0404
MAC5-4	0407
MAC5-5	0411
MAC5-6	0411
MAC5-7	OEM
MAC5-8	0418
MAC5-T	1050
MAC6-1	OEM
MAC6-2	OEM
MAC6-3	OEM
MAC6-4	OEM
MAC6-5	OEM
MAC6-6	OEM
MAC6-7	OEM
MAC6-8	OEM
MAC7C7.5D5	OEM
MAC7C7.5D10	OEM
MAC10-1	0588
MAC10-2	0588
MAC10-3	0948
MAC10-4	0567
MAC10-5	0951
MAC10-6	0954
MAC10-7	0955
MAC10-8	0960
MAC11-1	0588
MAC11-2	1081
MAC11-3	1085
MAC11-4	0407
MAC11-5	1087
MAC11-6	0411
MAC11-7	1091
MAC11-8	1092
MAC15-4	0767
MAC15-4FP	2188
MAC15-6	0739
MAC15-6FP	2188
MAC15-8	0612
MAC15-8FP	2188
MAC15-10	0869
MAC15-10FP	2188
MAC15A-4	0767
MAC15A4	0767
MAC15A4FP	2188
MAC15A-6	0739
MAC15A6	0739
MAC15A6FP	2188
MAC15A-8	0869
MAC15A8	0612
MAC15A8FP	2188
MAC15A-10	0869
MAC15A10	0869
MAC15A10FP	2188
MAC15A-B	OEM
MAC20-4	0902
MAC20-5	0902
MAC20-6	0902
MAC20-7	0902
MAC20-8	0902
MAC20-9	OEM
MAC20-10	OEM

DEVICE TYPE	REPL CODE
MAC20A-4	5567
MAC20A4	0902
MAC20A-5	5567
MAC20A5	0902
MAC20A-6	5567
MAC20A6	0902
MAC20A-7	5567
MAC20A7	0902
MAC20A-8	5567
MAC20A8	0902
MAC20A-9	OEM
MAC20A9	OEM
MAC20A-10	OEM
MAC20A10	OEM
MAC21-1	OEM
MAC21-2	OEM
MAC21-3	OEM
MAC21-4	OEM
MAC21-5	OEM
MAC21-6	OEM
MAC21-7	OEM
MAC25-4	2332
MAC25-5	2332
MAC25-6	2332
MAC25-7	0902
MAC25-8	0902
MAC25-9	OEM
MAC25-10	OEM
MAC25A-4	5567
MAC25A4	0902
MAC25A-5	5567
MAC25A5	2332
MAC25A-6	5567
MAC25A6	0902
MAC25A-7	5567
MAC25A7	0902
MAC25A-8	5567
MAC25A8	0902
MAC25A-9	OEM
MAC25A9	OEM
MAC25A-10	OEM
MAC25A10	OEM
MAC35-1	1058
MAC35-2	1058
MAC35-3	1058
MAC35-4	1058
MAC35-5	1307
MAC35-6	1307
MAC35-7	1880
MAC35-8	1880
MAC35-9	OEM
MAC35-10	OEM
MAC36-1	3117
MAC36-2	3118
MAC36-3	3119
MAC36-4	3121
MAC36-5	3122
MAC36-6	3123
MAC36-7	3124
MAC36-8	2007
MAC36-9	OEM
MAC36-10	OEM
MAC37-1	1058
MAC37-2	3124
MAC37-3	1058
MAC37-4	1058
MAC37-5	1307
MAC37-6	1307
MAC37-7	1880
MAC37-8	OEM
MAC37-9	OEM
MAC37-10	OEM
MAC38-1	3204
MAC38-2	2004
MAC38-3	2004
MAC38-4	2004
MAC38-5	2006
MAC38-6	2006
MAC38-7	2007
MAC38-8	3208
MAC38-9	OEM
MAC38-10	OEM
MAC50-4	0902
MAC50-5	0902
MAC50-6	0902
MAC50-7	0902
MAC50-8	0902
MAC50-9	OEM
MAC50-10	OEM
MAC50A-4	5567
MAC50A4	0902
MAC50A-5	5567
MAC50A5	0902
MAC50A-6	5567
MAC50A6	0902
MAC50A-7	5567
MAC50A7	0902
MAC50A-8	5567
MAC50A8	0902
MAC50A-9	OEM
MAC50A9	OEM
MAC50A-10	OEM
MAC50A10	OEM
MAC77-1	4341
MAC77-2	1744
MAC77-3	4343
MAC77-4	3458
MAC77-5	4058
MAC77-6	0480

If replacement code is OEM, contact original manufacturer for replacement.

DEVICE TYPE	REPL CODE	DEVICE TYPE	REPL CODE	DEVICE TYPE	REPL CODE	DEVICE TYPE	REPL CODE	DEVICE TYPE	REPL CODE	DEVICE TYPE	REPL CODE	DEVICE TYPE	REPL CODE
MAC77-7	4345	MAC95A7	4404	MAC223-8	1649	MAC525-4	OEM	MACZA9.1D10	0057	MACZA140D10	0252	MACZB91D	0156
MAC77-8	4346	MAC95A8	4404	MAC223-8FP	3430	MAC525-5	OEM	MACZA10D	0064	MACZA150D	0336	MACZB91D5	0156
MAC80-6	OEM	MAC96-1	OEM	MAC223-9	1956	MAC525-6	OEM	MACZA10D1010	OEM	MACZA150D5	0336	MACZB91D10	0156
MAC80-8	OEM	MAC96-2	OEM	MAC223-10	1956	MAC525-7	OEM	MACZA11D	0181	MACZA150D10	0336	MACZB100D	0189
MAC81-6	OEM	MAC96-3	OEM	MAC223-10FP	3430	MAC525-8	OEM	MACZA11D5	0181	MACZA160D	0366	MACZB100D5	0189
MAC81-8	OEM	MAC96-4	OEM	MAC223A-3	OEM	MAC525-9	OEM	MACZA11D10	0181	MACZA160D5	0366	MACZB100D10	0189
MAC91-1	OEM	MAC96-5	OEM	MAC223A3	5227	MAC525-10	OEM	MACZA12D	0052	MACZA160D10	0366	MACZB105D	0099
MAC91-2	OEM	MAC96-6	OEM	MAC223A-4	5227	MAC525A-4	OEM	MACZA12D5	0052	MACZA175D	0420	MACZB105D5	0099
MAC91-3	OEM	MAC96-7	OEM	MAC223A4	5227	MAC525A4	OEM	MACZA12D10	0052	MACZA175D5	0420	MACZB105D10	0099
MAC91-4	OEM	MAC96-8	OEM	MAC223A4FP	3430	MAC525A-5	OEM	MACZA13D	0053	MACZA175D10	0420	MACZB110D	0099
MAC91-5	OEM	MAC96A1	OEM	MAC223A-5	5230	MAC525A5	OEM	MACZA13D5	0053	MACZA180D	0420	MACZB110D5	0099
MAC91-6	OEM	MAC96A2	OEM	MAC223A5	5230	MAC525A-6	OEM	MACZA13D10	0053	MACZA180D5	0420	MACZB110D10	0099
MAC91-7	OEM	MAC96A3	OEM	MAC223A-6	5230	MAC525A6	OEM	MACZA14D	0873	MACZA180D10	0420	MACZB120D	0089
MAC91-8	OEM	MAC96A4	OEM	MAC223A6	5230	MAC525A-7	OEM	MACZA14D5	0873	MACZA200D	1464	MACZB120D5	0089
MAC91A-1	OEM	MAC96A5	OEM	MAC223A6FP	3430	MAC525A7	OEM	MACZA14D10	0873	MACZA200D5	1464	MACZB120D10	0089
MAC91A1	OEM	MAC96A6	OEM	MAC223A-7	OEM	MAC525A-8	OEM	MACZA15D	0681	MACZA200D10	1464	MACZB130D	0285
MAC91A-2	OEM	MAC96A7	OEM	MAC223A7	1649	MAC525A8	OEM	MACZA15D5	0681	MACZB6.8D	0062	MACZB130D5	0285
MAC91A2	OEM	MAC96A8	OEM	MAC223A-8	1956	MAC525A-9	OEM	MACZA15D10	0681	MACZB6.8D5	0062	MACZB130D10	0285
MAC91A-3	OEM	MAC97-4	4925	MAC223A8	1649	MAC525A9	OEM	MACZA16D	0440	MACZB6.8D10	0062	MACZB140D	0252
MAC91A3	OEM	MAC154	OEM	MAC223A8FP	3430	MAC525A-10	OEM	MACZA16D5	0440	MACZB7.5D	0077	MACZB140D5	0252
MAC91A-4	OEM	MAC156	OEM	MAC223A-9	1956	MAC525A10	OEM	MACZA16D10	0440	MACZB7.5D5	0077	MACZB140D10	0252
MAC91A4	OEM	MAC158	OEM	MAC223A9	1956	MAC800-02	OEM	MACZA17D	0210	MACZB7.5D10	0077	MACZB150D	0336
MAC91A-5	OEM	MAC216-4	OEM	MAC223A-10	1956	MAC800-05	OEM	MACZA17D5	0210	MACZB8.2D	0165	MACZB150D5	0336
MAC91A5	OEM	MAC216-6	OEM	MAC223A10	1956	MAC800-10	OEM	MACZA17D10	0210	MACZB8.2D5	0165	MACZB150D10	0336
MAC91A-6	OEM	MAC216-7	OEM	MAC223A10FP	0788	MAC800-20	OEM	MACZA18D	0371	MACZB8.2D10	0165	MACZB160D	0366
MAC91A6	OEM	MAC216-8	OEM	MAC224-4	1128	MAC800-40	OEM	MACZA18D5	0371	MACZB9.1D	0057	MACZB160D5	0366
MAC91A-7	OEM	MAC216A-4	OEM	MAC224-5	OEM	MAC800-60	OEM	MACZA18D10	0371	MACZB9.1D5	0057	MACZB160D10	0366
MAC91A7	OEM	MAC216A4	OEM	MAC224-6	1128	MAC800-80	OEM	MACZA19D	0666	MACZB9.1D10	0057	MACZB175D	0420
MAC91A-8	OEM	MAC216A-6	OEM	MAC224-7	OEM	MAC800A02	OEM	MACZA19D5	0666	MACZB10D	0064	MACZB175D5	0420
MAC91A8	OEM	MAC216A6	OEM	MAC224-8	1128	MAC800A05	OEM	MACZA19D10	0666	MACZB10D5	0064	MACZB175D10	0420
MAC92-1	4381	MAC216A-7	OEM	MAC224-9	OEM	MAC800A10	OEM	MACZA20D	0695	MACZB10D10	0064	MACZB180D	0420
MAC92-2	4381	MAC216A-8	OEM	MAC224-10	OEM	MAC800A20	OEM	MACZA20D5	0695	MACZB11D	0181	MACZB180D5	0420
MAC92-3	4381	MAC216A8	OEM	MAC224-A10	6013	MAC800A40	OEM	MACZA20D10	0695	MACZB11D5	0181	MACZB180D10	0420
MAC92-4	4381	MAC218-2	OEM	MAC224A-4	OEM	MAC800A60	OEM	MACZA22D	0700	MACZB11D10	0181	MACZB200D	1464
MAC92-5	4382	MAC218-3	OEM	MAC224A4	1128	MAC800A80	OEM	MACZA22D5	0700	MACZB12D	0052	MACZB200D5	1464
MAC92-6	4382	MAC218-4	0609	MAC224A-6	OEM	MAC800B02	OEM	MACZA22D10	0700	MACZB12D5	0052	MACZB200D10	1464
MAC92-7	4404	MAC218-5	OEM	MAC224A6	1128	MAC800B05	OEM	MACZA24D	0489	MACZB12D10	0052	MACZC6.8D	0062
MAC92-8	4404	MAC218-6	3205	MAC224A-7	OEM	MAC800B10	OEM	MACZA24D5	0489	MACZB13D	0053	MACZC6.8D5	0062
MAC92A-1	1923	MAC218-7	OEM	MAC224A7	OEM	MAC800B20	OEM	MACZA24D1010	0489	MACZB13D5	0053	MACZC6.8D10	0062
MAC92A1	4381	MAC218-8	2132	MAC224A-8	OEM	MAC800B40	OEM	MACZA25D	0709	MACZB13D10	0053	MACZC7.5D	0077
MAC92A-2	1923	MAC218-8FP	3549	MAC224A8	1128	MAC800B60	OEM	MACZA25D5	0709	MACZB14D	0873	MACZC8.2D	0165
MAC92A2	4381	MAC218-9	OEM	MAC224A-9	OEM	MAC800B80	OEM	MACZA25D10	0709	MACZB14D5	0873	MACZC8.2D5	0165
MAC92A-3	1923	MAC218-10	0591	MAC224A9	OEM	MAC3010-4	5475	MACZA27D	0450	MACZB14D10	0873	MACZC8.2D10	0165
MAC92A3	4381	MAC218-10FP	3549	MAC224A-10	OEM	MAC3010-8	5295	MACZA27D5	0450	MACZB15D	0681	MACZC9.1D	0057
MAC92A-4	1923	MAC218A2	OEM	MAC224A10	1128	MAC3010-15	3205	MACZA27D10	0450	MACZB15D5	0681	MACZC9.1D5	0057
MAC92A4	4381	MAC218A3	OEM	MAC225A5	OEM	MAC3010-25	0303	MACZA28D	0257	MACZB15D10	0681	MACZC9.1D10	0057
MAC92A-5	1924	MAC218A-4	OEM	MAC228-2	OEM	MAC3010-40	5550	MACZA28D10	0257	MACZB16D	0440	MACZC10D	0064
MAC92A5	4382	MAC218A4	0609	MAC228-3	OEM	MAC3010-40I	OEM	MACZA30D	0195	MACZB16D5	0440	MACZC10D5	0064
MAC92A-6	1924	MAC218A-5	OEM	MAC228-4	OEM	MAC3010-401	4270	MACZA30D5	0195	MACZB16D10	0440	MACZC10D10	0064
MAC92A6	4382	MAC218A5	OEM	MAC228-5	OEM	MAC3020-4	5475	MACZA30D10	0195	MACZB17D	0210	MACZC11D	0181
MAC92A-7	1926	MAC218A-6	OEM	MAC228-6	0567	MAC3020-8	4270	MACZA33D	0166	MACZB17D5	0210	MACZC11D10	0181
MAC92A7	4404	MAC218A6	3205	MAC228-7	OEM	MAC3020-15	3205	MACZA33D5	0166	MACZB17D10	0210	MACZC12D	0052
MAC92A-8	1926	MAC218A-7	OEM	MAC228-8	0929	MAC3020-25	0303	MACZA33D10	0166	MACZB18D	0371	MACZC12D5	0052
MAC92A8	4404	MAC218A7	OEM	MAC228-9	OEM	MAC3020-40	3215	MACZA36D	0010	MACZB18D5	0371	MACZC12D10	0052
MAC93-1	OEM	MAC218A-8	OEM	MAC228-10	0059	MAC3020-40I	OEM	MACZA36D5	0010	MACZB18D10	0371	MACZC13D	0053
MAC93-2	OEM	MAC218A8	2132	MAC228A2	OEM	MAC3020-401	4270	MACZA36D10	0010	MACZB19D	0666	MACZC13D5	0053
MAC93-3	OEM	MAC218A8FP	3549	MAC228A3	OEM	MAC3030-4	5475	MACZA39D	0032	MACZB19D5	0666	MACZC13D10	0053
MAC93-4	OEM	MAC218A-9	OEM	MAC228A4	5436	MAC3030-8	5295	MACZA39D5	0032	MACZB19D10	0666	MACZC14D	0873
MAC93-5	OEM	MAC218A9	OEM	MAC228A5	OEM	MAC3030-15	3205	MACZA39D10	0032	MACZB20D	0695	MACZC14D5	0873
MAC93-6	OEM	MAC218A-10	OEM	MAC228A6	5436	MAC3030-25	0303	MACZA43D	0054	MACZB20D5	0695	MACZC14D10	0873
MAC93-7	OEM	MAC218A10	0591	MAC228A7	OEM	MAC3030-40	3215	MACZA43D5	0054	MACZB20D10	0695	MACZC15D	0681
MAC93-8	OEM	MAC218A10FP	3549	MAC228A8	5999	MAC3030-40I	OEM	MACZA43D10	0054	MACZB22D	0700	MACZC15D5	0681
MAC93A-1	OEM	MAC220-2	5295	MAC228A9	OEM	MAC3030-401	4270	MACZA47D	0068	MACZB22D5	0700	MACZC15D10	0681
MAC93A1	OEM	MAC220-3	5295	MAC228A10	0059	MAC3040-4	5475	MACZA47D5	0068	MACZB22D10	0700	MACZC16D	0440
MAC93A-2	OEM	MAC220-5	5295	MAC229-4	5436	MAC3040-8	5295	MACZA47D10	0068	MACZB24D	0489	MACZC16D5	0440
MAC93A2	OEM	MAC220-7	0591	MAC229-6	5999	MAC3040-15	3205	MACZA51D	0092	MACZB24D5	0489	MACZC16D10	0440
MAC93A-3	OEM	MAC220-9	0591	MAC229-8	0845	MAC3040-25	0303	MACZA51D5	0092	MACZB24D10	0489	MACZC17D	0210
MAC93A3	OEM	MAC221-2	5295	MAC229-10	0845	MAC3040-40	3215	MACZA51D10	0092	MACZB25D	0709	MACZC17D5	0210
MAC93A-4	OEM	MAC221-3	5295	MAC229A4	5436	MAC3040-40I	OEM	MACZA56D	0125	MACZB25D5	0709	MACZC17D10	0210
MAC93A4	OEM	MAC221-5	5295	MAC229A6	5999	MAC3040-401	4270	MACZA56D5	0125	MACZB25D10	0709	MACZC18D	0371
MAC93A-5	OEM	MAC221-7	0591	MAC229A8	0845	MAC4688	3169	MACZA56D10	0125	MACZB27D	0450	MACZC18D5	0371
MAC93A5	OEM	MAC221-9	0591	MAC229A10	0059	MAC4689	3177	MACZA60D	2301	MACZB27D5	0450	MACZC18D10	0371
MAC93A-6	OEM	MAC222-1	OEM	MAC244A-5	OEM	MAC4690	3192	MACZA60D5	2301	MACZB27D10	0450	MACZC19D	0666
MAC93A6	OEM	MAC222-2	OEM	MAC320-4	5227	MAC5441	1058	MACZA60D10	2301	MACZB30D	0195	MACZC19D5	0666
MAC93A-7	OEM	MAC222-3	OEM	MAC320-4FP	0788	MAC5442	1307	MACZA62D	0152	MACZB30D5	0195	MACZC19D10	0666
MAC93A7	OEM	MAC222-4	OEM	MAC320-6	5230	MAC5443	1880	MACZA62D5	0152	MACZB30D10	0195	MACZC20D	0695
MAC93A-8	OEM	MAC222-5	OEM	MAC320-6FP	0788	MAC5444	2004	MACZA62D10	0152	MACZB33D	0166	MACZC20D5	0695
MAC93A8	OEM	MAC222-6	OEM	MAC320-8	1649	MAC5445	2006	MACZA68D	0173	MACZB33D5	0166	MACZC20D10	0695
MAC94-1	4381	MAC222-7	OEM	MAC320-8FP	0788	MAC5446	2007	MACZA68D5	0173	MACZB33D10	0166	MACZC22D	0700
MAC94-2	4381	MAC222-8	OEM	MAC320-10	1956	MAC5569	0154	MACZA68D10	0173	MACZB36D	0010	MACZC22D10	0700
MAC94-3	4381	MAC222-9	OEM	MAC320-10FP	0788	MAC5570	0147	MACZA75D	0094	MACZB36D5	0010	MACZC24D	0489
MAC94-4	4381	MAC222-10	OEM	MAC320A4	5227	MAC5573	0154	MACZA75D5	0094	MACZB36D10	0010	MACZC24D5	0489
MAC94-5	4404	MAC222A-1	OEM	MAC320A4FP	0788	MAC5574	0147	MACZA75D10	0094	MACZB39D	0032	MACZC24D10	0489
MAC94-6	4382	MAC222A1	OEM	MAC320A6	5230	MAC40688	3169	MACZA82D	0049	MACZB39D5	0032	MACZC25D	0709
MAC94-7	4404	MAC222A-2	OEM	MAC320A6FP	0788	MAC40689	3177	MACZA82D5	0049	MACZB39D10	0032	MACZC25D5	0709
MAC94-8	4404	MAC222A2	OEM	MAC320A8	1649	MAC40690	3192	MACZA82D1010	0049	MACZB43D	0054	MACZC25D10	0709
MAC94-A2	4381	MAC222A-3	OEM	MAC320A8FP	0788	MAC40795	1880	MACZA87D	0104	MACZB43D5	0054	MACZC27D	0450
MAC94A1	4381	MAC222A3	OEM	MAC320A10	1956	MAC40796	0278	MACZA87D5	0104	MACZB43D10	0054	MACZC27D5	0450
MAC94A2	4381	MAC222A-4	OEM	MAC320A10FP	0788	MAC40797	1880	MACZA87D10	0104	MACZB47D	0068	MACZC27D10	0450
MAC94A3	4381	MAC222A4	OEM	MAC515-4	OEM	MAC40798	0278	MACZA91D	0156	MACZB47D5	0068	MACZC30D	0195
MAC94A4	4381	MAC222A-5	OEM	MAC515-5	OEM	MAC40799	3169	MACZA91D5	0156	MACZB47D10	0068	MACZC30D5	0195
MAC94A5	4382	MAC222A5	OEM	MAC515-6	OEM	MAC40800	3177	MACZA91D10	0156	MACZB51D	0092	MACZC30D10	0195
MAC94A6	4382	MAC222A-6	OEM	MAC515-7	OEM	MAC40801	3192	MACZA100D	0189	MACZB51D5	0092	MACZC33D	0166
MAC94A7	4404	MAC222A6	OEM	MAC515-8	OEM	MACAZ28D5	OEM	MACZA100D5	0189	MACZB51D10	0092	MACZC33D5	0166
MAC94A8	4404	MAC222A-7	OEM	MAC515-9	OEM	MACCZA19D5	OEM	MACZA100D10	0189	MACZB56D	0125	MACZC33D10	0166
MAC95-1	4381	MAC222A7	OEM	MAC515-10	OEM	MACZ9.1D	0057	MACZA105D	0099	MACZB56D5	0125	MACZC36D	0010
MAC95-2	4381	MAC222A-8	OEM	MAC515A-4	OEM	MACZ9.1D5	0057	MACZA105D5	0099	MACZB56D10	0125	MACZC36D5	0010
MAC95-3	4381	MAC222A8	OEM	MAC515A4	OEM	MACZ9.1D10	0057	MACZA105D10	0099	MACZB62D	0152	MACZC36D10	0010
MAC95-4	4382	MAC222A-9	OEM	MAC515A-5	OEM	MACZA6.8D	0062	MACZA110D	0099	MACZB62D5	0152	MACZC39D	0032
MAC95-5	4382	MAC222A9	OEM	MAC515A5	OEM	MACZA6.8D5	0062	MACZA110D5	0099	MACZB62D10	0152	MACZC39D5	0032
MAC95-6	4404	MAC222A-10	OEM	MAC515A-6	OEM	MACZA6.8D10	0062	MACZA110D10	0099	MACZB68D	0173	MACZC39D10	0032
MAC95-7	4404	MAC222A10	OEM	MAC515A6	OEM	MACZA7.5D	0077	MACZA120D	0089	MACZB68D5	0173	MACZC43D	0054
MAC95-8	4404	MAC223-3	5227	MAC515A-7	OEM	MACZA7.5D5	0077	MACZA120D5	0089	MACZB68D10	0173	MACZC43D5	0054
MAC95A1	4381	MAC223-4	5227	MAC515A7	OEM	MACZA7.5D10	0077	MACZA120D10	0089	MACZB75D	0094	MACZC43D10	0054
MAC95A2	4381	MAC223-4FP	3430	MAC515A-8	OEM	MACZA8.2D	0165	MACZA130D	0450	MACZB75D5	0094	MACZC47D	0068
MAC95A3	4381	MAC223-5	5230	MAC515A8	OEM	MACZA8.2D5	0165	MACZA130D5	0450	MACZB75D10	0094	MACZC47D5	0068
MAC95A4	4381	MAC223-6	5230	MAC515A-9	OEM	MACZA8.2D10	0165	MACZA130D10	0450	MACZB82D	0049	MACZC47D10	0068
MAC95A5	4382	MAC223-6FP	3430	MAC515A9	OEM	MACZA9.1D	0057	MACZA140D	0252	MACZB82D5	0049	MACZC51D	0092
MAC95A6	4382	MAC223-7	1649	MAC515A-10	OEM	MACZA9.1D5	0057	MACZA140D5	0252	MACZB82D10	0049	MACZC51D5	0092

If replacement code is OEM, contact original manufacturer for replacement.

465

DEVICE TYPE	REPL CODE
MACZC51D10	0092
MACZC56D	0125
MACZC56D5	0125
MACZC56D10	0125
MACZC62D	0152
MACZC62D5	0152
MACZC62D10	0152
MACZC68D	0173
MACZC68D5	0173
MACZC68D10	0173
MACZC75D	0094
MACZC75D5	0094
MACZC75D10	0094
MACZC82D	0049
MACZC82D5	0049
MACZC82D10	0049
MACZC91D	0156
MACZC91D5	0156
MACZC91D10	0156
MACZC100D	0189
MACZC100D5	0189
MACZC100D10	0189
MACZC105D	0099
MACZC105D5	0099
MACZC105D10	0099
MACZC110D	0099
MACZC110D5	0099
MACZC110D10	0099
MACZC120D	0089
MACZC120D5	0089
MACZC120D10	0089
MACZC130D	0285
MACZC130D5	0285
MACZC130D10	0285
MACZC140D	0252
MACZC140D5	0252
MACZC140D10	0252
MACZC150D	0336
MACZC150D5	0336
MACZC150D10	0336
MACZC160D	0366
MACZC160D5	0366
MACZC160D10	0366
MACZC175D	0420
MACZC175D5	0420
MACZC175D10	0420
MACZC180D	0420
MACZC180D5	0420
MACZC180D10	0420
MACZC200D	1464
MACZC200D5	1464
MACZC200D10	1464
MACZC220D5	OEM
MACZD6.8D	0062
MACZD6.8D5	0062
MACZD6.8D10	0062
MACZD7.5D	0077
MACZD7.5D5	0077
MACZD7.5D10	0077
MACZD8.2D	0165
MACZD8.2D5	0165
MACZD8.2D10	0165
MACZD9.1D	0057
MACZD9.1D5	0057
MACZD9.1D10	0057
MACZD10D	0064
MACZD10D5	0064
MACZD10D10	0064
MACZD11D	0181
MACZD11D5	0181
MACZD11D10	0181
MACZD12D	0052
MACZD12D5	0052
MACZD12D10	0052
MACZD13D	0053
MACZD13D5	0053
MACZD13D10	0053
MACZD14D	0873
MACZD14D5	0873
MACZD14D10	0873
MACZD15D	0681
MACZD15D5	0681
MACZD15D10	0681
MACZD16D	0440
MACZD16D5	0440
MACZD16D10	0440
MACZD17D	0210
MACZD17D5	0210
MACZD17D10	0210
MACZD18D	0371
MACZD18D5	0371
MACZD18D10	0371
MACZD19D	0666
MACZD19D5	0666
MACZD19D10	0666
MACZD20D	0695
MACZD20D5	0695
MACZD20D10	0695
MACZD22D	0700
MACZD22D5	0700
MACZD22D10	0700
MACZD24D	0489
MACZD24D5	0489
MACZD24D10	0489
MACZD25D	0709
MACZD25D5	0709
MACZD25D10	0709
MACZD27D	0450
MACZD27D5	0450

DEVICE TYPE	REPL CODE
MACZD27D10	0450
MACZD28D	0257
MACZD28D10	0257
MACZD30D	0195
MACZD30D5	0195
MACZD30D10	0195
MACZD33D	0166
MACZD33D5	0166
MACZD33D10	0166
MACZD36D	0010
MACZD36D5	0010
MACZD36D10	0010
MACZD39D	0032
MACZD39D5	0032
MACZD39D10	0032
MACZD43D	0054
MACZD43D5	0054
MACZD43D10	0054
MACZD47D	0068
MACZD47D5	0068
MACZD47D10	0068
MACZD51D	0092
MACZD51D5	0092
MACZD51D10	0092
MACZD56D	0125
MACZD56D5	0125
MACZD56D10	0125
MACZD60D	2301
MACZD60D5	2301
MACZD60D10	2301
MACZD62D	0152
MACZD62D5	0152
MACZD62D10	0152
MACZD68D	0173
MACZD68D5	0173
MACZD68D10	0173
MACZD75D	0094
MACZD75D5	0094
MACZD75D10	0094
MACZD82D	0049
MACZD82D5	0049
MACZD82D10	0049
MACZD87D	0104
MACZD87D5	0104
MACZD87D10	0104
MACZD91D	0156
MACZD91D5	0156
MACZD91D10	0156
MACZD100D	0189
MACZD100D5	0189
MACZD100D10	0189
MACZD105D	0099
MACZD105D5	0099
MACZD105D10	0099
MACZD110D	0099
MACZD110D5	0099
MACZD110D10	0099
MACZD120D	0089
MACZD120D5	0089
MACZD120D10	0089
MACZD130D	0285
MACZD130D5	0285
MACZD130D10	0285
MACZD140D	0252
MACZD140D5	0252
MACZD140D10	0252
MACZD150D	0336
MACZD150D5	0336
MACZD150D10	0336
MACZD160D	0366
MACZD160D5	0366
MACZD160D10	0366
MACZD175D	0420
MACZD175D5	0420
MACZD175D10	0420
MACZD180D	0420
MACZD180D5	0420
MACZD180D10	0420
MACZD200D	1464
MACZD200D5	1464
MACZD200D10	1464
MACZD2805	0257
MACZE6.8D	0062
MACZE6.8D5	0062
MACZE6.8D10	0062
MACZE7.5D	0077
MACZE7.5D5	0077
MACZE7.5D10	0077
MACZE8.2D	0165
MACZE8.2D5	0165
MACZE8.2D10	0165
MACZE9.1D	0057
MACZE9.1D5	0057
MACZE9.1D10	0057
MACZE10D	0064
MACZE10D5	0064
MACZE10D10	0064
MACZE11D	0181
MACZE11D5	0181
MACZE11D10	0181
MACZE12D	0052
MACZE12D5	0052
MACZE12D10	0052
MACZE13D	0053
MACZE13D5	0053
MACZE13D10	0285
MACZE14D	0873
MACZE14D5	0873
MACZE14D10	0873

DEVICE TYPE	REPL CODE
MACZE15D	0681
MACZE15D5	0681
MACZE15D10	0681
MACZE16D	0440
MACZE16D5	0440
MACZE16D10	0440
MACZE17D	0210
MACZE17D5	0210
MACZE17D10	0210
MACZE18D	0371
MACZE18D5	0371
MACZE18D10	0371
MACZE19D	0666
MACZE19D5	0666
MACZE19D10	0666
MACZE20D	0695
MACZE20D5	0695
MACZE20D10	0695
MACZE22D	0700
MACZE22D5	0700
MACZE22D10	0700
MACZE24D	0489
MACZE24D5	0489
MACZE24D10	0489
MACZE25D	0709
MACZE25D5	0709
MACZE25D10	0709
MACZE27D	0450
MACZE27D5	0450
MACZE27D10	0450
MACZE30D	0195
MACZE30D5	0195
MACZE30D10	0195
MACZE33D	0166
MACZE33D5	0166
MACZE33D10	0166
MACZE36D	0010
MACZE36D5	0010
MACZE36D10	0010
MACZE39D	0032
MACZE39D5	0032
MACZE39D10	0032
MACZE43D	0054
MACZE43D5	0054
MACZE43D10	0054
MACZE47D	0068
MACZE47D5	0068
MACZE47D10	0068
MACZE51D	0092
MACZE51D5	0092
MACZE51D10	0092
MACZE56D	0125
MACZE56D5	0125
MACZE56D10	0125
MACZE62D	0152
MACZE62D5	0152
MACZE62D10	0152
MACZE68D	0173
MACZE68D5	0173
MACZE68D10	0173
MACZE75D	0094
MACZE75D5	0094
MACZE75D10	0094
MACZE82D	0049
MACZE82D5	0049
MACZE82D10	0049
MACZE91D	0156
MACZE91D5	0156
MACZE91D10	0156
MACZE100D	0189
MACZE100D5	0189
MACZE100D10	0189
MACZE105D	0099
MACZE105D5	0099
MACZE105D10	0099
MACZE110D	0099
MACZE110D5	0099
MACZE110D10	0099
MACZE120D	0089
MACZE120D5	0089
MACZE120D10	0089
MACZE130D	0285
MACZE130D5	0285
MACZE130D10	0285
MACZE140D	0252
MACZE140D5	0252
MACZE140D10	0252
MACZE150D	0336
MACZE150D5	0336
MACZE150D10	0336
MACZE160D	0366
MACZE160D5	0366
MACZE160D10	0366
MACZE175D	0420
MACZE175D5	0420
MACZE175D10	0420
MACZE180D	0420
MACZE180D5	0420
MACZE180D10	0420
MACZE200D	1464
MACZE200D5	1464
MACZE200D10	1464
MACZF1.8D	OEM
MACZF1.8D5	OEM
MACZF1.8D10	OEM
MACZF2.0D	OEM
MACZF2.0D5	OEM
MACZF2.0D10	OEM
MACZF2.2D	OEM

DEVICE TYPE	REPL CODE
MACZF2.2D5	OEM
MACZF2.2D10	OEM
MACZF2.4D	1266
MACZF2.4D5	1266
MACZF2.4D10	1266
MACZF2.7D	0755
MACZF2.7D5	0755
MACZF2.7D10	0755
MACZF3.0D	0118
MACZF3.0D5	0118
MACZF3.0D10	0118
MACZF3.3D	0296
MACZF3.3D5	0296
MACZF3.3D10	0296
MACZF3.6D	0372
MACZF3.6D5	0296
MACZF3.6D10	0372
MACZF3.9D	0036
MACZF3.9D5	0036
MACZF3.9D10	0036
MACZF4.3D	0274
MACZF4.3D5	0274
MACZF4.3D10	0274
MACZF4.7D	0140
MACZF4.7D5	0140
MACZF4.7D10	0140
MACZF5.1D	0041
MACZF5.1D5	0041
MACZF5.1D10	0041
MACZF5.6D	0253
MACZF5.6D5	0253
MACZF5.6D10	0253
MACZF6.2D	0466
MACZF6.2D5	0466
MACZF6.2D10	0466
MACZF6.8D	0062
MACZF6.8D5	0062
MACZF6.8D10	0062
MACZF7.5D	0077
MACZF7.5D5	0077
MACZF7.5D10	0077
MACZF8.2D	0165
MACZF8.2D5	0165
MACZF8.2D10	0165
MACZF9.1D	0057
MACZF9.1D5	0057
MACZF9.1D10	0057
MACZF10D	0064
MACZF10D5	0064
MACZF10D10	0064
MACZF12D	0052
MACZF12D5	0052
MACZF12D10	0052
MACZG2.4D	1266
MACZG2.4D5	1266
MACZG2.4D10	1266
MACZG2.7D	0755
MACZG2.7D5	0755
MACZG2.7D10	0755
MACZG3.0D	0118
MACZG3.0D5	0118
MACZG3.0D10	0118
MACZG3.3D	0296
MACZG3.3D5	0296
MACZG3.3D10	0296
MACZG3.6D	0372
MACZG3.6D5	0372
MACZG3.6D10	0372
MACZG3.9D	0036
MACZG3.9D5	0036
MACZG3.9D10	0036
MACZG4.3D	0274
MACZG4.3D5	0274
MACZG4.3D10	0274
MACZG4.7D	0140
MACZG4.7D5	0140
MACZG4.7D10	0140
MACZG5.1D	0041
MACZG5.1D5	0041
MACZG5.1D10	0041
MACZG5.6D	0253
MACZG5.6D5	0253
MACZG5.6D10	0253
MACZG5.8D5	OEM
MACZG6.2D	0466
MACZG6.2D5	0466
MACZG6.2D10	0466
MACZG6.8D	0062
MACZG6.8D10	0062
MACZG7.5D	0077
MACZG7.5D5	0077
MACZG7.5D10	0077
MACZG8.2D	0165
MACZG8.2D5	0165
MACZG8.2D10	0165
MACZG9.1D	0057
MACZG9.1D5	0057
MACZG9.1D10	0057
MACZG10D	0064
MACZG10D5	0064
MACZG10D10	0064
MACZG12D	0052
MACZG12D5	0052
MACZG12D10	0052
MAD-835	OEM
MAG001B	OEM
MAG15	OEM
MAG17	OEM
MAG19	OEM

DEVICE TYPE	REPL CODE
MAG20	OEM
MAG21A	OEM
MAG21B	OEM
MAG21C	OEM
MAG23A	OEM
MAG23C	OEM
MAG23D	OEM
MAH0801-2-2	OEM
MAI01	OEM
MAI02	OEM
MAI03	OEM
MAI04	OEM
MAI10	OEM
MAI11	OEM
MAI20	OEM
MAL100	OEM
MAN1A	4900
MAN2A	OEM
MAN10A	4900
MAN51A	5340
MAN52A	5342
MAN53A	OEM
MAN54A	5344
MAN58A	OEM
MAN71A	4783
MAN72A	4902
MAN73A	4784
MAN74	4786
MAN74A	4786
MAN78A	OEM
MAN81A	5037
MAN82A	5045
MAN83A	OEM
MAN84A	5040
MAN88A	OEM
MAN101A	4901
MAN1001A	4901
MAN2815	OEM
MAN3610A	5035
MAN3620A	5042
MAN3630A	OEM
MAN3640A	5038
MAN3680A	OEM
MAN3910A	OEM
MAN3920A	OEM
MAN3930A	OEM
MAN3940A	OEM
MAN3980A	OEM
MAN4505	OEM
MAN4510	OEM
MAN4540	OEM
MAN4580A	OEM
MAN4605	OEM
MAN4610	OEM
MAN4630	OEM
MAN4640	OEM
MAN4680A	OEM
MAN4705	OEM
MAN4710	6584
MAN4740	6589
MAN4780A	OEM
MAN4805	OEM
MAN4810	OEM
MAN4840	OEM
MAN4880A	OEM
MAN4905A	OEM
MAN4910A	OEM
MAN4940A	OEM
MAN4980A	OEM
MAN6410	OEM
MAN6610	OEM
MAN6630	OEM
MAN6640	OEM
MAN6650	OEM
MAN6660	OEM
MAN6680	OEM
MAN6710	4262
MAN6730	4266
MAN6740	4267
MAN6750	4268
MAN6760	2192
MAN6780	2185
MAN6910	OEM
MAN6930	OEM
MAN6940	OEM
MAN6950	OEM
MAN6960	OEM
MAN6980	OEM
MAN8610	2362
MAN8630	OEM
MAN8640	OEM
MAN8650	OEM
MAN8910	OEM
MAN8930	OEM
MAN8940	OEM
MAN8950	OEM
MAS20	0136
MAS21	0136
MAS22	0136
MAS23	0136
MAS32	OEM
MAS39	OEM
MAS-839	OEM
MAS-842	OEM
MAT0000100	OEM
MAT0000102	OEM
MAT0000133	OEM
MAT01AH	OEM
MAT01FH	OEM

DEVICE TYPE	REPL CODE
MAT01GH	OEM
MAT01H	OEM
MAY3877S	OEM
MAZCA10D5	OEM
MAg23B	OEM
MB-01	0276
MB01	0015
MB-02	0287
MB-04	0293
MB-06	0299
MB-08	0250
MB0103M	OEM
MB1B	0071
MB1C	OEM
MB-1D	0344
MB1D	0017
MB-1DS	OEM
MB1E	OEM
MB-1F	0182
MB1F	0344
MB-1FS	0017
MB1G	OEM
MB-4-01	0276
MB-4-02	0287
MB-4-04	0293
MB-4-06	0299
MB-4-08	0250
MB6Y	OEM
MB8A	OEM
MB-10	0102
MB10	0102
MB11A02V05	0319
MB11A02V10	0319
MB11A02V20	1404
MB11A02V30	0468
MB11A02V40	0468
MB11A02V60	0441
MB11A02V80	1412
MB11A02W10	2425
MB12A10V05	2347
MB12A10V10	2347
MB12A10V20	2347
MB12A10V30	2353
MB12A10V40	2353
MB12A10V60	2354
MB12A10V80	2356
MB12A10W10	2357
MB12A25V05	2347
MB12A25V10	2347
MB12A25V20	2347
MB12A25V30	2353
MB12A25V40	2353
MB12A25V60	2354
MB12A25V80	2356
MB12A25W10	2357
MB25-100	OEM
MB25-400	OEM
MB25-600	OEM
MB25-800	OEM
MB25-1000	OEM
MB25-1200	OEM
MB60BH302A	OEM
MB61	0319
MB62	1404
MB62H118	OEM
MB64	0468
MB64H153	OEM
MB64H303	OEM
MB66	0441
MB68	1412
MB74LS00	1519
MB74LS00M	1519
MB74LS00P	OEM
MB74LS01	1537
MB74LS01M	1537
MB74LS02	1550
MB74LS02M	1550
MB74LS03	1569
MB74LS03M	1569
MB74LS04	1585
MB74LS04M	1585
MB74LS05	1598
MB74LS05M	1598
MB74LS06	OEM
MB74LS08	1623
MB74LS08M	1623
MB74LS09	1632
MB74LS09M	1632
MB74LS10	1652
MB74LS10M	1652
MB74LS11	1657
MB74LS11M	1657
MB74LS12	1669
MB74LS12M	1669
MB74LS13	1678
MB74LS13M	1678
MB74LS14	1688
MB74LS14M	1688
MB74LS15	1697
MB74LS15M	1697
MB74LS20	0035
MB74LS20M	0035
MB74LS21	1752
MB74LS21M	1752
MB74LS22	1764
MB74LS22M	1764
MB74LS26	1372
MB74LS26M	1372
MB74LS27	0183

DEVICE TYPE	REPL CODE
MB74LS27M	0183
MB74LS28	0467
MB74LS28M	0467
MB74LS30	0822
MB74LS30M	0822
MB74LS32	0088
MB74LS32M	0088
MB74LS33	1821
MB74LS33M	1821
MB74LS37	1719
MB74LS37M	1719
MB74LS38	1828
MB74LS38M	1828
MB74LS38P	OEM
MB74LS40	0135
MB74LS40M	0135
MB74LS42	1830
MB74LS42M	1830
MB74LS47	1834
MB74LS47M	1834
MB74LS48	1838
MB74LS48M	1838
MB74LS49	1839
MB74LS49M	1839
MB74LS51	1027
MB74LS51M	1027
MB74LS54	1846
MB74LS54M	1846
MB74LS55	0452
MB74LS55M	0452
MB74LS73A	1856
MB74LS73AM	1856
MB74LS74A	0243
MB74LS74AM	0243
MB74LS76A	2166
MB74LS76AM	2166
MB74LS76P	2166
MB74LS78	1862
MB74LS78AM	1862
MB74LS83A	2204
MB74LS83AM	2204
MB74LS85	0426
MB74LS85M	0426
MB74LS86	0288
MB74LS86M	0288
MB74LS86P	0288
MB74LS107	1592
MB74LS107A	1592
MB74LS107AM	1592
MB74LS107M	1592
MB74LS109A	1895
MB74LS109AM	1895
MB74LS112A	2115
MB74LS112AM	2115
MB74LS113A	2241
MB74LS113AM	2241
MB74LS114A	2286
MB74LS114AM	2286
MB74LS122	1610
MB74LS122M	1610
MB74LS123	0973
MB74LS123M	0973
MB74LS125A	0075
MB74LS125AM	0075
MB74LS126A	2850
MB74LS126AM	2850
MB74LS132	1615
MB74LS132M	1615
MB74LS136	1618
MB74LS136M	1618
MB74LS138	0422
MB74LS138M	0422
MB74LS139	0153
MB74LS139M	0153
MB74LS145	1554
MB74LS145M	1554
MB74LS151	1636
MB74LS151M	1636
MB74LS153	0953
MB74LS153M	0953
MB74LS155	0209
MB74LS155M	0209
MB74LS156	1644
MB74LS156M	1644
MB74LS157	1153
MB74LS157M	1153
MB74LS158	1646
MB74LS158M	1646
MB74LS160A	0831
MB74LS160AM	0831
MB74LS161A	0852
MB74LS161AM	0852
MB74LS162A	0874
MB74LS162AM	0874
MB74LS163A	0887
MB74LS163AM	0887
MB74LS174	0260
MB74LS174M	0260
MB74LS175	1662
MB74LS175M	1662
MB74LS181	1668
MB74LS181M	1668
MB74LS183	OEM
MB74LS183M	OEM
MB74LS190	1676
MB74LS190M	1676
MB74LS191	1677
MB74LS191M	1677
MB74LS192	1679

466 If replacement code is OEM, contact original manufacturer for replacement.

DEVICE TYPE	REPL CODE
MB74LS192M	1679
MB74LS193	1682
MB74LS193M	1682
MB74LS221	1230
MB74LS221M	1230
MB74LS240	0447
MB74LS240M	0447
MB74LS241	1715
MB74LS242	1717
MB74LS242M	1717
MB74LS243	0900
MB74LS243M	0900
MB74LS244	0453
MB74LS244M	0453
MB74LS245	0458
MB74LS245M	0458
MB74LS247	1721
MB74LS247M	1721
MB74LS248	1723
MB74LS248M	1723
MB74LS249	1724
MB74LS249M	1724
MB74LS251	1726
MB74LS251M	1726
MB74LS253	1728
MB74LS253M	1728
MB74LS257	1733
MB74LS257M	1733
MB74LS258	1735
MB74LS258M	1735
MB74LS266	0587
MB74LS266M	0587
MB74LS273M	0888
MB74LS280	1762
MB74LS280M	1762
MB74LS283	1768
MB74LS283M	1768
MB74LS352	0756
MB74LS352M	0756
MB74LS353	0768
MB74LS353M	0768
MB74LS365A	0937
MB74LS365AM	0937
MB74LS366A	0950
MB74LS366AM	0950
MB74LS367A	0971
MB74LS367AM	0971
MB74LS368A	0985
MB74LS368AM	0985
MB74LS373	0704
MB74LS373P	0704
MB74LS374	0708
MB74LS386	1221
MB74LS386M	1221
MB74LS640	0664
MB74LS640M	0664
MB74LS641	0685
MB74LS641M	0685
MB74LS642	0714
MB74LS642M	0714
MB74LS643	2045
MB74LS643M	2045
MB74LS644	OEM
MB74LS644M	OEM
MB74LS645	0770
MB74LS645M	0770
MB74LS25858	OEM
MB74S00	0699
MB74S38	0775
MB75LS54	1846
MB75LS54M	1846
MB81	0319
MB81G	OEM
MB82	1404
MB82G	OEM
MB82HS181	OEM
MB82HS191	OEM
MB82HS321	OEM
MB82S131	OEM
MB82S321	OEM
MB84	0468
MB84G	OEM
MB84LS85M	OEM
MB86	0441
MB86G	OEM
MB88	1412
MB88G	OEM
MB101	OEM
MB101G	OEM
MB102	OEM
MB102G	OEM
MB104	OEM
MB104G	OEM
MB106	OEM
MB106G	OEM
MB108	OEM
MB108G	OEM
MB200	OEM
MB201	OEM
MB202	0133
MB204	OEM
MB206	OEM
MB207	OEM
MB208	OEM
MB209	OEM
MB211	OEM
MB211BAL2	OEM
MB213	OEM
MB244	0015
MB251	2347
MB251W	OEM
MB252	2347
MB252W	OEM
MB254	2353
MB254W	OEM
MB256	2354
MB256W	OEM
MB257	0015
MB258	2356
MB258W	OEM
MB269	0015
MB270	0015
MB335	OEM
MB336	OEM
MB337	OEM
MB338	OEM
MB339	OEM
MB340	OEM
MB351	1633
MB352	1633
MB354	1663
MB356	1663
MB358	1579
MB366	OEM
MB367	OEM
MB368	OEM
MB369	OEM
MB370	OEM
MB371	OEM
MB400	0232
MB400M	OEM
MB401	0507
MB401M	OEM
MB402	0692
MB402M	OEM
MB403	0867
MB403M	OEM
MB404	1018
MB404M	OEM
MB405	0738
MB405M	OEM
MB406	1265
MB406M	OEM
MB407	1417
MB407M	OEM
MB408	1527
MB408M	OEM
MB410	0936
MB410M	OEM
MB411	1177
MB411M	OEM
MB416	0268
MB416M	OEM
MB417	0310
MB417M	OEM
MB418	0357
MB418M	OEM
MB419	OEM
MB419M	OEM
MB420	1303
MB420M	OEM
MB421	OEM
MB421M	OEM
MB422	OEM
MB422M	OEM
MB423	OEM
MB423M	OEM
MB424	4437
MB424M	OEM
MB425	1852
MB425M	1852
MB426	OEM
MB426M	OEM
MB427	OEM
MB427M	OEM
MB428	OEM
MB428M	OEM
MB429	OEM
MB429M	OEM
MB430	OEM
MB430M	OEM
MB431	OEM
MB431M	OEM
MB432	OEM
MB432M	OEM
MB433	0990
MB433M	OEM
MB434	0990
MB434M	OEM
MB435	3478
MB435M	OEM
MB436	OEM
MB436M	OEM
MB437	OEM
MB437M	OEM
MB438	OEM
MB438M	OEM
MB439	OEM
MB439M	OEM
MB440	1149
MB440M	OEM
MB442	1046
MB442M	OEM
MB443	0614
MB443M	OEM
MB444	OEM
MB444M	OEM
MB445	1487
MB445M	OEM
MB446	OEM
MB446M	OEM
MB447	1818
MB447M	OEM
MB448	0370
MB448M	OEM
MB449	1358
MB449M	OEM
MB450	1635
MB450M	OEM
MB451	1621
MB451M	OEM
MB452	1705
MB453	1477
MB454	0974
MB455	1953
MB456	1906
MB456M	OEM
MB457	1901
MB457M	OEM
MB458	1831
MB458M	OEM
MB459	1845
MB459M	OEM
MB460	1711
MB513AR	0133
MB601	0232
MB602	0507
MB603	0692
MB604	0867
MB605	1018
MB605(BRIDGE)	0319
MB606	0738
MB607	1265
MB609	1417
MB610	2425
MB613	2090
MB614	4772
MB618	5320
MB805	0319
MB805G	OEM
MB810	2425
MB884-180J	OEM
MB1005	OEM
MB1005G	OEM
MB1010	OEM
MB1101	OEM
MB1151	OEM
MB2114A4	OEM
MB2114A5	OEM
MB2114AL1	OEM
MB2114AL2	OEM
MB2114AL3	OEM
MB2114AL4	OEM
MB2115A	OEM
MB2115A2	OEM
MB2115AL	OEM
MB2115H2	OEM
MB2115H3	OEM
MB2115H4	OEM
MB2118-10	OEM
MB2118-12	OEM
MB2118-15	OEM
MB2125A	OEM
MB2125A2	OEM
MB2125AL	OEM
MB2125AL2	OEM
MB2125H1	OEM
MB2125H2	OEM
MB2125H3	OEM
MB2125H4	OEM
MB2128-15	OEM
MB2128-20	OEM
MB2141-3	OEM
MB2141-4	OEM
MB2141-5	OEM
MB2141L3	OEM
MB2141L4	OEM
MB2141L5	OEM
MB2142-2	OEM
MB2142-3	OEM
MB2142L	OEM
MB2142L3	OEM
MB2147A(A)	OEM
MB2147A3(A)	OEM
MB2147AL(A)	OEM
MB2147AL3(A)	OEM
MB2147H	OEM
MB2147H1	OEM
MB2147H2	OEM
MB2147H3	OEM
MB2147HL	OEM
MB2147HL3	OEM
MB2148H	OEM
MB2148H2	OEM
MB2148H3	OEM
MB2148HL	OEM
MB2148HL3	OEM
MB2149H	OEM
MB2149H2	OEM
MB2149H3	OEM
MB2149HL	OEM
MB2149HL3	OEM
MB2164-15(A)	OEM
MB2164-20(A)	OEM
MB2164-25(A)	OEM
MB2167-10(A)	OEM
MB2167-70(A)	OEM
MB2167L70(A)	OEM
MB2186(A)	OEM
MB2505	2347
MB2505W	OEM
MB2510	2357
MB2510W	OEM
MB2716	OEM
MB2716-1	OEM
MB2716-2	OEM
MB2716-5	OEM
MB2716-6	OEM
MB2732A	OEM
MB2732A2	OEM
MB2732A3	OEM
MB2732A4	OEM
MB2732A20	OEM
MB2732A25	OEM
MB2732A30	OEM
MB2764-2	OEM
MB2764-3	OEM
MB2764-4	OEM
MB2764-25	OEM
MB2764-30	OEM
MB2764-45	OEM
MB2815	OEM
MB2815-3	OEM
MB2815-4	OEM
MB2816	OEM
MB2816-3	OEM
MB2816-4	OEM
MB2817(A)	OEM
MB2817-3(A)	OEM
MB2817-4(A)	OEM
MB3106M	OEM
MB3110	OEM
MB3110A	OEM
MB3110APS-G-SNY	OEM
MB3110A-SNY	OEM
MB3202	2246
MB3501K	OEM
MB3505	1633
MB3510	1579
MB3511	OEM
MB3511P-SH	OEM
MB3512PF-EF	OEM
MB3602C	OEM
MB3602K	OEM
MB3602M	OEM
MB3603C	OEM
MB3603K	OEM
MB3603M	OEM
MB3604C	OEM
MB3607C	OEM
MB3607K	OEM
MB3607M	OEM
MB3608C	OEM
MB3608K	OEM
MB3608M	OEM
MB3609C	OEM
MB3609M	OEM
MB3612C	OEM
MB3612M	OEM
MB3614	0656
MB3614C	OEM
MB3614M	OEM
MB3615M	OEM
MB3628A1	OEM
MB3628A3	OEM
MB3628A4(A)	OEM
MB3632	OEM
MB3632-1	OEM
MB3636B	OEM
MB3636B1	OEM
MB3636B2	OEM
MB3705M	OEM
MB3710	1805
MB3712	4227
MB3712HM	4227
MB3713	4399
MB3713HM	4399
MB3730M	OEM
MB3752C	OEM
MB3752K	OEM
MB3752M	OEM
MB3756	4567
MB3756M	OEM
MB3759	1813
MB3759C	OEM
MB3759M	OEM
MB3759P	1813
MB3760C	OEM
MB3760M	OEM
MB3761	OEM
MB3761M	OEM
MB3763	OEM
MB3763PF	OEM
MB3773	OEM
MB3773PS	OEM
MB3775PF	OEM
MB4001K	OEM
MB4002K	OEM
MB4111	OEM
MB4112	OEM
MB4204	0176
MB4204C	0176
MB4204F	OEM
MB4204M	0176
MB6001	OEM
MB6002	OEM
MB6356	1075
MB7051C	2161
MB7051G3	OEM
MB7052P	OEM
MB7052Z	2209
MB7053P	OEM
MB7053Z	2373
MB7054C	OEM
MB7055C	OEM
MB7056C	3139
MB7057P	OEM
MB7057Z	1907
MB7058P	OEM
MB7058Z	2372
MB7059C	OEM
MB7060C	OEM
MB7071ET	OEM
MB7071HT	OEM
MB7071NT	OEM
MB7072EC	OEM
MB7114-40	OEM
MB7114E	OEM
MB7121EC	2374
MB7121EP	OEM
MB7121HC	OEM
MB7121HP	OEM
MB7122EC	2376
MB7122EP	OEM
MB7122HC	OEM
MB7122HP	OEM
MB7123EZ	3257
MB7123HZ	OEM
MB7124EZ	2304
MB7124HZ	OEM
MB7127EP	OEM
MB7127EZ	OEM
MB7127HP	OEM
MB7127HZ	OEM
MB7128EP	OEM
MB7128EZ	3137
MB7128HP	OEM
MB7128HZ	3137
MB7128YP	OEM
MB7128YZ	OEM
MB7130EC	OEM
MB7130HC	OEM
MB7131EC	2835
MB7131HC	2835
MB7132EC	2881
MB7132HC	2881
MB7134EC	OEM
MB7134HC	OEM
MB7136E	OEM
MB7136ET	OEM
MB7136H	OEM
MB7136HT	OEM
MB7137EC	OEM
MB7137HC	OEM
MB7138EC	OEM
MB7138HC	OEM
MB7141EC	OEM
MB7141HC	OEM
MB7142EC	OEM
MB7142HC	OEM
MB7142NC	OEM
MB8116E	0518
MB8116EC	0518
MB8116EP	0518
MB8116EZ	OEM
MB8116HC	OEM
MB8116HP	OEM
MB8116HZ	OEM
MB8116NC	OEM
MB8116NP	OEM
MB8116NZ	OEM
MB8117-10P	OEM
MB8117-10Z	OEM
MB8117-12P	OEM
MB8117-12Z	OEM
MB8117-15C	OEM
MB8117-15P	OEM
MB8117-15Z(A)	OEM
MB8118-10P	OEM
MB8118-10Z	OEM
MB8118-12	OEM
MB8118-12P	OEM
MB8118-12Z	OEM
MB8118-15P	OEM
MB8118-15Z	OEM
MB8128-10C	OEM
MB8128-10P0P	OEM
MB8128-10Z	OEM
MB8128-15	1887
MB8128-15C	6041
MB8128-15P	OEM
MB8128-15Z	OEM
MB8148(A)	OEM
MB8167	OEM
MB8167-55C	OEM
MB8167-70C	OEM
MB8167A45Z	OEM
MB8167A55Z	OEM
MB8168-55Z	OEM
MB8168-70	OEM
MB8168-70Z	OEM
MB8168-90Z	OEM
MB8216E	OEM
MB8216EC	OEM
MB8216N	OEM
MB8264-15	OEM
MB8264-15C	OEM
MB8264-15Z	OEM
MB8264-20	OEM
MB8264-20C	OEM
MB8264-20Z	OEM
MB8264A10P	OEM
MB8264A10Z	OEM
MB8264A12P	OEM
MB8264A12Z	OEM
MB8265-15Z	OEM
MB8265-20Z	OEM
MB8265A10P	OEM
MB8265A10P(A)	OEM
MB8265A10Z	OEM
MB8265A12P	OEM
MB8265A12P(A)	OEM
MB8265A12Z	OEM
MB8266A10Z	OEM
MB8266A12Z	OEM
MB8364A	OEM
MB8364M	OEM
MB8404EC	OEM
MB8404EP	OEM
MB8414EC	OEM
MB8414EP	OEM
MB8416-15P	OEM
MB8416-15Z	OEM
MB8416-20LPF	OEM
MB8416-20P	OEM
MB8416-20Z	OEM
MB8416-25P	OEM
MB8416-25Z	OEM
MB8416A12P	OEM
MB8416A12Z	OEM
MB8416A15P	OEM
MB8416A15Z	OEM
MB8416P	OEM
MB8416XP	OEM
MB8416XZ	OEM
MB8416Z	OEM
MB8417-15P	OEM
MB8417-15Z	OEM
MB8417-20P	OEM
MB8417-20Z	OEM
MB8417-25P	OEM
MB8417-25Z	OEM
MB8417A12P	OEM
MB8417A12Z	OEM
MB8417A15P	OEM
MB8417A15Z	OEM
MB8417P	OEM
MB8417XP	OEM
MB8417XZ	OEM
MB8417Z	OEM
MB8418	OEM
MB8418-20P	OEM
MB8418-20Z	OEM
MB8418-25P	OEM
MB8418-25Z	OEM
MB8418A12P	OEM
MB8418A12Z	OEM
MB8418A15P	OEM
MB8418A15Z	OEM
MB8418B	OEM
MB8418P	OEM
MB8418XP	OEM
MB8418XZ	OEM
MB8418Z	OEM
MB8464-15L	OEM
MB8464-15LLP	OEM
MB8464A-15LL	OEM
MB8464A-15LLP-SK-G	OEM
MB8464A-80L-SK	OEM
MB8719	OEM
MB-8726	OEM
MB8726	OEM
MB8734	OEM
MB8747	OEM
MB8752	OEM
MB8758	OEM
MB8805-403N	OEM
MB8805-417	OEM
MB8805-417N	OEM
MB8841-180	OEM
MB8841-180J	OEM
MB8841-410J	OEM
MB8843	OEM
MB8844	OEM
MB8844-1436K	OEM
MB8845/529M	OEM
MB8845-495M	OEM
MB8845-527	OEM
MB8845-527M	OEM
MB8845-528	OEM
MB8845-528M	OEM
MB8845-549	OEM
MB8845-591	OEM
MB8845-592	OEM
MB8845-595	OEM
MB8847-1257K	OEM
MB8849	OEM
MB8851	OEM
MB8851-514L	OEM
MB8851A	OEM
MB-8851A-123A	OEM
MB8853	OEM
MB8854	OEM
MB8855-139M	OEM
MB8855-140	OEM
MB8855-141	OEM
MB8855-161	OEM
MB8855-176M	OEM
MB8855-333L	OEM
MB8855-406L	OEM
MB8866	OEM
MB8866C	OEM
MB8866M	OEM
MB8868AC	OEM
MB8868AM	OEM
MB8876	OEM
MB8876C	OEM
MB8876M	OEM
MB8877	OEM
MB8877C	OEM
MB8877M	OEM
MB8881	OEM
MB8881N	OEM
MB10101	OEM
MB10101M	OEM
MB10102	OEM
MB10102M	OEM
MB10103	OEM
MB10104	OEM
MB10104M	OEM
MB10105	OEM
MB10105M	OEM
MB10106	OEM
MB10106M	OEM
MB10107	OEM
MB10107M	OEM
MB10109	OEM
MB10109M	OEM
MB10110	OEM
MB10110M	OEM
MB10111	OEM
MB10111M	OEM
MB10115	OEM
MB10115M	OEM
MB10116	OEM
MB10116M	OEM
MB10117	OEM
MB10117M	OEM
MB10118	OEM
MB10118M	OEM
MB10119	OEM
MB10119M	OEM
MB10121	OEM
MB10121M	OEM
MB10124	OEM
MB10124M	OEM
MB10125	OEM
MB10125M	OEM
MB10130	OEM
MB10130M	OEM
MB10131	OEM
MB10131M	OEM
MB10133	OEM
MB10133M	OEM
MB10135	OEM
MB10135M	OEM
MB10136	OEM
MB10136M	OEM
MB10137	OEM
MB10137M	OEM
MB10160	OEM
MB10160M	OEM
MB10161	OEM
MB10161M	OEM
MB10162	OEM
MB10162M	OEM
MB10164	OEM
MB10164M	OEM
MB10174	OEM
MB10174M	OEM
MB10175	OEM
MB10175M	OEM
MB10179	OEM
MB10179M	OEM
MB10180	OEM
MB10180M	OEM
MB10181	OEM
MB10181M	OEM
MB27128-2(A)	1628
MB40176	OEM
MB40176P	OEM
MB40176PF-EF	OEM
MB40176P-SH	OEM
MB40576	OEM
MB62131	OEM
MB81256-15	1463
MB81416-12	OEM
MB81416-15	OEM
MB81461	OEM
MB81461-12	OEM
MB81461-12-PSZ-G-BF2	OEM
MB83256	OEM
MB84001B	0473
MB84001BM	0473
MB84002B	2044
MB84002BM	2044
MB84008B	0982
MB84008BM	0982
MB84011	0215
MB84011-U	0215
MB84011B	0215
MB84011BM	0215

If replacement code is OEM, contact original manufacturer for replacement.

DEVICE TYPE	REPL CODE	DEVICE TYPE	REPL CODE	DEVICE TYPE	REPL CODE	DEVICE TYPE	REPL CODE	DEVICE TYPE	REPL CODE	DEVICE TYPE	REPL CODE	DEVICE TYPE	REPL CODE
MB84011M	0215	MB90063-103K	OEM	MBCZA22D5	0700	MBCZB11D10	0181	MBCZB200D	1464	MBCZC120D10	0089	MBCZD62D5	0152
MB84011U	0215	MB653839	OEM	MBCZA22D10	0700	MBCZB12D	0052	MBCZB200D5	1464	MBCZC130D	0285	MBCZD62D10	0152
MB84011V	0473	MB654308	OEM	MBCZA24D	0489	MBCZB12D5	0052	MBCZB200D10	1464	MBCZC130D5	0285	MBCZD68D	0173
MB84012B	0493	MB654308-8825	OEM	MBCZA24D5	0489	MBCZB12D10	0052	MBCZC6.8D	0062	MBCZC130D10	0285	MBCZD68D5	0173
MB84012BM	0493	MB654839	OEM	MBCZA24D10	0489	MBCZB13D	0053	MBCZC6.8D5	0062	MBCZC140D	0252	MBCZD68D10	0173
MB84013B	0409	MB672312U	OEM	MBCZA25D	0709	MBCZB13D5	0053	MBCZC6.8D10	0062	MBCZC140D5	0252	MBCZD75D	0094
MB84013BM	0409	MB673198U	OEM	MBCZA25D5	0709	MBCZB13D10	0053	MBCZC7.5D	0077	MBCZC140D10	0252	MBCZD75D5	0094
MB84016B	1135	MB825191	OEM	MBCZA25D10	0709	MBCZB14D	0873	MBCZC7.5D5	0077	MBCZC150D	0336	MBCZD75D10	0094
MB84016BM	1135	MB885505-403N	OEM	MBCZA27D	0450	MBCZB14D5	0873	MBCZC7.5D10	0077	MBCZC150D5	0336	MBCZD82D	0049
MB84017B	0508	MB88201196L	OEM	MBCZA27D5	0450	MBCZB14D10	0873	MBCZC8.2D	0165	MBCZC150D10	0336	MBCZD82D5	0049
MB84017BM	0508	MBA7767S	OEM	MBCZA27D10	0450	MBCZB15D	0681	MBCZC8.2D5	0165	MBCZC160D	0366	MBCZD82D10	0049
MB84019B	1517	MBB11	OEM	MBCZA28D	0257	MBCZB15D5	0681	MBCZC8.2D10	0165	MBCZC160D5	0366	MBCZD87D	0104
MB84019BM	1517	MBB80	OEM	MBCZA28D5	0257	MBCZB15D10	0681	MBCZC9.1D	0057	MBCZC160D10	0366	MBCZD87D5	0104
MB84020B	1651	MBB88/01	OEM	MBCZA28D10	0257	MBCZB16D	0440	MBCZC9.1D5	0057	MBCZC175D	0420	MBCZD87D10	0104
MB84020BM	1651	MBB88/04	OEM	MBCZA30D	0195	MBCZB16D5	0440	MBCZC9.1D10	0057	MBCZC175D5	0420	MBCZD91D	0156
MB84022B	1247	MBB88/06	OEM	MBCZA30D5	0195	MBCZB16D10	0440	MBCZC10D	0064	MBCZC175D10	0420	MBCZD91D5	0156
MB84022BM	1247	MBB88/08	OEM	MBCZA30D10	0195	MBCZB17D	0210	MBCZC10D5	0064	MBCZC180D	0420	MBCZD91D10	0156
MB84023B	0515	MBB88/0202	OEM	MBCZA33D	0166	MBCZB17D5	0210	MBCZC10D10	0064	MBCZC180D5	0420	MBCZD100D	0189
MB84023BM	0515	MBB100	OEM	MBCZA33D5	0166	MBCZB17D10	0210	MBCZC11D	0181	MBCZC180D10	0420	MBCZD100D5	0189
MB84025B	2061	MBC008	OEM	MBCZA33D10	0166	MBCZB18D	0371	MBCZC11D5	0181	MBCZC200D	1464	MBCZD100D10	0189
MB84025BM	2061	MBC008L	OEM	MBCZA36D	0010	MBCZB18D5	0371	MBCZC11D10	0181	MBCZC200D5	1464	MBCZD105D	0099
MB84027B	1938	MBC008L3	OEM	MBCZA36D5	0010	MBCZB18D10	0371	MBCZC12D	0052	MBCZC200D10	1464	MBCZD105D5	0099
MB84027BM	OEM	MBC0083	OEM	MBCZA36D10	0010	MBCZB19D	0666	MBCZC12D5	0052	MBCZD6.8D	0062	MBCZD105D10	0099
MB84028B	2213	MBC01A2	OEM	MBCZA39D	0032	MBCZB19D5	0666	MBCZC12D10	0052	MBCZD6.8D5	0062	MBCZD110D	0099
MB84028BM	2213	MBC010-65	OEM	MBCZA39D5	0032	MBCZB19D10	0666	MBCZC13D	0053	MBCZD6.8D10	0062	MBCZD110D5	0099
MB84029B	2218	MBC010-68	OEM	MBCZA39D10	0032	MBCZB20D	0695	MBCZC13D5	0053	MBCZD7.5D	0077	MBCZD110D10	0099
MB84029BM	2218	MBC016	OEM	MBCZA43D	0054	MBCZB20D5	0695	MBCZC13D10	0053	MBCZD7.5D5	0077	MBCZD120D	0089
MB84040B	0056	MBC016D	OEM	MBCZA43D5	0054	MBCZB20D10	0695	MBCZC14D	0873	MBCZD7.5D10	0077	MBCZD120D5	0089
MB84040BM	0056	MBC016L	OEM	MBCZA43D10	0054	MBCZB22D	0700	MBCZC14D5	0873	MBCZD8.2D	0165	MBCZD120D10	0089
MB84049B	0001	MBC016L3	OEM	MBCZA47D	0068	MBCZB22D5	0700	MBCZC14D10	0873	MBCZD8.2D5	0165	MBCZD130D	0285
MB84049BM	0001	MBC020-65	OEM	MBCZA47D5	0068	MBCZB22D10	0700	MBCZC15D	0681	MBCZD8.2D10	0165	MBCZD130D5	0285
MB84050B	0394	MBC020-68	OEM	MBCZA47D10	0068	MBCZB24D	0489	MBCZC15D5	0681	MBCZD9.1D	0057	MBCZD130D10	0285
MB84050BM	0394	MBC-032/16	OEM	MBCZA51D	0092	MBCZB24D5	0489	MBCZC15D10	0681	MBCZD9.1D5	0057	MBCZD140D	0252
MB84051B	0362	MBC-032/16C	OEM	MBCZA51D5	0092	MBCZB24D10	0489	MBCZC16D	0440	MBCZD9.1D10	0057	MBCZD140D5	0252
MB84051BM	0362	MBC032D	OEM	MBCZA51D10	0092	MBCZB25D	0709	MBCZC16D5	0440	MBCZD10D	0064	MBCZD140D10	0252
MB84052B	0024	MBC048D	OEM	MBCZA56D	0125	MBCZB25D5	0709	MBCZC16D10	0440	MBCZD10D5	0064	MBCZD150D	0336
MB84052BM	0024	MBC-064/16	OEM	MBCZA56D5	0125	MBCZB25D10	0709	MBCZC17D	0210	MBCZD10D10	0064	MBCZD150D5	0336
MB84053B	0034	MBC-064/16C	OEM	MBCZA56D10	0125	MBCZB27D	0450	MBCZC17D5	0210	MBCZD11D5	0181	MBCZD150D10	0336
MB84053BM	0034	MBC064D	OEM	MBCZA60D	2301	MBCZB27D5	0450	MBCZC17D10	0210	MBCZD11D10	0181	MBCZD160D	0366
MB84060B	0146	MBC-096/16	OEM	MBCZA60D5	2301	MBCZB27D10	0450	MBCZC18D	0371	MBCZD12D	0052	MBCZD160D5	0366
MB84060BM	0146	MBC-096/16C	OEM	MBCZA60D10	2301	MBCZB30D	0195	MBCZC18D5	0371	MBCZD12D5	0052	MBCZD160D10	0366
MB84066B	0101	MBC0163	OEM	MBCZA62D	0152	MBCZB30D5	0195	MBCZC18D10	0371	MBCZD12D10	0052	MBCZD175D	0420
MB84066BM	0101	MBC11	OEM	MBCZA62D5	0152	MBCZB30D10	0195	MBCZC19D	0666	MBCZD13D	0053	MBCZD175D5	0420
MB84068B	0101	MBC-86/12(A)	OEM	MBCZA62D10	0152	MBCZB33D	0166	MBCZC19D5	0666	MBCZD13D5	0053	MBCZD175D10	0420
MB84068BM	2482	MBC86/12-032/5	OEM	MBCZA68D	0173	MBCZB33D5	0166	MBCZC19D10	0666	MBCZD13D10	0053	MBCZD180D	0420
MB84069B	0119	MBC-86/12-032/5(A)	OEM	MBCZA68D5	0173	MBCZB33D10	0166	MBCZC20D	0695	MBCZD14D	0873	MBCZD180D5	0420
MB84069BM	0119	MBC86/12-032/8	OEM	MBCZA68D10	0173	MBCZB36D	0010	MBCZC20D5	0695	MBCZD14D5	0873	MBCZD180D10	0420
MB84070B	2494	MBC-86/12-032/8(A)	OEM	MBCZA75D	0094	MBCZB36D5	0010	MBCZC20D10	0695	MBCZD14D10	0873	MBCZD200D	1464
MB84070BM	2494	MBC86/12-128/5	OEM	MBCZA75D5	0094	MBCZB36D10	0010	MBCZC22D	0700	MBCZD15D	0681	MBCZD200D5	1464
MB84071B	0129	MBC-86/12-128/5(A)	OEM	MBCZA75D10	0094	MBCZB39D	0032	MBCZC22D5	0700	MBCZD15D5	0681	MBCZD200D10	1464
MB84071BM	0129	MBC86/12-128/8	OEM	MBCZA82D	0049	MBCZB39D5	0032	MBCZC22D10	0700	MBCZD15D10	0681	MBCZE6.8D	0062
MB84072B	2502	MBC-86/12-128/8(A)	OEM	MBCZA82D5	0049	MBCZB39D10	0032	MBCZC24D	0489	MBCZD16D	0440	MBCZE6.8D5	0062
MB84072BM	2502	MBC100	OEM	MBCZA82D10	0049	MBCZB43D	0054	MBCZC24D5	0489	MBCZD16D5	0440	MBCZE6.8D10	0062
MB84073B	1528	MBC-128/16	OEM	MBCZA87D	0104	MBCZB43D5	0054	MBCZC24D10	0489	MBCZD16D10	0440	MBCZE7.5D	0077
MB84073BM	1528	MBC-128/16C	OEM	MBCZA87D5	0104	MBCZB43D10	0054	MBCZC25D	0709	MBCZD17D	0210	MBCZE7.5D5	0077
MB84075B	2518	MBC-256/16	OEM	MBCZA87D10	0104	MBCZB47D	0068	MBCZC25D5	0709	MBCZD17D5	0210	MBCZE7.5D10	0077
MB84075BM	2518	MBC-256/16C	OEM	MBCZA91D	0156	MBCZB47D5	0068	MBCZC25D10	0709	MBCZD17D10	0210	MBCZE8.2D	0165
MB84077B	2536	MBC-384/16	OEM	MBCZA91D5	0156	MBCZB47D10	0068	MBCZC27D	0450	MBCZD18D	0371	MBCZE8.2D5	0165
MB84077BM	2536	MBC-384/16C	OEM	MBCZA91D10	0156	MBCZB51D	0092	MBCZC27D5	0450	MBCZD18D5	0371	MBCZE8.2D10	0165
MB84078B	0915	MBC-512/16	OEM	MBCZA100D	0189	MBCZB51D5	0092	MBCZC27D10	0450	MBCZD18D10	0371	MBCZE9.1D	0057
MB84078BM	0915	MBC-512/16C	OEM	MBCZA100D5	0189	MBCZB51D10	0092	MBCZC30D	0195	MBCZD19D	0666	MBCZE9.1D5	0057
MB84081B	0621	MBCBCZC75D10	OEM	MBCZA100D10	0189	MBCZB56D	0125	MBCZC30D5	0195	MBCZD19D5	0666	MBCZE9.1D10	0057
MB84081BM	0621	MBCTF1	OEM	MBCZA105D	0099	MBCZB56D5	0125	MBCZC30D10	0195	MBCZD19D10	0666	MBCZE10D	0064
MB84082B	0297	MBCZA6.8D	0062	MBCZA105D5	0099	MBCZB56D10	0125	MBCZC33D	0166	MBCZD20D	0695	MBCZE10D5	0064
MB84082BM	0297	MBCZA6.8D5	0062	MBCZA105D10	0099	MBCZB62D	0152	MBCZC33D5	0166	MBCZD20D5	0695	MBCZE10D10	0064
MB84082BMBM	OEM	MBCZA6.8D10	0062	MBCZA110D	0099	MBCZB62D5	0152	MBCZC33D10	0166	MBCZD20D10	0695	MBCZE11D	0181
MB84518BM	OEM	MBCZA7.5D	0077	MBCZA110D5	0099	MBCZB62D10	0152	MBCZC36D	0010	MBCZD22D	0700	MBCZE11D5	0181
MB84520B	2650	MBCZA7.5D5	0077	MBCZA110D10	0099	MBCZB68D	0173	MBCZC36D5	0010	MBCZD22D5	0700	MBCZE11D10	0181
MB84520BM	OEM	MBCZA7.5D10	0077	MBCZA120D	0089	MBCZB68D5	0173	MBCZC36D10	0010	MBCZD22D10	0700	MBCZE12D	0052
MB84524B	OEM	MBCZA8.2D	0165	MBCZA120D5	0089	MBCZB68D10	0173	MBCZC39D	0032	MBCZD24D	0489	MBCZE12D5	0052
MB84524BM	OEM	MBCZA8.2D5	0165	MBCZA120D10	0089	MBCZB75D	0094	MBCZC39D5	0032	MBCZD24D5	0489	MBCZE12D10	0052
MB86140	OEM	MBCZA8.2D10	0165	MBCZA130D	0285	MBCZB75D5	0165	MBCZC39D10	0032	MBCZD24D10	0489	MBCZE13D	0053
MB86140P-SH	OEM	MBCZA9.1D	0057	MBCZA130D5	0285	MBCZB75D10	0094	MBCZC43D	0054	MBCZD25D	0709	MBCZE13D5	0053
MB86144B	OEM	MBCZA9.1D5	0057	MBCZA130D10	0285	MBCZB82D	0049	MBCZC43D5	0054	MBCZD25D5	0709	MBCZE13D10	0053
MB88201-128L	OEM	MBCZA9.1D10	0057	MBCZA140D	0252	MBCZB82D5	0049	MBCZC43D10	0054	MBCZD25D10	0709	MBCZE14D	0873
MB88201-196L	OEM	MBCZA10D	0064	MBCZA140D5	0252	MBCZB82D10	0049	MBCZC47D	0068	MBCZD27D	0450	MBCZE14D5	0873
MB88201-638L	OEM	MBCZA10D5	0064	MBCZA140D10	0252	MBCZB91D	0156	MBCZC47D5	0068	MBCZD27D5	0450	MBCZE14D10	0873
MB88201P-127K	OEM	MBCZA10D10	0064	MBCZA150D	0336	MBCZB91D5	0156	MBCZC47D10	0068	MBCZD27D10	0450	MBCZE15D	0681
MB88301A	OEM	MBCZA11D	0181	MBCZA150D5	0336	MBCZB91D10	0156	MBCZC51D	0092	MBCZD28D	0257	MBCZE15D5	0681
MB88303	OEM	MBCZA11D5	0181	MBCZA150D10	0336	MBCZB100D	0189	MBCZC51D5	0092	MBCZD28D5	0257	MBCZE15D10	0681
MB88303-P	OEM	MBCZA11D10	0181	MBCZA160D	0366	MBCZB100D5	0189	MBCZC51D10	0092	MBCZD28D10	0257	MBCZE16D	0440
MB88303P	OEM	MBCZA12D	0052	MBCZA160D5	0366	MBCZB100D10	0189	MBCZC56D	0125	MBCZD30D	0195	MBCZE16D5	0440
MB88323-K-1	OEM	MBCZA12D5	0052	MBCZA160D10	0366	MBCZB105D	0099	MBCZC56D5	0125	MBCZD30D5	0195	MBCZE16D10	0440
MB88341PFV	OEM	MBCZA12D10	0052	MBCZA175D	0420	MBCZB105D5	0099	MBCZC56D10	0125	MBCZD30D10	0195	MBCZE17D	0210
MB88421-147L	OEM	MBCZA13D	0053	MBCZA175D5	0420	MBCZB105D10	0099	MBCZC62D	0152	MBCZD33D	0166	MBCZE17D5	0210
MB88421-147P	OEM	MBCZA13D5	0053	MBCZA175D10	0420	MBCZB110D	0099	MBCZC62D5	0152	MBCZD33D5	0166	MBCZE17D10	0210
MB88501-114M	OEM	MBCZA13D10	0053	MBCZA180D	0420	MBCZB110D5	0099	MBCZC62D10	0152	MBCZD33D10	0166	MBCZE18D	0371
MB88501-120M	OEM	MBCZA14D	0873	MBCZA180D5	0420	MBCZB110D10	0099	MBCZC68D	0173	MBCZD36D	0010	MBCZE18D5	0371
MB88501-249L	OEM	MBCZA14D5	0873	MBCZA180D10	0420	MBCZB120D	0089	MBCZC68D5	0173	MBCZD36D5	0010	MBCZE18D10	0371
MB88503-115M	OEM	MBCZA14D10	0873	MBCZA200D	1464	MBCZB120D5	0089	MBCZC68D10	0173	MBCZD36D10	0010	MBCZE19D	0666
MB88503-119M	OEM	MBCZA15D	0681	MBCZA200D5	1464	MBCZB120D10	0089	MBCZC75D	0094	MBCZD39D	0032	MBCZE19D5	0666
MB88505-340N	OEM	MBCZA15D5	0681	MBCZA200D10	1464	MBCZB130D	0285	MBCZC75D5	0094	MBCZD39D5	0032	MBCZE19D10	0666
MB88505-403N	OEM	MBCZA15D10	0681	MBCZB6.8D	0062	MBCZB130D5	0285	MBCZC82D	0049	MBCZD39D10	0032	MBCZE20D	0695
MB88505-417N	OEM	MBCZA16D	0440	MBCZB6.8D5	0062	MBCZB130D10	0285	MBCZC82D5	0049	MBCZD43D	0054	MBCZE20D5	0695
MB88511-108N	OEM	MBCZA16D5	0440	MBCZB6.8D10	0062	MBCZB140D	0152	MBCZC82D10	0049	MBCZD43D5	0054	MBCZE20D10	0695
MB88514B-640L	OEM	MBCZA16D10	0440	MBCZB7.5D	0077	MBCZB140D5	0152	MBCZC91D	0156	MBCZD43D10	0054	MBCZE22D	0700
MB88541-130M	OEM	MBCZA17D	0210	MBCZB7.5D5	0077	MBCZB140D10	0152	MBCZC91D5	0156	MBCZD47D	0068	MBCZE22D5	0700
MB88733-123	OEM	MBCZA17D5	0210	MBCZB7.5D10	0077	MBCZB150D	0336	MBCZC91D10	0156	MBCZD47D5	0068	MBCZE22D10	0700
MB88733-137	OEM	MBCZA17D10	0210	MBCZB8.2D	0165	MBCZB150D5	0390	MBCZC100D	0189	MBCZD47D10	0068	MBCZE24D	0489
MB89009-107	OEM	MBCZA18D	0371	MBCZB8.2D5	0165	MBCZB150D10	0366	MBCZC100D5	0189	MBCZD51D	0092	MBCZE24D5	0489
MB89009F-102	OEM	MBCZA18D5	0371	MBCZB8.2D10	0165	MBCZB160D	0366	MBCZC100D10	0189	MBCZD51D5	0092	MBCZE24D10	0489
MB89009G-107	OEM	MBCZA18D10	0371	MBCZB9.1D	0057	MBCZB160D5	0366	MBCZC105D	0099	MBCZD51D10	0092	MBCZE25D	0709
MB89009P-102	OEM	MBCZA19D	0666	MBCZB9.1D5	0057	MBCZB160D10	0366	MBCZC105D5	0099	MBCZD56D	0125	MBCZE25D5	0709
MB89009PG-107	OEM	MBCZA19D5	0666	MBCZB9.1D10	0057	MBCZB175D	0420	MBCZC105D10	0099	MBCZD56D5	0125	MBCZE25D10	0709
MB89010-101	OEM	MBCZA19D10	0666	MBCZB10D	0064	MBCZB175D5	0420	MBCZC110D	0099	MBCZD56D10	0125	MBCZE27D	0450
MB89010A-112	OEM	MBCZA20D	0695	MBCZB10D5	0064	MBCZB175D10	0420	MBCZC110D5	0099	MBCZD60D	2301	MBCZE27D5	0450
MB89012-102	OEM	MBCZA20D5	0695	MBCZB10D10	0064	MBCZB180D	0420	MBCZC110D10	0099	MBCZD60D5	2301	MBCZE27D10	0450
MB90062-103A	OEM	MBCZA20D10	0695	MBCZB11D	0181	MBCZB180D5	0420	MBCZC120D	0089	MBCZD60D10	2301	MBCZE30D	0195
MB90062P-106	OEM	MBCZA22D	0700	MBCZB11D5	0181	MBCZB180D10	0420	MBCZC120D5	0089	MBCZD62D	0152	MBCZE30D5	0195

If replacement code is OEM, contact original manufacturer for replacement.

DEVICE TYPE	REPL CODE
MBCZE30D10	0195
MBCZE33D	0195
MBCZE33D5	0195
MBCZE33D10	0195
MBCZE36D	0010
MBCZE36D5	0010
MBCZE36D10	0010
MBCZE39D	0032
MBCZE39D5	0032
MBCZE39D10	0032
MBCZE43D	0054
MBCZE43D5	0054
MBCZE43D10	0054
MBCZE47D	0068
MBCZE47D5	0068
MBCZE47D10	0068
MBCZE51D	0092
MBCZE51D5	0092
MBCZE51D10	0092
MBCZE56D	0125
MBCZE56D5	0125
MBCZE56D10	0125
MBCZE62D	0152
MBCZE62D5	0152
MBCZE62D10	0152
MBCZE68D	0173
MBCZE68D5	0173
MBCZE68D10	0173
MBCZE75D	0094
MBCZE75D5	0094
MBCZE75D10	0094
MBCZE82D	0049
MBCZE82D5	0049
MBCZE82D10	0049
MBCZE91D	0156
MBCZE91D5	0156
MBCZE91D10	0156
MBCZE100D	0189
MBCZE100D5	0189
MBCZE100D10	0189
MBCZE105D	0099
MBCZE105D5	0099
MBCZE105D10	0099
MBCZE110D	0099
MBCZE110D5	0099
MBCZE110D10	0099
MBCZE120D	0089
MBCZE120D5	0089
MBCZE120D10	0089
MBCZE130D	0285
MBCZE130D5	0285
MBCZE130D10	0285
MBCZE140D	0252
MBCZE140D5	0252
MBCZE140D10	0252
MBCZE150D	0336
MBCZE150D5	0336
MBCZE150D10	0336
MBCZE160D	0366
MBCZE160D5	0366
MBCZE160D10	0366
MBCZE175D	0420
MBCZE175D5	0420
MBCZE175D10	0420
MBCZE180D	0420
MBCZE180D5	0420
MBCZE180D10	0420
MBCZE200D	1464
MBCZE200D5	1464
MBCZE200D10	1464
MBCZF1.8D	OEM
MBCZF1.8D5	OEM
MBCZF1.8D10	OEM
MBCZF2.0D	OEM
MBCZF2.0D5	OEM
MBCZF2.0D10	OEM
MBCZF2.2D	OEM
MBCZF2.2D5	OEM
MBCZF2.2D10	OEM
MBCZF2.4D	1266
MBCZF2.4D5	1266
MBCZF2.4D10	1266
MBCZF2.7D	0755
MBCZF2.7D5	0755
MBCZF2.7D10	0755
MBCZF3.0D	0118
MBCZF3.0D5	0118
MBCZF3.0D10	0118
MBCZF3.3D	0296
MBCZF3.3D5	0296
MBCZF3.3D10	0296
MBCZF3.6D	0372
MBCZF3.6D5	0372
MBCZF3.6D10	0372
MBCZF3.9D	0036
MBCZF3.9D5	0036
MBCZF3.9D10	0036
MBCZF4.3D	0274
MBCZF4.3D5	0274
MBCZF4.3D10	0274
MBCZF4.7D	0140
MBCZF4.7D5	0140
MBCZF4.7D10	0140
MBCZF5.1D	0041
MBCZF5.1D5	0041
MBCZF5.1D10	0041
MBCZF5.6D	0253
MBCZF5.6D5	0253
MBCZF5.6D10	0253
MBCZF6.2D	0466
MBCZF6.2D5	0466
MBCZF6.2D10	0466
MBCZF6.8D	0062
MBCZF6.8D5	0062
MBCZF6.8D10	0062
MBCZF7.5D	0077
MBCZF7.5D5	0165
MBCZF7.5D10	0077
MBCZF8.2D	0165
MBCZF8.2D5	0165
MBCZF8.2D10	0165
MBCZF9.1D	0057
MBCZF9.1D5	0057
MBCZF9.1D10	0057
MBCZF10D	0064
MBCZF10D5	0064
MBCZF10D10	0064
MBCZF12D	0052
MBCZF12D5	0052
MBCZF12D10	0052
MBCZG2.4D	1266
MBCZG2.4D5	1266
MBCZG2.4D10	1266
MBCZG2.7D	0755
MBCZG2.7D5	0755
MBCZG2.7D10	0755
MBCZG3.0D	0118
MBCZG3.0D5	0118
MBCZG3.0D10	0118
MBCZG3.3D	0296
MBCZG3.3D5	0296
MBCZG3.3D10	0296
MBCZG3.6D	0372
MBCZG3.6D5	0372
MBCZG3.6D10	0372
MBCZG3.9D	0036
MBCZG3.9D5	0036
MBCZG3.9D10	0036
MBCZG4.3D	0274
MBCZG4.3D5	0274
MBCZG4.3D10	0274
MBCZG4.7D	0140
MBCZG4.7D5	0140
MBCZG4.7D10	0140
MBCZG5.1D	0041
MBCZG5.1D5	0041
MBCZG5.1D10	0041
MBCZG5.6D	0253
MBCZG5.6D5	0253
MBCZG5.6D10	0253
MBCZG6.2D	0466
MBCZG6.2D5	0466
MBCZG6.2D10	0466
MBCZG6.8D	0062
MBCZG6.8D5	0062
MBCZG6.8D10	0062
MBCZG7.5D	0077
MBCZG7.5D5	OEM
MBCZG7.5D10	0077
MBCZG8.2D	0165
MBCZG8.2D5	0165
MBCZG8.2D10	0165
MBCZG9.1D	0057
MBCZG9.1D5	0057
MBCZG9.1D10	0057
MBCZG10D	0064
MBCZG10D5	0064
MBCZG10D10	0064
MBCZG12D	0052
MBCZG12D5	0052
MBCZG12D10	0052
MBCZZD11D	OEM
MBD101	0911
MBD102	0911
MBD201	OEM
MBD301	OEM
MBD501	OEM
MBD502	OEM
MBD701	OEM
MBD702	OEM
MBD5300	OEM
MBD5400	OEM
MBD5500	OEM
MBD5500A	OEM
MBD5550	OEM
MBD5550A	OEM
MBI-49-LPC	OEM
MBI-101	0911
MBI101	OEM
MBL6821N	0443
MBL8042H	OEM
MBL8049H	OEM
MBL8051AH	OEM
MBL8086-2	OEM
MBL8086-2P	OEM
MBL8088	OEM
MBL8088-1	OEM
MBL8259A-2	OEM
MBL8259A-2P	OEM
MBL8288	OEM
MBL82284-8	OEM
MBM27C64-20	OEM
MBM27C64-25CV	OEM
MBM27C64-25Z	OEM
MBM27C64-30CV	OEM
MBM27C64-30Z	OEM
MBM27C512-20	OEM
MBM2114A10LP	OEM
MBM2114A15LP	OEM
MBM2114A20LP	OEM
MBM2114A20P	OEM
MBM2147E	1683
MBM2147F35Z	OEM
MBM2147F45Z	OEM
MBM2147H35C	OEM
MBM2147H35F	OEM
MBM2147H35Z	OEM
MBM2147H45C	OEM
MBM2147H45F	OEM
MBM2147H45Z	OEM
MBM2147H55Z	1683
MBM2147H70Z	1683
MBM2148-55	OEM
MBM2148-55LZ	OEM
MBM2148-55Z(A)	OEM
MBM2148-70	OEM
MBM2148-70LZ	OEM
MBM2148-70Z(A)	OEM
MBM2149-45Z	OEM
MBM2149-55LZ	OEM
MBM2149-55Z	OEM
MBM2149-70LZ	OEM
MBM2149-70Z	OEM
MBM2716C	OEM
MBM2716HC	OEM
MBM2716HZ	OEM
MBM2716XZ	OEM
MBM2716Z	OEM
MBM2732-35Z	2672
MBM2732-45Z	2672
MBM2732A-20-QGA0-1	OEM
MBM2732A-20-QGA1	2672
MBM2732A20Z	2672
MBM2732A25	5829
MBM2732A25Z	2672
MBM2732A30	2672
MBM2732A30XZ	OEM
MBM2732A30Z	2672
MBM2732A35XZ	OEM
MBM2732A35Z	2672
MBM2764-20	0806
MBM2764-20Z	OEM
MBM2764-25	0806
MBM2764-25Z	OEM
MBM2764-30	0806
MBM2764-30XZ	OEM
MBM2764-30Z	OEM
MBM10415AC	OEM
MBM10415AHC	OEM
MBM10422A7C	OEM
MBM10422C	OEM
MBM10470-20	OEM
MBM10470A20C	OEM
MBM10474A15C	OEM
MBM10474C	OEM
MBM10480	OEM
MBM27128-25	1628
MBM27128-25TED-K	1628
MBM27256	OEM
MBM27256-20	OEM
MBM27256-XX	OEM
MBM93419C	OEM
MBM100422A7C	OEM
MBM100422C	OEM
MBM100422TF	OEM
MBM100470C	OEM
MBM100470CF	OEM
MBM100474-15C	OEM
MBM100474-20C	OEM
MBN101	OEM
MBR115P	1325
MBR120P	0730
MBR130P	0730
MBR140P	0730
MBR160	3834
MBR170	3834
MBR180	3834
MBR190	3834
MBR320M	OEM
MBR320P	OEM
MBR330M	OEM
MBR330P	OEM
MBR335M	OEM
MBR340M	OEM
MBR340P	OEM
MBR370	3559
MBR380	3559
MBR390	3559
MBR735	OEM
MBR745	OEM
MBR920	3338
MBR1020	OEM
MBR1035	OEM
MBR1045	OEM
MBR1060	OEM
MBR1100	OEM
MBR1520	0610
MBR1530	0610
MBR1535	0610
MBR1535CT	4249
MBR1540	0610
MBR1545CT	4249
MBR1635	OEM
MBR1645	OEM
MBR2035CT	4249
MBR2045CT	4249
MBR2060CT	OEM
MBR2520	OEM
MBR2530	OEM
MBR2535	OEM
MBR2535CT	2493
MBR2540	OEM
MBR2545CT	2493
MBR3020CT	OEM
MBR3035CT	OEM
MBR3035PT	5933
MBR3045CT	OEM
MBR3045HI	OEM
MBR3045PT	1931
MBR3100	OEM
MBR3520	5507
MBR3530	OEM
MBR3535	0610
MBR3545	0610
MBR3545H	OEM
MBR3545H1	OEM
MBR4020	1536
MBR4030	1536
MBR4030PF	OEM
MBR4035	1536
MBR4040	1536
MBR5825H	OEM
MBR5825H1	OEM
MBR5831H	OEM
MBR5831H1	OEM
MBR6020	1536
MBR6020B	OEM
MBR6020B0B	OEM
MBR6035	1536
MBR6035B	OEM
MBR6035CT	OEM
MBR6035PF	OEM
MBR6045	1536
MBR6045B	OEM
MBR6045CT	OEM
MBR6045H	OEM
MBR6045H1	OEM
MBR6045PF	OEM
MBR6535	OEM
MBR6545	OEM
MBR7535	OEM
MBR7545	OEM
MBR7545H	OEM
MBR7545H1	OEM
MBR8035	OEM
MBR8045	OEM
MBR12035CT	OEM
MBR12045CT	OEM
MBR20035CT	OEM
MBR20045CT	OEM
MBR30035CT	OEM
MBR30045CT	OEM
MBR583131H	OEM
MBRL030	OEM
MBRL040	OEM
MBS4C	OEM
MBS100	OEM
MBS4991	4169
MBS4992	4169
MC	OEM
MC001	OEM
MC001A	OEM
MC002	OEM
MC005	OEM
MC0	OEM
MC010	0015
MC015	0015
MC020	0604
MC020A	0604
MC021	1325
MC021A	1325
MC022	0080
MC022A	0080
MC023	0604
MC023A	0604
MC025	0015
MC030	0790
MC030A	0604
MC030B	0015
MC031	OEM
MC031A	OEM
MC032	OEM
MC032A	OEM
MC035	0015
MC040	0790
MC040A	0790
MC041	OEM
MC041A	OEM
MC042	OEM
MC042A	OEM
MC050	0015
MC050A	0015
MC051	OEM
MC051A	OEM
MC052	OEM
MC052A	OEM
MC060	0015
MC060A	0015
MC061	OEM
MC061A	OEM
MC062	OEM
MC062A	OEM
MC070	0071
MC070A	0071
MC080	0071
MC080A	0071
MC081	OEM
MC081A	OEM
MC082	OEM
MC082A	OEM
MC090	0071
MC090A	0071
MC091	OEM
MC092	OEM
MC092A	OEM
MC093	OEM
MC093A	OEM
MC094	OEM
MC094A	OEM
MC095	OEM
MC095A	OEM
MC096	OEM
MC096A	OEM
MC097A	OEM
MC098	OEM
MC098A	OEM
MC0101PD	OEM
MC02323	OEM
MC09797	OEM
MC1	OEM
MC1B	OEM
MC1C	OEM
MC1D	OEM
MC1E	OEM
MC1F	OEM
MC1G	OEM
MC2	0133
MC3	OEM
MC4B1	OEM
MC4B2	OEM
MC4C1	OEM
MC4C2	OEM
MC5	OEM
MC5B1	OEM
MC5B2	OEM
MC5C1	OEM
MC5C2	OEM
MC6A1	OEM
MC6A2	OEM
MC6B1	OEM
MC6B2	OEM
MC6C1	OEM
MC6C2	OEM
MC7	OEM
MC7A	OEM
MC7A1	OEM
MC7A2	OEM
MC7B	OEM
MC7B1	OEM
MC7B2	OEM
MC7C	OEM
MC7C1	OEM
MC7C2	OEM
MC7D	OEM
MC8A1	OEM
MC8A2	OEM
MC8B1	OEM
MC8B2	OEM
MC8T2LD	OEM
MC8T2LDS	OEM
MC8T13L	OEM
MC8T13LD	OEM
MC8T13LDS	OEM
MC8T13LS	OEM
MC8T13P	OEM
MC8T13PD	OEM
MC8T13PDS	OEM
MC8T13PS	OEM
MC8T14L	OEM
MC8T14LD	OEM
MC8T14LDS	OEM
MC8T14LS	OEM
MC8T14P	OEM
MC8T14PD	OEM
MC8T14PDS	OEM
MC8T14PS	OEM
MC8T23L	OEM
MC8T23LD	OEM
MC8T23LDS	OEM
MC8T23LS	OEM
MC8T23P	OEM
MC8T23PD	OEM
MC8T23PDS	OEM
MC8T23PS	OEM
MC8T24L	OEM
MC8T24LS	OEM
MC8T24P	OEM
MC8T24PD	OEM
MC8T24PDS	OEM
MC8T24PS	OEM
MC8T26AL	4437
MC8T26ALD	OEM
MC8T26ALDS	OEM
MC8T26ALS	OEM
MC8T26AP	4437
MC8T26APD	OEM
MC8T26APDS	OEM
MC8T26APS	OEM
MC8T28L	0576
MC8T28LD	OEM
MC8T28LDS	OEM
MC8T28LS	OEM
MC8T28P	0576
MC8T28PD	OEM
MC8T28PDS	OEM
MC8T28PS	OEM
MC8T95L	4566
MC8T95LD	OEM
MC8T95LDS	OEM
MC8T95LS	OEM
MC8T95P	4566
MC8T95PD	OEM
MC8T95PDS	OEM
MC8T95PS	OEM
MC8T96L	4570
MC8T96LD	OEM
MC8T96LDS	OEM
MC8T96LS	OEM
MC8T96P	4570
MC8T96PD	OEM
MC8T96PDS	OEM
MC8T96PS	OEM
MC8T97L	4577
MC8T97LD	OEM
MC8T97LDS	OEM
MC8T97LS	OEM
MC8T97P	4577
MC8T97PD	OEM
MC8T97PDS	OEM
MC8T97PS	OEM
MC8T98L	4586
MC8T98LD	OEM
MC8T98LDS	OEM
MC8T98LS	OEM
MC8T98P	4586
MC8T98PD	OEM
MC8T98PDS	OEM
MC8T98PS	OEM
MC9	OEM
MC9A1	OEM
MC9A2	OEM
MC9B1	OEM
MC9B2	OEM
MC10	0005
MC10A1	OEM
MC10A2	OEM
MC10B1	OEM
MC10B2	OEM
MC10F	OEM
MC10H016L	OEM
MC10H016P	OEM
MC10H100L	OEM
MC10H100P	OEM
MC10H101L	OEM
MC10H101P	OEM
MC10H102L	OEM
MC10H102P	OEM
MC10H103L	OEM
MC10H103P	OEM
MC10H104L	OEM
MC10H104P	OEM
MC10H105L	OEM
MC10H105P	OEM
MC10H106L	OEM
MC10H106P	OEM
MC10H107L	OEM
MC10H107P	OEM
MC10H109L	OEM
MC10H109P	OEM
MC10H115L	OEM
MC10H115P	OEM
MC10H116L	OEM
MC10H116P	OEM
MC10H117L	OEM
MC10H117P	OEM
MC10H118L	OEM
MC10H118P	OEM
MC10H119L	OEM
MC10H119P	OEM
MC10H121L	OEM
MC10H121P	OEM
MC10H124L	OEM
MC10H124P	OEM
MC10H125L	OEM
MC10H125P	OEM
MC10H130L	OEM
MC10H130P	OEM
MC10H131L	OEM
MC10H131P	OEM
MC10H136L	OEM
MC10H136P	OEM
MC10H141L	OEM
MC10H141P	OEM
MC10H145L	OEM
MC10H145P	OEM
MC10H155L	OEM
MC10H155P	OEM
MC10H158L	OEM
MC10H158P	OEM
MC10H159L	OEM
MC10H159P	OEM
MC10H160L	OEM
MC10H160P	OEM
MC10H161L	OEM
MC10H161P	OEM
MC10H162L	OEM
MC10H162P	OEM
MC10H164L	OEM
MC10H164P	OEM
MC10H165L	OEM
MC10H165P	OEM
MC10H166L	OEM
MC10H166P	OEM
MC10H173L	OEM
MC10H173P	OEM
MC10H174L	OEM
MC10H174P	OEM
MC10H175L	OEM
MC10H175P	OEM
MC10H176L	OEM
MC10H176P	OEM
MC10H179L	OEM
MC10H179P	OEM
MC10H180L	OEM
MC10H180P	OEM
MC10H181L	OEM
MC10H181P	OEM
MC10H186AL	OEM
MC10H186AP	OEM
MC10H188L	OEM
MC10H188P	OEM
MC10H189L	OEM
MC10H189P	OEM
MC10H209L	OEM
MC10H209P	OEM
MC10H210L	OEM
MC10H210P	OEM
MC10H211L	OEM
MC10H211P	OEM
MC10H330L	OEM
MC10H330P	OEM
MC10H332L	OEM
MC10H332P	OEM
MC10H334L	OEM
MC10H334P	OEM
MC10H350L	OEM
MC10H350P	OEM
MC10H424L	OEM
MC10H424P	OEM
MC11A1	OEM
MC11A2	OEM
MC11B1	OEM
MC11B2	OEM
MC12A1	OEM
MC12A2	OEM
MC12B1	OEM
MC12B2	OEM
MC13A1	OEM
MC13A2	OEM
MC13B1	OEM
MC13B2	OEM
MC14	OEM
MC14A1	OEM
MC14A2	OEM
MC14B1	OEM
MC14B2	OEM
MC14HC247ND	OEM
MC15	OEM
MC15A1	OEM
MC15A2	OEM
MC15B1	OEM
MC15B2	OEM
MC16	OEM
MC17	OEM
MC18	OEM
MC19	0604
MC20	OEM
MC20F	OEM
MC21	OEM
MC22	6964
MC22CL	OEM
MC22CP	OEM
MC22CS	OEM
MC22L	OEM
MC22P	OEM
MC22S	OEM
MC25	OEM
MC25F	OEM
MC26S10L	OEM
MC26S10P	OEM
MC30	0071
MC30F	OEM
MC34F19	OEM
MC34F19A	OEM
MC42	OEM
MC43	OEM
MC44	OEM
MC45	OEM
MC46	OEM
MC47	OEM
MC48	OEM
MC49	OEM
MC50	OEM
MC50F	OEM
MC51	0790
MC54F00J	OEM
MC54F00J(A)	OEM
MC54F00N	OEM
MC54F00N(A)	OEM
MC54F02J	OEM
MC54F02J(A)	OEM
MC54F02N	OEM
MC54F02N(A)	OEM
MC54F04J	OEM
MC54F04J(A)	OEM
MC54F04N	OEM
MC54F08J	OEM
MC54F08N	OEM
MC54F8N	OEM
MC54F10J	OEM
MC54F10J(A)	OEM
MC54F10N	OEM
MC54F10N(A)	OEM

If replacement code is OEM, contact original manufacturer for replacement. 469

DEVICE TYPE	REPL CODE
MC54F11J	OEM
MC54F11J(A)	OEM
MC54F11N	OEM
MC54F11N(A)	OEM
MC54F20J	OEM
MC54F20J(A)	OEM
MC54F20N	OEM
MC54F20N(A)	OEM
MC54F32J	OEM
MC54F32J(A)	OEM
MC54F32N	OEM
MC54F32N(A)	OEM
MC54F64J	OEM
MC54F64N	OEM
MC54F86J	OEM
MC54F86N	OEM
MC54F109J	OEM
MC54F109N	OEM
MC54F112	OEM
MC54F113	OEM
MC54F138J(A)	OEM
MC54F138N(A)	OEM
MC54F139J	OEM
MC54F139J(A)	OEM
MC54F139N	OEM
MC54F139N(A)	OEM
MC54F151	OEM
MC54F153J	OEM
MC54F153N	OEM
MC54F174	OEM
MC54F190J	OEM
MC54F190N	OEM
MC54F191J	OEM
MC54F191N	OEM
MC54F192	OEM
MC54F193	OEM
MC54F253J	OEM
MC54F253N	OEM
MC54F258J	OEM
MC54F258N	OEM
MC54F350J	OEM
MC54F350N	OEM
MC54F352J	OEM
MC54F352N	OEM
MC54F374J	OEM
MC54F374N	OEM
MC54F378	OEM
MC54F379	OEM
MC54F521J	OEM
MC54F521N	OEM
MC54F533J	OEM
MC54F533N	OEM
MC54HC00J	OEM
MC54HC02J	OEM
MC54HC03J	OEM
MC54HC03J(A)	OEM
MC54HC08BCAN(A)	OEM
MC54HC08J	OEM
MC54HC10J	OEM
MC54HC20J	OEM
MC54HC20J(A)	OEM
MC54HC27J	OEM
MC54HC30J	OEM
MC54HC42J	OEM
MC54HC42J(A)	OEM
MC54HC51J	OEM
MC54HC51J(A)	OEM
MC54HC58J	OEM
MC54HC58J(A)	OEM
MC54HC73J	OEM
MC54HC74J	OEM
MC54HC74J(A)	OEM
MC54HC75J	OEM
MC54HC76J	OEM
MC54HC85J	OEM
MC54HC86J	OEM
MC54HC107J	OEM
MC54HC109J	OEM
MC54HC109J(A)A)	OEM
MC54HC112J	OEM
MC54HC113J	OEM
MC54HC132J	OEM
MC54HC133J	OEM
MC54HC137J	OEM
MC54HC138J	OEM
MC54HC138J(A)	OEM
MC54HC139J	OEM
MC54HC139J(A)	OEM
MC54HC147J	OEM
MC54HC151J	OEM
MC54HC157J	OEM
MC54HC158J	OEM
MC54HC160J	OEM
MC54HC161J	OEM
MC54HC162J	OEM
MC54HC163J	OEM
MC54HC164J	OEM
MC54HC164J(A)	OEM
MC54HC165J	OEM
MC54HC165J(A)	OEM
MC54HC173J	OEM
MC54HC174J	OEM
MC54HC174J(A)	OEM
MC54HC175J(A)	OEM
MC54HC194J	OEM
MC54HC195J	OEM
MC54HC237J	OEM
MC54HC240J	OEM
MC54HC241J	OEM

DEVICE TYPE	REPL CODE
MC54HC242J	OEM
MC54HC242J(A)	OEM
MC54HC243J	OEM
MC54HC243J(A)	OEM
MC54HC244J	OEM
MC54HC251J	OEM
MC54HC257J	OEM
MC54HC266J	OEM
MC54HC273J	OEM
MC54HC273J(A)	OEM
MC54HC280J	OEM
MC54HC280J(A)	OEM
MC54HC365J	OEM
MC54HC366J	OEM
MC54HC367J	OEM
MC54HC368J	OEM
MC54HC373J	OEM
MC54HC374J	OEM
MC54HC374J(A)	OEM
MC54HC390J	OEM
MC54HC393J	OEM
MC54HC533J	OEM
MC54HC534J	OEM
MC54HC534J(A)	OEM
MC54HC595J	OEM
MC54HC4002J	OEM
MC54HC4017J	OEM
MC54HC4020J	OEM
MC54HC4020J(A)	OEM
MC54HC4024J	OEM
MC54HC4024J(A)	OEM
MC54HC4040J	OEM
MC54HC4040J(A)	OEM
MC54HC4049J	OEM
MC54HC4050J	OEM
MC54HC4075J	OEM
MC54HC4078J	OEM
MC54HC4511J	OEM
MC54HC4514J	OEM
MC54HC4514J(A)	OEM
MC54HC4538J	OEM
MC54HC4543J	OEM
MC54HC4543J(A)	OEM
MC54HCU04J	OEM
MC54HCU04J(A)	OEM
MC60	OEM
MC61	OEM
MC68A00CL	OEM
MC68A00CP	OEM
MC68A00Cs	OEM
MC68A00L	OEM
MC68A00P	OEM
MC68A00S	OEM
MC68A01L1	OEM
MC68A01P1	OEM
MC68A02CL	OEM
MC68A02CP	OEM
MC68A02L	OEM
MC68A02P	OEM
MC68A03G	OEM
MC68A03L	OEM
MC68A03P	OEM
MC68A05P6L	OEM
MC68A05P6P	OEM
MC68A05P6S	OEM
MC68A08L	OEM
MC68A08P	OEM
MC68A09CL	OEM
MC68A09CP	OEM
MC68A09CS	OEM
MC68A09ECL	OEM
MC68A09ECP	OEM
MC68A09ECS	OEM
MC68A09EL	OEM
MC68A09EP	OEM
MC68A09ES	OEM
MC68A09L	OEM
MC68A09P	OEM
MC68A09S	OEM
MC68A21CL	OEM
MC68A21CP	OEM
MC68A21CS	OEM
MC68A21L	OEM
MC68A21P	OEM
MC68A21S	OEM
MC68A22L	OEM
MC68A22P	OEM
MC68A29CL	OEM
MC68A29CP	OEM
MC68A29CS	OEM
MC68A29L	OEM
MC68A29P	OEM
MC68A29S	OEM
MC68A35CL	OEM
MC68A35CP	OEM
MC68A35CS	OEM
MC68A35L	OEM
MC68A35P	OEM
MC68A35S	OEM
MC68A39L	OEM
MC68A39P	OEM
MC68A40CL	OEM
MC68A40CP	OEM
MC68A40CS	OEM
MC68A40L	OEM
MC68A40P	OEM
MC68A40S	OEM
MC68A44CL	OEM
MC68A44CP	OEM

DEVICE TYPE	REPL CODE
MC68A44CS	OEM
MC68A44L	OEM
MC68A44P	OEM
MC68A44S	OEM
MC68A45CL	OEM
MC68A45CP	OEM
MC68A45CS	OEM
MC68A45L	OEM
MC68A45P	OEM
MC68A45R1CL	OEM
MC68A45R1CP	OEM
MC68A45R1CS	OEM
MC68A45R1L	OEM
MC68A45R1P	OEM
MC68A45R1S	OEM
MC68A45S	OEM
MC68A46L	OEM
MC68A46P	OEM
MC68A46S	OEM
MC68A50CL	OEM
MC68A50CP	OEM
MC68A50CS	OEM
MC68A50L	OEM
MC68A50P	OEM
MC68A50S	OEM
MC68A52CL	OEM
MC68A52CP	OEM
MC68A52CS	OEM
MC68A52L	OEM
MC68A52P	OEM
MC68A52S	OEM
MC68A54CL	OEM
MC68A54CP	OEM
MC68A54CS	OEM
MC68A54L	OEM
MC68A54P	OEM
MC68A54S	OEM
MC68A488L	OEM
MC68A488P	OEM
MC68A701L	OEM
MC68B00L	OEM
MC68B00P	OEM
MC68B00S	OEM
MC68B01L1	OEM
MC68B01P1	OEM
MC68B02L	OEM
MC68B02P	OEM
MC68B03G	OEM
MC68B03L	OEM
MC68B03P	OEM
MC68B05P6L	OEM
MC68B05P6P	OEM
MC68B05P6S	OEM
MC68B08L	OEM
MC68B08P	OEM
MC68B09CL	OEM
MC68B09CP	OEM
MC68B09CS	OEM
MC68B09ECL	OEM
MC68B09ECP	OEM
MC68B09ECS	OEM
MC68B09EL	OEM
MC68B09EP	OEM
MC68B09ES	OEM
MC68B09L	OEM
MC68B09P	OEM
MC68B09S	OEM
MC68B21L	OEM
MC68B21P	OEM
MC68B21S	OEM
MC68B22L	OEM
MC68B22P	OEM
MC68B29L	OEM
MC68B29P	OEM
MC68B29S	OEM
MC68B35CL	OEM
MC68B35CP	OEM
MC68B35CS	OEM
MC68B35L	OEM
MC68B35P	OEM
MC68B35S	OEM
MC68B39L	OEM
MC68B39P	OEM
MC68B40CL	OEM
MC68B40CP	OEM
MC68B40CS	OEM
MC68B40L	OEM
MC68B40P	OEM
MC68B40S	OEM
MC68B44L	OEM
MC68B44P	OEM
MC68B44S	OEM
MC68B45L	OEM
MC68B45P	OEM
MC68B45R1L	OEM
MC68B45R1P	OEM
MC68B45R1S	OEM
MC68B45S	OEM
MC68B50C	OEM
MC68B50L	OEM
MC68B50P	OEM
MC68B50S	OEM
MC68B52L	OEM
MC68B52P	OEM
MC68B52S	OEM
MC68B54L	OEM
MC68B54P	OEM
MC68B54S	OEM
MC68B488L	OEM

DEVICE TYPE	REPL CODE
MC68B488P	OEM
MC68B701L	OEM
MC68C68A1	OEM
MC68HC04P2P	OEM
MC68HC04P2Z	OEM
MC68HC05C4-SC403717	OEM
MC68HC05C4P	OEM
MC68HC05C4Z	OEM
MC68HC05N4-SC406656	OEM
MC68HC05T7	OEM
MC68HC05T7-LSC89919B	OEM
MC68HC09EL	OEM
MC68HC09EP	OEM
MC68HC51P	OEM
MC68HC53P	OEM
MC68HC68R1	OEM
MC68HC68R2	OEM
MC68HC68T1P	OEM
MC70	OEM
MC71	OEM
MC72	OEM
MC73	0052
MC73HC158JD	OEM
MC74D2970	OEM
MC74F00J	OEM
MC74F00J(A)	OEM
MC74F00N	OEM
MC74F00N(A)	OEM
MC74F02J	OEM
MC74F02J(A)	OEM
MC74F02N	OEM
MC74F02N(A)	OEM
MC74F04J	OEM
MC74F04N	OEM
MC74F08J	OEM
MC74F08J(A)	OEM
MC74F08N	OEM
MC74F08N(A)	OEM
MC74F0404N	OEM
MC74F10J	OEM
MC74F10J(A)	OEM
MC74F10N	OEM
MC74F10N(A)	OEM
MC74F11J	OEM
MC74F11J(A)	OEM
MC74F11N	OEM
MC74F11N(A)	OEM
MC74F20J	OEM
MC74F20J(A)	OEM
MC74F20N	OEM
MC74F20N(A)	OEM
MC74F32J	OEM
MC74F32J(A)	OEM
MC74F32N	OEM
MC74F32N(A)	OEM
MC74F64J	OEM
MC74F64N	OEM
MC74F74J	OEM
MC74F74N	OEM
MC74F86J	OEM
MC74F86N	OEM
MC74F109J	OEM
MC74F109N	OEM
MC74F112	OEM
MC74F112J	OEM
MC74F112N	OEM
MC74F113	OEM
MC74F113J	OEM
MC74F113N	OEM
MC74F114J	OEM
MC74F114N	OEM
MC74F138J	OEM
MC74F138J(A)	OEM
MC74F138N	OEM
MC74F138N(A)	OEM
MC74F139J	OEM
MC74F139J(A)	OEM
MC74F139N	OEM
MC74F139N(A)	OEM
MC74F151	OEM
MC74F151J	OEM
MC74F151N	OEM
MC74F153J	OEM
MC74F153N	OEM
MC74F157J	OEM
MC74F157N	OEM
MC74F158J	OEM
MC74F158N	OEM
MC74F160J	OEM
MC74F160N	OEM
MC74F161J	OEM
MC74F161N	OEM
MC74F162J	OEM
MC74F162N	OEM
MC74F163J	OEM
MC74F163N	OEM
MC74F168J	OEM
MC74F168N	OEM
MC74F169J	OEM
MC74F169N	OEM
MC74F174	OEM
MC74F174J	OEM
MC74F174N	OEM
MC74F175J	OEM
MC74F175N	OEM
MC74F181J	OEM

DEVICE TYPE	REPL CODE
MC74F181N	OEM
MC74F182J	OEM
MC74F182N	OEM
MC74F189J	OEM
MC74F189N	OEM
MC74F190J	OEM
MC74F190N	OEM
MC74F191J	OEM
MC74F191N	OEM
MC74F192	OEM
MC74F192J	OEM
MC74F192N	OEM
MC74F193	OEM
MC74F193J	OEM
MC74F193N	OEM
MC74F194J	OEM
MC74F194N	OEM
MC74F195J	OEM
MC74F195N	OEM
MC74F240J	OEM
MC74F240N	OEM
MC74F241J	OEM
MC74F241N	OEM
MC74F242J	OEM
MC74F242N	OEM
MC74F243J	OEM
MC74F243N	OEM
MC74F244J	OEM
MC74F244N	OEM
MC74F245J	OEM
MC74F245N	OEM
MC74F251J	OEM
MC74F251N	OEM
MC74F253J	OEM
MC74F253N	OEM
MC74F257J	OEM
MC74F257N	OEM
MC74F258J	OEM
MC74F258N	OEM
MC74F280J	OEM
MC74F280N	OEM
MC74F283J	OEM
MC74F283N	OEM
MC74F289J	OEM
MC74F289N	OEM
MC74F299J	OEM
MC74F299N	OEM
MC74F323J	OEM
MC74F323N	OEM
MC74F350J	OEM
MC74F350N	OEM
MC74F352J	OEM
MC74F352N	OEM
MC74F353J	OEM
MC74F353N	OEM
MC74F373J	OEM
MC74F373N	OEM
MC74F374J	OEM
MC74F374N	OEM
MC74F378	OEM
MC74F378J	OEM
MC74F378N	OEM
MC74F379	OEM
MC74F379J	OEM
MC74F379N	OEM
MC74F381J	OEM
MC74F381N	OEM
MC74F382J	OEM
MC74F382N	OEM
MC74F521J	OEM
MC74F521N	OEM
MC74F533J	OEM
MC74F533N	OEM
MC74F534J	OEM
MC74F534N	OEM
MC74F537J	OEM
MC74F537N	OEM
MC74F538J	OEM
MC74F538N	OEM
MC74F539J	OEM
MC74F539N	OEM
MC74F620J	OEM
MC74F620N	OEM
MC74F623J	OEM
MC74F623N	OEM
MC74F640J	OEM
MC74F640N	OEM
MC74F643J	OEM
MC74F643N	OEM
MC74F2960	OEM
MC74F2960J	OEM
MC74F2960N	OEM
MC74F2961J	OEM
MC74F2961N	OEM
MC74F2962J	OEM
MC74F2962N	OEM
MC74F2968	OEM
MC74F2968J	OEM
MC74F2968N	OEM
MC74F2969	OEM
MC74F2969J	OEM
MC74F2969N	OEM
MC74F2970J	OEM
MC74F2970N	OEM
MC74H58JS	OEM
MC74H74AF	2472
MC74H74AL	2472
MC74H74P	2472
MC74H87F	2557

DEVICE TYPE	REPL CODE
MC74H87L	2557
MC74H87P	2557
MC74H237JDS	OEM
MC74H237JS	OEM
MC74HC00F	OEM
MC74HC00J	OEM
MC74HC00JD	OEM
MC74HC00JDS	OEM
MC74HC00JS	OEM
MC74HC00N	1439
MC74HC00ND	OEM
MC74HC00NDS	OEM
MC74HC00NS	OEM
MC74HC02	OEM
MC74HC02J	OEM
MC74HC02JD	OEM
MC74HC02JDS	OEM
MC74HC02JS	OEM
MC74HC02N	1443
MC74HC02ND	OEM
MC74HC02NDS	OEM
MC74HC02NS	OEM
MC74HC03J	OEM
MC74HC03J(A)	OEM
MC74HC03JD	OEM
MC74HC03JDS	OEM
MC74HC03JS	OEM
MC74HC03N	1444
MC74HC03N(A)	OEM
MC74HC03ND	OEM
MC74HC03NDS	OEM
MC74HC03NS	OEM
MC74HC04F	1446
MC74HC08	4225
MC74HC08BCAJ(A)	OEM
MC74HC08BCAN(A)	OEM
MC74HC08J	OEM
MC74HC08JD	OEM
MC74HC08JDS	OEM
MC74HC08JS	OEM
MC74HC08N	2393
MC74HC08ND	OEM
MC74HC08NDS	OEM
MC74HC08NS	OEM
MC74HC10F	OEM
MC74HC10J	OEM
MC74HC10JD	OEM
MC74HC10JDS	OEM
MC74HC10JS	OEM
MC74HC10N	1453
MC74HC10ND	OEM
MC74HC10NDS	OEM
MC74HC10NS	OEM
MC74HC20J	OEM
MC74HC20J(A)	OEM
MC74HC20JD	OEM
MC74HC20JDS	OEM
MC74HC20N	1466
MC74HC20N(A)	OEM
MC74HC20ND	OEM
MC74HC20NDS	OEM
MC74HC20NS	OEM
MC74HC27J	OEM
MC74HC27JD	OEM
MC74HC27JS	OEM
MC74HC27N	1476
MC74HC27ND	OEM
MC74HC27NDS	OEM
MC74HC27NS	OEM
MC74HC30J	OEM
MC74HC30N	1480
MC74HC42J	OEM
MC74HC42J(A)	OEM
MC74HC42JD	OEM
MC74HC42JDS	OEM
MC74HC42JS	OEM
MC74HC42N	1507
MC74HC42N(A)	OEM
MC74HC42ND	OEM
MC74HC42NDS	OEM
MC74HC42NS	OEM
MC74HC51J	OEM
MC74HC51J(A)	OEM
MC74HC51JD	OEM
MC74HC51JDS	OEM
MC74HC51JS	OEM
MC74HC51N	OEM
MC74HC51N(A)	OEM
MC74HC51ND	OEM
MC74HC51NDS	OEM
MC74HC51NS	OEM
MC74HC58J	OEM
MC74HC58J(A)	OEM
MC74HC58JD	OEM
MC74HC58JDS	OEM
MC74HC58N	OEM
MC74HC58N(A)	OEM
MC74HC58ND	OEM
MC74HC58NDS	OEM
MC74HC58NS	OEM
MC74HC73J	OEM
MC74HC73JD	OEM
MC74HC73JDS	OEM
MC74HC73JS	OEM
MC74HC73N	1549
MC74HC73ND	OEM
MC74HC73NDS	OEM
MC74HC73NS	OEM
MC74HC74J	OEM

DEVICE TYPE	REPL CODE
MC74HC74J(A)	OEM
MC74HC74JD	OEM
MC74HC74JDS	OEM
MC74HC74JS	OEM
MC74HC74N	1552
MC74HC74N(A)	OEM
MC74HC74ND	OEM
MC74HC74NDS	OEM
MC74HC74NS	OEM
MC74HC75J	OEM
MC74HC75N	1555
MC74HC76J	OEM
MC74HC76JD	OEM
MC74HC76JDS	OEM
MC74HC76N	OEM
MC74HC76ND	OEM
MC74HC76NDS	OEM
MC74HC76NS	OEM
MC74HC85J	OEM
MC74HC85JD	OEM
MC74HC85JDS	OEM
MC74HC85JS	OEM
MC74HC85N	1573
MC74HC85ND	OEM
MC74HC85NDS	OEM
MC74HC85NS	OEM
MC74HC86J	OEM
MC74HC86JD	OEM
MC74HC86JDS	OEM
MC74HC86JS	OEM
MC74HC86N	1578
MC74HC86ND	OEM
MC74HC86NDS	OEM
MC74HC86NS	OEM
MC74HC107J	OEM
MC74HC107JD	OEM
MC74HC107JDS	OEM
MC74HC107JS	OEM
MC74HC107N	4611
MC74HC107ND	OEM
MC74HC107NDS	OEM
MC74HC107NS	OEM
MC74HC109J	OEM
MC74HC109J(A)	OEM
MC74HC109JD	OEM
MC74HC109JDS	OEM
MC74HC109JS	OEM
MC74HC109N	0115
MC74HC109N(A)	OEM
MC74HC109ND	OEM
MC74HC109NDS	OEM
MC74HC109NS	OEM
MC74HC112J	OEM
MC74HC112JD	OEM
MC74HC112JDS	OEM
MC74HC112JS	OEM
MC74HC112N	0214
MC74HC112ND	OEM
MC74HC112NDS	OEM
MC74HC112NS	OEM
MC74HC113J	OEM
MC74HC113JD	OEM
MC74HC113JDS	OEM
MC74HC113JS	OEM
MC74HC113N	OEM
MC74HC113ND	OEM
MC74HC113NDS	OEM
MC74HC113NS	OEM
MC74HC132J	OEM
MC74HC132JDS	OEM
MC74HC132JS	OEM
MC74HC132N	0675
MC74HC132ND	OEM
MC74HC132NDS	OEM
MC74HC132NS	OEM
MC74HC133J	OEM
MC74HC133N	OEM
MC74HC137J	OEM
MC74HC137JD	OEM
MC74HC137JDS	OEM
MC74HC137JS	OEM
MC74HC137N	0779
MC74HC137ND	OEM
MC74HC137NDS	OEM
MC74HC137NS	OEM
MC74HC138J	OEM
MC74HC138J(A)	OEM
MC74HC138JD	OEM
MC74HC138JDS	OEM
MC74HC138JS	OEM
MC74HC138N	0792
MC74HC138N(A)	OEM
MC74HC138ND	OEM
MC74HC138NDS	OEM
MC74HC138NS	OEM
MC74HC139J	OEM
MC74HC139JD	OEM
MC74HC139JDS	OEM
MC74HC139JS	OEM
MC74HC139N	0803
MC74HC139N(A)	OEM
MC74HC139ND	OEM
MC74HC139NDS	OEM
MC74HC139NS	OEM
MC74HC147J	OEM
MC74HC147N	0932
MC74HC151	OEM
MC74HC151J	OEM
MC74HC151JD	OEM

If replacement code is OEM, contact original manufacturer for replacement.

DEVICE TYPE	REPL CODE
MC74HC151JDS	OEM
MC74HC151JS	OEM
MC74HC151N	0997
MC74HC151NDS	OEM
MC74HC151NS	OEM
MC74HC157AN	OEM
MC74HC157J	OEM
MC74HC157JD	OEM
MC74HC157JDS	OEM
MC74HC157JS	OEM
MC74HC157N	1068
MC74HC157ND	OEM
MC74HC157NDS	OEM
MC74HC157NS	OEM
MC74HC158J	OEM
MC74HC158JDS	OEM
MC74HC158JS	OEM
MC74HC158N	1080
MC74HC158ND	OEM
MC74HC158NDS	OEM
MC74HC158NS	OEM
MC74HC160J	OEM
MC74HC160JD	OEM
MC74HC160JDS	OEM
MC74HC160JS	OEM
MC74HC160N	1109
MC74HC160ND	OEM
MC74HC160NDS	OEM
MC74HC160NS	OEM
MC74HC161	5315
MC74HC161J	OEM
MC74HC161JD	OEM
MC74HC161JDS	OEM
MC74HC161JS	OEM
MC74HC161N	1121
MC74HC161ND	OEM
MC74HC161NDS	OEM
MC74HC161NS	OEM
MC74HC162J	OEM
MC74HC162JD	OEM
MC74HC162JDS	OEM
MC74HC162JS	OEM
MC74HC162N	1134
MC74HC162ND	OEM
MC74HC162NDS	OEM
MC74HC162NS	OEM
MC74HC163J	OEM
MC74HC163JD	OEM
MC74HC163JDS	OEM
MC74HC163JS	OEM
MC74HC163N	1151
MC74HC163ND	OEM
MC74HC163NDS	OEM
MC74HC163NS	OEM
MC74HC164J	OEM
MC74HC164J(A)	OEM
MC74HC164JD	OEM
MC74HC164JDS	OEM
MC74HC164JS	OEM
MC74HC164N	1163
MC74HC164N(A)	OEM
MC74HC164ND	OEM
MC74HC164NDS	OEM
MC74HC164NS	OEM
MC74HC165J	OEM
MC74HC165J(A)	OEM
MC74HC165JD	OEM
MC74HC165JDS	OEM
MC74HC165JS	OEM
MC74HC165N	1175
MC74HC165N(A)	OEM
MC74HC165ND	OEM
MC74HC165NDS	OEM
MC74HC165NS	OEM
MC74HC173J	OEM
MC74HC173JD	OEM
MC74HC173JDS	OEM
MC74HC173JS	OEM
MC74HC173N	1271
MC74HC173ND	OEM
MC74HC173NDS	OEM
MC74HC173NS	OEM
MC74HC174J	OEM
MC74HC174J(A)	OEM
MC74HC174JD	OEM
MC74HC174JDS	OEM
MC74HC174JS	OEM
MC74HC174N	1287
MC74HC174N(A)	OEM
MC74HC174ND	OEM
MC74HC174NDS	OEM
MC74HC174NS	OEM
MC74HC175J	OEM
MC74HC175JD	OEM
MC74HC175JDS	OEM
MC74HC175JS	OEM
MC74HC175N	1295
MC74HC175N(A(	OEM
MC74HC175ND	OEM
MC74HC175NDS	OEM
MC74HC175NS	OEM
MC74HC194J	OEM
MC74HC194JD	OEM
MC74HC194JDS	OEM
MC74HC194JS	OEM
MC74HC194N	1548
MC74HC194ND	OEM
MC74HC194NDS	OEM
MC74HC194NS	OEM
MC74HC195J	OEM
MC74HC195JD	OEM
MC74HC195JDS	OEM
MC74HC195JS	OEM
MC74HC195N	1568
MC74HC195ND	OEM
MC74HC195NDS	OEM
MC74HC195NS	OEM
MC74HC237J	OEM
MC74HC237JD	OEM
MC74HC237N	1947
MC74HC237ND	OEM
MC74HC237NDS	OEM
MC74HC237NS	OEM
MC74HC240J	OEM
MC74HC240JD	OEM
MC74HC240JDS	OEM
MC74HC240JS	OEM
MC74HC240N	1968
MC74HC240ND	OEM
MC74HC240NDS	OEM
MC74HC240NS	OEM
MC74HC241J	OEM
MC74HC241JD	OEM
MC74HC241JDS	OEM
MC74HC241JS	OEM
MC74HC241N	1979
MC74HC241NDS	OEM
MC74HC241NS	OEM
MC74HC242J	OEM
MC74HC242J(A)	OEM
MC74HC242JDS	OEM
MC74HC242JS	OEM
MC74HC242N	1985
MC74HC242N(A)	OEM
MC74HC242ND	OEM
MC74HC242NDS	OEM
MC74HC242NS	OEM
MC74HC243J	OEM
MC74HC243J(A)	OEM
MC74HC243JD	OEM
MC74HC243JDS	OEM
MC74HC243JS	OEM
MC74HC243N	1990
MC74HC243N(A)	OEM
MC74HC243NDS	OEM
MC74HC243NS	OEM
MC74HC244J	OEM
MC74HC244JD	OEM
MC74HC244JDS	OEM
MC74HC244JS	OEM
MC74HC244N	1994
MC74HC244ND	OEM
MC74HC244NDS	OEM
MC74HC244NS	OEM
MC74HC245N	2003
MC74HC251J	OEM
MC74HC251JD	OEM
MC74HC251JDS	OEM
MC74HC251JS	OEM
MC74HC251N	2054
MC74HC251ND	OEM
MC74HC251NDS	OEM
MC74HC251NS	OEM
MC74HC257J	OEM
MC74HC257JD	OEM
MC74HC257JDS	OEM
MC74HC257JS	OEM
MC74HC257N	2103
MC74HC257NDS	OEM
MC74HC257NS	OEM
MC74HC266J	OEM
MC74HC266JD	OEM
MC74HC266JDS	OEM
MC74HC266JS	OEM
MC74HC266N	OEM
MC74HC266ND	OEM
MC74HC266NDS	OEM
MC74HC266NS	OEM
MC74HC273J	OEM
MC74HC273J(A)	OEM
MC74HC273JD	OEM
MC74HC273JDS	OEM
MC74HC273JS	OEM
MC74HC273N	2196
MC74HC273N(A)	OEM
MC74HC273ND	OEM
MC74HC273NDS	OEM
MC74HC273NS	OEM
MC74HC280J	OEM
MC74HC280J(A)	OEM
MC74HC280JD	OEM
MC74HC280JDS	OEM
MC74HC280JS	OEM
MC74HC280N	2234
MC74HC280N(A)	OEM
MC74HC280ND	OEM
MC74HC280NDS	OEM
MC74HC280NS	OEM
MC74HC365J	OEM
MC74HC365N	2853
MC74HC366J	OEM
MC74HC366N	2858
MC74HC367J	OEM
MC74HC367N	2867
MC74HC368J	OEM
MC74HC368N	2870
MC74HC373AN	OEM
MC74HC373J	OEM
MC74HC373JD	OEM
MC74HC373JDS	OEM
MC74HC373JS	OEM
MC74HC373N	2892
MC74HC373ND	OEM
MC74HC373NDS	OEM
MC74HC373NS	OEM
MC74HC374J	OEM
MC74HC374J(A)	OEM
MC74HC374JD	OEM
MC74HC374JDS	OEM
MC74HC374JS	OEM
MC74HC374N	2899
MC74HC374N(A)	OEM
MC74HC374ND	OEM
MC74HC374NDS	OEM
MC74HC374NS	OEM
MC74HC374P	OEM
MC74HC390J	OEM
MC74HC390N	3014
MC74HC393J	OEM
MC74HC393N	3035
MC74HC533J	OEM
MC74HC533JD	OEM
MC74HC533JDS	OEM
MC74HC533JS	OEM
MC74HC533N	3632
MC74HC533ND	OEM
MC74HC533NDS	OEM
MC74HC533NS	OEM
MC74HC534J	OEM
MC74HC534J(A)	OEM
MC74HC534JD	OEM
MC74HC534JDS	OEM
MC74HC534JS	OEM
MC74HC534N	3636
MC74HC534ND	OEM
MC74HC534NDS	OEM
MC74HC534NS	OEM
MC74HC589J	OEM
MC74HC589JD	OEM
MC74HC589JDS	OEM
MC74HC589JS	OEM
MC74HC589N	OEM
MC74HC589ND	OEM
MC74HC589NDS	OEM
MC74HC589NS	OEM
MC74HC595J	OEM
MC74HC595JD	OEM
MC74HC595JDS	OEM
MC74HC595JS	OEM
MC74HC595N	OEM
MC74HC595ND	OEM
MC74HC595NDS	OEM
MC74HC595NS	OEM
MC74HC597J	OEM
MC74HC597JD	OEM
MC74HC597JDS	OEM
MC74HC597JS	OEM
MC74HC4002J	OEM
MC74HC4002JD	OEM
MC74HC4002JDS	OEM
MC74HC4002N	5391
MC74HC4002ND	OEM
MC74HC4002NDS	OEM
MC74HC4017J	OEM
MC74HC4017JD	OEM
MC74HC4017JDS	OEM
MC74HC4017JS	OEM
MC74HC4017N	5414
MC74HC4017ND	OEM
MC74HC4017NDS	OEM
MC74HC4017NS	OEM
MC74HC4020J	OEM
MC74HC4020J(A)	OEM
MC74HC4020JD	OEM
MC74HC4020JDS	OEM
MC74HC4020JS	OEM
MC74HC4020N	6192
MC74HC4020N(A)	OEM
MC74HC4020ND	OEM
MC74HC4020NDS	OEM
MC74HC4020NS	OEM
MC74HC4024J	OEM
MC74HC4024J(A)	OEM
MC74HC4024JD	OEM
MC74HC4024JDS	OEM
MC74HC4024JS	OEM
MC74HC4024N	5418
MC74HC4024N(A)	OEM
MC74HC4024ND	OEM
MC74HC4024NDS	OEM
MC74HC4024NS	OEM
MC74HC4040J	OEM
MC74HC4040J(A)	OEM
MC74HC4040JD	OEM
MC74HC4040JDS	OEM
MC74HC4040JS	OEM
MC74HC4040N	6201
MC74HC4040N(A)	OEM
MC74HC4040ND	OEM
MC74HC4040NDS	OEM
MC74HC4040NS	OEM
MC74HC4049J	OEM
MC74HC4049N	5061
MC74HC4050J	OEM
MC74HC4050N	5443
MC74HC4053F	OEM
MC74HC4053N	3755
MC74HC4060J	OEM
MC74HC4060JD	OEM
MC74HC4060JDS	OEM
MC74HC4060JS	OEM
MC74HC4060N	6216
MC74HC4060ND	OEM
MC74HC4060NDS	OEM
MC74HC4060NS	OEM
MC74HC4066N	5471
MC74HC4075J	OEM
MC74HC4075JD	OEM
MC74HC4075JDS	OEM
MC74HC4075JS	OEM
MC74HC4075N	5476
MC74HC4075ND	OEM
MC74HC4075NDS	OEM
MC74HC4075NS	OEM
MC74HC4078J	OEM
MC74HC4078N	OEM
MC74HC4511J	OEM
MC74HC4511JD	OEM
MC74HC4511JDS	OEM
MC74HC4511JS	OEM
MC74HC4511N	5950
MC74HC4511ND	OEM
MC74HC4511NDS	OEM
MC74HC4511NS	OEM
MC74HC4514J	OEM
MC74HC4514J(A)	OEM
MC74HC4514JD	OEM
MC74HC4514JDS	OEM
MC74HC4514JS	OEM
MC74HC4514N	5955
MC74HC4514N(A)	OEM
MC74HC4514ND	OEM
MC74HC4514NDS	OEM
MC74HC4514NS	OEM
MC74HC4538J	OEM
MC74HC4538JD	OEM
MC74HC4538JDS	OEM
MC74HC4538JS	OEM
MC74HC4538N	5987
MC74HC4538ND	OEM
MC74HC4538NDS	OEM
MC74HC4538NS	OEM
MC74HC4543J	OEM
MC74HC4543J(A)	OEM
MC74HC4543JD	OEM
MC74HC4543JDS	OEM
MC74HC4543JS	OEM
MC74HC4543N	5998
MC74HC4543N(A)	OEM
MC74HC4543ND	OEM
MC74HC4543NDS	OEM
MC74HC4543NS	OEM
MC74HCU04J	OEM
MC74HCU04JD	OEM
MC74HCU04JDS	OEM
MC74HCU04JS	OEM
MC74HCU04N	4522
MC74HCU04N(A)	OEM
MC74HCU04ND	OEM
MC74HCU04NDS	OEM
MC74HCU04NS	OEM
MC74HD27JDS	OEM
MC75	3511
MC75F	OEM
MC75HC597N	OEM
MC75HC597ND	OEM
MC75HC597NDS	OEM
MC75HC597NS	OEM
MC75S110L	OEM
MC75S110P	OEM
MC78L02ACG	OEM
MC78L02ACP	OEM
MC78L05	1288
MC78L05,CP	1288
MC78L05ACG	1288
MC78L05ACP	1288
MC78L05C	1288
MC78L05CG	1288
MC78L05CP	1288
MC78L06AV	2285
MC78L08ACG	0083
MC78L08ACP	0083
MC78L08AGC	OEM
MC78L08CG	0083
MC78L08CP	0083
MC78L12ACG	1817
MC78L12ACP	1817
MC78L12CG	1817
MC78L12CP	1817
MC78L15ACG	3361
MC78L15ACP	3361
MC78L15CG	3361
MC78L15CP	3361
MC78L15CT	OEM
MC78L18ACG	OEM
MC78L18ACP	4427
MC78L18CG	OEM
MC78L18CP	4427
MC78L24ACG	OEM
MC78L24ACP	4430
MC78L24CG	OEM
MC78L24CP	4430
MC78L25ACP	OEM
MC78M05	OEM
MC78M05BT	OEM
MC78M05CG	OEM
MC78M05CT	0619
MC78M05CTD	OEM
MC78M06BT	OEM
MC78M06CG	OEM
MC78M06CT	0917
MC78M06CTD	OEM
MC78M08BT	OEM
MC78M08CG	OEM
MC78M08CT	1187
MC78M08CTD	OEM
MC78M12	0330
MC78M12BT	OEM
MC78M12CG	OEM
MC78M12CGCG	OEM
MC78M12CT	0330
MC78M12CTD	OEM
MC78M15BT	OEM
MC78M15CG	OEM
MC78M15CT	1311
MC78M15CTD	OEM
MC78M18BT	OEM
MC78M18CG	OEM
MC78M18CT	2244
MC78M18CTD	OEM
MC78M20BT	OEM
MC78M20CG	OEM
MC78M20CT	OEM
MC78M24BT	OEM
MC78M24CG	OEM
MC78M24CP	2224
MC78M24CT	2224
MC78M24CTD	OEM
MC78T05ACK	OEM
MC78T05ACT	OEM
MC78T05AK	OEM
MC78T05CK	1727
MC78T05CT	OEM
MC78T05K	1905
MC78T06CK	OEM
MC78T06CT	OEM
MC78T06K	OEM
MC78T08CK	OEM
MC78T08CT	OEM
MC78T08K	OEM
MC78T12ACK	OEM
MC78T12ACKCT	OEM
MC78T12ACT	OEM
MC78T12AK	OEM
MC78T12CK	2239
MC78T12CT	0330
MC78T12K	3359
MC78T15ACK	OEM
MC78T15ACT	OEM
MC78T15AK	OEM
MC78T15CK	2443
MC78T15CT	OEM
MC78T15K	OEM
MC78T18CK	OEM
MC78T18CT	OEM
MC78T18K	OEM
MC78T24CK	OEM
MC78T24CT	OEM
MC78T24K	OEM
MC79L00AC	OEM
MC79L03ACG	OEM
MC79L03ACP	OEM
MC79L03CG	OEM
MC79L03CP	OEM
MC79L05AC	4429
MC79L05ACG	4429
MC79L05ACP	4429
MC79L05ACPCP	OEM
MC79L05CG	4429
MC79L05CP	1275
MC79L06	OEM
MC79L12AC	1825
MC79L12ACG	1825
MC79L12ACP	1825
MC79L12CG	1825
MC79L12CP	1825
MC79L15AC	6387
MC79L15ACG	4952
MC79L15ACP	4952
MC79L15CG	4952
MC79L15CP	4952
MC79L18ACG	OEM
MC79L18ACP	4799
MC79L18CG	OEM
MC79L18CP	4799
MC79L24ACG	OEM
MC79L24ACP	1710
MC79L24CG	OEM
MC79L24CP	1710
MC82HS181	OEM
MC82HS191	OEM
MC82HS321	OEM
MC82S181	OEM
MC82S191	OEM
MC82S321	OEM
MC85-001	OEM
MC85-002	OEM
MC85-011	OEM
MC85-012	OEM
MC100	0071
MC100A	0087
MC100F	OEM
MC101	0050
MC103	0050
MC103A	0163
MC104	OEM
MC105	OEM
MC106	0549
MC110	0369
MC110A	0369
MC110AS	0369
MC110S	0369
MC120	0102
MC120A	0102
MC120AS	0102
MC120S	0102
MC125F	OEM
MC130	OEM
MC130A	OEM
MC130AS	OEM
MC130S	OEM
MC1330P	1797
MC140A	OEM
MC140AS	OEM
MC140S	OEM
MC145BL	OEM
MC150A	OEM
MC150AS	OEM
MC150F	OEM
MC150S	OEM
MC153	OEM
MC154	OEM
MC155	OEM
MC155DG	1070
MC156	OEM
MC157	OEM
MC158	OEM
MC159	OEM
MC160BCP	OEM
MC162	OEM
MC170	0133
MC200	OEM
MC201	0030
MC202	OEM
MC203	OEM
MC204	OEM
MC205	OEM
MC206	OEM
MC207	OEM
MC208	OEM
MC209	OEM
MC210	OEM
MC211	OEM
MC212	OEM
MC213	OEM
MC214	OEM
MC215	OEM
MC216	OEM
MC217	OEM
MC218	OEM
MC219	OEM
MC220	OEM
MC221	OEM
MC222	OEM
MC223	OEM
MC224	OEM
MC225	OEM
MC226	OEM
MC227	OEM
MC228	OEM
MC229	OEM
MC230	OEM
MC231	OEM
MC300	OEM
MC-301	0133
MC301	0163
MC302	0163
MC303	OEM
MC303P	2444
MC305	OEM
MC308	0143
MC328	OEM
MC338	OEM
MC350	1357
MC400	OEM
MC401	OEM
MC402	OEM
MC402L	OEM
MC403	OEM
MC405	OEM
MC407	0549
MC410	0005
MC415	OEM
MC422	OEM
MC433	OEM
MC456	1325
MC456A	0133
MC457	0080
MC457A	0133
MC458	0604
MC458A	0133
MC459	0133
MC459A	0133
MC461	0133
MC461A	0133
MC462	0133
MC462A	0080
MC463	0133
MC463A	0604
MC464	0133
MC464A	0604
MC482	0133
MC482A	0133
MC482B	0133
MC483	0133
MC483A	0133
MC483B	0124
MC484	0133
MC484A	0133
MC484B	0604
MC485	0133
MC485A	0133
MC485B	0604
MC486	0790
MC486A	0790
MC486B	0790
MC487	0790
MC487A	0790
MC487B	0790
MC488	0790
MC488A	0790
MC488B	0790
MC500A	OEM
MC500B	OEM
MC501A	OEM
MC501B	OEM
MC502A	OEM
MC502B	OEM
MC503A	OEM
MC503B	OEM
MC504A	OEM
MC504B	OEM
MC505A	OEM
MC505B	OEM
MC506A	OEM
MC506B	OEM
MC507A	OEM
MC507B	OEM
MC508A	OEM
MC508B	OEM
MC509A	OEM
MC509B	OEM
MC510A	OEM
MC510B	OEM
MC511A	OEM
MC511B	OEM
MC512A	OEM
MC512B	OEM
MC513A	OEM
MC513B	OEM
MC514A	OEM
MC514B	OEM
MC515A	OEM
MC515B	OEM
MC516A	OEM
MC516B	OEM
MC517A	OEM
MC517B	OEM
MC518A	OEM
MC518B	OEM
MC519A	OEM
MC519B	OEM
MC567	OEM
MC600	OEM
MC600L	OEM
MC600P	OEM
MC601	OEM
MC602	OEM
MC603	OEM
MC605	OEM
MC607	0549
MC610	0005
MC615	OEM
MC622	OEM
MC643	OEM
MC643A	OEM
MC656P	OEM
MC658	OEM
MC658A	OEM
MC659	OEM
MC659A	OEM
MC660	OEM
MC660A	OEM
MC660L	OEM
MC660P	0613
MC660TL	OEM
MC661	OEM
MC661A	OEM
MC661L	OEM
MC661P	2574
MC661TL	OEM
MC662	OEM
MC662A	OEM
MC662L	OEM
MC662P	2542
MC662TL	OEM
MC663	OEM
MC663A	OEM
MC663L	OEM
MC663P	2964
MC663TL	OEM
MC664	OEM
MC664L	OEM
MC664L4L	OEM
MC664P	3003
MC664TL	OEM
MC665L	OEM
MC665P	3025
MC665TL	OEM
MC666L	OEM
MC666P	4079
MC666TL	OEM
MC667	OEM

If replacement code is OEM, contact original manufacturer for replacement. 471

DEVICE TYPE	REPL CODE	DEVICE TYPE	REPL CODE	DEVICE TYPE	REPL CODE	DEVICE TYPE	REPL CODE	DEVICE TYPE	REPL CODE	DEVICE TYPE	REPL CODE	DEVICE TYPE	REPL CODE
MC667L	OEM	MC700G	3384	MC839P	OEM	MC914G	OEM	MC1091A	OEM	MC1372	0808	MC1436G	OEM
MC667P	3037	MC703G	3808	MC840	OEM	MC915G	OEM	MC1092	OEM	MC1372P	0808	MC1436U	OEM
MC667P7P	OEM	MC704G	3781	MC840L	1168	MC916	OEM	MC1092A	OEM	MC1373P	3266	MC1437L	OEM
MC667TL	OEM	MC705G	3669	MC840P	1168	MC916A	OEM	MC1093	OEM	MC1374P	OEM	MC1437P	OEM
MC668	OEM	MC706G	4170	MC841	OEM	MC921	3460	MC1093A	OEM	MC-1375P	1335	MC1438R	OEM
MC668L	OEM	MC707G	4172	MC841L	OEM	MC926G	OEM	MC1094	OEM	MC1375P	1335	MC1439G	OEM
MC668P	2417	MC708G	3793	MC841P	2598	MC927G	OEM	MC1094A	OEM	MC1375PQ	1335	MC1439L	OEM
MC668TL	OEM	MC709G	3797	MC842	OEM	MC930F	OEM	MC1095	OEM	MC1376	OEM	MC1439P1	OEM
MC669	OEM	MC710G	1248	MC843	OEM	MC930G	OEM	MC1095A	OEM	MC1376P	OEM	MC1439P2	OEM
MC669L	OEM	MC711G	1354	MC844	OEM	MC930L	OEM	MC1096	OEM	MC1377DW	OEM	MC1441P	OEM
MC669P	2986	MC712G	3843	MC844F	OEM	MC931	1083	MC1096A	OEM	MC1377P	3280	MC1444	OEM
MC670	OEM	MC713G	3847	MC844G	OEM	MC932F	OEM	MC1097	OEM	MC1385P	OEM	MC1444L	OEM
MC670L	OEM	MC714G	1063	MC844L	0033	MC932G	OEM	MC1097A	OEM	MC1391P	0842	MC1445	OEM
MC670P	2334	MC715G	3845	MC844P	0033	MC932L	OEM	MC1098	OEM	MC1393A	OEM	MC1445F	OEM
MC670TL	OEM	MC717P	OEM	MC845	OEM	MC933L	OEM	MC1098A	OEM	MC1393AP	3346	MC1445G	OEM
MC671	OEM	MC720	OEM	MC845F	OEM	MC934L	OEM	MC1125G	OEM	MC1393P	3346	MC1445J	OEM
MC671L	OEM	MC721G	3303	MC845G	OEM	MC935F	OEM	MC1158P	OEM	MC1394	0842	MC1445L	OEM
MC671P	4086	MC722	OEM	MC845L	0081	MC935L	OEM	MC1226	OEM	MC1394P	2473	MC1445W	OEM
MC671TL	OEM	MC723G	OEM	MC845P	0081	MC936F	OEM	MC1302P	OEM	MC1398	0850	MC1446L	OEM
MC672	0078	MC723P	OEM	MC846F	OEM	MC936L	OEM	MC1303	0687	MC1398P	0850	MC1454G	OEM
MC672L	OEM	MC723PQ	OEM	MC846G	OEM	MC937F	OEM	MC1303L	0687	MC1399P	3363	MC1455D	3589
MC672P	0078	MC724	OEM	MC846L	0141	MC937L	OEM	MC1303P	0687	MC1399PW	OEM	MC1455G	3592
MC672TL	OEM	MC724P	2840	MC846P	0141	MC938F	OEM	MC1304	0649	MC1400AG2	OEM	MC1455P	OEM
MC673	OEM	MC726	OEM	MC848F	OEM	MC938L	OEM	MC1304P	0649	MC1400AG5	OEM	MC1455P1	0967
MC673L	OEM	MC726G	3868	MC848G	OEM	MC939F	OEM	MC1304PQ	0649	MC1400AG6	OEM	MC1455P1D	OEM
MC673P	0795	MC727G	4154	MC848L	3365	MC939L	OEM	MC1305	0438	MC1400AG10	OEM	MC1455P1DS	OEM
MC673TL	OEM	MC728	OEM	MC848P	3365	MC940L	OEM	MC1305P	0438	MC1400AU2	OEM	MC1455P1S	OEM
MC674	OEM	MC730	OEM	MC849F	OEM	MC941L	OEM	MC1305P-C	0438	MC1400AU5	OEM	MC1455U	OEM
MC674L	OEM	MC732	OEM	MC849G	OEM	MC944F	OEM	MC1305PC	0438	MC1400AU6	OEM	MC1455UD	OEM
MC674P	4098	MC774G	1799	MC849L	1833	MC944G	OEM	MC1305PQ	0438	MC1400AU10	OEM	MC1455UDS	OEM
MC674RL	3393	MC776P	3393	MC849P	1833	MC944L	0033	MC1306P	2902	MC1400G2	OEM	MC1455US	OEM
MC674TL	OEM	MC778	OEM	MC850L	2595	MC945F	OEM	MC1307P	0696	MC1400G5	OEM	MC1456CG	OEM
MC675	OEM	MC779	OEM	MC850P	2595	MC945G	OEM	MC-1307-P	0696	MC1400G6	OEM	MC1456CL	OEM
MC675L	OEM	MC789	3395	MC851F	OEM	MC945L	OEM	MC1307P	0696	MC1400G10	OEM	MC1456CP1	OEM
MC675P	4101	MC789P	3395	MC851G	OEM	MC946F	OEM	MC1307PQ	0696	MC1400U2	OEM	MC1456CU	OEM
MC675TL	OEM	MC790P	OEM	MC851L	2067	MC946G	OEM	MC1309	0701	MC1400U5	OEM	MC1456CUCU	OEM
MC676	OEM	MC791P	OEM	MC851P	2067	MC946L	OEM	MC1309P	0701	MC1400U6	OEM	MC1456F	OEM
MC676L	OEM	MC794	OEM	MC852F	OEM	MC948F	OEM	MC1310	0514	MC1400U10	OEM	MC1456FE	OEM
MC676P	4107	MC795	OEM	MC852L	0329	MC948G	OEM	MC-1310P	0514	MC1401AU5	OEM	MC1456G	OEM
MC676TL	OEM	MC796	OEM	MC852P	0329	MC948L	OEM	MC1310P	0514	MC1403AU	OEM	MC1456L	OEM
MC677	OEM	MC797	OEM	MC853F	OEM	MC949F	OEM	MC1311	0627	MC1403D	OEM	MC1456N	OEM
MC677L	OEM	MC798	OEM	MC853P	0354	MC949G	OEM	MC1312P	1601	MC1403U	OEM	MC1456P1	OEM
MC677P	4108	MC799	OEM	MC855F	OEM	MC949L	OEM	MC1313P	OEM	MC1403UD	OEM	MC1456T	OEM
MC677TL	OEM	MC799P	OEM	MC855L	1472	MC950L	OEM	MC1314G	2600	MC1403UDS	OEM	MC1456U	OEM
MC678	0604	MC800	0264	MC855P	1472	MC951F	OEM	MC1314P	2958	MC1403US	OEM	MC1456V	OEM
MC678L	OEM	MC800G	3384	MC856F	OEM	MC951G	OEM	MC1315P	2967	MC1404AU5	OEM	MC1458	0356
MC678P	4110	MC801	OEM	MC856L	1622	MC951L	OEM	MC1316P	2977	MC1404AU6	OEM	MC1458A	OEM
MC678TL	OEM	MC802	OEM	MC856P	1622	MC952F	OEM	MC1317P	0696	MC1404AU10	OEM	MC1458CD	OEM
MC679	OEM	MC803	OEM	MC857F	OEM	MC952L	OEM	MC1324	0746	MC1404L	OEM	MC1458CG	2530
MC679B	OEM	MC803G	3808	MC857L	1424	MC953F	OEM	MC1324P	0746	MC1404U5	OEM	MC1458CL	OEM
MC679BL	OEM	MC804	0133	MC857P	1424	MC953L	OEM	MC-1326	0746	MC1404U6	OEM	MC1458CP	3974
MC679BP	OEM	MC804G	3781	MC-858	0461	MC955F	OEM	MC1326	0748	MC1404U10	OEM	MC1458CP1	0356
MC679L	OEM	MC805G	3669	MC858	0461	MC955L	OEM	MC1326P	0746	MC1405L	OEM	MC1458CP1D	OEM
MC679P	4112	MC806	OEM	MC858F	OEM	MC956F	OEM	MC1326PQ	0746	MC1406	OEM	MC1458CP1DS	OEM
MC679TL	OEM	MC806G	4170	MC858L	0461	MC956L	OEM	MC1327AP	OEM	MC1406L	OEM	MC1458CP1S	OEM
MC680	OEM	MC807	OEM	MC858P	0461	MC957L	OEM	MC1327P	OEM	MC1406LD	OEM	MC1458CP2	OEM
MC680L	OEM	MC807G	4172	MC861F	OEM	MC958F	OEM	MC1328	0661	MC1406LDS	OEM	MC1458CU	OEM
MC680P	4115	MC808	OEM	MC861G	OEM	MC958L	OEM	MC-1328G	0748	MC1406LS	OEM	MC1458CUD	OEM
MC680TL	OEM	MC808G	3793	MC861L	1848	MC961F	OEM	MC1328G	0748	MC1408-7F	OEM	MC1458CUDS	OEM
MC681L	OEM	MC809	OEM	MC861P	1848	MC961L	OEM	MC1328GT	OEM	MC1408-7N	4252	MC1458CUS	OEM
MC681P	3016	MC809G	3797	MC862F	OEM	MC962F	OEM	MC1328P	0345	MC1408-8D	OEM	MC1458D	OEM
MC681TL	OEM	MC810	OEM	MC862G	OEM	MC962G	OEM	MC1328PQ	0345	MC1408-8F	OEM	MC1458F	OEM
MC682	OEM	MC810G	1248	MC862L	0557	MC962L	OEM	MC1329P	0661	MC1408-8N	OEM	MC1458FE	OEM
MC682L	OEM	MC811G	1354	MC862P	0557	MC963F	OEM	MC1330	0438	MC1408D6	OEM	MC1458G	0356
MC682P	3010	MC812G	3843	MC863F	OEM	MC963G	OEM	MC1330A	1797	MC1408D7	OEM	MC1458H	OEM
MC682TL	OEM	MC813G	3847	MC863G	0337	MC963L	OEM	MC1330A1P	1797	MC1408D8	OEM	MC1458JG	OEM
MC683	OEM	MC814G	1063	MC863P	0337	MC981G	OEM	MC1330A2P	6817	MC1408L-6	OEM	MC1458L	3108
MC683L	OEM	MC815G	3845	MC870P	OEM	MC982G	OEM	MC1330P	1797	MC1408L6D	OEM	MC1458N	3406
MC683P	4122	MC816P	OEM	MC874G	1799	MC1017P	OEM	MC1331	OEM	MC1408L6DS	OEM	MC1458N-14	OEM
MC683TL	OEM	MC817P	OEM	MC876P	3393	MC1026	OEM	MC1331P	OEM	MC1408L6S	OEM	MC1458NG	OEM
MC684	OEM	MC821G	3303	MC886P	OEM	MC1031	OEM	MC1335P	OEM	MC1408L-7	OEM	MC1458NL	OEM
MC684L	OEM	MC823G	OEM	MC887P	OEM	MC1031A	OEM	MC1339P	2264	MC1408L7	OEM	MC1458NP1	OEM
MC684P	4124	MC824AP	OEM	MC889P	3395	MC1032	OEM	MC1344	0368	MC1408L7D	OEM	MC1458NP2	OEM
MC684TL	OEM	MC824P	2840	MC890	0133	MC1032A	OEM	MC1344P	0368	MC1408L7DS	OEM	MC1458NU	OEM
MC685	OEM	MC826G	3868	MC890P	OEM	MC1041	OEM	MC1345	0774	MC1408L7S	OEM	MC1458P	0356
MC685L	OEM	MC827G	4154	MC891	OEM	MC1041A	OEM	MC1345P	0368	MC1408L-8	OEM	MC1458P1	OEM
MC685P	4128	MC830F	OEM	MC892	OEM	MC1042	OEM	MC1345PQ	0368	MC1408L8D	OEM	MC1458P1D	OEM
MC685TL	OEM	MC830G	OEM	MC893	OEM	MC1042A	OEM	MC1346P	OEM	MC1408L8DS	OEM	MC1458P1DS	OEM
MC686	OEM	MC830L	1812	MC899G	OEM	MC1044P	0033	MC1349P	3166	MC1408L8S	OEM	MC1458P1S	OEM
MC686L	OEM	MC830P	1812	MC899P	OEM	MC1051	OEM	MC1350	0780	MC1408P6	OEM	MC1458P2	OEM
MC686P	4132	MC831L	3032	MC900G	OEM	MC1051A	OEM	MC1350P	0780	MC1408P7	OEM	MC1458SG	OEM
MC686TL	OEM	MC831P	3032	MC903	OEM	MC1052	OEM	MC1351	0784	MC1408P8	OEM	MC1458SL	OEM
MC688	OEM	MC832F	OEM	MC903A	OEM	MC1052A	OEM	MC1351N	0784	MC1411L	OEM	MC1458SP1	OEM
MC688L	OEM	MC832G	OEM	MC903G	OEM	MC1055A	OEM	MC1351P	0784	MC1411P	0839	MC1458SP2	OEM
MC688P	4136	MC832L	1035	MC904	OEM	MC1055B	OEM	MC1352	0391	MC1411P1P	OEM	MC1458SU	OEM
MC688TL	OEM	MC832N	1812	MC904A	OEM	MC1055C	OEM	MC1352P	0391	MC1412L	OEM	MC1458T	3108
MC689	OEM	MC832P	1035	MC904G	OEM	MC1055D	OEM	MC1353P	0849	MC1412P	1001	MC1458U	OEM
MC689L	OEM	MC833L	2086	MC905	OEM	MC1055E	OEM	MC1354	OEM	MC1413L	OEM	MC1458UD	OEM
MC689P	4137	MC833P	2086	MC905A	OEM	MC1055F	OEM	MC1355P	3189	MC1413P	1126	MC1458UDS	OEM
MC689TL	OEM	MC834L	OEM	MC906	OEM	MC1055G	OEM	MC-1356P	0659	MC1413PD	OEM	MC1458US	OEM
MC690	OEM	MC834P	OEM	MC906A	OEM	MC1055H	OEM	MC1356P	1434	MC1413PDS	OEM	MC1458V	0356
MC690L	OEM	MC835F	OEM	MC906G	OEM	MC1055I	OEM	MC1357	0659	MC1413PS	OEM	MC1461R	3618
MC690P	4140	MC835L	1168	MC907	OEM	MC1055J	OEM	MC1357A	0659	MC1413TL	OEM	MC1462	OEM
MC690TL	OEM	MC835P	1168	MC907A	OEM	MC1055K	OEM	MC1357P	0659	MC1413TP	OEM	MC1463G	OEM
MC691	OEM	MC836F	OEM	MC907G	OEM	MC1055L	OEM	MC1357PQ	0659	MC1414L	OEM	MC1463R	OEM
MC691L	OEM	MC836L	1820	MC908	OEM	MC1055M	OEM	MC1358	0167	MC1414LD	OEM	MC1465	OEM
MC691P	4143	MC836P	1820	MC908A	OEM	MC1055N	OEM	MC1358P	0167	MC1414LDS	OEM	MC1466L	OEM
MC691TL	OEM	MC837	OEM	MC908G	OEM	MC1061	OEM	MC1358PQ	0167	MC1414LS	OEM	MC1468BAL	OEM
MC693L	OEM	MC837A	OEM	MC909G	OEM	MC1061A	OEM	MC1362P	OEM	MC1414P	OEM	MC1468G	OEM
MC693P	OEM	MC837F	OEM	MC910G	OEM	MC1062	OEM	MC-1364	0797	MC1416L	OEM	MC1468L	3641
MC693TL	OEM	MC837L	1824	MC911	2189	MC1062A	OEM	MC1364	0797	MC1416P	1252	MC1468LD	OEM
MC696	OEM	MC837P	1824	MC911G	1354	MC1081	OEM	MC1364G	0360	MC1422P1	1534	MC1468LDS	OEM
MC696L	OEM	MC838	OEM	MC912G	OEM	MC1081A	OEM	MC1364P	0797	MC1435G	OEM	MC1468LS	OEM
MC696P	4157	MC838F	OEM	MC913G	OEM	MC1082	OEM	MC1364PQ	0797	MC1435L	OEM	MC1468R	OEM
MC696TL	OEM	MC838P	OEM	MC914	OEM	MC1082A	OEM	MC1370	0348	MC1436CD	OEM	MC1469G	OEM
MC697L	OEM	MC839	OEM	MC914A	OEM	MC1091	OEM	MC1370P	0348	MC1436CG	OEM	MC1469PS	OEM
MC697P	OEM	MC839F	OEM					MC1371	0350	MC1436CU	OEM	MC1469R	3618
MC697TL	OEM	MC839L	OEM					MC1371P	0350			MC1472P1	OEM
MC699L	OEM												

If replacement code is OEM, contact original manufacturer for replacement.

DEVICE TYPE	REPL CODE
MC1472U	OEM
MC1476G	OEM
MC1488	0503
MC1488F	0503
MC1488L	0503
MC1488LD	OEM
MC1488LDS	OEM
MC1488LS	OEM
MC1488N	0503
MC1488P	0503
MC1488PD	0503
MC1488PDS	OEM
MC1488PS	OEM
MC1489	0506
MC1489/SN75189N	0506
MC1489A	0506
MC1489AF	OEM
MC1489AL	OEM
MC1489ALD	OEM
MC1489ALDS	OEM
MC1489ALS	OEM
MC1489AN	OEM
MC1489AP	0506
MC1489APD	OEM
MC1489APDS	OEM
MC1489APS	OEM
MC1489F	0506
MC1489L	0506
MC1489LD	OEM
MC1489LDS	OEM
MC1489LS	OEM
MC1489N	0506
MC1489P	0506
MC1489PD	OEM
MC1489PDS	OEM
MC1489PS	OEM
MC1493BCLD	OEM
MC1494L	OEM
MC1495L	OEM
MC1496	0413
MC1496A	3751
MC1496D	OEM
MC1496G	0413
MC1496H	OEM
MC1496K	0413
MC1496L	3751
MC1496N	3751
MC1496P	3751
MC1500AG2	OEM
MC1500AG5	OEM
MC1500AG6	OEM
MC1500AU2	OEM
MC1500AU5	OEM
MC1500AU6	OEM
MC1500AU10	OEM
MC1500G2	OEM
MC1500G5	OEM
MC1500G6	OEM
MC1500G10	OEM
MC1500U2	OEM
MC1500U5	OEM
MC1500U6	OEM
MC1500U10	OEM
MC1503AU	OEM
MC1503U	OEM
MC1504AU5	OEM
MC1504AU6	OEM
MC1504AU10	OEM
MC1504U5	OEM
MC1504U6	OEM
MC1504U10	OEM
MC1505L	OEM
MC1506L	OEM
MC1508-8F	OEM
MC1508-8N	OEM
MC1508L-8	OEM
MC1508L8	OEM
MC1511	OEM
MC1512	OEM
MC1513	OEM
MC1514	OEM
MC1514L	OEM
MC1515	OEM
MC1519G	OEM
MC1520	0080
MC1521	0604
MC1522	0604
MC1523	0790
MC1524	0790
MC1525	0015
MC1526	0015
MC1527	0071
MC1528	0071
MC1529	0071
MC1536G	OEM
MC1536U	OEM
MC1537L	OEM
MC1538R	OEM
MC1539G	OEM
MC1539L	OEM
MC1545	OEM
MC1545F	OEM
MC1545G	OEM
MC1545L	OEM
MC1546	OEM
MC1546L	OEM
MC1547	OEM
MC1548	OEM
MC1549	OEM

DEVICE TYPE	REPL CODE
MC1550	1070
MC1550F	OEM
MC1550G	1070
MC-1550P	1902
MC1550P	1902
MC1554G	OEM
MC1555G	3592
MC1555U	3732
MC1556F	OEM
MC1556FE	OEM
MC1556G	OEM
MC1556L	OEM
MC1556N	OEM
MC1556T	OEM
MC1556U	OEM
MC1558	OEM
MC1558F	OEM
MC1558FE	OEM
MC1558G	0356
MC1558H	OEM
MC1558JG	OEM
MC1558L	OEM
MC1558N	OEM
MC1558N-14	OEM
MC1558NG	OEM
MC1558NL	OEM
MC1558NU	OEM
MC1558P	2377
MC1558SG	OEM
MC1558SL	OEM
MC1558SU	OEM
MC1558T	3108
MC1558U	OEM
MC1563G	OEM
MC1563R	OEM
MC1566L	OEM
MC1568G	OEM
MC1568L	OEM
MC1568R	OEM
MC1569G	OEM
MC1569R	OEM
MC1580L	OEM
MC1581L	OEM
MC1582L	OEM
MC1583L	OEM
MC1584L	OEM
MC1590G	OEM
MC1594L	OEM
MC1595L	OEM
MC1596F	OEM
MC1596G	OEM
MC1596H	OEM
MC1596L	4068
MC1600	OEM
MC1648F	OEM
MC1648L	OEM
MC1648LD	OEM
MC1648LDS	OEM
MC1648LS	OEM
MC1648ML	OEM
MC1648MLD	OEM
MC1648MLDS	OEM
MC1648MP	OEM
MC1648P	OEM
MC1648PD	OEM
MC1648PDS	OEM
MC1648PS	OEM
MC1650F	OEM
MC1650L	OEM
MC1650LD	OEM
MC1650LDS	OEM
MC1650LS	OEM
MC1651F	OEM
MC1651L	OEM
MC1651LD	OEM
MC1651LDS	OEM
MC1651LS	OEM
MC1654L	OEM
MC1654LD	OEM
MC1654LDS	OEM
MC1654LS	OEM
MC1658F	OEM
MC1658L	OEM
MC1658LD	OEM
MC1658LDS	OEM
MC1658LS	OEM
MC1658P	OEM
MC1658PD	OEM
MC1658PDS	OEM
MC1658PS	OEM
MC1660F	OEM
MC1660L	OEM
MC1660LD	OEM
MC1660LDS	OEM
MC1660LS	OEM
MC1662F	OEM
MC1662L	OEM
MC1662LD	OEM
MC1662LDS	OEM
MC1662LS	OEM
MC1664F	OEM
MC1664L	OEM
MC1664LD	OEM
MC1664LDS	OEM
MC1664LS	OEM
MC1666F	OEM
MC1666L	OEM
MC1666LD	OEM
MC1666LDS	OEM

DEVICE TYPE	REPL CODE
MC1666LS	OEM
MC1668F	OEM
MC1668L	OEM
MC1668LD	OEM
MC1668LDS	OEM
MC1668LS	OEM
MC1670F	OEM
MC1670L	OEM
MC1670LD	OEM
MC1670LDS	OEM
MC1670LS	OEM
MC1672F	OEM
MC1672L	OEM
MC1672LD	OEM
MC1672LDS	OEM
MC1672LS	OEM
MC1674F	OEM
MC1674L	OEM
MC1674LD	OEM
MC1674LDS	OEM
MC1674LS	OEM
MC1678L	OEM
MC1678LD	OEM
MC1678LDS	OEM
MC1678LS	OEM
MC1679L	OEM
MC1679LD	OEM
MC1679LDS	OEM
MC1679LS	OEM
MC1684MLS	OEM
MC1688F	OEM
MC1688L	OEM
MC1688LD	OEM
MC1688LDS	OEM
MC1688LS	OEM
MC1690F	OEM
MC1690L	OEM
MC1690LD	OEM
MC1690LDS	OEM
MC1690LS	OEM
MC1692F	OEM
MC1692L	OEM
MC1692LD	OEM
MC1692LDS	OEM
MC1692LS	OEM
MC1694L	OEM
MC1694LD	OEM
MC1694LDS	OEM
MC1694LS	OEM
MC1697L	OEM
MC1697LD	OEM
MC1697LDS	OEM
MC1697LS	OEM
MC1697P	OEM
MC1697PD	OEM
MC1697PDS	OEM
MC1697PS	OEM
MC1699F	OEM
MC1699L	OEM
MC1699LD	OEM
MC1699LDS	OEM
MC1699LS	OEM
MC1709AF	OEM
MC1709AG	OEM
MC1709AL	OEM
MC1709C	OEM
MC1709CF	OEM
MC1709CG	1291
MC1709CL	1695
MC1709CP1	1291
MC1709CP2	1695
MC1709F	OEM
MC1709G	1291
MC1709L	OEM
MC1710CF	OEM
MC1710CG	1786
MC1710CL	1789
MC1710CP	1789
MC1710F	OEM
MC1710G	OEM
MC1710L	OEM
MC1710P	1789
MC1711CF	OEM
MC1711CG	1879
MC1711CL	1886
MC1711CP	1886
MC1711F	OEM
MC1711G	OEM
MC1711L	1886
MC1723CD	OEM
MC1723CG	1183
MC1723CL	0026
MC1723CLD	OEM
MC1723CLDS	OEM
MC1723CLS	OEM
MC1723CP	0026
MC1723CPD	OEM
MC1723CPDS	OEM
MC1723CPS	OEM
MC1723G	1183
MC1723L	OEM
MC1731G	0406
MC1733CG	1113
MC1733CL	1110
MC1733CP	1110
MC1733G	1113
MC1733L	OEM
MC1741	0406
MC1741-5C	0406

DEVICE TYPE	REPL CODE
MC1741C2P	1971
MC1741CD	1965
MC1741CF	OEM
MC1741CG	0406
MC1741CL	1964
MC1741CP	0308
MC1741CP1	0308
MC1741CP1D	OEM
MC1741CP1DS	OEM
MC1741CP1S	OEM
MC1741CP2	1964
MC1741CPI	OEM
MC1741CU	OEM
MC1741CUCU	OEM
MC1741CUD	OEM
MC1741CUDS	OEM
MC1741CUS	OEM
MC1741F	OEM
MC1741G	0406
MC1741L	OEM
MC1741NCF	OEM
MC1741NCG	0406
MC1741NCL	OEM
MC1741NCP1	0308
MC1741NCP2	OEM
MC1741NCU	OEM
MC1741NF	OEM
MC1741NG	OEM
MC1741NL	OEM
MC1741NU	OEM
MC1741P1	0308
MC1741SCG	0406
MC1741SCP1	3752
MC1741SG	OEM
MC1741U	OEM
MC1747CG	2352
MC1747CL	2342
MC1747CLD	OEM
MC1747CLDS	OEM
MC1747CLS	OEM
MC1747CP2	2342
MC1747CP2D	OEM
MC1747CP2DS	OEM
MC1747CP2S	OEM
MC1747G	2352
MC1747L	2342
MC1748CG	4299
MC1748CP1	3861
MC1748CU	3861
MC1748G	2435
MC1748U	3861
MC1776CG	OEM
MC1776CP1	3885
MC1776CU	OEM
MC1776G	OEM
MC1776U	OEM
MC1800F	OEM
MC1800L	OEM
MC1800P	0844
MC1801F	OEM
MC1801L	OEM
MC1801P	0868
MC1802L	OEM
MC1802P	0882
MC1803L	OEM
MC1803P	0894
MC1804L	OEM
MC1804P	0913
MC1805	OEM
MC1805L	OEM
MC1805P	0923
MC1806L	OEM
MC1806P	0939
MC1807L	OEM
MC1807P	0956
MC1808L	OEM
MC1808P	0976
MC1809L	OEM
MC1809P	0992
MC1810L	OEM
MC1810P	1005
MC1811L	OEM
MC1811P	1019
MC1812L	OEM
MC1812P	1033
MC1813L	OEM
MC1813P	4458
MC1814L	OEM
MC1814P	4461
MC1816L	2931
MC1816P	2931
MC1818L	OEM
MC1818P	OEM
MC1820L	OEM
MC1820P	1918
MC1880P	OEM
MC1900F	OEM
MC1900L	OEM
MC1901F	OEM
MC1901L	OEM
MC1902F	OEM
MC1902L	OEM
MC1903F	OEM
MC1903L	OEM
MC1904F	OEM
MC1904L	OEM
MC1905F	OEM
MC1905L	OEM
MC1906F	OEM

DEVICE TYPE	REPL CODE
MC1906L	OEM
MC1907F	OEM
MC1907L	OEM
MC1908F	OEM
MC1908L	OEM
MC1909F	OEM
MC1909L	OEM
MC1910F	OEM
MC1910L	OEM
MC1911F	OEM
MC1911L	OEM
MC1912F	OEM
MC1912L	OEM
MC1914F	OEM
MC1914L	OEM
MC1918F	OEM
MC1918L	OEM
MC1920L	OEM
MC1946A	0413
MC2001	OEM
MC2114A4	OEM
MC2114A5	OEM
MC2114AL1	OEM
MC2114AL2	OEM
MC2114AL3	OEM
MC2114AL4	OEM
MC2115A	OEM
MC2115A2	OEM
MC2115AL	OEM
MC2115AL2	OEM
MC2115H2	OEM
MC2115H3	OEM
MC2115H4	OEM
MC2118-10	OEM
MC2118-12	OEM
MC2118-15	OEM
MC2125A	OEM
MC2125A2	OEM
MC2125AL	OEM
MC2125AL2	OEM
MC2125H1	OEM
MC2125H2	OEM
MC2125H3	OEM
MC2125H4	OEM
MC2128-15	OEM
MC2128-20	OEM
MC2141-2	OEM
MC2141-3	OEM
MC2141-4	OEM
MC2141-5	OEM
MC2141L3	OEM
MC2141L4	OEM
MC2141L5	OEM
MC2142	OEM
MC2142-2	OEM
MC2142-3	OEM
MC2142L	OEM
MC2142L3	OEM
MC2147A	OEM
MC2147A3	OEM
MC2147AL	OEM
MC2147AL3	OEM
MC2147H	OEM
MC2147H1	OEM
MC2147H2	OEM
MC2147H3	OEM
MC2147HL	OEM
MC2147HL3	OEM
MC2148H	OEM
MC2148H2	OEM
MC2148H3	OEM
MC2148HL	OEM
MC2148HL3	OEM
MC2149H	OEM
MC2149H2	OEM
MC2149H3	OEM
MC2149HL	OEM
MC2149HL3	OEM
MC2164-15	OEM
MC2164-20	OEM
MC2164-25	OEM
MC2167-10	OEM
MC2167-55	OEM
MC2167-70	OEM
MC2167L70	OEM
MC2186	OEM
MC2187	OEM
MC2315-3	2471
MC2321	0124
MC2325	0133
MC2326	0133
MC2335	0133
MC2336	0133
MC2338	0124
MC2355	0124
MC2356	0124
MC2501L	OEM
MC2502L	OEM
MC2503L	OEM
MC2525	0133
MC2526	0133
MC2535	0133
MC2536	0133
MC2555	0124
MC2556	0124
MC2625	0133
MC2626	0133
MC2635	0124
MC2636	0133

DEVICE TYPE	REPL CODE
MC2652L2(A)	OEM
MC2655	OEM
MC2656	OEM
MC2661A	OEM
MC2661B	OEM
MC2661C	OEM
MC2670L	OEM
MC2670P	OEM
MC2670S	OEM
MC2671L	OEM
MC2671P	OEM
MC2671S	OEM
MC2672L	OEM
MC2672P	OEM
MC2672S	OEM
MC2673L	OEM
MC2673P	OEM
MC2674L	OEM
MC2674P	OEM
MC2674S	OEM
MC2675L	OEM
MC2675P	OEM
MC2675S	OEM
MC2716	OEM
MC2716-1	OEM
MC2716-2	OEM
MC2716-5	OEM
MC2716-6	OEM
MC2732A	OEM
MC2732A2	OEM
MC2732A3	OEM
MC2732A4	OEM
MC2732A20	OEM
MC2732A25	OEM
MC2732A30	OEM
MC2764	OEM
MC2764-2	OEM
MC2764-3	OEM
MC2764-4	OEM
MC2764-25	OEM
MC2764-30	OEM
MC2764-45	OEM
MC2801P	OEM
MC2815	OEM
MC2815-3	OEM
MC2815-4	OEM
MC2816	OEM
MC2816-3	OEM
MC2816-4	OEM
MC2817	OEM
MC2817-3	OEM
MC2817-4	OEM
MC2833P	OEM
MC2836	OEM
MC2838	OEM
MC2870P	OEM
MC2871	OEM
MC2871A	OEM
MC3000L	0677
MC3000P	0677
MC3001	1532
MC3001L	5258
MC3001P	6178
MC3002	OEM
MC3002L	OEM
MC3002P	OEM
MC3004L	5241
MC3004P	5241
MC3005L	0680
MC3005P	0680
MC3006L	2382
MC3006P	2382
MC3008L	1896
MC3008P	1896
MC3009L	3221
MC3009P	3221
MC3010L	3670
MC3010P	3670
MC3011L	4772
MC3011P	4772
MC3012L	4516
MC3012P	4516
MC3015L	OEM
MC3015P	OEM
MC3016L	5284
MC3016P	5284
MC3018L	2705
MC3018P	2705
MC3019L	2638
MC3019P	2638
MC3020L	1781
MC3020P	1781
MC3021L	5680
MC3021P	5680
MC3022L	OEM
MC3022P	OEM
MC3023L	1933
MC3023P	1933
MC3024L	0554
MC3024P	0554
MC3025L	OEM
MC3025P	OEM
MC3026L	OEM
MC3026P	OEM
MC3028L	OEM
MC3028P	OEM
MC3029L	OEM
MC3029P	OEM
MC3030L	5312

DEVICE TYPE	REPL CODE
MC3030P	5312
MC3031L	2009
MC3031P	2009
MC3032L	2090
MC3032P	2090
MC3033L	2158
MC3033P	2158
MC3034L	3129
MC3034P	3129
MC3051L	OEM
MC3051P	OEM
MC3052L	OEM
MC3052P	OEM
MC3054L	3233
MC3054P	3233
MC3055L	3281
MC3055P	3281
MC3060L	OEM
MC3060P	OEM
MC3061L	OEM
MC3061P	1619
MC3062L	OEM
MC3062P	1613
MC3063L	2444
MC3101F	OEM
MC3101L	OEM
MC3102F	OEM
MC3102L	OEM
MC3103F	OEM
MC3103L	OEM
MC3107F	OEM
MC3107L	OEM
MC3115F	OEM
MC3115L	OEM
MC3121F	OEM
MC3121L	OEM
MC3122F	OEM
MC3122L	OEM
MC3125F	OEM
MC3125L	OEM
MC3126F	OEM
MC3126L	OEM
MC3128F	OEM
MC3128L	OEM
MC3129F	OEM
MC3129L	OEM
MC3151F	OEM
MC3151L	OEM
MC3152F	OEM
MC3152L	OEM
MC3160F	OEM
MC3160L	OEM
MC3161F	OEM
MC3161L	OEM
MC3162F	OEM
MC3162L	OEM
MC3232AL	OEM
MC3232AP	OEM
MC3242AL	OEM
MC3242ALD	OEM
MC3242AP	OEM
MC3242APD	OEM
MC3301P	2232
MC3302	0176
MC3302A	OEM
MC3302F	OEM
MC3302L	OEM
MC3302N	OEM
MC3302P	0176
MC3302PD	OEM
MC3302PDS	OEM
MC3302PS	OEM
MC3303	OEM
MC3303F	OEM
MC3303J	0823
MC3303L	0823
MC3303N	0823
MC3303P	0823
MC3310P	3915
MC3320P	3917
MC3321P	OEM
MC3324AL	OEM
MC3324AP	OEM
MC3324L	OEM
MC3324P	OEM
MC3325P	OEM
MC3333P	OEM
MC3334P	OEM
MC3340	1888
MC-3340P	1888
MC3340P	1888
MC3340P1	0618
MC3340PA	1888
MC3344L	OEM
MC3344P	OEM
MC3346P	1686
MC3350P	OEM
MC3356P	OEM
MC3357	2648
MC3357P	3742
MC3358P1	OEM
MC3359P	3746
MC3360P	0512
MC3361D	OEM
MC3361P	OEM
MC3370P	3887
MC3373	2661
MC3373P	OEM
MC3386P	1686

If replacement code is OEM, contact original manufacturer for replacement.

DEVICE TYPE	REPL CODE
MC3393P	OEM
MC3393PN	OEM
MC3396P	OEM
MC3401L	2232
MC3401P	2232
MC3403	2679
MC3403D	OEM
MC3403F	OEM
MC3403J	0823
MC3403L	0823
MC3403LD	OEM
MC3403LDS	OEM
MC3403LS	OEM
MC3403N	0823
MC3403P	6541
MC3403PD	OEM
MC3403PDS	OEM
MC3403PS	OEM
MC3405L	OEM
MC3405P	OEM
MC3408L	OEM
MC3410CF	OEM
MC3410CL	OEM
MC3410CN	OEM
MC3410F	OEM
MC3410L	OEM
MC3410N	OEM
MC3412L	OEM
MC3412P	OEM
MC3416L	OEM
MC3416P	OEM
MC3417L	OEM
MC3418L	OEM
MC3419AL	OEM
MC3419CL	OEM
MC3419L	OEM
MC3420L	OEM
MC3420P	OEM
MC3423	2692
MC3423JG	OEM
MC3423P	OEM
MC3423P1	2692
MC3423P1D	OEM
MC3423P1DS	OEM
MC3423P1S	OEM
MC3423U	2692
MC3423UDS	OEM
MC3423US	OEM
MC3424AL	OEM
MC3424AP	OEM
MC3424L	OEM
MC3424P	OEM
MC3425AP1	OEM
MC3425AU	OEM
MC3425P1	OEM
MC3425U	OEM
MC3430L	OEM
MC3430P	OEM
MC3431L	OEM
MC3431P	OEM
MC3432L	OEM
MC3432P	OEM
MC3433L	OEM
MC3433P	OEM
MC3437L	OEM
MC3437P	OEM
MC3438L	OEM
MC3438P	OEM
MC3440AP	OEM
MC3441AP	OEM
MC3443AP	OEM
MC3446	OEM
MC3446AP	OEM
MC3446J	OEM
MC3446N	OEM
MC3447L	OEM
MC3447P	OEM
MC3447P3	OEM
MC3448AL	OEM
MC3448AP	OEM
MC3450L	OEM
MC3450LD	OEM
MC3450LDS	OEM
MC3450LS	OEM
MC3450P	OEM
MC3450PD	OEM
MC3450PDS	OEM
MC3450PS	OEM
MC3452L	OEM
MC3452P	OEM
MC3453L	OEM
MC3453LD	OEM
MC3453P	OEM
MC3453PD	OEM
MC3456L	OEM
MC3456P	3254
MC3456PC	OEM
MC3456PD	OEM
MC3458G	3948
MC3458P1	2314
MC3458U	OEM
MC3459L	OEM
MC3459P	OEM
MC3460L	OEM
MC3460P	OEM
MC3467L	OEM
MC3467P	OEM
MC3468L	OEM
MC3468P	OEM

DEVICE TYPE	REPL CODE
MC3469P	OEM
MC3470	2732
MC3470AP	2732
MC3470N	2732
MC3470P	2732
MC3476G	3768
MC3476P1	3400
MC3476U	OEM
MC3476U6U	OEM
MC3479P	5711
MC3480L	OEM
MC3480P	OEM
MC3481L	OEM
MC3481P	OEM
MC3482AL	OEM
MC3482BL	OEM
MC3484V2	OEM
MC3484V4	OEM
MC3485L	OEM
MC3485P	OEM
MC3486	OEM
MC3486J	OEM
MC3486L	OEM
MC3486N	OEM
MC3486P	OEM
MC3487	OEM
MC3487J	OEM
MC3487L	OEM
MC3487LD	OEM
MC3487N	OEM
MC3487P	OEM
MC3487PD	OEM
MC3488AP1	OEM
MC3488AU	OEM
MC3488BU	OEM
MC3490P	4860
MC3491P	1866
MC3492P	1866
MC3492PD	OEM
MC3494P	4862
MC3503	OEM
MC3503F	OEM
MC3503J	OEM
MC3503L	OEM
MC3505L	OEM
MC3510F	OEM
MC3510L	OEM
MC3510N	OEM
MC3512L	OEM
MC3517L	OEM
MC3518L	OEM
MC3520L	OEM
MC3523JG	OEM
MC3523U	OEM
MC3524AL	OEM
MC3524L	OEM
MC3525AU	OEM
MC3525U	OEM
MC3556L	OEM
MC3558G	OEM
MC3558U	OEM
MC3628A1	OEM
MC3628A3	OEM
MC3628A4(A)	OEM
MC3632	OEM
MC3632-1	OEM
MC3636B	OEM
MC3636B1	OEM
MC3636B2	OEM
MC3870L	OEM
MC3870P	OEM
MC3870S	OEM
MC4000F	OEM
MC4000L	OEM
MC4000P	OEM
MC4001L	OEM
MC4001P	OEM
MC4002F	OEM
MC4002L	OEM
MC4002P	OEM
MC4004	3092
MC4004F	OEM
MC4004L	OEM
MC4004P	6973
MC4005L	OEM
MC4005P	6973
MC4006L	OEM
MC4006P	OEM
MC4007L	OEM
MC4007P	OEM
MC4008L	OEM
MC4008P	OEM
MC4010L	OEM
MC4010P	OEM
MC4012L	OEM
MC4012P	0493
MC4015L	OEM
MC4015P	OEM
MC4016L	OEM
MC4016P	1135
MC4017L	OEM
MC4017P	OEM
MC4018L	1381
MC4018P	1381
MC4019L	OEM
MC4019P	OEM
MC4021L	OEM
MC4021P	OEM
MC4022L	OEM

DEVICE TYPE	REPL CODE
MC4022P	OEM
MC4023L	OEM
MC4023P	OEM
MC4024	OEM
MC4024L	OEM
MC4024P	OEM
MC4026L	OEM
MC4026P	OEM
MC4028F	OEM
MC4028L	OEM
MC4028P	OEM
MC4030L	OEM
MC4030P	OEM
MC4032F	OEM
MC4032L	OEM
MC4032P	OEM
MC4035L	OEM
MC4037L	OEM
MC4037P	OEM
MC4038L	OEM
MC4038P	OEM
MC4039L	OEM
MC4039P	OEM
MC4040L	OEM
MC4040P	0011
MC4041P	OEM
MC4042L	OEM
MC4042P	0121
MC4044	0011
MC4044CP	0011
MC4044D	0011
MC4044F	OEM
MC4044L	0011
MC4044P	0011
MC4047	2315
MC4048L	OEM
MC4048P	OEM
MC4048P8P	OEM
MC4050	2016
MC4050L	OEM
MC4050P	OEM
MC4051B	0362
MC4051L	OEM
MC4051P	OEM
MC4056L	OEM
MC4056P	OEM
MC4060L	OEM
MC4060P	OEM
MC4062P	OEM
MC-4080	OEM
MC4300F	OEM
MC4300L	OEM
MC4301L	OEM
MC4302F	OEM
MC4302L	OEM
MC4304F	OEM
MC4304L	OEM
MC4305F	OEM
MC4305L	OEM
MC4306F	OEM
MC4306L	OEM
MC4307F	OEM
MC4307L	OEM
MC4308F	OEM
MC4308L	OEM
MC4310F	OEM
MC4310L	OEM
MC4312F	OEM
MC4312L	OEM
MC4315F	OEM
MC4315L	OEM
MC4316F	OEM
MC4316L	OEM
MC4317F	OEM
MC4317L	OEM
MC4318F	OEM
MC4318L	OEM
MC4319F	OEM
MC4319L	OEM
MC4321F	OEM
MC4321L	OEM
MC4322F	OEM
MC4322L	OEM
MC4323F	OEM
MC4323L	OEM
MC4324F	OEM
MC4324L	OEM
MC4326F	OEM
MC4326L	OEM
MC4328F	OEM
MC4328L	OEM
MC4330F	OEM
MC4330L	OEM
MC4332F	OEM
MC4332L	OEM
MC4335F	OEM
MC4335L	OEM
MC4337F	OEM
MC4337L	OEM
MC4342F	OEM
MC4342L	OEM
MC4344F	OEM
MC4344L	OEM
MC4348L	OEM
MC4350F	OEM
MC4350L	OEM
MC4356F	OEM
MC4356L	OEM
MC4360F	OEM

DEVICE TYPE	REPL CODE
MC4360L	OEM
MC4558ACP1	0356
MC4558C	3974
MC4558CD	5433
MC4558CG	OEM
MC4558CP	0356
MC4558CP1	0356
MC4558CU	0356
MC4558G	OEM
MC4558NCG	OEM
MC4558NCP1	OEM
MC4558NCU	OEM
MC4558NG	OEM
MC4558NU	OEM
MC4558S	OEM
MC4558U	OEM
MC4741CD	OEM
MC4741CL	2796
MC4741CLD	OEM
MC4741CP	2796
MC4741CPD	OEM
MC4741L	2796
MC4741LD	OEM
MC5201	3564
MC5223	OEM
MC5321	0124
MC5404F	OEM
MC5480L	OEM
MC5600	OEM
MC5601	OEM
MC5602	OEM
MC5603	OEM
MC5604	OEM
MC5605	OEM
MC5606	OEM
MC5607	OEM
MC5610	OEM
MC5611	OEM
MC5612	OEM
MC5613	OEM
MC5614	OEM
MC5615	OEM
MC5616	OEM
MC5617	OEM
MC5618	OEM
MC5619	OEM
MC6007	0157
MC6007A	0157
MC6008	0466
MC6008A	0466
MC6009	OEM
MC6009A	OEM
MC6010	0062
MC6010A	0062
MC6011	0077
MC6011A	0077
MC6012	0165
MC6012A	0165
MC6013	0057
MC6013A	0057
MC6014	0170
MC6014A	0170
MC6015	0181
MC6015A	0181
MC6016	0052
MC6016A	0052
MC6017	0053
MC6017A	0053
MC6018	0681
MC6018A	0681
MC6019	0440
MC6019A	0440
MC6020	0371
MC6020A	0371
MC6021	0695
MC6021A	0695
MC6022	0700
MC6022A	0700
MC6023	0489
MC6023A	0489
MC6024	0436
MC6024A	0436
MC6025	0195
MC6025A	0195
MC6026	0039
MC6026A	0039
MC6027	0010
MC6027A	0010
MC6028	0032
MC6028A	0032
MC6029	0054
MC6029A	0054
MC6030	0068
MC6030A	0068
MC6107	0157
MC6107A	0157
MC6108	0631
MC6108A	0631
MC6108L	OEM
MC6109	OEM
MC6109A	OEM
MC6110	0025
MC6110A	0025
MC6111	0644
MC6111A	0644
MC6112	0244
MC6112A	0244
MC6113	0012
MC6113A	0012

DEVICE TYPE	REPL CODE
MC6114	0170
MC6114A	0170
MC6115	0313
MC6115A	0313
MC6116	0137
MC6116A	0137
MC6117	0361
MC6117A	0361
MC6118	0002
MC6118A	0002
MC6119	0416
MC6119A	0416
MC6120	0490
MC6120A	0490
MC6121	0526
MC6121A	0526
MC6122	0560
MC6122A	0560
MC6123	0560
MC6123A	0398
MC6124	0436
MC6124A	0436
MC6125	0721
MC6125A	0721
MC6126	0039
MC6126A	0039
MC6127	0814
MC6127A	0814
MC6128	0346
MC6128A	0346
MC6129	0925
MC6129A	0925
MC6130	0993
MC6130A	0993
MC6172L	OEM
MC6172P	OEM
MC6173L	OEM
MC6173P	OEM
MC6187P	OEM
MC6190L	OEM
MC6190P	OEM
MC6191L	OEM
MC6191P	OEM
MC6192L	OEM
MC6192P	OEM
MC6193L	OEM
MC6193P	OEM
MC6194L	OEM
MC6194P	OEM
MC6195L	OEM
MC6195P	OEM
MC6196L	OEM
MC6196P	OEM
MC6308	0185
MC6308A	0185
MC6309	OEM
MC6309A	OEM
MC6310	0205
MC6310A	0205
MC6311	0475
MC6311A	0475
MC6312	0499
MC6312A	0499
MC6313	0679
MC6313A	0679
MC6314	0225
MC6314A	0225
MC6315	0230
MC6315A	0230
MC6316	0234
MC6316A	0234
MC6317	0237
MC6317A	0237
MC6318	0247
MC6318A	0247
MC6319	0251
MC6319A	0251
MC6320	0256
MC6320A	0256
MC6321	0262
MC6321A	0262
MC6322	0269
MC6322A	0269
MC6323	0273
MC6323A	0273
MC6324	0291
MC6324A	0291
MC6325	0305
MC6325A	0305
MC6326	0314
MC6326A	0314
MC6327	0316
MC6327A	0316
MC6328	0322
MC6328A	0322
MC6329	0333
MC6329A	0333
MC6330	0343
MC6330A	0343
MC6400	OEM
MC6400A	OEM
MC6400B	OEM
MC6400C	OEM
MC6401A	OEM
MC6401B	OEM
MC6401C	OEM
MC6402A	OEM
MC6402B	OEM
MC6402C	OEM

DEVICE TYPE	REPL CODE
MC6403A	OEM
MC6403B	OEM
MC6403C	OEM
MC6404A	OEM
MC6404B	OEM
MC6404C	OEM
MC6405A	OEM
MC6405B	OEM
MC6405C	OEM
MC6406A	OEM
MC6406B	OEM
MC6406C	OEM
MC6407A	OEM
MC6407B	OEM
MC6407C	OEM
MC6408A	OEM
MC6408B	OEM
MC6408C	OEM
MC6409A	OEM
MC6409B	OEM
MC6409C	OEM
MC6410A	OEM
MC6410B	OEM
MC6410C	OEM
MC6411A	OEM
MC6411B	OEM
MC6411C	OEM
MC6412A	OEM
MC6412B	OEM
MC6412C	OEM
MC6413A	OEM
MC6413B	OEM
MC6413C	OEM
MC6414A	OEM
MC6414B	OEM
MC6414C	OEM
MC6415B	OEM
MC6415C	OEM
MC6416	OEM
MC6416A	OEM
MC6416B	OEM
MC6416C	OEM
MC6417	OEM
MC6417A	OEM
MC6417B	OEM
MC6417C	OEM
MC6418	OEM
MC6418A	OEM
MC6418B	OEM
MC6418C	OEM
MC6419	OEM
MC6419A	OEM
MC6419B	OEM
MC6419C	OEM
MC6420	OEM
MC6420A	OEM
MC6420B	OEM
MC6420C	OEM
MC6421	OEM
MC6421A	OEM
MC6421B	OEM
MC6421C	OEM
MC6422	OEM
MC6422A	OEM
MC6422B	OEM
MC6422C	OEM
MC6423	OEM
MC6423A	OEM
MC6423B	OEM
MC6423C	OEM
MC6424	OEM
MC6424A	OEM
MC6424B	OEM
MC6424C	OEM
MC6425	OEM
MC6425A	OEM
MC6425B	OEM
MC6425C	OEM
MC6426	OEM
MC6426A	OEM
MC6426B	OEM
MC6426C	OEM
MC6427	OEM
MC6427A	OEM
MC6427B	OEM
MC6427C	OEM
MC6428	OEM
MC6428A	OEM
MC6428B	OEM
MC6428C	OEM
MC6429	OEM
MC6429A	OEM
MC6429B	OEM
MC6429C	OEM
MC6525P	OEM
MC6800BQCS	OEM
MC6800CL	0384
MC6800CP	0384
MC6800CQCS	OEM
MC6800CS	OEM
MC6800L	OEM
MC6800P	0384
MC6800S	OEM
MC6801-1G	OEM
MC6801-1L	OEM
MC6801C-1G	OEM
MC6801C-1L	OEM
MC6801CG	OEM
MC6801CL	OEM

DEVICE TYPE	REPL CODE
MC6801CL1	OEM
MC6801CL1-1	OEM
MC6801CP1	OEM
MC6801G	OEM
MC6801G1	OEM
MC6801L	OEM
MC6801L-1	OEM
MC6801L1	OEM
MC6801L1-1	OEM
MC6801P1	OEM
MC6801U4CL1	OEM
MC6801U4CP1	OEM
MC6801U4L1	OEM
MC6801U4L1-1	OEM
MC6801U4P1	OEM
MC6801U4P1-1	OEM
MC6801VL1	OEM
MC6801VP1	OEM
MC6802CL	OEM
MC6802CP	OEM
MC6802L	OEM
MC6802NSL	OEM
MC6802NSP	OEM
MC6802P	0389
MC6802P2P	OEM
MC6803-1L	OEM
MC6803C-1G	OEM
MC6803C-1L	OEM
MC6803CG	OEM
MC6803CL	OEM
MC6803CL-1	OEM
MC6803CP	OEM
MC6803CP-1	OEM
MC6803CP1-1	OEM
MC6803EG	OEM
MC6803EG-1	OEM
MC6803EL	OEM
MC6803EL-1	OEM
MC6803EP	OEM
MC6803EP-1	OEM
MC6803G	OEM
MC6803L	OEM
MC6803L-1	OEM
MC6803L1	OEM
MC6803P	OEM
MC6803P1	OEM
MC6803P1-1	OEM
MC6803U4CL1	OEM
MC6803U4CP1	OEM
MC6803U4L	OEM
MC6803U4L-1	OEM
MC6803U4P	OEM
MC6803U4P-1	OEM
MC6803VL	OEM
MC6803VP	OEM
MC6804	OEM
MC6805P2	OEM
MC6805P2L	OEM
MC6805P2L1	OEM
MC6805P2P	OEM
MC6805P2P1	OEM
MC6805P2S	OEM
MC6805P4L	OEM
MC6805P4P	OEM
MC6805P4S	OEM
MC6805P6L	OEM
MC6805P6P	OEM
MC6805P6S	OEM
MC6805R2L	OEM
MC6805R2L1	OEM
MC6805R2P	OEM
MC6805R2P1	OEM
MC6805R2S	OEM
MC6805R3L	OEM
MC6805R3P	OEM
MC6805R3S	OEM
MC6805T2L	OEM
MC6805T2P	OEM
MC6805U2G	OEM
MC6805U2L	OEM
MC6805U2L2	OEM
MC6805U2P	OEM
MC6805U2P2	OEM
MC6805U2S	OEM
MC6805U3L	OEM
MC6805U3P	OEM
MC6805U3S	OEM
MC6808L	OEM
MC6808P	OEM
MC6809CL	OEM
MC6809CP	OEM
MC6809CS	OEM
MC6809E	2105
MC6809ECL	OEM
MC6809ECP	OEM
MC6809ECS	OEM
MC6809EL	2105
MC6809EP	2105
MC6809ES	4287
MC6809L	5829
MC6809P	5829
MC6809S	6823
MC6820	0443
MC6821	0443
MC6821BQCS	OEM
MC6821CL	OEM
MC6821CP	0443
MC6821CQCS	OEM
MC6821CS	OEM

If replacement code is OEM, contact original manufacturer for replacement.

DEVICE TYPE	REPL CODE
MC6821L	OEM
MC6821P	0443
MC6821S	OEM
MC6822L	OEM
MC6822P	OEM
MC6822S	OEM
MC6828L	OEM
MC6828P	OEM
MC6829CL	OEM
MC6829CP	OEM
MC6829CS	OEM
MC6829L	OEM
MC6829P	OEM
MC6829S	OEM
MC6835CL	OEM
MC6835CP	OEM
MC6835CS	OEM
MC6835L	OEM
MC6835P	OEM
MC6835S	OEM
MC6840CL	OEM
MC6840CP	OEM
MC6840CS	OEM
MC6840L	OEM
MC6840P	OEM
MC6840S	OEM
MC6843	OEM
MC6843P	OEM
MC6844CL	OEM
MC6844CP	OEM
MC6844CS	OEM
MC6844L	OEM
MC6844P	OEM
MC6844S	OEM
MC6845	OEM
MC6845CL	OEM
MC6845CP	OEM
MC6845CS	OEM
MC6845L	OEM
MC6845P	OEM
MC6845R1CL	OEM
MC6845R1CP	OEM
MC6845R1CS	OEM
MC6845R1L	OEM
MC6845R1P	OEM
MC6845R1S	OEM
MC6845S	OEM
MC6846CL	OEM
MC6846CP	OEM
MC6846CS	OEM
MC6846L	OEM
MC6846L1	OEM
MC6846P	OEM
MC6846P1	OEM
MC6846P3	OEM
MC6846S	OEM
MC6847	OEM
MC6847L	OEM
MC6847P	OEM
MC6847S	OEM
MC6847YL	OEM
MC6847YP	OEM
MC6847YS	OEM
MC6850BJCS	OEM
MC6850CJCS	OEM
MC6850CL	OEM
MC6850CP	0509
MC6850CS	OEM
MC6850L	OEM
MC6850P	0509
MC6850S	OEM
MC6852CL	OEM
MC6852CP	OEM
MC6852CS	OEM
MC6852L	OEM
MC6852P	OEM
MC6852S	OEM
MC6854CL	OEM
MC6854CP	OEM
MC6854CS	OEM
MC6854L	OEM
MC6854P	OEM
MC6854S	OEM
MC6859L	OEM
MC6859L(A)	OEM
MC6859S(A)	OEM
MC6860CL	OEM
MC6860L	2667
MC6860P	2667
MC6860S	OEM
MC6862CL	OEM
MC6862CP	OEM
MC6862CS	OEM
MC6862L	OEM
MC6862P	OEM
MC6862S	OEM
MC6863L	OEM
MC6863P	OEM
MC6875	4118
MC6875AL	OEM
MC6875L	4118
MC6880AL	4437
MC6880AP	4437
MC6882AL	OEM
MC6882BL	OEM
MC6883	OEM
MC6883J(A)	OEM
MC6883L	OEM
MC6883N(A)	OEM
MC6883P	OEM
MC6885L	4566
MC6885P	4566
MC6886L	4570
MC6886P	4570
MC6887L	4577
MC6887P	4577
MC6888L	4586
MC6888P	4586
MC6889L	0576
MC6889P	0576
MC6890AL	OEM
MC6890AL(A)	OEM
MC6890L	OEM
MC6890L(A)	OEM
MC-7000	OEM
MC7000	OEM
MC7001	OEM
MC7002	OEM
MC7003	OEM
MC7004	OEM
MC7005	OEM
MC7006	OEM
MC7007	OEM
MC7008	OEM
MC7009	OEM
MC7400	0232
MC7400F	0232
MC7400L	0232
MC7400N	0232
MC7400P	0232
MC7401F	0268
MC7401L	0268
MC7401P	0268
MC-7402	0310
MC7402	4219
MC7402F	0310
MC7402L	0310
MC7402P	0310
MC7403L	0331
MC7403P	0331
MC7404F	OEM
MC7404L	0357
MC7404P	0357
MC7405L	0381
MC7405P	0381
MC7406L	1197
MC7406P	1197
MC7407L	1329
MC7407P	1329
MC7408L	0462
MC7408P	0462
MC7409L	0487
MC7409P	0487
MC7410F	0507
MC7410L	0507
MC7410P	0507
MC7416L	1339
MC7416P	1339
MC7417L	1342
MC7417P	1342
MC7420F	0692
MC7420L	0692
MC7420P	0692
MC7426L	0798
MC7426P	0798
MC7430F	0867
MC7430L	0867
MC7430P	0867
MC7437F	3478
MC7437L	3478
MC7437P	3478
MC7438F	0990
MC7438L	0990
MC7438P	0990
MC7440F	1018
MC7440L	1018
MC7440P	1018
MC7441AL	1032
MC7441AP	1032
MC7442L	1046
MC7442P	1046
MC7443L	1054
MC7443P	1054
MC7444L	1066
MC7444P	1066
MC7445L	1074
MC7445P	1074
MC7446L	1090
MC7446P	1090
MC7447L	1100
MC7447P	1100
MC7448L	1117
MC7448P	1117
MC7450F	0738
MC7450L	0738
MC7450P	0738
MC7451F	1160
MC7451L	1160
MC7451P	1160
MC7453F	1177
MC7453L	1177
MC7453P	1177
MC7454F	1193
MC7454L	1193
MC7454P	1193
MC7460F	1265
MC7460L	1265
MC7460P	1265
MC7470L	1394
MC7470P	1394
MC7472F	1417
MC7472L	1417
MC7472P	1417
MC7473F	1164
MC7473L	1164
MC7473P	1164
MC7474P	1303
MC7475L	1423
MC7475P	1423
MC7476L	1150
MC7476P	1150
MC7480L	1527
MC7480P	1527
MC7483L	0117
MC7483P	0117
MC7486F	1358
MC7486L	1358
MC7486P	1358
MC7490AP	1199
MC7490F	1199
MC7490L	1199
MC7490P	1199
MC7491AL	0974
MC7491AP	0974
MC7492F	0828
MC7492L	0828
MC7492P	0828
MC7493F	0564
MC7493L	0564
MC7493P	0564
MC7494L	1692
MC7494P	1692
MC7495L	1477
MC7495P	1477
MC7496L	1705
MC7496P	1705
MC7805	0619
MC7805ACK	1905
MC7805ACT	0619
MC7805AK	1905
MC7805BK	1905
MC7805BT	0619
MC7805C	0619
MC7805CK	1905
MC7805CP	0619
MC7805CT	0619
MC7805CTD	OEM
MC7805CTDS	0619
MC7805K	1905
MC7805UC	0619
MC7806ACK	OEM
MC7806ACT	0917
MC7806AK	OEM
MC7806BK	OEM
MC7806BT	0917
MC7806CK	OEM
MC7806CT	0917
MC7806CTD	OEM
MC7806CTS	OEM
MC7806K	OEM
MC7808ACK	OEM
MC7808ACT	6543
MC7808AK	OEM
MC7808BK	OEM
MC7808BT	1187
MC7808C	1187
MC7808CK	OEM
MC7808CP	5934
MC7808CT	1187
MC7808CTD	OEM
MC7808CTDS	OEM
MC7808CTS	OEM
MC7808K	OEM
MC7808UC	OEM
MC7809C	OEM
MC7809CT	1336
MC7812	0330
MC7812AC	0330
MC7812ACK	3359
MC7812ACT	0330
MC7812AK	3359
MC7812BK	3359
MC7812BT	0330
MC7812C	0330
MC7812CK	3359
MC7812CT	0330
MC7812CTD	OEM
MC7812CTDS	OEM
MC7812CTS	OEM
MC7812K	3359
MC7815	1311
MC7815ACK	1299
MC7815ACT	1311
MC7815AK	1299
MC7815BK	1299
MC7815BT	1311
MC7815C	4276
MC7815CK	1989
MC7815CP	1311
MC7815CT	1311
MC7815CTD	OEM
MC7815CTDS	OEM
MC7815CTS	OEM
MC7815K	1299
MC7815P	1311
MC7818A	4277
MC7818AC	4277
MC7818ACK	OEM
MC7818ACT	2244
MC7818AK	OEM
MC7818B	OEM
MC7818BK	OEM
MC7818BT	2244
MC7818C	4277
MC7818CK	3605
MC7818CT	2244
MC7818CTD	OEM
MC7818CTDS	OEM
MC7818CTS	OEM
MC7818K	OEM
MC7819CT	3774
MC7824	2224
MC7824ACK	OEM
MC7824ACT	2224
MC7824AK	OEM
MC7824BK	OEM
MC7824BT	2224
MC7824CK	3828
MC7824CT	2224
MC7824CTD	OEM
MC7824CTDS	OEM
MC7824CTS	OEM
MC7824K	OEM
MC7902CK	OEM
MC7902CT	OEM
MC7902CTD	OEM
MC7905	1275
MC7905ACK	OEM
MC7905ACT	1275
MC7905C	1275
MC7905CK	1993
MC7905CT	1275
MC7905CTD	OEM
MC7905CTDS	OEM
MC7905CTS	OEM
MC7905.2ACT	OEM
MC7905.2CK	OEM
MC7905.2CT	1275
MC7905.2CTD	OEM
MC7906ACT	2197
MC7906CK	OEM
MC7906CT	2624
MC7906CTD	OEM
MC7906CTDS	OEM
MC7908ACT	3390
MC7908CK	OEM
MC7908CT	2764
MC7908CTD	OEM
MC7908CTDS	OEM
MC7908CTS	OEM
MC7912ACK	OEM
MC7912ACT	1827
MC7912CK	5193
MC7912CT	1827
MC7912CTD	OEM
MC7912CTDS	OEM
MC7912CTS	OEM
MC7915ACK	OEM
MC7915ACT	3777
MC7915CK	5195
MC7915CP	3777
MC7915CT	3777
MC7915CTD	OEM
MC7915CTDS	OEM
MC7915CTS	OEM
MC7918	3312
MC7918ACT	3312
MC7918C	3312
MC7918CK	3777
MC7918CT	3774
MC7918CTD	OEM
MC7918CTDS	OEM
MC7918CTS	OEM
MC7924ACT	3554
MC7924CK	3529
MC7924CT	3531
MC7924CTD	OEM
MC7924CTDS	OEM
MC7924CTS	OEM
MC8035L	OEM
MC8048	OEM
MC8085A	OEM
MC8086	OEM
MC8088B	OEM
MC8148	OEM
MC8155	OEM
MC8180A	OEM
MC8212	OEM
MC8214	OEM
MC8216	OEM
MC8224	OEM
MC8226	OEM
MC8228	OEM
MC8251	OEM
MC8253	OEM
MC8255A	OEM
MC8257	OEM
MC8259A	OEM
MC8284	OEM
MC8288	OEM
MC8500	OEM
MC8500L	OEM
MC8500P	OEM
MC8501	OEM
MC8501L	OEM
MC8501P	OEM
MC8502	OEM
MC8502L	OEM
MC8502P	OEM
MC8503	OEM
MC8503L	OEM
MC8503P	OEM
MC8504L	OEM
MC8504P	OEM
MC8506	OEM
MC8506L	OEM
MC8506P	OEM
MC8507L	OEM
MC8507P	OEM
MC8520L	OEM
MC8601P	2252
MC8748	OEM
MC9346	OEM
MC9601L	2252
MC9930	1812
MC10100F	OEM
MC10100L	OEM
MC10100LD	OEM
MC10100LDS	OEM
MC10100LS	OEM
MC10100P	OEM
MC10100PD	OEM
MC10100PDS	OEM
MC10100PS	OEM
MC10101F	OEM
MC10101L	OEM
MC10101LD	OEM
MC10101LDS	OEM
MC10101LS	OEM
MC10101P	OEM
MC10101PDS	OEM
MC10101PS	OEM
MC10102	OEM
MC10102F	OEM
MC10102L	OEM
MC10102LD	OEM
MC10102LDS	OEM
MC10102LS	OEM
MC10102P	OEM
MC10102PD	OEM
MC10102PDS	OEM
MC10102PS	OEM
MC10103F	OEM
MC10103L	OEM
MC10103LD	OEM
MC10103LDS	OEM
MC10103LS	OEM
MC10103P	OEM
MC10103PD	OEM
MC10103PDS	OEM
MC10103PS	OEM
MC10104F	OEM
MC10104L	OEM
MC10104LD	OEM
MC10104LDS	OEM
MC10104LS	OEM
MC10104P	OEM
MC10104PD	OEM
MC10104PDS	OEM
MC10104PS	OEM
MC10105F	OEM
MC10105L	OEM
MC10105LD	OEM
MC10105LDS	OEM
MC10105LS	OEM
MC10105P	OEM
MC10105PD	OEM
MC10105PDS	OEM
MC10105PS	OEM
MC10106F	OEM
MC10106L	OEM
MC10106LD	OEM
MC10106LDS	OEM
MC10106LS	OEM
MC10106P	OEM
MC10106PD	OEM
MC10106PDS	OEM
MC10106PS	OEM
MC10107F	OEM
MC10107L	OEM
MC10107LD	OEM
MC10107LDS	OEM
MC10107LS	OEM
MC10107P	OEM
MC10107PD	OEM
MC10107PDS	OEM
MC10107PS	OEM
MC10109F	OEM
MC10109L	OEM
MC10109LD	OEM
MC10109LDS	OEM
MC10109LS	OEM
MC10109P	OEM
MC10109PD	OEM
MC10109PDS	OEM
MC10109PS	OEM
MC10110L	OEM
MC10110LD	OEM
MC10110LDS	OEM
MC10110LS	OEM
MC10110P	OEM
MC10110PD	OEM
MC10110PDS	OEM
MC10110PS	OEM
MC10111L	OEM
MC10111LD	OEM
MC10111LDS	OEM
MC10111LS	OEM
MC10111P	OEM
MC10111PD	OEM
MC10111PDS	OEM
MC10111PS	OEM
MC10113F	OEM
MC10113L	OEM
MC10113LD	OEM
MC10113LDS	OEM
MC10113LS	OEM
MC10113P	OEM
MC10113PD	OEM
MC10113PDS	OEM
MC10113PS	OEM
MC10114F	OEM
MC10114L	OEM
MC10114LD	OEM
MC10114LDS	OEM
MC10114LS	OEM
MC10114P	OEM
MC10114PD	OEM
MC10114PDS	OEM
MC10114PS	OEM
MC10115F	OEM
MC10115L	OEM
MC10115LD	OEM
MC10115LDS	OEM
MC10115LS	OEM
MC10115P	OEM
MC10115PD	OEM
MC10115PDS	OEM
MC10115PS	OEM
MC10116F	OEM
MC10116L	OEM
MC10116LD	OEM
MC10116LDS	OEM
MC10116LS	OEM
MC10116P	OEM
MC10116PD	OEM
MC10116PDS	OEM
MC10116PS	OEM
MC10117F	OEM
MC10117L	OEM
MC10117LD	OEM
MC10117LDS	OEM
MC10117LS	OEM
MC10117P	OEM
MC10117PD	OEM
MC10117PDS	OEM
MC10117PS	OEM
MC10118F	OEM
MC10118L	OEM
MC10118LD	OEM
MC10118LDS	OEM
MC10118LS	OEM
MC10118P	OEM
MC10118PD	OEM
MC10118PDS	OEM
MC10118PS	OEM
MC10119F	OEM
MC10119L	OEM
MC10119LD	OEM
MC10119LDS	OEM
MC10119LS	OEM
MC10119P	OEM
MC10119PD	OEM
MC10119PDS	OEM
MC10119PS	OEM
MC10121F	OEM
MC10121L	OEM
MC10121LD	OEM
MC10121LDS	OEM
MC10121LS	OEM
MC10121P	OEM
MC10121PD	OEM
MC10121PDS	OEM
MC10121PS	OEM
MC10123L	OEM
MC10123LD	OEM
MC10123LDS	OEM
MC10123LS	OEM
MC10123P	OEM
MC10123PD	OEM
MC10123PDS	OEM
MC10123PS	OEM
MC10124F	OEM
MC10124L	OEM
MC10124LD	OEM
MC10124LDS	OEM
MC10124LS	OEM
MC10124P	OEM
MC10124PD	OEM
MC10124PDS	OEM
MC10124PS	OEM
MC10125F	OEM
MC10125L	OEM
MC10125LD	OEM
MC10125LDS	OEM
MC10125LS	OEM
MC10125P	OEM
MC10125PD	OEM
MC10125PDS	OEM
MC10125PS	OEM
MC10128L	OEM
MC10128LD	OEM
MC10128LDS	OEM
MC10128LS	OEM
MC10129L	OEM
MC10129LD	OEM
MC10129LDS	OEM
MC10129LS	OEM
MC10130F	OEM
MC10130L	OEM
MC10130LD	OEM
MC10130LDS	OEM
MC10130LS	OEM
MC10130P	OEM
MC10130PD	OEM
MC10130PDS	OEM
MC10130PS	OEM
MC10131F	OEM
MC10131L	OEM
MC10131LD	OEM
MC10131LDS	OEM
MC10131LS	OEM
MC10131P	OEM
MC10131PD	OEM
MC10131PDS	OEM
MC10131PS	OEM
MC10132L	OEM
MC10132LD	OEM
MC10132LDS	OEM
MC10132LS	OEM
MC10132P	OEM
MC10132PD	OEM
MC10132PDS	OEM
MC10132PS	OEM
MC10133F	OEM
MC10133L	OEM
MC10133LD	OEM
MC10133LDS	OEM
MC10133LS	OEM
MC10133P	OEM
MC10133PD	OEM
MC10133PDS	OEM
MC10133PS	OEM
MC10134L	OEM
MC10134LD	OEM
MC10134LDS	OEM
MC10134LS	OEM
MC10134P	OEM
MC10134PD	OEM
MC10134PDS	OEM
MC10134PS	OEM
MC10135F	OEM
MC10135L	OEM
MC10135LD	OEM
MC10135LDS	OEM
MC10135LS	OEM
MC10135P	OEM
MC10135PD	OEM
MC10135PDS	OEM
MC10135PS	OEM
MC10136L	OEM
MC10136LD	OEM
MC10136LDS	OEM
MC10136LS	OEM
MC10136P	OEM
MC10136PD	OEM
MC10136PDS	OEM
MC10136PS	OEM
MC10137L	OEM
MC10137LD	OEM
MC10137LDS	OEM
MC10137LS	OEM
MC10137P	OEM
MC10137PD	OEM
MC10137PDS	OEM
MC10137PS	OEM
MC10138F	OEM
MC10138L	OEM
MC10138LD	OEM
MC10138LDS	OEM
MC10138LS	OEM
MC10138P	OEM
MC10138PD	OEM
MC10138PDS	OEM
MC10138PS	OEM
MC10141F	OEM
MC10141L	OEM
MC10141LD	OEM
MC10141LDS	OEM
MC10141LS	OEM
MC10141P	OEM
MC10141PD	OEM
MC10141PDS	OEM
MC10141PS	OEM
MC10153F	OEM
MC10153L	OEM
MC10153LD	OEM
MC10153LDS	OEM
MC10153LS	OEM
MC10153P	OEM
MC10153PD	OEM
MC10153PDS	OEM
MC10153PS	OEM
MC10154L	OEM
MC10154LD	OEM
MC10154LDS	OEM
MC10154LS	OEM
MC10154P	OEM
MC10154PD	OEM
MC10154PDS	OEM
MC10154PS	OEM
MC10158F	OEM
MC10158L	OEM

If replacement code is OEM, contact original manufacturer for replacement.

DEVICE TYPE	REPL CODE
MC10158LD	OEM
MC10158LDS	OEM
MC10158LS	OEM
MC10158P	OEM
MC10158PD	OEM
MC10158PDS	OEM
MC10158PS	OEM
MC10159L	OEM
MC10159LD	OEM
MC10159LDS	OEM
MC10159LS	OEM
MC10159P	OEM
MC10159PD	OEM
MC10159PDS	OEM
MC10159PS	OEM
MC10160F	OEM
MC10160L	OEM
MC10160LD	OEM
MC10160LDS	OEM
MC10160LS	OEM
MC10160P	OEM
MC10160PD	OEM
MC10160PDS	OEM
MC10160PS	OEM
MC10161F	OEM
MC10161L	OEM
MC10161LD	OEM
MC10161LDS	OEM
MC10161LS	OEM
MC10161P	OEM
MC10161PD	OEM
MC10161PDS	OEM
MC10161PS	OEM
MC10162F	OEM
MC10162L	OEM
MC10162LD	OEM
MC10162LDS	OEM
MC10162LS	OEM
MC10162P	OEM
MC10162PD	OEM
MC10162PDS	OEM
MC10162PS	OEM
MC10163F	OEM
MC10163L	OEM
MC10163LD	OEM
MC10163LDS	OEM
MC10163LS	OEM
MC10163P	OEM
MC10163PD	OEM
MC10163PDS	OEM
MC10163PS	OEM
MC10164F	OEM
MC10164L	OEM
MC10164LD	OEM
MC10164LDS	OEM
MC10164LS	OEM
MC10164P	OEM
MC10164PD	OEM
MC10164PDS	OEM
MC10164PS	OEM
MC10165F	OEM
MC10165L	OEM
MC10165LD	OEM
MC10165LDS	OEM
MC10165LS	OEM
MC10165P	OEM
MC10165PD	OEM
MC10165PDS	OEM
MC10165PS	OEM
MC10166L	OEM
MC10166LD	OEM
MC10166LDS	OEM
MC10166LS	OEM
MC10166P	OEM
MC10166PD	OEM
MC10166PDS	OEM
MC10166PS	OEM
MC10168F	OEM
MC10168L	OEM
MC10168LD	OEM
MC10168LDS	OEM
MC10168LS	OEM
MC10168P	OEM
MC10168PD	OEM
MC10168PDS	OEM
MC10168PS	OEM
MC10169F	OEM
MC10170L	OEM
MC10170LD	OEM
MC10170LDS	OEM
MC10170LS	OEM
MC10170P	OEM
MC10170PD	OEM
MC10170PDS	OEM
MC10170PS	OEM
MC10171F	OEM
MC10171L	OEM
MC10171LD	OEM
MC10171LDS	OEM
MC10171LS	OEM
MC10171P	OEM
MC10171PD	OEM
MC10171PDS	OEM
MC10171PS	OEM
MC10172F	OEM
MC10172L	OEM
MC10172LD	OEM
MC10172LDS	OEM
MC10172LS	OEM
MC10172P	OEM
MC10172PD	OEM
MC10172PDS	OEM
MC10172PS	OEM
MC10173L	OEM
MC10173LD	OEM
MC10173LDS	OEM
MC10173LS	OEM
MC10173P	OEM
MC10173PD	OEM
MC10173PDS	OEM
MC10173PS	OEM
MC10174F	OEM
MC10174L	OEM
MC10174LD	OEM
MC10174LDS	OEM
MC10174LS	OEM
MC10174P	OEM
MC10174PD	OEM
MC10174PDS	OEM
MC10174PS	OEM
MC10175F	OEM
MC10175L	OEM
MC10175LD	OEM
MC10175LDS	OEM
MC10175LS	OEM
MC10175P	OEM
MC10175PD	OEM
MC10175PDS	OEM
MC10175PS	OEM
MC10176F	OEM
MC10176L	OEM
MC10176LD	OEM
MC10176LDS	OEM
MC10176LS	OEM
MC10176P	OEM
MC10176PD	OEM
MC10176PDS	OEM
MC10176PS	OEM
MC10177L	OEM
MC10177LD	OEM
MC10177LDS	OEM
MC10177LS	OEM
MC10178F	OEM
MC10178L	OEM
MC10178LD	OEM
MC10178LDS	OEM
MC10178LS	OEM
MC10178P	OEM
MC10178PD	OEM
MC10178PDS	OEM
MC10178PS	OEM
MC10179F	OEM
MC10179L	OEM
MC10179LD	OEM
MC10179LDS	OEM
MC10179LS	OEM
MC10179P	OEM
MC10179PD	OEM
MC10179PDS	OEM
MC10179PS	OEM
MC10180F	OEM
MC10180L	OEM
MC10180LD	OEM
MC10180LDS	OEM
MC10180LS	OEM
MC10180P	OEM
MC10180PD	OEM
MC10180PDS	OEM
MC10180PS	OEM
MC10181F	OEM
MC10181L	OEM
MC10181LD	OEM
MC10181LDS	OEM
MC10181LS	OEM
MC10181P	OEM
MC10181PD	OEM
MC10181PDS	OEM
MC10181PS	OEM
MC10182F	OEM
MC10182L	OEM
MC10182LD	OEM
MC10182LDS	OEM
MC10182LS	OEM
MC10182P	OEM
MC10182PD	OEM
MC10182PDS	OEM
MC10182PS	OEM
MC10183L	OEM
MC10183LD	OEM
MC10183LDS	OEM
MC10183LS	OEM
MC10186F	OEM
MC10186L	OEM
MC10186LD	OEM
MC10186LDS	OEM
MC10186LS	OEM
MC10186P	OEM
MC10186PD	OEM
MC10186PDS	OEM
MC10186PS	OEM
MC10188L	OEM
MC10188LD	OEM
MC10188LDS	OEM
MC10188LS	OEM
MC10188P	OEM
MC10188PD	OEM
MC10188PDS	OEM
MC10188PS	OEM
MC10189L	OEM
MC10189LD	OEM
MC10189LDS	OEM
MC10189LS	OEM
MC10189P	OEM
MC10189PD	OEM
MC10189PDS	OEM
MC10189PS	OEM
MC10190F	OEM
MC10190L	OEM
MC10190LD	OEM
MC10190LDS	OEM
MC10190LS	OEM
MC10190P	OEM
MC10190PD	OEM
MC10190PDS	OEM
MC10190PS	OEM
MC10191F	OEM
MC10191L	OEM
MC10191LD	OEM
MC10191LDS	OEM
MC10191LS	OEM
MC10191P	OEM
MC10191PD	OEM
MC10191PDS	OEM
MC10191PS	OEM
MC10192L	OEM
MC10192LD	OEM
MC10192LDS	OEM
MC10192LS	OEM
MC10192P	OEM
MC10192PD	OEM
MC10192PDS	OEM
MC10192PS	OEM
MC10193F	OEM
MC10193L	OEM
MC10193LD	OEM
MC10193LDS	OEM
MC10193LS	OEM
MC10193P	OEM
MC10193PD	OEM
MC10193PDS	OEM
MC10193PS	OEM
MC10194F	OEM
MC10194L	OEM
MC10194LD	OEM
MC10194LDS	OEM
MC10194LS	OEM
MC10194P	OEM
MC10194PD	OEM
MC10194PDS	OEM
MC10194PS	OEM
MC10195F	OEM
MC10195L	OEM
MC10195LD	OEM
MC10195LDS	OEM
MC10195LS	OEM
MC10195P	OEM
MC10195PD	OEM
MC10195PDS	OEM
MC10195PS	OEM
MC10197F	OEM
MC10197L	OEM
MC10197LD	OEM
MC10197LDS	OEM
MC10197LS	OEM
MC10197P	OEM
MC10197PD	OEM
MC10197PDS	OEM
MC10197PS	OEM
MC10198L	OEM
MC10198LD	OEM
MC10198LDS	OEM
MC10198LS	OEM
MC10198P	OEM
MC10198PD	OEM
MC10198PDS	OEM
MC10198PS	OEM
MC10210F	OEM
MC10210L	OEM
MC10210LD	OEM
MC10210LDS	OEM
MC10210LS	OEM
MC10210P	OEM
MC10210PD	OEM
MC10210PDS	OEM
MC10210PS	OEM
MC10211F	OEM
MC10211L	OEM
MC10211LD	OEM
MC10211LDS	OEM
MC10211LS	OEM
MC10211P	OEM
MC10211PD	OEM
MC10211PDS	OEM
MC10211PS	OEM
MC10212F	OEM
MC10212L	OEM
MC10212LD	OEM
MC10212LDS	OEM
MC10212LS	OEM
MC10212P	OEM
MC10212PD	OEM
MC10212PDS	OEM
MC10212PS	OEM
MC10216F	OEM
MC10216L	OEM
MC10216LD	OEM
MC10216LDS	OEM
MC10216LS	OEM
MC10216P	OEM
MC10216PD	OEM
MC10216PDS	OEM
MC10216PS	OEM
MC10231F	OEM
MC10231L	OEM
MC10231LD	OEM
MC10231LDS	OEM
MC10231LS	OEM
MC10231P	OEM
MC10231PD	OEM
MC10231PDS	OEM
MC10231PS	OEM
MC10287F	OEM
MC10287L	OEM
MC10287LD	OEM
MC10287LDS	OEM
MC10287LS	OEM
MC10287P	OEM
MC10287PD	OEM
MC10287PDS	OEM
MC10287PS	OEM
MC10315L	OEM
MC10315L(A)	OEM
MC10317L	OEM
MC10317L(A)	OEM
MC10318CL6	OEM
MC10318CL7	OEM
MC10318L	OEM
MC10318L9	OEM
MC10425UBALD	OEM
MC10434BAL	OEM
MC10434BCL	OEM
MC10438BCP	OEM
MC10442BAL	OEM
MC10493BALD	OEM
MC10500F	OEM
MC10500L	OEM
MC10501F	OEM
MC10501L	OEM
MC10502F	OEM
MC10502L	OEM
MC10503F	OEM
MC10503L	OEM
MC10504F	OEM
MC10504L	OEM
MC10505F	OEM
MC10505L	OEM
MC10506F	OEM
MC10506L	OEM
MC10507F	OEM
MC10507L	OEM
MC10509F	OEM
MC10509L	OEM
MC10513F	OEM
MC10513L	OEM
MC10514F	OEM
MC10514L	OEM
MC10515F	OEM
MC10515L	OEM
MC10516F	OEM
MC10516L	OEM
MC10517F	OEM
MC10517L	OEM
MC10518F	OEM
MC10518L	OEM
MC10519F	OEM
MC10519L	OEM
MC10521F	OEM
MC10521L	OEM
MC10524F	OEM
MC10524L	OEM
MC10525F	OEM
MC10525L	OEM
MC10530F	OEM
MC10530L	OEM
MC10531F	OEM
MC10531L	OEM
MC10533F	OEM
MC10533L	OEM
MC10535F	OEM
MC10535L	OEM
MC10538F	OEM
MC10538L	OEM
MC10541F	OEM
MC10541L	OEM
MC10550	OEM
MC10553F	OEM
MC10553L	OEM
MC10558F	OEM
MC10558L	OEM
MC10560F	OEM
MC10560L	OEM
MC10561F	OEM
MC10562F	OEM
MC10563F	OEM
MC10563L	OEM
MC10564F	OEM
MC10564L	OEM
MC10565F	OEM
MC10565L	OEM
MC10568F	OEM
MC10568L	OEM
MC10570F	OEM
MC10570L	OEM
MC10571F	OEM
MC10571L	OEM
MC10572F	OEM
MC10572L	OEM
MC10574F	OEM
MC10574L	OEM
MC10575F	OEM
MC10575L	OEM
MC10578L	OEM
MC10579F	OEM
MC10579L	OEM
MC10580F	OEM
MC10580L	OEM
MC10581F	OEM
MC10581L	OEM
MC10582F	OEM
MC10582L	OEM
MC10590F	OEM
MC10590L	OEM
MC10591F	OEM
MC10591L	OEM
MC10593F	OEM
MC10593L	OEM
MC10594F	OEM
MC10594L	OEM
MC10595F	OEM
MC10595L	OEM
MC10597L	OEM
MC10616F	OEM
MC10616L	OEM
MC10631F	OEM
MC10631L	OEM
MC10800	OEM
MC10803L	OEM
MC10804L	OEM
MC10805L	OEM
MC10806	OEM
MC10807L	OEM
MC10808L	OEM
MC10900Z	OEM
MC10901Z	OEM
MC10902	OEM
MC10904	OEM
MC10905	OEM
MC10905(A)	OEM
MC12000L	OEM
MC12002L	OEM
MC12002LD	OEM
MC12002LDS	OEM
MC12002LS	OEM
MC12002P	OEM
MC12002PD	OEM
MC12002PDS	OEM
MC12002PS	OEM
MC12009L	OEM
MC12009LD	OEM
MC12009LDS	OEM
MC12009LS	OEM
MC12009P	OEM
MC12009PD	OEM
MC12009PDS	OEM
MC12009PS	OEM
MC12011L	OEM
MC12011LD	OEM
MC12011LDS	OEM
MC12011LS	OEM
MC12011P	OEM
MC12011PD	OEM
MC12011PDS	OEM
MC12011PS	OEM
MC12012L	OEM
MC12013L	OEM
MC12013LD	OEM
MC12013LDS	OEM
MC12013LS	OEM
MC12013P	OEM
MC12013PD	OEM
MC12013PDS	OEM
MC12013PS	OEM
MC12014L	OEM
MC12014LD	OEM
MC12014LDS	OEM
MC12014LS	OEM
MC12014P	OEM
MC12014PD	OEM
MC12014PDS	OEM
MC12015P	OEM
MC12015P(A)	OEM
MC12016P	OEM
MC12016P(A)	OEM
MC12017P	OEM
MC12017P(A)	OEM
MC12018P	OEM
MC12019P	OEM
MC12020L	OEM
MC12020P	OEM
MC12021L	OEM
MC12021P	OEM
MC12022P	OEM
MC12023P	OEM
MC12040L	OEM
MC12040LD	OEM
MC12040LDS	OEM
MC12040LS	OEM
MC12040P	OEM
MC12040PDS	OEM
MC12040PS	OEM
MC12060L	OEM
MC12060LS	OEM
MC12060P	OEM
MC12061L	OEM
MC12061LD	OEM
MC12061LDS	OEM
MC12061LS	OEM
MC12061P	OEM
MC12061PDS	OEM
MC12061PS	OEM
MC12071P	OEM
MC12071PD	OEM
MC12071PDS	OEM
MC12071PS	OEM
MC12073P	OEM
MC12074P	OEM
MC12075P	OEM
MC12090L	OEM
MC12090LD	OEM
MC12090LDS	OEM
MC12090LS	OEM
MC12104PS	OEM
MC12509L	OEM
MC12509P	OEM
MC12511L	OEM
MC12513L	OEM
MC12513P	OEM
MC12520L	OEM
MC12521L	OEM
MC12560L	OEM
MC12561L	OEM
MC12663	OEM
MC13001P	OEM
MC13001XP	OEM
MC13002P	OEM
MC13002XP	OEM
MC13010P	OEM
MC13010P(A)	OEM
MC13020P	OEM
MC13030P	OEM
MC13074P	OEM
MC13301P	3726
MC13503T4	OEM
MC13513T4	OEM
MC13528P	OEM
MC13580SP	OEM
MC14000	2013
MC14000ABCBS	OEM
MC14000ADCBS	OEM
MC14000BCL	OEM
MC14000UBAL	4231
MC14000UBALD	OEM
MC14000UBALDS	OEM
MC14000UBALS	OEM
MC14000UBCL	2013
MC14000UBCLD	OEM
MC14000UBCLDS	OEM
MC14000UBCLS	OEM
MC14000UBCP	2013
MC14000UBCPD	OEM
MC14000UBCPDS	OEM
MC14000UBCPS	OEM
MC14001	0473
MC14001ABCBS	OEM
MC14001ADCBS	OEM
MC14001B	0473
MC14001BAL	3214
MC14001BALD	OEM
MC14001BALDS	OEM
MC14001BALS	OEM
MC14001BBCBS	OEM
MC14001BCL	0473
MC14001BCP	0473
MC14001BCPD	OEM
MC14001BCPDS	OEM
MC14001BCPS	OEM
MC14001BDCBS	OEM
MC14001BP	3214
MC14001CP	0473
MC14001UBAL	OEM
MC14001UBALD	OEM
MC14001UBALDS	OEM
MC14001UBALS	OEM
MC14001UBCL	OEM
MC14001UBCLD	OEM
MC14001UBCLDS	OEM
MC14001UBCLS	OEM
MC14001UBCP	0473
MC14001UBCPD	OEM
MC14001UBCPDS	OEM
MC14001UBCPS	OEM
MC14002	2044
MC14002ABCBS	OEM
MC14002ADCBS	OEM
MC14002BAL	2044
MC14002BALD	OEM
MC14002BALDS	OEM
MC14002BALS	OEM
MC14002BBCBS	OEM
MC14002BCL	2044
MC14002BCLD	OEM
MC14002BCLDS	OEM
MC14002BCLS	OEM
MC14002BCP	2044
MC14002BCPD	OEM
MC14002BCPDS	OEM
MC14002BCPS	OEM
MC14002BDCBS	OEM
MC14002CP	2044
MC14002P	2044
MC14002UBAL	OEM
MC14002UBALD	OEM
MC14002UBALDS	OEM
MC14002UBALS	OEM
MC14002UBCL	OEM
MC14002UBCLD	OEM
MC14002UBCLDS	OEM
MC14002UBCLS	OEM
MC14002UBCP	OEM
MC14002UBCPD	OEM
MC14002UBCPDS	OEM
MC14002UBCPS	OEM
MC14006BAL	0641
MC14006BALD	OEM
MC14006BALDS	OEM
MC14006BALS	OEM
MC14006BBCBS	OEM
MC14006BCL	0641
MC14006BCLD	OEM
MC14006BCLDS	OEM
MC14006BCLS	OEM
MC14006BCP	0641
MC14006BCPD	OEM
MC14006BCPDS	OEM
MC14006BCPS	OEM
MC14006BDCBS	OEM
MC14007	2819
MC14007ABCBS	OEM
MC14007ADCBS	OEM
MC14007UBAL	2819
MC14007UBALD	OEM
MC14007UBALDS	OEM
MC14007UBALS	OEM
MC14007UBCL	4897
MC14007UBCLD	OEM
MC14007UBCLDS	OEM
MC14007UBCLS	OEM
MC14007UBCP	2819
MC14007UBCPD	OEM
MC14007UBCPDS	OEM
MC14007UBCPS	OEM
MC14007UBL	OEM
MC14007UBP	OEM
MC14008BAL	0982
MC14008BALD	OEM
MC14008BALDS	OEM
MC14008BCL	0982
MC14008BCLD	OEM
MC14008BCLDS	OEM
MC14008BCLS	OEM
MC14008BCP	0982
MC14008BCPD	OEM
MC14008BCPDS	OEM
MC14008BCPS	OEM
MC14008BDEBS	OEM
MC14008BEBS	OEM
MC14008CL	OEM
MC14011	0215
MC14011ABCBS	OEM
MC14011ADCBS	OEM
MC14011B	0215
MC14011BAL	0215
MC14011BALD	OEM
MC14011BALDS	OEM
MC14011BALS	OEM
MC14011BCL	0215
MC14011BCP	0215
MC14011BCPD	OEM
MC14011BDCBS	OEM
MC14011BF	OEM
MC-14011CP	0215
MC14011CP	0215
MC14011UB	OEM
MC14011UBAL	OEM
MC14011UBALD	OEM
MC14011UBALDS	OEM
MC14011UBALS	OEM
MC14011UBCL	OEM
MC14011UBCLD	OEM
MC14011UBCLDS	OEM
MC14011UBCLS	OEM
MC14011UBCP	OEM
MC14011UBCPD	OEM
MC14011UBCPDS	OEM
MC14011UBCPS	OEM
MC14012	0493
MC14012ABCBS	OEM
MC14012ADCBS	OEM
MC14012BAL	0493
MC14012BALD	OEM
MC14012BALDS	OEM
MC14012BALS	OEM
MC14012BBCBS	OEM
MC14012BCL	0493
MC14012BCLD	OEM
MC14012BCLDS	OEM
MC14012BCLS	OEM
MC14012BCP	0493
MC14012BCPD	OEM
MC14012BCPDS	OEM
MC14012BCPS	OEM
MC14012BDCBS	OEM
MC14012CP	0493
MC14012UBAL	OEM
MC14012UBALD	OEM
MC14012UBALDS	OEM
MC14012UBALS	OEM
MC14012UBCL	OEM
MC14012UBCLD	OEM
MC14012UBCLDS	OEM
MC14012UBCLS	OEM

If replacement code is OEM, contact original manufacturer for replacement.

DEVICE TYPE	REPL CODE
MC14012UBCP	OEM
MC14012UBCPD	OEM
MC14012UBCPDS	OEM
MC14012UBCPS	OEM
MC14013	0409
MC14013A1	0409
MC14013B	0409
MC14013BAL	0409
MC14013BALD	OEM
MC14013BALDS	OEM
MC14013BALS	OEM
MC14013BBCBS	OEM
MC14013BCL	0409
MC14013BCLD	OEM
MC14013BCLDS	OEM
MC14013BCLS	OEM
MC14013BCP	0409
MC14013BCPD	OEM
MC14013BCPDS	OEM
MC14013BCPS	OEM
MC14013BDCBS	OEM
MC14013BL	OEM
MC14013BP	OEM
MC14013CP	0409
MC14014BAL	0854
MC14014BALD	OEM
MC14014BALDS	OEM
MC14014BALS	OEM
MC14014BBEBS	OEM
MC14014BCL	0854
MC14014BCLD	OEM
MC14014BCLDS	OEM
MC14014BCLS	OEM
MC14014BCP	0854
MC14014BCPD	OEM
MC14014BCPS	OEM
MC14014BDEBS	OEM
MC14014BL	OEM
MC14014BP	OEM
MC14014CP	0854
MC14015	1008
MC14015BAL	1008
MC14015BALD	OEM
MC14015BALDS	OEM
MC14015BALS	OEM
MC14015BBEBS	OEM
MC14015BCL	1008
MC14015BCLD	OEM
MC14015BCLDS	OEM
MC14015BCLS	OEM
MC14015BCP	1008
MC14015BCPD	OEM
MC14015BCPDS	OEM
MC14015BCPS	OEM
MC14015BDEBS	OEM
MC14015BL	OEM
MC14015BP	OEM
MC14015CP	1008
MC14016	0101
MC14016B	4087
MC14016BAL	1135
MC14016BALD	OEM
MC14016BALDS	OEM
MC14016BALS	OEM
MC14016BBCBS	OEM
MC14016BCL	1135
MC14016BCLD	OEM
MC14016BCLDS	OEM
MC14016BCLS	OEM
MC14016BCP	1135
MC14016BCPDS	OEM
MC14016BCPS	OEM
MC14016BDCBS	OEM
MC14016CP	1135
MC14017	0508
MC14017BAL	0508
MC14017BALD	OEM
MC14017BALDS	OEM
MC14017BALS	OEM
MC14017BBEBS	OEM
MC14017BCL	0508
MC14017BCLD	OEM
MC14017BCLDS	OEM
MC14017BCLS	OEM
MC14017BCP	0508
MC14017BCPD	OEM
MC14017BCPDS	OEM
MC14017BCPS	OEM
MC14017BDEBS	OEM
MC14017CP	0508
MC14018BAL	1381
MC14018BALD	OEM
MC14018BALDS	OEM
MC14018BALS	OEM
MC14018BBEBS	OEM
MC14018BCL	1381
MC14018BCLS	OEM
MC14018BCP	1381
MC14018BCPD	OEM
MC14018BCPDS	OEM
MC14018BCPS	OEM
MC14018BDEBS	OEM
MC14018BL	3867
MC14018BP	OEM
MC14018CL	OEM
MC14018CLD	OEM
MC14018CLDS	OEM
MC14020	1651
MC14020BAL	1651

DEVICE TYPE	REPL CODE
MC14020BALD	OEM
MC14020BALDS	OEM
MC14020BALS	OEM
MC14020BBEBS	OEM
MC14020BCL	1651
MC14020BCLD	OEM
MC14020BCLDS	OEM
MC14020BCLS	OEM
MC14020BCP	1651
MC14020BCPD	OEM
MC14020BCPDS	OEM
MC14020BCPS	OEM
MC14020BDEBS	OEM
MC14020CP	1651
MC14021	1738
MC14021BAL	1738
MC14021BALD	OEM
MC14021BALDS	OEM
MC14021BALS	OEM
MC14021BBEBS	OEM
MC14021BCL	1738
MC14021BCLD	OEM
MC14021BCLDS	OEM
MC14021BCLS	OEM
MC14021BCP	1738
MC14021BCPD	OEM
MC14021BCPDS	OEM
MC14021BCPS	OEM
MC14021BDEBS	OEM
MC14021BL	OEM
MC14021BP	OEM
MC14021CP	1738
MC14022BAL	1247
MC14022BALD	OEM
MC14022BALDS	OEM
MC14022BALS	OEM
MC14022BBEBS	OEM
MC14022BCL	1247
MC14022BCLD	OEM
MC14022BCLDS	OEM
MC14022BCLS	OEM
MC14022BCP	1247
MC14022BCPD	OEM
MC14022BCPDS	OEM
MC14022BCPS	OEM
MC14022BDEBS	OEM
MC14023	0515
MC14023ABCBS	OEM
MC14023ADCBS	OEM
MC14023B	0515
MC14023BAL	0515
MC14023BALD	OEM
MC14023BALDS	OEM
MC14023BALS	OEM
MC14023BBCBS	OEM
MC14023BCL	0515
MC14023BCLD	OEM
MC14023BCLDS	OEM
MC14023BCLS	OEM
MC14023BCP	0515
MC14023BCPD	OEM
MC14023BCPDS	OEM
MC14023BCPS	OEM
MC14023BDCBS	OEM
MC14023CP	0515
MC14023UBAL	OEM
MC14023UBALD	OEM
MC14023UBALDS	OEM
MC14023UBALS	OEM
MC14023UBCL	OEM
MC14023UBCLD	OEM
MC14023UBCLDS	OEM
MC14023UBCLS	OEM
MC14023UBCP	OEM
MC14023UBCPD	OEM
MC14023UBCPDS	OEM
MC14023UBCPS	OEM
MC14024	1946
MC14024B	1946
MC14024BAL	1946
MC14024BALD	OEM
MC14024BALDS	OEM
MC14024BALS	OEM
MC14024BBCBS	OEM
MC14024BCL	1946
MC14024BCLD	OEM
MC14024BCLDS	OEM
MC14024BCLS	OEM
MC14024BCP	1946
MC14024BCPD	OEM
MC14024BCPDS	OEM
MC14024BCPS	OEM
MC14024BDCBS	OEM
MC14024CP	1946
MC14025	2061
MC14025ABCBS	OEM
MC14025ADCBS	OEM
MC14025AL	2061
MC14025B	2061
MC14025BAL	2061
MC14025BALD	OEM
MC14025BALDS	OEM
MC14025BALS	OEM
MC14025BBCBS	OEM
MC14025BCL	2061
MC14025BCLD	OEM
MC14025BCLDS	OEM
MC14025BCLS	OEM
MC14025BCP	2061

DEVICE TYPE	REPL CODE
MC14025BCPD	OEM
MC14025BCPDS	OEM
MC14025BCPS	OEM
MC14025BDCBS	OEM
MC14025CP	2061
MC14025UBAL	OEM
MC14025UBALDS	OEM
MC14025UBALS	OEM
MC14025UBCL	OEM
MC14025UBCLD	OEM
MC14025UBCLDS	OEM
MC14025UBCLS	OEM
MC14025UBCP	OEM
MC14025UBCPD	OEM
MC14025UBCPDS	OEM
MC14025UBCPS	OEM
MC14027	1938
MC14027BAL	1938
MC14027BALD	OEM
MC14027BALDS	OEM
MC14027BALS	OEM
MC14027BBEBS	OEM
MC14027BCL	1938
MC14027BCLD	OEM
MC14027BCLDS	OEM
MC14027BCLS	OEM
MC14027BCP	1938
MC14027BCPD	OEM
MC14027BCPDS	OEM
MC14027BCPS	OEM
MC14027BDEBS	OEM
MC14027CP	1938
MC14028	2213
MC14028B	4123
MC14028BAL	2213
MC14028BALD	OEM
MC14028BALDS	OEM
MC14028BALS	OEM
MC14028BBEBS	OEM
MC14028BCL	2213
MC14028BCLD	OEM
MC14028BCLDS	OEM
MC14028BCLS	OEM
MC14028BCP	2213
MC14028BCPD	OEM
MC14028BCPDS	OEM
MC14028BCPS	OEM
MC14028BDEBS	OEM
MC14028CP	2213
MC14029BAL	2218
MC14029BALD	OEM
MC14029BALDS	OEM
MC14029BALS	OEM
MC14029BBEBS	OEM
MC14029BCL	2218
MC14029BCLD	OEM
MC14029BCLDS	OEM
MC14029BCLS	OEM
MC14029BCP	2218
MC14029BCPD	OEM
MC14029BCPDS	OEM
MC14029BCPS	OEM
MC14029BDEBS	OEM
MC14029BL	OEM
MC14029BP	OEM
MC14029CP	2218
MC14032BAL	2509
MC14032BALD	OEM
MC14032BALS	OEM
MC14032BAL.DS	OEM
MC14032BBEBS	OEM
MC14032BCL	2509
MC14032BCLD	OEM
MC14032BCLDS	OEM
MC14032BCLS	OEM
MC14032BCP	2509
MC14032BCPDS	OEM
MC14032BCPS	OEM
MC14032BDEBS	OEM
MC14034BAL	3570
MC14034BALD	OEM
MC14034BALDS	OEM
MC14034BALS	OEM
MC14034BBJBS	OEM
MC14034BCL	5481
MC14034BCLD	OEM
MC14034BCLDS	OEM
MC14034BCLS	OEM
MC14034BCP	3570
MC14034BCPD	OEM
MC14034BCPDS	OEM
MC14034BDJBS	OEM
MC14035BAL	2750
MC14035BALD	OEM
MC14035BALDS	OEM
MC14035BALS	OEM
MC14035BBEBS	OEM
MC14035BCL	2750
MC14035BCLD	OEM
MC14035BCLDS	OEM
MC14035BCLS	OEM
MC14035BCP	2750
MC14035BCPD	OEM
MC14035BCPDS	OEM
MC14035BCPS	OEM
MC14035BDEBS	OEM
MC14038BAL	2953
MC14038BALD	OEM
MC14038BALDS	OEM

DEVICE TYPE	REPL CODE
MC14038BALS	OEM
MC14038BBEBS	OEM
MC14038BCL	2953
MC14038BCLD	OEM
MC14038BCLDS	OEM
MC14038BCLS	OEM
MC14038BCP	2953
MC14038BCPD	OEM
MC14038BCPS	OEM
MC14038BDEBS	OEM
MC14040	0056
MC14040B	0056
MC14040BAL	0056
MC14040BALD	OEM
MC14040BALDS	OEM
MC14040BALS	OEM
MC14040BBEBS	OEM
MC14040BCL	0056
MC14040BCLD	OEM
MC14040BCLDS	OEM
MC14040BCLS	OEM
MC14040BCP	0056
MC14040BCPD	OEM
MC14040BCPDS	OEM
MC14040BCPS	OEM
MC14040BDEBS	OEM
MC14040BL	OEM
MC14040BP	OEM
MC14040CP	0056
MC14042	0121
MC14042BAL	0121
MC14042BALD	OEM
MC14042BALDS	OEM
MC14042BALS	OEM
MC14042BB3EBS	OEM
MC14042BCL	0121
MC14042BCLD	OEM
MC14042BCLDS	OEM
MC14042BCLS	OEM
MC14042BCP	0121
MC14042BCPD	OEM
MC14042BCPDS	OEM
MC14042BCPS	OEM
MC14042BDEBS	OEM
MC14042CP	0121
MC14043BAL	1544
MC14043BALD	OEM
MC14043BALDS	OEM
MC14043BALS	OEM
MC14043BBEBS	OEM
MC14043BCL	1544
MC14043BCLD	OEM
MC14043BCLDS	OEM
MC14043BCLS	OEM
MC14043BCP	1544
MC14043BCPD	OEM
MC14043BCPDS	OEM
MC14043BCPS	OEM
MC14043BDEBS	OEM
MC14043BL	OEM
MC14043BP	OEM
MC14044BAL	2292
MC14044BALD	OEM
MC14044BALDS	OEM
MC14044BALS	OEM
MC14044BBEBS	OEM
MC14044BCL	2292
MC14044BCLD	OEM
MC14044BCLDS	OEM
MC14044BCLS	OEM
MC14044BCP	2292
MC14044BCPD	OEM
MC14044BCPDS	OEM
MC14044BCPS	OEM
MC14044BDEBS	OEM
MC14044BL	OEM
MC14044BP	OEM
MC14046BAL	3779
MC14046BALD	OEM
MC14046BALDS	OEM
MC14046BALS	OEM
MC14046BBEBS	OEM
MC14046BCL	6635
MC14046BCLD	OEM
MC14046BCLDS	OEM
MC14046BCLS	OEM
MC14046BCP	3394
MC14046BCPD	OEM
MC14046BCPDS	OEM
MC14046BCPS	OEM
MC14046BDEBS	OEM
MC14046BL	OEM
MC14046BP	OEM
MC14046CP	0056
MC14049	0001
MC14049ABEBS	OEM
MC14049ADEBS	OEM
MC14049B	0001
MC14049CP	0001
MC14049UB	0001
MC14049UBAL	0001
MC14049UBALD	OEM
MC14049UBALDS	OEM
MC14049UBALS	OEM
MC14049UBCL	0001
MC14049UBCLD	OEM
MC14049UBCLDS	OEM
MC14049UBCLS	OEM
MC14049UBCP	0001

DEVICE TYPE	REPL CODE
MC14049UBCPD	OEM
MC14049UBCPDS	OEM
MC14049UBCPS	OEM
MC14049UBL	OEM
MC14049UBP	OEM
MC14050	0394
MC14050B	0394
MC14050BAL	0394
MC14050BALD	OEM
MC14050BALDS	OEM
MC14050BALS	OEM
MC14050BBEBS	OEM
MC14050BCL	0394
MC14050BCLD	OEM
MC14050BCLDS	OEM
MC14050BCLS	OEM
MC14050BCP	0394
MC14050BCPD	OEM
MC14050BCPDS	OEM
MC14050BCPS	OEM
MC14050BDEBS	OEM
MC14050BL	OEM
MC14050BP	OEM
MC14050CP	0394
MC14051	0362
MC14051BAL	0362
MC14051BALD	OEM
MC14051BALDS	OEM
MC14051BALS	OEM
MC14051BBEBS	OEM
MC14051BCL	0362
MC14051BCLD	OEM
MC14051BCLDS	OEM
MC14051BCLS	OEM
MC14051BCP	0362
MC14051BCPD	OEM
MC14051BCPDS	OEM
MC14051BCPS	OEM
MC14051BDEBS	OEM
MC14051BL	OEM
MC14051BP	OEM
MC14052	0024
MC14052B	0024
MC14052BAL	0024
MC14052BALD	OEM
MC14052BALDS	OEM
MC14052BALS	OEM
MC14052BBEBS	OEM
MC14052BCL	0024
MC14052BCLD	OEM
MC14052BCLDS	OEM
MC14052BCLS	OEM
MC14052BCP	0024
MC14052BCPD	OEM
MC14052BCPDS	OEM
MC14052BCPS	OEM
MC14052BDEBS	OEM
MC14052BL	OEM
MC14052BP	OEM
MC14053	0034
MC14053B	0034
MC14053BAL	0034
MC14053BALD	OEM
MC14053BALDS	OEM
MC14053BALS	OEM
MC14053BBEBS	OEM
MC14053BCL	0034
MC14053BCLD	OEM
MC14053BCLDS	OEM
MC14053BCLS	OEM
MC14053BCP	0034
MC14053BCPD	OEM
MC14053BCPDS	OEM
MC14053BCPS	OEM
MC14053BDEBS	OEM
MC14053BL	OEM
MC14053BP	OEM
MC14060B	0146
MC14060BAL	0146
MC14060BALD	OEM
MC14060BALDS	OEM
MC14060BALS	OEM
MC14060BCL	4824
MC14060BCLD	OEM
MC14060BCLDS	OEM
MC14060BCLS	OEM
MC14060BCP	0146
MC14060BCPD	OEM
MC14060BCPDS	OEM
MC14060BCPS	OEM
MC14066	0101
MC14066B	0101
MC14066BAL	0101
MC14066BALD	OEM
MC14066BALDS	OEM
MC14066BALS	OEM
MC14066BBCBS	OEM
MC14066BCL	0101
MC14066BCLD	OEM
MC14066BCLDS	OEM
MC14066BCLS	OEM
MC14066BCP	0101
MC14066BCPD	OEM
MC14066BCPDS	OEM
MC14066BCPS	OEM
MC14066BDCBS	OEM
MC14066BF-T1	OEM
MC14066BL	OEM
MC14066BP	OEM

DEVICE TYPE	REPL CODE
MC14067BAL	3696
MC14067BALD	OEM
MC14067BALDS	OEM
MC14067BALS	OEM
MC14067BCL	OEM
MC14067BCLD	OEM
MC14067BCLDS	OEM
MC14067BCLS	OEM
MC14067BCP	4215
MC14067BCPD	OEM
MC14067BCPDS	OEM
MC14067BCPS	OEM
MC14067BL	OEM
MC14067BP	OEM
MC14068B	2482
MC14068BAL	2482
MC14068BALD	OEM
MC14068BALDS	OEM
MC14068BALS	OEM
MC14068BBCBS	OEM
MC14068BCL	2482
MC14068BCLD	OEM
MC14068BCLDS	OEM
MC14068BCLS	OEM
MC14068BCP	2482
MC14068BCPD	OEM
MC14068BCPDS	OEM
MC14068BCPS	OEM
MC14068BDCBS	OEM
MC14069ABCBS	OEM
MC14069ADCBS	OEM
MC14069B	3279
MC14069U	0119
MC14069UB	3279
MC14069UBAL	0119
MC14069UBALD	OEM
MC14069UBALDS	OEM
MC14069UBALS	OEM
MC14069UBAP	OEM
MC14069UBCL	0119
MC14069UBCLD	OEM
MC14069UBCLDS	OEM
MC14069UBCLS	OEM
MC14069UBCP	0119
MC14069UBCPD	OEM
MC14069UBCPDS	OEM
MC14069UBCPS	OEM
MC14069UBF	OEM
MC14070BAL	2494
MC14070BALD	OEM
MC14070BALDS	OEM
MC14070BALS	OEM
MC14070BBCBS	OEM
MC14070BCL	2494
MC14070BCLD	OEM
MC14070BCLDS	OEM
MC14070BCLS	OEM
MC14070BCP	2494
MC14070BCPD	OEM
MC14070BCPDS	OEM
MC14070BCPS	OEM
MC14070BDCBS	OEM
MC14070BL	5152
MC14070BP	OEM
MC14071	0129
MC14071BAL	0129
MC14071BALD	OEM
MC14071BALDS	OEM
MC14071BALS	OEM
MC14071BBCBS	OEM
MC14071BCL	0129
MC14071BCLD	OEM
MC14071BCLDS	OEM
MC14071BCLS	OEM
MC14071BCP	0129
MC14071BCPD	OEM
MC14071BCPDS	OEM
MC14071BCPS	OEM
MC14071BDCBS	OEM
MC14071CP	0129
MC14072BAL	2502
MC14072BALD	OEM
MC14072BALDS	OEM
MC14072BALS	OEM
MC14072BBCBS	OEM
MC14072BCL	6256
MC14072BCLD	OEM
MC14072BCLDS	OEM
MC14072BCLS	OEM
MC14072BCP	6256
MC14072BCPD	OEM
MC14072BCPDS	OEM
MC14072BCPS	OEM
MC14072BDCBS	OEM
MC14073B	1528
MC14073BAL	1528
MC14073BALD	OEM
MC14073BALDS	OEM
MC14073BALS	OEM
MC14073BBCBS	OEM
MC14073BCL	1528
MC14073BCLD	OEM
MC14073BCLDS	OEM
MC14073BCLS	OEM
MC14073BCP	1528
MC14073BCPD	OEM
MC14073BCPDS	OEM
MC14073BCPS	OEM
MC14073BDCBS	OEM

DEVICE TYPE	REPL CODE
MC14073BF	OEM
MC14075BAL	2518
MC14075BALD	OEM
MC14075BALDS	OEM
MC14075BALS	OEM
MC14075BBCBS	OEM
MC14075BCL	2518
MC14075BCLD	OEM
MC14075BCLDS	OEM
MC14075BCLS	OEM
MC14075BCP	2518
MC14075BCPD	OEM
MC14075BCPDS	OEM
MC14075BCPS	OEM
MC14075BDCBS	OEM
MC14076BAL	3455
MC14076BALD	OEM
MC14076BALDS	OEM
MC14076BALS	OEM
MC14076BBEBS	OEM
MC14076BCL	3455
MC14076BCLD	OEM
MC14076BCLDS	OEM
MC14076BCLS	OEM
MC14076BCP	3455
MC14076BCPD	OEM
MC14076BCPDS	OEM
MC14076BCPS	OEM
MC14076BDEBS	OEM
MC14077	OEM
MC14077BAL	2536
MC14077BALD	OEM
MC14077BALDS	OEM
MC14077BALS	OEM
MC14077BBCBS	OEM
MC14077BCL	2536
MC14077BCLD	OEM
MC14077BCLDS	OEM
MC14077BCLS	OEM
MC14077BCP	2536
MC14077BCPD	OEM
MC14077BCPDS	OEM
MC14077BCPS	OEM
MC14077BDCBS	OEM
MC14077BL	OEM
MC14077BP	OEM
MC14078B	4217
MC14078BAL	0915
MC14078BALD	OEM
MC14078BALDS	OEM
MC14078BALS	OEM
MC14078BBCBS	OEM
MC14078BCL	0915
MC14078BCLD	OEM
MC14078BCLDS	OEM
MC14078BCLS	OEM
MC14078BCP	0915
MC14078BCPD	OEM
MC14078BCPDS	OEM
MC14078BCPS	OEM
MC14078BDCBS	OEM
MC14081	0621
MC14081ABCBS	OEM
MC14081ADCBS	OEM
MC14081B	0621
MC14081BAL	0621
MC14081BALD	OEM
MC14081BALDS	OEM
MC14081BALS	OEM
MC14081BBCBS	OEM
MC14081BCL	0621
MC14081BCLD	OEM
MC14081BCLDS	OEM
MC14081BCLS	OEM
MC14081BCP	0328
MC14081BCPD	OEM
MC14081BCPDS	OEM
MC14081BCPS	OEM
MC14081BDCBS	OEM
MC14081CP	0621
MC14082B	0297
MC14082BAL	0297
MC14082BALD	OEM
MC14082BALDS	OEM
MC14082BALS	OEM
MC14082BBCBS	OEM
MC14082BCL	0297
MC14082BCLD	OEM
MC14082BCLDS	OEM
MC14082BCLS	OEM
MC14082BCP	0297
MC14082BCPD	OEM
MC14082BCPDS	OEM
MC14082BCPS	OEM
MC14082BDCBS	OEM
MC14088B	OEM
MC14093	2368
MC14093B	2368
MC14093BAL	2368
MC14093BALDS	OEM
MC14093BALS	OEM
MC14093BBCBS	OEM
MC14093BCL	2368
MC14093BCLDS	OEM
MC14093BCLS	OEM
MC14093BCP	2368
MC14093BCPD	OEM
MC14093BCPDS	OEM
MC14093BCPS	OEM

If replacement code is OEM, contact original manufacturer for replacement. 477

DEVICE TYPE	REPL CODE
MC14093BDCBS	OEM
MC14093BL	OEM
MC14093BP	OEM
MC14094BAL	1672
MC14094BALD	OEM
MC14094BALDS	OEM
MC14094BALS	OEM
MC14094BBEBS	OEM
MC14094BCL	1672
MC14094BCLD	OEM
MC14094BCLDS	OEM
MC14094BCLS	OEM
MC14094BCP	1672
MC14094BCPD	OEM
MC14094BCPDS	OEM
MC14094BCPS	OEM
MC14094BDEBS	OEM
MC14097BAL	3802
MC14097BALD	OEM
MC14097BALDS	OEM
MC14097BALS	OEM
MC14097BCL	OEM
MC14097BCLD	OEM
MC14097BCLDS	OEM
MC14097BCLS	OEM
MC14097BCP	5863
MC14097BCPD	OEM
MC14097BCPDS	OEM
MC14097BCPS	OEM
MC14097BL	OEM
MC14097BP	OEM
MC14099B	4248
MC14099BAL	3297
MC14099BALD	OEM
MC14099BALDS	OEM
MC14099BALS	OEM
MC14099BBEBS	OEM
MC14099BCL	3297
MC14099BCLD	OEM
MC14099BCLDS	OEM
MC14099BCLS	OEM
MC14099BCP	3297
MC14099BCPD	OEM
MC14099BCPDS	OEM
MC14099BCPS	OEM
MC14099BDEBS	OEM
MC14160BAL	1349
MC14160BALD	OEM
MC14160BALDS	OEM
MC14160BALS	OEM
MC14160BBEBS	OEM
MC14160BCL	1349
MC14160BCLD	OEM
MC14160BCLDS	OEM
MC14160BCLS	OEM
MC14160BCP	1349
MC14160BCPD	OEM
MC14160BCPDS	OEM
MC14160BCPS	OEM
MC14160BDEBS	OEM
MC14160BL	OEM
MC14160BP	OEM
MC14161BAL	1363
MC14161BALD	OEM
MC14161BALDS	OEM
MC14161BALS	OEM
MC14161BBEBS	OEM
MC14161BCL	1363
MC14161BCLD	OEM
MC14161BCLDS	OEM
MC14161BCLS	OEM
MC14161BCP	1363
MC14161BCPD	OEM
MC14161BCPDS	OEM
MC14161BCPS	OEM
MC14161BDEBS	OEM
MC14161BL	OEM
MC14161BP	OEM
MC14162BAL	1378
MC14162BALD	OEM
MC14162BALDS	OEM
MC14162BALS	OEM
MC14162BBEBS	OEM
MC14162BCL	1378
MC14162BCLD	OEM
MC14162BCLDS	OEM
MC14162BCLS	OEM
MC14162BCP	1378
MC14162BCPD	OEM
MC14162BCPDS	OEM
MC14162BCPS	OEM
MC14162BDEBS	OEM
MC14162BL	OEM
MC14162BP	OEM
MC14163BAL	1397
MC14163BALD	OEM
MC14163BALDS	OEM
MC14163BALS	OEM
MC14163BBEBS	OEM
MC14163BCL	1397
MC14163BCLD	OEM
MC14163BCLDS	OEM
MC14163BCLS	OEM
MC14163BCP	1397
MC14163BCPD	OEM
MC14163BCPDS	OEM
MC14163BCPS	OEM
MC14163BDEBS	OEM
MC14163BL	OEM

DEVICE TYPE	REPL CODE
MC14163BP	OEM
MC14174B	1542
MC14174BAL	1542
MC14174BALD	OEM
MC14174BALDS	OEM
MC14174BALS	OEM
MC14174BBEBS	OEM
MC14174BCL	1542
MC14174BCLD	OEM
MC14174BCLDS	OEM
MC14174BCLS	OEM
MC14174BCP	1542
MC14174BCPD	OEM
MC14174BCPDS	OEM
MC14174BCPS	OEM
MC14174BDEBS	OEM
MC14174BL	OEM
MC14174BP	OEM
MC14175BAL	OEM
MC14175BALD	OEM
MC14175BALDS	OEM
MC14175BALS	OEM
MC14175BBEBS	OEM
MC14175BCL	1520
MC14175BCLD	OEM
MC14175BCLDS	OEM
MC14175BCLS	OEM
MC14175BCP	1520
MC14175BCPD	OEM
MC14175BCPDS	OEM
MC14175BCPS	OEM
MC14175BDEBS	OEM
MC14175BL	OEM
MC14175BP	OEM
MC14194BAL	1758
MC14194BALD	OEM
MC14194BALDS	OEM
MC14194BALS	OEM
MC14194BBEBS	OEM
MC14194BCL	1758
MC14194BCLD	OEM
MC14194BCLDS	OEM
MC14194BCLS	OEM
MC14194BCP	1758
MC14194BCPD	OEM
MC14194BCPDS	OEM
MC14194BCPS	OEM
MC14194BDEBS	OEM
MC14194BL	OEM
MC14194BP	OEM
MC14400L	OEM
MC14401L	OEM
MC14402L	OEM
MC14402Z	OEM
MC14403L	OEM
MC14403L1(A)	OEM
MC14403L2(A)	OEM
MC14404L	OEM
MC14404P	OEM
MC14404Z	OEM
MC14405L	OEM
MC14406L	OEM
MC14406P	OEM
MC14407L	OEM
MC14407P	OEM
MC14407Z	OEM
MC14408L	OEM
MC14408LD	OEM
MC14408P	OEM
MC14408PD	OEM
MC14409L	OEM
MC14409LD	OEM
MC14409P	OEM
MC14409PD	OEM
MC14410ABEBS	OEM
MC14410ADEBS	OEM
MC14410L	OEM
MC14410LD	OEM
MC14410P	OEM
MC14410PD	OEM
MC14411BBJBS	OEM
MC14411BDJBS	OEM
MC14411L	OEM
MC14411LD	OEM
MC14411P	OEM
MC14411PD	OEM
MC14412FL	5216
MC14412FLD	OEM
MC14412FP	5216
MC14412FPD	OEM
MC14412L	5006
MC14412P	5006
MC14412VL	5216
MC14412VLD	OEM
MC14412VP	5216
MC14412VPD	OEM
MC14413-1L	OEM
MC14413-1P	OEM
MC14413-1S	OEM
MC14413-2L	OEM
MC14413-2P	OEM
MC14413-2S	OEM
MC14413L1	OEM
MC14413L2	OEM
MC14413P1	OEM
MC14413P2	OEM
MC14413Z1	OEM
MC14413Z2	OEM
MC14414-1L	OEM

DEVICE TYPE	REPL CODE
MC14414-1P	OEM
MC14414-1S	OEM
MC14414-2L	OEM
MC14414-2P	OEM
MC14414-2S	OEM
MC14414L1	OEM
MC14414L2	OEM
MC14414P1	OEM
MC14414P2	OEM
MC14414Z1	OEM
MC14414Z2	OEM
MC14415EFL	OEM
MC14415EFLD	OEM
MC14415EVL	OEM
MC14415EVLD	OEM
MC14415FL	OEM
MC14415FLD	OEM
MC14415FP	OEM
MC14415MC14415FPD	OEM
MC14415VL	OEM
MC14415VLD	OEM
MC14415VP	OEM
MC14415VPD	OEM
MC14416L	OEM
MC14416P	OEM
MC14417L	OEM
MC14417P	OEM
MC14418L	OEM
MC14418P	OEM
MC14419L	OEM
MC14419LD	OEM
MC14419P	OEM
MC14419PD	OEM
MC14424L	OEM
MC14424P	OEM
MC14433L	0482
MC14433LD	OEM
MC14433P	0482
MC14433PD	OEM
MC14435EFL	OEM
MC14435EVL	OEM
MC14435FL	OEM
MC14435FP	OEM
MC14435VL	OEM
MC14435VP	OEM
MC14440L	OEM
MC14442L	OEM
MC14442P	OEM
MC14443L	OEM
MC14443LD	OEM
MC14443P	OEM
MC14443PD	OEM
MC14444L	OEM
MC14444L(A)	OEM
MC14444P	OEM
MC14444P(A)	OEM
MC14447CP	OEM
MC14447L	OEM
MC14447LD	OEM
MC14447P	OEM
MC14447PD	OEM
MC14457L	OEM
MC14457LD	OEM
MC14457LDS	OEM
MC14457LS	OEM
MC14457P	OEM
MC14457PD	OEM
MC14457PDS	OEM
MC14457PS	OEM
MC14458L	OEM
MC14458P	OEM
MC14460L	OEM
MC14460LD	OEM
MC14460LDS	OEM
MC14460LS	OEM
MC14460P	OEM
MC14460PD	OEM
MC14460PDS	OEM
MC14460PS	OEM
MC14465-1P	OEM
MC14466P	OEM
MC14467L	OEM
MC14467P	OEM
MC14469L	OEM
MC14469LD	OEM
MC14469P	OEM
MC14469PD	OEM
MC14490ABEBS	OEM
MC14490ADEBS	OEM
MC14490EFL	OEM
MC14490EFLD	OEM
MC14490EFLDS	OEM
MC14490EFLS	OEM
MC14490EVL	OEM
MC14490EVLD	OEM
MC14490EVLDS	OEM
MC14490EVLS	OEM
MC14490FL	OEM
MC14490FLD	OEM
MC14490FLDS	OEM
MC14490FLS	OEM
MC14490FP	OEM
MC14490FPD	OEM
MC14490FPDS	OEM
MC14490FPS	OEM
MC14490L	OEM
MC14490LD	OEM
MC14490LDS	OEM
MC14490LS	OEM

DEVICE TYPE	REPL CODE
MC14490P	OEM
MC14490PD	OEM
MC14490PDS	OEM
MC14490PS	OEM
MC14490VL	OEM
MC14490VLD	OEM
MC14490VLDS	OEM
MC14490VLS	OEM
MC14490VP	OEM
MC14490VPD	OEM
MC14490VPDS	OEM
MC14490VPS	OEM
MC14495-1L	OEM
MC14495L1	OEM
MC14495P1	OEM
MC14500BAL	OEM
MC14500BALD	OEM
MC14500BCL	OEM
MC14500BCLD	OEM
MC14500BCP	OEM
MC14500BCPD	OEM
MC14500BL	OEM
MC14500BP	OEM
MC14501ABEBS	OEM
MC14501ADEBS	OEM
MC14501UBAL	OEM
MC14501UBALD	OEM
MC14501UBALDS	OEM
MC14501UBALS	OEM
MC14501UBCL	3758
MC14501UBCLD	OEM
MC14501UBCLDS	OEM
MC14501UBCLS	OEM
MC14501UBCP	3758
MC14501UBCPD	OEM
MC14501UBCPDS	OEM
MC14501UBCPS	OEM
MC14501UBD	OEM
MC14502BAL	1031
MC14502BALD	OEM
MC14502BALDS	OEM
MC14502BALS	OEM
MC14502BBEBS	OEM
MC14502BCL	1031
MC14502BCLD	OEM
MC14502BCLDS	OEM
MC14502BCLS	OEM
MC14502BCP	1031
MC14502BCPD	OEM
MC14502BCPDS	OEM
MC14502BCPS	OEM
MC14502BDEBS	OEM
MC14503BAL	2042
MC14503BALD	OEM
MC14503BALDS	OEM
MC14503BALS	OEM
MC14503BBEBS	OEM
MC14503BCL	2087
MC14503BCLD	OEM
MC14503BCLDS	OEM
MC14503BCLS	OEM
MC14503BCP	2042
MC14503BCPD	OEM
MC14503BCPDS	OEM
MC14503BCPS	OEM
MC14503BDEBS	OEM
MC14503BL	OEM
MC14503BP	6521
MC14504BAL	OEM
MC14504BALD	OEM
MC14504BALDS	OEM
MC14504BALS	OEM
MC14504BBEBS	OEM
MC14504BCL	OEM
MC14504BCLD	OEM
MC14504BCLDS	OEM
MC14504BCLS	OEM
MC14504BCP	OEM
MC14504BCPD	OEM
MC14504BCPDS	OEM
MC14504BCPS	OEM
MC14504BDEBS	OEM
MC14504BL	OEM
MC14504BP	OEM
MC14506	OEM
MC14506BAL	OEM
MC14506BALD	OEM
MC14506BALDS	OEM
MC14506BALS	OEM
MC14506BBEBS	OEM
MC14506BCL	3721
MC14506BCLD	OEM
MC14506BCLDS	OEM
MC14506BCLS	OEM
MC14506BCP	3721
MC14506BCPD	OEM
MC14506BCPDS	OEM
MC14506BCPS	OEM
MC14506BDEBS	OEM
MC14506UBCL	OEM
MC14506UBCP	3721
MC14506UBD	OEM
MC14508BAL	1800
MC14508BALD	OEM
MC14508BALDS	OEM
MC14508BALS	OEM
MC14508BBJBS	OEM
MC14508BCL	1800
MC14508BCP	1800

DEVICE TYPE	REPL CODE
MC14508BCPD	OEM
MC14508BCPDS	OEM
MC14508BCPS	OEM
MC14508BDJBS	OEM
MC14508CL	OEM
MC14508CLD	OEM
MC14508CLDS	OEM
MC14508CLS	OEM
MC14510BAL	1952
MC14510BALD	OEM
MC14510BALDS	OEM
MC14510BALS	OEM
MC14510BBEBS	OEM
MC14510BCL	4792
MC14510BCLD	OEM
MC14510BCLDS	OEM
MC14510BCLS	OEM
MC14510BCP	1952
MC14510BCPD	OEM
MC14510BCPDS	OEM
MC14510BCPS	OEM
MC14510BDEBS	OEM
MC14510CL	OEM
MC14511	1535
MC14511B	1535
MC14511B1	1535
MC14511BAL	1535
MC14511BALD	OEM
MC14511BALDS	OEM
MC14511BALS	OEM
MC14511BBEBS	OEM
MC14511BCL	1535
MC14511BCLD	OEM
MC14511BCLS	OEM
MC14511BCP	1535
MC14511BCPD	OEM
MC14511BCPDS	OEM
MC14511BCPS	OEM
MC14511BDEBS	OEM
MC14511BP	1535
MC14511L	1535
MC14512B	4153
MC14512BAL	2108
MC14512BALD	OEM
MC14512BALDS	OEM
MC14512BALS	OEM
MC14512BBEBS	OEM
MC14512BCL	2108
MC14512BCLD	OEM
MC14512BCLDS	OEM
MC14512BCLS	OEM
MC14512BCP	2108
MC14512BCPD	OEM
MC14512BCPDS	OEM
MC14512BCPS	OEM
MC14512BDEBS	OEM
MC14512BL	OEM
MC14512BP	OEM
MC14512CP	2108
MC14513BAL	OEM
MC14513BALD	OEM
MC14513BALDS	OEM
MC14513BALS	OEM
MC14513BCL	4889
MC14513BCLD	OEM
MC14513BCLDS	OEM
MC14513BCLS	OEM
MC14513BCP	4889
MC14513BCPD	OEM
MC14513BCPDS	OEM
MC14513BCPS	OEM
MC14514	1819
MC14514B	1819
MC14514BAL	1819
MC14514BALD	OEM
MC14514BALDS	OEM
MC14514BALS	OEM
MC14514BBJBS	OEM
MC14514BCL	1819
MC14514BCLD	OEM
MC14514BCLDS	OEM
MC14514BCLS	OEM
MC14514BCP	1819
MC14514BCPD	OEM
MC14514BCPDS	OEM
MC14514BCPS	OEM
MC14514BDJBS	OEM
MC14515	3555
MC14515BAL	3555
MC14515BALD	OEM
MC14515BALDS	OEM
MC14515BALS	OEM
MC14515BBJBS	OEM
MC14515BCL	3555
MC14515BCLD	OEM
MC14515BCLDS	OEM
MC14515BCLS	OEM
MC14515BCP	3555
MC14515BCPD	OEM
MC14515BCPDS	OEM
MC14515BCPS	OEM
MC14515BDJBS	OEM
MC14516BAL	2331
MC14516BALD	OEM
MC14516BALDS	OEM
MC14516BALS	OEM
MC14516BBEBS	OEM
MC14516BCL	2331
MC14516BCLD	OEM

DEVICE TYPE	REPL CODE
MC14516BCLDS	OEM
MC14516BCLS	OEM
MC14516BCP	2331
MC14516BCPD	OEM
MC14516BCPDS	OEM
MC14516BCPS	OEM
MC14516BDEBS	OEM
MC14516CP	2331
MC14517BAL	4220
MC14517BALD	OEM
MC14517BALDS	OEM
MC14517BALS	OEM
MC14517BBEBS	OEM
MC14517BCL	4220
MC14517BCLD	OEM
MC14517BCLDS	OEM
MC14517BCLS	OEM
MC14517BCP	4220
MC14517BCPD	OEM
MC14517BCPDS	OEM
MC14517BCPS	OEM
MC14517BDEBS	OEM
MC14518	1037
MC14518B	1037
MC14518BAL	1037
MC14518BALD	OEM
MC14518BALDS	OEM
MC14518BALS	OEM
MC14518BBEBS	OEM
MC14518BCL	1037
MC14518BCLD	OEM
MC14518BCLDS	OEM
MC14518BCLS	OEM
MC14518BCP	1037
MC14518BCPD	OEM
MC14518BCPDS	OEM
MC14518BCPS	OEM
MC14518BDEBS	OEM
MC14518BL	OEM
MC14518BP	OEM
MC14518CP	1037
MC14519BAL	1517
MC14519BALD	OEM
MC14519BALDS	OEM
MC14519BALS	OEM
MC14519BBEBS	OEM
MC14519BCL	OEM
MC14519BCLD	OEM
MC14519BCLDS	OEM
MC14519BCLS	OEM
MC14519BCP	1517
MC14519BCPD	OEM
MC14519BCPDS	OEM
MC14519BCPS	OEM
MC14519BDEBS	OEM
MC14520BAL	2650
MC14520BALD	OEM
MC14520BALDS	OEM
MC14520BALS	OEM
MC14520BBEBS	OEM
MC14520BCL	2650
MC14520BCLD	OEM
MC14520BCLDS	OEM
MC14520BCLS	OEM
MC14520BCP	2650
MC14520BCPD	OEM
MC14520BCPDS	OEM
MC14520BCPS	OEM
MC14520BDEBS	OEM
MC14520BL	OEM
MC14520BP	OEM
MC14520CP	5768
MC14521BAL	OEM
MC14521BALD	OEM
MC14521BALDS	OEM
MC14521BALS	OEM
MC14521BBEBS	OEM
MC14521BCL	4903
MC14521BCLD	OEM
MC14521BCLDS	OEM
MC14521BCLS	OEM
MC14521BCP	4903
MC14521BCPD	OEM
MC14521BCPDS	OEM
MC14521BCPS	OEM
MC14521BDEBS	OEM
MC14522BAL	OEM
MC14522BALD	OEM
MC14522BALDS	OEM
MC14522BALS	OEM
MC14522BBEBS	OEM
MC14522BCL	2810
MC14522BCLD	OEM
MC14522BCLDS	OEM
MC14522BCLS	OEM
MC14522BCP	2810
MC14522BCPD	OEM
MC14522BCPDS	OEM
MC14522BCPS	OEM
MC14522BDEBS	OEM
MC14522BL	OEM
MC14522BP	OEM
MC14526	3565
MC14526BAL	OEM
MC14526BALD	OEM
MC14526BALDS	OEM
MC14526BALS	OEM
MC14526BBEBS	OEM
MC14526BCL	3565
MC14526BCLD	OEM

DEVICE TYPE	REPL CODE
MC14526BCLDS	OEM
MC14526BCLS	OEM
MC14526BCP	3565
MC14526BCPD	OEM
MC14526BCPDS	OEM
MC14526BCPS	OEM
MC14526BDEBS	OEM
MC14526BL	OEM
MC14526BP	OEM
MC14527BAL	3116
MC14527BALD	OEM
MC14527BALDS	OEM
MC14527BALS	OEM
MC14527BBEBS	OEM
MC14527BCL	3116
MC14527BCLD	OEM
MC14527BCLDS	OEM
MC14527BCLS	OEM
MC14527BCP	3116
MC14527BCPD	OEM
MC14527BCPS	OEM
MC14527BDEBS	OEM
MC14527BL	OEM
MC14527BP	OEM
MC14527CP	3116
MC14528	3566
MC14528BAL	3168
MC14528BALD	OEM
MC14528BALDS	OEM
MC14528BALS	OEM
MC14528BCL	3168
MC14528BCLD	OEM
MC14528BCLDS	OEM
MC14528BCLS	OEM
MC14528BCP	3168
MC14528BCPD	OEM
MC14528BCPDS	OEM
MC14528BCPS	OEM
MC14528BL	OEM
MC14528BP	OEM
MC14529B	4451
MC14529BAL	OEM
MC14529BALD	OEM
MC14529BALDS	OEM
MC14529BALS	OEM
MC14529BBEBS	OEM
MC14529BCL	4451
MC14529BCLD	OEM
MC14529BCLDS	OEM
MC14529BCLS	OEM
MC14529BCP	4451
MC14529BCPD	OEM
MC14529BCPDS	OEM
MC14529BDEBS	OEM
MC14529PCPS	OEM
MC14530BAL	OEM
MC14530BALD	OEM
MC14530BALDS	OEM
MC14530BALS	OEM
MC14530BBEBS	OEM
MC14530BCL	OEM
MC14530BCLD	OEM
MC14530BCLDS	OEM
MC14530BCLS	OEM
MC14530BCP	OEM
MC14530BCPD	OEM
MC14530BCPDS	OEM
MC14530BCPS	OEM
MC14530BDEBS	OEM
MC14531BAL	OEM
MC14531BALD	OEM
MC14531BALDS	OEM
MC14531BALS	OEM
MC14531BBEBS	OEM
MC14531BCL	3292
MC14531BCLD	OEM
MC14531BCLDS	OEM
MC14531BCP	3292
MC14531BCPD	OEM
MC14531BCPDS	OEM
MC14531BCPS	OEM
MC14531BD	OEM
MC14531BDEBS	OEM
MC14532BAL	1010
MC14532BALD	OEM
MC14532BALDS	OEM
MC14532BALS	OEM
MC14532BBEBS	OEM
MC14532BCL	1010
MC14532BCLD	OEM
MC14532BCLDS	OEM
MC14532BCLS	OEM
MC14532BCP	1010
MC14532BCPD	OEM
MC14532BCPDS	OEM
MC14532BCPS	OEM
MC14532BDEBS	OEM
MC14534BAL	OEM
MC14534BALD	OEM
MC14534BALDS	OEM
MC14534BALS	OEM
MC14534BBJBS	OEM
MC14534BCL	OEM
MC14534BCLD	OEM
MC14534BCLDS	OEM
MC14534BCLS	OEM
MC14534BCP	OEM
MC14534BCPD	OEM
MC14534BCPDS	OEM

If replacement code is OEM, contact original manufacturer for replacement.

DEVICE TYPE	REPL CODE
MC14534BCPS	OEM
MC14534BDJBS	OEM
MC14536BAL	3659
MC14536BALD	OEM
MC14536BALDS	OEM
MC14536BALS	OEM
MC14536BBEBS	OEM
MC14536BCL	3714
MC14536BCLD	OEM
MC14536BCLDS	OEM
MC14536BCLS	OEM
MC14536BCP	3659
MC14536BCPD	OEM
MC14536BCPS	OEM
MC14536BDEBS	OEM
MC14536BL	OEM
MC14536BP	OEM
MC14538	3566
MC14538B	1057
MC14538BAL	1057
MC14538BALD	OEM
MC14538BALDS	OEM
MC14538BALS	OEM
MC14538BBEBS	OEM
MC14538BCL	4238
MC14538BCLD	OEM
MC14538BCLDS	OEM
MC14538BCLS	OEM
MC14538BCP	1057
MC14538BCPD	OEM
MC14538BCPDS	OEM
MC14538BCPS	OEM
MC14538BDEBS	OEM
MC14538BF	OEM
MC14538BL	OEM
MC14538BP	1057
MC14539BAL	OEM
MC14539BALD	OEM
MC14539BALDS	OEM
MC14539BALS	OEM
MC14539BBEBS	OEM
MC14539BCL	3611
MC14539BCLD	OEM
MC14539BCLDS	OEM
MC14539BCLS	OEM
MC14539BCP	3611
MC14539BCPD	OEM
MC14539BCPDS	OEM
MC14539BCPS	OEM
MC14539BD	OEM
MC14539BDEBS	OEM
MC14539CP	3611
MC14541BAL	4929
MC14541BALD	OEM
MC14541BALDS	OEM
MC14541BALS	OEM
MC14541BBCBS	OEM
MC14541BCL	4929
MC14541BCLD	OEM
MC14541BCLDS	OEM
MC14541BCLS	OEM
MC14541BCP	4929
MC14541BCPD	OEM
MC14541BCPDS	OEM
MC14541BCPS	OEM
MC14541BDCBS	OEM
MC14543BAL	4932
MC14543BALD	OEM
MC14543BALDS	OEM
MC14543BALS	OEM
MC14543BBEBS	OEM
MC14543BCL	4932
MC14543BCLD	OEM
MC14543BCLDS	OEM
MC14543BCLS	OEM
MC14543BCP	4932
MC14543BCPD	OEM
MC14543BCPDS	OEM
MC14543BCPS	OEM
MC14543BDEBS	OEM
MC14544BAL	OEM
MC14544BALD	OEM
MC14544BALDS	OEM
MC14544BALS	OEM
MC14544BCL	OEM
MC14544BCLD	OEM
MC14544BCLDS	OEM
MC14544BCLS	OEM
MC14544BCP	OEM
MC14544BCPD	OEM
MC14544BCPDS	OEM
MC14544BCPS	OEM
MC14547BAL	OEM
MC14547BALD	OEM
MC14547BALDS	OEM
MC14547BCL	4943
MC14547BCLD	OEM
MC14547BCP	4943
MC14547BCPD	OEM
MC14547BDW	OEM
MC14549BAL	OEM
MC14549BALD	OEM
MC14549BALDS	OEM
MC14549BALS	OEM
MC14549BBEBS	OEM
MC14549BCL	OEM
MC14549BCLD	OEM
MC14549BCLDS	OEM
MC14549BCLS	OEM

DEVICE TYPE	REPL CODE
MC14549BCP	OEM
MC14549BCPD	OEM
MC14549BCPDS	OEM
MC14549BCPS	OEM
MC14549BDEBS	OEM
MC14551BAL	OEM
MC14551BALD	OEM
MC14551BALDS	OEM
MC14551BALS	OEM
MC14551BBEBS	OEM
MC14551BCL	4950
MC14551BCLD	OEM
MC14551BCLDS	OEM
MC14551BCLS	OEM
MC14551BCP	4950
MC14551BCPD	OEM
MC14551BCPDS	OEM
MC14551BCPS	OEM
MC14551BD	OEM
MC14551BDEBS	OEM
MC14553BAL	OEM
MC14553BALD	OEM
MC14553BALDS	OEM
MC14553BALS	OEM
MC14553BBEBS	OEM
MC14553BCL	4951
MC14553BCLD	OEM
MC14553BCLDS	OEM
MC14553BCLS	OEM
MC14553BCP	4951
MC14553BCPD	OEM
MC14553BCPDS	OEM
MC14553BCPS	OEM
MC14553BDEBS	OEM
MC14553BDW	OEM
MC14554BAL	OEM
MC14554BALD	OEM
MC14554BALDS	OEM
MC14554BALS	OEM
MC14554BBEBS	OEM
MC14554BCL	OEM
MC14554BCLD	OEM
MC14554BCLDS	OEM
MC14554BCLS	OEM
MC14554BCP	OEM
MC14554BCPD	OEM
MC14554BCPDS	OEM
MC14554BCPS	OEM
MC14554BDEBS	OEM
MC14555BAL	2910
MC14555BALD	OEM
MC14555BALDS	OEM
MC14555BALS	OEM
MC14555BBEBS	OEM
MC14555BCL	2910
MC14555BCLD	OEM
MC14555BCLDS	OEM
MC14555BCLS	OEM
MC14555BCP	2910
MC14555BCPD	OEM
MC14555BCPDS	OEM
MC14555BCPS	OEM
MC14555BDEBS	OEM
MC14555CP	2910
MC14556	3397
MC14556BAL	3397
MC14556BALD	OEM
MC14556BALDS	OEM
MC14556BALS	OEM
MC14556BBEBS	OEM
MC14556BCL	3397
MC14556BCLD	OEM
MC14556BCLDS	OEM
MC14556BCLS	OEM
MC14556BCP	3397
MC14556BCPD	OEM
MC14556BCPDS	OEM
MC14556BCPS	OEM
MC14556BDEBS	OEM
MC14556CP	3397
MC14557BAL	OEM
MC14557BALD	OEM
MC14557BALDS	OEM
MC14557BALS	OEM
MC14557BBEBS	OEM
MC14557BCL	OEM
MC14557BCLD	OEM
MC14557BCLDS	OEM
MC14557BCP	OEM
MC14557BCPD	OEM
MC14557BCPDS	OEM
MC14557BCPS	OEM
MC14557BDEBS	OEM
MC14557BDLS	OEM
MC14558BAL	OEM
MC14558BALD	OEM
MC14558BALDS	OEM
MC14558BALS	OEM
MC14558BBEBS	OEM
MC14558BCL	4960
MC14558BCLD	OEM
MC14558BCLDS	OEM
MC14558BCLS	OEM
MC14558BCP	4960
MC14558BCPD	OEM
MC14558BCPDS	OEM
MC14558BCPS	OEM
MC14558BD	OEM
MC14558BDEBS	OEM

DEVICE TYPE	REPL CODE
MC14559BAL	OEM
MC14559BALD	OEM
MC14559BALDS	OEM
MC14559BALS	OEM
MC14559BBEBS	OEM
MC14559BCL	OEM
MC14559BCLD	OEM
MC14559BCLDS	OEM
MC14559BCLS	OEM
MC14559BCP	OEM
MC14559BCPD	OEM
MC14559BCPDS	OEM
MC14559BCPS	OEM
MC14559BDEBS	OEM
MC14560BAL	OEM
MC14560BALD	OEM
MC14560BALDS	OEM
MC14560BALS	OEM
MC14560BBEBS	OEM
MC14560BCL	6101
MC14560BCLDS	OEM
MC14560BCP	6101
MC14560BCPD	OEM
MC14560BCPDS	OEM
MC14560BCPS	OEM
MC14560BDEBS	OEM
MC14561BAL	OEM
MC14561BALD	OEM
MC14561BALDS	OEM
MC14561BALS	OEM
MC14561BBCBS	OEM
MC14561BCL	OEM
MC14561BCLD	OEM
MC14561BCLDS	OEM
MC14561BCLS	OEM
MC14561BCP	OEM
MC14561BCPD	OEM
MC14561BCPDS	OEM
MC14561BCPS	OEM
MC14561BDCBS	OEM
MC14562BAL	OEM
MC14562BALD	OEM
MC14562BALDS	OEM
MC14562BALS	OEM
MC14562BBCBS	OEM
MC14562BCL	1029
MC14562BCLD	OEM
MC14562BCLDS	OEM
MC14562BCLS	OEM
MC14562BCP	1029
MC14562BCPD	OEM
MC14562BCPDS	OEM
MC14562BCPS	OEM
MC14562BD	OEM
MC14562BDCBS	OEM
MC14566BAL	OEM
MC14566BALD	OEM
MC14566BALDS	OEM
MC14566BALS	OEM
MC14566BBEBS	OEM
MC14566BCL	3463
MC14566BCLD	OEM
MC14566BCLDS	OEM
MC14566BCLS	OEM
MC14566BCP	3463
MC14566BCPD	OEM
MC14566BCPDS	OEM
MC14566BCPS	OEM
MC14566BDEBS	OEM
MC14568	3573
MC14568B	3573
MC14568BALD	OEM
MC14568BALDS	OEM
MC14568BALS	OEM
MC14568BBEBS	OEM
MC14568BCL	3573
MC14568BCLD	OEM
MC14568BCLDS	OEM
MC14568BCLS	OEM
MC14568BCP	3573
MC14568BCPD	OEM
MC14568BCPDS	OEM
MC14568BCPS	OEM
MC14568BD	OEM
MC14568BDEBS	OEM
MC14568BL	OEM
MC14568BP	OEM
MC14568CP	3573
MC14569BAL	OEM
MC14569BALD	OEM
MC14569BALDS	OEM
MC14569BALS	OEM
MC14569BBEBS	OEM
MC14569BCL	4408
MC14569BCLD	OEM
MC14569BCLDS	OEM
MC14569BCLS	OEM
MC14569BCP	4408
MC14569BCPD	OEM
MC14569BCPDS	OEM
MC14569BCPS	OEM
MC14569BDEBS	OEM
MC14569BL	OEM
MC14569BP	OEM
MC14572ABEBS	OEM
MC14572ADEBS	OEM
MC14572UBAL	OEM
MC14572UBALD	OEM
MC14572UBALDS	OEM

DEVICE TYPE	REPL CODE
MC14572UBALS	OEM
MC14572UBCL	3440
MC14572UBCLD	OEM
MC14572UBCLDS	OEM
MC14572UBCLS	OEM
MC14572UBCP	3440
MC14572UBCPD	OEM
MC14572UBCPDS	OEM
MC14572UBCPS	OEM
MC14573CL	OEM
MC14573CLD	OEM
MC14573CP	OEM
MC14573CPD	OEM
MC14574CL	OEM
MC14574CLD	OEM
MC14574CP	OEM
MC14574CPD	OEM
MC14575CL	OEM
MC14575CLD	OEM
MC14575CP	OEM
MC14575CPD	OEM
MC14580BAL	OEM
MC14580BALD	OEM
MC14580BALDS	OEM
MC14580BALS	OEM
MC14580BBJBS	OEM
MC14580BCL	OEM
MC14580BCLD	OEM
MC14580BCLDS	OEM
MC14580BCLS	OEM
MC14580BCP	OEM
MC14580BCPD	OEM
MC14580BCPDS	OEM
MC14580BDJBS	OEM
MC14581BAL	3432
MC14581BALD	OEM
MC14581BALDS	OEM
MC14581BALS	OEM
MC14581BBJBS	OEM
MC14581BCL	5533
MC14581BCLD	OEM
MC14581BCLDS	OEM
MC14581BCLS	OEM
MC14581BCP	5533
MC14581BCPD	OEM
MC14581BCPDS	OEM
MC14581BCPSW	OEM
MC14581BDJBS	OEM
MC14582BAL	4579
MC14582BALD	OEM
MC14582BALDS	OEM
MC14582BALS	OEM
MC14582BBEBS	OEM
MC14582BCL	4579
MC14582BCLD	OEM
MC14582BCLDS	OEM
MC14582BCLS	OEM
MC14582BCP	4579
MC14582BCPD	OEM
MC14582BCPDS	OEM
MC14582BCPS	OEM
MC14582BDEBS	OEM
MC14583BAL	OEM
MC14583BALD	OEM
MC14583BALDS	OEM
MC14583BALS	OEM
MC14583BBEBS	OEM
MC14583BCL	1286
MC14583BCLD	OEM
MC14583BCLDS	OEM
MC14583BCLS	OEM
MC14583BCP	1286
MC14583BCPD	OEM
MC14583BCPDS	OEM
MC14583BCPS	OEM
MC14583BD	OEM
MC14583BDEBS	OEM
MC14584	3581
MC14584B	3581
MC14584BAL	3581
MC14584BALD	OEM
MC14584BALDS	OEM
MC14584BALS	OEM
MC14584BBCBS	OEM
MC14584BCL	3581
MC14584BCLD	OEM
MC14584BCLDS	OEM
MC14584BCLS	OEM
MC14584BCP	6438
MC14584BCPD	OEM
MC14584BCPDS	OEM
MC14584BCPS	OEM
MC14584BD	OEM
MC14584BDCBS	OEM
MC14584BL	OEM
MC14584BP	OEM
MC14585BAL	1365
MC14585BALD	OEM
MC14585BALDS	OEM
MC14585BALS	OEM
MC14585BBEBS	OEM
MC14585BCL	1365
MC14585BCLD	OEM
MC14585BCLDS	OEM
MC14585BCLS	OEM
MC14585BCP	3682
MC14585BCPD	OEM
MC14585BCPDS	OEM
MC14585BCPS	OEM

DEVICE TYPE	REPL CODE
MC14585BDEBS	OEM
MC14597BAL	OEM
MC14597BALD	OEM
MC14597BALDS	OEM
MC14597BALS	OEM
MC14597BCL	4048
MC14597BCLD	OEM
MC14597BCLDS	OEM
MC14597BCLS	OEM
MC14597BCP	4048
MC14597BCPD	OEM
MC14597BCPDS	OEM
MC14597BCPS	OEM
MC14597BDW	OEM
MC14597BL	OEM
MC14597BP	OEM
MC14598BAL	OEM
MC14598BALD	OEM
MC14598BALDS	OEM
MC14598BALS	OEM
MC14598BCL	4237
MC14598BCLD	OEM
MC14598BCLDS	OEM
MC14598BCLS	OEM
MC14598BCP	4237
MC14598BCPD	OEM
MC14598BCPDS	OEM
MC14598BCPS	OEM
MC14598BDW	OEM
MC14598BL	OEM
MC14598BP	OEM
MC14599BAL	OEM
MC14599BALD	OEM
MC14599BALDS	OEM
MC14599BALS	OEM
MC14599BCL	OEM
MC14599BCLD	OEM
MC14599BCLDS	OEM
MC14599BCLS	OEM
MC14599BCP	OEM
MC14599BCPD	OEM
MC14599BCPDS	OEM
MC14599BCPS	OEM
MC14669BCL	OEM
MC14669BCP	OEM
MC14669BDW	OEM
MC14681BP	OEM
MC27128-2	1628
MC33063P1	OEM
MC33063U	OEM
MC33423UD	OEM
MC34001AG	OEM
MC34001AP	OEM
MC34001AU	OEM
MC34001BG	OEM
MC34001BP	OEM
MC34001BU	OEM
MC34001D	OEM
MC34001G	OEM
MC34001P	5881
MC34001U	OEM
MC34002AG	OEM
MC34002AP	OEM
MC34002AU	OEM
MC34002BG	OEM
MC34002BP	OEM
MC34002BU	OEM
MC34002D	OEM
MC34002G	OEM
MC34002P	6170
MC34002U	OEM
MC34004BL	OEM
MC34004BP	OEM
MC34004D	OEM
MC34004L	OEM
MC34004P	6678
MC34012-1	OEM
MC34012-2	OEM
MC34012-3	OEM
MC34014P	OEM
MC34017	OEM
MC34018	OEM
MC34018P	OEM
MC34060L	5150
MC34060P	5150
MC34061AP	OEM
MC34061AP1	OEM
MC34061AU	OEM
MC34061P	OEM
MC34061P1	OEM
MC34061U	OEM
MC34062P1	OEM
MC34062U	OEM
MC34063P1	OEM
MC34063U	OEM
MC34065P	5693
MC34072P	OEM
MC34084	OEM
MC34084P	OEM
MC35001AG	OEM
MC35001AU	OEM
MC35001BG	OEM
MC35001BU	OEM
MC35002AG	OEM
MC35002AU	OEM
MC35002BG	OEM
MC35002BU	OEM
MC35004BL	OEM
MC35060L	OEM

DEVICE TYPE	REPL CODE
MC35061AU	OEM
MC35061U	OEM
MC35062U	OEM
MC35063U	OEM
MC38050N-25	OEM
MC41014BCPDS	OEM
MC41016BCPD	OEM
MC53200	0232
MC54802P	OEM
MC55107L	OEM
MC55108L	OEM
MC55325L	OEM
MC68000G6	OEM
MC68000G8	OEM
MC68000G10	OEM
MC68000L	OEM
MC68000L4	OEM
MC68000L6	OEM
MC68000L8	OEM
MC68000L10	OEM
MC68000L12	OEM
MC68000P8	OEM
MC68000Z	OEM
MC68020	OEM
MC68120-1L	OEM
MC68120L	OEM
MC68121-1	OEM
MC68121-1L	OEM
MC68121L	OEM
MC68153L	OEM
MC68153P	OEM
MC68230L8L	OEM
MC68230L8P	OEM
MC68230L10L	OEM
MC68230L10P	OEM
MC68451L4	OEM
MC68451L6	OEM
MC68451L8	OEM
MC68452L	OEM
MC68452P	OEM
MC68486	OEM
MC68488L	OEM
MC68488P	OEM
MC68652L(A)	OEM
MC68652L2(A)	OEM
MC68652P(A)	OEM
MC68652P2(A)	OEM
MC68652S(A)	OEM
MC68661A	OEM
MC68661B	OEM
MC68661C	OEM
MC68681	OEM
MC68701-1L	OEM
MC68701CL	OEM
MC68701CL-1	OEM
MC68701L	OEM
MC68701L-1	OEM
MC68701L1	OEM
MC68701U4L	OEM
MC68701U4L-1	OEM
MC68705P3L	OEM
MC68705P3S	OEM
MC68705PP	OEM
MC68705R3L	OEM
MC68705U3L	OEM
MC74107P	0936
MC74121P	0175
MC74145P	0614
MC74150P	1484
MC74152P	1509
MC74153P	1531
MC74155P	1566
MC74156P	1582
MC74164AP	0729
MC74165P	1675
MC74176P	1784
MC74177P	1792
MC74180P	1818
MC74181P	1831
MC74182P	1845
MC74192P	1910
MC74193P	1915
MC74195P	1932
MC74415P	1487
MC75107	OEM
MC75107L	OEM
MC75107P	OEM
MC75108L	OEM
MC75108P	OEM
MC75110L	OEM
MC75110P	OEM
MC75125L	OEM
MC75125P	OEM
MC75127L	OEM
MC75127P	OEM
MC75128L	OEM
MC75128P	OEM
MC75129L	OEM
MC75129P	OEM
MC75325L	OEM
MC75452P	1253
MC75452P1	1253
MC75462P	OEM
MC75463P	OEM
MC75491P	6222
MC75492P	6225
MC140007BCL	OEM
MC140008BALS	OEM
MC141000L	OEM

DEVICE TYPE	REPL CODE
MC141000P	OEM
MC141000S	OEM
MC141099L	OEM
MC141200L	OEM
MC141200P	OEM
MC141200S	OEM
MC142100AL	OEM
MC142100ALD	OEM
MC142100CL	OEM
MC142100CLD	OEM
MC142100CP	OEM
MC142100CPD	OEM
MC142100L	OEM
MC142100P	OEM
MC143403L	OEM
MC143403P	OEM
MC143404L	OEM
MC143404P	OEM
MC144111P	OEM
MC144115P	OEM
MC144143P1	OEM
MC145000	OEM
MC145000BCL	OEM
MC145000BCP	OEM
MC145000L	OEM
MC145000P	OEM
MC145001	OEM
MC145001BCL	OEM
MC145001BCP	OEM
MC145001L	OEM
MC145001P	OEM
MC145026L	OEM
MC145026P	OEM
MC145026PP	OEM
MC145027L	OEM
MC145027P	OEM
MC145028	OEM
MC145028L	OEM
MC145028P	OEM
MC145035CL	OEM
MC145100AL	OEM
MC145100ALD	OEM
MC145100CL	OEM
MC145100CLD	OEM
MC145100CP	OEM
MC145100CPD	OEM
MC145100L	OEM
MC145100P	OEM
MC145104	2592
MC145104L	OEM
MC145104P	2592
MC145104PD	OEM
MC145106	OEM
MC145106L	OEM
MC145106P	OEM
MC145106PD	OEM
MC145107L	OEM
MC145107P	OEM
MC145107PD	OEM
MC145109	1704
MC145109L	OEM
MC145109P	1704
MC145109PD	OEM
MC145112L	OEM
MC145112P	OEM
MC145112PD	OEM
MC145143L	OEM
MC145143P	OEM
MC145144L	OEM
MC145144P	OEM
MC145145L	OEM
MC145145P	OEM
MC145146L	OEM
MC145146P	OEM
MC145151L	OEM
MC145151P	OEM
MC145152L	OEM
MC145152P	OEM
MC145155L	OEM
MC145155P	OEM
MC145156L	OEM
MC145156P	OEM
MC145157L	OEM
MC145157P	OEM
MC145158L	OEM
MC145158P	OEM
MC145411P	OEM
MC145414L	OEM
MC145414P	OEM
MC145415L	OEM
MC145415P	OEM
MC145422L	OEM
MC145423L	OEM
MC145426L	OEM
MC145428L	OEM
MC145428P	OEM
MC145429L	OEM
MC145429P	OEM
MC145431L	OEM
MC145431P	OEM
MC145432L	OEM
MC145432P	OEM
MC145433L	OEM
MC145433P	OEM
MC145434L	OEM
MC145434P	OEM
MC145436BCPDS	OEM
MC145440L	OEM
MC145440P	OEM

DEVICE TYPE	REPL CODE
MC145441L	OEM
MC145441P	OEM
MC145445L	OEM
MC145445P	OEM
MC145450L	OEM
MC145450P	OEM
MC145668BCP	OEM
MC146805E2CL	OEM
MC146805E2CP	OEM
MC146805E2CS	OEM
MC146805E2CZ	OEM
MC146805E2L	OEM
MC146805E2P	OEM
MC146805E2S	OEM
MC146805E2Z	OEM
MC146805F2L	OEM
MC146805F2P	OEM
MC146805F2S	OEM
MC146805F2Z	OEM
MC146805G2L	OEM
MC146805G2P	OEM
MC146805G2S	OEM
MC146805G2Z	OEM
MC146805H2L	OEM
MC146805H2P	OEM
MC146805H2S	OEM
MC146805H2Z	OEM
MC146818AL	OEM
MC146818AP	OEM
MC146818APN	OEM
MC146818AS	OEM
MC146818L	OEM
MC146818P	OEM
MC146818S	OEM
MC146818Z	OEM
MC146823L	OEM
MC146823P	OEM
MC146823S	OEM
MC146823Z	OEM
MC147805	OEM
MC6800048	OEM
MCA	OEM
MCA7	OEM
MCA8	2612
MCA22CL	OEM
MCA22CP	OEM
MCA22CS	OEM
MCA22L	OEM
MCA22P	OEM
MCA22S	OEM
MCA81	2612
MCA230	1047
MCA231	0311
MCA255	1101
MCA2500ECL	OEM
MCB	OEM
MCB22CL	OEM
MCB22CP	OEM
MCB22CS	OEM
MCB22L	OEM
MCB22P	OEM
MCB22S	OEM
MCB-302	OEM
MCB-304	OEM
MCB-308	OEM
MCB-316	OEM
MCB-332	OEM
MCB-512-01	OEM
MCB-512-03	OEM
MCB-512-04	OEM
MCC	OEM
MCC-06I01	0647
MCC12	OEM
MCC15	OEM
MCC16	OEM
MCC17	OEM
MCC19	OEM
MCC20	OEM
MCC21	OEM
MCC555A	0967
MCC555B	0967
MCC670	OEM
MCC671	OEM
MCCZA6.8D	0062
MCCZA6.8D5	0062
MCCZA6.8D10	0062
MCCZA7.5D	0077
MCCZA7.5D5	0077
MCCZA7.5D10	0077
MCCZA8.2D	0165
MCCZA8.2D5	0165
MCCZA8.2D10	0165
MCCZA9.1D	0057
MCCZA9.1D5	0057
MCCZA9.1D10	0057
MCCZA10D	0064
MCCZA10D5	0064
MCCZA10D10	0064
MCCZA11D	0181
MCCZA11D5	0181
MCCZA11D10	0181
MCCZA12D	0052
MCCZA12D5	0052
MCCZA12D10	0052
MCCZA13D	0053
MCCZA13D5	0053
MCCZA13D10	0053
MCCZA14D	0873
MCCZA14D5	0873
MCCZA14D10	0873
MCCZA15D	0681
MCCZA15D5	0681
MCCZA15D10	0681
MCCZA16D	0440
MCCZA16D5	0440
MCCZA16D10	0440
MCCZA17D	0210
MCCZA17D5	0210
MCCZA17D10	0210
MCCZA18D	0371
MCCZA18D5	0371
MCCZA18D10	0371
MCCZA19D	0666
MCCZA19D10	0666
MCCZA20D	0695
MCCZA20D5	0695
MCCZA20D10	0695
MCCZA22D	0700
MCCZA22D5	0700
MCCZA22D10	0700
MCCZA24D	0489
MCCZA24D5	0489
MCCZA24D10	0489
MCCZA25D	0709
MCCZA25D5	0709
MCCZA25D10	0709
MCCZA27D	0450
MCCZA27D5	0450
MCCZA27D10	0450
MCCZA28D	0257
MCCZA28D5	0257
MCCZA28D10	0257
MCCZA30D	0195
MCCZA30D5	0195
MCCZA30D10	0195
MCCZA33D	0166
MCCZA33D5	0166
MCCZA33D10	0166
MCCZA36D	0010
MCCZA36D5	0010
MCCZA36D10	0010
MCCZA39D	0032
MCCZA39D5	0032
MCCZA39D10	0032
MCCZA43D	0054
MCCZA43D5	0054
MCCZA43D10	0054
MCCZA47D	0068
MCCZA47D5	0068
MCCZA47D10	0068
MCCZA51D	0092
MCCZA51D5	0092
MCCZA51D10	0092
MCCZA56D	0125
MCCZA56D5	0125
MCCZA56D10	0125
MCCZA60D	2301
MCCZA60D5	2301
MCCZA60D10	2301
MCCZA62D	0152
MCCZA62D5	0152
MCCZA62D10	0152
MCCZA68D	0173
MCCZA68D5	0173
MCCZA68D10	0173
MCCZA75D	0094
MCCZA75D5	0094
MCCZA75D10	0094
MCCZA82D	0049
MCCZA82D5	0049
MCCZA82D10	0049
MCCZA87D	0104
MCCZA87D5	0104
MCCZA87D10	0104
MCCZA91D	0156
MCCZA91D5	0156
MCCZA91D10	0156
MCCZA100D	0189
MCCZA100D5	0189
MCCZA100D10	0189
MCCZA105D	0099
MCCZA105D5	0099
MCCZA105D10	0099
MCCZA110D	0099
MCCZA110D5	0099
MCCZA110D10	0099
MCCZA120D	0089
MCCZA120D5	0089
MCCZA120D10	0089
MCCZA130D	0285
MCCZA130D5	0285
MCCZA130D10	0285
MCCZA140D	0252
MCCZA140D5	0252
MCCZA140D10	0252
MCCZA150D	0336
MCCZA150D5	0336
MCCZA150D10	0336
MCCZA160D	0366
MCCZA160D5	0366
MCCZA160D10	0366
MCCZA175D	0420
MCCZA175D5	0420
MCCZA175D10	0420
MCCZA180D	0420
MCCZA180D5	0420
MCCZA180D10	0420
MCCZA200D	1464
MCCZA200D5	1464
MCCZA200D10	1464
MCCZB6.8D	0062
MCCZB6.8D5	0062
MCCZB6.8D10	0062
MCCZB7.5D	0077
MCCZB7.5D5	0077
MCCZB7.5D10	0077
MCCZB8.2D	0165
MCCZB8.2D5	0165
MCCZB8.2D10	0165
MCCZB9.1D	0057
MCCZB9.1D5	0057
MCCZB9.1D10	0057
MCCZB10D	0064
MCCZB10D5	0064
MCCZB10D10	0064
MCCZB11D	0181
MCCZB11D5	0181
MCCZB11D10	0181
MCCZB12D	0052
MCCZB12D5	0052
MCCZB12D10	0052
MCCZB13D	0053
MCCZB13D5	0053
MCCZB13D10	0053
MCCZB14D	0873
MCCZB14D5	0873
MCCZB14D10	0873
MCCZB15D	0681
MCCZB15D5	0681
MCCZB15D10	0681
MCCZB16D	0440
MCCZB16D5	0440
MCCZB16D10	0440
MCCZB17D	0210
MCCZB17D5	0210
MCCZB17D10	0210
MCCZB18D	0371
MCCZB18D5	0371
MCCZB18D10	0371
MCCZB19D	0666
MCCZB19D5	0666
MCCZB19D10	0666
MCCZB20D	0695
MCCZB20D5	0695
MCCZB20D10	0695
MCCZB22D5	0700
MCCZB22D10	0700
MCCZB24D	0489
MCCZB24D5	0489
MCCZB24D10	0489
MCCZB25D	0709
MCCZB25D5	0709
MCCZB25D10	0709
MCCZB27D	0450
MCCZB27D5	0450
MCCZB27D10	0450
MCCZB30D	0195
MCCZB30D5	0195
MCCZB30D10	0195
MCCZB33D	0166
MCCZB33D5	0166
MCCZB33D10	0166
MCCZB36D	0010
MCCZB36D5	0010
MCCZB36D10	0010
MCCZB39D	0032
MCCZB39D5	0032
MCCZB39D10	0032
MCCZB43D	0054
MCCZB43D5	0054
MCCZB43D10	0054
MCCZB47D	0068
MCCZB47D5	0068
MCCZB47D10	0068
MCCZB51D	0092
MCCZB51D5	0092
MCCZB51D10	0092
MCCZB56D	0125
MCCZB56D5	0125
MCCZB56D10	0125
MCCZB62D	0152
MCCZB62D5	0152
MCCZB62D10	0152
MCCZB68D	0173
MCCZB68D5	0173
MCCZB68D10	0173
MCCZB75D	0094
MCCZB75D5	0094
MCCZB75D10	0094
MCCZB82D	0049
MCCZB82D5	0049
MCCZB82D10	0049
MCCZB91D	0156
MCCZB91D5	0156
MCCZB91D10	0156
MCCZB100D	0189
MCCZB100D5	0189
MCCZB100D10	0189
MCCZB105D	0099
MCCZB105D5	0099
MCCZB105D10	0099
MCCZB110D	0099
MCCZB110D5	0099
MCCZB110D10	0099
MCCZB120D	0089
MCCZB120D5	0089
MCCZB120D10	0089
MCCZB130D	0285
MCCZB130D5	0285
MCCZB130D10	0285
MCCZB140D	0252
MCCZB140D5	0252
MCCZB140D10	0252
MCCZB150D	0336
MCCZB150D5	0336
MCCZB150D10	0336
MCCZB160D	0366
MCCZB160D5	0366
MCCZB160D10	0366
MCCZB175D	0420
MCCZB175D5	0420
MCCZB175D10	0420
MCCZB180D	0420
MCCZB180D5	0420
MCCZB180D10	0420
MCCZB200D	1464
MCCZB200D5	1464
MCCZB200D10	1464
MCCZC6.8D	0062
MCCZC6.8D5	0062
MCCZC6.8D10	0062
MCCZC7.5D	0077
MCCZC7.5D5	0077
MCCZC7.5D10	0077
MCCZC8.2D	0165
MCCZC8.2D5	0165
MCCZC8.2D10	0165
MCCZC9.1D	0057
MCCZC9.1D5	0057
MCCZC9.1D10	0057
MCCZC10D	0064
MCCZC10D5	0064
MCCZC10D10	0064
MCCZC11D	0181
MCCZC11D5	0181
MCCZC11D10	0181
MCCZC12D	0052
MCCZC12D5	0052
MCCZC12D10	0052
MCCZC13D	0125
MCCZC13D5	0053
MCCZC13D10	0053
MCCZC14D	0873
MCCZC14D5	0873
MCCZC14D10	0873
MCCZC15D	0681
MCCZC15D5	0681
MCCZC15D10	0681
MCCZC16D	0440
MCCZC16D5	0440
MCCZC16D10	0440
MCCZC17D	0210
MCCZC17D5	0210
MCCZC17D10	0210
MCCZC18D	0371
MCCZC18D5	0371
MCCZC18D10	0371
MCCZC19D	0666
MCCZC19D5	0666
MCCZC19D10	0666
MCCZC20D	0695
MCCZC20D5	0695
MCCZC20D10	0695
MCCZC22D	0700
MCCZC22D5	0700
MCCZC22D10	0700
MCCZC24D	0489
MCCZC24D5	0489
MCCZC24D10	0489
MCCZC25D	0709
MCCZC25D5	0709
MCCZC25D10	0709
MCCZC27D	0450
MCCZC27D5	0450
MCCZC27D10	0450
MCCZC30D	0195
MCCZC30D5	0195
MCCZC30D10	0195
MCCZC33D	0166
MCCZC33D5	0166
MCCZC33D10	0166
MCCZC36D	0010
MCCZC36D5	0010
MCCZC36D10	0010
MCCZC39D	0032
MCCZC39D5	0032
MCCZC39D10	0032
MCCZC43D	0054
MCCZC43D5	0054
MCCZC43D10	0054
MCCZC47D	0068
MCCZC47D5	0068
MCCZC47D10	0068
MCCZC51D	0092
MCCZC51D5	0092
MCCZC51D10	0092
MCCZC56D	0125
MCCZC56D5	0125
MCCZC56D10	0125
MCCZC62D	0152
MCCZC62D5	0152
MCCZC62D10	0152
MCCZC68D	0173
MCCZC68D5	0173
MCCZC68D10	0173
MCCZC75D	0094
MCCZC75D5	0094
MCCZC75D10	0094
MCCZC82D	0049
MCCZC82D5	0049
MCCZC82D10	0049
MCCZC91D	0156
MCCZC91D10	0156
MCCZC92D5	0156
MCCZC100D	0189
MCCZC100D5	0189
MCCZC100D10	0064
MCCZC105D	0099
MCCZC105D5	0099
MCCZC105D10	0099
MCCZC110D	0099
MCCZC110D5	0099
MCCZC110D10	0099
MCCZC120D	0089
MCCZC120D5	0089
MCCZC120D10	0089
MCCZC130D	0285
MCCZC130D5	0285
MCCZC130D10	0285
MCCZC140D	0152
MCCZC140D5	0152
MCCZC140D10	0152
MCCZC150D	0336
MCCZC150D5	0336
MCCZC150D10	0336
MCCZC160D	0366
MCCZC160D5	0366
MCCZC160D10	0366
MCCZC175D	0420
MCCZC175D5	0420
MCCZC175D10	0420
MCCZC180D	0666
MCCZC180D5	0666
MCCZC180D10	0666
MCCZC200D	1464
MCCZC200D5	1464
MCCZC200D10	1464
MCCZD6.8D	0062
MCCZD6.8D5	0062
MCCZD6.8D10	0062
MCCZD7.5D	0077
MCCZD7.5D5	0077
MCCZD7.5D10	0077
MCCZD8.2D	0165
MCCZD8.2D5	0165
MCCZD8.2D10	0165
MCCZD9.1D	0057
MCCZD9.1D5	0057
MCCZD9.1D10	0057
MCCZD10D	0064
MCCZD10D5	0064
MCCZD10D10	0064
MCCZD11D	0181
MCCZD11D5	0181
MCCZD11D10	0181
MCCZD12D	0052
MCCZD12D5	0052
MCCZD12D10	0052
MCCZD13D	0053
MCCZD13D5	0053
MCCZD13D10	0053
MCCZD14D	0873
MCCZD14D5	0873
MCCZD14D10	0873
MCCZD15D	0681
MCCZD15D5	0681
MCCZD15D10	0681
MCCZD16D	0440
MCCZD16D5	0440
MCCZD16D10	0440
MCCZD17D	0210
MCCZD17D5	0210
MCCZD17D10	0210
MCCZD18D5	0371
MCCZD18D10	0371
MCCZD19D	0666
MCCZD19D5	0666
MCCZD19D10	0666
MCCZD20D	0695
MCCZD20D5	0695
MCCZD20D10	0695
MCCZD22D	0700
MCCZD22D5	0700
MCCZD22D10	0700
MCCZD24D	0489
MCCZD24D5	0489
MCCZD24D10	0489
MCCZD25D	0709
MCCZD25D5	0709
MCCZD25D10	0709
MCCZD27D	0450
MCCZD27D5	0450
MCCZD27D10	0450
MCCZD28D	0257
MCCZD28D5	0257
MCCZD28D10	0257
MCCZD30D	0195
MCCZD30D5	0195
MCCZD30D10	0195
MCCZD33D	0166
MCCZD33D5	0166
MCCZD33D10	0166
MCCZD36D	0010
MCCZD36D5	0010
MCCZD36D10	0010
MCCZD39D	0032
MCCZD39D5	0032
MCCZD39D10	0032
MCCZD43D	0054
MCCZD43D5	0054
MCCZD43D10	0054
MCCZD47D	0068
MCCZD47D5	0068
MCCZD47D10	0068
MCCZD51D	0092
MCCZD51D5	0092
MCCZD51D10	0092
MCCZD56D	0125
MCCZD56D5	0125
MCCZD56D10	0125
MCCZD60D	2301
MCCZD60D5	2301
MCCZD60D10	2301
MCCZD62D	0152
MCCZD62D5	0152
MCCZD62D10	0152
MCCZD68D	0173
MCCZD68D5	0173
MCCZD68D10	0173
MCCZD75D	0094
MCCZD75D5	0094
MCCZD75D10	0094
MCCZD82D	0049
MCCZD82D5	0049
MCCZD82D10	0049
MCCZD87D	0104
MCCZD87D5	0104
MCCZD87D10	0104
MCCZD91D	0156
MCCZD91D5	0156
MCCZD91D10	0156
MCCZD100D	0189
MCCZD100D5	0189
MCCZD100D10	0189
MCCZD105D	0099
MCCZD105D5	0099
MCCZD105D10	0099
MCCZD110D	0099
MCCZD110D5	0099
MCCZD110D10	0099
MCCZD120D	0089
MCCZD120D5	0089
MCCZD120D10	0089
MCCZD130D	0450
MCCZD130D5	0450
MCCZD130D10	0450
MCCZD140D	0252
MCCZD140D5	0252
MCCZD140D10	0252
MCCZD150D	0336
MCCZD150D5	0336
MCCZD150D10	0336
MCCZD160D	0366
MCCZD160D5	0366
MCCZD160D10	0366
MCCZD175D	0420
MCCZD175D5	0420
MCCZD175D10	0420
MCCZD180D	0420
MCCZD180D5	0420
MCCZD180D10	0420
MCCZD200D	1464
MCCZD200D5	1464
MCCZD200D10	1464
MCCZE6.8D	0062
MCCZE6.8D5	0062
MCCZE6.8D10	0062
MCCZE7.5D	0077
MCCZE7.5D5	0077
MCCZE7.5D10	0077
MCCZE8.2D	0165
MCCZE8.2D5	0165
MCCZE8.2D10	0165
MCCZE9.1D1D	0057
MCCZE9.1D5	0057
MCCZE9.1D10	0057
MCCZE10D	0064
MCCZE10D5	0064
MCCZE10D10	0064
MCCZE11D	0181
MCCZE11D5	0181
MCCZE11D10	0181
MCCZE12D	0052
MCCZE12D5	0052
MCCZE12D10	0052
MCCZE13D	0053
MCCZE13D5	0053
MCCZE13D10	0053
MCCZE14D	0873
MCCZE14D5	0873
MCCZE14D10	0873
MCCZE15D	0681
MCCZE15D5	0681
MCCZE15D10	0681
MCCZE16D	0440
MCCZE16D5	0440
MCCZE16D10	0440
MCCZE17D	0210
MCCZE17D5	0210
MCCZE17D10	0210
MCCZE18D	0371
MCCZE18D5	0371
MCCZE18D10	0371
MCCZE19D	0666
MCCZE19D5	0666
MCCZE19D10	0666
MCCZE20D	0695
MCCZE20D5	0695
MCCZE20D10	0695
MCCZE22D	0700
MCCZE22D5	0700
MCCZE22D10	0700
MCCZE24D	0489
MCCZE24D5	0489
MCCZE24D10	0489
MCCZE25D	0709
MCCZE25D5	0709
MCCZE25D10	0709
MCCZE27D	0450
MCCZE27D5	0450
MCCZE27D10	0450
MCCZE30D	0195
MCCZE30D5	0195
MCCZE30D10	0195
MCCZE33D	0166
MCCZE33D5	0166
MCCZE33D10	0166
MCCZE36D	0010
MCCZE36D5	0010
MCCZE36D10	0010
MCCZE39D	0032
MCCZE39D5	0032
MCCZE39D10	0032
MCCZE43D	0054
MCCZE43D5	0054
MCCZE43D10	0054
MCCZE47D	0068
MCCZE47D5	0068
MCCZE47D10	0068
MCCZE51D	0092
MCCZE51D5	0092
MCCZE51D10	0092
MCCZE56D	0125
MCCZE56D5	0125
MCCZE56D10	0125
MCCZE62D	0152
MCCZE62D5	0152
MCCZE62D10	0152
MCCZE68D	0173
MCCZE68D5	0173
MCCZE68D10	0173
MCCZE75D	0094
MCCZE75D5	0094
MCCZE75D10	0094
MCCZE82D	0049
MCCZE82D5	0049
MCCZE82D10	0049
MCCZE91D	0156
MCCZE91D5	0156
MCCZE91D10	0156
MCCZE100D	0189
MCCZE100D5	0189
MCCZE100D10	0189
MCCZE105D	0099
MCCZE105D5	0099
MCCZE105D10	0099
MCCZE110D	0099
MCCZE110D5	0099
MCCZE110D10	0099
MCCZE120D	0089
MCCZE120D5	0089
MCCZE120D10	0089
MCCZE130D	0285
MCCZE130D5	0285
MCCZE130D10	0285
MCCZE140D	0252
MCCZE140D5	0252
MCCZE140D10	0252
MCCZE150D	0336
MCCZE150D5	0336
MCCZE150D10	0336
MCCZE160D	0366
MCCZE160D5	0366
MCCZE160D10	0366
MCCZE175D	0420
MCCZE175D5	0420
MCCZE175D10	0420
MCCZE180D	0420
MCCZE180D5	0420
MCCZE180D10	0420
MCCZE200D	1464
MCCZE200D5	1464
MCCZE200D10	1464
MCCZF1.8D	OEM
MCCZF2.0D	OEM
MCCZF2.0D5	OEM
MCCZF2.0D10	OEM
MCCZF2.2D	OEM
MCCZF2.2D5	OEM
MCCZF2.2D10	OEM
MCCZF2.4D	OEM
MCCZF2.4D5	OEM
MCCZF2.4D10	OEM
MCCZF2.7D	0755
MCCZF2.7D5	0755
MCCZF2.7D10	0755
MCCZF2.8D5	0672
MCCZF2.8D10	0672
MCCZF3.0D	0118
MCCZF3.0D5	0118
MCCZF3.0D10	0118
MCCZF3.3D	0296
MCCZF3.3D5	0296

If replacement code is OEM, contact original manufacturer for replacement.

DEVICE TYPE	REPL CODE
MCCZF3.3D10	0296
MCCZF3.6D	0372
MCCZF3.6D5	0372
MCCZF3.6D10	0372
MCCZF3.9D	0036
MCCZF3.9D5	0036
MCCZF3.9D10	0036
MCCZF4.3D	0274
MCCZF4.3D5	OEM
MCCZF4.3D10	0274
MCCZF4.7D	0140
MCCZF4.7D5	0140
MCCZF4.7D10	0140
MCCZF5.1D	0041
MCCZF5.1D5	0041
MCCZF5.1D10	0041
MCCZF5.6D	0253
MCCZF5.6D5	0253
MCCZF5.6D10	0253
MCCZF6.2D	0466
MCCZF6.2D5	0466
MCCZF6.2D10	0466
MCCZF6.8D	0062
MCCZF6.8D5	0062
MCCZF6.8D10	0062
MCCZF7.5D	0077
MCCZF7.5D5	0077
MCCZF7.5D10	0077
MCCZF8.2D	0165
MCCZF8.2D5	0165
MCCZF8.2D10	0165
MCCZF9.1D	0057
MCCZF9.1D5	0057
MCCZF9.1D10	0057
MCCZF10D	0064
MCCZF10D5	0064
MCCZF12D	0052
MCCZF12D5	0052
MCCZF12D10	0052
MCCZG2.4D	1266
MCCZG2.4D5	1266
MCCZG2.4D10	1266
MCCZG2.7D	0755
MCCZG2.7D5	0755
MCCZG2.7D10	0755
MCCZG3.0D	0118
MCCZG3.0D5	0118
MCCZG3.0D10	0118
MCCZG3.3D	0296
MCCZG3.3D5	0296
MCCZG3.3D10	0296
MCCZG3.6D	0372
MCCZG3.6D5	0372
MCCZG3.6D10	0372
MCCZG3.9D	0036
MCCZG3.9D5	0036
MCCZG3.9D10	0036
MCCZG4.3D	0274
MCCZG4.3D5	0274
MCCZG4.3D10	0274
MCCZG4.7D	0140
MCCZG4.7D5	0140
MCCZG4.7D10	0140
MCCZG5.1D	0041
MCCZG5.1D5	0041
MCCZG5.1D10	0041
MCCZG5.6D	0253
MCCZG5.6D5	0253
MCCZG5.6D10	0253
MCCZG6.2D	0466
MCCZG6.2D5	0466
MCCZG6.2D10	0466
MCCZG6.8D	0062
MCCZG6.8D5	0062
MCCZG6.8D10	0062
MCCZG7.5D	0077
MCCZG7.5D5	0077
MCCZG7.5D10	0077
MCCZG8.2D	0165
MCCZG8.2D5	0165
MCCZG8.2D10	0165
MCCZG9.1D	0057
MCCZG9.1D5	0057
MCCZG9.1D10	0057
MCCZG10D	0064
MCCZG10D5	0064
MCCZG10D10	0064
MCCZG12D	0052
MCCZG12D5	0052
MCCZG12D10	0052
MCD	OEM
MCD521H	OEM
MCD521L	OEM
MCD522H	OEM
MCD522L	OEM
MCD526	OEM
MCD527	OEM
MCD537	OEM
MCD725	OEM
MCD735	OEM
MCF1145	OEM
MCF1165	OEM
MCF1166	OEM
MCF1327	OEM
MCF1329	OEM
MCF1330	OEM
MCF1331	OEM
MCF1492	OEM
MCF1493	OEM
MCF1510	OEM
MCF6021	1865
MCH-01	OEM
MCH2005F	2243
MCH5862	OEM
MCH5867	OEM
MCH5871	OEM
MCH5872	OEM
MCH5875	OEM
MCH5880	OEM
MCH5883	OEM
MCI00	OEM
MCI01	OEM
MCI12	OEM
MCL45	OEM
MCL601	OEM
MCL611	OEM
MCL701N	OEM
MCL702A	OEM
MCL702L	OEM
MCL703C	OEM
MCL703L	OEM
MCL716A	OEM
MCL723C	OEM
MCL1300	OEM
MCL1301	OEM
MCL1302	OEM
MCL1303	OEM
MCL1304	OEM
MCLTC6010	OEM
MCLTC6025	OEM
MCLTC6050	OEM
MCLTC6100	OEM
MCM10	OEM
MCM11	OEM
MCM20	OEM
MCM21	OEM
MCM21L14C20	OEM
MCM21L14C25	OEM
MCM21L14C30	OEM
MCM21L14C45	OEM
MCM21L14P20	OEM
MCM21L14P25	OEM
MCM21L14P30	OEM
MCM21L14P45	OEM
MCM21L15AC-45	OEM
MCM21L15AC-70	OEM
MCM21L25AC-45	OEM
MCM21L25AC-70	OEM
MCM27A08C	OEM
MCM27A08L	OEM
MCM27L16-25L	OEM
MCM27S19DC	OEM
MCM27S19PC	OEM
MCM27S25DC	OEM
MCM27S25PC	OEM
MCM27S27DC	OEM
MCM27S27PC	OEM
MCM27S29DC	OEM
MCM27S29PC	OEM
MCM27S31DC	OEM
MCM27S31PC	OEM
MCM27S35DC	OEM
MCM27S35PC	OEM
MCM27S37DC	OEM
MCM27S37PC	OEM
MCM27S45DC	OEM
MCM27S45PC	OEM
MCM27S47DC	OEM
MCM27S47PC	OEM
MCM27S181DC	OEM
MCM27S181PC	OEM
MCM27S191DC	OEM
MCM27S191PC	OEM
MCM27S281DC	OEM
MCM27S281PC	OEM
MCM27S291DC	OEM
MCM27S291PC	OEM
MCM40	OEM
MCM41	OEM
MCM51L01C45	OEM
MCM51L01C65	OEM
MCM51L01P45	OEM
MCM51L01P65	OEM
MCM66L41-20P	OEM
MCM66L41-25C	OEM
MCM66L41-25P	OEM
MCM66L41-30C	OEM
MCM66L41-30P	OEM
MCM66L41-45C	OEM
MCM66L41-45P	OEM
MCM68A	OEM
MCM68A10CL	OEM
MCM68A10CP	OEM
MCM68A10CS	OEM
MCM68A10L	OEM
MCM68A10P	OEM
MCM68A10S	OEM
MCM68A30AC	OEM
MCM68A30AP	OEM
MCM68A308C	OEM
MCM68A308P	OEM
MCM68A316E	OEM
MCM68A364	OEM
MCM68A708C	OEM
MCM68A708L	OEM
MCM68B10L	OEM
MCM68B10P	OEM
MCM68B10S	OEM
MCM68HC34L	OEM
MCM68HC34P	OEM
MCM80	OEM
MCM81	OEM
MCM93L422AD	OEM
MCM93L422AP	OEM
MCM93L422D	OEM
MCM93L422DC	OEM
MCM93L422P	OEM
MCM93L422PC	OEM
MCM101C80	OEM
MCM332	OEM
MCM364	OEM
MCM2016H	OEM
MCM2114	2037
MCM2114-20L	OEM
MCM2114-20P	OEM
MCM2114-25L	OEM
MCM2114-25P	OEM
MCM2114-30	2037
MCM2114-30L	OEM
MCM2114-30P	OEM
MCM2114-45	2037
MCM2114-45L	OEM
MCM2114-45P	OEM
MCM2114-P20	OEM
MCM2114C20	OEM
MCM2114C25	OEM
MCM2114C30	OEM
MCM2114C45	OEM
MCM2114P	5206
MCM2114P20	2037
MCM2114P25	OEM
MCM2114P-30	2037
MCM2114P30	OEM
MCM2114P-45	2037
MCM2114P45	2037
MCM2115AC-45	OEM
MCM2115AC-55	OEM
MCM2115AC-70	OEM
MCM2125AC-55	OEM
MCM2125AC-70	OEM
MCM2125AC-4545	OEM
MCM2147C55	1683
MCM2147C70	1683
MCM2147C85	1683
MCM2147C100	1683
MCM2167H-35L	OEM
MCM2167H-35P	OEM
MCM2167H-35Z	OEM
MCM2167H-45L	OEM
MCM2167H-45P	OEM
MCM2167H-45Z	OEM
MCM2167H-55L	OEM
MCM2167H-55P	OEM
MCM2167H-55Z	OEM
MCM2532C	5007
MCM2708C	4351
MCM2708L	4351
MCM2716C	2263
MCM2716L	6248
MCM2801	OEM
MCM2832-15L	OEM
MCM2832-15P	OEM
MCM2832-20L	OEM
MCM2832-20P	OEM
MCM2832P	OEM
MCM2833P	OEM
MCM4027AC2	OEM
MCM4027AC3	4887
MCM4027AC4	4887
MCM4116AC15	OEM
MCM4116AC20	0518
MCM4116AC25	0518
MCM4116AC30	0518
MCM4116BC15	OEM
MCM4116BC-20	OEM
MCM4116BC20	0518
MCM4116BC-25	OEM
MCM4116BC25	0518
MCM4116BC-30	OEM
MCM4116BC30	0518
MCM4116BC35	OEM
MCM4116BP-15	OEM
MCM4116BP15	OEM
MCM4116BP20	0518
MCM4116BP25	0518
MCM4116BP30	0518
MCM4116BP35	0518
MCM4517-12P	OEM
MCM4517-15P	OEM
MCM4517-20	OEM
MCM4517P	OEM
MCM4517P10	OEM
MCM4517P12	OEM
MCM4517P-15	OEM
MCM4517P15	OEM
MCM4517P15B1	OEM
MCM4517P20	OEM
MCM5101C65	OEM
MCM5101P65	OEM
MCM5101P80	OEM
MCM6116P15	OEM
MCM6116P20	OEM
MCM6256-10L	OEM
MCM6256-12L	OEM
MCM6256-15L	OEM
MCM6257L	OEM
MCM6257P	OEM
MCM6604L	OEM
MCM6604L2	OEM
MCM6604L4	OEM
MCM6604P	OEM
MCM6604P2	OEM
MCM6604P4	OEM
MCM6632AL15	OEM
MCM6632AL15(A)	OEM
MCM6632AL20	OEM
MCM6632AL20(A)	OEM
MCM6632AP12(A)	OEM
MCM6633AL	OEM
MCM6633AL15	OEM
MCM6633AL20	OEM
MCM6633AP	OEM
MCM6633AP12	OEM
MCM6641-20P	OEM
MCM6641-25P	OEM
MCM6641-30P	OEM
MCM6641-45P	OEM
MCM6664-20L	OEM
MCM6664A-12L	OEM
MCM6664A-12P	OEM
MCM6664A-15L	OEM
MCM6664A-15P	OEM
MCM6664A-20L	OEM
MCM6664A-20P	OEM
MCM6664AL	OEM
MCM6664AL15	OEM
MCM6664AL20	4251
MCM6664AL25	OEM
MCM6664AP	4251
MCM6664AP15	4251
MCM6664AP20	4251
MCM6664AP25	OEM
MCM6665	2341
MCM6665-20L	OEM
MCM6665A-12L	OEM
MCM6665A-12P	OEM
MCM6665A-15	OEM
MCM6665A-15L	OEM
MCM6665A-15P	OEM
MCM6665A-20	OEM
MCM6665A-20L	OEM
MCM6665A-20P	OEM
MCM6665AL15	2341
MCM6665AL20	2341
MCM6665AL25	OEM
MCM6665AP	4426
MCM6665AP15	2341
MCM6665AP20	2341
MCM6665AP25	OEM
MCM6665BP-20	OEM
MCM6665L25	2341
MCM6670L	OEM
MCM6670P	OEM
MCM6674P	OEM
MCM6810	4185
MCM6810BJCS	OEM
MCM6810CJCS	OEM
MCM6810CL	2075
MCM6810CP	2075
MCM6810CS	OEM
MCM6810L	OEM
MCM6810P	2075
MCM6810S	OEM
MCM7621AD	OEM
MCM7621ADC	OEM
MCM7621AP	OEM
MCM7621APC	OEM
MCM7621D	4996
MCM7621DC	OEM
MCM7621P	OEM
MCM7621PC	OEM
MCM7641AD	OEM
MCM7641ADC	OEM
MCM7641AP	OEM
MCM7641APC	OEM
MCM7641D	5017
MCM7641DC	OEM
MCM7641P	OEM
MCM7641PC	OEM
MCM7643AD	OEM
MCM7643ADC	OEM
MCM7643AP	OEM
MCM7643APC	OEM
MCM7643D	4275
MCM7643DC	OEM
MCM7643P	OEM
MCM7643PC	OEM
MCM7649ADC	OEM
MCM7649APC	OEM
MCM7649DC	OEM
MCM7649PC	OEM
MCM7681	2881
MCM7681A	OEM
MCM7681AD	OEM
MCM7681ADC	OEM
MCM7681AP	OEM
MCM7681APC	OEM
MCM7681D	5164
MCM7681DC	OEM
MCM7681P	2881
MCM7681PC	OEM
MCM7685AD	OEM
MCM7685ADC	OEM
MCM7685AP	OEM
MCM7685APC	OEM
MCM7685D	3137
MCM7685DC	OEM
MCM7685P	OEM
MCM7685PC	OEM
MCM10139L	OEM
MCM10143L	OEM
MCM10144L	OEM
MCM10145AL	OEM
MCM10145L	OEM
MCM10146L	OEM
MCM10147L	OEM
MCM10148L	OEM
MCM10149L	OEM
MCM10152L	OEM
MCM10415AF	OEM
MCM10415AP	OEM
MCM10415F	OEM
MCM10415L	OEM
MCM10422A	OEM
MCM10422F	OEM
MCM10422L	OEM
MCM10470AF	OEM
MCM10470AL	OEM
MCM10470F	OEM
MCM10470L	OEM
MCM10474AL	OEM
MCM10474L	OEM
MCM12090D	OEM
MCM12090P	OEM
MCM14505AL	OEM
MCM14505ALD	OEM
MCM14505CL	OEM
MCM14505CLD	OEM
MCM14505CP	OEM
MCM14505CPD	OEM
MCM14524AL	OEM
MCM14524CL	OEM
MCM14524CP	OEM
MCM14537AL	OEM
MCM14537ALD	OEM
MCM14537CL	OEM
MCM14537CLD	OEM
MCM14537CP	OEM
MCM14552AL	OEM
MCM14552ALD	OEM
MCM14552CL	OEM
MCM14552CLD	OEM
MCM14552CP	OEM
MCM14552CPD	OEM
MCM63128P	OEM
MCM63256P	OEM
MCM65116-12C(A)	OEM
MCM65116-12P(A)	OEM
MCM65116-15C(A)	OEM
MCM65116-15P(A)	OEM
MCM65116-20C(A)	OEM
MCM65116-20P(A)	OEM
MCM65116C	6041
MCM65116P	6041
MCM65116P15	1887
MCM65116P20	1887
MCM65147-55C(A)	OEM
MCM65147-55P(A)	OEM
MCM65147-70C	OEM
MCM65147-70P(A)	OEM
MCM65147C	OEM
MCM65147P	OEM
MCM65147P55	OEM
MCM65147P70	OEM
MCM65256P	OEM
MCM65256P(A)	OEM
MCM65516-43L	OEM
MCM65516-43P	OEM
MCM65516-55L	OEM
MCM65516-55P	OEM
MCM65516L	OEM
MCM65516L43M	OEM
MCM65516P	OEM
MCM65516P43M	OEM
MCM66320AL15	OEM
MCM66320AL15(A)	OEM
MCM66320AL20	OEM
MCM66320AL20(A)	OEM
MCM66321AL15	OEM
MCM66321AL15(A)	OEM
MCM66321AL20	OEM
MCM66321AL20(A)	OEM
MCM66330AL15	OEM
MCM66330AL20	OEM
MCM66331AL15	OEM
MCM66331AL20	OEM
MCM66700C	OEM
MCM66700P	OEM
MCM66710C	OEM
MCM66710P	OEM
MCM66714C	OEM
MCM66714P	OEM
MCM66720C	OEM
MCM66720P	OEM
MCM66730C	OEM
MCM66730P	OEM
MCM66734C	OEM
MCM66734P	OEM
MCM66740C	OEM
MCM66740P	OEM
MCM66750C	OEM
MCM66750P	OEM
MCM66760C	OEM
MCM66760P	OEM
MCM66770C	OEM
MCM66770P	OEM
MCM66780C	OEM
MCM66780P	OEM
MCM66790C	OEM
MCM66790P	OEM
MCM68364-20C	OEM
MCM68364-20L	OEM
MCM68364-20P	OEM
MCM68364-25C	OEM
MCM68364-25L	OEM
MCM68364-25P	OEM
MCM68364-30C	OEM
MCM68364-30L	OEM
MCM68364-30P	OEM
MCM68364C	OEM
MCM68364P	OEM
MCM68365-25C	OEM
MCM68365-25L	OEM
MCM68365-25P	OEM
MCM68365-35C	OEM
MCM68365-35L	OEM
MCM68365-35P	OEM
MCM68365P	OEM
MCM68366-25C	OEM
MCM68366-25L	OEM
MCM68366-25P	OEM
MCM68366-35C	OEM
MCM68366-35L	OEM
MCM68366-35P	OEM
MCM68366P	OEM
MCM68367P	OEM
MCM68368P	OEM
MCM68369P	OEM
MCM68370P	OEM
MCM68708C	OEM
MCM68708L	OEM
MCM68764C	OEM
MCM68764L	OEM
MCM68766-35C	OEM
MCM68766C	OEM
MCM68766C35	OEM
MCM68766L	OEM
MCM76161AD	OEM
MCM76161ADC	OEM
MCM76161AP	OEM
MCM76161APC	OEM
MCM76161D	OEM
MCM76161DC	OEM
MCM76161P	OEM
MCM76161PC	OEM
MCM76165ADC	OEM
MCM76165APC	OEM
MCM76165DC	OEM
MCM76165PC	OEM
MCM93415DC	OEM
MCM93415DM	OEM
MCM93415PC	OEM
MCM93422AD	OEM
MCM93422AP	OEM
MCM93422D	OEM
MCM93422DC	OEM
MCM93422P	OEM
MCM93422PC	OEM
MCM93425DC	OEM
MCM93425DM	OEM
MCM93425PC	OEM
MCN701A	OEM
MCN721A	OEM
MCP-893	OEM
MCPU-800	OEM
MCPU800-02	OEM
MCPU800-03	OEM
MCR051	OEM
MCR052	OEM
MCR053	OEM
MCR054	OEM
MCR16L4L6	OEM
MCR22-2	OEM
MCR22-3	OEM
MCR22-4	OEM
MCR22-5	OEM
MCR22-6	OEM
MCR22-7	OEM
MCR22-8	OEM
MCR23-2	OEM
MCR23-3	OEM
MCR23-4	OEM
MCR23-5	OEM
MCR23-6	OEM
MCR23-7	OEM
MCR23-8	OEM
MCR32-05	OEM
MCR32-20	OEM
MCR32-30	OEM
MCR32-40	OEM
MCR32-50	OEM
MCR32-60	OEM
MCR39-05	2396
MCR39-20	2396
MCR39-30	6235
MCR39-40	6235
MCR39-50	OEM
MCR39-60	OEM
MCR45-10	0217
MCR45-20	0217
MCR45-30	0217
MCR45-40	0217
MCR45-50	0217
MCR45-60	0217
MCR45-70	0653
MCR45-80	0653
MCR45-90	0653
MCR45-100	0653
MCR45-110	0653
MCR45-120	0653
MCR46-10	OEM
MCR46-20	OEM
MCR46-30	OEM
MCR46-40	OEM
MCR46-50	OEM
MCR46-60	OEM
MCR46-70	OEM
MCR46-80	OEM
MCR46-90	OEM
MCR46-100	OEM
MCR46-110	OEM
MCR46-120	OEM
MCR50-10	OEM
MCR50-20	OEM
MCR50-30	OEM
MCR50-40	OEM
MCR50-50	OEM
MCR50-60	OEM
MCR50-70	OEM
MCR50-80	OEM
MCR50-90	OEM
MCR50C-10	OEM
MCR50C-20	OEM
MCR50C-30	OEM
MCR50C-40	OEM
MCR50C-50	OEM
MCR50C-60	OEM
MCR50C-70	OEM
MCR50C-80	OEM
MCR50C-90	OEM
MCR50C-100	OEM
MCR50D-10	OEM
MCR50D-20	OEM
MCR50D-30	OEM
MCR50D-40	OEM
MCR50D-50	OEM
MCR50D-60	OEM
MCR50D-70	OEM
MCR50D-80	OEM
MCR50D-90	OEM
MCR50D-100	OEM
MCR50D-110	OEM
MCR50D-120	OEM
MCR52-10	OEM
MCR52-20	OEM
MCR52-30	OEM
MCR52-40	OEM
MCR52-50	OEM
MCR52-60	OEM
MCR52-70	OEM
MCR52-80	OEM
MCR52-90	OEM
MCR60-10	OEM
MCR60-20	OEM
MCR60-30	OEM
MCR60-40	OEM
MCR60-50	OEM
MCR62-10	OEM
MCR62-20	OEM
MCR62-30	OEM
MCR62-40	OEM
MCR62-50	OEM
MCR63-1	OEM
MCR63-2	OEM
MCR63-3	OEM
MCR63-4	OEM
MCR63-5	OEM
MCR63-6	OEM
MCR63-7	OEM
MCR63-8	OEM
MCR63-9	OEM
MCR63-10	OEM
MCR64-1	OEM
MCR64-2	6685
MCR64-3	6685
MCR64-4	6685
MCR64-5	OEM
MCR64-6	6686
MCR64-7	OEM
MCR64-8	6686
MCR64-9	OEM
MCR64-10	5945
MCR65-1	OEM
MCR65-2	OEM
MCR65-3	OEM
MCR65-4	OEM
MCR65-5	OEM
MCR65-6	OEM
MCR65-7	OEM
MCR65-8	OEM
MCR65-9	OEM
MCR65-10	OEM
MCR67-1	OEM
MCR67-2	OEM
MCR67-3	OEM
MCR68-1	6714
MCR68-2	6714
MCR68-3	6714
MCR69-1	OEM
MCR69-2	OEM
MCR69-3	OEM
MCR69-6	OEM
MCR70-1	OEM

If replacement code is OEM, contact original manufacturer for replacement.

481

DEVICE TYPE	REPL CODE
MCR70-2	OEM
MCR70-3	OEM
MCR70-6	OEM
MCR71-1	OEM
MCR71-2	OEM
MCR71-3	OEM
MCR72-1	1386
MCR72-2	1250
MCR72-3	0442
MCR72-4	0934
MCR72-5	1213
MCR72-6	0712
MCR72-7	0304
MCR72-8	0304
MCR80-0.5	OEM
MCR80-5	OEM
MCR80-10	OEM
MCR80-20	OEM
MCR80-30	OEM
MCR80-40	OEM
MCR80-50	OEM
MCR80-60	OEM
MCR80-70	OEM
MCR80-80	OEM
MCR81-0.5	OEM
MCR81-5	OEM
MCR81-10	OEM
MCR81-20	OEM
MCR81-30	OEM
MCR81-40	OEM
MCR81-50	OEM
MCR81-60	OEM
MCR81-70	OEM
MCR81-80	OEM
MCR82-0.5	OEM
MCR82-5	OEM
MCR82-10	OEM
MCR82-20	OEM
MCR82-30	OEM
MCR82-40	OEM
MCR82-50	OEM
MCR82-60	OEM
MCR82-70	OEM
MCR82-80	OEM
MCR83-5	OEM
MCR83-10	OEM
MCR83-20	OEM
MCR83-30	OEM
MCR83-40	OEM
MCR83-50	OEM
MCR83-60	OEM
MCR83-70	OEM
MCR83-80	OEM
MCR100-3	0895
MCR100-4	0058
MCR100-5	0403
MCR100-6	0403
MCR100-7	1673
MCR100-8	1673
MCR100-B	1673
MCR101	1129
MCR102	1129
MCR103	0340
MCR104	0895
MCR106-1	4384
MCR106-2	0174
MCR106-3	3801
MCR106-4	3575
MCR106-5	3291
MCR106-6	3291
MCR106-7	1494
MCR106-8	0304
MCR107-1	4384
MCR107-2	0174
MCR107-3	3801
MCR107-4	3575
MCR107-5	0712
MCR107-6	0705
MCR107-7	6561
MCR107-8	0304
MCR115	2326
MCR120	0058
MCR130	OEM
MCR150-10	OEM
MCR150-20	OEM
MCR150-30	OEM
MCR150-40	OEM
MCR150-50	0463
MCR150-60	0463
MCR150-70	0463
MCR150-80	0463
MCR150-90	0463
MCR150-100	0463
MCR150-110	0463
MCR150-120	0463
MCR150-130	OEM
MCR150-140	OEM
MCR150-150	OEM
MCR152-10	OEM
MCR152-20	OEM
MCR152-30	OEM
MCR152-40	OEM
MCR152-50	OEM
MCR152-60	OEM
MCR152-70	OEM
MCR152-80	OEM
MCR152-90	OEM
MCR152-100	OEM
MCR152-110	OEM

DEVICE TYPE	REPL CODE
MCR152-120	OEM
MCR152-130	OEM
MCR152-140	OEM
MCR152-150	OEM
MCR154-10	0521
MCR154-20	0521
MCR154-30	0521
MCR154-40	0521
MCR154-50	0521
MCR154-60	0521
MCR155-10	0521
MCR155-20	0521
MCR155-30	0521
MCR155-40	0521
MCR155-50	0521
MCR155-60	0521
MCR156-10	OEM
MCR156-20	OEM
MCR156-30	OEM
MCR156-40	OEM
MCR156-50	OEM
MCR156-60	OEM
MCR157-10	OEM
MCR157-20	OEM
MCR157-30	OEM
MCR157-40	OEM
MCR157-50	OEM
MCR157-60	OEM
MCR158-50	OEM
MCR158-60	OEM
MCR158-70	OEM
MCR158-80	OEM
MCR158-90	OEM
MCR158-100	OEM
MCR158-110	OEM
MCR158-120	OEM
MCR159-50	OEM
MCR159-60	OEM
MCR159-70	OEM
MCR159-80	OEM
MCR159-90	OEM
MCR159-100	OEM
MCR159-110	OEM
MCR159-120	OEM
MCR201	OEM
MCR202	3958
MCR203	3959
MCR204	0568
MCR205	OEM
MCR206	3963
MCR218-2	2084
MCR218-3	2078
MCR218-4	0500
MCR218-5	OEM
MCR218-6	0857
MCR218-7	OEM
MCR218-8	0323
MCR218-9	OEM
MCR218-10	0323
MCR220-5	0606
MCR220-7	0946
MCR220-9	3953
MCR221-5	3991
MCR221-7	3992
MCR221-9	3953
MCR225-2FP	2587
MCR225-4FP	2587
MCR225-5	3991
MCR225-6FP	OEM
MCR225-7	3992
MCR225-8FP	4496
MCR225-9	3953
MCR225-10FP	4496
MCR225-12	OEM
MCR235-10	OEM
MCR235-20	OEM
MCR235-30	OEM
MCR235-40	OEM
MCR235-50	OEM
MCR235-60	OEM
MCR235-70	OEM
MCR235-80	OEM
MCR235-90	OEM
MCR235-100	OEM
MCR235-110	OEM
MCR235-120	OEM
MCR235-130	OEM
MCR235-140	OEM
MCR235-150	OEM
MCR235A-10	OEM
MCR235A-20	OEM
MCR235A-30	OEM
MCR235A-40	OEM
MCR235A-50	OEM
MCR235A-60	OEM
MCR235B-10	OEM
MCR235B-20	OEM
MCR235B-30	OEM
MCR235B-40	OEM
MCR235B-50	OEM
MCR235B-60	OEM
MCR235B-80	OEM
MCR235C-10	OEM
MCR235C-20	OEM
MCR235C-30	OEM
MCR235C-40	OEM
MCR235C-50	OEM
MCR235C-60	OEM
MCR235C-70	OEM

DEVICE TYPE	REPL CODE
MCR235C-80	OEM
MCR235C-90	OEM
MCR235C-100	OEM
MCR251B-10	OEM
MCR251B-20	OEM
MCR251B-30	OEM
MCR251B-40	OEM
MCR251B-50	OEM
MCR251B-60	OEM
MCR251B-70	OEM
MCR251B-80	OEM
MCR251B-90	OEM
MCR251B-100	OEM
MCR251B-110	OEM
MCR251B-120	OEM
MCR251B-130	OEM
MCR251B-140	OEM
MCR251B-150	OEM
MCR251L-10	OEM
MCR251L-20	OEM
MCR251L-30	OEM
MCR251L-40	OEM
MCR251L-50	OEM
MCR251L-60	OEM
MCR251L-70	OEM
MCR251L-80	OEM
MCR251L-90	OEM
MCR251L-100	OEM
MCR251L-110	OEM
MCR251L-120	OEM
MCR251L-130	OEM
MCR251L-140	OEM
MCR251L-150	OEM
MCR264-2	4987
MCR264-3	4987
MCR264-4	4987
MCR264-6	4987
MCR264-8	4989
MCR264-10	4989
MCR264-12	OEM
MCR265-2	OEM
MCR265-4	OEM
MCR265-6	OEM
MCR265-8	OEM
MCR265-10	OEM
MCR320-1	OEM
MCR320-2	OEM
MCR320-3	OEM
MCR320-4	OEM
MCR320-5	OEM
MCR320-6	OEM
MCR320-7	OEM
MCR320-8	OEM
MCR380-10	OEM
MCR380-20	OEM
MCR380-30	OEM
MCR380-40	OEM
MCR380-50	OEM
MCR380-60	OEM
MCR380-70	OEM
MCR380-80	OEM
MCR380-90	OEM
MCR380-100	OEM
MCR380-110	OEM
MCR380-120	OEM
MCR380-130	OEM
MCR380-140	OEM
MCR380-150	OEM
MCR380B-10	OEM
MCR380B-20	OEM
MCR380B-30	OEM
MCR380B-40	OEM
MCR380B-50	OEM
MCR380B-60	OEM
MCR380B-70	OEM
MCR380B-80	OEM
MCR380C-10	OEM
MCR380C-20	OEM
MCR380C-30	OEM
MCR380C-40	OEM
MCR380C-50	OEM
MCR380C-60	OEM
MCR380C-70	OEM
MCR380C-80	OEM
MCR380C-90	OEM
MCR380C-100	OEM
MCR380D-10	OEM
MCR380D-20	OEM
MCR380D-30	OEM
MCR380D-40	OEM
MCR380D-50	OEM
MCR380D-60	OEM
MCR380D-70	OEM
MCR380D-80	OEM
MCR380D-90	OEM
MCR380D-100	OEM
MCR380D-110	OEM
MCR380D-120	OEM
MCR406-1	6030
MCR406-2	3253
MCR406-3	1912
MCR406-4	3575
MCR407-1	3252
MCR407-2	6032
MCR407-3	6033
MCR407-4	3575
MCR470-10	OEM
MCR470-20	OEM
MCR470-30	OEM

DEVICE TYPE	REPL CODE
MCR470-40	OEM
MCR470-50	OEM
MCR470-60	OEM
MCR470-70	OEM
MCR470-80	OEM
MCR470-90	OEM
MCR470-100	OEM
MCR470-110	OEM
MCR470-120	OEM
MCR470-130	OEM
MCR470-140	OEM
MCR470-150	OEM
MCR470C-10	OEM
MCR470C-20	OEM
MCR470C-30	OEM
MCR470C-40	OEM
MCR470C-50	OEM
MCR470C-60	OEM
MCR470C-70	OEM
MCR470C-80	OEM
MCR470D-10	OEM
MCR470D-20	OEM
MCR470D-30	OEM
MCR470D-40	OEM
MCR470D-50	OEM
MCR470D-60	OEM
MCR470D-70	OEM
MCR470D-80	OEM
MCR470D-90	OEM
MCR470D-100	OEM
MCR470E-10	OEM
MCR470E-20	OEM
MCR470E-30	OEM
MCR470E-40	OEM
MCR470E-50	OEM
MCR470E-60	OEM
MCR470E-70	OEM
MCR470E-80	OEM
MCR470E-90	OEM
MCR470E-100	OEM
MCR470E-110	OEM
MCR470E-120	OEM
MCR525-4	OEM
MCR525-5	OEM
MCR525-6	OEM
MCR525-7	OEM
MCR525-8	OEM
MCR525-9	OEM
MCR525-10	OEM
MCR568-1	OEM
MCR568-2	OEM
MCR568-3	OEM
MCR568-6	OEM
MCR569-1	OEM
MCR569-2	OEM
MCR569-3	OEM
MCR569-6	OEM
MCR606-2	OEM
MCR606-3	OEM
MCR606-4	OEM
MCR606-5	OEM
MCR606-6	OEM
MCR606-7	OEM
MCR606-8	OEM
MCR649-1	2497
MCR649-2	OEM
MCR649-3	1640
MCR649-4	1641
MCR649-5	1574
MCR649-6	OEM
MCR649-7	1655
MCR649-8	OEM
MCR649-9	OEM
MCR649-10	OEM
MCR649A1	OEM
MCR649A2	OEM
MCR649A3	OEM
MCR649A4	OEM
MCR649A5	OEM
MCR649A6	OEM
MCR649A7	OEM
MCR649A8	OEM
MCR649A9	OEM
MCR649A10	OEM
MCR649AP1	OEM
MCR649AP2	OEM
MCR649AP3	OEM
MCR649AP4	OEM
MCR649AP5	OEM
MCR649AP6	OEM
MCR649AP7	OEM
MCR649AP8	OEM
MCR649AP9	OEM
MCR649AP10	OEM
MCR649P1	OEM
MCR649P2	OEM
MCR649P3	OEM
MCR649P4	OEM
MCR649P5	OEM
MCR649P6	OEM
MCR649P7	OEM
MCR649P8	OEM
MCR649P9	OEM
MCR649P10	OEM
MCR729-5	OEM
MCR729-6	OEM
MCR729-7	OEM
MCR729-8	OEM
MCR729-9	OEM

DEVICE TYPE	REPL CODE
MCR729-10	OEM
MCR800-10	OEM
MCR800-20	OEM
MCR800-30	OEM
MCR800-40	OEM
MCR800-50	OEM
MCR800-60	OEM
MCR800-70	OEM
MCR800-80	OEM
MCR800-90	OEM
MCR800-100	OEM
MCR800-110	OEM
MCR800-120	OEM
MCR800-130	OEM
MCR800-140	OEM
MCR800-150	OEM
MCR808-1	OEM
MCR808-2	OEM
MCR808-3	OEM
MCR808-4	OEM
MCR808-5	OEM
MCR808-6	OEM
MCR846-1	1095
MCR846-2	1095
MCR846-3	0240
MCR846-4	0240
MCR914-1	OEM
MCR914-2	OEM
MCR914-3	OEM
MCR914-5	OEM
MCR914-6	OEM
MCR1000-4	OEM
MCR1000-6	OEM
MCR1000-8	OEM
MCR1304-1	OEM
MCR1304-2	OEM
MCR1304-3	OEM
MCR1304-4	OEM
MCR1304-5	OEM
MCR1305-6	OEM
MCR1305R1	OEM
MCR1305R2	OEM
MCR1305R3	OEM
MCR1305R4	OEM
MCR1305R5	OEM
MCR1305R6	OEM
MCR1308-1	0464
MCR1308-2	0464
MCR1308-3	0464
MCR1308-4	0464
MCR1308-5	0717
MCR1308-6	0717
MCR1336-5	OEM
MCR1336-6	OEM
MCR1336-7	OEM
MCR1336-8	OEM
MCR1336-9	OEM
MCR1336-10	OEM
MCR1604R1	OEM
MCR1604R2	OEM
MCR1604R3	OEM
MCR1604R4	OEM
MCR1604R5	OEM
MCR1604R6	OEM
MCR1605R1	OEM
MCR1605R2	OEM
MCR1605R3	OEM
MCR1605R4	OEM
MCR1605R5	OEM
MCR1605R6	OEM
MCR1718-5	0799
MCR1718-6	0799
MCR1718-7	0799
MCR1718-8	0799
MCR1819-8	OEM
MCR1906-1	0179
MCR1906-2	0179
MCR1906-3	0179
MCR1906-4	2396
MCR1906-5	0342
MCR1906-6	0342
MCR1907-1	0717
MCR1907-2	0717
MCR1907-3	0717
MCR1907-4	0717
MCR1907-5	0717
MCR1907-6	0717
MCR2064-6	1478
MCR2080-4	OEM
MCR2080-5	OEM
MCR2080-6	OEM
MCR2080-7	OEM
MCR2080-8	OEM
MCR2080-9	OEM
MCR2080-10	OEM
MCR2080A-4	OEM
MCR2080A4	OEM
MCR2080A-5	OEM
MCR2080A5	OEM
MCR2080A-6	OEM
MCR2080A6	OEM
MCR2080A-7	OEM
MCR2080A7	OEM
MCR2080A-8	OEM
MCR2080A8	OEM
MCR2080A-9	OEM
MCR2080A9	OEM
MCR2080A-10	OEM
MCR2080A10	OEM

DEVICE TYPE	REPL CODE
MCR2150-4	OEM
MCR2150-5	OEM
MCR2150-6	OEM
MCR2150-7	OEM
MCR2150-8	OEM
MCR2150-9	OEM
MCR2150-10	OEM
MCR2150A-4	OEM
MCR2150A4	OEM
MCR2150A-5	OEM
MCR2150A5	OEM
MCR2150A-6	OEM
MCR2150A6	OEM
MCR2150A-7	OEM
MCR2150A7	OEM
MCR2150A-8	OEM
MCR2150A8	OEM
MCR2150A-9	OEM
MCR2150A9	OEM
MCR2150A-10	OEM
MCR2150A10	OEM
MCR2305-1	0464
MCR2305-2	0240
MCR2305-3	0464
MCR2305-4	0240
MCR2305-5	0717
MCR2305-6	0717
MCR2305-7	OEM
MCR2305-8	OEM
MCR2305-9	OEM
MCR2305-10	OEM
MCR2315-1	3385
MCR2315-2	1095
MCR2315-3	0240
MCR2315-4	0240
MCR2315-5	2635
MCR2315-6	0671
MCR2604-1	1478
MCR2604-2	1478
MCR2604-3	1478
MCR2604-4	1574
MCR2604-5	1574
MCR2604-6	1574
MCR2604-7	OEM
MCR2604-8	OEM
MCR2605-1	1478
MCR2605-2	1478
MCR2605-3	1478
MCR2605-4	1478
MCR2605-5	1478
MCR2605-6	1478
MCR2605-7	OEM
MCR2605-8	OEM
MCR2614L1	OEM
MCR2614L2	OEM
MCR2614L3	OEM
MCR2614L-4	1574
MCR2614L4	OEM
MCR2614L-5	1574
MCR2614L5	OEM
MCR2614L-6	1574
MCR2818-1	OEM
MCR2818-2	OEM
MCR2818-3	OEM
MCR2818-4	OEM
MCR2818-5	OEM
MCR2818-6	OEM
MCR2818-7	OEM
MCR2818-8	OEM
MCR2819-1	OEM
MCR2819-2	OEM
MCR2819-3	OEM
MCR2819-4	OEM
MCR2819-5	OEM
MCR2819-6	OEM
MCR2819-7	OEM
MCR2835-1	1640
MCR2835-2	1640
MCR2835-3	1640
MCR2835-4	1640
MCR2835-5	2623
MCR2835-6	2623
MCR2835-7	2625
MCR2835-8	2625
MCR2918-1	0717
MCR2918-2	OEM
MCR2918-3	0717
MCR2918-4	OEM
MCR2918-5	0717
MCR2918-6	OEM
MCR2918-7	OEM
MCR2918-8	OEM
MCR2935-1	0464
MCR2935-2	0464
MCR2935-3	0464
MCR2935-4	0464
MCR2935-5	0717
MCR2935-6	0717
MCR2935-7	0720
MCR2935-8	0720
MCR3000-1	4508
MCR3000-2	2255
MCR3000-3	2255
MCR3000-4	2255
MCR3000-5	3368
MCR3000-6	3368
MCR3000-7	3370
MCR3000-8	3370
MCR3000-9	0323

DEVICE TYPE	REPL CODE
MCR3000-10	OEM
MCR3818-1	1641
MCR3818-2	1641
MCR3818-3	1641
MCR3818-4	1641
MCR3818-5	1574
MCR3818-6	1574
MCR3818-7	1655
MCR3818-8	1655
MCR3818-9	OEM
MCR3818-10	OEM
MCR3835-1	1640
MCR3835-2	1640
MCR3835-3	1640
MCR3835-4	1640
MCR3835-5	2623
MCR3835-6	2623
MCR3835-7	2625
MCR3835-8	2625
MCR3835-9	OEM
MCR3835-10	OEM
MCR3918-1	3275
MCR3918-2	2174
MCR3918-3	0562
MCR3918-4	0757
MCR3918-5	3240
MCR3918-6	0735
MCR3918-7	3260
MCR3918-8	0759
MCR3918-9	OEM
MCR3918-10	OEM
MCR3935-1	3246
MCR3935-2	0726
MCR3935-3	0707
MCR3935-4	0464
MCR3935-5	0716
MCR3935-6	0717
MCR3935-7	0773
MCR3935-8	0720
MCR3935-9	0745
MCR3935-10	0745
MCR3936-10	OEM
MCR4018-1	OEM
MCR4018-2	OEM
MCR4018-3	OEM
MCR4018-4	OEM
MCR4018-5	OEM
MCR4018-6	OEM
MCR4018-7	OEM
MCR4018-8	OEM
MCR4018-9	OEM
MCR4018-10	OEM
MCR4035-1	OEM
MCR4035-2	OEM
MCR4035-3	OEM
MCR4035-4	OEM
MCR4035-5	OEM
MCR4035-6	OEM
MCR4035-7	OEM
MCR4035-8	OEM
MCR4035-9	OEM
MCR4035-10	OEM
MCS00	OEM
MCS2	0235
MCS31	OEM
MCS35	OEM
MCS101	0133
MCS105	0133
MCS2027	OEM
MCS2114-30	2037
MCS2114-35	2037
MCS2114-45	OEM
MCS2114L-30	OEM
MCS2114L-35	OEM
MCS2114L-45	2037
MCS2135	0855
MCS2137	0855
MCS2316	OEM
MCS2332	OEM
MCS2400	2221
MCS6200	OEM
MCS6201	OEM
MCS8001	OEM
MCS8004	OEM
MCS8007	OEM
MCT00	OEM
MCT02	OEM
MCT2	0272
MCT-2E	0272
MCT2E	0272
MCT4	OEM
MCT4-R	OEM
MCT6	0294
MCT8	0302
MCT10	OEM
MCT11	OEM
MCT12	OEM
MCT15	OEM
MCT18	OEM
MCT19	OEM
MCT20	OEM
MCT21	OEM
MCT24	OEM
MCT26	0311
MCT27	OEM
MCT28	OEM
MCT29	OEM
MCT36	OEM
MCT38	OEM

If replacement code is OEM, contact original manufacturer for replacement.

DEVICE TYPE	REPL CODE
MCT40	OEM
MCT41	OEM
MCT43	OEM
MCT44	OEM
MCT45	OEM
MCT46	OEM
MCT66	1393
MCT78T08K	OEM
MCT81	1407
MCT210	4347
MCT271	OEM
MCT272	OEM
MCT273	4358
MCT274	OEM
MCT275	4358
MCT276	OEM
MCT277	OEM
MCT492P	0828
MCT2114-45	OEM
MCT2114L-45	OEM
MCT2201	4449
MCT3737	OEM
MCV	0015
MCV45	OEM
MCV1055E	OEM
MCV1055F5F	OEM
MCV1055G	OEM
MCV1125	OEM
MCV1170	OEM
MCV1300	OEM
MCV1352	OEM
MCV1353	OEM
MCV1420	OEM
MCV1421	OEM
MCX6809P	OEM
MCX14032BCPD	OEM
MD04	1325
MD06	OEM
MD08	OEM
MD0232	OEM
MD0233	OEM
MD0234	OEM
MD0235	OEM
MD1	OEM
MD1D914	OEM
MD1D914A	OEM
MD1D914B	OEM
MD1F3066	OEM
MD1F3067	OEM
MD1F3068	OEM
MD1F3069	OEM
MD1F3070	OEM
MD1F3071	OEM
MD1F3458	OEM
MD1F3459	OEM
MD1F3460	OEM
MD1F3823	OEM
MD1F4391	OEM
MD1F4392	OEM
MD1F4393	OEM
MD1F4416	OEM
MD1T918	OEM
MD1T1893	OEM
MD1T2222	OEM
MD1T2369	OEM
MD1T2484	OEM
MD1T2605	OEM
MD1T2907	OEM
MD1T3251	OEM
MD1T3704	OEM
MD2	OEM
MD2D914	OEM
MD2D914A	OEM
MD2D914B	OEM
MD2F	OEM
MD3	OEM
MD3F1	OEM
MD3H1	OEM
MD3N1	OEM
MD4	OEM
MD4F	OEM
MD-4H50	OEM
MD-4N50	OEM
MD5	OEM
MD6F	OEM
MD6F1	OEM
MD6H1	OEM
MD6N1	OEM
MD8F	OEM
MD-8H10	OEM
MD-8N10	OEM
MD10	OEM
MD10F	OEM
MD10F1	OEM
MD-10F10	OEM
MD10H1	OEM
MD10N1	OEM
MD-10N10	OEM
MD-12H10	OEM
MD12H10	OEM
MD-12N10	OEM
MD12N10	OEM
MD15F1	OEM
MD15H1	OEM
MD15N1	OEM
MD20	OEM
MD20F1	OEM
MD20H1	OEM
MD20N1	OEM
MD20SH05K	OEM
MD21SC14AE10	OEM
MD21SC14AE15	OEM
MD21SC14AE25	OEM
MD-22N01	OEM
MD22N01	OEM
MD23SC16AE	OEM
MD24	OEM
MD25	OEM
MD25-0	OEM
MD25-1	OEM
MD25-2	OEM
MD25-3	OEM
MD25-4	OEM
MD-25X1	OEM
MD25X1	OEM
MD-25X1-4-1-1	OEM
MD-25X1-5-1-1	OEM
MD-25X1-6-1-1	OEM
MD31	OEM
MD32	OEM
MD-34	0143
MD34	0143
MD34A	0143
MD34B	OEM
MD35	0143
MD-36N4	OEM
MD36SH05K	OEM
MD38	0143
MD-45H01	OEM
MD45H01	OEM
MD46	0143
MD50	0133
MD50SH05K	OEM
MD54	0143
MD54SC137AF	OEM
MD54SC138AF	OEM
MD54SC139AF	OEM
MD54SC237AF	OEM
MD54SC238AF	OEM
MD54SC239AF	OEM
MD54SC240AF	OEM
MD54SC241AF	OEM
MD54SC244AF	OEM
MD54SC245AF	OEM
MD54SC540AF	OEM
MD54SC541AF	OEM
MD54SC545AF	OEM
MD56	0143
MD58	OEM
MD60	0143
MD-60A	0123
MD60A	0123
MD-60E01	OEM
MD68SC02AC	OEM
MD68SC02AF	OEM
MD74HCT374	OEM
MD74LS37M	1719
MD74LS183M	OEM
MD74SC137AC	OEM
MD74SC138AC	OEM
MD74SC139AC	OEM
MD74SC237AC	OEM
MD74SC238AC	OEM
MD74SC239AC	OEM
MD74SC240AC	OEM
MD74SC241AC	OEM
MD74SC244AC	OEM
MD74SC245AC	OEM
MD74SC373AC	OEM
MD74SC373AE	OEM
MD74SC374AC	OEM
MD74SC374AE	OEM
MD74SC533AC	OEM
MD74SC533AE	OEM
MD74SC534AC	OEM
MD74SC534AE	OEM
MD74SC540AC	OEM
MD74SC541AC	OEM
MD74SC545AC	OEM
MD74SC563AC	OEM
MD74SC563AE	OEM
MD74SC564AC	OEM
MD74SC564AE	OEM
MD74SC573AE	OEM
MD74SC574AC	OEM
MD74SC574AE	OEM
MD82HS181	OEM
MD82HS191	OEM
MD82HS321	OEM
MD82S181	OEM
MD82S191	OEM
MD82S321	OEM
MD90	OEM
MD100	OEM
MD100-0	OEM
MD100-1	OEM
MD100-2	OEM
MD100-3	OEM
MD100-4	OEM
MD-100X08C	OEM
MD101	OEM
MD102	OEM
MD106	OEM
MD121	OEM
MD-125N08C	OEM
MD125N08C	OEM
MD134	0124
MD135	0124
MD136	0124
MD137	0023
MD138	0023
MD139	0023
MD189	OEM
MD189F	OEM
MD190	OEM
MD190F	OEM
MD191	OEM
MD191F	OEM
MD210CP	OEM
MD219	OEM
MD219F	OEM
MD220	OEM
MD220F	OEM
MD221	OEM
MD221F	OEM
MD234	0124
MD235	0124
MD236	0124
MD237	0023
MD238	0023
MD358	OEM
MD402	OEM
MD420	0050
MD-430	OEM
MD-430DP	OEM
MD-430PM	OEM
MD-440	OEM
MD-440DP	OEM
MD-440PM	OEM
MD-450	OEM
MD-450DP	OEM
MD-450PM	OEM
MD501	0004
MD501B	0004
MD630	OEM
MD-630DP	OEM
MD-630PM	OEM
MD631	OEM
MD632	OEM
MD633	OEM
MD634	OEM
MD635	OEM
MD636	OEM
MD640	OEM
MD-640DP	OEM
MD-640EW	OEM
MD-640LR	OEM
MD-640NS	OEM
MD-640PM	OEM
MD-640XY	OEM
MD650	OEM
MD-650DP	OEM
MD-650EW	OEM
MD-650LRLR	OEM
MD-650NS	OEM
MD-650PM	OEM
MD-650XY	OEM
MD695	5887
MD695A	5887
MD696	5888
MD696A	5888
MD697	5887
MD697A	5887
MD698	5888
MD698A	5888
MD700	OEM
MD700Y	OEM
MD701	OEM
MD701Y	OEM
MD702	OEM
MD702Y	OEM
MD703	OEM
MD703B	OEM
MD703Y	OEM
MD704	OEM
MD704Y	OEM
MD705	OEM
MD705Y	OEM
MD706	OEM
MD706Y	OEM
MD707	OEM
MD707Y	OEM
MD708	5279
MD708A	5279
MD708AF	5279
MD708B	5279
MD708BF	5279
MD708F	5279
MD708Y	OEM
MD709	OEM
MD709Y	OEM
MD710	OEM
MD710Y	OEM
MD711	OEM
MD711Y	OEM
MD712	OEM
MD712Y	OEM
MD713	OEM
MD713Y	OEM
MD714	OEM
MD714Y	OEM
MD715	OEM
MD715Y	OEM
MD752	0157
MD752A	0157
MD753	0631
MD753A	0631
MD757	0012
MD757A	0012
MD759	0137
MD759A	0137
MD918	2034
MD918A	2034
MD918AF	2034
MD918B	2034
MD918BF	2034
MD918F	2034
MD920A8	2384
MD981	OEM
MD981F	OEM
MD982	0037
MD982F	0037
MD984	2449
MD984F	OEM
MD985	4995
MD985F	OEM
MD986	OEM
MD986F	OEM
MD990	OEM
MD1120	OEM
MD1120F	OEM
MD1121	OEM
MD1121F	OEM
MD1122	2034
MD1122F	OEM
MD1123	5135
MD1123F	OEM
MD1124	OEM
MD1124F	OEM
MD1125	OEM
MD1125F	OEM
MD1126	2034
MD1127	2034
MD1128	OEM
MD1129	2034
MD1129F	OEM
MD1130	2449
MD1130F	OEM
MD1131	2034
MD1131F	OEM
MD1132	2034
MD1132F	OEM
MD1133	OEM
MD1133F	OEM
MD1134	OEM
MD1668	OEM
MD1670	OEM
MD1672	OEM
MD1674	OEM
MD1676	OEM
MD1678	OEM
MD1680	OEM
MD1682	OEM
MD1684	OEM
MD2060F	OEM
MD2114A4	OEM
MD2114A5	OEM
MD2114AL1	OEM
MD2114AL2	OEM
MD2114AL3	OEM
MD2114AL4	OEM
MD2114L	OEM
MD2114L2	OEM
MD2114L3	OEM
MD2114L4	OEM
MD2114L5	OEM
MD2115A	OEM
MD2115A2	OEM
MD2115AL	OEM
MD2115AL2	OEM
MD2115H2	OEM
MD2115H3	OEM
MD2115H4	OEM
MD2118-4	OEM
MD2118-7	OEM
MD2118-10	OEM
MD2118-12	OEM
MD2118-15	OEM
MD2125A	OEM
MD2125A2	OEM
MD2125AL	OEM
MD2125AL2	OEM
MD2125H1	OEM
MD2125H2	OEM
MD2125H3	OEM
MD2125H4	OEM
MD2128-15	OEM
MD2128-20	OEM
MD2141-2	OEM
MD2141-3	OEM
MD2141-4	OEM
MD2141-5	OEM
MD2141L3	OEM
MD2141L4	OEM
MD2141L5	OEM
MD2142	OEM
MD2142-2	OEM
MD2142-3	OEM
MD2142L	OEM
MD2142L3	OEM
MD2147	OEM
MD2147-3	OEM
MD2147A	OEM
MD2147A3	OEM
MD2147AL	OEM
MD2147AL3	OEM
MD2147H	OEM
MD2147H1	OEM
MD2147H2	OEM
MD2147H3	OEM
MD2147HL	OEM
MD2147HL3	OEM
MD2148	OEM
MD2148-3	OEM
MD2148H	OEM
MD2148H2	OEM
MD2148H3	OEM
MD2148HL	OEM
MD2148HL3	OEM
MD2149H	OEM
MD2149H2	OEM
MD2149H3	OEM
MD2149HL	OEM
MD2149HL3	OEM
MD2164-15	OEM
MD2164-20	OEM
MD2164-25	OEM
MD2167-10	OEM
MD2167-55	OEM
MD2167-70	OEM
MD2167L70	OEM
MD2186	OEM
MD2187	OEM
MD2218	2034
MD2218A	2034
MD2218AF	OEM
MD2218F	OEM
MD2219	2034
MD2219A	2034
MD2219AF	OEM
MD2219F	OEM
MD2363B	2034
MD2369	OEM
MD2369A	2034
MD2369B	6506
MD2716	OEM
MD2716-1	OEM
MD2716-2	OEM
MD2716-5	OEM
MD2716-6	OEM
MD2732A	OEM
MD2732A2	OEM
MD2732A3	OEM
MD2732A4	OEM
MD2732A20	OEM
MD2732A25	OEM
MD2732A30	OEM
MD2764	OEM
MD2764-2	OEM
MD2764-3	OEM
MD2764-4	OEM
MD2764-25	OEM
MD2764-30	OEM
MD2764-45	OEM
MD2815	OEM
MD2815-3	OEM
MD2815-4	OEM
MD2816	OEM
MD2816-3	OEM
MD2816-4	OEM
MD2817	OEM
MD2817-3	OEM
MD2817-4	OEM
MD2904	2449
MD2904A	2449
MD2904AF	OEM
MD2904F	OEM
MD2905	2449
MD2905A	2449
MD2905AF	OEM
MD2905F	OEM
MD2974	OEM
MD2975	OEM
MD2978	OEM
MD2979	OEM
MD3133	2449
MD3133F	0150
MD3134	2449
MD3134F	0150
MD3250	2449
MD3250A	2449
MD3250AF	OEM
MD3250F	OEM
MD3251	2449
MD3251A	2449
MD3251AF	OEM
MD3251F	OEM
MD3409	2034
MD3410	2034
MD3467	OEM
MD3467F	OEM
MD3628A1	OEM
MD3628A3	OEM
MD3628A4	OEM
MD3632	OEM
MD3632-1	OEM
MD3636B	OEM
MD3636B1	OEM
MD3636B2	OEM
MD3725	OEM
MD3725F	OEM
MD3762	OEM
MD3762F	OEM
MD4260	OEM
MD4261	OEM
MD4330BC	OEM
MD4330BE	OEM
MD4332BD	OEM
MD4332BE	4847
MD4957	OEM
MD5000	OEM
MD5000A	OEM
MD5000B	OEM
MD6001	OEM
MD6001F	OEM
MD6002	OEM
MD6002F	OEM
MD6003	OEM
MD6003F	OEM
MD6100	OEM
MD6100F	OEM
MD6900	OEM
MD7000	2034
MD7001	2449
MD7001F	OEM
MD7002	2034
MD7002A	4995
MD7002B	4995
MD7003	2449
MD7003A	OEM
MD7003AF	OEM
MD7003B	OEM
MD7003F	OEM
MD7004	OEM
MD7004F	OEM
MD7005	OEM
MD7005F	OEM
MD7007	OEM
MD7007A	OEM
MD7007B	OEM
MD7007BF	OEM
MD7007F	OEM
MD7021	OEM
MD7021F	OEM
MD8001	2034
MD8002	2034
MD8003	2034
MD8035L	OEM
MD8048	OEM
MD8085A	OEM
MD8086	OEM
MD8148	OEM
MD8155	OEM
MD8212	OEM
MD8214	OEM
MD8216	OEM
MD8224	OEM
MD8226	OEM
MD8228	OEM
MD8251	OEM
MD8253	OEM
MD8255A	OEM
MD8257	OEM
MD8259A	OEM
MD8284	OEM
MD8288	OEM
MD8748	OEM
MD27128-2	1628
MD50459	OEM
MDA3U3	OEM
MDA10Z-BIN	OEM
MDA65SN1K	OEM
MDA100	0276
MDA100A	0276
MDA101	0276
MDA101A	0276
MDA102	0287
MDA102A	0287
MDA104	0293
MDA104A	0293
MDA106	0299
MDA106A	0299
MDA108	0250
MDA108A	0250
MDA110	0250
MDA110A	0299
MDA200	0276
MDA201	0276
MDA202	0287
MDA204	0293
MDA206	0299
MDA208	0250
MDA210	0250
MDA220	OEM
MDA431	OEM
MDA431SMA	OEM
MDA435	OEM
MDA435SMA	OEM
MDA438	OEM
MDA438SMA	OEM
MDA800	2347
MDA801	0319
MDA802	1404
MDA804	0468
MDA806	0441
MDA-836-1	OEM
MDA-836-2	OEM
MDA920-1	0276
MDA920-2	0015
MDA920-4	0287
MDA920-5	0293
MDA920-6	0293
MDA920-7	0299
MDA920A1	OEM
MDA920A2	4129
MDA920A3	OEM
MDA920A4	OEM
MDA920A5	OEM
MDA920A6	0106
MDA920A7	1999
MDA920A8	2384
MDA920A9	3503
MDA942-1	0287
MDA942-2	0276
MDA942-3	0287
MDA942-4	0293
MDA942-5	0293
MDA942-6	0299
MDA942A-1	0276
MDA942A1	0276
MDA942A-2	0276
MDA942A2	0287
MDA942A-3	0287
MDA942A3	0287
MDA942A-4	0293
MDA942A4	OEM
MDA942A-5	0293
MDA942A5	0293
MDA942A-6	0299
MDA942A6	0299
MDA942A7	0250
MDA952FR-1	0319
MDA952FR-2	0319
MDA952FR-3	0287
MDA952FR-4	0468
MDA952FR-5	0468
MDA960-1	0319
MDA960-2	0319
MDA960-3	1404
MDA960-4	OEM
MDA960-5	0468
MDA970-1	OEM
MDA970-2	OEM
MDA970-3	OEM
MDA970-4	OEM
MDA970-5	OEM
MDA970A1	1036
MDA970A2	1036
MDA970A3	1036
MDA970A5	1039
MDA970A6	1039
MDA980-1	1633
MDA980-2	1633
MDA980-3	1633
MDA980-4	2353
MDA980-5	2353
MDA980-6	1579
MDA990-1	2347
MDA990-2	2347
MDA990-3	2347
MDA990-4	2353
MDA990-5	2353
MDA990-6	2354
MDA1200	2347
MDA1201	2347
MDA1202	2347
MDA1204	2353
MDA1206	2354
MDA1330H	OEM
MDA1331H	OEM
MDA2061	OEM
MDA2500	5386
MDA2501	2347
MDA2502	2353
MDA2504	2353
MDA2506	2354
MDA2550	2347
MDA2551	2347
MDA3500	1633
MDA3501	1633
MDA3502	1633
MDA3504	1663
MDA3506	1663
MDA3508	4096
MDA3510	1579
MDA3550	1633
MDA3551	1493
MDA3552	1493
MDA3661	0190
MDA3662	0190
MDA7705	OEM
MDA7705SMA	OEM
MDA7708	OEM
MDA7708SMA	OEM
MDA7709SMA	OEM
MDA7710	OEM
MDA9901	2347
MDA9902	2347
MDA9903	2347
MDA9905	2353
MDA9906	2354
MDAS-8D	OEM
MDAS-16	OEM
MDB-42XX	OEM
MDB-46-206	OEM
MDB510	OEM
MDB510-500	OEM
MDB510-1000	OEM
MDB511	OEM
MDB-CR11	OEM
MDB-DA11-B0I	OEM
MDB-DA11-BJ	OEM
MDB-DA528	OEM

If replacement code is OEM, contact original manufacturer for replacement.

DEVICE TYPE	REPL CODE
MDB-DT1711	OEM
MDB-DUP11	OEM
MDB-DZ11-A	OEM
MDB-DZ11-A/422	OEM
MDB-DZ11-B	OEM
MDB-DZ11-E	OEM
MDB-KW11-P	OEM
MDB-LP11/LLO	OEM
MDB-MDU11	OEM
MDB-PC11	OEM
MDB-TA528	OEM
MDB-XY11	OEM
MDC5FA2	1227
MDC11	OEM
MDC12FA2	2219
MDC20FA2	2219
MDCZ8.2D	0244
MDCZ8.2D10	0244
MDCZ15110UT	3381
MDCZ15109UL69-536	OEM
MDCZ15110UL	3381
MDCZA6.8D	0062
MDCZA6.8D5	0062
MDCZA6.8D10	0062
MDCZA7.5D	0077
MDCZA7.5D5	0077
MDCZA7.5D10	0077
MDCZA8.2D	0165
MDCZA8.2D5	0244
MDCZA8.2D10	0244
MDCZA9.1D	0057
MDCZA9.1D5	0057
MDCZA9.1D10	0057
MDCZA10D	0064
MDCZA10D5	0064
MDCZA10D10	0064
MDCZA11D	0181
MDCZA11D5	0181
MDCZA11D10	0181
MDCZA12D	0052
MDCZA12D5	0052
MDCZA12D10	0052
MDCZA13D	0053
MDCZA13D5	0053
MDCZA13D10	0053
MDCZA14D	0873
MDCZA14D5	0873
MDCZA14D10	0873
MDCZA15D	0681
MDCZA15D5	0681
MDCZA15D10	0681
MDCZA16D	0440
MDCZA16D5	0440
MDCZA16D10	0440
MDCZA17D	0210
MDCZA17D5	0210
MDCZA17D10	0210
MDCZA18D	0371
MDCZA18D5	0371
MDCZA18D10	0371
MDCZA19D	0666
MDCZA19D5	0666
MDCZA19D10	0666
MDCZA20D	0695
MDCZA20D5	0695
MDCZA20D10	0695
MDCZA22D	0700
MDCZA22D5	0700
MDCZA22D10	0700
MDCZA24D	OEM
MDCZA24D5	OEM
MDCZA24D10	OEM
MDCZA25D	0709
MDCZA25D5	0709
MDCZA25D10	0709
MDCZA27D	0450
MDCZA27D5	0450
MDCZA27D10	0450
MDCZA28D	0257
MDCZA28D5	0257
MDCZA28D10	0257
MDCZA30D	0195
MDCZA30D5	0195
MDCZA30D10	0195
MDCZA33D	0166
MDCZA33D5	0166
MDCZA33D10	0166
MDCZA36D	0010
MDCZA36D5	0010
MDCZA36D10	0010
MDCZA39D	0032
MDCZA39D5	0032
MDCZA39D10	0032
MDCZA43D	0054
MDCZA43D5	0054
MDCZA43D10	0054
MDCZA47D	0068
MDCZA47D5	0068
MDCZA47D10	0068
MDCZA51D	0092
MDCZA51D5	0092
MDCZA51D10	0092
MDCZA56D	0125
MDCZA56D5	0125
MDCZA56D10	0125
MDCZA60D	OEM
MDCZA60D5	2301
MDCZA60D10	2301
MDCZA62D	0152
MDCZA62D5	0152
MDCZA62D10	0152
MDCZA68D	0173
MDCZA68D5	0173
MDCZA68D10	0173
MDCZA75D	0094
MDCZA75D5	0094
MDCZA75D10	0094
MDCZA82D	0049
MDCZA82D5	0049
MDCZA82D10	0049
MDCZA87D	0104
MDCZA87D5	0104
MDCZA87D10	0104
MDCZA91D	0156
MDCZA91D5	0156
MDCZA91D10	0156
MDCZA100D	0189
MDCZA100D5	0189
MDCZA100D10	0189
MDCZA105D	OEM
MDCZA105D5	OEM
MDCZA105D10	OEM
MDCZA110D	0099
MDCZA110D5	0099
MDCZA110D10	0099
MDCZA120D	0089
MDCZA120D5	0089
MDCZA120D10	0089
MDCZA130D	0285
MDCZA130D5	0285
MDCZA130D10	0285
MDCZA140D	0252
MDCZA140D5	0252
MDCZA140D10	0252
MDCZA150D	0336
MDCZA150D5	0336
MDCZA150D10	0336
MDCZA160D	0366
MDCZA160D5	0366
MDCZA160D10	0366
MDCZA175D	OEM
MDCZA175D5	OEM
MDCZA175D10	OEM
MDCZA180D	0420
MDCZA180D5	0420
MDCZA180D10	0420
MDCZA200D	1464
MDCZA200D5	1464
MDCZA200D10	1464
MDCZB6.8D	0062
MDCZB6.8D5	0062
MDCZB6.8D10	0062
MDCZB7.5D	0077
MDCZB7.5D5	0077
MDCZB7.5D10	0077
MDCZB8.2D	0244
MDCZB8.2D5	0244
MDCZB8.2D10	0165
MDCZB9.1D	0057
MDCZB9.1D5	0057
MDCZB9.1D10	0057
MDCZB10D	0064
MDCZB10D5	0064
MDCZB10D10	0064
MDCZB11D	0052
MDCZB11D5	0052
MDCZB11D10	0052
MDCZB12D	0052
MDCZB12D5	0052
MDCZB12D10	0052
MDCZB13D	0053
MDCZB13D5	0053
MDCZB13D10	0053
MDCZB14D	0053
MDCZB14D5	0053
MDCZB14D10	0053
MDCZB15D	0681
MDCZB15D5	0681
MDCZB15D10	0681
MDCZB16D	0440
MDCZB16D5	0440
MDCZB16D10	0366
MDCZB17D	0210
MDCZB17D5	0210
MDCZB17D10	0210
MDCZB18D	0371
MDCZB18D5	0371
MDCZB18D10	0371
MDCZB19D	0666
MDCZB19D5	0666
MDCZB19D10	0666
MDCZB20D	0695
MDCZB20D5	0695
MDCZB20D10	0695
MDCZB22D	0700
MDCZB22D5	0700
MDCZB22D10	0700
MDCZB25D	0709
MDCZB25D5	0709
MDCZB25D10	0709
MDCZB27D	0450
MDCZB27D5	0450
MDCZB27D10	0450
MDCZB30D	0195
MDCZB30D5	0195
MDCZB30D10	0195
MDCZB33D	0166
MDCZB33D5	0166
MDCZB33D10	0166
MDCZB36D	0010
MDCZB36D5	0010
MDCZB36D10	0010
MDCZB39D	0032
MDCZB39D5	0032
MDCZB39D10	0032
MDCZB43D	0054
MDCZB43D5	0054
MDCZB43D10	0054
MDCZB47D	0068
MDCZB47D5	0068
MDCZB47D10	0068
MDCZB51D	0092
MDCZB51D5	0092
MDCZB51D10	0092
MDCZB56D	0125
MDCZB56D5	0125
MDCZB56D10	0125
MDCZB62D	0152
MDCZB62D5	0152
MDCZB62D10	0152
MDCZB68D	0173
MDCZB68D5	0173
MDCZB68D10	0173
MDCZB75D	0094
MDCZB75D5	0094
MDCZB75D10	0094
MDCZB82D	0049
MDCZB82D5	0049
MDCZB82D10	0049
MDCZB91D	0156
MDCZB91D5	OEM
MDCZB91D10	0156
MDCZB100D	0189
MDCZB100D5	0189
MDCZB100D10	0189
MDCZB105D	OEM
MDCZB105D5	OEM
MDCZB105D10	OEM
MDCZB110D	0099
MDCZB110D5	0099
MDCZB110D10	0099
MDCZB120D	0089
MDCZB120D5	0089
MDCZB120D10	0089
MDCZB130D	0285
MDCZB130D5	0285
MDCZB130D10	0285
MDCZB140D	0252
MDCZB140D5	0252
MDCZB140D10	0252
MDCZB150D	0336
MDCZB150D5	0336
MDCZB150D10	0336
MDCZB160D	0366
MDCZB160D5	0366
MDCZB160D10	OEM
MDCZB175D	OEM
MDCZB175D5	OEM
MDCZB175D10	OEM
MDCZB180D	0420
MDCZB180D5	0420
MDCZB180D10	0420
MDCZB200D	1464
MDCZB200D5	1464
MDCZB200D10	1464
MDCZC6.8D	0062
MDCZC6.8D5	0062
MDCZC6.8D10	0062
MDCZC7.5D	0077
MDCZC7.5D5	0077
MDCZC7.5D10	0077
MDCZC8.2D	0165
MDCZC8.2D5	0244
MDCZC8.2D10	0244
MDCZC9.1D	0057
MDCZC9.1D5	0057
MDCZC9.1D10	0057
MDCZC10D	0064
MDCZC10D5	0064
MDCZC10D10	0064
MDCZC11D	0181
MDCZC11D5	0181
MDCZC11D10	0181
MDCZC12D	0052
MDCZC12D5	0052
MDCZC12D10	0052
MDCZC13D	0053
MDCZC13D5	0053
MDCZC13D10	0053
MDCZC14D	0873
MDCZC14D5	0873
MDCZC14D10	0873
MDCZC15D	0681
MDCZC15D5	0681
MDCZC15D10	0681
MDCZC16D	0440
MDCZC16D5	0440
MDCZC16D10	0440
MDCZC17D	0210
MDCZC17D5	0210
MDCZC17D10	0210
MDCZC18D	0371
MDCZC18D5	0371
MDCZC18D10	0371
MDCZC19D	0666
MDCZC19D5	0666
MDCZC19D10	0666
MDCZC20D	0695
MDCZC20D5	0695
MDCZC20D10	0695
MDCZC22D	0700
MDCZC22D5	0700
MDCZC22D10	0700
MDCZC24D	0489
MDCZC24D5	0489
MDCZC24D10	0489
MDCZC25D	0709
MDCZC25D5	0709
MDCZC25D10	0709
MDCZC27D	0450
MDCZC27D5	0450
MDCZC27D10	0450
MDCZC30D	0195
MDCZC30D5	0195
MDCZC30D10	0195
MDCZC33D	0166
MDCZC33D5	0166
MDCZC33D10	0166
MDCZC36D	0010
MDCZC36D5	0010
MDCZC36D10	0010
MDCZC39D	0032
MDCZC39D5	0032
MDCZC39D10	0032
MDCZC43D	0054
MDCZC43D5	0054
MDCZC43D10	0054
MDCZC47D	0068
MDCZC47D5	0068
MDCZC47D10	0068
MDCZC51D	0092
MDCZC51D5	0092
MDCZC51D10	0092
MDCZC56D	0125
MDCZC56D5	0125
MDCZC56D10	0125
MDCZC62D	0152
MDCZC62D5	0152
MDCZC62D10	0152
MDCZC68D	0173
MDCZC68D5	0173
MDCZC68D10	0173
MDCZC75D	0094
MDCZC75D5	0094
MDCZC75D10	0094
MDCZC82D	0049
MDCZC82D5	0049
MDCZC82D10	0049
MDCZC91D	0156
MDCZC91D5	0156
MDCZC91D10	0156
MDCZC100D	0189
MDCZC100D5	0189
MDCZC100D10	0189
MDCZC105D	OEM
MDCZC105D5	OEM
MDCZC105D10	OEM
MDCZC110D	0099
MDCZC110D5	OEM
MDCZC110D10	0099
MDCZC120D	0089
MDCZC120D5	0089
MDCZC120D10	0089
MDCZC130D	0285
MDCZC130D5	0285
MDCZC130D10	0285
MDCZC140D	0252
MDCZC140D5	0252
MDCZC140D10	0252
MDCZC150D	0336
MDCZC150D5	0336
MDCZC150D10	0336
MDCZC160D	0366
MDCZC160D5	0366
MDCZC160D10	0366
MDCZC175D	OEM
MDCZC175D5	OEM
MDCZC175D10	OEM
MDCZC180D	0420
MDCZC180D5	0420
MDCZC180D10	0420
MDCZC200D	1464
MDCZC200D5	1464
MDCZC200D10	1464
MDCZD6.8D	0062
MDCZD6.8D5	0062
MDCZD6.8D10	0062
MDCZD7.5D	0077
MDCZD7.5D5	0077
MDCZD7.5D10	0077
MDCZD8.2D	0165
MDCZD8.2D5	0244
MDCZD8.2D10	0244
MDCZD9.1D	0057
MDCZD9.1D5	0057
MDCZD9.1D10	0057
MDCZD10D	0064
MDCZD10D5	0064
MDCZD10D10	0064
MDCZD11D	0181
MDCZD11D5	0181
MDCZD11D10	0181
MDCZD12D	0052
MDCZD12D5	0052
MDCZD12D10	0052
MDCZD13D	0053
MDCZD13D5	0053
MDCZD13D10	0053
MDCZD14D	0873
MDCZD14D5	0873
MDCZD14D10	0873
MDCZD15D	0681
MDCZD15D5	0681
MDCZD15D10	0681
MDCZD16D	0440
MDCZD16D5	0440
MDCZD16D10	0440
MDCZD17D	0210
MDCZD17D5	0210
MDCZD17D10	0210
MDCZD18D	0371
MDCZD18D5	0371
MDCZD18D10	0371
MDCZD19D	0666
MDCZD19D5	0666
MDCZD19D10	0666
MDCZD20D	0695
MDCZD20D5	0695
MDCZD20D10	0695
MDCZD22D	0700
MDCZD22D5	0700
MDCZD22D10	OEM
MDCZD24D	0489
MDCZD24D5	0489
MDCZD24D10	0489
MDCZD25D	0709
MDCZD25D5	0709
MDCZD25D10	0709
MDCZD27D	0450
MDCZD27D5	0450
MDCZD27D10	0450
MDCZD28D	0257
MDCZD28D5	0257
MDCZD28D10	0257
MDCZD30D	0195
MDCZD30D5	0195
MDCZD30D10	0195
MDCZD33D	0166
MDCZD33D5	0166
MDCZD33D10	0166
MDCZD36D	0010
MDCZD36D5	0010
MDCZD36D10	0010
MDCZD39D	0032
MDCZD39D5	0032
MDCZD39D10	0032
MDCZD43D	0054
MDCZD43D5	0054
MDCZD43D10	0054
MDCZD47D	0068
MDCZD47D5	0068
MDCZD47D10	0068
MDCZD51D	0092
MDCZD51D5	0092
MDCZD51D10	0092
MDCZD56D	0125
MDCZD56D5	0125
MDCZD56D10	0125
MDCZD60D	2301
MDCZD60D5	2301
MDCZD60D10	2301
MDCZD62D	0152
MDCZD62D5	0152
MDCZD62D10	0152
MDCZD68D	0173
MDCZD68D5	0173
MDCZD68D10	0173
MDCZD75D	0094
MDCZD75D5	0094
MDCZD75D10	0094
MDCZD82D	0049
MDCZD82D5	0049
MDCZD82D10	0049
MDCZD87D	0104
MDCZD87D5	0104
MDCZD87D10	0104
MDCZD91D	0156
MDCZD91D5	0156
MDCZD91D10	0156
MDCZD100D	0189
MDCZD100D5	0189
MDCZD100D10	0189
MDCZD105D	OEM
MDCZD105D5	OEM
MDCZD105D10	OEM
MDCZD110D	0099
MDCZD110D5	0099
MDCZD110D10	0099
MDCZD120D	0089
MDCZD120D5	0089
MDCZD120D10	0089
MDCZD130D	0285
MDCZD130D5	0285
MDCZD130D10	0285
MDCZD140D	0252
MDCZD140D5	0252
MDCZD140D10	0252
MDCZD150D	0336
MDCZD150D5	0336
MDCZD150D10	0336
MDCZD160D	0366
MDCZD160D5	0366
MDCZD160D10	0366
MDCZD175D	OEM
MDCZD175D5	OEM
MDCZD175D10	OEM
MDCZD180D	0420
MDCZD180D5	0420
MDCZD180D10	0420
MDCZD200D	1464
MDCZD200D5	1464
MDCZD200D10	1464
MDCZE6.8D	0062
MDCZE6.8D5	0062
MDCZE6.8D10	0062
MDCZE7.5D	0077
MDCZE7.5D5	0077
MDCZE7.5D10	0077
MDCZE8.2D	0165
MDCZE8.2D5	0244
MDCZE8.2D10	0244
MDCZE9.1D	0057
MDCZE9.1D5	0057
MDCZE9.1D10	0057
MDCZE10D	0064
MDCZE10D5	0064
MDCZE10D10	0064
MDCZE11D	0181
MDCZE11D5	0181
MDCZE11D10	0181
MDCZE12D	0052
MDCZE12D5	0052
MDCZE12D10	0052
MDCZE13D	0053
MDCZE13D5	0053
MDCZE13D10	0053
MDCZE14D	0873
MDCZE14D5	0873
MDCZE14D10	OEM
MDCZE15D	0681
MDCZE15D5	0681
MDCZE15D10	0681
MDCZE16D	0440
MDCZE16D5	0440
MDCZE16D10	0440
MDCZE17D	0210
MDCZE17D5	0210
MDCZE17D10	0210
MDCZE18D	0371
MDCZE18D5	0371
MDCZE18D10	0371
MDCZE19D	0666
MDCZE19D5	0666
MDCZE19D10	0666
MDCZE20D	0695
MDCZE20D5	0695
MDCZE20D10	0695
MDCZE22D	0700
MDCZE22D5	0700
MDCZE22D10	0700
MDCZE24D	0489
MDCZE24D5	0489
MDCZE24D10	0489
MDCZE25D	0709
MDCZE25D5	0709
MDCZE25D10	0709
MDCZE27D	0450
MDCZE27D5	0450
MDCZE27D10	0450
MDCZE30D	0195
MDCZE30D5	0195
MDCZE30D10	0195
MDCZE33D	0166
MDCZE33D5	0166
MDCZE33D10	0166
MDCZE36D	0010
MDCZE36D5	0010
MDCZE36D10	0010
MDCZE39D	0032
MDCZE39D5	0032
MDCZE39D10	0032
MDCZE43D	0054
MDCZE43D5	0054
MDCZE43D10	0054
MDCZE47D	0068
MDCZE47D5	0068
MDCZE47D10	0068
MDCZE51D	0092
MDCZE51D5	0092
MDCZE51D10	0092
MDCZE56D	0125
MDCZE56D5	0125
MDCZE56D10	0125
MDCZE62D	0152
MDCZE62D5	0152
MDCZE62D10	0152
MDCZE68D	0173
MDCZE68D5	0173
MDCZE68D10	0173
MDCZE75D	0094
MDCZE75D5	0094
MDCZE75D10	0094
MDCZE82D	0049
MDCZE82D5	0049
MDCZE82D10	0049
MDCZE91D	0156
MDCZE91D5	0156
MDCZE91D10	0156
MDCZE100D	0189
MDCZE100D10	0189
MDCZE105D	OEM
MDCZE105D5	OEM
MDCZE105D10	OEM
MDCZE110D	0099
MDCZE110D5	0099
MDCZE110D10	0099
MDCZE120D	0089
MDCZE120D5	0089
MDCZE120D10	0089
MDCZE130D	0285
MDCZE130D5	0285
MDCZE130D10	0285
MDCZE140D	0252
MDCZE140D5	0252
MDCZE140D10	0252
MDCZE150D	0336
MDCZE150D5	0336
MDCZE150D10	0336
MDCZE160D	0366
MDCZE160D5	0366
MDCZE160D10	0366
MDCZE175D	OEM
MDCZE175D5	OEM
MDCZE175D10	OEM
MDCZE180D	0420
MDCZE180D5	0420
MDCZE180D10	0420
MDCZE200D	1464
MDCZE200D10	1464
MDCZE200E5	1464
MDCZF1.8D	OEM
MDCZF1.8D5	OEM
MDCZF1.8D10	OEM
MDCZF2.0D	OEM
MDCZF2.0D5	OEM
MDCZF2.0D10	OEM
MDCZF2.2D	OEM
MDCZF2.2D5	OEM
MDCZF2.2D10	OEM
MDCZF2.4D	1266
MDCZF2.4D5	1266
MDCZF2.4D10	1266
MDCZF2.7D	0755
MDCZF2.7D5	0755
MDCZF2.7D10	0755
MDCZF3.0D	0118
MDCZF3.0D5	0118
MDCZF3.0D10	0118
MDCZF3.3D	0296
MDCZF3.3D5	0296
MDCZF3.3D10	0296
MDCZF3.6D	0372
MDCZF3.6D5	0372
MDCZF3.6D10	0296
MDCZF3.9D	0036
MDCZF3.9D5	0036
MDCZF3.9D10	0036
MDCZF4.3D	0274
MDCZF4.3D5	0274
MDCZF4.3D10	0274
MDCZF4.7D	0140
MDCZF4.7D5	0140
MDCZF4.7D10	0140
MDCZF5.1D	0041
MDCZF5.1D5	0041
MDCZF5.1D10	0041
MDCZF5.6D	0253
MDCZF5.6D5	0253
MDCZF5.6D10	0253
MDCZF6.2D	0466
MDCZF6.2D5	0466
MDCZF6.2D10	0466
MDCZF6.8D	0062
MDCZF6.8D5	0062
MDCZF6.8D10	0062
MDCZF7.5D	0077
MDCZF7.5D5	0077
MDCZF7.5D10	0077
MDCZF8.2D	0244
MDCZF8.2D5	0244
MDCZF8.2D10	0244
MDCZF9.1D	0057
MDCZF9.1D5	0057
MDCZF9.1D10	0057
MDCZF10D	0064
MDCZF10D5	0064
MDCZF10D10	0064
MDCZF12D	0052
MDCZF12D5	0052
MDCZF12D10	0052
MDCZG2.4D	1266
MDCZG2.4D5	1266
MDCZG2.7D	0755
MDCZG2.7D5	0755
MDCZG2.7D10	0755
MDCZG3.0D	0118
MDCZG3.0D5	0118
MDCZG3.0D10	0118
MDCZG3.3D	0296
MDCZG3.3D5	0296
MDCZG3.3D10	0296
MDCZG3.6D	0372
MDCZG3.6D5	0372
MDCZG3.6D10	0372
MDCZG3.9D	0036
MDCZG3.9D5	0036
MDCZG3.9D10	0036
MDCZG4.3D	0274
MDCZG4.3D5	0274
MDCZG4.3D10	0274
MDCZG4.7D	0140
MDCZG4.7D5	0140

If replacement code is OEM, contact original manufacturer for replacement.

DEVICE TYPE	REPL CODE
MDCZG4.7D10	0140
MDCZG5.1D	0041
MDCZG5.1D5	0041
MDCZG5.1D10	0041
MDCZG5.6D	0253
MDCZG5.6D5	0253
MDCZG5.6D10	0253
MDCZG6.2D	0466
MDCZG6.2D5	0466
MDCZG6.2D10	0466
MDCZG6.8D	0062
MDCZG6.8D5	0062
MDCZG6.8D10	0062
MDCZG7.5D	0077
MDCZG7.5D5	0077
MDCZG7.5D10	0077
MDCZG8.2D	0244
MDCZG8.2D5	0244
MDCZG8.2D10	0244
MDCZG9.1D	0057
MDCZG9.1D5	0057
MDCZG9.1D10	0057
MDCZG10D	0064
MDCZG10D5	0064
MDCZG10D10	0064
MDCZG12D	0052
MDCZG12D5	0052
MDCZG12D10	0052
MDD25-04N1	1787
MDD25-06N1	1787
MDD25-08N1	1787
MDD25-12N1	1787
MDD25-14N1	OEM
MDD25-16N1	OEM
MDD41-12N1	OEM
MDD42-04N1	1787
MDD42-06N1	1787
MDD42-08N1	1787
MDD42-14N1	OEM
MDD42-16N1	OEM
MDD-43	OEM
MDD-44	OEM
MDD-45	OEM
MDD-63	OEM
MDD-64	OEM
MDD-65	OEM
MDD-450	OEM
MDD-640	OEM
MDD-650	OEM
MDG-01	OEM
MDL-11	OEM
MDL-11W	OEM
MDL221	OEM
MDL235	OEM
MDL235-TV	OEM
MDL236-TV	OEM
MDL238	OEM
MDL255-TV	OEM
MDL258	OEM
MDL259	OEM
MDL420	OEM
MDL421	OEM
MDL422	OEM
MDL2255-TV	OEM
MDL2265-TV	OEM
MDL2788SKP	OEM
MDL4755SKP	OEM
MDL4777SKP	OEM
MDP173	0133
MDS-01	OEM
MDS20	0283
MDS21	0283
MDS26	0555
MDS27	0555
MDS31	0050
MDS32	0050
MDS33	0050
MDS33A	0050
MDS33C	0050
MDS33D	0050
MDS34	0050
MDS35	0136
MDS36	0050
MDS37	0050
MDS38	0050
MDS39	0050
MDS40	0050
MDS60	2186
MDS76	1257
MDS77	1257
MDS88	OEM
MDS503	OEM
MDS1678	0930
MDS6518	0786
MDS9400	0161
MDS9401	0161
MDS9450	0455
MDS9451	0455
MDX580C	OEM
MDX580D	OEM
MDX580M	OEM
MDX580N	OEM
MDX581C	OEM
MDX581D	OEM
MDX581M	OEM
MDX581N	OEM
MDX582C	OEM
MDX582D	OEM
MDX582M	OEM

DEVICE TYPE	REPL CODE
MDX582N	OEM
MDX583C	OEM
MDX583D	OEM
MDX583M	OEM
MDX583N3N	OEM
MDX584C	OEM
MDX584D	OEM
MDX584M	OEM
MDX584N	OEM
MDX585C	OEM
MDX585D	OEM
MDX585M	OEM
MDX585N	OEM
MDX586C	OEM
MDX586D	OEM
MDX586M	OEM
MDX586N	OEM
MDX587C	OEM
MDX587D	OEM
MDX587M	OEM
MDX587N	OEM
MDX588C	OEM
MDX588D	OEM
MDX588M	OEM
MDX588N	OEM
MDX589C	OEM
MDX589D	OEM
MDX589M	OEM
MDX589N	OEM
MDX590C	OEM
MDX590D	OEM
MDX590M	OEM
MDX590N	OEM
MDX591C	OEM
MDX591D	OEM
MDX591M	OEM
MDX591N	OEM
MDX592C	OEM
MDX592D	OEM
MDX592M	OEM
MDX592N	OEM
MDX593C	OEM
MDX593D	OEM
MDX593M	OEM
MDX593N	OEM
MDX594C4C	OEM
MDX594D	OEM
MDX594M	OEM
MDX594N	OEM
MDX595C	OEM
MDX595D	OEM
MDX595M	OEM
MDX595N	OEM
MDX596C	OEM
MDX596D	OEM
MDX596M	OEM
MDX596N	OEM
MDX597C	OEM
MDX597D	OEM
MDX597M	OEM
MDX597N	OEM
MDX598C	OEM
MDX598D	OEM
MDX598M	OEM
MDX598N	OEM
MDX599C	OEM
MDX599D	OEM
MDX599M	OEM
MDX599N	OEM
MDX623	OEM
MDX624	OEM
MDX625	OEM
MDX640	OEM
MDX641	OEM
MDX642	OEM
MDX643	OEM
MDX644	OEM
MDX645	OEM
MDX646	OEM
MDX647	OEM
MDX653	OEM
MDX654	OEM
MDX655	OEM
MDXP-32	OEM
MDXP-32-1	OEM
MDX-SV1-1	OEM
MDZ-01	OEM
MDZ-02	OEM
MDZ-03	OEM
MDZ-04	OEM
MDZ-05	OEM
MDZ-06	OEM
MDZ-07	OEM
MDZ-08	OEM
MDZ-09	OEM
MDZ-10	OEM
MDZ-11	OEM
MDZ-12	OEM
MDZ-13	OEM
MDZ-14	OEM
MDZ-15	OEM
MDZ-16	OEM
MDZ-17	OEM
MDZ-18	OEM
MDZ-19	OEM
MDZ-20	OEM
MDZ-21	OEM
MDZ-22	OEM
MDZ-23	OEM

DEVICE TYPE	REPL CODE
MDZ-24	OEM
MDZ-25	OEM
MDZ-26	OEM
MDZ-27	OEM
MDZ-28	OEM
MDZ-29	OEM
MDZ-30	OEM
MDZ-31	OEM
MDZ-32	OEM
MDZ-33	OEM
MDZG2.4D10	OEM
ME0401	0150
ME0402	0150
ME0404	0037
ME0404-1	0037
ME0404-2	0037
ME0404A	0006
ME0411	0855
ME0412	0855
ME0413	0855
ME0414	0855
ME0461	0037
ME0462	0037
ME0463	0150
ME0475	0855
ME-1	0016
ME1D821	0466
ME1D821A	0466
ME1D823	0466
ME1D823A	0466
ME1D825	0466
ME1D825A	0466
ME1D826	OEM
ME1D827	0466
ME1D827A	0466
ME1D828	OEM
ME1D829	0466
ME1D935	OEM
ME1D935A	OEM
ME1D935B	OEM
ME1D936	OEM
ME1D936A	OEM
ME1D936B	OEM
ME1D937	OEM
ME1D937A	OEM
ME1D937B	OEM
ME1D938	OEM
ME1D938A	OEM
ME1D938B	OEM
ME1D939	OEM
ME1D939A	OEM
ME1D939B	OEM
ME1D940	OEM
ME1D940A	OEM
ME1D940B	OEM
ME1D941	OEM
ME1D941A	OEM
ME1D941B	OEM
ME1D942	OEM
ME1D942A	OEM
ME1D942B	OEM
ME1D943	OEM
ME1D943A	OEM
ME1D943B	OEM
ME1D944	OEM
ME1D944A	OEM
ME1D944B	OEM
ME1D945	OEM
ME1D945A	OEM
ME1D945B	OEM
ME1D946	OEM
ME1D946A	OEM
ME1D946B	OEM
ME1D4565	OEM
ME1D4565A	OEM
ME1D4566	OEM
ME1D4566A	OEM
ME1D4567	OEM
ME1D4567A	OEM
ME1D4568	OEM
ME1D4568A	OEM
ME1D4569	OEM
ME1D4569A	OEM
ME1D4570	OEM
ME1D4570A	OEM
ME1D4571	OEM
ME1D4571A	OEM
ME1D4572	OEM
ME1D4572A	OEM
ME1D4573	OEM
ME1D4573A	OEM
ME1D4574	OEM
ME1D4574A	OEM
ME1D4575	OEM
ME1D4575A	OEM
ME1D4576	OEM
ME1D4576A	OEM
ME1D4577	OEM
ME1D4577A	OEM
ME1D4578	OEM
ME1D4578A	OEM
ME1D4579	OEM
ME1D4579A	OEM
ME1D4580	OEM
ME1D4580A	OEM
ME1D4581	OEM
ME1D4581A	OEM
ME1D4582	OEM
ME1D4582A	OEM

DEVICE TYPE	REPL CODE
ME1D4583	OEM
ME1D4583A	OEM
ME1D4584	OEM
ME1D4584A	OEM
ME1Z935	OEM
ME1Z935A	OEM
ME1Z935B	OEM
ME1Z936	OEM
ME1Z936A	OEM
ME1Z936B	OEM
ME1Z937	OEM
ME1Z937A	OEM
ME1Z937B	OEM
ME1Z938	OEM
ME1Z938A	OEM
ME1Z938B	OEM
ME1Z939	OEM
ME1Z939A	OEM
ME1Z939B	OEM
ME1Z940	OEM
ME1Z940A	OEM
ME1Z940B	OEM
ME1Z941	OEM
ME1Z941A	OEM
ME1Z941B	OEM
ME1Z942	OEM
ME1Z942A	OEM
ME1Z942B	OEM
ME1Z943	OEM
ME1Z943A	OEM
ME1Z943B	OEM
ME1Z944	OEM
ME1Z944A	OEM
ME1Z944B	OEM
ME1Z945	OEM
ME1Z945A	OEM
ME1Z945B	OEM
ME1Z946	OEM
ME1Z946A	OEM
ME1Z946B	OEM
ME1.2	OEM
ME1.5	OEM
ME-2	0079
ME2	OEM
ME-3	0079
ME-4	0139
ME-5	0561
ME30	OEM
ME60	5021
ME61	OEM
ME100	OEM
ME100D	OEM
ME-116	OEM
ME116R	OEM
ME120	OEM
ME200	OEM
ME209	OEM
ME213	0016
ME213A	0016
ME214	OEM
ME216	0016
ME217	0016
ME408-02C	0244
ME409-02B	0012
ME495	OEM
ME501	0037
ME502	0037
ME503	0150
ME504	OEM
ME509	OEM
ME510	OEM
ME511	0150
ME512	0150
ME513	0786
ME900	0079
ME900A	0016
ME901	0016
ME901A	0016
ME1001	0016
ME1002	0016
ME1013	OEM
ME1075	0086
ME1100	0855
ME1110	0233
ME1120	0233
ME1138	0224
ME1303	OEM
ME2001	0016
ME2002	0016
ME3001	0259
ME3002	0127
ME3011	0127
ME3440	0168
ME4001	0016
ME4002	0016
ME4003	0016
ME4003C	0016
ME4101	0016
ME4102	0016
ME4103	0016
ME4104	0016
ME5001	0144
ME6001	0016
ME6002	0016
ME6003	0016
ME6021	OEM
ME6022	OEM
ME6101	0037
ME7021	4120

DEVICE TYPE	REPL CODE
ME7024	OEM
ME7121	6713
ME7124	OEM
ME7161	5022
ME8001	0086
ME8002	0086
ME8003	0086
ME8101	0144
ME8201	0144
ME9001	0079
ME9002	0127
ME9003	0127
ME9021	0144
ME9022	0127
ME32865-00001-B	2674
MEE-888	OEM
MEF68	OEM
MEF69	OEM
MEF70	OEM
MEF101	OEM
MEF102	OEM
MEGA-4/64	OEM
MEGA-4/128	OEM
MEGA-4/256	OEM
MEGA-4/512	OEM
MEK6800D2	OEM
MEK6800D2AT	OEM
MEK6800D2C	OEM
MEK6800D2CAT	OEM
MEK6800D2D	OEM
MEK6800D2DAT	OEM
MEL11	OEM
MEL12	OEM
MEL31	OEM
MEL32	OEM
MEL100	OEM
MEM8N08	OEM
MEM11	OEM
MEM-88	OEM
MEM100	OEM
MEM101	OEM
MEM102	OEM
MEM200	OEM
MEM201	OEM
MEM202	OEM
MEM300	OEM
MEM301	OEM
MEM302	OEM
MEM400	OEM
MEM401	OEM
MEM402	OEM
MEM515	OEM
MEM519	OEM
MEM554	0212
MEM564C	0212
MEM620	OEM
MEM621	OEM
MEM622	OEM
MEM630	0212
MEM640	OEM
MEM641	OEM
MEM642	OEM
MEM656A	OEM
MEM680	0212
MEM680Y	0212
MEM803	OEM
MEM804	OEM
MEM805	OEM
MEM808	OEM
MEM809	OEM
MEM4001	0473
MEM4007	2819
MEM4011	0215
MEM4013	0409
MEM4016	1135
MEM4049	0001
MEM4050	0394
MEM4051	0362
MEMORY-32	OEM
MEP04	OEM
MEU21	OEM
MEU22	OEM
MEX27T10	0436
MEX68KDM	OEM
MEX68KECB	OEM
MEX848-22	OEM
MEX6801	OEM
MEX6801EVM	OEM
MEX6802-46	OEM
MEX6805	OEM
MEX6816-22D	OEM
MEX6816-22S	OEM
MEX6820	OEM
MEX6821-2	OEM
MEX6832-22	OEM
MEX6850	OEM
MEX6864-1HR	OEM
MEX6864-22	OEM
MEZ1-3.3	0289
MEZ1-3.6	0188
MEZ1-3.9	0451
MEZ1-4.3	0528
MEZ1-4.7	0446
MEZ1-5.1	0162
MEZ1-5.6	0157
MEZ1-6.2	0631
MEZ1-6.8	0025
MEZ1-7.5	0644
MEZ1-8.2	0244

DEVICE TYPE	REPL CODE
MEZ1-9.1	0012
MEZ1-10	0170
MEZ1-11	0313
MEZ1-12G	0137
MEZ1-14	0100
MEZ1-15	0002
MEZ1-20	0526
MEZ1-22	0560
MEZ1-24	0398
MEZ1-26	0436
MEZ1-27	0436
MEZ1-29	0721
MEZ1-33G	0039
MEZ1-36	0814
MEZ1-39	0925
MEZ1-43	0925
MEZ1-47	0993
MEZ1-51	0497
MEZ1-55	1823
MEZ1-56	0863
MEZ1-62	0778
MEZ1-68	1258
MEZ1-82	0327
MEZ1-91	1301
MEZ1-110F	0149
MEZ1-115	0789
MEZ1-120	0186
MEZ1-128	0361
MEZ1-130	0213
MEZ1-140	0245
MEZ1-150	0028
MEZ1-160	0255
MEZ1-162	0416
MEZ1-170	0871
MEZ1-178	0490
MEZ1-180	0363
MEZ1-190	2831
MEZ1-200	0417
MEZ1-200G	0417
MEZ5.6T5	0157
MEZ5.6T10	0157
MEZ12T5	0137
MEZ12T10	0137
MEZ15T5	0002
MEZ-15T5A	0002
MEZ15T10	0002
MEZ15T10C	0002
MEZ27T5	0436
MEZ27T5A	0436
MEZ27T10	0436
MEZ27T10A	0436
MF03104F	OEM
MF0C600	OEM
MF0D100	OEM
MF0D102F	OEM
MF0D104F	OEM
MF0D200	OEM
MF0D202F	OEM
MF0D300	OEM
MF0D302F	OEM
MF0D402F	OEM
MF0D404F	OEM
MF0D405F	OEM
MF0D624F	OEM
MF0D2202	OEM
MF0D2302	OEM
MF0D2404	OEM
MF0D2405	OEM
MF0E100	OEM
MF0E102F	OEM
MF0E103F	OEM
MF0E106F	OEM
MF0E107F	OEM
MF0E108F	OEM
MF0E200	OEM
MF0E1200	OEM
MF0L02R	OEM
MF0L02T	OEM
MF2/1B	OEM
MF2A40F	OEM
MF2A100F	OEM
MF2A103F	OEM
MF2A200F	OEM
MF2A203F	OEM
MF2A403F	OEM
MF2A600F	OEM
MF2A603F	OEM
MF2A800	OEM
MF2B100F	OEM
MF2B103F	OEM
MF2B200F	OEM
MF2B203F	OEM
MF2B400F	OEM
MF2B403F	OEM
MF2B600F	OEM
MF2B603F	OEM
MF2B800	OEM
MF2B800F	OEM
MF3CN1	OEM
MF3CN3	OEM
MF3M1	OEM
MF3M3	OEM
MF3N6	OEM
MF3N12	OEM
MF5CN1	OEM
MF5CN3	OEM
MF5M1	OEM
MF5M3	OEM
MF5N6	OEM

DEVICE TYPE	REPL CODE
MF5N12	OEM
MF7N6	OEM
MF7N12	OEM
MF9N6	OEM
MF9N12	OEM
MF10	OEM
MF10-100	OEM
MF10-200	OEM
MF10A103A	OEM
MF10A203A	OEM
MF10A403A	OEM
MF10A603A	OEM
MF10B103A	OEM
MF10B203A	OEM
MF10B403A	OEM
MF10B603A	OEM
MF10B803A	OEM
MF12/1B	0201
MF12/16	0201
MF-15/1B	0201
MF15/1B	0286
MF20/1B	0286
MF20/16	0286
MF25/1B	0752
MF25/16	0374
MF-30/1B	0374
MF30/1B	0374
MF-30/16	0374
MF35-600	OEM
MF35-800	OEM
MF35-1000	OEM
MF35-1200	OEM
MF-55-62	0160
MF71-100	OEM
MF71-200	OEM
MF71-600	OEM
MF71-800	OEM
MF71-1000	OEM
MF85	OEM
MF85MATH11A	OEM
MF85MATH12	OEM
MF100	OEM
MF101	OEM
MF201-02	OEM
MF201-03	OEM
MF201-04	OEM
MF201-05	OEM
MF201-06	OEM
MF201-07	OEM
MF201-08	OEM
MF201-10	OEM
MF201-11	OEM
MF201-12	OEM
MF433	OEM
MF434	OEM
MF435	OEM
MF521	0321
MF1161	0127
MF1162	0127
MF1163	0127
MF1164	0127
MF1237SB	OEM
MF2147	OEM
MF2147-3	OEM
MF2148	OEM
MF2148-3	OEM
MF3304	0037
MF4501B-F	OEM
MFC01	OEM
MFC04	OEM
MFC05D240M	OEM
MFC05D300M	OEM
MFC05D390M	OEM
MFC05D510M	OEM
MFC05D680M	OEM
MFC08D121M	OEM
MFC08D150M	OEM
MFC08D200M	OEM
MFC08D201K	OEM
MFC08D240M	OEM
MFC08D241K	OEM
MFC08D281K	OEM
MFC08D300M	OEM
MFC08D331K	OEM
MFC08D390M	OEM
MFC08D391K	OEM
MFC08D431K	OEM
MFC08D510M	OEM
MFC08D511K	OEM
MFC08D611K	OEM
MFC08D680M	OEM
MFC08D820M	OEM
MFC10D201K	OEM
MFC10D241K	OEM
MFC10D281K	OEM
MFC10D331K	OEM
MFC10D391K	OEM
MFC10D431K	OEM
MFC10D511K	OEM
MFC10D611K	OEM
MFC14D201K	OEM
MFC14D241K	OEM
MFC14D281K	OEM
MFC14D331K	OEM
MFC14D391K	OEM
MFC14D431K	OEM
MFC14D511K	OEM
MFC14D611K	OEM
MFC4000	0512

If replacement code is OEM, contact original manufacturer for replacement.

485

DEVICE TYPE	REPL CODE
MFC4000A	0512
MFC4000B	0512
MFC4010	3731
MFC4010A	3731
MFC4030	0718
MFC4040	0718
MFC4050	2016
MFC4052	2016
MFC4060	1178
MFC4060A	1178
MFC4062	1178
MFC4062A	1178
MFC4063	3875
MFC4063A	3875
MFC4064	1661
MFC4064A	1661
MFC6010	2089
MFC6020	1865
MFC6030	OEM
MFC6030A	OEM
MFC6032	2266
MFC6032A	2266
MFC6033	3879
MFC6033A	3879
MFC6034	3879
MFC6034A	3879
MFC6040	1888
MFC6050	0618
MFC6060	3884
MFC6080	2878
MFC8020	1969
MFC8021	1969
MFC8021A	1969
MFC8030	1674
MFC8070	3887
MFCH04D200	OEM
MFCH04D300	OEM
MFCH04D510	OEM
MFCH06D200	OEM
MFCH06D300	OEM
MFCH06D510	OEM
MFCH125A200	OEM
MFE16-50	OEM
MFE16-100	OEM
MFE16-150	OEM
MFE41-50	OEM
MFE41-100	OEM
MFE41-150	OEM
MFE71-50	OEM
MFE71-100	OEM
MFE71-150	OEM
MFE120	OEM
MFE121	0212
MFE122	OEM
MFE130	0212
MFE130-712	0212
MFE131	0212
MFE132	0212
MFE140	OEM
MFE521	OEM
MFE590	0212
MFE591	0212
MFE823	OEM
MFE825	OEM
MFE910	OEM
MFE930	OEM
MFE960	OEM
MFE990	OEM
MFE2000	0321
MFE2001	0321
MFE2004	1147
MFE2005	1147
MFE2006	1147
MFE2007	1147
MFE2008	OEM
MFE2009	OEM
MFE2010	OEM
MFE2011	OEM
MFE2012	OEM
MFE2093	0321
MFE2094	0321
MFE2095	0321
MFE2097	OEM
MFE2098	1147
MFE2133	OEM
MFE3001	4150
MFE3002	0843
MFE3003	OEM
MFE3004	0843
MFE3005	0349
MFE3006	0212
MFE3007	0212
MFE-3008	0212
MFE3008	0212
MFE3020	OEM
MFE3021	OEM
MFE3954	OEM
MFE3954A	OEM
MFE3955	OEM
MFE3955A	OEM
MFE3956	OEM
MFE3957	OEM
MFE3958	OEM
MFE4007	3350
MFE4008	0321
MFE4009	0321
MFE4010	0321
MFE4011	0321
MFE4012	0321
MFE4150	OEM
MFE6659	OEM
MFE6660	OEM
MFE6661	OEM
MFE9200	OEM
MFEC2010	OEM
MFEC3002	OEM
MFEC3003	OEM
MFJ1033S	0321
MFOD100	OEM
MFOD102F	OEM
MFOD200	OEM
MFOD202F	OEM
MFOD300	OEM
MFOD302F	OEM
MFOD402F	OEM
MFOD404F	OEM
MFOD405F	OEM
MFOE71&MFOD72	OEM
MFOE100	OEM
MFOE102F	OEM
MFOE103F	OEM
MFOE106F	OEM
MFOE200	OEM
MFP121	0212
MFPT100	OEM
MFPT100A	OEM
MFPT100B	OEM
MFQ930C	OEM
MFQ960C	OEM
MFQ990C	OEM
MFR221	OEM
MFR222	OEM
MFR224	OEM
MG15G1AL2	OEM
MG21D	OEM
MG30G1BL2	OEM
MG30G2CL2	OEM
MG31C	OEM
MG31D	OEM
MG31T	OEM
MG31W	OEM
MG32D	OEM
MG50G1BL2	OEM
MG50G2CL2	OEM
MG51C	OEM
MG51D	OEM
MG51T	OEM
MG51W	OEM
MG52C	OEM
MG52D	OEM
MG52T	OEM
MG52W	OEM
MG60T1	OEM
MG61D	OEM
MG62D	OEM
MG71D	OEM
MG81D	OEM
MG91T2	OEM
MG100G1AL2	OEM
MG131A	OEM
MG131AF	OEM
MG131C	OEM
MG131CF	OEM
MG132A	OEM
MG132C	OEM
MG133A	OEM
MG133C	OEM
MG134A	OEM
MG134C	OEM
MG141A	OEM
MG141C	OEM
MG143A	OEM
MG143C	OEM
MG151A	OEM
MG151C	OEM
MG200-1	OEM
MG200-2	OEM
MG241A	OEM
MG241C	OEM
MG251A	OEM
MG251C	OEM
MG5200	OEM
MG5201	OEM
MG5213	OEM
MG5222	OEM
MG5223	OEM
MG5239	OEM
MG5240	OEM
MG7712	OEM
MGA100	OEM
MGA300	OEM
MGA500	OEM
MGA600	OEM
MGA700	OEM
MGB51C	OEM
MGB51D	OEM
MGB51T	OEM
MGB51W	OEM
MGB52C	OEM
MGB52D	OEM
MGB52T	OEM
MGB52W	OEM
MGB61D	OEM
MGB71D	OEM
MGB81D	OEM
MGC31D	OEM
MGCS821-1	OEM
MGCS821-2	OEM
MGCS821-3	OEM
MGCS821-4	OEM
MGCS821-5	OEM
MGCS821-6	OEM
MGCS924-1	OEM
MGCS924-2	OEM
MGCS924-3	OEM
MGCS924-4	OEM
MGCS924-5	OEM
MGCS924-6	OEM
MGCS925-2	OEM
MGCS925-3	OEM
MGCS925-4	OEM
MGCS925-5	OEM
MGCS925-6	OEM
MGD25	OEM
MGD47	OEM
MGD50	OEM
MGD72	0124
MGD73	OEM
MGD91	OEM
MGF1202	OEM
MGF1400	OEM
MGF1402	OEM
MGF1403	OEM
MGF1404	OEM
MGF1412	OEM
MGF1801	OEM
MGF1802	OEM
MGF2116	OEM
MGF2117	OEM
MGF2124	OEM
MGF2124F	OEM
MGF2124G	OEM
MGF2148	OEM
MGF2148F	OEM
MGF2148G	OEM
MGF2172	OEM
MGF2205	OEM
MGF-X34M	OEM
MGKD72	OEM
MGLA8.2	0244
MGLA8.2A	0244
MGLA8.2B	0244
MGLA28	OEM
MGLA28A	OEM
MGLA28B	OEM
MGLA31	OEM
MGLA31A	OEM
MGLA31B	OEM
MGLA35	OEM
MGLA35A	OEM
MGLA35B	OEM
MGLA39	0188
MGLA39A	0451
MGLA39B	0188
MGLA43	0274
MGLA43A	0274
MGLA43B	0528
MGLA47	0162
MGLA47A	0446
MGLA47B	0162
MGLA51	0162
MGLA51A	0162
MGLA51B	0162
MGLA56	0157
MGLA56A	0157
MGLA56B	0157
MGLA62	0631
MGLA62A	0631
MGLA62B	0631
MGLA68	OEM
MGLA68A	OEM
MGLA68B	0025
MGLA75	OEM
MGLA75A	OEM
MGLA75B	OEM
MGLA82	0244
MGLA82A	0244
MGLA82B	0244
MGLA91	0012
MGLA91A	0012
MGLA91B	0012
MGLA100	0170
MGLA100A	0170
MGLA100B	0170
MGM5N45	OEM
MGM5N50	OEM
MGM20N45	OEM
MGM20N50	OEM
MGP00	OEM
MGP5N45	OEM
MGP5N50	OEM
MGP10N10	OEM
MGP20N45	OEM
MGP20N50	OEM
MGT108A	OEM
MGT108B	OEM
MGT108D	OEM
MGT108G	OEM
MGT108V	OEM
MH0007CH	OEM
MH0007H	OEM
MH0009CG	OEM
MH0009G	OEM
MH0012CG	OEM
MH0012G	OEM
MH0013CG	OEM
MH0013G	OEM
MH0810	OEM
MH0816	OEM
MH0818	OEM
MH0870	OEM
MH2F	OEM
MH4F	OEM
MH-5-015-D	0229
MH6F	OEM
MH8F	OEM
MH10F	OEM
MH12F	OEM
MH14F	OEM
MH16F	OEM
MH18F	OEM
MH20F	OEM
MH-26	3639
MH60	OEM
MH63	OEM
MH65	OEM
MH67	0015
MH68	0015
MH69	2621
MH70	0015
MH71	0015
MH72	0071
MH73	0087
MH100	OEM
MH104A	0161
MH110	OEM
MH111	OEM
MH-163	OEM
MH-166	OEM
MH-167	OEM
MH214	OEM
MH320	OEM
MH321F	OEM
MH321N	OEM
MH323	OEM
MH353	1986
MH353A	1986
MH353A01	1986
MH354	0190
MH383-B01	0190
MH383B01	0190
MH401	0344
MH500	0015
MH670	0015
MH680	0015
MH700	0015
MH710	0015
MH720	0071
MH730	0071
MH745	1275
MH746	1724
MH913	1493
MH913-5	OEM
MH913A01	1493
MH914	0190
MH914A01	0190
MH915	1061
MH915A01	0405
MH915A09	0405
MH915A12	2777
MH915A13	2777
MH915C	2777
MH915C01	0405
MH915C02	2777
MH915C04	2777
MH915G01	0405
MH915G02	2777
MH919	1493
MH919A01	1493
MH919D01	1493
MH920	0190
MH920A01	0190
MH920A06	0190
MH920A07	0190
MH920A10	3805
MH920G01	1493
MH931	1493
MH931A01	1493
MH931A04	1493
MH931A07	1493
MH932	0190
MH932A01	0190
MH943	2954
MH943A01	2954
MH955A01	1493
MH955B01	1493
MH966A01	0190
MH970A02	1700
MH970C01	1188
MH970C02	1700
MH970G01	1188
MH970G02	1700
MH-983	1493
MH983A01	1493
MH983A02	1493
MH983A03	1493
MH983A04	1493
MH983D	1493
MH983D-01	1493
MH983D-02	1493
MH983D-03	1493
MH983D-04	1493
MH983G01	1493
MH984	0405
MH984A01	0405
MH984C02	2777
MH984D	0405
MH984D-01	0405
MH-985	2954
MH985	2954
MH985A	2954
MH985A01	2954
MH985D-01	2954
MH985D-02	2954
MH985G01	2954
MH-987	0190
MH987	0190
MH987A01	0190
MH987A02	0190
MH987A03	0190
MH987A04	3805
MH987D-01	0190
MH987D-02	0190
MH987D-03	0190
MH987D-04	0190
MH987G01	0190
MH987G02	OEM
MH988A03	1986
MH988B03	1986
MH988G02	1986
MH1001	2956
MH1002	1493
MH1002A01	1493
MH1011	2956
MH1011B01	1048
MH1014	2956
MH1030	2956
MH1030A01	2956
MH1030A02	1048
MH1030A03	1048
MH1030B01	2956
MH1030D-01	2956
MH1030D-02	2956
MH1030D-03	2956
MH1030G01	2956
MH1030G02	1048
MH1031C01	1048
MH1200	OEM
MH1200G01	3610
MH1201	2524
MH1201A01	2524
MH1201A03	2524
MH1201C01	2524
MH1203	1061
MH1203A01	1061
MH1203A02	1061
MH1203B01	1061
MH1203B02	1061
MH1203B03	1061
MH1203B10	1061
MH1203B13	1061
MH1204	1061
MH1204A01	1061
MH1205	1061
MH1205A01	1061
MH1206	3610
MH1206A01	3610
MH1207	3610
MH1207A01	3610
MH1209	3610
MH1209A01	3610
MH1209H02	1048
MH-1220	3610
MH1220	3610
MH1220A01	3610
MH1220G01	3610
MH-1221	1061
MH1221	1061
MH1221A	1696
MH1221A01	1061
MH1221A02	1696
MH1221D-01	1061
MH1221D-02	1061
MH1221E02	1696
MH1221G01	OEM
MH1221G02	OEM
MH-1222	2524
MH1222	2524
MH1222A01	2524
MH1222A02	2524
MH1222A03	2957
MH1222D-01	2524
MH1222D-02	2524
MH1222D-03	2524
MH1222D-04	2524
MH1222D-05	2524
MH1222D-06	2524
MH1222G01	2524
MH1222G03	2957
MH1501	0590
MH1502	0786
MH7301	OEM
MH7302	OEM
MH7303	OEM
MH8100	OEM
MH8106	OEM
MH8108	OEM
MH8111	0161
MH8112	0161
MH8113	0161
MH8121	0161
MH8122	0161
MH8123	0161
MH8131	0161
MH8132	0161
MH8133	0161
MH8134	0161
MH8136	0161
MH8500	OEM
MH8700	OEM
MH9830A01	1493
MH987001	0190
MHD611	OEM
MHD612	OEM
MHD613	OEM
MHD614	OEM
MHD615	OEM
MHD616	OEM
MHD617	OEM
MHD618	OEM
MHD619	0124
MHF15-05D03	OEM
MHM1001	0144
MHM1101	0144
MHM1201	OEM
MHM2001	OEM
MHM2011	OEM
MHM2012	OEM
MHM2013	OEM
MHM2014	OEM
MHM2015	OEM
MHM2016	OEM
MHM2017	OEM
MHM2021	OEM
MHM2101	OEM
MHM2111	OEM
MHM2112	OEM
MHM2113	OEM
MHM2114	OEM
MHM2115	OEM
MHM2116	OEM
MHM2117	OEM
MHM2201	OEM
MHM2211	OEM
MHM2212	OEM
MHM2213	OEM
MHM2214	OEM
MHM2215	OEM
MHM2216	OEM
MHM2217	OEM
MH015-02D03	OEM
MH015-04D03	OEM
MH015-05D03	OEM
MH015-06D03	OEM
MH0811	0455
MH0812	0455
MH0813	0455
MH0821	0455
MH0822	0455
MH0823	0455
MH0831	0455
MH0832	0455
MH0833	0455
MH0834	0455
MH-OKOA	1986
MHQ918	OEM
MHQ2221	OEM
MHQ2222	0539
MHQ2369	OEM
MHQ2483	OEM
MHQ2484	OEM
MHQ2906	OEM
MHQ2907	OEM
MHQ3467	OEM
MHQ3546	OEM
MHQ3798	OEM
MHQ3799	OEM
MHQ4001A	OEM
MHQ4002A	OEM
MHQ4013	OEM
MHQ4014	3180
MHQ6001	OEM
MHQ6002	OEM
MHQ6100	OEM
MHQ6842	OEM
MHR	OEM
MHT180	0435
MHT181	0435
MHT230	0435
MHT-1802	0435
MHT1802	0435
MHT-1803	0435
MHT1803	0435
MHT-1804	0435
MHT1804	0435
MHT1807	0435
MHT1808	0435
MHT1809	0435
MHT2002	0595
MHT2003	0595
MHT2004	0595
MHT2008	0595
MHT2009	0595
MHT2010	0595
MHT2305	0435
MHT2414	0086
MHT2418	0086
MHT4401	0086
MHT4402	0233
MHT4411	0086
MHT4412	0086
MHT4413	0086
MHT4414	0168
MHT4415	0168
MHT4416	0168
MHT4417	0168
MHT4418	0168
MHT4419	0168
MHT4451	0086
MHT4452	0264
MHT4453	0283
MHT4454	0283
MHT4483	0086
MHT4511	0086
MHT4512	0086
MHT4513	0086
MHT5001	0283
MHT5002	0283
MHT5003	0283
MHT5004	0283
MHT5005	0283
MHT5501	0626
MHT5506	0626
MHT5507	0161
MHT5508	0161
MHT5511	0626
MHT5901	0178
MHT5906	0042
MHT5911	0178
MHT6901	OEM
MHT6902	OEM
MHT6903	OEM
MHT6904	OEM
MHT6905	OEM
MHT6906	OEM
MHT6907	OEM
MHT6908	OEM
MHT7206	0074
MHT7207	0074
MHT7208	0074
MHT7209	0637
MHT7401	0086
MHT7411	0086
MHT7412	0086
MHT7413	0283
MHT7414	0086
MHT7415	0283
MHT7416	0283
MHT7417	0086
MHT7601	0103
MHT7602	0103
MHT7603	0103
MHT7607	0103
MHT7608	0103
MHT7609	0103
MHT8920	OEM
MHT8921	OEM
MHT8922	OEM
MHT8923	OEM
MHT9001	0086
MHT9002	0086
MHT9003	0264
MHT9004	0086
MHT9005	0086
MHT9006	0264
MHT9007	0626
MHT9008	0283
MHT9009	0283
MHT9010	0626
MHT18010	0435
MHV1.5	OEM
MHV2	OEM
MHV2.5	OEM
MHV3	OEM
MHV3.5	OEM
MHV4	OEM
MHV5	OEM
MHV6	OEM
MHV7	OEM
MHV8	OEM
MHV9	OEM
MHV10	OEM
MHVG10	OEM
MHVG20	OEM
MHVG30	OEM
MHVG40	OEM
MHVG50	OEM
MHVG60	OEM
MHVS10	OEM
MHVS20	OEM
MHVS30	OEM
MHVS40	OEM
MHVS50	OEM
MHVS60	OEM
MHW252	OEM
MHW401-1	OEM
MHW401-2	OEM
MHW401-3	OEM
MHW590	OEM
MHW591	OEM
MHW592	OEM
MHW593	OEM
MHW612	OEM
MHW612A	OEM
MHW613A	OEM
MHW709-1	OEM
MHW709-2	OEM
MHW709-3	OEM
MHW710-1	OEM
MHW710-2	OEM
MHW710-3	OEM
MHW720-1	OEM
MHW720-2	OEM

If replacement code is OEM, contact original manufacturer for replacement.

DEVICE TYPE	REPL CODE
MHW1121	OEM
MHW1122	OEM
MHW1134	OEM
MHW1171	OEM
MHW1171R	OEM
MHW1172	OEM
MHW1172R	OEM
MHW1182	OEM
MHW1184	OEM
MHW1221	OEM
MHW1222	OEM
MHW1224	OEM
MHW1244	OEM
MHW1341	OEM
MHW1342	OEM
MHW1343	OEM
MHW1344	OEM
MHW2172	OEM
MHW4171	OEM
MHW4172	OEM
MHW5122	OEM
MHW5171	OEM
MHW5172	OEM
MHW5222	OEM
MHW5342	OEM
MHW6171	OEM
MHW6172	OEM
MHZ016	OEM
MHZ018	OEM
MHZ018Y	OEM
MI12	OEM
MI13	OEM
MI14	OEM
MI-15	1791
MI15	OEM
MI-15MR	1089
MI-15MS	1791
MI-15R	1089
MI15RC	0015
MI-15S	1791
MI15S	0015
MI15SC	0015
MI16	OEM
MI22	OEM
MI23	OEM
MI24	OEM
MI25	OEM
MI31T	OEM
MI51	OEM
MI51T	OEM
MI52	OEM
MI53	OEM
MI54	OEM
MI89	OEM
MI90	OEM
MI95	OEM
MI-101	0196
MI101	OEM
MI-101R	1089
MI101R	OEM
MI-102	1791
MI102	OEM
MI-102R	1089
MI102R	OEM
MI-104	0199
MI104	OEM
MI-104R	1009
MI104R	OEM
MI105	OEM
MI-106	0199
MI106	OEM
MI-106R	1009
MI106R	OEM
MI120	OEM
MI137	OEM
MI-151	0199
MI151	0196
MI-151R	1009
MI151R	1073
MI-152	0199
MI152	0199
MI-152A	0199
MI152A	0071
MI-152DR	3460
MI-152DS	0199
MI-152R	1009
MI152R	1089
MI-152RA	1009
MI152RA	0071
MI-154	0199
MI-154R	1009
MI154R	OEM
MI-156	0199
MI-156R	1009
MI156R	OEM
MI158-1	OEM
MI202	OEM
MI204	OEM
MI206	OEM
MI268	OEM
MI-301	0133
MI301	0133
MI303	OEM
MI308	OEM
MI402	0023
MI407	OEM
MI501M	OEM
MI505	OEM
MI507	OEM
MI508	OEM
MI509A	OEM
MI509B	OEM
MI509D	OEM
MI509E	OEM
MI509G	OEM
MI509V	OEM
MI521A2	OEM
MI521B2	OEM
MI521D2	OEM
MI521G2	OEM
MI521V2	OEM
MI522	OEM
MI588AM	OEM
MI589A	OEM
MI589B	OEM
MI589V	OEM
MI1546	0144
MI7001	OEM
MI7002	OEM
MI7022	OEM
MIC33T	OEM
MIC33TSA	OEM
MIC33TSB	OEM
MIC33TSC	OEM
MIC33TSD	OEM
MIC33TSE	OEM
MIC723-1	1183
MIC741-5C	0406
MIC930-5D	1812
MIC930-5P	1812
MIC931-5D	3032
MIC931-5P	3032
MIC932-5D	1035
MIC932-5P	1035
MIC933-5D	2086
MIC933-5P	2086
MIC935-5D	1168
MIC935-5P	1168
MIC936-5D	1820
MIC936-5P	1820
MIC937-5D	1824
MIC937-5P	1824
MIC941-5D	2598
MIC941-5P	2598
MIC944-5D	0033
MIC944-5P	0033
MIC945-5D	0081
MIC945-5P	0081
MIC946-5D	0141
MIC946-5P	0141
MIC948-5D	3365
MIC948-5P	3365
MIC949-5D	1833
MIC949-5P	1833
MIC950-5D	2595
MIC950-5P	2595
MIC951-5D	2067
MIC951-5P	2067
MIC961-5D	1848
MIC961-5P	1848
MIC962-5D	0557
MIC962-5P	0557
MIC963-5D	0337
MIC963-5P	0337
MIC7400J	0232
MIC7400N	0232
MIC7401J	0268
MIC7401N	0268
MIC7402J	0310
MIC7402N	0310
MIC7403J	0331
MIC7403N	0331
MIC7404J	0357
MIC7404N	0357
MIC7405J	0381
MIC7405N	0381
MIC7410J	0507
MIC7410N	0507
MIC7413J	1432
MIC7413N	1432
MIC7420J	0692
MIC7420N	0692
MIC7426J	0798
MIC7426N	0798
MIC7428J	4117
MIC7428N	4117
MIC7430J	0867
MIC7430N	0867
MIC7440J	1018
MIC7440N	1018
MIC7441AJ	1032
MIC7441AN	1032
MIC7442J	1046
MIC7442N	1046
MIC7443J	1054
MIC7443N	1054
MIC7444J	1066
MIC7444N	1066
MIC7445J	1074
MIC7445N	1074
MIC7450J	0738
MIC7450N	0738
MIC7451J	1160
MIC7451N	1160
MIC7453J	1177
MIC7453N	1177
MIC7454J	1193
MIC7454N	1193
MIC7460J	1265
MIC7460N	1265
MIC7470J	1394
MIC7470N	1394
MIC7472J	1417
MIC7472N	1417
MIC7473J	1164
MIC7473N	1164
MIC7474J	1303
MIC7474N	1303
MIC7475J	1423
MIC7475N	1423
MIC7476J	1150
MIC7476N	1150
MIC7481J	3092
MIC7481N	3092
MIC7482J	1564
MIC7482N	1564
MIC7483J	0117
MIC7483N	0117
MIC7486J	1358
MIC7486N	1358
MIC7490J	1199
MIC7490N	1199
MIC7491AJ	0974
MIC7491AN	0974
MIC7492J	0828
MIC7492N	0828
MIC7493J	0564
MIC7493N	0564
MIC7494J	1692
MIC7494N	1692
MIC7495J	1477
MIC7495N	1477
MIC7496J	1705
MIC9093-5D	0354
MIC9093-5P	0354
MIC9094-5D	1622
MIC9094-5P	1622
MIC9097-5D	1472
MIC9097-5P	1472
MIC9099-5D	0329
MIC9099-5P	0329
MIC74107J	0936
MIC74107N	0936
MIC74121J	0175
MIC74121N	0175
MIC74145J	0614
MIC74145N	0614
MIC74150J	1484
MIC74150N	1484
MIC74151J	1487
MIC74151N	1487
MIC74154J	1546
MIC74154N	1546
MIC74155J	1566
MIC74155N	1566
MIC74156J	1582
MIC74156N	1582
MIC74180J	1818
MIC74180N	1818
MIC77413J	1432
MID241	OEM
MID400	OEM
MII66003-001	OEM
MII66003-002	OEM
MII66003-003	OEM
MII66004-001	OEM
MII66004-002	OEM
MII66005-001	OEM
MII66005-002	OEM
MIKUL500	OEM
MIKUL509	OEM
MIKUL514M	OEM
MIKUL519	OEM
MIKUL576	OEM
MIKUL580	OEM
MIKUL598-4	OEM
MIKUL598-6	OEM
MIKUL598-8	OEM
MIKUL900-4	OEM
MIKUL900-6	OEM
MIKUL902	OEM
MIKUL991	OEM
MIKUL993	OEM
MIKUL995	OEM
MIKUL996	OEM
MIKUL997	OEM
MIKUL998	OEM
MIKUL6001	OEM
MIKUL6004	OEM
MIKUL6009-5	OEM
MIKUL6009-6	OEM
MIKUL6009-10	OEM
MIKUL6009-12	OEM
MIKUL6017	OEM
MIKUL6019	OEM
MIKUL6032	OEM
MIKUL6045	OEM
MIKUL6047	OEM
MIKUL6077	OEM
MIKUL6809-2	OEM
MIKUL6809-3	OEM
MIKUL6882	OEM
MIKUL60640	OEM
MIKUL60641	OEM
MINT-01-01	OEM
MINT-01-02	OEM
MIOV42092-056	OEM
MIOV42092-066	OEM
MIOV42092-076	OEM
MIOV42092-086	OEM
MIOV42092-096	OEM
MIOV42092-106	OEM
MIOV42092-126	OEM
MIOV42092-146	OEM
MIOV42092-166	OEM
MIOV42092-186	OEM
MIOV42092-206	OEM
MIOV42092-510	OEM
MIOV42092-515	OEM
MIOV42092-610	OEM
MIOV42092-615	OEM
MIOV42092-710	OEM
MIOV42092-715	OEM
MIOV42092-810	OEM
MIOV42092-815	OEM
MIOV42092-910	OEM
MIOV42092-915	OEM
MIOV42092-1010	OEM
MIOV42092-1015	OEM
MIOV42092-1210	OEM
MIOV42092-1215	OEM
MIOV42092-1410	OEM
MIOV42092-1415	OEM
MIOV42092-1610	OEM
MIOV42092-1615	OEM
MIOV42092-1810	OEM
MIOV42092-1815	OEM
MIOV42092-2010	OEM
MIOV42092-2015	OEM
MIOV42093-0520	OEM
MIOV42093-0525	OEM
MIOV42093-0530	OEM
MIOV42093-0535	OEM
MIOV42093-0620	OEM
MIOV42093-0625	OEM
MIOV42093-0630	OEM
MIOV42093-0635	OEM
MIOV42093-0720	OEM
MIOV42093-0725	OEM
MIOV42093-0730	OEM
MIOV42093-0735	OEM
MIOV42093-0820	OEM
MIOV42093-0825	OEM
MIOV42093-0830	OEM
MIOV42093-0835	OEM
MIOV42093-0920	OEM
MIOV42093-0925	OEM
MIOV42093-0930	OEM
MIOV42093-0935	OEM
MIOV42093-1020	OEM
MIOV42093-1025	OEM
MIOV42093-1030	OEM
MIOV42093-1035	OEM
MIOV42093-1220	OEM
MIOV42093-1225	OEM
MIOV42093-1230	OEM
MIOV42093-1235	OEM
MIOV42093-1420	OEM
MIOV42093-1425	OEM
MIOV42093-1430	OEM
MIOV42093-1435	OEM
MIOV42093-1620	OEM
MIOV42093-1625	OEM
MIOV42093-1630	OEM
MIOV42093-1635	OEM
MIOV42093-1820	OEM
MIOV42093-1825	OEM
MIOV42093-1830	OEM
MIOV42093-1835	OEM
MIOV42093-2020	OEM
MIOV42093-2025	OEM
MIOV42093-2030	OEM
MIOV42093-2035	OEM
MIS-181C1-4	1035
MIS-18101-3	1812
MIS-18101-5	0081
MIV-843	OEM
MIV42050-284	OEM
MIVR42050-055	OEM
MIVR42050-109	OEM
MIVR42050-128	OEM
MIVR42050-148	OEM
MIVR42050-158	OEM
MIVR42050-168	OEM
MIVR42050-188	OEM
MIVR42050-208	OEM
MIVR42050-224	OEM
MIVR42050-244	OEM
MIVR42050-264	OEM
MIVR42050-304	OEM
MIVR42050-324	OEM
MIVR42050-344	OEM
MIVR42050-510	OEM
MIVR42050-610	OEM
MIVR42050-710	OEM
MIVR42050-810	OEM
MIVR42050-910	OEM
MIVR42051-055	OEM
MIVR42051-065	OEM
MIVR42051-075	OEM
MIVR42051-085	OEM
MIVR42051-095	OEM
MIVR42051-105	OEM
MIVR42051-124	OEM
MIVR42051-144	OEM
MIVR42051-154	OEM
MIVR42051-164	OEM
MIVR42051-184	OEM
MIVR42051-204	OEM
MIVR42051-223	OEM
MIVR42051-243	OEM
MIVR42051-263	OEM
MIVR42051-283	OEM
MIVR42051-303	OEM
MIVR42051-323	OEM
MIVR42051-343	OEM
MIVR42052-055	OEM
MIVR42052-109	OEM
MIVR42052-128	OEM
MIVR42052-148	OEM
MIVR42052-158	OEM
MIVR42052-168	OEM
MIVR42052-188	OEM
MIVR42052-208	OEM
MIVR42052-224	OEM
MIVR42052-244	OEM
MIVR42052-264	OEM
MIVR42052-284	OEM
MIVR42052-304	OEM
MIVR42052-324	OEM
MIVR42052-344	OEM
MIVR42052-510	OEM
MIVR42052-610	OEM
MIVR42052-710	OEM
MIVR42052-810	OEM
MIVR42052-910	OEM
MIVR42055-0520	OEM
MIVR42055-0620	OEM
MIVR42055-0720	OEM
MIVR42055-0820	OEM
MIVR42055-0920	OEM
MIVR42055-1020	OEM
MIVR42055-1216	OEM
MIVR42055-1416	OEM
MIVR42055-1516	OEM
MIVR42055-1612	OEM
MIVR42055-1812	OEM
MIVR42055-2010	OEM
MIVR42055-2210	OEM
MIVR42055-2410	OEM
MIVR42055-2608	OEM
MIVR42055-2808	OEM
MIVR42094-005	OEM
MIVR42094-012	OEM
MIVR42094-015	OEM
MIVR42094-018	OEM
MIVR42094-024	OEM
MIVR42094-030	OEM
MIVR42095-005	OEM
MIVR42095-012	OEM
MIVR42095-015	OEM
MIVR42095-018	OEM
MIVR42095-024	OEM
MIVR42095-030	OEM
MJ105	0065
MJ139A	0155
MJ205	OEM
MJ320	OEM
MJ335	OEM
MJ340	0275
MJ400	0142
MJ410	0270
MJ411	0270
MJ413	0359
MJ420	0233
MJ420S	0233
MJ-421	0187
MJ421	0187
MJ421S	0187
MJ423	1955
MJ424	0637
MJ425	0637
MJ431	0359
MJ432	0359
MJ440	0626
MJ450	1671
MJ480	0103
MJ481	0103
MJ490	2002
MJ491	2002
MJ802	0130
MJ804	OEM
MJ900	2262
MJ901	2262
MJ920	2262
MJ921	2262
MJ1000	2411
MJ1001	2411
MJ1200	2411
MJ1201	2411
MJ1800	0270
MJ2249	0424
MJ2250	0424
MJ-2251	0086
MJ2251	0142
MJ2252	0142
MJ2253	0899
MJ2254	0899
MJ2267	1588
MJ2268	1588
MJ2300	OEM
MJ2305	OEM
MJ2500	3340
MJ2500M	OEM
MJ2501	3340
MJ2800	0103
MJ2801	0103
MJ2802	0103
MJ2840	0538
MJ2841	0538
MJ2901	0486
MJ2940	1671
MJ2941	1671
MJ2955	0486
MJ2955A	5371
MJ3000	3339
MJ3001	3339
MJ-3010	0074
MJ3010	0309
MJ3011	0309
MJ3026	0074
MJ3027	0074
MJ3028	0270
MJ3029	1980
MJ3030	0359
MJ3040	2602
MJ3042	2602
MJ3101	0424
MJ3201	0142
MJ3202	0142
MJ3237	OEM
MJ3238	OEM
MJ3247	OEM
MJ3248	OEM
MJ3260	0359
MJ3430	1955
MJ3480	0065
MJ3520	3339
MJ3521	3339
MJ3583	1021
MJ3584	1021
MJ3701	0899
MJ3738	OEM
MJ3739	OEM
MJ3760	0359
MJ3761	0359
MJ3771	0130
MJ3772	0130
MJ3773	0538
MJ4000	2411
MJ4001	2411
MJ4010	2262
MJ4011	2262
MJ4030	2429
MJ4031	2429
MJ4032	2429
MJ4033	1384
MJ4034	1384
MJ4035	1384
MJ4101	0178
MJ4102	0178
MJ4237	5534
MJ4238	5534
MJ4247	5535
MJ4248	5535
MJ4360	OEM
MJ4361	OEM
MJ4380	OEM
MJ4381	OEM
MJ4400	OEM
MJ4401	OEM
MJ4502	1671
MJ4645	0126
MJ4646	5606
MJ4648	5606
MJ5202	0178
MJ5203	0178
MJ5204	0178
MJ5257	0130
MJ5415	0434
MJ5416	0126
MJ5602	0538
MJ5603	0538
MJ6002	0538
MJ6257	0130
MJ6302	0177
MJ6502	3354
MJ6503	3354
MJ7160	0074
MJ7161	0074
MJ8100	1257
MJ8101	0617
MJ8400	0065
MJ8500	OEM
MJ8501	3446
MJ8502	3446
MJ8503	3446
MJ8504	0637
MJ8505	OEM
MJ9000	0359
MJ10000	2602
MJ10001	2602
MJ10002	1980
MJ10003	1980
MJ10004	2602
MJ10005	2602
MJ10006	1980
MJ10007	1980
MJ10008	2602
MJ10009	2602
MJ10010	OEM
MJ10011	4954
MJ10012	2602
MJ10013	OEM
MJ10014	OEM
MJ10015	3956
MJ10016	OEM
MJ10020	OEM
MJ10021	OEM
MJ10022	3956
MJ10023	3956
MJ10024	OEM
MJ10025	OEM
MJ10041	OEM
MJ10042	OEM
MJ10044	OEM
MJ10045	OEM
MJ10047	OEM
MJ10048	OEM
MJ10050	OEM
MJ10051	OEM
MJ10052	OEM
MJ10100	OEM
MJ10101	OEM
MJ10102	OEM
MJ10200	OEM
MJ10201	OEM
MJ10202	OEM
MJ11011	2404
MJ11012	2412
MJ11013	2404
MJ11014	2412
MJ11015	2404
MJ11016	2412
MJ11017	OEM
MJ11018	OEM
MJ11019	OEM
MJ11020	OEM
MJ11021	OEM
MJ11022	OEM
MJ11028	2412
MJ11029	2404
MJ11030	2412
MJ11031	2404
MJ11032	2412
MJ11033	2404
MJ12002	0309
MJ12003	0223
MJ12004	0309
MJ12005	0223
MJ12005D	OEM
MJ12010	3353
MJ12020	5316
MJ12021	5316
MJ12022	5316
MJ13014	1955
MJ13015	3354
MJ13070	4511
MJ13071	4511
MJ13080	3354
MJ13081	3354
MJ13090	3354
MJ13091	3354
MJ13100	OEM
MJ13101	OEM
MJ13330	4315
MJ13331	4315
MJ13332	1841
MJ13333	1841
MJ13334	1841
MJ13335	1841
MJ14000	OEM
MJ14001	OEM
MJ14002	OEM
MJ14003	OEM
MJ15001	0177
MJ15002	2002
MJ15003	3656
MJ15004	4081
MJ15011	0861
MJ15012	3561
MJ15015	2398
MJ15016	3561
MJ15022	0538
MJ15023	1588
MJ15024	2398
MJ15025	3561
MJ15026	OEM
MJ15027	OEM
MJ16002	5316
MJ16004	5316
MJ16006	3446
MJ16008	3446
MJ16010	5316
MJ16012	5316
MJ16014	OEM
MJ16016	OEM
MJ212007	OEM
MJ336941	OEM
MJ338978	OEM
MJ338986	OEM
MJ338987	OEM
MJ338995	OEM
MJ373034	OEM
MJA22219	OEM
MJC574J	1319
MJC10007	OEM
MJC10009	OEM
MJC10011	OEM
MJC10012	OEM
MJE29	0419
MJE29A	0419
MJE29B	0419

If replacement code is OEM, contact original manufacturer for replacement.

487

DEVICE TYPE	REPL CODE
MJE29C	0419
MJE30	0848
MJE30A	0848
MJE30B	0848
MJE30C	1190
MJE31	0419
MJE31A	0419
MJE31B	0419
MJE31C	0419
MJE32	0848
MJE32A	0848
MJE-32B	0848
MJE32B	0848
MJE32C	1190
MJE33	0419
MJE33A	0419
MJE33B	0419
MJE33C	0419
MJE34	0919
MJE34A	1190
MJE34B	1190
MJE34C	1190
MJE41	0419
MJE41A	0419
MJE41B	0419
MJE41C	0419
MJE-42	0848
MJE42	0848
MJE42A	0848
MJE42B	0848
MJE42C	1190
MJE-47	0388
MJE47	OEM
MJE-48	0388
MJE48	OEM
MJE-49	0168
MJE49	OEM
MJE-50	0168
MJE51T	2792
MJE52T	2792
MJE53T	2792
MJE101	0919
MJE102	0919
MJE103	0919
MJE104	1190
MJE105	1190
MJE105K	3136
MJE170	0848
MJE171	0455
MJE172	0676
MJE180	0161
MJE181	0556
MJE182	0556
MJE-200	0219
MJE200	0161
MJE-200E	0219
MJE200E	0161
MJE201	0042
MJE202	0042
MJE203	0556
MJE204	0556
MJE205	0556
MJE205K	2969
MJE210	0848
MJE-220	0161
MJE220	0161
MJE221	0161
MJE222	0161
MJE223	0161
MJE224	0161
MJE225	0161
MJE230	0455
MJE231	0455
MJE232	0455
MJE233	0455
MJE234	0455
MJE235	0455
MJE240	0060
MJE241	0060
MJE242	0060
MJE250	1298
MJE251	1298
MJE252	1298
MJE270	2529
MJE271	2533
MJE340	0275
MJE340K	0275
MJE341	0275
MJE341K	0275
MJE344	0275
MJE344D	0168
MJE344K	0275
MJE345	0283
MJE350	0520
MJE370	0455
MJE370K	3136
MJE371	0455
MJE371K	3136
MJE423	0074
MJE488	0161
MJE520	0161
MJE520K	0042
MJE-521	0161
MJE521	0161
MJE521K	2969
MJE700	2869
MJE700T	0597
MJE701	2869
MJE701T	0597
MJE702	2869
MJE702T	0597
MJE703	2869
MJE703T	0597
MJE710	0455
MJE711	0455
MJE712	1190
MJE720	0161
MJE721	0161
MJE722	0556
MJE800	0553
MJE800T	1203
MJE801	0553
MJE801T	1203
MJE802	0553
MJE802T	1203
MJE803	0553
MJE803T	1203
MJE1033G	OEM
MJE1090	3486
MJE1091	3486
MJE1092	3486
MJE1093	3486
MJE1100	3343
MJE1101	3343
MJE1102	3343
MJE1103	3343
MJE1290	1190
MJE1291	1190
MJE1305	OEM
MJE1660	0556
MJE1661	0556
MJE2010	0848
MJE-2011	0556
MJE2011	0556
MJE-2020	1190
MJE2020	1190
MJE2021	0419
MJE2050	0161
MJE2090	2222
MJE2091	0597
MJE2092	0597
MJE2093	0597
MJE2100	2220
MJE2101	2220
MJE2102	2220
MJE2103	2220
MJE2150	0455
MJE2360	0168
MJE2360T	0168
MJE2361	0168
MJE2361T	0168
MJE2370	3136
MJE2371	3136
MJE2380	0419
MJE2381	0419
MJE2382	0419
MJE2383	0419
MJE2480	2969
MJE2481	2969
MJE2482	2969
MJE2483	2969
MJE2490	3136
MJE2491	3136
MJE2520	2969
MJE2521	2969
MJE2522	2969
MJE2523	2969
MJE2801	0556
MJE2801K	0556
MJE2801T	0477
MJE2901	1190
MJE2901K	1190
MJE2901T	1359
MJE2940	0103
MJE2955	1190
MJE2955K	1190
MJE2955T	1359
MJE2995T	OEM
MJE3054	2969
MJE3055	0556
MJE3055K	0556
MJE3055T	0477
MJE3300	6432
MJE3301	6433
MJE3302	6433
MJE3310	6434
MJE3311	6434
MJE3312	6434
MJE3370	0455
MJE3371	0455
MJE3439	0841
MJE3440	0275
MJE3520	0042
MJE3521	0161
MJE3730	0388
MJE3738	0275
MJE3739	0275
MJE3740	3136
MJE3741	3136
MJE4340	3401
MJE4341	3401
MJE4342	3401
MJE4343	3401
MJE4350	3628
MJE4351	3628
MJE4352	3628
MJE4353	3628
MJE4918	1045
MJE4919	1045
MJE4920	0455
MJE4921	0161
MJE4922	0161
MJE4923	0161
MJE5170	OEM
MJE5171	OEM
MJE5172	OEM
MJE5180	OEM
MJE5181	OEM
MJE5182	OEM
MJE5190	0161
MJE5191	0161
MJE5192	0161
MJE5192J	OEM
MJE5193	0455
MJE5194	0455
MJE5195	0455
MJE5655	0275
MJE5656	0275
MJE5657	0168
MJE5740	OEM
MJE5741	OEM
MJE5742	OEM
MJE5850	5577
MJE5851	5577
MJE5852	5577
MJE5974	1190
MJE5975	1190
MJE5976	1190
MJE5977	0556
MJE5978	0556
MJE5979	0556
MJE5980	1190
MJE5981	1190
MJE5982	1190
MJE5983	0556
MJE5984	0556
MJE5985	0556
MJE6040	3488
MJE6041	3488
MJE6042	3488
MJE6043	3487
MJE6044	3487
MJE6045	3487
MJE8500	6819
MJE8501	OEM
MJE8502	OEM
MJE8503	OEM
MJE9400	0161
MJE9400-2	0161
MJE9411T	0144
MJE9730	0388
MJE9742	0275
MJE10000	OEM
MJE10001	OEM
MJE12004	OEM
MJE12007	2739
MJE13002	OEM
MJE13003	OEM
MJE13004	2985
MJE13005	0723
MJE13006	0723
MJE13007	0723
MJE13007A	2880
MJE13008	6582
MJE13009	0723
MJE13070	6587
MJE13071	6007
MJE15028	1157
MJE15029	6715
MJE15030	0388
MJE15031	0676
MJE16002	6007
MJE16002P	OEM
MJE16004	6007
MJE16004P	OEM
MJE16080	6007
MJE16081	4510
MJEC244	OEM
MJEC254	OEM
MJEC3302	OEM
MJEC3312	OEM
MJEC13009	OEM
MJEC15030	OEM
MJEC15031	OEM
MJF1033G	0321
MJF3370	0919
MJF10335	0321
MJG194	1190
MJM2229	OEM
MK-10	0321
MK10	0321
MK-10-2	0321
MK10-2	0321
MK-10-E	0321
MK10-E	0321
MK38C70/20J	OEM
MK38C70/20N	OEM
MK38C70/20P	OEM
MK38P70/02R-00	OEM
MK38P70/02R-05	OEM
MK38P70/02R-10	OEM
MK38P70/02R-15	OEM
MK38P73/02R-10	OEM
MK38P73/02R-15	OEM
MK102	0321
MK104	OEM
MK-111	OEM
MK279-14	0062
MK279-27	0490
MK433	OEM
MK585	0321
MK1002L	OEM
MK1002P	OEM
MK3805N	OEM
MK3807	OEM
MK3850N3F8	OEM
MK3850N13F8	OEM
MK3850P13F8	OEM
MK3850P23F8	OEM
MK3851N	OEM
MK3851P	OEM
MK3852N	OEM
MK3852N10	OEM
MK3852P	OEM
MK3852P10	OEM
MK3853N	OEM
MK3853N10	OEM
MK3853N20	OEM
MK3853P	OEM
MK3853P10	OEM
MK3853P20	OEM
MK3854N	OEM
MK3854N10	OEM
MK3854P	OEM
MK3854P10	OEM
MK3861	OEM
MK3870/10J-05	OEM
MK3870/10J-10	OEM
MK3870/10J-15	OEM
MK3870/10N-05	OEM
MK3870/10N-10	OEM
MK3870/10N-15	OEM
MK3870/10P-05	OEM
MK3870/10P-10	OEM
MK3870/10P-15	OEM
MK3870/12J-05	OEM
MK3870/12J-10	OEM
MK3870/12J-15	OEM
MK3870/12N-05	OEM
MK3870/12N-10	OEM
MK3870/12N-15	OEM
MK3870/12P-05	OEM
MK3870/12P-10	OEM
MK3870/12P-15	OEM
MK3870/20	OEM
MK3870/20J-05	OEM
MK3870/20J-10	OEM
MK3870/20J-15	OEM
MK3870/20N-05	OEM
MK3870/20N-10	OEM
MK3870/20N-15	OEM
MK3870/20P-05	OEM
MK3870/20P-10	OEM
MK3870/20P-15	OEM
MK3870/22J-05	OEM
MK3870/22J-10	OEM
MK3870/22J-15	OEM
MK3870/22N-05	OEM
MK3870/22N-10	OEM
MK3870/22N-15	OEM
MK3870/22P-05	OEM
MK3870/22P-10	OEM
MK3870/22P-15	OEM
MK3870/30J-05	OEM
MK3870/30J-10	OEM
MK3870/30J-15	OEM
MK3870/30N-05	OEM
MK3870/30N-10	OEM
MK3870/30N-15	OEM
MK3870/30P-05	OEM
MK3870/30P-10	OEM
MK3870/30P-15	OEM
MK3870/32J-05	OEM
MK3870/32J-10	OEM
MK3870/32J-15	OEM
MK3870/32N-05	OEM
MK3870/32N-10	OEM
MK3870/32N-15	OEM
MK3870/32P-05	OEM
MK3870/32P-10	OEM
MK3870/32P-15	OEM
MK3870/40J-05	OEM
MK3870/40J-10	OEM
MK3870/40J-15	OEM
MK3870/40N-05	OEM
MK3870/40N-15	OEM
MK3870/40N-1010	OEM
MK3870/40P-05	OEM
MK3870/40P-10	OEM
MK3870/40P-15	OEM
MK3870/42J-05	OEM
MK3870/42J-10	OEM
MK3870/42J-15	OEM
MK3870/42N-00	OEM
MK3870/42N-05	OEM
MK3870/42N-10	OEM
MK3870/42N-15	OEM
MK3870/42P-05	OEM
MK3870/42P-10	OEM
MK3870N	OEM
MK3870P	OEM
MK3870SCU1J-00	OEM
MK3870SCU1J-05	OEM
MK3870SCU1J-15	OEM
MK3870SCU1N-00	OEM
MK3870SCU1N-05	OEM
MK3870SCU1N-10	OEM
MK3870SCU1N-15	OEM
MK3870SCU1P-00	OEM
MK3870SCU1P-05	OEM
MK3870SCU1P-10	OEM
MK3870SCU1P-15	OEM
MK3871N	OEM
MK3871P	OEM
MK3873/10J-05	OEM
MK3873/10J-10	OEM
MK3873/10J-15	OEM
MK3873/10P-00	OEM
MK3873/10P-05	OEM
MK3873/10P-10	OEM
MK3873/10P-15	OEM
MK3873/12J-00	OEM
MK3873/12J-0505	OEM
MK3873/12J-10	OEM
MK3873/12J-15	OEM
MK3873/12N-00	OEM
MK3873/12N-05	OEM
MK3873/12N-15	OEM
MK3873/12P-05	OEM
MK3873/12P-10	OEM
MK3873/12P-15	OEM
MK3873/20J-00	OEM
MK3873/20J-05	OEM
MK3873/20J-10	OEM
MK3873/20J-15	OEM
MK3873/20P-00	OEM
MK3873/20P-05	OEM
MK3873/20P-10	OEM
MK3873/20P-15	OEM
MK3873/22P-00	OEM
MK3873/22P-05	OEM
MK3873/22P-15	OEM
MK3873EPC1J-00	OEM
MK3873EPC1N-00	OEM
MK3873EPC1P-00	OEM
MK3873SCU20N	OEM
MK3875/22J-00	OEM
MK3875/22J-05	OEM
MK3875/22J-10	OEM
MK3875/22J-15	OEM
MK3875/22N-00	OEM
MK3875/22N-05	OEM
MK3875/22N-10	OEM
MK3875/22N-15	OEM
MK3875/22P-00	OEM
MK3875/22P-05	OEM
MK3875/22P-10	OEM
MK3875/22P-15	OEM
MK3875/42J-00	OEM
MK3875/42J-05	OEM
MK3875/42J-10	OEM
MK3875/42J-15	OEM
MK3875/42N-00	OEM
MK3875/42N-05	OEM
MK3875/42N-10	OEM
MK3875/42N-15	OEM
MK3875/42P-00	OEM
MK3875/42P-05	OEM
MK3875/42P-10	OEM
MK3875/42P-15	OEM
MK3880N-4	6082
MK3880N4Z80	OEM
MK3880NZ80	OEM
MK3880P4Z80	OEM
MK3880P10Z80	OEM
MK3880P20Z80	OEM
MK3880PZ80	OEM
MK3881N	1893
MK3881N4	1893
MK3881P	6056
MK3881P4	OEM
MK3881P10	OEM
MK3881P20	OEM
MK3882N	5242
MK3882N4	OEM
MK3882N10	OEM
MK3882P	5242
MK3882P4	OEM
MK3882P10	OEM
MK3883N	OEM
MK3883N4	OEM
MK3883P	OEM
MK3883P4	OEM
MK3884N	OEM
MK3884N4	OEM
MK3884N10	OEM
MK3884P	OEM
MK3884P4	OEM
MK3884P10	OEM
MK3885N	OEM
MK3885N10	OEM
MK3885P	OEM
MK3885P10	OEM
MK3887N	OEM
MK3887N4	OEM
MK3887N10	OEM
MK3887P	OEM
MK3887P4	OEM
MK3887P10	OEM
MK4027J-1	OEM
MK4027J-2	OEM
MK4027J-3	4887
MK4027J-4	4887
MK4027N-1	OEM
MK4027N-2	OEM
MK4027N-3	4887
MK4027N-4	4887
MK4027P-1	OEM
MK4027P-2	OEM
MK4027P-3	4887
MK4104E-3	OEM
MK4104E-4	OEM
MK4104E-5	OEM
MK4104E-6	OEM
MK4104E-33	OEM
MK4104E-34	OEM
MK4104E-35	OEM
MK4104J-3	OEM
MK4104J-4	OEM
MK4104J-5	OEM
MK4104J-6	OEM
MK4104J-33	OEM
MK4104J-34	OEM
MK4104J-35	OEM
MK4104N-3	OEM
MK4104N-4	OEM
MK4104N-5	OEM
MK4104N-6	OEM
MK4104N-33	OEM
MK4104N-34	OEM
MK4104N-35	OEM
MK4116	0518
MK4116-4	0518
MK4116E-2	0518
MK4116E-3	0518
MK4116E-4	0518
MK4116J-2	0518
MK4116J-3	0518
MK4116J-4	0518
MK4116J44GP	OEM
MK4116J-53GP	0518
MK4116N-2	0518
MK4116N-3	0518
MK4116N-3GP	0518
MK4116N-4	0518
MK4116N-44GP	0518
MK4116P-2	0518
MK4116P-3	0518
MK4116P-4	0518
MK4118	OEM
MK4118AJ-1	OEM
MK4118AJ-2	OEM
MK4118AJ-3	OEM
MK4118AJ-4	OEM
MK4118AN-1	OEM
MK4118AN-2	OEM
MK4118AN-3	OEM
MK4118AN-4	OEM
MK4118AP-1	OEM
MK4118AP-2	OEM
MK4118AP-3	OEM
MK4118AP-4	OEM
MK4167P55	OEM
MK4332D-3	4847
MK4516E-15	OEM
MK4516J-12	OEM
MK4516N-12	OEM
MK4516N-15	OEM
MK4528D-15	OEM
MK4528D-20	OEM
MK4528D-25	OEM
MK4564J15	OEM
MK4564J20	OEM
MK4564J25	OEM
MK4564N-15	2341
MK4564N-20	OEM
MK4801AJ-55	OEM
MK4801AJ-70	OEM
MK4801AJ-90	OEM
MK4801AN-55	OEM
MK4801AN-70	OEM
MK4801AN-90	OEM
MK4801AP-55	OEM
MK4801AP-70	OEM
MK4801AP-90	OEM
MK4802J-1	OEM
MK4802J-3	OEM
MK4802J-70	OEM
MK4802J-90	OEM
MK4802N-1	OEM
MK4802N-3	OEM
MK4802N-70	OEM
MK4802N-90	OEM
MK4802P-1	OEM
MK4802P-3	1887
MK4802P-70	OEM
MK4802P-90	OEM
MK4808-5	OEM
MK4816J-3	OEM
MK4816J-4	OEM
MK4816J-5	OEM
MK4816N-4	OEM
MK4816N-5	OEM
MK5002N	OEM
MK5002P	OEM
MK5005N	OEM
MK5005P	OEM
MK5007N	OEM
MK5007P	OEM
MK5009N	OEM
MK5009P	OEM
MK5037N	OEM
MK5087J	OEM
MK5087N	OEM
MK5087P	OEM
MK5089J	0565
MK5089K	0565
MK5089N	OEM
MK5089P	0565
MK5091N	OEM
MK5092N	OEM
MK5094N	OEM
MK5099N	OEM
MK5102N-5	OEM
MK5103N-5	OEM
MK5116P	OEM
MK5151J	OEM
MK5151P	OEM
MK5156J	OEM
MK5156P	OEM
MK5168N-1	OEM
MK5173N(A)	OEM
MK5175N	OEM
MK5380J	OEM
MK5380N	OEM
MK5380P	OEM
MK5389J(A)	OEM
MK5389N(A)	OEM
MK5389P(A)	OEM
MK5912J3	OEM
MK9150-1	OEM
MK9150-2	OEM
MK9350-1	OEM
MK9350-2	OEM
MK12716J77	OEM
MK12716J78	OEM
MK14116J72	OEM
MK14116J73	OEM
MK14116J74	OEM
MK14680-00	OEM
MK14802J71	OEM
MK14802J73	OEM
MK14802J790	OEM
MK14802P71	OEM
MK14802P73	OEM
MK14802P790	OEM
MK18106-00	OEM
MK30884	OEM
MK34000	OEM
MK34000J-3	OEM
MK34000N-3	OEM
MK34000P-3	OEM
MK34073N-3	OEM
MK34073P-3	OEM
MK36000	OEM
MK36000J3	OEM
MK36000J4	OEM
MK36000J5	OEM
MK36000N3	OEM
MK36000N-4	OEM
MK36000N-5	OEM
MK36000P3	OEM
MK36000P-4	OEM
MK36000P-5	OEM
MK36906N-4	OEM
MK37000-4	OEM
MK37000J-4	OEM
MK37000J-5	OEM
MK37000N-4	OEM
MK37000N-5	OEM
MK37000P-5	OEM
MK38000N25	OEM
MK38000P25	OEM
MK38036N-25	OEM
MK38097N-21	OEM
MK41164-3GP	0518
MK50116J	OEM
MK50240N	4519
MK50240P	4519
MK50241N	4519
MK50241P	4519
MK50242N	OEM
MK50242P	OEM
MK50366N	OEM
MK50372	OEM
MK50372B	OEM
MK50372N	OEM
MK50375N	OEM
MK50395N	OEM
MK50396N	OEM
MK50397N	OEM
MK50398N	OEM
MK50399N	OEM
MK50808N	OEM
MK50808N-1	OEM
MK50808P	OEM
MK50808P-1	OEM
MK50816N	OEM
MK50816N-1	OEM
MK50816P	OEM
MK50816P-1	OEM
MK50981N	2658
MK50982N	OEM
MK50991N	OEM
MK50992N	2734
MK77650-4	OEM
MK77651-0	OEM
MK77651-4	OEM
MK77652-0	OEM
MK77653	OEM
MK77654	OEM
MK77655-0	OEM
MK77665-0	OEM

If replacement code is OEM, contact original manufacturer for replacement.

DEVICE TYPE	REPL CODE
MK77666-0	OEM
MK77669-0	OEM
MK77750-0	OEM
MK77751	OEM
MK77752-0	OEM
MK77752-4	OEM
MK77753-0	OEM
MK77753-4	OEM
MK77754-0	OEM
MK77754-4	OEM
MK77755	OEM
MK77756	OEM
MK77757	OEM
MK77758	OEM
MK77759	OEM
MK77760	OEM
MK77850-0	OEM
MK77850-4	OEM
MK77851-0	OEM
MK77851-4	OEM
MK77852-0	OEM
MK77853-0	OEM
MK77853-4	OEM
MK77950-0	OEM
MK77950-4	OEM
MK77958	OEM
MK77963-0	OEM
MK77963-4	OEM
MK77967	OEM
MK77969	OEM
MK77973	OEM
MK78033	OEM
MK78035	OEM
MK78106	OEM
MK78109	OEM
MK78110	OEM
MK78122	OEM
MK78124	OEM
MK78146	OEM
MK78172-42	OEM
MK78172-56	OEM
MK78175-40	OEM
MK78177-26	OEM
MK78182-1	OEM
MK78182-2	OEM
MK78192	OEM
MK78194	OEM
MK78198	OEM
MK78199	OEM
MK78207	OEM
MK776534	OEM
MKB1-2H49	OEM
MKB1-7H26P	OEM
MKB1-7H28P	OEM
MKB2-12H49	OEM
MKB4H38	OEM
MKB5H38	OEM
MKB5H69	OEM
MKB7H38	OEM
MKB7H69	OEM
MKB2716E88	OEM
MKB2716E90	OEM
MKB2716J-87	OEM
MKB2716J-88	OEM
MKB2716J-90	OEM
MKB4027F-84	OEM
MKB4027J-83	OEM
MKB4027J-84	OEM
MKB4104E-84(M)	OEM
MKB4104E-85	OEM
MKB4104E-86	OEM
MKB4104J-84(M)	OEM
MKB4104J-85	OEM
MKB4104J-86	OEM
MKB4104P-84(M)	OEM
MKB4104P-85	OEM
MKB4104P-86	OEM
MKB4116E-83	OEM
MKB4116E-84	OEM
MKB4116F-84	OEM
MKB4116J-82	OEM
MKB4116J-83	OEM
MKB4116J-84	OEM
MKB4116P-82	OEM
MKB4116P-83	OEM
MKB4116P-84	OEM
MKB4118AJ-82(MD)	OEM
MKB4118AJ-83(MD)	OEM
MKB4118AJ-84(MD)	OEM
MKB4118AP-82(MD)	OEM
MKB4118AP-83(MD)	OEM
MKB4118AP-84(MD)	OEM
MKB12040W	OEM
MKB12100W	OEM
MKB36000J-80(M)	OEM
MKB36000J-83(M)	OEM
MKB36000J-84(M)	OEM
MKB36000P-80	OEM
MKB36000P-83(M)	OEM
MKB36000P-84	OEM
MKB37000E-84(M)	OEM
MKB37000E-85(M)	OEM
MKB37000J-84(M)	OEM
MKB37000J-85(M)	OEM
MKB37000P-84(M)	OEM
MKB37000P-85(M)	OEM
MKB38000E-84(M)	OEM
MKB38000E-85(M)	OEM
MKB38000J-84(M)	OEM
MKB38000J-85(M)	OEM
MKB38000P-84(M)	OEM
MKB38000P-85(M)	OEM
MKK12	OEM
MKK16	OEM
MKK22	OEM
MKK25	OEM
MKK26	OEM
MKK26A	OEM
MKK29	OEM
MKK37	OEM
MKP9V120	OEM
MKP9V130	OEM
MKP9V240	OEM
MKP9V260	OEM
MKP9V270	OEM
MKT25	OEM
MKT27	OEM
MKT32	OEM
MKT33	OEM
MKT34	OEM
MKT35	OEM
MKT36	OEM
MKT37	OEM
MKT42	OEM
MKY1-4H37	OEM
MKY1-4H48	OEM
MKY1-5C38E	OEM
MKY1-5H26	OEM
MKY1-5H37	OEM
MKY1-5H38	OEM
MKY1-5H48	OEM
MKY1-5H49	OEM
MKY1-7C38E	OEM
MKY1-7H26	OEM
MKY1-7H37	OEM
MKY1-7H38	OEM
MKY1-7H39	OEM
MKY1-7H48	OEM
MKY1-7H49	OEM
ML	OEM
ML10A	OEM
ML20A	OEM
ML25	OEM
ML25P	OEM
ML25PS	OEM
ML25P-SF3	OEM
ML25P-TS	OEM
ML30A	OEM
ML33	OEM
ML37	OEM
ML39A	OEM
ML51A	OEM
ML60A	OEM
ML78L05	5538
ML78L05A	5416
ML78L12	5421
ML78L12A	5421
ML78L15	5425
ML78L15A	5425
ML78L18A	4427
ML78L24A	4430
ML78P05	OEM
ML78P05A	OEM
ML78P12	OEM
ML78P12A	OEM
ML78P15	OEM
ML78P15A	OEM
ML78P18	OEM
ML78P18A	OEM
ML79L24A	1710
ML82A	OEM
ML100A	OEM
ML101A	OEM
ML101B	OEM
ML102A	OEM
ML102B	OEM
ML103GM	OEM
ML103HM	OEM
ML110A	OEM
ML111B	OEM
ML120	OEM
ML131B	OEM
ML132A	OEM
ML132B	OEM
ML153A	OEM
ML153B	OEM
ML154A	OEM
ML154B	OEM
ML157A	OEM
ML157B	OEM
ML201AT	0093
ML231B-DG	OEM
ML231B-DP	OEM
ML232B-DG	OEM
ML232B-DP	OEM
ML236B-DP	OEM
ML237B-DP	OEM
ML238B-DP	OEM
ML239B-DP	OEM
ML301T	0093
ML307S	2267
ML530B	OEM
ML709CT	1291
ML723CM	0026
ML723CP	0026
ML723CT	1183
ML723T	1183
ML741CS	0308
ML741CT	0406
ML747CP	2342
ML747CT	2352
ML748CS	1290
ML920DP	OEM
ML922DG	OEM
ML923	OEM
ML924	3444
ML925	OEM
ML926	OEM
ML927	OEM
ML928DP	OEM
ML929DP	OEM
ML1307P	0696
ML1458S	0356
ML2201	OEM
ML2205	OEM
ML3001	OEM
ML3101	OEM
ML3401	OEM
ML4101	OEM
ML4202	OEM
ML4204	OEM
ML4206	OEM
ML4310	OEM
ML4311	OEM
ML4312	OEM
ML4313	OEM
ML4314	OEM
ML4315	OEM
ML4316	OEM
ML4317	OEM
ML4318	OEM
ML4319	OEM
ML4331	OEM
ML4332	OEM
ML4333	OEM
ML4334	OEM
ML4335	OEM
ML4336	OEM
ML4337	OEM
ML4338	OEM
ML4339	OEM
ML4340	OEM
ML4341	OEM
ML4342	OEM
ML4343	OEM
ML4351	OEM
ML4352	OEM
ML4353	OEM
ML4354	OEM
ML4355	OEM
ML4356	OEM
ML4357	OEM
ML4358	OEM
ML4359	OEM
ML4360	OEM
ML4361	OEM
ML4362	OEM
ML4363	OEM
ML4364	OEM
ML4365	OEM
ML4372	OEM
ML4373	OEM
ML4374	OEM
ML4375	OEM
ML4376	OEM
ML4377	OEM
ML4378	OEM
ML4379	OEM
ML4380	OEM
ML4381	OEM
ML4382	OEM
ML4383	OEM
ML4384	OEM
ML4385	OEM
ML4401	OEM
ML4402	OEM
ML4404	OEM
ML4405	OEM
ML4406	OEM
ML4407	OEM
ML4408	OEM
ML4409	OEM
ML4602	OEM
ML4603	OEM
ML4604	OEM
ML4605	OEM
ML4610	OEM
ML4611	OEM
ML4612	OEM
ML4613	OEM
ML4614	OEM
ML4615	OEM
ML4616	OEM
ML4617	OEM
ML4618	OEM
ML4619	OEM
ML4620	OEM
ML4621	OEM
ML4622	OEM
ML4623	OEM
ML4624	OEM
ML4625	OEM
ML4626	OEM
ML4627	OEM
ML4628	OEM
ML4629	OEM
ML4630	OEM
ML4631	OEM
ML4640	OEM
ML4641	OEM
ML4642	OEM
ML4643	OEM
ML4644	OEM
ML4645	OEM
ML4646	OEM
ML4647	OEM
ML4648	OEM
ML4649	OEM
ML4650	OEM
ML4651	OEM
ML4652	OEM
ML4653	OEM
ML4654	OEM
ML4655	OEM
ML4660-114	OEM
ML4660-115	OEM
ML4660-144	OEM
ML4661-114	OEM
ML4661-115	OEM
ML4661-144	OEM
ML4662-114	OEM
ML4662-115	OEM
ML4662-144	OEM
ML4663-114	OEM
ML4663-115	OEM
ML4663-144	OEM
ML4664-114	OEM
ML4664-115	OEM
ML4664-144	OEM
ML4665-114	OEM
ML4665-115	OEM
ML4665-144	OEM
ML4666-114	OEM
ML4666-115	OEM
ML4666-144	OEM
ML4667-114	OEM
ML4667-115	OEM
ML4667-144	OEM
ML4668-114	OEM
ML4668-115	OEM
ML4668-144	OEM
ML4669-114	OEM
ML4669-115	OEM
ML4669-144	OEM
ML4670-114	OEM
ML4670-115	OEM
ML4670-144	OEM
ML4671-114	OEM
ML4671-115	OEM
ML4671-144	OEM
ML4672-114	OEM
ML4672-115	OEM
ML4672-144	OEM
ML4673-114	OEM
ML4673-115	OEM
ML4673-144	OEM
ML4674-114	OEM
ML4674-115	OEM
ML4674-144	OEM
ML4703	OEM
ML4703S	OEM
ML4704	OEM
ML4704S	OEM
ML4705	OEM
ML4705S	OEM
ML4706	OEM
ML4707	OEM
ML4708	OEM
ML4709	OEM
ML4750	OEM
ML4803	OEM
ML4804	OEM
ML4805	OEM
ML5620C	OEM
ML5620CJ	OEM
ML5620J	OEM
ML5620PL	OEM
ML5620PS	OEM
ML5620S	OEM
ML5620X	OEM
ML5621C	OEM
ML5621CJ	OEM
ML5621J	OEM
ML5621PL	OEM
ML5621PS	OEM
ML5621S	OEM
ML5621X	OEM
ML5624C	OEM
ML5624J	OEM
ML5624PL	OEM
ML5624PS	OEM
ML5624S	OEM
ML5624SJ	OEM
ML5624X	OEM
ML5625C	OEM
ML5625J	OEM
ML5625PL	OEM
ML5625PS	OEM
ML5625S	OEM
ML5625SJ	OEM
ML5625X	OEM
ML5640C	OEM
ML5640J	OEM
ML5640PL	OEM
ML5640PS	OEM
ML5640S	OEM
ML5640X	OEM
ML5640XJ	OEM
ML5641C	OEM
ML5641J	OEM
ML5641PL	OEM
ML5641PS	OEM
ML5641S	OEM
ML5641X	OEM
ML5641XJ	OEM
ML5642J	OEM
ML5642X	OEM
ML5643J	OEM
ML5643X	OEM
ML5644C	OEM
ML5644J	OEM
ML5644PL	OEM
ML5644PS	OEM
ML5644S	OEM
ML5644X	OEM
ML5644XJ	OEM
ML5645C	OEM
ML5645J	OEM
ML5645PL	OEM
ML5645PS	OEM
ML5645S	OEM
ML5645X	OEM
ML5645XJ	OEM
ML5646J	OEM
ML5646X	OEM
ML5647J	OEM
ML5647X	OEM
ML5710C	OEM
ML5710J	OEM
ML5710LJ	OEM
ML5710PL	OEM
ML5710PX	OEM
ML5710S	OEM
ML5710X	OEM
ML5720C	OEM
ML5720J	OEM
ML5720LJ	OEM
ML5720PL	OEM
ML5720PX	OEM
ML5720S	OEM
ML5720X	OEM
ML5730C	OEM
ML5730J	OEM
ML5730PL	OEM
ML5730S	OEM
ML5730X	OEM
ML5740C	OEM
ML5740PL	OEM
ML5740S	OEM
ML5740X	OEM
ML7805	4273
ML7805A	4273
ML7812	1341
ML7812A	1341
ML7815	4276
ML7815A	4276
ML7815P	1311
ML7818	4277
ML7818A	4277
ML8204AE	6464
ML8205AE	OEM
ML17310M2	OEM
ML17310M3	OEM
ML17310M4	OEM
ML17320M2	OEM
ML17320M3	OEM
ML17320M4	OEM
ML17330M2	OEM
ML17330M3	OEM
ML17330M4	OEM
ML17340M2	OEM
ML17340M3	OEM
ML17340M4	OEM
ML17350M2	OEM
ML17350M3	OEM
ML17370M1	OEM
ML17370M2	OEM
ML17380M1	OEM
ML17380M2	OEM
MLA12	OEM
MLB.2A	OEM
MLC74HC00A	6468
MLC74HC00AM	OEM
MLC74HC02A	6476
MLC74HC02AM	OEM
MLC74HC03A	OEM
MLC74HC03AM	OEM
MLC74HC04A	6479
MLC74HC04AM	OEM
MLC74HC08A	4225
MLC74HC08AM	OEM
MLC74HC10	OEM
MLC74HC10M	OEM
MLC74HC11	5432
MLC74HC11M	OEM
MLC74HC14A	6493
MLC74HC14AM	OEM
MLC74HC20	OEM
MLC74HC20M	OEM
MLC74HC27	OEM
MLC74HC27M	OEM
MLC74HC30	OEM
MLC74HC30M	OEM
MLC74HC32A	6516
MLC74HC32AM	OEM
MLC74HC42	OEM
MLC74HC42M	OEM
MLC74HC51	OEM
MLC74HC51M	OEM
MLC74HC74	OEM
MLC74HC74AM	OEM
MLC74HC76	OEM
MLC74HC76M	OEM
MLC74HC86	5438
MLC74HC86M	OEM
MLC74HC107	OEM
MLC74HC107M	OEM
MLC74HC109	6484
MLC74HC109M	OEM
MLC74HCU04	OEM
MLC74HCU04M	OEM
MLC41005	OEM
MLE-7541	OEM
MLED15	OEM
MLED45	OEM
MLED50	OEM
MLED55	OEM
MLED60	OEM
MLED71	3203
MLED90	OEM
MLED92	3203
MLED93	OEM
MLED94	OEM
MLED95	OEM
MLED500	OEM
MLED600	OEM
MLED610	OEM
MLED630	OEM
MLED640	OEM
MLED650	1348
MLED655	2201
MLED660	OEM
MLED750	OEM
MLED900	OEM
MLED910	OEM
MLED930	0586
MLH5G	OEM
MLH5S	OEM
MLH5Y	OEM
MLH10G	OEM
MLH10S	OEM
MLH10Y	OEM
MLI8G	OEM
MLI8S	OEM
MLI8Y	OEM
MLI80G	OEM
MLI80S	OEM
MLI80Y	OEM
MLM101AG	1290
MLM111AG	1804
MLM139	0176
MLM139AL	0176
MLM139L	0176
MLM201AG	0093
MLM211AG	1804
MLM224L	0620
MLM224P	0620
MLM239AL	0176
MLM239L	0176
MLM239P	OEM
MLM301AG	0093
MLM301AU	1290
MLM307P1	2267
MLM307U	2267
MLM309K	1911
MLM311P1	2093
MLM324	0620
MLM324L	0620
MLM324P	0620
MLM324P1	0620
MLM339(P)	0176
MLM339AL	0176
MLM339L	0176
MLM339P	2753
MLM2901P	6099
MLNA328	2981
MLNA328A	2981
MLNA328B	OEM
MLNA331	1703
MLNA331A	OEM
MLNA331B	OEM
MLNA335	0188
MLNA335A	OEM
MLNA335B	OEM
MLNA339	0451
MLNA339A	0451
MLNA339B	0451
MLNA343	0528
MLNA343A	0528
MLNA343B	OEM
MLNA347	0446
MLNA347A	0446
MLNA347B	OEM
MLNA351	0162
MLNA351A	0162
MLNA351B	OEM
MLNA356	0157
MLNA356A	0157
MLNA356B	OEM
MLNA362	0631
MLNA362A	0631
MLNA362B	OEM
MLNA368	0025
MLNA368A	0025
MLNA368B	OEM
MLNA375	0644
MLNA375A	0644
MLNA375B	OEM
MLNA382	0244
MLNA382A	0244
MLNA382B	0244
MLNA391	0012
MLNA391A	0012
MLNA391B	OEM
MLNA3100	0170
MLNA3100A	0170
MLNA3100B	OEM
MLS101	OEM
MLS102	OEM
MLS103	OEM
MLS104	OEM
MLS105	OEM
MLS201	OEM
MLS202	OEM
MLS203	OEM
MLS204	OEM
MLS205	OEM
MLSI-11B	OEM
MLSI-512	OEM
MLSI-1710	OEM
MLSI2480	OEM
MLSI-BPA84	OEM
MLSI-CR11	OEM
MLSI-DLV11	OEM
MLSI-DLV11E	OEM
MLSI-DR11-B	OEM
MLSI-DRV11C	OEM
MLSI-DRV11P	OEM
MLSI-DT1761	OEM
MLSI-DUPV11	OEM
MLSI-DUV11	OEM
MLSI-DZ11-A	OEM
MLSI-DZ11-B	OEM
MLSI-IBV11	OEM
MLSI-LP11	OEM
MLSI-LP11-A	OEM
MLSI-MRV000	OEM
MLSI-MRV002	OEM
MLSI-MRV003	OEM
MLSI-MRV-004	OEM
MLSI-MRV-005	OEM
MLSI-PC11	OEM
MLSI-SMU	OEM
MLSI-TEV	OEM
MLSI-VRV001	OEM
MLSI-XYV11	OEM
MLT29	OEM
MLT33	OEM
MLT40	OEM
MLT47	OEM
MLT49	OEM
MLT438	OEM
MLT439	OEM
MLT478	OEM
MLV746A	0289
MLV747A	0372
MLV748A	0451
MLV749A	0528
MLV750A	0446
MLV751A	0162
MLV752A	0157
MLV753A	0631
MLV754A	0025
MLV755A	0644
MLV756A	0244
MLV757A	0012
MLV758A	0170
MLV759A	0137
MLV4370A	2975
MLV4371A	1302
MLV4372A	1703
MLZ-90	OEM
MLZ-90A-MF16C-1	OEM
MLZ-90A-MF16S-1	OEM
MLZ-90A-MF16S-2	OEM
MLZ-91A-32P-MFGDR	OEM
MLZ-91A-64P-MFGDR	OEM
MLZ-92A-16P-MFGDR	OEM
MLZ-92A-32P-MFGDR	OEM
MLZ-92A-64P-MFGDR	OEM
MLZ-93A	OEM
MLZ312	OEM
MLZ-DAQ	OEM
MM0	0015
MM1	OEM
MM1-A1	OEM
MM1-ACPU	OEM
MM1-AOS-4	OEM
MM1-AOS-8	OEM
MM1-CPU	OEM
MM1-DIO	OEM
MM1-ENC-RM	OEM
MM1-MSC	OEM
MM1-MVRAM-1	OEM
MM1-NVRAM-2	OEM
MM1-OPT	OEM
MM1-PBA	OEM
MM1-PROM	OEM
MM1-RAM	OEM
MM1-ZCPU	OEM
MM2	0015
MM3	0015
MM4	0015

If replacement code is OEM, contact original manufacturer for replacement.

DEVICE TYPE	REPL CODE
MM5	0015
MM6	0015
MM7	0071
MM8	0071
MM9	0071
MM10	0071
MM54C00	OEM
MM54C00D	OEM
MM54C02	OEM
MM54C02D	OEM
MM54C04	OEM
MM54C04J	OEM
MM54C04W	OEM
MM54C08	OEM
MM54C08D	OEM
MM54C10	OEM
MM54C10D	OEM
MM54C14J	OEM
MM54C14W	OEM
MM54C20	OEM
MM54C20D	OEM
MM54C30D	OEM
MM54C32D	OEM
MM54C42	OEM
MM54C42D	2100
MM54C42J	2100
MM54C42W	2100
MM54C48D	OEM
MM54C48N	OEM
MM54C73D	OEM
MM54C74	OEM
MM54C74D	OEM
MM54C76D	OEM
MM54C83D	OEM
MM54C85	OEM
MM54C85D	OEM
MM54C86	OEM
MM54C86D	OEM
MM54C89J	OEM
MM54C90	OEM
MM54C90D	OEM
MM54C93	OEM
MM54C93D	OEM
MM54C107D	OEM
MM54C150J	OEM
MM54C151J	OEM
MM54C151W	OEM
MM54C154J	OEM
MM54C157J	OEM
MM54C157W	OEM
MM54C160D	OEM
MM54C161D	OEM
MM54C162D	OEM
MM54C163D	OEM
MM54C173D	OEM
MM54C174D	OEM
MM54C175D	OEM
MM54C192D	OEM
MM54C193D	OEM
MM54C200J	OEM
MM54C221D	OEM
MM54C901J	OEM
MM54C901W	OEM
MM54HC14	OEM
MM54HCT00	OEM
MM74C00	2100
MM74C00N	2100
MM74C02	6067
MM74C02N	2102
MM74C04	6068
MM74C04J	2930
MM74C04N	2930
MM74C08	6069
MM74C08N	2106
MM74C10	6071
MM74C10N	2107
MM74C14J	3002
MM74C14N	3002
MM74C20	6073
MM74C20N	2110
MM74C30N	3100
MM74C32N	3105
MM74C42	6074
MM74C42J	2130
MM74C42N	2130
MM74C48N	2135
MM74C73N	2148
MM74C74	6075
MM74C74N	2149
MM74C76N	2150
MM74C83N	OEM
MM74C85	6077
MM74C85N	2157
MM74C86	6078
MM74C86N	2971
MM74C89J	OEM
MM74C89N	OEM
MM74C90	2160
MM74C90N	2160
MM74C93	2163
MM74C93N	2163
MM74C95N	3367
MM74C107N	3782
MM74C150J	OEM
MM74C150N	OEM
MM74C151J	3944
MM74C151N	3944
MM74C154J	3957
MM74C154N	3957

DEVICE TYPE	REPL CODE
MM74C157J	3972
MM74C157N	3972
MM74C160N	3983
MM74C161N	3984
MM74C162N	1134
MM74C163N	3995
MM74C164N	3999
MM74C173N	4026
MM74C174N	4030
MM74C175N	4034
MM74C192N	4056
MM74C193N	4059
MM74C200J	OEM
MM74C200N	OEM
MM74C221	3018
MM74C221N	3018
MM74C240N	2928
MM74C244N	4166
MM74C373N	4388
MM74C374N	4392
MM74C901N	4527
MM74C902N	4528
MM74C903N	4529
MM74C904N	4530
MM74C906	OEM
MM74C906N	OEM
MM74C922N	5496
MM74C923N	5498
MM74C925N	4540
MM74HC14	OEM
MM74HC240N	1968
MM74HC243N	1990
MM74HC245N	2003
MM74HC595	OEM
MM74HC595N	OEM
MM74HCT00	OEM
MM306	0086
MM380	0050
MM404	0164
MM404A	0136
MM420	0233
MM421	OEM
MM430	OEM
MM439	3562
MM440	OEM
MM486	0086
MM487	0086
MM488	0086
MM511	0086
MM512	0086
MM513	0086
MM709	0144
MM719	OEM
MM741	0308
MM799	OEM
MM800	OEM
MM801	OEM
MM869B	0079
MM999	0037
MM1002	OEM
MM1008	OEM
MM1028BF	OEM
MM1031	OEM
MM1031XS	OEM
MM1111XS	OEM
MM1114XEF	OEM
MM1114XFF	OEM
MM1139	0050
MM1151	0004
MM1152	0004
MM1153	0004
MM1154	0004
MM1161	OEM
MM1162	OEM
MM1163	OEM
MM1164	OEM
MM1199	0050
MM1367/2SC684	0144
MM1382	0144
MM1387	OEM
MM1461	OEM
MM1462	OEM
MM1500	0414
MM1501	0414
MM1501A	0414
MM1505	0079
MM1510	OEM
MM1511	OEM
MM1557	3542
MM1558	3543
MM1559	2485
MM1601	3532
MM1602	2156
MM1603	1966
MM1606	2156
MM1612	0693
MM1613	0079
MM1614	0037
MM1619	0042
MM1620	3524
MM1702AQ	OEM
MM1711	0079
MM1712	OEM
MM1736	OEM
MM1737	OEM
MM1738	OEM
MM1739	OEM
MM1742	0004
MM1748	0326

DEVICE TYPE	REPL CODE
MM1755	0016
MM1756	0016
MM1757	0016
MM1758	0016
MM1803	0488
MM1809	0086
MM1809A	0086
MM1810	0693
MM1810A	0086
MM1812	0283
MM1874A	OEM
MM1893	0626
MM1941	0488
MM1943	0086
MM1945	0144
MM2005-2	0016
MM2102	OEM
MM2103	0838
MM2112-2	OEM
MM2114N2L	OEM
MM2114N-3	2037
MM2193A	0590
MM2258	0168
MM2259	0168
MM2260	0233
MM2261	0590
MM2262	0626
MM2263	0168
MM2264	0626
MM2266	0086
MM2270	0590
MM2316ED	OEM
MM2316EN	OEM
MM2484	0016
MM2503	0050
MM2550	0050
MM2552	0050
MM2554	0050
MM2613	0079
MM2614	0037
MM2708Q	4351
MM2708Q-1	OEM
MM2711	0079
MM2712	0037
MM2716Q	2263
MM2716Q-1	OEM
MM2716Q-2	OEM
MM2716QE	OEM
MM2716QM	OEM
MM2758Q-A	OEM
MM2758Q-B	OEM
MM2894	0050
MM3000	0233
MM3001	0168
MM3002	0233
MM-3003	0233
MM3003	0283
MM3004	0555
MM3005	4161
MM3006	0016
MM3007	0617
MM3008	0264
MM-3009	0264
MM3009	0233
MM3014	0264
MM3025	OEM
MM3053	0626
MM3100	0233
MM3101	0233
MM3200-2C	OEM
MM3200-3C	OEM
MM3200-C	OEM
MM3724	0930
MM3725	0930
MM3726	0037
MM3734	0086
MM3735	0086
MM3736	0086
MM3737	0086
MM3903	0016
MM3904	0016
MM3905	0037
MM3906	0037
MM4000	0434
MM4000(IC)	2013
MM4001	0434
MM4002	0434
MM4003	0434
MM4005	0126
MM4006	0126
MM4007	2819
MM4008	0126
MM4009	1988
MM4010	0126
MM4011	0215
MM4012	0493
MM4013	0409
MM4015	1008
MM4016A	1135
MM4017	0508
MM4018	0126
MM4019	0126
MM4019(IC)	1517
MM4020	3536
MM4020(IC)	1651
MM4021	3538
MM4022	3539
MM4023	3540
MM4024	1946

DEVICE TYPE	REPL CODE
MM4025	2061
MM4027	1938
MM4030	0495
MM4031	0126
MM4032	0126
MM4033	0126
MM4036	0126
MM4037	0126
MM4040	0056
MM4042	0121
MM4048	0037
MM4049	0001
MM4050	0394
MM4051	0362
MM4052	0037
MM4052(IC)	0024
MM4257	3562
MM4258	3562
MM4429	0555
MM4430	0555
MM4511	1535
MM4518	1037
MM5000	0050
MM5001	0050
MM5002	0050
MM5005	0126
MM5006	0886
MM5007	0886
MM5107N	OEM
MM5189	0086
MM5262	0086
MM5290N-4	1276
MM5311N	OEM
MM5314N	OEM
MM5316	2279
MM5316D	OEM
MM5316N	2702
MM5322N	OEM
MM5369	OEM
MM5369AA/N	5731
MM5387	2279
MM5387/HD38991A	OEM
MM5387AA	2279
MM5387AA/N	2279
MM5387AA-N	2279
MM5387AAN	4308
MM5387AB/N	2279
MM5387ABN	OEM
MM5387N	2279
MM5402	2279
MM-5402N	OEM
MM5402N	2279
MM5407N	OEM
MM5415	5729
MM5416	0434
MM5430	OEM
MM5430N	OEM
MM5431N	OEM
MM5439N	OEM
MM5450N	OEM
MM5455N	OEM
MM5456N	OEM
MM5457N	OEM
MM5462N	OEM
MM5504D	OEM
MM5504F	OEM
MM5554N	OEM
MM5555N	OEM
MM5556N	OEM
MM5601AN	5442
MM5602AN	5460
MM5611AN	0215
MM5611BN	OEM
MM5612AN	5586
MM5613AN	OEM
MM5613BN	OEM
MM5617AN	5678
MM5619AN	4300
MM5620AN	5725
MM5622AN	5747
MM5623AN	5757
MM5624AN	5762
MM5625AN	5773
MM5627AN	1938
MM5628BN	OEM
MM5630AN	5834
MM5650BN	OEM
MM5660BN	6066
MM5673BN	OEM
MM5725N	OEM
MM5734N	OEM
MM5736N	OEM
MM5737N	OEM
MM5738N	OEM
MM5739N	OEM
MM5740AAC	OEM
MM5758N	OEM
MM5760N	OEM
MM5763N	OEM
MM5764N	OEM
MM5765N	OEM
MM5766N	OEM
MM5767N	OEM
MM5777N	OEM
MM5780N	OEM
MM5791N	OEM
MM5794N	OEM
MM5795N	OEM
MM5799N	OEM

DEVICE TYPE	REPL CODE
MM5823N	OEM
MM5824N	OEM
MM5829	OEM
MM5832N	OEM
MM5833N	OEM
MM5839	OEM
MM5840N	OEM
MM5841N	OEM
MM5860	OEM
MM5863N	OEM
MM5871N	OEM
MM5879	OEM
MM5880	OEM
MM5885	OEM
MM5886	OEM
MM5889	OEM
MM5889AB	OEM
MM5890	OEM
MM5899	OEM
MM6400A-C	OEM
MM6400C	OEM
MM6427	5841
MM6800	OEM
MM6800/16	OEM
MM6800D	OEM
MM7087	0233
MM7088	0233
MM7218BN	OEM
MM7317BN	OEM
MM8000	0414
MM8001	0414
MM8002	0414
MM8003	2059
MM8004	0693
MM8006	0007
MM8007	0007
MM8008	0414
MM8010	0414
MM8011	0414
MM8012	2059
MM8080/16	OEM
MM8080AL	OEM
MM8080B	OEM
MM8086	OEM
MM8086/16	OEM
MM8086D	OEM
MM14511BCN	1535
MM14511CN	1535
MM14538BCN	OEM
MM52116D	OEM
MM52116FDWD	OEM
MM52116FDWN	OEM
MM52116FDXD	OEM
MM52116FDXN	OEM
MM52116N	OEM
MM52132D	OEM
MM52132N	OEM
MM52164D	OEM
MM52164N	OEM
MM53100	OEM
MM53104	OEM
MM53105	OEM
MM53108N	OEM
MM53110AAN	OEM
MM53110ABN	OEM
MM53113N	2702
MM53118AA	OEM
MM53124N	OEM
MM53125N	OEM
MM53130N	OEM
MM53143J	OEM
MM53144J	OEM
MM53190N	OEM
MM53214NGQ/N	OEM
MM53224N	OEM
MM54240	OEM
MM55104	2592
MM55104N	2592
MM55106	OEM
MM55106N	OEM
MM55107N	OEM
MM55108	6605
MM55110	OEM
MM55114	OEM
MM55116	OEM
MM55116N	OEM
MM55121N	OEM
MM55122N	OEM
MM55123N	OEM
MM55124N	OEM
MM55126N	OEM
MM57103N	OEM
MM57104N	OEM
MM57123N	OEM
MM57135N	OEM
MM57136N	OEM
MM57140	OEM
MM57150	OEM
MM57150FHJ	OEM
MM57150N	OEM
MM57150PHJ	OEM
MM57409D	OEM
MM57409J	OEM
MM57409N	OEM
MM57455N	OEM
MM57459N	OEM
MM58104	OEM
MM58106N	OEM
MM58115	OEM

DEVICE TYPE	REPL CODE
MM58117	OEM
MM58118	OEM
MM58119	OEM
MM58120	OEM
MM58127	OEM
MM58128	OEM
MM58129	OEM
MM58130	OEM
MM58142N	OEM
MM58143N	OEM
MM58144N	OEM
MM58146N	OEM
MM58167AN	OEM
MM58174AJM	OEM
MM58174AN	OEM
MM58183N	OEM
MM58184N	OEM
MM58201N	OEM
MM58274N	OEM
MM58313N	OEM
MM58601	OEM
MM58801	OEM
MM587100N	OEM
MM681031	OEM
MMBA811C5	3832
MMBA811C6	3832
MMBA811C7	3832
MMBA811C8	OEM
MMBA812M3	3832
MMBA812M4	3832
MMBA812M5	3832
MMBA812M6	3832
MMBA812M7	3832
MMBA813S2	OEM
MMBA813S3	OEM
MMBA813S4	OEM
MMBA956H3	OEM
MMBA956H4	OEM
MMBA956H5	OEM
MMBA956H6	OEM
MMBC1009F1	5286
MMBC1009F2	5286
MMBC1009F3	5286
MMBC1009F4	5286
MMBC1009F5	5286
MMBC1321Q2	OEM
MMBC1321Q3	OEM
MMBC1321Q4	OEM
MMBC1321Q5	OEM
MMBC1621B2	OEM
MMBC1621B3	OEM
MMBC1621B4	OEM
MMBC1622D6	5286
MMBC1622D7	5286
MMBC1622D8	OEM
MMBC1623L3	5286
MMBC1623L4	5286
MMBC1623L5	5286
MMBC1623L6	5286
MMBC1623L7	5286
MMBC1653N2	2316
MMBC1653N3	2316
MMBC1653N4	2316
MMBC1654N5	2316
MMBC1654N6	2316
MMBC1654N7	2316
MMBC2107G3	OEM
MMBC2107G4	OEM
MMBC2107G5	OEM
MMBC2107G6	OEM
MMBD101	OEM
MMBD501	OEM
MMBD914	5396
MMBD2835	0897
MMBD2836	4830
MMBD2837	0901
MMBD2838	0901
MMBD6050	3703
MMBD6100	0901
MMBD7000	OEM
MMBF170	OEM
MMBF4393	OEM
MMBF4416	OEM
MMBF4860	OEM
MMBF5457	OEM
MMBF5459	OEM
MMBF5460	OEM
MMBF5484	OEM
MMBF5486	OEM
MMBFU310	OEM
MMBR901	3338
MMBR920	OEM
MMBR930	3338
MMBR931	3338
MMBR2060	OEM
MMBR2857	OEM
MMBR4957	OEM
MMBR5031	3338
MMBR5179	OEM
MMBS5060	OEM
MMBS5061	OEM
MMBS5062	OEM
MMBT290Z	OEM
MMBT404	1426
MMBT404A	1426
MMBT918	OEM
MMBT918R	OEM
MMBT2222	1722
MMBT2222A	1722

DEVICE TYPE	REPL CODE
MMBT2222AR	OEM
MMBT2222R	OEM
MMBT2369	1426
MMBT2369R	OEM
MMBT2907A	1491
MMBT2907AR	OEM
MMBT3014	OEM
MMBT3640	1491
MMBT3903	1426
MMBT3904	1426
MMBT3906	1491
MMBT3960	OEM
MMBT3960A	OEM
MMBT4260	OEM
MMBT4261	OEM
MMBT4403	1491
MMBT5086	1491
MMBT5087	1491
MMBT5088	1426
MMBT5089	1426
MMBT5401	1495
MMBT5550	2316
MMBT6427	OEM
MMBT6428	1426
MMBT6429	1426
MMBTA05	2316
MMBTA06	2316
MMBTA13	2322
MMBTA14	2322
MMBTA20	1426
MMBTA42	OEM
MMBTA42R	OEM
MMBTA43	OEM
MMBTA43R	OEM
MMBTA55	1495
MMBTA56	1495
MMBTA63	OEM
MMBTA64	OEM
MMBTA70	1491
MMBTA92	OEM
MMBTA93	OEM
MMBTH-10	OEM
MMBTH10	OEM
MMBTH-24	OEM
MMBTH24	OEM
MMBTH81	OEM
MMBV105G	OEM
MMBV109	OEM
MMBV2097	OEM
MMBV2098	OEM
MMBV2101	OEM
MMBV2103	OEM
MMBV2108	OEM
MMBV2109	OEM
MMBV3102	OEM
MMBV3401	OEM
MMBZ5226	OEM
MMBZ5227	OEM
MMBZ5228	OEM
MMBZ5229	OEM
MMBZ5230	OEM
MMBZ5231	OEM
MMBZ5232	OEM
MMBZ5233	OEM
MMBZ5234	0466
MMBZ5235	OEM
MMBZ5236	OEM
MMBZ5237	OEM
MMBZ5238	OEM
MMBZ5239	0057
MMBZ5240	OEM
MMBZ5241	OEM
MMBZ5242	0052
MMBZ5243	OEM
MMBZ5244	OEM
MMBZ5245	OEM
MMBZ5246	OEM
MMBZ5247	OEM
MMBZ5248	OEM
MMBZ5249	OEM
MMBZ5250	OEM
MMBZ5251	OEM
MMBZ5252	OEM
MMBZ5253	OEM
MMBZ5254	OEM
MMBZ5255	OEM
MMBZ5256	OEM
MMBZ5257	OEM
MMBZ5263	OEM
MMBZ5265	OEM
MMBZ5281	OEM
MMCM918	0144
MMCM930	0111
MMCM2221	OEM
MMCM2222	2427
MMCM2484	0855
MMCM2857	OEM
MMCM2906	OEM
MMCM2907	0150
MMCM3798	OEM
MMCM3799	OEM
MMCM3903	OEM
MMCM3904	OEM
MMCM3905	OEM
MMCM3906	OEM
MMCM3960A	OEM
MMD70	OEM
MMD6050	OEM
MMD6100	OEM

If replacement code is OEM, contact original manufacturer for replacement.

DEVICE TYPE	REPL CODE
MMD6150	OEM
MMD7000	OEM
MMH0026CG	OEM
MMH0026CL	OEM
MMH0026CPI	OEM
MMH0026CPID	OEM
MMH0026CPIDS	OEM
MMH0026CPIS	OEM
MMH0026G	OEM
MMH0026L	OEM
MM-S100	OEM
MM-SBC-80F	OEM
MM-SBC-80H	OEM
MMSD914	OEM
MMST918	OEM
MMST2222	OEM
MMST2222A	1426
MMST2907	1491
MMST2907A	OEM
MMST3903	OEM
MMST3904	OEM
MMST3905	OEM
MMST3906	OEM
MMST4123	OEM
MMST4124	OEM
MMST4125	OEM
MMST4126	OEM
MMST4400	OEM
MMST4401	OEM
MMST4402	OEM
MMST4403	OEM
MMST5086	OEM
MMST5087	OEM
MMST5088	OEM
MMST5089	OEM
MMST6428	OEM
MMST6429	OEM
MMSTA05	OEM
MMSTA06	OEM
MMSTA12	OEM
MMSTA13	OEM
MMSTA14	OEM
MMSTA20	OEM
MMSTA55	OEM
MMSTA56	OEM
MMSTA63	OEM
MMSTA64	OEM
MMSTA70	OEM
MMSTH24	OEM
MMT70	0111
MMT71	0855
MMT72	0079
MMT73	0079
MMT74	0414
MMT75	0855
MMT76	0855
MMT918	0224
MMT2060	OEM
MMT2222	0079
MMT2222A	OEM
MMT2857A	OEM
MMT2907	0527
MMT2907A	OEM
MMT3014	0079
MMT3546	4359
MMT3798	0786
MMT3799	0006
MMT3823	6457
MMT3903	0079
MMT3904	0079
MMT3905	0150
MMT3906	0527
MMT4123	OEM
MMT4124	OEM
MMT4125	OEM
MMT4126	OEM
MMT4261	OEM
MMT4400	OEM
MMT4401	OEM
MMT4402	OEM
MMT4403	OEM
MMT4416	OEM
MMT5031	OEM
MMT5031A	OEM
MMT5086	OEM
MMT5087	OEM
MMT5088	OEM
MMT5089	OEM
MMT6428	OEM
MMT6429	OEM
MMT8006	OEM
MMT8007	OEM
MMT8008	OEM
MMT8015	0127
MMTA05	OEM
MMTA06	OEM
MMTA12	OEM
MMTA13	OEM
MMTA14	OEM
MMTA20	OEM
MMTA55	OEM
MMTA56	OEM
MMTA63	OEM
MMTA64	OEM
MMTA70	OEM
MMTH24	OEM
MMZ3.3	0289
MMZ3.3-20	0289
MMZ3.3A	0289
MMZ3.6	0188
MMZ3.6-20	0188
MMZ3.6A	0188
MMZ3.9	0451
MMZ3.9-20	0451
MMZ3.9A	0451
MMZ4.3	0528
MMZ4.3-20	0528
MMZ4.3A	0528
MMZ4.7	0446
MMZ4.7-20	0446
MMZ4.7A	0446
MMZ5.1	0162
MMZ5.1-20	0162
MMZ5.1A	0162
MMZ5.6	0157
MMZ5.6-20	0157
MMZ5.6A	0157
MMZ6.2	0631
MMZ6.2-20	0631
MMZ6.2A	0631
MMZ6.8	0025
MMZ6.8-20	0025
MMZ6.8A	0025
MMZ7.5	0644
MMZ7.5-20	0644
MMZ7.5A	0644
MMZ8.2	0244
MMZ8.2-20	0244
MMZ8.2A	0244
MMZ9.1	0012
MMZ9.1-20	0012
MMZ9.1A	0012
MMZ10	0170
MMZ10-20	0170
MMZ10A	0170
MMZ11	0313
MMZ11-20	0313
MMZ11A	0313
MMZ12	0137
MMZ12(06)	0361
MMZ12-20	0137
MMZ12A	0137
MMZ13	0361
MMZ13-20	0361
MMZ13A	0361
MMZ15	0002
MMZ15-20	0002
MMZ15A	0002
MMZ15A-20	0002
MMZ16	0416
MMZ16-20	0416
MMZ16A	0416
MMZ18	0490
MMZ18-20	0490
MMZ18A	0490
MMZ20	0526
MMZ20-20	0526
MMZ20A	0526
MMZ22	0560
MMZ22-20	0560
MMZ22A	0560
MMZ24	0398
MMZ24-20	0398
MMZ24A	0398
MMZ27	0436
MMZ27-20	0436
MMZ27A	0436
MMZ30	0195
MMZ30-20	0195
MMZ30A	0195
MMZ33	0039
MMZ33-20	0039
MMZ33A	0039
MMZ36	0814
MMZ36-20	0814
MMZ36A	0814
MMZ39	0346
MMZ39-20	0346
MMZ39A	0346
MMZ43	0925
MMZ43-20	0925
MMZ43A	0925
MMZ47	0993
MMZ47-20	0993
MMZ47A	0993
MMZ51	0497
MMZ51-20	0497
MMZ51A	0497
MMZ56	0863
MMZ56-20	0863
MMZ56A	0863
MMZ62	0778
MMZ62-20	0778
MMZ62A	0778
MMZ68	2144
MMZ68-20	2144
MMZ68A	2144
MMZ75	1181
MMZ75-20	1181
MMZ75A	1181
MMZ82	0327
MMZ82-20	0327
MMZ82A	0327
MMZ91	1301
MMZ91-20	1301
MMZ91A	1301
MMZ100	0098
MMZ100-20	0098
MMZ100A	0098
MMZ110	OEM
MMZ110-20	0149
MMZ110A	0149
MMZ120	0186
MMZ120-20	0186
MMZ120A	0186
MMZ130	0213
MMZ130-20	0213
MMZ130A	0213
MMZ150	0028
MMZ150-20	0028
MMZ150A	0028
MMZ160	0255
MMZ160-20	0255
MMZ160A	0255
MMZ180	0363
MMZ180-20	0363
MMZ180A	0363
MMZ200	0417
MMZ200-20	0417
MMZ200A	0417
MN12C25	OEM
MN12C25D	OEM
MN12C201D	OEM
MN13A	OEM
MN13B	OEM
MN13C	OEM
MN19	OEM
MN21	0599
MN22	0160
MN23	0160
MN24	0160
MN25	0160
MN26	0160
MN28	OEM
MN29	0160
MN29BLK	0160
MN29GRN	0160
MN29PUR	0160
MN29WHT	0160
MN32	0160
MN34A	0143
MN46	0160
MN48	0160
MN49	0160
MN51	0143
MN52	0004
MN-53	0164
MN53	0004
MN53BLU	0004
MN53GRN	0004
MN53RED	0004
MN54	0079
MN60	0004
MN60(DIODE)	0143
MN61	0969
MN61A	0599
MN62A	0599
MN63	0969
MN63A	0599
MN64	0969
MN73	0160
MN73BLK	0160
MN73WHT	0160
MN74HC00	OEM
MN74HC04	OEM
MN74HC08	OEM
MN74HC14	OEM
MN74HC32	OEM
MN74HC138	OEM
MN74HC373	OEM
MN74HC4066S	OEM
MN76	0085
MN93C-46N	OEM
MN115P	OEM
MN194	0160
MN380	0375
MN380H	0375
MN512K	OEM
MN520	OEM
MN864A	OEM
MN1201A	OEM
MN1202	OEM
MN1203	OEM
MN1204B	OEM
MN1204E	OEM
MN1205A	OEM
MN1205D	OEM
MN1205E	OEM
MN1205F	OEM
MN1205H	OEM
MN1205P	OEM
MN1206A	5753
MN1207	OEM
MN1208	OEM
MN1215P	OEM
MN1217A	OEM
MN1218	OEM
MN1218A	OEM
MN1219	OEM
MN1224	OEM
MN1225	OEM
MN1226	OEM
MN1227(A)	OEM
MN1227A	OEM
MN1228	OEM
MN1228Q	OEM
MN1228T	OEM
MN1230	OEM
MN1257CQ	OEM
MN1280	3479
MN1280-K	3479
MN1280-L	4078
MN1280-M	OEM
MN1280-P	OEM
MN1280-Q	OEM
MN1280-R	3479
MN1280-S	OEM
MN1280L	4078
MN1280M	OEM
MN1280P	OEM
MN1280PQR	3479
MN1280R	3479
MN1280S	OEM
MN1297HNA	OEM
MN1301	4214
MN1380-M	OEM
MN1380-R	OEM
MN1381-Q	OEM
MN1400	OEM
MN1400ES	OEM
MN1400SE	OEM
MN1400VFA	OEM
MN1400VL	OEM
MN1400VN	OEM
MN1400VP	OEM
MN1402	OEM
MN1402ST0	OEM
MN1402STO	OEM
MN1403	OEM
MN1403-TN	OEM
MN1403SB	OEM
MN1403TN	OEM
MN1404	OEM
MN1405	OEM
MN1405GB	OEM
MN1405GH	OEM
MN1405MF	OEM
MN1405SF	OEM
MN1405SH	OEM
MN1405SHB	OEM
MN1405V1	OEM
MN1405VDG	OEM
MN1405VI	OEM
MN1405VK	OEM
MN1405VKL	OEM
MN1405VM	OEM
MN1405VS	OEM
MN1405VT	OEM
MN1405VXAO	OEM
MN1414HE	OEM
MN1414HF	OEM
MN1416SAA	OEM
MN1418BQR	OEM
MN1418BQS	OEM
MN1421FPC	OEM
MN1425VKI	OEM
MN1425VKL	OEM
MN1425VKM	OEM
MN1430	OEM
MN1432	OEM
MN1435	OEM
MN1450	OEM
MN1453	OEM
MN1454	OEM
MN1455	OEM
MN1455BVC	OEM
MN1483AH	OEM
MN1498	OEM
MN1499	OEM
MN1499A	OEM
MN1513VTF	1059
MN1527KMA	OEM
MN1534VRD	OEM
MN1542	OEM
MN1544	OEM
MN1547VSG	OEM
MN1550PDT	OEM
MN1550PEB	OEM
MN1551ASSA-1	OEM
MN1551KVA	OEM
MN1551SSA	OEM
MN1562	OEM
MN1564	OEM
MN1599	OEM
MN1610	OEM
MN1611	OEM
MN2020	OEM
MN2114	5206
MN2114-2	OEM
MN2200	OEM
MN2200H	OEM
MN2332	OEM
MN2716	6335
MN3001	5671
MN3002	OEM
MN3003	OEM
MN3004	OEM
MN3005	OEM
MN3006	OEM
MN3007	5109
MN3008	OEM
MN3009	OEM
MN3010	OEM
MN3011	5671
MN3012	OEM
MN3013	OEM
MN3101	4214
MN3102	OEM
MN3107CS	OEM
MN3204	OEM
MN3206	OEM
MN3207	OEM
MN3209	OEM
MN3210	OEM
MN3349	OEM
MN3349H	OEM
MN3412	OEM
MN3412H	OEM
MN3735F	OEM
MN3735FC	OEM
MN3735FCW	OEM
MN3735FS	OEM
MN3739FC	OEM
MN3810K	OEM
MN3810S	OEM
MN3817S	OEM
MN3818S	OEM
MN3830S	OEM
MN4001B	0473
MN4011B	0215
MN4011BS	OEM
MN4013B	0409
MN4013BS	OEM
MN4027B	1938
MN4030L	OEM
MN4040BS	OEM
MN4049B	5379
MN4052B	0024
MN4052BS	OEM
MN4053B	0034
MN4053BS	OEM
MN4053S	OEM
MN4066B	0101
MN4066BP	0101
MN4069UB	0119
MN4069UBS	0119
MN4071B	0129
MN4071BS	OEM
MN4081B	0621
MN4116	0518
MN4164P-12A	OEM
MN4164P-15A	2341
MN4264-15	OEM
MN4264P-15	OEM
MN4364-15	OEM
MN4503B	2042
MN4503BS	OEM
MN4528B	3168
MN4700	OEM
MN5101	4524
MN5104	OEM
MN5104S	OEM
MN5128	OEM
MN5150	OEM
MN5150H	OEM
MN5245	OEM
MN5260	OEM
MN5613AN	6497
MN6010	OEM
MN6010A	OEM
MN6013AS	OEM
MN6013BS	OEM
MN6013C	OEM
MN6013G	OEM
MN6013N	OEM
MN6014JS	OEM
MN6014W	OEM
MN6016A	4665
MN6016AK	OEM
MN6016AS	OEM
MN6021	OEM
MN6024	OEM
MN6025D	OEM
MN6027	OEM
MN6027B	OEM
MN6028	OEM
MN6028R	OEM
MN6030C	OEM
MN6030CA	OEM
MN6030HA	OEM
MN6030Z	OEM
MN6040	2592
MN6040A	2592
MN6044	OEM
MN6044A	OEM
MN6049	5182
MN6053	OEM
MN6054	OEM
MN6056	OEM
MN6057	OEM
MN6058	OEM
MN6059	OEM
MN6061A	4665
MN6062	OEM
MN6064	OEM
MN6064R	OEM
MN6069	OEM
MN6076	4669
MN6076L	OEM
MN6091	OEM
MN6092	OEM
MN6092A	OEM
MN6093	OEM
MN6163	5170
MN6163A	5170
MN6165VAA	OEM
MN6165VCA	OEM
MN6168IB	OEM
MN6168V1B	OEM
MN6168VIB	OEM
MN6168VIH	OEM
MN6175VCAK	OEM
MN6178CC	OEM
MN6178VAD	OEM
MN6178VAF	OEM
MN6179VBH	OEM
MN6221	OEM
MN6250	OEM
MN6251	OEM
MN6366	6175
MN6550B	OEM
MN6617	OEM
MN6617S	OEM
MN6618A	OEM
MN6623	OEM
MN6625	OEM
MN6632A	OEM
MN6632AK	OEM
MN6633	OEM
MN6634	OEM
MN6636	OEM
MN6636S	OEM
MN6712VLQ	OEM
MN6746VDAK	OEM
MN6746VDBK	OEM
MN6748FVAN	OEM
MN6790S	OEM
MN6790S-E2	OEM
MN6790S-T2	OEM
MN8027	OEM
MN8036	OEM
MN8303	0194
MN8303(IC)	OEM
MN12872A	OEM
MN12872FVAB	OEM
MN12973NAB	OEM
MN12973NAC	OEM
MN14821VVZ	OEM
MN14823QS	OEM
MN14823QSA	OEM
MN14823QU	OEM
MN14831JTD	OEM
MN14831JTZ	OEM
MN14833JTY	OEM
MN14834H	OEM
MN14834HH	OEM
MN14843JTX	OEM
MN14844HK	OEM
MN15151KWDC	OEM
MN15151Q14	OEM
MN15151Q14A	OEM
MN15151Q14N	OEM
MN15151Q14R	OEM
MN15151SAMA-2	OEM
MN15212HX	OEM
MN15221HP	OEM
MN15241QT	OEM
MN15241QTA	OEM
MN15241QTB2	OEM
MN15243VSN	OEM
MN15247Q10	OEM
MN15247Q10A	OEM
MN15247Q12	OEM
MN15261D01	OEM
MN15261D05	OEM
MN15261DO1	OEM
MN15261PDU	OEM
MN15261SVA	OEM
MN15263VAC	OEM
MN15266HM	OEM
MN15266HN	OEM
MN15266JMC	OEM
MN15266JMC-1	OEM
MN15281VAE	OEM
MN15283PER	OEM
MN15283PJG-2	OEM
MN15283PJL	OEM
MN15284HQ	OEM
MN15284HS	OEM
MN15286Q9	OEM
MN15286Q11	OEM
MN15287-SNE3	OEM
MN15287HM	OEM
MN15287HW	OEM
MN15287HY	OEM
MN15287JMM	OEM
MN15287SNE-4	OEM
MN15341-VKR	OEM
MN15522VLDS	OEM
MN15522VLMS	OEM
MN15831VSE	OEM
MN15832VRB	OEM
MN15832VSR	OEM
MN15841VKP	OEM
MN15841VKQ	OEM
MN15842-VXC	OEM
MN15842VUD	OEM
MN15842VXC	OEM
MN15843VRA	OEM
MN15844VSA	OEM
MN15844VSA-4	OEM
MN15844VSB	OEM
MN15844VSC	OEM
MN15845PEQ	OEM
MN15846VRC	OEM
MN15846VRG	OEM
MN15846VRG3	OEM
MN15847VSG	OEM
MN15847VSJ	OEM
MN15847VSL	OEM
MN15847VSL3	OEM
MN15847VSP	OEM
MN18781D22	OEM
MN18781D25	OEM
MN18781D26	OEM
MN18781D36	OEM
MN18788VRN2	OEM
MN18788VZL3	OEM
MN40098B	0427
MN41256-15	1463
MN41464-15	OEM
MN47464L-12	OEM
MN51003NJB	OEM
MN51003SVB	OEM
MN52040KVF	OEM
MN53015	OEM
MN53015XBM	OEM
MN53015XBR	OEM
MN60111AK	OEM
MN61753VCBK	OEM
MN61753VCEK	OEM
MN61754VCCK	OEM
MN67461VDFK	OEM
MN67461VDHK	OEM
MN67461VDLK	OEM
MN67461VDMF	OEM
MN67461VDNF	OEM
MN67512VLQ	OEM
MN67520IFVCS	OEM
MN67520VLS	OEM
MN67520VLT	OEM
MN67520VLW	OEM
MN67520VLX4	OEM
MN67603NS	OEM
MN152121JGM2	OEM
MN152121JM	OEM
MN152121JMT-3	OEM
MN152121JMT3	OEM
MN152121JMT-4	OEM
MN152121JMT4	OEM
MN152121JMT-5	OEM
MN152121JMT5	OEM
MN152121MTB-2	OEM
MN152121MTC	OEM
MN152611D07	OEM
MN152611PEN	OEM
MN152810Q16N	OEM
MN158241VAK	OEM
MN158461VAA2	OEM
MN158461VAL	OEM
MN158471VAB	OEM
MN187124FVCW	OEM
MN187129VLP	OEM
MN187164VRQ	OEM
MN188166VLC3	OEM
MN617531VCEK	OEM
MN617541VCDK	OEM
MN675201VZE	OEM
MN1872012AHHB-5	OEM
MN1872012HHB-1	OEM
MN1872012HHB-3	OEM
MN1872419Q17	OEM
MN1872432QAB	OEM
MN1872432QAD	OEM
MN1873234QAM	OEM
MNADC85C	OEM
MNADC87	OEM
MNADC87B	OEM
MNADC87H	OEM
MNADC87H/B	OEM
MO066A	OEM
MO101AL	OEM
MO101AM	OEM
MO101AS	OEM
MO101BL-FL	OEM
MO101BM-FM	OEM
MO101BS-FS	OEM
MO101GL	OEM
MO101GM	OEM
MO101GP	OEM
MO101GS	OEM
MO101HL	OEM
MO101HM	OEM
MO101HP	OEM
MO101HS	OEM
MO101JL-ML	OEM
MO101JM-MM	OEM
MO101JP-MP	OEM
MO101JS-MS	OEM
MO102AL	OEM
MO102AM	OEM
MO102AP	OEM
MO102AS	OEM
MO102BL-FL	OEM
MO102BM-FM	OEM
MO102BP	OEM
MO102BP-FP	OEM
MO102BS-FS	OEM
MO102GL	OEM
MO102GM	OEM
MO102GP	OEM
MO102GS	OEM
MO102HL	OEM

If replacement code is OEM, contact original manufacturer for replacement.

491

DEVICE TYPE	REPL CODE
MO102HM	OEM
MO102HP	OEM
MO102HS	OEM
MO102JL-LL	OEM
MO102JM-LM	OEM
MO102JP-LP	OEM
MO102JS-LS	OEM
MO103AL	OEM
MO103AM	OEM
MO103AP	OEM
MO103AS	OEM
MO103BL-FL	OEM
MO103BM-EM	OEM
MO103BP-FP	OEM
MO103BS-FS	OEM
MO103FM	OEM
MO103GL	OEM
MO103GP	OEM
MO103GS	OEM
MO103HL	OEM
MO103HP	OEM
MO103HS	OEM
MO111AJ	OEM
MO111AL	OEM
MO111AM	OEM
MO111BJ	OEM
MO111BL	OEM
MO111BM	OEM
MO112AJ	OEM
MO112AL	OEM
MO112AM	OEM
MO113AJ	OEM
MO113AL	OEM
MO113AM	OEM
MO114AJ	OEM
MO114AL	OEM
MO120AJ	OEM
MO120AL	OEM
MO120AM	OEM
MO120BJ	OEM
MO120BL	OEM
MO120BM	OEM
MO121AJ	OEM
MO121AL	OEM
MO121AM	OEM
MO121BJ	OEM
MO121BL	OEM
MO121BM	OEM
MO122AJ	OEM
MO122AL	OEM
MO122AM	OEM
MO122BJ	OEM
MO122BL	OEM
MO122BM	OEM
MO123AJ	OEM
MO123AL	OEM
MO123BJ	OEM
MO123BL	OEM
MO124AJ	OEM
MO124AL	OEM
MO124BJ	OEM
MO124BL	OEM
MO130C	OEM
MO130L	OEM
MO131C	OEM
MO131L	OEM
MO132C	OEM
MO132L	OEM
MO133C	OEM
MO133L	OEM
MO140C	OEM
MO140L	OEM
MO141C	OEM
MO141L	OEM
MO142C	OEM
MO142L	OEM
MO143C	OEM
MO143L	OEM
MO150C	OEM
MO150L	OEM
MO151C	OEM
MO151L	OEM
MO152C	OEM
MO152L	OEM
MO153C	OEM
MO153L	OEM
MO201AL	OEM
MO201AM	OEM
MO201AP	OEM
MO201AS	OEM
MO201BL-EL	OEM
MO201BM-EM	OEM
MO201BP-EP	OEM
MO201BS-ES	OEM
MO201FL	OEM
MO201FM	OEM
MO201FP	OEM
MO201FS	OEM
MO201GL	OEM
MO201GM-HM	OEM
MO201GP	OEM
MO201GS	OEM
MO201HL	OEM
MO201HP	OEM
MO201HS	OEM
MO201JL	OEM
MO201JM	OEM
MO201JP	OEM
MO201JS	OEM

DEVICE TYPE	REPL CODE
MO201KL-NL	OEM
MO201KM-NM	OEM
MO201KP-NP	OEM
MO201KS-NS	OEM
MO202AL	OEM
MO202AM	OEM
MO202AP	OEM
MO202AS	OEM
MO202BL-FL	OEM
MO202BM-FM	OEM
MO202BP-FP	OEM
MO202BS-FS	OEM
MO202GL	OEM
MO202GM	OEM
MO202GP	OEM
MO202GS	OEM
MO202HL	OEM
MO202HM	OEM
MO202HP	OEM
MO202HS	OEM
MO202JL-LL	OEM
MO202JM-LM	OEM
MO202JP-LP	OEM
MO202JS-LS	OEM
MO203AL	OEM
MO203AM	OEM
MO203AP	OEM
MO203AS	OEM
MO203BL-EL	OEM
MO203BM-EM	OEM
MO203BP-EP	OEM
MO203BS-ES	OEM
MO203FL-HL	OEM
MO203FM-HM	OEM
MO203FP-HP	OEM
MO203FS-HS	OEM
MO261C	OEM
MO261J	OEM
MO261L	OEM
MO262C	OEM
MO262J	OEM
MO262L	OEM
MO263C	OEM
MO263J	OEM
MO263L	OEM
MO264C	OEM
MO264J	OEM
MO264L	OEM
MO265C	OEM
MO265J	OEM
MO265L	OEM
MO266C	OEM
MO266J	OEM
MO266L	OEM
MO267C	OEM
MO267J	OEM
MO267L	OEM
MO268C	OEM
MO268J	OEM
MO268L	OEM
MO269C	OEM
MO269J	OEM
MO269L	OEM
MO270C	OEM
MO270J	OEM
MO270L	OEM
MO271C	OEM
MO271J	OEM
MO271L	OEM
MO272C	OEM
MO272J	OEM
MO272L	OEM
MO273C	OEM
MO273J	OEM
MO273L	OEM
MO274C	OEM
MO274J	OEM
MO274L	OEM
MO275C	OEM
MO275J	OEM
MO275L	OEM
MO276C	OEM
MO276J	OEM
MO276L	OEM
MO277C	OEM
MO277J	OEM
MO277L	OEM
MO280C	OEM
MO280J	OEM
MO280L	OEM
MO281C	OEM
MO281J	OEM
MO281L	OEM
MO282C	OEM
MO282J	OEM
MO282L	OEM
MO283C	OEM
MO283J	OEM
MO283L	OEM
MO284C	OEM
MO284J	OEM
MO284L	OEM
MO285C	OEM
MO285J	OEM
MO285L	OEM
MO286C	OEM
MO286J	OEM
MO286L	OEM
MO287C	OEM

DEVICE TYPE	REPL CODE
MO287J	OEM
MO287L	OEM
MO301AD	OEM
MO301AL	OEM
MO301AM	OEM
MO301AP	OEM
MO301AS	OEM
MO301BD-DD	OEM
MO301BL-DL	OEM
MO301BM-DM	OEM
MO301BP-DP	OEM
MO301BS-DS	OEM
MO302AD	OEM
MO302AL	OEM
MO302AM	OEM
MO302AP	OEM
MO302AS	OEM
MO302BD-DD	OEM
MO302BL-DL	OEM
MO302BM-DM	OEM
MO302BP-DP	OEM
MO302BS-DS	OEM
MO303AD	OEM
MO303AL	OEM
MO303AM	OEM
MO303AP	OEM
MO303AS	OEM
MO303BD	OEM
MO303BL	OEM
MO303BM	OEM
MO303BP	OEM
MO303BS	OEM
MO304AD	OEM
MO304AL	OEM
MO304AM	OEM
MO304AP	OEM
MO304AS	OEM
MO304BD	OEM
MO304BL	OEM
MO304BM	OEM
MO304BP	OEM
MO304BS	OEM
MO305AD	OEM
MO305AL	OEM
MO305AM	OEM
MO305AP	OEM
MO305AS	OEM
MO305BD	OEM
MO305BL	OEM
MO305BM	OEM
MO305BP	OEM
MO305BS	OEM
MO311AD	OEM
MO311AL	OEM
MO311AM	OEM
MO311AP	OEM
MO311AS	OEM
MO311BD-DD	OEM
MO311BL-DL	OEM
MO311BM-DM	OEM
MO311BP-DP	OEM
MO311BS-DS	OEM
MO312AD	OEM
MO312AL	OEM
MO312AM	OEM
MO312AP	OEM
MO312AS	OEM
MO312BD-DD	OEM
MO312BL-DL	OEM
MO312BM-DM	OEM
MO312BP-DP	OEM
MO312BS-DS	OEM
MO313AD	OEM
MO313AL	OEM
MO313AM	OEM
MO313AP	OEM
MO313AS	OEM
MO313BD	OEM
MO313BL	OEM
MO313BM	OEM
MO313BP	OEM
MO313BS	OEM
MO314AD	OEM
MO314AL	OEM
MO314AM	OEM
MO314AP	OEM
MO314AS	OEM
MO314BD	OEM
MO314BL	OEM
MO314BM	OEM
MO314BP	OEM
MO314BS	OEM
MO315AD	OEM
MO315AL	OEM
MO315AM	OEM
MO315AP	OEM
MO315AS	OEM
MO315BD	OEM
MO315BL	OEM
MO315BM	OEM
MO315BP	OEM
MO315BS	OEM
MO321AD	OEM
MO321AL	OEM
MO321AM	OEM
MO321AP	OEM
MO321AS	OEM
MO321BD	OEM
MO321BL	OEM

DEVICE TYPE	REPL CODE
MO321BM	OEM
MO321BP	OEM
MO321BS	OEM
MO321CD	OEM
MO321CL	OEM
MO321CM	OEM
MO321CP	OEM
MO321CS	OEM
MO322AD	OEM
MO322AL	OEM
MO322AM	OEM
MO322AP	OEM
MO322AS	OEM
MO322BD	OEM
MO322BL	OEM
MO322BM	OEM
MO322BP	OEM
MO322BS	OEM
MO322CD	OEM
MO322CL	OEM
MO322CM	OEM
MO322CP	OEM
MO322CS	OEM
MO323AD	OEM
MO323AL	OEM
MO323AM	OEM
MO323AP	OEM
MO323AS	OEM
MO323BD	OEM
MO323BL	OEM
MO323BM	OEM
MO323BS	OEM
MO323CD	OEM
MO323CL	OEM
MO323CM	OEM
MO323CP	OEM
MO323CS	OEM
MO324AD	OEM
MO324AL	OEM
MO324AM	OEM
MO324AP	OEM
MO324AS	OEM
MO324BD	OEM
MO324BL	OEM
MO324BM	OEM
MO324BP	OEM
MO324BS	OEM
MO325AD	OEM
MO325AL	OEM
MO325AM	OEM
MO325AP	OEM
MO325AS	OEM
MO325BD	OEM
MO325BL	OEM
MO325BM	OEM
MO325BP	OEM
MO325BS	OEM
MO326AD	OEM
MO326AL	OEM
MO326AM	OEM
MO326AP	OEM
MO326AS	OEM
MO326BD	OEM
MO326BL	OEM
MO326BM	OEM
MO326BP	OEM
MO326BS	OEM
MO327AD	OEM
MO327AL	OEM
MO327AM	OEM
MO327AP	OEM
MO327AS	OEM
MO327BD	OEM
MO327BL	OEM
MO327BM	OEM
MO327BP	OEM
MO327BS	OEM
MO328AD	OEM
MO328AL	OEM
MO328AM	OEM
MO328AP	OEM
MO328AS	OEM
MO328BD	OEM
MO328BL	OEM
MO328BM	OEM
MO328BS	OEM
MO331AD	OEM
MO331AL	OEM
MO331AM	OEM
MO331AP	OEM
MO331AS	OEM
MO331BD	OEM
MO331BL	OEM
MO331BM	OEM
MO331BP	OEM
MO331BS	OEM
MO331CD	OEM
MO331CL	OEM
MO331CM	OEM
MO331CP	OEM
MO331CS	OEM
MO332AD	OEM
MO332AL	OEM
MO332AM	OEM
MO332AP	OEM
MO332AS	OEM
MO332BD	OEM
MO332BL	OEM

DEVICE TYPE	REPL CODE
MO332BM	OEM
MO332BP	OEM
MO332BS	OEM
MO332CD	OEM
MO332CL	OEM
MO332CM	OEM
MO332CP	OEM
MO332CS	OEM
MO333AD	OEM
MO333AL	OEM
MO333AM	OEM
MO333AP	OEM
MO333AS	OEM
MO333BD	OEM
MO333BL	OEM
MO333BM	OEM
MO333BP	OEM
MO333BS	OEM
MO333CD	OEM
MO333CL	OEM
MO333CM	OEM
MO333CP	OEM
MO333CS	OEM
MO334AD	OEM
MO334AL	OEM
MO334AM	OEM
MO334AP	OEM
MO334AS	OEM
MO334BD	OEM
MO334BL	OEM
MO334BM	OEM
MO334BP	OEM
MO334BS	OEM
MO335AD	OEM
MO335AL	OEM
MO335AM	OEM
MO335AP	OEM
MO335AS	OEM
MO335BD	OEM
MO335BL	OEM
MO335BM	OEM
MO335BP	OEM
MO335BS	OEM
MO336AD	OEM
MO336AL	OEM
MO336AM	OEM
MO336AP	OEM
MO336AS	OEM
MO336BD	OEM
MO336BL	OEM
MO336BM	OEM
MO336BP	OEM
MO336BS	OEM
MO337AD	OEM
MO337AL	OEM
MO337AM	OEM
MO337AP	OEM
MO337AS	OEM
MO337BD	OEM
MO337BL	OEM
MO337BM	OEM
MO337BP	OEM
MO337BS	OEM
MO338AD	OEM
MO338AL	OEM
MO338AP	OEM
MO338AS	OEM
MO342AD	OEM
MO342AL	OEM
MO342AM	OEM
MO342AP	OEM
MO342AS	OEM
MO342BD	OEM
MO342BL	OEM
MO342BM	OEM
MO342BP	OEM
MO342BS	OEM
MO342CD	OEM
MO342CL	OEM
MO342CM	OEM
MO342CP	OEM
MO342CS	OEM
MO343AD	OEM
MO343AL	OEM
MO343AM	OEM
MO343AP	OEM
MO343AS	OEM
MO343BD	OEM
MO343BL	OEM
MO343BM	OEM
MO343BP	OEM
MO343BS	OEM
MO344AD	OEM
MO344AL	OEM
MO344AM	OEM
MO344AP	OEM
MO344AS	OEM
MO344BD	OEM
MO344BL	OEM
MO344BM	OEM
MO344BP	OEM
MO344BS	OEM
MO345AD	OEM
MO345AL	OEM
MO345AM	OEM
MO345AP	OEM
MO345AS	OEM
MO345BD	OEM
MO345BL	OEM

DEVICE TYPE	REPL CODE
MO345BM	OEM
MO345BP	OEM
MO345BS	OEM
MO346AD	OEM
MO346AL	OEM
MO346AM	OEM
MO346AP	OEM
MO346AS	OEM
MO346BD	OEM
MO346BL	OEM
MO346BM	OEM
MO346BP	OEM
MO346BS	OEM
MO347AD	OEM
MO347AL	OEM
MO347AM	OEM
MO347AP	OEM
MO347AS	OEM
MO347BD	OEM
MO347BL	OEM
MO347BM	OEM
MO347BP	OEM
MO347BS	OEM
MO348AD	OEM
MO348AL	OEM
MO348AP	OEM
MO348AS	OEM
MO352AD	OEM
MO352AL	OEM
MO352AM	OEM
MO352AP	OEM
MO352AS	OEM
MO352BD	OEM
MO352BL	OEM
MO352BM	OEM
MO352BP	OEM
MO352BS	OEM
MO353AD	OEM
MO353AL	OEM
MO353AM	OEM
MO353AP	OEM
MO353AS	OEM
MO353BD	OEM
MO353BL	OEM
MO353BM	OEM
MO353BP	OEM
MO353BS	OEM
MO354AD	OEM
MO354AL	OEM
MO354AM	OEM
MO354AP	OEM
MO354AS	OEM
MO354BD	OEM
MO354BL	OEM
MO354BM	OEM
MO354BP	OEM
MO354BS	OEM
MO355AD	OEM
MO355AL	OEM
MO355AM	OEM
MO355AP	OEM
MO355AS	OEM
MO355BD	OEM
MO355BM	OEM
MO355BO	OEM
MO355BP	OEM
MO355BS	OEM
MO356AD	OEM
MO356AL	OEM
MO356AM	OEM
MO356AP	OEM
MO356AS	OEM
MO356BD	OEM
MO356BL	OEM
MO356BM	OEM
MO356BP	OEM
MO356BS	OEM
MO357AD	OEM
MO357AL	OEM
MO357AM	OEM
MO357AP	OEM
MO357AS	OEM
MO357BD	OEM
MO357BL	OEM
MO357BM	OEM
MO357BP	OEM
MO357BS	OEM
MO358AD	OEM
MO358AL	OEM
MO358AP	OEM
MO358AS	OEM
MO358BD	OEM
MO358BL	OEM
MO358BM	OEM
MO358BP	OEM
MO358BS	OEM
MO362AD	OEM
MO362AL	OEM
MO362AM	OEM
MO362AP	OEM
MO362AS	OEM
MO362BD	OEM
MO362BL	OEM
MO362BM	OEM
MO362BP	OEM
MO362BS	OEM
MO363AD	OEM
MO363AL	OEM
MO363AM	OEM

DEVICE TYPE	REPL CODE
MO363AP	OEM
MO363AS	OEM
MO363BD	OEM
MO363BL	OEM
MO363BM	OEM
MO363BP	OEM
MO363BS	OEM
MO364AD	OEM
MO364AL	OEM
MO364AM	OEM
MO364AP	OEM
MO364AS	OEM
MO364BD	OEM
MO364BL	OEM
MO364BM	OEM
MO364BP	OEM
MO364BS	OEM
MO365AD	OEM
MO365AL	OEM
MO365AM	OEM
MO365AP	OEM
MO365AS	OEM
MO365BD	OEM
MO365BL	OEM
MO365BM	OEM
MO365BP	OEM
MO365BS	OEM
MO366AD	OEM
MO366AL	OEM
MO366AM	OEM
MO366AP	OEM
MO366AS	OEM
MO366BD	OEM
MO366BL	OEM
MO366BM	OEM
MO366BP	OEM
MO366BS	OEM
MO367AD	OEM
MO367AL	OEM
MO367AM	OEM
MO367AP	OEM
MO367AS	OEM
MO368AD	OEM
MO368AL	OEM
MO368AP	OEM
MO368AS	OEM
MO1124	OEM
MO1125	OEM
MO1126	OEM
MO1201	OEM
MO1202	OEM
MO1203	OEM
MO1204	OEM
MO1205	OEM
MO1206	OEM
MO1207	OEM
MO1208	OEM
MO1209	OEM
MO1210	OEM
MO1902	OEM
MO1902A	OEM
MO1902B	OEM
MO1903	OEM
MO1903A	OEM
MO1903B	OEM
MO1903C	OEM
MO-2001	OEM
MO2002B	OEM
MO2002C	OEM
MO2002D	OEM
MO2002E	OEM
MO2002F	OEM
MO2002G	OEM
MO2003B	OEM
MO2003C	OEM
MO2003D	OEM
MO2003E	OEM
MO2003F	OEM
MO2003G	OEM
MO2004	OEM
MO2004A	OEM
MO-2005	OEM
MO-2005A	OEM
MO2014	OEM
MO2014A	OEM
MO2014B	OEM
MO2014C	OEM
MO2014D	OEM
MO2014E	OEM
MO2014F	OEM
MO2111	OEM
MO2120B	OEM
MO2120C	OEM
MO2120D	OEM
MO2120E	OEM
MO2120F	OEM
MO2120G	OEM
MO2121B	OEM
MO2121C	OEM
MO2121D	OEM
MO2121F	OEM
MO2121G	OEM
MO2122	OEM
MO2123	OEM
MO2130B	OEM
MO2130C	OEM
MO2130D	OEM
MO2130E	OEM
MO2130F	OEM

If replacement code is OEM, contact original manufacturer for replacement.

DEVICE TYPE	REPL CODE
MO2130G	OEM
MO2131B	OEM
MO2131C	OEM
MO2131D	OEM
MO2131F	OEM
MO2131G	OEM
MO2132	OEM
MO2132A	OEM
MO2132B	OEM
MO2140	OEM
MO2140A	OEM
MO2141	OEM
MO2141A	OEM
MO2150	OEM
MO2151	OEM
MO2160	OEM
MO2160A	OEM
MO2170	OEM
MO2171	OEM
MO-2200	OEM
MO-2200A	OEM
MO-2201	OEM
MO-2201A	OEM
MO-2210A	OEM
MO-2211	OEM
MO-2211A	OEM
MO-2211B	OEM
MO-2212	OEM
MO-2212A	OEM
MO-2213	OEM
MO-2213A	OEM
MO-2220	OEM
MO-2220A	OEM
MO-2221	OEM
MO-2221A	OEM
MO-2230	OEM
MO-2230A	OEM
MO-2231	OEM
MO-2231A	OEM
MO-2231B	OEM
MO-2232	OEM
MO-2232A	OEM
MO-2233	OEM
MO-2233A	OEM
MO-2240	OEM
MO-2240A	OEM
MO-2241	OEM
MO-2241A	OEM
MO-2250	OEM
MO-2250A	OEM
MO-2250B	OEM
MO-2251	OEM
MO-2251A	OEM
MO-2251B	OEM
MO-2252	OEM
MO-2252A	OEM
MO-2253	OEM
MO-2253A	OEM
MO-2260	OEM
MO-2260A	OEM
MO-2261	OEM
MO-2261A	OEM
MO-2270	OEM
MO-2270A	OEM
MO-2270B	OEM
MO-2271	OEM
MO-2271A	OEM
MO-2271B	OEM
MO-2272	OEM
MO-2272A	OEM
MO-2273	OEM
MO-2273A	OEM
MO-2290	OEM
MO2301	OEM
MO2301A	OEM
MO2301B	OEM
MO2301C	OEM
MO2302	OEM
MO2302A	OEM
MO2302B	OEM
MO2302C	OEM
MO2303	OEM
MO2304	OEM
MO2305	OEM
MO2305A	OEM
MO-2306	OEM
MO-2306A	OEM
MO-2307	OEM
MO-2307A	OEM
MO2308	OEM
MO-2309	OEM
MO-2310	OEM
MO2360	OEM
MO2370	OEM
MO-2420	OEM
MO-2420A	OEM
MO-2460	OEM
MO-2470	OEM
MO2490	OEM
MO2491	OEM
MO2500	OEM
MO2500A	OEM
MO2500B	OEM
MO2500C	OEM
MO2501	OEM
MO2501A	OEM
MO2501B	OEM
MO2501C	OEM
MO2510	OEM
MO2510A	OEM
MO2510B	OEM
MO2510C	OEM
MO2511	OEM
MO2511A	OEM
MO2511B	OEM
MO2511C	OEM
MO-2620	OEM
MO-2620A	OEM
MO-2621	OEM
MO-2621A	OEM
MO-2630	OEM
MO-2630A	OEM
MO-2630B	OEM
MO-2631	OEM
MO-2631A	OEM
MO-2631B	OEM
MO2691	OEM
MO2701	OEM
MO2701A	OEM
MO2701B	OEM
MO2701C	OEM
MO2701D	OEM
MO2701E	OEM
MO2701F	OEM
MO2703	OEM
MO2703A	OEM
MO2703B	OEM
MO2703C	OEM
MO2703D	OEM
MO2703E	OEM
MO2703F	OEM
MO2707	OEM
MO2707B	OEM
MO2707C	OEM
MO2707D	OEM
MO2707E	OEM
MO2707F	OEM
MO2707G	OEM
MO2708B	OEM
MO2708C	OEM
MO2708D	OEM
MO2708E	OEM
MO2708F	OEM
MO2708G	OEM
MO2800	OEM
MO2800A	OEM
MO2800B	OEM
MO2800C	OEM
MO2800D	OEM
MO2801	OEM
MO2801A	OEM
MO2801B	OEM
MO2801C	OEM
MO2801D	OEM
MO2821	OEM
MO2822	OEM
MO2823	OEM
MO2824	OEM
MO2825	OEM
MOC31D	OEM
MOC31DR	OEM
MOC64A	OEM
MOC119	OEM
MOC601A	OEM
MOC602A	OEM
MOC603A	OEM
MOC604A	OEM
MOC622A	OEM
MOC623A	OEM
MOC624A	OEM
MOC625A	OEM
MOC626A	OEM
MOC627A	OEM
MOC628A	OEM
MOC629A	OEM
MOC633A	OEM
MOC635A	OEM
MOC640A	OEM
MOC1000	0536
MOC1001	0536
MOC1002	0536
MOC1003	0536
MOC1005	0311
MOC1006	0311
MOC1200	1047
MOC3002	0235
MOC3003	0235
MOC3007	0235
MOC3009	4961
MOC3010	4961
MOC3010MTE	4961
MOC3011	4961
MOC3020	4975
MOC3021	4975
MOC3022	4975
MOC3023	4975
MOC3030	5034
MOC3031	5034
MOC3032	5034
MOC3033	OEM
MOC3040	6379
MOC3041	5332
MOC3042	OEM
MOC3043	OEM
MOC5003	OEM
MOC5004	OEM
MOC5007	5328
MOC5008	5328
MOC5009	5328
MOC5010	OEM
MOC7811	1407
MOC7812	1407
MOC7813	1407
MOC7821	2616
MOC7822	2616
MOC7823	2616
MOC8020	OEM
MOC8021	OEM
MOC8030	4845
MOC8050	2096
MOC8100	5331
MOC8111	0536
MOC8112	0311
MOC8113	0311
MOC8204	OEM
MOC8205	OEM
MOC8206	OEM
MOD634A	OEM
MOS3635	0349
MOS6502	3036
MOS6502A	3036
MOS6510	OEM
MOS6510CBM	OEM
MOS6522	OEM
MOS6526	OEM
MOS6526R4	OEM
MOS6529B	OEM
MOS6551CBM	OEM
MOS6560-101	OEM
MOS6567R8	OEM
MOS6567R56A	OEM
MOS6581	OEM
MOS7360R7	OEM
MOS7501	OEM
MOS7712	1623
MOS8250P9	OEM
MOS8360R1	OEM
MOS8501R1	OEM
MOS8701	OEM
MOS8712	1623
MOS8713	1585
MOS65245	OEM
MOS251641-02	OEM
MOS318006-01	OEM
MOS901225-01	OEM
MOS901226-01	OEM
MOS901227-02	OEM
MOS901460-03	OEM
MOS901486-01	OEM
MOS901486-06	OEM
MOS906114-01	OEM
MOZ	0133
MP/100	OEM
MP/100-4K/8K	OEM
MP/100-8K	OEM
MP/100-16K/32K	OEM
MP/200	OEM
MP/200-8K	OEM
MP/200-16K/32K	OEM
MP/200MFC	OEM
MP-01	0015
MP01	0015
MP-02	0287
MP-04	0293
MP-06	0299
MP-08	0250
MP-055	OEM
MP066	OEM
MP067	OEM
MP067A	OEM
MP068	OEM
MP068A	OEM
MP0574J	1319
MP2	0124
MP-10	0250
MP20	OEM
MP40	OEM
MP50A	OEM
MP60	OEM
MP80	OEM
MP81	0319
MP82	1404
MP82HS181	OEM
MP82HS191	OEM
MP82HS321	OEM
MP82S181	OEM
MP82S191	OEM
MP82S321	OEM
MP84	0468
MP86	0441
MP88	1412
MP-100	OEM
MP100	0015
MP101	OEM
MP102	OEM
MP106	OEM
MP108	OEM
MP110	0160
MP110B	0599
MP110B-BLU	0599
MP110B-GRN	0599
MP110B-RED	0599
MP125	OEM
MP200DIAA	OEM
MP200DIAP	OEM
MP200DIBA	OEM
MP200DIBP	OEM
MP200DICJ	OEM
MP201DIAP	OEM
MP201DIBP	OEM
MP201DICJ	OEM
MP225	0015
MP249A	OEM
MP259	OEM
MP260	OEM
MP261	OEM
MP277	OEM
MP278	OEM
MP279	OEM
MP280	OEM
MP281	OEM
MP282	OEM
MP300	0015
MP301	OEM
MP302	OEM
MP303	OEM
MP310	OEM
MP311	OEM
MP312	OEM
MP313	OEM
MP318	OEM
MP-324	OEM
MP350	OEM
MP351	OEM
MP352	OEM
MP358	OEM
MP360	OEM
MP361	OEM
MP362	OEM
MP377B18	OEM
MP377C18	OEM
MP400	0015
MP500	0432
MP500(RECT.)	0015
MP500A	0435
MP501	0435
MP501A	0435
MP502	0435
MP502A	0435
MP503	0435
MP503A	0435
MP504	0435
MP504A	0435
MP505	0435
MP505A	0435
MP506	0435
MP506A	0435
MP507	0435
MP507A	0435
MP525	0085
MP525-1	0599
MP525-2	0599
MP525-3	0599
MP525-4	0599
MP525-5	0599
MP525-6	0599
MP549	0242
MP561JD	OEM
MP561JN	OEM
MP561KD	OEM
MP561KN	OEM
MP561SD	OEM
MP561TD	OEM
MP562ADBCD	OEM
MP562ADBIN	OEM
MP562KDBIN	OEM
MP562SDBCD	OEM
MP562SDBIN	OEM
MP600	0599
MP600A	OEM
MP601	0599
MP601A	OEM
MP602	0599
MP602A	OEM
MP603	0599
MP603A	OEM
MP651	0015
MP701	OEM
MP702	OEM
MP710	OEM
MP802	OEM
MP805	0319
MP810	2425
MP825	OEM
MP830	OEM
MP831	OEM
MP832	OEM
MP833	OEM
MP835	OEM
MP840	OEM
MP841	OEM
MP842	OEM
MP1003-1	0015
MP1003-2	0015
MP1003-4	0015
MP1005	OEM
MP1010	OEM
MP1014	0160
MP1014-1	0004
MP1014-2	0016
MP1014-4	0004
MP1014-5	0004
MP1014-6	0004
MP1077	OEM
MP1104	OEM
MP1111	OEM
MP1111B	OEM
MP1216	OEM
MP1304P	0649
MP1304PQ	0649
MP1509-1	0160
MP1509-2	0160
MP1509-3	0160
MP1529	0599
MP1529A	0599
MP1530	0599
MP1530A	0599
MP1531	0599
MP1531A	0599
MP1532	0160
MP1534	0599
MP1534A	0599
MP1535	0599
MP1535A	0599
MP1536	0599
MP1536A	0599
MP1537	0160
MP1537SL	OEM
MP1538SL	OEM
MP1539	OEM
MP1539A	0599
MP1539SL	OEM
MP1540	OEM
MP1540A	0599
MP1541	OEM
MP1541A	0599
MP1542	OEM
MP1542A	0160
MP1544	OEM
MP1544A	0599
MP1545	OEM
MP1545A	0599
MP1546	OEM
MP1546A	0599
MP1547	OEM
MP1547A	0160
MP1549	0599
MP1550	0599
MP1551	0599
MP1553	0599
MP1553A	0599
MP1554	0599
MP1554A	0599
MP1555	0599
MP1555A	0599
MP1557	0599
MP1557A	0599
MP1558	0599
MP1558A	0599
MP1559	0599
MP1559A	0599
MP1612	0969
MP1612A	0969
MP1612B	0969
MP1613	0969
MP2000A	0599
MP2000B	OEM
MP2060	0160
MP2060-1	0160
MP2060-2	OEM
MP2060-3	OEM
MP2060-4	OEM
MP2060-5	OEM
MP2060-6	OEM
MP2060-7	OEM
MP2061	0160
MP2061-1	OEM
MP2061-2	OEM
MP2061-3	OEM
MP2061-4	OEM
MP2061-5	OEM
MP2061-6	OEM
MP2061-7	OEM
MP2062	0160
MP2062-1	OEM
MP2062-3	OEM
MP2062-4	OEM
MP2062-5	OEM
MP2062-6	OEM
MP2062-7	OEM
MP2063	0599
MP2063-1	OEM
MP2063-2	OEM
MP2063-3	OEM
MP2063-4	OEM
MP2063-5	OEM
MP2063-6	OEM
MP2063-7	OEM
MP2100A	0599
MP2137	OEM
MP2137A	0160
MP2138	OEM
MP2138A	0160
MP2139	0160
MP2139A	0160
MP2140	0160
MP2140A	0599
MP2141	0160
MP2141-2	OEM
MP2141-3	OEM
MP2141-4	OEM
MP2141-5	OEM
MP2141A	0599
MP2141L3	OEM
MP2141L4	OEM
MP2141L5	OEM
MP2142	0085
MP2142-2	OEM
MP2142-3	OEM
MP2142A	0160
MP2142L	OEM
MP2142L3	OEM
MP2143	0160
MP2143A	0160
MP2144	0160
MP2144A	0160
MP2145	0160
MP2145A	0160
MP2146	0160
MP2146A	0160
MP2200A	0599
MP2200B	OEM
MP2216	OEM
MP2216-AO	OEM
MP2300A	0599
MP2526	0599
MP2810SL	OEM
MP2832	0599
MP3495A-N1LL	OEM
MP3495A-NILL	OEM
MP3611	0160
MP3612	0160
MP3613	0160
MP3614	0160
MP3615	0160
MP3616	0160
MP3617	0160
MP3618	0160
MP3730	0969
MP3730A	4233
MP3730B	4233
MP3731	0969
MP4001	OEM
MP4004	OEM
MP4301	OEM
MP5106P	3232
MP5113	0015
MP-5115	0015
MP5186AP	6975
MP5190P	0850
MP6359L	OEM
MP6566	0079
MP7572	OEM
MP8111	0042
MP8112	0042
MP8211	0930
MP8212	0930
MP8213	0930
MP8214	OEM
MP8216	OEM
MP8221	0930
MP8222	0930
MP8223	0930
MP8224	OEM
MP8226	OEM
MP8228	OEM
MP8231	0930
MP8232	0930
MP8251	OEM
MP8253	OEM
MP8255	OEM
MP8255A	OEM
MP8257	OEM
MP8259A	OEM
MP8284	OEM
MP8288	OEM
MP8304	OEM
MP8408	OEM
MP8416	OEM
MP8417	OEM
MP8418	OEM
MP8430	OEM
MP8608	OEM
MP8616	OEM
MP8632	OEM
MP8748	OEM
MP9377-16-4	OEM
MP9377-16-5	OEM
MP9377-16-6	OEM
MP13421	OEM
MP27128-2	1628
MP88303-P	OEM
MP88303P	OEM
MPB2-4H48	OEM
MPB2-5H49	OEM
MPB2-5H59	OEM
MPB2-7C39	OEM
MPB2-7C49	OEM
MPB2-7H39	OEM
MPB2-7H49	OEM
MPB2-12H49	OEM
MPB2-4859	OEM
MPB-100	OEM
MPB121D	2417
MPB123D	2574
MPB124D	4110
MPB125D	2542
MPC-4	OEM
MPC4D	OEM
MPC8D	OEM
MPC8S	OEM
MPC16S	OEM
MPC20C	0465
MPC23C	0523
MPC29C	0633
MPC29C2	0633
MPC30C	0648
MPC-31C	0668
MPC31C	0668
MPC33TS	OEM
MPC33TSAMPC800KG	OEM
MPC46C	0924
MPC47C	0940
MPC48C	0958
MPC100	OEM
MPC558C	3736
MPC561C	2569
MPC562C	2864
MPC566C	OEM
MPC566HB	1983
MPC566HC	1983
MPC566HD	1983
MPC570C	2860
MPC-574J	1319
MPC574J	1319
MPC575C	3788
MPC575C2	2845
MPC577H	2246
MPC595C	0846
MPC596C	0851
MPC596C2	0851
MPC596C2B	0851
MPC800SG	OEM
MPC801KG	OEM
MPC801SG	OEM
MPC1001	OEM
MPC1001H2	4348
MPC1003C2	OEM
MPC1051	OEM
MPC1052	OEM
MPC1053	OEM
MPC1054	OEM
MPC1094C	OEM
MPC1228H	OEM
MPC1352C	0485
MPC1355C	0391
MPC1356C	0859
MPC1356C2	0859
MPC1363	0678
MPC1363C	0678
MPC1367C	2888
MPC1368CA	OEM
MPC1372C	2599
MPC1373H	2015
MPC1373HA	2015
MPC1378	OEM
MPC1382C	2868
MPC1458C	0356
MPC1715FU	OEM
MPC1725MR	OEM
MPC1870CA-001	OEM
MPC3500	0133
MPC-5888	OEM
MPC7812H	0330
MPC7847	OEM
MPC14305	0619
MPD200	0133
MPD201	0133
MPD202	0133
MPD203	0133
MPD300	0133
MPD301	0133
MPD302	0133
MPD400	0133
MPD401	0133
MPD402	0133
MPD552C	OEM
MPD554C-118	OEM
MPD650C109	OEM
MPD858	2238
MPD858C	2238
MPD861C	3763
MPD861CE	3763
MPD1937	OEM
MPD1937C	2079
MPD1986C	OEM
MPD2801	OEM
MPD2801C	OEM
MPD4011B	OEM
MPD4011BC	0215
MPD4013BC	OEM
MPD4013C	OEM
MPD4049C	OEM
MPD4066BC	0101
MPD4066C	OEM
MPD4081C	OEM
MPD4093BC	2368
MPD4555	5583
MPD6104C	OEM
MPD6117C	OEM
MPD6145	OEM
MPD7801	OEM
MPD7810H	OEM
MPD14027BC	1938
MPD42274LE10	OEM
MPD42274LE12	OEM
MPDA	OEM
MPF101	0321
MPF102	1382
MPF103	0321
MPF104	0321
MPF105	0321
MPF-106	0321

If replacement code is OEM, contact original manufacturer for replacement.

493

DEVICE TYPE	REPL CODE
MPF106	1382
MPF107	0321
MPF108	0321
MPF109	3104
MPF109B	OEM
MPF109G	OEM
MPF109N	OEM
MPF109R	OEM
MPF109V	OEM
MPF109W	OEM
MPF109Y	OEM
MPF110	OEM
MPF111	2922
MPF112	0321
MPF120	0212
MPF-121	0212
MPF121	0212
MPF122	OEM
MPF130	0212
MPF131	0212
MPF132	0212
MPF161	2959
MPF201	OEM
MPF202	OEM
MPF203	OEM
MPF211	OEM
MPF212	OEM
MPF213	OEM
MPF230	OEM
MPF231	OEM
MPF232	OEM
MPF256	0321
MPF480	OEM
MPF481	OEM
MPF521	OEM
MPF820	0321
MPF910	OEM
MPF930	OEM
MPF960	OEM
MPF970	OEM
MPF971	OEM
MPF990	OEM
MPF1000	0212
MPF2608	OEM
MPF2609	OEM
MPF3330	OEM
MPF3821	OEM
MPF3822	OEM
MPF3823	OEM
MPF3824	OEM
MPF3970	OEM
MPF3971	OEM
MPF3972	OEM
MPF3993	OEM
MPF3994	OEM
MPF4091	OEM
MPF4092	OEM
MPF4093	OEM
MPF4117	OEM
MPF4117A	OEM
MPF4118	OEM
MPF4118A	OEM
MPF4119	OEM
MPF4119A	OEM
MPF4150	OEM
MPF4220	OEM
MPF4220A	OEM
MPF4221	OEM
MPF4221A	OEM
MPF4222	OEM
MPF4222A	OEM
MPF4223	OEM
MPF4224	OEM
MPF4391	OEM
MPF4392	OEM
MPF4393	OEM
MPF4416	OEM
MPF4416A	OEM
MPF4856	OEM
MPF4856A	OEM
MPF4857	OEM
MPF4857A	OEM
MPF4858	OEM
MPF4858A	OEM
MPF4859	OEM
MPF4859A	OEM
MPF4860	OEM
MPF4860A	OEM
MPF4861	OEM
MPF4861A	OEM
MPF6659	OEM
MPF6660	OEM
MPF6661	OEM
MPF9200	OEM
MPG06D	0023
MPG3877S	OEM
MPI3401	OEM
MPL1000	0037
MPM5006	0224
MPN3201	0133
MPN3202	OEM
MPN3208	OEM
MPN3209	OEM
MPN-3401	0133
MPN3401	2496
MPN3402	2496
MPN3404	OEM
MPN3411	OEM
MPN3412	0124

DEVICE TYPE	REPL CODE
MPN3500	OEM
MPN3503	OEM
MPN3504	OEM
MPQ918	0539
MPQ1500	6230
MPQ2221	0539
MPQ2221A	OEM
MPQ2222	0539
MPQ2222A	OEM
MPQ2369	0539
MPQ2483	2877
MPQ2483-1	OEM
MPQ2483-2	OEM
MPQ2484	OEM
MPQ2484-1	OEM
MPQ2484-2	OEM
MPQ2906	3628
MPQ2906A	OEM
MPQ2907	3628
MPQ2907A	OEM
MPQ3303	OEM
MPQ3467	6230
MPQ3546	OEM
MPQ3724	OEM
MPQ3725	0539
MPQ3725A	OEM
MPQ3762	OEM
MPQ3798	0281
MPQ3798-1	OEM
MPQ3798-2	OEM
MPQ3799	0281
MPQ3799-1	OEM
MPQ3799-2	OEM
MPQ3904	0539
MPQ3906	0281
MPQ6001	OEM
MPQ6002	OEM
MPQ6100	OEM
MPQ6100A	OEM
MPQ6426	OEM
MPQ6427	OEM
MPQ6501	6664
MPQ6502	2976
MPQ6600	OEM
MPQ6600-1	OEM
MPQ6600-2	OEM
MPQ6600A	OEM
MPQ6600A1	OEM
MPQ6600A2	OEM
MPQ6700	6664
MPQ6842	OEM
MPQ7041	5251
MPQ7042	6691
MPQ7043	5251
MPQ7051	OEM
MPQ7052	OEM
MPQ7053	OEM
MPQ7091	OEM
MPQ7092	OEM
MPQ7093	OEM
MPR10	OEM
MPR12	OEM
MPR15	OEM
MPR20	OEM
MPR40	OEM
MPR60	OEM
MPR80	OEM
MPR100	OEM
MPR125	OEM
MPR3877S	OEM
MPS-22	OEM
MPS25	0160
MPS-42	OEM
MPS-44	OEM
MPS-82	OEM
MPS-82-CL	OEM
MPS393	0079
MPS404	0037
MPS404A	0037
MPS407	OEM
MPS551M	0710
MPS654	0127
MPS-706	0079
MPS706	0079
MPS706A	0079
MPS706AK	OEM
MPS706AL	OEM
MPS706AM	OEM
MPS706K	OEM
MPS706L	OEM
MPS706M	OEM
MPS708	0144
MPS751	OEM
MPS751A	OEM
MPS805	0144
MPS834	0079
MPS835	0079
MPS918	0144
MPS929	0037
MPS929A	0037
MPS930	0037
MPS930A	0037
MPS960T	0079
MPS1097	0050
MPS1572	0037
MPS2114-30	2037
MPS2114-35	2037
MPS2114-45	2037
MPS2114-50	2037

DEVICE TYPE	REPL CODE
MPS2114L-30	OEM
MPS2114L-35	OEM
MPS2114L-45	OEM
MPS2221	0079
MPS2221A	0079
MPS2222	0079
MPS2222A	0079
MPS2222AK	OEM
MPS2222AL	OEM
MPS2222AM	OEM
MPS2222L	OEM
MPS2222M	OEM
MPS2223K	OEM
MPS2316	OEM
MPS2332	OEM
MPS2364	OEM
MPS2369	0079
MPS2369A	0734
MPS2369AK	OEM
MPS2369AL	OEM
MPS2369AM	OEM
MPS2369K	OEM
MPS2369L	OEM
MPS2369M	OEM
MPS2484	OEM
MPS2484K	OEM
MPS2484L	OEM
MPS2484M	OEM
MPS2709	0165
MPS2711	0079
MPS2711K	OEM
MPS2711L	OEM
MPS2711M	OEM
MPS2712	0079
MPS2712K	OEM
MPS2712L	OEM
MPS2712M	OEM
MPS2713	0079
MPS2713K	OEM
MPS2713L	OEM
MPS2713M	OEM
MPS2714	0079
MPS2714K	OEM
MPS2714L	OEM
MPS2714M	OEM
MPS2715	0079
MPS-2716	0079
MPS2716	0079
MPS2823	0127
MPS2894	0127
MPS2906	0079
MPS2907	0037
MPS2907A	0037
MPS2907AK	OEM
MPS2907AL	OEM
MPS2907AM	OEM
MPS2907K	OEM
MPS2907L	OEM
MPS2907M	OEM
MPS2923	0079
MPS2923K	OEM
MPS2923L	OEM
MPS2923M	OEM
MPS2924	0079
MPS2924K	OEM
MPS2924L	OEM
MPS2924M	OEM
MPS2925	0079
MPS2925K	OEM
MPS2925L	OEM
MPS2925M	OEM
MPS2926	0079
MPS2926-B	0086
MPS2926-BRN	0079
MPS2926-G	0079
MPS2926-GRN	0079
MPS2926-O	0086
MPS2926-ORG	0079
MPS2926-R	0086
MPS2926-RED	0079
MPS2926-Y	0086
MPS2926-YEL	0079
MPS2926BRN	0079
MPS2926GRN	0079
MPS2926ORN	0079
MPS2926RED	0079
MPS2926YEL	0079
MPS2990	OEM
MPS3013	0037
MPS3390	0079
MPS3391	0079
MPS3391A	0079
MPS3392	0079
MPS3392K	OEM
MPS3392L	OEM
MPS3392M	OEM
MPS3393	0079
MPS3393K	OEM
MPS3393L	OEM
MPS3393M	OEM
MPS3394	0079
MPS3394K	OEM
MPS3394L	OEM
MPS3394M	OEM
MPS3395	0079
MPS3395K	OEM
MPS3395L	OEM
MPS3395M	OEM
MPS3396	0079

DEVICE TYPE	REPL CODE
MPS3397	0111
MPS3398	0079
MPS3402	0590
MPS3403	0590
MPS3404	0590
MPS3405	0590
MPS3414	OEM
MPS3414K	OEM
MPS3414L	OEM
MPS3414M	OEM
MPS3415	OEM
MPS3415K	OEM
MPS3415L	OEM
MPS3415M	OEM
MPS3416	OEM
MPS3416K	OEM
MPS3416L	OEM
MPS3416M	OEM
MPS3417	OEM
MPS3417K	OEM
MPS3417L	OEM
MPS3417M	OEM
MPS3534	0150
MPS3536	0144
MPS-3563	0079
MPS3563	0007
MPS3564	OEM
MPS3565	0144
MPS3566	0079
MPS3567	0855
MPS3568	0855
MPS3569	0855
MPS3634	0126
MPS3638	0037
MPS-3638A	0037
MPS3638A	0037
MPS3638AK	OEM
MPS3638AL	OEM
MPS3638AM	OEM
MPS3638K	OEM
MPS3638L	3079
MPS3638M	OEM
MPS3639	0688
MPS-3640	0150
MPS3640	0037
MPS3641	OEM
MPS3641K	OEM
MPS3641L	OEM
MPS3641M	OEM
MPS3642	0079
MPS3642K	OEM
MPS3642L	OEM
MPS3642M	OEM
MPS3643	0016
MPS3644	0006
MPS3644K	OEM
MPS3644L	OEM
MPS3644M	OEM
MPS3645	0037
MPS3645K	OEM
MPS3645L	OEM
MPS3645M	OEM
MPS3646	0079
MPS3693	0144
MPS3693K	OEM
MPS3693L	OEM
MPS3693M	OEM
MPS3694	0076
MPS-3702	0037
MPS3702	0006
MPS3702K	OEM
MPS3702L	OEM
MPS3702M	OEM
MPS3703	0133
MPS3703K	OEM
MPS3703L	OEM
MPS3703M	OEM
MPS3704	0079
MPS3704K	OEM
MPS3704L	OEM
MPS3704M	OEM
MPS-3705	0079
MPS3705	0079
MPS3705K	OEM
MPS3705L	OEM
MPS3705M	OEM
MPS3706	0079
MPS3706K	OEM
MPS3706L	OEM
MPS3706M	OEM
MPS3707	1212
MPS3707K	OEM
MPS3707L	OEM
MPS3707M	OEM
MPS3708	0079
MPS3708K	OEM
MPS3708L	OEM
MPS3708M	OEM
MPS3709	0076
MPS3709K	OEM
MPS3709L	OEM
MPS3709M	OEM
MPS3710	0079
MPS3710K	OEM
MPS3710L	OEM
MPS3710M	OEM
MPS3711	0079
MPS3711K	OEM
MPS3711L	OEM

DEVICE TYPE	REPL CODE
MPS3711M	OEM
MPS3721	0079
MPS3731	0969
MPS3826	0079
MPS3827	0079
MPS3866	OEM
MPS3866A	OEM
MPS3900	0079
MPS3900A	0079
MPS3901	0079
MPS3903	0079
MPS3904	4305
MPS3905	0037
MPS3906	0037
MPS3992	0079
MPS4145	0016
MPS4248	0037
MPS4249	0037
MPS4250	0037
MPS4250A	0037
MPS4257	OEM
MPS4258	5530
MPS4274	0079
MPS4275	0079
MPS4354	0037
MPS4355	0037
MPS4356	0006
MPS4888	OEM
MPS4889	OEM
MPS5015	OEM
MPS5041	OEM
MPS5086	0037
MPS5127	0079
MPS5128	0144
MPS5129	0144
MPS5131	0144
MPS5132	0144
MPS5133	0079
MPS5134	0079
MPS5135	0079
MPS5136	0079
MPS5137	0079
MPS5138	0037
MPS5138K	OEM
MPS5139	OEM
MPS5142	0037
MPS5143	0037
MPS-5172	0111
MPS5172	0079
MPS5172K	OEM
MPS5172L	OEM
MPS5172M	OEM
MPS5179	OEM
MPS5192	OEM
MPS5306	0396
MPS5308	0396
MPS5551M	0710
MPS5668	0321
MPS5855	0037
MPS5856	OEM
MPS5857	0037
MPS5858	OEM
MPS6076	0037
MPS6134	0037
MPS6172	0037
MPS6351	0016
MPS6413	0016
MPS6434	0150
MPS6502	3036
MPS6502A	3036
MPS6507	0144
MPS6511	0144
MPS6511-S	0144
MPS6512	0076
MPS6513	0079
MPS6514	0076
MPS6515	0076
MPS6516	0006
MPS6517	0037
MPS6518	0006
MPS6519	0006
MPS6520	0079
MPS6521	0079
MPS6522	0037
MPS6522(IC)	OEM
MPS6523	0688
MPS6528	0127
MPS6529	0127
MPS6530	0076
MPS6530K	OEM
MPS6530L	OEM
MPS6530M	OEM
MPS6531	0079
MPS6531K	OEM
MPS6531L	OEM
MPS6531M	OEM
MPS6532	0076
MPS6532K	OEM
MPS6532L	OEM
MPS6532M	OEM
MPS6533	0037
MPS6533K	OEM
MPS6533L	OEM
MPS6533M	0037
MPS6534	0037
MPS6534K	OEM
MPS6534L	OEM
MPS6534M	0037
MPS6535	0006

DEVICE TYPE	REPL CODE
MPS6535K	OEM
MPS6535L	OEM
MPS6535M	0037
MPS6539	0224
MPS6540	0016
MPS6540-012	OEM
MPS6541	0224
MPS6542	0224
MPS6543	0224
MPS6544	0076
MPS6545	0076
MPS6546	0224
MPS6547	0144
MPS6548	0224
MPS6552	0079
MPS6553	0037
MPS6554	0079
MPS6555	0079
MPS6556	0079
MPS6560	0320
MPS6561	0320
MPS6562	0006
MPS6563	0006
MPS6564	0079
MPS6565	0076
MPS6565K	OEM
MPS6565L	OEM
MPS6565M	OEM
MPS6566	0079
MPS6566K	OEM
MPS6566L	OEM
MPS6566M	OEM
MPS6567	0079
MPS6568	0224
MPS6568A	0224
MPS6569	0224
MPS6569A	0326
MPS6570	0224
MPS6570A	0326
MPS-6571	0079
MPS6571	1212
MPS6572	0111
MPS6573	0079
MPS6574	0079
MPS6574-B	0086
MPS6574-BLUE	0086
MPS6574-G	0086
MPS6574-GREEN	0079
MPS6574-S	0086
MPS6574-SIL	0086
MPS6574-Y	0086
MPS6574-YEL	0086
MPS6575	0079
MPS6575GREEN	0155
MPS6576	0079
MPS6576-B	0079
MPS6576-BLUE	0079
MPS6576-G	0079
MPS6576-GREEN	0079
MPS6576-S	0079
MPS6576-SIL	0079
MPS6576-Y	0079
MPS6576-YEL	0155
MPS6576GREEN	0155
MPS6576SIL	0016
MPS6579	0037
MPS6580	0037
MPS6590	0086
MPS6591	0037
MPS6595	OEM
MPS6601	4945
MPS6602	4945
MPS6651	1587
MPS6652	1587
MPS6714	4945
MPS6715	4945
MPS6716	4945
MPS6717	4945
MPS6724	3749
MPS6725	3749
MPS6726	1587
MPS6727	1587
MPS6728	1587
MPS6729	1587
MPS6733	3718
MPS6734	3718
MPS6735	3718
MPS7156	OEM
MPS7418T	OEM
MPS7427B	OEM
MPS7751(A)	OEM
MPS7751B	3477
MPS8000	4389
MPS8001	0079
MPS8092	OEM
MPS8093	2245
MPS8097	0079
MPS8098	0079
MPS8099	0076
MPS8598	0037
MPS8599	0037
MPS9185	0016
MPS9246A.B	0079
MPS9406(C)	OEM
MPS9410	0086
MPS9410A	0086
MPS9410AJ	0086
MPS9410AK	0086
MPS9410H	0086

DEVICE TYPE	REPL CODE
MPS9411	2039
MPS9411(AI)	0710
MPS9411A	2039
MPS9411A1	0710
MPS9411AI	0710
MPS9411T	2039
MPS9412	OEM
MPS9412(J)	OEM
MPS9416	0320
MPS9416A	0320
MPS9416AS	0320
MPS9416AT	0320
MPS9416S	0320
MPS9417	5595
MPS9417A	0320
MPS9417AS	0320
MPS9417A-T	0079
MPS9417AT	0320
MPS9418	0086
MPS9418AS	0320
MPS9418AT	0320
MPS9418S	0320
MPS9418T	0086
MPS9423	0079
MPS9423G	0144
MPS9423H	0144
MPS9423I	0144
MPS9426	0224
MPS9426(B)	OEM
MPS9426-B	0224
MPS9426A.B	0079
MPS9426B	0224
MPS9426B,C	0224
MPS9426BC	0224
MPS9426C	0224
MPS9427	0224
MPS9427B	0224
MPS9427B.C	0079
MPS9427C	0224
MPS9433	0079
MPS9433I	0079
MPS9433J	0111
MPS9433K	0079
MPS9433S	0079
MPS9433T	0079
MPS9434	0079
MPS9434J	0079
MPS9434K	0079
MPS9440	OEM
MPS9444	0133
MPS9460	0126
MPS9460A	0126
MPS9460H	0126
MPS9461	OEM
MPS9461(AI)	OEM
MPS9461A1	0338
MPS9461AI	0338
MPS9462	OEM
MPS9466	2022
MPS9466A	0018
MPS9466AT	0431
MPS9467	2022
MPS9467A	0431
MPS9467AS	0431
MPS9467A-T	0037
MPS9467AT	0431
MPS9467T	0431
MPS9468	0431
MPS9468A	0037
MPS9468AS	0431
MPS9468AT	0431
MPS9468S	0431
MPS9468T	0037
MPS9483T	0006
MPS9484	0037
MPS9600	0079
MPS9600(G)	0079
MPS9600-5	0079
MPS9600F	0079
MPS9600G	0079
MPS9600G/H	0144
MPS9601	0144
MPS9602	0015
MPS9604	0224
MPS9604(E)	0079
MPS9604D	0079
MPS9604E	0079
MPS9604F	0079
MPS9604FG	0079
MPS9604I	0079
MPS9604R	0079
MPS9606(H)	0124
MPS9606(I)	0124
MPS9606I	0133
MPS9611-5	0079
MPS9616	0079
MPS9616A	0018
MPS9616J	0079
MPS9618	0079
MPS9618(J)	0079
MPS9618H	0079
MPS9618I	0079
MPS9618J	0079
MPS9623	0079
MPS9623C	0079
MPS9623C(F)	0079
MPS9623E	0079
MPS9623E.G	0079
MPS9623F	0079

494

If replacement code is OEM, contact original manufacturer for replacement.

DEVICE TYPE	REPL CODE
MPS-9623G	0079
MPS9623G	0079
MPS9623G/H	0079
MPS9623H	0079
MPS9623H/I	0079
MPS9623I	0079
MPS9623I/J	0079
MPS9623J	0079
MPS9624	OEM
MPS9625	0224
MPS9625D	0224
MPS9625E	0079
MPS9625F	0224
MPS9625G	0224
MPS9625H	0224
MPS9626	0079
MPS9626(E)	0079
MPS9626(F)	OEM
MPS9626G	0079
MPS9626H	0079
MPS9626I	0079
MPS9630	0079
MPS9630H	0079
MPS9630H.I	0079
MPS-9630I	0079
MPS9630I	0079
MPS9630K	1943
MPS9630T	0079
MPS9631	0079
MPS9631(I)	0016
MPS9631(S)	0079
MPS9631(T)	0079
MPS9631(U)	OEM
MPS9631I	0079
MPS9631J	0079
MPS9631K	0079
MPS9631S	0079
MPS9631T	0079
MPS9632	0079
MPS9632(I)	0079
MPS9632(K)	0079
MPS9632H	0079
MPS9632I	0079
MPS9632J	0079
MPS9632K	0079
MPS9632T	0079
MPS9633	0076
MPS9633B	0079
MPS9633C	0079
MPS9633D	0111
MPS9633G	0111
MPS9633X	0079
MPS9634	0079
MPS9634-O	1004
MPS9634B	0284
MPS9634C	0079
MPS9634D	0079
MPS9644	0133
MPS9646	0133
MPS9646G	0133
MPS9646H	0133
MPS9646I	0133
MPS9646J	0133
MPS9646V	OEM
MPS9666	0037
MPS9680	0037
MPS9680(T)	0037
MPS9680H	0037
MPS9680H/E	0688
MPS9680H/I	0037
MPS9680I	0037
MPS9680I/J	0037
MPS9680J	0037
MPS9680T	0037
MPS9681	0037
MPS9681(T)	0037
MPS9681J	0037
MPS9681K	0037
MPS9681T	0037
MPS9682(I)	0037
MPS9682I	0037
MPS9682J	0037
MPS9682K	0037
MPS9682T	0037
MPS9696	0079
MPS9696F	0079
MPS9696G	0155
MPS9696H	0079
MPS9700D	0079
MPS9700E	0079
MPS9700F	0079
MPS9700G	0079
MPS9700T	0079
MPS9700U	0079
MPS9750D	0037
MPS9750E	0037
MPS9750F	0037
MPS9750G	0037
MPS9750OF	0037
MPS9750T	0037
MPS96800	0037
MPS775113	OEM
MPS-A05	0111
MPSA05	0086
MPSA05K	OEM
MPSA05M	OEM
MPS-A06	0710
MPSA06	0079
MPSA06K	OEM
MPSA06L	OEM
MPSA06M	OEM
MPS-A09	0111
MPSA09	0079
MPSA2	OEM
MPS-A10	0016
MPSA10	0079
MPSA10-BLU	0079
MPSA10-GRN	0079
MPSA10-RED	0079
MPSA10-WHT	0079
MPSA10-YEL	0079
MPS-A12	3749
MPSA12	0016
MPSA12K	OEM
MPS-A13	2770
MPSA-13	2770
MPSA13	0396
MPSA13(11)	0396
MPSA13K	OEM
MPS-A14	3749
MPSA14	0396
MPSA14K	OEM
MPSA16	0111
MPSA17	0076
MPS-A18	2833
MPSA18	0111
MPS-A20	2427
MPSA20	0198
MPSA20-BLU	0111
MPSA20-GRN	0111
MPSA20-RED	0111
MPSA20-WHT	0111
MPSA20-YEL	0111
MPSA20K	OEM
MPSA20L	OEM
MPSA20M	OEM
MPS-A25	2996
MPSA25	2996
MPS-A26	2996
MPSA26	2996
MPS-A27	2996
MPSA27	2996
MPS-A28	2770
MPSA28	5841
MPS-A29	2770
MPSA29	2770
MPS-A42	0710
MPSA42	0710
MPS-A43	0710
MPSA43	0710
MPS-A44	OEM
MPSA44	OEM
MPS-A45	OEM
MPSA45	OEM
MPS-A55	0037
MPSA55	0037
MPSA55K	OEM
MPS-A56	0037
MPSA56	0037
MPSA56K	OEM
MPS-A62	3477
MPSA62	3477
MPS-A63	3477
MPSA-63	3477
MPSA63	3477
MPS-A64	3477
MPSA64	3477
MPS-A65	3477
MPSA65	3477
MPS-A66	3477
MPSA66	3477
MPS-A70	0037
MPSA70	0006
MPSA70-BLU	0855
MPSA70-GRN	0855
MPSA70-RED	0855
MPSA70-WHT	0855
MPSA70-YEL	0688
MPS-A75	3477
MPSA75	3477
MPS-A76	3477
MPSA76	3477
MPS-A77	3477
MPSA77	3477
MPS-A92	0338
MPSA92	0338
MPSA92K	OEM
MPS-A93	0338
MPSA93	0338
MPSA93K	OEM
MPSA9416A	OEM
MPSAY2	0710
MPS-D01	0710
MPSD01	0710
MPSD02	0710
MPSD03	0855
MPS-D04	0396
MPSD04	0396
MPSD05	0079
MPSD06	0079
MPS-D51	0338
MPSD51	0338
MPSD52	0338
MPSD53	0338
MPS-D54	3477
MPSD54	3477
MPSD55	0037
MPSD56	0037
MPSEL239	0079
MPSH02	0224
MPS-H04	0855
MPSH04	0855
MPSH05	0076
MPSH07	0144
MPSH08	0144
MPSH09	0127
MPSH10	0224
MPS-H11	0144
MPSH11	0224
MPS-H17	0224
MPSH17	0224
MPS-H19	0144
MPSH19	0224
MPS-H20	0144
MPSH20	0224
MPS-H24	0144
MPSH24	0144
MPSH30	0224
MPSH31	0224
MPS-H32	0079
MPSH32	0931
MPSH33	0488
MPS-H34	0224
MPSH34	0016
MPS-H37	0224
MPSH37	0224
MPSH54	0037
MPSH55	0037
MPSH69	2022
MPSH81	0037
MPS-H83	0150
MPSH85	0037
MPSHC05	OEM
MPSHC08	OEM
MPSHC17	OEM
MPSHC24	OEM
MPSHC55	OEM
MPSHC81	OEM
MPS-K20	0079
MPSK20	0079
MPS-K21	0079
MPSK21	0079
MPS-K22	0079
MPSK22	0079
MPSK70	0037
MPSK71	0037
MPSK72	0037
MPSL01	0076
MPS-L51	5392
MPSL51	0006
MPSM-10	OEM
MPSN-24	OEM
MPS-U01	0546
MPSU01	0546
MPS-U01A	4400
MPSU01A	0546
MPS-U02	5488
MPSU02	0546
MPS-U03	0264
MPSU03	0264
MPS-U04	0264
MPSU04	0264
MPS-U05	5488
MPSU05	0018
MPS-U06	5488
MPSU06	0546
MPS-U07	0546
MPSU07	0546
MPS-U10	0334
MPSU-10	0334
MPSU10	0334
MPS-U10F	0334
MPSU11	0334
MPS-U-31	OEM
MPS-U31	1165
MPSU31	1973
MPS-U45	3495
MPSU45	3495
MPS-U51	0378
MPSU51	0378
MPS-U51A	4504
MPSU51A	0378
MPS-U52	5491
MPSU52	0378
MPS-U55	0378
MPSU55	0148
MPS-U56	0378
MPSU56	0378
MPS-U57	4141
MPSU57	0378
MPS-U60	5492
MPSU60	3712
MPS-U95	5499
MPSU95	3496
MPSW01	4945
MPSW01A	4945
MPSW05	4945
MPSW06	4945
MPSW10	3718
MPSW13	3749
MPSW14	3749
MPSW42	3718
MPSW43	3718
MPSW45	3749
MPSW51	1587
MPSW51A	1587
MPSW55	1587
MPSW56	1587
MPSW60	OEM
MPSW63	OEM
MPSW64	OEM
MPSW92	OEM
MPSW93	OEM
MPT12N05	OEM
MPT12N10	OEM
MPT20	3603
MPT24	OEM
MPT28	3298
MPT32	2704
MPTE-5	OEM
MPTE-5C	5362
MPTE-8	OEM
MPTE-8C	OEM
MPTE-10	OEM
MPTE-10C	OEM
MPTE-12	OEM
MPTE-12C	OEM
MPTE-15	OEM
MPTE-15C	OEM
MPTE-18	OEM
MPTE-18C	OEM
MPTE-22	OEM
MPTE-22C	OEM
MPTE-36	OEM
MPTE-36C	OEM
MPTE-45	OEM
MPTE-45C	OEM
MPU-131	0312
MPU131	0312
MPU132	0312
MPU133	0312
MPU138	OEM
MPU231	OEM
MPU232	OEM
MPU233	OEM
MPU6027	0312
MPU6028	0312
MPV-131	OEM
MPV131	OEM
MPX-25	0015
MPX25	0015
MPX215	0015
MPX9623	0079
MPX9623H	0079
MPX9623H/I	0079
MPX9623I	0079
MPZ5-16A	OEM
MPZ5-16B	OEM
MPZ5-32A	OEM
MPZ5-32B	OEM
MPZ5-32C	OEM
MPZ5-180A	OEM
MPZ5-180B	OEM
MPZ5-180C	OEM
MQ1	0079
MQ1/1	OEM
MQ1/2	OEM
MQ1/3	OEM
MQ1/4	OEM
MQ1/5	OEM
MQ2	0079
MQ3/1	0015
MQ3/2	0015
MQ3/3	OEM
MQ3/4	OEM
MQ3/5	OEM
MQ6/1	0102
MQ6/2	0015
MQ6/3	OEM
MQ6/4	OEM
MQ6/5	OEM
MQ8/1	OEM
MQ8/2	0015
MQ8/3	OEM
MQ8/4	OEM
MQ32	0015
MQ62	0015
MQ82	0015
MQ918	OEM
MQ930	OEM
MQ982	OEM
MQ1120	OEM
MQ1129	OEM
MQ2218	OEM
MQ2219A	OEM
MQ2369	OEM
MQ2484	OEM
MQ2904	OEM
MQ2905A	OEM
MQ3251	OEM
MQ3467	OEM
MQ3725	OEM
MQ3798	OEM
MQ3799	OEM
MQ3799A	3066
MQ6001	OEM
MQ6002	OEM
MQ7001	OEM
MQ7003	OEM
MQ7004	OEM
MQ7005	OEM
MQ7007	OEM
MQ7021	OEM
MR05	OEM
MR-1	0015
MR1	1749
MR1-1000	1053
MR1-1200	0182
MR1-1400	0102
MR1-1600	0344
MR1A	OEM
MR-1C	0071
MR1C	0071
MR-1M	0071
MR1M	0071
MR2A	OEM
MR3A	OEM
MR4A	OEM
MR5	OEM
MR5-45B	OEM
MR5A	OEM
MR6A	OEM
MR7A	OEM
MR10	OEM
MR10A	OEM
MR11	OEM
MR11A	OEM
MR20	OEM
MR21	OEM
MR21CR	0058
MR30	OEM
MR31	OEM
MR33C-H	0296
MR35	OEM
MR36C-H	OEM
MR36E-H	OEM
MR36H	0188
MR39C-H	0188
MR40	0133
MR41	OEM
MR43C-H	OEM
MR43E-H	OEM
MR47C-H	0162
MR50	1627
MR51C-H	0162
MR51E-H	0162
MR54Z	OEM
MR56C-H	0157
MR60	0015
MR62C-H	0466
MR62E-H	0631
MR62H	0631
MR64Z	OEM
MR68C-H	OEM
MR70	0369
MR75C-H	OEM
MR75E-H	OEM
MR80	0369
MR82C-H	OEM
MR90	0369
MR91C-H	0057
MR91E-H	0057
MR100	0369
MR100C-H	0170
MR100H	0170
MR110C-H	OEM
MR1130R	0545
MR120C-H	0052
MR130C-H	OEM
MR132B	0087
MR-150-01	0015
MR150C-H	0681
MR160C-H	OEM
MR180C-H	OEM
MR200C-H	OEM
MR250-1	0102
MR322	4938
MR322R	2537
MR323	2591
MR323R	2544
MR324	2591
MR324R	2544
MR325	4938
MR325R	2537
MR326	4938
MR326R	2544
MR327	2591
MR327R	2591
MR328	2591
MR328R	2544
MR330	2591
MR330R	2544
MR331	OEM
MR331R	OEM
MR400	0581
MR-461	OEM
MR500	0110
MR501	0242
MR502	0242
MR504	0535
MR506	0959
MR508	0811
MR509	0916
MR510	0916
MR600	0581
MR750	1272
MR751	1272
MR752	1277
MR754	1277
MR756	1282
MR758	1285
MR760	1285
MR800	4193
MR801	0102
MR802	OEM
MR804	OEM
MR806	OEM
MR810	0102
MR811	0102
MR812	0102
MR813	0102
MR814	0102
MR816	0102
MR817	0102
MR818	0102
MR820	1352
MR821	1352
MR822	1352
MR824	1352
MR826	1362
MR830	1483
MR831	1483
MR832	1483
MR834	1483
MR836	1483
MR850	1137
MR851	1137
MR-852	0102
MR852	0023
MR854	1137
MR856	1483
MR860	1522
MR860R	4436
MR861	1522
MR861R	1512
MR862	1522
MR862R	1512
MR864	0029
MR864R	1836
MR866	0596
MR866R	1840
MR870	OEM
MR870R	OEM
MR871	OEM
MR871R	OEM
MR872	OEM
MR872R	OEM
MR874	OEM
MR874R	OEM
MR876	OEM
MR876R	OEM
MR910	0087
MR911	0031
MR912	0031
MR914	0031
MR916	0031
MR917	OEM
MR918	OEM
MR990	0071
MR990A	OEM
MR991	OEM
MR991A	OEM
MR992	OEM
MR992A	OEM
MR993	OEM
MR993A	OEM
MR994	OEM
MR994A	OEM
MR995A	OEM
MR996A	OEM
MR1030A	0087
MR1030AR	0087
MR1030B	0087
MR1030BR	0087
MR1031	0071
MR1031A	0087
MR1031AR	0087
MR1031B	0087
MR1031BR	0087
MR1032A	0087
MR1032AR	0087
MR1032B	0087
MR1032BR	0087
MR1033A	0087
MR1033AR	0087
MR1033B	0087
MR1033BR	0087
MR1034A	0087
MR1034AR	0087
MR1034B	0087
MR1034BR	0087
MR1035A	0087
MR1035AR	0087
MR1035B	0087
MR1035BR	0087
MR1036A	0087
MR1036AR	0087
MR1036B	0087
MR1036BR	0087
MR1038A	0087
MR1038AR	0087
MR1038B	0087
MR1038BR	0087
MR1040A	0087
MR1040AR	0087
MR1040B	0087
MR1040BR	0087
MR1120	0084
MR1120R	0529
MR1121	0090
MR1121R	0743
MR1122	0097
MR1122R	0760
MR1123	0105
MR1123R	0772
MR1124	0109
MR1124R	0533
MR1125	0116
MR1125R	0796
MR1126	0122
MR1126R	0810
MR1128	0131
MR1128R	0540
MR1130	0145
MR1130R	0545
MR1150A	OEM
MR1183	0315
MR1183R	0267
MR1184	0315
MR1184R	0267
MR1185	0315
MR1185R	0267
MR1186	0315
MR1186R	0267
MR1187	0315
MR1187R	0267
MR1188	0315
MR1188R	0267
MR1189	0315
MR1189R	0267
MR1190	0315
MR1190R	0267
MR1191	0315
MR1191R	0267
MR1192	0315
MR1192R	0267
MR1193	0315
MR1193R	0267
MR1194	0315
MR1194R	0267
MR1195	0315
MR1195A	0315
MR1195R	0267
MR1195RA	0267
MR1196	0315
MR1196A	0315
MR1196R	0267
MR1196RA	0267
MR1197	0315
MR1197A	0315
MR1197R	0267
MR1197RA	0267
MR1198	0315
MR1198A	0315
MR1198R	0267
MR1198RA	0267
MR1200	OEM
MR1200FL	OEM
MR1201	OEM
MR1201FL	OEM
MR1202	OEM
MR1202FL	OEM
MR1203	OEM
MR1203FL	OEM
MR1204	OEM
MR1205	OEM
MR1206	OEM
MR1207	OEM
MR1207FL	OEM
MR1208	OEM
MR1208FL	OEM
MR1209	OEM
MR1210SB	OEM
MR1210SL	OEM
MR1211SB	OEM
MR1211SL	OEM
MR1212SB	OEM
MR1212SL	OEM
MR1213SB	OEM
MR1213SL	OEM
MR1214SB	OEM
MR1214SL	OEM
MR1215SB	OEM
MR1216SB	OEM
MR1216SL	OEM
MR1217SB	OEM
MR1217SL	OEM
MR1218SB	OEM
MR1218SL	OEM
MR1219SB	OEM
MR1220R	1017
MR1220SB	1017
MR1220SL	OEM
MR1221FB	OEM
MR1221FL	OEM
MR1221R	0496
MR1221SB	1017
MR1221SL	OEM
MR1222FB	OEM
MR1222FL	OEM
MR1222R	0496
MR1222SB	1017
MR1222SL	OEM
MR1223FB	OEM
MR1223FL	OEM
MR1223R	0496
MR1223SB	1017
MR1223SL	OEM
MR1224FB	OEM
MR1224FL	OEM
MR1224SB	OEM
MR1224SL	OEM
MR1225FB	OEM

If replacement code is OEM, contact original manufacturer for replacement. 495

DEVICE TYPE	REPL CODE
MR1225FL	OEM
MR1225R	0496
MR1225SB	1017
MR1225SL	OEM
MR1226FB	OEM
MR1226FL	OEM
MR1226SB	OEM
MR1226SL	OEM
MR1227FB	OEM
MR1227FL	OEM
MR1227R	1766
MR1227SB	1030
MR1227SL	OEM
MR1228FB	OEM
MR1228FL	OEM
MR1228R	1766
MR1228SB	1030
MR1228SL	OEM
MR1229FB	OEM
MR1229FL	OEM
MR1229R	1766
MR1229SB	1030
MR1229SL	OEM
MR1230FB	OEM
MR1230FL	OEM
MR1230R	0496
MR1230SB	1017
MR1230SL	OEM
MR1231FB	OEM
MR1231FL	OEM
MR1231R	0496
MR1231SB	1017
MR1231SL	OEM
MR1232FB	OEM
MR1232FL	OEM
MR1232R	0496
MR1232SB	1017
MR1232SL	OEM
MR1233FB	OEM
MR1233FL	OEM
MR1233R	0496
MR1233SB	1017
MR1233SL	OEM
MR1234FB	OEM
MR1234FL	OEM
MR1234R	0496
MR1234SB	1017
MR1234SL	OEM
MR1235FB	OEM
MR1235FL	OEM
MR1235R	0496
MR1235SB	1017
MR1235SL	OEM
MR1236FB	OEM
MR1236FL	OEM
MR1236R	1766
MR1236SB	1030
MR1236SL	OEM
MR1237FB	0229
MR1237FL	0229
MR1237R	1766
MR1237SB	1017
MR1237SL	0229
MR1238FB	OEM
MR1238FL	OEM
MR1238R	1766
MR1238SB	1030
MR1238SL	OEM
MR1239FB	OEM
MR1239FL	OEM
MR1239R	1766
MR1239SB	1030
MR1239SL	OEM
MR1240FB	OEM
MR1240FL	OEM
MR1240SB	OEM
MR1240SL	OEM
MR1241FB	OEM
MR1241FL	OEM
MR1241SB	OEM
MR1241SL	OEM
MR1242FB	OEM
MR1242FL	OEM
MR1242SB	OEM
MR1242SL	OEM
MR1243FB	OEM
MR1243FL	OEM
MR1243SB	OEM
MR1243SL	OEM
MR1244FB	OEM
MR1244FL	OEM
MR1244SB	OEM
MR1244SL	OEM
MR1245FB	OEM
MR1245SB	OEM
MR1246FB	OEM
MR1246FL	OEM
MR1246SB	OEM
MR1246SL	OEM
MR1247FB	0229
MR1247FL	0229
MR1247SB	0229
MR1247SL	0229
MR1248FB	OEM
MR1248FL	OEM
MR1248SB	OEM
MR1248SL	OEM
MR1249FB	OEM
MR1249SB	OEM

DEVICE TYPE	REPL CODE
MR1260	OEM
MR1260FL	OEM
MR1261	OEM
MR1261FL	OEM
MR1262	OEM
MR1262FL	OEM
MR1263	OEM
MR1263FL	OEM
MR1264	OEM
MR1265	OEM
MR1266	OEM
MR1267	0229
MR1267FL	OEM
MR1268	OEM
MR1268FL	OEM
MR1269	OEM
MR1290	OEM
MR1291	OEM
MR1292	OEM
MR1293	OEM
MR1294	OEM
MR1295	OEM
MR1296	OEM
MR1297	OEM
MR1299	OEM
MR1337-1	0023
MR1337-2	0023
MR1337-3	0023
MR1337-4	0023
MR1337-5	0023
MR1366	0706
MR1366R	2939
MR1376	0706
MR1376R	2939
MR1386	0596
MR1386R	1840
MR1396	0596
MR1396R	1840
MR1810R	1337
MR1810SB	0594
MR1810SL	OEM
MR1811R	1337
MR1811SB	0594
MR1811SL	OEM
MR1812R	1337
MR1812SB	0594
MR1812SL	OEM
MR1813R	1337
MR1813SB	0594
MR1813SL	OEM
MR1814R	1337
MR1814SB	0594
MR1814SL	OEM
MR1815R	1337
MR1815SB	0594
MR1816R	1894
MR1816SB	1975
MR1816SL	OEM
MR1817R	1894
MR1817SB	1975
MR1817SL	OEM
MR1818R	1894
MR1818SB	1975
MR1818SL	OEM
MR1819R	1894
MR1819SB	1975
MR2000	1590
MR2000R	4917
MR2000S	1590
MR2000SR	1229
MR2001	OEM
MR2001R	OEM
MR2001S	0865
MR2001SR	1231
MR2002	0865
MR2002R	OEM
MR2002S	0865
MR2002SR	1625
MR2004	0847
MR2004R	1242
MR2004S	0847
MR2004SR	1242
MR2006	1599
MR2006R	OEM
MR2006S	1599
MR2006SR	1196
MR2008	1600
MR2008R	2124
MR2008S	1600
MR2008SR	2124
MR2010	1604
MR2010R	2236
MR2010S	1604
MR2010SR	2236
MR2064	0015
MR2065	0015
MR2066	OEM
MR2067	OEM
MR2068	OEM
MR2069	0087
MR2070	0087
MR2071	OEM
MR2072	OEM
MR2073	OEM
MR2074	OEM
MR2075	0087
MR2080HA	OEM
MR2081HA	OEM
MR2082HA	OEM

DEVICE TYPE	REPL CODE
MR2084HA	OEM
MR2100HA	OEM
MR2101HA	OEM
MR2102HA	OEM
MR2103HA	OEM
MR2104HA	OEM
MR2261	0015
MR2262	0229
MR2263	OEM
MR2264	OEM
MR2265	OEM
MR2266	0182
MR2271	0015
MR2272	1208
MR2273	0182
MR2360	0133
MR2361	OEM
MR2369	0087
MR2370	OEM
MR2371	OEM
MR2372	OEM
MR2373	OEM
MR2374	OEM
MR2375	0087
MR2400	OEM
MR2400F	OEM
MR2401	OEM
MR2401F	OEM
MR2402	OEM
MR2402F	OEM
MR2404	OEM
MR2404F	OEM
MR2406	OEM
MR2406F	OEM
MR2500	OEM
MR2501	OEM
MR2502	OEM
MR2504	OEM
MR2506	OEM
MR2508	OEM
MR2510	OEM
MR2525	2038
MR2525L	OEM
MR2525R	OEM
MR3932	0079
MR3933	0086
MR3934	0126
MR4001	OEM
MR4002	OEM
MR4003	OEM
MR4004	OEM
MR4005	OEM
MR4006	OEM
MR4007	OEM
MR5005	3475
MR5005R	4924
MR5010	3475
MR5010R	4924
MR5020	3475
MR5020R	4924
MR5030	3475
MR5030R	4924
MR5040	3475
MR5040R	4924
MR5059	OEM
MR5060	3498
MR5061	OEM
MR5102	3475
MR9600	0015
MR9601	0023
MR9602	0015
MR9803	0015
MRB-20C	0015
MRD14B	3156
MRD100	1489
MRD148	OEM
MRD150	0007
MRD160	OEM
MRD200	OEM
MRD210	OEM
MRD250	OEM
MRD300	3825
MRD310	2297
MRD360	3508
MRD370	3508
MRD450	0007
MRD500	OEM
MRD510	OEM
MRD601	OEM
MRD602	OEM
MRD603	OEM
MRD604	OEM
MRD611	OEM
MRD612	OEM
MRD613	OEM
MRD614	OEM
MRD701	OEM
MRD711	6317
MRD721	OEM
MRD821	0466
MRD823	OEM
MRD825	0466
MRD827	0466
MRD829	0466
MRD920	OEM
MRD921	0466
MRD923	0466
MRD925	0466
MRD927	0466

DEVICE TYPE	REPL CODE
MRD929	0466
MRD933	OEM
MRD3010	OEM
MRD3011	OEM
MRD3050	2297
MRD3051	2297
MRD3052	2297
MRD3053	2297
MRD3054	2297
MRD3055	2297
MRD3056	2297
MRF100	OEM
MRF134	OEM
MRF140	OEM
MRF148	OEM
MRF150	OEM
MRF171	OEM
MRF172	OEM
MRF174	OEM
MRF200	OEM
MRF207	2030
MRF208	1189
MRF209	1224
MRF212	1224
MRF216	3090
MRF221	5209
MRF222	OEM
MRF223	OEM
MRF224	2857
MRF225	0414
MRF227	2028
MRF229	3528
MRF230	3293
MRF231	3543
MRF232	1189
MRF233	1224
MRF234	1963
MRF237	3528
MRF238	3012
MRF239	6489
MRF240	OEM
MRF243	OEM
MRF244	3165
MRF245	3165
MRF247	3591
MRF250	OEM
MRF250A	OEM
MRF260	2693
MRF261	OEM
MRF262	2694
MRF264	OEM
MRF309	OEM
MRF313	OEM
MRF313A	OEM
MRF314	OEM
MRF314A	OEM
MRF315	OEM
MRF315A	OEM
MRF316	OEM
MRF317	OEM
MRF321	OEM
MRF323	OEM
MRF325	OEM
MRF326	OEM
MRF327	OEM
MRF328	OEM
MRF329	OEM
MRF331	OEM
MRF338	OEM
MRF340	OEM
MRF342	OEM
MRF344	OEM
MRF400	OEM
MRF402	3293
MRF404	2675
MRF406	5110
MRF412	2918
MRF412A	3519
MRF420	3521
MRF421	3586
MRF426	OEM
MRF426A	OEM
MRF427	OEM
MRF427A	OEM
MRF428	OEM
MRF428A	OEM
MRF429	OEM
MRF432	OEM
MRF433	5110
MRF435	OEM
MRF448	OEM
MRF449	2296
MRF449A	1189
MRF450	3521
MRF450A	1189
MRF452	2808
MRF452A	OEM
MRF453	2808
MRF453A	3519
MRF454	3521
MRF454A	3523
MRF455	2808
MRF455A	3519
MRF458	3521
MRF458A	3523
MRF460	2296
MRF463	2522
MRF464	2523
MRF464A	OEM

DEVICE TYPE	REPL CODE
MRF466	OEM
MRF472	1581
MRF475	0930
MRF476	0930
MRF477	OEM
MRF479	OEM
MRF485	2475
MRF486	OEM
MRF492	OEM
MRF492A	OEM
MRF497	OEM
MRF501	0007
MRF502	0007
MRF511	2059
MRF515	0684
MRF517	OEM
MRF519	OEM
MRF525	OEM
MRF526	OEM
MRF531	0086
MRF534	OEM
MRF536	OEM
MRF539	OEM
MRF559	OEM
MRF571	OEM
MRF572	OEM
MRF573	OEM
MRF580	OEM
MRF581	OEM
MRF587	OEM
MRF597	OEM
MRF600	OEM
MRF603	1189
MRF604	2675
MRF605	OEM
MRF606	2675
MRF607	3387
MRF618	2082
MRF619	3545
MRF620	3545
MRF621	2841
MRF626	2675
MRF627	OEM
MRF629	2028
MRF630	OEM
MRF641	2082
MRF644	3545
MRF646	2841
MRF648	3547
MRF652	OEM
MRF660	OEM
MRF750	OEM
MRF752	OEM
MRF754	OEM
MRF800	OEM
MRF817	3516
MRF835	OEM
MRF838	OEM
MRF838A	OEM
MRF840	OEM
MRF841	OEM
MRF842	OEM
MRF844	3599
MRF846	OEM
MRF870	OEM
MRF870A	OEM
MRF890	OEM
MRF892	OEM
MRF894	OEM
MRF901	2978
MRF904	OEM
MRF905	OEM
MRF911	2817
MRF914	OEM
MRF931	OEM
MRF961	OEM
MRF962	OEM
MRF965	OEM
MRF966	OEM
MRF967	OEM
MRF1000MA	OEM
MRF1000MB	OEM
MRF1002MA	OEM
MRF1002MB	OEM
MRF1004MA	OEM
MRF1004MB	OEM
MRF1008MA	OEM
MRF1008MB	OEM
MRF1015MA	OEM
MRF1015MB	OEM
MRF1035MA	OEM
MRF1035MB	OEM
MRF1090MA	OEM
MRF1090MB	OEM
MRF1150MA	OEM
MRF1150MB	OEM
MRF1250M	OEM
MRF1325M	OEM
MRF2001	OEM
MRF2001B	OEM
MRF2001M	OEM
MRF2003	OEM
MRF2003B	OEM
MRF2003M	OEM
MRF2005	OEM
MRF2005B	OEM
MRF2005M	OEM
MRF2010	OEM
MRF2010B	OEM

DEVICE TYPE	REPL CODE
MRF2010M	OEM
MRF2016M	OEM
MRF4070	3165
MRF5177A	OEM
MRF8003	2675
MRF8004	0693
MRS6548	0127
MRS-H10	OEM
MRV-20C	0015
MS-1	0080
MS1H	0015
MS-2	0015
MS2H	0015
MS3H	0015
MS-4	0790
MS4H	0015
MS5	0084
MS5H	0015
MS9/1X3	OEM
MS10	OEM
MS11H	0015
MS12H	0015
MS13H	0015
MS14H	0015
MS15	OEM
MS15/1C	0286
MS20	OEM
MS20K	OEM
MS21	OEM
MS22B	0016
MS30	OEM
MS30K	OEM
MS35H	0015
MS36H	0015
MS37H	0790
MS38H	0015
MS40	OEM
MS40K	OEM
MS41	OEM
MS50	0015
MS50K	OEM
MS51	OEM
MS60	1627
MS60K	OEM
MS80	OEM
MS80K	OEM
MS81-4	OEM
MS100	OEM
MS100A	OEM
MS115P	2289
MS120K	OEM
MS166	OEM
MS222	OEM
MS223	OEM
MS224	OEM
MS225	OEM
MS232	OEM
MS233	OEM
MS235	OEM
MS242	OEM
MS300	OEM
MS301	0392
MS302	0392
MS302M	OEM
MS303	OEM
MS303M	OEM
MS401	OEM
MS401M	OEM
MS500	OEM
MS501	OEM
MS510	0590
MS701T	0144
MS801X	OEM
MS802A	OEM
MS802B	OEM
MS802X	OEM
MS803X	OEM
MS804X	OEM
MS805X	OEM
MS806X	OEM
MS807X	OEM
MS808X	OEM
MS809X	OEM
MS810A	OEM
MS810B	OEM
MS812B	OEM
MS813A	OEM
MS813B	OEM
MS831A	OEM
MS831B	OEM
MS832A	OEM
MS832B	OEM
MS838A	OEM
MS838B	OEM
MS851X	OEM
MS852A	OEM
MS852B	OEM
MS852X	OEM
MS853X	OEM
MS854X	OEM
MS855X	OEM
MS856X	OEM
MS857A	OEM
MS857B	OEM
MS859B	OEM
MS874A	OEM
MS874B	OEM
MS893B	OEM
MS918F	OEM

DEVICE TYPE	REPL CODE
MS1005	OEM
MS1006	OEM
MS1007	OEM
MS1008	OEM
MS1010	0590
MS1015	OEM
MS1016	OEM
MS1020	OEM
MS1021	OEM
MS1022	OEM
MS1022A	OEM
MS1023	OEM
MS1023A	OEM
MS1035	OEM
MS1036	OEM
MS1037	OEM
MS1040	OEM
MS1041	OEM
MS1042	OEM
MS1043	OEM
MS1049	OEM
MS1050	OEM
MS1051	OEM
MS1052	OEM
MS1053	OEM
MS1054	OEM
MS1055	OEM
MS1056	OEM
MS1057	OEM
MS1058	OEM
MS1059	OEM
MS1080	OEM
MS1081	OEM
MS1081A	OEM
MS1082	OEM
MS1083	OEM
MS1083A	OEM
MS1084	OEM
MS1085	OEM
MS1085A	OEM
MS1086	OEM
MS1087	OEM
MS1087A	OEM
MS1088	OEM
MS1089	OEM
MS1090	OEM
MS1100	OEM
MS1101	OEM
MS1102	OEM
MS1103	OEM
MS1103A	OEM
MS1151	OEM
MS1153	OEM
MS1155	OEM
MS1156	OEM
MS1157	OEM
MS1158	OEM
MS1162	OEM
MS1164	OEM
MS1166	OEM
MS1168	OEM
MS1169	OEM
MS1170	OEM
MS1202	OEM
MS1203	OEM
MS1204	OEM
MS1205	OEM
MS1206	OEM
MS1207	OEM
MS1208	OEM
MS1209	OEM
MS1220	OEM
MS1221	OEM
MS1222	OEM
MS1223	OEM
MS1504	OEM
MS1505	OEM
MS1506	OEM
MS1507	OEM
MS1508	OEM
MS1509	OEM
MS1510	OEM
MS1511	OEM
MS1513A	OEM
MS1526A	OEM
MS1530	OEM
MS1530A	OEM
MS1531	OEM
MS1531A	OEM
MS1532	OEM
MS1532-16A	OEM
MS1532A	OEM
MS1533	OEM
MS1533A	OEM
MS1534	OEM
MS1534A	OEM
MS1535	OEM
MS1535A	OEM
MS1536A	OEM
MS1540	OEM
MS1541	OEM
MS1542	OEM
MS1550	OEM
MS1550A	OEM
MS1551	OEM
MS1551A	OEM
MS1552	OEM
MS1552A	OEM
MS1553	OEM

If replacement code is OEM, contact original manufacturer for replacement.

DEVICE TYPE	REPL CODE
MS1553A	OEM
MS1554	OEM
MS1554A	OEM
MS1555	OEM
MS1555A	OEM
MS1560	OEM
MS1561	OEM
MS1562	OEM
MS1563	OEM
MS1570	OEM
MS1571	OEM
MS1572	OEM
MS1573	OEM
MS1580	OEM
MS1620	OEM
MS1621	OEM
MS1625	OEM
MS1626	OEM
MS1700	OEM
MS1701	OEM
MS1702	OEM
MS1703	OEM
MS1704	OEM
MS1705	OEM
MS2022	OEM
MS2023	OEM
MS2024	OEM
MS2025	OEM
MS2501	OEM
MS2502	OEM
MS2503	OEM
MS2504	OEM
MS2505	OEM
MS2542	OEM
MS2543	OEM
MS2544	OEM
MS2545	OEM
MS2562	OEM
MS2562A	OEM
MS2563	OEM
MS2563A	OEM
MS2564	OEM
MS2564A	OEM
MS2565	OEM
MS2565A	OEM
MS2602	OEM
MS2603	OEM
MS2604	OEM
MS2605	OEM
MS2606	OEM
MS2620	OEM
MS2621	OEM
MS2623	OEM
MS2630	OEM
MS2631	OEM
MS2632	OEM
MS2991	0086
MS3001	OEM
MS3002	OEM
MS3003	OEM
MS3004	OEM
MS3005	OEM
MS3006	OEM
MS3012	OEM
MS3013	OEM
MS3014	OEM
MS3015	OEM
MS3016	OEM
MS3017	OEM
MS3062	OEM
MS3063	OEM
MS3064	OEM
MS3065	OEM
MS3130	OEM
MS3131	OEM
MS3132	OEM
MS3133	OEM
MS3134	OEM
MS3135	OEM
MS3136	OEM
MS3140	OEM
MS3141	OEM
MS3142	OEM
MS3143	OEM
MS3145	OEM
MS3146	OEM
MS3147	OEM
MS3150	OEM
MS3151-5	OEM
MS3160	OEM
MS3161-5	OEM
MS3166	OEM
MS3170	OEM
MS3171-5	OEM
MS3180	OEM
MS3181	OEM
MS3182	OEM
MS3183	OEM
MS3190	OEM
MS3191	OEM
MS3192	OEM
MS3200	OEM
MS3201-5	OEM
MS3210	OEM
MS3210-4	OEM
MS3220	OEM
MS3221	OEM
MS3222	OEM
MS3223	OEM

DEVICE TYPE	REPL CODE
MS3230	OEM
MS3231	OEM
MS3250	OEM
MS3251-5	OEM
MS3256	OEM
MS3260	OEM
MS3261-5	OEM
MS3266	OEM
MS3270	OEM
MS3271-4	OEM
MS3280	OEM
MS3281-2	OEM
MS3694	0079
MS4044	OEM
MS4108	OEM
MS4109	OEM
MS4110	OEM
MS4111	OEM
MS4112	OEM
MS4170	OEM
MS4171-4	OEM
MS4180	OEM
MS4181	OEM
MS4182	OEM
MS4220	OEM
MS4221-3	OEM
MS4230	OEM
MS4231	OEM
MS4232	OEM
MS4270	OEM
MS4271	OEM
MS4272	OEM
MS4273	OEM
MS4280	OEM
MS4281	OEM
MS4282	OEM
MS4320	OEM
MS4321	OEM
MS4322	OEM
MS4330	OEM
MS4331	OEM
MS4408	OEM
MS4409	OEM
MS4410	OEM
MS4411	OEM
MS4412	OEM
MS4500A	OEM
MS4500B-F	OEM
MS4500G	OEM
MS4501A	OEM
MS4501G	OEM
MS4502A	OEM
MS4502B-E	OEM
MS4503A	OEM
MS4503B	OEM
MS4503C	OEM
MS4510A	OEM
MS4510B-F	OEM
MS4510G	OEM
MS4511A	OEM
MS4511B-F	OEM
MS4511G	OEM
MS4512A	OEM
MS4512B-E	OEM
MS4513A	OEM
MS4513B	OEM
MS4513C	OEM
MS4520A	OEM
MS4520B-E	OEM
MS4520F	OEM
MS4520G	OEM
MS4521A	OEM
MS4521B-F	OEM
MS4522A	OEM
MS4522B-D	OEM
MS4523A	OEM
MS4523B	OEM
MS4523C	OEM
MS4530A	OEM
MS4530B-D	OEM
MS4531A	OEM
MS4531B-D	OEM
MS4532A	OEM
MS4532B	OEM
MS4532C	OEM
MS4533A	OEM
MS4533B	OEM
MS4540A	OEM
MS4540B	OEM
MS4540C	OEM
MS4541A	OEM
MS4541B	OEM
MS4541C	OEM
MS4542A	OEM
MS4542B	OEM
MS4542C	OEM
MS4543A	OEM
MS4543B	OEM
MS4543C	OEM
MS5000-8	OEM
MS5000-8A	OEM
MS5000-12	OEM
MS5000-16	OEM
MS5000-16A	OEM
MS5000A	OEM
MS5000B-F	OEM
MS5000G	OEM
MS5001A	OEM
MS5001B-F	OEM

DEVICE TYPE	REPL CODE
MS5001G	OEM
MS5002A	OEM
MS5002B-F	OEM
MS5002G	OEM
MS5003A	OEM
MS5003B-F	OEM
MS5003G	OEM
MS5010A	OEM
MS5010B-F	OEM
MS5010G	OEM
MS5011A	OEM
MS5011B-F	OEM
MS5011G	OEM
MS5012A	OEM
MS5012B-F	OEM
MS5012G	OEM
MS5013A	OEM
MS5013B-F	OEM
MS5013G	OEM
MS5015	OEM
MS5020A	OEM
MS5020B-F	OEM
MS5021A	OEM
MS5021B-F	OEM
MS5022A	OEM
MS5022B-F	OEM
MS5023A	OEM
MS5023B-F	OEM
MS5030A	OEM
MS5030B-D	OEM
MS5031A	OEM
MS5031B-D	OEM
MS5032A	OEM
MS5032B-D	OEM
MS5033A	OEM
MS5033B-D	OEM
MS5040A	OEM
MS5040B	OEM
MS5040C	OEM
MS5041A	OEM
MS5041B	OEM
MS5041C	OEM
MS5042A	OEM
MS5042B	OEM
MS5042C	OEM
MS5043A	OEM
MS5043B	OEM
MS5043C	OEM
MS5132-4A	OEM
MS5132-B	OEM
MS5133-4A	OEM
MS5133-8	OEM
MS5133-16A	OEM
MS5134-4A	OEM
MS5134-8	OEM
MS5134-16A	OEM
MS5142-8	OEM
MS5142-16A	OEM
MS5200-4A	OEM
MS5200-8	OEM
MS5200-8A	OEM
MS5240-4A	OEM
MS5240-8	OEM
MS5240-16A	OEM
MS5241-4A	OEM
MS5242-4A	OEM
MS5242-8	OEM
MS5242-16A	OEM
MS5243-4A	OEM
MS5243-8	OEM
MS5243-16A	OEM
MS5251-4A	OEM
MS5251-8	OEM
MS5251-16A	OEM
MS5252-4A	OEM
MS5252-8	OEM
MS5252-16A	OEM
MS5253-4A	OEM
MS5253-8	OEM
MS5253-16A	OEM
MS5254-4A	OEM
MS5254-8	OEM
MS5254-16A	OEM
MS6000	OEM
MS6001	OEM
MS6002	OEM
MS6003	OEM
MS6004	OEM
MS6005	OEM
MS6006	OEM
MS6007	OEM
MS6008	OEM
MS6009	OEM
MS6010	OEM
MS6011	OEM
MS6012	OEM
MS6013	OEM
MS6014	OEM
MS6015	OEM
MS6016	OEM
MS6017	OEM
MS6018	OEM
MS6019	OEM
MS6030-1	OEM
MS6030-8	OEM
MS6031-1	OEM
MS6031-8	OEM
MS6032-1	OEM
MS6032-8	OEM

DEVICE TYPE	REPL CODE
MS6033-1	OEM
MS6033-8	OEM
MS6034-1	OEM
MS6034-8	OEM
MS6035-1	OEM
MS6035-8	OEM
MS6040-1	OEM
MS6040-8	OEM
MS6041-1	OEM
MS6041-8	OEM
MS6042-1	OEM
MS6042-8	OEM
MS6043-1	OEM
MS6043-8	OEM
MS6044-1	OEM
MS6044-8	OEM
MS6045-1	OEM
MS6045-8	OEM
MS6101-8	OEM
MS6101-8A	OEM
MS6101-22	OEM
MS6101-23	OEM
MS6101-24	OEM
MS6103-8	OEM
MS6103-8A	OEM
MS6103-22	OEM
MS6103-23	OEM
MS6103-24	OEM
MS6105-8	OEM
MS6105-8A	OEM
MS6105-22	OEM
MS6105-23	OEM
MS6105-24	OEM
MS6107-8	OEM
MS6107-8A	OEM
MS6107-22	OEM
MS6107-23	OEM
MS6107-24	OEM
MS7000	OEM
MS7001	OEM
MS7101	OEM
MS7102	OEM
MS7111	OEM
MS7112	OEM
MS7500	0030
MS7501S	0144
MS7501T	0144
MS7502R	0016
MS7502S	0144
MS7502T	0144
MS7503R	0016
MS7504	0396
MS7505	0037
MS7506G	0126
MS7506H	0086
MS7506J	0086
MS8101	OEM
MS8102	OEM
MS8108	OEM
MS8112	OEM
MS8201	OEM
MS8202	OEM
MS8204	OEM
MS8208	OEM
MS8212	OEM
MSA137MS	OEM
MSA970A3	OEM
MSA7505	0042
MSA8503	0396
MSA8505	0042
MSA8506	0555
MSA8507	0396
MSA8508	0555
MSC6458-20SS	OEM
MSC6458-32SS	OEM
MSC645832SS	OEM
MSD601(R)	OEM
MSD601(S)	OEM
MSD6100	0196
MSD6101	1642
MSD6102	0196
MSD6150	1073
MSD7000	1642
MSG7506	0086
MSJ7505	0126
MSK110	OEM
MSK5405	0086
MSL915RS	OEM
MSL2301	OEM
MSL2514	OEM
MSL9371RS	OEM
MSL9372RS	OEM
MSL9373RS	OEM
MSL9378	OEM
MSL9378RS	5238
MSM63	0037
MSM74HC4094RS	OEM
MSM81C55RS	OEM
MSM311EL	2093
MSM561	OEM
MSM631	0037
MSM2114	2037
MSM2114L-3RS	2037
MSM2114L3RS	2037
MSM2764RS	0806
MSM3980	OEM
MSM3982	OEM
MSM4001	0473
MSM4002	2044

DEVICE TYPE	REPL CODE
MSM4008	0982
MSM4011	0215
MSM4011RS	0215
MSM4012	0493
MSM4013	0409
MSM4013RS	0409
MSM4016	1135
MSM4016B	OEM
MSM4016RS	1135
MSM4017	0508
MSM4017AN	0508
MSM4019	1517
MSM4020	1651
MSM4020RS	OEM
MSM4023	0515
MSM4025	2061
MSM4027	1938
MSM4028	2213
MSM4030	0495
MSM4040	0056
MSM4042	0121
MSM4043	1544
MSM4044	2292
MSM4050	0394
MSM4050RS	0394
MSM4064	0119
MSM4066RS	0101
MSM4068	2482
MSM4069	0119
MSM4069RS	0119
MSM4069UBRU	0119
MSM4071	0129
MSM4071BN	0129
MSM4072	2502
MSM4073	1528
MSM4075	2518
MSM4078	0915
MSM4081	0621
MSM4081RS	0621
MSM4082	0297
MSM4085	0300
MSM4086	0530
MSM4514RS	1819
MSM4518	1037
MSM4520	2650
MSM5258RS	OEM
MSM5550RSK	OEM
MSM5562	OEM
MSM5565-01RS	OEM
MSM5565RS	OEM
MSM5807	OEM
MSM5816RS	OEM
MSM5830RS	OEM
MSM5907	OEM
MSM5951	OEM
MSM6205GS	OEM
MSM6219AS	OEM
MSM6219GS-VK	OEM
MSM6234RS	OEM
MSM6404A-115RS	OEM
MSM6404A-120RS	OEM
MSM6404A-180RS	OEM
MSM6408-26SS	OEM
MSM6408-32SS	OEM
MSM6964	OEM
MSM6964-3RS	OEM
MSM6964MS	OEM
MSM6984	OEM
MSM6990-7203V1	OEM
MSM7400R	OEM
MSM7400RS	OEM
MSM16911RS	OEM
MSM40192	1753
MSM40193	1765
MSM55271RS	OEM
MSM58371RS	OEM
MSM84444Y	OEM
MSM87182	OEM
MSM512815RS	OEM
MSP3	OEM
MSP6	OEM
MSP10	0264
MSP10A	3249
MSP15	0264
MSP15A	3249
MSP20	0168
MSP20A	3249
MSP25	0168
MSP25A	3249
MSP30	0168
MSP31	OEM
MSP32	OEM
MSP33	OEM
MSP34	OEM
MSP1161	0432
MSP999058-1	0086
MSR2S28	OEM
MSR5	OEM
MSR10	OEM
MSR20	OEM
MSR40	OEM
MSR60	OEM
MSR80	OEM
MSR100	OEM
MSR-500	0015
MSR2502G	OEM
MSR2509A	OEM
MSR2520	OEM
MSR2528	OEM

DEVICE TYPE	REPL CODE
MSR2530	OEM
MSR7502	0144
MSR7503	0016
MSR-V5	0015
MSS100-4A	OEM
MSS-1000	0015
MSS1000	0015
MSS1001	OEM
MSS1002	OEM
MSS7501	0144
MSS7502	0144
MST001RS-KSS	OEM
MST-10	0086
MST10	0264
MST10S	0233
MST15	0264
MST16	OEM
MST20	0168
MST20B	0168
MST20S	0233
MST22	OEM
MST25	0168
MST30	0168
MST30B	0168
MST30S	0233
MST35	0168
MST40	0168
MST40B	0168
MST40S	0187
MST45	0168
MST48	OEM
MST50	0168
MST50B	0168
MST50S	0168
MST55	0168
MST105	0168
MST7501	0144
MSZ9.1	0057
MSZ10	OEM
MT01	OEM
MT020A	OEM
MT021	0015
MT021A	0015
MT022	0015
MT022A	0015
MT0404	0037
MT0404-1	0037
MT0404-2	0037
MT0411	0037
MT0412	0037
MT0413	0037
MT0414	0855
MT0461	0037
MT0462	0037
MT0463	0150
MT0493	0224
MT1	5030
MT2	5419
MT5	5417
MT10	OEM
MT14	0015
MT20	OEM
MT24	0015
MT30	OEM
MT30LA	OEM
MT32	OEM
MT44	0015
MT50	OEM
MT64	0015
MT84	0071
MT100	0144
MT101	0144
MT101B	OEM
MT102	0144
MT102B	OEM
MT104	0016
MT106	0144
MT107	0144
MT131B	OEM
MT132A	OEM
MT132B	OEM
MT170	0604
MT181	OEM
MT-301	0126
MT-302	0086
MT456	1325
MT456A	0133
MT457	0080
MT457A	0080
MT458	0604
MT458A	0133
MT459	0604
MT459A	0604
MT461	0133
MT461A	0133
MT462	0133
MT462A	0080
MT463	0604
MT463A	0604
MT464	0604
MT464A	0604
MT482	1325
MT482A	0133
MT482B	0133
MT483	0080
MT483A	0080
MT483B	0080
MT484	0604
MT484A	0133

DEVICE TYPE	REPL CODE
MT484B	0133
MT485	0604
MT485A	0604
MT485B	0604
MT486	0790
MT486A	0790
MT486B	0790
MT696	0016
MT697	0016
MT698	0233
MT699	0233
MT706	0016
MT706A	0016
MT706B	0016
MT707	0016
MT708	0016
MT726	0037
MT743	0144
MT744	0144
MT753	0144
MT869	0037
MT870	0233
MT871	0233
MT890	0080
MT910	0233
MT911	0233
MT912	0233
MT914	OEM
MT995	OEM
MT1038	0144
MT1038A	0144
MT1039	0144
MT1060	0259
MT1060A	0144
MT1061	0007
MT1061A	0144
MT1062	0414
MT1070	0555
MT1075	0855
MT1100	0855
MT1131	0037
MT1131A	0037
MT1132	0037
MT1132A	0037
MT1132B	0037
MT1254	0037
MT1255	0037
MT1256	0037
MT1257	0037
MT1258	0037
MT1259	0037
MT1259-12	OEM
MT1420	0037
MT1613	0086
MT1711	0086
MT1889	0143
MT1893	0233
MT1991	0037
MT2303	0037
MT2411	0037
MT2412	0037
MT3001	0007
MT3002	0007
MT3011	0144
MT3202	0142
MT4101	0079
MT4102	0079
MT4102A	0079
MT4103	0079
MT4104	0007
MT4264	OEM
MT4264-15	2341
MT4264-20	2341
MT5010	0080
MT5011	0080
MT5050	0015
MT5051	0015
MT5100	0604
MT5101	0604
MT5102	0080
MT5103	0080
MT6001	0079
MT6002	0079
MT6003	0079
MT6007	OEM
MT6011	OEM
MT6021	OEM
MT9001	0079
MT9002	0079
MT9003	0144
MT102351A	0050
MTA001	OEM
MTA001M	OEM
MTC1370PQ	0350
MTD1N40	OEM
MTD1N45	OEM
MTD2N50	OEM
MTD4N20	OEM
MTD4P05	OEM
MTD4P06	OEM
MTD5N05	OEM
MTD5N06	OEM
MTD6N08	OEM
MTD6N10	OEM
MTD6N15	OEM
MTD10N05E	OEM
MTD2972	OEM
MTD2973	OEM
MTD2974	OEM

If replacement code is OEM, contact original manufacturer for replacement.

497

DEVICE TYPE	REPL CODE
MTD2975	OEM
MTD2978	OEM
MTD2979	OEM
MTD3055E	OEM
MTE13B	OEM
MTF101	OEM
MTF102	OEM
MTH5N95	OEM
MTH5N100	OEM
MTH6N55	OEM
MTH6N60	OEM
MTH6N85	OEM
MTH6N90	OEM
MTH7N45	OEM
MTH7N50	OEM
MTH8N35	OEM
MTH8N40	OEM
MTH8N45	OEM
MTH8N55	OEM
MTH8N60	OEM
MTH8P18	OEM
MTH8P20	OEM
MTH13N45	OEM
MTH13N50	OEM
MTH15N20	OEM
MTH15N35	OEM
MTH15N40	OEM
MTH20N15	OEM
MTH20P08	OEM
MTH20P10	OEM
MTH25N08	OEM
MTH25N10	OEM
MTH25P05	OEM
MTH25P06	OEM
MTH30N20	OEM
MTH35N05	OEM
MTH35N06	OEM
MTH35N15	OEM
MTH40N05	OEM
MTH40N06	OEM
MTH40N08	OEM
MTH40N10	OEM
MTH50N05E	OEM
MTM1N95	OEM
MTM1N100	OEM
MTM2N45	OEM
MTM2N50	OEM
MTM2N55	OEM
MTM2N60	OEM
MTM2N85	OEM
MTM2N90	OEM
MTM2P45	5263
MTM2P50	OEM
MTM3N35	OEM
MTM3N40	OEM
MTM3N55	OEM
MTM3N60	OEM
MTM3N75	OEM
MTM3N80	OEM
MTM3N95	OEM
MTM3N100	OEM
MTM3P25	OEM
MTM4N45	OEM
MTM4N50	OEM
MTM4N85	OEM
MTM4N90	OEM
MTM5N18	OEM
MTM5N20	OEM
MTM5N35	1658
MTM5N40	1658
MTM5N45	OEM
MTM5N95	OEM
MTM5N100	OEM
MTM5P18	OEM
MTM5P20	OEM
MTM5P25	OEM
MTM6N55	OEM
MTM6N60	1658
MTM6N85	OEM
MTM6N90	OEM
MTM7N12	OEM
MTM7N15	OEM
MTM7N18	OEM
MTM7N20	OEM
MTM7N45	OEM
MTM7N50	OEM
MTM8N08	OEM
MTM8N10	OEM
MTM8N12	OEM
MTM8N15	OEM
MTM8N18	OEM
MTM8N20	OEM
MTM8N35	OEM
MTM8N40	OEM
MTM8N60	OEM
MTM8P08	OEM
MTM8P10	OEM
MTM8P18	OEM
MTM8P20	OEM
MTM8P25	OEM
MTM8P80	OEM
MTM8P08	OEM
MTM10N05	OEM
MTM10N06	OEM
MTM10N08	OEM
MTM10N5	OEM
MTM10N10	OEM
MTM10N12	OEM
MTM10N12L	OEM

DEVICE TYPE	REPL CODE
MTM10N15	OEM
MTM10N15L	OEM
MTM10N25	OEM
MTM12N05	OEM
MTM12N06	OEM
MTM12N08	OEM
MTM12N10	OEM
MTM12N12	OEM
MTM12N15	OEM
MTM12N18	OEM
MTM12N20	OEM
MTM12P05	OEM
MTM12P06	OEM
MTM12P08	OEM
MTM12P10	OEM
MTM15N05	OEM
MTM15N05L	OEM
MTM15N06	OEM
MTM15N06E	OEM
MTM15N06L	OEM
MTM15N08	OEM
MTM15N10	OEM
MTM15N12	OEM
MTM15N15	OEM
MTM15N18	OEM
MTM15N20	OEM
MTM15N35	OEM
MTM15N40	OEM
MTM15N45	OEM
MTM15N50	OEM
MTM20N08	OEM
MTM20N10	OEM
MTM20N12	OEM
MTM20N15	OEM
MTM20P05	OEM
MTM20P08	OEM
MTM20P10	OEM
MTM25N05	OEM
MTM25N05L	OEM
MTM25N06	OEM
MTM25N06L	OEM
MTM25N08	OEM
MTM25N10	OEM
MTM25N10E	OEM
MTM25P05	OEM
MTM25P06	OEM
MTM35N05	OEM
MTM35N06	OEM
MTM35N06E	OEM
MTM40N20	OEM
MTM45N05E	OEM
MTM45N15	OEM
MTM50N05E	OEM
MTM55N08	OEM
MTM55N10	OEM
MTM60N05	OEM
MTM60N06	OEM
MTM360	OEM
MTM474	OEM
MTM475	OEM
MTM564	1658
MTM565	1658
MTM814	2256
MTM815	OEM
MTM1034	OEM
MTM1035	OEM
MTM1224	OEM
MTM1225	OEM
MTMP5N35	OEM
MTN5N20	OEM
MTN6N55	OEM
MTN712	OEM
MTN1130-ASR	OEM
MTN1130-CSR	OEM
MTN2130-AG	OEM
MTN2130-CG	OEM
MTN3000-ASR	OEM
MTN3100-CSR	4127
MTN3200-AG	OEM
MTN3300-CG	OEM
MTN3600-AHR	OEM
MTN3600-AO	OEM
MTN3700-CHR	OEM
MTN3700-CO	OEM
MTN4130-AHR	OEM
MTN4130-AO	OEM
MTN4130-CHR	OEM
MTN4130-CO	OEM
MTP1N45	5649
MTP1N50	5649
MTP1N55	OEM
MTP1N60	OEM
MTP1N95	OEM
MTP1N100	OEM
MTP2N18	OEM
MTP2N20	OEM
MTP2N25	OEM
MTP2N35	OEM
MTP2N40	OEM
MTP2N45	1457
MTP2N50	1457
MTP2N55	OEM
MTP2N60	OEM
MTP2N85	3673
MTP2N90	OEM
MTP2P45	5263
MTP2P50	5263
MTP3N08L	OEM
MTP3N10L	OEM

DEVICE TYPE	REPL CODE
MTP3N12	OEM
MTP3N15	OEM
MTP3N18	OEM
MTP3N20	1456
MTP3N35	1456
MTP3N40	1456
MTP3N45	OEM
MTP3N50	OEM
MTP3N55	OEM
MTP3N60	3673
MTP3N75	3673
MTP3N80	3673
MTP3N95	OEM
MTP3N100	OEM
MTP3P25	OEM
MTP4N05L	OEM
MTP4N06L	OEM
MTP4N08	OEM
MTP4N10	OEM
MTP4N12	OEM
MTP4N15	1456
MTP4N25M	OEM
MTP4N45	6941
MTP4N50	1643
MTP4N50M	OEM
MTP4N85	3673
MTP4N90	OEM
MTP5N05	OEM
MTP5N06	OEM
MTP5N08	OEM
MTP5N10	OEM
MTP5N12	OEM
MTP5N18	OEM
MTP5N20	1456
MTP5N35	1456
MTP5N40	1456
MTP5N50	OEM
MTP5P18	OEM
MTP5P20	OEM
MTP5P25	OEM
MTP6N05	OEM
MTP6N06	OEM
MTP6N10	OEM
MTP6N55	1643
MTP6N60	OEM
MTP7N05	OEM
MTP7N06	2325
MTP7N12	OEM
MTP7N15	2162
MTP7N18	OEM
MTP7N20	OEM
MTP7N45	OEM
MTP7N50	OEM
MTP7P05	OEM
MTP7P06	OEM
MTP8N08	3059
MTP8N10	3059
MTP8N10E	OEM
MTP8N12	3063
MTP8N15	3063
MTP8N18	OEM
MTP8N20	OEM
MTP8N35	OEM
MTP8N40	OEM
MTP8N45	1643
MTP8N50	1643
MTP8N50M	OEM
MTP8P08	2256
MTP8P10	2256
MTP8P25	OEM
MTP10N05	5811
MTP10N06	5811
MTP10N06E	OEM
MTP10N08	OEM
MTP10N10	OEM
MTP10N10E	OEM
MTP10N10M	OEM
MTP10N12	3063
MTP10N12L	5618
MTP10N15	3063
MTP10N15L	5618
MTP10N25	OEM
MTP10N25M	OEM
MTP10N35	OEM
MTP10N40	OEM
MTP12N05	5264
MTP12N05E	OEM
MTP12N06	5264
MTP12N08	4970
MTP12N08L	OEM
MTP12N10	4970
MTP12N10L	OEM
MTP12N18	OEM
MTP12N20	5618
MTP12P05	OEM
MTP12P06	OEM
MTP12P08	OEM
MTP12P10	OEM
MTP14N05A	OEM
MTP15N05	5811
MTP15N05E	OEM
MTP15N05L	OEM
MTP15N06	5811
MTP15N06E	OEM
MTP15N06L	OEM
MTP15N12	OEM
MTP15N15	OEM
MTP16N05A	OEM
MTP20N08	OEM

DEVICE TYPE	REPL CODE
MTP20N10	OEM
MTP20N10E	OEM
MTP20P06	OEM
MTP25N05	OEM
MTP25N05E	OEM
MTP25N05L	OEM
MTP25N06	OEM
MTP25N06E	OEM
MTP25N06L	OEM
MTP25N10	OEM
MTP25N10E	OEM
MTP25N10M	OEM
MTP30N05E	OEM
MTP35N06E	OEM
MTP40N06M	OEM
MTP45N05E	OEM
MTP50N05E	OEM
MTP50N05M	OEM
MTP474	OEM
MTP475	OEM
MTP564	1456
MTP565	1456
MTP814	2256
MTP815	2256
MTP1034	OEM
MTP1035	OEM
MTP1224	4970
MTP1225	4970
MTP3055E	OEM
MTW8N50E	4944
MTZ3.6A	OEM
MTZ3.6B	OEM
MTZ4.7	0140
MTZ4.7A	OEM
MTZ4.7B	0140
MTZ4.7JA	OEM
MTZ5.1	0041
MTZ5.1(B)	0041
MTZ5.1(C)	0041
MTZ5.1-B	0582
MTZ5.1A	OEM
MTZ5.1B	0041
MTZ5.1B(TA)	0041
MTZ5.1BT-77	0041
MTZ5.1BTA	0582
MTZ5.1C	OEM
MTZ5.1TP	4049
MTZ5.6	0253
MTZ5.6B	0253
MTZ5.6B-T77	0253
MTZ5.6BT-77	0253
MTZ5.6C	OEM
MTZ5.6V	0253
MTZ6.2	0466
MTZ6.2(C)	0466
MTZ6.2A	0466
MTZ6.2A-T77	OEM
MTZ6.2B	0466
MTZ6.2B(TA)	OEM
MTZ6.2BT	0466
MTZ6.2BT-77	0466
MTZ6.2C	OEM
MTZ6.2CT	OEM
MTZ6.8	0062
MTZ6.8-C	OEM
MTZ6.8B	0062
MTZ6.8BT-77	0466
MTZ6.8C	0062
MTZ6.8JA	OEM
MTZ6.8JB	OEM
MTZ7.5	0077
MTZ7.5(C)	0077
MTZ7.5-C	0077
MTZ7.5A	OEM
MTZ7.5B	0077
MTZ7.5C	OEM
MTZ8.2	0244
MTZ8.2(C)	0165
MTZ8.2-C	0165
MTZ8.2B	OEM
MTZ8.2C	4245
MTZ8.2T-77	OEM
MTZ9.1	0057
MTZ9.1(C)	0057
MTZ9.1A	OEM
MTZ9.1B	0057
MTZ9.1C	OEM
MTZ9.1JA	OEM
MTZ9.1JC	OEM
MTZ9.1TP	5848
MTZ10	0532
MTZ10(C)	0064
MTZ10A	OEM
MTZ10B	OEM
MTZ10C	OEM
MTZ11	0181
MTZ11B	0181
MTZ11BT-77	0181
MTZ11TP	0181
MTZ12	0052
MTZ12B	0999
MTZ12BT-77	0999
MTZ12C	OEM
MTZ13	0053
MTZ13A	0053
MTZ13B	OEM
MTZ13BT	OEM
MTZ13C	OEM
MTZ15	0681

DEVICE TYPE	REPL CODE
MTZ15A	OEM
MTZ15B	OEM
MTZ15C	OEM
MTZ16	0440
MTZ16C	0440
MTZ18	0371
MTZ18A	OEM
MTZ20	0695
MTZ20-D	0695
MTZ20C	OEM
MTZ20D	OEM
MTZ22	0700
MTZ24	0489
MTZ24(C)	0489
MTZ24-C	0489
MTZ24A	OEM
MTZ24C	2448
MTZ27B	OEM
MTZ27C	OEM
MTZ27D	OEM
MTZ30A	0195
MTZ30B	0195
MTZ30B-T77	OEM
MTZ30D	OEM
MTZ33B	OEM
MTZ33B-T77	OEM
MTZ33C	OEM
MTZ39A	OEM
MTZ607	0157
MTZ607A	0157
MTZ608	0466
MTZ608A	0466
MTZ610	0062
MTZ610A	0025
MTZ611	0077
MTZ611A	0644
MTZ612	0165
MTZ612A	0244
MTZ613	0057
MTZ613A	0057
MTZ614	0170
MTZ614A	0170
MTZ615	0181
MTZ615A	0181
MTZ616	0052
MTZ616A	0052
MTZ617	0053
MTZ617A	0053
MTZ618	0681
MTZ618A	0681
MTZ619	0440
MTZ619A	0440
MTZ620	0371
MTZ620A	0371
MTZ621	0695
MTZ621A	0695
MTZ622A	0700
MTZ623	0489
MTZ623A	0489
MTZ624	0436
MTZ624A	0436
MTZ625	0195
MTZ625A	0721
MTZ626	0166
MTZ626A	0039
MTZ627	0010
MTZ627A	0814
MTZ628	0032
MTZ628A	0346
MTZ629	0054
MTZ629A	0925
MTZ630	0068
MTZ630A	0993
MTZ6722	OEM
MTZ-J3.6B	OEM
MTZJ4.3B	OEM
MTZJ4.7C	OEM
MTZ-J5.1C	OEM
MTZJ5.6B	OEM
MTZJ5.6C	OEM
MTZ-J6.2A	OEM
MTZJ6.2C	OEM
MTZJ6.8C	OEM
MTZJ7.5	OEM
MTZ-J7.5A	OEM
MTZJ7.5C	OEM
MTZJ8.2A	OEM
MTZJ8.2B	OEM
MTZJ9.1A	OEM
MTZ-J9.1C	OEM
MTZJ10A	0057
MTZ-J11A	OEM
MTZ-J11C	OEM
MTZJ12C	OEM
MTZJ13A	OEM
MTZJ13C	OEM
MTZJ16A	OEM
MTZ-J22B	OEM
MTZ-J33A	OEM
MU10	1882
MU20	1167
MU851	OEM
MU852	OEM
MU853	OEM
MU2646	2123
MU2646M	2123
MU3060PT	5856
MU4851	OEM
MU4852	OEM

DEVICE TYPE	REPL CODE
MU4853	OEM
MU4891	1882
MU4892	2123
MU4893	1882
MU4894	1882
MU9610T	0546
MU9611(G)	OEM
MU9611T	0546
MU9660T	0378
MU9661T	0378
MUR105	1082
MUR110	1082
MUR115	1082
MUR120	1082
MUR405	1356
MUR410	1356
MUR415	1356
MUR420	1356
MUR430	1356
MUR440	1356
MUR450	3833
MUR460	3833
MUR470	3833
MUR480	3833
MUR490	3833
MUR605CT	0903
MUR610CT	0903
MUR615CT	0903
MUR620CT	0903
MUR805	1119
MUR810	1119
MUR815	1119
MUR820	1119
MUR860	1654
MUR1505	3507
MUR1510	3507
MUR1515	3507
MUR1520	3507
MUR1605CT	1227
MUR1610CT	1227
MUR1615CT	1227
MUR1620CT	1227
MUR1630CT	0966
MUR1640CT	0966
MUR1650CT	0966
MUR1660CT	0966
MUR3005PT	2219
MUR3010PT	2219
MUR3015PT	2219
MUR3020PT	2219
MUR3030PT	5856
MUR3040PT	5856
MUR3050PT	5856
MUR3060PT	5856
MUR4100	3833
MUS4987	3373
MUS4988	3373
MUTE-X7B	OEM
MV0009	0030
MV009	0030
MV-1	0139
MV-1Y	0139
MV1Y	0139
MV-2	0139
MV-3	0139
MV3	0139
MV-4	1914
MV4	0133
MV-5	0015
MV5	0139
MV-5T	OEM
MV5T	OEM
MV-5W	OEM
MV5W	OEM
MV-5WY	OEM
MV-11	0139
MV11	0139
MV11T	5528
MV-12	0715
MV12A	0120
MV-12H	0139
MV12H	0139
MV-12NV	0120
MV-13	0120
MV13	0339
MV-13(BIAS)	0015
MV-13(DIO)	0133
MV-13(HV-46)	0535
MV13-YH	0120
MV-13H	0120
MV13Y	0120
MV-13YH	0120
MV13YH	0120
MV20C	0344
MV50	1970
MV52	1972
MV53	1974
MV-54	1978
MV54	1978
MV102	OEM
MV-103	OEM
MV103	OEM
MV104	OEM
MV104G	OEM
MV104GM2	OEM
MV104GM3	OEM
MV104GM4	OEM
MV104M2	OEM
MV104M3	OEM

DEVICE TYPE	REPL CODE
MV104M4	OEM
MV-104V	OEM
MV109	OEM
MV121LF	0139
MV201	0005
MV202	OEM
MV-203	OEM
MV203	OEM
MV209	0030
MV209M2	OEM
MV209M3	OEM
MV209M4	OEM
MV-303	OEM
MV306	OEM
MV830	OEM
MV831	OEM
MV832	0623
MV833	OEM
MV834	0030
MV835	OEM
MV836	OEM
MV837	OEM
MV838	OEM
MV839	OEM
MV840	OEM
MV1002	OEM
MV1211F	OEM
MV1212F	0139
MV1401	OEM
MV1403H	OEM
MV1404	OEM
MV1404H	OEM
MV1405	1023
MV1405H	OEM
MV1405VT	1023
MV1410	0623
MV1410A	0623
MV1620	0549
MV1620A	OEM
MV1622	OEM
MV1622A	OEM
MV1624	0005
MV1624A	OEM
MV1626	0715
MV1626A	OEM
MV1628	OEM
MV1628A	OEM
MV1630	OEM
MV1630A	OEM
MV1632	OEM
MV1634	0623
MV1634A	OEM
MV1636	OEM
MV1636A	OEM
MV1638	0030
MV1638A	OEM
MV1640	OEM
MV1640A	OEM
MV1642	OEM
MV1642A	OEM
MV1644	OEM
MV1644A	OEM
MV1646	OEM
MV1646A	OEM
MV1648	OEM
MV1648A	OEM
MV1650	OEM
MV1650A	OEM
MV1652	OEM
MV1654	OEM
MV1656	OEM
MV1658	OEM
MV1660	OEM
MV1662	OEM
MV1664	OEM
MV1666	OEM
MV1720A	0549
MV1724	0005
MV1724A	0005
MV1726	0715
MV1726A	0715
MV1734	0623
MV1734A	0623
MV1738	0030
MV1738A	0030
MV1805C	OEM
MV1805J	OEM
MV1806C	OEM
MV1807C1	OEM
MV1807J	OEM
MV1808A	OEM
MV1808B	OEM
MV1808B1	OEM
MV1808C	OEM
MV1808C1	OEM
MV1809C	OEM
MV1809C1	OEM
MV1810A	OEM
MV1810B	OEM
MV1810B1	OEM
MV1812A	OEM
MV1812B	OEM
MV1816A1	OEM
MV1816B	OEM
MV1816B1	OEM
MV1817A	OEM
MV1817A1	OEM
MV1817B	OEM
MV1817B1	OEM

DEVICE TYPE	REPL CODE
MV1866	OEM
MV1868	OEM
MV1870	OEM
MV1871	OEM
MV1872	OEM
MV1874	OEM
MV1876	OEM
MV1877	OEM
MV1878	OEM
MV2101	0549
MV2102	OEM
MV2103	0005
MV2104	0715
MV2105	0715
MV2106	OEM
MV2107	0623
MV2108	OEM
MV2109	0030
MV2110	OEM
MV2111	0030
MV2112	OEM
MV2113	OEM
MV2114	OEM
MV-2115	OEM
MV2115	OEM
MV2201	0549
MV2203	0005
MV2205	0030
MV2205(8)	0030
MV2207	OEM
MV-2209	0549
MV2209	0030
MV2209VVC	0030
MV2211	OEM
MV2213	OEM
MV2215	OEM
MV2301	OEM
MV2302	OEM
MV2303	OEM
MV2304	OEM
MV2305	OEM
MV2306	OEM
MV2307	OEM
MV2308	OEM
MV2401	OEM
MV2402	OEM
MV2403	OEM
MV3007	0549
MV3007E	0549
MV3010	0005
MV3010E	0005
MV3012	0715
MV3012E	0715
MV3015	0715
MV3015E	0715
MV3020	0623
MV3020E	0623
MV3027	0623
MV3027E	0623
MV3033	0030
MV3033E	0030
MV3039	0030
MV3039E	0030
MV3047	OEM
MV3047E	OEM
MV3056	OEM
MV3056E	OEM
MV3068	OEM
MV3082	OEM
MV3100	OEM
MV3102	OEM
MV3103	OEM
MV3140	OEM
MV3141	OEM
MV3142	OEM
MV5023	1605
MV5024	5027
MV5053	1348
MV5054-2	3153
MV5074B	2990
MV5153	3245
MV5174B	5023
MV5253	1767
MV5274B	0835
MV5353	3128
MV5374B	3095
MV5491	2181
MV5753	1951
MV5774B	3067
MV6113	0623
MV6114	OEM
MV6202	OEM
MV8066	OEM
MV8092A	OEM
MV8094	OEM
MV8096	OEM
MV8103B	OEM
MV8103C	OEM
MV8103D	OEM
MV8107B	OEM
MV8107C	OEM
MV8122	OEM
MV8122A	OEM
MV8124	OEM
MV8152	OEM
MV8152A	OEM
MV8153B	OEM
MV8153C	OEM
MV8153D	OEM
MV8154	OEM
MV8157B	OEM
MV8157C	OEM
MV8202	OEM
MV8203A	OEM
MV8203B	OEM
MV8203C	OEM
MV8203D	OEM
MV8207B	OEM
MV8207C	OEM
MV8253A	OEM
MV8253B	OEM
MV8253C	OEM
MV8253D	OEM
MV8303A	OEM
MV8303B	OEM
MV8303C	OEM
MV8303D	OEM
MV9051	0005
MV9052	0549
MV9053	0549
MV9054	0549
MV9111S	OEM
MV9112S	OEM
MV9151	0715
MV9152	0715
MV9153	0715
MV9154	0715
MV9251	0623
MV9252	0623
MV9253	0623
MV9254	0030
MV9351	0030
MV9352	0030
MV9353	0030
MV9354	0030
MV9600	0030
MV9601	0030
MV9602	0030
MV12097	OEM
MV12098	OEM
MV12099	OEM
MV12100	OEM
MV12101	OEM
MV12102	OEM
MV12103	OEM
MV12104	OEM
MV12105	OEM
MV12106	OEM
MV12107	OEM
MV12108	OEM
MV12109	OEM
MV53173	5351
MV54173	6469
MV57164	5062
MV57173	5349
MVA-05A	0015
MVA-05A(DIO)	0015
MVA-05A(RECT)	0015
MVAM1	OEM
MVAM109	OEM
MVB6113	0623
MVB6114	OEM
MVB6116	0623
MVB6117	OEM
MVB6118	OEM
MVB6124	0715
MVB6125	0715
MVB6126	0715
MVE6003	OEM
MVE6005	OEM
MVE6115	6640
MVE6117	OEM
MVE6118	OEM
MVS240	OEM
MVS460	5909
MVT210	4449
MWA110	4533
MWA110H	OEM
MWA120	4537
MWA120H	OEM
MWA130	OEM
MWA130H	OEM
MWA210	OEM
MWA210H	OEM
MWA220	4585
MWA220H	OEM
MWA230	OEM
MWA230H	OEM
MWA310	OEM
MWA310H	OEM
MWA320	OEM
MWA320H	OEM
MWA330	OEM
MWA330H	OEM
MWS5101AE3	OEM
MWS5101D	4524
MWS5101E	4524
MWS5101EL3	6054
MWS5105EL2	OEM
MX06092	OEM
MX-201	0136
MX-2269	2641
MX-2273	2015
MX-2279	OEM
MX-2986	OEM
MX-3013	0574
MX3057	2346
MX-3059	1899
MX3059	1899
MX-3108	0079
MX-3122	0224
MX-3123	0224
MX3138	OEM
MX3139	1635
MX-3198	1288
MX-3235	3763
MX-3240	4588
MX-3243	0514
MX-3256	1805
MX3256	1532
MX-3260	1532
MX-3267	0079
MX-3276	0320
MX3336	0780
MX-3364	1239
MX-3369	3751
MX-3370	4145
MX-3372	1805
MX-3379	4405
MX-3389	2246
MX-3393	2845
MX-3399	2238
MX-3452	1187
MX-3481	0320
MX-3540	4558
MX-3545	1532
MX-3587	1805
MX3587	1805
MX3619	2801
MX-3631	2801
MX-3632	3753
MX-3634	0215
MX3634	0215
MX-3733	0224
MX3733	0224
MX-3734	0320
MX-3735	0431
MX3735	0431
MX-3743	0079
MX-3808	0243
MX-3820	OEM
MX-3937	0079
MX-3944	0006
MX-3948	2512
MX-3976	1251
MX-3977	4647
MX-3978	0079
MX-3979	3028
MX3979	3028
MX-4158	1004
MX-4160	0079
MX-4234	OEM
MX-4264	OEM
MX-4294	OEM
MX-4295	0888
MX-4297	0798
MX-4313	1339
MX-4314	0153
MX-4339	2779
MX4340	3206
MX-4342	OEM
MX-4376	0024
MX-4404	3726
MX-4465	4216
MX-4476	2898
MX-4478	1319
MX-4479	4554
MX-4491	0079
MX-4492	0037
MX-4493	0320
MX-4504	0155
MX-4539	0224
MX-4540	0224
MX-4541	0079
MX-4542	3764
MX-4712	5080
MX-4821	1126
MX-4873	0155
MX-4875	4747
MX-4969	4843
MX-4972	0079
MX-4973	0037
MX-4974	0701
MX-5200	5101
MX5200	OEM
MX-5201	3564
MX5201	3564
MX-5202	2008
MX5202	2008
MX-5279	0485
MX-5280	0906
MX-5281	0328
MX-5352	2630
MX-5367	5935
MX-5368	0155
MX-5369	0006
MX-5370	0155
MX-5371	0155
MX-5372	0079
MX-5375	2599
MX-5389	3925
MX-5421	3299
MX-5429	3764
MX-5430	1251
MX-5435	OEM
MX-5436	2052
MX-5451	5096
MX-5452	OEM
MX5452	OEM
MX-5473	OEM
MX-5474	4336
MX-5475	2370
MX-5476	4750
MX5560	2105
MX-5594	1251
MX-5595	2572
MX-5596	0358
MX-5679	0765
MX5741	0967
MX-5925	2732
MX-5926	0826
MX-5927	OEM
MX-6092	2180
MX-6093	3640
MX-6159	1022
MX-6160	2031
MX6198	OEM
MX6199	OEM
MX6200	OEM
MX6201	OEM
MX6202	OEM
MX6203	OEM
MX6211	OEM
MX-6387	2180
MX-6406	2428
MX-6452	1420
MX-6536	3403
MX-6829	4047
MX-6973	OEM
MX-6974	OEM
MXC-1312	1601
MXC1312A	1601
MXF-5375	2599
MXR3866	OEM
MXR5160	OEM
MXR5583	OEM
MXR5943	OEM
MXT3904	5413
MXT3906	5308
MXTA14	OEM
MXTA27	OEM
MXTA42	4433
MXTA43	OEM
MXTA44	OEM
MXTA64	OEM
MXTA77	OEM
MXTA92	4435
MXTA93	4435
MY-1	0015
MZ-00	0133
MZ-08	0244
MZ090	0012
MZ3.9T5	0451
MZ3.9T10	0451
MZ3.9T20	0451
MZ4A	0140
MZ-4HV	OEM
MZ4.3T5	0528
MZ4.3T10	0528
MZ4.3T20	0528
MZ4.7T5	0446
MZ4.7T10	0446
MZ4.7T20	0446
MZ-5	0157
MZ5A	0157
MZ5.1T5	0162
MZ5.1T10	0162
MZ5.1T20	0162
MZ5.6T5	0157
MZ5.6T10	0157
MZ5.6T20	0157
MZ-6	0025
MZ6	0025
MZ-6HV	OEM
MZ6.2	0631
MZ6.2A	0466
MZ6.2B	0631
MZ6.2T5	0631
MZ6.2T10	0631
MZ6.2T20	0631
MZ6.8T5	0025
MZ6.8T10	0025
MZ6.8T20	0025
MZ-7	0025
MZ7.5T5	0644
MZ7.5T10	0644
MZ7.5T20	0644
MZ-8	0244
MZ8	0244
MZ-8HTE1	OEM
MZ-8HV	OEM
MZ8.2T5	0244
MZ8.2T10	0244
MZ8.2T20	0244
MZ8.6	0318
MZ-9	0012
MZ9	0222
MZ9.1B	0012
MZ9.1T5	0012
MZ9.1T10	0012
MZ9.1T20	0012
MZ-10	0170
MZ10	0170
MZ10A	0170
MZ-10HV	OEM
MZ10T5	0170
MZ10T20	0170
MZ-11	0137
MZ11	0313
MZ11B	OEM
MZ11T5	0313
MZ11T10	0313
MZ11T20	0313
MZ-12	0137
MZ12	0137
MZ12A	0137
MZ-12B	0137
MZ12B	0137
MZ12T5	0137
MZ12T10	0137
MZ12T20	0137
MZ13T5	0361
MZ13T10	0361
MZ13T20	0361
MZ14	0100
MZ15A	0002
MZ15T5	0002
MZ15T10	0002
MZ15T20	0002
MZ16T5	0416
MZ16T10	0416
MZ16T20	0416
MZ18T5	0490
MZ18T10	0490
MZ18T20	0490
MZ20T5	0526
MZ20T10	0526
MZ20T20	0526
MZ22T5	0560
MZ22T10	0560
MZ22T20	0560
MZ24T5	0398
MZ24T10	0398
MZ24T20	0398
MZ27	0436
MZ27A	0436
MZ27T5	0436
MZ27T10	0436
MZ27T20	0436
MZ30T5	0721
MZ30T10	0721
MZ30T20	0721
MZ33A	0039
MZ70-2.4	1266
MZ70-2.4A	1266
MZ70-2.4B	1266
MZ70-2.5	2847
MZ70-2.5A	2847
MZ70-2.5B	2847
MZ70-2.7	0755
MZ70-2.7A	0755
MZ70-2.7B	0755
MZ70-2.8	0672
MZ70-2.8A	0672
MZ70-2.8B	0672
MZ70-3.0	0118
MZ70-3.0A	0118
MZ70-3.0B	0118
MZ70-3.3	0296
MZ70-3.3A	0296
MZ70-3.3B	0296
MZ70-3.6	0372
MZ70-3.6A	0372
MZ70-3.6B	0372
MZ70-3.9	0036
MZ70-3.9A	0036
MZ70-3.9B	0036
MZ70-4.3	0274
MZ70-4.3A	0274
MZ70-4.3B	0274
MZ70-4.7	0140
MZ70-4.7A	0140
MZ70-5.1	0041
MZ70-5.1A	0041
MZ70-5.1B	0041
MZ70-5.6	0253
MZ70-5.6A	0253
MZ70-5.6B	0253
MZ70-6.0	0091
MZ70-6.0A	0091
MZ70-6.0B	0091
MZ70-6.2	0466
MZ70-6.2A	0466
MZ70-6.2B	0466
MZ70-6.8	0062
MZ70-6.8A	0062
MZ70-6.8B	0062
MZ70-7.5	0077
MZ70-7.5A	0077
MZ70-7.5B	0077
MZ70-8.2	0165
MZ70-8.2A	0165
MZ70-8.2B	0165
MZ70-8.7	0318
MZ70-8.7A	0318
MZ70-8.7B	0318
MZ70-9.1	0057
MZ70-9.1A	0057
MZ70-9.1B	0057
MZ70-10	0064
MZ70-10A	0064
MZ70-10B	0064
MZ70-11	0181
MZ70-11A	0181
MZ70-11B	0181
MZ70-12	0052
MZ70-12A	0052
MZ70-12B	0052
MZ70-13	0053
MZ70-13A	0053
MZ70-13B	0053
MZ70-14	0873
MZ70-14A	0873
MZ70-14B	0873
MZ70-15	0681
MZ70-15A	0681
MZ70-15B	0681
MZ70-16	0440
MZ70-16A	0440
MZ70-16B	0440
MZ70-17	0210
MZ70-17A	0210
MZ70-17B	0210
MZ70-18	0371
MZ70-18A	0371
MZ70-18B	0371
MZ70-19	0666
MZ70-19A	0666
MZ70-19B	0666
MZ70-20	0695
MZ70-20A	0695
MZ70-20B	0695
MZ70-22	0700
MZ70-22A	0700
MZ70-22B	0700
MZ70-24	0489
MZ70-24A	0489
MZ70-24B	0489
MZ70-25	0709
MZ70-25A	0709
MZ70-25B	0709
MZ70-27	OEM
MZ70-27A	0450
MZ70-27B	0450
MZ70-28	0257
MZ70-28A	0257
MZ70-28B	0257
MZ70-30	0195
MZ70-30A	0195
MZ70-30B	0195
MZ70-33	0166
MZ70-33A	0166
MZ70-33B	0166
MZ70-36	0010
MZ70-36A	0010
MZ70-36B	0010
MZ70-39	0032
MZ70-39A	0032
MZ70-39B	0032
MZ70-43	0054
MZ70-43A	0054
MZ70-43B	0054
MZ70-47	0068
MZ70-47A	0068
MZ70-47B	0068
MZ70-51	0092
MZ70-51A	0092
MZ70-51B	0092
MZ70-56	0125
MZ70-56A	0125
MZ70-56B	0125
MZ70-60	2301
MZ70-60A	2301
MZ70-60B	2301
MZ70-62	0152
MZ70-62A	OEM
MZ70-62B	0152
MZ70-68	0173
MZ70-68A	0173
MZ70-68B	0173
MZ70-75	0094
MZ70-75A	0094
MZ70-75B	0094
MZ70-82	0049
MZ70-82A	0049
MZ70-82B	0049
MZ70-87	0104
MZ70-87A	0104
MZ70-87B	0104
MZ70-91	0156
MZ70-91A	0156
MZ70-91B	0156
MZ70-100	0189
MZ70-100A	0189
MZ70-100B	0189
MZ70-110	0099
MZ70-110A	0099
MZ70-110B	0099
MZ70-120	0089
MZ70-120A	0089
MZ70-120B	0089
MZ70-130	0285
MZ70-130A	0285
MZ70-130B	0285
MZ70-140	0252
MZ70-140A	0252
MZ70-140B	0252
MZ70-150	0336
MZ70-150A	0336
MZ70-150B	0336
MZ70-160	0366
MZ70-160A	0366
MZ70-160B	0366
MZ70-170	0390
MZ70-170A	OEM
MZ70-170B	0390
MZ70-180	0420
MZ70-180A	0420
MZ70-180B	0420
MZ70-190	0448
MZ70-190A	0448
MZ70-190B	0448
MZ70-200	1464
MZ70-200A	1464
MZ70-200B	1464
MZ70MA	0298
MZ82A	0327
MZ92-2.4	1266
MZ92-2.4A	1266
MZ92-2.4B	1266
MZ92-2.5	2847
MZ92-2.5A	2847
MZ92-2.5B	2847
MZ92-2.7	0755
MZ92-2.7A	0755
MZ92-2.7B	0755
MZ92-2.8	0672
MZ92-2.8A	0672
MZ92-2.8B	0672
MZ92-3.0	0118
MZ92-3.0A	0118
MZ92-3.0B	0118
MZ92-3.3	0296
MZ92-3.3A	0296
MZ92-3.3B	0296
MZ92-3.6	0372
MZ92-3.6A	0372
MZ92-3.6B	0372
MZ92-3.9	0036
MZ92-3.9A	0188
MZ92-3.9B	0036
MZ92-4.3	0274
MZ92-4.3A	0274
MZ92-4.3B	0274
MZ92-4.7	0140
MZ92-4.7A	0446
MZ92-4.7B	0140
MZ92-5.1	0041
MZ92-5.1A	0162
MZ92-5.1B	0041
MZ92-5.6	0253
MZ92-5.6A	0157
MZ92-6,0B	0631
MZ92-6.0	0091
MZ92-6.0A	0091
MZ92-6.0B	0298
MZ92-6.2	0466
MZ92-6.2A	0466
MZ92-6.2B	0466
MZ92-6.8	0062
MZ92-6.8A	0062
MZ92-6.8B	0062
MZ92-7.5	0077
MZ92-7.5A	0077
MZ92-7.5B	0077
MZ92-8.2	0165
MZ92-8.2A	0165
MZ92-8.2B	0244
MZ92-8.7	0318
MZ92-8.7A	0318
MZ92-8.7B	0318
MZ92-9.1	0057
MZ92-9.1A	0057
MZ-92-9.1B	0012
MZ92-9.1B	0057
MZ92-10	0064
MZ92-10A	0170
MZ92-10B	0064
MZ92-11	0181
MZ92-11A	0181
MZ92-11B	0181
MZ92-12	0052
MZ92-12A	0052
MZ92-12B	0137
MZ92-13	0053
MZ92-13A	0053
MZ92-13B	0053
MZ92-14	0873
MZ92-14A	0873
MZ92-14B	0873
MZ92-15	0681
MZ92-15A	0681
MZ92-15B	0681
MZ92-16	0440
MZ92-16A	0440
MZ92-16B	0416
MZ92-17	0210
MZ92-17A	0210
MZ92-17B	0210
MZ92-18	0371
MZ92-18A	0371
MZ92-18B	0371
MZ92-19	0666
MZ92-19A	0666
MZ92-19B	0666
MZ92-20	0695
MZ92-20A	0695
MZ92-20B	0695
MZ92-22	0700
MZ92-22A	0700
MZ92-22B	0700
MZ92-24	0489
MZ92-24A	0489

If replacement code is OEM, contact original manufacturer for replacement. 499

DEVICE TYPE	REPL CODE
MZ92-24B	0560
MZ92-25	0440
MZ92-25A	0440
MZ92-25B	0440
MZ92-27	0450
MZ92-27A	0436
MZ92-27B	0450
MZ92-28	0257
MZ92-28A	0257
MZ92-28B	0257
MZ92-30	0195
MZ92-30A	0195
MZ92-30B	0195
MZ92-33	0166
MZ92-33A	0166
MZ92-33B	0166
MZ92-36	0010
MZ92-36A	0010
MZ92-36B	0814
MZ92-39	0032
MZ92-39A	0032
MZ92-39B	0032
MZ92-43	0054
MZ92-43A	0054
MZ92-43B	0054
MZ92-47	0068
MZ92-47A	0068
MZ92-47B	0068
MZ92-51	0092
MZ92-51A	0092
MZ92-51B	0092
MZ92-56	0125
MZ92-56A	0125
MZ92-56B	0125
MZ92-60	2301
MZ92-60A	2301
MZ92-60B	2301
MZ92-62	0152
MZ92-62A	0152
MZ92-62B	0152
MZ92-68	0173
MZ92-68A	0173
MZ92-68B	0173
MZ92-75	0094
MZ92-75A	0094
MZ92-75B	0094
MZ92-82	0049
MZ92-82A	0049
MZ92-82B	0049
MZ92-87	0104
MZ92-87A	0104
MZ92-87B	0104
MZ92-91	0156
MZ92-91A	0156
MZ92-91B	0156
MZ92-100	0189
MZ92-100A	0189
MZ92-100B	OEM
MZ92-110	0099
MZ92-110A	0099
MZ92-110B	0099
MZ92-120	0089
MZ92-120A	0089
MZ92-120B	0089
MZ92-130	0285
MZ92-130A	0285
MZ92-140	0252
MZ92-140A	0252
MZ92-140B	0252
MZ92-150	0336
MZ92-150A	0336
MZ92-150B	0336
MZ92-160	0366
MZ92-160A	0366
MZ92-160B	0366
MZ92-170	0390
MZ92-170A	0390
MZ92-170B	0390
MZ92-180	0420
MZ92-180A	0420
MZ92-180B	0420
MZ92-190	0448
MZ92-190A	OEM
MZ92-190B	0448
MZ92-200	1464
MZ92-200A	1464
MZ92-200B	1464
MZ110	1172
MZ111	1182
MZ112	1198
MZ113	1209
MZ114	1870
MZ115	0642
MZ116	1246
MZ117	2091
MZ118	1269
MZ120	0600
MZ130	OEM
MZ203	0118
MZ204	0036
MZ-204B	0036
MZ204B	0451
MZ204S	0451
MZ205	0041
MZ-206	0157
MZ206	0091
MZ207	0062
MZ207-02A	0025
MZ207A	0025
MZ207B	0025
MZ207C	0025
MZ208	0165
MZ-209	0012
MZ209	0057
MZ209A	0012
MZ209B	0012
MZ209C	0012
MZ210	0064
MZ-210B	0170
MZ-212	0137
MZ212	0052
MZ214	0873
MZ215	OEM
MZ216	0440
MZ218	0371
MZ220	0695
MZ222	0700
MZ224	0489
MZ224A	0489
MZ250	0057
MZ303	0118
MZ303A	0118
MZ303B	0118
MZ303C	0296
MZ304	0036
MZ304A	0372
MZ304B	0036
MZ304C	0372
MZ305	0041
MZ305A	0582
MZ-305B	0041
MZ305B	0041
MZ305C	0041
MZ306	0091
MZ306-A1	0091
MZ306-A2	0091
MZ306-B2	0091
MZ306A	0091
MZ306B	0091
MZ306B2	OEM
MZ306C	0298
MZ306C3	0091
MZ307	0062
MZ307-A1	0062
MZ307A	0062
MZ307A1	0062
MZ307B	0062
MZ307C	0062
MZ308	0165
MZ308-B2	OEM
MZ308A	0165
MZ308B	0165
MZ308C	0165
MZ309	0057
MZ309-B2	OEM
MZ309A	0057
MZ309B	0012
MZ309B2	0057
MZ309C	0057
MZ310	0064
MZ310-B	0064
MZ310A	0064
MZ310B	0064
MZ310C	0064
MZ310C1	0064
MZ311	1182
MZ312	0052
MZ312A	0052
MZ312B	0052
MZ312C	0052
MZ313	1209
MZ314	0873
MZ314A	0873
MZ314B	0873
MZ314C	0873
MZ315	0642
MZ316	0440
MZ316A	0440
MZ316B	0440
MZ316C	0440
MZ317	2091
MZ318	0371
MZ318A	0371
MZ318B	0371
MZ319	2210
MZ320	0695
MZ320A	0695
MZ320B	0695
MZ322	0700
MZ322A	0700
MZ322B	0700
MZ324	0489
MZ-324A	0489
MZ324A	0489
MZ324B	0489
MZ327	0450
MZ330	0195
MZ-330-23-B	0721
MZ330-23-B	0195
MZ330A	0195
MZ330B	0195
MZ333	0166
MZ333A	0166
MZ333B	0166
MZ336	0010
MZ339	0032
MZ343	0054
MZ406	0298
MZ407	0025
MZ408	0244
MZ408-02C	0165
MZ408A	0244
MZ408B	0244
MZ408C	0244
MZ409	0012
MZ409-02B	0012
MZ409A	0012
MZ409B	0012
MZ409C	0012
MZ410	0170
MZ410A	0170
MZ410B	0170
MZ410C	0170
MZ412	0137
MZ412A	0137
MZ412B	0137
MZ412C	0137
MZ414	0100
MZ414-B	0100
MZ414-B3	0100
MZ414A	0100
MZ414B	0100
MZ414C	0002
MZ416	0416
MZ416A	0416
MZ416B	0416
MZ416C	0416
MZ418	0490
MZ418A	0490
MZ418B	0490
MZ420	0526
MZ420A	0526
MZ420B	0526
MZ422	0560
MZ422A	0560
MZ422B	0560
MZ424	0398
MZ424A	0398
MZ424B	0398
MZ500(5.1V)	OEM
MZ500(10V)	OEM
MZ500-1	1266
MZ500-2	0755
MZ500-3	0118
MZ500-4	0296
MZ500-5	0188
MZ500-6	0036
MZ500-7	0274
MZ500-8	0140
MZ500-9	0041
MZ500-10	0253
MZ500-11	0466
MZ500-12	0062
MZ500-13	0077
MZ500-14	0165
MZ500-15	0057
MZ500-16	0064
MZ500-17	0181
MZ500-18	0052
MZ500-19	0053
MZ500-20	0681
MZ500-21	0440
MZ500-22	0371
MZ500-23	0695
MZ500-24	0700
MZ500-25	0489
MZ500-26	0450
MZ500-27	0195
MZ500-28	0166
MZ500-29	0010
MZ500-30	0032
MZ500-31	0054
MZ500-32	0068
MZ500-33	0092
MZ500-34	0125
MZ500-35	0152
MZ500-36	0173
MZ500-37	0094
MZ500-38	0049
MZ500-39	0156
MZ500-40	0189
MZ500.5	0188
MZ500.9	0162
MZ500.10	0157
MZ500.15	0012
MZ500.16	0170
MZ500.18	0137
MZ500.20	0526
MZ500.26	0436
MZ605	0466
MZ610	0466
MZ620	0466
MZ640	0466
MZ706	0205
MZ707	0475
MZ708	0499
MZ709	0679
MZ710	0225
MZ711	0230
MZ712	0234
MZ713	0237
MZ714	1387
MZ715	0247
MZ716	0251
MZ718	0256
MZ720	0262
MZ722	0269
MZ724	0273
MZ727	0291
MZ730	0305
MZ733	0314
MZ736	0316
MZ739	0322
MZ743	0333
MZ747	0343
MZ751	0027
MZ756	0266
MZ760	2829
MZ762	0382
MZ768	0401
MZ775	0421
MZ782	0439
MZ791	0238
MZ829	0466
MZ829A	0466
MZ920-130B	OEM
MZ939	0057
MZ939A	0057
MZ939B	0057
MZ943	0313
MZ945	0181
MZ945A	0181
MZ945B	0181
MZ946	0064
MZ946A	0173
MZ946B	0181
MZ1000-1	0289
MZ1000-2	0188
MZ1000-3	0451
MZ1000-4	0528
MZ1000-5	0446
MZ1000-6	0162
MZ1000-7	0157
MZ1000-8	0631
MZ1000-9	0025
MZ1000-10	0644
MZ1000-11	0244
MZ1000-12	0012
MZ1000-13	0170
MZ1000-14	0313
MZ-1000-15	0137
MZ1000-15	0137
MZ1000-16	0361
MZ1000-17	0002
MZ1000-18	0416
MZ1000-19	0490
MZ1000-20	0526
MZ1000-21	0560
MZ1000-22	0398
MZ1000-23	0436
MZ1000-24	0721
MZ1000-25	0039
MZ1000-26	0316
MZ1000-27	0346
MZ1000-28	0925
MZ1000-29	0993
MZ1000-30	0497
MZ1000-31	0863
MZ1000-32	0778
MZ1000-33	2144
MZ1000-34	1181
MZ1000-35	2997
MZ1000-36	1301
MZ1000-37	0098
MZ1002	OEM
MZ1003	0118
MZ1004	0036
MZ1005	0162
MZ1006	0298
MZ1007	0062
MZ1008	0165
MZ1009	0057
MZ1010	0064
MZ1012	0052
MZ1014	0873
MZ1016	0440
MZ1018	0371
MZ1020	0695
MZ1022	0700
MZ2360	0133
MZ2361	0133
MZ2362	1266
MZ3154	0165
MZ3154A	0165
MZ3155	0165
MZ3155A	0165
MZ3156	0165
MZ3156A	0165
MZ3157	0165
MZ3157A	0165
MZ4617	1266
MZ4618	2847
MZ4619	0118
MZ4620	0188
MZ4621	0372
MZ4622	0188
MZ4623	0274
MZ4624	0162
MZ4625	0162
MZ4626	0157
MZ4627	0631
MZ4682	0755
MZ5110	1172
MZ5111	1182
MZ5112	1198
MZ5113	1209
MZ5114	1870
MZ5115	0642
MZ5116	1246
MZ5117	2091
MZ5119	2210
MZ5120	0600
MZ5706	0205
MZ5707	0475
MZ5708	0499
MZ5709	0679
MZ5710	0225
MZ5712	0234
MZ5713	0237
MZ5714	1387
MZ5715	0247
MZ5716	0251
MZ5718	0256
MZ5720	0262
MZ5722	0269
MZ5724	0273
MZ5727	0291
MZ5730	0305
MZ5733	0314
MZ5736	0316
MZ5760	2829
MZ5766	OEM
MZ5775	0421
MZ5915	0247
MZ5918	0256
MZ5922	0269
MZ5927	0291
MZ5933	0314
MZ5956	0266
MZ7002.4B	OEM
MZ10510	OEM
MZC25B10	1596
MZC28B10	1664
MZC87B10	2997
MZG746	OEM
MZG746A	OEM
MZG747	OEM
MZG747A	OEM
MZG748	OEM
MZG748A	OEM
MZG749	OEM
MZG749A	OEM
MZG750	OEM
MZG750A	OEM
MZG751	OEM
MZG751A	OEM
MZG752	OEM
MZG752A	OEM
MZG753	OEM
MZG753A	OEM
MZG754	OEM
MZG754A	OEM
MZG755	OEM
MZG755A	OEM
MZG756	OEM
MZG756A	OEM
MZG757	OEM
MZG757A	OEM
MZG758	OEM
MZG758A	OEM
MZG759	OEM
MZG759A	OEM
MZG957	OEM
MZG957A	OEM
MZG957B	OEM
MZG958	OEM
MZG958A	OEM
MZG958B	OEM
MZG959	OEM
MZG959A	OEM
MZG959B	OEM
MZG960	OEM
MZG960A	OEM
MZG960B	OEM
MZG961	OEM
MZG961A	OEM
MZG961B	OEM
MZG962	OEM
MZG962A	OEM
MZG962B	OEM
MZG963	OEM
MZG963A	OEM
MZG963B	OEM
MZG964	OEM
MZG964A	OEM
MZG964B	OEM
MZG965	OEM
MZG965A	OEM
MZG965B	OEM
MZG966	OEM
MZG966A	OEM
MZG966B	OEM
MZG967	OEM
MZG967A	OEM
MZG967B	OEM
MZG968	OEM
MZG968A	OEM
MZG968B	OEM
MZG969	OEM
MZG969A	OEM
MZG969B	OEM
MZG970	OEM
MZG970A	OEM
MZG970B	OEM
MZG971	OEM
MZG971A	OEM
MZG971B	OEM
MZG972	OEM
MZG972A	OEM
MZG972B	OEM
MZG973	OEM
MZG973A	OEM
MZG973B	OEM
MZG974	OEM
MZG974A	OEM
MZG974B	OEM
MZG975	OEM
MZG975A	OEM
MZG975B	OEM
MZG976	OEM
MZG976A	OEM
MZG976B	OEM
MZG977	OEM
MZG977A	OEM
MZG977B	OEM
MZG978	OEM
MZG978A	OEM
MZG978B	OEM
MZG979	OEM
MZG979A	OEM
MZG979B	OEM
MZG980	OEM
MZG980A	OEM
MZG980B	OEM
MZG981	OEM
MZG981A	OEM
MZG981B	OEM
MZG982	OEM
MZG982A	OEM
MZG982B	OEM
MZG983	OEM
MZG983A	OEM
MZG983B	OEM
MZG984	OEM
MZG984A	OEM
MZG984B	OEM
MZG4370	OEM
MZG4370A	OEM
MZG4371	OEM
MZG4371A	OEM
MZG4372	OEM
MZG4372A	OEM
MZL1.8B10	OEM
MZL2.0B10	OEM
MZL2.2B10	OEM
MZL2.4A10	1266
MZL2.4B10	1266
MZL2.5A10	2847
MZL2.7A10	0755
MZL2.7B10	0755
MZL2.8A10	0672
MZL3.0A10	0118
MZL3.0B10	0118
MZL3.3A10	0296
MZL3.3B10	0296
MZL3.6A10	0372
MZL3.6B10	0372
MZL3.9A10	0036
MZL3.9B10	0036
MZL4.3A10	0274
MZL4.3B10	0274
MZL4.7A10	0140
MZL4.7B10	0140
MZL5.1A10	0041
MZL5.1B10	0041
MZL5.6A10	0253
MZL5.6B10	0253
MZL6.0A10	0091
MZL6.2A10	0466
MZL6.2B10	0466
MZL6.8A10	0062
MZL6.8B10	0062
MZL7.5A10	0077
MZL7.5B10	0077
MZL8.2A10	0165
MZL8.2B10	0165
MZL8.7A10	0318
MZL8.7B10	0318
MZL9.1A10	0057
MZL9.1B10	0057
MZL10A10	0064
MZL10B10	0064
MZL11A10	0181
MZL11B10	0181
MZL12A10	0052
MZL12B10	0052
MZL13A10	0053
MZL13B10	0053
MZL14A10	0873
MZL14B10	0873
MZL15A10	0681
MZL15B10	0681
MZL16A10	0440
MZL16B10	0440
MZL17A10	0210
MZL17B10	0210
MZL18A10	0371
MZL18B10	0371
MZL19A10	0666
MZL19B10	0666
MZL20A10	0695
MZL20B10	0695
MZL22A10	0700
MZL22B10	0700
MZL24A10	0489
MZL24B10	0489
MZL25A10	0709
MZL25B10	0709
MZL27A10	0450
MZL27B10	0450
MZL28A10	0257
MZL28B10	0257
MZL30A10	0195
MZL30B10	0195
MZL33A10	0166
MZL33B10	0166
MZL36A10	0010
MZL36B10	0010
MZL39A10	0032
MZL39B10	0032
MZL43A10	0054
MZL43B10	0054
MZL47A10	0068
MZL47B10	0068
MZL51A10	0092
MZL51B10	0092
MZL56A10	0125
MZL56B10	0125
MZL60A10	2301
MZL60B10	2301
MZL62A10	0152
MZL62B10	0152
MZL68A10	0173
MZL68B10	0173
MZL75A10	0094
MZL75B10	0094
MZL82A10	0049
MZL82B10	0049
MZL87A10	0104
MZL87B10	0104
MZL91A10	0156
MZL91B10	0156
MZL100A10	0189
MZL100B10	0189
MZL110A10	0099
MZL110B10	0099
MZL120A10	0089
MZL120B10	0089
MZL130A10	0285
MZL130B10	0285
MZL140A10	0252
MZL140B10	0252
MZL150A10	0336
MZL150B10	0336
MZL160A10	0366
MZL160B10	0366
MZL170A10	0390
MZL170B10	0390
MZL180A10	0420
MZL180B10	0420
MZL190A10	0448
MZL190B10	0448
MZL200A10	1464
MZL200B10	1464
MZL306	0091
MZL307	0062
MZL308	0165
MZL309	0057
MZL310	0064
MZL312	0052
MZL314	0873
MZL316	0681
MZL318	0371
MZL320	0695
MZL322	0700
MZL324	0489
MZL327	0450
MZL330	0195
MZL333	0166
MZL336	0010
MZL339	0032
MZL343	0054
MZ-00	0124
MZS1282L	OEM
MZT33-01	3417
MZT39B	OEM
MZT39C	OEM
MZU1.8B10	OEM
MZU2.0B10	OEM
MZU2.2B10	OEM
MZU2.4A10	1266
MZU2.4B10	1266
MZU2.5A10	2847
MZU2.7A10	0755
MZU2.7B10	0755
MZU2.8A10	0672
MZU3.0A10	0118
MZU3.0B10	0118
MZU3.3A10	0296
MZU3.3B10	0296
MZU3.6A10	0372
MZU3.6B10	0372
MZU3.9A10	0036
MZU3.9B10	0036
MZU4.3A10	0274
MZU4.3B10	0274
MZU4.7A10	0140
MZU4.7B10	0140
MZU5.1A10	0041
MZU5.1B10	0041
MZU5.6A10	0253
MZU5.6B10	0253
MZU6.0A10	0091

If replacement code is OEM, contact original manufacturer for replacement.

DEVICE TYPE	REPL CODE
MZU6.2A10	0466
MZU6.2B10	0466
MZU6.8A10	0062
MZU6.8B10	0062
MZU7.5A10	0077
MZU7.5B10	0077
MZU8.2A10	0165
MZU8.2B10	0165
MZU8.7A10	0318
MZU8.7B10	0318
MZU9.1A10	0057
MZU9.1B10	0057
MZU10A10	0064
MZU10B10	0064
MZU11A10	0181
MZU11B10	0181
MZU12A10	0052
MZU12B10	0052
MZU13A10	0053
MZU13B10	0053
MZU14A10	0873
MZU14B10	0873
MZU15A10	0681
MZU15B10	0681
MZU16A10	0440
MZU16B10	0440
MZU17A10	0210
MZU17B10	0210
MZU18A10	0371
MZU18B10	0371
MZU19A10	0666
MZU19B10	0666
MZU20A10	0695
MZU20B10	0695
MZU22A10	0700
MZU22B10	0700
MZU24A10	0489
MZU24B10	0489
MZU25A10	0709
MZU25B10	0709
MZU27A10	0450
MZU27B10	0450
MZU28A10	0257
MZU28B10	0257
MZU30B10	0195
MZU33A10	0166
MZU33B10	0166
MZU36A10	0010
MZU36B10	0010
MZU39A10	0032
MZU39B10	0032
MZU43A10	0054
MZU43B10	0054
MZU47A10	0068
MZU47B10	0068
MZU51A10	0092
MZU51B10	0092
MZU56A10	0125
MZU56B10	0125
MZU60A10	2301
MZU60B10	2301
MZU62A10	0152
MZU62B10	0152
MZU68A10	0173
MZU68B10	0173
MZU75A10	0094
MZU75B10	0094
MZU82A10	0318
MZU82B10	0049
MZU87A10	0104
MZU87B10	0104
MZU91A10	0156
MZU91B10	0156
MZU100A10	0189
MZU100B10	0189
MZU110A10	0099
MZU110B10	0099
MZU120A10	0089
MZU120B10	0089
MZU130A10	0285
MZU130B10	0285
MZU140A10	0252
MZU140B10	0252
MZU150A10	0336
MZU150B10	0336
MZU160A10	0366
MZU160B10	0366
MZU170A10	0390
MZU170B10	0390
MZU180A10	0420
MZU180B10	0420
MZU190A10	0448
MZU190B10	0448
MZU200A10	1464
MZU200B10	1464
MZX9.1	0012
MZZ3.6-20	OEM
Ma408	OEM
Mc1496F	OEM
Mc10561L	OEM
Mc10562L	OEM
Mc10578F	OEM
Mc10597F	OEM
Mk3870/42P-15	OEM
Mk3873/12N-10	OEM
N	OEM
N-020	0050
N020	0136
N1S7261A	OEM
N1X	0086
N2A	0143
N2A(DIODE)	0143
N2A(TRIPLER)	2957
N2A-1	2524
N2A-2	2524
N2XA	0233
N5	OEM
N5C2U	OEM
N7N	OEM
N8H80A	0677
N8H80J	0677
N8T13	OEM
N8T14	OEM
N8T22A	2252
N8T22N	1131
N8T23	OEM
N8T24	OEM
N8T26	4022
N8T26A	4022
N8T26AB	OEM
N8T26AF	4437
N8T26AN	4437
N8T28F	0576
N8T28N	0576
N8T95B	4565
N8T95F	4566
N8T95N	4566
N8T96B	4565
N8T96F	4570
N8T96N	4570
N8T97	4577
N8T97B	4574
N8T97F	4577
N8T97N	4577
N8T98F	4586
N8T98N	4586
N9HHB	0143
N9NDO	0182
N9NUS	0133
N9T22F	OEM
N10	OEM
N10R	OEM
N13T	0312
N13T1	0312
N13T2	0312
N19C	OEM
N19E	OEM
N19G	OEM
N19J	OEM
N20	OEM
N20C	OEM
N20E	OEM
N20G	OEM
N20J	OEM
N24	OEM
N25	OEM
N35A	OEM
N-41	0015
N48	0143
N57B2-3	0004
N57B2-6	0004
N57B2-7	0004
N57B2-8	0208
N57B2-11	0050
N57B2-13	0050
N57B2-14	0050
N57B2-15	0004
N57B2-17	0136
N57B2-18	0136
N57B2-19	0136
N57B2-22	0050
N57B2-23	0136
N57B2-25	0004
N57B4-2	0160
N57B4-4	0160
N60R006B	OEM
N60R006B16	OEM
N74H00A	0677
N74H00F	0677
N74H00N	0677
N74H01A	5241
N74H01F	5241
N74H01N	5241
N74H04A	1896
N74H04F	1896
N74H04N	1896
N74H05A	3221
N74H05F	3221
N74H05N	3221
N74H08A	5258
N74H08F	5258
N74H08N	5258
N74H10A	0680
N74H10F	0680
N74H10N	0680
N74H11A	2382
N74H11F	2382
N74H11N	2382
N74H20A	3670
N74H20F	3670
N74H20N	3670
N74H21A	4772
N74H21F	4772
N74H21N	4772
N74H22A	4516
N74H22F	4516
N74H22N	4516
N74H30A	5284
N74H30F	5284
N74H30N	5284
N74H30W	5284
N74H40A	0554
N74H40F	0554
N74H40N	0554
N74H50A	1781
N74H50F	1781
N74H50N	1781
N74H51A	1933
N74H51F	1933
N74H51N	1933
N74H52A	2009
N74H52F	2009
N74H52N	2009
N74H53A	2090
N74H53F	2090
N74H53N	2090
N74H54A	2158
N74H54F	2158
N74H54N	2158
N74H55A	3129
N74H55F	3129
N74H55N	3129
N74H60A	5312
N74H60F	5312
N74H60N	5312
N74H61A	2638
N74H61F	2638
N74H61N	2638
N74H62A	2705
N74H62F	2705
N74H62N	2705
N74H71A	3233
N74H71F	3233
N74H71N	3233
N74H72A	3281
N74H72F	3281
N74H72N	3281
N74H73A	2444
N74H73F	2444
N74H73N	2444
N74H74A	2472
N74H74F	2472
N74H74N	2472
N74H76B	5208
N74H76F	5208
N74H76N	5208
N74H101A	5424
N74H101F	5424
N74H101N	5424
N74H102A	5426
N74H102F	5426
N74H102N	5426
N74H103A	2941
N74H103F	2941
N74H103N	2941
N74H106B	5159
N74H106F	5159
N74H106N	5159
N74H108A	0180
N74H108F	0180
N74H108N	0180
N74LS00	1519
N74LS00F	1519
N74LS00N	1519
N74LS01F	1537
N74LS01N	1537
N74LS02F	1550
N74LS02N	1550
N74LS03F	1569
N74LS03N	1569
N74LS04F	1585
N74LS04N	1585
N74LS05F	1598
N74LS05N	1598
N74LS08F	1623
N74LS08N	1623
N74LS09F	1632
N74LS09N	1632
N74LS10F	1652
N74LS10N	1652
N74LS11F	1657
N74LS11N	1657
N74LS12F	1669
N74LS12N	1669
N74LS13F	1678
N74LS13N	1678
N74LS14F	1688
N74LS14N	1688
N74LS15F	1697
N74LS15N	1697
N74LS20F	0035
N74LS20N	0035
N74LS21F	1752
N74LS21N	1752
N74LS22F	1764
N74LS22N	1764
N74LS26F	1372
N74LS26N	1372
N74LS27F	0183
N74LS27N	0183
N74LS28F	0467
N74LS28N	0467
N74LS30F	0822
N74LS30N	0822
N74LS32F	0088
N74LS32N	0088
N74LS33F	1821
N74LS33N	1821
N74LS37F	1719
N74LS37N	1719
N74LS38F	1828
N74LS38N	1828
N74LS40F	0135
N74LS40N	0135
N74LS42F	1830
N74LS42N	1830
N74LS51F	1027
N74LS51N	1027
N74LS54F	1846
N74LS54N	1846
N74LS55F	0452
N74LS55N	0452
N74LS73F	1856
N74LS73N	1856
N74LS74AF	0243
N74LS74AN	0243
N74LS74F	0243
N74LS74N	0243
N74LS75F	1859
N74LS75N	1859
N74LS76F	2166
N74LS76N	2166
N74LS78F	1862
N74LS78N	1862
N74LS83AF	2204
N74LS83AN	2204
N74LS83F	2204
N74LS85F	0426
N74LS85N	0426
N74LS86F	0288
N74LS86N	0288
N74LS89F	OEM
N74LS89N	OEM
N74LS90F	1871
N74LS90N	1871
N74LS92F	1876
N74LS92N	1876
N74LS93F	1877
N74LS93N	1877
N74LS95BF	0766
N74LS95BN	0766
N74LS96F	OEM
N74LS96N	OEM
N74LS107F	1592
N74LS107N	1592
N74LS109AF	1895
N74LS109AN	1895
N74LS109F	1895
N74LS109N	1895
N74LS112F	2115
N74LS112N	2115
N74LS113F	2241
N74LS113N	2241
N74LS114F	2286
N74LS114N	2286
N74LS123AF	0973
N74LS123AN	0973
N74LS125F	0075
N74LS125N	0075
N74LS126F	2850
N74LS126N	2850
N74LS132F	1615
N74LS132N	1615
N74LS136F	1618
N74LS136N	1618
N74LS138F	0422
N74LS138N	0422
N74LS139F	0153
N74LS139N	0153
N74LS145F	1554
N74LS145N	1554
N74LS151F	1636
N74LS151N	1636
N74LS153F	0953
N74LS153N	0953
N74LS154F	4956
N74LS154N	4956
N74LS155F	0209
N74LS155N	0209
N74LS156F	1644
N74LS156N	1644
N74LS157D	OEM
N74LS157F	1153
N74LS157N	1153
N74LS158F	1646
N74LS158N	1646
N74LS160AF	0831
N74LS160AN	0831
N74LS161AF	0852
N74LS161AN	0852
N74LS162AF	0874
N74LS162AN	0874
N74LS163AF	0887
N74LS163AN	0887
N74LS164F	4274
N74LS164N	4274
N74LS168AF	0961
N74LS168AN	0961
N74LS169AF	0980
N74LS169AN	0980
N74LS170B	2605
N74LS170F	2605
N74LS170N	2605
N74LS173D	OEM
N74LS173N	6681
N74LS174B	0260
N74LS174F	0260
N74LS174N	0260
N74LS175B	1662
N74LS175F	1662
N74LS175N	1662
N74LS181F	1668
N74LS181N	1668
N74LS190F	1676
N74LS190N	1676
N74LS191F	1677
N74LS191N	1677
N74LS192F	1679
N74LS192N	1679
N74LS193F	1682
N74LS193N	1682
N74LS194AF	1294
N74LS194AN	1294
N74LS195AF	1305
N74LS195AN	1305
N74LS196F	2807
N74LS196N	2807
N74LS197F	2450
N74LS197N	2450
N74LS221F	1230
N74LS221N	1230
N74LS240F	0447
N74LS240N	0447
N74LS241F	1715
N74LS241N	1715
N74LS242F	1717
N74LS242N	1717
N74LS243F	0900
N74LS243N	0900
N74LS244F	0453
N74LS244N	0453
N74LS245F	0458
N74LS245N	0458
N74LS251AF	1726
N74LS251AN	1726
N74LS253F	1728
N74LS253N	1728
N74LS256F	OEM
N74LS256N	OEM
N74LS257AF	1733
N74LS257AN	1733
N74LS258AF	1735
N74LS258AN	1735
N74LS259F	3175
N74LS259N	3175
N74LS260F	5859
N74LS260N	5859
N74LS261F	OEM
N74LS261N	OEM
N74LS266F	0587
N74LS266N	0587
N74LS273F	0888
N74LS273N	0888
N74LS279F	3259
N74LS279N	3259
N74LS283F	1768
N74LS283N	1768
N74LS289N	OEM
N74LS290F	4352
N74LS290N	4352
N74LS293F	0082
N74LS293N	0082
N74LS295BF	2212
N74LS295BN	2212
N74LS298F	3337
N74LS298N	3337
N74LS299F	4353
N74LS299N	4353
N74LS301F	OEM
N74LS301N	OEM
N74LS323F	OEM
N74LS323N	OEM
N74LS352N	0756
N74LS353N	0768
N74LS363F	5869
N74LS363N	5869
N74LS364F	5870
N74LS364N	5870
N74LS365AD	OEM
N74LS365AF	0937
N74LS365AN	0937
N74LS366AN	6942
N74LS367AD	OEM
N74LS367AF	0971
N74LS367AN	0971
N74LS368AD	OEM
N74LS368AF	0985
N74LS368AN	0985
N74LS373F	0704
N74LS373N	0704
N74LS374F	0708
N74LS374N	0708
N74LS375F	OEM
N74LS375N	OEM
N74LS377F	1112
N74LS377N	1112
N74LS378F	1125
N74LS378N	1125
N74LS379F	1143
N74LS379N	1143
N74LS386F	1221
N74LS386N	1221
N74LS390F	1278
N74LS390N	1278
N74LS393F	0813
N74LS393N	0813
N74LS395AF	1320
N74LS395AN	1320
N74LS398F	1373
N74LS398N	1373
N74LS399F	1388
N74LS399N	1388
N74LS445F	OEM
N74LS445N	OEM
N74LS490F	2199
N74LS490N	2199
N74LS568F	OEM
N74LS568N	OEM
N74LS569F	OEM
N74LS569N	OEM
N74LS640-1F	0664
N74LS640-1N	0664
N74LS640F	0664
N74LS640N	0664
N74LS641-1F	0685
N74LS641-1N	0685
N74LS641F	0685
N74LS641N	0685
N74LS642-1N	0714
N74LS642F	0714
N74LS642N	0714
N74LS645-1F	0770
N74LS645F	0770
N74LS645N	0770
N74LS670B	1122
N74LS670F	1122
N74LS670N	1122
N74S00A	0699
N74S00F	0699
N74S00N	0699
N74S02F	2223
N74S02N	2223
N74S03A	2203
N74S03F	2203
N74S03N	2203
N74S04A	2248
N74S04F	2248
N74S04N	2248
N74S05A	2305
N74S05F	2305
N74S05N	2305
N74S08F	2547
N74S08N	2547
N74S09F	2642
N74S09N	2642
N74S10A	2426
N74S10F	2426
N74S10N	2426
N74S11A	2428
N74S11F	2428
N74S11N	2428
N74S15A	2432
N74S15F	2432
N74S15N	2432
N74S20A	1011
N74S20F	1011
N74S20N	1011
N74S22A	2442
N74S22F	2442
N74S22N	2442
N74S32F	OEM
N74S32N	OEM
N74S37F	5648
N74S37N	OEM
N74S38F	0775
N74S38N	OEM
N74S40A	2456
N74S40F	2456
N74S40N	2456
N74S51F	4241
N74S51N	4241
N74S64A	2476
N74S64F	2476
N74S64N	2476
N74S65A	2477
N74S65F	2477
N74S65N	2477
N74S74A	2483
N74S74F	2483
N74S74N	2483
N74S85F	5664
N74S85N	5664
N74S86A	2489
N74S86F	2489
N74S86N	2489
N74S86W	2489
N74S89F	OEM
N74S89N	OEM
N74S112B	1607
N74S112F	1607
N74S112N	1607
N74S113A	1613
N74S113F	1613
N74S113N	1613
N74S114A	1619
N74S114F	1619
N74S114N	1619
N74S133B	1808
N74S133F	1808
N74S133N	1808
N74S133W	1808
N74S134B	1816
N74S134F	1816
N74S134N	1816
N74S134W	1816
N74S135F	OEM
N74S135N	OEM
N74S138B	2125
N74S138F	2125
N74S138N	2125
N74S139F	OEM
N74S139N	OEM
N74S140A	1875
N74S140F	1875
N74S140N	1875
N74S151B	1944
N74S151F	1944
N74S151N	2151
N74S153F	2138
N74S153J	2138
N74S153N	2138
N74S157B	1685
N74S157F	1685
N74S157N	1685
N74S158B	2141
N74S158F	2141
N74S158N	2141
N74S158d	OEM
N74S172F	OEM
N74S172N	OEM
N74S174B	2119
N74S174F	2119
N74S174N	2119
N74S175B	2128
N74S175F	2128
N74S175N	2128
N74S178A	OEM
N74S178F	OEM
N74S179B	OEM
N74S179F	OEM
N74S181F	2151
N74S181J	2151
N74S181N	2151
N74S181W	2151
N74S182F	2152
N74S182N	2152
N74S189F	OEM
N74S189N	OEM
N74S189W	OEM
N74S194B	1920
N74S194F	1920
N74S194J	1920
N74S194N	1920
N74S194W	1920
N74S195B	OEM
N74S195F	OEM
N74S195J	OEM
N74S195N	OEM
N74S195W	OEM
N74S196F	OEM
N74S197F	OEM
N74S200F	OEM
N74S200I	OEM
N74S200N	OEM
N74S206B	OEM
N74S206I	OEM
N74S251B	2184
N74S251F	2184
N74S251N	2184
N74S253F	OEM
N74S253N	OEM
N74S257F	OEM
N74S257N	OEM
N74S258B	2191
N74S258F	2191
N74S258J	2191
N74S258N	2191
N74S260F	OEM
N74S260N	OEM
N74S273F	OEM
N74S273N	OEM
N74S280F	2205
N74S280N	2205
N74S301	OEM
N74S301N	OEM
N74S301R	OEM
N74S350F	OEM
N74S350N	OEM
N74S373F	2249
N74S373N	2249
N74S374F	2251
N74S374N	2251
N74S534F	OEM
N74S534N	OEM
N74S551F	4241
N74SL289F	OEM
N75E	OEM
N82S123F	OEM
N82S123N	2161
N82S129N	2209
N82S137BN	2376
N82S153N	OEM
N104B	OEM
N110-2	OEM
N110-3	OEM
N203A	0895
N203B	0058
N203C	0403
N203D	1673
N203YY	0340
N413	OEM
N413L	3298
N450CH06	OEM

If replacement code is OEM, contact original manufacturer for replacement.

DEVICE TYPE	REPL CODE
N-756A	0318
N874S40F	OEM
N1112	1026
N1212	0881
N1213	0892
N3563	0016
N4000	2013
N4001	0473
N4002	2044
N4007	2819
N4009	1988
N4011	0215
N4012	0493
N4013	0409
N4015	1008
N4016	1135
N4019	1517
N4021	1738
N4023	0515
N4025	2061
N4027	1938
N4030	0495
N4049	0001
N4050	0394
N4081	0621
N4111	4109
N4114	OEM
N4212	0881
N4213	0892
N4214	OEM
N4770F	OEM
N5065A	0167
N5070B	0348
N5070N	0348
N5071A	0350
N5072A	0661
N5111	0659
N5111A	0659
N5406	0133
N5596K	0413
N5723T	1183
N5741V	0308
N-7400A	0232
N7400A	0232
N7400F	0232
N7400N	0232
N7401	0268
N7401A	0232
N7401F	0232
N7401N	0268
N7402A	0310
N7402F	0310
N7402N	0310
N7403A	0331
N7403F	0331
N7403N	0331
N-7404A	0357
N7404A	0357
N7404F	0357
N7404N	0357
N7405A	0381
N7405F	0381
N7405N	0381
N7406A	1197
N7406F	1197
N7406N	1197
N7407A	1329
N7407F	1329
N7407N	1329
N-7408A	0462
N7408A	0462
N7408F	0462
N7408N	0462
N7409A	0487
N7409F	0487
N7409N	0487
N7410A	0507
N7410F	0507
N7410N	0507
N7411A	0522
N7411F	0522
N7411N	0522
N7412F	2227
N7412N	2227
N7413A	1432
N7413F	1432
N7413N	1432
N7414B	2228
N7414F	2228
N7414N	2228
N7416A	1339
N7416F	1339
N7416N	1339
N7417A	1342
N7417F	1342
N7417N	1342
N7420A	0692
N7420F	0692
N7420N	0692
N7421A	1347
N7421F	1347
N7421N	1347
N7423F	3429
N7423N	3429
N7425F	3438
N7425N	3438
N7426A	0798
N7426F	0798
N7426N	0798
N7427A	0812
N7427F	0812
N7427N	0812
N7428F	4117
N7428N	4117
N7430A	0867
N7430F	0867
N7430N	0867
N7432A	0893
N7432F	0893
N7432N	0893
N7433F	4130
N7433N	4130
N7437A	3478
N7437F	3478
N7437N	3478
N7438A	0990
N7438F	0990
N7438N	0990
N7439A	5722
N7439F	5722
N7439N	5722
N7440A	1018
N7440F	1018
N7440N	1018
N7441B	1032
N7441F	1032
N7442A	1046
N7442B	OEM
N7442BA	1046
N7442BF	1046
N7442F	1046
N7442N	1046
N7443A	1054
N7443F	1054
N7443N	1054
N7444B	1066
N7444F	1066
N7444N	1066
N7445B	1074
N7445F	1074
N7445N	1074
N7446AF	1090
N7446AN	1090
N7446B	1090
N7447A	1100
N7447AF	1100
N7447B	1100
N7447F	1100
N7448A	1117
N7448B	1117
N7448F	1117
N7448N	1117
N7450A	0738
N7450F	0738
N7450N	0738
N7451A	1160
N7451F	1160
N7451N	1160
N7453A	1177
N7453F	1177
N7453N	1177
N7454A	1193
N7454F	1193
N7454N	1193
N7460A	1265
N7460F	1265
N7460N	1265
N7470A	1394
N7470F	1394
N7470N	1394
N7472A	1417
N7472F	1417
N7472N	1417
N7473	1164
N-7473A	1164
N7473A	1164
N7473F	1164
N7473N	1164
N7474A	1303
N7474F	1303
N7474N	1303
N7475A	1423
N7475B	1423
N7475F	1423
N7475N	1423
N7476A	1150
N7476B	1150
N7476F	1150
N7476N	1150
N7480A	1527
N7480F	1527
N7480N	1527
N7483B	0117
N7483F	0117
N7483N	0117
N7485A	0370
N7485B	0370
N7485F	0370
N7485N	0370
N7486A	1358
N7486F	1358
N7486N	1358
N7488B	OEM
N7488W	OEM
N7489B	5358
N7490A	1199
N7490F	1199
N7490N	1199
N7491A	0974
N7491AF	0974
N7491AN	0974
N7491F	0974
N7492A	0828
N7492F	0828
N7492N	0828
N7493A	0564
N7493F	0564
N7493N	0564
N7494B	1692
N7494F	1692
N7494N	1692
N7495A	1477
N7495AF	1477
N7495AN	1477
N7495F	1477
N7495N	1477
N7496B	1705
N7496F	1705
N7496N	1705
N8233F	2063
N8233N	2063
N8234F	2069
N8234N	2069
N8235F	2076
N8235N	2076
N8250F	2173
N8250N	2173
N8252F	2182
N8252N	2182
N8259A-2	OEM
N8266F	2260
N8266N	2260
N8268F	1527
N8270F	1802
N8270N	1802
N8271N	1809
N8280F	1784
N8280N	1784
N8281F	1792
N8281N	1792
N8290F	1939
N8290N	1939
N8291F	1945
N8293F	2450
N8293N	2450
N8455F	1018
N8470F	0507
N8526AN	OEM
N8598F	OEM
N8815N	3438
N8828F	1303
N8840F	0738
N8848F	2472
N8875F	0268
N8881F	0268
N8881N	0268
N9308F	1064
N9308N	1064
N9309F	5430
N9309N	5430
N9314F	2468
N9314N	2468
N9334N	5465
N9602B	2270
N9602N	2270
N74107A	0936
N74107F	0936
N74107N	0936
N74109B	0962
N74109F	0962
N74109N	0962
N74109W	OEM
N74116F	4365
N74116N	6386
N74121A	0175
N74121F	0175
N74121N	0175
N74121W	OEM
N74122A	1131
N74122F	1131
N74122N	1131
N74123A	1149
N74123B	1149
N74123F	1149
N74123N	1149
N74125F	1174
N74125N	1174
N74126F	1184
N74126N	1184
N74128F	1210
N74129N	OEM
N74132B	1261
N74132F	1261
N74132N	1261
N74141B	1367
N74145	0614
N74145A	0614
N74145B	0614
N74145F	0614
N74145N	0614
N74147F	1442
N74147N	1442
N74148	1455
N74148F	1455
N74148N	1455
N74150A	1484
N74150B	1484
N74150F	1484
N74150N	1484
N74151A	1487
N74151B	1487
N74151F	1487
N74151N	1487
N74152F	1509
N74152N	1509
N74153B	1531
N74153F	1531
N74153N	1531
N74154A	1546
N74154F	1546
N74154N	1546
N74155B	1566
N74155F	1566
N74155N	1566
N74156B	1582
N74156F	1582
N74156N	1582
N74157F	1595
N74157N	1595
N74158F	4372
N74158N	4372
N74160B	1621
N74160F	1621
N74160N	1621
N74161B	1635
N74161F	1635
N74161N	1635
N74162B	1007
N74162F	1007
N74162N	1007
N74163B	1656
N74163F	1656
N74163N	1656
N74164A	0729
N74164F	0729
N74164N	0729
N74165B	1675
N74165F	1675
N74165N	1675
N74166B	0231
N74166F	0231
N74166N	0231
N74170B	1711
N74170F	1711
N74170N	1711
N74172F	OEM
N74172N	OEM
N74173N	1755
N74174	1759
N74174F	1759
N74174N	1759
N74175B	1776
N74175F	1776
N74175N	1776
N74178A	1802
N74178F	1802
N74179B	1809
N74179F	1809
N74180A	1818
N74180F	1818
N74180N	1818
N74181F	1831
N74181N	1831
N74182B	1845
N74182F	1845
N74182N	1845
N74190B	1901
N74190F	1901
N74190N	1901
N74190W	OEM
N74191B	1906
N74191F	1906
N74191N	1906
N74191W	OEM
N74192A	1910
N74192B	1910
N74192F	1910
N74192N	1910
N74192P	1910
N74193A	1915
N74193B	1915
N74193F	1915
N74193N	1915
N74194B	OEM
N74194F	OEM
N74194N	OEM
N74195B	1932
N74195F	1932
N74195N	1932
N74196A	1939
N74198F	1953
N74198N	1953
N74199F	1960
N74199N	1960
N74221D	OEM
N74221F	2129
N74221N	2129
N74279F	OEM
N74279N	OEM
N74298F	OEM
N74298N	OEM
N74365AF	1450
N74365AN	1450
N74366AF	1462
N74366AN	1462
N74367AF	1462
N74367AN	1479
N74368AF	1500
N74368AN	1500
N74478AN	OEM
N80286-8	OEM
N1716580001	OEM
N5301571130	0053
N5301571220	0700
N5301571330	0166
N5301571399	0036
N5301571439	0274
N5301571569	0253
N5301810001	0124
N5301811001	0124
N5302300003	OEM
N5302350001	2604
N5302470001	0911
N5302471001	0911
N5302491160	0440
N5302491519	0582
N5302491759	0077
N5302541039	0466
N5302600001	0031
N5302600002	0031
N5302620001	0071
N5302660001	0124
N5302740001	0511
N5302980001	OEM
N5302990001	1082
N5302990002	1082
N5303010002	OEM
N5303020003	0052
N5303040001	OEM
N5303051003	0031
N5303100001	0023
N5303100003	0031
N5303101003	0031
N5303150001	OEM
N5303150002	OEM
N5303150003	OEM
N5303260003	0541
N6101580003	0126
N6102230001	0037
N6102240001	0076
N6102320002	0198
N6102500003	0283
N6103600001	0338
N6103620001	OEM
N6103690001	0037
N6104330002	5248
N6104340001	0037
N6104350001	0079
N6104350004	0079
N6104420001	0008
N6104430001	0016
N6104980001	0037
N6105000001	0079
N6105000004	0079
N6105150002	OEM
N6105210001	OEM
N6105310001	0168
N6105320003	1503
N6105360001	OEM
N6105510001	2985
N6110180001	0857
N6110190001	0612
N6121860001	1135
N6123270001	4521
N6123700001	0347
N6124120002	3132
N6124400001	OEM
N6124440001	2164
N6124670001	3453
N6124720001	OEM
N6124790001	0619
N6124850002	OEM
N6124930001	0034
N6124990002	OEM
N6125070001	3015
N6125080001	5292
N6125450001	3352
N6125560002	OEM
N6125590001	OEM
N6125630001	3331
N6125640001	3830
N6125660001	OEM
N6125790001	OEM
N6125880001	OEM
N6125990001	OEM
NA0305	1991
NA0505	1991
NA1	1991
NA11	0575
NA-13	0015
NA13	0015
NA20	0595
NA21	0575
NA22	0015
NA25	0015
NA30	0208
NA-32	0015
NA32	0015
NA33	0015
NA-35	0015
NA35	0015
NA36	0015
NA-42	0015
NA42	0015
NA-45	0015
NA45	0015
NA46	0015
NA-62	0015
NA62	0229
NA-63	0015
NA63	0229
NA-65	0015
NA65	0229
NA-66	0015
NA66	0229
NA-74	0071
NA74	0071
NA-75	0071
NA75	0071
NA-76	0071
NA76	0071
NA-84	0071
NA84	0071
NA-85	0071
NA85	0071
NA-86	0071
NA86	0071
NA-104	0071
NA104	0071
NA-105	0071
NA105	0071
NA603	0964
NA615	0983
NA1005	1241
NA1022-1001	0050
NA1022-1007	0004
NA-1114-1001	0050
NA-1114-1002	0050
NA-1114-1004	0004
NA-1114-1005	0004
NA-1114-1006	0004
NA-1114-1007	0004
NA-1114-1008	0004
NA-1114-1009	0004
NA-1114-1010	0004
NA-1114-1011	0004
NA1302	2674
NA1505	1241
NA2002	1042
NA2005	1241
NA5015-1012	0136
NA5018-1001	0050
NA5018-1002	0136
NA5018-1003	0136
NA5018-1004	0136
NA5018-1005	0136
NA5018-1006	0136
NA5018-1007	0136
NA5018-1008	0136
NA5018-1009	0136
NA5018-1010	0136
NA5018-1011	0136
NA5018-1012	0136
NA5018-1013	0004
NA5018-1014	0004
NA5018-1015	0004
NA5018-1016	0004
NA5018-1219	0136
NA5018-1220	0136
NAM383	1042
NAP-TZ-8	0160
NAP-T-Z-10	0004
NAP-TZ-10	0004
NAS29	0168
NAS29A	0168
NAS29B	0168
NAS29C	0168
NAS815R	0740
NB011	0527
NB011EN	0079
NB013	0111
NB021	0527
NB021EV	0037
NB021EV(N.S.)	0037
NB-07014	0167
NB121	0037
NB211	0320
NB211E1	0320
NB211EI	0320
NB211ET	OEM
NC29	0143
NC30	0004
NC32	0164
NC33	0208
NC34	0841
NC-629	OEM
NCB14	1581
NCB35	0930
NCBJ35	0833
NCBV14	2684
NCBW35	0930
NCF150E	OEM
NCF200E	OEM
NCF250E	OEM
NCF300E	OEM
NCF400E	OEM
NCF600E	OEM
NCM5A	OEM
NCM6A	OEM
NCM7A	OEM
NCM8A	OEM
NCM9A	OEM
NCP704	OEM
NCR022D	OEM
NCR025D	OEM
NCR050D	OEM
NCR052B	OEM
NCR052D	OEM
NCR100D	OEM
NCR102B	OEM
NCR102D	OEM
NCR150D	OEM
NCR200D	OEM
NCR202D	OEM
NCR250D	OEM
NCR300D	OEM
NCR302B	OEM
NCR302D	OEM
NCR400D	OEM
NCR402B	OEM
NCR402D	OEM
NCR609-0380855	OEM
NCR2364-30	OEM
NCR23128-30	OEM
NCRF811521A	OEM
NCRF815103G	OEM
NCS9018D	0127
NCT200	0311
NCT260	0311
ND-07001	0232
ND10	0369
ND10A	0369
ND16AT	OEM
ND16BT	OEM
ND16DT	OEM
ND16GT	OEM
ND16JT	OEM
ND16KT	OEM
ND16MT	OEM
ND30AM	OEM
ND30BM	OEM
ND30DM	OEM
ND30GM	OEM
ND30JM	OEM
ND30KM	OEM
ND30MM	OEM
ND74LS01F	1537
ND487C1-3P	OEM
ND487C1-3R	OEM
ND487C2-3P	OEM
ND487C2-3R	OEM
ND487R1-3P	OEM
ND487R1-3R	OEM
ND487R2-3P	OEM
ND487R2-3R	OEM
ND587R-3P	OEM
ND587R-3R	OEM
ND587T-3P	OEM
ND587T-3R	OEM
ND5558-00	OEM
ND9862	OEM
NDAN601	OEM
NDC40013	OEM
NE02112	OEM
NE02132	OEM
NE02133	OEM
NE02135	OEM
NE02137	OEM
NE106J	OEM
NE112J	OEM
NE116J	OEM
NE124J	OEM
NE156J	OEM
NE161J	OEM
NE170J	OEM
NE180J	OEM
NE527H	3230
NE532AN	0765
NE532AT	1667
NE532N	0765
NE532T	1667
NE536T	1908
NE542N	3676
NE545B	3684
NE550A	0026
NE550F	0026
NE550N	0026
NE555	0967
NE555C	3732
NE555JG	0967
NE555N	0967
NE555P	0967
NE555V	0967
NE556	3254
NE556A	3254
NE556N	3254
NE558	3748
NE558CP	3748
NE558N	3748
NE565A	3347
NE566T	3773
NE566V	3775
NE567N	3733
NE571	OEM
NE571N	OEM
NE575D	OEM
NE575N	OEM
NE591A	OEM
NE592	1110
NE592A	1110
NE592D	1110
NE592D14	4209
NE592F	1110

If replacement code is OEM, contact original manufacturer for replacement.

DEVICE TYPE	REPL CODE
NE592FH	OEM
NE592H	1113
NE592K	1113
NE592N	1110
NE592N14	1110
NE645(B)	4045
NE645BN	4045
NE646B	OEM
NE646N	4045
NE657N	OEM
NE4304	0321
NE5532AP	OEM
NE5534	OEM
NE5534A	OEM
NE5534N	OEM
NE5560D	OEM
NE5560F	5772
NE5560N	5120
NE5568N	OEM
NE8131	OEM
NE21935	OEM
NE21937	OEM
NE22120	2059
NE41137	OEM
NE41612	OEM
NE41632	OEM
NE41635	OEM
NE46734	OEM
NE49433	OEM
NE59312	OEM
NE64535	OEM
NE64614B	OEM
NE66912	OEM
NE68033	OEM
NE68035	OEM
NE68037	OEM
NE68132	OEM
NE68133	OEM
NE68135	OEM
NE68137	OEM
NE68333	OEM
NE68337	OEM
NE71111	OEM
NE73412	OEM
NE73432	OEM
NE73433	OEM
NE73435	OEM
NE73437	OEM
NE74014	0414
NE85632	OEM
NE85633	OEM
NE85634	OEM
NE85635	OEM
NE85637	OEM
NE87112	OEM
NE88912	OEM
NE88933	OEM
NE88935	OEM
NE99532	OEM
N-EA15X130	0127
N-EA15X131	0144
N-EA15X132	0144
N-EA15X133	0136
N-EA15X134	0127
N-EA15X135	0127
N-EA15X136	0016
N-EA15X137	0016
N-EA15X138	0016
N-EA15X139	0816
N-EA16X27	0123
N-EA16X29	0137
N-EA16X30	0015
N-EA2136	0164
NEC303-1	OEM
NEZ0910-2A	OEM
NEZ0910-4A	OEM
NEZ0910-6A	OEM
NEZ1011-2A	OEM
NEZ1011-4A	OEM
NEZ1011-6A	OEM
NEZ1414-2A	OEM
NEZ1414-4A	OEM
NF520	0321
NF522	0321
NF523	0321
NF531	0321
NF533	0321
NF550	0015
NF580	OEM
NF581	OEM
NF582	OEM
NF583	OEM
NF584	OEM
NF3819	OEM
NF4302	2922
NF4303	2922
NF4304	5545
NF5163	OEM
NF5457	OEM
NF5458	OEM
NF5459	OEM
NF5485	0321
NF5486	0321
NF5638	OEM
NF5639	OEM
NF5640	OEM
NF5653	OEM
NF5654	OEM
NGP3002	0143

DEVICE TYPE	REPL CODE
NGP3003	0242
NGP5002	0631
NGP5007	0012
NGP5010	0137
NHM78M05A	OEM
NIM4558D	0356
NIS7261A	OEM
NIS7264	OEM
NIS7264B	OEM
NJ100A	0127
NJ100B	0016
NJ-101B	OEM
NJ101B	0037
NJ102C	0016
NJ107	0086
NJ181B	0004
NJ-202B	OEM
NJ202B	0127
NJ703N	0627
NJD6505S	OEM
NJD6506S	OEM
NJL1102L	OEM
NJL5121DC	0311
NJL5141EA	5556
NJL5141E-AB	OEM
NJL5141F-AB	OEM
NJL5161K	OEM
NJL6130A	OEM
NJL6145L	OEM
NJM072	OEM
NJM072-FP	OEM
NJM072D	6170
NJM082	OEM
NJM082M	4044
NJM58L05	2995
NJM78L02AA	OEM
NJM78L05	1288
NJM78L05A	1288
NJM78L05AV	1288
NJM78L05UA	OEM
NJM78L06A	2285
NJM78L08A	6061
NJM78L09	1775
NJM78L09A	1775
NJM78L09K	4403
NJM78L12A	4424
NJM78M05	0619
NJM78M05A	5908
NJM78M05FA	0619
NJM78M09A	OEM
NJM78M09E	OEM
NJM78M12	0330
NJM78M12A	6110
NJM78M13A	OEM
NJM78M15	OEM
NJM78M18A	2244
NJM78M93D	OEM
NJM78M93FD	OEM
NJM79L05A	4797
NJM79L06A	OEM
NJM79L12A	6892
NJM79M05A	6949
NJM79M05FA	OEM
NJM79M06A	6717
NJM79M06FA	OEM
NJM79M09A	OEM
NJM79M12A	6512
NJM386	OEM
NJM386BS	OEM
NJM386D	6450
NJM387A	OEM
NJM387DA	OEM
NJM555D	0967
NJM703	0627
NJM-703N	4039
NJM703N	0627
NJM2041DD	OEM
NJM2043S	OEM
NJM2043SE	OEM
NJM2058D	OEM
NJM2061D	OEM
NJM2068	OEM
NJM2068DD	OEM
NJM2068S	OEM
NJM2068SD	OEM
NJM2068SDN	OEM
NJM2074	OEM
NJM2074AD	OEM
NJM2074D	OEM
NJM2100MAT1	OEM
NJM2201	2246
NJM2207	OEM
NJM2207S	OEM
NJM2217L	OEM
NJM2220S	OEM
NJM2225M	OEM
NJM2225S	OEM
NJM2227AL	OEM
NJM2227L	OEM
NJM2229S	OEM
NJM-2233BS	OEM
NJM2233BS	OEM
NJM2234	OEM
NJM2234D	OEM
NJM2234L	OEM
NJM2234S	OEM
NJM2235M	OEM
NJM2245S	OEM
NJM2248S	OEM

DEVICE TYPE	REPL CODE
NJM2249L	OEM
NJM2355	OEM
NJM2406FTE1	OEM
NJM2901	0624
NJM2901D	0624
NJM2901M	4189
NJM2901MB	OEM
NJM2901N	0176
NJM2902M	4190
NJM2902N	4191
NJM2903	OEM
NJM2903D	0624
NJM2903M	OEM
NJM2903S	4194
NJM2904	0765
NJM2904D	0765
NJM2904M	4195
NJM2904MTE2	OEM
NJM3404AD	OEM
NJM3404S	OEM
NJM3414M	OEM
NJM3414MT1	OEM
NJM3415D	OEM
NJM4556D	OEM
NJM4556M	OEM
NJM4558C	0356
NJM4558D	0356
NJM4558D-1	0356
NJM4558DD	0356
NJM4558D-K	0356
NJM4558DM	0356
NJM4558DMA	0356
NJM4558DV	0356
NJM4558DX	0356
NJM4558K	0356
NJM4558M	5433
NJM4558MDA	0356
NJM-4558S	2884
NJM4558S	2884
NJM4558SD	2884
NJM4559D	0356
NJM4559S	OEM
NJM4560D	OEM
NJM4560DD	OEM
NJM4560F	OEM
NJM4560M	OEM
NJM4560S	OEM
NJM4562DDR	OEM
NJM4562S	OEM
NJM4562SD	OEM
NJM4565SB	OEM
NJM5532	OEM
NJM5532DD	OEM
NJM7805A	6654
NJM7805FA	0619
NJM7812A	3445
NJM7812B	OEM
NJM7812FA	0330
NJM7818FA	2244
NJM7905FA	OEM
NJM7906A	6717
NJM7906FA	OEM
NJM7912	OEM
NJU74HC04M	OEM
NJU74HCU04D	OEM
NJU4051BD	OEM
NJU4053B	OEM
NJU4053BM	OEM
NK1302	0050
NK1404	0050
NK5252	OEM
NKT4	0004
NKT5	0004
NKT11	0004
NKT12	0004
NKT24	0004
NKT25	0004
NKT32	0004
NKT33	0004
NKT42	0279
NKT43	0279
NKT52	0004
NKT53	0004
NKT54	0004
NKT62	0279
NKT63	0279
NKT64	0279
NKT72	0279
NKT73	0279
NKT74	0279
NKT101	OEM
NKT102	0164
NKT103	0136
NKT104	0164
NKT105	0164
NKT106	0164
NKT107	0164
NKT108	0164
NKT109	0164
NKT121	0050
NKT122	0050
NKT123	0004
NKT124	0050
NKT125	0050
NKT126	0004
NKT127	0136
NKT128	0279
NKT129	0279
NKT131	0136

DEVICE TYPE	REPL CODE
NKT132	0136
NKT133	0211
NKT141	0279
NKT142	0279
NKT143	0279
NKT144	0279
NKT151	0136
NKT152	0136
NKT153/25	0164
NKT154/25	0164
NKT162	0279
NKT163	0279
NKT163/25	0164
NKT164	0279
NKT164/25	0164
NKT201	OEM
NKT202	0279
NKT203	0279
NKT204	0279
NKT205	0279
NKT206	0279
NKT207	0279
NKT208	0004
NKT211	0164
NKT212	0164
NKT213	0164
NKT214	0164
NKT215	0164
NKT216	0164
NKT217	0164
NKT218	0164
NKT219	0164
NKT221	0211
NKT222	0211
NKT222S1	0279
NKT222S2	0279
NKT223	0211
NKT223A	0004
NKT224	0211
NKT225	0211
NKT226	0211
NKT227	0211
NKT228	0211
NKT229	0164
NKT231	0211
NKT232	0211
NKT240	0841
NKT241	0841
NKT242	0136
NKT243	0279
NKT244	0004
NKT245	0211
NKT246	0004
NKT247	0211
NKT249	0136
NKT251	0050
NKT252	0136
NKT253	0136
NKT254	0136
NKT255	0136
NKT261	0279
NKT262	0279
NKT263	0279
NKT264	0279
NKT265	0136
NKT270	0136
NKT271	0164
NKT272	0164
NKT273	0004
NKT274	0164
NKT275	0164
NKT275A	0164
NKT275E	0164
NKT275J	0164
NKT278	0004
NKT281	0164
NKT301A	OEM
NKT302A	OEM
NKT303	0004
NKT351	0164
NKT352	0164
NKT361	OEM
NKT362	OEM
NKT-401	0160
NKT401	0160
NKT-402	0160
NKT402	0160
NKT-403	0160
NKT403	0160
NKT-404	0160
NKT404	0160
NKT-405	0160
NKT405	0160
NKT406	0160
NKT-415	0160
NKT415	0160
NKT-416	0160
NKT416	0160
NKT450	0160
NKT450X2	OEM
NKT-451	0160
NKT451	0222
NKT-452	0160
NKT452	0222
NKT452-S1	0222
NKT452S1	OEM
NKT-453	0160
NKT453	0222
NKT-454	0160

DEVICE TYPE	REPL CODE
NKT454	0160
NKT-501	0160
NKT501	0160
NKT502	OEM
NKT-503	0160
NKT503	0160
NKT-504	0160
NKT504	0160
NKT618	0136
NKT674F	0136
NKT675	0136
NKT676	0136
NKT677	0136
NKT677F	0136
NKT701	0208
NKT703	0208
NKT713	0208
NKT717	0208
NKT732	0038
NKT734	0595
NKT735	OEM
NKT736	0595
NKT738	0595
NKT751	0208
NKT752	0208
NKT753	0595
NKT773	0208
NKT774	0595
NKT781	0208
NKT4054	0178
NKT4055	0486
NKT10339	0016
NKT10419	0016
NKT10439	0016
NKT10519	0016
NKT12329	0016
NKT12429	0016
NKT13329	0016
NKT13429	0016
NKT15325	0136
NKT15425	0136
NKT16229	0007
NKT16325	0279
NKT16425	0279
NKT20329	0037
NKT20339	0037
NKT35219	0007
NKT80111	2922
NKT80112	2922
NKT80113	2922
NKT80211	0321
NKT80212	0321
NKT80213	0321
NKT80214	0321
NKT80215	2922
NKT80216	2922
NKT800112	0321
NKT800113	0321
NL-2N683	0151
NL-2N684	3227
NL-2N685	0757
NL-2N686	3237
NL-2N687	3240
NL-2N688	0735
NL-2N689	3260
NL-2N690	0759
NL-2N691	2848
NL-2N692	0761
NL2N2023	OEM
NL2N2024	OEM
NL2N2025	OEM
NL2N2026	OEM
NL2N2027	OEM
NL2N2028	OEM
NL2N2029	OEM
NL2N2030	OEM
NL5	0015
NL10	0015
NL15	0015
NL20	0015
NL25	0015
NL30	0015
NL40	0015
NL50	0015
NL60	0015
NL100B	0127
NL-511-3	0674
NL-511-4	0674
NL-511-6	0674
NL516M	OEM
NL516S	OEM
NL548A	OEM
NL548B	OEM
NL548C	0650
NL548D	OEM
NL548E	OEM
NL548M	OEM
NL548N	OEM
NL548S	OEM
NL549A	OEM
NL549B	OEM
NL549C	OEM
NL549D	OEM
NL549E	OEM
NL549M	OEM
NL549N	OEM
NL549P	OEM
NL549S	OEM
NL549T	OEM

DEVICE TYPE	REPL CODE
NL551A	OEM
NL551B	OEM
NL551C	OEM
NL551D	OEM
NL551E	OEM
NL551M	OEM
NL551N	OEM
NL551S	OEM
NL552A	OEM
NL552B	OEM
NL552C	OEM
NL552D	OEM
NL552E	OEM
NL552M	OEM
NL552N	OEM
NL552P	OEM
NL552S	OEM
NL552T	OEM
NL555A	0463
NL555B	0463
NL555C	0463
NL555D	0463
NL555E	0463
NL555F	OEM
NL555G	OEM
NL555H	OEM
NL555M	0463
NL555N	0463
NL555P	0463
NL555PA	0463
NL555PB	0463
NL555PC	OEM
NL555R	OEM
NL555S	0653
NL556A	0653
NL556B	0217
NL556C	0217
NL556D	0217
NL556E	0217
NL556F	OEM
NL556G	OEM
NL556H	OEM
NL556M	0217
NL556N	0463
NL556P	OEM
NL556PA	OEM
NL556PB	OEM
NL556PC	OEM
NL556S	0463
NL556T	OEM
NL570A	OEM
NL570B	OEM
NL570C	OEM
NL570D	0735
NL570E	0759
NL570M	0759
NL571A	OEM
NL571B	OEM
NL571C	OEM
NL571D	OEM
NL571E	OEM
NL571F	OEM
NL571M	OEM
NL576B	1694
NL576C	3970
NL576D	3970
NL576E	3970
NL576M	3970
NL576N	0674
NL576P	0674
NL576PA	0674
NL576PB	0674
NL576S	0674
NL576T	0674
NL577B	1694
NL577C	3970
NL577D	3970
NL577E	3970
NL577M	3970
NL577N	0674
NL577P	0674
NL577P7P	OEM
NL577PA	0674
NL577PB	0674
NL577S	0674
NL577T	0674
NL-578	OEM
NL578B	1694
NL578C	3970
NL578D	3970
NL578E	3970
NL578M	3970
NL578N	0674
NL578P	0674
NL578PA	0674
NL578PB	0674
NL578S	0674
NL578T	0674
NL-579	OEM
NL579B	1694
NL579C	3970
NL579D	3970
NL579E	3970
NL579M	3970
NL579N	0674
NL579P	0674
NL579PA	0674
NL579PB	0674
NL579S	0674

DEVICE TYPE	REPL CODE
NL579T	0674
NL-1580	OEM
NL1580A	2816
NL1580B	2816
NL1580D	1754
NL1580E	1754
NL1580M	1754
NL1580N	1803
NL1580P	1803
NL1580PA	1803
NL1580PB	1803
NL1580S	1803
NL1580T	1803
NL-C35A	0707
NLC35A	0707
NL-C35B	0464
NLC35B	0464
NL-C35C	0773
NLC35C	0716
NL-C35D	0717
NLC35D	0717
NL-C35E	0720
NLC35E	0720
NL-C35F	0726
NL-C35G	0464
NLC35G	0726
NL-C35H	0716
NLC35H	0717
NL-C35M	0720
NLC35M	0720
NLC35N	0745
NLC35S	0745
NL-C35U	3246
NL-C36A	0717
NLC36A	0736
NL-C36A/2N1844	0736
NL-C36B	0717
NLC36B	0740
NL-C36B/2N1846	0740
NL-C36C	0717
NLC36C	0742
NL-C36C/2N1848	2889
NL-C36D	0717
NLC36D	0742
NL-C36D/2N1849	0742
NLC36E	0747
NL-C36E/2N1850	3213
NL-C36F	0717
NLC36F	0464
NL-C36G	0717
NLC36G	0740
NL-C36G2N1845	3076
NLC36H	0742
NLC36M	0759
NLC36N	0761
NLC36S	0761
NL-C36U	0717
NLC36U	0464
NL-C37A	0562
NLC37A	0562
NL-C37B	0757
NLC37B	0757
NL-C37C	3240
NLC37C	0735
NL-C37D	0735
NLC37D	0735
NL-C37E	3260
NLC37E	0759
NL-C37F	0717
NLC37F	0464
NL-C37G	0717
NL-C37M	0759
NLC37M	0759
NL-C37N	0761
NLC37N	0674
NL-C37S	2848
NLC37S	0674
NL-C37U	0717
NLC37U	0464
NL-C38A	0726
NLC38A	0726
NL-C38B	0464
NLC38B	0464
NL-C38C	0773
NLC38C	0717
NL-C38D	0717
NLC38D	0717
NL-C38E	0720
NLC38E	0773
NLC38F	OEM
NL-C38G	0464
NLC38G	0464
NL-C38H	0716
NLC38H	0717
NL-C38M	0720
NL-C38U	3246
NLC38U	0726
NLC40E	0799
NL-C45	OEM
NLC45A	0603
NLC45B	0603
NLC45C	0605
NLC45D	0605
NLC45E	0605
NL-C45F	OEM
NLC45G	0603
NLC45H	0605
NLC45M	0605
NLC45N	0463

If replacement code is OEM, contact original manufacturer for replacement.

503

DEVICE TYPE	REPL CODE
NLC45P	0463
NLC45PA	0463
NLC45PB	0463
NLC45S	0463
NLC45T	0463
NL-C45U	OEM
NL-C46	OEM
NLC46A	0636
NLC46B	0636
NLC46C	0217
NLC46D	0217
NLC46E	0217
NL-C46F	OEM
NLC46G	0636
NLC46H	0217
NLC46M	0217
NLC46N	0653
NLC46P	0653
NLC46PA	0653
NLC46PB	0653
NLC46S	0653
NLC46T	0653
NL-C46U	OEM
NL-C50	OEM
NLC50A	0217
NLC50B	0217
NLC50C	0217
NLC50D	0217
NLC50E	0217
NLC50G	0217
NLC50H	0217
NLC50M	0217
NLC50N	0463
NLC50S	0463
NL-C52	OEM
NLC52A	0217
NLC52B	0217
NLC52C	0217
NLC52D	0217
NLC52E	0217
NLC52G	0217
NLC52H	0217
NLC52M	0217
NLC52N	0653
NLC52S	0653
NL-C52U	OEM
NL-C55	OEM
NL-C55F	OEM
NL-C55U	OEM
NL-C56	OEM
NL-C56F	OEM
NL-C56U	OEM
NL-C60	OEM
NL-C62	OEM
NL-C135A2N3754	0707
NL-C135B2N3755	0464
NL-C135C2N3756	0716
NL-C135D2N3757	0717
NL-C135E2N3758	0773
NL-C135F2N3759	0726
NL-C135M2N3760	0720
NLC135N	OEM
NL-C137E	0773
NL-C137M	0720
NL-C150	OEM
NLC150E	0463
NLC150M	0463
NLC150N	0463
NLC150P	0463
NLC150PA	0463
NLC150PB	0463
NLC150S	0463
NLC150T	0463
NL-C151	OEM
NL-C151PA	OEM
NL-C151PB	OEM
NL-C151PC	OEM
NL-C152	OEM
NL-C153	OEM
NL-C153PA	OEM
NL-C153PB	OEM
NL-C153PC	OEM
NL-C154	OEM
NL-C154/C155B	OEM
NL-C155	OEM
NL-C156	OEM
NL-C157	OEM
NL-C178	OEM
NLC178A	0733
NLC178B	0733
NLC178C	0733
NLC178D	0733
NLC178E	0733
NLC178M	0733
NLC178N	0733
NLC178P	0733
NLC178PA	0733
NLC178PAA	OEM
NLC178PB	0733
NLC178S	0733
NLC178T	0733
NL-C180	OEM
NLC180A	0733
NLC180B	0733
NLC180C	0733
NLC180D	0733
NLC180E	0733
NLC180M	0733
NLC180M0M	OEM

DEVICE TYPE	REPL CODE
NLC180N	0733
NLC180P	0733
NLC180P0P	OEM
NLC180PA	0733
NLC180PB	0733
NLC180PC	OEM
NLC180S	0733
NLC180T	0733
NL-C181	OEM
NLC181A	1076
NLC181B	1076
NLC181C	1078
NLC181D	1078
NLC181E	1078
NLC181M	1078
NLC181N	1094
NLC181P	1094
NLC181S	1094
NLC181T	1094
NL-C185	OEM
NLC290A	1889
NLC290B	1889
NLC290C	1889
NLC290D	0733
NLC290E	0733
NLC290G	1889
NLC290H	1889
NLC290M	0733
NLC290N	0733
NLC290P	0733
NLC290PA	0733
NLC290PB	0733
NLC290S	0733
NLC290T	0733
NL-C350	OEM
NLC350A	0192
NLC350B	0192
NLC350C	0096
NLC350D	0096
NLC350E	0096
NLC350M	0096
NLC350N	0096
NLC350P	0096
NLC350PA	0096
NLC350PB	0096
NLC350S	0096
NLC350T	0096
NL-C354	OEM
NL-C354/C355M	OEM
NL-C355	OEM
NL-C380	OEM
NLC380A	0192
NLC380B	0192
NLC380C	0096
NLC380D	0096
NLC380E	0096
NLC380M	0096
NLC380N	2816
NLC380P	2816
NLC380PA	2816
NLC380PB	2816
NLC380S	2816
NLC380T	2816
NL-C385	OEM
NL-C501	OEM
NLC501A	2816
NLC501B	2816
NLC501C	1754
NLC501D	1754
NLC501E	1754
NLC501M	1754
NLC501N	1803
NLC501P	1803
NLC501PA	1803
NLC501PB	1803
NLC501S	1803
NLC501T	1803
NL-C601	OEM
NLC601N	1714
NLC601P	1714
NLC601T	1714
NLE45B	OEM
NLE45C	OEM
NLE45D	OEM
NLE45E	OEM
NLE45M	OEM
NLE45N	OEM
NLE45S	OEM
NLE45T	OEM
NLE46B	OEM
NLE46C	OEM
NLE46D	OEM
NLE46M	OEM
NLE46N	OEM
NLE46S	OEM
NLE46T	OEM
NLE150B	OEM
NLE150C	OEM
NLE150D	OEM
NLE150E	OEM
NLE150M	OEM
NLE150N	OEM
NLE150P	OEM
NLE150S	OEM
NLE150T	OEM
NLE151E	OEM
NLE151M	OEM
NLE151N	OEM
NLE151P	OEM

DEVICE TYPE	REPL CODE
NLE151S	OEM
NLE151T	OEM
NLE152B	OEM
NLE152C	OEM
NLE152D	OEM
NLE152E	OEM
NLE152M	OEM
NLE152N	OEM
NLE152P	OEM
NLE152S	OEM
NLE152T	OEM
NLE153E	OEM
NLE153M	OEM
NLE153N	OEM
NLE153P	OEM
NLE153S	OEM
NLE153T	OEM
NLE155A	OEM
NLE155B	OEM
NLE155C	OEM
NLE155D	OEM
NLE155E	OEM
NLE157A	OEM
NLE157B	OEM
NLE157C	OEM
NLE157D	OEM
NLE157E	OEM
NLF45B	OEM
NLF45C	OEM
NLF45D	OEM
NLF45E	OEM
NLF45M	OEM
NLF45N	OEM
NLF45S	OEM
NLF45T	OEM
NLF46B	OEM
NLF46C	OEM
NLF46D	OEM
NLF46E	OEM
NLF46M	OEM
NLF46N	OEM
NLF46S	OEM
NLF46T	OEM
NL-F150	OEM
NLF150B	0603
NLF150C	0605
NLF150D	0605
NLF150E	0605
NLF150M	0605
NLF150N	0463
NLF150P	0463
NLF150S	0463
NLF150T	0463
NL-F151	OEM
NLF151B	0521
NLF151C	0521
NLF151D	0521
NLF151E	0521
NLF151M	0521
NLF151N	0108
NLF151P	0108
NLF151PA	OEM
NLF151S	0108
NLF151T	0108
NL-F152	OEM
NLF152B	0636
NLF152C	0217
NLF152D	0217
NLF152E	0217
NLF152M	0217
NLF152N	0653
NLF152P	0653
NLF152S	0653
NLF152T	0653
NL-F153	OEM
NLF153B	0650
NLF153C	0650
NLF153D	0650
NLF153E	0650
NLF153M	0650
NLF153P	0650
NL-F153PA	OEM
NLF153S	0650
NLF153T	0650
NL-F154	OEM
NL-F154/F155D	OEM
NL-F155	OEM
NL-F156	OEM
NL-F157	OEM
NL-F158	OEM
NLF158A	0521
NLF158B	0521
NLF158C	0521
NLF158D	0521
NLF158E	0521
NLF158M	0521
NL-F159	OEM
NLF159A	0650
NLF159B	0650
NLF159C	0650
NLF159D	0650
NLF159E	0650
NLF159M	0650
NLF159N	0020
NLF159P	0020
NLF159S	0020
NLF159T	0020
NL-F180	OEM
NLF180A	1076

DEVICE TYPE	REPL CODE
NLF180B	1076
NLF180C	1078
NLF180D	1078
NLF180E	1078
NLF180M	1078
NLF180N	1094
NLF180P	1094
NLF180PA	OEM
NLF180PB	OEM
NLF180PC	OEM
NLF180S	1094
NLF180T	1094
NL-F185	OEM
NLF290A	1889
NLF290B	1889
NLF290C	1889
NLF290D	1889
NLF290E	1889
NLF290M	1889
NLF290N	0733
NLF290P	0733
NLF290PA	OEM
NLF290PB	OEM
NLF290S	0733
NLF290T	0733
NLF291PA	OEM
NLF291PB	OEM
NLF350A	0192
NLF350B	0192
NLF350C	0159
NLF350D	0159
NLF350E	0159
NLF350M	0159
NLF350N	0096
NLF350P	0096
NLF350S	0096
NLF350T	0096
NL-F358	OEM
NLF358A	0454
NLF358B	0454
NLF358C	0454
NLF358D	0454
NLF358E	0454
NLF358M	0454
NLF358N	0584
NLF358P	0584
NLF358S	0584
NLF358T	0584
NL-F380	OEM
NLF380A	0192
NLF380B	0192
NLF380C	0096
NLF380D	0096
NLF380E	0096
NLF380M	0096
NLF380N	2816
NLF380P	2816
NLF380S	2816
NL-F385	OEM
NL-F390	OEM
NLF390E	1754
NLF390M	1754
NLF390N	1803
NLF390P	1803
NLF390PA	1803
NLF390PB	1803
NLF390S	1803
NLF390T	1803
NL-F394	OEM
NL-F395	OEM
NL-F397	OEM
NL-F398	OEM
NL-F701	OEM
NLF701E	4085
NLF701M	4085
NLF701N	1714
NLF701P	1714
NLF701PA	1714
NLF701PB	1714
NLF701S	1714
NLF701T	1714
NLH150B	OEM
NLH150C	OEM
NLH150D	OEM
NLH150E	OEM
NLH150M	OEM
NLH150N	OEM
NLH150P	OEM
NLH150S	OEM
NLH150T	OEM
NLH152B	OEM
NLH152C	OEM
NLH152D	OEM
NLH152E	OEM
NLH152M	OEM
NLH152N	OEM
NLH152P	OEM
NLH152S	OEM
NLH152T	OEM
NM93C46	OEM
NMC93C-46N	OEM
NMC2147H-3	1683
NMC2148HJ-3	OEM
NMC2148HN-3	OEM
NMC2148J-3	OEM
NMC6508J-5	3164
NMC6508J-9	3164
NMC6508N-5	3164
NMC6508N-9	3164

DEVICE TYPE	REPL CODE
NMC9306M	OEM
NMC9306N	OEM
NMC9313BN	OEM
NMC9346	OEM
NMC9346N	OEM
NMJ2245S	OEM
NML16L8LNC	OEM
NML16L8LNJ	OEM
NN16AT	1716
NN16BT	1716
NN16DT	1716
NN16GT	1716
NN16JT	OEM
NN16KT	OEM
NN16MT	OEM
NN30AM	OEM
NN30BM	OEM
NN30DM	OEM
NN30GM	OEM
NN30JM	OEM
NN30KM	OEM
NN30MM	OEM
NN50	0015
NN650	0037
NN1199	0224
NN5762N	OEM
NN7000	0590
NN7001	0218
NN7002	0590
NN7003	0590
NN7004	0590
NN7005	0590
NN7500	0786
NN7501	0786
NN7502	0786
NN7503	0786
NN7504	0786
NN7505	0786
NN7511	1233
NN9017	0079
NP04S49	0710
NP16AT	1227
NP16BT	1227
NP16DT	1227
NP16GT	1227
NP16JT	OEM
NP16KT	OEM
NP16MT	OEM
NP30AM	2219
NP30AP	3631
NP30BM	2219
NP30BP	3631
NP30DM	2219
NP30DP	3631
NP30GM	2219
NP30GP	3634
NP30JM	6441
NP30KM	OEM
NP30KP	OEM
NP30MM	OEM
NP30MP	OEM
NP50A	0015
NP60A	0015
NP389	0015
NP1000	OEM
NP1001	OEM
NP2000	OEM
NP2001	OEM
NP2222AP	0079
NP3000	OEM
NP4510	2592
NP5114	OEM
NP5116	OEM
NPC00050	OEM
NPC0010	0015
NPC0050	0015
NPC069	0079
NPC069-98	0079
NPC079	0037
NPC079-98	0855
NPC0100	0015
NPC0200	OEM
NPC0400	OEM
NPC0600	OEM
NPC0800	OEM
NPC06998	0007
NPC12-1A	0178
NPC12-1B	0178
NPC12-2	0142
NPC108	1382
NPC108A	1382
NPC115	0086
NPC151	OEM
NPC167	0007
NPC173	0144
NPC187	0086
NPC188	0144
NPC189	0086
NPC200C	OEM
NPC211N	2922
NPC212N	2922
NPC213N	2922
NPC214N	2922
NPC215N	2922
NPC216N	2922
NPC290	0086
NPC312N	0321
NPC544	3946
NPC634	0455

DEVICE TYPE	REPL CODE
NPC636	0455
NPC737	0016
NPC750	0688
NPC1000	OEM
NPC1075	0326
NPC1096	0161
NPC1098	0161
NPC1500	OEM
NPC5104	OEM
NPC5107	OEM
NPC6069S	OEM
NPC7629	1704
NPC7837	OEM
NPC8021	OEM
NPC76315	4160
NPC76365	2592
NPC-C1006A	OEM
NPD0531	0133
NPQ199	OEM
NPQ300	OEM
NPQ6261	OEM
NPQ8317	OEM
NPS404	0037
NPS404A	0037
NPS6512	0079
NPS6513	0079
NPS6514	0079
NPS6516	0150
NPS6517	0150
NPS6518	0919
NPS6519	0079
NPS6520	0079
NPS6522	0079
NPS6523	0079
NPSA20	0111
NPT800	OEM
NR05	0595
NR041	0079
NR041E	0079
NR-071AU	0016
NR091ET	0079
NR5	0595
NR8AT	OEM
NR8BT	OEM
NR8DT	OEM
NR8GT	OEM
NR8JT	OEM
NR8KT	OEM
NR8MT	OEM
NR10	0595
NR20	0038
NR30	0595
NR201AY	0016
NR-261AS	0079
NR261AS	0016
NR271AY	0016
NR401	0016
NR401EG	0016
NR401EH	0016
NR421	0127
NR421DG	0127
NR-431AS	0016
NR441	0016
NR441EG	0016
NR441EN	0016
NR461	0079
NR461AA	0007
NR461AF	0127
NR-461AS	0016
NR461EG	0079
NR461EH	0079
NR601BT	0037
NR621AT	0037
NR621EU	0037
NR631AY	0037
NR700	0595
NR7916	0321
NR49333	OEM
NS8AT	1137
NS8BT	1137
NS8DT	1137
NS8GT	1137
NS8JT	1958
NS8KT	OEM
NS8MT	OEM
NS20-42	0233
NS32	0211
NS100	OEM
NS101	OEM
NS121	0211
NS142	0167
NS200	0016
NS316	0321
NS345	0007
NS381	0144
NS382	0144
NS383	0016
NS384	0016
NS404	0037
NS430	1471
NS431	1471
NS432	1471
NS433	1471
NS434	1471
NS435	1471
NS436	1471
NS437	1471
NS438	1471
NS475	0016

DEVICE TYPE	REPL CODE
NS476	0016
NS477	0016
NS478	0016
NS479	0016
NS480	0016
NS500	OEM
NS501	OEM
NS502	OEM
NS503	OEM
NS504	OEM
NS505	OEM
NS506	OEM
NS507	OEM
NS508	OEM
NS661	0037
NS662	0037
NS663	0037
NS664	0037
NS665	0037
NS666	0037
NS667	0037
NS668	0037
NS731	0016
NS731A	0016
NS732	0037
NS732A	0037
NS733	0016
NS733A	0016
NS734	0016
NS734A	0016
NS746	0661
NS792	0930
NS793	0930
NS949	0016
NS950	0590
NS1000	1325
NS1001	0037
NS1002	OEM
NS1110	0142
NS1111	OEM
NS1112	OEM
NS1116	OEM
NS1234	OEM
NS1355	0590
NS1356	0144
NS1500	0016
NS1510	0127
NS1672	0037
NS1673	0037
NS1674	0037
NS1675	0037
NS1861	0037
NS1862	0037
NS1863	0037
NS1864	0037
NS1900	0590
NS1960	0590
NS1972	0016
NS1973	0016
NS1974	0016
NS1975	0016
NS2000	0071
NS2006	0087
NS2007	0087
NS2008	0087
NS2100	0086
NS2101	0086
NS2310	OEM
NS2311	OEM
NS2525	OEM
NS3000	0087
NS3001	0087
NS3006	0087
NS3007	0087
NS3008	0087
NS3039	0127
NS3040	0127
NS3041	0127
NS3050	OEM
NS3051	OEM
NS3052	OEM
NS3053	OEM
NS3108	OEM
NS3109	OEM
NS3110	OEM
NS3300	0144
NS3762	0886
NS3763	0886
NS3903	0016
NS3904	0016
NS3905	0037
NS3906	0037
NS5387	OEM
NS6000	1557
NS6001	0037
NS6002	1557
NS6003	2140
NS6004	2140
NS6062	0037
NS6063	0037
NS6064	0037
NS6065	0037
NS6112	0144
NS6113	0144
NS6114	0016
NS6115	0016
NS6201	OEM
NS6203	OEM
NS6205	OEM

If replacement code is OEM, contact original manufacturer for replacement.

DEVICE TYPE	REPL CODE
NS6207	0016
NS6208	OEM
NS6209	OEM
NS6210	0016
NS6211	0037
NS6212	0233
NS6213	OEM
NS6214	OEM
NS6241	0037
NS7000	OEM
NS7001	OEM
NS7070	OEM
NS7100	OEM
NS7200	OEM
NS7201	OEM
NS7261	0144
NS7262	0016
NS7267	0144
NS7300	OEM
NS7301	OEM
NS7302	OEM
NS7303	OEM
NS7304	OEM
NS7305	OEM
NS7630	OEM
NS8000	OEM
NS8003	OEM
NS8250AN	OEM
NS8250AV	OEM
NS8250N-B	OEM
NS9210	OEM
NS9211	OEM
NS9400	0086
NS9420	0086
NS9500	0086
NS9540	0086
NS9608	OEM
NS9609	OEM
NS9609A	OEM
NS9710	0144
NS9713	OEM
NS9726	OEM
NS9728	0086
NS9729	0086
NS9730	0086
NS9731	0086
NS12000	2140
NS12001	2140
NS12002	2140
NS12006	0706
NS16450N	OEM
NS16550V	OEM
NS45006	0008
NS48004	0233
NSD102	0818
NSD103	0818
NSD104	0818
NSD105	0818
NSD106	0818
NSD131	0283
NSD132	0283
NSD133	0283
NSD134	0283
NSD151	3492
NSD152	3492
NSD202	0164
NSD203	0164
NSD204	3294
NSD205	3294
NSDU01	0555
NSDU01A	0555
NSDU05	0818
NSDU07	0818
NSDU51	1357
NSDU51A	1357
NSDU52	3294
NSDU55	3294
NSDU57	3294
NSE170	1257
NSE-181	0219
NSL5023	1605
NSL5024	5027
NSL5027	3153
NSL5053	3153
NSL5057	1951
NSL5076A	2990
NSL5253	1767
NSL5253A	1767
NSL5274	0835
NSL5353	0835
NSL5353A	3128
NSL5374	3095
NSL5753	3153
NSL5774	3067
NS060	OEM
NS061	OEM
NS063	OEM
NS064	OEM
NS066	OEM
NS067	OEM
NS069	OEM
NS070	OEM
NS072	OEM
NS073	OEM
NS075	OEM
NS078	OEM
NSQ4110L1	0411
NSS1021	0071
NT0.6C0	OEM

DEVICE TYPE	REPL CODE
NT0.6C12	0137
NT0.6C13	OEM
NT0.6C15	0002
NT0.6C16	OEM
NT0.6C18	OEM
NT0.6C20	OEM
NT0.6C22	OEM
NT0.6C24	OEM
NT0.6C27	OEM
NT0.6C30	OEM
NT0.6C33	OEM
NT0.6C36	OEM
NT0.6C39	OEM
NT0.6C43	OEM
NT0.6C47	OEM
NT0.6C51	OEM
NT0.6C56	OEM
NT3C10	0986
NT3C11	0989
NT3C12	1254
NT3C13	1240
NT3C15	1693
NT3C16	1693
NT3C18	1706
NT3C20	1720
NT3C22	0722
NT3C24	1745
NT3C27	1771
NT3C30	1761
NT3C33	1788
NT3C36	1798
NT3C39	1806
NT3C43	1815
NT3C47	1842
NT3C51	1855
NT3C56	1873
NT3C62	1884
NT3C68	1891
NT3C75	0731
NT3C82	1898
NT3C91	1903
NT3C100	0433
NT50C4V7	0446
NT55C3V3	0289
NT55C3V6	0188
NT55C3V9	0451
NT55C4V3	0528
NT55C4V7	0446
NT101	0340
NT102	0312
NT161	OEM
NT162	OEM
NT163	OEM
NT164	OEM
NT165	OEM
NT251	OEM
NT252	OEM
NT253	OEM
NT254	OEM
NT255	OEM
NT481EY	0710
NT826AB	4022
NT1056	0016
NT1503	0111
NT2222A	0079
NT2907	2245
NT3000	2293
NT5007	0037
NT5508	0289
NT5509	0188
NT5510	0451
NT5511	0528
NT5512	0446
NT6034	0111
NTC-4	0224
NTC-5	0127
NTC-6	0037
NTC-7	0076
NTC-8	0066
NTC-9	0949
NTC-10	0006
NTC-11	0076
NTC-12	0065
NTC-13	0019
NTC-14	0143
NTC-15	0124
NTC-16	0286
NTC-17	0023
NTC-18	0102
NTC-19	0015
NTC-20	0313
NTC-21	0167
NTE1V010	1681
NTE1V014	1997
NTE1V015	1304
NTE1V017	2309
NTE1V020	2763
NTE1V025	4297
NTE1V030	5638
NTE1V035	2907
NTE1V040	4199
NTE1V050	4395
NTE1V075	4834
NTE1V095	5066
NTE1V115	4072
NTE1V130	1364
NTE1V150	0246
NTE1V250	1322
NTE1V275	1648

DEVICE TYPE	REPL CODE
NTE1V300	4394
NTE2V010	1684
NTE2V014	1998
NTE2V015	1309
NTE2V017	2310
NTE2V020	2769
NTE2V025	3044
NTE2V030	3046
NTE2V035	2913
NTE2V040	3049
NTE2V050	3056
NTE2V075	3075
NTE2V095	3087
NTE2V115	3094
NTE2V130	0832
NTE2V150	1982
NTE2V250	1324
NTE2V275	1650
NTE2V300	2023
NTE2V420	3226
NTE2V480	1093
NTE10	2824
NTE11	1492
NTE12	3954
NTE13	0014
NTE14	4971
NTE15	2208
NTE16	0577
NTE17	2464
NTE18	2452
NTE19	0355
NTE20	0009
NTE21	4043
NTE22	3563
NTE23	1795
NTE24	3882
NTE25	4468
NTE26	1260
NTE27	4037
NTE28	3955
NTE29	4280
NTE30	4279
NTE31	1553
NTE32	1514
NTE33	0044
NTE34	3585
NTE35	4966
NTE36	0194
NTE36MP	5294
NTE37	3082
NTE37MCP	4398
NTE38	0787
NTE39	4402
NTE40	2896
NTE41	4967
NTE42	2395
NTE43	4968
NTE44	2919
NTE45	4969
NTE46	2770
NTE47	2833
NTE48	3749
NTE49	0818
NTE50	3294
NTE51	2985
NTE52	2885
NTE53	3009
NTE54	1157
NTE54MP	5502
NTE55	0713
NTE55MCP	3740
NTE56	2058
NTE57	0625
NTE58	3196
NTE59	3601
NTE60	3656
NTE60MP	5587
NTE61	4081
NTE61MCP	2000
NTE61MP	5599
NTE62	2820
NTE63	2817
NTE64	2978
NTE65	1332
NTE66	4970
NTE67	1456
NTE68	3561
NTE68MCP	4778
NTE69	2293
NTE70	3449
NTE71	3470
NTE72	0933
NTE73	2637
NTE74	2846
NTE74C00	2100
NTE74C02	2102
NTE74C04	2930
NTE74C08	2106
NTE74C10	2107
NTE74C14	3002
NTE74C20	2110
NTE74C30	3100
NTE74C32	3105
NTE74C42	2130
NTE74C48	2135
NTE74C73	2148
NTE74C74	2149
NTE74C76	2150
NTE74C85	2157

DEVICE TYPE	REPL CODE
NTE74C90	2160
NTE74C93	2163
NTE74C95	3367
NTE74C107	3782
NTE74C151	3944
NTE74C154	3957
NTE74C157	3972
NTE74C160	3983
NTE74C161	3984
NTE74C164	3999
NTE74C173	4026
NTE74C174	4030
NTE74C175	4034
NTE74C192	4056
NTE74C193	4059
NTE74C221	3018
NTE74C240	2928
NTE74C244	4166
NTE74C373	4388
NTE74C374	4392
NTE74C901	4527
NTE74C902	4528
NTE74C903	4529
NTE74C904	4530
NTE74C922	5496
NTE74C923	5498
NTE74C925	4540
NTE74H00	0677
NTE74H01	5241
NTE74H04	1896
NTE74H05	3221
NTE74H08	5258
NTE74H10	0680
NTE74H11	2382
NTE74H20	3670
NTE74H21	4772
NTE74H22	4516
NTE74H30	5284
NTE74H40	0554
NTE74H50	1781
NTE74H51	1933
NTE74H52	2009
NTE74H53	2090
NTE74H54	2158
NTE74H55	3129
NTE74H60	5312
NTE74H61	2638
NTE74H62	2705
NTE74H71	3233
NTE74H72	3281
NTE74H73	2444
NTE74H74	2472
NTE74H76	5208
NTE74H78	5320
NTE74H87	2557
NTE74H101	5424
NTE74H102	5426
NTE74H103	2941
NTE74H106	5159
NTE74H108	0180
NTE74H183	4329
NTE74L93	0651
NTE74LS00	1519
NTE74LS01	1537
NTE74LS02	1550
NTE74LS03	1569
NTE74LS04	1585
NTE74LS05	1598
NTE74LS08	1623
NTE74LS09	1632
NTE74LS10	1652
NTE74LS11	1657
NTE74LS12	1669
NTE74LS13	1678
NTE74LS14	1688
NTE74LS15	1697
NTE74LS20	0035
NTE74LS21	1752
NTE74LS22	1764
NTE74LS26	1372
NTE74LS27	0183
NTE74LS28	0467
NTE74LS30	0822
NTE74LS32	0088
NTE74LS33	1821
NTE74LS37	1719
NTE74LS38	1828
NTE74LS40	0135
NTE74LS42	1830
NTE74LS47	1834
NTE74LS48	1838
NTE74LS49	1839
NTE74LS51	1027
NTE74LS54	1846
NTE74LS55	0452
NTE74LS63	1853
NTE74LS73	1856
NTE74LS74A	0243
NTE74LS75	1859
NTE74LS76A	2166
NTE74LS77	1861
NTE74LS78	1862
NTE74LS83A	2204
NTE74LS85	0426
NTE74LS86	0288
NTE74LS90	1871
NTE74LS91	1874
NTE74LS92	1876
NTE74LS93	1877

DEVICE TYPE	REPL CODE
NTE74LS95B	0766
NTE74LS107	1592
NTE74LS109A	1895
NTE74LS112A	2115
NTE74LS113	2241
NTE74LS114	2286
NTE74LS122	1610
NTE74LS123	0973
NTE74LS124	5851
NTE74LS125A	0075
NTE74LS126A	2850
NTE74LS132	1615
NTE74LS133	3366
NTE74LS136	1618
NTE74LS138	0422
NTE74LS139	0153
NTE74LS145	1554
NTE74LS147	4330
NTE74LS148	3856
NTE74LS151	1636
NTE74LS153	0953
NTE74LS155	0209
NTE74LS156	1644
NTE74LS157	1153
NTE74LS158	1646
NTE74LS160A	0831
NTE74LS161A	0852
NTE74LS162A	0874
NTE74LS163A	0887
NTE74LS164	4274
NTE74LS164A	OEM
NTE74LS165	4289
NTE74LS166	4301
NTE74LS168A	0961
NTE74LS169A	0980
NTE74LS170	2605
NTE74LS173A	5125
NTE74LS174	0260
NTE74LS175	1662
NTE74LS181	1668
NTE74LS190	1676
NTE74LS191	1677
NTE74LS192	1679
NTE74LS193	1682
NTE74LS194	1294
NTE74LS194A	1294
NTE74LS195A	1305
NTE74LS196	2807
NTE74LS197	2450
NTE74LS221	1230
NTE74LS240	0447
NTE74LS241	1715
NTE74LS242	1717
NTE74LS243	0900
NTE74LS244	0453
NTE74LS245	0458
NTE74LS246A	OEM
NTE74LS247	1721
NTE74LS248	1723
NTE74LS249	1724
NTE74LS251	1726
NTE74LS253	1728
NTE74LS257	1733
NTE74LS258	1735
NTE74LS259	3175
NTE74LS260	5859
NTE74LS266	0587
NTE74LS273	0888
NTE74LS279	3259
NTE74LS280	1762
NTE74LS283	5861
NTE74LS290	4352
NTE74LS293	0082
NTE74LS295	5862
NTE74LS295A	2212
NTE74LS298	3337
NTE74LS299	4353
NTE74LS324	5864
NTE74LS327	5866
NTE74LS348	0660
NTE74LS352	0756
NTE74LS353	0768
NTE74LS363	5869
NTE74LS364	5870
NTE74LS365A	0937
NTE74LS366A	0950
NTE74LS367	0971
NTE74LS368	0985
NTE74LS373	0704
NTE74LS374	0708
NTE74LS377	1112
NTE74LS378	1125
NTE74LS379	1143
NTE74LS386	1221
NTE74LS390	1278
NTE74LS393	0813
NTE74LS395A	1320
NTE74LS396	5872
NTE74LS398	1373
NTE74LS445	5875
NTE74LS490	2199
NTE74LS540	2519
NTE74LS541	2525
NTE74LS624	3112
NTE74LS625	3120
NTE74LS626	3125
NTE74LS627	3133
NTE74LS629	3146
NTE74LS640	0664

DEVICE TYPE	REPL CODE
NTE74LS641	0685
NTE74LS642	0714
NTE74LS643	2045
NTE74LS645	0770
NTE74LS670	1122
NTE74S00	0699
NTE74S02	2223
NTE74S03	2203
NTE74S04	2248
NTE74S05	2305
NTE74S08	2547
NTE74S09	2642
NTE74S10	2426
NTE74S11	2428
NTE74S15	2432
NTE74S20	1011
NTE74S22	2442
NTE74S30	3681
NTE74S37	5648
NTE74S38	0775
NTE74S40	2456
NTE74S51	4241
NTE74S64	2476
NTE74S65	2477
NTE74S74	2483
NTE74S85	5664
NTE74S86	2489
NTE74S112	1607
NTE74S113	1613
NTE74S114	1619
NTE74S124	2113
NTE74S132	2121
NTE74S133	1808
NTE74S134	1816
NTE74S138	2125
NTE74S140	1875
NTE74S151	1944
NTE74S153	2138
NTE74S157	1685
NTE74S158	2141
NTE74S163	2143
NTE74S174	2119
NTE74S175	2128
NTE74S181	2151
NTE74S182	2152
NTE74S194	1920
NTE74S251	2184
NTE74S257	2190
NTE74S258	2191
NTE74S260	2193
NTE74S280	2205
NTE74S287	2209
NTE74S288	2161
NTE74S373	2249
NTE74S374	2251
NTE74S387	1907
NTE74S472	2304
NTE74S474	2306
NTE74S475	2308
NTE74S570	2372
NTE74S571	2373
NTE74S572	2374
NTE74S573	2376
NTE75	2936
NTE76	2059
NTE76MP	5819
NTE77	2194
NTE78	4972
NTE79	3747
NTE80	2575
NTE80C95	3148
NTE80C96	3150
NTE80C97	3151
NTE81	2034
NTE82	2449
NTE83	4930
NTE84	4974
NTE85	0284
NTE86	2526
NTE87	0861
NTE87MP	5896
NTE88	3459
NTE88MCP	4420
NTE88MP	5903
NTE89	0055
NTE90	0525
NTE91	0643
NTE92	2261
NTE93	3537
NTE93L08	2114
NTE93L16	2660
NTE93MCP	3271
NTE94	0270
NTE95	4187
NTE96	3969
NTE96L02	1459
NTE96LS02	2906
NTE96S02	4228
NTE97	1980
NTE98	2602
NTE99	3956
NTE100	0279
NTE101	0595
NTE102	0211
NTE102A	0004
NTE103	0038
NTE103A	0208
NTE104	0085
NTE104MP	3004

DEVICE TYPE	REPL CODE
NTE105	0435
NTE106	0150
NTE107	0127
NTE108	0144
NTE108-1	3729
NTE109	0143
NTE110MP	0123
NTE112	0911
NTE113A	0196
NTE114	0479
NTE115	1073
NTE116	0015
NTE116(4)	OEM
NTE117	4549
NTE118	0769
NTE119	OEM
NTE120	0469
NTE121	0160
NTE121MP	0265
NTE123	0198
NTE123A	0016
NTE123AP	0076
NTE124	0142
NTE125	0071
NTE125(2)	OEM
NTE126	0050
NTE126A	0628
NTE127	0969
NTE128	0086
NTE128P	4945
NTE129	0126
NTE129MCP	4100
NTE129P	1587
NTE130	0103
NTE130MP	1506
NTE131	0222
NTE131MP	0816
NTE132	3667
NTE133	3443
NTE134A	0188
NTE135A	0162
NTE136A	0157
NTE137A	0631
NTE138A	0644
NTE139A	0012
NTE140A	0170
NTE141A	0789
NTE142A	0137
NTE143A	0361
NTE144A	0100
NTE145A	0002
NTE146A	0436
NTE147A	0039
NTE148A	1823
NTE149A	0778
NTE150A	0327
NTE151A	0149
NTE152	0236
NTE152MP	4998
NTE153	0919
NTE153MCP	4156
NTE154	0233
NTE155	2736
NTE156	0087
NTE156A	5098
NTE157	0275
NTE158	0164
NTE159	0037
NTE159MCP	1371
NTE160	0050
NTE161	0007
NTE162	0074
NTE163A	0637
NTE164	0003
NTE165	0065
NTE166	0276
NTE167	0287
NTE168	0293
NTE169	0299
NTE170	0250
NTE171	0283
NTE172A	0396
NTE173BP	0290
NTE174	0918
NTE175	0178
NTE176	0841
NTE177	0133
NTE178MP	0907
NTE179	0599
NTE179MP	5439
NTE180	1671
NTE180MCP	3093
NTE181	0130
NTE181MP	5377
NTE182	0556
NTE183	1190
NTE184	0161
NTE184MP	5494
NTE185	0455
NTE185MCP	4525
NTE186	0555
NTE186A	0219
NTE187	1257
NTE187A	1045
NTE188	0546
NTE189	0378
NTE190	0264
NTE191	0334
NTE192	0590

If replacement code is OEM, contact original manufacturer for replacement.

505

DEVICE TYPE	REPL CODE
NTE192A	0218
NTE193	0786
NTE193A	1233
NTE194	0855
NTE195A	0693
NTE196	0419
NTE197	0848
NTE198	0168
NTE199	0111
NTE209	3467
NTE210	0561
NTE211	1357
NTE213	0432
NTE214	3700
NTE215	3702
NTE216	1518
NTE217	3704
NTE218	0899
NTE219	0486
NTE219MCP	5401
NTE220	0843
NTE221	0349
NTE222	0212
NTE224	0626
NTE225	3249
NTE226	1004
NTE226MP	1851
NTE227	3708
NTE228A	1698
NTE229	0224
NTE230	0239
NTE231	0061
NTE232	3477
NTE233	0326
NTE234	0688
NTE235	0930
NTE236	0830
NTE237	1401
NTE238	0309
NTE239	2320
NTE240	3712
NTE241	2969
NTE242	3136
NTE243	2411
NTE244	2262
NTE245	3339
NTE246	3340
NTE247	2422
NTE248	2415
NTE249	1384
NTE250	2429
NTE251	3483
NTE252	3484
NTE253	0553
NTE253MCP	6603
NTE254	2869
NTE255	3718
NTE256	3719
NTE257	3343
NTE258	3486
NTE259	3487
NTE260	3488
NTE261	1203
NTE262	0597
NTE263	2220
NTE264	2222
NTE265	2243
NTE266	3490
NTE267	3491
NTE268	3492
NTE269	3493
NTE270	0134
NTE271	0073
NTE272	3495
NTE273	3496
NTE274	3336
NTE275	3497
NTE276	1642
NTE277	2200
NTE278	0414
NTE280	0177
NTE280MP	2127
NTE281	2002
NTE281MCP	5669
NTE282	0617
NTE283	0359
NTE284	0538
NTE284MP	2355
NTE285	1588
NTE285MCP	6002
NTE286	1021
NTE287	0710
NTE288	0338
NTE289	0155
NTE289A	0155
NTE289AMP	1215
NTE289MP	2740
NTE290	0006
NTE290A	0006
NTE290AMCP	3644
NTE291	0236
NTE292	0676
NTE292MCP	3224
NTE293	0018
NTE293MP	3020
NTE294	0527
NTE295	1581
NTE296	2186
NTE297	0320
NTE297MP	3217
NTE298	0431
NTE299	2039
NTE300	2035
NTE300MP	3342
NTE302	1165
NTE306	1935
NTE307	1421
NTE308	1702
NTE308P	4534
NTE309K	1911
NTE310	2313
NTE310P	4526
NTE311	0488
NTE312	0321
NTE313	0470
NTE314	1814
NTE315	1967
NTE316	0259
NTE317	2918
NTE318	2296
NTE319	0008
NTE319P	0008
NTE320	1963
NTE320F	2857
NTE321	1740
NTE322	1973
NTE323	0886
NTE324	1471
NTE325	1189
NTE326	2959
NTE327	2465
NTE328	0615
NTE329	2675
NTE330	3517
NTE331	0477
NTE331MP	4121
NTE332	1359
NTE332MCP	3892
NTE333	2808
NTE334	3519
NTE335	3521
NTE336	3523
NTE337	3524
NTE338	3525
NTE338F	5110
NTE339	3526
NTE340	2699
NTE341	3528
NTE342	2693
NTE343	2694
NTE344	2504
NTE345	3012
NTE346	2030
NTE347	3532
NTE348	3534
NTE349	2156
NTE350	1224
NTE350F	5209
NTE351	1966
NTE352	3165
NTE353	3536
NTE354	3538
NTE355	3539
NTE356	3540
NTE357	3542
NTE358	1024
NTE358A	4391
NTE358B	4947
NTE358C	5406
NTE359	3543
NTE360	2485
NTE361	2028
NTE362	3516
NTE363	2080
NTE364	1410
NTE365	2082
NTE366	3545
NTE367	2841
NTE368	3547
NTE369	2085
NTE373	0558
NTE374	0520
NTE375	0388
NTE376	1077
NTE377	0060
NTE378	1298
NTE379	0723
NTE380	2911
NTE380MP	2708
NTE381	3527
NTE382	1376
NTE383	0472
NTE384	0424
NTE385	1955
NTE386	1841
NTE387	2416
NTE387MP	3158
NTE388	2398
NTE389	0223
NTE390	3052
NTE391	0853
NTE392	3557
NTE393	3558
NTE394	2589
NTE395	3562
NTE396	0187
NTE397	0434
NTE398	1638
NTE399	0261
NTE451	1382
NTE452	2861
NTE453	3043
NTE454	2439
NTE455	0367
NTE456	3577
NTE457	2922
NTE458	1747
NTE459	3104
NTE460	1133
NTE461	2917
NTE462	3583
NTE464	0838
NTE465	0977
NTE466	1147
NTE467	3102
NTE470	3586
NTE471	2523
NTE472	3387
NTE473	3293
NTE474	3587
NTE475	3289
NTE476	3290
NTE477	3090
NTE478	3591
NTE480	3593
NTE481	3595
NTE482	3596
NTE483	3597
NTE484	3598
NTE485	3599
NTE486	0684
NTE488	2677
NTE500A	0190
NTE502	0201
NTE503	0286
NTE504	0374
NTE505	0752
NTE506	0102
NTE507	0914
NTE508	1296
NTE509	2072
NTE510	2073
NTE511	1440
NTE512	2074
NTE513	1313
NTE514	3604
NTE515	1208
NTE518	1780
NTE519	0124
NTE521	3805
NTE522	1493
NTE523	1061
NTE524V13	0824
NTE524V15	3381
NTE524V25	1326
NTE524V27	4780
NTE524V30	4785
NTE524V42	3806
NTE524V48	0776
NTE525	0344
NTE526A	1696
NTE527A	5625
NTE528	2097
NTE529	2524
NTE530	3610
NTE531	2777
NTE532	0405
NTE533	1700
NTE534	2954
NTE535	2957
NTE536A	1986
NTE537	1188
NTE538	2956
NTE539	1048
NTE541	3613
NTE542	3614
NTE544	3615
NTE546	3616
NTE548	3617
NTE549	6429
NTE551	0182
NTE552	3494
NTE553	0163
NTE555	2496
NTE556	3621
NTE557	3622
NTE558	0017
NTE559	3818
NTE565	3624
NTE568	2647
NTE568A	5704
NTE578	3834
NTE579	3559
NTE580	0031
NTE581	1137
NTE582	3835
NTE583	3837
NTE584	0335
NTE585	0730
NTE586	2520
NTE587	1082
NTE588	0541
NTE590	3163
NTE591	3840
NTE592	3841
NTE593	3703
NTE594	3842
NTE595	0901
NTE596	0897
NTE597	1119
NTE598	1654
NTE599	3507
NTE600	1914
NTE601	0139
NTE604	3638
NTE605	0120
NTE605A	0339
NTE606	3639
NTE607	3407
NTE610	0549
NTE611	0005
NTE612	0715
NTE613	0623
NTE614	0030
NTE615	3417
NTE615A	OEM
NTE615P	1319
NTE616	1023
NTE617	3642
NTE618	3643
NTE684	0301
NTE700	3674
NTE701	3675
NTE702	2774
NTE703	0627
NTE703A	5849
NTE704	2600
NTE705A	2147
NTE706	2549
NTE707	0748
NTE708	0659
NTE709	0673
NTE710	0823
NTE711	2689
NTE712	0167
NTE713	0661
NTE714	0348
NTE715	0350
NTE716	3677
NTE718	0649
NTE720	0438
NTE721	2264
NTE722	0696
NTE723	1335
NTE724	0817
NTE725	0687
NTE726	2593
NTE727	2507
NTE728	2527
NTE729	0324
NTE730	2716
NTE731	2438
NTE734	6448
NTE736	1748
NTE737	1434
NTE738	0850
NTE739	0746
NTE740A	0375
NTE742	3690
NTE743	1385
NTE744	1411
NTE745	2902
NTE746	0780
NTE747	1797
NTE748	0784
NTE749	0391
NTE750	3189
NTE754	0718
NTE760	2089
NTE778A	0356
NTE778S	1689
NTE778SM	5433
NTE780	0360
NTE781	2720
NTE783	0797
NTE784	2674
NTE785	2681
NTE786	2688
NTE787	2242
NTE788	2728
NTE789	1832
NTE790	0345
NTE791	1327
NTE793	2032
NTE795	3166
NTE797	0516
NTE798	1742
NTE799	1601
NTE801	0514
NTE802	3715
NTE803	3717
NTE804	2535
NTE806	3388
NTE807	3720
NTE809	2663
NTE810A	2460
NTE815	0842
NTE818	2480
NTE819	1867
NTE820	2790
NTE821	2804
NTE822	2785
NTE823	3034
NTE824	3050
NTE825	3070
NTE826	3905
NTE828	3057
NTE829	1888
NTE832	3733
NTE832SM	5943
NTE834	0176
NTE834SM	2715
NTE835	3363
NTE836	2473
NTE841	3735
NTE842	3919
NTE843	2481
NTE844	3920
NTE845	3921
NTE846	1508
NTE848	3924
NTE849	3739
NTE850	3926
NTE851	3741
NTE852	2011
NTE853	3742
NTE854	3929
NTE855	0808
NTE856	3744
NTE857M	3627
NTE857SM	6209
NTE858M	3695
NTE858SM	4044
NTE859	3357
NTE859SM	4073
NTE860	3746
NTE861	3932
NTE862	3027
NTE863	3933
NTE864	0301
NTE867	3938
NTE868	3940
NTE869	2866
NTE871	3360
NTE873	2095
NTE874	3945
NTE875	1096
NTE876	3033
NTE877	3948
NTE878	1415
NTE887M	3152
NTE888M	3885
NTE889M	3288
NTE900	2662
NTE901	2664
NTE902	2721
NTE903	2515
NTE904	1843
NTE905	2673
NTE906	2676
NTE907	2685
NTE908	2680
NTE909	1291
NTE909D	1695
NTE910	1786
NTE910D	1789
NTE911	1879
NTE911D	1886
NTE912	1686
NTE913	3757
NTE914	2701
NTE915	1545
NTE916	2722
NTE917	2696
NTE918	2540
NTE918M	2545
NTE918SM	2543
NTE919	2552
NTE919D	2548
NTE921	3641
NTE922	1804
NTE922M	2093
NTE922SM	4106
NTE923	1183
NTE923D	0026
NTE924	2207
NTE924M	2495
NTE925	2863
NTE926	3748
NTE927	1113
NTE927D	1110
NTE927SM	4209
NTE928	1667
NTE928M	0765
NTE928S	3202
NTE928SM	2854
NTE929	2724
NTE930	2755
NTE931	1905
NTE932	2836
NTE933	3359
NTE934	3761
NTE935	2710
NTE936	3762
NTE937	3576
NTE937M	5901
NTE938	0890
NTE938M	2231
NTE939	3766
NTE940	1908
NTE941	0406
NTE941D	1964
NTE941M	0308
NTE941S	6045
NTE941SM	1965
NTE942	3000
NTE943	3767
NTE943M	0624
NTE943SM	3089
NTE944	3768
NTE944M	3400
NTE946	3618
NTE947	2352
NTE947D	2342
NTE948	2796
NTE948SM	2789
NTE949	2530
NTE950	1817
NTE951	3361
NTE952	3769
NTE953	3771
NTE954	3772
NTE955M	0967
NTE955MC	0580
NTE955S	3899
NTE955SM	2744
NTE956	2541
NTE957	2709
NTE958	2244
NTE959	3774
NTE960	0619
NTE961	1275
NTE962	0917
NTE963	2624
NTE964	1187
NTE965	2764
NTE966	0330
NTE967	1827
NTE968	1311
NTE969	3777
NTE970	2811
NTE971	3531
NTE972	2224
NTE973	0413
NTE973D	3751
NTE974	0011
NTE975	1290
NTE975SM	2339
NTE976	2267
NTE977	1288
NTE978	3254
NTE978C	2842
NTE978SM	2583
NTE979	OEM
NTE980	3779
NTE981	0083
NTE982	2803
NTE983	3391
NTE984	3239
NTE985	3780
NTE986	3060
NTE987	0620
NTE987SM	3172
NTE988	2285
NTE989	3347
NTE990	1482
NTE991	3550
NTE992	2232
NTE993	3783
NTE994M	3775
NTE995	2302
NTE995M	4471
NTE996	3784
NTE997	2995
NTE998	3996
NTE1000	1226
NTE1002	0383
NTE1003	0574
NTE1004	0872
NTE1005	2546
NTE1006	1206
NTE1008	OEM
NTE1009	0837
NTE1010	0858
NTE1011	0876
NTE1012	0021
NTE1013	0138
NTE1014	0351
NTE1015	2388
NTE1016	2390
NTE1017	2423
NTE1018	2457
NTE1019	2487
NTE1022	4476
NTE1023	4477
NTE1024	3506
NTE1025	1179
NTE1027	2849
NTE1028	4479
NTE1029	2247
NTE1030	4481
NTE1031	4482
NTE1032	4483
NTE1033	4484
NTE1034	2862
NTE1035	4485
NTE1036	4486
NTE1037	4031
NTE1038	4338
NTE1039	1611
NTE1040	4489
NTE1041	4490
NTE1042	4491
NTE1043	4320
NTE1045	2377
NTE1046	0523
NTE1047	2855
NTE1048	0668
NTE1049	0648
NTE1050	2864
NTE1051	3736
NTE1052	0428
NTE1053	2551
NTE1054	2554
NTE1055	2556
NTE1056	1826
NTE1057	2555
NTE1058	2111
NTE1060	2559
NTE1061	2560
NTE1062	0399
NTE1064	2563
NTE1065	2564
NTE1066	2565
NTE1067	2566
NTE1068	2567
NTE1069	2576
NTE1070	4014
NTE1071	2580
NTE1072	2568
NTE1073	2573
NTE1074	2569
NTE1075A	0465
NTE1078	3318
NTE1079	4495
NTE1080	0849
NTE1081A	1152
NTE1082	2246
NTE1083	2827
NTE1084	2859
NTE1085	2607
NTE1086	2860
NTE1087	1012
NTE1089	0633
NTE1090	2834
NTE1091	0958
NTE1092	2300
NTE1093	4498
NTE1094	0043
NTE1095	OEM
NTE1096	1624
NTE1097	3232
NTE1098	3901
NTE1099	4196
NTE1100	0905
NTE1101	2610
NTE1102	2608
NTE1103	1983
NTE1104	2046
NTE1105	4502
NTE1106	2606
NTE1107	3625
NTE1108	1383
NTE1109	2615
NTE1110	2289
NTE1112	2462
NTE1114	4506
NTE1115	1239
NTE1115A	3866
NTE1116	4084
NTE1117	3946
NTE1119	4509
NTE1120	2020
NTE1121	0385
NTE1122	0602
NTE1123	3973
NTE1124	4463
NTE1126	4513
NTE1127	4348
NTE1128	3859
NTE1130	1316
NTE1131	4514
NTE1132	4515
NTE1133	2216
NTE1134	2921
NTE1135	2051
NTE1137	2571
NTE1139	3880
NTE1140	2845
NTE1141	3788
NTE1142	1469
NTE1148	2837
NTE1149	4517
NTE1150	4518
NTE1151	4990
NTE1152	2484
NTE1153	3332
NTE1154	4520
NTE1155	1044
NTE1156	2988
NTE1158	0875
NTE1159	0878
NTE1160	3650
NTE1161	2914
NTE1162	3977
NTE1162A	OEM
NTE1163	2581
NTE1164	4992
NTE1165	2746
NTE1166	2754
NTE1167	1704
NTE1168	2579
NTE1169	4331

If replacement code is OEM, contact original manufacturer for replacement.

Original Device Types

DEVICE TYPE	REPL CODE
NTE1170	2512
NTE1171	0093
NTE1172	1369
NTE1173	3242
NTE1174	2038
NTE1175	2759
NTE1176	2762
NTE1177	2771
NTE1178	3660
NTE1179	2550
NTE1180	2590
NTE1181	2570
NTE1183	4133
NTE1184	4532
NTE1185	1470
NTE1186	0846
NTE1187	0851
NTE1188	2594
NTE1189	4325
NTE1191	4025
NTE1192	1532
NTE1193	3286
NTE1194	1805
NTE1195	4145
NTE1196	1049
NTE1197	4539
NTE1198	2238
NTE1199	3754
NTE1200	4174
NTE1201	4541
NTE1202	2364
NTE1203	2290
NTE1204	4405
NTE1205	2903
NTE1206	4542
NTE1209	4544
NTE1210	2609
NTE1211	2179
NTE1212	4545
NTE1213	4546
NTE1214	0646
NTE1215	2510
NTE1216	0910
NTE1217	0412
NTE1218	1561
NTE1219	1602
NTE1221	4550
NTE1223	1516
NTE1224	4024
NTE1226	0701
NTE1227	0616
NTE1228	3161
NTE1229	4551
NTE1230	2644
NTE1231	1162
NTE1231A	1051
NTE1232	1042
NTE1233	4160
NTE1234	2008
NTE1235	4552
NTE1236	2268
NTE1237	3606
NTE1239	3231
NTE1240	4006
NTE1241	2614
NTE1242	1501
NTE1243	4553
NTE1245	0898
NTE1246	4554
NTE1247	4555
NTE1248	1251
NTE1249	3980
NTE1250	4010
NTE1251	4556
NTE1252	4557
NTE1254	3763
NTE1255	2592
NTE1256	4559
NTE1257	4560
NTE1258	4561
NTE1260	4563
NTE1261	1120
NTE1262	4564
NTE1263	2932
NTE1264	4001
NTE1265	4002
NTE1266	4004
NTE1267	4007
NTE1268	4008
NTE1269	4017
NTE1271	4567
NTE1272	3515
NTE1273	4568
NTE1278	4571
NTE1281	4572
NTE1282	4573
NTE1283	4575
NTE1284	4576
NTE1285	0749
NTE1286	0751
NTE1287	4578
NTE1288	4493
NTE1289	4580
NTE1290	4027
NTE1291	4582
NTE1292	3416
NTE1293	4584
NTE1294	3949
NTE1295	5003

DEVICE TYPE	REPL CODE
NTE1296	0067
NTE1297	4319
NTE1298	4591
NTE1299	5004
NTE1300	3877
NTE1301	4588
NTE1302	3935
NTE1303	4589
NTE1304	3939
NTE1305	3941
NTE1306	3943
NTE1307	3947
NTE1308	3891
NTE1309	4590
NTE1310	3931
NTE1311	3876
NTE1312	3927
NTE1313	3928
NTE1319	OEM
NTE1320	4592
NTE1321	4593
NTE1322	4594
NTE1323	4595
NTE1324	4596
NTE1325	4597
NTE1326	4599
NTE1327	4600
NTE1328	4601
NTE1329	4602
NTE1330	4603
NTE1331	4604
NTE1332	4605
NTE1333	4606
NTE1334	4607
NTE1335	4608
NTE1336	4609
NTE1337	4610
NTE1338	1428
NTE1339	4612
NTE1340	4613
NTE1341	4614
NTE1342	4615
NTE1343	4617
NTE1344	4618
NTE1345	1892
NTE1346	4620
NTE1347	4621
NTE1348	4622
NTE1349	4623
NTE1350	4624
NTE1351	4625
NTE1352	4626
NTE1354	4627
NTE1355	4629
NTE1356	5008
NTE1357	5009
NTE1358	4088
NTE1359	5010
NTE1361	4632
NTE1362	5013
NTE1363	4633
NTE1364	4634
NTE1365	4635
NTE1366	4636
NTE1367	4637
NTE1368	4638
NTE1369	4639
NTE1370	4641
NTE1371	4642
NTE1372	4643
NTE1373	3860
NTE1374	3665
NTE1375	2767
NTE1376	3666
NTE1377	3299
NTE1378	4644
NTE1379	4645
NTE1380	4646
NTE1381	4647
NTE1382	1940
NTE1383	4648
NTE1384	4649
NTE1385	4651
NTE1386	3209
NTE1387	4302
NTE1388	4653
NTE1389	4654
NTE1390	5015
NTE1391	4655
NTE1392	4656
NTE1393	4658
NTE1394	4659
NTE1395	4035
NTE1396	0491
NTE1397	5016
NTE1398	5018
NTE1399	5019
NTE1400	1572
NTE1401	3317
NTE1402	3809
NTE1403	3325
NTE1404	4662
NTE1405	4663
NTE1406	3997
NTE1407	4664
NTE1408	4665
NTE1409	0678
NTE1409N	1934
NTE1410	2599

DEVICE TYPE	REPL CODE
NTE1411	0762
NTE1412	4666
NTE1413	0069
NTE1414	4669
NTE1415	4416
NTE1416	0485
NTE1417	2601
NTE1418	4102
NTE1419	4670
NTE1420	0548
NTE1421	4671
NTE1422	1575
NTE1423	4227
NTE1424	4399
NTE1425	4677
NTE1426	0670
NTE1427	4678
NTE1428	1570
NTE1429	4679
NTE1430	0912
NTE1431	4680
NTE1432	5026
NTE1433	4681
NTE1434	0866
NTE1435	4682
NTE1436	4355
NTE1437	4469
NTE1438	4683
NTE1439	3074
NTE1440	3692
NTE1441	4684
NTE1442	4685
NTE1443	5029
NTE1444	4005
NTE1445	1016
NTE1446	4000
NTE1447	4687
NTE1448	3989
NTE1449	4689
NTE1450	3985
NTE1451	4690
NTE1452	4692
NTE1453	2492
NTE1454	3216
NTE1455	4694
NTE1457	4695
NTE1458	4696
NTE1459	2508
NTE1460	4697
NTE1461	2686
NTE1462	4698
NTE1463	3167
NTE1464	4699
NTE1465	0358
NTE1466	2052
NTE1467	4676
NTE1468	3923
NTE1469	4700
NTE1470	3198
NTE1471	1192
NTE1472	4703
NTE1473	4705
NTE1474	4707
NTE1475	4708
NTE1476	4710
NTE1477	4711
NTE1478	4712
NTE1479	1437
NTE1480	4480
NTE1481	4714
NTE1482	4715
NTE1483	0859
NTE1484	4716
NTE1485	3564
NTE1486	3671
NTE1487	3982
NTE1488	2237
NTE1489	4719
NTE1490	4721
NTE1491	4723
NTE1492	4724
NTE1493	4725
NTE1494	4726
NTE1495	4727
NTE1496	4071
NTE1497	4728
NTE1498	4729
NTE1499	4730
NTE1500	4731
NTE1501	4733
NTE1502	4735
NTE1503	4736
NTE1504	4737
NTE1505	4739
NTE1507	4740
NTE1508	3039
NTE1509	3040
NTE1510	0804
NTE1511	4741
NTE1512	4216
NTE1513	4742
NTE1514	4743
NTE1515	4746
NTE1516	4747
NTE1517	4750
NTE1518	4751
NTE1519	4752
NTE1520	1617
NTE1521	3888

DEVICE TYPE	REPL CODE
NTE1522	2511
NTE1523	4754
NTE1525	2669
NTE1526	4757
NTE1527	4758
NTE1528	2312
NTE1529	2884
NTE1530	4760
NTE1531	4762
NTE1532	2043
NTE1533	4763
NTE1534	4765
NTE1535	5065
NTE1536	4766
NTE1537	4767
NTE1538	0328
NTE1539	1580
NTE1540	4285
NTE1541	2668
NTE1542	4243
NTE1543	4769
NTE1544	4770
NTE1545	0906
NTE1546	3462
NTE1547	0658
NTE1548	3461
NTE1549	3042
NTE1550	1420
NTE1551	3698
NTE1552	2888
NTE1553	3476
NTE1554	5067
NTE1556	5068
NTE1557	3764
NTE1558	2094
NTE1559	5069
NTE1560	1308
NTE1561	5070
NTE1562	5071
NTE1563	2898
NTE1564	OEM
NTE1565	3028
NTE1566	4521
NTE1567	3668
NTE1568	5077
NTE1569	0107
NTE1570	4899
NTE1571	5080
NTE1572	4047
NTE1573	1666
NTE1575	2170
NTE1576	3726
NTE1577	5083
NTE1578	3389
NTE1579	5085
NTE1580	0347
NTE1581	4050
NTE1582	3916
NTE1583	OEM
NTE1584	OEM
NTE1585	5088
NTE1586	OEM
NTE1588	OEM
NTE1589	0445
NTE1590	OEM
NTE1591	5089
NTE1593	5090
NTE1594	OEM
NTE1595	OEM
NTE1596	3907
NTE1597	5091
NTE1598	OEM
NTE1599	OEM
NTE1600	5093
NTE1601	OEM
NTE1602	5095
NTE1603	OEM
NTE1604	0460
NTE1605	OEM
NTE1606	5096
NTE1607	5097
NTE1608	0657
NTE1609	2513
NTE1610	3055
NTE1611	5099
NTE1612	2760
NTE1613	5100
NTE1615	4773
NTE1616	2868
NTE1617	OEM
NTE1618	3045
NTE1619	2772
NTE1620	5101
NTE1621	5102
NTE1624	5103
NTE1625	3707
NTE1626	4756
NTE1627	2781
NTE1628	2062
NTE1629	3713
NTE1630	0754
NTE1631	5105
NTE1632	5106
NTE1633	4210
NTE1634	2572
NTE1635	5107
NTE1636	2983
NTE1637	5108
NTE1639	4214

DEVICE TYPE	REPL CODE
NTE1641	5109
NTE1648	5111
NTE1649	5112
NTE1650	2109
NTE1651	4441
NTE1654	5113
NTE1655	2815
NTE1656	1433
NTE1657	4339
NTE1658	2641
NTE1659	5114
NTE1660	2632
NTE1661	4284
NTE1662	5115
NTE1663	5116
NTE1664	5117
NTE1666	5118
NTE1667	2370
NTE1668	3728
NTE1669	3250
NTE1670	4473
NTE1671	3640
NTE1672	5120
NTE1673	1977
NTE1674	0970
NTE1675	3329
NTE1676	2031
NTE1677	4923
NTE1678	4959
NTE1679	2409
NTE1680	3098
NTE1681	5122
NTE1682	5123
NTE1683	3800
NTE1684	4840
NTE1685	3223
NTE1686	OEM
NTE1687	2288
NTE1688	5126
NTE1689	0694
NTE1690	5127
NTE1691	5128
NTE1692	5129
NTE1693	5130
NTE1700	5132
NTE1701	5133
NTE1702	5134
NTE1703	3686
NTE1704	5136
NTE1705	0484
NTE1706	OEM
NTE1707	3301
NTE1708	4313
NTE1709	5137
NTE1710	2055
NTE1711	2531
NTE1712	2056
NTE1713	2057
NTE1714M	2661
NTE1714S	2015
NTE1715	2014
NTE1716	3776
NTE1717	5139
NTE1718	4194
NTE1719	2092
NTE1720	5140
NTE1721	2802
NTE1722	2814
NTE1723	2812
NTE1724	4713
NTE1725	2104
NTE1726	5141
NTE1727	3701
NTE1728	0534
NTE1729	1813
NTE1730	5143
NTE1731	5144
NTE1732	1562
NTE1733	2358
NTE1734	5145
NTE1735	2369
NTE1736	3327
NTE1737	1586
NTE1738	2852
NTE1739	1379
NTE1740	4083
NTE1741	4569
NTE1742	1631
NTE1743	3410
NTE1744	3403
NTE1745	5146
NTE1747	4281
NTE1748	3314
NTE1749	5148
NTE1750	5149
NTE1751	2180
NTE1752	3481
NTE1753	5150
NTE1754	2164
NTE1755	1086
NTE1757	5151
NTE1758	4706
NTE1759	2079
NTE1761	5153
NTE1762	5155
NTE1764	5156
NTE1771	0387
NTE1772	4286
NTE1773	0727

DEVICE TYPE	REPL CODE
NTE1774	5157
NTE1775	4074
NTE1776	3897
NTE1777	2348
NTE1778	3902
NTE1779	3848
NTE1780	1521
NTE1781	1022
NTE1782	4066
NTE1783	4131
NTE1785	5160
NTE1786	3352
NTE1787	3130
NTE1788	4314
NTE1789	4349
NTE1790	3206
NTE1791	5162
NTE1792	4009
NTE1794	2254
NTE1795	1594
NTE1796	5163
NTE1797	2929
NTE1798	3068
NTE1799	2998
NTE1800	3331
NTE1801	3830
NTE1803	3132
NTE1804	1245
NTE1805	4306
NTE1808	5165
NTE1809	5166
NTE1810	3869
NTE1811	5167
NTE1812	5168
NTE1813	5169
NTE1814	5170
NTE1815	2490
NTE1816	5172
NTE1817	5174
NTE1818	5175
NTE1819	5176
NTE1820	5177
NTE1822	2389
NTE1823	2402
NTE1824	3306
NTE1826	4312
NTE1827	3765
NTE1828	4838
NTE1829	5178
NTE1830	5179
NTE1831	5180
NTE1834	4054
NTE1835	4246
NTE1836	4310
NTE1838	0457
NTE1839	3896
NTE1840	3530
NTE1842	3680
NTE1843	4955
NTE1844	3220
NTE1845	0552
NTE1847	2099
NTE1848	2893
NTE1849	5182
NTE1852	3453
NTE1855	2330
NTE1856	0481
NTE1859	3054
NTE1860	2843
NTE1861	3871
NTE1863	4032
NTE1871	5183
NTE1872	2403
NTE1874	5184
NTE1875	5185
NTE1876	5186
NTE1877	1474
NTE1879	1430
NTE1900	5187
NTE1901	5188
NTE1902	1775
NTE1903	1825
NTE1905	4952
NTE1906	4427
NTE1907	4799
NTE1908	4430
NTE1909	1710
NTE1911	2697
NTE1912	2239
NTE1913	1993
NTE1914	3906
NTE1915	5193
NTE1916	1989
NTE1917	4429
NTE1918	2443
NTE1919	5195
NTE1920	3605
NTE1923	5196
NTE1924	3828
NTE1925	3529
NTE1926	5197
NTE1927	5198
NTE1928	2451
NTE1930	2155
NTE1932	2779
NTE1934	5199
NTE1934X	2517
NTE1936	4264
NTE1938	5202

DEVICE TYPE	REPL CODE
NTE1940	5203
NTE2000	5211
NTE2001	3684
NTE2003	4846
NTE2004	4045
NTE2011	0839
NTE2012	1001
NTE2013	1126
NTE2014	1252
NTE2015	4848
NTE2016	4849
NTE2017	4850
NTE2018	4852
NTE2019	4853
NTE2020	4854
NTE2021	3839
NTE2022	3864
NTE2023	2723
NTE2024	2800
NTE2025	4856
NTE2026	4019
NTE2027	1691
NTE2028	1782
NTE2029	4860
NTE2030	1866
NTE2031	4862
NTE2032	4863
NTE2047	5216
NTE2050	4864
NTE2051	4865
NTE2053	3743
NTE2054	4867
NTE2055	0482
NTE2056	5217
NTE2060	2279
NTE2061	2702
NTE2062	3925
NTE2070	4868
NTE2071	4869
NTE2072	4870
NTE2073	4872
NTE2074	4456
NTE2075	4874
NTE2076	4875
NTE2077	4876
NTE2078	4878
NTE2079	0963
NTE2080	4879
NTE2081	4880
NTE2082	4881
NTE2083	4882
NTE2084	4075
NTE2085	4781
NTE2086	5218
NTE2087	4883
NTE2088	5219
NTE2090	OEM
NTE2102	4886
NTE2104	4887
NTE2107	4815
NTE2114	2037
NTE2117	0518
NTE2128	1887
NTE2147	1683
NTE2164	2341
NTE2300	3326
NTE2301	3437
NTE2302	1533
NTE2303	2739
NTE2304	2351
NTE2305	3401
NTE2306	3628
NTE2307	2973
NTE2308	2171
NTE2309	2757
NTE2310	4376
NTE2311	1498
NTE2312	2880
NTE2313	3504
NTE2314	5244
NTE2315	1503
NTE2316	5245
NTE2317	4269
NTE2318	5248
NTE2319	3354
NTE2320	2976
NTE2321	0539
NTE2322	0281
NTE2323	5251
NTE2324	3454
NTE2325	3323
NTE2326	OEM
NTE2327	3187
NTE2328	3402
NTE2329	5252
NTE2330	3474
NTE2331	2116
NTE2332	0277
NTE2334	2350
NTE2336	3678
NTE2338	1055
NTE2340	5253
NTE2349	2412
NTE2350	2404
NTE2351	5255
NTE2352	5256
NTE2355	0826
NTE2356	4109
NTE2357	0881

If replacement code is OEM, contact original manufacturer for replacement.

DEVICE TYPE	REPL CODE
NTE2358	3114
NTE2359	0892
NTE2360	4067
NTE2361	2926
NTE2362	0013
NTE2380	1457
NTE2381	5263
NTE2382	3059
NTE2383	2256
NTE2386	1658
NTE2390	5264
NTE2392	5266
NTE2401	4410
NTE2402	4419
NTE2403	4419
NTE2404	5267
NTE2405	5268
NTE2406	1722
NTE2407	1741
NTE2408	0719
NTE2409	1731
NTE2410	OEM
NTE2411	5269
NTE2412	3345
NTE2413	5271
NTE2414	3442
NTE2415	1881
NTE2416	0975
NTE2417	0698
NTE2418	3439
NTE2419	3241
NTE2426	5272
NTE2427	5273
NTE2428	0662
NTE2429	3600
NTE2430	3433
NTE2431	5274
NTE2532	5007
NTE2708	4351
NTE2716	2263
NTE2732	2672
NTE2732A	6283
NTE2764	0806
NTE2800	1835
NTE2909	OEM
NTE3000	1970
NTE3001	1978
NTE3002	1974
NTE3003	1972
NTE3004	5020
NTE3005	5021
NTE3006	5022
NTE3007	2990
NTE3008	3067
NTE3009	5023
NTE3010	0835
NTE3011	3095
NTE3012	5024
NTE3012A	OEM
NTE3013	5025
NTE3014	3420
NTE3015	3421
NTE3016	3693
NTE3018	1605
NTE3019	5027
NTE3020	1348
NTE3021	3128
NTE3022	1951
NTE3023	3245
NTE3024	1767
NTE3025	3153
NTE3026	2181
NTE3027	4120
NTE3028	0586
NTE3029	3203
NTE3029A	3203
NTE3030	3965
NTE3031	5030
NTE3032	2297
NTE3033	2604
NTE3034	3825
NTE3034A	3825
NTE3035	3156
NTE3035A	3156
NTE3036	3508
NTE3037	5031
NTE3038	5032
NTE3039	5033
NTE3040	0536
NTE3041	0311
NTE3042	0272
NTE3043	4358
NTE3044	4845
NTE3045	2096
NTE3046	2221
NTE3047	4961
NTE3048	4975
NTE3049	5034
NTE3050	4900
NTE3051	4901
NTE3052	4783
NTE3053	5035
NTE3054	5036
NTE3055	5037
NTE3056	4786
NTE3057	4127
NTE3058	5038
NTE3059	5039
NTE3060	5040

DEVICE TYPE	REPL CODE
NTE3061	4902
NTE3062	5042
NTE3063	5043
NTE3064	5045
NTE3065	4784
NTE3068	5046
NTE3069	5047
NTE3070	5048
NTE3071	5049
NTE3074	4262
NTE3075	4267
NTE3076	4266
NTE3077	4268
NTE3078	2192
NTE3079	2185
NTE3080	2362
NTE3081	3333
NTE3082	5050
NTE3083	1101
NTE3084	1047
NTE3085	5323
NTE3086	1393
NTE3087	5325
NTE3088	5326
NTE3089	5327
NTE3090	5328
NTE3091	0235
NTE3092	1281
NTE3093	5329
NTE3095	5330
NTE3096	5331
NTE3097	5332
NTE3098	0112
NTE3099	2678
NTE3100	1407
NTE3101	2612
NTE3102	2616
NTE3103	5335
NTE3111	5336
NTE3112	5337
NTE3113	5338
NTE3114	5060
NTE3115	5062
NTE3116	5063
NTE3117	5064
NTE3120	2083
NTE3121	3930
NTE3130	5341
NTE3131	4928
NTE3150	5073
NTE3151	5075
NTE3152	5076
NTE3153	5078
NTE3154	5119
NTE3155	5079
NTE3160	5082
NTE3161	1069
NTE3162	5084
NTE3163	4686
NTE3164	3450
NTE3165	5086
NTE3166	3990
NTE3167	1123
NTE3168	5087
NTE3169	5346
NTE3170	5347
NTE3171	4973
NTE3180	5349
NTE3181	5350
NTE3182	5351
NTE3470	2732
NTE3880	3441
NTE3881	1893
NTE3882	5242
NTE4000	2013
NTE4001B	0473
NTE4002B	2044
NTE4006B	0641
NTE4007	2819
NTE4008B	0982
NTE4011B	0215
NTE4012B	0493
NTE4013B	0409
NTE4014B	0854
NTE4015B	1008
NTE4016B	1135
NTE4017B	0508
NTE4018B	1381
NTE4019B	1517
NTE4020B	1651
NTE4021B	1738
NTE4022B	1247
NTE4023B	0515
NTE4024B	1946
NTE4025B	2061
NTE4026B	2139
NTE4027B	1938
NTE4028B	2213
NTE4029B	2218
NTE4030B	0495
NTE4031B	2943
NTE4032B	2509
NTE4033B	2611
NTE4034B	3570
NTE4035B	2750
NTE4038B	2953
NTE4040B	0056
NTE4041	3145
NTE4042B	0121

DEVICE TYPE	REPL CODE
NTE4043B	1544
NTE4044B	2292
NTE4045B	3408
NTE4046B	3394
NTE4047B	2315
NTE4048B	3423
NTE4049	0001
NTE4050B	0394
NTE4051B	0362
NTE4052B	0024
NTE4053B	0034
NTE4055B	3272
NTE4056B	3661
NTE4060B	0146
NTE4063B	3682
NTE4066B	0101
NTE4067B	3696
NTE4068B	2482
NTE4069	0119
NTE4070B	2494
NTE4071B	0129
NTE4072B	2502
NTE4073B	1528
NTE4075B	2518
NTE4076B	3455
NTE4077B	2536
NTE4078B	0915
NTE4081B	0621
NTE4082B	0297
NTE4085B	0300
NTE4086B	0530
NTE4089B	3778
NTE4093B	2368
NTE4094B	1672
NTE4095B	3796
NTE4096B	3798
NTE4097B	3802
NTE4098B	3566
NTE4099B	3297
NTE4164	5473
NTE4501	3758
NTE4502B	1031
NTE4503B	2042
NTE4506B	3721
NTE4508B	1800
NTE4510B	1952
NTE4511B	1535
NTE4512B	2108
NTE4513B	4889
NTE4514B	1819
NTE4515B	3555
NTE4516B	2331
NTE4517B	4220
NTE4518B	1037
NTE4520B	2650
NTE4521B	4903
NTE4522B	2810
NTE4526B	3565
NTE4527B	3116
NTE4528B	3168
NTE4529B	4451
NTE4531B	3292
NTE4532B	1010
NTE4536B	3659
NTE4538B	1057
NTE4539B	3611
NTE4541B	4929
NTE4543B	4932
NTE4547B	4943
NTE4551B	4950
NTE4553B	4951
NTE4555B	2910
NTE4556B	3397
NTE4558B	4960
NTE4566B	3463
NTE4569B	4408
NTE4583B	1286
NTE4584B	5000
NTE4585B	1365
NTE4597B	4048
NTE4598B	4237
NTE4900	2380
NTE4902	3085
NTE4903	2120
NTE4918	3143
NTE4919	1161
NTE4926	3162
NTE4927	1756
NTE4928	3171
NTE4929	1921
NTE4934	1904
NTE4935	1941
NTE4950	0563
NTE4951	1961
NTE4958	0825
NTE4959	1976
NTE4988	1395
NTE4989	1398
NTE5000A	1266
NTE5001A	2847
NTE5002A	0755
NTE5003A	0672
NTE5004A	0118
NTE5005A	0296
NTE5006A	0372
NTE5007A	0036
NTE5008A	0274
NTE5009A	0140
NTE5010A	0041

DEVICE TYPE	REPL CODE
NTE5010T1	0582
NTE5011A	0253
NTE5011T1	0877
NTE5012A	0091
NTE5013A	0466
NTE5013T1	0292
NTE5014A	0062
NTE5015A	0077
NTE5016A	0165
NTE5017A	0318
NTE5018A	0057
NTE5019A	0064
NTE5019T1	0248
NTE5020A	0181
NTE5021A	0052
NTE5021T1	0999
NTE5022A	0053
NTE5023A	0873
NTE5024A	0681
NTE5025A	0440
NTE5026A	0210
NTE5027A	0371
NTE5028A	0666
NTE5029A	0695
NTE5030A	0700
NTE5031A	0489
NTE5032A	0709
NTE5033A	0450
NTE5034A	0257
NTE5034C	OEM
NTE5035A	0195
NTE5036A	0166
NTE5037A	0010
NTE5038A	0032
NTE5039A	0054
NTE5040A	0068
NTE5041A	0092
NTE5042A	0125
NTE5043A	2301
NTE5044A	0152
NTE5045A	0173
NTE5046A	0094
NTE5047A	0049
NTE5048A	0104
NTE5049A	0156
NTE5050A	0189
NTE5051A	0099
NTE5052A	0089
NTE5053A	0285
NTE5054A	0252
NTE5055A	0336
NTE5056A	0366
NTE5057A	0390
NTE5058A	0420
NTE5059A	0448
NTE5060A	1464
NTE5061A	2975
NTE5062A	5740
NTE5063A	1302
NTE5064A	2981
NTE5065A	1703
NTE5066A	0289
NTE5067A	0451
NTE5068A	0528
NTE5069A	0446
NTE5070A	0298
NTE5071A	0025
NTE5072A	0244
NTE5073A	1075
NTE5074A	0313
NTE5075A	0416
NTE5076A	1639
NTE5077A	0490
NTE5078A	0943
NTE5079A	0526
NTE5080A	0560
NTE5081A	0398
NTE5082A	1596
NTE5083A	1664
NTE5084A	0721
NTE5085A	0814
NTE5086A	0346
NTE5087A	0925
NTE5088A	0993
NTE5089A	0497
NTE5090A	0863
NTE5091A	1148
NTE5092A	1258
NTE5093A	1181
NTE5093T	OEM
NTE5094A	2997
NTE5095A	1301
NTE5096A	0098
NTE5097A	0186
NTE5098A	0213
NTE5099A	0245
NTE5100A	0028
NTE5101A	0255
NTE5102A	0871
NTE5103A	0363
NTE5104A	2831
NTE5105A	0417
NTE5111A	0777
NTE5112A	0791
NTE5113A	0801
NTE5114A	0815
NTE5115A	0827
NTE5116A	0437
NTE5117A	0870

DEVICE TYPE	REPL CODE
NTE5118A	3099
NTE5119A	0185
NTE5120A	0205
NTE5121A	0475
NTE5122A	0499
NTE5123A	3285
NTE5124A	0679
NTE5125A	0225
NTE5126A	0230
NTE5127A	0234
NTE5128A	0237
NTE5129A	1387
NTE5130A	0247
NTE5131A	0251
NTE5132A	1170
NTE5133A	0256
NTE5134A	2379
NTE5135A	0262
NTE5136A	0269
NTE5137A	0273
NTE5138A	2383
NTE5139A	0291
NTE5140A	1169
NTE5141A	0305
NTE5142A	0314
NTE5143A	0316
NTE5144A	0322
NTE5145A	0333
NTE5146A	0343
NTE5147A	0027
NTE5148A	0266
NTE5149A	2829
NTE5150A	0382
NTE5151A	0401
NTE5152A	0421
NTE5153A	0439
NTE5154A	2999
NTE5155A	0238
NTE5156A	1172
NTE5157A	1182
NTE5158A	1198
NTE5159A	1209
NTE5160A	1870
NTE5161A	0642
NTE5162A	1246
NTE5163A	2091
NTE5164A	1269
NTE5165A	2210
NTE5166A	0600
NTE5172A	4167
NTE5172AK	1000
NTE5173A	2381
NTE5173AK	1370
NTE5174A	2024
NTE5174AK	0542
NTE5175A	2385
NTE5175AK	2387
NTE5176A	1429
NTE5176AK	2101
NTE5177A	2391
NTE5177AK	2394
NTE5178A	1436
NTE5178AK	1890
NTE5179A	2399
NTE5179AK	2400
NTE5180A	2206
NTE5180AK	0691
NTE5181A	1449
NTE5181AK	1591
NTE5182A	0221
NTE5182AK	1606
NTE5183A	1481
NTE5183AK	1612
NTE5184A	2406
NTE5184AK	2408
NTE5185A	1608
NTE5185AK	0622
NTE5186A	0505
NTE5186AK	0986
NTE5187A	0686
NTE5187AK	0989
NTE5188A	0864
NTE5188AK	1254
NTE5189A	1014
NTE5189AK	1240
NTE5190A	1145
NTE5190AK	1626
NTE5191A	1264
NTE5191AK	1629
NTE5192A	1392
NTE5192AK	1693
NTE5193A	1524
NTE5193AK	1630
NTE5194A	1071
NTE5194AK	1706
NTE5195A	1701
NTE5195AK	1709
NTE5196A	1707
NTE5196AK	1720
NTE5197A	1712
NTE5197AK	0722
NTE5198A	1725
NTE5198AK	1745
NTE5199A	1737
NTE5199AK	1757
NTE5200A	1750
NTE5200AK	1771
NTE5201A	2431
NTE5201AK	2434

DEVICE TYPE	REPL CODE
NTE5202A	1761
NTE5202AK	1783
NTE5203A	1777
NTE5203AK	1788
NTE5204A	1785
NTE5204AK	1798
NTE5205A	1793
NTE5205AK	1806
NTE5206A	1185
NTE5206AK	1815
NTE5207A	1810
NTE5207AK	1829
NTE5208A	0022
NTE5208AK	1842
NTE5209A	0070
NTE5209AK	1850
NTE5210A	0132
NTE5210AK	1855
NTE5211A	0172
NTE5211AK	1863
NTE5212A	0207
NTE5212AK	1873
NTE5213A	0227
NTE5213AK	2455
NTE5214A	0263
NTE5214AK	1884
NTE5215A	0306
NTE5215AK	1891
NTE5216A	0325
NTE5216AK	0731
NTE5217A	0352
NTE5217AK	1898
NTE5218A	0377
NTE5218AK	2459
NTE5219A	0408
NTE5219AK	1903
NTE5220A	0433
NTE5220AK	1155
NTE5221A	0459
NTE5221AK	1913
NTE5222A	0483
NTE5222AK	1922
NTE5223A	0504
NTE5223AK	1930
NTE5224A	0519
NTE5224AK	1936
NTE5225A	0537
NTE5225AK	1942
NTE5226A	0063
NTE5226AK	1950
NTE5227A	0397
NTE5227AK	0353
NTE5228A	0593
NTE5228AK	2479
NTE5229A	0611
NTE5229AK	0665
NTE5230A	0629
NTE5230AK	0771
NTE5231A	0645
NTE5231AK	2486
NTE5232A	0663
NTE5232AK	1065
NTE5240A	0809
NTE5240AK	2695
NTE5241A	0821
NTE5241AK	2698
NTE5242A	0840
NTE5242AK	2700
NTE5243A	0862
NTE5243AK	2703
NTE5244A	0879
NTE5244AK	2706
NTE5245A	0891
NTE5245AK	2707
NTE5246A	0908
NTE5246AK	2711
NTE5247A	0920
NTE5247AK	2713
NTE5248A	0938
NTE5248AK	2717
NTE5249A	0952
NTE5249AK	1216
NTE5250A	0972
NTE5250AK	2719
NTE5251A	0988
NTE5251AK	1228
NTE5252A	1003
NTE5252AK	1243
NTE5253A	1013
NTE5253AK	1259
NTE5254A	0883
NTE5254AK	1267
NTE5255A	1043
NTE5255AK	1283
NTE5256A	1052
NTE5256AK	2725
NTE5257A	0926
NTE5257AK	1292
NTE5258A	1072
NTE5258AK	1300
NTE5259A	1088
NTE5259AK	2729
NTE5260A	1098
NTE5260AK	1314
NTE5261A	1115
NTE5261AK	2731
NTE5262A	1127
NTE5262AK	1323
NTE5263A	1144

DEVICE TYPE	REPL CODE
NTE5263AK	1334
NTE5264A	1156
NTE5264AK	1346
NTE5265A	1166
NTE5265AK	2733
NTE5266A	1176
NTE5266AK	1361
NTE5267A	1191
NTE5267AK	2735
NTE5268A	1201
NTE5268AK	1377
NTE5269A	1214
NTE5269AK	1396
NTE5270A	1223
NTE5270AK	1405
NTE5271A	1237
NTE5271AK	1419
NTE5272A	1256
NTE5272AK	1431
NTE5273A	1263
NTE5273AK	2745
NTE5274A	1280
NTE5274AK	1438
NTE5275A	1289
NTE5275AK	2749
NTE5276A	1297
NTE5276AK	1452
NTE5277A	1312
NTE5277AK	2752
NTE5278A	1321
NTE5278AK	1465
NTE5279A	1330
NTE5279AK	2756
NTE5280A	1343
NTE5280AK	0608
NTE5281A	1355
NTE5281AK	1502
NTE5282A	1374
NTE5282AK	1515
NTE5283A	1391
NTE5283AK	1529
NTE5284A	1402
NTE5284AK	1541
NTE5285A	1413
NTE5285AK	1565
NTE5286A	1427
NTE5286AK	2775
NTE5287A	1435
NTE5287AK	2776
NTE5288A	1448
NTE5288AK	1499
NTE5289A	1461
NTE5289AK	2778
NTE5290A	1475
NTE5290AK	2780
NTE5291A	1497
NTE5291AK	2783
NTE5292A	1513
NTE5292AK	2788
NTE5293A	1523
NTE5293AK	2791
NTE5294A	1539
NTE5294AK	2793
NTE5295A	1558
NTE5295AK	2795
NTE5296A	1577
NTE5296AK	2797
NTE5304	0106
NTE5305	1999
NTE5306	2384
NTE5307	0782
NTE5309	0724
NTE5310	0732
NTE5311	0737
NTE5312	0319
NTE5313	1404
NTE5314	0468
NTE5315	0441
NTE5316	1412
NTE5317	2425
NTE5318	2994
NTE5319	3006
NTE5320	3021
NTE5322	2347
NTE5322W	OEM
NTE5324	2353
NTE5324W	OEM
NTE5326	2354
NTE5326W	OEM
NTE5327	2356
NTE5327W	OEM
NTE5328	2357
NTE5328W	OEM
NTE5329	1036
NTE5330	1039
NTE5332	1864
NTE5334	3503
NTE5335	5629
NTE5338	5631
NTE5340	1633
NTE5342	1663
NTE5344	1579
NTE5346	5633
NTE5348	5634
NTE5351	4272
NTE5360	0799
NTE5368	0650
NTE5369	0020
NTE5371	0521

If replacement code is OEM, contact original manufacturer for replacement.

DEVICE TYPE	REPL CODE	DEVICE TYPE	REPL CODE	DEVICE TYPE	REPL CODE	DEVICE TYPE	REPL CODE	DEVICE TYPE	REPL CODE	DEVICE TYPE	REPL CODE	DEVICE TYPE	REPL CODE
NTE5372	0108	NTE5546	0773	NTE5705	5701	NTE5919	5398	NTE6118	2126	NTE7451	1160	NTE9689	4137
NTE5374	0423	NTE5547	0720	NTE5710	0647	NTE5920	0847	NTE6154	0594	NTE7453	1177	NTE9691	4143
NTE5375	1860	NTE5548	0745	NTE5711	4295	NTE5921	1242	NTE6155	1337	NTE7454	1193	NTE9800	0844
NTE5377	1690	NTE5550	2499	NTE5712	4494	NTE5922	5192	NTE6156	1975	NTE7460	1265	NTE9801	0868
NTE5378	0341	NTE5552	0393	NTE5720	2295	NTE5923	5399	NTE6157	1894	NTE7470	1394	NTE9802	0882
NTE5380	0454	NTE5554	0606	NTE5721	2966	NTE5924	1599	NTE6158	0652	NTE7472	1417	NTE9803	0894
NTE5381	0584	NTE5556	0946	NTE5722	2851	NTE5925	1196	NTE6159	0193	NTE7473	1164	NTE9804	0913
NTE5386	0764	NTE5558	1504	NTE5800	0110	NTE5928	1600	NTE6162	3277	NTE7474	1303	NTE9805	0923
NTE5387	0478	NTE5562	1837	NTE5801	0947	NTE5929	2124	NTE6163	0202	NTE7475	1423	NTE9806	0939
NTE5400	1129	NTE5564	1844	NTE5802	0242	NTE5932	1604	NTE6200	3631	NTE7476	1150	NTE9807	0956
NTE5401	0340	NTE5566	3185	NTE5803	1736	NTE5933	2236	NTE6202	3634	NTE7480	1527	NTE9808	0976
NTE5402	0895	NTE5567	1694	NTE5804	0535	NTE5940	1991	NTE6204	3635	NTE7481	3092	NTE9809	0992
NTE5403	2326	NTE5568	3970	NTE5805	1760	NTE5941	1992	NTE6206	2809	NTE7482	1564	NTE9810	1005
NTE5404	0058	NTE5569	0674	NTE5806	0959	NTE5942	0585	NTE6208	4125	NTE7483	0117	NTE9811	1019
NTE5405	0403	NTE5570	0603	NTE5808	0811	NTE5943	3234	NTE6210	4134	NTE7485	0370	NTE9812	1033
NTE5406	1673	NTE5572	0605	NTE5809	0916	NTE5944	1241	NTE6220	1787	NTE7486	1358	NTE9813	4458
NTE5408	0179	NTE5574	0463	NTE5812	1272	NTE5945	1567	NTE6230	2178	NTE7488A	4817	NTE9814	4461
NTE5409	0342	NTE5575	0636	NTE5814	1277	NTE5946	5487	NTE6240	1227	NTE7489	5358	NTE9910	1248
NTE5410	3315	NTE5577	0217	NTE5815	1282	NTE5947	3244	NTE6244	1716	NTE7490	1199	NTE9924	2840
NTE5411	4384	NTE5579	0653	NTE5817	1285	NTE5948	1571	NTE6246	2219	NTE7491	0974	NTE9926	3868
NTE5412	0174	NTE5580	1076	NTE5818	1557	NTE5949	3251	NTE6354	1017	NTE7492	0828	NTE9930	1812
NTE5413	3801	NTE5582	1078	NTE5819	1538	NTE5950	5489	NTE6355	0496	NTE7493A	0564	NTE9932	1035
NTE5414	3575	NTE5584	1094	NTE5820	2140	NTE5951	3256	NTE6356	1030	NTE7494	1692	NTE9933	2086
NTE5415	3291	NTE5587	1889	NTE5821	3110	NTE5952	1576	NTE6357	1766	NTE7495	1477	NTE9935	1168
NTE5416	1494	NTE5589	0733	NTE5822	0706	NTE5953	3263	NTE6358	1040	NTE7496	1705	NTE9936	1820
NTE5417	0998	NTE5590	0192	NTE5823	2939	NTE5962	4938	NTE6359	1778	NTE7497	2912	NTE9937	1824
NTE5418	1028	NTE5591	0159	NTE5826	3475	NTE5963	2537	NTE6362	2805	NTE7785M	OEM	NTE9944	0033
NTE5419	1140	NTE5592	0096	NTE5827	4924	NTE5966	2591	NTE6363	3138	NTE8070	2915	NTE9945	0081
NTE5424	1981	NTE5594	2816	NTE5828	3498	NTE5967	2544	NTE6400	5774	NTE8076	2916	NTE9946	0141
NTE5426	1038	NTE5595	1754	NTE5829	5477	NTE5980	3160	NTE6400A	1659	NTE8080A	4467	NTE9948	3365
NTE5427	5643	NTE5596	1803	NTE5830	0703	NTE5981	1620	NTE6401	2123	NTE8081	2920	NTE9949	1833
NTE5428	5644	NTE5598	4085	NTE5831	0927	NTE5982	2873	NTE6402	0312	NTE8085	2923	NTE9950	2595
NTE5429	5373	NTE5599	1714	NTE5832	4077	NTE5983	0254	NTE6403	4169	NTE8090	2927	NTE9951	2067
NTE5437	0712	NTE5600	4341	NTE5833	5420	NTE5986	1116	NTE6404	3373	NTE8096	2933	NTE9961	1848
NTE5438	0304	NTE5601	1744	NTE5834	0575	NTE5987	1099	NTE6405	4335	NTE8098	2363	NTE9962	0557
NTE5442	4508	NTE5602	4343	NTE5835	0941	NTE5988	1118	NTE6406	3603	NTE8103	2935	NTE9963	0337
NTE5444	2255	NTE5603	3458	NTE5836	2049	NTE5989	1103	NTE6407	3298	NTE8108	2940	NTE9989	3395
NTE5446	3368	NTE5604	4058	NTE5837	4443	NTE5990	0800	NTE6408	5776	NTE8115	2944	NTE15005	3130
NTE5448	3370	NTE5605	0480	NTE5838	0994	NTE5991	0258	NTE6409	1167	NTE8118	2945	NTE15019E	1796
NTE5452	1386	NTE5606	4345	NTE5839	1006	NTE5992	1186	NTE6410	1882	NTE8123	5801	NTE15020E	3858
NTE5453	1250	NTE5607	4346	NTE5840	2065	NTE5993	1634	NTE6411	5290	NTE8125	2948	NTE15027	4312
NTE5454	0442	NTE5608	0567	NTE5841	5467	NTE5994	0315	NTE6412	5537	NTE8139	2962	NTE15030	OEM
NTE5455	0934	NTE5609	0929	NTE5842	2070	NTE5995	0267	NTE6415	5539	NTE8149	2970	NTE15038	4213
NTE5456	1213	NTE5610	0059	NTE5843	1067	NTE5998	1124	NTE6416	5540	NTE8167	3005	NTE15039	4842
NTE5457	0095	NTE5611	5452	NTE5846	2077	NTE5999	1111	NTE6417	5542	NTE8181	3007	NTE15040	3896
NTE5458	1234	NTE5612	5453	NTE5847	1130	NTE6002	0045	NTE6418	5543	NTE8212	1849	NTE15041	3900
NTE5461	2084	NTE5613	0948	NTE5848	0607	NTE6003	0280	NTE6419	5544	NTE8213	2972	NTE15042	4843
NTE5462	2078	NTE5614	4366	NTE5849	1180	NTE6006	1522	NTE6502	3036	NTE8214	5927	NTE15043	4844
NTE5463	0500	NTE5615	0951	NTE5850	0964	NTE6007	1512	NTE6507	3041	NTE8216	1852	NTE15044	3479
NTE5465	0705	NTE5616	0954	NTE5851	0979	NTE6008	0029	NTE6508	3164	NTE8219	5930	NTE15045	4417
NTE5466	0857	NTE5617	0955	NTE5852	3688	NTE6009	1836	NTE6532	1962	NTE8223	5814	NTE15046	3871
NTE5468	0323	NTE5618	0960	NTE5853	0904	NTE6010	0596	NTE6800	0384	NTE8224	1699	NTE16007	5012
NTE5470	1102	NTE5621	5454	NTE5854	0983	NTE6011	1840	NTE6802	0389	NTE8226	2984	NTE17145	OEM
NTE5471	2904	NTE5622	1081	NTE5855	0984	NTE6020	3716	NTE6809	5829	NTE8228	1858	NTE21128	1628
NTE5472	0957	NTE5623	1085	NTE5856	3697	NTE6021	2640	NTE6809E	2105	NTE8234	2069	NTE30001	2678
NTE5473	2905	NTE5624	0407	NTE5857	0987	NTE6022	2629	NTE6810	2075	NTE8235	2076	NTE40085B	3415
NTE5474	2908	NTE5625	1087	NTE5858	0197	NTE6023	2670	NTE6821	0443	NTE8242	2992	NTE40097B	4367
NTE5475	3626	NTE5626	0411	NTE5859	0991	NTE6026	2633	NTE6850	0509	NTE8255	0051	NTE40098B	0427
NTE5476	3405	NTE5627	1091	NTE5860	0200	NTE6027	2741	NTE6860	2667	NTE8266	2260	NTE40100B	3895
NTE5480	3385	NTE5628	1092	NTE5861	0995	NTE6030	2639	NTE6875	4118	NTE8301	2182	NTE40106B	3581
NTE5481	1095	NTE5629	2284	NTE5862	0204	NTE6031	2828	NTE6880	4437	NTE8308	1064	NTE40160B	1349
NTE5482	2471	NTE5631	0573	NTE5863	0510	NTE6034	1995	NTE6885	4566	NTE8309	5430	NTE40161B	1363
NTE5483	0240	NTE5632	0566	NTE5866	0206	NTE6035	2879	NTE6886	4570	NTE8314	2468	NTE40162B	1378
NTE5484	2635	NTE5633	0588	NTE5867	1002	NTE6038	2652	NTE6887	4577	NTE8316	5820	NTE40163B	1397
NTE5485	0671	NTE5634	0569	NTE5868	0583	NTE6039	2946	NTE6888	4586	NTE8318	4082	NTE40174B	1542
NTE5486	2782	NTE5635	0571	NTE5869	0942	NTE6040	2657	NTE6889	0576	NTE8321	5821	NTE40175B	1520
NTE5487	0332	NTE5636	0572	NTE5870	0084	NTE6041	3022	NTE7010	3473	NTE8328	5822	NTE40182B	4579
NTE5491	2430	NTE5637	0589	NTE5871	0529	NTE6042	3846	NTE7214	5858	NTE8345M	OEM	NTE40192B	1753
NTE5492	0430	NTE5638	5226	NTE5872	0090	NTE6043	3088	NTE7400	0232	NTE8368	5825	NTE40193B	1765
NTE5494	1478	NTE5640	2367	NTE5873	0743	NTE6044	2631	NTE7401	0268	NTE8370	5826	NTE40194B	1758
NTE5496	0682	NTE5641	2378	NTE5874	0097	NTE6045	3178	NTE7402	0310	NTE8374	5827	NTE40195B	1773
NTE5500	3073	NTE5642	1403	NTE5875	0760	NTE6048	4242	NTE7403	0331	NTE8520	5837	NTE56004	0767
NTE5501	2497	NTE5643	2371	NTE5876	0105	NTE6049	3725	NTE7404	0357	NTE8542	5838	NTE56006	0739
NTE5502	0736	NTE5645	0550	NTE5877	0772	NTE6050	1551	NTE7405	0381	NTE8546	5839	NTE56008	0612
NTE5503	3076	NTE5646	1447	NTE5878	0109	NTE6051	2165	NTE7406	1197	NTE8556	5840	NTE56010	0869
NTE5504	0740	NTE5649	5456	NTE5879	0533	NTE6054	2813	NTE7407	1329	NTE8613	5953	NTE56014	6185
NTE5505	3080	NTE5650	2336	NTE5880	0116	NTE6055	2168	NTE7408	0462	NTE9093	0354	NTE56015	5227
NTE5506	2889	NTE5651	2337	NTE5881	0796	NTE6058	4244	NTE7409	0487	NTE9094	1622	NTE56016	5230
NTE5507	0742	NTE5652	2340	NTE5882	0122	NTE6059	3556	NTE7410	0507	NTE9097	1472	NTE56017	1649
NTE5508	3213	NTE5653	5457	NTE5883	0810	NTE6060	2823	NTE7411	0522	NTE9099	0329	NTE56018	1956
NTE5509	0747	NTE5655	4381	NTE5886	0131	NTE6061	2177	NTE7412	2227	NTE9135	1609	NTE56019	6000
NTE5511	3651	NTE5656	4382	NTE5887	0540	NTE6064	2844	NTE7413	1432	NTE9157	1424	NTE56020	5511
NTE5512	3349	NTE5657	4404	NTE5890	0145	NTE6065	2183	NTE7414	2228	NTE9158	0461	NTE56022	3169
NTE5513	3579	NTE5661	0400	NTE5891	0545	NTE6068	2806	NTE7416	1339	NTE9200	4095	NTE56024	3177
NTE5514	1641	NTE5665	5687	NTE5892	5417	NTE6069	2202	NTE7417	1342	NTE9221	OEM	NTE56026	3192
NTE5515	1574	NTE5673	0154	NTE5893	1229	NTE6072	2454	NTE7420	0692	NTE9285	OEM	NTE65101	4524
NTE5516	1655	NTE5675	0147	NTE5894	5482	NTE6073	2324	NTE7421	1347	NTE9370	1284	NTE74100	4474
NTE5517	1640	NTE5676	4465	NTE5895	1231	NTE6074	2751	NTE7422	4523	NTE9402	4099	NTE74101	OEM
NTE5518	2623	NTE5677	0278	NTE5896	2872	NTE6075	1734	NTE7423	3429	NTE9403	1589	NTE74105	4475
NTE5519	2625	NTE5679	0902	NTE5897	1232	NTE6076	2786	NTE7425	3438	NTE9415	OEM	NTE74107	0936
NTE5520	3275	NTE5680	3117	NTE5898	5483	NTE6077	1772	NTE7426	0798	NTE9601	2252	NTE74109	0962
NTE5521	2174	NTE5681	3118	NTE5899	1236	NTE6078	2619	NTE7427	0812	NTE9602	2270	NTE74110	0981
NTE5522	0562	NTE5682	3119	NTE5900	3705	NTE6079	1807	NTE7428	4117	NTE9660	0613	NTE74111	0996
NTE5523	3227	NTE5683	3121	NTE5901	2349	NTE6084	0610	NTE7430	0867	NTE9661	2574	NTE74116	4365
NTE5524	0757	NTE5684	3122	NTE5902	3711	NTE6085	1015	NTE7432	0893	NTE9663	2964	NTE74120	1108
NTE5525	3237	NTE5685	3123	NTE5903	1244	NTE6087	2493	NTE7433	4130	NTE9664	3003	NTE74121	0175
NTE5526	3240	NTE5686	3124	NTE5904	1104	NTE6090	1931	NTE7437	3478	NTE9666	4079	NTE74122	1131
NTE5527	0735	NTE5687	4038	NTE5905	2360	NTE6094	1536	NTE7438	0990	NTE9668	2417	NTE74123	1149
NTE5528	3260	NTE5688	1058	NTE5908	3722	NTE6102	4957	NTE7439	5722	NTE9669	2986	NTE74125	1174
NTE5529	0759	NTE5689	1307	NTE5909	1255	NTE6103	2299	NTE7440	1018	NTE9670	2334	NTE74126	1184
NTE5530	2848	NTE5690	1880	NTE5910	2982	NTE6104	0744	NTE7441	1032	NTE9671	4086	NTE74128	1210
NTE5531	0761	NTE5693	2004	NTE5911	0444	NTE6105	2765	NTE7442	1046	NTE9672	0078	NTE74132	1261
NTE5534	0226	NTE5695	2006	NTE5912	1590	NTE6106	4222	NTE7443	1054	NTE9675	4101	NTE74134	OEM
NTE5540	3246	NTE5697	2007	NTE5913	4917	NTE6107	4221	NTE7444	1066	NTE9676	4107	NTE74136	1306
NTE5541	0726	NTE5700	1425	NTE5914	5189	NTE6110	1217	NTE7445	1074	NTE9678	4110	NTE74138	OEM
NTE5542	0707	NTE5701	1670	NTE5915	5394	NTE6112	1195	NTE7446	1090	NTE9679	4112	NTE74141	1367
NTE5543	0464	NTE5702	2278	NTE5916	0865	NTE6113	2146	NTE7447	1100	NTE9680	4115	NTE74142	1380
NTE5544	0716	NTE5703	2282	NTE5917	1625	NTE6115	0474	NTE7448	1117	NTE9681	3016	NTE74143	1399
NTE5545	0717	NTE5704	5700	NTE5918	5190	NTE6116	4835	NTE7450	0738	NTE9682	3010	NTE74144	1408

If replacement code is OEM, contact original manufacturer for replacement.

DEVICE TYPE	REPL CODE
NTE74145	0614
NTE74147	1442
NTE74148	1455
NTE74150	1484
NTE74151	1487
NTE74152	1509
NTE74153	1531
NTE74154	1546
NTE74155	1566
NTE74156	1582
NTE74157	1595
NTE74158	4372
NTE74160	1621
NTE74161	1635
NTE74162	1007
NTE74163	1656
NTE74164	0729
NTE74165	1675
NTE74166	0231
NTE74170	1711
NTE74173	1755
NTE74174	1759
NTE74175	1776
NTE74176	1784
NTE74177	1792
NTE74178	1802
NTE74179	1809
NTE74180	1818
NTE74181	1831
NTE74182	1845
NTE74185	1857
NTE74190	1901
NTE74191	1906
NTE74192	1910
NTE74193	1915
NTE74195	1932
NTE74196	1939
NTE74197	1945
NTE74198	1953
NTE74199	1960
NTE74221	2129
NTE74249	2274
NTE74251	2283
NTE74265	4531
NTE74278	4536
NTE74279	4538
NTE74290	2588
NTE74293	2620
NTE74298	4547
NTE74365	1450
NTE74366	1462
NTE74367	1479
NTE74368	1500
NTE74374	4581
NTE74376	4583
NTE74390	3210
NTE74393	3225
NTE74426	4616
NTE74490	3619
NTE75188	0503
NTE75189	0506
NTE75322	4913
NTE75450B	1222
NTE75451B	1235
NTE75452B	1253
NTE75453B	1262
NTE75454B	1279
NTE75491B	1718
NTE75492B	1729
NTE75493	4933
NTE75494	4934
NTE75498	4936
NTM3906	OEM
NTP5V6	OEM
NTP6V2	0466
NTP6V8	OEM
NTP7V5	OEM
NTP8V2	3071
NTP9V1	0057
NTP10	OEM
NTP11	OEM
NTP12	0052
NTP13	OEM
NTP15	0681
NTT275	0004
NU34	0143
NV004	0030
NV009	0030
NV-8B	OEM
NV10A	0369
NV-11-B	OEM
NV20	OEM
NV20A	OEM
NV20F	OEM
NV30	OEM
NV30A	OEM
NV30F	OEM
NV40A	OEM
NV200DIO	OEM
NX25A	OEM
NX50	OEM
NZ309	OEM
02Z5.6A	0157
02Z6.2A	0466
02Z-10A	0170
02Z12A	0137
02Z12GR	0052
03P2M	0058
04-8054-3	0015

DEVICE TYPE	REPL CODE
04-8054-4	0015
04-8054-7	0015
05Z6.2Y	6716
05Z8.2U	0244
0-43	OEM
043	OEM
0-44	OEM
0-45	OEM
055C	0320
0-63	OEM
063	OEM
0-64	OEM
064	OEM
0-65	OEM
065	OEM
0101	0015
0200	1241
0201	1241
0210	1241
0211	1241
0220	1241
0221	1241
0573510	0007
0575005	0143
OA2	0914
OA6	0143
OA7	0143
OA9	0143
OA9D	0143
OA10	0110
OA47	0143
OA50	0143
OA-70	0019
OA70	0143
OA71	0143
OA71C	0143
OA72	0143
OA73	0143
OA73C	0143
OA74	0143
OA74A	0143
OA79	0143
OA81	0143
OA81C	0143
OA85	0143
OA85C	0143
OA86	1925
OA-90	0143
OA90	0143
OA-90(G)	0143
OA90-FM	0143
OA90-G	0143
OA90-M	0143
OA90-R	0143
OA90A-G	0019
OA90AG	0019
OA90A-M	0143
OA90A-R	0143
OA90FM	0123
OA90FV	0143
OA90G	0019
OA90GA	0143
OA90LF	0143
OA90M	0143
OA90MLF	0143
OA90S-G	0143
OA90S-R	0143
OA90Z	0143
OA91	0019
OA91A	0019
OA92	0143
OA-95	0133
OA95	0143
OA95A	0143
OA99	0019
OA99A	0143
OA126/5	0446
OA126/10	0181
OA126/12	0137
OA126/14	0100
OA127	0015
OA128	0015
OA129	0015
OA130	0015
OA131	0015
OA132	0015
OA134Q	0143
OA150	0143
OA159	0143
OA160	0143
OA161	0143
OA172	0143
OA174	0143
OA180	0015
OA182	0143
OA200	0133
OA201	OEM
OA202	0133
OA205	0133
OA210	0015
OA211	0015
OA214	0015
OA541	0143
OA626-50	OEM
OA626-300	OEM
OA626-500	OEM
OA626-600	OEM
OA636-600	OEM
OA645-100	OEM

DEVICE TYPE	REPL CODE
OA645-200	OEM
OA645-300	OEM
OA645-400	OEM
OA645-500	OEM
OA909	0143
OA2002	0133
OA2005	0133
OA7812UC	OEM
OA12610	0170
OA12612	0137
OAZ200	0446
OAZ201	0162
OAZ202	0157
OAZ203	0631
OAZ204	0025
OAZ206	0244
OAZ207	0012
OAZ209	0162
OAZ210	0631
OAZ212	0012
OAZ213	0137
OAZ222	1890
OAZ223	0691
OAZ224	1449
OAZ225	1606
OAZ227	1608
OAZ228	0505
OAZ230	0864
OAZ232	1264
OAZ234	1071
OAZ236	1712
OAZ240	0140
OAZ241	0041
OAZ242	0253
OAZ243	0466
OAZ244	0062
OAZ245	0077
OAZ246	0165
OAZ247	0057
OAZ268	0274
OAZ269	0041
OAZ270	0466
OAZ271	0077
OAZ272	0057
OAZ273	0052
OAZ290	0691
OAZ291	1606
OAZ292	1608
OB2764K-2	0806
OC3H	0004
OC3K	OEM
OC3L	OEM
OC3LP	OEM
OC3LR	OEM
OC3N	OEM
OC4-0	OEM
OC4H	0004
OC4K	0004
OC4L	OEM
OC4LP	OEM
OC4LR	OEM
OC4N	OEM
OC5-0	OEM
OC5K	OEM
OC5L	OEM
OC5LP	OEM
OC5LR	OEM
OC5N	OEM
OC-16	0160
OC16	0085
OC19	0160
OC20	0160
OC-22	0160
OC22	0085
OC-23	0160
OC23	0085
OC-24	0160
OC24	0085
OC-25	0160
OC25	0085
OC-26	0160
OC26	0085
OC27	0085
OC-28	0160
OC28	0085
OC-29	0160
OC29	0085
OC30	0222
OC-30A	0222
OC30A	0222
OC30B	0222
OC32	0211
OC33	0004
OC34	0004
OC-35	0160
OC35	0085
OC-36	0160
OC36	0085
OC38	0004
OC40	0136
OC41	0211
OC41N	0004
OC42	0136
OC42N	0004
OC43	0136
OC43N	0136
OC44	0136
OC44N	0136
OC45	0004

DEVICE TYPE	REPL CODE
OC45N	0136
OC46	0004
OC46N	0136
OC47	0004
OC47N	0136
OC50	0136
OC53	0050
OC54	0050
OC55	0050
OC56	0004
OC57	0004
OC58	0004
OC59	0004
OC60	0004
OC65	0004
OC66	0004
OC70	0004
OC70N	0004
OC71	0004
OC71A	0004
OC71N	0004
OC72	0004
OC73	0004
OC74	0004
OC74N	0004
OC75	0004
OC75N	0004
OC76	0004
OC77	0004
OC77M	0004
OC78	0004
OC79	0004
OC80	0004
OC81	0004
OC81D	0004
OC81DD	0004
OC81DN	0004
OC81N	0164
OC83	0164
OC83N	0164
OC84	0164
OC84N	0164
OC110	0004
OC120	0004
OC122	0004
OC123	0004
OC130	0136
OC139	0208
OC140	0208
OC141	0595
OC169	0050
OC169R	0050
OC170	0050
OC170N	0050
OC170R	0050
OC170V	0050
OC171	0050
OC171N	0050
OC171R	0050
OC171V	0050
OC174	0050
OC200	0037
OC201	0037
OC202	0037
OC203	0037
OC204	0037
OC205	0037
OC206	0037
OC207	0037
OC302	0004
OC303	0004
OC304	0004
OC304/1	0004
OC304/2	OEM
OC304/3	0004
OC304-1	0004
OC304-2	0004
OC304-3	0004
OC304N	0004
OC305	0004
OC305/1	0164
OC305/2	OEM
OC305-1	0004
OC305-2	0004
OC306	0004
OC306/1	0004
OC306/2	0004
OC306/3	0004
OC306-1	0004
OC306-2	0004
OC306-3	0004
OC307	0004
OC307-1	0004
OC307-2	0004
OC307-3	0004
OC308	0004
OC309	0004
OC309-1	0004
OC309-2	0004
OC309-3	0004
OC318	0004
OC320	0050
OC330	0004
OC331	0136
OC340	0004
OC341	0136
OC342	0136
OC343	0136
OC350	0004

DEVICE TYPE	REPL CODE
OC351	0136
OC360	0004
OC361	0136
OC362	0136
OC363	0136
OC364	0004
OC390	0136
OC400	0050
OC410	0050
OC430	0037
OC430K	0037
OC440	0037
OC440K	0037
OC443	0037
OC443K	0037
OC445	0037
OC445K	0037
OC449	0037
OC449K	0037
OC450	0037
OC450K	OEM
OC460	0037
OC460K	0037
OC463	0037
OC463K	0037
OC465	0037
OC465K	0037
OC466	0037
OC466K	0037
OC467	0037
OC467K	0037
OC468	0037
OC468K	0037
OC469	0037
OC469K	0037
OC470	0037
OC470K	0037
OC480	OEM
OC480K	OEM
OC601	0004
OC602	0004
OC602-SPEZ	0164
OC602SP	0004
OC602SQ	0004
OC603	0004
OC604	0004
OC604-SPEZ	0164
OC604SP	0004
OC612	0136
OC613	0136
OC614	0136
OC615	0136
OC615N	0050
OC622	OEM
OC623	OEM
OC624	OEM
OC700	0037
OC700A	0037
OC700B	0037
OC701	OEM
OC702	0037
OC702A	0037
OC702B	0037
OC703	OEM
OC703A	OEM
OC704	0037
OC711	0004
OC740	0037
OC740G	0037
OC740M	0037
OC7400	0037
OC740Q	OEM
OC742	0037
OC742G	0037
OC742M	0037
OC7420	0037
OC800	OEM
OC810	0004
OC975	0628
OC3403Z1	OEM
OC7400	0037
OC7420	0037
OCD81DN	0164
OCP71	OEM
OD650	OEM
OD650B	OEM
OD651	OEM
OD651A	OEM
OD652	OEM
ODD247109AA	OEM
ODG-204A	OEM
OEC0010C	OEM
OEC0015B	OEM
OEC1011	4444
OEC2012A	OEM
OEC3006	OEM
OEC3008	OEM
OEC3011	OEM
OEC5003	OEM
OEC6007A	OEM
OEC6010B	OEM
OEC6015C	OEM
OEC6015C911E	OEM
OEC6015C911EAI	OEM
OEC6015C9111EAI	OEM
OEC6015C9115EA1	OEM
OEC7002	OEM
OEC8002	OEM
OEC8031B	OEM

DEVICE TYPE	REPL CODE
OEC9001	OEM
OEC9005	OEM
OEC9008B	OEM
OECA001	OEM
OF66	0102
OF-129	0004
OF129	0004
OF156	0133
OF160	0015
OF162	0133
OF164	0015
OF173	0143
OF305	0019
OF449	0124
OF612	OEM
OF643	OEM
OFWM1953	OEM
OG336938	OEM
OG372884	OEM
OG851380	OEM
OG851794	6064
OGA00300	OEM
O-I5551	0855
OIS67	OEM
OLD-415	OEM
OMK7003/TK140	OEM
OMK7004/6940/TK76	OEM
ON67A	0143
ON74LS03N	1569
ON74LS05N	OEM
ON74LS08N	1623
ON74LS125AN	OEM
ON74LS145N	1554
ON74LS163AN	0887
ON74LS174N	0260
ON74LS175N	1662
ON74LS240N	0447
ON74LS244N	0453
ON74LS245N	0458
ON74LS373N	0704
ON74LS374N	0708
ON74LS670N	1122
ON74S00N	0699
ON74S10N	2426
ON74S20N	1011
ON74S138N	0422
ON74S240N	OEM
ON74S241N	OEM
ON150NV	OEM
ON174	0050
ON271	0079
ON274	0016
ON285A	OEM
ON769	2833
ON1102	OEM
ON1105	OEM
ON1301	OEM
ON1350	OEM
ON2160	OEM
ON2170-R	OEM
ON2170-RLF	OEM
ON2170-RS	OEM
ON2170-S	OEM
ON2170LH	OEM
ON2170L-R	OEM
ON2170R	OEM
ON3111	0112
ON3111Q	OEM
ON3111R	4837
ON3131	OEM
ON3131S	OEM
ON3161	0112
ON3161(Q)	0112
ON3161(R)	0112
ON3161-Q	OEM
ON3161-QR	0112
ON3161-R	0112
ON3161QR	OEM
ON3161R	0317
ON4047	5248
ON7406N	OEM
ON7407N	1329
ON7438N	0990
OP-05ADE	OEM
OP-05ADE/883B	OEM
OP-05AT	OEM
OP-05AT/883B	OEM
OP-05CDE	2231
OP-05CNB	2231
OP-05CT	0890
OP-05DE	OEM
OP-05DE/883B	OEM
OP-05EDE	2231
OP-05ENB	2231
OP-05ET	0890
OP-05T	OEM
OP-05T/883B	OEM
OP-07/883B	OEM
OP-07ADE	OEM
OP-07ADE/883B	OEM
OP-07AT	OEM
OP-07AT/883B	OEM
OP-07C	OEM
OP-07CDE	2231
OP-07CNB	2231
OP-07CT	0890
OP-07D	OEM
OP-07DDE	2231
OP-07DE	OEM

DEVICE TYPE	REPL CODE
OP-07DNB	2231
OP-07DT	0890
OP-07E	OEM
OP-07EDE	2231
OP-07ENB	2231
OP-07ET	0890
OP-07T	OEM
OP-07T/883B	OEM
OP-27ADE	OEM
OP-27ADE/883B	OEM
OP-27AT	OEM
OP-27AT/883B	OEM
OP-27BDE	OEM
OP-27BDE/883B	OEM
OP-27BT	OEM
OP-27BT/883B	OEM
OP-27CDE	OEM
OP-27CDE/883B	OEM
OP-27CT	OEM
OP-27CT/883B	OEM
OP-27EDE	2231
OP-27ENB	2231
OP-27ET	0890
OP-27FDE	2231
OP-27FNB	2231
OP-27FT	0890
OP-27GDE	2231
OP-27GNB	2231
OP-27GT	0890
OP-37ADE	OEM
OP-37ADE/883B	OEM
OP-37AT	OEM
OP-37AT/883B	OEM
OP-37BDE	OEM
OP-37BDE/883B	OEM
OP-37BT	OEM
OP-37BT/883B	OEM
OP-37CDE	OEM
OP-37CDE/883B	OEM
OP-37CT	OEM
OP-37CT/883B	OEM
OP-37EDE	2231
OP-37ENB	2231
OP-37ET	0890
OP-37FDE	2231
OP-37FNB	2231
OP-37FT	0890
OP-37GDE	2231
OP-37GNB	2231
OP-37GT	0890
OP-47BT	OEM
OP-47BT/883B	OEM
OP-47FT	0890
OP-47GNB	2231
OP-47GT	0890
OP130	0586
OP130W	0586
OP131	0586
OP131W	0586
OP132	0586
OP132W	0586
OP133	0586
OP133W	0586
OP135	0586
OP135W	0586
OP136	0586
OP136W	0586
OP137	0586
OP137W	0586
OP215BZ/883	OEM
OP800	2297
OP801	2297
OP811	2297
OP812	3825
OP813	2297
OP8242A	OEM
OP13152	1047
OP13153	2096
OP13251	2096
OP13252	2096
OP13253	1047
OPB814	1407
OPF54	OEM
OPF56	OEM
OPI1264A	OEM
OPI2100	0311
OPI2150	0311
OPI2151	0311
OPI2152	0536
OPI2153	0311
OPI2154	0536
OPI2155	0536
OPI2250	0311
OPI2251	0311
OPI2252	0536
OPI2253	0311
OPI2254	0536
OPI2255	0311
OPI2500	5327
OPI3009	6286
OPI3010	4961
OPI3011	6286
OPI3150	0311
OPI3151	0311
OPI3152	1101
OPI3153	1047
OPI3250	1047
OPI3251	1047
OPI3252	1101

If replacement code is OEM, contact original manufacturer for replacement.

DEVICE TYPE	REPL CODE
OPI3253	1047
OPI5000	0311
OPI6100	6598
OPI7002	3333
OPI7010	3333
OPL-211	OEM
OPP28	OEM
OR06NXZ31	0201
OR06YXZ31	0374
OR6JXZ33A	OEM
OR6LXZ33A	OEM
OR6QXZ33A	OEM
OR6UXZ33A	OEM
ORP30	OEM
ORP50	OEM
ORP63	OEM
ORP94	OEM
OS-1D	0015
OS-4D	0015
OS-6D	0015
OS-8D	0071
OS13	OEM
OS15	OEM
OS16	OEM
OS17	OEM
OS70	0143
OS-100A	OEM
OS492	0841
OS536G	0079
OS643	OEM
OS16308	0015
OSD	OEM
OSD-0033	0644
OSD0033	0644
OSF02	OEM
OSF03	OEM
OSF04	OEM
OSF05	OEM
OSI5JHGA	OEM
OSL3-1	OEM
OSL3-2	OEM
OSL3-3	OEM
OSL3L1	OEM
OSL3L2	OEM
OSL3L3	OEM
OSL6-1	OEM
OSL6L1	OEM
OSL6L2	OEM
OSL6L3	OEM
OSL16-1	OEM
OSL16-2	OEM
OSL16-3	OEM
OSL16L1	OEM
OSL16L2	OEM
OSL16L3	OEM
OSL26-1	OEM
OSL26L1	OEM
OSL50	OEM
OSM9510-12	OEM
OSS-16308	0015
OSS16308	0143
OSS-16685	0143
OSS16685	0143
OSS36503	0015
OSS36685	0015
OSS-36885	0015
OSS36885	0015
OV02	0102
OV-1	OEM
OV-2	OEM
OV-2-1	OEM
OV-2-2	OEM
OV-2-3	OEM
OV2764KFA552	0806
OVSSAC431-1	OEM
OY101	0015
OY1011	OEM
OY1021	OEM
OY5061	0015
OY5062	0015
OY5063	0015
OY5064	0015
OY5065	0015
OY5066	0015
OY5067	0071
OZ3.6T5	0188
OZ3.6T10	0188
OZ5.1T5	0162
OZ5.1T10	0162
OZ5.6T5	0157
OZ5.6T10	0157
OZ6.2T5	0631
OZ6.2T10	0631
OZ10T5	0170
OZ10T10	0170
OZ12T5	0137
OZ12T10	0137
OZ15T5	0002
OZ15T10	0002
OZ27T5	0436
OZ27T10	0436
P	OEM
P006001D	OEM
P006001E-H	OEM
P006004D	OEM
P006004E-H	OEM
P006010D	OEM
P006010E	OEM
P006010F	OEM

DEVICE TYPE	REPL CODE
P006010G	OEM
P027PH02F20	OEM
P027QH05FR0	OEM
P055I	0806
P056I	0806
P093	0170
P095PH04FG0	OEM
P0100AD	0895
P0100BA	0058
P0100BB	0058
P0100BD	0058
P0100CD	0403
P0100DA	0403
P0100DB	0403
P0100DD	0403
P0100MA	1673
P0100MB	1673
P0100NA	OEM
P0100NB	OEM
P0102AA	0895
P0102AB	0895
P0102BA	0058
P0102BB	0058
P0102CA	0403
P0102CB	0403
P0102DA	0403
P0102DB	0403
P0103AD	0895
P0103BA	0058
P0103BB	0058
P0103BD	0058
P0103CD	0403
P0103DA	0403
P0103DB	0403
P0103DD	0403
P0103MA	1673
P0103MB	1673
P0103NA	OEM
P0103NB	OEM
P0108EXP03A	OEM
P0117RD01B	OEM
P0165STD01E	2672
P015010D	OEM
P015010E	OEM
P015010F	OEM
P015010G	OEM
P015020C	OEM
P015020D	OEM
P015020E	OEM
P024020C	OEM
P024020D	OEM
P024020E	OEM
P030010C	OEM
P030010D	OEM
P030010E	OEM
P030010F	OEM
P045010B	OEM
P045010C-F	OEM
P045020B	OEM
P045020C	OEM
P045020D	OEM
P060003-1R	OEM
P060003-2R	OEM
P060003-3R	OEM
P060005-1R	OEM
P060005-2R	OEM
P060005-3R	OEM
P060007-1R	OEM
P060007-2R	OEM
P060010A	OEM
P060010B-E	OEM
P090020A	OEM
P090020B	OEM
P090020C	OEM
P1/1H	OEM
P1/2H	OEM
P1/3H	OEM
P1/4H	OEM
P1/5H	OEM
P1A	0160
P1A5	0015
P1B	0037
P1B5	0015
P1C	0037
P1C5	0015
P1CG	0037
P1D	0037
P1D5	0015
P1E	0486
P1E-1	0160
P1E-1BLK	0486
P1E-1BLU	0486
P1E-1GRN	0486
P1E-1RED	0486
P1E-1V10	1671
P1E-1VIO	0486
P1E-2BLK	0486
P1E-2BLU	0486
P1E-2GRN	0486
P1E-2RED	0486
P1E-2V10	1671
P1E-2VIO	0486
P1E-3BLK	0486
P1E-3BLU	0486
P1E-3GRN	0486
P1E-3RED	0486
P1E-3V10	1671
P1E-3VIO	0486
P1F	0969

DEVICE TYPE	REPL CODE
P1G	0160
P1H	0037
P1J	0037
P1K	0160
P1KBLK	0160
P1KBLU	0160
P1KBRN	0160
P1KGRN	0160
P1KORN	0160
P1KRED	0160
P1KYEL	0160
P1L	0004
P1L4956	0004
P1M	0126
P1N	0037
P1N-1	0037
P1N-2	0037
P1N-3	0037
P1P	0037
P1P-1	0037
P1R	0085
P1RF100	OEM
P1RP15	OEM
P1RP24	OEM
P1RP36	OEM
P1RP48	OEM
P1RP60	OEM
P1RP72	OEM
P1RP80	OEM
P1RP100	OEM
P1T	0160
P1V	0455
P1V-2	0455
P1V-3	0455
P1V-4	0919
P1W	0037
P1Y	0969
P2A	0037
P2A5	0015
P2B	0919
P2B5	0015
P2C	0085
P2C5	0015
P2D	0160
P2D5	0015
P2DBLU	0160
P2DBRN	0160
P2DGRN	0160
P2DORN	0160
P2DRED	0160
P2DYEL	0160
P2E	0037
P2F	0841
P2G	0037
P2GE	0037
P2H	0037
P2J	1671
P2K	0919
P2L	0037
P2M	0058
P2M-1	0037
P2M-2	0037
P2M-3	0037
P2M3Z	0058
P2M49	OEM
P2P	0037
P2R	0085
P2S	0037
P2T	0455
P2T-1	0455
P2T-2	0455
P2T-3	0455
P2T-4	0455
P2U	0378
P2U-1	0378
P2U-2	1357
P2V	0378
P2W	0037
P2Y	0037
P2Z	0599
P3/1H	OEM
P3/2H	0015
P3/3H	OEM
P3/4H	OEM
P3/5H	OEM
P3A	0848
P3A5	0015
P3B	0164
P3B5	0015
P3C	0037
P3C5	0015
P3D	0004
P3D5	0015
P3E	0222
P3E5	OEM
P3EBLK	0085
P3EBLU	0085
P3EGRN	0085
P3ERED	0085
P3H	0969
P3J	0969
P3K	0378
P3M	0455
P3N-1	0455
P3N-2	0455
P3N-3	0455
P3N-4	0455
P3N-5	1190
P3N45	OEM

DEVICE TYPE	REPL CODE
P3P	0455
P3P-1	0455
P3P-2	0455
P3P-3	0455
P3P-4	0455
P3P-5	0455
P3R	0222
P3R-1	0222
P3R-2	0222
P3R-3	0222
P3R-4	0222
P3S	0455
P3T	0222
P3T-1	0222
P3T-2	0222
P3U	0848
P3V	3136
P3W	0486
P3Y	0378
P3Z	0037
P4A5	0015
P4B	0786
P4B5	0015
P4C	0037
P4C5	0015
P4D	0085
P4D5	0015
P4E	0455
P4E-1	1190
P4E-2	1190
P4E-3	3136
P4E-4	3136
P4E5	OEM
P4F	0969
P4G	0037
P4G2X	OEM
P4H	0969
P4J	3136
P4J/48	0455
P4J148	0042
P4K	0037
P4L	0085
P4M	0160
P4N	0085
P4P	0037
P4R	0037
P4S	0455
P4T	1190
P4U	0455
P4V	0455
P4V-1	0455
P4V-2	1190
P4W	0919
P4W-1	0455
P4W-2	0455
P4Y	0037
P4Z	0086
P5A	OEM
P5A5	0015
P5B	0037
P5B5	0015
P5C	0037
P5C5	0015
P5D	0037
P5D5	0015
P5E5	OEM
P5F	3136
P5H	0919
P5L	0455
P5M	1257
P5R	0455
P5S	3136
P5U	0919
P6/1H	OEM
P6/2H	0015
P6/3H	OEM
P6/4H	OEM
P6/5H	OEM
P6A5	0015
P6B5	0015
P6C5	0015
P6D5	0015
P6E5	OEM
P6KE6.8	3085
P6KE6.8A	3085
P6KE6.8C	2120
P6KE6.8CA	2120
P6KE7.5	OEM
P6KE7.5A	OEM
P6KE7.5C	OEM
P6KE7.5CA	OEM
P6KE8.2	OEM
P6KE8.2A	OEM
P6KE8.2C	OEM
P6KE8.2CA	OEM
P6KE9.1	OEM
P6KE9.1A	OEM
P6KE9.1C	OEM
P6KE9.1CA	OEM
P6KE10	OEM
P6KE10A	OEM
P6KE10C	OEM
P6KE10CA	OEM
P6KE11	OEM
P6KE11A	OEM
P6KE11C	OEM
P6KE11CA	OEM
P6KE12	OEM
P6KE12A	OEM

DEVICE TYPE	REPL CODE
P6KE12C	OEM
P6KE12CA	OEM
P6KE13	3143
P6KE13A	3143
P6KE13C	1161
P6KE13CA	1161
P6KE15	OEM
P6KE15A	OEM
P6KE15C	OEM
P6KE15CA	OEM
P6KE16	OEM
P6KE16A	OEM
P6KE16C	OEM
P6KE16CA	OEM
P6KE18	3162
P6KE18A	3162
P6KE18C	1756
P6KE18CA	1756
P6KE20	3171
P6KE20A	3171
P6KE20C	1921
P6KE20CA	1921
P6KE22	OEM
P6KE22A	OEM
P6KE22C	OEM
P6KE22CA	OEM
P6KE24	OEM
P6KE24A	OEM
P6KE24C	OEM
P6KE24CA	OEM
P6KE27	1904
P6KE27A	1904
P6KE27C	1941
P6KE27CA	1941
P6KE30	OEM
P6KE30A	OEM
P6KE30C	OEM
P6KE30CA	OEM
P6KE33	OEM
P6KE33A	OEM
P6KE33C	OEM
P6KE33CA	OEM
P6KE36	OEM
P6KE36A	OEM
P6KE36C	OEM
P6KE36CA	OEM
P6KE39	OEM
P6KE39A	OEM
P6KE39C	OEM
P6KE39CA	OEM
P6KE43	OEM
P6KE43A	OEM
P6KE43C	OEM
P6KE43CA	OEM
P6KE47	OEM
P6KE47A	OEM
P6KE47C	OEM
P6KE47CA	OEM
P6KE51	0563
P6KE51A	0563
P6KE51C	1961
P6KE51CA	1961
P6KE56	OEM
P6KE56A	OEM
P6KE56C	OEM
P6KE56CA	OEM
P6KE62	OEM
P6KE62A	OEM
P6KE62C	OEM
P6KE62CA	OEM
P6KE68	0825
P6KE68A	0825
P6KE68C	1976
P6KE68CA	1976
P6KE75	OEM
P6KE75A	OEM
P6KE75C	OEM
P6KE75CA	OEM
P6KE82	OEM
P6KE82A	OEM
P6KE82C	OEM
P6KE82CA	OEM
P6KE91	OEM
P6KE91A	OEM
P6KE91C	OEM
P6KE91CA	OEM
P6KE100	OEM
P6KE100A	OEM
P6KE100C	OEM
P6KE100CA	OEM
P6KE110	OEM
P6KE110A	OEM
P6KE110C	OEM
P6KE110CA	OEM
P6KE120	OEM
P6KE120A	OEM
P6KE120C	OEM
P6KE120CA	OEM
P6KE130	OEM
P6KE130A	OEM
P6KE130C	OEM
P6KE130CA	OEM
P6KE150	OEM
P6KE150A	OEM
P6KE150C	OEM
P6KE150CA	OEM
P6KE160	OEM
P6KE160A	OEM
P6KE160C	OEM

DEVICE TYPE	REPL CODE
P6KE160CA	OEM
P6KE170	OEM
P6KE170A	OEM
P6KE170C	OEM
P6KE170CA	OEM
P6KE180	OEM
P6KE180A	OEM
P6KE180C	OEM
P6KE180CA	OEM
P6KE200	1395
P6KE200A	1395
P6KE200C	1398
P6KE200CA	1398
P6KE220A	OEM
P6KE250A	OEM
P6KE300A	OEM
P6KE350A	OEM
P6KE400A	OEM
P6RP8	0071
P6RP10	0071
P6RP12	OEM
P6SE6.8	OEM
P6SE6.8A	6609
P6SE7.5	OEM
P6SE7.5A	OEM
P6SE8.2	OEM
P6SE8.2A	OEM
P6SE9.1	OEM
P6SE9.1A	OEM
P6SE10	OEM
P6SE10A	OEM
P6SE11	OEM
P6SE11A	OEM
P6SE12	OEM
P6SE12A	OEM
P6SE13	OEM
P6SE13A	6472
P6SE15	OEM
P6SE15A	OEM
P6SE16	OEM
P6SE16A	OEM
P6SE18	OEM
P6SE18A	6483
P6SE20	OEM
P6SE20A	6486
P6SE22	OEM
P6SE22A	OEM
P6SE24	OEM
P6SE24A	OEM
P6SE27	OEM
P6SE27A	6495
P6SE30	OEM
P6SE30A	OEM
P6SE33	OEM
P6SE33A	OEM
P6SE36	OEM
P6SE36A	OEM
P6SE39	OEM
P6SE39A	OEM
P6SE43	OEM
P6SE43A	OEM
P6SE47	OEM
P6SE47A	OEM
P6SE51	OEM
P6SE51A	6520
P6SE56	OEM
P6SE56A	OEM
P6SE62	OEM
P6SE62A	OEM
P6SE68	OEM
P6SE68A	6536
P6SE75	OEM
P6SE75A	OEM
P6SE82	OEM
P6SE82A	OEM
P6SE91	OEM
P6SE91A	OEM
P6SE100	OEM
P6SE100A	OEM
P6SE110	OEM
P6SE110A	OEM
P6SE120	OEM
P6SE120A	OEM
P6SE130	OEM
P6SE130A	OEM
P6SE150	OEM
P6SE150A	OEM
P6SE160	OEM
P6SE160A	OEM
P6SE170	OEM
P6SE170A	OEM
P6SE180	OEM
P6SE180A	OEM
P6SE200	OEM
P6SE200A	6240
P7A5	0015
P7B5	0015
P7C5	0015
P7D5	0015
P8/1H	OEM
P8/2H	0015
P8/3H	OEM
P8/4H	OEM
P8/5H	OEM
P8B	0848
P8C	0676
P8H	0919
P13T1	0312
P13T2	0312

DEVICE TYPE	REPL CODE
P15	0196
P16	0479
P17	1073
P19C	1099
P19E	0258
P19G	0267
P19J	1111
P20	0015
P20C	1116
P20E	0800
P20G	0315
P20J	1124
P24	OEM
P32H	0015
P44	OEM
P51A	1512
P51B	1512
P51C	1512
P52A	1522
P52B	1522
P52C	1522
P61AM6116H	1887
P61CP7811N	OEM
P61LS00**H	1519
P61LS06**H	OEM
P61LS14**H	1688
P61LS32**H	0088
P61LS74**H	0243
P61LS139*H	0153
P61LS373*H	0704
P61LS374*H	0708
P61XX0002	0967
P61XX0026	OEM
P61XX0027	0176
P62D1S1588	0133
P62H	0015
P62T2B920	0713
P62X005	OEM
P62X010	OEM
P62X011	0023
P62X018	OEM
P62X020	0148
P62X045	0319
P62X046	0319
P62X048	0436
P62X049	0296
P62X050	4109
P67	0037
P82A05	OEM
P82A203	OEM
P82A204	OEM
P82A205	OEM
P82C201	OEM
P82C202	OEM
P82H	0015
P100	0015
P100A	0015
P100B	0015
P100D	0015
P100G	0015
P100J	0015
P101	1425
P101K	OEM
P101KW	OEM
P101W	1425
P102	1425
P102K	OEM
P102KW	OEM
P102W	1425
P103	1425
P103K	OEM
P103KW	OEM
P103W	1425
P104	1425
P104K	OEM
P104KW	OEM
P104W	1425
P105	1425
P105K	OEM
P105KW	OEM
P105W	1425
P111	1670
P111K	OEM
P111KW	OEM
P111W	1670
P112	1670
P112K	OEM
P112KW	OEM
P112W	1670
P113	1670
P113K	OEM
P113KW	OEM
P113W	1670
P114	1670
P114K	OEM
P114KW	OEM
P114W	1670
P115	1670
P115K	OEM
P115KW	OEM
P115W	1670
P121	OEM
P121K	OEM
P121KW	OEM
P121W	OEM
P122	OEM
P122K	OEM
P122KW	OEM
P122W	OEM

If replacement code is OEM, contact original manufacturer for replacement.

511

DEVICE TYPE	REPL CODE
P123	OEM
P123K	OEM
P123KW	OEM
P123W	OEM
P124	OEM
P124K	OEM
P124KW	OEM
P124W	OEM
P125	OEM
P125K	OEM
P125KW	OEM
P125W	OEM
P131	6810
P131K	OEM
P132	6810
P132K	OEM
P133	6810
P133K	OEM
P134	6810
P134K	OEM
P135	6810
P135K	2278
P141	6811
P141K	OEM
P142	6811
P142K	OEM
P143	6811
P143K	OEM
P144	6811
P144K	OEM
P145	6811
P145K	2282
P150A	0015
P150B	0015
P150D	0015
P150G	0015
P150J	0015
P161	6812
P162	6812
P163	6812
P164	6812
P165	5700
P171	6814
P172	6814
P173	6814
P174	6814
P175	5701
P200	0015
P200A	0015
P201D-5R	OEM
P218-1	0546
P218-2	0378
P300A	0110
P300B	0947
P300D	0242
P300DL	OEM
P300G	0535
P300GG1	0015
P300J	0959
P300K	0811
P300M	0916
P346	0144
P346A	0144
P400	0015
P400A	0015
P401	OEM
P401K	OEM
P401KW	OEM
P401W	OEM
P402	OEM
P402K	OEM
P402KW	OEM
P402W	OEM
P403	OEM
P403K	OEM
P403KW	OEM
P403W	OEM
P404	OEM
P404K	OEM
P404KW	OEM
P404W	OEM
P405	OEM
P405K	OEM
P405KW	OEM
P405W	OEM
P411	OEM
P411K	OEM
P411KW	OEM
P411W	OEM
P412	OEM
P412K	OEM
P412KW	OEM
P412W	OEM
P413	OEM
P413K	OEM
P413KW	OEM
P413W	OEM
P414	OEM
P414K	OEM
P414KW	OEM
P414W	OEM
P415	OEM
P415K	OEM
P415KW	OEM
P415W	OEM
P421	OEM
P421K	OEM
P421KW	OEM
P421W	OEM
P422	OEM
P422K	OEM
P422KW	OEM
P422W	OEM
P423	OEM
P423K	OEM
P423KW	OEM
P423W	OEM
P424	OEM
P424K	OEM
P424KW	OEM
P424W	OEM
P425	OEM
P425K	OEM
P425KW	OEM
P425W	OEM
P431	OEM
P431K	OEM
P432	OEM
P432K	OEM
P433	OEM
P433K	OEM
P434	OEM
P434K	OEM
P435	OEM
P435K	OEM
P441	OEM
P441K	OEM
P442	OEM
P442K	OEM
P443	OEM
P443K	OEM
P444	OEM
P444K	OEM
P445	OEM
P445K	OEM
P461	OEM
P462	OEM
P463	OEM
P464	OEM
P465	OEM
P471	OEM
P472	OEM
P473	OEM
P474	OEM
P475	OEM
P504	1991
P506	1991
P521	3333
P580	0071
P600	0015
P600A	1272
P600B	1272
P600D	1277
P600G	1277
P600J	1282
P600K	1285
P600M	1285
P621	0112
P621B	4837
P621GB	1158
P800	0071
P800A	0071
P850	OEM
P1000	0071
P1000A	0037
P1003	OEM
P1004	0585
P1005	OEM
P1006	0585
P1027	OEM
P1028	OEM
P1029	OEM
P1055	0143
P1062-02	0311
P1087	0321
P1087E	0321
P1103	3515
P1172	0133
P1172-1	0133
P1201-01	OEM
P1603-02	0311
P1760	OEM
P2004	0585
P2006	0585
P2010	3862
P2114	2037
P2114-3	2037
P2163	OEM
P2221	0079
P2221A	0079
P2222	0079
P2222A	0079
P2271	0103
P2440	0087
P2906	0037
P2906A	0037
P2907	0037
P2907A	0037
P3139	0103
P3172	0178
P3309	0526
P4069	0086
P4326	0133
P5034H080S	OEM
P5058H	OEM
P5058H-546	OEM
P5100	0071
P5148	0178
P5149	0103
P5152	0016
P5153	0016
P-6006	0133
P6009	3136
P6502B	3036
P6520A	OEM
P7109	0087
P7394	0133
P7776	0229
P8035	OEM
P8048AH	OEM
P8049AH	OEM
P8051	OEM
P8051AH	OEM
P8051AH-0178	OEM
P8051AH-0552	OEM
P8088	OEM
P8088-2	OEM
P8212	1849
P8216	1852
P8224	1699
P8226	2984
P8237A-4	OEM
P8237A-5	OEM
P8237A5	OEM
P8253-5	OEM
P8254	OEM
P8254-2	OEM
P8255A-5	0051
P8257-5	OEM
P8259A	OEM
P8272A	OEM
P8314	OEM
P8393	0016
P8394	0016
P8412A	OEM
P8452	OEM
P8612	OEM
P8748	OEM
P8870	0160
P8890	0160
P8890A	0160
P8890L	0160
P9459	0015
P9797	2296
P10115	0015
P10115A	0071
P10155	0143
P10156	0015
P10156A	0071
P21309	0911
P21316	0015
P21317	0015
P21344	0012
P21443	0015
P25011LB	OEM
P-31898	0160
P31898	0160
P38103/507-10	0002
P75534	0160
P75534-1	0160
P75534-2	0085
P75534-3	0085
P75534-4	0160
P75534-5	0160
P633024C(SYLVANIA)	0086
P633024G	0086
P86421505	OEM
PA0011	OEM
PA0016	OEM
PA0017	OEM
PA0021	OEM
PA0021A	OEM
PA0022	OEM
PA0030	OEM
PA0034	OEM
PA0034A	OEM
PA069	0015
PA070	0015
PA071	0015
PA2	OEM
PA2C	OEM
PA3	0015
PA4	OEM
PA4C	OEM
PA5	OEM
PA5C	OEM
PA7-703E	OEM
PA9D522/1	0276
PA40N200	OEM
PA40N300	OEM
PA53C	4075
PA54H	OEM
PA56C	OEM
PA75N85	OEM
PA75N120	OEM
PA75N150	OEM
PA125N40	OEM
PA125N60	OEM
PA200	0015
PA234	3679
PA239	2264
PA277	2535
PA300	0015
PA305	0015
PA305A	0015
PA306	2535
PA310	0015
PA310A	0015
PA315	0015
PA315A	0015
PA-320	0015
PA320	0015
PA320A	0015
PA320B	0015
PA325	0015
PA325A	0015
PA325B	0015
PA330	0015
PA330A	0015
PA330B	0015
PA340	0015
PA340A	0015
PA340B	0015
PA350	0015
PA350A	0015
PA360	0015
PA360A	0015
PA380	0071
PA400	0015
PA401	2834
PA401X	2834
PA-500	2834
PA500	2834
PA501	2837
PA501X	2834
PA600	0015
PA1000	0037
PA1001	0037
PA2002	OEM
PA2017	OEM
PA4009-A	OEM
PA4010	OEM
PA5010	OEM
PA5012	OEM
PA6015C	OEM
PA7001/518	0867
PA7001/519	0692
PA7001/520	0507
PA7001/521	0232
PA7001/522	1018
PA7001/523	1160
PA7001/524	1177
PA7001/525	0310
PA7001/526	0268
PA7001/527	0357
PA7001/528	0381
PA7001/529	1303
PA7001/530	1394
PA7001/531	1164
PA7001/532	1417
PA7001/533	1265
PA7001/539	1193
PA7001/593	0614
PA7615	0015
PA7703	0627
PA7703E	0627
PA8260	0111
PA8261	0002
PA8543	0111
PA8645	0015
PA8900	0555
PA9004	0111
PA9005	0111
PA9006	0016
PA9154	0050
PA9155	0050
PA9156	0004
PA9157	0004
PA9158	0164
PA9160	0015
PA9267	0631
PA9483	0590
PA10556	0015
PA10880	0050
PA10887	0015
PA-10889-1	0160
PA10889-1	0164
PA-10889-2	0160
PA10889-2	0164
PA-10890	0160
PA10890	0085
PA-10890-1	0160
PA10890-1	0160
PADT20	0050
PADT21	0050
PADT22	0050
PADT23	0050
PADT24	0050
PADT25	0050
PADT26	0050
PADT27	0050
PADT28	0050
PADT29	OEM
PADT30	0050
PADT31	0050
PADT35	0050
PADT40	0050
PADT50	0085
PADT51	0050
PAL10L8CN	OEM
PAL12L6NC	OEM
PAL12L10CNS	OEM
PAL14H4CN	OEM
PAL14L8CNS	OEM
PAL16L8	OEM
PAL16L8ACN	OEM
PAL16L8CN	OEM
PAL16R4CN	OEM
PAL20L10	OEM
PAL20X8CNS	OEM
PAR-12	0160
PAR12	0160
PAVIMB625167	OEM
PAVITD62083A	OEM
PAWI1W1510MA	OEM
PAWI2W1500C	OEM
PB	0208
PB2	OEM
PB4	OEM
PB5	OEM
PB40N280	OEM
PB40N400	OEM
PB61	0319
PB61G	OEM
PB62	1404
PB62G	OEM
PB64	0468
PB64G	OEM
PB66	0441
PB66G	OEM
PB68	1412
PB68G	OEM
PB75N140	OEM
PB75N180	OEM
PB-99S005	0136
PB110	0160
PB125N60	OEM
PB125N80	OEM
PB401	0319
PB553(C)	OEM
PB605	0319
PB605G	OEM
PB610	2425
PB610G	OEM
PB6013	0037
PB6013A	0037
PB6013B	0037
PB6014	0037
PB6014A	0037
PB6015C	OEM
PBC107	0111
PBC107A	0111
PBC107B	0111
PBC108	0111
PBC108A	0111
PBC108B	0111
PBC108C	0111
PBC109	0111
PBC109B	0111
PBC109C	0111
PBC182	0144
PBC183	0155
PBC184	0590
PBE3014-1	0164
PBE3014-2	0164
PBE3020-1	0164
PBE3020-2	0208
PBE3162	0164
PBE3162-1	0004
PBE3162-2	0004
PBE3322	0143
PBL3717	OEM
PBL3717A	OEM
PBM74LS30P	0822
PBM74LS74AP	0243
PBM74LS86P	0288
PBM74LS244P	0453
PBM74LS375P	OEM
PBM74LS393P	0813
PBM152	OEM
PBM6004	0037
PBT5504	0647
PBU05	OEM
PBU10	OEM
PBU20	OEM
PBU40	OEM
PBU60	OEM
PBU80	OEM
PBU100	OEM
PBX103	0211
PBX113	0211
PC02P1/2	0015
PC0211/2	0015
PC0600A	0549
PC0601A	0005
PC0603A	0623
PC0604A	0030
PC0610A	0549
PC0611A	0005
PC0620A	0549
PC0.2P11/2	0015
PC2	OEM
PC4	OEM
PC5	OEM
PC40N500	OEM
PC40N800	OEM
PC50B187-27	OEM
PC74HC157P	OEM
PC74HC4046AP	OEM
PC74HC4053P	OEM
PC74HCT164P	OEM
PC74HCT244P	OEM
PC74HCT245P	OEM
PC75N250	OEM
PC75N400	OEM
PC78L05	1288
PC78L05A	OEM
PC78M08H	OEM
PC78M12H	OEM
PC100	0419
PC110	0419
PC111	4449
PC125N130	OEM
PC125N180	OEM
PC127	0030
PC127A	0030
PC127B	OEM
PC127C	OEM
PC127D	OEM
PC128	0030
PC128A	0030
PC128B	OEM
PC128C	OEM
PC128D	OEM
PC133	0623
PC133A	0623
PC133B	OEM
PC133C	OEM
PC133D	OEM
PC135	0005
PC135A	0005
PC135B	OEM
PC135C	OEM
PC135D	OEM
PC136	0623
PC136A	0623
PC136B	OEM
PC136C	OEM
PC136D	OEM
PC138	0549
PC138A	0549
PC138B	OEM
PC138C	OEM
PC138D	OEM
PC139	0549
PC139A	0549
PC139B	OEM
PC139C	OEM
PC139D	OEM
PC140	0549
PC140A	0549
PC140B	OEM
PC140C	OEM
PC140D	OEM
PC141	0549
PC141A	0549
PC141B	OEM
PC141C	OEM
PC141D	OEM
PC200	0848
PC210	0848
PC339C	0176
PC358C	OEM
PC393C	0624
PC563H2	1152
PC574J	1319
PC702V	OEM
PC713	0311
PC-713U	0311
PC713U	0311
PC713V	0741
PC714	0311
PC714U	OEM
PC814	OEM
PC817	1158
PC817-B	1158
PC817-C	1158
PC817A	1158
PC817B	1158
PC-817BC	1158
PC817BC	1158
PC817C	1158
PC900	OEM
PC1007	0037
PC1007A	0037
PC1008	0037
PC1008A	0037
PC1008B	0037
PC1026C	0701
PC1066T	0164
PC1067T	0164
PC1068T	0164
PC1167C2	2237
PC1228H	OEM
PC1363C	0678
PC1873CT	OEM
PC1879-004	0170
PC-2007D	OEM
PC3002	0164
PC3003	0164
PC3004	0160
PC3005	0164
PC3006	0164
PC3007	0164
PC3009	0164
PC3010	0222
PC3345	OEM
PC3346	OEM
PC-3350	OEM
PC4004	0015
PC4558C	0356
PC7327C	1063
PC7805H	0619
PC7805HF	0619
PC7812H	OEM
PC7812HF	0330
PC17805H	0619
PC20003	0574
PC-20004	2142
PC20004	2142
PC-20005	2849
PC-20006	3506
PC-20007	1206
PC-20008	0438
PC-20009	OEM
PC-20010	OEM
PC-20011	OEM
PC-20012	4481
PC-20015	3724
PC-20018	0438
PC20018	1206
PC-20022	OEM
PC-20023	0858
PC-20024	0696
PC-20030	0696
PC-20045	0514
PC-20046	3050
PC-20051	2246
PC-20066	0144
PC-20069	2559
PC-20071	2051
PC-20082	0412
PC-20083	1602
PC-20084	OEM
PC-20085	2008
PC-20086	6048
PC-20087	2279
PC-20110	0358
PC-20143	2279
PC-20151	0701
PCB17A	OEM
PCD5582	OEM
PCD8582	OEM
PCF2N05	OEM
PCF2N08	OEM
PCF2N12	OEM
PCF2N18	OEM
PCF3N45	OEM
PCF5P12	OEM
PCF6P08	OEM
PCF8N18	OEM
PCF8P08	OEM
PCF10N12	OEM
PCF10N45	OEM
PCF12N08	OEM
PCF12N18	OEM
PCF12P08	OEM
PCF15N05	OEM
PCF15N12	OEM
PCF18N08	OEM
PCF25N18	OEM
PCF30N12	OEM
PCF35N08	OEM
PCF45N05	OEM
PCF2111P	OEM
PCF8571P	OEM
PCF8573P	OEM
PCF8583P	OEM
PCM53JP-V-2	OEM
PCM54HP	OEM
PCM54HP-V	OEM
PCM55HP-S	OEM
PCM56P	OEM
PCM56P(RED)	OEM
PCM56P-S	OEM
PCMB74LS00M	1519
PCMB74LS02M	1550
PCMB74LS04M	1585
PCMB74LS05M	1598
PCMB74LS10M	1652
PCMB74LS32M	0088
PCV50	OEM
PCV50A	OEM
PCV56	OEM
PCV58	OEM
PCV60	OEM
PCV61	OEM
PCV62	OEM
PCV63	OEM
PCV67	OEM
PCV68	OEM
PCV69	OEM
PCV70	OEM
PCV71	OEM
PCV73	OEM
PCV76	OEM
PCV84	OEM
PCV85	OEM
PCV88	OEM
PCV97	OEM
PCV104	OEM
PCX-010	OEM
PCX010	OEM
PD0011A	OEM
PD0012A	OEM
PD0026A	OEM
PD0031	OEM
PD0034	OEM
PD05	0276
PD2	OEM
PD3L	OEM
PD4	OEM
PD5	OEM

If replacement code is OEM, contact original manufacturer for replacement.

DEVICE TYPE	REPL CODE
PD6	OEM
PD10	0276
PD20	0287
PD31	OEM
PD32	OEM
PD40	0293
PD49P1	OEM
PD49PI	OEM
PD60	0299
PD80	0250
PD100	0250
PD101	4176
PD102	4176
PD103	0015
PD104	0015
PD105	0015
PD106	0015
PD107	0015
PD107A	0015
PD108	0015
PD110	0015
PD111	0015
PD114	0071
PD115	0071
PD116	0071
PD122	0015
PD125	0015
PD129	0015
PD130	0015
PD131	0015
PD132	0015
PD133	0015
PD134	0015
PD135	0015
PD151	OEM
PD154	0015
PD155	0015
PD301	OEM
PD302	OEM
PD303	OEM
PD304	OEM
PD305	OEM
PD306	OEM
PD307	OEM
PD308	OEM
PD309	OEM
PD310	OEM
PD311	OEM
PD323BHT	OEM
PD401	OEM
PD546C037	OEM
PD553C042	OEM
PD651G-517	OEM
PD651G-518	OEM
PD910	0015
PD913	0071
PD914	0071
PD915	0071
PD916	0071
PD1001	0079
PD1002	0079
PD1011	0276
PD1020	0299
PD-1567	0299
PD1703(C)	OEM
PD1705C	OEM
PD1913C	OEM
PD3068-B	OEM
PD3068B	OEM
PD3089A	OEM
PD3093	OEM
PD3093A	OEM
PD3095	OEM
PD3113	OEM
PD3113A	OEM
PD4035(C)	OEM
PD4051	OEM
PD4066BC	0101
PD4073A	OEM
PD4073B	OEM
PD4113A	OEM
PD4132	OEM
PD4150	OEM
PD4150A	OEM
PD4151A	OEM
PD4151B	OEM
PD4175B	OEM
PD4184	OEM
PD4185	OEM
PD4185A	OEM
PD4192	OEM
PD4193	OEM
PD4199	OEM
PD5030	OEM
PD5039	OEM
PD5039-A	OEM
PD5039A	OEM
PD5068-A	OEM
PD5068A	OEM
PD5115	OEM
PD6000	0755
PD6000A	0755
PD6001	0118
PD6001A	0118
PD6002	0296
PD6002A	0188
PD6003	0188
PD6003A	0188
PD6004	0188

DEVICE TYPE	REPL CODE
PD6004A	0451
PD6005	0274
PD6005A	0528
PD6006	0162
PD6006A	0446
PD6007	0162
PD6007A	0162
PD6008	0157
PD6008A	0157
PD6009	0466
PD6009A	0466
PD6010	0062
PD6010A	0062
PD6011	0077
PD6011A	0077
PD6012	0165
PD6012A	0165
PD6013	0057
PD6013A	0057
PD6014	0170
PD6014A	0170
PD6015	0181
PD6015A	0181
PD6016	0052
PD6016A	0052
PD6017	0053
PD6017A	0053
PD6018	0681
PD6018A	0681
PD6019	0440
PD6019A	0440
PD6020	0371
PD6020A	0371
PD6037	OEM
PD6041	0755
PD6042	0118
PD6043	0296
PD6044	0188
PD6045	0451
PD6046	0274
PD6047	0446
PD6048	0162
PD6049	0157
PD6049C	0157
PD6050	0631
PD6051	0062
PD6052	0077
PD6053	0165
PD6054	0057
PD6055	0170
PD6056	0181
PD6057	0052
PD6058	0053
PD6059	0681
PD6060	0440
PD6061	0371
PD6064A	OEM
PD6105	OEM
PD6105C	OEM
PD6201	0274
PD6202	0140
PD6209	0057
PD6336C	OEM
PD7507G-514	OEM
PD9093-59	0354
PD9094-59	1622
PD9097-59	1472
PD9099-59	0329
PD9930-59	1812
PD9932-59	1035
PD9933-59	2086
PD9935-59	1168
PD9936-59	1820
PD9937-59	1824
PD9944-59	0033
PD9945-59	0081
PD9946-59	0141
PD9948-59	3365
PD9949-59	1833
PD9950-59	2595
PD9951-59	2067
PD9961-59	1848
PD9962-59	0557
PD9963-59	0337
PDB004	OEM
PDE001	OEM
PDE003	OEM
PDE009	OEM
PDE018	OEM
PDE018B	OEM
PDE024	OEM
PDG002B	OEM
PDG005C	OEM
PDG013-A	OEM
PDG017-A	OEM
PDG017A	OEM
PDG023-A	OEM
PDG023A	OEM
PDG035	OEM
PDG037	OEM
PDG041	OEM
PDJ002	OEM
PDR25	1325
PDR50	1325
PE40	0468
PE55ST3	OEM
PE210	0224
PE210C	0224
PE254A	0224

DEVICE TYPE	REPL CODE
PE254B	0224
PE254C	0224
PE401	0015
PE401N	0015
PE402	0015
PE403	0015
PE404	0015
PE405	0015
PE406	0015
PE407	0071
PE408	0071
PE409	0071
PE410	0071
PE501	0015
PE502	0015
PE503	0015
PE504	0015
PE505	0015
PE506	0015
PE507	0071
PE508	0071
PE509	0071
PE510	0071
PE3001	0079
PE3002	0007
PE3015	0079
PE3100	0414
PE5010	0079
PE5013	0079
PE5015	0079
PE5025	0326
PE5029	0414
PE5030	0155
PE5030A	0155
PE5030B	0155
PE5031	0127
PE8050B	0018
PE8550B	0527
PE9093-59	0354
PE9094-59	1622
PE9097-59	1472
PE9099-59	0329
PE9930-59	1812
PE9932-59	1035
PE9933-59	2086
PE9935-59	1168
PE9936-59	1820
PE9937-59	1824
PE9944-59	0033
PE9945-59	0081
PE9946-59	0141
PE9948-59	3365
PE9949-59	1833
PE9950-59	2595
PE9951-59	2067
PE9961-59	1848
PE9962-59	0557
PE9963-59	0337
PEB79	OEM
PEL1009	OEM
PEL1018	OEM
PEL1021	OEM
PEL1022	OEM
PEP2	0016
PEP5	0016
PEP6	0016
PEP7	0016
PEP8	0016
PEP9	0016
PEP95	0396
PEP1001	0144
PEP2001	0086
PET0404	0855
PET0404-1	OEM
PET0404-2	0855
PET-101-1	0144
PET1001	0590
PET1002	0016
PET1075	0144
PET1075A	0233
PET2001	0016
PET2002	0016
PET3001	0144
PET3002	0007
PET3702	0037
PET3703	0037
PET3704	0016
PET3705	0079
PET3706	0016
PET3903	0079
PET3904	0079
PET3905	0037
PET3906	0037
PET4001	0016
PET4002	0016
PET4003	0111
PET4058	0037
PET4059	0037
PET4060	0037
PET4061	0037
PET4062	0037
PET4123	OEM
PET4124	0079
PET4125	0037
PET4126	0037
PET6001	0016
PET6002	0016
PET6003	1471
PET8000	0016

DEVICE TYPE	REPL CODE
PET8001	0016
PET8002	0016
PET8003	0016
PET8004	0016
PET8005	0016
PET8005A	0016
PET8006	0016
PET8006A	0016
PET8007	0016
PET8007A	0016
PET8101	0007
PET8200	0086
PET8201	0144
PET8202	0086
PET8203	0086
PET8204	0155
PET8250	0144
PET8251	0144
PET8300	0144
PET8301	0037
PET8302	OEM
PET8303	0037
PET8304	0037
PET8350	OEM
PET8351	OEM
PET8352	OEM
PET8353	OEM
PET9001	0079
PET9001A	OEM
PET9002	0016
PET9002A	OEM
PET9003	OEM
PET9004	OEM
PET9021	0086
PET9022	0086
PF110R	OEM
PF110S	OEM
PF125R	OEM
PF125S	OEM
PF140R	OEM
PF140S	OEM
PF310R	OEM
PF310S	OEM
PF325R	OEM
PF325S	OEM
PF340R	OEM
PF340S	OEM
PF510	OEM
PF810R	OEM
PF820R	OEM
PF825R	OEM
PFB1400	OEM
PFIGD	OEM
PFN3066	OEM
PFN3069	OEM
PFN3458	OEM
PFR851	4042
PFR856	0071
PFWB2	OEM
PFZ6V8	3085
PFZ6V8A	3085
PFZ13	3143
PFZ13A	3143
PFZ18	3162
PFZ18A	3162
PFZ20	3171
PFZ20A	3171
PFZ27	1904
PFZ27A	1904
PFZ51	0563
PFZ51A	0563
PFZ68	0825
PFZ68A	0825
PFZ200	1395
PFZ200A	1395
PG010	OEM
PG107A	0549
PG152R	OEM
PG207A	0549
PG307A	0549
PG310A	0005
PG322A	0623
PG333A	0030
PG2232SY-B1	OEM
PG3433SX	OEM
PG4001	1325
PG4002	0080
PG4003	0604
PG4004	0790
PG4005	0015
PG4006	0072
PG4007	0071
PG5531K	OEM
PG5533KY-GR	OEM
PG5553K-RE	OEM
PG5553KY	OEM
PG5628SY	OEM
PG5638SY	OEM
PG5724SY	OEM
PG6100A	OEM
PG6100B	OEM
PG6100C	OEM
PG6100D	OEM
PG6101A	OEM
PG6101B	OEM
PG6101C	OEM
PG6101D	OEM
PG6150A	OEM
PG6150B	OEM

DEVICE TYPE	REPL CODE
PG6150C	OEM
PG6150D	OEM
PG6151A	OEM
PG6151B	OEM
PG6151C	OEM
PG6151D	OEM
PG6220A	OEM
PG6220B	OEM
PG6220C	OEM
PG6220D	OEM
PG6221A	OEM
PG6221B	OEM
PG6221C	OEM
PG6221D	OEM
PG6330A	OEM
PG6330B	OEM
PG6330C	OEM
PG6330D	OEM
PG6331A	OEM
PG6331B	OEM
PG6331C	OEM
PG6331D	OEM
PG6470A	OEM
PG6470B	OEM
PG6470C	OEM
PG6470D	OEM
PG6680A	OEM
PG6680B	OEM
PG6680C	OEM
PG6680D	OEM
PG22225X	OEM
PGM1	OEM
PGM2	OEM
PGMI	OEM
PGR-24	0242
PH-1	OEM
PH9-221	0276
PH9D5	0071
PH9D522/1	0299
PH9D522/11	0293
PH9D522M	0276
PH9D5221	0276
PH9DS22	0015
PH9DS221	0276
PH11C22/1	0535
PH25C22	0015
PH25C22/1	0015
PH25C22/21	0015
PH25C221	0276
PH-70	OEM
PH101	OEM
PH101T	OEM
PH103	OEM
PH108	0102
PH109	0071
PH110	OEM
PH204	0015
PH208	0015
PH244N	OEM
PH-302	2604
PH302	2604
PH302B	OEM
PH302B(1)	OEM
PH309	OEM
PH310	OEM
PH310A-C	OEM
PH404	0015
PH421-6	1359
PH1021	0015
PH2222A	0079
PH2907A	0037
PH6659	OEM
PH6660	OEM
PH6661	OEM
PIC	0037
PIC500	OEM
PIC501	OEM
PIC502	OEM
PIC1640	OEM
PIC1650	OEM
PIK	0160
PIL/4956	0050
PIL74956	0050
PIP8.4	OEM
PIP24	OEM
PIP30	OEM
PIP60	OEM
PIP120	OEM
PIP208	OEM
PIP250	OEM
PIP440	OEM
PIP500	OEM
PJVD05AZ12	OEM
PJVD05AZ24	OEM
PJVIBA12003	OEM
PJVIHD63B3XP	OEM
PJVIL78LR05C	OEM
PJVIM70H036	OEM
PJVIM5165LL	OEM
PJVIM7032H	OEM
PJVIM54532P	OEM
PJVIMSM5299A	OEM
PJVISED1330F	OEM
PJWI1W1000M	OEM
PJWI2XR430M	OEM
PJWI2XR440M	OEM
PJWIR440M	OEM
PJWIXR340M	OEM
PJWIXR350M	OEM

DEVICE TYPE	REPL CODE
PJWIXR430M	OEM
PL3V6Z	OEM
PL4V3Z	0528
PL6V2Z	0631
PL9V1Z	0012
PL12Z	0137
PL15Z	0002
PL51Z	0497
PL56Z	0863
PL62Z	0778
PL68Z	1258
PL75Z	1181
PL82Z	0327
PL91Z	1301
PL100Z	0098
PL102	1704
PL110Z	0149
PL130Z	0213
PL-150-001-9-00	0143
PL-150-001-9-005	0019
PL-150-006-9-001	0123
PL-151-032-9-004	0120
PL-151-035-9-001	0133
PL-151-040-9-001	0133
PL-151-040-9-002	0133
PL-151-040-9-003	0015
PL-151-045-9-001	0015
PL-151-045-9-002	0133
PL-151-045-9-003	0143
PL-151-045-9-004	0015
PL-152-044-9-001	0012
PL-152-051-9-001	0012
PL-152-052-9-002	0091
PL-152-054-9-001	0244
PL-154-001-9-001	0030
PL160Z	0255
PL-172-010-9-001	0042
PL-172-014-9-001	0042
PL-172-014-9-002	0617
PL-172-024-9-004	0386
PL-176-025-9-001	0076
PL-176-029-9-001	0016
PL-176-029-9-002	0693
PL-176-042-9-001	0155
PL-176-042-9-002	0076
PL-176-042-9-003	0076
PL-176-042-9-004	0111
PL-176-042-9-005	0219
PL-176-042-9-006	0191
PL-176-047-9-002	0364
PL-176-049-9-002	0076
PL-177-006-9-002	0006
PL180Z	0363
PL-182-014-9-002	3017
PL-182-014-9-002(FET	0321
PL-307-047-9-001	0413
PL-307-047-9-002	0817
PL1021	0007
PL1022	0007
PL1023	0007
PL1024	0127
PL1025	0127
PL1026	0127
PL1031	0037
PL1032	0855
PL1033	0037
PL1033-1	OEM
PL1034	0037
PL1036-1	OEM
PL1051	0144
PL1052	0016
PL1053	0144
PL1054	0016
PL1055	0144
PL1061	0144
PL1062	0144
PL1063	0144
PL1064	0144
PL1065	0144
PL1066	0007
PL1067	0007
PL1068	OEM
PL1081	0144
PL1082	0144
PL1083	0086
PL1084	0086
PL1085	0283
PL1091	0321
PL1092	0321
PL1093	0321
PL1094	0321
PL1101	0037
PL1102	0037
PL1103	0037
PL1104	0037
PL1111	0007
PL1112	0007
PL1113	0127
PL4001	OEM
PL4001L	1325
PL4002	OEM
PL4002L	OEM
PL4003	OEM
PL4003L	0604
PL4004	OEM
PL4004L	0790
PL4005	OEM
PL4005L	OEM
PL4006	OEM

DEVICE TYPE	REPL CODE
PL4006L	0072
PL4007	OEM
PL4007L	0369
PL4021	0079
PL4023	0414
PL4031	0150
PL4032	0150
PL4033	0150
PL4034	0150
PL4051	0079
PL4052	0079
PL4053	0079
PL4054	0079
PL4055	0079
PL4061	0111
PL4062	0111
PL4112	0414
PL20015	3724
PLA552	OEM
PLE-48	0042
PLE202	1581
PLE534N	OEM
PLL01A	OEM
PLL02	1704
PLL02A	1704
PLL02A-C	1704
PLL02A-F	1704
PLL02A-G	4160
PLL02AG	4160
PLL03	3515
PLL03A	3515
PLQ0.8	0080
PLR501	OEM
PLR1001	OEM
PLR2001	OEM
PLR3001	OEM
PLR4001	OEM
PLS153	OEM
PLS153N	OEM
PLS173	OEM
PLS173N	OEM
PM0001	OEM
PM-3	OEM
PM3	OEM
PM-4	OEM
PM8	OEM
PM-9	OEM
PM9	OEM
PM101-1	4640
PM101-2	4640
PM101-4	4640
PM101-6	4640
PM102-1	4701
PM102-2	4701
PM102-4	4701
PM102-6	4701
PM194	0127
PM195	0127
PM308AP	2231
PM355AJ	3576
PM355J	3576
PM356AJ	3576
PM356J	3576
PM357AJ	3576
PM357J	3576
PM725CJ	2863
PM741CJ	0406
PM741CY	1964
PM1210B	OEM
PM1220B	OEM
PM4550C	OEM
PM5006	0079
PMBT2222	1426
PMBT2222A	1426
PMBT2369	1426
PMBT2907	OEM
PMBT2907A	1491
PMBT3640	OEM
PMBT3903	1426
PMBT3904	1426
PMBT3906	1491
PMBT4401	1426
PMBT4403	1491
PMBT5086	OEM
PMBT5087	OEM
PMBT5088	5286
PMBT5089	OEM
PMBT5401	1495
PMBT5550	2316
PMBT5551	2316
PMBT6427	OEM
PMBT6428	OEM
PMBT6429	OEM
PMBTA05	1426
PMBTA06	1426
PMBTA13	OEM
PMBTA14	OEM
PMBTA20	OEM
PMBTA42	OEM
PMBTA43	OEM
PMBTA55	1491
PMBTA56	1495
PMBTA63	OEM
PMBTA64	OEM
PMBTA70	OEM
PMBTA92	OEM
PMBTA93	OEM
PMC1367P	2888
PMD10K40	2422

If replacement code is OEM, contact original manufacturer for replacement. 513

DEVICE TYPE	REPL CODE
PMD10K60	2422
PMD10K80	2422
PMD10K100	2422
PMD11K40	2415
PMD11K60	2415
PMD11K80	2415
PMD11K100	2415
PMD12K40	2411
PMD12K60	2411
PMD12K80	2411
PMD12K100	2422
PMD13K40	2262
PMD13K60	2262
PMD13K80	2262
PMD13K100	2415
PMD16K60	3483
PMD16K80	3483
PMD16K100	3483
PMD17K40	3484
PMD17K60	3484
PMD17K80	3484
PMD17K100	3484
PMK16D40	OEM
PMM8713	OEM
PMP-G12S	OEM
PMT011	0086
PMT012	0086
PMT013	0079
PMT014	0079
PMT015	OEM
PMT016	0086
PMT018	0086
PMT019	0086
PMT020	0086
PMT021	OEM
PMT022	OEM
PMT023	0007
PMT024	0086
PMT025	OEM
PMT111	0079
PMT112	0086
PMT113	0079
PMT114	0086
PMT115	OEM
PMT116	0086
PMT117	OEM
PMT118	0086
PMT119	0086
PMT120	0086
PMT121	OEM
PMT122	OEM
PMT123	OEM
PMT124	OEM
PMT125	OEM
PMT211	OEM
PMT212	OEM
PMT213	OEM
PMT214	OEM
PMT215	OEM
PMT216	OEM
PMT217	OEM
PMT218	OEM
PMT219	OEM
PMT220	OEM
PMT221	OEM
PMT222	OEM
PMT223	OEM
PMT224	OEM
PMT225	OEM
PMT1767	0144
PMT1767M	OEM
PMT1767P	OEM
PMT1767T	OEM
PMT1787M	OEM
PMT1787P	OEM
PMT1787T	OEM
PMTT18501	OEM
PMV107	OEM
PMV107A	OEM
PMV112	OEM
PMV112A	OEM
PMV113	OEM
PMV113A	OEM
PMV114	OEM
PMV114A	OEM
PMV115	OEM
PMV115A	OEM
PMV116	OEM
PMV116A	OEM
PMV117	OEM
PMV117A	OEM
PMV122	OEM
PMV122A	OEM
PMV123	OEM
PMV123A	OEM
PMV124	OEM
PMV124A	OEM
PMV125	OEM
PMV125A	OEM
PMV126	OEM
PMV126A	OEM
PMV127	OEM
PMV127A	OEM
PMV128	OEM
PMV128A	OEM
PMV129	OEM
PMV129A	OEM
PMV130	OEM
PMV130A	OEM
PMV132	OEM
PMV132A	OEM
PMV133	OEM
PMV133A	OEM
PMV134	OEM
PMV134A	OEM
PMV135	OEM
PMV135A	OEM
PMV136	OEM
PMV136A	OEM
PMV137	OEM
PMV137A	OEM
PMV138	OEM
PMV138A	OEM
PMV139	OEM
PMV139A	OEM
PMV140	OEM
PMV140A	OEM
PMV141	OEM
PMV141A	OEM
PN2	OEM
PN26	0178
PN66	0042
PN70	0037
PN71	0037
PN72	0037
PN107	0016
PN108	0079
PN109	0079
PN111W	OEM
PN150	2083
PN150-TV	OEM
PN150NV	2083
PN150SAN	OEM
PN150TV	2083
PN158	OEM
PN158NV	OEM
PN204	0015
PN205	3930
PN268R-NC	OEM
PN302	OEM
PN303	OEM
PN313	2604
PN323	OEM
PN323B-HT	OEM
PN323BHT	OEM
PN350	0103
PN917	0144
PN918	0144
PN929	0111
PN930	0079
PN930(NSC)	0079
PN930(NTLB)	0079
PN1185	OEM
PN1190	OEM
PN1613	0086
PN1711	0086
PN2025	OEM
PN2218A	0734
PN2219A	0734
PN2221	0018
PN2221A	0079
PN2222	0079
PN2222A	0079
PN2369	0079
PN2369A	0079
PN2484	0127
PN2904	0037
PN2904A	0037
PN2905	0150
PN2905A	0037
PN2906	0037
PN2906A	0037
PN2907	0037
PN2907A	0037
PN2908	0037
PN3054	0556
PN3238-HT	OEM
PN3250	0037
PN3250A	0037
PN3251	0037
PN3251A	0037
PN3548	OEM
PN3563	0144
PN3564	0144
PN3565	0079
PN3566	0079
PN3567	0855
PN3568	0855
PN3569	0855
PN3638	0037
PN3638A	0037
PN3639	6435
PN3640	6435
PN3641	0079
PN3642	0079
PN3643	0079
PN3644	0037
PN3645	0037
PN3646	0079
PN3662	0144
PN3663	0144
PN3684	OEM
PN3685	OEM
PN3686	OEM
PN3687	OEM
PN3691	0079
PN3692	0079
PN3693	OEM
PN3694	0079
PN3946	OEM
PN3947	OEM
PN3962	OEM
PN4013	0079
PN4014	OEM
PN4054	0676
PN4121	0037
PN4122	0037
PN4140	0079
PN4141	0079
PN4142	0037
PN4143	0037
PN4248	0037
PN4249	0037
PN4258	0037
PN4275	0079
PN4302	OEM
PN4302-18	OEM
PN4303	OEM
PN4303-18	OEM
PN4304	OEM
PN4304-18	OEM
PN4342	OEM
PN4354	0037
PN4355	0037
PN4356	0037
PN4391	6498
PN4392	OEM
PN4393	OEM
PN4416	0321
PN4423	0037
PN4916	0037
PN4917	OEM
PN5127	0079
PN5128	0079
PN5129	0079
PN5130	0144
PN5131	0079
PN5132	0079
PN5133	0079
PN5134	0079
PN5135	0079
PN5136	0079
PN5137	0079
PN5138	0037
PN5139	0144
PN5142	0037
PN5143	0037
PN5179	0224
PO74LS04	1585
PO74LS368A	0985
PO93	0143
PO117RD01B	OEM
POSN74ALS08N	OEM
POSN74LS14N	1688
POSN74LS123N	0973
POSN74LS138N	0422
POSN74LS157N	1153
POSN74LS161AN	0852
POSN74LS166N	4301
POSN74LS221N	1230
POSN74LS245N	0458
POSN74LS368AN	0985
POSN74LS373N	0704
POSN74LS628N	OEM
POSN74S153N	2138
POSN7407N	1329
POSN7416N	1339
POSN7417N	1342
POSN7445N	1074
POSN74145N	0614
POSN74159N	OEM
POWER-12	0160
POWER12	0160
POWER-25	0160
POWER25	0160
POWER-40	0435
POWER40	0435
POWER-60	0435
POWER60	0435
POWER-80	0435
POWER80	0435
POWER-99	0160
POWER99	0160
POWER-299	0160
POWER299	0160
POWER500	0435
PP74F153	OEM
PP3000	0103
PP3001	0130
PP3002	0130
PP3003	0103
PP3004	0130
PP3006	0103
PP3007	0130
PP3008	0177
PP3083	0556
PP3084	0556
PP3085	0556
PP3086	0556
PP3087	0556
PP3088	0556
PP3250	0042
PP3310	0042
PP3312	0042
PP3647	0130
PPC1	OEM
PPR1006	0555
PPR1008	0555
PPT720	0016
PQ05R04	OEM
PQ05R041	OEM
PQ27	0050
PQ28	0164
PQ29	0164
PQ30	0050
PQ31	0085
PR3-3	0222
PR515	0162
PR605	0162
PR617	0137
PR620	0002
PR804	0162
PR9010R	0545
PR3423S	OEM
PR3433S	OEM
PR4524K	OEM
PR5400	0087
PR5401	0087
PR5402	0087
PR5403	0087
PR5404	0087
PR5405	0087
PR5406	0087
PR5407	0087
PR5408	0087
PR5505S	OEM
PR5532B	OEM
PR5533K-RE	OEM
PR-5534S	5560
PR5534S	5560
PR5553K	OEM
PR5608S	OEM
PR5628S	OEM
PR5638S	OEM
PR5704S	OEM
PR5705S-BS	OEM
PR5724S	OEM
PR9000	2077
PR9000R	1130
PR9001	2077
PR9001R	1130
PR9002	0607
PR9002R	1180
PR9003	0607
PR9003R	1180
PR9004	0206
PR9004R	1002
PR9005	0206
PR9005R	1002
PR9006	0583
PR9006R	0942
PR9007	0583
PR9007R	0942
PR9008	0131
PR9008R	0540
PR9009	0131
PR9009R	0540
PR9010R	0545
PR9011	0145
PR9011R	0545
PR9012	1124
PR9012R	1111
PR9013	1124
PR9013R	1111
PR9014	0045
PR9014R	0280
PR9015	0045
PR9015R	0280
PR9023	1124
PR9024	1124
PR9025	0045
PR9026	0045
PR9034	3716
PR9034R	2640
PR9035	2633
PR9035R	2741
PR9036	2633
PR9036R	2741
PR9037	1995
PR9037R	2879
PR9038	1995
PR9038R	2879
PR9039	2657
PR9039R	3022
PR9040	2657
PR9040R	3022
PR9041	3846
PR9041R	3088
PR9042	3846
PR9042R	3088
PR9043	2631
PR9043R	3178
PR9044	2631
PR9044R	3178
PRB738	OEM
PRB8128	OEM
PRC2A	0240
PRC5A	0240
PRC10A	0240
PRC15A	0240
PRC20A	0240
PRF851	OEM
PRO-050	OEM
PRO5	OEM
PRS3017	0162
PRT-101	0016
PRT101	0233
PRT-104	0016
PRT-104-1	0016
PRT-104-2	0016
PRT-104-3	0016
PRT-104-4	0086
PRV94	OEM
PRV100	OEM
PS	OEM
PS005	0015
PS08	1641
PS010	0015
PS015	0015
PS020	0015
PS025	0015
PS030	0015
PS035	0015
PS040	0015
PS050	0015
PS060	0015
PS0125	0015
PS-1	0160
PS1	0160
PS1A	0023
PS-1.5-2	0071
PS12	OEM
PS18	1641
PS24	OEM
PS28	1641
PS28(SCR)	1641
PS38	1574
PS48	1574
PS58	1655
PS68	1655
PS105	0015
PS110	0015
PS120	0015
PS125	0015
PS130	0015
PS135	0015
PS140	0015
PS150	0015
PS152R	0102
PS152RL	0071
PS160	0015
PS220	1641
PS320	1574
PS330	2623
PS405	0015
PS410	0015
PS415	0015
PS420	0015
PS425	0015
PS430	0015
PS435	0015
PS440	0015
PS450	0015
PS460	0015
PS520	1655
PS530	2625
PS603	0015
PS604	0015
PS605	0015
PS609	0015
PS610	0015
PS611	0015
PS615	0015
PS616	0015
PS617	0015
PS620	1655
PS621	0015
PS622	0015
PS623	0015
PS627	0015
PS628	0015
PS629	0015
PS630	2625
PS632	0015
PS633	0015
PS636	0015
PS637	0015
PS1140	0071
PS1325	0466
PS1511	0170
PS1512	0170
PS1513	0170
PS1514	0170
PS1515	0170
PS1516	0170
PS1517	0170
PS2001B	0272
PS2006B	1281
PS2021	0311
PS2207	0080
PS2208	0080
PS2209	0080
PS2247	0015
PS2249	0015
PS2346	0087
PS2347	0087
PS2401-2	OEM
PS2411	0015
PS2412	0015
PS2413	0015
PS2414	OEM
PS2415	0015
PS2416	0071
PS2417	0071
PS2501	OEM
PS2501-1	OEM
PS2501-1LB	OEM
PS3534	2847
PS3534A	2847
PS4005	OEM
PS4559	0080
PS4560	0790
PS4725	0080
PS5175	0326
PS5300	0790
PS5301	0790
PS5302	0790
PS5303	0015
PS5304	0015
PS6325	0327
PS6326	OEM
PS6327	OEM
PS6465	0755
PS6466	OEM
PS6467	OEM
PS6468	0162
PS6469	3099
PS6470	OEM
PS7267	OEM
PS7268	OEM
PS7269	OEM
PS7270	OEM
PS8900	1703
PS8901	0296
PS8902	0372
PS8903	0036
PS8904	0274
PS8905	0446
PS8906	0162
PS8907	0157
PS8908	0466
PS8909	0062
PS8910	0644
PS8911	0165
PS8912	0057
PS8913	0170
PS8914	0313
PS8915	0052
PS8916	0361
PS8917	0681
PS8918	0416
PS8919	0371
PS10016B	0025
PS10017B	0644
PS10018B	0244
PS10019B	0012
PS10020B	0170
PS10021B	0313
PS10022B	0137
PS10023B	0361
PS10024B	0002
PS10025B	0361
PS10026B	0490
PS10060	0025
PS10061	0644
PS10062	0644
PS10063	0012
PS10064	0170
PS10065	0313
PS10066	0137
PS10067	0361
PS10068	0002
PS10070	0490
PS25011LB	OEM
PSA06	0855
PSA20	0079
PSA56	0037
PSA70	0037
PSIB110	OEM
PSIBD125	0594
PSIBD150	0594
PSIC160	OEM
PSIC235	OEM
PSICD160	1017
PSICD250	1017
PSIF180	OEM
PSIF220	OEM
PSIF300	OEM
PSIF400	OEM
PSIF500	OEM
PSIF600	OEM
PSIFD600	OEM
PSIFD750	OEM
PSIFD900	OEM
PSIFT1000	OEM
PSIG300	OEM
PSIG400	OEM
PSIG500	OEM
PSIG650	OEM
PSIG850	OEM
PSIG950	OEM
PSIGD800	OEM
PSIGD1400	OEM
PSIGD1500	OEM
PSIH800	OEM
PSIH1000	OEM
PSIH1200	OEM
PSIH1400	OEM
PSIH1600	OEM
PSIH1600-16	OEM
PSIH1600-18	OEM
PSIH1800	OEM
PSIH1800-8	OEM
PSIH1800-10	OEM
PSIH1800-12	OEM
PSIH1800-14	OEM
PSIH1800-16	OEM
PSIH1800-18	OEM
PSIH2000	OEM
PSIH2000-1	OEM
PSIH2000-2	OEM
PSIH2000-3	OEM
PSIH2000-4	OEM
PSIH2000-5	OEM
PSIH2000-6	OEM
PSIH2300-1	OEM
PSIH2300-2	OEM
PSIH2300-3	OEM
PSIH2300-4	OEM
PSIHD1500	OEM
PSIHD2000	OEM
PSIHD2500	OEM
PSIHD3000	OEM
PSIHH1400-1	OEM
PSIHH1400-2	OEM
PSIHH1400-3	OEM
PSIHH1400-4	OEM
PSIHH1400-5	OEM
PSIHH1400-6	OEM
PSIHH1400-7	OEM
PSIHH1400-8	OEM
PSIHH1400-10	OEM
PSIHH1400-12	OEM
PSIHH1600-1	OEM
PSIHH1600-2	OEM
PSIHH1600-3	OEM
PSIHH1600-4	OEM
PSIHH1600-5	OEM
PSIHH1600-6	OEM
PSIHH1600-7	OEM
PSIHH1600-8	OEM
PSIHH1600-10	OEM
PSIHH1600-12	OEM
PSIHH1800-1	OEM
PSIHH1800-2	OEM
PSIHH1800-3	OEM
PSIHH1800-4	OEM
PSIHH1800-5	OEM
PSIHH1800-6	OEM
PSIHH1800-7	OEM
PSIHH1800-8	OEM
PSIHH1800-10	OEM
PSIHH1800-12	OEM
PSIHH2000-1	OEM
PSIHH2000-2	OEM
PSIHH2000-3	OEM
PSIHH2000-4	OEM
PSIHH2000-5	OEM
PSIHH2000-6	OEM
PSIHH2000-7	OEM
PSIHH2000-8	OEM
PSIHH2000-10	OEM
PSIHH2000-12	OEM
PSIHH2200-1	OEM
PSIHH2200-2	OEM
PSIHH2200-3	OEM
PSIHH2200-4	OEM
PSIHH2200-5	OEM
PSIHH2200-6	OEM
PSIHH2200-7	OEM
PSIHH2200-8	OEM
PSIHH2200-10	OEM
PSIHH2200-12	OEM
PSIJ3900-1	OEM
PSIJ3900-2	OEM
PSIJ3900-3	OEM
PSIJ3900-4	OEM
PSIJ3900-5	OEM
PSIJ3900-6	OEM
PSIJ4000-1	OEM
PSIJ4000-2	OEM
PSIJ4000-3	OEM
PSIJ4000-4	OEM
PSIJ4000-5	OEM
PSIJ4000-6	OEM
PSIJ4200-1	OEM
PSIJ4200-2	OEM
PSIJ4200-3	OEM
PSIJ4200-4	OEM
PSIJ4200-5	OEM
PSIJ4200-6	OEM
PSIJ4900-1	OEM
PSIJ4900-2	OEM
PSIJ4900-3	OEM
PSIJ4900-4	OEM
PSIK2500-2	OEM
PSIK2500-4	OEM
PSIK2500-6	OEM
PSIK3500-2	OEM
PSIK3500-4	OEM
PSIK3500-6	OEM
PSL11A	OEM
PSL12A	OEM
PST518	OEM
PST519A	OEM
PST520	OEM
PST520E	OEM
PST520G	OEM
PST523C	OEM
PST523D	OEM
PST523E	OEM
PST523E-2	OEM
PST523G	OEM

If replacement code is OEM, contact original manufacturer for replacement.

DEVICE TYPE	REPL CODE	DEVICE TYPE	REPL CODE	DEVICE TYPE	REPL CODE	DEVICE TYPE	REPL CODE	DEVICE TYPE	REPL CODE	DEVICE TYPE	REPL CODE	DEVICE TYPE	REPL CODE
PST523H-2	OEM	PT242	0160	PT898	0016	PTC104	0142	PTC214M	0133	PTC1645	OEM	PZT33	1777
PST524D	OEM	PT250	0435	PT900	OEM	PTC105	0160	PTC215	0162	PTC1667	OEM	PZT2222A	OEM
PST524D2	OEM	PT-255	0160	PT900-1	OEM	PTC105A	0160	PTC216	0102	PTC1689	OEM	PZT2907A	OEM
PST529C2	OEM	PT255	0160	PT901	OEM	PTC106	0435	PTC217	0911	PTC1701	OEM	PZT3904	OEM
PST529D	OEM	PT-256	0160	PT901-1	OEM	PTC107	0050	PTC218	0290	PTC1723	OEM	PZT3906	OEM
PST529D-2	OEM	PT256	0160	PT902	OEM	PTC108	0595	PTC219	OEM	PTC1745	0212	PZTA13	OEM
PST529E	OEM	PT-285	0160	PT902-1	OEM	PTC109	0211	PTC301	0139	PTC1778	OEM	PZTA14	OEM
PST529H2	OEM	PT285	0160	PT903	OEM	PTC110	0161	PTC302	0120	PTC1956	2720	PZTA42	OEM
PST532	OEM	PT-285A	0160	PT903-1	OEM	PTC111	0455	PTC311	0005	PTC1978	0378	PZTA43	OEM
PST532A	OEM	PT285A	0160	PT1515	0168	PTC112	0178	PTC401	0293	PTC6000	OEM	PZTA63	OEM
PSU06	0264	PT-301	0160	PT1544	0086	PTC113	0899	PTC402	0299	PTC6001	OEM	PZTA64	OEM
PSV111-08	0005	PT301	0160	PT1545	0086	PTC114	0085	PTC403	0015	PTC6002	OEM	PZTA92	OEM
PSV111-14	0005	PT-301A	0160	PT1558	0016	PTC115	0079	PTC404	0469	PTC6003	OEM	PZTA93	OEM
PSV111-16	0005	PT301A	0160	PT1559	0016	PTC116	0130	PTC405	2938	PTC6060	2602	Q001	2171
PSV114-06	0623	PT-307	0160	PT1610	0016	PTC117	0233	PTC406	0907	PTC6061	2602	Q-00169C	1270
PSV114-14	0623	PT307	0160	PT1835	0016	PTC118	0074	PTC407	0196	PTC6062	OEM	Q00169C	0321
PSV123-08	0005	PT-307A	0160	PT1836	0016	PTC119	0103	PTC501	0188	PTC6063	OEM	Q-00184R	1270
PSV123-14	0005	PT307A	0160	PT1837	0016	PTC120	0222	PTC502	0157	PTC7000	3956	Q00184R	0321
PSV123-16	0005	PT310	1307	PT1941	0103	PTC121	0079	PTC503	0466	PTC7001	3956	Q-00269C	0076
PSV126-06	0623	PT315	1307	PT2040A	6893	PTC122	0969	PTC504	0644	PTC7002	3956	Q-00284R	0127
PSV126-14	0623	PT320	OEM	PT2523	0283	PTC123	1471	PTC505	0057	PTC7003	3956	Q-00369C	0191
PT06	0160	PT325	1307	PT2524	0283	PTC124	1698	PTC506	0170	PTC8080	OEM	Q-00384R	0151
PT08	1058	PT330	1307	PT2525	0283	PTC125	0855	PTC507	0052	PTC8081	OEM	Q-00469C	0076
PT010	1058	PT336B	0085	PT2525A	0168	PTC126	0007	PTC508	0361	PTC8082	OEM	Q-00484R	0076
PT015	1058	PT340	1307	PT2540	0590	PTC127	0855	PTC509	0681	PTC8083	OEM	Q-00569C	0076
PT025	1058	PT-350C	OEM	PT2575	0016	PTC128	0617	PTC510	0490	PTC9045	OEM	Q-00584R	0151
PT-029	0042	PT-350D	OEM	PT2600	OEM	PTC128-RT	OEM	PTC511	0100	PTCL11	OEM	Q-00669C	1409
PT030	1058	PT360FS	OEM	PT2620	0555	PTC129	0637	PTC512	0039	PT-H3	OEM	Q-00769C	1139
PT040	1058	PT366B	0160	PT2630	0168	PTC129A	0065	PTC513	0863	PTH631D01	OEM	Q-00784R	0076
PT0139	0164	PT410	1307	PT2634	OEM	PTC130	0003	PTC514	0778	PTIN141S	OEM	Q-00869C	0016
PT2A	0050	PT415	1307	PT2635	0042	PTC131	0037	PTC515	0327	PT-L3	OEM	Q-00969C	0693
PT2S	0050	PT421FH	OEM	PT2640	0555	PTC132	0007	PTC516	0149	PT-M3	OEM	Q-00984R	0037
PT-3	0015	PT421FI-F	OEM	PT2660	0555	PTC133	2503	PTC517	0346	PTO-6	0160	Q0-419	0037
PT3	0015	PT425	1307	PT2670	0168	PTC134	0208	PTC518	0993	PT0139	0004	Q01E	0847
PT-3A	0160	PT430	1307	PT-2677C	2156	PTC135	0164	PTC601	1986	PTS520G	OEM	Q02E	0847
PT3A	0160	PT431	OEM	PT2677C	0693	PTC136	0016	PTC602	0128	PTSN7417N	1342	Q05B	OEM
PT4	2736	PT440	1307	PT2760	0016	PTC137	0556	PTC603	1493	PU2	OEM	Q05C	OEM
PT5	0015	PT481F	OEM	PT3141	0016	PTC137-RT	OEM	PTC604	1024	PU6C22	0015	Q05D	OEM
PT-5B	0015	PT483F1	OEM	PT3141A	0016	PTC138	0599	PTC605	1024	PU42C26	OEM	Q06B	OEM
PT5B	0015	PT483FI	OEM	PT3141B	0016	PTC139	0079	PTC606	4391	PU42C26NC	OEM	Q06C	OEM
PT-6	0160	PT501	0160	PT3151A	0079	PTC140	0103	PTC607	OEM	PU131	0312	Q06D	OEM
PT6	0160	PT-505	0015	PT3151B	0016	PTC141	0378	PTC608	1700	PU4120	OEM	Q-0115C	0079
PT6D22/1	0276	PT505	0015	PT3151C	0016	PTC142	1257	PTC651	0895	PU-4120A	OEM	Q-01069C	1401
PT6D22-1	0276	PT-510	0015	PT3473	OEM	PTC143	0555	PTC658	OEM	PU4120A	OEM	Q-01084R	0222
PT9C22/1	0071	PT510	0015	PT3500	0016	PTC144	0626	PTC660	OEM	PU4120B	OEM	Q-01115C	0364
PT-12	0160	PT-515	0015	PT3501	3293	PTC145	0136	PTC665	OEM	PU4124	OEM	Q-01169C	0086
PT12	0160	PT515	0435	PT3502	0086	PTC146	0065	PTC666	OEM	PU4320	OEM	Q-01184R	0016
PT13	OEM	PT515(SEMITRON)	0432	PT3503	0555	PTC147	0599	PTC701	0659	PU4411A	OEM	Q-01269C	0178
PT16	1058	PT516	OEM	PT3539	OEM	PTC148	0178	PTC703	0673	PU4411B	OEM	Q-01284R	0617
PT18	1058	PT517	OEM	PT3540	OEM	PTC149	0486	PTC705	0661	PU4417	OEM	Q-01369	2046
PT23	OEM	PT518	OEM	PT3760	OEM	PTC150	0334	PTC707	0748	PU4520	OEM	Q-01384R	1401
PT23F	OEM	PT519	OEM	PT4144	OEM	PTC151	3667	PTC708	2147	PU22106A	OEM	Q-02115C	0364
PT23F/WITHHOLDER	OEM	PT-520	0015	PT4579	0414	PTC152	0321	PTC709	0649	PU22198-2A	OEM	Q-03115C	0364
PT-23F-F	5589	PT520	0015	PT4690	0555	PTC153	0396	PTC711	1929	PUA3228	OEM	Q-04115C	0364
PT-23F-HLD	3156	PT522	OEM	PT4800	0016	PTC154	0419	PTC713	0438	PV-8	0015	Q-05115C	0364
PT-25	0160	PT523	OEM	PT4816	0127	PTC155	0164	PTC715	0348	PV8	0015	Q-06115C	0364
PT25	0160	PT-525	0015	PT4830	0127	PTC156	0164	PTC717	2264	PV509	OEM	Q-07115C	0364
PT26	1058	PT525	0015	PT5690	OEM	PTC157	0919	PTC719	0350	PV1043	0124	Q-08115C	0376
PT28	1058	PT-530	0015	PT5692	OEM	PTC158	0693	PTC721	0696	PV1500	OEM	Q-09115C	0376
P-T-30	0160	PT530	0015	PT5693	0042	PTC160	0050	PTC723	1335	PV1503	OEM	Q-013696	2046
PT30	0160	PT530-1	OEM	PT5694	OEM	PTC161	0321	PTC726	0167	PV1506	OEM	Q0V60526	0004
PT32	0222	PT-530A	0279	PT6001	OEM	PTC162	0919	PTC728	0345	PV1511	OEM	Q0V60528	0004
PT36	1307	PT530A	0004	PT6007	OEM	PTC163	0042	PTC729	1385	PVGA-1A	OEM	Q0V60538	0016
PT38	1307	PT531	0626	PT6011	OEM	PTC164	1190	PTC730	0797	PW300	OEM	Q-1	0211
PT-40	0160	PT-540	0015	PT6021	OEM	PTC165	0556	PTC731	2438	PW400	OEM	Q1	0004
PT40	0160	PT540	0015	PT6022/1	0299	PTC166	0848	PTC732	2535	PX0016CE	OEM	Q1/1	OEM
PT46	1307	PT-550	0015	PT6618	0555	PTC167	0419	PTC733	1327	PX0020GE	OEM	Q1/2	OEM
PT48	1307	PT550	0015	PT6669	0555	PTC168	1190	PTC734	1411	PX0032GE	OEM	Q1/3	OEM
PT-50	0160	PT-554	0160	PT6696	0555	PTC169	0419	PTC735	0514	PX0207CE	OEM	Q1/4	OEM
PT50	0160	PT554	0085	PT6905	OEM	PTC170	0710	PTC736	0356	PX0219CE	OEM	Q1/5	OEM
PT52	OEM	PT-555	0160	PT6905A	OEM	PTC171	0338	PTC737	1434	PX0226CE	OEM	Q1-7C	0004
PT53	OEM	PT555	0160	PT6905B	OEM	PTC172	1671	PTC738	2535	PX0238CE	OEM	Q-1A	0279
PT56	1880	PT-560	0015	PT6905C	OEM	PTC173	0130	PTC739	0746	PX0242CE	OEM	Q1B	0015
PT58	1880	PT560	0015	PT6941	0615	PTC174	1671	PTC740	5224	PXB-103	0004	Q1H	0015
PT60	OEM	PT580	0071	PT6942	0615	PTC175	0130	PTC741	0850	PXB103	0211	Q-1N914	0124
PT66	1880	PT600	0555	PT6994	0615	PTC176	0626	PTC742	2535	PXB-113	0004	Q-2	0595
PT68	1880	PT601	0555	PT6995	0615	PTC177	0786	PTC743	0627	PXB113	0211	Q2	0007
PT110	1058	PT610	1880	PT6996	2465	PTC178	0590	PTC744	0817	PXC-101	0004	Q2-7C	0004
PT115	1058	PT612	0086	PT7015	OEM	PTC179	0142	PTC745	0784	PXC101	0211	Q2N406	0004
PT125	1058	PT615	1880	PT7016	OEM	PTC180	1581	PTC746	0391	PXC101A	0211	Q2N1526	0050
PT130	1058	PT622/1	0299	PT7903	0615	PTC181	0212	PTC747	5225	PXC-101AB	0004	Q2N2428	0004
PT140	1058	PT625	1880	PT7904	0615	PTC182	0212	PTC754	0872	PXC101AB	0211	Q2N2613	0004
PT-150	0160	PT627	0016	PT7905	0615	PTC183	0843	PTC756	OEM	PXT2222A	OEM	Q2N4105	0038
PT150	0160	PT630	1880	PT7906	0615	PTC184	0212	PTC757	2111	PXT2907A	OEM	Q2N4106	0164
PT-155	0160	PT640	1880	PT7907	0615	PTC186	0830	PTC758	OEM	PXT3904	OEM	Q2N4107	2839
PT155	0160	PT657	OEM	PT7908	0615	PTC191	0693	PTC759	OEM	PXT3906	OEM	Q-2N5225	0076
PT-176	0160	PT665	0042	PT7909	2465	PTC192	2035	PTC762	OEM	PXT4401	OEM	Q-2N5226	0037
PT176	0160	PT703	0016	PT7910	2465	PTC193	2035	PTC765	0687	PXT4403	OEM	Q2T2222	0539
PT200	OEM	PT706	OEM	PT7930	0130	PTC194	0222	PTC767	2728	PXTA14	OEM	Q2T2905	0281
PT201	0435	PT706-1	OEM	PT7931	0130	PTC195	0236	PTC769	0516	PXTA42	OEM	Q2T3725	0539
PT210	1058	PT706A	OEM	PT8809	3516	PTC196	0676	PTC776	0324	PXTA64	OEM	Q2Z10A	0064
PT215	1058	PT706A-1	OEM	PT8810	2080	PTC197	0546	PTC780	1044	PXTA92	OEM	Q-3	0595
PT225	1058	PT709	OEM	PT8811	1410	PTC198	0378	PTC781	0905	PY-5	0015	Q3	0007
PT230	1058	PT720	0016	PT8838	1963	PTC201	0535	PTC787	2728	PY5608S	OEM	Q3/1	OEM
PT-234	0160	PT801	OEM	PT8874F	2857	PTC202	0015	PTC801	OEM	PZ10A	0505	Q3/2	0015
PT234	0160	PT802	OEM	PT9784	2296	PTC203	0071	PTC802	OEM	PZ18A	1071	Q3/3	OEM
PT-235	0160	PT822	OEM	PT9795	2296	PTC204	0071	PTC803	OEM	PZ22A	1712	Q3/4	OEM
PT235	0160	PT850	0086	PT9796	2296	PTC205	0071	PTC804	OEM	PZ140B	OEM	Q3/5	OEM
PT-235A	0160	PT850A	0086	PT9796A	1963	PTC206	0143	PTC805	OEM	PZ140D	OEM	Q-4	0211
PT235A	0085	PT851	0016	PT9799	2296	PTC206M	0123	PTC806	OEM	PZ140F	OEM	Q4	0004
PT-236	0160	PT852	OEM	PT9803	2296	PTC207	0143	PTC809	OEM	PZ140H	OEM	Q4B	0015
PT236	0085	PT853	OEM	PT-9816	1963	PTC207M	0143	PTC810	OEM	PZ140K	OEM	Q4S4	OEM
PT-236A	0160	PT855	0050	PT31961	0693	PTC208	0769	PTC904	0561	PZT8.2	OEM	Q-5	0595
PT236A	0085	PT856	0050	PT72130	0015	PTC209	1293	PTC905	1357	PZT10	OEM	Q5	0007
PT-236B	0160	PT886	0016	PT-72130-1	0535	PTC210	0201	PTC906	0236	PZT12	OEM	Q-6	0004
PT236B	0160	PT887	0016	PT1011601-A	OEM	PTC211	0286	PTC1101	0780	PZT15	OEM	Q6	0164
PT236C	0160	PT888	0086	PTC101	0086	PTC212	0752	PTC1123	OEM	PZT18	1071	Q6/1	OEM
PT240	1058	PT896	0086	PTC102	0279	PTC213	0752	PTC1423	2411	PZT22	1712	Q6/2	0015
PT-242	0160	PT897	0016	PTC103	0037	PTC214	0162	PTC1623	0780	PZT27	1750	Q6/3	OEM

If replacement code is OEM, contact original manufacturer for replacement.

515

DEVICE TYPE	REPL CODE
Q6/4	OEM
Q6/5	OEM
Q-7	0004
Q7	0164
Q7-C0710XBE	0364
Q7-C0735XBT	0191
Q7-C1318XDN	0086
Q7-K0033XBE	1270
Q-8	0004
Q8	0164
Q8/1	OEM
Q8/2	0015
Q8/3	OEM
Q8/4	OEM
Q8/5	OEM
Q-9	0595
Q10	OEM
Q-16	0004
Q16	0164
Q19C	4905
Q19D	6913
Q19E	4906
Q19G	4907
Q19J	4908
Q19L	4909
Q20C	OEM
Q20D	6914
Q20E	6915
Q20G	4914
Q20J	4915
Q20L	4916
Q32	0015
Q-35	0016
Q-36	0037
Q49	0143
Q50	0143
Q51	0143
Q52	1325
Q53	0015
Q54	0015
Q55	0015
Q56	0015
Q57	0015
Q58	0015
Q59	0015
Q59A	OEM
Q60	0015
Q61	0015
Q62	0015
Q70-500	OEM
Q70-500A	OEM
Q80-500	OEM
Q80-500A	OEM
Q80-750	OEM
Q80-950	OEM
Q82	0015
Q90-500	OEM
Q100-500	OEM
Q100-500A	OEM
Q100-750	OEM
Q100-950	OEM
Q110-500	OEM
Q205	0696
Q301	0127
Q402	OEM
Q506R4	OEM
Q510ZQ	0150
Q2001LT	5296
Q2001MS2	1403
Q2001P	2378
Q2001PT	2378
Q2003L3	0550
Q2003L4	5226
Q2003L5	OEM
Q2003LT	5296
Q2004A	0902
Q2004B	3169
Q2004F31	2284
Q2004F41	2284
Q2004FT1	OEM
Q2004L3	5226
Q2004L4	0550
Q2004LT	1447
Q2004R4	OEM
Q2004RT	OEM
Q2006	OEM
Q2006A	0902
Q2006AT	0588
Q2006B	3169
Q2006BT	0588
Q2006F41	OEM
Q2006FT1	OEM
Q2006G	1058
Q2006H	0154
Q2006L4	0550
Q2006LT	1447
Q2006N	3169
Q2006R4	5161
Q2006RT	OEM
Q2006T	0588
Q2008	OEM
Q2008A	0902
Q2008AT	OEM
Q2008B	3169
Q2008F41	OEM
Q2008FT1	OEM
Q2008G	1058
Q2008H	0154
Q2008L4	0550
Q2008L4A	0550
Q2008LT	1447
Q2008LTA	OEM
Q2008N	3169
Q2008R4	5161
Q2008RT	OEM
Q2008T	OEM
Q2010	OEM
Q2010A	0902
Q2010AT	OEM
Q2010B	3169
Q2010F41	OEM
Q2010F51	OEM
Q2010FT1	OEM
Q2010G	1058
Q2010H	0154
Q2010L4	0550
Q2010L5	0550
Q2010LT	5296
Q2010N	3169
Q2010R4	5226
Q2010R5	OEM
Q2010RT	OEM
Q2010T	OEM
Q2012L5	0753
Q2012R5	0767
Q2015	OEM
Q2015A	0902
Q2015B	3169
Q2015G	1058
Q2015H	0154
Q2015L5	0767
Q2015LT	OEM
Q2015N	3169
Q2015R5	0767
Q2015RT	OEM
Q2015U	OEM
Q2025	OEM
Q2025C	0902
Q2025D	3169
Q2025G	1058
Q2025H	2004
Q2025J6	5509
Q2025K6	5509
Q2025L6	6000
Q2025N	3169
Q2025P	0902
Q2025R6	0295
Q2025U	OEM
Q2040	OEM
Q2040C	0902
Q2040D	3169
Q2040J7	5509
Q2040K7	5509
Q2040P	1058
Q2040U	OEM
Q2040W7	5509
Q4001L3	5226
Q4001L4	0480
Q4001LT	1447
Q4001M	1403
Q4001P	0480
Q4003L3	0550
Q4003L4	5226
Q4003LT	OEM
Q4003P3	0480
Q4004A	0902
Q4004B	3177
Q4004F41	2284
Q4004FT1	OEM
Q4004L3	5226
Q4004L4	0550
Q4004LT	1447
Q4004R4	OEM
Q4004RT	OEM
Q4006	OEM
Q4006A	0902
Q4006AT	OEM
Q4006B	3177
Q4006F41	2284
Q4006FT1	OEM
Q4006G	1307
Q4006H	0147
Q4006L4	0550
Q4006L5	OEM
Q4006LT	5296
Q4006N	3177
Q4006R4	5295
Q4006RT	OEM
Q4006T	OEM
Q4008	OEM
Q4008A	0902
Q4008AT	OEM
Q4008B	3177
Q4008F41	OEM
Q4008FT1	OEM
Q4008G	1307
Q4008H	0902
Q4008L4	0550
Q4008L4A	0550
Q4008LT	1447
Q4008N	3177
Q4008R4	5295
Q4008RT	OEM
Q4008T	OEM
Q4010	OEM
Q4010A	0902
Q4010AT	OEM
Q4010B	3177
Q4010F41	OEM
Q4010F51	OEM
Q4010FT1	OEM
Q4010G	1307
Q4010H	0902
Q4010L4	0550
Q4010L5	0550
Q4010LT	1447
Q4010N	3177
Q4010R4	OEM
Q4010R5	OEM
Q4010RT	OEM
Q4010T	OEM
Q4012L5	5363
Q4012R5	0739
Q4015	OEM
Q4015A	0902
Q4015B	3177
Q4015G	1307
Q4015H	0147
Q4015L5	0739
Q4015LT	OEM
Q4015N	3177
Q4015R5	0739
Q4015RT	OEM
Q4015U	OEM
Q4025	OEM
Q4025C	0902
Q4025D	3177
Q4025G	1307
Q4025H	2006
Q4025J6	5509
Q4025K6	5509
Q4025L6	5511
Q4025N	3177
Q4025P	0902
Q4025R6	0303
Q4025U	OEM
Q4040	OEM
Q4040C	0902
Q4040D	3177
Q4040J7	5509
Q4040K7	5745
Q4040P	0902
Q4040U	OEM
Q4040W7	3709
Q4994F31	OEM
Q5004A	0902
Q5004B	3192
Q5004F41	OEM
Q5004FT1	OEM
Q5004L4	0550
Q5004LT	1447
Q5004R4	OEM
Q5004RT	OEM
Q5006	OEM
Q5006A	0902
Q5006AT	OEM
Q5006B	3192
Q5006FT1	OEM
Q5006G	1880
Q5006H	0278
Q5006L4	0550
Q5006LT	1447
Q5006N	3192
Q5006R4	0589
Q5006RT	OEM
Q5006T	OEM
Q5008	OEM
Q5008A	0902
Q5008AT	OEM
Q5008B	3192
Q5008FT1	OEM
Q5008G	1880
Q5008H	0278
Q5008L4	0550
Q5008LT	1447
Q5008N	3192
Q5008R4	0589
Q5008RT	OEM
Q5008T	OEM
Q5010	OEM
Q5010A	0902
Q5010AT	OEM
Q5010B	3192
Q5010F51	OEM
Q5010FT1	OEM
Q5010G	1880
Q5010H	0278
Q5010L4	0705
Q5010L5	0550
Q5010LT	1447
Q5010N	3192
Q5010R4	OEM
Q5010R5	2026
Q5010RT	OEM
Q5010T	OEM
Q5012L5	2132
Q5012R5	0612
Q5015	OEM
Q5015A	0902
Q5015B	3192
Q5015G	1880
Q5015H	0278
Q5015L5	0612
Q5015LT	OEM
Q5015N	3192
Q5015R5	0612
Q5015RT	OEM
Q5015U	OEM
Q5025	OEM
Q5025C	0902
Q5025D	3192
Q5025G	1880
Q5025H	2007
Q5025J6	3011
Q5025K6	3011
Q5025L6	1649
Q5025N	3192
Q5025P	0902
Q5025R6	0307
Q5025U	OEM
Q5040	OEM
Q5040C	0902
Q5040D	3192
Q5040J7	3011
Q5040K7	3011
Q5040P	0902
Q5040U	OEM
Q5040W7	3709
Q5044	0050
Q5053	0532
Q5053A	0532
Q5053C	0079
Q5053D	0532
Q5053E	0532
Q5053F	0532
Q5053G	0532
Q5055	OEM
Q5073D	0079
Q5073E	0079
Q5073F	0079
Q5075C	0142
Q5075CLY	0142
Q-5075CXY	0142
Q5075D	0142
Q5075DLY	0142
Q5075DXY	0142
Q5075E	0142
Q5075ELY	0142
Q5075EXY	0142
Q5075F	0142
Q5075FXY	0142
Q5075K	0142
Q5075X	0142
Q5075Y	0142
Q5075ZMY	0142
Q5077	0006
Q5077A	0006
Q5077E	0006
Q5077EA	0006
Q5078Z	0076
Q5083B	0103
Q5083C	0074
Q5094Z	0003
Q5095ZEE	0003
Q5099E	0086
Q5099F	0086
Q5100A	0126
Q5101D	0178
Q5102	0203
Q5102A	0203
Q5102P	0203
Q5102Q	0203
Q5102QA	0203
Q5102R	0203
Q5104K	0142
Q5104Z	0142
Q5104ZXF	0142
Q5110Z	0103
Q5111ZK	0309
Q5113ZLM	0142
Q5113ZMM	0142
Q5116C	0148
Q5116CA	0148
Q5119	0220
Q5119D	0220
Q5120P	0042
Q5120Q	0042
Q5120R	0074
Q51210	0111
Q5121Q	0076
Q5121R	0111
Q5123E	0076
Q5123F	0076
Q5124	0155
Q5132Z	0885
Q5135	0006
Q5135-OY	0006
Q5137BA	0388
Q5137CA	0388
Q5138	0949
Q5138K	0949
Q5138L	0949
Q5138M	0949
Q5140XP	2040
Q5140Z	0065
Q5140ZX-O	0065
Q5140ZXP	2040
Q5140ZXQ	2040
Q5140ZXR	0065
Q5141ZM	0142
Q5149	0042
Q5160	0320
Q5160-0	0168
Q5160-O	0638
Q5160R	0638
Q5160Y	0638
Q5161Z	0309
Q5163	0388
Q5163D	0388
Q5169Z	OEM
Q5175	0638
Q5175TM	0638
Q5178	0949
Q5180	0547
Q5182	0016
Q5183	0076
Q5183C	0076
Q5183P	0076
Q5196	0527
Q5199	0220
Q5202	0388
Q5205	0006
Q5206	0270
Q5207	0309
Q5207Z	0309
Q5209	0527
Q5210	0066
Q5217	0261
Q6004A	0902
Q6004B	3192
Q6004F41	OEM
Q6004FT1	OEM
Q6004L4	0705
Q6004LT	1447
Q6004R4	OEM
Q6004RT	OEM
Q6006	OEM
Q6006A	0902
Q6006AT	OEM
Q6006B	3192
Q6006FT1	OEM
Q6006G	1880
Q6006H	0278
Q6006L4	0705
Q6006LT	1447
Q6006N	3192
Q6006R4	OEM
Q6006RT	OEM
Q6006T	OEM
Q6008	OEM
Q6008A	0902
Q6008B	3192
Q6008F51	OEM
Q6008FT1	OEM
Q6008G	1880
Q6008H	0278
Q6008L4	0705
Q6008LT	1447
Q6008N	3192
Q6008R4	0550
Q6008RT	OEM
Q6010	OEM
Q6010A	0902
Q6010AT	OEM
Q6010B	3192
Q6010F51	OEM
Q6010FT1	OEM
Q6010G	1880
Q6010H	0278
Q6010L4	0705
Q6010L5	0550
Q6010LT	1447
Q6010N	3192
Q6010R4	OEM
Q6010R5	2026
Q6010RT	OEM
Q6010T	OEM
Q6012L5	2132
Q6012R5	0612
Q6015	OEM
Q6015A	0902
Q6015B	3192
Q6015G	1880
Q6015H	0278
Q6015L5	0612
Q6015LT	OEM
Q6015N	3192
Q6015R5	0612
Q6015RT	OEM
Q6015U	OEM
Q6025	OEM
Q6025C	0902
Q6025D	3192
Q6025G	1880
Q6025H	2007
Q6025J6	3011
Q6025K6	3011
Q6025L6	1649
Q6025N	3192
Q6025P	0902
Q6025R6	0307
Q6025U	OEM
Q6040	OEM
Q6040C	0902
Q6040D	3192
Q6040J7	3011
Q6040K7	3663
Q6040P	0902
Q6040U	OEM
Q6040W7	3709
Q6521	0338
Q6522	0338
Q6526Z	0261
Q6531	1317
Q6531ZM	1317
Q6536	0261
Q6536P	0261
Q6536Q	0261
Q6536R	0261
Q6541	0066
Q6541ZM	0066
Q6543	0261
Q6543A	0261
Q6562	0148
Q6562G	0148
Q6565	0076
Q6582Z	2824
Q6597	0055
Q6597Z	0055
Q6609	0638
Q6609Z	0638
Q6627	1382
Q6640Z	2885
Q6649	0558
Q6649Z	0558
Q6650	0520
Q6650Z	0520
Q6651Z	3827
Q6697	3017
Q6730D	1553
Q6730R	1553
Q6780	2874
Q6780Z	2874
Q6783	0275
Q6783Z	0275
Q6784	0275
Q6784K	0275
Q6784L	0275
Q6784M	0275
Q6785	0055
Q6793	2882
Q6803	0261
Q6805	0275
Q6805R	0275
Q6829	2171
Q6831	3236
Q7010L5	5314
Q7010R5	0591
Q7012L5	5314
Q7012R5	0869
Q7015L5	0869
Q7015R5	0869
Q7025J6	OEM
Q7025K6	OEM
Q7025L6	3430
Q7025P	OEM
Q7025R6	5506
Q7040J7	OEM
Q7040K7	OEM
Q7040P	OEM
Q7040W7	OEM
Q7219	0356
Q7220	OEM
Q7227	0328
Q7227R	0328
Q7256	2641
Q7293	3461
Q7296	3461
Q7327A	0034
Q7350	0288
Q7368	5124
Q7372A	0034
Q7393	0409
Q7402	0288
Q7406	0024
Q7424	4307
Q7448	0034
Q7478A	0101
Q7652	0101
Q7653A	0101
Q7668	0412
Q7672	OEM
Q7682	3726
Q7748	0616
Q8004	OEM
Q8004A	OEM
Q8004AT	OEM
Q8004B	OEM
Q8004BT	OEM
Q8004L5	OEM
Q8004LT	OEM
Q8004R5	OEM
Q8004RT	OEM
Q8004T	OEM
Q8006	OEM
Q8006A	OEM
Q8006AT	OEM
Q8006B	OEM
Q8006BT	OEM
Q8006G	OEM
Q8006H	OEM
Q8006L5	OEM
Q8006LT	OEM
Q8006N	OEM
Q8006R5	OEM
Q8006RT	OEM
Q8006T	OEM
Q8008	OEM
Q8008A	OEM
Q8008AT	OEM
Q8008B	OEM
Q8008BT	OEM
Q8008G	OEM
Q8008H	OEM
Q8008L5	6281
Q8008LT	OEM
Q8008N	OEM
Q8008R5	OEM
Q8008RT	OEM
Q8008T	OEM
Q8010	OEM
Q8010A	OEM
Q8010AT	OEM
Q8010B	OEM
Q8010BT	OEM
Q8010G	OEM
Q8010H	OEM
Q8010L5	5314
Q8010LT	OEM
Q8010N	OEM
Q8010R5	0869
Q8010RT	OEM
Q8010T	OEM
Q8012L5	5314
Q8012R5	0869
Q8015	OEM
Q8015A	OEM
Q8015AT	OEM
Q8015B	OEM
Q8015BT	OEM
Q8015G	OEM
Q8015H	OEM
Q8015L5	0869
Q8015LT	OEM
Q8015N	OEM
Q8015R5	0869
Q8015RT	OEM
Q8015U	OEM
Q8025	OEM
Q8025C	OEM
Q8025D	OEM
Q8025G	OEM
Q8025H	OEM
Q8025J6	OEM
Q8025K6	OEM
Q8025L6	3430
Q8025N	OEM
Q8025P	OEM
Q8025R6	5506
Q8025U	OEM
Q8040	OEM
Q8040C	OEM
Q8040D	OEM
Q8040J7	OEM
Q8040K7	OEM
Q8040P	OEM
Q8040U	OEM
Q8040W7	OEM
Q8266R	0155
Q8266S	0155
Q8266T	0155
Q-10115C	0284
Q-11115C	0042
Q-12115C	0042
Q-13115C	0376
Q-14115C	0364
Q-15115C	0364
Q-16115C	0076
Q-17115C	2039
Q-18115C	2280
Q-20115C	0143
Q-21115C	0133
Q-22115C	0019
Q-23115C	0133
Q-24115C	0133
Q-25115C	0012
Q-26115C	0015
Q34450	0142
Q35218	0004
Q35242	0079
Q35259	0007
Q40263	0004
Q40359	0050
Q50782	OEM
Q50787	0326
Q50787Z	0326
Q51112K	OEM
Q51210	0111
Q500614	0550
QA01-06SB	0298
QA01-07R	0002
QA01-07RE	0025
QA01-08R	0244
QA01-11SE	0313
QA01-11.5E	0313
QA01-12S	0137
QA01-14RD	0100
QA01-25A	0398
QA01-25R	0398
QA01-25R-A	0398
QA01-25RA	0398
QA01-25RB	OEM
QA0313AB	OEM
QA0313B	4877
QA-1	0050
QA1-11M	0313
QA-8	0086
QA8	0086
QA-9	0126
QA-10	0086
QA-11	0126
QA11	0142
QA-12	0016

If replacement code is OEM, contact original manufacturer for replacement.

DEVICE TYPE	REPL CODE
QA-13	0016
QA-14	0016
QA-15	0016
QA-16	0016
QA-17	0126
QA-18	0321
QA-19	0016
QA-20	0321
QA-21	0037
QA105R	0041
QA105RA	0582
QA105S	0582
QA106S	0292
QA106SB	0298
QA106SBV	0466
QA107R3	OEM
QA107RA	0062
QA107RE	0025
QA107REV	0025
QA107SP	0062
QA108SH	0165
QA111M	0313
QA111SE	0313
QA111SEV	0313
QA112R1	0137
QA112RI	0137
QA112RN-1	0052
QA112RN-2	0052
QA116R	0440
QA121R2	0700
QA135R2	0032
QA205AB	0140
QA205ABV	0140
QA205C	0041
QA205D	0041
QA205E	0041
QA205F	0041
QA205G	0041
QA205GV3	0041
QA206A	0091
QA206AB	0253
QA206B	0091
QA206BV3	0091
QA206CD	0091
QA206G	0292
QA206M	0091
QA206MV	0091
QA207D	0077
QA207M	0062
QA207M3	0062
QA208	0165
QA208C	0165
QA208G	0165
QA208GV3	0165
QA208M	OEM
QA209B	0057
QA209C	0057
QA209M	0057
QA209M9	0057
QA210D	0248
QA211B	0181
QA211CD	0999
QA211N1	0181
QA212B	0053
QA213A	0053
QA213B	0053
QA213M2	0053
QA220AB	0695
QA225	0709
QA225A	0709
QA225ABC	0709
QA225B	0709
QA225C	0709
QA228B	0257
QA230B	0195
QA230C	0195
QA232M2	OEM
QA232RC	OEM
QA233C	0166
QA233CV	0166
QA233G	0010
QA235A	0709
QA235AC	0709
QA235C	0010
QA235G	0010
QA703E	0627
QA2086M	OEM
QB01-05M	0162
QB01-11ZB	0313
QB01-15ZB	0002
QB01-18	0490
QB105M	0162
QB105N	0162
QB106P	0298
QB106PV	0298
QB107D	0025
QB107S	0025
QB107SV	0025
QB109SA	6564
QB110D	0313
QB110DV	0170
QB111	0313
QB111Z	0313
QB112	0137
QB115ZB	0002
QB115ZBV	0002
QB115ZD	0002
QB118	0490
QB400428	1063
QC	OEM
QC0008	OEM
QC0009	OEM
QC0011	1022
QC0014	OEM
QC0031A	1433
QC0032	4782
QC0042	0330
QC0048	OEM
QC0063	OEM
QC0065	4569
QC0069	0765
QC0073	4286
QC0074	4066
QC0080	3223
QC0081	0024
QC0085	0534
QC0093	1977
QC0234	0129
QC0235	0129
QC0237	OEM
QC0239	0129
QC0253	OEM
QC0275	0552
QC0291	4923
QC0300	0727
QC0309	OEM
QC0343	0409
QC0351	OEM
QC0352	3068
QC0353	OEM
QC0353(LA7018)	OEM
QC0380	3403
QC0543	3857
QC0554	0387
QC0554(LA7621)	OEM
QC0573	2929
QC0587	OEM
QC0679	OEM
QC0680	3054
QC0713	2099
QC0840	OEM
QC0846	1521
QC0852	0457
QC0908	OEM
QC-1	1024
QC1074	OEM
QC1238	OEM
QC1258	OEM
QC1280	OEM
QC1400	OEM
QC1872D1709ACT755	OEM
QCPL-3209	OEM
QD-2M205XE	0041
QD100-71	OEM
QD100-78	OEM
QD101-71	OEM
QD101-78	OEM
QD102-71	OEM
QD102-78	OEM
QD103-71	OEM
QD103-78	OEM
QD104-78	OEM
QD150-71	OEM
QD150-78	OEM
QD200-71	OEM
QD200-78	OEM
QD201-71	OEM
QD201-78	OEM
QD203-71	OEM
QD203-78	OEM
QD204-71	OEM
QD204-78	OEM
QD400-71	OEM
QD400-78	OEM
QD401-71	OEM
QD401-78	OEM
QD402-71	OEM
QD402-78	OEM
QD403-71	OEM
QD403-78	OEM
QD404-71	OEM
QD404-78	OEM
QD-CS2688D1	OEM
QD-CS2688DJ	0030
QD-CTT310XQ	0623
QDCTT410XQ	0030
QD-G1N60PXT	0123
QD-G1N60XXT	0019
QD-G1S32XXT	0143
QD-S1S953XA	0133
QD-SMA150XN	0133
QD-SS1555XT	0133
QD-SS1885XT	0023
QD-SS15555XT	OEM
QD-SSR1KX4P	0023
QDSSR3AMBE	0031
QD-SSS53XXA	0133
QD-SV06CXXB	0023
QDY31	OEM
QD-ZBZ102XJ	0416
QD-ZBZ162XJ	0416
QD-ZMZ205XE	0041
QDZMZ205XE	0041
QD-ZMZ306CE	0298
QD-ZMZ408CE	0165
QD-ZMZ409BE	0012
QD-ZRD9EXAA	0057
QD-ZRD56EAA	0091
QD-ZRD56FAA	0253
QG-0074	0160
QG0074	0160
QG-0076	0004
QG0076	0004
QG0254	0079
QGE-1	OEM
QH3091	OEM
QKH1199	OEM
QKH1214	OEM
QKH1302	OEM
QKH1325	OEM
QKH1374	OEM
QKH1381	OEM
QKH1448	OEM
QKH1495	OEM
QKH1512	OEM
QKH1516	OEM
QKH1527	OEM
QKH1528	OEM
QKH1535	OEM
QKH1553	OEM
QKH1560	OEM
QKH1569	OEM
QKH1578	OEM
QKH1579	OEM
QKH1589	OEM
QKH1592	OEM
QKH1599	OEM
QKH1663	OEM
QKH1665	OEM
QKH1666	OEM
QKH1667	OEM
QKH1693	OEM
QKH1708	OEM
QKH1709	OEM
QKH1744	OEM
QKH1757	OEM
QKH1763	OEM
QKH1777	OEM
QKH1793	OEM
QKH1811	OEM
QKH1817	OEM
QKH1820	OEM
QKH1832	OEM
QKH1833	OEM
QKH1850	OEM
QKH1851	OEM
QKH1865	OEM
QKH1866	OEM
QKH1977	OEM
QKH1978	OEM
QKH1982	OEM
QKH1990	OEM
QKH2039	OEM
QKH2040	OEM
QKK404	OEM
QKK412	OEM
QKK531	OEM
QKK532	OEM
QKK549	OEM
QKK623	OEM
QKK752	OEM
QKK753	OEM
QKK754A	OEM
QKK755A	OEM
QKK756A	OEM
QKK758A	OEM
QKK759A	OEM
QKK822	OEM
QKK826	OEM
QKK833A	OEM
QKK860	OEM
QKK869	OEM
QKK873	OEM
QKK877	OEM
QKK878	OEM
QKK879	OEM
QKK910	OEM
QKK965	OEM
QKK967	OEM
QKK968	OEM
QKK978	OEM
QKT-0033XBE	1270
QKT0033XBE	0321
QLMP-D268	OEM
QN2613	0211
QNJ937	OEM
Q01C	0865
Q01D	0847
Q02C	0865
Q02D	0847
Q07E	0847
Q08E	0847
Q0V60526	0164
Q0V60527	0208
Q0V60528	0004
Q0V60529	0079
Q0V60530	0016
Q0V60537	0208
Q0V60538	0164
Q0V60539	0004
QP-1	0599
QP1	0599
QP-1A	0599
QP1A	0599
QP-2	0599
QP2	0599
QP-3	0599
QP-3L	0919
QP-4	0599
QP-5	0599
QP-6	0599
QP6	0599
QP-7	0599
QP7	0599
QP-8	0103
QP8	0103
QP8-6623N	0435
QP-8-P	0103
QP-10	0599
QP-11	0103
QP-12	0103
QP-13	0455
QP-14	0161
QP-31	0848
QPCL-3209	OEM
QQ-0PLL01A0	OEM
QQ-0PLL01AO	OEM
QQ0PLL02AN	1704
QQ-0PPL02A0	1704
QQ-5311NA1	OEM
QQ-5311NAL	OEM
QQC61210	0004
QQ-M07205AT	1044
QQM07205AT	1044
QQ-MAN612AN	3980
QQMAN612AN	3980
QQ-MBA511BX	2746
QQ-MBA521AX	2754
QQ-MC3001AN	1532
QQ-MC3001AT	1532
QQ-MC3001DT	1532
QQ-M07205AT	1044
QQ-0PLL02A0	1704
QQ-0PLL02AN	1704
QQ-0PLL02AO	1704
QQ-0PLL020A	4160
QQ-0PLL02AN	1704
QQ0PLL02AN	4160
QQ-0PPL02A0	1704
QQ-PLL02A0	OEM
QQV60528	0004
QQV60529	0086
QQV60539	0004
QR2378	0004
QRF-2	0086
QRF3	0321
QRG-3	0321
QRT-100	0198
QRT-100A	6571
QRT-101	0006
QRT-101A	0431
QRT-102	0016
QRT-102A	0016
QRT-103	0037
QRT-103A	0037
QRT-104	0111
QRT-105	0111
QRT-106	0006
QRT-107	0079
QRT-107A	0320
QRT-108	0007
QRT-108A	0079
QRT-109	0079
QRT-110	0233
QRT-111	OEM
QRT-112	0111
QRT-113	0326
QRT-114	0617
QRT-115	OEM
QRT-116	0178
QRT-117	0004
QRT-118	0150
QRT-119	0038
QRT-120	0150
QRT-121	1233
QRT-122	0164
QRT-123	0164
QRT-124	0085
QRT-125	0435
QRT-126	0037
QRT-126A	0037
QRT-127	0085
QRT-127A	OEM
QRT-128	0178
QRT-129	0208
QRT-130	0969
QRT-131	0103
QRT-132	OEM
QRT-133	OEM
QRT-134	0127
QRT-135	0127
QRT-136	0164
QRT-137	2035
QRT-139	0309
QRT-140	0309
QRT-141	0320
QRT-143	2035
QRT-144	0396
QRT-145	0178
QRT-146	0042
QRT-147	0599
QRT-148	1671
QRT-149	0130
QRT-150	0556
QRT-151	1190
QRT-152	0042
QRT-153	0919
QRT-154	0236
QRT-155	0676
QRT-156	0419
QRT-157	0848
QRT-158	0419
QRT-159	0334
QRT-159A	0334
QRT-160	0930
QRT-162	OEM
QRT-163	OEM
QRT-164	1351
QRT-164A	OEM
QRT-165	1359
QRT-165A	OEM
QRT-166	1351
QRT-167	1359
QRT-172	0016
QRT-174	1897
QRT-175	0321
QRT-176	0321
QRT-177	2959
QRT-180	0349
QRT-181	0212
QRT-182	4070
QRT-183	0136
QRT-185	0886
QRT-186	0334
QRT-187	0155
QRT-188	0136
QRT-189	0899
QRT-190	0178
QRT-191	0930
QRT-192	0312
QRT-193	2123
QRT-194	1351
QRT-195	1359
QRT-196	1190
QRT-197	0556
QRT-200	0143
QRT-201	0916
QRT-202	0911
QRT-203	0071
QRT-204	0374
QRT-206	OEM
QRT-210	0071
QRT-212	0015
QRT-213	0015
QRT-214	0015
QRT-215	0015
QRT-216	0290
QRT-216D	0290
QRT-218	0133
QRT-220	0469
QRT-221	0196
QRT-222	0479
QRT-223	1073
QRT-224	1293
QRT-225	0769
QRT-226	0201
QRT-227	0239
QRT-228	0747
QRT-229	0286
QRT-230	0287
QRT-231	0299
QRT-232	0250
QRT-234	0188
QRT-235	0162
QRT-236	0157
QRT-237	0631
QRT-238	0025
QRT-239	0644
QRT-240	0012
QRT-241	0170
QRT-242	0313
QRT-243	0137
QRT-244	0361
QRT-245	0002
QRT-246	0416
QRT-247	0526
QRT-248	0560
QRT-249	0436
QRT-250	0039
QRT-251	0346
QRT-252	0993
QRT-253	0863
QRT-254	0778
QRT-255	0327
QRT-256	0149
QRT-257	0244
QRT-258	0490
QRT-259	0398
QRT-260	0186
QRT-261	0028
QRT-262	0030
QRT-263	0143
QRT-264	1780
QRT-265	1313
QRT-266	0417
QRT-267	0016
QRT-268	0016
QRT-269	0037
QRT-270	0037
QRT-271	0006
QRT-272	1879
QRT-300	0079
QRT-301	0590
QRT-302	0079
QRT-303	0037
QRT-304	0320
QRT-305	0431
QRT-306	5758
QRT-306F	0626
QRT-307	0626
QRT-308	0079
QRT-309	0079
QRT-310	1973
QRT-311	0786
QRT-312	0016
QRT-313	0144
QRT-314	0338
QRT-315	0710
QRT-600	1296
QRT-601	2072
QRT-602	2073
QRT-603	1440
QRT-604	2074
QRT-605	3604
QRT-700	OEM
QRT-701	OEM
QRT-702	OEM
QRT-703	OEM
QRT-704	OEM
QRT-705	OEM
QRT-708	OEM
QRT-709	OEM
QRT-710	OEM
QRT-711	OEM
QRT-712	OEM
QRT-713	OEM
QRT-714	OEM
QRT-715	OEM
QRT-716	OEM
QRT-717	OEM
QRT-718	OEM
QRT-719	OEM
QRT-720	OEM
QS054	0079
QS-0254	0155
QS0254	0079
QS23	OEM
QS24	OEM
QS25	0286
QS33	OEM
QS34	OEM
QS102AA	0015
QS102BA	0015
QS102CA	0015
QS102DA	0015
QS102EA	0015
QS102FA	0015
QS102GA	0015
QS102HA	0015
QS102KA	0015
QS102MA	0015
QS102PA	0071
QS102RA	0071
QS102TA	0071
QS102VA	0071
QS132AA	0071
QS132BA	0071
QS132CA	0071
QS132DA	0071
QS132EA	0071
QS132FA	0071
QS132GA	0071
QS132HA	0071
QS132KA	0071
QS132MA	0071
QS132PA	0071
QS132RA	0071
QS132TA	0071
QS132VA	0071
QS316	0037
QS317	OEM
QS318	OEM
QS319	OEM
QS320	OEM
QS751AA	0015
QS751BA	0015
QS751CA	0015
QS751DA	0015
QS751EA	0015
QS751FA	0015
QS751GA	0015
QS751HA	0015
QS751KA	0015
QS751MA	0015
QS751PA	0071
QS751RA	0071
QS751TA	0071
QS751VA	0071
QS1018	2039
QS1306	0930
QSC372	0527
QSC380	0079
QSC509	0320
QSC784	0079
QSE1001	0079
QSE3001	0144
QSE5020	0007
QSI-5022	3898
QT0013Z	1533
QT0036	1533
QT0036Z	1533
QT0072Z	3474
QT0074Z	1533
QT0085	0551
QT0085Z	0551
QT0095	0148
QT0100	0151
QT0100R	0151
QT0144Z	1533
QT0185R	OEM
QT0190Z	1498
QT0191	0558
QT0192	0520
QT0226R	1376
QT0226S	1376
QT0267Q	0042
QT0267R	0042
QT0267S	0042
QT0268Z	1498
QT-A0719AXN	0006
QT-A0719XAN	0006
QT-A0719XCN	0006
QT-A0719XHN	0006
QT-A0733XAA	0006
QT-A0733XDN	0006
QT-A0733XON	0006
QTA562	0037
QT-A0719XAN	0006
QT-C0372XAT	0076
QT-C0460CBB	0151
QT-C0710XAE	0364
QT-C0710XBE	0364
QT-C0710XEE	0364
QT-C0735XBT	0191
QT-C0828XAN	1211
QT-C0828XDN	1211
QT-C0829XAN	0151
QT-C0829XBN	0151
QT-C0829XON	0151
QT-C0839XDA	0076
QT-C0900XBA	1212
QT-C0900XBD	1212
QT-C0900XCA	0111
QT-C0945ACA	0076
QT-C0945AGA	0076
QT-C131BXDN	0155
QT-C1047SAN	0113
QT-C1047XAN	0113
QT-C1047XBN	0113
QT-C1306	0833
QT-C1306XZA	0833
QT-C1307XZA	0830
QT-C1307ZXA	0830
QT-C1318XAN	0284
QT-C1318XDN	0155
QT-C1318XON	0320
QT-C1359XAN	0151
QT-C1687XAN	0224
QT-C1760XAS	1935
QT-C1760XCS	1935
QT-C1846XAN	0781
QT-CBC546AA	0111
QT-CO372XAT	0144
QT-CO710XBE	0079
QT-CO828XDN	0144
QT-CO900XCA	0111
QT-CO945ACA	0111
QT-CQ460CBB	0151
QT-D0313XAC	0042
QT-D0325XAC	0042
QT-D0525XDT	0419
QTD0704XAE	0060
QT-K0023AAS	0321
QT-K0033XAE	0321
QT-K0033XBE	1270
QT-R0033XBE	OEM
QTVCM-5	0673
QTVCM-16	1335
QTVCM-44	0627
QTVCM-45	0687
QTVCM-48	0817
QTVCM-59	0780
QTVCM-73	0514
QTVCM-75	0574
QTVCM-77	2046
QTVCM-78	0905
QTVCM-79	1983
QTVCM-81	1044
QTVCM-500	0232
QTVCM-502	1303
QTVCM-505	1199
QU01-20	OEM
QU01-24	OEM
QU01-27	OEM
QV3508	OEM
QV3512	OEM
QV3518	OEM
QV3522	OEM
QV3530	OEM
QV3540	OEM
QV4508	OEM
QV4512	OEM
QV4518	OEM
QV4522	OEM
QV4530	OEM
QV4540	OEM
QV6008	OEM
QV6012	OEM
QV6018	OEM
QV6022	OEM
QV6030	OEM
QV6040	OEM
QV9008	OEM

If replacement code is OEM, contact original manufacturer for replacement. 517

DEVICE TYPE	REPL CODE
QV9012	OEM
QV9018	OEM
QV9025	OEM
QV9035	OEM
QV9045	OEM
QV-BD11246A	0139
QVD1KF114	0143
QVI1330	OEM
QVIM51181L	OEM
QVM800B	0143
QVM8513ART	0139
QZ3.6T5	0188
QZ3.6T10	0188
QZ5.1T5	0162
QZ5.1T10	0162
QZ5.6T5	0157
QZ5.6T10	0157
QZ6.2T5	0631
QZ6.2T10	0631
QZ10T5	0170
QZ10T10	0170
QZ12T5	0137
QZ12T10	0137
QZ14T5	0100
QZ14T10	0100
QZ15T5	0002
QZ15T10	0002
QZ27T5	0436
QZ27T10	0436
QZ1575	0002
R002Z	0071
R0050	0071
R0051	0071
R0052	0071
R0053	3855
R0054	0229
R0055	0072
R0056	0369
R0070	0947
R0071	0242
R0072	0535
R0074	0811
R0076	0811
R0078	0916
R0080	0087
R0081	0087
R0082	0087
R0084	OEM
R0086	0087
R0090	0087
R0091	0087
R0092	0222
R0094	0087
R0096	0087
R0097	0087
R0098	0087
R0-2AV	0071
R02	0959
R02A	0559
R02AU	0071
R02AV	0071
R02B	0087
R02C	0071
R02K	0071
R02Z	OEM
R06-1001	0144
R06-1002	0144
R06-1003	0144
R06-1004	0144
R06-1005	0144
R06-1006	0144
R06-1007	0004
R06-1008	0004
R06-1009	0004
R06-1010	0004
R07A	0025
R080	0071
R0100	OEM
R0100(HEP)	1272
R0101	OEM
R0101(HEP)	1272
R0102	0023
R0102(HEP)	1272
R0103AA	4381
R0103BA	4381
R0103CA	4382
R0103DA	4382
R0104	OEM
R0104(HEP)	1277
R0106	OEM
R0106(HEP)	1282
R0106AA	4381
R0106BA	4381
R0106CA	4382
R0106DA	4382
R0107AA	4381
R0107BA	4381
R0107CA	4382
R0107DA	4382
R0130	0122
R0130(HEP)	1590
R0131	0122
R0132	0122
R0132(HEP)	0865
R0134	0122
R0134(HEP)	0847
R0136	0122
R0137	OEM
R0138	OEM
R0160	0315
R0161	0315
R0162	0315
R0164	0315
R0166	6051
R0186	OEM
R0250	0315
R0251	0315
R0253	0315
R0254	0315
R0255	0315
R0256	0315
R0257	0315
R0801	6370
R0802	6370
R0803	6370
R0804	0106
R0805	0782
R0851	0276
R0852	0276
R0853	0287
R0855	0293
R0856	0299
R0861	OEM
R0862	OEM
R0863	OEM
R0865	OEM
R0866	OEM
R0875	2347
R0876	2347
R0877	2347
R0878	OEM
R0879	OEM
R0880	OEM
R0881	OEM
R0882	OEM
R0883	OEM
R0884	OEM
R0890	OEM
R0891	OEM
R0892	OEM
R0894	OEM
R0896	OEM
R07105	0789
R-1	0015
R1	0015
R1/1H	OEM
R1/2H	OEM
R1/3H	OEM
R1/4H	OEM
R-1A	0015
R1A	0015
R-1B	0242
R1B	0015
R1C	0604
R-1S188	0143
R-1S333Y	0244
R1Z	0102
R2	1293
R-2A	1241
R-2AV2	1440
R-2B	1241
R2D	0137
R2E	0002
R2H	0604
R2KN	OEM
R2M	5408
R-2SA222	0136
R-2SB186	0004
R-2SB187	0004
R-2SB303	0004
R-2SB405	0164
R-2SB474	1004
R-2SB492	0841
R2SB492	0841
R-2SC535	0127
R-2SC537	0191
R-2SC545	0127
R-2SC668	0127
R-2SC772	1136
R-2SC858	0111
R-2SD187	0208
R2SZ	0015
R3	0469
R3/1H	OEM
R3/2H	0015
R3/3H	OEM
R3/4H	OEM
R-3A	1241
R-3A3	1296
R-3AT2	2072
R-3DB3	2073
R4	OEM
R-4A	0535
R4A	0015
R4HZ	0800
R5	0071
R-5B	0242
R5B	0071
R-5C	0242
R5C	0071
R5.1JSB2X	OEM
R6	0071
R6/1H	OEM
R6/2H	0015
R6/3H	OEM
R6/4H	OEM
R-6A	1241
R-6B	1241
R6HZ	0315
R8	0071
R8/1H	OEM
R8/2H	0071
R8/3H	OEM
R8/4H	OEM
R9-56	2181
R9A	0015
R9H02015	OEM
R9H02024	OEM
R9H02215	OEM
R9H02415	OEM
R9H02615	OEM
R9H02815	OEM
R10D1	0015
R10DC	0015
R10G	OEM
R10J	0023
R12	0595
R14	0595
R15	0142
R16	0004
R18S12A	OEM
R18S12A2	OEM
R18S12A3	OEM
R18S12B	3277
R18S12B2	OEM
R18S12B3	OEM
R18S14A	OEM
R18S14A2	OEM
R18S14A3	OEM
R18S14B	3277
R18S14B2	OEM
R18S14B3	OEM
R18S16A	OEM
R18S16A2	OEM
R18S16A3	OEM
R18S18A	OEM
R18S18A2	OEM
R18S18A3	OEM
R18SG4A	OEM
R18SG4A2	OEM
R18SG4A3	OEM
R18SG4B	OEM
R18SG4B2	OEM
R18SG4B3	OEM
R18SG6A	OEM
R18SG6A2	OEM
R18SG6A3	OEM
R18SG6B	OEM
R18SG6B2	OEM
R18SG6B3	OEM
R18SG8A	OEM
R18SG8A2	OEM
R18SG8A3	OEM
R18SG8B	OEM
R18SG8B2	OEM
R18SG8B3	OEM
R18SG10A	OEM
R18SG10A2	OEM
R18SG10A3	OEM
R18SG10B	OEM
R18SG10B2	OEM
R18SG10B3	OEM
R18SGR4A	OEM
R18SGR4B	OEM
R18SGR6A	OEM
R18SGR6B	OEM
R18SGR8A	OEM
R18SGR8B	OEM
R18SGR10A	OEM
R18SGR10B	OEM
R18SR12A	OEM
R18SR12B	0202
R18SR14A	OEM
R18SR14B	0202
R18SR16A	OEM
R18SR18A	OEM
R23-1003	0004
R23-1004	0004
R23A4A	OEM
R23A4B	1217
R23A6A	OEM
R23A6B	1217
R23A8A	OEM
R23A8B	OEM
R23A10A	OEM
R23A10B	OEM
R23A12A	OEM
R23A12B	1195
R23A14A	OEM
R23A14B	OEM
R23A16A	OEM
R23A16B	OEM
R23A18A	OEM
R23A18B	OEM
R23A20A	OEM
R23A20B	OEM
R23A22A	OEM
R23A22B	OEM
R23A24A	OEM
R23A26A	OEM
R23D16A	OEM
R23DR16A	5298
R24-1001	0004
R24-1002	0004
R24-1003	0004
R24-1004	0004
R30D20B	OEM
R30DR20B	6017
R30E4A	OEM
R30E4B	OEM
R30E6A	OEM
R30E6B	OEM
R30E8A	OEM
R30E8B	OEM
R30E10A	OEM
R30E10B	OEM
R30E12A	OEM
R30E12B	OEM
R30E14A	OEM
R30E14B	OEM
R30E16A	OEM
R30E16B	OEM
R30E18A	OEM
R30E18B	OEM
R30E20A	OEM
R30E20B	OEM
R30E22A	OEM
R30E22B	OEM
R30E24A	OEM
R30E24B	OEM
R30E26A	OEM
R30E26B	OEM
R30E28A	OEM
R30E30A	OEM
R33	0208
R34	0208
R34B4A	OEM
R34B4B	2146
R34B6A	OEM
R34B6B	2146
R34B8A	OEM
R34B8B	OEM
R34B10A	OEM
R34B10B	OEM
R34B12A	OEM
R34B12B	0474
R34B14A	OEM
R34B14B	OEM
R34B16A	OEM
R34B16B	OEM
R34B18A	OEM
R34B18B	OEM
R34B20A	OEM
R34B20B	OEM
R34B22A	OEM
R34B22B	OEM
R34B24A	OEM
R34B24B	OEM
R34B26A	OEM
R34B26B	OEM
R34B28A	OEM
R34B30A	OEM
R35	0004
R38B4A	OEM
R38B4B	OEM
R38B6A	OEM
R38B6B	OEM
R38B8A	OEM
R38B8B	OEM
R38B10A	OEM
R38B10B	OEM
R38B12A	OEM
R38B12B	OEM
R38B14A	OEM
R38B14B	OEM
R38B16A	OEM
R38B16B	OEM
R38B18A	OEM
R38B18B	OEM
R38B20A	OEM
R38B20B	OEM
R38B22A	OEM
R38B22B	OEM
R38B24A	OEM
R38B24B	OEM
R38B26A	OEM
R38B26B	OEM
R38B28A	OEM
R38B28B	OEM
R38B30A	OEM
R38B30B	OEM
R38B32A	OEM
R38B34A	OEM
R38B36B	OEM
R38B38B	OEM
R38B40A	OEM
R38B42A	OEM
R38B44B	OEM
R38B46B	OEM
R38B48A	OEM
R38B50A	OEM
R41	0595
R43HZ	0800
R46	0211
R52	0004
R52K4A	OEM
R52K4B	4835
R52K6A	OEM
R52K6B	4835
R52K8A	OEM
R52K8B	2126
R52K10A	OEM
R52K10B	2126
R52K12A	2126
R52K12B	OEM
R52K14A	OEM
R52K14B	OEM
R52K16A	OEM
R52K16B	OEM
R52K18A	OEM
R52K18B	OEM
R52K20A	OEM
R52K20B	OEM
R52K22A	OEM
R52K22B	OEM
R52K24A	OEM
R52K24B	OEM
R52K26A	OEM
R52K26B	OEM
R52K28A	OEM
R52K28B	OEM
R52K30A	OEM
R52K30B	OEM
R52K32A	OEM
R52K34A	OEM
R52K36B	OEM
R52K38B	OEM
R52K40A	OEM
R52K42A	OEM
R52K44B	OEM
R52K46B	OEM
R52K48A	OEM
R52K50A	OEM
R56	0004
R60-1001	0136
R60-1002	0050
R60-1003	0050
R60-1004	0004
R60-1005	0004
R60-1006	0004
R60-1007	0143
R61	0208
R62	0208
R63	0208
R-63HZ	0315
R64	0004
R65	0004
R66	0004
R66-8504	0015
R67	0004
R79	0208
R80	0208
R83	0004
R87	0004
R98	0004
R100-1	0004
R100-8	0004
R100-9	0004
R101-2	0004
R101-3	0004
R101-4	0004
R104-5	0136
R104-6	0136
R104-7	0136
R104-8	0136
R117	0595
R118	0127
R119	0279
R120	0004
R122C	0015
R123	0086
R125	0595
R135	0595
R136	0595
R137	0595
R142	0133
R145B	0299
R152	0004
R154B	0276
R163	0279
R164	0004
R177	0208
R186	0279
R200	OEM
R202	0595
R203	0595
R204B	0276
R205	0071
R210	0087
R212	OEM
R220	OEM
R227	0279
R242	0004
R244	0279
R245	0004
R250	0087
R250-H	OEM
R250F	0087
R255	0004
R258	0279
R265A	0160
R289	0004
R290	0004
R291	0004
R324	0004
R336	0136
R337	0136
R338	0050
R339	0050
R340	0016
R341	0050
R350	0087
R350F	0087
R364	0004
R400	OEM
R-424	0279
R424	0050
R424-1	0050
R425	0050
R428	0004
R440M	OEM
R488	0279
R497	0050
R499-01-C	0079
R506	0279
R515	0050
R515A	0050
R516	0160
R516(T.I.)	0050
R516A	0050
R530	0004
R537	0004
R539	0050
R558	0050
R558(T.I.)	0004
R563	0050
R563(T.I.)	0004
R564	0050
R565	0050
R579	0050
R579(T.I.)	0004
R581	0136
R582	0016
R592	0595
R593	0050
R593A	0050
R600**20	1017
R600**25	1017
R608	0004
R608A	0004
R610**20	1017
R610**25	1017
R621-1	0042
R623-1	0419
R684	0136
R702	OEM
R704	OEM
R706	OEM
R710XPT	2219
R-711	0120
R711XPT	2219
R712XPT	2219
R713XPT	OEM
R714	0136
R714XPT	2219
R715	0136
R855-2	0015
R868	0004
R895	0079
R1000	0087
R1001	1129
R1002	0340
R1003	0895
R1004	2326
R1005	0058
R1019	0037
R1035	0015
R1106	0143
R1107	0143
R1109	0143
R1117-1	0142
R1202	1574
R1205	1574
R1215	OEM
R1215(HEP)	1386
R1216	OEM
R1217	OEM
R1217(HEP)	0442
R1218	3575
R1219	OEM
R1220	4508
R1220(HEP)	2084
R1221	2255
R1221(HEP)	0500
R1222	3368
R1223	3370
R1241	0759
R1242	0759
R1243	0759
R1243(MOTOROLA)	0240
R1244	0759
R1245	0759
R1246	0759
R1247	0759
R1273	0004
R1274	0004
R1300	0759
R1301	0759
R1302	0759
R1303	0759
R1304	0740
R1305	1620
R1306	0759
R1307	0759
R1329	0015
R1331	OEM
R1332	OEM
R1333	OEM
R1334	OEM
R1335	OEM
R1336	OEM
R1337	OEM
R-1348	0137
R1471	0720
R1472	0707
R1473	0720
R1475	0720
R1530	0208
R1531	0208
R1532	0208
R1533	0595
R1534	0208
R1537	0208
R1538	0208
R1539	0050
R1540	0004
R1541	0004
R1542	0004
R1543	0004
R1544	0004
R1545	0208
R1546	0004
R1547	0208
R1548	0004
R1549	0208
R1550	0050
R1553	0208
R1554	0050
R1555	0004
R1667	0143
R1701	OEM
R1702	OEM
R1703	OEM
R1711	1744
R1712	4343
R1713	3458
R1715	0480
R1721	1081
R1722	1085
R1723	0588
R1725	0411
R1750	0147
R1751	0147
R1752	0147
R1781	3123
R1782	3123
R1783	3123
R1785	3123
R1889	0143
R1901C-6L31	OEM
R1903	OEM
R1903-7609	OEM
R2001	0969
R2003	0969
R2005	4917
R2010	1625
R2015	1625
R2020	1625
R2025	1242
R2030	1242
R2035	1242
R2040	1242
R2045	1196
R2050	1196
R2060	1196
R2070	2124
R2080	2124
R2090	2236
R2096	0178
R2105	4917
R2110	1625
R2115	1625
R2120	1625
R2125	1242
R2130	2124
R2135	1242
R2140	1242
R2145	1196
R2150	1196
R2159	0015
R2160	1196
R2164	0143
R2170	2124
R2180	2124
R2190	2236
R2252	0015
R2270-7693	0126
R2350	0004
R2351	0004
R2352	0004
R2353	0004
R2355	0004
R2356	0208
R2359	0208
R2360	0208
R2364	0208
R2365	0208
R2366	0004
R2367	0004
R2373	0004
R2374	0208
R2375	0208
R2432-1	0823
R2434-1	2549
R-2436	0309
R2442	0015
R2444	0142
R2445-1	2689
R2460-1	0229
R-2460-3	0969
R2460-3	0969
R2460-4	0229
R2460-9(RCA)	0969

If replacement code is OEM, contact original manufacturer for replacement.

DEVICE TYPE	REPL CODE
R2473	0144
R2474-2	0233
R2476	0144
R2477	0144
R2482-1	0004
R2516	1335
R2516-1	0167
R2675	0004
R2677	0004
R2683	0050
R2684	0050
R2685	0050
R2686	0050
R2687	0050
R2688	0050
R2689	0004
R2694	0050
R2695	0050
R2696	0050
R2697	0050
R2749	0004
R2749M	0004
R2964	0969
R2982	0103
R3012	0102
R3012(HEP)	0102
R3057	0196
R3105	0267
R3110	1099
R3115	1099
R3120	1099
R3125	0258
R3130	0258
R3135	0258
R3140	0258
R3145	0267
R3150	0267
R3160	0267
R3170	1111
R3180	1111
R3190	0280
R3205	1620
R3210	1099
R3215	1099
R3220	1099
R3225	0258
R3230	0258
R3235	0258
R3240	0258
R3245	0267
R3250	0267
R3260	0267
R3270	1111
R3275	0004
R3276	0004
R3277	0050
R3278	0050
R3279	0050
R3279-13	OEM
R3280	1111
R3280(RCA)	0004
R3282	0004
R3283	0016
R3284	0004
R3285	0015
R3286	0004
R3287	0050
R3288	0050
R3290	0280
R3293	0208
R3293(GE)	0016
R3299	0004
R3301	0004
R3309	0050
R3314	0196
R3405	2640
R3410	2741
R3415	2741
R3420	2741
R3425	2879
R3430	2879
R3435	2879
R3440	2879
R3445	3022
R3450	3022
R3460	3022
R3470	3088
R3480	3088
R3490	3178
R3503	0142
R3505	1772
R3508	0086
R3510	1772
R3514-1	0969
R3515	0085
R3515(RCA)	0160
R3515(RECT)	1772
R3520	0142
R3520(RECT)	1772
R3520-1	0142
R3525	1772
R3530	1772
R3533	0196
R3535	1772
R3540	1772
R3545	1772
R3550	1772
R3560	1772
R3573-1	0208

DEVICE TYPE	REPL CODE
R3578-1	0004
R3583-7	0239
R3583-8	0239
R3585-5	0239
R3585-6	0061
R3585-7	0239
R3585-8	0061
R3598-2	0004
R3605	2640
R3608	0086
R3608-1	0086
R3608-2	0086
R3610	2168
R3613-3(RCA)	0334
R3615	2168
R3619-3	2378
R3620	2168
R3625	2177
R3630	2177
R3635	2177
R3640	2177
R3645	2183
R3650	2183
R3651-1	0212
R3660	2183
R3670	2202
R3680	2202
R3690	2324
R3705	1772
R3710	1772
R3715	1772
R3720	1772
R3725	1772
R3730	1772
R3740	1772
R3750	1772
R3760	1772
R3780	1807
R4057	0016
R4105	1337
R4110	1337
R4115	1337
R4120	1337
R4125	1337
R4130	1337
R4135	1894
R4140	1894
R4145	1894
R4150	1894
R4160	1894
R4170	0193
R4180	0193
R4190	0193
R4192	0142
R4193	0142
R4194	0142
R4195	0142
R4196	0142
R4210	1337
R4215	1337
R4220	1337
R4225	1337
R4230	1337
R4235	1894
R4240	1894
R4245	1894
R4250	1894
R4260	1894
R4270	0193
R4280	0193
R4290	0193
R4295-1	1178
R4295-1(RCA)	1178
R4295-2	1178
R4305	1337
R4310	1337
R4315	1337
R4320	1337
R4325	1337
R4330	1337
R4335	1894
R4340	1894
R4345	1894
R4348	0004
R4349	0004
R4350	1894
R4360	1894
R4369	0103
R4370	0193
R4380	0193
R4390	0193
R4409	0196
R4439-1	1832
R4439-1(RCA)	1832
R4439-2	1832
R4439-2(RCA)	1832
R4666	0196
R5048	0086
R5050	0208
R5051	0004
R5052	0004
R5053	0004
R5054	0208
R5055	0004
R5056	0208
R5096	0143
R5097	0004
R5098	0004
R5099	0004

DEVICE TYPE	REPL CODE
R5100	0004
R5101	0164
R5102	0050
R5103	0050
R5105	0496
R5110	0496
R5115	0496
R5120	0496
R5125	0496
R5130	0496
R5135	1766
R5140	1766
R5150	1766
R5160	1766
R5170	1778
R5179	0208
R5180	0208
R5181	0004
R5182	0164
R5190	1778
R5221AD	OEM
R5305	0496
R5310	0496
R5315	0496
R5320	0496
R5325	0496
R5330	0496
R5335	1766
R5340	1766
R5345	1766
R5350	1766
R5360	1766
R5370	1778
R5380	1778
R5390	1778
R5405	0496
R5410	0496
R5415	0496
R5420	0496
R5425	0496
R5430	0496
R5435	1766
R5440	1766
R5450	1766
R5460	1766
R5470	1778
R5480	1778
R5490	1778
R5522	0143
R5523	0004
R5524	0004
R5525	0004
R5708	0004
R5740-1	0279
R5862	0123
R5970	0015
R5971	0015
R5983	0030
R6048	0015
R6109	0123
R6110	0015
R6171-11	1208
R6171-12	1208
R6171-19	1208
R6171-20	1208
R6422	0015
R6502-40	3036
R6502C	3036
R6502E	OEM
R6502P	3036
R6507C	3041
R6507P	3041
R6520-13	OEM
R6520-26	OEM
R6520AP	OEM
R6532-12	OEM
R6532P	1962
R6551-11	OEM
R6551P	OEM
R6553	0004
R6765-5P	OEM
R6765P	OEM
R6789	0030
R6922	0004
R-7026	0133
R-7027	0133
R7028	0143
R-7029	0143
R7029	0143
R-7030	0644
R7030	0644
R7048	0004
R-7051	0143
R-7056	OEM
R-7092	0139
R-7093	0466
R-7094	0077
R-7096	0023
R-7097	0064
R-7103	0137
R-7110	0139
R7124	0004
R7127	0004
R7162	0015
R7163	0016
R7164	0004
R7165	0016
R7166	0004
R7167	0085

DEVICE TYPE	REPL CODE
R7248	0015
R7249	0016
R7253	0160
R7271	0015
R7343	0016
R7359	0016
R7360	0016
R7361	0016
R7362	0208
R7363	0004
R7489	0004
R7490	0004
R7491	0004
R7582	0016
R7612	0004
R7613	0086
R7615	0087
R7620	0085
R7682	0015
R7743	0143
R7885	0050
R7886	0050
R7887	0016
R7888	0004
R7889	0004
R7890	0435
R7891	0050
R7892	0143
R7893	0143
R7894	0137
R7953	0016
R7954	0015
R7962	0050
R8022	0133
R8023	0133
R8024	0015
R8060	0143
R8061	0143
R8066	0016
R8067	0016
R8068	0016
R8069	0016
R8070	0016
R8115	0016
R8116	0016
R8117	0016
R8118	0016
R8119	0016
R8120	0016
R8121	0004
R8158	0142
R8219	0143
R8223	0016
R8224	0016
R8225	0016
R8240	0050
R8241	0050
R8242	0050
R8243	0016
R8244	0016
R8257	0143
R8259	0016
R8260	0016
R8261	0016
R8305	0016
R8310	0004
R8311	0004
R8312	0016
R8313	0085
R8314	0133
R8364	0137
R8470	0015
R8471	0769
R8472	1293
R8473	0015
R8474	0196
R8475	0143
R8477	0469
R8528	0016
R8529	0127
R8530	0016
R8543	0016
R8551	0016
R8552	0016
R8553	0016
R8554	0016
R8555	0016
R8556	0016
R8557	0016
R8559	0050
R8560	0469
R8620	0016
R8645	0087
R8646	0016
R8647	0016
R8648	0016
R8649	0086
R8658	0016
R8659	0160
R8685	0050
R8686	0050
R8687	0004
R8688	0004
R8692	0050
R8693	0050
R8694	0050
R8695	0004
R8697	0004
R8703	0050

DEVICE TYPE	REPL CODE
R8704	0050
R8705	0050
R8706	0004
R8707	0004
R8721	0229
R8881	0050
R8882	0050
R8883	0004
R8884	0004
R8885	0004
R8886	0004
R8887	0143
R8889	0016
R8900	0016
R8914	0016
R8915	0086
R8916	0016
R8963	0016
R8964	0016
R8965	0016
R8966	0016
R8967	0037
R8968	0016
R8969	0037
R8970	0143
R8971	0004
R8989	0142
R9004	0016
R9005	0016
R9006	0016
R9025	0016
R9071	0016
R9381	0526
R9382	0283
R9383	0283
R9384	0016
R9385	0016
R9470	0015
R9483	0016
R9531	0050
R9532	0050
R9533	0164
R9534	0164
R9590	0143
R9597	0015
R9600	0224
R9601	0050
R9602	0050
R9603	0164
R9604	0164
R10254P936	1820
R10254P945	0081
R10254P945B	0081
R10254P946	0141
R10255P946B	0141
R10256P962	0557
R10256P962B	0557
R10564	0469
R20100	2236
R21100	2236
R24451	2689
R31100	0280
R32100	0280
R34100	3178
R36100	2324
R37100	1807
R41100	0193
R42100	0193
R43100	0193
R50305	0496
R50310	0496
R50315	1766
R50320	0496
R50325	0496
R50330	0496
R50335	1766
R50340	1766
R50345	1766
R50350	1766
R50360	1766
R50370	1778
R50380	1778
R50390	1778
R50405	0496
R50410	0496
R50415	0496
R50420	0496
R50425	0496
R50430	0496
R50435	1766
R50440	1766
R50445	1030
R50450	1766
R50460	1766
R50470	1778
R50480	1778
R50490	1778
R51100	1778
R53100	1778
R54100	1778
R80286-8	OEM
R105064	0769
R105330	1024
R106379	0015
R109180	0196
R109328	0196
R109474	0196
R112524	0143
R113321	0015

DEVICE TYPE	REPL CODE
R113391	1293
R113392	0015
R113397	0769
R503100	1778
R504100	1778
R600428R	0496
R1500715	0087
R2400730	0087
R3020506	0706
R3020512	0706
R3020606	0706
R3020612	0706
R3030506	2939
R3030512	2939
R3030606	2939
R3030612	2939
R4020520	0596
R4020530	0596
R4020620	0596
R4020630	0596
R4030520	1840
R4030530	1840
R4030620	1840
R4030630	1840
R4040060	2786
R4040070	2786
R4040160	2786
R4040170	2786
R4040260	2786
R4040270	2786
R4040360	2786
R4040370	2786
R4040460	2786
R4040470	2786
R4040560	2786
R4040570	2786
R4040660	2786
R4040670	2786
R4040760	2818
R4040770	2818
R4040860	2818
R4040870	2818
R4040960	2818
R4040970	2818
R4041060	2818
R4041070	2818
R4050060	1772
R4050070	1772
R4050160	1772
R4050170	1772
R4050260	1772
R4050270	1772
R4050360	1772
R4050370	1772
R4050460	1772
R4050470	1772
R4050560	1772
R4050570	1772
R4050660	1772
R4050670	1772
R4050760	1807
R4050770	1807
R4050860	1807
R4050870	1807
R4050960	1807
R4050970	1807
R4051060	1807
R4051070	1807
R4100022	0315
R4100025	3160
R4100040	2786
R4100070	2813
R4100122	0315
R4100140	2786
R4100170	2813
R4100222	0315
R4100225	1116
R4100240	2786
R4100322	0315
R4100325	0800
R4100340	2786
R4100422	0315
R4100425	0800
R4100440	2786
R4100522	0315
R4100540	2786
R4100622	0315
R4100640	2786
R4100822	1124
R4100840	1124
R4100860	3846
R4101022	0045
R4101040	0045
R4101060	2631
R4101070	2454
R4101822	1111
R4108070	2806
R4110022	0267
R4110040	1772
R4110070	2168
R4110122	0267
R4110140	1772
R4110170	2168
R4110222	0267
R4110240	1772
R4110322	0267
R4110340	1772
R4110422	0267
R4110440	1772

DEVICE TYPE	REPL CODE
R4110522	0267
R4110540	1772
R4110622	0267
R4110640	1772
R4110822	0280
R4110840	1111
R4110860	3088
R4111022	0280
R4111040	0280
R4111060	3178
R4111070	2324
R4118070	2202
R4140060	3716
R4140070	3725
R4140160	2629
R4140170	1551
R4140260	2633
R4140270	2813
R4140360	OEM
R4140370	OEM
R4140460	1995
R4140470	2823
R4140560	2652
R4140570	2844
R4140660	2657
R4140670	2844
R4140760	3846
R4140770	2806
R4140860	3846
R4140870	2806
R4140960	2631
R4140970	2454
R4141060	2631
R4141070	2454
R5000110	0594
R5000110XXWA	0594
R5000110XXWC	0594
R5000115	0594
R5000115XXWA	0594
R5000115XXWC	0594
R5000210	0594
R5000210XXWA	0594
R5000210XXWC	0594
R5000215	0594
R5000215XXWA	0594
R5000215XXWC	0594
R5000310	0594
R5000310XXWA	0594
R5000315	0594
R5000315XXWA	0594
R5000315XXWC	0594
R5000410	1975
R5000410XXWA	1975
R5000410XXWC	1975
R5000415	1975
R5000415XXWA	1975
R5000415XXWC	1975
R5000510	1975
R5000510XXWA	1975
R5000510XXWC	1975
R5000515	1975
R5000515XXWA	1975
R5000515XXWC	1975
R5000610	1975
R5000610XXWA	1975
R5000610XXWC	1975
R5000615	1975
R5000615WA	1975
R5000615XXWA	1975
R5000615XXWC	1975
R5000710	0652
R5000710XXWA	0652
R5000710XXWC	0652
R5000715	0652
R5000715XXWA	0652
R5000715XXWC	0652
R5000810	0652
R5000810XXWA	0652
R5000810XXWC	0652
R5000815	0652
R5000815XXWA	0652
R5000815XXWC	0652
R5000910	0652
R5000910XXWA	0652
R5000910XXWC	0652
R5000915	0652
R5000915XXWA	0652
R5000915XXWC	0652
R5001010	0652
R5001010XXWA	0652
R5001010XXWC	0652
R5001015	0652
R5001015XXWA	0652
R5001015XXWC	0652
R5010110	1337
R5010110XXWA	1337
R5010110XXWC	1337
R5010115	1337
R5010115XXWA	1337
R5010115XXWC	1337
R5010210	1337
R5010210XXWA	1337
R5010210XXWC	1337
R5010215	1337
R5010215XXWA	1337
R5010215XXWC	1337
R5010310	1337
R5010310XXWA	1337
R5010310XXWC	1337

If replacement code is OEM, contact original manufacturer for replacement.

DEVICE TYPE	REPL CODE
R5010315	1337
R5010315XXWA	1337
R5010315XXWC	1337
R5010410	1894
R5010410XXWA	1894
R5010410XXWC	1894
R5010415	1894
R5010415XXWA	1894
R5010415XXWC	1894
R5010510	1894
R5010510XXWA	1894
R5010510XXWC	1894
R5010515	1894
R5010515XXWA	1894
R5010515XXWC	1894
R5010610	1894
R5010610XXWA	1894
R5010610XXWC	1894
R5010615	1894
R5010615XXWA	1894
R5010615XXWC	1894
R5010710	0193
R5010710XXWA	0193
R5010710XXWC	0193
R5010715	0193
R5010715XXWA	0193
R5010715XXWC	0193
R5010810	0193
R5010810XXWA	0193
R5010810XXWC	0193
R5010815	0193
R5010815XXWA	0193
R5010815XXWC	0193
R5010910	0193
R5010910XXWA	0193
R5010910XXWC	0193
R5010915	0193
R5010915XXWA	0193
R5010915XXWC	0193
R5011010	0193
R5011010XXWA	0193
R5011010XXWC	0193
R5011015	0193
R5011015XXWA	0193
R5011015XXWC	0193
R5020108CJ	OEM
R5020108CJWA	OEM
R5020108EJ	OEM
R5020108EJWA	OEM
R5020108FJ	OEM
R5020108FJWA	OEM
R5020110CJ	OEM
R5020110EJ	OEM
R5020110FJ	OEM
R5020208CJ	OEM
R5020208EJ	OEM
R5020208FJ	OEM
R5020210CJ	OEM
R5020210EJ	OEM
R5020210FJ	OEM
R5020308CJ	OEM
R5020308EJ	OEM
R5020308FJ	OEM
R5020310CJ	OEM
R5020310EJ	OEM
R5020310FJ	OEM
R5020408CJ	OEM
R5020408EJ	OEM
R5020408FJ	OEM
R5020410CJ	OEM
R5020410EJ	OEM
R5020410FJ	OEM
R5020508CJ	OEM
R5020508EJ	OEM
R5020508FJ	OEM
R5020510CJ	OEM
R5020510EJ	OEM
R5020510FJ	OEM
R5020608CJ	OEM
R5020608EJ	OEM
R5020608FJ	OEM
R5020610CJ	OEM
R5020610EJ	OEM
R5020610FJ	OEM
R5020708CJ	OEM
R5020708EJ	OEM
R5020708FJ	OEM
R5020710CJ	OEM
R5020710EJ	OEM
R5020710FJ	OEM
R5020808CJ	OEM
R5020808EJ	OEM
R5020808FJ	OEM
R5020810CJ	OEM
R5020810EJ	OEM
R5020810FJ	OEM
R5020908CJ	OEM
R5020908EJ	OEM
R5020908FJ	OEM
R5020910CJ	OEM
R5020910EJ	OEM
R5020910FJ	OEM
R5021008CJ	OEM
R5021008EJ	OEM
R5021008FJ	OEM
R5021010CJ	OEM
R5021010EJ	OEM
R5021010FJ	OEM
R5021108CJ	OEM

DEVICE TYPE	REPL CODE
R5021108EJ	OEM
R5021108FJ	OEM
R5021110CJ	OEM
R5021110EJ	OEM
R5021110FJ	OEM
R5021208CJ	OEM
R5021208EJ	OEM
R5021208FJ	OEM
R5021210CJ	OEM
R5021210EJ	OEM
R5021210FJ	OEM
R5021408CJ	OEM
R5021408EJ	OEM
R5021408FJ	OEM
R5021410CJ	OEM
R5021410EJ	OEM
R5021410FJ	OEM
R5021608CJ	OEM
R5021608EJ	OEM
R5021608FJ	OEM
R5021610CJ	OEM
R5021610EJ	OEM
R5021610FJ	OEM
R5030108CJ	OEM
R5030108EJ	OEM
R5030108FJ	OEM
R5030110CJ	OEM
R5030110EJ	OEM
R5030110FJ	OEM
R5030208CJ	OEM
R5030208EJ	OEM
R5030208FJ	OEM
R5030210CJ	OEM
R5030210EJ	OEM
R5030210FJ	OEM
R5030308CJ	OEM
R5030308EJ	OEM
R5030308FJ	OEM
R5030310CJ	OEM
R5030310EJ	OEM
R5030310FJ	OEM
R5030408CJ	OEM
R5030408EJ	OEM
R5030408FJ	OEM
R5030410CJ	OEM
R5030410EJ	OEM
R5030410FJ	OEM
R5030508CJ	OEM
R5030508EJ	OEM
R5030508FJ	OEM
R5030510CJ	OEM
R5030510EJ	OEM
R5030510FJ	OEM
R5030608CJ	OEM
R5030608EJ	OEM
R5030608FJ	OEM
R5030610CJ	OEM
R5030610EJ	OEM
R5030610FJ	OEM
R5030708CJ	OEM
R5030708EJ	OEM
R5030708FJ	OEM
R5030710CJ	OEM
R5030710EJ	OEM
R5030710FJ	OEM
R5030808CJ	OEM
R5030808EJ	OEM
R5030808FJ	OEM
R5030810CJ	OEM
R5030810EJ	OEM
R5030810FJ	OEM
R5030908CJ	OEM
R5030908EJ	OEM
R5030908FJ	OEM
R5030910CJ	OEM
R5030910EJ	OEM
R5030910FJ	OEM
R5031008CJ	OEM
R5031008EJ	OEM
R5031008FJ	OEM
R5031010CJ	OEM
R5031010EJ	OEM
R5031010FJ	OEM
R5031108CJ	OEM
R5031108EJ	OEM
R5031108FJ	OEM
R5031110CJ	OEM
R5031110EJ	OEM
R5031110FJ	OEM
R5031208CJ	OEM
R5031208EJ	OEM
R5031208FJ	OEM
R5031210CJ	OEM
R5031210EJ	OEM
R5031210FJ	OEM
R5031408CJ	OEM
R5031408EJ	OEM
R5031408FJ	OEM
R5031410CJ	OEM
R5031410EJ	OEM
R5031410FJ	OEM
R5031608CJ	OEM
R5031608EJ	OEM
R5031608FJ	OEM
R5031610CJ	OEM
R5031610EJ	OEM
R5031610FJ	OEM
R5100110	0594
R5100110XXWA	0594

DEVICE TYPE	REPL CODE
R5100110XXWC	0594
R5100115	0594
R5100115XXWA	0594
R5100115XXWC	0594
R5100210	0594
R5100210XXWA	0594
R5100210XXWC	0594
R5100215	0594
R5100215WA	0594
R5100215XXWA	0594
R5100215XXWC	0594
R5100310	0594
R5100310XXWA	0594
R5100310XXWC	0594
R5100315	0594
R5100315XXWA	0594
R5100315XXWC	0594
R5100410	1975
R5100410XXWA	1975
R5100410XXWC	1975
R5100415	1975
R5100415XXWA	1975
R5100415XXWC	1975
R5100510	1975
R5100510XXWA	1975
R5100510XXWC	1975
R5100515	1975
R5100515XXWA	1975
R5100515XXWC	1975
R5100610	1975
R5100610XXWA	1975
R5100610XXWC	1975
R5100615	1975
R5100615XXWA	1975
R5100615XXWC	1975
R5100710	0652
R5100710XXWA	0652
R5100710XXWC	0652
R5100715	0652
R5100715XXWA	0652
R5100715XXWC	0652
R5100810	0652
R5100810XXWA	0652
R5100810XXWC	0652
R5100815	0652
R5100815XXWA	0652
R5100815XXWC	0652
R5100910	0652
R5100910XXWA	0652
R5100910XXWC	0652
R5100915	0652
R5100915XXWA	0652
R5100915XXWC	0652
R5101010	0652
R5101010XXWA	0652
R5101010XXWC	0652
R5101015	0652
R5101015XXWA	0652
R5101015XXWC	0652
R5110110	1337
R5110110XXWA	1337
R5110110XXWC	1337
R5110115	1337
R5110115XXWA	1337
R5110115XXWC	1337
R5110210	1337
R5110210XXWA	1337
R5110210XXWC	1337
R5110215	1337
R5110215XXWA	1337
R5110215XXWC	1337
R5110310	1337
R5110310XXWA	1337
R5110310XXWC	1337
R5110315	1337
R5110315XXWA	1337
R5110315XXWC	1337
R5110410	1894
R5110410XXWA	1894
R5110410XXWC	1894
R5110415	1894
R5110415XXWA	1894
R5110415XXWC	1894
R5110510	1894
R5110510XXWA	1894
R5110510XXWC	1894
R5110515	1894
R5110515XXWA	1894
R5110515XXWC	1894
R5110610	1894
R5110610XXWA	1894
R5110610XXWC	1894
R5110615	1894
R5110615XXWA	1894
R5110615XXWC	1894
R5110710	0193
R5110710XXWA	0193
R5110710XXWC	0193
R5110715	0193
R5110715XXWA	0193
R5110715XXWC	0193
R5110810	0193
R5110810XXWA	0193
R5110810XXWC	0193
R5110815	0193
R5110815XXWA	0193
R5110815XXWC	0193
R5110910	0193
R5110910XXWA	0193

DEVICE TYPE	REPL CODE
R5110910XXWC	0193
R5110915	0193
R5110915XXWA	0193
R5110915XXWC	0193
R5111010	0193
R5111010XXWA	0193
R5111015	0193
R5111015XXWA	0193
R5111015XXWC	0193
R6000124	1017
R6000124R	0496
R6000128	1017
R6000128R	0496
R6000224	1017
R6000224R	0496
R6000228	1017
R6000228R	0496
R6000324	1017
R6000324R	0496
R6000328	1017
R6000328R	0496
R6000424	1017
R6000424R	0496
R6000428	1017
R6000524	1030
R6000524R	1766
R6000528	1030
R6000528R	1766
R6000624	1030
R6000624R	1766
R6000628	1030
R6000628R	1766
R6000724	1040
R6000724R	1778
R6000728	1040
R6000728R	1778
R6000824	1040
R6000824R	1778
R6000828	1040
R6000828R	1778
R6000924	1040
R6000924R	1778
R6000928	1040
R6000928R	1778
R6001024	1040
R6001024R	1778
R6001028	1040
R6001028R	1778
R6001220	3872
R6001220YA	2805
R6001225	3872
R6001225YA	2805
R6001230	3872
R6001230YA	2805
R6001420	2805
R6001420YA	2805
R6001425	2805
R6001430YA	2805
R6001620	OEM
R6001625	OEM
R6001820	OEM
R6001825	OEM
R6002020	OEM
R6002025	OEM
R6002220	OEM
R6002420	OEM
R6002620	OEM
R6002820	OEM
R6002830YA	OEM
R6003020	OEM
R6003030YA	OEM
R6011220	3489
R6011225	3489
R6011230	3489
R6011420	3138
R6011425	3138
R6011620	OEM
R6011625	OEM
R6011820	OEM
R6011825	OEM
R6012020	OEM
R6012025	OEM
R6012220	OEM
R6012420	OEM
R6012620	OEM
R6012820	OEM
R6013020	OEM
R6020108CJ	OEM
R6020108EJ	OEM
R6020108FJ	OEM
R6020110CJ	OEM
R6020110EJ	OEM
R6020110FJ	OEM
R6020208CJ	OEM
R6020208EJ	OEM
R6020208FJ	OEM
R6020210CJ	OEM
R6020210EJ	OEM
R6020210FJ	OEM
R6020225CJ	OEM
R6020225EJ	OEM
R6020225FJ	OEM
R6020308CJ	OEM
R6020308EJ	OEM
R6020308FJ	OEM
R6020310CJ	OEM
R6020310EJ	OEM
R6020310FJ	OEM
R6020408CJ	OEM

DEVICE TYPE	REPL CODE
R6020408EJ	OEM
R6020408FJ	OEM
R6020410CJ	OEM
R6020410EJ	OEM
R6020410FJ	OEM
R6020425CJ	OEM
R6020425EJ	OEM
R6020425FJ	OEM
R6020508CJ	OEM
R6020508EJ	OEM
R6020508FJ	OEM
R6020510CJ	OEM
R6020510EJ	OEM
R6020510FJ	OEM
R6020608CJ	OEM
R6020608EJ	OEM
R6020608FJ	OEM
R6020610CJ	OEM
R6020610EJ	OEM
R6020610FJ	OEM
R6020625CJ	OEM
R6020625EJ	OEM
R6020625FJ	OEM
R6020708CJ	OEM
R6020708EJ	OEM
R6020708FJ	OEM
R6020710CJ	OEM
R6020710EJ	OEM
R6020710FJ	OEM
R6020808CJ	OEM
R6020808EJ	OEM
R6020808FJ	OEM
R6020810CJ	OEM
R6020810EJ	OEM
R6020810FJ	OEM
R6020825CJ	OEM
R6020825EJ	OEM
R6020825FJ	OEM
R6020908CJ	OEM
R6020908EJ	OEM
R6020908FJ	OEM
R6020910CJ	OEM
R6020910EJ	OEM
R6020910FJ	OEM
R6021008CJ	OEM
R6021008EJ	OEM
R6021008FJ	OEM
R6021010CJ	OEM
R6021010EJ	OEM
R6021010FJ	OEM
R6021025CJ	OEM
R6021025EJ	OEM
R6021025FJ	OEM
R6021108CJ	OEM
R6021108EJ	OEM
R6021108FJ	OEM
R6021110CJ	OEM
R6021110EJ	OEM
R6021110FJ	OEM
R6021208CJ	OEM
R6021208EJ	OEM
R6021208FJ	OEM
R6021210CJ	OEM
R6021210EJ	OEM
R6021210FJ	OEM
R6021225CJ	OEM
R6021225EJ	OEM
R6021225FJ	OEM
R6021408CJ	OEM
R6021408EJ	OEM
R6021408FJ	OEM
R6021410CJ	OEM
R6021410EJ	OEM
R6021410FJ	OEM
R6021420FJYA	OEM
R6021425FJYA	OEM
R6021608CJ	OEM
R6021608EJ	OEM
R6021608FJ	OEM
R6021610CJ	OEM
R6021610EJ	OEM
R6021610FJ	OEM
R6021620FJYA	OEM
R6021625FJYA	OEM
R6030108CJ	OEM
R6030108EJ	OEM
R6030108FJ	OEM
R6030110CJ	OEM
R6030110EJ	OEM
R6030110FJ	OEM
R6030208CJ	OEM
R6030208EJ	OEM
R6030208FJ	OEM
R6030210CJ	OEM
R6030210EJ	OEM
R6030210FJ	OEM
R6030308CJ	OEM
R6030308EJ	OEM
R6030308FJ	OEM
R6030310CJ	OEM
R6030310EJ	OEM
R6030310FJ	OEM
R6030408CJ	OEM
R6030408EJ	OEM
R6030408FJ	OEM
R6030410CJ	OEM
R6030410EJ	OEM
R6030410FJ	OEM
R6030508CJ	OEM

DEVICE TYPE	REPL CODE
R6030508EJ	OEM
R6030508FJ	OEM
R6030510CJ	OEM
R6030510EJ	OEM
R6030510FJ	OEM
R6030608CJ	OEM
R6030608EJ	OEM
R6030608FJ	OEM
R6030610CJ	OEM
R6030610EJ	OEM
R6030610FJ	OEM
R6030708CJ	OEM
R6030708EJ	OEM
R6030708FJ	OEM
R6030710CJ	OEM
R6030710EJ	OEM
R6030710FJ	OEM
R6030808CJ	OEM
R6030808EJ	OEM
R6030808FJ	OEM
R6030810CJ	OEM
R6030810EJ	OEM
R6030810FJ	OEM
R6030908CJ	OEM
R6030908EJ	OEM
R6030908FJ	OEM
R6030910CJ	OEM
R6030910EJ	OEM
R6030910FJ	OEM
R6031008CJ	OEM
R6031008EJ	OEM
R6031008FJ	OEM
R6031010CJ	OEM
R6031010EJ	OEM
R6031010FJ	OEM
R6031108CJ	OEM
R6031108EJ	OEM
R6031108FJ	OEM
R6031110CJ	OEM
R6031110EJ	OEM
R6031110FJ	OEM
R6031208CJ	OEM
R6031208EJ	OEM
R6031208FJ	OEM
R6031210CJ	OEM
R6031210EJ	OEM
R6031210FJ	OEM
R6031408CJ	OEM
R6031408EJ	OEM
R6031408FJ	OEM
R6031410CJ	OEM
R6031410EJ	OEM
R6031410FJ	OEM
R6031608CJ	OEM
R6031608EJ	OEM
R6031608FJ	OEM
R6031610CJ	OEM
R6031610EJ	OEM
R6031610FJ	OEM
R6100120	1017
R6100120XXYA	1017
R6100120YA	1017
R6100125	1017
R6100125XXYA	1017
R6100125YA	1017
R6100130	1017
R6100130XXYA	1017
R6100130YA	1017
R6100220	1017
R6100220XXYA	1017
R6100220YA	1017
R6100225	1017
R6100225XXYA	1017
R6100225YA	1017
R6100230	1017
R6100230XXYA	1017
R6100230YA	1017
R6100320	1017
R6100325	1017
R6100330	1017
R6100420	1017
R6100420XXYA	1030
R6100420YA	1017
R6100425	1030
R6100425XXYA	1030
R6100425YA	1017
R6100430	1017
R6100430XXYA	1030
R6100430YA	1017
R6100520	1030
R6100525	1030
R6100530	1030
R6100620	1030
R6100620XXYA	1030
R6100620YA	1030
R6100625	1030
R6100625XXYA	1030
R6100625YA	1030
R6100630	1030
R6100630XXYA	1030
R6100630YA	1030
R6100720	1040
R6100725	1040
R6100730	1040
R6100820	1040
R6100820XXYA	1040
R6100820YA	1040
R6100825	1040
R6100825XXYA	1040

DEVICE TYPE	REPL CODE
R6100825YA	1040
R6100830	1040
R6100830XXYA	1040
R6100830YA	1040
R6100920	1040
R6100925	1040
R6100930	1040
R6101020	1040
R6101020XXYA	1040
R6101020YA	1040
R6101025	1040
R6101025XXYA	1040
R6101025YA	1040
R6101030	1040
R6101030XXYA	1040
R6101030YA	1040
R6110120	0496
R6110120XXYA	0496
R6110125	0496
R6110125XXYA	0496
R6110130	0496
R6110130XXYA	0496
R6110220	0496
R6110220XXYA	0496
R6110225	0496
R6110225XXYA	0496
R6110230	0496
R6110230XXYA	0496
R6110320	0496
R6110325	0496
R6110330	0496
R6110420	1766
R6110420XXYA	1766
R6110425	0496
R6110425XXYA	1766
R6110430	0496
R6110430XXYA	1766
R6110520	1766
R6110525	1766
R6110530	1766
R6110620	1766
R6110620XXYA	1766
R6110625	1766
R6110625XXYA	1766
R6110630	1766
R6110630XXYA	1766
R6110720	1778
R6110725	1778
R6110730	1778
R6110820	1778
R6110820XXYA	1778
R6110825	1778
R6110825XXYA	1778
R6110830	1778
R6110830XXYA	1778
R6110920	1778
R6110925	1778
R6110930	1778
R6111020	1778
R6111020XXYA	1778
R6111025	1778
R6111025XXYA	1778
R6111030	1778
R6111030XXYA	1778
R6200130	1217
R6200140	1217
R6200150	1217
R6200230	1217
R6200240	1217
R6200250	1217
R6200330	1217
R6200340	1217
R6200350	1217
R6200430	1217
R6200440	1217
R6200450	1217
R6200530	1217
R6200540	1217
R6200550	1217
R6200630	1217
R6200640	1217
R6200650	1217
R6200830	1195
R6200840	1195
R6200850	1195
R6201030	1195
R6201040	1195
R6201050	1195
R6201230	1195
R6201240	1195
R6201250	1195
R6201430	OEM
R6201440	OEM
R6201630	OEM
R6201640	OEM
R6201830	OEM
R6201840	OEM
R6202030	OEM
R6202040	OEM
R6202230	OEM
R6202430	OEM
R6202630	OEM
R6202830	OEM
R6203030	OEM
R6220135CJ	OEM
R6220135EJ	OEM
R6220135FJ	OEM
R6220140CJ	OEM
R6220140EJ	OEM

If replacement code is OEM, contact original manufacturer for replacement.

DEVICE TYPE	REPL CODE
R6220140FJ	OEM
R6220235CJ	OEM
R6220235EJ	OEM
R6220235FJ	OEM
R6220240CJ	OEM
R6220240EJ	OEM
R6220240FJ	OEM
R6220335CJ	OEM
R6220335EJ	OEM
R6220335FJ	OEM
R6220340CJ	OEM
R6220340EJ	OEM
R6220340FJ	OEM
R6220435CJ	OEM
R6220435EJ	OEM
R6220435FJ	OEM
R6220440CJ	OEM
R6220440EJ	OEM
R6220440FJ	OEM
R6220535CJ	OEM
R6220535EJ	OEM
R6220535FJ	OEM
R6220540CJ	OEM
R6220540EJ	OEM
R6220540FJ	OEM
R6220635CJ	OEM
R6220635EJ	OEM
R6220635FJ	OEM
R6220640CJ	OEM
R6220640EJ	OEM
R6220640FJ	OEM
R6220735CJ	OEM
R6220735EJ	OEM
R6220735FJ	OEM
R6220740CJ	OEM
R6220740EJ	OEM
R6220740FJ	OEM
R6220835CJ	OEM
R6220835EJ	OEM
R6220835FJ	OEM
R6220840CJ	OEM
R6220840EJ	OEM
R6220840FJ	OEM
R6220935CJ	OEM
R6220935EJ	OEM
R6220935FJ	OEM
R6220940CJ	OEM
R6220940EJ	OEM
R6220940FJ	OEM
R6221035CJ	OEM
R6221035EJ	OEM
R6221035FJ	OEM
R6221040CJ	OEM
R6221040EJ	OEM
R6221040FJ	OEM
R6221135CJ	OEM
R6221135EJ	OEM
R6221135FJ	OEM
R6221140CJ	OEM
R6221140EJ	OEM
R6221140FJ	OEM
R6221235CJ	OEM
R6221235EJ	OEM
R6221235FJ	OEM
R6221240CJ	OEM
R6221240EJ	OEM
R6221240FJ	OEM
R6221435CJ	OEM
R6221435EJ	OEM
R6221435FJ00	OEM
R6221440CJ	OEM
R6221440EJ	OEM
R6221440FJ00	OEM
R6221635CJ	OEM
R6221635EJ	OEM
R6221635FJ00	OEM
R6221640CJ	OEM
R6221640EJ	OEM
R6221640FJ00	OEM
R7000103	4222
R7000103UA	4957
R7000104	4222
R7000104UA	4957
R7000105	4957
R7000203	4222
R7000203UA	4957
R7000204	4222
R7000204UA	4957
R7000205	4957
R7000205UA	4957
R7000303	4222
R7000304	4222
R7000305	4957
R7000403	4222
R7000403UA	4957
R7000404	4222
R7000404UA	4957
R7000405	4957
R7000405UA	4957
R7000503	4222
R7000503UA	OEM
R7000504	4222
R7000504UA	OEM
R7000505	4957
R7000505UA	OEM
R7000603	4222
R7000603UA	4957
R7000604	4222
R7000604UA	4957
R7000605	4957
R7000605UA	4957
R7000703	4222
R7000704	4222
R7000705	0744
R7000803	4222
R7000804	4222
R7000805	0744
R7000903	4222
R7000904	4222
R7000905	0744
R7001003	4222
R7001003UA	0744
R7001004	4222
R7001004UA	0744
R7001005	0744
R7001005UA	0744
R7001203	4222
R7001203UA	0744
R7001204	4222
R7001204UA	0744
R7001205	0744
R7001205UA	0744
R7001403	4222
R7001403UA	4222
R7001404	4222
R7001404UA	4222
R7001603	4222
R7001603UA	4222
R7001604	4222
R7001604UA	4222
R7001803	OEM
R7001804	OEM
R7002003	OEM
R7002004	OEM
R7002203	OEM
R7002403	OEM
R7002603	OEM
R7002803	OEM
R7003003	OEM
R7003203	OEM
R7003403	OEM
R7003603	OEM
R7003803	OEM
R7004003	OEM
R7010103	4221
R7010104	4221
R7010105	2299
R7010203	4221
R7010204	4221
R7010205	2299
R7010303	4221
R7010304	4221
R7010305	2299
R7010403	4221
R7010404	4221
R7010405	2299
R7010503	4221
R7010504	4221
R7010505	2299
R7010603	4221
R7010604	4221
R7010605	2299
R7010703	4221
R7010704	4221
R7010705	2765
R7010803	4221
R7010804	4221
R7010805	2765
R7010903	4221
R7010904	4221
R7010905	2765
R7011003	4221
R7011004	4221
R7011005	2765
R7011203	4221
R7011204	4221
R7011205	2765
R7011403	4221
R7011404	4221
R7011603	4221
R7011604	4221
R7011803	OEM
R7011804	OEM
R7012003	OEM
R7012004	OEM
R7012203	OEM
R7012403	OEM
R7012603	OEM
R7012803	OEM
R7013003	OEM
R7013203	OEM
R7013403	OEM
R7013603	OEM
R7013803	OEM
R7014003	OEM
R7200105	OEM
R7200106	2146
R7200108	OEM
R7200109	2146
R7200110	OEM
R7200112	2146
R7200205	OEM
R7200206	2146
R7200208	OEM
R7200209	2146
R7200210	OEM
R7200212	2146
R7200305	OEM
R7200306	2146
R7200308	OEM
R7200309	2146
R7200310	OEM
R7200312	2146
R7200405	OEM
R7200406	2146
R7200408	OEM
R7200409	2146
R7200410	OEM
R7200412	2146
R7200505	OEM
R7200506	2146
R7200508	OEM
R7200509	2146
R7200510	OEM
R7200512	2146
R7200605	OEM
R7200606	2146
R7200608	OEM
R7200609	2146
R7200610	OEM
R7200612	2146
R7200705	OEM
R7200708	OEM
R7200710	OEM
R7200805	OEM
R7200806	0474
R7200808	OEM
R7200809	0474
R7200810	OEM
R7200812	0474
R7200905	OEM
R7200908	OEM
R7200910	OEM
R7201005	OEM
R7201006	0474
R7201008	OEM
R7201009	0474
R7201010	OEM
R7201012	0474
R7201205	OEM
R7201206	0474
R7201208	OEM
R7201209	0474
R7201210	OEM
R7201212	0474
R7201405	OEM
R7201406	OEM
R7201408	OEM
R7201409	OEM
R7201605	OEM
R7201606	OEM
R7201608	OEM
R7201609	OEM
R7201805	OEM
R7201806	OEM
R7201808	OEM
R7201809	OEM
R7202005	OEM
R7202006	OEM
R7202008	OEM
R7202009	OEM
R7202205	OEM
R7202206	OEM
R7202405	OEM
R7202406	OEM
R7202605	OEM
R7202606	OEM
R7202805	OEM
R7202806	OEM
R7203005	OEM
R7203006	OEM
R7203015	OEM
R7203205	OEM
R7203405	OEM
R7203605	OEM
R7203805	OEM
R7204005	OEM
R7220105AJ	OEM
R7220105CJ	OEM
R7220105EJ	OEM
R7220106CJ	OEM
R7220106EJ	OEM
R7220108CJ	OEM
R7220108EJ	OEM
R7220205AJ	OEM
R7220205CJ	OEM
R7220205EJ	OEM
R7220206CJ	OEM
R7220206EJ	OEM
R7220208CJ	OEM
R7220208EJ	OEM
R7220305AJ	OEM
R7220305CJ	OEM
R7220305EJ	OEM
R7220306CJ	OEM
R7220306EJ	OEM
R7220308CJ	OEM
R7220308EJ	OEM
R7220405AJ	OEM
R7220405CJ	OEM
R7220405EJ	OEM
R7220406CJ	OEM
R7220406EJ	OEM
R7220408CJ	OEM
R7220408EJ	OEM
R7220505AJ	OEM
R7220505CJ	OEM
R7220505EJ	OEM
R7220506CJ	OEM
R7220506EJ	OEM
R7220508CJ	OEM
R7220508EJ	OEM
R7220605AJ	OEM
R7220605CJ	OEM
R7220605EJ	OEM
R7220606CJ	OEM
R7220606EJ	OEM
R7220608CJ	OEM
R7220608EJ	OEM
R7220705AJ	OEM
R7220705CJ	OEM
R7220705EJ	OEM
R7220706CJ	OEM
R7220706EJ	OEM
R7220708CJ	OEM
R7220708EJ	OEM
R7220805AJ	OEM
R7220805CJ	OEM
R7220805EJ	OEM
R7220806CJ	OEM
R7220806EJ	OEM
R7220808CJ	OEM
R7220808EJ	OEM
R7220905AJ	OEM
R7220905CJ	OEM
R7220905EJ	OEM
R7220906CJ	OEM
R7220906EJ	OEM
R7220908CJ	OEM
R7220908EJ	OEM
R7221005AJ	OEM
R7221005CJ	OEM
R7221005EJ	OEM
R7221006CJ	OEM
R7221006EJ	OEM
R7221008CJ	OEM
R7221008EJ	OEM
R7221105AJ	OEM
R7221105CJ	OEM
R7221105EJ	OEM
R7221106CJ	OEM
R7221106EJ	OEM
R7221108CJ	OEM
R7221108EJ	OEM
R7221205AJ	OEM
R7221205CJ	OEM
R7221205EJ	OEM
R7221206CJ	OEM
R7221206EJ	OEM
R7221208CJ	OEM
R7221208EJ	OEM
R7221305EJ	OEM
R7221306EJ	OEM
R7221308EJ	OEM
R7221405AJ	OEM
R7221405CJ	OEM
R7221405EJ	OEM
R7221406CJ	OEM
R7221406EJ	OEM
R7221408CJ	OEM
R7221408EJ	OEM
R7221505EJ	OEM
R7221506EJ	OEM
R7221508EJ	OEM
R7221605AJ	OEM
R7221605CJ	OEM
R7221605EJ	OEM
R7221606CJ	OEM
R7221606EJ	OEM
R7221608CJ	OEM
R7221608EJ	OEM
R7221705CJ	OEM
R7221705EJ	OEM
R7221706AJ	OEM
R7221706CJ	OEM
R7221706EJ	OEM
R7221708AJ	OEM
R7221708CJ	OEM
R7221708EJ	OEM
R7221805AJ	OEM
R7221805CJ	OEM
R7221805EJ	OEM
R7221806AJ	OEM
R7221806CJ	OEM
R7221806EJ	OEM
R7221808AJ	OEM
R7221808CJ	OEM
R7221808EJ	OEM
R7221905CJ	OEM
R7221905EJ	OEM
R7221906AJ	OEM
R7221906CJ	OEM
R7221906EJ	OEM
R7221908AJ	OEM
R7221908CJ	OEM
R7221908EJ	OEM
R7222005AJ	OEM
R7222005CJ	OEM
R7222005EJ	OEM
R7222006AJ	OEM
R7222006CJ	OEM
R7222006EJ	OEM
R7222008AJ	OEM
R7222008CJ	OEM
R7222008EJ	OEM
R7222105CJ	OEM
R7222105EJ	OEM
R7222106AJ	OEM
R7222106CJ	OEM
R7222106EJ	OEM
R7222108AJ	OEM
R7222108CJ	OEM
R7222108EJ	OEM
R7222205AJ	OEM
R7222205CJ	OEM
R7222205EJ	OEM
R7222206AJ	OEM
R7222206CJ	OEM
R7222206EJ	OEM
R7222208AJ	OEM
R7222208CJ	OEM
R7222208EJ	OEM
R7222305CJ	OEM
R7222305EJ	OEM
R7222306AJ	OEM
R7222306CJ	OEM
R7222306EJ	OEM
R7222308AJ	OEM
R7222308CJ	OEM
R7222308EJ	OEM
R7222405AJ	OEM
R7222405CJ	OEM
R7222405EJ	OEM
R7222406AJ	OEM
R7222406CJ	OEM
R7222406EJ	OEM
R7222408AJ	OEM
R7222408CJ	OEM
R7222408EJ	OEM
R7222505AJ	OEM
R7222505CJ	OEM
R7222505EJ	OEM
R7222506AJ	OEM
R7222506CJ	OEM
R7222506EJ	OEM
R7222508AJ	OEM
R7222508CJ	OEM
R7222508EJ	OEM
R9200116	OEM
R9200120	OEM
R9200216	OEM
R9200220	OEM
R9200316	OEM
R9200320	OEM
R9200416	OEM
R9200420	OEM
R9200516	OEM
R9200520	OEM
R9200616	OEM
R9200620	OEM
R9200816	OEM
R9200820	OEM
R9201016	OEM
R9201020	OEM
R9201216	OEM
R9201220	OEM
R9201416	OEM
R9201420	OEM
R9201616	OEM
R9201620	OEM
R9201816	OEM
R9201820	OEM
R9202016	OEM
R9202020	OEM
R40501060	1807
R40501070	1807
R620013000	1217
R620014000	1217
R620015000	1217
R620023000	1217
R620024000	1217
R620025000	1217
R620043000	1217
R620044000	1217
R620045000	1217
R620063000	1217
R620064000	1217
R620065000	1217
R620083000	1195
R620085000	1195
R620103000	1195
R620104000	1195
R620105000	1195
R620124000	1195
R620125000	1195
R620145000	OEM
R620165000	OEM
R620185000	OEM
R620205000	OEM
R620224000	OEM
R620225000	OEM
R620244000	OEM
R620245000	OEM
R620264000	OEM
R620265000	OEM
R620284000	OEM
R620285000	OEM
R620304000	OEM
R620305000	OEM
R720010600	2146
R720010900	2146
R720011200	2146
R720020600	2146
R720021200	2146
R720040600	2146
R720040900	2146
R720041200	2146
R720060600	2146
R720060900	2146
R720061200	2146
R720080600	0474
R720080900	0474
R720081200	0474
R720100600	0474
R720100900	0474
R720101200	0474
R720120900	0474
R720121200	0474
R720141200	OEM
R720161200	OEM
R720181200	OEM
R720201200	OEM
R720220900	OEM
R720221200	OEM
R720240900	OEM
R720241200	OEM
R720260900	OEM
R720261200	OEM
R720280900	OEM
R720281200	OEM
R720300900	OEM
R720301200	OEM
R920211200	OEM
R920211600	OEM
R920221600	OEM
R920222000	OEM
R920231600	OEM
R920232000	OEM
R920241600	OEM
R920242000	OEM
R920251600	OEM
R920252000	OEM
R920261600	OEM
R920262000	OEM
R920271600	OEM
R920281600	OEM
R920282000	OEM
R920291600	OEM
R920292000	OEM
R920301600	OEM
R920302000	OEM
RA-1	0015
RA1	0102
RA-1A	0015
RA1A	0133
RA-1B	0072
RA1B	0015
RA-1C	0071
RA1C	0071
RA-1D	0102
RA-1E	0102
RA-1F	0344
RA-1Y	0080
RA-1Z	0023
RA1Z	0023
RA-1ZC	0015
RA1ZC	0015
RA-2	0071
RA2	0497
RA2A	0071
RA2B	OEM
RA-2C	0071
RA2C	0071
RA3	OEM
RA-3-9600	OEM
RA-3-9600A	OEM
RA3A	OEM
RA3B	OEM
RA4	OEM
RA5E	0705
RA21	0497
RA25	0497
RA-26	1823
RA26	0497
RA26(50V)	0526
RA102AA	0015
RA102BA	0015
RA102CA	0015
RA102DA	0015
RA102EA	0015
RA102FA	0015
RA102GA	0015
RA102HA	0015
RA102KA	0015
RA102MA	0015
RA102PA	0071
RA102RA	0071
RA102TA	0071
RA102VA	0071
RA132AA	0071
RA132BA	0071
RA132CA	0071
RA132DA	0071
RA132EA	0071
RA132FA	0071
RA132GA	0071
RA132HA	0071
RA132JA	OEM
RA132KA	0071
RA132MA	0071
RA132PA	0071
RA132RA	0071
RA132TA	0071
RA132VA	0071
RA162AA	0071
RA162BA	0071
RA162CA	0071
RA162DA	0071
RA162EA	0071
RA162FA	0071
RA162GA	0071
RA162HA	0071
RA162KA	0071
RA162MA	0071
RA162PA	0071
RA162RA	0071
RA162TA	0071
RA162VA	0071
RA251	OEM
RA252	OEM
RA254	OEM
RA256	OEM
RA258	OEM
RA751AA	0015
RA751BA	0015
RA751CA	0015
RA751DA	0015
RA751EA	0015
RA751FA	0015
RA751GA	0015
RA751HA	0015
RA751KA	0015
RA751MA	0015
RA751PA	0071
RA751RA	0071
RA751TA	0071
RA751VA	0071
RA2505	OEM
RA2510	OEM
RA4153DC	OEM
RA39600	OEM
RA-Z	0102
RB7-M331	OEM
RB7M-17	OEM
RB7M-37	OEM
RB40	0468
RB-40C	0468
RB40C	0468
RB40N	0468
RB60	OEM
RB-150	0106
RB150	0106
RB150Z	OEM
RB-151	0106
RB151	0106
RB151Z	OEM
RB-152	0106
RB152	0106
RB-152LF-F	OEM
RB152LF-F	OEM
RB152Z	OEM
RB153	0106
RB-154	0196
RB154	0106
RB154Z	OEM
RB155	1999
RB-156	2384
RB156	2384
RB-156-LFB	2384
RB156LB	2384
RB-156LFB	2384
RB156LFB	1999
RB156Z	OEM
RB157	0782
RB158	OEM
RB158Z	OEM
RB401	0319
RB402	1404
RB-402U	1404
RB404	0468
RB-404N	0468
RB406	0441
RB-406N	0441
RB406N	0441
RB406NH	0468
RB-601	0319
RB601	OEM
RB-602	1404
RB602	5588
RB602-A	1404
RB602A	OEM
RB-602U	1404
RB-604	0468
RB-606	0441
RBA-401	OEM
RBA402	OEM
RBA406B	OEM
RBS520T	OEM
RBS530T	OEM
RBS535T	OEM
RBS540T	OEM
RBS545T	OEM
RBS820T	OEM
RBS830T	OEM
RBS835T	OEM
RBS840T	OEM
RBS845T	OEM
RBS850T	OEM
RBS860T	OEM
RBS1020T	OEM
RBS1030T	OEM
RBS1035T	OEM
RBS1040T	OEM

If replacement code is OEM, contact original manufacturer for replacement.

DEVICE TYPE	REPL CODE
RBS1045T	OEM
RBV-40C	0737
RBV-401	0724
RBV-402	2078
RBV402	OEM
RBV-402L	OEM
RBV402L	OEM
RBV-406	1039
RBV406	1039
RBV-406H	1039
RBV406H	5364
RBV-406H-01	1039
RBV-406M	1039
RBV406M	1039
RBV406M-LAF	1763
RBV-406M-LFA	1039
RBV-406MLFA	1763
RBV406M-LFA	1039
RBV-408	0737
RBV-602	1034
RBV602	OEM
RBV602-01	OEM
RBV-604	1763
RBV-606	1039
RBV606	1039
RBV606LF-A	OEM
RBV-608	OEM
RC	OEM
RC080	0071
RC-2	0344
RC2	0344
RC-2V	0344
RC2V	0344
RC78L05A	1288
RC78L09A	OEM
RC78L12A	1817
RC78M05A	OEM
RC78M05E	OEM
RC78M05FA	0619
RC78M09A	OEM
RC78M09FA	OEM
RC78M93FD	OEM
RC185-6	3494
RC201	OEM
RC202	OEM
RC203	OEM
RC204	OEM
RC205	OEM
RC206	OEM
RC207	OEM
RC529	OEM
RC529A	OEM
RC529B	OEM
RC529C	OEM
RC555	0967
RC555DE	0967
RC555NB	0967
RC555T	6612
RC556DB	3254
RC556DC	3254
RC709D	1695
RC709DC	1695
RC709T	1291
RC710DC	1789
RC710T	1786
RC714CDE	2231
RC714CH	0890
RC714EDE	2231
RC714EH	0890
RC714LDE	2231
RC714LH	0890
RC723D	0026
RC723T	1183
RC741D	1971
RC741DC	1971
RC741DE	0308
RC741DN	0308
RC741H	0406
RC741N	0308
RC741NB	0308
RC741T	0406
RC747DB	2342
RC747DC	2342
RC747T	2352
RC1458DE	0356
RC1458DN	0356
RC1458H	3108
RC1458NB	0356
RC1458T	3108
RC1700	0103
RC2041M	0356
RC2041NB	OEM
RC2043M	OEM
RC2043NB	0356
RC2403M	OEM
RC2403NB	0624
RC3078DE	OEM
RC3078NB	OEM
RC3078T	OEM
RC3302DB	0176
RC3403ADB	OEM
RC3403ADC	OEM
RC3414M	OEM
RC4136	2995
RC4136DB	2995
RC4136DC	2995
RC4151DE	OEM
RC4151NB	OEM
RC4151T	OEM
RC4152DE	OEM
RC4152NB	OEM
RC4152T	OEM
RC4153ADC	OEM
RC4153DC	OEM
RC4156DB	2796
RC4156DC	2796
RC4191DE	OEM
RC4191NB	OEM
RC4192DE	OEM
RC4192NB	OEM
RC4193DE	OEM
RC4193NB	OEM
RC4194DB	OEM
RC4194DC	OEM
RC4194TK	OEM
RC4195NB	5723
RC4195T	OEM
RC4195TK	OEM
RC4200ADE	OEM
RC4200ANB	OEM
RC4200DE	OEM
RC4200NB	OEM
RC4260DB	OEM
RC4260DC	OEM
RC4391DE	OEM
RC4391NB	OEM
RC4444PU	OEM
RC4444R	OEM
RC4556M	OEM
RC4556NB	OEM
RC4558	0356
RC4558DE	0356
RC4558DQ	0356
RC4558JG	0356
RC4558M	OEM
RC4558NB	0356
RC4558P	0356
RC4558PS	OEM
RC4558T	3108
RC4559DE	0356
RC4559M	OEM
RC4559N	OEM
RC4559NB	0356
RC4559T	3108
RC4560M	OEM
RC4560NB	OEM
RC4562M	OEM
RC4562NB	OEM
RC4739DB	0687
RC4739DP	0687
RC4805DE	OEM
RC4805EDE	OEM
RC4805ET	OEM
RC4805T	OEM
RC5258	OEM
RC5532ADE	OEM
RC5532ANB	OEM
RC5532AT	OEM
RC5532DE	OEM
RC5532NB	OEM
RC5532T	OEM
RC5534ADE	OEM
RC5534ANB	OEM
RC5534AT	OEM
RC5534DE	OEM
RC5534NB	OEM
RC5534T	OEM
RC7809FA	OEM
RC7812FA	0330
RCA1A01	0086
RCA1A02	0126
RCA1A03	3296
RCA1A04	4507
RCA1A05	0126
RCA1A06	0086
RCA1A07	0086
RCA1A08	0126
RCA1A09	0187
RCA1A10	0434
RCA1A11	0187
RCA1A15	0187
RCA1A16	0434
RCA1A17	0086
RCA1A18	0086
RCA1A19	0126
RCA1B01	0538
RCA1B04	0359
RCA1B05	0359
RCA1B06	0177
RCA1B07	3339
RCA1B08	3340
RCA1B09	0359
RCA1C03	0236
RCA1C04	0676
RCA1C05	0419
RCA1C06	0848
RCA1C07	0419
RCA1C08	1190
RCA1C09	0419
RCA1C10	0419
RCA1C11	0848
RCA1C12	0236
RCA1C13	0676
RCA1C14	0419
RCA1C15	2220
RCA1C16	2222
RCA1E02	0178
RCA1E03	0787
RCA29	0042
RCA29A	0042
RCA29ASDH	0419
RCA29B	0236
RCA29BSDH	0236
RCA29C	0236
RCA29CSDH	0236
RCA29SDH	0419
RCA30	0919
RCA30A	0919
RCA30B	0676
RCA30C	0676
RCA31	0419
RCA31A	0419
RCA31ASDH	0419
RCA31B	0419
RCA31BSDH	0419
RCA31C	0419
RCA31CSDH	0419
RCA31SDH	0419
RCA32	0848
RCA32A	0848
RCA32C	1190
RCA41	0556
RCA41A	0419
RCA41B	0419
RCA41C	0419
RCA41DSH	0556
RCA41SDH	5630
RCA42	1190
RCA42A	1190
RCA42B	1190
RCA42C	1190
RCA105	1298
RCA120	1203
RCA121	1203
RCA125	0597
RCA126	0597
RCA205	1298
RCA370	1298
RCA371	1298
RCA410	0103
RCA411	0270
RCA413	0074
RCA423	0074
RCA431	0074
RCA508	4704
RCA520	0060
RCA521	0060
RCA900	2262
RCA901	2262
RCA-1000	3339
RCA1000	2411
RCA-1001	3339
RCA1001	2411
RCA3054	0419
RCA3055	0419
RCA3517	0004
RCA3773	6294
RCA3858	0004
RCA6263	3084
RCA6340	6565
RCA6341	6565
RCA8203	0597
RCA8203A	2222
RCA8203B	2222
RCA8350	3340
RCA8350A	3340
RCA8350B	3340
RCA8638C	3656
RCA8638D	3656
RCA8638E	3656
RCA8766	5321
RCA8766A	5321
RCA8766B	5321
RCA8766C	5321
RCA8766D	5321
RCA8766E	5321
RCA9116C	4081
RCA9116D	4081
RCA9116E	4081
RCA9213A	1456
RCA9213B	1456
RCA9213C	OEM
RCA34098	0136
RCA34099	0136
RCA34100	0136
RCA34101	0004
RCA34106	0004
RCA35953	0004
RCA35954	0004
RCA40231	0208
RCA40245	0007
RCA40246	0007
RCA40250	0178
RCA40395	0004
RCA40396N	0208
RCA40396P	0004
RCA44098	0136
RCA45190	0556
RCA45191	0556
RCA45192	0556
RCA45193	1190
RCA45194	1190
RCA45195	1190
RCA1466860-2	1188
RCC7022	0469
RCL10580	OEM
RCP111A	0283
RCP111B	0283
RCP111C	0283
RCP111D	0283
RCP113A	0283
RCP113B	0283
RCP113C	0283
RCP113D	0283
RCP115	0283
RCP115B	0283
RCP117	0283
RCP117B	0283
RCP700A	3294
RCP700B	3294
RCP700C	0164
RCP700D	0164
RCP701A	0818
RCP701B	0818
RCP701C	0818
RCP701D	0818
RCP702A	0164
RCP702B	3294
RCP702C	3294
RCP702D	3294
RCP703A	0818
RCP703B	0818
RCP703C	0818
RCP703D	0818
RCP704	3294
RCP704B	3294
RCP705	0818
RCP705B	0818
RCP706	3294
RCP706B	3294
RCP707	0818
RCP707B	0818
RCR43U05JM	OEM
RCR70AX12	OEM
RCR70AX16	OEM
RCR70AX20	OEM
RCR70AY4	OEM
RCR70AY6	OEM
RCR70AY8	OEM
RCR70AY10	OEM
RCR70AY12	OEM
RCR150AX12	OEM
RCR150AX16	OEM
RCR150AX20	OEM
RCR150AX24	OEM
RCR150AY4	OEM
RCR150AY6	OEM
RCR150AY10	OEM
RCR150AY12	OEM
RCR300AX12	OEM
RCR300AX16	OEM
RCR300AX20	OEM
RCR300AX24	OEM
RCR300AY4	OEM
RCR300AY6	OEM
RCR300AY8	OEM
RCR300AY10	OEM
RCR300AY12	OEM
RCS29	0928
RCS29A	0178
RCS29B	0178
RCS29C	0178
RCS30	0899
RCS30A	0899
RCS30B	0899
RCS30C	1190
RCS31	0178
RCS31A	0178
RCS31B	0178
RCS31C	0178
RCS32	1190
RCS32A	1190
RCS32B	1190
RCS32C	1190
RCS242	0103
RCS258	0130
RCS559	0787
RCS560	0787
RCS564	0074
RCS579	0637
RCS617	OEM
RCS618	1671
RCS880	0434
RCS881	0434
RCS882	0723
RCV2	0102
RD,11EBTA21R	0181
RD027	0436
RD082	0244
RD10E-N1	0064
RD2R4E	2847
RD2R4ESB1	OEM
RD2R7EB1	0755
RD2R7EB2	0755
RD2.0E	OEM
RD2.0EB	OEM
RD2.0EC	OEM
RD2.0EK	OEM
RD2.0ES	OEM
RD2.0ES-B1	OEM
RD2.0ESB1	OEM
RD2.0F	OEM
RD2.0FB	OEM
RD2.0FC	OEM
RD2.0M	OEM
RD2.0P	OEM
RD-2.2E	0244
RD2.2E	OEM
RD2.2EB	OEM
RD2.2EC	OEM
RD2.2EK	OEM
RD2.2ES	OEM
RD2.2F	OEM
RD2.2FB	OEM
RD2.2FC	OEM
RD2.2M	OEM
RD2.2P	OEM
RD2.4E	1266
RD2.4EB	OEM
RD2.4EB2	OEM
RD2.4EC	OEM
RD2.4EK	OEM
RD2.4ES	1266
RD2.4ESB1	OEM
RD2.4F	1268
RD2.4FB	1268
RD2.4FC	OEM
RD2.4M	OEM
RD2.4MB	OEM
RD2.4P	OEM
RD2.7E	0755
RD2.7E-B	0755
RD2.7EB	0755
RD2.7EB1	0755
RD2.7E-B2	0755
RD2.7EB2	0755
RD2.7EC	OEM
RD2.7EL	OEM
RD2.7EL1	0755
RD2.7EL2	OEM
RD2.7EN	OEM
RD2.7EN-1	0755
RD2.7EN1	0755
RD2.7EN2	OEM
RD2.7ES	0755
RD2.7ESAB1	OEM
RD2.7ESB	OEM
RD2.7F	1302
RD2.7FB	1302
RD2.7FB1	OEM
RD2.7FB2	OEM
RD2.7FC	OEM
RD2.7M	OEM
RD2.7MB	OEM
RD2.7MB1	OEM
RD2.7MB2	OEM
RD2.7P	OEM
RD-3	0015
RD3A/-1B4	OEM
RD3A-1B4	0015
RD3R0EB	0118
RD3R3EB	0296
RD3R6EB	0372
RD3R9EC	0036
RD3.0BB	0118
RD3.0E	0118
RD3.0E-B	0289
RD3.0EB	0118
RD3.0EB1	0118
RD3.0EB2	0118
RD3.0EC	OEM
RD3.0EL	OEM
RD3.0EL-1	0118
RD3.0EL1	0118
RD3.0EL2	OEM
RD3.0EN	0118
RD3.0EN2	0118
RD3.0ES	0118
RD3.0ESB	0118
RD3.0ES-B1	0118
RD3.0F	1703
RD3.0FB	5906
RD3.0FB1	OEM
RD3.0FB2	OEM
RD3.0FC	OEM
RD3.0M	OEM
RD3.0MB	OEM
RD3.0MB1	OEM
RD3.0MB2	OEM
RD3.0P	OEM
RD3.3E	0296
RD3.3E-B	0296
RD3.3EB	0296
RD3.3EB1	0296
RD3.3EB2	0296
RD-3.3EC	0372
RD3.3EC	OEM
RD3.3EL	OEM
RD3.3EL1	OEM
RD3.3EL2	OEM
RD3.3EN	OEM
RD3.3EN1	OEM
RD3.3EN2	OEM
RD3.3ES	0296
RD3.3ESB2	OEM
RD3.3F	0289
RD3.3FB	0289
RD3.3FB1	OEM
RD3.3FB2	OEM
RD3.3M	OEM
RD3.3MB	OEM
RD3.3MB1	OEM
RD3.3MB2	OEM
RD3.3P	OEM
RD3.6E	0372
RD3.6E-B	0188
RD3.6EB	0372
RD3.6EB1	0372
RD3.6EB2	OEM
RD3.6EB2HF	OEM
RD3.6EC	0372
RD3.6EL	0372
RD3.6E-L1	0372
RD3.6EL1	0372
RD3.6EL1T	0372
RD3.6EL1Z	0372
RD3.6E-L2	0372
RD3.6EL2	0372
RD3.6EN	0372
RD3.6E-N1	0372
RD3.6EN1	0372
RD3.6E-N2	0372
RD3.6EN2	0372
RD3.6ES	0372
RD3.6ES-B1	0372
RD3.6ESB1	0372
RD3.6ES-B2	0372
RD3.6ES-L1	OEM
RD3.6ESL1	OEM
RD3.6ES-T1B1	0372
RD3.6EST2L	0372
RD3.6F	0188
RD3.6FB	0372
RD3.6FB1	0372
RD3.6FB2	OEM
RD3.6FBI	0372
RD3.6FC	OEM
RD3.6M	OEM
RD3.6MB	OEM
RD3.6M-B1	OEM
RD3.6MB1	OEM
RD3.6MB2	OEM
RD3.6P	OEM
RD3.8E-B	OEM
RD3.9E	0036
RD3.9E-B	0036
RD3.9EB	0036
RD3.9E-B1	0036
RD3.9EB1	OEM
RD3.9EB2	OEM
RD3.9EC	0036
RD3.9EL	0036
RD3.9EL1	0036
RD3.9EL2	0036
RD3.9EN	0036
RD3.9EN1	OEM
RD3.9E-N2	0036
RD3.9EN2	0036
RD3.9E-N3	0036
RD3.9EN3	OEM
RD3.9ES	0036
RD3.9ES-B1	OEM
RD3.9ESB1	OEM
RD3.9ES-B2	0036
RD3.9F	0451
RD3.9FB	0036
RD3.9FB1	OEM
RD3.9FB2	OEM
RD3.9FC	OEM
RD3.9M	OEM
RD3.9MB	OEM
RD3.9MB1	OEM
RD3.9MB2	OEM
RD3.9P	OEM
RD-4A	0188
RD4A	0036
RD-4AM	0188
RD4AM	0036
RD4B	0451
RD4R5ESB2	OEM
RD4R7	0140
RD4R7EB	0140
RD4R7EB2	0140
RD4R7JB2	0140
RD4R7JB3	0140
RD4R7JSB1	OEM
RD4R7JSB2	0140
RD4R7JSB3	0140
RD4.3B	0274
RD4.3E	0274
RD4.3E-B	0274
RD4.3EB	0528
RD4.3EB1	0274
RD4.3EB2	0274
RD4.3EB3	OEM
RD4.3EC	0446
RD4.3EL	0274
RD4.3EL2	OEM
RD4.3EL3	OEM
RD4.3EN	OEM
RD4.3EN1	OEM
RD4.3EN2	OEM
RD4.3EN3	OEM
RD4.3ES	0274
RD4.3ESB	0274
RD4.3ES-B1	0274
RD4.3ESB1	0274
RD4.3ESB2	OEM
RD4.3ES-T1B1	0274
RD4.3E.1	OEM
RD4.3F	0528
RD4.3FB	6746
RD4.3FB1	OEM
RD4.3FB2	OEM
RD4.3FB3	OEM
RD4.3FC	OEM
RD4.3M	OEM
RD4.3MB	OEM
RD4.3MB1	OEM
RD4.3MB2	OEM
RD4.3MB3	OEM
RD4.5ESB2	OEM
RD4.7BE	0446
RD4.7E	0140
RD-4.7EB	0140
RD4.7EB	0140
RD4.7EB1	0140
RD4.7E-B2	0140
RD4.7EB2	0140
RD4.7EB3	0140
RD4.7EB3T	0140
RD4.7EB23	0140
RD4.7EC	0140
RD4.7EL	OEM
RD4.7EL1	OEM
RD4.7EL2	OEM
RD4.7EL3	OEM
RD4.7EN	OEM
RD4.7EN-1	0140
RD4.7EN1	0140
RD4.7EN2	OEM
RD4.7EN3	OEM
RD4.7ES	0140
RD4.7ESAB2	OEM
RD4.7ESB	6974
RD4.7ES-B1	0140
RD4.7ESB1	0140
RD4.7ES-B2	0140
RD4.7ESB2	0140
RD4.7F	0446
RD4.7FB	0446
RD4.7FB1	OEM
RD4.7FB2	OEM
RD4.7FB3	OEM
RD4.7FC	OEM
RD4.7J	0140
RD4.7JB	0140
RD4.7J-B1	0140
RD4.7JB1	0140
RD4.7J-B2	0140
RD4.7JB2	0140
RD4.7JB3	0140
RD4.7JS	0140
RD4.7JSB1	OEM
RD4.7JSB2	0140
RD4.7JSB3	0140
RD4.7M	0140
RD4.7MB	OEM
RD4.7MB1	OEM
RD4.7MB2	OEM
RD4.7MB3	OEM
RD4.7P	0446
RD-5A	0162
RD5A	0041
RD5AK	5883
RD5AL	0140
RD5AM	0140
RD5AN	0041
RD5B	0162
RD5BK	OEM
RD5BL	OEM
RD5BM	OEM
RD5BN	OEM
RD5C	2394
RD5CK	OEM
RD5CL	2387
RD5CM	2387
RD5CN	2101
RD5D	2394
RD5DK	OEM
RD5DL	2387
RD5DLM	OEM
RD5DM	2101
RD5DMN	OEM
RD5DN	2101
RD5E-C	0041
RD5H32A	OEM
RD5H32C	OEM
RD5R1EB	0041
RD5R1EB2	0041
RD5R1EBB1	0041
RD5R1JB	0041
RD5R1JB1	0041
RD5R1JB3	0041
RD5R6EB	0253
RD5R6EB2	0253
RD5R6JB	0253
RD5R6JB2	0253
RD5R6JB3	0253
RD5.1(E)B3	0041
RD5.1E	0041
RD-5.1EB	0041
RD5.1E-B	0041
RD5.1EB	0041
RD5.1EB(2)	0041
RD5.1EB(2)-T4	0041
RD5.1EB(3)	0041
RD5.1EB1	0041
RD5.1E-B2	0041
RD5.1EB-2	0041
RD5.1EB2	0041
RD5.1E-B3	0041
RD5.1EB3	0041

If replacement code is OEM, contact original manufacturer for replacement.

DEVICE TYPE	REPL CODE
RD-5.1EC	0162
RD5.1E-C	0041
RD5.1EC	0041
RD5.1EL	OEM
RD5.1EL1	0041
RD5.1EL2	OEM
RD5.1EL2Z	0582
RD5.1EN	OEM
RD5.1E-N1	0041
RD5.1EN1	0041
RD5.1E-N2	0041
RD5.1EN2	0041
RD5.1E-N3	0041
RD5.1EN3	0041
RD5.1ES	0041
RD5.1ES(B3)	0582
RD5.1ES(B3)-Y	0582
RD5.1ESB	0041
RD5.1ES-B1	0041
RD5.1ESB1	0041
RD5.1ES-B2	0041
RD5.1ESB2	0041
RD5.1ES-B3	0582
RD5.1ESB3	0582
RD5.1ES-L2	OEM
RD5.1ES-T1B	0582
RD5.1ES-T1B1	0582
RD5.1ES-T2B2	0041
RD5.1ES-TIB	0582
RD5.1EV	0041
RD5.1E.3	OEM
RD5.1F	0162
RD5.1FB	0041
RD5.1FB1	0162
RD5.1FB2	0041
RD5.1F-B3	0162
RD5.1FB3	OEM
RD5.1FC	OEM
RD5.1J	0041
RD5.1JB	0041
RD5.1JB1	0041
RD5.1JB2	0041
RD5.1JB3	OEM
RD5.1JS	OEM
RD5.1JS2	OEM
RD5.1JSAB2	OEM
RD5.1JSAB2X	0041
RD5.1JSB2	5816
RD5.1JSB2X	0041
RD5.1M	OEM
RD5.1MB	OEM
RD5.1MB1	OEM
RD5.1M-B2	OEM
RD5.1MB2	OEM
RD5.1MB2-3	OEM
RD5.1P	OEM
RD5.2EC	OEM
RD5.2MB3	OEM
RD5.6-B2Z	0253
RD5.6B	0157
RD5.6E	0253
RD-5.6EB	0253
RD5.6E-B	0253
RD5.6EB	0253
RD5.6EB(1)	0253
RD5.6EB(2)	0253
RD5.6EB(2)-T4	0253
RD5.6EB1	0041
RD5.6E-B2	0253
RD5.6EB2	0253
RD5.6E-B2Z	0253
RD5.6EB2Z	0253
RD5.6E-B3	0253
RD5.6EB3	0253
RD5.6EB7ZS	0253
RD5.6EB23	0253
RD5.6EB-T4	0253
RD5.6E-BZ	0253
RD5.6EBZ	OEM
RD5.6E-BZ7	0253
RD5.6E-BZ7S	0253
RD5.6EB-Z7S	0253
RD5.6EBZ7S	0253
RD5.6EBZ7S1	0253
RD5.6EBZ7STN	0253
RD5.6E-C	0253
RD5.6EC	0091
RD5.6ED	0253
RD5.6EK	0253
RD5.6EL	OEM
RD5.6EL1	OEM
RD5.6E-L2	0253
RD5.6EL2	0253
RD5.6EL3	OEM
RD5.6EN	OEM
RD5.6E-N1	0253
RD5.6EN1	0253
RD5.6E-N1TN	0253
RD5.6E-N2	0253
RD5.6EN2	0253
RD5.6E-N2TN	0253
RD5.6E-N3	0253
RD5.6EN3	0253
RD5.6ER2TA21R	0253
RD5.6ES	0253
RD5.6ESAB1	OEM
RD5.6ESAB2	OEM
RD5.6ESB	OEM
RD5.6ES-B1	0253
RD5.6ESB1	0253
RD5.6ES-B2	0253
RD5.6ESB2	0253
RD5.6ES-B3	0253
RD5.6ESB3	0253
RD5.6ES-T1B1	0253
RD5.6ES-T1B2	0253
RD5.6ES-T1B3	0253
RD5.6ES-T2B	0253
RD5.6ES-T2B2	0253
RD5.6ES-T2B3	0253
RD5.6ES-TIB3	OEM
RD5.6EZ7S	0253
RD5.6F	0157
RD5.6FA	0157
RD5.6FB	0157
RD5.6FB1	0157
RD5.6FB2	OEM
RD5.6FB3	OEM
RD5.6F-BZ7STN	0253
RD5.6J	0253
RD5.6JB	0253
RD5.6JB1	OEM
RD5.6JB2	0253
RD5.6JB3	OEM
RD5.6JB-3B	OEM
RD5.6JB-B3	OEM
RD5.6JS	0253
RD5.6JSB2	0253
RD5.6M	0253
RD5.6MB	OEM
RD5.6MB1	OEM
RD5.6M-B2	OEM
RD5.6MB2	OEM
RD5.6MB3	OEM
RD5.6P	OEM
RD5.7FC	OEM
RD6	0157
RD-6A	0157
RD6A	0091
RD-6A(M)	0157
RD6A(M)	0157
RD6AK	OEM
RD6AL	0253
RD-6AM	0157
RD6AM	0157
RD6AN	0298
RD6B	0298
RD6BK	OEM
RD6BL	OEM
RD6BM	OEM
RD6BN	OEM
RD6C	2400
RD6CK	OEM
RD6CL	1890
RD6CM	1890
RD6CN	2400
RD6D	2400
RD6DK	OEM
RD6DL	1890
RD6DLM	OEM
RD6DM	1890
RD6DN	2400
RD6R2B2	0466
RD6R2EB	0466
RD6R2EB1	0466
RD6R2JSB1	OEM
RD6R2JSB2	OEM
RD6R8EB	0062
RD6R8EE	0025
RD6R8JSB1	OEM
RD6R8JSB3	OEM
RD6.2-EM	0466
RD6.2B2	0091
RD6.2E	0466
RD6.2E(4)	0466
RD6.2E(B1-B3)	0466
RD6.2E(B2)	0466
RD6.2E(B3)	0466
RD6.2E(FA-1)	0466
RD-6.2EB	0466
RD6.2E-B	0466
RD6.2EB	0466
RD6.2EB(1)	0466
RD6.2EB(3)	0466
RD6.2EB(3)-T4	0466
RD6.2E-B1	0466
RD6.2EB1	0091
RD6.2EB1Z	0091
RD6.2E-B2	0466
RD6.2EB2	0466
RD6.2EB2-0.4W	0466
RD6.2EB-2-TA11R	0466
RD6.2E-B3	0466
RD6.2EB-3	0466
RD6.2EB3	0466
RD6.2EB23	0466
RD6.2EC	0466
RD6.2EFA-1	0466
RD6.2EFA1	0466
RD6.2EL	OEM
RD6.2EL1	OEM
RD6.2EL2	0466
RD6.2EL3	OEM
RD6.2EN	OEM
RD6.2E-N1	0466
RD6.2EN1	OEM
RD6.2E-N1TN	0466
RD6.2E-N2	0466
RD6.2EN2	0466
RD6.2EN3	OEM
RD6.2ES	0466
RD6.2ESA2	OEM
RD6.2ESAB3	OEM
RD6.2ESB	0466
RD6.2ES-B1	0466
RD6.2ESB1	0091
RD6.2ES-B2	0466
RD6.2ESB2	0466
RD6.2ES-B3	0466
RD6.2ESB3	OEM
RD6.2F	0631
RD6.2FA-1	0466
RD6.2FB	0631
RD6.2FB1	0631
RD6.2FB2	0466
RD6.2FB-3	0631
RD6.2FB3	OEM
RD6.2FC	OEM
RD6.2J	0466
RD6.2JB	0466
RD6.2JB1	OEM
RD6.2JB2	0466
RD6.2JB3	OEM
RD6.2JS	0466
RD6.2JSB1	OEM
RD6.2JSB2	OEM
RD6.2L	0466
RD6.2M	0466
RD6.2MB	0466
RD6.2MB1	OEM
RD6.2MB2	OEM
RD6.2MB3	OEM
RD6.2P	OEM
RD6.3EB1	0466
RD6.5EB	OEM
RD6.8E	0062
RD6.8E8	0062
RD-6.8EB	0025
RD6.8E-B	0062
RD6.8EB	0062
RD6.8EB(3)	0062
RD6.8EB(3)-T4	0062
RD6.8E-B1	0025
RD6.8EB1	0466
RD6.8EB2	0062
RD6.8EB3	0062
RD6.8EBZ	OEM
RD6.8E-C	0062
RD6.8EC	0062
RD6.8EL	OEM
RD6.8EL1	0062
RD6.8EL2	0062
RD6.8EL3	OEM
RD6.8EN	OEM
RD6.8E-N1	0062
RD6.8EN1	0466
RD6.8EN2	0062
RD6.8EN3	OEM
RD6.8ENZ	0062
RD6.8ES	0062
RD6.8ESAB2	0062
RD6.8ESB	OEM
RD6.8ES-B1	0292
RD6.8ESB1	0292
RD6.8ES-B2	0062
RD6.8ESB2	0062
RD6.8ES-B3	0062
RD6.8ESB3	OEM
RD6.8ES-T1B1	0292
RD6.8ES-T1B2	0062
RD6.8ES-TIB2	OEM
RD6.8E-V3-Y	0062
RD6.8F	0025
RD6.8FA	0025
RD6.8FB	0025
RD6.8FB1	OEM
RD6.8FB2	OEM
RD6.8FB3	OEM
RD6.8FC	OEM
RD6.8J	0062
RD6.8JB	OEM
RD6.8JB1	OEM
RD6.8JB2	0062
RD6.8JB3	0062
RD6.8J-N3	0062
RD6.8JS	0062
RD6.8JSB1	OEM
RD6.8JSB2	0062
RD6.8JSB3	OEM
RD6.8M	OEM
RD6.8MB	OEM
RD6.8M-B1	OEM
RD6.8MB1	OEM
RD6.8MB2	0062
RD6.8MB3	OEM
RD6.8N2	OEM
RD6.8P	OEM
RD6.ESB2	OEM
RD-7A	0644
RD7A	0062
RD7AK	OEM
RD-7AM	0025
RD7AM	0062
RD7AN	0062
RD7B	0025
RD7BK	OEM
RD7BL	OEM
RD7BM	OEM
RD7BN	OEM
RD7C	1606
RD7CK	OEM
RD7CL	0691
RD7CM	1591
RD7CN	1606
RD7D	1606
RD7DK	OEM
RD7DL	0691
RD7DLM	OEM
RD7DM	1591
RD7DMN	OEM
RD7DN	1606
RD-7E	0025
RD7H	0062
RD7R5EB	0644
RD7R5EB2	0077
RD7R5EB3	0077
RD7R5FB	0077
RD7R5JB2	0077
RD7R5JSB2	0077
RD7.0EB	0062
RD7.2EB	0077
RD7.5B2	0644
RD7.5E	0077
RD7.5E(B3)	0077
RD-7.5EB	0077
RD7.5E-B	0077
RD7.5EB	0077
RD7.5E-B1	0077
RD7.5EB-1	0077
RD7.5EB1	0077
RD7.5EB2	0077
RD7.5E-B3	0077
RD7.5EB3	0077
RD7.5E-B3Z	0077
RD7.5EBM	0077
RD7.5EBMV	0077
RD7.5EB-Y	0077
RD7.5EC	0077
RD7.5ED	0077
RD7.5EL	OEM
RD7.5EL1	OEM
RD7.5E-L2	0077
RD7.5EL2	OEM
RD7.5EL3	OEM
RD7.5EN	OEM
RD7.5EN1	OEM
RD7.5EN2	OEM
RD7.5EN3	0077
RD7.5ES	0077
RD7.5ES(B2)-T2	OEM
RD7.5ES(B3)	0077
RD7.5ES(B3)-T2	0077
RD7.5ES(B3)-Y	0077
RD7.5ES-B2	OEM
RD7.5F	0644
RD7.5FA	0644
RD7.5FB	0644
RD7.5FB1	OEM
RD7.5FB2	0644
RD7.5FB3	OEM
RD7.5FC	OEM
RD7.5J	0077
RD7.5JB	0077
RD7.5JB1	OEM
RD7.5JB2	0077
RD7.5JB3	OEM
RD7.5JS	0077
RD7.5JSB2	0077
RD7.5M	0644
RD7.5MB	OEM
RD7.5MB1	OEM
RD7.5MB2	OEM
RD7.5MB3	OEM
RD7.5P	OEM
RD7.6E-B	0077
RD8	0244
RD8H	0165
RD8R2EV	0165
RD8R2FB3	0244
RD8R2JB1	0165
RD8.2	0165
RD-8.2#E	0244
RD-8.2-E	0165
RD-8.2A	0165
RD8.2A	0244
RD-8.2E	0165
RD8.2E	0165
RD-8.2E(B)	0165
RD8.2E(B1)	0165
RD8.2E(B3)	0165
RD-8.2E(C)	0165
RD-8.2EB	0165
RD8.2E-B	0165
RD8.2EB	0165
RD8.2EB1	0077
RD8.2EB2	0165
RD8.2EB2Z	0165
RD8.2EB3	0165
RD8.2EB3T	0165
RD-8.2EC	0165
RD8.2EC	0165
RD8.2EK	0165
RD8.2EL	OEM
RD8.2EL1	OEM
RD8.2EL2	OEM
RD8.2EL3	OEM
RD8.2EN	OEM
RD8.2EN1	OEM
RD8.2EN2	OEM
RD8.2EN3	OEM
RD8.2ES	0165
RD8.2ES(B1)	0165
RD8.2ES(B1)-T2	0165
RD8.2ES(B1)-Y	0165
RD8.2ESB	OEM
RD8.2ES-B1	OEM
RD8.2ESB1	OEM
RD8.2ESB3	0165
RD8.2EV	0165
RD8.2EW	0165
RD8.2F	1075
RD-8.2FB	0165
RD8.2FB	0165
RD8.2FB1	OEM
RD8.2FB2	0244
RD8.2FB3	0244
RD8.2FC	0244
RD8.2J	0165
RD8.2JB	0165
RD8.2JB1	0165
RD8.2JB2	OEM
RD8.2JB3	OEM
RD8.2JS	0165
RD8.2JSB1	0165
RD8.2M	0165
RD8.2MB	OEM
RD8.2MB1	OEM
RD8.2MB3	OEM
RD8.2M-T2BB3	OEM
RD8.2P	OEM
RD8.2V	0165
RD8.3EB	0165
RD9	0012
RD-9A	0012
RD9A	0057
RD9A(10)	0012
RD9AK	OEM
RD-9AL	0012
RD9AL	1075
RD9AM	0057
RD9A-N	0012
RD9AN	0057
RD9B	1075
RD9BK	OEM
RD9BL	OEM
RD9BM	OEM
RD9BN	OEM
RD9C	1612
RD9CK	OEM
RD9CL	1612
RD9CM	2408
RD9CN	0622
RD9D	1612
RD9DK	OEM
RD9DL	1612
RD9DLM	OEM
RD9DM	2408
RD9DN	0622
RD-9E	0170
RD9R1EB	0057
RD9R1EW	0057
RD9R1JSB1	OEM
RD-9.1	0012
RD-9.1E	0012
RD9.1E	0057
RD9.1EB	0057
RD-9.1EB(1)	0012
RD9.1EB1	0057
RD9.1EB2	0057
RD9.1E-B3	0057
RD9.1EB3	0057
RD-9.1EBD	0057
RD9.1EBD	0057
RD9.1EBT	0057
RD9.1EC	0057
RD9.1ED	0012
RD9.1EK	0057
RD9.1EL	OEM
RD9.1EL1	OEM
RD9.1EL2	OEM
RD9.1EL3	0057
RD9.1EN	OEM
RD9.1EN1	OEM
RD9.1EN2	OEM
RD9.1E-N3	0057
RD9.1EN3	0057
RD9.1ES	0057
RD9.1ESAB3	OEM
RD9.1ESB	OEM
RD9.1ES-B1	OEM
RD9.1ESB1	OEM
RD9.1ES-B2	0057
RD9.1ESB2	5848
RD9.1ES-B3	OEM
RD9.1ESB3	OEM
RD9.1EW	0057
RD9.1F	0012
RD9.1FA	0012
RD-9.1FB	0012
RD9.1FB	0012
RD9.1FB1	OEM
RD9.1FB2	OEM
RD9.1F-B3	0057
RD9.1FB3	0012
RD9.1FC	0057
RD9.1J	0057
RD9.1JB	0057
RD9.1JB1	OEM
RD9.1JB2	0057
RD9.1JB3	0057
RD9.1JS	0057
RD9.1JSAB1	OEM
RD9.1JSAB3	OEM
RD9.1JSB	OEM
RD9.1JSB1	OEM
RD9.1JSB2	OEM
RD9.1JSB3	OEM
RD9.1M	0057
RD9.1MB	0057
RD9.1M-B1	OEM
RD9.1MB1	OEM
RD9.1MB2	OEM
RD9.1MB3	OEM
RD9.1P	OEM
RD10(E)B3	0064
RD10E	0064
RD-10E(B)	0064
RD10EA	0064
RD-10EB	0064
RD10E-B	0064
RD10EB	0064
RD10EB(2)	0064
RD10EB-0.4W	5546
RD10E-B1	0064
RD10EB1	0057
RD10EB-2	0170
RD10EB2	0064
RD10E-B3	0064
RD10EB3	0064
RD10EB23	0064
RD10EB23T	0064
RD10EC	OEM
RD10EL	OEM
RD10EL1	OEM
RD10EL2	OEM
RD10EL3	0248
RD10EL4	OEM
RD10EN	OEM
RD10E-N1	0064
RD10EN1	0064
RD10EN1T	0057
RD10E-N2	0064
RD10EN2	0064
RD10E-N3	0064
RD10EN3	0064
RD10E-N3TN	0064
RD10ENI	OEM
RD10ES	0064
RD10ESB	OEM
RD10ES-B1	0064
RD10ESB1	0057
RD10ES-B2	0064
RD10ESB2	0064
RD10ES-B3	0064
RD10ESB3	0064
RD10ES-T1B1	OEM
RD10ES-T1B2	0064
RD10ES-T2B2	0064
RD10ES-TIB2	0064
RD10E-T1B1	0064
RD10E-TIBI	OEM
RD10F	0170
RD10FA	0170
RD10FB	0170
RD10FB1	OEM
RD10FB2	0170
RD10FB3	OEM
RD10FBD	0170
RD10FC	0170
RD10H	0064
RD10J	0064
RD10JB	OEM
RD10JB(2)	0064
RD10JB(3)	0064
RD10JB1	OEM
RD10JB2	0064
RD10JB3	0064
RD10JS	0064
RD10JSAB3	0064
RD10JSB	0064
RD10JSB(2)	0064
RD10JSB(3)	0064
RD10JSB2	0064
RD10JSB2T	0064
RD10JSB3	0064
RD10M	0170
RD10MB	OEM
RD10MB1	OEM
RD10MB2	OEM
RD10MB3	OEM
RD10P	OEM
RD10S-B	OEM
RD10.0E	0170
RD11A	0181
RD11AK	OEM
RD11AL	0064
RD11AM	0064
RD11AN	0181
RD-11B	0181
RD11B	0313
RD11BK	OEM
RD11BL	OEM
RD11BM	OEM
RD11BN	OEM
RD11C	0989
RD11CK	OEM
RD11CL	0986
RD11CM	0986
RD11CN	0989
RD11D	0989
RD11DK	OEM
RD11DL	0986
RD11DLM	OEM
RD11DM	0986
RD11DMN	OEM
RD11DN	0989
RD-11E	0313
RD11E	0181
RD11E(B)	0181
RD11E(B3)	0181
RD-11EB	0181
RD11EB	0181
RD11E-B1	0181
RD11EB1	0064
RD11E-B2	0181
RD11EB2	0181
RD11EB2-TA21R	0181
RD11EB2-TR21R	0181
RD11EB2TA21R	0181
RD-11EB3	0181
RD11EB3	0181
RD11EB-Y	0181
RD11EC	0052
RD11EE	0023
RD11EL	OEM
RD11EL1	OEM
RD11EL2	0181
RD11EL3	OEM
RD11EM	0313
RD11EN	OEM
RD11EN1	OEM
RD11EN2	0313
RD11EN3	OEM
RD11ES	0181
RD11ESB2	0181
RD11F	0313
RD11F(B)	0313
RD11FB	0313
RD11FB02-TA21-R	0313
RD11FB1	OEM
RD11FB2	0313
RD11FB3	OEM
RD11FBD2	0313
RD11FBD3	OEM
RD11FC	OEM
RD11GB02	0023
RD11J	0181
RD11JB	0313
RD11JB1	OEM
RD11JB2	OEM
RD11JB3	OEM
RD11JD	0181
RD11JS	0181
RD11M	0181
RD11MB	OEM
RD11MB1	OEM
RD11MB2	OEM
RD11M-B3	OEM
RD11MB3	OEM
RD11P	OEM
RD12	0137
RD12-OF	0137
RD12B	0052
RD12E	0052
RD12E(B1)	0052
RD12EA	0052
R-D12EB	0052
RD-12EB	0052
RD12E-B	0052
RD12EB	0999
RD12EB(1)	0052
RD-12EB(3)	0052
RD12EB(3)	0052
RD12EB(3)-T4	0052
RD12EB(AU)	0052
RD12EB0(2)	0052
RD12E-B1	0052
RD12EB-1	0052
RD12EB1	0052
RD12E-B1Z	0052
RD12EB1Z	0052
RD12E-B2	0052
RD12EB-2	0052
RD12EB2	0999
RD12EB2M	0052
RD12E-B2Z	0052
RD12E-B3	0052
RD12EB3	0052
RD12EBD	0052
RD12EBH	0137
RD12EBM	0052
RD12EB-T4	0052
RD12EC	0137
RD12EL	OEM
RD12EL1	OEM
RD12EL2	OEM
RD12EL3	OEM
RD12EN	OEM
RD12EN1	OEM
RD12EN2	0999
RD12EN3	OEM
RD12ES	0052
RD12ESAB1	0999

If replacement code is OEM, contact original manufacturer for replacement.

523

DEVICE TYPE	REPL CODE
RD12ES-B2	0052
RD12ESB2	3295
RD12ES-B3	0052
RD12ESB3	0052
RD12ES-T2B2	0052
RD12E-T2	0052
RD12F	0137
RD12F(B1)	0137
RD12FA	0137
RD12FB	0137
RD12FB1	0137
RD12FB2	0137
RD12FB3	0137
RD12FBD	0137
RD12FBT	0137
RD12FC	OEM
RD12J	0052
RD12JB	0052
RD12JB1	OEM
RD12JB2	0052
RD12JB3	OEM
RD12JS	OEM
RD12JSB1	OEM
RD12JSB2	0999
RD12M	0052
RD12MB	0052
RD12M-B1	OEM
RD12MB1	OEM
RD12MB2	OEM
RD12MB3	OEM
RD12P	OEM
RD13	0361
RD13(E)B2	0053
RD-13A	0361
RD13A	0053
RD-13A(M)	0361
RD-13A(N)	OEM
RD-13AD	0361
RD-13AK	0361
RD13AK	0361
RD-13AL	0244
RD13AL	0052
RD-13AM	0361
RD13AM	0053
RD-13AN	0137
RD13AN	0361
RD13ANP	0361
RD13B	0361
RD13BK	OEM
RD13BL	0052
RD13BM	OEM
RD13BN	OEM
RD13C	0237
RD13CK	OEM
RD13CL	0052
RD13CM	1240
RD13CN	1240
RD13D	0237
RD13DK	OEM
RD13DL	1254
RD13DLM	OEM
RD13DM	1240
RD13DMN	OEM
RD13DN	1240
RD-13E	0053
RD13E	0053
RD13E-B	0053
RD13EB	0053
RD13EB(2)	0053
RD13EB-1	0053
RD13EB1	0053
RD13E-B1Z8	0053
RD-13EB2	0053
RD13E-B2	0053
RD13EB2	0053
RD13E-B2TN	0053
RD13E-B2Z	0053
RD13EB2Z	0053
RD13EB3	0053
RD13EC	0053
RD13ED1	0053
RD13EL	OEM
RD13EL1	0053
RD13EL2	0053
RD13EL3	OEM
RD13EN	0053
RD13E-N1	0053
RD13EN1	0053
RD13E-N2	0053
RD13EN2	0053
RD13EN3	OEM
RD13ES	0053
RD13ES-B	0053
RD13ESB	0053
RD13ES-B1	OEM
RD13ESB1	OEM
RD13ESB1M4	OEM
RD13ES-B2	0053
RD13ESB2	OEM
RD13ESB3	OEM
RD13ES-T1B2	0053
RD13ES-TIB2	OEM
RD13F	0361
RD13FB	0361
RD13FB1	OEM
RD13FB2	OEM
RD13FB3	OEM
RD13FC	OEM
RD13H	OEM
RD13J	0053
RD13JB	OEM
RD13JB1	OEM
RD13JB2	OEM
RD13JB3	OEM
RD13JS	0053
RD13JSB3	OEM
RD13JS-Y	0053
RD13K	0137
RD13M	0361
RD13MB	OEM
RD13MB1	OEM
RD13MB2	OEM
RD13MB3	OEM
RD13P	OEM
RD15E	0002
RD15EA	0681
RD15EB	0873
RD15EB1	OEM
RD15EB2	4446
RD15E-B3	0681
RD15EB3	0681
RD15EB3-0.4W	0681
RD15EB3Z	0681
RD15EB23	0681
RD15EC	0681
RD15EL	OEM
RD15EN	OEM
RD15E-N1	0681
RD15EN1	OEM
RD15EN2	OEM
RD15E-N3	0681
RD15EN3	0681
RD15ES	0681
RD15ESB	OEM
RD15ESB2	0681
RD15F	0002
RD15F1	0002
RD15FA	0002
RD15FB	0002
RD15FB1	OEM
RD15FB3	0002
RD15FC	OEM
RD15FM	0002
RD15FMZ	0002
RD15J	0681
RD15JB1	OEM
RD15JB2	OEM
RD15JB3	0681
RD15JS	0681
RD15JS(B2)-T	0681
RD15JSB2	OEM
RD15JSB3	OEM
RD15L	OEM
RD15M	0681
RD15MB	0681
RD15MB1	OEM
RD15MB2	OEM
RD15MB3	OEM
RD15P	OEM
RD16A	0440
RD16AK	OEM
RD16AL	0873
RD16AM	0681
RD16AN	0210
RD16AT	OEM
RD16B	0416
RD16BK	OEM
RD16BL	OEM
RD16BM	OEM
RD16BN	OEM
RD16BT	OEM
RD16C	1693
RD16CK	OEM
RD16CL	1626
RD16CM	1629
RD16CN	1630
RD16C-Y	0416
RD16D	1693
RD16DK	OEM
RD16DL	1626
RD16DLM	OEM
RD16DM	1629
RD16DMN	OEM
RD16DN	1630
RD16DT	OEM
RD16E	0440
RD16E(B3)	0440
RD16EB	0440
RD16EB1	0440
RD16EB2	0440
RD16E-B3	0440
RD16EB3	0440
RD16EBS	OEM
RD16EC	1639
RD16EL	OEM
RD16EL1	OEM
RD16EL2	OEM
RD16EL3	0440
RD16E-M	0416
RD16EN	0440
RD16EN1	4999
RD16E-N2	0416
RD16EN2	OEM
RD16E-N3	0416
RD16EN3	OEM
RD16ES	0440
RD16ESB	OEM
RD16F	0416
RD16FB	0440
RD16FB1	0416
RD16FB2	OEM
RD16FB3	OEM
RD16FC	OEM
RD16GT	OEM
RD-16H	0002
RD16H	0002
RD16J	0440
RD16JB	OEM
RD16JB1	0440
RD16JB2	0440
RD16JB3	OEM
RD16JS	0440
RD16JSAB2	0077
RD16JT	OEM
RD16KT	OEM
RD16M	0440
RD16MB	OEM
RD16MB1	OEM
RD16MB2	OEM
RD16MB3	OEM
RD16P	OEM
RD18E	0371
RD18EB	0371
RD18E-B1	0371
RD18EB1	0371
RD18EB2	OEM
RD18EB3	0371
RD18EC	0371
RD18EL	OEM
RD18EL1	OEM
RD18EL2	OEM
RD18EL3	OEM
RD18EN	OEM
RD18EN1	OEM
RD18EN2	OEM
RD18EN3	OEM
RD18ES	0371
RD18ESB	OEM
RD18ES-B1	0210
RD18ESB1	0210
RD18ES-B2	0371
RD18ES-T1B1	OEM
RD18EST1B1	0210
RD18ES-TIBI	OEM
RD18F	0490
RD18FA	0490
RD18FB	0490
RD18FB1	OEM
RD18FB2	0490
RD18FB3	0490
RD18FC	OEM
RD18J	0371
RD18JB	OEM
RD18JB1	OEM
RD18JB2	OEM
RD18JB3	OEM
RD18JB-B3	OEM
RD18JS	0371
RD18M	OEM
RD18MB	OEM
RD18MB1	OEM
RD18M-B3	OEM
RD18MB3	OEM
RD18P	OEM
RD19	0943
RD19A	0666
RD19AK	OEM
RD19AL	0666
RD19AM	0666
RD19B	0943
RD19BK	OEM
RD19BL	OEM
RD19BM	OEM
RD19C	1709
RD19CK	OEM
RD19CL	1706
RD19CM	1720
RD19D	1709
RD19DK	OEM
RD19DL	1706
RD19DLM	OEM
RD19DM	1720
RD-20E	0526
RD20E	0695
RD20E(B1)	0695
RD20EB	0695
RD20EB1	OEM
RD20EB2	0666
RD20EB3	0210
RD20EC	OEM
RD20EL	OEM
RD20EL1	OEM
RD20EL2	OEM
RD20EL3	OEM
RD20EL4	OEM
RD20EN	OEM
RD20EN1	OEM
RD20EN2	OEM
RD20EN3	OEM
RD20EN4	OEM
RD20ES	0695
RD20ES-B1	0666
RD20ESB1	0666
RD20ES-B2	0666
RD20ESB2	0666
RD20ES-T1B2	0666
RD20ES-TIB2	OEM
RD20EV2	0695
RD20EV2-Y	0695
RD20F	0526
RD20FB	0526
RD20FB1	OEM
RD20FB2	0526
RD20FB3	OEM
RD20FC	OEM
RD20J	0695
RD20JB	OEM
RD20JB1	OEM
RD20JB2	OEM
RD20JB3	OEM
RD20JS	0695
RD20JSB2	6385
RD20M	OEM
RD20MB	OEM
RD20MB1	OEM
RD20MB2	OEM
RD20MB3	OEM
RD20P	OEM
RD22E	0700
RD22E-B	0700
RD22EB	0700
RD22EB1	0700
RD22EB2	OEM
RD22EB3	OEM
RD22EB4	OEM
RD22EC	0205
RD22EL	OEM
RD22EL1	OEM
RD22EL2	OEM
RD22EL3	OEM
RD22EL4	OEM
RD22ES	0700
RD22F	0560
RD22FA	0560
RD22FB	0560
RD22FB1	OEM
RD22FB2	5857
RD22FC	0560
RD22J	0695
RD22JB	OEM
RD22JB1	OEM
RD22JB2	OEM
RD22JB3	OEM
RD22JS	0695
RD22M	OEM
RD22MB	OEM
RD22MB1	OEM
RD22MB2	OEM
RD22MB3	OEM
RD22P	OEM
RD23D12A	OEM
RD23D12A3	OEM
RD23D12AF	OEM
RD23D12B	OEM
RD23D12B3	OEM
RD23D12BF	OEM
RD23D14A	OEM
RD23D14A3	OEM
RD23D14AF	OEM
RD23D14B	OEM
RD23D14B3	OEM
RD23D14BF	OEM
RD23D16A	OEM
RD23D16A3	OEM
RD23D16AF	OEM
RD23D16B	OEM
RD23D16B3	OEM
RD23D16BF	OEM
RD23D18A	OEM
RD23D18A3	OEM
RD23D18AF	OEM
RD23D18B	OEM
RD23D18B3	OEM
RD23D18BF	OEM
RD23D20A	OEM
RD23D20A3	OEM
RD23D20AF	OEM
RD23D20B	OEM
RD23D20B3	OEM
RD23D20BF	OEM
RD23D22A	OEM
RD23D22A3	OEM
RD23D22AF	OEM
RD23D22B	OEM
RD23D22B3	OEM
RD23D22BF	OEM
RD23D24A	OEM
RD23D24A3	OEM
RD23D24AF	OEM
RD23D26A	OEM
RD23D26A3	OEM
RD23D26AF	OEM
RD23DG4A	OEM
RD23DG4A3	OEM
RD23DG4AF	OEM
RD23DG4B	OEM
RD23DG4B3	OEM
RD23DG4BF	OEM
RD23DG6A	OEM
RD23DG6A3	OEM
RD23DG6AF	OEM
RD23DG6B	OEM
RD23DG6B3	OEM
RD23DG6BF	OEM
RD23DG8A	OEM
RD23DG8A3	OEM
RD23DG8AF	OEM
RD23DG8B	OEM
RD23DG8B3	OEM
RD23DG8BF	OEM
RD23DG10A	OEM
RD23DG10A3	OEM
RD23DG10AF	OEM
RD23DG10B	OEM
RD23DG10B3	OEM
RD23DG10BF	OEM
RD23DR12A	OEM
RD23DR12B	OEM
RD23DR14A	OEM
RD23DR14B	OEM
RD23DR16A	OEM
RD23DR16B	OEM
RD23DR18A	OEM
RD23DR18B	OEM
RD23DR20A	OEM
RD23DR20B	OEM
RD23DR22A	OEM
RD23DR22B	OEM
RD23DR24A	OEM
RD23DR26A	OEM
RD23DRG4A	OEM
RD23DRG4B	OEM
RD23DRG6A	OEM
RD23DRG6B	OEM
RD23DRG8A	OEM
RD23DRG8B	OEM
RD23DRG10A	OEM
RD23DRG10B	OEM
RD-24A	0398
RD24A	0489
RD24AK	OEM
RD24AL	0489
RD24AM	0489
RD24AN	0489
RD24B	0398
RD24BK	OEM
RD24BL	OEM
RD24BM	OEM
RD24BN	OEM
RD24C	1745
RD24CK	OEM
RD24CL	0722
RD24CM	0722
RD24CN	1757
RD24D	1745
RD24DK	OEM
RD24DL	0722
RD24DLM	OEM
RD24DM	0722
RD24DMN	OEM
RD24DN	1757
RD24E	0489
RD24E(B2)	0489
RD24E(B3)	0489
RD24E-B	0489
RD24EB	0489
RD24EB1	0489
RD24EB2	0489
RD24EB2VF	OEM
RD24EB3	0489
RD24EB4	OEM
RD24EB23	0489
RD24E-B27	0489
RD24E-BZ7	0489
RD24EB-Z7	0489
RD24EBZ7	0489
RD24E-BZ7TN	0489
RD24EC	1596
RD24EE	OEM
RD24EL	OEM
RD24EL1	OEM
RD24EL2	OEM
RD24EL3	OEM
RD24EL4	OEM
RD24ES	0489
RD24ESB	OEM
RD24ES-B1	0489
RD24F	0398
RD24FB	0273
RD24FB1	OEM
RD24FB2	OEM
RD24FB3	OEM
RD24F-BS	0398
RD24FC	1596
RD24J	0489
RD24JB	OEM
RD24JB1	OEM
RD24JB2	OEM
RD24JB3	OEM
RD24JS	0489
RD24M	0489
RD24MB	OEM
RD24MB1	OEM
RD24MB2	OEM
RD24MB3	OEM
RD24P	OEM
RD27	0436
RD27B1	OEM
RD27E	0450
RD27E(B4)	0436
RD27EB	0436
RD27EB1	0450
RD27EB2	0450
RD27E-B2Z	0450
RD27EB3	0450
RD27E-B4	0436
RD27EB4	0450
RD27EB4TN	0450
RD27EC	OEM
RD27ED	0436
RD27EL	OEM
RD27EL1	OEM
RD27EL2	OEM
RD27EL3	OEM
RD27EL4	OEM
RD27ES	0450
RD27ES-B1	0709
RD27ESB1	0709
RD27F	0436
RD27FA	0436
RD27FB	0436
RD27FB1	1596
RD27FB2	0436
RD27FB3	OEM
RD27FC	0436
RD27FCD	0436
RD27J	0257
RD27JB	OEM
RD27JB1	OEM
RD27JB2	OEM
RD27JB3	OEM
RD27JS	0450
RD27JS-B3	0450
RD27JST	0436
RD27JS-T1	0450
RD27JST1	0450
RD27M	0450
RD27P	OEM
RD29A	0257
RD29AK	OEM
RD29AL	0450
RD29AM	0257
RD29AN	0195
RD29B	1664
RD29BK	OEM
RD29BL	OEM
RD29BM	OEM
RD29BN	OEM
RD29C	2434
RD29CK	OEM
RD29CL	1771
RD29CM	2434
RD29CN	1783
RD29D	2434
RD29DK	OEM
RD29DL	1771
RD29DLM	OEM
RD29DM	2434
RD29DMN	OEM
RD29DN	1788
RD30AM	OEM
RD30B3	OEM
RD30BM	OEM
RD30D4A	OEM
RD30D4A3	OEM
RD30D4AF	OEM
RD30D4B	OEM
RD30D4B3	OEM
RD30D4BF	OEM
RD30D6A	OEM
RD30D6A3	OEM
RD30D6AF	OEM
RD30D6B	OEM
RD30D6B3	OEM
RD30D6BF	OEM
RD30D8A	OEM
RD30D8A3	OEM
RD30D8AF	OEM
RD30D8B	OEM
RD30D8B3	OEM
RD30D8BF	OEM
RD30D10A	OEM
RD30D10A3	OEM
RD30D10AF	OEM
RD30D10B	OEM
RD30D10B3	OEM
RD30D10BF	OEM
RD30D12A	OEM
RD30D12A3	OEM
RD30D12AF	OEM
RD30D12B	OEM
RD30D12B3	OEM
RD30D12BF	OEM
RD30D14A	OEM
RD30D14A3	OEM
RD30D14AF	OEM
RD30D14B	OEM
RD30D14B3	OEM
RD30D14BF	OEM
RD30D16A	OEM
RD30D16A3	OEM
RD30D16AF	OEM
RD30D16B	OEM
RD30D16B3	OEM
RD30D16BF	OEM
RD30D18A	OEM
RD30D18A3	OEM
RD30D18AF	OEM
RD30D18B	OEM
RD30D18B3	OEM
RD30D18BF	OEM
RD30D20A	OEM
RD30D20A3	OEM
RD30D20AF	OEM
RD30D20B	6016
RD30D20B3	OEM
RD30D20BF	OEM
RD30D22A	OEM
RD30D22A3	OEM
RD30D22AF	OEM
RD30D22B	OEM
RD30D22B3	OEM
RD30D22BF	OEM
RD30D24A	OEM
RD30D24A3	OEM
RD30D24AF	OEM
RD30D24B	OEM
RD30D24B3	OEM
RD30D24BF	OEM
RD30D26A	OEM
RD30D26A3	OEM
RD30D26AF	OEM
RD30D26B	OEM
RD30D26B3	OEM
RD30D26BF	OEM
RD30D28A	OEM
RD30D28A3	OEM
RD30D28AF	OEM
RD30D30A	OEM
RD30D30A3	OEM
RD30D30AF	OEM
RD30DM	OEM
RD30DR4A	OEM
RD30DR4B	OEM
RD30DR6A	OEM
RD30DR6B	OEM
RD30DR8A	OEM
RD30DR8B	OEM
RD30DR10A	OEM
RD30DR10B	OEM
RD30DR12A	OEM
RD30DR12B	OEM
RD30DR14A	OEM
RD30DR14B	OEM
RD30DR16A	OEM
RD30DR16B	OEM
RD30DR18A	OEM
RD30DR18B	OEM
RD30DR20A	OEM
RD30DR20B	OEM
RD30DR22A	OEM
RD30DR22B	OEM
RD30DR24A	OEM
RD30DR24B	OEM
RD30DR26A	OEM
RD30DR26B	OEM
RD30DR28A	OEM
RD30DR30A	OEM
RD30E	0721
RD-30EB	0166
RD30EB	0195
RD30EB1	OEM
RD30E-B2	0195
RD30EB2	0195
RD30E-B2Z	0195
RD30EB3	0195
RD30EB4	0195
RD30EC	OEM
RD30EL	OEM
RD30EL1	OEM
RD30EL2	OEM
RD30EL3	OEM
RD30EL4	OEM
RD30ES	0195
RD30ESB1	0195
RD30ES-B2	0195
RD30ESB2	OEM
RD30ESB4	0195
RD30F	0721
RD30FB	0721
RD30FB(1)	1664
RD30FB(2)	0721
RD30FB(3)	0721
RD30FB-1	1664
RD30FB1	1664
RD30FB2	0721
RD30FB3	0721
RD30FB3-1	OEM
RD30FB3-2	OEM
RD30FB31	OEM
RD30FB32	OEM
RD30FC	OEM
RD30GM	OEM
RD30J	0195
RD30JB	OEM
RD30JB1	OEM
RD30JB2	OEM
RD30JB3	OEM
RD30JM	OEM
RD30JS	0195
RD30KM	OEM
RD30M	0195
RD30MM	OEM
RD30P	OEM
RD33	0166
RD33B-E1	0166
RD33E	0166
RD33E(B1)-Y	OEM
RD33EB	0166
RD33EB*5*	0166
RD33EB(5)	0166
RD33E-B1	0166
RD33EB1	0195

If replacement code is OEM, contact original manufacturer for replacement.

DEVICE TYPE	REPL CODE
RD33E-B2	0166
RD33EB2	0166
RD33EB2T	0166
RD33E-B2TN	0166
RD33EB3	0166
RD33EB-4	0166
RD33EB4	0166
RD33EB5	0166
RD33EC	0814
RD33EL	OEM
RD33EL1	OEM
RD33EL2	OEM
RD33EL3	OEM
RD33EL4	OEM
RD33ES	0166
RD33ESB1	OEM
RD33ES-B2	0166
RD33ESB2	0166
RD33ESB3	0166
RD33ES-L3	OEM
RD33ES-T1B2	0195
RD33ES-TIB2	OEM
RD33F	0039
RD33FA	0039
RD33FB	0039
RD33FB1	0166
RD33FB2	0039
RD33FB3	OEM
RD33FC	OEM
RD33J	0166
RD33JB	OEM
RD33JB1	OEM
RD33JB2	OEM
RD33JB3	OEM
RD33JS	0166
RD33JSB1	0166
RD33JSB2	0166
RD33M	0166
RD33P	OEM
RD-35	0814
RD-35A	0039
RD35A	0010
RD35AE	0032
RD35AK	OEM
RD35AL	0166
RD35AM	0010
RD35AN	OEM
RD35B	0814
RD35BK	OEM
RD35BL	OEM
RD35BM	OEM
RD35BN	OEM
RD35C	1798
RD35CK	OEM
RD35CL	1788
RD35CLM	OEM
RD35CM	1798
RD35CN	1806
RD35D	1798
RD35DK	OEM
RD35DL	1788
RD35DM	1798
RD35DMN	OEM
RD35DN	1806
RD36E	0166
RD-36EB	OEM
RD36E-B	0010
RD36EB	0010
RD36E-B1	0010
RD36EB1	0010
RD36EB2	0166
RD36EB3	0010
RD36EB3V	0010
RD36EB4	OEM
RD36EB-T1	0010
RD36EB-TA11R	0010
RD36EC	OEM
RD36EL	OEM
RD36EL1	OEM
RD36EL2	OEM
RD36EL3	OEM
RD36EL4	OEM
RD36ES	0010
RD36ES-B-T1	0010
RD36ES-T1	0010
RD36EV3	0166
RD36EV8	0010
RD36F	0814
RD36FB	0814
RD36FB1	OEM
RD36FB2	OEM
RD36FB3	OEM
RD36FC	OEM
RD36J	0010
RD36JB	OEM
RD36JB1	OEM
RD36JB2	OEM
RD36JB3	OEM
RD36JS	0010
RD36M	0010
RD36P	OEM
RD39E	0032
RD39EB	0032
RD39E-B1	0032
RD39EB1	0032
RD39EB2	0032
RD39EB3	OEM
RD39EB4	OEM
RD39EC	OEM

DEVICE TYPE	REPL CODE
RD39EC1	OEM
RD39E-C2	0032
RD39EC2	OEM
RD39EC3	OEM
RD39EL	OEM
RD39EL1	OEM
RD39EL2	OEM
RD39EL3	OEM
RD39EL4	OEM
RD39EL5	OEM
RD39EL6	OEM
RD39EL7	OEM
RD39ES	0032
RD39ES-B4	OEM
RD39ESB4	OEM
RD39F	0346
RD39FA	0346
RD39FB	0346
RD39FB1	OEM
RD39FB2	OEM
RD39FB3	OEM
RD39FC	OEM
RD39J	0032
RD39JB	OEM
RD39JB1	OEM
RD39JB2	OEM
RD39JB3	OEM
RD39JS	0032
RD39M	0032
RD39P	OEM
RD-41PI	OEM
RD42EB	0274
RD43E	0054
RD43EB	3379
RD43F	0925
RD43FB	3386
RD43M	OEM
RD47D	OEM
RD47E	0068
RD47EB	3548
RD47EB2	0993
RD47EL1	OEM
RD47F	0993
RD47FB	3551
RD47FBD	0993
RD47F-TB	0068
RD47M	OEM
RD47P	OEM
RD51E	0092
RD51EB	0162
RD51E-B2	OEM
RD51F	0497
RD51FB	3710
RD51P	OEM
RD56B	0863
RD56E	0125
RD56EB	0125
RD56E-B2Z	0253
RD56E-BZ7S	0253
RD56F	0863
RD56FB	0863
RD56P	OEM
RD62E	0152
RD62EB	0152
RD62F	0778
RD62FB	4065
RD62P	OEM
RD68E	0173
RD68EB	0173
RD68F	1258
RD68FB	4188
RD68P	OEM
RD75E	0094
RD75E(B)	OEM
RD75EB	4292
RD75F	1181
RD75FB	4294
RD75P	OEM
RD82E	0049
RD82EB	4431
RD82EC	OEM
RD82F	0327
RD82FB	4434
RD-91	0012
RD-91E	0012
RD91E	1301
RD91EB	0156
RD-91F	OEM
RD91P	OEM
RD92EB	OEM
RD100E	0189
RD100EB	6891
RD100P	OEM
RD110E	0099
RD110EB	6954
RD110P	OEM
RD120E	0089
RD120EB	0697
RD120P	OEM
RD130E	0285
RD140E	0252
RD150E	0336
RD151	0106
RD152	0106
RD153	0106
RD154	0106
RD155	1999
RD156	2384
RD157	0782

DEVICE TYPE	REPL CODE
RD160E	0336
RD165S	OEM
RD170E	0390
RD180E	0420
RD190E	0448
RD200E	1464
RD250	0015
RD316	OEM
RD362EB2	0166
RD515	0133
RD900	OEM
RD1015	OEM
RD1212EB-T4	0052
RD2015	OEM
RD2512	OEM
RD3015	OEM
RD3472	0015
RD4015	OEM
RD4258	OEM
RD4502	OEM
RD6551-11	OEM
RD9037	0015
RD26235-1	0015
RD29799P	0015
RD31903P	0015
RD-EX0096CEZZ	0700
RDF02M	OEM
RDG.2EBZ	OEM
RDI2E-B	0052
RDR.1JB3	OEM
RDS5.6EB3	OEM
R-DW4	2074
RE-1	0279
RE1	0279
RE-2	0595
RE2	0015
RE-3	0211
RE3	0015
RE-4	0136
RE4	0004
RE-5	0038
RE5	0038
RE-6	0208
RE6	0208
RE7	0085
RE-7MP	3004
RE7MP	3004
RE-8	0435
RE8	0435
RE-9	0127
RE9	0127
RE-10	0144
RE10	0144
RE11	0160
RE-11MP	0160
RE11MP	0160
RE-12	0198
RE12	0198
RE-13	0016
RE13	0016
RE-14	0142
RE14	0142
RE15	0136
RE-16	0969
RE16	0969
RE-17	0086
RE17	0086
RE-18	0126
RE18	0126
RE-19	0103
RE19	0103
RE-20	0222
RE20	0222
RE-20MP	0816
RE20MP	0222
RE-21	0419
RE21	0419
RE-22	0848
RE22	0848
RE-23	0233
RE23	0233
RE-24	0187
RE24	0275
RE-25	0164
RE25	0164
RE-26	0037
RE26	0037
RE-27	0050
RE27	0050
RE-28	0007
RE28	0007
RE-29	0074
RE29	0074
RE-30	0637
RE30	0637
RE-31	0287
RE31	0003
RE-32	0065
RE32	0065
RE-33	0396
RE33	0396
RE-34	0178
RE34	0178
RE-35	0841
RE35	0841
RE-36	0599
RE36	0599
RE-37	0130
RE37	0130

DEVICE TYPE	REPL CODE
RE38	0556
RE39	1190
RE-40	0161
RE40	0161
RE-41	0455
RE41	0455
RE-42	0555
RE42	0555
RE-43	1257
RE43	1257
RE44	0264
RE45	0321
RE46	0321
RE-47	0015
RE47	0143
RE-48	0911
RE48	0911
RE-49	0015
RE49	0015
RE-50	0229
RE50	0229
RE-51	0071
RE51	0071
RE-52	0015
RE52	0133
RE-53	0150
RE53	0150
RE-54	2736
RE54	2736
RE-55	0102
RE55	0102
RE56	0787
RE57	0886
RE58	0886
RE59	1471
RE60	0710
RE-61	2002
RE61	2002
RE62	0688
RE63	0006
RE64	0111
RE65	0349
RE66	0079
RE-67	0111
RE67	0111
RE-68	0222
RE68	0899
RE69	0050
RE-70	0590
RE70	0086
RE71	0617
RE72	0037
RE-73	0222
RE73	0283
RE-74	1671
RE74	1671
RE-75	0546
RE75	0546
RE-76	0378
RE76	0378
RE-77	0334
RE77	0334
RE78	0855
RE-79	0150
RE79	0693
RE79A	0693
RE-80	2039
RE80	0561
RE81	1357
RE-82	0486
RE82	0486
RE-83	1004
RE83	1004
RE83MP	1004
RE85	1851
RE86	0123
RE-87	0196
RE87	0196
RE-88	0479
RE88	0479
RE-89	1073
RE89	1073
RE-90	2613
RE90	0071
RE-91	0469
RE91	0469
RE-92	0916
RE92	0087
RE-93	0290
RE93	0290
RE93P	0290
RE-94	0124
RE94	0124
RE95	2975
RE96	OEM
RE97	1302
RE98	2981
RE99	1703
RE-100	0289
RE100	0289
RE-101	0188
RE101	0188
RE-102	0451
RE102	0451
RE-103	0528
RE103	0528
RE-104	0446
RE104	0446
RE-105	0162

DEVICE TYPE	REPL CODE
RE105	0162
RE106	0157
RE-107	0157
RE107	0157
RE-108	0298
RE108	0298
RE-109	0631
RE109	0631
RE-110	0025
RE110	0025
RE-111	0644
RE111	0644
RE-112	0244
RE112	0244
RE113	1075
RE-114	0012
RE114	0012
RE-115	0170
RE115	0170
RE-116	0313
RE116	0313
RE-117	0789
RE117	0789
RE-118	0137
RE118	0137
RE-119	0361
RE119	0361
RE-120	0100
RE120	0100
RE-121	0002
RE121	0002
RE-122	0416
RE122	0416
RE-123	1639
RE123	1639
RE-124	0490
RE124	0490
RE-125	0943
RE125	0943
RE-126	0526
RE126	0526
RE-127	0560
RE127	0560
RE-128	0398
RE128	0398
RE-129	1596
RE129	1596
RE-130	0039
RE130	0039
RE-131	0346
RE131	0346
RE-132	0778
RE132	0778
RE-133	0098
RE133	0098
RE134	4167
RE135	2381
RE136	2024
RE137	2385
RE138	1429
RE140	2391
RE141	1436
RE142	2399
RE143	2206
RE144	1449
RE145	0221
RE146	1481
RE147	2406
RE148	1608
RE149	0505
RE150	0686
RE152	0864
RE153	1014
RE154	1145
RE155	1264
RE156	1392
RE157	1524
RE158	1071
RE159	1701
RE160	1707
RE161	1712
RE162	1725
RE163	1737
RE164	1761
RE165	1793
RE166	0070
RE-167	0769
RE167	0769
RE-168	0442
RE168	0442
RE169	2471
RE170	0707
RE-171	0934
RE171	0934
RE172	0240
RE-173	0464
RE173	0464
RE174	0095
RE-175	0671
RE175	0671
RE-176	0717
RE176	0717
RE177	0332
RE178	0720
RE179	2367
RE180	0404
RE181	3119
RE182	2378
RE183	0407

DEVICE TYPE	REPL CODE
RE184	3121
RE185	1403
RE186	0411
RE187	3123
RE188	2371
RE189	0418
RE-190	2704
RE190	5776
RE-191	0168
RE191	0168
RE-192	0111
RE192	0111
RE-193	0688
RE193	0688
RE-194	0930
RE194	0930
RE-195	0549
RE195	0623
RE196	0590
RE197	0786
RE198	1401
RE199	0212
RE200	0286
RE201	0830
RE202	0626
RE203	0930
RE204	1165
RE205	0419
RE206	0617
RE207	0710
RE208	0338
RE209	1581
RE210	0320
RE211	0431
RE212	2039
RE213	2035
RE214	0190
RE215	1061
RE216	0201
RE217	0374
RE218	0058
RE219	0527
RE220	0018
RE221	0848
RE222	0236
RE223	0676
RE224	1935
RE225	1313
RE226	2123
RE227	0312
RE228	0396
RE229	0219
RE230	0843
RE231	0239
RE232	0061
RE233	0309
RE234	1642
RE235	0006
RE236	1702
RE237	2313
RE238	1967
RE239	1973
RE240	5893
RE241	5894
RE242	1189
RE243	3805
RE244	1914
RE245	OEM
RE246	1129
RE247	0895
RE248	0895
RE249	3370
RE250	0139
RE251	0436
RE252	1823
RE253	0327
RE254	0149
RE255	0276
RE256	0899
RE257	0349
RE258	0103
RE259	3249
RE260	0224
RE261	0326
RE262	0615
RE263	0155
RE264	0488
RE265	1024
RE266	0715
RE-300-IC	0627
RE300-IC	0627
RE301-IC	0673
RE302-IC	2147
RE-303-IC	0797
RE303-IC	0797
RE-304-IC	0391
RE304-IC	0391
RE-305-IC	0167
RE305-IC	0167
RE-306-IC	0661
RE306-IC	0661
RE-307-IC	0348
RE307-IC	0348
RE308-IC	0350
RE309-IC	0696
RE-310-IC	1797
RE310-IC	1797
RE-311-IC	0659
RE311-IC	0659

DEVICE TYPE	REPL CODE
RE-312-IC	0746
RE312-IC	0746
RE-313-IC	0850
RE313-IC	0850
RE-314-IC	3690
RE314-IC	3690
RE-315-IC	1434
RE315-IC	1434
RE-316-IC	1748
RE316-IC	1748
RE-317-IC	1385
RE317-IC	1385
RE-318-IC	2264
RE318-IC	2264
RE-319-IC	0649
RE319-IC	0649
RE-320-IC	0438
RE320-IC	0438
RE-321-IC	0375
RE321-IC	0375
RE-322-IC	2535
RE322-IC	2535
RE-323-IC	0345
RE323-IC	0345
RE324-IC	1327
RE325-IC	0872
RE326-IC	1206
RE327-IC	0428
RE328-IC	0849
RE329-IC	1983
RE330-IC	1469
RE331-IC	0784
RE332-IC	2728
RE333-IC	0516
RE334-IC	0514
RE335-IC	0574
RE336-IC	2546
RE337-IC	0523
RE338-IC	2111
RE339-IC	1152
RE340-M	1012
RE340M	1012
RE341-M	2246
RE342-M	2300
RE343-IC	1624
RE344-M	0905
RE345-IC	1335
RE346-IC	0324
RE347-IC	6544
RE347M	3506
RE348-IC	1179
RE348-M	1179
RE348M	1179
RE349-IC	2849
RE349-M	2849
RE350M	OEM
RE351-IC	4031
RE352-IC	2573
RE353-M	2834
RE354-IC	1316
RE355-IC	2216
RE356-IC	2921
RE357-IC	1044
RE358-IC	2746
RE359-IC	2754
RE360-IC	4160
RE361-IC	2438
RE362-IC	1411
RE363-IC	OEM
RE364-IC	0360
RE367-IC	2864
RE368-IC	1826
RE369-IC	OEM
RE370-IC	2608
RE371-IC	OEM
RE372-IC	3859
RE373-IC	4514
RE374-IC	4515
RE375-IC	2051
RE376-IC	3332
RE377-IC	2914
RE378-IC	0167
RE379-IC	OEM
RE380-IC	3238
RE382-IC	0232
RE383-IC	1164
RE384-IC	1303
RE385-IC	1164
RE386-IC	1635
RE387-IC	1288
RE388-IC	1149
RE389-IC	2038
RE390-IC	1532
RE504	0229
RE664	OEM
RE670	OEM
RE896	OEM
RE1001	0144
RE1002	0144
RE2001	0007
RE2002	0007
RE3001	0127
RE3002	0127
RE4001	0111
RE4002	0111
RE4010	0111
RE5001	0007
RE5002	0007
RE136137	OEM

If replacement code is OEM, contact original manufacturer for replacement.

525

DEVICE TYPE	REPL CODE
REC86345	OEM
RECT-SI-154	0023
RECT-SI-154(AU)	0023
RECT-SI-1001	0790
RECT-SI-1001(AU)	0790
RECT-SI-1002	0023
RECT-SI-1002(AU)	0023
RECT-SI-1005	0023
RECT-SI-1019	0344
RECT-SI-1020	0023
RECT-SI-1021	0023
RECT-SI-1021(AU)	0023
RECT-SI-1026(AU)	0023
RECT-SI-1030	0015
RECT-SI-1039	0790
RECT-SI-1039(AU)	0790
RECT-SI-1044	0015
RECT-SI-1044(AU)	0015
RECT-U-007	OEM
RECT-U-1001	OEM
RECT-U-1002	OEM
RECT-U-1003	OEM
RECT-U-1004	OEM
RECT-U-1012	1999
RECT-UG-1002	1999
RECT-UG-1003	0276
RECT-UG-1004	0106
REF-01ADE	OEM
REF-01ADE/883B	OEM
REF-01AT	OEM
REF-01AT/883B	OEM
REF-01CDE	OEM
REF-01CT	OEM
REF-01DDE	OEM
REF-01DE	OEM
REF-01DE/883B	OEM
REF-01DT	OEM
REF-01EDE	OEM
REF-01ET	OEM
REF-01HDE	OEM
REF-01HT	OEM
REF-01T	OEM
REF-01T/883B	OEM
REF-02ADE	OEM
REF-02ADE/883B	OEM
REF-02AT	OEM
REF-02AT/883B	OEM
REF-02CDE	OEM
REF-02CT	OEM
REF-02DDE	OEM
REF-02DE	OEM
REF-02DE/883B	OEM
REF-02DT	OEM
REF-02EDE	OEM
REF-02ET	OEM
REF-02HDE	OEM
REF-02HT	OEM
REF-02T	OEM
REF-02T/883B	OEM
REF-03CDE	OEM
REF-03CNB	OEM
REF-03CT	OEM
REF-03DDE	OEM
REF-03DE/883B	OEM
REF-03DNB	OEM
REF-03DT	OEM
REF-03T	OEM
REF-03T/883B	OEM
REJ70148	0196
REJ70432	OEM
REJ70643	0015
REJ70931	0015
REJ71253	0133
REN56	2085
REN57	0886
REN58	0886
REN59	1471
REN60	0710
REN61	2002
REN62	0688
REN63	0006
REN64	0111
REN65	0349
REN66	0855
REN67	0111
REN68	0899
REN69	0050
REN70	0086
REN71	0617
REN72	0126
REN85	2959
REN90	0071
REN94	0124
REN100	0279
REN101	0595
REN102	0211
REN102A	0004
REN103	0038
REN103A	0208
REN104	0085
REN104MP	3004
REN105	0435
REN106	0150
REN107	0127
REN108	0144
REN109	0143
REN110	1106
REN112	0911
REN113	0196
REN114	0479
REN115	1073
REN116	0015
REN117	0229
REN118	0769
REN120	0469
REN121	0160
REN121MP	0265
REN123	0198
REN123A	0079
REN124	0142
REN125	0071
REN126	0136
REN127	0969
REN128	0086
REN129	0126
REN130	0103
REN131	0222
REN131MP	0816
REN132	0321
REN133	3443
REN134	0188
REN135	0162
REN136	0157
REN137	0631
REN138	0644
REN139	0012
REN140	0170
REN141	0789
REN142	0137
REN143	0361
REN144	0100
REN145	0002
REN146	0436
REN147	0039
REN148	1823
REN149	0778
REN150	0327
REN151	0149
REN152	0042
REN153	0919
REN154	0233
REN155	2736
REN156	0087
REN157	0275
REN158	0164
REN159	0037
REN160	0050
REN161	0007
REN162	0074
REN163	0637
REN164	0003
REN165	0065
REN166	0276
REN171	0283
REN172	0396
REN172A	0396
REN173	0290
REN173A	0290
REN173P	0290
REN175	0178
REN176	0841
REN177	0133
REN179	0599
REN180	1671
REN181	0130
REN182	0556
REN183	1190
REN184	0161
REN185	0455
REN186	0555
REN186A	0219
REN187	1257
REN188	0546
REN189	0378
REN190	0264
REN191	0334
REN192	0590
REN193	0786
REN194	0855
REN195A	0693
REN196	0419
REN197	0848
REN198	0168
REN199	0111
REN203	OEM
REN209	3467
REN210	0561
REN211	1357
REN218	0899
REN219	0486
REN220	0843
REN221	0349
REN222	0212
REN223	0103
REN224	0626
REN225	3249
REN226	1004
REN226MP	1851
REN229	0224
REN230	0239
REN231	0061
REN233	0326
REN234	0688
REN235	0930
REN236	0830
REN237	1401
REN238	0309
REN276	1642
REN280	0177
REN282	0617
REN287	0710
REN288	0338
REN289	0155
REN290	0006
REN291	0236
REN292	0676
REN293	0018
REN294	0527
REN295	1581
REN297	0320
REN298	0431
REN299	2039
REN300	2035
REN302	1165
REN311	0488
REN315	1967
REN322	1973
REN323	0886
REN324	1471
REN325	1189
REN358	1024
REN500A	0190
REN502	0201
REN503	0286
REN504	0374
REN506	0102
REN513	1313
REN521	3805
REN522	1493
REN523	1061
REN526A	1696
REN600	1914
REN601	0139
REN604	3638
REN612	0715
REN614	0030
REN703A	5849
REN705A	2147
REN708	0659
REN709	0673
REN712	0167
REN713	0661
REN714	0348
REN715	0350
REN718	0649
REN720	0438
REN721	2264
REN722	0696
REN723	1335
REN729	0324
REN731	2438
REN736	1748
REN737	1434
REN738	0850
REN739	0746
REN740	0375
REN742	3690
REN743	1385
REN744	1411
REN747	1797
REN748	0784
REN749	0391
REN755	2016
REN780	0360
REN783	0797
REN788	2728
REN790	0345
REN791	1327
REN797	0516
REN801	0514
REN804	2535
REN977	1288
REN1003	0574
REN1004	0872
REN1005	2546
REN1006	1206
REN1024	3506
REN1025	1179
REN1027	2849
REN1028	4479
REN1037	4031
REN1046	0523
REN1050	2864
REN1052	0428
REN1056	1826
REN1058	2111
REN1073	2573
REN1080	0849
REN1081A	1152
REN1082	2246
REN1087	1012
REN1090	2834
REN1092	2300
REN1096	1624
REN1099	4196
REN1100	0905
REN1102	2608
REN1103	1983
REN1127	4348
REN1128	3859
REN1130	1316
REN1131	4514
REN1132	4515
REN1133	2216
REN1134	2921
REN1135	2051
REN1142	1469
REN1153	3332
REN1155	1044
REN1161	2914
REN1162	3977
REN1163	2581
REN1164	3238
REN1165	2746
REN1166	2754
REN1167	1704
REN1174	2038
REN1192	1532
REN5061	2975
REN5062	OEM
REN5063	1302
REN5064	2981
REN5065	1703
REN5066	0289
REN5067	0451
REN5068	0528
REN5069	0446
REN5070	0298
REN5071	0025
REN5072	0244
REN5073	1075
REN5074	0313
REN5075	0416
REN5076	1639
REN5077	0490
REN5078	0943
REN5079	0526
REN5080	0560
REN5081	0398
REN5082	1596
REN5086	0346
REN5096	0098
REN5174	2024
REN5175	2385
REN5176	1429
REN5177	2391
REN5178	1436
REN5179	2399
REN5180	2206
REN5181	1449
REN5182	0221
REN5183	1481
REN5184	2406
REN5185	1608
REN5186	0505
REN5187	0686
REN5188	0864
REN5189	1014
REN5190	1145
REN5191	1264
REN5192	1392
REN5193	1524
REN5194	1071
REN5195	1701
REN5196	1707
REN5197	1712
REN5198	1725
REN5199	1737
REN5202	1761
REN5205	1793
REN5209	0070
REN5400	1129
REN5401	0340
REN5402	0895
REN5403	2326
REN5404	0058
REN5448	3370
REN5454	0442
REN5455	0934
REN5457	0095
REN5482	2471
REN5483	0240
REN5485	0671
REN5487	0332
REN5542	0707
REN5543	0464
REN5545	0717
REN5547	0720
REN5640	2367
REN5641	2378
REN5642	1403
REN5643	2371
REN5662	0404
REN5663	0407
REN5665	0411
REN5667	0418
REN5682	3119
REN5683	3121
REN5685	3123
REN6401	2123
REN6402	0312
REN6406	OEM
REN6408	5776
REN7400	0232
REN7473	1164
REN7474	1303
REN7493A	0564
REN74123	1149
REN74161	1635
RER-023	0907
RER023	0196
RET20	0015
RET-UG-1004	OEM
RF01F	0017
RF03C06	0286
RF-1	0023
RF1	0023
RF-1A	0023
RF1A	0023
RF1AV	0102
RF1B	0023
RF-1Z	0023
RF1Z	0023
RF10K35	0102
RF100	OEM
RF101	1325
RF200	0007
RF300	0604
RF414	OEM
RF1811	0143
RF2065	3528
RF2073	OEM
RF2084	OEM
RF3160	0015
RF3472	0015
RF5464-1P	0196
RF5465	0196
RF5465-1&	0196
RF5465-1P	0196
RF5794	0479
RF-6235-1	0015
RF7313	0142
RF26231-1	0015
RF26234-1	0015
RF26235-1	0015
RF26235-2	0015
RF26235-5	0015
RF29799P	0015
RF31903P	0015
RF32101-8	0015
RF32101-9	0015
RF32101R	0015
RF32102R	1293
RF32103-1	0769
RF32103R	0769
RF32412-3	0015
RF32426-7	0907
RF32645	0015
RF33426-7	0196
RF33550-1	0143
RF33976	0015
RF34383	0015
RF34661	0133
RF34720	0015
RF35123	0143
RF60034	0143
RFA70597	0015
RFA70600	0015
RFC61197	0015
RFC86345	OEM
RFH10N45	OEM
RFH12N35	OEM
RFH25N18	OEM
RFH25N20	OEM
RFH25P08	OEM
RFH25P10	OEM
RFH30N12	OEM
RFH30N15	OEM
RFH45N05	OEM
RFJ6134	0015
RFJ30704	0015
RFJ31218	0015
RFJ31362	0015
RFJ31363	0015
RFJ33292	0015
RFJ60033	0911
RFJ60172	0143
RFJ60173	0015
RFJ60174	0015
RFJ60286	0015
RFJ60313	0196
RFJ60366	0015
RFJ60614	0143
RFJ60869	0015
RFJ70147	0535
RFJ70148	0196
RFJ70149	0102
RFJ70161	OEM
RFJ70431	0196
RFJ70432	0015
RFJ70487	0015
RFJ70643	1073
RFJ70703	0015
RFJ70931	0015
RFJ70970	0015
RFJ70971	0102
RFJ70974	0015
RFJ70976	0102
RFJ70977	0015
RFJ71122	0015
RFJ71123	0087
RFJ71480	0012
RFJ72360	0015
RFJ72787	0015
RFK10N45	OEM
RFK10N50	OEM
RFK12N35	OEM
RFK12N40	OEM
RFK25N18	OEM
RFK25N20	OEM
RFK25P08	OEM
RFK25P10	OEM
RFK30N12	OEM
RFK30N15	OEM
RFK35N08	OEM
RFK35N10	OEM
RFK45N05	OEM
RFK45N06	OEM
RFL1N08	OEM
RFL1N08L	OEM
RFL1N10	OEM
RFL1N10L	OEM
RFL1N12	OEM
RFL1N12L	OEM
RFL1N15	OEM
RFL1N15L	OEM
RFL1N18	OEM
RFL1N18L	OEM
RFL1N20	OEM
RFL1N20L	OEM
RFL1P08	5778
RFL1P10	5778
RFL2N05	OEM
RFL2N06	OEM
RFL2N06L	OEM
RFL4N12	OEM
RFL4N15	OEM
RFL30596	0015
RFM3N45	OEM
RFM3N50	OEM
RFM4N35	OEM
RFM4N40	OEM
RFM5P12	OEM
RFM5P15	OEM
RFM6N45	OEM
RFM6N50	OEM
RFM6P08	OEM
RFM6P10	OEM
RFM8N18	OEM
RFM8N18L	OEM
RFM8N20	OEM
RFM8N20L	OEM
RFM8P08	OEM
RFM8P10	OEM
RFM10N12	OEM
RFM10N12L	OEM
RFM10N15	OEM
RFM10N15L	OEM
RFM10P12	OEM
RFM10P15	OEM
RFM12N08	OEM
RFM12N08L	OEM
RFM12N10	OEM
RFM12N10L	OEM
RFM12N18	2162
RFM12N20	2162
RFM12P08	OEM
RFM12P10	OEM
RFM15N05	OEM
RFM15N05L	OEM
RFM15N06	OEM
RFM15N06L	OEM
RFM15N12	OEM
RFM15N15	OEM
RFM18N08	4492
RFM18N10	4492
RFM25N05	5266
RFM25N06	5266
RFM33160	0015
RFP1N35	OEM
RFP1N40	OEM
RFP2N05L	OEM
RFP2N08	OEM
RFP2N08L	OEM
RFP2N10	OEM
RFP2N10L	OEM
RFP2N12	OEM
RFP2N12L	OEM
RFP2N15	6682
RFP2N15L	OEM
RFP2N18	OEM
RFP2N18L	OEM
RFP2N20	OEM
RFP2N20L	OEM
RFP2P08	2256
RFP2P10	3059
RFP3N45	5649
RFP3N50	5649
RFP4N05	OEM
RFP4N05L	OEM
RFP4N06	OEM
RFP4N06L	OEM
RFP4N35	OEM
RFP4N40	OEM
RFP5P12	6188
RFP5P15	6188
RFP6N45	6941
RFP6N50	1643
RFP6P08	6888
RFP6P10	3059
RFP8N18	2162
RFP8N18L	OEM
RFP8N20	2162
RFP8N20L	OEM
RFP8P08	2256
RFP8P10	2256
RFP10N12	2256
RFP10N12L	OEM
RFP10N15	2162
RFP10N15L	OEM
RFP10P12	OEM
RFP10P15	OEM
RFP12N08	4970
RFP12N08L	OEM
RFP12N10	4970
RFP12N10L	OEM
RFP12N18	2162
RFP12N20	2162
RFP12P08	5427
RFP12P10	5427
RFP15N05	5811
RFP15N05L	OEM
RFP15N06	5811
RFP15N06L	OEM
RFP15N12	OEM
RFP15N15	OEM
RFP18N08	OEM
RFP18N10	OEM
RFP25N05	OEM
RFP25N06	OEM
RFP33118	0015
RFS61436	0229
RFV60500	0015
RG010G	0023
RG1	0015
RG1A	0023
RG1B	0023
RG1D	0023
RG1G	0023
RG1J	0023
RG1K	0017
RG1M	0017
RG-2	0031
RG2	0031
RG2A	0031
RG2B	0031
RG2D	0031
RG2G	0031
RG2J	0031
RG2K	0102
RG2M	0102
RG-2V	0031
RG2V	0031
RG-2Y	0031
RG2Y	0031
RG2Z	0031
RG3	0031
RG3A	0031
RG3B	0031
RG3D	0031
RG3G	0031
RG3G-5007L	0031
RG3J	0031
RG3K	3159
RG3M	3159
RG4	0031
RG4A	0031
RG4B	0031
RG4C	3833
RG4D	0031
RG4G	0031
RG4J	0031
RG4K	3159
RG4LF-M1	OEM
RG4LFM1	0031
RG4M	3159
RG4Y	0031
RG4Z	0031
RG5LFM1	0031
RG100B	0015
RG100D	0015
RG100G	0015
RG100J	0015
RG600	OEM
RG601	OEM
RG602	3720
RG602T	3720
RG604	2663
RG604T	2663
RG606	0110
RG606T	0110
RG608	3846
RG608T	3846
RG610	2631
RG610T	2631
RG1004	0015
RG1127	0015
RGL27A	OEM
RGL27B	OEM
RGL27D	OEM
RGL27G	OEM
RGL27J	OEM
RGL27K	OEM
RGL27M	OEM
RGL41A	OEM
RGL41B	OEM
RGL41D	OEM
RGL41G	OEM
RGL41J	OEM
RGL41K	OEM
RGL41M	OEM
RGP01-08	0023
RGP01-10	0017
RGP01-12	0017
RGP01-14	0017
RGP01-16	0344
RGP01-17	0344
RGP01-17PKG23	0017
RGP01-18	0344
RGP01-20	0344
RGP02-17	OEM
RGP02-17EL	OEM
RGP10	0023

526

If replacement code is OEM, contact original manufacturer for replacement.

DEVICE TYPE	REPL CODE
RGP10-DG1	0080
RGP10A	3048
RGP-10B	0023
RGP10B	0023
RGP-10D	0023
RGP10D	3048
RGP10DG1	0604
RGP-10DGI	OEM
RGP-10G	0023
RGP10G	0023
RGP10GL	OEM
RGP10GL-6391	OEM
RGP10GPKG3	OEM
RGP10GPKG23	0023
RGP-10J	0023
RGP10J	0023
RGP10J,G23	0023
RGP10JG23	0023
RGP10J-T3	0023
RGP10J-Z	0023
RGP10K	0017
RGP10M	0017
RGP15-10	0017
RGP15-12	0017
RGP15-14	0017
RGP15-15	0017
RGP15-16	0344
RGP15-18	0344
RGP15-20	0344
RGP15A	0031
RGP15B	0031
RGP15D	0023
RGP-15G	2505
RGP15G	0031
RGP15GPKG23	0031
RGP15J	0031
RGP15K	0102
RGP15K-6179	OEM
RGP15M	0102
RGP18G	OEM
RGP20A	0031
RGP20B	0031
RGP20D	0031
RGP20G	0031
RGP20GL	0071
RGP20J	0031
RGP20K	0102
RGP20M	0102
RGP25A	0031
RGP25B	0031
RGP25D	0031
RGP25G	0031
RGP25J	0031
RGP25K	0071
RGP25M	0071
RGP30A	0541
RGP30B	0541
RGP30D	0541
RGP30G	0017
RGP30G-015	0031
RGP30G-5001L	0017
RGP30GJ	OEM
RGP30J	0031
RGP30K	3159
RGP30M	3159
RGP-100	0023
RGP100	0023
RGP150	OEM
RGP5040	0023
RGP5080	0071
RGP01-17PKG23	0017
RGPP1A	OEM
RGPP1B	OEM
RGPP1D	OEM
RGPP1G	OEM
RGPP1J	OEM
RGPP1K	OEM
RGPP5A	OEM
RGPP5B	OEM
RGPP5D	OEM
RGPP5G	OEM
RGPP5J	OEM
RGPP5K	OEM
RGPP10A	2068
RGPP10B	2068
RGPP10D	2068
RGPP10G	OEM
RGPP10J	0023
RGPP10K	0017
RGPP10M	0017
RGPP15A	2068
RGPP15B	2068
RGPP15D	2068
RGPP15G	OEM
RGPP15J	0031
RGPP15K	0102
RGPP15M	0102
RGPP30A	OEM
RGPP30B	OEM
RGPP30D	OEM
RGPP30G	OEM
RGPP30J	0031
RGPP30K	1917
RGPP30M	1917
RGPP60A	OEM
RGPP60B	OEM
RGPP60D	OEM
RGPP60G	OEM
RGPP60J	OEM

DEVICE TYPE	REPL CODE
RGPP60K	OEM
RGPP60M	OEM
RH-1	0023
RH1	0023
RH-1A	0023
RH1A	0023
RH-1AV1	0023
RH-1B	0102
RH1B	0102
RH-1BV	0023
RH-1B-Z	0102
RH-1C	0102
RH1C	0102
RH-1K0027CEZZ	OEM
RH-1M	0023
RH1M	0023
RH-1MV	0023
RH-1S	0023
RH1S	0023
RH1S-FAL	0023
RH1S-LFA1	0023
RH1S-T3	0023
RH1SV	0023
RH-1S-Z	0023
RH1S-Z	0023
RH-1V	0023
RH-1X0001TAZZ	0784
RH-1X0004CEZZ	0391
RH-1X0005PAZZ	1150
RH-1X0015TAZZ	0898
RH-1X0018TAZZ	2268
RH-1X0020CEZZ	0872
RH-1X0021CEZZ	0849
RH-1X0022CEZZ	3736
RH-1X0032CEZZ	0633
RH-1X0038CEZZ	0167
RH-1X0043CEZZ	0167
RH-1X0047CEZZ	4325
RH-1X0092CEZZ	0906
RH-1X1020AFZZ	1239
RH-1X1039AFZZ	4539
RH-1X1311AF	OEM
RH-1X1465AF	OEM
RH-1Z	0494
RH1Z	0023
RH-1ZM	0023
RH-1ZV	0023
RH1ZV	OEM
RH-2	OEM
RH-2D	0541
RH2D	0541
RH-2F	0017
RH2F	0017
RH2FM	0344
RH-2FS	0017
RH2FV	0017
RH10FV1	OEM
RH-12	OEM
RH-13	0581
RH120	0016
RH3761	0414
RH-DX0004TAZZ	6295
RH-DX0008CEZZ	0015
RH-DX0014-CEZZ	0023
RH-DX0017CEZZ	0102
RH-DX0025CEZZ	0023
RH-DX0026AGZZ	0015
RH-DX0028CEZZ	0182
RH-DX0029CEZZ	0182
RH-DX0033TAZZ	0133
RH-DX0038CEZZ	0023
RH-DX0039TAZZ	0102
RH-DX0041CEZZ	0196
RH-DX0042CEZZ	0015
RH-DX0043TAZZ	0023
RH-DX0045CEZZ	0124
RH-DX0045GEZZ	0124
RH-DX0046CEZZ	0133
RH-DX0047GEZZ	0730
RH-DX0048CEZZ	0133
RH-DX0048GEZZ	0133
RH-DX0049GEZZ	0494
RH-DX0051CEZZ	0102
RH-DX0052GEZZ	0023
RH-DX0053GEZZ	0124
RH-DX0054CEZZ	0133
RH-DX0055TAZZ	0015
RH-DX0056CEZZ	0015
RH-DX0056TAZZ	0102
RH-DX0059TAZZ	0015
RH-DX0062CEZZ	0102
RH-DX0063CEZZ	0102
RH-DX0064CEZZ	0023
RH-DX0065CEZZ	0102
RH-DX0065CZZ	0015
RH-DX0066TAZZ	0015
RH-DX0067TAZZ	0023
RH-DX0068TAZZ	0015
RH-DX0069TAZZ	0790
RH-DX0072CEZZ	0015
RH-DX0072TAZZ	OEM
RH-DX0073CEZZ	0023
RH-DX0073TAZZ	1404
RH-DX0077CEZZ	0344
RH-DX0079TAZZ	0015
RH-DX0081CEZZ	0015
RH-DX0081TAZZ	0015
RH-DX0083CEZZ	0015
RH-DX0085TAZZ	0023

DEVICE TYPE	REPL CODE
RH-DX0086TAZZ	0023
RHDX0086TAZZ	0023
RH-DX0090CEZZ	0344
RH-DX0091CEZZ	0087
RH-DX0092CEZZ	0071
RH-DX0094CEZZ	OEM
RH-DX0096CEZZ	0344
RH-DX0100CEZZ	0344
RH-DX0101-CEZZ	0023
RH-DX0101CEZZ	0023
RHDX0101CEZZ	0023
RH-DX0103CEZZ	OEM
RH-DX0104CEZZ	0182
RH-DX0105TAZZ	0023
RH-DX0105TEZZ	OEM
RH-DX0106CEZZ	0023
RH-DX0110CEZZ	0790
RH-DX0114CEZZ	0023
RH-DX0115CEZZ	0023
RH-DX0115TAZZ	0071
RH-DX0117TAZZ	0023
RH-DX0123CEZZ	0023
RHDX0123CEZZ	0023
RH-DX0126CEZZ	0023
RH-DX0130CEZZ	0023
RH-DX0131CEZZ	0023
RH-DX0132CEZZ	6198
RH-DX0136TAZZ	0071
RH-DX0142CEZZ	0133
RH-DX0152CEZZ	0468
RH-DX0154CEZZ	0023
RH-DX0155CEZZ	0023
RH-DX0179CEZZ	0124
RH-DX0181CEZZ	0031
RH-DX0190CEZZ	0017
RH-DX0200CEZZ	1864
RH-DX0202CEZZ	0023
RH-DX0203CEZZ	0031
RH-DX0204CEZZ	1083
RH-DX0208CEZZ	1864
RH-DX0214CEZZ	OEM
RH-DX0220CEZZ	0604
RH-DX0226CEZZ	0023
RH-DX0229CEZZ	0102
RH-DX0234CEZZ	0031
RH-DX0235CEZZ	0023
RH-DX0236CEZZ	0133
RH-DX0237CEZZ	0124
RH-DX0247CEZZ	0282
RH-DX0248CEZZ	0023
RH-DX0255CEZZ	OEM
RH-DX0259CEZZ	OEM
RH-DX0284CEZZ	OEM
RH-DX0302CEZZ	OEM
RH-DX0382CEZZ	OEM
RH-DXOL05TAZZ	1208
RH-DX1005AFZZ	0015
RH-DX0045GEZZ	OEM
RH-DY0003SEZZ	0015
RH-DZA008WRE0	OEM
RH-EX0002AEZZ	5900
RH-EX0003CEZZ	OEM
RH-EX002YTAZZ	0162
RH-EX0010GEZZ	0253
RH-EX0011CEZZ	0361
RH-EX0011GEZZ	0681
RH-EX0012CEZZ	0398
RH-EX0013CEZZ	0943
RH-EX0015CEZZ	0137
RH-EX0017CEZZ	0137
RH-EX0019CEZZ	0025
RH-EX0019GEZZ	0681
RH-EX0019TAZZ	0053
RH-EX0020CEZZ	OEM
RH-EX0020GEZZ	0041
RH-EX0021TAZZ	0181
RH-EX0022CEZZ	0943
RH-EX0022TAZZ	0181
RH-EX0023GEZZ	0170
RH-EX0024CEZZ	0466
RH-EX0024GEZZ	2500
RH-EX0024TAZZ	5770
RH-EX0033CEZZ	0039
RH-EX0034CEZZ	0398
RH-EX0037CEZZ	0526
RH-EX0038CEZZ	0137
RH-EX0041TAZZ	0062
RH-EX0042TAZZ	0140
RH-EX0043CEZZ	0195
RH-EX0043TAZZ	0041
RH-EX0044CEZZ	0064
RH-EX0045GEZZ	OEM
RH-EX0045TAZZ	OEM
RH-EX0046TAZZ	0077
RH-EX0047CEZZ	0999
RH-EX0047GEZZ	0140
RH-EX0047TAZZ	0064
RH-EX0048CEZZ	0466
RH-EX0049CEZZ	0041
RH-EX0049TAZZ	0877
RH-EX0053CEZZ	0010
RH-EX0053GEZZ	0253
RH-EX0053TAZZ	0466
RH-EX0054CEZZ	0186
RH-EX0057CEZZ	1823
RH-EX0057GEZZ	0466
RH-EX0061CEZZ	0137
RH-EX0062CEZZ	0102
RH-EX0063GEZZ	OEM

DEVICE TYPE	REPL CODE
RH-EX0065CEZZ	0440
RH-EX0072CEZZ	0526
RH-EX0074CEZZ	0642
RH-EX0084CEZZ	1181
RH-EX0084GEZZ	OEM
RH-EX0085CEZZ	0062
RH-EX0088CEZZ	0062
RH-EX0089CEZZ	0165
RH-EX0091CEZZ	0700
RH-EX0092CEZZ	0372
RH-EX0094CEZZ	4497
RH-EX0095GEZZ	OEM
RH-EX0098CEZZ	0700
RH-EX013CEZZ	0943
RH-EX022CEZZ	0943
RH-EX0101CEZZ	0755
RH-EX0102CEZZ	6652
RH-EX0103CEZZ	0253
RH-EX0106CEZZ	0049
RH-EX0112CEZZ	0371
RH-EX0116CEZZ	OEM
RH-EX0116GEZZ	0062
RH-EX0130CEZZ	0695
RH-EX0130GEZZ	0140
RH-EX0131CEZZ	0041
RH-EX0136CEZZ	0814
RH-EX0137CEZZ	0041
RH-EX0137GEZZ	OEM
RH-EX0137TAZZ	0140
RH-EX0138CEZZ	0062
RH-EX0139CEZZ	0162
RH-EX0140CEZZ	0062
RH-EX0145CEZZ	OEM
RH-EX0152CEZZ	OEM
RH-EX0152GEZZ	OEM
RH-EX0153CEZZ	OEM
RH-EX0154CEZZ	4448
RH-EX0155CEZZ	0062
RH-EX0156CEZZ	OEM
RH-EX0161CEZZ	0077
RH-EX0163CEZZ	0156
RH-EX0163GEZZ	0999
RH-EX0166CEZZ	0681
RH-EX0188GEZZ	OEM
RH-EX0192CEZZ	0631
RH-EX0193CEZZ	0181
RH-EX0198GEZZ	OEM
RH-EX0200CEZZ	0052
RH-EX0206CEZZ	OEM
RH-EX0207CEZZ	0195
RH-EX0217CEZZ	0873
RH-EX0219CEZZ	0166
RH-EX0223CEZZ	OEM
RH-EX0232CEZZ	1266
RH-EX0238CEZZ	OEM
RH-EX0247CEZZ	0631
RH-EX0255CEZZ	4999
RH-EX0294CEZZ	OEM
RH-EX0296CEZZ	5594
RH-EX0297CEZZ	OEM
RH-EX0300CEZZ	OEM
RH-EX0300CEZZ0	OEM
RH-EX0302CEZZ	OEM
RH-EX0309CEZZ	OEM
RH-EX0311CEZZ	OEM
RH-EX0313CEZZ	OEM
RH-EX0314CEZZ	OEM
RH-EX0322CEZZ	OEM
RH-EX0375GEZZ	0877
RH-EX0397CEZZ	OEM
RH-EX0398CEZZ	OEM
RH-EX0413GEZZ	OEM
RH-EX0417GEZZ	OEM
RH-EX0443CEZZ	0036
RH-EX0444CEZZ	0372
RH-EX0586CEZZ	4171
RH-EX0592CEZZ	4168
RH-EX0598CEZZ	OEM
RH-EX0625GEZZ	OEM
RH-EX0664GEZZ	0195
RH-FX0003CEZZ	0311
RH-FX0007CEZZ	1158
RH-FX0008CEZZ	1281
RH-FX0011CEZZ	1158
RH-FX0014CEZZ	1281
RH-FX0018CEZZ	0112
RH-I2157CEN1	OEM
RH-I2157CEZZ	OEM
RH-IX00004CEZZ	0391
RH-IX0001PAZZ	0851
RH-IX0001TAZZ	0784
RH-IX0004CE	0391
RH-IX0004CEZZ	0391
RH-IX0005PAZZ	1150
RH-IX0007TAZZ	OEM
RH-IX0012PAZZ	0357
RH-IX0013AEZZ	OEM
RH-IX0014PAZZ	0619
RH-IX0015TAZZ	4539
RH-IX0017AAZZ	OEM
RH-IX0017TAZZ	0167
RH-IX0018TAZZ	2268
RH-IX0020CE	0872
RH-IX0020CEZZ	0872
RH-IX0021CEZZ	0849
RH-IX0021PAZZ	OEM
RH-IX0022CEZZ	3736
RH-IX0022PAZZ	OEM
RH-IX0023CEZZ	2569

DEVICE TYPE	REPL CODE
RH-IX0023PAZZ	OEM
RH-IX0024CEZZ	4899
RH-IX0024PAZZ	3865
RH-IX0025CEZZ	2864
RH-IX0025PAZZ	2131
RH-IX0027CEZZ	OEM
RH-IX0027PAZZ	OEM
RH-IX0028CEZZ	OEM
RH-IX0028PAZZ	2122
RH-IX0032CEZZ	0633
RH-IX0034PAZZ	OEM
RH-IX0035GAZZ	0898
RH-IX0035PAZZ	OEM
RH-IX0035TAZZ	0898
RH-IX0037CEZZ	1319
RH-IX0038CEZZ	OEM
RH-IX0038PAZZ	1197
RH-IX0039PAZZ	0936
RH-IX0040PAZZ	0175
RH-IX0041PAZZ	1149
RH-IX0042PAZZ	1261
RH-IX0043CE	0167
RH-IX0043CEZZ	0167
RH-IX0045CEZZ	OEM
RH-IX0047CE	4325
RH-IX0047CEZZ	4325
RH-IX0047PAZZ	OEM
RH-IX0048CEZZ	4535
RH-IX0050PAZZ	OEM
RH-IX0054CEZZ	2845
RH-IX0056CEZZ	OEM
RH-IX0058GEZZ	OEM
RH-IX0061CEZZ	OEM
RH-IX0065CEZZ	1420
RH-IX0069CEZZ	0473
RH-IX0072CEZZ	0215
RH-IX0072PAZZ	1569
RH-IX0092CEZZ	0069
RH-IX0092CFZZ	OEM
RH-IX0093CEZZ	2043
RH-IX0094CEZZ	4071
RH-IX0108CEZZ	OEM
RH-IX0111CEZZ	1288
RH-IX0111CFZZ	OEM
RH-IX0113CEZZ	OEM
RH-IX0114PAZZ	1819
RH-IX0116CEZZ	1329
RH-IX0130CEZZ	OEM
RH-iX0137CEZZ	2180
RH-IX0144CEZZ	OEM
RH-IX0199CEZZ	2079
RH-IX0200CEZZ	OEM
RH-IX0203GEZZ	2641
RH-IX0205GEZZ	OEM
RH-IX0212CEZZ	3640
RH-IX0212GEZZ	OEM
RH-IX0213CEZZ	2868
RH-IX0214CEZZ	3726
RH-IX0223CEZZ	4047
RH-IX0224CEZZ	4899
RH-IX0225CEZZ	3299
RH-IX0228CEZZ	OEM
RH-IX0234GEZZ	OEM
RH-IX0238CEZZ	2031
RH-IX0252CEZZ	0069
RH-IX0258GEZZ	OEM
RH-IX0260CEZZ	2641
RH-IX0269CEZZ	OEM
RH-IX0270CEZZ	OEM
RH-IX0275CEZZ	4047
RH-IX0280CEZZ	OEM
RH-IX0308CEZZ	OEM
RH-IX0314CEZZ	OEM
RH-IX0321CEZZ	OEM
RH-IX0325CEZZ	6047
RH-IX0359CEZZ	OEM
RH-IX0360PAZZ	OEM
RH-IX0406GEZZ	OEM
RH-IX0416CEZZ	4009
RH-IX0424CEZZ	OEM
RH-IX0430GEZZ	OEM
RH-IX0450CEZZ	4246
RH-IX0453CEZZ	OEM
RH-IX0454CEZZ	OEM
RH-IX0468GEZZ	OEM
RH-IX0470GEZZ	OEM
RH-IX0474GEZZ	OEM
RH-IX0478PAZZ	OEM
RH-IX0487CEZZ	2254
RH-IX0488CEZZ	0412
RH-IX0499CEZZ	1594
RH-IX0508GEZZ	OEM
RH-IX0528GEZZ	OEM
RH-IX0539CEZZ	OEM
RH-IX0550GEZZ	OEM
RHIX0550GEZZ	OEM
RH-IX0564CEZZ	OEM
RH-IX0579CEZZ	OEM
RH-IX0580CEZZ	OEM
RH-IX0581CEZZ	OEM
RH-IX0600CEZZ	3206
RH-IX0614CEZZ	OEM
RH-IX0633CEZZ	4271
RH-IX0634CEZZ	OEM
RH-IX0669CEZZ	OEM
RH-IX0692CEZZ	OEM
RH-IX0715CEZZ	OEM
RH-IX0717CEZZ	OEM
RH-IX0733PAZZ	OEM

DEVICE TYPE	REPL CODE
RH-IX0735CEZZ	OEM
RH-IX0740CEZZ	OEM
RH-IX0740PAZZ	OEM
RH-IX0758CEZZ	OEM
RH-IX0800CEZZ	OEM
RH-IX0820CEZZ	OEM
RH-IX0854CEZZ	OEM
RH-IX0920PAZZ	OEM
RH-IX0930CEZZ	OEM
RH-IX0943CEZZ	OEM
RH-IX0948CEZZ	4066
RH-IX0950CEZZ	OEM
RH-IX0996CEZZ	OEM
RH-IX212CEZZ	OEM
RH-IX1016AFZZ	OEM
RH-IX1018AFZZ	4710
RH-IX1020AFZZ	1239
RH-IX1023CEZZ	OEM
RH-IX1030AFZZ	3606
RH-IX1030CEZZ	OEM
RH-IX1031AFZZ	OEM
RH-IX1036AFZZ	OEM
RH-IX1037AFZZ	OEM
RH-IX1038AFZZ	3262
RH-IX1039AFZZ	4543
RH-IX1067AFZZ	OEM
RH-IX1068AFZZ	1532
RH-IX1077CEZZ	OEM
RH-IX1078CEZZ	OEM
RH-IX1112CEZZ	6648
RH-IX1113CEZZ	OEM
RH-IX1132CEZZ	OEM
RH-IX1169CEZZ	OEM
RH-IX1190CEZZ	3473
RH-IX1231CEZZ	OEM
RH-IX1247CEZZ	OEM
RH-IX1311AF	OEM
RHIX1311AF	OEM
RHIX1311AFZZ	OEM
RH-IX1332AFZZ	OEM
RH-IX1505CEZZ	OEM
RH-IX1535CEZZ	OEM
RH-IX1553CEZZ	OEM
RH-IX1590CEZZ	OEM
RH-IX1675CEZZ	OEM
RH-IX1676CEZZ	OEM
RH-IX1705CEZZ	OEM
RH-IX1709CEZZ	OEM
RH-IX1712CEZZ	3473
RH-IX1750CEZZ	OEM
RH-iX2092CEZZ	OEM
RH-iX2157CEN1	OEM
RH-iX2157CEN2	OEM
RH-iX2157CEN3	OEM
RH-iX2157CEZZ	OEM
RH-iX2163CEZZ	OEM
RH-IX2195CEZZ	OEM
RH-iX2281CEZZ	OEM
RH-IX0137CEZZ	OEM
RH-IZ0008CEZZ	OEM
RH-IZ008CEZZ	OEM
RH-IZ0027CEZZ	OEM
RH-IZ0073CEZZ	OEM
RH-PH0167CEZZ	OEM
RH-PX0003GEZZ	OEM
RH-PX0012CEZZ	OEM
RH-PX0016CEZZ	OEM
RH-PX0033GEZZ	OEM
RH-PX0034GEZZ	OEM
RH-PX0040GEZZ	OEM
RH-PX0053GEZZ	OEM
RH-PX0068PAZZ	OEM
RH-PX0069CEZZ	OEM
RH-PX0085CEZZ	OEM
RH-PX0092CEZZ	OEM
RH-PX0095CEZZ	OEM
RH-PX0097PAZZ	OEM
RH-PX0102CEZZ	OEM
RH-PX0109PAZZ	OEM
RH-PX0119CEZZ	OEM
RH-PX0127CEZZ	OEM
RH-PX0133CEZZ	OEM
RH-PX0135GEZZ	OEM
RH-PX0140CEZZ	OEM
RH-PX0142PAZZ	OEM
RH-PX0143CEZZ	OEM
RH-PX0153CEZZ	OEM
RH-PX0159GEZZ	OEM
RH-PX0161CEZZ	OEM
RH-PX0167CEZZ	OEM
RH-PX0168CEZZ	OEM
RH-PX0183CEZZ	OEM
RH-PX0195CEZZ	OEM
RH-PX0207CEZZ	OEM
RH-PX0218CEZZ	OEM
RH-PX0219CEZZ	OEM
RH-PX0222CEZZ	OEM
RH-PX0223CEZZ	OEM
RH-PX0226CEZZ	OEM
RH-PX0238CEZZ	OEM
RH-PX0242CEZZ	OEM
RH-PX0265CEZZ	OEM
RH-PX0304CEZZ	OEM
RH-VX0004TAZZ	0120
RH-VX0006CEZZ	OEM
RH-VX0009TAZZ	0139
RH-VX0014TAZZ	0139
RI1A	0023
RI1B	OEM

DEVICE TYPE	REPL CODE
RI1C	OEM
RI2	OEM
RI2B	OEM
RI4010658	0124
RJF60313	0196
RK-13	2520
RK13	2520
RK14	2520
RK34	2520
RK39	3559
RK43	0031
RK44	0031
RK46	3559
RK46LF-L1	3559
RKBP005	OEM
RKBP01	OEM
RKBP02	OEM
RKBP04	OEM
RKBP06	OEM
RKBP08	OEM
RKBP10	OEM
RKBPC101	OEM
RKBPC102	OEM
RKBPC104	OEM
RKBPC106	OEM
RKBPC108	OEM
RKBPC110	OEM
RKBPC601	OEM
RKBPC602	OEM
RKBPC604	OEM
RKBPC606	OEM
RKBPC608	OEM
RKBPC610	OEM
RKBPC801	OEM
RKBPC802	OEM
RKBPC804	OEM
RKBPC806	OEM
RKBPC808	OEM
RKBPC810	OEM
RKBPC1005	OEM
RKBPC6005	OEM
RKBPC8005	OEM
RL005	0071
RL010	0071
RL020	0071
RL040	0071
RL060	0071
RL1N4002	0080
RL-2Z	0541
RL2Z	0541
RL31	0143
RL32	0143
RL32G	0143
RL34	0143
RL34G	0143
RL41	0143
RL41G	0143
RL42	0143
RL43	0143
RL43G	0143
RL44	OEM
RL44G	0143
RL52	0143
RL55-5	1978
RL101F	0023
RL101G	0015
RL102F	0023
RL102G	0015
RL103F	0023
RL103G	0015
RL104F	0023
RL104G	0015
RL105F	0023
RL105G	0015
RL106F	0017
RL106G	0087
RL107F	0017
RL107G	0087
RL151	0102
RL151G	OEM
RL-152	0947
RL152	0102
RL152G	OEM
RL153	0102
RL153G	OEM
RL154	0102
RL154G	OEM
RL155	0102
RL155G	OEM
RL156	0102
RL156G	OEM
RL157	0102
RL157G	OEM
RL201	0102
RL201G	0087
RL202	0102
RL202-M11	OEM
RL202G	0087
RL203	0102
RL203G	0087
RL204	0102
RL204G	0087
RL205	0102
RL205G	0087
RL206	0102
RL206G	0087
RL207	0102
RL207G	0087
RL209-1	2990

If replacement code is OEM, contact original manufacturer for replacement.

527

DEVICE TYPE	REPL CODE
RL232	OEM
RL232B	OEM
RL232G	0143
RL246	0143
RL247	0143
RL247G	0143
RL251	0071
RL252	0071
RL253	0071
RL254	0071
RL255	0071
RL256	0071
RL257	0071
RL709T	1291
RLC312	OEM
RLF1G	0015
RLH111	0507
RLM2902M	OEM
RLM2904M	OEM
RLR4001	OEM
RLR4002	OEM
RLR4003	OEM
RLR4004	OEM
RLS-71	OEM
RLS-72	OEM
RLS72	OEM
RLS-73	OEM
RLS73	OEM
RLS73TE11	OEM
RLS-92	OEM
RLS-93	OEM
RLS-94	OEM
RLS-135	OEM
RLS135	OEM
RLS-139	OEM
RLS-140	OEM
RLS-141	OEM
RLS-142	OEM
RLS-143	OEM
RLS-144	OEM
RLS914	OEM
RLS914A	OEM
RLS914B	OEM
RLS916	OEM
RLS916A	OEM
RLS916B	OEM
RLS3064	OEM
RLS3600	OEM
RLS3604	OEM
RLS3605	OEM
RLS3606	OEM
RLS-4148	OEM
RLS4148	OEM
RLS-4149	OEM
RLS4149	OEM
RLS-4150	OEM
RLS4150	OEM
RLS-4151	OEM
RLS4151	OEM
RLS-4152	OEM
RLS4152	OEM
RLS-4153	OEM
RLS4153	OEM
RLS-4154	OEM
RLS4154	OEM
RLS-4446	OEM
RLS4446	OEM
RLS-4447	OEM
RLS4447	OEM
RLS-4448	OEM
RLS4448	OEM
RLS-4449	OEM
RLS4449	OEM
RLS-4450	OEM
RLS4450	OEM
RLS-4454	OEM
RLS4454	OEM
RLS-4606	OEM
RLS4606	OEM
RLV11	OEM
RLZ-4.7	OEM
RLZ-5.1	OEM
RLZ5.1B	OEM
RLZ5.1B-TE-11	OEM
RLZ-5.6	OEM
RLZ5.6B	OEM
RLZ5.6B-TE-11	OEM
RLZ-6.2	OEM
RLZ-6.8	OEM
RLZ6.8B	OEM
RLZ6.8B-TE-11	OEM
RLZ-7.5	OEM
RLZ-8.2	OEM
RLZ8.2	OEM
RLZ8.2-TE-11	OEM
RLZ8.2A	OEM
RLZ8.2A-TE-11	OEM
RLZ8.2ATE-11	OEM
RLZ-9.1	OEM
RLZ9.1A	OEM
RLZ-10	OEM
RLZ-11	OEM
RLZ-12	OEM
RLZ-13	OEM
RLZ-15	OEM
RLZ-16	OEM
RLZ-18	OEM
RLZ-20	OEM
RLZ-22	OEM
RLZ-24	OEM
RLZ746	OEM
RLZ746A	OEM
RLZ747	OEM
RLZ747A	OEM
RLZ748	OEM
RLZ748A	OEM
RLZ749	OEM
RLZ749A	OEM
RLZ750	OEM
RLZ750A	OEM
RLZ751	OEM
RLZ751A	OEM
RLZ752	OEM
RLZ752A	OEM
RLZ753	OEM
RLZ753A	OEM
RLZ754	OEM
RLZ754A	OEM
RLZ755	OEM
RLZ755A	OEM
RLZ756	OEM
RLZ756A	OEM
RLZ757	OEM
RLZ757A	OEM
RLZ758	OEM
RLZ758A	OEM
RLZ759	OEM
RLZ759A	OEM
RLZ957	OEM
RLZ957A	OEM
RLZ957B	OEM
RLZ958	OEM
RLZ958A	OEM
RLZ958B	OEM
RLZ959	OEM
RLZ959A	OEM
RLZ959B	OEM
RLZ960	OEM
RLZ960A	OEM
RLZ960B	OEM
RLZ961	OEM
RLZ961A	OEM
RLZ961B	OEM
RLZ962	OEM
RLZ962A	OEM
RLZ962B	OEM
RLZ963	OEM
RLZ963A	OEM
RLZ963B	OEM
RLZ964	OEM
RLZ964A	OEM
RLZ964B	OEM
RLZ965	OEM
RLZ965A	OEM
RLZ965B	OEM
RLZ966	OEM
RLZ966A	OEM
RLZ966B	OEM
RLZ967	OEM
RLZ967A	OEM
RLZ967B	OEM
RLZ968	OEM
RLZ968A	OEM
RLZ968B	OEM
RLZ969	OEM
RLZ969A	OEM
RLZ969B	OEM
RLZ970	OEM
RLZ970A	OEM
RLZ970B	OEM
RLZ971	OEM
RLZ971A	OEM
RLZ971B	OEM
RLZ972	OEM
RLZ972A	OEM
RLZ972B	OEM
RLZ973	OEM
RLZ973A	OEM
RLZ973B	OEM
RLZ5226	OEM
RLZ5226A	OEM
RLZ5226B	OEM
RLZ5226C	OEM
RLZ5226D	OEM
RLZ5227	OEM
RLZ5227A	OEM
RLZ5227B	OEM
RLZ5227C	OEM
RLZ5227D	OEM
RLZ5228	OEM
RLZ5228A	OEM
RLZ5228B	OEM
RLZ5228C	OEM
RLZ5228D	OEM
RLZ5229	OEM
RLZ5229A	OEM
RLZ5229B	OEM
RLZ5229C	OEM
RLZ5229D	OEM
RLZ5230	OEM
RLZ5230A	OEM
RLZ5230B	OEM
RLZ5230C	OEM
RLZ5230D	OEM
RLZ5231	OEM
RLZ5231A	OEM
RLZ5231B	OEM
RLZ5231C	OEM
RLZ5231D	OEM
RLZ5232	OEM
RLZ5232A	OEM
RLZ5232B	OEM
RLZ5232C	OEM
RLZ5232D	OEM
RLZ5233	OEM
RLZ5233A	OEM
RLZ5233B	OEM
RLZ5233C	OEM
RLZ5233D	OEM
RLZ5234	OEM
RLZ5234A	OEM
RLZ5234B	OEM
RLZ5234C	OEM
RLZ5234D	OEM
RLZ5235	OEM
RLZ5235A	OEM
RLZ5235B	OEM
RLZ5235C	OEM
RLZ5235D	OEM
RLZ5236	OEM
RLZ5236A	OEM
RLZ5236B	OEM
RLZ5236C	OEM
RLZ5236D	OEM
RLZ5237	OEM
RLZ5237A	OEM
RLZ5237B	OEM
RLZ5237C	OEM
RLZ5237D	OEM
RLZ5238	OEM
RLZ5238A	OEM
RLZ5238B	OEM
RLZ5238C	OEM
RLZ5238D	OEM
RLZ5239	OEM
RLZ5239A	OEM
RLZ5239B	OEM
RLZ5239C	OEM
RLZ5239D	OEM
RLZ5240	OEM
RLZ5240A	OEM
RLZ5240B	OEM
RLZ5240C	OEM
RLZ5240D	OEM
RLZ5241	OEM
RLZ5241A	OEM
RLZ5241B	OEM
RLZ5241C	OEM
RLZ5241D	OEM
RLZ5242	OEM
RLZ5242A	OEM
RLZ5242B	OEM
RLZ5242C	OEM
RLZ5242D	OEM
RLZ5243	OEM
RLZ5243A	OEM
RLZ5243B	OEM
RLZ5243C	OEM
RLZ5243D	OEM
RLZ5244	OEM
RLZ5244A	OEM
RLZ5244B	OEM
RLZ5244C	OEM
RLZ5244D	OEM
RLZ5245	OEM
RLZ5245A	OEM
RLZ5245B	OEM
RLZ5245C	OEM
RLZ5245D	OEM
RLZ5246	OEM
RLZ5246A	OEM
RLZ5246B	OEM
RLZ5246C	OEM
RLZ5246D	OEM
RLZ5247	OEM
RLZ5247A	OEM
RLZ5247B	OEM
RLZ5247C	OEM
RLZ5247D	OEM
RLZ5248	OEM
RLZ5248A	OEM
RLZ5248B	OEM
RLZ5248C	OEM
RLZ5248D	OEM
RLZ5249	OEM
RLZ5249A	OEM
RLZ5249B	OEM
RLZ5249C	OEM
RLZ5249D	OEM
RLZ5250	OEM
RLZ5250A	OEM
RLZ5250B	OEM
RLZ5250C	OEM
RLZ5250D	OEM
RLZ5251	OEM
RLZ5251A	OEM
RLZ5251B	OEM
RLZ5251C	OEM
RLZ5251D	OEM
RLZ5252	OEM
RLZ5252A	OEM
RLZ5252B	OEM
RLZ5252C	OEM
RLZ5252D	OEM
RLZ5253	OEM
RLZ5253A	OEM
RLZ5253B	OEM
RLZ5253C	OEM
RLZ5253D	OEM
RLZ5254	OEM
RLZ5254A	OEM
RLZ5254B	OEM
RLZ5254C	OEM
RLZ5254D	OEM
RLZ5255	OEM
RLZ5255A	OEM
RLZ5255B	OEM
RLZ5255C	OEM
RLZ5255D	OEM
RLZ5256	OEM
RLZ5256A	OEM
RLZ5256B	OEM
RLZ5256C	OEM
RLZ5256D	OEM
RLZ5257	OEM
RLZ5257A	OEM
RLZ5257B	OEM
RLZ5257C	OEM
RLZ5257D	OEM
RLZ5258	OEM
RLZ5258A	OEM
RLZ5258B	OEM
RLZ5258C	OEM
RLZ5258D	OEM
RLZ5259	OEM
RLZ5259A	OEM
RLZ5259B	OEM
RLZ5259C	OEM
RLZ5259D	OEM
RLZ5260	OEM
RLZ5260A	OEM
RLZ5260B	OEM
RLZ5260C	OEM
RLZ5260D	OEM
RLZ5261	OEM
RLZ5261A	OEM
RLZ5261B	OEM
RLZ5261C	OEM
RLZ5261D	OEM
RLZ5262	OEM
RLZ5262A	OEM
RLZ5262B	OEM
RLZ5262C	OEM
RLZ5262D	OEM
RLZ5263	OEM
RLZ5263A	OEM
RLZ5263B	OEM
RLZ5263C	OEM
RLZ5263D	OEM
RLZ5264	OEM
RLZ5264A	OEM
RLZ5264B	OEM
RLZ5264C	OEM
RLZ5264D	OEM
RLZ5265	OEM
RLZ5265A	OEM
RLZ5265B	OEM
RLZ5265C	OEM
RLZ5265D	OEM
RLZ5266	OEM
RLZ5266A	OEM
RLZ5266B	OEM
RLZ5266C	OEM
RLZ5266D	OEM
RM01	OEM
RM-1	0023
RM1	0023
RM-1A	0023
RM1A	0023
RM-1AV	0015
RM-1B	0072
RM1B	0072
RM1C	0071
RM1D	0102
RM1E	0102
RM1F	0017
RM1S	0023
RM-1V	0015
RM1V	0023
RM-1Z	0015
RM1Z	0023
RM1ZM	0015
RM-1ZMV	0023
RM1ZMV	0023
RM-1ZV	0023
RM1ZV	0015
RM-2	0071
RM2	0071
RM2-C-Z	0071
RM-2A	0559
RM2A	0559
RM-2AV	0559
RM2AV	0071
RM-2AVTA	0559
RM2B	0071
RM-2C	2613
RM2C	0023
RM2C-LAF1	OEM
RM2C-LFA1	0071
RM2CS	0071
RM2CV	0071
RM2C-Z	0071
RM-2SC	0071
RM-2V	0071
RM2Z	0015
RM2ZLFB1	OEM
RM-4	OEM
RM4	0071
RM-4A	0959
RM4A	4052
RM4B	0071
RM4C	0071
RM4Y	0071
RM4Z	0071
RM4Z-LFK5	OEM
RM10	0023
RM10A	0071
RM10B	0071
RM10F	OEM
RM10M	0071
RM10MV	0071
RM10N	OEM
RM10TA-H	OEM
RM10TA-M	OEM
RM10Z	0071
RM11	0559
RM11A	0559
RM-11B	0071
RM11B	0071
RM11BV	0559
RM11C	0071
RM12M	OEM
RM15	0023
RM15TA-H	OEM
RM15TA-M	OEM
RM23T	OEM
RM-25	0497
RM25	0497
RM25V	0497
RM-26	2144
RM26	1258
RM26(50V)	0497
RM-26(ZENER)	2144
RM26(ZENER)	0497
RM26V	1258
RM78M93FD	OEM
RM-103	0071
RM103	0133
RM257	1823
RM555DE	3732
RM555DE/883B	OEM
RM555T	3592
RM555T/883B	OEM
RM556DC	OEM
RM556DC/883B	OEM
RM714DE	OEM
RM714DE/883B	OEM
RM714H	OEM
RM714H/883B	OEM
RM723T	1183
RM725DE	OEM
RM741DC	OEM
RM741DC/883B	OEM
RM741DE	OEM
RM741DE/883B	OEM
RM741T	4198
RM741T/883B	OEM
RM741TE	0406
RM747DC	OEM
RM747DC/883B	OEM
RM747T	4208
RM747T/883B	OEM
RM1558DE	OEM
RM1558DE/883B	OEM
RM1558T	3108
RM1558T/883B	OEM
RM3001	OEM
RM3002	OEM
RM3005	0042
RM3010	OEM
RM3022	2243
RM3036	OEM
RM3078ADE	OEM
RM3078AT	OEM
RM3078AT/883B	OEM
RM3503ADC	OEM
RM3503ADE/883	OEM
RM4136	OEM
RM4136DC	OEM
RM4136DC/883B	OEM
RM4151DE	OEM
RM4151DE/883B	OEM
RM4151T	OEM
RM4151T/883B	OEM
RM4152DE	OEM
RM4152DE/883B	OEM
RM4152T	OEM
RM4152T/883B	OEM
RM4153DC	OEM
RM4153DE/883B	OEM
RM4156DC	OEM
RM4156DC/883B	OEM
RM4191DE	OEM
RM4191DE/883B	OEM
RM4192DE	OEM
RM4192DE/883B	OEM
RM4193DE	OEM
RM4193DE/883B	OEM
RM4194DC	OEM
RM4194DC/883B	OEM
RM4194TK	OEM
RM4195T	OEM
RM4195TK	OEM
RM4200ADE	OEM
RM4200DE	OEM
RM4260DC	OEM
RM4260DC/883B	OEM
RM4391DE/883B	OEM
RM4558	0356
RM4558DE	OEM
RM4558DE/883B	OEM
RM4558T	OEM
RM4558T/883B	OEM
RM4559DE	OEM
RM4559DE/883B	OEM
RM4559T	OEM
RM4559T/883B	OEM
RM4805ADE	OEM
RM4805ADE/883B	OEM
RM4805AT	OEM
RM4805AT/883B	OEM
RM4805DE	OEM
RM4805DE/883B	OEM
RM4805T	OEM
RM4805T/883B	OEM
RM5008D	OEM
RM5532ADE	OEM
RM5532ADE/883B	OEM
RM5532AT	OEM
RM5532AT/883B	OEM
RM5532DE	OEM
RM5532DE/883B	OEM
RM5532T	OEM
RM5532T/883B	OEM
RM5534ADE	OEM
RM5534ADE/883B	OEM
RM5534AT	OEM
RM5534AT/883B	OEM
RM5534DE	OEM
RM5534DE/883B	OEM
RM5534T	OEM
RM5534T/883B	OEM
RM8007D	OEM
RM9391DE	OEM
RMIV	0015
RMP5020	0015
RMPG06D	1082
RMPG06G	0023
RMPTC0028CEZZ	3799
RMPTC0059CEZZ	6288
RMPTC0128CEZZ	OEM
RMPTC0135CEZZ	OEM
RMPTJ0027CEZZ	OEM
RMPTJ0028CEZZ	3799
RMPTJ0029CEZZ	5769
RMPTJ0037CEZZ	3789
RMVTC00921-3	0479
RN0008	OEM
RN0018	OEM
RN0020	OEM
RN0029	OEM
RN16AT	1716
RN16BT	1716
RN16DT	1716
RN16GT	OEM
RN16JT	OEM
RN16KT	OEM
RN30AM	OEM
RN30BM	OEM
RN30DM	OEM
RN30GM	OEM
RN30JM	OEM
RN30KM	OEM
RN30MM	OEM
RN515	1991
RN835	OEM
RN1001	OEM
RN1002	0826
RN1003	0881
RN1004	0892
RN1015	1241
RN1020	OEM
RN1030	OEM
RN1030A	OEM
RN1115	OEM
RN1120	1116
RN1135	OEM
RN1201	OEM
RN1202	0826
RN1203	0881
RN1204	0892
RN1205	OEM
RN1206	OEM
RN1403	5154
RN2003	1026
RN2005	OEM
RN2006	OEM
RN2015	1241
RN2201	OEM
RN2202	4109
RN2202TPE4	4109
RN2203	1026
RN2204	4067
RN2206	OEM
RN3015	1571
RN3020	OEM
RN3020R	OEM
RN3030	OEM
RN3030R	OEM
RN4015	1571
RN5015	1576
RN5016	1576
RN6015	1576
RN8015	OEM
RNUR8558571	0848
RO2	0071
RO2A	0071
RO2AV	0071
RO2Z	0071
RO-3-9502-011	OEM
RO-3-9502-025-8223	OEM
RO-3-9503	OEM
RO-3-9503-003	OEM
RO-3-9504-026-8210	OEM
RO-3-9504-026-8211	OEM
RO-3-9506	OEM
RO-3-9506-010	OEM
RO102	0015
RO130	0122
RO131	0122
RO132	0122
RO134	0122
RO136	0122
ROA-12015	OEM
RP1A	0102
RP1H	OEM
RP4Z	0071
RP16AT	1227
RP16BT	1227
RP16DT	1227
RP16GT	0903
RP16JT	OEM
RP16KT	OEM
RP30AM	2219
RP30AP	OEM
RP30BM	2219
RP30BP	OEM
RP30DM	2219
RP30DP	OEM
RP30GM	2219
RP30GP	OEM
RP30JM	2683
RP30JP	OEM
RP30KM	OEM
RP30KP	OEM
RP30MM	OEM
RP30MP	OEM
RP104	OEM
RP300G	0031
RP520	OEM
RP1020	2873
RP1040	2873
RP1120	0045
RP1140	0045
RP2020	1116
RP2040	1116
RP3020	OEM
RP4040	0800
RP5020	OEM
RP6020	0315
RP6040	0315
RP8020	1124
RP8040	1124
RP23256E	OEM
RP23256E-2110	OEM
RPG10J	0023
RPG15G	OEM
RPR540	1522
RPR1040	1522
RPR2040	1522
RPR3040	0029
RPR4040	0029
RPX50	OEM
RPX100	OEM
RPX200	OEM
RPX400	OEM
RPX600	OEM
RPX800	OEM
RPY13	OEM
RPY14	OEM
RPY17	OEM
RPY23	OEM
RPY41	OEM
RQ-409S	0015
RQ-444S	0151
RR0102DM	1272
RR0104DM	1282
RR-1	0031
RR-1Z	0031
RR8AT	OEM
RR8BT	OEM
RR8DT	OEM
RR8GT	OEM
RR8JT	OEM
RR8KT	OEM
RR7504	0016
RR8068	0016
RR8070	0144
RR8116	0144
RR8118	0144
RR8119	0144
RR8914	0016
RR8989	0144
RR8999	0144
RR9036R	2741
RRB24-06	0015
RRET-0004CEZZ	OEM
RRET-0006CEZZ	OEM
RRET-0011CEZZ	OEM
RRET-0021CEZZ	OEM
RRET-0025CEZZ	OEM
RRET-0033CEZZ	OEM
RS-05	0110

528 If replacement code is OEM, contact original manufacturer for replacement.

DEVICE TYPE	REPL CODE
RS05	0110
RS1	0023
RS1A	0017
RS1B	0017
RS1C	0182
RS1FM-12	0015
RS1Z	0023
RS3FS	1416
RS4F	0344
RS4FS	1560
RS6	OEM
RS8AT	1137
RS8BT	1137
RS8DT	1137
RS8GT	1137
RS8JT	1958
RS8KT	OEM
RS10	0015
RS20	OEM
RS30	OEM
RS-35	0039
RS40	OEM
RS50	OEM
RS52	OEM
RS52B	OEM
RS53B	OEM
RS60	OEM
RS80	OEM
RS100	OEM
RS-101	0050
RS101	0276
RS-102	0164
RS102	0276
RS-103	0050
RS103	0287
RS-104	0595
RS104	0293
RS-105	0085
RS105	0299
RS-106	0435
RS106	0250
RS-107	0016
RS107	0250
RS-108	0016
RS-109	0144
RS-110	0037
RS128	0016
RS132	0086
RS136	0016
RS201	0276
RS202	0276
RS203	0287
RS204	0293
RS205	0299
RS206	0250
RS207	0250
RS220AF	0015
RS230AF	0015
RS-253C	0133
RS-253S	0133
RS-267S	0133
RS-272US	0133
RS-279US	0111
RS-280S	0133
RS322	0004
RS372	OEM
RS380	0375
RS401	0724
RS401L	0724
RS402	0724
RS402L	0724
RS403	0724
RS403L	2994
RS404	0732
RS404L	0732
RS405	0732
RS405L	3006
RS406	0737
RS406L	0737
RS407	0737
RS407L	3021
RS501	OEM
RS502	OEM
RS503	OEM
RS504	OEM
RS505	OEM
RS506	OEM
RS507	OEM
RS555	0967
RS593	0050
RS601	1034
RS602	1034
RS603	1036
RS604	1039
RS605	1039
RS606	1041
RS607	1041
RS684	0050
RS685	0050
RS686	0050
RS687	0050
RS723	1183
RS741	0406
RS-805US	1211
RS-862S	2569
RS1049	0016
RS1059	0016
RS1192	0004
RS1234	0229

DEVICE TYPE	REPL CODE
R-S1264	0015
RS1264	0015
RS1290	1328
RS1296	0015
RS-1347	0015
RS1347	0015
RS1348	0137
RS1428	0133
RS1458	0356
RS1513	0595
RS1524	0208
RS1530	0595
RS1531	0595
RS1532	0595
RS1533	0208
RS1534	0595
RS1536	0595
RS1537	0595
RS1538	0595
RS1539	0050
RS1540	0004
RS1541	0004
RS1542	0004
RS1543	0004
RS1544	0004
RS1545	0004
RS1546	0004
RS1547	0595
RS1548	0004
RS1549	0208
RS1550	0050
RS1553	0595
RS1554	0050
RS1555	0004
R-S-1720	0015
RS1720	0015
RS1726	0144
RS1749	0015
R-S1805	0535
RS1805	0015
RS1811	0143
RS1823	0229
RS1832	0015
RS-2001	0595
RS2001	0595
RS-2002	0050
RS-2003	0136
RS2003	0050
RS-2004	0211
RS-2005	0211
RS-2006	0085
RS-2007	0164
RS-2008	0233
RS2008	0710
RS-2009	0079
RS2009	0016
RS-2010	0079
RS2010	0079
RS-2011	0007
RS-2012	0710
RS2012	0710
RS-2013	0079
RS2013	0079
RS-2014	0086
RS-2015	0144
RS-2016	0079
RS2016	0079
RS-2017	0161
RS2017	0042
RS-2018	0561
RS2018	0042
RS-2019	0556
RS2019	1351
RS-2020	0161
RS-2021	0037
RS-2022	0037
RS2022	0037
RS-2023	0037
RS-2024	0037
RS-2025	0455
RS2025	0919
RS-2026	1357
RS2026	1357
RS-2027	1190
RS2027	1359
RS-2028	0321
RS-2029	1167
RS-2030	0016
RS-2031	0326
RS-2032	0037
RS-2033	0016
RS-2034	0037
RS2038	0488
RS2039	0103
RS2040	0486
RS2041	0103
RS2042	1384
RS2043	0486
RS2350	0004
RS2351	0004
RS2352	0004
RS2353	0004
RS2354	0004
RS2355	0004
RS2356	0595
RS2359	0595
RS2360	0595
RS2364	0595
RS2365	0595

DEVICE TYPE	REPL CODE
RS2366	0595
RS2367	0004
RS2373	0004
RS2374	0004
RS2375	0595
RS2675	0004
RS2677	0004
RS2679	0050
RS2680	0050
RS2683	0050
RS2684	0050
RS2685	0050
RS2686	0050
RS2687	0050
RS2688	0050
RS2689	0004
RS2690	0279
RS2691	0279
RS2692	0279
RS2694	0050
RS2695	0050
RS2696	0279
RS2697	0004
RS2801	0143
RS2867	0004
RS2914	0016
RS3211	0004
RS3275	0004
RS3276	0211
RS3277	0050
RS3278	0050
RS3279	0050
RS3280	0004
RS3281	0279
RS3282	0004
RS3283	0004
RS3284	0004
RS3285	0004
RS3286	0004
RS3287	0279
RS3288	0050
RS3289	0004
RS3293	0004
RS3299	0004
RS3301	0004
RS3306	0595
RS3308	0004
RS3309	0050
RS3310	0004
RS3316	0004
RS3316-1	0004
RS3316-2	0004
RS3318	0004
RS3322	0050
RS3323	0050
RS3324	0050
RS3358-1	0160
RS3359-1	0160
RS3570	0015
RS3668	0050
RS3717	0004
RS3726	0004
RS3727	0015
RS3857	0004
RS3858	0160
RS-3858-1	0160
RS3858-1	0160
RS3862	0050
RS3863	0050
RS3864	0050
RS3866	0004
RS3867	0164
RS3868	0050
RS3880	0004
RS3892	0279
RS3897	0004
RS3898	0050
RS3900	0050
RS-3901	0050
RS3901	0050
RS3902	0050
RS3903	0050
RS3904	0004
RS3905	0050
RS3906	0050
RS3907	0050
RS3911	0050
RS3912	0050
RS3913	0004
RS-3914	0279
RS3914	0279
RS-3915	0279
RS3915	0279
RS3925	0004
RS-3926	0004
RS3926	0004
RS-3929	0279
RS3929	0050
RS3931	0208
RS3959	0160
RS3959-1	0160
RS3986	0050
RS3995	0050
RS4001	0473
RS4011	0215
RS4013	0409
RS4017	0508
RS4020	1651
RS4027	1938

DEVICE TYPE	REPL CODE
RS4049	0001
RS4050	0394
RS4518	1037
RS5008	0004
RS5101	0050
RS5102	0004
RS5103	0004
RS5104	0279
RS5105	0279
RS5106	0050
RS5107	0050
RS5108	0050
RS5109	0050
RS5201	0050
RS5202	0004
RS5203	0004
RS5204	0050
RS5205	0050
RS5206	0050
RS5207	0050
RS5208	0050
RS5209	0050
RS5243-2	0004
RS5301	0050
RS5302	0279
RS5303	0279
RS5305	0050
RS5306	0050
RS5311	0050
RS5312	0050
RS5313	0050
RS5314	0050
RS5317	0050
RS5401	0004
RS5402	0279
RS5403	0279
RS5406	0004
RS5502	0004
RS5503	0004
RS5504	0279
RS5505	0004
RS5506	0004
RS5507	0004
RS5511	0279
RS5530	0004
RS5531	0004
RS5532	0004
RS5533	0004
RS5534	0004
RS5535	0004
RS5536	0004
RS5540	0279
RS5541	0004
RS5542	0004
RS5543	0004
RS5544	0004
RS5545	0004
RS5551	0004
RS5552	0004
RS5553	0004
RS5554	0004
RS5555	0004
RS5556	0004
RS5557	0004
RS5558	0004
RS5563	0004
RS5564	0004
RS5565	0004
RS5566	0004
RS5567	0004
RS5568	0004
RS5602	0004
RS5603	0004
RS5605	0004
RS5607	0004
RS5608	0004
RS5610	0004
RS5612	0160
RS-5613	0160
RS5613	0160
RS5614	0160
RS5616	0160
RS5704	0004
RS5704-2	0004
RS5708	0004
RS5708-2	0004
RS5709	0004
RS5711	0004
RS5717	0004
RS5717-1	0004
RS5717-3	0004
RS5717-6	0004
RS5720	0004
RS5731	0004
RS5732	0004
RS5733	0004
RS5734	0004
RS5735	0004
RS5736	0004
RS5737	0004
RS5738	0004
RS5740	0004
RS5740-1	0004
RS5742	0004
RS5743	0004
RS-5743-1	0004
RS5743-1	0004
RS-5743-2	0004
RS5743-2	0004

DEVICE TYPE	REPL CODE
RS-5743-3	0004
RS5743-3	0004
RS5743.3	0279
RS-5744	0004
RS5744	0004
RS-5744-3	0004
RS5744-3	0004
RS5745	0004
RS5746	0004
RS5747	0004
RS5748	0004
RS5749	0004
RS5750	0004
RS5751	0004
RS5752	0004
RS5753	0136
RS-5753-2	0211
RS5753-2	0136
RS5754	0136
RS-5755	0136
RS5755	0136
RS5756	0136
RS5757	0136
RS5758	0136
RS5759	0136
RS5760	0136
RS5761	0136
RS5762	0136
RS5765	0004
RS5766	0004
RS5767	0004
RS5768	0004
RS5788	0841
RS5802	0136
RS5818	0050
RS5825	0211
RS-5835	0160
RS5835	0160
RS5851	0016
RS-5852	0004
RS5852	0004
RS5853	0016
RS5854	0004
RS-5855	0160
RS5855	0265
RS5856	0079
RS5857	0079
RS6344	0015
RS6461	0015
RS6471	0015
RS6523	0144
RS6705	0015
RS6821	0136
RS6822	0136
RS6824	0279
RS6840	0004
RS6843	0211
RS6846	0211
RS7101	0144
RS7102	0144
RS7103	0016
RS7104	0144
RS7105	0016
RS7106	0144
RS7107	0144
RS-7108	0144
RS7108	0016
RS7109	0144
RS7110	0144
RS7111	0016
RS7112	0144
RS7113	0144
RS7114	0224
RS7115	0144
RS7116	0144
RS7117	0144
RS7118	0144
RS7119	0144
RS7120	0144
RS7121	0016
RS7122	0144
RS7123	0144
RS-7124	0079
RS7124	0144
RS7125	0144
RS7126	0144
RS-7127	0079
RS7127	0079
RS7128	0144
RS-7129	0079
RS7129	0079
RS7132	0016
RS7133	0016
RS7135	0144
RS7136	0016
RS7138	0144
RS7139	0144
RS7140	0144
RS7141	0144
RS7142	0144
RS7143	0127
RS7144	0144
RS7145	0144
RS7160	0016
RS7161	0144
RS7162	0144
RS7163	0144
RS7164	0144
RS7165	0144

DEVICE TYPE	REPL CODE
RS7166	0144
RS7167	0144
RS7168	0144
RS7169	0144
RS7170	0144
RS7173	0224
RS7174	0144
RS7175	0144
RS7176	0144
RS7177	0144
RS-7201	0127
RS7201	0144
RS-7202	0144
RS7202	0144
RS7209	0144
RS7210	0144
RS7211	0144
RS-7212	0127
RS7212	0144
RS7214	0144
RS7215	0144
RS7216	0144
RS7217	0144
RS7218	0144
RS7219	0144
RS7220	0144
RS7221	0144
RS7222	0127
RS7223	0016
RS7224	0016
RS7225	0144
RS7226	0016
RS7227	0144
RS7228	0144
RS7229	0144
RS7230	0144
RS7231	0144
RS7232	0016
RS7233	0224
RS7234	0079
RS7235	0079
RS7236	0016
RS7237	0144
RS7238	0079
RS7241	0079
RS7242	0079
RS7310	0142
RS7311	0142
RS7312	0142
RS7313	0142
RS7315	0142
RS7316	0142
RS7317	0142
RS7318	0142
RS7320	0142
RS7321	0142
RS7327	0142
RS7328	0142
RS7329	0142
RS7330	0142
RS7333	0144
RS7334	0144
RS7365	0142
RS7366	0142
RS7367	0142
RS7368	0142
RS7400	0232
RS7402	0310
RS7404	0357
RS7405	0016
RS7406	0016
RS7406(IC)	1197
RS7407	0016
RS7408	0016
RS7408(IC)	0462
RS7409	0016
RS7410	0016
RS7410(IC)	0507
RS7411	0016
RS7412	0016
RS7413	0016
RS7413(IC)	1432
RS7415	0016
RS7420	0692
RS7421	0016
RS7427	0812
RS7432	0893
RS7441	1032
RS7447	1100
RS7448	1117
RS7451	1160
RS7473	1164
RS7474	1303
RS7475	1423
RS7476	1150
RS7485	0370
RS7486	1358
RS7490	1199
RS7492	0828
RS7504	0016
RS7510	0016
RS7511	0144
RS7512	0144
RS7513	0079
RS7513-15	0079
RS7514	0079
RS7515	0079
RS7516	0079
RS7517	0079

DEVICE TYPE	REPL CODE
RS7517-19	0079
RS7518	0079
RS7519	0079
RS7520	0144
RS7521	0079
RS7522	0144
RS7523	0127
RS7524	0144
RS7525	0079
RS7526	0079
RS7527	0079
RS7528	0079
RS7529	0079
RS7530	0079
RS7532	0144
RS7533	0144
RS7542	0079
RS7543	0079
RS7544	0079
RS7555	0079
RS7568	0004
RS7606	0016
RS7607	0016
RS7609	0016
RS7610	0016
RS7611	0016
RS7612	0016
RS7613	0016
RS7614	0016
RS7620	0016
RS7621	0016
RS7622	0016
RS7623	0016
RS7624	0079
RS7625	0079
RS7626	0079
RS7627	0079
RS7628	0079
RS7634	0079
RS7635	0079
RS7636	0079
RS7637	0079
RS7638	0079
RS7639	0079
RS7640	0079
RS7641	0079
RS7642	0079
RS7643	0079
RS7665	0037
RS7678	0086
RS7814	0079
RS7916	0321
RS8100	0126
RS8101	0086
RS8102	0126
RS8103	0086
RS8104	0126
RS8105	0086
RS8106	0126
RS8107	0086
RS8108	0126
RS8109	0086
RS8110	0126
RS8111	0086
RS8112	0126
RS8113	0086
RS8406	0164
RS8407	0208
RS8420	0208
RS8421	0004
RS8424	0164
RS8430	0015
RS8441	0208
RS8442	0079
RS8443	0208
RS8444	0004
RS8446	0164
RS8470	OEM
RS8471	OEM
RS8476	OEM
RS8478	OEM
RS8487	OEM
RS8493	OEM
RS8503	0079
RS8609	OEM
RS9510	0127
RS9511	0127
RS9512	0127
RS57042	0004
RS57062	0004
RS57433	0004
RS74123	1149
RS74145	0614
RS74150	1484
RS74154	1546
RS74192	1910
RS74193	1915
RS74196	1939
RSL0003F	OEM
RSL0004-F	OEM
RSL0007F	OEM
RSL0014-F	OEM
RSL0014F	OEM
RSLNA0004CEZZ	0469
RS-LNB0001CEZZ	0196
RSLNB0001CEZZ	0196
RSLND0003CEZZ	0102
RSWY/16L7Z	0143
RT05	OEM

If replacement code is OEM, contact original manufacturer for replacement. 529

DEVICE TYPE	REPL CODE
RT1N241S	2307
RT1N441C	3987
RT1N441C-T12-A1	OEM
RT1N441S	OEM
RT1P241S	1026
RT1P441S	OEM
RT6	OEM
RT10	OEM
RT20	OEM
RT30	OEM
RT40	OEM
RT60	OEM
RT80	OEM
RT-100	0016
RT100	0016
RT-100A	OEM
RT-101	0016
RT-101A	0431
RT-102	0079
RT102	0320
RT-102A	0320
RT-103	0037
RT103	0016
RT-103A	0431
RT-104	0111
RT104	0079
RT-105	0111
RT105	0016
RT-106	0855
RT106	0037
RT-107	0111
RT107	0144
RT-107A	0320
RT-108	0111
RT108	0144
RT-108A	0015
RT-109	0855
RT109	0855
RT-110	0233
RT110	0233
RT-111	0283
RT-112	0111
RT112	0127
RT-113	0007
RT113	0016
RT-114	0086
RT114	0016
RT-115	0150
RT115	0150
RT-116	0178
RT116	1680
RT-117	0004
RT-118	0855
RT-119	0038
RT119	0038
RT-120	0855
RT-121	0786
RT121	0164
RT-122	0038
RT-123	0164
RT-124	0085
RT124	0160
RT-125	0435
RT-126	0150
RT126	0016
RT-126A	0037
RT-127	0085
RT127	0160
RT-128	0142
RT128	0142
RT-129	0208
RT-130	0969
RT-131	0103
RT131	0103
RT-133	0042
RT133	0556
RT-134	0127
RT-135	0168
RT135	1698
RT-136	0164
RT-137	2035
RT-139	0003
RT-140	0065
RT-141	0086
RT141	0086
RT-143	2035
RT-144	0396
RT-145	0178
RT-146	0930
RT-147	0599
RT-148	1671
RT-149	0130
RT-150	0042
RT150	0042
RT150A	OEM
RT150B	OEM
RT-151	0919
RT151	0919
RT-152	0555
RT152	0555
RT-153	0848
RT-154	0103
RT154	0086
RT-155	0919
RT155	0919
RT-156	0168
RT156	0161
RT-157	1357
RT157	0455
RT-158	0419
RT-159	0283
RT159	0283
RT-159A	0334
RT-160	0930
RT-164	1351
RT-165	1359
RT-166	1351
RT-167	1359
RT-172	0015
RT-174	1897
RT-175	0321
RT175	0321
RT-176	3667
RT176	0321
RT-177	3350
RT-180	0212
RT180	0212
RT-181	0212
RT-182	0693
RT-183	0136
RT-185	0004
RT185	0004
RT-186	0334
RT-187	0155
RT-188	0086
RT188	0086
RT-189	0899
RT-190	0178
RT-191	0930
RT-192	0312
RT-193	2123
RT-194	0103
RT-195	1359
RT-196	1359
RT-197	1351
RT-200	0143
RT-201	0916
RT-202	0911
RT-203	0071
RT-204	0374
RT-206	OEM
RT-210	0071
RT210	0071
RT-212	0015
RT-213	0015
RT213	0015
RT-214	0015
RT214	0015
RT-215	0015
RT215	0015
RT-216	0290
RT-216D	0290
RT-218	0133
RT218	0133
RT-220	0469
RT-221	0196
RT-222	0479
RT-223	1073
RT-224	1293
RT-225	0769
RT-226	0201
RT-227	0239
RT-228	0747
RT-229	0286
RT-230	0287
RT-231	0299
RT-232	0250
RT-234	0188
RT-235	0162
RT235	0162
RT-236	0157
RT-237	0631
RT-238	0025
RT-239	0644
RT-240	0012
RT-241	0170
RT-242	0313
RT-243	0137
RT-244	0361
RT-245	0002
RT-246	0416
RT-247	0526
RT-248	0560
RT248	0560
RT-249	0436
RT-250	0039
RT-251	0346
RT-252	0993
RT-253	0863
RT-254	0778
RT-255	0327
RT-256	0149
RT-257	0244
RT-258	0490
RT-259	0398
RT-260	0186
RT-261	0028
RT-262	0030
RT-263	0143
RT-264	1780
RT-265	1313
RT-266	0417
RT-267	0016
RT-268	0016
RT-269	0037
RT-270	0037
RT-271	1879
RT-272	1879
RT-300	0320
RT-301	0590
RT-302	0155
RT-303	0006
RT-304	0320
RT304	0079
RT-305	0431
RT-306	2675
RT-306F	0626
RT-307	0626
RT-308	0111
RT-309	2064
RT-310	1973
RT-311	0786
RT-312	0016
RT-313	0144
RT-314	0338
RT-315	0710
RT409E	1471
RT476	0079
RT482	0086
RT483	0086
RT484	0086
RT497M	OEM
RT498M	OEM
RT-600	1296
RT-601	2072
RT601	2072
RT-602	2073
RT602	2073
RT-603	1440
RT603	1440
RT-604	2074
RT604	2074
RT-605	3604
RT656M	OEM
RT657M	OEM
RT679M	OEM
RT696AM	1471
RT696M	OEM
RT697AM	OEM
RT697M	0016
RT698	OEM
RT698M	OEM
RT699AM	OEM
RT699M	0086
RT-700	OEM
RT-701	OEM
RT-702	OEM
RT-703	OEM
RT-704	4232
RT-705	OEM
RT-709	OEM
RT-710	OEM
RT-711	OEM
RT-712	OEM
RT-713	OEM
RT-714	OEM
RT-715	OEM
RT-716	OEM
RT-717	OEM
RT717M	OEM
RT-718	OEM
RT718AM	OEM
RT718M	OEM
RT-719	OEM
RT719M	OEM
RT-720	OEM
RT720M	OEM
RT730M	1471
RT731M	1471
RT910M	1471
RT-929-H	0016
RT929H	0016
RT930H	0144
RT1008	0143
RT1106	0143
RT1108	0143
RT1110	OEM
RT1111	OEM
RT1115	0855
RT1116	0283
RT1184	0143
RT1210	0233
RT1252M	1471
RT1253M	1471
RT1306	0157
RT1306(G.E.)	0157
RT1395	0016
RT1409M	1471
RT1410M	1471
RT1420M	OEM
RT1595	0015
RT1613M	OEM
RT1667	0123
RT1669	0133
RT1686	0102
RT-1689	0143
RT1689	0133
RT1840	0015
RT1893	0283
RT1899	OEM
RT2016	0016
RT2061(G.E.)	0133
RT2221	OEM
RT2230	0004
RT2309	0547
RT2329	0004
RT2330	0004
RT2331	0004
RT2332	0016
RT2334	0143
RT2451	0123
RT2452	0143
RT2459	OEM
RT2460	OEM
RT2461	OEM
RT2462	OEM
RT2463	OEM
RT2669	0015
RT2694	0143
RT2709	0004
RT2914	0079
RT2915	0144
RT3061	OEM
RT3062	OEM
RT3063	0016
RT3064	0016
RT3065	0037
RT3069	0144
RT3070	0144
RT3071	0037
RT3072	0143
RT3095	0144
RT3096	0208
RT3097	0004
RT3098	0004
RT3099	0143
RT3101	OEM
RT3103	OEM
RT3111	OEM
RT3170	OEM
RT3171	OEM
RT3225	0144
RT3226	0144
RT3227	0144
RT3228	0016
RT3229	0004
RT3230	0004
RT3231	0004
RT3232	0144
RT3233	0143
RT3336	0143
RT3361	0136
RT3362	0136
RT3363	0004
RT3364	0004
RT3365	0004
RT3443	0015
RT3449	0004
RT3466	0050
RT3467	0004
RT3468	0004
RT3469	0143
RT3500	OEM
RT3501	OEM
RT3558	0015
RT3564	0004
RT3565	0016
RT3566	0004
RT3567	0079
RT3568	0004
RT3574	0644
RT3585	0015
RT3671	0002
RT3858	0015
RT3981	0015
RT4050	0015
RT4069	0015
RT4230	OEM
RT4232	0015
RT4293	0143
RT4525	0050
RT4584	OEM
RT4624	0004
RT4625	0164
RT4644	0143
RT4760	0111
RT4761	0191
RT4762	0222
RT4762MHF25	0085
RT-4764	0087
RT4764	0015
RT4767	0015
RT4880	0123
RT5001	0626
RT5002	0626
RT5003	0626
RT5004	0626
RT5061	0144
RT5063	0136
RT5070	0015
RT5108	0626
RT5151	0086
RT5152	0086
RT5200	0144
RT5201	0144
RT5202	0079
RT5203	0086
RT5204	0284
RT5205	0144
RT5206	0079
RT5207	0006
RT5208	0111
RT5211	0030
RT5212	0123
RT5213	0019
RT5214	0143
RT5215	0025
RT5216	0229
RT5217	0133
RT5230	0126
RT5321AD	OEM
RT5379	0123
RT5385	0015
RT5401	0086
RT5402	0086
RT5403	0086
RT5404	0086
RT5411	OEM
RT5412	OEM
RT5413	OEM
RT5418	OEM
RT5435	0111
RT5464	0127
RT5465	0127
RT5466	0136
RT5467	0136
RT5468	0004
RT5470	0123
RT5471	0025
RT5472	0015
RT5473	0030
RT5520	0136
RT5521	0004
RT5522	0004
RT5551	0079
RT5554	0133
RT5637	0004
RT5738	0123
RT5765	OEM
RT5793	0631
RT5804	1471
RT5900	0076
RT5901	0016
RT5902	0144
RT5903	0144
RT5904	0144
RT5905	0076
RT5906	0086
RT5907	0086
RT5908	0143
RT5909	0133
RT5911	0015
RT5912	0123
RT5939	0143
RT6105	0244
RT6119	0143
RT6157	0144
RT6158	0144
RT6159	0144
RT6160	0144
RT6178	0030
RT6179	0143
RT6180	0143
RT6181	0143
RT6182	0143
RT6183	0143
RT6184	0143
RT6189	0143
RT6201	0224
RT6202	0224
RT6203	0144
RT-6204	0191
RT6204	0151
RT6205	0004
RT6322	0015
RT6332	0015
RT6600	0127
RT6600MHF25	0079
RT6601	1136
RT6602	1136
RT6603	0030
RT6604	0004
RT6605	0071
RT6619	0143
RT6728	0123
RT6729	0015
RT6731	0123
RT6732	0151
RT6733	0151
RT6734	0004
RT6735	0103
RT6736	0004
RT6737	1211
RT6787	2195
RT6789	0030
RT6790	0574
RT6791	0015
RT6921	0191
RT6921MHF25	0079
RT-6922	0162
RT6922	0041
RT6923	0244
RT6988	0136
RT6989	0079
RT6990	0004
RT6991	0144
RT7007E	OEM
RT7320	0144
RT7321	0144
RT7322	0079
RT7323	0144
RT7324	0144
RT7325	0079
RT7326	0532
RT7327	0079
RT7329	0030
RT7330	0143
RT-7399	0574
RT7399	0574
RT7400	0208
RT7401	0004
RT7402	0276
RT7511	0016
RT7514	0079
RT7515	0016
RT7517	0016
RT7518	0016
RT7528	0016
RT7538	0123
RT7539	0631
RT7557	0076
RT7558	0164
RT7559	0111
RT7634	0015
RT7636	0143
RT7638	0016
RT7689	0143
RT7703	2195
RT7704	0127
RT7705	OEM
RT7845	0016
RT7846	1056
RT7848	0110
RT7849	0015
RT7850	0015
RT7851	0143
RT7943	0191
RT7944	0208
RT7945	0086
RT7946	0133
RT8047	0111
RT8101-2	OEM
RT8193	0016
RT8195	0016
RT8197	0191
RT8198	0076
RT8199	0229
RT8200	0053
RT8201	0079
RT8231	0015
RT8330	0079
RT8331	0321
RT8332	0016
RT8333	2195
RT8334	OEM
RT8335	0042
RT8336	0919
RT8337	0111
RT8338	0919
RT8339	0057
RT8340	0015
RT8442	0004
RT8527	0113
RT8528	OEM
RT8601-2	OEM
RT8602	0004
RT8664	OEM
RT8665	0071
RT8666	0111
RT-8667	0321
RT8667	0683
RT8668	1136
RT8669	0113
RT8670	0006
RT8671	0143
RT8701-2	OEM
RT8779	0030
RT8801-2	OEM
RT8838	OEM
RT8839	0015
RT8840	0015
RT8841	0015
RT8842	0164
RT8863	0111
RT8895	0037
RT8901-2	OEM
RT61012	0143
RT-61014	0136
RT61014	0136
RT-61015	0164
RT61015	0004
RT-61016	0164
RT61016	0004
RTB0103	1129
RTB0106	0340
RTB0110	0895
RTB0120	0058
RTB0130	0403
RTB0140	OEM
RTC05	OEM
RTC0103	1129
RTC0106	0340
RTC0110	0895
RTC0120	0058
RTC0130	0403
RTC0140	OEM
RTC10	OEM
RTC20	OEM
RTC40	OEM
RTC60	OEM
RTC80	OEM
RTC101L	OEM
RTC102L	OEM
RTC103L	OEM
RTC106L	OEM
RTC107L	OEM
RTC114L	OEM
RTC115L	OEM
RTC1001	OEM
RTC1002	OEM
RTC1003	OEM
RTC1005	OEM
RTC1100	OEM
RTC3001	OEM
RTC3003	OEM
RTC3005	OEM
RTF0101	OEM
RTF0103	OEM
RTF0106	OEM
RTF0110	OEM
RTF0115	OEM
RTF0120	OEM
RTF0125	OEM
RTF0130	OEM
RTF0135	OEM
RTF0140	OEM
RTF0201	OEM
RTF0203	OEM
RTF0206	OEM
RTF0210	OEM
RTF0215	OEM
RTF0220	OEM
RTF0225	OEM
RTF0230	OEM
RTF0235	OEM
RTF0240	OEM
RTF0301	OEM
RTF0303	OEM
RTF0306	OEM
RTF0310	OEM
RTF0315	OEM
RTF0320	OEM
RTF0325	OEM
RTF0330	OEM
RTF0335	OEM
RTF0340	OEM
RTF0401	OEM
RTF0403	OEM
RTF0406	OEM
RTF0410	OEM
RTF0415	OEM
RTF0420	OEM
RTF0425	OEM
RTF0430	OEM
RTF0435	OEM
RTF0440	OEM
RTF0501	OEM
RTF0503	OEM
RTF0506	OEM
RTF0510	OEM
RTF0515	OEM
RTF0520	OEM
RTF0525	OEM
RTF0530	OEM
RTF0535	OEM
RTF0540	OEM
RTF0601	OEM
RTF0603	OEM
RTF0606	OEM
RTF0610	OEM
RTF0615	OEM
RTF0620	OEM
RTGC0101	OEM
RTGC0103	OEM
RTGC0106	OEM
RTGC0110	OEM
RTGC0115	OEM
RTGC0120	OEM
RTGD0101	OEM
RTGD0103	OEM
RTGD0106	OEM
RTGD0110	OEM
RTGD0115	OEM
RTGD0120	OEM
RTGD0125	OEM
RTGD0130	OEM
RTH0101	OEM
RTH0103	OEM
RTH0106	OEM
RTH0110	OEM
RTH0115	OEM
RTH0120	OEM
RTH0125	OEM
RTH0130	OEM
RTH0201	OEM
RTH0203	OEM
RTH0206	OEM
RTH0210	OEM
RTH0215	OEM
RTH0220	OEM
RTH0225	OEM
RTH0230	OEM
RTH0301	OEM
RTH0303	OEM
RTH0306	OEM
RTH0310	OEM
RTH0315	OEM
RTH0320	OEM
RTH0325	OEM
RTH0330	OEM
RTH0401	OEM
RTH0403	OEM
RTH0406	OEM

530 If replacement code is OEM, contact original manufacturer for replacement.

DEVICE TYPE	REPL CODE
RTH0410	OEM
RTH0415	OEM
RTH0420	OEM
RTH0425	OEM
RTH0430	OEM
RTH0501	OEM
RTH0503	OEM
RTH0506	OEM
RTH0510	OEM
RTH0515	OEM
RTH0520	OEM
RTH0525	OEM
RTH0530	OEM
RTH0601	OEM
RTH0603	OEM
RTH0606	OEM
RTH0610	OEM
RTH0615	OEM
RTH0620	OEM
RTIN241S	2307
RTIP241S	1026
RTJ0103	1129
RTJ0106	0340
RTJ0110	0895
RTJ0120	0895
RTJ0130	0403
RTJ0140	0403
RTJ0201	1129
RTJ0203	1129
RTJ0206	0340
RTJ0210	0895
RTJ0215	0403
RTJ0220	0058
RTJ0225	0403
RTJ0230	0403
RTL0605	2084
RTL0610	2078
RTL0620	0500
RTL0640	0705
RTL0660	OEM
RTL0805	2084
RTL0810	2078
RTL0820	0500
RTL0840	0089
RTL0860	OEM
RTL1005	OEM
RTL1010	OEM
RTL1020	OEM
RTL1040	OEM
RTL1060	OEM
RTL1510	OEM
RTL1520	OEM
RTL1540	OEM
RTL1560	OEM
RTL1610	OEM
RTL1620	OEM
RTL1640	OEM
RTL1660	OEM
RTN0102	1095
RTN0105	1095
RTN0110	2471
RTN0120	0240
RTN0130	0671
RTN0140	0671
RTN0150	0332
RTN0160	0332
RTN0202	2430
RTN0205	2430
RTN0210	2430
RTN0220	0430
RTN0230	1478
RTN0240	1478
RTN0250	0682
RTN0260	0682
RTN0302	2430
RTN0305	2430
RTN0310	2430
RTN0320	0430
RTN0330	1478
RTN0340	1478
RTN0350	0682
RTN0360	0682
RTN0802	1095
RTN0805	1095
RTN0810	2471
RTN0820	0240
RTN0840	0671
RTN0860	0332
RTPC0103	OEM
RTPC0103-1	OEM
RTPC0106	OEM
RTPC0106-1	OEM
RTPC0110	OEM
RTPC0110-1	OEM
RTPC0115	OEM
RTPC0115-1	OEM
RTPC0120	OEM
RTPC0120-1	OEM
RTR0202	0998
RTR0205	2084
RTR0210	2078
RTR0220	0500
RTR0230	0705
RTR0240	0705
RTR0250	0857
RTR0260	0857
RTR0302	0998
RTR0305	2084
RTR0310	2078
RTR0320	0500
RTR0330	0705
RTR0340	0705
RTR0350	0857
RTR0360	0857
RTR0620	0500
RTR0660	OEM
RTR1005	OEM
RTR1010	OEM
RTR1020	OEM
RTR1040	OEM
RTR1060	OEM
RTS0202	1641
RTS0205	1641
RTS0210	1641
RTS0220	1641
RTS0230	1574
RTS0240	1574
RTS0250	1655
RTS0260	1655
RTS0702	1640
RTS0705	1640
RTS0710	1640
RTS0720	1640
RTS0730	2623
RTS0740	2623
RTS0750	2625
RTS0760	2625
RTS1002	1641
RTS1005	1641
RTS1010	1641
RTS1020	1641
RTS1040	1574
RTS1060	1655
RTS2505	1640
RTS2510	1640
RTS2520	1640
RTS2540	2623
RTS2560	2625
RTT0102	0464
RTT0105	0464
RTT0110	0464
RTT0120	0464
RTT0130	0717
RTT0140	0717
RTT0150	0720
RTT0160	0720
RTT0202	0464
RTT0205	0464
RTT0210	0464
RTT0220	0464
RTT0230	0717
RTT0240	0717
RTT0250	0720
RTT0260	0720
RTT0302	0464
RTT0305	0464
RTT0310	0464
RTT0320	0464
RTT0330	0717
RTT0340	0717
RTT0350	0720
RTT0360	0720
RTT0402	0464
RTT0405	0464
RTT0410	0464
RTT0420	0464
RTT0430	0717
RTT0440	0717
RTT0450	0720
RTT0460	0720
RTT0502	0799
RTT0505	0799
RTT0510	0799
RTT0520	0799
RTT0530	0799
RTT0540	0799
RTT0550	0799
RTT0560	0799
RTT0602	0464
RTT0605	0464
RTT0610	0464
RTT0620	0464
RTT0630	0717
RTT0640	0717
RTT0650	0720
RTT0660	0720
RTT2505	0726
RTT2510	0707
RTT2520	0464
RTT2540	0717
RTT2560	0720
RTU023#	0742
RTU0102	2497
RTU0105	2497
RTU0110	6787
RTU0120	0740
RTU0130	0742
RTU0140	0735
RTU0150	0747
RTU0160	0759
RTU0202	3275
RTU0205	2174
RTU0210	0562
RTU0220	0757
RTU0230	0735
RTU0240	0735
RTU0250	0759
RTU0260	0759
RTU0302	0464
RTU0305	0464
RTU0310	0464
RTU0320	0464
RTU0330	0717
RTU0340	0717
RTU0350	0720
RTU0360	0720
RTU0402	0464
RTU0405	0464
RTU0410	0464
RTU0420	0464
RTU0430	0717
RTU0440	0717
RTU0450	0720
RTU0460	0720
RTU0502	0464
RTU0505	0464
RTU0510	0464
RTU0520	0464
RTU0530	0717
RTU0540	0717
RTU0550	0720
RTU0560	0720
RTU0705	0726
RTU0710	0707
RTU0720	0464
RTU0730	0717
RTU0740	0717
RTU0750	0720
RTU0760	0720
RTU102	2497
RTU1005	2430
RTU1010	2430
RTU1020	0430
RTU1040	1478
RTU1060	0682
RTU2505	0726
RTU2510	0707
RTU2520	0464
RTU2540	0717
RTU2560	0720
RTV0102	OEM
RTV0105	OEM
RTV0110	OEM
RTV0120	OEM
RTV0130	OEM
RTV0140	OEM
RTV0150	OEM
RTV0160	OEM
RTV0202	OEM
RTV0205	4332
RTV0210	OEM
RTV0220	OEM
RTV0230	OEM
RTV0240	OEM
RTV0250	OEM
RTV0260	OEM
RTV0302	OEM
RTV0305	OEM
RTV0310	OEM
RTV0320	OEM
RTV0330	OEM
RTV0340	OEM
RTV0350	OEM
RTV0360	OEM
RTV0402	OEM
RTV0405	OEM
RTV0410	OEM
RTV0420	OEM
RTV0430	OEM
RTV0440	OEM
RTV0450	OEM
RTV0460	OEM
RTV0502	OEM
RTV0505	OEM
RTV0510	OEM
RTV0520	OEM
RTV0530	OEM
RTV0540	OEM
RTV0550	OEM
RTV0560	OEM
RTV0602	OEM
RTV0605	OEM
RTV0610	OEM
RTV0620	OEM
RTV0630	OEM
RTV0640	OEM
RTV0650	OEM
RTV0660	OEM
RU-1	0023
RU1	0023
RU-1A	0023
RU1A	0023
RU-1AV	0023
RU1B	0017
RU1C	0017
RU-1P	0023
RU1P	0023
RU-1V	0023
RU1V	0023
RU1Z	0023
RU-2	0023
RU2	0023
RU2-LFA1	0023
RU2AM	0023
RU2AN	0023
RU-2AV	0023
RU2B	0023
RU2C	0023
RU-2M	0023
RU2M	0023
RU-2M(V)	0023
RU-2M(V)TA	0023
RU-2MV	0023
RU2MV	0023
RU-2MVTA	0023
RU2N	0023
RU-2V	0023
RU2V	0102
RU2YX	0541
RU2Z	0023
RU-3	0282
RU3	0111
RU3-AM	0282
RU3A	0282
RU3AH	0282
RU-3AM	0282
RU3AM	0282
RU3AM-LFB1	0282
RU3AN	0023
RU-3B	0635
RU3B	0635
RU-3M	0282
RU3M	0282
RU3N	0031
RU3V	0282
RU3YX	3097
RU3YX-M	OEM
RU3YX-MLF-C2	OEM
RU3YX-MLF-C4	OEM
RU4	0102
RU-4A	0102
RU4A	0102
RU4A-J1	0102
RU-4AM	0031
RU4AM	0031
RU4AM(LF-L1)	0031
RU4AM-K1	0031
RU4AMK1	0031
RU4AM-LF-J3	0031
RU4AMLF-J3	0031
RU4AM-LFK2	OEM
RU4AMLF-K2	0031
RU4AM-T3	0031
RU4B	0102
RU4C	0102
RU-4D	0102
RU4D	0102
RU-4DS	0031
RU4DS	0102
RU4DS-LFK2	0102
RU4H	OEM
RU4M	0031
RU4M-LF-J3	0031
RU4MLF-K2	0031
RU4Y	0102
RU4YX	0541
RU4YX-LF-J3	0541
RU4YXLF-J3	0541
RU4YX-LFK2	OEM
RU4YXLF-K2	0541
RU-4Z	0031
RU4Z	0031
RU4ZLF-L1	0031
RU30A	OEM
RU800	OEM
RU801	OEM
RU802	OEM
RU803	OEM
RU804	OEM
RU805	OEM
RU806	OEM
RU808	OEM
RU810	OEM
RUD2DP22/1B	0015
RUNTK0152CEZZ	OEM
RUTFK505	OEM
RUZYX	OEM
RV06	0015
RV1	0023
RV1BA1330	0412
RV1LA3301	1206
RV1LA4126	1940
RV1S1998	2279
RV1SM5104	2592
RV2	0023
RV6.2	0466
RV15	OEM
RV101	OEM
RV555NB	0967
RV556DB	3254
RV741NB	0308
RV1017	0133
RV1059	0006
RV1068	0127
RV1180	0004
RV1181	0157
RV1189	0023
RV1226	0133
RV1395	0191
RV1424	0015
RV1458NB	3108
RV1467	0144
RV1468	0144
RV1469	0144
RV1470	0144
RV1471	0079
RV1472	0126
RV1473	0086
RV1474	0079
RV1475	0004
RV1476	0535
RV1477	0030
RV1478	0015
RV1479	0143
RV2068	0018
RV2069	0126
RV2070	0111
RV2071	0133
RV2072	0015
RV2213	0057
RV2248	0111
RV2249	0079
RV2250	0015
RV2260	0006
RV-2289	0015
RV2289	0015
RV2351	0037
RV2353	0203
RV2354	1211
RV2355	0006
RV2356	1257
RV3403ADB	OEM
RV4136DB	2995
RV4136DC	2995
RV4143NB	OEM
RV4144NB	OEM
RV4151DE	OEM
RV4151NB	OEM
RV4152DE	OEM
RV4153DC	OEM
RV4156DC	2796
RV4191DE	OEM
RV4191NB	OEM
RV4192DE	OEM
RV4192NB	OEM
RV4193DE	OEM
RV4193NB	OEM
RV4200ADE	OEM
RV4200ANB	OEM
RV4200DE	OEM
RV4200NB	OEM
RV4391DE	OEM
RV4391NB	OEM
RV4558DE	0356
RV4558NB	0356
RV4559DE	0356
RV4559NB	0356
RV2347042	OEM
RV2347043	OEM
RVB406	OEM
RVB-406MLFA	OEM
RVCFV-212A	0120
RVD0.8C22/1A	0015
RVD1E1LF	0015
RVD1K110	0143
RVD1N34A	0143
RVD1N4733A	0437
RVD1N4738	0244
RVD1N4739	0012
RVD1N4740	0170
RVD1SS54	0133
RVD1SV50S	0030
RVD1SV505	0030
RVD2-1K110	0143
RVD2DP	0015
RVD2DP22/1B	0015
RVD2DP22/1C	0276
RVD2DP22/18	0015
RVD2DP221B	0276
RVD2DP221P	0015
RVD2P22/1B	0015
RVD4B265J2	0015
RVD8MB4	0276
RVD8MBA	0015
RVD10D1	0015
RVD10DC1	0015
RVD10DC1R	0015
RVD10E1	0015
RVD10E1LF	0015
RVD10E11F	0015
RVD12B-1	0276
RVD1051	OEM
RVD14740	0170
RVDC08P1	0015
RVDC08P1R	0196
RVDCD0033	0298
RVDD124B	0276
RVDD1245	0276
RVDDS-410	0015
RVDEQA0106S	0298
RVDEQA0107S	0644
RVDEQA0108S	0644
RVDFV211	0139
RVDFV-212	0120
RVDFV212	0120
RVDFV214	0120
RVDGP05A	0015
RVDHZ3C1	0296
RVDK	0120
RVDKB162A	0133
RVDKB162C5	0133
RVDKB167	1914
RVDKB265J2	0139
RVDKB265J3	OEM
RVDMZ206	0091
RVDMZ208	0165
RVDMZ209	0057
RVD0.8C2211A	0535
RVDR5R6EB	0298
RVDR154B	0276
RVDRD5A1E	0041
RVDRD5R1EB	0041
RVDRD5R1EBB1	0041
RVDRD5R6EB	0253
RVDRD7AN	0062
RVDRD7R5E	0077
RVDRD7R5EB	0644
RVDRD7R5FB	0077
RVDRD9R1E	0057
RVDRD11AN	0181
RVDRD11EB	0064
RVDRD11EB,1	0181
RVDRD11EB1	0064
RVDS5277B	0015
RVDSC-15	0623
RVDSC20	3613
RVDSC-L5	0030
RVDSD-1	0102
RVDSD-1U	0015
RVDSD-1Y	0015
RVDSD113	0030
RVDSD113TA	0030
RVDSG-5N	0087
RVDSG-5P	0087
RVDSL55VR3FT	OEM
RVDSMIA02TPA	0015
RVDSR3AM2N	0071
RVDVD1150L	0139
RVDVD1150M	0139
RVDVD1210L	0120
RVDVD1210M	0120
RVDVD1211L	0120
RVDVD1212L	0120
RVDVD1213	0120
RVDVD1250M	0133
RVDVD1251L	0139
RVDVD1253	3638
RVDVD1260L	0139
RVDVD1262MF	0139
RVDVD12102	OEM
RVIBA328MR	2512
RVIBA338	2630
RVIBA532S	2767
RVIBA1330	0412
RVIBA6133	OEM
RVIHD36990	OEM
RVIHD38980A	2702
RVILM703	0627
RVILM8364DH	OEM
RVIM5102L	1899
RVIM51182	4676
RVIM51202	1899
RVIM51502L	1899
RVIMC4080	2827
RVIMK50372N	OEM
RVIS1998	2279
RVITK3200	OEM
RVITMS1943	2279
RVITMS1943N2	2279
RVITMS3451NC	OEM
RVITMS3451NL	OEM
RVITMS3454NR	OEM
RVIUPC20C2	0465
RVIUPC22C	3318
RVIUPC78L05	1288
RVIUPC575	2845
RVIUPC1018CE	2898
RVIUPD861	3763
RVS2SC645	0144
RVTCS1381	0016
RVTCS1382	0037
RVTCS1383	0016
RVTCS1384	0144
RVTCS1473	0111
RVTM51202	1899
RVTMC00921-3	0479
RVTMK10-2	0321
RVTMK10-E	0321
RVTS22410	0016
RVTS22411	0037
RW005M	OEM
RW01M	OEM
RW02M	OEM
RW04M	OEM
RW06M	OEM
RW08M	OEM
RW10M	OEM
RW15	OEM
RX-0034	OEM
RX-0043	OEM
RX090	0012
RX15	OEM
RXC192	OEM
RX-DX0041CEZZ	0196
RX-DX0131CEZZ	0023
RX-EX0019CEZZ	0025
RX-IX0035GAZZ	0898
RY10U	OEM
RY15	OEM
RY23	0604
RY24	0790
RZ08	OEM
RZ-3	0087
RZ3	OEM
RZ3.3	0289
RZ3.6	0188
RZ3.9	0451
RZ4.7	0446
RZ5.1	0041
RZ5.6	0157
RZ6.2	0631
RZ6.8	0025
RZ8.2	0244
RZ9.1	0012
RZ10	0170
RZ12	0137
RZ12A	0052
RZ14	0873
RZ15	0002
RZ15A	0681
RZ16	0440
RZ18	0490
RZ20	0695
RZ22	0560
RZ22A	0700
RZ25	0709
RZ27	0436
RZ27A	0436
RZ30	0195
RZ33A	0166
RZ39A	0032
RZ40	OEM
RZ47A	0068
RZ50	0092
RZ56A	0125
RZ68A	0173
RZ82A	0049
RZZ3.6	0188
RZZ3.9	0451
RZZ4.7	0446
RZZ5.1	0041
RZZ5.6	0157
RZZ6.2	0631
RZZ6.8	0025
RZZ8.2	0244
RZZ9.1	0012
RZZ10	0170
RZZ12	0137
RZZ15	0873
RZZ18	0371
RZZ22	0700
RZZ27	0450
S	0012
S0012	0126
S0013	0037
S0019	3066
S0026	0037
S0028	0338
S0029	0338
S0031	3078
S0032	3079
S0037	OEM
S00601DF	1557
S00602DF	1557
S00603DF	2140
S00604DF	2140
S00605DF	0706
S00606DF	0706
S001683	0086
S0-632	OEM
S0-4295-10	0103
S01	0050
S01E	0847
S02	0133
S02C	0865
S02D	0847
S02E	0847
S03	0050
S04	0133
S-05	0015
S05	OEM
S-05/01	0071
S-05-005	0015
S-05-01	0015
S05-01	OEM
S-05-02	0015
S05-02	OEM
S-05-04	0015
S05-04	OEM
S-05-06	0015
S05-06	OEM
S-05-08	0071
S05-08	OEM
S05-1	OEM
S-05-10	0071
S05-10	OEM
S-05-12	0102
S05K60	4158
S05K75	4834
S05K95	5066
S05K130	1364
S05K140	OEM
S05K150	0246
S05K175	OEM
S05K230	OEM
S05K250	1322
S05K275	1648
S05K300	4394
S07K60	4158
S07K75	4834
S07K95	5066
S07K130	1364
S07K140	OEM

If replacement code is OEM, contact original manufacturer for replacement.

531

DEVICE TYPE	REPL CODE
S07K150	0246
S07K175	OEM
S07K230	OEM
S07K250	1322
S07K275	1648
S07K300	4394
S010G	0071
S025	0004
S028	0595
S031A	0016
S035	OEM
S035AADF	1522
S037	0016
S042F	OEM
S042P	0321
S056F3	0464
S058F3	0464
S065	0164
S065A	0004
S074-007-001	0133
S082A	0911
S088	0004
S0300KS2	1129
S0301K	OEM
S0301M	2396
S0301MS2	1129
S0301MS3	OEM
S0303MS2	1386
S0303MS3	1386
S0303RS1	OEM
S0303RS2	1386
S0303RS3	1386
S0304F1	1386
S0306B	OEM
S0306G	1641
S0306H	2430
S0306L	0998
S0306LS2	1038
S0306RS2	OEM
S0306RS3	OEM
S0308B	OEM
S0308G	1641
S0308H	2430
S0308L	0998
S0308LS2	1038
S0308LS3	1038
S0308RS2	OEM
S0308RS3	OEM
S0310B	OEM
S0310G	1641
S0310H	2430
S0310L	0998
S0310LS2	1038
S0310LS3	1038
S0310RS2	OEM
S0310RS3	OEM
S0315G	1641
S0315H	2497
S0315L	2499
S0316B	OEM
S0316G	2497
S0316H	2497
S0316L	OEM
S0320L	2499
S0325B	OEM
S0325C	0226
S0325D	1837
S0325G	2497
S0325H	2174
S0325L	2587
S0325R	2597
S0325V	OEM
S0325Y	OEM
S0325Z	OEM
S0335C	0226
S0335D	1837
S0335G	1640
S0335H	0726
S0335J	2665
S0335K	2665
S0335W	2671
S0402BH	0712
S0402DH	0712
S0402MH	0304
S0402NH	0323
S0405BH	0712
S0405DH	0712
S0405MH	0304
S0405NH	0323
S0407BH	0712
S0407DH	0712
S0407MH	0304
S0407NH	0323
S0410BH	0712
S0410DH	0712
S0410MH	0304
S0410NH	0323
S0500KS2	0340
S-0501	0015
S0501	0015
S0501K	OEM
S0501L	0015
S0501LS1	1038
S0501LS2	1038
S0501LS3	5014
S0501M	0179
S0501MS2	1129
S0501MS3	OEM
S0503L	0998
S0503LS1	1038
S0503LS2	1038
S0503LS3	4549
S0503M	0179
S0503MS2	1250
S0503MS3	1250
S0503RS1	OEM
S0503RS2	1250
S0503RS3	0174
S0504F1	1250
S0506B	OEM
S0506G	1641
S0506H	2430
S0506L	2084
S0506LS2	1038
S0506LS3	1038
S0506RS2	OEM
S0506RS3	OEM
S0508B	OEM
S0508G	1641
S0508H	2430
S0508L	2084
S0508RS2	OEM
S0508RS3	OEM
S0510B	OEM
S0510F3	0464
S0510G	1641
S0510H	2430
S0510L	0998
S0510LS2	1038
S0510LS3	1038
S0510RS2	OEM
S0510RS3	OEM
S0515G	3575
S0515H	0340
S0515L	2499
S0516B	OEM
S0516G	2499
S0516H	2497
S0516L	OEM
S0520F4	0464
S0520L	2499
S0525B	OEM
S0525C	0226
S0525D	1837
S0525G	1640
S0525H	2174
S0525L	2587
S0525R	2597
S0525V	OEM
S0525Y	OEM
S0525Z	OEM
S0535	OEM
S0535C	0226
S0535D	1837
S0535G	1640
S0535H	0726
S0535J	2665
S0535K	2665
S0535W	2671
S0555M	2671
S0555W	2671
S0565J	OEM
S0565K	OEM
S0570W	OEM
S0602BH	0712
S0602DH	0712
S0602MH	0304
S0602NH	0323
S0605BH	0712
S0605DH	0712
S0605MH	0304
S0605NH	0323
S0607BH	0712
S0607DH	0712
S0607MH	0304
S0607NH	0323
S0610BH	0712
S0610DH	0712
S0610MH	0304
S0610NH	0323
S0702	0012
S0704	0016
S0802BH	0712
S0802DH	0712
S0802MH	0304
S0802NH	0323
S0805BH	0712
S0805DH	0712
S0805MH	0304
S0805NH	0323
S0807BH	0712
S0807DH	0712
S0807MH	0304
S0807NH	0323
S0810BH	0712
S0810DH	0712
S0810MH	0304
S0810NH	0323
S02501DF	6459
S02502DF	6459
S02503DF	6480
S02504DF	6480
S02505DF	6507
S02506DF	6507
S020803	OEM
S1	0023
S1-1	0015
S1-RECT-35	0133
S1-RECT-102	0015
S1A	0015
S1A05F	2068
S1A06	0015
S1A060	0015
S1A1F	2068
S1A2F	2068
S1A3	1328
S1A3F	0023
S1A4F	0023
S1A5F	0023
S1A6F	0023
S1A8F	0017
S1A10	OEM
S1A10F	0017
S1A12F	0017
S1A20	OEM
S1A40	OEM
S1A60	0015
S1A80	0071
S1A100	0071
S1A150	0102
S1AN6	0983
S1AN12	0097
S1AN15	0865
S1AN15R	1625
S1AN20	0865
S1AN20R	1625
S1AN31	1116
S1AN31R	1099
S1AN40	1116
S1AN40R	1099
S1AN41	OEM
S1AN55	2633
S1AN55R	2741
S1AN70	OEM
S1AN71	OEM
S1AR1	0015
S1AR2	0015
S1B	0015
S1B01	0015
S1B01-01	0015
S1B-01-02	0015
S1B01-02	0015
S1B01-04	0959
S1B01-0226	0015
S1B01-1	0015
S1B02	0015
S1B02-0	0015
S1B02-03C	0087
S1B02-06CE	0015
S1B02-06CRE	0015
S1B02-C	0015
S1B02-CR	0015
S1B02-O	0015
S1B02C	0164
S1B0101CR	0015
S1B0102	0015
S1B0201B	0276
S1B0201CR	0015
S1B-0306	0071
S1B1	0015
S1BD1-02	0015
S1BN15	0865
S1BN15R	1625
S1BN20	0865
S1BN20R	1625
S1BN31	1116
S1BN31R	1099
S1BN40	1116
S1BN40R	1099
S1BN55	2633
S1BN55R	2741
S1BR2	0983
S1BR5	1241
S1BR30	OEM
S1BR70	OEM
S1BR512	OEM
S1C	0071
S1CN1	0015
S1CR5	1241
S1CR8	OEM
S1CR25	OEM
S1CR30	OEM
S1D	0071
S1D2A-1	0907
S1D2A-3	0907
S1D23-13	0102
S1D23-15	0102
S1D26	0102
S1D30-13	0102
S1D50B851-A	0133
S1D51C052-19	0015
S1D51C169-1	0015
S1D153	0042
S1DR5	1241
S1DR8	OEM
S1DR25	OEM
S1DR30	OEM
S1ER5	1241
S1ER8	OEM
S1ER25	OEM
S1ER30	OEM
S1F	0017
S1FN270	OEM
S1FN290	OEM
S1G1	OEM
S1G2	OEM
S1G4	OEM
S1G6Z	OEM
S1G8Z	OEM
S1G10	0023
S1G20	0015
S1G40	0015
S1G40Z	0015
S1G60Z	0015
S1G80Z	0072
S1GN270	OEM
S1GR2	0947
S1K20	0023
S1K20H	0023
S1K40	0023
S1L200	0015
S1M	0110
S1M1	0110
S1M2	0110
S1N1189	OEM
S1N1204A	OEM
S1N1616	OEM
S1N3911	OEM
S1OAN6	0145
S1P	0102
S1P20	0102
S1P20Z	0102
S1P40Z	0102
S1P60	0017
S1P80	0017
S1P100	0017
S1P150	0017
S1PB15	0287
S1Q20Z	0287
S1QB10	0276
S1QB20	0287
S1QB20Z	0287
S1QB40	0293
S1QB40Z	0293
S1QB60	0299
S1R12B	0137
S1R13B	0137
S1R20	0133
S1R20Z	0102
S1R40Z	0102
S1R50	OEM
S1R60	0023
S1R80	2506
S1R100	0017
S1R150	0017
S1RB	0276
S1RB-10	0276
S1RB10	0276
S1RB20	0287
S1RB20Z	0287
S1RB40	0293
S1RB40Z	0293
S1RB60	0299
S1RBA	0276
S1RBA-10	6509
S1RBA10	0106
S1RBA10-F10	OEM
S1RBA20	0106
S1RBA20Z	0106
S1RBA40	0106
S1RBA40Z	0106
S1RBA60	1999
S1RBA80	2384
S1RC20	0015
S1RC20R	0015
S1S	OEM
S1S2	0133
S1S3H	0023
S1S4M	0023
S1S11	0143
S1S20	0143
S1SD-1	0015
S1SD-1HF	0015
S1SD-1X	0015
S1SM-150-01	0015
S1SM-150-02	0015
S1SS	OEM
S1T20H	5975
S1T40H	OEM
S1T60H	5890
S1U-1N	OEM
S1U-1P	OEM
S1U-12	OEM
S1V1D	OEM
S1V20	OEM
S1VB	0287
S1VB-10	0276
S1VB10	0276
S1VB10-S	0276
S1VB10S	0276
S1VB20	0287
S1VB20Z	0287
S1VB40	0293
S1VB40Z	0293
S1VB60	0299
S1VB60Z	0299
S1VN0104	OEM
S1WB	0241
S1WB(A)10	0241
S1WB(A)10D	0241
S1WB10	0241
S1WB20	0241
S1WB40	4501
S1WB60	1864
S1WBA40	1864
S1WBA40A	1864
S1WBA60	1864
S1WBS10	0241
S1WBS40	OEM
S1WBS4095	OEM
S1Y	1129
S1Y1D	OEM
S1YB10	OEM
S1YB20	OEM
S1YB40	OEM
S1YB60	OEM
S1Z	1293
S1.5	0015
S-1.5-0	0015
S1.5-01	0015
S-1.5-01FR	0102
S-1.5-02	0015
S1.5-02	OEM
S-1.5-02FR	0102
S-1.5-04	0015
S1.5-04	OEM
S-1.5-04FR	0102
S-1.5-06	0015
S1.5-06	OEM
S-1.5-06FR	0102
S-1.5-08	0071
S1.5-08	OEM
S-1.5-08FR	0102
S-1.5-10	0071
S1.5-10	OEM
S-1.5-10FR	0102
S-2	0015
S2	0150
S2A06	0015
S2A2F	OEM
S2A10	0015
S2A20	0242
S2A30	0535
S2A40	0535
S2A42	OEM
S2A50	0959
S2A60	0959
S2A80	0811
S2A100	0916
S2AN6	0097
S2AN12	0097
S2AN31	OEM
S2AN40	OEM
S2AN41	OEM
S2AN55	OEM
S2AN70	OEM
S2AN71	OEM
S2AO6	0110
S2AR1	0015
S2AR2	0015
S2BR30	OEM
S2BR70	OEM
S2BR512	OEM
S2C-10	OEM
S2C30	0015
S2C40	0015
S2C40A	0015
S2CN1	0242
S2CR8	OEM
S2CR25	OEM
S2CR30	OEM
S2DR8	OEM
S2DR25	OEM
S2DR30	OEM
S2E20	0015
S2E60	0015
S2E60-1	0015
S2E100	0071
S2ER8	OEM
S2ER25	OEM
S2ER30	OEM
S2F10	0015
S2F20	0015
S2FN270	OEM
S2FN290	OEM
S2GN270	OEM
S2GN290	OEM
S2GR2	0242
S2HB20Z	OEM
S2K-20	OEM
S2K20	0635
S2K20H	0541
S2K40	0604
S2K45	0031
S2K49	0087
S2L20UF	OEM
S2LA20	0541
S2LA20F	OEM
S2M1	0947
S2M2	0110
S2PB	0276
S2PB10	0276
S2PB20	0287
S2PB40	0293
S2Q20	0015
S2Q40	0015
S2Q60	0015
S2Q80	0071
S2Q100	0071
S2RB40	0293
S2TB	0293
S2TB10	0276
S2TB20	0287
S2TB40	0293
S2TB80	0250
S2V	0071
S2V2D	OEM
S2V3D	OEM
S2V10	0071
S2V20	0559
S2V40	0071
S2V60	0071
S2VB	1404
S2VB10	0319
S2VB-10-1	0319
S2VB20	1404
S2VB40	0468
S2VB60	0441
S2VC	0015
S2VC10	0071
S2VC10R	0071
S2Y1D	OEM
S2Z20	0242
S2Z40	0535
S2Z60	0959
S2Z80	0811
S2Z100	0916
S3	0150
S3-3AT2	2072
S3A05	0110
S3A05F	0541
S3A06	0015
S3A025	0110
S3A1	0947
S3A1F	0541
S3A2	0242
S3A2F	0541
S-3A3	1296
S3A3	0535
S3A3F	1352
S3A4	0535
S3A4F	1352
S3A5	0959
S3A5F	0031
S3A6	0959
S3A6F	0031
S3A7	0811
S3A8	0811
S3A8F	1362
S3A9	0916
S3A10	0916
S3A10F	1362
S3A12	OEM
S3A12F	OEM
S3A15	OEM
S3AN6	0109
S3AN12	0109
S3AN15	OEM
S3AN20	OEM
S3AN31	OEM
S3AN40	OEM
S3AN41	OEM
S3AN55	OEM
S3AN70	OEM
S3AN71	OEM
S3AR1	0015
S3AR2	OEM
S-3AT2	2072
S3B20Z	OEM
S3B40-02	OEM
S3B40-04	OEM
S3B40-06	OEM
S3B40-08	OEM
S3B40-10	OEM
S3B40-12	OEM
S3B40Z	OEM
S3BA05	0110
S3BN15	OEM
S3BN20	OEM
S3BN31	OEM
S3BN40	OEM
S3BN55	OEM
S3BN71	OEM
S3BR30	OEM
S3BR70	OEM
S3BR502	OEM
S3BR511	OEM
S3BR512	OEM
S3C321	OEM
S3C471	OEM
S3C661	OEM
S3CN1	0535
S3CN3	OEM
S3CR8	OEM
S3CR25	OEM
S3CR30	OEM
S-3DB3	2073
S3DR8	OEM
S3DR25	OEM
S3DR30	OEM
S3DR601	OEM
S3EN310	OEM
S3ER8	OEM
S3ER25	OEM
S3ER30	OEM
S3FN270	OEM
S3FN290	OEM
S3FN310	OEM
S3FN350	OEM
S3G1	OEM
S3G2	OEM
S3G4	0071
S3G4Z	OEM
S3G6Z	OEM
S3G8	OEM
S3G8Z	OEM
S3G10	0947
S3G20	0242
S3G40	0535
S3G40Z	0535
S3G41	0705
S3G60Z	0959
S3G80Z	0811
S3GN55	OEM
S3GN71	OEM
S3GN270	OEM
S3GN290	OEM
S3GN310	OEM
S3GN350	OEM
S3GR2	0535
S3GR311	OEM
S3H-02	OEM
S3HN310	OEM
S3HR311	OEM
S3K40	0031
S3M1	0242
S3M2	OEM
S3M3	OEM
S3MX	0015
S3S3M	2520
S3S4M	0559
S3S6M	3559
S3V1D	OEM
S3V-10	0087
S3V10	0087
S3V10SS	OEM
S3V20	0559
S3V40	0087
S3V60	0087
S3V60Z	0031
S3VC10	0199
S3VC10R	1009
S3VC20	0199
S3VC20R	1009
S3VC40	0199
S3VC40R	1009
S3VC60	OEM
S3WB	0441
S3WB10	0724
S3WB20	0724
S3WB40	0732
S3WB60	0732
S3WB60Z	0732
S4	0150
S4A06	0015
S4AN6	0109
S4AN12	0109
S4AN31	OEM
S4AN40	OEM
S4AN41	OEM
S4AN55	OEM
S4AN70	OEM
S4AN71	OEM
S4AO6	0015
S4AR1	0015
S4AR2	0015
S4AR30	0015
S4B01	OEM
S4BR30	OEM
S4BR70	OEM
S4BR502	OEM
S4BR512	OEM
S-4C	0017
S4C	0015
S4CN1	0242
S4CR8	OEM
S4CR25	OEM
S4CR30	OEM
S4DR8	OEM
S4DR25	OEM
S4DR30	OEM
S4ER8	OEM
S4ER25	OEM
S4ER30	OEM
S4FN270	OEM
S4FN290	OEM
S4FN300	0015
S4GN270	OEM
S4GN290	OEM
S4GR2	0242
S4LS132N	1615
S4LS221N	1230
S4LS374N	0708
S4M1	0535
S4M2	OEM
S4VB	1404
S4VB-10	0319
S4VB10	0319
S4VB-10-1	0319
S4VB20	1404
S4VB20A	OEM
S4VB20F	1404
S4VB40	0468
S4VB40F1	0468
S4VB60	0441
S-5A05	1272
S5A05	1272
S5A05F	1352
S5A025	1272
S-5A1	1272
S5A1	1272
S5A1F	1352
S-5A2	1272

If replacement code is OEM, contact original manufacturer for replacement.

DEVICE TYPE	REPL CODE
S5A2	1272
S5A2F	1352
S-5A3	1277
S5A3	1277
S5A3F	1352
S-5A4	1277
S5A4	1277
S5A4F	1352
S-5A5	1282
S5A5	1282
S5A5F	1362
S-5A6	1282
S5A6	1282
S5A6F	1362
S-5A8	1285
S5A8	1285
S5A8F	1362
S-5A10	1285
S5A10	1285
S5A10F	1362
S5A12	OEM
S5A12F	OEM
S5A15	OEM
S5AN6	0122
S5AN12	0122
S5AN15	OEM
S5AN20	OEM
S5AN31	OEM
S5AN40	OEM
S5AN41	OEM
S5AN55	OEM
S5AN70	OEM
S5AN71	OEM
S5AR1	0015
S5AR2	0015
S5B-01	OEM
S5B10	OEM
S5B20	OEM
S5B30	OEM
S5B40	OEM
S5B50	OEM
S5B60	OEM
S5B80	OEM
S5B100	OEM
S5BN15	OEM
S5BN20	OEM
S5BN31	OEM
S5BN40	OEM
S5BN55	OEM
S5BN71	OEM
S5BR30	OEM
S5BR70	OEM
S5BR502	OEM
S5BR511	OEM
S5BR512	OEM
S5C321	OEM
S5C471	OEM
S5C661	OEM
S5CN1	0535
S5CN3	OEM
S5CR8	OEM
S5CR25	OEM
S5CR30	OEM
S5DR8	OEM
S5DR25	OEM
S5DR30	OEM
S5DR601	OEM
S5EN310	OEM
S5ER8	OEM
S5ER25	OEM
S5ER30	OEM
S5FN270	OEM
S5FN290	OEM
S5FN310	OEM
S5FN350	OEM
S5GN55	OEM
S5GN71	OEM
S5GN270	OEM
S5GN290	OEM
S5GN310	OEM
S5GN350	OEM
S5GR2	0959
S5GR311	OEM
S5HN310	OEM
S5HN311	OEM
S5HR311	OEM
S5KC20	1227
S5KC20H	1227
S5KC20R	1716
S5KC20RH	1716
S5KC40	OEM
S5KC40R	OEM
S5KD20	OEM
S5KD20H	OEM
S5KD40	OEM
S5KP5.0	OEM
S5KP5.0A	OEM
S5KP6.0	OEM
S5KP6.0A	OEM
S5KP6.5	OEM
S5KP6.5A	OEM
S5KP7.0	OEM
S5KP7.0A	OEM
S5KP7.5	OEM
S5KP7.5A	OEM
S5KP8.0	OEM
S5KP8.0A	OEM
S5KP8.5	OEM
S5KP8.5A	OEM

DEVICE TYPE	REPL CODE
S5KP9.0	OEM
S5KP9.0A	OEM
S5KP10	OEM
S5KP10A	OEM
S5KP11	OEM
S5KP11A	OEM
S5KP12	OEM
S5KP12A	OEM
S5KP13	OEM
S5KP13A	OEM
S5KP14	OEM
S5KP14A	OEM
S5KP15	OEM
S5KP15A	OEM
S5KP16	OEM
S5KP16A	OEM
S5KP17	OEM
S5KP17A	OEM
S5KP18	OEM
S5KP18A	OEM
S5KP20	OEM
S5KP20A	OEM
S5KP22	OEM
S5KP22A	OEM
S5KP24	OEM
S5KP24A	OEM
S5KP26	OEM
S5KP26A	OEM
S5KP28	OEM
S5KP28A	OEM
S5KP30	OEM
S5KP30A	OEM
S5KP33	OEM
S5KP33A	OEM
S5KP36	OEM
S5KP36A	OEM
S5KP40	OEM
S5KP40A	OEM
S5KP43	OEM
S5KP43A	OEM
S5KP45	OEM
S5KP45A	OEM
S5KP48	OEM
S5KP48A	OEM
S5KP51	OEM
S5KP51A	OEM
S5KP54	OEM
S5KP54A	OEM
S5KP58	OEM
S5KP58A	OEM
S5KP60	OEM
S5KP60A	OEM
S5KP64	OEM
S5KP64A	OEM
S5KP70	OEM
S5KP70A	OEM
S5KP75	OEM
S5KP75A	OEM
S5KP78	OEM
S5KP78A	OEM
S5KP85	OEM
S5KP85A	OEM
S5KP90	OEM
S5KP90A	OEM
S5KP100	OEM
S5KP100A	OEM
S5KP110	OEM
S5KP110A	OEM
S5M1	0535
S5M2	OEM
S5M3	OEM
S5S	0015
S5S3	2066
S5S3M	OEM
S5S4	2066
S5S4M	OEM
S5SR	0015
S5VB	1404
S5VB-10	1404
S5VB10	0319
S5VB10F	OEM
S5VB20	1404
S5VB40	0468
S5VB40-F1	0468
S5VB60	0441
S6-3	0276
S6-10	0170
S6-103A	2872
S6-103K	2275
S6-203A	2872
S6-203K	2275
S6-403A	1104
S6-403K	0471
S6-603A	1104
S6-603K	0471
S6-803A	2982
S6-803K	0444
S6-1003A	2982
S6-1003K	0444
S6-1203K	OEM
S6-Z603A	1104
S6-Z603K	0471
S6-Z803A	2982
S6-Z803K	0444
S6-Z1003A	2982
S6-Z1003K	0444
S6A05	1272
S6A1	1272
S6A2	1277

DEVICE TYPE	REPL CODE
S6A3	1277
S6A4	1277
S6A5	1282
S6A6	1282
S6A8	1285
S6A10	1285
S6AN6	0122
S6AN12	0122
S6AN31	OEM
S6AN40	OEM
S6AN41	OEM
S6AN55	OEM
S6AN70	OEM
S6AN71	OEM
S6AR1	0015
S6AR2	0015
S6BR30	OEM
S6BR70	OEM
S6BR512	OEM
S6CR8	OEM
S6CR25	OEM
S6CR30	OEM
S6DR8	OEM
S6DR25	OEM
S6DR30	OEM
S6ER8	OEM
S6ER25	OEM
S6ER30	OEM
S6FN270	OEM
S6GN270	OEM
S6GR2	0959
S6K20	5779
S6K20H	1119
S6K20R	OEM
S6K40	5779
S6K40R	OEM
S6M1	0959
S6M2	OEM
S6Z803A	OEM
S6Z1003A	OEM
S6Z1203A	OEM
S7	OEM
S7-8	0133
S7AN6	0131
S7AN12	0131
S7AN15	OEM
S7AN20	OEM
S7AN31	OEM
S7AN40	OEM
S7AN55	OEM
S7AN70	OEM
S7AN71	OEM
S7AR1	0071
S7BN15	OEM
S7BN20	OEM
S7BN31	OEM
S7BN40	OEM
S7BN55	OEM
S7BN200	OEM
S7BR30	OEM
S7BR70	OEM
S7BR125	OEM
S7BR502	OEM
S7BR511	OEM
S7BR512	OEM
S7C321	OEM
S7C452	OEM
S7C471	OEM
S7C661	OEM
S7CN3	OEM
S7CR8	OEM
S7CR25	OEM
S7CR30	OEM
S7DR8	OEM
S7DR25	OEM
S7DR30	OEM
S7DR601	OEM
S7EN310	OEM
S7ER8	OEM
S7ER25	OEM
S7ER30	OEM
S7FN270	OEM
S7FN290	OEM
S7FN310	OEM
S7FN350	OEM
S7GN55	OEM
S7GN71	OEM
S7GN270	OEM
S7GN290	OEM
S7GN310	OEM
S7GN350	OEM
S7GR311	OEM
S7HN310	OEM
S7HR311	OEM
S7KN125	OEM
S7LN125	OEM
S7PN125	OEM
S-8-01	0865
S8-01	1241
S8-01F	OEM
S-8-01FR	0865
S-8-02	0865
S8-02	OEM
S8-02F	OEM
S-8-02FR	0865
S-8-03	0847
S8-03	OEM
S8-03F	OEM
S-8-04	0847

DEVICE TYPE	REPL CODE
S8-04	OEM
S8-04F	OEM
S-8-04FR	0847
S-8-06	4257
S8-06	0087
S8-06F	OEM
S-8-06FR	OEM
S-8-08	4258
S8-08	OEM
S8-08F	OEM
S-8-08FR	OEM
S8-10	0087
S8-10F	OEM
S-8-10FR	OEM
S-8-12	OEM
S8AN6	0131
S8AN12	0131
S8AN31	OEM
S8AN40	OEM
S8AN55	OEM
S8AN70	OEM
S8AN71	OEM
S8AR1	0071
S8AR2	0071
S8B10	OEM
S8B20	OEM
S8B30	OEM
S8B40	OEM
S8B50	OEM
S8B60	OEM
S8B80	OEM
S8B100	OEM
S8BN200	OEM
S8BR30	OEM
S8BR70	OEM
S8BR503	OEM
S8BR512	OEM
S8CN1	0811
S8CR8	OEM
S8CR25	OEM
S8CR30	OEM
S8DR8	OEM
S8DR25	OEM
S8DR30	OEM
S8ER8	OEM
S8ER25	OEM
S8ER30	OEM
S8GN270	OEM
S8GR2	0811
S8H80J	0677
S8M1	0959
S8M2	OEM
S-8R-01	5805
S-8R-01FR	OEM
S-8R-02	5805
S-8R-02FR	OEM
S-8R-03	OEM
S-8R-04	5806
S-8R-04FR	OEM
S-8R-06	5808
S-8R-06FR	OEM
S-8R-08	5809
S-8R-08FR	OEM
S-8R-10	5810
S-8R-10FR	OEM
S-8R-12	OEM
S8T28F	0576
S8T95F	OEM
S8T97F	OEM
S8T98F	OEM
S9AH12	0145
S9AN6	0145
S9AN12	0145
S9AN15	OEM
S9AN20	OEM
S9AN31	OEM
S9AN40	OEM
S9AN55	OEM
S9AN70	OEM
S9AN71	OEM
S9AR1	0071
S9BN15	OEM
S9BN20	OEM
S9BN31	OEM
S9BN40	OEM
S9BN55	OEM
S9BN71	OEM
S9BN200	OEM
S9BR30	OEM
S9BR70	OEM
S9BR125	OEM
S9BR502	OEM
S9BR503	OEM
S9BR511	OEM
S9BR512	OEM
S9C321	OEM
S9C452	OEM
S9C471	OEM
S9C661	OEM
S9CN3	OEM
S9CR8	OEM
S9CR25	OEM
S9CR30	OEM
S9DR8	OEM
S9DR25	OEM
S9DR30	OEM
S9DR601	OEM
S9EN310	OEM
S9ER8	OEM

DEVICE TYPE	REPL CODE
S9ER25	OEM
S9ER30	OEM
S9FN270	OEM
S9FN290	OEM
S9FN310	OEM
S9FN350	OEM
S9GN55	OEM
S9GN71	OEM
S9GN270	OEM
S9GN290	OEM
S9GN310	OEM
S9GN350	OEM
S9GR311	OEM
S9HN310	OEM
S9HR311	OEM
S9K1003K3	OEM
S9K1003K4	OEM
S9K1003K5	OEM
S9K1003K35	OEM
S9K1003K45	OEM
S9K1103K3	OEM
S9K1103K4	OEM
S9K1103K5	OEM
S9K1103K35	OEM
S9K1103K45	OEM
S9K1203K3	OEM
S9K1203K4	OEM
S9K1203K5	OEM
S9K1203K35	OEM
S9K1203K45	OEM
S9K1303K3	OEM
S9K1303K4	OEM
S9K1303K5	OEM
S9K1303K35	OEM
S9K1303K45	OEM
S9K1403K3	OEM
S9K1403K4	OEM
S9K1403K5	OEM
S9K1403K35	OEM
S9K1403K45	OEM
S9K1503K3	OEM
S9K1503K4	OEM
S9K1503K5	OEM
S9K1503K35	OEM
S9K1503K45	OEM
S9K1603K3	OEM
S9K1603K4	OEM
S9K1603K5	OEM
S9K1603K35	OEM
S9K1603K45	OEM
S9K1703K3	OEM
S9K1703K4	OEM
S9K1703K5	OEM
S9K1703K35	OEM
S9K1703K45	OEM
S9K1803K3	OEM
S9K1803K4	OEM
S9K1803K5	OEM
S9K1803K35	OEM
S9K1803K45	OEM
S9K2003K4	OEM
S9K2003K5	OEM
S9K2003K35	OEM
S9K2003K45	OEM
S9K2103K4	OEM
S9K2103K5	OEM
S9K2103K45	OEM
S9K2203K4	OEM
S9K2203K5	OEM
S9K2203K45	OEM
S9K2303K4	OEM
S9K2303K5	OEM
S9K2303K45	OEM
S9K2403A4	OEM
S9K2403K5	OEM
S9K2403K45	OEM
S9K2503K5	OEM
S9K2503K45	OEM
S9K2603K5	OEM
S9K2703K5	OEM
S9K2803K5	OEM
S9K2903K5	OEM
S9K3003K5	OEM
S9KN125	OEM
S9LN125	OEM
S9PN125	OEM
S10	0015
S10-12	2296
S10A	0015
S10AN6	0145
S10AN12	0145
S10AN31	OEM
S10AN40	OEM
S10AN55	OEM
S10AN70	OEM
S10AN71	OEM
S10AR1	0071
S10AR2	0071
S10BN200	OEM
S10BR30	OEM
S10BR70	OEM
S10BR503	OEM
S10BR512	OEM
S10BV1069	0319
S10C	0865
S10CN1	0811
S10CR8	OEM
S10CR25	OEM
S10CR30	OEM

DEVICE TYPE	REPL CODE
S10DR8	OEM
S10DR25	OEM
S10DR30	OEM
S10E	0847
S10ER8	OEM
S10ER25	OEM
S10ER30	OEM
S10FFD01	OEM
S10FFD02	OEM
S10FFD04	OEM
S10FFD06	OEM
S10FFD08	OEM
S10FFD10	OEM
S10FFD12	OEM
S10FHD01	OEM
S10FHD02	OEM
S10FHD04	OEM
S10FHD06	OEM
S10FHD08	OEM
S10FN270	OEM
S10FND02	OEM
S10FND04	OEM
S10FND06	OEM
S10FND08	OEM
S10FND10	OEM
S10FND12	OEM
S10FUD01	OEM
S10FUD02	OEM
S10FUD04	OEM
S10GN270	OEM
S10GN302	OEM
S10GR2	0916
S10GR302	OEM
S10HN302	OEM
S10HR302	OEM
S-10K	OEM
S10K14	1998
S10K17	2310
S10K20	2769
S10K25	3044
S10K30	3046
S10K35	2913
S10K40	3049
S10K50	3056
S10K60	3061
S10K75	3075
S10K95	3087
S10K130	0832
S10K140	OEM
S10K150	1982
S10K175	OEM
S10K230	OEM
S10K250	1324
S10K275	1650
S10K300	2023
S10K385	OEM
S10K420	3226
S10K460	OEM
S10K510	OEM
S10K550	OEM
S10K625	OEM
S10K680	OEM
S10M1	0811
S10M2	OEM
S10N500E	OEM
S10N500E3	OEM
S10N500E4	OEM
S10N500E5	OEM
S10N600E	OEM
S10N600E3	OEM
S10N600E4	OEM
S10N600E5	OEM
S10N700E	OEM
S10N700E3	OEM
S10N700E4	OEM
S10N700E5	OEM
S10N800E	OEM
S10N800E3	OEM
S10N800E4	OEM
S10N800E5	OEM
S10N900E	OEM
S10N900E3	OEM
S10N900E4	OEM
S10N900E5	OEM
S10N1000E	OEM
S10N1000E3	OEM
S10N1000E4	OEM
S10N1000E5	OEM
S10N1100E	OEM
S10N1100E3	OEM
S10N1100E4	OEM
S10N1100E5	OEM
S10N1200E	OEM
S10N1200E3	OEM
S10N1200E4	OEM
S10N1200E5	OEM
S10N1300E	OEM
S10N1300E3	OEM
S10N1300E4	OEM
S10N1300E5	OEM
S10N1400E	OEM
S10N1400E3	OEM
S10N1400E4	OEM
S10N1400E5	OEM
S10N1500E	OEM
S10N1500E3	OEM
S10N1500E4	OEM
S10N1500E5	OEM
S10N1600E	OEM

DEVICE TYPE	REPL CODE
S10N1600E3	OEM
S10N1600E4	OEM
S10N1600E5	OEM
S10N1700E	OEM
S10N1800E	OEM
S10SC3	OEM
S10SC3M	1227
S10SC3MR	1716
S10SC4	OEM
S10SC4M	1227
S10SC4MR	1716
S10VB	0319
S10VB10	0319
S10VB20	1404
S10VB40	0468
S10VB60	0441
S10V-S05K150	0246
S11	0133
S11AN15	OEM
S11AN20	OEM
S11AN31	OEM
S11AN40	OEM
S11AN55	OEM
S11AN70	OEM
S11AN71	OEM
S11AN125	OEM
S11B	OEM
S11BN15	OEM
S11BN20	OEM
S11BN31	OEM
S11BN40	OEM
S11BN55	OEM
S11BN71	OEM
S11BN200	OEM
S11BR125	OEM
S11BR502	OEM
S11BR503	OEM
S11BR511	OEM
S11BR512	OEM
S11C	OEM
S11C321	OEM
S11C452	OEM
S11C471	OEM
S11C661	OEM
S11D	OEM
S11DR601	OEM
S11EN310	OEM
S11FN270	OEM
S11FN290	OEM
S11FN310	OEM
S11FN350	OEM
S11GN55	OEM
S11GN71	OEM
S11GN270	OEM
S11GN290	OEM
S11GN302	OEM
S11GN310	OEM
S11GN350	OEM
S11GR302	OEM
S11GR311	OEM
S11HN302	OEM
S11HN310	OEM
S11HR302	OEM
S11HR311	OEM
S11KN125	OEM
S11LN125	OEM
S11P500E	OEM
S11P600E	OEM
S11P700E	OEM
S11P800E	OEM
S11P900E	OEM
S11P1000E	OEM
S11P1100E	OEM
S11P1200E	OEM
S11P1300E	OEM
S11P1400E	OEM
S11P1500E	OEM
S11P1600E	OEM
S11P1700E	OEM
S11P1800E	OEM
S11PN125	OEM
S-12	0242
S-12A	0242
S12AN6	OEM
S12AN31	OEM
S12AN40	OEM
S12AN55	OEM
S12AN70	OEM
S12AN71	OEM
S12AR2	OEM
S12B	OEM
S12BN200	OEM
S12BR30	OEM
S12BR70	OEM
S12BR503	OEM
S12C	OEM
S12C20	OEM
S12C40	OEM
S12C60	OEM
S12C80	OEM
S12C100	OEM
S12CN1	0811
S12CR8	OEM
S12CR25	OEM
S12CR30	OEM
S12D	OEM
S12DR8	OEM
S12DR25	OEM
S12DR30	OEM

If replacement code is OEM, contact original manufacturer for replacement. 533

DEVICE TYPE	REPL CODE
S12ER8	OEM
S12ER25	OEM
S12ER30	OEM
S12FN270	OEM
S12GN270	OEM
S12GN302	OEM
S12GR2	OEM
S12GR302	OEM
S12HN302	OEM
S12HR302	OEM
S12KC20	2219
S12KC20H	2219
S12KC40	4409
S12M1	0916
S12M2	OEM
S12P500E	OEM
S12P600E	OEM
S12P700E	OEM
S12P800E	OEM
S12P900E	OEM
S12P1000E	OEM
S12P1100E	OEM
S12P1200E	OEM
S12P1300E	OEM
S12P1400E	OEM
S12P1500E	OEM
S12P1600E	OEM
S12P1700E	OEM
S12P1800E	OEM
S13	0015
S13A	0535
S13AN15	OEM
S13AN20	OEM
S13AN31	OEM
S13AN40	OEM
S13AN70	OEM
S13AN125	OEM
S13BN15	OEM
S13BN20	OEM
S13BN31	OEM
S13BN40	OEM
S13BN55	OEM
S13BN71	OEM
S13BN200	OEM
S13BR125	OEM
S13BR503	OEM
S13BR512	OEM
S13C322	OEM
S13C453	OEM
S13C472	OEM
S13C661	OEM
S13DR601	OEM
S13EN310	OEM
S13FN270	OEM
S13FN290	OEM
S13FN310	OEM
S13FN350	OEM
S13GN55	OEM
S13GN71	OEM
S13GN270	OEM
S13GN290	OEM
S13GN302	OEM
S13GN310	OEM
S13GN350	OEM
S13GR302	OEM
S13GR312	OEM
S13GR313	OEM
S13HN302	OEM
S13HN310	OEM
S13HR302	OEM
S13HR312	OEM
S13HR313	OEM
S13KN125	OEM
S13KV	0201
S13LN125	OEM
S13N500E	OEM
S13N600E	OEM
S13N700E	OEM
S13N800E	OEM
S13N900E	OEM
S13N1000E	OEM
S13N1100E	OEM
S13N1200E	OEM
S13N1300E	OEM
S13N1400E	OEM
S13N1500E	OEM
S13N1600E	OEM
S13N1700E	OEM
S13N1800E	OEM
S13PN125	OEM
S14	0015
S14A	0535
S14AN31	OEM
S14AN40	OEM
S14AN70	OEM
S14AN125	OEM
S14BN200	OEM
S14BR125	OEM
S14C322	OEM
S14FN270	OEM
S14GN270	OEM
S14GN302	OEM
S14GR302	OEM
S14GR312	OEM
S14HN302	OEM
S14HR302	OEM
S14HR312	OEM
S14K14	1998
S14K17	2310
S14K20	2769
S14K25	3044
S14K30	3046
S14K35	2913
S14K40	3049
S14K50	3056
S14K60	3061
S14K75	3075
S14K95	3087
S14K130	0832
S14K140	OEM
S14K150	1982
S14K175	OEM
S14K230	OEM
S14K250	1324
S14K275	1650
S14K300	2023
S14K385	OEM
S14K420	3226
S14K460	OEM
S14K510	OEM
S14K550	OEM
S14K625	OEM
S14K680	OEM
S14K1000	OEM
S14KN125	OEM
S14LN125	OEM
S14PN125	OEM
S-15	0015
S15	0102
S-15-10	0015
S15A	0015
S15AN6	OEM
S15AN31	OEM
S15AN40	OEM
S15AN70	OEM
S15AR2	OEM
S15AR504	OEM
S15B	OEM
S15BN200	OEM
S15BR30	OEM
S15BR512	OEM
S-15C	0017
S15C	1053
S15C322	OEM
S15C323	OEM
S15C453	OEM
S15C472	OEM
S15CN1	OEM
S15CN3	OEM
S15CR8	OEM
S15CR25	OEM
S15CR30	OEM
S15D	OEM
S15DR8	OEM
S15DR25	OEM
S15DR30	OEM
S15ER8	OEM
S15ER25	OEM
S15ER30	OEM
S15FN270	OEM
S15GN270	OEM
S15GN302	OEM
S15GR2	OEM
S15GR302	OEM
S15GR312	OEM
S15GR313	OEM
S-15H	0102
S15H	0133
S15HN302	OEM
S15HR302	OEM
S15HR312	OEM
S15HR313	OEM
S15M1	OEM
S15M3	OEM
S15S3	0610
S15S4	0610
S15S6	OEM
S15SC3M	1931
S15SC4M	1931
S15VB10	2347
S15VB20	2347
S15VB40	2353
S15VB60	2354
S16	0015
S16A	0015
S16AR504	OEM
S16B	0015
S16B10	OEM
S16B20	OEM
S16B30	OEM
S16B40	OEM
S16B50	OEM
S16B60	OEM
S16B80	OEM
S16B100	OEM
S16C	OEM
S16C322	OEM
S16D	OEM
S16EN270	OEM
S16EN290	OEM
S16EN310	OEM
S16F3	0464
S16FN270	OEM
S16FN290	OEM
S16FN310	OEM
S16GN270	OEM
S16GN290	OEM
S16GN302	OEM
S16GN310	OEM
S16GR302	OEM
S16GR312	OEM
S16HN270	OEM
S16HN290	OEM
S16HN302	OEM
S16HN310	OEM
S16HN350	OEM
S16HR302	OEM
S16HR312	OEM
S17	0015
S17A	0015
S17AR504	OEM
S17BR503	OEM
S17BR512	OEM
S17C322	OEM
S17C323	OEM
S17C453	OEM
S17C472	OEM
S17C662	OEM
S17DR602	OEM
S17GN302	OEM
S17GR302	OEM
S17GR312	OEM
S17GR313	OEM
S17HN302	OEM
S17HR302	OEM
S17HR312	OEM
S17HR313	OEM
S18	0015
S18A	0015
S18AR2	OEM
S18B	0015
S18C322	OEM
S18F3	0464
S18GN302	OEM
S18GR2	OEM
S18GR302	OEM
S18GR312	OEM
S18HN302	OEM
S18HR302	OEM
S18HR312	OEM
S18KV	0374
S19	0015
S19A	0015
S19AR505	OEM
S19BR512	OEM
S19C	1099
S19C322	OEM
S19C323	OEM
S19C454	OEM
S19C472	OEM
S19C662	OEM
S19D	1103
S19DR602	OEM
S19E	0258
S19G	0267
S19GN302	OEM
S19GR302	OEM
S19GR312	OEM
S19GR313	OEM
S19HN302	OEM
S19HR302	OEM
S19HR312	OEM
S19HR313	OEM
S19J	1111
S19L	0280
S20	0071
S-20-01	0865
S20-01	OEM
S20-01F	OEM
S-20-01FR	0865
S-20-02	0865
S20-02	OEM
S20-02F	OEM
S-20-02FR	0865
S-20-04	0847
S20-04	OEM
S20-04F	OEM
S-20-04FR	0847
S-20-06	4914
S20-06	OEM
S20-06F	OEM
S-20-06FR	OEM
S-20-08	4915
S20-08	OEM
S20-08F	OEM
S-20-08FR	OEM
S-20-10	4916
S20-10	OEM
S-20-10-FR	OEM
S20-10F	OEM
S20AR505	OEM
S20C	1116
S20C322	OEM
S20D	1118
S20E	0800
S20FFA01	OEM
S20FFA02	OEM
S20FFA04	OEM
S20FFA06	OEM
S20FFA08	OEM
S20FFA10	OEM
S20FFA12	OEM
S20FFD01	OEM
S20FFD02	OEM
S20FFD04	OEM
S20FFD06	OEM
S20FFD08	OEM
S20FFD10	OEM
S20FFD12	OEM
S20FFK01	OEM
S20FFK02	OEM
S20FFK04	OEM
S20FFK06	OEM
S20FFK08	OEM
S20FFK10	OEM
S20FFK12	OEM
S20FHA01	OEM
S20FHA02	OEM
S20FHA04	OEM
S20FHA06	OEM
S20FHA08	OEM
S20FHD01	OEM
S20FHD02	OEM
S20FHD04	OEM
S20FHD06	OEM
S20FHD08	OEM
S20FHK01	OEM
S20FHK02	OEM
S20FHK04	OEM
S20FHK06	OEM
S20FHK08	OEM
S20FNA02	OEM
S20FNA04	OEM
S20FNA06	OEM
S20FNA08	OEM
S20FNA10	OEM
S20FNA12	OEM
S20FND02	OEM
S20FND04	OEM
S20FND06	OEM
S20FND08	OEM
S20FND10	OEM
S20FND12	OEM
S20FNK02	OEM
S20FNK04	OEM
S20FNK06	OEM
S20FNK08	OEM
S20FNK10	OEM
S20FNK12	OEM
S20FUA01	OEM
S20FUA02	OEM
S20FUA04	OEM
S20FUD01	OEM
S20FUD02	OEM
S20FUD04	OEM
S20FUK01	OEM
S20FUK02	OEM
S20FUK04	OEM
S20G	0315
S20GN302	OEM
S20GR302	OEM
S20GR312	OEM
S20HN302	OEM
S20HR302	OEM
S20HR312	OEM
S20J	1124
S20K60	OEM
S20K75	OEM
S20K95	OEM
S20K130	0824
S20K140	OEM
S20K150	3381
S20K175	OEM
S20K230	OEM
S20K250	1326
S20K275	4780
S20K300	4785
S20K385	OEM
S20K420	3806
S20K460	OEM
S20K510	OEM
S20K550	OEM
S20K625	OEM
S20K680	OEM
S20K1000	OEM
S20KV	0374
S20L	0045
S20N400D3	OEM
S20N400D4	OEM
S20N400D5	OEM
S20N400G3	OEM
S20N400G4	OEM
S20N400G5	OEM
S20N400H	OEM
S20N500J3	OEM
S20N500J4	OEM
S20N500J5	OEM
S20N600J3	OEM
S20N600J4	OEM
S20N600J5	OEM
S20N700J3	OEM
S20N700J4	OEM
S20N700J5	OEM
S20N750D3	OEM
S20N750D4	OEM
S20N750D5	OEM
S20N750G3	OEM
S20N750G4	OEM
S20N750G5	OEM
S20N800J3	OEM
S20N800J4	OEM
S20N800J5	OEM
S20N900J3	OEM
S20N900J4	OEM
S20N900J5	OEM
S20N1000D3	OEM
S20N1000D4	OEM
S20N1000D5	OEM
S20N1000G3	OEM
S20N1000G4	OEM
S20N1000G5	OEM
S20N1000J3	OEM
S20N1000J4	OEM
S20N1000J5	OEM
S20N1100J3	OEM
S20N1100J4	OEM
S20N1100J5	OEM
S20N1200J3	OEM
S20N1200J4	OEM
S20N1200J5	OEM
S20N1250D3	OEM
S20N1250D4	OEM
S20N1250D5	OEM
S20N1250G3	OEM
S20N1250G4	OEM
S20N1250G5	OEM
S20N1300J3	OEM
S20N1300J4	OEM
S20N1300J5	OEM
S20N1400J3	OEM
S20N1400J4	OEM
S20N1400J5	OEM
S20N1500D3	OEM
S20N1500D4	OEM
S20N1500D5	OEM
S20N1500G3	OEM
S20N1500G4	OEM
S20N1500G5	OEM
S20N1500J3	OEM
S20N1500J4	OEM
S20N1500J5	OEM
S20N1600J3	OEM
S20N1600J4	OEM
S20N1600J5	OEM
S20ND400	0015
S20NH400	0015
S-20R-01	4904
S-20R-01FR	OEM
S-20R-02	4905
S-20R-02FR	OEM
S-20R-04	4906
S-20R-04FR	OEM
S-20R-06	4907
S-20R-06FR	OEM
S-20R-08	4908
S-20R-08FR	OEM
S-20R-10	4909
S-20R-10FR	OEM
S21	0015
S21AR505	OEM
S21BR512	OEM
S21C322	OEM
S21C323	OEM
S21C454	OEM
S21C472	OEM
S21C662	OEM
S21DR602	OEM
S21GN302	OEM
S21GR302	OEM
S21GR312	OEM
S21GR313	OEM
S21H4302	OEM
S21HN302	OEM
S21HR313	OEM
S21N100H	OEM
S21N200H	OEM
S21N300H	OEM
S21N400H	OEM
S21N500H	OEM
S21N600H	OEM
S21N700H	OEM
S21N800H	OEM
S22	0015
S22A	0015
S22C322	OEM
S22GN302	OEM
S22GR302	OEM
S22GR312	OEM
S22HN302	OEM
S22HR302	OEM
S22HR312	OEM
S22MD1	0235
S23	0015
S23A	0015
S23C322	OEM
S23C455	OEM
S23C662	OEM
S23DR602	OEM
S23GR312	OEM
S23HR312	OEM
S24	0071
S24AR506	OEM
S25A05	3160
S25A1	2873
S25A2	1116
S25A3	1118
S25A4	0800
S25A6	0315
S25A7	OEM
S25A8	1124
S25A10	0045
S25AR506	OEM
S25C424	OEM
S25C455	OEM
S25GR314	OEM
S25HR314	OEM
S25VB10	2347
S25VB20	2347
S25VB40	2353
S25VB60	2354
S25X01D	OEM
S25X02D	OEM
S25X2	OEM
S25X15D	OEM
S26	0015
S26F3	0464
S27AR506	OEM
S27C424	OEM
S27C456	OEM
S27C663	OEM
S27CN506	OEM
S27CR506	OEM
S27GR314	OEM
S27HR314	OEM
S28	0071
S28CN506	OEM
S28CR506	OEM
S28F3	0464
S29AR506	OEM
S29C424	OEM
S29C456	OEM
S29C663	OEM
S29CN506	OEM
S29CR506	OEM
S29GR314	OEM
S29HR314	OEM
S30	0015
S30-12	2296
S30CN506	OEM
S30CR506	OEM
S30N500JA3	OEM
S30N600JA3	OEM
S30N700JA3	OEM
S30N800JA3	OEM
S30N900JA3	OEM
S30N1000JA3	OEM
S30N1100JA3	OEM
S30N1200JA3	OEM
S30N1300JA3	OEM
S30N1400JA3	OEM
S30N1500JA3	OEM
S30N1600JA3	OEM
S30S3	4250
S30S3A	1536
S30S4	OEM
S30S4A	1536
S30S6	OEM
S30SC3	OEM
S30SC3F	OEM
S30SC3M	1931
S30SC4	OEM
S30SC4F	OEM
S30SC4M	1931
S31	0015
S31AR506	OEM
S31C456	OEM
S31C663	OEM
S31CN506	OEM
S31CR506	OEM
S32	0015
S32CN506	OEM
S32CR506	OEM
S33	0015
S33AR506	OEM
S33C456	OEM
S33C663	OEM
S33CN506	OEM
S33CR506	OEM
S-34	0102
S34	0023
S34AR507	OEM
S34CN506	OEM
S34CR506	OEM
S35	0015
S35AR506	OEM
S35AR507	OEM
S35C456	OEM
S35CN506	OEM
S35CR506	OEM
S36	0015
S36CN506	OEM
S36CR506	OEM
S36F3	0717
S37	0084
S37C457	OEM
S38	0084
S38DC014PG02	OEM
S38F3	0717
S39	0097
S39AR507	OEM
S39C457	OEM
S-39T	0160
S40	0015
S40A	0015
S40A05	3160
S40A1	2873
S40A2	1116
S40A3	1118
S40A4	0800
S40A5	0315
S40A6	0315
S40A8	1124
S40A10	0045
S40FFA01	OEM
S40FFA02	OEM
S40FFA04	OEM
S40FFA06	OEM
S40FFA08	OEM
S40FFA10	OEM
S40FFA12	OEM
S40FFK01	OEM
S40FFK02	OEM
S40FFK04	OEM
S40FFK06	OEM
S40FFK08	OEM
S40FFK10	OEM
S40FFK12	OEM
S40FHA01	OEM
S40FHA02	OEM
S40FHA04	OEM
S40FHA06	OEM
S40FHA08	OEM
S40FHK04	OEM
S40FHK06	OEM
S40FHK08	OEM
S40FNA02	OEM
S40FNA04	OEM
S40FNA06	OEM
S40FNA08	OEM
S40FNA10	OEM
S40FNA12	OEM
S40FNK02	OEM
S40FNK04	OEM
S40FNK06	OEM
S40FNK08	OEM
S40FNK10	OEM
S40FNK12	OEM
S40FUA01	OEM
S40FUA02	OEM
S40FUA04	OEM
S40FUK01	OEM
S40FUK02	OEM
S40FUK04	OEM
S-40T	0160
S-40TB	0160
S41AR507	OEM
S41C457	OEM
S-41T	0160
S-42T	0160
S43	0015
S-43T	0160
S44	0015
S45AR508	OEM
S45C458	OEM
S46	0015
S-46T	0160
S47	0015
S47AR508	OEM
S47C458	OEM
S48	0015
S48F3	0717
S-48T	0160
S49	0015
S49AR508	OEM
S49C458	OEM
S-49T	0160
S50	0131
S50-12	3521
S50-28	2918
S51	0131
S51A	1512
S51AR508	OEM
S51B	1512
S51C	1512
S51C458	OEM
S52	0097
S52A	1522
S52B	1522
S52C	1522
S53	0109
S53A	1538
S53B	1538
S54	OEM
S54A	1557
S54B	1557
S54B-10	1404
S54LS20F	OEM
S54LS20W	OEM
S54S20F	OEM
S54S20W	OEM
S55	0122
S-55TB	0136
S56	0122
S56F3	0720
S57	0131
S58	0131
S58F3	0720
S-58TB	0160
S59	0145
S-60	OEM
S60	OEM
S60FFN01	OEM
S60FFN02	OEM
S60FFN04	OEM
S60FFN06	OEM
S60FFN08	OEM
S60FFN10	OEM
S60FFN12	OEM
S60FFR01	OEM
S60FFR02	OEM
S60FFR04	OEM
S60FFR06	OEM
S60FFR08	OEM

If replacement code is OEM, contact original manufacturer for replacement.

DEVICE TYPE	REPL CODE	DEVICE TYPE	REPL CODE	DEVICE TYPE	REPL CODE	DEVICE TYPE	REPL CODE	DEVICE TYPE	REPL CODE	DEVICE TYPE	REPL CODE	DEVICE TYPE	REPL CODE
S60FFR10	OEM	S106-05	1250	S210F3	0464	S508	0133	S813SDU15	OEM	S903SAU19	OEM	S904SFU27	OEM
S60FFR12	OEM	S106-1	0442	S210S	0154	S509	0133	S813SDU16	OEM	S903SAU20	OEM	S904SFU28	OEM
S60FHN01	OEM	S106-2	0934	S215	1058	S510F3	0720	S813SDU17	OEM	S903SAU21	OEM	S904SFU29	OEM
S60FHN02	OEM	S106-4	0095	S215S	0154	S518T	0065	S813SDU18	OEM	S903SAU22	OEM	S913	0769
S60FHN04	OEM	S106A	0442	S217	0015	S520	0037	S813SDU19	OEM	S903SAU23	OEM	S926	0769
S60FHN06	OEM	S106A1	0442	S218	0015	S520F4	0720	S813SDU20	OEM	S903SBU10	OEM	S939	OEM
S60FHN08	OEM	S106A2	0442	S219	0015	S525	OEM	S813SDU21	OEM	S903SBU11	OEM	S951SAU01	OEM
S60FHR01	OEM	S106B1	0934	S220	0015	S535	OEM	S813SDU22	OEM	S903SBU12	OEM	S951SAU02	OEM
S60FHR02	OEM	S106B2	0934	S220F4	0464	S541	OEM	S813SHU01	OEM	S903SBU13	OEM	S951SAU03	OEM
S60FHR04	OEM	S106C	0095	S221	0015	S542	OEM	S813SHU02	OEM	S903SBU14	OEM	S951SAU04	OEM
S60FHR06	OEM	S106C1	0095	S222	0015	S550	OEM	S813SHU03	OEM	S903SBU15	OEM	S951SAU05	OEM
S60FHR08	OEM	S106C2	0095	S223	0015	S551	OEM	S813SHU04	OEM	S903SBU16	OEM	S951SAU06	OEM
S60FUN01	OEM	S106D	0095	S224	0015	S552	OEM	S813SHU05	OEM	S903SBU17	OEM	S951SAU07	OEM
S60FUN02	OEM	S106D1	0095	S225	1058	S575A	OEM	S813SHU06	OEM	S903SBU18	OEM	S951SAU08	OEM
S60FUN04	OEM	S106D2	0095	S225S	3121	S600	0122	S813SHU07	OEM	S903SBU19	OEM	S951SAU09	OEM
S60FUR01	OEM	S106E	0304	S227	1083	S601T	OEM	S813SHU08	OEM	S903SBU20	OEM	S951SAU10	OEM
S60FUR02	OEM	S106E1	0304	S227(JAPAN)	1083	S608L	OEM	S813SHU09	OEM	S903SBU21	OEM	S951SAU11	OEM
S60FUR04	OEM	S106E2	OEM	S229	0242	S610	OEM	S813SHU10	OEM	S903SBU22	OEM	S951SAU12	OEM
S60S3	1536	S106F	1250	S230	0015	S610F3	0720	S813SHU11	OEM	S903SBU23	OEM	S951SBU01	OEM
S60S4	1536	S106F1	1250	S231	OEM	S611F	OEM	S813SHU12	OEM	S903SCU10	OEM	S951SBU02	OEM
S60S6	OEM	S106F2	1250	S232	0015	S612F	OEM	S813SHU13	OEM	S903SCU11	OEM	S951SBU03	OEM
S61	0071	S106M	0304	S233	0015	S613F	OEM	S813SHU14	OEM	S903SCU12	OEM	S951SBU04	OEM
S62	0071	S106M1	0304	S234	0015	S614F	OEM	S813SHU15	OEM	S903SCU13	OEM	S951SBU05	OEM
S63	0071	S106M2	OEM	S235	0015	S620	OEM	S813SHU16	OEM	S903SCU14	OEM	S951SBU06	OEM
S66F3	0720	S106N1	OEM	S236	0242	S620F4	0720	S813SHU17	OEM	S903SCU15	OEM	S951SBU07	OEM
S68F3	0720	S106N2	OEM	S238	0015	S622F	OEM	S813SHU18	OEM	S903SCU17	OEM	S951SBU08	OEM
S70-12	2918	S106P1	OEM	S239	0015	S625	OEM	S813SHU19	OEM	S903SCU18	OEM	S951SBU09	OEM
S70FNN-02	OEM	S106P2	OEM	S240	0015	S630T	0065	S813SHU20	OEM	S903SCU19	OEM	S951SBU10	OEM
S70FNN-04	OEM	S106Q	1386	S241	0015	S635	OEM	S813SHU21	OEM	S903SCU20	OEM	S951SBU11	OEM
S70FNN-06	OEM	S106Y	1386	S243	0015	S637T	3311	S813SHU22	OEM	S903SCU21	OEM	S951SBU12	OEM
S70FNN-08	OEM	S106Y1	1386	S250	0015	S641	1616	S814SDU01	OEM	S903SCU22	OEM	S951SCU01	OEM
S70FNN-10	OEM	S106Y2	1386	S251	0015	S642	OEM	S814SDU02	OEM	S903SCU23	OEM	S951SCU02	OEM
S70FNN-12	OEM	S107	0015	S252	0015	S651	OEM	S814SDU03	OEM	S904SAU10	OEM	S951SCU03	OEM
S70FNR-02	OEM	S107-05	1250	S253	0015	S652	OEM	S814SDU04	OEM	S904SAU11	OEM	S951SCU04	OEM
S70FNR-04	OEM	S107-1	0442	S254	0015	S653	OEM	S814SDU05	OEM	S904SAU12	OEM	S951SCU05	OEM
S70FNR-06	OEM	S107-2	0934	S255	0015	S671T	0275	S814SDU06	OEM	S904SAU13	OEM	S951SCU06	OEM
S70FNR-08	OEM	S107-4	0095	S256	0015	S673	OEM	S814SDU07	OEM	S904SAU14	OEM	S951SCU07	OEM
S70FNR-10	OEM	S107A1	0442	S257	0071	S673T	4402	S814SDU08	OEM	S904SAU15	OEM	S951SCU08	OEM
S70FNR-12	OEM	S107A2	0442	S258	0071	S684	0050	S814SDU09	OEM	S904SAU16	OEM	S951SCU09	OEM
S-70T	0136	S107B1	5147	S260	0071	S685	0004	S814SDU10	OEM	S904SAU17	OEM	S951SCU10	OEM
S70T	0050	S107B2	0934	S262	0015	S686	0004	S814SDU11	OEM	S904SAU18	OEM	S951SCU11	OEM
S72	0015	S107C1	0095	S-277B	OEM	S687	0004	S814SDU12	OEM	S904SAU19	OEM	S951SCU12	OEM
S73	0015	S107C2	0095	S298	0133	S708	1293	S814SDU13	OEM	S904SAU20	OEM	S951SFU01	OEM
S75	0015	S107D1	0095	S300	OEM	S715	0555	S814SDU14	OEM	S904SAU21	OEM	S951SFU02	OEM
S77	0015	S107D2	0095	S305	0071	S750	0071	S814SDU15	OEM	S904SAU22	OEM	S951SFU03	OEM
S78-06H02	OEM	S107E1	0304	S305A	0103	S750C	0071	S814SDU16	OEM	S904SAU23	OEM	S951SFU04	OEM
S79	0015	S107E2	OEM	S306A	0178	S-789	1293	S814SDU17	OEM	S904SAU24	OEM	S951SFU05	OEM
S80-12	3521	S107F1	1250	S310F3	0717	S-798	0015	S814SDU18	OEM	S904SAU25	OEM	S951SFU06	OEM
S-80T	0136	S107F2	1250	S320F4	0717	S800	0131	S814SDU19	OEM	S904SAU26	OEM	S951SFU07	OEM
S81	0015	S107M1	0304	S321	0133	S801	0555	S814SDU20	OEM	S904SAU27	OEM	S951SFU08	OEM
S82	0015	S107M2	OEM	S322	0133	S-810	0015	S814SDU21	OEM	S904SAU28	OEM	S951SFU09	OEM
S83	0015	S107N1	OEM	S324	0133	S812SDU01	OEM	S814SDU22	OEM	S904SAU29	OEM	S951SFU10	OEM
S84	0015	S107N2	OEM	S325	0133	S812SDU02	OEM	S814SDU23	OEM	S904SBU10	OEM	S951SFU11	OEM
S-85	0161	S107P1	OEM	S334	0133	S812SDU04	OEM	S814SDU24	OEM	S904SBU11	OEM	S951SFU12	OEM
S85	0015	S107P2	OEM	S337	0133	S812SDU05	OEM	S814SDU25	OEM	S904SBU12	OEM	S953SAU01	OEM
S-86	0161	S107Y1	1386	S353	0103	S812SDU06	OEM	S814SDU26	OEM	S904SBU13	OEM	S953SAU02	OEM
S86	0015	S107Y2	1386	S354	0178	S812SDU07	OEM	S814SDU27	OEM	S904SBU14	OEM	S953SAU03	OEM
S-87TB	0136	S108	0015	S364S	2844	S812SDU08	OEM	S814SDU28	OEM	S904SBU15	OEM	S953SAU04	OEM
S87TB	0050	S109	OEM	S380	0375	S812SDU09	OEM	S814SDU29	OEM	S904SBU16	OEM	S953SAU05	OEM
S-88TB	0136	S110	0921	S398	0133	S812SDU10	OEM	S814SDU30	OEM	S904SBU17	OEM	S953SAU06	OEM
S88TB	0050	S110A	0916	S400	0133	S812SDU11	OEM	S814SHU01	OEM	S904SBU18	OEM	S953SAU07	OEM
S90SC4M	OEM	S110F3	0464	S401	0133	S812SDU12	OEM	S814SHU02	OEM	S904SBU19	OEM	S953SAU08	OEM
S91	0015	S115	0015	S402	0133	S812SDU13	OEM	S814SHU03	OEM	S904SBU20	OEM	S953SAU09	OEM
S91-A	0015	S118	0124	S403	0133	S812SDU14	OEM	S814SHU04	OEM	S904SBU21	OEM	S953SAU10	OEM
S91-H	0015	S120	OEM	S406	1307	S812SDU15	OEM	S814SHU05	OEM	S904SBU22	OEM	S953SAU11	OEM
S91A	0110	S120-1/4	OEM	S406S	0147	S812SDU16	OEM	S814SHU06	OEM	S904SBU23	OEM	S953SAU12	OEM
S91B	0947	S120F4	0464	S409F	0086	S812SDU17	OEM	S814SHU07	OEM	S904SBU24	OEM	S953SAU13	OEM
S91H	0015	S125	OEM	S410	1307	S812SDU18	OEM	S814SHU08	OEM	S904SBU25	OEM	S953SAU14	OEM
S92	0015	S129	0015	S410F3	0717	S812SDU19	OEM	S814SHU10	OEM	S904SBU26	OEM	S953SAU15	OEM
S92-A	0015	S130	OEM	S410S	0147	S812SDU20	OEM	S814SHU11	OEM	S904SBU27	OEM	S953SAU16	OEM
S92-H	0015	S130-138	0007	S411	0097	S812SDU21	OEM	S814SHU12	OEM	S904SBU28	OEM	S953SAU17	OEM
S92A	0110	S130-251	0007	S413	0109	S812SDU22	OEM	S814SHU13	OEM	S904SBU29	OEM	S953SAU18	OEM
S92H	0015	S133-1	0016	S415	1307	S812SDU23	OEM	S814SHU14	OEM	S904SCU10	OEM	S953SAU19	OEM
S93	0015	S135	OEM	S415S	0147	S812SHU01	OEM	S814SHU15	OEM	S904SCU11	OEM	S953SAU20	OEM
S93A	0015	S154	0102	S417	0131	S812SHU02	OEM	S814SHU16	OEM	S904SCU12	OEM	S953SAU21	OEM
S93H	0015	S160	0133	S420	0097	S812SHU03	OEM	S814SHU17	OEM	S904SCU13	OEM	S953SAU22	OEM
S93SE133	0103	S169N	0016	S420F4	0717	S812SHU04	OEM	S814SHU18	OEM	S904SCU14	OEM	S953SAU23	OEM
S93SE140	1506	S182SDU03	OEM	S421	0097	S812SHU05	OEM	S814SHU19	OEM	S904SCU15	OEM	S953SBU01	OEM
S93SE165	0103	S184SHU09	OEM	S423	0109	S812SHU06	OEM	S814SHU20	OEM	S904SCU16	OEM	S953SBU02	OEM
S93.20.709	0287	S191G	0015	S425	1307	S812SHU07	OEM	S814SHU21	OEM	S904SCU17	OEM	S953SBU03	OEM
S93.20.714	0287	S200	0015	S425S	3123	S812SHU08	OEM	S814SHU22	OEM	S904SCU18	OEM	S953SBU04	OEM
S94	0015	S-200-02	OEM	S427	0131	S812SHU09	OEM	S814SHU23	OEM	S904SCU19	OEM	S953SBU05	OEM
S95	0015	S-200-02F	OEM	S428	0015	S812SHU10	OEM	S814SHU24	OEM	S904SCU20	OEM	S953SBU06	OEM
S-99	0023	S-200-02FR	OEM	S431	0015	S812SHU11	OEM	S814SHU25	OEM	S904SCU21	OEM	S953SBU07	OEM
S99	0133	S-200-03	3109	S435	OEM	S812SHU12	OEM	S814SHU26	OEM	S904SCU22	OEM	S953SBU08	OEM
S-99(DIODE)	0133	S200-03F	OEM	S481	1082	S812SHU13	OEM	S814SHU27	OEM	S904SCU23	OEM	S953SBU09	OEM
S100	0071	S-200-04	3109	S-500	0071	S812SHU14	OEM	S814SHU28	OEM	S904SCU24	OEM	S953SBU10	OEM
S-100-01	6477	S200-04F	OEM	S500	0133	S812SHU15	OEM	S814SHU29	OEM	S904SCU25	OEM	S953SBU11	OEM
S-100-01FR	OEM	S-200-04FR	OEM	S500-2	OEM	S812SHU16	OEM	S814SHU30	OEM	S904SCU26	OEM	S953SBU12	OEM
S-100-02	6477	S-200-06	3111	S500-3	OEM	S812SHU17	OEM	S842G	OEM	S904SCU27	OEM	S953SBU13	OEM
S-100-02FR	OEM	S200-06F	OEM	S500-4	OEM	S812SHU18	OEM	S855	0469	S904SCU28	OEM	S953SBU14	OEM
S-100-03	6477	S-200-08	3113	S500-5	OEM	S812SHU19	OEM	S-870R	OEM	S904SCU29	OEM	S953SBU15	OEM
S-100-04	6477	S200-08F	OEM	S500-6	OEM	S812SHU20	OEM	S870R	OEM	S904SFU10	OEM	S953SBU16	OEM
S-100-04FR	OEM	S-200-10	3113	S500-7	OEM	S812SHU21	OEM	S-870S	OEM	S904SFU11	OEM	S953SBU17	OEM
S-100-06	5939	S200-10F	OEM	S500-8	OEM	S812SHU22	OEM	S870S	OEM	S904SFU12	OEM	S953SBU18	OEM
S-100-08	6478	S201	0015	S500-10	OEM	S812SHU23	OEM	S872A	OEM	S904SFU13	OEM	S953SBU19	OEM
S-100-10	6478	S201MN2B-02	OEM	S-500B	0015	S813SDU01	OEM	S-873TB	0050	S904SFU14	OEM	S953SBU20	OEM
S100-12	3586	S201MN2B-04	OEM	S500B	0535	S813SDU02	OEM	S873TB	0178	S904SFU15	OEM	S953SBU21	OEM
S100-28	2523	S201MN2B-06	OEM	S-500C	0015	S813SDU03	OEM	S-874TB	0050	S904SFU16	OEM	S953SBU22	OEM
S101	0015	S201MN2B-08	OEM	S500C	0535	S813SDU04	OEM	S-880	0769	S904SFU17	OEM	S953SBU23	OEM
S102	0015	S201MN2B-10	OEM	S501	0133	S813SDU05	OEM	S903SAU10	OEM	S904SFU18	OEM	S953SCU01	OEM
S102P	OEM	S202	0015	S502	0133	S813SDU06	OEM	S903SAU11	OEM	S904SFU19	OEM	S953SCU02	OEM
S-102V	0015	S203	0015	S502-23X1	0190	S813SDU07	OEM	S903SAU12	OEM	S904SFU20	OEM	S953SCU03	OEM
S103	0015	S204	0015	S502-23XL	0190	S813SDU08	OEM	S903SAU13	OEM	S904SFU21	OEM	S953SCU04	OEM
S104	0015	S205	0015	S502J	OEM	S813SDU09	OEM	S903SAU14	OEM	S904SFU22	OEM	S953SCU05	OEM
S104P	OEM	S206	1058	S504	0133	S813SDU10	OEM	S903SAU15	OEM	S904SFU23	OEM	S953SCU06	OEM
S105	0023	S206S	0154	S505	0133	S813SDU11	OEM	S903SAU16	OEM	S904SFU24	OEM	S953SCU07	OEM
S105A	0110	S208	0071	S506	0133	S813SDU12	OEM	S903SAU17	OEM	S904SFU25	OEM	S953SCU08	OEM
S106	0015	S210	1058	S507	0133	S813SDU14	OEM	S903SAU18	OEM	S904SFU26	OEM	S953SCU09	OEM

If replacement code is OEM, contact original manufacturer for replacement.

535

DEVICE TYPE	REPL CODE
S953SCU10	OEM
S953SCU11	OEM
S953SCU12	OEM
S953SCU13	OEM
S953SCU14	OEM
S953SCU15	OEM
S953SCU16	OEM
S953SCU17	OEM
S953SCU18	OEM
S953SCU19	OEM
S953SCU20	OEM
S953SCU21	OEM
S953SCU22	OEM
S953SCU23	OEM
S953SFU10	OEM
S953SFU11	OEM
S953SFU12	OEM
S953SFU13	OEM
S953SFU14	OEM
S953SFU15	OEM
S953SFU16	OEM
S953SFU17	OEM
S953SFU18	OEM
S953SFU19	OEM
S953SFU20	OEM
S953SFU21	OEM
S953SFU22	OEM
S953SFU23	OEM
S954SAU01	OEM
S954SAU02	OEM
S954SAU03	OEM
S954SAU04	OEM
S954SAU05	OEM
S954SAU06	OEM
S954SAU07	OEM
S954SAU08	OEM
S954SAU09	OEM
S954SAU10	OEM
S954SAU11	OEM
S954SAU12	OEM
S954SAU13	OEM
S954SAU14	OEM
S954SAU15	OEM
S954SAU16	OEM
S954SAU17	OEM
S954SAU18	OEM
S954SAU19	OEM
S954SAU20	OEM
S954SAU21	OEM
S954SAU22	OEM
S954SAU23	OEM
S954SAU24	OEM
S954SAU25	OEM
S954SAU26	OEM
S954SAU27	OEM
S954SAU28	OEM
S954SAU29	OEM
S954SBU01	OEM
S954SBU02	OEM
S954SBU03	OEM
S954SBU04	OEM
S954SBU05	OEM
S954SBU06	OEM
S954SBU07	OEM
S954SBU08	OEM
S954SBU09	OEM
S954SBU10	OEM
S954SBU11	OEM
S954SBU12	OEM
S954SBU13	OEM
S954SBU14	OEM
S954SBU15	OEM
S954SBU16	OEM
S954SBU17	OEM
S954SBU18	OEM
S954SBU19	OEM
S954SBU20	OEM
S954SBU21	OEM
S954SBU22	OEM
S954SBU23	OEM
S954SBU24	OEM
S954SBU25	OEM
S954SBU26	OEM
S954SBU27	OEM
S954SBU28	OEM
S954SBU29	OEM
S954SCU01	OEM
S954SCU02	OEM
S954SCU03	OEM
S954SCU04	OEM
S954SCU05	OEM
S954SCU06	OEM
S954SCU07	OEM
S954SCU08	OEM
S954SCU09	OEM
S954SCU10	OEM
S954SCU11	OEM
S954SCU12	OEM
S954SCU13	OEM
S954SCU14	OEM
S954SCU15	OEM
S954SCU16	OEM
S954SCU17	OEM
S954SCU18	OEM
S954SCU19	OEM
S954SCU20	OEM
S954SCU21	OEM
S954SCU22	OEM
S954SCU23	OEM
S954SCU24	OEM
S954SCU25	OEM
S954SCU26	OEM
S954SCU27	OEM
S954SCU28	OEM
S954SCU29	OEM
S954SFU10	OEM
S954SFU11	OEM
S954SFU12	OEM
S954SFU13	OEM
S954SFU14	OEM
S954SFU15	OEM
S954SFU16	OEM
S954SFU17	OEM
S954SFU18	OEM
S954SFU19	OEM
S954SFU20	OEM
S954SFU21	OEM
S954SFU22	OEM
S954SFU23	OEM
S954SFU24	OEM
S954SFU25	OEM
S954SFU26	OEM
S954SFU27	OEM
S954SFU28	OEM
S954SFU29	OEM
S962SJU25	OEM
S962SJU26	OEM
S962SJU27	OEM
S962SJU28	OEM
S962SJU29	OEM
S962SJU30	OEM
S962SJU31	OEM
S962SJU32	OEM
S962SJU33	OEM
S962SJU34	OEM
S962SJU35	OEM
S962SJU36	OEM
S962SJU37	OEM
S962SJU38	OEM
S962SJU39	OEM
S962SJU40	OEM
S962SJU41	OEM
S962SJU42	OEM
S962SJU43	OEM
S962SJU44	OEM
S962SJU45	OEM
S962SJU46	OEM
S962SJU47	OEM
S962SJU48	OEM
S962SJU49	OEM
S962SJU50	OEM
S962SJU51	OEM
S962SJU52	OEM
S962SJU53	OEM
S962SJU54	OEM
S962SJU55	OEM
S962SJU56	OEM
S1000	0607
S1000-1	0071
S1000KS2	0895
S1001K	OEM
S1001L	0998
S1001LS2	1038
S1001LS3	4937
S1001M	0179
S1001MS2	0340
S1001MS3	0179
S1003L	0998
S1003LS1	1038
S1003LS2	1038
S1003LS3	1038
S1003M	0179
S1003MS2	0442
S1003MS3	0442
S1003RS1	OEM
S1003RS2	0442
S1003RS3	0442
S1004F1	0442
S1005BH	0500
S1005DH	0705
S1005MH	0857
S1005NH	0323
S1006B	3458
S1006G	1641
S1006H	2430
S1006L	2078
S1006LS2	1038
S1006LS3	1038
S1006RS2	0442
S1006RS3	3801
S1007BH	0998
S1007DH	1028
S1007MH	1140
S1007NH	0323
S1008B	3458
S1008G	1641
S1008H	2430
S1008L	2078
S1008LS2	1038
S1008LS3	1038
S1008RS2	OEM
S1008RS3	OEM
S1009	0144
S1010	0947
S1010B	3458
S1010BH	0500
S1010DH	0705
S1010G	1641
S1010H	2430
S1010L	0998
S1010LS2	1038
S1010LS3	1038
S1010MH	0857
S1010NH	0323
S1010RS2	OEM
S1010RS3	OEM
S1016	0016
S1016B	1837
S1016G	1640
S1016H	4926
S1016L	OEM
S-1019	0127
S1019	0144
S-1019(UHF)	0127
S1020	0242
S1020L	0393
S1025B	OEM
S1025C	0226
S1025D	1837
S1025G	1640
S1025H	4941
S1025L	2587
S1025R	4942
S1025V	OEM
S1025Y	OEM
S1025Z	OEM
S1030	1736
S1035C	0226
S1035D	1837
S1035G	1640
S1035H	0707
S1035J	OEM
S1035K	2665
S1035W	2671
S1037	0144
S1040	0535
S1041	0127
S1041-16GN	0127
S1044	0144
S1050	1760
S1055M	2671
S1055W	2671
S1058	0144
S1059	0144
S1060	0959
S1061	0016
S1062	0144
S1063	OEM
S1064	OEM
S1065	0016
S1065J	OEM
S1065K	OEM
S1066	0016
S1068	0016
S1069	0016
S1070	0811
S1070W	OEM
S1074(R)	0016
S1074(X)	0934
S1076	0144
S1078	0144
S1079	0144
S1080	0811
S1090	0916
S1101SCU11	OEM
S1101SFU01	OEM
S1101SFU02	OEM
S1101SFU03	OEM
S1101SFU04	OEM
S1101SFU05	OEM
S1101SFU06	OEM
S1101SFU07	OEM
S1101SFU08	OEM
S1101SFU09	OEM
S1101SFU10	OEM
S1101SFU11	OEM
S1101SFU12	OEM
S1104SAU01	OEM
S1104SAU02	OEM
S1104SAU03	OEM
S1104SAU04	OEM
S1104SAU05	OEM
S1104SAU06	OEM
S1104SAU07	OEM
S1104SAU08	OEM
S1104SAU09	OEM
S1104SAU10	OEM
S1104SAU11	OEM
S1104SAU12	OEM
S1104SAU13	OEM
S1104SAU14	OEM
S1104SAU15	OEM
S1104SAU16	OEM
S1104SAU17	OEM
S1104SAU18	OEM
S1104SAU19	OEM
S1104SAU20	OEM
S1104SAU21	OEM
S1104SAU22	OEM
S1104SAU23	OEM
S1104SAU24	OEM
S1104SAU25	OEM
S1104SAU26	OEM
S1104SAU27	OEM
S1104SAU28	OEM
S1104SAU29	OEM
S1104SBU01	OEM
S1104SBU02	OEM
S1104SBU03	OEM
S1104SBU04	OEM
S1104SBU05	OEM
S1104SBU06	OEM
S1104SBU07	OEM
S1104SBU08	OEM
S1104SBU09	OEM
S1104SBU10	OEM
S1104SBU11	OEM
S1104SBU12	OEM
S1104SBU13	OEM
S1104SBU14	OEM
S1104SBU15	OEM
S1104SBU16	OEM
S1104SBU17	OEM
S1104SBU18	OEM
S1104SBU19	OEM
S1104SBU20	OEM
S1104SBU21	OEM
S1104SBU22	OEM
S1104SBU23	OEM
S1104SBU24	OEM
S1104SBU25	OEM
S1104SBU26	OEM
S1104SBU27	OEM
S1104SBU28	OEM
S1104SBU29	OEM
S1104SCU01	OEM
S1104SCU02	OEM
S1104SCU03	OEM
S1104SCU04	OEM
S1104SCU05	OEM
S1104SCU06	OEM
S1104SCU07	OEM
S1104SCU08	OEM
S1104SCU09	OEM
S1104SCU10	OEM
S1104SCU11	OEM
S1104SCU12	OEM
S1104SCU13	OEM
S1104SCU14	OEM
S1104SCU15	OEM
S1104SCU16	OEM
S1104SCU17	OEM
S1104SCU18	OEM
S1104SCU19	OEM
S1104SCU20	OEM
S1104SCU21	OEM
S1104SCU22	OEM
S1104SCU23	OEM
S1104SCU24	OEM
S1104SCU25	OEM
S1104SCU26	OEM
S1104SCU27	OEM
S1104SCU28	OEM
S1104SCU29	OEM
S1104SFU10	OEM
S1104SFU11	OEM
S1104SFU12	OEM
S1104SFU13	OEM
S1104SFU14	OEM
S1104SFU15	OEM
S1104SFU16	OEM
S1104SFU17	OEM
S1104SFU18	OEM
S1104SFU19	OEM
S1104SFU20	OEM
S1104SFU21	OEM
S1104SFU22	OEM
S1104SFU23	OEM
S1104SFU24	OEM
S1104SFU25	OEM
S1104SFU27	OEM
S1104SFU28	OEM
S1104SFU29	OEM
S1107SAU01	OEM
S1107SAU02	OEM
S1107SAU03	OEM
S1107SAU04	OEM
S1107SAU05	OEM
S1107SAU06	OEM
S1107SAU07	OEM
S1107SAU08	OEM
S1107SAU09	OEM
S1107SAU10	OEM
S1107SAU11	OEM
S1107SAU12	OEM
S1107SAU13	OEM
S1107SAU14	OEM
S1107SAU15	OEM
S1107SAU16	OEM
S1107SAU17	OEM
S1107SAU18	OEM
S1107SAU19	OEM
S1107SAU20	OEM
S1107SAU21	OEM
S1107SAU22	OEM
S1107SAU23	OEM
S1107SAU24	OEM
S1107SAU25	OEM
S1107SAU26	OEM
S1107SAU27	OEM
S1107SAU28	OEM
S1107SAU29	OEM
S1107SAU30	OEM
S1107SAU31	OEM
S1107SAU32	OEM
S1107SAU33	OEM
S1107SAU34	OEM
S1107SBU01	OEM
S1107SBU02	OEM
S1107SBU03	OEM
S1107SBU04	OEM
S1107SBU05	OEM
S1107SBU06	OEM
S1107SBU07	OEM
S1107SBU08	OEM
S1107SBU09	OEM
S1107SBU10	OEM
S1107SBU11	OEM
S1107SBU12	OEM
S1107SBU13	OEM
S1107SBU14	OEM
S1107SBU15	OEM
S1107SBU16	OEM
S1107SBU17	OEM
S1107SBU18	OEM
S1107SBU19	OEM
S1107SBU20	OEM
S1107SBU21	OEM
S1107SBU22	OEM
S1107SBU23	OEM
S1107SBU24	OEM
S1107SBU25	OEM
S1107SBU26	OEM
S1107SBU27	OEM
S1107SBU28	OEM
S1107SBU29	OEM
S1107SBU30	OEM
S1107SBU31	OEM
S1107SBU32	OEM
S1107SBU33	OEM
S1107SBU34	OEM
S1107SCU01	OEM
S1107SCU02	OEM
S1107SCU03	OEM
S1107SCU04	OEM
S1107SCU05	OEM
S1107SCU06	OEM
S1107SCU07	OEM
S1107SCU08	OEM
S1107SCU09	OEM
S1107SCU10	OEM
S1107SCU11	OEM
S1107SCU12	OEM
S1107SCU13	OEM
S1107SCU14	OEM
S1107SCU15	OEM
S1107SCU16	OEM
S1107SCU17	OEM
S1107SCU18	OEM
S1107SCU19	OEM
S1107SCU20	OEM
S1107SCU21	OEM
S1107SCU22	OEM
S1107SCU23	OEM
S1107SCU24	OEM
S1107SCU25	OEM
S1107SCU26	OEM
S1107SCU27	OEM
S1107SCU28	OEM
S1107SCU29	OEM
S1107SCU30	OEM
S1107SCU31	OEM
S1107SCU32	OEM
S1107SCU33	OEM
S1107SCU34	OEM
S1107SJU24	OEM
S1107SJU25	OEM
S1107SJU26	OEM
S1107SJU27	OEM
S1107SJU28	OEM
S1107SJU29	OEM
S1107SJU30	OEM
S1107SJU31	OEM
S1107SJU32	OEM
S1107SJU33	OEM
S1107SJU34	OEM
S1107SJU35	OEM
S1107SJU36	OEM
S1109SJU30	OEM
S1109SJU31	OEM
S1109SJU32	OEM
S1109SJU33	OEM
S1109SJU34	OEM
S1109SJU35	OEM
S1109SJU36	OEM
S1109SJU37	OEM
S1109SJU38	OEM
S1109SJU40	OEM
S1109SJU41	OEM
S1109SJU42	OEM
S1109SJU43	OEM
S1109SJU44	OEM
S1122	0127
S1126	0127
S1128	0016
S1142	0144
S1143	0016
S1153	0144
S1158	OEM
S1200-1	1293
S1205BH	0393
S1205DH	0606
S1205MH	0946
S1205NH	1504
S1207BH	0393
S1207DH	0606
S1207MH	0946
S1207NH	1504
S-1210	0139
S1210	0947
S1210-3	OEM
S1210BH	0393
S1210DH	0606
S1210MH	0946
S1210NH	1504
S1211N	0321
S1212N	0321
S1213N	0321
S1214N	0321
S1215-3	OEM
S1215N	0321
S1216N	0321
S1220	0242
S1220-3	OEM
S1221	0016
S1221A	0016
S1221N	0321
S1222N	0321
S1223N	0321
S1224N	0321
S1225N	0321
S1226	0016
S1226N	0321
S1227	0144
S1230	1736
S1231N	0321
S1232N	0321
S1233N	0321
S1234N	0321
S1235N	0321
S1236N	0321
S1240	0535
S1241	0016
S1242	0016
S1243	0016
S1245	0016
S1250	1760
S1260	0959
S1270	0811
S1272	0016
S-1276	0144
S1276	0144
S1280	0811
S1286	0007
S1290	0916
S-1296	0144
S1296	0144
S1298	0283
S1307	0016
S1308	0127
S1309	0016
S-1313	0127
S1313	0144
S-1316	0127
S1316	0144
S1317	0144
S-1318	0127
S1318	0144
S1331	0016
S1331N	0016
S1331W	0016
S1332	0136
S1341P	0855
S1342P	0855
S1343P	0855
S1348	0004
S1349	0004
S1350	0037
S1351	OEM
S1351P	0855
S1352P	0855
S1353P	0855
S1360	0144
S1361	0144
S1362	0144
S1363	0016
S1364	0016
S1366	0233
S1367	0037
S1368	0086
S1369	0016
S1373	0016
S1374	0016
S1382	OEM
S1384	0123
S1400-1	0102
S1403	0016
S1405	0016
S1407	0233
S1408	0144
S1409	0144
S1419	0016
S1420	0016
S1421	0086
S1428	0133
S1429-3	0016
S1430	0126
S1431	0126
S1432	0016
S1443	0016
S-1453	0038
S1453	0016
S1475	0079
S1476	0016
S1477	0037
S1487	0016
S1502	0016
S1510	0016
S1512	0016
S1514	0086
S1516	0086
S1517	0086
S1520	0126
S1523	0086
S1525	0086
S1526	0016
S1527	0016
S1529	0016
S1530	0016
S1533	0016
S1556-2	0160
S1559	0016
S1568	0016
S1570	0016
S1600	0015
S1610BH	0393
S1610DH	0606
S1610MH	0946
S1610NH	1504
S1612BH	0393
S1612DH	0606
S1612MH	0946
S1612NH	1504
S1619	0016
S1620	0016
S1629	0016
S1636	0144
S1639	0004
S1640	0050
S1642	0086
S1644	0086
S1671	0086
S1672	0164
S1674	0144
S1674A	0144
S1682	0144
S1683	0086
S1685	0103
S1689	0086
S1691	0103
S1692	0103
S1697	0016
S1698	0126
S1715	OEM
S1761	0016
S1761A	0016
S1761B	0016
S1761C	0016
S1762	0086
S1764	0016
S1765	0016
S1766	0016
S1768	0016
S1769	0233
S1770	0016
S1772	0016
S1773	0086
S1777	0086
S1784	0016
S1785	0016
S1788	0079
S1801-02	0015
S1810-3	OEM
S1815-3	OEM
S1835	0016
S1854	OEM
S1854(FA2)	OEM
S1854-2	OEM
S1854FA	OEM
S1854FA-1	OEM
S1854FA-2	OEM
S1854FA2	OEM
S1854LBM-4	OEM
S1854M4	OEM
S1863	0126
S1864	0086
S1865	0103
S1871	0016
S1874	0086
S1878	0079
S1880	OEM
S1889	0037
S1891	0016
S1891A	0016
S1891B	0016
S1897	0127
S1905	0103
S1905A	0103
S1907	0103
S1955	0016
S1970	OEM
S1983	0126
S1993	0016
S1998	2279
S1998A	2279
S2000A3	OEM
S2000KS2	0058
S2001K	OEM
S2001L	0998
S2001LS1	1038
S2001LS2	1038
S2001LS3	4937
S2001M	0179

If replacement code is OEM, contact original manufacturer for replacement.

DEVICE TYPE	REPL CODE
S2001MS1	OEM
S2001MS2	0058
S2001MS3	0179
S2002	0007
S2002SPU23	OEM
S2003-1	0103
S2003L	0998
S2003LS1	1038
S2003LS2	1038
S2003LS3	4937
S2003MS2	0934
S2003MS3	0934
S2003RS1	OEM
S2003RS2	0934
S2003RS3	3575
S2004F1	0934
S2004SPU10	OEM
S2004SPU11	OEM
S2004SPU12	OEM
S2004SPU13	OEM
S2004SPU14	OEM
S2004SPU15	OEM
S2004SPU16	OEM
S2004SPU17	OEM
S2004SPU18	OEM
S2004SPU19	OEM
S2004SPU20	OEM
S2004SPU21	OEM
S2004SPU22	OEM
S2004SPU24	OEM
S2005	1590
S2006B	1837
S2006G	1641
S2006H	0430
S2006L	0500
S2006LS2	1038
S2006LS3	1038
S2006RS2	OEM
S2006RS3	OEM
S2008B	1837
S2008G	1641
S2008H	0430
S2008L	0500
S2008LS2	1038
S2008LS3	1038
S2008RS2	OEM
S2008RS3	OEM
S2010	0865
S2010B	1837
S2010G	1641
S2010H	0430
S2010L	0998
S2010LS2	1038
S2010LS3	1038
S2010RS2	OEM
S2010RS3	OEM
S2012BH	0393
S2012DH	0606
S2012MH	0946
S2012NH	1504
S2014BH	0393
S2014DH	0606
S2014MH	0946
S2014NH	1504
S2015	0865
S2015G	1641
S2015H	0740
S2015L	0393
S2016B	OEM
S2016G	1641
S2016H	0740
S2016L	OEM
S2020	0865
S2020L	4496
S2025	0847
S2025B	OEM
S2025C	0226
S2025D	1837
S2025G	0998
S2025H	0757
S2025L	OEM
S2025R	OEM
S2025V	OEM
S2025Y	OEM
S2025Z	OEM
S2030	0847
S2030G	1640
S2030H	0464
S2034	0016
S2035	0847
S2035C	0226
S2035D	1837
S2035G	1640
S2035H	0464
S2035J	2665
S2035K	2665
S2035W	2671
S2038	0111
S2040	0847
S2041	0919
S-2041-8661	0033
S2042	0042
S2043	0016
S2044	0016
S2045	1599
S2050	1599
S2055M	2671
S2055W	2671
S2059	0142
S2060	1599
S2060A	0442
S2060B	0934
S2060C	1213
S2060D	0095
S2060E	0304
S2060F	2084
S2060M	0304
S2060Q	2084
S2060Y	2084
S2061A	0442
S2061B	0934
S2061C	1213
S2061D	0095
S2061E	0304
S2061F	2084
S2061M	0304
S2061Q	2084
S2061Y	2084
S2062A	0442
S2062B	0934
S2062C	0095
S2062D	0095
S2062E	0304
S2062F	1250
S2062M	0304
S2062Q	0712
S2062Y	1386
S2065J	OEM
S2065K	OEM
S2070	1600
S2070W	OEM
S2080	1600
S2085	0143
S2090	1604
S2091	0037
S2104	0590
S2105	1590
S2110	0865
S2114-2CE	OEM
S2114UCB	OEM
S2115	0865
S2117	0126
S2118	0086
S2120	0865
S2121	0016
S2122	0016
S2123	0016
S2124	0016
S2125	0847
S2128	0037
S2129	0037
S2130	0847
S2131	0127
S2132	0127
S2133	0127
S2134	0127
S2135	0847
S2139B	0030
S2140	0847
S2140(RECTIFIER)	0847
S2145	1599
S2150	1599
S2150A	OEM
S2152	OEM
S2159	0144
S2160	1599
S2170	1600
S2171	0016
S2172	0016
S2180	1600
S2190	1604
S2200	OEM
S-2200-1135	1896
S2200A	OEM
S2209	0086
S2210	OEM
S2224	0144
S2225	0016
S2241	0103
S2274	0126
S2321	0178
S2350	OEM
S2368	0126
S2369	0086
S2370	0126
S2371	0086
S2392	0103
S2397	0016
S2398C	0126
S2400	0086
S2400A	0086
S2400B	0086
S2400D	OEM
S2400M	OEM
S2401	0086
S2401A	0086
S2401B	0086
S2401C	0086
S2402	0086
S2402A	0086
S2402B	0086
S2402C	0086
S2403B	0103
S2403C	0103
S2427	0086
S2438	0224
S2471	0103
S2486	0178
S2487	0086
S2501DF	1522
S2502DF	1522
S2503DF	0029
S2504DF	0029
S2505DF	0596
S2506DF	0596
S2512BK	1526
S2512DK	1526
S2512MK	1526
S2512NK	OEM
S2514BK	OEM
S2514DK	1526
S2514MK	1526
S2514NK	OEM
S2525	0037
S2526	0086
S2527	0178
S2536A	OEM
S2537A	OEM
S2581	0016
S2582	0016
S2590	0016
S2593	0016
S2600B	0500
S2600D	0705
S2600M	0857
S2610D	0742
S2610M	0759
S-2617	0127
S2617	3356
S2617(UHF)	0127
S2620B	0500
S2620D	0705
S2620M	0857
S2635	0016
S2636	0016
S2645	0037
S2648	0086
S2710B	3579
S2710D	3579
S2710M	3579
S2716	0224
S2718	0224
S2719	0144
S2741	0103
S2771	0126
S2775	0023
S2794	0086
S2800A	2078
S2800B	0500
S2800C	0705
S2800D	0705
S2800E	6788
S2800F	2084
S2800M	6788
S2800S	0323
S2935	0016
S-2940I	OEM
S2944	0016
S2984	0016
S2985	0016
S2986	0233
S2988	0037
S2989	0016
S2991	0126
S2992	0086
S2993	0126
S2994	0126
S2995	0126
S2996	0016
S2997	0016
S2998	0016
S2999	0016
S3001	0693
S3001(HEP)	0693
S3002	0233
S3002(HEP)	0233
S3003	3653
S3004	0037
S3004(HEP)	0037
S3004-1715	0631
S3004-1716	0133
S3004-1718	0631
S3005	4135
S3005(HEP)	3532
S3006	1963
S3006(HEP)	1963
S3006C	OEM
S3006D	OEM
S3006E	OEM
S3006S	OEM
S3007	1966
S3007(HEP)	1963
S3008	0488
S3008(HEP)	0414
S3009	OEM
S3009(HEP)	1963
S3010	3296
S3010-3	OEM
S3011	OEM
S3011(HEP)	1215
S3012	0126
S3013	0488
S3014	0488
S3015-3	OEM
S3015A	OEM
S3015B	OEM
S3016	0139
S3016-R	0139
S3016R	0139
S3019	0144
S3019(DIODE)	OEM
S3019A	OEM
S3019B	OEM
S3020	0144
S3020-3	OEM
S3020A	OEM
S3021	0334
S3023	4138
S3024	4139
S3027C	OEM
S3028	4141
S3030G	0143
S3032	0378
S3033	0233
S3034	0233
S3035	0233
S3036	OEM
S3037	OEM
S3038	OEM
S3039	OEM
S3039(HEP)	1189
S3040	1963
S3040(HEP)	1963
S3041	OEM
S3041(HEP)	1963
S3042	0086
S3042(HEP)	0414
S3043	1973
S3043(HEP)	1973
S3044	OEM
S3044(HEP)	1581
S3045	0930
S3045(HEP)	0930
S3046	OEM
S3047	OEM
S3047(HEP)	0561
S3048(HEP)	0334
S3049	1581
S3049(HEP)	0334
S3050	OEM
S3050(HEP)	1357
S3051	OEM
S3051(HEP)	0334
S3052	1189
S3053	OEM
S3054	OEM
S3054(HEP)	0848
S3055	OEM
S3055(HEP)	0848
S3060	OEM
S3060(HEP)	0419
S3060D	OEM
S3060E	OEM
S3060S	OEM
S3061	OEM
S3061(HEP)	0419
S3062	OEM
S3062(HEP)	0930
S3066	OEM
S3072	0139
S3072C	0133
S3073	0030
S3087B	2313
S3105	3160
S3106	OEM
S3110	2873
S3115	1116
S3120	1116
S3125	1118
S3130	1118
S3135	0800
S3140	0800
S3145	1186
S3150	1186
S3160	0315
S3170	1124
S3180	1124
S3190	0045
S3205	3160
S3210	2873
S3215	1116
S3220	1116
S3225	1118
S3230	1118
S3235	0800
S3240	0800
S3245	1186
S3250	0315
S3260	1186
S3270	1124
S3280	1124
S3290	0045
S3295G-TPA2	OEM
S3295GTPA2	0023
S3372G	0019
S3386	0126
S3405	3716
S3410	2629
S3415	2633
S3420	2633
S3425	2639
S3430	2639
S3435	1995
S3440	1995
S3445	2657
S3450	2652
S3460	2657
S3470	3846
S3480	3846
S3490	2631
S3505	2786
S3510	2786
S3515	2786
S3515G	OEM
S3520	2786
S3525	2786
S3530	2786
S3535	2786
S3540	2786
S3545	2786
S3550	2786
S3560	2786
S3603G	0143
S3605	4242
S3610	1551
S3615	2813
S3620	2813
S3625	4244
S3630	4244
S3635	2823
S3639	0037
S3640	2823
S3645	2844
S3650	2844
S3655	0037
S3660	2844
S3670	2806
S3680	2806
S3690	2454
S3700B	0239
S3700D	0239
S3700M	0239
S3701M	OEM
S3702S	0061
S3702SF	0061
S3703SF	0239
S3704A	0061
S3704B	0061
S3704D	0061
S3704M	0061
S3704S	0061
S3704SD	0239
S3705	2786
S3705M	0239
S3706E	0061
S3706M	OEM
S3708G	OEM
S3710	2786
S3714A	OEM
S3714B	OEM
S3714D	OEM
S3714M	OEM
S3714S	OEM
S3715	2786
S3720	2786
S3725	2786
S3730	2786
S3735	2786
S3740	2786
S3745	2786
S3750	2786
S3760	2786
S3770	2818
S3771	0103
S3780	2818
S3790	2818
S3800D	OEM
S3800E	OEM
S3800EF	OEM
S3800M	OEM
S3800MF	OEM
S3800S	1702
S3800SF	2313
S3838G	OEM
S3838GA	0143
S3900E	4526
S3900MF	4526
S3900S	4526
S3900SF	4526
S3901M	4534
S3901MF	4534
S3901S	4534
S3902DF	OEM
S3903MF	OEM
S3953G	OEM
S3961G	0143
S3967G	OEM
S3969G	OEM
S3972G	OEM
S4000KS2	0403
S4001	0015
S4001K	OEM
S4001L	1028
S4001LS1	1038
S4001LS2	1038
S4001LS3	1038
S4001M	0342
S4001MS1	OEM
S4001MS2	OEM
S4001MS3	0342
S4002	0007
S4003	0015
S4003L	1028
S4003LS1	1038
S4003LS2	1038
S4003LS3	1038
S4003M	0342
S4003MS2	0095
S4003MS3	0095
S4003RS1	OEM
S4003RS2	0095
S4003RS3	0095
S4004F1	0095
S4006B	1844
S4006G	1574
S4006H	1478
S4006J	OEM
S4006L	0705
S4006LS2	1038
S4006LS3	1038
S4006RS2	OEM
S4006RS3	OEM
S4008B	1844
S4008F1	OEM
S4008G	1574
S4008H	1478
S4008L	0705
S4008LS2	1038
S4008LS3	1038
S4008RS2	OEM
S4008RS3	OEM
S4010	OEM
S4010-3	OEM
S4010B	1844
S4010G	1574
S4010H	1478
S4010L	1028
S4010RS2	OEM
S4010RS3	OEM
S4012BK	OEM
S4012DK	1526
S4012MK	1526
S4012NK	OEM
S4014BK	1526
S4014DK	1526
S4014MK	1526
S4014NK	OEM
S4015-3	OEM
S4015L	0606
S4016B	1844
S4016G	OEM
S4016H	0735
S4016L	OEM
S4020-3	OEM
S4025B	1844
S4025C	0226
S4025D	1844
S4025G	2623
S4025H	0735
S4025L	2587
S4025R	3991
S4025V	OEM
S4025Y	OEM
S4025Z	OEM
S4035C	0226
S4035D	1844
S4035G	2623
S4035H	0717
S4035J	2665
S4035K	2665
S4035W	2671
S4055M	4988
S4055W	2671
S4065J	OEM
S4065K	OEM
S4070W	OEM
S4105	0594
S4110	0594
S4115	0594
S4120	0594
S4125	0594
S4130	0594
S4135	1975
S4140	1975
S4145	1975
S4150	1975
S4160	1975
S4170	0652
S4180	0652
S4190	0652
S4205	0594
S4210	0594
S4215	0594
S4220	0594
S4225	0594
S4230	0594
S4235	1975
S4240	1975
S4245	1975
S4248	0004
S4249	0037
S4250	1975
S4260	1975
S4270	0652
S4280	0652
S4290	0652
S4305	0594
S4310	0594
S4315	0594
S4320	0594
S4325	0594
S4330	0594
S4335	1975
S4340	1975
S4345	1975
S4350	1975
S4360	1975
S4370	0652
S4380	0652
S4390	0652
S5000	4500
S5004	0556
S5005	4503
S5006	2558
S5010B	OEM
S5010D	OEM
S5010M	OEM
S5012	3509
S5013	4507
S5014	4138
S5014(HEP)	0086
S5015	0275
S5018	0899
S5019	0178
S5020	0007
S5021	0007
S5022	OEM
S5023	3653
S5024	0187
S5025	0725
S5026	3392
S5027(HEP)	0161
S5028	OEM
S5028(HEP)	1045
S5041T951	OEM
S5089-A	0015
S5092-4B	OEM
S5092-6A	OEM
S5102	OEM
S5103	OEM
S5104	OEM
S5105	1017
S5105R	0496
S5106	OEM
S5110	1017
S5110R	0496
S5115	1017
S5115R	0496
S5120	1017
S5120R	0496
S5125	1017
S5125R	0496
S5130	1017
S5135	1017
S5135R	0496
S5140	1017
S5140R	0496
S5145	1030
S5145R	1766
S5150	1030
S5150R	1766
S5151	1272
S5151R	1272
S5160	1030
S5160R	1766
S5162	OEM
S5166	OEM
S5170	1040
S5170R	1778
S5177B	0015
S5180	1040
S5180R	1778
S5188	2347
S5190	1040
S5190R	1778
S5226	0296
S5226A	0296
S5226B	0296
S5227	0372
S5227A	0372
S5227B	0372
S5228	0036
S5228A	0036
S5228B	0036
S5229	0274
S5229A	0274
S5229B	0274
S5230	0140
S5230A	0140
S5230B	0140
S5241	OEM
S-5277B	0015
S5277B	0023
S5277D	0023
S5277G	0790
S5277J	0023
S5277L	0072
S5277N	0071
S5295	0133
S5295-G	0023
S5295B	0023
S5295D	0023
S5295G	0023
S5295GTPA2	0023
S5295I	0023
S5295J	0023
S5295JTPA2	0023
S5305	1017
S5305R	0496
S5310	1017
S5310R	0496
S5315	1017
S5315R	0496

If replacement code is OEM, contact original manufacturer for replacement. 537

DEVICE TYPE	REPL CODE
S5320	1017
S5320R	0496
S5325	1017
S5325R	0496
S5327E	0144
S5328E	0144
S5330	1017
S5330R	0496
S5335	1017
S5335R	0496
S5340	1017
S5340R	0496
S5343	OEM
S5344	OEM
S5345	1030
S5345R	1766
S5347	OEM
S5350	1030
S5350R	1766
S5360	1030
S5360R	1766
S5367	OEM
S5370	1040
S5370R	1778
S5373	OEM
S5380	1040
S5380R	1778
S5390	1040
S5390R	1778
S5405	1017
S5410	1017
S5415	1017
S5420	1017
S5420F	OEM
S5420W	OEM
S5425	1017
S5430	1017
S5435	1030
S5440	1030
S5440-5	3825
S5445	1030
S5450	1030
S5456J	0559
S5460	1030
S5470	1040
S5480	1040
S5490	1040
S5500	0015
S5500-D	0015
S5500B	0080
S5500D	0015
S5500DTF	OEM
S5500DTP	0080
S5500G	0790
S5566	OEM
S5566B	0015
S5566G	0790
S5566J	0015
S5566N	0071
S5670E	0144
S5688B	0015
S5688G-TPA3	OEM
S5723T	1183
S5800B	OEM
S5800C	OEM
S5800D	OEM
S5800E	OEM
S5800M	OEM
S5801B	OEM
S5801C	OEM
S5801D	OEM
S5801E	OEM
S5801M	OEM
S5802B	OEM
S5802C	OEM
S5802D	OEM
S5802E	OEM
S5802M	OEM
S5907	OEM
S6000	0769
S6000C	0606
S6000E	0946
S6000KS2	OEM
S6000KS3	OEM
S6000S	OEM
S6001K	OEM
S6001L	1140
S6001M	3315
S6001MS2	0304
S6001MS3	0304
S6003L	1140
S6003M	3315
S6003MS2	0304
S6003MS3	0304
S6003RS1	OEM
S6003RS2	0304
S6003RS3	0304
S6004F1	0095
S6005	0015
S6006B	3185
S6006G	1655
S6006H	0682
S6006L	0857
S6006RS2	OEM
S6006RS3	OEM
S6008B	3185
S6008G	1655
S6008H	0682
S6008L	1140

DEVICE TYPE	REPL CODE
S6008RS2	OEM
S6008RS3	OEM
S6010	OEM
S6010B	3185
S6010G	1655
S6010H	0682
S6010L	1140
S6010RS2	OEM
S6010RS3	OEM
S6015	OEM
S6015G	1655
S6015H	0759
S6015L	0946
S6016B	OEM
S6016G	1655
S6016H	0759
S6016L	OEM
S6020	OEM
S6022	OEM
S6022B	OEM
S6025B	OEM
S6025C	0226
S6025D	1140
S6025G	2625
S6025H	0759
S6025L	2587
S6025R	3992
S6026H	0720
S6030	4896
S6035	OEM
S6035C	0226
S6035D	3185
S6035G	2625
S6035H	0720
S6035J	2665
S6035K	2665
S6035W	6172
S6040	OEM
S6045	OEM
S6050	OEM
S6055M	6172
S6055W	6172
S6060	OEM
S6065J	OEM
S6065K	OEM
S6070	OEM
S6070W	OEM
S6080	OEM
S6080A	0061
S6080B	0061
S6080C	OEM
S6087A	1702
S6087B	2313
S6089	0239
S6090	OEM
S6100C	6983
S6100E	6984
S6100S	OEM
S6121-1	0287
S6121-3	0468
S6121-5	0441
S6132A	OEM
S6132B	OEM
S6142	0095
S6142C	0095
S6142G	0095
S6200A	1640
S6200B	1641
S6200D	1574
S6200M	1655
S6210A	0736
S6210B	0740
S6210D	0742
S6210M	0759
S6220A	1837
S6220B	OEM
S6220D	1844
S6220M	OEM
S6230-AH	0287
S6230-AH1	0468
S6230-AH2	0441
S6230A	OEM
S6230B	OEM
S6230D	OEM
S6230M	OEM
S6240A	0226
S6240B	0226
S6240D	0226
S6240M	0226
S6250A	OEM
S6250B	OEM
S6250D	OEM
S6250M	OEM
S6321F	1981
S6321FLC6	6006
S6340G	0095
S6344G	2712
S6394GL6	0750
S6394GLC6	0750
S6410A	0464
S6410B	0464
S6410D	0717
S6410M	0720
S6413M	3157
S6420A	1837
S6420B	1837
S6420D	3182
S6420M	3185
S6430A	OEM

DEVICE TYPE	REPL CODE
S6430B	OEM
S6430D	OEM
S6430M	OEM
S6430N	OEM
S6431M	0720
S6440A	0226
S6440B	0226
S6440D	0226
S6440M	0226
S6440N	OEM
S6450A	OEM
S6450B	OEM
S6450D	OEM
S6450M	OEM
S6450N	OEM
S6493M	OEM
S6500	0769
S6508	3164
S6508-1	3164
S6508A	3164
S6508E	3164
S6508P	3164
S6565(LB)	OEM
S6565(OEC)	OEM
S6565G	1981
S6565G-(LB)	1981
S6565G(LB)	OEM
S6565G-(OEC)	1981
S6565G(OEC)	OEM
S-6700A	OEM
S6700A	OEM
S6785G	OEM
S6800	0384
S6801	0016
S6802	0389
S6804	0086
S6810P	2075
S6821P	0443
S6850	0509
S6850P	0509
S6856DL	OEM
S7000	0130
S7001	OEM
S7002	5056
S7003	OEM
S7004	0103
S7005	4873
S7006	OEM
S7006(HEP)	0919
S7007	OEM
S7007(HEP)	1671
S7008	OEM
S7008(HEP)	0130
S7230B	OEM
S7310B	OEM
S7310C	OEM
S7310D	OEM
S7310E	OEM
S7310M	OEM
S7410M	0799
S7412M	0799
S7430M	0799
S7502	0403
S7503	0403
S8001L	OEM
S8001M	6095
S8003L	OEM
S8003M	OEM
S8006B	OEM
S8006G	OEM
S8006H	0761
S8006L	6096
S8008B	OEM
S8008G	OEM
S8008H	0761
S8008L	OEM
S8010B	OEM
S8010G	OEM
S8010H	0761
S8010L	1504
S8015L	1504
S8016B	OEM
S8016G	OEM
S8016H	0761
S8016L	OEM
S8020L	1504
S8025	OEM
S8025C	OEM
S8025D	OEM
S8025G	OEM
S8025H	0761
S8025L	2587
S8025R	3953
S8033HA	OEM
S8035	OEM
S8035C	OEM
S8035D	OEM
S8035G	OEM
S8035H	0745
S8035J	2665
S8035K	2665
S8035W	OEM
S8040R	4989
S8049H4	OEM
S8050K	5836
S8052ALR	OEM
S8052ALY	OEM
S8053ALB	OEM
S-8053ALR	OEM

DEVICE TYPE	REPL CODE
S8053ALR	OEM
S8054ALB	OEM
S8054ALB-LM-S	OEM
S-8054ALR	OEM
S8054ALR	OEM
S8054ALRS-LN	OEM
S8055M	3246
S8055W	6172
S8056H	OEM
S8056H1	OEM
S8065J	OEM
S8065K	OEM
S8070W	OEM
S8201	OEM
S8201A	OEM
S8202	OEM
S8202A	OEM
S8205	OEM
S8206	OEM
S8250	OEM
S8250A	OEM
S8250B	OEM
S8251	OEM
S8252	OEM
S8660	0161
S8851	0190
S8856	0911
S9100	0396
S9101	0553
S9101(HEP)	0553
S9102	3343
S9102(HEP)	3343
S9103	OEM
S9120	3477
S9121	2869
S9122	3486
S9123	OEM
S9140	2411
S9140(HEP)	2411
S9141	2262
S9141(HEP)	2262
S9142	OEM
S9143	OEM
S9144	OEM
S9144(HEP)	2262
S9145	OEM
S9145(HEP)	2411
S9146	OEM
S9146(HEP)	3339
S9147	OEM
S9147(HEP)	3340
S9148	OEM
S9148(HEP)	2422
S9149	OEM
S9149(HEP)	2415
S9150	OEM
S9151	OEM
S9152	OEM
S9153	OEM
S9308F	1064
S9314F	2468
S9516	0050
S9524	0004
S9602F	2270
S9631	0079
S9923	0004
S10001D	OEM
S10002D	OEM
S10015D	OEM
S10100	0916
S10110	0102
S10129	OEM
S10130	OEM
S10131	OEM
S10149	0015
S10153	0161
S-10386	3392
S11042FU26	OEM
S12100	0916
S12110	0102
S12120	0102
S12130	0102
S12140	0102
S12150	OEM
S15001D	OEM
S15002D	OEM
S15015D	OEM
S15649	0016
S15650	0007
S15657	0007
S15658	0007
S15659	0007
S15660	0086
S16901	OEM
S17074	0196
S17862	0233
S17900	0086
S18000	0086
S18100	0037
S18200	0086
S19386	0086
S20005	5417
S20100	2982
S20405	0084
S20410	0097
S20415	0097
S20420	0097
S20425	0109
S20430	0109

DEVICE TYPE	REPL CODE
S20435	0109
S20445	1390
S-20446	0693
S20446	1401
S20450	0122
S20460	0122
S21100	1604
S21271	0143
S21520	0178
S21549	0086
S21639	0012
S21648	0127
S22543	0016
S23130	0037
S23579	0079
S24226	0037
S24591	0016
S24592	0111
S24594	0126
S24596	0016
S24597	0126
S24598	0086
S24612	0126
S24614	0086
S24615	0126
S24616	0086
S25261	0007
S25805	0144
S25941	0127
S26822	0079
S27233	0086
S27604	0007
S27893	0224
S29956	0111
S30001D	OEM
S30002D	OEM
S30015D	OEM
S30405	3160
S30410	1116
S30415	1116
S30420	1116
S30425	1118
S30430	1118
S30435	0800
S30440	0800
S30445	1186
S30450	1186
S30460	0315
S31100	0045
S31160	OEM
S31551	0037
S31866	0079
S32417	0144
S32550	0086
S32669	0144
S32903	0161
S33291	0142
S33529	0919
S33530	0228
S33755	0079
S33886	0126
S33990	0144
S34100	2631
S34540	0016
S35232	0007
S35233	0144
S35487	0130
S36100	2454
S36951	0155
S37100	2818
S37110	2818
S37120	2619
S37162	0419
S37165	0919
S37166	0042
S37182	0079
S37214	0079
S37423	0079
S38280	OEM
S38763	0079
S38787	0079
S38789	0016
S38854	0079
S39094	0037
S39261	0919
S39262	0042
S39509	0378
S39560	0233
S39868	0264
S40204	0007
S40205	0233
S41100	0652
S42100	0652
S42110	3277
S42120	3277
S42130	3277
S42140	3277
S43100	0652
S43110	3277
S43120	3277
S43130	3277
S43140	3277
S50305	1017
S50310	1017
S50315	1017
S50320	1017
S50325	1017
S50330	1017
S50335	1030

DEVICE TYPE	REPL CODE
S50340	1030
S50345	1030
S50350	1030
S50360	1030
S50370	1040
S50380	1040
S50390	1040
S50410	1017
S50415	1017
S50420	1017
S50425	1017
S50430	1017
S50435	1030
S50440	1030
S50445	1030
S50450	1030
S50460	1030
S50470	1040
S50480	1040
S50490	1040
S51100	1040
S51100R	1778
S53100	1040
S53100R	1778
S53110	1040
S53120	3872
S53130	2805
S53140	2805
S54100	1040
S60100	OEM
S60252	OEM
S63512D	OEM
S67794	0142
S67809	0160
S-81230AG	OEM
S81230AG	OEM
S81250HG	OEM
S81350AG	OEM
S-88509	2955
S88509	0190
S88568	OEM
S-88569	0190
S-88569S	OEM
S-88570	0190
S88570	0190
S-88571	0190
S88571	0190
S-88576	0911
S88576	0911
S95101	0050
S95102	0050
S95103	0050
S95104	0050
S95106	0050
S95125	0144
S95125A	0144
S95126	0144
S95126A	0144
S95201	0004
S95202	0016
S95203	0004
S95204	0004
S95206	0004
S95207	0004
S95214	0004
S95218	0004
S95252	0275
S-95253	0160
S95253	0160
S-95253-1	0160
S95253-1	0160
S97520	OEM
S97539	OEM
S99101	0050
S99102	0050
S99103	0050
S99104	0050
S99201	0004
S99203	0004
S99218	0004
S99252	0275
S326690	0144
S413796	0211
S503100	1040
S503110	5423
S503120	5423
S504100	1040
S504110	5423
S504120	5423
S1977634	0103
S2041635	0004
S2042634	0208
SA0419	0126
SA1AN12	2872
SA1CN3	OEM
SA1M1	0947
SA-2	0087
SA2	5470
SA-2A	0087
SA2AN12	2872
SA-2B	0087
SA2B	0015
SA-2C	0087
SA2CN3	OEM
SA2H	0071
SA2M1	0242
SA-2Z	0087
SA2Z	0071
SA3B	0015

DEVICE TYPE	REPL CODE
SA3M1	0535
SA4AN12	1104
SA5AN12	OEM
SA5CN3	OEM
SA5M1	0959
SA5M3	OEM
SA5.0A(DIO)	2380
SA6AN12	1104
SA6CN3	OEM
SA6M1	0959
SA6.0A(DIO)	3085
SA6.5A(DIO)	OEM
SA7	0595
SA7CN3	OEM
SA7M3	OEM
SA7.0A(DIO)	OEM
SA7.5A(DIO)	OEM
SA8AN12	2982
SA8CN3	OEM
SA8M1	0811
SA8.0A(DIO)	OEM
SA8.5A(DIO)	OEM
SA9CN3	OEM
SA9.0A(DIO)	OEM
SA10A(DIO)	OEM
SA10AN12	2982
SA10CN3	OEM
SA10M1	0916
SA11A(DIO)	3143
SA12A	0279
SA12A(DIO)	OEM
SA12B	0279
SA12C	0279
SA12D	0279
SA12E	0279
SA12F	0279
SA12G	0279
SA12L	0279
SA12M	0279
SA12M1	OEM
SA12R	0279
SA12T	0279
SA12X	0279
SA12Y	0279
SA13A	0279
SA13A(DIO)	OEM
SA13B	0279
SA13C	0279
SA13D	0279
SA13E	0279
SA13F	0279
SA13G	0279
SA13L	0279
SA13M	0279
SA13R	0279
SA13T	0279
SA13X	0279
SA13Y	0279
SA14A	0279
SA14A(DIO)	OEM
SA14B	0279
SA14C	0279
SA14D	0279
SA14E	0279
SA14F	0279
SA14G	0279
SA14L	0279
SA14M	0279
SA14R	0279
SA14T	0279
SA14X	0279
SA14Y	0279
SA15A	0050
SA15A(DIO)	3162
SA15B	0050
SA15C	0050
SA15D	0050
SA15E	0050
SA15F	0050
SA15G	0050
SA15L	0050
SA15M	0050
SA15N	0050
SA15R	0050
SA15T	0050
SA15X	0050
SA15Y	0050
SA16A	0279
SA16A(DIO)	OEM
SA16B	0279
SA16C	0279
SA16D	0279
SA16E	0279
SA16F	0279
SA16G	0279
SA16L	0279
SA16M	0279
SA16R	0279
SA16T	0279
SA16X	0279
SA16Y	0279
SA17A	0279
SA17A(DIO)	3171
SA17B	0279
SA17C	0279
SA17D	0279
SA17E	0279
SA17F	0279
SA17G	0279

If replacement code is OEM, contact original manufacturer for replacement.

DEVICE TYPE	REPL CODE
SA17L	0279
SA17M	0279
SA17R	0279
SA17T	0279
SA17X	0279
SA17Y	0279
SA18A	0136
SA18A(DIO)	OEM
SA18B	0136
SA18C	0136
SA18D	0136
SA18E	0136
SA18F	0136
SA18G	0136
SA18L	0136
SA18M	0136
SA18R	0136
SA18T	0136
SA18X	0136
SA18Y	0136
SA19A	0136
SA19B	0136
SA19C	0136
SA19D	0136
SA19E	0136
SA19F	0136
SA19G	0136
SA19L	0136
SA19M	0136
SA19R	0136
SA19T	0136
SA19X	0136
SA19Y	0136
SA20	OEM
SA20A	0136
SA20A(DIO)	OEM
SA20B	0136
SA20C	0136
SA20D	0136
SA20E	0136
SA20F	0136
SA20G	0136
SA20L	0136
SA20M	0136
SA20R	0136
SA20T	0136
SA20X	0136
SA20Y	0136
SA21	OEM
SA21A	0136
SA21B	0136
SA21C	0136
SA21D	0136
SA21E	0136
SA21F	0136
SA21G	0136
SA21L	0136
SA21M	0136
SA21R	0136
SA21T	0136
SA21X	0136
SA21Y	0136
SA22A(DIO)	1904
SA24A(DIO)	OEM
SA26A	0279
SA26A(DIO)	OEM
SA26B	0279
SA26C	0279
SA26D	0279
SA26E	0279
SA26F	0279
SA26G	0279
SA26L	0279
SA26M	0279
SA26R	0279
SA26T	0279
SA26X	0279
SA26Y	0279
SA-28	OEM
SA28A	0279
SA28A(DIO)	OEM
SA28B	0279
SA28C	0279
SA28D	0279
SA28E	0279
SA28F	0279
SA28G	0279
SA28L	0279
SA28M	0279
SA28R	0279
SA28T	0279
SA28X	0279
SA28Y	0279
SA29	0164
SA29A	0136
SA29B	0136
SA29C	0136
SA29D	0136
SA29E	0136
SA29F	0136
SA29G	0136
SA29L	0136
SA29M	0136
SA29R	0136
SA29T	0136
SA29X	0136
SA29Y	0136
SA30A	0279
SA30A(DIO)	OEM

DEVICE TYPE	REPL CODE
SA30B	0279
SA30C	0279
SA30D	0279
SA30E	0279
SA30F	0279
SA30G	0279
SA30L	0279
SA30M	0279
SA30R	0279
SA30T	0279
SA30X	0279
SA30Y	0279
SA31A	0279
SA31B	0279
SA31C	0279
SA31D	0279
SA31E	0279
SA31F	0279
SA31G	0279
SA31L	0279
SA31M	0279
SA31R	0279
SA31T	0279
SA31X	0279
SA31Y	0279
SA32A	0279
SA32B	0279
SA32C	0279
SA32D	0279
SA32E	0279
SA32F	0279
SA32G	0279
SA32L	0279
SA32M	0279
SA32R	0279
SA32T	0279
SA32X	0279
SA32Y	0279
SA33	0004
SA33A(DIO)	OEM
SA33BRN	0004
SA33RED	0004
SA35A	0279
SA35B	0279
SA35C	0279
SA35E	0279
SA35F	0279
SA35G	0279
SA35L	0279
SA35M	0279
SA35R	0279
SA35T	0279
SA35X	0279
SA35Y	0279
SA36A	0279
SA36A(DIO)	OEM
SA36B	0279
SA36C	0279
SA36D	0279
SA36E	0279
SA36F	0279
SA36G	0279
SA36L	0279
SA36M	0279
SA36R	0279
SA36T	0279
SA36X	0279
SA36Y	0279
SA37A	0279
SA37B	0279
SA37C	0279
SA37D	0279
SA37E	0279
SA37F	0279
SA37G	0279
SA37L	0279
SA37M	0279
SA37R	0279
SA37T	0279
SA37X	0279
SA37Y	0279
SA38A	0279
SA38B	0279
SA38C	0279
SA38D	0279
SA38E	0279
SA38F	0279
SA38G	0279
SA38L	0279
SA38M	0279
SA38R	0279
SA38T	0279
SA38X	0279
SA38Y	0279
SA39A	0279
SA39B	0279
SA39C	0279
SA39D	0279
SA39E	0279
SA39F	0279
SA39G	0279
SA39L	0279
SA39M	0279
SA39R	0279
SA39T	0279
SA39X	0279
SA39Y	0279
SA40	OEM
SA40A	0279

DEVICE TYPE	REPL CODE
SA40A(DIO)	OEM
SA40B	0279
SA40C	0279
SA40D	0279
SA40E	0279
SA40F	0279
SA40G	0279
SA40L	0279
SA40M	0279
SA40R	0279
SA40T	0279
SA40X	0279
SA40Y	0279
SA41A	0279
SA41B	0279
SA41C	0279
SA41D	0279
SA41E	0279
SA41F	0279
SA41G	0279
SA41L	0279
SA41M	0279
SA41R	0279
SA41T	0279
SA41X	0279
SA41Y	0279
SA42A	0841
SA42B	0841
SA42C	0841
SA42D	0841
SA42E	0841
SA42F	0841
SA42G	0841
SA42L	0841
SA42M	0841
SA42R	0841
SA42T	0841
SA42X	0841
SA42Y	0841
SA43A	0050
SA43A(DIO)	0563
SA43B	0050
SA43C	0050
SA43D	0050
SA43E	0050
SA43F	0050
SA43G	0050
SA43L	0050
SA43M	0050
SA43R	0050
SA43T	0050
SA43X	0050
SA43Y	0050
SA44A	0279
SA44B	0279
SA44C	0279
SA44D	0279
SA44E	0279
SA44F	0279
SA44G	0279
SA44L	0279
SA44M	0279
SA44R	0279
SA44T	0279
SA44X	0279
SA44Y	0279
SA45A	0050
SA45A(DIO)	OEM
SA45B	0050
SA45C	0050
SA45D	0050
SA45E	0050
SA45F	0050
SA45G	0050
SA45L	0050
SA45M	0050
SA45R	0050
SA45T	0050
SA45X	0050
SA45Y	0050
SA48A(DIO)	OEM
SA49A	0279
SA49B	0279
SA49C	0279
SA49D	0279
SA49E	0279
SA49F	0279
SA49G	0279
SA49L	0279
SA49M	0279
SA49R	0279
SA49T	0279
SA49X	0279
SA49Y	0279
SA50	0037
SA51	0037
SA51A	0037
SA51A(DIO)	OEM
SA52	0037
SA52A	0037
SA52B	0037
SA53	0037
SA54	0037
SA54A	0037
SA54A(DIO)	OEM
SA55	0037
SA56	0037
SA58A(DIO)	0825
SA60A(DIO)	OEM

DEVICE TYPE	REPL CODE
SA64A(DIO)	OEM
SA70	0037
SA70A(DIO)	OEM
SA71A	0050
SA71B	0050
SA71C	0050
SA71D	0050
SA71E	0050
SA71F	0050
SA71G	0050
SA71L	0050
SA71M	0050
SA71R	0050
SA71T	0050
SA71X	0050
SA71Y	0050
SA72A	0050
SA72B	0050
SA72C	0050
SA72D	0050
SA72E	0050
SA72F	0050
SA72G	0050
SA72L	0050
SA72M	0050
SA72R	0050
SA72T	0050
SA72X	0050
SA72Y	0050
SA73A	0050
SA73B	0050
SA73C	0050
SA73D	0050
SA73E	0050
SA73F	0050
SA73G	0050
SA73L	0050
SA73M	0050
SA73R	0050
SA73T	0050
SA73X	0050
SA73Y	0050
SA74A	0050
SA74B	0050
SA74C	0050
SA74D	0050
SA74E	0050
SA74F	0050
SA74G	0050
SA74L	0050
SA74M	0050
SA74R	0050
SA74T	0050
SA74X	0050
SA74Y	0050
SA75A	0279
SA75A(DIO)	OEM
SA75B	0279
SA75C	0279
SA75D	0279
SA75E	0279
SA75F	0279
SA75G	0279
SA75L	0279
SA75M	0279
SA75R	0279
SA75T	0279
SA75X	0279
SA75Y	0279
SA76A	0050
SA76B	0050
SA76C	0050
SA76D	0050
SA76E	0050
SA76F	0050
SA76G	0050
SA76L	0050
SA76M	0050
SA76R	0050
SA76T	0050
SA76X	0050
SA76Y	0050
SA77A	0050
SA77B	0050
SA77C	0050
SA77D	0050
SA77E	0050
SA77F	0050
SA77G	0050
SA77L	0050
SA77M	0050
SA77R	0050
SA77T	0050
SA77X	0050
SA77Y	0050
SA78A	0050
SA78A(DIO)	OEM
SA78B	0050
SA78C	0050
SA78D	0050
SA78E	0050
SA78F	0050
SA78G	0050
SA78HV05CDA	1905
SA78HV05CU	0619
SA78HV12CDA	3359
SA78HV12CU	0330
SA78L	0050
SA78M	0050

DEVICE TYPE	REPL CODE
SA78R	0050
SA78T	0050
SA78X	0050
SA78Y	0050
SA79A	0841
SA79B	0841
SA79C	0841
SA79D	0841
SA79E	0841
SA79F	0841
SA79G	0841
SA79L	0841
SA79M	0841
SA79R	0841
SA79T	0841
SA79X	0841
SA79Y	0841
SA80A	0050
SA80B	0050
SA80C	0050
SA80D	0050
SA80E	0050
SA80F	0050
SA80G	0050
SA80L	0050
SA80M	0050
SA80R	0050
SA80T	0050
SA80X	0050
SA80Y	0050
SA81A	0136
SA81B	0136
SA81C	0136
SA81D	0136
SA81E	0136
SA81F	0136
SA81G	0136
SA81L	0136
SA81M	0136
SA81R	0136
SA81T	0136
SA81X	0136
SA81Y	0136
SA82A	0136
SA82B	0136
SA82C	0136
SA82D	0136
SA82E	0136
SA82F	0136
SA82G	0136
SA82L	0136
SA82M	0136
SA82R	0136
SA82T	0136
SA83A	0050
SA83B	0050
SA83C	0050
SA83D	0050
SA83E	0050
SA83F	0050
SA83G	0050
SA83L	0050
SA83M	0050
SA83R	0050
SA83T	0050
SA83X	0050
SA83Y	0050
SA84A	0050
SA84B	0050
SA84C	0050
SA84D	0050
SA84E	0050
SA84F	0050
SA84G	0050
SA84L	0050
SA84M	0050
SA84R	0050
SA84T	0050
SA84X	0050
SA84Y	0050
SA85A	0136
SA85A(DIO)	OEM
SA85B	0136
SA85C	0136
SA85D	0136
SA85E	0136
SA85F	0136
SA85G	0136
SA85L	0136
SA85M	0136
SA85R	0136
SA85T	0136
SA85X	0136
SA85Y	0136
SA86A	0841
SA86B	0841
SA86C	0841
SA86D	0841
SA86E	0841
SA86F	0841
SA86G	0841
SA86L	0841
SA86M	0841
SA86R	0841
SA86T	0841
SA86X	0841
SA86Y	0841
SA87A	0050
SA87B	0050

DEVICE TYPE	REPL CODE
SA87C	0050
SA87D	0050
SA87E	0050
SA87F	0050
SA87G	0050
SA87L	0050
SA87M	0050
SA87R	0050
SA87T	0050
SA87X	0050
SA87Y	0050
SA90A	0050
SA90A(DIO)	OEM
SA90B	0050
SA90C	0050
SA90D	0050
SA90E	0050
SA90F	0050
SA90G	0050
SA90L	0050
SA90M	0050
SA90R	0050
SA90T	0050
SA90X	0050
SA90Y	0050
SA92A	0050
SA92B	0050
SA92C	0050
SA92D	0050
SA92E	0050
SA92F	0050
SA92G	0050
SA92L	0050
SA92M	0050
SA92R	0050
SA92T	0050
SA92X	0050
SA92Y	0050
SA93A	0050
SA93B	0050
SA93C	0050
SA93D	0050
SA93E	0050
SA93F	0050
SA93G	0050
SA93L	0050
SA93M	0050
SA93R	0050
SA93T	0050
SA93X	0050
SA93Y	0050
SA94A	0136
SA94B	0136
SA94C	0136
SA94D	0136
SA94E	0136
SA94F	0136
SA94G	0136
SA94L	0136
SA94M	0136
SA94R	0136
SA94T	0136
SA94X	0136
SA94Y	0136
SA95A	0037
SA95B	0037
SA95C	0037
SA95D	0037
SA95E	0037
SA95F	0037
SA95G	0037
SA95L	0037
SA95M	0037
SA95R	0037
SA95T	0037
SA95X	0037
SA95Y	0037
SA100	OEM
SA100A	0279
SA100A(DIO)	OEM
SA100B	0279
SA100C	0279
SA100D	0279
SA100E	0279
SA100F	0279
SA100G	0279
SA100L	0279
SA100M	0279
SA100R	0279
SA100T	0279
SA100X	0279
SA100Y	0279
SA101A	0050
SA101B	0050
SA101C	0050
SA101D	0050
SA101E	0050
SA101F	0050
SA101G	0050
SA101L	0050
SA101M	0050
SA101R	0050
SA101T	0050
SA101X	0050
SA101Y	0050
SA102	0136
SA102A	0050
SA102B	0050
SA102C	0050

DEVICE TYPE	REPL CODE
SA102D	0050
SA102E	0050
SA102F	0050
SA102G	0050
SA102L	0050
SA102M	0050
SA102R	0050
SA102T	0050
SA102X	0050
SA102Y	0050
SA103A	0050
SA103B	0050
SA103C	0050
SA103D	0050
SA103E	0050
SA103F	0050
SA103G	0050
SA103L	0050
SA103M	0050
SA103R	0050
SA103T	0050
SA103X	0050
SA103Y	0050
SA104A	0050
SA104B	0050
SA104C	0050
SA104D	0050
SA104E	0050
SA104F	0050
SA104G	0050
SA104L	0050
SA104M	0050
SA104R	0050
SA104T	0050
SA104X	0050
SA104Y	0050
SA105A	0136
SA105B	0136
SA105C	0136
SA105D	0136
SA105E	0136
SA105F	0136
SA105G	0136
SA105L	0136
SA105M	0136
SA105R	0136
SA105T	0136
SA105X	0136
SA105Y	0136
SA106A	0050
SA106B	0050
SA106C	0050
SA106D	0050
SA106E	0050
SA106F	0050
SA106G	0050
SA106L	0050
SA106M	0050
SA106R	0050
SA106T	0050
SA106X	0050
SA106Y	0050
SA107	OEM
SA107B	0050
SA107C	0050
SA107D	0050
SA107E	0050
SA107F	0050
SA107G	0050
SA107L	0050
SA107M	0050
SA107R	0050
SA107T	0050
SA107X	0050
SA107Y	0050
SA108A	0050
SA108B	0050
SA108C	0050
SA108D	0050
SA108E	0050
SA108F	0050
SA108G	0050
SA108L	0050
SA108M	0050
SA108R	0050
SA108T	0050
SA108X	0050
SA108Y	0050
SA109A	0050
SA109B	0050
SA109C	0050
SA109D	0050
SA109E	0050
SA109F	0050
SA109G	0050
SA109L	0050
SA109M	0050
SA109R	0050
SA109T	0050
SA109X	0050
SA109Y	0050
SA110A	0050
SA110A(DIO)	OEM
SA110B	0050
SA110C	0050
SA110D	0050
SA110E	0050
SA110F	0050
SA110G	0050

If replacement code is OEM, contact original manufacturer for replacement.

539

DEVICE TYPE	REPL CODE	DEVICE TYPE	REPL CODE	DEVICE TYPE	REPL CODE	DEVICE TYPE	REPL CODE	DEVICE TYPE	REPL CODE	DEVICE TYPE	REPL CODE	DEVICE TYPE	REPL CODE
SA110L	0050	SA118Y	0050	SA132A	0279	SA142F	0050	SA150R	0136	SA160A	0279	SA168E	0279
SA110M	0050	SA120A(DIO)	OEM	SA132B	0279	SA142G	0050	SA150T	0136	SA160A(DIO)	OEM	SA168F	0279
SA110R	0050	SA121A	0050	SA132C	0279	SA142L	0050	SA150X	0136	SA160B	0279	SA168G	0279
SA110T	0050	SA121B	0050	SA132D	0279	SA142M	0050	SA150Y	0136	SA160C	0279	SA168L	0279
SA110X	0050	SA121C	0050	SA132E	0279	SA142R	0050	SA151A	0279	SA160D	0279	SA168M	0279
SA110Y	0050	SA121D	0050	SA132F	0279	SA142T	0050	SA151B	0279	SA160E	0279	SA168R	0279
SA111A	0050	SA121E	0050	SA132G	0279	SA142X	0050	SA151C	0279	SA160F	0279	SA168T	0279
SA111B	0050	SA121F	0050	SA132L	0279	SA142Y	0050	SA151D	0279	SA160G	0279	SA168X	0279
SA111C	0050	SA121G	0050	SA132M	0279	SA143A	0050	SA151E	0279	SA160L	0279	SA168Y	0279
SA111D	0050	SA121L	0050	SA132R	0279	SA143B	0050	SA151F	0279	SA160M	0279	SA169A	0279
SA111E	0050	SA121M	0050	SA132T	0279	SA143C	0050	SA151G	0279	SA160R	0279	SA169B	0279
SA111F	0050	SA121R	0050	SA132X	0279	SA143D	0050	SA151L	0279	SA160T	0279	SA169C	0279
SA111G	0050	SA121T	0050	SA132Y	0279	SA143E	0050	SA151M	0279	SA160X	0279	SA169D	0279
SA111L	0050	SA121X	0050	SA133A	0050	SA143F	0050	SA151R	0279	SA160Y	0279	SA169E	0279
SA111M	0050	SA121Y	0050	SA133B	0050	SA143G	0050	SA151T	0279	SA161A	0050	SA169F	0279
SA111R	0050	SA122A	0050	SA133C	0050	SA143L	0050	SA151X	0279	SA161B	0050	SA169G	0279
SA111T	0050	SA122B	0050	SA133D	0050	SA143M	0050	SA151Y	0279	SA161C	0050	SA169L	0279
SA111X	0050	SA122C	0050	SA133E	0050	SA143R	0050	SA152A	0279	SA161D	0050	SA169M	0279
SA111Y	0050	SA122D	0050	SA133F	0050	SA143T	0050	SA152B	0279	SA161E	0050	SA169R	0279
SA112A	0050	SA122E	0050	SA133G	0050	SA143X	0050	SA152C	0279	SA161F	0050	SA169T	0279
SA112B	0050	SA122F	0050	SA133L	0050	SA143Y	0050	SA152D	0279	SA161G	0050	SA169X	0279
SA112C	0050	SA122G	0050	SA133M	0050	SA144A	0279	SA152E	0279	SA161L	0050	SA169Y	0279
SA112D	0050	SA122L	0050	SA133R	0050	SA144B	0279	SA152F	0279	SA161M	0050	SA170A	0279
SA112E	0050	SA122M	0050	SA133T	0050	SA144C	0279	SA152G	0279	SA161R	0050	SA170A(DIO)	1395
SA112F	0050	SA122R	0050	SA133X	0050	SA144D	0279	SA152L	0279	SA161T	0050	SA170B	0279
SA112G	0050	SA122T	0050	SA133Y	0050	SA144E	0279	SA152M	0279	SA161X	0050	SA170C	0279
SA112L	0050	SA122X	0050	SA134A	0050	SA144F	0279	SA152R	0279	SA161Y	0050	SA170D	0279
SA112M	0050	SA122Y	0050	SA134B	0050	SA144G	0279	SA152T	0279	SA162A	0050	SA170E	0279
SA112R	0050	SA123A	0050	SA134C	0050	SA144L	0279	SA152X	0279	SA162B	0050	SA170F	0279
SA112T	0050	SA123B	0050	SA134D	0050	SA144M	0279	SA152Y	0279	SA162C	0050	SA170G	0279
SA112X	0050	SA123C	0050	SA134E	0050	SA144R	0279	SA153A	0050	SA162D	0050	SA170L	0279
SA112Y	0050	SA123D	0050	SA134F	0050	SA144T	0279	SA153B	0050	SA162E	0050	SA170M	0279
SA113A	0050	SA123E	0050	SA134G	0050	SA144X	0279	SA153C	0050	SA162F	0050	SA170R	0279
SA113B	0050	SA123F	0050	SA134L	0050	SA144Y	0279	SA153D	0050	SA162G	0050	SA170T	0279
SA113C	0050	SA123G	0050	SA134M	0050	SA145A	0279	SA153E	0050	SA162L	0050	SA170X	0279
SA113D	0050	SA123L	0050	SA134R	0050	SA145B	0279	SA153F	0050	SA162M	0050	SA170Y	0279
SA113E	0050	SA123M	0050	SA134T	0050	SA145C	0279	SA153G	0050	SA162R	0050	SA171A	0279
SA113F	0050	SA123R	0050	SA134X	0050	SA145D	0279	SA153L	0050	SA162T	0050	SA171B	0279
SA113G	0050	SA123T	0050	SA134Y	0050	SA145E	0279	SA153M	0050	SA162X	0050	SA171C	0279
SA113L	0050	SA123X	0050	SA135A	0279	SA145F	0279	SA153R	0050	SA162Y	0050	SA171D	0279
SA113M	0050	SA123Y	0050	SA135B	0279	SA145G	0279	SA153T	0050	SA163A	0050	SA171E	0279
SA113R	0050	SA124A	0050	SA135C	0279	SA145L	0279	SA153X	0050	SA163B	0050	SA171F	0279
SA113T	0050	SA124B	0050	SA135D	0279	SA145M	0279	SA153Y	0050	SA163C	0050	SA171G	0279
SA113X	0050	SA124C	0050	SA135E	0279	SA145R	0279	SA154A	0050	SA163D	0050	SA171L	0279
SA113Y	0050	SA124D	0050	SA135F	0279	SA145T	0279	SA154B	0050	SA163E	0050	SA171M	0279
SA114A	0050	SA124E	0050	SA135G	0279	SA145X	0279	SA154C	0050	SA163F	0050	SA171R	0279
SA114B	0050	SA124F	0050	SA135L	0279	SA145Y	0279	SA154D	0050	SA163G	0050	SA171T	0279
SA114C	0050	SA124G	0050	SA135M	0279	SA146A	0279	SA154E	0050	SA163L	0050	SA171X	0279
SA114D	0050	SA124L	0050	SA135R	0279	SA146B	0279	SA154F	0050	SA163M	0050	SA171Y	0279
SA114E	0050	SA124M	0050	SA135T	0279	SA146C	0279	SA154G	0050	SA163R	0050	SA172A	0279
SA114F	0050	SA124R	0050	SA135X	0279	SA146D	0279	SA154L	0050	SA163T	0050	SA172B	0279
SA114G	0050	SA124T	0050	SA135Y	0279	SA146E	0279	SA154M	0050	SA163X	0050	SA172C	0279
SA114L	0050	SA124X	0050	SA136A	0050	SA146F	0279	SA154R	0050	SA163Y	0050	SA172D	0279
SA114M	0050	SA124Y	0050	SA136B	0050	SA146G	0279	SA154T	0050	SA164A	0050	SA172E	0279
SA114R	0050	SA125A	0050	SA136C	0050	SA146L	0279	SA154X	0050	SA164B	0050	SA172F	0279
SA114T	0050	SA125B	0050	SA136D	0050	SA146M	0279	SA154Y	0050	SA164C	0050	SA172G	0279
SA114X	0050	SA125C	0050	SA136E	0050	SA146R	0279	SA155A	0050	SA164D	0050	SA172L	0279
SA114Y	0050	SA125D	0050	SA136F	0050	SA146T	0279	SA155B	0050	SA164E	0050	SA172M	0279
SA115A	0050	SA125E	0050	SA136G	0050	SA146X	0279	SA155C	0050	SA164F	0050	SA172R	0279
SA115B	0050	SA125F	0050	SA136L	0050	SA146Y	0279	SA155D	0050	SA164G	0050	SA172T	0279
SA115C	0050	SA125G	0050	SA136M	0050	SA147A	0279	SA155E	0050	SA164L	0050	SA172X	0279
SA115D	0050	SA125L	0050	SA136R	0050	SA147B	0279	SA155F	0050	SA164M	0050	SA172Y	0279
SA115E	0050	SA125M	0050	SA136T	0050	SA147C	0279	SA155G	0050	SA164R	0050	SA173A	0279
SA115F	0050	SA125R	0050	SA136X	0050	SA147D	0279	SA155L	0050	SA164T	0050	SA173B	0279
SA115G	0050	SA125T	0050	SA136Y	0050	SA147E	0279	SA155M	0050	SA164X	0050	SA173C	0279
SA115L	0050	SA125X	0050	SA137A	0279	SA147F	0279	SA155R	0050	SA164Y	0050	SA173D	0279
SA115M	0050	SA125Y	0050	SA137B	0279	SA147G	0279	SA155T	0050	SA165A	0050	SA173E	0279
SA115R	0050	SA128	0004	SA137C	0279	SA147L	0279	SA155X	0050	SA165B	0050	SA173F	0279
SA115T	0050	SA128-1	0004	SA137D	0279	SA147M	0279	SA155Y	0050	SA165C	0050	SA173G	0279
SA115X	0050	SA129A	0136	SA137E	0279	SA147R	0279	SA156A	0050	SA165D	0050	SA173L	0279
SA115Y	0050	SA129B	0136	SA137F	0279	SA147T	0279	SA156B	0050	SA165E	0050	SA173M	0279
SA116A	0050	SA129C	0136	SA137G	0279	SA147X	0279	SA156C	0050	SA165F	0050	SA173R	0279
SA116B	0050	SA129D	0136	SA137L	0279	SA147Y	0279	SA156D	0050	SA165G	0050	SA173T	0279
SA116C	0050	SA129E	0136	SA137M	0279	SA148A	0279	SA156E	0050	SA165L	0050	SA173X	0279
SA116D	0050	SA129F	0136	SA137R	0279	SA148B	0279	SA156F	0050	SA165M	0050	SA173Y	0279
SA116E	0050	SA129G	0136	SA137T	0279	SA148C	0279	SA156G	0050	SA165R	0050	SA174A	0279
SA116F	0050	SA129L	0136	SA137X	0279	SA148D	0279	SA156L	0050	SA165T	0050	SA174B	0279
SA116G	0050	SA129M	0136	SA137Y	0279	SA148E	0279	SA156M	0050	SA165X	0050	SA174C	0279
SA116L	0050	SA129R	0136	SA139A	0050	SA148F	0279	SA156R	0050	SA165Y	0050	SA174D	0279
SA116M	0050	SA129T	0136	SA139B	0050	SA148G	0279	SA156T	0050	SA166A	0050	SA174E	0279
SA116R	0050	SA129X	0136	SA139C	0050	SA148L	0279	SA156X	0050	SA166B	0050	SA174F	0279
SA116T	0050	SA129Y	0136	SA139D	0050	SA148M	0279	SA156Y	0050	SA166C	0050	SA174G	0279
SA116X	0050	SA130A	0050	SA139E	0050	SA148R	0279	SA157A	0050	SA166D	0050	SA174L	0279
SA116Y	0050	SA130A(DIO)	OEM	SA139F	0050	SA148T	0279	SA157B	0050	SA166E	0050	SA174M	0279
SA117A	0050	SA130B	0050	SA139G	0050	SA148X	0279	SA157C	0050	SA166F	0050	SA174R	0279
SA117B	0050	SA130C	0050	SA139L	0050	SA148Y	0279	SA157D	0050	SA166G	0050	SA174T	0279
SA117C	0050	SA130D	0050	SA139M	0050	SA149A	0279	SA157E	0050	SA166L	0050	SA174X	0279
SA117D	0050	SA130E	0050	SA139R	0050	SA149B	0279	SA157F	0050	SA166M	0050	SA174Y	0279
SA117E	0050	SA130F	0050	SA139T	0050	SA149C	0279	SA157G	0050	SA166R	0050	SA175A	0050
SA117F	0050	SA130G	0050	SA139X	0050	SA149D	0279	SA157L	0050	SA166T	0050	SA175B	0050
SA117G	0050	SA130L	0050	SA139Y	0050	SA149E	0279	SA157M	0050	SA166X	0050	SA175C	0050
SA117L	0050	SA130M	0050	SA141A	0050	SA149F	0279	SA157R	0050	SA166Y	0050	SA175D	0050
SA117M	0050	SA130R	0050	SA141B	0050	SA149G	0279	SA157T	0050	SA167A	0279	SA175E	0050
SA117R	0050	SA130T	0050	SA141C	0050	SA149L	0279	SA157X	0050	SA167B	0279	SA175F	0050
SA117T	0050	SA130X	0050	SA141D	0050	SA149M	0279	SA157Y	0050	SA167C	0279	SA175G	0050
SA117X	0050	SA130Y	0050	SA141E	0050	SA149R	0279	SA159A	0050	SA167D	0279	SA175L	0050
SA117Y	0050	SA131A	0279	SA141F	0050	SA149T	0279	SA159B	0050	SA167E	0279	SA175M	0050
SA118A	0050	SA131B	0279	SA141G	0050	SA149X	0279	SA159C	0050	SA167F	0279	SA175R	0050
SA118B	0050	SA131C	0279	SA141L	0050	SA149Y	0279	SA159D	0050	SA167G	0279	SA175T	0050
SA118C	0050	SA131D	0279	SA141M	0050	SA150A	0136	SA159E	0050	SA167L	0279	SA175X	0050
SA118D	0050	SA131E	0279	SA141R	0050	SA150A(DIO)	OEM	SA159F	0050	SA167M	0279	SA175Y	0050
SA118E	0050	SA131F	0279	SA141T	0050	SA150B	0136	SA159G	0050	SA167R	0279	SA176A	0136
SA118F	0050	SA131G	0279	SA141X	0050	SA150C	0136	SA159L	0050	SA167T	0279	SA176B	0136
SA118G	0050	SA131L	0279	SA141Y	0050	SA150D	0136	SA159M	0050	SA167X	0279	SA176C	0136
SA118L	0050	SA131M	0279	SA142A	0050	SA150E	0136	SA159R	0050	SA167Y	0279	SA176D	0136
SA118M	0050	SA131R	0279	SA142B	0050	SA150F	0136	SA159T	0050	SA168A	0279	SA176E	0136
SA118R	0050	SA131T	0279	SA142C	0050	SA150G	0136	SA159X	0050	SA168B	0279	SA176F	0136
SA118T	0050	SA131X	0279	SA142D	0050	SA150L	0136	SA159Y	0050	SA168C	0279	SA176G	0136
SA118X	0050	SA131Y	0279	SA142E	0050	SA150M	0136	SA160	0279	SA168D	0279	SA176L	0136

If replacement code is OEM, contact original manufacturer for replacement.

DEVICE TYPE	REPL CODE
SA176M	0136
SA176R	0136
SA176T	0136
SA176X	0136
SA176Y	0136
SA180A	0279
SA180B	0279
SA180C	0279
SA180D	0279
SA180E	0279
SA180F	0279
SA180G	0279
SA180L	0279
SA180M	0279
SA180R	0279
SA180T	0279
SA180X	0279
SA180Y	0279
SA181A	0279
SA181B	0279
SA181C	0279
SA181D	0279
SA181E	0279
SA181F	0279
SA181G	0279
SA181L	0279
SA181M	0279
SA181R	0279
SA181T	0279
SA181X	0279
SA181Y	0279
SA182A	0279
SA182B	0279
SA182C	0279
SA182D	0279
SA182E	0279
SA182F	0279
SA182G	0279
SA182L	0279
SA182M	0279
SA182R	0279
SA182T	0279
SA182X	0279
SA182Y	0279
SA183A	0279
SA183B	0279
SA183C	0279
SA183D	0279
SA183E	0279
SA183F	0279
SA183G	0279
SA183L	0279
SA183M	0279
SA183R	0279
SA183T	0279
SA183X	0279
SA183Y	0279
SA188A	0279
SA188B	0279
SA188C	0279
SA188D	0279
SA188E	0279
SA188F	0279
SA188G	0279
SA188L	0279
SA188M	0279
SA188R	0279
SA188T	0279
SA188X	0279
SA188Y	0279
SA189A	0279
SA189B	0279
SA189C	0279
SA189D	0279
SA189E	0279
SA189F	0279
SA189G	0279
SA189L	0279
SA189M	0279
SA189R	0279
SA189T	0279
SA189X	0279
SA189Y	0279
SA197	0004
SA197-1	0004
SA197-2	0004
SA197-3	0004
SA198A	0279
SA198B	0279
SA198C	0279
SA198D	0279
SA198E	0279
SA198F	0279
SA198G	0279
SA198L	0279
SA198M	0279
SA198R	0279
SA198T	0279
SA198X	0279
SA198Y	0279
SA201A	0279
SA201B	0279
SA201C	0279
SA201D	0279
SA201E	0279
SA201F	0279
SA201G	0279
SA201L	0279
SA201M	0279
SA201R	0279
SA201T	0279
SA201X	0279
SA201Y	0279
SA202A	0136
SA202B	0136
SA202C	0136
SA202D	0136
SA202E	0136
SA202F	0136
SA202G	0136
SA202L	0136
SA202M	0136
SA202R	0136
SA202T	0136
SA202X	0136
SA202Y	0136
SA203A	0279
SA203B	0279
SA203C	0279
SA203D	0279
SA203E	0279
SA203F	0279
SA203G	0279
SA203L	0279
SA203M	0279
SA203R	0279
SA203T	0279
SA203X	0279
SA203Y	0279
SA204	0004
SA205BLU	0004
SA205BRN	0004
SA205GRN	0004
SA205ORN	0004
SA205RED	0004
SA205VIO	0004
SA205WHT	0004
SA205YEL	0004
SA206A	0279
SA206B	0279
SA206C	0279
SA206D	0279
SA206E	0279
SA206F	0279
SA206G	0279
SA206L	0279
SA206M	0279
SA206R	0279
SA206T	0279
SA206X	0279
SA206Y	0279
SA207A	0279
SA207B	0279
SA207C	0279
SA207D	0279
SA207E	0279
SA207F	0279
SA207G	0279
SA207L	0279
SA207M	0279
SA207R	0279
SA207T	0279
SA207X	0279
SA207Y	0279
SA208A	0279
SA208B	0279
SA208C	0279
SA208D	0279
SA208E	0279
SA208F	0279
SA208G	0279
SA208L	0279
SA208M	0279
SA208R	0279
SA208T	0279
SA208X	0279
SA208Y	0279
SA209A	0279
SA209B	0279
SA209C	0279
SA209D	0279
SA209E	0279
SA209F	0279
SA209G	0279
SA209L	0279
SA209M	0279
SA209R	0279
SA209T	0279
SA209X	0279
SA209Y	0279
SA210A	0279
SA210B	0279
SA210C	0279
SA210D	0279
SA210E	0279
SA210F	0279
SA210G	0279
SA210L	0279
SA210M	0279
SA210R	0279
SA210T	0279
SA210X	0279
SA210Y	0279
SA211A	0279
SA211B	0279
SA211C	0279
SA211D	0279
SA211E	0279
SA211F	0279
SA211G	0279
SA211L	0279
SA211M	0279
SA211R	0279
SA211T	0279
SA211X	0279
SA211Y	0279
SA212A	0279
SA212B	0279
SA212C	0279
SA212D	0279
SA212E	0279
SA212F	0279
SA212G	0279
SA212L	0279
SA212M	0279
SA212R	0279
SA212T	0279
SA212X	0279
SA212Y	0279
SA213A	0050
SA213B	0050
SA213C	0050
SA213D	0050
SA213E	0050
SA213F	0050
SA213G	0050
SA213L	0050
SA213M	0050
SA213R	0050
SA213T	0050
SA213X	0050
SA213Y	0050
SA214A	0050
SA214B	0050
SA214C	0050
SA214D	0050
SA214E	0050
SA214F	0050
SA214G	0050
SA214L	0050
SA214M	0050
SA214R	0050
SA214T	0050
SA214X	0050
SA214Y	0050
SA215A	0050
SA215B	0050
SA215C	0050
SA215D	0050
SA215E	0050
SA215F	0050
SA215G	0050
SA215L	0050
SA215M	0050
SA215R	0050
SA215T	0050
SA215X	0050
SA215Y	0050
SA216A	0050
SA216B	0050
SA216C	0050
SA216D	0050
SA216E	0050
SA216F	0050
SA216G	0050
SA216L	0050
SA216M	0050
SA216R	0050
SA216T	0050
SA216X	0050
SA216Y	0050
SA217A	0050
SA217B	0050
SA217C	0050
SA217D	0050
SA217E	0050
SA217F	0050
SA217G	0050
SA217L	0050
SA217M	0050
SA217R	0050
SA217T	0050
SA217X	0050
SA217Y	0050
SA218A	0136
SA218B	0136
SA218C	0136
SA218D	0136
SA218E	0136
SA218F	0136
SA218G	0136
SA218L	0136
SA218M	0136
SA218R	0136
SA218T	0136
SA218X	0136
SA218Y	0136
SA219A	0050
SA219B	0050
SA219C	0050
SA219D	0050
SA219E	0050
SA219F	0050
SA219G	0050
SA219L	0050
SA219M	0050
SA219R	0050
SA219T	0050
SA219X	0050
SA219Y	0050
SA220A	0136
SA220B	0136
SA220C	0136
SA220D	0136
SA220E	0136
SA220F	0136
SA220G	0136
SA220L	0136
SA220M	0136
SA220R	0136
SA220T	0136
SA220X	0136
SA220Y	0136
SA221A	0136
SA221B	0136
SA221C	0136
SA221D	0136
SA221E	0136
SA221F	0136
SA221G	0136
SA221L	0136
SA221M	0136
SA221R	0136
SA221T	0136
SA221X	0136
SA221Y	0136
SA222A	0136
SA222B	0136
SA222C	0136
SA222D	0136
SA222E	0136
SA222F	0136
SA222G	0136
SA222L	0136
SA222M	0136
SA222R	0136
SA222T	0136
SA222X	0136
SA222Y	0136
SA223A	0050
SA223B	0050
SA223C	0050
SA223D	0050
SA223E	0050
SA223F	0050
SA223G	0050
SA223L	0050
SA223M	0050
SA223R	0050
SA223T	0050
SA223X	0050
SA223Y	0050
SA224A	0136
SA224B	0136
SA224C	0136
SA224D	0136
SA224E	0136
SA224F	0136
SA224G	0136
SA224L	0136
SA224M	0136
SA224X	0136
SA224Y	0136
SA225A	0050
SA225B	0050
SA225C	0050
SA225D	0050
SA225E	0050
SA225F	0050
SA225G	0050
SA225M	0050
SA225R	0050
SA225T	0050
SA225X	0050
SA225Y	0050
SA227A	0050
SA227B	0050
SA227C	0050
SA227D	0050
SA227E	0050
SA227F	0050
SA227G	0050
SA227L	0050
SA227M	0050
SA227R	0050
SA227T	0050
SA227X	0050
SA227Y	0050
SA229A	0050
SA229B	0050
SA229C	0050
SA229D	0050
SA229E	0050
SA229F	0050
SA229G	0050
SA229L	0050
SA229M	0050
SA229R	0050
SA229T	0050
SA229X	0050
SA229Y	0050
SA230A	0050
SA230B	0050
SA230C	0050
SA230D	0050
SA230E	0050
SA230F	0050
SA230G	0050
SA230L	0050
SA230M	0050
SA230R	0050
SA230T	0050
SA230X	0050
SA230Y	0050
SA231A	0841
SA231B	0841
SA231C	0841
SA231D	0841
SA231E	0841
SA231F	0841
SA231G	0841
SA231L	0841
SA231M	0841
SA231R	0841
SA231T	0841
SA231X	0841
SA231Y	0841
SA233A	0050
SA233B	0050
SA233C	0050
SA233D	0050
SA233E	0050
SA233F	0050
SA233G	0050
SA233L	0050
SA233M	0050
SA233R	0050
SA233T	0050
SA233X	0050
SA233Y	0050
SA234A	0136
SA234B	0136
SA234C	0136
SA234D	0136
SA234E	0136
SA234F	0136
SA234G	0136
SA234L	0136
SA234M	0136
SA234R	0136
SA234T	0136
SA234X	0136
SA234Y	0136
SA235A	0050
SA235B	0050
SA235C	0050
SA235D	0050
SA235E	0050
SA235F	0050
SA235G	0050
SA235L	0050
SA235M	0050
SA235R	0050
SA235T	0050
SA235X	0050
SA235Y	0050
SA236A	0050
SA236B	0050
SA236C	0050
SA236D	0050
SA236E	0050
SA236F	0050
SA236G	0050
SA236L	0050
SA236M	0050
SA236R	0050
SA236T	0050
SA236X	0050
SA236Y	0050
SA237A	0136
SA237B	0136
SA237C	0136
SA237D	0136
SA237E	0136
SA237F	0136
SA237G	0136
SA237L	0136
SA237M	0136
SA237R	0136
SA237T	0136
SA237X	0136
SA237Y	0136
SA238A	0050
SA238B	0050
SA238C	0050
SA238D	0050
SA238E	0050
SA238F	0050
SA238G	0050
SA238L	0050
SA238M	0050
SA238R	0050
SA238T	0050
SA238X	0050
SA238Y	0050
SA239A	0050
SA239B	0050
SA239C	0050
SA239D	0050
SA239E	0050
SA239F	0050
SA239G	0050
SA239L	0050
SA239M	0050
SA239R	0050
SA239T	0050
SA239X	0050
SA239Y	0050
SA240	0004
SA241A	0050
SA241B	0050
SA241C	0050
SA241D	0050
SA241E	0050
SA241F	0050
SA241G	0050
SA241L	0050
SA241M	0050
SA241R	0050
SA241T	0050
SA241X	0050
SA241Y	0050
SA246A	0050
SA246B	0050
SA246C	0050
SA246D	0050
SA246E	0050
SA246F	0050
SA246G	0050
SA246L	0050
SA246M	0050
SA246R	0050
SA246T	0050
SA246X	0050
SA246Y	0050
SA247A	0050
SA247B	0050
SA247C	0050
SA247D	0050
SA247E	0050
SA247F	0050
SA247G	0050
SA247L	0050
SA247M	0050
SA247R	0050
SA247T	0050
SA247X	0050
SA247Y	0050
SA248A	0279
SA248B	0279
SA248C	0279
SA248D	0279
SA248E	0279
SA248F	0279
SA248G	0279
SA248L	0279
SA248M	0279
SA248R	0279
SA248T	0279
SA248X	0279
SA248Y	0279
SA249A	0136
SA249B	0136
SA249C	0136
SA249D	0136
SA249E	0136
SA249F	0136
SA249G	0136
SA249L	0136
SA249M	0136
SA249R	0136
SA249T	0136
SA249X	0136
SA249Y	0136
SA250A	0136
SA250B	0136
SA250C	0136
SA250D	0136
SA250E	0136
SA250F	0136
SA250G	0136
SA250L	0136
SA250M	0136
SA250R	0136
SA250T	0136
SA250X	0136
SA250Y	0136
SA251A	0050
SA251B	0050
SA251C	0050
SA251D	0050
SA251E	0050
SA251F	0050
SA251G	0050
SA251L	0050
SA251M	0050
SA251R	0050
SA251T	0050
SA251X	0050
SA251Y	0050
SA252A	0050
SA252B	0050
SA252C	0050
SA252D	0050
SA252E	0050
SA252F	0050
SA252G	0050
SA252L	0050
SA252M	0050
SA252R	0050
SA252T	0050
SA252X	0050
SA252Y	0050
SA253A	0050
SA253B	0050
SA253C	0050
SA253D	0050
SA253E	0050
SA253F	0050
SA253G	0050
SA253L	0050
SA253M	0050
SA253R	0050
SA253T	0050
SA253X	0050
SA253Y	0050
SA254A	0279
SA254B	0279
SA254C	0279
SA254D	0279
SA254E	0279
SA254F	0279
SA254G	0279
SA254L	0279
SA254M	0279
SA254R	0279
SA254T	0279
SA254X	0279
SA254Y	0279
SA255A	0279
SA255B	0279
SA255C	0279
SA255D	0279
SA255E	0279
SA255F	0279
SA255G	0279
SA255L	0279
SA255M	0279
SA255R	0279
SA255T	0279
SA255X	0279
SA255Y	0279
SA256A	0136
SA256B	0136
SA256C	0136
SA256D	0136
SA256E	0136
SA256F	0136
SA256G	0136
SA256L	0136
SA256M	0136
SA256R	0136
SA256T	0136
SA256X	0136
SA256Y	0136
SA257A	0050
SA257B	0050
SA257C	0050
SA257D	0050
SA257E	0050
SA257F	0050
SA257G	0050
SA257L	0050
SA257M	0050
SA257R	0050
SA257T	0050
SA257X	0050
SA257Y	0050
SA258A	0050
SA258B	0050
SA258C	0050
SA258D	0050
SA258E	0050
SA258F	0050
SA258G	0050
SA258L	0050
SA258M	0050
SA258R	0050
SA258T	0050
SA258X	0050
SA258Y	0050
SA259A	0136
SA259B	0136
SA259C	0136
SA259D	0136
SA259E	0136
SA259F	0136
SA259G	0136
SA259L	0136
SA259M	0136
SA259R	0136
SA259T	0136
SA259X	0136
SA259Y	0136
SA260A	0050
SA260B	0050
SA260C	0050
SA260D	0050
SA260E	0050
SA260F	0050
SA260G	0050
SA260L	0050
SA260M	0050
SA260R	0050
SA260T	0050
SA260X	0050
SA260Y	0050
SA261A	0050
SA261B	0050
SA261C	0050
SA261D	0050
SA261E	0050
SA261F	0050

If replacement code is OEM, contact original manufacturer for replacement.

541

DEVICE TYPE	REPL CODE	DEVICE TYPE	REPL CODE	DEVICE TYPE	REPL CODE	DEVICE TYPE	REPL CODE	DEVICE TYPE	REPL CODE	DEVICE TYPE	REPL CODE	DEVICE TYPE	REPL CODE
SA261G	0050	SA269X	0136	SA279D	0279	SA287G	0136	SA295X	0050	SA309G	0050	SA330B	0279
SA261L	0050	SA269Y	0136	SA279E	0279	SA287L	0136	SA295Y	0050	SA309L	0050	SA330C	0279
SA261M	0050	SA270A	0050	SA279F	0279	SA287M	0136	SA296A	0279	SA309M	0050	SA330D	0279
SA261R	0050	SA270B	0050	SA279G	0279	SA287R	0136	SA296B	0279	SA309R	0050	SA330E	0279
SA261T	0050	SA270C	0050	SA279L	0279	SA287T	0136	SA296C	0279	SA309T	0050	SA330F	0279
SA261X	0050	SA270D	0050	SA279M	0279	SA287X	0136	SA296D	0279	SA309X	0050	SA330G	0279
SA261Y	0050	SA270E	0050	SA279R	0279	SA287Y	0136	SA296E	0279	SA309Y	0050	SA330L	0279
SA262A	0050	SA270F	0050	SA279T	0279	SA288A	0136	SA296F	0279	SA310	0037	SA330M	0279
SA262B	0050	SA270G	0050	SA279X	0279	SA288B	0136	SA296G	0279	SA311	0037	SA330R	0279
SA262C	0050	SA270L	0050	SA279Y	0279	SA288C	0136	SA296L	0279	SA312	0037	SA330T	0279
SA262D	0050	SA270M	0050	SA280A	0050	SA288D	0136	SA296M	0279	SA313	0037	SA330X	0279
SA262E	0050	SA270R	0050	SA280B	0050	SA288E	0136	SA296R	0279	SA313A	0037	SA330Y	0279
SA262F	0050	SA270T	0050	SA280C	0050	SA288F	0136	SA296T	0279	SA314	0037	SA331A	0050
SA262G	0050	SA270X	0050	SA280D	0050	SA288G	0136	SA296X	0279	SA315	0037	SA331B	0050
SA262L	0050	SA270Y	0050	SA280E	0050	SA288L	0136	SA296Y	0279	SA316	0037	SA331C	0050
SA262M	0050	SA271A	0136	SA280F	0050	SA288M	0136	SA297A	0279	SA318-2	0164	SA331D	0050
SA262R	0050	SA271B	0136	SA280G	0050	SA288R	0136	SA297B	0279	SA318-3	0164	SA331E	0050
SA262T	0050	SA271C	0136	SA280L	0050	SA288T	0136	SA297C	0279	SA321A	0050	SA331F	0050
SA262X	0050	SA271D	0136	SA280M	0050	SA288X	0136	SA297E	0279	SA321B	0050	SA331G	0050
SA262Y	0050	SA271E	0136	SA280R	0050	SA288Y	0136	SA297F	0279	SA321C	0050	SA331L	0050
SA263A	0050	SA271F	0136	SA280T	0050	SA289A	0050	SA297G	0279	SA321D	0050	SA331M	0050
SA263B	0050	SA271G	0136	SA280X	0050	SA289B	0050	SA297L	0279	SA321E	0050	SA331R	0050
SA263C	0050	SA271L	0136	SA280Y	0050	SA289C	0050	SA297M	0279	SA321F	0050	SA331T	0050
SA263D	0050	SA271M	0136	SA281A	0050	SA289D	0050	SA297R	0279	SA321G	0050	SA331X	0050
SA263E	0050	SA271R	0136	SA281B	0050	SA289E	0050	SA297T	0279	SA321L	0050	SA331Y	0050
SA263F	0050	SA271T	0136	SA281C	0050	SA289F	0050	SA297X	0279	SA321M	0050	SA332A	0136
SA263G	0050	SA271X	0136	SA281D	0050	SA289G	0050	SA297Y	0279	SA321R	0050	SA332B	0136
SA263L	0050	SA271Y	0136	SA281E	0050	SA289L	0050	SA298A	0136	SA321T	0050	SA332C	0136
SA263M	0050	SA272A	0136	SA281F	0050	SA289M	0050	SA298B	0136	SA321X	0050	SA332D	0136
SA263R	0050	SA272B	0136	SA281G	0050	SA289R	0050	SA298C	0136	SA321Y	0050	SA332E	0136
SA263T	0050	SA272C	0136	SA281L	0050	SA289T	0050	SA298D	0136	SA322A	0136	SA332F	0136
SA263X	0050	SA272D	0136	SA281M	0050	SA289X	0050	SA298E	0136	SA322B	0136	SA332G	0136
SA263Y	0050	SA272E	0136	SA281R	0050	SA289Y	0050	SA298L	0136	SA322C	0136	SA332L	0136
SA264A	0050	SA272F	0136	SA281T	0050	SA290A	0050	SA298M	0136	SA322D	0136	SA332M	0136
SA264B	0050	SA272G	0136	SA281X	0050	SA290B	0050	SA298R	0136	SA322E	0136	SA332R	0136
SA264C	0050	SA272L	0136	SA281Y	0050	SA290C	0050	SA298T	0136	SA322F	0136	SA332T	0136
SA264D	0050	SA272M	0136	SA282	0133	SA290D	0050	SA298X	0136	SA322G	0136	SA332X	0136
SA264E	0050	SA272R	0136	SA282A	0279	SA290E	0050	SA298Y	0136	SA322L	0136	SA332Y	0136
SA264F	0050	SA272T	0136	SA282B	0279	SA290F	0050	SA301	OEM	SA322M	0136	SA334A	0050
SA264G	0050	SA272X	0136	SA282C	0279	SA290G	0050	SA301A	0050	SA322R	0136	SA334B	0050
SA264L	0050	SA272Y	0136	SA282D	0279	SA290L	0050	SA301B	0050	SA322T	0136	SA334C	0050
SA264M	0050	SA273A	0136	SA282E	0279	SA290M	0050	SA301C	0050	SA322X	0136	SA334D	0050
SA264R	0050	SA273B	0136	SA282F	0279	SA290R	0050	SA301D	0050	SA322Y	0136	SA334E	0050
SA264T	0050	SA273C	0136	SA282G	0279	SA290T	0050	SA301E	0050	SA323A	0136	SA334F	0050
SA264X	0050	SA273D	0136	SA282L	0279	SA290X	0050	SA301F	0050	SA323B	0136	SA334G	0050
SA264Y	0050	SA273E	0136	SA282M	0279	SA290Y	0050	SA301G	0050	SA323C	0136	SA334L	0050
SA265A	0050	SA273F	0136	SA282R	0279	SA291A	0050	SA301L	0050	SA323D	0136	SA334M	0050
SA265B	0050	SA273G	0136	SA282T	0279	SA291B	0050	SA301M	0050	SA323E	0136	SA334R	0050
SA265C	0050	SA273L	0136	SA282X	0279	SA291C	0050	SA301R	0050	SA323F	0136	SA334T	0050
SA265D	0050	SA273M	0136	SA282Y	0279	SA291D	0050	SA301T	0050	SA323G	0136	SA334X	0050
SA265E	0050	SA273R	0136	SA283	0133	SA291E	0050	SA301X	0050	SA323L	0136	SA334Y	0050
SA265F	0050	SA273T	0136	SA283A	0279	SA291F	0050	SA301Y	0050	SA323M	0136	SA335A	0050
SA265G	0050	SA273X	0136	SA283B	0279	SA291G	0050	SA303AY	OEM	SA323R	0136	SA335B	0050
SA265L	0050	SA273Y	0136	SA283C	0279	SA291L	0050	SA304A	0841	SA323T	0136	SA335C	0050
SA265M	0050	SA274A	0136	SA283D	0279	SA291M	0050	SA304B	0841	SA323X	0136	SA335D	0050
SA265R	0050	SA274B	0136	SA283E	0279	SA291R	0050	SA304C	0841	SA323Y	0136	SA335E	0050
SA265T	0050	SA274C	0136	SA283F	0279	SA291T	0050	SA304D	0841	SA324A	0050	SA335F	0050
SA265X	0050	SA274D	0136	SA283G	0279	SA291X	0050	SA304E	0841	SA324B	0050	SA335G	0050
SA265Y	0050	SA274E	0136	SA283L	0279	SA291Y	0050	SA304F	0841	SA324C	0050	SA335L	0050
SA266A	0136	SA274F	0136	SA283M	0279	SA292A	0050	SA304G	0841	SA324D	0050	SA335M	0050
SA266B	0136	SA274G	0136	SA283R	0279	SA292B	0050	SA304L	0841	SA324E	0050	SA335R	0050
SA266C	0136	SA274L	0136	SA283T	0279	SA292C	0050	SA304M	0841	SA324F	0050	SA335T	0050
SA266D	0136	SA274M	0136	SA283X	0279	SA292D	0050	SA304R	0841	SA324G	0050	SA335X	0050
SA266E	0136	SA274R	0136	SA283Y	0279	SA292E	0050	SA304T	0841	SA324L	0050	SA335Y	0050
SA266F	0136	SA274T	0136	SA284A	0279	SA292F	0050	SA304X	0841	SA324M	0050	SA337A	0050
SA266G	0136	SA274X	0136	SA284B	0279	SA292G	0050	SA304Y	0841	SA324R	0050	SA337B	0050
SA266L	0136	SA274Y	0136	SA284C	0279	SA292L	0050	SA305A	0279	SA324T	0050	SA337C	0050
SA266M	0136	SA275A	0136	SA284D	0279	SA292M	0050	SA305B	0279	SA324X	0050	SA337D	0050
SA266R	0136	SA275B	0136	SA284E	0279	SA292R	0050	SA305C	0279	SA324Y	0050	SA337E	0050
SA266T	0136	SA275C	0136	SA284F	0279	SA292T	0050	SA305D	0279	SA325A	0050	SA337F	0050
SA266X	0136	SA275D	0136	SA284G	0279	SA292X	0050	SA305E	0279	SA325B	0050	SA337G	0050
SA266Y	0136	SA275E	0136	SA284L	0279	SA292Y	0050	SA305F	0279	SA325C	0050	SA337L	0050
SA267A	0050	SA275F	0136	SA284M	0279	SA293A	0050	SA305G	0279	SA325D	0050	SA337M	0050
SA267B	0050	SA275G	0136	SA284R	0279	SA293B	0050	SA305L	0279	SA325E	0050	SA337R	0050
SA267C	0050	SA275L	0136	SA284T	0279	SA293C	0050	SA305M	0279	SA325F	0050	SA337T	0050
SA267D	0050	SA275M	0136	SA284X	0279	SA293D	0050	SA305R	0279	SA325G	0050	SA337X	0050
SA267E	0050	SA275R	0136	SA284Y	0279	SA293E	0050	SA305T	0279	SA325L	0050	SA337Y	0050
SA267F	0050	SA275T	0136	SA285A	0136	SA293F	0050	SA305X	0279	SA325M	0050	SA338A	0136
SA267G	0050	SA275X	0136	SA285B	0136	SA293G	0050	SA305Y	0279	SA325R	0050	SA338B	0136
SA267L	0050	SA275Y	0136	SA285C	0136	SA293L	0050	SA307A	0136	SA325T	0050	SA338C	0136
SA267M	0050	SA277A	0279	SA285D	0136	SA293M	0050	SA307B	0136	SA325X	0050	SA338D	0136
SA267R	0050	SA277B	0279	SA285E	0136	SA293R	0050	SA307C	0136	SA325Y	0050	SA338E	0136
SA267T	0050	SA277C	0279	SA285F	0136	SA293T	0050	SA307D	0136	SA326A	0050	SA338F	0136
SA267X	0050	SA277D	0279	SA285G	0136	SA293X	0050	SA307E	0136	SA326B	0050	SA338G	0136
SA267Y	0050	SA277E	0279	SA285L	0136	SA293Y	0050	SA307F	0136	SA326C	0050	SA338L	0136
SA268A	0050	SA277F	0279	SA285M	0136	SA294A	0050	SA307G	0136	SA326D	0050	SA338M	0136
SA268B	0050	SA277G	0279	SA285R	0136	SA294B	0050	SA307L	0136	SA326E	0050	SA338R	0136
SA268C	0050	SA277L	0279	SA285T	0136	SA294C	0050	SA307M	0136	SA326F	0050	SA338T	0136
SA268D	0050	SA277M	0279	SA285X	0136	SA294D	0050	SA307R	0136	SA326G	0050	SA338X	0136
SA268E	0050	SA277R	0279	SA285Y	0136	SA294E	0050	SA307T	0136	SA326L	0050	SA338Y	0136
SA268F	0050	SA277T	0279	SA286A	0136	SA294F	0050	SA307X	0136	SA326M	0050	SA339A	0136
SA268G	0050	SA277X	0279	SA286B	0136	SA294G	0050	SA307Y	0136	SA326R	0050	SA339B	0136
SA268L	0050	SA277Y	0279	SA286C	0136	SA294L	0050	SA308A	0050	SA326T	0050	SA339C	0136
SA268M	0050	SA278A	0279	SA286D	0136	SA294M	0050	SA308B	0050	SA326X	0050	SA339D	0136
SA268R	0050	SA278B	0279	SA286E	0136	SA294R	0050	SA308C	0050	SA326Y	0050	SA339E	0136
SA268T	0050	SA278C	0279	SA286F	0136	SA294T	0050	SA308D	0050	SA329A	0050	SA339F	0136
SA268X	0050	SA278D	0279	SA286G	0136	SA294X	0050	SA308E	0050	SA329B	0050	SA339G	0136
SA268Y	0050	SA278E	0279	SA286L	0136	SA294Y	0050	SA308F	0050	SA329C	0050	SA339L	0136
SA269A	0136	SA278F	0279	SA286M	0136	SA295A	0050	SA308G	0050	SA329D	0050	SA339M	0136
SA269B	0136	SA278G	0279	SA286R	0136	SA295B	0050	SA308R	0050	SA329E	0050	SA339R	0136
SA269C	0136	SA278L	0279	SA286T	0136	SA295C	0050	SA308T	0050	SA329F	0050	SA339T	0136
SA269D	0136	SA278M	0279	SA286X	0136	SA295D	0050	SA308X	0050	SA329G	0050	SA339X	0136
SA269E	0136	SA278R	0279	SA286Y	0136	SA295E	0050	SA308Y	0050	SA329L	0050	SA339Y	0136
SA269F	0136	SA278T	0279	SA287A	0136	SA295F	0050	SA309A	0050	SA329M	0050	SA341A	0136
SA269G	0136	SA278X	0279	SA287B	0136	SA295G	0050	SA309B	0050	SA329R	0050	SA341B	0136
SA269L	0136	SA278Y	0279	SA287C	0136	SA295L	0050	SA309C	0050	SA329T	0050	SA341C	0136
SA269M	0136	SA279A	0279	SA287D	0136	SA295M	0050	SA309D	0050	SA329X	0050	SA341D	0136
SA269R	0136	SA279B	0279	SA287E	0136	SA295R	0050	SA309E	0050	SA329Y	0050	SA341E	0136
SA269T	0136	SA279C	0279	SA287F	0136	SA295T	0050	SA309F	0050	SA330A	0279	SA341F	0136

If replacement code is OEM, contact original manufacturer for replacement.

DEVICE TYPE	REPL CODE
SA341G	0136
SA341L	0136
SA341M	0136
SA341R	0136
SA341T	0136
SA341X	0136
SA341Y	0136
SA342A	0136
SA342B	0136
SA342C	0136
SA342D	0136
SA342E	0136
SA342F	0136
SA342G	0136
SA342L	0136
SA342M	0136
SA342R	0136
SA342T	0136
SA342X	0136
SA342Y	0136
SA343A	0050
SA343B	0050
SA343C	0050
SA343D	0050
SA343E	0050
SA343F	0050
SA343G	0050
SA343L	0050
SA343M	0050
SA343R	0050
SA343T	0050
SA343X	0050
SA343Y	0050
SA344A	0050
SA344B	0050
SA344C	0050
SA344D	0050
SA344E	0050
SA344F	0050
SA344G	0050
SA344L	0050
SA344M	0050
SA344R	0050
SA344T	0050
SA344X	0050
SA344Y	0050
SA348A	0050
SA348B	0050
SA348C	0050
SA348D	0050
SA348E	0050
SA348F	0050
SA348G	0050
SA348L	0050
SA348M	0050
SA348R	0050
SA348T	0050
SA348X	0050
SA348Y	0050
SA350A	0050
SA350B	0050
SA350C	0050
SA350D	0050
SA350E	0050
SA350F	0050
SA350G	0050
SA350L	0050
SA350M	0050
SA350R	0050
SA350T	0050
SA350X	0050
SA350Y	0050
SA351A	0050
SA351B	0050
SA351C	0050
SA351D	0050
SA351E	0050
SA351F	0050
SA351G	0050
SA351L	0050
SA351M	0050
SA351R	0050
SA351T	0050
SA351X	0050
SA351Y	0050
SA352A	0050
SA352B	0050
SA352C	0050
SA352D	0050
SA352E	0050
SA352F	0050
SA352G	0050
SA352L	0050
SA352M	0050
SA352R	0050
SA352T	0050
SA352X	0050
SA352Y	0050
SA353A	0050
SA353B	0050
SA353C	0050
SA353D	0050
SA353E	0050
SA353F	0050
SA353G	0050
SA353L	0050
SA353M	0050
SA353R	0050
SA353T	0050
SA353X	0050
SA353Y	0050
SA354B	0038
SA355A	0050
SA355B	0050
SA355C	0050
SA355D	0050
SA355E	0050
SA355F	0050
SA355G	0050
SA355L	0050
SA355M	0050
SA355R	0050
SA355T	0050
SA355X	0050
SA355Y	0050
SA356A	0136
SA356B	0136
SA356C	0136
SA356D	0136
SA356E	0136
SA356F	0136
SA356G	0136
SA356L	0136
SA356M	0136
SA356R	0136
SA356T	0136
SA356X	0136
SA356Y	0136
SA357A	0136
SA357B	0136
SA357C	0136
SA357D	0136
SA357E	0136
SA357F	0136
SA357G	0136
SA357L	0136
SA357M	0136
SA357R	0136
SA357T	0136
SA357X	0136
SA357Y	0136
SA358A	0050
SA358B	0050
SA358C	0050
SA358D	0050
SA358E	0050
SA358F	0050
SA358G	0050
SA358L	0050
SA358M	0050
SA358R	0050
SA358T	0050
SA358X	0050
SA358Y	0050
SA359A	0050
SA359B	0050
SA359C	0050
SA359D	0050
SA359E	0050
SA359F	0050
SA359G	0050
SA359L	0050
SA359M	0050
SA359R	0050
SA359T	0050
SA359X	0050
SA359Y	0050
SA360A	0050
SA360B	0050
SA360C	0050
SA360D	0050
SA360E	0050
SA360F	0050
SA360G	0050
SA360L	0050
SA360M	0050
SA360R	0050
SA360T	0050
SA360X	0050
SA360Y	0050
SA361A	0050
SA361B	0050
SA361C	0050
SA361D	0050
SA361E	0050
SA361F	0050
SA361G	0050
SA361L	0050
SA361M	0050
SA361R	0050
SA361T	0050
SA361X	0050
SA361Y	0050
SA364A	0050
SA364B	0050
SA364C	0050
SA364D	0050
SA364E	0050
SA364F	0050
SA364G	0050
SA364L	0050
SA364M	0050
SA364R	0050
SA364T	0050
SA364X	0050
SA364Y	0050
SA365A	0050
SA365B	0050
SA365C	0050
SA365D	0050
SA365E	0050
SA365F	0050
SA365G	0050
SA365L	0050
SA365M	0050
SA365R	0050
SA365T	0050
SA365X	0050
SA365Y	0050
SA366A	0050
SA366B	0050
SA366C	0050
SA366D	0050
SA366E	0050
SA366F	0050
SA366G	0050
SA366L	0050
SA366M	0050
SA366R	0050
SA366T	0050
SA366X	0050
SA366Y	0050
SA367A	0050
SA367B	0050
SA367C	0050
SA367D	0050
SA367E	0050
SA367F	0050
SA367G	0050
SA367L	0050
SA367M	0050
SA367R	0050
SA367T	0050
SA367X	0050
SA367Y	0050
SA368A	0050
SA368B	0050
SA368C	0050
SA368D	0050
SA368E	0050
SA368F	0050
SA368G	0050
SA368L	0050
SA368M	0050
SA368R	0050
SA368T	0050
SA368X	0050
SA368Y	0050
SA369A	0136
SA369B	0136
SA369C	0136
SA369D	0136
SA369E	0136
SA369F	0136
SA369G	0136
SA369L	0136
SA369M	0136
SA369R	0136
SA369T	0136
SA369X	0136
SA369Y	0136
SA375A	0841
SA375B	0841
SA375C	0841
SA375D	0841
SA375E	0841
SA375F	0841
SA375G	0841
SA375L	0841
SA375M	0841
SA375R	0841
SA375T	0841
SA375X	0841
SA375Y	0841
SA376A	0050
SA376B	0050
SA376C	0050
SA376D	0050
SA376E	0050
SA376F	0050
SA376G	0050
SA376L	0050
SA376M	0050
SA376R	0050
SA376T	0050
SA376X	0050
SA376Y	0050
SA377A	0050
SA377B	0050
SA377C	0050
SA377D	0050
SA377E	0050
SA377F	0050
SA377G	0050
SA377L	0050
SA377M	0050
SA377R	0050
SA377T	0050
SA377X	0050
SA377Y	0050
SA378A	0050
SA378B	0050
SA378C	0050
SA378D	0050
SA378E	0050
SA378F	0050
SA378G	0050
SA378L	0050
SA378M	0050
SA378R	0050
SA378T	0050
SA378X	0050
SA378Y	0050
SA379A	0050
SA379B	0050
SA379C	0050
SA379D	0050
SA379E	0050
SA379F	0050
SA379G	0050
SA379L	0050
SA379M	0050
SA379R	0050
SA379T	0050
SA379X	0050
SA379Y	0050
SA380A	0050
SA380B	0050
SA380C	0050
SA380D	0050
SA380E	0050
SA380F	0050
SA380G	0050
SA380L	0050
SA380M	0050
SA380R	0050
SA380T	0050
SA380X	0050
SA380Y	0050
SA381A	0136
SA381B	0136
SA381C	0136
SA381D	0136
SA381E	0136
SA381F	0136
SA381G	0136
SA381L	0136
SA381M	0136
SA381R	0136
SA381T	0136
SA381X	0136
SA381Y	0136
SA382A	0136
SA382B	0136
SA382C	0136
SA382D	0136
SA382E	0136
SA382F	0136
SA382G	0136
SA382L	0136
SA382M	0136
SA382R	0136
SA382T	0136
SA382X	0136
SA382Y	0136
SA384A	0136
SA384B	0136
SA384C	0136
SA384D	0136
SA384E	0136
SA384F	0136
SA384G	0136
SA384L	0136
SA384M	0136
SA384R	0136
SA384T	0136
SA384X	0136
SA384Y	0136
SA385A	0050
SA385B	0050
SA385C	0050
SA385D	0050
SA385E	0050
SA385F	0050
SA385G	0050
SA385L	0050
SA385M	0050
SA385R	0050
SA385T	0050
SA385X	0050
SA385Y	0050
SA391A	0050
SA391B	0050
SA391C	0050
SA391D	0050
SA391E	0050
SA391F	0050
SA391G	0050
SA391L	0050
SA391M	0050
SA391R	0050
SA391T	0050
SA391X	0050
SA391Y	0050
SA392A	0050
SA392B	0050
SA392C	0050
SA392D	0050
SA392E	0050
SA392F	0050
SA392G	0050
SA392L	0050
SA392M	0050
SA392R	0050
SA392T	0050
SA392X	0050
SA392Y	0050
SA393A	0050
SA393B	0050
SA393C	0050
SA393D	0050
SA393E	0050
SA393F	0050
SA393G	0050
SA393L	0050
SA393M	0050
SA393R	0050
SA393T	0050
SA393X	0050
SA393Y	0050
SA394A	0050
SA394B	0050
SA394C	0050
SA394D	0050
SA394E	0050
SA394F	0050
SA394G	0050
SA394L	0050
SA394M	0050
SA394R	0050
SA394T	0050
SA394X	0050
SA394Y	0050
SA395A	0050
SA395B	0050
SA395C	0050
SA395D	0050
SA395E	0050
SA395F	0050
SA395G	0050
SA395L	0050
SA395M	0050
SA395R	0050
SA395T	0050
SA395X	0050
SA395Y	0050
SA398A	0050
SA398B	0050
SA398C	0050
SA398D	0050
SA398E	0050
SA398F	0050
SA398G	0050
SA398L	0050
SA398M	0050
SA398R	0050
SA398T	0050
SA398X	0050
SA398Y	0050
SA399A	0050
SA399B	0050
SA399C	0050
SA399D	0050
SA399E	0050
SA399F	0050
SA399G	0050
SA399L	0050
SA399M	0050
SA399R	0050
SA399T	0050
SA399X	0050
SA399Y	0050
SA400A	0136
SA400B	0136
SA400C	0136
SA400D	0136
SA400E	0136
SA400F	0136
SA400G	0136
SA400L	0136
SA400M	0136
SA400R	0136
SA400T	0136
SA400X	0136
SA400Y	0136
SA403A	0050
SA403B	0050
SA403C	0050
SA403D	0050
SA403E	0050
SA403F	0050
SA403G	0050
SA403L	0050
SA403M	0050
SA403R	0050
SA403T	0050
SA403X	0050
SA403Y	0050
SA404A	0050
SA404B	0050
SA404C	0050
SA404D	0050
SA404E	0050
SA404F	0050
SA404G	0050
SA404L	0050
SA404M	0050
SA404R	0050
SA404T	0050
SA404X	0050
SA404Y	0050
SA406A	0279
SA406B	0279
SA406C	0279
SA406D	0279
SA406E	0279
SA406F	0279
SA406G	0279
SA406L	0279
SA406M	0279
SA406R	0279
SA406T	0279
SA406X	0279
SA406Y	0279
SA407A	0279
SA407B	0279
SA407C	0279
SA407D	0279
SA407E	0279
SA407F	0279
SA407G	0279
SA407L	0279
SA407M	0279
SA407R	0279
SA407T	0279
SA407X	0279
SA407Y	0279
SA408A	0841
SA408B	0841
SA408C	0841
SA408D	0841
SA408E	0841
SA408F	0841
SA408G	0841
SA408L	0841
SA408M	0841
SA408R	0841
SA408T	0841
SA408X	0841
SA408Y	0841
SA409A	0841
SA409B	0841
SA409C	0841
SA409D	0841
SA409E	0841
SA409F	0841
SA409G	0841
SA409L	0841
SA409M	0841
SA409R	0841
SA409T	0841
SA409X	0841
SA409Y	0841
SA410	0037
SA411	0037
SA412	0037
SA413	0037
SA414	0037
SA415	0037
SA416	0037
SA420A	0050
SA420B	0050
SA420C	0050
SA420D	0050
SA420E	0050
SA420F	0050
SA420G	0050
SA420L	0050
SA420M	0050
SA420R	0050
SA420T	0050
SA420X	0050
SA420Y	0050
SA426A	0050
SA426B	0050
SA426C	0050
SA426D	0050
SA426E	0050
SA426F	0050
SA426G	0050
SA426L	0050
SA426M	0050
SA426R	0050
SA426T	0050
SA426X	0050
SA426Y	0050
SA427A	0050
SA427B	0050
SA427C	0050
SA427D	0050
SA427E	0050
SA427F	0050
SA427G	0050
SA427L	0050
SA427M	0050
SA427R	0050
SA427T	0050
SA427X	0050
SA427Y	0050
SA428A	0050
SA428B	0050
SA428C	0050
SA428D	0050
SA428E	0050
SA428F	0050
SA428G	0050
SA428L	0050
SA428M	0050
SA428R	0050
SA428T	0050
SA428X	0050
SA428Y	0050
SA429A	0037
SA429B	0037
SA429C	0037
SA429D	0037
SA429E	0037
SA429F	0037
SA429G	0037
SA429L	0037
SA429M	0037
SA429R	0037
SA429T	0037
SA429X	0037
SA429Y	0037
SA432A	0050
SA432B	0050
SA432C	0050
SA432D	0050
SA432E	0050
SA432F	0050
SA432G	0050
SA432L	0050
SA432M	0050
SA432R	0050
SA432T	0050
SA432X	0050
SA432Y	0050
SA433A	0050
SA433B	0050
SA433C	0050
SA433D	0050
SA433E	0050
SA433F	0050
SA433G	0050
SA433L	0050
SA433M	0050
SA433R	0050
SA433T	0050
SA433X	0050
SA433Y	0050
SA434A	0050
SA434B	0050
SA434C	0050
SA434D	0050
SA434E	0050
SA434F	0050
SA434G	0050
SA434L	0050
SA434M	0050
SA434R	0050
SA434T	0050
SA434X	0050
SA434Y	0050
SA435A	0136
SA435B	0136
SA435C	0136
SA435D	0136
SA435E	0136
SA435F	0136
SA435G	0136
SA435L	0136
SA435M	0136
SA435R	0136
SA435T	0136
SA435X	0136
SA435Y	0136
SA436A	0050
SA436B	0050
SA436C	0050
SA436D	0050
SA436E	0050
SA436F	0050
SA436G	0050
SA436L	0050
SA436M	0050
SA436R	0050
SA436T	0050
SA436X	0050
SA436Y	0050
SA437A	0050
SA437B	0050
SA437C	0050
SA437D	0050
SA437E	0050
SA437F	0050
SA437G	0050
SA437L	0050
SA437M	0050
SA437R	0050
SA437T	0050
SA437X	0050
SA437Y	0050
SA438A	0050
SA438B	0050
SA438C	0050
SA438D	0050
SA438E	0050
SA438F	0050
SA438G	0050
SA438L	0050
SA438M	0050
SA438R	0050
SA438T	0050
SA438X	0050
SA438Y	0050
SA440A	0050
SA440B	0050
SA440C	0050
SA440D	0050
SA440E	0050
SA440F	0050
SA440G	0050

If replacement code is OEM, contact original manufacturer for replacement.

543

DEVICE TYPE	REPL CODE	DEVICE TYPE	REPL CODE	DEVICE TYPE	REPL CODE	DEVICE TYPE	REPL CODE	DEVICE TYPE	REPL CODE	DEVICE TYPE	REPL CODE	DEVICE TYPE	REPL CODE
SA440L	0050	SA465Y	0037	SA474M	0050	SA484A	0126	SA497D	0126	SA505M	0455	SA518A	0050
SA440M	0050	SA466A	0050	SA474R	0050	SA484B	0126	SA497E	0126	SA505R	0455	SA518B	0050
SA440R	0050	SA466B	0050	SA474T	0050	SA484C	0126	SA497F	0126	SA505T	0455	SA518C	0050
SA440T	0050	SA466C	0050	SA474X	0050	SA484D	0126	SA497G	0126	SA505X	0455	SA518D	0050
SA440X	0050	SA466D	0050	SA474Y	0050	SA484E	0126	SA497L	0126	SA505Y	0455	SA518E	0050
SA440Y	0050	SA466E	0050	SA475A	0050	SA484F	0126	SA497M	0126	SA507A	0050	SA518F	0050
SA446A	0050	SA466F	0050	SA475B	0050	SA484G	0126	SA497R	0126	SA507B	0050	SA518G	0050
SA446B	0050	SA466G	0050	SA475C	0050	SA484L	0126	SA497T	0126	SA507C	0050	SA518L	0050
SA446C	0050	SA466L	0050	SA475D	0050	SA484M	0126	SA497X	0126	SA507D	0050	SA518M	0050
SA446D	0050	SA466M	0050	SA475E	0050	SA484R	0126	SA497Y	0126	SA507E	0050	SA518R	0050
SA446E	0050	SA466R	0050	SA475F	0050	SA484T	0126	SA498A	0126	SA507F	0050	SA518T	0050
SA446F	0050	SA466T	0050	SA475G	0050	SA484X	0126	SA498B	0126	SA507G	0050	SA518X	0050
SA446G	0050	SA466X	0050	SA475L	0050	SA484Y	0126	SA498C	0126	SA507L	0050	SA518Y	0050
SA446L	0050	SA466Y	0050	SA475M	0050	SA485A	0126	SA498D	0126	SA507M	0050	SA522A	0037
SA446M	0050	SA467A	0037	SA475R	0050	SA485B	0126	SA498E	0126	SA507R	0050	SA522B	0037
SA446R	0050	SA467B	0037	SA475T	0050	SA485C	0126	SA498F	0126	SA507T	0050	SA522C	0037
SA446T	0050	SA467C	0037	SA475X	0050	SA485D	0126	SA498G	0126	SA507X	0050	SA522D	0037
SA446X	0050	SA467D	0037	SA475Y	0050	SA485E	0126	SA498L	0126	SA507Y	0050	SA522E	0037
SA446Y	0050	SA467E	0037	SA476A	0136	SA485F	0126	SA498M	0126	SA509A	0037	SA522F	0037
SA447A	0050	SA467F	0037	SA476B	0136	SA485G	0126	SA498R	0126	SA509B	0037	SA522G	0037
SA447B	0050	SA467L	0037	SA476C	0136	SA485L	0126	SA498T	0126	SA509C	0037	SA522L	0037
SA447C	0050	SA467M	0037	SA476D	0136	SA485M	0126	SA498X	0126	SA509D	0037	SA522M	0037
SA447D	0050	SA467R	0037	SA476E	0136	SA485R	0126	SA498Y	0126	SA509E	0037	SA522R	0037
SA447E	0050	SA468A	0050	SA476F	0136	SA485T	0126	SA499A	0037	SA509F	0037	SA522T	0037
SA447F	0050	SA468B	0050	SA476G	0136	SA485X	0126	SA499B	0037	SA509G	0037	SA522X	0037
SA447G	0050	SA468C	0050	SA476L	0136	SA485Y	0126	SA499C	0037	SA509L	0037	SA522Y	0037
SA447L	0050	SA468D	0050	SA476M	0136	SA489A	0848	SA499D	0037	SA509M	0037	SA525A	0037
SA447M	0050	SA468E	0050	SA476R	0136	SA489B	0848	SA499E	0037	SA509R	0037	SA525B	0037
SA447R	0050	SA468F	0050	SA476T	0136	SA489C	0848	SA499F	0037	SA509T	0037	SA525C	0037
SA447T	0050	SA468G	0050	SA476X	0136	SA489D	0848	SA499G	0037	SA509X	0037	SA525D	0037
SA447X	0050	SA468L	0050	SA476Y	0136	SA489E	0848	SA499L	0037	SA509Y	0037	SA525E	0037
SA447Y	0050	SA468M	0050	SA477A	0050	SA489F	0848	SA499M	0037	SA510A	0126	SA525F	0037
SA453A	0050	SA468R	0050	SA477B	0050	SA489G	0848	SA499R	0037	SA510B	0126	SA525G	0037
SA453B	0050	SA468T	0050	SA477C	0050	SA489L	0848	SA499T	0037	SA510C	0126	SA525L	0037
SA453C	0050	SA468X	0050	SA477D	0050	SA489M	0848	SA499X	0037	SA510D	0126	SA525M	0037
SA453D	0050	SA468Y	0050	SA477E	0050	SA489R	0848	SA499Y	0037	SA510E	0126	SA525R	0037
SA453E	0050	SA469A	0050	SA477F	0050	SA489T	0848	SA500A	0037	SA510F	0126	SA525T	0037
SA453F	0050	SA469B	0050	SA477G	0050	SA489X	0848	SA500B	0037	SA510G	0126	SA525X	0037
SA453G	0050	SA469C	0050	SA477L	0050	SA489Y	0848	SA500C	0037	SA510L	0126	SA525Y	0037
SA453L	0050	SA469D	0050	SA477M	0050	SA490A	0848	SA500D	0037	SA510M	0126	SA527A	0126
SA453M	0050	SA469E	0050	SA477R	0050	SA490B	0848	SA500E	0037	SA510R	0126	SA527B	0126
SA453R	0050	SA469F	0050	SA477T	0050	SA490C	0848	SA500F	0037	SA510T	0126	SA527C	0126
SA453T	0050	SA469G	0050	SA477X	0050	SA490D	0848	SA500G	0037	SA510X	0126	SA527D	0126
SA453X	0050	SA469L	0050	SA477Y	0050	SA490E	0848	SA500L	0037	SA510Y	0126	SA527E	0126
SA453Y	0050	SA469M	0050	SA478A	0050	SA490F	0848	SA500M	0037	SA511A	0037	SA527F	0126
SA454A	0050	SA469R	0050	SA478B	0050	SA490G	0848	SA500R	0037	SA511B	0037	SA527G	0126
SA454B	0050	SA469T	0050	SA478C	0050	SA490L	0848	SA500T	0037	SA511C	0037	SA527L	0126
SA454C	0050	SA469X	0050	SA478D	0050	SA490M	0848	SA500X	0037	SA511D	0037	SA527M	0126
SA454D	0050	SA469Y	0050	SA478E	0050	SA490R	0848	SA500Y	0037	SA511E	0037	SA527R	0126
SA454E	0050	SA470A	0050	SA478F	0050	SA490T	0848	SA501A	0126	SA511F	0037	SA527T	0126
SA454F	0050	SA470B	0050	SA478G	0050	SA490X	0848	SA501B	0126	SA511G	0037	SA527X	0126
SA454G	0050	SA470C	0050	SA478L	0050	SA490Y	0848	SA501C	0126	SA511L	0037	SA527Y	0126
SA454L	0050	SA470D	0050	SA478M	0050	SA493A	0037	SA501D	0126	SA511M	0037	SA528A	0126
SA454M	0050	SA470E	0050	SA478R	0050	SA493B	0037	SA501E	0126	SA511R	0037	SA528B	0126
SA454R	0050	SA470F	0050	SA478T	0050	SA493C	0037	SA501F	0126	SA511T	0037	SA528C	0126
SA454T	0050	SA470G	0050	SA478X	0050	SA493D	0037	SA501G	0126	SA511X	0037	SA528D	0126
SA454X	0050	SA470L	0050	SA478Y	0050	SA493E	0037	SA501L	0126	SA511Y	0037	SA528E	0126
SA454Y	0050	SA470M	0050	SA479A	0050	SA493F	0037	SA501M	0126	SA512A	0126	SA528F	0126
SA455A	0050	SA470R	0050	SA479B	0050	SA493G	0037	SA501R	0126	SA512B	0126	SA528G	0126
SA455B	0050	SA470T	0050	SA479C	0050	SA493L	0037	SA501T	0126	SA512C	0126	SA528L	0126
SA455C	0050	SA470X	0050	SA479D	0050	SA493M	0037	SA501X	0126	SA512D	0126	SA528M	0126
SA455D	0050	SA470Y	0050	SA479E	0050	SA493R	0037	SA501Y	0126	SA512E	0126	SA528R	0126
SA455E	0050	SA471A	0050	SA479F	0050	SA493T	0037	SA502A	0126	SA512F	0126	SA528T	0126
SA455F	0050	SA471B	0050	SA479G	0050	SA493X	0037	SA502B	0126	SA512G	0126	SA528X	0126
SA455G	0050	SA471C	0050	SA479L	0050	SA493Y	0037	SA502C	0126	SA512L	0126	SA528Y	0126
SA455L	0050	SA471D	0050	SA479M	0050	SA494A	0037	SA502D	0126	SA512M	0126	SA529	0004
SA455M	0050	SA471E	0050	SA479R	0050	SA494B	0037	SA502E	0126	SA512R	0126	SA530A	0037
SA455R	0050	SA471F	0050	SA479T	0050	SA494C	0037	SA502F	0126	SA512T	0126	SA530B	0037
SA455T	0050	SA471G	0050	SA479X	0050	SA494D	0037	SA502G	0126	SA512X	0126	SA530C	0037
SA455X	0050	SA471L	0050	SA479Y	0050	SA494E	0037	SA502L	0126	SA512Y	0126	SA530D	0037
SA455Y	0050	SA471M	0050	SA480A	0037	SA494F	0037	SA502M	0126	SA513A	0037	SA530E	0037
SA456A	0050	SA471R	0050	SA480B	0037	SA494G	0037	SA502R	0126	SA513B	0037	SA530F	0037
SA456B	0050	SA471T	0050	SA480C	0037	SA494L	0037	SA502T	0126	SA513C	0037	SA530G	0037
SA456C	0050	SA471X	0050	SA480D	0037	SA494M	0037	SA502X	0126	SA513D	0037	SA530L	0037
SA456D	0050	SA471Y	0050	SA480E	0037	SA494R	0037	SA502Y	0126	SA513E	0037	SA530M	0037
SA456E	0050	SA472A	0050	SA480F	0037	SA494T	0037	SA503A	0126	SA513F	0037	SA530R	0037
SA456F	0050	SA472B	0050	SA480G	0037	SA494X	0037	SA503B	0126	SA513G	0037	SA530T	0037
SA456G	0050	SA472C	0050	SA480L	0037	SA494Y	0037	SA503C	0126	SA513L	0037	SA530X	0037
SA456L	0050	SA472D	0050	SA480M	0037	SA495	0150	SA503D	0126	SA513M	0037	SA530Y	0037
SA456M	0050	SA472E	0050	SA480R	0037	SA495A	0037	SA503E	0126	SA513R	0037	SA532A	0126
SA456R	0050	SA472F	0050	SA480T	0037	SA495B	0037	SA503F	0126	SA513T	0037	SA532B	0126
SA456T	0050	SA472G	0050	SA480X	0037	SA495C	0037	SA503G	0126	SA513X	0037	SA532C	0126
SA456X	0050	SA472L	0050	SA480Y	0037	SA495D	0037	SA503L	0126	SA513Y	0037	SA532D	0126
SA456Y	0050	SA472M	0050	SA482A	0037	SA495E	0037	SA503M	0126	SA516A	0126	SA532E	0126
SA457A	0050	SA472R	0050	SA482B	0037	SA495F	0037	SA503R	0126	SA516B	0126	SA532F	0126
SA457B	0050	SA472T	0050	SA482C	0037	SA495G	0037	SA503T	0126	SA516C	0126	SA532G	0126
SA457C	0050	SA472X	0050	SA482D	0037	SA495L	0037	SA503X	0126	SA516D	0126	SA532L	0126
SA457D	0050	SA472Y	0050	SA482E	0037	SA495M	0037	SA503Y	0126	SA516E	0126	SA532M	0126
SA457E	0050	SA473A	0848	SA482F	0037	SA495R	0037	SA504A	0126	SA516F	0126	SA532R	0126
SA457F	0050	SA473B	0848	SA482G	0037	SA495T	0037	SA504B	0126	SA516G	0126	SA532T	0126
SA457G	0050	SA473C	0848	SA482L	0037	SA495X	0037	SA504C	0126	SA516L	0126	SA532X	0126
SA457L	0050	SA473D	0848	SA482M	0037	SA495Y	0037	SA504D	0126	SA516M	0126	SA532Y	0126
SA457M	0050	SA473E	0848	SA482R	0037	SA496	0150	SA504E	0126	SA516R	0126	SA537	0150
SA457R	0050	SA473F	0848	SA482T	0037	SA496A	0150	SA504F	0126	SA516T	0126	SA537A	0126
SA457T	0050	SA473G	0848	SA482X	0037	SA496B	0150	SA504G	0126	SA516X	0126	SA537B	0126
SA457X	0050	SA473L	0848	SA482Y	0037	SA496C	0848	SA504L	0126	SA516Y	0126	SA537C	0126
SA457Y	0050	SA473M	0848	SA483A	0848	SA496D	0848	SA504M	0126	SA517A	0136	SA537D	0126
SA465A	0037	SA473R	0848	SA483B	0848	SA496E	0848	SA504R	0126	SA517B	0136	SA537E	0126
SA465B	0037	SA473T	0848	SA483C	0848	SA496F	0848	SA504T	0126	SA517C	0136	SA537F	0126
SA465C	0037	SA473X	0848	SA483D	0848	SA496G	0848	SA504X	0126	SA517D	0136	SA537G	0126
SA465D	0037	SA473Y	0848	SA483E	0848	SA496L	0848	SA504Y	0126	SA517E	0136	SA537L	0126
SA465E	0037	SA474A	0050	SA483F	0848	SA496M	0848	SA505A	0455	SA517F	0136	SA537M	0126
SA465F	0037	SA474B	0050	SA483G	0848	SA496R	0848	SA505B	0455	SA517G	0136	SA537R	0126
SA465G	0037	SA474C	0050	SA483L	0848	SA496T	0848	SA505C	0455	SA517L	0136	SA537T	0126
SA465L	0037	SA474D	0050	SA483M	0848	SA496X	0848	SA505D	0455	SA517M	0136	SA537X	0126
SA465M	0037	SA474E	0050	SA483R	0848	SA496Y	0848	SA505E	0455	SA517R	0136	SA537Y	0126
SA465R	0037	SA474F	0050	SA483T	0848	SA497A	0126	SA505F	0455	SA517T	0136	SA538	0150
SA465T	0037	SA474G	0050	SA483X	0848	SA497B	0126	SA505G	0455	SA517X	0136	SA539	0150
SA465X	0037	SA474L	0050	SA483Y	0848	SA497C	0126	SA505L	0455	SA517Y	0136	SA539A	0037

If replacement code is OEM, contact original manufacturer for replacement.

DEVICE TYPE	REPL CODE	DEVICE TYPE	REPL CODE	DEVICE TYPE	REPL CODE	DEVICE TYPE	REPL CODE	DEVICE TYPE	REPL CODE	DEVICE TYPE	REPL CODE	DEVICE TYPE	REPL CODE
SA539B	0037	SA551F	0037	SA567L	0037	SA603Y	0150	SA616F	0848	SA641B	0037	SA661E	0037
SA539C	0037	SA551G	0037	SA567M	0037	SA604A	0126	SA616G	0848	SA641C	0037	SA661F	0037
SA539D	0037	SA551L	0037	SA567R	0037	SA604B	0126	SA616L	0848	SA641D	0037	SA661G	0037
SA539E	0037	SA551M	0037	SA567T	0037	SA604C	0126	SA616M	0848	SA641E	0037	SA661L	0037
SA539F	0037	SA551R	0037	SA567X	0037	SA604D	0126	SA616R	0848	SA641F	0037	SA661M	0037
SA539G	0037	SA551T	0037	SA567Y	0037	SA604E	0126	SA616T	0848	SA641G	0037	SA661R	0037
SA539L	0037	SA551X	0037	SA568A	0150	SA604F	0126	SA616X	0848	SA641L	0037	SA661T	0037
SA539M	0037	SA551Y	0037	SA568B	0150	SA604G	0126	SA616Y	0848	SA641M	0037	SA661X	0037
SA539R	0037	SA552A	0126	SA568C	0150	SA604L	0126	SA623A	0848	SA641R	0037	SA661Y	0037
SA539T	0037	SA552B	0126	SA568D	0150	SA604M	0126	SA623B	0848	SA641T	0037	SA663A	0486
SA539X	0037	SA552C	0126	SA568E	0150	SA604R	0126	SA623C	0848	SA641X	0037	SA663B	0486
SA539Y	0037	SA552D	0126	SA568F	0150	SA604T	0126	SA623D	0848	SA641Y	0037	SA663C	0486
SA540	0150	SA552E	0126	SA568G	0150	SA604X	0126	SA623E	0848	SA642A	0848	SA663D	0486
SA542A	0037	SA552F	0126	SA568L	0150	SA604Y	0126	SA623F	0848	SA642B	0848	SA663E	0486
SA542B	0037	SA552G	0126	SA568M	0150	SA606A	0126	SA623G	0848	SA642C	0848	SA663F	0486
SA542C	0037	SA552L	0126	SA568R	0150	SA606B	0126	SA623L	0848	SA642D	0848	SA663G	0486
SA542D	0037	SA552M	0126	SA568T	0150	SA606C	0126	SA623M	0848	SA642E	0848	SA663L	0486
SA542E	0037	SA552R	0126	SA568X	0150	SA606D	0126	SA623R	0848	SA642F	0848	SA663M	0486
SA542F	0037	SA552T	0126	SA568Y	0150	SA606E	0126	SA623T	0848	SA642G	0848	SA663R	0486
SA542G	0037	SA552X	0126	SA569A	0037	SA606F	0126	SA623X	0848	SA642L	0848	SA663T	0486
SA542L	0037	SA552Y	0126	SA569B	0037	SA606G	0126	SA623Y	0848	SA642M	0848	SA663X	0486
SA542M	0037	SA555	OEM	SA569C	0037	SA606L	0126	SA624A	0848	SA642R	0848	SA663Y	0486
SA542R	0037	SA556	OEM	SA569D	0037	SA606M	0126	SA624B	0848	SA642T	0848	SA666A	0037
SA542T	0037	SA560A	0126	SA569E	0037	SA606R	0126	SA624C	0848	SA642X	0848	SA666B	0037
SA542X	0037	SA560B	0126	SA569F	0037	SA606T	0126	SA624D	0848	SA642Y	0848	SA666C	0037
SA542Y	0037	SA560C	0126	SA569G	0037	SA606X	0126	SA624E	0848	SA643A	0071	SA666D	0037
SA543A	0126	SA560D	0126	SA569L	0037	SA606Y	0126	SA624F	0848	SA643B	0071	SA666E	0037
SA543B	0126	SA560E	0126	SA569M	0037	SA607A	0126	SA624G	0848	SA643C	0071	SA666F	0037
SA543C	0126	SA560F	0126	SA569R	0037	SA607B	0126	SA624L	0848	SA643D	0071	SA666G	0037
SA543D	0126	SA560G	0126	SA569T	0037	SA607C	0126	SA624M	0848	SA643E	0071	SA666L	0037
SA543E	0126	SA560L	0126	SA569X	0037	SA607D	0126	SA624R	0848	SA643F	0071	SA666M	0037
SA543F	0126	SA560M	0126	SA569Y	0037	SA607E	0126	SA624T	0848	SA643G	0071	SA666R	0037
SA543G	0126	SA560R	0126	SA570A	0037	SA607F	0126	SA624X	0848	SA643L	0071	SA666T	0037
SA543L	0126	SA560T	0126	SA570B	0037	SA607G	0126	SA624Y	0848	SA643M	0071	SA666X	0037
SA543M	0126	SA560X	0126	SA570C	0037	SA607L	0126	SA628A	0037	SA643R	0071	SA666Y	0037
SA543R	0126	SA560Y	0126	SA570D	0037	SA607M	0126	SA628B	0037	SA643T	0071	SA670A	0848
SA543T	0126	SA561A	0037	SA570E	0037	SA607R	0126	SA628C	0037	SA643X	0071	SA670B	0848
SA543X	0126	SA561B	0037	SA570F	0037	SA607T	0126	SA628D	0037	SA643Y	0071	SA670C	0848
SA543Y	0126	SA561C	0037	SA570G	0037	SA607X	0126	SA628E	0037	SA645A	0561	SA670D	0848
SA544A	0037	SA561D	0037	SA570L	0037	SA607Y	0126	SA628F	0037	SA645B	0561	SA670E	0848
SA544B	0037	SA561E	0037	SA570M	0037	SA608A	0037	SA628G	0037	SA645C	0561	SA670F	0848
SA544C	0037	SA561F	0037	SA570R	0037	SA608B	0037	SA628L	0037	SA645D	0561	SA670G	0848
SA544D	0037	SA561G	0037	SA570T	0037	SA608C	0037	SA628M	0037	SA645E	0561	SA670L	0848
SA544E	0037	SA561L	0037	SA570X	0037	SA608D	0037	SA628R	0037	SA645F	0561	SA670M	0848
SA544F	0037	SA561M	0037	SA570Y	0037	SA608E	0037	SA628T	0037	SA645G	0561	SA670R	0848
SA544G	0037	SA561R	0037	SA571A	0126	SA608F	0037	SA628X	0037	SA645L	0561	SA670T	0848
SA544L	0037	SA561T	0037	SA571B	0126	SA608G	0037	SA628Y	0037	SA645M	0561	SA670X	0848
SA544M	0037	SA561X	0037	SA571C	0126	SA608L	0037	SA629A	0037	SA645R	0561	SA670Y	0848
SA544R	0037	SA561Y	0037	SA571D	0126	SA608M	0037	SA629B	0037	SA645T	0561	SA671A	0848
SA544T	0037	SA562A	0037	SA571E	0126	SA608R	0037	SA629C	0037	SA645X	0561	SA671B	0848
SA544X	0037	SA562B	0037	SA571F	0126	SA608T	0037	SA629D	0037	SA645Y	0561	SA671C	0848
SA544Y	0037	SA562C	0037	SA571G	0126	SA608X	0037	SA629E	0037	SA646	0004	SA671D	0848
SA545A	0037	SA562D	0037	SA571L	0126	SA608Y	0037	SA629F	0037	SA646A	1045	SA671E	0848
SA545B	0037	SA562E	0037	SA571M	0126	SA609A	0037	SA629G	0037	SA646B	1045	SA671F	0848
SA545C	0037	SA562F	0037	SA571R	0126	SA609B	0037	SA629L	0037	SA646C	1045	SA671G	0848
SA545D	0037	SA562G	0037	SA571T	0126	SA609C	0037	SA629M	0037	SA646D	1045	SA671L	0848
SA545E	0037	SA562L	0037	SA571X	0126	SA609D	0037	SA629R	0037	SA646E	1045	SA671M	0848
SA545F	0037	SA562M	0037	SA571Y	0126	SA609E	0037	SA629T	0037	SA646F	1045	SA671R	0848
SA545G	0037	SA562R	0037	SA592A	0037	SA609F	0037	SA634A	0848	SA646G	1045	SA671T	0848
SA545L	0037	SA562T	0037	SA592B	0037	SA609G	0037	SA634B	0848	SA646L	1045	SA671X	0848
SA545M	0037	SA562X	0037	SA592C	0037	SA609L	0037	SA634C	0848	SA646M	1045	SA671Y	0848
SA545R	0037	SA562Y	0037	SA592D	0037	SA609M	0037	SA634D	0848	SA646R	1045	SA672A	0037
SA545T	0037	SA564A	0037	SA592E	0037	SA609R	0037	SA634E	0848	SA646T	1045	SA672B	0037
SA545X	0037	SA564B	0037	SA592F	0037	SA609T	0037	SA634F	0848	SA646X	1045	SA672C	0037
SA545Y	0037	SA564C	0037	SA592G	0037	SA609X	0037	SA634G	0848	SA646Y	1045	SA672D	0037
SA546A	0126	SA564D	0037	SA592L	0037	SA609Y	0037	SA634L	0848	SA649	2002	SA672E	0037
SA546B	0126	SA564E	0037	SA592M	0037	SA610A	0126	SA634M	0848	SA657A	0486	SA672F	0037
SA546C	0126	SA564F	0037	SA592R	0037	SA610B	0126	SA634R	0848	SA657B	0486	SA672G	0037
SA546D	0126	SA564G	0037	SA592T	0037	SA610C	0126	SA634T	0848	SA657C	0486	SA672L	0037
SA546E	0126	SA564L	0037	SA592X	0037	SA610E	0126	SA634X	0848	SA657D	0486	SA672M	0037
SA546F	0126	SA564M	0037	SA592Y	0037	SA610F	0126	SA634Y	0848	SA657E	0486	SA672R	0037
SA546G	0126	SA564R	0037	SA594A	0126	SA610G	0126	SA636A	0848	SA657F	0486	SA672T	0037
SA546L	0126	SA564T	0037	SA594B	0126	SA610L	0126	SA636B	0848	SA657G	0486	SA672X	0037
SA546M	0126	SA564X	0037	SA594C	0126	SA610M	0126	SA636C	0848	SA657L	0486	SA672Y	0037
SA546R	0126	SA564Y	0037	SA594D	0126	SA610R	0126	SA636D	0848	SA657M	0486	SA673A	0037
SA546T	0126	SA565	0004	SA594E	0126	SA610T	0126	SA636E	0848	SA657R	0486	SA673B	0037
SA546X	0126	SA565A	0037	SA594F	0126	SA610X	0126	SA636F	0848	SA657T	0486	SA673C	0037
SA546Y	0126	SA565B	0037	SA594G	0126	SA610Y	0126	SA636G	0848	SA657X	0486	SA673D	0037
SA548A	0150	SA565C	0037	SA594L	0126	SA611A	0126	SA636L	0848	SA657Y	0486	SA673E	0037
SA548B	0150	SA565D	0037	SA594M	0126	SA611B	0126	SA636M	0848	SA658A	0486	SA673F	0037
SA548C	0150	SA565E	0037	SA594R	0126	SA611C	0126	SA636R	0848	SA658B	0486	SA673G	0037
SA548D	0150	SA565F	0037	SA594T	0126	SA611D	0126	SA636T	0848	SA658C	0486	SA673L	0037
SA548E	0150	SA565G	0037	SA594X	0126	SA611E	0126	SA636X	0848	SA658D	0486	SA673R	0037
SA548F	0150	SA565L	0037	SA594Y	0126	SA611F	0126	SA636Y	0848	SA658E	0486	SA673T	0037
SA548G	0150	SA565M	0037	SA597A	0126	SA611G	0126	SA639A	0037	SA658F	0486	SA673X	0037
SA548L	0150	SA565R	0037	SA597B	0126	SA611L	0126	SA639B	0037	SA658G	0486	SA673Y	0037
SA548M	0150	SA565T	0037	SA597C	0126	SA611M	0126	SA639C	0037	SA658L	0486	SA677A	0150
SA548R	0150	SA565X	0037	SA597D	0126	SA611R	0126	SA639D	0037	SA658M	0486	SA677B	0150
SA548T	0150	SA565Y	0037	SA597E	0126	SA611T	0126	SA639E	0037	SA658R	0486	SA677C	0150
SA548X	0150	SA566A	0848	SA597F	0126	SA611X	0126	SA639F	0037	SA658T	0486	SA677D	0150
SA548Y	0150	SA566B	0848	SA597G	0126	SA611Y	0126	SA639G	0037	SA658X	0486	SA677E	0150
SA550A	0126	SA566C	0848	SA597L	0126	SA612A	0126	SA639L	0037	SA658Y	0486	SA677F	0150
SA550B	0126	SA566D	0848	SA597M	0126	SA612B	0126	SA639M	0037	SA659A	0037	SA677G	0150
SA550C	0126	SA566E	0848	SA597R	0126	SA612C	0126	SA639R	0037	SA659B	0037	SA677L	0150
SA550D	0126	SA566F	0848	SA597T	0126	SA612D	0126	SA639T	0037	SA659C	0037	SA677M	0150
SA550E	0126	SA566G	0848	SA597X	0126	SA612E	0126	SA640A	0150	SA659D	0037	SA677R	0150
SA550F	0126	SA566L	0848	SA597Y	0126	SA612F	0126	SA640B	0150	SA659E	0037	SA677T	0150
SA550G	0126	SA566M	0848	SA603A	0150	SA612G	0126	SA640C	0150	SA659F	0037	SA677X	0150
SA550L	0126	SA566R	0848	SA603B	0150	SA612L	0126	SA640D	0150	SA659G	0037	SA677Y	0150
SA550M	0126	SA566T	0848	SA603C	0150	SA612M	0126	SA640E	0150	SA659L	0037	SA678A	0150
SA550R	0126	SA566X	0848	SA603D	0150	SA612R	0126	SA640F	0150	SA659M	0037	SA678B	0150
SA550T	0126	SA566Y	0848	SA603E	0150	SA612T	0126	SA640G	0150	SA659R	0037	SA678C	0150
SA550X	0126	SA567A	0037	SA603F	0150	SA612X	0126	SA640L	0150	SA659T	0037	SA678D	0150
SA550Y	0126	SA567B	0037	SA603G	0150	SA612Y	0126	SA640M	0150	SA659X	0037	SA678E	0150
SA551A	0037	SA567C	0037	SA603L	0150	SA616A	0848	SA640R	0150	SA659Y	0037	SA678F	0150
SA551B	0037	SA567D	0037	SA603M	0150	SA616B	0848	SA640T	0150	SA661A	0037	SA678G	0150
SA551C	0037	SA567E	0037	SA603R	0150	SA616C	0848	SA640X	0150	SA661B	0037	SA678L	0150
SA551D	0037	SA567F	0037	SA603T	0150	SA616D	0848	SA640Y	0150	SA661C	0037	SA678M	0150
SA551E	0037	SA567G	0037	SA603X	0150	SA616E	0848	SA641A	0037	SA661D	0037	SA678R	0150

If replacement code is OEM, contact original manufacturer for replacement.

DEVICE TYPE	REPL CODE
SA678T	0150
SA678X	0150
SA678Y	0150
SA680A	0486
SA680B	0486
SA680C	0486
SA680D	0486
SA680E	0486
SA680F	0486
SA680G	0486
SA680L	0486
SA680M	0486
SA680R	0486
SA680T	0486
SA680X	0486
SA680Y	0486
SA681	0164
SA682A	0126
SA682B	0126
SA682C	0126
SA682D	0126
SA682E	0126
SA682F	0126
SA682G	0126
SA682L	0126
SA682M	0126
SA682R	0126
SA682T	0126
SA682X	0126
SA682Y	0126
SA683A	0126
SA683B	0126
SA683C	0126
SA683D	0126
SA683E	0126
SA683F	0126
SA683G	0126
SA683L	0126
SA683M	0126
SA683R	0126
SA683T	0126
SA683X	0126
SA683Y	0126
SA684A	0126
SA684B	0126
SA684C	0126
SA684D	0126
SA684E	0126
SA684F	0126
SA684G	0126
SA684L	0126
SA684M	0126
SA684R	0126
SA684T	0126
SA684X	0126
SA684Y	0126
SA685A	0037
SA685B	0037
SA685C	0037
SA685D	0037
SA685E	0037
SA685F	0037
SA685G	0037
SA685L	0037
SA685M	0037
SA685R	0037
SA685T	0037
SA685X	0037
SA685Y	0037
SA695A	0126
SA695B	0126
SA695C	0126
SA695D	0126
SA695E	0126
SA695F	0126
SA695G	0126
SA695L	0126
SA695M	0126
SA695R	0126
SA695T	0126
SA695X	0126
SA695Y	0126
SA696A	0150
SA696B	0150
SA696C	0150
SA696D	0150
SA696E	0150
SA696F	0150
SA696G	0150
SA696L	0150
SA696M	0150
SA696R	0150
SA696T	0150
SA696X	0150
SA696Y	0150
SA697A	0037
SA697B	0037
SA697C	0037
SA697D	0037
SA697E	0037
SA697F	0037
SA697G	0037
SA697L	0037
SA697M	0037
SA697R	0037
SA697T	0037
SA697X	0037
SA697Y	0037
SA699A	0848
SA699B	0848
SA699C	0848
SA699D	0848
SA699E	0848
SA699F	0848
SA699G	0848
SA699L	0848
SA699M	0848
SA699R	0848
SA699T	0848
SA699X	0848
SA699Y	0848
SA700A	0848
SA700B	0848
SA700C	0848
SA700D	0848
SA700E	0848
SA700F	0848
SA700G	0848
SA700L	0848
SA700M	0848
SA700R	0848
SA700T	0848
SA700X	0848
SA700Y	0848
SA701A	0150
SA701B	0150
SA701C	0150
SA701D	0150
SA701E	0150
SA701F	0150
SA701G	0150
SA701L	0150
SA701M	0150
SA701R	0150
SA701T	0150
SA701X	0150
SA701Y	0150
SA704A	0150
SA704B	0150
SA704C	0150
SA704D	0150
SA704E	0150
SA704F	0150
SA704G	0150
SA704L	0150
SA704M	0150
SA704R	0150
SA704T	0150
SA704X	0150
SA704Y	0150
SA705A	0150
SA705B	0150
SA705C	0150
SA705D	0150
SA705E	0150
SA705F	0150
SA705G	0150
SA705L	0150
SA705M	0150
SA705R	0150
SA705T	0150
SA705X	0150
SA705Y	0150
SA707A	0037
SA707B	0037
SA707C	0037
SA707D	0037
SA707E	0037
SA707F	0037
SA707G	0037
SA707L	0037
SA707M	0037
SA707R	0037
SA707T	0037
SA707X	0037
SA707Y	0037
SA708A	1357
SA708B	1357
SA708C	1357
SA708D	1357
SA708E	1357
SA708F	1357
SA708G	1357
SA708L	1357
SA708M	1357
SA708R	1357
SA708T	1357
SA708X	1357
SA708Y	1357
SA715A	0455
SA715B	0455
SA715C	0455
SA715D	0455
SA715E	0455
SA715F	0455
SA715G	0455
SA715L	0455
SA715M	0455
SA715R	0455
SA715T	0455
SA715X	0455
SA715Y	0455
SA717A	1357
SA717B	1357
SA717C	1357
SA717D	1357
SA717E	1357
SA717F	1357
SA717G	1357
SA717L	1357
SA717M	1357
SA717R	1357
SA717T	1357
SA717X	1357
SA717Y	1357
SA719A	0126
SA719B	0126
SA719C	0126
SA719D	0126
SA719E	0126
SA719F	0126
SA719G	0126
SA719L	0126
SA719M	0126
SA719R	0126
SA719T	0126
SA719X	0126
SA719Y	0126
SA720A	0037
SA720B	0037
SA720C	0037
SA720D	0037
SA720E	0037
SA720F	0037
SA720G	0037
SA720L	0037
SA720M	0037
SA720R	0037
SA720T	0037
SA720X	0037
SA720Y	0037
SA721A	0037
SA721B	0037
SA721C	0037
SA721D	0037
SA721E	0037
SA721F	0037
SA721G	0037
SA721L	0037
SA721M	0037
SA721R	0037
SA721T	0037
SA721X	0037
SA721Y	0037
SA723CN	0026
SA733A	0126
SA733B	0126
SA733C	0126
SA733D	0126
SA733E	0126
SA733F	0126
SA733G	0126
SA733L	0126
SA733M	0126
SA733R	0126
SA733T	0126
SA733X	0126
SA733Y	0126
SA736A	0150
SA736B	0150
SA736C	0150
SA736D	0150
SA736E	0150
SA736F	0150
SA736G	0150
SA736L	0150
SA736M	0150
SA736R	0150
SA736T	0150
SA736X	0150
SA736Y	0150
SA738A	0848
SA738B	0848
SA738C	0848
SA738D	0848
SA738E	0848
SA738F	0848
SA738G	0848
SA738L	0848
SA738M	0848
SA738R	0848
SA738T	0848
SA738X	0848
SA738Y	0848
SA741A	0037
SA741B	0037
SA741C	0037
SA741D	0037
SA741E	0037
SA741F	0037
SA741G	0037
SA741L	0037
SA741M	0037
SA741R	0037
SA741T	0037
SA741X	0037
SA741Y	0037
SA742A	0126
SA742B	0126
SA742C	0126
SA742D	0126
SA742E	0126
SA742F	0126
SA742G	0126
SA742L	0126
SA742M	0126
SA742R	0126
SA742T	0126
SA742X	0126
SA742Y	0126
SA743A	0126
SA743B	0126
SA743C	0126
SA743D	0126
SA743E	0126
SA743F	0126
SA743G	0126
SA743L	0126
SA743M	0126
SA743R	0126
SA743T	0126
SA743X	0126
SA743Y	0126
SA751A	0126
SA751B	0126
SA751C	0126
SA751D	0126
SA751E	0126
SA751F	0126
SA751G	0126
SA751L	0126
SA751M	0126
SA751R	0126
SA751T	0126
SA751X	0126
SA751Y	0126
SA754A	0848
SA754B	0848
SA754C	0848
SA754D	0848
SA754E	0848
SA754F	0848
SA754G	0848
SA754L	0848
SA754M	0848
SA754R	0848
SA754T	0848
SA754X	0848
SA754Y	0848
SA755A	0848
SA755B	0848
SA755C	0848
SA755D	0848
SA755E	0848
SA755F	0848
SA755G	0848
SA755L	0848
SA755M	0848
SA755T	0848
SA755X	0848
SA755Y	0848
SA756A	0486
SA756B	0486
SA756C	0486
SA756D	0486
SA756E	0486
SA756F	0486
SA756G	0486
SA756L	0486
SA756M	0486
SA756R	0486
SA756T	0486
SA756X	0486
SA756Y	0486
SA766A	0848
SA766B	0848
SA766C	0848
SA766D	0848
SA766E	0848
SA766F	0848
SA766G	0848
SA766L	0848
SA766M	0848
SA766R	0848
SA766T	0848
SA766X	0848
SA766Y	0848
SA773A	0037
SA773B	0037
SA773C	0037
SA773D	0037
SA773E	0037
SA773F	0037
SA773G	0037
SA773L	0037
SA773M	0037
SA773R	0037
SA773T	0037
SA773X	0037
SA773Y	0037
SA775A	0848
SA775B	0848
SA775C	0848
SA775D	0848
SA775E	0848
SA775F	0848
SA775G	0848
SA775L	0848
SA775M	0848
SA775R	0848
SA775T	0848
SA775X	0848
SA775Y	0848
SA778A	0037
SA778B	0037
SA778C	0037
SA778D	0037
SA778E	0037
SA778F	0037
SA778G	0037
SA778L	0037
SA778M	0037
SA778R	0037
SA778T	0037
SA778Y	0037
SA779A	0848
SA779B	0848
SA779C	0848
SA779D	0848
SA779E	0848
SA779F	0848
SA779G	0848
SA779L	0848
SA779M	0848
SA779R	0848
SA779T	0848
SA779X	0848
SA779Y	0848
SA780A	0848
SA780B	0848
SA780C	0848
SA780D	0848
SA780E	0848
SA780F	0848
SA780G	0848
SA780L	0848
SA780M	0848
SA780R	0848
SA780T	0848
SA780X	0848
SA780Y	0848
SA816A	0848
SA816B	0848
SA816C	0848
SA816D	0848
SA816E	0848
SA816F	0848
SA816G	0848
SA816L	0848
SA816M	0848
SA816R	0848
SA816T	0848
SA816X	0848
SA816Y	0848
SA821	0631
SA821A	0631
SA823	0631
SA823A	0631
SA825	0631
SA825A	0631
SA827	0631
SA827A	0631
SA829	0631
SA829A	0631
SA836A	0037
SA836B	0037
SA836C	0037
SA836D	0037
SA836E	0037
SA836F	0037
SA836G	0037
SA836L	0037
SA836M	0037
SA836R	0037
SA836T	0037
SA836X	0037
SA836Y	0037
SA841A	0037
SA841B	0037
SA841C	0037
SA841D	0037
SA841E	0037
SA841F	0037
SA841G	0037
SA841L	0037
SA841M	0037
SA841R	0037
SA841T	0037
SA841X	0037
SA841Y	0037
SA842A	0037
SA842B	0037
SA842C	0037
SA842D	0037
SA842E	0037
SA842F	0037
SA842G	0037
SA842L	0037
SA842M	0037
SA842R	0037
SA842T	0037
SA842X	0037
SA842Y	0037
SA909A	0037
SA909B	0037
SA909C	0037
SA909D	0037
SA909E	0037
SA909F	0037
SA909G	0037
SA909L	0037
SA909M	0037
SA909R	0037
SA909T	0037
SA909X	0037
SA909Y	0037
SA1054P	OEM
SA1270	OEM
SA2002R	OEM
SA2004R	OEM
SA2006R	OEM
SA2008R	OEM
SA2913	OEM
SA2914	OEM
SA2915	OEM
SA2916	OEM
SA2917	OEM
SA2918	OEM
SA2919	OEM
SA2920	OEM
SA7805CDA	1905
SA7805CU	0619
SA7812CDA	3359
SA7812CU	0330
SA334490	OEM
SA334498	OEM
SA338979	OEM
SA338981	OEM
SA764059	OEM
SA878163	OEM
SA879849	OEM
SAA07347	OEM
SAA2-036	OEM
SAA4-001	OEM
SAA1000	OEM
SAA1004-N	OEM
SAA1005	OEM
SAA1005-P	OEM
SAA1008	OEM
SAA1010	OEM
SAA1020	OEM
SAA1021	OEM
SAA1022	OEM
SAA1024	3865
SAA1025	2131
SAA1030	OEM
SAA1042	OEM
SAA1043P	OEM
SAA1050	OEM
SAA1051	OEM
SAA1061	OEM
SAA1071	OEM
SAA1072	OEM
SAA1073	OEM
SAA1074	OEM
SAA1075	OEM
SAA1076	OEM
SAA1080	OEM
SAA-1124	OEM
SAA1124	3865
SAA1130	OEM
SAA1350	OEM
SAA1351	OEM
SAA2008	OEM
SAA3000	OEM
SAA3010P	OEM
SAA3027P	OEM
SAA3037	OEM
SAA3100	OEM
SAA6000	OEM
SAA6001	OEM
SAA6002	OEM
SAA7000	OEM
SAA7010	OEM
SAA7020	OEM
SAA7030	OEM
SAA7210P	OEM
SAA7220	5709
SAA7220N	5709
SAA7220PA	OEM
SAA9010P	OEM
SAA60425	OEM
SAB1018P	OEM
SAB1044	0007
SAB3034	OEM
SAB3035	OEM
SAB3036	OEM
SAB3037	3352
SAB3037N	3352
SAB3469	0007
SAB8086-2-P	OEM
SAB8237A5P	OEM
SAB8259AP	OEM
SAB80513	OEM
SAC40	0150
SAC40A	0150
SAC40B	0150
SAC42	0150
SAC42A	0150
SAC42B	0150
SAC44	0150
SAC431-1	OEM
SAC-1843	0127
SADBG497ZSK	OEM
SAF0300	OEM
SAF45MJ	OEM
SAF45MS	OEM
SAF1032PN	OEM
SAF1039P	0944
SAF1039PN	0944
SAF1055	OEM
SAH190	OEM
SAH215	OEM
SAJ110	4290
SAJ270E	OEM
SAJ300R	OEM
SAJ300S	OEM
SAJ300T	OEM
SAJ2160	2860
SAJ72155	0940
SAJ72156	0958
SAJ72157	0523
SAJ72158	2855
SAJ72159	0924
SAJ72160	2860
SAJ72161	0633
SAJ72162	0668
SAJ72184	OEM
SAK115	OEM
SAK215	OEM
SANY0002	OEM
SANYO-002	OEM
SANYO002	OEM
SANYO-003	OEM
SANYO003	OEM
SANYO-004	OEM
SANYO004	OEM
SANYO-012	OEM
SANYO-051	OEM
SANYO-091	OEM
SAO403	OEM
SAO403A	OEM
SAO419	OEM
SAW-1S1941	0023
SAW-1S1944	0023
SAW-2SB56	0004
SAW-2SC372GR	0079
SAW-2SC372Y	0076
SAW-2SC945R	0076
SAY115X	OEM
SAY115Y	OEM
SB007-03SPA	OEM
SB0015-03A	OEM
SB-01	0276
SB01	0015
SB01-02	0133
SB01-05CP	OEM
SB-02	0287
SB-03	0015
SB-04	0293
SB05-05CP	OEM
SB-06	0299
SB07-03	OEM
SB07-03N	OEM
SB-08	0250
SB0319	0042
SB0419	0899
SB-1	0102
SB1-01-04	0015
SB-1AHF	0790
SB-1B	0102
SB-1Z	0015
SB1Z	0110
SB-2	0102
SB2	OEM
SB-2(CENTERING-58	0914
SB-2B	0102
SB-2C	0344
SB2C	1053
SB-2C-GL	OEM
SB-2CGL	0344
SB-2CH	0102
SB2CH	OEM
SB2G	0102
SB-2T	0102
SB-2Y	0344
SB-3	0015
SB-3-02	0015
SB-3F	0087
SB-3F01	0015
SB-3N	0015
SB-10	0250
SB-15	0030
SB100	0136
SB101	0050
SB102	0050
SB103	0050
SB120	1325
SB130	1325
SB140	1325
SB150	1325
SB160	0080
SB168	0004
SB169	0004
SB170	0080
SB180	0080
SB190	3834
SB200	0136
SB302	0015
SB-309A	0015
SB309A	0276
SB-309C	0015
SB309C	0276
SB315	0015
SB320	0087
SB330	0087
SB332	0015
SB333	0015
SB340	0087
SB350	0087
SB360	0087
SB370	0087
SB380	0087

If replacement code is OEM, contact original manufacturer for replacement.

DEVICE TYPE	REPL CODE	DEVICE TYPE	REPL CODE	DEVICE TYPE	REPL CODE	DEVICE TYPE	REPL CODE	DEVICE TYPE	REPL CODE	DEVICE TYPE	REPL CODE	DEVICE TYPE	REPL CODE
SB390	3559	SBP3030M	OEM	SBX1618-51	OEM	SC60D13	3123	SC141E2	0572	SC148M3	OEM	SC241D	1307
SB393	0015	SBP3030P	1931	SBX1637-11	OEM	SC60E	3123	SC141E3	0572	SC148M5	OEM	SC241D12	OEM
SB520	OEM	SBP3035M	OEM	SBX1637A	OEM	SC60E13	3123	SC141E4	0572	SC148M6	OEM	SC241D13	OEM
SB530	OEM	SBP3035P	1931	SBX1653-01	OEM	SC60F	6626	SC141E5	0572	SC149	0111	SC241D14	OEM
SB540	OEM	SBP3040M	OEM	SBX1681-01	OEM	SC60F13	3118	SC141E6	0572	SC149B	0111	SC241E	1880
SB550	OEM	SBP3040P	1931	SC	0030	SC61	OEM	SC141F	0573	SC149B(TRIAC)	0767	SC241E12	OEM
SB560	OEM	SBP3045M	OEM	SC05	0015	SC63	0004	SC141F1	0573	SC149C	0079	SC241E13	OEM
SB561	0037	SBP3045P	1931	SC05E	0015	SC65	0016	SC141F2	0573	SC149D	0739	SC241E14	OEM
SB570	OEM	SBP3050M	OEM	SC-05M	OEM	SC-66	0004	SC141F3	0573	SC149E	0612	SC241M	1880
SB580	OEM	SBP3050P	OEM	SC-080	OEM	SC66	0004	SC141F4	0573	SC149M	0612	SC241M12	OEM
SB821	0631	SBP3060M	OEM	SC-080U	OEM	SC68	0004	SC141F5	0573	SC150	OEM	SC241M13	OEM
SB821A	0631	SBP3060P	OEM	SC0321	0130	SC69	0004	SC141F6	0573	SC150B	0753	SC245B	0154
SB823	0631	SBP9900A	OEM	SC0328	0130	SC-70	0160	SC141M	0589	SC150B3	OEM	SC245B2	3169
SB823A	0631	SBP9900ANJ-1	OEM	SC0421	1671	SC70	3613	SC141N	0591	SC150B5	OEM	SC245B3	3169
SB825	0631	SBP9989	OEM	SC0428	1671	SC70F	OEM	SC141S	OEM	SC150B6	OEM	SC245B12	OEM
SB825A	0631	SBP9989NJ	OEM	SC0515	1590	SC71	0050	SC142B	0588	SC150C20	OEM	SC245B13	0154
SB827	0631	SBR05	0276	SC1	0015	SC72	0050	SC142B2	OEM	SC150C30	OEM	SC245B14	OEM
SB827A	0631	SBR6A05	2347	SC2	0015	SC73	0004	SC142B5	OEM	SC150C40	OEM	SC245B22	OEM
SB829	0631	SBR6A1	2347	SC2C	0015	SC74	0050	SC142B6	OEM	SC150C40J	OEM	SC245B23	OEM
SB829A	0631	SBR6A2	2347	SC3	OEM	SC75	OEM	SC142D	0588	SC150C50	OEM	SC245B24	OEM
SB840	OEM	SBR6A3	2353	SC-4	0015	SC78	0050	SC142D3	OEM	SC150C60	OEM	SC245B32	OEM
SB1000	0015	SBR6A4	2353	SC4	0015	SC79	0050	SC142D5	OEM	SC150C80	OEM	SC245B33	OEM
SB5021	OEM	SBR6A5	2354	SC5	OEM	SC80	3613	SC142D6	OEM	SC150C100	OEM	SC245D	0147
SB5122	0136	SBR6A6	2354	SC-6	0143	SC80F	OEM	SC142E	0550	SC150C120	OEM	SC245D2	3177
SBA10L	OEM	SBR6A8	2356	SC6	0229	SC82	OEM	SC142E3	OEM	SC150D	0758	SC245D3	3177
SBD1620T	OEM	SBR6A10	2357	SC-7	0095	SC91	0012	SC142E5	OEM	SC150D3	OEM	SC245D12	OEM
SBD1630T	OEM	SBR10A05	2347	SC7	OEM	SC92A	4925	SC142E6	OEM	SC150D5	OEM	SC245D13	0278
SBD1635T	OEM	SBR10A1	2347	SC-7(PHILCO)	0095	SC92B	4925	SC142M	0550	SC150D6	OEM	SC245D14	OEM
SBD1640T	OEM	SBR10A2	2347	SC7C	OEM	SC92D	6645	SC142M3	OEM	SC150E	OEM	SC245D22	OEM
SBD1645T	OEM	SBR10A3	2353	SC7D	OEM	SC92F	4925	SC142M5	OEM	SC150E3	OEM	SC245D23	OEM
SBD1650T	OEM	SBR10A4	2353	SC7S08F	OEM	SC100	OEM	SC142M6	OEM	SC150E5	OEM	SC245D24	OEM
SBD1660T	OEM	SBR10A5	2354	SC8	0071	SC107	0079	SC143B	0609	SC150E6	OEM	SC245D32	OEM
SBD3020M	OEM	SBR10A6	2354	SC8A	0071	SC107A	0079	SC143D	0588	SC150M	OEM	SC245D33	OEM
SBD3020P	OEM	SBR10A8	2356	SC9	OEM	SC107B	0079	SC143E	0612	SC150M3	OEM	SC245E	0278
SBD3030M	OEM	SBR10A10	2357	SC10	0071	SC108	0079	SC143M	0589	SC150M5	OEM	SC245E2	3192
SBD3030P	OEM	SBR15	OEM	SC10A	0071	SC108A	0079	SC146A	0566	SC150M6	OEM	SC245E3	3192
SBD3035M	OEM	SBR-260	0015	SC11	OEM	SC108B	0079	SC146A1	0566	SC151B	0767	SC245E12	OEM
SBD3035P	OEM	SBR520T	OEM	SC12	0004	SC108C	0079	SC146A2	0566	SC151D	0739	SC245E13	0278
SBD3040M	OEM	SBR530T	OEM	SC12(DIODE)	0133	SC109	0079	SC146A3	0566	SC151E	0612	SC245E22	OEM
SBD3040P	OEM	SBR535T	OEM	SC-15	0623	SC109A	0079	SC146A4	0566	SC151M	0612	SC245E23	OEM
SBD3045M	OEM	SBR540T	OEM	SC15	0030	SC109B	0079	SC146A5	0566	SC157	0855	SC245E24	OEM
SBD3045P	OEM	SBR545T	OEM	SC-16	0015	SC109C	OEM	SC146A6	0566	SC157A	0855	SC245E32	OEM
SBD3050M	OEM	SBR820T	OEM	SC16	0015	SC110	0015	SC146B	0588	SC157V1	0037	SC245E33	OEM
SBD3050P	OEM	SBR830T	OEM	SC16C5	OEM	SC115	0865	SC146B1	0588	SC157VI	0855	SC245M	0278
SBD3060M	OEM	SBR835T	OEM	SC16N	OEM	SC116D	0588	SC146B2	0588	SC158	0855	SC245M2	3192
SBD3060P	OEM	SBR840T	OEM	SC-20	0623	SC120	OEM	SC146B3	0588	SC158A	0855	SC245M3	3192
SBEB05	0276	SBR845T	OEM	SC20	3613	SC126A	OEM	SC146B4	0588	SC158B	0688	SC245M12	OEM
SBEB6	0299	SBR850T	OEM	SC20F	OEM	SC126B	OEM	SC146B5	0588	SC158V1	0037	SC245M13	OEM
SBL-121	OEM	SBR860T	OEM	SC25	OEM	SC126C	OEM	SC146B6	0588	SC158VI	0855	SC245M22	OEM
SBL-122	OEM	SBR1020T	OEM	SC-29	0196	SC126D	OEM	SC146C	0569	SC159	0855	SC245M23	OEM
SBL-221	OEM	SBR1030T	OEM	SC29	0907	SC126E	OEM	SC146C1	0569	SC159A	0855	SC245M32	OEM
SBL-801	OEM	SBR1035T	OEM	SC30	3613	SC126F	OEM	SC146C2	0569	SC159B	0688	SC245M33	OEM
SBL-801(A)	OEM	SBR1040T	OEM	SC30F	OEM	SC126M	OEM	SC146C3	0569	SC160B	0902	SC246B	1058
SBL-801(Q)	OEM	SBR1045T	OEM	SC35A	0154	SC129B	0295	SC146C4	0569	SC160D	0902	SC246B12	OEM
SBL-801(S)	OEM	SBR1620T	OEM	SC35B	0154	SC129D	0303	SC146C5	0569	SC160E	0909	SC246B13	OEM
SBL-802	OEM	SBR1630T	OEM	SC35D	0147	SC129E	0307	SC146C6	OEM	SC160M	OEM	SC246B14	OEM
SBL-802(A)	OEM	SBR1635T	OEM	SC35F	0154	SC129M	0307	SC146D	0571	SC174	0079	SC246D	1307
SBL-802(Q)	OEM	SBR1640T	OEM	SC36B	1058	SC136A	OEM	SC146D1	0571	SC174A	0079	SC246D12	OEM
SBL-802(S)	OEM	SBR1645T	OEM	SC36D	1307	SC136B	0476	SC146D2	0571	SC174B	0079	SC246D13	OEM
SBL-803	OEM	SBS520T	OEM	SC40	3613	SC136C	OEM	SC146D3	0571	SC180	OEM	SC246D14	OEM
SBL-803(A)	OEM	SBS530T	OEM	SC40B	0154	SC136D	0480	SC146D4	0571	SC200	OEM	SC246E	1880
SBL-803(Q)	OEM	SBS535T	OEM	SC40B-1	0147	SC136E	OEM	SC146D5	0571	SC215	0865	SC246E12	OEM
SBL-803(S)	OEM	SBS540T	OEM	SC40B23	OEM	SC136M	OEM	SC146D6	0571	SC240B	0154	SC246E13	OEM
SBL-804	OEM	SBS545T	OEM	SC40B33	OEM	SC140B	0550	SC146E	0572	SC240B2	3169	SC246E14	OEM
SBL-804(A)	OEM	SBS820T	OEM	SC40D	0147	SC140B3	OEM	SC146E1	0572	SC240B3	3169	SC246F13	OEM
SBL-804(Q)	OEM	SBS830T	OEM	SC40E	0278	SC140B5	OEM	SC146E3	0572	SC240B12	OEM	SC246M	1880
SBL-804(S)	OEM	SBS835T	OEM	SC40F	6608	SC140B6	OEM	SC146E4	0572	SC240B13	0154	SC246M12	OEM
SBL1030CT	1015	SBS840T	OEM	SC41B	1058	SC140D	0550	SC146E5	0572	SC240B14	OEM	SC246M13	1880
SBL1040CT	1015	SBS845T	OEM	SC41D	1307	SC140D3	OEM	SC146E6	0572	SC240B22	OEM	SC250	OEM
SBN1020T	OEM	SBS850T	OEM	SC41E	1880	SC140D5	OEM	SC146F	0573	SC240B22/32	OEM	SC250B	0154
SBN1030T	OEM	SBS860T	OEM	SC43	0279	SC140D6	OEM	SC146F1	0573	SC240B23	OEM	SC250B2	3169
SBN1035T	OEM	SBS1020T	OEM	SC44	0279	SC140E	0550	SC146F2	0573	SC240B24	OEM	SC250B3	3169
SBN1040T	OEM	SBS1030T	OEM	SC45	0004	SC140E3	OEM	SC146F3	0573	SC240B32	OEM	SC250B12	OEM
SBN1045T	OEM	SBS1035T	OEM	SC45A	0147	SC140E5	OEM	SC146F4	0573	SC240B33	OEM	SC250B13	0154
SBN1620T	OEM	SBS1040T	OEM	SC45B	0154	SC140E6	OEM	SC146F5	0573	SC240D	0147	SC250B14	OEM
SBN1630T	OEM	SBS1045T	OEM	SC45B13	0154	SC140M	0550	SC146F6	0573	SC240D2	3177	SC250B22	OEM
SBN1635T	OEM	SBS1620T	OEM	SC45D	0147	SC140M3	OEM	SC146M	0589	SC240D3	3177	SC250B23	OEM
SBN1640T	OEM	SBS1630T	OEM	SC45D13	0147	SC140M5	OEM	SC146N	OEM	SC240D12	OEM	SC250B24	OEM
SBN1645T	OEM	SBS1635T	OEM	SC45E	0278	SC140M6	OEM	SC146S	OEM	SC240D13	0147	SC250B32	OEM
SBN1650T	OEM	SBS1640T	OEM	SC45E13	0278	SC141A	0566	SC147	0079	SC240D14	OEM	SC250D	0147
SBN1660T	OEM	SBS1645T	OEM	SC45F	0147	SC141A1	0566	SC147A	0111	SC240D22	OEM	SC250D2	3177
SBN3020M	OEM	SBT-101A+	2786	SC46	0279	SC141A2	0566	SC147B	0111	SC240D23	OEM	SC250D3	3177
SBN3020P	OEM	SBT-101K+	1772	SC46B	1058	SC141A3	0566	SC147B3	OEM	SC240D24	OEM	SC250D12	OEM
SBN3030M	OEM	SBT-201A+	2786	SC46D	1307	SC141A4	0566	SC147B5	OEM	SC240D32	OEM	SC250D13	0147
SBN3030P	OEM	SBT-201K+	1772	SC46E	1880	SC141A5	0566	SC147B6	OEM	SC240D33	OEM	SC250D14	OEM
SBN3035M	OEM	SBT-401A+	2786	SC47	OEM	SC141A6	0566	SC147D	0550	SC240E	0278	SC250D22	OEM
SBN3035P	OEM	SBT-401K+	1772	SC50	3613	SC141B	0567	SC147D3	OEM	SC240E2	3192	SC250D23	OEM
SBN3040M	OEM	SBT-601A+	2786	SC50A	0147	SC141B1	0588	SC147D5	OEM	SC240E3	3192	SC250D24	OEM
SBN3040P	OEM	SBT-601K+	1772	SC50B	0154	SC141B2	0588	SC147D6	OEM	SC240E12	OEM	SC250D32	OEM
SBN3045M	OEM	SBT-801A+	2818	SC50B13	0154	SC141B3	0588	SC147E	0550	SC240E13	0278	SC250D33	OEM
SBN3045P	OEM	SBT-801K+	1807	SC50D	0147	SC141B4	0588	SC147M	0550	SC240E14	OEM	SC250E	0278
SBN3050M	OEM	SBT-1001A+	2818	SC50D13	0147	SC141B5	0588	SC147M3	OEM	SC240E22	OEM	SC250E2	3192
SBN3050P	OEM	SBT-1001K+	1807	SC50E	0278	SC141B6	0588	SC147M5	OEM	SC240E23	OEM	SC250E3	3192
SBN3060M	OEM	SBX1435	OEM	SC50E13	0278	SC141C	0569	SC147M6	OEM	SC240E24	OEM	SC250E12	OEM
SBN3060P	OEM	SBX1435-01	OEM	SC50F	6619	SC141C1	0569	SC148	0111	SC240E32	OEM	SC250E13	0278
SBP1020T	1015	SBX1475	OEM	SC51	OEM	SC141C2	0569	SC148A	0111	SC240E33	OEM	SC250E14	OEM
SBP1030T	1015	SBX1483-51	OEM	SC51D	1307	SC141C3	0569	SC148B	0111	SC240M	0278	SC250E22	OEM
SBP1035T	1015	SBX1483-59	OEM	SC51E	1880	SC141C4	0569	SC148B3	OEM	SC240M2	3192	SC250E23	OEM
SBP1040T	1015	SBX1492-51	OEM	SC54	0143	SC141C5	0569	SC148B5	OEM	SC240M3	3192	SC250E24	OEM
SBP1045T	2493	SBX1505-01	OEM	SC-56	0208	SC141C6	0569	SC148B6	OEM	SC240M12	OEM	SC250E32	OEM
SBP1620T	2493	SBX1535-02	OEM	SC56	0208	SC141D	0571	SC148C	0111	SC240M13	OEM	SC250E33	OEM
SBP1630T	2493	SBX1535-04	OEM	SC60	3613	SC141D1	0571	SC148D	OEM	SC240M22	OEM	SC250M	0278
SBP1635T	2493	SBX1535-51	OEM	SC60A	3119	SC141D2	0571	SC148D3	OEM	SC240M23	OEM	SC250M2	3192
SBP1640T	2493	SBX1535-52	OEM	SC60A13	3119	SC141D3	0571	SC148D5	OEM	SC240M32	OEM	SC250M3	3192
SBP1645T	2493	SBX1535-54	OEM	SC60B	3121	SC141D4	0571	SC148D6	OEM	SC240M33	OEM	SC250M12	OEM
SBP1650T	OEM	SBX1535-54V	OEM	SC60B13	3121	SC141D5	0571	SC148E	OEM	SC241B	1058	SC250M13	OEM
SBP1660T	OEM	SBX1568-5	OEM	SC60C	3122	SC141D6	0571	SC148E5	OEM	SC241B12	OEM	SC250M22	OEM
SBP3020M	OEM	SBX1568-51	OEM	SC60C13	3122	SC141E	0572	SC148E6	OEM	SC241B13	OEM	SC250M23	OEM
SBP3020P	1931	SBX1618-11	OEM	SC60D	3123	SC141E1	0572	SC148M	OEM	SC241B14	OEM	SC250M23/33	OEM

If replacement code is OEM, contact original manufacturer for replacement.

547

DEVICE TYPE	REPL CODE
SC250M32	OEM
SC250M33	OEM
SC251B	1058
SC251B12	OEM
SC251B13	OEM
SC251B14	OEM
SC251D	1307
SC251D12	OEM
SC251D13	OEM
SC251D14	OEM
SC251E	1880
SC251E12	OEM
SC251E13	OEM
SC251E14	OEM
SC251M	1880
SC251M12	OEM
SC251M13	OEM
SC256	0855
SC256A	0855
SC256B	0786
SC257	0855
SC257A	0855
SC257V1	0037
SC257VI	0855
SC258	0855
SC258A	0855
SC258B	0688
SC258V1	0037
SC258VI	0855
SC259	0855
SC259A	0855
SC259B	0688
SC260B	2004
SC260B2	3169
SC260B3	3169
SC260B12	OEM
SC260B13	OEM
SC260B22	OEM
SC260B23	OEM
SC260B32	OEM
SC260B33	OEM
SC260D	2006
SC260D2	3177
SC260D3	3177
SC260D12	OEM
SC260D13	OEM
SC260D22	OEM
SC260D23	OEM
SC260D32	OEM
SC260D33	OEM
SC260E	2007
SC260E2	3192
SC260E3	3192
SC260E12	OEM
SC260E13	OEM
SC260E22	OEM
SC260E23	OEM
SC260E32	OEM
SC260E33	OEM
SC260M	2007
SC260M2	3192
SC260M3	3192
SC260M12	OEM
SC260M13	OEM
SC260M22	OEM
SC260M23	OEM
SC260M32	OEM
SC260M33	OEM
SC261B	1058
SC261B12	OEM
SC261B13	OEM
SC261D	1307
SC261D12	OEM
SC261D13	OEM
SC261E	1880
SC261E12	OEM
SC261E13	OEM
SC261M	1880
SC261M12	OEM
SC261M13	OEM
SC265B	2004
SC265B2	3169
SC265B3	3169
SC265D	2006
SC265D2	3177
SC265D3	3177
SC265E	2007
SC265E2	3192
SC265E3	3192
SC265M	2007
SC265M2	3192
SC265M3	3192
SC266B	1058
SC266D	1307
SC266E	1880
SC266M	1880
SC305	0015
SC315	OEM
SC350	0016
SC365	0126
SC400Y	0142
SC415	OEM
SC441	0168
SC4960B	OEM
SC515	OEM
SC570A	OEM
SC727	0142
SC777	0142
SC785	0198
SC786	0007
SC821	0631
SC821A	0631
SC823	0631
SC823A	0631
SC825	0631
SC825A	0631
SC827	0631
SC827A	0631
SC829	0631
SC829A	0631
SC832	0016
SC842	0016
SC843	0126
SC843(T.I.)	0233
SC902	OEM
SC902A	OEM
SC969	OEM
SC1001	0016
SC1007	0050
SC1010	0016
SC1148-4	0344
SC1168G	0016
SC1168H	0016
SC1227F	0144
SC1227G	0144
SC1229E	0086
SC1229G	0016
SC1294H	0126
SC1600	OEM
SC1601	OEM
SC1611	0838
SC1612	0838
SC1613	0838
SC1614	0838
SC1625	OEM
SC3162	OEM
SC4001BH	0473
SC4001UBC	0473
SC4004	0142
SC4010	0016
SC4044	0016
SC4073	0208
SC4116	0015
SC4131	0086
SC4131-1	0086
SC4132	0142
SC4133	0161
SC4135	0086
SC4162	OEM
SC4163	OEM
SC4164	OEM
SC4167	0086
SC4195	OEM
SC4244	0086
SC4274	0222
SC4277	OEM
SC4303	0042
SC4303-1	0042
SC4303-2	0042
SC4308	0042
SC5087	OEM
SC5088	OEM
SC5117	0649
SC5118P	0438
SC5150P	2979
SC5172P	1929
SC5172PC	1929
SC5172PQ	1929
SC5175G	0406
SC5177P	0649
SC5199P	0649
SC5204P	1742
SC5219P	0350
SC5220P	0167
SC5221P	5001
SC5245P	0784
SC5282P	1902
SC5454P	OEM
SC5858	3675
SC5896	2480
SC5898	1162
SC6394GLC6	OEM
SC8705P	0696
SC8709P	0661
SC8723P	0345
SC9314P	0649
SC9341P	OEM
SC9430P	1797
SC9431P	0391
SC9436P	0167
SC9438P	0167
SC9961P	OEM
SC9963P	2840
SC9964P	3393
SC9965P	3395
SC11007	OEM
SC11014	OEM
SC41342P	OEM
SC41843P	OEM
SC42502P	3550
SC42530P	OEM
SC42682P	OEM
SC51750	0406
SC67331	OEM
SC67331P	OEM
SC68681C5140(A)	OEM
SC68681CSN40(A)	OEM
SC74186	OEM
SC77526	OEM
SC77527	OEM
SC77527P	OEM
SC77562P	OEM
SC78130U	OEM
SC80240P	OEM
SC80444P	OEM
SC80756P	OEM
SC82165FN	OEM
SC84251P	OEM
SC87898P	OEM
SC88639B	OEM
SC88658B	OEM
SC93870P	OEM
SC94815P	OEM
SC99616P	OEM
SC99630P	OEM
SC99642P	OEM
SC99643P	OEM
SC99659P	OEM
SC99666B	OEM
SC99669P	OEM
SC403602P	OEM
SC403603P	OEM
SC403604P	OEM
SC403737P	OEM
SC409006B	OEM
SC411733B	OEM
SC420111P	OEM
SC4036037P	OEM
SCA05	0015
SCA1	0015
SCA2	0015
SCA3	0015
SCA4	0015
SCA5	0015
SCA6	0015
SCA8	0071
SCA10	0071
SCA42	0710
SCA43	0710
SCA44	0710
SCA45	0710
SCA-45A	1313
SCA45A	6060
SCA92	0338
SCA95	0472
SCA1103	0015
SCA3021	0259
SCA3022	0007
SCA3023	0414
SCA3235	0007
SCA3236	0007
SCA3237	0007
SCA3238	0007
SCA3239	0007
SCA3240	0007
SCA3242	0050
SCA3243	0007
SCA3244	0007
SCA3246	0007
SCAJ2	1404
SCAJ4	0468
SCAJ6	0441
SCBA2	2347
SCBA6	2354
SCBR05F	0071
SCBR1F	0071
SCBR6	0087
SCBR6F	0071
SCBR15	OEM
SCBR35F	0071
SCC321	0130
SCC421	1671
SCC8530	OEM
SCD11B1	1047
SCD11B2	1047
SCD11B3	1047
SCD255	1101
SCD321	0130
SCD421	1671
SCD1181	OEM
SCD1182	OEM
SCD1183	OEM
SCD-1062013	0461
SCE1	0015
SCE2	0015
SCE3	0015
SCE4	0015
SCE6	0015
SCE8	0071
SCE10	0071
SCE15	OEM
SCE20	OEM
SCE25	OEM
SCE25A	OEM
SCE30	OEM
SCE30A	OEM
SCE40	OEM
SCE40A	OEM
SCE50	OEM
SCE50A	OEM
SCE75	OEM
SCE100	OEM
SCE321	0130
SCE421	1671
SCF40501	2016
SCH120	OEM
SCH130	OEM
SCH140	OEM
SCH150	OEM
SCH160	OEM
SCH320	OEM
SCH330	OEM
SCH340	OEM
SCH350	OEM
SCH360	OEM
SCH520	OEM
SCH530	OEM
SCH540	OEM
SCH550	OEM
SCH560	OEM
SCH1020	OEM
SCH1030	OEM
SCH1040	OEM
SCH1050	OEM
SCH1060	OEM
SCI148-4	0102
SCITT310YXXXX	0030
SCITT410STXX	0030
SCITT410STXXX	0030
SCL5.0A	2380
SCL6.0A	3085
SCL6.5A	OEM
SCL7.0A	OEM
SCL7.5A	OEM
SCL8.0A	OEM
SCL8.5A	OEM
SCL9.0A	OEM
SCL10A	OEM
SCL11A	3143
SCL12A	OEM
SCL13A	OEM
SCL14A	OEM
SCL15A	3162
SCL16A	OEM
SCL17A	3171
SCL18A	OEM
SCL20A	OEM
SCL22A	1904
SCL24A	OEM
SCL26A	OEM
SCL28A	OEM
SCL30A	OEM
SCL33A	OEM
SCL36A	OEM
SCL40A	OEM
SCL43A	0563
SCL45A	OEM
SCL48A	OEM
SCL51A	OEM
SCL54A	OEM
SCL58A	0825
SCL60A	OEM
SCL64A	OEM
SCL70A	OEM
SCL75A	OEM
SCL78A	OEM
SCL85A	OEM
SCL90A	OEM
SCL100A	OEM
SCL110A	OEM
SCL120A	OEM
SCL130A	OEM
SCL150A	OEM
SCL160A	OEM
SCL170A	1395
SCL4000	2013
SCL4000B	2013
SCL4000BC	2013
SCL4000BD	2013
SCL4000BE	2013
SCL4000BF	2013
SCL4000BH	2013
SCL4001	0473
SCL4001B	0473
SCL4001BC	0473
SCL4001BD	0473
SCL4001BE	0473
SCL4001BF	0473
SCL4001UB	OEM
SCL4001UBD	0473
SCL4001UBE	0473
SCL4001UBF	0473
SCL4001UBH	0473
SCL4002	2044
SCL4002B	2044
SCL4002BC	2044
SCL4002BD	2044
SCL4002BE	2044
SCL4002BF	2044
SCL4002BH	2044
SCL4006BC	0641
SCL4006BD	0641
SCL4006BE	0641
SCL4006BF	0641
SCL4007	2819
SCL4007UBC	2819
SCL4007UBD	2819
SCL4007UBE	2819
SCL4007UBHN	OEM
SCL4008B	0982
SCL4008BC	0982
SCL4008BD	0982
SCL4008BE	0982
SCL4008BF	0982
SCL4008BH	0982
SCL4008BP	0982
SCL4009	1988
SCL4009UBC	1988
SCL4009UBD	1988
SCL4009UBE	0001
SCL4009UBHN	OEM
SCL4010BC	3222
SCL4010BD	3222
SCL4010BE	0394
SCL4010BHN	OEM
SCL4011	0215
SCL4011B	0215
SCL4011BC	0215
SCL4011BD	0215
SCL4011BE	0215
SCL4011BF	0215
SCL4011BH	0215
SCL4011UB	OEM
SCL4011UBC	0215
SCL4011UBD	0215
SCL4011UBE	0215
SCL4011UBF	0215
SCL4011UBH	0215
SCL4012	0493
SCL4012B	0493
SCL4012BC	0493
SCL4012BD	0493
SCL4012BE	0493
SCL4012BF	0493
SCL4012BH	0493
SCL4013	0409
SCL4013AC	0409
SCL4013AD	0409
SCL4013AE	0409
SCL4013AF	0409
SCL4013AH	0409
SCL4013BC	0409
SCL4013BD	0409
SCL4013BE	0409
SCL4013BF	0409
SCL4013BH	0409
SCL4013BP	0409
SCL4014BC	0854
SCL4014BD	0854
SCL4014BE	0854
SCL4014BF	OEM
SCL4014BHN	OEM
SCL4015	1008
SCL4015BC	1008
SCL4015BD	1008
SCL4015BE	1008
SCL4015BF	OEM
SCL4015BHN	OEM
SCL4016	1135
SCL4016BH	OEM
SCL4016BHN	OEM
SCL4017	0508
SCL4017ABC	0508
SCL4017ABD	0508
SCL4017ABE	0508
SCL4017ABF	0508
SCL4017ABH	0508
SCL4017AC	0508
SCL4017AD	0508
SCL4017AE	0508
SCL4017AF	0508
SCL4017AH	0508
SCL4017B	0508
SCL4017BC	0508
SCL4017BD	0508
SCL4017BE	0508
SCL4017BF	0508
SCL4017BH	0508
SCL4018AC	1381
SCL4018AD	1381
SCL4018AE	1381
SCL4018AF	1381
SCL4018AH	1381
SCL4018B	1381
SCL4018BD	1381
SCL4018BE	1381
SCL4018BF	1381
SCL4018BH	1381
SCL4019	1517
SCL4020	1651
SCL4020ABC	1651
SCL4020ABD	1651
SCL4020ABE	1651
SCL4020ABF	1651
SCL4020ABH	1651
SCL4020AC	1651
SCL4020AD	1651
SCL4020AE	1651
SCL4020AF	1651
SCL4020AH	1651
SCL4020B	1651
SCL4021	1738
SCL4021BC	1738
SCL4021BD	1738
SCL4021BE	1738
SCL4021BF	OEM
SCL4021BHN	OEM
SCL4022ABC	1247
SCL4022ABD	1247
SCL4022ABE	1247
SCL4022ABF	1247
SCL4022ABH	1247
SCL4022AC	1247
SCL4022AD	1247
SCL4022AE	1247
SCL4022AF	1247
SCL4022AH	1247
SCL4022B	1247
SCL4022BC	1247
SCL4022BD	1247
SCL4022BE	1247
SCL4022BF	1247
SCL4022BH	1247
SCL4023	0515
SCL4023AC	0515
SCL4023AD	0515
SCL4023AE	0515
SCL4023AF	0515
SCL4023AH	0515
SCL4023B	0515
SCL4023BC	0515
SCL4023BD	0515
SCL4023BE	0515
SCL4023BF	0515
SCL4023BH	0515
SCL4024	1946
SCL4024AC	1946
SCL4024AD	1946
SCL4024AE	1946
SCL4024AF	1946
SCL4024AH	1946
SCL4024AT	1946
SCL4024B	1946
SCL4024BC	1946
SCL4024BD	1946
SCL4024BE	1946
SCL4024BF	1946
SCL4024BH	1946
SCL4025	2061
SCL4025AC	2061
SCL4025AD	2061
SCL4025AE	2061
SCL4025AF	2061
SCL4025AH	2061
SCL4025B	2061
SCL4025BC	2061
SCL4025BD	2061
SCL4025BE	2061
SCL4025BF	2061
SCL4025BH	2061
SCL4026AB	2139
SCL4026ABC	2139
SCL4026ABD	2139
SCL4026ABE	2139
SCL4027	1938
SCL4027B	1938
SCL4027BC	1938
SCL4027BD	1938
SCL4027BE	1938
SCL4027BF	1938
SCL4027BH	1938
SCL4028AC	2213
SCL4028AD	2213
SCL4028AE	2213
SCL4028AF	2213
SCL4028AH	2213
SCL4028B	2213
SCL4028BC	2213
SCL4028BD	2213
SCL4028BE	2213
SCL4028BF	2213
SCL4028BH	2213
SCL4029AC	2218
SCL4029AD	2218
SCL4029AE	2218
SCL4029AF	2218
SCL4029AH	2218
SCL4029B	2218
SCL4029BC	2218
SCL4029BD	2218
SCL4029BE	2218
SCL4029BH	2218
SCL4030	0495
SCL4030AC	0495
SCL4030AD	0495
SCL4030AE	0495
SCL4030AF	0495
SCL4030AH	0495
SCL4030B	0495
SCL4030BC	0495
SCL4030BD	0495
SCL4030BE	0495
SCL4030BF	0495
SCL4030BH	0495
SCL4033AB	2611
SCL4033ABC	2611
SCL4033ABD	2611
SCL4033ABE	2611
SCL4034BC	3570
SCL4034BD	3570
SCL4034BE	3570
SCL4034BH	OEM
SCL4035BC	2750
SCL4035BD	2750
SCL4035BE	2750
SCL4035BF	OEM
SCL4035BHN	OEM
SCL4040	0056
SCL4040ABC	0056
SCL4040ABD	0056
SCL4040AC	0056
SCL4040AD	0056
SCL4040AE	0056
SCL4040AF	0056
SCL4040AH	0056
SCL4040B	0056
SCL4041UBC	3145
SCL4041UBD	3145
SCL4041UBE	3145
SCL4041UBHN	OEM
SCL4042	0121
SCL4042B	0121
SCL4042BC	0121
SCL4042BD	0121
SCL4042BE	0121
SCL4042BF	0121
SCL4042BH	0121
SCL4042BHN	OEM
SCL4043ABC	1544
SCL4043ABD	1544
SCL4043ABE	1544
SCL4043ABF	1544
SCL4043ABH	1544
SCL4043B	1544
SCL4043BC	1544
SCL4043BD	1544
SCL4043BE	1544
SCL4043BF	1544
SCL4043BH	1544
SCL4044ABC	2292
SCL4044ABE	2292
SCL4044ABF	2292
SCL4044ABH	2292
SCL4044B	2292
SCL4044BC	2292
SCL4044BD	2292
SCL4044BE	2292
SCL4044BF	2292
SCL4044BH	2292
SCL4047B	2315
SCL4047BC	2315
SCL4047BD	2315
SCL4047BE	2315
SCL4047BF	2315
SCL4047BH	2315
SCL4049	0001
SCL4049UBH	OEM
SCL4049UBHN	OEM
SCL4050	0394
SCL4050BH	OEM
SCL4050BHN	OEM
SCL4051	0362
SCL4051BH	OEM
SCL4051BHN	OEM
SCL4052	0024
SCL4053BH	OEM
SCL4053BHN	OEM
SCL4060ABC	0146
SCL4060ABD	0146
SCL4060ABE	0146
SCL4060ABF	0146
SCL4060ABH	0146
SCL4060AC	0146
SCL4060AD	0146
SCL4060AE	0146
SCL4060AF	0146
SCL4060AH	0146
SCL4060B	0146
SCL4066BH	OEM
SCL4066BHN	OEM
SCL4068B	2482
SCL4068BC	2482
SCL4068BD	2482
SCL4068BE	2482
SCL4068BF	2482
SCL4068BH	2482
SCL4070B	2494
SCL4070BC	2494
SCL4070BD	2494
SCL4070BE	2494
SCL4070BF	2494
SCL4070BH	2494
SCL4071AC	0129
SCL4071AD	0129
SCL4071AE	0129
SCL4071AF	0129
SCL4071AH	0129
SCL4071B	0129
SCL4071BC	0129
SCL4071BD	0129
SCL4071BE	0129
SCL4071BF	0129
SCL4071BH	0129
SCL4072AC	2502
SCL4072AD	2502
SCL4072AE	2502
SCL4072AF	2502
SCL4072AH	2502
SCL4072B	2502
SCL4072BC	2502
SCL4072BD	2502
SCL4072BE	2502
SCL4072BF	2502
SCL4072BH	2502
SCL4073AC	1528
SCL4073AD	1528
SCL4073AE	1528
SCL4073AF	1528
SCL4073AH	1528
SCL4073B	1528
SCL4073BC	1528
SCL4073BD	1528

If replacement code is OEM, contact original manufacturer for replacement.

DEVICE TYPE	REPL CODE
SCL4073BE	1528
SCL4073BF	1528
SCL4073BH	1528
SCL4075AC	2518
SCL4075AD	2518
SCL4075AE	2518
SCL4075AF	2518
SCL4075AH	2518
SCL4075B	2518
SCL4075BC	2518
SCL4075BD	2518
SCL4075BE	2518
SCL4075BF	2518
SCL4075BH	2518
SCL4076BC	3455
SCL4076BD	3455
SCL4076BE	3455
SCL4076BF	OEM
SCL4076BHN	OEM
SCL4077B	2536
SCL4077BC	2536
SCL4077BD	2536
SCL4077BE	2536
SCL4077BF	2536
SCL4077BH	2536
SCL4078B	0915
SCL4078BC	0915
SCL4078BD	0915
SCL4078BE	0915
SCL4078BF	0915
SCL4078BH	0915
SCL4081	0621
SCL4081AC	0621
SCL4081AD	0621
SCL4081AE	0621
SCL4081AF	0621
SCL4081AH	0621
SCL4081B	0621
SCL4081BC	0621
SCL4081BD	0621
SCL4081BE	0621
SCL4081BF	0621
SCL4081BH	0621
SCL4082B	0297
SCL4082BC	0297
SCL4082BD	0297
SCL4082BE	0297
SCL4082BF	0297
SCL4082BH	0297
SCL4085B	0300
SCL4085BC	0297
SCL4085BD	0300
SCL4085BE	0300
SCL4085BF	0300
SCL4085BH	0300
SCL4086B	0530
SCL4086BC	0530
SCL4086BD	0530
SCL4086BE	0530
SCL4086BF	0530
SCL4086BH	0530
SCL4094BD	1672
SCL4094BE	1672
SCL4160B	1349
SCL4161B	1363
SCL4162B	1378
SCL4163B	1397
SCL4174B	1542
SCL4416	OEM
SCL4416ABE	OEM
SCL4449UBE	0001
SCL4502BE	1031
SCL4510AC	1952
SCL4510AD	1952
SCL4510AE	1952
SCL4510AF	1952
SCL4510AH	1952
SCL4510B	1952
SCL4510BC	1952
SCL4510BD	1952
SCL4510BE	1952
SCL4510BF	1952
SCL4510BH	1952
SCL4511AC	1535
SCL4511AD	1535
SCL4511AE	1535
SCL4511AF	1535
SCL4511AH	1535
SCL4511BC	1535
SCL4511BD	1535
SCL4511BE	1535
SCL4511BF	1535
SCL4511BH	1535
SCL4512BC	2108
SCL4512BD	2108
SCL4512BE	2108
SCL4512BHN	OEM
SCL4514B	1819
SCL4514BD	1819
SCL4514BE	1819
SCL4514BH	1819
SCL4515B	3555
SCL4515BD	3555
SCL4515BE	3555
SCL4515BH	3555
SCL4516AC	2331
SCL4516AD	2331
SCL4516AE	2331
SCL4516AF	2331
SCL4516AH	2331
SCL4516B	2331
SCL4516BC	2331
SCL4516BD	2331
SCL4516BE	2331
SCL4516BF	2331
SCL4516BH	2331
SCL4518	1037
SCL4518AC	1037
SCL4518AD	1037
SCL4518AE	1037
SCL4518AF	1037
SCL4518AH	1037
SCL4518B	1037
SCL4518BC	1037
SCL4518BD	1037
SCL4518BE	1037
SCL4518BF	1037
SCL4518BH	1037
SCL4520AC	2650
SCL4520AD	2650
SCL4520AE	2650
SCL4520AF	2650
SCL4520AH	2650
SCL4520B	2650
SCL4520BC	2650
SCL4520BD	2650
SCL4520BE	2650
SCL4520BF	2650
SCL4520BH	2650
SCL4522B	OEM
SCL4522BC	2810
SCL4522BD	2810
SCL4522BE	2810
SCL4522BF	2810
SCL4522BH	2810
SCL4526B	3565
SCL4527B	3116
SCL4527BC	3116
SCL4527BD	3116
SCL4527BE	3116
SCL4527BF	3116
SCL4527BH	3116
SCL4528B	3566
SCL4531B	OEM
SCL4543BC	4929
SCL4543BD	OEM
SCL4543BE	4932
SCL4555B	2910
SCL4555BC	2910
SCL4555BD	2910
SCL4555BE	2910
SCL4555BF	2910
SCL4555BH	2910
SCL4556BC	3397
SCL4556BD	3397
SCL4556BE	3397
SCL4556BF	3397
SCL4556BH	3397
SCM5.0A	2380
SCM6.0A	3085
SCM6.5A	OEM
SCM7.0A	OEM
SCM7.5A	OEM
SCM8.0A	OEM
SCM8.5A	OEM
SCM9.0A	OEM
SCM10	OEM
SCM10A	OEM
SCM11A	3143
SCM12A	OEM
SCM13A	OEM
SCM14A	OEM
SCM15	OEM
SCM15A	3162
SCM16A	OEM
SCM17A	3171
SCM18A	OEM
SCM20	OEM
SCM20A	OEM
SCM22A	1904
SCM24A	OEM
SCM25	OEM
SCM26A	OEM
SCM28A	OEM
SCM30A	OEM
SCM33A	OEM
SCM36A	OEM
SCM40A	OEM
SCM43A	0563
SCM45A	OEM
SCM48A	OEM
SCM51A	OEM
SCM54A	OEM
SCM58A	0825
SCM60A	OEM
SCM64A	OEM
SCM70A	OEM
SCM75A	OEM
SCM78A	OEM
SCM85A	OEM
SCM90A	OEM
SCM100A	OEM
SCM110A	OEM
SCM120A	OEM
SCM130A	OEM
SCM150A	OEM
SCM160A	OEM
SCM170A	1395
SCM90072C	0518
SCM90072P	0518
SCM90522P	OEM
SCM90590P	OEM
SCM91248C	OEM
SCM91619P	OEM
SCM91665P	OEM
SCM91692P	OEM
SCM92135P	OEM
SCM93007P	OEM
SCM93008P	OEM
SCM95987P	OEM
SCN8048AC6N40-A	OEM
SCN68000C8N64	OEM
SC0321	OEM
SC0328	OEM
SC0421	OEM
SC0428	OEM
SCP5E	0015
SCPH3	OEM
SCPH5	OEM
SCPH7	OEM
SCPH15	OEM
SCPH25	OEM
SCPH35	OEM
SCPH45	OEM
SCQ38068PB01	OEM
SCQ38068PB02	OEM
SCR-01	1095
SCR-01-B	1095
SCR01C	1095
SCR-02	0240
SCR-02-C	0240
SCR02C	1067
SCR-03	2497
SCR03	0717
SCR-03-C	2174
SCR-04	0740
SCR04	0740
SCR-04-C	0757
SCR04C	0740
SCR5P-05M	0500
SCR10A	OEM
SCR11A	OEM
SCR12A	OEM
SCR13A	OEM
SCR14A	OEM
SCR15	0340
SCR15A	OEM
SCR16A	OEM
SCR17A	OEM
SCR18A	OEM
SCR30A	OEM
SCR31A	OEM
SCR32A	OEM
SCR33A	OEM
SCR34A	OEM
SCR35A	OEM
SCR36A	OEM
SCR37A	OEM
SCR38A	OEM
SCR50A	OEM
SCR51	OEM
SCR51A	OEM
SCR52	OEM
SCR52(ELCOM)	2174
SCR52A	OEM
SCR53A	OEM
SCR54	OEM
SCR54A	OEM
SCR55	1095
SCR55A	OEM
SCR56A	OEM
SCR57A	OEM
SCR58A	OEM
SCR71	OEM
SCR72	OEM
SCR74	OEM
SCR76	OEM
SCR92	OEM
SCR102	0736
SCR102(ELCOM)	0562
SCR104	2255
SCR104(ELCOM)	1912
SCR108	0895
SCR108(ELCOM)	0895
SCR111	OEM
SCR112	OEM
SCR118	0740
SCR118(ELCOM)	2471
SCR122(ELCOM)	1641
SCR150	OEM
SCR160	OEM
SCR160A	OEM
SCR161A	OEM
SCR162A	OEM
SCR163A	OEM
SCR164A	OEM
SCR165A	OEM
SCR166A	OEM
SCR167A	OEM
SCR168A	OEM
SCR200	0058
SCR202	0740
SCR202(ELCOM)	0757
SCR204	2255
SCR207	0740
SCR207(ELCOM)	0430
SCR208	0740
SCR208(ELCOM)	0240
SCR218	0058
SCR218(ELCOM)	0058
SCR222(ELCOM)	1641
SCR255	0726
SCR303	OEM
SCR315	OEM
SCR325	OEM
SCR335	OEM
SCR345	OEM
SCR350	OEM
SCR355	OEM
SCR360	OEM
SCR370	OEM
SCR380	OEM
SCR402	0742
SCR402(ELCOM)	0735
SCR404(ELCOM)	0095
SCR408	0742
SCR408(ELCOM)	0671
SCR422(ELCOM)	1574
SCR502	2497
SCR505	2782
SCR505(ELCOM)	2782
SCR508	2497
SCR508(ELCOM)	1095
SCR520	0240
SCR535	OEM
SCR535A	OEM
SCR538	2255
SCR545	OEM
SCR545A	OEM
SCR550A	OEM
SCR555	OEM
SCR555A	OEM
SCR560A	OEM
SCR570	OEM
SCR570A	OEM
SCR580	OEM
SCR580A	OEM
SCR604(ELCOM)	3370
SCR605(ELCOM)	3579
SCR608(ELCOM)	0332
SCR613	2255
SCR635(ELCOM)	0720
SCR805(ELCOM)	0061
SCR816(ELCOM)	0761
SCR835	OEM
SCR845	OEM
SCR855	OEM
SCR860	OEM
SCR865	OEM
SCR870	OEM
SCR875	OEM
SCR880	OEM
SCR1635	OEM
SCR1635A	OEM
SCR1645	OEM
SCR1645A	OEM
SCR1655	OEM
SCR1655A	OEM
SCR1660A	OEM
SCR1670A	OEM
SCR1680A	OEM
SCR2520	0464
SCRF10A	OEM
SCRF11A	OEM
SCRF12A	OEM
SCRF13A	OEM
SCRF14A	OEM
SCRF15A	OEM
SCRF16A	OEM
SCRF17A	OEM
SCRF18A	OEM
SCRF30A	OEM
SCRF31A	OEM
SCRF32A	OEM
SCRF33A	OEM
SCRF34A	OEM
SCRF35A	OEM
SCRF36A	OEM
SCRF37A	OEM
SCRF38A	OEM
SCRF50A	OEM
SCRF51A	OEM
SCRF52A	OEM
SCRF53A	OEM
SCRF54A	OEM
SCRF55A	OEM
SCRF56A	OEM
SCRF57A	OEM
SCRF58A	OEM
SCRF160A	OEM
SCRF161A	OEM
SCRF162A	OEM
SCRF163A	OEM
SCRF164A	OEM
SCRF165A	OEM
SCRF166A	OEM
SCRF167A	OEM
SCRF168A	OEM
SCRF503	OEM
SCRF505	OEM
SCRF510	OEM
SCRF515	OEM
SCRF520	OEM
SCRF525	OEM
SCRF530	OEM
SCRF535	OEM
SCRF540	OEM
SCRF545	OEM
SCRF550	OEM
SCRF555	OEM
SCRF560	OEM
SCRF570	OEM
SCRF580	OEM
SCRF1603	OEM
SCRF1605	OEM
SCRF1610	OEM
SCRF1615	OEM
SCRF1620	OEM
SCRF1625	OEM
SCRF1630	OEM
SCRF1635	OEM
SCRF1640	OEM
SCRF1645	OEM
SCRF1650	OEM
SCRF1655	OEM
SCRF1660	OEM
SCRF1665	OEM
SCRF1670	OEM
SCRF1680	OEM
SCRFL03	OEM
SCRFL05	OEM
SCRFL10	OEM
SCRFL15	OEM
SCRFL20	OEM
SCRFL25	OEM
SCRFL30	OEM
SCRFL35	OEM
SCRFL40	OEM
SCRFL45	OEM
SCRFL50	OEM
SCRFL55	OEM
SCRFL60	OEM
SCRFL70	OEM
SCRFL80	OEM
SCRJ03	OEM
SCRJ05	OEM
SCRJ10	OEM
SCRJ15	OEM
SCRJ20	OEM
SCRJ25	OEM
SCRJ30	OEM
SCRJ35	OEM
SCRJ40	OEM
SCRJ45	OEM
SCRJ50	OEM
SCRJ55	OEM
SCRJ60	OEM
SCRJ70	OEM
SCRJ80	OEM
SCRJL01	OEM
SCRJL03	OEM
SCRJL05	OEM
SCRJL15	OEM
SCRJL20	OEM
SCRJL25	OEM
SCRJL30	OEM
SCRJL35	OEM
SCRJL40	OEM
SCRJL45	OEM
SCRJL50	OEM
SCRJL55	OEM
SCRJL60	OEM
SCRJL70	OEM
SCRJL80	OEM
SCRL35	OEM
SCRL40	OEM
SCRL45	OEM
SCRL50	OEM
SCRL55	OEM
SCRL60	OEM
SCRL70	OEM
SCRL80	OEM
SCT1	0071
SCT2	0071
SCT3	0071
SCT4	0071
SCT5	0071
SCT-24	2503
SD-0033	0025
SD05	0015
SD-07	0015
SD07	0015
SD014	OEM
SD020	0123
SD040	0015
SD0345	0060
SD0445	1298
SD-1	0102
SD1	0023
SD1-1	0015
SD1-11	0102
SD-1-30DA	0102
SD1-30DA	0102
SD-1-211B	0015
SD1-211B	0015
SD-1-211C	0015
SD1-X	0015
SD1-Z	0015
SD-1A	0015
SD1A	0102
SD1A(UF)	OEM
SD-1AHF	0914
SD1AHF	1293
SD-1AUF	0133
SD-1B	0015
SD1B	0102
SD-1B(HF)	0102
SD-1BHF	0102
SD1BHF	0102
SD-1C	0102
SD1C	0071
SD-1C-4F	0015
SD-1C-UF	0015
SD-1CUF	0015
SD1CUF	0015
SD1DM-4	0015
SD-1HF	0015
SD1HF	0015
SD-1L	0015
SD1L	OEM
SD-1LA	0015
SD1LA	0015
SD-1N34A	0123
SD-1N60	0019
SD-1N60P	0123
SD-1N60S	0019
SD-1N4148	0124
SD1P60XXXXFXT	0019
SD-1S295	1898
SD-1S1555	0133
SD-1S1925	0911
SD-1S2076	0133
SD-1S2207	0030
SD-1S2339	0549
SD-1S2692	2496
SD-1SS16	0911
SD-1SV58	1023
SD-1SV59	1023
SD-1SV70	1023
SD-1U	0015
SD-1UF	0015
SD-1VHF	0102
SD1W	OEM
SD-1X	0015
SD1X	0015
SD-1Y	0015
SD1Y	0023
SD-1Z	0015
SD1Z	0023
SD-1ZHF	0015
SD1ZHF	0015
SD-2	0015
SD2	0071
SD2A	0015
SD2B	0015
SD2C	0071
SD2L	OEM
SD2LE	OEM
SD2LEE	OEM
SD-2N5062	0895
SD2WE	OEM
SD4	0015
SD4(DUAL)	0196
SD-5	0133
SD5	0015
SD5(DUAL)	0479
SD-5(PHILCO)	0133
SD-6	0162
SD6	0015
SD6(DUAL)	0242
SD-7	4051
SD7	5474
SD-7(PHILCO)	0133
SD-8	0012
SD8	0071
SD-8(PHILCO)	0012
SD-8(RECTIFIER)	0811
SD10	0015
SD-11	0490
SD11F	0123
SD-12	0143
SD12	0143
SD12B	0143
SD12E	0143
SD12M	0143
SD12V	0143
SD-13	0015
SD13	0143
SD-14	0143
SD14	0143
SD-15	0012
SD15	0143
SD-16	0143
SD16	0143
SD-16A	0015
SD-16D	0015
SD17	0143
SD-18	0015
SD18	0143
SD-19	0276
SD19	0030
SD20	0015
SD21	0143
SD21A	0143
SD-22	0102
SD22	0102
SD23	0015
SD24	0030
SD-27	0012
SD30	OEM
SD-31	0526
SD31	0560
SD-32	0157
SD32	0253
SD-33	0361
SD33	0137
SD-34	0133
SD34	0143
SD38	0143
SD-39	0030
SD39	0030
SD41	OEM
SD42	0025
SD-43	0133
SD43	0133
SD45	0015
SD-46	0143
SD46	0143
SD46(4)	0123
SD-46-2	0143
SD46-2	0143
SD46R	0123
SD-49	0025
SD49	0025
SD50	1325
SD-51	0911
SD51	0911
SD53	0137
SD54	0143
SD-56	0143
SD56	0143
SD-60	0143
SD60	0143
SD-60P	0015
SD60P	1325
SD-61P	0015
SD61P	0790
SD-80	0015
SD80	0015
SD82	0911
SD82A	0911
SD82AG	0911
SD-91	0015
SD91	0110
SD-91A	0015
SD91A	0242
SD-91S	0015
SD91S	0242
SD-92	0015
SD92	0242
SD-92A	0015
SD92A	0242
SD-92S	0015
SD92S	0242
SD-93	0015
SD93	0535
SD-93A	0015
SD93A	0535
SD93S	0015
SD-94	0015
SD94	0535
SD-94A	0015
SD94A	0535
SD-94AB	0015
SD94AB	0015
SD94B	0015
SD94S	0015
SD-95	0015
SD95	0015
SD-95A	0015
SD95A	0015
SD96	0015
SD96A	0015
SD96S	0015
SD98	0071
SD98A	0071
SD98S	0071
SD100	0133
SD-101	0015
SD101	0124
SD102	0124
SD103	0124
SD103B	0911
SD103C	OEM
SD104	0023
SD105	0023
SD-109	0079
SD109	0079
SD-110	0133
SD111	0715
SD112	OEM
SD113	0030
SD113TA	0030
SD115	0755
SD-116	0005
SD116	0005
SD120	OEM
SD122	OEM
SD141	0178
SD-150	0143
SD160	0133
SD165	0133
SD184-1	OEM
SD190	3834
SD200	OEM
SD-201	0015
SD201	0015
SD202	0015
SD218	0615
SD241	OEM
SD241P	0579
SD282A	0911
SD300C02C	OEM

If replacement code is OEM, contact original manufacturer for replacement.

DEVICE TYPE	REPL CODE
SD300C04C	OEM
SD300C06C	OEM
SD300C08C	OEM
SD300C10C	OEM
SD300C12C	OEM
SD300C14C	OEM
SD300C16C	OEM
SD300C18C	OEM
SD300C20C	OEM
SD300C22C	OEM
SD300C24C	OEM
SD300C26C	OEM
SD300C28C	OEM
SD300C30C	OEM
SD345	0042
SD390	3559
SD400C02C	OEM
SD400C04C	OEM
SD400C06C	OEM
SD400C08C	OEM
SD400C10C	OEM
SD400C12C	OEM
SD400C14C	OEM
SD400C16C	OEM
SD400C18C	OEM
SD400C20C	OEM
SD400C22C	OEM
SD400C24C	OEM
SD400N02MC	OEM
SD400N02PC	OEM
SD400N04MC	OEM
SD400N04PC	OEM
SD400N06MC	OEM
SD400N06PC	OEM
SD400N08MC	OEM
SD400N08PC	OEM
SD400N10MC	OEM
SD400N10PC	OEM
SD400N12MC	OEM
SD400N12PC	OEM
SD400N14MC	OEM
SD400N14PC	OEM
SD400N16MC	OEM
SD400N16PC	OEM
SD400N18MC	OEM
SD400N18PC	OEM
SD400N20MC	OEM
SD400N20PC	OEM
SD400N22MC	OEM
SD400N22PC	OEM
SD400N24MC	OEM
SD400N24PC	OEM
SD400R02PC	OEM
SD400R04PC	OEM
SD400R06PC	OEM
SD400R08PC	OEM
SD400R10PC	OEM
SD400R12PC	OEM
SD400R14PC	OEM
SD400R16PC	OEM
SD400R18PC	OEM
SD400R20PC	OEM
SD400R22PC	OEM
SD400R24PC	OEM
SD-404	0911
SD404	0911
SD445	0919
SD461	0143
SD467	0284
SD-470	0015
SD470	0015
SD471CG	OEM
SD500	0133
SD500C	0015
SD500KD	1658
SD501	0015
SD503K	OEM
SD600	0133
SD600C	0015
SD600N02P	4957
SD600N04P	4957
SD600N06P	4957
SD600N06PC	4957
SD600N08P	0744
SD600N10P	0744
SD600N12P	0744
SD600N12PC	OEM
SD600N14P	OEM
SD600N16P	OEM
SD600N18PC	OEM
SD600N20PC	OEM
SD600N22PC	OEM
SD600N24PC	OEM
SD600R02P	2299
SD600R04P	2299
SD600R06P	2299
SD600R06PC	2299
SD600R08P	2765
SD600R10P	2765
SD600R12P	2765
SD600R12PC	2765
SD600R14P	OEM
SD600R16P	OEM
SD600R18PC	OEM
SD600R20PC	OEM
SD600R22PC	OEM
SD600R24PC	OEM
SD603K	OEM
SD-630	0133

DEVICE TYPE	REPL CODE
SD630	0133
SD-632	0012
SD632	0012
SD632(10)	0012
SD701-02	0133
SD703K	OEM
SD800	0071
SD803K	OEM
SD838	0911
SD903K	OEM
SD910	0071
SD910A	0071
SD910S	0071
SD950	0015
SD974	0133
SD1002KD	OEM
SD1003K	OEM
SD1005	2059
SD1005KD	OEM
SD1006	2194
SD1011KD	1658
SD1012	0284
SD1012KD	1658
SD1013	1189
SD1014	1224
SD1014-1	5209
SD1014KD	OEM
SD1015KD	OEM
SD1018	1963
SD1020	0488
SD1021KD	1658
SD1023	0555
SD1069	1224
SD1074	2296
SD1076	3521
SD1077	2675
SD1078	OEM
SD1080	2030
SD1080-2	2030
SD1080-4	2030
SD1080-7	2030
SD1088	3545
SD1089	2841
SD1094	OEM
SD1095	OEM
SD1096	OEM
SD1098	3598
SD1100C02C	OEM
SD1100C04C	OEM
SD1100C06C	OEM
SD1100C08C	OEM
SD1100C10C	OEM
SD1100C12C	OEM
SD1100C14C	OEM
SD1100C16C	OEM
SD1100C18C	OEM
SD1100C20C	OEM
SD1100C22C	OEM
SD1100C24C	OEM
SD1101	0015
SD1102	0015
SD1103	0015
SD1103K	OEM
SD1115-4	0414
SD1127	3528
SD1133	1224
SD1134	3516
SD1134-1	3387
SD1135	2080
SD1136	1410
SD1143	1224
SD1144	3516
SD1144-1	0414
SD1145	2080
SD1146	1410
SD1169	3526
SD1203K	OEM
SD1212-7	3587
SD1214	1189
SD1214-6	3747
SD1216	1966
SD1229	1966
SD1270	3387
SD1272	3012
SD1278	OEM
SD1285	5110
SD1288	3523
SD1290	3526
SD1300	0259
SD1301	0259
SD1303K	OEM
SD1335	0060
SD1345	0042
SD1347-7	6044
SD1403K	OEM
SD1405	3521
SD1407	2523
SD1410	3595
SD1412	3597
SD1416	3165
SD1418	3596
SD1428	3090
SD1433	1410
SD1434	2841
SD1444	2028
SD1445	0919
SD1451	2296
SD1479	2156
SD1484	2030

DEVICE TYPE	REPL CODE
SD1503K	OEM
SD1556-3	0599
SD1603K	OEM
SD1703K	OEM
SD1803K	OEM
SD3621A	OEM
SD5010	OEM
SD5011	OEM
SD5012	OEM
SD5013	OEM
SD5014	OEM
SD5015	OEM
SD5050	OEM
SD5051	OEM
SD5171	OEM
SD5410-1	3508
SD5410-2	3508
SD5410-3	3508
SD5440-1	2297
SD5440-2	2297
SD5440-3	2297
SD5440-4	3825
SD5443-1	2297
SD5443-2	2297
SD11441	0007
SD58655	OEM
SDA345	0042
SDA445	0919
SDA980-1	2347
SDA980-1F	2347
SDA980-2	2347
SDA980-2F	2347
SDA980-3	2347
SDA980-3F	2347
SDA980-4	2353
SDA980-4F	2353
SDA980-5	2353
SDA980-5F	2353
SDA980-6	2354
SDA980-6F	2354
SDA980-8	2356
SDA980-10	2357
SDA990-1	2347
SDA990-1F	1633
SDA990-2	1633
SDA990-2F	1633
SDA990-3	1633
SDA990-3F	1633
SDA990-4	1663
SDA990-4F	1663
SDA990-5	1663
SDA990-5F	1663
SDA990-6	1663
SDA990-6F	1663
SDA990-8	1579
SDA990-10	1579
SDA3202	OEM
SDB345	0042
SDB445	0919
SDB501B-GD	OEM
SD-BA244	0163
SD-BA244A	0133
SD-BB409	OEM
SD-BZX9V1	2458
SDD4	0196
SDD5	0479
SDD6	1073
SDD320	OEM
SDD420	0086
SDD421	0016
SDD820	0127
SDD821	0016
SDD1220	0086
SDD3000	0016
SDD-C05	OEM
SDD-C10	0196
SDDS442XXXXXX	0124
SDDSF10XCXXXXT	0023
SD-ERB24-04D	0023
SD-ERB26-20	0344
SD-ERC26-13	0102
SDF10	OEM
SDF20	OEM
SDF30	OEM
SDF40	OEM
SDF50	OEM
SDF60	OEM
SDF9401F	OEM
SDG600	0599
SDG601	0599
SDG602	0599
SDG603	0599
SDGMA01XXXXXT	0124
SDGZA033XXXXX	0296
SDGZA062YXXXX	0466
SDH-2	0143
SDH-2HC	0911
SD-HV23GBL	1914
SDI345	0042
SDI445	0919
SD-IN4148	0124
SDJ345	0042
SDJ445	0919
SDK345	0042
SDK445	0919
SDL345	0042
SDL445	0919
SDM345	0042
SDM402	OEM

DEVICE TYPE	REPL CODE
SDM445	0919
SDM4001	1384
SDM4002	1384
SDM4003	1384
SDM4004	1384
SDM4005	1384
SDM4006	1384
SDM4010	2422
SDM5001	3483
SDM5002	3483
SDM5003	3483
SDM5004	3483
SDM5005	3483
SDM5006	3483
SDM5010	2602
SDM5011	2602
SDM5012	2602
SDM5013	2602
SDN201	1203
SDN345	0042
SDN401	3336
SDN445	0919
SDN501	2220
SDN601	3340
SDN6000	2602
SDN6060	2602
SDN6061	2602
SDN6062	2602
SDN6251	1980
SDN6252	2602
SDN6253	2602
SDN22311	1980
SDN22312	1980
SDN22313	1980
SDO345	0236
SDO445	0676
SDP251	0597
SDP345	0419
SDP445	1190
SDP451	3497
SDP502	OEM
SDR3A	0087
SDR-25	0015
SDR25	0015
SDR2712	OEM
SDR2713	OEM
SDR2720	OEM
SDR2721	OEM
SDR2722	OEM
SDR2723	OEM
SDR3001	0087
SDR3002	0087
SDS113	0015
SDS240	0007
SDT234A	OEM
SDT401	0074
SDT402	0223
SDT-410	0074
SDT410	0270
SDT-411	1955
SDT411	0270
SDT-413	0359
SDT413	0074
SDT-423	0637
SDT423	1955
SDT424	0223
SDT425	0309
SDT430	0359
SDT431	1955
SDT445	0919
SDT520	OEM
SDT521	OEM
SDT522	0617
SDT525	OEM
SDT526	OEM
SDT527	0359
SDT530	OEM
SDT531	OEM
SDT532	0359
SDT535	OEM
SDT536	OEM
SDT537	0359
SDT540	OEM
SDT541	OEM
SDT542	0359
SDT545	OEM
SDT547	0359
SDT550	OEM
SDT551	OEM
SDT552	OEM
SDT555	OEM
SDT556	OEM
SDT557	OEM
SDT560	OEM
SDT561	OEM
SDT562	OEM
SDT565	OEM
SDT566	OEM
SDT567	OEM
SDT570	OEM
SDT571	OEM
SDT572	OEM
SDT1000	OEM
SDT1001	0359
SDT1002	0359
SDT1003	0359
SDT1004	0359
SDT1005	0359
SDT1006	0309

DEVICE TYPE	REPL CODE
SDT1007	0309
SDT1011	0359
SDT1012	0359
SDT1013	0359
SDT1014	0359
SDT1015	0359
SDT1016	0309
SDT1017	0309
SDT1051	0359
SDT1055	0359
SDT1056	0359
SDT1060	0359
SDT1061	0359
SDT1611	1955
SDT1612	1955
SDT1613	1955
SDT1614	1955
SDT1615	1955
SDT1616	1955
SDT1617	1955
SDT1618	1955
SDT1621	0130
SDT1622	0130
SDT1623	0130
SDT1631	0130
SDT1632	0130
SDT1633	0130
SDT3321	0126
SDT3322	0126
SDT3325	1257
SDT3326	0555
SDT3421	6241
SDT3422	0617
SDT3423	0617
SDT3424	0617
SDT3425	6241
SDT3426	6241
SDT3427	0617
SDT3428	0617
SDT3429	0617
SDT3501	0126
SDT3502	0126
SDT3503	0126
SDT3504	6250
SDT3505	0378
SDT3506	0378
SDT3507	4507
SDT3508	4507
SDT3509	0919
SDT3510	0919
SDT3513	0919
SDT3514	0919
SDT3550	0378
SDT3552	0378
SDT3553	0378
SDT3575	0899
SDT3576	0899
SDT3577	0899
SDT3578	0899
SDT3579	0899
SDT3701	0919
SDT3702	0919
SDT3703	0919
SDT3704	0919
SDT3706	0919
SDT3707	0919
SDT3708	0919
SDT3709	0919
SDT3710	0919
SDT3711	0919
SDT3712	0919
SDT3713	0919
SDT3715	0919
SDT3716	0919
SDT3717	0919
SDT3718	1190
SDT3719	1190
SDT3720	0919
SDT3721	0919
SDT3722	0919
SDT3723	1190
SDT3724	1190
SDT3725	0919
SDT3726	0919
SDT3727	0919
SDT3728	1190
SDT3729	0919
SDT3730	0919
SDT3731	1190
SDT3732	1190
SDT3733	0919
SDT3750	1588
SDT3751	1588
SDT3752	1588
SDT3753	1588
SDT3754	1671
SDT3755	1671
SDT3756	1588
SDT3757	1588
SDT3758	1588
SDT3759	1671
SDT3760	1671
SDT3761	1588
SDT3762	1588
SDT3763	1588
SDT3764	1671
SDT3765	1671
SDT3766	1671
SDT3775	1257

DEVICE TYPE	REPL CODE
SDT3776	1257
SDT3778	1257
SDT3801	1190
SDT3802	1190
SDT3803	1190
SDT3804	1190
SDT3805	1190
SDT3806	1190
SDT3807	1190
SDT3825	1588
SDT3826	1671
SDT3827	1671
SDT3850	1190
SDT3851	1190
SDT3852	1190
SDT3875	1671
SDT3876	1671
SDT3877	1671
SDT4301	6241
SDT4302	6241
SDT4304	6241
SDT4305	6241
SDT4306	0617
SDT4307	6241
SDT4308	6241
SDT4309	0617
SDT4310	6241
SDT4311	6241
SDT4312	0617
SDT4455	0555
SDT4483	0555
SDT4551	0555
SDT4553	0555
SDT4583	0555
SDT4611	0555
SDT4612	0555
SDT4614	0555
SDT4615	0555
SDT4813	OEM
SDT4814	OEM
SDT5001	6241
SDT5002	3296
SDT5003	3296
SDT5006	6241
SDT5007	3296
SDT5008	3296
SDT5011	0555
SDT5012	3296
SDT5013	3296
SDT5102	0042
SDT5112	0919
SDT5501	6241
SDT5502	3296
SDT5503	3296
SDT5504	0617
SDT5506	6241
SDT5507	3296
SDT5508	3296
SDT5509	0617
SDT5511	0555
SDT5512	3296
SDT5513	3296
SDT5635	OEM
SDT5636	OEM
SDT5901	0555
SDT5902	0555
SDT5903	2526
SDT5906	0555
SDT5907	0042
SDT5908	2526
SDT5911	2526
SDT5912	2526
SDT5913	2526
SDT6001	0042
SDT6011	0042
SDT6013	0042
SDT6031	0042
SDT6101	0555
SDT6102	0555
SDT6103	0042
SDT6104	0555
SDT6105	0555
SDT6106	0555
SDT6383	OEM
SDT6417	OEM
SDT6418	OEM
SDT6419	OEM
SDT6420	OEM
SDT6901	0178
SDT6905	0178
SDT7011	2637
SDT7012	2637
SDT7013	2637
SDT7014	2637
SDT7015	2637
SDT7016	2637
SDT7140	2637
SDT7141	2637
SDT7150	2637
SDT7151	2637
SDT7152	2637
SDT7154	2637
SDT7155	2637
SDT7206	2258
SDT7401	6241
SDT7402	0617
SDT7403	0617
SDT7411	6241
SDT7412	0617

DEVICE TYPE	REPL CODE
SDT7413	0617
SDT7414	0617
SDT7415	0617
SDT7416	0617
SDT7417	0617
SDT7418	0617
SDT7419	0617
SDT7471	OEM
SDT7472	OEM
SDT7473	OEM
SDT7474	OEM
SDT7475	OEM
SDT7476	OEM
SDT7477	OEM
SDT7478	OEM
SDT7511	0042
SDT7512	0042
SDT7514	0042
SDT7515	0042
SDT7530	OEM
SDT7531	OEM
SDT7601	0103
SDT7602	0103
SDT7603	0103
SDT7604	2416
SDT7607	0103
SDT7608	0103
SDT7609	0103
SDT7610	6377
SDT7611	6377
SDT7612	6377
SDT7618	OEM
SDT7619	OEM
SDT7731	0103
SDT7732	0103
SDT7733	0103
SDT7734	4704
SDT7735	4704
SDT8002	3470
SDT8003	3470
SDT8012	3470
SDT8013	3470
SDT8015	3470
SDT8016	3470
SDT8045	3470
SDT8070	3470
SDT8071	3470
SDT8301	3449
SDT8302	3449
SDT8303	3449
SDT8304	3449
SDT9001	0555
SDT9002	0555
SDT9003	0555
SDT9004	1257
SDT9005	0555
SDT9006	0555
SDT9007	0555
SDT9008	0555
SDT9009	0042
SDT9113	OEM
SDT9201	0103
SDT9202	0538
SDT9203	6725
SDT9204	0538
SDT9205	0103
SDT9206	0103
SDT9207	0538
SDT9208	0538
SDT9209	0538
SDT9210	0103
SDT9261	0103
SDT9301	0103
SDT9302	0103
SDT9303	0103
SDT9304	0103
SDT9305	0359
SDT9306	0103
SDT9307	0103
SDT9308	0103
SDT9309	0103
SDT9701	0130
SDT9702	2465
SDT9703	4704
SDT9704	0130
SDT9705	2465
SDT9706	4704
SDT9707	0130
SDT9804	4704
SDT9901	0538
SDT9902	0538
SDT9903	0538
SDT9904	0538
SDT12201	OEM
SDT12202	OEM
SDT12203	OEM
SDT12301	1841
SDT12302	1841
SDT12303	1841
SDT13201	OEM
SDT13202	OEM
SDT13203	OEM
SDT13204	OEM
SDT13205	OEM
SDT13301	1841
SDT13302	1841
SDT13303	1841
SDT13304	OEM
SDT13305	OEM

If replacement code is OEM, contact original manufacturer for replacement.

DEVICE TYPE	REPL CODE
SDT14304	OEM
SDT14305	OEM
SD-W005M	0106
SD-W04	0287
SD-Y	0015
SE0001	0076
SE002(1)	0127
SE-05	0015
SE05	0015
SE-05-01	0015
SE-05-02	0015
SE-05-2	0229
SE-05-A	0015
SE-05-B	0015
SE-05-C	0071
SE-05-D	0071
SE-05A	0015
SE05A	0535
SE05B	0015
SE-05C	0087
SE05C	0071
SE05D	0015
SE05S	0015
SE05SS	0015
SE-05X	0015
SE0555	OEM
SE-0.5A	0535
SE-0.5B	0015
SE-1.5A	0087
SE1.5A	OEM
SE1.5B	OEM
SE1.5C	OEM
SE1.5D	OEM
SE1.5S	OEM
SE1.5SS	OEM
SE-2	0015
SE-5	0015
SE-5-0399	0969
SE-5-0819	0211
SE5-0930	2803
SE5-0933	0167
SE5-0996	0321
SE5U4GE	OEM
SE6(DUAL)	1073
SE6X4	OEM
SE19	OEM
SE21	OEM
SE30B26A	0015
SE46	0015
SE106J	OEM
SE111J	OEM
SE112J	OEM
SE116J	OEM
SE120	OEM
SE120N	OEM
SE125J	OEM
SE130N	OEM
SE130NH	OEM
SE135	OEM
SE-135N	OEM
SE-135NS	OEM
SE136	OEM
SE136N	OEM
SE140	OEM
SE140N	OEM
SE140NL	OEM
SE155J	OEM
SE156J	OEM
SE161J	OEM
SE170J	OEM
SE180J	OEM
SE303	OEM
SE303A	0511
SE303AC	OEM
SE303ACK	0511
SE303ANC	OEM
SE303AX	OEM
SE303AX2	OEM
SE303AY	OEM
SE304	OEM
SE393A	OEM
SE416J	OEM
SE424J	OEM
SE455J	OEM
SE480J	OEM
SE500G	0144
SE504	0144
SE521	0144
SE555	3732
SE555V	0967
SE556	6737
SE592F	OEM
SE592FH	OEM
SE592K	OEM
SE-705G	0187
SE724J	OEM
SE1000C	OEM
SE1000P	OEM
SE1001	0076
SE1001-1	0224
SE1001-2	0224
SE-1002	0016
SE1002	0076
SE1002-1	0007
SE1002-2	0007
SE1003	OEM
SE1004C	OEM
SE-1010	0127
SE1010	0007
SE1012	0590
SE1019	0144
SE1044	0007
SE1100C	OEM
SE1331	0016
SE1400P	OEM
SE1419	0144
SE1730	0071
SE1731	OEM
SE1732	OEM
SE1733	OEM
SE1734	OEM
SE2001	0007
SE2002	0007
SE2020	0127
SE2100P	OEM
SE2130P	OEM
SE2200P	OEM
SE2382	OEM
SE2383	OEM
SE2384	OEM
SE2385	OEM
SE2397	0127
SE2400	0050
SE2400P	OEM
SE2401	0016
SE2402	0016
SE-3001	0144
SE3001	0007
SE3001R	0144
SE3002	0007
SE3003	0144
SE3005	0007
SE3019	0007
SE3030	0074
SE3031	0074
SE3032	0177
SE3033	0103
SE3034	0626
SE3035	0103
SE3036	0103
SE3040	0424
SE3041	0424
SE3100	0326
SE3450-1	0586
SE3450-2	0586
SE3450-3	0586
SE3451-1	0586
SE3451-2	0586
SE3451-3	0586
SE3453-1	0586
SE3453-2	0586
SE3453-3	0586
SE3453-4	0586
SE3455-1	0586
SE3455-2	0586
SE3455-3	OEM
SE3455-4	OEM
SE3646	0007
SE3819	0321
SE-4001	0079
SE4001	0016
SE4002	1212
SE-4010	0016
SE4010	1212
SE-4020	0086
SE4020	1212
SE4020/6-04	0007
SE4021	1212
SE4022	0007
SE4172	0016
SE4329	OEM
SE-5001	0144
SE5001	0224
SE5002	0076
SE5003	0007
SE5004	0007
SE-5006	0016
SE5006	0144
SE5010	0144
SE5015	0144
SE5020	0007
SE5021	0007
SE5022	0007
SE-5023	0007
SE5023	0007
SE-5024	0007
SE5024	0007
SE-5025	0007
SE5025	0144
SE5029	0144
SE5030	0144
SE5030A	0076
SE5030B	0016
SE5031	0144
SE5032	0007
SE5035	0007
SE5036	0144
SE5040	0144
SE5050	0007
SE5051	0007
SE5052	0007
SE5055	0224
SE5056	0144
SE5151	0016
SE5315	0212
SE5450-1	0586
SE5450-2	0586
SE5450-3	0586
SE5451-1	0586
SE5451-2	0586
SE5451-3	0586
SE5453-1	0586
SE5453-2	0586
SE5453-3	0586
SE5453-4	0586
SE5455-1	0586
SE5455-2	0586
SE5455-3	0586
SE5455-4	0586
SE5534	OEM
SE5560F	OEM
SE5560N	OEM
SE-6001	0016
SE6001	0076
SE-6002	0016
SE6002	0076
SE6006	0086
SE6010	0016
SE6020	0016
SE6020A	0086
SE6021	0086
SE6021A	0086
SE6022	0086
SE6023	0086
SE6452-3	OEM
SE6550	OEM
SE7001	0076
SE7002	0233
SE7005	0086
SE7006	0142
SE7010	0233
SE7015	0086
SE7016	0233
SE7017	0233
SE7020	0142
SE7030	0142
SE7050	0233
SE7055	0233
SE7056	0233
SE8001	0086
SE8002	0076
SE8010	0086
SE8012	0086
SE8040	0016
SE8041	0086
SE8042	0086
SE8510	0086
SE8520	0086
SE8521	3392
SE8540	0126
SE8541	0126
SE8542	0126
SE9002	0103
SE9020	0074
SE9060	0178
SE9061	0178
SE9062	0178
SE9063	0178
SE9070	2526
SE9071	2526
SE9080	0103
SE9081	2526
SE9200	OEM
SE9201	OEM
SE9202	OEM
SE9203	OEM
SE9205	OEM
SE9206	OEM
SE9207	OEM
SE9208	OEM
SE9220	OEM
SE9221	OEM
SE9222	OEM
SE9223	OEM
SE9225	OEM
SE9226	OEM
SE9227	OEM
SE9228	OEM
SE9230	OEM
SE9231	OEM
SE9232	OEM
SE9233	OEM
SE9235	OEM
SE9236	OEM
SE9237	OEM
SE9238	OEM
SE9300	2220
SE9301	2220
SE9302	2220
SE9303	3339
SE9304	3339
SE9305	1980
SE9331	1021
SE9400	2222
SE9401	2222
SE9402	2222
SE9403	3340
SE9404	3339
SE9405	2415
SE9560	0899
SE9561	0899
SE9562	0899
SE9563	0899
SE9570	0455
SE9571	0455
SE9572	0455
SE9573	0455
SE-40022	0160
SE40022	0160
SE50399	0969
SEB1000C	OEM
SEB1000P	OEM
SEB1004C	OEM
SEB1100C	OEM
SEB1100P	OEM
SEB1400P	OEM
SEB2100P	OEM
SEB2130P	OEM
SEB2400P	OEM
SEC1077	OEM
SEC1078	0590
SEC1079	0590
SEC1080	OEM
SEC1477	0590
SEC1478	OEM
SEC1479	0590
SEC1480	OEM
SED1330F	OEM
SED9420C	OEM
SEL-101C	OEM
SEL101R	OEM
SEL102R	OEM
SEL-103R	OEM
SEL103RF	OEM
SEL112NP-N	OEM
SEL162B	OEM
SEL550S	OEM
SEL550ST	OEM
SEL650ST	OEM
SEL1112R	OEM
SEL-1120R	3990
SEL1120R	3990
SEL1210R	OEM
SEL1210S	OEM
SEL1210SC	OEM
SEL1210W	OEM
SEL1222R-C	OEM
SEL1222R-D	OEM
SEL1320G	1123
SEL1410E	OEM
SEL1410G	OEM
SEL-1413(GRN)	OEM
SEL1413E	OEM
SEL1910D	OEM
SEL1910W	OEM
SEL2110R	OEM
SEL2110S	OEM
SEL2201WC	OEM
SEL2210R	OEM
SEL2210S	OEM
SEL2210S-C	OEM
SEL2213C	OEM
SEL2213E	OEM
SEL2310E	OEM
SEL2413E	OEM
SEL2510C-C	OEM
SEL2810A-C	OEM
SEL2910A	OEM
SEL2910A-C	OEM
SEL2910AX	OEM
SEL2910AY	OEM
SEL2910D	OEM
SEL2910GW-C	OEM
SEL2910W-C	OEM
SEL4214R	OEM
SEL4214S	OEM
SEL4214W	OEM
SEL4410E	OEM
SEL4414E	OEM
SEL4910A-C	OEM
SEL4914A-X	OEM
SEL4914AX	OEM
SEL4914AY	OEM
SEL5500ST	OEM
SELEN-26	0196
SELEN-30	0201
SELEN30	0201
SELEN-36	OEM
SELEN-38	0196
SELEN-40	0752
SELEN-42	0469
SELEN-44	0276
SELEN-48	1293
SELEN48	1293
SELEN-52	0286
SELEN-58	0201
SELEN-64	0087
SELEN-70	0015
SELEN-92	0102
SELEN-701	0015
SEN2A1	0276
SEN2A2	0287
SEN2A4	0293
SEN2A6	0299
SEN2A8	0250
SEN2A10	0250
SEN105	1325
SEN105FR	OEM
SEN110	0080
SEN110FR	OEM
SEN120	0604
SEN120FR	OEM
SEN130	0790
SEN130FR	OEM
SEN140	0790
SEN140FR	OEM
SEN150	0015
SEN150FR	OEM
SEN160	0015
SEN160FR	OEM
SEN170FR	OEM
SEN180	0072
SEN180FR	OEM
SEN205	0087
SEN205FR	OEM
SEN210	0087
SEN210FR	OEM
SEN220	0087
SEN220FR	OEM
SEN230	0087
SEN230FR	OEM
SEN240	0087
SEN240FR	OEM
SEN250	0087
SEN250FR	OEM
SEN260	0087
SEN260FR	OEM
SEN270FR	OEM
SEN280	0087
SEN305	0087
SEN310	0087
SEN320	0087
SEN330	0087
SEN340	0087
SEN350	0087
SEN360	0087
SEN380	0087
SEN480	OEM
SEN480FR	OEM
SEN1100	0071
SEN2100	0087
SEN3100	0087
SES632	0103
SES881	0103
SES3819	0321
SES5001	0071
SF0R1A41	0895
SF0R1B42	0895
SF0R1B42IG1	0895
SF0R3G42	0403
SF0R3G42(G5H1)	0403
SF0R3G42-1G5	0403
SF0R3G42-IG5	0403
SF-1	0344
SF1	0102
SF1A11	0174
SF1A11A	0174
SF1AN6	OEM
SF1AN12	OEM
SF1AR6	OEM
SF1AR12	OEM
SF1B11	3801
SF1B11A	3801
SF1C11	OEM
SF1C11A	OEM
SF1CN1	0071
SF1D11	3575
SF1D11A	3575
SF1E11	OEM
SF1E11A	OEM
SF1F11	OEM
SF1F11A	OEM
SF1G11	OEM
SF1G11A	OEM
SF1GH315	OEM
SF1GR316	OEM
SF1HN315	OEM
SF1HR316	OEM
SF1R-3B41	2255
SF1R3B41	0442
SF1R3D41	0934
SF1Z11	OEM
SF1Z11A	OEM
SF2AN6	OEM
SF2AN12	OEM
SF2AR6	OEM
SF2AR12	OEM
SF2B41	0442
SF2D41	0934
SF2G41	0095
SF2GR316	OEM
SF2HN315	OEM
SF2K212XXX3XX	1382
SF3	OEM
SF3AN6	OEM
SF3AN12	OEM
SF3AN126	OEM
SF3AR6	OEM
SF3AR12	OEM
SF3B12	2471
SF3B41	2078
SF3BR64	OEM
SF3C325	OEM
SF3CN1	0071
SF3D12	0240
SF3D41	0934
SF3G4L	0705
SF3G12	2782
SF3G14	3349
SF3G41	0705
SF3GN315	OEM
SF3GR64	OEM
SF3GR315	OEM
SF3GR316	OEM
SF3HN315	OEM
SF3HR315	OEM
SF3HR316	OEM
SF3J41	0857
SF4	0071
SF4AN6	OEM
SF4AN12	OEM
SF4AR6	OEM
SF4AR12	OEM
SF4CN1	0071
SF4GN315	OEM
SF4GR316	OEM
SF4H4316	OEM
SF4HN315	OEM
SF5	0071
SF5A11	1095
SF5AN12	OEM
SF5AN126	OEM
SF5AR6	OEM
SF5AR12	OEM
SF5B11	2471
SF5B12	2471
SF5B13	2471
SF5B41	2078
SF5BR64	OEM
SF5C11	OEM
SF5C325	OEM
SF5D11	0240
SF5D12	0240
SF5D13	0240
SF5D41	0500
SF5E11	OEM
SF5F11	2635
SF5F12	0671
SF5G11	0671
SF5G12	0671
SF5G13	0671
SF5G41	0705
SF5GN315	OEM
SF5GR315	OEM
SF5GR316	OEM
SF5H11	OEM
SF5HN315	OEM
SF5HR315	OEM
SF5HR316	OEM
SF5J11	0332
SF5J12	0332
SF5J13	0332
SF5J41	0857
SF5Z11	1095
SF6	0071
SF6AN6	OEM
SF6AN12	OEM
SF6AR6	OEM
SF6AR12	OEM
SF6GN315	OEM
SF6GR64	OEM
SF6GR316	OEM
SF6HN315	OEM
SF6HR316	OEM
SF7AN126	OEM
SF7BR64	OEM
SF7C325	OEM
SF7GN315	OEM
SF7GR64	OEM
SF7GR315	OEM
SF7GR316	OEM
SF7HN315	OEM
SF7HR315	OEM
SF7HR316	OEM
SF8	OEM
SF8B41	2078
SF8D41	0500
SF8G41	0705
SF8GN315	OEM
SF8GR316	OEM
SF8HN315	OEM
SF8HR316	OEM
SF8J41	0857
SF9AN126	OEM
SF9BR64	OEM
SF9C325	OEM
SF9GN315	OEM
SF9GR64	OEM
SF9GR315	OEM
SF9GR316	OEM
SF9HN315	OEM
SF9HR315	OEM
SF9HR316	OEM
SF10	OEM
SF10A11	2497
SF10B11	0736
SF10B12	0562
SF10B13	0736
SF10C11	0740
SF10D11	0740
SF10D12	0757
SF10D13	0740
SF10E11	0742
SF10F11	2889
SF10G11	0742
SF10G12	0735
SF10GN315	OEM
SF10GZ47	3852
SF10H11	0747
SF10HN315	OEM
SF10J11	0759
SF10J12	0759
SF10JZ47	3852
SF10L11	0761
SF10L12	0761
SF10N11	OEM
SF10N12	OEM
SF10Z11	2497
SF11	1082
SF11AN126	OEM
SF11BR64	OEM
SF11C325	OEM
SF11GN315	OEM
SF11GR64	OEM
SF11GR315	OEM
SF11GR316	OEM
SF11HN315	OEM
SF11HR315	OEM
SF11HR316	OEM
SF12	1082
SF12GN315	OEM
SF12HN315	OEM
SF13	1082
SF13GR316	OEM
SF13HR316	OEM
SF14	1082
SF15GR316	OEM
SF15HR316	OEM
SF16A11	2174
SF16B11	0562
SF16B12	0562
SF16B13	0562
SF16B14	0562
SF16C11	0757
SF16D11	0757
SF16D12	0442
SF16D13	0757
SF16D14	0393
SF16E11	0757
SF16F11	3240
SF16F12	0735
SF16G11	0735
SF16G12	0735
SF16G13	0735
SF16G14	0606
SF16J11	0759
SF16J12	0735
SF16J13	0759
SF16L11	0761
SF16L12	0761
SF16L13	0761
SF16N11	OEM
SF16N12	OEM
SF16Q12	OEM
SF16R11	OEM
SF16Z11	2174
SF17GR316	OEM
SF17HR316	OEM
SF22	0541
SF23	0541
SF24	0541
SF30	OEM
SF30D11	OEM
SF30F11	OEM
SF30G11	OEM
SF30J11	OEM
SF30L11	OEM
SF30N11	OEM
SF31	0541
SF32	0541
SF33	0541
SF34	0541
SF35	1352
SF36	1352
SF47C	OEM
SF50	OEM
SF50D11	OEM
SF50G11	OEM
SF50J11	OEM
SF50L11	OEM
SF50N11	OEM
SF50R11	OEM
SF51	1356
SF52	1356
SF53	1356
SF54	1356
SF55	1356
SF56	1356
SF60	OEM
SF61	OEM
SF62	OEM
SF63	OEM
SF80	OEM
SF80D15	0603
SF80G15	0605
SF80L13	0463
SF80N13	0463
SF80Q13	0463
SF81	1119
SF81R	OEM
SF82	1119
SF82R	OEM
SF83	1119
SF83R	OEM
SF84	1119
SF84R	OEM
SF85	4104
SF85R	OEM
SF86	4104
SF86R	OEM
SF91	OEM
SF93	OEM
SF100	OEM

If replacement code is OEM, contact original manufacturer for replacement. 551

DEVICE TYPE	REPL CODE
SF100G21	0159
SF100J21	0159
SF100Q21	0096
SF101	OEM
SF102	OEM
SF103	OEM
SF110	OEM
SF111	OEM
SF112	OEM
SF113	OEM
SF115	0224
SF115A	0224
SF115B	0224
SF115C	0224
SF115D	0224
SF115E	0224
SF120	OEM
SF121	OEM
SF122	OEM
SF123	OEM
SF130	OEM
SF131	OEM
SF132	OEM
SF133	OEM
SF150G15	1078
SF150J15	1078
SF150L13	1094
SF150N13	1094
SF150Q13	1094
SF161A	0896
SF161C	0903
SF161D	OEM
SF162A	0896
SF162C	OEM
SF162D	OEM
SF163A	0896
SF163C	0903
SF163D	OEM
SF164A	0896
SF164C	0903
SF164D	OEM
SF165A	OEM
SF165C	0966
SF165D	OEM
SF166A	OEM
SF166C	0966
SF166D	OEM
SF167	0007
SF173	0007
SF194	0007
SF194B	0007
SF195	0007
SF195C	0007
SF195D	0007
SF196	0007
SF197	0007
SF200	OEM
SF201	OEM
SF202	OEM
SF203	OEM
SF210	OEM
SF211	OEM
SF212	OEM
SF213	OEM
SF251	0410
SF280	OEM
SF281	OEM
SF282	OEM
SF283	OEM
SF294	0007
SF294B	0007
SF295	0007
SF295C	0007
SF295D	0007
SF300G15	1889
SF300J15	1889
SF300L13	0733
SF300N13	0733
SF300Q13	0733
SF301A	OEM
SF301C	2259
SF301D	OEM
SF302A	OEM
SF302C	2259
SF302D	OEM
SF303A	OEM
SF303C	2259
SF303D	OEM
SF304A	OEM
SF304C	2259
SF304D	OEM
SF310	0007
SF313	OEM
SF314	0007
SF334	0007
SF334B	0007
SF335	0007
SF335C	0007
SF335D	0007
SF500EX22	OEM
SF500U22	OEM
SF500Y22	OEM
SF703SF	0239
SF800J22	OEM
SF800J25	4085
SF800L21	OEM
SF800L22	OEM
SF800L25	1714
SF800N21	OEM
SF800N22	OEM
SF800N25	1714
SF800R21	OEM
SF800R22	OEM
SF1001	0016
SF1220	OEM
SF1713	0016
SF1714	0016
SF1726	0016
SF1730	0016
SF12412	OEM
SF12413	OEM
SFB8970	0212
SFC400E	0232
SFC401E	0268
SFC402E	0310
SFC408E	0462
SFC409E	0487
SFC420E	0692
SFC426E	0798
SFC430E	0867
SFC437E	3478
SFC438E	0990
SFC440E	1018
SFC442E	1046
SFC450E	0738
SFC451E	1160
SFC453E	1177
SFC454E	1193
SFC460E	1265
SFC472E	1417
SFC473E	1164
SFC474E	1303
SFC475E	1423
SFC476E	1150
SFC485E	0370
SFC486E	1358
SFC492E	0828
SFC899S	0212
SFC-1616	0212
SFC-1617	0212
SFC2109RM	1905
SFC2209R	1905
SFC2301A	0093
SFC2309R	1905
SFC2458DC	0356
SFC2709C	1291
SFC2710C	1786
SFC2711C	1879
SFC2741C	0406
SFC2748C	0093
SFC2748M	0093
SFC2805EC	0619
SFC2805RC	1911
SFC2806EC	0917
SFC2808EC	1187
SFC2812EC	0330
SFC2812RC	3359
SFC2815EC	1311
SFC2824EC	2224
SFC3012	0007
SFC3020	0007
SFC4050	2016
SFC4052	2016
SFC4107E	0936
SFC4121E	0175
SFC4122E	1131
SFC4123E	1149
SFC4141E	1367
SFC4155E	1566
SFC4156E	1582
SFC4180E	1818
SFC4181E	1831
SFC4182E	1845
SFC4192E	1910
SFC4193E	1915
SFC6050	0618
SFC8544	OEM
SFC8999	0212
SFD037A	0019
SFD12	0143
SFD43	0133
SFD46	0133
SFD48	0133
SFD79	0133
SFD83	0133
SFD102	OEM
SFD103	0143
SFD104	0019
SFD107	0143
SFD111	0143
SFD112	0143
SFD161	OEM
SFD162	OEM
SFD163	OEM
SFD164	0133
SFD165	OEM
SFD166	OEM
SFD180	0133
SFD181	0133
SFD182	0124
SFD400B	OEM
SFD400E	OEM
SFD400F	OEM
SFD400G	OEM
SFD400H	OEM
SFD401E	OEM
SFD401F	OEM
SFD401G	OEM
SFD401H	OEM
SFD401K	OEM
SFD402E	OEM
SFD402F	OEM
SFD402G	OEM
SFD402H	OEM
SFD410E	OEM
SFD410F	OEM
SFD410G	OEM
SFD410H	OEM
SFD411B	OEM
SFD411E	OEM
SFD411F	OEM
SFD411G	OEM
SFD411H	OEM
SFD412E	OEM
SFD412F	OEM
SFD412G	OEM
SFD412H	OEM
SFD420C	OEM
SFD420D	OEM
SFD420E	OEM
SFD420F	OEM
SFD421C	OEM
SFD421D	OEM
SFD421E	OEM
SFD421F	OEM
SFD421G	OEM
SFD422C	OEM
SFD422D	OEM
SFD422E	OEM
SFD422F	OEM
SFD422G	OEM
SFD423C	OEM
SFD423D	OEM
SFD423E	OEM
SFD423F	OEM
SFD430A	OEM
SFD430B	OEM
SFD430C	OEM
SFD430D	OEM
SFD431A	OEM
SFD431B	OEM
SFD431C	OEM
SFD431D	OEM
SFD432A	OEM
SFD432B	OEM
SFD432C	OEM
SFD432D	OEM
SFD433A	OEM
SFD433B	OEM
SFD433C	OEM
SFD433D	OEM
SFD440A	OEM
SFD441A	OEM
SFD450A	OEM
SFD460	OEM
SFD2285	0212
SFD4160	OEM
SFD4161	OEM
SFD4162	OEM
SFD4163	OEM
SFD4164	OEM
SFD4165	OEM
SFD4166	OEM
SFE145	0321
SFE253	0212
SFE303	0349
SFE425	1441
SFE427	0212
SFE303424	0212
SFF103	OEM
SFF121	OEM
SFH205	OEM
SFIR3B41	0442
SFIR3D41	0934
SFM10	OEM
SFM15	OEM
SFM20	OEM
SFM25	OEM
SFOR1A41	0895
SFOR1B41	0895
SFOR1B42	4790
SFOR1B42(IG1)	0895
SFOR1B421G1	OEM
SFOR2B41	0895
SFOR2D41	0058
SFOR2G2	OEM
SFOR2G41	0403
SFOR3G42	6911
SFOR3G42-IG5	OEM
SFOR3G42IG5	0403
SFOR3J42	OEM
SFORIB42IG1	OEM
SFPB-54VL	OEM
SFPB54VL	OEM
SFPM-52V	OEM
SFPM52V	OEM
SFR135	0015
SFR135/2	OEM
SFR151	0015
SFR152	0015
SFR153	0015
SFR154	0015
SFR155	0015
SFR156	0015
SFR164	0015
SFR251	0015
SFR252	0015
SFR253	0015
SFR254	0015
SFR255	0015
SFR256	0015
SFR258	0071
SFR264	0015
SFR266	0015
SFR268	0071
SFT104	0143
SFT106	OEM
SFT107	OEM
SFT108	0143
SFT113	OEM
SFT114	OEM
SFT115	OEM
SFT120	0050
SFT121	0164
SFT122	0164
SFT123	0164
SFT124	0164
SFT125	0164
SFT125P	0164
SFT126	OEM
SFT127	OEM
SFT128	OEM
SFT130	0164
SFT131	0164
SFT131P	0164
SFT135	OEM
SFT136	OEM
SFT141	OEM
SFT142	OEM
SFT143	0164
SFT144	0164
SFT145	0164
SFT146	0164
SFT150	OEM
SFT151	0004
SFT152	0004
SFT153	OEM
SFT155	OEM
SFT162	0050
SFT163	0050
SFT171	0050
SFT172	0050
SFT173	0050
SFT174	0050
SFT184	0595
SFT185	OEM
SFT186	0233
SFT187	0233
SFT190	0160
SFT191	0160
SFT192	0160
SFT211	OEM
SFT212	0160
SFT213	0160
SFT214	0160
SFT220	OEM
SFT221	0211
SFT221A	0004
SFT222	0211
SFT223	0279
SFT226	0279
SFT227	0279
SFT228	0279
SFT229	0279
SFT232	0004
SFT233	OEM
SFT234	OEM
SFT235	OEM
SFT237	0279
SFT238	0160
SFT239	0160
SFT240	0160
SFT241	0164
SFT242	0164
SFT243	0164
SFT244	OEM
SFT245	OEM
SFT250	0160
SFT251	0279
SFT252	0279
SFT253	0279
SFT259	0595
SFT260	0595
SFT261	0595
SFT264	0435
SFT265	0435
SFT266	0435
SFT267	0435
SFT268	0050
SFT288	0279
SFT298	0595
SFT306	0004
SFT307	0136
SFT308	0136
SFT315	0050
SFT316	0050
SFT317	0136
SFT318	0136
SFT319	0136
SFT320	0136
SFT321	0004
SFT322	0004
SFT323	0004
SFT325	0164
SFT327	0004
SFT337	0004
SFT337B	0004
SFT337V	0004
SFT351	0004
SFT352	0004
SFT353	0004
SFT354	0136
SFT357	0136
SFT357P	0136
SFT358	0050
SFT367	0164
SFT377	0208
SFT440	0086
SFT443	0086
SFT443A	0086
SFT445	0086
SFT523	0164
SFT526	0004
SFT601	OEM
SFT602	OEM
SFT603	OEM
SFT604	OEM
SFT713	0016
SFT714	0016
SFT714A	OEM
SFT715	OEM
SFT715A	OEM
SFT918	OEM
SFT918B	OEM
SFTAN6	OEM
SFZ708	0157
SFZ716	0052
SFZ720	OEM
SFZ722	OEM
SF.T124	0164
SF.T125	0004
SF.T125P	0164
SF.T130	0164
SF.T131	0004
SF.T131P	0164
SF.T163	0050
SF.T171	0279
SF.T172	0279
SF.T173	0279
SF.T174	0279
SF.T184	0595
SF.T186	0233
SF.T187	0283
SF.T191	0085
SF.T212	0969
SF.T213	0969
SF.T214	0969
SF.T221	0164
SF.T222	0211
SF.T223	0164
SF.T227	0211
SF.T228	0279
SF.T237	0004
SF.T238	0969
SF.T239	0969
SF.T240	0969
SF.T250	0969
SF.T251	0004
SF.T252	0004
SF.T253	0004
SF.T264	0435
SF.T265	0435
SF.T266	0435
SF.T306	0004
SF.T307	0136
SF.T315	0050
SF.T316	0050
SF.T317	0050
SF.T318	0211
SF.T319	0050
SF.T320	0050
SF.T321	0164
SF.T322	0164
SF.T323	0004
SF.T337	0004
SF.T351	0164
SF.T352	0164
SF.T353	0841
SF.T354	0050
SF.T357	0050
SF.T358	0050
SF.T377	0208
SF.T440	0590
SF.T443	0590
SF.T443A	0590
SF.T445	0590
SF.T714	0590
SG	OEM
SG-005	0015
SG005	0535
SG011	OEM
SG-2BC	OEM
SG-5(-)	OEM
SG-5(+)	OEM
SG-5AR	OEM
SG-5AS	OEM
SG-5BR	OEM
SG-5BS	OEM
SG-5F	OEM
SG5F	OEM
SG-5FR	OEM
SG-5FS	OEM
SG-5L(-)	OEM
SG-5L(+)	OEM
SG-5N	0087
SG-5P	0087
SG-5T	0015
SG-5T(-)	OEM
SG-5T(+)	OEM
SG-6(-)	OEM
SG-6(+)	OEM
SG-6AR	OEM
SG-6AS	OEM
SG-6BR	OEM
SG-6BS	OEM
SG-6LR	OEM
SG-6LS	OEM
SG16H11	OEM
SG-21R	OEM
SG-21S	OEM
SG-22R	OEM
SG-22S	OEM
SG-23R	OEM
SG-23S	OEM
SG40	OEM
SG41	OEM
SG42	OEM
SG43	OEM
SG50	OEM
SG51	OEM
SG52	OEM
SG53	OEM
SG-53R	OEM
SG-53S	OEM
SG-56R	OEM
SG-56S	OEM
SG60	OEM
SG61	OEM
SG62	OEM
SG63	OEM
SG-63R	OEM
SG-66R	OEM
SG-66S	OEM
SG70	OEM
SG71	OEM
SG72	OEM
SG73	OEM
SG90	OEM
SG91	OEM
SG92	OEM
SG93	OEM
SG100	OEM
SG101	OEM
SG102	OEM
SG103	OEM
SG-105	0015
SG105	0023
SG110	OEM
SG111	OEM
SG112	OEM
SG113	OEM
SG120	OEM
SG121	OEM
SG122	OEM
SG123	0655
SG130	OEM
SG131	OEM
SG132	OEM
SG133	OEM
SG140	OEM
SG141	OEM
SG142	OEM
SG143	OEM
SG150	OEM
SG151	OEM
SG152	OEM
SG153	OEM
SG160	OEM
SG161	OEM
SG162	OEM
SG163	OEM
SG170	OEM
SG171	OEM
SG172	OEM
SG173	OEM
SG180	OEM
SG181	OEM
SG182	OEM
SG183	OEM
SG190	OEM
SG191	OEM
SG192	OEM
SG193	OEM
SG200	OEM
SG201	OEM
SG201AT	0093
SG202	OEM
SG203	OEM
SG-205	0015
SG205	0242
SG210	OEM
SG211	OEM
SG212	OEM
SG213	OEM
SG213T	OEM
SG220	OEM
SG221	OEM
SG222	OEM
SG223	0655
SG224J	0620
SG224N	0620
SG230	OEM
SG231	OEM
SG232	OEM
SG233	OEM
SG240	OEM
SG240D	OEM
SG241	OEM
SG242	OEM
SG243	OEM
SG250	OEM
SG251	OEM
SG252	OEM
SG253	OEM
SG260	OEM
SG261	OEM
SG262	OEM
SG263	OEM
SG-264A	1642
SG264A	1642
SG270	OEM
SG271	OEM
SG272	OEM
SG273	OEM
SG290	OEM
SG291	OEM
SG292	OEM
SG293	OEM
SG300	OEM
SG301	OEM
SG301AM	1290
SG301AT	0093
SG302	OEM
SG303	OEM
SG-305	0015
SG305	0535
SG308AM	2231
SG308AT	0890
SG308AY	2231
SG308M	2231
SG308T	0890
SG308Y	2231
SG309K	1911
SG310	OEM
SG310M	2495
SG310T	2207
SG311	OEM
SG312	OEM
SG313	OEM
SG320	OEM
SG321	OEM
SG322	OEM
SG323	0015
SG323K	1905
SG324N	0620
SG330	OEM
SG331	OEM
SG332	OEM
SG333	OEM
SG340	OEM
SG340-05K	1905
SG340-12K	3359
SG341	OEM
SG342	OEM
SG343	OEM
SG351	OEM
SG353	OEM
SG370	OEM
SG371	OEM
SG372	OEM
SG373	OEM
SG380	OEM
SG381	OEM
SG382	OEM
SG383	OEM
SG505	0015
SG555CM	0967
SG555M	0967
SG-608	OEM
SG609	2321
SG609-3	2321
SG613	1642
SG613-A	OEM
SG710CN	1789
SG710CT	1786
SG711CN	1886
SG711CT	1879
SG723CN	0026
SG723CT	1183
SG723T	1183
SG733CJ	1110
SG733CT	1110
SG741CM	0308
SG741CN	1964
SG741CT	0406
SG741SCT	0406
SG747CT	2352
SG-805	0015
SG805	0811
SG-870	OEM
SG1009	0586
SG1009/F	0586
SG1009A	0586
SG1009A/F	0586
SG1010	0586
SG1010/F	0586
SG1010A	0586
SG1010A/F	0586
SG-1198	0015
SG1198	0015
SG1458M	0356
SG1488J	0503
SG1489J	0506

If replacement code is OEM, contact original manufacturer for replacement.

DEVICE TYPE	REPL CODE
SG1495N	OEM
SG1496	0413
SG1496T	0413
SG1691	OEM
SG1910	OEM
SG1911	OEM
SG1912	OEM
SG1920	OEM
SG1921	OEM
SG1922	OEM
SG1930	OEM
SG1931	OEM
SG1932	OEM
SG1940	OEM
SG1941	OEM
SG1942	OEM
SG2182	2839
SG2183	2839
SG3081N	2722
SG3400	0015
SG3524	5140
SG3524N	OEM
SG3525A	2802
SG3526N	2814
SG3527A	2812
SG5000	OEM
SG5009	0133
SG5013	0086
SG5018	OEM
SG5100	OEM
SG5200	OEM
SG5250	OEM
SG5260	OEM
SG5270	OEM
SG5300	OEM
SG5400	0133
SG5717	0133
SG5777	OEM
SG5800	OEM
SG5811	OEM
SG6476	OEM
SG7400N	0232
SG7402N	0310
SG7410N	0507
SG7420N	0692
SG7430N	0867
SG7440N	1018
SG7450N	0738
SG7451N	1160
SG7453N	1177
SG7454N	1193
SG7460N	1265
SG7812	0330
SG7812CK	3359
SG7812T	1817
SG7815T	3361
SG7818ACP	2244
SG7818CK	3605
SG7818CP	2244
SG7824CK	3828
SG7908ACP	2764
SG7908CP	2764
SG7918ACP	3774
SG7918CK	5196
SG7918CP	0023
SG9012I	0037
SG9072	OEM
SG-9150	0133
SG9150	0133
SG9600	OEM
SGA-2	OEM
SGA-2CN	OEM
SGA-2CP	OEM
SGA-4	OEM
SGA-4CN	OEM
SGA-4CP	OEM
SGA-5	OEM
SGA-5CN	OEM
SGA-5CP	OEM
SGB-2	OEM
SGB-2CN	OEM
SGB-2CP	OEM
SGB-4	OEM
SGB-4CN	OEM
SGB-4CP	OEM
SGB-5	OEM
SGB-5CN	OEM
SGB-5CP	OEM
SGB-8CN	OEM
SGB-8CP	OEM
SGB-9742	0144
SGC-7202	0079
SGC7202	0086
SGF-2	OEM
SGF-4	OEM
SGF-5	OEM
SGI5001	0031
SGI5002	0031
SGI5003	0031
SGI5004	0031
SGI5301	OEM
SGI5302	OEM
SGI5303	OEM
SGI5304	OEM
SGI5401	1137
SGI5401C	1227
SGI5401CR	1716
SGI5401R	OEM
SGI5402	1137
SGI5402C	1227
SGI5402CR	1716
SGI5402R	OEM
SGI5403	1137
SGI5403C	1227
SGI5403CR	1716
SGI5403R	OEM
SGI5404	1137
SGI5404C	1227
SGI5404CR	1716
SGI5404R	OEM
SGI5601C	OEM
SGI5601CR	OEM
SGI5602C	OEM
SGI5602CR	OEM
SGI5603C	OEM
SGI5603CR	OEM
SGI5604C	OEM
SGI5604CR	OEM
SGM-12R	OEM
SGM-12S	OEM
SGM-13	OEM
SGM-22	OEM
SGM-52	OEM
SGM-53	OEM
SGM-54	OEM
SGM182BL	OEM
SGR100	0015
SGS1	OEM
SGS17139XRH	2145
SGS87231	0007
SGSIF461	3468
SGT03U13	OEM
SGT06U13	OEM
SGT10S10	OEM
SGT23B13	OEM
SGT23U13	OEM
SH-1	0023
SH1	0015
SH-1A	0023
SH1A	0015
SH-1B	0017
SH1B	0071
SH1B42	OEM
SH-1C	0017
SH1C	0071
SH-1D	0017
SH-1DE	0015
SH1DE	0015
SH-1E	0017
SH-1S	0015
SH1S	0242
SH-1Z	0023
SH4D05	0015
SH4D1	0015
SH4D2	0015
SH4D3	0015
SH4D4	0015
SH4D5	OEM
SH4D6	0015
SH4D8	0071
SH5A	OEM
SH5B11	0404
SH5B12	OEM
SH5D11	OEM
SH5D12	OEM
SH5F11	0418
SH5F12	OEM
SH5G11	0418
SH5G12	OEM
SH5H11	0418
SH5H12	OEM
SH5J11	0418
SH5J12	OEM
SH-6K	0201
SH6K	OEM
SH-8K	0201
SH8K	OEM
SH-10K	0201
SH10K	OEM
SH-12K	0201
SH12K	OEM
SH15	0015
SH16B11	3119
SH16B12	OEM
SH16D11	3121
SH16D12	OEM
SH16F11	3122
SH16F12	OEM
SH16G11	3123
SH16G12	OEM
SH16H11	3124
SH16H12	OEM
SH16J11	2007
SH16J12	OEM
SH80U12A	OEM
SH200	1325
SH200A	1325
SH202	0133
SH202A	0133
SH212	0133
SH212A	0133
SH222	0133
SH222A	0133
SH242	0133
SH242A	0133
SH252	0133
SH252A	0133
SH300	0133
SH300A	0133
SH301	0133
SH301A	0133
SH302	0133
SH302A	0133
SH323SC	1905
SH400L21	OEM
SH400N21	OEM
SH400R21	OEM
SH400U23	OEM
SH1064	0016
SH5000	OEM
SH7500	OEM
SH10000	OEM
SH12500	OEM
SH15000	OEM
SH20000	OEM
SH25000	OEM
SH764059	OEM
SH779567	OEM
SHA7520	0786
SHA7521	0786
SHA7522	0786
SHA7523	0786
SHA7524	0786
SHA7526	0786
SHA7527	0786
SHA7528	0786
SHA7530	0037
SHA7531	0037
SHA7532	0037
SHA7533	0037
SHA7534	0037
SHA7535	0338
SHA7536	0037
SHA7537	0037
SHA7538	0037
SHA7539	0338
SHA7597	0786
SHA7598	0786
SHA7599	0786
SHAD-1	0015
SHF5000	OEM
SHF7500	OEM
SHF10000	OEM
SHF12500	OEM
SHF15000	OEM
SHF20000	OEM
SHF25000	OEM
SHOR3D42	OEM
SHV-03	OEM
SHV-06	OEM
SHV-06UN	OEM
SHV-08	OEM
SHV-08UN	OEM
SHV-10	OEM
SHV-12	OEM
SHV-12U	OEM
SHV-16	OEM
SHV-16U	OEM
SHV-20	OEM
SHV-24	OEM
SHVF2500	OEM
SHVF5000	OEM
SHVF7500	OEM
SHVF10000	OEM
SHVF12500	OEM
SHVF15000	OEM
SHVF20000	OEM
SHVF25000	OEM
SI03E	OEM
SI03K	OEM
SI03L	OEM
SI03N	OEM
SI05	0110
SI-05A	0071
SI05A	0110
SI0V-S05K150	0246
SI1	0947
SI-1A	0071
SI1A	0242
SI1SS54	0133
SI2	0242
SI-2A	0071
SI2A	OEM
SI3	0535
SI-3A	0071
SI3A	OEM
SI4	0535
SI-4A	0071
SI4A	OEM
SI5	0959
SI-5A	0071
SI5A	OEM
SI6	0959
SI-6A	0071
SI6A	OEM
SI7	0811
SI-7A	0071
SI7A	OEM
SI8	0811
SI-8A	0071
SI8A	0087
SI9	0916
SI10	0916
SI-10A	0071
SI10A	0087
SI11E	OEM
SI11K	OEM
SI11L	OEM
SI11N	OEM
SI12	OEM
SI12A	OEM
SI15	OEM
SI21E	OEM
SI21K	OEM
SI21L	OEM
SI21N	OEM
SI50E	0015
SI61E	OEM
SI61K	OEM
SI61L	OEM
SI61N	OEM
SI91E	OEM
SI91G	0015
SI91K	OEM
SI91L	OEM
SI91N	OEM
SI100E	0015
SI-154	0023
SI211N	OEM
SI212N	OEM
SI213N	OEM
SI214N	OEM
SI215N	OEM
SI216N	OEM
SI221N	OEM
SI222N	OEM
SI223N	OEM
SI224N	OEM
SI225N	OEM
SI226N	OEM
SI231N	OEM
SI232N	OEM
SI233N	OEM
SI234N	OEM
SI235N	OEM
SI236N	OEM
SI244N	OEM
SI245N	OEM
SI246N	OEM
SI250P12K38	OEM
SI250P14K38	OEM
SI250P16K38	OEM
SI250P20K38	OEM
SI300P10K35	OEM
SI300P12K35	OEM
SI300P14K35	OEM
SI300P16K35	OEM
SI300P16K44	OEM
SI300P18K35	OEM
SI300P18K44	OEM
SI300P20K35	OEM
SI300P20K44	OEM
SI300P22K44	OEM
SI300P26K44	OEM
SI300P28K44	OEM
SI300P30K44	OEM
SI341P	0150
SI342P	0150
SI343P	0150
SI345P	OEM
SI346P	OEM
SI351P	0150
SI352P	0150
SI353P	0150
SI-600	0299
SI1000E	0071
SI-1002	0023
SI-1006	0023
SI-1014	0023
SI-1019	0344
SI-1020	0023
SI-1021	0023
SI-1030	0015
SI-3052P	6394
SI-3052V	2517
SI3052V	2517
SI-3122P	4264
SI-3122V	4264
SI-3152P	6482
SI-3152V	OEM
SI-3242P	6570
SI4101	OEM
SI-4102	5183
SI4102	3001
SI-6102	OEM
SI-6901	OEM
SI-6901A	OEM
SI-7115B	2893
SI7115B	2893
SI-7200E	OEM
SI-7200M	OEM
SI-7230E	OEM
SI-7230M	OEM
SI-7300A	OEM
SI-7301A	OEM
SI-7330A	OEM
SI-7500A	OEM
SIB01	0015
SIB01-01	0023
SIB01-01V	4333
SIB01-01W	0023
SIB-01-02	0015
SIB01-02	0080
SIB01-02TP1	0604
SIB01-02U	0604
SIB01-02VI	0604
SIB01-04	0023
SIB01-04VI	0959
SIB01-06	0023
SIB01-06B	OEM
SIB-01-022	0015
SIB01-022	0015
SIB01-2	0023
SIB02-03C	0015
SIB02-03CR	0015
SIB02-CR	0023
SIB02-CR1	0907
SIB03-08	0071
SIB03-10	0071
SIB03-12	0102
SIB020-1B	0276
SIB0101	4333
SIB0102	0015
SIB-0306	0071
SIB0306	0071
SIB0L-02	0015
SIB1	0015
SIB50B794-1	0276
SIB1014D	OEM
SIB01	OEM
SI-CA3064E	0797
SI-CA3065E	0167
SICGJ-1	0344
SICT-5	6739
SICT-8	OEM
SICT-10	OEM
SICT-12	OEM
SICT-15	6483
SICT-18	OEM
SICT-22	6495
SICT-36	OEM
SICT-45	OEM
SICTE-5	OEM
SICTE-8	OEM
SICTE-10	OEM
SICTE-12	OEM
SICTE-15	OEM
SICTE-18	OEM
SICTE-22	OEM
SICTE-36	OEM
SICTE-45	OEM
SID01-01	0529
SID01-02	0015
SID01-03	0533
SID01-06	0540
SID01-09	0545
SID01-12	OEM
SID01E	0015
SID01K	0071
SID01L	0015
SID01N	OEM
SID02E	0015
SID02K	0071
SID02L	0015
SID02N	OEM
SID03E	OEM
SID03K	OEM
SID03L	OEM
SID03N	OEM
SID2A-1	0196
SID2A1	OEM
SID2A2	OEM
SID2A-3	0196
SID2A3	OEM
SID2A4	OEM
SID2A6	OEM
SID2A11	OEM
SID2A12	OEM
SID2A13	OEM
SID2A14	OEM
SID2A16	OEM
SID2B1	OEM
SID2B2	OEM
SID2B3	OEM
SID2B11	OEM
SID2B12	OEM
SID2B13	OEM
SID3A1	OEM
SID3A2	OEM
SID3A3	OEM
SID3A4	OEM
SID3A6	OEM
SID3B1	OEM
SID3B2	OEM
SID3B-3	1073
SID3B3	OEM
SID20E	OEM
SID20K	OEM
SID20L	OEM
SID20N	OEM
SID23-13	0102
SID23-15	0102
SID26-12	0102
SID26-15	0102
SID30-1	0102
SID30-13	0182
SID30-15	5104
SID50B851	0133
SID51C052-19	0087
SID51C169	0015
SID300P16K44	OEM
SID300P18K44	OEM
SID300P20K44	OEM
SID300P22K44	OEM
SID300P24K44	OEM
SID300P26K44	OEM
SID300P28K44	OEM
SID300P30K44	OEM
SID500P40K62	OEM
SID500P42K62	OEM
SID500P44K62	OEM
SID500P46K62	OEM
SID500P48K62	OEM
SID500P50K62	OEM
SID500P52K62	OEM
SID500P54K62	OEM
SID500P56K62	OEM
SID500P58K62	OEM
SID50894	0133
SID51169-2	OEM
SIDA02K	OEM
SIDA02N	OEM
SIDA02P	OEM
SIDA0.5K	0959
SIDA0.5N	0811
SIDA0.5P	0916
SIE01-01	0865
SIE01-03	0847
SIE01-06	0267
SIE01-09	0280
SIE01-12	OEM
SIE03-30	OEM
SIF4	0023
SIF14A-P	0015
SIF114E	0102
SIFN270	OEM
SIG01-01	0254
SIG01-03	0258
SIG01-06	0267
SIG01-09	0280
SIG01-12	OEM
SIG03-30	OEM
SIG1/100	0242
SIG1/200	0242
SIG1/400	0015
SIG1/600	0015
SIG1/800	0811
SIG300P10K35	OEM
SIG300P12K35	OEM
SIG300P14K35	OEM
SIG300P16K35	OEM
SIG300P18K35	OEM
SIH31-01	1337
SIH31-01R	0594
SIH31-03	1337
SIH31-03R	0594
SIH31-06	1894
SIH31-06R	1975
SIH31-10	0193
SIH31-10R	0652
SIH31-12	0202
SIH31-12R	3277
SI-HA11580	1049
SIIR3N05XXXXX	6629
SIIR3N06XXXXX	OEM
SIL	0071
SIL1	OEM
SIL31-01	0496
SIL31-01R	1017
SIL31-03	0496
SIL31-03R	1017
SIL31-06	1766
SIL31-06R	1030
SIL31-10	1778
SIL31-10R	1040
SIL31-12	3138
SIL31-12R	6724
SIL200	0015
SILC4001BXXXX	0473
SILC4069UBXXX	0119
SI-LM3065N	0167
SILM8560BXXXX	5935
SIM2	OEM
SIM3	OEM
SIM5	OEM
SIM6	OEM
SIM8	OEM
SIM9	OEM
SIM-20ST	OEM
SI-MC1352P	0391
SI-MC1358P	0167
SI-MC1362P	OEM
SI-MC1364P	0797
SIN01-12	4221
SIN01-12R	4222
SIN03-30	OEM
SIOV-S05K150	OEM
SIPI8.4	OEM
SIPI-24	OEM
SIPI30	OEM
SIPI60	OEM
SIPI120	OEM
SIPI208	OEM
SIPI250	OEM
SIPI440	OEM
SIPI500	OEM
SIPS08	1837
SIPS010	1837
SIPS020	1837
SIPS025	1837
SIPS030	OEM
SIPS035	1837
SIPS18	1837
SIPS28	1837
SIPS38	1844
SIPS48	1844
SIPS58	3185
SIPS68	3185
SIPS110	1837
SIPS120	1837
SIPS125	1837
SIPS130	OEM
SIPS135	1837
SIPS210	1837
SIPS220	1837
SIPS225	1837
SIPS230	OEM
SIPS235	1837
SIPS310	1844
SIPS320	1844
SIPS325	1844
SIPS330	OEM
SIPS335	1844
SIPS410	1844
SIPS420	1844
SIPS425	1844
SIPS430	OEM
SIPS435	1844
SIPS510	3185
SIPS520	3185
SIPS525	3185
SIPS530	OEM
SIPS535	3185
SIPS610	3185
SIPS620	3185
SIPS625	3185
SIPS630	OEM
SIPS635	3185
SIPT06	3169
SIPT08	3169
SIPT010	3169
SIPT015	3169
SIPT025	3169
SIPT030	3169
SIPT040	3169
SIPT16	3169
SIPT18	3169
SIPT26	3169
SIPT28	3169
SIPT36	3177
SIPT38	3177
SIPT46	3177
SIPT48	3177
SIPT56	3192
SIPT58	3192
SIPT66	3192
SIPT68	3192
SIPT110	3169
SIPT115	3169
SIPT125	3169
SIPT130	3169
SIPT140	3169
SIPT210	3169
SIPT215	3169
SIPT225	3169
SIPT230	3169
SIPT240	3169
SIPT310	3177
SIPT315	3177
SIPT325	3177
SIPT330	3177
SIPT340	3177
SIPT410	3177
SIPT415	3177
SIPT425	3177
SIPT430	3177
SIPT440	3177
SIPT510	3192
SIPT515	3192
SIPT525	3192
SIPT530	3192
SIPT540	3192
SIPT610	3192
SIPT615	3192
SIPT625	3192
SIPT630	3192
SIPT640	3192
SIR20	0015
SIR-34ST3	OEM
SIR-56ST3	OEM
SIR60	0023
SIR-80	0015
SIR80	0023
SIR150	0102
SIR-562ST	OEM
SIRB-10	0276
SIRB10	0087
SIRBA00	0106
SIRBA10	0106
SI-REC-73	0015
SI-RECT-044	0015
SI-RECT-2	0015
SIRECT-2	0015
SI-RECT-20	0015
SI-RECT-23	0030
SI-RECT-25	0015
SI-RECT-27	0015
SI-RECT-33	0015
SI-RECT-34	0015
SI-RECT-35	0133
SI-RECT-36	0102
SIRECT-36	0015

If replacement code is OEM, contact original manufacturer for replacement. 553

DEVICE TYPE	REPL CODE	DEVICE TYPE	REPL CODE	DEVICE TYPE	REPL CODE	DEVICE TYPE	REPL CODE	DEVICE TYPE	REPL CODE	DEVICE TYPE	REPL CODE	DEVICE TYPE	REPL CODE
SI-RECT-37	0015	SIT95-500	OEM	SJ820	0103	SJE403	0455	SK7C02	1443	SK7C4046A	5061	SK7CT365	6658
SI-RECT-39	0015	SIT95-600	OEM	SJ821	0486	SJE404	0161	SK7C03	1444	SK7C4049	5441	SK7CT366	6661
SI-RECT-44	0102	SIT180-50	OEM	SJ822	0899	SJE405	0161	SK7C04	1446	SK7C4050	5443	SK7CT367	6662
SI-RECT-48	0015	SIT180-100	OEM	SJ1000F	0916	SJE407	0161	SK7C08	1451	SK7C4051	5446	SK7CT368	6663
SIRECT-48	0015	SIT180-200	OEM	SJ1003E	OEM	SJE408	0455	SK7C10	1453	SK7C4052	5448	SK7CT373	5984
SI-RECT-49	0015	SIT180-500	OEM	SJ1003F	0087	SJE513	0042	SK7C11	1454	SK7C4053	3755	SK7CT374	6917
SI-RECT-50	0087	SIT180-600	OEM	SJ1003H	OEM	SJE514	0919	SK7C14	1458	SK7C4059	5459	SK7CT377	6670
SI-RECT-53	0015	SI-TA7074P	0391	SJ1003K	OEM	SJE515	0042	SK7C20	1466	SK7C4060	6216	SK7CT390	6675
SI-RECT-59	0015	SI-TA7075P	0849	SJ1106	0103	SJE527	0161	SK7C21	1468	SK7C4066	5471	SK7CT393	6679
SI-RECT-69	0015	SITA7640APIXX	3680	SJ1152	0919	SJE583	0161	SK7C27	1476	SK7C4067	6601	SK7CT423	4386
SI-RECT-73	0015	SITO.8-50	OEM	SJ1165	0142	SJE584	0455	SK7C30	1480	SK7C4075	5476	SK7CT533	5614
SI-RECT-75	0015	SITO.8-100	OEM	SJ1171	0919	SJE633	0455	SK7C32	1486	SK7C4094	5495	SK7CT534	5632
SI-RECT-77	0015	SITO.8-200	OEM	SJ1172	0178	SJE634	0161	SK7C42	1507	SK7C4316	5818	SK7CT540	6791
SI-RECT-84	0015	SITO.8-300	OEM	SJ1201	0142	SJE-649	0161	SK7C73	1549	SK7C4351	5843	SK7CT541	6792
SI-RECT-92	0015	SITR-300	OEM	SJ1203E	OEM	SJE649	0161	SK7C74	1552	SK7C4352	5844	SK7CT563	6799
SIRECT-92	0015	SITVR-06G	0015	SJ1203F	OEM	SJE669	0161	SK7C75	1555	SK7C4353	5846	SK7CT564	6800
SI-RECT-94	0015	SITVR-066	0015	SJ1203H	OEM	SJE677	0919	SK7C85	1573	SK7C4510	5949	SK7CT573	6927
SI-RECT-98	0918	SI-UPC574J	1319	SJ1203K	OEM	SJE678	0042	SK7C86	1578	SK7C4511	5950	SK7CT574	6928
SI-RECT-100	0015	SI-UPC580C	1049	SJ1284	0919	SJE687	0378	SK7C93	1584	SK7C4514	5955	SK7CT583	6813
SI-RECT-100-102	0015	SI-UPC1031H	0898	SJ1286	0142	SJE694	0042	SK7C107	4611	SK7C4515	5956	SK7CT597	6818
SI-RECT-102	0015	SIV20	OEM	SJ1403H	OEM	SJE695	0919	SK7C109	0115	SK7C4516	5959	SK7CT640	6859
SI-RECT102	0015	SIVN0104	OEM	SJ1470	0103	SJE721	0161	SK7C112	0214	SK7C4518	5964	SK7CT643	6866
SIRECT-102	0015	SJ051A	1991	SJ1902	2422	SJE723	0455	SK7C123	4628	SK7C4520	5968	SK7CT646	6869
SI-RECT-110	0087	SJ051E	0015	SJ1903	2415	SJE724	0161	SK7C125	4630	SK7C4538	5987	SK7CT648	4428
SI-RECT-110/SB-3F	0015	SJ051F	0015	SJ1925	0321	SJE736	0455	SK7C126	4631	SK7C4543	5998	SK7CT670	6898
SI-RECT-112	0015	SJ052A	1991	SJ2000	0103	SJE737	0161	SK7C132	0675	SK7C7030	5422	SK7CT688	3378
SI-RECT-112/SB-3	0087	SJ052E	0015	SJ2001	0486	SJE743	0455	SK7C137	0779	SK7C7046	5057	SK7CT4002	3330
SI-RECT-114	0102	SJ052F	0015	SJ2008	0103	SJE764	1671	SK7C138	0792	SK7C7046A	5057	SK7CT4015	3371
SI-RECT-122	0015	SJ053	OEM	SJ2009	0899	SJE768	0455	SK7C139	0803	SK7C7266	5754	SK7CT4016	3375
SI-RECT-126	0015	SJ053E	0964	SJ2031	0126	SJE769	0161	SK7C147	0932	SK7C22106	6305	SK7CT4017	3383
SI-RECT-136	0102	SJ053EK	0084	SJ2032	0086	SJE781	0161	SK7C151	0997	SK7C40102	4982	SK7CT4020	3396
SI-RECT-140	0091	SJ053F	0110	SJ2095	0424	SJE783	0042	SK7C153	4650	SK7C40103	4983	SK7CT4024	3413
SI-RECT-140/TR-6	0631	SJ053K	0964	SJ3408	0178	SJE784	0161	SK7C154	4652	SK7C40104	4984	SK7CT4040	3464
SI-RECT-140/TR6S	0298	SJ054E	0084	SJ3423	0074	SJE785	0161	SK7C157	1068	SK7C40105	4985	SK7CT4046A	5054
SI-RECT-144	0015	SJ054EK	0084	SJ3447	0178	SJE797	0455	SK7C158	1080	SK7CT00	5780	SK7CT4051	3512
SI-RECT-152	0133	SJ054F	OEM	SJ3477	0074	SJE799	0455	SK7C160	1109	SK7CT02	4823	SK7CT4052	3514
SI-RECT-154	0015	SJ054K	0084	SJ3478	0074	SJE1032	0264	SK7C161	4657	SK7CT03	5781	SK7CT4053	3520
SI-RECT-155	0015	SJ60F	0015	SJ3604	0103	SJE1518	0455	SK7C162	1134	SK7CT04	3265	SK7CT4059	3560
SI-RECT-156	0015	SJ101A	0575	SJ3629	0079	SJE1519	0161	SK7C163	1151	SK7CT08	3268	SK7CT4060	3569
SI-RECT-158	0102	SJ101F	0015	SJ3648	0178	SJE1520	0161	SK7C164	1163	SK7CT10	5782	SK7CT4066	3584
SI-RECT-162	0102	SJ102A	0575	SJ3678	0103	SJE2112	OEM	SK7C165	1175	SK7CT11	5783	SK7CT4067	3588
SI-RECT-168	0041	SJ102F	0015	SJ4076	OEM	SJE2123	OEM	SK7C166	4660	SK7CT14	3269	SK7CT4075	3620
SI-RECT-169	OEM	SJ103E	0983	SJ5525	0003	SJE2789	6183	SK7C173	1271	SK7CT20	5785	SK7CT4094	3691
SI-RECT-170	0102	SJ103EK	0090	SJ5526	0065	SJE3478	0074	SK7C174	1287	SK7CT21	5786	SK7CT4316	4259
SI-RECT-174	0196	SJ103F	0947	SJ6351	0065	SJE5018	0556	SK7C175	1295	SK7CT27	5787	SK7CT4351	4322
SI-RECT-178	1073	SJ103H	OEM	SJ8701	0103	SJE5019	0556	SK7C181	4667	SK7CT30	5789	SK7CT4352	4324
SI-RECT-178B	1073	SJ103K	0983	SJ9110	0103	SJE-5038	0555	SK7C182	4668	SK7CT32	3274	SK7CT4353	4326
SI-RECT-178BF	0196	SJ104E	0084	SJ10003EK	0145	SJE5402	0161	SK7C190	4672	SK7CT42	5792	SK7CT4510	4804
SI-RECT-182	0102	SJ104EK	0090	SJE42	0042	SJE8621	0919	SK7C191	4673	SK7CT73	5796	SK7CT4511	4807
SI-RECT-204	0071	SJ104F	OEM	SJE100	0161	SJE8635	0042	SK7C192	4674	SK7CT74	5797	SK7CT4514	4816
SI-RECT-206	0102	SJ104K	0084	SJE103	0264	SJN2M100/08	OEM	SK7C193	4675	SK7CT75	5798	SK7CT4515	4821
SI-RECT-208	0087	SJ130	0142	SJE106	0161	SK01	4193	SK7C194	1548	SK7CT85	5799	SK7CT4516	4822
SI-RECT-218	0015	SJ201A	0575	SJE108	0455	SK04	0071	SK7C195	1568	SK7CT86	5800	SK7CT4518	4826
SI-RECT-220	0015	SJ201F	0015	SJE111	0455	SK06M6	OEM	SK7C221	4693	SK7CT93	5802	SK7CT4520	4831
SI-RECT-222	0015	SJ202A	0575	SJE112	0455	SK08	0071	SK7C237	1947	SK7CT107	6454	SK7CT4538	4871
SI-RECT-224	0102	SJ202F	0015	SJE113	0161	SK1-K2	0604	SK7C238	4702	SK7CT109	6455	SK7CT4543	4892
SI-RECT-226	0015	SJ203E	0983	SJE114	0455	SK1K-2	0015	SK7C240	1968	SK7CT112	6456	SK7CT7030	3427
SI-RECT-228	0137	SJ203EK	0097	SJE133	0161	SK-1W50	0497	SK7C241	1979	SK7CT123	6460	SK7CT7046	3485
SI-RECT-230	0137	SJ203F	0242	SJE202	0455	SK-1W-55	1823	SK7C242	1985	SK7CT125	6461	SK7CT7046A	3485
SIRK514	OEM	SJ203H	OEM	SJE203	0161	SK2A4	1266	SK7C243	1990	SK7CT126	6462	SK7CT7266	4184
SIRM-2C	0023	SJ203K	0983	SJE205	0275	SK2A5	2847	SK7C244	4709	SK7CT132	6466	SK7CT22106	6302
SIR-RECT-44	0015	SJ204E	0084	SJE210	0455	SK2A7	0755	SK7C245	2003	SK7CT137	4328	SK7CT40102	4977
SIS2	0143	SJ204EK	0097	SJE211	0161	SK2A8	0672	SK7C251	2054	SK7CT138	6821	SK7CT40103	4978
SIS4M	0023	SJ204F	OEM	SJE218	0275	SK2V4	2975	SK7C253	4717	SK7CT139	6471	SK7CT40104	4979
SIS11	0143	SJ204K	0084	SJE220	0556	SK2V7	1302	SK7C257	4718	SK7CT147	6487	SK7CT40105	4980
SISD-1	0102	SJ301F	0015	SJE221	0455	SK2V8	2981	SK7C258	4720	SK7CT151	6492	SK7CU04	4522
SISD-1HF	0071	SJ302F	0015	SJE222	0161	SK3A0	0118	SK7C259	4722	SK7CT153	6494	SK7V5	0644
SISD-1X	0015	SJ303E	OEM	SJE227	0455	SK3A3	0296	SK7C273	4738	SK7CT154	4956	SK7X5	0475
SISD-K	0015	SJ303F	OEM	SJE228	0161	SK3A6	0372	SK7C280	2234	SK7CT157	6499	SK8A2	0165
SISM-150-01	0015	SJ303K	OEM	SJE229	0161	SK3A9	0036	SK7C283	4744	SK7CT158	5957	SK8A7	0318
SI-SN76650N	0391	SJ304E	OEM	SJE231	0455	SK3F01	OEM	SK7C297	4759	SK7CT160	6505	SK8V2	0244
SI-SN76730N	OEM	SJ304EK	0109	SJE232	0275	SK3F02	OEM	SK7C299	4761	SK7CT161	6900	SK8V7	1075
SISW-05-02	0015	SJ304F	OEM	SJE237	0161	SK3F04	OEM	SK7C354	4776	SK7CT162	6901	SK8X2	0499
SISW-0502	0015	SJ304K	OEM	SJE241	0455	SK3F06	OEM	SK7C356	4777	SK7CT163	6902	SK8X7	3285
SIT4-50	OEM	SJ401F	0015	SJE242	0161	SK3F08	OEM	SK7C365	2853	SK7CT164	6510	SK9A1	0057
SIT4-100	OEM	SJ402F	0015	SJE243	0455	SK3F10	OEM	SK7C366	2858	SK7CT165	6511	SK9V1	0012
SIT4-200	OEM	SJ403E	OEM	SJE244	0161	SK3V0	1703	SK7C367	2867	SK7CT166	6513	SK9X1	0679
SIT14-50	OEM	SJ403F	0535	SJE245	0455	SK3V3	0289	SK7C368	2870	SK7CT173	6517	SK10A	0064
SIT14-100	OEM	SJ403H	OEM	SJE246	0161	SK3V6	0188	SK7C373	2892	SK7CT174	6903	SK10V	0170
SIT14-200	OEM	SJ403K	OEM	SJE248	0161	SK3V9	0451	SK7C374	2899	SK7CT175	6519	SK10X	0225
SIT14-400	OEM	SJ404E	OEM	SJE253	0161	SK3X3	0777	SK7C377	4779	SK7CT181	6522	SK11A	0181
SIT18-50	OEM	SJ404EK	0109	SJE254	0161	SK3X6	0791	SK7C390	3014	SK7CT182	5981	SK11V	0313
SIT18-100	OEM	SJ404F	OEM	SJE255	0161	SK3X9	0801	SK7C393	3035	SK7CT190	6528	SK11V5	0789
SIT18-200	OEM	SJ404K	OEM	SJE256	0455	SK4A3	0274	SK7C404	OEM	SK7CT191	6529	SK11X	0230
SIT18-400	OEM	SJ501F	0015	SJE257	0455	SK4A7	0140	SK7C423	4789	SK7CT192	6532	SK12	OEM
SIT18-500	OEM	SJ570	0016	SJE261	0161	SK4V3	0528	SK7C533	3632	SK7CT193	6533	SK12A	0052
SIT18-600	OEM	SJ601F	0015	SJE262	0161	SK4V7	0446	SK7C534	3636	SK7CT194	6535	SK12V	0137
SIT20-50	OEM	SJ603	0122	SJE265	0455	SK4X3	0815	SK7C540	4801	SK7CT195	5962	SK12V5	0361
SIT20-100	OEM	SJ603E	0122	SJE267	0455	SK4X7	0827	SK7C541	4802	SK7CT221	6562	SK12X	0234
SIT20-200	OEM	SJ603EK	0122	SJE271	0161	SK5A1	0041	SK7C563	4805	SK7CT237	6573	SK13A	0053
SIT20-300	OEM	SJ603F	0959	SJE272	0161	SK5A6	0253	SK7C564	4806	SK7CT238	6574	SK13V	0361
SIT30-100	OEM	SJ603H	OEM	SJE273	0455	SK5V1	0162	SK7C573	4809	SK7CT240	6909	SK13X	0237
SIT30-200	OEM	SJ603K	0122	SJE274	0161	SK5V6	0157	SK7C574	4810	SK7CT241	6577	SK14A	0873
SIT30-400	OEM	SJ604	0122	SJE275	0161	SK5X1	0437	SK7C583	4812	SK7CT242	6578	SK14V	0100
SIT30-500	OEM	SJ604E	0122	SJE276	0455	SK5X6	0870	SK7C597	4814	SK7CT243	6581	SK14X	1387
SIT30-600	OEM	SJ604EK	0122	SJE277	0455	SK6A0	0091	SK7C640	4825	SK7CT244	5969	SK15A	0681
SIT50-50	OEM	SJ604F	OEM	SJE278	0161	SK6A2	0466	SK7C643	4827	SK7CT245	4013	SK15V	0002
SIT50-100	OEM	SJ604K	0122	SJE279	0455	SK6A8	0062	SK7C646	4828	SK7CT251	6588	SK15X	0247
SIT50-200	OEM	SJ619	0103	SJE280	0161	SK6AB	OEM	SK7C648	4829	SK7CT253	6590	SK16	1997
SIT50-400	OEM	SJ619-1	0103	SJE283	0455	SK6V0	0298	SK7C670	4832	SK7CT257	6592	SK16A	0440
SIT50-500	OEM	SJ652	0899	SJE284	0161	SK6V2	0631	SK7C688	4836	SK7CT258	6593	SK16V	0416
SIT50-600	OEM	SJ803E	OEM	SJE288	0455	SK6V8	0025	SK7C4002	5391	SK7CT259	6595	SK16V2	6278
SIT80-50	OEM	SJ803F	0811	SJE289	0161	SK6VB	OEM	SK7C4015	5409	SK7CT273	6910	SK16X	0251
SIT80-100	OEM	SJ803H	OEM	SJE305	0161	SK6X0	3099	SK7C4016	5410	SK7CT280	6618	SK17A	0210
SIT80-200	OEM	SJ803K	OEM	SJE320	0161	SK6X2	0185	SK7C4017	5414	SK7CT283	6621	SK17V	1639
SIT80-300	OEM	SJ805	0142	SJE340	0161	SK6X8	0205	SK7C4020	6192	SK7CT297	6631	SK17V7	0490
SIT95-50	OEM	SJ806	0142	SJE400	0275	SK7	0595	SK7C4024	5418	SK7CT299	6632	SK17X	1170
SIT95-100	OEM	SJ807	OEM	SJE401	0161	SK7A5	0077	SK7C4040	6201	SK7CT354	0785	SK18A	0371
SIT95-400	OEM	SJ811	0178	SJE402	0161	SK7C00	1439	SK7C4046	5061	SK7CT356	0807	SK18V	0490

If replacement code is OEM, contact original manufacturer for replacement.

DEVICE TYPE	REPL CODE
SK18X	0256
SK19	0321
SK19A	0666
SK19V	0943
SK19X	2379
SK20A	0695
SK20V	0526
SK20X	0262
SK22	2763
SK22A	0700
SK22V	0560
SK22X	0269
SK24	OEM
SK24A	0489
SK24V	0398
SK24X	0273
SK25A	0709
SK25V	1596
SK25X	2383
SK26	3046
SK26V	2553
SK27A	1266
SK27V	0436
SK27X	0291
SK28A	0257
SK28V	1664
SK28X	1169
SK29V	2585
SK30	4199
SK30A	0195
SK30V	0721
SK30X	0305
SK31	3049
SK33A	0166
SK33V	0039
SK33X	0314
SK36A	0010
SK36V	0814
SK36X	0316
SK39A	0032
SK39V	0346
SK39X	0322
SK43A	0054
SK43V	0925
SK43X	0333
SK47A	0068
SK47V	0993
SK47X	0343
SK50	0834
SK51	1364
SK51A	0092
SK51V	0497
SK51X	0027
SK52	0832
SK53	0824
SK54	4204
SK55V	1823
SK56A	0125
SK56V	0863
SK56X	0266
SK60	0246
SK60A	2301
SK60V	1148
SK60X	2829
SK62A	0152
SK62V	0778
SK62X	0382
SK63	3381
SK68A	0173
SK68V	1258
SK68X	0401
SK73	1324
SK74C02	2102
SK74C04	2930
SK74C10	2107
SK74C20	2110
SK74C30	3100
SK74C32	3105
SK74C48	2135
SK74C73	2148
SK74C76	2150
SK74C93	2163
SK74C95	3367
SK74C107	3782
SK74C151	3944
SK74C154	3957
SK74C157	3972
SK74C161	3984
SK74C164	3999
SK74C173	4026
SK74C174	4030
SK74C175	4034
SK74C192	4056
SK74C193	4059
SK74C221	3018
SK74C240	2928
SK74C244	4166
SK74C245	6321
SK74C373	4388
SK74C374	4392
SK74C901	4527
SK74C902	4528
SK74C903	4529
SK74C904	4530
SK74C922	5496
SK74C923	5498
SK74C925	4540
SK74H00	0677
SK74H04	1896

DEVICE TYPE	REPL CODE
SK74LS00	1519
SK74LS01	1537
SK74LS02	1550
SK74LS03	1569
SK74LS04	1585
SK74LS05	1598
SK74LS08	1623
SK74LS10	1652
SK74LS11	1657
SK74LS12	1669
SK74LS13	1678
SK74LS14	1688
SK74LS15	1697
SK74LS20	0035
SK74LS22	1764
SK74LS26	1372
SK74LS27	0183
SK74LS28	0467
SK74LS30	0822
SK74LS32	0088
SK74LS33	1821
SK74LS37	1719
SK74LS38	1828
SK74LS40	0135
SK74LS42	1830
SK74LS47	1834
SK74LS48	1838
SK74LS49	1839
SK74LS51	1027
SK74LS54	1846
SK74LS55	0452
SK74LS73	1856
SK74LS73A	1856
SK74LS74	0243
SK74LS74A	0243
SK74LS75	1859
SK74LS76A	2166
SK74LS77	1861
SK74LS78	1862
SK74LS83	2204
SK74LS83A	2204
SK74LS85	0426
SK74LS86	0288
SK74LS90	1871
SK74LS92	1876
SK74LS93	1877
SK74LS107	1592
SK74LS109	1895
SK74LS113	2241
SK74LS114	2286
SK74LS122	1610
SK74LS123	0973
SK74LS123P	0973
SK74LS125A	0075
SK74LS133	3366
SK74LS136	1618
SK74LS138	0422
SK74LS139	0153
SK74LS145	1554
SK74LS148	3856
SK74LS151	1636
SK74LS153	0953
SK74LS155	0209
SK74LS156	1644
SK74LS157	1153
SK74LS161	0852
SK74LS163	0887
SK74LS164	4274
SK74LS168A	0961
SK74LS169A	0980
SK74LS174	0260
SK74LS175	1662
SK74LS191	1677
SK74LS193	1682
SK74LS194	1294
SK74LS194A	1294
SK74LS195	1305
SK74LS196	2807
SK74LS221	1230
SK74LS240	0447
SK74LS241	1715
SK74LS242	1717
SK74LS243	0900
SK74LS244	0453
SK74LS245	0458
SK74LS247	1721
SK74LS248	1723
SK74LS249	1724
SK74LS253	1728
SK74LS257	1733
SK74LS258	1735
SK74LS259	3175
SK74LS260	5859
SK74LS266	0587
SK74LS273	0888
SK74LS279	3259
SK74LS280	1762
SK74LS290	4352
SK74LS293	0082
SK74LS298	3337
SK74LS322	1794
SK74LS348	0660
SK74LS352	0756
SK74LS353	0768
SK74LS364	5870
SK74LS367	0971
SK74LS373	0704
SK74LS377	1112
SK74LS378	1125

DEVICE TYPE	REPL CODE
SK74LS379	1143
SK74LS386	1221
SK74LS393	0813
SK74LS398	1373
SK74LS399	1388
SK74LS490	2199
SK74LS624	3112
SK74LS625	3120
SK74LS626	3125
SK74LS627	3133
SK74LS629	3146
SK74LS641	0685
SK74LS642	0714
SK74LS645	0770
SK74S00	0699
SK74S04	2248
SK74S11	2428
SK74S20	1011
SK74S22	2442
SK74S32	3795
SK74S74	2483
SK74S86	2489
SK74S112	1607
SK74S174	2119
SK75A	0094
SK75V	1181
SK75X	0421
SK82A	0049
SK82V	0327
SK82X	0439
SK87A	0104
SK87V	2997
SK87X	2999
SK91A	0156
SK91V	1301
SK91X	0238
SK100A	0189
SK100V	0098
SK100X	1172
SK103K	OEM
SK107-4	0321
SK110A	0099
SK110V	0149
SK110V151A	OEM
SK110X	1182
SK112	2381
SK113	1370
SK114	2024
SK115	0542
SK116	2385
SK117	2387
SK118	1429
SK119	2101
SK120	2391
SK120A	0089
SK120V	0186
SK120X	1198
SK121	2394
SK122	1436
SK123	1890
SK124	2399
SK125	2400
SK126	2206
SK127	0691
SK128	1449
SK129	1591
SK130	0221
SK130A	0285
SK130V	0213
SK130X	1209
SK131	1606
SK132	1481
SK133	1612
SK134	2406
SK135	2408
SK136	1608
SK137	0622
SK138	0505
SK139	0986
SK140	0686
SK140A	0252
SK140V	0245
SK140X	1870
SK141	0989
SK142	0864
SK143	1254
SK144	1014
SK145	1240
SK146	1145
SK147	1626
SK148	1264
SK149	1629
SK150	1392
SK150A	0336
SK150V	0028
SK150X	0642
SK151	1693
SK152	1524
SK153	1630
SK154	1071
SK155	1706
SK156	1701
SK157	1709
SK158	1707
SK159	1720
SK160	1712
SK160A	0366
SK160V	0255
SK160X	1246

DEVICE TYPE	REPL CODE
SK161	0722
SK162	1725
SK163	1745
SK164	1737
SK165	1757
SK166	1750
SK167	1771
SK168	2431
SK169	2434
SK170	1761
SK170A	0390
SK170V	0871
SK170X	2091
SK171	1783
SK172	1777
SK173	1788
SK174	1785
SK175	1798
SK176	1793
SK177	1806
SK178	1185
SK179	1815
SK180	1810
SK180A	0420
SK180V	0363
SK180X	1269
SK181	1829
SK182	0022
SK183	1842
SK184	0070
SK185	1850
SK186	0132
SK187	1855
SK188	0172
SK189	1863
SK190	0207
SK190A	0448
SK190V	2831
SK190X	2210
SK191	1873
SK192	0227
SK193	2455
SK194	0263
SK195	1884
SK196	0306
SK197	1891
SK198	0325
SK199	0731
SK200	0352
SK200A	1464
SK200V	0417
SK200X	0600
SK201	1898
SK202	0377
SK203	2459
SK203K	OEM
SK204	0408
SK205	1903
SK206	0433
SK207	1155
SK208	0459
SK209	1913
SK210	0483
SK211	1922
SK212	0504
SK213	1930
SK214	0519
SK215	1936
SK216	0537
SK217	1942
SK-218	0015
SK218	0063
SK219	1950
SK220	0397
SK221	0353
SK222	0593
SK223	2479
SK224	0611
SK225	0665
SK226	0629
SK227	0771
SK228	0645
SK229	2486
SK230	0663
SK231	1065
SK301	2521
SK342	1843
SK350	2577
SK372	2603
SK379	2344
SK400	2627
SK401	2627
SK401B	2627
SK403	2628
SK403B	2628
SK403K	OEM
SK404EK	0109
SK510	0809
SK511	2695
SK512	0821
SK513	2698
SK514	0840
SK515	2700
SK516	0862
SK517	2703
SK518	0879
SK519	2706
SK520	0891
SK521	2707

DEVICE TYPE	REPL CODE
SK522	0908
SK523	2711
SK524	0920
SK525	2713
SK526	0938
SK527	2717
SK528	0952
SK529	1216
SK530	0972
SK531	2719
SK532	0988
SK533	1228
SK534	1003
SK535	1243
SK536	1013
SK537	1259
SK538	0883
SK539	1267
SK540	1043
SK541	1283
SK542	1052
SK543	2725
SK544	0926
SK545	1292
SK546	1072
SK547	1300
SK548	1088
SK549	2729
SK550	1098
SK551	1314
SK552	1115
SK553	2731
SK554	1127
SK555	1323
SK556	1144
SK557	1334
SK558	1156
SK559	1346
SK560	1166
SK561	2733
SK562	1176
SK563	1361
SK564	1191
SK565	2735
SK566	1201
SK567	1377
SK568	1214
SK569	1396
SK570	1223
SK571	1405
SK572	1237
SK573	1419
SK574	1256
SK575	1431
SK576	1263
SK577	2745
SK578	1280
SK579	1438
SK580	1289
SK581	2749
SK582	1297
SK583	1452
SK584	1312
SK585	2752
SK586	1321
SK587	1465
SK588	1330
SK589	2756
SK590	1343
SK591	0608
SK592	1355
SK593	1502
SK594	1374
SK595	1515
SK596	1391
SK597	1529
SK598	1402
SK599	1541
SK600	1413
SK601	1565
SK602	1427
SK603	2775
SK603K	OEM
SK604	1435
SK605	2776
SK606	1448
SK607	1499
SK608	1461
SK609	2778
SK610	1475
SK611	2780
SK612	1497
SK613	2783
SK614	1513
SK615	2788
SK616	1523
SK617	2791
SK618	1539
SK619	2793
SK620	1558
SK621	2795
SK622	1577
SK623	2797
SK803K	OEM
SK814	2909
SK821	2915
SK827	2916
SK832	2920
SK836	2923

DEVICE TYPE	REPL CODE
SK841	2927
SK847	2933
SK849	2363
SK854	2935
SK859	2940
SK866	2944
SK869	2945
SK876	2948
SK890	2962
SK900	2970
SK901	2972
SK914	2984
SK930	2992
SK948	3005
SK952	3007
SK1002K	OEM
SK1203K	OEM
SK1320	0144
SK1403K	OEM
SK1639	0037
SK1640	0037
SK1641	0016
SK1802	3193
SK1805	3322
SK1806	6244
SK1822	3981
SK1823	4021
SK1824	4041
SK1826	6247
SK1851	4587
SK1852	4661
SK1853	4732
SK1854	4361
SK1855	4793
SK1856	6249
SK1857	OEM
SK1858	OEM
SK1859	OEM
SK1861	4921
SK1862	4931
SK1863	OEM
SK1864	4963
SK1866	4997
SK1867	OEM
SK1868	OEM
SK1869	5053
SK1870	OEM
SK1871	5138
SK1872	5173
SK1873	5194
SK1874	5213
SK1875	5221
SK1876	5234
SK1877	5246
SK1878	6251
SK1879	6252
SK1881	6253
SK1882	6254
SK1883	6255
SK1900	0443
SK1901	0384
SK1911	3743
SK1912	2672
SK1914	1685
SK1915	2138
SK1917	2223
SK1918	0708
SK1919	1726
SK1920	1752
SK1921	2450
SK1922	5125
SK1923	1646
SK1924	1632
SK2000	1970
SK2001	1978
SK2002	1974
SK2003	1972
SK2004	5020
SK2005	5021
SK2006	5022
SK2006A	5022
SK2007	2990
SK2008	3067
SK2009	5023
SK2009A	5023
SK2010	0835
SK2010A	0835
SK2011	3095
SK2018	1605
SK2019	5027
SK2020	1348
SK2021	3128
SK2022	1951
SK2023	3245
SK2024	1767
SK2025	3153
SK2026	2181
SK2027	4120
SK2027A	4120
SK2031	5030
SK2032	2297
SK2035	3156
SK2035A	3156
SK2040	0536
SK2041	0311
SK2042	0272
SK2043	4358
SK2046	2221
SK2048	4975

DEVICE TYPE	REPL CODE
SK2049	5034
SK2052	4783
SK2053	5035
SK2054	5036
SK2055	5037
SK2056	4786
SK2058	5038
SK2059	5039
SK2060	5040
SK2061	4902
SK2062	5042
SK2063	5043
SK2064	5045
SK2065	4784
SK2068	5046
SK2069	5047
SK2070	5048
SK2071	5049
SK2074	4262
SK2075	4267
SK2076	4266
SK2077	4268
SK2078	2192
SK2079	2185
SK2083	1101
SK2084	1047
SK2086	1393
SK2087	5325
SK2111	5336
SK2112	5337
SK2113	5338
SK2114	5060
SK2115	5062
SK2116	5063
SK2117	5064
SK2131	6267
SK2132	6269
SK2150	5073
SK2151	5075
SK2152	5076
SK2153	5078
SK2154	5119
SK2160	5082
SK2161	1069
SK2162	5084
SK2163	4686
SK2164	3450
SK2165	5086
SK2166	3990
SK2167	1123
SK2168	5087
SK2169	3965
SK2170	4928
SK2171	5341
SK2214	2037
SK2222	OEM
SK2604	0037
SK2716	2263
SK2880	3441
SK2881	1893
SK2882	5242
SK3003	0004
SK3003A	0628
SK3004	0004
SK3005	5121
SK3006	0050
SK3007	0050
SK3007A	1056
SK3008	6354
SK3009	2687
SK3010	0208
SK3011	0595
SK3011A	4362
SK3012	0435
SK3013	0265
SK3014	6355
SK3015	6356
SK3016	0015
SK3016A	0959
SK3017	0229
SK3017A	0015
SK3017B	1345
SK3018	2503
SK3019	2503
SK3020	0198
SK3021	0142
SK3022	2594
SK3023	2600
SK3024	0086
SK3025	0126
SK3026	6358
SK3027	0103
SK3028	6359
SK3029	1506
SK3030	0015
SK3031	0015
SK3031A	3855
SK3032	0071
SK3032A	0072
SK3033	0071
SK3033A	2613
SK3034	0969
SK3035	1665
SK3036	2187
SK3037	6361
SK3038	6362
SK3039	0259
SK3040	0725
SK3041	0456

If replacement code is OEM, contact original manufacturer for replacement.

555

DEVICE TYPE	REPL CODE	DEVICE TYPE	REPL CODE	DEVICE TYPE	REPL CODE	DEVICE TYPE	REPL CODE	DEVICE TYPE	REPL CODE	DEVICE TYPE	REPL CODE	DEVICE TYPE	REPL CODE
SK3042	0239	SK3142	6278	SK3245	0111	SK3350	0028	SK3458	1826	SK3567	1804	SK3671	1275
SK3043	1208	SK3143	2716	SK3246	0224	SK3351	0255	SK3459	2111	SK3567A	1804	SK3672	2624
SK3043A	4423	SK3144	1335	SK3246A	0224	SK3352	0871	SK3460	2559	SK3568	2755	SK3673	1827
SK3043B	4423	SK3145	0490	SK3247	0688	SK3353	0363	SK3461	2246	SK3569	0176	SK3674	3777
SK3044	0233	SK3146	2242	SK3248	0386	SK3354	2831	SK3462	1288	SK3570	6417	SK3675	3531
SK3045	3249	SK3147	2728	SK3249	0428	SK3355	0417	SK3463	0139	SK3571	5626	SK3676	1999
SK3046	6363	SK3148	6375	SK3250	1967	SK3356	6393	SK3464	2035	SK3572	0500	SK3677	2384
SK3047	0086	SK3149	1327	SK3251	1935	SK3357	0219	SK3465	0356	SK3573	0857	SK3678	0299
SK3047A	0086	SK3150	6376	SK3252	1165	SK3358	1206	SK3466	0037	SK3574	4411	SK3679	5386
SK3048	2675	SK3151	0398	SK3253	1581	SK3359	2002	SK3467	0359	SK3575	6418	SK3680	2347
SK3049	0626	SK3152	3506	SK3254	2681	SK3360	2127	SK3468	1470	SK3576	6419	SK3681	2353
SK3050	0349	SK3153	2849	SK3255	0842	SK3361	4490	SK3469	4145	SK3577	5643	SK3682	2354
SK3051	0087	SK3154	4595	SK3256	0456	SK3362	4489	SK3470	0648	SK3578	5644	SK3683	3651
SK3052	6364	SK3155	1179	SK3257	6368	SK3363	4220	SK3471	0523	SK3579	0740	SK3684	3349
SK3053	5606	SK3156	0396	SK3258	4296	SK3364	2632	SK3472	2300	SK3580	0742	SK3685	2084
SK3054	0419	SK3157	0627	SK3259	4296	SK3365	0872	SK3473	2845	SK3581	0464	SK3686	2078
SK3055	0188	SK3158	0516	SK3260	4704	SK3366	1611	SK3474	1152	SK3582	0717	SK3687	0705
SK3056	0162	SK3159	0649	SK3261	0178	SK3367	4491	SK3475	2864	SK3583	2378	SK3688	2232
SK3057	0157	SK3160	0514	SK3262	0126	SK3368	2247	SK3476	2607	SK3584	0204	SK3689	3254
SK3058	0631	SK3161	0696	SK3263	6378	SK3369	4485	SK3477	1012	SK3585	1576	SK3690	1770
SK3059	0644	SK3162	0687	SK3264	6378	SK3370	4486	SK3478	1316	SK3586	1557	SK3691	1667
SK3060	0012	SK3163	1748	SK3265	2214	SK3371	4031	SK3479	2257	SK3586A	1557	SK3692	0765
SK3061	0170	SK3164	1183	SK3266	3296	SK3372	4481	SK3480	3660	SK3587	0706	SK3693	3592
SK3062	0137	SK3165	0026	SK3267	6380	SK3373	3961	SK3481	6402	SK3587A	0706	SK3694	2723
SK3063	0002	SK3166	2530	SK3268	6381	SK3374	6397	SK3482	2903	SK3588	4148	SK3695	2724
SK3064	0436	SK3167	0850	SK3269	6377	SK3375	1434	SK3483	1501	SK3588A	4148	SK3696	6431
SK3065	0212	SK3168	0391	SK3270	6382	SK3376	0858	SK3484	1805	SK3589	5521	SK3697	2478
SK3066	0769	SK3169	2720	SK3271	0142	SK3377	0777	SK3485	1469	SK3589A	5521	SK3698	1099
SK3067	0201	SK3170	2438	SK3272	6383	SK3378	0791	SK3486	4532	SK3590	1695	SK3699	2244
SK3068	0286	SK3171	1411	SK3273	6384	SK3379	0801	SK3487	2008	SK3591	0619	SK3700	0412
SK3069	0128	SK3172	1385	SK3274	0919	SK3380	0815	SK3488	3859	SK3592	0330	SK3701	3286
SK3070	2689	SK3173	0486	SK3275	0855	SK3381	0827	SK3489	2921	SK3593	1311	SK3702	2492
SK3071	2507	SK3174	0015	SK3276	2902	SK3382	0437	SK3490	2216	SK3594	2679	SK3703	1624
SK3072	0167	SK3175	0102	SK3277	3715	SK3383	0870	SK3491	0673	SK3595	3347	SK3704	4546
SK3073	2527	SK3175A	2506	SK3278	3717	SK3384	3099	SK3492	0876	SK3596	2267	SK3705	4325
SK3074	0324	SK3176	1224	SK3279	1797	SK3385	0185	SK3493	1516	SK3597	0934	SK3706	2570
SK3075	0348	SK3177	1966	SK3280	3189	SK3386	0205	SK3494	2556	SK3598	0095	SK3707	3606
SK3076	0350	SK3178B	0818	SK3281	1983	SK3387	0475	SK3495	2569	SK3599	0197	SK3708	4331
SK3077	0661	SK3179	4888	SK3282	3332	SK3388	0499	SK3496	2573	SK3600	0983	SK3709	0123
SK3078	1832	SK3179B	4888	SK3283	2610	SK3389	3285	SK3497	1251	SK3601	0964	SK3710	0309
SK3079	6367	SK3180	2220	SK3284	0849	SK3390	0679	SK3498	3318	SK3602	0109	SK3711	2615
SK3080	0369	SK3181	2222	SK3285	4502	SK3391	0225	SK3499	0837	SK3603	0097	SK3712	4543
SK3081	0071	SK3181A	2222	SK3286	4514	SK3392	0230	SK3500	0122	SK3604	0084	SK3713	4619
SK3082	1004	SK3182	2411	SK3287	4515	SK3393	0234	SK3501	0315	SK3605	1571	SK3714	4174
SK3083	0848	SK3183	3340	SK3288	0574	SK3394	0237	SK3502	3579	SK3606	1241	SK3715	5270
SK3084	0848	SK3183A	2262	SK3289	0875	SK3395	1387	SK3503	3315	SK3607	1991	SK3716	0007
SK3085	6368	SK3184	1239	SK3290	0878	SK3396	0247	SK3504	3213	SK3608	0800	SK3716A	0007
SK3086	1851	SK3185	3239	SK3291	2834	SK3397	0251	SK3505	0720	SK3609	1116	SK3717	0160
SK3087	2217	SK3186	2038	SK3292	2837	SK3398	1170	SK3506	1403	SK3610	3160	SK3718	0265
SK3088	0019	SK3187	4432	SK3293	0127	SK3399	0256	SK3507	6406	SK3611	4180	SK3719	0085
SK3089	0911	SK3188	0556	SK3294	6085	SK3400	2379	SK3508	0147	SK3612	4180	SK3720	3004
SK3090	0143	SK3188A	0556	SK3295	2568	SK3401	0262	SK3509	2006	SK3613	1641	SK3721	0279
SK3091	0143	SK3189	1190	SK3296	1642	SK3402	0269	SK3510	0103	SK3614	1837	SK3722	0211
SK3092	0789	SK3189A	1190	SK3297	0177	SK3403	0273	SK3511	0130	SK3615	1640	SK3723	2546
SK3093	0361	SK3190	0161	SK3298	2039	SK3404	2383	SK3512	3296	SK3616	6423	SK3724	0083
SK3094	0100	SK3191	0455	SK3299	1401	SK3405	0291	SK3513	6409	SK3617	2993	SK3725	1049
SK3095	0039	SK3192	0555	SK3300	2777	SK3406	1169	SK3514	0406	SK3618	OEM	SK3726	4571
SK3096	1823	SK3193	1257	SK3301	0405	SK3407	0305	SK3515	2506	SK3619	3510	SK3727	3238
SK3097	0778	SK3194	1021	SK3302	1700	SK3408	0314	SK3516	2077	SK3620	1351	SK3728	2579
SK3098	0327	SK3195	0488	SK3303	1493	SK3409	0316	SK3517	0810	SK3621	6425	SK3729	3242
SK3099	0149	SK3196	2313	SK3304	0190	SK3410	0322	SK3518	0267	SK3622	6426	SK3730	5592
SK3100	0124	SK3197	0930	SK3305	2954	SK3411	0333	SK3519	2371	SK3623	0787	SK3730(TRANS)	0050
SK3101	2549	SK3198	0222	SK3306	1061	SK3412	0343	SK3520	0278	SK3624	0787	SK3731	4553
SK3102	0823	SK3199	0546	SK3307	2524	SK3413	0027	SK3520A	0278	SK3625	0899	SK3732	1704
SK3103	0187	SK3200	0378	SK3308	3610	SK3414	0266	SK3521	4038	SK3626	0928	SK3733	4539
SK3103A	0187	SK3201	0283	SK3309	1048	SK3415	2829	SK3522	2007	SK3627	0058	SK3734	3388
SK3104	2626	SK3202	0561	SK3310	2956	SK3416	0382	SK3523	3298	SK3628	0312	SK3735	0910
SK3104A	2626	SK3203	1357	SK3311	0604	SK3417	0401	SK3524	2674	SK3629	1911	SK3736	0646
SK3105	6370	SK3204	2438	SK3312	0790	SK3418	0421	SK3525	0817	SK3630	1187	SK3737	2550
SK3106	0106	SK3205	2803	SK3313	0015	SK3419	0439	SK3526	2352	SK3631	1085	SK3738	2510
SK3107	0782	SK3206	2473	SK3314	1917	SK3420	2999	SK3527	3979	SK3632	0407	SK3739	2179
SK3108	0752	SK3207	2480	SK3315	0914	SK3421	0238	SK3528	0434	SK3633	0411	SK3740	1561
SK3109	1293	SK3208	2481	SK3315A	2501	SK3422	1172	SK3529	4182	SK3634	2255	SK3741	1602
SK3110	0469	SK3209	2538	SK3316	3048	SK3423	1182	SK3530	0626	SK3635	3368	SK3742	0851
SK3111	6371	SK3210	2762	SK3316A	3048	SK3424	1198	SK3531	OEM	SK3636	3370	SK3743	3973
SK3112	3350	SK3211	0516	SK3317	0635	SK3425	1209	SK3532	0411	SK3637	4552	SK3744	4563
SK3113	OEM	SK3212	2759	SK3317A	0635	SK3426	1870	SK3533	0571	SK3638	0895	SK3745	6437
SK3114	0006	SK3213	2771	SK3318	2505	SK3427	0642	SK3534	1351	SK3639	1272	SK3746	2959
SK3114A	0006	SK3214	3780	SK3318A	2505	SK3428	1246	SK3535	0130	SK3640	1282	SK3747	0275
SK3115	0065	SK3215	0797	SK3319	5529	SK3429	2091	SK3536	OEM	SK3641	1290	SK3748	0617
SK3116	3219	SK3216	1742	SK3320	1023	SK3430	1269	SK3537	OEM	SK3642	0599	SK3749	1075
SK3117	0047	SK3217	6377	SK3322	6390	SK3431	2210	SK3538	6411	SK3643	0620	SK3750	0361
SK3118	4359	SK3218	0414	SK3323	0549	SK3432	0600	SK3539	2680	SK3644	2433	SK3751	0416
SK3119	0196	SK3219	0949	SK3324	0005	SK3433	0710	SK3540	2515	SK3645	2435	SK3752	0490
SK3120	0479	SK3220	0168	SK3325	0715	SK3434	0338	SK3541	2701	SK3646	3360	SK3753	1596
SK3121	1073	SK3221	2222	SK3326	0623	SK3435	6399	SK3542	1843	SK3647	0287	SK3754	1664
SK3122	0191	SK3222	2220	SK3327	0030	SK3436	4479	SK3543	1686	SK3648	0293	SK3755	0721
SK3123	6372	SK3223	0905	SK3328	0375	SK3437	1671	SK3544	2696	SK3649	0250	SK3756	1296
SK3124	0155	SK3224	2608	SK3329	3607	SK3438	5604	SK3545	2685	SK3650	4089	SK3757	2072
SK3124A	0155	SK3225	2046	SK3330	0289	SK3439	0637	SK3546	2673	SK3651	4096	SK3758	2073
SK3125	0182	SK3226	2580	SK3331	0451	SK3439A	0637	SK3547	2662	SK3652	2004	SK3759	1440
SK3125A	0182	SK3227	2576	SK3332	0528	SK3440	0236	SK3548	2676	SK3653	2623	SK3760	2074
SK3126	0623	SK3228	2560	SK3333	0446	SK3441	0676	SK3549	2664	SK3654	2625	SK3761	3604
SK3127	1208	SK3229	2289	SK3334	0025	SK3442	4534	SK3550	2722	SK3655	1837	SK3762	0616
SK3128	1208	SK3230	4520	SK3335	0526	SK3443	1313	SK3551	3108	SK3656	1844	SK3763	0701
SK3129	2593	SK3231	1044	SK3336	0560	SK3444	0016	SK3552	0308	SK3657	3185	SK3764	0969
SK3130	2784	SK3232	0334	SK3337	0814	SK3445	1532	SK3553	0406	SK3658	0767	SK3765	0693
SK3131	2085	SK3233	0413	SK3338	0346	SK3446	3232	SK3555	3108	SK3659	0739	SK3766	1266
SK3131A	2085	SK3234	0780	SK3339	0925	SK3447	6048	SK3556	2342	SK3660	0612	SK3767	2847
SK3132	6374	SK3235	0746	SK3340	0993	SK3448	3672	SK3557	6412	SK3661	3169	SK3768	0755
SK3133	0003	SK3236	0784	SK3341	0497	SK3449	0320	SK3558	0705	SK3662	3177	SK3769	0672
SK3134	2147	SK3237	3166	SK3342	0863	SK3450	0431	SK3559	0074	SK3663	3192	SK3770	0118
SK3135	0659	SK3238	1601	SK3343	1258	SK3451	3720	SK3560	4097	SK3664	4343	SK3771	0296
SK3136	0244	SK3239	0830	SK3344	1181	SK3452	0144	SK3561	3510	SK3665	3458	SK3772	0372
SK3137	0590	SK3240	0368	SK3345	1301	SK3453	3690	SK3562	6414	SK3666	0480	SK3773	0036
SK3138	1233	SK3241	3477	SK3346	0098	SK3454	0345	SK3563	6415	SK3667	2800	SK3774	0274
SK3139	0313	SK3242	1070	SK3347	0186	SK3455	2535	SK3564	0967	SK3668	2093	SK3775	0140
SK3140	2688	SK3243	3650	SK3348	0213	SK3456	3689	SK3565	0093	SK3669	0917	SK3776	0041
SK3141	0360	SK3244	6057	SK3349	0245	SK3457	2554	SK3566	1885	SK3670	2224	SK3777	0253

If replacement code is OEM, contact original manufacturer for replacement.

DEVICE TYPE	REPL CODE
SK3778	0091
SK3779	0466
SK3780	0062
SK3781	0077
SK3782	0165
SK3783	0318
SK3784	0057
SK3785	0064
SK3786	0181
SK3787	0052
SK3788	0053
SK3789	0873
SK3790	0681
SK3791	0440
SK3792	0210
SK3793	0371
SK3794	0666
SK3795	0695
SK3796	0700
SK3797	0489
SK3798	0709
SK3799	0450
SK3800	0257
SK3801	0195
SK3802	0166
SK3803	0010
SK3804	0032
SK3805	0054
SK3806	0068
SK3807	0092
SK3808	0125
SK3809	2301
SK3810	0152
SK3811	0173
SK3812	0094
SK3813	0049
SK3814	0104
SK3815	0156
SK3816	0189
SK3817	0099
SK3818	0089
SK3819	0285
SK3820	0252
SK3821	0336
SK3822	0366
SK3823	0390
SK3824	0420
SK3825	0448
SK3826	1464
SK3827	2754
SK3828	2614
SK3829	2728
SK3830	2801
SK3831	4018
SK3832	1162
SK3833	3891
SK3834	3667
SK3835	0208
SK3836	0538
SK3837	1302
SK3838	1703
SK3839	2736
SK3840	0816
SK3841	0527
SK3842	6444
SK3843	6445
SK3844	1740
SK3845	0841
SK3846	1588
SK3847	5922
SK3848	0959
SK3849	0018
SK3850	5643
SK3851	5373
SK3852	1042
SK3853	3665
SK3854	0079
SK3855	1702
SK3856	2313
SK3857	0061
SK3858	3483
SK3859	3484
SK3860	2243
SK3861	0595
SK3862	0038
SK3863	1914
SK3864	0120
SK3865	5873
SK3865A	5873
SK3866	1553
SK3866A	1553
SK3867	1514
SK3867A	1514
SK3868	2949
SK3869	2950
SK3870	2952
SK3871	2951
SK3872	1120
SK3873	4559
SK3874	2512
SK3875	4582
SK3876	2051
SK3877	0465
SK3878	0898
SK3879	4554
SK3880	3763
SK3881	2312
SK3882	2804
SK3883	2346
SK3884	4766
SK3885	4469
SK3887	3391
SK3888	2590
SK3889	3161
SK3890	4518
SK3891	1888
SK3892	3751
SK3893	0042
SK3894	0424
SK3895	0615
SK3896	1203
SK3897	0597
SK3898	1814
SK3899	2446
SK3900	1986
SK3901	3814
SK3902	2957
SK3903	1188
SK3904	3622
SK3905	3621
SK3906	2097
SK3909	2647
SK3910	6449
SK3911	0667
SK3912	0819
SK3913	0625
SK3914	0358
SK3915	5517
SK3916	4568
SK3917	3866
SK3918	3060
SK3919	2785
SK3920	2932
SK3921	4008
SK3922	0749
SK3923	0751
SK3924	3000
SK3925	0344
SK3926	3409
SK3927	2790
SK3928	1867
SK3929	2883
SK3930	5370
SK3931	0525
SK3932	0643
SK3933	2911
SK3934	3527
SK3935	0134
SK3936	0073
SK3937	0566
SK3938	0588
SK3939	0572
SK3940	1095
SK3941	2471
SK3942	0240
SK3943	0671
SK3944	0332
SK3945	2465
SK3946	1955
SK3947	2398
SK3948	2422
SK3949	2415
SK3950	1129
SK3951	0403
SK3952	1673
SK3953	0174
SK3954	3575
SK3955	3291
SK3956	1494
SK3957	2820
SK3958	3052
SK3959	0853
SK-3960	OEM
SK3960	3557
SK3961	3558
SK3962	1775
SK3963	3980
SK3964	3074
SK3965	0011
SK3966	2279
SK3967	5029
SK3968	2914
SK3969	4084
SK3970	3753
SK3971	3230
SK3973	2285
SK3974	3346
SK3975	0839
SK3976	OEM
SK3977	3577
SK3978	3487
SK3979	3488
SK3980	2975
SK3982	2981
SK3983	2589
SK3984	0150
SK3985	0319
SK3986	1404
SK3987	0468
SK3988	0441
SK3989	1412
SK3990	0843
SK3991	2439
SK3992	6185
SK3993	6185
SK3994	0902
SK3995	2900
SK3996	0553
SK3997	2869
SK3998	0017
SK3999	0290
SK4000	5970
SK4000B	5970
SK4000UB	2013
SK4001	0473
SK4001B	0473
SK4002	2044
SK4002B	2044
SK4006B	0641
SK4007	2819
SK4007UB	2819
SK4008B	0982
SK4009	1988
SK4009UB	1988
SK4010	3222
SK4010B	3222
SK4011	0215
SK4011B	0215
SK4012	0493
SK4012B	0493
SK4013	0409
SK4013B	0409
SK4014B	0854
SK4015	1008
SK4015B	1008
SK4016	1135
SK4016B	1135
SK4017	0508
SK4017B	0508
SK4018B	1381
SK4019	1517
SK4019B	1517
SK4020	1651
SK4020B	1651
SK4021	1738
SK4021B	1738
SK4022B	1247
SK4023	0515
SK4023B	0515
SK4024	1946
SK4024B	1946
SK4025	2061
SK4025B	2061
SK4026B	2139
SK4027	1938
SK4027B	1938
SK4028B	2213
SK4029	2218
SK4029B	2218
SK4030	0495
SK4030B	0495
SK4031B	2943
SK4032B	2509
SK4033B	2611
SK4034B	3570
SK4035	2750
SK4035B	2750
SK4037A	OEM
SK4037B	OEM
SK4038B	2953
SK4040	0056
SK4040B	0056
SK4041UB	3145
SK4042	0121
SK4042B	0121
SK4043B	1544
SK4044B	2292
SK4045B	3408
SK4046	3779
SK4046B	3779
SK4047	2315
SK4047B	2315
SK4048B	3423
SK4049	0001
SK4049UB	0001
SK4050	0394
SK4050B	0394
SK4051	0362
SK4051B	0362
SK4052	0024
SK4052B	0024
SK4053B	0034
SK4054	4450
SK4054B	4450
SK4055B	3272
SK4056	3661
SK4056B	3661
SK4059A	3276
SK4059B	OEM
SK4060	0146
SK4060B	0146
SK4063B	3682
SK4066	0101
SK4066B	0101
SK4067B	3696
SK4068	2482
SK4068B	2482
SK4069	0119
SK4069UB	0119
SK4070	2494
SK4070B	2494
SK4071	0129
SK4071B	0129
SK4072	2502
SK4072B	2502
SK4073	1528
SK4073B	1528
SK4075	2518
SK4075B	2518
SK4076	3455
SK4076B	3455
SK4077	2536
SK4077B	2536
SK4078	0915
SK4078B	0915
SK4081	0621
SK4081B	0621
SK4082	0297
SK4082B	0297
SK4085B	0300
SK4086	0530
SK4086B	0530
SK4089B	3778
SK4093	2368
SK4093B	2368
SK4094	1672
SK4094B	1672
SK4095B	3796
SK4096B	3798
SK4097B	3802
SK4098	3566
SK4098B	3566
SK4099	3297
SK4099B	3297
SK4311	6470
SK4320	6473
SK4325	6474
SK4326	6475
SK4332	4847
SK4368	5825
SK4501UB	3758
SK4502B	1031
SK4503	2042
SK4503B	2042
SK4506UB	3721
SK4508B	1800
SK4510	1952
SK4510B	1952
SK4511	1535
SK4511B	1535
SK4512	2108
SK4512B	2108
SK4513B	4889
SK4514	1819
SK4514B	1819
SK4515	3555
SK4515B	3555
SK4516B	2331
SK4517B	4220
SK4518	1037
SK4518B	1037
SK4520	2650
SK4520B	2650
SK4521B	4903
SK4522B	2810
SK4526B	3565
SK4527B	3116
SK4529B	4451
SK4531B	3292
SK4532B	1010
SK4536B	3659
SK4538B	1057
SK4539B	3611
SK4541B	4929
SK4543B	4932
SK4547B	4943
SK4551B	4950
SK4553B	4951
SK4555B	2910
SK4556B	3397
SK4558B	4960
SK4560B	6101
SK4562B	1029
SK4566B	3463
SK4568B	3573
SK4569B	4408
SK4572UB	3440
SK4583B	1286
SK4584B	6438
SK4585B	1365
SK4597B	4048
SK4598B	4237
SK4724B	3432
SK4801	0412
SK4802	4533
SK4803	4585
SK4804	4537
SK4812	5106
SK4814	1415
SK4815	1114
SK4816	4284
SK4821	4641
SK4822	3860
SK4825	4047
SK4826	3357
SK4828	5096
SK4831	2370
SK4832	2362
SK4833	5117
SK4834	2062
SK4835	0460
SK4837	4285
SK4838	4708
SK4839	4676
SK4843	3932
SK4900	4037
SK4903	3628
SK4904	3401
SK4906	3749
SK4907	3343
SK4908	2171
SK4909	1503
SK4910	4075
SK4911	1931
SK4914	2320
SK4915	0367
SK4916	5335
SK4918	2284
SK4919	4376
SK4920	5544
SK4921	5543
SK4922	5290
SK4928	3930
SK4929	0235
SK4930	1407
SK4931	2612
SK4932	2616
SK4933	5328
SK4934	5050
SK4935	4845
SK4936	3508
SK4937	0586
SK4939	0470
SK5000	OEM
SK5001	1137
SK5002	0494
SK5003	6296
SK5006	6546
SK5010	4549
SK5010A	4549
SK5012	3211
SK5014	2501
SK5016	6451
SK5020	0702
SK5028	0724
SK5030	0732
SK5031	0737
SK5032	6548
SK5036	0031
SK5040	1917
SK5042	6549
SK5044	6550
SK5046	6552
SK5048	6553
SK5050	6554
SK5051	0015
SK5052	6555
SK5053	6556
SK5054	6557
SK5060	1227
SK5101	6054
SK5114	6560
SK5131	0573
SK5137	0589
SK5173	0154
SK5176	4465
SK5184A	0142
SK5188	0503
SK5189	0506
SK5191	OEM
SK5236	6567
SK5237	0712
SK5238	0304
SK5538	5226
SK5545	0550
SK5550	2336
SK5551	2337
SK5552	2340
SK5555	4381
SK5556	4382
SK5557	4404
SK5579	0902
SK5588	1058
SK5589	1307
SK5590	1880
SK5704	6615
SK5797	0037
SK5798	0037
SK5801	0016
SK5814A	0142
SK5915	0016
SK6006	OEM
SK6117	6642
SK6118	6643
SK6345	0037
SK6346	0037
SK6347	0037
SK6347A	0037
SK6402	5523
SK6477	OEM
SK6502	0736
SK6554	1017
SK6555	0496
SK6556	1030
SK6557	1766
SK6558	1040
SK6559	1778
SK6560	3872
SK6561	3489
SK6601	1744
SK6606	4345
SK6607	4346
SK6615	1574
SK6616	1655
SK6621	2174
SK6622	0562
SK6624	0757
SK6627	0735
SK6629	0759
SK6630	1081
SK6631	0761
SK6632	4455
SK6634	1091
SK6635	1092
SK6641	0726
SK6642	0707
SK6648	0745
SK6649	4771
SK6650	2499
SK6651	6665
SK6652	0393
SK6654	0606
SK6656	0946
SK6658	1504
SK6681	3118
SK6682	3119
SK6683	3121
SK6685	3123
SK6686	3124
SK6703	1076
SK6707	6672
SK6708	0567
SK6709	0929
SK6717	1694
SK6718	3970
SK6719	0674
SK6720	0603
SK6722	0605
SK6724	0463
SK6725	0636
SK6727	0217
SK6729	0653
SK6730	1076
SK6732	1078
SK6734	1094
SK6736	1878
SK6740	2367
SK6744	2816
SK6745	1754
SK6746	1803
SK6747	5223
SK6748	4085
SK6749	1714
SK6752	1386
SK6753	1250
SK6754	0442
SK6760	0192
SK6761	0159
SK6762	0096
SK6768	0650
SK6769	0020
SK6771	0521
SK6772	0108
SK6774	0423
SK6775	1860
SK6777	1889
SK6778	0733
SK6780	0454
SK6781	0584
SK6786	0764
SK6787	0478
SK6788	6673
SK6791	2430
SK6792	0430
SK6794	1478
SK6796	0682
SK6810	2075
SK6848	OEM
SK7003	OEM
SK7038	0994
SK7039	4443
SK7042	2070
SK7043	1067
SK7046	2077
SK7047	1130
SK7048	0607
SK7049	1180
SK7051	0979
SK7055	0984
SK7059	0991
SK7063	0510
SK7066	0206
SK7067	1002
SK7068	0583
SK7069	0942
SK7074	2751
SK7075	1734
SK7076	2786
SK7077	1772
SK7078	2818
SK7079	1807
SK7086	0131
SK7087	0540
SK7090	0145
SK7091	0545
SK7092	5417
SK7093	1229
SK7096	2872
SK7097	1232
SK7100	3705
SK7101	2349
SK7104	1104
SK7105	2360
SK7108	3722
SK7109	1255
SK7110	2982
SK7111	0444
SK7145	1567
SK7153	3263
SK7171	0529
SK7175	0760
SK7179	0533
SK7181	1620
SK7182	2873
SK7183	0254
SK7191	0258
SK7198	1124
SK7199	1111
SK7202	0045
SK7203	0280
SK7206	1522
SK7207	1512
SK7208	0029
SK7209	1836
SK7210	0596
SK7211	1840
SK7220	3716
SK7221	2640
SK7222	2629
SK7223	2670
SK7226	2633
SK7227	2741
SK7234	1995
SK7235	2879
SK7240	2657
SK7241	3022
SK7242	3846
SK7243	3088
SK7244	2631
SK7245	3178
SK7248	4242
SK7249	3725
SK7250	1551
SK7251	2165
SK7254	2813
SK7255	2168
SK7260	2823
SK7261	2177
SK7264	2844
SK7265	2183
SK7268	2806
SK7269	2202
SK7272	2454
SK7273	2324
SK7301	6701
SK7303	5634
SK7305	6702
SK7307	6703
SK7313	5631
SK7315	5642
SK7317	6708
SK7330	5771
SK7331	4884
SK7332	3835
SK7333	5625
SK7352	5633
SK7353	5629
SK7354	0594
SK7355	1337
SK7356	1975
SK7357	1894
SK7358	0652
SK7359	0193
SK7362	4938
SK7363	2537
SK7366	2591
SK7367	2544
SK7376	3475
SK7377	4924
SK7378	3498
SK7379	5477
SK7400	0232
SK7401	0268
SK7402	0310
SK7403	0331
SK7404	0357
SK7405	0381
SK7406	1197
SK7407	1329
SK7408	0462
SK7409	0487
SK7410	0507
SK7411	0522
SK7412	2227
SK7413	1432
SK7414	2228
SK7416	1339
SK7417	1342
SK7420	0692
SK7422	4523
SK7423	3429
SK7425	3438
SK7426	0798
SK7427	0812
SK7428	4117
SK7430	0867
SK7432	0893
SK7433	4130
SK7437	3478
SK7438	0990
SK7439	5722
SK7440	1018
SK7441	1032

If replacement code is OEM, contact original manufacturer for replacement.

DEVICE TYPE	REPL CODE
SK7442	1046
SK7443	1054
SK7444	1066
SK7445	1074
SK7446	1090
SK7447	1100
SK7448	1117
SK7450	0738
SK7451	1160
SK7453	1177
SK7454	1193
SK7460	1265
SK7470	1394
SK7472	1417
SK7473	1164
SK7474	1303
SK7475	1423
SK7476	1150
SK7480	1527
SK7481	3092
SK7483	0117
SK7485	0370
SK7486	1358
SK7489	5358
SK7490	1199
SK7492	0828
SK7493	0564
SK7494	1692
SK7495	1477
SK7496	1705
SK7497	2912
SK7600	4227
SK7601	4399
SK7602	5089
SK7603	5016
SK7604	2669
SK7605	3764
SK7606	2109
SK7607	3671
SK7608	2767
SK7609	2630
SK7610	5070
SK7611	5103
SK7612	2702
SK7613	6728
SK7614	3917
SK7615	3641
SK7616	0808
SK7617	1110
SK7618	3701
SK7619	4281
SK7620	1308
SK7621	6693
SK7622	4647
SK7623	4226
SK7626	3800
SK7627	1572
SK7628	6623
SK7629	5447
SK7630	4633
SK7632	5676
SK7633	5742
SK7634	0866
SK7635	2799
SK7636	4472
SK7637	3040
SK7638	3039
SK7641	3695
SK7642	2451
SK7643	2155
SK7644	5187
SK7645	3742
SK7646	3461
SK7647	3462
SK7648	2898
SK7649	4584
SK7650	4713
SK7651	4935
SK7652	4756
SK7653	2031
SK7654	3209
SK7655	1238
SK7656	4746
SK7657	5068
SK7658	1940
SK7659	4599
SK7660	4600
SK7661	4572
SK7662	4607
SK7663	4645
SK7664	6731
SK7665	4302
SK7666	0794
SK7667	4729
SK7668	4734
SK7669	4336
SK7670	5113
SK7671	6732
SK7672	3726
SK7673	4339
SK7674	3680
SK7675	5971
SK7676	0658
SK7677	5080
SK7678	1666
SK7679	4441
SK7680	6733
SK7681	4899
SK7682	1885

DEVICE TYPE	REPL CODE
SK7683	1868
SK7686	3919
SK7687	2815
SK7690	4965
SK7691	4962
SK7692	3940
SK7693	5996
SK7694	6004
SK7695	6168
SK7696	6167
SK7697	6003
SK7698	1872
SK7699	6734
SK7700	6229
SK7701	6660
SK7702	6735
SK7703	1562
SK7704	4750
SK7705	2104
SK7706	4644
SK7707	3666
SK7708	3744
SK7709	6736
SK7710	2692
SK7711	2288
SK7712	2071
SK7713	5123
SK7714	5464
SK7715	2029
SK7717	3945
SK7718	2095
SK7719	2092
SK7720	3476
SK7721	3748
SK7722	4561
SK7723	4556
SK7724	4560
SK7725	1096
SK7726	4521
SK7727	2663
SK7728	0399
SK7729	4210
SK7730	2460
SK7731	3746
SK7732	2732
SK7733	3910
SK7734	1433
SK7735	2868
SK7736	2641
SK7737	3929
SK7738	6738
SK7739	5199
SK7740	4264
SK7741	5202
SK7742	5203
SK7743	0347
SK7744	5515
SK7747	2264
SK7751	1534
SK7752	3769
SK7753	1226
SK7754	2388
SK7755	2390
SK7756	2487
SK7757	4477
SK7758	4483
SK7759	4484
SK7760	2855
SK7761	2551
SK7762	2555
SK7763	2562
SK7764	2565
SK7765	2566
SK7766	4495
SK7767	0633
SK7768	0958
SK7769	0043
SK7770	3901
SK7771	2606
SK7772	3625
SK7773	0385
SK7774	4513
SK7775	4348
SK7776	2571
SK7778	2581
SK7779	3993
SK7781	4550
SK7782	4024
SK7783	4551
SK7784	2268
SK7785	4006
SK7786	4557
SK7787	4002
SK7789	4567
SK7790	5601
SK7791	3941
SK7792	6740
SK7793	4680
SK7794	4682
SK7795	4684
SK7796	4692
SK7797	2508
SK7798	4697
SK7799	3198
SK7800	4703
SK7801	4480
SK7802	4736
SK7803	4752
SK7804	2884

DEVICE TYPE	REPL CODE
SK7805	3668
SK7806	3771
SK7807	3772
SK7808	3299
SK7809	2358
SK7810	5145
SK7811	2369
SK7812	0696
SK7813	3905
SK7814	4655
SK7815	5015
SK7816	5755
SK7817	4083
SK7827	0754
SK7841	3640
SK7900	3373
SK7901	5776
SK7951	6751
SK7952	0339
SK8223	OEM
SK8251	0016
SK8261	0233
SK8604	OEM
SK8937	0224
SK9000	0023
SK9001	1791
SK9002	1089
SK9003	0110
SK9004	0947
SK9005	0242
SK9006	1736
SK9007	0535
SK9008	1760
SK9009	0811
SK9010	0916
SK9011	2294
SK9012	1482
SK9013	3050
SK9014	0438
SK9015	2888
SK9016	2599
SK9017	1113
SK9018	4663
SK9019	3864
SK9020	3839
SK9021	0298
SK9022	1639
SK9023	0943
SK9024	2997
SK9025	2774
SK9026	3675
SK9027	3739
SK9028	3674
SK9029	2815
SK9030	1318
SK9031	6825
SK9032	6826
SK9033	3656
SK9034	4081
SK9035	3807
SK9036	2317
SK9037	2425
SK9038	2030
SK9039	1841
SK9040	2416
SK9041	0558
SK9042	0520
SK9043	3809
SK9044	4981
SK9045	4666
SK9046	4670
SK9047	3738
SK9048	1570
SK9049	4677
SK9050	4678
SK9051	4671
SK9052	OEM
SK9053	6464
SK9054	4017
SK9055	5463
SK9056	3692
SK9057	6828
SK9058	4416
SK9059	3997
SK9060	6829
SK9061	3564
SK9062	4099
SK9063	1589
SK9064	4665
SK9065	6830
SK9067	1905
SK9068	6832
SK9069	1473
SK9070	1879
SK9071	1886
SK9072	2861
SK9073	1899
SK9074	2609
SK9075	0276
SK9076	1045
SK9077	4849
SK9078	4850
SK9079	4852
SK9080	4853
SK9081	4854
SK9082	3603
SK9082A	4505
SK9083A	4512
SK9084	2704

DEVICE TYPE	REPL CODE
SK9084A	2704
SK9085	0723
SK9086	1780
SK9087	2356
SK9088	2357
SK9089	3733
SK9090	1545
SK9091	0133
SK9092	1001
SK9093	1126
SK9094	1252
SK9095	4848
SK9096	1277
SK9097	1295
SK9098	1208
SK9099	5469
SK9100	5469
SK9101	1633
SK9102	5503
SK9103	1663
SK9104	6834
SK9105	1579
SK9106	5265
SK9107	3336
SK9108	3497
SK9109	1980
SK9110	3956
SK9111	2602
SK9112	0060
SK9113	1298
SK9114	2034
SK9115	2449
SK9116	6835
SK9117	6836
SK9118	0388
SK9119	0055
SK9120	4169
SK9121	1882
SK9122	1659
SK9123	2123
SK9124	1167
SK9125	4335
SK9126	3070
SK9127	3057
SK9128	2207
SK9129	2495
SK9130	3389
SK9131	1498
SK9132	0148
SK9133	3029
SK9134	0130
SK9136	1671
SK9137	1376
SK9138	0472
SK9139	2824
SK9140	1331
SK9141	0270
SK9142	0590
SK9143	0786
SK9144	2540
SK9145	2545
SK9146	3576
SK9147	5901
SK9148	2917
SK9149	3104
SK9150	2496
SK9150A	2496
SK9152	6839
SK9153	6786
SK9154	6840
SK9155	6219
SK9156	6217
SK9157	0321
SK9158	0977
SK9159	0838
SK9160	3583
SK9161	2922
SK9162	3102
SK9163	1147
SK9164	1382
SK9165	4970
SK9166	0890
SK9167	2231
SK9168	2764
SK9169	1817
SK9170	3361
SK9171	1908
SK9172	2995
SK9173	2796
SK9174	2863
SK9175	1786
SK9176	1789
SK9177	1291
SK9178	1508
SK9179	1319
SK9180	0548
SK9181	3416
SK9182	4580
SK9183	4027
SK9184	3216
SK9185	0898
SK9186	4653
SK9187	1016
SK9188	1437
SK9189	4604
SK9190	2145
SK9191	5018
SK9192	3028
SK9193	4770

DEVICE TYPE	REPL CODE
SK9194	1192
SK9195	2170
SK9196	4724
SK9197	2511
SK9198	0678
SK9199	0670
SK9200	2721
SK9201	3784
SK9202	3735
SK9203	4863
SK9204	4867
SK9205	3101
SK9206	3741
SK9207	3933
SK9208	3167
SK9209	2302
SK9210	3034
SK9211	0859
SK9212	2052
SK9213	5892
SK9214	4102
SK9215	2541
SK9216	2709
SK9217	2552
SK9218	2548
SK9219	4429
SK9221	1825
SK9222	4952
SK9224	3775
SK9225	0491
SK9226	3946
SK9227	5698
SK9228	4578
SK9229	0284
SK9230	0241
SK9231	4501
SK9232	1864
SK9233	3503
SK9234	0477
SK9236	1359
SK9237	0861
SK9239	3459
SK9241	2838
SK9242	2748
SK9243	2761
SK9244	2094
SK9245	2983
SK9246	0762
SK9247	0912
SK9248	2011
SK9249	1420
SK9250	4742
SK9251	4646
SK9252	4493
SK9253	3490
SK9254	3491
SK9255	3492
SK9256	3493
SK9257	3948
SK9258	2314
SK9259	3969
SK9260	4402
SK9261	3031
SK9262	4460
SK9263	6845
SK9264	5321
SK9265	4319
SK9266	3977
SK9267	4575
SK9268	4576
SK9269	5019
SK9270	3449
SK9271	3470
SK9272	0933
SK9273	2637
SK9274	2846
SK9275	2936
SK9276	3239
SK9277	6430
SK9278	6847
SK9279	6848
SK9280	6849
SK9281	3363
SK9282	6850
SK9283	3774
SK9284	2140
SK9285	3110
SK9286	1538
SK9287	2939
SK9288	6851
SK9289	6852
SK9290	2084
SK9291	2078
SK9292	0500
SK9293	0705
SK9294	0857
SK9295	4187
SK9296	0479
SK9297	2526
SK9298	3698
SK9299	5003
SK9300	3616
SK9301	6853
SK9302	6854
SK9303	3812
SK9304	3813
SK9305	3617
SK9306	3613
SK9307	3614

DEVICE TYPE	REPL CODE
SK9308	3811
SK9311	0067
SK9312	4721
SK9313	4035
SK9314	5004
SK9315	2601
SK9316	6855
SK9317	3081
SK9318	6857
SK9319	6858
SK9320	2043
SK9321	4071
SK9322	3923
SK9323	6860
SK9324	5116
SK9325	0970
SK9326	4669
SK9327	OEM
SK9328	1024
SK9329	4391
SK9330	4947
SK9331	3906
SK9332	1989
SK9333	2697
SK9334	1993
SK9335	5193
SK9336	5195
SK9337	2239
SK9338	2443
SK9339	2811
SK9340	2836
SK9341	3359
SK9342	3761
SK9343	5905
SK9344	2710
SK9345	6861
SK9346	6862
SK9347	6863
SK9348	6864
SK9349	OEM
SK9350	6865
SK9351	3712
SK9352	0261
SK9353	3325
SK9354	3317
SK9355	4705
SK9356	4700
SK9357	0963
SK9358	6496
SK9359	2852
SK9360	4050
SK9361	4632
SK9362	1077
SK9362A	1077
SK9363	1638
SK9364	2058
SK9365	3561
SK9366	1157
SK9367	0713
SK9368	1471
SK9369	0886
SK9370	3658
SK9371	2817
SK9372	2978
SK9373	1332
SK9374	2965
SK9375	6003
SK9376	4965
SK9377	4401
SK9378	4396
SK9379	0906
SK9380	0069
SK9381	3920
SK9382	3921
SK9383	3926
SK9384	1051
SK9385	OEM
SK9386	3938
SK9387	0326
SK9388	6870
SK9389	3248
SK9390	5380
SK9391	3086
SK9392	0219
SK9393	6871
SK9394	3949
SK9395	4634
SK9396	5013
SK9397	3899
SK9398	4591
SK9399	4356
SK9400	OEM
SK9401	4803
SK9402	1977
SK9403	0328
SK9404	1580
SK9405	0598
SK9406	4603
SK9407	6872
SK9408	3316
SK9409	3457
SK9410	6616
SK9411	0223
SK9412	3718
SK9413	0194
SK9415	3082
SK9417	3195
SK9418	3372
SK9419	4930

DEVICE TYPE	REPL CODE
SK9420	4974
SK9421	3582
SK9422	1533
SK9423	2896
SK9424	4967
SK9425	2395
SK9426	4968
SK9427	2919
SK9428	4969
SK9429	0044
SK9430	3585
SK9431	5212
SK9432	0008
SK9433	3173
SK9434	3572
SK9435	0264
SK9436	3495
SK9437	3496
SK9438	3339
SK9439	3340
SK9440	1384
SK9441	2429
SK9442	2996
SK9443	3477
SK9444	2366
SK9445	6876
SK9446	2261
SK9447	3537
SK9448	3196
SK9449	3601
SK9450	2969
SK9451	3136
SK9452	2985
SK9453	6877
SK9454	6878
SK9455	0396
SK9455A	0396
SK9456	0630
SK9456A	0630
SK9457	5353
SK9458	5367
SK9459	2833
SK9460	1747
SK9461	2770
SK9462	1698
SK9463	6880
SK9464	0805
SK9465	6881
SK9466	6882
SK9467	5382
SK9468	4945
SK9469	1587
SK9470	1518
SK9471	3704
SK9472	3708
SK9473	6883
SK9474	6884
SK9475	2350
SK9476	3326
SK9477	1260
SK9478	3474
SK9479	5253
SK9480	1055
SK9481	3678
SK9482	5244
SK9483	2973
SK9484	3009
SK9485	2739
SK9486	6885
SK9487	5384
SK9488	2757
SK9489	5252
SK9495	0323
SK9500	6682
SK9501	5621
SK9502	6887
SK9503	5811
SK9504	5778
SK9505	6188
SK9506	6888
SK9507	2256
SK9508	5427
SK9509	1456
SK9600	2059
SK9601	5819
SK9602	2194
SK9603	2918
SK9604	2296
SK9605	1963
SK9606	2857
SK9607	1189
SK9608	6896
SK9609	2808
SK9610	3519
SK9611	3521
SK9612	3523
SK9613	3524
SK9614	3525
SK9615	5110
SK9616	3526
SK9617	3528
SK9618	2693
SK9619	2694
SK9620	2504
SK9621	3012
SK9622	6899
SK9623	3534
SK9624	2156
SK9625	5209

If replacement code is OEM, contact original manufacturer for replacement.

DEVICE TYPE	REPL CODE
SK9626	3165
SK9627	3536
SK9628	3538
SK9629	3539
SK9630	3540
SK9631	3542
SK9632	3543
SK9633	2485
SK9634	2028
SK9635	3516
SK9636	2080
SK9637	1410
SK9638	2082
SK9639	3545
SK9640	2841
SK9641	3547
SK9642	3586
SK9643	2523
SK9644	3387
SK9645	3293
SK9646	3587
SK9647	3289
SK9648	3290
SK9649	3090
SK9650	3591
SK9651	1344
SK9652	3593
SK9653	3595
SK9654	3596
SK9655	3597
SK9656	3598
SK9657	3599
SK9658	0684
SK9659	2677
SK9660	3532
SK9661	0014
SK9662	4971
SK9663	2208
SK9664	0577
SK9665	2464
SK9666	2452
SK9667	0355
SK9668	0009
SK9669	4043
SK9670	3563
SK9671	1795
SK9672	6905
SK9700	4577
SK9701	4437
SK9702	0509
SK9703	2881
SK9704	1613
SK9705	5033
SK9706	5107
SK9707	0657
SK9708	4961
SK9709	0610
SK9710	5229
SK9711	1447
SK9712	5707
SK9713	4040
SK9715	2015
SK9716	0578
SK9717	5162
SK9718	1869
SK9719	5238
SK9720	0640
SK9721	5210
SK9722	5165
SK9723	5232
SK9724	5166
SK9725	5126
SK9726	3848
SK9727	3869
SK9728	4246
SK9729	4840
SK9730	4066
SK9731	1521
SK9732	3403
SK9733	5167
SK9734	5168
SK9735	5169
SK9736	4838
SK9737	5178
SK9738	4078
SK9739	5170
SK9740	4054
SK9741	1026
SK9742	0881
SK9743	3897
SK9744	3902
SK9745	3068
SK9746	1022
SK9747	4202
SK9748	0534
SK9749	0387
SK9750	0457
SK9751	4111
SK9752	0727
SK9753	2929
SK9754	4307
SK9755	4309
SK9756	4310
SK9757	1428
SK9758	6263
SK9759	6261
SK9760	1525
SK9761	2718
SK9762	3314

DEVICE TYPE	REPL CODE
SK9763	1158
SK9764	4417
SK9765	4312
SK9766	3130
SK9767	4074
SK9768	6144
SK9769	4923
SK9770	1281
SK9771	3635
SK9772	3634
SK9773	3631
SK9774	1536
SK9775	2493
SK9776	2219
SK9777	1716
SK9778	4134
SK9779	4125
SK9780	2809
SK9781	2160
SK9782	2157
SK9783	2149
SK9784	2130
SK9785	2106
SK9786	1718
SK9787	4367
SK9788	1472
SK9789	1622
SK9790	1852
SK9791	4586
SK9792	4570
SK9793	4566
SK9794	4118
SK9795	2667
SK9796	5829
SK9797	0389
SK9798	1015
SK9799	6209
SK9800	3627
SK9805	3002
SK9806	2100
SK9807	1235
SK9808	5511
SK9809	0576
SK9810	2619
SK9811	1425
SK9812	2380
SK9813	4883
SK9814	1782
SK9815	3329
SK9816	2781
SK9817	2760
SK9818	2237
SK9822	3027
SK9823	3486
SK9825	4934
SK9827	1262
SK9828	1222
SK9829	4524
SK9830	1649
SK9831	4082
SK9832	0518
SK9833	1306
SK9834	1253
SK9835	3225
SK9837	1347
SK9838	4306
SK9839	5228
SK9840	3882
SK9841	4468
SK9842	1133
SK9843	5542
SK9844	5540
SK9846	5539
SK9847	3639
SK9848	3407
SK9849	6265
SK9850	3206
SK9851	0301
SK9852	1400
SK9853	0321
SK9854	3479
SK9855	3323
SK9856	5255
SK9857	5256
SK9858	1119
SK9859	1654
SK9860	3507
SK9861	1234
SK9862	3152
SK9863	3885
SK9864	3288
SK9866	4286
SK9867	5157
SK9868	4074
SK9870	2348
SK9871	3857
SK9873	4131
SK9874	3352
SK9875	4314
SK9876	4349
SK9877	4009
SK9878	2254
SK9879	1594
SK9880	5163
SK9881	2998
SK9882	3331
SK9883	3830
SK9884	3132
SK9885	3765

DEVICE TYPE	REPL CODE
SK9886	6182
SK9888	5703
SK9889	5177
SK9890	5174
SK9891	2490
SK9892	5176
SK9893	5175
SK9894	1245
SK9895	5180
SK9896	5179
SK9897	5172
SK9898	3321
SK9899	3306
SK9902	2389
SK9903	4881
SK9906	4882
SK9907	5218
SK9908	5219
SK9911	0445
SK9912	1813
SK9913	4781
SK9914	4280
SK9915	4279
SK9916	3700
SK9918	1492
SK9919	3954
SK9920	5294
SK9921	4398
SK9922	5502
SK9923	3740
SK9924	5587
SK9925	2000
SK9926	5599
SK9927	4778
SK9928	5896
SK9929	4420
SK9930	5903
SK9931	3271
SK9932	4100
SK9933	4156
SK9934	0730
SK9935	2520
SK9936	4998
SK9937	1082
SK9938	0541
SK9939	3163
SK9940	2189
SK9941	3841
SK9942	3703
SK9943	3842
SK9944	0901
SK9945	2843
SK9946	3054
SK9947	4959
SK9948	3223
SK9949	0694
SK9950	0484
SK9951	2055
SK9952	2531
SK9953	2056
SK9954	2057
SK9955	5143
SK9957	0826
SK9958	4109
SK9959	0892
SK9960	4067
SK9961	3442
SK9962	1881
SK9963	0662
SK9964	3600
SK9965	3333
SK9967	0582
SK9968	0877
SK9969	0292
SK9970	0248
SK9971	0999
SK9972	1039
SK9975	0163
SK9976	1319
SK9977	4773
SK9978	3728
SK9980	5132
SK9981	5136
SK9982	5681
SK9983	5140
SK9984	5377
SK9985	2351
SK9986	5248
SK9987	4088
SK9989	2686
SK9990	5099
SK9991	3402
SK9992	2154
SK9993	0624
SK9994	4569
SK9995	1631
SK9996	3410
SK9997	4612
SK9998	1892
SK10000	2880
SK10001	5148
SK10002	2164
SK10003	2079
SK10004	3504
SK10005	3892
SK10006	4121
SK10007	4594
SK10008	5133
SK10010	5100

DEVICE TYPE	REPL CODE
SK10012	3776
SK10013	5134
SK10015	3354
SK10016	3686
SK10017	4313
SK10018	3301
SK10019	2661
SK10021	2014
SK10022	5139
SK10023	4194
SK10024	2802
SK10025	2814
SK10026	2812
SK10028	5141
SK10029	3327
SK10030	1586
SK10031	1379
SK10032	OEM
SK10033	5146
SK10035	5149
SK10036	3481
SK10037	5150
SK10038	1086
SK10041	4706
SK10042	0944
SK10044	5155
SK10045	5692
SK10047	5188
SK10048	4427
SK10049	4799
SK10050	4430
SK10051	1710
SK10052	2697
SK10053	3605
SK10054	5196
SK10055	3828
SK10056	3529
SK10058	5723
SK10059	3806
SK10060	4780
SK10061	5433
SK10062	5943
SK10063	2715
SK10064	4044
SK10065	4073
SK10066	2866
SK10067	3033
SK10069	2543
SK10070	4106
SK10071	4209
SK10072	3202
SK10073	2854
SK10074	1965
SK10075	3089
SK10076	3768
SK10077	3400
SK10079	2789
SK10080	5137
SK10081	0107
SK10082	0552
SK10083	3309
SK10084	2099
SK10085	2330
SK10086	4782
SK10087	2517
SK10088	2116
SK10089	3838
SK10090	3836
SK10091	1948
SK10092	1957
SK10093	2926
SK10094	0013
SK10095	2891
SK10096	4419
SK10097	1722
SK10098	1741
SK10099	0719
SK10100	1731
SK10101	5977
SK10102	5269
SK10103	4410
SK10104	5267
SK10105	5268
SK10106	3431
SK10107	3345
SK10108	0975
SK10109	0698
SK10110	3439
SK10111	3241
SK10112	5272
SK10113	5273
SK10114	3433
SK10115	5274
SK10116	5245
SK10117	4269
SK10118	2976
SK10119	0539
SK10120	4015
SK10121	4016
SK10122	2412
SK10123	2404
SK10124	2307
SK10125	3114
SK10126	1457
SK10127	5263
SK10128	3059
SK10129	5764
SK10130	1658
SK10131	2162

DEVICE TYPE	REPL CODE
SK10132	5264
SK10133	5266
SK10134	0281
SK10136	3454
SK10137	3107
SK10138	3187
SK10139	1689
SK10140	5183
SK10141	5184
SK10142	5706
SK10143	3896
SK10144	3530
SK10145	3273
SK10146	4955
SK10147	3220
SK10148	2893
SK10149	5182
SK10150	3127
SK10151	3453
SK10152	5709
SK10153	5983
SK10154	5960
SK10155	0481
SK10156	5711
SK10158	3871
SK10159	3727
SK10161	3448
SK10162	3834
SK10163	3559
SK10164	2403
SK10165	2994
SK10166	5185
SK10168	1474
SK10169	1430
SK10170	2287
SK10171	2397
SK10172	4080
SK10173	2318
SK10174	2401
SK10175	2738
SK10176	3785
SK10177	2678
SK10178	0112
SK10179	5556
SK10180	5989
SK10181	5259
SK10182	4912
SK10183	4548
SK10184	5575
SK10185	1796
SK10186	3858
SK10187	5990
SK10188	5991
SK10189	5993
SK10190	5733
SK10191	1463
SK10192	5994
SK10193	3085
SK10194	2120
SK10195	3143
SK10196	1161
SK10197	3162
SK10198	1756
SK10199	3171
SK10200	1921
SK10201	1904
SK10202	1941
SK10203	0563
SK10204	1961
SK10205	0825
SK10206	1976
SK10207	1395
SK10208	1398
SK10209	4957
SK10210	2299
SK10211	0744
SK10212	2765
SK10213	1217
SK10214	1195
SK10215	2146
SK10216	0474
SK10217	4835
SK10219	3277
SK10220	0202
SK10221	5093
SK10223	5095
SK10226	2513
SK10230	5102
SK10232	3707
SK10233	5105
SK10234	2572
SK10238	5671
SK10239	5109
SK10241	4473
SK10242	5120
SK10243	3021
SK10244	2409
SK10246	5122
SK10247	5679
SK10252	5675
SK10253	2126
SK10254	1036
SK10255	0998
SK10256	1028
SK10257	1102
SK10258	1140
SK10259	2904
SK10260	0957
SK10261	2908

DEVICE TYPE	REPL CODE
SK10262	3405
SK10263	3024
SK10264	3026
SK10265	0869
SK10266	5227
SK10267	5230
SK10268	1956
SK10269	6000
SK10271	3006
SK10272	5052
SK10273	1371
SK10274	4243
SK10275	5066
SK10276	4019
SK10277	1691
SK10278	0501
SK10279	4864
SK10280	4865
SK10281	5732
SK10282	0482
SK10283	5734
SK10284	5735
SK10285	5736
SK10286	4868
SK10287	4869
SK10288	4870
SK10289	4872
SK10290	4456
SK10291	4874
SK10292	4875
SK10293	4876
SK10294	4878
SK10295	3925
SK10296	1683
SK10297	2341
SK10298	5753
SK10299	4510
SK10300	3426
SK10301	3424
SK10302	0277
SK10303	5661
SK10304	5005
SK10305	2961
SK10309	2355
SK10310	6002
SK10311	1215
SK10312	3644
SK10313	3224
SK10314	3020
SK10315	3217
SK10316	3342
SK10317	3134
SK10318	3140
SK10320	3693
SK10321	0511
SK10322	3203
SK10324	2604
SK10325	5031
SK10326	5032
SK10327	2096
SK10328	4901
SK10330	5323
SK10331	5326
SK10332	5327
SK10334	5329
SK10335	5330
SK10336	5332
SK10337	5331
SK10400	1041
SK10401	3852
SK10402	4496
SK10403	4900
SK10404	5568
SK10405	4989
SK10406	5836
SK10407	4988
SK10408	3246
SK10409	5745
SK10410	3663
SK10411	6012
SK10412	6013
SK10413	0059
SK10414	1670
SK10415	5701
SK10416	0647
SK10417	2295
SK10418	4295
SK10419	2966
SK10420	4494
SK10421	2851
SK10422	1590
SK10423	4917
SK10424	0865
SK10425	1625
SK10426	0847
SK10427	1242
SK10428	1599
SK10429	1196
SK10430	1600
SK10431	2124
SK10432	1604
SK10433	2236
SK10434	1787
SK10435	2178
SK10436	2278
SK10437	2282
SK10438	5700
SK10439	5347
SK10440	4973

DEVICE TYPE	REPL CODE
SK10441	5350
SK10442	5351
SK10443	6015
SK10444	5298
SK10445	5346
SK10446	5349
SK10447	4095
SK10448	4105
SK10449	0580
SK10450	2744
SK10451	4471
SK10452	3172
SK10453	2583
SK10454	2842
SK10455	2339
SK10456	2105
SK10457	6016
SK10458	6017
SK10459	0418
SK10460	6018
SK10460-5668A	OEM
SK10461	3425
SK10462	3790
SK10463	3791
SK10464	3794
SK10465	2436
SK10466	3549
SK10467	2188
SK10468	0788
SK10469	6020
SK10470	5639
SK10471	4126
SK10472	4177
SK10473	5891
SK10474	4866
SK10475	6021
SK10476	4452
SK10477	0517
SK10478	3645
SK10479	3473
SK10480	6022
SK10481	3344
SK10482	4470
SK10483	6023
SK10484	3590
SK10485	6024
SK10486	6025
SK10488	4843
SK10489	6026
SK10493	4288
SK10494	5694
SK10496	5714
SK10499	4055
SK10500	5715
SK10501	5719
SK10502	3051
SK10505	3894
SK10507	5720
SK10508	5721
SK10509	5713
SK10510	1356
SK10511	3833
SK10512	5684
SK10513	5856
SK10514	3280
SK10515	5204
SK10516	5200
SK10518	2083
SK10519	1887
SK10520	5292
SK22100	3013
SK22101	3019
SK22102	3023
SK22859	5215
SK-31024-3	0144
SK31024-3	0144
SK40061	1811
SK40098B	0427
SK40100B	3895
SK40101B	3960
SK40102B	3998
SK40103B	4029
SK40104B	4046
SK40105B	4060
SK40106B	3581
SK40107B	4090
SK40108B	4119
SK40109B	4146
SK40110B	4165
SK40114B	4234
SK40116	3077
SK40117B	6357
SK40147B	5011
SK40160B	1349
SK40161	1363
SK40161B	1363
SK40162B	1378
SK40163B	1397
SK40174B	1542
SK40175B	1520
SK40181B	5533
SK40182B	4579
SK40192B	1753
SK40193B	1765
SK40194B	1758
SK40195B	1773
SK40208B	5879
SK40251B	OEM
SK40257B	6260

If replacement code is OEM, contact original manufacturer for replacement.

559

DEVICE TYPE	REPL CODE
SK74107	0936
SK74109	0962
SK74110	0981
SK74111	0996
SK74121	0175
SK74122	1131
SK74123	1149
SK74125	1174
SK74126	1184
SK74128	1210
SK74132	1261
SK74141	1367
SK74142	1380
SK74143	1399
SK74144	1408
SK74145	0614
SK74146	1784
SK74147	1442
SK74150	1484
SK74151	1487
SK74153	1531
SK74154	1546
SK74155	1566
SK74156	1582
SK74157	1595
SK74158	4372
SK74160	1621
SK74161	1635
SK74162	1007
SK74163	1656
SK74164	0729
SK74165	1675
SK74166	0231
SK74170	1711
SK74173	1755
SK74174	1759
SK74175	1776
SK74176	1784
SK74177	1792
SK74178	1802
SK74179	1809
SK74180	1818
SK74181	1831
SK74182	1845
SK74190	1901
SK74191	1906
SK74192	1910
SK74193	1915
SK74195	1932
SK74196	1939
SK74197	1945
SK74198	1953
SK74199	1960
SK74221	2129
SK74251	2283
SK74290	2588
SK74293	2620
SK74365	1450
SK74366	1462
SK74367	1479
SK74368	1500
SK74390	3210
SK74500	OEM
SK74511	OEM
SK74574	OEM
SK75454B	1279
SK75493	4933
SK92189	OEM
SK707380	0588
SKA0030	0079
SKA13	OEM
SKA17	OEM
SKA1079	0126
SKA1080	0016
SKA1117	0016
SKA1279	0037
SKA1395	0016
SKA1416	0127
SKA-4061	0037
SKA-4074	0127
SKA4074	0144
SKA-4075	0127
SKA4075	0144
SKA-4076	0224
SKA4076	0144
SKA4129	0037
SKA4141	0016
SKA4410	0590
SKA4525	0144
SKA-4590	0224
SKA4616	0086
SKA4621	0126
SKA4768	0007
SKA-4802	0111
SKA-5248	0127
SKA5248	0144
SKA-5541	0007
SKA5571	0283
SKA-5658	0264
SKA-5886	0144
SKA5886	0144
SKA6250	0037
SKA-6256	0079
SKA-6437	0079
SKA6556	0016
SKA-8105	0079
SKA9013	0144
SKA9096	0144
SKB8339	0016

DEVICE TYPE	REPL CODE
SKH866A	OEM
SKLS30	OEM
SKMV10B	1681
SKMV10C	1684
SKMV14B	1997
SKMV14C	1998
SKMV15B	1304
SKMV15C	1309
SKMV17B	2309
SKMV17C	2310
SKMV18A	2577
SKMV20B	2763
SKMV20C	2769
SKMV25A	4297
SKMV25B	3044
SKMV30A	5638
SKMV30C	3046
SKMV35B	2907
SKMV35C	2913
SKMV40B	4199
SKMV40C	3049
SKMV50B	4395
SKMV50C	3056
SKMV60A	4158
SKMV60B	3061
SKMV75A	4834
SKMV75B	3075
SKMV95A	5066
SKMV95B	3087
SKMV115B	4072
SKMV115C	3094
SKMV130G	0834
SKMV130H	1364
SKMV130J	0832
SKMV130K	0824
SKMV130L	4204
SKMV130P	2521
SKMV132A	2603
SKMV150H	0246
SKMV150J	1982
SKMV150K	3381
SKMV250H	1322
SKMV250J	1324
SKMV250K	1326
SKMV275A	1648
SKMV275B	1650
SKMV300	4394
SKMV320B	2023
SKMV373A	2344
SKMV420	3226
SKMV480G	1093
SKMV480H	0776
SKN4F1-01	OEM
SKN4F1-02	OEM
SKN4F1-03	OEM
SKN4F1-04	OEM
SKN4F1-06	OEM
SKN4F1-08	OEM
SKN4F1-11	OEM
196433	1772
SKT1-01A	OEM
SKT1-01G	OEM
SKT1-02A	OEM
SKT1-02G	OEM
SKT1-04A	OEM
SKT1-04B	OEM
SKT1-04G	OEM
SKT1-06A	OEM
SKT1-06B	OEM
SKT1-06G	OEM
SKT1-07A	OEM
SKT1-07G	OEM
SKT1-08B	OEM
SKT1-10B	OEM
SKT1-12B	OEM
SKT3-01A	OEM
SKT3-01G	OEM
SKT3-02A	OEM
SKT3-02G	OEM
SKT3-04A	OEM
SKT3-04B	OEM
SKT3-04G	OEM
SKT3-06A	OEM
SKT3-06B	OEM
SKT3-06G	OEM
SKT3-07A	OEM
SKT3-07G	OEM
SKT3-08B	OEM
SKT3-10B	OEM
SKT3-12B	OEM
SKT12-01CR	OEM
SKT12-02C	OEM
SKT12-02CQ	OEM
SKT12-02CR	OEM
SKT12-02CS	OEM
SKT12-04C	OEM
SKT12-04CQ	OEM
SKT12-04CR	OEM
SKT12-04CS	OEM
SKT12-06C	OEM
SKT12-06CQ	OEM
SKT12-06CR	OEM
SKT12-06CS	OEM
SKT12-08C	OEM
SKT12-08CR	OEM
SKT12-08CS	OEM
SKT12-10C	OEM
SKT12-10CR	OEM
SKT12-10CS	OEM

DEVICE TYPE	REPL CODE
SKT12-12C	OEM
SKT12-12CS	OEM
SKT16-01CS	OEM
SKT16-02C	OEM
SKT16-02CR	OEM
SKT16-02CS	OEM
SKT16-04C	OEM
SKT16-04CR	OEM
SKT16-04CS	OEM
SKT16-06CR	OEM
SKT16-06CS	OEM
SKT16-08C	OEM
SKT16-08CR	OEM
SKT16-08CS	OEM
SKT16-10CR	OEM
SKT16-10CS	OEM
SKT16-10E	OEM
SKT16-12CS	OEM
SKT24-02C	OEM
SKT24-04C	OEM
SKT24-06C	OEM
SKT24-08C	OEM
SKT24-08C#	0674
SKT24-10E	OEM
SKT36-02C	OEM
SKT36-04C	OEM
SKT36-06C	OEM
SKT36-08C	OEM
SKT36-10C	OEM
SKT36-10E	OEM
SKT36-12C	OEM
SKT36-12E	OEM
SKT45-02C	OEM
SKT45-04C	OEM
SKT45-06C	OEM
SKT45-08C	OEM
SKT45-10C	OEM
SKT45-10E	OEM
SKT45-12C	OEM
SKT45-12E	OEM
SKT45-14C	OEM
SKT45-14E	OEM
SKT45-16C	OEM
SKT45-16E	OEM
SKT46-09	OEM
SKT55-02C	OEM
SKT55-04C	OEM
SKT55-06C	OEM
SKT55-08C	OEM
SKT55-10C	OEM
SKT55-10E	OEM
SKT55-12C	OEM
SKT71-09	OEM
SKT80-02C	OEM
SKT80-04C	OEM
SKT80-06C	OEM
SKT80-08C	OEM
SKT80-10C	OEM
SKT80-10E	OEM
SKT90-0F	OEM
SKT100-10E	OEM
SKT111-09	OEM
SKT130-02C	OEM
SKT130-04C	OEM
SKT130-06C	OEM
SKT130-08C	OEM
SKT130-10C	OEM
SKT130-10E	OEM
SKT130-12C	OEM
SKT140-02CV	OEM
SKT140-04CV	OEM
SKT140-06CV	OEM
SKT140-08CV	OEM
SKT140-10CV	OEM
SKT140-12CV	OEM
SKT141-09	OEM
SKT160-02C	1076
SKT160-04C	1078
SKT160-06C	OEM
SKT160-08C	OEM
SKT160-10C	OEM
SKT160-10E	OEM
SKT160-12C	OEM
SKT171-09	OEM
SKT180-02CT	OEM
SKT180-02CU	OEM
SKT180-02CV	OEM
SKT180-04CT	OEM
SKT180-04CU	OEM
SKT180-04CV	OEM
SKT180-06CT	OEM
SKT180-06CU	OEM
SKT180-06CV	OEM
SKT180-08CT	OEM
SKT180-08CU	OEM
SKT180-08CV	OEM
SKT180-10CU	OEM
SKT180-10CV	OEM
SKT180-12CU	OEM
SKT180-12CV	OEM
SKT215-02C	OEM
SKT215-04C	OEM
SKT215-06C	OEM
SKT215-08C	OEM
SKT215-10C	OEM
SKT215-10E	OEM
SKT215-12C	OEM
SKT216-02C	OEM
SKT216-04C	OEM

DEVICE TYPE	REPL CODE
SKT216-06C	OEM
SKT216-08C	OEM
SKT216-10C	OEM
SKT216-10E	OEM
SKT216-12C	OEM
SKT216-12E	OEM
SKT216-14C	OEM
SKT216-14E	OEM
SKT216-16C	OEM
SKT216-16E	OEM
SKT220-02F	OEM
SKT220-04F	OEM
SKT220-06F	OEM
SKT220-08F	OEM
SKT220-10	OEM
SKT220-12	OEM
SKT220-14	OEM
SKT220-16	OEM
SKT221-09	OEM
SKT230-02C	OEM
SKT230-04C	OEM
SKT230-06C	OEM
SKT230-08C	OEM
SKT230-10C	OEM
SKT230-10E	OEM
SKT230-12C	OEM
SKT240-02CT	OEM
SKT240-02CU	OEM
SKT240-02CV	OEM
SKT240-04CT	OEM
SKT240-04CU	OEM
SKT240-04CV	OEM
SKT240-06CT	OEM
SKT240-06CU	OEM
SKT240-06CV	OEM
SKT240-08CT	OEM
SKT240-08CU	OEM
SKT240-08CV	OEM
SKT240-10CU	OEM
SKT240-10CV	OEM
SKT240-12CU	OEM
SKT240-12CV	OEM
SKT250-02C	OEM
SKT250-06C	OEM
SKT250-08C	OEM
SKT250-10C	OEM
SKT250-10E	OEM
SKT250-12C	OEM
SKT251-02C	OEM
SKT251-04C	OEM
SKT251-06C	OEM
SKT251-08C	OEM
SKT251-10C	OEM
SKT251-10E	OEM
SKT251-12C	OEM
SKT251-12E	OEM
SKT251-14C	OEM
SKT251-14E	OEM
SKT251-16C	OEM
SKT251-16E	OEM
SKT300-02C	OEM
SKT300-04C	OEM
SKT300-06C	OEM
SKT300-08C	OEM
SKT300-10C	OEM
SKT300-12C	OEM
SKT301-02C	OEM
SKT301-04C	OEM
SKT301-06C	OEM
SKT301-08C	OEM
SKT301-10C	OEM
SKT301-10E	OEM
SKT301-12C	OEM
SKT301-12E	OEM
SKT301-14C	OEM
SKT301-14E	OEM
SKT301-16C	OEM
SKT301-16E	OEM
SKT330-10E	OEM
SKT450-02C	OEM
SKT450-06C	OEM
SKT450-10C	OEM
SKT450-12C	OEM
SKT300102C+	OEM
SKT300104C+	0733
SKT300106C+	0733
SKT300108C+	0733
SKT300110C+	0733
SKT300112C+	0733
SKX75000	OEM
SKX100000	OEM
SKX125000	OEM
SKX150000	OEM
SL-030	0015
SL030S	0015
SL-030T	0015
SL030T	0015
SL051A	1991
SL0305,T	0015
SL0307	OEM
SL0315	OEM
SL0325	OEM
SL0335	OEM
SL0507	OEM
SL0515	OEM
SL0525	OEM
SL0535	OEM
SL01640	1063
SL02518	3384

DEVICE TYPE	REPL CODE
SL02519	1063
SL02734	1063
SL02779	1063
SL02781	OEM
SL03019	1063
SL03021	OEM
SL03667	3847
SL03911	1833
SL03912	1848
SL03913	0337
SL03914	1035
SL03915	0033
SL03916	1824
SL03917	2067
SL04194	1248
SL04217	3384
SL04218	1063
SL04563	1812
SL04567	1820
SL04568	1035
SL04570	2067
SL04732	1063
SL-2	0015
SL2	0015
SL-3	0015
SL3	0109
SL-3R	OEM
SL-5	0242
SL5	0015
SL-5R	OEM
SL10	0145
SL-25R	OEM
SL50	0084
SL53URT	OEM
SL55VR3FT	OEM
SL91	0015
SL92	0015
SL93	0015
SL100	0144
SL-103	0242
SL103	0015
SL103K	OEM
SL119	0037
SL136-6	OEM
SL200	0150
SL201	0150
SL203A	OEM
SL203K	OEM
SL203M	OEM
SL300	0016
SL301A	0414
SL301AE	0414
SL301B	0414
SL301BE	0414
SL301C	0086
SL301CE	0086
SL301E	0414
SL301EE	0414
SL302A	OEM
SL303A	OEM
SL303AE	0414
SL303AT	0414
SL303B	OEM
SL303BE	0414
SL303BT	0414
SL354BE	0414
SL354BF	0414
SL360	OEM
SL400	0109
SL403	0155
SL403A	OEM
SL403K	OEM
SL404	OEM
SL-425G	OEM
SL-425R	OEM
SL500	0122
SL600	0122
SL603A	OEM
SL603K	OEM
SL603M	OEM
SL608	0071
SL610	0071
SL708	0071
SL710	0071
SL800	0131
SL800X	0131
SL803A	OEM
SL803K	OEM
SL803M	OEM
SL-833	0015
SL833	0015
SL-833A	0015
SL833A	0015
SL918	0144
SL1000	0145
SL1000X	0145
SL1003A	OEM
SL1003K	OEM
SL1003M	OEM
SL1041	OEM
SL1049A	OEM
SL1199	OEM
SL-1203	OEM
SL1203	OEM
SL-1203-20	OEM
SL1203-20	OEM
SL1203A	OEM
SL-1203H	OEM
SL1203K	OEM

DEVICE TYPE	REPL CODE
SL1203M	OEM
SL1233A	OEM
SL1252	OEM
SL1255	OEM
SL1256	OEM
SL1259A	OEM
SL1263	OEM
SL-1263H	OEM
SL1403A	OEM
SL1424-11B	OEM
SL1424-11U	OEM
SL1462-11C	OEM
SL1489A	OEM
SL1498	OEM
SL1498IIT	OEM
SL1611C	OEM
SL1611C/DP	OEM
SL1621C	OEM
SL1622C	1635
SL1626C	1635
SL1626K	OEM
SL1640C	OEM
SL1641C	OEM
SL2010	OEM
SL-2243T	OEM
SL2243T	OEM
SL2272-05K	OEM
SL2283	OEM
SL2444-04K	OEM
SL2444-04KUL	OEM
SL2475-04K	OEM
SL2713-01K	OEM
SL3101	0126
SL3111	0126
SL3693	0144
SL7059	0627
SL7283	0627
SL7308	0627
SL7531	0627
SL7593	0627
SL8020	0627
SL8110	OEM
SL11877	1812
SL11878	1820
SL11879	0141
SL11880	3365
SL11881	0557
SL14959	0680
SL14960	2382
SL14971	0462
SL14972	0990
SL16121	OEM
SL16122	1248
SL16201	1812
SL16203	2067
SL16204	0141
SL16206	1035
SL16208	1824
SL16209	0329
SL16210	1820
SL16211	0081
SL16212	0557
SL16215	0033
SL16216	1833
SL16218	0337
SL16516	1812
SL16517	2086
SL16518	1820
SL16519	0141
SL16520	0557
SL16521	0081
SL16522	0329
SL16584	1812
SL16585	3032
SL16586	1035
SL16587	1820
SL16588	0081
SL16589	0141
SL16590	3365
SL16591	0557
SL16793	0232
SL16794	0268
SL16795	0310
SL16796	0357
SL16797	0381
SL16798	0462
SL16799	0522
SL16800	0692
SL16801	0507
SL16802	0867
SL16803	1018
SL16804	0738
SL16805	1177
SL16806	1164
SL16807	1303
SL16808	1150
SL16809	0828
SL16810	1705
SL16811	0033
SL17242	1164
SL17284	1035
SL17289	1820
SL17869	0462
SL17887	0522
SL18386	0117
SL18387	0936
SL18699	1354
SL20721	2147
SL20755	0661

DEVICE TYPE	REPL CODE
SL21017	0350
SL21122	0348
SL21384	1545
SL21441	0748
SL21577	1545
SL21654	0167
SL21864	0696
SL24618	4506
SL53424	1812
SL53425	1035
SL53426	1168
SL53427	1820
SL53428	0033
SL53429	0141
SL53431	0268
SL146211C	OEM
SLA007-1	OEM
SLA009	OEM
SLA-01	3835
SLA01	0071
SLA-02	3835
SLA02	OEM
SLA-02-HC	0344
SLA-02-HF	3835
SLA02HC	OEM
SLA02HF	OEM
SLA-03	3835
SLA03	OEM
SLA-03-HC	OEM
SLA-03-HF	3835
SLA03HC	OEM
SLA03HF	OEM
SLA-04	3835
SLA04	OEM
SLA-04-HC	OEM
SLA-04-HF	3835
SLA04HC	OEM
SLA04HF	OEM
SLA-05	3835
SLA05	OEM
SLA-05-HC	OEM
SLA-05-HF	3835
SLA05HC	OEM
SLA05HF	OEM
SLA-06	3835
SLA06	OEM
SLA-08	OEM
SLA08	OEM
SLA-010	OEM
SLA010	OEM
SLA-012	OEM
SLA012	OEM
SLA-014	OEM
SLA014	OEM
SLA-016	OEM
SLA016	OEM
SLA-018	OEM
SLA018	OEM
SLA-020	OEM
SLA020	OEM
SLA-11	1325
SLA11AB	0015
SLA11C	0015
SLA-12	0080
SLA12	OEM
SLA12AB	0015
SLA12C	0015
SLA-13	0604
SLA13AB	0015
SLA13C	0015
SLA-14	0790
SLA14	OEM
SLA14AB	0015
SLA14C	0015
SLA-15	0790
SLA15AB	0015
SLA15C	0015
SLA-16	0015
SLA16	OEM
SLA16AB	0015
SLA16C	0015
SLA-17	0015
SLA17AB	0015
SLA17C	0015
SLA-18	0072
SLA18	OEM
SLA18AB	0071
SLA18C	0071
SLA-19	0071
SLA19AB	0071
SLA19C	0071
SLA-20	0182
SLA20AB	OEM
SLA20C	OEM
SLA-21	0071
SLA21A	0110
SLA21B	0110
SLA21C	0110
SLA-22	0071
SLA22A	0947
SLA22B	0947
SLA22C	0947
SLA-23	0071
SLA23A	OEM
SLA23B	0242
SLA23C	0947
SLA-24	0071
SLA24A	0535
SLA24B	0535

If replacement code is OEM, contact original manufacturer for replacement.

DEVICE TYPE	REPL CODE
SLA24C	0535
SLA-25	0071
SLA25A	0535
SLA25B	0535
SLA25C	0535
SLA-26	0071
SLA26A	0959
SLA26B	0959
SLA26C	0959
SLA-27	0071
SLA27A	0959
SLA27B	0959
SLA27C	0959
SLA-28	0071
SLA28A	0811
SLA28B	0811
SLA28C	0811
SLA-29	0071
SLA29A	0916
SLA29B	0916
SLA29C	0916
SLA-30	0102
SLA30A	OEM
SLA30B	OEM
SLA30C	OEM
SLA-31	0102
SLA31A	OEM
SLA31B	OEM
SLA31C	OEM
SLA-32	0344
SLA32A	OEM
SLA32B	OEM
SLA32C	OEM
SLA-33	0344
SLA33A	OEM
SLA33B	OEM
SLA33C	OEM
SLA-34	0344
SLA34A	OEM
SLA34B	OEM
SLA34C	OEM
SLA-50-LCD	0276
SLA-100-LCD	0276
SLA-200	1404
SLA-200-LCD	0287
SLA-300	0468
SLA-400	0468
SLA-400-LCD	0293
SLA440	0015
SLA440B	0015
SLA441	0015
SLA441B	0015
SLA442	0015
SLA442B	0015
SLA443	0015
SLA443B	0015
SLA444	0015
SLA444A	0015
SLA444B	0015
SLA445	0015
SLA445B	0015
SLA-500	0441
SLA536	0015
SLA537	0015
SLA538	0015
SLA539	0015
SLA540	0015
SLA547	0015
SLA560	0071
SLA561	0071
SLA591LT3	4240
SLA599	0015
SLA599A	0015
SLA-600	0441
SLA600	0015
SLA-600-LCD	0299
SLA600A	0015
SLA601	0015
SLA601A	0015
SLA602	0015
SLA602A	0015
SLA603	0015
SLA603A	0015
SLA604	0015
SLA604A	0015
SLA605	0015
SLA605A	0015
SLA606	0015
SLA606A	0015
SLA-700	1412
SLA-800	1412
SLA-800-LCD	0250
SLA-900	2425
SLA-1000	2425
SLA-1000-LCD	0250
SLA1095	0015
SLA1096	0015
SLA1100	0015
SLA1101	0015
SLA1102	0015
SLA1103	0535
SLA1104	0015
SLA1105	0015
SLA-1400	0344
SLA1400A	OEM
SLA1400B	OEM
SLA1400C	OEM
SLA1487	0015
SLA1488	0015

DEVICE TYPE	REPL CODE
SLA1489	0015
SLA1490	0015
SLA1491	0015
SLA1492	0015
SLA-1600	0344
SLA1600A	OEM
SLA1600B	OEM
SLA1600C	OEM
SLA1692	0015
SLA1693	0015
SLA1694	0015
SLA1695	0015
SLA1696	0015
SLA1697	0015
SLA-1800	0344
SLA1800A	OEM
SLA1800B	OEM
SLA1800C	OEM
SLA-2000	0344
SLA2000A	OEM
SLA2000B	OEM
SLA2000C	OEM
SLA2610	0015
SLA2611	0015
SLA2612	0015
SLA2613	0015
SLA2614	0015
SLA2615	0015
SLA2616	0071
SLA2617	0071
SLA3193	0015
SLA3194	0015
SLA3195	0015
SLA3196	0071
SLA4030C0B	OEM
SLA4061	OEM
SLA5197	0110
SLA5197HF	OEM
SLA5198	0947
SLA5198HF	OEM
SLA5199	0242
SLA5199HF	OEM
SLA5200	0535
SLA5200HF	OEM
SLA5201	0959
SLA5201HF	OEM
SLA5202	0811
SLA5202HF	OEM
SLA5203	0916
SLA5203HF	OEM
SLA5204	OEM
SLA5204HF	OEM
SLA5205	OEM
SLA5205HF	OEM
SLA6140J1P	OEM
SLA6330JOL	OEM
SLA6330JOM	OEM
SLA6430J1S	OEM
SLA6430J2A	OEM
SLA7020	OEM
SLA7020M	OEM
SLA9030M	OEM
SLA01	0071
SLB-15DU3	OEM
SLB15DU3	OEM
SLB-22DU	OEM
SLB-22GG	OEM
SLB-22UR	OEM
SLB-22YY	OEM
SLB-25DU	OEM
SLB25DU	OEM
SLB-25DU3	OEM
SLB25DU3	OEM
SLB-25MG	OEM
SLB-25MG3	OEM
SLB25MG3	OEM
SLB-25VR	OEM
SLB25VR	OEM
SLB-25VR3	OEM
SLB25VR3	OEM
SLB-26GG	OEM
SLB-26UR	OEM
SLB26UR5	OEM
SLB-26UU	OEM
SLB-26YY	OEM
SLB-55DU3	OEM
SLB55DU3	OEM
SLB55MG3	OEM
SLB55VR3	OEM
SLB-72GG5HL	OEM
SLB72UR5HL	OEM
SLB74UR3GH	OEM
SLC6.5	OEM
SLC6.5A	OEM
SLC7.0	OEM
SLC7.0A	OEM
SLC7.5	OEM
SLC7.5A	OEM
SLC8.0	OEM
SLC8.0A	OEM
SLC8.5	OEM
SLC8.5A	OEM
SLC9.0	OEM
SLC9.0A	OEM
SLC10	OEM
SLC10A	OEM
SLC11	OEM
SLC11A	OEM
SLC12	OEM

DEVICE TYPE	REPL CODE
SLC12A	OEM
SLC13	OEM
SLC13A	OEM
SLC14	OEM
SLC14A	OEM
SLC15	OEM
SLC15A	OEM
SLC16	OEM
SLC16A	OEM
SLC17	OEM
SLC17A	OEM
SLC18	OEM
SLC18A	OEM
SLC20	OEM
SLC20A	OEM
SLC22	OEM
SLC22A	OEM
SLC-22DU	OEM
SLC-22GG	OEM
SLC-22UR	OEM
SLC-22YY	OEM
SLC24	OEM
SLC24A	OEM
SLC-26	OEM
SLC26	OEM
SLC26A	OEM
SLC-26GC14	OEM
SLC-26GG	OEM
SLC-26UR	OEM
SLC-26UR14	OEM
SLC26UR14	OEM
SLC-26UU	OEM
SLC-26VR5F	OEM
SLC26VR5F	OEM
SLC-26YY	OEM
SLC28	OEM
SLC28A	OEM
SLC30	OEM
SLC30A	OEM
SLC33	OEM
SLC33A	OEM
SLC36	OEM
SLC36A	OEM
SLC40	OEM
SLC40A	OEM
SLC43	OEM
SLC43A	OEM
SLC45	OEM
SLC45A	OEM
SLC48	OEM
SLC48A	OEM
SLC51	OEM
SLC51A	OEM
SLC54	OEM
SLC54A	OEM
SLC58	OEM
SLC58A	OEM
SLC60	OEM
SLC60A	OEM
SLC64	OEM
SLC64A	OEM
SLC70	OEM
SLC70A	OEM
SLC75	OEM
SLC75A	OEM
SLC90	OEM
SLC90A	OEM
SLC100	OEM
SLC100A	OEM
SLC110	OEM
SLC110A	OEM
SLC120	OEM
SLC120A	OEM
SLC130	OEM
SLC130A	OEM
SLC150	OEM
SLC150A	OEM
SLC160	OEM
SLC160A	OEM
SLC170	OEM
SLC170A	OEM
SLC50155RSN	OEM
SLCE6.5	OEM
SLCE6.5A	OEM
SLCE7.0	OEM
SLCE7.0A	OEM
SLCE7.5	OEM
SLCE7.5A	OEM
SLCE8.0	OEM
SLCE8.0A	OEM
SLCE8.5	OEM
SLCE8.5A	OEM
SLCE9.0	OEM
SLCE9.0A	OEM
SLCE10	OEM
SLCE10A	OEM
SLCE11	OEM
SLCE11A	OEM
SLCE12	OEM
SLCE12A	OEM
SLCE13	OEM
SLCE13A	OEM
SLCE14	OEM
SLCE14A	OEM
SLCE15	OEM
SLCE15A	OEM
SLCE16	OEM
SLCE16A	OEM
SLCE17	OEM

DEVICE TYPE	REPL CODE
SLCE17A	OEM
SLCE18	OEM
SLCE18A	OEM
SLCE20	OEM
SLCE20A	OEM
SLCE22	OEM
SLCE22A	OEM
SLCE24	OEM
SLCE24A	OEM
SLCE26	OEM
SLCE26A	OEM
SLCE28	OEM
SLCE28A	OEM
SLCE30	OEM
SLCE30A	OEM
SLCE33	OEM
SLCE33A	OEM
SLCE36	OEM
SLCE36A	OEM
SLCE40	OEM
SLCE40A	OEM
SLCE43	OEM
SLCE43A	OEM
SLCE45	OEM
SLCE45A	OEM
SLCE48	OEM
SLCE48A	OEM
SLCE51	OEM
SLCE51A	OEM
SLCE54	OEM
SLCE54A	OEM
SLCE58	OEM
SLCE58A	OEM
SLCE60	OEM
SLCE60A	OEM
SLCE64	OEM
SLCE64A	OEM
SLCE70	OEM
SLCE70A	OEM
SLCE75	OEM
SLCE75A	OEM
SLCE90	OEM
SLCE90A	OEM
SLCE100	OEM
SLCE100A	OEM
SLCE110	OEM
SLCE110A	OEM
SLCE120	OEM
SLCE120A	OEM
SLCE130	OEM
SLCE130A	OEM
SLCE150	OEM
SLCE150A	OEM
SLCE160	OEM
SLCE160A	OEM
SLCE170	OEM
SLCE170A	OEM
SLD30AR	OEM
SLD30UR	OEM
SLEA05	2347
SLEA1	2347
SLEA2	2347
SLEA3	2353
SLEA4	2353
SLEA6	2354
SLEA8	2356
SLEA10	2357
SLED-G	OEM
SLED-R	OEM
SLG5553KB++GR	OEM
SLG5553KB++RE	OEM
SLH-34DC3	OEM
SLH-34DT3	OEM
SLH-34DU3	OEM
SLH-34MC3	OEM
SLH-34MC3F	OEM
SLH-34MG3	OEM
SLH-34MT3	OEM
SLH34MT3	OEM
SLH-34PC3	OEM
SLH-34PT3	OEM
SLH-34UR3	OEM
SLH-34URC3	OEM
SLH-34UT3	OEM
SLH-34VC3	OEM
SLH-34VR3	OEM
SLH-34VT3	OEM
SLH-34YC3	OEM
SLH-34YC3F	OEM
SLH-34YT3	OEM
SLH-34YY3	OEM
SLH54MT4	OEM
SLH-56DC3	OEM
SLH-56DT3	OEM
SLH-56DU3	OEM
SLH-56MC3	OEM
SLH56MC4F	OEM
SLH-56MC77F	OEM
SLH-56MG3	OEM
SLH-56MT3	OEM
SLH-56PC3	OEM
SLH-56PT3	OEM
SLH-56UR3	OEM
SLH-56URC3	OEM
SLH-56UT3	OEM
SLH-56VC3	OEM
SLH56VC3	OEM
SLH56VC4F	OEM
SLH56VC5	OEM

DEVICE TYPE	REPL CODE
SLH-56VC77F	OEM
SLH-56VR3	OEM
SLH-56VT3	OEM
SLH-56YC3	OEM
SLH56YC3	OEM
SLH-56YT3	OEM
SLH-56YY3	OEM
SLJ-265MGHL	OEM
SLJ-265URHL	OEM
SLK2442-01	OEM
SLN2020P	OEM
SLN2030P	OEM
SLN2035P	OEM
SLN2040P	OEM
SLN2045P	OEM
SLN3020P	OEM
SLN3030P	OEM
SLN3035P	OEM
SLN3040P	OEM
SLN3045P	OEM
SLP24B	OEM
SLP-34UR5	OEM
SLP114	OEM
SLP114A	OEM
SLP114B	OEM
SLP-115R	OEM
SLP115R	OEM
SLP-123B	OEM
SLP123B	OEM
SLP131	OEM
SLP131B	OEM
SLP133B	OEM
SLP133P	OEM
SLP135A50	OEM
SLP135B	OEM
SLP135B-55	OEM
SLP135BA	OEM
SLP135BB	OEM
SLP135BC	OEM
SLP136B	OEM
SLP-136B-50	OEM
SLP136B-50	OEM
SLP136BA	OEM
SLP-136B-B	OEM
SLP136BB	OEM
SLP136BC	OEM
SLP137B	OEM
SLP-138C-50	OEM
SLP138C-50	OEM
SLP-138C-51	OEM
SLP138C-51	OEM
SLP138C-51B	OEM
SLP-138CB-50	OEM
SLP138CB-50	OEM
SLP-141B	OEM
SLP141B	OEM
SLP144B	OEM
SLP-144B-40	OEM
SLP144B-40	OEM
SLP-144B-51	OEM
SLP144B-51	OEM
SLP-145B	OEM
SLP145B	OEM
SLP146B	OEM
SLP-146B-50	OEM
SLP146B-50	OEM
SLP-151B	5082
SLP151B	5082
SLP-151B-50	5040
SLP151B-50	OEM
SLP152B	6904
SLP152B-02	OEM
SLP-153B	OEM
SLP153B	OEM
SLP-153B-01	OEM
SLP153B-40	OEM
SLP154B	6907
SLP154B-60	OEM
SLP-155B	3990
SLP155B	6908
SLP-155B-50	3990
SLP155B-50	OEM
SLP155BRE	OEM
SLP156B	OEM
SLP-159B	OEM
SLP159B	OEM
SLP159B-50	OEM
SLP159BA	OEM
SLP159BB	OEM
SLP159BC	OEM
SLP-160C	OEM
SLP-161B	OEM
SLP161B	OEM
SLP-162B	OEM
SLP162B	OEM
SLP164BA	OEM
SLP165B	OEM
SLP166B	OEM
SLP166B-03	OEM
SLP167B	OEM
SLP167B-02	OEM
SLP167B-03	OEM
SLP167B-70	OEM
SLP169B	OEM
SLP171D	OEM
SLP171E	OEM
SLP-173	OEM
SLP173	OEM
SLP-173B-01	OEM

DEVICE TYPE	REPL CODE
SLP173B-01	OEM
SLP-173B-50	3990
SLP173B-50	OEM
SLP174B	OEM
SLP175B	OEM
SLP-175B-50	OEM
SLP175B-50	OEM
SLP-177B-60	OEM
SLP177B-60	OEM
SLP-178B	OEM
SLP178B	OEM
SLP-178C-A	OEM
SLP178CA	OEM
SLP-180C-AB	OEM
SLP-181B	OEM
SLP181B	OEM
SLP181B-50	OEM
SLP181B-50A	OEM
SLP181B-50B	OEM
SLP183B-09	OEM
SLP224B	OEM
SLP-235B	0835
SLP235B	OEM
SLP-235B(GR)	0835
SLP-236B	0856
SLP-236B(G)	4598
SLP-236B(GR)	4598
SLP-236B(GREEN)	4598
SLP-236B(Y)	0856
SLP-236B(YEL)	0856
SLP-236B(YELLOW)	0856
SLP236B-50	OEM
SLP-236B-A	OEM
SLP-236P(GR)	4598
SLP237B	OEM
SLP239B	OEM
SLP244B	OEM
SLP-251B	1069
SLP251B	6960
SLP251B-50	OEM
SLP252B	6961
SLP252B-03	OEM
SLP253B	OEM
SLP-255B	1123
SLP255B	6963
SLP258B	OEM
SLP-261B	OEM
SLP261B	OEM
SLP-262B	OEM
SLP262B	OEM
SLP265B	OEM
SLP267B	OEM
SLP267B-03	OEM
SLP271D	OEM
SLP-273	OEM
SLP-273B-01	OEM
SLP273B-01	OEM
SLP273B-50U	OEM
SLP274B	OEM
SLP275B	OEM
SLP-277B-60	OEM
SLP277B-60	OEM
SLP-278C	OEM
SLP278C	OEM
SLP280F-50U	OEM
SLP280F-51	OEM
SLP280F-51P	OEM
SLP280F-51U	OEM
SLP282F-50P	OEM
SLP355B-51A	OEM
SLP355B-51B	OEM
SLP-373B-50	OEM
SLP373B-50	OEM
SLP382F-50	OEM
SLP382F-51	OEM
SLP451B	1984
SLP453B	OEM
SLP455B	2012
SLP466B	OEM
SLP475B	OEM
SLP531D	OEM
SLP651B-50A	OEM
SLP651B-50B	OEM
SLP-655B	OEM
SLP655B	OEM
SLP-662B-A	OEM
SLP662B-A	OEM
SLP-662B-B	OEM
SLP662B-B	OEM
SLP-673B-51-A	OEM
SLP-673B-51-B	OEM
SLP673B-51A	OEM
SLP673B-51B	OEM
SLP674B-50A	OEM
SLP674B-50B	OEM
SLP-678B-A	OEM
SLP678B-A	OEM
SLP678B-B	OEM
SLP-873B-51-A	OEM
SLP-888A	4298
SLP955B-50	OEM
SLP973B	OEM
SLP978C	OEM
SLP980C-51	OEM
SLP980F-51	OEM
SLP981C-50	OEM
SLP-982A-50	OEM
SLP982A-50	OEM
SLP982A-51	OEM

DEVICE TYPE	REPL CODE
SLP982C	OEM
SLP982C-50	OEM
SLP2020P	1931
SLP2030P	0579
SLP2035P	1931
SLP2040P	1931
SLP2045P	1931
SLP3020P	1931
SLP3030P	1931
SLP3035P	1931
SLP3040P	1931
SLP3045P	1931
SLP3070K	OEM
SLP4070	OEM
SLP9070	OEM
SLR30UR	OEM
SLR-34DC3	OEM
SLR-34DU3	OEM
SLR-34GG3	OEM
SLR34MC	OEM
SLR-34MC3	OEM
SLR34MC3F	OEM
SLR34MC5	OEM
SLR-34MG3	OEM
SLR-34MT3	OEM
SLR-34PT3	OEM
SLR-34UR3	OEM
SLR-34UR3F	OEM
SLR34UR3F	OEM
SLR-34UR5	OEM
SLR34UR5	OEM
SLR-34UR5F	OEM
SLR-34URC3	OEM
SLR34URC3	OEM
SLR34URC5	OEM
SLR-34URS	OEM
SLR34UW5	OEM
SLR-34VC3	OEM
SLR34VC3F	OEM
SLR34VC3N	OEM
SLR-34VR3	OEM
SLR-34VT3	OEM
SLR-34YC3	OEM
SLR-34YY3	OEM
SLR-40MC3F	OEM
SLR40MC3F	OEM
SLR-40UR3F	OEM
SLR40UR3F	OEM
SLR-40UR5F	OEM
SLR40UR5F	OEM
SLR53GC	OEM
SLR-53GG	OEM
SLR53GG	OEM
SLR53URC	OEM
SLR-53URT	OEM
SLR53URT-1	OEM
SLR-54MC	OEM
SLR-54MT4	OEM
SLR54MT4	OEM
SLR54NPQ	OEM
SLR-54UR	OEM
SLR54UR	OEM
SLR-54UR4	OEM
SLR54UR4	OEM
SLR54URC	OEM
SLR54URC-4	OEM
SLR-54UR-H	OEM
SLR54UR-H	OEM
SLR-54URT	OEM
SLR-54UT4	OEM
SLR54VC	OEM
SLR54VC3F	OEM
SLR54VR4	OEM
SLR55GC5	OEM
SLR-55MC	OEM
SLR55MC	OEM
SLR55MC3F	OEM
SLR-55MC-H	OEM
SLR-56DC3	OEM
SLR-56DU3	OEM
SLR-56GG3	OEM
SLR-56MC3	OEM
SLR-56MG3	OEM
SLR-56MT3	OEM
SLR-56PT3	OEM
SLR-56UR3	OEM
SLR-56URC3	OEM
SLR-56UT3	OEM
SLR-56UW3	OEM
SLR-56VC3	OEM
SLR-56VR3	OEM
SLR-56VT3	OEM
SLR-56YC3	OEM
SLR-56YY3	OEM
SLR-320PG3K	OEM
SLR-320VR3K	OEM
SLR331MC70F070	OEM
SLR534RT	OEM
SLR-932A	OEM
SLR932A	OEM
SLR-933A	OEM
SLR933A	OEM
SLR-938C	OEM
SLR938C	OEM
SLR980C1	OEM
SLT-35GG	OEM
SLT-35UR	OEM
SLT-35UU	OEM
SLT-35YY	OEM

If replacement code is OEM, contact original manufacturer for replacement. 561

DEVICE TYPE	REPL CODE
SLV56DC3	OEM
SLV56URC	OEM
SLZ-136C-07-T1	OEM
SLZ136C-14-AB-T1	OEM
SLZ146B	OEM
SLZ151B	OEM
SLZ167B	OEM
SLZ177BA	OEM
SLZ177BB	OEM
SLZ177BC	OEM
SLZ183B	OEM
SLZ-603A+	1104
SLZ-603K+	0471
SLZ-803A+	2982
SLZ-803K+	0444
SLZ-1003A+	2982
SLZ-1003K+	0444
SM-05-16FR	0344
SM-05-20FRZ	0344
SM-05A-16FR	0344
SM0843	0004
SM07275	0079
SM07286	0079
SM-1	0015
SM1	OEM
SM-1-005	0015
SM1-01C	OEM
SM-1-02	0023
SM1-02	0023
SM-1-02FR	0023
SM1-02FR	OEM
SM-1-02FRA	0023
SM-1-04	0023
SM-1-04FR	0023
SM1-04FR	OEM
SM-1-04FRA	0023
SM-1-06FRA	0023
SM-1-08	0071
SM-1-08FR	0071
SM-1-08FRA	0071
SM-1-10FR	0071
SM-1-10FRA	0071
SM-1-12	0102
SM1-12	OEM
SM-1-47	0015
SM-1A	0023
SM-1A-01	0015
SM-1A-01Z	0080
SM-1A-02	0023
SM1A-02	OEM
SM-1A-02FR	0023
SM-1A-02FRA	0023
SM-1A-02LFD	OEM
SM1A-02LFD	OEM
SM1A-02LFE	OEM
SM-1A-02Z	0604
SM-1A-04	0023
SM-1A-04FR	0023
SM-1A-04FRA	0023
SM-1A-04Z	0790
SM-1A-06	0023
SM-1A-06FR	0023
SM-1A-06FRA	0023
SM-1A-06Z	0015
SM-1A-08	0017
SM-1A-12	0017
SM-1A-15	0017
SM-1A-200	0015
SM-1K	0015
SM1K	0535
SM-1XF08	OEM
SM-1XH02	0023
SM-1XH04	0023
SM-1XH06	0023
SM-1XM02	0023
SM-1XM04	0023
SM-1XM06	0023
SM-1XM08	0017
SM-1XM10	0017
SM-1XN02	0023
SM-1XN04	0023
SM-1XN06	0023
SM-1XN08	0017
SM-1XN12	0017
SM-1XN15	0017
SM-1.5-02	0031
SM-1.5-02FR	0031
SM1.5-02FRT	OEM
SM-1.5-04	0031
SM-1.5-04FR	0031
SM-1.5-08	0071
SM-1.5-08FR	0071
SM-1.5-10	0071
SM-1.5-10FR	0071
SM-1.5-10Z1	0015
SM2B41	0948
SM2B42	OEM
SM2D41	4366
SM2D42	OEM
SM-3-02	0031
SM-3-02FR	0031
SM-3-04	0031
SM-3-04FR	0031
SM-3-06	0031
SM-3-06FR	0031
SM-3-08	0071
SM-3-08FR	0071
SM3G41	0480
SM3G41-LC2	0480

DEVICE TYPE	REPL CODE
SM4	0015
SM5	0015
SM5B12	0404
SM5D12	0407
SM10	0015
SM10B11	0404
SM10B12	0154
SM10D11	0407
SM10D12	0154
SM10G12	0278
SM11	0015
SM12	OEM
SM12D41	0767
SM12G41	0739
SM12J41	0612
SM13	OEM
SM20	0015
SM21	OEM
SM22	OEM
SM23	OEM
SM30	0015
SM30D11	2004
SM30G11	2006
SM31	0015
SM33	OEM
SM40	0015
SM41	OEM
SM42	OEM
SM43	OEM
SM45	OEM
SM50	0015
SM51	0015
SM60	0015
SM61	OEM
SM63	1423
SM70	0071
SM71	0071
SM72	OEM
SM73	0071
SM73(I.C.)	1423
SM75	OEM
SM80	0071
SM80B11	OEM
SM80D11	OEM
SM80G11	OEM
SM81	0071
SM82	OEM
SM83	0071
SM90	OEM
SM91	OEM
SM92	OEM
SM93	OEM
SM100	0071
SM101	0071
SM103	0071
SM105	0015
SM110	0015
SM112	0015
SM113-02	OEM
SM113-03	OEM
SM118	OEM
SM118F	OEM
SM120	0015
SM121	OEM
SM121-02	OEM
SM121-03	OEM
SM123	OEM
SM123-02	OEM
SM123-03	OEM
SM130	0015
SM131-02	OEM
SM131-03	OEM
SM133-02	OEM
SM133-03	OEM
SM140	0015
SM143-02	OEM
SM150	0071
SM-150-005	0071
SM-150-01	0071
SM-150-02	0071
SM150-02	0071
SM-150-02(CENTERING)	0914
SM-150-04	0015
SM150-04	OEM
SM-150-06	0015
SM150-06	OEM
SM-150-08	0071
SM150-08	OEM
SM150-6	0071
SM-150-10	0071
SM150-10	OEM
SM150-11	0071
SM-150-12	0102
SM-150-A	0015
SM-150-B	0015
SM-150-C	0071
SM-150-D	0071
SM-150A	0071
SM150A	0071
SM150B	0071
SM150C	0071
SM150D	0071
SM150S	0071
SM150SS	0071
SM153-02	OEM
SM153-03	OEM
SM153A	OEM
SM153AH	OEM
SM153B	OEM

DEVICE TYPE	REPL CODE
SM153BM	OEM
SM153C	OEM
SM153CH	OEM
SM160	0015
SM163-02	OEM
SM163-03	OEM
SM170	0071
SM173-02	OEM
SM173-03	OEM
SM180	0071
SM182-02	OEM
SM182-03	OEM
SM192-02	OEM
SM192-03	OEM
SM200	0071
SM205	0015
SM210	0015
SM211-02	OEM
SM211-03	OEM
SM213-02	OEM
SM213-03	OEM
SM215A	0604
SM217	0050
SM220	0015
SM221-02	OEM
SM221-03	OEM
SM223-02	OEM
SM223-03	OEM
SM230	0015
SM240	0015
SM249I	0050
SM250	0015
SM260	0015
SM270	0071
SM280	0071
SM300	0071
SM483	0015
SM486	0015
SM487	0015
SM488	0015
SM505	0015
SM510	0015
SM512	0015
SM513	0015
SM514	0015
SM515	0015
SM516	0015
SM517	0071
SM518	0071
SM520	0071
SM576-1	0016
SM576-2	0016
SM645	0015
SM646	0015
SM705	0015
SM710	0015
SM-716	0016
SM716	0016
SM720	0015
SM730	0015
SM740	0015
SM750	0015
SM760	0015
SM770	0071
SM780	0071
SM800	0071
SM843	0004
SM862	0136
SM906	OEM
SM1297	0050
SM1507	0037
SM1600	0050
SM2491	0050
SM2492	0050
SM2700	0016
SM2701	0016
SM3014	0050
SM3104	0016
SM3117A	0016
SM3505	0016
SM3978	0086
SM3986	0016
SM3987	0126
SM-4304-S	0007
SM4304-S	0224
SM4508	OEM
SM4508-B	0016
SM4547	0037
SM4719	0037
SM5104	2592
SM5104F	2592
SM5104G	2592
SM5104P	2592
SM5107	OEM
SM5109	1704
SM5118	OEM
SM5118G	OEM
SM5205A	OEM
SM5379	0016
SM5502A	OEM
SM5564	0079
SM5601	OEM
SM5602	OEM
SM5602C	OEM
SM5643	0079
SM5796	0144
SM5807EP	OEM
SM5807ESET	OEM
SM5807FP	OEM

DEVICE TYPE	REPL CODE
SM6251	0086
SM6430B	OEM
SM6442A	OEM
SM6442B	OEM
SM6727	0233
SM6728	0126
SM6762	0079
SM6773	0079
SM6814	0168
SM7545	0079
SM7815	0079
SM7836	0079
SM-7991	0693
SM7991	0036
SM8112	0079
SM8113	0079
SM8341	0004
SM8471	OEM
SM8472	OEM
SM8473	OEM
SM8475	OEM
SM8476	OEM
SM8477	OEM
SM8978	0079
SM9008	0079
SM9135	0079
SM9253	0079
SM47145	OEM
SM55450BJ	OEM
SM62186	0150
SM64442B	OEM
SM74177	OEM
SM76115N	OEM
SMA7023M	OEM
SMB-01	0276
SMB-02	0287
SMB-04	0293
SMB-08	0250
SMB-10	0250
SMB454549	0211
SMB454760	0050
SMC7400N	0232
SMC7402N	0310
SMC7408N	0462
SMC7410N	0507
SMC7420N	0692
SMC7430N	0867
SMC7440N	1018
SMC7451N	1160
SMC7473N	1164
SMC7474N	1303
SMC7475N	1423
SMC7476N	1150
SMC7490N	1199
SMC7493N	0564
SMF-7-2	OEM
SMF7-2	OEM
SMF-13-2	OEM
SMF13-2	OEM
SMH-08	OEM
SMH08	OEM
SMH-10	OEM
SMH10	OEM
SMH-16	OEM
SMH16	OEM
SMH-20	OEM
SMH-25ED	OEM
SMH204	OEM
SMHD-08	OEM
SMHD08	OEM
SMHD2-08	OEM
SMHD2-10	OEM
SMHD2-16	OEM
SMHD2-20	OEM
SMHD2-25ED	OEM
SMHD-10	OEM
SMHD10	OEM
SMHD-16	OEM
SMHD16	OEM
SMHD-20	OEM
SMHR-110	OEM
SMHR110	OEM
SMHR-135	OEM
SMHR135	OEM
SMHR-165	OEM
SMHR165	OEM
SMPAL16L8NC	OEM
SMPT-5	OEM
SMPT-8	OEM
SMPT-8C	OEM
SMPT-10	OEM
SMPT-10C	OEM
SMPT-12	OEM
SMPT-12C	OEM
SMPT-15	OEM
SMPT-15C	OEM
SMPT-18	OEM
SMPT-18C	OEM
SMPT-22	OEM
SMPT-22C	OEM
SMPT-36	OEM
SMPT-36C	OEM
SMPT-45	OEM
SMPT-45C	OEM
SMPTE-5	OEM
SMPTE-8	OEM
SMPTE-8C	OEM
SMPTE-10	OEM
SMPTE-10C	OEM

DEVICE TYPE	REPL CODE
SMPTE-12	OEM
SMPTE-12C	OEM
SMPTE-15	OEM
SMPTE-15C	OEM
SMPTE-18	OEM
SMPTE-18C	OEM
SMPTE-22	OEM
SMPTE-22C	OEM
SMPTE-36	OEM
SMPTE-36C	OEM
SMPTE-45	OEM
SMT100	OEM
SMT101	OEM
SMT102	OEM
SMT103	OEM
SMT104	OEM
SMT105	OEM
SMU1275	0623
SMU1398	OEM
SMV589	OEM
SMV807	OEM
SMV1172	0549
SMZ206A	OEM
SN0303	0015
SN-1	0015
SN1	0015
SN-1Z	0015
SN7ALS12ND	OEM
SN7ALS28NDS	OEM
SN7ALS642N	OEM
SN7LS02J	OEM
SN7LS02ND	OEM
SN7S32F	OEM
SN10	0369
SN20	OEM
SN30	OEM
SN40	OEM
SN54ALS00A	OEM
SN54ALS01	OEM
SN54ALS02	OEM
SN54ALS03A	OEM
SN54ALS04	OEM
SN54ALS05	OEM
SN54ALS08	OEM
SN54ALS09	OEM
SN54ALS10	OEM
SN54ALS11	OEM
SN54ALS12	OEM
SN54ALS15	OEM
SN54ALS20A	OEM
SN54ALS21	OEM
SN54ALS22A	OEM
SN54ALS27	OEM
SN54ALS28	OEM
SN54ALS30	OEM
SN54ALS32	OEM
SN54ALS33	OEM
SN54ALS37	OEM
SN54ALS38	OEM
SN54ALS40	OEM
SN54ALS74	OEM
SN54ALS109	OEM
SN54ALS112	OEM
SN54ALS113	OEM
SN54ALS114	OEM
SN54ALS133	OEM
SN54ALS137	OEM
SN54ALS138	OEM
SN54ALS139	OEM
SN54ALS151	OEM
SN54ALS153	OEM
SN54ALS157	OEM
SN54ALS158	OEM
SN54ALS160	OEM
SN54ALS161	OEM
SN54ALS162	OEM
SN54ALS163	OEM
SN54ALS168	OEM
SN54ALS169	OEM
SN54ALS174	OEM
SN54ALS175	OEM
SN54ALS190	OEM
SN54ALS191	OEM
SN54ALS192	OEM
SN54ALS192FH	OEM
SN54ALS192J	OEM
SN54ALS193	OEM
SN54ALS193FH	OEM
SN54ALS193J	OEM
SN54ALS240	OEM
SN54ALS241	OEM
SN54ALS242	OEM
SN54ALS243	OEM
SN54ALS244	OEM
SN54ALS245	OEM
SN54ALS251	OEM
SN54ALS253	OEM
SN54ALS257	OEM
SN54ALS258	OEM
SN54ALS259	OEM
SN54ALS273	OEM
SN54ALS299	OEM
SN54ALS323	OEM
SN54ALS352	OEM
SN54ALS353	OEM
SN54ALS373	OEM
SN54ALS374	OEM
SN54ALS465	OEM
SN54ALS466	OEM

DEVICE TYPE	REPL CODE
SN54ALS467	OEM
SN54ALS468	OEM
SN54ALS521	OEM
SN54ALS538	OEM
SN54ALS540	OEM
SN54ALS541	OEM
SN54ALS560	OEM
SN54ALS561	OEM
SN54ALS563	OEM
SN54ALS564	OEM
SN54ALS568	OEM
SN54ALS569	OEM
SN54ALS573	OEM
SN54ALS574	OEM
SN54ALS576	OEM
SN54ALS580	OEM
SN54ALS620	OEM
SN54ALS621	OEM
SN54ALS622	OEM
SN54ALS623	OEM
SN54ALS636	OEM
SN54ALS637	OEM
SN54ALS638	OEM
SN54ALS639	OEM
SN54ALS640	OEM
SN54ALS641	OEM
SN54ALS642	OEM
SN54ALS643	OEM
SN54ALS644	OEM
SN54ALS645	OEM
SN54ALS688	OEM
SN54ALS689	OEM
SN54ALS804	OEM
SN54ALS1000	OEM
SN54ALS1002	OEM
SN54ALS1003	OEM
SN54ALS1004	OEM
SN54ALS1005	OEM
SN54ALS1008	OEM
SN54ALS1010	OEM
SN54ALS1011	OEM
SN54ALS1020	OEM
SN54ALS1032	OEM
SN54ALS1034	OEM
SN54ALS1035	OEM
SN54ALS1240	OEM
SN54ALS1241	OEM
SN54ALS1242	OEM
SN54ALS1243	OEM
SN54ALS1244	OEM
SN54ALS1245	OEM
SN54ALS1616	OEM
SN54ALS1620	OEM
SN54ALS1621	OEM
SN54ALS1622	OEM
SN54ALS1623	OEM
SN54ALS1638	OEM
SN54ALS1639	OEM
SN54ALS1640	OEM
SN54ALS1641	OEM
SN54ALS1642	OEM
SN54ALS1643	OEM
SN54ALS1644	OEM
SN54ALS1645	OEM
SN54AS194FH	OEM
SN54AS194J	OEM
SN54AS805	OEM
SN54AS805A	OEM
SN54AS808	OEM
SN54AS808A	OEM
SN54AS830	OEM
SN54AS832	OEM
SN54AS832A	OEM
SN54AS836	OEM
SN54AS850	OEM
SN54AS857	OEM
SN54AS859	OEM
SN54AS866	OEM
SN54AS867	OEM
SN54AS869	OEM
SN54AS870	OEM
SN54AS871	OEM
SN54AS872	OEM
SN54AS873	OEM
SN54AS874	OEM
SN54AS875	OEM
SN54AS876	OEM
SN54AS877	OEM
SN54AS880	OEM
SN54AS881A	OEM
SN54AS882	OEM
SN54AS883	OEM
SN54AS884	OEM
SN54AS885	OEM
SN54AS886	OEM
SN54AS888	OEM
SN54AS889	OEM
SN54AS890	OEM
SN54AS891	OEM
SN54AS894	OEM
SN54H00	OEM
SN54H01	OEM
SN54H04	OEM
SN54H05	OEM
SN54H10	OEM
SN54H11	OEM
SN54H15	OEM
SN54H20	OEM
SN54H21	OEM

DEVICE TYPE	REPL CODE
SN54H21J	OEM
SN54H21W	OEM
SN54H22	OEM
SN54H30	OEM
SN54H40	OEM
SN54H50	OEM
SN54H51	OEM
SN54H52	OEM
SN54H53	OEM
SN54H54	OEM
SN54H55	OEM
SN54H60	OEM
SN54H61	OEM
SN54H62	OEM
SN54H71	OEM
SN54H72	OEM
SN54H73	OEM
SN54H74	OEM
SN54H76	OEM
SN54H78	OEM
SN54H87	OEM
SN54H101	OEM
SN54H102	OEM
SN54H103	OEM
SN54H106	OEM
SN54H108	OEM
SN54H183	OEM
SN54L02J	OEM
SN54L90	OEM
SN54L91	OEM
SN54L93	OEM
SN54L96	OEM
SN54L98	OEM
SN54L99	OEM
SN54L153J	OEM
SN54L164	OEM
SN54L192	OEM
SN54L192J	OEM
SN54L193	OEM
SN54L193J	OEM
SN54LS00	OEM
SN54LS01	OEM
SN54LS02FK	OEM
SN54LS02J	OEM
SN54LS02W	OEM
SN54LS03	OEM
SN54LS04	OEM
SN54LS05	OEM
SN54LS08	OEM
SN54LS09	OEM
SN54LS09J	OEM
SN54LS09N	OEM
SN54LS10	OEM
SN54LS11	OEM
SN54LS12	OEM
SN54LS13	OEM
SN54LS14	OEM
SN54LS15	OEM
SN54LS18	OEM
SN54LS19	OEM
SN54LS20	OEM
SN54LS21	OEM
SN54LS21FK	OEM
SN54LS21J	OEM
SN54LS21W	OEM
SN54LS22	OEM
SN54LS24	OEM
SN54LS26	OEM
SN54LS27	OEM
SN54LS28	OEM
SN54LS30	OEM
SN54LS32	OEM
SN54LS33	OEM
SN54LS37	OEM
SN54LS38	OEM
SN54LS38J	OEM
SN54LS40	OEM
SN54LS42	OEM
SN54LS47	OEM
SN54LS48	OEM
SN54LS49	OEM
SN54LS51	OEM
SN54LS54	OEM
SN54LS55	OEM
SN54LS63	OEM
SN54LS73A	OEM
SN54LS74A	OEM
SN54LS75	OEM
SN54LS76A	OEM
SN54LS77	OEM
SN54LS78A	OEM
SN54LS83A	OEM
SN54LS86	OEM
SN54LS90	OEM
SN54LS91	OEM
SN54LS92	OEM
SN54LS93	OEM
SN54LS96	OEM
SN54LS107A	OEM
SN54LS109A	OEM
SN54LS112A	OEM
SN54LS113A	OEM
SN54LS113AFK	OEM
SN54LS113AJ	OEM
SN54LS113AW	OEM
SN54LS114A	OEM
SN54LS122	OEM
SN54LS123	OEM
SN54LS125A	OEM

562 If replacement code is OEM, contact original manufacturer for replacement.

DEVICE TYPE	REPL CODE
SN54LS126A	OEM
SN54LS132	OEM
SN54LS136	OEM
SN54LS136FK	OEM
SN54LS136J	OEM
SN54LS136W	OEM
SN54LS137	OEM
SN54LS138	OEM
SN54LS139	OEM
SN54LS145	OEM
SN54LS147	OEM
SN54LS148	OEM
SN54LS151	OEM
SN54LS152	OEM
SN54LS153	OEM
SN54LS153FK	OEM
SN54LS153J	OEM
SN54LS153W	OEM
SN54LS155	OEM
SN54LS156	OEM
SN54LS157	OEM
SN54LS157FK	OEM
SN54LS157J	OEM
SN54LS157W	OEM
SN54LS158	OEM
SN54LS158FK	OEM
SN54LS158J	OEM
SN54LS158N	OEM
SN54LS158W	OEM
SN54LS160A	OEM
SN54LS161A	OEM
SN54LS162A	OEM
SN54LS163A	OEM
SN54LS164	OEM
SN54LS165A	OEM
SN54LS166A	OEM
SN54LS169B	OEM
SN54LS170	OEM
SN54LS173A	OEM
SN54LS173AFK	OEM
SN54LS173AJ	OEM
SN54LS173AW	OEM
SN54LS174	OEM
SN54LS175	OEM
SN54LS181	OEM
SN54LS183	OEM
SN54LS190	OEM
SN54LS191	OEM
SN54LS192	OEM
SN54LS192FH	OEM
SN54LS192J	OEM
SN54LS193	OEM
SN54LS193FH	OEM
SN54LS193J	OEM
SN54LS194A	OEM
SN54LS194AFH	OEM
SN54LS194AJ	OEM
SN54LS195A	OEM
SN54LS196	OEM
SN54LS196J	OEM
SN54LS196W	OEM
SN54LS197	OEM
SN54LS197J	OEM
SN54LS197W	OEM
SN54LS221	OEM
SN54LS222	OEM
SN54LS224	OEM
SN54LS227	OEM
SN54LS228	OEM
SN54LS240	OEM
SN54LS241	OEM
SN54LS242	OEM
SN54LS243	OEM
SN54LS244	OEM
SN54LS245	OEM
SN54LS247	OEM
SN54LS248	OEM
SN54LS249	OEM
SN54LS251	OEM
SN54LS253	OEM
SN54LS257	OEM
SN54LS258	OEM
SN54LS259	OEM
SN54LS261	OEM
SN54LS266	OEM
SN54LS273	OEM
SN54LS275	OEM
SN54LS279	OEM
SN54LS280	OEM
SN54LS283	OEM
SN54LS290	OEM
SN54LS292	OEM
SN54LS293	OEM
SN54LS294	OEM
SN54LS295B	OEM
SN54LS297	OEM
SN54LS298	OEM
SN54LS299	OEM
SN54LS320	OEM
SN54LS321	OEM
SN54LS322A	OEM
SN54LS323	OEM
SN54LS347	OEM
SN54LS348	OEM
SN54LS352	OEM
SN54LS353	OEM
SN54LS354	OEM
SN54LS355	OEM
SN54LS356	OEM

DEVICE TYPE	REPL CODE
SN54LS357	OEM
SN54LS365A	OEM
SN54LS366A	OEM
SN54LS367A	OEM
SN54LS368A	OEM
SN54LS373	OEM
SN54LS373FK	OEM
SN54LS373J	OEM
SN54LS374	OEM
SN54LS374FK	OEM
SN54LS374J	OEM
SN54LS375	OEM
SN54LS377	OEM
SN54LS378	OEM
SN54LS379	OEM
SN54LS381A	OEM
SN54LS382	OEM
SN54LS384	OEM
SN54LS385	OEM
SN54LS386	OEM
SN54LS390	OEM
SN54LS390J	OEM
SN54LS390W	OEM
SN54LS393	OEM
SN54LS393J	OEM
SN54LS393W	OEM
SN54LS395A	OEM
SN54LS396	OEM
SN54LS398	OEM
SN54LS399	OEM
SN54LS422	OEM
SN54LS423	OEM
SN54LS424	OEM
SN54LS440	OEM
SN54LS441	OEM
SN54LS442	OEM
SN54LS443	OEM
SN54LS444	OEM
SN54LS445	OEM
SN54LS446	OEM
SN54LS447	OEM
SN54LS448	OEM
SN54LS449	OEM
SN54LS465	OEM
SN54LS466	OEM
SN54LS467	OEM
SN54LS468	OEM
SN54LS490	OEM
SN54LS540	OEM
SN54LS541	OEM
SN54LS590	OEM
SN54LS591	OEM
SN54LS592	OEM
SN54LS593	OEM
SN54LS595	OEM
SN54LS596	OEM
SN54LS597	OEM
SN54LS598	OEM
SN54LS600	OEM
SN54LS601	OEM
SN54LS602	OEM
SN54LS603	OEM
SN54LS604	OEM
SN54LS605	OEM
SN54LS606	OEM
SN54LS607	OEM
SN54LS608	OEM
SN54LS610	OEM
SN54LS611	OEM
SN54LS612	OEM
SN54LS613	OEM
SN54LS620	OEM
SN54LS621	OEM
SN54LS622	OEM
SN54LS623	OEM
SN54LS624	OEM
SN54LS625	OEM
SN54LS626	OEM
SN54LS627	OEM
SN54LS628	OEM
SN54LS629	OEM
SN54LS630	OEM
SN54LS631	OEM
SN54LS636	OEM
SN54LS637	OEM
SN54LS638	OEM
SN54LS639	OEM
SN54LS640	OEM
SN54LS641	OEM
SN54LS642	OEM
SN54LS643	OEM
SN54LS644	OEM
SN54LS645	OEM
SN54LS646	OEM
SN54LS647	OEM
SN54LS648	OEM
SN54LS649	OEM
SN54LS651	OEM
SN54LS652	OEM
SN54LS668	OEM
SN54LS669	OEM
SN54LS670	OEM
SN54LS671	OEM
SN54LS672	OEM
SN54LS673	OEM
SN54LS674	OEM
SN54LS681	OEM
SN54LS682	OEM
SN54LS683	OEM

DEVICE TYPE	REPL CODE
SN54LS684	OEM
SN54LS685	OEM
SN54LS686	OEM
SN54LS687	OEM
SN54LS688	OEM
SN54LS689	OEM
SN54LS690	OEM
SN54LS691	OEM
SN54LS692	OEM
SN54LS693	OEM
SN54LS696	OEM
SN54LS697	OEM
SN54LS698	OEM
SN54LS699	OEM
SN54LS1245	OEM
SN54PL16L8	OEM
SN54PL16R4	OEM
SN54PL16R6	OEM
SN54PL16R8	OEM
SN54PL333	OEM
SN54PL335	OEM
SN54PL839	OEM
SN54PL840	OEM
SN54S00	OEM
SN54S02	OEM
SN54S02FK	OEM
SN54S02J	OEM
SN54S02W	OEM
SN54S03	OEM
SN54S04	OEM
SN54S05	OEM
SN54S08	OEM
SN54S09	OEM
SN54S10	OEM
SN54S11	OEM
SN54S15	OEM
SN54S20	OEM
SN54S22	OEM
SN54S30	OEM
SN54S32	OEM
SN54S37	OEM
SN54S38	OEM
SN54S40	OEM
SN54S51	OEM
SN54S64	OEM
SN54S65	OEM
SN54S74	OEM
SN54S85	OEM
SN54S86	OEM
SN54S112	OEM
SN54S113	OEM
SN54S113FK	OEM
SN54S113J	OEM
SN54S113W	OEM
SN54S114	OEM
SN54S124	OEM
SN54S132	OEM
SN54S133	OEM
SN54S134	OEM
SN54S135	OEM
SN54S138	OEM
SN54S139	OEM
SN54S140	OEM
SN54S151	OEM
SN54S153	OEM
SN54S153FK	OEM
SN54S153J	OEM
SN54S153W	OEM
SN54S157	OEM
SN54S157FK	OEM
SN54S157J	OEM
SN54S157W	OEM
SN54S158	OEM
SN54S158FK	OEM
SN54S158J	OEM
SN54S158W	OEM
SN54S162	OEM
SN54S163	OEM
SN54S168	OEM
SN54S169	OEM
SN54S174	OEM
SN54S175	OEM
SN54S181	OEM
SN54S182	OEM
SN54S194	OEM
SN54S194FH	OEM
SN54S194J	OEM
SN54S195	OEM
SN54S196	OEM
SN54S196J	OEM
SN54S196W	OEM
SN54S197	OEM
SN54S197J	OEM
SN54S197W	OEM
SN54S226	OEM
SN54S240	OEM
SN54S241	OEM
SN54S244	OEM
SN54S251	OEM
SN54S257	OEM
SN54S260	OEM
SN54S274	OEM
SN54S275	OEM
SN54S280	OEM
SN54S281	OEM
SN54S283	OEM
SN54S299	OEM
SN54S340	OEM
SN54S341	OEM

DEVICE TYPE	REPL CODE
SN54S344	OEM
SN54S373	OEM
SN54S373FK	OEM
SN54S373J	OEM
SN54S374	OEM
SN54S374FK	OEM
SN54S374J	OEM
SN54S381	OEM
SN54S412	OEM
SN54S428	OEM
SN54S436	OEM
SN54S437	OEM
SN54S438	OEM
SN54S481	OEM
SN54S482	OEM
SN54S484	OEM
SN54S485	OEM
SN60	0595
SN74ALS00A	OEM
SN74ALS00AFN	OEM
SN74ALS00AJ	OEM
SN74ALS00AN	2392
SN74ALS00J	OEM
SN74ALS00N	OEM
SN74ALS00ND	OEM
SN74ALS00NDS	OEM
SN74ALS00NS	OEM
SN74ALS01	OEM
SN74ALS01FN	OEM
SN74ALS01J	OEM
SN74ALS01N	OEM
SN74ALS01ND	OEM
SN74ALS01NDS	OEM
SN74ALS01NS	OEM
SN74ALS02	OEM
SN74ALS02FN	OEM
SN74ALS02J	OEM
SN74ALS02N	OEM
SN74ALS03A	OEM
SN74ALS03AFN	OEM
SN74ALS03AJ	OEM
SN74ALS03AN	5552
SN74ALS03J	OEM
SN74ALS03N	OEM
SN74ALS03ND	OEM
SN74ALS03NDS	OEM
SN74ALS03NS	OEM
SN74ALS04	OEM
SN74ALS04AFN	OEM
SN74ALS04AJ	OEM
SN74ALS04AN	OEM
SN74ALS04J	OEM
SN74ALS04N	OEM
SN74ALS04ND	OEM
SN74ALS04NS	OEM
SN74ALS05	OEM
SN74ALS05AFN	OEM
SN74ALS05AJ	OEM
SN74ALS05AN	OEM
SN74ALS05J	OEM
SN74ALS05N	OEM
SN74ALS05ND	OEM
SN74ALS05NDS	OEM
SN74ALS05NS	OEM
SN74ALS08	OEM
SN74ALS08FN	OEM
SN74ALS08J	OEM
SN74ALS08N	OEM
SN74ALS08ND	OEM
SN74ALS08NDS	OEM
SN74ALS08NS	OEM
SN74ALS09	OEM
SN74ALS09FN	OEM
SN74ALS09J	OEM
SN74ALS09N	OEM
SN74ALS0NDS	OEM
SN74ALS10	OEM
SN74ALS10AN	OEM
SN74ALS10FN	OEM
SN74ALS10J	OEM
SN74ALS10N	OEM
SN74ALS10ND	OEM
SN74ALS10NDS	OEM
SN74ALS10NS	OEM
SN74ALS11	OEM
SN74ALS11FN	OEM
SN74ALS11J	OEM
SN74ALS11N	OEM
SN74ALS11NDS	OEM
SN74ALS11NS	OEM
SN74ALS12	OEM
SN74ALS12FN	OEM
SN74ALS12J	OEM
SN74ALS12N	OEM
SN74ALS12NDS	OEM
SN74ALS12NS	OEM
SN74ALS13J	OEM
SN74ALS13N	OEM
SN74ALS14J	OEM
SN74ALS14N	OEM
SN74ALS15	OEM
SN74ALS15FN	OEM
SN74ALS15J	OEM
SN74ALS15N	OEM
SN74ALS15ND	OEM
SN74ALS15NDS	OEM
SN74ALS15NS	OEM
SN74ALS20A	OEM
SN74ALS20AFN	OEM

DEVICE TYPE	REPL CODE
SN74ALS20AJ	OEM
SN74ALS20AN	OEM
SN74ALS20J	OEM
SN74ALS20N	OEM
SN74ALS20ND	OEM
SN74ALS20NDS	OEM
SN74ALS20NS	OEM
SN74ALS21	OEM
SN74ALS21FN	OEM
SN74ALS21J	OEM
SN74ALS21N	OEM
SN74ALS21ND	OEM
SN74ALS21NDS	OEM
SN74ALS21NS	OEM
SN74ALS22A	OEM
SN74ALS22AFN	OEM
SN74ALS22AJ	OEM
SN74ALS22AN	OEM
SN74ALS22J	OEM
SN74ALS22N	OEM
SN74ALS22ND	OEM
SN74ALS22NDS	OEM
SN74ALS22NS	OEM
SN74ALS27	OEM
SN74ALS27FN	OEM
SN74ALS27J	OEM
SN74ALS27N	OEM
SN74ALS27ND	OEM
SN74ALS27NDS	OEM
SN74ALS27NS	OEM
SN74ALS28	OEM
SN74ALS28AFN	OEM
SN74ALS28AJ	OEM
SN74ALS28AN	OEM
SN74ALS28J	OEM
SN74ALS28N	OEM
SN74ALS28ND	OEM
SN74ALS28NS	OEM
SN74ALS30	OEM
SN74ALS30AN	OEM
SN74ALS30FN	OEM
SN74ALS30J	OEM
SN74ALS30N	OEM
SN74ALS32	OEM
SN74ALS32FN	OEM
SN74ALS32J	OEM
SN74ALS32N	2646
SN74ALS32ND	OEM
SN74ALS32NDS	OEM
SN74ALS32NS	OEM
SN74ALS33	OEM
SN74ALS33AFN	OEM
SN74ALS33AJ	OEM
SN74ALS33AN	OEM
SN74ALS33J	OEM
SN74ALS33N	OEM
SN74ALS34FN	OEM
SN74ALS34J	OEM
SN74ALS34N	OEM
SN74ALS35FN	OEM
SN74ALS35J	OEM
SN74ALS35N	OEM
SN74ALS37	OEM
SN74ALS37AFN	OEM
SN74ALS37AJ	OEM
SN74ALS37AN	OEM
SN74ALS37J	OEM
SN74ALS37N	OEM
SN74ALS38	OEM
SN74ALS38AFN	OEM
SN74ALS38AJ	OEM
SN74ALS38AN	OEM
SN74ALS38J	OEM
SN74ALS38N	3750
SN74ALS40	OEM
SN74ALS40AFN	OEM
SN74ALS40AJ	OEM
SN74ALS40AN	OEM
SN74ALS40J	OEM
SN74ALS40N	OEM
SN74ALS51J	OEM
SN74ALS51N	OEM
SN74ALS55IN	OEM
SN74ALS55IND	OEM
SN74ALS55INDS	OEM
SN74ALS55INS	OEM
SN74ALS55J	OEM
SN74ALS55N	OEM
SN74ALS55ND	OEM
SN74ALS55NDS	OEM
SN74ALS55NS	OEM
SN74ALS74	OEM
SN74ALS74AN	OEM
SN74ALS74FN	OEM
SN74ALS74J	OEM
SN74ALS74N	OEM
SN74ALS86	OEM
SN74ALS86FN	OEM
SN74ALS86J	OEM
SN74ALS86N	OEM
SN74ALS91J	OEM
SN74ALS91N	OEM
SN74ALS109	OEM
SN74ALS109AN	OEM
SN74ALS109FN	OEM
SN74ALS109J	OEM
SN74ALS109N	OEM
SN74ALS112	OEM
SN74ALS112AFN	OEM

DEVICE TYPE	REPL CODE
SN74ALS112AJ	OEM
SN74ALS112AN	OEM
SN74ALS112N	OEM
SN74ALS113	OEM
SN74ALS113AFN	OEM
SN74ALS113AJ	OEM
SN74ALS113AN	OEM
SN74ALS114	OEM
SN74ALS114AFN	OEM
SN74ALS114AJ	OEM
SN74ALS114AN	OEM
SN74ALS131FN	OEM
SN74ALS131J	OEM
SN74ALS131N	OEM
SN74ALS132J	OEM
SN74ALS132N	OEM
SN74ALS133	OEM
SN74ALS133FN	OEM
SN74ALS133J	OEM
SN74ALS133N	OEM
SN74ALS137	OEM
SN74ALS137FN	OEM
SN74ALS137J	OEM
SN74ALS137N	OEM
SN74ALS138	OEM
SN74ALS138FN	OEM
SN74ALS138J	OEM
SN74ALS138N	5655
SN74ALS139	OEM
SN74ALS139FN	OEM
SN74ALS139J	OEM
SN74ALS139N	OEM
SN74ALS151	OEM
SN74ALS151FN	OEM
SN74ALS151J	OEM
SN74ALS151N	OEM
SN74ALS153	OEM
SN74ALS153FN	OEM
SN74ALS153J	OEM
SN74ALS153N	5682
SN74ALS157	OEM
SN74ALS157FN	OEM
SN74ALS157J	OEM
SN74ALS157N	5690
SN74ALS157ND	OEM
SN74ALS157NDS	OEM
SN74ALS157NS	OEM
SN74ALS158	OEM
SN74ALS158FN	OEM
SN74ALS158J	OEM
SN74ALS158N	OEM
SN74ALS158ND	OEM
SN74ALS158NDS	OEM
SN74ALS158NS	OEM
SN74ALS160	OEM
SN74ALS160AFN	OEM
SN74ALS160AJ	OEM
SN74ALS160AN	OEM
SN74ALS160J	OEM
SN74ALS160N	OEM
SN74ALS160ND	OEM
SN74ALS160NDS	OEM
SN74ALS160NS	OEM
SN74ALS161	OEM
SN74ALS161AFN	OEM
SN74ALS161AJ	OEM
SN74ALS161AN	OEM
SN74ALS161BN	OEM
SN74ALS161J	OEM
SN74ALS161N	OEM
SN74ALS161ND	OEM
SN74ALS161NDS	OEM
SN74ALS161NS	OEM
SN74ALS162	OEM
SN74ALS162AFN	OEM
SN74ALS162AJ	OEM
SN74ALS162AN	OEM
SN74ALS162J	OEM
SN74ALS162N	OEM
SN74ALS162ND	OEM
SN74ALS162NDS	OEM
SN74ALS162NS	OEM
SN74ALS163	OEM
SN74ALS163AFN	OEM
SN74ALS163AJ	OEM
SN74ALS163AN	OEM
SN74ALS163J	OEM
SN74ALS163N	OEM
SN74ALS163ND	OEM
SN74ALS163NDS	OEM
SN74ALS163NS	OEM
SN74ALS164FN	OEM
SN74ALS164J	OEM
SN74ALS164N	OEM
SN74ALS165FN	OEM
SN74ALS165J	OEM
SN74ALS165N	OEM
SN74ALS166FN	OEM
SN74ALS166J	OEM
SN74ALS166N	OEM
SN74ALS168	OEM
SN74ALS168AFN	OEM
SN74ALS168AJ	OEM
SN74ALS168AN	OEM
SN74ALS168J	OEM
SN74ALS168N	OEM
SN74ALS169	OEM
SN74ALS169AFN	OEM
SN74ALS169AJ	OEM

DEVICE TYPE	REPL CODE
SN74ALS169AN	OEM
SN74ALS169J	OEM
SN74ALS169N	OEM
SN74ALS174	OEM
SN74ALS174FN	OEM
SN74ALS174J	OEM
SN74ALS174N	OEM
SN74ALS175	OEM
SN74ALS175FN	OEM
SN74ALS175J	OEM
SN74ALS175N	OEM
SN74ALS190	OEM
SN74ALS190FN	OEM
SN74ALS190J	OEM
SN74ALS190N	OEM
SN74ALS190ND	OEM
SN74ALS190NDS	OEM
SN74ALS190S	OEM
SN74ALS191	OEM
SN74ALS191FN	OEM
SN74ALS191J	OEM
SN74ALS191N	OEM
SN74ALS191ND	OEM
SN74ALS191NDS	OEM
SN74ALS191NS	OEM
SN74ALS192	OEM
SN74ALS192FN	OEM
SN74ALS192J	OEM
SN74ALS192N	OEM
SN74ALS192ND	OEM
SN74ALS192NDS	OEM
SN74ALS192S	OEM
SN74ALS193	OEM
SN74ALS193FN	OEM
SN74ALS193J	OEM
SN74ALS193N	5744
SN74ALS193ND	OEM
SN74ALS193NDS	OEM
SN74ALS193NS	OEM
SN74ALS217	OEM
SN74ALS218	OEM
SN74ALS238J	OEM
SN74ALS238N	OEM
SN74ALS239J	OEM
SN74ALS239N	OEM
SN74ALS240	OEM
SN74ALS240AFN	OEM
SN74ALS240AJ	OEM
SN74ALS240AN	OEM
SN74ALS240J	OEM
SN74ALS240N	5794
SN74ALS241	OEM
SN74ALS241AFN	OEM
SN74ALS241AJ	OEM
SN74ALS241AN	OEM
SN74ALS241J	OEM
SN74ALS241N	OEM
SN74ALS242	OEM
SN74ALS242AFN	OEM
SN74ALS242AJ	OEM
SN74ALS242AN	OEM
SN74ALS242J	OEM
SN74ALS242N	OEM
SN74ALS243	OEM
SN74ALS243AFN	OEM
SN74ALS243AJ	OEM
SN74ALS243AN	OEM
SN74ALS243J	OEM
SN74ALS243N	OEM
SN74ALS244	OEM
SN74ALS244AFN	OEM
SN74ALS244AJ	OEM
SN74ALS244AN	OEM
SN74ALS244J	OEM
SN74ALS244N	5803
SN74ALS245	OEM
SN74ALS245AFN	OEM
SN74ALS245AJ	OEM
SN74ALS245AN	OEM
SN74ALS245J	OEM
SN74ALS245N	OEM
SN74ALS251	OEM
SN74ALS251FN	OEM
SN74ALS251J	OEM
SN74ALS251N	OEM
SN74ALS253	OEM
SN74ALS253FN	OEM
SN74ALS253J	OEM
SN74ALS253N	OEM
SN74ALS257	OEM
SN74ALS257FN	OEM
SN74ALS257J	OEM
SN74ALS257N	OEM
SN74ALS258	OEM
SN74ALS258FN	OEM
SN74ALS258J	OEM
SN74ALS258N	OEM
SN74ALS259	OEM
SN74ALS259FN	OEM
SN74ALS259J	OEM
SN74ALS259N	OEM
SN74ALS273	OEM
SN74ALS273FN	OEM
SN74ALS273J	OEM
SN74ALS273N	OEM
SN74ALS299	OEM
SN74ALS299FN	OEM
SN74ALS299J	OEM
SN74ALS299N	OEM

If replacement code is OEM, contact original manufacturer for replacement.

DEVICE TYPE	REPL CODE
SN74ALS317	OEM
SN74ALS318	OEM
SN74ALS323	OEM
SN74ALS323FN	OEM
SN74ALS323J	OEM
SN74ALS323N	OEM
SN74ALS352	OEM
SN74ALS352FN	OEM
SN74ALS352J	OEM
SN74ALS352N	OEM
SN74ALS353	OEM
SN74ALS353FN	OEM
SN74ALS353J	OEM
SN74ALS353N	OEM
SN74ALS365FN	OEM
SN74ALS365J	OEM
SN74ALS365N	OEM
SN74ALS366FN	OEM
SN74ALS366J	OEM
SN74ALS366N	OEM
SN74ALS367FN	OEM
SN74ALS367J	OEM
SN74ALS367N	5895
SN74ALS368FN	OEM
SN74ALS368J	OEM
SN74ALS368N	OEM
SN74ALS373	OEM
SN74ALS373FN	OEM
SN74ALS373J	OEM
SN74ALS373N	OEM
SN74ALS374	OEM
SN74ALS374FN	OEM
SN74ALS374J	OEM
SN74ALS374N	OEM
SN74ALS377J	OEM
SN74ALS377N	OEM
SN74ALS465	OEM
SN74ALS465AFN	OEM
SN74ALS465AJ	OEM
SN74ALS465AN	OEM
SN74ALS466	OEM
SN74ALS466AFN	OEM
SN74ALS466AJ	OEM
SN74ALS466AN	OEM
SN74ALS467	OEM
SN74ALS467AFN	OEM
SN74ALS467AJ	OEM
SN74ALS467AN	OEM
SN74ALS468	OEM
SN74ALS468AFN	OEM
SN74ALS468AJ	OEM
SN74ALS468AN	OEM
SN74ALS518FN	OEM
SN74ALS518J	OEM
SN74ALS518N	OEM
SN74ALS519FN	OEM
SN74ALS519J	OEM
SN74ALS519N	OEM
SN74ALS520FN	OEM
SN74ALS520J	OEM
SN74ALS520N	OEM
SN74ALS521	OEM
SN74ALS521FN	OEM
SN74ALS521J	OEM
SN74ALS521N	OEM
SN74ALS522FN	OEM
SN74ALS522J	OEM
SN74ALS522N	OEM
SN74ALS526FN	OEM
SN74ALS526J	OEM
SN74ALS526N	OEM
SN74ALS527FN	OEM
SN74ALS527J	OEM
SN74ALS527N	OEM
SN74ALS528FN	OEM
SN74ALS528J	OEM
SN74ALS528N	OEM
SN74ALS533FN	OEM
SN74ALS533J	OEM
SN74ALS533N	OEM
SN74ALS534FN	OEM
SN74ALS534J	OEM
SN74ALS534N	OEM
SN74ALS537J	OEM
SN74ALS537N	OEM
SN74ALS538	OEM
SN74ALS538FN	OEM
SN74ALS538J	OEM
SN74ALS538N	OEM
SN74ALS539FN	OEM
SN74ALS539J	OEM
SN74ALS539N	OEM
SN74ALS540	OEM
SN74ALS540FN	OEM
SN74ALS540J	OEM
SN74ALS540N	OEM
SN74ALS541	OEM
SN74ALS541FN	OEM
SN74ALS541J	OEM
SN74ALS541N	OEM
SN74ALS560	OEM
SN74ALS560AFN	OEM
SN74ALS560AJ	OEM
SN74ALS560AN	OEM
SN74ALS560J	OEM
SN74ALS560N	OEM
SN74ALS561	OEM
SN74ALS561AFN	OEM
SN74ALS561AJ	OEM
SN74ALS561AN	OEM
SN74ALS561J	OEM
SN74ALS561N	OEM
SN74ALS563	OEM
SN74ALS563FN	OEM
SN74ALS563J	OEM
SN74ALS563N	OEM
SN74ALS564	OEM
SN74ALS564FN	OEM
SN74ALS564J	OEM
SN74ALS564N	OEM
SN74ALS568	OEM
SN74ALS568AFN	OEM
SN74ALS568AJ	OEM
SN74ALS568AN	OEM
SN74ALS568J	OEM
SN74ALS568N	OEM
SN74ALS569	OEM
SN74ALS569AFN	OEM
SN74ALS569AJ	OEM
SN74ALS569AN	OEM
SN74ALS569J	OEM
SN74ALS569N	OEM
SN74ALS573	OEM
SN74ALS573BN	OEM
SN74ALS573FN	OEM
SN74ALS573J	OEM
SN74ALS573N	OEM
SN74ALS574	OEM
SN74ALS574FN	OEM
SN74ALS574J	OEM
SN74ALS574N	OEM
SN74ALS575FN	OEM
SN74ALS575J	OEM
SN74ALS575N	OEM
SN74ALS576	OEM
SN74ALS576FN	OEM
SN74ALS576J	OEM
SN74ALS576N	OEM
SN74ALS577FN	OEM
SN74ALS577J	OEM
SN74ALS577N	OEM
SN74ALS580	OEM
SN74ALS580FN	OEM
SN74ALS580J	OEM
SN74ALS580N	OEM
SN74ALS612N	OEM
SN74ALS620	OEM
SN74ALS620AFN	OEM
SN74ALS620AJ	OEM
SN74ALS620AN	OEM
SN74ALS620J	OEM
SN74ALS620N	OEM
SN74ALS621	OEM
SN74ALS621AFN	OEM
SN74ALS621AJ	OEM
SN74ALS621AN	OEM
SN74ALS621J	OEM
SN74ALS621N	OEM
SN74ALS622	OEM
SN74ALS622AFN	OEM
SN74ALS622AJ	OEM
SN74ALS622AN	OEM
SN74ALS622J	OEM
SN74ALS622N	OEM
SN74ALS623	OEM
SN74ALS623AFN	OEM
SN74ALS623AJ	OEM
SN74ALS623AN	OEM
SN74ALS623J	OEM
SN74ALS623N	OEM
SN74ALS632JD	OEM
SN74ALS633JD	OEM
SN74ALS634JD	OEM
SN74ALS635JD	OEM
SN74ALS636	OEM
SN74ALS637	OEM
SN74ALS638	OEM
SN74ALS638AFN	OEM
SN74ALS638AJ	OEM
SN74ALS638AN	OEM
SN74ALS638J	OEM
SN74ALS638N	OEM
SN74ALS639	OEM
SN74ALS639AFN	OEM
SN74ALS639AJ	OEM
SN74ALS639AN	OEM
SN74ALS639J	OEM
SN74ALS639N	OEM
SN74ALS640	OEM
SN74ALS640AFN	OEM
SN74ALS640AJ	OEM
SN74ALS640AN	OEM
SN74ALS640J	OEM
SN74ALS640N	OEM
SN74ALS641	OEM
SN74ALS641AFN	OEM
SN74ALS641AJ	OEM
SN74ALS641AN	OEM
SN74ALS641J	OEM
SN74ALS641N	OEM
SN74ALS642	OEM
SN74ALS642AFN	OEM
SN74ALS642AJ	OEM
SN74ALS642AN	OEM
SN74ALS642J	OEM
SN74ALS642N	OEM
SN74ALS643	OEM
SN74ALS643AFN	OEM
SN74ALS643AJ	OEM
SN74ALS643AN	OEM
SN74ALS643J	OEM
SN74ALS643N	OEM
SN74ALS644	OEM
SN74ALS644AFN	OEM
SN74ALS644AJ	OEM
SN74ALS644AN	OEM
SN74ALS644J	OEM
SN74ALS644N	OEM
SN74ALS645	OEM
SN74ALS645AFN	OEM
SN74ALS645AJ	OEM
SN74ALS645AN	OEM
SN74ALS646FN	OEM
SN74ALS646J	OEM
SN74ALS646JT	OEM
SN74ALS646N	OEM
SN74ALS646NT	OEM
SN74ALS647FN	OEM
SN74ALS647J	OEM
SN74ALS647JT	OEM
SN74ALS647N	OEM
SN74ALS647NT	OEM
SN74ALS648FN	OEM
SN74ALS648J	OEM
SN74ALS648JT	OEM
SN74ALS648N	OEM
SN74ALS648NT	OEM
SN74ALS649FN	OEM
SN74ALS649J	OEM
SN74ALS649JT	OEM
SN74ALS649N	OEM
SN74ALS649NT	OEM
SN74ALS651FN	OEM
SN74ALS651J	OEM
SN74ALS651JT	OEM
SN74ALS651N	OEM
SN74ALS651NT	OEM
SN74ALS652FN	OEM
SN74ALS652J	OEM
SN74ALS652JT	OEM
SN74ALS652N	OEM
SN74ALS652NT	OEM
SN74ALS653FN	OEM
SN74ALS653J	OEM
SN74ALS653JT	OEM
SN74ALS653N	OEM
SN74ALS653NT	OEM
SN74ALS654FN	OEM
SN74ALS654J	OEM
SN74ALS654JT	OEM
SN74ALS654N	OEM
SN74ALS654NT	OEM
SN74ALS671J	OEM
SN74ALS671N	OEM
SN74ALS672J	OEM
SN74ALS672N	OEM
SN74ALS677FN	OEM
SN74ALS677JT	OEM
SN74ALS677NT	OEM
SN74ALS678FN	OEM
SN74ALS678JT	OEM
SN74ALS678NT	OEM
SN74ALS679FN	OEM
SN74ALS679J	OEM
SN74ALS679N	OEM
SN74ALS680FN	OEM
SN74ALS680J	OEM
SN74ALS680N	OEM
SN74ALS688	OEM
SN74ALS688FN	OEM
SN74ALS688J	OEM
SN74ALS688N	OEM
SN74ALS689	OEM
SN74ALS689FN	OEM
SN74ALS689J	OEM
SN74ALS689N	OEM
SN74ALS690J	OEM
SN74ALS690N	OEM
SN74ALS691J	OEM
SN74ALS691N	OEM
SN74ALS692J	OEM
SN74ALS692N	OEM
SN74ALS693J	OEM
SN74ALS693N	OEM
SN74ALS694J	OEM
SN74ALS694N	OEM
SN74ALS695J	OEM
SN74ALS695N	OEM
SN74ALS696J	OEM
SN74ALS696N	OEM
SN74ALS697J	OEM
SN74ALS697N	OEM
SN74ALS698J	OEM
SN74ALS698N	OEM
SN74ALS699J	OEM
SN74ALS699N	OEM
SN74ALS790J	OEM
SN74ALS790N	OEM
SN74ALS804	OEM
SN74ALS804FN	OEM
SN74ALS804J	OEM
SN74ALS804N	OEM
SN74ALS805	OEM
SN74ALS805FN	OEM
SN74ALS805J	OEM
SN74ALS805N	OEM
SN74ALS808	OEM
SN74ALS808FN	OEM
SN74ALS808J	OEM
SN74ALS808N	OEM
SN74ALS832	OEM
SN74ALS832FN	OEM
SN74ALS832J	OEM
SN74ALS832N	OEM
SN74ALS841FN	OEM
SN74ALS841JT	OEM
SN74ALS841NT	OEM
SN74ALS842FN	OEM
SN74ALS842JT	OEM
SN74ALS842NT	OEM
SN74ALS843FN	OEM
SN74ALS843JT	OEM
SN74ALS843NT	OEM
SN74ALS844FN	OEM
SN74ALS844JT	OEM
SN74ALS844NT	OEM
SN74ALS845FN	OEM
SN74ALS845JT	OEM
SN74ALS845NT	OEM
SN74ALS846FN	OEM
SN74ALS846JT	OEM
SN74ALS846NT	OEM
SN74ALS857	OEM
SN74ALS857FN	OEM
SN74ALS857JT	OEM
SN74ALS857NT	OEM
SN74ALS873	OEM
SN74ALS873FN	OEM
SN74ALS873J	OEM
SN74ALS873JT	OEM
SN74ALS873N	OEM
SN74ALS873NT	OEM
SN74ALS874	OEM
SN74ALS874FN	OEM
SN74ALS874J	OEM
SN74ALS874JT	OEM
SN74ALS874N	OEM
SN74ALS874NT	OEM
SN74ALS876	OEM
SN74ALS876FN	OEM
SN74ALS876J	OEM
SN74ALS876JT	OEM
SN74ALS876N	OEM
SN74ALS876NT	OEM
SN74ALS878FN	OEM
SN74ALS878J	OEM
SN74ALS878JT	OEM
SN74ALS878N	OEM
SN74ALS878NT	OEM
SN74ALS879FN	OEM
SN74ALS879J	OEM
SN74ALS879JT	OEM
SN74ALS879N	OEM
SN74ALS879NT	OEM
SN74ALS880	OEM
SN74ALS880FN	OEM
SN74ALS880J	OEM
SN74ALS880JT	OEM
SN74ALS880N	OEM
SN74ALS880NT	OEM
SN74ALS1000	OEM
SN74ALS1000AFN	OEM
SN74ALS1000AJ	OEM
SN74ALS1000AN	OEM
SN74ALS1002	OEM
SN74ALS1002AFN	OEM
SN74ALS1002AJ	OEM
SN74ALS1002AN	OEM
SN74ALS1003	OEM
SN74ALS1003AFN	OEM
SN74ALS1003AJ	OEM
SN74ALS1003AN	OEM
SN74ALS1004	OEM
SN74ALS1004FN	OEM
SN74ALS1004J	OEM
SN74ALS1004N	OEM
SN74ALS1005	OEM
SN74ALS1005FN	OEM
SN74ALS1005J	OEM
SN74ALS1005N	OEM
SN74ALS1008	OEM
SN74ALS1008AFN	OEM
SN74ALS1008AJ	OEM
SN74ALS1008AN	OEM
SN74ALS1010	OEM
SN74ALS1010AFN	OEM
SN74ALS1010AJ	OEM
SN74ALS1010AN	OEM
SN74ALS1011	OEM
SN74ALS1011AFN	OEM
SN74ALS1011AJ	OEM
SN74ALS1011AN	OEM
SN74ALS1020	OEM
SN74ALS1020AFN	OEM
SN74ALS1020AJ	OEM
SN74ALS1020AN	OEM
SN74ALS1032	OEM
SN74ALS1032AFN	OEM
SN74ALS1032AJ	OEM
SN74ALS1032AN	OEM
SN74ALS1034	OEM
SN74ALS1034FN	OEM
SN74ALS1034J	OEM
SN74ALS1034N	OEM
SN74ALS1035	OEM
SN74ALS1035FN	OEM
SN74ALS1035J	OEM
SN74ALS1035N	OEM
SN74ALS1240	OEM
SN74ALS1240FN	OEM
SN74ALS1240J	OEM
SN74ALS1240N	OEM
SN74ALS1241	OEM
SN74ALS1241FN	OEM
SN74ALS1241J	OEM
SN74ALS1241N	OEM
SN74ALS1242	OEM
SN74ALS1242FN	OEM
SN74ALS1242J	OEM
SN74ALS1242N	OEM
SN74ALS1243	OEM
SN74ALS1243FN	OEM
SN74ALS1243J	OEM
SN74ALS1243N	OEM
SN74ALS1244	OEM
SN74ALS1244AFN	OEM
SN74ALS1244AJ	OEM
SN74ALS1244AN	OEM
SN74ALS1245	OEM
SN74ALS1245FN	OEM
SN74ALS1245J	OEM
SN74ALS1245N	OEM
SN74ALS1616	OEM
SN74ALS1620	OEM
SN74ALS1620FN	OEM
SN74ALS1620J	OEM
SN74ALS1620N	OEM
SN74ALS1621	OEM
SN74ALS1621FN	OEM
SN74ALS1621J	OEM
SN74ALS1621N	OEM
SN74ALS1622	OEM
SN74ALS1622FN	OEM
SN74ALS1622J	OEM
SN74ALS1622N	OEM
SN74ALS1623	OEM
SN74ALS1623FN	OEM
SN74ALS1623J	OEM
SN74ALS1623N	OEM
SN74ALS1638	OEM
SN74ALS1638FN	OEM
SN74ALS1638J	OEM
SN74ALS1638N	OEM
SN74ALS1639	OEM
SN74ALS1639FN	OEM
SN74ALS1639J	OEM
SN74ALS1639N	OEM
SN74ALS1640	OEM
SN74ALS1640AFN	OEM
SN74ALS1640AJ	OEM
SN74ALS1640AN	OEM
SN74ALS1641	OEM
SN74ALS1641FN	OEM
SN74ALS1641J	OEM
SN74ALS1641N	OEM
SN74ALS1642	OEM
SN74ALS1642FN	OEM
SN74ALS1642J	OEM
SN74ALS1642N	OEM
SN74ALS1643	OEM
SN74ALS1643FN	OEM
SN74ALS1643J	OEM
SN74ALS1643N	OEM
SN74ALS1644	OEM
SN74ALS1644FN	OEM
SN74ALS1644J	OEM
SN74ALS1644N	OEM
SN74ALS1645	OEM
SN74ALS1645AFN	OEM
SN74ALS1645AJ	OEM
SN74ALS1645AN	OEM
SN74ALS1670N	OEM
SN74ALS8003FN	OEM
SN74ALS8003JG	OEM
SN74ALSL191N	OEM
SN74AS00FN	OEM
SN74AS00J	OEM
SN74AS00N	OEM
SN74AS02FN	OEM
SN74AS02J	OEM
SN74AS02N	OEM
SN74AS04FN	OEM
SN74AS04J	OEM
SN74AS04N	OEM
SN74AS08FN	OEM
SN74AS08J	OEM
SN74AS08N	OEM
SN74AS10FN	OEM
SN74AS10J	OEM
SN74AS10N	OEM
SN74AS11FN	OEM
SN74AS11J	OEM
SN74AS11N	OEM
SN74AS20FN	OEM
SN74AS20J	OEM
SN74AS20N	OEM
SN74AS21FN	OEM
SN74AS21J	OEM
SN74AS21N	OEM
SN74AS27FN	OEM
SN74AS27J	OEM
SN74AS27N	OEM
SN74AS30FN	OEM
SN74AS30J	OEM
SN74AS30N	OEM
SN74AS32FN	OEM
SN74AS32J	OEM
SN74AS32N	OEM
SN74AS34FN	OEM
SN74AS34J	OEM
SN74AS34N	OEM
SN74AS74	OEM
SN74AS74FN	OEM
SN74AS74J	OEM
SN74AS74N	OEM
SN74AS94FN	OEM
SN74AS94J	OEM
SN74AS94N	OEM
SN74AS109	OEM
SN74AS109FN	OEM
SN74AS109J	OEM
SN74AS109N	OEM
SN74AS112	OEM
SN74AS112FN	OEM
SN74AS112J	OEM
SN74AS112N	OEM
SN74AS113	OEM
SN74AS113FN	OEM
SN74AS113J	OEM
SN74AS113N	OEM
SN74AS114	OEM
SN74AS114FN	OEM
SN74AS114J	OEM
SN74AS114N	OEM
SN74AS131FN	OEM
SN74AS131J	OEM
SN74AS131N	OEM
SN74AS137FN	OEM
SN74AS137J	OEM
SN74AS137N	OEM
SN74AS138FN	OEM
SN74AS138J	OEM
SN74AS138N	OEM
SN74AS139FN	OEM
SN74AS139J	OEM
SN74AS139N	OEM
SN74AS151	OEM
SN74AS151FN	OEM
SN74AS151J	OEM
SN74AS151N	OEM
SN74AS153	OEM
SN74AS153FN	OEM
SN74AS153J	OEM
SN74AS153N	OEM
SN74AS157FN	OEM
SN74AS157J	OEM
SN74AS157N	OEM
SN74AS158FN	OEM
SN74AS158J	OEM
SN74AS158N	OEM
SN74AS160	OEM
SN74AS160FN	OEM
SN74AS160J	OEM
SN74AS160N	OEM
SN74AS161	OEM
SN74AS161FN	OEM
SN74AS161J	OEM
SN74AS161N	OEM
SN74AS162	OEM
SN74AS162FN	OEM
SN74AS162J	OEM
SN74AS162N	OEM
SN74AS163	OEM
SN74AS163FN	OEM
SN74AS163J	OEM
SN74AS163N	OEM
SN74AS168	OEM
SN74AS168FN	OEM
SN74AS168J	OEM
SN74AS168N	OEM
SN74AS169	OEM
SN74AS169FN	OEM
SN74AS169J	OEM
SN74AS169N	OEM
SN74AS174	OEM
SN74AS174FN	OEM
SN74AS174J	OEM
SN74AS174N	OEM
SN74AS175	OEM
SN74AS175FN	OEM
SN74AS175J	OEM
SN74AS175N	OEM
SN74AS181A	OEM
SN74AS181AFN	OEM
SN74AS181AJ	OEM
SN74AS181AN	OEM
SN74AS181ANT	OEM
SN74AS182FN	OEM
SN74AS182J	OEM
SN74AS182N	OEM
SN74AS194FN	OEM
SN74AS194J	OEM
SN74AS194N	OEM
SN74AS195FN	OEM
SN74AS195J	OEM
SN74AS195N	OEM
SN74AS230	OEM
SN74AS230FN	OEM
SN74AS230J	OEM
SN74AS230N	OEM
SN74AS231	OEM
SN74AS231FN	OEM
SN74AS231J	OEM
SN74AS231N	OEM
SN74AS240	OEM
SN74AS240FN	OEM
SN74AS240J	OEM
SN74AS240N	OEM
SN74AS241	OEM
SN74AS241FN	OEM
SN74AS241J	OEM
SN74AS241N	OEM
SN74AS242	OEM
SN74AS242FN	OEM
SN74AS242J	OEM
SN74AS242N	OEM
SN74AS243	OEM
SN74AS243FN	OEM
SN74AS243J	OEM
SN74AS243N	OEM
SN74AS244	OEM
SN74AS244FN	OEM
SN74AS244J	OEM
SN74AS244N	OEM
SN74AS245FN	OEM
SN74AS245J	OEM
SN74AS245N	OEM
SN74AS250FN	OEM
SN74AS250J	OEM
SN74AS250N	OEM
SN74AS251	OEM
SN74AS251FN	OEM
SN74AS251J	OEM
SN74AS251N	OEM
SN74AS253	OEM
SN74AS253FN	OEM
SN74AS253J	OEM
SN74AS253N	OEM
SN74AS257FN	OEM
SN74AS257J	OEM
SN74AS257N	OEM
SN74AS258FN	OEM
SN74AS258J	OEM
SN74AS258N	OEM
SN74AS264FN	OEM
SN74AS264J	OEM
SN74AS264N	OEM
SN74AS280	OEM
SN74AS280FN	OEM
SN74AS280J	OEM
SN74AS280N	OEM
SN74AS282FN	OEM
SN74AS282J	OEM
SN74AS282N	OEM
SN74AS286FN	OEM
SN74AS286J	OEM
SN74AS286N	OEM
SN74AS298FN	OEM
SN74AS298J	OEM
SN74AS298N	OEM
SN74AS299FN	OEM
SN74AS299J	OEM
SN74AS299N	OEM
SN74AS323FN	OEM
SN74AS323J	OEM
SN74AS323N	OEM
SN74AS352	OEM
SN74AS352FN	OEM
SN74AS352J	OEM
SN74AS352N	OEM
SN74AS353	OEM
SN74AS353FN	OEM
SN74AS353J	OEM
SN74AS353N	OEM
SN74AS373	OEM
SN74AS373FN	OEM
SN74AS373J	OEM
SN74AS373N	OEM
SN74AS374	OEM
SN74AS374FN	OEM
SN74AS374J	OEM
SN74AS374N	OEM
SN74AS395FN	OEM
SN74AS395J	OEM
SN74AS395N	OEM
SN74AS533	OEM
SN74AS533FN	OEM
SN74AS533J	OEM
SN74AS533N	OEM
SN74AS534	OEM
SN74AS534FN	OEM
SN74AS534J	OEM
SN74AS534N	OEM
SN74AS573	OEM
SN74AS573FN	OEM
SN74AS573J	OEM
SN74AS573N	OEM
SN74AS574	OEM
SN74AS574FN	OEM
SN74AS574J	OEM
SN74AS574N	OEM
SN74AS575FN	OEM
SN74AS575J	OEM
SN74AS575N	OEM
SN74AS576	OEM
SN74AS576FN	OEM
SN74AS576J	OEM
SN74AS576N	OEM
SN74AS577FN	OEM
SN74AS577J	OEM
SN74AS577N	OEM
SN74AS580	OEM
SN74AS580FN	OEM

If replacement code is OEM, contact original manufacturer for replacement.

DEVICE TYPE	REPL CODE
SN74AS580J	OEM
SN74AS580N	OEM
SN74AS598	OEM
SN74AS620FN	OEM
SN74AS620J	OEM
SN74AS620N	OEM
SN74AS621FN	OEM
SN74AS621J	OEM
SN74AS621N	OEM
SN74AS622FN	OEM
SN74AS622J	OEM
SN74AS622N	OEM
SN74AS623FN	OEM
SN74AS623J	OEM
SN74AS623N	OEM
SN74AS638FN	OEM
SN74AS638J	OEM
SN74AS638N	OEM
SN74AS639FN	OEM
SN74AS639J	OEM
SN74AS639N	OEM
SN74AS640	OEM
SN74AS640FN	OEM
SN74AS640J	OEM
SN74AS640N	OEM
SN74AS641	OEM
SN74AS641FN	OEM
SN74AS641J	OEM
SN74AS641N	OEM
SN74AS642	OEM
SN74AS642FN	OEM
SN74AS642J	OEM
SN74AS642N	OEM
SN74AS643	OEM
SN74AS643FN	OEM
SN74AS643J	OEM
SN74AS643N	OEM
SN74AS644	OEM
SN74AS644FN	OEM
SN74AS644J	OEM
SN74AS644N	OEM
SN74AS645	OEM
SN74AS645FN	OEM
SN74AS645J	OEM
SN74AS645N	OEM
SN74AS646FN	OEM
SN74AS646JT	OEM
SN74AS646NT	OEM
SN74AS648FN	OEM
SN74AS648JT	OEM
SN74AS648NT	OEM
SN74AS651FN	OEM
SN74AS651JT	OEM
SN74AS651NT	OEM
SN74AS652FN	OEM
SN74AS652JT	OEM
SN74AS652NT	OEM
SN74AS756FN	OEM
SN74AS756J	OEM
SN74AS756N	OEM
SN74AS757FN	OEM
SN74AS757J	OEM
SN74AS757N	OEM
SN74AS758FN	OEM
SN74AS758J	OEM
SN74AS758N	OEM
SN74AS759FN	OEM
SN74AS759J	OEM
SN74AS759N	OEM
SN74AS760FN	OEM
SN74AS760J	OEM
SN74AS760N	OEM
SN74AS762FN	OEM
SN74AS762J	OEM
SN74AS762N	OEM
SN74AS763FN	OEM
SN74AS763J	OEM
SN74AS763N	OEM
SN74AS800	OEM
SN74AS800FN	OEM
SN74AS800J	OEM
SN74AS800N	OEM
SN74AS801	OEM
SN74AS802	OEM
SN74AS802FN	OEM
SN74AS802J	OEM
SN74AS802N	OEM
SN74AS804	OEM
SN74AS804A	OEM
SN74AS804AFN	OEM
SN74AS804AJ	OEM
SN74AS804AN	OEM
SN74AS805	OEM
SN74AS805A	OEM
SN74AS805AFN	OEM
SN74AS805AJ	OEM
SN74AS805AN	OEM
SN74AS808	OEM
SN74AS808A	OEM
SN74AS808AFN	OEM
SN74AS808AJ	OEM
SN74AS808AN	OEM
SN74AS821FN	OEM
SN74AS821JT	OEM
SN74AS821NT	OEM
SN74AS822FN	OEM
SN74AS822JT	OEM
SN74AS822NT	OEM
SN74AS823FN	OEM

DEVICE TYPE	REPL CODE
SN74AS823JT	OEM
SN74AS823NT	OEM
SN74AS824FN	OEM
SN74AS824JT	OEM
SN74AS824NT	OEM
SN74AS825FN	OEM
SN74AS825JT	OEM
SN74AS825NT	OEM
SN74AS826FN	OEM
SN74AS826JT	OEM
SN74AS826NT	OEM
SN74AS830	OEM
SN74AS832	OEM
SN74AS832A	OEM
SN74AS832AFN	OEM
SN74AS832AJ	OEM
SN74AS832AN	OEM
SN74AS836	OEM
SN74AS841FN	OEM
SN74AS841JT	OEM
SN74AS841NT	OEM
SN74AS842FN	OEM
SN74AS842J	OEM
SN74AS842N	OEM
SN74AS843FN	OEM
SN74AS843JT	OEM
SN74AS843NT	OEM
SN74AS844FN	OEM
SN74AS844JT	OEM
SN74AS844NT	OEM
SN74AS845FN	OEM
SN74AS845JT	OEM
SN74AS845NT	OEM
SN74AS846FN	OEM
SN74AS846JT	OEM
SN74AS846NT	OEM
SN74AS850	OEM
SN74AS850FN	OEM
SN74AS850JD	OEM
SN74AS850N	OEM
SN74AS851FN	OEM
SN74AS851JD	OEM
SN74AS851N	OEM
SN74AS852FN	OEM
SN74AS852JT	OEM
SN74AS852NT	OEM
SN74AS856FN	OEM
SN74AS856JT	OEM
SN74AS856NT	OEM
SN74AS857	OEM
SN74AS857FN	OEM
SN74AS857J	OEM
SN74AS857N	OEM
SN74AS859	OEM
SN74AS866	OEM
SN74AS866FN	OEM
SN74AS866JD	OEM
SN74AS866N	OEM
SN74AS867	OEM
SN74AS867FN	OEM
SN74AS867JT	OEM
SN74AS867NT	OEM
SN74AS869	OEM
SN74AS869FN	OEM
SN74AS869JT	OEM
SN74AS869NT	OEM
SN74AS870	OEM
SN74AS870FN	OEM
SN74AS870JT	OEM
SN74AS870NT	OEM
SN74AS871	OEM
SN74AS871FN	OEM
SN74AS871JD	OEM
SN74AS871N	OEM
SN74AS872	OEM
SN74AS873	OEM
SN74AS873FN	OEM
SN74AS873JT	OEM
SN74AS873NT	OEM
SN74AS874	OEM
SN74AS874FN	OEM
SN74AS874JT	OEM
SN74AS874NT	OEM
SN74AS875	OEM
SN74AS876	OEM
SN74AS876FN	OEM
SN74AS876JT	OEM
SN74AS876NT	OEM
SN74AS877	OEM
SN74AS877FN	OEM
SN74AS877JT	OEM
SN74AS877NT	OEM
SN74AS878FN	OEM
SN74AS878JT	OEM
SN74AS878NT	OEM
SN74AS879FN	OEM
SN74AS879JT	OEM
SN74AS879NT	OEM
SN74AS880	OEM
SN74AS880FN	OEM
SN74AS880JT	OEM
SN74AS880NT	OEM
SN74AS881A	OEM
SN74AS881AFN	OEM
SN74AS881AJT	OEM
SN74AS881ANT	OEM
SN74AS882	OEM
SN74AS882FN	OEM
SN74AS882JT	OEM

DEVICE TYPE	REPL CODE
SN74AS882NT	OEM
SN74AS883	OEM
SN74AS884	OEM
SN74AS885	OEM
SN74AS885FN	OEM
SN74AS885JT	OEM
SN74AS885NT	OEM
SN74AS886	OEM
SN74AS888	OEM
SN74AS889	OEM
SN74AS890	OEM
SN74AS891	OEM
SN74AS894	OEM
SN74AS1000FN	OEM
SN74AS1000J	OEM
SN74AS1000N	OEM
SN74AS1004	OEM
SN74AS1004FN	OEM
SN74AS1004J	OEM
SN74AS1004N	OEM
SN74AS1008FN	OEM
SN74AS1008J	OEM
SN74AS1008N	OEM
SN74AS1032FN	OEM
SN74AS1032J	OEM
SN74AS1032N	OEM
SN74AS1034FN	OEM
SN74AS1034J	OEM
SN74AS1034N	OEM
SN74AS1036FN	OEM
SN74AS1036J	OEM
SN74AS1036N	OEM
SN74AS2620FN	OEM
SN74AS2620J	OEM
SN74AS2620N	OEM
SN74AS2623FN	OEM
SN74AS2623J	OEM
SN74AS2623N	OEM
SN74AS2640FN	OEM
SN74AS2640J	OEM
SN74AS2640N	OEM
SN74AS2645FN	OEM
SN74AS2645J	OEM
SN74AS2645N	OEM
SN74H00	0677
SN74H00J	0677
SN74H00N	0677
SN74H01	5241
SN74H01J	5241
SN74H01N	5241
SN74H04	1896
SN74H04J	1896
SN74H04N	1896
SN74H05	3221
SN74H05J	3221
SN74H05N	3221
SN74H10	0680
SN74H10J	0680
SN74H10N	0680
SN74H11	2382
SN74H11J	2382
SN74H11N	2382
SN74H15	OEM
SN74H15J	OEM
SN74H15N	OEM
SN74H20	3670
SN74H20J	3670
SN74H20N	3670
SN74H21	4772
SN74H21J	4772
SN74H21N	4772
SN74H22	4516
SN74H22J	4516
SN74H22N	4516
SN74H30	5284
SN74H30J	5284
SN74H30N	5284
SN74H40	0554
SN74H40J	0554
SN74H40N	0554
SN74H50	1781
SN74H50J	1781
SN74H50N	1781
SN74H51	1933
SN74H51J	1933
SN74H51N	1933
SN74H52	2009
SN74H52J	2009
SN74H52N	2009
SN74H53	2090
SN74H53J	2090
SN74H53N	2090
SN74H54	2158
SN74H54DC	2158
SN74H54J	2158
SN74H54N	2158
SN74H55	3129
SN74H55J	3129
SN74H55N	3129
SN74H60	5312
SN74H60J	5312
SN74H60N	5312
SN74H61	2638
SN74H61J	2638
SN74H61N	2638
SN74H62	2705
SN74H62J	2705
SN74H62N	2705
SN74H71	3233

DEVICE TYPE	REPL CODE
SN74H71J	3233
SN74H71N	3233
SN74H72	3281
SN74H72J	3281
SN74H72N	3281
SN74H73	2444
SN74H73J	2444
SN74H73N	2444
SN74H74	2472
SN74H74J	2472
SN74H74N	2472
SN74H76	5208
SN74H76J	5208
SN74H76N	5208
SN74H78	5320
SN74H78J	5320
SN74H78N	5320
SN74H87	2557
SN74H87J	2557
SN74H87N	2557
SN74H101	5424
SN74H101J	5424
SN74H101N	5424
SN74H102	5426
SN74H102J	5426
SN74H102N	5426
SN74H103	2941
SN74H103J	2941
SN74H103N	2941
SN74H106	5159
SN74H106J	5159
SN74H106N	5159
SN74H108	0180
SN74H108J	0180
SN74H108N	0180
SN74H183	4329
SN74H183J	4329
SN74H183N	4329
SN74HC00NS	OEM
SN74HC02N	5285
SN74HC03N	1444
SN74HC04ANS	1446
SN74HC86N	1578
SN74HC240N	1968
SN74L00N	OEM
SN74L03	1569
SN74L04J	OEM
SN74L04N	OEM
SN74L46J	OEM
SN74L46N	OEM
SN74L47J	OEM
SN74L47N	OEM
SN74L77W	OEM
SN74L91J	OEM
SN74L91N	OEM
SN74L93J	0651
SN74L93N	0651
SN74L95J	OEM
SN74L95N	OEM
SN74L96J	OEM
SN74L96N	OEM
SN74L98J	OEM
SN74L98N	OEM
SN74L99J	OEM
SN74L99N	OEM
SN74L153J	OEM
SN74L153N	OEM
SN74L154J	OEM
SN74L154N	OEM
SN74L157J	OEM
SN74L157N	OEM
SN74L164J	OEM
SN74L164N	OEM
SN74L164T	OEM
SN74LD247D	OEM
SN74LD247FN	OEM
SN74LS00	1519
SN74LS00J	1519
SN74LS00JD	1519
SN74LS00JDS	1519
SN74LS00JS	1519
SN74LS00N	1519
SN74LS00ND	1519
SN74LS00NDS	1519
SN74LS00NS	1519
SN74LS00W	1519
SN74LS01	1537
SN74LS01J	1537
SN74LS01JD	1537
SN74LS01JDS	1537
SN74LS01JS	1537
SN74LS01N	1537
SN74LS01ND	1537
SN74LS01NDS	1537
SN74LS01NS	1537
SN74LS02	1550
SN74LS02D	OEM
SN74LS02FN	OEM
SN74LS02J	1550
SN74LS02JD	1550
SN74LS02JDS	1550
SN74LS02JS	1550
SN74LS02N	1550
SN74LS02NDS	1550
SN74LS02NS	1550
SN74LS02W	1550
SN74LS03	4152
SN74LS03J	1569
SN74LS03JD	1569

DEVICE TYPE	REPL CODE
SN74LS03JDS	1569
SN74LS03JS	1569
SN74LS03N	1569
SN74LS03ND	1569
SN74LS03NDS	1569
SN74LS03NS	1569
SN74LS03W	1569
SN74LS04	1585
SN74LS04J	1585
SN74LS04JD	1585
SN74LS04JDS	1585
SN74LS04JS	1585
SN74LS04N	1585
SN74LS04ND	1585
SN74LS04NDS	1585
SN74LS04NS	1585
SN74LS05	1598
SN74LS05J	1598
SN74LS05JD	1598
SN74LS05JDS	1598
SN74LS05JS	1598
SN74LS05N	1598
SN74LS05ND	1598
SN74LS05NDS	1598
SN74LS05NS	1598
SN74LS06N	OEM
SN74LS07N	OEM
SN74LS08	1623
SN74LS08J	1623
SN74LS08JD	1623
SN74LS08JDS	1623
SN74LS08JS	1623
SN74LS08N	1623
SN74LS08ND	1623
SN74LS08NDS	1623
SN74LS08NS	1623
SN74LS08W	1623
SN74LS09	1632
SN74LS09J	1632
SN74LS09JD	1632
SN74LS09JDS	1632
SN74LS09JS	1632
SN74LS09N	1632
SN74LS09ND	1632
SN74LS09NDS	1632
SN74LS09NS	1632
SN74LS10	1652
SN74LS10J	1652
SN74LS10JD	1652
SN74LS10JDS	1652
SN74LS10JS	1652
SN74LS10N	1652
SN74LS10ND	1652
SN74LS10NDS	1652
SN74LS10NS	1652
SN74LS10W	1652
SN74LS11	1657
SN74LS11J	1657
SN74LS11JD	1657
SN74LS11JDS	1657
SN74LS11JS	1657
SN74LS11N	1657
SN74LS11ND	1657
SN74LS11NDS	1657
SN74LS11NS	1657
SN74LS11W	1657
SN74LS12	1669
SN74LS12J	1669
SN74LS12JD	1669
SN74LS12JDS	1669
SN74LS12JS	1669
SN74LS12N	1669
SN74LS12ND	1669
SN74LS12NDS	1669
SN74LS12NS	1669
SN74LS13	1678
SN74LS13J	1678
SN74LS13JD	1678
SN74LS13JDS	1678
SN74LS13JS	1678
SN74LS13N	1678
SN74LS13ND	1678
SN74LS13NDS	1678
SN74LS13NS	1678
SN74LS14	1688
SN74LS14J	1688
SN74LS14JD	1688
SN74LS14JDS	1688
SN74LS14JS	1688
SN74LS14N	1688
SN74LS14ND	1688
SN74LS14NDS	1688
SN74LS14NS	1688
SN74LS15	1697
SN74LS15J	1697
SN74LS15JD	1697
SN74LS15JDS	1697
SN74LS15JS	1697
SN74LS15N	1697
SN74LS15ND	1697
SN74LS15NDS	1697
SN74LS15NS	1697
SN74LS18	OEM
SN74LS18J	OEM
SN74LS18N	OEM
SN74LS19	OEM
SN74LS19AN	OEM
SN74LS19J	OEM
SN74LS19N	OEM

DEVICE TYPE	REPL CODE
SN74LS20	0035
SN74LS20J	0035
SN74LS20JD	0035
SN74LS20JDS	0035
SN74LS20JS	0035
SN74LS20N	0035
SN74LS20ND	0035
SN74LS20NDS	0035
SN74LS20NS	0035
SN74LS20W	0035
SN74LS21	1752
SN74LS21D	OEM
SN74LS21FN	OEM
SN74LS21J	1752
SN74LS21JD	1752
SN74LS21JDS	1752
SN74LS21JS	1752
SN74LS21N	1752
SN74LS21ND	1752
SN74LS21NDS	1752
SN74LS21NS	1752
SN74LS22	1764
SN74LS22J	1764
SN74LS22JD	1764
SN74LS22JDS	1764
SN74LS22JS	1764
SN74LS22N	1764
SN74LS22ND	1764
SN74LS22NDS	1764
SN74LS22NS	1764
SN74LS24	OEM
SN74LS24J	OEM
SN74LS24N	OEM
SN74LS26	1372
SN74LS26J	1372
SN74LS26JD	1372
SN74LS26JDS	1372
SN74LS26JS	1372
SN74LS26N	1372
SN74LS26ND	1372
SN74LS26NS	1372
SN74LS27J	0183
SN74LS27JD	0183
SN74LS27JDS	0183
SN74LS27N	0183
SN74LS27ND	0183
SN74LS27NDS	0183
SN74LS27NS	0183
SN74LS27W	0183
SN74LS28	0467
SN74LS28J	0467
SN74LS28JD	0467
SN74LS28JDS	0467
SN74LS28JS	0467
SN74LS28N	0467
SN74LS28ND	0467
SN74LS28NDS	0467
SN74LS28NS	0467
SN74LS30	0822
SN74LS30J	0822
SN74LS30JD	0822
SN74LS30JDS	0822
SN74LS30JS	0822
SN74LS30N	0822
SN74LS30ND	0822
SN74LS30NDS	0822
SN74LS30NS	0822
SN74LS30W	0822
SN74LS31N	OEM
SN74LS32	0088
SN74LS32J	0088
SN74LS32JD	0088
SN74LS32JDS	0088
SN74LS32JS	0088
SN74LS32N	0088
SN74LS32ND	0088
SN74LS32NDS	0088
SN74LS32NS	0088
SN74LS32W	0088
SN74LS33	1821
SN74LS33J	1821
SN74LS33JD	OEM
SN74LS33JDS	OEM
SN74LS33JS	OEM
SN74LS33N	1821
SN74LS33ND	OEM
SN74LS33NDS	OEM
SN74LS33NS	1310
SN74LS37	1719
SN74LS37J	1719
SN74LS37JD	1719
SN74LS37JDS	1719
SN74LS37JS	1719
SN74LS37N	1719
SN74LS37ND	1719
SN74LS37NDS	1719
SN74LS37NS	1719
SN74LS38	1828
SN74LS38J	1828
SN74LS38JD	1828
SN74LS38JDS	1828
SN74LS38JS	1828
SN74LS38N	1828
SN74LS38ND	1828
SN74LS38NS	1828
SN74LS40	0135
SN74LS40J	0135
SN74LS40JD	0135

DEVICE TYPE	REPL CODE
SN74LS40JDS	0135
SN74LS40JS	0135
SN74LS40N	0135
SN74LS40ND	0135
SN74LS40NDS	0135
SN74LS40NS	0135
SN74LS42	1830
SN74LS42J	1830
SN74LS42JD	1830
SN74LS42JDS	1830
SN74LS42JS	1830
SN74LS42N	1830
SN74LS42ND	1830
SN74LS42NDS	1830
SN74LS42NS	1830
SN74LS42W	1830
SN74LS47	1834
SN74LS47J	1834
SN74LS47JD	1834
SN74LS47JDS	1834
SN74LS47JS	1834
SN74LS47N	1834
SN74LS47ND	1834
SN74LS47NDS	1834
SN74LS47NS	1834
SN74LS48J	1838
SN74LS48JD	1838
SN74LS48JDS	1838
SN74LS48JS	1838
SN74LS48N	1838
SN74LS48ND	1838
SN74LS48NDS	1838
SN74LS48NS	1838
SN74LS49	1839
SN74LS49J	1839
SN74LS49JD	1839
SN74LS49JDS	1839
SN74LS49JS	1839
SN74LS49N	1839
SN74LS49ND	1839
SN74LS49NDS	1839
SN74LS49NS	1839
SN74LS51	1027
SN74LS51J	1027
SN74LS51JD	1027
SN74LS51JDS	1027
SN74LS51JS	1027
SN74LS51N	1027
SN74LS51ND	1027
SN74LS51NDS	1027
SN74LS51NS	1027
SN74LS51W	1027
SN74LS54	1846
SN74LS54J	1846
SN74LS54JD	1846
SN74LS54JDS	1846
SN74LS54JS	1846
SN74LS54N	1846
SN74LS54ND	1846
SN74LS54NDS	1846
SN74LS54NS	1846
SN74LS55	0452
SN74LS55J	0452
SN74LS55JD	0452
SN74LS55JDS	0452
SN74LS55JS	0452
SN74LS55N	0452
SN74LS55ND	0452
SN74LS55NDS	0452
SN74LS55NS	0452
SN74LS63	OEM
SN74LS63J	OEM
SN74LS63N	OEM
SN74LS68JDS	OEM
SN74LS73A	1856
SN74LS73AJ	1856
SN74LS73AJD	1856
SN74LS73AJDS	1856
SN74LS73AJS	1856
SN74LS73AN	1856
SN74LS73AND	1856
SN74LS73ANDS	1856
SN74LS73ANS	1856
SN74LS73AW	1856
SN74LS73J	1856
SN74LS73N	1856
SN74LS74	0243
SN74LS74A	0243
SN74LS74AJ	0243
SN74LS74AJDS	0243
SN74LS74AJS	0243
SN74LS74AN	0243
SN74LS74AND	0243
SN74LS74ANDS	0243
SN74LS74ANS	0243
SN74LS74AW	0243
SN74LS74N	0243
SN74LS75	1859
SN74LS75J	1859
SN74LS75JD	1859
SN74LS75JDS	1859
SN74LS75JS	1859
SN74LS75N	1859
SN74LS75ND	1859
SN74LS75NDS	1859
SN74LS75NS	1859
SN74LS75W	1859
SN74LS76A	2166

If replacement code is OEM, contact original manufacturer for replacement.

DEVICE TYPE	REPL CODE
SN74LS76AJ	2166
SN74LS76AJD	2166
SN74LS76AJDS	2166
SN74LS76AJS	2166
SN74LS76AN	2166
SN74LS76AND	2166
SN74LS76ANDS	2166
SN74LS76ANS	2166
SN74LS77J	1861
SN74LS77JD	1861
SN74LS77JDS	1861
SN74LS77JS	1861
SN74LS77N	1861
SN74LS77ND	1861
SN74LS77NDS	1861
SN74LS77NS	3936
SN74LS78A	1862
SN74LS78AJ	1862
SN74LS78AJD	1862
SN74LS78AJDS	1862
SN74LS78AJS	1862
SN74LS78AN	1862
SN74LS78AND	1862
SN74LS78ANDS	1862
SN74LS78ANS	1862
SN74LS83A	2204
SN74LS83AJ	2204
SN74LS83AJD	2204
SN74LS83AJDS	2204
SN74LS83AJS	2204
SN74LS83AN	2204
SN74LS83AND	2204
SN74LS83ANDS	2204
SN74LS83ANS	2204
SN74LS83AW	2204
SN74LS83N	2204
SN74LS85J	0426
SN74LS85JD	0426
SN74LS85JDS	0426
SN74LS85JS	0426
SN74LS85N	0426
SN74LS85ND	0426
SN74LS85NDS	0426
SN74LS85NS	0426
SN74LS85W	0426
SN74LS86	0288
SN74LS86AN	0288
SN74LS86J	0288
SN74LS86JD	0288
SN74LS86JDS	0288
SN74LS86JS	0288
SN74LS86N	0288
SN74LS86ND	0288
SN74LS86NDS	0288
SN74LS86NS	0288
SN74LS86W	0288
SN74LS90	1871
SN74LS90J	1871
SN74LS90JD	1871
SN74LS90JDS	1871
SN74LS90JS	1871
SN74LS90N	1871
SN74LS90ND	1871
SN74LS90NDS	1871
SN74LS90NS	1871
SN74LS91	1874
SN74LS91J	1874
SN74LS91JD	1874
SN74LS91JDS	1874
SN74LS91JS	1874
SN74LS91N	1874
SN74LS91ND	1874
SN74LS91NDS	1874
SN74LS91NS	1874
SN74LS92	1876
SN74LS92J	1876
SN74LS92JD	1876
SN74LS92JDS	1876
SN74LS92JS	1876
SN74LS92N	1876
SN74LS92ND	1876
SN74LS92NDS	1876
SN74LS92NS	1876
SN74LS93	1877
SN74LS93J	1877
SN74LS93JD	1877
SN74LS93JDS	1877
SN74LS93N	1877
SN74LS93ND	1877
SN74LS93NDS	1877
SN74LS93NS	1877
SN74LS93W	1877
SN74LS95AJ	OEM
SN74LS95AN	OEM
SN74LS95AW	OEM
SN74LS95BJ	0766
SN74LS95BJD	0766
SN74LS95BJDS	0766
SN74LS95BJS	0766
SN74LS95BN	0766
SN74LS95BND	0766
SN74LS95BNDS	0766
SN74LS95BNS	0766
SN74LS95N	OEM
SN74LS96	OEM
SN74LS96J	OEM
SN74LS96N	OEM
SN74LS107A	1592
SN74LS107AJ	1592
SN74LS107AJD	1592
SN74LS107AJDS	1592
SN74LS107AJS	1592
SN74LS107AN	1592
SN74LS107AND	1592
SN74LS107ANDS	1592
SN74LS107ANS	1592
SN74LS107AW	1592
SN74LS107N	1592
SN74LS109A	1895
SN74LS109AJ	1895
SN74LS109AJD	1895
SN74LS109AJDS	1895
SN74LS109AJS	1895
SN74LS109AN	1895
SN74LS109AND	1895
SN74LS109ANDS	1895
SN74LS109ANS	1895
SN74LS109AW	1895
SN74LS109N	1895
SN74LS112A	2115
SN74LS112AJ	2115
SN74LS112AJD	2115
SN74LS112AJDS	2115
SN74LS112AJS	2115
SN74LS112AN	2115
SN74LS112AND	2115
SN74LS112ANDS	2115
SN74LS112ANS	2115
SN74LS112N	1607
SN74LS113A	2241
SN74LS113AD	OEM
SN74LS113AFN	OEM
SN74LS113AJ	2241
SN74LS113AJD	2241
SN74LS113AJDS	2241
SN74LS113AJS	2241
SN74LS113AN	2241
SN74LS113AND	2241
SN74LS113ANDS	2241
SN74LS113ANS	2241
SN74LS114A	2286
SN74LS114AJ	2286
SN74LS114AJD	2286
SN74LS114AJDS	2286
SN74LS114AJS	2286
SN74LS114AN	2286
SN74LS114AND	2286
SN74LS114ANDS	2286
SN74LS114ANS	2286
SN74LS122	1610
SN74LS122J	1610
SN74LS122JD	1610
SN74LS122JDS	1610
SN74LS122JS	1610
SN74LS122N	1610
SN74LS122ND	1610
SN74LS122NDS	1610
SN74LS122NS	1610
SN74LS123	0973
SN74LS123J	0973
SN74LS123JD	0973
SN74LS123JDS	0973
SN74LS123JS	0973
SN74LS123N	0973
SN74LS123ND	0973
SN74LS123NDS	0973
SN74LS123NS	0973
SN74LS123W	0973
SN74LS124J	3146
SN74LS124N	3146
SN74LS125A	0075
SN74LS125AJ	0075
SN74LS125AJD	0075
SN74LS125AJDS	0075
SN74LS125AJS	0075
SN74LS125AN	0075
SN74LS125AND	0075
SN74LS125ANDS	0075
SN74LS125ANS	0075
SN74LS126A	2850
SN74LS126AJ	2850
SN74LS126AJD	2850
SN74LS126AJDS	2850
SN74LS126AJS	2850
SN74LS126AN	2850
SN74LS126AND	2850
SN74LS126ANDS	2850
SN74LS126ANS	2850
SN74LS126J	2850
SN74LS126N	2850
SN74LS132	1615
SN74LS132J	1615
SN74LS132JD	1615
SN74LS132JDS	1615
SN74LS132JS	1615
SN74LS132N	1615
SN74LS132ND	1615
SN74LS132NDS	1615
SN74LS132NS	1615
SN74LS133J	3366
SN74LS133JD	3366
SN74LS133JDS	3366
SN74LS133JS	3366
SN74LS133N	3366
SN74LS133ND	3366
SN74LS133NDS	3366
SN74LS133NS	3366
SN74LS136	1618
SN74LS136D	OEM
SN74LS136J	1618
SN74LS136JD	1618
SN74LS136JDS	1618
SN74LS136JS	1618
SN74LS136N	1618
SN74LS136ND	1618
SN74LS136NDS	1618
SN74LS136NS	1618
SN74LS136W	1618
SN74LS137	4328
SN74LS137J	4328
SN74LS137JD	4328
SN74LS137JDS	4328
SN74LS137JS	4328
SN74LS137N	4328
SN74LS137ND	4328
SN74LS137NDS	4328
SN74LS137NS	4328
SN74LS138	0422
SN74LS138J	0422
SN74LS138JD	0422
SN74LS138JDS	0422
SN74LS138JS	0422
SN74LS138N	0422
SN74LS138ND	0422
SN74LS138NDS	0422
SN74LS138NS	0422
SN74LS138X	0422
SN74LS139	0153
SN74LS139AN	0153
SN74LS139J	0153
SN74LS139JD	0153
SN74LS139JDS	0153
SN74LS139JS	0153
SN74LS139N	0153
SN74LS139ND	0153
SN74LS139NDS	0153
SN74LS139NS	0153
SN74LS139X	0153
SN74LS145	1554
SN74LS145J	1554
SN74LS145JD	1554
SN74LS145JDS	1554
SN74LS145JS	1554
SN74LS145N	1554
SN74LS145ND	1554
SN74LS145NDS	1554
SN74LS145NS	1554
SN74LS147	4330
SN74LS147J	4330
SN74LS147JD	4330
SN74LS147JDS	4330
SN74LS147JS	4330
SN74LS147N	4330
SN74LS147ND	4330
SN74LS147NDS	4330
SN74LS147NS	4330
SN74LS148	3856
SN74LS148AJ	3856
SN74LS148AJD	3856
SN74LS148AJDS	3856
SN74LS148AJS	3856
SN74LS148AN	3856
SN74LS148AND	3856
SN74LS148ANDS	3856
SN74LS148ANS	3856
SN74LS148J	3856
SN74LS148JD	3856
SN74LS148JDS	3856
SN74LS148JS	3856
SN74LS148N	3856
SN74LS148ND	3856
SN74LS148NDS	3856
SN74LS148NS	3856
SN74LS151	1636
SN74LS151J	1636
SN74LS151JD	1636
SN74LS151JDS	1636
SN74LS151JS	1636
SN74LS151N	1636
SN74LS151ND	1636
SN74LS151NDS	1636
SN74LS151NS	1636
SN74LS151X	1636
SN74LS153	0953
SN74LS153D	OEM
SN74LS153FN	OEM
SN74LS153J	0953
SN74LS153JD	0953
SN74LS153JDS	0953
SN74LS153JS	0953
SN74LS153N	0953
SN74LS153ND	0953
SN74LS153NDS	0953
SN74LS153NS	0953
SN74LS154N	OEM
SN74LS155	0209
SN74LS155AN	0209
SN74LS155J	0209
SN74LS155JD	0209
SN74LS155JDS	0209
SN74LS155JS	0209
SN74LS155N	0209
SN74LS155ND	0209
SN74LS155NDS	0209
SN74LS155NS	0209
SN74LS156	1644
SN74LS156J	1644
SN74LS156JD	1644
SN74LS156JDS	1644
SN74LS156JS	1644
SN74LS156N	1644
SN74LS156ND	1644
SN74LS156NDS	1644
SN74LS156NS	1644
SN74LS157	1153
SN74LS157D	OEM
SN74LS157FN	OEM
SN74LS157J	1153
SN74LS157JD	1153
SN74LS157JDS	1153
SN74LS157JS	1153
SN74LS157N	1153
SN74LS157ND	1153
SN74LS157NDS	1153
SN74LS157NS	1153
SN74LS158	1646
SN74LS158D	OEM
SN74LS158FN	OEM
SN74LS158J	1646
SN74LS158JD	1646
SN74LS158JDS	1646
SN74LS158JS	1646
SN74LS158N	1646
SN74LS158ND	1646
SN74LS158NDS	1646
SN74LS158NS	1646
SN74LS160A	0831
SN74LS160AJ	0831
SN74LS160AJD	0831
SN74LS160AJDS	0831
SN74LS160AJS	0831
SN74LS160AN	0831
SN74LS160AND	0831
SN74LS160ANDS	0831
SN74LS160ANS	0831
SN74LS160J	0831
SN74LS160N	0831
SN74LS161A	0852
SN74LS161AJ	0852
SN74LS161AJD	0852
SN74LS161AJDS	0852
SN74LS161AJS	0852
SN74LS161AN	0852
SN74LS161AND	0852
SN74LS161ANDS	0852
SN74LS161ANS	0852
SN74LS161AW	0852
SN74LS161J	0852
SN74LS161N	0852
SN74LS162A	0874
SN74LS162AJ	0874
SN74LS162AJD	0874
SN74LS162AJDS	0874
SN74LS162AJS	0874
SN74LS162AN	0874
SN74LS162AND	0874
SN74LS162ANDS	0874
SN74LS162ANS	0874
SN74LS162J	0874
SN74LS162N	0874
SN74LS163A	0887
SN74LS163AJ	0887
SN74LS163AJD	0887
SN74LS163AJDS	0887
SN74LS163AJS	0887
SN74LS163AN	0887
SN74LS163AND	0887
SN74LS163ANDS	0887
SN74LS163ANS	0887
SN74LS163AW	0887
SN74LS163J	0887
SN74LS163N	0887
SN74LS164	4274
SN74LS164AN	OEM
SN74LS164J	4274
SN74LS164JD	4274
SN74LS164JDS	4274
SN74LS164JS	4274
SN74LS164N	4274
SN74LS164ND	4274
SN74LS164NDS	4274
SN74LS164NS	4274
SN74LS165A	4289
SN74LS165J	4289
SN74LS165JD	4289
SN74LS165JDS	4289
SN74LS165JS	4289
SN74LS165N	4289
SN74LS165ND	4289
SN74LS165NDS	4289
SN74LS165NS	4289
SN74LS166	4301
SN74LS166A	4301
SN74LS166AN	4301
SN74LS166J	4301
SN74LS166JD	4301
SN74LS166JDS	4301
SN74LS166JS	4301
SN74LS166N	4301
SN74LS166ND	4301
SN74LS166NDS	4301
SN74LS166NS	4301
SN74LS168N	0961
SN74LS169AJ	0980
SN74LS169AN	0980
SN74LS169B	0980
SN74LS169BN	OEM
SN74LS169J	0980
SN74LS169N	0980
SN74LS170	2605
SN74LS170J	2605
SN74LS170JD	2605
SN74LS170JDS	2605
SN74LS170JS	2605
SN74LS170N	2605
SN74LS170ND	2605
SN74LS170NDS	2605
SN74LS170NS	2605
SN74LS173A	5125
SN74LS173AD	OEM
SN74LS173AFN	OEM
SN74LS173AJ	5125
SN74LS173AJD	5125
SN74LS173AJDS	5125
SN74LS173AJS	5125
SN74LS173AN	5125
SN74LS173AND	5125
SN74LS173ANDS	5125
SN74LS173ANS	5125
SN74LS174	0260
SN74LS174J	0260
SN74LS174JD	0260
SN74LS174JDS	0260
SN74LS174JS	0260
SN74LS174N	0260
SN74LS174ND	0260
SN74LS174NDS	0260
SN74LS174NS	0260
SN74LS175	1662
SN74LS175J	1662
SN74LS175JD	1662
SN74LS175JDS	1662
SN74LS175JS	1662
SN74LS175N	1662
SN74LS175ND	1662
SN74LS175NDS	1662
SN74LS175NS	1662
SN74LS178N	OEM
SN74LS181	1668
SN74LS181J	1668
SN74LS181JD	1668
SN74LS181JDS	1668
SN74LS181JS	1668
SN74LS181N	1668
SN74LS181ND	1668
SN74LS181NDS	1668
SN74LS181NS	1668
SN74LS182J	5981
SN74LS182JD	5981
SN74LS182JDS	5981
SN74LS182JS	5981
SN74LS182N	5981
SN74LS182ND	5981
SN74LS182NDS	5981
SN74LS182NS	5981
SN74LS183	OEM
SN74LS183J	OEM
SN74LS183JD	OEM
SN74LS183JDS	OEM
SN74LS183JS	OEM
SN74LS183N	OEM
SN74LS183ND	OEM
SN74LS183NDS	OEM
SN74LS183NS	OEM
SN74LS189A	OEM
SN74LS189N	OEM
SN74LS190	1676
SN74LS190J	1676
SN74LS190JD	1676
SN74LS190JDS	1676
SN74LS190JS	1676
SN74LS190N	1676
SN74LS190ND	1676
SN74LS190NDS	1676
SN74LS190NS	1676
SN74LS191	1677
SN74LS191J	1677
SN74LS191JD	1677
SN74LS191JDS	1677
SN74LS191JS	1677
SN74LS191N	1677
SN74LS191ND	1677
SN74LS191NDS	1677
SN74LS191NS	1677
SN74LS191W	1677
SN74LS192	1679
SN74LS192FN	OEM
SN74LS192J	1679
SN74LS192JD	1679
SN74LS192JDS	1679
SN74LS192JS	1679
SN74LS192N	1679
SN74LS192ND	1679
SN74LS192NDS	1679
SN74LS192NS	1679
SN74LS193	1682
SN74LS193FN	OEM
SN74LS193J	1682
SN74LS193JD	1682
SN74LS193JDS	1682
SN74LS193JS	1682
SN74LS193N	1682
SN74LS193ND	1682
SN74LS193NDS	1682
SN74LS193NS	1682
SN74LS193W	1682
SN74LS194A	1294
SN74LS194AFN	OEM
SN74LS194AJ	1294
SN74LS194AJD	1294
SN74LS194AJDS	1294
SN74LS194AJS	1294
SN74LS194AN	1294
SN74LS194AND	1294
SN74LS194ANDS	1294
SN74LS194ANS	1294
SN74LS194FN	OEM
SN74LS195	1305
SN74LS195A	1305
SN74LS195AJ	1305
SN74LS195AJD	1305
SN74LS195AJDS	1305
SN74LS195AJS	1305
SN74LS195AN	1305
SN74LS195AND	1305
SN74LS195ANDS	1305
SN74LS195ANS	1305
SN74LS195N	1305
SN74LS196	2807
SN74LS196D	OEM
SN74LS196FK	OEM
SN74LS196FN	OEM
SN74LS196J	2807
SN74LS196JD	2807
SN74LS196JDS	2807
SN74LS196JS	2807
SN74LS196N	2807
SN74LS196ND	2807
SN74LS196NS	2807
SN74LS197	2450
SN74LS197AN	OEM
SN74LS197D	OEM
SN74LS197FK	OEM
SN74LS197FN	OEM
SN74LS197J	2450
SN74LS197JD	2450
SN74LS197JDS	2450
SN74LS197JS	2450
SN74LS197N	2450
SN74LS197ND	2450
SN74LS197NDS	2450
SN74LS197NS	2450
SN74LS202J	OEM
SN74LS202N	OEM
SN74LS210J	OEM
SN74LS210N	OEM
SN74LS219A	OEM
SN74LS219J	OEM
SN74LS219N	OEM
SN74LS221	1230
SN74LS221J	1230
SN74LS221JD	1230
SN74LS221JDS	1230
SN74LS221JS	1230
SN74LS221N	1230
SN74LS221ND	1230
SN74LS221NDS	1230
SN74LS221NS	1230
SN74LS221W	1230
SN74LS222	OEM
SN74LS224	OEM
SN74LS227	OEM
SN74LS228	OEM
SN74LS240	0447
SN74LS240J	0447
SN74LS240JD	0447
SN74LS240JDS	0447
SN74LS240JS	0447
SN74LS240N	0447
SN74LS240ND	0447
SN74LS240NDS	0447
SN74LS240NS	0447
SN74LS241	1715
SN74LS241J	1715
SN74LS241JD	1715
SN74LS241JDS	1715
SN74LS241JS	1715
SN74LS241N	1715
SN74LS241ND	1715
SN74LS241NDS	1715
SN74LS241NS	1715
SN74LS242	1717
SN74LS242J	1717
SN74LS242JD	1717
SN74LS242JDS	1717
SN74LS242JS	1717
SN74LS242N	1717
SN74LS242ND	1717
SN74LS242NDS	1717
SN74LS242NS	1717
SN74LS243	0900
SN74LS243J	0900
SN74LS243JD	0900
SN74LS243JDS	0900
SN74LS243JS	0900
SN74LS243N	0900
SN74LS243ND	0900
SN74LS243NDS	0900
SN74LS243NS	0900
SN74LS244	0453
SN74LS244J	0453
SN74LS244JD	0453
SN74LS244JDS	0453
SN74LS244JS	0453
SN74LS244N	0453
SN74LS244ND	0453
SN74LS244NDS	0453
SN74LS244NS	0453
SN74LS245	0458
SN74LS245J	0458
SN74LS245JD	0458
SN74LS245JDS	0458
SN74LS245JS	0458
SN74LS245N	0458
SN74LS245ND	0458
SN74LS245NDS	0458
SN74LS245NS	0458
SN74LS247	1721
SN74LS247J	1721
SN74LS247JD	1721
SN74LS247JDS	1721
SN74LS247JS	1721
SN74LS247N	1721
SN74LS247ND	1721
SN74LS247NDS	1721
SN74LS247NS	1721
SN74LS248	1723
SN74LS248D	OEM
SN74LS248FN	OEM
SN74LS248J	1723
SN74LS248JD	1723
SN74LS248JDS	1723
SN74LS248JS	1723
SN74LS248N	1723
SN74LS248ND	1723
SN74LS248NDS	1723
SN74LS248NS	1723
SN74LS249	1724
SN74LS249D	OEM
SN74LS249FN	OEM
SN74LS249J	1724
SN74LS249JD	1724
SN74LS249JDS	1724
SN74LS249JS	1724
SN74LS249N	1724
SN74LS249ND	1724
SN74LS249NDS	1724
SN74LS249NS	1724
SN74LS251	1726
SN74LS251D	OEM
SN74LS251FN	OEM
SN74LS251J	1726
SN74LS251JD	1726
SN74LS251JDS	1726
SN74LS251JS	1726
SN74LS251N	1726
SN74LS251ND	1726
SN74LS251NDS	1726
SN74LS251NS	1726
SN74LS251X	1726
SN74LS253	1728
SN74LS253J	1728
SN74LS253JD	1728
SN74LS253JDS	1728
SN74LS253JS	1728
SN74LS253N	1728
SN74LS253ND	1728
SN74LS253NDS	1728
SN74LS253NS	1728
SN74LS256J	OEM
SN74LS256JD	OEM
SN74LS256JDS	OEM
SN74LS256JS	OEM
SN74LS256N	OEM
SN74LS256ND	OEM
SN74LS256NDS	OEM
SN74LS256NS	OEM
SN74LS257	1733
SN74LS257AJ	1733
SN74LS257AJD	1733
SN74LS257AJDS	1733
SN74LS257AJS	1733
SN74LS257AN	1733
SN74LS257AND	1733
SN74LS257ANDS	1733
SN74LS257ANS	1733
SN74LS257BN	1733
SN74LS257J	1733
SN74LS257N	1733
SN74LS257X	1733
SN74LS258	1735
SN74LS258AJ	1735
SN74LS258AJD	1735
SN74LS258AJDS	1735
SN74LS258AJS	1735
SN74LS258AN	1735
SN74LS258AND	1735
SN74LS258ANDS	1735
SN74LS258ANS	1735
SN74LS258B	OEM
SN74LS258BN	OEM
SN74LS258J	1735
SN74LS258N	1735
SN74LS258X	1735
SN74LS259	3175
SN74LS259J	3175
SN74LS259JD	3175
SN74LS259JDS	3175
SN74LS259JS	3175
SN74LS259N	3175
SN74LS259ND	3175
SN74LS259NDS	3175

If replacement code is OEM, contact original manufacturer for replacement.

DEVICE TYPE	REPL CODE
SN74LS259NS	3175
SN74LS259W	3175
SN74LS260J	5859
SN74LS260JD	5859
SN74LS260JDS	5859
SN74LS260JS	5859
SN74LS260N	5859
SN74LS260ND	5859
SN74LS260NDS	5859
SN74LS260NS	5859
SN74LS261	OEM
SN74LS261J	OEM
SN74LS261N	OEM
SN74LS266	0587
SN74LS266J	0587
SN74LS266JD	0587
SN74LS266JDS	0587
SN74LS266JS	0587
SN74LS266N	0587
SN74LS266ND	0587
SN74LS266NDS	0587
SN74LS266NS	0587
SN74LS266W	0587
SN74LS267NDS	OEM
SN74LS273	0888
SN74LS273J	0888
SN74LS273JD	0888
SN74LS273JDS	0888
SN74LS273JS	0888
SN74LS273N	0888
SN74LS273ND	0888
SN74LS273NDS	0888
SN74LS273NS	0888
SN74LS275	OEM
SN74LS275J	OEM
SN74LS275N	OEM
SN74LS279	3259
SN74LS279J	3259
SN74LS279JD	3259
SN74LS279JDS	3259
SN74LS279JS	3259
SN74LS279N	3259
SN74LS279ND	3259
SN74LS279NDS	3259
SN74LS279NS	3259
SN74LS280	1762
SN74LS280J	1762
SN74LS280JD	1762
SN74LS280JDS	1762
SN74LS280JS	1762
SN74LS280N	1762
SN74LS280ND	1762
SN74LS280NDS	1762
SN74LS280NS	1762
SN74LS280W	1762
SN74LS283	1768
SN74LS283J	1768
SN74LS283JD	1768
SN74LS283JDS	1768
SN74LS283JS	1768
SN74LS283N	5861
SN74LS283ND	1768
SN74LS283NDS	1768
SN74LS283NS	1768
SN74LS289A	OEM
SN74LS289J	OEM
SN74LS289N	OEM
SN74LS290	4352
SN74LS290D	OEM
SN74LS290FN	OEM
SN74LS290J	4352
SN74LS290JD	4352
SN74LS290JDS	4352
SN74LS290JS	4352
SN74LS290N	4352
SN74LS290ND	4352
SN74LS290NDS	4352
SN74LS290NS	4352
SN74LS292	OEM
SN74LS292J	OEM
SN74LS292N	OEM
SN74LS293	0082
SN74LS293D	OEM
SN74LS293FN	OEM
SN74LS293J	0082
SN74LS293JD	0082
SN74LS293JDS	0082
SN74LS293JS	0082
SN74LS293N	0082
SN74LS293ND	0082
SN74LS293NDS	0082
SN74LS293NS	0082
SN74LS294	OEM
SN74LS294J	OEM
SN74LS294N	OEM
SN74LS295AJ	2212
SN74LS295AJD	2212
SN74LS295AJDS	2212
SN74LS295AJS	2212
SN74LS295AN	2212
SN74LS295AND	2212
SN74LS295ANDS	2212
SN74LS295ANS	2212
SN74LS295B	2212
SN74LS295BJ	2212
SN74LS295BN	2212
SN74LS297	OEM
SN74LS298	3337
SN74LS298J	3337
SN74LS298JD	3337
SN74LS298JDS	3337
SN74LS298JS	3337
SN74LS298N	3337
SN74LS298ND	3337
SN74LS298NDS	3337
SN74LS298NS	3337
SN74LS299	4353
SN74LS299J	4353
SN74LS299JD	4353
SN74LS299JDS	4353
SN74LS299JS	4353
SN74LS299N	4353
SN74LS299ND	4353
SN74LS299NDS	4353
SN74LS299NS	4353
SN74LS302J	OEM
SN74LS302N	OEM
SN74LS310J	OEM
SN74LS310N	OEM
SN74LS319A	OEM
SN74LS319J	OEM
SN74LS319N	OEM
SN74LS320	OEM
SN74LS320J	OEM
SN74LS320N	OEM
SN74LS321	OEM
SN74LS321J	OEM
SN74LS321N	OEM
SN74LS322A	1794
SN74LS322AJ	1794
SN74LS322AJD	1794
SN74LS322AJDS	1794
SN74LS322AJS	1794
SN74LS322AN	1794
SN74LS322AND	1794
SN74LS322ANDS	1794
SN74LS322ANS	1794
SN74LS322J	1794
SN74LS322N	1794
SN74LS322P	OEM
SN74LS323	OEM
SN74LS323J	OEM
SN74LS323JD	OEM
SN74LS323JDS	OEM
SN74LS323JS	OEM
SN74LS323N	OEM
SN74LS323ND	OEM
SN74LS323NDS	OEM
SN74LS323NS	OEM
SN74LS340J	OEM
SN74LS340N	OEM
SN74LS341J	OEM
SN74LS341N	OEM
SN74LS344J	OEM
SN74LS344N	OEM
SN74LS347	OEM
SN74LS347J	OEM
SN74LS347N	OEM
SN74LS348	0660
SN74LS348AJ	0660
SN74LS348AJD	0660
SN74LS348AJDS	0660
SN74LS348AJS	0660
SN74LS348AN	0660
SN74LS348AND	0660
SN74LS348ANDS	0660
SN74LS348ANS	0660
SN74LS348J	0660
SN74LS348JD	0660
SN74LS348JDS	0660
SN74LS348JS	0660
SN74LS348N	0660
SN74LS348ND	0660
SN74LS348NDS	0660
SN74LS348NS	0660
SN74LS352	0756
SN74LS352J	0756
SN74LS352JD	0756
SN74LS352JDS	0756
SN74LS352JS	0756
SN74LS352N	0756
SN74LS352ND	0756
SN74LS352NDS	0756
SN74LS352NS	0756
SN74LS353	0768
SN74LS353J	0768
SN74LS353JD	0768
SN74LS353JDS	0768
SN74LS353JS	0768
SN74LS353N	0768
SN74LS353ND	0768
SN74LS353NDS	0768
SN74LS353NS	0768
SN74LS354	0785
SN74LS354J	0785
SN74LS354N	0785
SN74LS355	OEM
SN74LS355J	OEM
SN74LS355N	OEM
SN74LS356	0807
SN74LS356J	0807
SN74LS356N	0807
SN74LS357	OEM
SN74LS357J	OEM
SN74LS357N	OEM
SN74LS361N	OEM
SN74LS365A	0937
SN74LS365AJ	0937
SN74LS365AJD	0937
SN74LS365AJDS	0937
SN74LS365AJS	0937
SN74LS365AN	0937
SN74LS365AND	0937
SN74LS365ANDS	0937
SN74LS365ANS	0937
SN74LS365J	0937
SN74LS365N	0937
SN74LS366A	0950
SN74LS366AJ	0950
SN74LS366AJD	0950
SN74LS366AJDS	0950
SN74LS366AJS	0950
SN74LS366AN	0950
SN74LS366AND	0950
SN74LS366ANDS	0950
SN74LS366ANS	0950
SN74LS366J	0950
SN74LS366N	0950
SN74LS367	0971
SN74LS367A	0971
SN74LS367AJ	0971
SN74LS367AJD	0971
SN74LS367AJDS	0971
SN74LS367AJS	0971
SN74LS367AN	0971
SN74LS367AND	0971
SN74LS367ANDS	0971
SN74LS367ANS	0971
SN74LS367AN-X	0971
SN74LS367J	0971
SN74LS367N	0971
SN74LS368A	0985
SN74LS368AJ	0985
SN74LS368AJD	0985
SN74LS368AJDS	0985
SN74LS368AJS	0985
SN74LS368AN	0985
SN74LS368AND	0985
SN74LS368ANDS	0985
SN74LS368ANS	0985
SN74LS368J	0985
SN74LS368N	0985
SN74LS373	0704
SN74LS373DW	OEM
SN74LS373FN	OEM
SN74LS373J	0704
SN74LS373JD	0704
SN74LS373JDS	0704
SN74LS373JS	0704
SN74LS373N	0704
SN74LS373ND	0704
SN74LS373NDS	0704
SN74LS373NS	0704
SN74LS374	0708
SN74LS374DW	OEM
SN74LS374FN	OEM
SN74LS374J	0708
SN74LS374JD	0708
SN74LS374JDS	0708
SN74LS374JS	0708
SN74LS374N	0708
SN74LS374ND	0708
SN74LS374NDS	0708
SN74LS374NS	0708
SN74LS375	OEM
SN74LS375J	OEM
SN74LS375JD	OEM
SN74LS375JDS	OEM
SN74LS375JS	OEM
SN74LS375N	OEM
SN74LS375ND	OEM
SN74LS375NDS	OEM
SN74LS375NS	OEM
SN74LS377	1112
SN74LS377J	1112
SN74LS377JD	1112
SN74LS377JDS	1112
SN74LS377JS	1112
SN74LS377N	1112
SN74LS377ND	1112
SN74LS377NDS	1112
SN74LS377NS	1112
SN74LS378	1125
SN74LS378J	1125
SN74LS378JD	1125
SN74LS378JDS	1125
SN74LS378JS	1125
SN74LS378N	1125
SN74LS378ND	1125
SN74LS378NDS	1125
SN74LS378NS	1125
SN74LS379	1143
SN74LS379J	1143
SN74LS379JD	1143
SN74LS379JDS	1143
SN74LS379JS	1143
SN74LS379N	1143
SN74LS379ND	1143
SN74LS379NDS	1143
SN74LS379NS	1143
SN74LS381A	OEM
SN74LS382	OEM
SN74LS384	OEM
SN74LS385	OEM
SN74LS385J	OEM
SN74LS385JD	OEM
SN74LS385JDS	OEM
SN74LS385JS	OEM
SN74LS385N	OEM
SN74LS385ND	OEM
SN74LS385NDS	OEM
SN74LS385NS	OEM
SN74LS386	1221
SN74LS386J	1221
SN74LS386JD	1221
SN74LS386JDS	1221
SN74LS386JS	1221
SN74LS386N	1221
SN74LS386ND	1221
SN74LS386NDS	1221
SN74LS386NS	1221
SN74LS390	1278
SN74LS390D	OEM
SN74LS390FK	OEM
SN74LS390FN	OEM
SN74LS390J	1278
SN74LS390JD	1278
SN74LS390JDS	1278
SN74LS390JS	1278
SN74LS390N	1278
SN74LS390ND	1278
SN74LS390NDS	1278
SN74LS390NS	1278
SN74LS393	0813
SN74LS393D	OEM
SN74LS393FK	OEM
SN74LS393FN	OEM
SN74LS393J	0813
SN74LS393JD	0813
SN74LS393JDS	0813
SN74LS393JS	0813
SN74LS393N	0813
SN74LS393ND	0813
SN74LS393NDS	0813
SN74LS393NS	0813
SN74LS395A	1320
SN74LS395AN	1320
SN74LS395J	1320
SN74LS395JD	1320
SN74LS395JDS	1320
SN74LS395JS	1320
SN74LS395N	1320
SN74LS395ND	1320
SN74LS395NDS	1320
SN74LS395NS	1320
SN74LS396	OEM
SN74LS398J	1373
SN74LS398JD	1373
SN74LS398JDS	1373
SN74LS398JS	1373
SN74LS398N	1373
SN74LS398ND	1373
SN74LS398NDS	1373
SN74LS398NS	1373
SN74LS399	1388
SN74LS399J	1388
SN74LS399JD	1388
SN74LS399JDS	1388
SN74LS399JS	1388
SN74LS399N	1388
SN74LS399ND	1388
SN74LS399NDS	1388
SN74LS399NS	1388
SN74LS422	1699
SN74LS423	4386
SN74LS424	4387
SN74LS424J	1699
SN74LS424N	1699
SN74LS440	OEM
SN74LS441	OEM
SN74LS442	OEM
SN74LS443	OEM
SN74LS444	OEM
SN74LS445	OEM
SN74LS446	OEM
SN74LS447	OEM
SN74LS448	OEM
SN74LS465	OEM
SN74LS466	OEM
SN74LS467	OEM
SN74LS468	OEM
SN74LS478	OEM
SN74LS479J	OEM
SN74LS481	OEM
SN74LS490	2199
SN74LS490J	2199
SN74LS490JD	2199
SN74LS490JDS	2199
SN74LS490JS	2199
SN74LS490N	2199
SN74LS490ND	2199
SN74LS490NDS	2199
SN74LS490NS	2199
SN74LS540	2519
SN74LS540J	2519
SN74LS540JD	2519
SN74LS540JDS	2519
SN74LS540JS	2519
SN74LS540N	2519
SN74LS540ND	2519
SN74LS540NDS	2519
SN74LS540NS	2519
SN74LS541	2525
SN74LS541J	2525
SN74LS541JD	2525
SN74LS541JDS	2525
SN74LS541JS	2525
SN74LS541N	2525
SN74LS541ND	2525
SN74LS541NDS	2525
SN74LS541NS	2525
SN74LS568J	OEM
SN74LS568JD	OEM
SN74LS568JDS	OEM
SN74LS568JS	OEM
SN74LS568N	OEM
SN74LS568ND	OEM
SN74LS568NDS	OEM
SN74LS568NS	OEM
SN74LS569J	OEM
SN74LS569JD	OEM
SN74LS569JDS	OEM
SN74LS569JS	OEM
SN74LS569N	OEM
SN74LS569ND	OEM
SN74LS569NDS	OEM
SN74LS569NS	OEM
SN74LS590	OEM
SN74LS590N	OEM
SN74LS591	OEM
SN74LS592	OEM
SN74LS593	OEM
SN74LS595	OEM
SN74LS596	OEM
SN74LS597	OEM
SN74LS598	OEM
SN74LS600	OEM
SN74LS601	OEM
SN74LS602	OEM
SN74LS603	OEM
SN74LS604	OEM
SN74LS604N	OEM
SN74LS604ND	OEM
SN74LS604NS	OEM
SN74LS605	OEM
SN74LS605N	OEM
SN74LS605ND	OEM
SN74LS605NDS	OEM
SN74LS605NS	OEM
SN74LS606	OEM
SN74LS606N	OEM
SN74LS606ND	OEM
SN74LS606NDS	OEM
SN74LS606NS	OEM
SN74LS607	OEM
SN74LS607N	OEM
SN74LS607ND	OEM
SN74LS607NDS	OEM
SN74LS607NS	OEM
SN74LS608	OEM
SN74LS610	OEM
SN74LS611	OEM
SN74LS612	OEM
SN74LS612N	OEM
SN74LS613	OEM
SN74LS620	OEM
SN74LS620J	OEM
SN74LS620JD	OEM
SN74LS620JDS	OEM
SN74LS620JS	OEM
SN74LS620N	OEM
SN74LS620ND	OEM
SN74LS620NDS	OEM
SN74LS620NS	OEM
SN74LS621	OEM
SN74LS621J	OEM
SN74LS621JD	OEM
SN74LS621JDS	OEM
SN74LS621JS	OEM
SN74LS621N	OEM
SN74LS621ND	OEM
SN74LS621NDS	OEM
SN74LS621NS	OEM
SN74LS622	OEM
SN74LS622N	OEM
SN74LS622ND	OEM
SN74LS622NDS	OEM
SN74LS622NS	OEM
SN74LS623	OEM
SN74LS623J	OEM
SN74LS623JD	OEM
SN74LS623JDS	OEM
SN74LS623JS	OEM
SN74LS623N	OEM
SN74LS623ND	OEM
SN74LS623NDS	OEM
SN74LS623NS	OEM
SN74LS624	3112
SN74LS624J	3112
SN74LS624N	3112
SN74LS625	3120
SN74LS625J	3120
SN74LS625N	3125
SN74LS626	3125
SN74LS626J	3125
SN74LS626N	3125
SN74LS627	3133
SN74LS627J	3133
SN74LS627N	3133
SN74LS628	OEM
SN74LS628N	OEM
SN74LS629	3146
SN74LS629J	3146
SN74LS629N	3146
SN74LS630	OEM
SN74LS631	OEM
SN74LS636	OEM
SN74LS637	OEM
SN74LS638	OEM
SN74LS639	OEM
SN74LS640	0664
SN74LS640J	0664
SN74LS640JD	0664
SN74LS640JDS	0664
SN74LS640JS	0664
SN74LS640N	0664
SN74LS640ND	0664
SN74LS640NDS	0664
SN74LS640NS	0664
SN74LS641	0685
SN74LS641J	0685
SN74LS641JD	0685
SN74LS641JDS	0685
SN74LS641JS	0685
SN74LS641N	0685
SN74LS641ND	0685
SN74LS641NDS	0685
SN74LS641NS	0685
SN74LS642	0714
SN74LS642J	0714
SN74LS642JD	0714
SN74LS642JDS	0714
SN74LS642JS	0714
SN74LS642N	0714
SN74LS642ND	0714
SN74LS642NDS	0714
SN74LS642NS	0714
SN74LS643	2045
SN74LS643J	2045
SN74LS643JD	2045
SN74LS643JDS	2045
SN74LS643JS	2045
SN74LS643N	2045
SN74LS643ND	2045
SN74LS643NDS	2045
SN74LS643NS	2045
SN74LS644	OEM
SN74LS644J	OEM
SN74LS644JD	OEM
SN74LS644JDS	OEM
SN74LS644JS	OEM
SN74LS644N	OEM
SN74LS645	0770
SN74LS645J	0770
SN74LS645JD	0770
SN74LS645JDS	0770
SN74LS645JS	0770
SN74LS645N	0770
SN74LS645ND	0770
SN74LS645NDS	0770
SN74LS645NS	0770
SN74LS646	OEM
SN74LS646NT	OEM
SN74LS647	OEM
SN74LS648	4428
SN74LS649	OEM
SN74LS651	OEM
SN74LS652	OEM
SN74LS668	OEM
SN74LS668N	OEM
SN74LS669	OEM
SN74LS669N	OEM
SN74LS670	1122
SN74LS670J	1122
SN74LS670JD	1122
SN74LS670JDS	1122
SN74LS670JS	1122
SN74LS670N	1122
SN74LS670ND	1122
SN74LS670NDS	1122
SN74LS670NS	1122
SN74LS671	OEM
SN74LS672	OEM
SN74LS673	OEM
SN74LS673N	OEM
SN74LS674	OEM
SN74LS674N	OEM
SN74LS681	OEM
SN74LS682	OEM
SN74LS682J	OEM
SN74LS682JD	OEM
SN74LS682JDS	OEM
SN74LS682JS	OEM
SN74LS682N	OEM
SN74LS682ND	OEM
SN74LS682NDS	OEM
SN74LS682NS	OEM
SN74LS683	OEM
SN74LS683J	OEM
SN74LS683JD	OEM
SN74LS683JDS	OEM
SN74LS683JS	OEM
SN74LS683N	OEM
SN74LS683ND	OEM
SN74LS683NDS	OEM
SN74LS683NS	OEM
SN74LS684	OEM
SN74LS684J	OEM
SN74LS684JD	OEM
SN74LS684JS	OEM
SN74LS684N	OEM
SN74LS684ND	OEM
SN74LS684NDS	OEM
SN74LS684NS	OEM
SN74LS685	OEM
SN74LS685J	OEM
SN74LS685JD	OEM
SN74LS685JDS	OEM
SN74LS685JS	OEM
SN74LS685N	OEM
SN74LS685ND	OEM
SN74LS685NDS	OEM
SN74LS685NS	OEM
SN74LS686	OEM
SN74LS686J	OEM
SN74LS686JD	OEM
SN74LS686JDS	OEM
SN74LS686JS	OEM
SN74LS686N	OEM
SN74LS686ND	OEM
SN74LS686NDS	OEM
SN74LS686NS	OEM
SN74LS687	OEM
SN74LS687J	OEM
SN74LS687JD	OEM
SN74LS687JDS	OEM
SN74LS687JS	OEM
SN74LS687N	OEM
SN74LS688	3378
SN74LS688J	3378
SN74LS688JD	3378
SN74LS688JDS	3378
SN74LS688JS	3378
SN74LS688N	3378
SN74LS688ND	3378
SN74LS688NDS	3378
SN74LS688NS	3378
SN74LS689	OEM
SN74LS689J	OEM
SN74LS689JD	OEM
SN74LS689JDS	OEM
SN74LS689JS	OEM
SN74LS689N	OEM
SN74LS689ND	OEM
SN74LS689NDS	OEM
SN74LS689NS	OEM
SN74LS690	OEM
SN74LS691	OEM
SN74LS692	OEM
SN74LS693	OEM
SN74LS696	OEM
SN74LS697	OEM
SN74LS698	OEM
SN74LS699	OEM
SN74LS716J	OEM
SN74LS716JD	OEM
SN74LS716JDS	OEM
SN74LS716JS	OEM
SN74LS716N	OEM
SN74LS716ND	OEM
SN74LS716NDS	OEM
SN74LS716NS	OEM
SN74LS718J	OEM
SN74LS718JD	OEM
SN74LS718JDS	OEM
SN74LS718JS	OEM
SN74LS718N	OEM
SN74LS718ND	OEM
SN74LS718NDS	OEM
SN74LS718NS	OEM
SN74LS724J	OEM
SN74LS724N	OEM
SN74LS748J	OEM
SN74LS748JD	OEM
SN74LS748JDS	OEM
SN74LS748JS	OEM
SN74LS748N	OEM
SN74LS748ND	OEM
SN74LS748NDS	OEM
SN74LS748NS	OEM
SN74LS783N	OEM
SN74LS795J	OEM
SN74LS795JD	OEM
SN74LS795JDS	OEM
SN74LS795JS	OEM
SN74LS795N	OEM
SN74LS795ND	OEM
SN74LS795NDS	OEM
SN74LS795NS	OEM
SN74LS796J	OEM
SN74LS796JD	OEM
SN74LS796JDS	OEM
SN74LS796JS	OEM
SN74LS796N	OEM
SN74LS796ND	OEM
SN74LS796NDS	OEM
SN74LS796NS	OEM
SN74LS797J	OEM
SN74LS797JD	OEM
SN74LS797JDS	OEM
SN74LS797JS	OEM
SN74LS797N	OEM
SN74LS797ND	OEM
SN74LS797NDS	OEM
SN74LS797NS	OEM
SN74LS798J	OEM
SN74LS798JD	OEM
SN74LS798JDS	OEM
SN74LS798JS	OEM
SN74LS798N	OEM
SN74LS798ND	OEM
SN74LS798NDS	OEM
SN74LS798NS	OEM

If replacement code is OEM, contact original manufacturer for replacement.

DEVICE TYPE	REPL CODE
SN74LS848J	OEM
SN74LS848JD	OEM
SN74LS848JDS	OEM
SN74LS848JS	OEM
SN74LS848N	OEM
SN74LS848ND	OEM
SN74LS848NDS	OEM
SN74LS848NS	OEM
SN74LS1245	OEM
SN74PL16L8	OEM
SN74PL16R4	OEM
SN74PL16R6	OEM
SN74PL16R8	OEM
SN74PL333	OEM
SN74PL335	OEM
SN74PL839	OEM
SN74PL840	OEM
SN74S00	0699
SN74S00J	0699
SN74S00N	0699
SN74S02	2223
SN74S02D	OEM
SN74S02FN	OEM
SN74S02J	2223
SN74S02N	2223
SN74S03	2203
SN74S03J	2203
SN74S03N	2203
SN74S04	2248
SN74S04AN	OEM
SN74S04J	2248
SN74S04N	2248
SN74S05	2305
SN74S05J	2305
SN74S05N	2305
SN74S08	2547
SN74S08J	2547
SN74S08N	2547
SN74S09	2642
SN74S09J	2642
SN74S09N	2642
SN74S10	2426
SN74S10J	2426
SN74S10N	2426
SN74S11	2428
SN74S11J	2428
SN74S11N	2428
SN74S15	2432
SN74S15J	2432
SN74S15N	2432
SN74S20	1011
SN74S20J	1011
SN74S20N	1011
SN74S22	2442
SN74S22J	2442
SN74S22N	2442
SN74S30	3681
SN74S30J	3681
SN74S30N	3681
SN74S32	3795
SN74S32J	OEM
SN74S32N	3795
SN74S37	OEM
SN74S37J	OEM
SN74S37N	OEM
SN74S38	OEM
SN74S38J	OEM
SN74S38N	OEM
SN74S40	2456
SN74S40J	2456
SN74S40N	2456
SN74S51	4241
SN74S51J	4241
SN74S51N	4241
SN74S64	2476
SN74S64J	2476
SN74S64N	2476
SN74S65	2477
SN74S65J	2477
SN74S65N	2477
SN74S74	2483
SN74S74J	2483
SN74S74N	2483
SN74S85	OEM
SN74S85J	OEM
SN74S85N	OEM
SN74S86	2489
SN74S86J	2489
SN74S86N	2489
SN74S112	1607
SN74S112AN	OEM
SN74S112J	1607
SN74S112N	1607
SN74S113	1613
SN74S113D	OEM
SN74S113FN	OEM
SN74S113J	1613
SN74S113N	1613
SN74S114	1619
SN74S114J	1619
SN74S114N	1619
SN74S124	2113
SN74S124J	2113
SN74S124N	2113
SN74S132	2121
SN74S132J	2121
SN74S132N	2121
SN74S133	1808
SN74S133J	1808

DEVICE TYPE	REPL CODE
SN74S133N	1808
SN74S134	1816
SN74S134J	1816
SN74S134N	1816
SN74S135	OEM
SN74S135J	OEM
SN74S135N	OEM
SN74S137N	OEM
SN74S138	2125
SN74S138J	2125
SN74S138N	2125
SN74S138X	2125
SN74S139	OEM
SN74S139J	OEM
SN74S139N	OEM
SN74S139X	OEM
SN74S140	1875
SN74S140J	1875
SN74S140N	1875
SN74S151	1944
SN74S151J	1944
SN74S151N	1944
SN74S151X	1944
SN74S153	2138
SN74S153D	OEM
SN74S153FN	OEM
SN74S153J	2138
SN74S153N	2138
SN74S153X	2138
SN74S157	1685
SN74S157D	OEM
SN74S157FN	OEM
SN74S157J	1685
SN74S157N	1685
SN74S158	2141
SN74S158D	OEM
SN74S158FN	OEM
SN74S158J	2141
SN74S158N	2141
SN74S160J	OEM
SN74S160N	OEM
SN74S161J	OEM
SN74S161N	OEM
SN74S162	OEM
SN74S162J	OEM
SN74S162N	OEM
SN74S163	0887
SN74S163J	0887
SN74S163N	OEM
SN74S168	OEM
SN74S168J	OEM
SN74S168N	OEM
SN74S169	OEM
SN74S169J	OEM
SN74S169N	OEM
SN74S174	2119
SN74S174J	2119
SN74S174N	2119
SN74S175	2128
SN74S175J	2128
SN74S175N	2128
SN74S181	2151
SN74S181J	2151
SN74S181N	2151
SN74S182	2152
SN74S182D	OEM
SN74S182FN	OEM
SN74S182J	2152
SN74S182J16	2152
SN74S182N	OEM
SN74S188	3139
SN74S189AJ	OEM
SN74S189AW	OEM
SN74S189B	OEM
SN74S189J	OEM
SN74S189N	OEM
SN74S194	1920
SN74S194FN	OEM
SN74S194J	1920
SN74S194N	1920
SN74S195	OEM
SN74S195J	OEM
SN74S195N	OEM
SN74S196	OEM
SN74S196D	OEM
SN74S196FK	OEM
SN74S196FN	OEM
SN74S196J	OEM
SN74S196N	OEM
SN74S197	OEM
SN74S197D	OEM
SN74S197FK	OEM
SN74S197FN	OEM
SN74S197J	OEM
SN74S197N	OEM
SN74S201	OEM
SN74S201J	OEM
SN74S201N	OEM
SN74S209J	OEM
SN74S209N	OEM
SN74S210J	OEM
SN74S210N	OEM
SN74S225	OEM
SN74S226	OEM
SN74S226J	OEM
SN74S226N	OEM
SN74S240	OEM
SN74S240J	OEM
SN74S240N	OEM

DEVICE TYPE	REPL CODE
SN74S241	OEM
SN74S241J	OEM
SN74S241N	OEM
SN74S244	OEM
SN74S244J	OEM
SN74S244N	OEM
SN74S251	2184
SN74S251D	OEM
SN74S251FN	OEM
SN74S251J	2184
SN74S251N	2184
SN74S251X	OEM
SN74S253J	OEM
SN74S253N	OEM
SN74S253X	OEM
SN74S257	OEM
SN74S257J	OEM
SN74S257N	2190
SN74S257X	OEM
SN74S258J	2191
SN74S258N	2191
SN74S260	OEM
SN74S270B	OEM
SN74S274	OEM
SN74S275	OEM
SN74S280	2205
SN74S280N	2205
SN74S281	OEM
SN74S283	OEM
SN74S287	2209
SN74S288	2161
SN74S289B	OEM
SN74S299	OEM
SN74S299N	OEM
SN74S301	OEM
SN74S340	OEM
SN74S341	OEM
SN74S344	OEM
SN74S373	2249
SN74S373DW	OEM
SN74S373FN	OEM
SN74S373J	OEM
SN74S373N	OEM
SN74S374	2251
SN74S374DW	OEM
SN74S374FN	OEM
SN74S374J	OEM
SN74S374N	OEM
SN74S381	OEM
SN74S387	1907
SN74S412	4260
SN74S412J	1849
SN74S412N	1849
SN74S428	4263
SN74S428N	1858
SN74S436	OEM
SN74S437	OEM
SN74S438	OEM
SN74S452	OEM
SN74S453	OEM
SN74S454	3137
SN74S455	OEM
SN74S470	OEM
SN74S472	2304
SN74S473	3257
SN74S474	2306
SN74S475	2308
SN74S476	4275
SN74S477	2374
SN74S478	2881
SN74S479	2835
SN74S481	OEM
SN74S482	OEM
SN74S484	OEM
SN74S485	OEM
SN74SLA11ND	OEM
SN80	0595
SN101	OEM
SN102	OEM
SN109	OEM
SN110	OEM
SN118	OEM
SN166	0086
SN167	0086
SN171	OEM
SN172	OEM
SN173	OEM
SN200	OEM
SN201	OEM
SN202	OEM
SN204	OEM
SN230	OEM
SN231	OEM
SN232	OEM
SN234	OEM
SN270	OEM
SN271	OEM
SN272	OEM
SN274	OEM
SN423	OEM
SN500	OEM
SN545LS481	OEM
SN674LS604NDS	OEM
SN746AN	OEM
SN784LS367AN-X	OEM
SN962-2M	0557
SN2222	OEM
SN2222A	OEM
SN2222AP	0079

DEVICE TYPE	REPL CODE
SN2243	OEM
SN2243A	OEM
SN2270	OEM
SN2432	OEM
SN2432A	OEM
SN2484	OEM
SN4311N	OEM
SN4448	0124
SN5211P	2093
SN5400	OEM
SN5401	OEM
SN5402	OEM
SN5402J	OEM
SN5402W	OEM
SN5403	OEM
SN5404	OEM
SN5405	OEM
SN5406	OEM
SN5407	OEM
SN5408	OEM
SN5409	OEM
SN5410	OEM
SN5412	OEM
SN5413	OEM
SN5414	OEM
SN5416	OEM
SN5417	OEM
SN5420	OEM
SN5422	OEM
SN5425	OEM
SN5426	OEM
SN5427	OEM
SN5428	OEM
SN5430	OEM
SN5432	OEM
SN5433	OEM
SN5437	OEM
SN5438	OEM
SN5440	OEM
SN5442A	OEM
SN5443A	OEM
SN5444A	OEM
SN5445	OEM
SN5446A	OEM
SN5447A	OEM
SN5448	OEM
SN5449	OEM
SN5450	OEM
SN5451	OEM
SN5453	OEM
SN5454	OEM
SN5460	OEM
SN5470	OEM
SN5472	OEM
SN5473	OEM
SN5474	OEM
SN5475	OEM
SN5476	OEM
SN5477	OEM
SN5480	OEM
SN5482	OEM
SN5483A	OEM
SN5485	OEM
SN5486	OEM
SN5490A	OEM
SN5491A	OEM
SN5492A	OEM
SN5493A	OEM
SN5493N	OEM
SN5494	OEM
SN5496	OEM
SN5497	OEM
SN6285	3483
SN7248L	2435
SN7400	0232
SN7400A	0232
SN7400J	0232
SN7400N	0232
SN7400N-10	0232
SN7401	0268
SN7401J	0268
SN7401N	0268
SN7402	0310
SN7402J	0310
SN7402N	0310
SN7402N-10	0310
SN7403	0331
SN7403J	0331
SN7403N	0331
SN7404	0357
SN7404J	0357
SN7404N	0357
SN7404N-10	0357
SN7405	0381
SN7405A	0381
SN7405J	0381
SN7405N	0381
SN7406	1197
SN7406J	1197
SN7406N	1197
SN7406N-10	1197
SN7407	1329
SN7407J	1329
SN7407N	1329
SN7408	0462
SN7408J	0462
SN7408N	0462
SN7408N-10	0462
SN7409	0487

DEVICE TYPE	REPL CODE
SN7409J	0487
SN7409N	0487
SN7410	0507
SN7410J	0507
SN7410N	0507
SN7410N-10	0507
SN7412	2227
SN7412J	2227
SN7412N	2227
SN7412W	2227
SN7413	1432
SN7413J	1432
SN7413N	1432
SN7413N-10	1432
SN7414	2228
SN7414J	2228
SN7414N	2228
SN7415AN	OEM
SN7415N	OEM
SN7416	1339
SN7416J	1339
SN7416N	1339
SN7417	1342
SN7417(SM)	OEM
SN7417J	1342
SN7417N	1342
SN7417NS(SM)	OEM
SN7420	0692
SN7420J	0692
SN7420N	0692
SN7420N-10	0692
SN7422	4523
SN7422J	4523
SN7422N	4523
SN7423	3429
SN7423J	3429
SN7423N	3429
SN7425	3438
SN7425J	3438
SN7425N	3438
SN-7426	0798
SN7426	0798
SN7426J	0798
SN7426N	0798
SN7427	0812
SN7427J	0812
SN7427N	0812
SN7427N-10	0812
SN7428	4117
SN7428J	4117
SN7428N	4117
SN7430	0867
SN7430J	0867
SN7430N	0867
SN7432	0893
SN7432J	0893
SN7432N	0893
SN7432N-10	0893
SN7433	4130
SN7433J	4130
SN7433N	4130
SN7437	3478
SN7437J	3478
SN7437N	3478
SN7438	0990
SN7438J	0990
SN7438N	0990
SN7439N	5722
SN7440	1018
SN7440J	1018
SN7440N	1018
SN7441N-10	1032
SN7442A	1046
SN7442AJ	1046
SN7442AN	1046
SN7442N	1046
SN7443A	1054
SN7443AJ	1054
SN7443AN	1054
SN7443N	1054
SN7444A	1066
SN7444AJ	1066
SN7444AN	1066
SN7444N	1066
SN7445	1074
SN7445J	1074
SN7445N	1074
SN7446A	1090
SN7446AJ	1090
SN7446AN	1090
SN7447A	1100
SN7447AJ	1100
SN7447AM	OEM
SN7447AN	1100
SN7447J	1100
SN7447N	1100
SN7447N-10	1100
SN7448	1117
SN7448J	1117
SN7448N	1117
SN7448N-10	1117
SN7449	OEM
SN7450	0738
SN7450J	0738
SN7450N	0738
SN7451	1160
SN7451J	1160
SN7451N	1160
SN7451N-10	1160

DEVICE TYPE	REPL CODE
SN7453	1177
SN7453J	1177
SN7453N	1177
SN7454	1193
SN7454J	1193
SN7454N	1193
SN7460	1265
SN7460J	1265
SN7460N	1265
SN7470	1394
SN7470J	1394
SN7470N	1394
SN7472	1417
SN7472J	1417
SN7472N	1417
SN7473	1164
SN7473J	1164
SN7473N	1164
SN7473N-10	1164
SN-7474	1303
SN7474	1303
SN7474J	1303
SN7474M	1303
SN7474N	1303
SN7474N-10	1303
SN7475	1423
SN7475J	1423
SN7475N	1423
SN7475N-10	1423
SN7476	1150
SN7476B	1150
SN7476J	1150
SN7476N	1150
SN7476N-10	1150
SN7477	OEM
SN7480	1527
SN7480J	1527
SN7480N	1527
SN7481A	3092
SN7481AJ	OEM
SN7481AN	3092
SN7482	1564
SN7482J	1564
SN7482N	1564
SN7483A	0117
SN7483AJ	3092
SN7483AN	0117
SN7484A	OEM
SN7484AJ	OEM
SN7484AN	OEM
SN7485	0370
SN7485J	0370
SN7485N	0370
SN7485N-10	0370
SN7486	1358
SN7486J	1358
SN7486N	1358
SN7486N-10	1358
SN7488AN	4817
SN7489	5358
SN7489N	5358
SN7490A	1199
SN7490AJ	1199
SN7490AN	1199
SN7490N	1199
SN7490N-10	1199
SN7491A	0974
SN7491AJ	0974
SN7491AN	0974
SN7492A	0828
SN7492AJ	0828
SN7492AN	0828
SN7492N	0828
SN7492N-10	0828
SN7493	0564
SN7493A	0564
SN7493AJ	0564
SN7493AN	0564
SN7493N	0564
SN7494	1692
SN7494J	1692
SN7494N	1692
SN7495AJ	1477
SN7495AN	1477
SN7496J	1705
SN7496N	1705
SN7497	2912
SN7497J	2912
SN7497N	2912
SN7506NE	4781
SN7604	OEM
SN7630N	OEM
SN7666	0167
SN7666N	0167
SN7668IN	OEM
SN15830J	1812
SN15830N	1812
SN15831J	3032
SN15831N	3032
SN15832J	1035
SN15832N	1035
SN15833J	2086
SN15833N	2086
SN15835J	1168
SN15835N	1168
SN15836J	1820
SN15836N	1820
SN15837J	1824
SN15837N	1824

DEVICE TYPE	REPL CODE
SN15838J	1609
SN15838N	1609
SN15844J	0033
SN15844N	0033
SN15845J	0081
SN15845N	0081
SN15846J	0141
SN15846N	0141
SN15848J	3365
SN15848N	3365
SN15849J	1833
SN15849N	1833
SN15850J	2595
SN15850N	2595
SN15851J	2067
SN15851N	2067
SN15857J	1424
SN15857N	1424
SN15858J	0461
SN15858N	0461
SN15861F	OEM
SN15861J	1848
SN15861N	1848
SN15861R	OEM
SN15862J	0557
SN15862N	0557
SN15863F	OEM
SN15863J	0337
SN15863N	0337
SN15863R	OEM
SN16704C	1319
SN16706N	0167
SN16726N	0350
SN16727N	0345
SN16827	OEM
SN16840C	1327
SN16859	1327
SN16869A	1327
SN16869A#	2460
SN16887A	OEM
SN16889	OEM
SN16889P	OEM
SN16890	0618
SN16901	OEM
SN29764N	OEM
SN47191	OEM
SN47248	OEM
SN52101AL	0093
SN52101L	0093
SN52301	1290
SN52723L	1183
SN52723N	0026
SN52741	0406
SN52741L	0406
SN52741P	0406
SN52747L	2352
SN52748J	2433
SN52748L	2435
SN52748N	2433
SN52748P	2433
SN54100	OEM
SN54107	OEM
SN54109	OEM
SN54110	OEM
SN54111	OEM
SN54116	OEM
SN54116J	OEM
SN54116W	OEM
SN54120	OEM
SN54120J	OEM
SN54120W	OEM
SN54121	OEM
SN54121J	OEM
SN54121W	OEM
SN54122	OEM
SN54122J	OEM
SN54122W	OEM
SN54123	OEM
SN54123J	OEM
SN54123W	OEM
SN54125	OEM
SN54125J	OEM
SN54125W	OEM
SN54126	OEM
SN54126J	OEM
SN54126W	OEM
SN54128	OEM
SN54128J	OEM
SN54128W	OEM
SN54132	OEM
SN54132J	OEM
SN54132W	OEM
SN54136	OEM
SN54136J	OEM
SN54136W	OEM
SN54141	OEM
SN54143	OEM
SN54143J	OEM
SN54143W	OEM
SN54144	OEM
SN54144J	OEM
SN54144W	OEM
SN54145	OEM
SN54145J	OEM
SN54145W	OEM
SN54147	OEM
SN54147J	OEM
SN54147W	OEM
SN54148	OEM

If replacement code is OEM, contact original manufacturer for replacement.

DEVICE TYPE	REPL CODE
SN54148J	OEM
SN54148W	OEM
SN54150	OEM
SN54150J	OEM
SN54150W	OEM
SN54151A	OEM
SN54151AJ	OEM
SN54151AW	OEM
SN54152A	OEM
SN54152AW	OEM
SN54153	OEM
SN54153J	OEM
SN54153W	OEM
SN54154	OEM
SN54154J	OEM
SN54154W	OEM
SN54155	OEM
SN54155J	OEM
SN54155W	OEM
SN54156	OEM
SN54156J	OEM
SN54156W	OEM
SN54157	OEM
SN54157J	OEM
SN54157W	OEM
SN54159	OEM
SN54159J	OEM
SN54159W	OEM
SN54160	OEM
SN54160J	OEM
SN54160W	OEM
SN54161	OEM
SN54161J	OEM
SN54161W	OEM
SN54162	OEM
SN54162J	OEM
SN54162W	OEM
SN54163	OEM
SN54163J	OEM
SN54163W	OEM
SN54164	OEM
SN54164J	OEM
SN54164W	OEM
SN54165	OEM
SN54165J	OEM
SN54165W	OEM
SN54166	OEM
SN54166J	OEM
SN54166W	OEM
SN54167	OEM
SN54167J	OEM
SN54167W	OEM
SN54170	OEM
SN54170J	OEM
SN54170W	OEM
SN54173	OEM
SN54173J	OEM
SN54173W	OEM
SN54174	OEM
SN54174J	OEM
SN54174W	OEM
SN54175	OEM
SN54175J	OEM
SN54175W	OEM
SN54176	OEM
SN54176J	OEM
SN54176W	OEM
SN54177	OEM
SN54177J	OEM
SN54177W	OEM
SN54178	OEM
SN54178J	OEM
SN54179	OEM
SN54179J	OEM
SN54179W	OEM
SN54180	OEM
SN54180J	OEM
SN54180W	OEM
SN54181	OEM
SN54181J	OEM
SN54181W	OEM
SN54182	OEM
SN54182J	OEM
SN54182W	OEM
SN54184	OEM
SN54184J	OEM
SN54184W	OEM
SN54185A	OEM
SN54185AJ	OEM
SN54190	OEM
SN54191	OEM
SN54192	OEM
SN54192FH	OEM
SN54192J	OEM
SN54193	OEM
SN54193FH	OEM
SN54193J	OEM
SN54194	OEM
SN54194FH	OEM
SN54194J	OEM
SN54195	OEM
SN54196	OEM
SN54196J	OEM
SN54196W	OEM
SN54197	OEM
SN54197J	OEM
SN54197W	OEM
SN54198	OEM
SN54199	OEM
SN54221	OEM
SN54246	OEM
SN54247	OEM
SN54248	OEM
SN54249	OEM
SN54251	OEM
SN54259	OEM
SN54265	OEM
SN54273	OEM
SN54276	OEM
SN54278	OEM
SN54279	OEM
SN54283	OEM
SN54284	OEM
SN54285	OEM
SN54290	OEM
SN54293	OEM
SN54298	OEM
SN54365A	OEM
SN54366A	OEM
SN54367A	OEM
SN54376	OEM
SN54390	OEM
SN54390J	OEM
SN54390W	OEM
SN54393	OEM
SN54393J	OEM
SN54393W	OEM
SN54425	OEM
SN54490	OEM
SN55107A	OEM
SN55107B	OEM
SN55108A	OEM
SN55108B	OEM
SN55109A	OEM
SN55110A	OEM
SN55113	OEM
SN55114	OEM
SN55115	OEM
SN55116	OEM
SN55117	OEM
SN55118	OEM
SN55119	OEM
SN55121	OEM
SN55122	OEM
SN55138	OEM
SN55140	OEM
SN55141	OEM
SN55142A	OEM
SN55143A	OEM
SN55152	OEM
SN55154	OEM
SN55158	OEM
SN55160A	OEM
SN55161A	OEM
SN55182	OEM
SN55183	OEM
SN55189	OEM
SN55189A	OEM
SN55325	OEM
SN55326	OEM
SN55327	OEM
SN55426B	OEM
SN55427B	OEM
SN55446	OEM
SN55450B	OEM
SN55450BFK	OEM
SN55450J	OEM
SN55451B	OEM
SN55451BFK	OEM
SN55451BJG	OEM
SN55452B	OEM
SN55452BFK	OEM
SN55452BJG	OEM
SN55453B	OEM
SN55453BFK	OEM
SN55453BJG	OEM
SN55454B	OEM
SN55454BFK	OEM
SN55454BJG	OEM
SN55461	OEM
SN55462	OEM
SN55463	OEM
SN55464	OEM
SN55471	OEM
SN55472	OEM
SN55473	OEM
SN55474	OEM
SN57207B	OEM
SN72301	1290
SN72301AL	0093
SN72301AN	0093
SN72301AP	1290
SN72307	2267
SN72307JA	2267
SN72307JP	2267
SN72307N	2267
SN72307P	2267
SN72311P	2093
SN72555JP	0967
SN72555P	0967
SN72558L	1879
SN72709	1695
SN72709J	1695
SN72709T	1291
SN72723J	0026
SN72723L	1183
SN72723N	0026
SN72741J	1964
SN72741P	0308
SN72747	2352
SN72747J	2342
SN72747JA	2342
SN72747L	2352
SN72747N	2342
SN72748J	2433
SN72748JG	1290
SN72748L	2435
SN72748N	2433
SN72748P	2433
SN72905	1275
SN72906	2624
SN72912	1827
SN72915	3777
SN72924	2224
SN74100	OEM
SN74107	0936
SN74107N	0936
SN74109	0962
SN74109J	0962
SN74109N	0962
SN74110J	0981
SN74110N	0981
SN74111	0996
SN74111J	0996
SN74111N	0996
SN74116	1064
SN74116J	OEM
SN74116N	1064
SN74120	1108
SN74120J	1108
SN74120N	1108
SN74121	0175
SN74121J	0175
SN74121N	0175
SN74122	1131
SN74122J	1131
SN74122N	1131
SN74123	1149
SN74123J	1149
SN74123N	1149
SN74123N-10	1149
SN74125	1174
SN74125J	1174
SN74125N	1174
SN74126	1184
SN74126J	1184
SN74126N	1184
SN74128	1210
SN74128J	1210
SN74128N	1210
SN74132	1261
SN74132J	1261
SN74132N	1261
SN74136	1306
SN74136J	1306
SN74136N	1306
SN74141	1367
SN74141J	1367
SN74141N	1367
SN74142	1380
SN74142J	1380
SN74142N	1380
SN74143	1399
SN74143J	1399
SN74143N	1399
SN74144	1408
SN74144J	1408
SN74144N	1408
SN74145	0614
SN74145J	0614
SN74145N	0614
SN74145N-10	0614
SN74147	1442
SN74147J	1442
SN74147N	1442
SN74148	1455
SN74148J	1455
SN74148N	1455
SN74150	1484
SN74150J	1484
SN74150N	1484
SN74150N-10	1484
SN74151A	1487
SN74151AJ	1487
SN74151AN	1487
SN74151N	1487
SN74152A	1509
SN74152N	1509
SN74152S	1509
SN74153	1531
SN74153J	1531
SN74153N	1531
SN74154	1546
SN74154J	1546
SN74154N	1546
SN74154N-10	1546
SN74155	1566
SN74155J	1566
SN74155N	1566
SN74156	1582
SN74156J	1582
SN74156N	1582
SN74157	1595
SN74157J	1595
SN74157N	1595
SN74159	OEM
SN74159J	OEM
SN74159N	OEM
SN74160	1621
SN74160J	1621
SN74160N	1621
SN74161	1635
SN74161AN	OEM
SN74161J	1635
SN74161N	1635
SN74162	1007
SN74162J	1007
SN74162N	1007
SN74163	1656
SN74163J	1656
SN74163N	1656
SN74164	0729
SN74164J	0729
SN74164N	0729
SN74165	1675
SN74165J	1675
SN74165N	1675
SN74166	0231
SN74166J	0231
SN74166N	0231
SN74167	OEM
SN74167J	OEM
SN74167N	OEM
SN74170	1711
SN74170J	1711
SN74170N	1711
SN74172	OEM
SN74172J	OEM
SN74172N	OEM
SN74173	1755
SN74173J	1751
SN74173N	1755
SN74174	1759
SN74174J	1759
SN74174N	1759
SN74175	1776
SN74175AN	OEM
SN74175J	1776
SN74175N	1776
SN74176	1784
SN74176J	1784
SN74176N	1784
SN74177J	1792
SN74177N	1792
SN74178	1802
SN74178J	1802
SN74178N	1802
SN74179	1809
SN74179J	1809
SN74179N	1809
SN74180	1818
SN74180J	1818
SN74180N	1818
SN74181	1831
SN74181J	1831
SN74181N	1831
SN74182	1845
SN74182J	1845
SN74182N	1845
SN74184	OEM
SN74184J	OEM
SN74184N	OEM
SN74185A	1857
SN74185AJ	1857
SN74185AN	1857
SN74190	1901
SN74190J	1901
SN74190N	1901
SN74191J	1906
SN74191N	1906
SN74192	1910
SN74192J	1910
SN74192N	1910
SN74192N-10	1910
SN74193	1915
SN74193J	1915
SN74193N	1915
SN74193N-10	1915
SN74194	OEM
SN74194FN	OEM
SN74194J	OEM
SN74194N	OEM
SN74195	1932
SN74195J	1932
SN74195N	1932
SN74195W	OEM
SN74196	1939
SN74196J	1939
SN74196N	1939
SN74196N-10	1939
SN74197	1945
SN74197J	1945
SN74197N	1945
SN74198	1953
SN74198J	1953
SN74198N	1953
SN74199	1960
SN74199J	1960
SN74199N	1960
SN74221	2129
SN74221J	2129
SN74221N	2129
SN74246	OEM
SN74246J	OEM
SN74246N	OEM
SN74247	OEM
SN74247J	OEM
SN74247N	OEM
SN74248J	OEM
SN74248N	OEM
SN74249	2274
SN74249J	2274
SN74249N	2277
SN74251	2283
SN74251J	2283
SN74251N	2283
SN74259	OEM
SN74265	4531
SN74273	OEM
SN74276	OEM
SN74278	4536
SN74279	4538
SN74279N	OEM
SN74283	OEM
SN74283N	OEM
SN74284	OEM
SN74285	OEM
SN74290	2588
SN74290J	2588
SN74290N	2588
SN74293	2620
SN74293J	2620
SN74293N	2620
SN74298	4547
SN74351	OEM
SN74365A	1450
SN74365AJ	1450
SN74365AN	1450
SN74365J	1450
SN74365N	1450
SN74366A	1462
SN74366AJ	1462
SN74366AN	1462
SN74366J	1462
SN74366N	1462
SN74367A	1479
SN74367AJ	1479
SN74367AN	1479
SN74367J	1479
SN74367N	1479
SN74368A	1500
SN74368AJ	1500
SN74368AN	1500
SN74368J	1500
SN74368N	1500
SN74376	OEM
SN74390	3210
SN74390J	3210
SN74390N	3210
SN74393	3225
SN74393J	3225
SN74393N	3225
SN74425	OEM
SN74426	4616
SN74490	3619
SN74490J	3619
SN74490N	3619
SN74500N	0699
SN74741L	0406
SN74915N	OEM
SN74921-10	0828
SN75064	OEM
SN75065	OEM
SN75066	OEM
SN75067	OEM
SN75067NE	5218
SN75068	OEM
SN75068NE	4883
SN75069	OEM
SN75069NE	4883
SN75074	OEM
SN75075	OEM
SN75107A	OEM
SN75107B	OEM
SN75108A	OEM
SN75108B	OEM
SN75109A	OEM
SN75110A	OEM
SN75112	OEM
SN75113	OEM
SN75114	OEM
SN75115	OEM
SN75115J	5220
SN75115N	5220
SN75116	OEM
SN75117	OEM
SN75118	OEM
SN75119	OEM
SN75121	OEM
SN75122	OEM
SN75123	OEM
SN75124	OEM
SN75125	OEM
SN75126	OEM
SN75127	OEM
SN75128	OEM
SN75129	OEM
SN75130	OEM
SN75136	OEM
SN75138	OEM
SN75140	OEM
SN75141	OEM
SN75142A	OEM
SN75143A	OEM
SN75150	OEM
SN75150P	OEM
SN75151	OEM
SN75152	OEM
SN75153	OEM
SN75154	OEM
SN75154D(SM)	OEM
SN75154N	OEM
SN75157	OEM
SN75158	OEM
SN75159	OEM
SN75160A	OEM
SN75161A	OEM
SN75162A	OEM
SN75163A	OEM
SN75172	OEM
SN75173	OEM
SN75173J	OEM
SN75173N	OEM
SN75174	OEM
SN75175	OEM
SN75175J	OEM
SN75175N	OEM
SN75176	OEM
SN75177	OEM
SN75178	OEM
SN75182	OEM
SN75183	OEM
SN75188	0503
SN75188J	0503
SN75188N	0503
SN75189	0506
SN75189A	0506
SN75189AN	0506
SN75189N	0506
SN75207	OEM
SN75208	OEM
SN75208B	OEM
SN75322	OEM
SN75325	OEM
SN75326	OEM
SN75327	OEM
SN75328	OEM
SN75330	OEM
SN75350	OEM
SN75357	OEM
SN75361A	OEM
SN75363	OEM
SN75365	OEM
SN75366	OEM
SN75367	OEM
SN75368	OEM
SN75369	OEM
SN75370	OEM
SN75375	OEM
SN75401	OEM
SN75402	OEM
SN75403	OEM
SN75404	OEM
SN75411	OEM
SN75412	OEM
SN75413	OEM
SN75414	OEM
SN75416	OEM
SN75417	OEM
SN75417B	OEM
SN75418	OEM
SN75419	OEM
SN75426B	OEM
SN75430	OEM
SN75431	OEM
SN75432	OEM
SN75433	OEM
SN75434	OEM
SN75436	OEM
SN75437A	OEM
SN75438	OEM
SN75441	OEM
SN75446	OEM
SN75447	OEM
SN75448	OEM
SN75449	OEM
SN75450B	1222
SN75450BN	1222
SN75451B	1235
SN75451BD	OEM
SN75451BP	1235
SN75452B	1253
SN75452BD	OEM
SN75452BP	1253
SN75452P	1253
SN75453B	1262
SN75453BD	OEM
SN75453BP	1262
SN75454BD	OEM
SN75454BN	1279
SN75454BP	OEM
SN75460	OEM
SN75461	OEM
SN75462	OEM
SN75463	OEM
SN75463P	OEM
SN75464	OEM
SN75466	OEM
SN75467	OEM
SN75468	OEM
SN75469	OEM
SN75470	OEM
SN75471	OEM
SN75472	OEM
SN75473	OEM
SN75474	OEM
SN75476	OEM
SN75477	OEM
SN75477P	OEM
SN75478	OEM
SN75479	OEM
SN75480N	1782
SN75491AN	1718
SN75491N	1718
SN75492N	1729
SN75493N	4933
SN75494N	4934
SN75497N	5726
SN75498N	4936
SN75500A	OEM
SN75501A	OEM
SN75502A	OEM
SN75503A	OEM
SN76001	2145
SN76001A	2145
SN76001AN	2145
SN-76001N	2145
SN76001N	2145
SN76007	3724
SN76007N	3724
SN76008	0780
SN76104N	0649
SN76105N	0438
SN76107	0696
SN76110	0696
SN76110N	0696
SN76110N-07	0696
SN76111	1929
SN76111N	1929
SN76113N	0696
SN76115	0514
SN76115N	0514
SN76116N	1385
SN76130	2264
SN76130N	2264
SN76131M	0687
SN76131N	0687
SN76177ND	2535
SN76242N	0348
SN76243AN	0350
SN76243N	0350
SN76246A	6366
SN76246N	0661
SN76298	0850
SN76298N	0850
SN76333	OEM
SN76334	OEM
SN76477	OEM
SN76487	OEM
SN76488	OEM
SN76489	OEM
SN76489A	OEM
SN76493	OEM
SN76494	OEM
SN76495	OEM
SN76496	OEM
SN76496N	OEM
SN76514	3942
SN76514N	OEM
SN76524N	OEM
SN76550	OEM
SN76564	0797
SN76565N	0797
SN76566	OEM
SN76591P	0842
SN76594	2473
SN76600	0780
SN76600P	0780
SN76602	OEM
SN76604	OEM
SN76635N	1411
SN76642	0673
SN76642N	0673
SN76642P	0673
SN76643	0659
SN76643A	0659
SN76643N	0659
SN76645	OEM
SN76650	0391
SN76650N	0391
SN76651N	0784
SN76653N	0659
SN76664N	0167
SN76665	0167
SN76665N	0167
SN76666	0167
SN76666N	0167
SN76666N-S	0167
SN76666NS	0167
SN76669N	1434
SN76670N	6011
SN76675	0391
SN76676HC	2720
SN76678	1748
SN76678P	1748
SN76681N	OEM
SN76689	2728
SN76689N	2728
SN76730	OEM
SN76730N	OEM
SN76760N	OEM
SN76832A	OEM
SN76873N	5647

If replacement code is OEM, contact original manufacturer for replacement.

DEVICE TYPE	REPL CODE
SN76873NT	OEM
SN76881	OEM
SN76882	OEM
SN76889	OEM
SN76891	OEM
SN76940	OEM
SN94017P	1748
SN94018N	1335
SN94041N	OEM
SN94041NL	OEM
SN94042N	OEM
SN94042NL	OEM
SN94043N	OEM
SN94066	OEM
SN94105AN	OEM
SN94174	1327
SN94281	OEM
SN94302N	OEM
SN94310N	OEM
SN94311N	OEM
SN94312N	OEM
SN94313N	OEM
SN94314N	OEM
SN94315N	OEM
SN94316N	OEM
SN94510CN	OEM
SN94624N	OEM
SN102977AN	OEM
SN151800J	0844
SN151800N	0844
SN151801J	0868
SN151801N	0868
SN151802J	0882
SN151802N	0882
SN151803J	0894
SN151803N	0894
SN151804J	0913
SN151804N	0913
SN151805J	0923
SN151805N	0923
SN151806J	0939
SN151806N	0939
SN151807J	0956
SN151807N	0956
SN151808J	0976
SN151808N	0976
SN151809J	0992
SN151809N	0992
SN151810J	1005
SN151810N	1005
SN151811J	1019
SN151811N	1019
SN151812J	1033
SN151812N	1033
SN151910N	OEM
SN151911N	OEM
SN158093J	0354
SN158093N	0354
SN158093R	OEM
SN158094F	OEM
SN158094J	1622
SN158094N	1622
SN158094R	OEM
SN158097F	OEM
SN158097J	1472
SN158097N	1472
SN158097R	OEM
SN158099F	OEM
SN158099J	0329
SN158099N	0329
SN297654N	OEM
SN400091N	OEM
SN490300N	OEM
SN742471	OEM
SN745064NE	4781
SN745065NE	4781
SN745066NE	5218
SN745067NE	5218
SN745068NE	4883
SN745069NE	4883
SN764246N	0345
SN765241N	OEM
SN766008	0780
SNC5476J	OEM
SNJ54LS125AJ	OEM
SNM74S251J	2184
SNN74LS189J	OEM
SNR-7A130K	1364
SNR-7A150K	0246
SNR-7A250K	1322
SNR-7D18L	1681
SNR-7D22L	1997
SNR-7D24L	1304
SNR-7D27L	2309
SNR-7D33K	2763
SNR-7D56K	2907
SNR-7D82K	4395
SNR-14A115K	4072
SNR-14A130K	0832
SNR14A130K	0832
SNR-14A150K	1982
SNR-14A480K	1093
SNR-14D18L	1684
SNR-14D22L	1998
SNR-14D24L	1309
SNR-14D33K	2769
SNR-14D56K	2913
SNR-14D82K	3056
SNR20A130K	0824
SNR-20A150K	0824
SNR-20A250K	1326
SNR-20A480K	0776
SNR-A130L2	1364
SNR-A130L10	0832
SNR-A130L20	1364
SNR-A150L2	0246
SNR-A150L10	1982
SNR-A150L20	3381
SNR-A250L4	1322
SNR-A250L20	1324
SNR-A250L40	1326
SNR-A480L40	1093
SNR-A480L80	0776
SNR-D18M1	1681
SNR-D18M3	1684
SNR-D22L1	1997
SNR-D22L3	1998
SNR-D24K1	1304
SNR-D24K4	1309
SNR-D27L1	2309
SNR-D27L4	2310
SNR-D33K1	2763
SNR-D33K5	2769
SNR-D56K2	2907
SNR-D56K8	2913
SNR-D82K2	4395
SNR-D82K12	3056
SNR-D180K1	4072
SNR-D180K10	3094
SNT204	0037
SNW-Q-1	0211
SNW-Q-2	0038
SNW-Q-3	0038
SNW-Q-4	0211
SNW-Q-5	0038
SNW-Q-6	0211
SO-1	0050
SO1	0050
SO1C	0865
SO1D	0847
SO-2	0050
SO2	0050
SO2C	0865
SO-3	0050
SO3	0050
SO10G	0071
SO25	0004
SO42P	OEM
SO46	0123
SO65	0004
SO65A	0136
SO88	0004
SO501	0015
SO-632	0012
SOA	0071
SOC532A	OEM
SOD20AS	0703
SOD20BS	1991
SOD30AL	0110
SOD30AS	0703
SOD30BL	0110
SOD30BS	0703
SOD30CS	0703
SOD30DL	0110
SOD30DS	0703
SOD50AL	0110
SOD50AS	0703
SOD50BL	0110
SOD50BS	0703
SOD50CL	0110
SOD50DL	0110
SOD50DS	0703
SOD100AL	0242
SOD100AS	0575
SOD100BL	0242
SOD100BS	0575
SOD100CL	0242
SOD100CS	0575
SOD100DS	0242
SOD200AL	0242
SOD200BL	0242
SOD200BS	0575
SOD200CL	0242
SOD200CS	0575
SOD-200D	0087
SOD200D	0015
SOD200DL	0242
SOD200DS	0575
SOS0121	0126
SP-01	0319
SP-02	1404
SP-03	0468
SP-04	0468
SP-06	0441
SP0256	OEM
SP0256-AL2	OEM
SP-1	0015
SP1	0015
SP1K	0229
SP1K-1	0015
SP1K-2	0023
SP-1.5A	0110
SP2	0279
SP2-01	0276
SP2-02	0287
SP2-04	0293
SP2-06	0299
SP2-08	0250
SP2-10	0250
SP3	0160
SP4	0435
SP5-1	OEM
SP5-2	OEM
SP5-3	OEM
SP6	0595
SP6GC1	0196
SP6GD1	0479
SP6GX1	1073
SP7	0595
SP9	0050
SP10	0079
SP11	0127
SP12	0142
SP13MP	0265
SP14	0103
SP15MP	1506
SP16	0160
SP17	0016
SP18	0086
SP26	0085
SP34AS	0143
SP39	0969
SP44UD	0085
SP44US	0085
SP47	0085
SP60	0143
SP62	0969
SP-70	0168
SP70	0037
SP74ALS8003P	OEM
SP82	0911
SP82A	0911
SP-89RW	0160
SP89UG	0160
SP90	0037
SP100	OEM
SP101	0133
SP102	OEM
SP103	OEM
SP104	OEM
SP105	OEM
SP-148-3	0160
SP148-3	0160
SP176	0085
SP180CI	1843
SP230	0085
SP295	0143
SP334	0160
SP404	0160
SP-404T	0160
SP404T	0160
SP441	0160
SP441D	0085
SP441G	0160
SP441S	0085
SP-485	0160
SP485	0160
SP485B	0160
SP485BLK	0160
SP485BLU	0160
SP485BRN	0160
SP485W	0160
SP485WHT	0160
SP-486	0160
SP486	0160
SP486W	0160
SP486WHT	0160
SP-634	0160
SP634	0160
SP-649	0160
SP649	0160
SP-649-1	0160
SP649-1	0160
SP706F	OEM
SP708F	OEM
SP744	0160
SP819R	0160
SP-834	0160
SP834	0160
SP838	0599
SP838-1	0599
SP875	0160
SP880	0085
SP880-1	0160
SP880-3	0160
SP891	0085
SP891-B	0085
SP891B	0160
SP891BLU	0160
SP891G	0160
SP891GRN	0160
SP891R	0160
SP891W	0160
SP891WHT	0160
SP1013B	0085
SP-1108	0160
SP1108	0085
SP1118	0160
SP1137	0085
SP1271	0160
SP1273	0160
SP-1278	0160
SP1278	0841
SP1323	0085
SP1403	0085
SP1481	0160
SP1481-1	0160
SP1481-2	0160
SP1481-3	0160
SP1481-4	0160
SP1481-5	0160
SP1482	0160
SP1482-2	0160
SP1482-3	0160
SP1482-4	0160
SP-1482-5	0160
SP1482-5	0160
SP1482-6	0160
SP1482-7	0160
SP1483	0160
SP1483-1	0160
SP1483-2	0160
SP1483-3	0160
SP-1484	0160
SP1484	0160
SP1484-1	0599
SP1484-2	0599
SP1484-3	0599
SP1484-4	0599
SP1484-5	0599
SP1550-3	0160
SP1556	0160
SP1556-1	0160
SP1556-2	0160
SP1556-3	0160
SP1556-4	0160
SP1563-2	0160
SP1595BLK	0160
SP1595BLU	0160
SP1595GRN	0160
SP1595RED	0160
SP1596BLK	0160
SP1596BLU	0160
SP1596GRN	0160
SP1596RED	0160
SP1600	0085
SP-1603	0160
SP1603	0160
SP-1603-1	0160
SP1603-1	0160
SP-1603-2	0160
SP1603-2	0160
SP1603-3	0160
SP1619	0085
SP1650	0599
SP1651	0085
SP1657	0160
SP1742	0969
SP1801	0160
SP1817	0599
SP1844	0160
SP1927	0085
SP1938	0160
SP1950	0160
SP2034	OEM
SP2045	0160
SP2046	0160
SP2048	0160
SP2072	0160
SP2076	0160
SP2077	0599
SP2094	0160
SP2155	0160
SP2158	0208
SP2188	0208
SP2200	OEM
SP2234	0085
SP2247	0085
SP2341	0160
SP2358	0085
SP2361	0160
SP2361BLU	0160
SP2361BRN	0160
SP2361GRN	0160
SP2361ORN	0160
SP2361RED	0160
SP2361YEL	0160
SP2395	0160
SP2411	0969
SP2431	0085
SP2431P	0435
SP2493	0160
SP2512	0969
SP2541	0160
SP2551	0222
SP2610	0599
SP2946F	OEM
SP3003	0004
SP3004	0004
SP3005	0279
SP3006	0050
SP3007	0050
SP3008	0136
SP3009	0160
SP3010	0208
SP3011	0595
SP3012	0435
SP3013	0265
SP3014	0160
SP3015	0265
SP3016	0015
SP3017A	0229
SP3018	0144
SP3019	0144
SP3020	0198
SP3020F	OEM
SP3021	0142
SP3024	0086
SP3025	0126
SP3026	0178
SP3027	0103
SP3028	0178
SP3029	1506
SP3030	0015
SP3031	3855
SP3032	0071
SP3033	0071
SP3035	0969
SP3036	2002
SP3037	5377
SP3038	0079
SP3039	0259
SP3040	0233
SP3041	0042
SP3042	0239
SP3044	0233
SP3045	3249
SP3046	0079
SP3047	0086
SP3048	2675
SP3049	0626
SP3050	0349
SP3051	0087
SP3052	0222
SP3053	0334
SP3054	0419
SP3055	0188
SP3056	0162
SP3057	0157
SP3058	0631
SP3059	0644
SP3060	0012
SP3061	0170
SP3062	0137
SP3063	0002
SP3064	0436
SP3065	0212
SP3066	0769
SP3067	0201
SP3068	0286
SP3079	0074
SP3080	0071
SP3081	0071
SP3082	1004
SP3083	0848
SP3084	0848
SP3085	0848
SP3086	1851
SP3087	0143
SP3088	0143
SP3089	0911
SP3090	0143
SP3091	0143
SP3092	0789
SP3093	0361
SP3094	0100
SP3095	0039
SP3096	3517
SP3096(ZENER)	0002
SP3097	0778
SP3098	0327
SP3099	0149
SP3100	0286
SP3103	3517
SP3105	0276
SP3106	0106
SP3109	1293
SP3112	0321
SP3114	0006
SP3115F	OEM
SP3116	0321
SP3116F	OEM
SP3117	0144
SP3118	0150
SP3119	0196
SP3120	0479
SP3121	1073
SP3122	0079
SP3133F	OEM
SP3134F	OEM
SP3135F	OEM
SP3136F	OEM
SP3253QD	OEM
SP3500	0122
SP3501	0315
SP3502	3651
SP3504	3213
SP3505	0720
SP3507	0411
SP3508	0147
SP3510	0103
SP3511	0130
SP3512	0086
SP3513	0126
SP3515	1760
SP3516	2077
SP4436	0007
SP4552	OEM
SP4632	OEM
SP4634	OEM
SP4653	OEM
SP4654	OEM
SP7056	0283
SP8300	OEM
SP8302	OEM
SP8303	OEM
SP8304	OEM
SP8307	OEM
SP8309	OEM
SP8310	OEM
SP8311	OEM
SP8400	0233
SP8401	0233
SP8402	0590
SP8411	OEM
SP8411A	OEM
SP8412	OEM
SP8412A	OEM
SP8413	OEM
SP8414	OEM
SP8414A	OEM
SP8416	0042
SP8588	OEM
SP8588A	OEM
SP8629	OEM
SP-8660	0161
SP8660	0042
SP8918	0161
SP10800	OEM
SP10801	OEM
SP10810	OEM
SP10811	OEM
SP22001	OEM
SPB-26MUW	OEM
SPC40	0016
SPC42	0016
SPC50	0016
SPC51	0016
SPC52	0016
SPC401	0270
SPC402	0270
SPC410	0309
SPC411	0270
SPC413	0309
SPC423	0309
SPC423M	OEM
SPC424	0309
SPC425	0309
SPC430	0270
SPC431	0359
SPC40411	0130
SPD110	OEM
SPD-121	OEM
SPD-121(A)	OEM
SPD-121(Q)	OEM
SPD-121(S)	OEM
SPD-121(T)	OEM
SPD-221	OEM
SPD-221(A)	OEM
SPD-221(Q)	OEM
SPD-221(S)	OEM
SPD-221(T)	OEM
SPD510	OEM
SPD521	OEM
SPD550	OEM
SPD560	OEM
SPD605	1557
SPD610	1557
SPD620	1557
SPD630	1557
SPD1205	1557
SPD1210	1266
SPD1220	1557
SPD1230	2140
SPF024	0321
SPF168	3017
SPF215	0212
SPF274	0212
SPF512	0212
SPF530	0224
SPF609	0212
SPI-06FC	OEM
SPI-06PF	2604
SPI201-20	OEM
SPI1050-01	OEM
SPN-01	0015
SPN01	0015
SPN-02	0287
SPN-03	0468
SPN-04	0468
SPN-06	0441
SPR-54MUW	OEM
SPR-54MVW3F	OEM
SPR1050-01	OEM
SPR4652	OEM
SPR4652REC	OEM
SPS08	2430
SPS010	0464
SPS020	2174
SPS025	0464
SPS030	0726
SPS035	0726
SPS0121	0126
SPS0122	0086
SPS4	0144
SPS12	0037
SPS18	2430
SPS20	0144
SPS22	0037
SPS28	0430
SPS38	0127
SPS40	0144
SPS41	0016
SPS42	0037
SPS43-1	0127
SPS47	0037
SPS48	1478
SPS49	0086
SPS58	0682
SPS68	0682
SPS91	0160
SPS110	0464
SPS120	4941
SPS125	0464
SPS130	0707
SPS135	0707
SPS167	OEM
SPS210	0464
SPS220	0144
SPS220#	0464
SPS225	0464
SPS230	0464
SPS235	0464
SPS310	0717
SPS320	0735
SPS325	0717
SPS330	0717
SPS335	0464
SPS401K	0037
SPS410	0717
SPS420	0735
SPS425	0735
SPS426	OEM
SPS428	0144
SPS429	0127
SPS430	0717
SPS435	0717
SPS477	0079
SPS-501C-1	OEM
SPS-503C-3	OEM
SPS510	0720
SPS514	0037
SPS520	0759
SPS525	0720
SPS530	0720
SPS535	0720
SPS610	0720
SPS620	0759
SPS625	0720
SPS627	0037
SPS630	0720
SPS635	0720
SPS668	0037
SPS699	0079
SPS816	OEM
SPS817	0079
SPS817N	0016
SPS-856	0127
SPS856	0127
SPS-860	0127
SPS860	0127
SPS868	0016
SPS871	0136
SPS906	0007
SPS907	0079
SPS915	0144
SPS-917	0224
SPS917	0144
SPS918	0079
SPS919	0007
SPS920	0224
SPS-934	0079
SPS934	0016
SPS-952	0079
SPS952	0079
SPS-952-2	0079
SPS952-2	0008
SPS1045	0016
SPS1082	0079
SPS1097	0037
SPS1107	0546
SPS-1351	0127
SPS1351	0144
SPS-1352	0127
SPS1352	0144
SPS-1353	0127
SPS1353	0144
SPS1359	0037
SPS1436	0546
SPS1437	0527
SPS-1473	0127
SPS1473	0144
SPS-1473RT	0224
SPS-1475(YT)	0079
SPS-1475YT	0079
SPS-1476	0111
SPS1523	0037
SPS-1539	0037
SPS-1539(WT)	0111
SPS-1539WT	0037
SPS1593WT	0037
SPS1802	0079
SPS1817	0079
SPS1846	0224
SPS1977	0079
SPS1978	0037
SPS2003	1518
SPS2104	0079
SPS2110	0144
SPS2111	0144
SPS2129	0079
SPS2130	0086
SPS2131	0126

If replacement code is OEM, contact original manufacturer for replacement.

DEVICE TYPE	REPL CODE
SPS2134	0855
SPS2135	0224
SPS2142	0079
SPS2164	0079
SPS2167	0127
SPS2194	0079
SPS2195	OEM
SPS2208-1	0008
SPS2216	0111
SPS2217	0111
SPS2224	0144
SPS2225	0079
SPS2226	0126
SPS-2265	0127
SPS2265	0144
SPS2265-2	0144
SPS-2266	0127
SPS2266	0144
SPS2269	0037
SPS2270	1212
SPS2271	0111
SPS2272	0006
SPS2274	0037
SPS2279	0037
SPS2320	0144
SPS2323	3495
SPS2403	OEM
SPS2415	0079
SPS2425	0127
SPS2526	0150
SPS3003	0144
SPS3015	0079
SPS3329	0037
SPS3370	0144
SPS3438	0037
SPS3724	0037
SPS3735	0079
SPS3786	0037
SPS3787	0127
SPS3900	0079
SPS3907	0079
SPS3908	0079
SPS3909	0079
SPS3910	OEM
SPS3912	0086
SPS3914	0086
SPS3915	0079
SPS3922	OEM
SPS3923	0079
SPS3924	0037
SPS3925	0079
SPS3926	0079
SPS3927	0037
SPS3929	0144
SPS3930	0079
SPS3931	0037
SPS3936	0079
SPS3937	0144
SPS3938	0079
SPS3940	0079
SPS3948	0144
SPS3951	0079
SPS3952	0144
SPS3957C	0079
SPS3967	0079
SPS3968	0144
SPS3971	0144
SPS3972	0079
SPS3973	0079
SPS3987	0037
SPS3988	0037
SPS3990	0037
SPS3999	0079
SPS4000	0037
SPS4002	0144
SPS4003	0079
SPS4004	0079
SPS4005	0144
SPS4006	0079
SPS4007	0037
SPS4008	0144
SPS4009	0079
SPS4010	0126
SPS4013	0037
SPS4014	0037
SPS4016	0144
SPS4017	0079
SPS4018	0037
SPS4019	0037
SPS4020	0079
SPS4025	0037
SPS4026	0037
SPS4027	0037
SPS4028	0037
SPS4029	0079
SPS4030	0144
SPS4031	0037
SPS4032	0079
SPS4034	0079
SPS4037	0079
SPS4038	0086
SPS4039	0079
SPS4040	0079
SPS4041	0079
SPS4042	0079
SPS4043	0144
SPS4044	0079
SPS4045	0079
SPS4049	0079

DEVICE TYPE	REPL CODE
SPS4050	0144
SPS4051	0144
SPS4052	0079
SPS4053	0079
SPS4054	0037
SPS4055	0079
SPS4056	0037
SPS4059	0079
SPS4060	0079
SPS4061	0079
SPS4062	0079
SPS4063	0079
SPS4064	0037
SPS4066	0079
SPS4067	0079
SPS4068	0144
SPS4069	0079
SPS4072	0037
SPS4073	0037
SPS4074	0079
SPS4075	0079
SPS4076	0037
SPS4076A	0037
SPS4077	0079
SPS4078	0037
SPS4079	0144
SPS4080	0144
SPS4081	0079
SPS4082	0037
SPS4083	0079
SPS4084	0079
SPS4085	0079
SPS4086	0037
SPS4087	0037
SPS4088	0079
SPS4089	0079
SPS4090	0037
SPS4091	0144
SPS4092	1357
SPS4095	0079
SPS4099	0378
SPS4143	0127
SPS-4145	0127
SPS4145	0144
SPS4149	OEM
SPS4167	0224
SPS4168	0144
SPS4169	0144
SPS4199	0079
SPS4201	OEM
SPS4213	OEM
SPS4236	0079
SPS4300	0086
SPS4301	0126
SPS4302	0037
SPS4303	0079
SPS4309	0086
SPS4310	0126
SPS4311	0086
SPS4312	0126
SPS4313	0079
SPS4314	0037
SPS4330	0037
SPS4331	0224
SPS4338	0037
SPS4343	0007
SPS4344	0079
SPS4345	0079
SPS4347	0079
SPS4348	0037
SPS4354	0037
SPS4355	0037
SPS4356	0079
SPS4359	0079
SPS4360	0079
SPS4361	0086
SPS4363	0079
SPS4365	0037
SPS4367	0079
SPS4368	0079
SPS4382	0079
SPS4390	0079
SPS4391	0086
SPS4392	0079
SPS-4396	0079
SPS4397	0037
SPS4399	0144
SPS4401	0150
SPS-4423	0127
SPS4423	0144
SPS4436	0224
SPS4439	OEM
SPS4443	0079
SPS4446	0079
SPS4450	0079
SPS4451	0079
SPS4452	0037
SPS4453	0079
SPS4455	0079
SPS4456	0079
SPS4457	0079
SPS4458	0037
SPS4459	0079
SPS4460	0037
SPS4461	0086
SPS4462	0126
SPS4472	0079
SPS4473	0037
SPS4476	0079

DEVICE TYPE	REPL CODE
SPS4477	0126
SPS4478	0079
SPS4480	0037
SPS4489	0037
SPS4490	0086
SPS4491	0079
SPS4492	0126
SPS4493	0079
SPS4494	0079
SPS4495	0086
SPS4497	0126
SPS4498	0079
SPS4610	0144
SPS4813	0037
SPS4814	0111
SPS4815	0037
SPS4920	0079
SPS5000	0079
SPS5006	0079
SPS5006-1	0079
SPS5006-2	0079
SPS5007	0037
SPS5007-1	0037
SPS5007-2	0037
SPS5008	0037
SPS5328	0050
SPS5349	OEM
SPS5450	0855
SPS5450S	0855
SPS5451	0676
SPS5569	0127
SPS5809	0086
SPS6109	0037
SPS6111	0079
SPS6112	0079
SPS6113	0079
SPS6124	0086
SPS6125	0126
SPS6155	0224
SPS6185	0264
SPS6571	0079
SPS6682	0127
SPS6953	0037
SPS7303	OEM
SPS7359	0079
SPS7652	0079
SPS8870	0144
SPS8871	0037
SPSB1001-01	OEM
SPT06	0154
SPT08	0154
SPT010	0154
SPT015	0154
SPT025	3118
SPT040	2004
SPT16	0154
SPT18	0154
SPT26	0154
SPT28	0154
SPT36	0147
SPT38	0147
SPT46	0147
SPT48	0147
SPT56	0278
SPT58	0278
SPT66	0278
SPT68	0278
SPT110	0154
SPT115	0154
SPT125	3119
SPT130	2004
SPT140	2004
SPT201	OEM
SPT210	0154
SPT215	0154
SPT225	3121
SPT230	2004
SPT240	2004
SPT260	OEM
SPT310	0147
SPT315	0147
SPT325	3122
SPT330	2006
SPT340	2006
SPT360	OEM
SPT410	0147
SPT415	0147
SPT425	3123
SPT430	2006
SPT440	2006
SPT460	OEM
SPT510	0278
SPT515	0278
SPT525	2007
SPT530	2007
SPT540	2007
SPT560	OEM
SPT610	0278
SPT615	0278
SPT625	2007
SPT630	2007
SPT640	2007
SPT2300L01	OEM
SPT2370H07	OEM
SPT2370H08	OEM
SPT3240L05	OEM
SPT3440	0168
SPT3713	0103
SPT5303	0130

DEVICE TYPE	REPL CODE
SPT6402L04	OEM
SPT9020	OEM
SPT640203	OEM
SPX2	0311
SPX2E	0311
SPX4	0311
SPX5	0311
SPX6	0311
SPX26	0311
SPX28	0311
SPX33	0311
SPX35	0311
SPX36	0311
SPX37	0311
SPX53	0311
SPX103	0311
SPX7110	0536
SPX7130	0536
SPX7150	0311
SPX7270	0536
SPX7271	0536
SPX7272	0311
SPX7273	0311
SPX7530	0536
SPX7550	0536
SPX7590	0311
SQ7	0595
SQ46	0143
SQ1220A	0549
SQ1220B	OEM
SQ1220C	OEM
SQ1224A	0005
SQ1224B	OEM
SQ1224C	OEM
SQ1226A	0715
SQ1226B	OEM
SQ1226C	OEM
SQ1234A	0623
SQ1234B	OEM
SQ1234C	OEM
SQ1238A	0030
SQ1238B	OEM
SQ1238C	OEM
SQ1270A	0549
SQ1270B	OEM
SQ1270C	OEM
SQ1274A	0005
SQ1274B	OEM
SQ1274C	OEM
SQ1276A	0715
SQ1276B	OEM
SQ1276C	OEM
SQ1284A	0623
SQ1284B	OEM
SQ1284C	OEM
SQ1288A	0030
SQ1288B	OEM
SQ1288C	OEM
SQ1716	OEM
SQ1716A	OEM
SQ1717	OEM
SQ1717A	OEM
SQ1718	OEM
SQ1718A	OEM
SQ1719	OEM
SQ1719A	OEM
SQ1720	0549
SQ1720A	OEM
SQ1720B	OEM
SQ1720C	OEM
SQ1722	OEM
SQ1722A	OEM
SQ1724	0005
SQ1724A	0005
SQ1724B	OEM
SQ1724C	OEM
SQ1726	0715
SQ1726A	0715
SQ1726B	OEM
SQ1726C	OEM
SQ1728	OEM
SQ1728A	OEM
SQ1730	OEM
SQ1730A	OEM
SQ1732	OEM
SQ1732A	OEM
SQ1734	0623
SQ1734A	OEM
SQ1734B	OEM
SQ1734C	OEM
SQ1736	OEM
SQ1736A	OEM
SQ1738	0030
SQ1738A	OEM
SQ1738B	OEM
SQ1738C	OEM
SQ1740	OEM
SQ1740A	OEM
SQ1742	OEM
SQ1742A	OEM
SQ1744	OEM
SQ1744A	OEM
SQ1746	OEM
SQ1746A	OEM
SQ1748	OEM
SQ1748A	OEM
SQ1750	OEM
SQ1750A	OEM
SQ2502	OEM

DEVICE TYPE	REPL CODE
SQ2503	OEM
SQ2508	OEM
SQ2519	OEM
SQ2520	OEM
SQ2521	OEM
SQ2526	OEM
SQ2527	OEM
SQ2529	OEM
SQ2534	OEM
SQ2535	OEM
SQ2536	OEM
SQ2543	OEM
SQ2544	OEM
SQ2544V1	OEM
SQ2545	OEM
SQ2545V1	OEM
SQ2546	OEM
SQ2554	OEM
SQ2555	OEM
SQ2556	OEM
SQ2557	OEM
SQ2558	OEM
SQ5441A	OEM
SQ5441B	OEM
SQ5441C	OEM
SQ5442A	OEM
SQ5442B	OEM
SQ5442C	OEM
SQ5443A	OEM
SQ5443B	OEM
SQ5443C	OEM
SQ5444A	OEM
SQ5444B	OEM
SQ5444C	OEM
SQ5445A	OEM
SQ5445B	OEM
SQ5445C	OEM
SQ5446A	OEM
SQ5446B	OEM
SQ5446C	OEM
SQ5447A	OEM
SQ5447B	OEM
SQ5447C	OEM
SQ5448A	OEM
SQ5448B	OEM
SQ5448C	OEM
SQ5449A	OEM
SQ5449B	OEM
SQ5449C	OEM
SQ5450A	OEM
SQ5450B	OEM
SQ5450C	OEM
SQ5451A	OEM
SQ5451B	OEM
SQ5451C	OEM
SQ5452A	OEM
SQ5452B	OEM
SQ5452C	OEM
SQ5453A	OEM
SQ5453B	OEM
SQ5453C	OEM
SQ5454A	OEM
SQ5454B	OEM
SQ5454C	OEM
SQ5455A	OEM
SQ5455B	OEM
SQ5455C	OEM
SQ5456A	OEM
SQ5456B	OEM
SQ5456C	OEM
SQ5461A	0549
SQ5463A	0005
SQ5464A	0715
SQ5468A	0623
SQ5470A	0030
SQB501B-GD	OEM
SR-0004	0196
SR-0005	0015
SR-0006	0196
SR-0007	0015
SR-0008	0015
SR-05K-2	0015
SR05K-2	0023
SR05K-4	0023
SR05K-8	0023
SR05K-12	0023
SR05K-16	0017
SR05K-20	0017
SR-1	0080
SR1	0004
SR1-2	0015
SR1A-1	0015
SR1A1	0015
SR1A-2	0015
SR1A2	0015
SR1A-4	0015
SR1A4	0015
SR1A-8	0015
SR1A8	0015
SR1A-12	0229
SR1A12	0015
SR1B	0276
SR1C1	OEM
SR1C-2	0604
SR1C2	OEM
SR1C-4	0790
SR1C4	OEM
SR1C-6	0790
SR1C6	OEM

DEVICE TYPE	REPL CODE
SR1C-8	0015
SR1C8	OEM
SR1C-12	0015
SR1C12	OEM
SR1C-16	0071
SR1C16	OEM
SR1C-20	0071
SR1C20	OEM
SR1C-24	0102
SR1C24	OEM
SR1D-1	0015
SR1D1M	0015
SR1D-2	0015
SR1D-4	0015
SR1D-6	0015
SR1D-8	0015
SR1DM	0015
SR1DM-1	0015
SR1DM1	0015
SR1DM-2	0110
SR1DM-4	0015
SR1DM-6	0015
SR1DM-8	0015
SR1DM-10	0015
SR1DMX	0015
SR1E	0015
SR1EM	0015
SR1EM-1	0015
SR1EM1	0015
SR1EM-2	0015
SR1EM2	0015
SR1EM-4	0087
SR1EM4	0087
SR1EM-6	0015
SR1EM6	OEM
SR1EM-8	0015
SR1EM8	OEM
SR1EM-10	0015
SR1EM10	OEM
SR1EM-12	0015
SR1EM12	OEM
SR1EM-16	0071
SR1EM-20	0071
SR1EM20	OEM
SR1FM	0015
SR1FM-0	OEM
SR1FM-1	0015
SR1FM1	0015
SR1FM-2	0102
SR1FM2	0015
SR1FM-4	0015
SR1FM4	0015
SR1FM6	0015
SR1FM-8	0015
SR1FM8	0535
SR1FM-12	0071
SR1FM12	0015
SR1FM-16	0071
SR1FM16	0071
SR1FM-20	0071
SR1FM20	0071
SR1G-4	0102
SR1G4	OEM
SR1G-8	0102
SR1G8	OEM
SR1G-12	0102
SR1G12	OEM
SR1G-16	0102
SR1G16	OEM
SR1G20	OEM
SR1G24	OEM
SR-1HM-2	0015
SR1HM-2	0102
SR1HM-4	0102
SR1HM-8	0023
SR1HM-12	0102
SR1HM-16	0102
SR1K	0015
SR1K-0	0015
SR1K-1	0023
SR1K1	0015
SR1K-1K	0015
SR1K-2	0015
SR1K2	0015
SR-1K-2A	0071
SR1K-4	0023
SR1K4	0015
SR1K-8	0023
SR1K8	0015
SR1K-12	0015
SR1K-16	0071
SR1K-20	0071
SR1K-24	0344
SR1K-4100-521	OEM
SR-1K-0	OEM
SR1K-Z	0015
SR1KZ	0015
SR1S-1	1325
SR1S-2	OEM
SR1S-4	OEM
SR1S-8	OEM
SR1T	0015
SR-1Z	0015
SR1Z	0015
SR-2	0080
SR2A-1	0015
SR2A1	0015
SR2A-2	0015
SR2A2	0015

DEVICE TYPE	REPL CODE
SR2A-4	0015
SR2A4	0015
SR2A-8	0071
SR2A8	0015
SR2A-12	0071
SR2A12	0015
SR2B1	OEM
SR2B2	OEM
SR2B4	OEM
SR2B6	OEM
SR2B8	OEM
SR2B-12	2070
SR2B12	0087
SR2B-16	2077
SR2B16	0087
SR2B-20	0607
SR2B20	0087
SR2B-24	OEM
SR2B24	OEM
SR2C-1	0703
SR2C1	OEM
SR2C-2	0575
SR2C2	OEM
SR2C-4	0575
SR2C4	OEM
SR2C-6	0994
SR2C6	OEM
SR2C-8	0994
SR2C8	OEM
SR2C-12	2070
SR2C12	OEM
SR2C-16	2077
SR2C16	OEM
SR2C-20	0607
SR2C20	OEM
SR2C-24	OEM
SR2C24	OEM
SR2GH315	OEM
SR2HR316	OEM
SR2K	0023
SR2KL	OEM
SR2KN	OEM
SR-2M	3829
SR2M	3829
SR-2S	OEM
SR2S	OEM
SR-2T	0080
SR-3	0015
SR3	0015
SR3AM	0133
SR3AM-1	0031
SR3AM1	0110
SR3AM-2	0031
SR3AM2	0071
SR3AM-3	0947
SR3AM3	0398
SR3AM-4	0031
SR3AM4	0071
SR3AM-6	0031
SR3AM6	0535
SR3AM-8	0031
SR3AM8	0535
SR3AM-10	0031
SR3AM10	0959
SR3AM-12	0031
SR3AM12	0959
SR3BM-6	0015
SR3U-2	0031
SR3U-4	0031
SR-4	0015
SR4	0015
SR-5	0015
SR5	0015
SR6	0196
SR-9	0015
SR10	0479
SR10-4S	0865
SR10A-2R	0760
SR10A-2S	0097
SR10A-4R	0760
SR10A-4S	0097
SR10A-6R	0533
SR10A-6S	0109
SR10A-8R	0533
SR10A-8S	0109
SR10A-10R	0810
SR10A-10S	0122
SR10A-12R	0810
SR10A-12S	0122
SR10A-16R	0540
SR10A-16S	0131
SR10A-20R	0545
SR10A-20S	0145
SR10A-24R	OEM
SR10A-24S	OEM
SR10C-2R	OEM
SR10C-2S	OEM
SR10C-4R	OEM
SR10C-4S	OEM
SR10C-8R	OEM
SR10C-8S	OEM
SR10D1	0084
SR10D2	0097
SR10D4	0585
SR10D6	OEM
SR10D8	OEM
SR10D-10	OEM
SR10D10	OEM
SR10D-12	OEM

If replacement code is OEM, contact original manufacturer for replacement. 571

DEVICE TYPE	REPL CODE
SR10D12	OEM
SR10D-14	OEM
SR10D14	OEM
SR10D-16	OEM
SR10D16	OEM
SR10D-18	OEM
SR10D18	OEM
SR10D-20	OEM
SR10D20	OEM
SR10D-24	OEM
SR10D24	OEM
SR10F-1R	2537
SR10F-1S	4938
SR10F1S	OEM
SR10F-2R	2537
SR10F-2S	4938
SR10F2S	OEM
SR10F-4R	2537
SR10F-4S	4938
SR10F4S	OEM
SR10F-6R	2537
SR10F-6S	4938
SR10F6S	OEM
SR10F-8R	2537
SR10F-8S	4938
SR10F8S	OEM
SR10F10S	OEM
SR10H-1	1590
SR10H-2	0865
SR10H-4	0865
SR10H-6	0847
SR10H-8	0847
SR10J-1	1590
SR10J1S	OEM
SR10J-2	0865
SR10J2S	OEM
SR10J-4	0865
SR10J4S	OEM
SR10J-6	0847
SR10J6S	OEM
SR10J-8	0847
SR10J8S	OEM
SR10K2S	OEM
SR10K6S	OEM
SR10K10S	OEM
SR10L-1S	1590
SR10L-2R	1567
SR10L-2S	1241
SR10L-4S	0865
SR10L-6S	0847
SR10L-8S	0847
SR10N-2R	OEM
SR10N-2S	OEM
SR10N-4R	OEM
SR10N-4S	OEM
SR10N-6R	OEM
SR10N-6S	OEM
SR10N-8R	OEM
SR10N-8S	OEM
SR10N-10R	OEM
SR10N-10S	OEM
SR-13	2875
SR13	0196
SR13H	0015
SR-14	0015
SR14	0479
SR-15	0102
SR15	0479
SR16	0229
SR-16(PHILCO)	1208
SR16DM-2R	OEM
SR16DM-2S	OEM
SR16DM-4R	OEM
SR16DM-4S	OEM
SR16DM-6R	OEM
SR16DM-6S	OEM
SR17	0015
SR-17(PHILCO)	1208
SR-18	0015
SR18	0811
SR-20	0907
SR20	0196
SR20F1S	OEM
SR20F-2R	OEM
SR20F-2S	OEM
SR20F2S	OEM
SR20F-4R	OEM
SR20F-4S	OEM
SR20F4S	OEM
SR20F-6R	OEM
SR20F-6S	OEM
SR20F6S	OEM
SR20F-8R	OEM
SR20F-8S	OEM
SR20F8S	OEM
SR20F10S	OEM
SR20N-2R	OEM
SR20N-2S	OEM
SR20N-4R	OEM
SR20N-4S	OEM
SR20N-6R	OEM
SR20N-6S	OEM
SR20N-8R	OEM
SR20N-8S	OEM
SR20N-10R	OEM
SR20N-10S	OEM
SR20N12S	OEM
SR21	0196
SR22	0015
SR23	0015
SR24	0015
SR25	0102
SR25A-1R	OEM
SR25A-1S	OEM
SR25A1S	OEM
SR25A-2R	OEM
SR25A-2S	OEM
SR25A2S	OEM
SR25A-4R	OEM
SR25A-4S	OEM
SR25A4S	OEM
SR25A-6R	OEM
SR25A-6S	OEM
SR25A6S	OEM
SR25A-8R	OEM
SR25A-8S	OEM
SR25A8S	OEM
SR25A-10R	OEM
SR25A-10S	OEM
SR25A10S	OEM
SR25B-2R	0254
SR25B-2S	2873
SR25B-4R	1099
SR25B-4S	1116
SR25B-6R	1103
SR25B-6S	1118
SR25B-8R	0258
SR25B-8S	0800
SR25B-10R	1634
SR25B-10S	1186
SR25B12S	OEM
SR-27	0015
SR27	0015
SR-28	0015
SR28	0015
SR-29	0196
SR29	0196
SR-30	0469
SR30	0015
SR30A-2R	0254
SR30A-2S	2873
SR30A2S	OEM
SR30A-4R	1099
SR30A-4S	1116
SR30A4S	OEM
SR30A6S	OEM
SR30A-8R	0258
SR30A-8S	0800
SR30A8S	0800
SR30A10S	OEM
SR30A-12R	0267
SR30A-12S	0315
SR30A12S	OEM
SR30A-16R	1111
SR30A-16S	1124
SR30A16S	1124
SR30A-20R	0280
SR30A-20S	0045
SR30A20S	0280
SR30A-24R	OEM
SR30A-24S	OEM
SR30A24S	OEM
SR30B-1	OEM
SR30B1	OEM
SR30B-2	OEM
SR30B2	OEM
SR30B-4	OEM
SR30B4	OEM
SR30B-6	OEM
SR30B6	OEM
SR30B-8	OEM
SR30B8	OEM
SR30B-10	OEM
SR30B10	OEM
SR30B-12	OEM
SR30B12	OEM
SR30B-14	OEM
SR30B14	OEM
SR30B-16	OEM
SR30B16	OEM
SR30B-18	OEM
SR30B18	OEM
SR30B-20	OEM
SR30B20	OEM
SR30B-24	OEM
SR30B24	OEM
SR30C-2R	1512
SR30C-2S	1522
SR30C-4R	1512
SR30C-4S	1522
SR30C-6R	1836
SR30C-6S	0029
SR30C-8R	1836
SR30C-8S	0029
SR30C-10R	1840
SR30C-10S	0596
SR30C-12R	1840
SR30C-12S	0596
SR30C-16R	OEM
SR30C-16S	OEM
SR30C-20R	OEM
SR30C-20S	OEM
SR30D-8R	OEM
SR30D-8S	OEM
SR30D-16R	OEM
SR30D-16S	OEM
SR30D-24R	OEM
SR30D-24S	OEM
SR-31	1293
SR31	1293
SR-32	0769
SR32	0769
SR35	0015
SR-37	0469
SR37	0469
SR40	0015
SR40K-2R	OEM
SR40K-2S	OEM
SR40K-4R	OEM
SR40K-4S	OEM
SR40K-6R	OEM
SR40K-6S	OEM
SR40K-8R	OEM
SR40K-8S	OEM
SR40K-10R	OEM
SR40K-10S	OEM
SR40K-12R	OEM
SR40K-12S	OEM
SR50	0015
SR50A8S	2823
SR50A10S	2844
SR50A12S	2844
SR50A16S	2806
SR50A20S	2454
SR50A24S	OEM
SR60	0015
SR70C-10	2183
SR70C10	2183
SR70C-12	2165
SR70C12	2183
SR70C-16	2202
SR70C16	2202
SR70C-20	2324
SR70C20	2324
SR70C-24	OEM
SR70C24	OEM
SR70C-28	OEM
SR70C28	OEM
SR70C30	OEM
SR70C-32	OEM
SR70C32	OEM
SR70C-36	OEM
SR70C36	OEM
SR70C-40	OEM
SR70C40	OEM
SR70E2S	OEM
SR70E4S	OEM
SR70E6S	OEM
SR70E8S	OEM
SR70F12R	OEM
SR70F16R	OEM
SR70F20R	OEM
SR70K-2R	OEM
SR70K-2S	OEM
SR70K-4R	OEM
SR70K-4S	OEM
SR70K-6R	OEM
SR70K-6S	OEM
SR70K-8R	OEM
SR70K-8S	OEM
SR70K-10R	OEM
SR70K-10S	OEM
SR70K-12R	OEM
SR70K-12S	OEM
SR-76	0015
SR76	0015
SR-100	0242
SR100	0015
SR100AM-10	OEM
SR100AM-12	OEM
SR100AM-16	OEM
SR100AM-20	OEM
SR100AM-24	OEM
SR100AM-32	OEM
SR100AM-36	OEM
SR100AM-40	OEM
SR100K-2R	OEM
SR100K-2S	OEM
SR100K-4R	OEM
SR100K-4S	OEM
SR100K-6R	OEM
SR100K-6S	OEM
SR100K-8R	OEM
SR100K-8S	OEM
SR100K-10R	OEM
SR100K-10S	OEM
SR100K-12R	OEM
SR100K-12S	OEM
SR100L2S	OEM
SR100L4S	OEM
SR100L6S	OEM
SR100L8S	OEM
SR101-1	0015
SR101-2	0015
SR102	0730
SR103	0730
SR103D	3153
SR103W	1348
SR104	0730
SR105	0015
SR106	3834
SR106C	1970
SR106C4	OEM
SR106D	1970
SR108	3834
SR108D	OEM
SR112	0015
SR-114	0242
SR114	0015
SR-120	0015
SR120	0015
SR-130-1	0015
SR130-1	0144
SR131-1	0015
SR-132-1	0015
SR132-1	0110
SR135-1	0015
SR-136	0015
SR136	0110
SR144	0015
SR145	0015
SR150	0071
SR-150-1	0015
SR151	0015
SR152	0015
SR153	1991
SR200	1345
SR200B	1345
SR200DL-12R	OEM
SR200DL-12S	OEM
SR200DL-16R	OEM
SR200DL-16S	OEM
SR200DL-20R	OEM
SR200DL-20S	OEM
SR200DL-24R	OEM
SR200DL-24S	OEM
SR200DM-28R	OEM
SR200DM-28S	OEM
SR200DM-32R	OEM
SR200DM-32S	OEM
SR200DM-36R	OEM
SR200DM-36S	OEM
SR200DM-40R	OEM
SR200DM-40S	OEM
SR200H10	OEM
SR200H-12	OEM
SR200H12	OEM
SR200H-14	OEM
SR200H14	OEM
SR200H-16	OEM
SR200H16	OEM
SR200H-18	OEM
SR200H18	OEM
SR200H-20	OEM
SR200H20	OEM
SR200H-24	OEM
SR200H24	OEM
SR200P-10	OEM
SR200P-12	OEM
SR200P12	OEM
SR200P-16	OEM
SR200P16	OEM
SR200P-20	OEM
SR200P20	OEM
SR200P-24	OEM
SR200P24	OEM
SR200P-30	OEM
SR200P30	OEM
SR200P-36	OEM
SR200P36	OEM
SR200P-40	OEM
SR200P40	OEM
SR200P50	OEM
SR200P60	OEM
SR200PH-28R	4221
SR200PH-28S	4222
SR200PH-32R	4221
SR200PH-32S	4222
SR200PH-36R	OEM
SR200PH-36S	OEM
SR200PH-40R	OEM
SR200PH-40S	OEM
SR200PL-12R	1766
SR200PL-12S	1030
SR200PL-16R	1778
SR200PL-16S	1040
SR200PL-20R	1778
SR200PL-20S	1040
SR200PL-24R	4221
SR200PL-24S	4222
SR200T-12R	OEM
SR200T-12S	OEM
SR200T12S	OEM
SR200T-16R	OEM
SR200T-16S	OEM
SR200T16S	OEM
SR200T-20R	OEM
SR200T-20S	OEM
SR200T20S	OEM
SR205	0015
SR210	0242
SR220	0242
SR300A1	OEM
SR300A2	OEM
SR300A3	OEM
SR300A4	OEM
SR300A6	OEM
SR300A8	OEM
SR300A10	OEM
SR300A-12	OEM
SR300A12	OEM
SR300A-14	OEM
SR300A14	OEM
SR300A-16	OEM
SR300A16	OEM
SR300A-18	OEM
SR300A18	OEM
SR300A-20	OEM
SR300A20	OEM
SR300A-24	OEM
SR300A24	OEM
SR302	2520
SR303	2520
SR304	2520
SR305	3559
SR306	4187
SR308	OEM
SR-390	0015
SR390	0015
SR390-2	0229
SR400A30	OEM
SR400A-40	OEM
SR400A40	OEM
SR400A-50	OEM
SR400A50	OEM
SR400A-60	OEM
SR400A60	OEM
SR400A-70	OEM
SR400A70	OEM
SR400A-80	OEM
SR400A80	OEM
SR400C-10	OEM
SR400C10	OEM
SR400C-12	OEM
SR400C12	OEM
SR400C-16	OEM
SR400C16	OEM
SR400C-20	OEM
SR400C20	OEM
SR400C-24	OEM
SR400C24	OEM
SR400C28	OEM
SR400C-30	OEM
SR400C30	OEM
SR400C32	OEM
SR400C36	OEM
SR400C-40	OEM
SR400C40	OEM
SR400C-50	OEM
SR400C50	OEM
SR400C-60	OEM
SR400C60	OEM
SR400C70	OEM
SR400C80	OEM
SR400D10	OEM
SR400D12	OEM
SR400D16	OEM
SR400D20	OEM
SR400D24	OEM
SR400D30	OEM
SR400D40	OEM
SR400D50	OEM
SR400D60	OEM
SR400D70	OEM
SR400DH-28	4221
SR400DH-32	4221
SR400DH-36	OEM
SR400DH-40	OEM
SR400DH-50	OEM
SR400DH-60	OEM
SR400DL-10	4221
SR400DL-12	4221
SR400DL-16	4221
SR400DL-20	4221
SR400DL-24	4221
SR400DV-70	OEM
SR400DV-80	OEM
SR400EL-10	OEM
SR400EL-12	OEM
SR400EL-16	OEM
SR400EL-20	OEM
SR400EL-24	OEM
SR400FH-28	OEM
SR400FH-32	OEM
SR400FH-36	OEM
SR400FH-40	OEM
SR400FH-50	OEM
SR400FH-60	OEM
SR400FV-70	OEM
SR400FV-80	OEM
SR401	0015
SR405	0015
SR475	0110
SR499	0087
SR500	0015
SR500B	0015
SR502	OEM
SR503	OEM
SR503D	OEM
SR504	OEM
SR505	OEM
SR506	OEM
SR506D	OEM
SR507	0242
SR508	OEM
SR513D	OEM
SR605	0015
SR605D	2990
SR606C	OEM
SR632D	OEM
SR632D-R	OEM
SR710	3631
SR710A	OEM
SR710CT	2219
SR710CTE	OEM
SR710CTR	2219
SR710E	OEM
SR710F	2809
SR710FA	OEM
SR710FE	OEM
SR710SD	OEM
SR711	3631
SR711A	OEM
SR711CT	2219
SR711CTE	OEM
SR711CTR	2219
SR711E	OEM
SR711F	2809
SR711FA	OEM
SR711FE	OEM
SR711SD	OEM
SR712	3631
SR712A	OEM
SR712CT	2219
SR712CTE	OEM
SR712CTR	2219
SR712E	OEM
SR712F	2809
SR712FA	OEM
SR712FE	OEM
SR712SD	OEM
SR713	3634
SR713A	OEM
SR713E	OEM
SR713F	4125
SR713FA	OEM
SR713FE	OEM
SR714	3634
SR714A	OEM
SR714CT	OEM
SR714CTE	OEM
SR714CTR	4409
SR714E	OEM
SR714F	4125
SR714FA	OEM
SR714FE	OEM
SR714SD	OEM
SR716	3635
SR716A	OEM
SR716E	OEM
SR716F	4134
SR716FA	OEM
SR716FD	OEM
SR716FE	OEM
SR718CT	OEM
SR718CTE	OEM
SR718CTR	OEM
SR718SD	OEM
SR720CT	OEM
SR720CTE	OEM
SR720CTR	OEM
SR720SD	OEM
SR802	1137
SR802R	OEM
SR803	1137
SR803R	OEM
SR804	1137
SR804R	OEM
SR805	1137
SR805R	OEM
SR806	1137
SR806-126	0015
SR806R	OEM
SR808	1137
SR808R	OEM
SR846-2	0015
SR851	0015
SR851-121	0015
SR889	0015
SR1001	1991
SR1002	OEM
SR1002R	OEM
SR1003	OEM
SR1003R	OEM
SR1004	OEM
SR1004R	OEM
SR1005	OEM
SR1005R	OEM
SR1006	OEM
SR1006R	OEM
SR1024	0015
SR1104	0015
SR1266	0015
SR1378-2	0535
SR1422	0110
SR1493	0015
SR1549	0015
SR1598	0110
SR1602A	1716
SR1602C	1227
SR1602D	OEM
SR1603A	1716
SR1603C	1227
SR1603D	OEM
SR1604A	1716
SR1604C	1227
SR1604D	OEM
SR1605A	1716
SR1605C	1227
SR1605D	OEM
SR1606A	1716
SR1606C	1227
SR1606D	OEM
SR1643A	0110
SR1650	0811
SR-1668	0015
SR1668	0015
SR1692	0015
SR1693	0015
SR1694	0015
SR1695	0015
SR1731-1	0015
SR1731-2	0015
SR1731-3	0015
SR1731-4	0015
SR1731-5	0015
SR1742	0015
SR1762	0242
SR1766	0015
SR-1849-1	0015
SR1984	0015
SR2121	0015
SR2301	0015
SR2301A	0015
SR3002A	OEM
SR3002C	1931
SR3003A	OEM
SR3003C	1931
SR3004A	OEM
SR3004C	1931
SR3005A	OEM
SR3005C	2219
SR3006A	OEM
SR3006C	2219
SR3010	0015
SR3582	0015
SR3943	0015
SR4500D80	OEM
SR5005	3399
SR5010	3399
SR5020	3399
SR5030	3399
SR5040	3399
SR5700	OEM
SR5701	OEM
SR5702	OEM
SR5703	OEM
SR5704	OEM
SR5705	OEM
SR6134	0015
SR6324	0015
SR6325	0015
SR6385	0015
SR6415	0015
SR6560	0015
SR6567	0015
SR6617	0015
SR-9000	0769
SR9000	0769
SR-9001	1293
SR9001	1293
SR-9002	0196
SR9002	0196
SR9003	0015
SR-9005	0469
SR9005	0015
SR20226	0224
SR20234	0079
SR50253-2	0287
SR50411-1	0015
SR50517	0229
SR63197	0037
SR75844	0016
SRA989A-1	OEM
SRAM2064C15	OEM
SRB-1	OEM
SRB-2	OEM
SRB-3	OEM
SRB-4	OEM
SRC220	OEM
SRC221	OEM
SRC230	OEM
SRC260	OEM
SRC290	OEM
SRC600	OEM
SRC740	OEM
SRC9231	OEM
SRC9261	OEM
SRE4-05	OEM
SRE7-05	OEM
SRE9A05	OEM
SRE12B05	OEM
SRE17A05	OEM
SRE23B05	OEM
SRE33-05	OEM
SRE86A05	OEM
SRE115B05	OEM
SREA4-05	OEM
SREA7-05	OEM
SREA9A05	OEM
SREA12B05	OEM
SREA17A05	OEM
SREA23B05	OEM
SREA33-05	OEM
SREA86A05	OEM
SREA115B05	OEM
S-RECT-174	0196
SRF-1	OEM
SRF-2	OEM
SRF-3	OEM
SRF-4	OEM
SRF2017	2296
SRH25C	OEM

DEVICE TYPE	REPL CODE
SRI-155740B	0720
SRIDM	0015
SRIDM-1	0015
SRIDM-4	0015
SRIEM-1	0015
SRIEM-2	0015
SRIEM-4	0015
SRIFM-2	0102
SRIFM-4	0102
SRIFM-12	0102
SRIHM-8	0102
SR-IK-2	0015
SRIK-2	0015
SRIK-8	0015
SRK1	0015
SRK-2	0015
SRK-11ZC	OEM
SRLP1004	0886
SRM-2064C	OEM
SRM2064C	OEM
SRM2064C15	OEM
SRM2114C3	2037
SRM2264LC12	OEM
SRM2264M12	OEM
SRN02	OEM
SRN02-100	1009
SRN02-200	1009
SRN02-400	1009
SRP02	OEM
SRP02-100	0199
SRP02-200	0199
SRP02-400	0199
SRP100A	0023
SRP100B	0023
SRP100D	0023
SRP100G	0023
SRP100J	0023
SRP100K	0023
SRP300A	0031
SRP300B	0031
SRP300D	0031
SRP300G	0031
SRP300J	0031
SRP300K	1362
SRP600A	OEM
SRP600B	OEM
SRP600D	OEM
SRP600G	OEM
SRP600J	OEM
SRP600K	OEM
SRQ02-100	6301
SRQ02-200	6301
SRQ02-400	6301
SR-R13	0196
SRR13	0196
SRS105	1325
SRS1004	0264
SRS1100	OEM
SRS2004	0168
SRS2504	0168
SRS2804S	0168
SRS3014	0168
SRS3100	OEM
SRS3204S	0168
SRS3504	0168
SRS3604S	0168
SRS4014	0168
SRS4014S	0168
SRS4404S	0168
SRS4504	0168
SRS5014	0168
SRS5504	0168
SRUF15	OEM
SRUN15	OEM
SRUN38T	OEM
SRUN50T	OEM
SS0001	0004
SS0002	0004
SS0003	0164
SS0004	0004
SS0005	0004
SS0007	0143
SS0008	0143
SS0009	0015
SS00010	0015
SS000I	0004
SS-1	0015
SS1.5J4	2520
SS2J4	OEM
SS-2N5062	0895
SS-3	OEM
SS3J4	OEM
SS-3R	OEM
SS-5	OEM
SS-5R	OEM
SS-7	OEM
SS-7R	OEM
SS29A4	0688
SS29A5	0688
SS101A	OEM
SS101B	OEM
SS101C	OEM
SS151	OEM
SS151R	OEM
SS155	0050
SS201	OEM
SS277G	0790
SS301	OEM
SS321	0604

DEVICE TYPE	REPL CODE
SS322	0604
SS324	0604
SS325	1325
SS334	0604
SS337	0604
SS455	0015
SS524	0233
SS1001	4610
SS1002	OEM
SS1003	OEM
SS1004	OEM
SS1005	OEM
SS1010	OEM
SS1011	OEM
SS1012	OEM
SS1015	OEM
SS1020	OEM
SS1030	OEM
SS1040	OEM
SS1123	0334
SS1202	OEM
SS1601	OEM
SS1602	OEM
SS1603	OEM
SS1606	0037
SS1621	OEM
SS1623	OEM
SS1906	3079
SS1912	0233
SS2002	OEM
SS2005	OEM
SS2010	OEM
SS2015	OEM
SS2020	OEM
SS2030	OEM
SS2040	OEM
SS2308	0016
SS2503	0037
SS2504	0016
SS3534-4	0321
SS3586	0321
SS3638	0037
SS3638A	0037
SS3672	0321
SS3694	0016
SS-3704	0321
SS3704	0321
SS3735	0321
SS3935	0693
SS4001AE	0473
SS4002AE	2044
SS4011AE	0215
SS4012AE	0493
SS4013AE	0409
SS4023AE	0515
SS4025AE	2061
SS4027AE	1938
SS4028AE	2213
SS4030AE	0495
SS4042	0007
SS6111	0233
SS6724	0037
SS9101	OEM
SS9327	0264
SS9328	0079
SSA5.0	OEM
SSA5.0A	OEM
SSA6.0	OEM
SSA6.0A	OEM
SSA6.5	OEM
SSA6.5A	OEM
SSA7.0	OEM
SSA7.0A	OEM
SSA7.5	OEM
SSA7.5A	OEM
SSA8.0	OEM
SSA8.0A	OEM
SSA8.5	OEM
SSA8.5A	OEM
SSA9.0	OEM
SSA9.0A	OEM
SSA10	OEM
SSA10A	OEM
SSA11	OEM
SSA11A	OEM
SSA12	OEM
SSA12A	OEM
SSA13	OEM
SSA13A	OEM
SSA14	OEM
SSA14A	OEM
SSA15	OEM
SSA15A	OEM
SSA16	OEM
SSA16A	OEM
SSA17	OEM
SSA17A	OEM
SSA18	OEM
SSA18A	OEM
SSA20	OEM
SSA20A	OEM
SSA22	OEM
SSA22A	OEM
SSA24	OEM
SSA24A	OEM
SSA26	OEM
SSA26A	OEM
SSA28	OEM
SSA28A	OEM

DEVICE TYPE	REPL CODE
SSA30	OEM
SSA30A	OEM
SSA33	OEM
SSA33A	OEM
SSA36	OEM
SSA36A	OEM
SSA40	OEM
SSA40A	OEM
SSA43	0037
SSA43A	0037
SSA45	OEM
SSA45A	OEM
SSA46	0037
SSA46A	0037
SSA48	0037
SSA48A	0037
SSA51	OEM
SSA51A	OEM
SSA54	OEM
SSA54A	OEM
SSA58	OEM
SSA58A	OEM
SSA60	OEM
SSA60A	OEM
SSA64	OEM
SSA64A	OEM
SSA70	OEM
SSA70A	OEM
SSA75	OEM
SSA75A	OEM
SSA78	OEM
SSA78A	OEM
SSA85	OEM
SSA85A	OEM
SSA90	OEM
SSA90A	OEM
SSA100	OEM
SSA100A	OEM
SSA110	OEM
SSA110A	OEM
SSA120	OEM
SSA120A	OEM
SSA130	OEM
SSA130A	OEM
SSA150	OEM
SSA150A	OEM
SSA160	OEM
SSA160A	OEM
SSA170	OEM
SSA170A	OEM
SSB3020CT	1931
SSB3020SD	OEM
SSB3030CT	1931
SSB3030SD	OEM
SSB3040CT	1931
SSB3040SD	OEM
SSB3050CT	OEM
SSB3050SD	OEM
SSB3060CT	OEM
SSB3060SD	OEM
SSB3080CT	OEM
SSB3080SD	OEM
SSC600	OEM
SSD708	0133
SSD974	0015
SSD2404	OEM
SSF15	OEM
SSF20	OEM
SSF25	OEM
SSF30	OEM
SSF40A	OEM
SSF50A	OEM
SSF60A	OEM
SSF200	OEM
SSF201	OEM
SSF202	OEM
SSF203	OEM
SSH1A020	1325
SSH1A040	1325
SSH1A060	0080
SSH1A080	0080
SSH3A020	0087
SSH3A030	0087
SSH3A040	0087
SSH3A050	0087
SSH3A060	0087
SSH5A020	OEM
SSH5A030	OEM
SSH5A040	OEM
SSH5A050	OEM
SSH5A060	OEM
SSH30A03D	0579
SSH30A04D	0579
SSH30A020D	0579
SSH30A020S	0610
SSH30A020T	OEM
SSH30A030D	OEM
SSH30A030S	0610
SSH30A030T	OEM
SSH30A040D	OEM
SSH30A040S	0610
SSH30A040T	OEM
SSH30A050D	OEM
SSH30A050S	OEM
SSH30A050T	OEM
SSH30A060D	OEM
SSH30A060S	OEM
SSH30A060T	OEM
SSH75A020	OEM

DEVICE TYPE	REPL CODE
SSH75A020V	OEM
SSH75A030	OEM
SSH75A030V	OEM
SSH75A040	OEM
SSH75A040V	OEM
SSH75A050	OEM
SSH75A050V	OEM
SSH75A060	OEM
SSH75A060V	OEM
SSH2500	OEM
SSH5000	OEM
SSH7500	OEM
SSH10000	OEM
SSH12500	OEM
SSH15000	OEM
SSH20000	OEM
SSHF2500	OEM
SSHF5000	OEM
SSHF7500	OEM
SSHF10000	OEM
SSHF12500	OEM
SSHF15000	OEM
SSHF20000	OEM
SSI202	OEM
SSI1120	0535
SSIB0140	0087
SSIB0180	0087
SSIB0640	0087
SSIB0680	0087
SSIB0710	OEM
SSIB0720	OEM
SSIB0740	OEM
SSIB0780	OEM
SSIC0810	0242
SSIC0820	0535
SSIC0840	0087
SSIC0860	0916
SSIC0880	0087
SSIC1110	0242
SSIC1140	0959
SSIC1160	0087
SSIC1180	0916
SSIC1210	0242
SSIC1220	0535
SSIC1240	0087
SSIC1260	0916
SSIC1280	0087
SSIC1660A	0916
SSIC1740	0087
SSIC1780	0087
SSIC1960A	0087
SSIC15100A	OEM
SSIC16100A	OEM
SSIC19100A	OEM
SSIC20100A	OEM
SSIE0810	OEM
SSIE0820	OEM
SSIE0840	OEM
SSIE0860	OEM
SSIE2060A	OEM
SSIE2080	OEM
SSIE2702	OEM
SSIE2705	OEM
SSIE2710	OEM
SSIE2715	OEM
SSIE2802	OEM
SSIE2805	OEM
SSIE2810	OEM
SSIE2815	OEM
SSIF0320	OEM
SSIF0340	OEM
SSIF0360	OEM
SSIH0220	OEM
SSIH0240	OEM
SSIH0260	OEM
SSIK0210	OEM
SSIK0220	OEM
SSIK0240	OEM
SSIK0260	OEM
SSIK0270	OEM
SSIK0420	OEM
SSIK0440	OEM
SSIK0460	OEM
SSIK0480	OEM
SSIK2020	OEM
SSIK2040	OEM
SSIK2060	OEM
SSIK2060A	OEM
SSIK2080	OEM
SSIK2080A	OEM
SSIL0520	OEM
SSIL0540	OEM
SSIL0560	OEM
SSIL0570	OEM
SSIL1080	OEM
SSIL1080A	OEM
SSIL1280	OEM
SSIL10100	OEM
SSIL10100A	OEM
SSIL12100	OEM
SSIL12120	OEM
SSIN2060	OEM
SSIN2080	OEM
SSIN2080A	OEM
SSIN2360	OEM
SSIN2380	OEM
SSIN2460	OEM
SSIN2483	OEM
SSIN20100	OEM

DEVICE TYPE	REPL CODE
SSIN20100A	OEM
SSIN20120	OEM
SSIN23100	OEM
SSIN23120	OEM
SSIN24100	OEM
SSIN24120	OEM
SSIN98100	OEM
SSIN98110	OEM
SSIN98120	OEM
SSIN98135	OEM
SSIN98145	OEM
SSIN98155	OEM
SSIP0160	OEM
SSIP0180	OEM
SSIP01100	OEM
SSIP30120	OEM
SSIP30135	OEM
SSIP30150	OEM
SSIR-5	OEM
SSIR-5D	OEM
SSIR-SC	OEM
SSM20	OEM
SSM30	OEM
SSM40	OEM
SSM50A	OEM
SSM60A	OEM
SSM410	OEM
SSM510	OEM
SSM920SSM1020	OEM
SSN74LS243	0900
SSP310	0610
SSP320	0610
SSP330	0610
SSP340	0610
SSP840	0610
SSP1530	0610
SSP1540	0610
SSP2020	0610
SSP2030	0610
SSP2040	0610
SSP2848	0617
SSP2849	0617
SSP2850	0617
SSP2851	0617
SSP2852	0617
SSP3005	1536
SSP3010	1536
SSP3030	1536
SSP3040	1536
SSP3051	OEM
SSRC9-001	OEM
SST610	OEM
ST/217/Q	0016
ST01	0016
ST02	0016
ST03	0016
ST04	0016
ST05	0016
ST06	0016
ST07279	0050
ST07430	0111
ST1	OEM
ST-2	3298
ST2	2137
ST2(GE)	3298
ST2-10	0097
ST2-20	0097
ST2-30	0109
ST2-40	0109
ST2B	4350
ST-2N6558	0638
ST-2SA562Y	0006
ST-2SA673C	0148
ST-2SA715C	0520
ST-2SA733Q	0006
ST-2SA844C	0688
ST-2SA1015Y	0148
ST-2SB568C	1900
ST-2SC287A	0470
ST-2SC288A	1332
ST-2SC383W	0076
ST-2SC454C	0076
ST-2SC458C	0076
ST-2SC460	0151
ST-2SC535	0127
ST-2SC535B	0127
ST-2SC605	0470
ST-2SC606	0470
ST-2SC681AYL	2420
ST-2SC1070	0007
ST-2SC1106	0220
ST-2SC1106A	0220
ST-2SC1213C	0191
ST-2SC1213D	0191
ST-2SC1213D-24	0191
ST-2SC1317Q	0155
ST-2SC1514	1077
ST-2SC1514-05	1077
ST-2SC1730	0127
ST-2SC1815GR	5580
ST-2SC1855	0224
ST-2SC1906	0127
ST-2SC1923-O	2666
ST-2SC2371L	0275
ST-2SC2371M	0275
ST-2SC2735	2891
ST-2SC2756	OEM
ST-2SC2757	OEM
ST-2SD235Y	0228

DEVICE TYPE	REPL CODE
ST-2SD467B	0945
ST-2SD467C	0945
ST-2SD478C	0388
ST-2SD748A	3197
ST-2SD748A-01	3197
ST-2SD748A-01A	3197
ST-2SD781	0558
ST3	OEM
ST3-10	0800
ST3-20	0800
ST3-30	0800
ST3-40	0800
ST3A10N	0267
ST3A10P	0315
ST3A20N	0267
ST3A20P	0315
ST3A30N	0267
ST3A30P	0315
ST3A40N	0267
ST3A40P	0315
ST3A50N	0267
ST3A50P	0315
ST3A60N	0267
ST3A60P	0315
ST3B10N	0267
ST3B10P	0315
ST3B20N	0267
ST3B20P	0315
ST3B30N	0267
ST3B30P	0315
ST3B40N	0267
ST3B40P	0315
ST3B50N	0267
ST3B50P	0315
ST3B60N	0267
ST3B60P	0315
ST-3SK53	0212
ST-3SK60	2439
ST-3SK80	0367
ST-3SK87	0367
ST-4	4335
ST4	4335
ST4-10	1116
ST4-20	1116
ST4-30	0800
ST4-40	0800
ST5	OEM
ST5-	OEM
ST5A10N	1772
ST5A10P	2786
ST5A20N	1772
ST5A20P	2786
ST5A30N	1772
ST5A30P	2786
ST5A40N	1772
ST5A40P	2786
ST5A50N	1772
ST5A50P	2786
ST5A60N	1807
ST5A60P	2818
ST6	OEM
ST9	0144
ST10	0144
ST11	0127
ST12	0144
ST13	0144
ST14	0144
ST15	0144
ST16	0015
ST18	0071
ST20	OEM
ST22-05	OEM
ST22-10	OEM
ST22-20	OEM
ST22-30	OEM
ST22-40	OEM
ST22-60	OEM
ST22-80	OEM
ST22-100	OEM
ST22-120	OEM
ST24C02AB1	OEM
ST25A	0016
ST25B	0016
ST25C	0016
ST28A	0004
ST28B	0004
ST28C	0004
ST29	0144
ST30	0144
ST31	0144
ST32	0144
ST33	0144
ST34	0144
ST35	0144
ST37C	0004
ST37D	0004
ST37E	0004
ST37O	0841
ST39	0036
ST40	0144
ST41	0144
ST42	0144
ST43	0144
ST44	0144
ST45	0144
ST47	0911
ST50	0016
ST51	0016
ST53	0016

DEVICE TYPE	REPL CODE
ST54	0016
ST55	0016
ST56	0016
ST57	0016
ST58	0016
ST59	0016
ST60	0144
ST61	0144
ST62	0144
ST63	0016
ST64	0016
ST66	OEM
ST70	0144
ST71	0144
ST72	0144
ST80	0144
ST82	0144
ST101	0130
ST106	0435
ST107	0435
ST108	0435
ST109	0435
ST110	0435
ST111	0435
ST112	0435
ST122	0004
ST123	0004
ST150	0016
ST151	0016
ST152	0016
ST153	0016
ST154	0016
ST155	0016
ST156	0016
ST157	0016
ST160	0016
ST161	0016
ST162	0016
ST163	0016
ST172	0595
ST175	0016
ST176	0016
ST177	0016
ST178	0016
ST180	0016
ST181	0016
ST182	0016
ST185	OEM
ST186	OEM
ST187	OEM
ST210N	2275
ST210P	2872
ST220N	0471
ST220P	1104
ST230N	0471
ST230P	1104
ST235	0160
ST240N	0471
ST240P	1104
ST250	0016
ST250N	0471
ST250P	1104
ST251	0016
ST260N	0444
ST260P	2982
ST280N	0444
ST280P	2982
ST301	0004
ST302	0004
ST303	0004
ST304	0004
ST310N	0267
ST310P	0315
ST320N	0267
ST320P	0315
ST330N	0267
ST330P	0315
ST332	0004
ST340N	0267
ST340P	0315
ST350N	0267
ST350P	0315
ST360N	0280
ST360P	0045
ST382	0004
ST402	0590
ST403	0016
ST410	OEM
ST410N	1772
ST410P	2786
ST411	OEM
ST414	OEM
ST415	0144
ST420N	1772
ST420P	2786
ST430N	1772
ST430P	2786
ST440N	1772
ST440P	2786
ST450N	1772
ST450P	2786
ST460N	1807
ST460P	2818
ST480N	1807
ST480P	2818
ST501	0016
ST502	0016
ST503	0016
ST504	0016

If replacement code is OEM, contact original manufacturer for replacement.

573

DEVICE TYPE	REPL CODE
ST510	OEM
ST510N	1337
ST510P	0594
ST520N	1894
ST520P	1975
ST530N	1894
ST530P	1975
ST540N	1894
ST540P	1975
ST550N	1894
ST550P	1975
ST560N	1975
ST560P	0193
ST610N	0652
ST610P	1337
ST615	OEM
ST620N	1337
ST620P	1337
ST630N	1337
ST630P	1894
ST640N	1975
ST640P	1975
ST650N	1894
ST650P	1975
ST660N	0193
ST660P	0193
ST710N	0496
ST710P	1017
ST720N	1766
ST720P	1030
ST721	OEM
ST722	0086
ST723	0086
ST730N	1766
ST730P	1030
ST740N	1766
ST740P	1030
ST750N	1766
ST750P	1030
ST760N	1778
ST760P	1040
ST903	0144
ST904	0144
ST904A	0144
ST905	0144
ST910	0144
ST910N	0496
ST910P	1017
ST920N	1766
ST920P	1030
ST930N	1766
ST930P	1030
ST940N	1766
ST940P	1030
ST950N	1766
ST950P	1030
ST960N	1778
ST960P	1040
ST980N	1778
ST980P	1040
ST1010N	1337
ST1010P	0594
ST1020N	1894
ST1020P	1975
ST1026	0144
ST1030N	1894
ST1030P	1975
ST1040N	1894
ST1040P	1975
ST1042	0079
ST1042C	0079
ST1050	0144
ST1050N	1894
ST1050P	1975
ST1051	0144
ST-1060	OEM
ST1060N	0193
ST1060P	0652
ST1110N	1772
ST1110P	2786
ST1120N	1772
ST1120P	1772
ST1130N	1772
ST1130P	2786
ST1140N	1772
ST1140P	2786
ST1150N	1772
ST1150P	2786
ST1160N	1807
ST1160P	2818
ST1180N	1807
ST1180P	2818
ST1242	0016
ST1243	0016
ST1244	0016
ST1290	0016
ST1336	0144
ST1402C	0016
ST1402D	0076
ST1402E	0079
ST1502B	0127
ST1502C	3756
ST1502CD	3756
ST1502D	0127
ST-1502L	0079
ST1502L	0079
ST1504	0590
ST1505	0590
ST1506	0016
ST1523	OEM
ST1524	OEM
ST1525	OEM
ST1527	OEM
ST1528	OEM
ST1543	0079
ST1602D	0037
ST1607	0016
ST1610N	1337
ST1610P	0594
ST1620N	1894
ST1620P	1975
ST1630N	1894
ST1630P	1975
ST1633	OEM
ST1640N	1894
ST1640P	1975
ST1650N	1894
ST1650P	1975
ST1660N	0193
ST1660P	0652
ST1680N	0193
ST1680P	0652
ST1694	0016
ST1700	0079
ST1702L	0079
ST1702M	0079
ST1702N	0284
ST1802M	0527
ST1802N	0527
ST1902D	OEM
ST2040P	0015
ST2110	0144
ST2120	0007
ST2130	0007
ST3030	0198
ST3031	0198
ST3042	2602
ST3043	OEM
ST4044	OEM
ST4045	OEM
ST4080	OEM
ST4081	OEM
ST4150	0086
ST4201	0086
ST4202	0086
ST4203	0086
ST4204	0086
ST4341	0086
ST4402	OEM
ST5060	0016
ST5061	0590
ST5641	0007
ST6008	OEM
ST6010	OEM
ST6110	0016
ST6120	0144
ST6125	0144
ST6130	0079
ST6398B1	OEM
ST6398B1/A	OEM
ST6398B1/B	OEM
ST6497B1	OEM
ST6510	0127
ST6511	0016
ST6512	0016
ST6573	0086
ST6574	0086
ST6593	0016
ST6594	0016
ST6600	0016
ST6601	0086
ST7100	0111
ST8014	0037
ST8033	0037
ST8034	0037
ST8035	0037
ST8036	0037
ST8065	0037
ST8181	0037
ST8182	0037
ST8183	0126
ST8184	0126
ST8190	0037
ST8191	0126
ST8500	0037
ST8509	0037
ST8700	0037
ST8704	0037
ST8705	0037
ST8709	0037
ST9001	OEM
ST9008	OEM
ST9045	OEM
ST9046	OEM
ST9047	OEM
ST10000	2602
ST10001	2602
ST10007	1980
ST10008	2602
ST10009	2602
ST27020	0919
ST29045	1671
ST29046	1671
ST29047	1671
ST47025	0144
ST48119	OEM
ST61000	0786
ST62180	0037
ST72039	0126
ST72040	0126
ST74000	0168
ST78020	OEM
ST83255	0037
ST84000	0168
ST84027	0168
ST84028	0168
ST84029	0168
ST984539-006	3365
STA301A	OEM
STA302A	OEM
STA303	OEM
STA311A	OEM
STA321A	OEM
STA341M	OEM
STA401A	OEM
STA403	OEM
STA403A	3910
STA404A	OEM
STA405A	OEM
STA434A	OEM
STA437A	OEM
STA451C	OEM
STA455C	OEM
STA608XFXXXXI	0006
STA901M	OEM
STA7604	2465
STA8012	OEM
STA8341	0359
STA9364	0074
STAR-IFPH	OEM
STB01-02	0133
STB0101	4333
STB3	OEM
STB4	0755
STB567	OEM
STB568	0133
STB569	0133
STB576	0133
STB598XEXXXXX	3760
ST-BF422	0261
ST-BF459	0275
STBF459	0275
ST-BF960	0367
ST-BU208	0065
STC389	OEM
STC536XFXXUB	0532
STC536XFXXXUB	5239
STC930XEXXXRI	2195
STC1001	OEM
STC1035	0103
STC1035A	0103
STC1036	0103
STC1036A	0103
STC1080	0103
STC1081	0103
STC1082	0103
STC1083	0103
STC1084	0103
STC-1085	0103
STC1085	0074
STC1094	0130
STC1101	OEM
STC1102	OEM
STC1103	OEM
STC1104	OEM
STC1105	OEM
STC1105A	OEM
STC1106	OEM
STC1106A	OEM
STC1300	0042
STC1311	OEM
STC1312	OEM
STC1313	OEM
STC1314	OEM
STC1331	OEM
STC1332	OEM
STC1336	0590
STC1674LXXXXX	1060
STC1725	OEM
STC1727	OEM
STC1729	OEM
STC1730	OEM
STC1732	OEM
STC1734	OEM
STC1735	OEM
STC1737	OEM
STC1739	OEM
STC1750	OEM
STC1751	OEM
STC1777	OEM
STC1800	0555
STC1850	0042
STC1860	0042
STC1862	0555
STC2100	OEM
STC2101	OEM
STC2220	0130
STC2221	0130
STC2224	0130
STC2225	0130
STC2228	0130
STC2229	0130
STC4252	0103
STC4253	0103
STC4254	0103
STC4255	0103
STC-4401	0178
STC4401	0178
STC5080	OEM
STC5081	OEM
STC5082	OEM
STC5083	OEM
STC5084	OEM
STC5085	OEM
STC5109/1	OEM
STC5110/1	OEM
STC5111/1	OEM
STC5112/1	OEM
STC5113/1	OEM
STC5114/1	OEM
STC5202	0919
STC5203	0919
STC5205	0919
STC5206	0919
STC5303	0919
STC5519/1	OEM
STC5520/1	OEM
STC5521/1	OEM
STC5522/1	OEM
STC5523/1	OEM
STC5524/1	OEM
STC5550	OEM
STC5551	OEM
STC5552	OEM
STC5553	OEM
STC5554	OEM
STC5555	OEM
STC5606	OEM
STC5608	OEM
STC5610	0126
STC5611	0126
STC5612	0126
STC5648	OEM
STC5649	OEM
STC5650	OEM
STC5651	OEM
STC5652	OEM
STC5802	0919
STC5803	0919
STC5805	0919
STC5806	0919
STD28	OEM
STD30	OEM
STD33	OEM
STD36	OEM
STD39	OEM
STD43	OEM
STD47	OEM
STD51	OEM
STD56	OEM
STD62	OEM
STD68	OEM
STD75	OEM
STD82	OEM
STD91	OEM
STD100	OEM
STD110	OEM
STD330XEXXXXX	1597
STD545XEXXXXX	0018
STD580	OEM
STD734FXFXXXX	1505
STD9007	0555
STD13301	1841
STD13302	1841
STD13303	1841
STD40304	1955
STE400	0144
STE401	2427
STFCN10	0015
ST-HIT9012H	1359
STHIT9012H	0006
ST-HIT9013H	0079
STHIT9013H	0079
ST-HIT9014C	0079
STHIT9014C	0079
ST-HIT9016G	0224
STI-10	0488
STI10	0168
STI-20	0233
STI20	0168
STI-30	0233
STI30	0168
STI40	0168
STI50	0168
STI-105	0142
STI-205	0142
STI-305	0142
STI401	0223
STI410	0223
STI411	0223
STI413	0223
STI431	0223
STI701	0003
STI1506	0142
STI2006	0142
STI2506	0142
STI3006	0142
STI3007	0142
STIP-10	0886
STIP10	0886
STIP20	0434
ST-JE9014C	4811
STK-0029	OEM
STK0050	6747
STK0050-II	OEM
STK0080	4594
STK0080-II	OEM
STK00502	OEM
STK00802	OEM
STK-011	3506
STK011	3506
STK013	4545
STK-015	2849
STK015	2849
STK016	4595
STK-018	6530
STK020	1179
STK020F	1179
STK031	4605
STK-036	2837
STK040	4596
STK041	4597
STK043	4597
STK050	4609
STK058	4613
STK070	4609
STK-075	2837
STK075	4614
STK077	4599
STK078	4599
STK080	4600
STK-082	4600
STK082	4600
STK083	4601
STK-084	4601
STK084	4601
STK086	4610
STK0100	OEM
STK01002	OEM
STK-154	4479
STK401	4990
STK413	1561
STK415	1561
STK430	4617
STK-433	1561
STK433	1561
STK435	1561
STK-436	OEM
STK436	OEM
STK436TV	OEM
STK-437	1602
STK437	1602
STK439	1602
STK441	4602
STK443	4612
STK457	4603
STK459	4603
STK460	4621
STK461	4604
STK463	4604
STK465	1892
STK465A	1892
STK561	OEM
STK561E	OEM
STK561EA	OEM
STK-561F	1525
STK561F	2532
STK561FA	OEM
STK563A	1562
STK-563F	1562
STK563F	1562
STK583F	2718
STK-583FST	OEM
STK583FST	1562
STK-711	OEM
STK711	OEM
STK720A	OEM
STK720B	OEM
STK720C	OEM
STK730-010	OEM
STK740B	OEM
STK740C	OEM
STK743B	OEM
STK752	OEM
STK756	OEM
STK-756A	OEM
STK760	OEM
STK770	OEM
STK772B	OEM
STK-780	OEM
STK780	OEM
STK795	OEM
STK1050	4088
STK1050A	4088
STK2230	5185
STK2250	OEM
STK3042	1428
STK3042II	OEM
STK3042III	1428
STK3042MK2	OEM
STK3062	OEM
STK3062III	6265
STK3082	4612
STK3082II	4612
STK3102II	1400
STK3102III	1400
STK3122III	6263
STK3152III	6261
STK3633	OEM
STK4021	1114
STK4021M	1114
STK4024II	2490
STK4024V	OEM
STK4026II	OEM
STK4026V	OEM
STK4028II	OEM
STK4028V	OEM
STK4030	OEM
STK4030-2	OEM
STK4030II	OEM
STK4030V	OEM
STK4032II	OEM
STK4032V	OEM
STK4034II	OEM
STK4034V	OEM
STK4036-II	OEM
STK4036II	OEM
STK4036V	OEM
STK4038II	OEM
STK4038V	OEM
STK4040-V	OEM
STK4040II	OEM
STK4040V	OEM
STK4042II	OEM
STK4042V	OEM
STK4044-V	OEM
STK4044II	3571
STK4044V	4080
STK4046II	OEM
STK4046V	OEM
STK4046XI	OEM
STK4048-V	OEM
STK4048II	OEM
STK4048V	OEM
STK4050V	OEM
STK4112II	OEM
STK4121-II	OEM
STK4121II	5184
STK4131-II	OEM
STK4132	OEM
STK4132-II	OEM
STK4141-II	OEM
STK4141II	5645
STK4142-II	OEM
STK4142II	5645
STK4151	OEM
STK4151-II	OEM
STK4152	OEM
STK4152-2M	OEM
STK4152II	5176
STK4171-2S	OEM
STK4171II	5942
STK4181	OEM
STK4182II	3001
STK4192-II	OEM
STK4192II	5183
STK4211-5P	OEM
STK4231-5	OEM
STK4231II	OEM
STK4231M-1	OEM
STK4231MK2	OEM
STK4273	1430
STK4311	1474
STK4332	OEM
STK4362	1561
STK4362TV	OEM
STK4372	OEM
STK4392	1602
STK5314	OEM
STK5321SL	OEM
STK5322	2281
STK5322H	OEM
STK5327SL	OEM
STK5332	2287
STK5333	OEM
STK5342	OEM
STK5346	OEM
STK5352	OEM
STK5364	OEM
STK5372	2318
STK5422	OEM
STK5431	2358
STK5431SL	2358
STK5431ST	2358
STK5436	OEM
STK5443	OEM
STK5451	2369
STK5461ST	OEM
STK5464	OEM
STK5464ST	OEM
STK5466	OEM
STK5466ST	5705
STK5468	OEM
STK5468S	OEM
STK5471	2389
STK5476	2397
STK5478	OEM
STK5479	2401
STK5481	2402
STK5482	2403
STK5483	OEM
STK5487	OEM
STK5490	2410
STK5633F	OEM
STK5883F	OEM
STK-6011	OEM
STK-6021	OEM
STK6722H	2738
STK6722HZ	OEM
STK6922	OEM
STK6940	3306
STK6941	3307
STK6942	3307
STK6950	OEM
STK6951	OEM
STK6952	OEM
STK6960	3313
STK6960H	OEM
STK6961	3313
STK6961H	OEM
STK6962	3314
STK6962H	3314
STK6965	OEM
STK6965H	OEM
STK6966	OEM
STK6966H	OEM
STK6967	OEM
STK6967H	OEM
STK6968	OEM
STK6970	3319
STK6970H	OEM
STK6971	3319
STK6971H	OEM
STK6972	3321
STK6972H	OEM
STK6981B	3327
STK6982	3327
STK6982B	3327
STK7216	OEM
STK7216S	OEM
STK7217	OEM
STK7231	OEM
STK7308	3448
STK7309	3448
STK7310	OEM
STK7348	OEM
STK7356	OEM
STK7358	OEM
STK7360	OEM
STK7402	OEM
STK7402-105	OEM
STK7404	OEM
STK7406	OEM
STK7408	OEM
STK7410	OEM
STK7451	OEM
STK7452	OEM
STK7453	OEM
STK7457	OEM
STK7458	OEM
STK7459	OEM
STK7462	OEM
STK7468	OEM
STK7554	OEM
STK7563F	1586
STK7563FE	1586
STK7563GII	OEM
STK40362	OEM
STK40405	OEM
STK40442M	OEM
STK40445	OEM
STK41212	OEM
STK41312	OEM
STK66083P	OEM
STK73012	OEM
STK73405II	OEM
STK73408II	OEM
STK73409II	OEM
STK73410II	OEM
STK73605I	OEM
STK73606I	OEM
STL6961	3313
ST-LM1274	OEM
ST-LM2152	0079
ST-LM2682	0079
STM101	0190
STM-204	OEM
STM204	OEM
STM-204-1	OEM
STM204-1	OEM
STM204-8088	OEM
STM206Z86C27	OEM
STM208	OEM
STM401	2777
STM2047C432N-8097	OEM
STM20247C432-8086	OEM
STM20247C432-8097	OEM
STM-20247C432AN-8098	OEM
STM20247C432AN-8098	OEM
STM20247C432N-8086	OEM
STM20247C432N8086	OEM
STM20247C432N-8097	OEM
STM20247C432N8097	OEM
ST-MJE9742	0275
ST-MPS9410AJ	0086
ST-MPS9410AK	0086
ST-MPS9418AS	0320
ST-MPS9418AT	0320
ST-MPS9433	0079
ST-MPS9433S	0079
ST-MPS9433T	0079
ST-MPS9632J	0079
ST-MPS9633C	0079
ST-MPS9682J	0037
ST-MPS9700D	0079
ST-MPS9700E	0079
ST-MPS9700F	0079
ST-MPS9700G	0079
ST-MPS9750D	0037
ST-MPS9750F	0037
ST-MPS9750G	0037

If replacement code is OEM, contact original manufacturer for replacement.

DEVICE TYPE	REPL CODE
ST-MPSH10	0224
ST-MPSH24	0144
STPT260	3508
STR101(ELCOM)	2367
STR103(ELCOM)	2367
STR106(ELCOM)	0154
STR117	3119
STR117(ELCOM)	0154
STR125	3119
STR201(ELCOM)	2378
STR202(ELCOM)	2378
STR203(ELCOM)	2378
STR206(ELCOM)	0154
STR217	3121
STR217(ELCOM)	0154
STR225	3121
STR225(ELCOM)	0154
STR230(ELCOM)	0154
STR-300	OEM
STR370	OEM
STR371	OEM
STR-380	3461
STR380	3461
STR-381	3462
STR381	3462
STR381A	3462
STR382	3476
STR383	2092
STR-384A	OEM
STR384A	OEM
STR385	3476
STR403(ELCOM)	1403
STR406(ELCOM)	0147
STR411(ELCOM)	0954
STR417	3123
STR417(ELCOM)	0147
STR418(ELCOM)	0571
STR425	3123
STR425(ELCOM)	3123
STR430(ELCOM)	0147
STR729	5674
STR2005	OEM
STR2012	1159
STR2012A	1159
STR2013	4795
STR2015	OEM
STR2024	OEM
STR-2124	OEM
STR2124	OEM
STR3030	OEM
STR3035	3410
STR3105	OEM
STR3110	OEM
STR3115	4083
STR3118	OEM
STR3123	4569
STR-3125	4569
STR3125	4569
STR3127	OEM
STR3130	1631
STR3135	3410
STR-3220	OEM
STR3220	OEM
STR3225	3278
STR-3230	OEM
STR3230	1631
STR3335	OEM
STR4142	OEM
STR5100	4782
STR-5241	OEM
STR5314	OEM
STR6431L959	OEM
STR9005	OEM
STR9012	OEM
STR9015	OEM
STR10130	OEM
STR11006	OEM
STR12006	OEM
STR13006	OEM
STR20005	OEM
STR20012	OEM
STR30110	OEM
STR30112	OEM
STR30113	OEM
STR30115	3894
STR-30120	2092
STR30120	3896
STR-30123	3897
STR30123	3897
STR30125	3900
STR30130	2348
STR30130-A	2348
STR30130A	2348
STR30134	3902
STR30135	3857
STR30135F	3857
STR50041	3310
STR50041A	3310
STR50092	OEM
STR-50092K	OEM
STR50092K	OEM
STR51041	2273
STR52100	OEM
STR52100A	OEM
STR53041	3530
STR53043	3273
STR53043A	3273
STR54041	5163
STR57051	OEM

DEVICE TYPE	REPL CODE
STR60001	OEM
STR60001F51	OEM
STR90050	OEM
STR90090	OEM
STR90120	OEM
STR90150	OEM
STR-D1005	OEM
STR-D1005T	OEM
STRD1005T	OEM
STR-D1206	OEM
STR-D3030	OEM
STRD3030	OEM
STR-D3035	OEM
STRD3035	OEM
STRD6602	OEM
STRM6513	OEM
STR-S5041	OEM
STRS5041	OEM
STR-S5041G	OEM
STR-S5041T	OEM
STRS5041T	OEM
STRS5041T951	OEM
STR-S5141G	OEM
STRS5141G	OEM
STR-S5241	OEM
STRS5241	OEM
STR-S6301	5500
STRS6301	6277
STRS6301-LF953	5500
STR-S6301A	OEM
STRS-6301A	OEM
STRS6301A	OEM
STR-S6302	OEM
STR-S6309	OEM
STRS6309S	OEM
STRS6421	OEM
STRS6431L959	OEM
STS104	0538
STS105	0538
STS106	0538
STS107	0538
STS401	0359
STS402	0359
STS403	0359
STS409	0359
STS410	0270
STS-411	0074
STS411	0270
STS413	0359
STS423	0223
STS424	0223
STS425	0223
STS430	1955
STS431	1955
STS1121	0074
STS1131	0074
STS1132	0074
STT2300	0130
STT2405	0830
STT2406	0830
STT3500	0130
STT4451	0555
STT4483	0830
STT9001	0830
STT9002	0830
STT9004	0830
STT9005	0830
STV-2H	OEM
STV-3	0015
STV-3H	0120
STV3H	OEM
STV-4H	OEM
STX0010	0178
STX0011	0126
STX0013	0161
STX0014	0103
STX0015	0142
STX0016	0178
STX0020	0455
STX0026	0161
STX0027	0103
STX0028	0233
STX0029	0919
STX0030	0919
STX0032	0103
STX0033	0136
STX0034	0136
STX0036	0050
STX0085	0050
STX0087	0050
STX0089	0050
STX0090	0050
STX0096	0004
STX0099	0004
STX0104	0004
STX0105	0004
STX0110	0004
STX0114	0004
STX0121	0164
STX0123	0004
STX0224	0164
STX0260	0004
STX0263	0004
STX0264	0004
STX0265	0004
STX0268	0004
STX0269	0004
STX5/3010	OEM
STX5/3025	OEM

DEVICE TYPE	REPL CODE
STX5/5010	OEM
STX5/5025	OEM
STX5/6010	OEM
STX5/6025	OEM
STX5/7010	OEM
STX5/7025	OEM
SU012	OEM
SU26HZ	OEM
SU44	1167
SU101A	OEM
SU101K	OEM
SU110	2123
SU112	1882
SU201A	OEM
SU201K	OEM
SU212	OEM
SU300	OEM
SU305	OEM
SU306	OEM
SU312	OEM
SU314	OEM
SU315	OEM
SU316	OEM
SU320	OEM
SU331	OEM
SU332	OEM
SU401A	OEM
SU401K	OEM
SU412	OEM
SU512	OEM
SU601A	OEM
SU601K	OEM
SU801A	OEM
SU801K	OEM
SU1001A	OEM
SU1001K	OEM
SU2000	OEM
SU2002	OEM
SU2004	OEM
SU2006	OEM
SU2008	OEM
SU2010	OEM
SU2020	OEM
SU2021	OEM
SU2022	OEM
SU2023	OEM
SU2024	OEM
SU2025	OEM
SU2026	OEM
SU2027	OEM
SU2028	OEM
SU2029	OEM
SU2032	OEM
SU2034	OEM
SU2037	OEM
SU2074	OEM
SU2075	OEM
SU2076	0321
SU2077	0321
SU2080	0321
SU2081	0321
SUC650	0631
SUES501	OEM
SUES502	OEM
SUES503	OEM
SUES504	OEM
SUES505	OEM
SUES601	OEM
SUES602	OEM
SUES603	OEM
SUES604	OEM
SUES605	OEM
SUES606	OEM
SUES607	OEM
SUES608	OEM
SUES609	OEM
SUES610	OEM
SUES611	OEM
SUES701	OEM
SUES702	OEM
SUES703	OEM
SUES704	OEM
SUES705	OEM
SUES706	OEM
SUES707	OEM
SUES708	OEM
SUES709	OEM
SUES710	OEM
SUES711	OEM
SUES801	OEM
SUES802	OEM
SUES803	OEM
SUES804	OEM
SUES805	OEM
SUES806	OEM
SUES807	OEM
SUES808	OEM
SUES809	OEM
SUES810	OEM
SUES811	OEM
SUES1101	0541
SUES1102	0541
SUES1103	0541
SUES1104	1082
SUES1105	1352
SUES1106	1352
SUES1107	OEM
SUES1108	OEM
SUES1109	OEM

DEVICE TYPE	REPL CODE
SUES1110	OEM
SUES1111	OEM
SUES1301	OEM
SUES1302	OEM
SUES1303	OEM
SUES1304	0541
SUES1305	1352
SUES1306	1352
SUES1307	OEM
SUES1308	OEM
SUES1309	OEM
SUES1310	OEM
SUES1311	OEM
SUES2601	OEM
SUES2602	OEM
SUES2603	OEM
SUES2604	OEM
SUES2605	OEM
SUES2606	OEM
SUES2607	OEM
SUES2608	OEM
SUES2609	OEM
SUES2610	OEM
SUES2611	OEM
SUM6010	0631
SUM6011	0631
SUM6020	0631
SUM6021	0631
SUR3005CT	2219
SUR3005CTE	OEM
SUR3005CTR	OEM
SUR3005SD	OEM
SUR3010CT	2219
SUR3010CTE	OEM
SUR3010CTR	OEM
SUR3010SD	OEM
SUR3015CT	2219
SUR3015CTE	OEM
SUR3015CTR	OEM
SUR3015SD	OEM
SUR3020CT	2219
SUR3020CTE	OEM
SUR3020CTR	OEM
SUR3020SD	OEM
SUR3030CT	OEM
SUR3030CTE	OEM
SUR3030CTR	OEM
SUR3040CT	4409
SUR3040CTE	OEM
SUR3040CTR	OEM
SUR3040SD	OEM
SUR3050CT	OEM
SUR3050CTE	OEM
SUR3050CTR	OEM
SUR3060CT	4409
SUR3060CTE	OEM
SUR3060CTR	OEM
SUR3060SD	OEM
SUR3070CT	OEM
SUR3070CTE	OEM
SUR3070CTR	OEM
SUR3080CT	OEM
SUR3080SD	OEM
SUR3100CT	OEM
SUR3100SD	OEM
SUT-101A	0315
SUT-101K	0267
SUT-201A	0315
SUT-201K	0267
SUT-401A	0315
SUT-401K	0267
SUT-601A	0315
SUT-601K	0267
SUT-801A	0045
SUT-801K	0280
SUT-1001A	0045
SUT-1001K	0280
SV-01A	0015
SV01A	0015
SV-01B	0015
SV-02	0120
SV02	0015
SV02A	0015
SV-02Y	0120
SV02YS	OEM
SV-03	0120
SV03	0120
SV-03S	0120
SV-03Y	3407
SV03YS	3639
SV-04	0120
SV-04S	3407
SV-04Y	3407
SV04YS	3407
SV-05	0015
SV05	0015
SV-05Y	OEM
SV05YS	OEM
SV-06	OEM
SV-06Y	OEM
SV06YS	OEM
SV-07	OEM
SV-08	OEM
SV-1	0080
SV1	OEM
SV-1R	0015
SV-2	0604
SV2	OEM
SV2SS	OEM

DEVICE TYPE	REPL CODE
SV-3	0790
SV3	OEM
SV-3A	0120
SV3SS	OEM
SV-4R	0015
SV4SS	OEM
SV-6R	0015
SV-7	0644
SV-8R	0071
SV-9	0012
SV14B	0124
SV14C	0124
SV24A	OEM
SV24B	OEM
SV30	0143
SV-31	0143
SV31	0164
SV-31(DIODE)	0143
SV36C	OEM
SV55A	OEM
SV55B	OEM
SV55C	OEM
SV55C-6	OEM
SV55D	OEM
SV56A	OEM
SV56B	OEM
SV56C	OEM
SV56D	OEM
SV66B	OEM
SV66B-8	OEM
SV66C	OEM
SV66D	OEM
SV67C	OEM
SV67D	OEM
SV70-14	OEM
SV77D	OEM
SV77E	OEM
SV77F	OEM
SV77G	OEM
SV77H	OEM
SV87A	OEM
SV87A(1)	OEM
SV87B	OEM
SV87B(1)	OEM
SV87C	OEM
SV87D	OEM
SV88A	OEM
SV88B	OEM
SV88C	OEM
SV88D	OEM
SV89D	OEM
SV89E	OEM
SV110	OEM
SV111	OEM
SV112	OEM
SV113	OEM
SV114	OEM
SV121	0162
SV122	0162
SV123	0157
SV135	0137
SV138	0002
SV146E	OEM
SV220	OEM
SV230	OEM
SV240	OEM
SV513C	OEM
SV513D	OEM
SV513E	OEM
SV514B	OEM
SV514C	OEM
SV514D	OEM
SV514E	OEM
SV533C	OEM
SV533D	OEM
SV533E	OEM
SV534E	OEM
SV543C	OEM
SV543D	OEM
SV543E	OEM
SV544C	OEM
SV544D	OEM
SV544E	OEM
SV566D-2	OEM
SV566D-4	OEM
SV794AN	OEM
SV800	OEM
SV826AN	OEM
SV910	0989
SV1000	OEM
SV1004	OEM
SV1005	OEM
SV1006	OEM
SV1007	OEM
SV1008	OEM
SV1009	OEM
SV1010	OEM
SV1011	OEM
SV1012	OEM
SV1013	OEM
SV1014	OEM
SV1015	OEM
SV1016	OEM
SV1017	0137
SV1018	OEM
SV1019	0100
SV1020	0002
SV1021	OEM
SV1022	OEM

DEVICE TYPE	REPL CODE
SV1023	OEM
SV1024	OEM
SV1025	OEM
SV1033	OEM
SV1034	OEM
SV1035	OEM
SV2002	1017
SV2004	1017
SV2006	1030
SV2008	1040
SV2010	1040
SV2052	0070
SV2058	1626
SV3140	OEM
SV3141	OEM
SV3142	OEM
SV3143	OEM
SV3144	0755
SV3145	OEM
SV3170	OEM
SV3171	OEM
SV3173	OEM
SV3174	OEM
SV3175	OEM
SV3176	OEM
SV3206	OEM
SV3207	OEM
SV4010	OEM
SV4010A	OEM
SV4011	OEM
SV4011A	OEM
SV4012	0137
SV4012A	0137
SV4013	OEM
SV4013A	OEM
SV4014	0100
SV4014A	0100
SV4015	0002
SV4015A	0002
SV4016	OEM
SV4016A	OEM
SV4017	OEM
SV4017A	OEM
SV4018	0371
SV4018A	0371
SV4019	OEM
SV4019A	OEM
SV4020	OEM
SV4020A	OEM
SV4021	OEM
SV4021A	OEM
SV4022	OEM
SV4022A	OEM
SV4023	OEM
SV4023A	OEM
SV4024	OEM
SV4024A	OEM
SV4025	OEM
SV4025A	OEM
SV4026	OEM
SV4026A	OEM
SV4027	0436
SV4027A	0436
SV4028	OEM
SV4028A	OEM
SV4029	OEM
SV4029A	OEM
SV4030	OEM
SV4030A	OEM
SV4031	OEM
SV4031A	OEM
SV4032	OEM
SV4032A	OEM
SV4033	0039
SV4033A	0039
SV4034	OEM
SV4034A	OEM
SV4035	OEM
SV4035A	OEM
SV4036	OEM
SV4036A	OEM
SV4037	OEM
SV4037A	OEM
SV4038	OEM
SV4038A	OEM
SV4039	OEM
SV4039A	OEM
SV4040	OEM
SV4040A	OEM
SV4041	OEM
SV4041A	OEM
SV4042	OEM
SV4042A	OEM
SV4043	OEM
SV4043A	OEM
SV4044	OEM
SV4044A	OEM
SV4045	OEM
SV4045A	OEM
SV4046	OEM
SV4046A	OEM
SV4047	OEM
SV4047A	OEM
SV4048	OEM
SV4048A	OEM
SV4049	OEM
SV4049A	OEM
SV4050	OEM
SV4050A	OEM

DEVICE TYPE	REPL CODE
SV4051	OEM
SV4051A	OEM
SV4052	OEM
SV4052A	OEM
SV4053	OEM
SV4053A	OEM
SV4054A	OEM
SV4055	1823
SV4055A	1823
SV4056	OEM
SV4056A	OEM
SV4057	OEM
SV4057A	OEM
SV4058	OEM
SV4058A	OEM
SV4059	OEM
SV4059A	OEM
SV4060	OEM
SV4060A	OEM
SV4061	OEM
SV4061A	OEM
SV4062	0778
SV4062A	0778
SV4063	OEM
SV4063A	OEM
SV4064	OEM
SV4064A	OEM
SV4065	OEM
SV4065A	OEM
SV4066	OEM
SV4066A	OEM
SV4067	OEM
SV4067A	OEM
SV4068	OEM
SV4068A	OEM
SV4069	OEM
SV4069A	OEM
SV4070	OEM
SV4070A	OEM
SV4071	OEM
SV4071A	OEM
SV4072	OEM
SV4072A	OEM
SV4073	OEM
SV4073A	OEM
SV4074	OEM
SV4074A	OEM
SV4075	OEM
SV4075A	OEM
SV4076	OEM
SV4076A	OEM
SV4077	OEM
SV4077A	OEM
SV4078	OEM
SV4078A	OEM
SV4079	OEM
SV4079A	OEM
SV4080	OEM
SV4080A	OEM
SV4081	OEM
SV4081A	OEM
SV4082	0327
SV4082A	0327
SV4083	OEM
SV4083A	OEM
SV4084	OEM
SV4084A	OEM
SV4085	OEM
SV4085A	OEM
SV4086	OEM
SV4086A	OEM
SV4087	OEM
SV4087A	OEM
SV4088	OEM
SV4088A	OEM
SV4089	OEM
SV4089A	OEM
SV4090	OEM
SV4090A	OEM
SV4091	OEM
SV4091A	OEM
SV4092	OEM
SV4092A	OEM
SV4093	OEM
SV4093A	OEM
SV4094	OEM
SV4094A	OEM
SV4095	OEM
SV4095A	OEM
SV4096	OEM
SV4096A	OEM
SV4097	OEM
SV4097A	OEM
SV4098	OEM
SV4098A	OEM
SV4099	OEM
SV4099A	OEM
SV4100	OEM
SV4100A	OEM
SV5054	OEM
SV7031AN	OEM
SV7031BN	OEM
SV7031CN	OEM
SV7032AN	OEM
SV7032CN	OEM
SV7033AN	OEM
SV7034CN	OEM
SV7302AN	OEM
SV7307AN	OEM

If replacement code is OEM, contact original manufacturer for replacement.

575

DEVICE TYPE	REPL CODE
SV9785	OEM
SV9786	OEM
SV10052	OEM
SV12388	0015
SV12388E	0015
SVB10-100	0276
SVB10-200	0287
SVB15-100	0276
SVB15-200	0287
SV-BZX79C10V	0064
SVC0053	0030
SVC101	0030
SVC112	1023
SVC151	OEM
SVC-201	0030
SVC201	0030
SVC201SP	OEM
SVC201SP-BJ	OEM
SVC201Y	0623
SVC201Y-AG	OEM
SVC201Y-BW	OEM
SVC202	OEM
SVC202AF	OEM
SVC203	OEM
SVC211	1023
SVC211SP	OEM
SVC211SP-B	OEM
SVC211SP-B2	OEM
SVC211SP-C	OEM
SVC212	OEM
SVC-241	OEM
SVC251	0030
SVC251SP	OEM
SVC251Y	OEM
SVC303Y	3643
SVC311	3643
SVC321	3643
SVC321-C2	3643
SVC321C	OEM
SVC321C2	OEM
SVC321D2	OEM
SVC321SP	OEM
SVC321SP-C2	OEM
SVC321Y	3643
SVC333	OEM
SVC625	0631
SVD02Z8	0244
SVD02Z8.2	0244
SVD02Z8.2A	0244
SVD02Z9.5A	0012
SVD0278.2A	0244
SVD0279.5A	0012
SVD0A70	0143
SVD0A79	0143
SVD0A90	0019
SVD1S1717	1075
SVD1S1850	0023
SVD-1S1850R	0015
SVD1S1850R	0023
SVD1S2076AT	OEM
SVD1SR35200A	OEM
SVD10D-1	0015
SVD12B2B1P-M	0276
SVD20A70	0143
SVD20A79	0143
SVDAS2HB10	0087
SVDGP1S53	OEM
SVDMA26	0139
SVDMA26-1	0139
SVDMA26-2	0139
SVD0A70	0143
SVD0A90	0143
SVDS1RB10	0276
SVDS-1S1850	0015
SVDS3V20	OEM
SVDS3V40	OEM
SVDS5688GT3	OEM
SVDSC20	3613
SVDV1121	OEM
SVDVD1121	0139
SVDVD1223	0120
SVI3102B	OEM
SVI3105A	OEM
SVI3105B	OEM
SVI3203	OEM
SVI3204	OEM
SVI3205	OEM
SVI3206	OEM
SVIBA4558F	OEM
SVIBA4560F	OEM
SVIBA6218	OEM
SVICXK5816M	OEM
SVIH8DN2041	OEM
SVIH8DN2175	OEM
SVIK4152-2M	OEM
SVILC6526CPA	OEM
SVI-LD3120	2487
SVILM833M	OEM
SVINJM4560M	OEM
SVIPCM55HP	OEM
SVI-STK018	3880
SVISTK020F	1179
SVIUPC1161C3	OEM
SV-KB262	0120
SVM61	0631
SVM601	0631
SVM602	0631
SVM605	0631
SVM6010	0466

DEVICE TYPE	REPL CODE
SVM7962CBR	OEM
SVR12A	OEM
SVR12B	OEM
SVR12C	OEM
SVR19A	OEM
SVR19B	OEM
SVR34B	OEM
SVT400-3	0074
SVT450-5	OEM
SVT6000	2602
SVT6001	2602
SVT6002	2602
SVT6060	2602
SVT6061	2602
SVT6062	2602
SVT6251	1980
SVT6252	2602
SVT6253	2602
SVT6546	OEM
SVT6547	OEM
SVT7574	1841
SVVD1220XXXXX	0120
SVVD1221LXXXX	0120
SW01	0137
SW-05	0110
SW05	0015
SW-05-005	0015
SW05-005	0015
SW-05-01	0015
SW05-01	0015
SW-05-02	0015
SW05-02	0015
SW-05-A	0015
SW-05-B	0015
SW-05-C	0071
SW-05-D	0071
SW05A	0015
SW05B	0015
SW05C	0071
SW05D	0071
SW05S	0015
SW05SS	1345
SW05V	0015
SW0501	0015
SW1	0087
SW-1-01	0087
SW-1-02	0087
SW-1-03	0015
SW-1-04	0015
SW-1-06	0015
SW-1-08	0071
SW-1-10	0071
SW-1A	0015
SW1A	OEM
SW1B	OEM
SW1C	0071
SW1D	0071
SW1S	OEM
SW1SS	OEM
SW-5-005	0015
SW10	OEM
SW11	OEM
SW30	OEM
SW74LS247	1721
SW705-2M	0354
SW705-2P	0354
SW706-2M	0329
SW706-2P	0329
SW708-2M	1622
SW708-2P	1622
SW709-2M	1472
SW709-2P	1472
SW930-2M	1812
SW930-2P	1812
SW932-2M	1035
SW932-2P	1035
SW933-2M	2086
SW933-2P	2086
SW935-2M	1168
SW935-2P	1168
SW936-2M	1820
SW936-2P	1820
SW937-2M	1824
SW937-2P	1824
SW941-2M	2598
SW941-2P	2598
SW944-2M	0033
SW944-2P	0033
SW945-2M	0081
SW945-2P	0081
SW946-2M	0141
SW946-2P	0141
SW948-2M	3365
SW948-2P	3365
SW949-2M	1833
SW949-2P	1833
SW950-2M	2595
SW950-2P	2595
SW951-2M	2067
SW951-2P	2067
SW957-2M	1424
SW957-2P	1424
SW958-2M	0461
SW958-2P	0461
SW961-2M	1848
SW961-2P	1848
SW962-2P	0557
SW963-2M	0337
SW963-2P	0337

DEVICE TYPE	REPL CODE
SW4001	0473
SW4002	2044
SW4011	0215
SW4012	0493
SW4013	0409
SW4015	1008
SW4016	1135
SW4017	0508
SW4019	1517
SW4020	1651
SW4021	1738
SW4023	0515
SW4024	1946
SW4025	2061
SW4027	1938
SW4030	0495
SW4049	0001
SW4050	0394
SW-10548	1824
SW-10549	0461
SWC	0071
SWD	0071
SWH-08	OEM
SWH08	OEM
SWH2-16	OEM
SWH2-20	OEM
SWH2-25ED	OEM
SWH-10	OEM
SWHD-08	OEM
SWHD2-16	OEM
SWHD2-20	OEM
SWHD2-25	OEM
SWHD3-16	OEM
SWHD3-20	OEM
SWHD-10	OEM
SWHD-16	OEM
SWHD-20	OEM
SW0.5A	0015
SWT622	2497
SWT1032	0037
SWT1042	0079
SWT1728	0136
SWT2188	0050
SWT3588	0050
SX-1.5-01	0947
SX-1.5-02	0242
SX-1.5-04	0535
SX-1.5-06	0959
SX-1.5-08	0811
SX-1.5-10	0916
SX6.8	0205
SX9.1	0679
SX10	0225
SX11	0230
SX12	0234
SX13	0237
SX15	0247
SX16	0251
SX18	0256
SX20	0262
SX22	0269
SX24	0273
SX27	0291
SX30	0305
SX33	0314
SX36	0316
SX39	0322
SX40	OEM
SX43	0333
SX47	0343
SX50	OEM
SX51	0027
SX55	0079
SX56	0266
SX-58Y	0321
SX60	OEM
SX60M	0233
SX61	0126
SX61M	0037
SX62	0382
SX64-KERN	OEM
SX68	0401
SX75	0421
SX80	OEM
SX82	0439
SX91	0238
SX100	1172
SX110	1182
SX120	1198
SX623	0015
SX631	0015
SX633	0015
SX641	0604
SX642	1345
SX643	0604
SX644	3855
SX645	3855
SX751	0090
SX752	0097
SX753	0109
SX754	0109
SX780	0124
SX781	OEM
SX782	OEM
SX3001	0144
SX3702	0037
SX3709	0079
SX3711	0079
SX3819	0321

DEVICE TYPE	REPL CODE
SX3825	0144
SX3826	0224
SX3827	0144
SY20	1707
SY22	1712
SY-23	0015
SY23	0790
SY-24	0015
SY24	0790
SY27	1750
SY30	1761
SY101	0595
SY432D	OEM
SY2114AL-3	OEM
SY2128	1887
SY4320	OEM
SY6502	3036
SY6530	OEM
SY6991	OEM
SY6992	OEM
SY23128	OEM
SY68045	OEM
SYC68B20	OEM
SYC68B21	OEM
SYC1791-02	OEM
SYC1793-02	OEM
SYC2101-1	OEM
SYC2101A	OEM
SYC2101A-2	OEM
SYC2101A-4	OEM
SYC2114	2037
SYC2114-3	2037
SYC2147	1683
SYC2147-3	1683
SYC2147-6	1683
SYC2147H	OEM
SYC2147H-1	OEM
SYC2147H-2	OEM
SYC2147H-3	OEM
SYC2147HL	OEM
SYC2147HL-3	OEM
SYC2147L	1683
SYC2148H	OEM
SYC2148H-2	OEM
SYC2148H-3	OEM
SYC2148HL	OEM
SYC2148HL-3	OEM
SYC2149H	OEM
SYC2149H-2	OEM
SYC2149H-3	OEM
SYC2149HL	OEM
SYC2149HL-3	OEM
SYC2332-3	OEM
SYC2333-3	OEM
SYC2661-1	OEM
SYC2661-2	OEM
SYC2661-3	OEM
SYC3308	OEM
SYC3316	OEM
SYC3316A	OEM
SYC6502	3036
SYC6502A	OEM
SYC6502B	OEM
SYC6502C	OEM
SYC6503	OEM
SYC6503A	OEM
SYC6503B	OEM
SYC6503C	OEM
SYC6504	OEM
SYC6504A	OEM
SYC6504B	OEM
SYC6504C	OEM
SYC6505	OEM
SYC6505A	OEM
SYC6505B	OEM
SYC6505C	OEM
SYC6506	OEM
SYC6506A	OEM
SYC6506B	OEM
SYC6506C	OEM
SYC6507	3041
SYC6507A	OEM
SYC6507B	OEM
SYC6507C	OEM
SYC6512	OEM
SYC6512A	OEM
SYC6512B	OEM
SYC6512C	OEM
SYC6513	OEM
SYC6513A	OEM
SYC6513B	OEM
SYC6513C	OEM
SYC6514	OEM
SYC6514A	OEM
SYC6514B	OEM
SYC6514C	OEM
SYC6515	OEM
SYC6515A	OEM
SYC6515B	OEM
SYC6515C	OEM
SYC6520	OEM
SYC6520A	OEM
SYC6521	OEM
SYC6521A	OEM
SYC6522	OEM
SYC6522A	OEM
SYC6532	1962
SYC6532A	OEM
SYC6545	OEM

DEVICE TYPE	REPL CODE
SYC6545-1	OEM
SYC6545A	OEM
SYC6545A-1	OEM
SYC6551	OEM
SYC6551A	OEM
SYC6591	OEM
SYC6591A	OEM
SYC6820	OEM
SYC6821	OEM
SYD68B20	OEM
SYD68B21	OEM
SYD1791-02	OEM
SYD1793-02	OEM
SYD2111-1	OEM
SYD2111A	OEM
SYD2112-1	OEM
SYD2112A	OEM
SYD2112A-2	OEM
SYD2112A-4	OEM
SYD2114	2037
SYD2114-1	OEM
SYD2114-2	2037
SYD2114-3	2037
SYD2114L	2037
SYD2114L-1	OEM
SYD2114L-2	2037
SYD2114L-3	2037
SYD2114LV	OEM
SYD2114LV-2	OEM
SYD2114LV-3	OEM
SYD2142	OEM
SYD2142-2	OEM
SYD2142-3	OEM
SYD2142L	OEM
SYD2142L-2	OEM
SYD2142L-3	OEM
SYD2147	1683
SYD2147-3	1683
SYD2147-6	1683
SYD2147H	OEM
SYD2147H-1	OEM
SYD2147H-2	OEM
SYD2147H-3	OEM
SYD2147HL	OEM
SYD2147HL-3	OEM
SYD2147L	1683
SYD2148H	OEM
SYD2148H-2	OEM
SYD2148H-3	OEM
SYD2148HL	OEM
SYD2148HL-3	OEM
SYD2149H	OEM
SYD2149H-2	OEM
SYD2149H-3	OEM
SYD2149HL	OEM
SYD2149HL-3	OEM
SYD2164	OEM
SYD2164-2	OEM
SYD2164-3	OEM
SYD2164A	OEM
SYD2164A-2	OEM
SYD2164A-3	OEM
SYD2316A	OEM
SYD2316B	OEM
SYD2316B-2	OEM
SYD2316B-3	OEM
SYD2332	OEM
SYD2333	OEM
SYD2365	OEM
SYD2365-2	OEM
SYD2365-3	OEM
SYD2365A	OEM
SYD2365A-2	OEM
SYD2365A-3	OEM
SYD2661-1	OEM
SYD2661-2	OEM
SYD2661-3	OEM
SYD3308	OEM
SYD3316	OEM
SYD3316A	OEM
SYD6502	3036
SYD6502A	OEM
SYD6502B	OEM
SYD6502C	OEM
SYD6503	OEM
SYD6503A	OEM
SYD6503B	OEM
SYD6503C	OEM
SYD6504	OEM
SYD6504A	OEM
SYD6504B	OEM
SYD6504C	OEM
SYD6505	OEM
SYD6505A	OEM
SYD6505B	OEM
SYD6505C	OEM
SYD6506	OEM
SYD6506A	OEM
SYD6506B	OEM
SYD6506C	OEM
SYD6507	3041
SYD6507A	OEM
SYD6507B	OEM
SYD6507C	OEM
SYD6512	OEM
SYD6512A	OEM
SYD6512B	OEM
SYD6512C	OEM
SYD6513	OEM

DEVICE TYPE	REPL CODE
SYD6513A	OEM
SYD6513B	OEM
SYD6513C	OEM
SYD6514	OEM
SYD6514A	OEM
SYD6514B	OEM
SYD6514C	OEM
SYD6515	OEM
SYD6515A	OEM
SYD6515B	OEM
SYD6515C	OEM
SYD6520	OEM
SYD6520A	OEM
SYD6521	OEM
SYD6521A	OEM
SYD6532	1962
SYD6532A	OEM
SYD6545	OEM
SYD6545-1	OEM
SYD6545A	OEM
SYD6545A-1	OEM
SYD6551	OEM
SYD6551A	OEM
SYD6591	OEM
SYD6591A	OEM
SYD6820	OEM
SYD6821	OEM
SYEC68B20	OEM
SYEC68B21	OEM
SYEC6502	OEM
SYEC6502A	OEM
SYEC6503	OEM
SYEC6503A	OEM
SYEC6504	OEM
SYEC6504A	OEM
SYEC6505	OEM
SYEC6505A	OEM
SYEC6506	OEM
SYEC6506A	OEM
SYEC6507	OEM
SYEC6507A	OEM
SYEC6512	OEM
SYEC6512A	OEM
SYEC6513	OEM
SYEC6513A	OEM
SYEC6514	OEM
SYEC6514A	OEM
SYEC6515	OEM
SYEC6515A	OEM
SYEC6520	OEM
SYEC6520A	OEM
SYEC6521	OEM
SYEC6521A	OEM
SYEC6522	OEM
SYEC6532	OEM
SYEC6532A	OEM
SYEC6551	OEM
SYEC6551A	OEM
SYEC6820	OEM
SYEC6821	OEM
SYED68B20	OEM
SYED68B21	OEM
SYED6502	OEM
SYED6502A	OEM
SYED6503	OEM
SYED6503A	OEM
SYED6504	OEM
SYED6504A	OEM
SYED6505	OEM
SYED6505A	OEM
SYED6506	OEM
SYED6506A	OEM
SYED6507	OEM
SYED6507A	OEM
SYED6512	OEM
SYED6512A	OEM
SYED6513	OEM
SYED6513A	OEM
SYED6514	OEM
SYED6514A	OEM
SYED6515	OEM
SYED6515A	OEM
SYED6520	OEM
SYED6520A	OEM
SYED6521	OEM
SYED6521A	OEM
SYED6522	OEM
SYED6532	OEM
SYED6532A	OEM
SYED6551	OEM
SYED6551A	OEM
SYED6820	OEM
SYED6821	OEM
SYEP68B20	OEM
SYEP68B21	OEM
SYEP6502	OEM
SYEP6502A	OEM
SYEP6503	OEM
SYEP6503A	OEM
SYEP6504	OEM
SYEP6504A	OEM
SYEP6505	OEM
SYEP6505A	OEM
SYEP6506	OEM
SYEP6506A	OEM
SYEP6507	OEM
SYEP6507A	OEM
SYEP6512	OEM
SYEP6512A	OEM

DEVICE TYPE	REPL CODE
SYEP6513	OEM
SYEP6513A	OEM
SYEP6514	OEM
SYEP6514A	OEM
SYEP6515	OEM
SYEP6515A	OEM
SYEP6520	OEM
SYEP6520A	OEM
SYEP6521	OEM
SYEP6521A	OEM
SYEP6522	OEM
SYEP6532	OEM
SYEP6532A	OEM
SYEP6551	OEM
SYEP6551A	OEM
SYEP6820	OEM
SYEP6821	OEM
SYK4332	5404
SYL101	0595
SYL102	0595
SYL103	0038
SYL104	0038
SYL105	0279
SYL106	0279
SYL107	0211
SYL108	0211
SYL109	0160
SYL128	0123
SYL152	0198
SYL160	0279
SYL792	0595
SYL1182	0016
SYL1279	0595
SYL1297	0038
SYL1310	0595
SYL1311	0595
SYL1312	0595
SYL1313	0595
SYL1326	0595
SYL1327	0595
SYL1329	0038
SYL1380	0595
SYL1396	0038
SYL1408	0595
SYL1430	0211
SYL1454	0595
SYL1468	0208
SYL1524	0038
SYL1536	0038
SYL1537	0595
SYL1538	0038
SYL1539	0038
SYL1547	0038
SYL1583	0211
SYL1588	0279
SYL1591	0595
SYL1592	OEM
SYL1608	0279
SYL1617	0595
SYL1655	0211
SYL1665	0211
SYL1668	0211
SYL1684	OEM
SYL1690	0279
SYL1697	0279
SYL1717	0279
SYL1750	0595
SYL1986	OEM
SYL1987	0595
SYL2120	0279
SYL2130	0595
SYL2131	0595
SYL2132	0595
SYL2134	0038
SYL2135	0038
SYL2136	0038
SYL2189	0050
SYL2245	0595
SYL2246	0595
SYL2247	0279
SYL2248	0211
SYL2249	0211
SYL2250	0279
SYL2300	0211
SYL2301	OEM
SYL2494	OEM
SYL2650	0038
SYL3013	OEM
SYL3613	0211
SYL4131	0144
SYL4224	OEM
SYL4225	OEM
SYL4275	0037
SYL4280	0086
SYL4312	OEM
SYL4315	0038
SYL-4339	0038
SYL4339	0595
SYMC2147	OEM
SYMC2147-6	OEM
SYMC2148	OEM
SYMC2148-6	OEM
SYMC2149H	OEM
SYMC2149H-3	OEM
SYMC3316	OEM
SYMC3316A	OEM
SYMD2147	OEM
SYMD2147-6	OEM
SYMD2148	OEM

If replacement code is OEM, contact original manufacturer for replacement.

DEVICE TYPE	REPL CODE
SYMD2148-6	OEM
SYMD2149H	OEM
SYMD2149H-3	OEM
SYMD3316	OEM
SYMD3316A	OEM
SYMF2147	OEM
SYMF2147-6	OEM
SYMF2148	OEM
SYMF2148-6	OEM
SYN600	OEM
SYP68B20	OEM
SYP68B21	OEM
SYP1791-02	OEM
SYP1793-02	OEM
SYP2101-1	OEM
SYP2101A	OEM
SYP2101A-2	OEM
SYP2101A-4	OEM
SYP2111-1	OEM
SYP2111A	OEM
SYP2111A-2	OEM
SYP2111A-4	OEM
SYP2112-1	OEM
SYP2112A	OEM
SYP2112A-2	OEM
SYP2112A-4	OEM
SYP2114	2037
SYP2114-1	OEM
SYP2114-2	2037
SYP2114-3	2037
SYP2114L	2037
SYP2114L-1	OEM
SYP2114L-2	2037
SYP2114L-3	2037
SYP2114LV	OEM
SYP2114LV-2	OEM
SYP2114LV-3	OEM
SYP2142	OEM
SYP2142-2	OEM
SYP2142-3	OEM
SYP2142L	OEM
SYP2142L-2	OEM
SYP2142L-3	OEM
SYP2142LV	OEM
SYP2142LV-2	OEM
SYP2142LV-3	OEM
SYP2164	OEM
SYP2164-2	OEM
SYP2164-3	OEM
SYP2164A	OEM
SYP2164A-2	OEM
SYP2164A-3	OEM
SYP2316A	OEM
SYP2316B	OEM
SYP2316B-2	OEM
SYP2316B-3	OEM
SYP2332	OEM
SYP2332-3	OEM
SYP2333	OEM
SYP2333-3	OEM
SYP2365	OEM
SYP2365-2	OEM
SYP2365-3	OEM
SYP2365A	OEM
SYP2365A-2	OEM
SYP2365A-3	OEM
SYP2661-1	OEM
SYP2661-2	OEM
SYP2661-3	OEM
SYP6502	3036
SYP6502A	OEM
SYP6502B	OEM
SYP6502C	OEM
SYP6503	OEM
SYP6503A	OEM
SYP6503B	OEM
SYP6503C	OEM
SYP6504	OEM
SYP6504A	OEM
SYP6504B	OEM
SYP6504C	OEM
SYP6505	OEM
SYP6505A	OEM
SYP6505B	OEM
SYP6505C	OEM
SYP6506	OEM
SYP6506A	OEM
SYP6506B	OEM
SYP6506C	OEM
SYP6507	3041
SYP6507A	OEM
SYP6507B	OEM
SYP6507C	OEM
SYP6512	OEM
SYP6512A	OEM
SYP6512B	OEM
SYP6512C	OEM
SYP6513	OEM
SYP6513A	OEM
SYP6513B	OEM
SYP6513C	OEM
SYP6514	OEM
SYP6514A	OEM
SYP6514B	OEM
SYP6514C	OEM
SYP6515	OEM
SYP6515A	OEM
SYP6515B	OEM
SYP6515C	OEM

DEVICE TYPE	REPL CODE
SYP6520	OEM
SYP6520A	OEM
SYP6521	OEM
SYP6521A	OEM
SYP6522	OEM
SYP6522A	OEM
SYP6532	1962
SYP6532A	OEM
SYP6545	OEM
SYP6545-1	OEM
SYP6545A	OEM
SYP6545A-1	OEM
SYP6551	OEM
SYP6551A	OEM
SYP6591	OEM
SYP6591A	OEM
SYP6820	OEM
SYP6821	OEM
SZ090	0016
SZ1.0	0007
SZ2.4	2975
SZ2.7	1302
SZ3.0	1703
SZ3.3	0289
SZ3.6	0188
SZ3.9	0451
SZ4.3	0528
SZ4.7	0162
SZ5	0162
SZ5.1	0162
SZ5.6	0157
SZ6	0298
SZ6.2	0631
SZ6.2A	0631
SZ6.8	0025
SZ-7	0062
SZ7	0062
SZ7.5	0644
SZ8	0244
SZ8.2	0244
SZ-9	0057
SZ9	0012
SZ9.1	0012
SZ10	0170
SZ10C	0225
SZ-11	0181
SZ11	0313
SZ11C	0230
SZ11.0	0789
SZ12	0052
SZ12C	0234
SZ12.0	0137
SZ-13	0053
SZ13	0361
SZ13C	0237
SZ13.0	0361
SZ14	0100
SZ15	0681
SZ15B	OEM
SZ15C	0247
SZ15.0	0002
SZ-16	0440
SZ16	0244
SZ16C	0251
SZ16.0	0416
SZ17	0210
SZ18	0371
SZ18B	0490
SZ18C	0256
SZ19	0666
SZ20	0695
SZ22B	0560
SZ22C	0269
SZ24C	0273
SZ-25	0709
SZ27B	0436
SZ27C	0291
SZ30C	0305
SZ31	OEM
SZ33B	0039
SZ33C	0314
SZ39B	OEM
SZ47B	OEM
SZ56A	0870
SZ56B	OEM
SZ62A	0185
SZ68A	0205
SZ68B	OEM
SZ75A	0475
SZ82A	0499
SZ91A	0679
SZ119	0398
SZ200	0162
SZ200-4	0036
SZ200-5	0162
SZ200-6	0091
SZ200-7	0062
SZ-200-8	0012
SZ200-8	0012
SZ200-8.2	0244
SZ-200-9	0012
SZ200-9	0057
SZ-200-9V	0012
SZ-200-10	0170
SZ-200-11	0313
SZ200-11	0181
SZ-200-12	0137
SZ-200-13	0361
SZ200-13	0137

DEVICE TYPE	REPL CODE
SZ-200-14	0100
SZ-200-15	0002
SZ-200-16	0244
SZ200-16	0440
SZ-200-17	0210
SZ200-17	1639
SZ-200-18	0371
SZ-200-19	0666
SZ-200-20	0695
SZ671-B	0137
SZ671-G	0137
SZ671-O	0313
SZ671-W	0313
SZ720C	OEM
SZ961-B	0002
SZ961-R	0100
SZ961-V	0361
SZ961-Y	0100
SZ1200	1823
SZ11763	0149
SZ14138	OEM
SZ51398	OEM
SZA-6	0298
SZA-13	0361
SZ-AW01-11	0313
SZ-BEX9V1	OEM
SZ-BZ-110	0313
SZ-BZ-120	0137
SZ-BZX9V1	OEM
SZC9	0012
SZ-EQB01-12A	0137
SZ-HZ4B	0274
SZ-HZ4B3	0036
SZ-HZ9B3	0318
SZ-HZ43	0274
SZL9	0170
SZL10	0505
SZ-LA4102	3161
SZM-206	OEM
SZM206	OEM
SZM206A	OEM
SZM-214	OEM
SZM-214D	OEM
SZM-226EC	OEM
SZP-9	0012
SZP-105	OEM
SZ-RD3.9EB2	0036
SZ-RD6.2E	0466
SZ-RD6.2EB	0466
SZ-RD6.2EB3	0466
SZ-RD9.1FB	0012
SZ-RD11FB	0313
SZ-RD12EB	0999
SZ-RD12FB	0137
SZT8	0137
SZT9	0012
SZ-US-4.0C	0274
SZ-UZ-4.0C	0274
SZ-UZ-6.2B	0466
SZ-UZ6.2B	0466
SZ-UZ-12B	0052
SZ-UZP-11B	0313
SZ-UZP-12B	0137
SZ-WZ-040	0036
SZ-WZ-063	0466
SZ-WZ-120	0052
SZ-YZ-063	0466
SZ-YZ063	0466
SZ-ZD-4A2	0274
SZ-ZD-4A3	0274
T0003	0004
T0004	0004
T0005	0004
T00014	0004
T0012	0004
T0014	0004
T0015	0004
T0031	0004
T0033	0004
T0038	0004
T0039	0004
T0040	0004
T0041	0004
T0051	0004
T0-101	0279
T0-102	0279
T01-044	0321
T01-101	0016
T01-104	0016
T01-105	0016
T08N5A00	OEM
T033Z3	0279
T053A2	OEM
T054B7T	OEM
T056B7T	OEM
T058B7T	OEM
T-065	0015
T065	0015
T072F	OEM
T-075	0015
T075	0015
T082	OEM
T0101	0279
T0102	0279
T-0150	0015
T0150	0015
T0505BH	0567
T0505DH	0567
T0505MH	0929

DEVICE TYPE	REPL CODE
T0505NH	0059
T0509BH	0567
T0509DH	0567
T0509MH	0929
T0509NH	0059
T0510B7T	OEM
T0510BH	0567
T0510DH	0567
T0510MH	0929
T0510NH	0059
T0512BH	0567
T0512DH	0567
T0512MH	0929
T0512NH	0059
T0515B7T	OEM
T0530G8	OEM
T0530H8	OEM
T0530J8	OEM
T0540G8	OEM
T0540H8	OEM
T0540J8	OEM
T0605BH	0567
T0605DH	0567
T0605MH	0929
T0605NH	0059
T0609BH	0567
T0609DH	0567
T0609MH	0929
T0609NH	0059
T0610BH	0567
T0610BJ	0567
T0610DH	0567
T0610DJ	0567
T0610MH	0929
T0610MJ	0929
T0610NH	0059
T0610NJ	0059
T0612BJ	0567
T0612DJ	0567
T0612MJ	0929
T0612NJ	0059
T0805BH	0567
T0805DH	0567
T0805MH	0929
T0805NH	0059
T0809BH	0567
T0809DH	0567
T0809MH	0929
T0809NH	0059
T0810BH	0567
T0810BJ	0567
T0810DH	0567
T0810DJ	0567
T0810MH	0929
T0810MJ	0929
T0810NH	0059
T0810NJ	0059
T0812BH	0567
T0812BJ	0567
T0812DH	0567
T0812DJ	0567
T0812MH	0929
T0812MJ	0929
T0812NH	0059
T0812NJ	0059
T0813BJ	0567
T0813DJ	0567
T0813MJ	0929
T0813NJ	0059
T0B	0627
T0.8/50	OEM
T0.8/100	OEM
T0.8/200	OEM
T0.8/300	OEM
T0.8/400	OEM
T0.8N0.6A00	0179
T0.8N1A00	0179
T0.8N2A00	0179
T0.8N3A00	0342
T0.8N4A00	0342
T0.8N5A00	3315
T0.8N50	OEM
T0.8N100	OEM
T0.8N200	OEM
T0.8N300	OEM
T0.8N400	OEM
T0.8N500	OEM
T1/1	OEM
T1/2	OEM
T1/3	OEM
T1/4	OEM
T1/5	OEM
T1-1A6	0016
T1-55	OEM
T1A	2600
T1B	0627
T1E	0696
T1F	0784
T1G	0143
T1H	0823
T1J	0649
T1J6G	0015
T1M	3679
T1N	0649
T1N300	0342
T1N400	0342
T1P29	0042
T1P29X	0042
T1P31	0042

DEVICE TYPE	REPL CODE
T1P31A	0236
T1P33	3052
T1P33A	3052
T1S14	0321
T1S-18	0224
T1S18	0224
T1S86	0127
T1S88	0321
T1S92	0079
T1S93	0037
T1S94	0144
T1S94(PENNCREST)	0030
T1S95	0079
T1S97	0079
T1S98	0144
T1SDS1K	0015
T1T	2016
T1V-3	0623
T1XM05	0050
T1X-M14	0007
T1X-M15	0007
T1XM15	0144
T1X-M16	0007
T1XM17	0144
T1Z	0696
T2A	0696
T2B	OEM
T2C	0696
T2D	1335
T2E	3731
T2G	1335
T2J	0659
T2K	OEM
T2L	1969
T2M	2720
T2N	1832
T2N-1	1832
T2N1	1832
T2R	0356
T2SA495-O	0006
T2SA562-O	0006
T2SA940	1900
T2SA945-O	0164
T2SC388A	0836
T2SC1195S	0103
T2SC1829S	2596
T2SC1893S	2643
T2SC1894S	0309
T2SC2068	0638
T2SC2068-1	0638
T2SC2073	1274
T2SC2120Y	0860
T2SC2229-O	0066
T2SC2229Y	0066
T2SC2230AY	0261
T2SD657S	0074
T2T	2728
T2T-1	2728
T2T-2	2728
T2V	1748
T3/1	OEM
T3/2	0015
T3/3	OEM
T3/4	OEM
T3/5	OEM
T3A	1385
T3A-1	1385
T3A-2	1385
T3B	0308
T3D	OEM
T3D-1	OEM
T3E	OEM
T3G	0143
T3H-2	OEM
T3N0.6C00	OEM
T3N1C00	OEM
T3N2C00	OEM
T3N4C00	OEM
T3N5C00	OEM
T3N6C00	OEM
T3N50	1102
T3N100	2904
T3N200	0957
T3N300	2908
T3N400	2908
T3N500	3405
T3N600	3405
T4G	OEM
T4.5/100	2471
T4.5/200	0240
T4.5/300	0671
T4.5/400	0671
T5G	OEM
T6/1	OEM
T6/2	OEM
T6/3	OEM
T6/4	OEM
T6/5	OEM
T6K40	OEM
T6N100BOC	0464
T6N200BOC	0464
T6N300BOC	0720
T6N400BOC	0720
T6N500BOC	0720
T6N600BOC	0720
T6N700BOC	0674
T6N800BOC	0674
T6.5N100	OEM
T6.5N200	OEM

DEVICE TYPE	REPL CODE
T6.5N300	OEM
T6.5N400	OEM
T6.5N500	OEM
T6.5N600	OEM
T6.5N700	OEM
T6.5N800	OEM
T6.5N900	OEM
T7	0143
T8/1	OEM
T8/2	0015
T8/3	OEM
T8/4	OEM
T8/5	OEM
T8F100CCC	OEM
T8F100HCC	OEM
T8F700CCC	OEM
T8F700HCC	OEM
T8G	0143
T8N100BOC	0464
T8N200BOC	0464
T8N300BOC	0720
T8N400BOC	0720
T8N500BOC	0720
T8N600BOC	0720
T8N700BOC	0674
T8N800BOC	0674
T9	0143
T9G	0143
T9G0060803DH	4085
T9G0061003DH	4085
T9G0061203DH	4085
T9G0080803DH	1714
T9G0081003DH	1714
T9G0100803DH	1714
T9G0101003DH	1714
T9G0101203DH	1714
T9G0120803DH	1714
T9G0121003DH	1714
T9G0121203DH	1714
T9H0200603	OEM
T9H0220603	OEM
T9H0240603	OEM
T9H0260603	OEM
T9H0280603	OEM
T9H0300603	OEM
T10N100BOC+	0464
T10N200BOC+	0464
T10N300BOC+	0717
T10N400BOC+	0720
T10N500BOC+	0720
T10N600BOC+	0720
T10N700BOC+	2025
T10N800BOC+	2025
T11	0019
T12	0143
T12A6F	OEM
T12G	0143
T12N100BOC+	0464
T12N100COB	0707
T12N200BOC+	0464
T12N400BOC+	0720
T12N500BOC+	0720
T12N600BOC+	0720
T12N700BOC+	2025
T12N800BOC+	2025
T12N900BOC+	2025
T13	0143
T13A2	OEM
T13G	0143
T14	0143
T14/50	OEM
T14/100	OEM
T14/200	OEM
T14/400	OEM
T14B7T	OEM
T14F100C	OEM
T14F100E	OEM
T14F200C	OEM
T14F200E	OEM
T14F300C	OEM
T14F300E	OEM
T14F400C	OEM
T14F400E	OEM
T14F500C	OEM
T14F500E	OEM
T14F600C	OEM
T14F600E	OEM
T14F700C	OEM
T14F700E	OEM
T14F800C	OEM
T14F800E	OEM
T14F900C	OEM
T14F900E	OEM
T14G	0143
T14N100	OEM
T14N200	OEM
T14N400	OEM
T14N500	OEM
T14N600	OEM
T14N700	OEM
T15	OEM
T15G	OEM
T15N400C	OEM
T15N500C	OEM
T15N500E	OEM
T15N600C	OEM
T15N600E	OEM
T15N700C	OEM
T15N700E	OEM

DEVICE TYPE	REPL CODE
T15N800C	OEM
T15N800E	OEM
T15N900C	OEM
T15N900E	OEM
T15N1000C	OEM
T15N1000E	OEM
T15N1100C	OEM
T15N1100E	OEM
T15N1200C	OEM
T15N1200E	OEM
T15N1300C	OEM
T15N1300E	OEM
T15.LN100BOC+	0464
T15.LN200BOC+	0464
T15.LN400BOC+	0720
T15.LN500BOC+	0720
T15.LN600BOC+	0720
T15.LN700BOC+	2025
T15.LN800BOC+	2025
T15.LN900BOC+	2025
T16	0133
T16B7T	OEM
T16X19	0143
T17	0143
T17-A	0644
T17A	0644
T18	0143
T18/50	OEM
T18/100	OEM
T18/200	OEM
T18/400	OEM
T18/500	OEM
T18/600	OEM
T18/700	OEM
T18B7T	OEM
T18F100	OEM
T18F100C	OEM
T18F100E	OEM
T18F200	OEM
T18F200C	OEM
T18F200E	OEM
T18F300C	OEM
T18F300E	OEM
T18F400	OEM
T18F400C	OEM
T18F400E	OEM
T18F500	OEM
T18F500C	OEM
T18F500E	OEM
T18F600	OEM
T18F600C	OEM
T18F600E	OEM
T18F700	OEM
T18F700C	OEM
T18F700E	OEM
T18F800	OEM
T18F800C	OEM
T18F800E	OEM
T18F900	OEM
T18F900C	OEM
T18F900E	OEM
T19	0143
T19G	0143
T20	0143
T20A6	OEM
T20A6F	OEM
T20F50	OEM
T20F100	OEM
T20F150	OEM
T20F200	OEM
T20F300	OEM
T20F400	OEM
T20F500	OEM
T20F600	OEM
T20F700	OEM
T20F800	OEM
T20G	0143
T20N50R3	OEM
T20N100R3	OEM
T20N150R3	OEM
T20N200R3	OEM
T20N250R3	OEM
T20N300R3	OEM
T21	0143
T21F5	OEM
T21F10	OEM
T21F15	OEM
T21F20	OEM
T21F25	OEM
T21F30	OEM
T21F35	OEM
T21F40	OEM
T21F50	OEM
T21F60	OEM
T21G	0143
T22	0143
T22G	0143
T22N400	OEM
T22N400C	OEM
T22N400E	OEM
T22N500	OEM
T22N500C	OEM
T22N500E	OEM
T22N600	OEM
T22N600C	OEM
T22N600E	OEM
T22N700	OEM
T22N700C	OEM
T22N700E	OEM

If replacement code is OEM, contact original manufacturer for replacement. 577

DEVICE TYPE	REPL CODE
T22N800	OEM
T22N800C	OEM
T22N800E	OEM
T22N900	OEM
T22N900C	OEM
T22N900E	OEM
T22N1000	OEM
T22N1000C	OEM
T22N1000E	OEM
T22N1100	OEM
T22N1100C	OEM
T22N1100E	OEM
T22N1200	OEM
T22N1200C	OEM
T22N1200E	OEM
T22N1300	OEM
T22N1300C	OEM
T22N1300E	OEM
T-23	0004
T23	0143
T23A2	OEM
T23G	0143
T24	OEM
T24B7T	OEM
T24G	0143
T25	OEM
T25T002080	OEM
T25T117GR5	3104
T26	OEM
T26B7T	OEM
T26G	0143
T27G	0143
T28G	0050
T30/50	OEM
T30/100	OEM
T30/200	OEM
T30/400	OEM
T30/500	OEM
T30/600	OEM
T30/700	OEM
T30A6F	OEM
T30F100	OEM
T30F100C	OEM
T30F100E	OEM
T30F200	OEM
T30F200C	OEM
T30F200E	OEM
T30F300E	OEM
T30F400	OEM
T30F400C	OEM
T30F400E	OEM
T30F500	OEM
T30F500C	OEM
T30F500E	OEM
T30F600	OEM
T30F600C	OEM
T30F600E	OEM
T30F700	OEM
T30F700C	OEM
T30F800	OEM
T30F800C	OEM
T30F800E	OEM
T30F900	OEM
T30F900C	OEM
T30F900E	OEM
T31	OEM
T31F5	OEM
T31F10	OEM
T31F15	OEM
T31F20	OEM
T31F25	OEM
T31F30	OEM
T31F35	OEM
T31F40	OEM
T31F50	OEM
T31F60	OEM
T32	OEM
T33	OEM
T33A2	OEM
T-33Z1	0004
T-33Z3	0004
T34	OEM
T34B7T	OEM
T35	OEM
T35N400B0B+	0463
T35N600B0B+	0463
T35N800B0B+	0463
T35N1000B0B+	0463
T35N1100B0B+	0463
T35N1200B0B+	0463
T36	OEM
T36B7T	OEM
T38B7T	OEM
T39	0004
T40	0150
T40R062202	OEM
T40R062203	OEM
T40R062204	OEM
T40R082202	OEM
T40R082203	OEM
T40R082204	OEM
T40R102202	OEM
T40R102203	OEM
T40R102204	OEM
T43A2	OEM
T44B7T	OEM
T45	0004
T45N400B0B+	0463
T45N600B0B+	0463
T45N800B0B+	0463
T45N1000B0B+	0463
T45N1100B0B+	0463
T45N1200B0B+	0463
T46	0004
T46B7T	OEM
T47	0004
T47C231AN4943	OEM
T48	0004
T48B7T	OEM
T-50	0015
T50	0004
T50/50	OEM
T50/100	OEM
T50/200	OEM
T50/400	OEM
T50/500	OEM
T50/600	OEM
T50/700	OEM
T50F100	OEM
T50F200	OEM
T50F300	OEM
T50F400	OEM
T50F500	OEM
T50F600	OEM
T50F700	OEM
T50F800	OEM
T50F900	OEM
T50N400	OEM
T50N500	OEM
T50N600	OEM
T50N700	OEM
T50N800	OEM
T50N900	OEM
T50N1000	OEM
T50N1100	OEM
T50N1200	OEM
T50N1300	OEM
T51A	1512
T51B	1512
T51C	1512
T51N400B0B+	0733
T51N600B0B+	0733
T51N800B0B+	0733
T51N1000B0B+	0733
T51N1100B0B+	0733
T51N1200B0B+	0733
T52A	1522
T52B	1522
T52C	1522
T53A	1538
T53A1	OEM
T53A2	OEM
T53A3	OEM
T53B	1538
T53T	1538
T54A	1557
T54B	1557
T54B7T	OEM
T54T	1557
T56B7T	OEM
T58B7T	OEM
T59	0004
T60	0004
T61	0004
T62J011022DN	OEM
T62J011032DN	OEM
T62J011033DN	OEM
T62J011042DN	OEM
T62J011043DN	OEM
T62J011052DN	OEM
T62J011053DN	OEM
T62J011062DN	OEM
T62J011063DN	OEM
T62J011072DN	OEM
T62J011073DN	OEM
T62J011082DN	OEM
T62J011083	OEM
T62J011083DN	OEM
T62J011522DN	OEM
T62J011532DN	OEM
T62J011533DN	OEM
T62J011542DN	OEM
T62J011543DN	OEM
T62J011552DN	OEM
T62J011553DN	OEM
T62J011562DN	OEM
T62J011563DN	OEM
T62J011572DN	OEM
T62J011573	OEM
T62J011573DN	OEM
T62J011582DN	OEM
T62J011583DN	OEM
T62J012022DN	OEM
T62J012032DN	OEM
T62J012033DN	OEM
T62J012042DN	OEM
T62J012043DN	OEM
T62J012052DN	OEM
T62J012053DN	OEM
T62J012062DN	OEM
T62J012063	OEM
T62J012063DN	OEM
T62J012072DN	OEM
T62J012073DN	OEM
T62J012082DN	OEM
T62J012083DN	OEM
T62J021022DN	OEM
T62J021032DN	OEM
T62J021033DN	OEM
T62J021042DN	OEM
T62J021043DN	OEM
T62J021052DN	OEM
T62J021053DN	OEM
T62J021062DN	OEM
T62J021063DN	OEM
T62J021072DN	OEM
T62J021073DN	OEM
T62J021082DN	OEM
T62J021083	OEM
T62J021083DN	OEM
T62J021522DN	OEM
T62J021532DN	OEM
T62J021533DN	OEM
T62J021542DN	OEM
T62J021543DN	OEM
T62J021552DN	OEM
T62J021553DN	OEM
T62J021562DN	OEM
T62J021563DN	OEM
T62J021572DN	OEM
T62J021573	OEM
T62J021573DN	OEM
T62J021582DN	OEM
T62J021583DN	OEM
T62J022022DN	OEM
T62J022032DN	OEM
T62J022033DN	OEM
T62J022042DN	OEM
T62J022043DN	OEM
T62J022052DN	OEM
T62J022053DN	OEM
T62J022062DN	OEM
T62J022063	OEM
T62J022063DN	OEM
T62J022072DN	OEM
T62J022073DN	OEM
T62J022082DN	OEM
T62J022083DN	OEM
T62J031022DN	OEM
T62J031032DN	OEM
T62J031033DN	OEM
T62J031042DN	OEM
T62J031043DN	OEM
T62J031052DN	OEM
T62J031053DN	OEM
T62J031062DN	OEM
T62J031063DN	OEM
T62J031072DN	OEM
T62J031073DN	OEM
T62J031082DN	OEM
T62J031083	OEM
T62J031083DN	OEM
T62J031522DN	OEM
T62J031532DN	OEM
T62J031533DN	OEM
T62J031542DN	OEM
T62J031543DN	OEM
T62J031552DN	OEM
T62J031553DN	OEM
T62J031562DN	OEM
T62J031563DN	OEM
T62J031572DN	OEM
T62J031573	OEM
T62J031573DN	OEM
T62J031582DN	OEM
T62J031583DN	OEM
T62J032022DN	OEM
T62J032032DN	OEM
T62J032033DN	OEM
T62J032042DN	OEM
T62J032043DN	OEM
T62J032052DN	OEM
T62J032053DN	OEM
T62J032062DN	OEM
T62J032063	OEM
T62J032063DN	OEM
T62J032072DN	OEM
T62J032073DN	OEM
T62J032082DN	OEM
T62J032083DN	OEM
T62J041022DN	OEM
T62J041032DN	OEM
T62J041033DN	OEM
T62J041042DN	OEM
T62J041043DN	OEM
T62J041052DN	OEM
T62J041053DN	OEM
T62J041062DN	OEM
T62J041063DN	OEM
T62J041072DN	OEM
T62J041073DN	OEM
T62J041082DN	OEM
T62J041083	OEM
T62J041083DN	OEM
T62J041522DN	OEM
T62J041532DN	OEM
T62J041533DN	OEM
T62J041542DN	OEM
T62J041543DN	OEM
T62J041552DN	OEM
T62J041553DN	OEM
T62J041562DN	OEM
T62J041563DN	OEM
T62J041572DN	OEM
T62J041573	OEM
T62J041573DN	OEM
T62J041582DN	OEM
T62J041583DN	OEM
T62J042022DN	OEM
T62J042032DN	OEM
T62J042033DN	OEM
T62J042042DN	OEM
T62J042043DN	OEM
T62J042052DN	OEM
T62J042053DN	OEM
T62J042062DN	OEM
T62J042063	OEM
T62J042063DN	OEM
T62J042072DN	OEM
T62J042073DN	OEM
T62J042082DN	OEM
T62J042083DN	OEM
T62J051022DN	OEM
T62J051032DN	OEM
T62J051033DN	OEM
T62J051042DN	OEM
T62J051043DN	OEM
T62J051052DN	OEM
T62J051053DN	OEM
T62J051062DN	OEM
T62J051063DN	OEM
T62J051072DN	OEM
T62J051073DN	OEM
T62J051082DN	OEM
T62J051083	OEM
T62J051083DN	OEM
T62J051522DN	OEM
T62J051532DN	OEM
T62J051533DN	OEM
T62J051542DN	OEM
T62J051543DN	OEM
T62J051552DN	OEM
T62J051553DN	OEM
T62J051562DN	OEM
T62J051563DN	OEM
T62J051572DN	OEM
T62J051573	OEM
T62J051573DN	OEM
T62J051582DN	OEM
T62J051583DN	OEM
T62J052022DN	OEM
T62J052032DN	OEM
T62J052033DN	OEM
T62J052042DN	OEM
T62J052043DN	OEM
T62J052052DN	OEM
T62J052053DN	OEM
T62J052062DN	OEM
T62J052063	OEM
T62J052063DN	OEM
T62J052072DN	OEM
T62J052073DN	OEM
T62J052082DN	OEM
T62J052083DN	OEM
T62J061022DN	OEM
T62J061032DN	OEM
T62J061033DN	OEM
T62J061042DN	OEM
T62J061043DN	OEM
T62J061052DN	OEM
T62J061053DN	OEM
T62J061062DN	OEM
T62J061063DN	OEM
T62J061072DN	OEM
T62J061073DN	OEM
T62J061082DN	OEM
T62J061083	OEM
T62J061083DN	OEM
T62J061522DN	OEM
T62J061532DN	OEM
T62J061533DN	OEM
T62J061542DN	OEM
T62J061543DN	OEM
T62J061552DN	OEM
T62J061553DN	OEM
T62J061562DN	OEM
T62J061563DN	OEM
T62J061572DN	OEM
T62J061573	OEM
T62J061573DN	OEM
T62J061582DN	OEM
T62J061583DNDN	OEM
T62J062022DN	OEM
T62J062032DN	OEM
T62J062033DN	OEM
T62J062042DN	OEM
T62J062043DN	OEM
T62J062052DN	OEM
T62J062053DN	OEM
T62J062062DN	OEM
T62J062063	OEM
T62J062063DN	OEM
T62J062072DN	OEM
T62J062073DN	OEM
T62J062082DN	OEM
T62J062083DN	OEM
T62J071022DN	OEM
T62J071032DN	OEM
T62J071033DN	OEM
T62J071042DN	OEM
T62J071043DN	OEM
T62J071052DN	OEM
T62J071053DN	OEM
T62J071062DN	OEM
T62J071063DN	OEM
T62J071072DN	OEM
T62J071073DN	OEM
T62J071083	OEM
T62J071083DN	OEM
T62J071522DN	OEM
T62J071532DN	OEM
T62J071533DN	OEM
T62J071542DN	OEM
T62J071543DN	OEM
T62J071552DN	OEM
T62J071553DN	OEM
T62J071562DN	OEM
T62J071563DN	OEM
T62J071572DN	OEM
T62J071573	OEM
T62J071573DN	OEM
T62J071582DN	OEM
T62J071583DN	OEM
T62J072022DN	OEM
T62J072032DN	OEM
T62J072033DN	OEM
T62J072042DN	OEM
T62J072043DN	OEM
T62J072052DN	OEM
T62J072053DN	OEM
T62J072062DN	OEM
T62J072063	OEM
T62J072063DN	OEM
T62J072072DN	OEM
T62J072073DN	OEM
T62J072082DN	OEM
T62J072083DN	OEM
T62J081022DN	OEM
T62J081032DN	OEM
T62J081033DN	OEM
T62J081042DN	OEM
T62J081043DN	OEM
T62J081052DN	OEM
T62J081053DN	OEM
T62J081062DN	OEM
T62J081063DN	OEM
T62J081072DN	OEM
T62J081073DN	OEM
T62J081082DN	OEM
T62J081083	OEM
T62J081083DN	OEM
T62J081522DN	OEM
T62J081532DN	OEM
T62J081533DN	OEM
T62J081542DN	OEM
T62J081543DN	OEM
T62J081552DN	OEM
T62J081553DN	OEM
T62J081562DN	OEM
T62J081563DN	OEM
T62J081572DN	OEM
T62J081573	OEM
T62J081573DN	OEM
T62J081582DN	OEM
T62J081583DN	OEM
T62J082022DN	OEM
T62J082032DN	OEM
T62J082033DN	OEM
T62J082042DN	OEM
T62J082043DN	OEM
T62J082052DN	OEM
T62J082053DN	OEM
T62J082062DN	OEM
T62J082063	OEM
T62J082063DN	OEM
T62J082072DN	OEM
T62J082073DN	OEM
T62J082082DN	OEM
T62J082083DN	OEM
T62J091022DN	OEM
T62J091032DN	OEM
T62J091033DN	OEM
T62J091042DN	OEM
T62J091043DN	OEM
T62J091052DN	OEM
T62J091053DN	OEM
T62J091062DN	OEM
T62J091063DN	OEM
T62J091072DN	OEM
T62J091073DN	OEM
T62J091083	OEM
T62J091083DN	OEM
T62J091522DN	OEM
T62J091532DN	OEM
T62J091533DN	OEM
T62J091542DN	OEM
T62J091543DN	OEM
T62J091552DN	OEM
T62J091553DN	OEM
T62J091562DN	OEM
T62J091563DN	OEM
T62J091572DN	OEM
T62J091573	OEM
T62J091573DN	OEM
T62J091583DN	OEM
T62J092022DN	OEM
T62J092032DN	OEM
T62J092033DN	OEM
T62J092042DN	OEM
T62J092043DN	OEM
T62J092052DN	OEM
T62J092053DN	OEM
T62J092062DN	OEM
T62J092063	OEM
T62J092063DN	OEM
T62J092073DN	OEM
T62J092083DN	OEM
T62J101022DN	OEM
T62J101032DN	OEM
T62J101033DN	OEM
T62J101042DN	OEM
T62J101043DN	OEM
T62J101052DN	OEM
T62J101053DN	OEM
T62J101062DN	OEM
T62J101063DN	OEM
T62J101072DN	OEM
T62J101073DN	OEM
T62J101083	OEM
T62J101083DN	OEM
T62J101522DN	OEM
T62J101532DN	OEM
T62J101533DN	OEM
T62J101542DN	OEM
T62J101543DN	OEM
T62J101552DN	OEM
T62J101553DN	OEM
T62J101562DN	OEM
T62J101563DN	OEM
T62J101572DN	OEM
T62J101573	OEM
T62J101573DN	OEM
T62J101583DN	OEM
T62J102022DN	OEM
T62J102032DN	OEM
T62J102033DN	OEM
T62J102042DN	OEM
T62J102043DN	OEM
T62J102052DN	OEM
T62J102053DN	OEM
T62J102062DN	OEM
T62J102063	OEM
T62J102063DN	OEM
T62J102072DN	OEM
T62J102073DN	OEM
T62J102083DN	OEM
T62J111022DN	OEM
T62J111032DN	OEM
T62J111033DN	OEM
T62J111042DN	OEM
T62J111043DN	OEM
T62J111052DN	OEM
T62J111053DN	OEM
T62J111062DN	OEM
T62J111063	OEM
T62J111063DN	OEM
T62J111073DN	OEM
T62J111083DN	OEM
T62J111522DN	OEM
T62J111532DN	OEM
T62J111533DN	OEM
T62J111542DN	OEM
T62J111543DN	OEM
T62J111552DN	OEM
T62J111553DN	OEM
T62J111562DN	OEM
T62J111563	OEM
T62J111563DN	OEM
T62J111573DN	OEM
T62J111583DN	OEM
T62J112022DN	OEM
T62J112032DN	OEM
T62J112033DN	OEM
T62J112042DN	OEM
T62J112043DN	OEM
T62J112052DN	OEM
T62J112053DN	OEM
T62J112062DN	OEM
T62J112063	OEM
T62J112063DN	OEM
T62J112073DN	OEM
T62J112083DN	OEM
T62J121022DN	OEM
T62J121032DN	OEM
T62J121033DN	OEM
T62J121042DN	OEM
T62J121043DN	OEM
T62J121052DN	OEM
T62J121053DN	OEM
T62J121062DN	OEM
T62J121063	OEM
T62J121063DN	OEM
T62J121073DN	OEM
T62J121083DN	OEM
T62J121522DN	OEM
T62J121532DN	OEM
T62J121533DN	OEM
T62J121542DN	OEM
T62J121543DN	OEM
T62J121552DN	OEM
T62J121553DN	OEM
T62J121562DN	OEM
T62J121563	OEM
T62J121563DN	OEM
T62J121573DN	OEM
T62J121583DN	OEM
T62J122022DN	OEM
T62J122032DN	OEM
T62J122033DN	OEM
T62J122042DN	OEM
T62J122043DN	OEM
T62J122052DN	OEM
T62J122053DN	OEM
T62J122062DN	OEM
T62J122063	OEM
T62J122063DN	OEM
T62J122073DN	OEM
T62J122083DN	OEM
T63A011790	1741
T63A1	OEM
T63A2	OEM
T63A3	OEM
T64B7T	OEM
T66B7T	OEM
T67A1037K0	1731
T68B7T	OEM
T70F200EEB	OEM
T70F200EEC	OEM
T70F200EFB	OEM
T70F200EFC	OEM
T70F200EGB	OEM
T70F200EGC	OEM
T70F400EEB	OEM
T70F400EEC	OEM
T70F400EFB	OEM
T70F400EFC	OEM
T70F400EGB	OEM
T70F400EGC	OEM
T70F500EEB	OEM
T70F500EEC	OEM
T70F500EFB	OEM
T70F500EFC	OEM
T70F500EGB	OEM
T70F500EGC	OEM
T70F600EEB	OEM
T70F600EEC	OEM
T70F600EFB	OEM
T70F600EFC	OEM
T70F600EGB	OEM
T70F600EGC	OEM
T70F700EEB	OEM
T70F700EEC	OEM
T70F700EFB	OEM
T70F700EFC	OEM
T70F700EGB	OEM
T70F700EGC	OEM
T70F800EEB	OEM
T70F800EEC	OEM
T70F800EFB	OEM
T70F800EFC	OEM
T70F800EGB	OEM
T70F800EGC	OEM
T70F900EFB	OEM
T70F900EFC	OEM
T70F900EGB	OEM
T70F900EGC	OEM
T70F1000EFB	OEM
T70F1000EFC	OEM
T70F1000EGB	OEM
T70F1000EGC	OEM
T70F1100EFB	OEM
T70F1100EFC	OEM
T70F1100EGB	OEM
T70F1100EGC	OEM
T70F1200EFB	OEM
T70F1200EFC	OEM
T70F1200EGB	OEM
T70F1200EGC	OEM
T70F1300EFB	OEM
T70F1300EFC	OEM
T70F1300EGB	OEM
T70F1300EGC	OEM
T70N400EOB	OEM
T70N400EOC	OEM
T70N400EOF	OEM
T70N600EOB	OEM
T70N600EOC	OEM
T70N600EOF	OEM
T70N800EOB	OEM
T70N800EOC	OEM
T70N800EOF	OEM
T70N1000EOB	OEM
T70N1000EOC	OEM
T70N1000EOF	OEM
T70N1100EOB	OEM
T70N1100EOC	OEM
T70N1100EOF	OEM
T70N1200EOB	OEM
T70N1200EOC	OEM
T70N1200EOF	OEM
T70N1300EOB	OEM
T70N1300EOC	OEM
T70N1300EOF	OEM
T70N1400EOB	OEM
T70N1400EOC	OEM
T70N1400EOF	OEM
T70N1500EOB	OEM
T70N1500EOC	OEM
T70N1500EOF	OEM
T70N1600EOB	OEM
T70N1600EOC	OEM
T70N1600EOF	OEM
T71N400B0B+	0733
T71N600B0B+	0733
T71N800B0B+	0733
T71N1000B0B+	0733
T71N1100B0B+	0733
T71N1200B0B+	0733
T72	0004
T72H012524DN	OEM
T72H012534DN	OEM
T72H012544DN	OEM
T72H012554DN	OEM
T72H012564	OEM

If replacement code is OEM, contact original manufacturer for replacement.

DEVICE TYPE	REPL CODE
T72H012564DN	OEM
T72H012574DN	OEM
T72H012584	OEM
T72H012584DN	OEM
T72H013524DN	OEM
T72H013534DN	OEM
T72H013544DN	OEM
T72H013554DN	OEM
T72H013564DN	OEM
T72H013574	OEM
T72H013574DN	OEM
T72H013584DN	OEM
T72H014524DN	OEM
T72H014534DN	OEM
T72H014544DN	OEM
T72H014554	OEM
T72H014554DN	OEM
T72H014564DN	OEM
T72H014574DN	OEM
T72H014584DN	OEM
T72H022524DN	OEM
T72H022534DN	OEM
T72H022544DN	OEM
T72H022554DN	OEM
T72H022564DN	OEM
T72H022574DN	OEM
T72H022584	OEM
T72H022584DN	OEM
T72H023524DN	OEM
T72H023534DN	OEM
T72H023544DN	OEM
T72H023554DN	OEM
T72H023564DN	OEM
T72H023574	OEM
T72H023574DN	OEM
T72H023584DN	OEM
T72H024524DN	OEM
T72H024534DN	OEM
T72H024544DN	OEM
T72H024554	OEM
T72H024554DN	OEM
T72H024564DN	OEM
T72H024574DN	OEM
T72H024584DN	OEM
T72H032524DN	OEM
T72H032534DN	OEM
T72H032544DN	OEM
T72H032554DN	OEM
T72H032564DN	OEM
T72H032574DN	OEM
T72H032584	OEM
T72H032584DN	OEM
T72H033524DN	OEM
T72H033534DN	OEM
T72H033544DN	OEM
T72H033554DN	OEM
T72H033564DN	OEM
T72H033574	OEM
T72H033574DN	OEM
T72H033584DN	OEM
T72H034524DN	OEM
T72H034534DN	OEM
T72H034544DN	OEM
T72H034554	OEM
T72H034554DN	OEM
T72H034564DN	OEM
T72H034574DN	OEM
T72H034584DN	OEM
T72H042524DN	OEM
T72H042534DN	OEM
T72H042544DN	OEM
T72H042554DN	OEM
T72H042564DN	OEM
T72H042574DN	OEM
T72H042584	OEM
T72H042584DN	OEM
T72H043524DN	OEM
T72H043534DN	OEM
T72H043544DN	OEM
T72H043554DN	OEM
T72H043564DN	OEM
T72H043574	OEM
T72H043574DN	OEM
T72H043584DN	OEM
T72H044524DN	OEM
T72H044534DN	OEM
T72H044544DN	OEM
T72H044554	OEM
T72H044554DN	OEM
T72H044564DN	OEM
T72H044574DN	OEM
T72H044584DN	OEM
T72H052524DN	OEM
T72H052534DN	OEM
T72H052544DN	OEM
T72H052554DN	OEM
T72H052564DN	OEM
T72H052574DN	OEM
T72H052584	OEM
T72H052584DN	OEM
T72H053524DN	OEM
T72H053534DN	OEM
T72H053544DN	OEM
T72H053554DN	OEM
T72H053564DN	OEM
T72H053574	OEM
T72H053574DN	OEM
T72H053584DN	OEM
T72H054524DN	OEM

DEVICE TYPE	REPL CODE
T72H054534DN	OEM
T72H054544DN	OEM
T72H054554	OEM
T72H054554DN	OEM
T72H054564DN	OEM
T72H054574DN	OEM
T72H054584DN	OEM
T72H062524DN	OEM
T72H062534DN	OEM
T72H062544DN	OEM
T72H062554DN	OEM
T72H062564DN	OEM
T72H062574DN	OEM
T72H062584	OEM
T72H062584DN	OEM
T72H063524DN	OEM
T72H063534DN	OEM
T72H063544DN	OEM
T72H063554DN	OEM
T72H063564DN	OEM
T72H063574	OEM
T72H063574DN	OEM
T72H063584DN	OEM
T72H064524DN	OEM
T72H064534DN	OEM
T72H064544DN	OEM
T72H064554	OEM
T72H064554DN	OEM
T72H064564DN	OEM
T72H064574DN	OEM
T72H064584DN	OEM
T72H072524DN	OEM
T72H072534DN	OEM
T72H072544DN	OEM
T72H072554DN	OEM
T72H072564DN	OEM
T72H072574	OEM
T72H072574DN	OEM
T72H072584DN	OEM
T72H073524DN	OEM
T72H073534DN	OEM
T72H073544DN	OEM
T72H073554DN	OEM
T72H073564DN	OEM
T72H073574	OEM
T72H073574DN	OEM
T72H073584DN	OEM
T72H074524DN	OEM
T72H074534DN	OEM
T72H074544DN	OEM
T72H074554	OEM
T72H074554DN	OEM
T72H074564DN	OEM
T72H074574DN	OEM
T72H074584DN	OEM
T72H082524DN	OEM
T72H082534DN	OEM
T72H082544DN	OEM
T72H082554DN	OEM
T72H082564DN	OEM
T72H082574	OEM
T72H082574DN	OEM
T72H082584DN	OEM
T72H083524DN	OEM
T72H083534DN	OEM
T72H083544DN	OEM
T72H083554DN	OEM
T72H083564DN	OEM
T72H083574	OEM
T72H083574DN	OEM
T72H083584DN	OEM
T72H084524DN	OEM
T72H084534DN	OEM
T72H084544DN	OEM
T72H084554	OEM
T72H084554DN	OEM
T72H084564DN	OEM
T72H084574DN	OEM
T72H084584DN	OEM
T72H092524DN	OEM
T72H092534DN	OEM
T72H092544DN	OEM
T72H092554DN	OEM
T72H092564	OEM
T72H092564DN	OEM
T72H092574DN	OEM
T72H092584DN	OEM
T72H093524DN	OEM
T72H093534DN	OEM
T72H093544DN	OEM
T72H093554DN	OEM
T72H093564	OEM
T72H093564DN	OEM
T72H093574DN	OEM
T72H093584DN	OEM
T72H094524DN	OEM
T72H094534DN	OEM
T72H094544DN	OEM
T72H094554	OEM
T72H094554DN	OEM
T72H094564DN	OEM
T72H094574DN	OEM
T72H094584DN	OEM
T72H102524DN	OEM
T72H102534DN	OEM
T72H102544DN	OEM
T72H102554DN	OEM
T72H102564DN	OEM
T72H102574DN	OEM

DEVICE TYPE	REPL CODE
T72H102584DN	OEM
T72H103524DN	OEM
T72H103534DN	OEM
T72H103544DN	OEM
T72H103554DN	OEM
T72H103564	OEM
T72H103564DN	OEM
T72H103574DN	OEM
T72H103584DN	OEM
T72H104524DN	OEM
T72H104534DN	OEM
T72H104544DN	OEM
T72H104554	OEM
T72H104554DN	OEM
T72H104564DN	OEM
T72H104574DN	OEM
T72H104584DN	OEM
T72H112524DN	OEM
T72H112534DN	OEM
T72H112544DN	OEM
T72H112554DN	OEM
T72H112564	OEM
T72H112564DN	OEM
T72H112574DN	OEM
T72H112584DN	OEM
T72H113524DN	OEM
T72H113534DN	OEM
T72H113544DN	OEM
T72H113554DN	OEM
T72H113564DN	OEM
T72H113574DN	OEM
T72H113584DN	OEM
T72H114524DN	OEM
T72H114534DN	OEM
T72H114544DN	OEM
T72H114554	OEM
T72H114554DN	OEM
T72H114564DN	OEM
T72H114574DN	OEM
T72H114584DN	OEM
T72H122524DN	OEM
T72H122534DN	OEM
T72H122544DN	OEM
T72H122554DN	OEM
T72H122564	OEM
T72H122564DN	OEM
T72H122574DN	OEM
T72H122584DN	OEM
T72H123524DN	OEM
T72H123534DN	OEM
T72H123544DN	OEM
T72H123554DN	OEM
T72H123564DN	OEM
T72H123574DN	OEM
T72H123584DN	OEM
T72H124524DN	OEM
T72H124534DN	OEM
T72H124544DN	OEM
T72H124554	OEM
T72H124554DN	OEM
T74	0004
T74H00B1	0677
T74H00D1	0677
T74H00D2	0677
T74H10B1	0680
T74H10D1	0680
T74H10D2	0680
T74H11B1	2382
T74H11D1	2382
T74H11D2	2382
T74H20B1	3670
T74H20D1	3670
T74H20D2	3670
T74H21B1	4772
T74H21D1	4772
T74H21D2	4772
T74H40B1	0554
T74H40D1	0554
T74H40D2	0554
T74H50B1	1781
T74H50D1	1781
T74H50D2	1781
T74H51B1	1933
T74H51D1	1933
T74H51D2	1933
T74H52B1	2009
T74H52D1	2009
T74H52D2	2009
T74H53B1	2090
T74H53D1	2090
T74H53D2	2090
T74H54B1	2158
T74H54D1	2158
T74H54D2	2158
T74H61B1	2638
T74H61D1	2638
T74H61D2	2638
T74H62B1	2705
T74H62D1	2705
T74H62D2	2705
T74H71B1	3233
T74H71D2	3233
T74H72B1	3281
T74H72D1	3281
T74H72D2	3281
T74LS00B1	1519
T74LS00D1	1519
T74LS01B1N	1537
T74LS02B1	1550

DEVICE TYPE	REPL CODE
T74LS02D1	1550
T74LS03B1	1569
T74LS03D1	1569
T74LS04B1	1585
T74LS08B1	1623
T74LS08D1	1623
T74LS09B1	1632
T74LS09D1	1632
T74LS10B1	1652
T74LS10D1	1652
T74LS11B1	1657
T74LS11D1	1657
T74LS13B1	1678
T74LS14B1	1688
T74LS14BI	1688
T74LS15B1	1697
T74LS15D1	1697
T74LS20B1	0035
T74LS20D1	0035
T74LS21B1	1752
T74LS21D1	1752
T74LS22B1	1764
T74LS22D1	1764
T74LS26B1	1372
T74LS26D1	1372
T74LS27B1	0183
T74LS27BI	0183
T74LS27D1	0183
T74LS28B1	0467
T74LS30B1	0822
T74LS30D1	0822
T74LS32B1	0088
T74LS32BI	0088
T74LS32D1	0088
T74LS40B1	0135
T74LS40C1	OEM
T74LS40D1	OEM
T74LS40M1	OEM
T74LS51B1	1027
T74LS51D1	1027
T74LS54B1	1846
T74LS54D1	1846
T74LS55B1	0452
T74LS55B1N	0452
T74LS55C1	OEM
T74LS55D1	0452
T74LS55M1	OEM
T74LS74B1	0243
T74LS74D1	0243
T74LS83B1	2204
T74LS83D1	2204
T74LS86B1	0288
T74LS86D1	0288
T74LS109B1	1895
T74LS109D1	1895
T74LS112B1	2115
T74LS112D1	2115
T74LS113B1	2241
T74LS113D1	2241
T74LS114B1	2286
T74LS114D1	2286
T74LS125AB1	OEM
T74LS132P	OEM
T74LS136B1	1618
T74LS136D1	1618
T74LS138B1	0422
T74LS151B1	5044
T74LS155B1	0209
T74LS157B1	1153
T74LS161B1	0852
T74LS164B1	6741
T74LS174B1	0260
T74LS175B1	1662
T74LS193B1	5744
T74LS244B1	0453
T74LS257B1	1733
T74LS273B1	OEM
T74LS279B1	3259
T74LS283D1	OEM
T74LS352B1	0756
T74LS352C1	OEM
T74LS352D1	OEM
T74LS352M1	OEM
T74LS353B1	0768
T74LS353C1	OEM
T74LS353D1	OEM
T74LS353M1	OEM
T74LS373B1	0704
T74LS374B1	0708
T74LS386AB1	OEM
T74LS393B1	0813
T74LS398B1	1373
T74LS399B1	1388
T74LS399C1	OEM
T74LS399D1	OEM
T74LS399M1	OEM
T74LS670B1	1122
T76	0016
T77	0004
T78	0004
T81	0208
T-82	0279
T82	0004
T83	0004
T83A028120	0719
T83A028127	0719
T83A028140	0719
T84	0004
T84B7T	OEM

DEVICE TYPE	REPL CODE
T86B7T	OEM
T87	0004
T87A	0604
T87A02412K	0719
T88B7T	OEM
T95	0004
T95/50	OEM
T95/100	OEM
T95/200	OEM
T95/400	OEM
T95/500	OEM
T95/600	OEM
T95/700	OEM
T95F100	OEM
T95F200	OEM
T95F300	OEM
T95F400	OEM
T95F500	OEM
T95F600	OEM
T95F700	OEM
T95F800	OEM
T95F900	OEM
T99	0004
T99N400BOB+	0733
T99N600BOB+	0733
T99N800BOB+	0733
T99N1000BOB+	0733
T99N1100BOB+	0733
T99N1200BOB+	0733
T-100	0015
T100	0004
T100F200EEB	OEM
T100F200EEC	OEM
T100F200EFB	OEM
T100F200EFC	OEM
T100F200EGB	OEM
T100F200EGC	OEM
T100F400EEB	OEM
T100F400EEC	OEM
T100F400EFB	OEM
T100F400EFC	OEM
T100F400EGB	OEM
T100F400EGC	OEM
T100F500EEB	OEM
T100F500EEC	OEM
T100F500EFB	OEM
T100F500EFC	OEM
T100F500EGB	OEM
T100F500EGC	OEM
T100F600EEB	OEM
T100F600EEC	OEM
T100F600EFB	OEM
T100F600EFC	OEM
T100F600EGB	OEM
T100F600EGC	OEM
T100F700EEB	OEM
T100F700EEC	OEM
T100F700EFB	OEM
T100F700EFC	OEM
T100F700EGB	OEM
T100F700EGC	OEM
T100F800EEB	OEM
T100F800EEC	OEM
T100F800EFB	OEM
T100F800EFC	OEM
T100F800EGB	OEM
T100F800EGC	OEM
T100F900EFB	OEM
T100F900EFC	OEM
T100F900EGB	OEM
T100F900EGC	OEM
T100F1000EFB	OEM
T100F1000EFC	OEM
T100F1000EGB	OEM
T100F1000EGC	OEM
T100F1100EFB	OEM
T100F1100EFC	OEM
T100F1100EGB	OEM
T100F1100EGC	OEM
T100F1200EFB	OEM
T100F1200EFC	OEM
T100F1200EGB	OEM
T100F1200EGC	OEM
T100F1300EFB	OEM
T100F1300EFC	OEM
T100F1300EGB	OEM
T100F1300EGC	OEM
T100N400BOC	OEM
T100N400EOC	OEM
T100N600BOC	OEM
T100N600EOC	OEM
T100N800BOC	OEM
T100N800EOC	OEM
T100N1000BOC	OEM
T100N1000EOC	OEM
T100N1200BOC	OEM
T100N1200EOC	OEM
T100N1400BOC	OEM
T100N1400EOC	OEM
T100N1600BOC	OEM
T100N1600EOC	OEM
T100N1800BOC	OEM
T100N1800EOC	OEM
T-101	0160
T101	0004
T102A	0004
T104B7T	OEM
T106A1	0442
T106A1SC	2284

DEVICE TYPE	REPL CODE
T106A1SD	2284
T106A1SG	2284
T106A1SH	2284
T106A1SS	2284
T106A2SC	2284
T106A2SD	2284
T106A2SG	2284
T106A2SH	2284
T106A2SS	2284
T106B1	0934
T106B1SC	2284
T106B1SD	2284
T106B1SG	2284
T106B1SH	2284
T106B1SS	2284
T106B2SC	2284
T106B2SD	2284
T106B2SG	2284
T106B2SH	2284
T106B2SS	2284
T106B7T	OEM
T106C1	0095
T106C1SC	2284
T106C1SD	2284
T106C1SG	2284
T106C1SH	2284
T106C1SS	2284
T106C2SC	2284
T106C2SD	2284
T106C2SG	2284
T106C2SH	2284
T106C2SS	2284
T106D1	0095
T106D1SC	2284
T106D1SD	2284
T106D1SG	2284
T106D1SH	2284
T106D1SS	2284
T106D2SC	2284
T106D2SD	2284
T106D2SG	2284
T106D2SH	2284
T106D2SS	2284
T106F1	1250
T106F1SC	2284
T106F1SD	2284
T106F1SG	2284
T106F1SH	2284
T106F1SS	2284
T106F2SC	2284
T106F2SD	2284
T106F2SG	2284
T106F2SH	2284
T106F2SS	2284
T106Q1	1386
T106Y1	1386
T107A1	0442
T107B1	0934
T107C1	0095
T107D1	0095
T107F1	1250
T107Q1	1386
T107Y1	1386
T108	0004
T108B7T	OEM
T109	0004
T110F200TEC	OEM
T110F800TEC	OEM
T110F900TFC	OEM
T110F1300TFC	OEM
T-112	0037
T116	0004
T125N400	OEM
T125N500	OEM
T125N600	OEM
T125N700	OEM
T125N800	OEM
T125N900	OEM
T125N1000	OEM
T125N1100	OEM
T125N1200	OEM
T125N1300	OEM
T126	0004
T-127	0160
T127	0004
T129	0004
T129N400BOB+	0733
T129N600BOB+	0733
T129N800BOB+	0733
T129N1000BOB+	0733
T129N1100BOB+	0733
T129N1200BOB+	0733
T130	0004
T130G8	OEM
T130H8	OEM
T130J8	OEM
T130N400EOC	OEM
T130N600EOC	OEM
T130N800EOC	OEM
T130N1000EOC	OEM
T130N1200EOC	OEM
T130N1400EOC	OEM
T130N1600EOC	OEM
T-131	0164
T131	0164
T139	0085
T140G8	OEM
T140H8	OEM
T140J8	OEM

DEVICE TYPE	REPL CODE
T142	0160
T143	0016
T150F200TEC	OEM
T150F800TEC	OEM
T150F900TFC	OEM
T150F1300TFC	OEM
T151	0133
T152	0133
T153	0133
T154	0133
T155	0133
T155N1600	OEM
T155N1800	OEM
T155N2000	OEM
T155N2200	OEM
T156	0604
T157	0016
T158	0079
T159	0015
T159N400BOB+	0733
T159N600BOB+	0733
T159N800BOB+	0733
T159N1000BOB+	0733
T159N1100BOB+	0733
T160	0004
T160N400	OEM
T160N500	OEM
T160N600	OEM
T160N700	OEM
T160N800	OEM
T160N900	OEM
T160N1000	OEM
T160N1100	OEM
T160N1200	OEM
T160N1300	OEM
T160N1400	OEM
T160N1500	OEM
T161N400EOC	OEM
T161N600EOC	OEM
T161N800EOC	OEM
T161N1000EOC	OEM
T161N1200EOC	OEM
T161N1400EOC	OEM
T161N1600EOC	OEM
T-163	0050
T163	0050
T-164	OEM
T165N400TOC	OEM
T165N400TOF	OEM
T165N1800TOC	OEM
T165N1800TOF	OEM
T170	0079
T170F100	OEM
T170F200	OEM
T170F300	OEM
T170F400	OEM
T170F500	OEM
T170F600	OEM
T170F700	OEM
T170F800	OEM
T170F900	OEM
T170N400	OEM
T170N500	OEM
T170N600	OEM
T170N700	OEM
T170N800	OEM
T170N900	OEM
T170N1000	OEM
T170N1100	OEM
T170N1200	OEM
T170N1300	OEM
T171	0079
T180/50	OEM
T180/100	OEM
T180/200	OEM
T180/400	OEM
T180/500	OEM
T180/600	OEM
T180/700	OEM
T185	0079
T200	0015
T200N400TOC	OEM
T200N400TOF	OEM
T200N1800TOC	OEM
T200N1800TOF	OEM
T-203	0127
T210B7T	OEM
T215B7T	OEM
T220N400	OEM
T220N500	OEM
T220N600	OEM
T220N700	OEM
T220N800	OEM
T220N900	OEM
T220N1000	OEM
T220N1100	OEM
T220N1200	OEM
T220N1300	OEM
T220N1400	OEM
T220N1500	OEM
T222	0074
T225	0074
T226	OEM
T230G8	OEM
T230H8	OEM
T230J8	OEM
T-235	0160
T-235A	OEM
T235N1600	OEM

If replacement code is OEM, contact original manufacturer for replacement.

579

DEVICE TYPE	REPL CODE
T235N1800	OEM
T235N2000	OEM
T237	0016
T240G8	OEM
T240H8	OEM
T240J8	OEM
T-246	0037
T246	0126
T247	0086
T-251	0037
T253	0050
T253(SEARS)	0050
T-255	0079
T255	0079
T256	0079
T257	0142
T260F100	OEM
T260F200	OEM
T260F300	OEM
T260F400	OEM
T260F500	OEM
T260F600	OEM
T260F700	OEM
T260F800	OEM
T260F900	OEM
T261	0142
T271	0178
T276	0037
T277	0079
T-278	0050
T278	0050
T-279	0050
T279	0050
T280	0050
T280(SEARS)	0136
T281	0050
T281(SEARS)	0136
T282	0050
T282(SEARS)	0004
T287	0275
T-291	0086
T291	0079
T300	0015
T300N400	OEM
T300N500	OEM
T300N600	OEM
T300N700	OEM
T300N800	OEM
T300N900	OEM
T300N1000	OEM
T300N1100	OEM
T300N1200	OEM
T300N1300	OEM
T301N400	OEM
T301N500	OEM
T301N600	OEM
T301N700	OEM
T301N800	OEM
T301N900	OEM
T301N1000	OEM
T301N1100	OEM
T301N1200	OEM
T301N1300	OEM
T301N1400	OEM
T302N400EOC	OEM
T302N600EOC	OEM
T302N800EOC	OEM
T302N1000EOC	OEM
T302N1200EOC	OEM
T302N1400EOC	OEM
T302N1600EOC	OEM
T308	0144
T310B7T	OEM
T313	OEM
T315B7T	OEM
T327	0079
T327-2	0079
T328	0079
T330F200TEC	OEM
T330F200TFC	OEM
T330F1200TEC	OEM
T330F1200TFC	OEM
T330G8	OEM
T330H8	OEM
T330J8	OEM
T334-2	0126
T336-2	0086
T338	0018
T-339	0086
T339	0079
T-340	0126
T340	0037
T340G8	OEM
T340H8	OEM
T340J8	OEM
T-342	0161
T342	0079
T-344	0161
T344	0161
T-345	0455
T345	0455
T346	0279
T-348	0136
T348	0050
T350N400TOC	OEM
T350N400TOF	OEM
T350N1600TOC	OEM
T350N1600TOF	OEM
T367	0050

DEVICE TYPE	REPL CODE
T-368	0050
T368	0050
T370	0599
T373	0050
T374	0050
T381	0007
T381(SEARS)	0007
T386	0016
T386(SEARS)	0127
T-396	0455
T396	0455
T-399	0079
T399	0079
T400	0015
T410B7T	OEM
T411A	0404
T411F	0395
T415B7T	OEM
T416-16(SEARS)	0079
T417	0079
T422	0546
T423	0378
T430G8	OEM
T430H8	OEM
T430J8	OEM
T440G8	OEM
T440H8	OEM
T440J8	OEM
T449	0050
T449(SEARS)	0136
T450	0015
T450N400TOC	OEM
T450N400TOF	OEM
T450N1600TOC	OEM
T450N1600TOF	OEM
T452	0086
T457-16	0079
T457-16(SEARS)	0079
T458-16	0079
T459	0126
T459(SEARS)	0079
T460	0079
T460(SEARS)	0037
T461-16	0079
T461-16(SEARS)	0016
T462	0079
T462(SEARS)	0079
T464	0212
T472	0079
T472(SEARS)	0079
T475	0126
T475(SEARS)	0037
T480F100TDC	OEM
T480F500TDC	OEM
T480F600TDC	OEM
T-481	0233
T481(SEARS)	0233
T482(SEARS)	0037
T483(SEARS)	0079
T484(SEARS)	0079
T485(SEARS)	0079
T-486	0144
T486(SEARS)	0079
T500	0015
T508N1000TOB	OEM
T508N1000TOC	OEM
T508N1000TOF	OEM
T508N1100TOB	OEM
T508N1100TOC	OEM
T508N1100TOF	OEM
T508N1200TOB	OEM
T508N1200TOC	OEM
T508N1200TOF	OEM
T508N1400TOB	OEM
T508N1400TOC	OEM
T508N1400TOF	OEM
T508N1600TOB	OEM
T508N1600TOC	OEM
T508N1600TOF	OEM
T510B7T	OEM
T511F	1425
T512F	1425
T513	0212
T513F	OEM
T514F	OEM
T515B7T	OEM
T518B	OEM
T520C	OEM
T520D	OEM
T520E	OEM
T520G	OEM
T520N1100TOC	OEM
T521N800TOF	OEM
T522F	1670
T523C	OEM
T524D	OEM
T529C	OEM
T529H	OEM
T530G8	OEM
T530H8	OEM
T530J8	OEM
T540G8	OEM
T540H8	OEM
T540J8	OEM
T541	2278
T542	2278
T542-6	OEM
T550	0015
T551	2282

DEVICE TYPE	REPL CODE
T552	2282
T576-1	0007
T597-1	0037
T600	0015
T600*1804	OEM
T600F600TEC	OEM
T600F800TEC	OEM
T600F1000TEC	OEM
T600F1100TEC	OEM
T600F1200TEC	OEM
T600F1300TEC	OEM
T610B7T	OEM
T611-1	0042
T611-1(RCA)	0161
T611F	OEM
T612-1	0042
T612-1(RCA)	0161
T612F	OEM
T613F	OEM
T615B7T	OEM
T621-1	0161
T621M	OEM
T625N3600TOF	OEM
T625N3800TOF	OEM
T625N4000TOF	OEM
T625N4400TOF	OEM
T630G8	OEM
T630H8	OEM
T630J8	OEM
T640G8	OEM
T640H8	OEM
T640J8	OEM
T650	0015
T651	OEM
T652	OEM
T653	OEM
T670F1600TMC	OEM
T670F1800TMC	OEM
T670F2000TMC	OEM
T671N3000TOF	OEM
T671N3200TOF	OEM
T671N3400TOF	OEM
T671N3600TOF	OEM
T698F200TCC	OEM
T698F400TCC	OEM
T698F500TCC	OEM
T699	OEM
T-700-709	0143
T700-709	0143
T700N1800TOB	OEM
T700N1800TOC	OEM
T700N1800TOF	OEM
T700N2000TOB	OEM
T700N2000TOC	OEM
T700N2000TOF	OEM
T700N2200TOB	OEM
T700N2200TOC	OEM
T700N2200TOF	OEM
T700N2400TOB	OEM
T700N2400TOC	OEM
T700N2400TOF	OEM
T700N2600TOB	OEM
T700N2600TOC	OEM
T700N2600TOF	OEM
T-750-713	0143
T-750-714	0057
T760F2000TUC	OEM
T760F2200TUC	OEM
T760F2400TUC	OEM
T800	0071
T800X	0071
T810B7T	OEM
T811	0050
T814	0164
T815	0164
T815B7T	OEM
T819	OEM
T841	0130
T842	0130
T843	0130
T844	0130
T900B1	OEM
T900B1-K	OEM
T900BI-K	OEM
T911B1-T	5103
T911BIT	5103
T916BI	OEM
T951HL	OEM
T975	OEM
T-1000	0071
T1000	0164
T-1000X	0071
T1000X	0071
T1001	0004
T1002	0004
T1002A	0004
T1003	0004
T1003-521	0144
T1004	0004
T1005	0004
T1006	0004
T1007	0004
T1007(ZENITH)	0111
T1008	0004
T1008-834	0079
T1009	0004
T1010	0004
T1010B7T	OEM
T1010BH	0588

DEVICE TYPE	REPL CODE
T1010BJ	0588
T1010DH	0571
T1010DJ	0571
T1010MH	0589
T1010MJ	0589
T1010NH	0869
T1010NJ	0869
T1011	0050
T1012	0050
T1012BH	0588
T1012BJ	0588
T1012DH	0571
T1012DJ	0571
T1012MH	0589
T1012MJ	0929
T1012NH	0869
T1012NJ	0059
T1013	0004
T1013BH	0588
T1013BJ	0588
T1013DH	0571
T1013DJ	0571
T1013MH	0589
T1013MJ	0589
T1013NH	0869
T1013NJ	0869
T1015B7T	OEM
T1023	0004
T1025	OEM
T1028	0050
T1032	0050
T1033	0050
T-1034	0050
T1034	0050
T1036	0004
T1037	0004
T1038	0050
T1039	OEM
T1040	0085
T1041	0085
T1042	0004
T1043	0004
T1046	0004
T1047	0004
T1050	OEM
T1076	0004
T1085	0015
T1106	0007
T1159	OEM
T1166	0050
T1167	0160
T1168	0160
T1200N1200TOF	OEM
T1200N1400TOF	OEM
T1200N1600TOF	OEM
T1202	0004
T1202(GE)	0007
T1203	0004
T1208	0321
T1210BH	0767
T1210DH	0739
T1210MH	0612
T1210NH	0869
T1212BH	0767
T1212BJ	0767
T1212DH	0739
T1212DJ	0739
T1212MH	0612
T1212MJ	0612
T1212NH	0869
T1212NJ	0869
T1213BH	0767
T1213BJ	0767
T1213DH	0739
T1213DJ	0739
T1213MH	0612
T1213MJ	0612
T1213NH	0869
T1213NJ	0869
T1224	0050
T1225	0050
T1232	0050
T1233	0050
T1250	0050
T1251	0050
T1275	0126
T1276	0126
T1282	OEM
T1289	0279
T1291	0279
T1298	0050
T1299	0050
T1300	0004
T1305	0050
T1306	0050
T1310	0004
T1312	0279
T1314	0050
T1317	OEM
T1322	0279
T1326	0279
T1327	0004
T1328	0004
T1334	0004
T1340A3H	0086
T1340A3I	0016
T1340A3J	0016
T1340A3K	0016
T1340A31	0016

DEVICE TYPE	REPL CODE
T1341A3K	0111
T1342	0004
T1343	OEM
T1344	OEM
T1346	0004
T1352	0004
T1363	0004
T1364	0004
T1366	0085
T1366A	0085
T1367	0085
T1367A	0085
T1368	0085
T1368A	0085
T1369	0085
T1369A	0085
T1370	0085
T1370A	0085
T1381	OEM
T1382	OEM
T1383	OEM
T1387	0050
T1388	0136
T1389	0050
T1390	0050
T1391	0050
T1396	0841
T1397	0841
T1400	0050
T1401	0050
T1402	0111
T1403	0050
T1408	0224
T1410	0007
T1413	0016
T1414	0016
T1415	0079
T1416	0079
T1417	0016
T1447	OEM
T1450	0015
T1454	0050
T1459	0050
T1460	0136
T1461	0050
T1474	0279
T1480E	0102
T1486	0042
T1487	0042
T1495	0016
T1501	OEM
T1510	0279
T1512BJ	0767
T1512DJ	0739
T1512MJ	0612
T1512NJ	0869
T1513BJ	0767
T1513DJ	0739
T1513MJ	0612
T1513NJ	0869
T1524BRN	0136
T1524BRN/RED	0136
T1546	0004
T1548	0050
T1558	OEM
T1559	0004
T1573	0004
T1574	0004
T1577	0004
T1581	OEM
T1583	0004
T1591	OEM
T1593	0004
T1594	0004
T1595	0004
T1596	0004
T1597	0004
T1598	0004
T1599	0004
T1601	0160
T1602	0037
T1612BH	5227
T1612DH	5230
T1612MH	1649
T1612NH	1956
T1613BH	5227
T1613DH	5230
T1613MH	1649
T1613NH	1956
T1618	0050
T1623	OEM
T1642B	0016
T1654	0136
T1654BLU	0136
T1655	OEM
T1656	OEM
T1657	0050
T1670	OEM
T1684	OEM
T1685	OEM
T1686	OEM
T1687	OEM
T1688	OEM
T1689	OEM
T1690	0050
T1691	0050
T1692	0050
T1706	0086
T1706A	0086

DEVICE TYPE	REPL CODE
T1706B	0086
T1706C	0086
T1711A	0136
T1731	0212
T1737	0050
T1738	0050
T1740	0004
T1746	0016
T1746A	0016
T1746B	0016
T1746C	0016
T1748	0016
T1748A	0016
T1748B	0016
T1748C	0016
T1756	OEM
T1788	0050
T1789	OEM
T1796	OEM
T1802	0016
T1802A	0016
T1802B	0016
T1804	0016
T1805	0016
T1806	OEM
T1807	OEM
T1808	0126
T1808A	0126
T1808B	0126
T1808C	0126
T1808D	0126
T1808E	0126
T1810	0016
T1810B	0016
T1811	0086
T1811E	0086
T1811G	0086
T1814	0050
T1822	OEM
T1826	OEM
T1831	0050
T1832	OEM
T1833	OEM
T1850	OEM
T1851	OEM
T1851M	OEM
T1858	OEM
T1859	OEM
T1866	OEM
T1871	OEM
T-1877	0279
T1877	0279
T1885	OEM
T1886	OEM
T1887	OEM
T1888	OEM
T1889	OEM
T1890	OEM
T1891	OEM
T1892	OEM
T1893	OEM
T1895	OEM
T1902	0279
T1903	0004
T1904	0004
T1905	0050
T1909	0016
T1930	0050
T1937	OEM
T1947	OEM
T1961	0004
T1967	OEM
T1973	OEM
T1992	OEM
T2015	0050
T2016	0050
T2017	0050
T2018	OEM
T2019	0050
T2020	0050
T2021	0050
T2022	0050
T2023	OEM
T2024	0050
T2025	0050
T2026	0050
T-2028	0050
T2028	0050
T-2029	0050
T2029	0050
T-2030	0050
T2030	0050
T-2038	0279
T2038	0279
T-2039	0279
T2039	0279
T-2040	0279
T2040	0279
T2050	OEM
T2057	OEM
T2058	OEM
T2059	OEM
T2060	OEM
T2061	OEM
T-2062	0102
T2062	0797
T2071	OEM
T2088	OEM
T2089	OEM

DEVICE TYPE	REPL CODE
T-2091	0279
T2091	0279
T2110	OEM
T2119	OEM
T-2122	0211
T2122	0279
T2144	OEM
T2145	OEM
T2159	0004
T2172	0279
T2173	0279
T2186	OEM
T2187	OEM
T2191	0050
T2198	OEM
T2211	OEM
T2256	0279
T2257	0279
T2258	0279
T2259	0279
T2260	0279
T2261	0279
T2299	OEM
T2300A	2336
T2300B	2337
T2300C	2340
T2300D	2340
T2300E	OEM
T2300F	2336
T2300PA	2336
T2300PB	2337
T2300PC	2340
T2300PD	2340
T2300PF	2336
T2301A	2336
T2301B	2337
T2301C	OEM
T2301D	2340
T2301E	OEM
T2301F	2336
T2301G	OEM
T2301PA	2336
T2301PA5	OEM
T2301PB	2337
T2301PB5	2337
T2301PC	OEM
T2301PC5	OEM
T2301PD	2340
T2301PD5	2340
T2301PE	OEM
T2301PE5	OEM
T2301PF	OEM
T2301PM	OEM
T2301PM5	OEM
T2302A	2336
T2302B	2337
T2302C	2340
T2302D	2340
T2302E	OEM
T2302F	2336
T2302PA	2336
T2302PA5	2336
T2302PB	2337
T2302PB5	2337
T2302PC	OEM
T2302PC5	OEM
T2302PD	2340
T2302PD5	2340
T2302PE	OEM
T2302PE5	OEM
T2302PF	OEM
T2302PF5	OEM
T2302PM	OEM
T2302PM5	OEM
T2303C	OEM
T2303E	OEM
T2303F	2367
T2304B	2337
T2304D	2371
T2305B	2378
T2305D	1403
T2306A	2367
T2306B	2378
T2306D	1403
T2310A	2367
T2310B	2337
T2310D	1403
T2312A	2336
T2312B	2378
T2312D	1403
T2312F	2367
T2313A	2367
T2313B	2378
T2313D	1403
T2313F	OEM
T2313M	2371
T2320A	2284
T2320B	2284
T2320C	2284
T2320D	2284
T2320E	OEM
T2320F	2284
T2322	0050
T2322A	2284
T2322B	2284
T2322C	2284
T2322D	2284
T2322E	OEM
T2322F	2284

580

If replacement code is OEM, contact original manufacturer for replacement.

DEVICE TYPE	REPL CODE
T2323	0050
T2323A	2284
T2323B	2284
T2323C	2284
T2323D	2284
T2323E	OEM
T2323F	2284
T2323M	OEM
T2324	0050
T2327	OEM
T2327A	2284
T2327B	2284
T2327C	2284
T2327D	2284
T2327E	OEM
T2327F	2284
T2329	OEM
T2330	OEM
T2331	OEM
T2340	OEM
T2351	OEM
T2352	OEM
T-2357	0150
T2357	0150
T2363	OEM
T2364	0050
T2370	2480
T2379	0050
T2384	0050
T2392	OEM
T2393	OEM
T2401PF5	OEM
T2415	OEM
T2417	OEM
T2418	OEM
T2439	0004
T2440	0004
T2441	0004
T2446	0016
T2448	OEM
T2452	OEM
T2453	OEM
T2454	OEM
T2455	OEM
T2469	OEM
T2470	OEM
T2471	OEM
T2472	OEM
T2478	OEM
T2479	OEM
T2490	OEM
T2491	OEM
T2492	OEM
T2500B	0550
T2500D	0550
T2500E	OEM
T2500M	OEM
T2500N	OEM
T2500S	OEM
T2506B	OEM
T2506D	OEM
T-2508	2180
T2508	2180
T2512BH	5227
T2512BK	OEM
T2512DH	5230
T2512DK	OEM
T2512MH	1649
T2512MK	OEM
T2512NH	1956
T2512NK	OEM
T2513BH	5227
T2513BK	OEM
T2513DH	5230
T2513DK	OEM
T2513MH	1649
T2513MK	OEM
T2513NH	1956
T2513NK	OEM
T2515	0004
T2517	0004
T2560	OEM
T2578	OEM
T2579	OEM
T2580	OEM
T2588	OEM
T2589	OEM
T2606B	OEM
T2606D	OEM
T2606DF	OEM
T2610	OEM
T2611	OEM
T2616DF	OEM
T2634	0144
T2679	OEM
T2691	OEM
T2700B	0407
T2700D	0571
T2706B	4159
T2706D	4159
T2710B	0407
T2710D	0411
T2716B	4159
T2716D	4159
T2788	0050
T2800A	OEM
T2800B	0567
T2800C	0550
T2800D	0550

DEVICE TYPE	REPL CODE
T2800E	0550
T2800F	OEM
T2800M	0550
T2801A	OEM
T2801B	0588
T2801C	0569
T2801D	0571
T2801DF	0572
T2801E	0572
T2801F	OEM
T2801M	0589
T2802A	OEM
T2802B	0588
T2802C	0569
T2802D	0571
T2802E	0572
T2802F	OEM
T2802M	0589
T2806B	0588
T2806C	OEM
T2806D	0571
T2806M	OEM
T2850A	0550
T2850B	0550
T2850D	0550
T2850E	OEM
T2850F	OEM
T2850M	OEM
T2851B	0550
T2851C	0550
T2851D	0550
T2851DF	OEM
T2851E	0550
T2856B	OEM
T2856C	OEM
T2856D	OEM
T2856E	OEM
T2856M	OEM
T2857	0144
T2878	0050
T2896	0050
T2945	0050
T2946	0050
T3000	OEM
T3002	OEM
T3003	OEM
T3004	OEM
T3005	0004
T3321	0004
T3322	0004
T3530	0144
T3536	0144
T3539	0144
T3565	0079
T-3568	0007
T3568	0127
T3568(RCA)	0144
T3570	0037
T3601	0079
T3601(RCA)	0127
T3889	OEM
T3890	OEM
T3891	OEM
T3892	OEM
T3893	OEM
T3899	OEM
T3900	OEM
T3901	OEM
T3902	OEM
T3902B	OEM
T3903	OEM
T3909	OEM
T3910	OEM
T3911	OEM
T3912	OEM
T3913	OEM
T4012BK	OEM
T4012DK	OEM
T4012MK	OEM
T4012NK	OEM
T4013BK	OEM
T4013DK	OEM
T4013MK	OEM
T4013NK	OEM
T4100E	1880
T4100F	1880
T4100M	1880
T4101E	1880
T4101F	1058
T4101M	1880
T4103B	OEM
T4103D	OEM
T4104B	OEM
T4104D	OEM
T4105B	OEM
T4105D	OEM
T4106B	OEM
T4106D	OEM
T4106M	OEM
T4107B	OEM
T4107D	OEM
T4110E	OEM
T4110F	OEM
T4110M	0278
T4111E	OEM
T4111F	OEM
T4111M	0278
T4113B	0154
T4113D	0147

DEVICE TYPE	REPL CODE
T4113E	OEM
T4113M	OEM
T4114B	0154
T4114D	0147
T4114E	OEM
T4114M	OEM
T4115B	0154
T4115D	0147
T4115E	OEM
T4115M	OEM
T4116B	0154
T4116D	0147
T4116M	OEM
T4117B	0154
T4117D	0147
T4117M	OEM
T4120B	3169
T4120D	3177
T4120E	OEM
T4120F	OEM
T4120M	3192
T4120N	OEM
T4120S	OEM
T4121B	OEM
T4121D	OEM
T4121E	OEM
T4121F	OEM
T4121M	0278
T4121N	OEM
T4121S	OEM
T4126B	OEM
T4126D	OEM
T4126M	OEM
T4127B	OEM
T4127D	OEM
T4127M	OEM
T4130B	5343
T4130D	OEM
T4130M	OEM
T4131B	OEM
T4131D	OEM
T4131M	OEM
T4140B	0902
T4140D	0902
T4140M	0902
T4141B	5343
T4141D	5343
T4141M	5567
T4150B	0902
T4150D	0902
T4150M	5567
T4151B	5343
T4151D	5343
T4151M	OEM
T4446	OEM
T4590	0123
T4700B	4180
T4700D	4159
T4700E	OEM
T4700F	OEM
T4706B	OEM
T4706D	0147
T5135-5	OEM
T5135-6	OEM
T5135-G	OEM
T5135-M	OEM
T5135-X	OEM
T5140-5	OEM
T5140-6	OEM
T5140-G	OEM
T5140-M	OEM
T5140-X	OEM
T5145-5	OEM
T5145-6	OEM
T5145-G	OEM
T5145-M	OEM
T5145-X	OEM
T5627	OEM
T5901	OEM
T5902	OEM
T5903	OEM
T5909	OEM
T6000B	0588
T6000C	0571
T6000D	4893
T6000E	4894
T6000F	4895
T6000M	0589
T6001B	OEM
T6001C	OEM
T6001D	OEM
T6001E	OEM
T6001F	OEM
T6001M	OEM
T6006B	0588
T6006C	0571
T6006D	0571
T6006E	0589
T6006M	OEM
T6028	0136
T6029	0136
T6030	0136
T6031	0136
T6032	0136
T6058	0050
T6260B	5343
T6260C	5343
T6260D	5343
T6260E	OEM

DEVICE TYPE	REPL CODE
T6260M	0902
T6261B	0902
T6261C	0902
T6261D	0902
T6261E	0902
T6261M	0902
T6400B	1058
T6400D	1307
T6400M	1880
T6400N	OEM
T6400S	OEM
T6401B	1058
T6401D	1880
T6401E	OEM
T6401F	OEM
T6401M	1880
T6401N	OEM
T6401S	OEM
T6404B	OEM
T6404D	OEM
T6404E	OEM
T6405B	OEM
T6405D	OEM
T6405E	OEM
T6406B	OEM
T6406D	OEM
T6406E	OEM
T6406M	OEM
T6407B	OEM
T6407D	OEM
T6407E	OEM
T6407M	OEM
T6410B	OEM
T6410D	OEM
T6410M	5524
T6410N	5525
T6411B	2006
T6411D	2006
T6411E	5524
T6411F	5527
T6411M	2007
T6411N	OEM
T6411S	OEM
T6414B	2004
T6414D	2006
T6415B	3121
T6415D	2007
T6416B	2004
T6416D	2006
T6416M	2007
T6417B	2004
T6417D	2006
T6417M	2007
T6420	2007
T6420B	3169
T6420D	3177
T6420E	3192
T6420F	3169
T6420M	3192
T6420N	OEM
T6421B	3169
T6421D	3177
T6421E	3192
T6421F	3169
T6421M	3192
T6421N	OEM
T6421S	OEM
T6426B	OEM
T6426D	OEM
T6426M	OEM
T6427B	OEM
T6427D	OEM
T6427M	OEM
T6430B	OEM
T6430D	OEM
T6430M	OEM
T6431B	OEM
T6431D	OEM
T6431M	OEM
T6440B	5567
T6440D	5567
T6440M	5567
T6441B	0902
T6441D	0902
T6441M	5567
T6450B	5567
T6450D	5567
T6450M	OEM
T6451B	5567
T6451D	0902
T6451M	5567
T6506B	OEM
T6676AS	OEM
T7400B1	0232
T7400D1	0232
T7400D2	0232
T7401B1	0268
T7401D1	0268
T7401D2	0268
T7402B1	0310
T7402D1	0310
T7402D2	0310
T7403B1	0331
T7403D1	0331
T7403D2	0331
T7404B1	0357
T7405B1	0381
T7406B1	1197
T7407B1	1329

DEVICE TYPE	REPL CODE
T7408B1	0462
T7408D1	0462
T7408D2	0462
T7409B1	0487
T7409D1	0487
T7409D2	0487
T7410B1	0507
T7410D1	0507
T7410D2	0507
T7416B1	1339
T7420B1	0692
T7420D1	0692
T7420D2	0692
T7426B1	0798
T7426D1	0798
T7426D2	0798
T7428B1	4117
T7428D1	4117
T7428D2	4117
T7430B1	0867
T7430D1	0867
T7430D2	0867
T7433B1	4130
T7433D1	4130
T7433D2	4130
T7440B1	1018
T7440D1	1018
T7440D2	1018
T7441AB1	1032
T7441AD1	1032
T7441AD2	1032
T7442B1	1046
T7442D1	1046
T7442D2	1046
T7443B1	1054
T7443D1	1054
T7443D2	1054
T7444B1	1066
T7444D1	1066
T7444D2	1066
T7450B1	0738
T7450D1	0738
T7450D2	0738
T7451B1	1160
T7451D1	1160
T7451D2	1160
T7453B1	1177
T7453D1	1177
T7453D2	1177
T7454B1	1193
T7454D1	1193
T7454D2	1193
T7460B1	1265
T7460D1	1265
T7460D2	1265
T7472B1	1417
T7472D1	1417
T7472D2	1417
T7473B1	1164
T7473D1	1164
T7473D2	1164
T7474B1	1303
T7474D1	1303
T7474D2	1303
T7475B1	1423
T7476B1	1150
T7476D1	1150
T7476D2	1150
T7481B1	3092
T7483B1	0117
T7484B1	OEM
T7486B1	1358
T7486D1	1358
T7486D2	1358
T7490B1	1199
T7490D1	1199
T7490D2	1199
T7492B1	0828
T7492D1	0828
T7492D2	0828
T7493B1	0564
T7493D1	0564
T7493D2	0564
T7815A-0102	OEM
T8150	OEM
T8401B	OEM
T8401D	OEM
T8401M	OEM
T8430B	OEM
T8430D	OEM
T8430M	OEM
T8889A	OEM
T9011A1C	0079
T9011A1G	0079
T9011AZ	0079
T9011EF	0144
T9011G	0144
T9011G(CD)	0079
T9011G(EF)	0079
T9011GEF	0144
T9011H	0144
T9011H(EF)	0079
T9011I(EF)	0079
T9011J(GH)	0079
T9016F	0144
T9016H	0144
T9418	0018
T9423	0224
T9468	0527

DEVICE TYPE	REPL CODE
T9631	0079
T9681	0037
T10010	0004
T10085	0004
T10144	0015
T10175	0015
T10185	0015
T10195	0276
T10453	0015
T11087T	OEM
T11618	0004
T13000	0004
T13015	0086
T13029	0160
T14881	0023
T18218	OEM
T18231	OEM
T21237	0143
T21238	0143
T21271	0143
T21312	0015
T21313	0143
T21333	0015
T21334	0012
T21507	0015
T21600	0133
T21601	0030
T21602	0015
T21638	0229
T21639	0012
T21649	0015
T21679	0015
T30155	0229
T30155-001	0015
T30155-1	0015
T42692-001	0015
T42692-1R	0015
T50339A	0004
T50631	0004
T50818	0136
T50931B	0211
T50933B	0164
T50944	0279
T51573A	0211
T52054	0136
T52147	0279
T52147Z	0279
T52148Z	0279
T-52149	0279
T52149	0279
T52149Z	0279
T52150	0004
T52150Z	0004
T52151	0004
T52151Z	0004
T52159	0004
T59235A	0016
T59247	0004
T59249	0004
T59276	0595
T59277	0595
T69901	OEM
T74107B1	0936
T74180B1	1818
T74193B1	1915
T78010AP	2779
T78012AP	OEM
T81901	OEM
T152148	0279
T164213	0086
T250117GR5	3104
T1003521	0144
T1004671	0016
T1008834	0016
T4080016	0464
T4080116	0464
T4080216	0464
T4080316	0720
T4080416	0720
T4080516	0720
T5070140B4AQ	0521
T5070170B4AQ	0521
T5070240B4AQ	OEM
T5070270B4AQ	0521
T5070280B4AQ	0521
T5070340B4AQ	0521
T5070370B4AQ	0521
T5070380B4AQ	0521
T5070440B4AQ	0521
T5070470B4AQ	0521
T5070480B4AQ	0521
T5070540B4AQ	0521
T5070570B4AQ	0521
T5070580B4AQ	0521
T5070640B4AQ	0521
T5070670B4AQ	0521
T5070680B4AQ	0521
T5070740B4AQ	0108
T5070770B4AQ	0108
T5070780B4AQ	0108
T5070840B4AQ	0108
T5070870B4AQ	0108
T5070880B4AQ	0108
T5070940B4AQ	0108
T5070970B4AQ	0108
T5070980B4AQ	0108
T5071040B4AQ	0108
T5071070B4AQ	0108
T5071080B4AQ	0108

DEVICE TYPE	REPL CODE
T5071140B4AQ	0108
T5071170B4AQ	0108
T5071180B4AQ	0108
T5071240B4AQ	0108
T5071270B4AQ	0108
T5071280B4AQ	0108
T6000713	0733
T6000715	0733
T6000813	0733
T6000815	0733
T6000913	0733
T6000915	0733
T6001013	0733
T6001015	0733
T6001113	0733
T6001115	0733
T6001213	0733
T6001215	0733
T6070113B4BT	0423
T6070115B4BT	0423
T6070118B4BT	0423
T6070213B4BT	0423
T6070215B4BT	0423
T6070218B4BT	0423
T6070313B4BT	0423
T6070315B4BT	0423
T6070413B4BT	0423
T6070415B4BT	0423
T6070418B4BT	0423
T6070513B4BT	0423
T6070515B4BT	0423
T6070613B4BT	0423
T6070615B4BT	0423
T6070618B4BT	0423
T6071013B4BT	1860
T6071015B4BT	1860
T6071113B4BT	1860
T6071115B4BT	1860
T6071118B4BT	1860
T6071213B4BT	1860
T6071215B4BT	1860
T6071218B4BT	1860
T6100113	0733
T6100115	0733
T6100213	0733
T6100215	0733
T6100313	0733
T6100315	0733
T6100413	0733
T6100415	0733
T6100513	0733
T6100515	0733
T6100613	0733
T6100615	0733
T7000125	1889
T7000130	1889
T7000225	1889
T7000230	1889
T7000425	0733
T7000430	0733
T7000625	0733
T7000630	0733
T7000825	0733
T7000830	0733
T7000835	0733
T7001025	0733
T7001030	0733
T7001225	0733
T7001230	0733
T7070128B4BY	1690
T7070228B4BY	1690
T7070328B4BY	1690
T7070428B4BY	1690
T7070528B4BY	1690
T7070625B4BY	1690
T7070628B4BY	1690
T7070630B4BY	1690
T7070725B4BY	0341
T7070728B4BY	0341
T7070730B4BY	0341
T7070825B4BY	0341
T7070828B4BY	0341
T7070830B4BY	0341
T7070925B4BY	0341
T7070930B4BY	0341
T7071025B4BY	0341
T7071030B4BY	0341
T7071125B4BY	0341
T7071130B4BY	0341
T7071225B4BY	0341
T7071230B4BY	0341
T7270135B4DN	0764
T7270235B4DN	0764
T7270335B4DN	0764
T7270435B4DN	0764
T7270535B4DN	0764
T7270635B4DN	0764
T7270735B4DN	0478
T7270835B4DN	0478
T7270935B4DN	0478
T7271035B4DN	OEM
T7271135B4DN	0478
T7271235B4DN	0478
T22000104E	0321
T107108064AQ	OEM
T107108074AQ	OEM
T107114034AQ	OEM
T220001040	0321
T400001006	0464

If replacement code is OEM, contact original manufacturer for replacement. 581

DEVICE TYPE	REPL CODE
T400001008	2497
T400001606	2174
T400001608	2174
T400002206	0726
T400002208	0726
T400011006	0736
T400011008	0736
T400011606	0562
T400011608	0562
T400012206	1574
T400012208	0707
T400021006	0464
T400021008	0740
T400021606	0757
T400021608	0757
T400022206	OEM
T400022208	0464
T400031006	0717
T400031008	0742
T400031606	0735
T400031608	0735
T400032206	OEM
T400032208	0717
T400041006	0717
T400041008	0742
T400041606	0735
T400041608	0735
T400042206	OEM
T400042208	0717
T400051006	0720
T400051008	0747
T400051606	0759
T400051608	0759
T400052206	OEM
T400052208	0720
T400061006	0759
T400061008	0747
T400061606	0759
T400061608	0759
T400062206	OEM
T400062208	0720
T400071006	0674
T400071008	0674
T400071606	0674
T400071608	0674
T400072206	OEM
T400072208	0745
T400081006	0761
T400081008	0674
T400081606	0761
T400081608	0674
T400082206	OEM
T400082208	0745
T400091006	0674
T400091008	0674
T400091606	0674
T400091608	0674
T400092208	OEM
T400101006	0674
T400101008	0674
T400101600	OEM
T400101606	0674
T400101608	0674
T400102208	OEM
T400111006	0674
T400111008	0674
T400111606	0674
T400111608	0674
T400112208	OEM
T400121006	0674
T400121008	0674
T400121606	0674
T400121608	0674
T400122208	OEM
T407185152	0037
T408001006	OEM
T408002206	OEM
T408011006	OEM
T408012206	OEM
T408021006	OEM
T408022206	OEM
T408031006	OEM
T408032206	OEM
T408041006	OEM
T408042206	OEM
T408051006	OEM
T408052206	OEM
T408061006	OEM
T408062206	OEM
T408071008	OEM
T408072206	OEM
T408081008	OEM
T408082206	OEM
T500014005(T083)	0650
T500014005(T094)	0521
T500014005AA	OEM
T500014005AQ	OEM
T500018005(T083)	0636
T500018005(T094)	0603
T500018005AA	OEM
T500018005AQ	OEM
T500024005(T083)	0650
T500024005(T094)	0521
T500024005AQ	OEM
T500028005(T083)	0636
T500028005(T094)	0603
T500028005AA	OEM
T500028005AQ	OEM
T500034005(T083)	0650
T500034005(T094)	0521
T500034005AA	OEM
T500034005AQ	OEM
T500038005(T083)	0217
T500038005(T094)	0605
T500038005AA	OEM
T500038005AQ	OEM
T500044005(T083)	0650
T500044005(T094)	0521
T500044005AA	OEM
T500044005AQ	OEM
T500048005(T083)	0217
T500048005(T094)	0605
T500048005AA	OEM
T500048005AQ	OEM
T500054005(T083)	0650
T500054005(T094)	0521
T500054005AA	OEM
T500054005AQ	OEM
T500058005(T083)	0217
T500058005(T094)	0605
T500058005AA	OEM
T500058005AQ	OEM
T500064005(T083)	0650
T500064005(T094)	0521
T500064005AA	OEM
T500064005AQ	OEM
T500068005(T083)	0217
T500068005(T094)	0605
T500068005AA	OEM
T500068005AQ	OEM
T500074004AQ	0463
T500074005(T083)	0020
T500074005(T094)	0108
T500074005AB	0653
T500074005AQ	0463
T500078004AQ	0463
T500078005(T083)	0653
T500078005(T094)	0463
T500078005AB	0653
T500078005AQ	0463
T500084004AQ	0463
T500084005(T083)	0020
T500084005(T094)	0108
T500084005AB	0653
T500084005AQ	0463
T500088004AQ	0463
T500088005(T083)	0653
T500088005(T094)	0463
T500088005AB	0653
T500088005AQ	0463
T500094004AQ	0463
T500094005(T083)	0020
T500094005(T094)	0108
T500094005AB	0653
T500094005AQ	0463
T500098004AQ	0463
T500098005(T083)	0653
T500098005(T094)	0463
T500098005AB	0653
T500098005AQ	0463
T500104004AQ	0463
T500104005(T083)	0020
T500104005(T094)	0108
T500104005AB	0653
T500104005AQ	0463
T500108004AQ	0463
T500108005(T083)	0653
T500108005(T094)	0463
T500108005AB	0653
T500108005AQ	0463
T500114004AQ	0463
T500114005AB	0653
T500114005AQ	0463
T500118004AQ	0463
T500118005AB	0653
T500118005AQ	0463
T500124004AQ	0463
T500124005(T083)	OEM
T500124005(T094)	0108
T500124005AB	0653
T500124005AQ	0463
T500128004AQ	0463
T500128005(T083)	0653
T500128005(T094)	0463
T500128005AA	OEM
T500128005AB	0653
T500128005AQ	0463
T500144005(T083)	OEM
T500144005(T094)	OEM
T500148005(T083)	OEM
T500148005(T094)	OEM
T500164005(T083)	OEM
T500164005(T094)	OEM
T500168005(T083)	OEM
T500168005(T094)	OEM
T504017043AA	OEM
T504017043AQ	OEM
T504017073AA	OEM
T504017073AQ	OEM
T504027043AA	OEM
T504027043AQ	OEM
T504027073AA	OEM
T504027073AQ	OEM
T504037043AA	OEM
T504037043AQ	OEM
T504037073AA	OEM
T504037073AQ	OEM
T504047043AA	OEM
T504047043AQ	OEM
T504047073AA	OEM
T504047073AQ	OEM
T504057043AA	OEM
T504057043AQ	OEM
T504057073AA	OEM
T504057073AQ	OEM
T504067043AQ	OEM
T504067073AA	OEM
T504067073AQ	OEM
T504077043AA	OEM
T504077043AQ	OEM
T504077073AA	OEM
T504077073AQ	OEM
T504087043AA	OEM
T504087043AQ	OEM
T504087073AA	OEM
T504087073AQ	OEM
T504097043AA	OEM
T504097043AQ	OEM
T504107043AA	OEM
T504107043AQ	OEM
T505014005AA	OEM
T507014024AA	0650
T507014024AQ	0521
T507014034AA	0650
T507014034AQ	0521
T507014044AA	0650
T507014044AQ	0521
T507014054AA	0650
T507014054AQ	0521
T507014064AA	0650
T507014064AQ	0521
T507014074AA	0650
T507014074AQ	0521
T507014084AA	0650
T507014084AQ	0521
T507017024AA	0650
T507017024AQ	0521
T507017034AA	0650
T507017034AQ	0521
T507017044AA	0650
T507017044AQ	0521
T507017054AA	0650
T507017054AQ	0521
T507017064AA	0650
T507017064AQ	0521
T507017074AA	0650
T507017074AQ	0521
T507017084AA	0650
T507017084AQ	0521
T507018024AA	0650
T507018024AQ	0521
T507018034AA	0650
T507018034AQ	0521
T507018044AA	0650
T507018044AQ	0521
T507018054AA	0650
T507018054AQ	0521
T507018064AA	0650
T507018064AQ	0521
T507018074AA	0650
T507018074AQ	0521
T507018084AA	0650
T507018084AQ	0521
T507024024AA	0650
T507024024AQ	0521
T507024034AA	0650
T507024034AQ	0521
T507024044AA	0650
T507024044AQ	0521
T507024054AA	0650
T507024054AQ	0521
T507024064AA	0650
T507024064AQ	0521
T507024074AA	0650
T507024074AQ	0521
T507024084AA	0650
T507024084AQ	0521
T507027024AA	0650
T507027024AQ	0521
T507027034AA	0650
T507027034AQ	0521
T507027044AA	0650
T507027044AQ	0521
T507027054AA	0650
T507027054AQ	0521
T507027064AA	0650
T507027064AQ	0521
T507027074AA	0650
T507027074AQ	0521
T507027084AA	0650
T507027084AQ	0521
T507028024AA	0650
T507028024AQ	0521
T507028034AA	0650
T507028034AQ	0521
T507028044AA	0650
T507028044AQ	0521
T507028054AA	0650
T507028054AQ	0521
T507028064AA	0650
T507028064AQ	0521
T507028074AA	0650
T507028074AQ	0521
T507028084AA	0650
T507028084AQ	0521
T507034024AA	0650
T507034024AQ	0521
T507034034AA	0650
T507034034AQ	0521
T507034044AA	0650
T507034044AQ	0521
T507034054AA	0650
T507034054AQ	0521
T507034064AA	0650
T507034064AQ	0521
T507034074AA	0650
T507034074AQ	0521
T507034084AA	0650
T507034084AQ	0521
T507037024AA	0650
T507037024AQ	0521
T507037034AA	0650
T507037034AQ	0521
T507037044AA	0650
T507037044AQ	0521
T507037054AA	0650
T507037054AQ	0521
T507037064AA	0650
T507037064AQ	0521
T507037074AA	0650
T507037074AQ	0521
T507037084AA	0650
T507037084AQ	0521
T507038024AA	0650
T507038024AQ	0521
T507038034AA	0650
T507038034AQ	0521
T507038044AA	0650
T507038044AQ	0521
T507038054AA	0650
T507038054AQ	0521
T507038064AA	0650
T507038064AQ	0521
T507038074AA	0650
T507038074AQ	0521
T507038084AA	0650
T507038084AQ	0521
T507044024AA	0650
T507044024AQ	0521
T507044034AA	0650
T507044034AQ	0521
T507044044AA	0650
T507044044AQ	0521
T507044054AA	0650
T507044054AQ	0521
T507044064AA	0650
T507044064AQ	0521
T507044074AA	0650
T507044074AQ	0521
T507044084AA	0650
T507044084AQ	0521
T507047024AA	0650
T507047024AQ	0521
T507047034AA	0650
T507047034AQ	0521
T507047044AA	0650
T507047044AQ	0521
T507047054AA	0650
T507047054AQ	0521
T507047064AA	0650
T507047064AQ	0521
T507047074AA	0650
T507047074AQ	0521
T507047084AA	0650
T507047084AQ	0521
T507048024AA	0650
T507048024AQ	0521
T507048034AA	0650
T507048034AQ	0521
T507048044AA	0650
T507048044AQ	0521
T507048054AA	0650
T507048054AQ	0521
T507048064AA	0650
T507048064AQ	0521
T507048074AA	0650
T507048074AQ	0521
T507048084AA	0650
T507048084AQ	0521
T507054024AA	0650
T507054024AQ	0521
T507054034AA	0650
T507054034AQ	0521
T507054044AA	0650
T507054044AQ	0521
T507054054AA	0650
T507054054AQ	0521
T507054064AA	0650
T507054064AQ	0521
T507054074AA	0650
T507054074AQ	0521
T507054084AA	0650
T507054084AQ	0521
T507057024AA	0650
T507057024AQ	0521
T507057034AA	0650
T507057034AQ	0521
T507057044AA	0650
T507057044AQ	0521
T507057054AA	0650
T507057054AQ	0521
T507057064AA	0650
T507057064AQ	0521
T507057074AA	0650
T507057074AQ	0521
T507057084AA	0650
T507057084AQ	0521
T507058024AA	0650
T507058024AQ	0521
T507058034AA	0650
T507058034AQ	0521
T507058044AA	0650
T507058044AQ	0521
T507058054AA	0650
T507058054AQ	0521
T507058064AA	0650
T507058064AQ	0521
T507058074AA	0650
T507058074AQ	0521
T507058084AA	0650
T507058084AQ	0521
T507064024AA	0650
T507064024AQ	0521
T507064034AA	0650
T507064034AQ	0521
T507064044AA	0650
T507064044AQ	0521
T507064054AA	0650
T507064054AQ	0521
T507064064AA	0650
T507064064AQ	0521
T507064074AA	0650
T507064074AQ	0521
T507064084AA	0650
T507064084AQ	0521
T507067024AA	0650
T507067024AQ	0521
T507067034AA	0650
T507067034AQ	0521
T507067044AA	0650
T507067044AQ	0521
T507067054AA	0650
T507067054AQ	0521
T507067064AA	0650
T507067064AQ	0521
T507067074AA	0650
T507067074AQ	0521
T507067084AA	0650
T507067084AQ	0521
T507068024AA	0650
T507068024AQ	0521
T507068034AA	0650
T507068034AQ	0521
T507068044AA	0650
T507068044AQ	0521
T507068054AA	0650
T507068054AQ	0521
T507068064AA	0650
T507068064AQ	0521
T507068074AA	0650
T507068074AQ	0521
T507068084AA	0650
T507068084AQ	0521
T507074024AA	0020
T507074024AQ	0108
T507074034AA	0020
T507074034AQ	0108
T507074044AA	0020
T507074044AQ	0108
T507074054AA	0020
T507074054AQ	0108
T507074064AA	0020
T507074064AQ	0108
T507074074AA	0020
T507074074AQ	0108
T507074084AQ	0108
T507077024AA	0020
T507077024AQ	0108
T507077034AA	0020
T507077034AQ	0108
T507077044AA	0020
T507077044AQ	0108
T507077054AA	0020
T507077054AQ	0108
T507077064AA	0020
T507077064AQ	0108
T507077074AA	0020
T507077074AQ	0108
T507077084AQ	0108
T507078024AA	0020
T507078024AQ	0108
T507078034AA	0020
T507078034AQ	0108
T507078044AA	0020
T507078044AQ	0108
T507078054AA	0020
T507078054AQ	0108
T507078064AA	0020
T507078064AQ	0108
T507078074AA	0020
T507078074AQ	0108
T507078084AQ	0108
T507084024AA	0020
T507084024AQ	0108
T507084034AA	0020
T507084034AQ	0108
T507084044AA	0020
T507084044AQ	0108
T507084054AA	0020
T507084054AQ	0108
T507084064AA	0020
T507084064AQ	0108
T507084074AA	0020
T507084074AQ	0108
T507087024AA	0020
T507087024AQ	0108
T507087034AA	0020
T507087034AQ	0108
T507087044AA	0020
T507087044AQ	0108
T507087054AA	0020
T507087054AQ	0108
T507087064AA	0020
T507087064AQ	0108
T507087074AA	0020
T507087074AQ	0108
T507087084AQ	0108
T507088024AA	0020
T507088024AQ	0108
T507088034AA	0020
T507088034AQ	0108
T507088044AA	0020
T507088044AQ	0108
T507088054AA	0020
T507088054AQ	0108
T507088064AA	0020
T507088064AQ	0108
T507088074AA	0020
T507088074AQ	0108
T507088084AQ	0108
T507094024AA	0020
T507094024AQ	0108
T507094034AA	0020
T507094034AQ	0108
T507094044AA	0020
T507094044AQ	0108
T507094054AA	0020
T507094054AQ	0108
T507094064AA	0020
T507094064AQ	0108
T507094074AA	0020
T507094074AQ	0108
T507094084AQ	0108
T507097024AA	0020
T507097024AQ	0108
T507097034AA	0020
T507097034AQ	0108
T507097044AA	0020
T507097044AQ	0108
T507097054AA	0020
T507097054AQ	0108
T507097064AA	0020
T507097064AQ	0108
T507097074AA	0020
T507097074AQ	0108
T507097084AQ	0108
T507098024AA	0020
T507098024AQ	0108
T507098034AA	0020
T507098034AQ	0108
T507098044AA	0020
T507098044AQ	0108
T507098054AA	0020
T507098054AQ	0108
T507098064AA	0020
T507098064AQ	0108
T507098074AA	0020
T507098074AQ	0108
T507104024AA	0020
T507104024AQ	0108
T507104034AA	0020
T507104034AQ	0108
T507104044AA	0020
T507104044AQ	0108
T507104054AA	0020
T507104054AQ	0108
T507104064AA	0020
T507104064AQ	0108
T507104074AA	0020
T507104074AQ	0108
T507107024AA	0020
T507107024AQ	0108
T507107034AA	0020
T507107034AQ	0108
T507107044AA	0020
T507107044AQ	0108
T507107054AA	0020
T507107054AQ	0108
T507107064AA	0020
T507107064AQ	0108
T507107074AA	0020
T507107074AQ	0108
T507108024AA	0020
T507108024AQ	0108
T507108034AA	0020
T507108034AQ	0108
T507108044AA	0020
T507108044AQ	0108
T507108054AA	0020
T507108054AQ	0108
T507108064AA	0020
T507108064AQ	0108
T507108074AA	0020
T507108074AQ	0108
T507114024AA	0020
T507114024AQ	0108
T507114034AA	0020
T507114034AQ	0108
T507114044AA	0020
T507114044AQ	0108
T507114054AA	0020
T507114054AQ	0108
T507114064AA	0020
T507114064AQ	0108
T507114074AQ	0108
T507117024AA	0020
T507117024AQ	0108
T507117034AA	0020
T507117034AQ	0108
T507117044AA	0020
T507117044AQ	0108
T507117054AA	0020
T507117054AQ	0108
T507117064AA	0020
T507117064AQ	0108
T507117074AQ	0108
T507118024AA	0020
T507118024AQ	0108
T507118034AA	0020
T507118034AQ	0108
T507118044AA	0020
T507118044AQ	0108
T507118054AA	0020
T507118054AQ	0108
T507118064AA	0020
T507118064AQ	0108
T507118074AQ	0108
T507124024AA	0020
T507124024AQ	0108
T507124034AA	0020
T507124034AQ	0108
T507124044AA	0020
T507124044AQ	0108
T507124054AA	0020
T507124054AQ	0108
T507124064AA	0020
T507124064AQ	0108
T507124074AQ	0108
T507127024AA	0020
T507127024AQ	0108
T507127034AA	0020
T507127034AQ	0108
T507127044AA	0020
T507127044AQ	0108
T507127054AA	0020
T507127054AQ	0108
T507127064AA	0020
T507127064AQ	0108
T507127074AQ	0108
T507128024AA	0020
T507128024AQ	0108
T507128034AA	0020
T507128034AQ	0108
T507128044AA	0020
T507128044AQ	0108
T507128054AA	0020
T507128054AQ	0108
T507128064AA	0020
T507128064AQ	0108
T507128074AQ	0108
T507138044AB	OEM
T507138044AQ	OEM
T507144024AA	OEM
T507144024AQ	OEM
T507144034AA	OEM
T507144034AB	OEM
T507144034AQ	OEM
T507144044AA	OEM
T507144044AQ	OEM
T507144054AA	OEM
T507144054AB	OEM
T507144054AQ	OEM
T507144064AA	OEM
T507144064AQ	OEM
T507147024AA	OEM
T507147024AQ	OEM
T507147034AA	OEM
T507147034AB	OEM
T507147034AQ	OEM
T507147044AA	OEM
T507147044AB	OEM
T507147044AQ	OEM
T507147054AA	OEM
T507147054AB	OEM
T507147054AQ	OEM
T507147064AA	OEM
T507147064AQ	OEM
T507148024AA	OEM
T507148024AQ	OEM
T507148034AA	OEM
T507148034AQ	OEM
T507148044AA	OEM
T507148044AQ	OEM
T507148054AA	OEM
T507148054AQ	OEM
T507148064AA	OEM
T507148064AQ	OEM
T507154024AA	OEM
T507154024AQ	OEM
T507154034AA	OEM
T507154034AQ	OEM
T507154044AA	OEM
T507154044AQ	OEM
T507154054AA	OEM
T507154054AQ	OEM
T507157024AA	OEM
T507157024AQ	OEM
T507157034AA	OEM
T507157034AQ	OEM
T507157044AA	OEM
T507157044AQ	OEM
T507157054AA	OEM
T507157054AQ	OEM

If replacement code is OEM, contact original manufacturer for replacement.

Original Device Types

DEVICE TYPE	REPL CODE
T507158024AA	OEM
T507158024AQ	OEM
T507158034AA	OEM
T507158034AQ	OEM
T507158044AA	OEM
T507158044AQ	OEM
T507158054AA	OEM
T507158054AQ	OEM
T508097007AA	OEM
T508107007AA	OEM
T508257007AA	OEM
T510005004AB	0217
T510005004AQ	0217
T510005005AB	0217
T510005005AQ	0217
T510005007(T083)	0650
T510005007(T094)	0521
T510005007AB	0217
T510008004AB	0217
T510008004AQ	0636
T510008005AB	0217
T510008005AQ	0217
T510008007(T083)	0650
T510008007(T094)	0521
T510008007AB	0217
T510008007AQ	0217
T510015004AB	0217
T510015004AQ	0217
T510015005AB	0217
T510015005AQ	0217
T510015007(T083)	0650
T510015007(T094)	0521
T510015007AB	0217
T510015007AQ	0217
T510018004AB	0217
T510018004AQ	0217
T510018005AB	0217
T510018005AQ	0217
T510018007(T083)	0650
T510018007(T094)	0521
T510018007AB	0217
T510018007AQ	0217
T510025004AB	0217
T510025004AQ	0217
T510025005AB	0217
T510025005AQ	0217
T510025007(T083)	0650
T510025007(T094)	0521
T510025007AB	0217
T510025007AQ	0217
T510028004AB	0217
T510028004AQ	0217
T510028005AB	0217
T510028005AQ	0217
T510028007(T083)	0650
T510028007(T094)	0521
T510028007AB	0217
T510028007AQ	0217
T510035004AB	0217
T510035004AQ	0217
T510035005AB	0217
T510035005AQ	0217
T510035007(T083)	0650
T510035007(T094)	0521
T510035007AB	0217
T510035007AQ	0217
T510038004AB	0217
T510038004AQ	0217
T510038005AB	0217
T510038005AQ	0217
T510038007(T083)	0650
T510038007(T094)	0521
T510038007AB	0217
T510038007AQ	0217
T510045004AB	0217
T510045004AQ	0217
T510045005AB	0217
T510045005AQ	0217
T510045007(T083)	0650
T510045007(T094)	0521
T510045007AB	0217
T510045007AQ	0217
T510048004AB	0217
T510048004AQ	0217
T510048005AB	0217
T510048005AQ	0217
T510048007(T083)	0650
T510048007(T094)	0521
T510048007AB	0217
T510048007AQ	0217
T510055004AB	0217
T510055004AQ	0217
T510055005AB	0217
T510055005AQ	0217
T510055007(T083)	0650
T510055007(T094)	0521
T510055007AB	0217
T510055007AQ	0217
T510058004AB	0217
T510058004AQ	0217
T510058005AB	0217
T510058005AQ	0217
T510058007(T083)	0650
T510058007(T094)	0521
T510058007AB	0217
T510058007AQ	0217
T510065004AB	0217
T510065004AQ	0217
T510065005AB	0217
T510065005AQ	0217
T510065007(T083)	0650
T510065007(T094)	0521
T510065007AB	0217
T510065007AQ	0217
T510068004AB	0217
T510068004AQ	0217
T510068005AB	0217
T510068005AQ	0217
T510068007(T083)	0650
T510068007(T094)	0521
T510068007AB	0217
T510068007AQ	0217
T520011305	0192
T520021305	0192
T520031305	0159
T520041305	0159
T520051305	0159
T520061305	0159
T520071305	0096
T520081305	0096
T520091305	0096
T520101305	0096
T520121305	0096
T520141305	OEM
T520161305	OEM
T527011324DN	0454
T527011334DN	0454
T527011344DN	0454
T527011354DN	0454
T527011364DN	0454
T527011374DN	0454
T527011384DN	0454
T527021324DN	0454
T527021334DN	0454
T527021344DN	0454
T527021354DN	0454
T527021364DN	0454
T527021374DN	0454
T527021384DN	0454
T527031324DN	0454
T527031334DN	0454
T527031344DN	0454
T527031354DN	0454
T527031364DN	0454
T527031374DN	0454
T527031384DN	0454
T527041324DN	0454
T527041334DN	0454
T527041344DN	0454
T527041354DN	0454
T527041364DN	0454
T527041374DN	0454
T527041384DN	0454
T527051324DN	0454
T527051334DN	0454
T527051344DN	0454
T527051354DN	0454
T527051364DN	0454
T527051374DN	0454
T527051384DN	0454
T527061324DN	0454
T527061334DN	0454
T527061344DN	0454
T527061354DN	0454
T527061364DN	0454
T527061374DN	0454
T527061384DN	0454
T527071324DN	0584
T527071334DN	0584
T527071344DN	0584
T527071354DN	0584
T527071364DN	0584
T527071374DN	0584
T527081324DN	0584
T527081334DN	0584
T527081344DN	0584
T527081354DN	0584
T527081364DN	0584
T527081374DN	0584
T527091324DN	0584
T527091334DN	0584
T527091344DN	0584
T527091354DN	0584
T527091364DN	0584
T527091374DN	0584
T527101324DN	0584
T527101334DN	0584
T527101344DN	0584
T527101354DN	0584
T527101364DN	0584
T527101374DN	0584
T527111324DN	0584
T527111334DN	0584
T527111344DN	0584
T527111354DN	0584
T527111364DN	0584
T527121284DN	0584
T527121324DN	0584
T527121334DN	0584
T527121344DN	0584
T527121354DN	0584
T527121364DN	0584
T527141324DN	OEM
T527141334DN	OEM
T527141344DN	OEM
T527141354DN	OEM
T527141364DN	OEM
T527151324DN	OEM
T527151334DN	OEM
T527151344DN	OEM
T527151354DN	OEM
T600011304	1076
T600011504	1076
T600011804	1076
T600021304	1076
T600021504	1076
T600021804	1076
T600031304	1078
T600031504	1078
T600031804	1078
T600041304	1078
T600041504	1078
T600041804	1078
T600051304	1078
T600051504	1078
T600051804	1078
T600061304	1078
T600061504	1078
T600061804	1078
T600071304	1094
T600071304BT	0733
T600071504	1094
T600071504BT	0733
T600071804	1094
T600081304	1094
T600081304BT	0733
T600081504	1094
T600081504BT	0733
T600081804	1094
T600081804BT	1094
T600091304	1094
T600091304BT	0733
T600091504	1094
T600091804	1094
T600091804BT	1094
T600101304	1094
T600101304BT	0733
T600101504	1094
T600101504BT	0733
T600101804	1094
T600101804BT	1094
T600111304BT	0733
T600111504BT	0733
T600111804BT	1094
T600121304	1094
T600121304BT	0733
T600121504	1094
T600121504BT	0733
T600121804	1094
T600121804BT	1094
T600141304	OEM
T600141504	OEM
T600141804	OEM
T600161304	OEM
T600161504	OEM
T600161804	OEM
T604011842BT	OEM
T604011852BT	OEM
T604021842BT	OEM
T604021852BT	OEM
T604031842BT	OEM
T604031852BT	OEM
T604041842BT	OEM
T604041852BT	OEM
T604051842BT	OEM
T604051852BT	OEM
T604061842BT	OEM
T604061852BT	OEM
T604071842BT	OEM
T604071852BT	OEM
T604081842BT	OEM
T604081852BT	OEM
T604091842BT	OEM
T604101842BT	OEM
T607011324BT	0423
T607011334BT	0423
T607011344BT	0423
T607011354BT	0423
T607011364BT	0423
T607011374BT	0423
T607011384BT	0423
T607011524BT	0423
T607011534BT	0423
T607011544BT	0423
T607011554BT	0423
T607011564BT	0423
T607011574BT	0423
T607011584BT	0423
T607011824BT	0423
T607011834BT	0423
T607011844BT	0423
T607011854BT	0423
T607011864BT	0423
T607011874BT	0423
T607011884BT	0423
T607017084BT	0423
T607021324BT	0423
T607021334BT	0423
T607021344BT	0423
T607021354BT	0423
T607021364BT	0423
T607021374BT	0423
T607021384BT	0423
T607021524BT	0423
T607021534BT	0423
T607021544BT	0423
T607021554BT	0423
T607021564BT	0423
T607021574BT	0423
T607021584BT	0423
T607021824BT	0423
T607021834BT	0423
T607021844BT	0423
T607021854BT	0423
T607021864BT	0423
T607021874BT	0423
T607021884BT	0423
T607031324BT	0423
T607031334BT	0423
T607031344BT	0423
T607031354BT	0423
T607031364BT	0423
T607031374BT	0423
T607031384BT	0423
T607031524BT	0423
T607031534BT	0423
T607031544BT	0423
T607031554BT	0423
T607031564BT	0423
T607031574BT	0423
T607031584BT	0423
T607031824BT	0423
T607031834BT	0423
T607031844BT	0423
T607031854BT	0423
T607031864BT	0423
T607031874BT	0423
T607031884BT	0423
T607041324BT	0423
T607041334BT	0423
T607041344BT	0423
T607041354BT	0423
T607041364BT	0423
T607041374BT	0423
T607041384BT	0423
T607041524BT	0423
T607041534BT	0423
T607041544BT	0423
T607041554BT	0423
T607041564BT	0423
T607041574BT	0423
T607041584BT	0423
T607041824BT	0423
T607041834BT	0423
T607041844BT	0423
T607041854BT	0423
T607041864BT	0423
T607041874BT	0423
T607041884BT	0423
T607051324BT	0423
T607051334BT	0423
T607051344BT	0423
T607051354BT	0423
T607051364BT	0423
T607051374BT	0423
T607051384BT	0423
T607051524BT	0423
T607051534BT	0423
T607051544BT	0423
T607051554BT	0423
T607051564BT	0423
T607051574BT	0423
T607051584BT	0423
T607051824BT	0423
T607051834BT	0423
T607051844BT	0423
T607051854BT	0423
T607051864BT	0423
T607051874BT	0423
T607051884BT	0423
T607061324BT	0423
T607061334BT	0423
T607061344BT	0423
T607061354BT	0423
T607061364BT	0423
T607061374BT	0423
T607061384BT	0423
T607061524BT	0423
T607061534BT	0423
T607061544BT	0423
T607061554BT	0423
T607061564BT	0423
T607061574BT	0423
T607061584BT	0423
T607061824BT	0423
T607061834BT	0423
T607061844BT	0423
T607061854BT	0423
T607061864BT	0423
T607061874BT	0423
T607061884BT	0423
T607071324BT	1860
T607071334BT	1860
T607071344BT	1860
T607071354BT	1860
T607071364BT	1860
T607071374BT	1860
T607071384BT	1860
T607071524BT	1860
T607071534BT	1860
T607071544BT	1860
T607071554BT	1860
T607071564BT	1860
T607071574BT	1860
T607071584BT	1860
T607071824BT	1860
T607071834BT	1860
T607071844BT	1860
T607071854BT	1860
T607071864BT	1860
T607071874BT	1860
T607071884BT	1860
T607081324BT	1860
T607081334BT	1860
T607081344BT	1860
T607081354BT	1860
T607081364BT	1860
T607081374BT	1860
T607081384BT	1860
T607081524BT	1860
T607081534BT	1860
T607081544BT	1860
T607081554BT	1860
T607081564BT	1860
T607081574BT	1860
T607081584BT	1860
T607081824BT	1860
T607081834BT	1860
T607081844BT	1860
T607081854BT	1860
T607081864BT	1860
T607081874BT	1860
T607081884BT	1860
T607091324BT	1860
T607091334BT	1860
T607091344BT	1860
T607091354BT	1860
T607091364BT	1860
T607091374BT	1860
T607091384BT	1860
T607091524BT	1860
T607091534BT	1860
T607091544BT	1860
T607091554BT	1860
T607091564BT	1860
T607091574BT	1860
T607091584BT	1860
T607091824BT	1860
T607091834BT	1860
T607091844BT	1860
T607091854BT	1860
T607091864BT	1860
T607091874BT	1860
T607091884BT	1860
T607101324BT	1860
T607101334BT	1860
T607101344BT	1860
T607101354BT	1860
T607101364BT	1860
T607101374BT	1860
T607101524BT	1860
T607101534BT	1860
T607101544BT	1860
T607101554BT	1860
T607101564BT	1860
T607101574BT	1860
T607101824BT	1860
T607101834BT	1860
T607101844BT	1860
T607101854BT	1860
T607101864BT	1860
T607101874BT	1860
T607111324BT	1860
T607111334BT	1860
T607111344BT	1860
T607111354BT	1860
T607111364BT	1860
T607111524BT	1860
T607111534BT	1860
T607111544BT	1860
T607111554BT	1860
T607111564BT	1860
T607111824BT	1860
T607111834BT	1860
T607111844BT	1860
T607111854BT	1860
T607111864BT	1860
T607121324BT	1860
T607121334BT	1860
T607121344BT	1860
T607121354BT	1860
T607121364BT	1860
T607121524BT	1860
T607121534BT	1860
T607121544BT	1860
T607121554BT	1860
T607121564BT	1860
T607121824BT	1860
T607121834BT	1860
T607121844BT	1860
T607121854BT	1860
T607121864BT	1860
T607141324BT	OEM
T607141334BT	OEM
T607141344BT	OEM
T607141354BT	OEM
T607141364BT	OEM
T607141524BT	OEM
T607141534BT	OEM
T607141544BT	OEM
T607141554BT	OEM
T607141564BT	OEM
T607141824BT	OEM
T607141834BT	OEM
T607141844BT	OEM
T607141854BT	OEM
T607141864BT	OEM
T607151324BT	OEM
T607151334BT	OEM
T607151344BT	OEM
T607151354BT	OEM
T607151524BT	OEM
T607151534BT	OEM
T607151544BT	OEM
T607151554BT	OEM
T607151824BT	OEM
T607151834BT	OEM
T607151844BT	OEM
T607151854BT	OEM
T610011304BT	1076
T610011304DT	0733
T610011504BT	1076
T610011504DT	0733
T610011804BT	1076
T610021304BT	1076
T610021304DT	0733
T610021504BT	1076
T610021504DT	0733
T610021804BT	1076
T610031304BT	1078
T610031304DT	0733
T610031504BT	1078
T610031504DT	0733
T610031804BT	1078
T610041304BT	1078
T610041304DT	0733
T610041504BT	1078
T610041504DT	0733
T610041804BT	1078
T610051304BT	0733
T610051504BT	0733
T610051804BT	1078
T610061304BT	0733
T610061504BT	0733
T610061804BT	1078
T620011304	0192
T620012004	0192
T620013004	0192
T620021304	0192
T620022004	0192
T620023004	0192
T620031304	0159
T620032004	0159
T620033004	0159
T620041304	0159
T620042004	0159
T620043004	0159
T620051304	0159
T620052004	0159
T620053004	0159
T620061304	0159
T620062004	0159
T620063004	0159
T620071304	0096
T620071504DN	0096
T620072004	0096
T620072004DN	0096
T620073004	0096
T620073004DN	0096
T620081304	0096
T620082004	0096
T620082004DN	0096
T620083004	0096
T620083004DN	0096
T620091304	0096
T620091504DN	0096
T620092004	0096
T620092004DN	0096
T620093004	0096
T620093004DN	0096
T620101304	0096
T620101504DN	0096
T620102004	0096
T620102004DN	0096
T620103004	0096
T620103004DN	0096
T620111504DN	0096
T620112004DN	0096
T620113004DN	0096
T620121304	0096
T620121504DN	0096
T620122004	0096
T620122004DN	0096
T620123004	0096
T620123004DN	0096
T620141304	OEM
T620142004	OEM
T620143004	OEM
T620161304	OEM
T620162004	OEM
T620163004	OEM
T627011524DN	0454
T627011534DN	0454
T627011544DN	0454
T627011554DN	0454
T627011564DN	0454
T627011574DN	0454
T627011584DN	0454
T627012024DN	0454
T627012034DN	0454
T627012044DN	0454
T627012054DN	0454
T627012064DN	0454
T627012074DN	0454
T627012084DN	0454
T627012524DN	0454
T627012534DN	0454
T627012544DN	0454
T627012554DN	0454
T627012564DN	0454
T627012574DN	0454
T627012584DN	0454
T627021524DN	0454
T627021534DN	0454
T627021544DN	0454
T627021554DN	0454
T627021564DN	0454
T627021574DN	0454
T627021584DN	0454
T627022024DN	0454
T627022034DN	0454
T627022044DN	0454
T627022054DN	0454
T627022064DN	0454
T627022074DN	0454
T627022084DN	0454
T627022524DN	0454
T627022534DN	0454
T627022544DN	0454
T627022554DN	0454
T627022564DN	0454
T627022574DN	0454
T627022584DN	0454
T627031524DN	0454
T627031534DN	0454
T627031544DN	0454
T627031554DN	0454
T627031564DN	0454
T627031574DN	0454
T627031584DN	0454
T627032024DN	0454
T627032034DN	0454
T627032044DN	0454
T627032054DN	0454
T627032064DN	0454
T627032074DN	0454
T627032084DN	0454
T627032524DN	0454
T627032534DN	0454
T627032544DN	0454
T627032554DN	0454
T627032564DN	0454
T627032574DN	0454
T627032584DN	0454
T627041524DN	OEM
T627041534DN	0454
T627041544DN	0454
T627041554DN	0454
T627041564DN	0454
T627041574DN	0454
T627041584DN	0454
T627042024DN	0454
T627042034DN	0454
T627042044DN	0454
T627042054DN	0454
T627042064DN	0454
T627042074DN	0454
T627042084DN	0454
T627042524DN	0454
T627042534DN	0454
T627042544DN	0454
T627042554DN	0454
T627042564DN	0454
T627042574DN	0454
T627042584DN	0454
T627051524DN	0454
T627051534DN	0454
T627051544DN	0454
T627051554DN	0454
T627051564DN	0454
T627051574DN	0454
T627051584DN	0454
T627052024DN	0454
T627052034DN	0454
T627052044DN	0454
T627052054DN	0454
T627052064DN	0454
T627052074DN	0454
T627052084DN	0454
T627052524DN	0454
T627052534DN	0454
T627052544DN	0454
T627052554DN	0454
T627052564DN	0454
T627052574DN	0454
T627052584DN	0454
T627061524DN	0454
T627061534DN	0454
T627061544DN	0454
T627061554DN	0454
T627061564DN	0454
T627061574DN	0454
T627061584DN	0454
T627062024DN	0454
T627062034DN	0454
T627062044DN	0454
T627062054DN	0454
T627062064DN	0454
T627062074DN	0454
T627062084DN	0454
T627062524DN	0454
T627062534DN	0454
T627062544DN	0454

If replacement code is OEM, contact original manufacturer for replacement.

DEVICE TYPE	REPL CODE
T627062554DN	0454
T627062564DN	0454
T627062574DN	0454
T627062584DN	0454
T627071524DN	0584
T627071534DN	0584
T627071544DN	0584
T627071554DN	0584
T627071564DN	0584
T627071574DN	0584
T627071584DN	0584
T627072024DN	0584
T627072034DN	0584
T627072044DN	0584
T627072054DN	0584
T627072064DN	0584
T627072074DN	0584
T627072084DN	0584
T627072524DN	0584
T627072534DN	0584
T627072544DN	0584
T627072554DN	0584
T627072564DN	0584
T627072574DN	0584
T627072584DN	0584
T627081524DN	0584
T627081534DN	0584
T627081544DN	0584
T627081554DN	0584
T627081564DN	0584
T627081574DN	0584
T627081584DN	0584
T627082024DN	0584
T627082034DN	0584
T627082044DN	0584
T627082054DN	0584
T627082064DN	0584
T627082074DN	0584
T627082084DN	0584
T627082524DN	0584
T627082534DN	0584
T627082544DN	0584
T627082554DN	0584
T627082564DN	0584
T627082574DN	0584
T627082584DN	0584
T627091524DN	0584
T627091534DN	0584
T627091544DN	0584
T627091554DN	0584
T627091564DN	0584
T627091574DN	0584
T627091584DN	0584
T627092024DN	0584
T627092034DN	0584
T627092044DN	0584
T627092054DN	0584
T627092064DN	0584
T627092074DN	0584
T627092084DN	0584
T627092524DN	0584
T627092534DN	0584
T627092544DN	0584
T627092554DN	0584
T627092564DN	0584
T627092574DN	0584
T627092584DN	0584
T627101524DN	0584
T627101534DN	0584
T627101544DN	0584
T627101554DN	0584
T627101564DN	0584
T627101574DN	0584
T627101584DN	0584
T627102024DN	0584
T627102034DN	0584
T627102044DN	0584
T627102054DN	0584
T627102064DN	0584
T627102074DN	0584
T627102084DN	0584
T627102524DN	0584
T627102534DN	0584
T627102544DN	0584
T627102554DN	0584
T627102564DN	0584
T627102574DN	0584
T627102584DN	0584
T627111524DN	0584
T627111534DN	0584
T627111544DN	0584
T627111554DN	0584
T627111564DN	0584
T627111574DN	0584
T627111584DN	0584
T627112024DN	0584
T627112034DN	0584
T627112044DN	0584
T627112054DN	0584
T627112064DN	0584
T627112074DN	0584
T627112084DN	0584
T627112524DN	0584
T627112534DN	0584
T627112544DN	0584
T627112554DN	0584
T627112564DN	0584
T627112574DN	0584
T627112584DN	0584

DEVICE TYPE	REPL CODE
T627121524DN	0584
T627121534DN	0584
T627121544DN	0584
T627121554DN	0584
T627121564DN	0584
T627121574DN	0584
T627121584DN	0584
T627122024DN	0584
T627122034DN	0584
T627122044DN	0584
T627122054DN	0584
T627122064DN	0584
T627122074DN	0584
T627122084DN	0584
T627122524DN	0584
T627122534DN	0584
T627122544DN	0584
T627122554DN	0584
T627122564DN	0584
T627122574DN	0584
T627122584DN	0584
T627141524DN	OEM
T627141534DN	OEM
T627141544DN	OEM
T627141554DN	OEM
T627141564DN	OEM
T627142024DN	OEM
T627142034DN	OEM
T627142044DN	OEM
T627142054DN	OEM
T627142064DN	OEM
T627142524DN	OEM
T627142534DN	OEM
T627142544DN	OEM
T627142554DN	OEM
T627142564DN	OEM
T627151524DN	OEM
T627151534DN	OEM
T627151544DN	OEM
T627151554DN	OEM
T627152024DN	OEM
T627152034DN	OEM
T627152044DN	OEM
T627152054DN	OEM
T627152524DN	OEM
T627152534DN	OEM
T627152544DN	OEM
T627152554DN	OEM
T630011504DN	0159
T630012004DN	0159
T630013004DN	0192
T630021504DN	0192
T630022004DN	0159
T630023004DN	0192
T630031504DN	0159
T630032004DN	0159
T630033004DN	0159
T630041504DN	0159
T630042004DN	0159
T630043004DN	0159
T630051504DN	0159
T630052004DN	0159
T630053004DN	0159
T630061504DN	0159
T630062004DN	0159
T630063004DN	0159
T660013004BY	OEM
T660023004BY	OEM
T660033004BY	OEM
T660043004BY	OEM
T660053004BY	OEM
T660063004BY	OEM
T660073004BY	OEM
T660083004BY	OEM
T660093004BY	OEM
T660103004BY	OEM
T660113004BY	OEM
T660123004BY	OEM
T660133004BY	OEM
T660143004BY	OEM
T700012504	1889
T700012504BY	1889
T700013004	1889
T700013004BY	1889
T700013504	1889
T700022504	1889
T700022504BY	1889
T700023004	1889
T700023004BY	1889
T700023504	1889
T700032504	1889
T700033004	1889
T700033504	1889
T700042504	1889
T700042504BY	0733
T700043004	1889
T700043004BY	0733
T700043504	1889
T700052504	1889
T700053004	1889
T700053504	1889
T700062504	1889
T700062504BY	0733
T700063004	1889
T700063004BY	0733
T700063504	1889
T700072504	0733
T700073004	0733
T700073504	0733

DEVICE TYPE	REPL CODE
T700082504	0733
T700082504BY	0733
T700083004	0733
T700083004BY	0733
T700083504	0733
T700092504	0733
T700093004	0733
T700093504	0733
T700102504	0733
T700102504BY	0733
T700103004	0733
T700103004BY	0733
T700103504	0733
T700122504	0733
T700122504BY	0733
T700123004	0733
T700123004BY	0733
T700123504	0733
T700123504BY	0733
T700142504	OEM
T700143004	OEM
T700143504	OEM
T700162504	OEM
T700163004	OEM
T700163504	OEM
T700182504	OEM
T700183004	OEM
T700202504	OEM
T700203004	OEM
T700222504	OEM
T700222504BY	OEM
T700223004BY	OEM
T700242504	OEM
T707011324BT	1690
T707011334BT	1690
T707011344BT	1690
T707011354BT	1690
T707011364BT	1690
T707011374BT	OEM
T707011384BT	OEM
T707011524BT	1690
T707011534BT	1690
T707011544BT	1690
T707011554BT	1690
T707011564BT	1690
T707011574BT	OEM
T707011824BT	1690
T707011834BT	1690
T707011844BT	1690
T707011854BT	1690
T707011864BT	1690
T707011874BT	OEM
T707011884BT	OEM
T707012524BY	1690
T707012534BY	1690
T707012544BY	1690
T707012834BY	1690
T707012844BY	1690
T707012854BY	1690
T707013024BY	1690
T707013034BY	1690
T707013044BY	1690
T707013054BY	1690
T707017084BT	OEM
T707021324BT	1690
T707021334BT	1690
T707021344BT	1690
T707021354BT	1690
T707021364BT	1690
T707021374BT	OEM
T707021384BT	OEM
T707021524BT	1690
T707021534BT	1690
T707021544BT	1690
T707021554BT	1690
T707021564BT	1690
T707021574BT	OEM
T707021584BT	OEM
T707021824BT	1690
T707021834BT	1690
T707021844BT	1690
T707021854BT	1690
T707021864BT	1690
T707021874BT	OEM
T707021884BT	OEM
T707022524BY	1690
T707022534BY	1690
T707022544BY	1690
T707022554BY	1690
T707022834BY	1690
T707022844BY	1690
T707022854BY	1690
T707023024BY	1690
T707023034BY	1690
T707023044BY	1690
T707023054BY	1690
T707031324BT	1690
T707031334BT	1690
T707031344BT	1690
T707031354BT	1690
T707031364BT	1690
T707031374BT	OEM
T707031384BT	OEM
T707031524BT	1690
T707031534BT	1690
T707031544BT	1690
T707031554BT	1690
T707031564BT	1690
T707031574BT	OEM

DEVICE TYPE	REPL CODE
T707031584BT	OEM
T707031824BT	1690
T707031834BT	1690
T707031844BT	1690
T707031854BT	1690
T707031864BT	1690
T707031874BT	OEM
T707031884BT	OEM
T707032524BY	1690
T707032534BY	1690
T707032544BY	1690
T707032554BY	1690
T707032834BY	OEM
T707032844BY	OEM
T707032854BY	1690
T707033024BY	1690
T707033034BY	1690
T707033044BY	1690
T707033054BY	1690
T707041324BT	1690
T707041334BT	1690
T707041344BT	1690
T707041354BT	1690
T707041364BT	1690
T707041374BT	OEM
T707041384BT	OEM
T707041524BT	1690
T707041534BT	1690
T707041544BT	1690
T707041554BT	1690
T707041564BT	1690
T707041574BT	OEM
T707041584BT	OEM
T707041824BT	1690
T707041834BT	1690
T707041844BT	1690
T707041854BT	1690
T707041864BT	1690
T707041874BT	OEM
T707041884BT	OEM
T707042524BY	1690
T707042534BY	1690
T707042544BY	1690
T707042554BY	1690
T707042834BY	1690
T707042844BY	1690
T707042854BY	1690
T707043024BY	1690
T707043034BY	1690
T707043044BY	1690
T707043054BY	1690
T707051324BT	1690
T707051334BT	1690
T707051344BT	1690
T707051354BT	1690
T707051364BT	1690
T707051374BT	OEM
T707051384BT	OEM
T707051524BT	1690
T707051534BT	1690
T707051544BT	1690
T707051554BT	1690
T707051564BT	1690
T707051574BT	OEM
T707051584BT	OEM
T707051824BT	1690
T707051834BT	1690
T707051844BT	1690
T707051854BT	1690
T707051864BT	1690
T707051874BT	OEM
T707051884BT	OEM
T707052524BY	1690
T707052534BY	1690
T707052544BY	1690
T707052834BY	1690
T707052844BY	1690
T707052854BY	1690
T707053024BY	1690
T707053034BY	1690
T707053044BY	1690
T707053054BY	1690
T707061324BT	1690
T707061334BT	1690
T707061344BT	1690
T707061354BT	1690
T707061364BT	1690
T707061374BT	OEM
T707061384BT	OEM
T707061524BT	1690
T707061534BT	1690
T707061544BT	1690
T707061554BT	1690
T707061564BT	1690
T707061574BT	OEM
T707061584BT	OEM
T707061824BT	1690
T707061834BT	1690
T707061844BT	1690
T707061854BT	1690
T707061864BT	1690
T707061874BT	OEM
T707061884BT	OEM
T707062524BY	1690
T707062534BY	1690
T707062544BY	1690
T707062554BY	1690
T707062834BY	1690
T707062844BY	1690

DEVICE TYPE	REPL CODE
T707062854BY	1690
T707063024BY	1690
T707063034BY	1690
T707063044BY	1690
T707063054BY	1690
T707071324BT	0341
T707071334BT	0341
T707071344BT	0764
T707071354BT	0341
T707071364BT	0341
T707071374BT	OEM
T707071524BT	0341
T707071534BT	0341
T707071544BT	0341
T707071554BT	0341
T707071564BT	0341
T707071574BT	OEM
T707071824BT	0341
T707071834BT	0341
T707071844BT	0341
T707071854BT	0341
T707071864BT	0341
T707071874BT	OEM
T707072524BY	0341
T707072534BY	0341
T707072544BY	0341
T707072554BY	0341
T707072834BY	0341
T707072844BY	0341
T707072854BY	0341
T707073024BY	0341
T707073034BY	0341
T707073044BY	0341
T707073054BY	0341
T707081324BT	0341
T707081334BT	0341
T707081344BT	0341
T707081354BT	0341
T707081364BT	0341
T707081374BT	OEM
T707081524BT	0341
T707081534BT	0341
T707081544BT	0341
T707081554BT	0341
T707081564BT	0341
T707081574BT	OEM
T707081824BT	0341
T707081834BT	0341
T707081844BT	0341
T707081854BT	0341
T707081864BT	0341
T707081874BT	OEM
T707082524BY	0341
T707082534BY	0341
T707082544BY	0341
T707082554BY	0341
T707082834BY	0341
T707082844BY	0341
T707082854BY	0341
T707083024BY	0341
T707083034BY	0341
T707083044BY	0341
T707083054BY	0341
T707091324BT	0341
T707091334BT	0341
T707091344BT	0341
T707091354BT	0341
T707091364BT	0341
T707091374BT	OEM
T707091524BT	0341
T707091534BT	0341
T707091544BT	0341
T707091554BT	0341
T707091564BT	0341
T707091574BT	OEM
T707091824BT	0341
T707091834BT	0341
T707091844BT	0341
T707091854BT	0341
T707091864BT	0341
T707091874BT	OEM
T707092524BY	0341
T707092534BY	0341
T707092544BY	0341
T707092554BY	0341
T707093024BY	0341
T707093034BY	0341
T707093044BY	0341
T707093054BY	0341
T707101324BT	0341
T707101334BT	0341
T707101344BT	0341
T707101354BT	0341
T707101364BT	0341
T707101374BT	OEM
T707101524BT	0341
T707101534BT	0341
T707101544BT	0341
T707101554BT	0341
T707101564BT	0341
T707101574BT	OEM
T707101824BT	0341
T707101834BT	0341
T707101844BT	0341
T707101854BT	0341
T707101864BT	0341
T707101874BT	OEM
T707102524BY	0341
T707102534BY	0341

DEVICE TYPE	REPL CODE
T707102544BY	0341
T707102554BY	0341
T707103024BY	0341
T707103034BY	0341
T707103044BY	0341
T707103054BY	0341
T707111324BT	0341
T707111334BT	0341
T707111344BT	0341
T707111354BT	0341
T707111364BT	0341
T707111524BT	0341
T707111534BT	0341
T707111544BT	0341
T707111554BT	0341
T707111564BT	0341
T707111824BT	0341
T707111834BT	0341
T707111844BT	0341
T707111854BT	0341
T707111864BT	0341
T707112524BY	0341
T707112534BY	0341
T707112544BY	0341
T707112554BY	0341
T707113024BY	0341
T707113034BY	0341
T707113044BY	0341
T707113054BY	0341
T707121324BT	0341
T707121334BT	0341
T707121344BT	0341
T707121354BT	OEM
T707121364BT	0341
T707121524BT	0341
T707121534BT	0341
T707121544BT	0341
T707121554BT	0341
T707121564BT	0341
T707121824BT	0341
T707121834BT	0341
T707121844BT	0341
T707121854BT	0341
T707121864BT	0341
T707122524BY	0341
T707122534BY	0341
T707122544BY	0341
T707122554BY	0341
T707123024BY	0341
T707123034BY	0341
T707123044BY	0341
T707123054BY	0341
T707141324BT	OEM
T707141334BT	OEM
T707141344BT	OEM
T707141354BT	OEM
T707141364BT	OEM
T707141524BT	OEM
T707141534BT	OEM
T707141544BT	OEM
T707141554BT	OEM
T707141564BT	OEM
T707141824BT	OEM
T707141834BT	OEM
T707141844BT	OEM
T707141854BT	OEM
T707141864BT	OEM
T720013504	2816
T720014504	2816
T720015504	2816
T720023504	2816
T720024504	2816
T720025504	2816
T720033504	1754
T720034504	1754
T720035504	1754
T720043504	1754
T720044504	1754
T720045504	1754
T720053504	1754
T720054504	1754
T720055504	1754
T720063504	1754
T720064504	1754
T720065504	1754
T720073504	1803
T720074504	1803
T720075504	1803
T720083504	1803
T720083504DN	1803
T720084504	1803
T720084504DN	1803
T720085504	1803
T720085504DN	1803
T720093504	1803
T720094504	1803
T720095504	1803
T720103504	1803
T720103504DN	1803
T720104504	1803
T720104504DN	1803
T720105504	1803
T720105504DN	1803
T720123504	1803
T720124504	1803
T720125504	1803
T720143504	OEM
T720144504	OEM
T720145504	OEM

DEVICE TYPE	REPL CODE
T720163504	OEM
T720164504	OEM
T720165504	OEM
T720183504	OEM
T720184504	OEM
T720203504	OEM
T720204504	OEM
T720223504	OEM
T720243504	OEM
T727012524DN	0764
T727012534DN	0764
T727012544DN	0764
T727012554DN	0764
T727012564DN	0764
T727012574DN	OEM
T727012584DN	OEM
T727013524DN	0764
T727013534DN	0764
T727013544DN	0764
T727013554DN	0764
T727013564DN	0764
T727013574DN	OEM
T727013584DN	OEM
T727014524DN	0764
T727014534DN	0764
T727014544DN	0764
T727014554DN	0764
T727014564DN	0478
T727014574DN	OEM
T727014584DN	OEM
T727022524DN	0764
T727022534DN	0764
T727022544DN	0764
T727022554DN	0764
T727022564DN	0764
T727022574DN	OEM
T727022584DN	OEM
T727023524DN	0764
T727023534DN	0764
T727023544DN	0764
T727023554DN	0764
T727023564DN	0764
T727023574DN	OEM
T727023584DN	OEM
T727024524DN	0764
T727024534DN	0764
T727024544DN	0764
T727024554DN	0764
T727024564DN	0764
T727024574DN	OEM
T727024584DN	OEM
T727032524DN	0764
T727032534DN	0764
T727032544DN	0764
T727032554DN	0764
T727032564DN	0764
T727032574DN	OEM
T727032584DN	OEM
T727033524DN	0764
T727033534DN	0764
T727033544DN	0764
T727033554DN	0764
T727033564DN	0764
T727033574DN	OEM
T727033584DN	OEM
T727034524DN	0764
T727034534DN	0764
T727034544DN	0764
T727034554DN	0764
T727034564DN	0764
T727034574DN	OEM
T727034584DN	OEM
T727042524DN	0764
T727042534DN	0764
T727042544DN	0764
T727042554DN	0764
T727042564DN	0764
T727042574DN	OEM
T727042584DN	OEM
T727043524DN	0764
T727043534DN	0764
T727043544DN	0764
T727043554DN	0764
T727043564DN	0764
T727043574DN	OEM
T727043584DN	OEM
T727044524DN	0764
T727044534DN	0764
T727044544DN	0764
T727044554DN	0764
T727044564DN	0764
T727044574DN	OEM
T727044584DN	OEM
T727052524DN	0764
T727052534DN	0764
T727052544DN	0764
T727052554DN	0764
T727052564DN	0764
T727052574DN	OEM
T727052584DN	OEM
T727053524DN	0764
T727053534DN	0764
T727053544DN	0764
T727053554DN	0764
T727053564DN	0764
T727053574DN	OEM
T727053584DN	OEM
T727054524DN	0764
T727054534DN	0764

If replacement code is OEM, contact original manufacturer for replacement.

DEVICE TYPE	REPL CODE
T727054544DN	0764
T727054554DN	0764
T727054564DN	0764
T727054574DN	OEM
T727054584DN	OEM
T727062524DN	0764
T727062534DN	0764
T727062544DN	0764
T727062554DN	0764
T727062564DN	0764
T727062574DN	OEM
T727062584DN	OEM
T727063524DN	0764
T727063534DN	0764
T727063544DN	0764
T727063554DN	0764
T727063564DN	0764
T727063574DN	OEM
T727063584DN	OEM
T727064524DN	0764
T727064534DN	0764
T727064544DN	0764
T727064554DN	0764
T727064564DN	0764
T727064574DN	OEM
T727064584DN	OEM
T727072524DN	0478
T727072534DN	0478
T727072544DN	0478
T727072554DN	0478
T727072564DN	0478
T727072574DN	OEM
T727073524DN	0478
T727073534DN	0478
T727073544DN	0478
T727073554DN	0478
T727073564DN	0478
T727073574DN	OEM
T727074524DN	0478
T727074534DN	0478
T727074544DN	0478
T727074554DN	0478
T727074564DN	0478
T727074574DN	OEM
T727082524DN	0478
T727082534DN	0478
T727082544DN	0478
T727082554DN	0478
T727082564DN	0478
T727082574DN	OEM
T727083524DN	0478
T727083534DN	0478
T727083544DN	0478
T727083554DN	0478
T727083564DN	0478
T727083574DN	OEM
T727084524DN	0478
T727084534DN	0478
T727084544DN	0478
T727084554DN	0478
T727084564DN	0478
T727084574DN	OEM
T727092524DN	0478
T727092534DN	0478
T727092544DN	0478
T727092554DN	0478
T727092564DN	0478
T727093524DN	0478
T727093534DN	0478
T727093544DN	0478
T727093554DN	0478
T727093564DN	0478
T727094524DN	0478
T727094534DN	0478
T727094544DN	0478
T727094554DN	0478
T727094564DN	0478
T727102524DN	0478
T727102534DN	0478
T727102544DN	0478
T727102554DN	0478
T727102564DN	0478
T727103524DN	0478
T727103534DN	0478
T727103544DN	0478
T727103554DN	0478
T727103564DN	0478
T727104524DN	0478
T727104534DN	0478
T727104544DN	0478
T727104554DN	0478
T727104564DN	0478
T727112524DN	0478
T727112534DN	0478
T727112544DN	0478
T727112554DN	0478
T727113524DN	0478
T727113534DN	0478
T727113544DN	0478
T727113554DN	0478
T727114524DN	0478
T727114534DN	0478
T727114544DN	0478
T727114554DN	0478
T727122524DN	0478
T727122534DN	0478
T727122544DN	0478
T727122554DN	0478
T727123524DN	0478

DEVICE TYPE	REPL CODE
T727123534DN	0478
T727123544DN	0478
T727123554DN	0478
T727124524DN	0478
T727124534DN	0478
T727124544DN	0478
T727124554DN	0478
T727142524DN	OEM
T727142534DN	OEM
T727142544DN	OEM
T727143524DN	OEM
T727143534DN	OEM
T727143544DN	OEM
T727144524DN	OEM
T727144534DN	OEM
T727144544DN	OEM
T730013504DN	2816
T730023504DN	2816
T730024504DN	2816
T730025504DN	2816
T730043504DN	2816
T730044504DN	1754
T730045504DN	1754
T730063504DN	1754
T730064504DN	1754
T730065504DN	1754
T920010603	OEM
T920010703	OEM
T920010803	OEM
T920010903	OEM
T920011003	OEM
T920020603	OEM
T920020703	OEM
T920020803	OEM
T920020903	OEM
T920021003	OEM
T920030603	OEM
T920030703	OEM
T920030803	OEM
T920030903	OEM
T920031003	OEM
T920040603	OEM
T920040703	OEM
T920040803	OEM
T920040903	OEM
T920041003	OEM
T920050603	OEM
T920050703	OEM
T920050803	OEM
T920050903	OEM
T920051003	OEM
T920060603	OEM
T920060703	OEM
T920060803	OEM
T920060903	OEM
T920061003	OEM
T920070603	OEM
T920070703	OEM
T920070803	OEM
T920070903	OEM
T920071003	OEM
T920080603	OEM
T920080703	OEM
T920080803	OEM
T920080903	OEM
T920081003	OEM
T920090603	OEM
T920090703	OEM
T920090803	OEM
T920090903	OEM
T920091003	OEM
T920100603	OEM
T920100703	OEM
T920100803	OEM
T920100903	OEM
T920101003	OEM
T920120603	OEM
T920120703	OEM
T920120803	OEM
T920120903	OEM
T920121003	OEM
T920140603	OEM
T920140703	OEM
T920140803	OEM
T920140903	OEM
T920141003	OEM
T920160603	OEM
T920160703	OEM
T920160803	OEM
T920160903	OEM
T920161003	OEM
T920180603	OEM
T920180703	OEM
T920180803	OEM
T920180903	OEM
T920200603	OEM
T920200703	OEM
T920200803	OEM
T920220603	OEM
T920220703	OEM
T920220803	OEM
T920240603	OEM
T920260603	OEM
T920280603	OEM
T920300603	OEM
T40000100600	0464
T40000100800	0464
T40000101600	OEM
T40000101800	OEM

DEVICE TYPE	REPL CODE
T40000160600	0464
T40000160800	0464
T40000161600	OEM
T40000161800	OEM
T40000220600	OEM
T40000220800	OEM
T40000221600	OEM
T40000221800	OEM
T40001100600	0464
T40001100800	0464
T40001101600	OEM
T40001101800	OEM
T40001160600	0464
T40001160800	0464
T40001161600	OEM
T40001161800	OEM
T40001220600	OEM
T40001220800	OEM
T40001221600	OEM
T40001221800	OEM
T40002100600	0464
T40002100800	0464
T40002101600	OEM
T40002101800	OEM
T40002160600	0464
T40002160800	0464
T40002161600	OEM
T40002161800	OEM
T40002220600	OEM
T40002220800	OEM
T40002221600	OEM
T40002221800	OEM
T40003100600	0717
T40003100800	0717
T40003101600	OEM
T40003101800	OEM
T40003160600	0717
T40003160800	0717
T40003161600	OEM
T40003161800	OEM
T40003220600	OEM
T40003220800	OEM
T40003221600	OEM
T40003221800	OEM
T40004100600	0717
T40004100800	0717
T40004101600	OEM
T40004101800	OEM
T40004160600	0717
T40004160800	0717
T40004161600	OEM
T40004161800	OEM
T40004220600	OEM
T40004220800	OEM
T40004221600	OEM
T40004221800	OEM
T40005100600	0720
T40005100800	0720
T40005101600	OEM
T40005101800	OEM
T40005160600	0720
T40005160800	0720
T40005161600	OEM
T40005161800	OEM
T40005220600	OEM
T40005220800	OEM
T40005221600	OEM
T40005221800	OEM
T40006100600	0720
T40006100800	0720
T40006101600	OEM
T40006101800	OEM
T40006160600	0720
T40006160800	0720
T40006161600	OEM
T40006161800	OEM
T40006220600	OEM
T40006220800	OEM
T40006221600	OEM
T40006221800	OEM
T40007100600	0674
T40007100800	0674
T40007101600	OEM
T40007101800	OEM
T40007160600	0674
T40007160800	0674
T40007161600	OEM
T40007161800	OEM
T40007220600	OEM
T40007220800	OEM
T40007221600	OEM
T40007221800	OEM
T40008100600	0674
T40008100800	0674
T40008101600	OEM
T40008101800	OEM
T40008160600	0674
T40008160800	OEM
T40008161600	OEM
T40008161800	OEM
T40008220600	OEM
T40008220800	OEM
T40008221600	OEM
T40008221800	OEM
T40009100600	0674
T40009100800	0674
T40009101600	OEM
T40009101800	OEM
T40009160600	0674

DEVICE TYPE	REPL CODE
T40009160800	0674
T40009161600	OEM
T40009161800	OEM
T40009220600	OEM
T40009220800	OEM
T40009221600	OEM
T40009221800	OEM
T40010100600	0674
T40010100800	0674
T40010101600	OEM
T40010101800	OEM
T40010160600	0674
T40010160800	0674
T40010161600	OEM
T40010161800	OEM
T40010220600	OEM
T40010220800	OEM
T40010221600	OEM
T40010221800	OEM
T40011100600	0674
T40011100800	0674
T40011101600	OEM
T40011101800	OEM
T40011160600	0674
T40011160800	0674
T40011161600	OEM
T40011161800	OEM
T40011220600	OEM
T40011220800	OEM
T40011221600	OEM
T40011221800	OEM
T40012100600	0674
T40012100800	0674
T40012101600	OEM
T40012101800	OEM
T40012160600	0674
T40012160800	0674
TA1Z	0086
TA-2	0160
TA2A	0079
TA2SA817	0431
TA2T00733Q	0006
TA2T00952L	0006
TA2T007330	0006
TA-3	0435
TA3	0071
TA3T006080	0006
TA3T0608K0	0006
TA3T0608KF	0006
TA3T0984K0	0006
TA3T016240	0338
TA3T017060	OEM
TA3T0116240	0338
TA3T1371A0	OEM
TA-4	0004
TA-5	0136
TA5	0071
TA5Q1306Y0	OEM
TA5T010154	0148
TA5T013200	0338
TA5T013210	0338
TA-6	0016
TA6	0016
TA-7	0144
TA7	0016
TA7T009330	0148
TA10E	0571
TA21R	0181
TA50	0015
TA54	OEM
TA57	OEM
TA58	OEM
TA60	4206
TA61	OEM
TA70L9&	2610
TA76	OEM
TA78	OEM
TA78L	1288
TA78L005	1288
TA78L-005AP	OEM
TA78L005AP	1288
TA78L005AP-Y	1288
TA78L005P	1288
TA78L006AP	4018
TA78L007P	OEM
TA78L008P	0083
TA78L009AP	4403
TA78L009P	1775
TA78L010AP	OEM
TA78L010P	OEM
TA78L012AP	1817
TA78L018AP	4427
TA78L024P	4430
TA78M	OEM
TA79L024P	1710
TA-98	OEM
TA100	0015
TA115	0918
TA200	0015
TA300	0015
TA304A-1L	OEM
TA310P	1532
TA320	OEM
TA400	0015
TA500	0015
TA600	0015
TA611CS	OEM
TA-705M	2689
TA721KP	0087

DEVICE TYPE	REPL CODE
TA766P	4074
TA800	0071
TA991D	OEM
TA1000	0369
TA1008	OEM
TA1050G	OEM
TA1056M	OEM
TA1062	0015
TA1063	0015
TA1064	0015
TA1222	3651
TA1225	3349
TA1575	0004
TA1575B	0004
TA-1614	0160
TA1614	0160
TA1620A	0038
TA1620B	0038
TA1628	0050
TA1650A	0050
TA1655B	0004
TA1658	0050
TA1659	0050
TA1660	0050
TA1662	0050
TA-1682	0160
TA1682	0160
TA-1682A	0160
TA1682A	0160
TA1697	0004
TA1703B	OEM
TA1704	0279
TA-1705	0160
TA1705	0160
TA1706	0004
TA1730	0004
TA1731	0050
TA1755	0050
TA1756	0050
TA1757	0050
TA1759	0595
TA1763	0279
TA1763A	0279
TA1763B	OEM
TA-1765	0160
TA1765	0160
TA-1766	0160
TA1766	0160
TA1767	0595
TA1771	0595
TA1772	0595
TA-1773	0160
TA1773	0160
TA1778	0279
TA1782	0279
TA1783	0279
TA-1794	0160
TA1794	0160
TA1796	0050
TA1797	0050
TA1798	0050
TA1828	0050
TA1829	0050
TA1830	0050
TA1846	0050
TA1847	0050
TA1860	0050
TA1861	0050
TA-1881	0160
TA1881	0160
TA1882	OEM
TA-1890	0160
TA1890	0160
TA-1891	0160
TA1891	0160
TA1920	OEM
TA1920A	OEM
TA1920B	OEM
TA1928A	0969
TA1938	OEM
TA1939	OEM
TA1990	0050
TA-2003	OEM
TA2083	0969
TA2084	OEM
TA2090A	OEM
TA2124P	3859
TA2188	0969
TA2235A	3392
TA2275	OEM
TA2276	OEM
TA2277	1510
TA2278	OEM
TA2279	OEM
TA2280	OEM
TA2301	0160
TA2307	OEM
TA2322	0050
TA2333	3568
TA2359A	OEM
TA2388	OEM
TA2401	0144
TA2402A	0178
TA2403A	1822
TA2404	OEM
TA2442	0740
TA2444	0740
TA2458	6287
TA2462	OEM

DEVICE TYPE	REPL CODE
TA2468A	2258
TA2469A	OEM
TA2470	5914
TA2492	OEM
TA2493	OEM
TA2494	3470
TA2495	3470
TA2501	3392
TA2503	0144
TA2510	3792
TA2511	3792
TA2512	3792
TA2513	OEM
TA2514	OEM
TA2529	OEM
TA2551	OEM
TA2554	0007
TA2555	0007
TA2577A	0103
TA2606	6293
TA2616	OEM
TA2626	OEM
TA2644	0212
TA2652	OEM
TA2653	3903
TA2654	3903
TA2655	3903
TA2672	0160
TA2700	OEM
TA2701	OEM
TA2735	OEM
TA2736	OEM
TA2750	OEM
TA2758	OEM
TA2761	2194
TA2773	3579
TA2786	OEM
TA2787	OEM
TA2800	0414
TA2840	0843
TA2871	3792
TA2888	0934
TA2889	0934
TA2892	1403
TA2911	0042
TA3002R	OEM
TA3002RF	OEM
TA3003RF	OEM
TA3004R	OEM
TA3004RF	OEM
TA3006RF	OEM
TA3008RF	OEM
TA3010RF	OEM
TA3137P-ST	OEM
TA4001	OEM
TA4004	OEM
TA4005	OEM
TA4006S	OEM
TA4017	OEM
TA4123	OEM
TA4124	OEM
TA4131	OEM
TA4163	OEM
TA4164A	OEM
TA4166	OEM
TA4168-1L	OEM
TA4301-1L1	OEM
TA4302	OEM
TA4304A-1L	OEM
TA4305A-1L	OEM
TA4306A-1K5	OEM
TA4307A-1L5	OEM
TA4308A-1L	OEM
TA4309-1L	OEM
TA4309A-1L	OEM
TA4310	OEM
TA4310-1L	OEM
TA4312A	OEM
TA4313	OEM
TA4313A	OEM
TA4313A-1L	OEM
TA4314	OEM
TA4314-1L	OEM
TA4315A	OEM
TA4316A	OEM
TA4316A-1L1	OEM
TA4317B-1L	OEM
TA4328	OEM
TA4335	OEM
TA4336	OEM
TA4337A	OEM
TA4338	OEM
TA4340A	OEM
TA4341	OEM
TA4342A	OEM
TA4343A	OEM
TA4344	OEM
TA4345	OEM
TA4351	OEM
TA4352	OEM
TA4372	OEM
TA4373	OEM
TA4374A	OEM
TA4375A-2M	OEM
TA4377A	OEM
TA4381E	OEM
TA4384	OEM
TA4385	OEM
TA4385-3D	OEM

DEVICE TYPE	REPL CODE
TA4386A	OEM
TA4386B	OEM
TA4387A	OEM
TA4387B	OEM
TA4390A	OEM
TA4396	OEM
TA4398	OEM
TA4398A	OEM
TA4398A-5A	OEM
TA-4846	0050
TA5628	2728
TA5649	0348
TA5649A	0348
TA5702	0350
TA-5702B	0350
TA5702B	0350
TA5814	0167
TA5912	0661
TA6200	0086
TA6462	OEM
TA6472	3239
TA6480	2759
TA6699B	2481
TA6896	2480
TA7021P	OEM
TA-7027M	2593
TA7027M	2593
TA7028M	2594
TA7038M#	2600
TA-7045	0817
TA7045	0817
TA-7045M	0817
TA7045M	0817
TA-7046	1383
TA7046P	1383
TA7047	1843
TA7047M	1843
TA-7050M	2689
TA7050M	2689
TA7051/01	0102
TA7051P	0823
TA-7053M	0748
TA7053M	0748
TA7054	2606
TA7054P	2606
TA-7055P	2903
TA7055P	2903
TA7055P-D	2903
TA-7055P-E	2903
TA7055P-E	2903
TA7055P-F	2903
TA7057M	2673
TA-7060	2046
TA7060	2046
TA-7060P	2046
TA7060P	2046
TA-7061AP	0905
TA7061AP	0905
TA-7061B	0905
TA7061BP	OEM
TA-7061P	0905
TA7062P	2608
TA-7063	1983
TA7063	1983
TA7063P	1983
TA7063P-C	1983
TA7064P	4552
TA7064P-JA	4552
TA7066P	3923
TA7069	OEM
TA-7069P	2610
TA7069P	OEM
TA7070A	0872
TA7070B	0872
TA7070FA-1	0872
TA7070P	0872
TA7070PFA-1	0872
TA7070PFA1	0872
TA7070PGL	0872
TA7071GL	0167
TA7071P	0167
TA7072P	0784
TA7073AP	0784
TA7073P	0784
TA7074GL	0391
TA7074P	0391
TA7074PGL	0391
TA7075B	0849
TA7075P	0849
TA7075PL	0849
TA7076	2615
TA7076AP	2615
TA-7076P	2615
TA7076P	2615
TA7089P	OEM
TA-7092-P	3625
TA7092AP-B	4477
TA7092C	3625
TA7092P	3625
TA7092P-C	3625
TA-7102P	4502
TA7102P	4502
TA7103	3660
TA7103P	0399
TA7104P	OEM
TA7108P	5640
TA7109P	OEM
TA7115P	2737
TA7117P	4476

If replacement code is OEM, contact original manufacturer for replacement.

585

DEVICE TYPE	REPL CODE
TA7119A	OEM
TA7119P	OEM
TA-7120P	1012
TA7120P	1012
TA7120P-A	OEM
TA7120P-B	1012
TA7120PB	1012
TA7120P-C	1012
TA7120PC	1012
TA7120P-D	1012
TA7120PD	OEM
TA7120P-E	1012
TA7122	2607
TA7122AP	2607
TA7122AR	2607
TA7124P	3859
TA7124P(FA-2)	OEM
TA7124PFA-3	3859
TA7124PFA-4	3859
TA7125P	OEM
TA7129AP	OEM
TA7129P	OEM
TA7130	6689
TA7130A	OEM
TA7130A3	OEM
TA7130P	2008
TA7130P-8	OEM
TA7130P-B	2008
TA7130PB	2008
TA7130P-C	2008
TA7130PC	2008
TA7133P	OEM
TA7137	0042
TA7137(IC)	2609
TA7137P	2052
TA7137P-ST	2052
TA7140P	3923
TA7140PC	3923
TA7142P	OEM
TA7145P	2921
TA7146P	2216
TA7147P	OEM
TA7148P	4514
TA7149	0349
TA7149P	4515
TA7150	0349
TA7150P	1316
TA7151	0349
TA7152P	6085
TA7153P	OEM
TA7154P	OEM
TA7155P	0412
TA7156	0042
TA7157AP	OEM
TA7157P	4542
TA7158P	OEM
TA7159P	4553
TA7167	4174
TA7167P	4174
TA7174P	6092
TA7176AP	0167
TA7176AP(FA-1)	2268
TA7176AP(FA1)	OEM
TA7176APFA	0167
TA7176APFA-1	2268
TA7176P	2268
TA7176P(FA1)	OEM
TA7176PFA-1	0167
TA7177P	OEM
TA7178P	OEM
TA7184P	OEM
TA7187AP	OEM
TA7189	0212
TA7192P	1049
TA7199	0103
TA7200	0103
TA7200P	OEM
TA7201	0103
TA7202	0103
TA7202P	5517
TA7203P	4520
TA7204P	3332
TA7205	1044
TA7205A	1044
TA7205AP	1044
TA7205AT	1044
TA-7205P	1044
TA7205P	1044
TA7207P	4710
TA7209P	5592
TA7215P	4645
TA7220P	1012
TA7222	4571
TA7222AP	4571
TA7222P	4571
TA7223P	5240
TA7230	OEM
TA7230P	4302
TA7232P	0794
TA7233P	OEM
TA7236AP	OEM
TA7236BP	OEM
TA7244P	OEM
TA7245BP	OEM
TA7245P	OEM
TA7250P	OEM
TA7252P	OEM
TA7256P	OEM
TA7257P	OEM

DEVICE TYPE	REPL CODE
TA7259P	OEM
TA7262	0042
TA7262(RCA)	0349
TA7267P	OEM
TA7269P	OEM
TA7270P	5179
TA7273P	OEM
TA7274	0212
TA7274P	5706
TA7280P	5720
TA7281P	5721
TA7282AP	OEM
TA7283AP	OEM
TA7288	OEM
TA7288P	OEM
TA7291P	OEM
TA7291S	OEM
TA7299	OEM
TA7299P	OEM
TA7302P	4707
TA7303P	2669
TA7310	1532
TA7310P	1532
TA7310P-B	OEM
TA7310P-U	1532
TA7310P-Y	1532
TA7311	0556
TA7312	0556
TA7313	0556
TA7313(IC)	0358
TA7313AP	0358
TA7313F	0358
TA7313P	0358
TA7313P(IC)	0358
TA7314	0556
TA7314P	3888
TA7315	0556
TA7315AP	OEM
TA7315BP	OEM
TA7315P	OEM
TA7316	0556
TA7317P	OEM
TA7318	0556
TA7318P	4729
TA7319P	0358
TA7320	3753
TA7320P	3753
TA7320PD1626	OEM
TA7321P	OEM
TA7323P	0794
TA7324	OEM
TA7324P	OEM
TA7325P	5143
TA7328	4734
TA7328AP	4734
TA7328P	4734
TA7335P	4336
TA7337	OEM
TA7337P	OEM
TA7339P	OEM
TA7340P	OEM
TA7341P	6243
TA7342P	OEM
TA7343AP	4339
TA7343P	4339
TA7343PS	4339
TA7347	4417
TA7347AP	OEM
TA7347P	4417
TA7348AP	4312
TA7348P	4312
TA7350P	OEM
TA7354P	OEM
TA7357AP	OEM
TA7358AP	4955
TA7358F	OEM
TA-7358P	4955
TA7358P	4955
TA7360P	OEM
TA7361	3130
TA7361AP	3130
TA7361P	3130
TA7363	0042
TA7365P	OEM
TA7366P	OEM
TA7368P	OEM
TA7370P	OEM
TA7374	0212
TA7375P	OEM
TA7378P	OEM
TA7399	0212
TA7404	0500
TA7405	0705
TA7405P	OEM
TA7417AP	OEM
TA7420	0359
TA7461	2007
TA7462	2007
TA7500	2367
TA7501	2378
TA7502	1403
TA7503	2371
TA7504	0308
TA7504M	0406
TA7504P	0308
TA7504S	0308
TA7513	0359
TA7520	0455
TA7530	OEM

DEVICE TYPE	REPL CODE
TA7554	0042
TA7555	0042
TA7556	0919
TA7557	0919
TA7557S	OEM
TA7579	2371
TA7580	2371
TA7581	2371
TA7582	2371
TA7584	2007
TA-7603	OEM
TA7604	OEM
TA7604AP	OEM
TA7604CP	OEM
TA7604P	OEM
TA7606AP	6307
TA7607	0906
TA7607A	0906
TA7607AP	0906
TA7607BP	0906
TA7607P	0906
TA7608AP	2043
TA7608BP	2043
TA7608BR	2043
TA7608CP	2043
TA7608CP(FA-5)	2043
TA7608CPFA-5	2043
TA7608CPFA-6	2043
TA7608CP-GS-4	2043
TA7608CP-GS-5	2043
TA7608P	2043
TA7608P(FA-3)	OEM
TA7608P(FA-5)	OEM
TA7608P(FA-6)	OEM
TA7608PFA-5	2043
TA7608PFA-6	2043
TA7608PGS-4	2043
TA7608PGS-5	2043
TA7609	4071
TA7609AP	4071
TA7609BP	OEM
TA7609GS-2	4071
TA7609P	4071
TA7609P(FA-2)	4071
TA7609P-FA2	OEM
TA7609PFA-2	4071
TA7609PFA2	4071
TA7609PFA-5	OEM
TA7609P-GS-2	4071
TA7609PGS-2	4071
TA7611AP	0069
TA7611AP-S	0069
TA7614	OEM
TA7614AP	5113
TA7614AP-Y	5113
TA7614P	5113
TA7619AP	OEM
TA7619P	OEM
TA7623AP	4734
TA7623P	OEM
TA7628AP	OEM
TA7628HP	OEM
TA7629P	OEM
TA7629P-DD	OEM
TA7630	3726
TA76300	OEM
TA7630P	3726
TA7631P	OEM
TA7632	OEM
TA7632FA-1	5971
TA7632P	5971
TA7632PFA-1	5971
TA7634AP	OEM
TA7634P	OEM
TA7636P(FA-1)	OEM
TA7636P(FA-2)	OEM
TA7637P	OEM
TA7639P	OEM
TA7640	OEM
TA-7640AP	3680
TA7640AP	3680
TA7640AP1	5926
TA7640AP2	OEM
TA7640P	3680
TA7643P	5666
TA7644AP	0658
TA7644BP	0658
TA7644BPFA-1	0658
TA7644P	6531
TA7658P	5080
TA7660	4074
TA7660P	4074
TA7660P(FA)	OEM
TA7660P(FA-1)	4074
TA7660PFA	4074
TA7660PFA-1	4074
TA7661P	OEM
TA7662P	1049
TA7664P	1666
TA7664P(FA-1)	1666
TA7664P(FA1)	OEM
TA7664PFA-1	1666
TA7664PFA1	1666
TA7665P	OEM
TA7666P	OEM
TA7668AP	4441
TA7668BP	6558
TA7668P	6558
TA7669	0212

DEVICE TYPE	REPL CODE
TA7670P	3640
TA7671P	2268
TA7671P(FA-1)	2268
TA7671PFA-1	2268
TA7672P	OEM
TA7673	5099
TA7673P	5099
TA7676AP	OEM
TA7678AP	OEM
TA7678P	OEM
TA7680AP	4047
TA7680P	4047
TA7681AP	4899
TA7681P	4899
TA7683P	OEM
TA7684	0212
TA7685P	OEM
TA7688F	OEM
TA7688P	OEM
TA7691P	OEM
TA7693P	OEM
TA7705P	OEM
TA7717AP	OEM
TA7717P	OEM
TA7725P	OEM
TA7739	1698
TA7739F	OEM
TA7740	1698
TA7741	1257
TA7750P	3344
TA7757F	OEM
TA7757P	OEM
TA7758P	OEM
TA7763P	OEM
TA7764P	OEM
TA7769P	OEM
TA7772P	OEM
TA7774P	4866
TA7777N	3206
TA7777P	3206
TA7777P(FA-1)	3206
TA7777P(FA-3)	3206
TA7777PFA-1	3206
TA7777PFA-3	3206
TA7778AP	OEM
TA7778P	OEM
TA7784P	OEM
TA7805S	OEM
TA7809S	OEM
TA7840AP1	OEM
TA8102P	OEM
TA8110AP	OEM
TA8110P	OEM
TA8127NX	OEM
TA8135P	OEM
TA8158	0239
TA8159	2311
TA8160	1208
TA8161	1208
TA8162	1208
TA8164P	OEM
TA8200	OEM
TA8200AH	6275
TA8200H	OEM
TA8207K	OEM
TA8210AH	OEM
TA8210H	OEM
TA8210P	OEM
TA8211AH	OEM
TA8211H	OEM
TA8213K	OEM
TA8214K	OEM
TA8215H	OEM
TA8216H	OEM
TA8218H	OEM
TA8242	0212
TA8400P	OEM
TA8403K	OEM
TA8406P	OEM
TA8410K	OEM
TA8432K	OEM
TA8445K	OEM
TA8515F	OEM
TA8601AN	OEM
TA8601BN	OEM
TA8601BN-FA-1	OEM
TA8601BNV	OEM
TA8601CN	OEM
TA8601CN(FA-1)	OEM
TA8603	OEM
TA8603P	OEM
TA8604	OEM
TA8604F	OEM
TA8604N	OEM
TA8606F	OEM
TA8607P	OEM
TA8609P	OEM
TA8611AN	OEM
TA8618S	OEM
TA8619P	OEM
TA8620P	OEM
TA8622N	OEM
TA8624F	OEM
TA8628N	OEM
TA8644N	OEM
TA8647S	OEM
TA8654AN	OEM
TA8654N	OEM
TA8655AN	OEM

DEVICE TYPE	REPL CODE
TA-8677N	OEM
TA8677N	3206
TA8680AN	3473
TA8680BN	3473
TA8680BNFA-1	3473
TA8680N	3473
TA8703S	3578
TA8720AN	OEM
TA8723N	OEM
TA8725AN	OEM
TA8725N	OEM
TA8725N-J	OEM
TA8728P	OEM
TA8745N	OEM
TA8747N	OEM
TA8782N	OEM
TA8785N	OEM
TA8801AN	OEM
TA8801N(FA)	OEM
TA8870N	OEM
TA8879N	OEM
TA8991	0065
TA-9014P	OEM
TA9106	OEM
TA9112A	3059
TA9112B	2162
TA9192B	OEM
TA9193	OEM
TA9195B	OEM
TA9232	OEM
TA9437A	OEM
TA9437B	OEM
TA9438A	OEM
TA9438B	OEM
TA10072	OEM
TA10086B	OEM
TA10086C	OEM
TA10535	OEM
TA10641-1	OEM
TA10642	OEM
TA11868A	OEM
TA13280A	OEM
TA17044	0279
TA31002P	OEM
TA31032P	OEM
TA57745	OEM
TA70639	0428
TA75324P	OEM
TA75339	0176
TA75339P	0176
TA75358P	0765
TA75393	0624
TA75393P	0624
TA75393S	OEM
TA75458P	0356
TA75458S	OEM
TA75557P	0356
TA75557S	2884
TA75558P	0356
TA75558S	0765
TA75558S-1	0765
TA75559P	0356
TA75559P(FA-1)	0356
TA75559PFA-1	0356
TA75902	0656
TA75902P	0823
TA78005AP	0619
TA78005P	0619
TA78009AP	OEM
TA78010AP	2779
TA78012A	0330
TA78012AP	0330
TA78012M	3906
TA78055	OEM
TA78607AP	OEM
TA78805	OEM
TA20007330	0006
TA30016060	0713
TA50013040	1638
TAA320	0321
TAA500-B	OEM
TAA521	1291
TAA521A	1695
TAA522	1291
TAA550	4688
TAA550-B	1319
TAA550B	4688
TAA611A12	2145
TAA611B	2145
TAA611B1Z	OEM
TAA611B12	2145
TAA611C11	1909
TAA621	2453
TAA621A11	2453
TAA621A12	2462
TAA780	OEM
TAA790	OEM
TAA890	OEM
TAB101	OEM
TAC010	OEM
TAC047	0016
TA-D93	OEM
TAD93	OEM
TAG0630	OEM
TAG0660	OEM
TAG0690	OEM
TAG1-200	0179
TAG1-400	0342
TAG1-500	3315

DEVICE TYPE	REPL CODE
TAG2-100	0179
TAG2-200	0179
TAG2-300	0342
TAG2-400	0342
TAG2N400	0179
TAG2.5-100	0179
TAG2.5-200	0179
TAG2.5-300	0342
TAG2.5-400	0342
TAG3-50	OEM
TAG3-300	OEM
TAG7-50R	2430
TAG7-100R	2430
TAG7-200R	0430
TAG7-300R	1478
TAG7-400R	1478
TAG7-500R	1478
TAG7-600R	0682
TAG7-700R	OEM
TAG7-800R	OEM
TAG7S50R	OEM
TAG7S100R	OEM
TAG7S200R	OEM
TAG7S300R	OEM
TAG7S400R	OEM
TAG7S500R	OEM
TAG7S600R	OEM
TAG7S700R	OEM
TAG7S800R	OEM
TAG10-50R	2430
TAG10-100R	2430
TAG10-200R	0430
TAG10-300R	1478
TAG10-400R	1478
TAG10-500R	0682
TAG10-600R	0682
TAG10-700R	OEM
TAG10-800R	OEM
TAG10S50R	OEM
TAG10S100R	OEM
TAG10S200R	OEM
TAG10S300R	OEM
TAG10S400R	OEM
TAG10S500R	OEM
TAG10S600R	OEM
TAG10S700R	OEM
TAG10S800R	OEM
TAG19F800DU	0745
TAG19F4000DU	0717
TAG20-50R	0726
TAG20-100R	0707
TAG20-200R	0464
TAG20-300R	0717
TAG20-400R	0717
TAG20-500R	0720
TAG20-600R	0720
TAG20-700R	OEM
TAG20-800R	OEM
TAG20S50R	OEM
TAG20S100R	OEM
TAG20S200R	OEM
TAG20S300R	OEM
TAG20S400R	OEM
TAG20S500R	OEM
TAG20S600R	OEM
TAG20S700R	OEM
TAG20S800R	OEM
TAG92-1	4381
TAG92-2	4381
TAG92-3	4381
TAG92-4	4381
TAG92-5	4382
TAG92-6	4382
TAG200-100	2367
TAG200-200	2378
TAG200-400	1403
TAG200-600	2371
TAG201-100	2336
TAG201-200	2337
TAG201-400	2340
TAG201-600	5804
TAG220-200	0550
TAG220-400	0550
TAG220-600	0550
TAG222-400	0567
TAG222-600	0929
TAG222-800	0059
TAG224-200	0767
TAG224-600	0612
TAG225-200	0550
TAG225-600	0550
TAG230-200	0550
TAG230-400	0550
TAG230-600	0550
TAG240-200	0550
TAG240-400	0550
TAG240-600	0550
TAG241-200	0550
TAG241-400	0550
TAG241-600	0550
TAG245-200	0550
TAG245-400	0550
TAG245-600	0550
TAG246-200	0550
TAG246-400	0550
TAG246-600	0550
TAG250-200	0767
TAG250-400	0739
TAG250-600	0612

DEVICE TYPE	REPL CODE
TAG251-200	0767
TAG251-400	0739
TAG251-600	0612
TAG252-200	0550
TAG252-400	0550
TAG252-600	0550
TAG255-200	0767
TAG255-400	0739
TAG255-600	0612
TAG256-200	0767
TAG256-400	0739
TAG256-600	0612
TAG257-200	0550
TAG257-400	0550
TAG257-600	0550
TAG280-200	0767
TAG280-400	0739
TAG280-600	0612
TAG420-200	0550
TAG420-400	0550
TAG420-600	0550
TAG421-200	0550
TAG421-400	0550
TAG421-600	0550
TAG425-200	0550
TAG425-400	0550
TAG425-600	0550
TAG426-200	0550
TAG426-400	0550
TAG611-100	0179
TAG611-200	0179
TAG611-400	0342
TAG611-600	3315
TAG612-100	0179
TAG612-200	0179
TAG612-400	0342
TAG612-600	3315
TAG620-100	2078
TAG620-200	0500
TAG620-400	0705
TAG620-600	0857
TAG622-200	0712
TAG622-400	0712
TAG622-600	0304
TAG623-200	0712
TAG623-400	0712
TAG623-600	0304
TAG625-100	2078
TAG625-200	0500
TAG625-400	0705
TAG625-600	0857
TAG625-800	0323
TAG627-100	0712
TAG627-200	0712
TAG627-400	0712
TAG627-600	0304
TAG628-200	0712
TAG628-400	0712
TAG628-600	0304
TAG630-200	0500
TAG630-400	0705
TAG630-600	0857
TAG630-800	0323
TAG632-200	0712
TAG632-400	0712
TAG632-600	0304
TAG633-200	0712
TAG633-400	0712
TAG633-600	0712
TAG655S200	0500
TAG655S300	0705
TAG655S400	0705
TAG655S500	0857
TAG655S600	0857
TAG670-100	2078
TAG670-200	0500
TAG670-400	0705
TAG670-600	0857
TAG670-800	0323
TAG675-100	0393
TAG675-200	0393
TAG675-400	0606
TAG675-600	0946
TAG675-800	1504
TAG6151	0767
TAG6152	0739
TAG6153	0612
TAG6154	0767
TAG6155	0739
TAG6156	0612
TAIT00101P	0006
TAL004	OEM
TALT00952L	0006
TALT007330	0006
TALT009520	0006
TA-M93	OEM
TAM93	OEM
TASCA3137	2762
TAT004	OEM
TAT008	OEM
TAT010	OEM
TAT020	OEM
TAT328AP	OEM
TAT1371A0	OEM
TAU051A/AN3231K	OEM
TAU1765	OEM
TAV	4549
TB-1	0276
TB-2	0287

If replacement code is OEM, contact original manufacturer for replacement.

DEVICE TYPE	REPL CODE
TB3G0632KE	0455
TB3G01134R	0919
TB3T006980	0006
TB3T009260	3954
TB-4	0293
TB4B	1864
TB4H	1864
TB4.1	0604
TB5	0110
TB5-1	1864
TB6.B	0241
TB-15H	0344
TB100	0242
TB200	0242
TB410FA	OEM
TB410FB	OEM
TB410V	OEM
TB412	OEM
TB413	OEM
TB414	OEM
TB415	OEM
TB416	OEM
TB417	OEM
TB418	OEM
TB419	OEM
TB420FA	OEM
TB420FB	OEM
TB420V	OEM
TB430FA	OEM
TB430FB	OEM
TB440FA	OEM
TB440FB	OEM
TB440V	OEM
TB450FA	OEM
TB450FB	OEM
TB460FA	OEM
TB460FB	OEM
TB460V	OEM
TB470FA	OEM
TB470FB	OEM
TB480FA	OEM
TB480FB	OEM
TB480V	OEM
TB490FA	OEM
TB490FB	OEM
TB820	OEM
TB1203BP	OEM
TB1203P	OEM
TB1207N-BA1	OEM
TB4100FA	OEM
TB4100FB	OEM
TB4100V	OEM
TB4110	OEM
TB4120V	OEM
TB4130	OEM
TB4140V	OEM
TB4150	OEM
TB4160V	OEM
TB200546AL	1638
TB3000632E	0455
TB3001134R	0919
TB30006320	0455
TBA10S-H	1239
TBA120	6037
TBA120AS	3416
TBA120S	3416
TBA120U	0347
TBA180S	OEM
TBA221	0406
TBA222	0406
TBA281	1183
TBA396	OEM
TBA641B11	4506
TBA-800	4084
TBA800	4084
TBA800C	OEM
TBA806	OEM
TBA810	1239
TBA810AS	1239
TBA810AT	OEM
TBA810DS	1239
TBA810P	3866
TBA-810S	1239
TBA810S	1239
TBA810S-H	1239
TBA-820	3946
TBA820	3946
TBA820L	3946
TBA820M	3949
TBA820MT	2599
TBA840	OEM
TBA890	OEM
TBA920MT	OEM
TBA940	OEM
TBA950	OEM
TBA950F	OEM
TBA1204B	OEM
TBA1440G	OEM
TBA1441GN	OEM
TBA2214	1971
TBA6003	OEM
TBAB10S	OEM
TBB0747	2352
TBB0747A	2342
TBB0748	0093
TBB0748B	1290
TBB1458B	0356
TBC337	0111
TBC338	0111

DEVICE TYPE	REPL CODE
TBC414C	0079
TBC547	0111
TBC548	0111
TBC549	0111
TBC550	0111
TBG625	OEM
TBG625A	OEM
TBG630	OEM
TBG820	OEM
TBG820A	OEM
TBG825	OEM
TBG825A	OEM
TBG830	OEM
TBG920	OEM
TBG920A	OEM
TBG925	OEM
TBG925A	OEM
TBG930	OEM
TBG1020	OEM
TBG1020A	OEM
TBG1025	OEM
TBG1025A	OEM
TBG1030	OEM
TBI010	OEM
TBI110	OEM
TBI208	OEM
TBI210	OEM
TBI308	OEM
TBI310	OEM
TBI408	OEM
TBI410	OEM
TBI608	OEM
TBI610	OEM
TBI708	OEM
TBI808	OEM
TBI810	OEM
TBI1008	OEM
TBL005	OEM
TBL005A	OEM
TBL105	OEM
TBL105A	OEM
TBL205	OEM
TBL205A	OEM
TBL305	OEM
TBL305A	OEM
TBL405	OEM
TBL405A	OEM
TBL605	OEM
TBL605A	OEM
TBL805	OEM
TBL805A	OEM
TBL905	OEM
TBL905A	OEM
TBM54578P	OEM
TBP14S10	2209
TBP14S10J	2209
TBP14S10MJ	OEM
TBP14S10N	2209
TBP14SA10	1907
TBP14SA10J	1907
TBP14SA10MJ	OEM
TBP14SA10N	1907
TBP18S030	2161
TBP18S030J	2161
TBP18S030MJ	OEM
TBP18S030N	2161
TBP18S22	OEM
TBP18S22J	OEM
TBP18S22MJ	OEM
TBP18S22N	OEM
TBP18S42	2304
TBP18S42J	2304
TBP18S42MJ	OEM
TBP18S42N	2304
TBP18S46	2306
TBP18S46J	2306
TBP18S46MJ	OEM
TBP18S46N	2306
TBP18SA030	3139
TBP18SA030J	3139
TBP18SA030MJ	OEM
TBP18SA030N	3139
TBP18SA22	OEM
TBP18SA22J	OEM
TBP18SA22MJ	OEM
TBP18SA22N	OEM
TBP18SA42	3257
TBP18SA42J	3257
TBP18SA42MJ	OEM
TBP18SA42N	3257
TBP18SA46	2308
TBP18SA46J	2308
TBP18SA46MJ	OEM
TBP18SA46N	2308
TBP24S10	OEM
TBP24S10J	OEM
TBP24S10MJ	OEM
TBP24S10N	OEM
TBP24S41	2376
TBP24S41J	2376
TBP24S41MJ	OEM
TBP24S41N	2376
TBP24S81	3137
TBP24S81-55	OEM
TBP24S81J	3137
TBP24S81N	3137
TBP24SA10	OEM
TBP24SA10J	OEM
TBP24SA10MJ	OEM

DEVICE TYPE	REPL CODE
TBP24SA10N	OEM
TBP24SA41	2374
TBP24SA41J	2374
TBP24SA41N	2374
TBP24SA81	OEM
TBP24SA81-55	OEM
TBP24SA81J	OEM
TBP24SA81MJ	OEM
TBP24SA81N	OEM
TBP28L22	OEM
TBP28L22J	OEM
TBP28L22MJ	OEM
TBP28L22N	OEM
TBP28L42	OEM
TBP28L42J	OEM
TBP28L42MJ	OEM
TBP28L42N	OEM
TBP28L45J	OEM
TBP28L45MJ	OEM
TBP28L45N	OEM
TBP28L46	OEM
TBP28L85J	OEM
TBP28L85N	OEM
TBP28L86A	OEM
TBP28L86J	OEM
TBP28L86MJ	OEM
TBP28L86N	OEM
TBP28L166	OEM
TBP28L166J	OEM
TBP28L166N	OEM
TBP28LA22	OEM
TBP28P42J	OEM
TBP28P42N	OEM
TBP28P45J	OEM
TBP28P45N	OEM
TBP28P85J	OEM
TBP28P85N	OEM
TBP28P166J	OEM
TBP28P166N	OEM
TBP28R45J	OEM
TBP28R45N	OEM
TBP28R85J	OEM
TBP28R85N	OEM
TBP28R166	OEM
TBP28R166J	OEM
TBP28R166N	OEM
TBP28S42	OEM
TBP28S42J	OEM
TBP28S42MJ	OEM
TBP28S42N	OEM
TBP28S45J	OEM
TBP28S45N	OEM
TBP28S46	OEM
TBP28S46J	OEM
TBP28S46MJ	OEM
TBP28S46N	OEM
TBP28S85J	OEM
TBP28S85MJ	OEM
TBP28S85N	OEM
TBP28S86A	OEM
TBP28S86J	OEM
TBP28S86MJ	OEM
TBP28S86N	OEM
TBP28S166	OEM
TBP28S166-55	OEM
TBP28S166J	OEM
TBP28S166MJ	OEM
TBP28S166N	OEM
TBP28S2708	OEM
TBP28S2708J	OEM
TBP28S2708MJ	OEM
TBP28S2708N	OEM
TBP28SA86J	OEM
TBP28SA86MJ	OEM
TBP28SA86N	OEM
TBRC147B	0079
TBS20A	OEM
TBS20AS	OEM
TBS20B	OEM
TBS20BS	OEM
TBS30A	OEM
TBS30B	OEM
TBS30C	OEM
TBS40AS	OEM
TBS40BS	OEM
TBS50CS	OEM
TC-0-2P11/1	0102
TC02P12	0015
TC02P112	0015
TC-0363	OEM
TC0914	0144
TC0918	0144
TC-0.09M21/3	0196
TC0.09M21/3	0479
TC-0.09M21/5	0479
TC0.09M22/1	0276
TC-0.2	0102
TC-0.2P11/1	0102
TC0.2P11/2	0015
TC0.2P11/12	0914
TC1T013170	0155
TC2T009450	0076
TC3F03789E	0275
TC3F017560	0638
TC3F035030	0275
TC3F042170	0275
TC3Q026210	0275
TC3Q040750	1077
TC3R022710	0261

DEVICE TYPE	REPL CODE
TC3T005360	0532
TC3T0536K0	0532
TC3T0536KF	0532
TC3T0536S0	0532
TC3T022710	0261
TC3T022740	0155
TC3T023620	1218
TC3T030000	0284
TC3T034680	0261
TC3T2274K0	0155
TC3T2362K0	1218
TC4S69	OEM
TC5F03620S	0275
TC5Q3298Y0	OEM
TC5T0388A0	0836
TC5T018154	0076
TC5T021204	0860
TC5T022294	0066
TC8A5A	OEM
TC8A50A	OEM
TC10A5A	0170
TC10A50A	OEM
TC10LB2	0934
TC12.4A5A	OEM
TC14.6A5A	OEM
TC15G008AP-0023	OEM
TC15G022AP-0013	OEM
TC15G022AP-0014	OEM
TC16.8A5A	OEM
TC17G014AP-0012	OEM
TC18.5A5A	OEM
TC21A5A	OEM
TC21SC160AT	OEM
TC23A5A	OEM
TC27A5A	0436
TC30A5A	0721
TC33A5A	0039
TC37A5A	OEM
TC40H000P	OEM
TC40H004P	OEM
TC40H032P	OEM
TC40H074P	OEM
TC40H244P	OEM
TC40H373P	OEM
TC40HC04	OEM
TC40HC032P	OEM
TC43A5A	0925
TC47A5A	0993
TC50	0110
TC51A5B	0497
TC56A5B	0863
TC62A5B	0778
TC68A5B	2144
TC74HC00	OEM
TC74HC00F	OEM
TC74HC02	1443
TC74HC02F	OEM
TC74HC02P	1443
TC74HC03P	1444
TC74HC04	1446
TC74HC04F	OEM
TC74HC04P	1446
TC74HC040P	OEM
TC74HC14	OEM
TC74HC14P	3817
TC74HC30P	1480
TC74HC123F	OEM
TC74HC123P	3851
TC74HC139P	3893
TC74HC157AP	OEM
TC74HC157P	OEM
TC74HC240P	4163
TC74HC4094AP	OEM
TC74HCT244P	6950
TC74HCU04P	4522
TC75A5B	1181
TC82A5B	0327
TC87A5B	2997
TC91A5B	1301
TC100	0242
TC100A5B	OEM
TC101	OEM
TC102	OEM
TC105A5B	OEM
TC106A1	0442
TC106A2	0442
TC106A3	0442
TC106A4	0442
TC106B	0934
TC106B1	0934
TC106B2	0934
TC106B3	0934
TC106B4	0934
TC106C1	1213
TC106C2	1213
TC106C3	1213
TC106C4	1213
TC106D1	0095
TC106D2	0095
TC106D3	0095
TC106D4	0095
TC106F1	1250
TC106F2	1250
TC106F3	1250
TC106F4	1250
TC106Q1	1386
TC106Q2	1386
TC106Q3	1386
TC106Q4	1386

DEVICE TYPE	REPL CODE
TC106Y1	1386
TC106Y2	1386
TC106Y3	1386
TC106Y4	1386
TC110A5B	0149
TC120A5B	0186
TC130A5C	0213
TC136	0015
TC150A5C	0028
TC175A5C	OEM
TC200	0242
TC200A5C	OEM
TC261	OEM
TC301	OEM
TC302	OEM
TC303	OEM
TC304	OEM
TC306	OEM
TC2126	OEM
TC2369A	0144
TC2483	0144
TC2484	0144
TC3001	1532
TC3114	0144
TC4000BP	2013
TC4001B	OEM
TC4001BP	0473
TC4001P	0473
TC4001UBP	0473
TC4002BP	2044
TC4002P	2044
TC4007BP	0649
TC4008BP	0982
TC4009UBP	0001
TC4010BP	0394
TC4011	0215
TC4011B	0215
TC4011BP	0215
TC4011P	0215
TC4011UBP	0215
TC4012BP	0493
TC4013	OEM
TC4013B	0409
TC4013BAP	OEM
TC4013BCP	0409
TC4013BP	0409
TC4013P	0409
TC4015BP	1008
TC4015P	1008
TC4016BB	1135
TC4016BP	0101
TC4017BP	0508
TC4017P	0508
TC4018BP	1381
TC4019BP	1517
TC4019P	1517
TC4020BP	1651
TC4021P	1738
TC4022BP	1247
TC4023BP	0515
TC4023P	0515
TC4024BP	1946
TC4025BP	2061
TC4025P	2061
TC4027	1938
TC4027B	1938
TC4027BP	1938
TC4027P	1938
TC4028B	2213
TC4028BP	2213
TC4028P	2213
TC4029BP	2218
TC4030BP	0495
TC4030P	0495
TC4032BP	2509
TC4038BP	2953
TC4040B	0056
TC4040BP	0056
TC4040P	0056
TC4042BP	0121
TC4042P	0121
TC4043BP	1544
TC4044BP	2292
TC4047BP	2315
TC4049	0001
TC4049BF	OEM
TC4049BP	0001
TC4049P	0001
TC4050BP	0394
TC4050CP	0394
TC4050P	0394
TC4051BP	0362
TC4052	0024
TC4052BP	0024
TC4052BP-1	0024
TC4053BF	OEM
TC4053BP	0034
TC4053BP-1	OEM
TC4053BPHB	OEM
TC4054BP	4450
TC4055BP	3272
TC4056BP	3661
TC4063BP	3682
TC4066	0101
TC4066B	0101
TC4066BC	0101
TC4066BP	0101
TC4066P	0101
TC4068BP	2482

DEVICE TYPE	REPL CODE
TC4069B	3279
TC4069BP	0119
TC4069P	0119
TC4069UB	3279
TC4069UBP	0119
TC4069UPB	0119
TC4069UPN	0119
TC4071BP	0129
TC4071P.JA	0129
TC4072BP	2502
TC4073BP	1528
TC4075BP	2518
TC4077BP	OEM
TC4078BP	0915
TC4081	0621
TC4081BP	0328
TC4081P	0621
TC4082BP	0297
TC4082P	0297
TC4085BP	0300
TC4086BP	0530
TC4093BP	2368
TC4094BP	1672
TC4099BP	3297
TC4502BP	OEM
TC4508BP	1800
TC4510BP	1952
TC4511BP	1535
TC4512BP	2108
TC4512P	2108
TC4514BP	1819
TC4514P	1819
TC4515BP	2269
TC4516BP	2331
TC4518BP	1037
TC4519BP	OEM
TC4520BP	2650
TC4521BP	OEM
TC4522BP	2810
TC4526BP	OEM
TC4527BP	3116
TC4528BP	3168
TC4531BP	3292
TC4532BP	3334
TC4538BP	1057
TC4539BP	3611
TC4539P	3611
TC4555BP	2910
TC4556BP	3397
TC4584	3581
TC4584BP	3581
TC5003P	OEM
TC5012BP	2042
TC5018P	OEM
TC5030BP	OEM
TC5036P	OEM
TC5064BP	OEM
TC5066BP	OEM
TC5067BP	OEM
TC5069BP	OEM
TC5080	4539
TC5080P	4619
TC5081	4543
TC5081AP	OEM
TC5081P	4543
TC5082	4539
TC5082P	4539
TC5082P-L	4539
TC5508P	3164
TC5508P-1	3164
TC5514AP	OEM
TC5514AP3	OEM
TC5516AFL-2T	OEM
TC5516AP	OEM
TC5518BF-25	OEM
TC5565	1887
TC5565-LL	OEM
TC5565AFL-15L	OEM
TC5565APL-15L	OEM
TC5565PL-15	OEM
TC7400	0232
TC7400BP	2100
TC7476BP	2150
TC8601F	OEM
TC9002AP	OEM
TC9002BP	OEM
TC9002DP	OEM
TC9002P	OEM
TC9003AP	OEM
TC9012	OEM
TC9012F	OEM
TC9012F-001	OEM
TC9012F-011	OEM
TC9020P	OEM
TC9020P-003	OEM
TC9029P-002	OEM
TC9029P-SPEC	OEM
TC9100C	1704
TC9100P	1704
TC9102P	OEM
TC9103P	OEM
TC9106BP	OEM
TC9106D	2801
TC9106P	2801
TC9107P	OEM
TC9109P	OEM
TC9112	OEM
TC9112P	OEM
TC9116P	OEM

DEVICE TYPE	REPL CODE
TC9125BP	OEM
TC9125P	OEM
TC9126N	OEM
TC9132P	OEM
TC9137BP	OEM
TC9137P	OEM
TC9138AP	OEM
TC9143P	OEM
TC9145P	6144
TC9147BP	OEM
TC9148P	OEM
TC9149P	OEM
TC9150P	OEM
TC9152P	OEM
TC9153AP	OEM
TC9153P	OEM
TC9154AP	OEM
TC9154P	OEM
TC9157AP	OEM
TC9157P	OEM
TC9158P	OEM
TC9159P	OEM
TC9160F	OEM
TC9160P	OEM
TC9162N	OEM
TC9163N	OEM
TC9164N	OEM
TC9171P	OEM
TC9172P	OEM
TC9174P	OEM
TC9176P	OEM
TC9177P	OEM
TC9183F	OEM
TC9184P	OEM
TC9188N	OEM
TC9212P	OEM
TC9214P	OEM
TC9302AF-005	OEM
TC9302AF-008	OEM
TC9302AF-012	OEM
TC9302AF-035	OEM
TC9303AN001	OEM
TC9304F-013	OEM
TC9304F-024	OEM
TC9306F-024	OEM
TC9310N-014	OEM
TC9310N-023	OEM
TC40160BP	1349
TC40161BP	1363
TC40162BP	1378
TC40163BP	1397
TC40174BP	1542
TC40175BP	1520
TC40192BP	3831
TC40193BP	1765
TC51832SPL-12	OEM
TC53257P-6887	OEM
TC53257P-6888	OEM
TC89101P	OEM
TC500388A0	0836
TC3002271D	0261
TC3002344E	1274
TC3002621E	0275
TC10013170	0155
TC20009450	0076
TC20019410	1317
TC30005360	0532
TC30022710	0261
TC30024560	0275
TC30031560	3351
TC30034670	0261
TC30039020	0558
TC30041590	1157
TC50018154	0076
TC50032960	0388
TC311200600	0143
TC312307222	0079
TC3112006000	0143
TC3112319300	0015
TC3123036722	0016
TC3123036900	0016
TC3123037111	0016
TC3123037222	0016
TC3123037412	0016
TC3123041557	0004
TCA0372DP2	3730
TCA250	OEM
TCA350	OEM
TCA350X	OEM
TCA350Y	OEM
TCA350Z	OEM
TCA380	0375
TCA420A	OEM
TCA430-N	OEM
TCA440	OEM
TCA440N	OEM
TCA700	OEM
TCA700Y	OEM
TCA710A	OEM
TCA720	OEM
TCA830	3866
TCA830A	1239
TCA830S	3866
TCA860	OEM
TCB0331	0142
TCE1A66102-04E	OEM
TCG1V010	1681
TCG1V014	1997
TCG1V015	1304

If replacement code is OEM, contact original manufacturer for replacement.

587

DEVICE TYPE	REPL CODE
TCG1V017	2309
TCG1V020	2763
TCG1V035	2907
TCG1V050	4395
TCG1V115	4072
TCG1V130	1364
TCG1V150	0246
TCG1V250	1322
TCG2V010	1684
TCG2V014	1998
TCG2V015	1309
TCG2V017	2310
TCG2V020	2769
TCG2V035	2913
TCG2V050	3056
TCG2V115	3094
TCG2V130	0832
TCG2V150	1982
TCG2V250	1324
TCG2V480	1093
TCG33	0044
TCG34	3585
TCG35	4966
TCG36	0194
TCG36MP	5294
TCG37	3082
TCG37MCP	4398
TCG38	0787
TCG39	4402
TCG40	2896
TCG40-45B	3408
TCG41	4967
TCG42	2395
TCG43	4968
TCG44	2919
TCG45	4969
TCG46	2770
TCG47	2833
TCG48	3749
TCG49	0818
TCG50	3294
TCG51	2985
TCG52	4511
TCG53	3009
TCG54	1157
TCG54MP	5502
TCG55	0713
TCG55MCP	3740
TCG56	2058
TCG57	0625
TCG58	3196
TCG59	3601
TCG60	3656
TCG60MP	5587
TCG61	4081
TCG61MCP	2000
TCG61MP	5599
TCG62	2820
TCG63	2817
TCG64	2978
TCG65	1332
TCG66	4970
TCG67	1456
TCG68	3561
TCG68MCP	4778
TCG70	3449
TCG71	3470
TCG72	0933
TCG73	2637
TCG74	2846
TCG74C00	2100
TCG74C02	2102
TCG74C04	2930
TCG74C08	2106
TCG74C10	2107
TCG74C14	3002
TCG74C20	2110
TCG74C30	3100
TCG74C32	3105
TCG74C42	2130
TCG74C48	2135
TCG74C74	2149
TCG74C76	2150
TCG74C85	2150
TCG74C90	2160
TCG74C95	3367
TCG74C107	3782
TCG74C154	3957
TCG74C157	3972
TCG74C160	3983
TCG74C161	3984
TCG74C164	3999
TCG74C173	4026
TCG74C174	4030
TCG74C175	4034
TCG74C192	4056
TCG74C193	4059
TCG74C221	3018
TCG74C240	2928
TCG74C244	4166
TCG74C901	4527
TCG74C902	4528
TCG74C903	4529
TCG74C904	4530
TCG74C925	4540
TCG74H00	0677
TCG74H01	5241
TCG74H04	1896
TCG74H05	3221

DEVICE TYPE	REPL CODE
TCG74H08	5258
TCG74H10	0680
TCG74H11	2382
TCG74H20	3670
TCG74H21	4772
TCG74H22	4516
TCG74H30	5284
TCG74H40	0554
TCG74H50	1781
TCG74H51	1933
TCG74H52	2009
TCG74H53	2090
TCG74H54	2158
TCG74H55	3129
TCG74H60	5312
TCG74H61	2638
TCG74H62	2705
TCG74H71	3233
TCG74H72	3281
TCG74H73	2444
TCG74H74	2472
TCG74H76	5208
TCG74H78	5320
TCG74H87	2557
TCG74H101	5424
TCG74H102	5426
TCG74H103	2941
TCG74H106	5159
TCG74H108	0180
TCG74H183	4329
TCG74L93	0651
TCG74LS00	1519
TCG74LS01	1537
TCG74LS02	1550
TCG74LS03	1569
TCG74LS04	1585
TCG74LS05	1598
TCG74LS08	1623
TCG74LS09	1632
TCG74LS10	1652
TCG74LS11	1657
TCG74LS12	1669
TCG74LS13	1678
TCG74LS14	1688
TCG74LS15	1697
TCG74LS20	0035
TCG74LS21	1752
TCG74LS22	1764
TCG74LS26	1372
TCG74LS27	0183
TCG74LS30	0822
TCG74LS32	0088
TCG74LS37	1719
TCG74LS38	1828
TCG74LS40	0135
TCG74LS42	1830
TCG74LS47	1834
TCG74LS48	1838
TCG74LS49	1839
TCG74LS51	1027
TCG74LS54	1846
TCG74LS55	0452
TCG74LS73	1856
TCG74LS74A	0243
TCG74LS75	1859
TCG74LS76A	2166
TCG74LS78	1862
TCG74LS83A	2204
TCG74LS85	0426
TCG74LS86	0288
TCG74LS90	1871
TCG74LS92	1876
TCG74LS93	1877
TCG74LS107	1592
TCG74LS109A	1895
TCG74LS112A	2115
TCG74LS113	2241
TCG74LS114	2286
TCG74LS123	0973
TCG74LS124	5851
TCG74LS125A	0075
TCG74LS126A	2850
TCG74LS132	1615
TCG74LS136	1618
TCG74LS138	0422
TCG74LS139	0153
TCG74LS145	1554
TCG74LS151	1636
TCG74LS153	0953
TCG74LS155	0209
TCG74LS156	1644
TCG74LS157	1153
TCG74LS158	1646
TCG74LS160A	0831
TCG74LS161A	0852
TCG74LS162A	0874
TCG74LS163A	0887
TCG74LS164	4274
TCG74LS170	2605
TCG74LS173A	5125
TCG74LS174	0260
TCG74LS175	1662
TCG74LS190	1676
TCG74LS191	1677
TCG74LS192	1679
TCG74LS193	1682
TCG74LS194	1294
TCG74LS195A	1305
TCG74LS196	2807

DEVICE TYPE	REPL CODE
TCG74LS197	2450
TCG74LS221	1230
TCG74LS240	0447
TCG74LS241	1715
TCG74LS242	1717
TCG74LS243	0900
TCG74LS244	0453
TCG74LS245	0458
TCG74LS247	1721
TCG74LS248	1723
TCG74LS249	1724
TCG74LS251	1726
TCG74LS253	1728
TCG74LS257	1733
TCG74LS258	1735
TCG74LS259	3175
TCG74LS266	0587
TCG74LS273	0888
TCG74LS279	3259
TCG74LS280	1762
TCG74LS283	1768
TCG74LS290	4352
TCG74LS293	0082
TCG74LS296	OEM
TCG74LS298	3337
TCG74LS324	5864
TCG74LS327	5866
TCG74LS348	0660
TCG74LS352	0756
TCG74LS353	0768
TCG74LS363	5869
TCG74LS364	5870
TCG74LS365A	0937
TCG74LS366A	0950
TCG74LS367	0971
TCG74LS368	0985
TCG74LS373	0704
TCG74LS374	0708
TCG74LS377	1112
TCG74LS378	1125
TCG74LS379	1143
TCG74LS393	0813
TCG74LS395A	1320
TCG74LS490	2199
TCG74LS540	2519
TCG74LS541	2525
TCG74LS624	3112
TCG74LS625	3120
TCG74LS626	3125
TCG74LS627	3133
TCG74LS629	3146
TCG74LS640	0664
TCG74LS641	0685
TCG74LS642	0714
TCG74LS643	2045
TCG74LS645	0770
TCG74LS670	1122
TCG74S00	0699
TCG74S02	2223
TCG74S03	2203
TCG74S04	2248
TCG74S05	2305
TCG74S08	2547
TCG74S09	2642
TCG74S10	2426
TCG74S11	2428
TCG74S15	2432
TCG74S20	1011
TCG74S22	2442
TCG74S30	3681
TCG74S37	5648
TCG74S38	0775
TCG74S40	2456
TCG74S51	4241
TCG74S64	2476
TCG74S65	2477
TCG74S74	2483
TCG74S85	5664
TCG74S86	2489
TCG74S112	1607
TCG74S113	1613
TCG74S114	1619
TCG74S124	2113
TCG74S132	2121
TCG74S133	1808
TCG74S134	1816
TCG74S138	2125
TCG74S140	1875
TCG74S151	1944
TCG74S153	2138
TCG74S157	1685
TCG74S158	2141
TCG74S163	0887
TCG74S174	2119
TCG74S175	2128
TCG74S181	2151
TCG74S182	2152
TCG74S194	1920
TCG74S251	2184
TCG74S258	2191
TCG74S280	1762
TCG74S373	2249
TCG74S374	2251
TCG75	2936
TCG76	2059
TCG76MP	5819
TCG77	2194
TCG78	4972
TCG79	3747

DEVICE TYPE	REPL CODE
TCG80	2575
TCG80C95	3148
TCG80C96	3150
TCG80C97	3151
TCG81	2034
TCG82	2449
TCG83	4930
TCG84	4974
TCG85	0284
TCG86	2526
TCG87	0861
TCG87MP	5896
TCG88	3459
TCG88MCP	4420
TCG88MP	5903
TCG89	0055
TCG90	0861
TCG91	0643
TCG92	2261
TCG93	3537
TCG93L08	2114
TCG93L16	2660
TCG93MCP	3271
TCG94	0270
TCG95	4187
TCG96	3969
TCG96L02	1459
TCG96LS02	2906
TCG96S02	4228
TCG97	1980
TCG98	2602
TCG99	3956
TCG100	0279
TCG101	0595
TCG102	0211
TCG102A	0004
TCG103	0038
TCG103A	0208
TCG104	0085
TCG104MP	3004
TCG105	0435
TCG106	0150
TCG107	0127
TCG108	0144
TCG108-1	3729
TCG109	0143
TCG110	1106
TCG110MP	0123
TCG112	0911
TCG113A	0196
TCG114	0479
TCG116	0015
TCG117	0229
TCG117A	4549
TCG118	0769
TCG120	0469
TCG121	0160
TCG121MP	0265
TCG122	0240
TCG123	0198
TCG123A	0016
TCG123AP	0079
TCG124	0142
TCG125	0071
TCG126	0136
TCG126A	0628
TCG127	0969
TCG128	0086
TCG129	0126
TCG129MCP	4100
TCG130	0103
TCG130MP	1506
TCG131	0222
TCG131MP	0816
TCG132	0321
TCG133	3443
TCG134A	0188
TCG135A	0162
TCG136A	0157
TCG137A	0631
TCG138A	0644
TCG139A	0012
TCG140A	0170
TCG141A	0789
TCG142A	0137
TCG143A	0361
TCG144A	0100
TCG145A	0002
TCG146A	0436
TCG147A	0039
TCG148A	1823
TCG149A	0778
TCG150A	0327
TCG151A	0149
TCG152	0042
TCG152MP	4998
TCG153	0919
TCG153MCP	4156
TCG154	0233
TCG155	2736
TCG156	0087
TCG157	0275
TCG158	0164
TCG159	0037
TCG159MCP	1371
TCG160	0050
TCG161	0007
TCG162	0074
TCG163A	0637

DEVICE TYPE	REPL CODE
TCG164	0003
TCG165	0065
TCG166	0276
TCG167	0287
TCG168	0293
TCG169	0299
TCG170	0250
TCG171	0283
TCG172A	0396
TCG173BP	0290
TCG174	0918
TCG175	0178
TCG176	0841
TCG177	0133
TCG178MP	0907
TCG179	0599
TCG179MP	5439
TCG180	1671
TCG180MCP	3093
TCG181	0130
TCG181MP	5377
TCG182	0556
TCG183	1190
TCG184	0161
TCG184MP	5494
TCG185	0455
TCG185MCP	4525
TCG186	0555
TCG186A	0219
TCG187	1257
TCG187A	1045
TCG188	0546
TCG189	0378
TCG190	0264
TCG191	0334
TCG192	0590
TCG192A	0218
TCG193	0786
TCG193A	1233
TCG194	0855
TCG195A	0693
TCG196	0419
TCG197	0848
TCG198	0168
TCG199	0111
TCG209	3467
TCG210	0561
TCG211	1357
TCG213	0432
TCG218	0899
TCG219	0486
TCG219MCP	5401
TCG220	0843
TCG221	0349
TCG222	0212
TCG224	0626
TCG225	3249
TCG226	1004
TCG226MP	1851
TCG228A	1698
TCG229	0224
TCG230	0239
TCG231	0061
TCG232	3477
TCG233	0326
TCG234	0688
TCG235	0930
TCG236	0830
TCG237	1401
TCG238	0309
TCG239	2320
TCG241	2969
TCG242	3136
TCG243	2411
TCG244	2262
TCG245	3339
TCG246	3340
TCG247	2422
TCG248	2415
TCG249	1384
TCG250	2429
TCG251	3483
TCG252	3484
TCG253	0553
TCG254	2869
TCG257	3343
TCG258	3486
TCG259	3487
TCG260	3488
TCG261	1203
TCG262	0597
TCG263	2220
TCG264	2222
TCG265	2243
TCG266	3490
TCG267	3491
TCG268	3492
TCG269	3493
TCG270	0134
TCG271	0073
TCG272	3495
TCG273	3496
TCG274	3336
TCG275	3497
TCG276	1642
TCG277	2200
TCG278	0414
TCG280	0177
TCG280MP	2127

DEVICE TYPE	REPL CODE
TCG281	2002
TCG281MCP	5669
TCG282	0617
TCG283	0359
TCG284	0538
TCG284MP	2355
TCG285	1588
TCG285MCP	6002
TCG286	1021
TCG287	0710
TCG288	0338
TCG289	0155
TCG289A	0155
TCG289AMP	1215
TCG289MP	2740
TCG290	0006
TCG290A	0006
TCG290AMCP	3644
TCG290AMP	OEM
TCG290Q	OEM
TCG291	0236
TCG292	0676
TCG292MCP	3224
TCG293	0018
TCG293MP	3020
TCG294	0527
TCG295	1581
TCG297	0320
TCG297MP	3217
TCG298	0431
TCG299	2039
TCG300	2035
TCG300MP	3342
TCG302	1165
TCG304Q	OEM
TCG306	1935
TCG307	1421
TCG308	1702
TCG308P	4534
TCG309K	1911
TCG310	2313
TCG310P	4526
TCG311	0488
TCG312	0321
TCG313	0470
TCG314	1814
TCG315	1967
TCG316	0259
TCG317	2918
TCG318	2296
TCG319	0008
TCG319P	0008
TCG320	1963
TCG320F	2857
TCG321	1740
TCG322	1973
TCG323	0886
TCG324	1471
TCG325	1189
TCG326	2959
TCG327	2465
TCG328	0615
TCG329	2675
TCG330	3517
TCG331	0477
TCG331MP	4121
TCG332	1359
TCG332MPC	3892
TCG333	2808
TCG334	3519
TCG335	3521
TCG336	3523
TCG337	3524
TCG338	3525
TCG338F	5110
TCG339	3526
TCG340	2699
TCG341	3528
TCG342	2693
TCG343	2694
TCG344	2504
TCG345	3012
TCG346	2030
TCG347	3532
TCG348	3534
TCG349	2156
TCG350	1224
TCG350F	5209
TCG351	1966
TCG352	3165
TCG353	3536
TCG354	3538
TCG355	3539
TCG356	3540
TCG357	3542
TCG358	1024
TCG358A	4391
TCG358B	4947
TCG359	3543
TCG360	2485
TCG361	2028
TCG362	3516
TCG363	2080
TCG364	1410
TCG365	2082
TCG366	3545
TCG367	2841
TCG368	3547
TCG369	2085

DEVICE TYPE	REPL CODE
TCG373	0558
TCG374	0520
TCG375	0388
TCG376	1077
TCG377	0060
TCG378	1298
TCG379	0723
TCG380	2911
TCG380MP	2708
TCG381	3527
TCG382	1376
TCG383	0472
TCG384	0424
TCG385	1955
TCG386	1841
TCG387	2416
TCG387MP	3158
TCG388	2398
TCG389	0223
TCG390	3052
TCG391	0853
TCG392	3557
TCG393	3558
TCG394	2589
TCG395	3562
TCG396	0187
TCG397	0434
TCG398	1638
TCG399	0261
TCG451	1382
TCG452	2861
TCG453	3043
TCG454	2439
TCG455	0367
TCG456	3577
TCG457	2922
TCG458	1747
TCG459	3104
TCG460	1133
TCG461	2917
TCG462	3583
TCG464	0838
TCG465	0977
TCG466	1147
TCG467	3102
TCG470	3586
TCG471	2523
TCG472	3387
TCG473	3293
TCG474	3587
TCG475	3289
TCG476	3290
TCG477	3090
TCG478	3591
TCG480	3593
TCG481	3595
TCG482	3596
TCG483	3597
TCG484	3598
TCG485	3599
TCG486	0684
TCG500A	0190
TCG502	0201
TCG503	0286
TCG504	0374
TCG505	0752
TCG506	0102
TCG507	0914
TCG508	1296
TCG509	2072
TCG510	2073
TCG511	1440
TCG512	2074
TCG513	1313
TCG514	3604
TCG516	OEM
TCG519	0124
TCG521	2955
TCG522	1493
TCG523	1061
TCG524	3607
TCG524V13	0824
TCG524V15	3381
TCG524V25	1326
TCG524V48	0776
TCG525	0344
TCG526A	1696
TCG529	2524
TCG530	3610
TCG531	2777
TCG532	0405
TCG533	1700
TCG534	2954
TCG535	2957
TCG536A	1986
TCG537	1188
TCG538	2956
TCG539	1048
TCG541	3613
TCG542	3614
TCG544	3615
TCG546	3616
TCG548	3617
TCG551	0182
TCG552	0023
TCG555	2496
TCG556	3621
TCG557	3622
TCG558	0017

If replacement code is OEM, contact original manufacturer for replacement.

Original Device Types

DEVICE TYPE	REPL CODE
TCG565	3624
TCG600	1914
TCG601	0139
TCG604	3638
TCG605	0120
TCG606	3639
TCG607	3407
TCG610	0549
TCG611	0005
TCG612	0715
TCG613	0623
TCG614	0030
TCG617	3642
TCG618	3643
TCG700	3674
TCG701	3675
TCG702	2774
TCG703A	0627
TCG704	2600
TCG705A	2147
TCG706	2549
TCG707	0748
TCG708	0659
TCG709	0673
TCG710	0823
TCG711	2689
TCG712	0167
TCG714	0348
TCG715	0350
TCG716	3677
TCG717	3679
TCG718	0649
TCG720	0438
TCG721	2264
TCG722	0696
TCG723	1335
TCG724	0817
TCG725	0687
TCG726	2593
TCG727	2507
TCG728	2527
TCG729	0324
TCG730	2716
TCG731	2438
TCG736	1748
TCG737	1434
TCG738	0850
TCG740A	0375
TCG741	3689
TCG742	3690
TCG743	1385
TCG744	1411
TCG745	2902
TCG746	0780
TCG747	1797
TCG748	0784
TCG749	0391
TCG750	3189
TCG754	0718
TCG762	OEM
TCG768	1742
TCG778A	0356
TCG780	0360
TCG781	2720
TCG783	0797
TCG784	2674
TCG785	2681
TCG786	2688
TCG787	2242
TCG788	2728
TCG789	1832
TCG790	0345
TCG791	1327
TCG797	0516
TCG798	1742
TCG799	1601
TCG801	0514
TCG802	3715
TCG803	3717
TCG804	2535
TCG805	3376
TCG807	3720
TCG812	3724
TCG815	0842
TCG818	2480
TCG819	1867
TCG820	2790
TCG821	2804
TCG822	2785
TCG823	3034
TCG824	3050
TCG825	3070
TCG828	3057
TCG829	1888
TCG832	3733
TCG834	0176
TCG836	2473
TCG841	3735
TCG843	2481
TCG846	1508
TCG849	3739
TCG851	3741
TCG852	2011
TCG853	3742
TCG855	0808
TCG856	3744
TCG857M	3627
TCG859	3357
TCG860	3746

DEVICE TYPE	REPL CODE
TCG900	2662
TCG901	2664
TCG902	2721
TCG903	2515
TCG904	1843
TCG905	2673
TCG906	2676
TCG907	2685
TCG908	2680
TCG909	1291
TCG909D	1695
TCG910	1786
TCG910D	1786
TCG911	1879
TCG911D	1886
TCG912	1686
TCG913	3757
TCG914	2701
TCG915	1545
TCG916	2722
TCG917	2696
TCG918	2540
TCG918M	2545
TCG919	2552
TCG919D	2548
TCG922	1804
TCG922M	2093
TCG923	1183
TCG923D	0026
TCG924	2207
TCG924M	2495
TCG925	2863
TCG926	3748
TCG927	1113
TCG927D	1110
TCG928	1667
TCG928M	0765
TCG930	2755
TCG931	1905
TCG932	2836
TCG933	3359
TCG934	3761
TCG935	2710
TCG936	3762
TCG937	3576
TCG937M	5901
TCG938	0890
TCG938M	0890
TCG939	3766
TCG940	1908
TCG941	0406
TCG941D	1971
TCG941M	0308
TCG942	3000
TCG943	3767
TCG943M	0624
TCG944	3768
TCG944M	3400
TCG946	3618
TCG947	2352
TCG947D	2342
TCG948	2796
TCG949	2530
TCG950	1817
TCG951	3361
TCG952	3769
TCG953	3771
TCG954	3772
TCG955M	0967
TCG956	2541
TCG957	2709
TCG958	2244
TCG959	3774
TCG960	0619
TCG961	1275
TCG962	0917
TCG963	2624
TCG964	1187
TCG965	2764
TCG966	0330
TCG967	1827
TCG968	1311
TCG969	3777
TCG970	2811
TCG971	3531
TCG972	2224
TCG973	0413
TCG973D	3751
TCG974	0011
TCG975	1290
TCG976	2267
TCG977	1288
TCG978	3254
TCG979	OEM
TCG980	3779
TCG981	0083
TCG984	3239
TCG985	3780
TCG986	3060
TCG987	0620
TCG988	2285
TCG989	3347
TCG990	1482
TCG991	3550
TCG992	2232
TCG993	3783
TCG994M	3775
TCG995	2302
TCG996	3784

DEVICE TYPE	REPL CODE
TCG997	2995
TCG1000	1226
TCG1002	0383
TCG1003	0574
TCG1004	0872
TCG1005	2546
TCG1006	1206
TCG1009	0837
TCG1010	0858
TCG1011	0876
TCG1012	0021
TCG1013	0138
TCG1014	0351
TCG1015	2388
TCG1016	2390
TCG1017	2423
TCG1018	2457
TCG1019	2487
TCG1020	OEM
TCG1021	2142
TCG1022	4476
TCG1023	4477
TCG1024	3506
TCG1025	1179
TCG1027	2849
TCG1028	4479
TCG1029	2247
TCG1030	4481
TCG1031	4482
TCG1032	4483
TCG1033	4484
TCG1034	2862
TCG1035	4485
TCG1036	4486
TCG1037	4031
TCG1038	4338
TCG1039	1611
TCG1040	4489
TCG1041	4490
TCG1042	4491
TCG1043	4320
TCG1045	2377
TCG1046	0523
TCG1047	2855
TCG1048	0668
TCG1049	0648
TCG1050	2864
TCG1051	3736
TCG1052	0428
TCG1053	2551
TCG1054	2554
TCG1055	2556
TCG1056	1826
TCG1057	2555
TCG1058	2111
TCG1060	2559
TCG1061	2560
TCG1062	0399
TCG1064	2563
TCG1065	2564
TCG1066	2565
TCG1067	2566
TCG1068	2567
TCG1069	2576
TCG1070	4014
TCG1071	2580
TCG1072	2568
TCG1073	2573
TCG1074	2569
TCG1075A	0465
TCG1077	0924
TCG1078	3318
TCG1079	4495
TCG1080	0849
TCG1081A	1152
TCG1082	2246
TCG1083	2827
TCG1084	2859
TCG1085	2607
TCG1086	2860
TCG1087	1012
TCG1089	0633
TCG1090	2834
TCG1091	0958
TCG1092	2300
TCG1093	4498
TCG1094	0043
TCG1096	1624
TCG1097	3232
TCG1098	3901
TCG1099	4196
TCG1100	0905
TCG1101	2610
TCG1102	2608
TCG1103	1983
TCG1104	2046
TCG1105	4502
TCG1106	2606
TCG1107	3625
TCG1108	1383
TCG1109	2615
TCG1110	2289
TCG1110R	6098
TCG1114	4506
TCG1115	1239
TCG1115A	3866
TCG1116	4084
TCG1117	3946
TCG1119	4509

DEVICE TYPE	REPL CODE
TCG1120	2020
TCG1121	0385
TCG1122	0602
TCG1123	3973
TCG1124	4463
TCG1126	4513
TCG1127	4348
TCG1128	3859
TCG1130	1316
TCG1131	4514
TCG1132	4515
TCG1133	2216
TCG1134	2921
TCG1135	2051
TCG1137	2571
TCG1139	3880
TCG1140	2845
TCG1141	3788
TCG1142	1469
TCG1148	2837
TCG1149	4517
TCG1150	4518
TCG1152	2484
TCG1153	3332
TCG1154	4520
TCG1155	1044
TCG1156	2988
TCG1158	0875
TCG1159	0878
TCG1160	3650
TCG1161	2914
TCG1162	3977
TCG1163	2581
TCG1164	3238
TCG1165	2746
TCG1166	2754
TCG1167	1704
TCG1168	2579
TCG1169	4331
TCG1170	2512
TCG1171	0093
TCG1172	1369
TCG1173	3242
TCG1174	2038
TCG1175	2759
TCG1176	2762
TCG1178	3660
TCG1179	2550
TCG1180	2590
TCG1181	2570
TCG1183	4133
TCG1184	4532
TCG1185	1470
TCG1186	0846
TCG1187	0851
TCG1188	2594
TCG1189	4325
TCG1190	4535
TCG1191	4025
TCG1192	1532
TCG1193	3286
TCG1194	1805
TCG1195	4145
TCG1196	1049
TCG1197	4539
TCG1198	2238
TCG1199	3754
TCG1200	4174
TCG1201	4541
TCG1202	2364
TCG1203	2290
TCG1204	4405
TCG1205	2903
TCG1206	4542
TCG1208	4543
TCG1209	4544
TCG1210	2609
TCG1211	2179
TCG1212	4545
TCG1213	4546
TCG1214	0646
TCG1215	2510
TCG1216	0910
TCG1217	0412
TCG1218	1561
TCG1219	1602
TCG1221	4550
TCG1223	1516
TCG1224	4024
TCG1226	0701
TCG1227	0616
TCG1228	3161
TCG1229	4551
TCG1230	2644
TCG1231	1162
TCG1231A	1051
TCG1232	1042
TCG1233	4160
TCG1234	2008
TCG1235	4552
TCG1236	2268
TCG1237	3606
TCG1238	3961
TCG1239	3231
TCG1240	4006
TCG1241	2614
TCG1242	1501
TCG1243	4553
TCG1245	0898

DEVICE TYPE	REPL CODE
TCG1246	4554
TCG1247	4555
TCG1248	1251
TCG1249	3980
TCG1250	4010
TCG1251	4556
TCG1252	4557
TCG1253	4558
TCG1254	3763
TCG1256	4559
TCG1257	4560
TCG1258	4561
TCG1260	4563
TCG1261	1120
TCG1262	4564
TCG1263	2932
TCG1264	4001
TCG1265	4002
TCG1266	4004
TCG1267	4007
TCG1268	4008
TCG1269	4017
TCG1271	4567
TCG1272	3515
TCG1273	4568
TCG1278	4571
TCG1281	4572
TCG1282	4573
TCG1283	4575
TCG1284	4576
TCG1285	0749
TCG1286	0751
TCG1287	4578
TCG1288	4493
TCG1289	4580
TCG1290	4027
TCG1291	4582
TCG1292	3416
TCG1293	4584
TCG1300	3877
TCG1301	4588
TCG1302	3935
TCG1303	4589
TCG1304	3939
TCG1305	3941
TCG1306	3943
TCG1307	3947
TCG1308	3891
TCG1309	4590
TCG1310	3931
TCG1311	3876
TCG1312	3927
TCG1313	3928
TCG1320	4592
TCG1321	4593
TCG1322	4594
TCG1323	4595
TCG1324	4596
TCG1325	4597
TCG1326	4599
TCG1327	4600
TCG1328	4601
TCG1329	4602
TCG1330	4603
TCG1331	4604
TCG1332	4605
TCG1333	4606
TCG1334	4607
TCG1335	4608
TCG1336	4609
TCG1337	4610
TCG1338	1428
TCG1339	4612
TCG1340	4613
TCG1341	4614
TCG1342	4615
TCG1343	4617
TCG1344	4618
TCG1345	1892
TCG1346	4620
TCG1347	4621
TCG1348	4622
TCG1349	4623
TCG1350	4624
TCG1351	4625
TCG1352	4626
TCG1354	4627
TCG1355	4629
TCG1361	4632
TCG1363	4633
TCG1364	4634
TCG1365	4635
TCG1366	4636
TCG1367	4637
TCG1368	4638
TCG1369	4639
TCG1370	4641
TCG1371	4642
TCG1372	4643
TCG1373	3860
TCG1374	3665
TCG1375	2767
TCG1376	3666
TCG1377	3299
TCG1378	4644
TCG1379	4645
TCG1380	4646
TCG1381	4647
TCG1382	1940

DEVICE TYPE	REPL CODE
TCG1383	4648
TCG1384	4649
TCG1385	4651
TCG1386	3209
TCG1387	4302
TCG1388	4653
TCG1389	4654
TCG1391	4655
TCG1392	4656
TCG1393	4658
TCG1394	4659
TCG1395	4035
TCG1396	0491
TCG1400	1572
TCG1401	3317
TCG1403	3325
TCG1404	4662
TCG1405	4663
TCG1406	3997
TCG1407	4664
TCG1408	4665
TCG1409	0678
TCG1410	2599
TCG1411	0762
TCG1412	4666
TCG1413	0069
TCG1414	4669
TCG1415	4416
TCG1416	0485
TCG1417	2601
TCG1419	4670
TCG1420	0548
TCG1421	4671
TCG1422	1575
TCG1423	4227
TCG1424	4399
TCG1425	4677
TCG1426	0670
TCG1427	4678
TCG1428	1570
TCG1429	4679
TCG1430	0912
TCG1431	4680
TCG1433	4681
TCG1434	0866
TCG1435	4682
TCG1436	4355
TCG1437	4469
TCG1438	4683
TCG1439	3074
TCG1440	3692
TCG1441	4684
TCG1442	4685
TCG1445	1016
TCG1446	4000
TCG1447	4687
TCG1448	3989
TCG1449	4689
TCG1450	3985
TCG1451	4690
TCG1452	4692
TCG1453	2492
TCG1454	3216
TCG1455	4694
TCG1457	4695
TCG1458	4696
TCG1459	2508
TCG1460	4697
TCG1461	2686
TCG1462	4698
TCG1463	3167
TCG1464	4699
TCG1465	0358
TCG1466	2052
TCG1467	4676
TCG1468	3923
TCG1469	4700
TCG1470	3198
TCG1471	1192
TCG1472	4703
TCG1473	4705
TCG1474	4707
TCG1475	4708
TCG1476	4710
TCG1477	4711
TCG1478	4712
TCG1479	1437
TCG1480	4480
TCG1481	4714
TCG1482	4715
TCG1483	0859
TCG1484	4716
TCG1486	3671
TCG1487	3982
TCG1488	2237
TCG1489	4719
TCG1490	4721
TCG1491	4723
TCG1492	4724
TCG1493	4725
TCG1494	4726
TCG1495	4727
TCG1496	4071
TCG1497	4728
TCG1498	4729
TCG1499	4730
TCG1500	4731
TCG1501	4733
TCG1502	4735

DEVICE TYPE	REPL CODE
TCG1503	4736
TCG1504	4737
TCG1505	4739
TCG1507	4740
TCG1508	3039
TCG1509	3040
TCG1510	0804
TCG1511	4741
TCG1512	4216
TCG1513	4742
TCG1514	4743
TCG1515	4746
TCG1516	4747
TCG1517	4750
TCG1518	4751
TCG1519	4752
TCG1520	1617
TCG1521	3888
TCG1522	2511
TCG1523	4754
TCG1525	2669
TCG1526	4757
TCG1527	4758
TCG1528	2312
TCG1529	2884
TCG1530	4760
TCG1531	4762
TCG1532	2043
TCG1533	4763
TCG1534	4765
TCG1536	4766
TCG1537	4767
TCG1538	0328
TCG1539	1580
TCG1540	4285
TCG1541	2668
TCG1543	4769
TCG1544	4770
TCG1545	0906
TCG1935	OEM
TCG2003	4846
TCG2004	4045
TCG2011	0839
TCG2012	1001
TCG2013	1126
TCG2014	1252
TCG2015	4848
TCG2016	4849
TCG2017	4850
TCG2018	4852
TCG2019	4853
TCG2020	4854
TCG2021	3839
TCG2022	3864
TCG2023	2723
TCG2025	4856
TCG2026	4019
TCG2027	1691
TCG2028	1782
TCG2029	4860
TCG2030	1866
TCG2031	4862
TCG2032	4863
TCG2050	4864
TCG2051	4865
TCG2053	3743
TCG2054	4867
TCG2060	2279
TCG2061	2702
TCG2070	4868
TCG2071	4869
TCG2072	4870
TCG2073	4872
TCG2074	4456
TCG2075	4874
TCG2076	4875
TCG2077	4876
TCG2078	4878
TCG2079	0963
TCG2080	4879
TCG2081	4880
TCG2082	4881
TCG2083	4882
TCG2084	4075
TCG2085	4781
TCG2087	4883
TCG2102	4886
TCG2104	4887
TCG2114	2037
TCG2117	0518
TCG2147	1683
TCG2708	4351
TCG2716	2263
TCG3000	1970
TCG3001	1978
TCG3002	1974
TCG3003	1972
TCG3004	5020
TCG3005	5021
TCG3006	5022
TCG3007	2990
TCG3008	3067
TCG3009	5023
TCG3010	0835
TCG3011	3095
TCG3012	5024
TCG3013	5025
TCG3014	3420
TCG3015	3421

If replacement code is OEM, contact original manufacturer for replacement.

DEVICE TYPE	REPL CODE
TCG3016	3693
TCG3018	1605
TCG3019	5027
TCG3020	1348
TCG3021	3128
TCG3022	1951
TCG3023	3245
TCG3024	1767
TCG3025	3153
TCG3026	2181
TCG3027	4120
TCG3028	0586
TCG3029	3203
TCG3031	5030
TCG3032	2297
TCG3034	3825
TCG3035	3156
TCG3037	5031
TCG3038	5032
TCG3039	5033
TCG3040	0536
TCG3041	0311
TCG3042	0272
TCG3043	4358
TCG3044	4845
TCG3045	2096
TCG3046	2221
TCG3047	4961
TCG3048	4975
TCG3049	5034
TCG3050	4900
TCG3051	4901
TCG3052	4783
TCG3053	5035
TCG3054	5036
TCG3055	5037
TCG3056	4786
TCG3057	4127
TCG3058	5038
TCG3059	5039
TCG3060	5040
TCG3061	4902
TCG3062	5042
TCG3063	5043
TCG3064	5045
TCG3065	4784
TCG3068	5046
TCG3069	5047
TCG3070	5048
TCG3071	5049
TCG3074	4262
TCG3075	4267
TCG3076	4266
TCG3077	4268
TCG3078	2192
TCG3079	2185
TCG3080	2362
TCG3081	3333
TCG3082	5050
TCG3083	1101
TCG3084	1047
TCG3114	5060
TCG3115	5062
TCG3116	5063
TCG3117	5064
TCG3150	5073
TCG3151	5075
TCG3152	5076
TCG3153	5078
TCG3155	5079
TCG3160	5082
TCG3161	1069
TCG3162	5084
TCG3163	4686
TCG3164	3450
TCG3165	5086
TCG3166	3990
TCG3167	1123
TCG3168	5087
TCG3880	3441
TCG3881	1893
TCG3882	5242
TCG4000	2013
TCG4001B	0473
TCG4002B	2044
TCG4006B	0641
TCG4007	2819
TCG4007B	2819
TCG4008B	0982
TCG4011B	0215
TCG4012B	0493
TCG4013B	0409
TCG4014B	0854
TCG4015B	1008
TCG4016B	1135
TCG4017B	0508
TCG4018B	1381
TCG4019B	1517
TCG4020B	1651
TCG4021B	1738
TCG4022B	1247
TCG4023B	0515
TCG4024B	1946
TCG4025B	2061
TCG4026B	2139
TCG4027B	1938
TCG4028B	2213
TCG4029B	2218
TCG4030B	0495

DEVICE TYPE	REPL CODE
TCG4031B	2943
TCG4032B	2509
TCG4033B	2611
TCG4034B	3570
TCG4035B	2750
TCG4038B	2953
TCG4040B	0056
TCG4041	3145
TCG4042B	0121
TCG4043B	1544
TCG4044B	2292
TCG4047B	2315
TCG4048B	3422
TCG4049	0001
TCG4049B	0001
TCG4050B	0394
TCG4051B	0362
TCG4052B	0024
TCG4053B	0034
TCG4055B	3272
TCG4056B	3661
TCG4060B	0146
TCG4063B	3682
TCG4066B	0101
TCG4067B	3696
TCG4068B	2482
TCG4069	0119
TCG4069B	0119
TCG4070B	2494
TCG4071B	0129
TCG4072B	2502
TCG4073B	1528
TCG4075B	2518
TCG4076B	3455
TCG4077B	2536
TCG4078B	0915
TCG4081	0621
TCG4081B	0621
TCG4082B	0297
TCG4085B	0300
TCG4086B	0530
TCG4089B	3778
TCG4093B	2368
TCG4094B	1672
TCG4095B	3796
TCG4096B	3798
TCG4097B	3802
TCG4098B	3566
TCG4099B	3297
TCG4501	3758
TCG4502B	1031
TCG4503B	2042
TCG4506B	3721
TCG4508B	1800
TCG4510B	1952
TCG4511B	1535
TCG4512B	2108
TCG4514B	1819
TCG4515B	3555
TCG4516B	2331
TCG4517B	4220
TCG4518B	1037
TCG4520B	2650
TCG4521B	4903
TCG4522B	2810
TCG4526B	3565
TCG4527B	3116
TCG4528B	3168
TCG4529B	4451
TCG4531B	3292
TCG4532B	1010
TCG4536B	4708
TCG4539B	3611
TCG4541B	4929
TCG4543B	4932
TCG4547B	4943
TCG4551B	4950
TCG4555B	2910
TCG4556B	3397
TCG4558B	4960
TCG4566B	3463
TCG4583B	1286
TCG4585B	1365
TCG4900	2380
TCG4902	3085
TCG4918	3143
TCG4926	3162
TCG4928	3171
TCG4934	1904
TCG4950	0563
TCG4958	0825
TCG4988	1395
TCG5000A	1266
TCG5001A	2847
TCG5002A	0755
TCG5003A	0672
TCG5004A	0118
TCG5005A	0296
TCG5006A	0372
TCG5007A	0036
TCG5008A	0274
TCG5009A	0140
TCG5010A	0041
TCG5010T1	0582
TCG5011A	0253
TCG5011T1	0877
TCG5012A	0091
TCG5013A	0466
TCG5013T1	0292

DEVICE TYPE	REPL CODE
TCG5014A	0062
TCG5015A	0077
TCG5016A	0165
TCG5017A	0318
TCG5018A	0057
TCG5019A	0064
TCG5019T1	0248
TCG5020A	0181
TCG5021A	0052
TCG5021T1	0999
TCG5022A	0053
TCG5023A	0873
TCG5024A	0681
TCG5025A	0440
TCG5026A	0210
TCG5027A	0371
TCG5028A	0666
TCG5029A	0695
TCG5030A	0700
TCG5031A	0489
TCG5032A	0709
TCG5033A	0450
TCG5034A	0257
TCG5035A	0195
TCG5036A	0166
TCG5037A	0010
TCG5038A	0032
TCG5039A	0054
TCG5040A	0068
TCG5041A	0092
TCG5042A	0125
TCG5043A	2301
TCG5044A	0152
TCG5045A	0173
TCG5046A	0094
TCG5047A	0049
TCG5048A	0104
TCG5049A	0156
TCG5050A	0189
TCG5051A	0099
TCG5052A	0089
TCG5053A	0285
TCG5054A	0252
TCG5055A	0336
TCG5056A	0366
TCG5057A	0390
TCG5058A	0420
TCG5059A	0448
TCG5060A	1464
TCG5061A	2975
TCG5063A	1302
TCG5064A	2981
TCG5065A	1703
TCG5066A	0289
TCG5067A	0451
TCG5068A	0528
TCG5069A	0446
TCG5070A	0298
TCG5071A	0025
TCG5072A	0244
TCG5073A	1075
TCG5074A	0313
TCG5075A	0416
TCG5076A	1639
TCG5077A	0490
TCG5078A	0943
TCG5079A	0526
TCG5080A	0560
TCG5081A	0398
TCG5082A	1596
TCG5083A	1664
TCG5084A	0721
TCG5085A	0814
TCG5086A	0346
TCG5087A	0925
TCG5088A	0993
TCG5089A	0497
TCG5090A	0863
TCG5091A	1148
TCG5092A	2144
TCG5093A	1181
TCG5094A	2997
TCG5095A	1301
TCG5096A	0098
TCG5097A	0186
TCG5098A	0213
TCG5099A	0245
TCG5100A	0028
TCG5101A	0255
TCG5102A	0871
TCG5103A	0363
TCG5104A	2831
TCG5105A	0417
TCG5111A	0777
TCG5112A	0791
TCG5113A	0801
TCG5114A	0815
TCG5115A	0827
TCG5116A	0437
TCG5117A	0870
TCG5118A	3099
TCG5119A	0185
TCG5120A	0205
TCG5121A	0475
TCG5122A	0499
TCG5123A	3285
TCG5124A	0679
TCG5125A	0225
TCG5126A	0230

DEVICE TYPE	REPL CODE
TCG5127A	0234
TCG5128A	0237
TCG5129A	1387
TCG5130A	0247
TCG5131A	0251
TCG5132A	1170
TCG5133A	0256
TCG5134A	2379
TCG5135A	0262
TCG5136A	0269
TCG5137A	0273
TCG5138A	2383
TCG5139A	0291
TCG5140A	1169
TCG5141A	0305
TCG5142A	0314
TCG5143A	0316
TCG5144A	0322
TCG5145A	0333
TCG5146A	0343
TCG5147A	0027
TCG5148A	0266
TCG5149A	2829
TCG5150A	0382
TCG5151A	0401
TCG5152A	0421
TCG5153A	0439
TCG5154A	2999
TCG5155A	0238
TCG5156A	1172
TCG5157A	1182
TCG5158A	1198
TCG5159A	1209
TCG5160A	1870
TCG5161A	0642
TCG5162A	1246
TCG5163A	2091
TCG5164A	1269
TCG5165A	2210
TCG5166A	0600
TCG5174A	2024
TCG5174AK	0542
TCG5175A	2385
TCG5175AK	2387
TCG5176A	1429
TCG5176AK	2101
TCG5177A	2391
TCG5177AK	2394
TCG5178A	1436
TCG5178AK	1890
TCG5179A	2399
TCG5179AK	2400
TCG5180A	2206
TCG5180AK	0691
TCG5181A	1449
TCG5181AK	1591
TCG5182A	0221
TCG5182AK	1606
TCG5183A	1481
TCG5183AK	1612
TCG5184A	2406
TCG5184AK	2408
TCG5185A	1608
TCG5185AK	0622
TCG5186	0505
TCG5186A	0505
TCG5186AK	0986
TCG5187A	0686
TCG5187AK	0989
TCG5188A	0864
TCG5188AK	1254
TCG5189A	1014
TCG5189AK	1240
TCG5190A	1145
TCG5190AK	1626
TCG5191A	1264
TCG5191AK	1629
TCG5192A	1392
TCG5192AK	1693
TCG5193A	1524
TCG5193AK	1630
TCG5194A	1071
TCG5194AK	1706
TCG5195A	1701
TCG5195AK	1709
TCG5196A	1707
TCG5196AK	1720
TCG5197A	1712
TCG5197AK	0722
TCG5198A	1725
TCG5198AK	1745
TCG5199A	1737
TCG5199AK	1757
TCG5200A	1750
TCG5200AK	1771
TCG5201A	2431
TCG5201AK	2434
TCG5202A	1761
TCG5202AK	1783
TCG5203A	1777
TCG5203AK	1788
TCG5204A	1785
TCG5204AK	1798
TCG5205A	1793
TCG5205AK	1806
TCG5206A	1185
TCG5206AK	1815
TCG5207A	1810
TCG5207AK	1829

DEVICE TYPE	REPL CODE
TCG5208A	0022
TCG5208AK	1842
TCG5209A	0070
TCG5209AK	1850
TCG5210A	0132
TCG5210AK	1855
TCG5211A	0172
TCG5211AK	1863
TCG5212A	0207
TCG5212AK	1873
TCG5213A	0227
TCG5213AK	2455
TCG5214A	0263
TCG5214AK	1884
TCG5215A	0306
TCG5215AK	1891
TCG5216A	0325
TCG5216AK	0731
TCG5217A	0352
TCG5217AK	1898
TCG5218A	0377
TCG5218AK	2459
TCG5219A	0408
TCG5219AK	1903
TCG5220A	0433
TCG5220AK	1155
TCG5221A	0459
TCG5221AK	1913
TCG5222A	0483
TCG5222AK	1922
TCG5223A	0504
TCG5223AK	1930
TCG5224A	0519
TCG5224AK	1936
TCG5225A	0537
TCG5225AK	1942
TCG5226A	0063
TCG5226AK	1950
TCG5227A	0397
TCG5227AK	0353
TCG5228A	0593
TCG5228AK	2479
TCG5229A	0611
TCG5229AK	0665
TCG5230A	0629
TCG5230AK	0771
TCG5231A	0645
TCG5231AK	2486
TCG5232A	0663
TCG5232AK	1065
TCG5234A	OEM
TCG5240A	0809
TCG5240AK	2695
TCG5241A	0821
TCG5241AK	2698
TCG5242A	0840
TCG5242AK	2700
TCG5243A	0862
TCG5243AK	2703
TCG5244A	0879
TCG5244AK	2706
TCG5245A	0891
TCG5245AK	2707
TCG5246A	0908
TCG5246AK	2711
TCG5247A	0920
TCG5247AK	2713
TCG5248A	0938
TCG5248AK	2717
TCG5249A	0952
TCG5249AK	1216
TCG5250A	0972
TCG5250AK	2719
TCG5251A	0988
TCG5251AK	1228
TCG5252A	1003
TCG5252AK	1243
TCG5253A	1013
TCG5253AK	1259
TCG5254A	0883
TCG5254AK	1267
TCG5255A	1043
TCG5255AK	1283
TCG5256A	1052
TCG5256AK	1292
TCG5257A	0926
TCG5257AK	1292
TCG5258A	1072
TCG5258AK	1300
TCG5259A	1088
TCG5259AK	2729
TCG5260A	1098
TCG5260AK	1314
TCG5261A	1115
TCG5261AK	2731
TCG5262A	1127
TCG5262AK	1323
TCG5263A	1144
TCG5263AK	1334
TCG5264A	1156
TCG5264AK	1346
TCG5265A	1166
TCG5265AK	2733
TCG5266A	1176
TCG5266AK	1361
TCG5267A	1191
TCG5267AK	2735
TCG5268A	1201
TCG5268AK	1377

DEVICE TYPE	REPL CODE
TCG5269A	1214
TCG5269AK	1396
TCG5270A	1223
TCG5270AK	1405
TCG5271A	1237
TCG5271AK	1419
TCG5272A	1256
TCG5272AK	1431
TCG5273A	1263
TCG5273AK	2745
TCG5274A	1280
TCG5274AK	1438
TCG5275A	1289
TCG5275AK	2749
TCG5276A	1297
TCG5276AK	1452
TCG5277A	1312
TCG5277AK	1465
TCG5278A	1321
TCG5278AK	1465
TCG5279A	1330
TCG5279AK	2756
TCG5280A	1343
TCG5280AK	0608
TCG5281A	1355
TCG5281AK	1502
TCG5282A	1374
TCG5282AK	1515
TCG5283A	1391
TCG5283AK	1529
TCG5284A	1402
TCG5284AK	1541
TCG5285A	1413
TCG5285AK	1565
TCG5286A	1427
TCG5286AK	2775
TCG5287A	1435
TCG5287AK	2776
TCG5288A	1448
TCG5288AK	1499
TCG5289A	1461
TCG5289AK	2778
TCG5290A	1475
TCG5290AK	2780
TCG5291A	1497
TCG5291AK	2783
TCG5292A	1513
TCG5292AK	2788
TCG5293A	1523
TCG5293AK	2791
TCG5294A	1539
TCG5294AK	2793
TCG5295A	1558
TCG5295AK	2795
TCG5296A	1577
TCG5296AK	2797
TCG5304	0106
TCG5305	1999
TCG5306	2384
TCG5307	0782
TCG5312	0319
TCG5313	1404
TCG5314	0468
TCG5315	0441
TCG5316	1412
TCG5317	2425
TCG5322	2347
TCG5324	2353
TCG5326	2354
TCG5327	2356
TCG5328	2357
TCG5332	1864
TCG5334	3503
TCG5340	1633
TCG5342	1663
TCG5344	1579
TCG5351	4272
TCG5360	0799
TCG5368	0650
TCG5369	0020
TCG5371	0521
TCG5372	0108
TCG5374	0423
TCG5375	1860
TCG5377	1690
TCG5378	0341
TCG5380	0454
TCG5381	0584
TCG5386	0764
TCG5387	0478
TCG5400	1129
TCG5401	0340
TCG5402	0895
TCG5403	2326
TCG5404	0058
TCG5405	0403
TCG5406	1673
TCG5407	OEM
TCG5408	0179
TCG5409	0342
TCG5410	3315
TCG5411	4384
TCG5412	0174
TCG5413	3801
TCG5414	3575
TCG5415	3291
TCG5416	1494
TCG5417	0998
TCG5418	1028

DEVICE TYPE	REPL CODE
TCG5419	1140
TCG5425	5429
TCG5426	1038
TCG5437	0712
TCG5438	0304
TCG5442	4508
TCG5444	2255
TCG5446	3368
TCG5448	3370
TCG5452	1386
TCG5453	1250
TCG5454	0442
TCG5455	0934
TCG5456	1213
TCG5457	0095
TCG5461	2084
TCG5462	2078
TCG5463	2084
TCG5465	0705
TCG5466	0857
TCG5468	0323
TCG5470	1102
TCG5471	2904
TCG5472	0957
TCG5473	2905
TCG5474	2908
TCG5475	3626
TCG5476	3405
TCG5480	3385
TCG5481	1095
TCG5482	2471
TCG5483	0240
TCG5484	2635
TCG5485	0671
TCG5486	2782
TCG5487	0332
TCG5491	2430
TCG5492	0430
TCG5494	1478
TCG5496	0682
TCG5500	3073
TCG5501	2497
TCG5502	0736
TCG5503	3076
TCG5504	0740
TCG5505	3080
TCG5506	2889
TCG5507	0742
TCG5508	3213
TCG5509	0747
TCG5511	3651
TCG5512	3349
TCG5513	3579
TCG5514	1641
TCG5515	1574
TCG5516	1655
TCG5517	1640
TCG5518	2623
TCG5520	3275
TCG5521	2174
TCG5522	0562
TCG5523	3227
TCG5524	0757
TCG5525	3237
TCG5526	3240
TCG5527	0735
TCG5528	3260
TCG5529	0759
TCG5530	2848
TCG5531	0761
TCG5534	0226
TCG5540	3246
TCG5541	0726
TCG5542	0707
TCG5543	0464
TCG5544	0716
TCG5545	0717
TCG5546	0773
TCG5547	0720
TCG5548	0745
TCG5550	2499
TCG5552	0393
TCG5554	0606
TCG5556	0946
TCG5558	1504
TCG5562	1837
TCG5564	1844
TCG5566	3185
TCG5567	1694
TCG5568	3970
TCG5569	0674
TCG5570	0603
TCG5572	0605
TCG5574	0463
TCG5575	0636
TCG5577	0217
TCG5579	0653
TCG5580	1076
TCG5582	1078
TCG5584	1094
TCG5600	4341
TCG5601	1744
TCG5602	4343
TCG5603	3458
TCG5604	4058
TCG5605	0480
TCG5606	4345
TCG5607	4346
TCG5608	0567

If replacement code is OEM, contact original manufacturer for replacement.

DEVICE TYPE	REPL CODE
TCG5609	0929
TCG5610	0059
TCG5611	5452
TCG5612	5453
TCG5614	4366
TCG5615	0951
TCG5616	0954
TCG5617	0955
TCG5618	0960
TCG5621	5454
TCG5622	1081
TCG5623	0948
TCG5624	0407
TCG5625	1087
TCG5626	0411
TCG5627	0480
TCG5628	1092
TCG5631	0573
TCG5632	0566
TCG5633	0588
TCG5634	0569
TCG5635	0571
TCG5636	0572
TCG5637	0589
TCG5638	5226
TCG5640	2367
TCG5641	2378
TCG5642	1403
TCG5643	2371
TCG5645	0550
TCG5646	1447
TCG5649	5456
TCG5650	2336
TCG5651	2337
TCG5652	2340
TCG5653	5457
TCG5655	4381
TCG5656	4382
TCG5657	4404
TCG5660	0395
TCG5661	0400
TCG5662	0404
TCG5665	0418
TCG5666	0418
TCG5667	0418
TCG5672	5461
TCG5673	0154
TCG5675	0147
TCG5676	4465
TCG5677	0278
TCG5679	0902
TCG5680	3117
TCG5681	3118
TCG5682	3119
TCG5683	3121
TCG5684	3122
TCG5685	3123
TCG5686	3124
TCG5687	4038
TCG5688	1058
TCG5689	1307
TCG5690	1880
TCG5693	2004
TCG5695	2006
TCG5697	2007
TCG5800	0110
TCG5801	0947
TCG5802	0242
TCG5803	1736
TCG5804	0535
TCG5805	1760
TCG5806	0959
TCG5808	0811
TCG5809	0916
TCG5812	1272
TCG5814	1277
TCG5815	1282
TCG5817	1285
TCG5818	1557
TCG5819	1538
TCG5820	2140
TCG5821	3110
TCG5822	0706
TCG5823	2939
TCG5826	3475
TCG5827	4924
TCG5828	3498
TCG5829	5477
TCG5830	0703
TCG5831	0927
TCG5832	4077
TCG5833	5420
TCG5834	0575
TCG5835	0941
TCG5836	2049
TCG5837	4443
TCG5838	0994
TCG5839	1006
TCG5840	2065
TCG5841	5467
TCG5842	2070
TCG5843	1067
TCG5846	2077
TCG5847	1130
TCG5848	0607
TCG5849	1180
TCG5850	0964
TCG5851	0979
TCG5852	3688

DEVICE TYPE	REPL CODE
TCG5853	0904
TCG5854	0983
TCG5855	0984
TCG5856	3697
TCG5857	0987
TCG5858	0197
TCG5859	0991
TCG5860	0200
TCG5861	0995
TCG5862	0204
TCG5863	0510
TCG5866	0206
TCG5867	1002
TCG5868	0583
TCG5869	0942
TCG5870	0084
TCG5871	0529
TCG5872	0090
TCG5873	0743
TCG5874	0097
TCG5875	0760
TCG5876	0105
TCG5877	0540
TCG5878	0109
TCG5879	0533
TCG5880	0116
TCG5881	0796
TCG5882	0122
TCG5883	0810
TCG5886	0131
TCG5887	0540
TCG5890	0145
TCG5891	0545
TCG5892	5417
TCG5893	1229
TCG5894	5482
TCG5895	1231
TCG5896	2872
TCG5897	1232
TCG5898	5483
TCG5899	1236
TCG5900	3705
TCG5901	2349
TCG5902	3711
TCG5903	1244
TCG5904	1104
TCG5905	2360
TCG5908	3722
TCG5909	1255
TCG5910	2982
TCG5911	0444
TCG5912	1590
TCG5913	4917
TCG5914	5189
TCG5915	5394
TCG5916	0865
TCG5917	1625
TCG5918	5190
TCG5919	5398
TCG5920	0847
TCG5921	1242
TCG5922	5192
TCG5923	5399
TCG5924	1599
TCG5925	1196
TCG5928	1600
TCG5929	2124
TCG5932	1604
TCG5933	2236
TCG5940	1991
TCG5941	1992
TCG5942	0585
TCG5943	3234
TCG5944	1241
TCG5945	1567
TCG5946	5487
TCG5947	3244
TCG5948	1571
TCG5949	3251
TCG5950	5489
TCG5951	3256
TCG5952	1576
TCG5953	3263
TCG5960	OEM
TCG5962	4938
TCG5963	2537
TCG5966	2591
TCG5967	2544
TCG5980	3160
TCG5981	1620
TCG5982	2873
TCG5983	0254
TCG5986	1116
TCG5987	1099
TCG5988	1118
TCG5989	1103
TCG5990	0800
TCG5991	0258
TCG5992	1186
TCG5993	1634
TCG5994	0315
TCG5995	0267
TCG5998	1124
TCG5999	1111
TCG6002	0045
TCG6003	0280
TCG6006	1522
TCG6008	0029
TCG6009	1836

DEVICE TYPE	REPL CODE
TCG6010	0596
TCG6011	1840
TCG6020	3716
TCG6021	2640
TCG6022	2629
TCG6023	2670
TCG6026	2633
TCG6027	2741
TCG6030	2639
TCG6031	2828
TCG6034	1995
TCG6035	2879
TCG6038	2652
TCG6039	2946
TCG6040	2657
TCG6041	3022
TCG6042	3846
TCG6043	3088
TCG6044	2631
TCG6045	3178
TCG6048	4242
TCG6049	3725
TCG6050	1551
TCG6051	2165
TCG6054	2813
TCG6055	2168
TCG6058	4244
TCG6059	3556
TCG6060	2823
TCG6061	2177
TCG6064	2844
TCG6065	2183
TCG6068	2806
TCG6069	2202
TCG6072	2454
TCG6073	2324
TCG6074	2751
TCG6075	1734
TCG6076	2786
TCG6077	1772
TCG6078	2619
TCG6079	1807
TCG6084	0610
TCG6094	1536
TCG6154	0594
TCG6155	1337
TCG6156	1975
TCG6157	1894
TCG6158	0652
TCG6159	0193
TCG6354	1017
TCG6355	0496
TCG6356	1030
TCG6357	1766
TCG6358	1040
TCG6359	1778
TCG6400	1659
TCG6400A	1659
TCG6401	2123
TCG6402	0312
TCG6403	4169
TCG6404	3373
TCG6405	4335
TCG6406	3603
TCG6407	3298
TCG6408	2704
TCG6409	1167
TCG6410	1882
TCG6411	5290
TCG6412	5537
TCG6415	5539
TCG6416	5540
TCG6417	5542
TCG6418	5543
TCG6419	5544
TCG6502	3036
TCG6507	3041
TCG6508	3164
TCG6532	1962
TCG6800	0384
TCG6802	0389
TCG6810	2075
TCG6821	0443
TCG6850	0509
TCG6875	4118
TCG6880	4437
TCG6885	4566
TCG6886	4570
TCG6887	4577
TCG6888	4586
TCG6889	0576
TCG7400	0232
TCG7401	0268
TCG7402	0310
TCG7403	0331
TCG7404	0357
TCG7405	0381
TCG7406	1197
TCG7407	1329
TCG7408	0462
TCG7409	0487
TCG7410	0507
TCG7411	0522
TCG7412	2227
TCG7413	1432
TCG7414	2228
TCG7416	1339
TCG7417	1342
TCG7420	0692

DEVICE TYPE	REPL CODE
TCG7421	1347
TCG7422	4523
TCG7423	3429
TCG7425	3438
TCG7426	0798
TCG7427	0812
TCG7428	4117
TCG7430	0867
TCG7432	0893
TCG7433	4130
TCG7437	3478
TCG7438	0990
TCG7439	5722
TCG7440	1018
TCG7441	1032
TCG7442	1046
TCG7443	1054
TCG7444	1066
TCG7445	1074
TCG7446	1090
TCG7447	1100
TCG7448	1117
TCG7450	0738
TCG7451	1160
TCG7453	1177
TCG7454	1193
TCG7460	1265
TCG7470	1394
TCG7472	1417
TCG7473	1164
TCG7474	1303
TCG7475	1423
TCG7476	1150
TCG7480	1527
TCG7481	3092
TCG7482	1564
TCG7483	0117
TCG7485	0370
TCG7486	1358
TCG7486A	1358
TCG7488A	4817
TCG7489	5358
TCG7490	1199
TCG7491	0974
TCG7492	0828
TCG7493A	0564
TCG7494	1692
TCG7495	1477
TCG7496	1705
TCG7497	2912
TCG8070	2915
TCG8076	2916
TCG8080A	4467
TCG8081	2920
TCG8085	2923
TCG8090	2927
TCG8096	2933
TCG8098	2363
TCG8108	2940
TCG8115	2944
TCG8118	2945
TCG8123	5801
TCG8125	2948
TCG8139	2962
TCG8149	2970
TCG8167	3005
TCG8181	3007
TCG8212	1849
TCG8213	2972
TCG8216	1852
TCG8223	5814
TCG8224	1699
TCG8226	2984
TCG8228	1858
TCG8242	2992
TCG8255	0051
TCG8301	2182
TCG8308	1064
TCG8309	5430
TCG8314	2468
TCG8316	5820
TCG8318	4082
TCG8321	5821
TCG8328	5822
TCG8368	5825
TCG8370	5826
TCG8374	5827
TCG8520	5837
TCG8542	5838
TCG8546	5839
TCG8556	5840
TCG9093	0354
TCG9094	1622
TCG9097	1472
TCG9099	0329
TCG9135	1609
TCG9157	1424
TCG9158	0461
TCG9200	4095
TCG9370	1284
TCG9402	4099
TCG9403	1589
TCG9601	2252
TCG9602	2270
TCG9660	0613
TCG9661	2574
TCG9663	2964
TCG9664	3003
TCG9666	4079

DEVICE TYPE	REPL CODE
TCG9668	2417
TCG9669	2986
TCG9670	2334
TCG9671	4086
TCG9672	0078
TCG9673	0795
TCG9675	4101
TCG9676	4107
TCG9678	4110
TCG9679	4112
TCG9680	4115
TCG9681	3016
TCG9682	3010
TCG9689	4137
TCG9691	4143
TCG9800	0844
TCG9801	0868
TCG9802	0882
TCG9803	0894
TCG9804	0913
TCG9805	0923
TCG9806	0939
TCG9807	0956
TCG9808	0976
TCG9809	0992
TCG9810	1005
TCG9811	1019
TCG9812	1033
TCG9813	4458
TCG9814	4461
TCG9904	1622
TCG9910	1248
TCG9917	OEM
TCG9923	OEM
TCG9924	2840
TCG9926	2232
TCG9930	1812
TCG9932	1035
TCG9933	2086
TCG9935	1168
TCG9936	1820
TCG9937	1824
TCG9944	0033
TCG9945	0081
TCG9946	0141
TCG9948	3365
TCG9949	1833
TCG9950	2595
TCG9951	2067
TCG9961	1848
TCG9962	0557
TCG9963	0337
TCG9969	OEM
TCG9989	3395
TCG32154	5119
TCG40085B	3415
TCG40097B	4367
TCG40098B	0427
TCG40100B	3895
TCG40106B	3581
TCG40160B	1349
TCG40161B	1363
TCG40162B	1378
TCG40163B	1397
TCG40174B	1542
TCG40175B	1520
TCG40182B	4579
TCG40192B	1753
TCG40193B	1765
TCG40194B	1758
TCG40195B	1773
TCG47368	OEM
TCG56004	0767
TCG56006	0739
TCG56008	0612
TCG56010	0869
TCG56022	3169
TCG56024	3177
TCG56026	3192
TCG65101	4524
TCG74100	4474
TCG74105	4475
TCG74107	0936
TCG74109	0962
TCG74110	0981
TCG74111	0996
TCG74116	4365
TCG74120	1108
TCG74121	0175
TCG74122	1131
TCG74123	1149
TCG74125	1174
TCG74126	1184
TCG74128	1210
TCG74132	1261
TCG74136	1306
TCG74141	1367
TCG74144	1408
TCG74145	0614
TCG74147	1442
TCG74148	1455
TCG74150	1484
TCG74151	1487
TCG74152	1509
TCG74153	1531
TCG74154	1546
TCG74155	1566
TCG74156	1582
TCG74157	1595

DEVICE TYPE	REPL CODE
TCG74158	4372
TCG74160	1621
TCG74161	1635
TCG74162	1007
TCG74163	1656
TCG74164	0729
TCG74165	1675
TCG74166	0231
TCG74170	1759
TCG74173	1755
TCG74174	1759
TCG74175	1776
TCG74176	1784
TCG74177	1792
TCG74178	1802
TCG74179	1809
TCG74180	1818
TCG74181	1831
TCG74182	1845
TCG74185	1857
TCG74190	1901
TCG74191	1906
TCG74192	1910
TCG74193	1915
TCG74195	1932
TCG74196	1939
TCG74197	1945
TCG74198	1953
TCG74199	1960
TCG74221	2129
TCG74249	2274
TCG74251	2283
TCG74265	4531
TCG74278	4536
TCG74279	4538
TCG74290	2588
TCG74293	2620
TCG74298	4547
TCG74365	1450
TCG74366	1462
TCG74367	1479
TCG74368	1500
TCG74390	3210
TCG74393	3225
TCG74426	4616
TCG74490	3619
TCG75188	0503
TCG75189	0506
TCG75450B	1222
TCG75451B	1235
TCG75452B	1253
TCG75453B	1262
TCG75454B	1279
TCG75491B	1718
TCG75492B	1729
TCG75493	4933
TCG75494	4934
TCGHIDIV-1	2949
TCGHIDIV-2	2950
TCGHIDIV-3	2952
TCGHIDIV-4	2951
TCGHIDIV-12	5265
TCH98	0037
TCH99	0037
TCH99B	0037
TCIT00501P	0076
TCK1509	OEM
TCL0009450	0076
TCLT009450	0076
TCM1501	OEM
TCM1504	OEM
TCM1505	OEM
TCM1512A	OEM
TCM1701	OEM
TCM1702	OEM
TCM1703	OEM
TCM2101	OEM
TCM2401	OEM
TCM2910A	OEM
TCM2911A	OEM
TCM2912	OEM
TCM2913	OEM
TCM2914	OEM
TCM4110	OEM
TCM4910	OEM
TCM5087	OEM
TCM5089	5127
TCM5089N	OEM
TCM5091	OEM
TCM5092	OEM
TCN3C00	OEM
TC02P112	0015
TC0914	0079
TC0.09M22/1	0276
TC-0.2	0102
TCP4621AF-6002	OEM
TCP4633BN9503	OEM
TCP4633BN9905	OEM
TCP4633BN9907	OEM
TCP4633BN9908	OEM
TCP4633BN9912	OEM
TCP46307311	OEM
TCP46307311B	OEM
TCP46307322B	OEM
TCP46339903X	OEM
TCP46339904X	OEM
TCP46339905	OEM
TCR3	1095
TCR8	1095

DEVICE TYPE	REPL CODE
TCR13	0240
TCR18	0240
TCR23	0240
TCR28	0240
TCR38	2635
TCR48	0671
TCR50	1095
TCR51	2471
TCR52	0240
TCR53	0240
TCR54	2635
TCR55	2635
TCR56	0671
TCR70	1095
TCR71	2471
TCR72	0240
TCR74	2635
TCR75	2635
TCR82	OEM
TCR85	OEM
TCR86	OEM
TCR102	OEM
TCR152	OEM
TCR202	OEM
TCR252	OEM
TCR302	OEM
TCR352	OEM
TCR402	OEM
TCR503	OEM
TCR505	1095
TCR510	1095
TCR550	OEM
TCR730	1095
TCR731	2471
TCR732	0240
TCR733	2635
TCR734	0671
TCR742	1095
TCR743	2471
TCR744	0240
TCR745	0240
TCR746	2635
TCR747	2635
TCR748	0671
TCR1005	0240
TCR1010	2471
TCR1050	OEM
TCR1503	OEM
TCR1505	0240
TCR1510	0240
TCR1520	OEM
TCR1550	OEM
TCR2003	OEM
TCR2005	0240
TCR2010	0240
TCR2050	OEM
TCR2503	OEM
TCR2505	2635
TCR2510	2635
TCR2550	OEM
TCR3003	OEM
TCR3005	2635
TCR3010	2635
TCR3050	OEM
TCR3503	OEM
TCR3505	0671
TCR3510	0671
TCR3550	OEM
TCR4003	OEM
TCR4005	0671
TCR4010	0671
TCR5275	OEM
TCR5276	OEM
TCR5277	OEM
TCR5278	OEM
TCR5279	OEM
TCR5280	OEM
TCR5281	OEM
TCR5282	OEM
TCR5283	OEM
TCR5284	OEM
TCR5285	OEM
TCR5286	OEM
TCR5287	OEM
TCR5288	OEM
TCR5289	OEM
TCR5290	OEM
TCR5291	OEM
TCR5292	OEM
TCR5293	OEM
TCR5294	OEM
TCR5295	OEM
TCR5296	OEM
TCR5297	OEM
TCR5298	OEM
TCR5300	OEM
TCR5301	OEM
TCR5302	OEM
TCR5303	OEM
TCR5304	OEM
TCR5305	OEM
TCR5306	OEM
TCR5307	OEM
TCR5308	OEM
TCR5309	OEM
TCR5310	OEM
TCR5311	OEM
TCR5312	OEM
TCR5313	OEM

DEVICE TYPE	REPL CODE
TCR5314	OEM
TCR5315	OEM
TCS100	0590
TCS101	0472
TCS102	0590
TCS103	0472
TCT009450	0076
TCXB003H	OEM
TCXQ88535-119S	OEM
TD2SC2334	2253
TD3F012070	3882
TD3F013970	1533
TD3F013980	1533
TD3G0612KE	1779
TD3H018250	3107
TD3T00863E	1376
TD3T007340	1505
TD3T011110	OEM
TD3T012070	3882
TD4G	1864
TD5	3315
TD5F014260	1533
TD5F014270	1533
TD5F015550	0551
TD5G015540	1533
TD5Q01555S	0551
TD5Q015460	3326
TD5Q015470	3326
TD5Q015560	1533
TD5U015460	3326
TD5.B	1864
TD5.F	1864
TD5.G	1864
TD5.K	1864
TD5.L	1864
TD6	3315
TD6F	1864
TD6.B	1864
TD6.C	1864
TD7	OEM
TD7.C	1864
TD7.J	1864
TD8	OEM
TD8.A	1864
TD8.B	1864
TD8.C	1864
TD8.E	1864
TD8.I	1864
TD8.K	1864
TD8.L	1864
TD-9	OEM
TD9	OEM
TD9.C	1864
TD-13	0182
TD-15	0182
TD15	0182
TD-15-BL	0133
TD-15H	0182
TD15H	0102
TD15M	0102
TD-20W	0139
TD-25	OEM
TD-25-0	OEM
TD52	OEM
TD55	OEM
TD64	OEM
TD-80	OEM
TD80	OEM
TD-100	4930
TD100	0079
TD-101	4930
TD101	3873
TD-102	4930
TD102	0079
TD110	OEM
TD-200	4930
TD200	0079
TD-201	4930
TD201	0079
TD201A	OEM
TD-202	4930
TD202	0079
TD202A	OEM
TD203	OEM
TD203A	OEM
TD204	OEM
TD204A	OEM
TD205	OEM
TD205A	OEM
TD206	OEM
TD-250	4930
TD250	0079
TD251	OEM
TD251A	OEM
TD252	OEM
TD252A	OEM
TD253	OEM
TD253A	OEM
TD253B	OEM
TD254	OEM
TD254A	OEM
TD255	OEM
TD255A	OEM
TD256	OEM
TD256A	OEM
TD-261	OEM
TD261	OEM
TD-261A	OEM
TD261A	OEM

DEVICE TYPE	REPL CODE
TD-262	OEM
TD262	OEM
TD-262A	OEM
TD262A	OEM
TD-263	OEM
TD263	OEM
TD-263A	OEM
TD263A	OEM
TD-263B	OEM
TD263B	OEM
TD-264	OEM
TD264	OEM
TD-264A	OEM
TD264A	OEM
TD-265	OEM
TD265	OEM
TD-265A	OEM
TD265A	OEM
TD-266	OEM
TD266	OEM
TD-266A	OEM
TD266A	OEM
TD271	OEM
TD271A	OEM
TD272	OEM
TD272A	OEM
TD273	OEM
TD273A	OEM
TD273B	OEM
TD274	OEM
TD274A	OEM
TD275A	OEM
TD276	OEM
TD276A	OEM
TD-400	4974
TD400	0037
TD-401	4974
TD401	0037
TD-402	4974
TD402	0037
TD-500	4974
TD500	0037
TD-501	4974
TD501	0037
TD501(SCR)	OEM
TD501F	OEM
TD501J	OEM
TD501S	OEM
TD-502	4974
TD502	0037
TD503	0179
TD510	OEM
TD-550	4974
TD550	0037
TD554	OEM
TD-600	3863
TD-601	3863
TD-602	3863
TD-700	3863
TD-701	3863
TD-702	3863
TD710	OEM
TD712	OEM
TD713	OEM
TD714	OEM
TD715	OEM
TD716	OEM
TD717	OEM
TD718	OEM
TD719	OEM
TD1001F	OEM
TD1001J	OEM
TD1001S	OEM
TD1003	0179
TD1053	OEM
TD1060	1812
TD1060P	1812
TD1061	1168
TD1061P	1168
TD1062	1035
TD1062P	1035
TD1063	2086
TD1063P	2086
TD1064	0033
TD1064P	0033
TD1065	0141
TD1065P	0141
TD1066	0557
TD1066P	0557
TD1067	3365
TD1067P	3365
TD1070	0081
TD1070P	0081
TD1072	1820
TD1072P	1820
TD1073	0354
TD1073P	0354
TD1074	0329
TD1074P	0329
TD1080	1848
TD1080P	1848
TD1083A	OEM
TD1085	1833
TD1085P	1833
TD1086	0337
TD1086P	0337
TD1401	0232
TD1401P	0232
TD1402	0507

DEVICE TYPE	REPL CODE
TD1402P	0507
TD1403	0692
TD1403P	0692
TD1404	0867
TD1404P	0867
TD1405	1018
TD1405P	1018
TD1406	0738
TD1406P	0738
TD1407	1265
TD1407P	1265
TD1408	1417
TD1408P	1417
TD1409	1164
TD1409P	1164
TD1419	1160
TD1419P	1160
TD2001F	OEM
TD2001J	OEM
TD2001P	2574
TD2001S	OEM
TD2002P	2334
TD2003	0179
TD2003P	2417
TD2004P	3003
TD2005P	2964
TD2006P	2986
TD2008P	0613
TD2009P	4086
TD2010P	0078
TD2011P	2542
TD2012P	4115
TD2013P	4108
TD2015P	3037
TD-2219	4930
TD2219	0079
TD2400	OEM
TD-2905	4974
TD2905	0037
TD3001F	OEM
TD3001J	OEM
TD3001S	OEM
TD3003	0342
TD3168	OEM
TD3169	OEM
TD3171	OEM
TD3172	OEM
TD3173	OEM
TD3174	OEM
TD3400A	0232
TD3400AP	0232
TD3400P	0232
TD3401A	0268
TD3401AP	0268
TD3402A	0310
TD3402AP	0310
TD3404A	0357
TD3404AP	0357
TD3405A	0381
TD3405AP	0381
TD3409A	0487
TD3409AP	0487
TD3410A	0507
TD3410AP	0507
TD3410P	0507
TD3420A	0692
TD3420AP	0692
TD3420P	0692
TD3430A	0867
TD3430AP	0867
TD3430P	0867
TD3440A	1018
TD3440AP	1018
TD3440P	1018
TD3441A	1032
TD3441AP	1032
TD3442	OEM
TD3442A	1046
TD3442AP	1046
TD3447A	1100
TD3447AP	1100
TD3450A	0738
TD3450AP	0738
TD3450P	0738
TD3451A	1160
TD3451AP	1160
TD3451P	1160
TD3460A	1265
TD3460AP	1265
TD3460P	1265
TD3472A	1417
TD3472AP	1417
TD3473A	1164
TD3473AP	1164
TD3474A	1303
TD3474AP	1303
TD3474P	1303
TD3475A	1423
TD3475AP	1423
TD3480A	1527
TD3480AP	1527
TD3482P	1564
TD3483P	0117
TD3490	OEM
TD3490A	1199
TD3490AP	1199
TD3490P	1199
TD3491A	0974
TD3491AP	0974

DEVICE TYPE	REPL CODE
TD3492A	0828
TD3492AP	0828
TD3492P	0828
TD3493A	0564
TD3493AP	0564
TD3493BP	0564
TD3493P	0564
TD3495A	1477
TD3495AP	1477
TD3503A	0729
TD3503AP	0729
TD4001F	OEM
TD4001J	OEM
TD4001S	OEM
TD4003	0342
TD5001J	OEM
TD5003	3315
TD6001J	OEM
TD-6012P	OEM
TD6103P(FA-1)	OEM
TD6104P	OEM
TD6107P	OEM
TD6110P	OEM
TD6133F	OEM
TD6301AN	OEM
TD6301AP	OEM
TD6301P	OEM
TD6306FA-1	OEM
TD6306P	5124
TD6306PFA-1	5124
TD6312P	4923
TD6314P	OEM
TD6350P	4923
TD6358P	OEM
TD6359N	OEM
TD6359P	OEM
TD6360N-02	OEM
TD6360N-04	OEM
TD6360P	OEM
TD6361N-C1	OEM
TD6365N-A1	OEM
TD6530	OEM
TD7001	OEM
TD7001J	OEM
TD7001S	OEM
TD8001	OEM
TD8001J	OEM
TD8001S	OEM
TD34121A	0175
TD34121AP	0175
TD34192A	1910
TD34192AP	1910
TD62003P	1126
TD62006P	4876
TD62007P	OEM
TD62083AP	OEM
TD62103P	OEM
TD62104P	0963
TD62107P	OEM
TD62307P	OEM
TD62308AP	OEM
TD62308BP	OEM
TD62501P	OEM
TD62504	OEM
TD62504P	OEM
TD62507P	OEM
TD62553S	OEM
TD62555S	OEM
TD81515	0133
TD81518	0133
TD200401A0	1274
TD200401AL	1274
TD501052A0	2058
TD960016-1M	0133
TD3214738	3071
TD3214739	0012
TD3214740	OEM
TD3214741	OEM
TD3214742	0137
TD3214743	OEM
TD3214744	0002
TD3214745	OEM
TD3214746	OEM
TD3214747	OEM
TD3214748	OEM
TD3214749	OEM
TD3214750	OEM
TD3214751	OEM
TD3214752	OEM
TD3907562	3071
TD3907572	0057
TD3907582	OEM
TD3907592	0052
TD3909622	OEM
TD3909632	0052
TD3909642	OEM
TD3909652	0681
TD3909662	OEM
TD3909672	OEM
TD3909682	OEM
TD3909692	OEM
TD3909702	OEM
TD3909712	OEM
TD3909722	OEM
TD3909732	OEM
TD20004710	0018
TD20008820	0161
TD30006120	1779
TD30011590	2985

DEVICE TYPE	REPL CODE
TD30012070	3882
TD30016660	0060
TD30018250	3107
TD50014260	1533
TDA0470	OEM
TDA0470-D	OEM
TDA152AN	3132
TDA407	0414
TDA412	OEM
TDA420	0414
TDA1013A	3453
TDA1013AU	3453
TDA1013B	3453
TDA1032	OEM
TDA1034B	OEM
TDA1035	OEM
TDA1043	OEM
TDA1044	OEM
TDA1044F	OEM
TDA1057	OEM
TDA1060	5120
TDA1083	5103
TDA-1083/2	4986
TDA1083A	5103
TDA1151	OEM
TDA1151M	OEM
TDA-1170	4580
TDA1170	4580
TDA1170A	OEM
TDA1170D	OEM
TDA1170N	OEM
TDA1170S	4580
TDA1177	OEM
TDA1180P	6971
TDA1190P	1051
TDA1190Z	1162
TDA1200	2728
TDA1220B	OEM
TDA1330P	1797
TDA1412	0330
TDA1415	1311
TDA1424A	OEM
TDA1458D	0356
TDA1504P	OEM
TDA1506	OEM
TDA1510	OEM
TDA1512	OEM
TDA1520A	OEM
TDA1521	3127
TDA1521U	3127
TDA1524	3132
TDA1524A	3132
TDA1524AN	3132
TDA1524PN	3132
TDA1526	OEM
TDA1533	OEM
TDA1540	OEM
TDA1540D	OEM
TDA1540P	OEM
TDA1541	3207
TDA1541A	OEM
TDA1541AN	3207
TDA1541N	3207
TDA1543	OEM
TDA1559	OEM
TDA1576	OEM
TDA1578	OEM
TDA1594(A)	OEM
TDA1670A	3727
TDA1675	OEM
TDA1770A	OEM
TDA1872A	OEM
TDA1905	6020
TDA1908	OEM
TDA1908A	OEM
TDA1910	OEM
TDA1940	OEM
TDA1940F	OEM
TDA1950	OEM
TDA2002	1042
TDA2003	4493
TDA2003V	4493
TDA2004	0491
TDA2005M	0491
TDA2006	4644
TDA2007	OEM
TDA2008	6089
TDA2009	OEM
TDA2009A	OEM
TDA2030	4646
TDA2052	OEM
TDA2170	OEM
TDA2190	OEM
TDA2270	OEM
TDA2518Q	OEM
TDA2540	2799
TDA-2541	3692
TDA2541	2799
TDA2541Q	2799
TDA2544	0906
TDA2545A	OEM
TDA2546A	3481
TDA2548	OEM
TDA2575AQ	OEM
TDA2577	5106
TDA2577A	5106
TDA2577AS2	5106
TDA2579	OEM
TDA2581Q	OEM

DEVICE TYPE	REPL CODE
TDA2593	5639
TDA2593N	5639
TDA2595	OEM
TDA2611	4521
TDA2611A	4521
TDA2611AQ	4521
TDA2653A	1245
TDA2653AN	1245
TDA2653AU	1245
TDA2730	OEM
TDA2758A	OEM
TDA2791	5675
TDA2822	OEM
TDA2822M	OEM
TDA2824	OEM
TDA3047	5153
TDA3048	5155
TDA3048D	OEM
TDA3048N	5155
TDA3190	1051
TDA3190P	OEM
TDA3333	OEM
TDA3333P	OEM
TDA3500	OEM
TDA3505	OEM
TDA3507	OEM
TDA3563	OEM
TDA3564	5292
TDA3566	OEM
TDA3568	OEM
TDA3569	OEM
TDA3569B	OEM
TDA3570	0485
TDA3651A	3668
TDA3651A2	OEM
TDA3651AQ	3668
TDA3652	2164
TDA3653B	OEM
TDA3654	2164
TDA3654AQ	2164
TDA3654Q	2164
TDA3654U	2164
TDA3810	OEM
TDA3830/V1	OEM
TDA4504	OEM
TDA4504A	OEM
TDA4505	3015
TDA4505A	3015
TDA4505B	3015
TDA4510	OEM
TDA4555	OEM
TDA4600-2	4126
TDA4601	4126
TDA4601D	OEM
TDA4605	OEM
TDA5030A	OEM
TDA5208T	OEM
TDA5582	OEM
TDA5708	OEM
TDA5709T	OEM
TDA6306P	OEM
TDA6350P	OEM
TDA7000	OEM
TDA7052	6500
TDA7053	OEM
TDA7056	6145
TDA7262	OEM
TDA7263	OEM
TDA7318	OEM
TDA8170	OEM
TDA8172	4314
TDA8173	OEM
TDA8174	5712
TDA8175	6025
TDA8176	OEM
TDA8178FS	OEM
TDA8178S	OEM
TDA8179FS	OEM
TDA8179S	OEM
TDA8189	OEM
TDA8198	OEM
TDA8199	OEM
TDA8302	OEM
TDA8305	OEM
TDA8305A	OEM
TDA8425	OEM
TDA8426	OEM
TDA8444	OEM
TDA8702	OEM
TDA8808T	OEM
TDA8809T	OEM
TDA9400	OEM
TDA9500	OEM
TDA11907	1162
TDAL110	OEM
TDAL113	OEM
TDAL116	OEM
TDAL220	OEM
TDAL223	OEM
TDAL226	OEM
TDAL381S	OEM
TDAL383S	OEM
TDAL601A	OEM
TDAL601B	OEM
TDAL603A	OEM
TDAL603B	OEM
TDAL603S	OEM
TDAL606	OEM
TDAV190Z	1162

DEVICE TYPE	REPL CODE
TDB0117	6779
TDB0124DP	0620
TDB0193DP	0624
TDB0555B	0967
TDB0555DP	0967
TDB0556A	3254
TDB0723	1183
TDB0723A	0026
TDB2033	OEM
TDB2905SP	1275
TDB2912SP	1827
TDB2915SP	3777
TDB7805	1911
TDB7805T	0619
TDB7806T	0917
TDB7808T	1187
TDB7812	3359
TDB7812T	0330
TDB7815T	1311
TDB7824T	2224
TDD1605S	OEM
TDD1606S	OEM
TDD1608S	OEM
TDD1610S	OEM
TDD1612S	OEM
TDD1615S	OEM
TDD1618S	OEM
TDD1624S	OEM
TDF014270	1533
TDH05	OEM
TDH1	OEM
TDH2	OEM
TDH3	OEM
TDH4	OEM
TDR05	OEM
TDR1	OEM
TDR2	OEM
TDR3	OEM
TDR4	OEM
TDRA05	OEM
TDRA1	OEM
TDRA2	OEM
TDRA3	OEM
TDRA4	OEM
T-E0137	1024
T-E0317	1024
TE35	1129
TE55	0340
TE105	0895
TE155	OEM
TE205	0895
TE305	0403
TE405	0403
TE500	0321
TE-500-E	0321
TE697	0016
TE706	0144
TE1010	0015
T-E1011	0015
TE-1011	0015
TE1011	0015
T-E1014	0143
TE-1014	0143
TE1014	0143
T-E1024	0015
TE1024	0015
T-E1024C	0015
TE1024C	0015
T-E1024D	0023
TE1024D	0015
T-E1029	0914
TE-1029	0133
TE1029	0015
T-E1031	0143
TE-1031	0143
TE1031	0143
T-E1042	0276
TE1042	0015
T-E1050	0015
TE-1050	0015
TE1050	0015
T-E1061	0196
TE-1061	0196
TE1061	0196
T-E1061A	0196
TE-1061A	0196
TE1061A	0196
T-E1064	0015
TE1064	0102
T-E1068	0137
TE1068	0137
T-E1077	0137
TE1077	0137
T-E1078	0015
TE1078	0015
T-E1078A	0015
T-E1080	0015
TE1080	0015
T-E1086	0196
TE1086	0196
T-E1086A	0196
T-E1088	0015
TE1088	0015
T-E1089	0015
TE1089	0015
T-E1090	0015
TE1090	0087
T-E1095	0769
TE1095	0769

592

If replacement code is OEM, contact original manufacturer for replacement.

DEVICE TYPE	REPL CODE	DEVICE TYPE	REPL CODE	DEVICE TYPE	REPL CODE	DEVICE TYPE	REPL CODE	DEVICE TYPE	REPL CODE	DEVICE TYPE	REPL CODE	DEVICE TYPE	REPL CODE
T-E1097	0015	TE5086	0786	TER502RA	0267	TG2SB375A	1665	TG52	0015	TI40A0	1095	TI391	0050
TE1097	0015	TE5087	0786	TER503	0315	TG2SB511-1	0919	TG61	0015	TI-40A1	0240	TI-393	0050
T-E1098	0133	TE5088	0111	TER503R	0267	TG2SB511-12SD325-1	OEM	TG62	0015	TI40A1	2471	TI-395	0050
TE1098	0143	TE5089	0111	TER601	0315	TG2SB544E	0527	T-G1138	0143	TI-40A2	0240	TI395	0050
T-E1102	0015	TE5249	0111	TER601R	0267	TG2SB560E	0472	T-G5033	0086	TI40A2	0240	TI-396	0050
T-E1102A	0015	TE5309	0111	TER602	0315	TG2SB598	3760	T-G5055	0086	TI40A3	2635	TI396	0050
T-E1105	0123	TE5310	0111	TER602R	0267	TG2SB698	0006	TGB0331	0079	TI40A4	0671	TI-397	0050
TE1105	0143	TE5311	0111	TER602RA	0267	TG2SB698F	0006	TGL-102	OEM	TI40A5	OEM	TI397	0050
T-E1106	0137	TE5365	0037	TER603	0315	TG2SB764	0472	T-GMP5	OEM	TI40A6	OEM	TI-398	0050
T-E1107	1293	TE5366	0037	TER603R	0267	TG2SC2SC1175-E	OEM	T-GMP5A	OEM	TI42	3298	TI398	0050
T-E1108	0914	TE5367	0786	TF5QS6565G	1981	TG2SC65(Y)	0233	T-GMP5B	OEM	TI42A	2704	TI-399	0050
TE1108	0015	TE5368	0016	TF7	0142	TG2SC536	0532	TGZSA608(C)	0150	TI43	OEM	TI399	0050
T-E1114	0769	TE5369	0016	TF20	0015	TG2SC536(C)	0532	T-H1S557	0023	TI43A	2704	TI-400	0050
TE1114	0769	TE5370	0016	TF21	0015	TG2SC536(E)	0532	TH1S557	0015	TI-51	0133	TI400	0050
T-E1116	0143	TE5371	0016	TF22	0015	TG2SC536-D-A	0532	T-H1S750	0911	TI51	0133	TI401	0050
T-E1118	0133	TE5376	0016	TF23	0015	TG2SC536-E	0532	TH-1S750	0911	TI52	0015	TI-402	0050
T-E1119	0133	TE5377	0016	TF-30	0004	TG2SC536-E-A	0532	T-H2SC313	3356	TI53	1325	TI402	0050
T-E1121	0133	TE5378	0037	TF30	0004	TG2SC536-E-B	0532	T-H2SC387	0144	TI54	1325	TI-403	0050
T-E1122	0087	TE5379	0037	TF44	0133	TG2SC536-F	0532	TH2SC535	0127	TI54A	0016	TI403	0050
T-E1124	0015	TE5447	0037	TF49	0004	TG2SC536-F-A	0532	T-H2SC536	0532	TI54D	0111	TI-407	0007
T-E1127	0087	TE5448	0037	TF50S6344G	2712	TG2SC536E	0532	TH2SC536	0079	TI54E	0016	TI407	0144
T-E1133	0015	TE5449	0016	TF50S6565G	1981	TG2SC536KN	0532	T-H2SC693	0547	TI-55	0015	TI-408	0007
T-E1138	0015	TE5450	0016	TF65	0004	TG2SC536NP	0532	TH2SC693	0079	TI55	0015	TI408	0144
T-E1140	0137	TE5451	0016	TF65/30	0004	TG2SC536NPF	0532	T-H2SC715	0284	TI-56	0110	TI-409	0007
T-E1144	0015	TE13002	OEM	TF65/M	0004	TG2SC536SP	0532	TH2SC715	0079	TI56	0015	TI409	0144
T-E1145	0102	TE13003	OEM	TF65/S/30	0004	TG2SC536SPF	0532	TH3C10	OEM	TI57	0604	TI410	0144
T-E1146	0102	TE13004	0037	TF65M	0164	TG2SC927(C)	0007	TH3J10	OEM	TI58	0790	TI-411	0079
T-E1148	0015	TE13005	0037	TF66	0004	TG2SC927-C-A	0007	TH3L10	OEM	TI59	0015	TI411	0016
T-E1153	0102	TE13006	0723	TF66/30	0004	TG2SC927-D-A	0007	TH3L10Z	OEM	TI60	0790	TI412	0016
T-E1155	0015	TE13007	0723	TF66/60	0004	TG2SC927-E-A	0007	TH35	OEM	TI-71	0015	TI-413	0016
T-E1157	0015	TEA0657	OEM	TF70	0595	TG2SC983-0	0066	TH35S	OEM	TI71	0015	TI413	0016
T-E1171	0015	TEA1009	5692	TF71	0595	TG2SC983-Y	0066	TH40A	OEM	TI-92	0016	TI-414	0016
T-E1176	0015	TEA2014A	OEM	TF72	0595	TG2SC983R	0066	TH50	0015	TI92	0016	TI414	0016
T-E1177	0123	TEA2025	OEM	TF75	0004	TG2SC1025(D)	0928	TH55	OEM	TI116	OEM	TI-415	0111
T-E1184	OEM	TEA2025A	OEM	TF77	0004	TG2SC1175	0191	TH55S	OEM	TI117	OEM	TI415	0016
TE1420	0016	TEA2261	OEM	TF77/30	OEM	TG2SC1175(C)	0191	TH75	OEM	TI118	OEM	TI-416	0111
TE1990	0086	TEA3718	OEM	TF-78	0016	TG2SC1175-	0191	TH105	OEM	TI-132	0240	TI416	0016
TE2484	0144	TEA5120	OEM	TF78	0085	TG2SC1175-C	0191	TH105S	OEM	TI-136	0240	TI-417	0144
TE2711	0111	TEA5570	OEM	TF78/30	0085	TG2SC1175-D	0191	TH155S	OEM	TI136	0240	TI417	0016
TE2712	0111	TEA5582	OEM	TF78/30Z	0160	TG2SC1175-E	0191	TH205S	OEM	TI137	2635	TI-418	0111
TE2713	0396	TEA5591-4527	OEM	TF78/60	0160	TG2SC1293	1060	TH252B	OEM	TI138	0671	TI418	0016
TE2714	0396	TEA5591A	OEM	TF80	0284	TG2SC1293(A)	1060	TH305S	OEM	TI140A3	0671	TI-419	0111
TE2715	0144	TEA37185	OEM	TF-80/30	0160	TG2SC1293-	0284	TH400	0015	TI140A4	0671	TI419	0016
TE2716	0144	TECEC-0913	OEM	TF80/30	0160	TG2SC1293-A-A	1060	TH405S	OEM	TI140A5	OEM	TI-420	0144
TE2921	0111	TECEC-0933	OEM	TF80/30Z	0160	TG2SC1293-B-A	1060	TH600	0015	TI140A6	OEM	TI420	0016
TE2922	0111	TEG0129	0007	TF80/60	OEM	TG2SC1293-C-A	1060	TH800	0071	TI145A5	OEM	TI-421	0111
TE2923	0111	TEH0143	0233	TF80/80	OEM	TG2SC1293-D-A	1060	TH801	0015	TI145A6	OEM	TI421	0111
TE2924	0111	TEH0147	OEM	TF80/302	0004	TG2SC1293A	1060	TH802	0015	TI150	OEM	TI-422	0016
TE2925	0111	TEH0149	0326	TF90/30	OEM	TG2SC1295(0)	1142	TH803	0015	TI152	0015	TI422	0016
TE2926	0111	TER51	0315	TF90/60	OEM	TG2SC1295-0	1142	TH804	0015	TI154	OEM	TI-423	0016
TE3390	0111	TER51R	0267	TF251	OEM	TG2SC1755-C-A	1077	TH805	0015	TI155	OEM	TI423	0016
TE3391	0111	TER52	0315	TF260	0168	TG2SC1756	0638	TH806	0015	TI158	OEM	TI-424	0086
TE3391A	0111	TER52A	0315	TF320M-A	OEM	TG2SC1756-	0168	TH808	0071	TI158A	OEM	TI424	0016
TE3392	0111	TER52R	0267	TF320MA	0705	TG2SC1756-2SC1756	OEM	TH810	0071	TI158AL	OEM	TI-425	0086
TE3393	0111	TER52RA	0267	TF320M-AZ	0705	TG2SC1756-C	0638	TH1000	0071	TI158L	OEM	TI425	0086
TE3394	0111	TER53	0315	TF861S	3852	TG2SC1756-C-A	0638	TH1003	OEM	TI159	0604	TI426	OEM
TE3395	0111	TER53R	0267	TFH340M	0705	TG2SC1756-C-B	0638	TH1004	OEM	TI-266A	0160	TI427	OEM
TE3396	0111	TER101	0315	TFH340MF	0705	TG2SC1756-D	0638	TH1005	OEM	TI266A	0160	TI-428	0037
TE3397	0111	TER101R	0267	TFH340MFLC6	0750	TG2SC1756-D-B	0638	TH1006	OEM	TI-269	0160	TI428	0037
TE3398	0111	TER102	0315	TFK162-12	OEM	TG2SC1756-E	0638	TH1007	OEM	TI269	0160	TI-429	0037
TE3414	0016	TER102A	0315	TFK613	0017	TG2SC1756-E-A	0638	TH1008	OEM	TI320	OEM	TI429	0037
TE3415	0016	TER102R	0267	TFR105	0071	TG2SC1756-E-B	0638	TH2369	OEM	TI321	OEM	TI-430	0016
TE3416	0086	TER102RA	0267	TFR110	0071	TG2SC2057-C	0224	TH3638	OEM	TI338	0050	TI430	0144
TE3417	0590	TER103	0315	TFR-120	0015	TG2SC2057-D	0224	TH4148	OEM	TI-363	0279	TI-431	0144
TE3605	0016	TER103R	0267	TFR120	0015	TG2SC2057-E1	0224	TH4258	OEM	TI363	0050	TI431	0016
TE3605A	0016	TER151	0315	TFR140	0071	TG2SC2057C	0224	TH9008P	OEM	TI-364	0279	TI-432	0016
TE3606	0079	TER151R	0267	TFR305	OEM	TG2SC2057D	0224	TH-9014P	OEM	TI364	0050	TI432	0016
TE3606A	0079	TER152	0315	TFR310	OEM	TG2SC2228	1317	TH9015P	OEM	TI-365	0050	TI-433	0016
TE3607	0016	TER152A	0315	TFR320	OEM	TG2SC2274	0155	THD3600	0080	TI365	0050	TI433	0016
TE3662	0007	TER152R	0267	TFR340	OEM	TG2SC2274E	0155	THF05002	OEM	TI-365A	0276	TI440	OEM
TE3663	0007	TER152RA	0267	TFR605	OEM	TG2SC2274F	0155	TH-H2SC313	0007	TI-366	0160	TI442	OEM
TE3702	0786	TER153	0315	TFR610	OEM	TG2SC2999	0127	THP35	OEM	TI366	0160	TI443	OEM
TE3703	0786	TER153R	0267	TFR620	OEM	TG2SC3399	0892	THP36	OEM	TI-366A	0160	TI444	OEM
TE3704	0016	TER201	0315	TFR640	OEM	TG2SC3400	2307	THP45	OEM	TI366A	0160	TI445	OEM
TE3705	0016	TER201R	0267	TFR1205	OEM	TG2SC3402	0826	THP46	OEM	TI-367	0160	TI446	OEM
TE3707	0144	TER202	0315	TFR1210	OEM	TG2SD24(Y)	0142	THP47	OEM	TI367	0160	TI447	OEM
TE3708	0144	TER202A	0315	TFR1220	OEM	TG2SD313	0042	THP61	OEM	TI-367A	0160	TI448	OEM
TE3709	0144	TER202R	0267	TFR1240	OEM	TG2SD313E	0042	THP62	OEM	TI367A	0160	TI450	OEM
TE3710	0144	TER202RA	0267	TFS340M	0750	TG2SD325-1	0555	THP106	OEM	TI-368	0160	TI451	OEM
TE3711	0144	TER203	0315	TFS340MX	0750	TG2SD386Y-D-A	0388	THP169	OEM	TI368	0160	TI457	OEM
TE3843	0111	TER203R	0267	TG1A	OEM	TG2SD386Y-E-A	0388	THP170	OEM	TI-368A	0160	TI458	OEM
TE3844	0111	TER251	0315	TG2A	OEM	TG2SD400E	2882	THP171	OEM	TI368A	0160	TI459	OEM
TE3845	0111	TER251R	0267	TG2SA201(C)	0050	TG2SD438E	0191	THP172	OEM	TI-369	0160	TI460	OEM
TE3854	0111	TER252	0315	TG2SA201(O)	0136	TG2SD545	0018	THP501	0050	TI369	0160	TI461	OEM
TE3854A	0111	TER252A	0315	TG2SA201-0	0136	TG2SD612E	1779	THP502	0050	TI-369A	0160	TI462	OEM
TE3855	0111	TER252R	0267	TG2SA201-N	0136	TG2SD613D	0060	THS103A	OEM	TI369A	0160	TI-474	0144
TE3855A	0111	TER252RA	0267	TG2SA608	0006	TG2SD613E	0060	T-HS6105	0015	TI-370	0160	TI474	0144
TE3859	0111	TER253	0315	TG2SA608(C)	0006	TG2SD734	1505	T-HSG105	0015	TI370	0085	TI-475	0086
TE3859A	0590	TER301	0315	TG2SA608-D	0006	TG2SD894	0553	THSG105	0015	TI-370A	0160	TI475	0086
TE3860	0111	TER301R	0267	TG2SA608-E	0006	TG3A	OEM	T-HU60U	0150	TI370A	0085	TI-480	0016
TE3900	0111	TER302	0315	TG2SA608C	0037	TG4A	OEM	THU60U	0004	TI376	OEM	TI480	0016
TE3900A	0111	TER302A	0315	TG2SA608F	0006	TG4.C	1864	THZ821	0466	TI-378	OEM	TI-481	0086
TE3901	0111	TER302R	0267	TG2SA608K	0006	TG5A	OEM	THZ823	0466	TI378	OEM	TI481	0016
TE3903	0016	TER302RA	0267	TG2SA608NP	0006	TG6A	OEM	THZ825	0466	TI379	OEM	TI-482	0086
TE3904	0016	TER303	0315	TG2SA608NPF	0006	TG7A	OEM	THZ827	0466	TI380	OEM	TI482	0016
TE3905	0037	TER303R	0267	TG2SA608NPG	0006	TG8A	OEM	THZ829	0466	TI382	OEM	TI-483	0086
TE3906	0016	TER401	0315	TG2SA608SP	0006	TG11	0841	TI010	OEM	TI383	OEM	TI483	0016
TE4123	0016	TER401R	0267	TG2SA608SPF	0006	TG12	0015	TI025	OEM	TI384	OEM	TI-484	0086
TE4124	0016	TER402	0315	TG2SA659	0006	TG21	0015	TI031	0133	TI385	0050	TI484	0016
TE4125	0037	TER402A	0315	TG2SA953	1338	TG22	0015	TI050	OEM	TI386	0050	TI-485	0590
TE4126	0037	TER402R	0267	TG2SA984	0006	TG31	0015	TI-1A6	0222	TI387	0050	TI485	0016
TE4256	0111	TER402RA	0267	TG2SA984E	0006	TG32	0015	TI1A6	0016	TI-388	0050	TI-486	0042
TE4409	0079	TER403	0315	TG2SA984K	0006	TG41	0015	TI2	OEM	TI388	0050	TI486	0042
TE4424	0016	TER403R	0267	TG2SA984KE	0006	TG42	0015	TI6	OEM	TI-389	0050	TI487	0042
TE4425	0590	TER501	0315	TG2SA1016	0688	TG-48	0143	TI-7A	0222	TI389	0050	TI-490	0144
TE4951	0016	TER501R	0267	TG2SA1345	4067	TG48	0164	TI24A	0016	TI-390	0050	TI490	0144
TE4952	0016	TER502	0315	TG2SA1346	3114	TG51	0015	TI24B	0016	TI390	0050		
TE4953	0016	TER502A	0315					TI25A	0144	TI-391	0050		
TE4954	0016	TER502R	0267					TI25B	0144				

If replacement code is OEM, contact original manufacturer for replacement.

DEVICE TYPE	REPL CODE
TI-492	0007
TI492	0016
TI-493	0007
TI493	0016
TI-494	0007
TI494	0016
TI-495	0144
TI495	0016
TI-496	0086
TI496	0016
TI-503	0037
TI503	0037
TI539	OEM
TI540	OEM
TI550	OEM
TI551	OEM
TI602	OEM
TI605	OEM
TI607	OEM
TI607A	OEM
TI608	OEM
TI609	OEM
TI610	OEM
TI611	OEM
TI612	OEM
TI613	OEM
TI614	OEM
TI615	OEM
TI616	OEM
TI617	OEM
TI618	OEM
TI619	OEM
TI620	OEM
TI621	OEM
TI622	OEM
TI623	OEM
TI624	OEM
TI625	OEM
TI642B	0079
TI693	OEM
TI694	OEM
TI695	OEM
TI696	OEM
TI697	OEM
TI711A	OEM
TI712	OEM
TI-714	0016
TI714	0016
TI-714A	0016
TI-722	0233
TI722	0283
TI741	0321
TI-743	0037
TI743	0037
TI-744	0037
TI744	0037
TI-751	0016
TI751	0016
TI-752	0037
TI752	0037
TI801	OEM
TI802	OEM
TI802B	0016
TI803	OEM
TI803B	0016
TI804	OEM
TI805	OEM
TI806	OEM
TI-806G	0016
TI807	OEM
TI808	OEM
TI808E	0126
TI809	OEM
TI810	OEM
TI810B	0016
TI811	OEM
TI811G	0086
TI812	OEM
TI813	OEM
TI814	OEM
TI815	OEM
TI874	OEM
TI876	OEM
TI884	OEM
TI885	OEM
TI886	OEM
TI887	OEM
TI888	OEM
TI-890	0037
TI890	0037
TI-891	0218
TI891	0786
TI896	OEM
TI897	OEM
TI898	OEM
TI899	OEM
TI903	OEM
TI904	0016
TI-905	0037
TI905	0037
TI-907	0016
TI907	0016
TI-908	0016
TI908	0016
TI910	OEM
TI951	OEM
TI952	OEM
TI953	OEM
TI1121	OEM

DEVICE TYPE	REPL CODE
TI1122	OEM
TI1123	OEM
TI1124	OEM
TI1125	OEM
TI1126	OEM
TI1141	OEM
TI1142	OEM
TI1143	OEM
TI1144	OEM
TI1145	OEM
TI1146	OEM
TI1151	2637
TI1152	2637
TI1153	2637
TI1154	2637
TI1155	2637
TI1156	2637
TI1392	OEM
TI1599-5	OEM
TI1599-6	OEM
TI1722A	OEM
TI1724A	OEM
TI1779	OEM
TI1935	OEM
TI1936	OEM
TI1937	OEM
TI2150	OEM
TI2151	OEM
TI3000	OEM
TI3001	OEM
TI3010	0050
TI3011	0050
TI3012	0160
TI3013	OEM
TI3014	OEM
TI3015	0086
TI-3016	0127
TI3016	0144
TI3018	OEM
TI3027	0160
TI3028	0160
TI-3029	0160
TI3029	0160
TI-3030	0599
TI3030	0160
TI-3031	0599
TI3033	OEM
TI3034	OEM
TI3035	OEM
TI3036	OEM
TI3037	OEM
TI3038	OEM
TI3039	OEM
TI3040	OEM
TI3041	OEM
TI3042	OEM
TI8003B	0079
TI8419	0284
TI8423	OEM
TI64213	0086
TIA01	0004
TIA02	0050
TIA03	0279
TIA04	0211
TIA05	0279
TIA06	0016
TIA042	0240
TIA102	0016
TIA7630	3726
TIC01	OEM
TIC02	OEM
TIC03	OEM
TIC04	OEM
TIC05	OEM
TIC11	OEM
TIC12	OEM
TIC13	OEM
TIC14	OEM
TIC15	OEM
TIC26	OEM
TIC27	OEM
TIC29	OEM
TIC30	OEM
TIC31	OEM
TIC44	1129
TIC45	0340
TIC46	0895
TIC47	0058
TIC54	3298
TIC55	3603
TIC56	3298
TIC57	3603
TIC106A	0712
TIC106B	0712
TIC106C	0712
TIC106D	0712
TIC106E	0304
TIC106F	0304
TIC106M	0304
TIC106Y	1386
TIC116A	2078
TIC116B	0500
TIC116C	0705
TIC116D	0705
TIC116E	0857
TIC116F	2084
TIC116M	0857
TIC122B	OEM
TIC122D	OEM

DEVICE TYPE	REPL CODE
TIC122E	OEM
TIC122F	OEM
TIC126A	0393
TIC126B	0393
TIC126C	0606
TIC126D	0606
TIC126E	0946
TIC126F	2499
TIC126M	0946
TIC126N	OEM
TIC126S	OEM
TIC201	OEM
TIC201A	0567
TIC201B	0567
TIC201C	0567
TIC201D	0567
TIC201E	0929
TIC201M	0929
TIC201N	0059
TIC201S	0059
TIC205A	2336
TIC205B	2337
TIC205D	2340
TIC206A	0567
TIC206B	0567
TIC206C	0567
TIC206D	0567
TIC206E	0929
TIC206M	0929
TIC206N	0059
TIC206S	0059
TIC215A	OEM
TIC215B	OEM
TIC215D	OEM
TIC216A	0567
TIC216B	0567
TIC216C	0567
TIC216D	0567
TIC216E	0929
TIC216M	0929
TIC216N	0059
TIC216S	0059
TIC220B	OEM
TIC220D	OEM
TIC220E	OEM
TIC221B	OEM
TIC221D	OEM
TIC221E	OEM
TIC222B	0154
TIC222D	0147
TIC222E	0278
TIC225A	0567
TIC225B	0567
TIC225C	0567
TIC225D	0567
TIC225E	0929
TIC225M	0929
TIC225N	0059
TIC225S	0059
TIC226A	0567
TIC226B	0567
TIC226C	0567
TIC226D	0567
TIC226E	0929
TIC226M	0929
TIC226N	0059
TIC226S	0059
TIC230B	OEM
TIC230D	OEM
TIC230E	OEM
TIC231B	OEM
TIC231D	OEM
TIC231E	OEM
TIC232B	0154
TIC232D	0147
TIC232E	0278
TIC235M	OEM
TIC236A	0767
TIC236B	0767
TIC236C	0739
TIC236D	0739
TIC236E	0612
TIC236M	0612
TIC236N	0869
TIC236S	0869
TIC240B	OEM
TIC240D	OEM
TIC240E	OEM
TIC241B	OEM
TIC241D	OEM
TIC241E	OEM
TIC242B	0154
TIC242D	0147
TIC242E	0278
TIC246A	5227
TIC246B	5227
TIC246C	5230
TIC246D	5230
TIC246E	1649
TIC246M	1649
TIC246N	1956
TIC246S	1956
TIC250B	OEM
TIC250D	OEM
TIC250E	OEM
TIC250M	OEM
TIC252B	3121
TIC252D	3123
TIC252E	3124

DEVICE TYPE	REPL CODE
TIC252M	4038
TIC253A	0767
TIC253B	0767
TIC253C	0739
TIC253D	0739
TIC253E	0612
TIC253M	0612
TIC253N	0869
TIC253S	0869
TIC260B	OEM
TIC260D	OEM
TIC260E	OEM
TIC260M	OEM
TIC262B	3121
TIC262D	3123
TIC262E	3124
TIC262M	4038
TIC263A	5227
TIC263B	5227
TIC263C	5230
TIC263D	5230
TIC263E	1649
TIC263M	1649
TIC263N	1956
TIC263S	1956
TIC270B	OEM
TIC270D	OEM
TIC270E	OEM
TIC270M	OEM
TIC272B	2004
TIC272D	2006
TIC272E	2007
TIC272M	2007
TIC536F	0532
TIC2420	0278
TIC3010	1641
TIC3011	1641
TIC3012	1641
TIC3013	1574
TIC3014	1574
TICP100D	OEM
TICP106A	OEM
TICP106B	OEM
TICP106C	OEM
TICP106D	OEM
TICP106E	OEM
TICP106M	OEM
TICP108A	OEM
TICP108B	OEM
TICP108C	OEM
TICP108D	OEM
TICP108E	OEM
TICP108M	OEM
TICP206A	OEM
TICP206B	OEM
TICP206C	OEM
TICP206D	OEM
TICP206E	OEM
TICP206M	OEM
TID21A	OEM
TID22A	OEM
TID23A	OEM
TID24A	OEM
TID25A	OEM
TID26A	OEM
TID29A	OEM
TID30A	OEM
TID31	OEM
TID32	OEM
TID33	OEM
TID34	OEM
TID35	OEM
TID36	OEM
TID37	OEM
TID38	OEM
TID39	OEM
TID40	OEM
TID41	OEM
TID42	OEM
TID43	OEM
TID44	OEM
TID45	OEM
TID121	OEM
TID122	OEM
TID123	OEM
TID124	OEM
TID125	OEM
TID126	OEM
TID129	OEM
TID130	OEM
TID131	OEM
TID132	OEM
TID133	OEM
TID134	OEM
TID135N	OEM
TID136N	OEM
TID139N	OEM
TID140F	OEM
TID140N	OEM
TID141F	OEM
TID141N	OEM
TID142F	OEM
TID142N	OEM
TID143F	OEM
TID143N	OEM
TID144F	OEM
TID144N	OEM
TID381	1325
TID382	OEM

DEVICE TYPE	REPL CODE
TID383	OEM
TID384	OEM
TID385	OEM
TID777	OEM
TID778	OEM
TID1111	OEM
TIDM155F	OEM
TIDM155J	OEM
TIDM166F	OEM
TIDM166J	OEM
TIDM168F	OEM
TIDM168J	OEM
TIDM185F	OEM
TIDM185J	OEM
TIDM186F	OEM
TIDM186J	OEM
TIDM255F	OEM
TIDM255J	OEM
TIDM266F	OEM
TIDM266J	OEM
TIDM268F	OEM
TIDM268J	OEM
TIDM285F	OEM
TIDM285J	OEM
TIDM286F	OEM
TIDM286J	OEM
TIE	0649
TIED55	OEM
TIED56	OEM
TIED59	OEM
TIED69	OEM
TIED80	OEM
TIED82	OEM
TIED83	OEM
TIED84	OEM
TIED85	OEM
TIED86	OEM
TIED87	OEM
TIED88	OEM
TIED89	OEM
TIED90	OEM
TIED91	OEM
TIED92	OEM
TIED93	OEM
TIED94	OEM
TIED95	OEM
TIED96	OEM
TIED97	OEM
TIED98	OEM
TIED451	OEM
TIED452	OEM
TIEF150	OEM
TIEF151	OEM
TIEF152	OEM
TIES06	OEM
TIES12	OEM
TIES13	OEM
TIES13A	OEM
TIES14	OEM
TIES15	OEM
TIES16A	OEM
TIES16B	OEM
TIES16C	OEM
TIES27	OEM
TIES35	OEM
TIES36	OEM
TIES471	OEM
TIES472	OEM
TIJ	0649
TIJ132-5C	OEM
TIJ132-5D	OEM
TIJ132-6A	OEM
TIJ132-6C	OEM
TIJ132-6D	OEM
TIJ132-7A	OEM
TIJ132-7C	OEM
TIJ132-7D	OEM
TIJ132-8A	OEM
TIJ132-8C	OEM
TIJ132-8D	OEM
TIJ132-9A	OEM
TIJ132-9C	OEM
TIJ132-9D	OEM
TIJ132-10A	OEM
TIJ132-10C	OEM
TIJ132-10D	OEM
TIL01	OEM
TIL09	OEM
TIL23	OEM
TIL24	OEM
TIL25	OEM
TIL26	OEM
TIL31	0586
TIL31A	OEM
TIL32	OEM
TIL33	0586
TIL33A	OEM
TIL34	0586
TIL34A	OEM
TIL38	OEM
TIL39	OEM
TIL-40	OEM
TIL40	OEM
TIL58	OEM
TIL63	OEM
TIL64	2297
TIL65	OEM
TIL66	2297
TIL67	2297

DEVICE TYPE	REPL CODE
TIL77	OEM
TIL78	OEM
TIL81	5419
TIL99	OEM
TIL100	OEM
TIL102	OEM
TIL103	OEM
TIL107	OEM
TIL108	OEM
TIL111	0272
TIL112	0311
TIL113	0311
TIL114	0272
TIL115	0311
TIL116	4358
TIL117	0311
TIL118	0311
TIL119	4845
TIL120	OEM
TIL121	OEM
TIL124	0311
TIL125	0311
TIL126	0311
TIL127	1047
TIL128	1047
TIL131	OEM
TIL132	OEM
TIL133	OEM
TIL134	OEM
TIL135	OEM
TIL136	OEM
TIL137	OEM
TIL138	OEM
TIL139	OEM
TIL141	OEM
TIL142	OEM
TIL143	2612
TIL144	2612
TIL145	1407
TIL146	1407
TIL147	OEM
TIL148	OEM
TIL149	OEM
TIL153	0311
TIL154	0311
TIL155	0311
TIL156	1047
TIL157	1047
TIL158	OEM
TIL159	OEM
TIL160	OEM
TIL161	OEM
TIL201	OEM
TIL202	OEM
TIL209	OEM
TIL209A	2990
TIL210	OEM
TIL212-1	5023
TIL212-2	OEM
TIL216-1	3067
TIL216-2	OEM
TIL220	1605
TIL221	OEM
TIL224-1	3128
TIL224-2	OEM
TIL227-1	OEM
TIL227-2	OEM
TIL228-1	OEM
TIL228-2	6072
TIL231-1	OEM
TIL231-2	OEM
TIL232-1	OEM
TIL232-2	OEM
TIL234-1	1767
TIL234-2	OEM
TIL236-1	OEM
TIL236-2	OEM
TIL282	OEM
TIL302	4900
TIL303	OEM
TIL304	4901
TIL305	OEM
TIL306	OEM
TIL307	OEM
TIL308	OEM
TIL309	OEM
TIL311	OEM
TIL312	4902
TIL313	OEM
TIL321A	OEM
TIL322A	OEM
TIL327	OEM
TIL330A	OEM
TIL339	OEM
TIL340	OEM
TIL341	OEM
TIL345	OEM
TIL346	OEM
TIL347	OEM
TIL393-6	OEM
TIL393-8	OEM
TIL393-9	OEM
TIL401	OEM
TIL402	OEM
TIL403	OEM
TIL404	OEM
TIL405	OEM
TIL406	OEM
TIL411	OEM

DEVICE TYPE	REPL CODE
TIL412	OEM
TIL413	OEM
TIL413S	OEM
TIL414	4918
TIL504	OEM
TIL505	OEM
TIL506	OEM
TIL507	OEM
TIL560	OEM
TIL601	OEM
TIL602	OEM
TIL603	OEM
TIL604	OEM
TIL605	OEM
TIL606	OEM
TIL607	OEM
TIL608	OEM
TIL804	OEM
TIL804-8	OEM
TIL804-10	OEM
TIL804-12	OEM
TIL804-B	OEM
TIL807	OEM
TIL808	OEM
TIL829	OEM
TIL830	OEM
TIL831	OEM
TIL832	OEM
TIL833	OEM
TIL834	OEM
TIL835	OEM
TIL836	OEM
TIL837	OEM
TIL838	OEM
TIL839	OEM
TIL840	OEM
TIL841	OEM
TIL842	OEM
TIL844	OEM
TIL906-1	6711
TIM-01	0050
TIM-1/MX	OEM
TIM-10	0050
TIM-11	0050
TIM9904ANL	OEM
TIM9905	OEM
TIM9906	OEM
TIM9907	OEM
TIM9908	OEM
TIN	0649
TIP04	0359
TIP11	OEM
TIP-14	0042
TIP14	0161
TIP24	0042
TIP27	0275
TIP-29	0042
TIP29	0042
TIP29A	0236
TIP29B	0061
TIP29C	2985
TIP29D	2985
TIP29E	2985
TIP29F	2985
TIP-29T	0168
TIP-30	0919
TIP30	0676
TIP30A	0676
TIP30B	0676
TIP30C	0676
TIP30D	OEM
TIP30E	OEM
TIP30F	OEM
TIP31	0042
TIP31A	0042
TIP31B	0236
TIP31C	0236
TIP31D	2985
TIP31E	2985
TIP31F	2985
TIP32	0676
TIP32A	0676
TIP32B	0676
TIP32C	0676
TIP32D	OEM
TIP32E	OEM
TIP32F	OEM
TIP-33	3052
TIP33	3052
TIP33A	3052
TIP33B	3052
TIP33C	3401
TIP33D	3401
TIP33E	1498
TIP33F	1498
TIP34	0853
TIP34A	0853
TIP34B	3628
TIP34C	3628
TIP34D	3628
TIP34E	OEM
TIP34F	OEM
TIP35	3557
TIP35A	3557
TIP35B	3557
TIP35C	3557
TIP35D	OEM
TIP35E	OEM
TIP35F	OEM

If replacement code is OEM, contact original manufacturer for replacement.

DEVICE TYPE	REPL CODE
TIP36	3558
TIP36A	3558
TIP36B	3558
TIP36C	3558
TIP36D	OEM
TIP36E	OEM
TIP36F	OEM
TIP37B	OEM
TIP41	0477
TIP41(B)	0723
TIP41A	0477
TIP41B	1274
TIP41C	0477
TIP41D	OEM
TIP41E	OEM
TIP41F	OEM
TIP42	1359
TIP42(B)	1359
TIP42/A	1359
TIP42/B	1359
TIP42/C	1359
TIP42A	1359
TIP42B	1359
TIP42C	1359
TIP42D	OEM
TIP42E	OEM
TIP42F	OEM
TIP42M	OEM
TIP47	0168
TIP48	0168
TIP49	0168
TIP50	0168
TIP51	2589
TIP52	2589
TIP52(A)	OEM
TIP53	2589
TIP54	2589
TIP54(A)	OEM
TIP55A	1498
TIP56A	1498
TIP57A	1498
TIP58A	1498
TIP59	OEM
TIP60	OEM
TIP62	OEM
TIP62A	OEM
TIP62B	OEM
TIP62C	OEM
TIP63	OEM
TIP64	OEM
TIP65	OEM
TIP66	OEM
TIP73	0477
TIP73A	0477
TIP73B	0477
TIP73C	0477
TIP74	1359
TIP74A	1359
TIP74B	1359
TIP74C	1359
TIP75	2985
TIP75A	2985
TIP75B	2985
TIP75C	2985
TIP100	1203
TIP101	1203
TIP102	1203
TIP105	0597
TIP106	0597
TIP107	0597
TIP110	4265
TIP111	1203
TIP112	1203
TIP115	0597
TIP116	0597
TIP117	0597
TIP120	2220
TIP121	2220
TIP122	1203
TIP125	0597
TIP126	0597
TIP127	0597
TIP130	1203
TIP131	1203
TIP132	1203
TIP135	0597
TIP136	0597
TIP137	0597
TIP140	0134
TIP140T	1948
TIP141	0134
TIP141T	1948
TIP142	0134
TIP142T	1948
TIP145	0073
TIP145T	1957
TIP146	0073
TIP146T	1957
TIP147	0073
TIP147T	1957
TIP150	OEM
TIP151	OEM
TIP152	OEM
TIP160	5245
TIP161	5245
TIP162	5245
TIP501	0617
TIP502	1588
TIP503	0178

DEVICE TYPE	REPL CODE
TIP504	0178
TIP505	4187
TIP506	4187
TIP509	0615
TIP510	0615
TIP515	0615
TIP516	0615
TIP525	1331
TIP526	2637
TIP527	1588
TIP530	0424
TIP531	1841
TIP532	1841
TIP535	1955
TIP536	1955
TIP537	1841
TIP538	1841
TIP539	1841
TIP540	1841
TIP541	0617
TIP544	1671
TIP545	1588
TIP546	1588
TIP550	5375
TIP551	0065
TIP552	0065
TIP553	0309
TIP554	1955
TIP555	1955
TIP556	4327
TIP558	0359
TIP559	1955
TIP560	1955
TIP561	1841
TIP562	0359
TIP563	0359
TIP564	OEM
TIP565	OEM
TIP575	OEM
TIP575A	OEM
TIP575B	OEM
TIP575C	OEM
TIP600	3339
TIP601	3339
TIP602	2422
TIP605	3340
TIP606	3340
TIP607	2415
TIP620	2411
TIP621	2411
TIP622	2422
TIP625	2262
TIP626	2262
TIP627	2415
TIP640	0134
TIP641	0134
TIP642	0134
TIP645	0073
TIP646	0073
TIP647	0073
TIP660	1980
TIP661	1980
TIP662	1980
TIP663	2602
TIP664	2602
TIP665	2602
TIP666	1980
TIP667	1980
TIP668	2602
TIP773B	OEM
TIP2955	3558
TIP3055	0477
TIPC47	OEM
TIPC100	OEM
TIPC102	OEM
TIPC105	OEM
TIPC106	OEM
TIPC107	OEM
TIPL751	1841
TIPL751A	4376
TIPL752	1841
TIPL752A	4376
TIPL753	3009
TIPL753A	1498
TIPL755	1841
TIPL755A	OEM
TIPL757	OEM
TIPL757A	OEM
TIPL760	4376
TIPL760A	4376
TIPL761	4376
TIPL761A	4376
TIPL762	1498
TIPL762A	1498
TIPL763	1498
TIPL763A	1498
TIPL765	OEM
TIPL765A	OEM
TIPL773	OEM
TIPL773A	OEM
TIPL774	3956
TIPL775	3956
TIPL775A	3956
TIPL777	OEM
TIPL777A	OEM
TIPL777B	OEM
TIPL780	OEM
TIPL780A	OEM
TIPL781	OEM

DEVICE TYPE	REPL CODE
TIPL781A	OEM
TIPL784	OEM
TIPL785	3719
TIPL785A	3719
TIPL790	OEM
TIPL790A	OEM
TIPL790A(A)	OEM
TIR01	0015
TIR02	0015
TIR03	0015
TIR04	0015
TIR05	0015
TIR06	0015
TIR07	0071
TIR08	0071
TIR09	0071
TIR10	0071
TIR101A	OEM
TIR101B	OEM
TIR101C	OEM
TIR101D	OEM
TIR102A	OEM
TIR102B	OEM
TIR102C	OEM
TIR102D	OEM
TIR105C	OEM
TIR105D	OEM
TIR106D	OEM
TIR201A	OEM
TIR201B	OEM
TIR201C	OEM
TIR201D	OEM
TIR202A	OEM
TIR202B	OEM
TIR202C	OEM
TIR202D	OEM
TIR206A	OEM
TIR206B	OEM
TIR206C	OEM
TIR206D	OEM
TIS01	OEM
TIS02	OEM
TIS-03	0037
TIS03	0037
TIS04	0037
TIS05	OEM
TIS06	OEM
TIS07	OEM
TIS06701D20G	OEM
TIS06702D20G	OEM
TIS06704D20G	OEM
TIS06706D20G	OEM
TIS06708D20G	OEM
TIS06710D20G	OEM
TIS06712D20G	OEM
TIS06714D20G	OEM
TIS06716D20G	OEM
TIS06718D20G	OEM
TIS06720D20G	OEM
TIS06722D20G	OEM
TIS08001D20	OEM
TIS08001D20A	OEM
TIS08001D20B	OEM
TIS08001D20Y	OEM
TIS08001D20Z	OEM
TIS08002D20A	OEM
TIS08002D20B	OEM
TIS08002D20Y	OEM
TIS08002D20Z	OEM
TIS08004D20A	OEM
TIS08004D20B	OEM
TIS08004D20Y	OEM
TIS08004D20Z	OEM
TIS08006D20A	OEM
TIS08006D20B	OEM
TIS08006D20Y	OEM
TIS08006D20Z	OEM
TIS08008D20A	OEM
TIS08008D20B	OEM
TIS08008D20Y	OEM
TIS08008D20Z	OEM
TIS08010D20A	OEM
TIS08010D20B	OEM
TIS08010D20Y	OEM
TIS08010D20Z	OEM
TIS08012D20A	OEM
TIS08012D20B	OEM
TIS08012D20Y	OEM
TIS08012D20Z	OEM
TIS-1B	0127
TIS11	OEM
TIS14	0321
TIS15	OEM
TIS16	OEM
TIS17	OEM
TIS-18	0007
TIS18	0127
TIS22	0016
TIS23	0016
TIS24	0144
TIS25	OEM
TIS26	OEM
TIS27	OEM
TIS34	0321
TIS37	0037
TIS38	0037
TIS39	0488
TIS41	OEM
TIS42	0321

DEVICE TYPE	REPL CODE
TIS43	1167
TIS44	0016
TIS45	0016
TIS46	0016
TIS47	0016
TIS48	0016
TIS49	0016
TIS50	0037
TIS51	0016
TIS52	0016
TIS53	0037
TIS54	0037
TIS55	0016
TIS56	0007
TIS57	0007
TIS58	0321
TIS59	0321
TIS60	0155
TIS60A	0086
TIS60B	0086
TIS60C	0086
TIS60D	0086
TIS60E	0086
TIS60M	0086
TIS61	0037
TIS61A	0126
TIS61B	0126
TIS61C	0126
TIS61D	0126
TIS61E	0126
TIS61M	0126
TIS-62	0079
TIS62	0144
TIS62A	0144
TIS63	0144
TIS63A	0144
TIS64	0144
TIS64A	0144
TIS71	0016
TIS72	0016
TIS73	OEM
TIS74	OEM
TIS75	OEM
TIS78	0321
TIS79	0321
TIS82	0555
TIS83	0079
TIS84	0224
TIS85	0144
TIS86	0224
TIS87	0224
TIS-88	0321
TIS88	0321
TIS88A	OEM
TIS89	0079
TIS90	0320
TIS90-BLU	0855
TIS90-GRN	0155
TIS90-GRY	0016
TIS90-VIO	0855
TIS90-YEL	0155
TIS90M	1967
TIS90M-BLU	0855
TIS90M-GRN	0155
TIS90M-GRY	0016
TIS90M-VIO	0016
TIS90M-YEL	0155
TIS91	0006
TIS91-BLU	0037
TIS91-GRN	0037
TIS91-GRY	5504
TIS91-VIO	0037
TIS91-YEL	0037
TIS91M	0037
TIS91M-BLU	0037
TIS91M-GRN	0037
TIS91M-GRY	0016
TIS91M-VIO	0037
TIS91M-YEL	0037
TIS92	0079
TIS92-B	0016
TIS92-BLU	0079
TIS92-G	0016
TIS92-GRN	0079
TIS92-GRY	0079
TIS92-V	0016
TIS92-VIO	0079
TIS92-Y	0016
TIS92-YEL	0079
TIS92M	0086
TIS92M-BLU	0855
TIS92M-GRN	0155
TIS92M-GRY	0016
TIS92M-VIO	0855
TIS92M-YEL	0155
TIS93	0037
TIS93-B	0037
TIS93-BLU	0037
TIS93-G	0037
TIS93-GRN	0037
TIS93-GRY	0037
TIS93-V	0037
TIS93-VIO	0037
TIS93-YEL	0037
TIS93M	0126
TIS93M-BLU	0037
TIS93M-GRN	0037
TIS93M-GRY	0597
TIS93M-VIO	0037

DEVICE TYPE	REPL CODE
TIS93M-YEL	0037
TIS-94	0111
TIS94	0079
TIS94(AFAMP)	0079
TIS94(AFC)	0030
TIS94(DIO)	0030
TIS94(XSTR)	0079
TIS95	0018
TIS96	0018
TIS-97	0111
TIS97	0079
TIS-98	0079
TIS98	0127
TIS99	0127
TIS100	0710
TIS101	0710
TIS102	0233
TIS103	0233
TIS104	0037
TIS105	0224
TIS106	0855
TIS107	0086
TIS108	0224
TIS109	0693
TIS110	0086
TIS111	0086
TIS112	0037
TIS113	0016
TIS114	0016
TIS-125	0079
TIS125	0224
TIS126	0224
TIS128	0150
TIS129	0224
TIS130	OEM
TIS132	0283
TIS133	0079
TIS134	0079
TIS135	0086
TIS136	0086
TIS137	0037
TIS138	0150
TIS150	OEM
TIS151	2770
TIS175	OEM
TIS176	OEM
TIS180	OEM
TIS412	0127
TIS991	0037
TIS992	0079
TIS993	0037
TISA02	0279
TISM74LS00N	1519
TIUC226N	OEM
TI-UG-1888	0133
TI-UG1888	0133
TIV21	1023
TIV22	OEM
TIV23	OEM
TIV24	OEM
TIV25	OEM
TIV305	OEM
TIV306	0549
TIV307	OEM
TIV308	OEM
TIX09	OEM
TIX10	OEM
TIX90	0004
TIX91	0050
TIX92	0050
TIX93	OEM
TIX94	OEM
TIX95	OEM
TIX120A0	OEM
TIX120A1	OEM
TIX120A2	OEM
TIX155	OEM
TIX316	0050
TIX440	1991
TIX441	1241
TIX442	1241
TIX608	OEM
TIX609	OEM
TIX610	OEM
TIX611	OEM
TIX612	OEM
TIX613	OEM
TIX614	OEM
TIX615	OEM
TIX616	OEM
TIX617	OEM
TIX618	OEM
TIX619	OEM
TIX620	OEM
TIX621	OEM
TIX622	OEM
TIX623	OEM
TIX624	OEM
TIX690	OEM
TIX712	0079
TIX802	OEM
TIX803	OEM
TIX804	0037
TIX805	0037
TIX806	OEM
TIX807	OEM
TIX808	OEM
TIX809	OEM
TIX810	OEM

DEVICE TYPE	REPL CODE
TIX811	OEM
TIX812	OEM
TIX813	OEM
TIX814	OEM
TIX815	OEM
TIX876	0144
TIX880	0144
TIX881	OEM
TIX882	OEM
TIX883	OEM
TIX888	0693
TIX890	0037
TIX891	0037
TIX895	0279
TIX896	0595
TIX1392	0693
TIX1393	0693
TIX2000	OEM
TIX2150	OEM
TIX2151	OEM
TIX3011	OEM
TIX3012	OEM
TIX3015	OEM
TIX3016	0050
TIX3016A	0050
TIX3023	OEM
TIX3032	0050
TIX3033	0161
TIX3035	0161
TIXA01	0279
TIXA02	0279
TIXA03	0279
TIXA04	0279
TIXA05	0279
TIXD747	0188
TIXD753	0631
TIXD758	0170
TIXL02	OEM
TIXL03	OEM
TIXL05	OEM
TIXL08	OEM
TIXL09	OEM
TIXL10	OEM
TIXL17	OEM
TIXL18	OEM
TIXL19	OEM
TIXL20	OEM
TIXL21	OEM
TIXL22	OEM
TIXL26	OEM
TIXL28	OEM
TIXL29	OEM
TIXL30	OEM
TIXL51	OEM
TIXL52	OEM
TIXL53	OEM
TIXL54	OEM
TIXL58	OEM
TIXL101	OEM
TIXL113	OEM
TIXL146	OEM
TIX-M01	0050
TIXM01	0050
TIX-M02	0050
TIXM02	0050
TIX-M03	0050
TIXM03	0050
TIX-M04	0050
TIXM04	0050
TIX-M05	0050
TIXM05	0050
TIX-M06	0050
TIXM06	0050
TIX-M07	0050
TIXM07	0050
TIX-M08	0050
TIXM08	0050
TIXM10	0050
TIX-M11	0050
TIXM11	0050
TIXM12	OEM
TIXM13	0050
TIX-M14	0007
TIXM14	0050
TIX-M15	0007
TIXM15	0050
TIX-M16	0007
TIXM16	0050
TIX-M17	0050
TIXM17	0050
TIXM18	0050
TIXM19	0050
TIX-M101	0050
TIXM101	0050
TIXM103	0050
TIXM104	0050
TIXM105	0050
TIXM106	0050
TIXM107	0050
TIXM108	0050
TIX-M201	0050
TIXM-201	0050
TIXM201	0050
TIX-M202	0050
TIXM202	0050
TIX-M203	0050
TIXM203	0050
TIX-M204	0050
TIXM204	0050

DEVICE TYPE	REPL CODE
TIX-M205	0050
TIXM205	0050
TIX-M206	0050
TIXM206	0050
TIX-M207	0050
TIXM207	0050
TIXM301	OEM
TIXM07	OEM
TIXP39	OEM
TIXP40	OEM
TIXS09	0144
TIXS10	0144
TIXS11	OEM
TIXS12	0079
TIXS13	0079
TIXS28	0144
TIXS29	0144
TIXS30	0144
TIXS31	0144
TIXS33	OEM
TIXS37	OEM
TIXS41	OEM
TIXS42	OEM
TIXS67	OEM
TIXS78	OEM
TIXS79	OEM
TIXV01	OEM
TIXV02	OEM
TIXV03	OEM
TIXV04	OEM
TIXV06	OEM
TIXV07	OEM
TIXV08	OEM
TIXV09	OEM
TIXV10	OEM
TIXV11	OEM
TIXV12	OEM
TIXV13	OEM
TIXV14	OEM
TIXV15	OEM
TIXV16	OEM
TIXV17	OEM
TIXV18	OEM
TIXV19	OEM
TIXV304	OEM
TJ1	OEM
TJ2	OEM
TJ3	OEM
TJ5A	0015
TJ10A	0015
TJ15A	0015
TJ20A	0015
TJ25A	0015
TJ30A	0015
TJ35A	0015
TJ40A	0015
TJ60A	0015
TJ132-0A	OEM
TJ132-0C	OEM
TJ132-0D	OEM
TJ132-1A	OEM
TJ132-1C	OEM
TJ132-1D	OEM
TJ132-2A	OEM
TJ132-2C	OEM
TJ132-2D	OEM
TJ132-3A	OEM
TJ132-3C	OEM
TJ132-3D	OEM
TJ132-4A	OEM
TJ132-4C	OEM
TJ132-4D	OEM
TJ132-5A	OEM
TJ366	OEM
TJ405	OEM
TJ703DFA	OEM
TJ705DFA	OEM
TJ707DFA	OEM
TJ709DFA	OEM
TJ711DFA	OEM
TK	OEM
TK05	OEM
TK1	0463
TK1FA	OEM
TK1FB	OEM
TK2	0463
TK2FA	OEM
TK2FB	OEM
TK3FA	OEM
TK3FB	OEM
TK3L10	OEM
TK3V	OEM
TK4	0463
TK4FA	OEM
TK4FB	OEM
TK5	0604
TK5FA	OEM
TK5FB	OEM
TK6	0463
TK6FA	OEM
TK6FB	OEM
TK7	OEM
TK7FA	OEM
TK7FB	OEM
TK8	0463
TK8FA	OEM
TK8FB	OEM
TK9	OEM
TK9FA	OEM

If replacement code is OEM, contact original manufacturer for replacement.

595

Original Device Types

DEVICE TYPE	REPL CODE
TK9FB	OEM
TK10	0015
TK10FA	OEM
TK10FB	OEM
TK11	0015
TK12	0463
TK13	OEM
TK15	OEM
TK20	0015
TK20A	OEM
TK20B	OEM
TK20C	OEM
TK21	0015
TK21A	OEM
TK21B	OEM
TK21C	OEM
TK23	OEM
TK23A	OEM
TK23C	0004
TK24	OEM
TK24A	OEM
TK24B	OEM
TK24C	OEM
TK25	OEM
TK25A	0004
TK25B	0004
TK25C	OEM
TK26	OEM
TK26A	OEM
TK26B	OEM
TK27	OEM
TK27A	OEM
TK27B	OEM
TK28	0004
TK28C	OEM
TK30	0015
TK30C	OEM
TK31	OEM
TK31C	OEM
TK33C	0595
TK34C	0004
TK35	OEM
TK35C	0004
TK36	OEM
TK36C	0004
TK37	OEM
TK37C	0004
TK38	OEM
TK38C	OEM
TK-40	0015
TK40	0211
TK40A	0004
TK40C	0211
TK-41	0015
TK41	0211
TK41C	0050
TK42	0211
TK42C	0050
TK44	OEM
TK44C	OEM
TK45	OEM
TK45C	0211
TK46	OEM
TK46C	OEM
TK47C	OEM
TK48C	OEM
TK49C	0004
TK50	1345
TK60	1345
TK61	0015
TK70	OEM
TK71	OEM
TK72	OEM
TK76	OEM
TK-80	OEM
TK82	0855
TK105	OEM
TK110	0463
TK110FA	OEM
TK110FB	OEM
TK110FX	OEM
TK120	0463
TK120FA	OEM
TK120FB	OEM
TK120FX	OEM
TK130	OEM
TK130FA	OEM
TK130FB	OEM
TK130FX	OEM
TK140	0463
TK140FA	OEM
TK140FB	OEM
TK140FX	OEM
TK150	OEM
TK150FA	OEM
TK150FB	OEM
TK150FX	OEM
TK160	0463
TK160FA	OEM
TK160FB	OEM
TK160FX	OEM
TK170	OEM
TK170FA	OEM
TK170FB	OEM
TK170FX	OEM
TK180	0463
TK180FA	OEM
TK180FB	OEM
TK180FX	OEM
TK190	OEM
TK190FA	OEM
TK190FB	OEM
TK190FX	OEM
TK200A	0236
TK201A	0236
TK202A	OEM
TK203A	OEM
TK210	0733
TK220	0733
TK240	0733
TK250A	0855
TK251A	0855
TK252A	OEM
TK253A	OEM
TK254A	0016
TK255A	0016
TK256A	0016
TK257A	0016
TK258A	0016
TK259A	0016
TK260	0733
TK264A	0016
TK280	0733
TK310	1889
TK320	1889
TK340	0733
TK360	0733
TK380	0733
TK400	0015
TK400A	0160
TK401A	0160
TK402A	0160
TK403A	0160
TK582	0527
TK600	0015
TK-705M	0196
TK705M	0196
TK705M12/1	0196
TK800	0071
TK1000	0071
TK1100FA	OEM
TK1100FB	OEM
TK1100FX	OEM
TK1100V	0463
TK1110	OEM
TK1120V	0463
TK1130	OEM
TK1150	OEM
TK1201	OEM
TK1202	OEM
TK1204	OEM
TK1206	OEM
TK1208	OEM
TK1210	OEM
TK1212	OEM
TK1214	OEM
TK1216	OEM
TK1228-001	0050
TK1228-1001	0136
TK1228-1002	0004
TK1228-1003	0004
TK1228-1004	0004
TK1228-1005	0004
TK1228-1006	0004
TK1228-1007	0004
TK1228-1008	0198
TK1228-1009	0198
TK1228-1010	0016
TK1228-1011	0016
TK1228-1012	0016
TK1401	OEM
TK1401FA	OEM
TK1401FB	OEM
TK1402	OEM
TK1402FA	OEM
TK1402FB	OEM
TK1403	OEM
TK1403FA	OEM
TK1403FB	OEM
TK1404	OEM
TK1404FA	OEM
TK1404FB	OEM
TK1405	OEM
TK1405FA	OEM
TK1405FB	OEM
TK1406	OEM
TK1406FA	OEM
TK1406FB	OEM
TK1407	OEM
TK1407FA	OEM
TK1407FB	OEM
TK1408	OEM
TK1408FA	OEM
TK1408FB	OEM
TK1409	OEM
TK1409FA	OEM
TK1409FB	OEM
TK1410	OEM
TK1410FA	OEM
TK1410FB	OEM
TK1411	OEM
TK1412	OEM
TK1413	OEM
TK1414	OEM
TK1415	OEM
TK1416	OEM
TK1701	0733
TK1702	0733
TK1703	OEM
TK1704	0733
TK1705	OEM
TK1706	0733
TK1707	OEM
TK1708	0733
TK1709	OEM
TK1710	0733
TK1712	0733
TK1802	OEM
TK1804	OEM
TK1806	OEM
TK1808	OEM
TK1810	OEM
TK1812	OEM
TK1814	OEM
TK2100	0733
TK2120	0733
TK2601	OEM
TK2602	OEM
TK2604	OEM
TK2606	OEM
TK2608	OEM
TK2610	OEM
TK2612	OEM
TK2614	OEM
TK2616	OEM
TK3001	OEM
TK3002	OEM
TK3004	OEM
TK3006	OEM
TK3008	OEM
TK3010	OEM
TK3012	OEM
TK3014	OEM
TK3016	OEM
TK3055	OEM
TK3100	0733
TK3120	0733
TK3601	OEM
TK3602	OEM
TK3604	OEM
TK3606	OEM
TK3608	OEM
TK3610	OEM
TK3612	OEM
TK9201	0130
TK10170	OEM
TK10280	OEM
TK10311	OEM
TK10320	OEM
TK10321	OEM
TK10360	OEM
TK10466-10A	OEM
TK10500M	OEM
TK10580M	OEM
TK15021Z	OEM
TK15050	OEM
TK19080L	OEM
TK30551	0130
TK30552	0130
TK30553	0130
TK30555	0130
TK30556	0130
TK30557	0130
TK30558	0130
TK30560	0130
TK55303	OEM
TKAL110	OEM
TKAL120	OEM
TKAL130	OEM
TKAL140	OEM
TKAL150	OEM
TKAL160	OEM
TKAL170	OEM
TKAL180	OEM
TKAL190	OEM
TKAL210	OEM
TKAL220	OEM
TKAL240	OEM
TKAL260	OEM
TKAL280	OEM
TKAL1100	OEM
TKAL1110	OEM
TKAL1120	OEM
TKAL2100	OEM
TKAL2120	OEM
TKE801	0603
TKE802	0603
TKE804	0605
TKE806	0605
TKE808	0463
TKE810	0463
TKE1201	0603
TKE1202	0603
TKE1204	0605
TKE1206	0605
TKE1208	0463
TKE1210	0463
TKF5	0015
TKF10	1345
TKF20	1345
TKF40	1345
TKF60	1345
TKF80	0072
TKF100	2613
TKTA562-0	0006
TKTA1015Y	0006
TKTC1815Y	0284
TKTC2120Y	0155
TL010	OEM
TL010A	OEM
TL011C	OEM
TL012C	OEM
TL014C	OEM
TL021C	OEM
TL022C	OEM
TL022CGJ	OEM
TL022CP	OEM
TL022M	OEM
TL022MJG	OEM
TL022MP	OEM
TL044CJ	OEM
TL044CN	OEM
TL044M	OEM
TL044MJ	OEM
TL060AC	OEM
TL060ACJG	OEM
TL060ACP	OEM
TL060AGJG	OEM
TL060BC	OEM
TL060C	OEM
TL060CJG	OEM
TL060CP	OEM
TL060I	OEM
TL060IJG	OEM
TL060IP	OEM
TL060MJG	OEM
TL061AC	OEM
TL061ACJG	OEM
TL061ACP	3152
TL061AMJG	OEM
TL061BC	OEM
TL061BCJG	OEM
TL061BCP	OEM
TL061C	OEM
TL061CJG	OEM
TL061CP	3152
TL061I	OEM
TL061IJG	OEM
TL061IP	OEM
TL061M	OEM
TL061MJG	OEM
TL061MU	OEM
TL062AC	3288
TL062ACJG	OEM
TL062ACP	3288
TL062AMJG	OEM
TL062BC	OEM
TL062BCJG	OEM
TL062BCP	OEM
TL062C	3288
TL062CJG	OEM
TL062CP	OEM
TL062I	OEM
TL062IJG	OEM
TL062IP	OEM
TL062M	OEM
TL062MJG	OEM
TL062MU	OEM
TL064AC	OEM
TL064ACJ	OEM
TL064ACN	OEM
TL064AMJ	OEM
TL064BC	OEM
TL064BCJ	OEM
TL064BCN	OEM
TL064C	OEM
TL064CJ	OEM
TL064CN	OEM
TL064I	OEM
TL064IJ	OEM
TL064IN	OEM
TL064M	OEM
TL064MJ	OEM
TL064MW	OEM
TL066AC	OEM
TL066ACJG	OEM
TL066ACP	OEM
TL066AMJG	OEM
TL066BC	OEM
TL066BCJG	OEM
TL066BCP	OEM
TL066C	OEM
TL066CJG	OEM
TL066CP	OEM
TL066I	OEM
TL066IJG	OEM
TL066IP	OEM
TL066MJG	OEM
TL068C	OEM
TL068CLP	OEM
TL068ILP	OEM
TL070AC	OEM
TL070ACJG	OEM
TL070ACP	OEM
TL070BC	OEM
TL070CJG	OEM
TL070CP	OEM
TL070IJG	OEM
TL070IP	OEM
TL070MJG	OEM
TL071ACJG	OEM
TL071ACP	3627
TL071AMJG	OEM
TL071BCJG	OEM
TL071BCP	OEM
TL071C	OEM
TL071CJG	OEM
TL071CP	3627
TL071I	OEM
TL071IJG	OEM
TL071IP	OEM
TL071M	OEM
TL071MJG	OEM
TL072AC	OEM
TL072ACJG	OEM
TL072ACP	OEM
TL072AMJG	OEM
TL072BC	OEM
TL072BCJG	OEM
TL072C	OEM
TL072CJG	OEM
TL072CP	3695
TL072I	OEM
TL072IJG	OEM
TL072IP	OEM
TL072M	OEM
TL072MJG	OEM
TL072ML	OEM
TL074AC	OEM
TL074ACJ	OEM
TL074ACN	OEM
TL074AMJ	OEM
TL074BC	OEM
TL074BCJ	OEM
TL074BCN	OEM
TL074C	OEM
TL074CJ	OEM
TL074CN	3357
TL074I	OEM
TL074IJ	OEM
TL074IN	OEM
TL074M	OEM
TL074MJ	OEM
TL074MW	OEM
TL075ACJ	OEM
TL075ACN	OEM
TL075BCJ	OEM
TL075BCN	OEM
TL075C	OEM
TL075CJ	OEM
TL075CN	OEM
TL075IJ	OEM
TL075IN	OEM
TL075MJ	OEM
TL080AC	OEM
TL080ACJG	OEM
TL080ACP	OEM
TL080C	OEM
TL080CJG	OEM
TL080CP	OEM
TL080I	OEM
TL080IJG	OEM
TL080IP	OEM
TL080MJG	OEM
TL081	3627
TL081AC	OEM
TL081ACJG	OEM
TL081ACP	OEM
TL081AMJG	OEM
TL081BC	OEM
TL081BCDP	OEM
TL081BCJG	OEM
TL081BCP	OEM
TL081C	OEM
TL081CDP	OEM
TL081CFP	6209
TL081CJG	OEM
TL081CP	3627
TL081I	OEM
TL081IDP	OEM
TL081IJG	OEM
TL081IP	OEM
TL081M	OEM
TL081MGC	OEM
TL081MH	OEM
TL081MJG	OEM
TL082AC	OEM
TL082ACJG	OEM
TL082ACP	OEM
TL082AMJG	OEM
TL082BC	OEM
TL082BCJG	OEM
TL082BCP	OEM
TL082C	OEM
TL082CD	4044
TL082CJG	OEM
TL082CN	OEM
TL082CP	OEM
TL082I	OEM
TL082IJG	OEM
TL082IP	OEM
TL082M	OEM
TL082MJG	OEM
TL083AC	OEM
TL083ACN	OEM
TL083C	OEM
TL083CJ	OEM
TL083CN	OEM
TL083I	OEM
TL083IJ	OEM
TL083IN	OEM
TL083MJ	OEM
TL084	3357
TL084AC	OEM
TL084ACDP	OEM
TL084ACJ	OEM
TL084ACN	OEM
TL084AMJ	OEM
TL084BC	OEM
TL084BCDP	OEM
TL084BCJ	OEM
TL084BCN	OEM
TL084C	OEM
TL084CD	4073
TL084CDP	3357
TL084CFP	OEM
TL084CJ	OEM
TL084CN	3357
TL084I	OEM
TL084IDP	OEM
TL084IJ	OEM
TL084IN	OEM
TL084M	OEM
TL084MDG	OEM
TL084MGC	OEM
TL084MJ	OEM
TL084MW	OEM
TL085C	OEM
TL085CJ	OEM
TL085CN	OEM
TL085MJ	OEM
TL087C	OEM
TL087CJG	OEM
TL087CP	OEM
TL087I	OEM
TL087IJG	OEM
TL087IP	OEM
TL087MJG	OEM
TL088C	OEM
TL088CJG	OEM
TL088CP	OEM
TL088CU	OEM
TL088I	OEM
TL088IJG	OEM
TL088IP	OEM
TL088IU	OEM
TL088M	OEM
TL088MJG	OEM
TL091C	OEM
TL091CJG	OEM
TL091CP	OEM
TL091MJG	OEM
TL092C	OEM
TL092CJG	OEM
TL092CP	OEM
TL092MJG	OEM
TL094C	OEM
TL094CJ	OEM
TL094CN	OEM
TL094IN	OEM
TL094M	OEM
TL094MJ	OEM
TL094MW	OEM
TL0250	OEM
TL1	0015
TL2	0015
TL2SA881Q	0006
TL2SA881R	0006
TL2SC2021R	1132
TL4	OEM
TL6	OEM
TL11	0015
TL12	0015
TL21	0015
TL22	0015
TL31	0015
TL32	0015
TL41	0015
TL42	0015
TL51	0015
TL61	0015
TL74H87N	2557
TL74H183N	4329
TL106-05	1250
TL106-1	0442
TL106-2	0934
TL106-4	0095
TL106-6	OEM
TL107-05	1250
TL107-1	0442
TL107-2	0934
TL107-4	0095
TL107-6	OEM
TL111	OEM
TL111J	OEM
TL111JG	OEM
TL170	OEM
TL170CLP	OEM
TL172	OEM
TL172CLP	OEM
TL173CLP	OEM
TL182C	OEM
TL182CL	OEM
TL182CN	OEM
TL182I	OEM
TL182IL	OEM
TL182IN	OEM
TL182MJ	OEM
TL185C	OEM
TL185CJ	OEM
TL185CN	OEM
TL185I	OEM
TL185IJ	OEM
TL185IN	OEM
TL185MJ	OEM
TL188C	OEM
TL188CL	OEM
TL188CN	OEM
TL188I	OEM
TL188IL	OEM
TL188IN	OEM
TL188MJ	OEM
TL188ML	OEM
TL191C	OEM
TL191CJ	OEM
TL191CN	OEM
TL191I	OEM
TL191IJ	OEM
TL191IN	OEM
TL191MJ	OEM
TL195C	OEM
TL287C	OEM
TL287CJG	OEM
TL287CP	OEM
TL287I	OEM
TL287IJG	OEM
TL287IP	OEM
TL287MJG	OEM
TL288C	OEM
TL288CJG	OEM
TL288CP	OEM
TL288CU	OEM
TL288I	OEM
TL288IJG	OEM
TL288IP	OEM
TL288IU	OEM
TL288MJG	OEM
TL311	OEM
TL311AJ	OEM
TL311AJG	OEM
TL311AN	OEM
TL311AP	OEM
TL311J	OEM
TL311JG	OEM
TL311N	OEM
TL311P	OEM
TL317	5187
TL317JG	OEM
TL317LP	5187
TL317P	OEM
TL321C	OEM
TL321CJG	OEM
TL321CP	OEM
TL321IJG	OEM
TL321IP	OEM
TL321MJG	OEM
TL321MP	OEM
TL322C	OEM
TL322I	OEM
TL331C	OEM
TL331CJG	OEM
TL331CP	OEM
TL331I	OEM
TL331IJG	OEM
TL331IP	OEM
TL331M	OEM
TL331MJG	OEM
TL336	OEM
TL368A	OEM
TL369	OEM
TL371	OEM
TL375	OEM
TL376	OEM
TL376C	OEM
TL376CNE	OEM
TL378	OEM
TL379	OEM
TL382	OEM
TL413	4918
TL430C	OEM
TL430CJG	OEM
TL431	OEM
TL431ACD	5200
TL431ACLP	OEM
TL431ACP	5204
TL431AILP	OEM
TL431AIP	OEM
TL431C	OEM
TL431CD	5200
TL431CJG	OEM
TL431CLP	OEM
TL431CLPB	OEM
TL431CP	5204
TL431I	OEM
TL431IJG	OEM
TL431ILP	OEM
TL431IP	OEM
TL431MJG	OEM
TL440C	OEM
TL440CJ	OEM
TL440CN	OEM
TL441C	OEM
TL441CJ	OEM
TL441CN	OEM
TL441MJ	OEM
TL441MN	OEM
TL442C	OEM
TL480CJ	OEM
TL480CN	OEM
TL481CNG	OEM
TL487C	4737
TL487CJG	OEM
TL487CP	4737

If replacement code is OEM, contact original manufacturer for replacement.

DEVICE TYPE	REPL CODE	DEVICE TYPE	REPL CODE	DEVICE TYPE	REPL CODE	DEVICE TYPE	REPL CODE	DEVICE TYPE	REPL CODE	DEVICE TYPE	REPL CODE	DEVICE TYPE	REPL CODE
TL489	OEM	TL702MU	OEM	TL7705CP-B	OEM	TLG2167	OEM	TLR302	OEM	TM31R	0471	TM115	1073
TL489C	4739	TL710CJ	OEM	TL8505P	OEM	TLG2168	OEM	TLR312	4786	TM32	0097	TM116	0015
TL489CP	4739	TL710CJG	OEM	TL8506P	OEM	TLG2259	OEM	TLR313	4783	TM32R	0471	TM117	0229
TL490C	5615	TL710CN	OEM	TL8608AP	OEM	TLH340MF	0705	TLR314	4784	TM33	0015	TM118	0769
TL490CJ	OEM	TL710CP	OEM	TL8608P	OEM	TLN103	OEM	TLR321	OEM	TM33R	0471	TM119	1293
TL490CN	5615	TL710CU	OEM	TL8608P(FV)	OEM	TLN104-B	OEM	TLR324	OEM	TM34	0097	TM120	0469
TL491C	4740	TL710MJ	OEM	TL8703P	OEM	TLN105A	OEM	TLR325	OEM	TM34R	0471	TM121	0160
TL491CJ	OEM	TL710MJG	OEM	TL8707P	OEM	TLN105B	OEM	TLR325(US)	OEM	TM35	0097	TM121MP	0265
TL491CN	4740	TL710MN	OEM	TL8708P	OEM	TLN110	OEM	TLR332	4127	TM36	0097	TM122	0240
TL493AC	OEM	TL710MP	OEM	TL8803P	OEM	TLN111	OEM	TLR-333	OEM	TM37	0097	TM123	0198
TL494	1813	TL710MU	OEM	TL74107N	0936	TL072BCP	OEM	TLR-334	OEM	TM37R	0471	TM123A	0016
TL494AC	OEM	TL711CJ	OEM	TL74121N	0175	TL082CN	OEM	TLR-335	OEM	TM38	0097	TM123AP	0079
TL494C	4349	TL711CN	OEM	TL74122N	1131	TL0113A	OEM	TLR2047	OEM	TM38R	0471	TM124	0142
TL494CJ	1813	TL720CJ	OEM	TL74123N	1149	TL0153	OEM	TLR2098	OEM	TM39	0097	TM125	0071
TL494CN	4349	TL720CN	OEM	TL74141N	1367	TL0153FA	OEM	TLR2098A	OEM	TM39R	0471	TM126	0136
TL494IJ	OEM	TL780-00C	OEM	TL74145N	0614	TL0200	OEM	TLR-2168	OEM	TM41	0109	TM127	0969
TL494IN	OEM	TL780-05C	OEM	TL74150N	1484	TL0208	OEM	TLR2168	OEM	TM41R	0471	TM128	0086
TL494MJ	OEM	TL780-12C	OEM	TL74151N	1487	TL0221	OEM	TLR2177	OEM	TM42	0109	TM129	0126
TL495AC	OEM	TL780-15C	OEM	TL74153N	1531	TL0251	OEM	TLR2718	OEM	TM42R	0471	TM130	0103
TL495CJ	OEM	TL783	OEM	TL74154N	1546	TL0253	OEM	TLR-3168	OEM	TM43	0015	TM130MP	1506
TL495CN	OEM	TL783C	OEM	TL74155N	1566	TL0257	OEM	TLRC221	OEM	TM43R	0471	TM131	0222
TL495IJ	OEM	TL810C	OEM	TL74156N	1582	TL0258	OEM	TLRG101	3693	TM44	0097	TM131MP	0816
TL495IN	OEM	TL810CJ	OEM	TL74162N	1007	TL0259	OEM	TLS113	OEM	TM44R	0471	TM132	3667
TL496	OEM	TL810CJG	OEM	TL74163N	1656	TLOG116	OEM	TLS134A	OEM	TM45	0097	TM133	3443
TL496C	OEM	TL810CN	OEM	TL74164N	0729	TLOG205	OEM	TLS200	OEM	TM46	0097	TM134	0188
TL496CJG	OEM	TL810CP	OEM	TL74165N	1675	TLOG208	OEM	TLS221	OEM	TM47	0097	TM134A	0188
TL496CP	OEM	TL810CU	OEM	TL74166N	0231	TLP521	3333	TLS226	OEM	TM47R	0471	TM135	0162
TL497AC	OEM	TL810MJ	OEM	TL74180N	1818	TLP521(YG)	OEM	TLS251	OEM	TM48	0097	TM135A	0162
TL497ACJ	OEM	TL810MJG	OEM	TL74181N	1831	TLP521-1	6729	TLS253	OEM	TM48R	0471	TM136	0157
TL497ACN	OEM	TL810MN	OEM	TL74182N	1845	TLP521-1(A)	OEM	TLS257	OEM	TM49	0097	TM136A	0157
TL497AI	OEM	TL810MP	OEM	TL74190N	1901	TLP521-1(FA)	3333	TLS258	OEM	TM49R	0471	TM137	0631
TL497AMJ	OEM	TL810MU	OEM	TL74191N	1906	TLP521-1(G)	OEM	TLS259	OEM	TM51	0122	TM137A	0631
TL497MN	OEM	TL811C	OEM	TL74192N	1910	TLP521-1(Y)	OEM	TLSG116	OEM	TM51R	0471	TM138	0644
TL500C	OEM	TL811CJ	OEM	TL74193N	1915	TLP521-1(YG)	OEM	TLSG205	OEM	TM52	0122	TM138A	0644
TL500CN	OEM	TL811CN	OEM	TL74196N	1939	TLP521-1-BL	1158	TLSG208	OEM	TM52R	0471	TM139	0012
TL501C	OEM	TL811CU	OEM	TL74197N	1945	TLP521-1-YG	0112	TLSG222	OEM	TM53	1104	TM139A	0012
TL501CN	OEM	TL811MJ	OEM	TL74198N	1953	TLP521-1FA	0317	TLUG163	OEM	TM53R	0471	TM140	0170
TL502C	OEM	TL811MN	OEM	TL74199N	1960	TLP521-2	OEM	TLUR121	OEM	TM54	1104	TM140A	0170
TL502CN	OEM	TL811MU	OEM	TLA7601G	1977	TLP521-YG	OEM	TLUR122	OEM	TM54R	0471	TM141	0789
TL503C	OEM	TL820CJ	OEM	TLA78601G	1977	TLP521YG	OEM	TLUR153	OEM	TM55	0122	TM141A	0789
TL503CN	OEM	TL820CN	OEM	TLB20C	OEM	TLP531	0311	TLUR163	OEM	TM55R	0471	TM142	0137
TL505C	OEM	TL820MJ	OEM	TLB20M	OEM	TLP531-AUDIO	0311	TLY102	OEM	TM56	0122	TM142A	0137
TL505CN	OEM	TL820MN	OEM	TLBG5400	OEM	TLP541G	0235	TLY113A	OEM	TM56R	0471	TM143	0361
TL506C	OEM	TL1003	OEM	TLBG5410	4928	TLP550	OEM	TLY124	3095	TM57	1104	TM143A	0361
TL506CJ	OEM	TL1006	OEM	TLBO5160	OEM	TLP551	1281	TLY153	OEM	TM57R	0471	TM144	0100
TL506CN	OEM	TL1451ACNS	OEM	TLBO5400	OEM	TLP551(FA)	OEM	TLY153FA	OEM	TM58	1104	TM144A	0100
TL506CW	OEM	TL1555P	0967	TLBO5410	OEM	TLP551-2	OEM	TLY200	OEM	TM58R	0471	TM145	0002
TL506MJ	OEM	TL2003	OEM	TLBR5400	OEM	TLP551FA-1	1281	TLY206	OEM	TM59	1104	TM145A	0002
TL506MN	OEM	TL2006	OEM	TLBR5410	3965	TLP551FA-2	1281	TLY221	OEM	TM59R	0471	TM146	0436
TL507C	OEM	TL3400	OEM	TLBV5380	OEM	TLP560G	OEM	TLY250	OEM	TM61	0087	TM146A	0436
TL507CP	OEM	TL4003	OEM	TLBY5400	OEM	TLP621	0112	TLY251	OEM	TM61R	0471	TM147	0039
TL507P	OEM	TL4558P	0356	TLBY5410	5341	TLP621(GRL)	0112	TLY253	OEM	TM62	0015	TM147A	0039
TL510CJ	OEM	TL4558PA	OEM	TLC27M2	OEM	TLP621-1	1158	TLY257	OEM	TM62R	0471	TM148	1823
TL510CJG	OEM	TL7400N	0232	TLC27M4	OEM	TLP-621-1-GB	1158	TLY258	OEM	TM63	0015	TM148A	1823
TL510CN	OEM	TL7401N	0268	TLC271	OEM	TLP-621-1-GB	1158	TLY259	OEM	TM64	1104	TM149	0778
TL510CP	OEM	TL7402N	0310	TLC374	OEM	TLP621-2	OEM	TLYG116	OEM	TM64R	0471	TM149A	0778
TL510MJ	OEM	TL7403N	0331	TLC548	OEM	TLP621-4	OEM	TLYG205	OEM	TM65	0015	TM150A	0327
TL510MJG	OEM	TL7404N	0357	TLC555	0580	TLP621G	OEM	TLYG208	OEM	TM65R	0471	TM151	0149
TL510MN	OEM	TL7405N	0381	TLC555CP	0580	TLP621GB	0112	TM1	0084	TM66	0015	TM151A	0149
TL510MP	OEM	TL7406N	1197	TLC556	OEM	TLP621GR	0112	TM1R	2275	TM66R	0471	TM152	0042
TL510MU	OEM	TL7407N	1329	TLC556CP	2842	TLP631	0311	TM2	0703	TM67	1104	TM153	0919
TL514C	OEM	TL7409N	0487	TLFG2100	OEM	TLP634	OEM	TM2R	2275	TM67R	0471	TM154	0233
TL514CJ	OEM	TL7410N	0507	TLFG3100	OEM	TLP636	OEM	TM2SC1685	0284	TM68	1104	TM155	2736
TL514CN	OEM	TL7412N	2227	TLFO2100	OEM	TLP651	OEM	TM2SC1686	0284	TM68R	0471	TM156	0087
TL514M	OEM	TL7413N	1432	TLFO3100	OEM	TLP802	OEM	TM3	0097	TM69	1104	TM157	0275
TL514MJ	OEM	TL7416N	1339	TLFR2100	OEM	TLP-809	OEM	TM3R	2275	TM69R	0471	TM158	0164
TL514MN	OEM	TL7420N	0692	TLFR3100	OEM	TLP850	OEM	TM4	0097	TM74	2982	TM159	0037
TL520C	OEM	TL7423N	3429	TLFY2100	OEM	TLP907-0	OEM	TM4R	2275	TM74R	0444	TM160	0050
TL520N(A)	OEM	TL7425N	3438	TLFY3100	OEM	TLP5211YG	OEM	TM5	0703	TM75	2982	TM161	0007
TL521N(A)	OEM	TL7426N	0798	TLG-102	OEM	TLPS604	5031	TM5R	2275	TM75R	0444	TM162	0074
TL531IN(A)	OEM	TL7430N	0867	TLG102	OEM	TLR102	OEM	TM6	0097	TM76	2982	TM163A	0637
TL532N(A)	OEM	TL7437N	3478	TLG-103	OEM	TLR102C	OEM	TM6R	2275	TM76R	0444	TM164	0003
TL533N(A)	OEM	TL7438N	0990	TLG103	3420	TLR-103	OEM	TM7	1991	TM78	2982	TM165	0065
TL560C	OEM	TL7440N	1018	TLG105	3421	TLR103	OEM	TM7R	2275	TM78R	0444	TM166	0276
TL560CJG	OEM	TL7442N	1046	TLG113	OEM	TLR-104	OEM	TM8	1991	TM79	2982	TM167	0287
TL560CL	OEM	TL7443N	1054	TLG113A	OEM	TLR104	5024	TM8R	2275	TM79R	0444	TM168	0293
TL560CP	OEM	TL7444N	1066	TLG113AE	OEM	TLR105	5025	TM9	1590	TM84	0087	TM169	0299
TL601C	OEM	TL7445N	1074	TLG113A-F	OEM	TLR-106	OEM	TM11	0090	TM84R	0444	TM170	0250
TL601CJG	OEM	TL7446AN	1090	TLG-114	1767	TLR-107	5024	TM11R	2275	TM85	0087	TM171	0283
TL601CP	OEM	TL7447AN	1100	TLG121	OEM	TLR111	OEM	TM12	0090	TM85R	0444	TM172A	0396
TL601I	OEM	TL7448N	1117	TLG122	1972	TLR112	OEM	TM12R	2275	TM86	0071	TM173BP	0290
TL601IJG	OEM	TL7450N	0738	TLG-123A	OEM	TLR113	3153	TM13	0575	TM86R	0444	TM174	0918
TL601IP	OEM	TL7451N	1160	TLG123A	OEM	TLR113A	OEM	TM13R	2275	TM88	2982	TM175	0178
TL601MJG	OEM	TL7453N	1177	TLG124	0835	TLR-113AD	OEM	TM14	0097	TM88R	0444	TM176	0841
TL604C	OEM	TL7454N	1193	TLG124A	0835	TLR113DFA	OEM	TM15	0097	TM89	2982	TM177	0133
TL604CJG	OEM	TL7460N	1265	TLG124A-E	OEM	TLR-114	1605	TM16	0097	TM89R	0444	TM178MP	0907
TL604CP	OEM	TL7470N	1394	TLG143	OEM	TLR114	1605	TM17	1241	TM92	2275	TM179	0599
TL604I	OEM	TL7472N	1417	TLG153	OEM	TLR114A	OEM	TM17R	2275	TM100	0279	TM180	1671
TL604IJG	OEM	TL7473N	1164	TLG153FA	OEM	TLR-121	1970	TM18	1241	TM101	0595	TM181	0130
TL604IP	OEM	TL7474N	1303	TLG200	OEM	TLR121	1970	TM18R	2275	TM102	0211	TM182	0556
TL604MJG	OEM	TL7475N	1423	TLG205	OEM	TLR122	5020	TM19	0865	TM102A	0004	TM183	1190
TL607C	OEM	TL7476N	1150	TLG206	OEM	TLR123	2990	TM19R	2275	TM103	0038	TM184	0161
TL607CJG	OEM	TL7480N	1527	TLG208	3450	TLR124	2990	TM21	0097	TM103A	0208	TM185	0455
TL607CP	OEM	TL7481N	3092	TLG211	OEM	TLR140	OEM	TM21R	2275	TM104	0087	TM186	0555
TL607I	OEM	TL7482N	1564	TLG221	OEM	TLR143	OEM	TM22	0097	TM104MP	3004	TM186A	0219
TL607IJG	OEM	TL7483N	0117	TLG250	OEM	TLR144	3134	TM22R	2275	TM104R	0444	TM187	1257
TL607IP	OEM	TL7485N	0370	TLG251	OEM	TLR145	3140	TM23	0575	TM105	0087	TM187A	1045
TL607MJG	OEM	TL7486N	1358	TLG253	OEM	TLR146	OEM	TM23R	2275	TM105R	0444	TM188	0546
TL610C	OEM	TL7489N	5358	TLG257	OEM	TLR-147	5024	TM24	1241	TM106	0150	TM189	0378
TL610CJG	OEM	TL7490N	1199	TLG258	OEM	TLR147	OEM	TM24R	2275	TM106R	0444	TM190	0264
TL610CP	OEM	TL7491N	0974	TLG259	OEM	TLR200	OEM	TM25	0941	TM107	0127	TM191	0334
TL610I	OEM	TL7492N	0828	TLG321	OEM	TLR205	OEM	TM26	1241	TM108	0144	TM192	0590
TL610IJG	OEM	TL7493N	0564	TLG325	OEM	TLR206	OEM	TM27	1241	TM109	0143	TM193	0786
TL610IP	OEM	TL7494N	1692	TLG325(TCL)	OEM	TLR208	4686	TM27R	2275	TM110	1106	TM194	0855
TL610MJG	OEM	TL7495AN	1477	TLG332	OEM	TLR210	OEM	TM28	1241	TM110MP	0123	TM195A	0693
TL702CJ	OEM	TL7496N	1705	TLG333	OEM	TLR211	OEM	TM28R	2275	TM112	0911	TM196	0419
TL702CN	OEM	TL7497N	2912	TLG334	OEM	TLR218RD	OEM	TM29	0865	TM113	0196	TM197	0848
TL702CU	OEM	TL7601G	OEM	TLG335	OEM	TLR221	OEM	TM29R	2275	TM113A	0196	TM198	0168
TL702MJ	OEM	TL7705CP	OEM	TLG367	OEM	TLR250	OEM	TM31	0994	TM114	0479	TM199	0111

If replacement code is OEM, contact original manufacturer for replacement.

DEVICE TYPE	REPL CODE
TM209	OEM
TM210	0561
TM211	1357
TM213	0432
TM218	0899
TM219	0486
TM220	0843
TM221	0349
TM222	0212
TM223	0538
TM224	0626
TM225	3249
TM226	1004
TM226MP	1851
TM228	1698
TM229	0224
TM230	0239
TM231	0061
TM232	3477
TM233	0326
TM234	0688
TM235	0930
TM236	0830
TM237	1401
TM238	0309
TM239	2320
TM241	2969
TM242	0309
TM243	2411
TM244	2262
TM245	3339
TM246	3340
TM247	2422
TM248	2415
TM249	1384
TM250	2429
TM251	3483
TM252	3484
TM253	0553
TM254	2869
TM257	3343
TM258	3486
TM259	3487
TM260	3488
TM261	1203
TM262	0597
TM263	2220
TM264	2222
TM265	2243
TM266	3490
TM267	3491
TM268	3492
TM269	3493
TM270	0134
TM271	0073
TM272	3495
TM273	3496
TM274	3336
TM275	3497
TM276	5710
TM277	2200
TM278	0414
TM279	2321
TM280	0177
TM280MP	2127
TM281	2002
TM282	0617
TM283	0359
TM284	0538
TM284MP	2355
TM285	1588
TM286	1021
TM287	0710
TM288	0338
TM289	0155
TM289MP	2740
TM290	0006
TM291	0236
TM292	0676
TM293	0018
TM293MP	3020
TM294	0527
TM295	1581
TM297	0320
TM297MP	3217
TM298	0431
TM299	2039
TM300	2035
TM300MP	3342
TM302	1165
TM306	1935
TM307	1421
TM308	1702
TM309K	1911
TM310	2313
TM311	0488
TM312	0321
TM313	0470
TM314	1814
TM315	1967
TM316	0259
TM317	2918
TM318	2296
TM319	0008
TM320	1963
TM321	1740
TM322	1973
TM323	0886
TM324	1471

DEVICE TYPE	REPL CODE
TM325	1189
TM326	2959
TM327	2465
TM328	0615
TM329	2675
TM330	3517
TM330W	5867
TM331	0477
TM332	1359
TM333	2808
TM334	3519
TM336	3523
TM337	3524
TM338	3525
TM339	3526
TM340	2699
TM341	3528
TM342	2693
TM343	2694
TM344	2504
TM345	3012
TM346	2030
TM347	3532
TM348	3534
TM349	2156
TM350	1224
TM351	1966
TM353	3536
TM354	3538
TM355	3539
TM356	3540
TM357	3542
TM358	1024
TM358A	4391
TM358B	4947
TM359	3543
TM360	2485
TM361	2028
TM362	3516
TM363	2080
TM364	1410
TM365	2082
TM366	3545
TM367	2841
TM368	3547
TM369	2085
TM370	3759
TM373	0558
TM374	0520
TM375	0388
TM376	1077
TM377	0060
TM378	1298
TM379	0723
TM380	2911
TM381	3527
TM382	1376
TM383	0472
TM384	0424
TM385	1955
TM386	1841
TM387	2416
TM388	2398
TM389	0223
TM390	3052
TM391	0853
TM392	0853
TM393	3558
TM394	2589
TM395	3562
TM396	0187
TM397	0434
TM401	OEM
TM402	OEM
TM403	OEM
TM404	OEM
TM405	OEM
TM409	OEM
TM410	OEM
TM412	OEM
TM413	OEM
TM415	OEM
TM416	OEM
TM417	OEM
TM418	OEM
TM419	OEM
TM420	OEM
TM421	OEM
TM422	OEM
TM423	OEM
TM500A	0190
TM501A	0128
TM501B	0128
TM502	0201
TM503	0286
TM504	0374
TM505	0752
TM506	0102
TM507	0914
TM507(SCR)	1095
TM507F	OEM
TM507S	OEM
TM510	2073
TM513	1313
TM515	1208
TM516	OEM
TM518	1780
TM519	0124
TM520	2956

DEVICE TYPE	REPL CODE
TM521	3805
TM522	1493
TM523	1061
TM524	3607
TM525	0344
TM526	1696
TM526A	1696
TM527	3807
TM528	2097
TM529	2524
TM530	3610
TM531	1048
TM532	0405
TM533	1700
TM534	2954
TM535	2957
TM536A	1986
TM537	1188
TM538	2956
TM539	1048
TM551	0182
TM552	0023
TM605	0120
TM703A	5849
TM704	2600
TM705A	2147
TM706	2549
TM707	0748
TM708	0659
TM709	0673
TM710	0823
TM711	2689
TM712	0167
TM713	0661
TM714	0348
TM715	0350
TM716	3677
TM717	3679
TM718	0649
TM719	1929
TM720	0438
TM721	2264
TM722	0696
TM723	1335
TM724	0817
TM725	0687
TM726	2593
TM727	2507
TM729	0324
TM730	2716
TM731	2438
TM735	2979
TM736	1748
TM737	1434
TM738	0850
TM739	0746
TM740A	0375
TM741	3689
TM742	3690
TM743	1385
TM744	1411
TM745	2902
TM747	1797
TM748	0784
TM749	0391
TM750	3189
TM752	0512
TM753	3731
TM754	0718
TM756	1178
TM757	1178
TM758	3875
TM759	1661
TM760	2089
TM761	1865
TM763	2266
TM764	3879
TM765	3879
TM767	0618
TM768	3884
TM770	2878
TM772A	1969
TM773	1674
TM776	3887
TM778	0356
TM778A	0356
TM779-1	0368
TM780	0360
TM781	2720
TM782	0373
TM783	0797
TM784	2674
TM785	2681
TM786	2688
TM787	2242
TM788	2728
TM789	1832
TM790	0345
TM791	1327
TM793	2032
TM795	3166
TM796	1969
TM797	0516
TM799	1601
TM801	0514
TM802	3715
TM803	3717
TM804	2535
TM805	3376

DEVICE TYPE	REPL CODE
TM806	3388
TM807	3720
TM808	2584
TM809	2663
TM810	2460
TM812	3724
TM813	3898
TM814	2977
TM815	0842
TM816	1070
TM817	1902
TM818	2480
TM819	1867
TM820	2790
TM821	2804
TM822	2785
TM823	3034
TM824	3050
TM825	3070
TM826	3905
TM830	1318
TM832	3733
TM833	1534
TM834	0176
TM900	2662
TM901	2664
TM903	2515
TM904	1843
TM905	2673
TM906	2676
TM907	2685
TM908	2680
TM909	1291
TM909D	1695
TM910	1786
TM910D	1789
TM911	1879
TM912	1686
TM913	3757
TM914	2701
TM915	1545
TM916	2722
TM917	2696
TM923	1183
TM923D	0026
TM925	2863
TM940	1908
TM941	0406
TM941D	1964
TM941M	0308
TM946	3618
TM947	2352
TM947D	2342
TM949	2530
TM955M	0967
TM960	0619
TM961	1275
TM962	0917
TM963	2624
TM964	1187
TM966	0330
TM967	1827
TM968	1311
TM969	3777
TM971	3531
TM972	2224
TM973	0413
TM973D	3751
TM974	0011
TM975	1290
TM976	2267
TM977	1288
TM978	3254
TM980	3779
TM981	0083
TM982	2803
TM983	3391
TM984	3239
TM985	3780
TM986	3060
TM987	0620
TM988	2285
TM989	3347
TM990	1482
TM990/4XX	OEM
TM990/56X	OEM
TM990/100MA	OEM
TM990/101MA	OEM
TM990/102	OEM
TM990/201	OEM
TM990/202-X	OEM
TM990/203	OEM
TM990/203A-XX	OEM
TM990/204	OEM
TM990/303A	OEM
TM990/306	OEM
TM990/307	OEM
TM990/308	OEM
TM990/309	OEM
TM990/310	OEM
TM990/311	OEM
TM990/314	OEM
TM990/315	OEM
TM990/317	OEM
TM990/601	OEM
TM990/602	OEM
TM990/1241	OEM
TM990/1481	OEM
TM990/C101MA	OEM

DEVICE TYPE	REPL CODE
TM990/C201	OEM
TM990/C307	OEM
TM990/C308	OEM
TM990/C310	OEM
TM991	3550
TM992	2232
TM1000	1226
TM1001	4363
TM1002	0383
TM1003	0574
TM1004	0872
TM1005	2546
TM1006	1206
TM1007	2471
TM1007(SCR)	2471
TM1007F	OEM
TM1007S	OEM
TM1008	2991
TM1009	0837
TM1010	0858
TM1011	0876
TM1012	0021
TM1013	0138
TM1014	0351
TM1015	2388
TM1016	2390
TM1017	2423
TM1018	2457
TM1019	2487
TM1020	OEM
TM1021	2142
TM1022	0240
TM1023	4477
TM1024	3506
TM1025	1179
TM1026	2445
TM1027	2849
TM1028	4479
TM1029	2247
TM1030	4481
TM1031	4482
TM1032	4483
TM1033	4484
TM1034	2862
TM1035	4485
TM1036	4486
TM1037	4031
TM1039	1611
TM1040	4489
TM1041	4490
TM1042	4491
TM1043	4320
TM1045	2377
TM1046	0523
TM1047	2855
TM1048	0668
TM1049	0648
TM1050	2864
TM1051	3736
TM1052	0428
TM1053	2551
TM1054	2554
TM1055	2556
TM1056	1826
TM1057	2555
TM1058	2111
TM1059	3966
TM1060	2559
TM1061	2560
TM1062	0399
TM1063	2562
TM1064	2563
TM1065	2564
TM1066	2565
TM1067	2566
TM1068	2567
TM1069	2576
TM1070	4014
TM1071	2580
TM1072	2568
TM1073	2573
TM1074	2569
TM1075A	0465
TM1076	0940
TM1078	3318
TM1079	4495
TM1080	0849
TM1081A	1152
TM1082	2246
TM1083	2827
TM1084	2859
TM1085	2607
TM1086	2860
TM1087	1012
TM1088	5576
TM1089	0633
TM1090	2834
TM1091	0958
TM1092	2300
TM1093	4498
TM1094	0043
TM1095	4406
TM1096	1624
TM1097	3232
TM1098	3901
TM1099	4196
TM1100	0905
TM1101	2610
TM1102	2608

DEVICE TYPE	REPL CODE
TM1103	1983
TM1104	2046
TM1105	4502
TM1106	2606
TM1107	3625
TM1108	1383
TM1109	2615
TM1110	2289
TM1111	2453
TM1112	2462
TM1113	2145
TM1114	4506
TM1115	1239
TM1115A	3866
TM1116	4084
TM1117	3946
TM1118	1909
TM1119	4509
TM1120	2020
TM1121	0385
TM1122	0602
TM1123	3973
TM1124	4463
TM1125	3968
TM1126	4513
TM1127	4348
TM1128	3859
TM1130	1316
TM1131	4514
TM1132	4515
TM1133	2216
TM1134	2921
TM1135	2051
TM1136	3106
TM1137	2571
TM1139	3880
TM1140	2845
TM1141	3788
TM1142	1469
TM1149	4517
TM1150	4518
TM1152	2484
TM1153	3332
TM1154	4520
TM1155	1044
TM1156	2988
TM1158	0875
TM1159	0878
TM1160	3650
TM1161	2914
TM1162	3977
TM1163	2581
TM1164	3238
TM1165	2746
TM1166	2754
TM1167	1704
TM1168	2579
TM1169	4331
TM1170	2512
TM1171	0093
TM1172	1369
TM1173	3242
TM1174	2038
TM1175	2759
TM1176	2762
TM1177	2771
TM1178	3660
TM1179	2550
TM1180	2590
TM1181	2570
TM1182	3993
TM1183	4133
TM1184	4532
TM1185	1470
TM1186	0846
TM1187	0851
TM1188	2594
TM1189	4325
TM1190	4535
TM1191	4025
TM1192	1532
TM1193	3286
TM1194	1805
TM1195	4145
TM1196	1049
TM1197	4539
TM1200	4174
TM1201	4541
TM1202	2364
TM1203	2290
TM1204	4405
TM1205	2903
TM1206	4542
TM1207	4619
TM1208	4543
TM1209	4544
TM1210	2609
TM1211	2179
TM1212	4545
TM1213	4546
TM1214	0646
TM1215	2510
TM1216	0910
TM1217	0412
TM1218	1561
TM1219	1602
TM1221	4550
TM1222	5592
TM1223	1516

DEVICE TYPE	REPL CODE
TM1224	4024
TM1225	2645
TM1226	0701
TM1227	0616
TM1228	3161
TM1229	4551
TM1230	2644
TM1231	1162
TM1232	1042
TM1233	4160
TM1234	2008
TM1235	4552
TM1236	2268
TM1237	3606
TM1238	3961
TM1239	3231
TM1240	4006
TM1241	2614
TM1242	1501
TM1243	4553
TM1244	2737
TM1245	0898
TM1246	4554
TM1247	4555
TM1248	1251
TM1249	3980
TM1250	4010
TM1251	4556
TM1252	4557
TM1253	4558
TM1254	3763
TM1255	2592
TM1256	4559
TM1257	4560
TM1258	4561
TM1259	5517
TM1260	4563
TM1261	1120
TM1262	4564
TM1263	2932
TM1264	4001
TM1265	4002
TM1266	4004
TM1267	4007
TM1268	4008
TM1269	4017
TM1270	5463
TM1271	4567
TM1272	3515
TM1273	4568
TM1274	5600
TM1300	3877
TM1301	4588
TM1302	3935
TM1303	4589
TM1304	3939
TM1305	3941
TM1306	3943
TM1307	3947
TM1308	3891
TM1309	4590
TM1310	3931
TM1311	3876
TM1312	3927
TM1313	3928
TM1613	0016
TM1614	0037
TM1711	0016
TM1712	0037
TM1814	0855
TM2004	4045
TM2007F	OEM
TM2007S	OEM
TM2010	OEM
TM2011	0839
TM2012	1001
TM2013	1126
TM2014	1252
TM2015	4848
TM2016	4849
TM2017	4850
TM2018	4852
TM2019	4853
TM2020	4854
TM2021	3839
TM2022	3864
TM2023	2723
TM2024	2800
TM2040	4290
TM2613	0079
TM2614	0037
TM2711	0079
TM2712	0037
TM3004	5020
TM3007F	OEM
TM3007S	OEM
TM3010	0835
TM4000	2013
TM4001B	0473
TM4002B	2044
TM4004	OEM
TM4006B	0641
TM4007B	2819
TM4007F	OEM
TM4007S	OEM
TM4008B	0982
TM4010	OEM
TM4011B	0215
TM4012B	0493

If replacement code is OEM, contact original manufacturer for replacement.

DEVICE TYPE	REPL CODE
TM4013B	0409
TM4014B	0854
TM4015B	1008
TM4016B	1135
TM4017B	0508
TM4018B	1381
TM4019B	1517
TM4020B	1651
TM4021B	1738
TM4022B	1247
TM4023B	0515
TM4024B	1946
TM4025B	2061
TM4027B	1938
TM4028B	2213
TM4029B	2218
TM4030B	0495
TM4034B	3570
TM4035B	2750
TM4040B	0056
TM4042B	0121
TM4043B	1544
TM4044B	2292
TM4049B	0001
TM4050B	0394
TM4051B	0362
TM4052B	0024
TM4053B	0034
TM4055B	3272
TM4060B	0146
TM4063B	3682
TM4066B	0101
TM4068B	2482
TM4069	0119
TM4071B	0129
TM4072B	2502
TM4073B	1528
TM4075B	2518
TM4076B	3455
TM4077B	2536
TM4078B	0915
TM4081B	0621
TM4082B	0297
TM4085B	0300
TM4086B	0530
TM4093B	2368
TM4098B	3566
TM4099B	3297
TM4216P	OEM
TM4217P	OEM
TM4500BP	OEM
TM4510B	1952
TM4511B	1535
TM4512B	2108
TM4514B	1819
TM4515B	3555
TM4516B	2331
TM4518B	1037
TM4520B	2650
TM4522B	2810
TM4527B	3116
TM4539B	3611
TM4555B	2910
TM4556B	3397
TM4801P	OEM
TM5000A	1266
TM5001A	2847
TM5002A	0755
TM5003A	0672
TM5004	0118
TM5004A	0118
TM5005A	0296
TM5006A	0372
TM5007A	0036
TM5008A	0274
TM5009A	0140
TM5010	0041
TM5010A	0041
TM5011A	0253
TM5012A	0091
TM5013A	0466
TM5014A	0062
TM5015A	0077
TM5016	0165
TM5016A	0165
TM5017A	0318
TM5018A	0057
TM5019A	0064
TM5020A	0181
TM5021A	0052
TM5022	0053
TM5022A	0053
TM5023	0873
TM5023A	0873
TM5024A	0681
TM5025A	0440
TM5026A	0210
TM5027A	0371
TM5028A	0666
TM5029A	0695
TM5030A	0700
TM5031A	0489
TM5032A	0709
TM5033A	0450
TM5034A	0257
TM5035A	0195
TM5036A	0166
TM5037A	0010
TM5038A	0032

DEVICE TYPE	REPL CODE
TM5039A	0054
TM5040A	0068
TM5041A	0092
TM5042A	0125
TM5043A	2301
TM5044A	2301
TM5045A	0173
TM5046A	0094
TM5047A	0049
TM5048A	0104
TM5049A	0156
TM5050	OEM
TM5050A	0189
TM5051A	0099
TM5052A	0089
TM5053A	0285
TM5054A	0252
TM5055A	0336
TM5056A	0366
TM5057A	0390
TM5058A	0420
TM5059A	0448
TM5060A	1464
TM5061	2975
TM5061A	2975
TM5062A	OEM
TM5063A	1302
TM5064A	2981
TM5065A	1703
TM5066A	0289
TM5067A	0451
TM5068	0528
TM5068A	0528
TM5069A	0446
TM5070	0298
TM5070A	0298
TM5071	0025
TM5071A	0025
TM5072	0244
TM5072A	0244
TM5073	1075
TM5073A	1075
TM5074	0313
TM5074A	0313
TM5075	0416
TM5075A	0416
TM5076	1639
TM5076A	1639
TM5077	0490
TM5077A	0490
TM5078A	0943
TM5079	0526
TM5079A	0526
TM5080	0560
TM5080A	0560
TM5081	0398
TM5081A	0398
TM5082	1596
TM5082A	1596
TM5083	1664
TM5083A	1664
TM5084	0721
TM5084A	0721
TM5085A	0814
TM5086	0346
TM5086A	0346
TM5087A	0925
TM5088A	0993
TM5089A	0497
TM5090A	0863
TM5091A	1148
TM5092A	2144
TM5093A	1181
TM5094A	2997
TM5095	1301
TM5095A	1301
TM5096	0098
TM5096A	0098
TM5097	0186
TM5097A	0186
TM5098	0213
TM5098A	0213
TM5099	0245
TM5099A	0245
TM5100	0028
TM5101	0255
TM5101A	0255
TM5102A	0871
TM5103A	0363
TM5104A	2831
TM5105	0417
TM5105A	0417
TM5111A	0777
TM5112A	0791
TM5113A	0801
TM5114A	0815
TM5115A	0827
TM5116	0437
TM5116A	0437
TM5117A	0870
TM5118A	3099
TM5119A	0185
TM5120A	0205
TM5121A	0475
TM5122A	0499
TM5123A	3285
TM5124A	0679
TM5125A	0225
TM5126A	0230

DEVICE TYPE	REPL CODE
TM5127A	0234
TM5128A	0237
TM5129A	1387
TM5130	0247
TM5130A	0247
TM5131A	0251
TM5132A	1170
TM5133A	0256
TM5134A	2379
TM5135	0262
TM5135A	0262
TM5136	0269
TM5136A	0269
TM5137A	0273
TM5138	2383
TM5138A	2383
TM5139A	0291
TM5140A	1169
TM5141A	0305
TM5142A	0314
TM5143A	0316
TM5144A	0322
TM5145A	0333
TM5146A	0343
TM5147A	0027
TM5148A	0266
TM5149A	2829
TM5150A	0382
TM5151A	0401
TM5152A	0421
TM5153A	0439
TM5154A	2999
TM5155A	0238
TM5156A	1172
TM5157A	1182
TM5158A	1198
TM5159A	1209
TM5160	1870
TM5160A	1870
TM5161A	0642
TM5162A	1246
TM5163A	2091
TM5164A	1269
TM5165A	2210
TM5166A	0600
TM5172A	4167
TM5172AK	1000
TM5173A	2381
TM5173AK	1370
TM5174A	2024
TM5174AK	0542
TM5175A	2385
TM5175AK	2387
TM5176A	1429
TM5176AK	2101
TM5177A	2391
TM5177AK	2394
TM5178A	1436
TM5178AK	1890
TM5179A	2399
TM5179AK	2400
TM5180A	2206
TM5180AK	0691
TM5181A	1449
TM5181AK	1591
TM5182A	0221
TM5182AK	1606
TM5183A	1481
TM5183AK	1612
TM5184A	2406
TM5184AK	2408
TM5185A	1608
TM5185AK	0622
TM5186A	0505
TM5186AK	0986
TM5187A	0686
TM5187AK	0989
TM5188A	0864
TM5188AK	1254
TM5189A	1014
TM5189AK	1240
TM5190A	1145
TM5190AK	1626
TM5191A	1264
TM5191AK	1629
TM5192A	1392
TM5192AK	1693
TM5193A	1524
TM5193AK	1630
TM5194A	1071
TM5194AK	1706
TM5195A	1701
TM5195AK	1709
TM5196A	1707
TM5196AK	1720
TM5197A	1712
TM5197AK	0722
TM5198A	1725
TM5198AK	1745
TM5199A	1737
TM5199AK	1757
TM5200A	1750
TM5200AK	1771
TM5201A	2431
TM5201AK	2434
TM5202A	1761
TM5202AK	1783
TM5203A	1777
TM5203AK	1788

DEVICE TYPE	REPL CODE
TM5204A	1785
TM5204AK	1798
TM5205A	1793
TM5205AK	1806
TM5206A	1185
TM5206AK	1815
TM5207A	1810
TM5207AK	1829
TM5208A	0022
TM5208AK	1842
TM5209A	0070
TM5209AK	1850
TM5210A	0132
TM5210AK	1855
TM5211A	0172
TM5211AK	1863
TM5212A	0207
TM5212AK	1873
TM5213A	0227
TM5213AK	2455
TM5214A	0263
TM5214AK	1884
TM5215A	0306
TM5215AK	1891
TM5216A	0325
TM5216AK	0731
TM5217A	0352
TM5217AK	1898
TM5218A	0377
TM5218AK	2459
TM5219A	0408
TM5219AK	1903
TM5220A	0433
TM5220AK	1155
TM5221A	0459
TM5221AK	1913
TM5222A	0483
TM5222AK	1922
TM5223A	0504
TM5223AK	1930
TM5224A	0519
TM5224AK	1936
TM5225A	0537
TM5225AK	1942
TM5226A	0063
TM5226AK	1950
TM5227A	0397
TM5227AK	0353
TM5228A	0593
TM5228AK	2479
TM5229A	0611
TM5229AK	0665
TM5230A	0629
TM5230AK	0771
TM5231A	0645
TM5231AK	2486
TM5232A	0663
TM5232AK	1065
TM5240A	0809
TM5240AK	2695
TM5241A	0821
TM5241AK	2698
TM5242A	0840
TM5242AK	2700
TM5243A	0862
TM5243AK	2703
TM5244A	0879
TM5244AK	2706
TM5245A	0891
TM5245AK	2707
TM5246A	0908
TM5246AK	2711
TM5247A	0920
TM5247AK	2713
TM5248A	0938
TM5248AK	2717
TM5249A	0952
TM5249AK	1216
TM5250A	0972
TM5250AK	2719
TM5251A	0988
TM5251AK	1228
TM5252A	1003
TM5252AK	1243
TM5253A	1013
TM5253AK	1259
TM5254A	0883
TM5254AK	1267
TM5255A	1043
TM5255AK	1283
TM5256A	1052
TM5256AK	2725
TM5257A	0926
TM5257AK	1292
TM5258A	0926
TM5258AK	1300
TM5259A	1088
TM5259AK	2729
TM5260A	1098
TM5260AK	1314
TM5261A	1115
TM5261AK	2731
TM5262A	1127
TM5262AK	1323
TM5263A	1144
TM5263AK	1334
TM5264A	1156
TM5264AK	1346
TM5265A	1166

DEVICE TYPE	REPL CODE
TM5265AK	2733
TM5266A	1176
TM5266AK	1361
TM5267A	1191
TM5267AK	2735
TM5268A	1201
TM5268AK	1377
TM5269A	1214
TM5269AK	1396
TM5270A	1223
TM5270AK	1405
TM5271A	1237
TM5271AK	1419
TM5272A	1256
TM5272AK	1431
TM5273A	1263
TM5273AK	2745
TM5274A	1280
TM5274AK	1438
TM5275A	1289
TM5275AK	2749
TM5276A	1297
TM5276AK	1452
TM5277A	1312
TM5277AK	2752
TM5278A	1321
TM5278AK	1465
TM5279A	1330
TM5279AK	2756
TM5280A	1343
TM5280AK	0608
TM5281A	1355
TM5281AK	1502
TM5282A	1374
TM5282AK	1515
TM5283A	1391
TM5283AK	1529
TM5284A	1402
TM5284AK	1541
TM5285A	1413
TM5285AK	1565
TM5286A	1427
TM5286AK	2775
TM5287A	1435
TM5287AK	2776
TM5288A	1448
TM5288AK	1499
TM5289A	1461
TM5289AK	2778
TM5290A	1475
TM5290AK	2780
TM5291A	1497
TM5291AK	2783
TM5292A	1513
TM5292AK	2788
TM5293A	1523
TM5293AK	2791
TM5294A	1539
TM5294AK	2793
TM5295A	1558
TM5295AK	2795
TM5296A	1577
TM5296AK	2797
TM5404	0058
TM5414	3575
TM5444	2255
TM5448	3370
TM5452	1386
TM5454	0442
TM5455	0934
TM5800	0110
TM5802	0242
TM5804	0535
TM5806	0959
TM5982	2873
TM5984	OEM
TM5986	1116
TM5987	1099
TM5990	0800
TM5994	0315
TM6004	OEM
TM6010	0596
TM6402	0312
TM6407	3298
TM7004	OEM
TM7007	OEM
TM7010	OEM
TM7492	0828
TM7493A	0564
TM8004	OEM
TM8010	OEM
TM59090	OEM
TMAL110	OEM
TMAL113	OEM
TMAL116	OEM
TMAL220	OEM
TMAL223	OEM
TMAL226	OEM
TMAM4004-6	OEM
TMAM4004-10	OEM
TMAM4008-6	OEM
TMAM4008-10	OEM
TMAM4011	OEM
TMAM4014-21	OEM
TMAM4015-21	OEM
TMAM4016-21	OEM
TMAM4017-21	OEM
TMAM6001	OEM
TMAM6002	OEM

DEVICE TYPE	REPL CODE
TMAM6003	OEM
TMAM6004	OEM
TMAM6058	OEM
TMAM6059	OEM
TMAM6070	OEM
TMAM6071	OEM
TMAM6073	OEM
TMAM6075	OEM
TMAM6081	OEM
TMAM6095	OEM
TMAM7001	OEM
TMAM7002	OEM
TMAM7003	OEM
TMAM7005	OEM
TMAM7010	OEM
TMAM9000	OEM
TMAM9010	OEM
TMAM9020	OEM
TMAM9040	OEM
TMD01	0162
TMD01A	0162
TMD02	0157
TMD02A	0157
TMD03	0631
TMD03A	0631
TMD04	0062
TMD04A	0062
TMD05	OEM
TMD05A	OEM
TMD06	0165
TMD06A	0165
TMD07	0057
TMD07A	0057
TMD08	0170
TMD08A	0170
TMD09	OEM
TMD09A	OEM
TMD10	0052
TMD10A	0052
TMD20	OEM
TMD20A	OEM
TMD24	OEM
TMD25	OEM
TMD27	OEM
TMD40	OEM
TMD40A	OEM
TMD41	0133
TMD42	0604
TMD45	0604
TMD50	OEM
TMD914	OEM
TMD916	OEM
TMM314AP	2037
TMM314APL-3	2037
TMM315D	1683
TMM315D-1	1683
TMM323D	OEM
TMM416D-3	0518
TMM416D-4	0518
TMM416P-3	0518
TMM841P	OEM
TMM2016	1887
TMM2016AP	1887
TMM2016AP-10	OEM
TMM2016AP-12	1887
TMM2016BP-10	OEM
TMM2016BP-12	OEM
TMM2016BP-15	1887
TMM2016BP-90	OEM
TMM2016P	1887
TMM2016P-1	1887
TMM2016P-2	1887
TMM2016P-7	1887
TMM2063AP-10	OEM
TMM2063P-10	OEM
TMM2063P-15	OEM
TMM2063P-150	OEM
TMM2064P-15	OEM
TMM2114AP-15	5206
TMM2116AP-15	OEM
TMM2764D-2	0806
TMM4164AP-15	OEM
TMM4164P-3	2341
TMM10010-01	OEM
TMM10010-02	OEM
TMM10010-03	OEM
TMM10010-04	OEM
TMM10010-05	OEM
TMM10010-06	OEM
TMM20000-01	OEM
TMM20000-02	OEM
TMM20000-03	OEM
TMM20000-04	OEM
TMM20000-05	OEM
TMM23256P	OEM
TMM23256P-5879	OEM
TMM24512AP-25	OEM
TMM27128AD-20	1628
TMM27256AD	OEM
TMM27256AD-20	OEM
TMM27256AD-XX	OEM
TMM27512AD-15	OEM
TMM30000-01	OEM
TMM30000-02	OEM
TMM30000-03	OEM
TMM40010-01	OEM
TMM40010-02	OEM
TMM40010-04	OEM
TMM40010-07	OEM

DEVICE TYPE	REPL CODE
TMM41256CP-12	1463
TMM41257P-15	OEM
TMM41464AP-12	OEM
TMMS27256JL	OEM
TMP42C40P-10	OEM
TMP42C40P1007	OEM
TMP42C40P-1367	OEM
TMP47C00AF-68572	OEM
TMP47C25N-3055	OEM
TMP47C40P	OEM
TMP47C40P-SA6201	OEM
TMP47C40P-SB6204	OEM
TMP47C40P-SC	OEM
TMP47C200AN-2567	OEM
TMP47C200AN-2574	OEM
TMP47C200AN-2575	OEM
TMP47C200N-2572	OEM
TMP47C231AN4942	OEM
TMP47C231AN-4942Z	OEM
TMP47C231AN4943	OEM
TMP47C231AN-4943Z	OEM
TMP47C231AN4951	OEM
TMP47C231AN-4951Z	OEM
TMP47C232	OEM
TMP47C232-4981	OEM
TMP47C232-4989	OEM
TMP47C232AN-4989	OEM
TMP47C232AN-4989Z	OEM
TMP47C232N-4981	OEM
TMP47C232N4981	OEM
TMP47C232N-4989	OEM
TMP47C232N8893	OEM
TMP47C236AN-R702	OEM
TMP47C236ANR702	OEM
TMP47C337AN	OEM
TMP47C400-6764	OEM
TMP47C400AF-6857	OEM
TMP47C400AN-6265Z	OEM
TMP47C400AN-6403	OEM
TMP47C400AN-6404	OEM
TMP47C400AN-6405	OEM
TMP47C400CN-6452	OEM
TMP47C400F-6442	OEM
TMP47C400N	OEM
TMP47C400N-6402	OEM
TMP47C400N-6403	OEM
TMP47C400N-6452	OEM
TMP47C400N-6454	OEM
TMP47C400N-6455	OEM
TMP47C420AF8352	OEM
TMP47C432-8857	OEM
TMP47C432AN	OEM
TMP47C432AN-8088	OEM
TMP47C432AN-8088Z	OEM
TMP47C432AN-8098	OEM
TMP47C432AN-8382	OEM
TMP47C432AN-8497	OEM
TMP47C432AN8699	OEM
TMP47C432AN-8734	OEM
TMP47C432AN-8939Z	OEM
TMP47C432AN8939Z	OEM
TMP47C432N(8083)	OEM
TMP47C432N(8091)	OEM
TMP47C432N88	OEM
TMP47C432N-8083	OEM
TMP47C432N-8091	OEM
TMP47C432N8784	OEM
TMP47C432N-8857	OEM
TMP47C432N-8858	OEM
TMP47C432N-8859	OEM
TMP47C432N-8861	OEM
TMP47C432N8861	OEM
TMP47C432N-8890	OEM
TMP47C432N8890	OEM
TMP47C432N-8989	OEM
TMP47C434N-3404	OEM
TMP47C434N-3464	OEM
TMP47C434N-3509Z	OEM
TMP47C434N3594	OEM
TMP47C441AN-1662	OEM
TMP47C460-9242	OEM
TMP47C634N	OEM
TMP47C634N(GS8108-01	
	OEM
TMP47C634N-2402	OEM
TMP47C634N-2409	OEM
TMP47C634N-2417	OEM
TMP47C634N-2418	OEM
TMP47C634N-2427Z	OEM
TMP47C634N2427Z	OEM
TMP47C634N-2438	OEM
TMP47C634N2438	OEM
TMP47C634N2453	OEM
TMP47C634N-2453Z	OEM
TMP47C634N2454	OEM
TMP47C634N2454Z	OEM
TMP47C634N2651	OEM
TMP47C634N-2654Z	OEM
TMP47C634N-2663	OEM
TMP47C634N-2679	OEM
TMP47C634N-2687	OEM
TMP47C634N-2689	OEM
TMP47C634N-R075	OEM
TMP47C634N-R301	OEM
TMP47C634NR357	OEM
TMP47C634NR357(Z)	OEM
TMP47C634N-R357Z	OEM
TMP47C634NR357Z	OEM
TMP47C634N-R401	OEM

If replacement code is OEM, contact original manufacturer for replacement.

599

DEVICE TYPE	REPL CODE
TMP47C634N-R402	OEM
TMP47C634N-R417	OEM
TMP47C660N-1454	OEM
TMP47C670N-1264	OEM
TMP47C670N-1282	OEM
TMP47C670N-1283	OEM
TMP47C834N-R075	OEM
TMP47C870N-4627	OEM
TMP47C1237NU132	OEM
TMP47C1237N-U132(Z)	OEM
TMP47C1638NU311(F)Z	OEM
TMP47C1638NU312(F)Z	OEM
TMP47C2314951	OEM
TMP47C2324981	OEM
TMP47C2324989	OEM
TMP47C4328784	OEM
TMP47C4328857	OEM
TMP47C4328858	OEM
TMP47C4328859	OEM
TMP47C4328861	OEM
TMP47C4328890	OEM
TMP47C4328989	OEM
TMP47C6342427	OEM
TMP47P860N	OEM
TMP87CH33N-3014	OEM
TMP90C041N	OEM
TMP4240P-1603	OEM
TMP4315BN0422	OEM
TMP4315BN0433	OEM
TMP4320-6214A	OEM
TMP4320-6422A	OEM
TMP4320-6432	OEM
TMP4320AN-6462	OEM
TMP4320AN6462	OEM
TMP4320AP-6201	OEM
TMP4320AP-6226A	OEM
TMP4320AP-6401A	OEM
TMP4320AP-6422	OEM
TMP4320AP-6433	OEM
TMP4320P-6202	OEM
TMP4320P-6203	OEM
TMP4320P-6204	OEM
TMP4320P-6205	OEM
TMP4321AP-FA	OEM
TMP4321AP-SA9002	OEM
TMP4321AP-SC	OEM
TMP4321AP-SC9007	OEM
TMP4323AN-8124	OEM
TMP4323AP-8605	OEM
TMP4501	OEM
TMP4720P-1802	OEM
TMP4740P	OEM
TMP4740P-5403	OEM
TMP4740P-5404	OEM
TMP4740P-5411	OEM
TMP4740P-5541	OEM
TMP4740P5541	OEM
TMP4740P-5543	OEM
TMP4740P5543	OEM
TMP4740P5659	OEM
TMP4740P-5702	OEM
TMP4746N	OEM
TMP8039P	OEM
TMP8048P-1877	OEM
TMP8049AP-6	OEM
TMP8085AP	OEM
TMP8155P	OEM
TMP8155P-2	OEM
TMP8155P2	OEM
TMP43103312A	OEM
TMP43103323A	OEM
TMP43150414B	OEM
TMP43206432A	OEM
TMP43206462AN	OEM
TMP47201802	OEM
TMP47405541	OEM
TMP47405543	OEM
TMP47405702	OEM
TMP47465759	OEM
TMP47465768	OEM
TMP47465775	OEM
TMPD459	3841
TMPD914	OEM
TMPD2835	OEM
TMPD2836	OEM
TMPD2837	0901
TMPD2838	0901
TMPD4148	OEM
TMPD4150	3703
TMPD4153	OEM
TMPD4154	3703
TMPD4448	OEM
TMPD5711	OEM
TMPD6050	0080
TMPD6100	0080
TMPD6914	OEM
TMPD6916	OEM
TMPD6919	OEM
TMPD7000	OEM
TMS0117	OEM
TMS25L32-45	OEM
TMS27C128JL	OEM
TMS27C256-20JL	OEM
TMS27L08-45	OEM
TMS27PC512NL	OEM
TMS40L44-12	OEM
TMS40L44-20	OEM
TMS40L44-25	OEM
TMS40L44-45	OEM

DEVICE TYPE	REPL CODE
TMS70E40	OEM
TMS70L22	OEM
TMS1000	OEM
TMS1000C	OEM
TMS1000N	OEM
TMS1000NLL	OEM
TMS1004C	OEM
TMS1018	OEM
TMS1020	OEM
TMS1023NL	OEM
TMS1024	OEM
TMS1024NLL	OEM
TMS1025	OEM
TMS1025N	OEM
TMS1025N2LC	OEM
TMS1025N2LL	OEM
TMS1050	OEM
TMS1070	OEM
TMS1070C	OEM
TMS1100	OEM
TMS1100C	OEM
TMS1100N2LL	OEM
TMS1100NLL	OEM
TMS1117	OEM
TMS1121	OEM
TMS1152NL	OEM
TMS1170	OEM
TMS1170NLHL	OEM
TMS1200	OEM
TMS1200C	OEM
TMS1270	OEM
TMS1270C	OEM
TMS1300	OEM
TMS1300C	OEM
TMS1370	OEM
TMS1400	OEM
TMS1470	OEM
TMS1600	OEM
TMS1670	OEM
TMS1670MP7572A	OEM
TMS1700	OEM
TMS1943	2279
TMS1943A2	2279
TMS1943N2	2279
TMS1943N2L	2279
TMS1943N21	2279
TMS1943NL	2279
TMS1944N2	OEM
TMS1944N2L	OEM
TMS-1952	2702
TMS1952NL	2702
TMS2016	OEM
TMS2100	OEM
TMS2114-15	5206
TMS2114-20	2037
TMS2114-25	2037
TMS2114-45	2037
TMS2114L-15	5206
TMS2114L-20	2037
TMS2114L-25	2037
TMS2114L-45	2037
TMS2132	OEM
TMS2147H-3	OEM
TMS2147H-4	OEM
TMS2147H-5	OEM
TMS2147H-7	OEM
TMS2149-3	OEM
TMS2149-4	OEM
TMS2149-5	OEM
TMS2149-7	OEM
TMS2170	OEM
TMS2220	OEM
TMS2240	OEM
TMS2300	OEM
TMS2370	OEM
TMS2372	OEM
TMS2400	OEM
TMS2470	OEM
TMS2516-30	OEM
TMS2516-35	OEM
TMS2516-45	OEM
TMS2516JL-45	5485
TMS2532-30	5007
TMS2532-35	5007
TMS2532-45	5007
TMS2532JL-45	OEM
TMS2564-35	0806
TMS2564-45	0806
TMS2564JL	OEM
TMS2600	OEM
TMS2670	OEM
TMS2708-35	OEM
TMS2708-45	OEM
TMS2716-30	OEM
TMS2716-45	OEM
TMS2732AJL-30	2672
TMS2732AJL-35	2672
TMS2764JL-25	0806
TMS3450N1	OEM
TMS3450NL	3925
TMS3451NL	OEM
TMS3452N2L	OEM
TMS3453N2L	OEM
TMS3454NR	OEM
TMS3614NC	OEM
TMS3763CNL28	OEM
TMS3763CNL8805	OEM
TMS4016-12	OEM
TMS4016-15	1887

DEVICE TYPE	REPL CODE
TMS4016-20	1887
TMS4016-25	1887
TMS4044-12	OEM
TMS4044-20	OEM
TMS4044-25	OEM
TMS4044-45	OEM
TMS4116-15	OEM
TMS4116-20	0518
TMS4116-25	0518
TMS4164-15	2341
TMS4164-15NLJ	2341
TMS4164-20	2341
TMS4164-20NL	2341
TMS4164-25	2341
TMS4164NLJ	2341
TMS4256	OEM
TMS4256-15	OEM
TMS4256-15NL	1463
TMS4256FML	OEM
TMS4416	OEM
TMS4416-12NL	OEM
TMS4416-15	OEM
TMS4416-15NL	OEM
TMS4416-20	OEM
TMS4416-20NL	OEM
TMS4416-25	OEM
TMS4464-12NL	OEM
TMS4732	OEM
TMS4764	OEM
TMS4764-30NL	OEM
TMS5027	OEM
TMS5037	OEM
TMS5100	OEM
TMS5100N	OEM
TMS5100NL	OEM
TMS5110	OEM
TMS5220	OEM
TMS6100	OEM
TMS6125	OEM
TMS7000	OEM
TMS7020	OEM
TMS7040	OEM
TMS7041	OEM
TMS8080AN	4467
TMS9900-40	OEM
TMS9900NL	OEM
TMS9901	OEM
TMS9901NL	OEM
TMS9902A	OEM
TMS9903	OEM
TMS9909	OEM
TMS9914A	OEM
TMS9918A	OEM
TMS9919	OEM
TMS9927	OEM
TMS9928A	OEM
TMS9929A	OEM
TMS9937	OEM
TMS9940M	OEM
TMS9980A	OEM
TMS9981	OEM
TMS9995	OEM
TMS27128-20JL	OEM
TMS27128AD-200	OEM
TMS27128D-15	OEM
TMS27256JL	OEM
TMS27256JL-XX	OEM
TMS99105	OEM
TMS99110	OEM
TMS99531	OEM
TMS99532	OEM
TMS99541	OEM
TMS99650	OEM
TMSK101	OEM
TMSK101A	OEM
TMSK202	OEM
TMSW330R-6	OEM
TMSW330R-10	OEM
TMSW330R-21	OEM
TMSW334H-21	OEM
TMSW340F-21	OEM
TMSW340R-6	OEM
TMSW340R-10	OEM
TMSW348E-21	OEM
TMSW352M-21	OEM
TMSW356I-21	OEM
TMSW511F-21	OEM
TMSW600P-3	OEM
TMSW754P-6	OEM
TMSW754P-10	OEM
TMSW755P-21	OEM
TMT696	0144
TMT697	0144
TMT839	0144
TMT840	0144
TMT841	0144
TMT842	0144
TMT843	0144
TMT1131	OEM
TMT1132	OEM
TMT1543	0016
TMT2427	0144
TN0102N2	OEM
TN0102N3	OEM
TN0102ND	OEM
TN0104N2	OEM
TN0104N3	OEM
TN0104ND	OEM
TN0106N2	OEM

DEVICE TYPE	REPL CODE
TN0106N3	OEM
TN0106ND	OEM
TN0110N2	OEM
TN0110N3	OEM
TN0110ND	OEM
TN0202N2	OEM
TN0202N3	OEM
TN0202ND	OEM
TN0204N2	OEM
TN0204N3	OEM
TN0204ND	OEM
TN0520N2	OEM
TN0520N3	OEM
TN0520ND	OEM
TN0524N2	OEM
TN0524N3	OEM
TN0524ND	OEM
TN0602N2	OEM
TN0602N3	OEM
TN0602ND	OEM
TN0604N2	OEM
TN0604N3	OEM
TN0604ND	OEM
TN0606N2	OEM
TN0606N3	OEM
TN0606N5	OEM
TN0606N6	OEM
TN0606N7	OEM
TN0606ND	OEM
TN0610N2	OEM
TN0610N3	OEM
TN0610N5	OEM
TN0610ND	OEM
TN0620N2	OEM
TN0620N3	OEM
TN0620N5	OEM
TN0620ND	OEM
TN0624N2	OEM
TN0624N3	OEM
TN0624N5	OEM
TN0624ND	OEM
TN2SA643	1233
TN2SA733	0006
TN2SA733-4	0006
TN2SA733-Q	0006
TN-2SA733-Q-B	0006
TN2SA733-Q-B	0006
TN2SA733-R	0006
TN2SA733-R-A	0006
TN2SA733K	0006
TN2SA733P	0006
TN2SA733Q	0006
TN2SA733R	0006
TN2SA817Y	0431
TN2SA952L	0006
TN2SA953	1338
TN2SA953K	1338
TN2SA1175	3580
TN2SB810E	0527
TN2SB810H	0527
TN2SC495-R	0781
TN2SC945	0076
TN2SC945-Q	0076
TN2SC945-R	0076
TN2SC945K	0076
TN2SC945R	0076
TN2SC1449K	0161
TN2SC1507	0949
TN2SC1507-K	0949
TN2SC1507-K-A	0949
TN2SC1507-L	0949
TN2SC1507-L-A	0949
TN2SC1507-M	0949
TN2SC1507-M-A	0949
TN2SC1507L	0949
TN2SC1520-1	0168
TN2SC1520-1-1A	0168
TN2SC1520-K-1	0168
TN2SC1520-K-1A	0168
TN2SC1520-K-3A	0168
TN2SC1520-L-1	0168
TN2SC1520-L-1A	0168
TN2SC1520-L-3A	0168
TN2SC1520-M-1	0168
TN2SC1520-M-1A	0168
TN2SC1520-M-3A	0168
TN2SC1845	0525
TN2SC1941	1317
TN2SC1941-	0710
TN2SC1941-2SC1941	OEM
TN2SC2002	0945
TN2SC2002K	0945
TN2SC2002L	0945
TN2SC2785	0249
TN2SC2785E	0249
TN2SC2785H	0249
TN2SD471K	0018
TN2SD568K	0419
TN2SK68A	3308
TN3TB03001	0826
TN3TC03001	2307
TN3TC05001	0975
TN3TD03001	0892
TN7TB03001	0826
TN7TC03001	0881
TN7TC05001	3442
TN7TD03001	0892
TN10	0369
TN12	0344

DEVICE TYPE	REPL CODE
TN15	OEM
TN41A	0312
TN51	OEM
TN52	OEM
TN-53	0016
TN53	0016
TN-54	0016
TN54	0320
TN55	0016
TN56	0016
TN-59	0016
TN59	0016
TN-60	0016
TN60	0016
TN-61	0016
TN61	0016
TN-62	0016
TN62	0016
TN-63	0016
TN63	0016
TN-64	0016
TN64	0016
TN71	2526
TN72	2526
TN79	0590
TN80	0016
TN81	0590
TN237	0016
TN238	0016
TN301	OEM
TN302	OEM
TN303	OEM
TN304	OEM
TN421	0086
TN591	0004
TN2001	OEM
TN2001A	OEM
TN-3200	0007
TN3200	0007
TN3866	1344
TN-3903	0016
TN3903	0016
TN-3904	0016
TN3904	0016
TN-3905	2449
TN3905	0855
TN3906	0855
TN4338	OEM
TN4339	OEM
TNC61688	0396
TNC61689	0016
TNC61690	0037
TNC61702	0016
TNC61703	0037
TNF10	OEM
TNF12	OEM
TNF15	OEM
TNH11304	5823
TNH11304EZ	OEM
TNH11306	OEM
TNH11309	OEM
TNJ6I672(RECT)	0015
TNJ1034	0111
TNJ1036	0079
TNJ60063	0050
TNJ60064	0050
TNJ60065	0050
TNJ60066	1332
TNJ60067	0050
TNJ60068	0050
TNJ60069	0050
TNJ60069(2SC74)	0127
TNJ60070	0004
TNJ60071	0050
TNJ60072	0233
TNJ60073	0136
TNJ60074	0004
TNJ60075	0160
TNJ60076	0155
TNJ60077	0136
TNJ60078	0168
TNJ60079	0004
TNJ60080	0599
TNJ60279	0050
TNJ60280	0050
TNJ60281	0050
TNJ-60282	0004
TNJ60282	0004
TNJ60283	0004
TNJ-60362	0050
TNJ60362	0136
TNJ-60363	0050
TNJ60363	0136
TNJ-60364	0050
TNJ60364	0136
TNJ-60365	0050
TNJ60365	0004
TNJ60447	0127
TNJ60448	0127
TNJ60449	0127
TNJ60450	0050
TNJ60451	0178
TNJ60453	0178
TNJ60454	0160
TNJ60455	0074
TNJ60456	0050
TNJ60457	0918
TNJ-60604	0079
TNJ60604	0127

DEVICE TYPE	REPL CODE
TNJ-60605	0127
TNJ60605	0127
TNJ-60606	0079
TNJ60606	0127
TNJ-60607	0079
TNJ60607	0127
TNJ-60608	0050
TNJ60608	0279
TNJ-60610	0279
TNJ60610	0004
TNJ-60611	0279
TNJ60611	0004
TNJ-60612	0279
TNJ60612	0164
TNJ60728	0004
TNJ61217	0127
TNJ61218	0127
TNJ61219	0079
TNJ61220	0016
TNJ61221	0211
TNJ61222	0004
TNJ61223	0841
TNJ61282	0004
TNJ61671	0595
TNJ61671(2SC688)	0127
TNJ61671(2SD72)	0208
TNJ61672(2SK25)	0321
TNJ61673	0321
TNJ61673(2SB186)	0004
TNJ61673(2SK24)	0321
TNJ61674	0164
TNJ61679	0127
TNJ61730	0127
TNJ61731	0127
TNJ61734	0208
TNJ70450	0555
TNJ70478	0144
TNJ70478-1	0144
TNJ70479	0144
TNJ70479-1	0079
TNJ70480	0144
TNJ70481	0786
TNJ70482	0086
TNJ70483	0222
TNJ70484	0144
TNJ70537	0016
TNJ70539	0016
TNJ70540	0161
TNJ70541	0222
TNJ70634	0004
TNJ70635	0004
TNJ70637	0079
TNJ70638	1136
TNJ70639	0155
TNJ70640	0284
TNJ70641	0136
TNJ70688	0164
TNJ70691	0111
TNJ71034	0111
TNJ71035	0086
TNJ71036	0079
TNJ71037	0037
TNJ71143	0007
TNJ71173	0144
TNJ71234	0086
TNJ71248	0136
TNJ71252	0590
TNJ71271	0111
TNJ71277	0111
TNJ71498	0113
TNJ71629	0127
TNJ71773	0037
TNJ71774	0037
TNJ71937	0127
TNJ71963	0127
TNJ71964	0007
TNJ71965	0111
TNJ72146	0003
TNJ72147	0142
TNJ72148	0103
TNJ72149	0065
TNJ72150	0007
TNJ72151	0007
TNJ72152	0786
TNJ72153	0142
TNJ72154	0037
TNJ72275	0007
TNJ72276	0326
TNJ72277	0127
TNJ72278	0004
TNJ72279	0127
TNJ72280	0079
TNJ72281	0016
TNJ72282	0233
TNJ72283	0004
TNJ72284	0208
TNJ72285	0004
TNJ72286	0178
TNJ72287	0004
TNJ72288	0086
TNJ72289	0004
TNJ72318	0160
TNJ72319	0637
TNJ72320	0074
TNJ72368	0007
TNJ72701	0007
TNJ72774	1257
TNJ72775	0555
TNJ72783	0016

DEVICE TYPE	REPL CODE
TNJ72784	0016
TNP47C231AN4943	OEM
TNP47C634N2427Z	OEM
TNQ2621	OEM
TNQ2682	OEM
TNQ2682B	OEM
TNQ2683	OEM
TNT839	0144
TNT840	0144
TNT841	0144
TNT842	0016
TNT843	0144
TNT1131	OEM
TNT1132	OEM
TNV76601G2	OEM
TNYTD03001	0892
T0-003	0050
T0-004	0050
T0-005	0004
T0-012	0160
T0-014	0004
T0-015	0160
T0-033	0016
T0-038	0016
T0-039	0016
T0-040	0016
T0-041	0004
T01-101	0016
T01-104	0016
T01-105	0016
T0-36	OEM
T0-101	0279
T0101	0004
T0-102	0279
T0102	0004
T0-103	0004
T0103	0004
T0-104	0004
T0104	0004
T0507	OEM
T01007	OEM
T02007	OEM
T03007	OEM
T04007	OEM
T05007	OEM
T06007	OEM
TOAL113	OEM
TOAL116	OEM
TOAL223	OEM
TOAL226	OEM
TOTX172	OEM
TP0102N2	OEM
TP0102N3	OEM
TP0102ND	OEM
TP0104N2	OEM
TP0104N3	OEM
TP0104ND	OEM
TP0202N2	OEM
TP0202N3	OEM
TP0202ND	OEM
TP0204N2	OEM
TP0204N3	OEM
TP0204ND	OEM
TP0602N2	OEM
TP0602N3	OEM
TP0602ND	OEM
TP0604N2	OEM
TP0604N3	OEM
TP0604ND	OEM
TP0616N2	OEM
TP0616N3	OEM
TP0616N5	OEM
TP0616ND	OEM
TP0620N2	OEM
TP0620N3	OEM
TP0620N5	OEM
TP0620ND	OEM
TP1	OEM
TP2	OEM
TP3TC03001	3114
TP3TD06001	4067
TP5	OEM
TP7TC03001	1026
TP7TC05001	0698
TP7TD03002	4067
TP10	OEM
TP20	OEM
TP20-0284	0631
TP30	OEM
TP34	0143
TP34A	0143
TP40	OEM
TP100	0097
TP100R	2275
TP101	0015
TP107	0079
TP107A	0079
TP107B	0079
TP108	0079
TP108A	0079
TP108B	0079
TP108C	0079
TP109	0079
TP109A	0079
TP109B	0079
TP109C	0079
TP200	0097
TP200R	2275
TP201	0015

600 If replacement code is OEM, contact original manufacturer for replacement.

DEVICE TYPE	REPL CODE
TP251A	0037
TP252A	0037
TP253A	0037
TP300	0097
TP300R	0471
TP302	0015
TP400	0097
TP400R	0471
TP402	0015
TP504	OEM
TP506	OEM
TP551	OEM
TP1004	OEM
TP1006	OEM
TP2004	OEM
TP2006	OEM
TP3004	OEM
TP3006	OEM
TP3566	0079
TP3638	0037
TP3638A	0786
TP3644	0037
TP3645	0037
TP3702	0037
TP3703	0037
TP3704	0111
TP3705	0111
TP3706	0111
TP3707	0155
TP3708	0155
TP3709	0155
TP3710	0155
TP3711	0155
TP4000	2013
TP4001	0473
TP4001AN	0473
TP4001B	OEM
TP4001BN	0473
TP4001BP	0473
TP4002	2044
TP4002AN	2044
TP4004	OEM
TP4006	OEM
TP4007	2819
TP4007UBN	2819
TP4008AN	0982
TP4008BN	0982
TP4009	1988
TP4009UBN	0001
TP4010BN	0394
TP4011	0215
TP4011AN	0215
TP4011B	0215
TP4011BN	0215
TP4011BP	0215
TP4012	0493
TP4012AN	0493
TP4013	0409
TP4013AN	0409
TP4013B	OEM
TP4013BE	0409
TP4013BN	0409
TP4014AN	0854
TP4015	1008
TP4015AN	1008
TP4016	4087
TP4016A	0101
TP4016AN	1135
TP4016BN	1135
TP4016UBN	1135
TP4017	0508
TP4017AN	0508
TP4018AN	1381
TP4018BN	1381
TP4019	1517
TP4019AN	1517
TP4019BN	1517
TP4020	1651
TP4020AN	1651
TP4020BN	1651
TP4021	1738
TP4021AN	1738
TP4022AN	1247
TP4023	0515
TP4023AN	0515
TP4024	1946
TP4024AN	1946
TP4024BN	1946
TP4025	2061
TP4025AN	2061
TP4027	1938
TP4027AN	1938
TP4027BN	1938
TP4028AN	2213
TP4028BN	2213
TP4029AN	2218
TP4030AN	0495
TP4040	0056
TP4040AN	0056
TP4040B	OEM
TP4040BN	0056
TP4042	0121
TP4042AN	0121
TP4042BN	0121
TP4043AN	1544
TP4043BN	1544
TP4044AN	2292
TP4044BN	2292
TP4049	0001

DEVICE TYPE	REPL CODE
TP4049AN	0001
TP4049UBN	0001
TP4050	0394
TP4050AN	0394
TP4051	0362
TP4051BN	0362
TP4052	0024
TP4052BN	0024
TP4053BN	0034
TP4058	3477
TP4059	1401
TP4060	3477
TP4061	3477
TP4062	3477
TP4067-409	0015
TP4067-410	0111
TP4067-411	0111
TP4068BN	2482
TP4069UBN	0119
TP4069UPN	0119
TP4071BN	0129
TP4072BN	2502
TP4073BN	1528
TP4075BN	2518
TP4078BN	0915
TP4081	0621
TP4081BN	0621
TP4082BN	0297
TP4123	0016
TP4124	0016
TP4125	0037
TP4126	0037
TP4257	0037
TP4258	0037
TP4274	0595
TP4275	0144
TP4512	2108
TP4512AN	2108
TP4518	1037
TP4518AN	1037
TP4520AN	2650
TP4522AN	2810
TP5004	OEM
TP5006	OEM
TP5135	0079
TP5136	0079
TP5142	0037
TP6004	OEM
TP6006	OEM
TP8004	OEM
TP8006	OEM
TPA2	0023
TPA2006	OEM
TPA5000B	OEM
TPA5001A	OEM
TPA5004C	OEM
TPA5004F	OEM
TPD3004K	OEM
TPL1	OEM
TPL2	OEM
TPL3	OEM
TPL521-YG	OEM
TPLD3	OEM
TPLD3E	OEM
TPLD4	OEM
TPLD4E	OEM
TPM1	OEM
TPM2	OEM
TPM3	OEM
TPM4	OEM
TPMD4	OEM
TPMD5	OEM
TPMD6	OEM
TPND1	OEM
TPND2	OEM
TPND3	OEM
TPND4	OEM
TPQ2221	0539
TPQ2222	0539
TPQ2483	0539
TPQ2484	0539
TPQ2906	OEM
TPQ2907	OEM
TPQ2907A	OEM
TPQ3724	OEM
TPQ3725	OEM
TPQ3725A	OEM
TPQ3798	0281
TPQ3799	OEM
TPQ3904	0539
TPQ3906	OEM
TPQ4258	OEM
TPQ4354	OEM
TPQ5400	OEM
TPQ5401	OEM
TPQ5550	OEM
TPQ5551	OEM
TPQ6001	OEM
TPQ6002	OEM
TPQ6100	OEM
TPQ6100A	OEM
TPQ6501	OEM
TPQ6502	2976
TPQ6600	OEM
TPQ6600A	OEM
TPQ6700	OEM
TPQA05	OEM
TPQA06	OEM
TPQA55	OEM

DEVICE TYPE	REPL CODE
TPQA56	OEM
TPS20	OEM
TPS50	OEM
TPS98	0855
TPS603	OEM
TPS604	5031
TPS605	5032
TPS606	OEM
TPS606-C	OEM
TPS703	2604
TPS703A	OEM
TPS6512	0016
TPS6513	0016
TPS6514	0016
TPS6515	0016
TPS6516	0037
TPS6517	0037
TPS6518	0037
TPS6519	0037
TPS6520	0016
TPS6521	0016
TPS6522	0037
TPS6523	0037
TPYTD03002	4067
TQ1	0144
TQ2	0144
TQ3	0144
TQ4	0016
TQ5	0144
TQ6	0144
TQ6A	OEM
TQ7	0144
TQ8	0144
TQ9	0144
TQ53	0786
TQ53A	0037
TQ54	0786
TQ54A	0037
TQ55	0786
TQ56	0527
TQ57	0786
TQ58	0786
TQ-59	0037
TQ59	0786
TQ59A	0786
TQ-60	0037
TQ60	0786
TQ60A	0786
TQ-61	0037
TQ61	0037
TQ61A	0037
TQ-62	0037
TQ62	0037
TQ62A	0037
TQ-63	0037
TQ63	0126
TQ63A	0126
TQ-64	0037
TQ64	0126
TQ64A	0126
T-Q5019	0637
T-Q5020	0136
TQ5020	0279
TQ5020(SANYO)	0196
T-Q5021	0136
TQ5021	0050
T-Q5022	0136
TQ5022	0050
T-Q5023	0628
TQ5023	0004
T-Q5025	0164
TQ5025	0004
T-Q5026	0004
TQ5026	0004
T-Q5027	0004
TQ5027	0211
T-Q5028	0160
TQ5028	0004
T-Q5030	1665
TQ5030	0599
T-Q5031	0208
TQ5031	0595
T-Q5032	0233
TQ-5032	2839
TQ5032	0595
T-Q5034	0050
TQ-5034	0050
TQ5034	0050
T-Q5035	0050
TQ5035	0050
T-Q5036	0160
TQ5036	0160
T-Q5038	0050
TQ5038	0050
T-Q5039	0208
TQ5039	0595
TQ-5044	2839
TQ5044	0208
T-Q5049	0007
TQ5049	0144
T-Q5050	0208
TQ-5050	2839
TQ5050	0208
TQ-5051	0164
TQ5051	0004
TQ-5052	0079
TQ5052	0079
T-Q5053	0079
TQ-5053	0079

DEVICE TYPE	REPL CODE
TQ5053	0079
T-Q5053C	0079
TQ-5054	0079
TQ5054	0079
T-Q5055	0144
TQ-5055	0086
TQ5055	0086
T-Q5057	0142
TQ-5060	0079
TQ5060	0079
TQ-5061	0164
TQ5061	0004
TQ-5062	2839
TQ5062	0208
TQ-5062(NPN	0038
T-Q5063	0086
TQ-5063	0283
TQ5063	0233
TQ-5064	0160
TQ5064	0160
T-Q5071	0007
T-Q5073	0016
T-Q5075	0142
T-Q5077	0037
T-Q5078	0326
T-Q5079	0127
T-Q5080	0178
T-Q5081	0086
TQ5081	0086
T-Q5082	0233
T-Q5083	0003
T-Q5084	0065
T-Q5086	0007
T-Q5087	0037
T-Q5093	0111
T-Q5099	0086
T-Q5104	0142
T-Q5105	0103
T-Q5106	0127
T-Q7037	0872
TQ7037	0872
T-Q7038	0872
TQ7038	0872
TR0055	0037
TR0-1064-5	2422
TR0-1064-6	2422
TR0-1064-7	2422
TR0-1064-8	2422
TR0-2012	0050
TR0-2028-5	1190
TR0-2064-5	2415
TR0-2064-6	2415
TR0-2064-7	2415
TR0-2064-8	2415
TR0-9022	2834
TR-01	0160
TR01	0085
TR-01(PENNCREST)	0086
TR-01B	0144
TR-01B(PENNCREST)	0016
TR-01C	0160
TR01C	0160
TR-01C(PENNCREST)	0016
TR-01E	0086
TR-01E(PENNCREST)	0086
TR-01MP	0085
TR01MP	0085
TR-02	0085
TR02	0160
TR02C	0160
TR-02E	0015
TR-03	0435
TR03	0435
TR03C	0435
TR-04	0004
TR04	0211
TR04C	0004
TR-04C(PENNCREST)	0126
TR-05	0279
TR05	0211
TR05C	0279
TR-06	0279
TR06	0050
TR-06(PENNCREST)	0016
TR06C	0050
TR-07	0050
TR07	0595
TR-07(PENNCREST)	0086
TR07C	0279
TR-08	0595
TR08	0595
TR-08(PENNCREST)	0126
TR-08C	0595
TR-09	0595
TR09	0038
TR-09C	0595
TR09C	0595
TR0140A	OEM
TR0140B	OEM
TR0140D	OEM
TR0140M	OEM
TR0141A	OEM
TR0141B	OEM
TR0141D	OEM
TR0141M	OEM
TR0142A	OEM
TR0142B	OEM
TR0142D	OEM
TR0142M	OEM

DEVICE TYPE	REPL CODE
TR0146A	OEM
TR0146B	OEM
TR0146D	OEM
TR0146M	OEM
TR0911	0438
TR01014	0111
TR01015	0079
TR01026	0144
TR01027	OEM
TR01037	0086
TR01040	0111
TR01042	0007
TR01045	0161
TR01051-5	6506
TR01053-1	0037
TR01054-1	3392
TR01054-5	OEM
TR01054-7	0086
TR01056-5	0161
TR01057-1	OEM
TR01057-3	0161
TR01059-5	OEM
TR01062-1	0086
TR01062-7	0018
TR01065	0208
TR01073	0079
TR01074	0079
TR02012	0136
TR02020-2	0037
TR02051-1	0037
TR02051-5	0037
TR02051-6	0037
TR02053-5	0378
TR02053-7	0378
TR02054-1	3079
TR02054-7	0126
TR02057-1	OEM
TR02057-3	0455
TR02059-5	OEM
TR02062-1	0037
TR02062-6	0037
TR02063-1	0136
TR02063-8	0037
TR06011	0321
TR06014	0321
TR08004	0212
TR09004	0649
TR09005	0627
TR09006	0627
TR09007	3189
TR09008	2089
TR09009	2089
TR09010	0780
TR09011	0438
TR09018	2728
TR09019	0514
TR09022	2834
TR09023	2834
TR09024	2834
TR010602-1	0144
TR0573486	0151
TR0573491	0076
TR0573507	0151
TR0575002	0123
TR0575005	0123
TR1	OEM
TR1AC	0588
TR1N4002	0080
TR-1R26	0050
TR1R26	0050
TR-1R31	0144
TR-1R33	0079
TR-1R35	0144
TR2	OEM
TR2A	0015
TR2N2614C	0004
TR-2R26	0050
TR2R26	0050
TR-2R31	0144
TR-2R33	0144
TR-2R35	0144
TR2S1570LH	0111
TR2SA763	0688
TR-2SC367	0284
TR-2SC371	0191
TR-2SC372	0076
TR-2SC373	0076
TR2SC373	0076
TR-2SC384	0127
TR-2SC482	1583
TR2SC535	0127
TR-2SC735	0191
TR2SC1342	0127
TR2SC1570LH	0111
TR2SD330E	1597
TR-2SK55	6457
TR2SK55	0321
TR-3	0160
TR3	OEM
TR-3R26	0050
TR3R26	0050
TR-3R31	0144
TR-3R33	0144
TR-3R35	0144
TR-3R38	0016
TR4	OEM
TR-4R26	0050
TR4R26	0050
TR-4R31	0086

DEVICE TYPE	REPL CODE
TR-4R33	0016
TR-4R35	0144
TR-4R38	0037
TR4S	0036
TR5	0160
TR-5R26	0004
TR5R26	0211
TR-5R31	0086
TR-5R33	0016
TR-5R35	0016
TR-5R38	0016
TR5S	0140
TR6	OEM
TR-6R26	0004
TR6R26	0211
TR-6R33	0016
TR-6R35	0037
TR6S	0091
TR7	OEM
TR-7GS	0644
TR-7R31	0086
TR-7R35	0016
TR7S	0062
TR-7SA	0644
TR7SA	0062
TR-7SB	0137
TR7SB	0025
TR8	OEM
TR-8R35	0016
TR9	OEM
TR-9GS	0012
T-R9S	0012
TR-9S	0012
TR9S	0057
TR-9SA	0012
TR-9SB	0012
TR9SB	0012
TR-10	0595
TR10	0595
TR-10C	0595
TR-11	0136
TR11	0279
TR-11C	0050
TR11E	OEM
TR-12	0050
TR12	0050
TR-12C	0050
TR12EBM	0052
TR12S	0053
TR12SA	0052
TR12SB	0053
TR12SC	0873
TR12.5	OEM
TR12.75	OEM
TR-13	0050
TR13	0050
TR-13C	0050
TR-14	0004
TR14	0004
TR-14C	0004
TR-15	0004
TR15	0004
TR-15C	0004
TR-16	0085
TR16	0969
TR-16C	0085
TR16C	0160
TR16H	OEM
TR16X2	3004
TR-17	0050
TR17	0050
TR-17A	0050
TR-17C	0050
TR-18	0050
TR18	0050
TR-18C	0050
TR18E	OEM
TR-19	0037
TR19	0037
TR-20	0037
TR20	0037
TR-20A	0037
TR-21	0016
TR21	0016
TR-21C	0079
TR21R	0181
TR-22	0079
TR22	0126
TR-22C	0079
TR22E	OEM
TR-23	0142
TR23	0086
TR23A	0126
TR-24	0144
TR24	0144
TR-24(PHILCO)	0079
TR-25	0086
TR25	0086
TR-26	0103
TR26	0103
TR-27	0969
TR27	0969
TR-28	0126
TR28	0037
TR-29	0486
TR-30	0037
TR30	0037
TR-30A	0037
TR-31	0037

DEVICE TYPE	REPL CODE
TR31	0037
TR-31(IR)	0855
TR-32	0855
TR32	0855
TR-33	0018
TR33	0111
TR-34	0969
TR34	0969
TR-35	0599
TR35	0599
TR-36	0130
TR36	0130
TR36(IR)	0130
TR-36MP	0130
TR-36MP(IR)	0130
TR-37	0899
TR38	0144
TR43	0004
TR43A	0164
TR-43B	0160
TR44	0004
TR45	0004
TR-50	0222
TR50	0222
TR50R	0267
TR-51	0079
TR51	0050
TR-52	0527
TR52	0050
TR52(IR)	0050
TR-53	0086
TR53	0279
TR53R	0267
TR-54	0527
TR54	0004
TR-55	0555
TR55	0279
TR-55(IR)	0219
TR-56	1257
TR56	0085
TR-56(IR)	1421
TR56(IR)	1421
TR-57	0178
TR57	0435
TR-58	0848
TR58	0899
TR-59	0103
TR59	0103
TR-60	0187
TR60	0187
TR60-2	0315
TR-61	0074
TR61	0074
TR-61MP	0074
TR-62	0079
TR62	0050
TR-63	0626
TR63	0136
TR-64	0626
TR64	0279
TR-65	0693
TR65	0279
TR-66	2156
TR-67	0637
TR67	0065
TR67(IR)	0637
TR-68	0065
TR68	0074
TR68(IR)	0003
TR-69	0396
TR69	0396
TR-69(IR)	0396
TR69(IR)	0396
TR-70	0224
TR70	0224
TR71	0004
TR71(IR)	0004
TR-72	0264
TR72	0004
TR-73	0378
TR-73(IR)	0378
TR73(IR)	0378
TR-74	0264
TR-75	0137
TR75	0137
TR-76	0161
TR76	0161
TR-76(IR)	0042
TR76(IR)	0042
TR-77	0015
TR77	0050
TR-77(IR)	0919
TR77(IR)	0919
TR-77(XSTR)	0455
TR-78	0283
TR-78(IR)	0283
TR78(IR)	0283
TR-79	0283
TR79	0283
TR-79(IR)	0283
TR79(IR)	0283
TR-80	0144
TR80	0144
TR-81	0178
TR81	0004
TR-81MP	0178
TR-82	0841
TR82	0841
TR-83	0144

If replacement code is OEM, contact original manufacturer for replacement.

601

DEVICE TYPE	REPL CODE
TR83	0144
TR-84	0164
TR84	0164
TR-84(IR)	0164
TR84(IR)	0164
TR-85	0164
TR85	0164
TR-86	0079
TR86	0079
TR-87	0086
TR87	0050
TR-88	0126
TR88	0050
TR-91	2736
TR91(IR)	2736
TR-92	0830
TR-92(IR)	0830
TR92(IR)	0830
TR92-1	4381
TR92-2	4381
TR92-3	4381
TR92-4	4381
TR92-5	4382
TR92-6	4382
TR-93	0065
TR93	0065
TR93-1	4381
TR93-2	4381
TR93-3	4381
TR93-4	4381
TR93-5	4382
TR93-6	4382
TR94-1	4381
TR94-2	4381
TR94-3	4381
TR94-4	4381
TR94-5	4382
TR94-6	4382
TR-94MP	0816
TR94MP	0816
TR-95	0012
TR95	0007
TR-95(B)	0012
TR-95(IR)	0007
TR-95(XSTR)	0007
TR-95B	0012
TR100	2873
TR100A	OEM
TR100R	0267
TR103	2813
TR103R	0267
TR104	0279
TR105	0050
TR106A41#	OEM
TR109	0279
TR123	0050
TR125	0002
TR125B	0002
TR136A	0550
TR136B	0550
TR136D	0550
TR136M	0550
TR139	0050
TR147A	0550
TR147B	0550
TR147D	0550
TR147M	0550
TR150	2872
TR150A	OEM
TR150R	0267
TR151	1116
TR151R	0267
TR152	0865
TR152R	0267
TR153	2813
TR153R	0267
TR-157(OLSON)	0164
TR-158(OLSON)	0164
TR-159(OLSON)	0595
TR-160(OLSON)	0595
TR-161(OLSON)	0050
TR-162(OLSON)	0016
TR-163(OLSON)	0144
TR-164(OLSON)	0086
TR-165(OLSON)	0126
TR-166(OLSON)	0050
TR167	0595
TR-167(OLSON)	0037
TR-168(OLSON)	0136
TR-169(OLSON)	0004
TR-170(OLSON)	0164
TR-171	0007
TR-172(OLSON)	0085
TR-174(OLSON)	0435
TR-175(OLSON)	0142
TR-176(OLSON)	0130
TR-178(OLSON)	0160
TR-180(OLSON)	0178
TR182	0595
TR-182(OLSON)	0455
TR183	0595
TR-183(OLSON)	0969
TR184	0595
TR-184(OLSON)	0222
TR-185(OLSON)	0327
TR-186(OLSON)	0074
TR-187(OLSON)	0637
TR-188(OLSON)	0178
TR193	0595

DEVICE TYPE	REPL CODE
TR194	0595
TR200	1116
TR200R	0267
TR203	2813
TR203R	0267
TR209T2	1075
TR211	0595
TR212	0595
TR213	0595
TR214	0595
TR215	0279
TR216	0595
TR217	0279
TR218	0050
TR251	0800
TR251R	0267
TR252	0800
TR252R	0267
TR253	0800
TR253R	0267
TR262-2	0142
TR266-2	0142
TR269	0050
TR271TR26	0103
TR300	0800
TR300R	0267
TR301	0233
TR301R	0267
TR302	0016
TR302R	0267
TR303	2823
TR303R	0267
TR320	0211
TR320A	0211
TR321	0211
TR321(HFGH1)	0279
TR321A	0211
TR322	OEM
TR323	0211
TR323A	0211
TR324	OEM
TR325	OEM
TR326	OEM
TR331	0050
TR332	0211
TR333	0160
TR334	0435
TR335	0595
TR336	0595
TR337	0595
TR338	0038
TR351	0800
TR351R	0267
TR352	0800
TR352R	0267
TR353	2823
TR353R	0267
TR381	0164
TR382	0164
TR383	0211
TR383(HGFH-2)	0211
TR400	0800
TR400R	0267
TR401	0800
TR401R	0267
TR402	0800
TR402R	0267
TR403	2823
TR403R	0267
TR460	0164
TR461	0164
TR482	0279
TR482A	0279
TR500	0315
TR500R	0267
TR501	1576
TR501R	0267
TR502	1186
TR502R	0267
TR503	0315
TR503R	0267
TR506	OEM
TR508	0211
TR508A	0211
TR515	OEM
TR515S	OEM
TR560	OEM
TR563	OEM
TR600	0315
TR600R	0267
TR601	0016
TR601R	0267
TR602	0315
TR602R	0267
TR603	0315
TR603R	0267
TR650	0211
TR650A	0004
TR653	0211
TR701	0045
TR701R	0280
TR702	0045
TR702R	0280
TR721	0211
TR722	0211
TR758A	0279
TR759	0279
TR760	0279
TR761	0136

DEVICE TYPE	REPL CODE
TR762	0136
TR763	0211
TR763A	0004
TR764	0279
TR792	0279
TR800	0045
TR800R	0280
TR801	0279
TR801R	0280
TR802	0279
TR802R	0280
TR803	0050
TR1000	0126
TR-1000-2	0037
TR-1000-3	0086
TR-1000-7	0103
TR-1001	OEM
TR1001	0086
TR1001-2	0855
TR1002	0126
TR1003	0086
TR1004	0126
TR1005	0086
TR1007	0103
TR1009	0074
TR1009A	0130
TR1010	4771
TR1011	0079
TR1012	0126
TR1015	OEM
TR1015S	OEM
TR1025	0103
TR1030	0037
TR-1030-1	0037
TR1030-1	0037
TR-1030-2	0037
TR1030-2	0037
TR1031	0079
TR-1031-1	0155
TR1031-1	0855
TR-1031-2	0155
TR1031-2	0855
TR1032	0037
TR-1032-1	0150
TR1032-1	0037
TR-1032-2	0037
TR1033	0016
TR-1033-1	0016
TR1033-1	0264
TR-1033-2	0016
TR-1033-3	0016
TR1033-3	0016
TR1033-4	0264
TR1033-5	0264
TR1033-6	0264
TR1034	0037
TR-1035-3	OEM
TR1036	0599
TR-1036-1	1190
TR-1036-2	1190
TR1036-2	1190
TR-1036-3	1257
TR1036-3	1190
TR-1037-1	0556
TR1037-1	1190
TR-1037-2	0556
TR1037-2	0556
TR-1037-3	0555
TR1037-3	0556
TR1038	0599
TR-1038-4	1671
TR1038-4	0486
TR1038-5	2002
TR1038-6	1190
TR-1039-4	0103
TR1039-4	0103
TR1039-5	0177
TR1039-6	0103
TR1077	0103
TR1110	OEM
TR1120	0084
TR1120R	2275
TR1121	0090
TR1121R	2275
TR1122	0097
TR1122R	2275
TR1123	0109
TR1123R	0471
TR1124	0109
TR1124R	0471
TR1125	0122
TR1125R	0471
TR1126	0122
TR1126R	0471
TR1128	0131
TR1128R	0444
TR1130	0145
TR1130R	0444
TR1210	OEM
TR1402A	OEM
TR1402B	OEM
TR1490	0103
TR1491	0103
TR1492	0103
TR1493	0103
TR1512-80	0144
TR1591	0178
TR1593	0178
TR1602A	4361

DEVICE TYPE	REPL CODE
TR1602B	OEM
TR1605LP	0142
TR1863A	OEM
TR1863B	OEM
TR1865-PL	OEM
TR1865A	OEM
TR1865B	OEM
TR1983E	OEM
TR1983F	OEM
TR1993-2	0016
TR2007	OEM
TR2015	OEM
TR2015S	OEM
TR2083-40	0030
TR2083-41	0143
TR2083-42	0133
TR2083-44	0133
TR2083-70	0321
TR2083-71	0079
TR2083-72	0079
TR2083-73	0079
TR2083-74	0007
TR2083-75	0211
TR2880	0015
TR3015	OEM
TR3015S	OEM
TR4010-2	0016
TR4015	OEM
TR4015S	OEM
TR4083-23273	1611
TR4083-2327311	1611
TR4083-2327312	1611
TR5015	OEM
TR5528	0321
TR6010	0720
TR6015	OEM
TR7010	0674
TR7015	OEM
TR-8001	0050
TR8001	0050
TR-8002	0050
TR8002	0050
TR-8003	0050
TR8003	0050
TR-8004	0079
TR8004	0144
TR-8004-4	0144
TR8004-4	0079
TR-8004-5	0144
TR-8005	0142
TR8005	0142
TR-8006	0160
TR8006	0160
TR-8007	0037
TR8007	0211
TR-8007(FISHER)	0037
TR-8010	0127
TR8010	0079
TR-8014	0016
TR8014	0016
TR8015	2503
TR-8018	0130
TR8018	0130
TR-8019	0919
TR8019	0919
TR-8020	0126
TR8020	0037
TR-8021	0086
TR8021	0016
TR-8022	0264
TR8022	0264
TR-8023	0086
TR8023	0264
TR-8024	0086
TR8024	0264
TR-8025	0079
TR8025	0079
TR-8026	0037
TR-8027	0321
TR8027	0321
TR-8028	0144
TR8028	0016
TR-8029	0144
TR8029	0016
TR-8030	0144
TR8030	0016
TR-8031	0144
TR8031	0016
TR-8032	0144
TR-8034	0111
TR8034	0079
TR-8035	0079
TR8035	0079
TR-8036	0086
TR8036	0086
TR-8037	0037
TR8037	0126
TR-8038	0144
TR8038	0079
TR-8039	0079
TR8039	0079
TR-8040	0111
TR8040	0079
TR-8042	0016
TR8042	0144
TR-8043	0127
TR8043	0016
TR8053	0016
TR8330	0079

DEVICE TYPE	REPL CODE
TR9010	0674
TR9100	0016
TR-9100-18	0016
TR10076B	OEM
TR10076C	OEM
TR12001-4	0143
TR14001-1	0398
TR-14001-2	0247
TR-14001-4	0262
TR14002-6	0137
TR-14002-10	0039
TR14002-12	0002
TR14002-13	0526
TR19001	OEM
TR35144	0160
TR35524	0160
TR36643	0086
TR38117	0004
TR39453	0349
TR40603	0349
TR310011	0004
TR310012	0004
TR310015	0279
TR310017	0004
TR310018	0004
TR310019	0050
TR310025	0050
TR310026	0004
TR310065	0050
TR310068	0050
TR310069	0050
TR310075	0004
TR310107	0004
TR310123	0050
TR310125	0004
TR310136	0004
TR310139	0050
TR310147	0050
TR310150	0050
TR310153	0004
TR310155	0050
TR310156	0050
TR310157	0050
TR310158	0050
TR310159	0004
TR310160	0208
TR310161	0279
TR310164	0004
TR310224	0050
TR310225	0211
TR310230	0144
TR310231	0016
TR310232	0050
TR310235	0004
TR310236	0208
TR310243	0016
TR310244	0144
TR310245	0016
TR310249	0144
TR310250	0144
TR310251	0004
TR310252	0004
TR310255	0004
TR320007	0123
TR320008	0143
TR320020	0015
TR320022	0015
TR320039	0143
TR320041	0143
TR320048	0143
TR330027	0015
TR330028	0170
TR2320063	0076
TR2327031	0023
TR2327041	0023
TR2327203	0042
TR2327293	0191
TR2327312	1611
TR2327333	0191
TR2327363	0547
TR2327393	0016
TR2327411	4490
TR2327422	0438
TR2327431	0410
TR2327443	0547
TR2327444	0547
TR2327574	2766
TR2327603	0558
TR2327607	0558
TR2327723	0919
TR2327733	0062
TR2327743	0688
TR2327841	3459
TR2327852	1139
TR2337011	0133
TR2337063	0560
TR2337101	0052
TR2337103	0052
TR2337123	0091
TR2347041	0139
TR2367151	4480
TR2367161	4463
TR2367171	0514
TR3100227	0211
TR5320326	0127
TR10000102	OEM
TR20000014	OEM
TR20000040	OEM
TR30000467	OEM

DEVICE TYPE	REPL CODE
TR40000021	OEM
TR40000094	OEM
TR22873700104	0438
TR228723002003	OEM
TR228735045311	0144
TR228735046011	0127
TR228735048617	0144
TR228735048618	0144
TR228735120325	0321
TR228736002003	0143
TR228736002004	0123
TR228736003026	0170
TR228779905696	0574
TRA05	OEM
TRA05D	OEM
TRA1	OEM
TRA1D	OEM
TRA-2	0136
TRA2	0628
TRA2D	OEM
TRA3	OEM
TRA3D	OEM
TRA-4	0016
TRA4	0016
TRA-4A	0016
TRA4A	0016
TRA-4B	0076
TRA4B	0016
TRA4D	OEM
TRA-7R	0160
TRA7R	0160
TRA-7RM	0160
TRA-8R	0160
TRA8R	0160
TRA9LC1013	OEM
TRA-9R	0076
TRA9R	0016
TRA-10R	0050
TRA10R	0050
TRA11	1641
TRA11D	1641
TRA-11R	0136
TRA11R	0050
TRA12	1641
TRA12D	0740
TRA-12R	0136
TRA12R	0050
TRA13	OEM
TRA13D	OEM
TRA14	1641
TRA14D	1574
TRA21	OEM
TRA21D	OEM
TRA-22	0136
TRA22	0628
TRA-22A	0136
TRA22A	0050
TRA-22B	0050
TRA22B	0050
TRA22D	OEM
TRA-23	0136
TRA23	0050
TRA-23A	0136
TRA23A	0050
TRA-23B	0136
TRA23B	0050
TRA23D	OEM
TRA-24	0136
TRA24	0050
TRA-24A	0136
TRA24A	0050
TRA-24B	0136
TRA24D	OEM
TRA32	0004
TRA33	0004
TRA34	0016
TRA36	0016
TRA71	1641
TRA71D	2430
TRA72	1641
TRA72D	0430
TRA73	OEM
TRA73D	OEM
TRA74	1574
TRA74D	1478
TRA75	OEM
TRA75D	OEM
TRA76	OEM
TRA76D	OEM
TRA105	1641
TRA105D	2497
TRA205	OEM
TRA205D	OEM
TRA516DFX	OEM
TRA516DFZ	OEM
TRA705	1641
TRA705D	2430
TRA1016DFX	OEM
TRA1016DFZ	OEM
TRA2016DFX	OEM
TRA2016DFZ	OEM
TRA3016DFX	OEM
TRA3016DFZ	OEM
TRA4016DFX	OEM
TRA4016DFZ	OEM
TRA5016DFX	OEM
TRA5016DFZ	OEM
TRA6016DFX	OEM
TRA6016DFZ	OEM

DEVICE TYPE	REPL CODE
TRAL110	OEM
TRAL110D	OEM
TRAL116	OEM
TRAL116D	OEM
TRAL220	OEM
TRAL220D	OEM
TRAL226	OEM
TRAL226D	OEM
TRAL610D	OEM
TRAL615D	OEM
TRAL625D	OEM
TRAL630D	OEM
TRAL640D	OEM
TRAL1025D	OEM
TRAL1110	OEM
TRAL1110D	OEM
TRAL1115	OEM
TRAL1115D	0154
TRAL1125D	2004
TRAL1130D	OEM
TRAL1135D	2004
TRAL1225D	OEM
TRAL2210	OEM
TRAL2210D	OEM
TRAL2215	OEM
TRAL2215D	0147
TRAL2225D	2006
TRAL2230D	OEM
TRAL2235D	2006
TRAL3810D	OEM
TRAL3815D	OEM
TRAL3825D	OEM
TRAL3830D	OEM
TRAL3835D	OEM
TRANSMITTER	OEM
TRAPLC711	0016
TRAPLC871	0016
TRAPLC1013	0555
TR-BC147B	0016
TRBC147B	0016
TR-BC149C	0111
TRC15-050A	OEM
TRC15-050B	OEM
TR-C44	0279
TRC44	0279
TR-C44A	0279
TRC44A	0279
TR-C45	0211
TRC45	0279
TR-C45A	0279
TRC45A	0279
TR-C70	0211
TRC70	0211
TR-C71	0211
TRC71	0211
TR-C72	0211
TRC72	0211
TRC-P4	0196
TRDV125	OEM
TRDV225	OEM
TRDV425	OEM
TRDV625	OEM
TRDV825	OEM
TRDV1025	OEM
TRDV1226	OEM
TRF401	OEM
TRF450	OEM
TRF450A	OEM
TRF454	OEM
TRF454A	OEM
TRF641	OEM
TRF644	OEM
TRF646	OEM
TRF648	OEM
TR-FE100	0321
TRG-103	OEM
TRHA1151	3606
TR-I1835E	OEM
TRL104LED	5024
TRL2255	OEM
TRLA1230	2474
TRLA3350	0412
TRLP2004	0434
TRLP3034S	OEM
TRM13	0050
TRM14	0050
TRM15	0279
TRM16	0136
TRM17	0136
TRM21	0279
TRM34	0164
TRM81	0050
TRM1201	OEM
TRM-1202	OEM
TRM-1203	OEM
TRM-1204	OEM
TRM-1205	OEM
TRM1205	OEM
TRM-1206	OEM
TRM1206	OEM
TRM-1207	OEM
TRM-1208	OEM
TRM-1209	OEM
TRM1212	OEM
TRO2E	OEM
TRO5E	OEM
TRO1015	OEM
TRO1026	0079
TRO1027	OEM

If replacement code is OEM, contact original manufacturer for replacement.

DEVICE TYPE	REPL CODE
TRO1037	0111
TRO1042	0007
TRO1045	OEM
TRO1047	OEM
TRO1048	OEM
TRO1051-5	0079
TRO1053-1	0150
TRO1053-6	OEM
TRO1054-1	0086
TRO1054-7	OEM
TRO1056-5	OEM
TRO1064-9	OEM
TRO1065	OEM
TRO1073	OEM
TRO1074	OEM
TRO2012	OEM
TRO2020-2	OEM
TRO2047	OEM
TRO2051-1	0150
TRO2054-1	0126
TRO2062-1	0150
TRO2063-8	OEM
TRO2064-9	OEM
TRO6011	0321
TRO6014	OEM
TRO6015	OEM
TRO8004	OEM
TRO-9004	0649
TRO9004	0649
TRO-9005	0627
TRO9005	0627
TRO-9006	0627
TRO9006	0627
TRO-9011	0438
TRO9018	2474
TRO9023	OEM
TRO9024	2834
TRO9027	OEM
TRO9032	4003
TRO9033	OEM
TRO9034	OEM
TRO9035	OEM
TRO10602-1	0079
TRPLC711	0111
TRPW5B0M050A	OEM
TRR6	0631
TR-RR38	0016
TRS02101D09A	OEM
TRS02101D09B	OEM
TRS02101D09W	OEM
TRS02101D09X	OEM
TRS02101D09Y	OEM
TRS02101D09Z	OEM
TRS02102D09A	OEM
TRS02102D09B	OEM
TRS02102D09Q	OEM
TRS02102D09W	OEM
TRS02102D09X	OEM
TRS02102D09Y	OEM
TRS02102D09Z	OEM
TRS02104D09A	OEM
TRS02104D09Q	OEM
TRS02104D09W	OEM
TRS02104D09X	OEM
TRS02104D09Z	OEM
TRS02106D09A	OEM
TRS02106D09Q	OEM
TRS02106D09W	OEM
TRS02106D09X	OEM
TRS02106D09Z	OEM
TRS02108D09A	OEM
TRS02108D09W	OEM
TRS02108D09X	OEM
TRS02108D09Z	OEM
TRS02110D09A	OEM
TRS02110D09W	OEM
TRS02110D09X	OEM
TRS02110D09Z	OEM
TRS02112D09A	OEM
TRS02112D09X	OEM
TRS02112D09Z	OEM
TRS02114D09Z	OEM
TRS02301D09Y	OEM
TRS02302D09A	OEM
TRS02302D09Q	OEM
TRS02302D09W	OEM
TRS02302D09X	OEM
TRS02302D09Z	OEM
TRS02304D09A	OEM
TRS02304D09Q	OEM
TRS02304D09W	OEM
TRS02304D09X	OEM
TRS02304D09Z	OEM
TRS02306D09A	OEM
TRS02306D09Q	OEM
TRS02306D09W	OEM
TRS02306D09X	OEM
TRS02306D09Z	OEM
TRS02308D09A	OEM
TRS02308D09W	OEM
TRS02308D09X	OEM
TRS02308D09Z	OEM
TRS02312D09Z	OEM
TRS02602D09A	OEM
TRS02602D09Q	OEM
TRS02602D09W	OEM
TRS02602D09X	OEM
TRS02602D09Z	OEM
TRS02604D09A	OEM
TRS02604D09Q	OEM
TRS02604D09W	OEM
TRS02604D09X	OEM
TRS02604D09Z	OEM
TRS02606D09A	OEM
TRS02606D09Q	OEM
TRS02606D09W	OEM
TRS02606D09X	OEM
TRS02606D09Y	OEM
TRS02606D09Z	OEM
TRS02608D09A	OEM
TRS02608D09W	OEM
TRS02608D09Z	OEM
TRS02610D09A	OEM
TRS02610D09X	OEM
TRS02610D09Z	OEM
TRS02612D09Z	OEM
TRS03802D13A	OEM
TRS03802D13B	OEM
TRS03802D13W	OEM
TRS03802D13X	OEM
TRS03802D13Y	OEM
TRS03804D13A	OEM
TRS03804D13B	OEM
TRS03804D13Q	OEM
TRS03804D13W	OEM
TRS03804D13X	OEM
TRS03804D13Y	OEM
TRS03806D13A	OEM
TRS03806D13W	OEM
TRS03806D13X	OEM
TRS03806D13Y	OEM
TRS03808D13A	OEM
TRS03808D13W	OEM
TRS03808D13X	OEM
TRS03808D13Y	OEM
TRS03810D13A	OEM
TRS03810D13B	OEM
TRS03810D13X	OEM
TRS03810D13Y	OEM
TRS03812D13B	OEM
TRS04002D13A	OEM
TRS04002D13B	OEM
TRS04002D13Q	OEM
TRS04002D13W	OEM
TRS04002D13X	OEM
TRS04002D13Y	OEM
TRS04004D13A	OEM
TRS04004D13Q	OEM
TRS04004D13W	OEM
TRS04004D13X	OEM
TRS04006D13A	OEM
TRS04006D13B	OEM
TRS04006D13Q	OEM
TRS04006D13W	OEM
TRS04006D13X	OEM
TRS04006D13Y	OEM
TRS04008D13A	OEM
TRS04008D13B	OEM
TRS04008D13W	OEM
TRS04008D13X	OEM
TRS04008D13Y	OEM
TRS04010D13A	OEM
TRS04010D13B	OEM
TRS04010D13X	OEM
TRS04010D13Y	OEM
TRS04012D13B	OEM
TRS04302D13A	OEM
TRS04302D13Q	OEM
TRS04306D13Y	OEM
TRS04308D13X	OEM
TRS04310D13Z	OEM
TRS06602D17B	OEM
TRS06610D17B	OEM
TRS06610D17Y	OEM
TRS06610D17Z	OEM
TRS06612D17B	OEM
TRS06612D17Y	OEM
TRS06612D17Z	OEM
TRS06614D17B	OEM
TRS06614D17Y	OEM
TRS06614D17Z	OEM
TRS15X5	OEM
TRS25X	0168
TRS30X	0168
TRS35X	0168
TRS100	0233
TRS100A	0233
TRS100HC	0617
TRS101	0233
TRS120	0233
TRS125HC	0617
TRS140	0233
TRS140HP	0283
TRS140MP	0168
TRS160	0233
TRS160HP	0283
TRS160MP	0168
TRS180	0233
TRS180HP	0283
TRS180MP	0168
TRS200	0233
TRS200HP	0283
TRS200MP	0168
TRS225	0233
TRS225HP	0283
TRS225MP	0168
TRS250	0233
TRS250HP	0283
TRS250MP	0168
TRS275	0233
TRS275HP	0283
TRS275MP	0168
TRS301	0233
TRS301HP	0283
TRS301LC	0168
TRS301MP	0168
TRS325	0710
TRS325HP	0283
TRS325MP	0168
TRS350	0187
TRS350HP	0187
TRS350MP	0187
TRS375	0187
TRS375HP	0187
TRS375MP	0187
TRS401	0187
TRS401HP	0187
TRS401LC	0187
TRS401MP	0187
TRS425	0187
TRS425HP	0187
TRS425MP	0187
TRS450	0187
TRS451	0187
TRS451MP	0168
TRS475	0168
TRS475MP	0168
TRS501	0168
TRS501C	OEM
TRS501LC	0168
TRS501MP	0168
TRS525	0168
TRS525MP	0168
TRS550	0168
TRS550MP	0168
TRS1004	0264
TRS1004LP	0264
TRS1005	0142
TRS1005LP	0142
TRS1204	0168
TRS1204LP	0264
TRS1205	0142
TRS1205LP	0142
TRS1404	0168
TRS1404LP	0264
TRS1405	0142
TRS1405LP	0142
TRS1604	0168
TRS1604LP	0264
TRS1605	0142
TRS1605LP	0264
TRS1804	0168
TRS1804LP	0264
TRS1805	0142
TRS1805LP	0142
TRS2004	0168
TRS2004LP	0168
TRS2005	0142
TRS2005LP	0142
TRS2006	0168
TRS2254	0168
TRS2254LP	0168
TRS2255	0142
TRS2255LP	0142
TRS2504	0168
TRS2504LP	0168
TRS2505	0142
TRS2505LP	0142
TRS2754	0168
TRS2754LP	0168
TRS2755	0142
TRS2755LP	0142
TRS2804S	0168
TRS2805S	0168
TRS3006	0168
TRS3011	0233
TRS3012	0233
TRS3012C#	2985
TRS3014	0283
TRS3014LP	0168
TRS3015	0168
TRS3015LP	0142
TRS3016LC	0142
TRS3204S	0168
TRS3205S	0168
TRS3254	0168
TRS3254LP	0168
TRS3255	0168
TRS3501	0187
TRS3502	0187
TRS3504	0168
TRS3504LP	0168
TRS3604S	0168
TRS3742	0168
TRS3754	0168
TRS3754LP	0168
TRS4001	0187
TRS4002	0187
TRS4004	0168
TRS4006S	OEM
TRS4014	0168
TRS4014LP	0168
TRS4014S	0168
TRS4016LC	0142
TRS4254	0168
TRS4254LP	0168
TRS4296	0168
TRS4297	0168
TRS4404S	0168
TRS4405S	OEM
TRS4501	0187
TRS4504	0168
TRS4504LP	0168
TRS4754	0168
TRS4754LP	0168
TRS4926	0168
TRS4927	0168
TRS5006A	OEM
TRS5014	0168
TRS5016LC	0142
TRS5254	0168
TRS5504	0168
TRS6016LC	0142
TRS11002D25B	OEM
TRS11004D25B	OEM
TRS11006D25B	OEM
TRS11008D25B	OEM
TRS11010D25B	OEM
TRS11012D25B	OEM
TRSP2254	0434
TRSP2254S	0434
TRSP3738	OEM
TRSP3739	OEM
TRSP4000	0126
TRSP4001	0434
TRSP4002	0434
TRSR3AM	0133
TRT	OEM
TRT-1301	OEM
TR-TR38	0016
TR-U1650E	0321
TR-U1650E-1	0321
TR-U1835E	0321
TRW2307	OEM
TRW6259	OEM
TRW54001	OEM
TRW54101	OEM
TRW54201	OEM
TRW54401	OEM
TRW54501	OEM
TRW54601	OEM
TRW62601	OEM
TRW62602	OEM
TRW63601	OEM
TRW63602	OEM
TRW64601	OEM
TRW64602	OEM
TRY-1002	OEM
TS05	0015
TS035	OEM
TS035FA	0799
TS035FB	OEM
TS04700	OEM
TS05100	OEM
TS05600	OEM
TS06000	OEM
TS06200	0466
TS06800	OEM
TS07100	OEM
TS07500	OEM
TS08200	OEM
TS08700	OEM
TS09100	0057
TS-1	0004
TS1	0015
TS-2	0004
TS2	0015
TS2A	0015
TS-3	0004
TS3	0071
TS4	0535
TS5	0015
TS6	0015
TS6.8	OEM
TS7	OEM
TS7.5	OEM
TS8	0071
TS8.2	OEM
TS9	OEM
TS9.1	OEM
TS10	OEM
TS10A	OEM
TS11	OEM
TS12	OEM
TS-13	0004
TS13	0211
TS-14	0004
TS14	0211
TS-15	0004
TS15	0211
TS16	OEM
TS17	OEM
TS18	OEM
TS20	OEM
TS22	OEM
TS24	OEM
TS27	OEM
TS30	OEM
TS30A	OEM
TS33	OEM
TS36	OEM
TS39	OEM
TS39A	OEM
TS40	OEM
TS43	OEM
TS47	OEM
TS50	OEM
TS51	OEM
TS51A	OEM
TS56	OEM
TS60	OEM
TS60A	OEM
TS62	OEM
TS68	OEM
TS75	OEM
TS80	OEM
TS82	OEM
TS82A	OEM
TS91	OEM
TS97-1	0037
TS100	OEM
TS100A	OEM
TS110	OEM
TS110A	OEM
TS120	OEM
TS135	0464
TS135FA	0799
TS135FB	OEM
TS-162	0004
TS162	0164
TS-163	0004
TS163	0164
TS-164	0211
TS164	0164
TS-165	0004
TS165	0164
TS-166	0004
TS166	0164
TS-173	0160
TS173	0160
TS-176	0160
TS176	0160
TS187	OEM
TS235	0464
TS235FA	0799
TS235FB	OEM
TS322-3	OEM
TS322-3-0	OEM
TS322-3IR	OEM
TS322-3LED	OEM
TS335	OEM
TS335FA	OEM
TS335FB	OEM
TS-337	0137
TS435	0720
TS435FA	0799
TS435FB	OEM
TS511-3	OEM
TS511-4	OEM
TS511-6	OEM
TS535	OEM
TS535FA	OEM
TS535FB	OEM
TS555A	OEM
TS555B	OEM
TS555C	OEM
TS555CD	2744
TS555CN	0580
TS555D	OEM
TS555E	OEM
TS555F	OEM
TS555G	OEM
TS555H	OEM
TS555M	OEM
TS555N	OEM
TS555P	OEM
TS555PA	OEM
TS555PB	OEM
TS555PC	OEM
TS555S	OEM
TS555T	OEM
TS556A	OEM
TS556B	OEM
TS556C	OEM
TS556CD	OEM
TS556CJ	OEM
TS556CN	2842
TS556D	OEM
TS556E	OEM
TS556F	OEM
TS556G	OEM
TS556H	OEM
TS556ID	OEM
TS556IJ	OEM
TS556IN	OEM
TS556M	OEM
TS556MD	OEM
TS556MJ	OEM
TS556MN	OEM
TS556N	OEM
TS556P	OEM
TS556PA	OEM
TS556PB	OEM
TS556PC	OEM
TS556S	OEM
TS556T	OEM
TS560	OEM
TS-601	0279
TS601	0164
TS-602	0279
TS602	0164
TS-603	0004
TS603	0164
TS-604	0004
TS604	0164
TS605	0004
TS606	0004
TS-609	0435
TS609	0435
TS-610	0085
TS610	0160
TS-612	0085
TS612	0160
TS-613	0085
TS613	0160
TS-614	0085
TS614	0160
TS-615	0050
TS615	0279
TS-616	0004
TS616	0164
TS-617	0004
TS617	0164
TS-618	0004
TS618	0164
TS619	0164
TS-620	0050
TS620	0164
TS-621	0050
TS621	0164
TS-627	0004
TS627	0164
TS-627A	0050
TS627A	0211
TS-627B	0050
TS627B	0211
TS-629	0004
TS629	0164
TS-630	0050
TS630	0050
TS635	0720
TS635FA	0799
TS635FB	OEM
TS669A	0279
TS669B	0279
TS669C	0050
TS669D	0279
TS669E	0279
TS669F	0279
TS-672A	0050
TS672A	0211
TS-672B	0050
TS672B	0050
TS-673A	0050
TS673A	0050
TS-673B	0050
TS673B	0050
TS735	OEM
TS735FA	OEM
TS735FB	OEM
TS-739	0004
TS739	0164
TS-739B	0004
TS739B	0164
TS-740	0004
TS740	0164
TS748	OEM
TS-765	0004
TS765	0164
TS835	0674
TS835FA	OEM
TS835FB	OEM
TS935	OEM
TS1000	OEM
TS-1007	0004
TS1007	0164
TS1035	0674
TS1060	OEM
TS-1134	OEM
TS1135	OEM
TS1235	0674
TS-1266	0004
TS1266	0164
TS-1657	0160
TS1657	0160
TS-1727	0004
TS1727	0164
TS-1728	0004
TS1728	0164
TS1792	0004
TS2000	OEM
TS2000/883B	OEM
TS2000PT	OEM
TS2060	OEM
TS2218	0086
TS2219	0086
TS2221	0016
TS2222	0016
TS2427	OEM
TS2427-1	OEM
TS2776	0233
TS2779	0326
TS2904	0037
TS2905	0037
TS2906	0037
TS2907	0037
TS3060	OEM
TS4060	OEM
TS4078BP	0915
TS9013	0144
TS10000	OEM
TSA551T/C2B	OEM
TSA5510T/C2B	OEM
TSB-245	0015
TSB245	0015
TSB-1000	0015
TSB1204L	OEM
TSB3055	3052
TSC36M	OEM
TSC36N	OEM
TSC36S	OEM
TSC40A	OEM
TSC40B	OEM
TSC40C	OEM
TSC40D	OEM
TSC40E	OEM
TSC40F	OEM
TSC40G	OEM
TSC40H	OEM
TSC40U	OEM
TSC45A	OEM
TSC45B	OEM
TSC45C	OEM
TSC45D	OEM
TSC45E	OEM
TSC45F	OEM
TSC45G	OEM
TSC45H	OEM
TSC45M	OEM
TSC45N	OEM
TSC45S	OEM
TSC45T	OEM
TSC45U	OEM
TSC46A	OEM
TSC46B	OEM
TSC46C	OEM
TSC46D	OEM
TSC46E	OEM
TSC46F	OEM
TSC46G	OEM
TSC46H	OEM
TSC46M	OEM
TSC46N	OEM
TSC46S	OEM
TSC46T	OEM
TSC46U	OEM
TSC50N	OEM
TSC50T	OEM
TSC52U	OEM
TSC136	0133
TSC150E	OEM
TSC150M	OEM
TSC150N	OEM
TSC150P	OEM
TSC150PA	OEM
TSC150PB	OEM
TSC150PC	OEM
TSC150S	OEM
TSC150T	OEM
TSC152E	OEM
TSC152M	OEM
TSC152N	OEM
TSC152P	OEM
TSC152PA	OEM
TSC152PB	OEM
TSC152PC	OEM
TSC152S	OEM
TSC152T	OEM
TSC159	0015
TSC350AL	OEM
TSC350CL	OEM
TSC351AL	OEM
TSC351CJ	OEM
TSC351CL	OEM
TSC361AJ	OEM
TSC361CJ	OEM
TSC361CL	OEM
TSC362AJ	OEM
TSC362AL	OEM
TSC362CJ	OEM
TSC362CL	OEM
TSC363AL	OEM
TSC363CJ	OEM
TSC363CL	OEM
TSC367AJ	OEM
TSC367AL	OEM
TSC367CJ	OEM
TSC367CL	OEM
TSC368AJ	OEM
TSC368AL	OEM
TSC368CJ	OEM
TSC368CL	OEM
TSC380AJ	OEM
TSC380AL	OEM
TSC380CJ	OEM
TSC380CL	OEM
TSC381AJ	OEM
TSC381AL	OEM
TSC381CJ	OEM
TSC381CL	OEM
TSC382AJ	OEM
TSC382AL	OEM
TSC382CJ	OEM
TSC382CL	OEM
TSC383AJ	OEM
TSC383AL	OEM
TSC383BL	OEM
TSC383CJ	OEM
TSC383CL	OEM
TSC383ML	OEM
TSC390AL	OEM
TSC390CL	OEM

If replacement code is OEM, contact original manufacturer for replacement. 603

DEVICE TYPE	REPL CODE
TSC391AL	OEM
TSC391CL	OEM
TSC392AL	OEM
TSC392CL	OEM
TSC393AL	OEM
TSC393CL	OEM
TSC394AL	OEM
TSC394CL	OEM
TSC395AL	OEM
TSC395CL	OEM
TSC396AJ	OEM
TSC396AL	OEM
TSC396CJ	OEM
TSC396CL	OEM
TSC450ACPE(M)	OEM
TSC450AIJE(M)	OEM
TSC450AMJE(M)	OEM
TSC450BCPE(M)	OEM
TSC450BIJE(M)	OEM
TSC450BMJE(M)	OEM
TSC-499	0111
TSC499	0016
TSC614	0144
TSC695	0016
TSC700A/Y(A)	OEM
TSC700AIJL(A)	OEM
TSC700AMJL(MA)	OEM
TSC-722	0086
TSC722	0086
TSC767	0111
TSC4728CHIP	OEM
TSC4729CHIP	OEM
TSC4730CHIP	OEM
TSC4731CHIP	OEM
TSC4732CHIP	OEM
TSC4733CHIP	OEM
TSC4734CHIP	OEM
TSC4735CHIP	OEM
TSC4736CHIP	OEM
TSC4737CHIP	OEM
TSC4738CHIP	OEM
TSC4739CHIP	OEM
TSC4740CHIP	OEM
TSC6082CHIP	OEM
TSC6083CHIP	OEM
TSC6084CHIP	OEM
TSC6085CHIP	OEM
TSC6086CHIP	OEM
TSC6087CHIP	OEM
TSC6088CHIP	OEM
TSC6089CHIP	OEM
TSC6090CHIP	OEM
TSC6091CHIP	OEM
TSC7106CDL	OEM
TSC7106CPL	4865
TSC7106RCPL	OEM
TSC7107CDL	OEM
TSC7107CPL	4864
TSC7107RCPL	OEM
TSC7109CPL	OEM
TSC7109IPL	OEM
TSC7109MDL	OEM
TSC7116CDL	OEM
TSC7116CPL	OEM
TSC7117CDL	OEM
TSC7117CPL	OEM
TSC7126CDL	OEM
TSC7126CPL	OEM
TSC7135CJI(A)	OEM
TSC7135CPI(A)	OEM
TSC7541AD	OEM
TSC7541BD	OEM
TSC7541JN	OEM
TSC7541KN	OEM
TSC7541SD	OEM
TSC7541TD	OEM
TSC8640BN	OEM
TSC8640CJ	OEM
TSC8640CN	OEM
TSC8641BN	OEM
TSC8641CJ	OEM
TSC8641CN	OEM
TSC8700CJ	OEM
TSC8700CN	OEM
TSC8701CN	OEM
TSC8702CN	OEM
TSC8703BH	OEM
TSC8703BN	OEM
TSC8703CJ	OEM
TSC8703CN	OEM
TSC8704BH	OEM
TSC8704BN	OEM
TSC8704CJ	OEM
TSC8704CN	OEM
TSC8705BH	OEM
TSC8705BN	OEM
TSC8705CJ	OEM
TSC8705CN	OEM
TSC8750BH	OEM
TSC8750BN	OEM
TSC8750CJ	OEM
TSC8750CN	OEM
TSC9012F-001	OEM
TSC9403CJ(A)	OEM
TSC9403IL(A)	OEM
TSC9404CJ(A)	OEM
TSC9404IL(A)	OEM
TSC14433ACJ	OEM
TSC14433ACN	OEM

DEVICE TYPE	REPL CODE
TSC14433CJ	OEM
TSC14433CN	OEM
TSD035	OEM
TSD135	OEM
TSD235	OEM
TSD335	OEM
TSD435	OEM
TSD536	OEM
TSD635	OEM
TSD835	OEM
TSD1035	OEM
TSD6100	OEM
TSD7000	OEM
TSF1202	OEM
TSF1202C	OEM
TSF1203	OEM
TSF1203M	OEM
TSF1204B	OEM
TSF1212M	OEM
TSF1213A	OEM
TSF1216A	OEM
TSF1218	OEM
TSF1220	OEM
TSF1220M	OEM
TSF1227L	OEM
TSF1228L	OEM
TSF1230L	OEM
TSF2202A	OEM
TSF2203	OEM
TSF3201	OEM
TSH1202C	OEM
TSI1/50	OEM
TSI1/100	OEM
TSI1/150	OEM
TSI1/200	OEM
TSI5/50	OEM
TSI5/100	OEM
TSI5/200	OEM
TSI5/400	OEM
TSK10/06	OEM
TSK10-01	OEM
TSK10-02	OEM
TSK10-04	OEM
TSK10-08	OEM
TSK10-09	OEM
TSK10-10	OEM
TSK25-01	OEM
TSK25-02	OEM
TSK25-04	OEM
TSK25-06	OEM
TSK25-08	OEM
TSK25-09	OEM
TSK25-10	OEM
TSK35-01	OEM
TSK35-02	OEM
TSK35-04	OEM
TSK35-06	OEM
TSK35-08	OEM
TSK35-09	OEM
TSK35-10	OEM
TSK50-01	OEM
TSK50-02	OEM
TSK50-04	OEM
TSK50-06	OEM
TSK50-08	OEM
TSK50-10	OEM
TSK65-01	OEM
TSK65-02	OEM
TSK65-04	OEM
TSK65-06	OEM
TSK65-08	OEM
TSK65-09	OEM
TSK65-10	OEM
TSO5400	OEM
TSO5500	OEM
TSP150	OEM
TSP400	OEM
TSP1000A	OEM
TSP1000B	OEM
TSQ-2222F/C	OEM
TSQ-2907D/C	OEM
TSQ-2907F/C	OEM
TSQ-3467D/C	OEM
TSQ-3467F/C	OEM
TSQ-3725D/C	OEM
TSQ-3725F/C	OEM
TSQ-3762D/C	OEM
TSQ-3762F/C	OEM
TSS-616-1	1024
TSTD-15	0102
TSV	OEM
TSV-1000	0015
TSW61A	OEM
TSW101A	OEM
TSW201A	OEM
TSY65YN	OEM
TSZ5.1	0162
TSZ5.6	0157
TSZ6.2	0631
TSZ6.8	0025
TSZ7.5	0475
TSZ8.2	0244
TSZ9.1	0057
TSZ10	0170
TSZ11	0313
TSZ12	0137
TT05	OEM
TT1	OEM
TT1FA	OEM

DEVICE TYPE	REPL CODE
TT1FB	OEM
TT2	OEM
TT2FA	OEM
TT2FB	OEM
TT2SA495-0	0006
TT2SA495-0-A	0006
TT2SA495-O	0006
TT2SA495-O-A	0006
TT2SA495-Y	0006
TT2SA495-Y-A	0006
TT2SA817Y	0431
TT2SA950	1338
TT2SA9500	1338
TT2SA965Y	5233
TT2SA1015	0148
TT2SA1015G	0148
TT2SC496Y	0781
TT2SC983	0066
TT2SC983-0-A	0066
TT2SC983-O-A	0066
TT2SC983-R-A	0066
TT2SC983-Y-A	0066
TT2SC1627(Y)	0728
TT2SC1627Y	0728
TT2SC1815	0076
TT2SC1815G	0076
TT2SC22360	2882
TT2SC2458G	0076
TT2SD843Y	0060
TT3	OEM
TT3FA	OEM
TT3FB	OEM
TT4	OEM
TT4FA	OEM
TT4FB	OEM
TT5	OEM
TT5FA	OEM
TT5FB	OEM
TT6	OEM
TT6FA	OEM
TT6FB	OEM
TT7	OEM
TT7FA	OEM
TT7FB	OEM
TT8	OEM
TT8FA	OEM
TT8FB	OEM
TT9	OEM
TT9FA	OEM
TT9FB	OEM
TT10	OEM
TT10FA	OEM
TT10FB	OEM
TT11	OEM
TT12	OEM
TT13	OEM
TT14	OEM
TT15	OEM
TT16	OEM
TT18F400KCC	OEM
TT18F600KCC	OEM
TT18F800KCC	OEM
TT18F1000KCC	OEM
TT18F1200KCC	OEM
TT18N400	OEM
TT18N600	OEM
TT18N800	OEM
TT18N1000	OEM
TT18N1100	OEM
TT18N1200	OEM
TT18N1300	OEM
TT18N1400	OEM
TT25F400KCC	OEM
TT25F600KCC	OEM
TT25F800KCC	OEM
TT25F1000KCC	OEM
TT25F1200KCC	OEM
TT25N400	OEM
TT25N600	OEM
TT25N800	OEM
TT25N1000	OEM
TT25N1100	OEM
TT25N1200	OEM
TT25N1300	OEM
TT25N1400	OEM
TT32N400KOF	OEM
TT32N600KOF	OEM
TT32N800KOF	OEM
TT32N1000KOF	OEM
TT32N1200KOF	OEM
TT32N1600KOF	OEM
TT45N400KOF	OEM
TT45N600KOF	OEM
TT45N800KOF	OEM
TT45N1000KOF	OEM
TT45N1200KOF	OEM
TT45N1400KOF	OEM
TT60N60CK	0647
TT60N600KOF	OEM
TT60N800KOF	OEM
TT60N1000KOF	OEM
TT60N1200KOF	OEM
TT60N1400KOF	OEM
TT66X26	0015
TT204	0144
TT204A	0144
TT204AB	0144
TT204B	0144
TT204C	0144

DEVICE TYPE	REPL CODE
TT205	OEM
TT210	OEM
TT210FA	OEM
TT210FB	OEM
TT210FX	OEM
TT220	OEM
TT220FA	OEM
TT220FB	OEM
TT220FX	OEM
TT230	OEM
TT230FA	OEM
TT230FB	OEM
TT230FX	OEM
TT240	OEM
TT240FA	OEM
TT240FB	OEM
TT240FX	OEM
TT250	OEM
TT250FA	OEM
TT250FB	OEM
TT250FX	OEM
TT260	OEM
TT260FA	OEM
TT260FB	OEM
TT260FX	OEM
TT270	OEM
TT270FA	OEM
TT270FB	OEM
TT270FX	OEM
TT280	OEM
TT280FA	OEM
TT280FB	OEM
TT280FX	OEM
TT290	OEM
TT290FA	OEM
TT290FB	OEM
TT290FX	OEM
TT310FA	OEM
TT310FB	OEM
TT310V	OEM
TT320FA	OEM
TT320FB	OEM
TT320V	OEM
TT330	OEM
TT330FA	OEM
TT330FB	OEM
TT340FA	OEM
TT340FB	OEM
TT340V	OEM
TT350	OEM
TT350FA	OEM
TT350FB	OEM
TT360FA	OEM
TT360FB	OEM
TT360V	OEM
TT370	OEM
TT370FA	OEM
TT370FB	OEM
TT380FA	OEM
TT380FB	OEM
TT380V	OEM
TT390	OEM
TT390FA	OEM
TT390FB	OEM
TT500	OEM
TT501	OEM
TT502	OEM
TT590I	OEM
TT590J	OEM
TT590K	OEM
TT590L	OEM
TT590M	OEM
TT-1083	0160
TT1083	0160
TT1097	0016
TT2100	OEM
TT2100FA	OEM
TT2100FB	OEM
TT2100FX	OEM
TT2110	OEM
TT2120	OEM
TT2130	OEM
TT2140	OEM
TT2150	OEM
TT2160	OEM
TT3100FA	OEM
TT3100FB	OEM
TT3100V	OEM
TT3110	OEM
TT3120V	OEM
TT3130	OEM
TT3140V	OEM
TT3150	OEM
TT3160V	OEM
TT3180V	OEM
TT3200V	OEM
TTAL210	OEM
TTAL220	OEM
TTAL230	OEM
TTAL240	OEM
TTAL250	OEM
TTAL260	OEM
TTAL270	OEM
TTAL280	OEM
TTAL290	OEM
TTAL2100	OEM
TTAL2110	OEM
TTAL2120	OEM
TTS2C983-Y-A	OEM

DEVICE TYPE	REPL CODE
TTT-2SC1000GB	0111
TTT-2SC1000GBL	0111
TTT-2SK30A--O	3017
TTT-2SK30A-OO	3017
TU000	0164
TU1B	OEM
TU3F700H	0239
TU7F	OEM
TU10/1	OEM
TU10/2	OEM
TU11/1	OEM
TU11/2	OEM
TU12/1	OEM
TU12/2	OEM
TU13/1	OEM
TU13/2	OEM
TU14/1	OEM
TU14/2	OEM
TU25F	OEM
TU30	OEM
TU36HZ	OEM
TU101	OEM
TU102	OEM
TU105	OEM
TU110	OEM
TU120	OEM
TU220	OEM
TU420	OEM
TU620	OEM
TU820	OEM
TU920	OEM
TU1020	OEM
TU3002	OEM
TU3004	OEM
TUA008	OEM
TUA108	OEM
TUA208	OEM
TUA308	OEM
TUA408	OEM
TUA600C	OEM
TUA608	OEM
TUI1	OEM
TUI1R	OEM
TUM835	OEM
TUM1035	OEM
TUP3	OEM
TUP3S	OEM
TUP4	OEM
TUP13	OEM
TV2RD16EB2	OEM
TV2SB126	0160
TV2SB126F	0160
TV2SB126V	0160
TV2SB448	0222
TV2SC208	0007
TV4	0015
TV-6	0079
TV6	0079
TV6.5	0769
TV-7	0144
TV7	0079
TV8	0071
TV9SI	OEM
TV10SI	OEM
TV-11	0201
TV11-S	0201
TV13-11K60	0201
TV13-12K60	0286
TV13-S	0286
TV13SI	OEM
TV15	0007
TV-15A	0007
TV15A	0007
TV-15B	0144
TV15B	0007
TV15C	0007
TV-16	0007
TV16	0144
TV16SI	OEM
TV-17	0079
TV17	0016
TV-18	0016
TV18	0144
TV18-S	0374
TV18B	0079
TV18SI	OEM
TV-19	0233
TV19	0233
TV-20	0326
TV20	0007
TV20-S	0752
TV-21	0016
TV21	0590
TV-22	0144
TV22	0334
TV-23	0016
TV23	0086
TV-25	0334
TV25	0086
TV-26	0086
TV26	0590
TV-27	0208
TV27	0038
TV-28	0086
TV28	0590
TV-29	0126
TV29	0126
TV-32	0079
TV32	0144

DEVICE TYPE	REPL CODE
TV-33	0008
TV33	0007
TV-34	0008
TV34	0102
TV-35	0008
TV35	0007
TV-36	0007
TV36	0079
TV-37	0007
TV37	0008
TV-38	0007
TV38	0016
TV-39	0007
TV39	0016
TV-40	0016
TV40	0016
TV-41	0086
TV41	0086
TV-42	0079
TV42	0086
TV-43	0086
TV43	0079
TV-44	0037
TV44	0037
TV-45	0086
TV45	0086
TV-46	0016
TV46	0016
TV-47	0037
TV47	0164
TV-48	0224
TV48	0016
TV-49	0233
TV49	0334
TV-50	0008
TV50	0007
TV-51	0079
TV51	0086
TV-52	0079
TV52	0086
TV-53	0016
TV53	0086
TV-54	0326
TV54	0007
TV-55	0326
TV55	0144
TV55E	OEM
TV55F	OEM
TV-56	0016
TV56	0016
TV-57	0037
TV57	0127
TV-58	0079
TV58	0127
TV-59	0086
TV59	0086
TV-60	0079
TV60	0127
TV-61	0211
TV61	0164
TV-62	0079
TV62	0396
TV-65	0079
TV65	0079
TV-66	0079
TV66	0079
TV-67	0086
TV67	0079
TV-68	0079
TV68	0079
TV-70	0233
TV70B	0233
TV-71	0150
TV-73	0555
TV-74	1257
TV74	0555
TV-75	0555
TV-77	0326
TV80	0321
TV81	0326
TV-82	0555
TV82	0161
TV-83	0321
TV83	0321
TV-84	0079
TV84	0079
TV85	0283
TV-87	0037
TV87	0037
TV-92	0079
TV92	0079
TV-93	0037
TV93	0037
TV105	0486
TV106	0969
TV108	0637
TV-109	0178
TV109	0178
TV110	2002
TV111	0969
TV-112	0419
TV112	0419
TV113	0142
TV114	0969
TV-115	0042
TV115	0144
TV-116	0919
TV116	0848
TV-117	0042

DEVICE TYPE	REPL CODE
TV117	0419
TV118	0637
TV119	1955
TV-120	0275
TV120	0161
TV121	0074
TV122	0142
TV-124	0065
TV124	0065
TV-125	0065
TV125	0637
TV210B	OEM
TV215	1313
TV217C	OEM
TV217CH	OEM
TV220A	OEM
TV220B	OEM
TV220C	OEM
TV220D	OEM
TV220E	OEM
TV220F	OEM
TV220G	OEM
TV220J	OEM
TV221A	OEM
TV221B	OEM
TV221C	OEM
TV221D	OEM
TV221E	OEM
TV221F	OEM
TV221G	OEM
TV221H	OEM
TV221K	OEM
TV222A	OEM
TV222B	OEM
TV222C	OEM
TV222D	OEM
TV222E	OEM
TV222F	OEM
TV222G	OEM
TV222Z	OEM
TV225A	OEM
TV232	OEM
TV242	OEM
TV244	OEM
TV259	OEM
TV262	OEM
TV313	OEM
TV514	OEM
TV695	0769
TV848	OEM
TV851	OEM
TV1000	0144
TV1255B	OEM
TV1505	OEM
TV1546	OEM
TV1547	OEM
TV2001W	OEM
TV2002	OEM
TV2011	OEM
TV2013	OEM
TV2015	OEM
TV2017	OEM
TV2018	OEM
TV2019W	OEM
TV2022	OEM
TV2028	OEM
TV2030	OEM
TV2032	OEM
TV2042	OEM
TV2053	OEM
TV2091	OEM
TV2092	OEM
TV2125CBA	OEM
TV2125CBB	OEM
TV2202F	OEM
TV2204F	OEM
TV2206F	OEM
TV2208F	OEM
TV2210F	OEM
TV2211A	OEM
TV2211B	OEM
TV2211C	OEM
TV2211D	OEM
TV2214F	OEM
TV2215A	OEM
TV2215F	OEM
TV2216A	OEM
TV2216B	OEM
TV2216C	OEM
TV2217H	OEM
TV2226	OEM
TV2246A	OEM
TV2246B	OEM
TV2246X	OEM
TV2350	OEM
TV2403	0144
TV2404	0144
TV2411	0004
TV2412M	OEM
TV2419	0015
TV2428	0004
TV2429	0004
TV2434	0004
TV2455	0050
TV2479	0050
TV2496	0015
TV3002	1017
TV3004	1017
TV3006	1030

DEVICE TYPE	REPL CODE	DEVICE TYPE	REPL CODE	DEVICE TYPE	REPL CODE	DEVICE TYPE	REPL CODE	DEVICE TYPE	REPL CODE	DEVICE TYPE	REPL CODE	DEVICE TYPE	REPL CODE
TV3008	1040	TV24383	0127	TVCM-47	2674	TVM1D246L	OEM	TVP519A	OEM	TVP1035	OEM	TVP5009A	OEM
TV3010	1040	TV24385	0127	TVCM-48	0817	TVM1D256L	OEM	TVP520	OEM	TVP1035A	OEM	TVP5010	OEM
TV3012	OEM	TV24387	0144	TVCM-49	2681	TVM1D267L	OEM	TVP520A	OEM	TVP1036	OEM	TVP5010A	OEM
TV3014	OEM	TV-24399	0007	TVCM-50	2549	TVM1D279L	OEM	TVP521	OEM	TVP1036A	OEM	TVP5011	OEM
TV3016	OEM	TV24399	0007	TVCM-51	0823	TVM1D292L	OEM	TVP521A	OEM	TVP1037	OEM	TVP5011A	OEM
TV3018	OEM	TV24435	0233	TVCM-52	2688	TVM1D2108L	OEM	TVP522	OEM	TVP1037A	OEM	TVP5012	OEM
TV3020	OEM	TV24436	0007	TVCM-53	2689	TVM2	OEM	TVP522A	OEM	TVP1038	OEM	TVP5012A	OEM
TV3301	OEM	TV24437	0007	TVCM-54	2507	TVM3	OEM	TVP523	OEM	TVP1038A	OEM	TVP5013	OEM
TV3304	OEM	TV24438	0127	TVCM-55	2716	TVM4	OEM	TVP523A	OEM	TVP1039	OEM	TVP5013A	OEM
TV3308	OEM	TV24453	0016	TVCM-56	2720	TVM5	OEM	TVP524	OEM	TVP1039A	OEM	TVP5014	OEM
TV3309	OEM	TV24454	0016	TVCM-57	2242	TVM7K705M	0196	TVP525	OEM	TVP1500	OEM	TVP5014A	OEM
TV3340	OEM	TV24458	0016	TVCM-58	1832	TVM35	0015	TVP525A	OEM	TVP1500A	OEM	TVP5015	OEM
TV3340A	OEM	TV24468	0969	TVCM-59	0780	TVM56	0015	TVP526	OEM	TVP1501	OEM	TVP5015A	OEM
TV3340B	OEM	TV24487	0178	TVCM-60	1469	TVM-153	1493	TVP526A	OEM	TVP1501A	OEM	TVP5016	OEM
TV9140	OEM	TV24495	0037	TVCM60	1797	TVM153	1493	TVP527	OEM	TVP1502	OEM	TVP5016A	OEM
TV19111	OEM	TV24499	0233	TVCM-61	0356	TVM511	0015	TVP527A	OEM	TVP1502A	OEM	TVP5017	OEM
TV19112C	OEM	TV24540	0286	TVCM-62	0368	TVM-526	0196	TVP528	OEM	TVP1503	OEM	TVP5017A	OEM
TV19114	OEM	TV24554	0133	TVCM-63	OEM	TVM526	0479	TVP528A	OEM	TVP1503A	OEM	TVP5018	OEM
TV24100	0015	TV24558	OEM	TVCM-64	OEM	TVM529	0276	TVP529	OEM	TVP1504	OEM	TVP5018A	OEM
TV24102	0144	TV24568	0969	TVCM-65	2535	TVM-530	0907	TVP529A	OEM	TVP1504A	OEM	TVP5019A	OEM
TV24103	0911	TV24571	0007	TVCM-66	1686	TVM530	0196	TVP530	OEM	TVP1505	OEM	TVP5020	OEM
TV24104	0015	TV24573	0144	TVCM-67	2696	TVM-531	0201	TVP530A	OEM	TVP1505A	OEM	TVP5020A	OEM
TV24115	0004	TV24574	0144	TVCM-68	3376	TVM531	0286	TVP531	OEM	TVP1506	OEM	TVP5021	OEM
TV24122	0019	TV24576	0016	TVCM-69	OEM	TVM533	0374	TVP531A	OEM	TVP1506A	OEM	TVP5021A	OEM
TV24124	0196	TV24582	0015	TVCM69	0413	TVM-535	0015	TVP532	OEM	TVP1507	OEM	TVP5022	OEM
TV24125	0015	TV24589	0144	TVCM-70	OEM	TVM535	0102	TVP532A	OEM	TVP1507A	OEM	TVP5022A	OEM
TV24130	0911	TV24599	0004	TVCM-71	OEM	TVM-537	1293	TVP533	OEM	TVP1508	OEM	TVP5023	OEM
TV24136	0015	TV24617	0102	TVCM-72	OEM	TVM537	0102	TVP533A	OEM	TVP1508A	OEM	TVP5023A	OEM
TV24137	0136	TV24648	0102	TVCM-73	0514	TVM-538	0196	TVP534	OEM	TVP1509	OEM	TVP5024	OEM
TV24142	0969	TV24649	0918	TVCM-74	2111	TVM538	0196	TVP534A	OEM	TVP1509A	OEM	TVP5024A	OEM
TV24143	0208	TV24650	0286	TVCM-75	0574	TVM540	0752	TVP535	OEM	TVP1510	OEM	TVP5025	OEM
TV24148	0050	TV24651	0110	TVCM-76	OEM	TVM540A	0374	TVP535A	OEM	TVP1510A	OEM	TVP5025A	OEM
TV24152	0136	TV24655	0016	TVCM-77	2046	TVM546	0914	TVP536	OEM	TVP1511	OEM	TVP5026	OEM
TV24154	0004	TV24678	0160	TVCM-78	0905	TVM550	0015	TVP536A	OEM	TVP1511A	OEM	TVP5026A	OEM
TV24155	0015	TV24681	0918	TVCM-79	1983	TVM553	0201	TVP537	OEM	TVP1512	OEM	TVP5027	OEM
TV24156	0004	TV24684	0144	TVCM-80	OEM	TVM-554	0479	TVP537A	OEM	TVP1512A	OEM	TVP5027A	OEM
TV24157	0211	TV24803	0015	TVCM-81	1044	TVM554	0196	TVP538	OEM	TVP1513	OEM	TVP5028	OEM
TV24158	0050	TV24806	0127	TVCM-82	0428	TVM554A	2875	TVP538A	OEM	TVP1513A	OEM	TVP5028A	OEM
TV24159	0911	TV24848	0150	TVCM-500	0232	TVM563	0015	TVP539	OEM	TVP1514	OEM	TVP5029	OEM
TV24160	0007	TV24941	0015	TVCM-501	4516	TVM567	0201	TVP539A	OEM	TVP1514A	OEM	TVP5029A	OEM
TV24161	0007	TV24942	0071	TVCM-502	1303	TVM569	0286	TVP1000	OEM	TVP1515	OEM	TVP5030A	OEM
TV24162	1004	TV24945	0004	TVCM-503	1100	TVM-778	0190	TVP1000A	OEM	TVP1515A	OEM	TVP5031	OEM
TV24163	0222	TV24979	0015	TVCM-504	0564	TVM-EH2C	0015	TVP1001	OEM	TVP1516	OEM	TVP5031A	OEM
TV24164	0233	TV24981	0025	TVCM-505	1199	TVM-EH2C11	0015	TVP1001A	OEM	TVP1516A	OEM	TVP5032	OEM
TV24165	0769	TV24983	0208	TVCM-506	1635	TVM-EH2C11/1	0015	TVP1002	OEM	TVP1517	OEM	TVP5032A	OEM
TV24166	0136	TV24984	0004	TVCM-551	0626	TVM-EH2C11/1+12/1	0015	TVP1002A	OEM	TVP1517A	OEM	TVP5033	OEM
TV24167	0015	TV24985	1073	TVCM-553	0086	TVM-EH2C12/1	0015	TVP1003	OEM	TVP1518	OEM	TVP5033A	OEM
TV24168	0102	TV24987	0196	TVC-MK3800	3106	TVM-HS15/1B	0201	TVP1003A	OEM	TVP1518A	OEM	TVP5034	OEM
TV24169	0102	TV34232	0015	TVCMK3800	3106	TVM-HS20/1B	0752	TVP1004	OEM	TVP1519	OEM	TVP5034A	OEM
TV24172	0136	TV241013	0123	TVDFV0212	0120	TVM-HS25/1G	0196	TVP1004A	OEM	TVP1519A	OEM	TVP5035	OEM
TV24176	1024	TV241072	0872	TVH05	OEM	TVM-K112C	0196	TVP1005	OEM	TVP1520	OEM	TVP5035A	OEM
TV24180	0015	TV241073	0015	TVH08	OEM	TVMK112C	0196	TVP1005A	OEM	TVP1520A	OEM	TVP5036	OEM
TV24181	0182	TV241074	0015	TVH3W250M	OEM	TVML00.09D1115	0015	TVP1006	OEM	TVP1521	OEM	TVP5036A	OEM
TV24182	0911	TV241077	0079	TVH3W265M	OEM	TVM-L00.09M1115	1293	TVP1006A	OEM	TVP1521A	OEM	TVP5037	OEM
TV24183	0015	TV241078	0079	TVH3W280M	OEM	TVML00.09M1115	0015	TVP1007	OEM	TVP1522	OEM	TVP5037A	OEM
TV24189	0004	TV242248	0015	TVH3W2100M	OEM	TVM-M204B	0015	TVP1007A	OEM	TVP1522A	OEM	TVP5038	OEM
TV24190	0196	TVA12W1100K	OEM	TVH3W2120M	OEM	TVMM204B	0015	TVP1008	OEM	TVP1523	OEM	TVP5038A	OEM
TV-24191	0015	TVA12W1120K	OEM	TVH3W2150L	OEM	TVM026	1986	TVP1008A	OEM	TVP1523A	OEM	TVP5039	OEM
TV24191	0015	TVA12W1140K	OEM	TVH3W2180L	OEM	TVM-PH9D22/1	0015	TVP1009	OEM	TVP1524	OEM	TVP5039A	OEM
TV24193	0015	TVA12W1160K	OEM	TVH3W2220L	OEM	TVMPH9DZ2/1	0015	TVP1009A	OEM	TVP1524A	OEM	TVPC520	OEM
TV24194	0004	TVA11393	OEM	TVH3W2270L	OEM	TVM-PT6D22/1	0276	TVP1010	OEM	TVP1525	OEM	TVPC502	OEM
TV24200	0015	TVAQA108SH	0165	TVH15	OEM	TVMTC00921-3	0479	TVP1010A	OEM	TVP1525A	OEM	TVPC502A	OEM
TV24203	0144	TVC-3	0015	TVH30	OEM	TVM-TC0.2P	0479	TVP1011A	OEM	TVP1526	OEM	TVPC503	OEM
TV24204	0144	TVC3	0469	TVH101	OEM	TVM-TC0.2P11/2	0015	TVP1012	OEM	TVP1526A	OEM	TVPC503A	OEM
TV24209	0007	TVC-6	0469	TVH102	OEM	TVM-TC0.2P	0479	TVP1012A	OEM	TVP1527	OEM	TVPC504	OEM
TV24210	0127	TVC6	0469	TVH103	OEM	TVM-TC0.2P1	0914	TVP1013	OEM	TVP1527A	OEM	TVPC504A	OEM
TV24211	0178	TVCM-1	2147	TVH104	OEM	TVM-TK-705M	0196	TVP1013A	OEM	TVP1528A	OEM	TVPC505	OEM
TV24214	0037	TVCM-2	0661	TVH201	OEM	TVM-TK705M	0196	TVP1014	OEM	TVP1529	OEM	TVPC505A	OEM
TV24215	0079	TVCM-3	0748	TVH202	OEM	TVN5201KND	OEM	TVP1014A	OEM	TVP1529A	OEM	TVPC506	OEM
TV24216	0079	TVCM-4	0659	TVH210	OEM	TVN6000KNS	OEM	TVP1015	OEM	TVP1530	OEM	TVPC506A	OEM
TV24217	0102	TVCM-5	0673	TVH211	OEM	TVP500	OEM	TVP1015A	OEM	TVP1530A	OEM	TVPC507	OEM
TV24218	0969	TVCM-6	0649	TVH212	OEM	TVP500A	OEM	TVP1016	OEM	TVP1531	OEM	TVPC507A	OEM
TV24219	0182	TVCM-7	0438	TVH213	OEM	TVP501	OEM	TVP1016A	OEM	TVP1531A	OEM	TVPC508	OEM
TV24220	OEM	TVCM-8	0348	TVH214	OEM	TVP501A	OEM	TVP1017	OEM	TVP1532	OEM	TVPC508A	OEM
TV24221	0015	TVCM-9	0350	TVH-526	0479	TVP502	OEM	TVP1017A	OEM	TVP1532A	OEM	TVPC509	OEM
TV24222	0102	TVCM-10	0696	TVH526	0479	TVP502A	OEM	TVP1018	OEM	TVP1533	OEM	TVPC509A	OEM
TV24224	1075	TVCM-11	0167	TVH538	0196	TVP503	OEM	TVP1018A	OEM	TVP1533A	OEM	TVPC510	OEM
TV24225	0087	TVCM-12	1929	TVH700	OEM	TVP503A	OEM	TVP1019	OEM	TVP1534	OEM	TVPC510A	OEM
TV24226	0196	TVCM-13	2264	TVHD3/2D2100L	OEM	TVP504	OEM	TVP1019A	OEM	TVP1534A	OEM	TVPC511	OEM
TV24229	0050	TVCM-14	1748	TVHD3/2D2140L	OEM	TVP504A	OEM	TVP1020	OEM	TVP1535	OEM	TVPC511A	OEM
TV24230	0050	TVCM-15	2438	TVHD3/2D2120L	OEM	TVP505	OEM	TVP1020A	OEM	TVP1535A	OEM	TVPC512	OEM
TV-24232	0015	TVCM-16	1335	TVHD10	OEM	TVP505A	OEM	TVP1021	OEM	TVP1536	OEM	TVPC512A	OEM
TV24232	0015	TVCM-17	2979	TVHD12	OEM	TVP506	OEM	TVP1021A	OEM	TVP1536A	OEM	TVPC513	OEM
TV24234	0015	TVCM-18	1434	TVHD14	OEM	TVP506A	OEM	TVP1022	OEM	TVP1537	OEM	TVPC513A	OEM
TV-24237	0469	TVCM-19	1411	TVHS1R31100K	OEM	TVP507	OEM	TVP1022A	OEM	TVP1537A	OEM	TVPC514	OEM
TV24237	0469	TVCM-20	1748	TVHS1R31300K	OEM	TVP507A	OEM	TVP1023	OEM	TVP1538	OEM	TVPC514A	OEM
TV24239	0050	TVCM-21	0746	TVHS150	OEM	TVP508	OEM	TVP1023A	OEM	TVP1538A	OEM	TVPC515	OEM
TV-24266	0015	TVCM21	0399	TVHS200	OEM	TVP508A	OEM	TVP1024	OEM	TVP1539	OEM	TVPC515A	OEM
TV24266	0015	TVCM-22	0345	TVHS260	OEM	TVP509	OEM	TVP1024A	OEM	TVP1539A	OEM	TVPC516	OEM
TV-24272	0644	TVCM-23	2535	TVHS330	OEM	TVP509A	OEM	TVP1025	OEM	TVP1728	OEM	TVPC516A	OEM
TV24272	0644	TVCM-24	OEM	TVHS400	OEM	TVP510	OEM	TVP1025A	OEM	TVP5000	OEM	TVPC517	OEM
TV24273	0123	TVCM-25	2535	TVHS480	OEM	TVP510A	OEM	TVP1026	OEM	TVP5000A	OEM	TVPC517A	OEM
TV24278	0015	TVCM-26	2535	TVHS580	OEM	TVP511	OEM	TVP1026A	OEM	TVP5001	OEM	TVPC518	OEM
TV24281	0016	TVCM-27	0850	TVHS700	OEM	TVP511A	OEM	TVP1027	OEM	TVP5001A	OEM	TVPC518A	OEM
TV24282	0015	TVCM-28	3690	TVHS840	OEM	TVP512	OEM	TVP1027A	OEM	TVP5002	OEM	TVPC519	OEM
TV24283	0015	TVCM-29	1385	TVK1D24M	OEM	TVP512A	OEM	TVP1028	OEM	TVP5002A	OEM	TVPC519A	OEM
TV24285	0276	TVCM-30	0797	TVK1D25M	OEM	TVP513	OEM	TVP1028A	OEM	TVP5003	OEM	TVPC520A	OEM
TV24292	0015	TVCM-31	0360	TVK1D26M	OEM	TVP513A	OEM	TVP1029	OEM	TVP5003A	OEM	TVPC521	OEM
TV24298	0015	TVCM-32	2527	TVK1D28M	OEM	TVP514	OEM	TVP1029A	OEM	TVP5004	OEM	TVPC521A	OEM
TV24313	0144	TVCM-33	0324	TVK-33	0128	TVP514A	OEM	TVP1030	OEM	TVP5004A	OEM	TVPC522	OEM
TV24337	0160	TVCM-34	1327	TVK-55	0128	TVP515	OEM	TVP1030A	OEM	TVP5005	OEM	TVPC522A	OEM
TV24341	0969	TVCM-35	0375	TVL0	OEM	TVP515A	OEM	TVP1031	OEM	TVP5005A	OEM	TVPC523	OEM
TV24351	0050	TVCM-39	2728	TVL1	OEM	TVP516	OEM	TVP1031A	OEM	TVP5006	OEM	TVPC523A	OEM
TV24363	0037	TVCM-41	0784	TVL2	OEM	TVP516A	OEM	TVP1032	OEM	TVP5006A	OEM	TVPC524	OEM
TV24370	0004	TVCM-42	0391	TVL3	OEM	TVP517	OEM	TVP1032A	OEM	TVP5007	OEM	TVPC524A	OEM
TV24372	0016	TVCM-43	0687	TVL4	OEM	TVP517A	OEM	TVP1033	OEM	TVP5007A	OEM	TVPC525	OEM
TV24378	0535	TVCM-44	0627	TVM0	OEM	TVP518	OEM	TVP1033A	OEM	TVP5008	OEM	TVPC525A	OEM
TV24380	0127	TVCM-45	2593	TVM-026	1986	TVP518A	OEM	TVP1034	OEM	TVP5008A	OEM	TVPC526	OEM
TV24382	0127	TVCM-46	2600	TVM1	OEM	TVP519	OEM	TVP1034A	OEM	TVP5009	OEM	TVPC526A	OEM

If replacement code is OEM, contact original manufacturer for replacement.

605

DEVICE TYPE	REPL CODE
TVPC527	OEM
TVPC527A	OEM
TVPC528	OEM
TVPC528A	OEM
TVPC529	OEM
TVPC529A	OEM
TVPC530	OEM
TVPC530A	OEM
TVPC531	OEM
TVPC531A	OEM
TVPC532	OEM
TVPC532A	OEM
TVPC533	OEM
TVPC533A	OEM
TVPC534	OEM
TVPC534A	OEM
TVPC535	OEM
TVPC535A	OEM
TVPC536	OEM
TVPC536A	OEM
TVPC537	OEM
TVPC537A	OEM
TVPC538	OEM
TVPC538A	OEM
TVPC539	OEM
TVPC539A	OEM
TVPC1002	OEM
TVPC1002A	OEM
TVPC1003	OEM
TVPC1003A	OEM
TVPC1004	OEM
TVPC1004A	OEM
TVPC1005	OEM
TVPC1005A	OEM
TVPC1006	OEM
TVPC1006A	OEM
TVPC1007	OEM
TVPC1007A	OEM
TVPC1008	OEM
TVPC1008A	OEM
TVPC1009	OEM
TVPC1009A	OEM
TVPC1010	OEM
TVPC1010A	OEM
TVPC1011	OEM
TVPC1011A	OEM
TVPC1012	OEM
TVPC1012A	OEM
TVPC1013	OEM
TVPC1013A	OEM
TVPC1014	OEM
TVPC1014A	OEM
TVPC1015	OEM
TVPC1015A	OEM
TVPC1016	OEM
TVPC1016A	OEM
TVPC1017	OEM
TVPC1017A	OEM
TVPC1018	OEM
TVPC1018A	OEM
TVPC1019	OEM
TVPC1019A	OEM
TVPC1020	OEM
TVPC1020A	OEM
TVPC1021	OEM
TVPC1021A	OEM
TVPC1022	OEM
TVPC1022A	OEM
TVPC1023	OEM
TVPC1023A	OEM
TVPC1024	OEM
TVPC1024A	OEM
TVPC1025	OEM
TVPC1025A	OEM
TVPC1026	OEM
TVPC1026A	OEM
TVPC1027	OEM
TVPC1027A	OEM
TVPC1028	OEM
TVPC1028A	OEM
TVPC1029	OEM
TVPC1029A	OEM
TVPC1030	OEM
TVPC1030A	OEM
TVPC1031	OEM
TVPC1031A	OEM
TVPC1032	OEM
TVPC1032A	OEM
TVPC1033	OEM
TVPC1033A	OEM
TVPC1034	OEM
TVPC1034A	OEM
TVPC1035	OEM
TVPC1035A	OEM
TVPC1036	OEM
TVPC1036A	OEM
TVPC1037	OEM
TVPC1037A	OEM
TVPC1038	OEM
TVPC1038A	OEM
TVPC1039	OEM
TVPC1039A	OEM
TVPC1502	OEM
TVPC1502A	OEM
TVPC1503	OEM
TVPC1503A	OEM
TVPC1504	OEM
TVPC1504A	OEM
TVPC1505	OEM
TVPC1505A	OEM
TVPC1506	OEM
TVPC1506A	OEM
TVPC1507	OEM
TVPC1507A	OEM
TVPC1508	OEM
TVPC1508A	OEM
TVPC1509	OEM
TVPC1509A	OEM
TVPC1510	OEM
TVPC1510A	OEM
TVPC1511	OEM
TVPC1511A	OEM
TVPC1512	OEM
TVPC1512A	OEM
TVPC1513	OEM
TVPC1513A	OEM
TVPC1514	OEM
TVPC1514A	OEM
TVPC1515	OEM
TVPC1515A	OEM
TVPC1516	OEM
TVPC1516A	OEM
TVPC1517	OEM
TVPC1517A	OEM
TVPC1518	OEM
TVPC1518A	OEM
TVPC1519	OEM
TVPC1519A	OEM
TVPC1520	OEM
TVPC1520A	OEM
TVPC1521	OEM
TVPC1521A	OEM
TVPC1522	OEM
TVPC1522A	OEM
TVPC1523	OEM
TVPC1523A	OEM
TVPC1524	OEM
TVPC1524A	OEM
TVPC1525	OEM
TVPC1525A	OEM
TVPC1526	OEM
TVPC1527	OEM
TVPC1527A	OEM
TVPC1528	OEM
TVPC1528A	OEM
TVPC1529	OEM
TVPC1529A	OEM
TVPC1530	OEM
TVPC1530A	OEM
TVPC1531	OEM
TVPC1531A	OEM
TVPC1532	OEM
TVPC1532A	OEM
TVPC1533	OEM
TVPC1533A	OEM
TVPC1534	OEM
TVPC1534A	OEM
TVPC1535	OEM
TVPC1535A	OEM
TVPC1536	OEM
TVPC1536A	OEM
TVPC1537	OEM
TVPC1537A	OEM
TVPC1538	OEM
TVPC1538A	OEM
TVPC1539	OEM
TVPC1539A	OEM
TVPC5002	OEM
TVPC5002A	OEM
TVPC5003	OEM
TVPC5003A	OEM
TVPC5004	OEM
TVPC5004A	OEM
TVPC5005	OEM
TVPC5005A	OEM
TVPC5006	OEM
TVPC5006A	OEM
TVPC5007	OEM
TVPC5007A	OEM
TVPC5008	OEM
TVPC5008A	OEM
TVPC5009	OEM
TVPC5009A	OEM
TVPC5010	OEM
TVPC5010A	OEM
TVPC5011	OEM
TVPC5011A	OEM
TVPC5012	OEM
TVPC5012A	OEM
TVPC5013	OEM
TVPC5013A	OEM
TVPC5014	OEM
TVPC5014A	OEM
TVPC5015	OEM
TVPC5015A	OEM
TVPC5016	OEM
TVPC5016A	OEM
TVPC5017	OEM
TVPC5017A	OEM
TVPC5018	OEM
TVPC5018A	OEM
TVPC5019	OEM
TVPC5019A	OEM
TVPC5020	OEM
TVPC5020A	OEM
TVPC5021	OEM
TVPC5021A	OEM
TVPC5022	OEM
TVPC5022A	OEM
TVPC5023	OEM
TVPC5023A	OEM
TVPC5024	OEM
TVPC5024A	OEM
TVPC5025	OEM
TVPC5025A	OEM
TVPC5026	OEM
TVPC5026A	OEM
TVPC5027	OEM
TVPC5027A	OEM
TVPC5028	OEM
TVPC5028A	OEM
TVPC5029	OEM
TVPC5029A	OEM
TVPC5030A	OEM
TVPC5031	OEM
TVPC5031A	OEM
TVPC5032	OEM
TVPC5032A	OEM
TVPC5033	OEM
TVPC5033A	OEM
TVPC5034	OEM
TVPC5034A	OEM
TVPC5035	OEM
TVPC5035A	OEM
TVPC5036	OEM
TVPC5036A	OEM
TVPC5037	OEM
TVPC5037A	OEM
TVPC5038	OEM
TVPC5038A	OEM
TVPC5039	OEM
TVPC5039A	OEM
TVR-06B	0015
TVR-06D	0023
TVR06D	0023
TVR-06G	0015
TVR06G	0015
TVR-06G23	0015
TVR-06GG23	0015
TVR-06K	0015
TVR06K	0023
TVR-060	OEM
TVR-1	0102
TVR-1B	0023
TVR1B	0023
TVR1D	0023
TVR1D(TP)	0023
TVR-1G	0023
TVR1G	0023
TVR1G(TP)	0023
TVR-1J	0023
TVR1J	0023
TVR1J(TP)	0023
TVR-2	0023
TVR2B	0023
TVR-2D	0023
TVR2D	0023
TVR-2G	0023
TVR2G	0023
TVR2J	0023
TVR4J	0102
TVR4J-TPA2	0102
TVR4L	0102
TVR4N	0102
TVR10D	OEM
TVR10G	0023
TVRAK002	OEM
TVS001-06SB	0298
TVS001-06SD	OEM
TVS00410	0071
TVS03P2M	0058
TVS010D1	0023
TVS-0A70	0143
TVS0A70	0143
TVS-0A71	0143
TVS0A71	0143
TVS-0A82G	0143
TVS-0A90	0143
TVS0A90	0019
TVS-0A91	0019
TVS0A91	0019
TVS-0A95	0143
TVS-0V-02	0102
TVS1/2D233M	OEM
TVS1CE2	0015
TVS1FSD-1	0015
TVS-1N82G	0911
TVS1N741A	0285
TVS1N741H	0285
TVS1N4148	0124
TVS1N4148TE	0124
TVS1N4148V	0124
TVS1N4150V	0133
TVS1N4741	0313
TVS1N4741A	0313
TVS1P20	0015
TVS1P80	0071
TVS1R80	0017
TVS-1S18	0143
TVS-1S750	0911
TVS1S750	0911
TVS1S954	0133
TVS-1S1211	0139
TVS1S1850	0023
TVS-1S1893	0549
TVS-1S1906	0015
TVS1S1906	0015
TVS-1S1922	0549
TVS1S1922G	0911
TVS1S1926K	0911
TVS1S1950	0015
TVS1S2076	0133
TVS1S2076MC	0124
TVS1S2339	0549
TVS1S2339K	0030
TVS1S2370	0017
TVS-2B-2C	0102
TVS-2B126F	0160
TVS2CS1256HG	0786
TVS2P5M	1234
TVS2PD56	OEM
TVS2PD57	OEM
TVS-2S172F	0004
TVS-2S288A	0127
TVS2S1664	3336
TVS-2SA71B	0050
TVS2SA71B	0050
TVS-2SA103	0136
TVS-2SA171	0279
TVS2SA171	0279
TVS-2SA385	0136
TVS-2SA385A	0136
TVS-2SA385L	0136
TVS2SA483	0899
TVS2SA543	0688
TVS2SA546	0126
TVS2SA546B	0126
TVS2SA546E	0126
TVS2SA546H	0126
TVS-2SA564	0203
TVS2SA564	0203
TVS-2SA564A	0203
TVS2SA564A	0203
TVS2SA564C	0203
TVS-2SA564P	0203
TVS2SA564P	0203
TVS2SA564Q	0203
TVS-2SB126	0160
TVS2SB126	0160
TVS-2SB126F	0160
TVS-2SB126V	0160
TVS2SB126V	0160
TVS-2SB171	0004
TVS2SB171	0004
TVS-2SB171A	0004
TVS2SB171A	0004
TVS-2SB171B	0004
TVS-2SB171F	0004
TVS-2SB172	0004
TVS2SB172	0004
TVS2SB172A	0004
TVS-2SB172F	0004
TVS-2SB176	0004
TVS-2SB234	0969
TVS-2SB324	1056
TVS-2SB448	0222
TVS2SB449	0160
TVS2SB449(F)	0160
TVS-2SB449F	0160
TVS2SB449F	0160
TVS2SB546	1638
TVS-2SC58	0233
TVS-2SC58A	0233
TVS2SC58A	0233
TVS-2SC183P	0470
TVS-2SC183Q	0470
TVS-2SC185A	0470
TVS-2SC206	0216
TVS-2SC208	0007
TVS-2SC208A	0007
TVS-2SC287A	0470
TVS2SC288A	1332
TVS-2SC313	3356
TVS-2SC429A	0470
TVS-2SC446	5468
TVS-2SC466	0259
TVS-2SC526	0233
TVS-2SC538	0079
TVS-2SC538A	0079
TVS2SC538A	0079
TVS-2SC562	0216
TVS2SC562	0216
TVS-2SC563	0829
TVS2SC563	0829
TVS-2SC563A	0829
TVS-2SC564	0016
TVS2SC564	0016
TVS2SC564-O	0016
TVS2SC5640	0016
TVS2SC564R	0016
TVS-2SC582	2634
TVS-2SC582A	2634
TVS-2SC605	0470
TVS-2SC606	0470
TVS-2SC644	0111
TVS2SC644	0111
TVS-2SC645	0669
TVS2SC645	0669
TVS-2SC645A	0669
TVS2SC645A	0669
TVS-2SC645B	0669
TVS2SC645B	0669
TVS-2SC645C	0669
TVS2SC645C	0669
TVS-2SC646	0615
TVS2SC647	4316
TVS-2SC683	0047
TVS2SC683	0047
TVS-2SC683V	0047
TVS-2SC684	0127
TVS2SC684	0127
TVS-2SC687	0177
TVS2SC696	0639
TVS-2SC762	1146
TVS2SC762	1146
TVS2SC783	1021
TVS-2SC828	1211
TVS2SC828	1211
TVS2SC828(Q)	1211
TVS-2SC828A	1211
TVS2SC828A	1211
TVS2SC828P	1211
TVS-2SC828Q	1211
TVS2SC828Q	1211
TVS2SC828R	1211
TVS2SC829(B)	0151
TVS2SC829B	0151
TVS-2SC840	2017
TVS2SC840	2017
TVS-2SC840A	2017
TVS2SC840A	2017
TVS2SC840C	2017
TVS-2SC901	0637
TVS2SC901	0637
TVS-2SC948	0216
TVS2SC968	2901
TVS2SC1129A	0224
TVS2SC1502	0949
TVS2SC1505	0949
TVS2SC1505(1)	0949
TVS2SC1505-1	0949
TVS2SC1505I	0949
TVS2SC1507	0949
TVS2SC1520	0168
TVS2SC1629A	0130
TVS2SC1664R	0625
TVS2SC1828	2085
TVS2SC1829	2596
TVS2SC1875Q	2636
TVS2SC1875R	2636
TVS2SC2199	0615
TVS2SC5640	0016
TVS-2SD226A	0178
TVS2SD226A	0178
TVS2SD226P	0178
TVS2SD401	1274
TVS2SD794	0161
TVS2SD794(2)	0161
TVS2SD794(2)P	0161
TVS2SD794(2)Q	0161
TVS2SD794-2	0161
TVS2SD794-2P	0161
TVS2SD794-2Q	0161
TVS2SD794-P	0161
TVS2SD794-Q	0161
TVS2SD794P	0161
TVS2SD794Q	0161
TVS2SD794R	0161
TVS2SD950	2643
TVS2SD950-Q	2643
TVS2SD950Q	2643
TVS3DL2	0023
TVS-5B-2-H5W	0015
TVS5B-2-H5W	0015
TVS-7C0.0911/10	1293
TVS8B2A	0071
TVS10D	0015
TVS10D1	0023
TVS10D2	0023
TVS-10D8	0023
TVS10D8	0023
TVS10DC4	0015
TVS10DC4R	0015
TVS10E1	0015
TVS10E2	0015
TVS10E4	0015
TVS15SB20R	0743
TVS25A103	0050
TVS25B172	0211
TVS25B448	0969
TVS25C208	0016
TVS25C562	0016
TVS25C645	0016
TVS30D1	0087
TVS45	OEM
TVS-82G	0911
TVS120Z	OEM
TVS-182G	0911
TVS-185D	0015
TVS185D	0015
TVS305	OEM
TVS310	OEM
TVS312	OEM
TVS315	OEM
TVS318	OEM
TVS324	OEM
TVS328	OEM
TVS340M	0750
TVS348	OEM
TVS360	OEM
TVS410	OEM
TVS420	OEM
TVS430	OEM
TVS505	OEM
TVS510	OEM
TVS512	OEM
TVS515	OEM
TVS518	OEM
TVS524	OEM
TVS528	OEM
TVS550	0015
TVS-828A	0016
TVS828A	0016
TVS-1303	0037
TVS-1850	0535
TVS2406M	0023
TVS3153GM1	3239
TVS25126F	0160
TVS81202	0015
TVSA81004	0730
TVSAFS01	0102
TVSAFSD1	0102
TVSAN155	0039
TVSAN225	0399
TVSAN227	2562
TVSAN230	2564
TVSAN241	3977
TVSAN5210	3738
TVSAW01-11	0313
TVSB01-02	0015
TVSB012-2	0133
TVSB0102	0604
TVSB0102V	0604
TVSB1-29	0436
TVSB24-06C	0023
TVSB24-06D	0102
TVSB1201	0015
TVSB1202	0604
TVSB1202V	0604
TVSB1204	0071
TVSB2404C	0023
TVSB2404D	0023
TVSB2406D	0102
TVSB2804D	0023
TVSB3015M	0017
TVSB4302	0023
TVSB4304	0023
TVSB4304V	0023
TVSB81004	0110
TVSB84009	OEM
TVSBA236	OEM
TVSBA526	2760
TVSBAX-13	0124
TVSBAX13	0124
TVSBB2	0102
TVSBB2A	0023
TVSBB10	0182
TVSBB21	0023
TVSBN5040A	OEM
TVSBN5111	3692
TVSBN5115	OEM
TVSBN5210	3738
TVSBN5416	3800
TVSBN5416A	3800
TVSC0102FL7	0071
TVSC0102L7	0071
TVSC0410	0071
TVSC0508	0071
TVSC0510	0071
TVSC1255H	0086
TVSC2406M	0023
TVSC2615A	0017
TVSC2715M	0102
TVSC4702	0031
TVSC65010042	OEM
TVSCA3126	0516
TVSCA3137	2762
TVSCA3139GM1	2038
TVSCA3139GMI	2038
TVSCA3151EM1	OEM
TVSCA3153GM1	3239
TVSCA3153GMI	3239
TVSCN5310	2599
TVSCN5310L	2599
TVSCN5310M	2599
TVSCN5311	2599
TVSCN5311CL	2599
TVSCN5311KL	2599
TVSCN5411	5004
TVSC0510	0071
TVS-CS1255H	0086
TVSCS1255H	0086
TVS-CS1255HF	0786
TVSCS1255HF	0786
TVS-CS1256HG	0590
TVSCS1256HG	0786
TVS-CS1303	0037
TVSCSC1255H	0848
TVSCSC1255HF	0590
TVSCSC1256HG	0126
TVSD1M	0157
TVS-DG1NR	0182
TVS-DS-1K	0023
TVS-DS1K	0023
TVSDS1K	0023
TVS-DS-1M	0023
TVS-DS1M	0023
TVSDS-1M	0015
TVSDS1M	0023
TVS-DS2K	0015
TVSDS-2K	0015
TVSDS2K	0015
TVSDS2M	0023
TVSEA01-07R	0002
TVSEGA010-ST	0162
TVSEM1	0015
TVSEM1Z	0023
TVSEM1ZV	0023
TVSEN1364	1162
TVSEN11235	1420
TVSEN11238	3250
TVSEN11301	1162
TVSEN11401	3317
TVSEN11414	3325
TVSEN11436	2109
TVSEN11438	3060
TVSEQA01-05T	0041
TVSEQA01-06S	0091
TVSEQB01-12	0137
TVSEQB01-15	0002
TVSEQB01-15Z	0002
TVSERA81-004	0023
TVSERB-04D	0023
TVSERB-06B	0015
TVSERB12-02	0023
TVSERB24-04D	0023
TVSERB24-06	0023
TVSERB24-06A	0015
TVSERB24-06B	0023
TVSERC05-08	0071
TVSERC0508	0071
TVSERC0510	0071
TVSERC0510V	0071
TVSERZC10ZK241U	1982
TVSES1	0023
TVSES1Z	0023
TVSESA06	0293
TVS-ET1P	0015
TVSEU1Z	0023
TVSEU2	0023
TVSEU2A	0023
TVSEU2V	0023
TVSFG2PC	0102
TVS-FR1MD	5307
TVS-FR1N	0015
TVS-FR-1P	0023
TVS-FR1P	0023
TVSFR1P	0023
TVS-FR-1P(FR1P)	0015
TVS-FR1PC	0015
TVSFR1PC	0023
TVSFR2-005	0102
TVSFR2-02	0023
TVSFR2-02C	0015
TVSFR2-02G	0023
TVSFR2-04	0102
TVSFR2-04(SD-1)	0102
TVSFR2-06	0023
TVSFR2-10	0102
TVS-FR-2M	0015
TVS-FR2M	0015
TVS-FR2P	5307
TVS-FR2PC	0535
TVSFR2PC	0535
TVS-FR10	0015
TVSFR202	2068
TVSFT1M	0102
TVS-FT1N	0015
TVS-FT-1P	0102
TVS-FT1P	0102
TVSFT-1P	0102
TVSFT1P	0102
TVS-FT1PC	0102
TVS-FT10	0071
TVS-FU1N	0102
TVSFU1N	0102
TVSFUIN	0102
TVSG4011BCM	0215
TVSG65020054	OEM
TVSGH3F	0158
TVSGH3FLF	0158
TVSGN2050	OEM
TVSGN3002U	OEM
TVSGN3100E	OEM
TVSGN3210	OEM
TVSGN3500	OEM
TVSGN3600	OEM
TVSGP2-354	0133
TVSGRU2A	0102
TVSH20/1D	OEM
TVS-H-339W	0752
TVS-H-399W	0752
TVSHA-1	0102
TVSHA1151	3606
TVSHF-1	0102
TVSHF1	0102
TVSHFD1Z	0102
TVSHFSD-1	0102
TVSHFSD-1A	0102
TVSHFSD-1C	0102
TVS-HFSD1Z	0102
TVSHFSD-1Z	0102
TVSHFSD1Z	0102
TVS-HF-SD-12	0102
TVS-HS7/1	0769
TVSHS7/1	0769
TVS-HS25/1B	0374
TVS-HS25/16	0374
TVSHZ5C1	0248
TVSHZ5C1TD	0041
TVSHZ6A1	0877
TVSHZ7B2	0062
TVSHZ9A1	0165

If replacement code is OEM, contact original manufacturer for replacement.

DEVICE TYPE	REPL CODE
TVSHZ11B1	0064
TVSHZ11C2	0181
TVSHZ11C3TE	0181
TVSHZ33S1	0166
TVSHZT33	3417
TVSHZT33S1	1319
TVSJA1200	0079
TVSJL41A	0015
TVSJL41AM	0015
TVSJN76664V	0167
TVS-K112C	0196
TVSK112C	0196
TVSKA1200	0007
TVSKB162D	0139
TVSKB265A	0133
TVSKB462F	3407
TVS-KC2-LP	0015
TVS-KC2CP12/1	0015
TVS-KC2DP12/2	0015
TVS-KC20P12/1	0015
TVSL78M12RL	0330
TVSL78N05	1288
TVSLA7530N	3765
TVSM5218L	1689
TVSM51247	3242
TVSM51247P	3242
TVSM51320P	OEM
TVSM51320P(M51320P)	OEM
TVSM51321P	OEM
TVSM51376SP	OEM
TVSM53216P	1339
TVSM58479P	OEM
TVSM58725P	1887
TVSMA26	0139
TVS-MA26A	0139
TVS-MA242C	0015
TVSMB-1F	0182
TVSMB1F	0344
TVSMI-15R	1089
TVSMI15RC	0015
TVSMI-15S	1791
TVSMI15SC	0015
TVSMP0574J	1319
TVS-MPC23C	0523
TVSMPC23C	0523
TVSMPC574J	1319
TVSMPC595C	0846
TVSMPC596C	0851
TVSMPC596C2	0851
TVSMPC596C2B	0851
TVSMPC596CE	0851
TVSMPC596CZ	0851
TVSMPC1355C	0391
TVSMPS596C2	0851
TVSMR1C	0071
TVSMR-1M	0071
TVSN13T1	0312
TVSN76665	0167
TVS-OA70	0143
TVSOA71	0143
TVS-OA81	0143
TVS-OA90	0143
TVSOA90	0143
TVS-OA91	0019
TVS-OA95	0143
TVS-OV-02	0102
TVS-PC02P11/2	0015
TVSPC-713U	0311
TVS-PCD2P11/2	0015
TVSPCD2P11/2	0015
TVSPH302	2604
TVSPH302B	OEM
TVSPH309	OEM
TVSQA01-06SB	0298
TVSQA01-07BE	0025
TVSQA01-07R	0002
TVSQA01-07RE	0025
TVSQA01-11SE	0313
TVSQA01-11.5E	0313
TVSQA01-12S	0137
TVSQA01-14RD	0100
TVSQA01-15S	0002
TVSQA01-25BA	0398
TVSQA01-25R	0398
TVSQA01-25RA	0398
TVSQA01-25RB	OEM
TVSQA105R	0041
TVSQA105RA	0582
TVSQA107RE	0025
TVSQA107SP	0062
TVSQA108SH	0165
TVSQA112R1	0137
TVSQA112RI	0137
TVSQA112RN-2	0052
TVSQA116R2	0440
TVSQA135R2	0032
TVSQA205AB	0140
TVSQA205C	0041
TVSQA205D	0041
TVSQA205E	0041
TVSQA205EV3	0041
TVSQA205F	0041
TVSQA205G	0041
TVSQA205GV3	0041
TVSQA206	0091
TVSQA206A	0091
TVSQA206AB	0253
TVSQA206B	0091
TVSQA206CD	0091
TVSQA206G	0292
TVSQA206M	0091
TVSQA206MV	0091
TVSQA206MV3	0091
TVSQA207D	0077
TVSQA207M	0062
TVSQA207M3	0062
TVSQA208	0165
TVSQA208C	0165
TVSQA208G	0165
TVSQA208GV3	0165
TVSQA208M	OEM
TVSQA209B	0057
TVSQA209C	0057
TVSQA209M	0057
TVSQA209M9	0057
TVSQA210D	0248
TVSQA211B	0181
TVSQA211N1	0181
TVSQA212B	0053
TVSQA213A	0053
TVSQA213B	0053
TVSQA213M2	0053
TVSQA225A	0709
TVSQA228B	0257
TVSQA230B	0195
TVSQA232M2	OEM
TVSQA233C	0166
TVSQA233CV	0166
TVSQA233CV3	0166
TVSQA233G	0010
TVSQA235AC	0709
TVSQA235C	0010
TVSQA235G	0010
TVSQB01-15ZB	0002
TVSQB01-18	0490
TVSQB105M	OEM
TVSQB105N	0162
TVSQB106P	0298
TVSQB107D	0025
TVSQB107S	0025
TVSQB107SV	0025
TVSQB109SA	6564
TVSQB110D	0313
TVSQB112	0137
TVSQB112ZE	0137
TVSQB115ZB	0002
TVSQB115ZBV	0002
TVSQB118	0490
TVSQR110D	0313
TVSRA1A	0133
TVSRA-1Z	0023
TVSRA1Z	0023
TVSRA-26	1823
TVSRA26	0497
TVSRC2	0344
TVSRD2R4E	2847
TVSRD2.7EB2	0755
TVSRD3R3EB	0296
TVSRD3R6EB2	0372
TVSRD3.0EB1	0118
TVSRD3.0EB1Z	0118
TVSRD3.0EB2	0118
TVSRD3.0EL1	0118
TVSRD3.0EL1Z	0118
TVSRD3.2EB1	OEM
TVSRD3.6EL	0372
TVSRD3.6EL1Z	0372
TVSRD4AM	0036
TVSRD4R7	0140
TVSRD4R7EB	0140
TVSRD4R7EB2	0140
TVSRD4.7EB2	0140
TVS-RD5A	0041
TVSRD5A	0041
TVSRD5AK	0041
TVSRD5R1EB2	0041
TVSRD5R1JB3	0041
TVSRD5.1EB	OEM
TVSRD5.1EB1	0041
TVSRD5.1EB1Z	0041
TVSRD5.1EB2	0041
TVSRD5.1EL2Z	0582
TVSRD5.6EB1	0041
TVSRD5.6EN3	0253
TVSRD5.6EN3Z	0253
TVSRD6A	0091
TVSRD6R8E	0062
TVSRD6R8EB	0062
TVSRD6.2EB	0466
TVSRD6.2EB1	0091
TVSRD6.2EB1Z	0091
TVSRD6.2EB3	0466
TVSRD6.2FB1	0631
TVSRD6.2FB2	0466
TVSRD6.8MB2X	0062
TVS-RD7A	0062
TVSRD7.5EB	0077
TVSRD7.5EBMV	0077
TVSRD8.2EB1	0077
TVSRD8.2EB2	0165
TVSRD9A1	OEM
TVSRD9AL	1075
TVSRD10FC	0170
TVS-RD11A	0181
TVSRD11A	0181
TVSRD11EB1	0064
TVSRD11EB3	0181
TVSRD12EB	0999
TVSRD12EB1	0052
TVSRD12EB1Z	0052
TVSRD12EB2M	0052
TVSRD12EBH	0999
TVSRD12EBM	0052
TVSRD12FB2	0137
TVSRD12FB3	0137
TVS-RD-13A	0053
TVS-RD13A	0053
TVSRD13AL	0052
TVSRD13EB2	0053
TVSRD13EB2Z	0053
TVSRD13EB3	0053
TVSRD13EL1	0053
TVSRD15EB2	0873
TVSRD15EB3	0681
TVSRD15FM	0002
TVSRD15FMZ	0002
TVSRD16EB2	0440
TVSRD22EB1	0700
TVSRD24EB1	0489
TVSRD27E	0450
TVSRD27EB	0436
TVSRD27EB4	0450
TVSRD27EB4TN	0450
TVSRD27EB4Z	0450
TVSRD27EBS	0436
TVSRD27RB4TN	OEM
TVS-RD29AN	0195
TVSRD33EB	0166
TVSRD36EB3	0010
TVSRD36EB3V	0010
TVSRD36EB3Z	0010
TVSRD47EB2	0140
TVSRF1	0023
TVSRF-1A	0023
TVSRF1A	0023
TVSRG2	0031
TVSRG4	0031
TVSRG4J5	0031
TVSRGP10J	0023
TVSRH-1	0023
TVSRH1	0023
TVSRH1M	0023
TVSRH1S	0023
TVSRH1SV	0023
TVSRH2F	0017
TVSRH2FM	0344
TVSRM1	0023
TVSRM1Z	0015
TVSRM1ZM	0015
TVSRM1ZMV	0023
TVSRM2C	0023
TVSRM10	0023
TVSRM10B	0071
TVSRM10M	0071
TVSRM10MV	0071
TVSRM11B	0071
TVSRM25	0497
TVSRM-26	2144
TVSRM26V	1258
TVSRMP5020	0015
TVSRP1A	0102
TVSRU-2	0023
TVSRU2	0023
TVSRU2AM	0023
TVSRU2AN	0023
TVSRU2M	0023
TVSRU3AM	0282
TVSRU3AN	0023
TVSRU3N	0031
TVSRVDFV211	0139
TVSRVDKB167	1914
TVS-S1B02-03C	0087
TVS-S1B02-03CR	0087
TVSS1P20	0102
TVSS1R8D	0015
TVSS1R20	0133
TVSS1R80	2506
TVSS1WB10	0241
TVSS1WBS10	0241
TVSS3-2	0015
TVSS3G4	0071
TVSS4C	0015
TVSS4LS221N	1230
TVSS4LS374N	0708
TVSS15	0102
TVSS-34	0102
TVSS34	0023
TVS-S82	0015
TVSS1854	OEM
TVSS6321FLC6	1981
TVSS6394GLC6	0750
TVSSA-2	0087
TVSSA-2B	0087
TVSSA2B	0015
TVSSA-2H	0071
TVSSA2H	0071
TVSSB-2	0102
TVSSB2-C	1053
TVS-SB-2C	0102
TVSSB-2C	5104
TVSSB2C	5214
TVSSB-2G	0102
TVSSB-2T	0102
TVS-SB-20	0071
TVS-SC15	0030
TVSSC15	0030
TVS-SD-1	0102
TVSSD1A	0102
TVS-SD-1B	0102
TVS-SD1B	0102
TVS-SD-1B(BOOST)	0015
TVSSD-1Y	0023
TVSSD-14	0143
TVS-SD82	0911
TVSSE303A	0511
TVSSEL1410G	OEM
TVS-SF-1	0344
TVSSF-1	0102
TVSSID30-15	5104
TVSSIR80	2506
TVSSJE5472-1	0275
TVSSN74LS09N	1632
TVSSN7403N	0331
TVSSN7409N	0487
TVSSN7666N	0167
TVSSN76002N	OEM
TVSSN76642N	0673
TVSSN76664N	0167
TVSSN76665	0167
TVS-SPN01	0015
TVSSR2K	0023
TVSSR2KL	OEM
TVSSR2KN	OEM
TVSSR2KN(SR2KN)	OEM
TVSSTK436TV	OEM
TVSSTK4362TV	OEM
TVSSTR371	OEM
TVSSTR380	3461
TVSSTR381	3462
TVSSTR381A	3462
TVSSTR3130	1631
TVSSTR3230	1631
TVSSTR30130	2348
TVSSV02	0015
TVSSV03	0120
TVSSV-04	0120
TVSSV-05	0015
TVSTA7676AP	OEM
TVSTA7717AP	OEM
TVS-TC009M11/10	0015
TVS-TC009M21/3	0479
TVS-TC0-09M21/3	0479
TVS-TC0.09M11/10	0015
TVS-TC-0.09M21/3	0196
TVS-TC0.09M21/3	0479
TVS-TC0.0911/10	1293
TVSTC4011BP	0215
TVSTC4052BP	0024
TVSTC4053BP	0034
TVSTC4066BP	0101
TVSTC4069UBP	0119
TVSTD15	0182
TVSTD-15H	0102
TVSTD15M	0102
TVSTDA1190Z	1162
TVSTFH340M	0750
TVSTFS340M	0750
TVSTFS340MX	0750
TVSTFS340MY	0750
TVSTLN105A	OEM
TVSTLR321	OEM
TVSTMS1943A2	2279
TVSTMS1943N2	2279
TVSTMSI943A2	OEM
TVSUA67	0696
TVSUC78M12H2	0330
TVSUF2	0023
TVSUF-2B	0017
TVS-UFSD-1	0102
TVSUFSD-1	0015
TVSUFSD1	0102
TVSUFSD-1F	0015
TVSUFSD1F	0015
TVSUP574J	1319
TVSUPC23	0523
TVS-UPC23C	0523
TVSUPC23C	0523
TVSUPC78M-12H2	0330
TVSUPC78M12H2	0330
TVSUPC339C	0176
TVSUPC574J	1319
TVSUPC595C	0846
TVSUPC596C2	0851
TVSUPC1363CA	1934
TVSUPC1380C	1049
TVSUPD4011BC	0215
TVSUPD4013BC	0409
TVSUPD4017BC	0508
TVSUPD4027BC	1938
TVSUPD4052BC	0024
TVSUPD4053BC	0034
TVSUPD4066BC	0101
TVSUZ6R8B	0025
TVSUZ18BS	0371
TVSVD1221L	0120
TVSVFSD1	0102
TVSW04	0287
TVSW04-M	0106
TVSW04M	0106
TVSW270	0450
TVSWF2	0321
TVSWZ061	0091
TVSWZ270	0450
TVSYZ065F	0025
TVSYZ-080	0244
TVSYZ080	0244
TVSZB	0789
TVSZB1-6	0298
TVS-ZB1-11	0789
TVSZB1-11	0789
TVS-ZB1-15	0002
TVSZB1-15	0002
TVSZB1-27	0436
TVSZB1-29	0436
TVSZB-29	0436
TW3	0604
TW5	1345
TW6N100CZ	0154
TW6N100HZ	OEM
TW6N200CZ	0154
TW6N200HZ	OEM
TW6N300CZ	0147
TW6N300HZ	OEM
TW6N400CZ	0147
TW6N400HZ	OEM
TW6N500CZ	0278
TW6N500HZ	OEM
TW6N600CZ	0278
TW6N600HZ	OEM
TW6N700CZ	OEM
TW6N700HZ	OEM
TW7N400FZ	OEM
TW7N600FZ	OEM
TW7N700FZ	OEM
TW7N800FZ	OEM
TW8N100CZ	3119
TW8N100HZ	OEM
TW8N200CZ	3121
TW8N200HZ	OEM
TW8N300CZ	3123
TW8N300HZ	OEM
TW8N400CZ	3123
TW8N400HZ	OEM
TW8N500CZ	2007
TW8N500HZ	OEM
TW8N600CZ	3208
TW8N600HZ	OEM
TW8N700CZ	OEM
TW8N700HZ	OEM
TW9N400FZ	OEM
TW9N600FZ	OEM
TW9N700FZ	OEM
TW9N800FZ	OEM
TW10	0015
TW10N100CZ	3119
TW10N100HZ	OEM
TW10N200CZ	3121
TW10N200HZ	OEM
TW10N300CZ	3123
TW10N300HZ	OEM
TW10N400CZ	3123
TW10N400HZ	OEM
TW10N500CZ	4038
TW10N500HZ	OEM
TW10N600CZ	2007
TW10N600HZ	OEM
TW10N700CZ	OEM
TW10N700HZ	OEM
TW11N400FZ	OEM
TW11N600FZ	OEM
TW11N700FZ	OEM
TW11N800FZ	OEM
TW12N400CX	2006
TW12N400HX	OEM
TW12N600CX	2007
TW12N600HX	OEM
TW12N800CX	OEM
TW12N800HX	OEM
TW12N1000CX	OEM
TW12N1000HX	OEM
TW12N1100CX	OEM
TW12N1100HX	OEM
TW18N400CT	OEM
TW18N500CT	OEM
TW18N600CT	OEM
TW18N700CT	OEM
TW18N800CT	OEM
TW18N900CT	OEM
TW18N1000CT	OEM
TW18N1100CT	OEM
TW20	1345
TW25N400CT	OEM
TW25N500CT	OEM
TW25N600CT	OEM
TW25N700CT	OEM
TW25N800CT	OEM
TW25N900CT	OEM
TW25N1000CT	OEM
TW25N1100CT	OEM
TW30	1345
TW40	1345
TW50	1345
TW60	1345
TW-80	0071
TW80	1345
TW-100	0071
TW100	0071
TW120	OEM
TW135	0150
TWC5	OEM
TWC5A	OEM
TWC5B	OEM
TWC5C	OEM
TWC14	OEM
TWC14A	OEM
TWC14B	OEM
TWC14C	OEM
TWC18	OEM
TWJ30	OEM
TWLC200	OEM
TWS6	OEM
TWS7	OEM
TWS10/7642	OEM
TWS12	OEM
TWS17	OEM
TWS36	OEM
TWV	0604
TWX8	OEM
TWX16	OEM
TWX19	OEM
TWX22	OEM
TWX34	OEM
TX-0018	OEM
TX1N645	0015
TX1N647	0015
TX1N3190	0015
TX1N3191	0015
TX27A	0436
TX75	2296
TX-100-1	0086
TX100-1	0016
TX-100-2	0086
TX100-2	0016
TX-100-3	0142
TX100-3	0016
TX-100-4	0233
TX100-4	0086
TX-100-5	0142
TX100-5	0142
TX-101-8	0086
TX101-8	0142
TX-101-9	0086
TX101-9	0086
TX-101-11	0142
TX101-11	0142
TX-101-12	0016
TX101-12	0016
TX-102-1	0079
TX102-1	0016
TX102-2	0016
TX-102-4	0142
TX102-4	0142
TX-103-1	0160
TX103-1	0085
TX-104-3	0164
TX104-3	0164
TX-106-1	0164
TX106-1	0004
TX-107-1	0016
TX107-1	0016
TX-107-3	0127
TX107-3	0016
TX-107-4	0016
TX107-4	0016
TX-107-5	0016
TX107-5	0016
TX-107-6	0016
TX107-6	0016
TX-107-10	0016
TX107-10	0016
TX-107-12	0127
TX107-12	0016
TX-107-13	0142
TX107-13	0142
TX-107-16	0016
TX107-16	0016
TX-108-1	0079
TX108-1	0016
TX-111-1	0142
TX111-1	0142
TX-112-1	0016
TX112-1	0016
TX116-1	OEM
TX116-2	OEM
TX116-3	OEM
TX-119-1	0016
TX120	0127
TX121	0037
TX122	0037
TX-122-1	0037
TX-123	0396
TX123-1	0396
TX-124	0086
TX124	0086
TX124-1	0016
TX-125	0126
TX125	0037
TX125-1	0126
TX-126-1	0208
TX-128-1	0016
TX128-1	0086
TX-134-1	0037
TX134-1	0126
TX-135	0086
TX135	0086
TX-136	0126
TX136	0126
TX-138	0016
TX138	0086
TX-139	0126
TX139	0126
TX-140	0086
TX140	0086
TX-141	0016
TX141	0127
TX-145	1386
TX-183S	0074
TX287	OEM
TX-429D	OEM
TX827	OEM
TX-1005	0178
TX1005	0142
TXAL116B	0550
TXAL116C	0550
TXAL116G	OEM
TXAL116M	0550
TXAL118B	0550
TXAL118C	0550
TXAL118G	OEM
TXAL118M	0550
TXAL226B	0550
TXAL226C	0550
TXAL226G	OEM
TXAL226M	0550
TXAL228B	0550
TXAL228C	0550
TXAL228G	OEM
TXAL228M	0550
TXAL386B	OEM
TXAL386C	OEM
TXAL386M	OEM
TXAL388B	OEM
TXAL388C	OEM
TXAL388M	OEM
TXAL606B	OEM
TXAL606C	OEM
TXAL606G	OEM
TXAL606M	OEM
TXAL608B	OEM
TXAL608C	OEM
TXAL608G	OEM
TXAL608M	OEM
TXAL610B	OEM
TXAL610C	OEM
TXAL610G	OEM
TXAL610M	OEM
TXAL615B	OEM
TXAL615C	OEM
TXAL615G	OEM
TXAL615M	OEM
TXAL1110B	0550
TXAL1110C	0550
TXAL1110G	OEM
TXAL1110M	0550
TXAL1115B	OEM
TXAL1115C	OEM
TXAL1115G	OEM
TXAL1115M	OEM
TXAL2210B	0550
TXAL2210C	0550
TXAL2210G	OEM
TXAL2210M	0550
TXAL2215B	OEM
TXAL2215C	OEM
TXAL2215G	OEM
TXAL2215M	OEM
TXAL3810B	OEM
TXAL3810C	OEM
TXAL3810M	OEM
TXAL3815B	OEM
TXAL3815M	OEM
TXB3518MA	0037
TXC0063	OEM
TXC01A10	OEM
TXC01A20	OEM
TXC01A40	OEM
TXC01A50	OEM
TXC01A60	OEM
TXC01C60	OEM
TXC02A10	OEM
TXC02A20	OEM
TXC02A40	OEM
TXC02A50	OEM
TXC02A60	OEM
TXC03A10	OEM
TXC03A20	OEM
TXC03A40	OEM
TXC03A50	OEM
TXC03A60	OEM
TXC10K80	0869
TXC30L70	OEM
TXC38D60	OEM
TXC38E40	OEM
TXC38G70	OEM
TXC38G80	OEM
TXC38H40	OEM
TXC38H60	OEM
TXC39D60	OEM
TXC39E40	OEM
TXC39E60	OEM
TXC39G80	OEM
TXC39H40	OEM
TXC39H60	OEM
TXD10K50M	0612
TXD98A20	OEM
TXD98A40	OEM
TXD98A50	OEM
TXD98A60	OEM
TXD99A20	OEM
TXD99A40	OEM
TXD99A50	OEM
TXD99A60	OEM
TXDV208	OEM

DEVICE TYPE	REPL CODE
TXDV408	OEM
TXDV608	OEM
TXDV808	OEM
TXE99A20	OEM
TXE99A40	OEM
TXE99A50	OEM
TXE99A60	OEM
TXED453C025	OEM
TXED453C050	OEM
TXED453C100	OEM
TXED455	OEM
TXED456	OEM
TXED457	OEM
TXEF402	OEM
TXEF402M001	OEM
TXEF402M003	OEM
TXEF402M006	OEM
TXEF402M010	OEM
TXEF402M020	OEM
TXEF402M030	OEM
TXEF402M040	OEM
TXEF402M050	OEM
TXES37	OEM
TXES475C025	OEM
TXES475C050	OEM
TXES475C100	OEM
TXES476C025	OEM
TXES476C050	OEM
TXES476C100	OEM
TXES478	OEM
TXES479	OEM
TXES480	OEM
TXES481	OEM
TXES482	OEM
TXES483	OEM
TXES488	OEM
TXES489	OEM
TXES490	OEM
TXES491	OEM
TXES492	OEM
TXES493	OEM
TXL-80	2296
TXL-100	2296
TXN0510	0998
TXN108(A)	OEM
TXN110	0998
TXN210	0998
TXN410	1028
TXN610	1140
TXN810	OEM
TXN1010	OEM
TXS607-8(A)	OEM
TXZ4206	0326
TY2SA933	0148
TY2SA1198E	0688
TY2SA1198S	0688
TY2SB822Q	4043
TY2SC1652(Q)	2452
TY2SC1652Q	2452
TY2SC1652R	2452
TY2SC1740	0151
TY105F	OEM
TY-107-4	0016
TY-107-12	0016
TY120SP8K2	OEM
TY120SP10K2	OEM
TY120SP12K2	OEM
TY120SP14K2	OEM
TY120SP16K2	OEM
TY120SP18K2	OEM
TY180NP2K2	OEM
TY180NP3K2	OEM
TY180NP4K2	OEM
TY180NP5K2	OEM
TY180NP6K2	OEM
TY180NP7K2	OEM
TY180NP8K2	OEM
TY180QP2K2	OEM
TY180QP3K2	OEM
TY180QP4K2	OEM
TY180QP5K2	OEM
TY180QP6K2	OEM
TY180QP7K2	OEM
TY180QP8K2	OEM
TY290SP8K2	OEM
TY290SP10K2	OEM
TY290SP12K2	OEM
TY290SP14K2	OEM
TY290SP16K2	OEM
TY290SP18K2	OEM
TY490SP8K2	OEM
TY490SP10K2	OEM
TY490SP12K2	OEM
TY490SP14K2	OEM
TY490SP16K2	OEM
TY490SP18K2	OEM
TY500SK2P8	OEM
TY500SK2P10	OEM
TY500SK2P12	OEM
TY500SK2P14	OEM
TY500SK2P16	OEM
TY500SK2P18	OEM
TY500SP8K2	OEM
TY500SP10K2	OEM
TY500SP12K2	OEM
TY500SP14K2	OEM
TY500SP16K2	OEM
TY500SP18K2	OEM
TY504	2084

DEVICE TYPE	REPL CODE
TY505F	OEM
TY507	OEM
TY508	2084
TY508FA	OEM
TY510	2499
TY718	OEM
TY1004	2078
TY1007	OEM
TY1008	2078
TY1010	0393
TY2004	0500
TY2005F	OEM
TY2007	OEM
TY2008	0500
TY2008FA	OEM
TY2010	0393
TY2010GH	OEM
TY3004	0705
TY3005F	OEM
TY3007	OEM
TY3008	0705
TY3010	0606
TY4004	0705
TY4005F	OEM
TY4007	OEM
TY4008	0705
TY4008FA	OEM
TY4010	0606
TY5004	0857
TY5005F	OEM
TY5007	OEM
TY5008	0857
TY5010	0946
TY6004	0857
TY6005F	OEM
TY6007	OEM
TY6008	0857
TY6008FA	OEM
TY6010	0946
TY8008	OEM
TY8010	OEM
TYA290SP8K2	OEM
TYA290SP10K2	OEM
TYA290SP12K2	OEM
TYA290SP14K2	OEM
TYA290SP16K2	OEM
TYA290SP18K2	OEM
TYA490SP8K2	OEM
TYA490SP10K2	OEM
TYA490SP12K2	OEM
TYA490SP14K2	OEM
TYA490SP16K2	OEM
TYA490SP18K2	OEM
TYAL113B	OEM
TYAL113C	OEM
TYAL113G	OEM
TYAL113M	OEM
TYAL114B	OEM
TYAL114C	OEM
TYAL114M	OEM
TYAL116C	0550
TYAL116G	OEM
TYAL116M	0550
TYAL118B	0550
TYAL118C	0550
TYAL118G	OEM
TYAL118M	0550
TYAL223B	OEM
TYAL223C	OEM
TYAL223G	OEM
TYAL223M	OEM
TYAL226B	0550
TYAL226C	0550
TYAL226G	OEM
TYAL226M	0550
TYAL228B	0550
TYAL228C	0550
TYAL228G	OEM
TYAL228M	0550
TYAL383B	OEM
TYAL383C	OEM
TYAL383M	OEM
TYAL386B	OEM
TYAL386C	OEM
TYAL386M	OEM
TYAL388B	OEM
TYAL388C	OEM
TYAL388M	OEM
TYAL603B	OEM
TYAL603C	OEM
TYAL603G	OEM
TYAL603M	OEM
TYAL606B	OEM
TYAL606C	OEM
TYAL606G	OEM
TYAL606M	OEM
TYAL608B	OEM
TYAL608C	OEM
TYAL608G	OEM
TYAL608M	OEM
TYAL610B	OEM
TYAL610C	OEM
TYAL610G	OEM
TYAL610M	OEM
TYAL615B	OEM
TYAL615C	OEM
TYAL615G	OEM
TYAL615M	OEM
TYAL1110B	0550

DEVICE TYPE	REPL CODE
TYAL1110C	0550
TYAL1110G	OEM
TYAL1110M	0550
TYAL1115B	OEM
TYAL1115C	OEM
TYAL1115G	OEM
TYAL1115M	OEM
TYAL2210B	0550
TYAL2210C	0550
TYAL2210G	OEM
TYAL2210M	0550
TYAL2215B	OEM
TYAL2215C	OEM
TYAL2215G	OEM
TYAL2215M	OEM
TYAL3810B	OEM
TYAL3810C	OEM
TYAL3810M	OEM
TYAL3815B	OEM
TYAL3815M	OEM
TYC300SK2P8	OEM
TYC300SK2P10	OEM
TYC300SK2P12	OEM
TYC300SK2P14	OEM
TYC300SK2P16	OEM
TYC300SK2P18	OEM
TYDTA124	1026
TYDTA124N	1026
TYDTA124S	1026
TYDTA144	4067
TYDTA144S	4067
TYDTC114ES	0826
TYDTC114Y	OEM
TYDTC124	0881
TYDTC124N	0881
TYDTC124S	0881
TYDTC144N	0892
TYDTC144S	0892
TYK8820	OEM
TYN058	2084
TYN0510	OEM
TYN104(A)	OEM
TYN110	OEM
TYN204(A)	OEM
TYN208	0500
TYN210	OEM
TYN404(A)	OEM
TYN408(A)	OEM
TYN410	0705
TYN604(A)	OEM
TYN608(A)	OEM
TYN610	OEM
TYN804(A)	OEM
TYN808(A)	OEM
TYN810	OEM
TYN1004(A)	OEM
TYN1008(A)	OEM
TYN1010	OEM
TYP212	OEM
TYP512	OEM
TYP1012	OEM
TYP2012	OEM
TYPD0312UAR	OEM
TYS406-05(A)	OEM
TYS407-05(A)	OEM
TZ4A326	0023
TZ4C254	0015
TZ4C284	0023
TZ4E254	0015
TZ4F339-4	OEM
TZ4.7	0140
TZ5.1	0041
TZ5.6	0253
TZ6	0160
TZ6.2	0466
TZ6.8	0062
TZ6.8A	0025
TZ6.8B	0025
TZ6.8C	0025
TZ6.8D	OEM
TZ7	0160
TZ7.5	0077
TZ7.5A	0644
TZ7.5B	0644
TZ7.5C	0644
TZ7.5D	OEM
TZ-8	0160
TZ8	0160
TZ8.2	0165
TZ8.2A	0244
TZ8.2B	0244
TZ8.2C	0244
TZ8.2D	3071
TZ9	0012
TZ9.1	0057
TZ9.1A	0012
TZ9.1B	0012
TZ9.1C	0012
TZ9.1D	0012
TZ10	0064
TZ10A	0170
TZ10B	0170
TZ10C	0170
TZ10D	OEM
TZ11	0181
TZ11A	0313
TZ11B	0313
TZ11C	0313
TZ11D	OEM

DEVICE TYPE	REPL CODE
TZ12	0052
TZ12A	0137
TZ12B	0137
TZ12C	0137
TZ12D	OEM
TZ13	0053
TZ13A	0361
TZ13B	0361
TZ13C	0361
TZ13D	OEM
TZ14	0100
TZ14A	0100
TZ14B	0100
TZ14C	0100
TZ14D	OEM
TZ15	0681
TZ15A	0002
TZ15B	0002
TZ15C	0002
TZ15D	OEM
TZ16	0440
TZ16A	0416
TZ16B	0416
TZ16C	0416
TZ16D	OEM
TZ17	1639
TZ17A	1639
TZ17B	1639
TZ17C	1639
TZ17D	OEM
TZ18	0371
TZ18A	0490
TZ18B	0490
TZ18C	0490
TZ18D	OEM
TZ19	0943
TZ19A	0943
TZ19B	0943
TZ19C	0943
TZ19D	OEM
TZ20	0695
TZ20A	0526
TZ20B	0526
TZ20C	0526
TZ20D	OEM
TZ22	0700
TZ22A	0560
TZ22B	0560
TZ22C	0560
TZ22D	OEM
TZ24	0489
TZ24A	0398
TZ24B	0398
TZ24C	0398
TZ24D	OEM
TZ25	1596
TZ25A	1596
TZ25B	1596
TZ25C	1596
TZ25D	OEM
TZ26	0436
TZ26A	0436
TZ27	0436
TZ27A	0436
TZ27AA	0436
TZ27B	0436
TZ27C	0436
TZ27D	OEM
TZ28	1664
TZ28A	1664
TZ30	0721
TZ30A	0721
TZ30B	0721
TZ30C	0721
TZ30D	OEM
TZ33	0039
TZ33A	0039
TZ33B	0039
TZ33C	0039
TZ33D	OEM
TZ36	0814
TZ36A	0814
TZ36B	0814
TZ36C	0814
TZ36D	OEM
TZ39	0346
TZ39A	0346
TZ39B	0346
TZ39C	0346
TZ39D	OEM
TZ40	OEM
TZ40A	0346
TZ43	0925
TZ43A	0925
TZ43B	0925
TZ43C	0925
TZ43D	OEM
TZ45	0993
TZ45A	0993
TZ45B	0993
TZ45C	0993
TZ45D	OEM
TZ47	0993
TZ47A	0993
TZ47B	0993
TZ47C	0993
TZ47D	OEM
TZ48	0993
TZ48A	0993

DEVICE TYPE	REPL CODE
TZ50	0497
TZ50A	0497
TZ50B	0497
TZ50C	0497
TZ50D	OEM
TZ51	0497
TZ51A	0497
TZ51B	0497
TZ51C	0497
TZ51D	OEM
TZ52	0497
TZ52A	0497
TZ52B	0497
TZ52C	0497
TZ52D	OEM
TZ54	0863
TZ54A	0863
TZ56	0863
TZ56A	0863
TZ56B	0863
TZ56C	0863
TZ56D	0863
TZ58	1148
TZ58A	1148
TZ60	1148
TZ60A	1148
TZ62	0778
TZ62A	0778
TZ62B	0778
TZ62C	0778
TZ62D	OEM
TZ64	0778
TZ64A	0778
TZ68	2144
TZ68A	2144
TZ68B	2144
TZ68C	2144
TZ68D	OEM
TZ75	1181
TZ75A	1181
TZ75B	1181
TZ75C	1181
TZ75D	OEM
TZ81	0111
TZ82	0111
TZ82A	0327
TZ82B	0439
TZ82C	0327
TZ82D	OEM
TZ85	2997
TZ85A	2997
TZ90	1301
TZ90A	1301
TZ91	1301
TZ91A	1301
TZ91B	1301
TZ91C	1301
TZ91D	OEM
TZ100	0098
TZ100A	0098
TZ100B	0098
TZ100C	0098
TZ100D	OEM
TZ105	0149
TZ105A	0149
TZ105B	0149
TZ105C	0149
TZ105D	OEM
TZ110	0149
TZ110A	0149
TZ110B	0149
TZ110C	0149
TZ110D	OEM
TZ120	0186
TZ120A	0186
TZ120B	0186
TZ120C	0186
TZ120D	OEM
TZ130	0213
TZ130A	0213
TZ130B	0213
TZ130C	0213
TZ130D	OEM
TZ140	0245
TZ140A	0245
TZ140B	0245
TZ140C	0245
TZ140D	OEM
TZ150	0028
TZ150A	0028
TZ150B	0028
TZ150C	0028
TZ150D	OEM
TZ160	0255
TZ160A	0255
TZ160B	0255
TZ160C	0255
TZ160D	OEM
TZ170	0871
TZ170A	0871
TZ175	0363
TZ175A	0363
TZ175B	0363
TZ175C	0363
TZ175D	OEM
TZ180	0363
TZ180A	0363
TZ180B	0363
TZ180C	0363

DEVICE TYPE	REPL CODE
TZ180D	OEM
TZ200	0417
TZ200A	0417
TZ200B	0417
TZ200C	OEM
TZ200D	OEM
TZ220	OEM
TZ220A	OEM
TZ220B	OEM
TZ220C	OEM
TZ220D	OEM
TZ240	OEM
TZ240A	OEM
TZ260	OEM
TZ260A	OEM
TZ270	OEM
TZ270A	OEM
TZ275	OEM
TZ275A	OEM
TZ278	OEM
TZ278A	OEM
TZ280	OEM
TZ280A	OEM
TZ543	0037
TZ-551	0037
TZ551	0037
TZ-552	0786
TZ552	0037
TZ-553	0786
TZ553	0786
TZ554	0786
TZ581	1357
TZ582	1357
TZ966-03	0042
TZ990	OEM
TZ992-01	OEM
TZ1029-01	0065
TZ1034	0283
TZ1037	0283
TZ1088	OEM
TZ1151	0111
TZ1152	0111
TZ1153	0133
TZ1160	0016
TZ1180	0016
TZ1182	0016
TZ2001	OEM
TZ2002	OEM
TZ2003	OEM
TZ7000	0086
TZ7001	0086
TZ7002	0079
TZ7003	0079
TZ7500	0037
TZ7501	0037
TZ7502	OEM
TZ7503	0037
TZB6.8A	0025
TZB6.8B	0025
TZB7.5A	0644
TZB7.5B	0644
TZB8.2A	0244
TZB8.2B	0244
TZB9.1A	0012
TZB9.1B	0012
TZB10A	0170
TZB10B	0170
TZB11A	0313
TZB11B	0313
TZB12A	0137
TZB12B	0137
TZB13A	0361
TZB13B	0361
TZB15A	0002
TZB15B	0002
TZB16A	0416
TZB16B	0416
TZB18A	0490
TZB18B	0490
TZB20A	0526
TZB20B	0526
TZB22A	0560
TZB22B	0560
TZB24A	0398
TZB24B	0398
TZB27A	0436
TZB27B	0436
TZB30A	0721
TZB30B	0721
TZB33A	0039
TZB33B	0039
TZB36A	0814
TZB36B	0814
TZB39A	0346
TZB39B	0346
TZB43A	0925
TZB43B	0925
TZB47A	0993
TZB47B	0993
TZB51A	0497
TZB51B	0497
TZB56A	0863
TZB56B	0863
TZB62A	0778
TZB62B	0778
TZB68A	2144
TZB68B	2144
TZB75A	1181
TZB75B	1181

DEVICE TYPE	REPL CODE
TZB82A	0327
TZB82B	0327
TZB91A	1301
TZB91B	1301
TZB100A	0098
TZB100B	0098
TZB110A	0149
TZB110B	0149
TZB120A	0186
TZB120B	0186
TZB130A	0213
TZB130B	0213
TZB150A	0028
TZB150B	0028
TZB160A	0255
TZB160B	0255
TZB170A	0871
TZB170B	0871
TZB180A	0363
TZB180B	0363
TZB200A	0417
TZB200B	0417
TZB220A	OEM
TZB220B	OEM
TZB250A	OEM
TZB250B	OEM
TZB300A	OEM
TZB300B	OEM
TZB350A	OEM
TZB350B	OEM
TZB400A	OEM
TZB400B	OEM
TZC6.8	0205
TZC6.8A	0205
TZC6.8B	0205
TZC6.8C	OEM
TZC6.8D	OEM
TZC6.8E	OEM
TZC7.5	0475
TZC7.5A	0475
TZC7.5B	0475
TZC7.5C	OEM
TZC7.5D	OEM
TZC7.5E	OEM
TZC8.2	0499
TZC8.2A	0499
TZC8.2B	0499
TZC8.2C	OEM
TZC8.2D	OEM
TZC8.2E	OEM
TZC9.1	0679
TZC9.1A	0679
TZC9.1B	0679
TZC9.1C	OEM
TZC9.1D	OEM
TZC9.1E	OEM
TZC10	0225
TZC10A	0225
TZC10B	0225
TZC10C	OEM
TZC10D	OEM
TZC10E	OEM
TZC11	0230
TZC11A	0230
TZC11B	0230
TZC11C	OEM
TZC11D	OEM
TZC11E	OEM
TZC12	0234
TZC12A	0234
TZC12B	0234
TZC12C	OEM
TZC12D	OEM
TZC12E	OEM
TZC13	0237
TZC13A	0237
TZC13B	0237
TZC13C	OEM
TZC13D	OEM
TZC13E	OEM
TZC14	1387
TZC14A	1387
TZC14B	1387
TZC14C	OEM
TZC14D	OEM
TZC14E	OEM
TZC15	0247
TZC15A	0247
TZC15B	0247
TZC15C	OEM
TZC15D	OEM
TZC15E	OEM
TZC17	1170
TZC17A	1170
TZC17B	1246
TZC17C	OEM
TZC17D	OEM
TZC17E	OEM
TZC18	0256
TZC18A	0256
TZC18B	0256
TZC18C	OEM
TZC18D	OEM
TZC18E	OEM
TZC19	2379
TZC19A	2379
TZC19B	2379
TZC19C	OEM
TZC19D	OEM

If replacement code is OEM, contact original manufacturer for replacement.

DEVICE TYPE	REPL CODE
TZC19E	OEM
TZC20	0262
TZC20A	0262
TZC20B	0262
TZC20C	OEM
TZC20D	OEM
TZC20E	OEM
TZC22	0269
TZC22A	0269
TZC22B	0269
TZC22C	OEM
TZC22D	OEM
TZC22E	OEM
TZC24	0273
TZC24A	0273
TZC24B	0273
TZC24C	OEM
TZC24D	OEM
TZC24E	OEM
TZC25	2383
TZC25A	2383
TZC25B	2383
TZC25C	OEM
TZC25D	OEM
TZC25E	OEM
TZC27	0291
TZC27A	0291
TZC27B	0291
TZC27C	OEM
TZC27D	OEM
TZC27E	OEM
TZC30	0305
TZC30A	0305
TZC30B	0305
TZC30C	OEM
TZC30D	OEM
TZC30E	OEM
TZC33	0314
TZC33A	0314
TZC33B	0314
TZC33C	OEM
TZC33D	OEM
TZC33E	OEM
TZC36	0316
TZC36A	0316
TZC36B	0316
TZC36C	OEM
TZC36D	OEM
TZC36E	OEM
TZC39	0322
TZC39A	0322
TZC39B	0322
TZC39C	OEM
TZC39D	OEM
TZC39E	OEM
TZC43	0333
TZC43A	0333
TZC43B	0333
TZC43C	OEM
TZC43D	0333
TZC43E	OEM
TZC45	0343
TZC45A	0343
TZC45B	0343
TZC45C	OEM
TZC45D	OEM
TZC45E	OEM
TZC47	0343
TZC47A	0343
TZC47B	0343
TZC47C	OEM
TZC47D	OEM
TZC47E	OEM
TZC50	0027
TZC50A	0027
TZC50B	0027
TZC50C	OEM
TZC50D	OEM
TZC50E	OEM
TZC51	0027
TZC51A	0027
TZC51B	0027
TZC51C	OEM
TZC51D	OEM
TZC51E	OEM
TZC52	0027
TZC52A	0027
TZC52B	0027
TZC52C	OEM
TZC52D	OEM
TZC52E	OEM
TZC56	0266
TZC56A	0266
TZC56B	0266
TZC56C	OEM
TZC56D	OEM
TZC56E	OEM
TZC62	0382
TZC62A	0382
TZC62B	0382
TZC62C	OEM
TZC62D	OEM
TZC62E	OEM
TZC63C	OEM
TZC68	0401
TZC68A	0401
TZC68B	0401
TZC68C	OEM
TZC68D	OEM

DEVICE TYPE	REPL CODE
TZC68E	OEM
TZC75	0421
TZC75A	0421
TZC75B	0421
TZC75C	OEM
TZC75D	OEM
TZC75E	OEM
TZC82	0439
TZC82A	0439
TZC82B	0439
TZC82C	OEM
TZC82D	OEM
TZC82E	OEM
TZC91	0238
TZC91A	0238
TZC91B	0238
TZC91C	OEM
TZC91D	OEM
TZC91E	OEM
TZC100	1172
TZC100A	1172
TZC100B	1172
TZC100C	OEM
TZC100D	OEM
TZC100E	OEM
TZC105	1182
TZC105A	1182
TZC105B	1182
TZC105C	OEM
TZC105D	OEM
TZC105E	OEM
TZC110	1182
TZC110A	1182
TZC110B	1182
TZC110C	OEM
TZC110D	OEM
TZC110E	OEM
TZC120	1198
TZC120A	1198
TZC120B	1198
TZC120C	OEM
TZC120D	OEM
TZC120E	OEM
TZC130	1209
TZC130A	1209
TZC130B	1209
TZC130C	OEM
TZC130D	OEM
TZC130E	OEM
TZC140	1870
TZC140A	1870
TZC140B	1870
TZC140C	OEM
TZC140D	OEM
TZC140E	OEM
TZC150	0642
TZC150A	0642
TZC150B	0642
TZC150C	OEM
TZC150D	OEM
TZC150E	OEM
TZC160	1246
TZC160A	1246
TZC160B	1246
TZC160C	OEM
TZC160D	OEM
TZC160E	OEM
TZC180	1269
TZC180A	1269
TZC180B	1269
TZC180C	OEM
TZC180D	OEM
TZC180E	OEM
TZC200	0600
TZC200A	0600
TZC200B	0600
TZC200C	OEM
TZC200D	OEM
TZC200E	OEM
TZPD3.9	0036
TZPD4.3	0274
TZPD4.7	0140
TZPD5.1	0041
TZPY3.9	0036
TZPY4.3	0274
TZPY4.7	0140
TZPY5.1	0041
TZV6.2	OEM
TZV6.2A	OEM
TZV6.8	OEM
TZV6.8A	OEM
TZV7.5	OEM
TZV7.5A	OEM
TZV8.2	OEM
TZV8.2A	OEM
TZV9.1	OEM
TZV9.1A	OEM
TZV10	OEM
TZV10A	OEM
TZV10.A	OEM
TZV11	OEM
TZV11A	OEM
TZV11.A	OEM
TZV12	OEM
TZV12A	OEM
TZV12.A	OEM
TZV13	OEM
TZV13A	OEM
TZV13.A	OEM

DEVICE TYPE	REPL CODE
TZV15	OEM
TZV15A	OEM
TZV15.A	OEM
TZV16	OEM
TZV16A	OEM
TZV16.A	OEM
TZV18	OEM
TZV18A	OEM
TZV18.A	OEM
TZV20	OEM
TZV20A	OEM
TZV20.A	OEM
TZV22	OEM
TZV22A	OEM
TZV22.A	OEM
TZV24	OEM
TZV24A	OEM
TZV24.A	OEM
TZV27	OEM
TZV27A	OEM
TZV27.A	OEM
TZV30	OEM
TZV30A	OEM
TZV30.A	OEM
TZV33	OEM
TZV33A	OEM
TZV33.A	OEM
TZV36	OEM
TZV36A	OEM
TZV36.A	OEM
TZV39	OEM
TZV39A	OEM
TZV39.A	OEM
TZV43	OEM
TZV43A	OEM
TZV43.A	OEM
TZV47	OEM
TZV47A	OEM
TZV47.A	OEM
TZV51	OEM
TZV51A	OEM
TZV51.A	OEM
TZV56	OEM
TZV56A	OEM
TZV56.A	OEM
TZV62	OEM
TZV62A	OEM
TZV62.A	OEM
TZV68	OEM
TZV68A	OEM
TZV68.A	OEM
TZV75	OEM
TZV75A	OEM
TZV75.A	OEM
TZV82	OEM
TZV82A	OEM
TZV82.A	OEM
TZV91	OEM
TZV91A	OEM
TZV91.A	OEM
TZV100	OEM
TZV100A	OEM
TZV100.A	OEM
TZV110	OEM
TZV110A	OEM
TZV110.A	OEM
TZV120	OEM
TZV120A	OEM
TZV120.A	OEM
TZV130	OEM
TZV130A	OEM
TZV130.A	OEM
TZV150	OEM
TZV150A	OEM
TZV150.A	OEM
TZV160	OEM
TZV160A	OEM
TZV160.A	OEM
TZV170	OEM
TZV170A	OEM
TZV170.A	OEM
TZV180	OEM
TZV180A	OEM
TZV180.A	OEM
TZV200	OEM
TZV200A	OEM
TZV200.A	OEM
T.4HP521	OEM
T.75F50	OEM
T.75F100	OEM
T.75F200	OEM
T.75F400	OEM
U	OEM
U0-5E	0535
U01R-24	OEM
U01R-30	OEM
U03C	0865
U03E	0847
U03R-2	0017
U03R-4	0017
U03R-8	0017
U03R-12	0017
U03R-16	0017
U03R-20	0017
U04C	0865
U04E	0847
U05-E	0072
U05B	0559
U05C	0087

DEVICE TYPE	REPL CODE
U05E	0535
U05ES	0087
U05G	0959
U05J	0811
U06B	0031
U06C	0023
U06CS	4833
U06E	0015
U06G	0959
U06J	0811
U07J	0017
U07L	0017
U07M	0017
U07N	0017
U0A	0023
U1	0023
U1B4B42	OEM
U1BZ41	OEM
U1D4B42	OEM
U1DZ41	OEM
U1G4B42	OEM
U1GZ41	OEM
U1J4B42	OEM
U1JZ41	OEM
U1S102	0015
U1Z	0023
U2	0023
U2A	0023
U2N34	0211
U2N96	0211
U2N474A	0198
U2S93	0136
U2SB267	0004
U2T85	0208
U2T101	OEM
U2T105	OEM
U2T151	OEM
U2T155	OEM
U2T201	OEM
U2T205	OEM
U2T251	OEM
U2T255	OEM
U2T301	OEM
U2T305	OEM
U2T351	OEM
U2T355	OEM
U2T401	OEM
U2T405	OEM
U2T451	OEM
U2T455	OEM
U2T501	OEM
U2T505	OEM
U2T601	OEM
U2T605	OEM
U2TA406	1203
U2TA408	1203
U2TA410	OEM
U2TA506	OEM
U2TA508	OEM
U2TA510	OEM
U2TB406	1203
U2TB408	1203
U2TB410	OEM
U2TD410	1203
U2TD420	OEM
U2TD430	OEM
U2TG406	1203
U2TG408	1203
U2TG410	OEM
U5B771739	OEM
U5B992328	OEM
U5D770331X	0627
U5D770339X	0627
U5D7703312	0627
U5D7703393	0627
U5D7703394	0627
U5E7746394	0748
U5L	0378
U5.6BSA	OEM
U6A7065354	0167
U6A7729394	0438
U6A7732394	0649
U6A7746394	0661
U6A7767394	0696
U6A7781394	0350
U6B7780394	0348
U6E7729394	0438
U7F7065354	0167
U7F7729394	0438
U7F7732394	0649
U7F7746394	0661
U7F7767394	0696
U7F7780394	0348
U7F7781394	0350
U8A992329	OEM
U8B770339	0627
U8B770339-825	0627
U8B770339X	0627
U8B7703394	0627
U8F7737394	2147
U8F7746394	2147
U9A7746394	0345
U9A7781394	0350
U9B7780394	0348
U9C7065354	0167
U13T1	OEM
U13T2	OEM
U13T3	OEM
U13T4	OEM

DEVICE TYPE	REPL CODE
U15B	0087
U15C	0087
U15E	0087
U15G	0087
U15J	0087
U17B	0031
U17C	0031
U17D	0031
U17E	0031
U19-E	0031
U19B	0031
U19C	0031
U19E	0031
U19E-F	0031
U19E-FK	0031
U22	OEM
U33N	0023
U47ZA1	OEM
U89	OEM
U90A	OEM
U106BS	OEM
U111B	OEM
U112BA	OEM
U114	OEM
U117	0321
U119	0071
U120	0071
U139	OEM
U139D	OEM
U182	OEM
U197	0321
U199	1147
U201	1147
U203	OEM
U204	OEM
U205	OEM
U206	OEM
U207	OEM
U212	0015
U212-25	0015
U213	1219
U214	0015
U222	1147
U235	0321
U244	OEM
U248	OEM
U248A	OEM
U249	OEM
U249A	OEM
U250	OEM
U250A	OEM
U251	OEM
U251A	0647
U252	OEM
U253	OEM
U254	OEM
U255	OEM
U256	OEM
U266	OEM
U273	OEM
U273A	OEM
U274	OEM
U274A	OEM
U275	OEM
U275A	OEM
U280	OEM
U281	OEM
U282	OEM
U283	OEM
U284	OEM
U285	OEM
U308	2861
U309	2861
U310	OEM
U311	2861
U312	2861
U318	OEM
U319	OEM
U328	OEM
U329	OEM
U330	OEM
U331	OEM
U361	0071
U401B	0647
U410	2917
U410B	OEM
U411	2917
U412	2917
U417B	5103
U418B	OEM
U420B	OEM
U-422	0015
U460A	0127
U460A,B	0127
U460B	0127
U535A	0224
U535A,B	0127
U535B	0224
U535C	0016
U535M	0016
U552D	4295
U574	1319
U574(IC)	1319
U574K	1319
U1001	OEM
U1002	OEM
U-1003	OEM
U1003	OEM
U-1004	OEM

DEVICE TYPE	REPL CODE
U1004	OEM
U1005	OEM
U1006	OEM
U1007	OEM
U1008	OEM
U1009	OEM
U1010	OEM
U1178	0321
U1180	3577
U1181	0321
U1285	0321
U1321	OEM
U1322	3577
U1323	0321
U1324	0321
U1420	0321
U1421	0321
U1422	0321
U1585E	0016
U1585F	0016
U1585F,H	0127
U1585G	0016
U1585H	0016
U1715	0321
U1837E	0321
U1897E	3102
U1916	0321
U1994E	0321
U2400-03	0015
U2848-1	0016
U8423	OEM
U8508E	OEM
U8514A	OEM
U8514B	OEM
U8516C	OEM
U8522A	OEM
UA0801ADM	OEM
UA0801AFM	OEM
UA0801CDC	OEM
UA0801CPC	OEM
UA0801DM	OEM
UA0801EDC	OEM
UA0801EPC	OEM
UA0801FM	OEM
UA0801HDC	OEM
UA0801HPC	OEM
UA0802ADC	OEM
UA0802APC	OEM
UA0802BDC	OEM
UA0802BPC	OEM
UA0802CDC	OEM
UA0802CPC	OEM
UA0802DM	OEM
UA0802FM	OEM
UA0802HDC	OEM
UA0802HPC	OEM
UA8T24DC	OEM
UA8T26	4437
UA8T26ADC	OEM
UA8T26ADM	OEM
UA8T26APC	OEM
UA8T26D	4437
UA8T26DC	4437
UA8T26P	4437
UA8T26PC	4437
UA8T28	0576
UA8T28D	0576
UA8T28DC	0576
UA8T28DM	0576
UA8T28P	0576
UA8T28PC	0576
UA67	0696
UA74H53A	OEM
UA78GC-U1	OEM
UA78GKC	5197
UA78GKM	OEM
UA78GU1C	3771
UA78H05KC	2836
UA78H12KC	3359
UA78H15KC	5905
UA78HGKC	2710
UA78L	0083
UA78L00AC	OEM
UA78L00C	OEM
UA78L02AC	OEM
UA78L02ACJG	OEM
UA78L02ACLP	OEM
UA78L02AS	OEM
UA78L02C	OEM
UA78L02CJG	OEM
UA78L02CLP	OEM
UA78L02S	OEM
UA78L05	1288
UA78L05AC	1288
UA78L05ACJG	OEM
UA78L05ACLP	1288
UA78L05ADB	OEM
UA78L05AHC	OEM
UA78L05AS	OEM
UA78L05AWC	1288
UA78L05AWV	OEM
UA78L05C	1288
UA78L05CJG	OEM
UA78L05CLP	1288
UA78L05DB	OEM
UA78L05HC	OEM
UA78L05HM	OEM
UA78L05S	1288
UA78L05WC	1288

DEVICE TYPE	REPL CODE
UA78L06	4018
UA78L06AC	OEM
UA78L06ACJG	OEM
UA78L06ACLP	2285
UA78L06AS	2285
UA78L06C	OEM
UA78L06CJG	OEM
UA78L06CLP	2285
UA78L06S	2285
UA78L08	0083
UA78L08AC	0083
UA78L08ACJG	OEM
UA78L08ACLP	0083
UA78L08AWC	0083
UA78L08C	0083
UA78L08CJG	OEM
UA78L08CLP	0083
UA78L08S	0083
UA78L08WC	0083
UA78L09AC	OEM
UA78L09ACJG	OEM
UA78L09ACLP	1775
UA78L09AWC	1775
UA78L09C	OEM
UA78L09CJG	OEM
UA78L09CLP	OEM
UA78L062WV	2285
UA78L6.2AHC	2285
UA78L-8.2AWC	0083
UA78L10	OEM
UA78L10AC	OEM
UA78L10ACJG	OEM
UA78L10ACLP	OEM
UA78L10C	OEM
UA78L10CJG	OEM
UA78L10CLP	OEM
UA78L12AC	1817
UA78L12ACJG	OEM
UA78L12ACLP	1817
UA78L12ADB	OEM
UA78L12AHC	OEM
UA78L12AS	OEM
UA78L12AWC	1817
UA78L12AWV	OEM
UA78L12BD	OEM
UA78L12C	1817
UA78L12CJG	OEM
UA78L12CLP	1817
UA78L12HM	OEM
UA78L12S	OEM
UA78L15AC	3361
UA78L15ACJG	OEM
UA78L15ACLP	3361
UA78L15ADB	OEM
UA78L15AHC	OEM
UA78L15AS	OEM
UA78L15AWC	5425
UA78L15AWV	OEM
UA78L15C	3361
UA78L15CJG	OEM
UA78L15CLP	3361
UA78L15DM	OEM
UA78L15HM	OEM
UA78L15S	OEM
UA78L62AHC	2285
UA78L62AWC	2285
UA78L62AWV	2285
UA78L62HC	OEM
UA78L82	0083
UA78L82AHC	OEM
UA78L82AWC	0083
UA78L82AWV	0083
UA78L82W	0083
UA78M00C	OEM
UA78M05C	0619
UA78M05CKC	0619
UA78M05CKD	OEM
UA78M05CLA	OEM
UA78M05HC	OEM
UA78M05HM	OEM
UA78M05MLA	OEM
UA78M05U1C	OEM
UA78M05UC	0619
UA78M05UV	OEM
UA78M06C	0917
UA78M06CKC	0917
UA78M06CKD	OEM
UA78M06CLA	OEM
UA78M06HC	OEM
UA78M06HM	OEM
UA78M06MLA	OEM
UA78M06U1C	OEM
UA78M06UC	0917
UA78M06UV	OEM
UA78M08C	1187
UA78M08CKC	1187
UA78M08CKD	1187
UA78M08CLA	OEM
UA78M08HC	OEM
UA78M08HM	OEM
UA78M08MLA	OEM
UA78M08U1C	OEM
UA78M08UC	1187
UA78M08UV	OEM
UA78M10C	OEM
UA78M10CKC	OEM
UA78M10CKD	OEM
UA78M10CLA	OEM
UA78M12	1341

If replacement code is OEM, contact original manufacturer for replacement. 609

DEVICE TYPE	REPL CODE	DEVICE TYPE	REPL CODE	DEVICE TYPE	REPL CODE	DEVICE TYPE	REPL CODE	DEVICE TYPE	REPL CODE	DEVICE TYPE	REPL CODE	DEVICE TYPE	REPL CODE
UA78M12C	0330	UA101AHM	OEM	UA703	0627	UA723CA	0026	UA741MJG	OEM	UA760RM	OEM	UA2656	OEM
UA78M12CKC	0330	UA101FM	OEM	UA703A	0627	UA723CD	OEM	UA741ML	0406	UA767	0696	UA2901DC	OEM
UA78M12CKD	0330	UA101HM	OEM	UA703C	0627	UA723CF	OEM	UA741MU	OEM	UA767PC	0696	UA2901PC	0176
UA78M12CLA	OEM	UA105HM	OEM	UA703CT	0627	UA723CH	OEM	UA741N	OEM	UA771ARC	3627	UA2902	0620
UA78M12HC	OEM	UA107HM	OEM	UA-703E	0627	UA723CJ	0026	UA741N-14	OEM	UA771ARM	OEM	UA2902DV	OEM
UA78M12HM	OEM	UA108AFM	OEM	UA703E	0627	UA723CL	1183	UA741PC	1964	UA771ATC	3627	UA2902PC	OEM
UA78M12RM	OEM	UA108AHM	OEM	UA703HC	0627	UA723CN	0026	UA741RC	OEM	UA771BRC	3627	UA2902PV	OEM
UA78M12U1C	OEM	UA108FM	OEM	UA703L	0627	UA723CP	OEM	UA741RM	OEM	UA771BRM	OEM	UA2903RC	OEM
UA78M12UC	0330	UA108HM	OEM	UA705	2535	UA723CT	1183	UA741T	OEM	UA771BTC	3627	UA2903TC	OEM
UA78M12UV	OEM	UA109HM	OEM	UA706	4506	UA723CU	OEM	UA741TC	0308	UA771LRC	OEM	UA3018AHM	1843
UA78M15C	1311	UA109KM	OEM	UA706BPC	OEM	UA723DC	0026	UA741V	OEM	UA771LTC	3627	UA3018H	1843
UA78M15CKC	1311	UA110FM	OEM	UA709A	1695	UA723DM	0026	UA746	0748	UA771RC	3627	UA3019HC	2673
UA78M15CKD	1311	UA111FM	OEM	UA709AF	OEM	UA723F	OEM	UA746(DIP)	0661	UA771TC	3627	UA3026HC	2676
UA78M15CLA	OEM	UA111HM	OEM	UA709AFM	OEM	UA723H	OEM	UA746(METAL-CAN)	0748	UA772ARC	3695	UA3039HC	2685
UA78M15HC	OEM	UA111RM	OEM	UA709AHM	OEM	UA723HC	1183	UA746C	0661	UA772ARM	OEM	UA3045DC	1686
UA78M15HM	OEM	UA117KM	OEM	UA709AMJ	OEM	UA723HM	0026	UA746DC	0661	UA772ATC	3695	UA3045PC	1686
UA78M15MLA	OEM	UA124DM	OEM	UA709AMJG	OEM	UA723J	OEM	UA746E	2147	UA772BRC	3695	UA3046DC	1686
UA78M15U1C	OEM	UA139ADM	OEM	UA709AML	OEM	UA723L	1183	UA746HC	0748	UA772BRM	OEM	UA3046PC	1686
UA78M15UC	1311	UA139DM	OEM	UA709AMU	OEM	UA723MJ	OEM	UA746PC	0661	UA772BTC	3695	UA3054DC	2696
UA78M20C	OEM	UA148DM	OEM	UA709AN	OEM	UA723ML	0026	UA747ADM	OEM	UA772RC	3695	UA3064	OEM
UA78M20CKC	OEM	UA148FM	OEM	UA709AN-14	OEM	UA723MU	OEM	UA747AFM	OEM	UA772TC	3695	UA3064HC	0360
UA78M20CKD	OEM	UA193ARM	OEM	UA709AT	OEM	UA723N	OEM	UA747AHM	OEM	UA774LDC	3357	UA3064PC	0797
UA78M20CLA	OEM	UA193RM	OEM	UA709C	1695	UA723P	OEM	UA747C	2352	UA774LPC	3357	UA3064TC	0360
UA78M20MLA	OEM	UA201AFM	OEM	UA709CJ	1695	UA723PC	0026	UA747CA	2342	UA776HC	OEM	UA3065	0167
UA78M22C	OEM	UA201AH	0093	UA709CJG	OEM	UA723T	OEM	UA747CD	OEM	UA776HM	OEM	UA3065P	0167
UA78M22CKC	OEM	UA201AHM	OEM	UA709CL	1291	UA725AFM	OEM	UA747CF	2342	UA776TC	3885	UA3065PC	0167
UA78M22CKD	OEM	UA201H	0093	UA709CN	1695	UA725AHM	OEM	UA747CH	OEM	UA777C	OEM	UA3066DC	2527
UA78M22CLA	OEM	UA201HC	0093	UA709CN-14	OEM	UA725ARM	OEM	UA747CJ	2342	UA777CJ	OEM	UA3066PC	2527
UA78M24C	2224	UA201TC	OEM	UA709CP	OEM	UA725BHC	OEM	UA747CK	2352	UA777CJG	OEM	UA3067DC	0324
UA78M24CKC	2224	UA207HM	OEM	UA709CT	1291	UA725EHC	OEM	UA747CL	2352	UA777CL	OEM	UA3075PC	1335
UA78M24CKD	2224	UA208AFM	OEM	UA709CU	OEM	UA725ERC	OEM	UA747CN	2342	UA777CN	OEM	UA3086DC	1686
UA78M24CLA	OEM	UA208AHM	OEM	UA709CV	OEM	UA725HC	2863	UA747CW	OEM	UA777CP	OEM	UA3086DM	1686
UA78M24HC	OEM	UA208FM	OEM	UA709DC	1695	UA725HM	OEM	UA747DC	2342	UA777CU	OEM	UA3086PC	1686
UA78M24HM	OEM	UA208HM	OEM	UA709F	OEM	UA725RC	OEM	UA747DM	OEM	UA777DC	OEM	UA3089E	2728
UA78M24MLA	OEM	UA209KM	1911	UA709FM	OEM	UA725RM	OEM	UA747EDC	OEM	UA777HC	OEM	UA3301P	2232
UA78M24U1C	OEM	UA217UV	OEM	UA709HC	1291	UA726HC	OEM	UA747EHC	OEM	UA777MJ	OEM	UA3302DC	OEM
UA78M24UC	2224	UA224DM	0620	UA709HM	1291	UA726HM	OEM	UA747F	OEM	UA777MJG	OEM	UA3302PC	OEM
UA78M85C	OEM	UA224DV	OEM	UA709M	OEM	UA729	0438	UA747FC	OEM	UA777ML	OEM	UA3303DC	OEM
UA78MGCH	OEM	UA224PV	OEM	UA709MJ	OEM	UA729CA	0438	UA747FM	OEM	UA777MU	OEM	UA3303PC	0620
UA78MGCU1	OEM	UA239ADC	OEM	UA709MJG	OEM	UA732	0649	UA747H(M)	OEM	UA777TC	OEM	UA3401PC	2232
UA78MGH	OEM	UA239APC	OEM	UA709ML	OEM	UA732PC	0649	UA747HC	2352	UA780	0348	UA3403DC	0620
UA78MGHC	OEM	UA239DC	OEM	UA709MU	OEM	UA733A	OEM	UA747HM	2352	UA780C	0348	UA3403PC	0620
UA78MGHM	OEM	UA239PC	OEM	UA709N	1695	UA733C	1113	UA747K	2352	UA780DC	0348	UA3503DC	OEM
UA78MGU1C	3771	UA248DC	OEM	UA709N-14	OEM	UA733CA	OEM	UA747M	OEM	UA780PC	0348	UA3525	OEM
UA78S40DC	OEM	UA248PC	OEM	UA709PC	1695	UA733CF	1110	UA747MJ	OEM	UA781	0350	UA3533	OEM
UA78S40DM	OEM	UA293ARC	OEM	UA709T	1291	UA733CH	1113	UA747ML	2352	UA781-8.2AWC	OEM	UA3548	OEM
UA78S40PC	OEM	UA293ATC	OEM	UA709TC	OEM	UA733CJ	1110	UA747MW	OEM	UA781C	0350	UA3572	OEM
UA79GC-U1	OEM	UA293RC	OEM	UA710	1786	UA733CK	OEM	UA747N	2342	UA781DC	0350	UA3596	OEM
UA79M00C	OEM	UA293TC	OEM	UA710A	1789	UA733CL	OEM	UA747PC	2342	UA781PC	0350	UA3656	OEM
UA79M05AHC	OEM	UA301AH	0093	UA710C	OEM	UA733CN	1110	UA748A	OEM	UA783P4C	OEM	UA3680DC	OEM
UA79M05AUC	1275	UA301AHC	0093	UA710CA	1789	UA733CU	OEM	UA748ADM	OEM	UA-785PC	OEM	UA3680PC	OEM
UA79M05C	1275	UA301AT	1290	UA710CF	OEM	UA733DC	1110	UA748AHM	OEM	UA786CKA	OEM	UA4031P	OEM
UA79M05CKC	1275	UA301ATC	1290	UA710CJ	1789	UA733DM	OEM	UA748C	OEM	UA787	0516	UA4136	2995
UA79M05CKD	OEM	UA305AHC	OEM	UA710CL	1786	UA733F	OEM	UA748CA	OEM	UA787PC	0516	UA4136DC	OEM
UA79M05CLA	OEM	UA305HC	6036	UA710CN	1789	UA733FC	OEM	UA748CD	OEM	UA788PC	OEM	UA4136DM	OEM
UA79M05HM	OEM	UA307HC	OEM	UA710CN-14	OEM	UA733FM	OEM	UA748CF	OEM	UA791KC	OEM	UA4136PC	2995
UA79M05MLA	OEM	UA307T	2267	UA710CT	1786	UA733H	OEM	UA748CFE	OEM	UA791KM	OEM	UA4188DC	0503
UA79M05U1C	OEM	UA307TC	2267	UA710DC	1789	UA733HC	1113	UA748CJ	2433	UA796	0413	UA4558T	0356
UA79M06AUC	2624	UA308AHC	0890	UA710DM	1789	UA733HM	OEM	UA748CJG	2433	UA796DC	3751	UA5116DC	OEM
UA79M06C	2624	UA308AHM	OEM	UA710F	OEM	UA733K	OEM	UA748CL	2435	UA796HC	0413	UA5116JC	OEM
UA79M06CKC	2624	UA308ATC	OEM	UA710FM	OEM	UA733MJ	OEM	UA748CN	2433	UA796PC	3751	UA5151DC	OEM
UA79M06CKD	OEM	UA308HC	0890	UA710HC	1786	UA733MN	OEM	UA748CN-14	OEM	UA798HM	1667	UA5151JC	OEM
UA79M06CLA	OEM	UA308HM	OEM	UA710HM	OEM	UA733N	OEM	UA748CP	2433	UA798TC	4356	UA5156DC	OEM
UA79M08AHC	OEM	UA308TC	2231	UA710MJ	OEM	UA733PC	1110	UA748CT	2435	UA824PC	OEM	UA5156JC	OEM
UA79M08AUC	2764	UA309K	1911	UA710MJG	OEM	UA734DC	OEM	UA748CU	OEM	UA915	0247	UA7094HC	1291
UA79M08C	2764	UA309KC	1911	UA710ML	OEM	UA734HC	OEM	UA748CV	OEM	UA1312PC	1601	UA7300	4155
UA79M08CKC	OEM	UA311HC	1804	UA710MU	OEM	UA734HM	OEM	UA748DC	2433	UA1314PC	3715	UA7351DC	OEM
UA79M08CKD	OEM	UA311RC	OEM	UA710N	OEM	UA737	0748	UA748DM	2433	UA1315PC	3717	UA7392DC	OEM
UA79M08CLA	OEM	UA311TC	2093	UA710N-14	OEM	UA737E	2147	UA748F	OEM	UA1391TC	0842	UA7392DM	OEM
UA79M08HM	OEM	UA317KC	OEM	UA710PC	1789	UA739DC	0687	UA748FE	OEM	UA1458CHC	OEM	UA7392PC	OEM
UA79M08MLA	OEM	UA317UC	OEM	UA710T	1786	UA739PC	0687	UA748FM	OEM	UA1458CP	0356	UA7508A	0619
UA79M08U1C	OEM	UA318HC	OEM	UA711A	1879	UA740AHM	OEM	UA748HC	0093	UA1458CRC	OEM	UA7703E	OEM
UA79M6MLA	OEM	UA324DC	0620	UA711C	OEM	UA740CT	1908	UA748HM	2435	UA1458CTC	0356	UA7800	OEM
UA79M12AHC	OEM	UA324PC	0620	UA711CA	1886	UA740EHC	1908	UA748M	OEM	UA1458CTE	OEM	UA7800C	OEM
UA79M12AUC	1827	UA339ADC	0176	UA711CF	OEM	UA740T	OEM	UA748MJ	2433	UA1458HC	3108	UA7805	0619
UA79M12AUV	OEM	UA339APC	OEM	UA711CJ	1886	UA741	0406	UA748MJG	2433	UA1458P	0356	UA7805A	0619
UA79M12C	1827	UA339DC	OEM	UA711CK	1879	UA741A	0308	UA748ML	2435	UA1458RC	OEM	UA7805C	0619
UA79M12CKC	1827	UA339PC	OEM	UA711CL	1879	UA741AFM	OEM	UA748MU	OEM	UA1458TC	0356	UA7805CDA	1911
UA79M12CKD	1827	UA348DC	2796	UA711CN	1886	UA741AHM	OEM	UA748N	2433	UA1488	0503	UA7805CKA	1911
UA79M12CLA	OEM	UA348PC	2796	UA711CU	OEM	UA741ARM	OEM	UA748N-14	OEM	UA1488D	0503	UA7805CKC	0619
UA79M12HM	OEM	UA376TC	OEM	UA711DC	1886	UA741C	1964	UA748T	2435	UA1488DC	0503	UA7805CU	0619
UA79M12MLA	OEM	UA393ARC	OEM	UA711DM	1886	UA741CA	1964	UA748TC	1290	UA1488P	0503	UA7805DA	1911
UA79M12U1C	OEM	UA393ATC	OEM	UA711F	OEM	UA741CD	1965	UA748V	1290	UA1488PC	0503	UA7805KC	1911
UA79M15AHC	OEM	UA393RC	OEM	UA711FM	OEM	UA741CF	OEM	UA749	2530	UA1489	0506	UA7805KM	1911
UA79M15AUC	3777	UA393TC	OEM	UA711HC	1879	UA741CFE	OEM	UA749D	2530	UA1489ADC	6285	UA7805MKA	1911
UA79M15C	3777	UA431AWC	OEM	UA711HM	1879	UA741CH	OEM	UA749DC	OEM	UA1489APC	0506	UA7805UC	0619
UA79M15CKC	3777	UA431HC	OEM	UA711K	1879	UA741CJ	1971	UA749DHC	6306	UA1489D	0506	UA7805UV	0619
UA79M15CKD	3777	UA431HM	OEM	UA711M	OEM	UA741CJG	0308	UA749DM	OEM	UA1489DC	0506	UA7806C	0917
UA79M15CLA	OEM	UA431WC	OEM	UA711MJ	OEM	UA741CL	0406	UA749PC	OEM	UA1489P	0506	UA7806CDA	OEM
UA79M15HM	OEM	UA431WV	OEM	UA711ML	OEM	UA741CN	1964	UA753TC	1748	UA1489PC	0506	UA7806CKC	0917
UA79M15MLA	OEM	UA438JC	OEM	UA711MU	OEM	UA741CN-14	OEM	UA757DC	OEM	UA1489PCQR	0506	UA7806CU	0917
UA79M15U1C	OEM	UA494DC	OEM	UA711N	OEM	UA741CP	0308	UA757DM	OEM	UA1558HM	3108	UA7806DA	OEM
UA79M20C	OEM	UA494DM	OEM	UA711PC	1886	UA741CT	0406	UA757DMQB	OEM	UA1558RM	OEM	UA7806KC	0917
UA79M20CKC	OEM	UA494PC	OEM	UA-714C	OEM	UA741CU	OEM	UA758	1385	UA1748G	0093	UA7806KM	OEM
UA79M20CKD	OEM	UA555	0967	UA-714E	OEM	UA741CV	0308	UA758A	OEM	UA2002	1042	UA7806MKA	OEM
UA79M20CLA	OEM	UA555HC	3592	UA714EHC	OEM	UA741DC	0308	UA758AP	OEM	UA2136P	1434	UA7806UC	0917
UA79M20MLA	OEM	UA555HM	3592	UA714HC	OEM	UA741DM	OEM	UA758B	1385	UA2136PC	1434	UA7806UV	0917
UA79M24AUC	3531	UA555IC	0967	UA714HM	OEM	UA741EHC	4198	UA758BA	1385	UA2240	OEM	UA7808	1187
UA79M24C	3531	UA555TC	0967	UA714LHC	OEM	UA741ERC	OEM	UA758N	1385	UA2240C	2071	UA7808C	1187
UA79M24CKC	3531	UA556DBC20	OEM	UA715(METAL-CAN)	1545	UA741ETC	OEM	UA758PC	1385	UA2240CJ	OEM	UA7808CKA	OEM
UA79M24CKD	3531	UA556DC	3254	UA715DC	OEM	UA741F	OEM	UA759HC	OEM	UA2240CN	OEM	UA7808CKC	1187
UA79M24CLA	OEM	UA556DM	3254	UA715DM	OEM	UA741FC	OEM	UA759HM	OEM	UA2240DC	2071	UA7808CU	1187
UA79M24MLA	OEM	UA556PC	3254	UA715HC	6930	UA741FE	OEM	UA759U1C	OEM	UA2240DM	OEM	UA7808DA	OEM
UA79MGCH	OEM	UA565JJC	OEM	UA715HM	6930	UA741FM	OEM	UA760	OEM	UA2240MJ	OEM	UA7808KC	1187
UA79MGCU1	OEM	UA565KJC	OEM	UA-719	OEM	UA741H	OEM	UA760DC	OEM	UA2240PC	2071	UA7808KM	OEM
UA79MGH	OEM	UA565SJM	OEM	UA720DC	1411	UA741HC	0406	UA760DM	OEM	UA2525	OEM	UA7808MKA	OEM
UA79MGHM	OEM	UA565TJM	OEM	UA723	1183	UA741HM	0308	UA760HC	3230	UA2548	OEM	UA7808UC	1187
UA79MGU1C	OEM	UA702MJ	OEM	UA723A	OEM	UA741M	OEM	UA760HM	3230	UA2572	OEM	UA7808UV	1187
UA101AFM	OEM	UA702ML	OEM	UA723C	OEM	UA741MJ	OEM	UA760RC	OEM	UA2596	OEM	UA7810CKA	OEM

If replacement code is OEM, contact original manufacturer for replacement.

DEVICE TYPE	REPL CODE
UA7810CKC	OEM
UA7810MKA	OEM
UA7812	1341
UA7812C	0330
UA7812CDA	5405
UA7812CKA	3906
UA7812CKC	0330
UA7812CU	0330
UA7812DA	3906
UA7812KC	3906
UA7812KM	3906
UA7812MKA	3906
UA7812UC	0330
UA7812UV	0330
UA7814CDA	OEM
UA7814CU	OEM
UA7814DA	OEM
UA7815	1311
UA7815C	1311
UA7815CDA	1989
UA7815CKA	1989
UA7815CKC	1311
UA7815CU	1311
UA7815DA	1989
UA7815KC	1989
UA7815KM	1989
UA7815MKA	1989
UA7815UC	1311
UA7815UV	4276
UA7818C	2244
UA7818CDA	OEM
UA7818CKA	3605
UA7818CKC	2244
UA7818CKG	2244
UA7818CU	2244
UA7818DA	OEM
UA7818KC	3605
UA7818KM	OEM
UA7818MKA	OEM
UA7818UC	2244
UA7818UV	2244
UA7822C	OEM
UA7822CKA	OEM
UA7822CKC	OEM
UA7822MKA	OEM
UA7824C	2224
UA7824CDA	OEM
UA7824CKA	3828
UA7824CKC	2224
UA7824CU	2224
UA7824DA	OEM
UA7824KC	3828
UA7824KM	OEM
UA7824MKA	OEM
UA7824UC	2224
UA7824UV	2224
UA7885C	OEM
UA7885CKA	OEM
UA7885CKC	OEM
UA7885MKA	OEM
UA7885UC	OEM
UA7900C	OEM
UA7905	1275
UA7905C	1275
UA7905CKA	1993
UA7905CKC	1275
UA7905KC	1275
UA7905KM	1993
UA7905MKA	1993
UA7905UC	1275
UA7906C	2624
UA7906CKA	OEM
UA7906CKC	2624
UA7906MKA	OEM
UA7906U	2624
UA7906UC	2624
UA7908C	2764
UA7908CKA	OEM
UA7908CKC	2764
UA7908KC	2764
UA7908KM	OEM
UA7908MKA	OEM
UA7908UC	2764
UA7912	1827
UA7912C	1827
UA7912CKA	5193
UA7912CKC	1827
UA7912KC	5193
UA7912KM	OEM
UA7912MKA	OEM
UA7912U	1827
UA7912UC	1827
UA7915C	3777
UA7915CKA	5195
UA7915CKC	3777
UA7915KC	5195
UA7915KM	5195
UA7915U	3777
UA7915UC	3777
UA7918C	3774
UA7918CKA	5196
UA7918CKC	3774
UA7918CKG	3774
UA7918MKA	OEM
UA7918UC	3774
UA7924C	3531
UA7924CKA	3529
UA7924CKC	3531
UA7924U	3531
UA7924UC	3531
UA7952C	OEM
UA8728DC	OEM
UA9636A	OEM
UA9637A	OEM
UA9637ACP	OEM
UA9638C	OEM
UA9638CP	OEM
UA9643	OEM
UA9644	OEM
UA78606	4018
UAA110	OEM
UAA170	OEM
UAA171	OEM
UAA180	OEM
UAA210	OEM
UAA1000	OEM
UAA1001	OEM
UAA1030	OEM
UAA4000	1086
UAB1010	OEM
UB-151	OEM
UB-152	OEM
UB-154	OEM
UBB770339X	0627
UBD203	0031
UBD204	0031
UBFY11	0144
UC	OEM
UC20	0321
UC22	OEM
UC23	OEM
UC40	OEM
UC41	OEM
UC42	OEM
UC43	OEM
UC78M12H2	0330
UC100	0321
UC105	0321
UC110	0321
UC115	0321
UC120	0321
UC125	0321
UC135	OEM
UC140	OEM
UC150	2861
UC155	0321
UC201	0321
UC210	0321
UC220	0321
UC241	0321
UC258	OEM
UC300	OEM
UC305	OEM
UC310	OEM
UC315	OEM
UC320	OEM
UC325	OEM
UC330	OEM
UC335	OEM
UC337K	2697
UC340	OEM
UC450	OEM
UC451	OEM
UC547C	0016
UC588	0321
UC701	0321
UC703	0321
UC704	3577
UC705	3577
UC707	1147
UC714	0321
UC714E	OEM
UC734	0321
UC734E	0321
UC750	0321
UC751	0321
UC752	0321
UC753	0321
UC756	0321
UC801	OEM
UC803	OEM
UC804	OEM
UC805	1133
UC850	OEM
UC852	OEM
UC900	OEM
UC-1001B	OEM
UC-1002B	OEM
UC-1003B	OEM
UC-1004B	OEM
UC-1005B	OEM
UC-1006B	OEM
UC1100	0037
UC1406HA	4009
UC1496A	OEM
UC1496N	OEM
UC1700	OEM
UC2136	0321
UC2138	0321
UC2139	0321
UC2147	2917
UC2148	0321
UC2149	0321
UC3525AN	2802
UC3842	OEM
UC3842AN	OEM
UC3843AN	OEM
UC4741	0406
UC4741C	0406
UC6550	OEM
UC7550	OEM
UC7805UC	0619
UC7933	0330
UCD125	0124
UCD227	0124
UCD329	OEM
UCR10	OEM
UCR10L	OEM
UCR20	OEM
UCR20L	OEM
UCR30	OEM
UCR30L	OEM
UCR40	OEM
UCR40L	OEM
UCR50	OEM
UCR50L	OEM
UCR60	OEM
UCR60L	OEM
UCX1702	OEM
UCX2700	OEM
UD5B	0087
UD6C	OEM
UD1000	OEM
UD1001	OEM
UD-2000	3020
UD2000	OEM
UD-3005	OEM
UD3005	OEM
UD-3006	OEM
UD3006	OEM
UD-3007	OEM
UD3007	OEM
UD3008	OEM
UD-4001	OEM
UD-4024	OEM
UD4174	OEM
UD4175	OEM
UDC40013	OEM
UDGE	OEM
UDN2841	OEM
UDN2845	OEM
UDN-3611M	1235
UDN-3612M	1253
UDN3612N	OEM
UDN-3613M	1262
UDN-3614M	1279
UDN-5703A	OEM
UDN-5706A	OEM
UDN-5707A	OEM
UDN-5711M	OEM
UDN-5712M	OEM
UDN-5713M	OEM
UDN5713M	OEM
UDN-5714M	OEM
UDN5722M	OEM
UDN-5733A	OEM
UDN-6116A	OEM
UDN-6116A-1	OEM
UDN6116A-1	4019
UDN-6116A-2	OEM
UDN-6116R	OEM
UDN-6116R-2	OEM
UDN-6118A	5777
UDN6118A	3839
UDN-6118A-1	OEM
UDN-6118A-2	OEM
UDN-6118R	5777
UDN-6118R-2	OEM
UDN-6128A	5795
UDN6128A	3864
UDN-6128A-1	OEM
UDN-6128A-2	OEM
UDN-6128R	5795
UDN6128R	OEM
UDN-6128R-2	OEM
UDN6128R-2	OEM
UDN-6138A	OEM
UDN6138A	OEM
UDN-6138A-2	OEM
UDN6138A2	OEM
UDN-6144A	4856
UDN6148A	OEM
UDN6148A2	OEM
UDN-6164A	4019
UDN6164A	4019
UDN-6184A	3839
UDN6184A	OEM
UDN6510A	OEM
UDN6510R	OEM
UDN6514A	OEM
UDN6514R	OEM
UDN7180A	OEM
UDN-7183A	3839
UDN7183A	OEM
UDN7184A	OEM
UDN-7186A	3864
UDN7186A	OEM
UDQ2956R	OEM
UDQ2957R	OEM
UDS2981H	OEM
UDS2982H	OEM
UDS2983H	OEM
UDS2984H	OEM
UDS3611H	OEM
UDS3612H	OEM
UDS3613H	OEM
UDS3614H	OEM
UDS5703H	OEM
UDS5706H	OEM
UDS5707H	OEM
UDS5711H	OEM
UDS5712H	OEM
UDS5713H	OEM
UDS5714H	OEM
UDS5733H	OEM
UDS5790H	OEM
UDS5791H	OEM
UDT450	OEM
UDT451	OEM
UDT452	OEM
UDT455	OEM
UDT500D	OEM
UDT600	OEM
UDZ110	OEM
UDZ122	OEM
UDZ130	OEM
UDZ210	OEM
UDZ222	OEM
UDZ230	OEM
UDZ707	0475
UDZ708	0499
UDZ709	0679
UDZ710	0225
UDZ712	0234
UDZ715	0247
UDZ718	0256
UDZ720	0262
UDZ724	0273
UDZ727	0291
UDZ730	0305
UDZ733	0314
UDZ736	0316
UDZ740	OEM
UDZ745	OEM
UDZ760	2829
UDZ807	OEM
UDZ808	OEM
UDZ809	OEM
UDZ810	OEM
UDZ812	OEM
UDZ815	OEM
UDZ818	OEM
UDZ820	OEM
UDZ824	OEM
UDZ827	OEM
UDZ830	OEM
UDZ833	OEM
UDZ836	OEM
UDZ840	OEM
UDZ845	OEM
UDZ860	OEM
UDZ5110	OEM
UDZ5122	OEM
UDZ5130	OEM
UDZ5210	OEM
UDZ5222	OEM
UDZ5230	OEM
UDZ5707	0475
UDZ5708	0499
UDZ5709	0679
UDZ5710	0225
UDZ5712	0234
UDZ5715	0247
UDZ5718	0256
UDZ5720	0262
UDZ5724	0273
UDZ5727	OEM
UDZ5730	OEM
UDZ5733	OEM
UDZ5736	OEM
UDZ5740	OEM
UDZ5745	OEM
UDZ5760	OEM
UDZ5807	OEM
UDZ5808	OEM
UDZ5809	OEM
UDZ5810	OEM
UDZ5812	OEM
UDZ5815	OEM
UDZ5818	OEM
UDZ5820	OEM
UDZ5824	0273
UDZ5827	OEM
UDZ5830	OEM
UDZ5833	OEM
UDZ5836	OEM
UDZ5840	OEM
UDZ5845	OEM
UDZ5860	OEM
UDZ7110	OEM
UDZ7210	OEM
UDZ7707	OEM
UDZ7708	OEM
UDZ7709	OEM
UDZ7710	OEM
UDZ7712	OEM
UDZ7715	OEM
UDZ7718	OEM
UDZ7720	OEM
UDZ7724	OEM
UDZ7727	OEM
UDZ7730	OEM
UDZ7733	OEM
UDZ7736	OEM
UDZ7740	OEM
UDZ7745	OEM
UDZ7760	OEM
UDZ7807	OEM
UDZ7808	OEM
UDZ7809	OEM
UDZ7810	OEM
UDZ7812	OEM
UDZ7815	OEM
UDZ7818	OEM
UDZ7820	OEM
UDZ7824	OEM
UDZ7827	OEM
UDZ7830	OEM
UDZ7833	OEM
UDZ7836	OEM
UDZ7840	OEM
UDZ7845	OEM
UDZ7860	OEM
UDZ8707	0644
UDZ8708	0244
UDZ8709	0012
UDZ8710	0170
UDZ8712	0137
UDZ8715	0002
UDZ8718	0490
UDZ8720	0526
UDZ8724	0398
UDZ8727	0436
UDZ8730	OEM
UDZ8733	OEM
UDZ8736	OEM
UDZ8740	OEM
UDZ8745	OEM
UDZ8760	OEM
UDZ8807	OEM
UDZ8808	OEM
UDZ8809	OEM
UDZ8810	OEM
UDZ8812	OEM
UDZ8815	OEM
UDZ8818	OEM
UDZ8820	OEM
UDZ8824	OEM
UDZ8827	OEM
UDZ8830	OEM
UDZ8833	OEM
UDZ8836	OEM
UDZ8840	OEM
UDZ8845	OEM
UDZ8860	OEM
UES101	0031
UES102	0031
UES103	0031
UES104	0031
UES201	OEM
UES202	OEM
UES203	OEM
UES204	OEM
UES301	OEM
UES302	OEM
UES303	OEM
UES304	OEM
UES501	OEM
UES502	OEM
UES503	OEM
UES504	OEM
UES505	OEM
UES601	OEM
UES602	OEM
UES603	OEM
UES604	OEM
UES605	OEM
UES606	OEM
UES701	OEM
UES702	OEM
UES703	OEM
UES704	OEM
UES705	OEM
UES706	OEM
UES801	OEM
UES802	OEM
UES803	OEM
UES804	OEM
UES805	OEM
UES806	OEM
UES1001	1325
UES1002	OEM
UES1003	OEM
UES1101	0541
UES1102	0541
UES1103	0541
UES1104	OEM
UES1105	OEM
UES1106	OEM
UES1301	OEM
UES1302	OEM
UES1303	OEM
UES1304	0541
UES1305	OEM
UES1306	OEM
UES1401	1119
UES1402	1119
UES1403	1119
UES2401	1227
UES2402	1227
UES2403	1227
UES2601	OEM
UES2602	OEM
UES2603	OEM
UES2604	OEM
UES2605	OEM
UES2606	OEM
UF-01	0050
UF01	0023
UF-1	0023
UF1	0541
UF-1A	0023
UF1A	0023
UF-1B	0017
UF1B	0541
UF-1C	0071
UF1C	0541
UF-1D	1760
UF-1E	1760
UF-1F	1760
UF-1V	0023
UF-2	0023
UF2	0023
UF-2B	0017
UF-3	0031
UF40A	OEM
UF40B	OEM
UF40C	OEM
UF55A	OEM
UF55B	OEM
UF55C	OEM
UF75A	OEM
UF75B	OEM
UF75C	OEM
UF100A	OEM
UF100B	OEM
UF100C	OEM
UF130A	OEM
UF130B	OEM
UF130C	OEM
UF160A	OEM
UF160B	OEM
UF160C	OEM
UF200A	OEM
UF200B	OEM
UF200C	OEM
UF250A	OEM
UF250B	OEM
UF250C	OEM
UF4001	1325
UF4002	0080
UF4003	0604
UF4004	0790
UF4005	0015
UF4006	0072
UF4007	0071
UF5400	0031
UF5401	0031
UF5402	0031
UF5403	0031
UF5404	0031
UF5404J	OEM
UF5405	0031
UF5406	0031
UFB2.5	OEM
UFB5	OEM
UFB7	OEM
UFS5	OEM
UFS7.5	OEM
UFS10	OEM
UF-SD1	0143
UFSD-1	0015
UFSD1	0102
UFSD-1A	0102
UFSD1A	0102
UFSD-1B	0071
UFSD1B	OEM
UFSD-1C	0102
UFSD1C	0102
UFSD1F	0015
UFSD-18	0071
UG3C	0023
UG-1002	1999
UG-1003	0276
UG-1004	0106
UG1888	0133
UGB5	OEM
UGB7.5	OEM
UGB10	OEM
UGB3132AD	OEM
UGB6124ADA	OEM
UGB6124AG	OEM
UGD5	OEM
UGD7.5	OEM
UGD10	OEM
UGE0221AY4	OEM
UGE0421AY4	OEM
UGE0501NY4B	OEM
UGE1112AY4	OEM
UGE3126AY4	OEM
UGF2.5	OEM
UGF5	OEM
UGF7.5	OEM
UGH7812	0330
UGJ7109393	1911
UGN3013T	OEM
UGN3019T	OEM
UGN3020T	OEM
UGN3030T	OEM
UGN3040T	OEM
UGN3201M	OEM
UGN3203M	OEM
UGN3220S	OEM
UGN3501C	OEM
UGN3501H	OEM
UGN3501M	OEM
UGN3501T	OEM
UGN3600M	OEM
UGN3601M	OEM
UGN30501M	OEM
UGS3019T	OEM
UGS3020T	OEM
UGS3030T	OEM
UHC-001	OEM
UHC-005	OEM
UHC-006	OEM
UHC-007	OEM
UHC-023	OEM
UHC-024	OEM
UHC-036	OEM
UHC-037	OEM
UHC-400	OEM
UHC400	OEM
UHC-400-1	OEM
UHC400-1	OEM
UHC-402	OEM
UHC402	OEM
UHC-402-1	OEM
UHC402-1	OEM
UHC-403	OEM
UHC403	OEM
UHC-403-1	OEM
UHC403-1	OEM
UHC-406	OEM
UHC406	OEM
UHC-406-1	OEM
UHC406-1	OEM
UHC-407	OEM
UHC407	OEM
UHC-407-1	OEM
UHC407-1	OEM
UHC-408	OEM
UHC408	OEM
UHC-408-1	OEM
UHC408-1	OEM
UHC-420	OEM
UHC-432	OEM
UHC432	OEM
UHC-432-1	OEM
UHC432-1	OEM
UHC-433	OEM
UHC433	OEM
UHC-433-1	OEM
UHC433-1	OEM
UHC-451	OEM
UHC-459	OEM
UHC-500	OEM
UHC500	OEM
UHC-502	OEM
UHC502	OEM
UHC-503	OEM
UHC503	OEM
UHC-506	OEM
UHC506	OEM
UHC-507	OEM
UHC507	OEM
UHC-508	OEM
UHC508	OEM
UHC-520	OEM
UHC-532	OEM
UHC532	OEM
UHC-533	OEM
UHC533	OEM
UHC-551	OEM
UHC-559	OEM
UHD-400	OEM
UHD400	OEM
UHD-400-1	OEM
UHD400-1	OEM
UHD-402	OEM
UHD402	OEM
UHD-402-1	OEM
UHD402-1	OEM
UHD-403	OEM
UHD403	OEM
UHD-403-1	OEM
UHD403-1	OEM
UHD-406	OEM
UHD406	OEM
UHD-406-1	OEM
UHD406-1	OEM
UHD-407	OEM
UHD407	OEM
UHD-407-1	OEM
UHD407-1	OEM
UHD-408	OEM
UHD408	OEM
UHD-408-1	OEM
UHD408-1	OEM
UHD-420	OEM
UHD-432	OEM
UHD432	OEM
UHD-432-1	OEM
UHD432-1	OEM
UHD-433	OEM
UHD433	OEM
UHD-433-1	OEM
UHD433-1	OEM
UHD-451	OEM
UHD-459	OEM
UHD-480	OEM
UHD-481	OEM
UHD-490	OEM

If replacement code is OEM, contact original manufacturer for replacement.

611

DEVICE TYPE	REPL CODE
UHD490	OEM
UHD-491	OEM
UHD491	OEM
UHD-500	OEM
UHD500	OEM
UHD-502	OEM
UHD502	OEM
UHD-503	OEM
UHD503	OEM
UHD-506	OEM
UHD506	OEM
UHD-507	OEM
UHD507	OEM
UHD-508	OEM
UHD508	OEM
UHD-520	OEM
UHD-532	OEM
UHD532	OEM
UHD-533	OEM
UHD533	OEM
UHD-551	OEM
UHD-559	OEM
UHIC-001	4541
UHIC001	4541
UHIC-003	2364
UHIC003	2364
UHIC-004	2290
UHIC004	2290
UHIC-004E	2290
UHIC-004F	OEM
UHIC-005	4405
UHIC005	4405
UHIC006	4555
UHIC-007	4564
UHIC007	4564
UHIC-131	OEM
UHM-412	OEM
UHM-500	OEM
UHM-505	OEM
UHP-004	0539
UHP-181	OEM
UHP-400	OEM
UHP400	OEM
UHP-400-1	OEM
UHP400-1	OEM
UHP-402	OEM
UHP402	OEM
UHP-402-1	OEM
UHP402-1	OEM
UHP-403	OEM
UHP403	OEM
UHP-403-1	OEM
UHP403-1	OEM
UHP-406	OEM
UHP406	OEM
UHP-406-1	OEM
UHP406-1	OEM
UHP-407	OEM
UHP407	OEM
UHP-407-1	OEM
UHP407-1	OEM
UHP-408	OEM
UHP408	OEM
UHP-408-1	OEM
UHP408-1	OEM
UHP-420	OEM
UHP-432	OEM
UHP432	OEM
UHP-432-1	OEM
UHP432-1	OEM
UHP-433	OEM
UHP433	OEM
UHP-433-1	OEM
UHP433-1	OEM
UHP-451	OEM
UHP-459	OEM
UHP-480	OEM
UHP480	OEM
UHP-481	OEM
UHP481	OEM
UHP-482	OEM
UHP-490	OEM
UHP490	OEM
UHP-491	OEM
UHP491	OEM
UHP-495	OEM
UHP495	OEM
UHP-500	OEM
UHP500	OEM
UHP-502	OEM
UHP502	OEM
UHP-503	OEM
UHP503	OEM
UHP-506	OEM
UHP506	OEM
UHP-507	OEM
UHP507	OEM
UHP-508	OEM
UHP508	OEM
UHP-520	OEM
UHP-532	OEM
UHP532	OEM
UHP-533	OEM
UHP533	OEM
UHP-551	OEM
UHP-559	OEM
UHV100	OEM
UHV125	OEM
UHV150	OEM

DEVICE TYPE	REPL CODE
UHV175	OEM
UHV200	OEM
UHV225	OEM
UHV250	OEM
UHV275	OEM
UHV300	OEM
UIU-.KO	0212
UL-914	1063
UL-923	OEM
UL923	OEM
UL2070B	OEM
ULA2C184E	OEM
ULA9RB015E	OEM
ULA1045E	OEM
ULC3037	0659
ULM2111A	0673
ULM2114A	0345
ULM2274P	2535
ULN-2001A	0839
ULN2001A	0839
ULN2001AJ	0839
ULN2001AN	0839
ULN2001R	OEM
ULN-2002A	1001
ULN2002A	1001
ULN2002AJ	1001
ULN2002AN	1001
ULN2002R	OEM
ULN2003	1126
ULN-2003A	1126
ULN2003A	1126
ULN2003AJ	1126
ULN2003AN	1126
ULN2003N	OEM
ULN2003R	OEM
ULN-2004A	1252
ULN2004A	1252
ULN2004AJ	1252
ULN2004AN	1252
ULN2004N	OEM
ULN2004R	OEM
ULN2005A	4848
ULN2005R	OEM
ULN2011A	0839
ULN2011R	OEM
ULN2012A	1001
ULN2013A	1126
ULN2013R	OEM
ULN2014A	1252
ULN2014R	OEM
ULN2015A	4848
ULN2015R	OEM
ULN2021A	OEM
ULN2022A	OEM
ULN2023A	OEM
ULN2024A	OEM
ULN2025A	OEM
ULN-2031A	OEM
ULN2031A	OEM
ULN-2032A	OEM
ULN2032A	OEM
ULN-2033A	OEM
ULN2033A	OEM
ULN-2046A	1686
ULN2046A	1686
ULN-2054A	4755
ULN2054A	OEM
ULN2061A	OEM
ULN2061M	OEM
ULN2062M	OEM
ULN2064	OEM
ULN-2064A	4781
ULN2064A	OEM
ULN2064B	4781
ULN2064NE	4781
ULN2065	OEM
ULN2065B	4781
ULN2065NE	4781
ULN2066	OEM
ULN2066B	5218
ULN2066NE	5218
ULN2067	OEM
ULN2067B	5218
ULN2067NE	5218
ULN2068	OEM
ULN2068B	4883
ULN2068NE	4883
ULN2069	OEM
ULN2069B	4883
ULN2071B	5219
ULN2074	OEM
ULN-2074A	OEM
ULN2074B	OEM
ULN2074NE	OEM
ULN2075	OEM
ULN2075B	OEM
ULN2075NE	OEM
ULN2076B	OEM
ULN2077B	OEM
ULN-2081A	2722
ULN2081A	2722
ULN-2082A	2723
ULN2082A	2723
ULN2083A	2724
ULN-2086A	1686
ULN2086A	1686
ULN-2103M	OEM
ULN2110(A)	0514
ULN2111	0659

DEVICE TYPE	REPL CODE
ULN-2111A	0659
ULN2111A	0659
ULN-2111N	0659
ULN2111N	0659
ULN2113	0673
ULN-2113A	0673
ULN2113A	0673
ULN-2113N	0673
ULN2113N	0673
ULN2114	0345
ULN-2114A	0345
ULN2114A	0661
ULN-2114K	0748
ULN2114K	0748
ULN-2114N	0345
ULN2114N	0345
ULN-2114W	2147
ULN2114W	0748
ULN-2120A	0649
ULN2120A	0649
ULN-2120N	0649
ULN-2121A	1929
ULN2121A	1929
ULN-2121N	1929
ULN2121N	1929
ULN-2122A	0438
ULN2122A	0438
ULN-2122N	0438
ULN2122N	0438
ULN2124	0348
ULN-2124A	0348
ULN2124A	0348
ULN2124N	0348
ULN-2125A	2438
ULN2125A	2438
ULN-2126A	2264
ULN2126A	2264
ULN-2126N	2264
ULN-2127A	0350
ULN2127A	0350
ULN-2127N	0350
ULN2127N	0350
ULN-2128	2264
ULN2128	0696
ULN-2128A	0696
ULN2128A	0696
ULN-2128N	0696
ULN2128N	0696
ULN-2129A	1335
ULN2129A	1335
ULN-2129N	1335
ULN-2136A	0659
ULN2136A	1434
ULN-2137A	1411
ULN2137A	1411
ULN-2139D	OEM
ULN-2139G	OEM
ULN-2139H	OEM
ULN-2139M	OEM
ULN-2140A	OEM
ULN2140A	OEM
ULN-2140H	OEM
ULN-2141A	OEM
ULN-2141H	OEM
ULN-2142A	OEM
ULN-2142H	OEM
ULN-2151D	0406
ULN-2151G	OEM
ULN-2151H	OEM
ULN-2151M	0308
ULN-2156D	0406
ULN-2156G	OEM
ULN-2156H	OEM
ULN-2156M	0308
ULN-2157A	2342
ULN-2157H	2342
ULN-2157K	2352
ULN-2158D	2540
ULN-2158G	OEM
ULN-2158H	OEM
ULN-2158M	2545
ULN-2159D	0406
ULN-2159G	OEM
ULN-2159H	1971
ULN-2159M	0308
ULN2165	6624
ULN-2165A	0167
ULN2165A	0167
ULN-2165N	0167
ULN2165N	0167
ULN-2171D	0406
ULN-2171G	OEM
ULN-2171H	OEM
ULN-2171M	0308
ULN-2172D	2540
ULN-2172G	OEM
ULN-2172H	OEM
ULN-2172M	2545
ULN-2173D	0406
ULN-2173G	OEM
ULN-2173H	OEM
ULN-2173M	0308
ULN-2174D	2540
ULN-2174G	OEM
ULN-2174H	OEM
ULN-2174M	2545
ULN-2175D	OEM
ULN-2175G	OEM
ULN-2175H	OEM

DEVICE TYPE	REPL CODE
ULN-2175M	OEM
ULN-2176D	2545
ULN-2176G	OEM
ULN-2176H	OEM
ULN-2176M	2545
ULN-2177D	0406
ULN-2177G	OEM
ULN-2177H	1971
ULN-2177M	0308
ULN-2178D	2540
ULN-2178G	OEM
ULN-2178H	OEM
ULN-2178M	2545
ULN2204A	5103
ULN-2208M	3376
ULN-2209M	1748
ULN2209M	1748
ULN2209V	OEM
ULN2210	0514
ULN-2210A	0514
ULN2211	3690
ULN2211A	3690
ULN2211B	3690
ULN2211N	5501
ULN-2211P	3690
ULN-2212A	3720
ULN2212B	3720
ULN2212N	OEM
ULN-2212P	3720
ULN-2216A	OEM
ULN2224	6894
ULN-2224A	0746
ULN2224A	3660
ULN-2228A	0345
ULN2228A	0345
ULN2231A	3391
ULN2240A	OEM
ULN2241A	OEM
ULN2242A	OEM
ULN2242N	0399
ULN2243A	3389
ULN2244	1385
ULN-2244A	1385
ULN2244A	1385
ULN2244N	1385
ULN2244R	1385
ULN2245A	OEM
ULN2249A	4027
ULN2261	2480
ULN2261A	2480
ULN2262	0516
ULN2264	0360
ULN-2264A	0797
ULN2264A	0797
ULN2264AN	0345
ULN2264K	0360
ULN2266A	2527
ULN2266N	2527
ULN2267	0324
ULN2267A	0324
ULN-2267N	0324
ULN2267N	0324
ULN2268A	2803
ULN-2269A	1327
ULN2269A	1327
ULN2270B	OEM
ULN2270Q	OEM
ULN2274B	2535
ULN-2274P	2535
ULN2274P	2535
ULN2275	2535
ULN-2275A	2535
ULN2275B	2535
ULN-2275P	2535
ULN2275P	2535
ULN2276B	2535
ULN2276P	2535
ULN2276Q	2535
ULN2277	2535
ULN2277B	2535
ULN-2277P	2535
ULN2277P	2535
ULN2278	2535
ULN2278B	2535
ULN-2278P	2535
ULN2278P	2535
ULN2278Q	2535
ULN-2280A	0375
ULN2280A	0375
ULN-2280B	0375
ULN2280B	0375
ULN2280N	0375
ULN-2280P	0375
ULN2280P	0375
ULN2280Q	0375
ULN-2281B	3027
ULN2281B	3689
ULN2283B	OEM
ULN2283B1	OEM
ULN2289	2728
ULN2289(A)	2728
ULN2289A	2728
ULN2290B	1051
ULN2290Q	1162
ULN2291M	0842
ULN2293A	OEM
ULN2294M	2473
ULN2296	3739
ULN2297A	3239

DEVICE TYPE	REPL CODE
ULN2298	0850
ULN-2298A	2032
ULN2298A	0850
ULN2298P	0850
ULN-2300M	OEM
ULN-2301M	OEM
ULN2401A	OEM
ULN2429A	OEM
ULN2430M	OEM
ULN-2709CM	0308
ULN-2709M	0308
ULN-2723A	0026
ULN-2723K	1183
ULN-2741D	0406
ULN2741D	0406
ULN-2747A	2342
ULN2801A	4849
ULN2801R	OEM
ULN2802A	4850
ULN2802R	OEM
ULN2803A	4852
ULN2803R	OEM
ULN2804A	4853
ULN2804R	OEM
ULN2805A	4854
ULN2805R	OEM
ULN2811A	4849
ULN2811R	OEM
ULN2812A	4850
ULN2813A	4852
ULN2813R	OEM
ULN2814A	4853
ULN2814R	OEM
ULN2815A	4854
ULN2815R	OEM
ULN2821A	OEM
ULN2822A	OEM
ULN2823A	OEM
ULN2824A	OEM
ULN2825A	OEM
ULN-3000M	OEM
ULN-3000R	OEM
ULN-3000S	OEM
ULN-3004M	OEM
ULN-3004S	OEM
ULN-3006M	OEM
ULN-3006S	OEM
ULN-3006T	OEM
ULN-3008M	OEM
ULN-3100M	OEM
ULN-3100R	OEM
ULN-3100S	OEM
ULN3262A	0516
ULN-3303M	OEM
ULN-3304M	OEM
ULN3304M	OEM
ULN-3305M	OEM
ULN3305M	OEM
ULN-3306M	OEM
ULN3306M	OEM
ULN-3330Y	5033
ULN3330Y	5033
ULN3701Z	1042
ULN3702Z	OEM
ULN3809A	6931
ULN3810A	OEM
ULN3810A1	OEM
ULN3838A1	OEM
ULN3838A2	OEM
ULN3838A3	OEM
ULN3859A	6958
ULN3889A	OEM
ULN3941A	OEM
ULN4436A	OEM
ULN8126A	2814
ULN8126R	OEM
ULN8160A	5120
ULN8160R	5120
ULPR73B-50	OEM
ULQ8126A	OEM
ULQ8126R	OEM
ULS2001H	OEM
ULS2001R	OEM
ULS2002H	OEM
ULS2002R	OEM
ULS2003H	OEM
ULS2003R	OEM
ULS2004H	OEM
ULS2004R	OEM
ULS2005H	OEM
ULS2005R	OEM
ULS2011H	OEM
ULS2011R	OEM
ULS2012H	OEM
ULS2012R	OEM
ULS2013H	OEM
ULS2013R	OEM
ULS2014H	OEM
ULS2014R	OEM
ULS2015H	OEM
ULS2015R	OEM
ULS2021H	OEM
ULS2022H	OEM
ULS2023H	OEM
ULS2024H	OEM
ULS2025H	OEM
ULS-2045H	1686
ULS2045H	1686
ULS2083H	OEM

DEVICE TYPE	REPL CODE
ULS-2139D	OEM
ULS-2139G	OEM
ULS-2139H	OEM
ULS-2139M	OEM
ULS-2140A	OEM
ULS-2140H	OEM
ULS2140H	OEM
ULS-2141A	OEM
ULS-2141H	OEM
ULS-2142A	OEM
ULS-2142H	OEM
ULS-2151D	0406
ULS-2151G	OEM
ULS-2151H	OEM
ULS-2151M	0308
ULS-2156D	0406
ULS-2156G	OEM
ULS-2156H	OEM
ULS-2156M	0308
ULS-2157A	2342
ULS-2157H	2342
ULS-2157K	2352
ULS-2158D	2540
ULS-2158G	OEM
ULS-2158H	OEM
ULS-2158M	2545
ULS-2159D	0406
ULS-2159G	OEM
ULS-2159H	1971
ULS-2159M	0308
ULS-2171D	0406
ULS-2171G	OEM
ULS-2171H	OEM
ULS-2171M	0308
ULS-2172D	2540
ULS-2172G	OEM
ULS-2172H	OEM
ULS-2172M	2545
ULS-2173D	0406
ULS-2173G	OEM
ULS-2173H	OEM
ULS-2173M	0308
ULS-2174D	2540
ULS-2174G	OEM
ULS-2174H	OEM
ULS-2174M	2545
ULS-2175D	OEM
ULS-2175G	OEM
ULS-2175H	OEM
ULS-2175M	OEM
ULS-2176D	2540
ULS-2176G	OEM
ULS-2176H	OEM
ULS-2176M	2545
ULS-2177D	0406
ULS-2177G	OEM
ULS-2177H	1971
ULS-2177M	0308
ULS-2178D	2545
ULS-2178G	OEM
ULS-2178H	OEM
ULS-2178M	2545
ULS-2723A	0026
ULS-2723K	1183
ULS-2741D	0406
ULS2741D	0406
ULS2801H	OEM
ULS2802H	OEM
ULS2802R	OEM
ULS2803H	OEM
ULS2803R	OEM
ULS2804H	OEM
ULS2804R	OEM
ULS2805H	OEM
ULS2805R	OEM
ULS2811H	OEM
ULS2811R	OEM
ULS2812H	OEM
ULS2812R	OEM
ULS2813H	OEM
ULS2813R	OEM
ULS2814H	OEM
ULS2814R	OEM
ULS2815H	OEM
ULS2815R	OEM
ULS2821H	OEM
ULS2822H	OEM
ULS2823H	OEM
ULS2824H	OEM
ULS2825H	OEM
ULS-3006M	OEM
ULS-3006S	OEM
ULS-3006T	OEM
ULS8126R	OEM
ULS8160R	OEM
ULT2260	3675
ULT3730	0969
ULT3731	0969
ULX2210	0514
ULX2210D	0514
ULX-2231A	3391
ULX2244	1385
ULX-2267A	0324
ULX2277P	OEM
ULX-2289A	2728
ULX2298	0850
ULX3701H	OEM
ULX3701Z	1042
ULX3701ZV	OEM

DEVICE TYPE	REPL CODE
ULX3788W	OEM
ULX3804A	OEM
ULX3840A	OEM
ULX8161M(A)	OEM
ULXX3777W	OEM
UM31AWC	OEM
UM1285-8	OEM
UM2010A	OEM
UM2010B	OEM
UM2010C	OEM
UM2012A	OEM
UM2012B	OEM
UM2012C	OEM
UM2014A	OEM
UM2014B	OEM
UM2016A	OEM
UM2016B	OEM
UM2016C	OEM
UM2018A	OEM
UM2018B	OEM
UM2018C	OEM
UM2020A	OEM
UM2020B	OEM
UM2020C	OEM
UM2301	OEM
UM2333-D201	OEM
UM3482	OEM
UM3482A	OEM
UM4000	OEM
UM4001A	OEM
UM4001B	OEM
UM4001C	OEM
UM4001CR	OEM
UM4001D	OEM
UM4001DR	OEM
UM4001E	OEM
UM4002A	OEM
UM4002B	OEM
UM4002C	OEM
UM4002CR	OEM
UM4002D	OEM
UM4002DR	OEM
UM4002E	OEM
UM4004A	OEM
UM4004B	OEM
UM4004C	OEM
UM4004CR	OEM
UM4004D	OEM
UM4004DR	OEM
UM4004E	OEM
UM4006A	OEM
UM4006B	OEM
UM4006C	OEM
UM4006CR	OEM
UM4006D	OEM
UM4006DR	OEM
UM4006E	OEM
UM4008A	OEM
UM4008B	OEM
UM4008C	OEM
UM4008CR	OEM
UM4008D	OEM
UM4008DR	OEM
UM4008E	OEM
UM4010A	OEM
UM4010B	OEM
UM4010C	OEM
UM4010CR	OEM
UM4010D	OEM
UM4010DR	OEM
UM4010E	OEM
UM4012A	OEM
UM4012B	OEM
UM4012C	OEM
UM4012CR	OEM
UM4012D	OEM
UM4012DR	OEM
UM4012E	OEM
UM4300	OEM
UM4301A	OEM
UM4301B	OEM
UM4301C	OEM
UM4301CR	OEM
UM4301D	OEM
UM4301DR	OEM
UM4301E	OEM
UM4302A	OEM
UM4302B	OEM
UM4302C	OEM
UM4302D	OEM
UM4302E	OEM
UM4304A	OEM
UM4304B	OEM
UM4304C	OEM
UM4304CR	OEM
UM4304D	OEM
UM4304DR	OEM
UM4304E	OEM
UM4306A	OEM
UM4306B	OEM
UM4306C	OEM
UM4306D	OEM
UM4306E	OEM
UM4310A	OEM
UM4310B	OEM
UM4310C	OEM
UM4310CR	OEM
UM4310D	OEM
UM4310DR	OEM

612

If replacement code is OEM, contact original manufacturer for replacement.

DEVICE TYPE	REPL CODE
UM4310E	OEM
UM4900	OEM
UM4901A	OEM
UM4901B	OEM
UM4901C	OEM
UM4901CR	OEM
UM4901D	OEM
UM4901DR	OEM
UM4901E	OEM
UM4902A	OEM
UM4902B	OEM
UM4902C	OEM
UM4904A	OEM
UM4904B	OEM
UM4904C	OEM
UM4904CR	OEM
UM4904D	OEM
UM4904DR	OEM
UM4904E	OEM
UM4906A	OEM
UM4906B	OEM
UM4906C	OEM
UM4906CR	OEM
UM4906D	OEM
UM4906DR	OEM
UM4906E	OEM
UM4910A	OEM
UM4910B	OEM
UM4910C	OEM
UM4910CR	OEM
UM4910D	OEM
UM4910DR	OEM
UM4910E	OEM
UM6000	OEM
UM6001A	OEM
UM6001B	OEM
UM6001C	OEM
UM6001CR	OEM
UM6001E	OEM
UM6001H	OEM
UM6002A	OEM
UM6002B	OEM
UM6002C	OEM
UM6002E	OEM
UM6002H	OEM
UM6004A	OEM
UM6004B	OEM
UM6004C	OEM
UM6004CR	OEM
UM6004E	OEM
UM6006A	OEM
UM6006B	OEM
UM6006C	OEM
UM6006CR	OEM
UM6006E	OEM
UM6010A	OEM
UM6010B	OEM
UM6010C	OEM
UM6010CR	OEM
UM6010E	OEM
UM6101A	OEM
UM6101B	OEM
UM6101C	OEM
UM6101CR	OEM
UM6101E	OEM
UM6104A	OEM
UM6104B	OEM
UM6104C	OEM
UM6104CR	OEM
UM6104E	OEM
UM6108A	OEM
UM6108B	OEM
UM6108C	OEM
UM6108CR	OEM
UM6108E	OEM
UM6200	OEM
UM6201A	OEM
UM6201B	OEM
UM6201C	OEM
UM6201CR	OEM
UM6201E	OEM
UM6202A	OEM
UM6202B	OEM
UM6202C	OEM
UM6202E	OEM
UM6204A	OEM
UM6204B	OEM
UM6204C	OEM
UM6204CR	OEM
UM6204E	OEM
UM6206A	OEM
UM6206B	OEM
UM6206C	OEM
UM6206CR	OEM
UM6206E	OEM
UM6600	OEM
UM6601A	OEM
UM6601B	OEM
UM6601C	OEM
UM6601CR	OEM
UM6601E	OEM
UM6601H	OEM
UM6602A	OEM
UM6602B	OEM
UM6602C	OEM
UM6602E	OEM
UM6602H	OEM
UM6604A	OEM
UM6604B	OEM
UM6604C	OEM
UM6604CR	OEM
UM6604E	OEM
UM6606A	OEM
UM6606B	OEM
UM6606C	OEM
UM6606CR	OEM
UM6606E	OEM
UM6606H	OEM
UM6610A	OEM
UM6610B	OEM
UM6610C	OEM
UM6610D	OEM
UM6610E	OEM
UM6845	OEM
UM6845E	OEM
UM7000	OEM
UM7001A	OEM
UM7001B	OEM
UM7001C	OEM
UM7001CR	OEM
UM7001D	OEM
UM7001DR	OEM
UM7001E	OEM
UM7002A	OEM
UM7002B	OEM
UM7002C	OEM
UM7004A	OEM
UM7004B	OEM
UM7004C	OEM
UM7004CR	OEM
UM7004D	OEM
UM7004DR	OEM
UM7004E	OEM
UM7006A	OEM
UM7006B	OEM
UM7006C	OEM
UM7006D	OEM
UM7006E	OEM
UM7010A	OEM
UM7010B	OEM
UM7010C	OEM
UM7010CR	OEM
UM7010D	OEM
UM7010DR	OEM
UM7010E	OEM
UM7016A	OEM
UM7016B	OEM
UM7016C	OEM
UM7016D	OEM
UM7016E	OEM
UM7020A	OEM
UM7020B	OEM
UM7020C	OEM
UM7020CR	OEM
UM7020D	OEM
UM7020DR	OEM
UM7020E	OEM
UM7100	OEM
UM7101A	OEM
UM7101B	OEM
UM7101C	OEM
UM7101CR	OEM
UM7101D	OEM
UM7101DR	OEM
UM7101E	OEM
UM7102A	OEM
UM7102B	OEM
UM7102C	OEM
UM7102D	OEM
UM7102E	OEM
UM7104A	OEM
UM7104B	OEM
UM7104C	OEM
UM7104CR	OEM
UM7104D	OEM
UM7104DR	OEM
UM7104E	OEM
UM7108A	OEM
UM7108B	OEM
UM7108C	OEM
UM7108CR	OEM
UM7108D	OEM
UM7108DR	OEM
UM7108E	OEM
UM7200	OEM
UM7201A	OEM
UM7201B	OEM
UM7201C	OEM
UM7201CR	OEM
UM7201D	OEM
UM7201DR	OEM
UM7201E	OEM
UM7202A	OEM
UM7202B	OEM
UM7202C	OEM
UM7202D	OEM
UM7202E	OEM
UM7204A	OEM
UM7204B	OEM
UM7204C	OEM
UM7204CR	OEM
UM7204D	OEM
UM7204DR	OEM
UM7204E	OEM
UM7206A	OEM
UM7206B	OEM
UM7206C	OEM
UM7206CR	OEM
UM7206D	OEM
UM7206DR	OEM
UM7206E	OEM
UM7300	OEM
UM7301A	OEM
UM7301B	OEM
UM7301C	OEM
UM7301CR	OEM
UM7301D	OEM
UM7301DR	OEM
UM7301E	OEM
UM7302A	OEM
UM7302B	OEM
UM7302C	OEM
UM7302D	OEM
UM7302E	OEM
UM7304A	OEM
UM7304B	OEM
UM7304C	OEM
UM7304CR	OEM
UM7304D	OEM
UM7304DR	OEM
UM7304E	OEM
UM7306A	OEM
UM7306B	OEM
UM7306C	OEM
UM7306D	OEM
UM7306E	OEM
UM7310A	OEM
UM7310B	OEM
UM7310C	OEM
UM7310CR	OEM
UM7310D	OEM
UM7310DR	OEM
UM7310E	OEM
UM8048-8-038	OEM
UM8326	OEM
UM9301	OEM
UM9302	OEM
UM9401	OEM
UM9402	OEM
UM9415	OEM
UM9441	OEM
UM9601	OEM
UM9602	OEM
UM9603	OEM
UM9604	OEM
UM9605	OEM
UM9606	OEM
UM9607	OEM
UM9608	OEM
UM20414C	OEM
UMT1006	1955
UMT1007	4327
UMT1008	1955
UMT1009	1841
UMT1011	1841
UMT1012	1841
UMT1203	OEM
UMT1204	OEM
UMT3202	0142
UMT3584	OEM
UMT3585	OEM
UMT13004	0723
UMT13005	0723
UMT13006	OEM
UMT13007	OEM
UMT13008	OEM
UMT13009	OEM
UMX520	OEM
UMX570	OEM
UMX2020	OEM
UN11A	OEM
UN11B	OEM
UN11C	OEM
UN11D	OEM
UN12A	OEM
UN12B	OEM
UN12C	OEM
UN12D	OEM
UN23	OEM
UN211F	OEM
UN411-D	OEM
UN421-D	OEM
UN521E	OEM
UN1111	4109
UN1112	1026
UN1113	4067
UN1210	OEM
UN1211	0826
UN1212	0881
UN1213	0892
UN1214	OEM
UN1216	OEM
UN1222	OEM
UN1231	OEM
UN2069NE	OEM
UN2111	1881
UN2113	5257
UN2117	OEM
UN2119	OEM
UN2124	OEM
UN2211	4457
UN2212	5154
UN2213	5278
UN2214	OEM
UN2215	OEM
UN2216	OEM
UN4066B	0101
UN4111	4109
UN4111TA	OEM
UN4112	1026
UN4112TA	OEM
UN4113	5486
UN4113TA	OEM
UN4114	OEM
UN4114TA	OEM
UN4115	OEM
UN4115TA	OEM
UN4211	2088
UN4211TA	OEM
UN4212	0881
UN4212TA	OEM
UN4213	0892
UN4213TA	OEM
UN4214	OEM
UN4214TA	OEM
UN4215	OEM
UN4215TA	OEM
UN4216	OEM
UN5112	OEM
UN5113	OEM
UN5115	OEM
UN5212	OEM
UN5213	OEM
UN5217	OEM
UN10015	OEM
UN05	OEM
UN06	OEM
U05E	0087
U05ES	0087
U05G	0015
U06C	4833
UP11A	OEM
UP11B	OEM
UP11C	OEM
UP11D	OEM
UP12A	OEM
UP12B	OEM
UP12C	OEM
UP12D	OEM
UP32C	2864
UP1706	0007
UP1706A	0007
UP1706B	0007
UP11303	0279
UP11305	0279
UP11307	0279
UP11309	0279
UP11345	0004
UP11347	0004
UP11352	0004
UP11353	0279
UP12217	0555
UP12218	0555
UP12222	0079
UP12222B	0079
UP14046	0555
UP14046-46	0079
UP14047	0555
UP14047-46	0079
UPA16	OEM
UPA33A	3787
UPA34A	OEM
UPA44D	OEM
UPA50A	OEM
UPA51B	OEM
UPA53C	4075
UPA54H	OEM
UPA56C	OEM
UPA60A	OEM
UPA61A	OEM
UPA62C	OEM
UPA63H	OEM
UPA64H	3098
UPA64HA	3098
UPA68H	OEM
UPA70A	OEM
UPA71A	OEM
UPA72H	OEM
UPA79C	5738
UPA80C	OEM
UPA81C	0963
UPA1428H	OEM
UPA1436H	OEM
UPA1437H	OEM
UPA1456H	OEM
UPA2003	1126
UPA2003C	1126
UPA2004C	1252
UPB74H04C	1896
UPB74H40C	0554
UPB201C	0232
UPB201D	0232
UPB202C	0507
UPB202D	0507
UPB203C	0692
UPB203D	0692
UPB204C	0867
UPB204D	0867
UPB205C	1018
UPB205D	1018
UPB206C	0738
UPB206D	0738
UPB207C	1160
UPB207D	1160
UPB208D	1177
UPB209D	1193
UPB210C	1265
UPB210D	1265
UPB211C	1417
UPB211D	1394
UPB212C	1164
UPB212D	1417
UPB213C	1303
UPB214C	1303
UPB214D	1303
UPB215C	0268
UPB215D	0268
UPB216C	2382
UPB216D	2382
UPB217C	1423
UPB217D	1423
UPB218C	1032
UPB218D	1032
UPB219C	1199
UPB219D	1199
UPB222C	0828
UPB222D	0828
UPB223C	0564
UPB223D	0564
UPB224C	1150
UPB224D	1150
UPB225C	1164
UPB225D	1164
UPB226C	1477
UPB226D	1477
UPB227D	1046
UPB230D	0117
UPB232C	0310
UPB232D	0310
UPB233C	4772
UPB233D	4772
UPB234C	0462
UPB234D	0462
UPB235D	0357
UPB236D	0381
UPB237D	3478
UPB238D	0990
UPB551C	OEM
UPB552C	OEM
UPB553	OEM
UPB553AC	OEM
UPB562	OEM
UPB562AC	OEM
UPB562C	OEM
UPB568	OEM
UPB568HA	OEM
UPB2047D	1100
UPB2080D	1527
UPB2085D	0370
UPB2086D	1358
UPB2091D	0974
UPB2150D	1484
UPB2151D	1487
UPB2154D	1546
UPB2161D	1635
UPB2170D	1711
UPB2180D	1818
UPB2181P	1831
UPB2182D	1845
UPB2192D	1910
UPB2193D	1915
UPB2195D	1932
UPB2198D	1953
UPB6101-009	OEM
UPB7400C	0232
UPB7402C	0310
UPB7404C	0357
UPB7405C	0381
UPB7410C	0507
UPB7413C	1432
UPB7420C	0692
UPB7430C	0867
UPB7437C	3478
UPB7438C	0990
UPB7440C	1018
UPB7442C	1046
UPB7445C	1074
UPB7447C	1100
UPB7450C	0738
UPB7451C	1160
UPB7453C	1177
UPB7454C	1193
UPB7460C	1265
UPB7473C	1164
UPB7474C	1303
UPB7476C	1150
UPB7480C	1527
UPB7485C	0370
UPB7486	1358
UPB7486C	1358
UPB7491C	0974
UPB8216C	1852
UPB8284AD	OEM
UPB8288D	OEM
UPB74107C	0936
UPB74123C	1149
UPB74141D	1367
UPB74150C	1484
UPB74151C	1487
UPB74153C	1531
UPB74154C	1546
UPB74155C	1566
UPB74156	1582
UPB74156C	1582
UPB74157C	1595
UPB74161C	1635
UPB74164C	0729
UPB74170D	1711
UPB74175C	1776
UPB74180C	1818
UPB74181D	1831
UPB74182C	1845
UPB74192C	1910
UPB74193C	1915
UPB74195C	1932
UPB74198D	1953
UPC15MA	0093
UPC-16	2377
UPC16	2377
UPC-16A	2377
UPC16A	2377
UPC-16C	2377
UPC16C	2377
UPC17C	2855
UPC20	OEM
UPC-20C	0465
UPC20C	0465
UPC20C1	0465
UPC20C2	0465
UPC22C	3318
UPC23C	0523
UPC27C	4463
UPC27CI	4463
UPC29C	0633
UPC29C2	0633
UPC29C3	0633
UPC30C	0648
UPC31C	0668
UPC32C	2864
UPC35C	OEM
UPC41C	4498
UPC46C	0924
UPC47C	0940
UPC48C1	0958
UPC49C	2860
UPC-50C	2859
UPC55D	OEM
UPC56C	OEM
UPC71A	1786
UPC78L05	1288
UPC78L05A	1288
UPC-78L-05AN	1288
UPC78L05J	1288
UPC78L05T	1288
UPC78L05T-E1	OEM
UPC78L08	0083
UPC78L12	1817
UPC78L15	3361
UPC78L24J	4430
UPC78M05	0619
UPC78M05H	0619
UPC78M08H	1187
UPC78M10H	2779
UPC78M12	0330
UPC78M12H	OEM
UPC78M12H2	0330
UPC78M15H	OEM
UPC78M18	2244
UPC78M18H	2244
UPC78N05	OEM
UPC78N05H	OEM
UPC78N12H	OEM
UPC81	0465
UPC81C	0465
UPC143-05	0619
UPC143C08	1187
UPC151A	0406
UPC151C	0308
UPC154A	2863
UPC157A	0093
UPC157C	1290
UPC159A	OEM
UPC177C	0176
UPC206	0465
UPC213C	1303
UPC215C	0268
UPC251A	2352
UPC251C	0356
UPC262C	2864
UPC271C	2093
UPC276	4463
UPC301AC	1290
UPC301AN	1290
UPC305(C)	2155
UPC305C	2155
UPC311	OEM
UPC311C	2093
UPC311G	4106
UPC311G2	4106
UPC317	OEM
UPC317H	OEM
UPC324	OEM
UPC324C	0620
UPC324G2	3172
UPC339C	0176
UPC339G2	2715
UPC358	0765
UPC358C	0765
UPC358G	6087
UPC358G2	OEM
UPC373C	0624
UPC380C	OEM
UPC393	0624
UPC393C	0624
UPC393G2	OEM
UPC451C	0620
UPC494C	1813
UPC539C	OEM
UPC544C	1206
UPC554	1469
UPC-554C	1469
UPC554C	1469
UPC554H	1469
UPC-555A	0627
UPC555A	0627
UPC555H	2300
UPC558	3736
UPC558C	3736
UPC561	3232
UPC561C	2569
UPC562C	2864
UPC563C	OEM
UPC563H	1152
UPC563H2	1152
UPC566	0428
UPC566H	0428
UPC566H2	0428
UPC566H3	0428
UPC566H-B	0428
UPC566H-L	0428
UPC566H-M	0428
UPC566H-N	0428
UPC569C2	4325
UPC570C	2860
UPC570G	2860
UPC571	3318
UPC-571C	3318
UPC571C	3318
UPC-573C	4532
UPC573C	4532
UPC-574	1319
UPC574	1319
UPC574-J	1319
UPC574I	1319
UPC-574J	1319
UPC574J	1319
UPC574J(L)	1319
UPC574J(M)	1319
UPC574J(V)	1319
UPC574JA	1319
UPC574JAG	1319
UPC574JC	1319
UPC574J-G	1319
UPC574JK	1319
UPC574J-KL	1319
UPC574JL	1319
UPC574JM	1319
UPC574J-T	1319
UPC574JT	1319
UPC574K	1319
UPC574K02L	1319
UPC574V	1319
UPC575	2845
UPC575C	2845
UPC575C2	2845
UPC-576H	1470
UPC576H	1470
UPC577	2246
UPC577A	2246
UPC577H	2246
UPC577N	2246
UPC580C	1049
UPC587C	0701
UPC587C2	0701
UPC592A2	4145
UPC592H	4145
UPC592H2	4145
UPC592HZ	4145
UPC592N	4145
UPC595C	0846
UPC595C2	0851
UPC596	0851
UPC-596C	0851
UPC596C	0851
UPC596C2	0851
UPC661CA	OEM
UPC661G	OEM
UPC741C	0308
UPC767PC	0696
UPC-781-05AN	1288
UPC858	2238
UPC858C	2238
UPC861C	3763
UPC861CE	3763
UPC1001	4084
UPC1001-H2	4348
UPC1001H	4348
UPC1001H2	4348
UPC1004C	OEM
UPC1008C	1369
UPC1018	2898
UPC1018C	2898
UPC1018CE	2898
UPC1018C-F	2898
UPC1020	3650
UPC1020H	3650
UPC1023H	2607
UPC1024H	OEM
UPC1025	1152
UPC1025H	6196
UPC1026	0701
UPC1026C	0701
UPC1028H	2008

If replacement code is OEM, contact original manufacturer for replacement. 613

DEVICE TYPE	REPL CODE
UPC1031B2	OEM
UPC1031H	0898
UPC1031H2	0898
UPC1032H	2512
UPC1032HA	OEM
UPC1037H	OEM
UPC1037HA	OEM
UPC1043C	OEM
UPC1057C	5099
UPC1154H	1805
UPC1155H	1805
UPC1156	1805
UPC1156H	1805
UPC1156H2	1805
UPC1158H2	4728
UPC1161(C)	4719
UPC1161C	4719
UPC1161C3	OEM
UPC1170H	OEM
UPC1171C	4723
UPC1173C	4697
UPC1177H	OEM
UPC1181	0749
UPC1181H	0749
UPC1182	0751
UPC1182A	0751
UPC1182H	0751
UPC1185H	4584
UPC1185H2	4584
UPC1186H	4696
UPC1187V	4725
UPC1188H	4713
UPC1191V	4727
UPC1197	5976
UPC1197C	1251
UPC1212C	OEM
UPC1213	OEM
UPC1213C	4747
UPC1216V	4751
UPC1217G	OEM
UPC1222C	4935
UPC1225H	OEM
UPC1228H	OEM
UPC1230H	4654
UPC1230H2	OEM
UPC1235C	OEM
UPC1237H	OEM
UPC1237HA	OEM
UPC1238	5982
UPC1238V	1042
UPC1241H	OEM
UPC1252H2	2254
UPC1252HA	2254
UPC1253H2	1594
UPC1253HA2	1594
UPC1263C2	OEM
UPC1270H	OEM
UPC1273H	OEM
UPC1277H	4756
UPC1278H	OEM
UPC1290C	OEM
UPC1298V	OEM
UPC1303G	OEM
UPC1342V	OEM
UPC1350C	4760
UPC1352	0485
UPC1352C	0485
UPC1352S	2599
UPC1353	2599
UPC1353C	4554
UPC1355C	0391
UPC1356C	0859
UPC1356C2	0859
UPC1358A	0548
UPC1358C	0548
UPC1358H	0548
UPC1358H2	0548
UPC1358HZ	0548
UPC1360	1617
UPC1360C	1617
UPC1362C	OEM
UPC1363C	0678
UPC1363CA	1934
UPC1365C	OEM
UPC1366C	2511
UPC1366C2	2511
UPC-1367C	2888
UPC1367C	2601
UPC1368H	0670
UPC1368H2	0670
UPC1368HR	0670
UPC1368HZ	0670
UPC1371	2599
UPC1371C	2599
UPC1372C	2599
UPC1372E	0485
UPC1373	2015
UPC1373-H	2015
UPC1373H	2015
UPC1373HA	2015
UPC1377C	5117
UPC1378	2031
UPC1378-H-L	2031
UPC1378H	2031
UPC1378H-L	2031
UPC1378H-P	2031
UPC1378JE	OEM
UPC-1379C	4284
UPC1379C	4284

DEVICE TYPE	REPL CODE
UPC1380	1049
UPC1380C	6524
UPC1382	OEM
UPC1382C	2868
UPC1391H	3728
UPC1391H-1	3728
UPC1391HA	3728
UPC1393C	OEM
UPC1393CA	OEM
UPC1394C	4959
UPC1394G	OEM
UPC1394G-T2	OEM
UPC1397C	OEM
UPC1401C	OEM
UPC1401CA	6028
UPC1402CA	0578
UPC1406HA	4009
UPC1458	0356
UPC1458C	0356
UPC1470H	3220
UPC1473HA	OEM
UPC1474-HA	OEM
UPC1474HA	5162
UPC1475HA	OEM
UPC1480CA	3331
UPC1481CA	3830
UPC1483CA	OEM
UPC1484CA	OEM
UPC1486	4843
UPC1486C	4843
UPC1487C	OEM
UPC1488H	OEM
UPC1490HA	4470
UPC1491HA	OEM
UPC1498H	6634
UPC1503C	OEM
UPC1504C	OEM
UPC1505C	OEM
UPC1513HA	3130
UPC1514CA	OEM
UPC1517CA	OEM
UPC1519HA	OEM
UPC1520CA	6026
UPC1524C	OEM
UPC1530CA	1059
UPC1531HA	OEM
UPC1536C	OEM
UPC1571C	OEM
UPC1651G	OEM
UPC1675G	OEM
UPC1705C-016	OEM
UPC1712G	OEM
UPC1870CA	OEM
UPC1870CA-001	OEM
UPC1870CA-001-L	OEM
UPC1870CA-002	OEM
UPC1870CA-003	OEM
UPC1870GH	OEM
UPC1870GH006	OEM
UPC1870GH007	OEM
UPC1871CU	OEM
UPC1873CT	OEM
UPC1880C	1049
UPC2002	1042
UPC2002V	1042
UPC2300ACA	OEM
UPC2300CA	OEM
UPC2300G	OEM
UPC2304CA	OEM
UPC2305GH	OEM
UPC2306AGH	OEM
UPC2308ACA	OEM
UPC2308BCA	OEM
UPC2308CA	OEM
UPC2308G	OEM
UPC2309GS	OEM
UPC2310C	OEM
UPC2311C	OEM
UPC2816C	2312
UPC4001C	0473
UPC4062	3288
UPC4066	0101
UPC4512C	OEM
UPC4539BC	OEM
UPC4556(C)	OEM
UPC4556C	OEM
UPC4558	0356
UPC4558/RC45	OEM
UPC4558C	0356
UPC4558D	0356
UPC4570C	OEM
UPC4570G	OEM
UPC4570G2	OEM
UPC4570G2-T1	OEM
UPC4570HA	3220
UPC4570HA-1	OEM
UPC4572C	OEM
UPC4572HA	OEM
UPC4741C	OEM
UPC5742	3417
UPC6105C	OEM
UPC7805	0619
UPC7805H	0619
UPC7812	0330
UPC7812H	0330
UPC7812HA	0330
UPC7812HF	0330
UPC7815H	3777
UPC7818HF	2244

DEVICE TYPE	REPL CODE
UPC7893H	OEM
UPC7893HF	OEM
UPC7912	OEM
UPC7912H	1827
UPC11564	OEM
UPC14305	1288
UPC14305H	0619
UPC14308	1187
UPC14308H	1187
UPC14312	0330
UPC14312H	0330
UPC14315	4276
UPC14315D	1311
UPC14315H	1311
UPC143150	OEM
UPD23C512EC-143	OEM
UPD23C512EC-185	OEM
UPD23C1000-1-539	OEM
UPD23C1000-1-580	OEM
UPD23C1000-1-629	OEM
UPD23C1000C-1-580	OEM
UPD23C1000C-135	OEM
UPD74HC02G	OEM
UPD74HC04	OEM
UPD74HC14	OEM
UPD74HC367G	OEM
UPD74HC373G	OEM
UPD74HCU04C	OEM
UPD78C10G	OEM
UPD82C43C	OEM
UPD236C-1	OEM
UPD416	0518
UPD416-3	0518
UPD416C	0518
UPD416C-1	0518
UPD416C-2	0518
UPD416D	0518
UPD416D-1	0518
UPD416D-2	0518
UPD444C	OEM
UPD446C-1	OEM
UPD446G-15	OEM
UPD446G-20	OEM
UPD449	OEM
UPD471C	0129
UPD546-037	OEM
UPD546C	OEM
UPD546C-037	OEM
UPD546C037	OEM
UPD546C-107	OEM
UPD547-060	OEM
UPD547C-049	OEM
UPD547C-060	OEM
UPD552C-083	OEM
UPD552C083	OEM
UPD553-020	OEM
UPD553C	OEM
UPD553C-020	OEM
UPD553C-042	OEM
UPD553C-149	OEM
UPD553C149	OEM
UPD553C-167	OEM
UPD554C062	OEM
UPD554C-118	OEM
UPD610BC003	OEM
UPD650C-024	OEM
UPD650C109	OEM
UPD651G-517	OEM
UPD651G-518	OEM
UPD652C-066	OEM
UPD751G-604	OEM
UPD761C	OEM
UPD765	OEM
UPD765A	OEM
UPD765AC	OEM
UPD780C	3441
UPD833G	OEM
UPD857C	3754
UPD858	2238
UPD-858C	2238
UPD858C	2238
UPD861	3763
UPD861C	3763
UPD861CE	3763
UPD861E	3763
UPD1511C-044	OEM
UPD1511C-072	OEM
UPD1511C-073	OEM
UPD1511C-074	OEM
UPD1511C-079	OEM
UPD1511C-133	OEM
UPD1511C-137	OEM
UPD1511C-144	OEM
UPD1511C-161	OEM
UPD1511C-179	OEM
UPD1512C-045	OEM
UPD1512C-061	OEM
UPD1514C-031	OEM
UPD1521	OEM
UPD1703C-011	OEM
UPD1704C-562	OEM
UPD1705C	OEM
UPD1705C-012	OEM
UPD1705C-016	OEM
UPD1705C-518	OEM
UPD1705C-520	OEM
UPD1708-G	OEM
UPD1709-113	OEM
UPD1709A-738	OEM

DEVICE TYPE	REPL CODE
UPD1709A-740	OEM
UPD1709AC530	OEM
UPD1709ACT-113	OEM
UPD1709ACT-128	OEM
UPD1709ACT-733	OEM
UPD1709ACT-736	OEM
UPD1709ACT-738	OEM
UPD1709ACT-740	OEM
UPD1709ACT-741	OEM
UPD1709ACT-746	OEM
UPD1709ACT-753	OEM
UPD1709ACT-755	OEM
UPD1709C-011	OEM
UPD1709C-014	OEM
UPD1709C-113	OEM
UPD1709C-511	OEM
UPD1709C-515	OEM
UPD1709C-518	OEM
UPD1709C-520	OEM
UPD1709C-521	OEM
UPD1709C-530	OEM
UPD1709C530	OEM
UPD1709C-535	OEM
UPD1709C-536	OEM
UPD1709C-538	OEM
UPD-1709CT	OEM
UPD1709CT-113	OEM
UPD1709CT-114	OEM
UPD1709CT-118	OEM
UPD1709CT-121	OEM
UPD1709CT-127	OEM
UPD1709CT-128	OEM
UPD1709CT-713	OEM
UPD-1709CT-715	OEM
UPD-1709CT715	OEM
UPD1709CT-715	OEM
UPD1709CT-722	OEM
UPD1710G-015	OEM
UPD1711CU-517	OEM
UPD1713AGE550	OEM
UPD1913C	OEM
UPD1913C-14	OEM
UPD1937C	2079
UPD1943	OEM
UPD1943G	OEM
UPD1986C	4706
UPD-1987C	OEM
UPD1987C	2079
UPD2102AL-4	4886
UPD2102ALC-4	4886
UPD2114LC	2037
UPD2114LC-1	2037
UPD2114LC-5	2037
UPD2147A-25	OEM
UPD2147A-35	OEM
UPD2147A-45	1683
UPD2364C-1	OEM
UPD2364EC-163	OEM
UPD2732	2672
UPD2732A	2672
UPD2732D	2672
UPD2732D-4	2672
UPD2764D-FC4-A2	0806
UPD2764D-FC5-A3	0806
UPD2801C	OEM
UPD2803C	OEM
UPD2810C	OEM
UPD2812C	OEM
UPD2814C	4558
UPD2816C	2312
UPD2861C	OEM
UPD3551D	OEM
UPD3551D-02	OEM
UPD4001BC	0473
UPD4001BG	OEM
UPD4001C	0473
UPD4002BC	2044
UPD4002C	2044
UPD4011	0215
UPD4011B	0215
UPD4011BC	0215
UPD4011BCG	OEM
UPD4011BCM	0215
UPD4011C	0215
UPD4012BC	0493
UPD4012C	0493
UPD4013BC	0409
UPD4013BG	0409
UPD4013C	0409
UPD4013G	OEM
UPD4015C	1008
UPD4016	1887
UPD4016C	1887
UPD4016C-2	1887
UPD4016CX	1887
UPD4016CX-20	OEM
UPD4016D-1	1887
UPD4017BC	0508
UPD4017C	0508
UPD4020C	1651
UPD4021C	1738
UPD4023BC	0515
UPD4023C	0515
UPD4024BC	OEM
UPD4025C	2061
UPD4027	1938
UPD4027BC	1938
UPD4027C	1938
UPD4028BC	OEM

DEVICE TYPE	REPL CODE
UPD4029	2218
UPD4029C	2218
UPD4030BC	0495
UPD4030C	0495
UPD4035C	2750
UPD4039C	OEM
UPD4040BC	0056
UPD4040C	0056
UPD4042C	0121
UPD4044BC	OEM
UPD4049	0001
UPD4049BC	OEM
UPD4049C	0001
UPD4049UBC	0001
UPD4050C	0394
UPD4051BC	0362
UPD4052	0024
UPD4052BC	0024
UPD4052BG	OEM
UPD4053	0034
UPD4053B	0034
UPD4053BC	0034
UPD4053BG	0034
UPD4053BP	0034
UPD4066	0101
UPD4066B	0101
UPD4066B-1	0101
UPD4066BC	0101
UPD4066BG	OEM
UPD4066BP	0101
UPD4066C	0101
UPD4066G	0101
UPD4069	0119
UPD4069BG	OEM
UPD4069C	0119
UPD4069UBC	0119
UPD4069UBP	OEM
UPD4071	0129
UPD4071BC	0129
UPD4078C	0915
UPD4081	OEM
UPD4081BC	0621
UPD4081C	0328
UPD4093BC	2368
UPD4094BC	OEM
UPD4099B	OEM
UPD4099BC	OEM
UPD4160BC	1349
UPD4164-3	2341
UPD4168C-20	OEM
UPD4364C	OEM
UPD4364C-15LL	OEM
UPD4364C-20L	OEM
UPD4364C-20LL	OEM
UPD4364C-LL	OEM
UPD4464C-15L	OEM
UPD4468-20	OEM
UPD4503BC	2042
UPD4503C	2042
UPD4512BC	OEM
UPD4518	1037
UPD4520C	2650
UPD4528B	3168
UPD4528BC	5028
UPD4528C	3168
UPD4538	1057
UPD4538BC	1057
UPD4538BG	OEM
UPD4538G	OEM
UPD4539C	3611
UPD4555C	2910
UPD4556C	3397
UPD4584BC	3581
UPD6102G	OEM
UPD6104	OEM
UPD6104C	OEM
UPD6104C-001	OEM
UPD6104C-021	OEM
UPD6105C	OEM
UPD6105C-002	OEM
UPD6105P	OEM
UPD6108C-003	OEM
UPD6108C003	OEM
UPD6108C-006	OEM
UPD6110CA	OEM
UPD6117C	OEM
UPD6121G-001	OEM
UPD6122	OEM
UPD6122G-001	OEM
UPD6122G001	OEM
UPD6122G-501	OEM
UPD6122G-504	OEM
UPD6124CA601	OEM
UPD6124CA-612	OEM
UPD6124G	OEM
UPD6125ACA-630	OEM
UPD6125AG-575	OEM
UPD6125G-531	OEM
UPD6128C-001	OEM
UPD6128C001	OEM
UPD6140-001	OEM
UPD6140C	OEM
UPD6140C-001	OEM
UPD6140C001	OEM
UPD6141C-001	OEM
UPD6143	OEM
UPD6143C	OEM
UPD6143G-602	OEM
UPD6145C-001	OEM

DEVICE TYPE	REPL CODE
UPD6145G-601	OEM
UPD6147G	OEM
UPD6163ACA	OEM
UPD6250C	OEM
UPD6251C	OEM
UPD6325C	1869
UPD6325G	OEM
UPD6326C	OEM
UPD6335C	OEM
UPD6335G	OEM
UPD6336C	OEM
UPD6376GSE1	OEM
UPD6460G-601	OEM
UPD6460GT-601	OEM
UPD6510-517	OEM
UPD6510-518	OEM
UPD6900C	OEM
UPD6901C	OEM
UPD6901G	OEM
UPD7051CU-538	OEM
UPD7225G	OEM
UPD7502G229	OEM
UPD7502G245	OEM
UPD7507C-053	OEM
UPD7507C107	OEM
UPD7507CU	OEM
UPD7507HC-033	OEM
UPD7507HC-035	OEM
UPD7507SC1	OEM
UPD7507SC2	OEM
UPD7508AC-018	OEM
UPD7508BGB-505	OEM
UPD7508C-A02	OEM
UPD7508C-A37	OEM
UPD7508C-B13	OEM
UPD7508H-519	OEM
UPD7508HC035	OEM
UPD7508HG-592	OEM
UPD7508HG51922	OEM
UPD7514G	OEM
UPD7514G-064	OEM
UPD7516HCW-279	OEM
UPD7516HCW-287	OEM
UPD7519G	OEM
UPD7519G-53	OEM
UPD7519G-109	OEM
UPD7519G-124	OEM
UPD7519G-530	OEM
UPD7519G-598	OEM
UPD7519G-59812	OEM
UPD7519G-60412	OEM
UPD7520C-055	OEM
UPD7520C-087	OEM
UPD7537C	OEM
UPD7538C-021	OEM
UPD7538C021	OEM
UPD7538C-028	OEM
UPD7538C-049	OEM
UPD7538L-021	OEM
UPD7564G511	OEM
UPD7564G513	OEM
UPD7566CS-041	OEM
UPD7800	OEM
UPD7800G	OEM
UPD7801	OEM
UPD7801G-141	OEM
UPD7801G-176	OEM
UPD7801G-176-36	OEM
UPD7801G-215	OEM
UPD7805	0619
UPD7809G-029	OEM
UPD7809G-050	OEM
UPD7810	OEM
UPD7810G	OEM
UPD7810H	OEM
UPD7810HCW	OEM
UPD7810HG	OEM
UPD7811	OEM
UPD7811G	OEM
UPD7811HG	OEM
UPD8080AFC	4467
UPD8085AC	OEM
UPD8155C	OEM
UPD8155HC-2	OEM
UPD8237AC-5	OEM
UPD8243HC	OEM
UPD8251AC	OEM
UPD8253	OEM
UPD8253-5	OEM
UPD8253C	OEM
UPD8253C-2	OEM
UPD8253C-5	OEM
UPD8255AC-2	OEM
UPD8255AC-5	0051
UPD8255AP-5	OEM
UPD8284A	OEM
UPD8585C	2238
UPD17008	OEM
UPD17008CW-514	OEM
UPD17051CU-538	OEM
UPD23128EC-088	1550
UPD27128D-2	OEM
UPD27256AD	OEM
UPD27256AD-X	OEM
UPD40666BC	OEM
UPD41221C	OEM
UPD41264C	OEM
UPD41264C-15	OEM
UPD41416C-20	OEM

DEVICE TYPE	REPL CODE
UPD41464L	OEM
UPD41647H-45	2341
UPD42272AGF	OEM
UPD42274LE10	OEM
UPD42832C-150	OEM
UPD65006-015	OEM
UPD65006-LC	OEM
UPD65006CW-230	OEM
UPD65006G-124	OEM
UPD65022	OEM
UPD65025GC-025	OEM
UPD75104G	OEM
UPD75108-709	OEM
UPD75108GF-718	OEM
UPD75108GF-720	OEM
UPD75206CW-025	OEM
UPD75206G-516	OEM
UPD75206G516	OEM
UPD75208CW-058	OEM
UPD75208CW-069	OEM
UPD75208CW257	OEM
UPD75216ACW-029	OEM
UPD75216ACW-095	OEM
UPD75216ACW-254	OEM
UPD75308GF4033B9	OEM
UPD75512GF-013	OEM
UPD75512GF-013-3B9	OEM
UPD75516GF-019	OEM
UPD75516GF-025	OEM
UPD75516GF-045	OEM
UPD75516GF-064-3B9	OEM
UPI404	0050
UPI706	0016
UPI706A	0016
UPI706B	0016
UPI718A	0016
UPI956	0086
UPI1301	0050
UPI1303	0211
UPI1305	0211
UPI1307	0211
UPI1309	0211
UPI1345	0164
UPI1347	0279
UPI1352	0004
UPI1353	0004
UPI1613	0086
UPI1711	0086
UPI2069	OEM
UPI2069A	OEM
UPI2070	OEM
UPI2070A	OEM
UPI2071	OEM
UPI2071A	OEM
UPI2217	0086
UPI2218	0086
UPI2222	0016
UPI2222B	0016
UPI2222P	0079
UPI4046	0016
UPI4046-46	0016
UPI4047	0016
UPI4047-46	0016
UPM5-250	OEM
UPM5-250E	OEM
UPM5-250J	OEM
UPM5-500	OEM
UPM5-500D5	OEM
UPM5-500D12	OEM
UPM5-500D28	OEM
UPM5-500E	OEM
UPM5-500J	OEM
UPM5-1000	OEM
UPM5-1000B	OEM
UPM5-1000BE	OEM
UPM5-1000BJ	OEM
UPM5-1000D12	OEM
UPM5-1000D28	OEM
UPM5-1000E	OEM
UPM5-1000J	OEM
UPM5-2000	OEM
UPM5-2000D12	OEM
UPM5-2000D28	OEM
UPM5-2000E	OEM
UPM5-2000J	OEM
UPM6-150A	OEM
UPM6-150AE	OEM
UPM6-150AJ	OEM
UPM9-100A	OEM
UPM9-100AE	OEM
UPM9-100AJ	OEM
UPM12-100A	OEM
UPM12-100AE	OEM
UPM12-100AJ	OEM
UPM15-100A	OEM
UPM15-100AE	OEM
UPM15-100AJ	OEM
UPO7500	OEM
UPS577H	OEM
UPS2003C	OEM
UPT011	0233
UPT012	0233
UPT013	0233
UPT014	0187
UPT015	0187
UPT021	0168
UPT022	0168
UPT023	0168
UPT024	0168

614 If replacement code is OEM, contact original manufacturer for replacement.

DEVICE TYPE	REPL CODE
UPT025	0168
UPT111	0086
UPT112	0086
UPT113	0086
UPT114	0187
UPT115	0187
UPT121	0424
UPT122	0424
UPT123	0424
UPT124	0424
UPT125	0424
UPT211	0617
UPT212	0617
UPT213	0617
UPT214	0617
UPT215	0617
UPT221	0178
UPT222	0178
UPT223	2085
UPT224	2085
UPT225	2085
UPT321	2085
UPT322	2085
UPT323	2085
UPT324	2085
UPT325	2085
UPT410	0538
UPT411	0359
UPT413	0359
UPT423	0359
UPT430	0359
UPT431	0359
UPT521	0424
UPT522	0424
UPT523	0424
UPT524	0424
UPT531	1955
UPT532	1955
UPT533	1955
UPT534	1955
UPT535	1841
UPT611	0617
UPT612	0617
UPT613	0617
UPT614	0617
UPT615	0617
UPT621	1955
UPT622	1955
UPT623	1955
UPT624	1955
UPT625	1955
UPT721	0424
UPT722	0424
UPT723	0424
UPT724	0424
UPT725	0424
UPT731	1955
UPT732	1955
UPT733	1955
UPT734	1955
UPT735	1955
UPT821	0424
UPT822	0424
UPT823	0424
UPT824	0424
UPT825	0424
UPT831	1955
UPT832	1955
UPT833	1955
UPT834	1955
UPT835	1955
UPT931	2465
UPT1021	0424
UPT1022	0424
UPT1023	0424
UPT1024	0424
UPT1025	0424
UPT1031	2465
UPT1032	2465
UPT1033	2465
UPT1034	2465
UPT1035	2465
UPT1131	0615
UPT1132	0615
UPT1133	0615
UPT1134	0615
UPT1135	0615
UPT1215	0617
UPTA510	OEM
UPTA520	OEM
UPTA530	OEM
UPTB520	OEM
UPTB530	OEM
UPTB540	OEM
UPTB550	OEM
UPTO21	0142
UPTO22	0142
UPTO23	0142
UPTO24	0142
UR105	0015
UR110	0015
UR115	0015
UR120	0015
UR123AA	0084
UR123BA	0090
UR123CA	0097
UR123DA	0097
UR123EA	0109
UR123FA	0109

DEVICE TYPE	REPL CODE
UR123GA	0109
UR123HA	0109
UR123KA	0109
UR123MA	0122
UR123PA	0131
UR123RA	0131
UR123VA	0145
UR125	0015
UR205	0110
UR210	0947
UR215	0242
UR220	0242
UR225	0535
UR710	OEM
URS-126-2	0074
US-0100	OEM
US-0101	OEM
US-0102	OEM
US-0103	OEM
US-0104	OEM
US-0105	OEM
US-0106	OEM
US-0107	OEM
US-0108	OEM
US-0109	OEM
US-0110	OEM
US-0111	OEM
US-0112	OEM
US-0113	OEM
US-0114	OEM
US-0115	OEM
US-0908D	3793
US-0908E	OEM
US-0909D	3384
US-0909E	OEM
US-0910D	1248
US-0910E	OEM
US-0911D	1354
US-0911E	OEM
US-0912D	3843
US-0912E	OEM
US-0913D	3847
US-0913E	OEM
US-0921D	3303
US-0921E	OEM
US-0940D	OEM
US-0960D	1063
US12	OEM
US15	OEM
US15/1	0201
US15/1B	0201
US15/1S	0201
US15/16	0286
US15-1	0286
US15-1B	0201
US18	OEM
US20	OEM
US20/1	0201
US-20/1A	OEM
US20/1A	0201
US20/1B	0201
US20/1B-S	0286
US20/1BS	0286
US20/1D	OEM
US20/1S	0201
US20-113	0201
US25	OEM
US25/1A	0286
US25/1AS	0286
US25/1CS	0374
US25/1D	OEM
US25-1B	0374
US30	OEM
US35	OEM
US40	OEM
US45	OEM
US45A	OEM
US50	OEM
US50A	OEM
US54H00A	OEM
US54H00J	OEM
US54H01A	OEM
US54H01J	OEM
US54H04A	OEM
US54H04J	OEM
US54H05A	OEM
US54H05J	OEM
US54H08A	OEM
US54H08J	OEM
US54H10A	OEM
US54H10J	OEM
US54H11A	OEM
US54H11J	OEM
US54H20A	OEM
US54H20J	OEM
US54H21A	OEM
US54H21J	OEM
US54H22A	OEM
US54H22J	OEM
US54H30A	OEM
US54H30J	OEM
US54H37A	OEM
US54H37J	OEM
US54H40A	OEM
US54H40J	OEM
US54H50A	OEM
US54H50J	OEM
US54H51A	OEM
US54H51J	OEM

DEVICE TYPE	REPL CODE
US54H52A	OEM
US54H52J	OEM
US54H53A	OEM
US54H53J	OEM
US54H54A	OEM
US54H54J	OEM
US54H55A	OEM
US54H55J	OEM
US54H60A	OEM
US54H60J	OEM
US54H61A	OEM
US54H61J	OEM
US54H62A	OEM
US54H62J	OEM
US54H71A	OEM
US54H71J	OEM
US54H72A	OEM
US54H72J	OEM
US54H73A	OEM
US54H73J	OEM
US54H76A	OEM
US54H76J	OEM
US54H78A	OEM
US54H78J	OEM
US60	OEM
US60A	OEM
US70	OEM
US70A	OEM
US74H00A	0677
US74H00J	0677
US74H01A	5241
US74H01J	5241
US74H04A	1896
US74H04J	1896
US74H05A	3221
US74H05J	3221
US74H08A	5258
US74H08J	5258
US74H10A	0680
US74H10J	0680
US74H11A	2382
US74H11J	2382
US74H20A	3670
US74H20J	3670
US74H21A	4772
US74H21J	4772
US74H22A	4516
US74H22J	4516
US74H30A	5284
US74H30J	5284
US74H37A	OEM
US74H37J	OEM
US74H40A	0554
US74H40J	0554
US74H50A	1781
US74H50J	1781
US74H51A	1933
US74H51J	1933
US74H52A	2009
US74H52J	2009
US74H53A	2090
US74H53J	2090
US74H54A	2158
US74H54J	2158
US74H55A	3129
US74H55J	3129
US74H60A	5312
US74H60J	5312
US74H61A	2638
US74H61J	2638
US74H62A	2705
US74H62J	2705
US74H71A	3233
US74H71J	3233
US74H72A	3281
US74H72J	3281
US74H73A	2444
US74H73J	2444
US74H74A	2472
US74H74J	2472
US74H76A	5208
US74H76J	1705
US74H78A	5320
US74H78J	5320
US78M12MLA	OEM
US80	OEM
US80A	OEM
US100	OEM
US100A	OEM
US120	OEM
US120A	OEM
US123AA	0084
US123BA	0097
US123CA	0097
US123DA	0097
US123EA	0109
US123FA	0109
US123GA	0109
US123HA	0109
US123KA	0122
US123MA	0122
US123PA	0131
US123RA	0131
US123TA	0145
US123VA	0145
US150	OEM
US150A	OEM
US180	OEM
US180A	OEM

DEVICE TYPE	REPL CODE
US183AA	1590
US183BA	0865
US183CA	0865
US183DA	0865
US183EA	0847
US183FA	0847
US183GA	0847
US183HA	0847
US183KA	1599
US183MA	1599
US183PA	1600
US183RA	1600
US183TA	1604
US183VA	1604
US200	OEM
US200A	OEM
US284HF	0752
US315HF	0752
US322-3	OEM
US322-3-0	OEM
US322-3IR	OEM
US322-3LED	OEM
US720J	OEM
US721J	OEM
US727J	OEM
US730J	OEM
US731J	OEM
US732J	OEM
US734DM	OEM
US824HFP	0752
US1020	0124
US1020M	0124
US1040	0133
US1040M	0133
US1040MT	0133
US1060	0124
US1060M	0124
US1090	0124
US1090M	0124
US1511S	0201
US5400A	OEM
US5400J	OEM
US5401A	OEM
US5401J	OEM
US5402A	OEM
US5402J	OEM
US5403A	OEM
US5403J	OEM
US5404A	OEM
US5404J	OEM
US5405A	OEM
US5405J	OEM
US5408A	OEM
US5408J	OEM
US5409A	OEM
US5409J	OEM
US5410A	OEM
US5410J	OEM
US5411A	OEM
US5411J	OEM
US5418A	OEM
US5418J	OEM
US5420A	OEM
US5420J	OEM
US5426A	OEM
US5430A	OEM
US5430J	OEM
US5432A	OEM
US5432J	OEM
US5440A	OEM
US5440J	OEM
US5441A	OEM
US5442A	OEM
US5443A	OEM
US5444A	OEM
US5445A	OEM
US5446A	OEM
US5447A	OEM
US5448A	OEM
US5450A	OEM
US5450J	OEM
US5451A	OEM
US5451J	OEM
US5453A	OEM
US5453J	OEM
US5454A	OEM
US5454J	OEM
US5459A	OEM
US5459J	OEM
US5460A	OEM
US5460J	OEM
US5470A	OEM
US5470J	OEM
US5472A	OEM
US5472J	OEM
US5473A	OEM
US5473J	OEM
US5474A	OEM
US5474J	OEM
US5475A	OEM
US5476A	OEM
US5476J	OEM
US5477J	OEM
US5480A	OEM
US5480J	OEM
US5482A	OEM
US5482J	OEM
US5483A	OEM
US5486A	OEM

DEVICE TYPE	REPL CODE
US5486J	OEM
US5490A	OEM
US5490J	OEM
US5491A	OEM
US5491J	OEM
US5492A	OEM
US5492J	OEM
US5493A	OEM
US5493J	OEM
US5494A	OEM
US5495A	OEM
US5495J	OEM
US5496A	OEM
US7051A	0041
US7082A	2975
US7091	0057
US7120B	0052
US7150	0681
US7400A	0232
US7400J	0232
US7401A	0268
US7401J	0268
US7402A	0310
US7402J	0310
US7403A	0331
US7403J	0331
US7404A	0357
US7404J	0357
US7405A	0381
US7405J	0381
US7408A	0462
US7408J	0462
US7409A	0487
US7409J	0487
US7410A	0507
US7410J	0507
US7411A	0522
US7411J	0522
US7418A	OEM
US7418J	OEM
US7420A	0692
US7420J	0692
US7426A	0798
US7427A	0812
US7430A	0867
US7430J	0867
US7432A	0893
US7432J	0893
US7438A	0990
US7438J	0990
US7440A	1018
US7440J	1018
US7441A	1032
US7442A	1046
US7443A	1054
US7444A	1066
US7445A	1074
US7446A	1090
US7447A	1100
US7448A	1117
US7450A	0738
US7450J	0738
US7451A	1160
US7451J	1160
US7453A	1177
US7453J	1177
US7454A	1193
US7454J	1193
US7459A	OEM
US7459J	OEM
US7460A	1265
US7460J	1265
US7470A	1394
US7470J	1394
US7472A	1417
US7472J	1417
US7473A	1164
US7473J	1164
US7474A	1303
US7474J	1303
US7475A	1423
US7475J	1423
US7476A	1150
US7476J	1150
US7477J	OEM
US7480A	1527
US7480J	OEM
US7482A	1564
US7482J	OEM
US7483A	0117
US7486A	1358
US7486J	1358
US7490A	1199
US7490J	1199
US7491A	0974
US7491J	OEM
US7492A	0828
US7492J	0828
US7493A	0564
US7493J	0564
US7494A	1692
US7495A	1477
US7495J	OEM
US7496A	1705
US54107A	OEM
US54107J	OEM
US54121A	OEM
US54121J	OEM
US54145A	OEM

DEVICE TYPE	REPL CODE
US54153A	OEM
US54154A	OEM
US54180A	OEM
US54180J	OEM
US74107A	0936
US74107J	0936
US74121A	0175
US74121J	0175
US74145A	0614
US74153A	1531
US74154A	1546
US74154AN	1546
US74180A	1818
US74180J	1818
US75324A	OEM
US75324G	OEM
US75324H	OEM
US75324J	OEM
USAF116ES571PML	OEM
USAF117ES552MML	OEM
USAF304	OEM
USAF377A	OEM
USAF501ES001M	1471
USAF505ES105	0004
USAF508ES020P	0855
USAF508ES021P	0855
USAF510ES030M	1471
USAF510ES031M	1471
USAF511ES035P	0018
USAF511ES036P	0018
USAF512ES040	0279
USAF515ES045M	0037
USAF515ES046M	0037
USAF516ES047M	0037
USAF516ES048M	0037
USAF518ES065M	0338
USAF519ES067M	0710
USAF519ES068M	0710
USB2.5	OEM
USB5	OEM
USB7.5	OEM
USB10	OEM
USC1420-2	OEM
USC1420-4	OEM
USC1420-6	OEM
USC1420-8	OEM
USC1440-2	OEM
USC1440-4	OEM
USC1440-6	OEM
USC1440-8	OEM
USC1470-2	OEM
USC1470-4	OEM
USC1470-6	OEM
USC1470-8	OEM
USC1490-2	OEM
USC1490-4	OEM
USC1490-6	OEM
USC1490-8	OEM
USC2120-2	OEM
USC2120-4	OEM
USC2120-6	OEM
USC2120-8	OEM
USC2140-2	OEM
USC2140-4	OEM
USC2140-6	OEM
USC2140-8	OEM
USC2250-2	OEM
USC2250-4	OEM
USC2250-6	OEM
USC2250-8	OEM
USC2270-2	OEM
USC2270-4	OEM
USC2270-6	OEM
USC2270-8	OEM
USD320C	OEM
USD335C	OEM
USD345C	OEM
USD420	OEM
USD435	OEM
USD445	OEM
USD520	OEM
USD535	OEM
USD545	OEM
USD545HR2	OEM
USD820	OEM
USD835	OEM
USD840	OEM
USD845	OEM
USD920	OEM
USD935	OEM
USD940	OEM
USD945	OEM
USD7703394	0627
USN2N1910W	OEM
USN2N1915W	OEM
USN2N1916W	OEM
USN2N2031W	OEM
USN-7441B	1032
USN-7480A	1527
USN-7480J	OEM
USN-7482A	1564
USN-7482J	OEM
USN-7483B	0117
USN-7490A	1199
USN-7490J	OEM
USN-7491A	0974
USN-7491J	OEM
USN-7492A	0828
USN-7492J	OEM

DEVICE TYPE	REPL CODE
USN-7493A	0564
USN-7493J	OEM
USR12	OEM
USR15	OEM
USR20	OEM
USR25	OEM
USR30	OEM
USR35	OEM
USR40	OEM
USR40A	OEM
USR45	OEM
USR45A	OEM
USR50	OEM
USR50A	OEM
USR60	OEM
USR60A	OEM
USR70	OEM
USR70A	OEM
USR80	OEM
USR80A	OEM
USR100	OEM
USR100A	OEM
USR120	OEM
USR120A	OEM
USR150	OEM
USR150A	OEM
USR180	OEM
USR180A	OEM
USR931	OEM
USR932	OEM
USR933	OEM
USR934	OEM
USR1171	0313
USR1172	0313
USR1173	0313
USR1174	0313
USS5	OEM
USS7.5	OEM
USS10	OEM
USS15	OEM
USS729J	OEM
UST10	OEM
UST19	OEM
UST81	OEM
UST87	OEM
UST88	OEM
UST722	OEM
UST760	OEM
UST761	OEM
UST762	OEM
UST763	OEM
UST764	OEM
UT7-242	OEM
UT11	0015
UT12	0242
UT12.8B	0361
UT13	0242
UT14	0015
UT15	0015
UT16	0015
UT17	0015
UT18	0015
UT21	0015
UT22	0015
UT23	0015
UT24	0015
UT25	0015
UT26	0015
UT26TRIAC	0767
UT27	0015
UT100	OEM
UT101	OEM
UT111	0015
UT112	0015
UT113	0015
UT114	0015
UT115	0015
UT116	0015
UT117	0015
UT118	0071
UT119	0811
UT120	0071
UT123AA	0529
UT123BA	0760
UT123CA	0760
UT123DA	0760
UT123EA	0533
UT123FA	0533
UT123GA	0533
UT123HA	0533
UT123KA	0810
UT123MA	0810
UT123PA	0540
UT123RA	0540
UT123TA	0545
UT123VA	0545
UT183AA	4917
UT183BA	1625
UT183CA	1625
UT183DA	1625
UT183EA	1242
UT183FA	1242
UT183GA	1242
UT183HA	1242
UT183KA	1196
UT183MA	1196
UT183PA	2124
UT183RA	2124
UT183TA	2236

If replacement code is OEM, contact original manufacturer for replacement.

DEVICE TYPE	REPL CODE
UT183VA	2236
UT211	1736
UT212	1736
UT213	0535
UT214	1760
UT215	0959
UT221	0015
UT222	0015
UT223	0015
UT224	0015
UT225	0015
UT226	0015
UT228	0015
UT229	0015
UT231	0015
UT232	0015
UT233	0015
UT234	0242
UT235	0535
UT236	0947
UT237	1760
UT238	0959
UT242	0242
UT244	0535
UT245	1760
UT247	0959
UT249	0947
UT251	0947
UT252	0242
UT254	0535
UT255	1760
UT257	0959
UT258	0811
UT261	0947
UT262	0242
UT264	0535
UT265	1760
UT267	0959
UT268	0811
UT345	0071
UT347	0916
UT361	0811
UT362	0811
UT363	0916
UT364	0916
UT905	1325
UT905A	0031
UT910	0080
UT910A	0031
UT920	0604
UT920A	0031
UT940	0790
UT940A	0031
UT950A	0031
UT-1000	OEM
UT1005	0031
UT1005A	0031
UT1010	0031
UT1010A	0031
UT1020	0031
UT1020A	0031
UT1040	0031
UT1040A	0031
UT1050A	0031
UT2005	0110
UT2010	0947
UT2020	0242
UT2040	0535
UT2060	0959
UT3005	0110
UT3010	0947
UT3020	0242
UT3040	0535
UT3060	0959
UT3080	0811
UT4005	OEM
UT4010	OEM
UT4020	OEM
UT4040	OEM
UT4060	OEM
UT5105	OEM
UT5110	OEM
UT5120	OEM
UT5140	OEM
UT5160	OEM
UT6105	OEM
UT6110	OEM
UT6120	OEM
UT6140	OEM
UT6160	OEM
UT8105	OEM
UT8110	OEM
UT8120	OEM
UT8140	OEM
UT8160	OEM
UTF015	OEM
UTF025	OEM
UTF040	OEM
UTL502	OEM
UTL1001	OEM
UTL1002	OEM
UT0161	OEM
UT0250	OEM
UT0310	OEM
UT0311	OEM
UT0410	OEM
UT0416	OEM
UT0421	OEM
UT0501	OEM

DEVICE TYPE	REPL CODE
UT0501R	OEM
UT0502	OEM
UT0502R	OEM
UT0503	OEM
UT0503R	OEM
UT0504	OEM
UT0504R	OEM
UT0505	OEM
UT0505R	OEM
UT0507	OEM
UT0508	OEM
UT0510	OEM
UT0510R	OEM
UT0511	OEM
UT0511R	OEM
UT0512	OEM
UT0512R	OEM
UT0513	OEM
UT0513R	OEM
UT0514	OEM
UT0515	OEM
UT0515R	OEM
UT0516	OEM
UT0516R	OEM
UT0517	OEM
UT0521	OEM
UT0521R	OEM
UT0523	OEM
UT0523R	OEM
UT0524	OEM
UT0533	OEM
UT0543	OEM
UT0544	OEM
UT0545	OEM
UT0546	OEM
UT0551	OEM
UT0551R	OEM
UT0561	OEM
UT01001	OEM
UT01001R	OEM
UT01002	OEM
UT01002R	OEM
UT01003	OEM
UT01003R	OEM
UT01004	OEM
UT01011	OEM
UT01012	OEM
UT01013	OEM
UT01021	OEM
UT01033	OEM
UT01043	OEM
UT01044	OEM
UT01045	OEM
UT01051	OEM
UT01051R	OEM
UT01501	OEM
UT01501R	OEM
UT01502	OEM
UT01502R	OEM
UT01503	OEM
UT01503R	OEM
UT01504	OEM
UT01511	OEM
UT01511R	OEM
UT01521	OEM
UT01522	OEM
UT02001	OEM
UT02001R	OEM
UT02002	OEM
UT02002R	OEM
UT02003	OEM
UT02003R	OEM
UT02011	OEM
UT02011R	OEM
UT02012	OEM
UT02013	OEM
UT02021	OEM
UT02022	OEM
UT02023	OEM
UT02031	OEM
UT02032	OEM
UT02033	OEM
UT02302	OEM
UT02302R	OEM
UT02303	OEM
UT02303R	OEM
UT02311	OEM
UT02311R	OEM
UT02321	OEM
UTR01	OEM
UTR02	OEM
UTR10	OEM
UTR11	OEM
UTR12	OEM
UTR20	OEM
UTR21	OEM
UTR22	OEM
UTR30	OEM
UTR31	OEM
UTR32	OEM
UTR40	OEM
UTR41	OEM
UTR42	OEM
UTR50	OEM
UTR51	OEM
UTR52	OEM
UTR60	OEM
UTR61	OEM
UTR62	OEM

DEVICE TYPE	REPL CODE
UTR511	OEM
UTR512	OEM
UTR905A	1137
UTR910A	1137
UTR920A	1137
UTR940A	1137
UTR950A	OEM
UTR1005A	1137
UTR1010A	1137
UTR1020A	1137
UTR1040A	1137
UTR1050A	OEM
UTR2305	OEM
UTR2310	OEM
UTR2320	OEM
UTR2340	OEM
UTR2350	OEM
UTR2360	OEM
UTR3305	OEM
UTR3310	OEM
UTR3320	OEM
UTR3340	OEM
UTR3350	OEM
UTR3360	OEM
UTR4305	OEM
UTR4310	OEM
UTR4320	OEM
UTR4340	OEM
UTR4350	OEM
UTR4360	OEM
UTR4405	OEM
UTR4410	OEM
UTR4420	OEM
UTR4440	OEM
UTR5405	OEM
UTR5410	OEM
UTR5420	OEM
UTR5440	OEM
UTR6405	OEM
UTR6410	OEM
UTR6420	OEM
UTR6440	OEM
UTS322-3	OEM
UTS322-3-0	OEM
UTS322-3IR	OEM
UTS322-3LED	OEM
UTX105	OEM
UTX110	OEM
UTX115	OEM
UTX120	OEM
UTX125	OEM
UTX205	OEM
UTX210	OEM
UTX215	OEM
UTX220	OEM
UTX225	OEM
UTX3105	OEM
UTX3110	OEM
UTX3115	OEM
UTX3120	OEM
UTX4105	OEM
UTX4110	OEM
UTX4115	OEM
UTX4120	OEM
UV040BQ	OEM
UV5	OEM
UV7-1	OEM
UV13	OEM
UV13-1	OEM
UV14	OEM
UV78	OEM
UV79	OEM
UV95M	OEM
UV100BQ	OEM
UV204	OEM
UV205	OEM
UV215BQ	OEM
UV229-1	OEM
UV250BQ	OEM
UV444BQ	OEM
UV1001	OEM
UV1002	OEM
UV1003	OEM
UV1004	OEM
UV1005	OEM
UV1010	OEM
UV1011	OEM
UZ1-3.3	0289
UZ1-3.4	0289
UZ1-3.6	0188
UZ1-3.9	0451
UZ1-4.3	0528
UZ1-4.7	0446
UZ1-5.1	0162
UZ1-5.6	0157
UZ1-6.2	0631
UZ1-6.8	0025
UZ1-7.5	0644
UZ1-8.2	0244
UZ1-9.1	0012
UZ1-10	0170
UZ1-11	0313
UZ1-11.5	0789
UZ1-12	0137
UZ1-14	0100
UZ1-15	0002
UZ1-20	0526
UZ1-22	0560
UZ1-24	0627

DEVICE TYPE	REPL CODE
UZ1-26	0436
UZ1-27	0436
UZ1-29	0721
UZ1-33	0039
UZ1-36	0814
UZ1-39	0346
UZ1-43	0925
UZ1-43G	0925
UZ1-47	0993
UZ1-47G	0993
UZ1-51	0497
UZ1-55	1823
UZ1-56	0863
UZ1-62	0778
UZ1-68	1258
UZ1-82	0327
UZ1-92	1301
UZ1-110	0149
UZ1-120	0186
UZ1-128	0361
UZ1-130	0213
UZ1-140	0245
UZ1-150	0028
UZ1-160	0255
UZ1-164	0416
UZ1-170	0871
UZ1-176	0490
UZ1-180	0363
UZ1-190	2831
UZ1-200	0417
UZ-2.0A	OEM
UZ-2.0B	OEM
UZ-2.2A	OEM
UZ-2.2B	OEM
UZ2.2BSB	OEM
UZ-2.4A	1266
UZ-2.4B	1266
UZ-2.7A	0755
UZ-2.7B	0755
UZ2.7BSA	OEM
UZ-3.0A	0118
UZ-3.0B	0118
UZ3.0B	OEM
UZ3.3	0289
UZ-3.3A	0296
UZ-3.3B	0296
UZ3.6	0188
UZ-3.6A	0372
UZ-3.6B	0372
UZ3.6B	OEM
UZ-3.9	0036
UZ3.9	0036
UZ-3.9A	0036
UZ-3.9B	0036
UZ3.9B	OEM
UZ-4.0C	0274
UZ-4.3A	0274
UZ-4.3B	0274
UZ4.3BSB	OEM
UZ4.7	0140
UZ-4.7A	0140
UZ-4.7B	0140
UZ4.7BCA	0140
UZ4.7BSB	OEM
UZ5.1	0162
UZ-5.1A	0041
UZ-5.1B	0041
UZ5.1B	0162
UZ5.1BSA	OEM
UZ5.1BSB	OEM
UZ-5.6B	0253
UZ5.6B	OEM
UZ-5.6BCC	OEM
UZ5.6BM	OEM
UZ5.6BSA	OEM
UZ5.6BSB	OEM
UZ6R8B	0025
UZ6.2	0466
UZ-6.2B	0466
UZ6.2B	0466
UZ6.2BSA	OEM
UZ6.2BSB	OEM
UZ6.2BSC	OEM
UZ6.2ESA	OEM
UZ-6.8B	0062
UZ6.8B	0062
UZ6.8BH	OEM
UZ6.8BM	OEM
UZ6.8BSB	0062
UZ6.8V	0062
UZ7.5	0644
UZ-7.5B	0077
UZ7.5B	OEM
UZ7.5BL	OEM
UZ7.5BM	OEM
UZ7.5BS	OEM
UZ8.2	0244
UZ-8.2B	0165
UZ8.2B	0244
UZ8.2BM	OEM
UZ8.2V	0165
UZ9B	0012
UZ9.1	0012
UZ-9.1B	0057
UZ9.1B	0012
UZ9.1BSC	OEM
UZ-10B	0064
UZ10B	OEM
UZ10BM	OEM

DEVICE TYPE	REPL CODE
UZ10BS	OEM
UZ-11B	0064
UZ-12B	0052
UZ12B	0052
UZ-12B(AU)	0052
UZ-12BCB	OEM
UZ12BSA	OEM
UZ-13B	0053
UZ13B	0137
UZ13BH	OEM
UZ13BL	OEM
UZ13BSB	OEM
UZ15	0002
UZ-15B	0681
UZ15BL	OEM
UZ15BSB	OEM
UZ-16B	0440
UZ16B	OEM
UZ16.2BH	OEM
UZ-18B	0371
UZ18B	OEM
UZ-20B	0695
UZ20B	OEM
UZ-22B	0700
UZ-24B	0489
UZ-27B	0450
UZ-30B	0195
UZ30BSB	OEM
UZ30BSC	0195
UZ-35B	0010
UZ36BSA	OEM
UZ-40B	0032
UZ91E	OEM
UZ91F	0012
UZ110	1172
UZ111	1182
UZ112	1198
UZ113	1209
UZ114	1870
UZ115	0642
UZ116	1246
UZ117	2091
UZ118	1269
UZ119	2210
UZ120	0600
UZ122	OEM
UZ124	OEM
UZ126	OEM
UZ128	OEM
UZ130	OEM
UZ132	OEM
UZ134	OEM
UZ136	OEM
UZ138	OEM
UZ140	OEM
UZ210	1172
UZ211	1182
UZ212	1198
UZ213	1209
UZ214	1870
UZ215	0642
UZ216	1246
UZ217	2091
UZ218	1269
UZ219	2210
UZ220	0600
UZ222	OEM
UZ224	OEM
UZ226	OEM
UZ228	OEM
UZ230	OEM
UZ232	OEM
UZ234	OEM
UZ236	OEM
UZ238	OEM
UZ240	OEM
UZ310	1172
UZ311	1182
UZ312	1198
UZ313	1209
UZ314	1870
UZ315	0642
UZ316	1246
UZ317	2091
UZ318	1269
UZ319	2210
UZ320	0600
UZ322	OEM
UZ324	OEM
UZ326	OEM
UZ328	OEM
UZ330	OEM
UZ332	OEM
UZ334	OEM
UZ336	OEM
UZ338	OEM
UZ340	OEM
UZ706	0205
UZ707	0475
UZ708	0499
UZ709	0679
UZ710	0225
UZ712	0234
UZ713	0237
UZ714	1387
UZ715	0247
UZ716	0251
UZ718	0256
UZ720	0262

DEVICE TYPE	REPL CODE
UZ722	0269
UZ724	0273
UZ727	0291
UZ730	0305
UZ733	0314
UZ736	0316
UZ740	0322
UZ745	0993
UZ750	0027
UZ756	0266
UZ760	2829
UZ770	2144
UZ775	0421
UZ780	0439
UZ790	0238
UZ806	0205
UZ807	0475
UZ808	0499
UZ809	0679
UZ810	0225
UZ812	0234
UZ813	0237
UZ814	1387
UZ815	0247
UZ816	0251
UZ818	0256
UZ820	0262
UZ822	0269
UZ824	0273
UZ827	0291
UZ830	0305
UZ833	0314
UZ836	0316
UZ840	0322
UZ845	0993
UZ850	0027
UZ856	0266
UZ860	2829
UZ870	2144
UZ875	0421
UZ880	0439
UZ890	0238
UZ906	0205
UZ907	0475
UZ908	0499
UZ909	0679
UZ910	0225
UZ912	0234
UZ913	0237
UZ914	1387
UZ915	0247
UZ916	0251
UZ918	0256
UZ920	0262
UZ922	0269
UZ924	0273
UZ927	0291
UZ930	0305
UZ933	0314
UZ936	0316
UZ940	0322
UZ945	OEM
UZ950	0027
UZ956	0266
UZ960	2829
UZ970	OEM
UZ975	0421
UZ980	0439
UZ990	0238
UZ3016	0025
UZ3016A	0025
UZ3016B	0025
UZ3017	0077
UZ3017A	0644
UZ3017B	0644
UZ3018	0244
UZ3018A	0244
UZ3018B	0244
UZ3019	0012
UZ3019A	0012
UZ3019B	0012
UZ3020	0170
UZ3020A	0170
UZ3020B	0170
UZ3021	0313
UZ3021A	0313
UZ3021B	0313
UZ3022	0137
UZ3022A	0137
UZ3022B	0137
UZ3023	0361
UZ3023A	0361
UZ3023B	0361
UZ3024	0002
UZ3024A	0002
UZ3024B	0002
UZ3025	0416
UZ3025A	0416
UZ3025B	0416
UZ3026	0490
UZ3026A	0490
UZ3026B	0490
UZ3027	0526
UZ3027A	0526
UZ3027B	0526
UZ3028	0560
UZ3028A	0560
UZ3028B	0560
UZ3029	0398

DEVICE TYPE	REPL CODE
UZ3029A	0398
UZ3029B	0398
UZ3030	0436
UZ3030A	0436
UZ3030B	0436
UZ3031	0721
UZ3031A	0721
UZ3031B	0721
UZ3032	0039
UZ3032A	0039
UZ3032B	0039
UZ3033	0814
UZ3033A	0814
UZ3033B	0814
UZ3034	0346
UZ3034A	0346
UZ3034B	0346
UZ3035	0925
UZ3035A	0925
UZ3035B	0925
UZ3036	0993
UZ3036A	0993
UZ3036B	0993
UZ3037	0497
UZ3037A	0497
UZ3037B	0497
UZ3038	0863
UZ3038A	0863
UZ3038B	0863
UZ3039	0778
UZ3039A	0778
UZ3039B	0778
UZ3040	2144
UZ3040A	2144
UZ3040B	2144
UZ3041	1181
UZ3041A	1181
UZ3041B	1181
UZ3042	0327
UZ3042A	0327
UZ3042B	0327
UZ3043	1301
UZ3043A	1301
UZ3043B	1301
UZ3044	0098
UZ3044A	0098
UZ3044B	0098
UZ3045	0149
UZ3045A	0149
UZ3045B	0149
UZ3046	0186
UZ3046A	0186
UZ3046B	0186
UZ3047	0213
UZ3047A	0213
UZ3047B	0213
UZ3048	0028
UZ3048A	0213
UZ3048B	0028
UZ3049	0255
UZ3049A	0255
UZ3049B	0255
UZ3050	0363
UZ3050A	0363
UZ3050B	0363
UZ3051	0417
UZ3051A	0417
UZ3051B	0417
UZ4110	1172
UZ4111	1182
UZ4112	1198
UZ4113	1209
UZ4115	0642
UZ4116	1246
UZ4118	1269
UZ4120	0600
UZ4210	1172
UZ4211	1182
UZ4212	1198
UZ4213	1209
UZ4215	0642
UZ4216	1246
UZ4218	1269
UZ4220	0600
UZ4706	0205
UZ4707	0475
UZ4708	0499
UZ4709	0679
UZ4710	0225
UZ4712	0234
UZ4713	0237
UZ4715	0247
UZ4716	0251
UZ4718	0256
UZ4720	0262
UZ4722	0269
UZ4724	0273
UZ4727	0291
UZ4730	0305
UZ4733	0314
UZ4736	0316
UZ4739	0322
UZ4743	0333
UZ4747	0343
UZ4751	0027
UZ4756	0266
UZ4762	0382
UZ4768	0401
UZ4775	0421

616 If replacement code is OEM, contact original manufacturer for replacement.

DEVICE TYPE	REPL CODE
UZ4782	0439
UZ4791	0238
UZ4806	0205
UZ4807	0475
UZ4808	0499
UZ4809	0679
UZ4810	0225
UZ4812	0234
UZ4813	0237
UZ4815	0247
UZ4816	0251
UZ4818	0256
UZ4820	0262
UZ4822	0269
UZ4824	0273
UZ4827	0291
UZ4830	0305
UZ4833	0314
UZ4836	0316
UZ4839	0322
UZ4843	0333
UZ4847	0343
UZ4851	0027
UZ4856	0266
UZ4862	0382
UZ4868	0401
UZ4875	0421
UZ4882	0439
UZ4891	0238
UZ5110	1172
UZ5111	1182
UZ5112	1198
UZ5113	1209
UZ5114	1870
UZ5115	0642
UZ5116	1246
UZ5117	2091
UZ5118	1269
UZ5119	2210
UZ5120	0600
UZ5122	OEM
UZ5124	OEM
UZ5126	OEM
UZ5128	OEM
UZ5130	OEM
UZ5132	OEM
UZ5134	OEM
UZ5136	OEM
UZ5138	OEM
UZ5140	OEM
UZ5210	1172
UZ5211	1182
UZ5212	1198
UZ5213	1209
UZ5214	1870
UZ5215	0642
UZ5216	1246
UZ5217	2091
UZ5218	1269
UZ5219	2210
UZ5220	0600
UZ5222	OEM
UZ5224	OEM
UZ5226	OEM
UZ5228	OEM
UZ5230	OEM
UZ5232	OEM
UZ5234	OEM
UZ5236	OEM
UZ5238	OEM
UZ5240	OEM
UZ5310	1172
UZ5311	1182
UZ5312	1198
UZ5313	1209
UZ5314	1870
UZ5315	0642
UZ5316	1246
UZ5317	2091
UZ5318	1269
UZ5319	2210
UZ5320	0600
UZ5322	OEM
UZ5324	OEM
UZ5326	OEM
UZ5328	OEM
UZ5330	OEM
UZ5332	OEM
UZ5334	OEM
UZ5336	OEM
UZ5338	OEM
UZ5340	OEM
UZ5706	0205
UZ5707	0475
UZ5708	0499
UZ5709	0679
UZ5710	0225
UZ5712	0234
UZ5713	0237
UZ5714	1387
UZ5715	0247
UZ5716	0251
UZ5718	0256
UZ5720	0262
UZ5722	0269
UZ5724	0273
UZ5727	0291
UZ5730	0305
UZ5733	0314
UZ5736	0316
UZ5740	0322
UZ5745	0343
UZ5750	0027
UZ5756	0266
UZ5760	2829
UZ5770	0401
UZ5775	0421
UZ5780	0439
UZ5790	0238
UZ5806	0205
UZ5807	0475
UZ5808	0499
UZ5809	0679
UZ5810	0225
UZ5812	0234
UZ5813	0237
UZ5814	1387
UZ5815	0247
UZ5816	0251
UZ5818	0256
UZ5820	0262
UZ5822	0269
UZ5824	0273
UZ5827	0291
UZ5830	0305
UZ5833	0314
UZ5836	0316
UZ5840	0322
UZ5845	0343
UZ5850	0027
UZ5856	0266
UZ5860	2829
UZ5870	0401
UZ5875	0421
UZ5880	0439
UZ5890	0238
UZ5906	0205
UZ5907	0475
UZ5908	0499
UZ5909	0679
UZ5910	0225
UZ5912	0234
UZ5913	0237
UZ5914	1387
UZ5915	0247
UZ5916	0251
UZ5918	0256
UZ5920	0262
UZ5922	0269
UZ5924	0273
UZ5927	0291
UZ5930	0305
UZ5933	0314
UZ5936	0316
UZ5940	0322
UZ5945	0343
UZ5950	0027
UZ5956	0266
UZ5960	2829
UZ5970	0401
UZ5975	0421
UZ5980	0439
UZ5990	0238
UZ7110	OEM
UZ7110L	OEM
UZ7210	OEM
UZ7210L	OEM
UZ7310	OEM
UZ7310L	OEM
UZ7706	OEM
UZ7706L	OEM
UZ7707	OEM
UZ7707L	OEM
UZ7708	OEM
UZ7708L	OEM
UZ7709	OEM
UZ7709L	OEM
UZ7710	OEM
UZ7710L	OEM
UZ7712	OEM
UZ7712L	OEM
UZ7713	OEM
UZ7713L	OEM
UZ7714	OEM
UZ7714L	OEM
UZ7715	OEM
UZ7715L	OEM
UZ7716	OEM
UZ7716L	OEM
UZ7718	OEM
UZ7718L	OEM
UZ7720	OEM
UZ7720L	OEM
UZ7722	OEM
UZ7722L	OEM
UZ7724	OEM
UZ7724L	OEM
UZ7727	OEM
UZ7727L	OEM
UZ7730	OEM
UZ7730L	OEM
UZ7733	OEM
UZ7733L	OEM
UZ7736	OEM
UZ7736L	OEM
UZ7740	OEM
UZ7740L	OEM
UZ7745	OEM
UZ7745L	OEM
UZ7750	OEM
UZ7750L	OEM
UZ7756	OEM
UZ7756L	OEM
UZ7760	OEM
UZ7760L	OEM
UZ7770	OEM
UZ7770L	OEM
UZ7775	OEM
UZ7775L	OEM
UZ7780	OEM
UZ7780L	OEM
UZ7790	OEM
UZ7790L	OEM
UZ7806	OEM
UZ7806L	OEM
UZ7807	OEM
UZ7807L	OEM
UZ7808	OEM
UZ7808L	OEM
UZ7809	OEM
UZ7809L	OEM
UZ7810	OEM
UZ7810L	OEM
UZ7812	OEM
UZ7812L	OEM
UZ7813	OEM
UZ7813L	OEM
UZ7814	OEM
UZ7814L	OEM
UZ7815	OEM
UZ7815L	OEM
UZ7816	OEM
UZ7816L	OEM
UZ7818	OEM
UZ7818L	OEM
UZ7820	OEM
UZ7820L	OEM
UZ7822	OEM
UZ7822L	OEM
UZ7824	OEM
UZ7824L	OEM
UZ7827	OEM
UZ7827L	OEM
UZ7830	OEM
UZ7830L	OEM
UZ7833	OEM
UZ7833L	OEM
UZ7836	OEM
UZ7836L	OEM
UZ7840	OEM
UZ7840L	OEM
UZ7845	OEM
UZ7845L	OEM
UZ7850	OEM
UZ7850L	OEM
UZ7856	OEM
UZ7856L	OEM
UZ7860	OEM
UZ7860L	OEM
UZ7870	OEM
UZ7870L	OEM
UZ7875	OEM
UZ7875L	OEM
UZ7880	OEM
UZ7880L	OEM
UZ7890	OEM
UZ7890L	OEM
UZ7906	OEM
UZ7906L	OEM
UZ7907	OEM
UZ7907L	OEM
UZ7908	OEM
UZ7908L	OEM
UZ7909	OEM
UZ7909L	OEM
UZ7910	OEM
UZ7910L	OEM
UZ7912	OEM
UZ7912L	OEM
UZ7913	OEM
UZ7913L	OEM
UZ7914	OEM
UZ7914L	OEM
UZ7915	OEM
UZ7915L	OEM
UZ7916	OEM
UZ7916L	OEM
UZ7918	OEM
UZ7918L	OEM
UZ7920	OEM
UZ7920L	OEM
UZ7922	OEM
UZ7922L	OEM
UZ7924	OEM
UZ7924L	OEM
UZ7927	OEM
UZ7927L	OEM
UZ7930	OEM
UZ7930L	OEM
UZ7933	OEM
UZ7933L	OEM
UZ7936	OEM
UZ7936L	OEM
UZ7940	OEM
UZ7940L	OEM
UZ7945	OEM
UZ7945L	OEM
UZ7950	OEM
UZ7950L	OEM
UZ7956	OEM
UZ7956L	OEM
UZ7960	OEM
UZ7960L	OEM
UZ7970	OEM
UZ7970L	OEM
UZ7975	OEM
UZ7975L	OEM
UZ7980	OEM
UZ7980L	OEM
UZ7990	OEM
UZ7990L	OEM
UZ8110	0098
UZ8111	0149
UZ8112	0186
UZ8113	0213
UZ8114	0245
UZ8115	0028
UZ8116	0255
UZ8117	0871
UZ8118	0363
UZ8119	2831
UZ8120	0417
UZ8210	0098
UZ8211	0149
UZ8212	0186
UZ8213	0213
UZ8214	0245
UZ8215	0028
UZ8216	0255
UZ8217	0871
UZ8218	0363
UZ8219	2831
UZ8220	0417
UZ8706	0025
UZ8707	0644
UZ8708	0244
UZ8709	0012
UZ8710	0170
UZ8712	0137
UZ8713	0361
UZ8714	0100
UZ8715	0002
UZ8716	0416
UZ8718	0490
UZ8720	0526
UZ8722	0560
UZ8724	0398
UZ8727	0436
UZ8730	0721
UZ8733	0039
UZ8736	0814
UZ8740	0346
UZ8745	0993
UZ8750	0497
UZ8756	0863
UZ8760	1148
UZ8770	2144
UZ8775	1181
UZ8780	0327
UZ8790	1301
UZ8806	0025
UZ8807	0644
UZ8808	0244
UZ8809	0012
UZ8810	0170
UZ8812	0137
UZ8813	0361
UZ8814	0012
UZ8815	0002
UZ8816	0416
UZ8818	0490
UZ8820	0526
UZ8822	0560
UZ8824	0398
UZ8827	0436
UZ8830	0721
UZ8833	0039
UZ8836	0814
UZ8840	0346
UZ8845	0993
UZ8850	0497
UZ8856	0863
UZ8860	1148
UZ8870	2144
UZ8875	1181
UZ8880	0327
UZ8890	1301
UZL-3.3	0289
UZL-3.4	0289
UZL-3.6	0188
UZL-3.9	0451
UZL-4.3	0528
UZL-4.7	0446
UZL-5.1	0162
UZL-5.6	0157
UZL-6H2	OEM
UZL-6.2	0631
UZL-6.8	0025
UZL7M3	OEM
UZL-7.5	0644
UZL-8.2	0244
UZL-9.1	0012
UZL-10	0170
UZL-11	0313
UZL-12	0137
UZL-14	0100
UZL-15	0002
UZL-22	0560
UZL-24	0398
UZL-26	0436
UZL-27	0436
UZL-29	0721
UZL-33	0039
UZL-36	0814
UZL-39	0346
UZL-51	0497
UZL-55	1823
UZL-56	0863
UZL-62	0778
UZL-68	1258
UZL-82	0327
UZL-91	1301
UZL-110	0149
UZL-115	0789
UZL-120	0186
UZL-128	0361
UZL-130	0213
UZL-140	0245
UZL-150	0028
UZL-160	0255
UZL-163	0416
UZL-170	0871
UZL-176	0490
UZL-180	0363
UZL-190	2831
UZL-200	0417
UZP3.3BB	OEM
UZP5.1B	OEM
UZP-5.6B	0157
UZP-6.2B	0631
UZP-6.8B	0025
UZP-7.5B	0644
UZP-8.2B	0244
UZP-9.1B	0012
UZP-10B	0170
UZP-11B	0313
UZP11B	0313
UZP-12B	0137
UZP-13B	0361
UZP-15B	0002
UZP-16B	0416
UZP-18B	0490
UZP-20B	0526
UZP-22B	0560
UZP-24B	0398
UZP-27B	0436
UZP-30B	0721
UZP-33B	0039
V0-3C	0071
V0-6B	0015
V0-6C	0015
V0-6C-401	0015
V0-9C	0071
V01C	0242
V01E	0535
V01G	0071
V01J	0811
V01L	0916
V03-C	0071
V03C	0015
V03D	OEM
V03E	0071
V03G	0071
V03J	0071
V05B	0087
V05E	0015
V06	0015
V06(DIO)	0015
V06(RECT)	0015
V06-C	0015
V06-E	0071
V06-G	0071
V06A	0023
V06B	0023
V06BX4	0015
V06C	0023
V06C(BOOST)	0102
V06C(LAFAYETTE)	0644
V06C(POWER-RECTIFIER	0015
V06C(S)	0023
V06C5	0015
V06CS	0023
V06E	0023
V06G	0023
V06J	0102
V07E	0071
V07G	0071
V07J	0071
V08E	0071
V08G	0071
V08J	0071
V09-E	0102
V09-E(CENT.)	0914
V09-G	0023
V09C	0023
V09E	0023
V09E-TA	OEM
V09ETA	0023
V09E-Z	0023
V09G	0023
V09G-F2	0023
V09G-TA	0023
V09GTA	0023
V0BX4	0549
V0G	0015
V-1	0290
V2I	OEM
V2SC1257-/11	OEM
V2SD669C	OEM
V5R5	OEM
V5R9	OEM
V5R12	OEM
V5R12-5	OEM
V5R12-12	OEM
V5R15	OEM
V5R15-15	OEM
V6/2R	0136
V6/2RC	0004
V6/2RJ	0004
V6/4R	0136
V6/4RC	0004
V6/4RJ	0004
V6/8R	0136
V6/8RJ	0004
V6/RC	0004
V7	OEM
V7A	OEM
V7B	OEM
V7C	OEM
V7D	OEM
V7E	OEM
V7EA	OEM
V7EB	OEM
V7EC	OEM
V7ED	OEM
V8ZA05	OEM
V8ZA1	OEM
V8ZA2	OEM
V10	0005
V10/1S	0136
V10/1SJ	0136
V10/2S	0279
V10/2SJ	0279
V10/15A	0211
V10/25	0279
V10/25J	0279
V10/30A	0211
V10/50A	0211
V10/50B	OEM
V10A	0005
V10B	OEM
V10C	OEM
V10D	OEM
V10E	OEM
V10EA	OEM
V10EB	OEM
V10EC	OEM
V10ED	OEM
V11-CA	0071
V11J	0102
V11L	0102
V11M	0102
V-11N	0102
V11N	0023
V12	0715
V12A	0715
V12A12-12	OEM
V12A15-15	OEM
V12B	OEM
V12C	OEM
V12D	OEM
V12E	OEM
V12EA	OEM
V12EB	OEM
V12EC	OEM
V12ED	OEM
V12P5	OEM
V12P12/12	OEM
V12P15/15	OEM
V12R5	OEM
V12R9	OEM
V12R12	OEM
V12R12-5	OEM
V12R12-12	OEM
V12R15	OEM
V12R15-15	OEM
V12ZA05	OEM
V12ZA1	OEM
V12ZA2	OEM
V13	OEM
V13/11	0279
V15	OEM
V15/10DP	0160
V15/10P	OEM
V15/15NP	0160
V15/20DP	0160
V15/20IP	OEM
V15/20P	OEM
V15/20R	0136
V15/30DP	0160
V15/30NP	0160
V15/30P	OEM
V15A	OEM
V15B	OEM
V15C	OEM
V15C200/80-V&	0015
V15C200/80-VF	0015
V15D	OEM
V15E	OEM
V15EA	OEM
V15EB	OEM
V15EC	OEM
V15ED	OEM
V17A	0031
V17B	0031
V17C	0031
V17D	0031
V17E	0031
V17L	0015
V18MA1A	OEM
V18Z-1	OEM
V18Z-3	OEM
V18ZA05	OEM
V18ZA1	1681
V18ZA2	OEM
V18ZA3	1684
V18ZA40	OEM
V19	0023
V19B	0023
V19C	0023
V19CS	0023
V19CSS	0023
V19C-T52	0023
V19E	0023
V19E-T52	0023
V19E-Z	0023
V19G	0017
V20	OEM
V20A	OEM
V20B	OEM
V20C	OEM
V20D	OEM
V20E	OEM
V20EA	OEM
V20EB	OEM
V20EC	OEM
V20ED	OEM
V20EG	OEM
V20G	OEM
V22	OEM
V22MA1A	OEM
V22Z-1	OEM
V22Z-3	OEM
V22ZA05	OEM
V22ZA1	1997
V22ZA2	OEM
V22ZA3	1998
V23	OEM
V24E	OEM
V24Z-1	OEM
V24Z-4	OEM
V24ZA1	1304
V24ZA4	1309
V24ZA50	OEM
V27	OEM
V27A	OEM
V27A-1	OEM
V27B	OEM
V27C	OEM
V27D	OEM
V27E	OEM
V27EA	OEM
V27EB	OEM
V27EC	OEM
V27ED	OEM
V27EG	OEM
V27G	OEM
V27MA1A	OEM
V27Z-1	OEM
V27Z-4	OEM
V27ZA05	OEM
V27ZA1	2309
V27ZA2	OEM
V27ZA3	OEM
V27ZA4	2310
V27ZA60	OEM
V30/10DP	0160
V30/10P	OEM
V30/15NP	0160
V30/20DP	0160
V30/20IP	OEM
V30/20P	OEM
V30/30DP	0085
V30/30NP	0160
V30/30P	OEM
V30J	0071
V30L	0344
V30M	0344
V30N	0023
V33	5444
V33A	0030
V33A-2	OEM
V33B	OEM
V33C	OEM
V33D	OEM
V33EG	0030
V33G	0030
V33MA1A	2577
V33MA1B	OEM
V33Z-1	OEM
V33Z-5	OEM
V33ZA05	OEM
V33ZA1	2763
V33ZA2	OEM
V33ZA3	OEM
V33ZA5	2769
V33ZA70	OEM
V36ZA80	OEM
V39	OEM
V39A	OEM
V39A-2	OEM
V39B	OEM
V39B/C	OEM

If replacement code is OEM, contact original manufacturer for replacement. 617

DEVICE TYPE	REPL CODE
V39C	OEM
V39D	OEM
V39E	OEM
V39EA	OEM
V39EB	OEM
V39EC	OEM
V39EG	OEM
V39G	OEM
V39MA2A	OEM
V39MA2B	OEM
V39Z-2	OEM
V39Z-6	OEM
V39ZA05	4297
V39ZA1	4297
V39ZA3	3044
V39ZA6	3044
V40B/C	OEM
V40LA2A	OEM
V40LA2B	OEM
V47	OEM
V47A	OEM
V47A-3	OEM
V47B	OEM
V47C	OEM
V47D	OEM
V47E	OEM
V47EA	OEM
V47EB	OEM
V47EC	OEM
V47ED	OEM
V47EG	OEM
V47G	OEM
V47MA2A	OEM
V47MA2B	OEM
V47Z-2	OEM
V47Z-7	OEM
V47ZA05	5638
V47ZA1	5638
V47ZA3	OEM
V47ZA7	3046
V50	OEM
V50A260-36	0143
V50A260-36(GE-DIO)	0143
V50A260-36(SI-DIO)	0133
V51	0004
V53B/C	OEM
V55B	OEM
V55D	OEM
V55E	OEM
V55F	OEM
V56	OEM
V56A	OEM
V56A-3	OEM
V56B	OEM
V56C	OEM
V56D	OEM
V56E	OEM
V56EA	OEM
V56EB	OEM
V56EC	OEM
V56ED	OEM
V56EG	OEM
V56G	OEM
V56MA2A	OEM
V56MA2B	OEM
V56Z-2	OEM
V56Z-8	OEM
V56ZA05	OEM
V56ZA2	2907
V56ZA3	OEM
V56ZA8	2913
V58	0050
V58C	OEM
V60/10DP	0160
V60/10P	0160
V60/20DP	0160
V60/20IP	OEM
V60/20P	0160
V60/30DP	0160
V60/30P	0160
V60LA3A	OEM
V60LA3B	OEM
V64	OEM
V68	OEM
V68A	OEM
V68A-3	OEM
V68B	OEM
V68C	OEM
V68D	OEM
V68E	OEM
V68EA	OEM
V68EB	OEM
V68EC	OEM
V68ED	OEM
V68G	OEM
V68MA3A	OEM
V68MA3B	OEM
V68Z-2	OEM
V68Z-10	OEM
V68ZA05	OEM
V68ZA2	4199
V68ZA3	OEM
V68ZA10	3049
V72	OEM
V74	0143
V75	0050
V77B	OEM
V77C	OEM
V78	0229
V82	OEM
V82A	OEM
V82A-5	OEM
V82B	OEM
V82C	OEM
V82D	OEM
V82E	OEM
V82EA	OEM
V82EB	OEM
V82EC	OEM
V82ED	OEM
V82G	OEM
V82MA3A	OEM
V82MA3B	OEM
V82Z-2	OEM
V82Z-12	OEM
V82ZA05	OEM
V82ZA2	4199
V82ZA4	OEM
V82ZA12	3056
V95LA7A	OEM
V95LA7B	OEM
V100	OEM
V100A	OEM
V100A-2	OEM
V100B	OEM
V100C	OEM
V100D	OEM
V100E	OEM
V100EA	OEM
V100EB	OEM
V100EC	OEM
V100ED	OEM
V100G	OEM
V100MA4A	OEM
V100MA4B	OEM
V100Z-3	OEM
V100Z-15	OEM
V100ZA05	4158
V100ZA3	4158
V100ZA4	3061
V100ZA15	3061
V115	0143
V117	0143
V117R-2	OEM
V117R-5	OEM
V117R-6	OEM
V117R-15	OEM
V118	0127
V119	0016
V120	0050
V120A-2	OEM
V120MA1A	OEM
V120MA2B	OEM
V120PH	0144
V120RH	0086
V120Z-3	OEM
V120Z-18	OEM
V120ZA05	4834
V120ZA1	4834
V120ZA4	3075
V120ZA6	3075
V126	0002
V129	0127
V130HE150	OEM
V130LA1	0834
V130LA2	1364
V130LA5	OEM
V130LA10	0832
V130LA10A	0832
V130LA20	0824
V130LA20A	0824
V130LA20B	4204
V130PA10A	OEM
V130PA20A	2521
V130PA20B	OEM
V130PA20C	OEM
V131P	OEM
V135	0143
V139	0086
V140	0644
V140LA2	OEM
V140LA5	OEM
V140LA10A	OEM
V143	0127
V144	0142
V145	0160
V146	0086
V148	0229
V150A-3	OEM
V150HE150	OEM
V150LA1	6628
V150LA2	0246
V150LA5	OEM
V150LA10	3381
V150LA10A	1982
V150LA20	3381
V150LA20A	3381
V150LA20B	3382
V150MA1A	OEM
V150MA2B	OEM
V150PA10A	OEM
V150PA20A	OEM
V150PA20B	OEM
V150PA20C	OEM
V150R-2	OEM
V150R-6	OEM
V150R-8	OEM
V150R-17	OEM
V150ZA05	OEM
V150ZA1	5066
V150ZA4	3087
V150ZA8	3087
V151(BENCO)	1063
V152	0037
V154	0086
V157	OEM
V159	0321
V160	0137
V162	0037
V166	0086
V167	0188
V168P	OEM
V169	0016
V170P	OEM
V171	0229
V172	0086
V174	0644
V175	0436
V175LA2	OEM
V175LA10A	OEM
V176	0161
V177	0086
V180	0126
V180A-3	OEM
V180MA1A	OEM
V180MA3B	OEM
V180ZA05	OEM
V180ZA1	4072
V180ZA5	OEM
V180ZA10	3094
V181(BENCO)	3395
V183	0321
V183R-2	OEM
V183R-7	OEM
V183R-9	OEM
V183R-20	OEM
V188	0162
V188P	OEM
V191	0087
V200	OEM
V205	0050
V-210C	0143
V210C	0015
V213P	OEM
V216R-3	OEM
V216R-7	OEM
V216R-10	OEM
V216R-20	OEM
V220	0144
V220A-4	OEM
V220MA2A	2603
V220MA4B	OEM
V220SM16	OEM
V220ZA05	OEM
V221	0144
V222	0144
V230LA4	OEM
V230LA10	OEM
V230LA20A	OEM
V237C/2K	OEM
V238A/1K	OEM
V239C/1K	OEM
V239C/2K	OEM
V241C/1K	OEM
V241C/2K	OEM
V250HE250	OEM
V250LA2	3737
V250LA4	1322
V250LA10	OEM
V250LA15	1324
V250LA15A	1324
V250LA20	1324
V250LA20A	1324
V250LA40	1326
V250LA40A	1326
V250LA40B	5171
V250PA10A	OEM
V250PA20A	OEM
V250PA40A	OEM
V250PA40B	OEM
V250PA40C	OEM
V250R-3	OEM
V250R-10	OEM
V250R-12	OEM
V250R-25	OEM
V262	OEM
V270	OEM
V270/6312	OEM
V270-D1	0015
V270-4	OEM
V270MA2A	OEM
V270MA4B	OEM
V270ZA05	OEM
V275C/3M	OEM
V275HE250	OEM
V275L2	OEM
V275LA2	1648
V275LA4	1648
V275LA10	6653
V275LA15A	1650
V275LA20A	1650
V275LA40A	4780
V275LA40B	4780
V275PA10A	OEM
V275PA20A	OEM
V275PA40B	OEM
V275PA40C	OEM
V283R-3	OEM
V283R-10	OEM
V283R-12	OEM
V283R-30	OEM
V290/6314	OEM
V290P	4120
V297	0016
V300	OEM
V300LA2	4394
V300LA4	4394
V310P	OEM
V311P	OEM
V312P	OEM
V313P	OEM
V320HE300	OEM
V320LA15A	OEM
V320LA20A	2023
V320LA40A	OEM
V320LA40B	OEM
V320P	OEM
V320PA40A	OEM
V320PA40B	OEM
V320PA40C	OEM
V321P	OEM
V322	OEM
V322P	OEM
V323P	OEM
V324	OEM
V326	OEM
V327	OEM
V328	OEM
V330	0110
V330A-5	OEM
V330MA2A	OEM
V330MA5B	OEM
V330P	OEM
V330R-4	OEM
V330R-11	OEM
V330R-13	OEM
V330R-34	OEM
V330X	0031
V330ZA05	OEM
V331	0947
V331P	OEM
V331X	0023
V332	0242
V332P	OEM
V332X	0031
V333P	OEM
V334	0535
V334X	0031
V336	0959
V336X	0031
V338	0811
V340P	OEM
V341P	OEM
V342	OEM
V342P	OEM
V343P	OEM
V344	OEM
V346	OEM
V348	OEM
V350	0087
V350R-4	OEM
V350R-11	OEM
V350R-13	OEM
V350R-36	OEM
V350X	OEM
V351	OEM
V351X	OEM
V352	OEM
V352X	OEM
V354	OEM
V354X	OEM
V356	OEM
V356X	OEM
V358	OEM
V370A-5	OEM
V383R-5	OEM
V383R-13	OEM
V383R-15	OEM
V383R-40	OEM
V390A-6	OEM
V390MA3A	OEM
V390MA6B	OEM
V390P	OEM
V390ZA05	OEM
V400	OEM
V405	0144
V405A	3562
V409	0042
V410	0037
V410A	0037
V412A	OEM
V412B	OEM
V412C	OEM
V413	2704
V413K	2704
V413L	3298
V413M	3298
V413N	2704
V415	0144
V416R-5	OEM
V416R-15	OEM
V416R-20	OEM
V416R-45	OEM
V417	0144
V420HE400	OEM
V420LA10	OEM
V420LA20A	3226
V420LA40A	3806
V420LA40B	3806
V420LB20	3226
V420LB20A	3226
V420LB40	3806
V420LB40A	3806
V420LB40B	OEM
V420PA20A	OEM
V420PA40A	OEM
V420PA40B	OEM
V420PA40C	OEM
V430A-7	OEM
V430MA3A	OEM
V430MA7B	2344
V430ZA05	1648
V433EJ	OEM
V433GZ	OEM
V433N	OEM
V433R	OEM
V433T	OEM
V433X	OEM
V433Y	OEM
V435	0144
V435A	0037
V442	0015
V450R-5	OEM
V450R-15	OEM
V450R-20	OEM
V450R-45	OEM
V460LA20A	OEM
V460LA40A	OEM
V460LA40B	OEM
V460LB20	OEM
V460LB20A	OEM
V460LB40	OEM
V460LB40A	OEM
V460LB40B	OEM
V460PA20A	OEM
V460PA40A	OEM
V460PA40B	OEM
V460PA40C	OEM
V470ZA05	OEM
V480HE450	OEM
V480LA20A	1093
V480LA40A	1093
V480LA80A	0776
V480LA80B	OEM
V480LB20	1093
V480LB20A	1093
V480LB40	1093
V480LB40A	1093
V480LB80	0776
V480LB80A	0776
V480LB80B	OEM
V480PA20A	OEM
V480PA40A	OEM
V480PA80A	OEM
V480PA80B	OEM
V480PA80C	OEM
V500	OEM
V500R-6	OEM
V500R-16	OEM
V500R-22	OEM
V500R-50	OEM
V510HE500	OEM
V510LA20A	OEM
V510LA40A	OEM
V510LA80A	OEM
V510LA80B	OEM
V510LB20	OEM
V510LB20A	OEM
V510LB40	OEM
V510LB40A	OEM
V510LB80	OEM
V510LB80A	OEM
V510LB80B	OEM
V510P	OEM
V510PA20A	OEM
V510PA40A	OEM
V510PA80A	OEM
V510PA80B	OEM
V510PA80C	OEM
V511P	OEM
V512P	OEM
V513P	OEM
V518P	OEM
V520P	OEM
V521P	OEM
V522P	OEM
V523P	OEM
V530P	OEM
V531P	OEM
V532P	OEM
V533P	OEM
V540P	OEM
V541P	OEM
V542P	OEM
V543P	OEM
V550LA20A	OEM
V550LA40A	OEM
V550LA80A	OEM
V550LA80B	OEM
V550LB20A	OEM
V550LB40A	OEM
V550LB80A	OEM
V550LB80B	OEM
V550P	OEM
V550PA20A	OEM
V550PA40A	OEM
V550PA80A	OEM
V550PA80B	OEM
V550PA80C	OEM
V550R-6	OEM
V550R-18	OEM
V550R-24	OEM
V550R-55	OEM
V551P	OEM
V552P	OEM
V553P	OEM
V575HE550	OEM
V575LA20A	OEM
V575LA40A	OEM
V575LA80A	OEM
V575LA80B	OEM
V575LB20A	OEM
V575LB40A	OEM
V575LB80A	OEM
V575LB80B	OEM
V575PA20A	OEM
V575PA40A	OEM
V575PA80A	OEM
V575PA80B	OEM
V575PA80C	OEM
V600	0086
V601	OEM
V602	OEM
V610	OEM
V611	OEM
V612	OEM
V622P	4928
V643	0264
V653	0855
V654	0786
V655	0786
V660HE600	OEM
V660LA50A	OEM
V660LA100B	OEM
V660PA100A	OEM
V660PA100B	OEM
V660PA100C	OEM
V680ZA05	OEM
V700R-70	OEM
V721	0037
V730R-70	OEM
V741	0786
V745	0126
V750HE700	OEM
V750ZA05	OEM
V751DA40	OEM
V761	0037
V763	0037
V765	0126
V765R-70	OEM
V800	OEM
V800R-80	OEM
V850R-80	OEM
V900	OEM
V900B	OEM
V900C	OEM
V900E	OEM
V900EA	OEM
V900EB	OEM
V900EC	OEM
V900ED	OEM
V907	OEM
V907A	OEM
V907B	OEM
V907C	OEM
V907D	OEM
V907E	OEM
V907EA	OEM
V907EB	OEM
V907EC	OEM
V907ED	OEM
V910	0005
V910A	0005
V910B	OEM
V910C	OEM
V910D	OEM
V910E	OEM
V910EA	OEM
V910EB	OEM
V910EC	OEM
V910ED	OEM
V912	0715
V912A	0715
V912D	OEM
V912E	OEM
V912EA	OEM
V912EB	OEM
V912EC	OEM
V912ED	OEM
V915	OEM
V915A	OEM
V915B	OEM
V915C	OEM
V915D	OEM
V915E	OEM
V915EA	OEM
V915EB	OEM
V915EC	OEM
V915ED	OEM
V918	1963
V920	OEM
V920A	OEM
V920B	OEM
V920C	OEM
V920D	OEM
V920E	OEM
V920EA	OEM
V920EB	OEM
V920EC	OEM
V920ED	OEM
V927	OEM
V927A	OEM
V927B	OEM
V927C	OEM
V927D	OEM
V927E	OEM
V927EA	OEM
V927EB	OEM
V927EC	OEM
V927ED	OEM
V933	0030
V933A	0030
V933B	OEM
V933C	OEM
V933D	OEM
V933E	OEM
V933EA	OEM
V933EB	OEM
V933EC	OEM
V933ED	OEM
V939	OEM
V939A	OEM
V939B	OEM
V939C	OEM
V939D	OEM
V939E	OEM
V939EA	OEM
V939EB	OEM
V939EC	OEM
V939ED	OEM
V947	OEM
V947A	OEM
V947B	OEM
V947C	OEM
V947D	OEM
V947E	OEM
V947EA	OEM
V947EB	OEM
V947EC	OEM
V947ED	OEM
V953A/B/G/H	OEM
V956	OEM
V956A	OEM
V956B	OEM
V956C	OEM
V956D	OEM
V956E	OEM
V956EA	OEM
V956EB	OEM
V956EC	OEM
V956ED	OEM
V968	OEM
V968A	OEM
V968B	OEM
V968C	OEM
V968D	OEM
V968EA	OEM
V968EB	OEM
V968EC	OEM
V968ED	OEM
V982	OEM
V982A	OEM
V982B	OEM
V982C	OEM
V982D	OEM
V982E	OEM
V982EA	OEM
V982EB	OEM
V982EC	OEM
V982ED	OEM
V1000	OEM
V1000LA80A	OEM
V1000LA160A	OEM
V1000LA160B	OEM
V1000LB80	OEM
V1000LB80A	OEM
V1000LB160	OEM
V1000LB160A	OEM
V1000LB160B	OEM
V1000R-100	OEM
V1112	0133
V1400R-100	OEM
V1650E-1	0321
V1650E-4	0321
V1833E	0321
V2051E	OEM
V2051H	OEM
V2051K	OEM
V2059EJ	OEM
V2059GZ	OEM
V2059N	OEM
V2059R	OEM
V2059X	OEM
V2059Z	OEM
V2060EJ	OEM
V2060M	OEM
V2060P	OEM
V2060X	OEM
V3074A20	0015
V3074A21	0015
V3310	0916
V3510	OEM

If replacement code is OEM, contact original manufacturer for replacement.

DEVICE TYPE	REPL CODE
V8634-3	0911
V9446-4	0015
V9646-4	0015
V10158	0015
V10916-1	0143
V-10916-3	0143
V10916-3	0143
V11189-1	0015
V15920	0015
V27001	0015
V50260-10	0133
V50260-16	0143
V50260-36	0133
VA2SC1815GRRW-1	0076
VA10	OEM
VA10X	OEM
VA12-12	OEM
VA15	0344
VA15-15	OEM
VA15X	OEM
VA20	OEM
VA20X	OEM
VA21	OEM
VA22	OEM
VA23	OEM
VA24	OEM
VA25	OEM
VA25X	OEM
VA30	OEM
VA30X	OEM
VA35	OEM
VA87E	OEM
VA92	OEM
VA92B	OEM
VA92H	OEM
VA94	OEM
VA94B	OEM
VA97	OEM
VA97B	OEM
VA98	OEM
VA98J	OEM
VA98M	OEM
VA107	OEM
VA112	OEM
VA113	OEM
VA114	OEM
VA115	OEM
VA116	OEM
VA117	OEM
VA118A	OEM
VA122	OEM
VA123	OEM
VA124	OEM
VA125	OEM
VA126	OEM
VA127	0030
VA128	0030
VA129	OEM
VA130	OEM
VA132	0005
VA133	OEM
VA134	OEM
VA135	0005
VA136	OEM
VA137	OEM
VA138	OEM
VA139	OEM
VA140	OEM
VA141	OEM
VA145B	OEM
VA145D	OEM
VA145E	OEM
VA145F	OEM
VA145H	OEM
VA145J	OEM
VA145UH	OEM
VA145UL	OEM
VA146	OEM
VA146C	OEM
VA146M	OEM
VA146N	OEM
VA150	OEM
VA151	OEM
VA152	OEM
VA153	OEM
VA154	OEM
VA155	OEM
VA156	OEM
VA157	0005
VA158	OEM
VA159	OEM
VA160	0030
VA160E	OEM
VA160M	OEM
VA160N	OEM
VA161	OEM
VA161F	OEM
VA161M	OEM
VA162	OEM
VA162F	OEM
VA162M	OEM
VA163	OEM
VA163M	OEM
VA164M	OEM
VA165	OEM
VA166	OEM
VA167	OEM
VA168	OEM
VA169	OEM

DEVICE TYPE	REPL CODE
VA170	OEM
VA171	OEM
VA172	OEM
VA173	OEM
VA173M	OEM
VA173T	OEM
VA173TA	OEM
VA175M	OEM
VA175T	OEM
VA177M	OEM
VA178M	OEM
VA183G	OEM
VA183GA	OEM
VA184F	OEM
VA184M	OEM
VA184T	OEM
VA185F	OEM
VA185M	OEM
VA187M	OEM
VA200	OEM
VA201	OEM
VA201B	OEM
VA202	OEM
VA203	OEM
VA203B	OEM
VA203B/6975	OEM
VA203C	OEM
VA203G	OEM
VA203H	OEM
VA203J	OEM
VA203K	OEM
VA203L	OEM
VA204	OEM
VA205	OEM
VA206	OEM
VA207	OEM
VA208	OEM
VA209	OEM
VA210	OEM
VA210B	OEM
VA210M	OEM
VA211	OEM
VA212	OEM
VA213	OEM
VA215H	OEM
VA217C	OEM
VA217HL	OEM
VA218	OEM
VA218B	OEM
VA220A	OEM
VA220B	OEM
VA220C	OEM
VA220D	OEM
VA220E	OEM
VA220F	OEM
VA220G	OEM
VA220J	OEM
VA220Z	OEM
VA221B	OEM
VA221C	OEM
VA221D	OEM
VA221E	OEM
VA221F	OEM
VA221G	OEM
VA221H	OEM
VA222A	OEM
VA222B8821	OEM
VA222C	OEM
VA222D	OEM
VA222E	OEM
VA222F	OEM
VA222G	OEM
VA222Z	OEM
VA225	OEM
VA232	OEM
VA237A	OEM
VA237B	OEM
VA237C	OEM
VA237D	OEM
VA237E	OEM
VA237F	OEM
VA240	OEM
VA240C	OEM
VA241	OEM
VA242	OEM
VA244	OEM
VA244K	OEM
VA246	OEM
VA249	OEM
VA253	OEM
VA259	OEM
VA259A	OEM
VA259AT	OEM
VA259B	OEM
VA259BT	OEM
VA259C	OEM
VA259CT	OEM
VA259DT	OEM
VA259E	OEM
VA259ET	OEM
VA259F	OEM
VA259FT	OEM
VA259J	OEM
VA259N	OEM
VA259P	OEM
VA259R	OEM
VA259T	OEM
VA264	OEM
VA265	OEM

DEVICE TYPE	REPL CODE
VA266A	OEM
VA270VP6915	OEM
VA272	OEM
VA273B	OEM
VA273D	OEM
VA273G	OEM
VA273H	OEM
VA275A	OEM
VA275B/C	OEM
VA275D	OEM
VA282	OEM
VA282AD	OEM
VA282D	OEM
VA282E	OEM
VA283	OEM
VA286	OEM
VA287	OEM
VA287A	OEM
VA287B	OEM
VA287C	OEM
VA287D	OEM
VA288A	OEM
VA297	OEM
VA297T	OEM
VA297U	OEM
VA297V	OEM
VA297W	OEM
VA297X	OEM
VA297Y	OEM
VA297Z	OEM
VA300	OEM
VA301	OEM
VA302	OEM
VA303	OEM
VA304	OEM
VA305	OEM
VA306	OEM
VA307	OEM
VA308	OEM
VA309	OEM
VA310	OEM
VA311	OEM
VA312	OEM
VA313	OEM
VA318	OEM
VA322	OEM
VA326	OEM
VA327	OEM
VA329	OEM
VA435M	OEM
VA436M	OEM
VA440M	OEM
VA440N	OEM
VA441F	OEM
VA441M	OEM
VA450C	OEM
VA450M	OEM
VA450N	OEM
VA451M	OEM
VA451N	OEM
VA460M	OEM
VA460N	OEM
VA461M	OEM
VA461N	OEM
VA462N	OEM
VA470M	OEM
VA470N	OEM
VA472M	OEM
VA480M	OEM
VA482M	OEM
VA490M	OEM
VA490N	OEM
VA503B	OEM
VA503C	OEM
VA504B	OEM
VA506	OEM
VA508	OEM
VA510B	OEM
VA510D	OEM
VA513	OEM
VA514	OEM
VA515B	OEM
VA516	OEM
VA517	OEM
VA518	OEM
VA519	OEM
VA520	OEM
VA521	OEM
VA522	OEM
VA523	OEM
VA524	OEM
VA531	OEM
VA531A	OEM
VA532	OEM
VA533	OEM
VA534	OEM
VA535	OEM
VA536	OEM
VA537	OEM
VA620A	OEM
VA621	OEM
VA622	OEM
VA623	OEM
VA624	OEM
VA625L	OEM
VA645G	OEM
VA651	OEM
VA664A	OEM
VA723	OEM

DEVICE TYPE	REPL CODE
VA724	OEM
VA800E	OEM
VA800H	OEM
VA802B	OEM
VA804	OEM
VA808	OEM
VA811	OEM
VA811B	OEM
VA811C	OEM
VA812D	OEM
VA812E	OEM
VA816J	OEM
VA820	OEM
VA820D	OEM
VA820E	OEM
VA820F	OEM
VA823	OEM
VA824	OEM
VA834B	OEM
VA838	OEM
VA838A	OEM
VA838B	OEM
VA839	OEM
VA842	OEM
VA845	OEM
VA846	OEM
VA853	OEM
VA853M	OEM
VA861	OEM
VA862A	OEM
VA862B	OEM
VA862C	OEM
VA864M	OEM
VA866	OEM
VA866S	OEM
VA869A	OEM
VA870	OEM
VA874B	OEM
VA874E	OEM
VA876	OEM
VA876A	OEM
VA879	OEM
VA879G	OEM
VA882	OEM
VA883	OEM
VA884B	OEM
VA884C	OEM
VA884D	OEM
VA888	OEM
VA888B	OEM
VA888D	OEM
VA888E	OEM
VA888H	OEM
VA890A	OEM
VA890H	OEM
VA891A	OEM
VA891H	OEM
VA892A	OEM
VA892H	OEM
VA896	OEM
VA896F	OEM
VA903	OEM
VA908	OEM
VA909	OEM
VA911	OEM
VA913A	OEM
VA914	OEM
VA914B	OEM
VA915A	OEM
VA917B	OEM
VA920A	OEM
VA920B	OEM
VA921	OEM
VA922	OEM
VA925	OEM
VA925B	OEM
VA925C	OEM
VA925E	OEM
VA926	OEM
VA927	OEM
VA928A	OEM
VA930	OEM
VA932	OEM
VA932B	OEM
VA934	OEM
VA935	OEM
VA936A	OEM
VA936B	OEM
VA936E	OEM
VA936G	OEM
VA936J	OEM
VA936K	OEM
VA936L	OEM
VA936N	OEM
VA938A	OEM
VA938C	OEM
VA938D	OEM
VA943A	OEM
VA943B	OEM
VA944A	OEM
VA944B	OEM
VA945A	OEM
VA945B	OEM
VA946A	OEM
VA946A/B	OEM
VA946C	OEM
VA946H	OEM
VA947/B	OEM
VA947A	OEM

DEVICE TYPE	REPL CODE
VA947C	OEM
VA947H	OEM
VA948A	OEM
VA948A/B	OEM
VA948C	OEM
VA949SERIES	OEM
VA950A	OEM
VA950G	OEM
VA951A	OEM
VA951G	OEM
VA952A	OEM
VA952G	OEM
VA953A/B	OEM
VA954A/B	OEM
VA954A/B/G/H	OEM
VA955A/B	OEM
VA955A/B/G	OEM
VA956	OEM
VA958A	OEM
VA961	OEM
VA962	OEM
VA963A	OEM
VA963D	OEM
VA988	OEM
VA988A	OEM
VA988B	OEM
VA988C	OEM
VA5139	0549
VA5139A	0549
VA5140	OEM
VA5140A	OEM
VA5141	OEM
VA5141A	OEM
VA5142	OEM
VA5142A	OEM
VA5143	OEM
VA5143A	OEM
VAAD009	0139
VAANZ2SC1096	0386
VAB11BN20	OEM
VAB803N20	OEM
VAB803N25	OEM
VAB814A3N44	OEM
VAB824N26	OEM
VAB825N20	OEM
VAB825N26	OEM
VAB1610AN28	OEM
VAC824N20	OEM
VAMV-1	0015
VA011A	OEM
VA011CN20	OEM
VA011DN20	OEM
VA012AN20	OEM
VA012BN20	OEM
VA012FN20	OEM
VA021CN19	OEM
VA021DN19	OEM
VAP81AEP	OEM
VAP81AM	OEM
VAP81AP	OEM
VAP81BEP	OEM
VAP81BM	OEM
VAP81BN19	OEM
VAP81BP	OEM
VAP81CEP	OEM
VAP81CM	OEM
VAP81CN9	OEM
VAP81CN15	OEM
VAP81CN20	OEM
VAP81CP	OEM
VAP81DM	OEM
VAP81DP	OEM
VAP81EEP	OEM
VAP81EM	OEM
VAP81EP	OEM
VAP81FEP	OEM
VAP81FM	OEM
VAP81FN19	OEM
VAP81FP	OEM
VAP81GEP	OEM
VAP81GM	OEM
VAP81GP	OEM
VAP81HEP	OEM
VAP81HM	OEM
VAP81HP	OEM
VAP81IEP	OEM
VAP81IM	OEM
VAP81IP	OEM
VAP82AEP	OEM
VAP82AM	OEM
VAP82AP	OEM
VAP82BEP	OEM
VAP82BM	OEM
VAP82BP	OEM
VAP82CEP	OEM
VAP82CM	OEM
VAP82CP	OEM
VAP82DEP	OEM
VAP82DM	OEM
VAP82DP	OEM
VAP82EEP	OEM
VAP82EM	OEM
VAP82EP	OEM
VAP83AEP	OEM
VAP83AM	OEM
VAP83AN9	OEM
VAP83AP	OEM
VAP83BEP	OEM
VAP83BM	OEM

DEVICE TYPE	REPL CODE
VAP83BP	OEM
VAP83CEP	OEM
VAP83CM	OEM
VAP83CP	OEM
VAP83DEP	OEM
VAR	0133
VAR-1R2	0133
VARIST-5	0015
VAS13	OEM
VAS23	OEM
VAS24	OEM
VAS33	OEM
VAS34	OEM
VAS44	OEM
VAS45	OEM
VAS54	OEM
VAS55	OEM
VAS62N10	OEM
VAS62N16	OEM
VAS62N18	OEM
VAS62N20	OEM
VAS64	OEM
VAS65	OEM
VAT11N16	OEM
VAT11N18	OEM
VAT11N20	OEM
VAT11N32	OEM
VAT12N32	OEM
VAT13AN9	OEM
VAT13AN11	OEM
VAT13N32	OEM
VAT14N32	OEM
VAT15N32	OEM
VAT16N32	OEM
VAT17N32	OEM
VAT18N32	OEM
VAT19N32	OEM
VAT51N32	OEM
VAT52N16	OEM
VAT52N18	OEM
VAT52N20	OEM
VAT52N32	OEM
VAT53N32	OEM
VAT54N32	OEM
VAT55N32	OEM
VAT56N32	OEM
VAT57N32	OEM
VAT58N32	OEM
VAT59N32	OEM
VAT71N32	OEM
VAT72N32	OEM
VAT73N32	OEM
VAT74N32	OEM
VAT75N32	OEM
VAT76N32	OEM
VAT77N32	OEM
VAT78N32	OEM
VAT79N32	OEM
VAT1002N9	OEM
VAV091	OEM
VAV092	OEM
VAV093	OEM
VAV094	OEM
VAV121	OEM
VAV122	OEM
VAV123	OEM
VAV124	OEM
VAV151	OEM
VAV152	OEM
VAV153	OEM
VAV154	OEM
VAV201	OEM
VAV202	OEM
VAV203	OEM
VAV204	OEM
VB	OEM
VB011	OEM
VB013-10N01	OEM
VB013-12N01	OEM
VB013-14N01	OEM
VB013-16N01	OEM
VB020-04N01	OEM
VB020-08N01	OEM
VB020-10N01	OEM
VB020-12N01	OEM
VB020-14N01	OEM
VB020-16N01	OEM
VB1B	OEM
VB2	OEM
VB3-80	OEM
VB10	OEM
VB10X	OEM
VB-11	0015
VB11	0004
VB12	OEM
VB13	0279
VB14	OEM
VB20	OEM
VB20X	OEM
VB30	OEM
VB30X	OEM
VB40	OEM
VB40X	OEM
VB50	OEM
VB50X	OEM
VB60	OEM
VB100	0015
VB100-1	OEM
VB100-2	OEM

DEVICE TYPE	REPL CODE
VB100-3	OEM
VB100-4	OEM
VB100-5	OEM
VB100-8	OEM
VB100-18	OEM
VB100X	OEM
VB150X	OEM
VB200	OEM
VB300	0015
VB400	0015
VB500	0015
VB600	0015
VB600A	0015
VB701	OEM
VB704	OEM
VB709	OEM
VBC89C	OEM
VBC89J	OEM
VBC99J	OEM
VBC119J	OEM
VBC7506M	OEM
VBE77M	OEM
VBH600	0015
VBO2.2-14N02	OEM
VBO2.2-14N04	OEM
VBO2.2-14N05	OEM
VBO2.2-14N06	OEM
VBO13-04N01	OEM
VBO13-08N01	OEM
VBX7504M	OEM
VBX7505M	OEM
VBX7521B	OEM
VC4S0006	OEM
VC6E	0015
VC7	OEM
VC7A	OEM
VC7B	OEM
VC10	0005
VC10A	0005
VC10B	OEM
VC12	0715
VC12A	0715
VC12B	OEM
VC15	OEM
VC15A	OEM
VC15B	OEM
VC20	3613
VC20A	OEM
VC20B	OEM
VC20X	OEM
VC27	OEM
VC27A	OEM
VC27B	OEM
VC30	3613
VC30X	OEM
VC33	0030
VC33A	0030
VC33B	OEM
VC39	OEM
VC39A	OEM
VC39B	OEM
VC40	3613
VC40X	OEM
VC47	OEM
VC47A	OEM
VC47B	OEM
VC50	4788
VC50A	OEM
VC50B	OEM
VC60	3613
VC60X	OEM
VC68	OEM
VC68A	OEM
VC68BB	OEM
VC70	3613
VC70X	OEM
VC80	3613
VC80X	OEM
VC82	OEM
VC82A	OEM
VC82B	OEM
VC99	OEM
VC99A	OEM
VC99B	OEM
VC102	OEM
VC103A	OEM
VC103B	OEM
VC103C	OEM
VC103D	OEM
VC103E	OEM
VC112	OEM
VC112A	OEM
VC112B	OEM
VC115	OEM
VC115A	OEM
VC115B	OEM
VC118	OEM
VC118A	OEM
VC118B	OEM
VC122	OEM
VC122A	OEM
VC122B	OEM
VC127	OEM
VC127A	OEM
VC127B	OEM
VC133	OEM
VC133A	OEM
VC133B	OEM
VC207	OEM

If replacement code is OEM, contact original manufacturer for replacement.

619

DEVICE TYPE	REPL CODE
VC207A	OEM
VC207B	OEM
VC210	0005
VC210A	0005
VC210B	OEM
VC212	0715
VC212A	0715
VC212B	OEM
VC215	OEM
VC215A	OEM
VC215B	OEM
VC220	OEM
VC220A	OEM
VC220B	OEM
VC227	OEM
VC227A	OEM
VC227B	OEM
VC233	0030
VC233A	0030
VC233B	OEM
VC239	OEM
VC239A	OEM
VC239B	OEM
VC247	OEM
VC247A	OEM
VC247B	OEM
VC256	OEM
VC256A	OEM
VC256B	OEM
VC268	OEM
VC268A	OEM
VC268B	OEM
VC282	OEM
VC282A	OEM
VC282B	OEM
VC299	OEM
VC299A	OEM
VC299B	OEM
VC306	OEM
VC306A	OEM
VC306B	OEM
VC307	OEM
VC307A	OEM
VC307B	OEM
VC309	0005
VC309A	0005
VC309B	OEM
VC310	OEM
VC310A	OEM
VC310B	OEM
VC314	OEM
VC314A	OEM
VC314B	OEM
VC315	OEM
VC315A	OEM
VC315B	OEM
VC321	0623
VC321A	0623
VC321B	OEM
VC322	OEM
VC322A	0030
VC322B	OEM
VC332	0030
VC332A	0030
VC332B	OEM
VC333	OEM
VC333A	OEM
VC333B	OEM
VC346	OEM
VC346A	OEM
VC346B	OEM
VC347	OEM
VC347A	OEM
VC347B	OEM
VC367	OEM
VC367A	OEM
VC367B	OEM
VC399	OEM
VC399A	OEM
VC399B	OEM
VC406	OEM
VC406A	OEM
VC406B	OEM
VC407	OEM
VC407A	OEM
VC407B	OEM
VC408	0549
VC408A	0549
VC408B	OEM
VC409	0005
VC409A	0005
VC409B	OEM
VC410	0005
VC410A	0005
VC410B	OEM
VC411	OEM
VC411A	OEM
VC411B	OEM
VC414	OEM
VC414A	OEM
VC414B	OEM
VC415	OEM
VC415A	OEM
VC415B	OEM
VC416	OEM
VC416A	OEM
VC416B	OEM
VC421	0623
VC421A	0623
VC421B	OEM
VC422	0623
VC422A	0623
VC422B	OEM
VC423	OEM
VC423A	OEM
VC423B	OEM
VC432	0030
VC432A	0030
VC432B	OEM
VC433	0030
VC433A	0030
VC433B	OEM
VC434	OEM
VC434A	OEM
VC434B	OEM
VC446	OEM
VC446A	OEM
VC446B	OEM
VC447	OEM
VC447A	OEM
VC447B	OEM
VC448	OEM
VC448A	OEM
VC448B	OEM
VC467	OEM
VC467A	OEM
VC467B	OEM
VC533	OEM
VC533B	OEM
VC533C	OEM
VC533D	OEM
VC539	OEM
VC539B	OEM
VC539C	OEM
VC539D	OEM
VC547	OEM
VC547B	OEM
VC547C	OEM
VC547D	OEM
VC556	OEM
VC556B	OEM
VC556C	OEM
VC556D	OEM
VC568	OEM
VC568A	OEM
VC568B	OEM
VC568C	OEM
VC568D	OEM
VC582	OEM
VC582B	OEM
VC582C	OEM
VC582D	OEM
VC599	OEM
VC599B	OEM
VC599C	OEM
VC599D	OEM
VC605	OEM
VC605A	OEM
VC605B	OEM
VC606	OEM
VC606A	OEM
VC606B	OEM
VC607	OEM
VC607A	OEM
VC607B	OEM
VC608	OEM
VC608A	OEM
VC608B	OEM
VC610	0005
VC610A	0005
VC610B	OEM
VC611	0005
VC611A	0005
VC611B	OEM
VC612	0715
VC612A	0715
VC612B	OEM
VC613	0715
VC613A	0623
VC613B	OEM
VC615	OEM
VC615A	OEM
VC615B	OEM
VC616	OEM
VC616A	OEM
VC616B	OEM
VC618	OEM
VC618A	OEM
VC618B	OEM
VC619	OEM
VC619A	OEM
VC619B	OEM
VC622	0623
VC622A	0623
VC622B	OEM
VC623	0623
VC623A	0623
VC623B	OEM
VC627	OEM
VC627A	OEM
VC627B	OEM
VC628	OEM
VC628A	OEM
VC628B	OEM
VC633	0030
VC633A	0030
VC633B	OEM
VC634	0030
VC634A	0030
VC634B	OEM
VC639	OEM
VC639A	OEM
VC639B	OEM
VC641	OEM
VC641A	OEM
VC641B	OEM
VC647	OEM
VC647A	OEM
VC647B	OEM
VC648	OEM
VC648A	OEM
VC648B	OEM
VC720	OEM
VC722	OEM
VC722A	OEM
VC724	OEM
VC726	OEM
VC728	OEM
VC730	OEM
VC732	OEM
VC734	OEM
VC736	OEM
VC740	OEM
VC742	OEM
VC744	OEM
VC746	OEM
VC748	OEM
VC752	OEM
VC821	OEM
VC821A	OEM
VC821B	OEM
VC822	0005
VC822A	0005
VC822B	OEM
VC823	0715
VC823A	0715
VC823B	OEM
VC824	OEM
VC824A	OEM
VC824B	OEM
VC825	OEM
VC825A	OEM
VC825B	OEM
VC826	OEM
VC826A	OEM
VC826B	OEM
VC827	0030
VC827A	0030
VC827B	OEM
VC828	OEM
VC828A	OEM
VC828B	OEM
VC829	OEM
VC829A	OEM
VC829B	OEM
VC831	OEM
VC831A	OEM
VC831B	OEM
VC832	OEM
VC832A	OEM
VC832B	OEM
VC833	OEM
VC833A	OEM
VC833B	OEM
VC834	OEM
VC834A	OEM
VC834B	OEM
VC841	0549
VC841A	0549
VC841B	OEM
VC842	OEM
VC842A	OEM
VC842B	OEM
VC843	OEM
VC843A	OEM
VC843B	OEM
VC844	OEM
VC844A	OEM
VC844B	OEM
VC845	OEM
VC845A	OEM
VC845B	OEM
VC846	OEM
VC846A	OEM
VC846B	OEM
VC847	OEM
VC847A	OEM
VC847B	OEM
VC848	OEM
VC848A	OEM
VC848B	OEM
VC849	OEM
VC849A	OEM
VC849B	OEM
VC851	OEM
VC851A	OEM
VC851B	OEM
VC852	OEM
VC852A	OEM
VC852B	OEM
VC853	OEM
VC853A	OEM
VC853B	OEM
VC854	OEM
VC854A	OEM
VC854B	OEM
VC2007	OEM
VC2008	OEM
VC2011	0230
VC2022A	OEM
VC2022C	OEM
VC2024Z	OEM
VC2070	OEM
VC2071	OEM
VC3001	OEM
VC6204	OEM
VC6233	OEM
VC6256	OEM
VC6299	OEM
VC6607	OEM
VC6615	OEM
VC6633	OEM
VCB102-1	OEM
VCB102-2	OEM
VCB104-1	OEM
VCB104-2	OEM
VCB207	OEM
VCB252-1	OEM
VCB252-2	OEM
VCB252-3	OEM
VCB252-4	OEM
VCB252-7	OEM
VCB252-9	OEM
VCB252-10	OEM
VCB252-12	OEM
VCB254-1	OEM
VCB254-2	OEM
VCB254-3	OEM
VCB254-4	OEM
VCB254-7	OEM
VCB254-9	OEM
VCB254-10	OEM
VCB254-12	OEM
VCB256-1	OEM
VCB256-2	OEM
VCB256-3	OEM
VCB256-4	OEM
VCB256-7	OEM
VCB256-9	OEM
VCB256-10	OEM
VCB256-12	OEM
VCB502-7	OEM
VCB502-8	OEM
VCB502-10	OEM
VCB502-11	OEM
VCB504-7	OEM
VCB504-8	OEM
VCB504-10	OEM
VCB504-11	OEM
VCB506-7	OEM
VCB506-8	OEM
VCB506-10	OEM
VCB506-11	OEM
VCP193	OEM
VCP200	OEM
VCR0006	OEM
VCR0014	OEM
VCR0018	OEM
VCR0019	OEM
VCR0019-1	OEM
VCR0069	OEM
VCR0087-1	OEM
VCR00871	OEM
VCR2N	OEM
VCR3P	1133
VCR4N	1147
VCR5P	OEM
VCR6P	OEM
VCR7N	OEM
VCR10N	OEM
VCR11N	OEM
VCR12N	OEM
VCR13N	OEM
VCR20N	OEM
VCRB307	OEM
VCRB407	OEM
VCRB607	OEM
VCRC201	OEM
VCRC301	OEM
VCRC401	OEM
VCRC601	OEM
VCRE210	OEM
VCRE235	OEM
VCRE310	OEM
VCRE335	OEM
VCRE410	OEM
VCRE435	OEM
VCRE610	OEM
VCRE635	OEM
VCRH208	OEM
VCRH216	OEM
VCRH308	OEM
VCRH316	OEM
VCRH408	OEM
VCRH416	OEM
VCRH608	OEM
VCRH616	OEM
VCRS0004	OEM
VCRS0006	OEM
VCRS0008	OEM
VCRS-0009	OEM
VCRS0009	OEM
VCRS0011	2531
VCRS0012	OEM
VCRS0014	OEM
VCRS0019	OEM
VCRS0020	OEM
VCRS0027	OEM
VCRS0030	OEM
VCRS0037	6199
VCRS0038	6200
VCRS0045	OEM
VCRS0046	OEM
VCRS0047	OEM
VCRS0048	OEM
VCRS0050	OEM
VCRS0051	OEM
VCRS0052	OEM
VCRS0053	OEM
VCRS0072	OEM
VCRS0076	OEM
VCRS0083	OEM
VCRS0084	OEM
VCRS0085	OEM
VCRS0093	OEM
VCRS0101-C	OEM
VCRS0101-T-2	OEM
VCRS0102	OEM
VCRS0104	OEM
VCRS0107	OEM
VCRS0107-T	OEM
VCRS0109	OEM
VCRS0109-T	OEM
VCRS0109A	OEM
VCRS0116-TA	OEM
VCRS0117	OEM
VCRS0131	OEM
VCRS0133	OEM
VCRS0137-A	OEM
VCRW0029	OEM
VCRW0030	OEM
VCS40	OEM
VCS50	OEM
VCS60	OEM
VCS70	OEM
VCS80	OEM
VCS90	OEM
VCV1500	OEM
VCZ80B	OEM
VD1E1////-1	0015
VD1R2JA	OEM
VD-1R4JA/B	OEM
VD-1R41B	OEM
VD3C	OEM
VD6	0015
VD6C	OEM
VD10E1////-1	0015
VD10E1LF	0015
VD10E11F	0015
VD11	0143
VD12	2217
VD13	0143
VD1150M	0133
VD-121C	0015
VD121C	0015
VD1120	0139
VD1121	0139
VD-1122	0015
VD1122	0139
VD-1123	0133
VD1123	0139
VD-1124	0139
VD1124	0139
VD1150L	0139
VD1150M	0139
VD1210	0120
VD1211	0120
VD1212	0120
VD1213	0120
VD1220	0120
VD1220-M	0120
VD-1221	0120
VD1221	0120
VD1221L	0120
VD1222	0120
VD1223	0120
VD1251L	0139
VD1260L	0139
VD1262MF	0139
VDB-8024	OEM
VDC11	OEM
VDC1006	OEM
VDC1008	OEM
VDC1020	OEM
VDC1025	OEM
VDC1026	OEM
VDC1029	OEM
VDC1032	OEM
VDI	OEM
VDI-K	OEM
VDK1000	OEM
VDS1006	OEM
VDS1007	OEM
VDS1011	OEM
VDS1013	OEM
VDS1014	OEM
VDS1015	OEM
VDS1018	OEM
VDS1019	OEM
VDS1020	OEM
VDS1021	OEM
VDS1022	OEM
VDS1023	OEM
VDS1028	OEM
VDS1032	OEM
VDU1001	OEM
VDU1002	OEM
VDU1014	OEM
VDU1015	OEM
VDU1046	OEM
VDX1001A	OEM
VDX1006	OEM
VDX1025	OEM
VDX1036	OEM
VDX1047	OEM
VDX1051	OEM
VDX1052	OEM
VDX1071	OEM
VDX1085	OEM
VDX1086	OEM
VDX1099	OEM
VDZ80B	OEM
VE08	0106
VE08X	OEM
VE18	0106
VE18X	OEM
VE27	0106
VE28	0106
VE28X	OEM
VE47	0106
VE48	0106
VE48X	OEM
VE67	1999
VE68	1999
VE68X	OEM
VE87	OEM
VE88	2384
VE108	0782
VE79092	1833
VE79093	0033
VE79141	1824
VEC87M	OEM
VEE77M	OEM
VEKW1212	OEM
VEPS2108A1	OEM
VEPS2108B1	OEM
VEPW0721	OEM
VEPW0743	OEM
VEPW0746	OEM
VEPW0747	OEM
VERSAFLOPPYII	OEM
VERSAFLOPY	OEM
VF01	OEM
VF1	OEM
VF1A	OEM
VF1B	OEM
VF1C	OEM
VF5	OEM
VF5-5	1780
VF5-5X	1780
VF5-7	1780
VF5-7X	1780
VF5-10	1780
VF5-10X	1780
VF5-12	OEM
VF5-12X	OEM
VF5-15	OEM
VF5-15X	OEM
VF5-20	OEM
VF5-20X	OEM
VF5-25	OEM
VF5-25X	OEM
VF5-30	OEM
VF5-30X	OEM
VF5-40	OEM
VF5-40X	OEM
VF5X	OEM
VF7	OEM
VF7X	OEM
VF10	OEM
VF10-5	1780
VF10-5X	1780
VF10-7	1780
VF10-7X	1780
VF10-10	1780
VF10-10X	1780
VF10-12	OEM
VF10-12X	OEM
VF10-15	OEM
VF10-15X	OEM
VF10-20	OEM
VF10-20X	OEM
VF10-25	OEM
VF10-25X	OEM
VF10-30	OEM
VF10-30X	OEM
VF10-40	OEM
VF10-40X	OEM
VF10X	OEM
VF12	OEM
VF12X	OEM
VF15	OEM
VF15X	OEM
VF20	OEM
VF20X	OEM
VF25	OEM
VF25-5	1780
VF25-5X	1780
VF25-7	1780
VF25-7X	1780
VF25-10	1780
VF25-10X	1780
VF25-12	OEM
VF25-12X	OEM
VF25-15	OEM
VF25-15X	OEM
VF25-20	OEM
VF25-20X	OEM
VF25-25	OEM
VF25-25X	OEM
VF25-30	OEM
VF25-30X	OEM
VF25-40	OEM
VF25-40X	OEM
VF25X	OEM
VF28	OEM
VF30	OEM
VF30X	OEM
VF40	OEM
VF40X	OEM
VF50	OEM
VF50X	OEM
VFA2745C	0015
VFC12	OEM
VFC12LD	OEM
VFC15	OEM
VFC15LD	OEM
VFC32BM	OEM
VFC32KP	OEM
VFC32SM	OEM
VFC42BM	OEM
VFC42BP	OEM
VFC42SM	OEM
VFC52BM	OEM
VFC52BP	OEM
VFC52SM	OEM
VFG2745B	0085
VFG-274513	0085
VFL-2744K	0136
VFL2744K	0050
VFP-2746C	0085
VFP2746C	0160
VFP6357C	0160
VFP-6537C	0160
VFP6537C	0160
VFQ-1C	OEM
VFQ-1R	OEM
VFQ2C	OEM
VFQ3C	OEM
VFQ2745F	0004
VFS5K	0136
VFS-2745	0004
VFS2745	0164
VFS-2745J	0004
VFS2745J	0164
VFSD1	0102
VF-SD1A	0102
VFSD-1A	1293
VFT-2745H	0004
VFT2745H	0211
VFU-2746B	0160
VFU2746B	0160
VFV100K	OEM
VFW2745D	0050
VFW-27450	0136
VFX9500	OEM
VFX9507	OEM
VFY-2745E	0279
VFY2745E	0279
VG1	OEM
VG1X	OEM
VG2	OEM
VG2X	4884
VG3	OEM
VG3X	OEM
VG4	OEM
VG4X	OEM
VG5	OEM
VG5X	OEM
VG7	OEM
VG7X	OEM
VG10	OEM
VG10X	OEM
VG12	OEM
VG12X	OEM
VG15	OEM
VG15X	OEM
VG20	OEM
VG20X	OEM
VGA919S	OEM
VGB0101CAA	OEM
VGB0102CAA	OEM
VGB0103AAA	OEM
VGB0103CAA	OEM
VGB0104AAA	OEM
VGB0104CAA	OEM
VGB0124AY7A	OEM
VGB0491MY7	OEM
VGB0492MY7	OEM
VGB0493MY7	OEM
VGB0494MY7	OEM
VGC7205-0409	OEM
VGT7702-4003	OEM
VH048	0319
VH107	OEM
VH138	OEM
VH139	OEM
VH140	OEM
VH141	OEM
VH148	0319
VH160	OEM
VH167	OEM
VH175	OEM

If replacement code is OEM, contact original manufacturer for replacement.

DEVICE TYPE	REPL CODE
VH183	OEM
VH191	OEM
VH200	OEM
VH201	OEM
VH225	OEM
VH226	OEM
VH227	OEM
VH228	OEM
VH229	OEM
VH230	OEM
VH231	OEM
VH247	1404
VH248	1404
VH447	0468
VH448	0468
VH647	0441
VH648	0441
VH848	1412
VH1048	2425
VHC1S2790-W-1	0623
VHC1S2790W-1	0623
VHCBB109G//-1	0030
VHCBB109G-1	0030
VHCBB1096//-1	0030
VHD02BZ2R7/1A	0755
VHD1A3-F///-1	OEM
VHD1N34///-1	0123
VHD1N34A///-1	0123
VHD1N34A///1	0123
VHD1N34A///1E	0123
VHD1N34A//-1	0123
VHD1N60////-1	0019
VHD1S34///-1	0143
VHD1S1553//-1	0133
VHD1S1555//-1	0133
VHD1S1555//1A	0133
VHD1S1555-R-1	0133
VHD1S1834	0023
VHD1S1834//-1	0023
VHD1S1885//-1	0023
VHD1S1885-1	0023
VHD1S1887//-1	0023
VHD1S2076//-1	0133
VHD1S2076//-U	0133
VHD1S2076-//-1	0133
VHD1S2076-1	0133
VHD1S2230//1E	0015
VHD1S2835//1E	0133
VHD1S2837//-1E	0901
VHD1S2837//1E	0901
VHD1SS82///1A	0023
VHD1SS119	0392
VHD1SS119//-1	0124
VHD1SS119//1E	0124
VHD1SS198//-1	0335
VHD1SS270//-1	0133
VHD1SS270//-F	OEM
VHD10E1////-1	0015
VHD10E-4///-1	0015
VHD151885-1	0015
VHDIS1555-R-1	0133
VHDMA151WK/-1	0901
VHEHZ6B3///1A	0157
VHERD6R8EE/-1	0025
VHERD27ED//-1	0436
VHEWZ-100//1F	0064
VHEWZ-100-1F	0064
VHEWZ-1001F	0064
VHEXZ-090-1	0012
VHF1S2076-1	0133
VHFRD6R8EE/-1	OEM
VHI51494L/-1	OEM
VHIAN3211K/-1	4306
VHIAN3321K/-1	OEM
VHIAN3990//-1	OEM
VHIAN6291//-1	3403
VHIBA6209//1E	3776
VHIBA6238AU1E	4054
VHIBA6405//-1	OEM
VHIBA7021//-1	OEM
VHIBA7244S/-1	OEM
VHIBA7252S/-1	OEM
VHIBA7280AS-1	OEM
VHIBA7280S/-1	OEM
VHIBA7765AS-1	OEM
VHIBU4011B/-1	0215
VHICXA1011P-1	3054
VHID74LS136P	1618
VHIHA11845NT1	OEM
VHIHA17812W-1	1341
VHIHD74LS00P/	1519
VHIHD74LS14-1	1688
VHIHD74LS136P	1618
VHIHD74LS221/	1230
VHIHD74S04/-1	2248
VHIHD7406//-1	1197
VHIHD7417//-1	1342
VHIHD7426//-1	0798
VHIHD14042P-1	0121
VHIIR2C32//-1	OEM
VHIIR2E01//-1	OEM
VHIIR3P42//-1	OEM
VHIIR3393//-1	0624
VHIIR3702//-1	OEM
VHIIR9358//-1	OEM
VHIIR94558/-1	OEM
VHILA7016//-1	1022
VHILA7838//-1	OEM
VHiLA7945//-1	OEM

DEVICE TYPE	REPL CODE
VHILC7458B/-1	OEM
VHILH5047//-1	OEM
VHILH5116N-2	OEM
VHILVA516S2-1	OEM
VHILVA519S2-1	OEM
VHILVA51952-1	OEM
VHIM5223P//-1	OEM
VHIM5224P//-1	0620
VHIM5228P//-1	OEM
VHIM51321P/-1	OEM
VHIM51329P/-1	OEM
VHIM51494L/-1	OEM
VHIM54641L/-	OEM
VHIM58659P/-1	OEM
VHIMC4558S/-	OEM
VHIMN3007//-1	5109
VHIMN3101//-1	4214
VHINJM2220S-1	OEM
VHINJM4558D-1	0356
VHINS74LS32-1	0088
VHIPA0030//-1	OEM
VHiPST529C2-1	OEM
VHIPST529H2-1	OEM
VHISN74LS08-1	1623
VHISN74LS32-1	0088
VHISN74S04/-1	2248
VHISN74S11/-1	2428
VHISTK4048V-	OEM
VHISTRM6513-1	OEM
VHISTRS6301-1	OEM
VHIT8889A//-1	OEM
VHITA6703S/-1	OEM
VHITA7130P2/F	2008
VHITA7133P/-1	OEM
VHITA7343P/-1	4339
VHITA7347/-1	4417
VHITA7347P/-1	4417
VHITA7348P/-1	4312
VHITA7378P/-	OEM
VHITA7764P/-1	OEM
VHiTA7809S/-1	OEM
VHITA8110AP-	OEM
VHITA8216H/-1	OEM
VHITA8644N/-1	OEM
VHITA8647S/-1	OEM
VHITA8703A/-1	OEM
VHITA8703S/-1	3578
VHITA75558S-1	0765
VHITA78010AP1	2779
VHITA78055/-1	OEM
VHITC4001BP-1	0473
VHITC4013BP-1	0409
VHITC4028BP-1	2213
VHITC4030BP-1	0495
VHITC4052BP-1	0024
VHITC4066BP-1	0101
VHITC4077BP-1	OEM
VHITC4081BP-1	0328
VHITD620304/-1	OEM
VHITDA3569/-1	OEM
VHiTDA7052/-1	6500
VHITDA7056/-1	OEM
VHITDA8305A-1	OEM
VHITEA5582/-1	OEM
VHITL8708P/-1	OEM
VHIUPC574JT-1	1319
VHIUPC1373H-1	2015
VHIUPC1373HA/	2015
VHIUPC1373HA1	2015
VHIUPC1391H-1	3728
VHiUPC1406HA1	4009
VHIUPC1486C	4843
VHIUPC1486C//	OEM
VHIUPC1486C-1	4843
VHIUPC1486C1	OEM
VHIUPC1513H-1	3130
VHIUPD4066B-1	0101
VHIUPD6104C-1	OEM
VHS2SF656//1E	0895
VHS2SF1422/1E	0239
VHS3S4M//LB1E	0095
VHS3S4M/LB1E	0095
VHS326	0133
VHSCR3AM28LB1	0095
VHSCR3AMZ8L81	0095
VHSCR3AMZ8LB1	0095
VHSCRAMZ8LB1	0095
VHSS6089///1B	0239
VHSS6089///1E	0239
VHSS6142GLB1E	0095
VHSS6304G//1E	OEM
VHSS6340G	0095
VHSS6340G//1E	0095
VHSS6340GLB1E	0095
VHSS6344GLB1E	2712
VHSS6758GLBIE	OEM
VHSS6785GLB1E	OEM
VHSS6785GLB2E	OEM
VHSS6785GLBIE	OEM
VHSSFOR1A411E	0895
VHSSFORIA411E	0895
VHSSH3D42//-1	OEM
VHV1S1209-1	0139
VHV3K121///1E	OEM
VHVTD80////1E	OEM
VI1010	OEM
VI1023	OEM
VIDIODE	0290
VJ148	0319

DEVICE TYPE	REPL CODE
VJ248	1404
VJ448	0468
VJ648	0441
VJ848	1412
VJ1048	2425
VL/8RJ	0279
VL16C450-PC	OEM
VL18RJ	0136
VL1772-02PC	OEM
VL6765-08PC	OEM
VLC9007A	OEM
VLFS0018	OEM
VLFS0031	OEM
VM08	1864
VM-0.09M	0196
VM-0.09M12/3	0196
VM18	1864
VM25	1864
VM-28	1864
VM28	1864
VM48	1864
VM68	1864
VM88	3503
VM108	3503
VM204	0549
VM204A	0549
VM205	0549
VM205A	0549
VM210	0549
VM210A	0549
VM211	0549
VM211A	0549
VM216	0549
VM216A	0549
VM217	0549
VM217A	0549
VM222	0549
VM222A	0549
VM223	0549
VM223A	0549
VM228	0549
VM228A	0549
VM229	0549
VM229A	0549
VM234	0549
VM234A	0549
VM235	0549
VM235A	0549
VM304	0005
VM304A	0005
VM305	0005
VM305A	0005
VM310	0005
VM310A	0005
VM311	0005
VM311A	0005
VM316	0005
VM316A	0005
VM317	0005
VM317A	0005
VM328	0005
VM328A	0005
VM329	0005
VM329A	0005
VM334	0005
VM334A	0005
VM335	0005
VM335A	0005
VM504	0623
VM504A	0623
VM505	0623
VM505A	0623
VM510	0623
VM510A	0623
VM511	0623
VM511A	0623
VM516	0623
VM516A	0623
VM517	0623
VM517A	0623
VM522	0623
VM522A	0623
VM523	0623
VM523A	0623
VM528	0623
VM528A	0623
VM529	0623
VM529A	0623
VM534	0623
VM534A	0623
VM535	0623
VM535A	0623
VM604	0030
VM604A	0030
VM605	0030
VM605A	0030
VM610	0030
VM610A	0030
VM611	0030
VM611A	0030
VM616	0030
VM616A	0030
VM617	0030
VM617A	0030
VM622	0030
VM622A	0030
VM623	0030
VM623A	0030
VM628	0030

DEVICE TYPE	REPL CODE
VM628A	0030
VM629	0030
VM629A	0030
VM634	0030
VM634A	0030
VM635	0030
VM20233	0142
VM-30203	0160
VM30203	0160
VM30209	0016
VM30233	0142
VM30234	0142
VM30241	0016
VM30242	0016
VM30244	0004
VM30245	0142
VM61001	OEM
VM61002	OEM
VM61003	OEM
VM61004	OEM
VM61005	OEM
VM71001	OEM
VM71002	OEM
VM71003	OEM
VM-HS9/1	0196
VMP1	OEM
VMP2	OEM
VMP4	OEM
VMP11	OEM
VMP12	OEM
VMP21	OEM
VMP22	OEM
VM-PH9D522/1	0015
VM-PH11D522/1	0015
VMPH11D522-1	0015
VM-PH90522/1	0015
VMT-01	0405
VMT-02	2777
VMT-03	0190
VMT-03-01	0190
VMT-03-02	0190
VMT-04	3805
VMT-05	1493
VMT-05-01	1493
VMT-05-02	1493
VMT-05-03	1493
VMT-06	1188
VMT-07	1700
VMT-08	1061
VMT-09	2524
VMT-09-01	2524
VMT-11	2954
VMT-12	2956
VMT-13	1048
VMT-14	1048
VMT-15	3610
VM-TC02P11/2	0015
VM-TC0.2P11/2	0015
VN011BB	OEM
VN011BD	OEM
VN0104	OEM
VN0104A	OEM
VN0104N2	OEM
VN0104N3	OEM
VN0104N5	OEM
VN0104N6	OEM
VN0104N7	OEM
VN0104N9	OEM
VN0104ND	OEM
VN0106N2	OEM
VN0106N3	OEM
VN0106N5	OEM
VN0106N6	OEM
VN0106N7	OEM
VN0106N9	OEM
VN0106ND	OEM
VN0109N2	OEM
VN0109N3	OEM
VN0109N5	OEM
VN0109N9	OEM
VN0109ND	OEM
VN0116N2	OEM
VN0116N3	OEM
VN0116N5	OEM
VN0116ND	OEM
VN0120N2	OEM
VN0120N3	OEM
VN0120N5	OEM
VN0120ND	OEM
VN0204N2	OEM
VN0204N5	OEM
VN0204N6	OEM
VN0204N7	OEM
VN0204ND	OEM
VN0206N2	OEM
VN0206N3	OEM
VN0206N5	OEM
VN0206N6	OEM
VN0206N7	OEM
VN0206ND	OEM
VN0210N2	OEM
VN0210N3	OEM
VN0210N5	OEM
VN0210ND	OEM
VN0216N2	OEM
VN0216N3	OEM
VN0216N5	OEM
VN0216ND	OEM
VN0220N2	OEM

DEVICE TYPE	REPL CODE
VN0220N3	OEM
VN0220N5	OEM
VN0220ND	OEM
VN0300B	OEM
VN0300D	OEM
VN0300L	OEM
VN0300M	OEM
VN0330N1	1658
VN0330N5	1456
VN0335B1	1658
VN0335C1	1658
VN0335N1	1658
VN0335N2	OEM
VN0335N5	1456
VN0335ND	OEM
VN0340B1	1658
VN0340C1	1658
VN0340N1	1658
VN0340N2	OEM
VN0340N5	1456
VN0340ND	OEM
VN0345B1	OEM
VN0345C1	OEM
VN0345N1	OEM
VN0345N2	OEM
VN0345N5	OEM
VN0345ND	OEM
VN0350B1	OEM
VN0350C1	OEM
VN0350N1	OEM
VN0350N2	OEM
VN0350N5	OEM
VN0350ND	OEM
VN0355N1	OEM
VN0355N5	OEM
VN0355ND	OEM
VN0360D	OEM
VN0400A	OEM
VN0400D	OEM
VN0401A	OEM
VN0401D	OEM
VN0435N1	OEM
VN0440N1	OEM
VN0535N2	OEM
VN0535N3	OEM
VN0535ND	OEM
VN0540N2	OEM
VN0540N3	OEM
VN0540ND	OEM
VN0555N2	OEM
VN0555N3	OEM
VN0555ND	OEM
VN0600A	OEM
VN0600D	OEM
VN0606M	OEM
VN0610L	OEM
VN0610LL	OEM
VN0635N2	OEM
VN0635N3	OEM
VN0635N5	OEM
VN0635ND	OEM
VN0640N2	OEM
VN0640N3	OEM
VN0640N5	OEM
VN0640ND	OEM
VN0645N2	OEM
VN0645N3	OEM
VN0645N5	OEM
VN0645ND	OEM
VN0650N2	OEM
VN0650N3	OEM
VN0650N5	OEM
VN0650ND	OEM
VN0655N2	OEM
VN0655N3	OEM
VN0655N5	OEM
VN0655ND	OEM
VN0660N2	OEM
VN0660N3	OEM
VN0660N5	OEM
VN0660ND	OEM
VN0800A	OEM
VN0800D	OEM
VN0801A	OEM
VN0801D	OEM
VN0808M	OEM
VN03601	OEM
VN03605	OEM
VN2SF1422	0239
VN10KE	6217
VN10KM	6219
VN10KN3	OEM
VN10KN9	OEM
VN10LE	OEM
VN10LM	OEM
VN10LP	OEM
VN30AA	OEM
VN30AB	OEM
VN33AJ	OEM
VN33AK	OEM
VN35AA	OEM
VN35AB	OEM
VN35AJ	OEM
VN35AK	OEM
VN40AF	OEM
VN46AF	OEM
VN64GA	OEM
VN66AD	OEM
VN66AF	OEM

DEVICE TYPE	REPL CODE
VN66AJ	OEM
VN66AK	OEM
VN67AA	OEM
VN67AB	OEM
VN67AD	OEM
VN67AF	OEM
VN67AJ	OEM
VN67AK	OEM
VN80AF	OEM
VN88AD	OEM
VN88AF	OEM
VN89AA	OEM
VN89AB	OEM
VN89AD	OEM
VN89AF	OEM
VN90AA	OEM
VN90AB	OEM
VN98AJ	OEM
VN98AK	OEM
VN99AA	OEM
VN99AB	OEM
VN99AJ	OEM
VN99AK	OEM
VN401D	OEM
VN1000A	OEM
VN1000D	OEM
VN1001A	OEM
VN1001D	OEM
VN1106N1	OEM
VN1106N2	OEM
VN1106N5	OEM
VN1106ND	OEM
VN1110N1	OEM
VN1110N2	OEM
VN1110N5	OEM
VN1110ND	OEM
VN1116N1	OEM
VN1116N2	OEM
VN1116N5	OEM
VN1116ND	OEM
VN1120N1	OEM
VN1120N2	OEM
VN1120N5	OEM
VN1120ND	OEM
VN1200A	OEM
VN1200D	OEM
VN1201A	OEM
VN1201D	OEM
VN1204N1	OEM
VN1204N2	OEM
VN1204N5	OEM
VN1204ND	OEM
VN1206B	OEM
VN1206D	OEM
VN1206L	OEM
VN1206M	OEM
VN1206N1	OEM
VN1206N2	OEM
VN1206N5	OEM
VN1206ND	OEM
VN1208N1	OEM
VN1209N1	OEM
VN1210L	OEM
VN1210M	OEM
VN1210N1	OEM
VN1210N2	OEM
VN1210N5	OEM
VN1210ND	OEM
VN1216N1	OEM
VN1216N2	OEM
VN1216N5	OEM
VN1216ND	OEM
VN1220N1	OEM
VN1220N2	OEM
VN1220N5	OEM
VN1220ND	OEM
VN1304N2	OEM
VN1304N3	OEM
VN1304N6	OEM
VN1304N7	OEM
VN1304ND	OEM
VN1306N2	OEM
VN1306N3	OEM
VN1306N6	OEM
VN1306N7	OEM
VN1306ND	OEM
VN1310N2	OEM
VN1310N3	OEM
VN1310ND	OEM
VN1316N2	OEM
VN1316N3	OEM
VN1316ND	OEM
VN1320N2	OEM
VN1320N3	OEM
VN1320ND	OEM
VN1706B	OEM
VN1706D	OEM
VN1706L	OEM
VN1706M	OEM
VN1710B	OEM
VN1710L	OEM
VN1710M	OEM
VN1720M	OEM
VN2020L	OEM
VN2222KM	OEM
VN2222L	OEM
VN2222LL	OEM
VN2222LM	OEM
VN2306N1	OEM

DEVICE TYPE	REPL CODE
VN2306N5	OEM
VN2306ND	OEM
VN2310N1	OEM
VN2310N5	OEM
VN2310ND	OEM
VN2316N1	OEM
VN2316N5	OEM
VN2316ND	OEM
VN2320N1	OEM
VN2320N5	OEM
VN2320ND	OEM
VN2335N1	OEM
VN2335N5	OEM
VN2335ND	OEM
VN2340N1	OEM
VN2340N5	OEM
VN2340ND	OEM
VN2345N1	OEM
VN2345N5	OEM
VN2345ND	OEM
VN2350N1	OEM
VN2350N5	OEM
VN2350ND	OEM
VN2406B	OEM
VN2406D	OEM
VN2406L	OEM
VN2406M	OEM
VN2410B	OEM
VN2410L	OEM
VN2410M	OEM
VN2420L	OEM
VN3500A	OEM
VN3500D	OEM
VN3501A	OEM
VN3501D	OEM
VN4000A	OEM
VN4000D	OEM
VN4001A	1658
VN4001D	OEM
VN4501A	OEM
VN4501D	OEM
VN4502A	OEM
VN4502D	OEM
VN5001A	OEM
VN5001D	OEM
VN5002A	OEM
VN5002D	OEM
VNC003A	OEM
VNC010B	OEM
VNC010D	OEM
VNC011B	OEM
VNC011D	OEM
VND010B	OEM
VND010D	OEM
VND011B	OEM
VND011D	OEM
VNE003A	OEM
VNE010B	OEM
VNE010D	OEM
VNG004A	OEM
VNJ004A	OEM
VNL001A	OEM
VNL005A	OEM
VNM001A	OEM
VNM005A	OEM
VNN002A	OEM
VNN006A	OEM
VNP002A	OEM
VNP006A	OEM
VNS008A	OEM
VNS008D	OEM
VNS009A	OEM
VNS009D	OEM
VNSS012A	OEM
VNSS013A	OEM
VNT008A	OEM
VNT008D	OEM
VNT009A	OEM
VNT009D	OEM
VNT012A	OEM
VNT013A	OEM
VO0220N2	OEM
VO0220N3	OEM
VO0220N5	OEM
VO0220ND	OEM
VO1G	1073
VO3-G	0071
VO3C	0947
VO3E	OEM
VO3G	0071
VO6-C	0015
VO6-G	0015
VO-6A	0015
VO6A	0535
VO-6B	0535
VO-6C	0015
VO6C	0015
VO-6C-401	0535
VO6E	0015
VO9-E	0535
VO9C	0023
VO9E	0102
VO9G	0023
VOG	0015
VP0104N2	OEM
VP0104N3	OEM
VP0104N5	OEM
VP0104N6	OEM
VP0104N7	OEM

If replacement code is OEM, contact original manufacturer for replacement.

DEVICE TYPE	REPL CODE
VP0104N9	OEM
VP0104ND	OEM
VP0106N2	OEM
VP0106N3	OEM
VP0106N5	OEM
VP0106N6	OEM
VP0106N7	OEM
VP0106N9	OEM
VP0106ND	OEM
VP0109N2	OEM
VP0109N3	OEM
VP0109N5	OEM
VP0109N9	OEM
VP0109ND	OEM
VP0116N2	OEM
VP0116N3	OEM
VP0116N5	OEM
VP0116ND	OEM
VP0120N2	OEM
VP0120N3	OEM
VP0120N5	OEM
VP0120ND	OEM
VP0204N2	OEM
VP0204N5	OEM
VP0204N6	OEM
VP0204N7	OEM
VP0204ND	OEM
VP0206N2	OEM
VP0206N3	OEM
VP0206N5	OEM
VP0206N6	OEM
VP0206N7	OEM
VP0206ND	OEM
VP0210N2	OEM
VP0210N3	OEM
VP0210N5	OEM
VP0210ND	OEM
VP0216N2	OEM
VP0216N3	OEM
VP0216N5	OEM
VP0216ND	OEM
VP0300B	OEM
VP0300L	OEM
VP0300M	OEM
VP0300P	OEM
VP0335N1	OEM
VP0335N2	OEM
VP0335N5	OEM
VP0335ND	OEM
VP0340N1	OEM
VP0340N2	OEM
VP0340N5	OEM
VP0340ND	OEM
VP0345N1	OEM
VP0345N2	OEM
VP0345N5	OEM
VP0345ND	OEM
VP0350N1	OEM
VP0350N2	OEM
VP0350N5	OEM
VP0350ND	OEM
VP0535N2	OEM
VP0535N3	OEM
VP0535ND	OEM
VP0540N2	OEM
VP0540N3	OEM
VP0540ND	OEM
VP0545N2	OEM
VP0545N3	OEM
VP0545ND	OEM
VP0550N2	OEM
VP0550N3	OEM
VP0550ND	OEM
VP0635N2	OEM
VP0635N3	OEM
VP0635N5	OEM
VP0635ND	OEM
VP0640N2	OEM
VP0640N3	OEM
VP0640N5	OEM
VP0640ND	OEM
VP0645N2	OEM
VP0645N3	OEM
VP0645N5	OEM
VP0645ND	OEM
VP0650N2	OEM
VP0650N3	OEM
VP0650N5	OEM
VP0650ND	OEM
VP0808B	OEM
VP0808L	OEM
VP0808M	OEM
VP16RP8MPC	OEM
VP130A10	1364
VP130A20	0832
VP150A10	0246
VP150A20	1982
VP250A20	1324
VP250A40	1324
VP420B40	3226
VP460B40	OEM
VP480B40	1093
VP480B80	1093
VP510B40	OEM
VP510B80	OEM
VP1000B80	OEM
VP1000B160	OEM
VP1008B	OEM
VP1008L	OEM
VP1008M	OEM
VP1106N1	OEM
VP1106N2	OEM
VP1106N5	OEM
VP1106ND	OEM
VP1110N1	OEM
VP1110N2	OEM
VP1110N5	OEM
VP1110ND	OEM
VP1116N1	OEM
VP1116N2	OEM
VP1116N5	OEM
VP1116ND	OEM
VP1120N1	OEM
VP1120N2	OEM
VP1120N5	OEM
VP1120ND	OEM
VP1204N1	OEM
VP1204N2	OEM
VP1204N5	OEM
VP1204ND	OEM
VP1206N1	OEM
VP1206N2	OEM
VP1206N5	OEM
VP1206ND	OEM
VP1210N1	OEM
VP1210N2	OEM
VP1210N5	OEM
VP1210ND	OEM
VP1216N1	OEM
VP1216N2	OEM
VP1216N5	OEM
VP1216ND	OEM
VP1220N1	OEM
VP1220N2	OEM
VP1220N5	OEM
VP1220ND	OEM
VP1304N2	OEM
VP1304N3	OEM
VP1304N6	OEM
VP1304N7	OEM
VP1304ND	OEM
VP1306N2	OEM
VP1306N3	OEM
VP1306N6	OEM
VP1306N7	OEM
VP1306ND	OEM
VP1310N2	OEM
VP1310N3	OEM
VP1310ND	OEM
VP1316N2	OEM
VP1316N3	OEM
VP1316ND	OEM
VP1320D	OEM
VP13202	OEM
VP13203	OEM
VPC1228H	OEM
VQ1000CJ	OEM
VQ1000J	OEM
VQ1000N6	OEM
VQ1000N7	OEM
VQ1000P	OEM
VQ1001J	OEM
VQ1001P	OEM
VQ1004J	OEM
VQ1004P	OEM
VQ1006J	OEM
VQ1006P	OEM
VQ2001J	OEM
VQ2001P	OEM
VQ2004J	OEM
VQ2004P	OEM
VQ2006J	OEM
VQ2006P	OEM
VQ3001J	OEM
VQ3001N6	OEM
VQ3001N7	OEM
VQ3001P	OEM
VQ7254J	OEM
VQ7254N6	OEM
VQ7254N7	OEM
VQ7254P	OEM
VR	OEM
VR1B	0023
VR1D	0023
VR1G	0023
VR1J	0023
VR5.6	0157
VR5.6A	0157
VR5.6B	0157
VR6.2	0631
VR6.2A	0631
VR6.2B	0631
VR7E	OEM
VR8E	OEM
VR9B	0012
VR9E	OEM
VR-9.1	0012
VR9.1	0012
VR9.1A	0012
VR9.1B	0012
VR10	0170
VR10A	0170
VR10B	0170
VR10E	0505
VR10F	0225
VR11	0789
VR11A	0789
VR11B	0313
VR11E	OEM
VR11F	0230
VR12	0137
VR12A	0137
VR12B	0137
VR12E	0864
VR12F	0234
VR13	0361
VR13A	0361
VR13B	0361
VR13E	OEM
VR13F	0237
VR-14	0002
VR14	0100
VR14A	0100
VR14B	0100
VR15	0002
VR15A	0002
VR15B	0002
VR15E	1264
VR15F	0247
VR16E	OEM
VR18	0490
VR18A	0490
VR18B	0490
VR18E	1071
VR18F	0256
VR20E	OEM
VR22E	1712
VR22F	0269
VR24E	OEM
VR27	0436
VR27A	0436
VR27B	0436
VR27E	1750
VR27F	0291
VR30E	OEM
VR33	0039
VR33A	0039
VR33B	0039
VR35E	OEM
VR56	1823
VR56A	1823
VR56B	0863
VR-60	OEM
VR-60B	OEM
VR-60BT	OEM
VR-60S	OEM
VR60SS	OEM
VR-60T	OEM
VR-60U	OEM
VR-61	OEM
VR-61B	OEM
VR-61S	OEM
VR61SS	OEM
VR-61T	OEM
VR-61U	OEM
VR62	0778
VR62A	0778
VR62B	0778
VR82	0327
VR82A	0327
VR82B	0327
VR110	0149
VR110A	0149
VR110B	0149
VR425E	OEM
VR475E	OEM
VR525E	OEM
VR575E	OEM
VR625E	OEM
VRBG5315S-B3	OEM
VS-0A70	0143
VS-1	0015
VS1	0015
VS-1N82AG	0911
VS2A71BS	0050
VS2C1740SQR1E	0151
VS2C1741-1	3392
VS2S669D//1E	0558
VS-2SA71	0050
VS-2SA71B	0050
VS2SA71B	0050
VS-2SA71BS	0050
VS2SA71BS	0050
VS-2SA103	0136
VS2SA103	0136
VS2SA128V	0164
VS-2SA288A	0136
VS-2SA358	0136
VS-2SA378	0050
VS2SA378	0050
VS-2SA379	0050
VS2SA379	0050
VS-2SA385	0136
VS2SA385	0136
VS2SA448	0050
VS2SA495-0/1E	0006
VS2SA495-0/-1	0006
VS2SA495-O/1E	0006
VS2SA495-Y/1E	0006
VS2SA562-0/1E	0006
VS2SA562-O/1E	0006
VS2SA562-Q/1E	0006
VS2SA562-Y/1E	0006
VS2SA562TO/-1	0006
VS2SA562T-O/1E	0006
VS2SA562T-Q/1E	0006
VS2SA673-B/1E	0148
VS2SA673-C/1A	0148
VS2SA673-C/1E	0148
VS2SA673A-B/1E	0148
VS2SA673A-C/1E	0148
VS2SA733AQ/-1	0006
VS2SA738-C/-1	0455
VS2SA740///1E	1638
VS2SA812-M51E	1731
VS2SA844-D/-1	0688
VS2SA844-D/-2	0688
VS2SA854-1/1E	OEM
VS2SA854-Q/1E	1338
VS2SA854TO/-1	1338
VS2SA933QR1E	0148
VS2SA933SQR1E	0148
VS2SA937-Q/-1	2464
VS2SA950-Y/1E	1338
VS2SA952LK/-1	0006
VS2SA966-Y/-1	0527
VS2SA968Y//-1	1638
VS2SA988///1E	0643
VS2SA1013//1E	1514
VS2SA1015/1E	0148
VS2SA1015G/1E	0148
VS2SA1015Y/-1E	0148
VS2SA1015Y/1E	0148
VS2SA1015Y/2E	0148
VS2SA1015YW-1	0148
VS2SA1020Y/-1	0429
VS2SA1037KQ-1	1731
VS2SA1271-Y-1	3154
VS-2SB126	0160
VS2SB126	0160
VS-2SB126F	0160
VS2SB126F	0160
VS-2SB126FV	0160
VS-2SB126V	0160
VS2SB126V	0160
VS-2SB128	0969
VS-2SB128V	0969
VS-2SB171	0004
VS2SB171	0004
VS-2SB172	0004
VS2SB172	0004
VS2SB172F	0004
VS-2SB172FN	0004
VS2SB172FN	0004
VS-2SB176	0004
VS2SB176	0004
VS-2SB178	0004
VS2SB178	0004
VS-2SB178A	0004
VS2SB178A	0004
VS-2SB324	1056
VS2SB324	1056
VS-2SB448	0222
VS2SB561-C/-1	0431
VS2SB561-C-1	0431
VS2SB568///-1	1900
VS2SB1212//1E	OEM
VS-2SC41	0615
VS-2SC58	0233
VS-2SC58A	0233
VS-2SC58B	0233
VS-2SC58C	0233
VS-2SC206	0216
VS2SC206	0216
VS-2SC208	0007
VS2SC208	0007
VS-2SC288A	1332
VS2SC288A	1332
VS-2SC324	0016
VS-2SC324H	0016
VS2SC324H	0016
VS-2SC371-R-1	0191
VS2SC371-R-1	0191
VS2SC372-0/1E	0076
VS2SC372-Y/1E	0076
VS2SC373//-1E	0076
VS-2SC373-//1E	0076
VS2SC373-G/-1	0076
VS2SC373G-1	0076
VS2SC374-B-1	0547
VS2SC383-W/1E	0076
VS2SC383-WT-1	0076
VS-2SC385	0544
VS-2SC385L	0544
VS2SC385L	0544
VS2SC394-0-1	0155
VS2SC394-O-1	0155
VS2SC394-Y-1	0155
VS-2SC446	0654
VS2SC454-B/1E	0076
VS2SC454-C/1A	0076
VS2SC454-C/1E	0076
VS2SC454-C/3A	0076
VS-2SC458	0076
VS2SC458	0076
VS2SC458-C/1E	0076
VS2SC458-D/-1	0076
VS2SC460B-1	0151
VS-2SC466	0259
VS2SC481-1	0693
VS2SC495T/-1	0781
VS2SC495T/1	0781
VS2SC495T-1	0781
VS-2SC526	0233
VS-2SC538	0079
VS2SC538	0079
VS-2SC563	0829
VS-2SC645	0669
VS-2SC645A	0669
VS2SC645A	0669
VS-2SC645B	0669
VS-2SC645C	0669
VS2SC669C//1E	0617
VS2SC669D/1E	0617
VS2SC681A-Y2E	2420
VS-2SC683	0047
VS-2SC683Y	0047
VS-2SC684	0127
VS2SC684	0127
VS-2SC687	0177
VS2SC717///-1	0127
VS2SC732-VIF	0076
VS2SC733B-1	0111
VS2SC735Y-1	0191
VS-2SC762	1146
VS2SC784R1F	1136
VS2SC900U-1	1212
VS2SC945A(Q)/-1	0076
VS2SC945AP/-1	0076
VS2SC945AQ/-1	0076
VS2SC945LK-1	0076
VS2SC945LP-1	0076
VS2SC983-0/2E	0066
VS2SC983-O/2E	0066
VS2SC1013//1E	OEM
VS2SC1166-0-1	0728
VS2SC1166-O-1	0728
VS2SC1166Y-1	0728
VS2SC1172-/1E	0309
VS2SC1174-/1E	0309
VS2SC1174-1E	0309
VS2SC1213-C/1A	0191
VS2SC1213AC/1A	0191
VS2SC1213AC1A	0191
VS2SC1237-/1F	0930
VS2SC1237-1F	0930
VS2SC1335D/-1	1212
VS2SC1335D/1	1212
VS2SC1335D/-1E	1212
VS2SC1447-/1E	0638
VS2SC1447LB1E	0638
VS2SC1509R/-1	0320
VS2SC1514//-1	1077
VS2SC1514/-1	1077
VS2SC1514BK-1E	1077
VS2SC1514BK1E	1077
VS2SC1569K/1E	0638
VS2SC1569K/1K	0638
VS2SC1623L51E	0719
VS2SC1627A	0728
VS2SC1627Y	0728
VS2SC1664//-1	0625
VS2SC1674L/-1	1060
VS2SC1675M-1	0076
VS2SC1681G/1E	1746
VS2SC1723//-1	1077
VS2SC1723-1	1077
VS2SC1723S/-1	1077
VS2SC1740SQR1E	0151
VS2SC1741-1	1505
VS2SC1815GR-1	0076
VS2SC1815GW-1	0076
VS2SC18150W-1	0076
VS2SC1815Y/-1	0076
VS2SC1815YW-1	0076
VS2SC1815YW1E	0076
VS2SC1826-Y1A	0419
VS2SC1827//1E	0236
VS2SC1827Y/1E	0236
VS2SC1829/1E	2596
VS2SC1829-/1E	2596
VS2SC1841-E-1	0525
VS2SC1841E1	0525
VS2SC1855//-1	0224
VS2SC1890A/1E	0525
VS2SC1890AD-1	0525
VS2SC1890AE-1	0525
VS2SC1906//1E	0127
VS2SC1906//E	1084
VS2SC1921//-1E	0261
VS2SC1921//1E	0261
VS2SC1923-O1E	2666
VS2SC1942//1E	2636
VS2SC1959Y/1E	0284
VS2SC1983//-1	2047
VS2SC1983//1E	2047
VS2SC1983//-2	2047
VS2SC2001-M-1	1505
VS2SC2001LK-1	1505
VS2SC2001LX-1	1505
VS2SC2002-K/A	0945
VS2SC2002-K1A	0945
VS2SC2021-Q-1	1132
VS2SC2023-/1E	2589
VS2SC2059KN1E	0719
VS2SC2068LB1E	0638
VS2SC2073	1274
VS2SC2073//1E	1274
VS2SC2073//3E	1274
VS2SC2073/3E	1274
VS2SC2073LB2E	1274
VS2SC2073LBE	1274
VS2SC2120Y/-1A	0860
VS2SC2120Y/1A	0860
VS2SC2120Y/-A	0860
VS2SC22290/-1	0066
VS2SC22290/1E	0066
VS2SC2231Y/1E	0168
VS2SC2236/-Y	2882
VS2SC22360/-1	2882
VS2SC2236Y/-1	2882
VS2SC2238Y/-1	3084
VS2SC2371K	0275
VS2SC2371K/1E	0275
VS2SC2371LK	0275
VS2SC2373L	0723
VS2SC2383//-1	1553
VS2SC2383//-1E	1553
VS2SC2383//1E	1553
VS2SC2412KQ-1	0719
VS2SC2458-C/1E	0076
VS2SC2458Y/-1	0076
VS2SC2462-C-1	0719
VS2SC2481-0	0558
VS2SC24810/1E	0558
VS2SC2481Y	0558
VS2SC2481Y/1E	0558
VS2SC2482//-1	0261
VS2SC2482//-1J	0261
VS2SC2555//-1	2171
VS2SC2610/-1E	0261
VS2SC2610BK/1E	0261
VS2SC2610K/1E	0261
VS2SC2610Y/-1	0261
VS2SC2611//-1	0275
VS2SC2611/-1	0275
VS2SC2611/-1E	0275
VS2SC2655(Y)	0018
VS2SC2655Y/-1	0018
VS2SC2712Y/-1	0719
VS2SC2735//-1	2891
VS2SC2794LB1E	0558
VS2SC2827//1E	0723
VS2SC3299Y/-1	0060
VS2SC3299Y/1E	0060
VS2SC3377-Q-1	OEM
VS2SC3886A/1E	5520
VS2SC3939QR-1	OEM
VS2SC4544LB1E	OEM
VS2SC4544LB2E	OEM
VS2SC4600B-1	OEM
VS2SC14471B1E	0168
VS2SC16742/-1	0224
VS2SC17235/-1	0168
VS2SC20731B2E	OEM
VS2SC22290/1E	0261
VS2SC24810/1E	0558
VS2SD227V-1	1409
VS2SD467-C/-1	0945
VS2SD468-C/-1	0018
VS2SD471-KL1E	0018
VS2SD471-S/-1	0018
VS2SD476-C/-1	0419
VS2SD478-YL-2E	0388
VS2SD478-YL2E	0388
VS2SD478-YL-ZE	0388
VS2SD478SYL2E	0388
VS2SD478YL2E	0388
VS2SD604-//1E	0074
VS2SD655-DE1E	1967
VS2SD666-C/-1	1376
VS2SD666A-C1A	1376
VS2SD669-C/1E	0558
VS2SD669-D/1E	0558
VS2SD669C	0558
VS2SD669C//1E	0558
VS2SD669D	0558
VS2SD669D//1E	0558
VS2SD669D/1E	0558
VS2SD699C	0558
VS2SD724///1A	0388
VS2SD758-C/1E	1077
VS2SD764///-1	0223
VS2SD794A//-1	0161
VS2SD794A//1E	0161
VS2SD794ALB1E	0161
VS2SD869//1E	0055
VS2SD869-//1E	0055
VS2SD870	0055
VS2SD870///-1	0055
VS2SD871///-1	0055
VS2SD898-/1E	0055
VS2SD898A-/1E	0055
VS2SD898A/1E	0055
VS2SD898B//1E	0055
VS2SD898B-/1E	0055
VS2SD898B-13//1E	0055
VS2SD906///-1	0055
VS2SD906///1E	0055
VS2SD975	0558
VS2SD975///-1	0558
VS2SD1190//1E	5360
VS2SD1264//1E	0388
VS2SD1267-P1E	0060
VS2SD1426//1E	1533
VS2SD1554//1E	1533
VS2SD1650//-1	1533
VS2SD1650CA1E	1533
VS2SD1812Q/-1	OEM
VS2SD2095//1E	2116
VS2SD2125//1E	2116
VS2SD2271-1	0016
VS2SF1422//1E	0239
VS2SK30AG//1E	3017
VS2SK30AG//2E	3017
VS2SK49F-1	1270
VS2SK532///-1	OEM
VS120	0015
VS202	0015
VS247	1404
VS248	1404
VS447	0468
VS449	1576
VS500	1576
VS600	1576
VS848	1412
VS1048	2425
VS2687	OEM
VSC2SC383-W/1E	OEM
VSCS0065	OEM
VSCS0075	OEM
VS-CS1255H	0086
VSCS1255H	0086
VS-CS1255HF	0086
VS-CS1256HG	0126
VSCS1256HG	0037
VSD101AN20	OEM
VSD101BN20	OEM
VSD101N19	OEM
VSD101N20	OEM
VSD102AN20	OEM
VSD102BN20	OEM
VSD102N10	OEM
VSD102N19	OEM
VSD102N20	OEM
VSD102N26	OEM
VSD103AN20	OEM
VSD103BN20	OEM
VSD103N10	OEM
VSD103N19	OEM
VSD103N20	OEM
VSD103N26	OEM
VSD104AN20	OEM
VSD104BN20	OEM
VSD111N10	OEM
VSD111N20	OEM
VSD111N26	OEM
VSD112N10	OEM
VSD112N20	OEM
VSD112N26	OEM
VSD121N10	OEM
VSD121N19	OEM
VSD121N20	OEM
VSD121N26	OEM
VSD122N19	OEM
VSD122N20	OEM
VSD201N10	OEM
VSD201N20	OEM
VSD201N26	OEM
VSD203N10	OEM
VSD203N20	OEM
VSD203N26	OEM
VSD204N20	OEM
VSD211N10	OEM
VSD501AN20	OEM
VSD501BN20	OEM
VSD501N10	OEM
VSD501N20	OEM
VSD501N26	OEM
VSD502AN20	OEM
VSD502BN20	OEM
VSD502N10	OEM
VSD502N20	OEM
VSD502N26	OEM
VSD503BN20	OEM
VSD503N10	OEM
VSD503N20	OEM
VSD503N26	OEM
VSD504AN20	OEM
VSD504BN20	OEM
VSD505AN20	OEM
VSD505BN20	OEM
VSD506AN20	OEM
VSD506BN20	OEM
VSD507AN20	OEM
VSD507BN20	OEM
VSD508AN20	OEM
VSD508BN20	OEM
VSD521N10	OEM
VSD521N20	OEM
VSD521N26	OEM
VSD522N10	OEM
VSD522N20	OEM
VSD522N26	OEM
VSD701N10	OEM
VSD701N19	OEM
VSD701N20	OEM
VSD701N26	OEM
VSD702N10	OEM
VSD702N19	OEM
VSD702N20	OEM
VSD702N26	OEM
VSD711N10	OEM
VSD711N20	OEM
VSD711N26	OEM
VSD712N10	OEM
VSD712N20	OEM
VSD712N26	OEM
VSD721N10	OEM
VSD721N19	OEM
VSD721N20	OEM
VSD721N26	OEM
VSD722N10	OEM

622 If replacement code is OEM, contact original manufacturer for replacement.

DEVICE TYPE	REPL CODE
VSD722N19	OEM
VSD722N20	OEM
VS-DG1N	0102
VS-DG1NR	0182
VSDTA114EK/-1	1881
VSDTA124EK/-1	0698
VSDTA124ES/-1	1026
VSDTA144EK/-1	3241
VSDTA144ES/-1	4067
VSDTC114EK/-1	3442
VSDTC114ES/-1	0826
VSDTC124ES/-1	0881
VSDTC124F//-1	0881
VSDTC144EK/-1	3439
VSDTC144ES/-1	0892
VSDTC144F//-1	0892
VSDTC363EK/-1	OEM
VSES0011	OEM
VSF204BN20	OEM
VSF2745	0279
VS-FR1	0015
VSFR1	0015
VS-FR1P	0015
VSFR1P	0015
VS-FR-1U	0015
VS-FT-1N	0015
VSFT1N	0015
VSG-20024	0015
VSGM380	0136
VSH200A	1325
VSH202A	0133
VSH212A	0133
VSH222A	0133
VSH242A	0133
VSH252A	0133
VSK120	1325
VSK130	1325
VSK140	1325
VSK320	0087
VSK330	0087
VSK340	0087
VSK1520	0610
VSK1530	0610
VSK1540	0610
VSK3020S	0610
VSK3030S	0610
VSK3040S	0610
VSK4020	1536
VSK4030	1536
VSK4040	1536
VS-MA102	0015
VS-MA103	OEM
VSOA70	0143
VS-PC02P11/2	0015
VSPH9D522/1	0015
VSQS0730	OEM
VS-RD11AM	0064
VSS6142GLB1E	0095
VS-SD1	0023
VS-SD-1B	0102
VS-SD1B	0102
VSSD1B	0015
VS-SD-1Z	0023
VSSD1Z	0015
VS-SD-13	0071
VS-SD-82A	0911
VS-SD82A	0911
VS-TC0-2P11/2	0015
VS-TC02P11/2	0015
VSTC02P11/2	0015
VS-TC0.2P11/2	0914
VSZS0065	OEM
VSZS0066	OEM
VSZS0075	OEM
VSZS0076	OEM
VT005-8	OEM
VT030-18A	OEM
VT1.5040	OEM
VT14LE	OEM
VT101	OEM
VT101E	OEM
VT101H	OEM
VT101HE	OEM
VT102	OEM
VT102E	OEM
VT102L	OEM
VT102L3	OEM
VT103	OEM
VT103L	OEM
VT104	OEM
VT111	OEM
VT111E	OEM
VT111H	OEM
VT111HE	OEM
VT112	OEM
VT112E	OEM
VT112L	OEM
VT112LE	OEM
VT113	OEM
VT113L	OEM
VT121	OEM
VT121E	OEM
VT121H	OEM
VT121HE	OEM
VT122	OEM
VT122E	OEM
VT122L	OEM
VT122LE	OEM
VT123	OEM

DEVICE TYPE	REPL CODE
VT123L	OEM
VT124	OEM
VT132	OEM
VT133	OEM
VT133E	OEM
VT133L	OEM
VT133LE	OEM
VT141	OEM
VT141E	OEM
VT141H	OEM
VT141HE	OEM
VT142	OEM
VT142L	OEM
VT142LE	OEM
VT143	OEM
VT143L	OEM
VT6005	OEM
VT10030	OEM
VT10150	OEM
VT120020N	OEM
VT120100N	OEM
VTA1112	3508
VTCL27-0602-01	OEM
VTCL27-0603-00	OEM
VTF200	OEM
VTF400	OEM
VTF600	OEM
VTM-01	OEM
VTM-02	OEM
VTM-03	OEM
VTM-03-01	OEM
VTM-04	OEM
VTM-05	OEM
VTM-05-01	OEM
VTM-05-02	OEM
VTM-05-03	OEM
VTM-06	OEM
VTM-07	OEM
VTM-08	OEM
VTM-09	OEM
VTM-10	OEM
VTM-11	OEM
VTM-12	OEM
VTM-13	OEM
VTM-14	OEM
VTM-15	OEM
VTR866	OEM
VTR867	OEM
VUAS0042	OEM
VVC201	0549
VVC203	0005
VVC205	0715
VVC205A	0715
VVC205B	OEM
VVC213	0030
VVC409	0030
VVC409A	0030
VVC409B	OEM
VVC410	0030
VVC410A	0030
VVC410B	OEM
VVC412	0005
VVC412A	0005
VVC413	0623
VVC415	0623
VVC415A	0623
VVC700	0549
VVC702	0549
VVC702A	0549
VVC704	0549
VVC704A	0549
VVC705	0005
VVC705A	0005
VVC706	0005
VVC706A	0005
VVC710	0623
VVC710A	0623
VVC712	0030
VVC712A	0030
VVC713	0030
VVC713A	0030
VVC726	0549
VVC729	0005
VVC730	0005
VVC731	0715
VVC732	0715
VVC741	0623
VVC742	0623
VVC743	0623
VVC747	0030
VVC748	0030
VVC749	0030
VVC789	0549
VVC790	0549
VVC791	0549
VVC792	0549
VVC795	0005
VVC796	0005
VVC797	0005
VVC798	0005
VVC799	0005
VVC810	0715
VVC811	0715
VVC822	0030
VVC823	0030
VVC824	0030
VVC825	0030
VVC847	0549
VVC848	0549

DEVICE TYPE	REPL CODE
VVC849	0549
VVC850	0005
VVC851	0005
VVC852	0005
VVC862	0623
VVC863	0623
VVC864	0623
VVC869	0030
VVC870	0030
VVC871	0030
VVC910	0005
VVC911	0005
VVC924	0623
VVC925	0623
VVC932	0030
VVC933	0030
VVC934	0030
VVC1003	0549
VVC1004	0005
VVC1005	0715
VVC1009	0623
VVC1011	0030
VVC1620	0549
VVC1624	0005
VVC1624A	0005
VVC1624B	OEM
VVC1624C	OEM
VVC1626	0715
VVC1634	0623
VVC1638	0030
VX0006CE	OEM
VX3375	0555
VX3733	0042
VX3866	OEM
VXEW0009	OEM
VZ-050A	0162
VZ-050B	0162
VZ-050C	0162
VZ-050D	0162
VZ-050E	0162
VZ-052A	0041
VZ-052B	0041
VZ-052C	0041
VZ-052D	0041
VZ-052E	0041
VZ-056A	0157
VZ-056B	0157
VZ-056C	0157
VZ-056D	0157
VZ-056E	0157
VZ061	0091
VZ-061A	0631
VZ-061B	0631
VZ-061C	0631
VZ-061D	0631
VZ-061E	0631
VZ-063A	0466
VZ-063B	0466
VZ-063C	0466
VZ-063D	0466
VZ-063E	0466
VZ-073A	0077
VZ-073B	0077
VZ-073C	0077
VZ-073D	0077
VZ-073E	0077
VZ-075A	0077
VZ-075B	0077
VZ-075C	0077
VZ-075D	0077
VZ-075E	0077
VZ-077A	0077
VZ-077B	0077
VZ-077C	0077
VZ-077D	0077
VZ-077E	0077
VZ-079A	0165
VZ-079B	0165
VZ-079C	0165
VZ-079D	0165
VZ-079E	0165
VZ-081A	0165
VZ-081B	0165
VZ-081C	0165
VZ-081D	0165
VZ-081E	0165
VZ-083A	0165
VZ-083B	0165
VZ-083C	0165
VZ-083D	0165
VZ-083E	0165
VZ-085A	0318
VZ-085B	0318
VZ-085C	0318
VZ-085D	0318
VZ-085E	0318
VZ-090A	0057
VZ-090B	0057
VZ-090C	0057
VZ-090D	0057
VZ-090E	0057
VZ-092A	0057
VZ-092B	0057
VZ-092C	0057
VZ-092D	0057
VZ-092E	0057
VZ-094A	0057
VZ-094B	0057
VZ-094C	0057

DEVICE TYPE	REPL CODE
VZ-094D	0057
VZ-096A	0064
VZ-096B	0064
VZ-096C	0064
VZ-096D	0064
VZ-096E	0064
VZ-098A	0064
VZ-098B	0064
VZ-098C	0064
VZ-098D	0064
VZ-098E	0064
VZ33CH	0289
VZ33DF	0777
VZ33EF	0777
VZ36CH	0188
VZ36DF	0791
VZ36EF	0791
VZ39CH	0451
VZ39DF	0801
VZ39EF	0801
VZ43CH	0528
VZ43DF	0815
VZ43EF	0815
VZ43F	0815
VZ47CH	0446
VZ47DF	0827
VZ47EF	0827
VZ47F	0827
VZ51CH	0162
VZ51D	0437
VZ51EF	0437
VZ51F	0437
VZ56CH	0157
VZ56DF	0870
VZ56EF	0870
VZ56F	0870
VZ62CH	0631
VZ62DF	0185
VZ62EF	0185
VZ62F	0185
VZ68CH	0025
VZ68DF	0205
VZ68EF	0205
VZ68F	0205
VZ75CH	0644
VZ75DF	0475
VZ75EF	0475
VZ75F	0475
VZ82CH	0244
VZ82DF	0499
VZ82EF	0499
VZ82F	0499
VZ91CH	0012
VZ91DF	0679
VZ91EF	0679
VZ91F	0679
VZ-100A	0064
VZ-100B	0064
VZ-100C	0064
VZ100CH	0170
VZ-100D	0064
VZ100DF	0225
VZ-100E	0064
VZ100EF	0225
VZ100F	0225
VZ-105A	0181
VZ-105B	0181
VZ-105C	0181
VZ-105D	0181
VZ-105E	0181
VZ110	OEM
VZ-110A	0181
VZ-110B	0181
VZ-110C	0181
VZ110CH	0313
VZ-110D	0181
VZ110DF	0230
VZ-110E	0181
VZ110EF	0230
VZ-110F	0181
VZ110F	0230
VZ-115A	0789
VZ-115B	0789
VZ-115C	0789
VZ-115D	0789
VZ-115E	0789
VZ-120A	0052
VZ-120B	0052
VZ-120C	0052
VZ120CH	0137
VZ-120D	0052
VZ120DF	0234
VZ-120E	0052
VZ120EF	0234
VZ120F	0234
VZ-125A	0361
VZ-125B	0361
VZ-125C	0361
VZ-125D	0361
VZ-125E	0361
VZ-130A	0053
VZ-130B	0053
VZ-130C	0053
VZ130CH	0361
VZ-130D	0053
VZ130DF	0237
VZ-130E	0053
VZ130EF	0237
VZ130F	0237

DEVICE TYPE	REPL CODE
VZ-135A	0873
VZ-135B	0873
VZ-135E	0873
VZ-140A	0873
VZ-140B	0873
VZ-140C	0873
VZ-140D	0873
VZ-140E	0873
VZ-145A	0681
VZ-145B	0681
VZ-145C	0681
VZ-145D	0681
VZ-145E	0681
VZ-150A	0681
VZ-150B	0681
VZ-150C	0681
VZ150CH	0002
VZ-150D	0681
VZ150DF	0247
VZ-150E	0681
VZ150EF	0247
VZ150F	0247
VZ-157	0440
VZ-157A	0440
VZ-157B	0440
VZ-157C	0440
VZ-157D	0440
VZ-157E	0440
VZ160CH	0416
VZ160DF	0251
VZ160EF	0251
VZ160F	0251
VZ-162	0440
VZ-162A	0440
VZ-162B	0440
VZ-162C	0440
VZ-162D	0440
VZ-162E	0440
VZ-167A	0210
VZ-167B	0210
VZ-167C	0210
VZ-167D	0210
VZ-167E	0210
VZ-172A	0210
VZ-172B	0210
VZ-172C	0210
VZ-172D	0210
VZ-172E	0210
VZ-177A	0490
VZ-177B	0490
VZ-177C	0490
VZ-177D	0490
VZ-177E	0490
VZ180CH	0490
VZ180DF	0256
VZ180EF	0256
VZ180F	0256
VZ-182A	0371
VZ-182B	0371
VZ-182C	0371
VZ-182D	0371
VZ-182E	0371
VZ-192A	0666
VZ-192B	0666
VZ-192C	0666
VZ-192D	0666
VZ-192E	0666
VZ200CH	0526
VZ200DF	0262
VZ200EF	0262
VZ200F	0262
VZ220CH	0560
VZ220DF	0269
VZ220EF	0269
VZ220F	0269
VZ-230	0398
VZ-230A	0398
VZ-230B	0398
VZ-230C	0398
VZ-230D	0398
VZ-230E	0398
VZ-240	0398
VZ-240A	0398
VZ-240B	0398
VZ-240C	0398
VZ240CH	0398
VZ-240D	0398
VZ240DF	0273
VZ-240E	0398
VZ240EF	0273
VZ240F	0273
VZ-250	0398
VZ-250A	0398
VZ-250B	0398
VZ-250C	0398
VZ-250D	0398
VZ-250E	0398
VZ-260	0436
VZ-260A	0436
VZ-260B	0436
VZ-260C	0436
VZ-260D	0436
VZ-260E	0436
VZ-270	0436
VZ-270A	0436
VZ-270B	0436
VZ-270C	0436
VZ270CH	0436
VZ-270D	0436

DEVICE TYPE	REPL CODE
VZ270DF	0291
VZ-270E	0436
VZ270EF	0291
VZ270F	0291
VZ-280	0721
VZ-280A	0721
VZ-280B	0721
VZ-280C	0721
VZ-280D	0721
VZ-280E	0721
VZ-290	0721
VZ-290A	0721
VZ-290B	0721
VZ-290C	0721
VZ-290D	0721
VZ-290E	0721
VZ-300	0721
VZ-300A	0721
VZ-300B	0721
VZ-300C	0721
VZ300CH	0721
VZ-300D	0721
VZ300DF	0305
VZ-300E	0721
VZ300EF	0305
VZ300F	0305
VZ-320	0039
VZ-320A	0039
VZ-320B	0039
VZ-320C	0039
VZ-320D	0039
VZ-320E	0039
VZ-330	0039
VZ-330A	0039
VZ-330B	0039
VZ-330C	0039
VZ330CH	0039
VZ-330D	0039
VZ330DF	0314
VZ-330E	0039
VZ330EF	0314
VZ330F	0314
VZ-340	0039
VZ-340A	0039
VZ-340B	0039
VZ-340C	0039
VZ-340D	0039
VZ-340E	0039
W/6A	0015
W0005M	0106
W-005	0276
W005	0106
W005L	0106
W005M	0106
W0-6A	0133
W0-6B	0604
W0-61	0631
W01	0106
W01L	0106
W01M	0106
W02	0106
W02L	0106
W02M	0106
W03A	0015
W03B	0023
W03BTA	4333
W03C	0023
W04	0287
W04L	0106
W04M	0106
W06	1999
W06-A	0015
W06-B	0015
W-06A	0015
W06A	0023
W06A-T3	0023
W06A-Z	0015
W06B	0023
W06C	0023
W06F	1999
W06L	1999
W06M	1999
W06MA	OEM
W08	2384
W08F	OEM
W08L	2384
W08M	2384
W08MA	OEM
W09A	0080
W09B	0604
W09C	0023
W010L	0782
W010M	0782
W075	0077
W081	OEM
W005	OEM
W1	0279
W1-050	0162
W1-052	0162
W1-054	0157
W1-056	0157
W1-058	0157
W1-061	0631
W1-063	0631
W1-065	0631
W1-071	0644
W1-073	0644
W1-075	0644
W1-077	0644

DEVICE TYPE	REPL CODE
W1-079	0244
W1-081	0244
W1-083	0244
W1-085	0244
W1-088	0012
W1-090	0012
W1-092	0012
W1-094	0012
W1-098	0170
W1-100	0170
W1-110	0313
W1-115	0789
W1-120	0137
W1-125	0361
W1-130	0361
W1-140	0100
W1-150	0002
W1-157	0416
W1-162	0416
W1-167	0416
W1-172	0490
W1-177	0490
W1-182	0490
W1-230	0398
W1-240	0398
W1-250	0398
W1-260	0436
W1-270	0436
W1-290	0721
W1-300	0721
W1-330	0039
W1-340	0039
W1A	0321
W1E	0843
W1L	0058
W1P	0321
W1R	0058
W1R(SCR)	0058
W1U	0212
W1U-1	0212
W1W	2255
W2	0595
W2-050	0162
W2-052	0157
W2-054	0157
W2-056	0157
W2-058	0157
W2-061	0631
W2-063	0631
W2-065	0631
W2-071	0644
W2-073	0644
W2-075	0644
W2-077	0644
W2-079	0244
W2-081	0244
W2-083	0244
W2-085	0244
W2-088	0012
W2-090	0012
W2-092	0012
W2-094	0012
W2-098	0170
W2-100	0170
W2-110	0313
W2-115	0789
W2-125	0361
W2-130	0361
W2-140	0100
W2-150	0002
W2-157	0416
W2-167	0416
W2-172	0490
W2-177	0490
W2-182	0490
W2-230	0398
W2-240	0398
W2-250	0398
W2-260	0436
W2-270	0436
W2-290	0721
W2-300	0721
W2-330	0039
W2-340	0436
W2AA50C	2282
W2AA50E	2282
W2B325C	OEM
W2BA25C	1425
W2BA25E	1425
W2BC25C	1425
W2BC25E	1425
W2BE25C	1425
W2BE25E	1425
W2BH25C	2278
W2BH25E	2278
W2BJ25C	1670
W2BJ25E	1670
W2BK25C	1670
W2BK25E	1670
W2CA25C	OEM
W2CA25E	OEM
W2DA25C	OEM
W2DA25E	OEM
W2DC25E	OEM
W2VB10	OEM
W3	0004
W3D	0588
W4	0208
W4-050	0162

If replacement code is OEM, contact original manufacturer for replacement.

623

DEVICE TYPE	REPL CODE
W4-052	0162
W4-054	0157
W4-056	0157
W4-058	0157
W4-061	0007
W4-063	0631
W4-065	0631
W4-071	0644
W4-073	0644
W4-075	0644
W4-077	0644
W4-079	0244
W4-081	0244
W4-083	0244
W4-085	0244
W4-088	0012
W4-090	0012
W4-092	0012
W4-094	0012
W4-098	0170
W4-100	0170
W4-110	0313
W4-115	0789
W4D45C	1787
W4D45D	1787
W4D45M	1787
W4D45N	1787
W4D45P	1787
W4D45PB	1787
W4D45PD	OEM
W4D45PM	OEM
W4D80C	2178
W4D80D	2178
W4D80M	2178
W4D80N	2178
W4D80P	2178
W4D80PB	2178
W4D80PD	OEM
W4D80PM	OEM
W4DA40C	4295
W4DA40D	4295
W4DA40M	4295
W4DA40N	4295
W4DA40P	4295
W4DA40PB	4295
W4DA40PD	OEM
W4DA55C	4295
W4DA55D	4295
W4DA55M	4295
W4DA55N	4295
W4DA55P	4295
W4DA55PB	4295
W4DA55PD	OEM
W4DB40C	4494
W4DB40D	4494
W4DB40M	4494
W4DB40N	4494
W4DB40P	4494
W4DB40PB	4494
W4DB40PD	OEM
W4DB55C	4295
W4DB55D	4295
W4DB55M	4295
W4DB55N	4295
W4DB55P	4295
W4DB55PB	4295
W4DB55PD	4295
W4DC40C	0647
W4DC40D	0647
W4DC40M	0647
W4DC40N	0647
W4DC40P	0647
W4DC40PB	0647
W4DC40PD	OEM
W4DC55C	0647
W4DC55D	0647
W4DC55M	0647
W4DC55N	0647
W4DC55P	0647
W4DC55PB	0647
W4DC55PD	OEM
W4H45C	OEM
W4H45D	OEM
W4H45M	OEM
W4H45N	OEM
W4H45P	OEM
W4H45PB	OEM
W4H45PD	OEM
W4H45PM	OEM
W4H80C	OEM
W4H80D	OEM
W4H80M	OEM
W4H80N	OEM
W4H80P	OEM
W4H80PB	OEM
W4H80PD	OEM
W4H80PM	OEM
W5	0085
W5-22	OEM
W5-23	OEM
W5MC/15D	OEM
W5MC/16B	OEM
W5MC/17D	OEM
W5MC/18M	OEM
W5MW1M	OEM
W5PA1M	OEM
W5R-12	OEM
W6	0435
W6-120	0137
W6-125	0361
W6-130	0361
W6-140	0100
W6-150	0002
W6-157	0416
W6-162	0416
W6-167	0416
W6-172	0490
W6-177	0490
W6-182	0490
W6-230	0398
W6-240	0398
W6-250	0398
W6-260	0436
W6-270	0436
W6-290	0721
W6-300	0721
W6-330	0039
W6-340	0039
W6MT/2A	OEM
W7	0150
W7/3G	OEM
W7/4G	OEM
W7/5GA	OEM
W7/5GC	OEM
W7/6GA	OEM
W7/6GC	OEM
W7/6GZ	OEM
W7-120	0137
W7-125	0361
W7-130	0361
W7-140	0100
W7-150	0002
W7-157	0416
W7-162	0416
W7-167	0416
W7-172	0490
W7-177	0490
W7-182	0490
W7-230	0398
W7-240	0398
W7-250	0398
W7-260	0436
W7-270	0436
W7-290	0721
W7-300	0721
W7-330	0039
W7-340	0039
W7MC/2R	OEM
W7MC/11C	OEM
W7MC/13B	OEM
W8	0144
W8-050	0162
W8-052	0162
W8-054	0157
W8-056	0157
W8-058	0157
W8-061	0631
W8-063	0631
W8-065	0631
W8-071	0644
W8-073	0644
W8-075	0644
W8-077	0644
W8-079	0244
W8-081	0244
W8-083	0244
W8-085	0244
W8-088	0012
W8-090	0012
W8-092	0012
W8-094	0012
W8-098	0170
W8-100	0170
W8-110	0313
W8-115	0789
W8-120	0137
W8-125	0361
W8-130	0361
W8-140	0100
W8-150	0002
W8-157	0416
W8-162	0416
W8-167	0416
W8-172	0490
W8-177	0490
W8-182	0490
W8-230	0398
W8-240	0398
W8-250	0398
W8-260	0436
W8-270	0436
W8-300	0721
W8-330	0039
W8-340	0039
W8-390	0721
W9	0160
W9/2E	OEM
W9/3E	OEM
W9/340	0039
W9-050	0162
W9-054	0157
W9-056	0157
W9-058	0157
W9-061	0631
W9-063	0631
W9-065	0631
W9-071	0644
W9-073	0644
W9-075	0644
W9-077	0644
W9-079	0244
W9-081	0244
W9-083	0244
W9-085	0244
W9-088	0012
W9-090	0012
W9-092	0012
W9-094	0012
W9-098	0170
W9-100	0170
W9-110	0313
W9-115	0789
W9-120	0137
W9-125	0361
W9-130	0361
W9-140	0100
W9-150	0002
W9-157	0490
W9-162	0490
W9-167	0490
W9-172	0490
W9-177	0490
W9-182	0490
W9-230	0398
W9-240	0398
W9-250	0398
W9-260	0436
W9-270	0436
W9-290	0721
W9-300	0039
W9ACW	0321
W10	0198
W10/3E	OEM
W10F	0782
W10M	0782
W11	0142
W12	0050
W13	0969
W14	0086
W15	0126
W16	0103
W16MP	1506
W17	0222
W17MP	0816
W18	0042
W19	0919
W20	0016
W21	0037
W22	0050
W23	0007
W24	0016
W25	0164
W26	0275
W27	2736
W28	0233
W29	0127
W45B/5E	OEM
W46D/2T	OEM
W48D/1T	OEM
W53-046-0	OEM
W55	1823
W103-254	0015
W106A1	0442
W106B1	0934
W106C1	1213
W106Y1	1386
W110	0106
W122A	2078
W122B	0500
W122C	0712
W122D	0705
W122F	2084
W208FS	OEM
W208FS-1	OEM
W208FSM	OEM
W208FSM-1	OEM
W208FSMZS	OEM
W208FSMZS-1	OEM
W208FSQ	OEM
W208FSQ-1	OEM
W208FSQZS	OEM
W208FSQZS-1	OEM
W208FST	OEM
W208FST-1	OEM
W208FSTZS	OEM
W208FSTZS-1	OEM
W208FSZS	OEM
W208FSZS-1	OEM
W264FS	OEM
W264FSQ	OEM
W264FSQZS	OEM
W264FST	OEM
W264FSTZS	OEM
W264FSZS	OEM
W265	1189
W463A	OEM
W463B	OEM
W463D	OEM
W463E	OEM
W463F	OEM
W464A	OEM
W464B	OEM
W464C	OEM
W464D	OEM
W465A	OEM
W465B	OEM
W465C	OEM
W465D	OEM
W466A	OEM
W466B	OEM
W466C	OEM
W466D	OEM
W467	OEM
W468	OEM
W469A	OEM
W469B	OEM
W469C	OEM
W470A	OEM
W470B	OEM
W470C	OEM
W470D	OEM
W496A	OEM
W496B	OEM
W496C	OEM
W496D	OEM
W496E	OEM
W497A	OEM
W497B	OEM
W497C	OEM
W497D	OEM
W497E	OEM
W498A	OEM
W498C	OEM
W498D	OEM
W498E	OEM
W498F	OEM
W498G	OEM
W498H	OEM
W498I	OEM
W498J	OEM
W498K	OEM
W498L	OEM
W806FS	OEM
W806FS-1	OEM
W806FSM	OEM
W806FSM-1	OEM
W806FSMZS	OEM
W806FSMZS-1	OEM
W806FSQ	OEM
W806FSQ-1	OEM
W806FSQZS	OEM
W806FSQZS-1	OEM
W806FST	OEM
W806FST-1	OEM
W806FSTZS	OEM
W806FSTZS-1	OEM
W806FSZS	OEM
W806FSZS-1	OEM
W812BS	OEM
W812BS-1	OEM
W812BSM	OEM
W812BSM-1	OEM
W812BSMZS	OEM
W812BSMZS-1	OEM
W812BSQ	OEM
W812BSQ-1	OEM
W812BSQZS	OEM
W812BSQZS-1	OEM
W812BST	OEM
W812BST-1	OEM
W812BSTZS	OEM
W812BSTZS-1	OEM
W812BSZS	OEM
W812BSZS-1	OEM
W4891	OEM
W4892	OEM
W4893	OEM
W4894	OEM
W5696A	0549
WA-050	0162
WA-050A	0162
WA-050B	0162
WA-050D	0162
WA-052	0162
WA-052A	0162
WA-052B	0162
WA-052C	0162
WA-052D	0162
WA-054	0157
WA-054A	0157
WA-054B	0157
WA-054C	0157
WA-054D	0157
WA-056	0157
WA-056A	0157
WA-056B	0157
WA-056C	0157
WA-056D	0157
WA-058	0157
WA-058A	0157
WA-058B	0157
WA-058C	0157
WA-058D	0157
WA-061	0631
WA-061A	0631
WA-061B	0631
WA-061C	0631
WA-063	0631
WA-063A	0631
WA-063B	0631
WA-063C	0631
WA-063D	0631
WA-065	0631
WA-065A	0631
WA-065B	0631
WA-065C	0631
WA-065D	0631
WA-071	0644
WA-071A	0644
WA-071B	0644
WA-071C	0644
WA-071D	0644
WA-073	0644
WA-073A	0644
WA-073B	0644
WA-073C	0644
WA-073D	0644
WA-075	0644
WA-075A	0644
WA-075B	0644
WA-075C	0644
WA-075D	0644
WA-077	0644
WA-077A	0644
WA-077B	0644
WA-077C	0644
WA-077D	0644
WA-079	0244
WA-079A	0244
WA-079B	0244
WA-079C	0244
WA-079D	0244
WA-081	0244
WA-081A	0244
WA-081B	0244
WA-081C	0244
WA-081D	0244
WA-083	0244
WA-083A	0244
WA-083B	0244
WA-083C	0244
WA-083D	0244
WA-085	0244
WA-085A	0244
WA-085B	0244
WA-085C	0244
WA-085D	0244
WA-088	0012
WA-088A	0012
WA-088B	0012
WA-088C	0012
WA-088D	0012
WA-090	0012
WA-090A	0012
WA-090B	0012
WA-090C	0012
WA-090D	0012
WA-092	0012
WA-092A	0012
WA-092B	0012
WA-092C	0012
WA-092D	0012
WA-094	0012
WA-094A	0012
WA-094B	0012
WA-094C	0012
WA-094D	0012
WA-098	0012
WA-098A	0012
WA-098B	0170
WA-098C	0170
WA-098D	0170
WA0A-90	0133
WA-26	0133
WA-100	0170
WA100	2363
WA-100A	0170
WA-100B	0170
WA-100C	0170
WA-100D	0170
WA-110	0313
WA-110A	0313
WA-110B	0313
WA-110C	0313
WA-110D	0313
WA-115	0789
WA-115A	0789
WA-115B	0789
WA-115C	0789
WA-115D	0789
WA-120	0137
WA-120A	0137
WA-120B	0137
WA-120C	0137
WA-120D	0137
WA-125	0361
WA-125A	0361
WA-125B	0361
WA-125C	0361
WA-125D	0361
WA-130	0361
WA-130A	0361
WA-130B	0361
WA-130C	0361
WA-130D	0361
WA-140	0100
WA-140A	0100
WA-140B	0100
WA-140C	0100
WA-140D	0100
WA-150	0002
WA-150A	0002
WA-150B	0002
WA-150C	0002
WA-150D	0002
WA-157	0416
WA-157A	0416
WA-157B	0416
WA-157C	0416
WA-157D	0416
WA-161D	0631
WA-162	0416
WA-162A	0416
WA-162B	0416
WA-162C	0416
WA-162D	0416
WA-167	0416
WA-167A	0416
WA-167B	0416
WA-167C	0416
WA-167D	0416
WA-172	0490
WA-172A	0490
WA-172B	0490
WA-172C	0490
WA-172D	0490
WA-177	0490
WA-177A	0490
WA-177B	0490
WA-177C	0490
WA-177D	0490
WA-182	0490
WA-182A	0490
WA-182B	0490
WA-182C	0490
WA-182D	0490
WA200	OEM
WA-230	0398
WA-230A	0398
WA-230B	0398
WA-230C	0398
WA-230D	0398
WA-240	0398
WA-240A	0398
WA-240B	0398
WA-240C	0398
WA-240D	0398
WA-250	0398
WA-250A	0398
WA-250B	0398
WA-250C	0398
WA-250D	0398
WA-260	0436
WA-260A	0436
WA-260B	0436
WA-260C	0436
WA-260D	0436
WA-270	0436
WA-270A	0436
WA-270B	0436
WA-270C	0436
WA-270D	0436
WA-290	0721
WA-290A	0721
WA-290B	0721
WA-290C	0721
WA-290D	0721
WA-300	0721
WA300	OEM
WA-300A	0721
WA-300B	0721
WA-300C	0721
WA-300D	0721
WA-330A	0039
WA-330B	0039
WA-330C	0039
WA-330D	0039
WA-340	0039
WA-340A	0039
WA-340B	0039
WA-340C	0039
WA-340D	0039
WA400	OEM
WA500	OEM
WA600	OEM
WAC1	OEM
WAC2	OEM
WAC3	OEM
WB-050	0162
WB-050A	0162
WB-050B	0162
WB-050C	0162
WB-050D	0162
WB-052	0162
WB-052A	0162
WB-052B	0162
WB-052C	0162
WB-052D	0162
WB-054	0157
WB-054A	0157
WB-054B	0157
WB-054C	0157
WB-054D	0157
WB-056	0157
WB-056A	0157
WB-056B	0157
WB-056C	0157
WB-056D	0157
WB-058	0157
WB-058A	0157
WB-058B	0157
WB-058C	0157
WB-058D	0157
WB-061	0631
WB-061A	0631
WB-061B	0631
WB-061C	0631
WB-061D	0631
WB-063	0631
WB-063A	0631
WB-063B	0631
WB-063C	0631
WB-063D	0631
WB-065	0631
WB-065A	0631
WB-065B	0631
WB-065C	0631
WB-065D	0631
WB-071	0644
WB-071A	0644
WB-071B	0644
WB-071C	0644
WB-071D	0644
WB-073	0644
WB-073A	0644
WB-073B	0644
WB-073C	0644
WB-073D	0644
WB-075	0644
WB-075A	0644
WB-075B	0644
WB-075C	0644
WB-075D	0644
WB-077	0644
WB-077A	0644
WB-077B	0644
WB-077C	0644
WB-077D	0644
WB-079	0244
WB-079A	0244
WB-079B	0244
WB-079C	0244
WB-081	0244
WB-081A	0244
WB-081B	0244
WB-081C	0244
WB-081D	0244
WB-083	0244
WB-083A	0244
WB-083B	0244
WB-083C	0244
WB-083D	0244
WB-085	0244
WB-085A	0244
WB-085B	0244
WB-085C	0244
WB-085D	0244
WB-088	0012
WB-088A	0012
WB-088B	0012
WB-088C	0012
WB-088D	0012
WB-090	0012
WB-090A	0012
WB-090B	0012
WB-090C	0012
WB-090D	0012
WB-092	0012
WB-092A	0012
WB-092B	0012
WB-092C	0012
WB-092D	0012
WB-094	0012
WB-094A	0012
WB-094B	0012
WB-094C	0012
WB-094D	0012
WB-098	0170
WB-098B	0170
WB-098C	0170
WB-098D	0170
WB9TUI	0321
WB23	OEM
WB-100	0170
WB-100A	0170
WB-100B	0170
WB-100C	0170
WB-100D	0170
WB-110	0313
WB-110A	0313
WB-110B	0313
WB-110C	0313
WB-110D	0313
WB-115	0789
WB-115A	0789
WB-115B	0789
WB-115C	0789
WB-115D	0789
WB-120	0137
WB-120A	0137
WB-120B	0137
WB-120C	0137
WB-120D	0137
WB-125	0361
WB-125A	0361
WB-125B	0361
WB-125C	0361
WB-125D	0361
WB-130	0361
WB-130A	0361
WB-130B	0361
WB-130C	0361
WB-130D	0361

624

If replacement code is OEM, contact original manufacturer for replacement.

DEVICE TYPE	REPL CODE	DEVICE TYPE	REPL CODE	DEVICE TYPE	REPL CODE	DEVICE TYPE	REPL CODE	DEVICE TYPE	REPL CODE	DEVICE TYPE	REPL CODE	DEVICE TYPE	REPL CODE
WB-140	0100	WC-056	0157	WC-120B	0137	WCN02	OEM	WD-092A	0012	WD-230D	0398	WD8250-PL	OEM
WB-140A	0100	WC-056A	0157	WC-120C	0137	WCN04	OEM	WD-092B	0012	WD-240	0398	WD8250A	OEM
WB-140B	0100	WC-056B	0157	WC-120D	0137	WCN06	OEM	WD-092C	0012	WD-240A	0398	WD8250B	OEM
WB-140C	0100	WC-056C	0157	WC-125	0361	WCN08	OEM	WD-092D	0012	WD-240B	0398	WD8250PL-00	OEM
WB-140D	0100	WC-056D	0157	WC-125A	0361	WCN10	OEM	WD-094	0012	WD-240C	0398	WD9216	OEM
WB-150	0002	WC-058	0157	WC-125B	0361	WD001	0604	WD-094A	0012	WD-240D	0398	WE-050	0162
WB-150A	0002	WC-058A	0157	WC-125C	0361	WD002	0604	WD-094B	0012	WD-250	0398	WE-050A	0162
WB-150B	0002	WC-058B	0157	WC-125D	0361	WD003	0015	WD-094C	0012	WD-250A	0398	WE-050B	0162
WB-150C	0002	WC-058C	0157	WC-130	0361	WD004	0604	WD-094D	0012	WD-250B	0398	WE-050C	0162
WB-150D	0002	WC-058D	0157	WC-130A	0361	WD005	0604	WD-098	0170	WD-250C	0398	WE-050D	0162
WB-157	0416	WC-061	0631	WC-130B	0361	WD006	0604	WD-098A	0170	WD-250D	0398	WE-052	0162
WB-157A	0416	WC-061A	0631	WC-130C	0361	WD007	0604	WD-098B	0170	WD-260	0436	WE-052A	0162
WB-157B	0416	WC-061B	0631	WC-130D	0361	WD008	0604	WD-098C	0170	WD-260A	0436	WE-052B	0162
WB-157C	0416	WC-061C	0631	WC-140	0100	WD009	0604	WD-098D	0170	WD-260B	0436	WE-052C	0162
WB-157D	0416	WC-061D	0631	WC-140A	0100	WD010	0604	WD1	0143	WD-260C	0436	WE-052D	0162
WB-162	0416	WC-063	0631	WC-140B	0100	WD011	0604	WD2	0911	WD-260D	0436	WE-054	0157
WB-162A	0416	WC-063A	0631	WC-140C	0100	WD012	0604	WD3	0123	WD-270	0436	WE-054A	0157
WB-162B	0416	WC-063B	0631	WC-140D	0170	WD013	3855	WD4	0133	WD-270A	0436	WE-054B	0157
WB-162C	0416	WC-063C	0631	WC-150	0002	WD014	0015	WD10	0196	WD-270B	0436	WE-054C	0157
WB-162D	0416	WC-063D	0631	WC-150A	0002	WD015	3855	WD10C20-PH	OEM	WD-270C	0436	WE-054D	0157
WB-167	0416	WC-065	0631	WC-150B	0002	WD-050	0162	WD10C20A-PH	OEM	WD-270D	0436	WE-056	0157
WB-167A	0416	WC-065A	0631	WC-150C	0002	WD-050A	0162	WD11	0479	WD-290	0721	WE-056A	0157
WB-167B	0416	WC-065B	0631	WC-150D	0002	WD-050C	0162	WD11C00-JT	OEM	WD-290A	0721	WE-056B	0157
WB-167C	0416	WC-065C	0631	WC-157	0416	WD-052	0162	WD11C00-JU	OEM	WD-290B	0721	WE-056C	0157
WB-167D	0416	WC-065D	0631	WC-157A	0416	WD-052A	0162	WD12	1073	WD-290C	0721	WE-056D	0157
WB-172	0490	WC-071	0644	WC-157B	0416	WD-052B	0162	WD16C92-PL	OEM	WD-290D	0721	WE-058	0157
WB-172A	0490	WC-071A	0644	WC-157C	0416	WD-052C	0162	WD22	0469	WD-300	0721	WE-058A	0157
WB-172B	0490	WC-071B	0644	WC-157D	0416	WD-052D	0162	WD37C65	OEM	WD-300B	0721	WE-058B	0157
WB-172C	0490	WC-071C	0644	WC-162	0416	WD-054	0157	WD51A	OEM	WD-300C	0721	WE-058C	0157
WB-172D	0490	WC-071D	0644	WC-162A	0416	WD-054A	0644	WD51B	OEM	WD-300D	0721	WE-058D	0157
WB-177	0490	WC-073	0644	WC-162B	0416	WD-054B	0157	WD55A	OEM	WD-330	0039	WE-061	0157
WB-177A	0490	WC-073A	0644	WC-162C	0416	WD-054C	0157	WD55B	OEM	WD-330A	0039	WE-061A	0631
WB-177B	0490	WC-073B	0644	WC-162D	0416	WD-054D	0157	WD61	0015	WD-330B	0039	WE-061B	0631
WB-177C	0490	WC-073C	0644	WC-167	0416	WD-056	0157	WD74HC200E	OEM	WD-330C	0039	WE-061C	0631
WB-177D	0490	WC-073D	0644	WC-167A	0416	WD-056A	0157	WD74HC200F	OEM	WD-330D	0039	WE-061D	0631
WB-182	0490	WC-075	0644	WC-167B	0416	WD-056B	0157	WD-100	0170	WD-340	0039	WE-063	0631
WB-182A	0490	WC-075A	0644	WC-167C	0416	WD-056C	0157	WD-100A	0170	WD-340A	0039	WE-063A	0631
WB-182B	0490	WC-075B	0644	WC-167D	0416	WD-056D	0157	WD-100B	0170	WD-340B	0039	WE-063B	0631
WB-182C	0490	WC-075C	0644	WC-172	0490	WD-058	0157	WD-100C	0170	WD-340C	0039	WE-063C	0631
WB-182D	0490	WC-075D	0644	WC-172A	0490	WD-058A	0157	WD-100D	0170	WD-340D	0039	WE-063D	0631
WB-230	0398	WC-077	0644	WC-172B	0490	WD-058B	0157	WD-110	0313	WD900	OEM	WE-065	0631
WB-230A	0398	WC-077A	0644	WC-172C	0490	WD-058C	0157	WD-110A	0313	WD1000	OEM	WE-065A	0631
WB-230B	0398	WC-077B	0644	WC-172D	0490	WD-058D	0157	WD-110B	0313	WD1010-PL	OEM	WE-065B	0631
WB-230C	0398	WC-077C	0644	WC-177	0490	WD-061	0631	WD-110C	0313	WD1010A-PL	OEM	WE-065C	0631
WB-230D	0398	WC-077D	0644	WC-177A	0490	WD-061A	0631	WD-110D	0313	WD1012	0143	WE-065D	0631
WB-240	0398	WC-079	0244	WC-177B	0490	WD-061B	0631	WD-115	0789	WD1014-CL	OEM	WE-071	0644
WB-240A	0398	WC-079A	0244	WC-177C	0490	WD-061C	0631	WD-115A	0789	WD1015-PL	OEM	WE-071A	0644
WB-240B	0398	WC-079B	0244	WC-177D	0490	WD-061D	0631	WD-115B	0789	WD1100-01U	OEM	WE-071B	0644
WB-240C	0398	WC-079C	0244	WC-182	0490	WD-063	0631	WD-115C	0789	WD1100-01V	OEM	WE-071C	0644
WB-240D	0398	WC-079D	0244	WC-182A	0490	WD-063A	0631	WD-115D	0789	WD1100-02U	OEM	WE-071D	0644
WB-250	0398	WC-081	0244	WC-182B	0490	WD-063B	0631	WD-120	0137	WD1100-02V	OEM	WE-073	0644
WB-250A	0398	WC-081A	0244	WC-182C	0490	WD-063C	0631	WD-120A	0137	WD1100-05U	OEM	WE-073A	0644
WB-250B	0398	WC-081B	0244	WC-182D	0398	WD-063D	0631	WD-120B	0137	WD1100-05V	OEM	WE-073B	0644
WB-250C	0398	WC-081C	0244	WC-230	0398	WD-065	0631	WD-120C	0137	WD1510E00	OEM	WE-073C	0644
WB-250D	0398	WC-081D	0244	WC-230A	0398	WD-065A	0631	WD-120D	0137	WD1510E01	OEM	WE-073D	0644
WB-260	0436	WC-083	0244	WC-230B	0398	WD-065B	0631	WD-125	0361	WD1510F00	OEM	WE-075	0644
WB-260A	0436	WC-083A	0244	WC-230C	0398	WD-065C	0631	WD-125A	0361	WD1510F01	OEM	WE-075A	0644
WB-260B	0436	WC-083B	0244	WC-230D	0398	WD-065D	0631	WD-125B	0361	WD1511E	OEM	WE-075B	0644
WB-260C	0436	WC-083C	0244	WC-240	0398	WD-071	0644	WD-125C	0361	WD1511F	OEM	WE-075C	0644
WB-260D	0436	WC-083D	0244	WC-240A	0398	WD-071A	0644	WD-125D	0361	WD1691PE-00-02	OEM	WE-075D	0644
WB-270	0436	WC-085	0244	WC-240B	0398	WD-071B	0644	WD-130	0361	WD1691U	OEM	WE-077	0644
WB-270A	0436	WC-085A	0244	WC-240C	0398	WD-071C	0644	WD-130A	0361	WD1691V	OEM	WE-077A	0644
WB-270B	0436	WC-085B	0244	WC-240D	0398	WD-071D	0644	WD-130B	0361	WD1770-PH	OEM	WE-077B	0644
WB-270C	0436	WC-085C	0244	WC-250	0398	WD-073	0644	WD-130C	0361	WD1772-PH	OEM	WE-077C	0644
WB-270D	0436	WC-085D	0244	WC-250A	0398	WD-073A	0644	WD-130D	0361	WD1773	OEM	WE-077D	0644
WB-290	0721	WC-088	0012	WC-250B	0398	WD-073B	0644	WD-140	0100	WD1773-PH	OEM	WE-079	0244
WB-290A	0721	WC-088A	0012	WC-250C	0398	WD-073C	0644	WD-140A	0100	WD1773PH-00	OEM	WE-079A	0244
WB-290B	0721	WC-088B	0012	WC-250D	0398	WD-073D	0644	WD-140B	0100	WD1793	OEM	WE-079B	0244
WB-290C	0721	WC-088C	0012	WC-260	0436	WD-075	0644	WD-140C	0100	WD1931A	OEM	WE-079C	0244
WB-290D	0721	WC-090	0012	WC-260A	0436	WD-075A	0644	WD-140D	0100	WD1931B	OEM	WE-079D	0244
WB-300	0721	WC-090A	0012	WC-260B	0436	WD-075B	0644	WD-150	0002	WD1933A	OEM	WE-081	0244
WB-300A	0721	WC-090B	0012	WC-260C	0436	WD-075C	0644	WD-150A	0002	WD1933B	OEM	WE-081A	0244
WB-300B	0721	WC-090C	0012	WC-260D	0436	WD-075D	0644	WD-150B	0002	WD1983E	OEM	WE-081B	0244
WB-300C	0721	WC-090D	0012	WC-270	0436	WD-077	0644	WD-150C	0002	WD1983F	OEM	WE-081C	0244
WB-300D	0721	WC-092	0012	WC-270A	0436	WD-077A	0644	WD-150D	0002	WD1984E	OEM	WE-081D	0244
WB-330	0039	WC-092A	0012	WC-270B	0436	WD-077B	0644	WD-157	0416	WD1984F	OEM	WE-083	0244
WB-330A	0039	WC-092B	0012	WC-270C	0436	WD-077C	0644	WD-157A	0416	WD1993	OEM	WE-083A	0244
WB-330B	0039	WC-092C	0012	WC-270D	0436	WD-077D	0644	WD-157B	0416	WD1993E	OEM	WE-083B	0244
WB-330C	0039	WC-092D	0012	WC-290	0721	WD-079	0244	WD-157C	0416	WD1993F	OEM	WE-083C	0244
WB-330D	0039	WC-094	0012	WC-290A	0721	WD-079A	0244	WD-157D	0416	WD2001E	OEM	WE-083D	0244
WB-340	0039	WC-094A	0012	WC-290B	0721	WD-079B	0244	WD-162	0416	WD2001F	OEM	WE-085	0244
WB-340A	0039	WC-094B	0012	WC-290C	0721	WD-079C	0244	WD-162A	0416	WD2002A	OEM	WE-085A	0244
WB-340B	0039	WC-094C	0012	WC-290D	0721	WD-079D	0244	WD-162B	0416	WD2002B	OEM	WE-085B	0244
WB-340C	0039	WC-094D	0012	WC-300	0721	WD-081	0244	WD-162C	0416	WD2010B-PL	OEM	WE-085C	0244
WB-340D	0039	WC-098	0170	WC-300A	0721	WD-081A	0244	WD-162D	0416	WD2123	OEM	WE-085D	0244
WBC1	OEM	WC-098A	0170	WC-300B	0721	WD-081B	0244	WD-167	0416	WD2123A	OEM	WE-088	0012
WBC2	OEM	WC-098B	0170	WC-300C	0721	WD-081C	0244	WD-167A	0416	WD2123B	OEM	WE-088A	0012
WBC3	OEM	WC-098C	0170	WC-300D	0721	WD-081D	0244	WD-167B	0416	WD2143-01	OEM	WE-088B	0012
WBC4	OEM	WC-098D	0170	WC-330	0039	WD-083	0244	WD-167C	0416	WD2143L01	OEM	WE-088C	0012
WBC5	OEM	WC6B	OEM	WC-330A	0039	WD-083A	0244	WD-167D	0416	WD2143M	OEM	WE-088D	0012
WBC6	OEM	WC-88D	0012	WC-330B	0039	WD-083B	0244	WD-172	0490	WD2143M01	OEM	WE-090	0012
WBC7	OEM	WC-100	0170	WC-330C	0039	WD-083C	0244	WD-172A	0490	WD2293-PE	OEM	WE-090A	0012
WBC8	OEM	WC-100A	0170	WC-330D	0039	WD-083D	0244	WD-172B	0490	WD2293A-PE	OEM	WE-090B	0012
WBC9	OEM	WC-100B	0170	WC-340	0039	WD-085	0244	WD-172C	0490	WD2501	OEM	WE-090C	0012
WC-050	0162	WC-100C	0170	WC-340A	0039	WD-085A	0244	WD-172D	0490	WD2501-11	OEM	WE-090D	0012
WC-050A	0162	WC-100D	0170	WC-340B	0039	WD-085B	0244	WD-177	0490	WD2511	OEM	WE-092	0012
WC-050B	0162	WC-110	0313	WC-340C	0039	WD-085C	0244	WD-177A	0490	WD2793A-PL	OEM	WE-092A	0012
WC-050C	0162	WC-110A	0313	WC-340D	0039	WD-085D	0244	WD-177B	0490	WD2793A-PL02-04	OEM	WE-092B	0012
WC-050D	0162	WC-110B	0313	WC501G	OEM	WD-088	0012	WD-177C	0490	WD4020A	OEM	WE-092C	0012
WC-052	0162	WC-110C	0313	WC501P	OEM	WD-088A	0012	WD-177D	0490	WD4020AE	OEM	WE-092D	0012
WC-052A	0162	WC-110D	0313	WC535P	OEM	WD-088B	0012	WD-182	0490	WD4020B	OEM	WE-094	0012
WC-052B	0162	WC-115	0789	WC14020	0015	WD-088C	0012	WD-182A	0490	WD4020BE	OEM	WE-094A	0012
WC-052C	0162	WC-115A	0789	WC14027	0015	WD-088D	0012	WD-182B	0490	WD4200E	OEM	WE-094B	0012
WC-052D	0162	WC-115B	0789	WC19862	0208	WD-090	0012	WD-182C	0490	WD4200F	OEM	WE-094C	0012
WC-054	0157	WC-115C	0789	WC19862A	0164	WD-090A	0012	WD-182D	0490	WD4210E	OEM	WE-094D	0012
WC-054A	0157	WC-115D	0789	WC19863	0004	WD-090B	0012	WD-230	0398	WD4210F	OEM	WE-098	0170
WC-054B	0157	WC-120	0137	WC19864	0004	WD-090C	0012	WD-230A	0398	WD5869J	OEM	WE-098A	0170
WC-054C	0157	WC120	0015	WC19865	0015	WD-090D	0012	WD-230B	0398	WD5869K	OEM	WE-098B	0170
WC-054D	0157	WC-120A	0137	WCN005	OEM	WD-092	0012	WD-230C	0398	WD8250	OEM	WE-098C	0170

If replacement code is OEM, contact original manufacturer for replacement. 625

DEVICE TYPE	REPL CODE
WE-098D	0170
WE-100	0170
WE-100A	0170
WE-100B	0170
WE-100C	0170
WE-100D	0170
WE-110	0313
WE-110A	0313
WE-110B	0313
WE-110C	0313
WE-110D	0170
WE-115	0789
WE-115A	0789
WE-115B	0789
WE-115C	0789
WE-115D	0789
WE-120	0137
WE-120A	0137
WE-120B	0137
WE-120C	0137
WE-120D	0137
WE-125	0361
WE-125A	0361
WE-125B	0361
WE-125C	0361
WE-125D	0361
WE-130	0361
WE-130A	0361
WE-130B	0361
WE-130C	0361
WE-130D	0361
WE-140	0100
WE-140A	0100
WE-140B	0100
WE-140C	0100
WE-140D	0100
WE-150	0002
WE-150A	0002
WE-150B	0002
WE-150C	0002
WE-150D	0002
WE-157	0416
WE-157A	0416
WE-157B	0416
WE-157C	0416
WE-157D	0416
WE-162	0416
WE-162A	0416
WE-162B	0416
WE-162C	0416
WE-162D	0416
WE-167	0416
WE-167A	0416
WE-167B	0416
WE-167C	0416
WE-167D	0416
WE-172	0490
WE-172A	0490
WE-172B	0490
WE-172C	0490
WE-172D	0490
WE-177	0490
WE-177A	0490
WE-177B	0490
WE-177C	0490
WE-177D	0490
WE-182	0490
WE-182A	0490
WE-182B	0490
WE-182C	0490
WE-182D	0490
WE183P	OEM
WE-230	0398
WE-230A	0398
WE-230B	0398
WE-230C	0398
WE-230D	0398
WE-240	0398
WE-240A	0398
WE-240B	0398
WE-240C	0398
WE-240D	0398
WE-250	0398
WE-250A	0398
WE-250B	0398
WE-250C	0398
WE-250D	0398
WE-260	0436
WE-260A	0436
WE-260B	0436
WE-260C	0436
WE-260D	0436
WE-270	0436
WE-270A	0436
WE-270B	0436
WE-270C	0436
WE-270D	0436
WE-290	0721
WE-290A	0721
WE-290B	0721
WE-290C	0721
WE-290D	0721
WE-300	0721
WE-300A	0721
WE-300B	0721
WE-300C	0721
WE-300D	0721
WE-330	0039
WE-330A	0039
WE-330C	0039
WE-330D	0039
WE-340	0039
WE-340A	0039
WE-340B	0039
WE-340C	0039
WE-340D	0039
WE530P	OEM
WE4110	0512
WE13400	OEM
WE0704/130	0103
WEP2	0279
WEP3	0050
WEP10	0628
WEP14	OEM
WEP15/512	2074
WEP16/511	1440
WEP17	1296
WEP17/508	1296
WEP18	2072
WEP18/509	2072
WEP19	2073
WEP19/510	2073
WEP50	0079
WEP51	0126
WEP52	0037
WEP53	0018
WEP54	2833
WEP55	2528
WEP56	0144
WEP56/108	0144
WEP57	0037
WEP58	0198
WEP58/123	0198
WEP59	0086
WEP59/128	0086
WEP60	0126
WEP60/129	0126
WEP61	0275
WEP61/157	0275
WEP62	0037
WEP62/159	0037
WEP63	0007
WEP63/161	0007
WEP64	0855
WEP64/194	0855
WEP65	0279
WEP66	0111
WEP66/199	0111
WEP67	3477
WEP67/232	3477
WEP68	0710
WEP68/287	0710
WEP89/89	0055
WEP93	OEM
WEP93/502	0201
WEP94	0286
WEP94/503	0286
WEP95	OEM
WEP95/504	0374
WEP100	0279
WEP100/100	0279
WEP101	0170
WEP102	0188
WEP103	0631
WEP103A	0644
WEP104	0012
WEP105	0137
WEP106	0150
WEP106/106	0150
WEP118	0769
WEP118/118	0769
WEP119	0102
WEP119/119	1293
WEP120	OEM
WEP125	OEM
WEP125/358	1024
WEP125/358B	4947
WEP126	OEM
WEP126/358A	4391
WEP134	0143
WEP134/109	0143
WEP138	0143
WEP139	0911
WEP139/112	0911
WEP152	0023
WEP152/552	0023
WEP154	1325
WEP155	0080
WEP156	0604
WEP157	0790
WEP158	0015
WEP158/116	0015
WEP158A	0071
WEP159	0072
WEP160	0071
WEP164	2934
WEP164/114	0479
WEP165	0196
WEP165/113	0196
WEP165A	0479
WEP166	1073
WEP166/115	1073
WEP167	2937
WEP168	0469
WEP168/120	0469
WEP169	2938
WEP170	0071
WEP170/125	0071
WEP172	0102
WEP172/506	0102
WEP173	0023
WEP175	0023
WEP177	0133
WEP177/525	0344
WEP178	1780
WEP178/518	1780
WEP179	OEM
WEP180	0290
WEP181	0190
WEP182	0290
WEP182/173AP	0290
WEP183	0286
WEP184	0374
WEP185	0752
WEP186	0102
WEP187	0004
WEP188	1493
WEP189	2949
WEP189/HI-DIV-1	2949
WEP190	2950
WEP190/HI-DIV-2	2950
WEP191	2951
WEP192	1061
WEP193	2952
WEP195	2954
WEP195/534	2954
WEP196	2955
WEP197	2956
WEP197/538	2956
WEP198	2957
WEP199	1493
WEP199/522	1493
WEP200	0030
WEP203	0405
WEP215	1313
WEP215/513	1313
WEP221	1671
WEP221/180	1671
WEP221MP	1671
WEP222	0130
WEP222/181	0130
WEP224	0626
WEP224/224	0626
WEP227	0164
WEP227/158	0164
WEP228	2736
WEP228/155	2736
WEP229	0222
WEP229/131	0222
WEP229MP	0816
WEP229MP/131MP	0816
WEP230	0085
WEP230MP	3004
WEP231	0435
WEP232	0160
WEP232MP	0265
WEP233	0435
WEP233/105	0435
WEP234	0160
WEP234/121	0160
WEP234MP	0265
WEP234MP/121MP	0265
WEP235	0969
WEP235/127	0969
WEP236	0432
WEP236/213	0432
WEP238	1414
WEP239	0841
WEP239/176	0841
WEP240	0142
WEP240/124	0142
WEP241	0178
WEP241/175	0178
WEP242	0126
WEP243	0086
WEP244	0275
WEP245	0161
WEP246	0455
WEP247	0538
WEP247MP	2355
WEP248	1588
WEP250	0211
WEP250/102	0211
WEP253	0164
WEP254	0208
WEP255	0787
WEP261/261	1203
WEP273	0558
WEP273/373	0558
WEP308	1659
WEP308/6400	1659
WEP309	2123
WEP310	1167
WEP310/6410	1167
WEP350	0916
WEP367	0222
WEP371	0191
WEP372	0076
WEP373	0076
WEP374/374	0520
WEP379/379	0723
WEP380	0284
WEP391/391	0853
WEP394	0155
WEP403	0155
WEP405	0164
WEP454	0076
WEP458	0076
WEP460	0151
WEP474	1004
WEP474/226	1004
WEP474MP	1851
WEP474MP/226MP	1851
WEP481	0222
WEP495	0006
WEP500	0627
WEP500/703A	0627
WEP501	2600
WEP501/704	2600
WEP502	2147
WEP502/705A	2147
WEP503	0748
WEP503/707	0748
WEP504	0659
WEP504/708	0659
WEP505	0673
WEP505/709	0673
WEP506	0823
WEP506/710	0823
WEP507	0167
WEP507/712	0167
WEP508	0661
WEP508/713	0661
WEP509	0348
WEP509/714	0348
WEP510	0350
WEP510/715	0350
WEP511	0649
WEP511/718	0649
WEP512	0438
WEP512/720	0438
WEP513	0696
WEP513/722	0696
WEP514	0687
WEP515	OEM
WEP515/725	0687
WEP517	1401
WEP535	0127
WEP535/107	0127
WEP536	0532
WEP537	0191
WEP538	0079
WEP564	0203
WEP568	0111
WEP601/601	0139
WEP602	0162
WEP603	0157
WEP604	0789
WEP605	0361
WEP605/605	0120
WEP606	0100
WEP607	0002
WEP608	0436
WEP609	0039
WEP610	1823
WEP611	0778
WEP612	0327
WEP613	0149
WEP615/615	1319
WEP620	0004
WEP620/102A	0004
WEP621	0050
WEP621/160	0050
WEP624	0085
WEP624/104	0085
WEP624MP	3004
WEP624MP/104MP	3004
WEP628	0085
WEP628MP	0085
WEP630	0164
WEP631	0211
WEP632	0004
WEP633	2064
WEP634	2064
WEP635	0136
WEP635/126	0136
WEP637	0050
WEP641	0595
WEP641/101	0595
WEP641A	0038
WEP641A/103	0038
WEP641B	0208
WEP641B/103A	0208
WEP642	0222
WEP642MP	0222
WEP643	0222
WEP643MP	OEM
WEP644	0111
WEP645	0599
WEP645/179	0599
WEP700	0455
WEP701	0161
WEP702	0283
WEP702/171	0283
WEP703	0178
WEP704	0103
WEP704/130	0103
WEP705	2427
WEP706	2427
WEP707	0074
WEP707/162	0074
WEP707MP	0074
WEP708	0224
WEP709	1136
WEP710	0364
WEP711	0414
WEP712	0488
WEP713	0233
WEP713/154	0233
WEP714	OEM
WEP714/321	0130
WEP715	0527
WEP716	0037
WEP717	0037
WEP719	0224
WEP720	0224
WEP723	0016
WEP724	0016
WEP728	0016
WEP729	0016
WEP735	0016
WEP735A	0191
WEP736	0079
WEP736/123A	0016
WEP740	0637
WEP740/163	0637
WEP740A	0003
WEP740A/164	0003
WEP740B	0065
WEP740B/165	0065
WEP741	0899
WEP741/218	0899
WEP744	1021
WEP744/286	1021
WEP744MP	OEM
WEP745	0042
WEP745/152	0042
WEP746	0919
WEP746/153	0919
WEP747	0556
WEP747/182	0556
WEP748	1190
WEP748/183	1190
WEP749	0264
WEP749/190	0264
WEP750	0164
WEP751	0555
WEP751/186	0555
WEP752	1257
WEP752/187	1257
WEP753	0590
WEP753/192	0590
WEP754	0786
WEP754/193	0786
WEP755	0693
WEP755/195A	0693
WEP756	0419
WEP756/196	0419
WEP757	0848
WEP757/197	0848
WEP758	0561
WEP758/210	0561
WEP759	1357
WEP759/211	1357
WEP760	0486
WEP760/219	0486
WEP761	2085
WEP761/369	2085
WEP762	3249
WEP762/225	3249
WEP763	0388
WEP763/375	0388
WEP764	0309
WEP764/238	0309
WEP765	3136
WEP765/242	3136
WEP766	2200
WEP766/277	2200
WEP767	0414
WEP767/278	0414
WEP768	0615
WEP768/280MP	2127
WEP768/328	0615
WEP768MP	2127
WEP769	2002
WEP769/281	2002
WEP770	0359
WEP770/283	0359
WEP771	1935
WEP771/306	1935
WEP772	1136
WEP773	0783
WEP774	3258
WEP775	0538
WEP775/284	0538
WEP775MP	2355
WEP775MP/284MP	2355
WEP776	1588
WEP776/285	1588
WEP777	1401
WEP778	1401
WEP779	0168
WEP779/198	0168
WEP780	0236
WEP780/291	0236
WEP781	0676
WEP781/292	0676
WEP782	2918
WEP782/317	2918
WEP783	2296
WEP783/318	2296
WEP784	1136
WEP785	0833
WEP785/235	0833
WEP799	1401
WEP799/237	1401
WEP801	3017
WEP801/133	3017
WEP802	0321
WEP802/132	3667
WEP803	OEM
WEP810	2156
WEP811	1189
WEP811/325	1189
WEP812	1963
WEP812/320	1963
WEP813	0488
WEP814	OEM
WEP821/821	2804
WEP822/822	2785
WEP828	1211
WEP829	0151
WEP838	0191
WEP840	0830
WEP840/236	0830
WEP850	2675
WEP850/329	2675
WEP851	0617
WEP852	0886
WEP853	1973
WEP853/322	1973
WEP854	0334
WEP854/191	0334
WEP855	0818
WEP856	3294
WEP857	0378
WEP857/189	0378
WEP858	0546
WEP858/188	0546
WEP880	0161
WEP880/184	0161
WEP881	0477
WEP882	1359
WEP883	0455
WEP883/185	0455
WEP900	0219
WEP900/186A	0219
WEP901	1421
WEP901/307	1421
WEP903	0843
WEP903/220	0843
WEP904	0349
WEP904/221	0349
WEP905	0212
WEP905/222	0212
WEP906	0326
WEP906/233	0326
WEP907	0688
WEP907/234	0688
WEP908	2969
WEP908/241	2969
WEP909	0617
WEP909/282	0617
WEP910	0155
WEP910/289	0155
WEP911	0006
WEP911/290	0006
WEP911/290A	0006
WEP912	0018
WEP912/293	0018
WEP913	1581
WEP913/295	1581
WEP914	0320
WEP914/297	0320
WEP915	0431
WEP915/298	0431
WEP916	0527
WEP916/294	0527
WEP917	2035
WEP917/300	2035
WEP918	1165
WEP918/302	1165
WEP920	0321
WEP920/312	0321
WEP921	0470
WEP921/313	0470
WEP922	1967
WEP922/315	1967
WEP923	0259
WEP923/316	0259
WEP924	2874
WEP924/319	2874
WEP925	0124
WEP925/519	0124
WEP926	0817
WEP926/724	0817
WEP927	2593
WEP927/726	2593
WEP928	0512
WEP929	0718
WEP930	1865
WEP931	1070
WEP933	0308
WEP933/941M	0308
WEP934	1226
WEP934/1000	1226
WEP935	0021
WEP935/1012	0021
WEP936	2390
WEP937	2111
WEP937/1058	2111
WEP938	0465
WEP938/1075A	0465
WEP939	2246
WEP939/1082	2246
WEP941	0905
WEP941/1100	0905
WEP942	2608
WEP942/1102	2608
WEP943	1983
WEP943/1103	1983
WEP944	2046
WEP944/1104	2046
WEP945	2145
WEP945/1113	2145
WEP946	1909
WEP946/1118	1909
WEP948	3332
WEP948/1153	3332
WEP949	1044
WEP949/1155	1044
WEP950	0508
WEP950/4017	0508
WEP953	0087
WEP954	0087
WEP955	3298
WEP955/6407	3298
WEP956	0224
WEP956/229	0224
WEP959	3336
WEP959/274	3336
WEP962	1272
WEP962/5812	1272
WEP963	1277
WEP963/5814	1277
WEP964	1282
WEP964/5815	1282
WEP965	1285
WEP966	1285
WEP966/5817	1285
WEP966L/966	0330
WEP968	0338
WEP968/288	0338
WEP969	0488
WEP969/311	0488
WEP970	OEM
WEP971	0396
WEP971/172	0396
WEP972	2411
WEP972/243	2411
WEP973	2262
WEP973/244	2262
WEP974	3339
WEP974/245	3339
WEP975	3340
WEP975/246	3340
WEP976	2422
WEP976/247	2422
WEP977	2415
WEP977/248	2415
WEP984	3343
WEP984/257	3343
WEP986/986	3060
WEP989	3347
WEP989/989	3347
WEP992	2243
WEP992/265	2243
WEP1008	0025
WEP1010	0244
WEP1014	2035
WEP1018	2039
WEP1018/299	2039
WEP1043	0319
WEP1044	1404
WEP1045	0468
WEP1046	0441
WEP1050	0276
WEP1051	0276
WEP1051/166	0276
WEP1052	0287
WEP1052/167	0287
WEP1053	0293
WEP1053/168	0293
WEP1054	0299
WEP1054/169	0299
WEP1056	0250
WEP1056/170	0250
WEP1060	0133
WEP1061	0907
WEP1061/178MP	0907
WEP1062	0133
WEP1062/177	0133
WEP1065	5386
WEP1066	2347
WEP1066/5322	1404
WEP1067	2353
WEP1067/5324	0468
WEP1075	0911
WEP1076	0312
WEP1076/6402	0312
WEP1077	4169
WEP1077/6403	4169
WEP1078	3373
WEP1078/6404	3373
WEP1079	4335
WEP1079/6405	4335
WEP1080	2704
WEP1080/6408	2704
WEP1082	0015
WEP1083	0015
WEP1096	0386
WEP1100	0451
WEP1100/5067	0451

If replacement code is OEM, contact original manufacturer for replacement.

DEVICE TYPE	REPL CODE
WEP1102	0446
WEP1102/5069	0446
WEP1103	0162
WEP1103/135	0162
WEP1104	0157
WEP1104/136	0157
WEP1106	0025
WEP1106/5071	0025
WEP1107	0644
WEP1107/138	0644
WEP1108	0244
WEP1108/5072	0244
WEP1109	0012
WEP1109/139	0012
WEP1110	0170
WEP1110/140	0170
WEP1112	0137
WEP1112/142	0137
WEP1114	0002
WEP1114/145	0002
WEP1116	0490
WEP1116/5077	0490
WEP1118	0560
WEP1118/5080	0560
WEP1120	0436
WEP1120/146	0436
WEP1122	0039
WEP1122/147	0039
WEP1124	0346
WEP1124/5086	0346
WEP1126	0993
WEP1126/5088	0993
WEP1128	0863
WEP1128/5090	0863
WEP1130	2144
WEP1130/5092	1258
WEP1132	0327
WEP1132/150	0327
WEP1134	0098
WEP1134/5096	0098
WEP1136	0186
WEP1136/5097	0186
WEP1138	0028
WEP1138/5100	0028
WEP1140	0363
WEP1140/5103	0363
WEP1145/5061	2975
WEP1147	1302
WEP1147/5063	1302
WEP1148	2981
WEP1148/5064	2981
WEP1149	1703
WEP1149/5065	1703
WEP1150	0289
WEP1150/5066	0289
WEP1151	0188
WEP1151/134	0188
WEP1152	0528
WEP1152/5068	0528
WEP1153	0298
WEP1153/5070	0298
WEP1154	0631
WEP1154/137	0631
WEP1155	1075
WEP1155/5073	1075
WEP1156	0313
WEP1156/5074	0313
WEP1157	0789
WEP1157/141	0789
WEP1158	0361
WEP1158/143	0361
WEP1159	0100
WEP1159/144	0100
WEP1160	0416
WEP1160/5075	0416
WEP1161	1639
WEP1161/5076	1639
WEP1162	0943
WEP1162/5078	0943
WEP1163	0526
WEP1163/5079	0526
WEP1164	0398
WEP1164/5081	0398
WEP1165	1596
WEP1165/5082	1596
WEP1166	1664
WEP1166/5083	1664
WEP1167	0721
WEP1167/5084	0721
WEP1168	0814
WEP1168/5085	0814
WEP1169	0925
WEP1169/5087	0925
WEP1172	0497
WEP1172/5089	0497
WEP1174	1823
WEP1174/148	1823
WEP1175	1148
WEP1175/5091	1148
WEP1176	0778
WEP1176/149	0778
WEP1177	1181
WEP1177/5093	1181
WEP1178	2997
WEP1178/5094	2997
WEP1179	1301
WEP1179/5095	1301
WEP1181	0149
WEP1181/151	0149
WEP1182	0213
WEP1182/5098	0213
WEP1183	0245
WEP1183/5099	0245
WEP1184	0255
WEP1184/5101	0255
WEP1185	0871
WEP1185/5102	0871
WEP1187	2831
WEP1187/5104	2831
WEP1188	0417
WEP1188/5105	0417
WEP1200	0801
WEP1204	0870
WEP1206	0205
WEP1208	0499
WEP1212	0234
WEP1214	0251
WEP1231/1231	1162
WEP1237	0930
WEP1239	1897
WEP1246/1246	4554
WEP1300	2024
WEP1300/5174	2024
WEP1300R	0542
WEP1300R/5174K	0542
WEP1302	1429
WEP1302/5176	1429
WEP1302R	2101
WEP1302R/5176K	2101
WEP1304	1436
WEP1304/5178	1436
WEP1304R	1890
WEP1304R/5178K	1890
WEP1306	1449
WEP1306/5181	1449
WEP1306R	1591
WEP1306R/5181K	1591
WEP1307	0830
WEP1308	1481
WEP1308/5183	1481
WEP1308R	1612
WEP1308R/5183R	1612
WEP1310	0505
WEP1310/5186	0505
WEP1310R	0986
WEP1310R/5186K	0986
WEP1312	0864
WEP1312/5188	0864
WEP1312R	1254
WEP1312R/5188K	1254
WEP1314	1264
WEP1314/5191	1264
WEP1314R	1629
WEP1314R/5191K	1629
WEP1316	1071
WEP1316/5194	1071
WEP1316R	1706
WEP1316R/5194K	1706
WEP1318	1712
WEP1318/5197	1712
WEP1318R	0722
WEP1318R/5197K	0722
WEP1320	1750
WEP1320/5200	1750
WEP1320R	1771
WEP1320R/5200K	1771
WEP1322	1750
WEP1322/5203	1777
WEP1322R	1788
WEP1322R/5203K	1788
WEP1324	1793
WEP1324/5205	1793
WEP1324R	1806
WEP1324R/5205K	1806
WEP1326	0022
WEP1326/5208	0022
WEP1326R	1842
WEP1326R/5208K	1842
WEP1328	0207
WEP1328/5212	0207
WEP1328R	1873
WEP1328R/5212K	1873
WEP1330	0306
WEP1330/5215	0306
WEP1330R	1891
WEP1330R/5215K	1891
WEP1332	0352
WEP1332/5217	0352
WEP1332R	1898
WEP1332R/5217K	1898
WEP1334	0433
WEP1334/5220	0433
WEP1334R	1155
WEP1334R/5220K	1155
WEP1336	0504
WEP1336/5223	0504
WEP1336R	1930
WEP1336R/5223K	1930
WEP1338	0063
WEP1338/5226	0063
WEP1338R	1950
WEP1338R/5226K	1950
WEP1340	0611
WEP1340/5230	0611
WEP1340R	0771
WEP1340R/5230K	0771
WEP1400	1266
WEP1400/5000	1266
WEP1401	2847
WEP1401/5001	2847
WEP1402	0755
WEP1402/5002	0755
WEP1403	0672
WEP1403/5003	0672
WEP1404	0118
WEP1404/5004	0118
WEP1405	0296
WEP1405/5005	0296
WEP1406	0372
WEP1406/5006	0372
WEP1407	0036
WEP1407/5007	0036
WEP1408	0274
WEP1408/5008	0274
WEP1409	0140
WEP1409/5009	0140
WEP1410	2599
WEP1410/1410	2599
WEP1411	0041
WEP1411/5010	0041
WEP1412	0253
WEP1412/5011	0253
WEP1413	0091
WEP1413/5012	0091
WEP1414	0466
WEP1414/5013	0466
WEP1415	0062
WEP1415/5014	0062
WEP1416	0077
WEP1416/5015	0077
WEP1416L/1416	0069
WEP1417	0165
WEP1417/5016	0165
WEP1417L/1417	2601
WEP1418	0318
WEP1418/5017	0318
WEP1419	0057
WEP1419/5018	0057
WEP1420	0064
WEP1420/5019	0064
WEP1421	0181
WEP1421/5020	0181
WEP1423	0052
WEP1423/5021	0052
WEP1424	0053
WEP1424/5022	0053
WEP1425	0873
WEP1425/5023	0873
WEP1426	0681
WEP1426/5024	0681
WEP1427	0440
WEP1427/5025	0440
WEP1428	6790
WEP1428/5026	0210
WEP1429	0371
WEP1429/5027	0371
WEP1430	0666
WEP1430/5028	0666
WEP1431	0695
WEP1431/5029	0695
WEP1432	0700
WEP1432/5030	0700
WEP1433	0489
WEP1433/5031	0489
WEP1434	0709
WEP1434/5032	0709
WEP1435	0450
WEP1435/5033	0450
WEP1436	0257
WEP1436/5034	0257
WEP1437	0195
WEP1437/5035	0195
WEP1438	0166
WEP1438/5036	0166
WEP1439	0010
WEP1439/5037	0010
WEP1440	0032
WEP1440/5038	0032
WEP1440L/1440	3692
WEP1441	0054
WEP1441/5039	0054
WEP1443	0068
WEP1443/5040	0068
WEP1445	0092
WEP1445/5041	0092
WEP1448	0125
WEP1448/5042	0125
WEP1449	2301
WEP1449/5043	2301
WEP1450	0152
WEP1450/5044	0152
WEP1451	0173
WEP1451/5045	0173
WEP1452	0094
WEP1452/5046	0094
WEP1453	0049
WEP1453/5047	0049
WEP1454	0104
WEP1454/5048	0104
WEP1455	0156
WEP1455/5049	0156
WEP1456	0189
WEP1456/5050	0189
WEP1458	0099
WEP1458/5051	0099
WEP1459	0089
WEP1459/5052	0089
WEP1460	0285
WEP1460/5053	0285
WEP1461	0252
WEP1461/5054	0252
WEP1462	0336
WEP1462/5055	0336
WEP1463	0366
WEP1463/5056	0366
WEP1464	0390
WEP1464/5057	0390
WEP1466	0420
WEP1466/5058	0420
WEP1467	0448
WEP1467/5059	0448
WEP1468	1464
WEP1468/50060	1464
WEP1504	0437
WEP1514	0225
WEP1518	0251
WEP1605	0777
WEP1605/5111	0777
WEP1606	0791
WEP1606/5112	0791
WEP1607	0801
WEP1607/5113	0801
WEP1607/5113A	0801
WEP1608	0815
WEP1608/5114	0815
WEP1609	0827
WEP1609/5115	0827
WEP1610	0437
WEP1610/5116	0437
WEP1611	0870
WEP1611/5117	0870
WEP1612	3099
WEP1612/5118	3099
WEP1613	0185
WEP1613/5119	0185
WEP1614	0205
WEP1614/5120	0205
WEP1615	0475
WEP1615/5121	0475
WEP1616	0499
WEP1616/5122	0499
WEP1617	3285
WEP1617/5123	3285
WEP1618	0679
WEP1618/5124	0679
WEP1619	0225
WEP1619/5125	0225
WEP1620	0230
WEP1620/5126	0230
WEP1621	0234
WEP1621/5127	0234
WEP1622	0237
WEP1622/5128	0237
WEP1623	1387
WEP1623/5129	1387
WEP1624	0247
WEP1624/5130	0247
WEP1625	0251
WEP1625/5131	0251
WEP1626	1170
WEP1626/5132	1170
WEP1627	0256
WEP1627/5133	0256
WEP1628	2379
WEP1628/5134	2379
WEP1629	0262
WEP1629/5135	0262
WEP1630	0269
WEP1630/5136	0269
WEP1631	0273
WEP1631/5137	0273
WEP1632	2383
WEP1632/5138	2383
WEP1633	0291
WEP1633/5139	0291
WEP1634	1169
WEP1634/5140	1169
WEP1635	0305
WEP1635/5141	0305
WEP1636	0314
WEP1636/5142	0314
WEP1637	0316
WEP1637/5143	0316
WEP1638	0322
WEP1638/5144	0322
WEP1639	0333
WEP1639/5145	0333
WEP1641	0343
WEP1641/5146	0343
WEP1643	0027
WEP1643/5147	0027
WEP1646	0266
WEP1646/5148	0266
WEP1647	2829
WEP1647/5149	2829
WEP1648	0382
WEP1648/5150	0382
WEP1649	0401
WEP1649/5151	0401
WEP1650	0421
WEP1650/5152	0421
WEP1651	0439
WEP1651/5153	0439
WEP1652	2999
WEP1652/5154	2999
WEP1653	0238
WEP1653/5155	0238
WEP1654	1172
WEP1654/5156	1172
WEP1656	1182
WEP1656/5157	1182
WEP1657	1198
WEP1657/5158	1198
WEP1658	1209
WEP1658/5159	1209
WEP1658/5169	OEM
WEP1659	1870
WEP1659/5160	1870
WEP1660	0642
WEP1660/5161	0642
WEP1661	1246
WEP1661/5162	1246
WEP1661/6162	3277
WEP1662	2091
WEP1662/5163	2091
WEP1664	1269
WEP1664/5164	1269
WEP1665	2210
WEP1665/5165	2210
WEP1666	0600
WEP1666/5166	0600
WEP1717	0127
WEP1860	0004
WEP1945	0076
WEP2000	2549
WEP2000/706	2549
WEP2001	2746
WEP2001/1165	2746
WEP2002	3677
WEP2002/716	3677
WEP2003	2754
WEP2003/717	5978
WEP2003/1166	2754
WEP2004	1929
WEP2004/719	1929
WEP2005	2264
WEP2005/721	2264
WEP2006	1335
WEP2006/723	1335
WEP2007	4160
WEP2007/1233	1704
WEP2008	2527
WEP2008/728	2527
WEP2009	0324
WEP2009/729	0324
WEP2010	2737
WEP2010/1244	2737
WEP2011	2438
WEP2011/731	2438
WEP2014	1748
WEP2014/736	1748
WEP2015	1434
WEP2015/737	1434
WEP2017	0746
WEP2017/739	0746
WEP2018	0375
WEP2018/740A	0375
WEP2020	3690
WEP2020/742	3690
WEP2021	1385
WEP2021/743	1385
WEP2022	1411
WEP2022/744	1411
WEP2024	0780
WEP2024/746	0780
WEP2026	0784
WEP2026/748	0784
WEP2027	0391
WEP2027/749	0391
WEP2028/370	3759
WEP2030	2689
WEP2030/711	2689
WEP2032	2507
WEP2032/727	2507
WEP2033	2716
WEP2033/730	2716
WEP2035	0850
WEP2035/738	0850
WEP2036	2902
WEP2036/745	2902
WEP2037	1797
WEP2037/747	1797
WEP2039	2681
WEP2039/785	2681
WEP2040	2728
WEP2040/788	2728
WEP2041	3166
WEP2041/795	3166
WEP2043	0516
WEP2043/797	0516
WEP2044	1742
WEP2044/798	1742
WEP2046	1742
WEP2046/804	2535
WEP2053	0356
WEP2053/778	0356
WEP2054	1291
WEP2054/909	1291
WEP2055	0360
WEP2055/780	0360
WEP2056	1695
WEP2056/909D	1695
WEP2057/782	0373
WEP2058	0797
WEP2058/783	0797
WEP2059	2674
WEP2059/784	2674
WEP2060	1786
WEP2060/910	1786
WEP2061	2688
WEP2061/786	2688
WEP2063	1971
WEP2063/941D	1971
WEP2064	1832
WEP2064/789	1832
WEP2065	0345
WEP2065/790	0345
WEP2066	1327
WEP2066/791	1327
WEP2067	0413
WEP2067/973	0413
WEP2072	3506
WEP2072/1024	3506
WEP2073	2849
WEP2073/1027	2849
WEP2074	4479
WEP2074/1028	4479
WEP2075	0514
WEP2075/801	0514
WEP2076	2247
WEP2076/1029	2247
WEP2077	4481
WEP2077/1030	4481
WEP2079	4031
WEP2079/1037	4031
WEP2080	2377
WEP2080/1045	2377
WEP2081	2864
WEP2081/1050	2864
WEP2082	0428
WEP2082/1052	0428
WEP2086	0399
WEP2086/1062	0399
WEP2087	3318
WEP2087/1078	3318
WEP2089	0849
WEP2089/1080	0849
WEP2090	1152
WEP2090/1081A	1152
WEP2093	3232
WEP2093/1097	3232
WEP2094	2615
WEP2094/1109	2615
WEP2095	2289
WEP2095/1110	2289
WEP2097	4506
WEP2097/1114	4506
WEP2098	1239
WEP2098/1115	1239
WEP2099	3866
WEP2099/1115A	3866
WEP2100	4348
WEP2100/1127	4348
WEP2102	2216
WEP2102/1133	2216
WEP2103	3106
WEP2103/1136	3106
WEP2104	1686
WEP2104/912	1686
WEP2105	2845
WEP2105/1140	2845
WEP2106	4518
WEP2106/1150	4518
WEP2107	4520
WEP2107/1154	4520
WEP2108	2988
WEP2108/1156	2988
WEP2109	0875
WEP2109/1158	0875
WEP2110	1183
WEP2110/923	1183
WEP2111	2914
WEP2111/1161	2914
WEP2112	3238
WEP2112/1164	3238
WEP2113	1369
WEP2113/1172	1369
WEP2114	0406
WEP2114/941	0406
WEP2115	3242
WEP2115/1173	3242
WEP2117	2352
WEP2117/947	2352
WEP2118	2530
WEP2118/949	2530
WEP2119	0967
WEP2119/955M	0967
WEP2120	1532
WEP2120/1192	1532
WEP2121	3286
WEP2121/1193	3286
WEP2122	0574
WEP2122/1003	0574
WEP2123	0872
WEP2123/1004	0872
WEP2124	2546
WEP2124/1005	2546
WEP2125	1206
WEP2125/1006	1206
WEP2126	1805
WEP2126/1194	1805
WEP2127	2238
WEP2127/1198	2238
WEP2129	0858
WEP2129/1010	0858
WEP2130	0876
WEP2130/1011	0876
WEP2131	4541
WEP2131/1201	4541
WEP2132	2364
WEP2132/1202	2364
WEP2133	2388
WEP2133/1015	2388
WEP2134	2423
WEP2134/1017	2423
WEP2135	2290
WEP2135/1203	2290
WEP2136	2487
WEP2136/1019	2487
WEP2138	2142
WEP2138/1021	2142
WEP2139	4405
WEP2139/1204	4405
WEP2141	2179
WEP2141/1211	2179
WEP2142	4545
WEP2142/1212	4545
WEP2143	0412
WEP2143/1217	0412
WEP2144	1561
WEP2144/1218	1561
WEP2145	1602
WEP2145/1219	1602
WEP2148	3161
WEP2148/1228	3161
WEP2150	1042
WEP2150/1232	1042
WEP2156	1611
WEP2156/1039	1611
WEP2160	4320
WEP2160/1043	4320
WEP2175	2759
WEP2175/1175	2759
WEP2176	2560
WEP2176/1061	2560
WEP2184	2576
WEP2184/1069	2576
WEP2185	4014
WEP2185/1070	4014
WEP2186	2580
WEP2186/1071	2580
WEP2195	OEM
WEP2207	0043
WEP2207/1094	0043
WEP2214	4502
WEP2214/1105	4502
WEP2215	2606
WEP2215/1106	2606
WEP2223	3973
WEP2223/1123	3973
WEP2228	0385
WEP2228/1121	0385
WEP2229	0602
WEP2229/1122	0602
WEP2242	2051
WEP2242/1135	2051
WEP2245	0898
WEP2245/1245	0898
WEP2248	1469
WEP2248/1142	1469
WEP2258	3650
WEP2258/1160	3650
WEP2259	0851
WEP2259/1187	0851
WEP2260	2559
WEP2260/1060	2559
WEP2261	1049
WEP2261/1196	1049
WEP2262	4006
WEP2262/1240	4006
WEP2265	1120
WEP2266	2932
WEP2266/1263	2932
WEP2268	4017
WEP2268/1269	4017
WEP2272	0473
WEP2272/4001B	0473
WEP2275	1135
WEP2275/4016	1135
WEP2279	0564
WEP2279/7493A	0564
WEP2281	2032
WEP2281/793	2032
WEP2285	2480
WEP2285/818	2480
WEP2286	0846
WEP2286/1186	0846
WEP2289	1187
WEP2289/964	1187
WEP2293	1012
WEP2293/1087	1012
WEP2294	3977
WEP2294/1162	3977
WEP2296	3660
WEP2296/1178	3660
WEP2297	4133
WEP2297/1183	4133
WEP2308	3891
WEP2308/1308	3891
WEP2319	OEM
WEP2319/309K	1911
WEP2331	0026
WEP2331/923D	0026

If replacement code is OEM, contact original manufacturer for replacement.

DEVICE TYPE	REPL CODE
WEP3021	0334
WEP3023	0477
WEP3305	0920
WEP3305/5247	0920
WEP3305R	2713
WEP3305R/5247K	2713
WEP3307	0952
WEP3307/5249	0952
WEP3307R	1216
WEP3307R/5249K	1216
WEP3309	1003
WEP3309/5252	1003
WEP3309R	1243
WEP3309R/5252K	1243
WEP3311	0883
WEP3311/5254	0883
WEP3311R	1267
WEP3311R/5254K	1267
WEP3314	0926
WEP3314/5257	0926
WEP3314R	1292
WEP3314R/5257K	1292
WEP3317	1098
WEP3317/5260	1098
WEP3317R	1314
WEP3317R/5260K	1314
WEP3320	1144
WEP3320/5263	1144
WEP3320R	1334
WEP3320R/5263K	1334
WEP3323	1176
WEP3323/5266	1176
WEP3323R	1361
WEP3323R/5266K	1361
WEP3325	1214
WEP3325/5269	1214
WEP3325R	1396
WEP3325R/5269K	1396
WEP3327	1237
WEP3327/5271	1237
WEP3327R	1419
WEP3327R/5271K	1419
WEP3334	1321
WEP3334/5278	1321
WEP3334R	1465
WEP3334R/5278K	1465
WEP3340	1427
WEP3340/5285	1427
WEP3340R	1565
WEP3340R/5285K	1565
WEP4000	0110
WEP4000/5800	0110
WEP4001	0947
WEP4001/5801	0947
WEP4002	0242
WEP4002/5802	0242
WEP4004	0535
WEP4004/5804	0535
WEP4006	0959
WEP4006/5806	0959
WEP4007	0811
WEP4007/5808	0811
WEP4008	0916
WEP4008/5809	0087
WEP4011B	0215
WEP4011B/4011B	0215
WEP4013B	0409
WEP4013B/4013B	0409
WEP4066B/4066B	0101
WEP4069	0119
WEP4069/4069	0119
WEP4081	0703
WEP4081/5912	0703
WEP4085	0575
WEP4085/5916	0575
WEP4089	0994
WEP4089/5920	0994
WEP5457	0095
WEP5457/5457	0095
WEP6097	1744
WEP6097/5633	1744
WEP6240	1386
WEP6240/5452	1386
WEP6242	1250
WEP6242/5454	1250
WEP6243	0934
WEP6243/5455	0934
WEP6244	1213
WEP6244/5456	1213
WEP6251	2084
WEP6251/5461	2084
WEP6252	2078
WEP6252/5462	2078
WEP6253	0500
WEP6253/5463	0500
WEP6254	0712
WEP6255	0705
WEP6255/5465	0705
WEP6271	1102
WEP6271/5481	1102
WEP6273	OEM
WEP6273/5483	2904
WEP6300	0061
WEP6300/231	0061
WEP6301	2311
WEP6301/230	0239
WEP6302	1702
WEP6302/308	1702
WEP6303	2313

DEVICE TYPE	REPL CODE
WEP6303/310	2313
WEP6304	0914
WEP6304/507	0914
WEP6305	OEM
WEP6305/516	OEM
WEP6307	OEM
WEP6310	2320
WEP6310/239	2320
WEP6311	1642
WEP6311/276	1642
WEP6312	2321
WEP6312/279	2321
WEP6313	1814
WEP6313/314	1814
WEP6320	1129
WEP6320/5400	1129
WEP6321	0340
WEP6321/5401	0340
WEP6322	0895
WEP6322/5402	0895
WEP6323	2326
WEP6323/5403	2326
WEP6324	0058
WEP6324/5404	0058
WEP6900	OEM
WEP6901	OEM
WEP6902	OEM
WEP7400	0232
WEP7400/7400	0232
WEP7401	0268
WEP7401/7401	0268
WEP7402	0310
WEP7402/7402	0310
WEP7408	0462
WEP7408/7408	0462
WEP7426	0798
WEP7426/7426	0798
WEP7473	1164
WEP7473/7473	1164
WEP7474	1303
WEP7474/7474	1303
WEP7476	1150
WEP7476/7476	1150
WEP7490	1199
WEP7490/7490	1199
WEP9158	0461
WEP9158/9158	0461
WEP9914	1063
WEP9917	OEM
WEP9917/9917	OEM
WEP9923	OEM
WEP9923/9923	OEM
WEP9924	2840
WEP9924/9924	2840
WEP9934	OEM
WEP9946	0141
WEP9946/9946	0141
WEP74145	0614
WEP74145/74145	0614
WEP74162	1007
WEP74162/74162	1007
WEPG6001	0599
WEPS13KV	0201
WEPS18KV	0374
WEPS20KV	0374
WEPS1000-1	0071
WEPS1200-1	1293
WEPS1400-1	0102
WEPS3000	0290
WEPS3001	0626
WEPS3002	0626
WEPS3003	0126
WEPS3020	0626
WEPS3021	0334
WEPS3023	0561
WEPS3027	1357
WEPS3031	0378
WEPS4000	0290
WEPS5000	0290
WEPS5003	0161
WEPS5004	0556
WEPS5005	1190
WEPS5007	0455
WEPS6000	0769
WEPS6500	0769
WEPS7000	0130
WEPS7001	1671
WEPS8000	0190
WEPS9100	0396
WEPSD4	0196
WEPSD5	0479
WEPSH3	2937
WEPSH4	0469
WEPSH5	2938
WF-050	0162
WF-050A	0162
WF-050B	0162
WF-050C	0162
WF-050D	0162
WF-052	0162
WF-052A	0162
WF-052B	0162
WF-052C	0162
WF-052D	0162
WF-054	0157
WF-054A	0157
WF-054B	0157
WF-054D	0157
WF-056	0157

DEVICE TYPE	REPL CODE
WF-056A	0157
WF-056B	0157
WF-056C	0157
WF-056D	0157
WF-058	0157
WF-058A	0157
WF-058B	0157
WF-058C	0157
WF-058D	0157
WF-061	0002
WF-061A	0002
WF-061B	0002
WF-061C	0002
WF-061D	0002
WF-063	0002
WF-063A	0002
WF-063B	0002
WF-063C	0002
WF-063D	0002
WF-065	0002
WF-065A	0002
WF-065B	0002
WF-065C	0002
WF-065D	0002
WF-071	0644
WF-071A	0644
WF-071B	0644
WF-071C	0644
WF-071D	0644
WF-073	0644
WF-073A	0644
WF-073B	0644
WF-073C	0644
WF-073D	0644
WF-075	0644
WF-075A	0644
WF-075B	0644
WF-075C	0644
WF-075D	0644
WF-077	0644
WF-077A	0644
WF-077B	0644
WF-077C	0644
WF-077D	0644
WF-079	0244
WF-079A	0244
WF-079B	0244
WF-079C	0244
WF-079D	0244
WF-081	0244
WF-081A	0244
WF-081B	0244
WF-081C	0244
WF-081D	0244
WF-083	0244
WF-083A	0244
WF-083B	0244
WF-083C	0244
WF-083D	0244
WF-085	0244
WF-085B	0244
WF-085C	0244
WF-085D	0244
WF-088	0012
WF-088A	0012
WF-088B	0012
WF-088C	0012
WF-088D	0012
WF-090	0012
WF-090A	0012
WF-090B	0012
WF-090C	0012
WF-090D	0012
WF-092	0012
WF-092A	0012
WF-092B	0012
WF-092C	0012
WF-092D	0012
WF-094	0012
WF-094A	0012
WF-094B	0012
WF-094C	0012
WF-094D	0012
WF-098	0170
WF-098A	0170
WF-098B	0170
WF-098C	0170
WF-098D	0170
WF1	0321
WF2	0321
WF5AM	OEM
WF5M	OEM
WF10AM	OEM
WF10M	OEM
WF15AM	OEM
WF15M	OEM
WF20	OEM
WF20A	OEM
WF20AM	OEM
WF20B	OEM
WF20M	OEM
WF21H	OEM
WF22A	OEM
WF22B	OEM
WF23A	OEM
WF23B	OEM
WF30	OEM
WF30A	OEM
WF30AM	OEM

DEVICE TYPE	REPL CODE
WF30B	OEM
WF30M	OEM
WF34E	OEM
WF40	OEM
WF40A	OEM
WF40AM	OEM
WF40B	OEM
WF40M	OEM
WF42	OEM
WF43	OEM
WF49A	OEM
WF50	OEM
WF50A	OEM
WF50AM	OEM
WF50B	OEM
WF50M	OEM
WF60	OEM
WF63L	OEM
WF70	OEM
WF71	OEM
WF-100	0170
WF100	OEM
WF-100A	0170
WF100A	OEM
WF100AM	OEM
WF-100B	0137
WF100B	OEM
WF-100C	0137
WF-100D	0137
WF100M	OEM
WF-110	0244
WF-110A	0313
WF-110B	0313
WF-110C	0313
WF-110D	0313
WF-115	0789
WF-115A	0789
WF-115B	0789
WF-115C	0789
WF-115D	0789
WF-120	0137
WF-120A	0137
WF-120B	0137
WF-120C	0137
WF-120D	0137
WF-125	0361
WF-125A	0361
WF-125B	0361
WF-125C	0361
WF-125D	0361
WF-130	0361
WF-130A	0361
WF-130B	0361
WF-130C	0361
WF-130D	0361
WF-140	0100
WF-140A	0100
WF-140B	0100
WF-140C	0100
WF-140D	0100
WF-150	0002
WF-150A	0002
WF-150B	0002
WF-150C	0002
WF-150D	0002
WF-157	0416
WF-157A	0416
WF-157B	0416
WF-157C	0416
WF-157D	0416
WF-162	0416
WF-162A	0416
WF-162B	0416
WF-162C	0416
WF-162D	0416
WF-167	0416
WF-167A	0416
WF-167B	0416
WF-167C	0416
WF-167D	0416
WF-172	0490
WF-172A	0490
WF-172B	0398
WF-172C	0398
WF-172D	0398
WF-177	0398
WF-177A	0398
WF-177B	0398
WF-177C	0398
WF-177D	0398
WF-182	0398
WF-182A	0398
WF-182B	0398
WF-182C	0398
WF-182D	0398
WF200	OEM
WF200A	OEM
WF200AM	OEM
WF200B	OEM
WF200M	OEM
WF-230	0398
WF-230A	0398
WF-230B	0398
WF-230C	0398
WF-230D	0398
WF-240	0398
WF-240A	0398
WF-240B	0398
WF-240C	0398

DEVICE TYPE	REPL CODE
WF-240D	0398
WF-250A	0398
WF-250B	0398
WF-250C	0398
WF-250D	0398
WF-260	0012
WF-260A	0436
WF-260B	0436
WF-260D	0436
WF-270	0436
WF-270A	0436
WF-270B	0436
WF-270C	0436
WF-270D	0436
WF-290	0436
WF-290A	0721
WF-290B	0721
WF-290C	0721
WF-290D	0721
WF-300	0721
WF-300A	0721
WF-300B	0721
WF-300C	0721
WF-300D	0721
WF-330	0039
WF-330A	0039
WF-330B	0039
WF-330C	0039
WF-330D	0039
WF-340	0039
WF-340A	0039
WF-340B	0039
WF-340C	0039
WF-340D	0039
WF402	OEM
WF402L	OEM
WF403	OEM
WF404L	OEM
WF405L	OEM
WF406L	OEM
WF409LC	OEM
WF412L	OEM
WF413L	OEM
WF414L	OEM
WF416	OEM
WF424	OEM
WF461	OEM
WF471	OEM
WG-050A	0162
WG-050B	0162
WG-050C	0162
WG-050D	0162
WG-052	0162
WG-052A	0162
WG-052B	0162
WG-052C	0162
WG-052D	0162
WG-054	0157
WG-054A	0157
WG-054B	0157
WG-054C	0157
WG-054D	0157
WG-056	0157
WG-056A	0157
WG-056B	0157
WG-056C	0157
WG-056D	0157
WG-058	0157
WG-058A	0157
WG-058B	0157
WG-058C	0157
WG-058D	0157
WG-061	0631
WG-061A	0631
WG-061B	0631
WG-061C	0631
WG-061D	0631
WG-063	0631
WG-063A	0631
WG-063B	0631
WG-063C	0631
WG-063D	0631
WG-065	0631
WG-065A	0631
WG-065B	0631
WG-065C	0631
WG-065D	0631
WG-071	0644
WG-071A	0644
WG-071B	0644
WG-071C	0644
WG-071D	0644
WG-073	0644
WG-073A	0644
WG-073B	0644
WG-073C	0644
WG-073D	0644
WG-075	0644
WG-075A	0644
WG-075B	0644
WG-075C	0644
WG-075D	0644
WG-077	0644
WG-077A	0644
WG-077B	0644
WG-077C	0644
WG-077D	0644
WG-079	0244
WG-079A	0244

DEVICE TYPE	REPL CODE
WG-079B	0244
WG-079C	0244
WG-079D	0244
WG-081	0244
WG-081A	0244
WG-081B	0244
WG-081C	0244
WG-081D	0244
WG-083	0244
WG-083A	0244
WG-083B	0244
WG-083C	0244
WG-083D	0244
WG-085	0244
WG-085A	0244
WG-085B	0244
WG-085C	0244
WG-085D	0244
WG-088	0012
WG-088A	0012
WG-088B	0012
WG-088C	0012
WG-088D	0012
WG-090	0012
WG-090A	0012
WG-090B	0012
WG-090C	0012
WG-090D	0012
WG-092	0012
WG-092A	0012
WG-092B	0012
WG-092C	0012
WG-092D	0012
WG-094	0012
WG-094A	0012
WG-094B	0012
WG-094C	0012
WG-094D	0012
WG-098	0170
WG-098A	0170
WG-098B	0170
WG-098C	0170
WG-098D	0170
WG0A-90	0133
WG-10AS	0133
WG91	0012
WG-100	0170
WG-100A	0170
WG-100B	0170
WG-100C	0170
WG-100D	0170
WG-110	0313
WG-110A	0313
WG-110B	0313
WG-110C	0313
WG-110D	0313
WG-115	0789
WG-115A	0789
WG-115B	0789
WG-115C	0789
WG-115D	0789
WG-120	0137
WG-120A	0137
WG-120B	0137
WG-120C	0137
WG-120D	0137
WG-125	0361
WG-125A	0361
WG-125B	0361
WG-125C	0361
WG-125D	0361
WG-130	0361
WG-130A	0361
WG-130B	0361
WG-130C	0361
WG-130D	0361
WG-140	0100
WG-140A	0100
WG-140B	0100
WG-140C	0100
WG-140D	0100
WG-150	0002
WG-150A	0002
WG-150B	0002
WG-150C	0002
WG-150D	0002
WG-157	0416
WG-157A	0416
WG-157B	0416
WG-157C	0416
WG-157D	0416
WG-162	0416
WG-162A	0416
WG-162B	0416
WG-162C	0416
WG-162D	0416
WG-167	0416
WG-167A	0416
WG-167B	0416
WG-167C	0416
WG-167D	0416
WG-172	0490
WG-172A	0490
WG-172B	0490
WG-172C	0490
WG-172D	0490
WG-177	0490
WG-177A	0490
WG-177B	0490

DEVICE TYPE	REPL CODE
WG-177C	0490
WG-177D	0490
WG-182	0490
WG-182A	0490
WG-182B	0490
WG-182C	0490
WG-182D	0490
WG-230	0398
WG-230A	0398
WG-230B	0398
WG-230C	0398
WG-230D	0398
WG-240	0398
WG-240A	0398
WG-240B	0398
WG-240C	0398
WG-240D	0398
WG-250	0398
WG-250A	0398
WG-250B	0398
WG-250C	0398
WG-250D	0398
WG-260	0436
WG-260A	0436
WG-260B	0436
WG-260C	0436
WG-260D	0436
WG-270	0436
WG-270A	0436
WG-270B	0436
WG-270C	0436
WG-270D	0436
WG-290	0721
WG-290A	0721
WG-290B	0721
WG-290C	0721
WG-290D	0721
WG-300	0721
WG-300A	0721
WG-300B	0721
WG-300C	0721
WG-300D	0721
WG-330	0039
WG-330A	0039
WG-330B	0039
WG-330C	0039
WG-330D	0039
WG-340	0039
WG-340A	0039
WG-340B	0039
WG-340C	0039
WG-340D	0039
WG-599	0133
WG-713	0133
WG713	0133
WG713A	0124
WG-713C	0133
WG714	0133
WG759-42	OEM
WG759-43	OEM
WG759-44	OEM
WG759-51	OEM
WG1010	0124
WG-1010A	0133
WG1010A	0133
WG1010B	0133
WG-1012	0133
WG1012	0133
WG1014A	0133
WG1021	0133
WG8038BC	OEM
WG8038BM	OEM
WG8038CC	OEM
WGOA-90	0124
WH-050	0398
WH-050A	0398
WH-050B	0398
WH-050C	0398
WH-050D	0398
WH-052	0398
WH-052A	0398
WH-052B	0398
WH-052C	0398
WH-052D	0398
WH-054	0157
WH-054A	0157
WH-054B	0157
WH-054C	0157
WH-054D	0157
WH-056	0157
WH-056A	0157
WH-056B	0157
WH-056C	0157
WH-056D	0157
WH-058	0157
WH-058A	0157
WH-058B	0157
WH-058C	0157
WH-058D	0157
WH-061	0631
WH-061A	0631
WH-061B	0631
WH-061C	0631
WH-061D	0631
WH-063	0631
WH-063A	0631
WH-063B	0631
WH-063C	0631
WH-063D	0631

If replacement code is OEM, contact original manufacturer for replacement.

DEVICE TYPE	REPL CODE	DEVICE TYPE	REPL CODE	DEVICE TYPE	REPL CODE	DEVICE TYPE	REPL CODE	DEVICE TYPE	REPL CODE	DEVICE TYPE	REPL CODE	DEVICE TYPE	REPL CODE
WH-065	0631	WH-150D	0002	WI-063B	0631	WI-150B	0002	WJ-063C	0631	WJ-150C	0002	WK-061C	0631
WH-065A	0631	WH-157	0416	WI-063C	0631	WI-150C	0002	WJ-063D	0631	WJ-150D	0002	WK-061D	0631
WH-065B	0631	WH-157A	0416	WI-063D	0631	WI-150D	0002	WJ-065	0631	WJ-157	0416	WK-063	0631
WH-065C	0631	WH-157B	0416	WI-065	0631	WI-157	0416	WJ-065A	0631	WJ-157A	0416	WK-063A	0631
WH-065D	0631	WH-157C	0416	WI-065A	0631	WI-157A	0416	WJ-065B	0631	WJ-157B	0416	WK-063B	0631
WH-071	0644	WH-157D	0416	WI-065B	0631	WI-157B	0416	WJ-065C	0631	WJ-157C	0416	WK-063C	0631
WH-071A	0644	WH-162	0416	WI-065C	0631	WI-157C	0416	WJ-065D	0631	WJ-157D	0416	WK-063D	0631
WH-071B	0644	WH-162A	0416	WI-065D	0631	WI-157D	0416	WJ-071	0644	WJ-162	0416	WK-065	0631
WH-071C	0644	WH-162B	0416	WI-071	0644	WI-162	0416	WJ-071A	0644	WJ-162A	0416	WK-065A	0631
WH-071D	0644	WH-162C	0416	WI-071A	0644	WI-162A	0416	WJ-071B	0644	WJ-162B	0416	WK-065B	0631
WH-073	0644	WH-162D	0416	WI-071B	0644	WI-162B	0416	WJ-071C	0644	WJ-162C	0416	WK-065C	0631
WH-073A	0644	WH-167	0416	WI-071C	0644	WI-162C	0416	WJ-071D	0644	WJ-162D	0416	WK-065D	0631
WH-073B	0644	WH-167A	0416	WI-071D	0644	WI-162D	0416	WJ-073	0644	WJ-167	0416	WK-071	0644
WH-073C	0644	WH-167B	0416	WI-073	0644	WI-167	0416	WJ-073A	0644	WJ-167A	0416	WK-071A	0644
WH-073D	0644	WH-167C	0416	WI-073A	0644	WI-167A	0416	WJ-073B	0644	WJ-167B	0416	WK-071B	0644
WH-075	0644	WH-167D	0490	WI-073B	0644	WI-167B	0416	WJ-073C	0644	WJ-167C	0416	WK-071C	0644
WH-075A	0644	WH-172	0490	WI-073C	0644	WI-167C	0416	WJ-073D	0644	WJ-167D	0416	WK-071D	0644
WH-075B	0644	WH-172A	0490	WI-073D	0644	WI-167D	0416	WJ-075	0644	WJ-172	0490	WK-073	0644
WH-075C	0644	WH-172B	0490	WI-075	0644	WI-172	0490	WJ-075A	0644	WJ-172A	0490	WK-073A	0644
WH-075D	0644	WH-172C	0490	WI-075A	0644	WI-172A	0490	WJ-075B	0644	WJ-172B	0490	WK-073B	0644
WH-077	0644	WH-172D	0490	WI-075B	0644	WI-172B	0490	WJ-075C	0644	WJ-172C	0490	WK-073C	0644
WH-077A	0644	WH-177	0490	WI-075C	0644	WI-172C	0490	WJ-075D	0644	WJ-172D	0490	WK-073D	0644
WH-077B	0644	WH-177A	0490	WI-075D	0644	WI-172D	0490	WJ-077	0644	WJ-177	0490	WK-075	0644
WH-077C	0644	WH-177B	0490	WI-077	0644	WI-177	0490	WJ-077A	0644	WJ-177A	0490	WK-075A	0644
WH-077D	0644	WH-177C	0490	WI-077A	0644	WI-177A	0490	WJ-077B	0644	WJ-177B	0490	WK-075B	0644
WH-079	0244	WH-177D	0490	WI-077B	0644	WI-177B	0490	WJ-077C	0644	WJ-177C	0490	WK-075C	0644
WH-079A	0244	WH-182	0490	WI-077C	0644	WI-177C	0490	WJ-077D	0644	WJ-177D	0490	WK-075D	0644
WH-079B	0244	WH-182A	0490	WI-077D	0644	WI-177D	0490	WJ-079	0244	WJ-182	0490	WK-077	0644
WH-079C	0244	WH-182B	0490	WI-079	0244	WI-182	0490	WJ-079A	0244	WJ-182A	0490	WK-077A	0644
WH-079D	0244	WH-182C	0490	WI-079A	0244	WI-182A	0490	WJ-079B	0244	WJ-182B	0490	WK-077C	0644
WH-081	0244	WH-182D	0490	WI-079B	0244	WI-182B	0490	WJ-079C	0244	WJ-182C	0490	WK-077D	0644
WH-081A	0244	WH-230	0398	WI-079C	0244	WI-182C	0490	WJ-079D	0244	WJ-182D	0490	WK-079	0244
WH-081B	0244	WH-230A	0398	WI-079D	0244	WI-182D	0490	WJ-081	0244	WJ-230	0398	WK-079A	0244
WH-081C	0244	WH-230B	0398	WI-081	0244	WI-230	0398	WJ-081A	0244	WJ-230A	0398	WK-079B	0244
WH-081D	0244	WH-230C	0398	WI-081A	0244	WI-230A	0398	WJ-081B	0244	WJ-230B	0398	WK-079C	0244
WH-083	0244	WH-230D	0398	WI-081B	0244	WI-230B	0398	WJ-081C	0244	WJ-230C	0398	WK-079D	0244
WH-083A	0244	WH-240	0398	WI-081C	0244	WI-230C	0398	WJ-081D	0244	WJ-230D	0398	WK-081	0244
WH-083B	0244	WH-240A	0398	WI-081D	0244	WI-230D	0398	WJ-083	0244	WJ-240	0398	WK-081A	0244
WH-083C	0244	WH-240B	0398	WI-083A	0244	WI-240	0398	WJ-083A	0244	WJ-240A	0398	WK-081B	0244
WH-083D	0244	WH-240C	0398	WI-083B	0244	WI-240A	0398	WJ-083B	0244	WJ-240B	0398	WK-081C	0244
WH-085	0244	WH-240D	0398	WI-083C	0244	WI-240B	0398	WJ-083C	0244	WJ-240C	0398	WK-081D	0244
WH-085A	0244	WH-250	0398	WI-083D	0244	WI-240C	0398	WJ-083D	0244	WJ-240D	0398	WK-083	0244
WH-085B	0244	WH-250A	0398	WI-085	0244	WI-240D	0398	WJ-085	0244	WJ-250	0398	WK-083A	0244
WH-085C	0244	WH-250B	0398	WI-085A	0244	WI-250A	0398	WJ-085B	0244	WJ-250A	0398	WK-083B	0244
WH-085D	0244	WH-250C	0398	WI-085B	0244	WI-250B	0398	WJ-085C	0244	WJ-250B	0398	WK-083C	0244
WH-088	0012	WH-250D	0398	WI-085C	0244	WI-250C	0398	WJ-085D	0244	WJ-250C	0398	WK-083D	0244
WH-088A	0012	WH-260	0436	WI-085D	0244	WI-250D	0398	WJ-088	0012	WJ-250D	0398	WK-085	0244
WH-088B	0012	WH-260A	0436	WI-088	0012	WI-260	0436	WJ-088A	0012	WJ-260	0436	WK-085A	0244
WH-088C	0012	WH-260B	0436	WI-088A	0012	WI-260A	0436	WJ-088B	0012	WJ-260A	0436	WK-085B	0244
WH-088D	0012	WH-260C	0436	WI-088B	0012	WI-260B	0436	WJ-088C	0012	WJ-260B	0436	WK-085C	0244
WH-090	0012	WH-260D	0436	WI-088C	0012	WI-260C	0436	WJ-088D	0012	WJ-260C	0436	WK-085D	0244
WH-090A	0012	WH-270	0436	WI-088D	0012	WI-260D	0436	WJ-090	0012	WJ-260D	0436	WK-088	0012
WH-090B	0012	WH-270A	0436	WI-090	0012	WI-270	0436	WJ-090A	0012	WJ-270	0436	WK-088A	0012
WH-090C	0012	WH-270B	0436	WI-090A	0012	WI-270A	0436	WJ-090B	0012	WJ-270A	0436	WK-088B	0012
WH-090D	0012	WH-270C	0436	WI-090B	0012	WI-270B	0436	WJ-090C	0012	WJ-270B	0436	WK-088C	0012
WH-092	0012	WH-270D	0436	WI-090C	0012	WI-270C	0436	WJ-090D	0012	WJ-270C	0436	WK-088D	0012
WH-092A	0012	WH-290	0721	WI-090D	0012	WI-270D	0436	WJ-092	0012	WJ-270D	0436	WK-090	0012
WH-092B	0012	WH-290A	0721	WI-092	0012	WI-290	0721	WJ-092A	0012	WJ-290	0721	WK-090A	0012
WH-092C	0012	WH-290B	0721	WI-092A	0012	WI-290A	0721	WJ-092B	0012	WJ-290A	0721	WK-090B	0012
WH-092D	0012	WH-290C	0721	WI-092B	0012	WI-290B	0721	WJ-092C	0012	WJ-290B	0721	WK-090C	0012
WH-094	0012	WH-290D	0721	WI-092C	0012	WI-290C	0721	WJ-092D	0012	WJ-290C	0721	WK-090D	0012
WH-094A	0012	WH-300	0721	WI-092D	0012	WI-290D	0721	WJ-094	0012	WJ-290D	0721	WK-092	0012
WH-094B	0012	WH-300A	0721	WI-094	0012	WI-300	0721	WJ-094A	0012	WJ-300	0721	WK-092A	0012
WH-094C	0012	WH-300B	0721	WI-094A	0012	WI-300B	0721	WJ-094B	0012	WJ-300A	0721	WK-092B	0012
WH-094D	0012	WH-300C	0721	WI-094B	0012	WI-300C	0721	WJ-094C	0012	WJ-300B	0721	WK-092C	0012
WH-098	0170	WH-300D	0721	WI-094C	0012	WI-300D	0721	WJ-094D	0012	WJ-300C	0721	WK-092D	0012
WH-098A	0170	WH-330	0039	WI-094D	0012	WI-330	0721	WJ-098	0170	WJ-300D	0721	WK-094	0012
WH-098B	0170	WH-330A	0039	WI-098	0170	WI-330A	0039	WJ-098A	0170	WJ-330	0039	WK-094A	0012
WH-098C	0170	WH-330B	0039	WI-098A	0170	WI-330B	0039	WJ-098B	0170	WJ-330A	0039	WK-094B	0012
WH-098D	0170	WH-330C	0039	WI-098B	0170	WI-330C	0039	WJ-098C	0170	WJ-330B	0039	WK-094C	0012
WH-100	0170	WH-330D	0039	WI-098C	0170	WI-340	0039	WJ-098D	0170	WJ-330C	0039	WK-094D	0012
WH-100A	0170	WH-340	0039	WI-098D	0170	WI-340A	0039	WJ-100	0170	WJ-330D	0039	WK-098	0170
WH-100B	0170	WH-340A	0039	WI-100	0170	WI-340B	0039	WJ-100A	0170	WJ-340	0039	WK-098A	0170
WH-100C	0170	WH-340B	0039	WI-100A	0170	WI-340C	0039	WJ-100B	0170	WJ-340A	0039	WK-098B	0170
WH-100D	0170	WH-340C	0039	WI-100B	0170	WI-340D	0039	WJ-100C	0170	WJ-340B	0039	WK-098C	0170
WH-110	0313	WH-340D	0039	WI-100C	0170	WIE	0843	WJ-100D	0170	WJ-340C	0039	WK-098D	0170
WH-110A	0313	WH1012	0133	WI-100D	0170	WJ-050	0162	WJ-110	0313	WJ-340D	0039	WK-100	0170
WH-110B	0313	WI-050	0162	WI-110	0313	WJ-050A	0162	WJ-110A	0313	WJ759-33	OEM	WK-100B	0170
WH-110C	0313	WI-050A	0162	WI-110A	0313	WJ-050B	0162	WJ-110B	0313	WJ759-34	OEM	WK-100C	0170
WH-110D	0313	WI-050B	0162	WI-110B	0313	WJ-050C	0162	WJ-110C	0313	WJ759-40	OEM	WK-100D	0170
WH-115	0789	WI-050C	0162	WI-110C	0313	WJ-050D	0162	WJ-110D	0313	WJ759-41	OEM	WK-110	0313
WH-115A	0789	WI-050D	0162	WI-110D	0313	WJ-052	0162	WJ-115	0789	WK-050	0162	WK-110A	0313
WH-115B	0789	WI-052	0162	WI-115	0789	WJ-052A	0162	WJ-115A	0789	WK-050A	0162	WK-110B	0313
WH-115C	0789	WI-052A	0162	WI-115A	0789	WJ-052B	0162	WJ-115B	0789	WK-050B	0162	WK-110C	0313
WH-115D	0789	WI-052B	0162	WI-115B	0789	WJ-052C	0162	WJ-115C	0789	WK-050C	0162	WK-110D	0313
WH-120	0137	WI-052C	0162	WI-115C	0789	WJ-052D	0162	WJ-115D	0789	WK-050D	0162	WK-115	0789
WH-120A	0137	WI-052D	0162	WI-115D	0789	WJ-054	0157	WJ-120	0137	WK-052	0162	WK-115A	0789
WH-120B	0137	WI-054	0157	WI-120	0137	WJ-054A	0157	WJ-120A	0137	WK-052A	0162	WK-115B	0789
WH-120C	0137	WI-054A	0157	WI-120A	0137	WJ-054B	0157	WJ-120B	0137	WK-052B	0162	WK-115C	0789
WH-120D	0137	WI-054B	0157	WI-120B	0137	WJ-054C	0157	WJ-120C	0137	WK-052C	0162	WK-115D	0789
WH-125	0361	WI-054C	0157	WI-120C	0137	WJ-054D	0157	WJ-120D	0137	WK-052D	0162	WK-120	0137
WH-125A	0361	WI-054D	0157	WI-120D	0137	WJ-056	0157	WJ-125	0361	WK-054	0157	WK-120A	0137
WH-125B	0361	WI-056	0157	WI-125	0361	WJ-056A	0157	WJ-125A	0361	WK-054A	0157	WK-120B	0137
WH-125C	0361	WI-056A	0157	WI-125A	0361	WJ-056B	0157	WJ-125B	0361	WK-054B	0157	WK-120C	0137
WH-125D	0361	WI-056B	0157	WI-125B	0361	WJ-056C	0157	WJ-125C	0361	WK-054C	0157	WK-120D	0137
WH-130	0361	WI-056C	0157	WI-125C	0361	WJ-056D	0157	WJ-125D	0361	WK-054D	0157	WK-125	0361
WH-130A	0361	WI-056D	0157	WI-125D	0361	WJ-058	0157	WJ-130	0361	WK-056	0157	WK-125A	0361
WH-130B	0361	WI-058	0157	WI-130	0361	WJ-058A	0157	WJ-130A	0361	WK-056A	0157	WK-125B	0361
WH-130C	0361	WI-058A	0157	WI-130A	0361	WJ-058B	0157	WJ-130B	0361	WK-056B	0157	WK-125C	0361
WH-130D	0361	WI-058B	0157	WI-130B	0361	WJ-058C	0157	WJ-130C	0361	WK-056C	0157	WK-125D	0361
WH-140	0100	WI-058C	0157	WI-130C	0361	WJ-058D	0157	WJ-130D	0361	WK-056D	0157	WK-130	0361
WH-140A	0100	WI-058D	0157	WI-130D	0361	WJ-061	0631	WJ-140	0100	WK-058	0157	WK-130A	0361
WH-140B	0100	WI-061	0631	WI-140	0100	WJ-061A	0631	WJ-140A	0100	WK-058A	0157	WK-130B	0361
WH-140C	0100	WI-061A	0631	WI-140A	0100	WJ-061B	0631	WJ-140B	0100	WK-058B	0157	WK-130C	0361
WH-140D	0100	WI-061B	0631	WI-140B	0100	WJ-061C	0631	WJ-140C	0100	WK-058C	0157	WK-130D	0361
WH-150	0002	WI-061C	0631	WI-140C	0100	WJ-061D	0631	WJ-140D	0100	WK-058D	0157	WK-140	0100
WH-150A	0002	WI-061D	0631	WI-140D	0100	WJ-063	0631	WJ-150	0002	WK-061	0631	WK-140A	0100
WH-150B	0002	WI-063	0631	WI-150	0002	WJ-063A	0631	WJ-150A	0002	WK-061A	0631	WK-140B	0100
WH-150C	0002	WI-063A	0631	WI-150A	0002	WJ-063B	0631	WJ-150B	0002	WK-061B	0631	WK-140C	0100

If replacement code is OEM, contact original manufacturer for replacement.

DEVICE TYPE	REPL CODE
WK-140D	0100
WK-150	0002
WK-150A	0002
WK-150B	0002
WK-150C	0002
WK-150D	0002
WK-157	0416
WK-157A	0416
WK-157B	0416
WK-157C	0416
WK-157D	0416
WK-162	0416
WK-162A	0416
WK-162B	0416
WK-162C	0416
WK-162D	0416
WK-167	0416
WK-167A	0416
WK-167B	0416
WK-167C	0416
WK-167D	0416
WK-172	0490
WK-172A	0490
WK-172B	0490
WK-172C	0490
WK-172D	0490
WK-177	0490
WK-177A	0490
WK-177B	0490
WK-177C	0490
WK-177D	0490
WK-182	0490
WK-182A	0490
WK-182B	0490
WK-182C	0490
WK-182D	0490
WK-230	0398
WK-230A	0398
WK-230B	0398
WK-230C	0398
WK-230D	0398
WK-240	0398
WK-240A	0398
WK-240B	0398
WK-240C	0398
WK-240D	0398
WK-250	0398
WK-250A	0398
WK-250B	0398
WK-250C	0398
WK-250D	0398
WK-260	0436
WK-260A	0436
WK-260B	0436
WK-260C	0436
WK-260D	0436
WK-270	0436
WK-270A	0436
WK-270B	0436
WK-270C	0436
WK-270D	0436
WK-290	0721
WK-290A	0721
WK-290B	0721
WK-290C	0721
WK-290D	0721
WK-300	0721
WK-300A	0721
WK-300B	0721
WK-300C	0721
WK-300D	0721
WK-330	0039
WK-330A	0039
WK-330B	0039
WK-330C	0039
WK-330D	0039
WK-340	0039
WK-340A	0039
WK-340B	0039
WK-340C	0039
WK-340D	0039
WK5457	OEM
WK5458	0435
WK5459	0435
WL005	OEM
WL005F	OEM
WL005M	0106
WL-01	0106
WL01	0106
WL01F	0106
WL02-5004-L	OEM
WL02-5004L	OEM
WL02F	0106
WL02M	0106
WL04F	0106
WL04M	0106
WL06F	1999
WL06M	1999
WL08F	2384
WL08M	2384
WL-050	0162
WL-050A	0162
WL-050B	0162
WL-050C	0162
WL-050D	0162
WL-052	0162
WL-052A	0162
WL-052B	0162
WL-052C	0162
WL-052D	0162
WL-054	0157
WL-054A	0157
WL-054B	0157
WL-054C	0157
WL-054D	0157
WL-056	0157
WL-056A	0157
WL-056B	0157
WL-056C	0157
WL-056D	0157
WL-058	0157
WL-058A	0157
WL-058B	0157
WL-058C	0157
WL-058D	0157
WL-061	0631
WL-061A	0631
WL-061B	0631
WL-061C	0631
WL-061D	0631
WL-063	0631
WL-063A	0631
WL-063B	0631
WL-063C	0631
WL-063D	0631
WL-065	0631
WL-065A	0631
WL-065B	0631
WL-065C	0631
WL-065D	0631
WL-071	0644
WL-071A	0644
WL-071B	0644
WL-071C	0644
WL-071D	0644
WL-073	0644
WL-073A	0644
WL-073B	0644
WL-073C	0644
WL-073D	0644
WL-075	0644
WL-075A	0644
WL-075B	0644
WL-075C	0644
WL-075D	0644
WL-077	0644
WL-077A	0644
WL-077B	0644
WL-077C	0644
WL-077D	0644
WL-079	0644
WL-079A	0244
WL-079B	0244
WL-079C	0244
WL-079D	0244
WL-081	0244
WL-081A	0244
WL-081B	0244
WL-081C	0244
WL-081D	0244
WL-083	0244
WL-083A	0244
WL-083B	0244
WL-083C	0244
WL-083D	0244
WL-085	0244
WL-085A	0244
WL-085B	0244
WL-085C	0244
WL-085D	0244
WL-088	0012
WL-088A	0012
WL-088B	0012
WL-088C	0012
WL-088D	0012
WL-090	0012
WL-090A	0012
WL-090B	0012
WL-090C	0012
WL-090D	0012
WL-092	0012
WL-092A	0012
WL-092B	0012
WL-092C	0012
WL-092D	0012
WL-094	0012
WL-094A	0012
WL-094B	0012
WL-094C	0012
WL-094D	0012
WL-098	0170
WL-098A	0170
WL-098B	0170
WL-098C	0170
WL-098D	0170
WL10F	0782
WL10M	0782
WL-100	0170
WL100	OEM
WL-100A	0170
WL-100B	0170
WL-100C	0170
WL-100D	0170
WL-110	0313
WL-110A	0313
WL-110B	0313
WL-110C	0313
WL-110D	0313
WL-115	0789
WL-115A	0789
WL-115B	0789
WL-115C	0789
WL-115D	0789
WL-120	0137
WL-120A	0137
WL-120B	0137
WL-120C	0137
WL-120D	0137
WL500	OEM
WL530P	OEM
WL900	OEM
WN-170D	0416
WO-005	0106
WO-01	OEM
WO-02	OEM
WO-04	OEM
WO-06	OEM
WO-08	OEM
WO-6A	0015
WO-6B	0023
WO6C	0015
WO68	OEM
WPC23C	0523
WPD858	2238
WR-006	0110
WR006	0015
WR011	0276
WR-013	0015
WR013	0015
WR-030	0110
WR030	0276
WR-040	0110
WR040	0276
WR1	0087
WR2	0087
WR3	0916
WR10	0430
WR30	0964
WR31	3688
WR32	0983
WR33	0197
WR34	0204
WR40	0084
WR41	0090
WR42	0097
WR43	0109
WR44	0122
WR50	3160
WR51	2873
WR52	1116
WR53	0800
WR54	0315
WR60	3160
WR61	2873
WR62	1116
WR63	0800
WR64	0315
WR100	0015
WR200	0015
WR300	0015
WR400	1345
WRE981	0015
WRR1952	0016
WRR1953	0016
WRR1954	0016
WRR1955	0535
WRR1956	0535
WRT1114	0211
WS20-1	0286
WS20-1B	0286
WS20-1S	0286
WS100	0124
WS200	0124
WS300	0124
WS531P	OEM
WS6945-2	0081
WSC2260	OEM
WSD002C	0133
WT-10C	0361
WT16X7	0196
WT16X8	0479
WT16X9	0479
WT635-01D	OEM
WT635-01M	OEM
WT635-02D	OEM
WT635-02M	OEM
WT4311	OEM
WT4312	OEM
WT4313	OEM
WT4314	OEM
WT4315	OEM
WT4316	OEM
WT4321	OEM
WT4322	OEM
WT4323	OEM
WT4324	OEM
WT4325	OEM
WT4331	OEM
WT4332	OEM
WT4333	OEM
WT4334	OEM
WT4411	OEM
WT4412	OEM
WT4413	OEM
WT4414	OEM
WT4415	OEM
WT4416	OEM
WT4421	OEM
WT4422	OEM
WT4423	OEM
WT4424	OEM
WT4425	OEM
WT4431	OEM
WT4432	OEM
WT4433	OEM
WT4434	OEM
WT5301	OEM
WT5303	OEM
WT5304	OEM
WT5305	OEM
WT5306	OEM
WT5308	OEM
WT5310	OEM
WT5503	OEM
WT5504	OEM
WT5505	OEM
WT5506	OEM
WT5510	OEM
WT5511	OEM
WT5603	OEM
WT5604	OEM
WT5605	OEM
WT5606	OEM
WT5611	OEM
WT5650	OEM
WT5651	OEM
WT5652	OEM
WT5703	OEM
WT5704	OEM
WT5705	OEM
WT5706	OEM
WT5750(A)	OEM
WT5751(A)	OEM
WT5752(A)	OEM
WTL1010	OEM
WTL1016	OEM
WTV008CL	OEM
WTV008CP	OEM
WTV008L	OEM
WTV008P	OEM
WTV3MC	0050
WTV6MC	0050
WTV6PWR	0160
WTV12MC	0050
WTV12PWR	0160
WTV15MG	0004
WTV15VMG	0004
WTV20MC	0050
WTV20MG	0004
WTV20VH6	0004
WTV20VHG	0004
WTV20VMG	0004
WTV25PWR	0160
WTV30VHG	0004
WTV30VLG	0004
WTV30VMG	0004
WTV40PWR	0160
WTV99PWR	0160
WTV129PWR	0435
WTV199PWR	0160
WTV299PWR	0435
WTVAT6	0004
WTVAT6A	0050
WTVB5	0050
WTVB5A	0004
WTVB6	0279
WTVB6A	0211
WTVBA6	0050
WTVBA6A	0004
WTVBE6	0050
WTVBE6A	0004
WTVBMC	0164
WTVL6	0038
WTVSA7	0595
WTVSK7	0595
WTVSQ7	0595
WU-054	0157
WU-056D	0631
WU-065D	0631
WV-1	0139
WV2AA50C	2282
WV2AA50E	2282
WV2B325E	OEM
WV2BA25C	OEM
WV2BA25E	OEM
WV2BC25C	1425
WV2BC25E	1425
WV2BE25C	1425
WV2BE25E	1425
WV2BH25C	2278
WV2BH25E	2278
WV2BJ25C	1670
WV2BJ25E	1670
WV2BK25C	1670
WV2BK25E	1670
WV2CA25C	OEM
WV2CA25E	OEM
WV2DA25C	OEM
WV2DA25E	OEM
WV2DC25C	OEM
WV2DC25E	OEM
WV530P	OEM
WV535P	OEM
WX-090	0012
WX090	0012
WX6	0143
WX115UA	OEM
WX115UB	OEM
WX115UC	OEM
WX115UD	OEM
WX115VA	OEM
WX115VB	OEM
WX115VC	OEM
WX115VD	OEM
WX115WA	OEM
WX115WB	OEM
WX115WC	OEM
WX115WD	OEM
WX115XA	OEM
WX115XB	OEM
WX115XC	OEM
WX115XD	OEM
WX1015	OEM
WX1015A	OEM
WX1015B	OEM
WX1015C	OEM
WX1015D	OEM
WX1015E	OEM
WX1015F	OEM
WX1016	OEM
WX1016A	OEM
WX1016B	OEM
WX1016C	OEM
WX1016D	OEM
WX1016E	OEM
WX1016F	OEM
WZ0-90	OEM
WZ09	0057
WZ030	0296
WZ-032	0296
WZ032	0296
WZ-034	0296
WZ034	0296
WZ-036	0372
WZ036	0372
WZ-038	0036
WZ038	0036
WZ-040	0036
WZ040	0036
WZ-042	0274
WZ042	0274
WZ-044	0274
WZ044	0274
WZ-046	0140
WZ046	0140
WZ-048	0140
WZ048	0140
WZ-049	0446
WZ-050	0041
WZ050	0041
WZ-052	0041
WZ052	0041
WZ-054	0253
WZ054	0253
WZ-056	0253
WZ056	0253
WZ-058	0157
WZ058	0157
WZ060	0157
WZ-061	0466
WZ061	0091
WZ-063	0466
WZ063	0466
WZ-065	0062
WZ065	0631
WZ-067	0062
WZ067	0062
WZ-069	0062
WZ069	0025
WZ-071	0062
WZ071	0062
WZ-073	0077
WZ073	0077
WZ-075	0077
WZ075	0077
WZ-077	0077
WZ077	0077
WZ-079	0165
WZ079	0165
WZ-081	0244
WZ081	0244
WZ-083	0165
WZ083	0165
WZ-085	0012
WZ085	1075
WZ-088	0318
WZ088	0318
WZ-090	0057
WZ090	0057
WZ-092	0012
WZ092	0012
WZ-094	0012
WZ094	0057
WZ-096	0064
WZ096	0170
WZ-098	0064
WZ098	0064
WZ5.6	0157
WZ7.5	0644
WZ9.1	0012
WZ10	0170
WZ12	0137
WZ13B	0361
WZ15	0002
WZ27	0436
WZ33	0039
WZ82	0327
WZ-90	0012
WZ-100	0170
WZ100	0064
WZ-105	0181
WZ105	0181
WZ-110	0181
WZ110	0181
WZ-115	0789
WZ115	0052
WZ-120	0052
WZ120	0052
WZ-120(AU)	0052
WZ-125	0053
WZ125	0361
WZ-130	0053
WZ130	0053
WZ-135	0873
WZ135	0873
WZ-140	0873
WZ140	0100
WZ-145	0681
WZ145	0681
WZ-150	0002
WZ150	0681
WZ-157	0440
WZ157	0440
WZ-162	0440
WZ162	0440
WZ-167	0210
WZ167	0210
WZ-172	0210
WZ172	0210
WZ-177	0490
WZ177	1639
WZ-182	0371
WZ182	0371
WZ-187	0666
WZ187	0666
WZ-192	0943
WZ192	0943
WZ-197	0695
WZ197	0695
WZ-210	0560
WZ210	0700
WZ-220	0700
WZ220	0700
WZ-230	0489
WZ230	0489
WZ-240	0398
WZ240	0398
WZ-250	0709
WZ250	0709
WZ-260	0450
WZ260	0450
WZ-270	0450
WZ270	0450
WZ-280	0257
WZ280	0257
WZ-290	0195
WZ290	0195
WZ-300	0195
WZ300	0195
WZ-310	0195
WZ310	0195
WZ-320	0166
WZ320	0166
WZ-330	0166
WZ330	0166
WZ-340	0166
WZ340	0166
WZ-350	0010
WZ350	0010
WZ360	0010
WZ522	0162
WZ523	0157
WZ524	0091
WZ525	0062
WZ526	0062
WZ527	0077
WZ528	0165
WZ529	0318
WZ531	0057
WZ532	0057
WZ533	0170
WZ534	0181
WZ535	0052
WZ536	0053
WZ537	0100
WZ538	0681
WZ539	0440
WZ541	0210
WZ542	0371
WZ543	0666
WZ544	0695
WZ904	0446
WZ905	0162
WZ906	0157
WZ907	0298
WZ908	0025
WZ909	0025
WZ910	0644
WZ911	0244
WZ912	1075
WZ913	0012
WZ914	0012
WZ915	0170
WZ916	0789
WZ917	0137
WZ918	0361
WZ919	0100
WZ920	0002
WZ921	0416
WZ922	1639
WZ923	0490
WZ924	0943
WZ925	0526
WZ926	0560
WZ927	1664
WZ928	1596
WZ3000	OEM
WZ3000A	OEM
WZ3000B	OEM
WZ3002	OEM
WZ3002A	OEM
WZ3002B	OEM
WZ3003	OEM
WZ3003A	OEM
WZ3003B	OEM
WZ3004	OEM
WZ3004A	OEM
WZ3004B	OEM
WZ3005	OEM
WZ3005A	OEM
WZ3005B	OEM
X0027CE	OEM
X0043CE	0167
X0054CE	2845
X0058GE	OEM
X0065CE	1420
X0069CE	0473
X0085TA	0598
X0087TA	4746
X0088TA	OEM
X0092CE	0069
X0093CE	2043
X0094CE	2043
X0094PA	OEM
X026BK	OEM
X030AK	OEM
X0100AA	0895
X0100AB	0895
X0100BA	0058
X0100BB	0058
X0100CA	0403
X0100CB	0403
X0100DA	0403
X0100DB	0403
X0101BA	0058
X0101BB	0058
X0101BD	0179
X0101DA	0403
X0101DB	0403
X0101DD	0342
X0101MA	1673
X0101MB	1673
X0101MD	3315
X0101NA	OEM
X0101NB	OEM
X0101ND	OEM
X0102AA	0895
X0102AB	0895
X0102BA	0058
X0102BB	0058
X0102CA	0403
X0102CB	0403
X0102DA	0403
X0102DB	0403
X0103BA	0058
X0103BB	0058
X0103BD	0179
X0103DA	0403
X0103DB	0403
X0103DD	0342
X0103MA	1673
X0103MB	1673
X0103MD	3315
X0103NA	OEM
X0103NB	OEM
X0103ND	OEM
X0137CE	2180
X0137E	OEM
X0178CE	1580
X0186GE	OEM
X0212CE	3640
X0213CE	2868
X0225C	3299
X0232CE	1835
X0233CE	OEM
X0238CE	2031
X0243CE	0167
X0249CE	1319
X0252CE	0069
X0260C	2641
X0260CE	OEM
X0268GE	OEM
X0275CE	4047
X0280C	OEM
X0301BG	0179
X0301DG	0342
X0301MG	3315
X0303BG	0179
X0303DG	0342
X0303MG	3315
X0304BG	0179
X0304DG	0342
X0304MG	3315

If replacement code is OEM, contact original manufacturer for replacement.

DEVICE TYPE	REPL CODE
X0308CE	OEM
X0314CE	OEM
X0359CE	OEM
X0403BE	0934
X0403BF	0934
X0403DE	0095
X0403DF	0095
X0403ME	1234
X0403MF	1234
X0403NE	OEM
X0403NF	OEM
X0404BE	0934
X0404BF	0934
X0404DE	0095
X0404DF	0934
X0404ME	OEM
X0404MF	OEM
X0404NE	OEM
X0404NF	OEM
X0424CE	OEM
X0424CE-1	OEM
X0539CE	OEM
X0564CE	OEM
X0579CE	OEM
X0580CE	OEM
X0581CE	OEM
X0600CE	3206
X0609BE	0934
X0609BF	0934
X0609DE	0095
X0609DF	0095
X0609ME	OEM
X0609MF	OEM
X0609NE	OEM
X0609NF	OEM
X0669CE	OEM
X0692CE	OEM
X0709BG	0179
X0709DG	0342
X0709MG	3315
X0735CE	OEM
X0735CE-542	OEM
X0800CE	OEM
X0820CE	OEM
X0943CE	OEM
X0950CE	OEM
X0D971	OEM
X0E861	OEM
X0E961	OEM
X0F751	OEM
X0F851	OEM
X0F951	OEM
X0G751	OEM
X0G851	OEM
X0H121	OEM
X0H131	OEM
X0H741	OEM
X1	OEM
X1C1644	0004
X1D971	OEM
X1E861	OEM
X1E961	OEM
X1F751	OEM
X1F851	OEM
X1F951	OEM
X1G751	OEM
X1G851	OEM
X1H121	OEM
X1H131	OEM
X1H741	OEM
X1RC2	OEM
X1RC3	OEM
X1RC5	OEM
X1RC7	OEM
X1RC10	OEM
X1RC20	OEM
X2	OEM
X2D971	OEM
X2E861	OEM
X2E961	OEM
X2F751	OEM
X2F851	OEM
X2F951	OEM
X2G751	OEM
X2G851	OEM
X2H121	OEM
X2H131	OEM
X2H741	OEM
X2I111	OEM
X3D971	OEM
X3E861	OEM
X3E961	OEM
X3F751	OEM
X3F851	OEM
X3F951	OEM
X3G751	OEM
X3G851	OEM
X3H741	OEM
X3I111	OEM
X4	OEM
X4B7.5	OEM
X4D971	OEM
X4E861	OEM
X4E961	OEM
X4F751	OEM
X4F851	OEM
X4F951	OEM
X4G751	OEM
X4G851	OEM

DEVICE TYPE	REPL CODE
X4H741	OEM
X5	OEM
X5D971	OEM
X5E861	OEM
X5E961	OEM
X5F751	OEM
X5F851	OEM
X5F951	OEM
X5G221	OEM
X5G551	OEM
X5G751	OEM
X5G851	OEM
X5H341	OEM
X5H541	OEM
X5H741	OEM
X5I111	OEM
X5I211	OEM
X5I331	OEM
X5I531	OEM
X5J201	OEM
X5J321	OEM
X5M6	0015
X6	OEM
X6A71	OEM
X6A72	OEM
X6A73	OEM
X6A74	OEM
X6A100	OEM
X6A101	OEM
X6A102	OEM
X6A103	OEM
X6A104	OEM
X6A105	OEM
X6A106	OEM
X6A107	OEM
X6D971	OEM
X6E861	OEM
X6E961	OEM
X6F751	OEM
X6F851	OEM
X6F951	OEM
X6G551	OEM
X6G751	OEM
X6G851	OEM
X6H341	OEM
X6H541	OEM
X6H741	OEM
X6I331	OEM
X6I531	OEM
X6J321	OEM
X6P1	OEM
X6P3	OEM
X6P10	OEM
X6P11	OEM
X8	OEM
X10-3	OEM
X10-4	OEM
X10-5	OEM
X10-6	OEM
X10-7	OEM
X10-8	OEM
X10-9	OEM
X10G1829	0016
X12	OEM
X13	OEM
X13B	OEM
X13C	OEM
X16	0143
X16A545-7	0016
X16A1938	0016
X16E3860	0016
X16E3890	0590
X16E3960	0016
X16N1485	0016
X18	0143
X24C00P	OEM
X-24C01P	OEM
X24C01P	OEM
X24C04	OEM
X24C04P	OEM
X25-3	OEM
X25-4	OEM
X25-5	OEM
X25-6	OEM
X25-7	OEM
X25-8	OEM
X25-9	OEM
X26	OEM
X30	OEM
X30A	OEM
X31	OEM
X31A	OEM
X32	OEM
X32A	OEM
X32A1389	0037
X32C4211	0079
X32C4293	0050
X32C4296	0079
X32C5099	0086
X32C5111	0086
X32C5198	0079
X32C6105	0079
X32D5422	0079
X32L4296	0079
X32M5026	0079
X32P5660	0144
X34E1226	0037
X34E2111	0079
X37C	1319

DEVICE TYPE	REPL CODE
X40N121	0283
X40Z113	0283
X42	0050
X43C248	0378
X44C358	0042
X44C758	0060
X45C359	0919
X50-3	OEM
X50-4	OEM
X50-5	OEM
X50-6	OEM
X50-7	OEM
X50-8	OEM
X50-9	OEM
X61P2	OEM
X-78	0004
X78	0279
X100KS	OEM
X110	0160
X113	OEM
X125KS	OEM
X133	OEM
X134	OEM
X137	0435
X150KS	OEM
X240P	OEM
X244P	OEM
X351A	OEM
X351B	OEM
X602K	OEM
X780	OEM
X841D	OEM
X881D	OEM
X1004	OEM
X1005	0160
X-1018	1024
X1018	1024
X1030CE	OEM
X1030CE-752	OEM
X1077CE	OEM
X1132CE	OEM
X1190CE	3473
X1231CE	OEM
X1247CE	OEM
X1535CE	OEM
X1712CE	OEM
X2402P	OEM
X2404P	OEM
X2444	OEM
X2444P	OEM
X2816BP	OEM
X3002	OEM
X3002A	OEM
X3030	OEM
X3033	OEM
X3060	OEM
X3066	OEM
X3068	OEM
X3070	OEM
X3070A	OEM
X3075	OEM
X3076	OEM
X4604	0015
X5004CE	OEM
X7070	0025
X-23305-3	0535
X-23305-4	0535
X24441	OEM
X53527AC(A)	OEM
X330302	0137
X-2408473	1063
X-2408784	2067
X300071592	0520
X300073360	0006
X300101502	0148
X300101509	0148
X300102009	0429
X300106930	3533
X300115080	0006
X300117500	3580
X300117593	3580
X300145009	0472
X301076530	1957
X301077251	0520
X301079400	2869
X301096530	1957
X301131809	OEM
X302056430	0527
X302094530	0076
X302116292	0558
X302138400	0018
X302164709	0277
X302181502	0076
X302181509	0076
X302181589	0076
X302183209	0042
X302183309	0042
X302251600	1157
X302278500	0249
X302278530	0249
X302278593	0249
X302278594	0249
X302329300	0261
X302369100	0060
X302374609	0060
X302374809	0060
X302398709	3678
X303056009	1203
X303088000	0456

DEVICE TYPE	REPL CODE
X303098600	2942
X303121800	2350
X303139200	2350
X303139500	2350
X303163000	1055
X303184309	OEM
X310090100	OEM
X320010070	0133
X320010079	0133
X320010080	0133
X320010190	2505
X320010240	0023
X320010380	0023
X320010390	0133
X320010430	0102
X320010450	0023
X320010452	0124
X320010460	0124
X320010470	0124
X320010480	0133
X320010512	0015
X320010939	0124
X320011201	0124
X330000059	0140
X330000068	0140
X330000230	0709
X330000320	1266
X330000342	0248
X330000422	0053
X330000442	0700
X330000492	0695
X330000522	0296
X330000542	0372
X330000550	0248
X330000560	0012
X330000570	0010
X330000582	0041
X330013009	0372
X330020020	0273
X330030288	0068
X330160109	0140
X330160209	0681
X330160309	0695
X330180069	0372
X340040030	0106
X340200010	OEM
X340200040	OEM
X340300010	0468
X340330017	0724
X340400030	0106
X340400040	0276
X340400060	0319
X350030030	0739
X350040090	OEM
X400004491	OEM
X400007650	OEM
X400007801	3441
X400014680	OEM
X400040161	1887
X400072010	OEM
X400072200	OEM
X400078010	OEM
X400078100	OEM
X400078101	OEM
X400081550	OEM
X400082371	OEM
X400082530	OEM
X400082550	0051
X400082591	OEM
X400104162	0518
X400120640	OEM
X400141640	2341
X400143644	OEM
X400244010	OEM
X400250300	OEM
X400662647	OEM
X420100030	0331
X420100060	1197
X420100070	1329
X420100160	1339
X420100170	1342
X420100380	0990
X420101230	1149
X420200020	2223
X420200040	2248
X420201610	0852
X420202410	OEM
X420202570	2190
X420300000	1519
X420300020	1550
X420300040	1585
X420300050	1598
X420300080	1623
X420300100	1652
X420300140	1688
X420300200	0035
X420300270	0183
X420300300	0822
X420300320	0088
X420300510	1027
X420300540	1846
X420300730	1856
X420300740	0243
X420300750	1859
X420300860	0288
X420300930	1877
X420301230	0973
X420301390	0153
X420301450	1554

DEVICE TYPE	REPL CODE
X420301540	4956
X420301560	1644
X420301610	0852
X420301630	0887
X420301640	4274
X420301750	1662
X420301950	1305
X420302210	1230
X420302440	0453
X420302450	0458
X420302730	0888
X420303730	0704
X420303740	0708
X420303930	0813
X420305410	2525
X420500000	2392
X420500020	OEM
X420500040	OEM
X420500080	OEM
X420500100	OEM
X420500110	OEM
X420500320	2646
X420500370	OEM
X420500400	OEM
X420500740	0243
X420501120	OEM
X420505730	OEM
X420505740	OEM
X440029020	0620
X440029040	0765
X440032060	1197
X440040030	OEM
X440041040	0963
X440045040	OEM
X440055560	3254
X440057330	1110
X440058120	0330
X440063050	0619
X440064940	1813
X440069050	1275
X440070490	0001
X440072350	OEM
X440072920	0624
X440073860	3034
X440075631	OEM
X440078051	1288
X440078054	1288
X440079120	1827
X440137140	OEM
X440140050	0619
X440150640	3098
X440150790	5738
X440160660	0101
X440167610	OEM
X440170070	OEM
X440193050	2155
X440200650	3877
X440212000	OEM
X440223110	2093
X440672200	2738
X440672210	2738
X440751880	0503
X440751890	0506
X440755400	1586
X440756330	1586
X440757110	OEM
X440757520	OEM
X440757600	OEM
X440759820	3327
X440762120	4264
X460405000	0394
X460406901	0119
X460409300	2368
X460458400	3581
X4700078101	OEM
XA/RA-1000	OEM
XA101	0050
XA102	0050
XA103	0050
XA104	0050
XA111	0050
XA112	0050
XA121	0015
XA122	0004
XA123	0050
XA124	0050
XA126	0050
XA131	0050
XA141	0050
XA142	0050
XA143	0050
XA151	0164
XA152	0164
XA161	0050
XA162	OEM
XA494	0037
XA-495	0037
XA495	0037
XA495(C)	0037
XA495AC	0037
XA495C	0037
XA495D	0006
XA701	0595
XA702	0595
XA703	0595
XAA104	0232
XAA105	0867
XAA106	1018
XAA107	1164

DEVICE TYPE	REPL CODE
XAA108	1150
XAA109	1199
XAN3061	4783
XAN3062	4784
XAN3063	OEM
XAN3064	4786
XB087A0	OEM
XB1	0211
XB2	0211
XB2/XB4	2839
XB2.XB4	2839
XB3	0211
XB3B	0211
XB3BN	0004
XB3C	0211
XB4	0038
XB-5	0160
XB5	0085
XB-7	0160
XB7	0085
XB8	0050
XB8C	OEM
XB8E	OEM
XB9	0279
XB10	0050
XB12	0086
XB13	0004
XB14	0160
XB102	0004
XB103	0004
XB104	0004
XB112	0004
XB113	0004
XB114	0004
XB121	OEM
XB152	0002
XB401	0555
XB404	0042
XB408	0042
XB413	1963
XB476	0042
XC55FA	OEM
XC55FB	OEM
XC55FC	OEM
XC55FD	OEM
XC55FDQ	OEM
XC55PA	OEM
XC55PC	OEM
XC55PD	OEM
XC55PDK	OEM
XC66-10	OEM
XC66-10K	OEM
XC66-25	OEM
XC66-25K	OEM
XC70	0025
XC88FA	OEM
XC88FAQ	OEM
XC88FB	OEM
XC88FBQ	OEM
XC88FC	OEM
XC88FCQ	OEM
XC88FD	OEM
XC88PA	OEM
XC88PAK	OEM
XC88PB	OEM
XC88PBK	OEM
XC88PC	OEM
XC88PCK	OEM
XC88PD	OEM
XC99-30	OEM
XC99-50K	OEM
XC101	0004
XC121	0004
XC131	0004
XC141	0160
XC142	0160
XC155	0085
XC156	0085
XC161	0279
XC163	OEM
XC171	0004
XC209-5VG	OEM
XC209-5VR	OEM
XC209-5VY	OEM
XC209G	0835
XC209R	OEM
XC209Y	3095
XC210G	OEM
XC210R	OEM
XC210Y	OEM
XC220G	OEM
XC220R	OEM
XC220Y	OEM
XC309	OEM
XC371	0127
XC372	0079
XC373	0079
XC374	0079
XC520R	OEM
XC521R	OEM
XC522G	OEM
XC522R	OEM
XC526G	OEM
XC526G2	OEM
XC526R	OEM
XC526R2	OEM
XC526Y	OEM
XC526Y2	OEM
XC554G	OEM

DEVICE TYPE	REPL CODE
XC554G6	OEM
XC554G15	OEM
XC554G24	OEM
XC554R	OEM
XC554R9	OEM
XC554R12	OEM
XC554Y	OEM
XC554Y12	OEM
XC556G	OEM
XC556G2	OEM
XC556G3	OEM
XC556R	OEM
XC556R2	OEM
XC556R3	OEM
XC556Y	OEM
XC556Y2	OEM
XC556Y3	OEM
XC703	OEM
XC713	OEM
XC723	0103
XC880A	OEM
XC880AE	OEM
XC880B	OEM
XC880BE	OEM
XC880C	OEM
XC880CE	OEM
XC880D	OEM
XC881A	OEM
XC881AE	OEM
XC881B	OEM
XC881BE	OEM
XC881C	OEM
XC881CE	OEM
XC940A	OEM
XC940AE	OEM
XC940B	OEM
XC940BE	OEM
XC940C	OEM
XC940CE	OEM
XC940D	OEM
XC940DE	OEM
XC941A	OEM
XC941AE	OEM
XC941B	OEM
XC941BE	OEM
XC941C	OEM
XC941CE	OEM
XC941D	OEM
XC941DE	OEM
XC944	OEM
XC945	OEM
XC1011	OEM
XC1017	OEM
XC1100G	OEM
XC1100R	OEM
XC1100Y	OEM
XC1101G	OEM
XC1101R	OEM
XC1101Y	OEM
XC1209A	OEM
XC1209AB	OEM
XC1209B	OEM
XC1209BB	OEM
XC1209C	OEM
XC1209CB	OEM
XC1209D	OEM
XC1209DB	OEM
XC1288A	OEM
XC1288AB	OEM
XC1288B	OEM
XC1288BB	OEM
XC1288C	OEM
XC1288CB	OEM
XC1288D	OEM
XC1312	1601
XC-1312A	1601
XC1510	OEM
XC2090	OEM
XC2201	OEM
XC4550	OEM
XC4555	OEM
XC4560	OEM
XC4655	OEM
XC4850-5VG	OEM
XC4850-5VR	OEM
XC4850-5VY	OEM
XC4850-12VG	OEM
XC4850-12VR	OEM
XC4850-12VY	OEM
XC4850G	OEM
XC4850R	OEM
XC4850Y	OEM
XC4950	OEM
XC4955	OEM
XC5053G	1767
XC5053R	OEM
XC5053Y	3128
XC5057R	OEM
XC5057R3	OEM
XC5059G	OEM
XC5059R	OEM
XC5059Y	OEM
XC-5491	5287
XC5491	OEM
XC5535	OEM
XC5547R	OEM
XC5547R9	OEM
XC5547R15	OEM
XC5549G	OEM
XC5549G6	OEM

If replacement code is OEM, contact original manufacturer for replacement. 631

DEVICE TYPE	REPL CODE
XC5549G15	OEM
XC5549G24	OEM
XC5549R	OEM
XC5549R9	OEM
XC5549R12	OEM
XC5549Y	OEM
XC5549Y6	OEM
XC5549Y12	OEM
XC5565	OEM
XC5567R	OEM
XC5567R2	OEM
XC5567R3	OEM
XC5569G	OEM
XC5569G2	OEM
XC5569G3	OEM
XC5569R	OEM
XC5569R2	OEM
XC5569R3	OEM
XC5569Y	OEM
XC5569Y2	OEM
XC5569Y3	OEM
XC89507P	OEM
XC99659P	OEM
XD/RD-1000	OEM
XD2A	0123
XD-258-42	0571
XD500	OEM
XD501	OEM
XD502	OEM
XD503	OEM
XD2201A	OEM
XD2210	OEM
XD2212D	OEM
XD-2581-42	0571
XD2804A	OEM
XD2816A	OEM
XD5081	OEM
XD5082	OEM
XDC14528-304	OEM
XDS2724P	OEM
XDS2724S	OEM
XE8340ENM	OEM
XE1503723	OEM
XF3-0.5	OEM
XF3-1.0	OEM
XF3-1.5	OEM
XF3-2.0	OEM
XF3-2.5	OEM
XF10-3	OEM
XF10-4	OEM
XF10-5	OEM
XF10-6	OEM
XF10-7	OEM
XF10-8	OEM
XF10-9	OEM
XF25-3	OEM
XF25-4	OEM
XF25-5	OEM
XF25-6	OEM
XF25-7	OEM
XF25-8	OEM
XF25-9	OEM
XF50-3	OEM
XF50-4	OEM
XF50-5	OEM
XF50-6	OEM
XF50-7	OEM
XF50-8	OEM
XF50-9	OEM
XFT2	OEM
XG1	0050
XG2	0050
XG3	0050
XG5	0050
XG8	0004
XG10	0050
XG11	0050
XG12	0050
XG24	0050
XG28	0208
XG29	0208
XG30	0016
XG32	0164
XG33	0208
XGS3025	OEM
XGS3030	OEM
XGS3035	OEM
XGS5025	OEM
XGS5030	OEM
XGS5035	OEM
XGS7001	OEM
XGS7002	0617
XGS410030	1841
XGS410035	1841
XGSA1530	OEM
XGSA1535	OEM
XGSA1540	OEM
XGSA3030	OEM
XGSA3035	OEM
XGSA3040	OEM
XGSA5030	OEM
XGSA5035	OEM
XGSA5040	OEM
XGSQ1530	OEM
XGSQ1535	OEM
XGSQ1540	OEM
XGSQ3030	OEM
XGSQ3035	OEM
XGSQ3040	OEM
XGSQ5030	OEM
XGSQ5035	OEM
XGSQ5040	OEM
XGSQ7530	OEM
XGSQ7535	OEM
XGSQ7540	OEM
XGSR3030	1955
XGSR3035	1955
XGSR3040	OEM
XGSR5030	1955
XGSR5035	1841
XGSR5040	1955
XGSR7530	OEM
XGSR7535	OEM
XGSR7540	OEM
XGSR10025	OEM
XGSR10030	OEM
XGSR10035	OEM
XGSR10040	1841
XGSR50020	OEM
XH10	OEM
XH20	OEM
XH20A	OEM
XI-548	0103
XI-549	0178
XJ13	0211
XJ71	0050
XJ72	0050
XJ73	0050
XM203	OEM
XM541	OEM
XM542	OEM
XM543	OEM
XM544	OEM
XMP1	OEM
XMP2	OEM
XMP3	OEM
XN1B301	OEM
XN12A	0085
XN12B	0085
XN12C	0085
XN12E	0085
XN1113	OEM
XN1212	OEM
XN1213	OEM
XN1215	OEM
XN1401	OEM
XN1501	OEM
XN4113	OEM
XN4213	OEM
XN4401	OEM
XN4501	OEM
XN4601	OEM
XNC101	0038
XO238CE	OEM
XP-258I-82	0571
XP-2581-82	0571
XR082CN	OEM
XR082CP	3695
XR082D	OEM
XR082DN	OEM
XR082DP	OEM
XR082N	OEM
XR082P	OEM
XR083CN	OEM
XR083CP	OEM
XR083D	OEM
XR083DN	OEM
XR083DP	OEM
XR083M	OEM
XR083N	OEM
XR083P	OEM
XR084CN	OEM
XR084CP	OEM
XR084D	OEM
XR084DN	OEM
XR084DP	OEM
XR084M	OEM
XR084N	OEM
XR084P	OEM
XR094CN	OEM
XR094CP	OEM
XR094M	OEM
XR094N	OEM
XR094P	OEM
XR095CN	OEM
XR095CP	OEM
XR095M	OEM
XR095N	OEM
XR095P	OEM
XR096CN	OEM
XR096CP	OEM
XR096N	OEM
XR096P	OEM
XR146M	OEM
XR205	OEM
XR210CN	OEM
XR210M	OEM
XR246N	OEM
XR246P	OEM
XR320P	OEM
XR340M	OEM
XR346-2CN	OEM
XR346-2CP	OEM
XR346CN	OEM
XR346CP	OEM
XR350M	OEM
XR430M	OEM
XR494CN	OEM
XR494CP	OEM
XR494M	OEM
XR495CN	OEM
XR495CP	OEM
XR495M	OEM
XR555CM	OEM
XR555CN	OEM
XR555CP	OEM
XR555M	OEM
XR556CN	OEM
XR556CP	OEM
XR556M	OEM
XR558CN	OEM
XR558CP	OEM
XR558M	OEM
XR559CN	OEM
XR559CP	OEM
XR559M	OEM
XR567CN	OEM
XR567CP	OEM
XR567M	6597
XR1310	6190
XR1458CP	0356
XR1468CN	OEM
XR1488N	0503
XR1488P	0503
XR1489AN	0506
XR1489AP	OEM
XR1524M	OEM
XR1525AN(A)	OEM
XR1527AN(A)	OEM
XR1543N(A)	OEM
XR1568M	OEM
XR1568N	OEM
XR2200	OEM
XR2200CP	OEM
XR2201CP	0839
XR2202CP	1001
XR2203CP	1126
XR2204CP	1252
XR-2206	OEM
XR2206	OEM
XR2206CN	OEM
XR2206CP	OEM
XR2206M	OEM
XR2206N	OEM
XR2206P	OEM
XR-2207CN	OEM
XR2207CN	OEM
XR2207CP	OEM
XR-2207M	OEM
XR2207M	OEM
XR-2207M/883B	OEM
XR-2207N	OEM
XR2207N	OEM
XR-2207P	OEM
XR2207P	OEM
XR2208CN	OEM
XR2208CP	OEM
XR2208M	OEM
XR2208N	OEM
XR2208P	OEM
XR2209CN	OEM
XR2209CP	OEM
XR2209M	OEM
XR-2211	OEM
XR2211	OEM
XR-2211CN	OEM
XR-2211CP	OEM
XR-2211M	OEM
XR-2211M/883B	OEM
XR-2211N	OEM
XR-2211P	OEM
XR2213CN	OEM
XR2213CP	OEM
XR2213M	OEM
XR2213P	OEM
XR2216CN	OEM
XR2216CP	OEM
XR2225AN(A)	OEM
XR2228CN	OEM
XR2228CP	OEM
XR2228M	OEM
XR2228N	OEM
XR2228P	OEM
XR2230CP	OEM
XR2235(A)	OEM
XR2240CN	OEM
XR2240CP	OEM
XR2240M	OEM
XR2240N	OEM
XR2240P	OEM
XR2242	OEM
XR2242CN	OEM
XR2242CP	OEM
XR2242M	OEM
XR2243CN	OEM
XR2243CP	OEM
XR2264CP	OEM
XR2265CP	OEM
XR2266	OEM
XR2271CN	OEM
XR2271CP	OEM
XR2272CN	OEM
XR2272CP	OEM
XR2276CP	OEM
XR2277P	OEM
XR2278P	OEM
XR2279CP	OEM
XR2284CP	OEM
XR2284P	OEM
XR2288CP	OEM
XR2288P	OEM
XR2524N	OEM
XR2524P	OEM
XR2525AC(A)	OEM
XR2527AC(A)	OEM
XR2527AN(A)	OEM
XR2556CN	OEM
XR2556CP	OEM
XR2556M	OEM
XR2567CN	OEM
XR2567CP	OEM
XR2567M	OEM
XR3403CN	OEM
XR3403CP	OEM
XR3503M	OEM
XR3524	5140
XR3524CN	OEM
XR3524CP	5140
XR3525AC(A)	OEM
XR3525AN(A)	OEM
XR3527AN(A)	OEM
XR3543N(A)	OEM
XR4136CN	OEM
XR4136CP	2995
XR4136M	OEM
XR4151CP	OEM
XR4151P	OEM
XR4194CN	OEM
XR4194M	OEM
XR4194MK	OEM
XR4195CK	OEM
XR4195CP	5723
XR4195MT	OEM
XR4202M	OEM
XR4202N	OEM
XR4202P	OEM
XR4212CN	OEM
XR4212CP	OEM
XR4212M	OEM
XR4558CP	0356
XR4739CN	OEM
XR4739CP	OEM
XR4741CN	OEM
XR4741CP	OEM
XR4741M	OEM
XR5532AN	OEM
XR5532N	OEM
XR5533AN	OEM
XR5533AP	OEM
XR5533N	OEM
XR5533P	OEM
XR5534ACN	OEM
XR5534ACP	OEM
XR5534AM	OEM
XR5534CN	OEM
XR5534CP	OEM
XR5534M	OEM
XR5534N	OEM
XR5534P	OEM
XR6118AP	OEM
XR6118P	OEM
XR6128AP	OEM
XR6128P	OEM
XR8038ACN(A)	OEM
XR8038ACP(A)	OEM
XR8038AM(A)	OEM
XR8038AN(A)	OEM
XR8038AP(A)	OEM
XR-8038CN	0301
XR8038CN	0301
XR-8038CP	0301
XR8038CP	0301
XR-8038M	OEM
XR8038M	OEM
XR-8038N	0301
XR8038N	OEM
XR-8038P	0301
XR8038P	0301
XR9201CP	OEM
XR13600AP	OEM
XR13600CP	OEM
XRA5114L	OEM
XRA6459P1	OEM
XRA7305AS	OEM
XRA7305BS	OEM
XRA15218N	OEM
XRL555CN	0580
XRL555CP	OEM
XRL555M	OEM
XRL556CN	2842
XRL556CP	2842
XRL556M	OEM
XR-S200	OEM
XRU2744S	OEM
XRU27745-1	OEM
XS1	0144
XS2	0144
XS3	0144
XS4	0144
XS6	0144
XS9.1B	0012
XS10	0015
XS12	OEM
XS14	0144
XS15	0144
XS16	0015
XS16A	0015
XS17	0015
XS17A	0015
XS18	0015
XS19	0037
XS21	0016
XS22	1325
XS22(RECT.)	0015
XS23	0015
XS23A	0015
XS26	0208
XS30	0086
XS30L	OEM
XS31	0015
XS31L	OEM
XS31P	OEM
XS32L	OEM
XS32P	OEM
XS36	0007
XS37	0007
XS38	0007
XS39	0007
XS40	0127
XS40A	0015
XS40L	OEM
XS40P	OEM
XS41L	OEM
XS41P	OEM
XS42L	OEM
XS42P	OEM
XS101	0164
XS104	0164
XS121	0164
XT1-24	OEM
XT1A	0334
XT1B	0334
XT1C	OEM
XT1D	OEM
XT1.24	OEM
XT2A	OEM
XT2B	OEM
XT2C	OEM
XT2D	OEM
XT15X3	0144
XT100	0164
XT200	0164
XT200A	OEM
XT300	0136
XT400	0136
XT515	0264
XT516	0264
XT517	0264
XT518	0264
XT519	0264
XT520	0264
XT2104-401	OEM
XT2104-501	OEM
XT2104-601	OEM
XT2104-701	OEM
XT2104-801	OEM
XT2105-601	OEM
XT2105-801	OEM
XT2105-1001	OEM
XT2105-1201	OEM
XT2105-1401	OEM
XTP10	OEM
XTP11	OEM
XU604	0015
XV541	OEM
XV542	OEM
XV543	OEM
XV544	OEM
XX	OEM
XX8	OEM
XX10	OEM
XX12	OEM
XX15	OEM
XX20	OEM
XX25	OEM
XX30	OEM
XX40	OEM
XXC	OEM
XXF8	OEM
XXF10	OEM
XXF12	OEM
XXF15	OEM
XXF20	OEM
XXF25	OEM
XXF30	OEM
XXF40	OEM
XZ045	OEM
XZ047	OEM
XZ-049	0162
XZ049	0041
XZ-051	0162
XZ051	4303
XZ055	0253
XZ057	0253
XZ060	0091
XZ062	0466
XZ-064	0244
XZ064	0244
XZ-070	0298
XZ-072	0644
XZ-076	0644
XZ076	0644
XZ084	0244
XZ-086	1075
XZ-090	0012
XZ090	0012
XZ-092	0012
XZ092	0012
XZ094	0012
XZ-096	0170
XZ098	0170
XZ-100	0170
XZ100	0170
XZ102	0170
XZ107	OEM
XZ-122	0137
XZ122	0137
XZ132	1389
XZ-152	0002
XZ152	0002
XZ495C	OEM
XZH24	OEM
XZ070	0025
Y	OEM
Y0-6A	0015
Y065	0025
Y068	0062
Y10EA	OEM
Y10GA	OEM
Y23	OEM
Y25	OEM
Y100	0479
Y363	0004
Y3015	OEM
Y29979	0144
Y56601-08	0016
Y56601-50	0037
Y1343773-1	0111
Y13175962	0124
Y13189245	1129
Y13238241	0326
Y13290333	0111
Y13297762	0037
Y13297763	0037
Y13298671	0133
Y13310137	0224
Y13310138	0144
Y13310139	0037
Y13310146	0102
Y13310147	0015
Y13331721	0102
Y13331741	0283
Y13331781	0786
Y13331799	OEM
Y13331813	0309
Y13331873	0695
Y13358072	0016
Y13390991	0042
Y13391001	0919
Y13391143	0590
Y13391153	0786
Y13398601	0015
Y13399701	0037
Y13411222	0015
Y13417381	0103
Y13430051	0236
Y13432501	0133
Y13437771	0023
Y13450181	1698
Y15310157	0167
Y15310158	1319
Y15310159	1239
Y15377001	2153
Y15390751	0850
Y15415451	3346
Y15416272	2804
Y15418561	3166
Y15432511	1797
Y15432512	1797
Y15437031	0850
Y15453001	0167
Y32390915	1061
Y130201002	0518
Y130213002	0898
Y130213003	0076
Y130213004	0275
Y130213005	0191
Y130213006	2420
Y130213007	0148
Y130213041	0133
Y130213042	4833
Y130213043	0023
Y130213044	0344
Y130213045	0023
Y130800501	OEM
Y130800701	2672
Y130801001	2263
Y130801301	OEM
Y130801401	2263
Y131759610	0124
Y132929871	0133
Y133101149	0077
Y133101310	0076
Y133101317	1045
Y133101318	1157
Y133101319	0037
Y133101321	0144
Y133101322	0079
Y133101326	0590
Y133101327	0710
Y133101328	0079
Y133101332	0527
Y133101333	0018
Y133101363	0155
Y133101410	0005
Y133101411	0133
Y133101412	0143
Y133101413	0133
Y133101414	0041
Y133101415	0005
Y133101417	0133
Y133101419	0015
Y133101440	0015
Y133318728	OEM
Y310502139	OEM
Y384456911	3381
Y435800501	OEM
Y435800701	OEM
Y435800702	OEM
Y435800801	OEM
Y440800001	OEM
Y440800101	2161
Y440800102	OEM
Y440800301	2263
Y440800601	0806
Y440800701	OEM
Y440800702	OEM
Y440801001	OEM
Y440801101	0806
Y440801301	OEM
Y440801501	2263
Y440802501	OEM
Y440803801	OEM
Y440804101	OEM
Y441800101	0806
Y441800102	0806
Y441800103	OEM
Y446800001	OEM
Y446800102	OEM
Y448800001	OEM
Y448800404	OEM
Y461800002	OEM
Y461800003	OEM
Y490801601	OEM
Y560800000	OEM
YAAD001	0244
YAAD004	0015
YAAD007	0139
YAAD009	0143
YAAD010	0133
YAAD017	0244
YAAD018	0133
YAAD019	0015
YAAD020	0015
YAAD021	0244
YAAD022	0015
YAAN2SC1096K	0555
YAAN2SC1096L	0555
YAAN2SC1096N	0555
YAAN2SD141	0178
YAANL2SC1096K	0386
YAANL2SC1096L	0386
YAANL2SC1096M	0386
YAANL2SC1096N	0386
YAANL2SC1096Q	0386
YAANL2SC1096R	0386
YAANZ2S1096	0555
YAANZ2SC1096	0386
YAANZ2SC1096K	0386
YAANZ2SC1096L	0386
YAG100	OEM
YAG444	OEM
YAG444-4	OEM
YANZ2SC1096	0386
YANZ2SC1096K	0386
YANZ2SC1096L	0386
YANZ2SC1096M	0386
YBAD009	0015
YBG1000	5064
YC02P11/2	0087
YD1121	0133
YEAD005	0005
YEAD009	OEM
YEAD010	0244
YEAD015	0012
YEAD022	OEM
YEAD024	0244
YEAD025	0012
YEAD029	0030
YEAD030	0015
YEAD032	0143
YEAD1N60P	0123
YEAD1SV53	0030
YEADAW01-06	0298
YEADISV53	0030
YEADUPC577H	2246
YEAM004	3901
YEAM53274P	1303
YEAMJM78L05	1288
YEAMLM2900N	2232
YEAMM5152L	2512
YEAMNJ58L05	1288
YEAMNJM58L05	2995
YEAMNJM78L05	1288
YEAMSCL4416	OEM
YEAMSM5118	6048
YEAMSN16889	OEM
YEAMUPC577H	2246
YEAN2SC941	0155
YEAN3SK39Q	0349
YH1000	OEM
YH1010	OEM
YH1012	OEM

632

If replacement code is OEM, contact original manufacturer for replacement.

DEVICE TYPE	REPL CODE
YH1014	OEM
YH1020	OEM
YH1041	OEM
YH1042	OEM
YH1043	OEM
YH1045	OEM
YH1047A1	OEM
YH1047A2	OEM
YH1048	OEM
YH1049	OEM
YH1050	OEM
YH1120	OEM
YH1150	OEM
YH1160	OEM
YH1162	OEM
YH1181	OEM
YH1190	OEM
YH1191	OEM
YH1193	OEM
YH1194	OEM
YH1196	OEM
YH1197	OEM
YH1202	OEM
YH1203	OEM
YH1204	OEM
YH1205	OEM
YH1206	OEM
YH1207	OEM
YH1208	OEM
YH1209	OEM
YH1300	OEM
YH1301	OEM
YH1420	OEM
YH1421	OEM
YH1422	OEM
YH1750	OEM
YJ1050	OEM
YJ1060	OEM
YJ1071	OEM
YJ1110	OEM
YJ1112	OEM
YJ1120	OEM
YJ1121	OEM
YJ1123	OEM
YJ1124	OEM
YJ1150	OEM
YJ1160	OEM
YJ1162	OEM
YJ1164	OEM
YJ1180	OEM
YJ1180H	OEM
YJ1180L	OEM
YJ1181	OEM
YJ1181H	OEM
YJ1181L	OEM
YJ1185	OEM
YJ1185H	OEM
YJ1185L	OEM
YJ1191	OEM
YJ1193	OEM
YJ1194	OEM
YJ1200	OEM
YJ1201	OEM
YJ1210	OEM
YJ1230	OEM
YJ1280	OEM
YJ1300	OEM
YJ1301	OEM
YJ1320	OEM
YJ1321	OEM
YJ1380	OEM
YJ1400	OEM
YJ1410	OEM
YJ1420	OEM
YJ1440	OEM
YJ1441	OEM
YJ1442	OEM
YJ1443	OEM
YJ1463	OEM
YJ1464	OEM
YJ1470	OEM
YJ1480	OEM
YJ1481	OEM
YJ1490	OEM
YJ1500	OEM
YK1000	OEM
YK1001	OEM
YK1002	OEM
YK1003	OEM
YK1004	OEM
YK1005	OEM
YK1010	OEM
YK1020	OEM
YK1021	OEM
YK1023	OEM
YK1030	OEM
YK1050	OEM
YK1081	OEM
YK1082	OEM
YK1100	OEM
YK1110	OEM
YK1120	OEM
YK1151	OEM
YK1190	OEM
YK1191	OEM
YK1192	OEM
YK1195	OEM
YK1196	OEM
YK1197	OEM

DEVICE TYPE	REPL CODE
YK1200	OEM
YK1210	OEM
YK1220	OEM
YK1230	OEM
YK1300	OEM
YL56	1974
YL212	3095
YL4484	3095
YL4550	3128
YL4850	3128
YM2149F	OEM
YM2201K	OEM
YM2601	OEM
YM3015	OEM
YM3015N000	OEM
YM3411	OEM
YM3428	OEM
YM3531	OEM
YM3805	OEM
YM3805N	OEM
YO	OEM
YOD4	0229
YR	OEM
YR-011	0015
YR011	0015
YS6-V139-2-2	0143
YSD2-11P4K32	OEM
YSD2-11P4K35	OEM
YSD2-11P6K32	OEM
YSD2-11P6K35	OEM
YSD2-11P8K38	OEM
YSD2-11P8K41	OEM
YSD2-11P10K38	OEM
YSD2-11P10K41	OEM
YSD2-11P12K38	OEM
YSD2-11P12K41	OEM
YSD2-11P14K38	OEM
YSD2-11P14K41	OEM
YSD2-12P4K32	OEM
YSD2-12P4K35	OEM
YSD2-12P6K32	OEM
YSD2-12P6K35	OEM
YSD2-12P8K38	OEM
YSD2-12P8K41	OEM
YSD2-12P10K38	OEM
YSD2-12P10K41	OEM
YSD2-12P12K38	OEM
YSD2-12P12K41	OEM
YSD2-12P14K38	OEM
YSD2-12P14K41	OEM
YSD5-41P10K44	OEM
YSD5-41P12K44	OEM
YSD5-41P14K44	OEM
YSD5-41P16K44	OEM
YSD5-41P18K44	OEM
YSD9-01P16K29	OEM
YSD9-01P16K32	OEM
YSD9-01P16K35	OEM
YSD9-01P18K29	OEM
YSD9-01P18K32	OEM
YSD9-01P18K35	OEM
YSD9-01P20K29	OEM
YSD9-01P20K32	OEM
YSD9-01P20K35	OEM
YSD9-02P24K38	OEM
YSD9-02P24K41	OEM
YSD9-02P24K44	OEM
YSD9-02P26K38	OEM
YSD9-02P26K41	OEM
YSD9-02P26K44	OEM
YSD9-02P28K38	OEM
YSD9-02P28K41	OEM
YSD9-02P28K44	OEM
YSD9-03P30K50	OEM
YSD9-03P30K53	OEM
YSD9-03P32K50	OEM
YSD9-03P32K53	OEM
YSD9-03P34K50	OEM
YSD9-03P34K53	OEM
YSD9-03P36K50	OEM
YSD9-03P36K53	OEM
YSD211P4K38	OEM
YSD211P6K38	OEM
YSD212P4K38	OEM
YSD902P22K38	OEM
YSG-20024	0015
YSG-V47-1-3	0102
YSG-V47-7-51	0479
YSG-V47-7-51-1	0015
YSG-V47-7-51-2	0015
YSG-V81-2-3	0907
YSG-V139-2-2	0143
YSG-V139-22	0143
YST2-01K2P8	OEM
YST2-01K2P10	OEM
YST2-01K2P12	OEM
YST2-01K2P14	OEM
YST2-01K2P16	OEM
YST2-02K1P2	OEM
YST2-02K1P4	OEM
YST2-02K1P6	OEM
YST2-02K1P8	OEM
YST3-41K3P2	OEM
YST3-41K3P4	OEM
YST3-41K3P6	OEM
YST3-41K3P8	OEM
YST3-42K3P2	OEM
YST3-42K3P4	OEM
YST3-42K3P6	OEM

DEVICE TYPE	REPL CODE
YST3-42K3P8	OEM
YST3-42K3P10	OEM
YST3-42K3P12	OEM
YST3-42K3P14	OEM
YST5-01K2P8	OEM
YST5-01K2P10	OEM
YST5-01K2P12	OEM
YST5-01K2P14	OEM
YST5-01K2P16	OEM
YST5-01K2P18	OEM
YST5-21K4P18	OEM
YST5-21K4P20	OEM
YST5-21K4P22	OEM
YST5-21K4P24	OEM
YST5-21K4P26	OEM
YST5-21K4P28	OEM
YST5-21K4P30	OEM
YST8-01K2P8	OEM
YST8-01K2P10	OEM
YST8-01K2P12	OEM
YST8-01K2P14	OEM
YST8-01K2P16	OEM
YST8-01K2P18	OEM
YST8-02K1P2	OEM
YST8-02K1P4	OEM
YST8-21K3P18	OEM
YST8-21K3P20	OEM
YST8-21K3P22	OEM
YST8-21K3P24	OEM
YST8-21K3P26	OEM
YST8-21K3P28	OEM
YST8-21K3P30	OEM
YST301QP2K3	OEM
YST301QP4K3	OEM
YST301QP6K3	OEM
YST301QP8K3	OEM
YST301QP10K3	OEM
YST302QP2K3	OEM
YST302QP4K3	OEM
YST302QP6K3	OEM
YST302QP8K3	OEM
YST302QP10K3	OEM
YST302QP12K3	OEM
YST302QP14K3	OEM
YST801SP8K2	OEM
YST801SP10K2	OEM
YST801SP12K2	OEM
YST801SP14K2	OEM
YST801SP16K2	OEM
YST801SP18K2K2	OEM
YV1	0004
YV1A	0004
YV2	0004
YYAAD007	0139
YZ030	0296
YZ-037	0188
YZ037	0451
YZ-047	0446
YZ047A	0446
YZ058	0157
YZ060	3428
YZ-063	0466
YZ063	0466
YZ065F	0025
YZ-080	0244
YZ080	0244
YZ088A	OEM
YZ-284	1664
YZ284	0721
Z/D27	0436
Z0008CE	OEM
Z-00	0914
Z0021-UA	OEM
Z0027CE	OEM
Z0035-UDC	OEM
Z0039-BCA	OEM
Z0047-UBA	OEM
Z0047-VBA	OEM
Z0047UBA	OEM
Z0063-UAA	2647
Z0063-UAB	2647
Z0064-UAA	2647
Z0065-UAA	OEM
Z0065-UAB	OEM
Z0069UAA	2647
Z0069UAB	2647
Z0073CE	OEM
Z0-12	0137
Z0-12A	0137
Z0-12B	0137
Z0-27	0436
Z0-27A	0436
Z0-27B	0436
Z01-13	0361
Z-08	0644
Z0101BA	4381
Z0101BB	4382
Z0101DA	4382
Z0101DB	4382
Z0101MA	4404
Z0101MB	4404
Z0101NA	OEM
Z0101NB	OEM
Z0102BA	OEM
Z0102DA	OEM
Z0102MA	OEM
Z0102NA	OEM
Z0104BA	4381
Z0104BB	4381

DEVICE TYPE	REPL CODE
Z0104DA	4382
Z0104DB	4382
Z0104MA	4404
Z0104MB	4404
Z0104NA	OEM
Z0104NB	OEM
Z0105BA	OEM
Z0105DA	OEM
Z0105MA	OEM
Z0105NA	OEM
Z0106BA	4381
Z0106BB	4381
Z0106DA	4382
Z0106DB	4382
Z0106MA	4404
Z0106MB	4404
Z0106NA	OEM
Z0106NB	OEM
Z0109BA	OEM
Z0109DA	OEM
Z0109MA	OEM
Z0109NA	OEM
Z0110BA	OEM
Z0110DA	OEM
Z0110MA	OEM
Z0110NA	OEM
Z0206	0188
Z0206A	OEM
Z0208A	OEM
Z0210A	OEM
Z0211A	OEM
Z0212A	OEM
Z0214A	OEM
Z0215A	OEM
Z0216A	OEM
Z0217A	OEM
Z0219A	OEM
Z0220A	OEM
Z0222A	OEM
Z0225A	OEM
Z0228A	OEM
Z0230A	OEM
Z0231A	OEM
Z0234A	OEM
Z0254A	OEM
Z0255A	OEM
Z0302BG	2337
Z0302DG	2340
Z0302MG	5457
Z0302NG	OEM
Z0305BG	2337
Z0305DG	2340
Z0305MG	5457
Z0305NG	OEM
Z0309BG	2337
Z0309DG	2340
Z0309MG	5457
Z0309NG	OEM
Z0310BG	2378
Z0310DG	1403
Z0310MG	2371
Z0310NG	OEM
Z0401	5553
Z0402	0188
Z0402BE	2284
Z0402BF	2284
Z0402DE	2284
Z0402DF	2284
Z0402ME	OEM
Z0402MF	OEM
Z0402NE	OEM
Z0402NF	OEM
Z0403	5554
Z0405	5555
Z0405BE	2284
Z0405BF	2284
Z0405DE	2284
Z0405DF	2284
Z0405ME	OEM
Z0405MF	OEM
Z0405NE	OEM
Z0405NF	OEM
Z0406	0162
Z0407	0157
Z0408	0631
Z0409	3428
Z0409BE	2284
Z0409BF	2284
Z0409DE	2284
Z0409DF	2284
Z0409ME	OEM
Z0409MF	OEM
Z0409NE	OEM
Z0409NF	OEM
Z0410	0644
Z0410BE	2284
Z0410BF	2284
Z0410DE	2284
Z0410DF	2284
Z0410ME	OEM
Z0410MF	OEM
Z0410NE	OEM
Z0410NF	OEM
Z0411	0244
Z0412	0012
Z0413	0170
Z0414	0313
Z0415	0137
Z0416	0361

DEVICE TYPE	REPL CODE
Z0417	0100
Z0418	0002
Z0419	0416
Z0420	0490
Z0421	5558
Z0422	5559
Z0423	0398
Z0424	0436
Z0425	OEM
Z0427	0814
Z0428	5561
Z0430	3551
Z0432	1823
Z0433	0778
Z0436	0327
Z0438	OEM
Z0439	0149
Z0440	5562
Z0442	5563
Z0444	5565
Z0445	5566
Z0765A08PSC	OEM
Z0A0.7	OEM
Z0A1.3	OEM
Z0A1.4	OEM
Z0A2.0	OEM
Z0A2.2	OEM
Z0A2.4	1266
Z0A2.7	OEM
Z0A3.0	OEM
Z0A3.3	0188
Z0A3.6	0372
Z0A3.9	0188
Z0A4.3	OEM
Z0A4.7	OEM
Z0A5.1	0582
Z0A5.6	0877
Z0A6.2	0292
Z0A6.8	OEM
Z0A7.5	OEM
Z0A8.2	3071
Z0A9.1	OEM
Z0A10	0248
Z0A11	OEM
Z0A12	0999
Z0A13	OEM
Z0A15	OEM
Z0A16	OEM
Z0A18	OEM
Z0A20	OEM
Z0A22	OEM
Z0A24	OEM
Z0A27	OEM
Z0A30	OEM
Z0A33	OEM
Z0B0.7	OEM
Z0B1.3	OEM
Z0B1.4	OEM
Z0B2.0	OEM
Z0B2.2	OEM
Z0B2.4	1266
Z0B2.7	0755
Z0B3.0	0118
Z0B3.3	0296
Z0B3.6	0372
Z0B3.9	0036
Z0B4.3	0274
Z0B4.7	0140
Z0B5.1	0041
Z0B5.6	0157
Z0B6.2	0466
Z0B6.8	0062
Z0B7.5	0077
Z0B8.2	0165
Z0B9.1	0057
Z0B10	0170
Z0B11	0181
Z0B12	0052
Z0B13	0053
Z0B15	0681
Z0B16	0440
Z0B18	0371
Z0B20	0695
Z0B22	0700
Z0B24	0489
Z0B27	0436
Z0B30	0195
Z0B33	0166
Z0C3.3	0188
Z0C4.7	0162
Z0C5.1	0162
Z0C5.6	0157
Z0C6.2	0631
Z0C6.8	0062
Z0C8.2	0165
Z0C9.1	0012
Z0C10	0170
Z0C12	0137
Z0C15	0002
Z0C18	0371
Z0C20	0695
Z0C22	0700
Z0C27	0436
Z0D3.3	0188
Z0D3.9	0188
Z0D4.7	0162
Z0D5.1	0162
Z0D5.6	0157
Z0D6.2	0631

DEVICE TYPE	REPL CODE
Z0D8.2	0165
Z0D9.1	0012
Z0D10	0170
Z0D12	0137
Z0D15	0002
Z0D20	0695
Z0D22	0700
Z0D27	0450
Z0D27B	0436
Z1	OEM
Z1A2.4	1266
Z1A2.7	0755
Z1A3.3	0188
Z1A3.9	0188
Z1A4.7	0140
Z1A8.2	0244
Z1B3.9	0451
Z1B4.7	0446
Z1B5.1	0162
Z1B5.6	0157
Z1B6.2	0631
Z1B6.8	0025
Z1B7.5	0644
Z1B8.2	0244
Z1B9.1	0012
Z1B10	0170
Z1B12	0137
Z1B15	0002
Z1B18	0490
Z1B20	0526
Z1B22	0560
Z1B27	0436
Z1C3.3	0188
Z1C3.9	0188
Z1C4.7	0162
Z1C5.1	0162
Z1C5.6	0162
Z1C6.2	0631
Z1C8.2	0165
Z1C9.1	0057
Z1C10	0170
Z1C12	0137
Z1C15	0002
Z1C18	0371
Z1C20	0695
Z1C22	0700
Z1C27	0436
Z1D3.3	0188
Z1D3.9	0036
Z1D4.7	0162
Z1D5.1	0162
Z1D5.6	0157
Z1D6.2	0631
Z1D7.5	0644
Z1D8.2	0165
Z1D9.1	0057
Z1D10	0170
Z1D12	0137
Z1D15	0002
Z1D18	0371
Z1D20	0695
Z1D22	0700
Z1D27	0450
Z1K	OEM
Z2A33F	0289
Z2A36F	0188
Z2A39F	0451
Z2A43F	0528
Z2A47F	0446
Z2A51F	0162
Z2A56CF	0157
Z2A56F	0157
Z2A62F	0631
Z2A68F	0025
Z2A75F	0644
Z2A82F	0244
Z2A91F	0012
Z2A100F	0170
Z2A110F	0313
Z2A120F	0137
Z2A130F	0361
Z2A150F	0002
Z2B3.0	OEM
Z2B3.3	0777
Z2B3.6	0791
Z2B3.9	0801
Z2B4.3	0815
Z2B4.7	0827
Z2B5.1	0437
Z2B5.6	0870
Z2B6.2	0185
Z2B6.8	0205
Z2B7.5	0475
Z2B8.2	0499
Z2B9.1	0679
Z2B10	0225
Z2B11	0230
Z2B12	0234
Z2B13	0237
Z2B15	0247
Z2B16	0251
Z2B18	0256
Z2B20	0262
Z2B22	0269
Z2B24	0273
Z2B27	0291
Z2B30	0305
Z2B33	0314
Z2B36	0316

DEVICE TYPE	REPL CODE
Z2B39	0322
Z2B43	0333
Z2B47	0343
Z2B51	0027
Z2B56	0266
Z2B62	0382
Z2B68	0401
Z2B75	0421
Z2B82	0439
Z2B91	0238
Z2B100	1172
Z2B110	1182
Z2B120	1198
Z2B130	1209
Z2B150	0777
Z2B160	1246
Z2B180	0600
Z2B200	0600
Z2B400	OEM
Z2C3.9	0801
Z2C4.7	0827
Z2C5.6	0870
Z2C6.2	0185
Z2C7.5	0475
Z2C9.1	0679
Z2C10	0225
Z2C12	0234
Z2C15	0247
Z2C18	0256
Z2C22	0269
Z2C33	0314
Z2D3.9	0801
Z2D5.6	0870
Z2D6.2	0185
Z2D7.5	0475
Z2D9.1	0679
Z2D10	0225
Z2D12	0234
Z2D15	0247
Z2D18	0256
Z2D22	0269
Z2D27	0291
Z2D33	0314
Z2.7	1302
Z3	0372
Z3A3.0	OEM
Z3A3.3	OEM
Z3A3.6	OEM
Z3A3.9	OEM
Z3A4.3	OEM
Z3A4.7	OEM
Z3A5.1	OEM
Z3A5.6	OEM
Z3A6.2	OEM
Z3A6.8	OEM
Z3A7.5	OEM
Z3A8.2	OEM
Z3A9.1	OEM
Z3A10	OEM
Z3A11	OEM
Z3A12	OEM
Z3A13	OEM
Z3A15	OEM
Z3A16	OEM
Z3A18	OEM
Z3A20	OEM
Z3A22	OEM
Z3A24	OEM
Z3A27	OEM
Z3A30	OEM
Z3A33	OEM
Z3A36	OEM
Z3A39	OEM
Z3A43	OEM
Z3A47	OEM
Z3A51	OEM
Z3A56	OEM
Z3A62	OEM
Z3A68	OEM
Z3A75	OEM
Z3A82	OEM
Z3A91	OEM
Z3A100	OEM
Z3A110	OEM
Z3A120	OEM
Z3A130	OEM
Z3A150	OEM
Z3A160	OEM
Z3A180	OEM
Z3A200	OEM
Z3B3.0	OEM
Z3B3.3	1000
Z3B3.6	1370
Z3B3.9	0542
Z3B4.3	2387
Z3B4.7	2101
Z3B5.1	2394
Z3B5.6	1890
Z3B6.2	1606
Z3B6.8	1591
Z3B7.5	1606
Z3B8.2	1612
Z3B9.1	0622
Z3B10	0986
Z3B11	0989
Z3B12	1254
Z3B13	1240
Z3B15	1629
Z3B16	1693

If replacement code is OEM, contact original manufacturer for replacement. 633

DEVICE TYPE	REPL CODE
Z3B18	1706
Z3B20	1720
Z3B22	0722
Z3B24	1745
Z3B27	1771
Z3B30	1783
Z3B33	1788
Z3B33CF	0777
Z3B36	6276
Z3B36CF	0791
Z3B39	1806
Z3B39CE	0801
Z3B39CF	0801
Z3B43	1815
Z3B43CF	0815
Z3B47	1842
Z3B47CF	0827
Z3B51	1855
Z3B51CF	0437
Z3B56	1396
Z3B56CF	0870
Z3B62	1884
Z3B62CF	0185
Z3B68	1891
Z3B68CF	0205
Z3B75	0731
Z3B75CF	0475
Z3B82CF	0499
Z3B91	1903
Z3B91CF	0679
Z3B100	1155
Z3B100CF	0225
Z3B110	1922
Z3B110CF	0230
Z3B120	1930
Z3B120CF	0234
Z3B130	1936
Z3B130CF	OEM
Z3B150	1950
Z3B150CF	0247
Z3B160	0353
Z3B160CF	0251
Z3B180	0771
Z3B180CF	0256
Z3B200	1065
Z3B200CF	0262
Z3B220CF	0269
Z3B240CF	0273
Z3B270CF	0291
Z3B300CF	0305
Z3B330CF	0314
Z3B360CF	0316
Z3B390CF	0322
Z3B430CF	0333
Z3B470CF	0343
Z3B510CF	0027
Z3B560CF	0266
Z3B620CF	0382
Z3B680CF	0401
Z3B750CF	0421
Z3B820CF	0439
Z3B910CF	0238
Z3B1000CF	1172
Z3K	OEM
Z3.0	1703
Z3.3	0289
Z3.6	0188
Z3.9	0188
Z4	0274
Z4A3.0	OEM
Z4A3.3	OEM
Z4A3.6	OEM
Z4A3.9	OEM
Z4A4.3	OEM
Z4A4.7	OEM
Z4A5.1	OEM
Z4A5.6	OEM
Z4A6.2	0631
Z4A6.8	OEM
Z4A7.5	OEM
Z4A8.2	0244
Z4A9.1	OEM
Z4A10	OEM
Z4A11	OEM
Z4A12	OEM
Z4A13	OEM
Z4A15	OEM
Z4A16	OEM
Z4A18	OEM
Z4A20	OEM
Z4A22	OEM
Z4A24	OEM
Z4A27	OEM
Z4A30	OEM
Z4A33	OEM
Z4A36	OEM
Z4A39	OEM
Z4A43	OEM
Z4A47	OEM
Z4A51	OEM
Z4A56	OEM
Z4A62	OEM
Z4A68	OEM
Z4A75	OEM
Z4A82	OEM
Z4A91	OEM
Z4A100	OEM
Z4A110	OEM
Z4A120	OEM

DEVICE TYPE	REPL CODE
Z4A130	OEM
Z4A150	OEM
Z4A160	OEM
Z4A180	OEM
Z4A200	OEM
Z4B	0036
Z4B3.0	1703
Z4B3.3	0289
Z4B3.6	0188
Z4B3.9	0451
Z4B4.3	0528
Z4B4.7	0446
Z4B5.1	0162
Z4B5.6	0157
Z4B6.2	0631
Z4B6.8	0025
Z4B8.2	0244
Z4B9.1	0012
Z4B10	0170
Z4B11	0313
Z4B12	0137
Z4B13	0361
Z4B15	0002
Z4B16	0416
Z4B18	0490
Z4B20	0526
Z4B22	0560
Z4B24	0398
Z4B27	0436
Z4B30	0721
Z4B33	0039
Z4B36	0814
Z4B43	0925
Z4B47	0993
Z4B51	0497
Z4B56	0863
Z4B62	0778
Z4B68	2144
Z4B75	1181
Z4B82	0327
Z4B91	1301
Z4B100	0098
Z4B110	0149
Z4B120	0186
Z4B130	0213
Z4B150	0028
Z4B180	0363
Z4B200	0417
Z4K	0140
Z4MW333	0016
Z4X5.1A	0162
Z4X5.1B	0162
Z4X5.6	0157
Z4X9.1	0012
Z4X11	0789
Z4X12	0137
Z4X13	0361
Z4X14	0100
Z4X14A	0100
Z4X14B	0100
Z4X15	0002
Z4XL6.2	0631
Z4XL6.2B	0631
Z4XL7.5	0644
Z4XL7.5B	0644
Z4XL9.1	0012
Z4XL9.1B	0012
Z4XL12	0137
Z4XL12B	0137
Z4XL14	0100
Z4XL16	0416
Z4XL16B	0416
Z4XL18	0490
Z4XL18B	0490
Z4XL20	0526
Z4XL20B	0526
Z4XL22	0560
Z4XL22B	0560
Z4XL75	0644
Z4.3	0528
Z4.7	0446
Z5	0253
Z5A3.0	OEM
Z5A3.3	0296
Z5A3.6	OEM
Z5A3.9	0188
Z5A4.3	OEM
Z5A4.7	OEM
Z5A5.1	0582
Z5A5.6	0877
Z5A6.2	0466
Z5A6.8	OEM
Z5A7.5	OEM
Z5A8.2	OEM
Z5A9.1	OEM
Z5A10	0248
Z5A11	OEM
Z5A12	0999
Z5A13	OEM
Z5A15	OEM
Z5A16	OEM
Z5A18	OEM
Z5A20	0526
Z5A22	OEM
Z5A24	OEM
Z5A27	OEM
Z5A30	OEM
Z5A33	OEM
Z5B3.0	0118

DEVICE TYPE	REPL CODE
Z5B3.3	0296
Z5B3.6	0188
Z5B3.9	0036
Z5B4.3	0274
Z5B4.7	0140
Z5B5.1	0162
Z5B5.6	0157
Z5B6.2	0466
Z5B6.8	0062
Z5B7.5	0077
Z5B8.2	0165
Z5B9.1	0057
Z5B10	0170
Z5B11	0181
Z5B12	0052
Z5B13	0053
Z5B-15	0002
Z5B15	0681
Z5B16	0440
Z5B18	0371
Z5B20	0695
Z5B22	0700
Z5B24	0489
Z5B27	0450
Z5B30	0195
Z5B33	0166
Z5C3.3	0188
Z5C3.9	0188
Z5C4.7	0162
Z5C5.1	0162
Z5C5.6	0157
Z5C6.2	0631
Z5C6.8	0062
Z5C8.2	0165
Z5C9.1	0012
Z5C10	0170
Z5C12	0137
Z5C15	0002
Z5C18	0371
Z5C20	0695
Z5C22	0700
Z5D3.3	0188
Z5D3.9	0188
Z5D4.7	0162
Z5D5.1	0162
Z5D5.6	0157
Z5D6.2	0631
Z5D6.8	0062
Z5D8.2	0165
Z5D9.1	0012
Z5D10	0170
Z5D12	0137
Z5D15	0002
Z5D18	0371
Z5D20	0695
Z5D22	0700
Z5D82CF	1481
Z5D91CF	1608
Z5D100CF	0505
Z5D110CF	0686
Z5D120CF	0864
Z5D130CF	1014
Z5D150CF	1264
Z5D160CF	1392
Z5D180CF	1071
Z5D200CF	1707
Z5D220CF	1712
Z5D240CF	1725
Z5D270CF	1750
Z5D300CF	1761
Z5D330CF	1777
Z5D360CF	1785
Z5D390CF	1793
Z5D430CF	1185
Z5D470CF	0022
Z5D560CF	0207
Z5D620CF	0263
Z5D680CF	0306
Z5D750CF	0325
Z5D820CF	0352
Z5D910CF	0408
Z5D1000CF	0433
Z5K	0253
Z5.1	0162
Z5.1(500MW)	0041
Z5.1B	0041
Z5.1BTA	0041
Z5.6	0157
Z5.6(500MW)	0253
Z5.6A	0157
Z5.6B	0157
Z5.6BM	0253
Z5.6BMTA	0253
Z5.6C	OEM
Z5.6D	OEM
Z6	0298
Z6A2	0091
Z6A3.6	OEM
Z6A3.9	OEM
Z6A4.3	OEM
Z6A4.7	OEM
Z6A5.1	OEM
Z6A5.6	OEM
Z6A6.2	OEM
Z6A6.8	OEM
Z6A7.5	OEM
Z6A8.2	OEM
Z6A9.1	OEM
Z6A10	OEM

DEVICE TYPE	REPL CODE
Z6A11	OEM
Z6A12	OEM
Z6A13	OEM
Z6A15	OEM
Z6A16	OEM
Z6A18	OEM
Z6A20	OEM
Z6A22	OEM
Z6A24	OEM
Z6A27	OEM
Z6A30	OEM
Z6A33	OEM
Z6A36	OEM
Z6A39	OEM
Z6A43	OEM
Z6A47	OEM
Z6A51	OEM
Z6A56	OEM
Z6A62	OEM
Z6A68	OEM
Z6A75	OEM
Z6A82	OEM
Z6A91	OEM
Z6A100	OEM
Z6A110	OEM
Z6A120	OEM
Z6A130	OEM
Z6A150	OEM
Z6A160	OEM
Z6A180	OEM
Z6A200	OEM
Z6B3.6	OEM
Z6B3.9	OEM
Z6B4.3	OEM
Z6B4.7	OEM
Z6B5.1	OEM
Z6B5.6	OEM
Z6B6.2	OEM
Z6B6.8	OEM
Z6B7.5	OEM
Z6B8.2	OEM
Z6B9.1	OEM
Z6B10	OEM
Z6B11	OEM
Z6B12	OEM
Z6B13	OEM
Z6B15	OEM
Z6B16	OEM
Z6B18	OEM
Z6B20	OEM
Z6B22	OEM
Z6B24	OEM
Z6B27	OEM
Z6B30	OEM
Z6B33	OEM
Z6B36	OEM
Z6B39	OEM
Z6B43	OEM
Z6B47	OEM
Z6B51	OEM
Z6B56	OEM
Z6B62	OEM
Z6B68	OEM
Z6B75	OEM
Z6B82	OEM
Z6B91	OEM
Z6B100	OEM
Z6B110	OEM
Z6B120	OEM
Z6B130	OEM
Z6B150	OEM
Z6B160	OEM
Z6B180	OEM
Z6B200	OEM
Z6K	0062
Z6P12	OEM
Z6.2	0631
Z6.2A	0631
Z6.2B	0631
Z6.2C	0631
Z6.2D	OEM
Z6.8	0025
Z6.8A	0025
Z6.8B	0025
Z6.8BHTA	0062
Z6.8C	OEM
Z6.8D	OEM
Z7	0077
Z7A1	0062
Z7A3.0	OEM
Z7A3.3	OEM
Z7A3.6	OEM
Z7A3.9	OEM
Z7A4.3	OEM
Z7A4.7	OEM
Z7A5.1	OEM
Z7A5.6	OEM
Z7A6.2	OEM
Z7A6.8	OEM
Z7A7.5	OEM
Z7A8.2	OEM
Z7A9.1	OEM
Z7A10	OEM
Z7A11	OEM
Z7A12	OEM
Z7A13	OEM
Z7A15	OEM
Z7A16	OEM
Z7A18	OEM

DEVICE TYPE	REPL CODE
Z7A20	OEM
Z7A22	OEM
Z7A24	OEM
Z7A27	OEM
Z7A30	OEM
Z7A33	OEM
Z7A36	OEM
Z7A39	OEM
Z7A43	OEM
Z7A51	OEM
Z7A56	OEM
Z7A62	OEM
Z7A68	OEM
Z7A75	OEM
Z7A82	OEM
Z7A91	OEM
Z7A100	OEM
Z7A110	OEM
Z7A120	OEM
Z7A130	OEM
Z7A150	OEM
Z7A160	OEM
Z7A180	OEM
Z7A200	OEM
Z7A400	OEM
Z7B3.0	OEM
Z7B3.3	OEM
Z7B3.7	OEM
Z7B3.9	OEM
Z7B4.3	OEM
Z7B4.7	OEM
Z7B5.1	OEM
Z7B5.6	OEM
Z7B6.2	OEM
Z7B6.8	OEM
Z7B7.5	OEM
Z7B8.2	OEM
Z7B9.1	OEM
Z7B10	OEM
Z7B11	OEM
Z7B12	OEM
Z7B13	OEM
Z7B15	OEM
Z7B16	OEM
Z7B18	OEM
Z7B20	OEM
Z7B22	OEM
Z7B24	OEM
Z7B27	OEM
Z7B30	OEM
Z7B33	OEM
Z7B36	OEM
Z7B39	OEM
Z7B43	OEM
Z7B47	OEM
Z7B51	OEM
Z7B56	OEM
Z7B62	OEM
Z7B68	OEM
Z7B75	OEM
Z7B82	OEM
Z7B91	OEM
Z7B100	OEM
Z7B110	OEM
Z7B120	OEM
Z7B130	OEM
Z7B150	OEM
Z7B160	OEM
Z7B180	OEM
Z7B200	OEM
Z7B400	OEM
Z7K	0077
Z7L101	OEM
Z7L102	OEM
Z7L121	OEM
Z7L151	OEM
Z7L181	OEM
Z7L201	OEM
Z7L220	OEM
Z7L221	OEM
Z7L270	OEM
Z7L271	OEM
Z7L330	OEM
Z7L331	OEM
Z7L390	OEM
Z7L391	OEM
Z7L441	OEM
Z7L470	OEM
Z7L471	OEM
Z7L560	OEM
Z7L561	OEM
Z7L680	OEM
Z7L681	OEM
Z7L820	OEM
Z7L821	OEM
Z7.5	0644
Z7.5A	0644
Z7.5B	0644
Z7.5BIS	0077
Z7.5BM	0077
Z7.5C	OEM
Z7.5D	OEM
Z8	0318
Z8-01CS	OEM
Z8-01PS	OEM
Z8-02QS	OEM
Z8-03RS	OEM
Z8.2	0244
Z8.2A	0244

DEVICE TYPE	REPL CODE
Z8.2B	0244
Z8.2C	0244
Z8.2D	0244
Z9.1	0012
Z9.1A	0012
Z9.1B	0012
Z9.1B1	0012
Z9.1BL	0057
Z9.1BLTA	0012
Z9.1C	0012
Z9.1D	OEM
Z10	0170
Z10A	0064
Z10B	0064
Z10C	OEM
Z10D	OEM
Z10K	0170
Z10L101	OEM
Z10L102	OEM
Z10L121	OEM
Z10L151	OEM
Z10L181	OEM
Z10L201	OEM
Z10L271	OEM
Z10L330	OEM
Z10L331	OEM
Z10L390	OEM
Z10L391	OEM
Z10L441	OEM
Z10L470	OEM
Z10L471	OEM
Z10L560	OEM
Z10L561	OEM
Z10L680	OEM
Z10L681	OEM
Z10L820	OEM
Z10L821	OEM
Z10.0	0170
Z-11	0137
Z11	0313
Z11A	0313
Z11B	0181
Z11B1	0181
Z11BA	OEM
Z11BL	0181
Z11BLTA	0181
Z11BM	0181
Z11BMTA	OEM
Z11C	OEM
Z11D	OEM
Z11.0	0313
Z-12	0137
Z12	0137
Z12(500MW)	0052
Z12A	0052
Z12B	0052
Z12BM	0052
Z12BMTA	0052
Z12C	0137
Z12D	OEM
Z12K	0052
Z12.0	0137
Z13	0361
Z13A	0361
Z13B	0361
Z13C	OEM
Z13D	OEM
Z13.0	0361
Z14	0100
Z14A	0100
Z14B	0100
Z14C	OEM
Z14D	OEM
Z15	0002
Z15A	0002
Z15B	0002
Z15C	0002
Z15D	OEM
Z15K	0681
Z15L101	OEM
Z15L102	OEM
Z15L121	OEM
Z15L151	OEM
Z15L181	OEM
Z15L201	OEM
Z15L221	OEM
Z15L271	OEM
Z15L331	OEM
Z15L390	OEM
Z15L391	OEM
Z15L441	OEM
Z15L470	OEM
Z15L471	OEM
Z15L560	OEM
Z15L561	OEM
Z15L680	OEM
Z15L681	OEM
Z15L820	OEM
Z15L821	OEM
Z15.0	0002
Z16	0416
Z16A	0416
Z16B	0416
Z16C	OEM
Z16D	OEM
Z16.0	0416
Z17	1639
Z17A	1639
Z17B	1639

DEVICE TYPE	REPL CODE
Z17C	OEM
Z17D	OEM
Z18	0490
Z18A	0490
Z18B	1639
Z18C	OEM
Z18D	OEM
Z18K	OEM
Z18.0	0490
Z19	0943
Z19A	0943
Z19B	0943
Z19C	OEM
Z19D	OEM
Z20	0526
Z20A	0526
Z20B	0526
Z20C	OEM
Z20D	OEM
Z20.0	0526
Z21L101	OEM
Z21L102	OEM
Z21L121	OEM
Z21L151	OEM
Z21L181	OEM
Z21L201	OEM
Z21L221	OEM
Z21L271	OEM
Z21L331	OEM
Z21L391	OEM
Z21L441	OEM
Z21L470	OEM
Z21L471	OEM
Z21L560	OEM
Z21L561	OEM
Z21L680	OEM
Z21L681	OEM
Z21L820	OEM
Z21L821	OEM
Z22	0560
Z22A	0560
Z22B	0560
Z22C	OEM
Z22D	OEM
Z22.0	0560
Z24	0489
Z24A	0398
Z24B	0398
Z24BL	5878
Z24BLTA	OEM
Z24C	OEM
Z24D	OEM
Z24.0	0398
Z25	1596
Z25A	1596
Z25B	1596
Z25C	OEM
Z25D	OEM
Z27	0436
Z27A	0436
Z27B	0436
Z27C	0436
Z27D	OEM
Z27.0	0436
Z30	0721
Z30(500MW)	0166
Z30A	0721
Z30B	0721
Z30BM	0195
Z30BMTA	0195
Z30C	OEM
Z30D	OEM
Z30.0	0721
Z33	0039
Z33A	0039
Z33B	0039
Z33C	OEM
Z33D	OEM
Z33M102	OEM
Z33M221	OEM
Z33M271	OEM
Z33M331	OEM
Z33M391	OEM
Z33M441	OEM
Z33M471	OEM
Z33M561	OEM
Z33M681	OEM
Z33M821	OEM
Z33.0	0039
Z36	0814
Z36A	0814
Z36B	0814
Z36C	OEM
Z36D	OEM
Z39	0346
Z39A	0346
Z39B	0346
Z39C	OEM
Z39D	OEM
Z43	0925
Z43A	0925
Z43B	0925
Z43C	OEM
Z43D	OEM
Z45	0925
Z45A	0252
Z45B	0925
Z45C	OEM
Z45D	OEM

634

If replacement code is OEM, contact original manufacturer for replacement.

DEVICE TYPE	REPL CODE	DEVICE TYPE	REPL CODE	DEVICE TYPE	REPL CODE	DEVICE TYPE	REPL CODE	DEVICE TYPE	REPL CODE	DEVICE TYPE	REPL CODE	DEVICE TYPE	REPL CODE
Z47	0993	Z120	0186	Z-1116	0490	Z2008A	0185	Z2506	OEM	Z6007U	0475	Z8010DS	OEM
Z47A	0993	Z120A	0186	Z1116	0490	Z2008B	0185	Z2508	OEM	Z6008	0499	Z8010PE	OEM
Z47B	0993	Z120B	0186	Z1116-C	0490	Z2008U	0244	Z2510	OEM	Z6008U	0499	Z8010PS	OEM
Z47C	OEM	Z120C	OEM	Z1118	0560	Z2009	0205	Z2513	OEM	Z6010	0225	Z8015	OEM
Z47D	OEM	Z120D	OEM	Z1118-C	0560	Z2009A	0205	Z2514	OEM	Z6010U	0225	Z8030ACE	OEM
Z50	0497	Z130	0213	Z-1120	0436	Z2009B	0205	Z2516	OEM	Z6012	0234	Z8030ACS	OEM
Z50A	0497	Z130A	0213	Z1120	0089	Z2010	0170	Z2519	OEM	Z6012U	0234	Z8030ADE	OEM
Z50B	0497	Z130B	0213	Z1120-C	0436	Z2010A	0475	Z2522	OEM	Z6015	0247	Z8030ADS	OEM
Z50C	OEM	Z130C	OEM	Z-1122	0039	Z2010B	0475	Z2525	0269	Z6015U	0247	Z8030APE	OEM
Z50D	OEM	Z130D	OEM	Z1122	0039	Z2010U	0170	Z2526	OEM	Z6018	0256	Z8030APS	OEM
Z51	0497	Z140	0245	Z1124	0346	Z2011	0499	Z2528	OEM	Z6018U	0256	Z8030CS	OEM
Z51A	0497	Z140A	0245	Z-1126	0993	Z2011A	0499	Z2530	0305	Z6022	0269	Z8030DE	OEM
Z51B	0497	Z140B	0245	Z1126	0993	Z2011B	0499	Z2531	OEM	Z6022U	0269	Z8030DS	OEM
Z51C	OEM	Z140C	OEM	Z1128	0863	Z2012	0137	Z2537	OEM	Z6027	0291	Z8030PE	OEM
Z51D	OEM	Z140D	OEM	Z1130	0778	Z2012A	3285	Z2542	OEM	Z6027U	0291	Z8030PS	OEM
Z52	0497	Z150	0028	Z-1132	0327	Z2012B	3285	Z2545	OEM	Z6033	0314	Z8036ACE	OEM
Z52A	0497	Z150A	0028	Z1132	0327	Z2012U	0137	Z2547	OEM	Z6033U	0314	Z8036ACS	OEM
Z52B	0497	Z150B	0028	Z-1134	0149	Z2013	0679	Z2548	1209	Z6039	0322	Z8036ADE	OEM
Z52C	OEM	Z150C	OEM	Z1134	0149	Z2013A	0679	Z2551	OEM	Z6039U	0322	Z8036ADS	OEM
Z52D	OEM	Z150D	OEM	Z1136	0186	Z2013B	0679	Z3305	0920	Z6047	0343	Z8036APE	OEM
Z56	0863	Z160	0255	Z1138	0028	Z2014	0225	Z3307	0952	Z6047U	0343	Z8036APS	OEM
Z56A	0863	Z160A	0255	Z-1140	0157	Z2014A	0225	Z3309	1003	Z6056	0266	Z8036CE	OEM
Z56B	0863	Z160B	0255	Z1140	0253	Z2014B	0225	Z3311	0883	Z6056U	0266	Z8036CS	OEM
Z56C	OEM	Z160C	OEM	Z-1145	0157	Z2015	0002	Z3314	0926	Z6068	0401	Z8036DE	OEM
Z56D	OEM	Z160D	OEM	Z1145	0253	Z2015A	0230	Z3317	1098	Z6068U	0401	Z8036DS	OEM
Z62	0778	Z175	0363	Z-1150	0157	Z2015B	0230	Z3320	1144	Z6082	0439	Z8036PE	OEM
Z62A	0778	Z175A	0363	Z1150	0336	Z2015U	0002	Z3323	1176	Z6082U	0439	Z8036PS	OEM
Z62B	0778	Z175B	0363	Z-1155	0157	Z2016	0234	Z3325	1214	Z6100	1172	Z8038ACE	OEM
Z62C	OEM	Z175C	OEM	Z1155	0253	Z2016A	0234	Z3327	1237	Z6100U	1172	Z8038ACS	OEM
Z62D	OEM	Z175D	OEM	Z-1160	0157	Z2016B	0234	Z3334	1321	Z6120	1198	Z8038ADE	OEM
Z-64	OEM	Z180	0363	Z1160	0253	Z2017	0237	Z3340	1413	Z6120U	1198	Z8038ADS	OEM
Z68	2144	Z180A	0363	Z-1165	0157	Z2017A	0237	Z3433	OEM	Z6132-3CS	OEM	Z8038APE	OEM
Z68A	2144	Z180B	0363	Z1165	0253	Z2017B	0237	Z3434	0036	Z6132-3DS	OEM	Z8038APS	OEM
Z68B	2144	Z180C	OEM	Z-1170	0157	Z2018	0100	Z3500	OEM	Z6132-3PS	OEM	Z8038CE	OEM
Z68C	OEM	Z180D	OEM	Z1170	0253	Z2018A	1387	Z3500(HEP)	0542	Z6132-4CS	OEM	Z8038CS	OEM
Z68D	OEM	Z200	0417	Z1200	0801	Z2018B	1387	Z3500R(HEP)	2024	Z6132-4DS	OEM	Z8038DE	OEM
Z75	1181	Z200A	0417	Z1202	0446	Z2018U	0490	Z3502	OEM	Z6132-4PS	OEM	Z8038DS	OEM
Z75A	1181	Z200B	0417	Z1203	0437	Z2019	0247	Z3502(HEP)	2101	Z6132-5CS	OEM	Z8038PE	OEM
Z75B	1181	Z200C	OEM	Z1204	0870	Z2019A	0247	Z3502R(HEP)	1429	Z6132-5DS	OEM	Z8038PS	OEM
Z75C	OEM	Z200D	OEM	Z1206	0205	Z2019B	0247	Z3504	OEM	Z6132-5PS	OEM	Z8052	OEM
Z75D	OEM	Z211/1G	OEM	Z1207	0475	Z2020	0526	Z3504(HEP)	1890	Z6132-6CS	OEM	Z8060	OEM
Z80	3441	Z220	OEM	Z1208	0499	Z2020A	0251	Z3504R(HEP)	1436	Z6132-6DS	OEM	Z8068	OEM
Z80-8420	OEM	Z220A	OEM	Z1209	0679	Z2020B	0251	Z3505	OEM	Z6132-6PS	OEM	Z8070	OEM
Z80-AIB	OEM	Z220B	OEM	Z1212	0137	Z2021	1170	Z3507	OEM	Z6150	0642	Z8090CE	OEM
Z80-AIBN	OEM	Z220C	OEM	Z1218	0269	Z2021A	1170	Z3511	OEM	Z6150U	0642	Z8090CS	OEM
Z80-AIO	OEM	Z220D	OEM	Z1238	0642	Z2021B	1170	Z3512	OEM	Z6180	1269	Z8090DE	OEM
Z80-AION	OEM	Z237/1KW	OEM	Z-1240	0157	Z2022	0256	Z3512R(HEP)	0505	Z6180U	1269	Z8090DS	OEM
Z80-IOB	OEM	Z501	OEM	Z1240	0253	Z2022A	0256	Z3514	OEM	Z6200	0600	Z8090PE	OEM
Z80-MCB4	OEM	Z501-4M	OEM	Z-1245	0157	Z2022B	0256	Z3514R(HEP)	1254	Z6200U	0600	Z8090PS	OEM
Z80-MCB16	OEM	Z537	0039	Z1245	0253	Z2022U	0560	Z3516	OEM	Z6220	OEM	Z8091QS	OEM
Z80-MDC	OEM	Z694	0012	Z-1250	0157	Z2023	2379	Z3516R(HEP)	1629	Z6220U	OEM	Z8092QS	OEM
Z80-PPB	OEM	Z714	0012	Z1250	0253	Z2023A	2379	Z3518	OEM	Z6250	OEM	Z8093RS	OEM
Z80-PPB/16	OEM	Z765A08PSC	OEM	Z-1255	0157	Z2023B	2379	Z3518R(HEP)	1706	Z6250U	OEM	Z8094RS	OEM
Z80-RMB	OEM	Z765APS	OEM	Z1255	0253	Z2024	0262	Z3520	OEM	Z6300	OEM	Z8400ACE	OEM
Z80-SCE4	OEM	Z801	0631	Z-1260	0157	Z2024A	0262	Z3520R(HEP)	0722	Z6300U	OEM	Z8400ACM	OEM
Z80-SIB	OEM	Z-963B	0137	Z1260	0253	Z2024B	0262	Z3522	OEM	Z6350	OEM	Z8400ACMB	OEM
Z80-VDB	OEM	Z1000	0296	Z-1265	0157	Z2025	0269	Z3522R(HEP)	1771	Z6350U	OEM	Z8400ACS	OEM
Z80A	3441	Z1002	0036	Z1265	0253	Z2025A	0269	Z3524	OEM	Z6400	OEM	Z8400ADE	OEM
Z80A/4MHZ	OEM	Z-1004	0446	Z-1270	0157	Z2025B	0269	Z3524R(HEP)	1788	Z6400U	OEM	Z8400ADS	OEM
Z80ACTCCE	OEM	Z1004	0140	Z1270	0253	Z2026	0273	Z3530	OEM	Z6440	OEM	Z8400APE	OEM
Z80ACTCCM	OEM	Z-1006	0157	Z1300	0542	Z2026A	0273	Z3530R(HEP)	1873	Z6440U	OEM	Z8400APS	3441
Z80ACTCCS	OEM	Z1006	0253	Z1302	2101	Z2026B	0273	Z3534	OEM	Z8000	OEM	Z8400BCE	OEM
Z80ACTCPS	OEM	Z1008	0062	Z1304	1890	Z2027	0436	Z3534R(HEP)	1898	Z8001ACE	OEM	Z8400BCM	OEM
Z80ADMACE	OEM	Z1010	0165	Z1306	1591	Z2027A	2383	Z3536	OEM	Z8001ACM	OEM	Z8400BCS	OEM
Z80ADMACM	OEM	Z-1012	0064	Z1308	1612	Z2027B	2383	Z3536R(HEP)	1913	Z8001ACMB	OEM	Z8400BDE	OEM
Z80ADMACS	OEM	Z1012	0064	Z1310	0505	Z2027U	0436	Z4026	OEM	Z8001ACS	OEM	Z8400BDS	OEM
Z80ADMAPS	OEM	Z-1014	0137	Z1312	0864	Z2028	0291	Z4729	0372	Z8001ADE	OEM	Z8400BPE	OEM
Z80APS	OEM	Z1014	0052	Z1314	1264	Z2028A	0291	Z4729A	0372	Z8001ADS	OEM	Z8400BPS	OEM
Z80B	OEM	Z1015	0681	Z1316	1071	Z2028B	0291	Z-5140	0157	Z8001APE	OEM	Z8400CE	OEM
Z80B/6MHZ	OEM	Z-1016	0002	Z1318	1712	Z2029	1169	Z5140	0253	Z8001APS	OEM	Z8400CM	OEM
Z80CTCCE	OEM	Z1016	0681	Z1320	1750	Z2029A	1169	Z-5145	0157	Z8001CE	OEM	Z8400CMB	OEM
Z80CTCCM	OEM	Z1018	0371	Z1322	1777	Z2029B	1169	Z5145	0253	Z8001CM	OEM	Z8400CS	OEM
Z80CTCCS	OEM	Z1020	0700	Z1324	1793	Z2030	0305	Z-5150	0157	Z8001CMB	OEM	Z8400DE	OEM
Z80CTCPS	OEM	Z-1022	0436	Z1326	0022	Z2030A	0305	Z5150	0253	Z8001CS	OEM	Z8400DS	OEM
Z82	0327	Z1022	0700	Z1328	0207	Z2030B	0305	Z-5155	0157	Z8001DE	OEM	Z8400PE	OEM
Z82A	0327	Z-1024	0039	Z1330	0306	Z2031	0314	Z5155	0253	Z8001DS	OEM	Z8400PS	OEM
Z82B	0327	Z1024	0166	Z1332	0352	Z2031A	0314	Z-5160	0157	Z8001PE	OEM	Z8410ACE	OEM
Z82C	OEM	Z1027	0450	Z1334	0433	Z2031B	0314	Z5160	0253	Z8001PS	OEM	Z8410ACM	OEM
Z82D	OEM	Z1033	0166	Z1336	0504	Z2033	0039	Z-5165	0157	Z8002ACE	OEM	Z8410ACMB	OEM
Z86C2704PSC	OEM	Z1039	0032	Z1338	0063	Z2033U	0039	Z5165	0253	Z8002ACM	OEM	Z8410ACS	OEM
Z86C2704PSCR390	OEM	Z1047	0068	Z1340	0629	Z2039	0346	Z-5170	0157	Z8002ACMB	OEM	Z8410ADS	OEM
Z86C2704PSC-R425	OEM	Z1056	0125	Z1528	0343	Z2039U	0032	Z5170	0253	Z8002ACS	OEM	Z8410APE	OEM
Z86C2704PSCR425	OEM	Z-1068	1976	Z1530	0027	Z2047	0993	Z-5240	0157	Z8002ADE	OEM	Z8410APS	OEM
Z86C2704PSC-R681	OEM	Z1068	0173	Z1532	1172	Z2047U	0993	Z5240	0253	Z8002ADS	OEM	Z8410CE	OEM
Z86C2704PSC-R1028	OEM	Z1082	0049	Z-1540	0157	Z2056	0863	Z-5245	0157	Z8002APE	OEM	Z8410CM	OEM
Z86C2704PS-R390	OEM	Z-1100	0188	Z1540	0253	Z2056U	0863	Z-5250	0157	Z8002APS	OEM	Z8410CMB	OEM
Z91	1301	Z1100	0189	Z-1545	0157	Z2068	2144	Z5250	0253	Z8002CE	OEM	Z8410CS	OEM
Z91A	1301	Z1100-C	0451	Z1545	0253	Z2068U	2144	Z-5255	0157	Z8002CM	OEM	Z8410DE	OEM
Z91B	1301	Z-1102	0446	Z-1550	0157	Z2082	0327	Z5255	0253	Z8002CMB	OEM	Z8410DS	OEM
Z91C	OEM	Z1102	0446	Z1550	0253	Z2082U	0327	Z-5260	0157	Z8002CS	OEM	Z8410PE	OEM
Z91D	OEM	Z1102-C	0446	Z-1555	0157	Z2100	0098	Z5260	0253	Z8002DE	OEM	Z8410PS	OEM
Z95LA7A	OEM	Z-1104	0157	Z1555	0253	Z2100U	0098	Z-5265	0157	Z8002DS	OEM	Z8420ACE	OEM
Z100	0098	Z1104	0157	Z-1560	0157	Z2120	0186	Z5265	0253	Z8002PE	OEM	Z8420ACM	OEM
Z100A	0098	Z1104-C	0157	Z1560	0253	Z2120U	0186	Z-5270	0157	Z8002PS	OEM	Z8420ACMB	OEM
Z100B	0098	Z-1106	0631	Z-1565	0157	Z2150	0028	Z5270	0253	Z8003	OEM	Z8420ACS	OEM
Z100C	OEM	Z1106	0025	Z1565	0253	Z2150U	0028	Z-5540	0157	Z8004	OEM	Z8420ADE	OEM
Z100D	OEM	Z1106-C	0025	Z-1570	0157	Z2180	0363	Z5540	0253	Z8010ACE	OEM	Z8420ADS	OEM
Z101	0244	Z1108	0244	Z1570	0253	Z2180U	0363	Z-5545	0157	Z8010ACM	OEM	Z8420APE	OEM
Z105	0149	Z-1110	0170	Z2005	0437	Z2200	0417	Z5545	0253	Z8010ACMB	OEM	Z8420APS	6102
Z105A	0149	Z1110	0170	Z2005A	0437	Z2200U	0417	Z-5550	0157	Z8010ACS	OEM	Z8420BCE	OEM
Z105B	0149	Z1110-C	0170	Z2005B	0437	Z2220	OEM	Z5550	0253	Z8010ADE	OEM	Z8420BCM	OEM
Z105C	OEM	Z-1112	0137	Z2006	0870	Z2220U	OEM	Z-5555	0157	Z8010ADS	OEM	Z8420BCMB	OEM
Z105D	OEM	Z1112	0137	Z2006A	0870	Z2250	OEM	Z5555	0253	Z8010APE	OEM	Z8420BCS	OEM
Z110	0149	Z1112-C	0137	Z2006B	0870	Z2250U	OEM	Z-5560	0157	Z8010APS	OEM	Z8420BDE	OEM
Z110A	0149	Z-1112C	0137	Z2007	3099	Z2360	0102	Z5560	0253	Z8010CE	OEM	Z8420BDS	OEM
Z110B	0149	Z1112C	0137	Z2007A	3099	Z2500	OEM	Z-5565	0157	Z8010CM	OEM	Z8420BPE	OEM
Z110C	OEM	Z-1114	0002	Z2007B	3099	Z2501-6L	OEM	Z5565	0253	Z8010CMB	OEM	Z8420BPS	OEM
Z110D	OEM	Z1114	0002	Z2007U	0644	Z2502	OEM	Z-5570	0157	Z8010CS	OEM	Z8420CE	OEM
Z111Z	0137	Z1114-C	0002	Z2008	0244	Z2504	OEM	Z5570	0253	Z8010DE	OEM	Z8420CM	OEM

If replacement code is OEM, contact original manufacturer for replacement.

DEVICE TYPE	REPL CODE
Z8420CMB	OEM
Z8420CS	OEM
Z8420DE	OEM
Z8420DS	OEM
Z8420PE	OEM
Z8420PS	OEM
Z8430AB1	6940
Z8430ACE	OEM
Z8430ACM	OEM
Z8430ACMB	OEM
Z8430ACS	OEM
Z8430ADE	OEM
Z8430ADS	OEM
Z8430APE	OEM
Z8430APS	6940
Z8430BCE	OEM
Z8430BCM	OEM
Z8430BCS	OEM
Z8430BDE	OEM
Z8430BDS	OEM
Z8430BPE	OEM
Z8430BPS	OEM
Z8430CE	OEM
Z8430CM	OEM
Z8430CMB	OEM
Z8430CS	OEM
Z8430DE	OEM
Z8430DS	OEM
Z8430PE	OEM
Z8430PS	OEM
Z8440ACE	OEM
Z8440ACM	OEM
Z8440ACMB	OEM
Z8440ACS	OEM
Z8440ADE	OEM
Z8440ADS	OEM
Z8440APE	OEM
Z8440APS	OEM
Z8440BCE	OEM
Z8440BCM	OEM
Z8440BCMB	OEM
Z8440BCS	OEM
Z8440BDE	OEM
Z8440BDS	OEM
Z8440BPE	OEM
Z8440BPS	OEM
Z8440CE	OEM
Z8440CM	OEM
Z8440CMB	OEM
Z8440CS	OEM
Z8440DE	OEM
Z8440DS	OEM
Z8440PE	OEM
Z8440PS	OEM
Z8441ACE	OEM
Z8441ACM	OEM
Z8441ACMB	OEM
Z8441ACS	OEM
Z8441ADE	OEM
Z8441ADS	OEM
Z8441APE	OEM
Z8441APS	OEM
Z8441BCE	OEM
Z8441CE	OEM
Z8441CM	OEM
Z8441CS	OEM
Z8441DE	OEM
Z8441DS	OEM
Z8441PE	OEM
Z8441PS	OEM
Z8442ACE	OEM
Z8442ACM	OEM
Z8442ACS	OEM
Z8442ADE	OEM
Z8442ADS	OEM
Z8442APE	OEM
Z8442APS	OEM
Z8442BCE	OEM
Z8442BCM	OEM
Z8442BCMB	OEM
Z8442BCS	OEM
Z8442BDE	OEM
Z8442BDS	OEM
Z8442BPE	OEM
Z8442BPS	OEM
Z8442CE	OEM
Z8442CM	OEM
Z8442CMB	OEM
Z8442DE	OEM
Z8442DS	OEM
Z8442PE	OEM
Z8442PS	OEM
Z8449ACE	OEM
Z8449ACM	OEM
Z8449ACMB	OEM
Z8449ACS	OEM
Z8449ADE	OEM
Z8449ADS	OEM
Z8449APE	OEM
Z8449APS	OEM
Z8449BCE	OEM
Z8449BCM	OEM
Z8449BCMB	OEM
Z8449BCS	OEM
Z8449BDE	OEM
Z8449BDS	OEM
Z8449BPE	OEM
Z8449BPS	OEM
Z8449CE	OEM
Z8449CM	OEM
Z8449CMB	OEM
Z8449DE	OEM
Z8449DS	OEM
Z8449PE	OEM
Z8449PS	OEM
Z8470ACE	OEM
Z8470ACM	OEM
Z8470ACMB	OEM
Z8470ACS	OEM
Z8470ADE	OEM
Z8470ADS	OEM
Z8470APE	OEM
Z8470APS	OEM
Z8470BCE	OEM
Z8470BCM	OEM
Z8470BCS	OEM
Z8470BDE	OEM
Z8470BDS	OEM
Z8470BPE	OEM
Z8470BPS	OEM
Z8470CE	OEM
Z8470CM	OEM
Z8470CMB	OEM
Z8470CS	OEM
Z8470DE	OEM
Z8470DS	OEM
Z8470PE	OEM
Z8470PS	OEM
Z8530ACE	OEM
Z8530ACS	OEM
Z8530ADE	OEM
Z8530ADS	OEM
Z8530APE	OEM
Z8530APS	OEM
Z8530CE	OEM
Z8530CS	OEM
Z8530PE	OEM
Z8530PS	OEM
Z8530SCCC	OEM
Z8530SCCP	OEM
Z8536ACE	OEM
Z8536ACS	OEM
Z8536ADE	OEM
Z8536ADS	OEM
Z8536APE	OEM
Z8536APS	OEM
Z8536CE	OEM
Z8536CS	OEM
Z8536DE	OEM
Z8536DS	OEM
Z8536PE	OEM
Z8536PS	OEM
Z8538ACE	OEM
Z8538ACS	OEM
Z8538ADE	OEM
Z8538ADS	OEM
Z8538APE	OEM
Z8538APS	OEM
Z8538CE	OEM
Z8538CS	OEM
Z8538DE	OEM
Z8538DS	OEM
Z8538PE	OEM
Z8538PS	OEM
Z8590CE	OEM
Z8590CS	OEM
Z8590DE	OEM
Z8590DS	OEM
Z8590PE	OEM
Z8590PS	OEM
Z8591QS	OEM
Z8592QS	OEM
Z8593RS	OEM
Z8594RS	OEM
Z8601CE	OEM
Z8601CS	OEM
Z8601DE	OEM
Z8601DS	OEM
Z8601PE	OEM
Z8601PS	OEM
Z8602QE	OEM
Z8602QS	OEM
Z8603RS	OEM
Z8611CE	OEM
Z8611CS	OEM
Z8611DE	OEM
Z8611DS	OEM
Z8611PE	OEM
Z8611PS	OEM
Z8611QE	OEM
Z8612QE	OEM
Z8612QS	OEM
Z8613RS	OEM
Z84008BCMB	OEM
Z86128	OEM
Z8612812PSC	OEM
ZA6.8	0025
ZA6.8A	0025
ZA6.8B	0025
ZA7.5	0644
ZA7.5A	0644
ZA7.5B	0644
ZA8.2	0244
ZA8.2A	0244
ZA8.2B	0244
ZA9.1	0012
ZA9.1A	0012
ZA9.1B	0012
ZA10	0170
ZA10A	0170
ZA10B	0170
ZA11	0789
ZA11A	0313
ZA11B	0313
ZA12	0137
ZA12A	0137
ZA12B	0137
ZA13	0361
ZA13A	0361
ZA13B	0361
ZA15	0002
ZA15A	0002
ZA-15B	0002
ZA15B	0002
ZA15V	0002
ZA16	0416
ZA16A	0416
ZA16B	0416
ZA18	0490
ZA18A	0490
ZA18B	0490
ZA20	0526
ZA20A	0526
ZA20B	0526
ZA21A	0560
ZA21B	0560
ZA22	0560
ZA22A	0560
ZA22B	0560
ZA24	0398
ZA24A	0398
ZA24B	0560
ZA27	0436
ZA27A	0436
ZA27B	0436
ZA30	0721
ZA30A	0721
ZA30B	0721
ZA31A	0721
ZA33	0039
ZA33A	0039
ZA33B	0039
ZA36	0814
ZA36A	0814
ZA36B	0814
ZA39	0346
ZA39A	0346
ZA39B	0346
ZA43	0925
ZA43A	0925
ZA43B	0925
ZA47	0993
ZA47A	0993
ZA47B	0993
ZA51	0497
ZA51A	0497
ZA51B	0497
ZA56	1823
ZA56A	1823
ZA56B	0863
ZA62	0778
ZA62A	0778
ZA62B	0778
ZA68	2144
ZA68A	2144
ZA68B	1258
ZA75	1181
ZA75A	1181
ZA75B	1181
ZA82	0327
ZA82A	0327
ZA82B	0327
ZA91	1301
ZA91A	1301
ZA91B	1301
ZA100	0098
ZA100A	0098
ZA100B	0098
ZA110	0149
ZA110A	0149
ZA110B	0149
ZA120	0186
ZA120A	0186
ZA120B	0186
ZA130	0213
ZA130A	0213
ZA130B	0213
ZA150	0028
ZA150A	0028
ZA150B	0028
ZA160	0255
ZA160A	0255
ZA160B	0255
ZA180	0363
ZA180A	0363
ZA180B	0363
ZA200	0417
ZA200A	0417
ZA200B	0417
ZA1250NL	OEM
ZAC6.8	0205
ZAC6.8A	0205
ZAC6.8B	0205
ZAC7.5	0475
ZAC7.5A	0475
ZAC7.5B	0475
ZAC9.1	0679
ZAC9.1A	0679
ZAC9.1B	0679
ZAC10	0225
ZAC10A	0225
ZAC10B	0225
ZAC11	0230
ZAC11A	0230
ZAC11B	0230
ZAC12	0234
ZAC12A	0234
ZAC12B	0234
ZAC13	0237
ZAC13A	0237
ZAC13B	0237
ZAC15	0247
ZAC15A	0247
ZAC15B	0247
ZAC16	0251
ZAC16A	0251
ZAC16B	0251
ZAC18	0256
ZAC18A	0256
ZAC18B	0256
ZAC20	0262
ZAC20A	0262
ZAC20B	0262
ZAC22	0269
ZAC22A	0269
ZAC22B	0269
ZAC24	0273
ZAC24A	0273
ZAC24B	0273
ZAC27	0291
ZAC27A	0291
ZAC27B	0291
ZAC30	0305
ZAC30A	0305
ZAC30B	0305
ZAC33	0314
ZAC33A	0314
ZAC33B	0314
ZAC36	0316
ZAC36A	0316
ZAC36B	0316
ZAC39	0322
ZAC39A	0322
ZAC39B	0322
ZAC43	0333
ZAC43A	0333
ZAC43B	0333
ZAC47	0343
ZAC47A	0343
ZAC47B	0343
ZAC51	0027
ZAC51A	0027
ZAC51B	0027
ZAC56	0266
ZAC56A	0266
ZAC56B	0266
ZAC62	0382
ZAC62A	0382
ZAC62B	0382
ZAC68	0401
ZAC68A	0401
ZAC68B	0401
ZAC75	0421
ZAC75A	0421
ZAC75B	0421
ZAC82	0439
ZAC82A	0439
ZAC82B	0439
ZAC91	0238
ZAC91A	0238
ZAC91B	0238
ZAC100	1172
ZAC100A	1172
ZAC100B	1172
ZAC110	1182
ZAC110A	1182
ZAC110B	1182
ZAC120	1198
ZAC120A	1198
ZAC120B	1198
ZAC130	1209
ZAC130A	1209
ZAC130B	1209
ZAC150	0642
ZAC150A	0642
ZAC150B	0642
ZAC160	1246
ZAC160A	1246
ZAC160B	1246
ZAC180	1269
ZAC180A	1269
ZAC180B	1269
ZAC200	0600
ZAC200A	0600
ZAC200B	0600
ZAM627-600	OEM
ZAR110	0916
ZAR210	0145
ZAR610	0916
ZAR710	0916
ZB-1	0789
ZB1	0526
ZB1-6	0298
ZB1-7	0025
ZB1-8	0244
ZB1-9	0012
ZB-1-9.5	0012
ZB1-10	0170
ZB1-10A	0170
ZB1-11	0789
ZB1-12	0137
ZB1-13	0361
ZB1-14	0100
ZB1-15	0002
ZB1-16	0416
ZB1-18	0490
ZB1-19	0943
ZB1-20	0526
ZB1-23	0398
ZB1-27	0436
ZB1-29	0436
ZB1-31	0721
ZB1-35	0039
ZB1-50	0497
ZB1-100	0098
ZB1-100-2	0098
ZB1-110	0149
ZB1-125	0213
ZB1-150	0028
ZB3.3	0188
ZB3.3A	0289
ZB3.3B	0289
ZB3.6	0188
ZB3.6A	0188
ZB3.6B	0188
ZB3.9	0451
ZB3.9A	0451
ZB3.9B	0451
ZB4.3	0528
ZB4.3A	0528
ZB4.3B	0528
ZB4.7	0162
ZB4.7A	0446
ZB4.7B	0446
ZB5.1	0162
ZB5.1A	0162
ZB5.1B	0162
ZB5.6	0157
ZB5.6A	0157
ZB5.6B	0157
ZB6-18	OEM
ZB6C2704PSC-R425	OEM
ZB6.2	0631
ZB6.2A	0631
ZB6.2B	0631
ZB6.8	0025
ZB6.8A	0025
ZB6.8B	0025
ZB7.5	0644
ZB7.5A	0644
ZB7.5B	0644
ZB8.2	0244
ZB8.2A	0244
ZB8.2B	0244
ZB9.1	0012
ZB9.1A	0012
ZB9.1B	0012
ZB10	0170
ZB10A	0170
ZB10B	0170
ZB10X	0170
ZB11	0313
ZB11A	0313
ZB11B	0313
ZB12	0137
ZB12A	0137
ZB12B	0137
ZB13	0361
ZB13A	0002
ZB13B	0361
ZB15	0002
ZB15A	0002
ZB15B	0002
ZB16	0416
ZB16A	0416
ZB16B	0416
ZB18	0490
ZB18A	0490
ZB18B	0490
ZB20	0526
ZB20A	0526
ZB20B	0526
ZB22	0560
ZB22A	0560
ZB22B	0560
ZB24	0398
ZB24A	0398
ZB24B	0398
ZB26B	OEM
ZB27	0436
ZB27A	0436
ZB27B	0436
ZB30	0721
ZB30A	0721
ZB30B	0721
ZB33	0039
ZB33A	0039
ZB33B	0039
ZB36	0814
ZB36A	0814
ZB36B	0814
ZB39	0346
ZB39A	0346
ZB39B	0346
ZB43	0925
ZB43A	0925
ZB43B	0925
ZB47	0993
ZB47A	0993
ZB47B	0993
ZB51	0497
ZB51A	0497
ZB51B	0497
ZB56	0863
ZB56A	0863
ZB56B	0863
ZB62	0778
ZB62A	0778
ZB62B	0778
ZB68	2144
ZB68A	1258
ZB68B	2144
ZB75	1181
ZB75A	1181
ZB75B	1181
ZB82	0327
ZB82A	0327
ZB82B	0327
ZB91	1301
ZB91A	1301
ZB91B	1301
ZB100	0098
ZB100A	0098
ZB100B	0098
ZB110	0149
ZB110A	0149
ZB110B	0149
ZB120	0186
ZB120A	0186
ZB120B	0186
ZB130	0213
ZB130A	0213
ZB130B	0213
ZB150	0028
ZB150A	0028
ZB150B	0028
ZB160	0255
ZB160A	0255
ZB160B	0255
ZB180	0363
ZB180A	0363
ZB180B	0363
ZB200	0417
ZB200A	0417
ZB200B	0417
ZB202	0755
ZB203	0188
ZB204	0528
ZB205	0157
ZB206	0631
ZB207	0644
ZB209	1075
ZB210	0170
ZB212	0137
ZB215	0244
ZB220	0526
ZB225	1596
ZB230	0721
ZB235	0814
ZB240	0925
ZB250	0497
ZB442ACMB	OEM
ZB442CS	OEM
ZBC-0128	OEM
ZBC-0128A	OEM
ZBC-0256	OEM
ZBC-0256A	OEM
ZBC-0384	OEM
ZBC-0384A	OEM
ZBC-0512	OEM
ZBC-0512A	OEM
ZBC3.3	0777
ZBC3.3A	0777
ZBC3.3B	0777
ZBC3.6	0791
ZBC3.6A	0791
ZBC3.6B	0791
ZBC3.9	0801
ZBC3.9A	0801
ZBC3.9B	0801
ZBC4.3	0815
ZBC4.3A	0815
ZBC4.3B	0815
ZBC4.7	0827
ZBC4.7A	0827
ZBC4.7B	0827
ZBC5.1	0437
ZBC5.1A	0437
ZBC5.1B	0437
ZBC5.6	0870
ZBC5.6A	0870
ZBC5.6B	0870
ZBC6.2	0185
ZBC6.2A	0185
ZBC6.2B	0185
ZBC6.8	0205
ZBC6.8A	0205
ZBC6.8B	0205
ZBC7.5	0475
ZBC7.5A	0475
ZBC7.5B	0475
ZBC8.2	0499
ZBC8.2A	0499
ZBC8.2B	0499
ZBC9.1	0679
ZBC9.1A	0679
ZBC9.1B	0679
ZBC10	0225
ZBC10A	0225
ZBC10B	0225
ZBC11	0230
ZBC11A	0230
ZBC11B	0230
ZBC12	0234
ZBC12A	0234
ZBC12B	0234
ZBC13	0237
ZBC13A	0237
ZBC13B	0237
ZBC14	1387
ZBC14A	1387
ZBC14B	1387
ZBC15	0247
ZBC15A	0247
ZBC15B	0247
ZBC17	1246
ZBC17A	1170
ZBC17B	1170
ZBC18	0256
ZBC18A	0256
ZBC18B	0256
ZBC19	2379
ZBC19A	2379
ZBC19B	2379
ZBC20	0262
ZBC20A	0262
ZBC20B	0262
ZBC22	0269
ZBC22A	0269
ZBC22B	0269
ZBC24	0273
ZBC24A	0273
ZBC24B	0273
ZBC25	2383
ZBC25A	2383
ZBC25B	2383
ZBC27	0291
ZBC27A	0291
ZBC27B	0291
ZBC30	0305
ZBC30A	0305
ZBC30B	0305
ZBC33	0314
ZBC33A	0314
ZBC33B	0314
ZBC36	0316
ZBC36A	0316
ZBC36B	0316
ZBC39	0322
ZBC39A	0322
ZBC39B	0322
ZBC43	0333
ZBC43A	0333
ZBC43B	0333
ZBC45	0333
ZBC45A	0333
ZBC45B	0333
ZBC47	0343
ZBC47A	0343
ZBC47B	0343
ZBC50	0027
ZBC50A	0027
ZBC50B	0027
ZBC51	0027
ZBC51A	0027
ZBC51B	0027
ZBC52	0027
ZBC52A	0027
ZBC52B	0027
ZBC56	0266
ZBC56A	0266
ZBC56B	0266
ZBC62	0382
ZBC62A	0382
ZBC62B	0382
ZBC68	0401
ZBC68A	0401
ZBC68B	0401
ZBC75	0421
ZBC75A	0421
ZBC75B	0421
ZBC-80	OEM
ZBC82	0439
ZBC82A	0439
ZBC82B	0439
ZBC91	0238
ZBC91A	0238
ZBC91B	0238
ZBC100	1172
ZBC100A	1172
ZBC100B	1172
ZBC105	1182
ZBC105A	1182
ZBC105B	1182
ZBC110	1182
ZBC110A	1182
ZBC110B	1182
ZBC120	1198
ZBC120A	1198
ZBC120B	1198
ZBC130	1209
ZBC130A	1209
ZBC130B	1209

If replacement code is OEM, contact original manufacturer for replacement.

DEVICE TYPE	REPL CODE
ZBC140	1870
ZBC140A	1870
ZBC140B	1870
ZBC150	0642
ZBC150A	0642
ZBC150B	0642
ZBC160	1246
ZBC160A	1246
ZBC160B	1246
ZBC180	1269
ZBC180A	1269
ZBC180B	1269
ZBC200	0600
ZBC200A	0600
ZBC200B	0600
ZBI-09	0012
ZBI-13	0157
ZBI-14	0002
ZBX218A	OEM
ZBX324	OEM
ZBX349	OEM
ZBX350	OEM
ZC008	0499
ZC009	0679
ZC01	OEM
ZC02	OEM
ZC02-3	0436
ZC06	OEM
ZC010	0170
ZC011	0313
ZC012	0137
ZC013	0361
ZC015	0002
ZC018	0490
ZC020	0526
ZC020A	OEM
ZC020B	OEM
ZC020C	OEM
ZC021A-25A	OEM
ZC021B-25B	OEM
ZC021C-25C	OEM
ZC022	0560
ZC024	0398
ZC027	0436
ZC030	0721
ZC033	0039
ZC0181	OEM
ZC0226	OEM
ZC-0226A	OEM
ZC0226A	OEM
ZC0227	OEM
ZC0227A	OEM
ZC0229X	OEM
ZC-0231X	OEM
ZC0231X	OEM
ZC0233X	OEM
ZC-0235BX	OEM
ZC0235BX	OEM
ZC0239X	OEM
ZC0240X	OEM
ZC0241	OEM
ZC-0247A	OEM
ZC-0247A(NTSC)	OEM
ZC0247A-N	OEM
ZC-0248	OEM
ZC0248	OEM
ZC-0250	OEM
ZC0250	OEM
ZC-0253BT	OEM
ZC0256SE	OEM
ZC0261A	OEM
ZC0262	OEM
ZC0263	OEM
ZC0266X	OEM
ZC0300	OEM
ZC0310	OEM
ZC1N34A	0143
ZC1S352M	0030
ZC1S358S	0133
ZC2SA70	0050
ZC2SA71	0050
ZC2SA71A	0050
ZC2SA101	0050
ZC2SA101BA	0050
ZC2SA102	0050
ZC2SA102CA	0050
ZC2SA103	0050
ZC2SA103CA	0050
ZC2SA377	0050
ZC2SA700A	0050
ZC2SA700B	0050
ZC2SB172	0164
ZC2SB172A	0164
ZC3.3	0777
ZC3.3A	0777
ZC3.3B	0777
ZC3.6	0791
ZC3.6A	0791
ZC3.6B	0791
ZC3.9	0801
ZC3.9A	0801
ZC3.9B	0801
ZC4.3	0815
ZC4.3A	0815
ZC4.3B	0815
ZC4.7	0827
ZC4.7A	0827
ZC4.7B	0827
ZC5.1	0437

DEVICE TYPE	REPL CODE
ZC5.1A	0437
ZC5.1B	0437
ZC5.6	0870
ZC5.6A	0870
ZC5.6B	0870
ZC6.2	0185
ZC6.2A	0185
ZC6.2B	0185
ZC6.8	0205
ZC6.8A	0205
ZC6.8B	0205
ZC7.5	0475
ZC7.5A	0475
ZC7.5B	0475
ZC8.2	0499
ZC8.2A	0499
ZC8.2B	0499
ZC9.1	0679
ZC9.1A	0679
ZC9.1B	0679
ZC10	0225
ZC10A	0098
ZC10B	0225
ZC11	0230
ZC11A	0230
ZC11B	0230
ZC12	0234
ZC12A	0234
ZC12B	0234
ZC13	0237
ZC13A	0237
ZC13B	0237
ZC14	1387
ZC14A	1870
ZC14B	1387
ZC15	0247
ZC15A	0247
ZC15B	0247
ZC17	1170
ZC17A	1170
ZC17B	1170
ZC18	0256
ZC18A	0256
ZC18B	0256
ZC19	2379
ZC19A	2379
ZC19B	2379
ZC20	0262
ZC20A	0262
ZC20B	0526
ZC21	0269
ZC22	0269
ZC22A	0269
ZC22B	0269
ZC24	0273
ZC24A	0273
ZC24B	0273
ZC25	2383
ZC25A	2383
ZC25B	2383
ZC27	0291
ZC27A	0291
ZC27B	0291
ZC29BF	OEM
ZC29BG-BI	OEM
ZC29BJ	OEM
ZC29BK	OEM
ZC29BL	OEM
ZC29CG-CI	OEM
ZC29CJ	OEM
ZC29CK	OEM
ZC29CL	OEM
ZC29EF	OEM
ZC29EG-EI	OEM
ZC29EJ	OEM
ZC29EK	OEM
ZC29EL	OEM
ZC30	0305
ZC30A	0305
ZC30B	0305
ZC30BF	OEM
ZC30BG-BI	OEM
ZC30BJ	OEM
ZC30BK	OEM
ZC30BL	OEM
ZC30CF	OEM
ZC30CG-CI	OEM
ZC30CJ	OEM
ZC30CK	OEM
ZC30CL	OEM
ZC30EF	OEM
ZC30EG-EI	OEM
ZC30EJ	OEM
ZC30EK	OEM
ZC30EL	OEM
ZC31BE-BH	OEM
ZC31CE-CH	OEM
ZC31EE-EH	OEM
ZC32B	OEM
ZC32BD-BG	OEM
ZC32C	OEM
ZC32CD-CG	OEM
ZC32ED-EG	OEM
ZC33	0314
ZC33A	0314
ZC33B	0314
ZC36	0316
ZC36A	0316
ZC36B	0316

DEVICE TYPE	REPL CODE
ZC39	0322
ZC39A	0322
ZC39B	0322
ZC43	0333
ZC43A	0333
ZC43B	0333
ZC45	0343
ZC45A	0343
ZC45B	0343
ZC47	0343
ZC47A	0343
ZC47B	0343
ZC50	0027
ZC50A	0027
ZC50B	0027
ZC50BB	OEM
ZC50BC-BE	OEM
ZC50BF	OEM
ZC50BG	OEM
ZC50BH	OEM
ZC50CB	OEM
ZC50CC-CE	OEM
ZC50CF	OEM
ZC50CG	OEM
ZC50CH	OEM
ZC50EC-EE	OEM
ZC50EF	OEM
ZC50EG	OEM
ZC50EH	OEM
ZC51	0027
ZC51A	0027
ZC51B	0027
ZC51BB	OEM
ZC51BC-BG	OEM
ZC51C	OEM
ZC51CB	OEM
ZC51CC-CG	OEM
ZC51EB	OEM
ZC51EC-EG	OEM
ZC52	0027
ZC52A	0027
ZC52B	0027
ZC52BB	OEM
ZC52BC-BF	OEM
ZC52C	OEM
ZC52CB	OEM
ZC52CC-CF	OEM
ZC52EB	OEM
ZC52EC-EF	OEM
ZC53B	OEM
ZC53BB	OEM
ZC53BC-BE	OEM
ZC53C	OEM
ZC53CB	OEM
ZC53CC-CE	OEM
ZC53EB	OEM
ZC53EC-EE	OEM
ZC54B	OEM
ZC54BB	OEM
ZC54BC	OEM
ZC54BD	OEM
ZC54C	OEM
ZC54CB	OEM
ZC54CC	OEM
ZC54CD	OEM
ZC54EB	OEM
ZC54EC	OEM
ZC54ED	OEM
ZC55PB	OEM
ZC56	0266
ZC56A	0266
ZC56B	0266
ZC62	0382
ZC62A	0382
ZC62B	0382
ZC68	0401
ZC68A	0401
ZC68B	0401
ZC70BB	OEM
ZC70BC-BE	OEM
ZC70BF	OEM
ZC70BG	OEM
ZC70BH	OEM
ZC70CB	OEM
ZC70CC-CE	OEM
ZC70CF	OEM
ZC70CG	OEM
ZC70CH	OEM
ZC70EB	OEM
ZC70EC-EE	OEM
ZC70EF	OEM
ZC70EG	OEM
ZC70EH	OEM
ZC71BB	OEM
ZC71BC-BG	OEM
ZC71CB	OEM
ZC71CC-CG	OEM
ZC71EB	OEM
ZC71EC-EG	OEM
ZC72B	OEM
ZC72BB	OEM
ZC72BC-BF	OEM
ZC72C	OEM
ZC72CB	OEM
ZC72CC-CF	OEM
ZC72EB	OEM
ZC72EC-EF	OEM
ZC73B	OEM
ZC73BB	OEM

DEVICE TYPE	REPL CODE
ZC73BC-BE	OEM
ZC73C	OEM
ZC73CB	OEM
ZC73CC-CE	OEM
ZC73EB	OEM
ZC73EC-EE	OEM
ZC74B	OEM
ZC74BB	OEM
ZC74BC	OEM
ZC74BD	OEM
ZC74C	OEM
ZC74CB	OEM
ZC74CC	OEM
ZC74CD	OEM
ZC74EB	OEM
ZC74EC	OEM
ZC74ED	OEM
ZC75	0421
ZC75A	0421
ZC75B	0421
ZC82	0439
ZC82A	0439
ZC82B	0439
ZC91	0238
ZC91A	0238
ZC91B	0238
ZC99-50	OEM
ZC100	1172
ZC100A	1172
ZC100B	1172
ZC101	OEM
ZC102	1302
ZC103	0188
ZC104	0528
ZC105	0157
ZC105A	1182
ZC105B	1182
ZC106	0631
ZC107	0644
ZC109	1075
ZC110	0170
ZC110A	1182
ZC110B	1182
ZC111	OEM
ZC112	0137
ZC112BI	OEM
ZC112BJ	OEM
ZC112BK	OEM
ZC112EI	OEM
ZC112EJ	OEM
ZC112EK	OEM
ZC115	0002
ZC120	1198
ZC120A	1198
ZC120B	1198
ZC125	1596
ZC130	0721
ZC130A	1209
ZC130B	1209
ZC130T	0721
ZC135	0814
ZC-140	0010
ZC140	0925
ZC-140(TRANS)	0042
ZC140(ZENER)	0925
ZC140A	1870
ZC140B	1870
ZC150	0497
ZC150A	0642
ZC150B	0777
ZC151	OEM
ZC160	0778
ZC160A	1246
ZC160B	0499
ZC170	2144
ZC180	0327
ZC180A	1269
ZC180B	1269
ZC200	0600
ZC200A	0600
ZC200B	0600
ZC201	OEM
ZC202	OEM
ZC209	OEM
ZC240	OEM
ZC620	OEM
ZC700	0549
ZC700B	OEM
ZC700C	OEM
ZC701	OEM
ZC701B	OEM
ZC701C	OEM
ZC702	0005
ZC702B	OEM
ZC702C	OEM
ZC703	0715
ZC703B	OEM
ZC703C	OEM
ZC704	OEM
ZC704B	OEM
ZC704C	OEM
ZC705	OEM
ZC705B	OEM
ZC705C	OEM
ZC706	OEM
ZC706B	OEM
ZC706C	OEM
ZC707	OEM
ZC707B	OEM

DEVICE TYPE	REPL CODE
ZC707C	OEM
ZC708	0165
ZC708B	OEM
ZC708C	OEM
ZC709	0057
ZC709B	OEM
ZC709C	OEM
ZC710	0157
ZC710B	OEM
ZC710C	OEM
ZC711	0181
ZC711B	OEM
ZC711C	OEM
ZC712	0052
ZC712B	OEM
ZC712C	OEM
ZC713	0053
ZC713B	OEM
ZC713C	OEM
ZC714	OEM
ZC714B	OEM
ZC714C	OEM
ZC715	0681
ZC716	0440
ZC718	0371
ZC720	0695
ZC721	OEM
ZC722	0700
ZC723	OEM
ZC724	0489
ZC725	0709
ZC726	OEM
ZC727	0450
ZC728	0244
ZC729	OEM
ZC730	0195
ZC731	OEM
ZC732	OEM
ZC733	0166
ZC736	0010
ZC739	0032
ZC740	OEM
ZC741	OEM
ZC742	OEM
ZC743	0054
ZC744	OEM
ZC745	OEM
ZC746	OEM
ZC747	0068
ZC748	OEM
ZC749	OEM
ZC751	0092
ZC753	OEM
ZC754	OEM
ZC756	0125
ZC762	0152
ZC768	0173
ZC775	OEM
ZC782	0049
ZC791	0156
ZC799	0189
ZC800	0005
ZC800A	0005
ZC800B	OEM
ZC801	OEM
ZC801A	OEM
ZC801B	OEM
ZC802	0623
ZC802A	0623
ZC802B	OEM
ZC803	OEM
ZC803A	OEM
ZC803B	OEM
ZC804	OEM
ZC804A	OEM
ZC804B	OEM
ZC805	OEM
ZC805A	OEM
ZC805B	OEM
ZC806	OEM
ZC806A	OEM
ZC806B	OEM
ZC807	OEM
ZC807A	OEM
ZC807B	OEM
ZC808	OEM
ZC808A	OEM
ZC808B	OEM
ZC809	OEM
ZC809A	OEM
ZC809B	OEM
ZC810	OEM
ZC811	OEM
ZC812	OEM
ZC813	OEM
ZC814	OEM
ZC815	OEM
ZC816	OEM
ZC820	OEM
ZC821	OEM
ZC822	OEM
ZC823	OEM
ZC824	OEM
ZC825	OEM
ZC826	OEM
ZC830A	OEM
ZC830B	OEM
ZC831A	OEM
ZC831B	OEM

DEVICE TYPE	REPL CODE
ZC833A	OEM
ZC833B	OEM
ZC834A	OEM
ZC834B	OEM
ZC835A	OEM
ZC835B	OEM
ZC836A	OEM
ZC836B	OEM
ZC898	OEM
ZC899	OEM
ZC2008	OEM
ZC2009	OEM
ZC2010	0225
ZC2011	0230
ZC2012	0234
ZC2013	0237
ZC2015	0247
ZC2016	0251
ZC2018	0256
ZC2020	0262
ZC2022	0269
ZC2024	0273
ZC2027	0291
ZC2030	0305
ZC2033	0314
ZC2800	OEM
ZC2800A	0080
ZC2800B	OEM
ZC2800E	OEM
ZC2800H	OEM
ZC2810	OEM
ZC2810B	OEM
ZC2810E	OEM
ZC2810H	OEM
ZC2811	OEM
ZC2811B	OEM
ZC2811E	OEM
ZC2811H	OEM
ZC2833B	OEM
ZC5008	1481
ZC5009	1608
ZC5010	0505
ZC5011	0686
ZC5012	0864
ZC5013	1014
ZC5015	1264
ZC5016	1392
ZC5018	1071
ZC5020	1707
ZC5022	1712
ZC5024	1725
ZC5027	1750
ZC5030	1761
ZC5033	1777
ZC5036	1785
ZC5039	1793
ZC5043	1185
ZC5047	0022
ZC5051	0132
ZC5056	0207
ZC5062	0263
ZC5068	0306
ZC5075	0325
ZC5082	0352
ZC5091	0408
ZC5099	0433
ZC5800	OEM
ZC5800E	OEM
ZC5800H	OEM
ZCC3.3	0777
ZCC3.3A	0777
ZCC3.3B	0777
ZCC3.6	0791
ZCC3.6A	0791
ZCC3.6B	0791
ZCC3.9	0801
ZCC3.9A	0801
ZCC3.9B	0801
ZCC4.3	0815
ZCC4.3A	0815
ZCC4.3B	0815
ZCC4.7	0827
ZCC4.7A	0827
ZCC4.7B	0827
ZCC5.1	0437
ZCC5.1A	0437
ZCC5.1B	0437
ZCC5.6	0870
ZCC5.6A	0870
ZCC5.6B	0870
ZCC6.2	0185
ZCC6.2A	0185
ZCC6.2B	0185
ZCC6.8	0205
ZCC6.8A	0205
ZCC6.8B	0205
ZCC7.5	0475
ZCC7.5A	0475
ZCC7.5B	0475
ZCC8.2	0499
ZCC8.2A	0499
ZCC8.2B	0499
ZCC9.1	0679
ZCC9.1A	0679
ZCC9.1B	0679
ZCC10	0225
ZCC10A	0225
ZCC10B	0225
ZCC11	0230

DEVICE TYPE	REPL CODE
ZCC11A	0230
ZCC11B	0230
ZCC12	0234
ZCC12A	0234
ZCC12B	0234
ZCC13	0237
ZCC13A	0237
ZCC13B	0237
ZCC14	1387
ZCC14A	1387
ZCC14B	1387
ZCC15	0247
ZCC15A	0247
ZCC15B	1870
ZCC17	1170
ZCC17A	1170
ZCC17B	1170
ZCC18	0256
ZCC18A	0256
ZCC18B	0256
ZCC19A	2379
ZCC19B	2379
ZCC20	0262
ZCC20A	0262
ZCC20B	0262
ZCC22	0269
ZCC22A	0269
ZCC22B	0269
ZCC24	0273
ZCC24A	0273
ZCC24B	0273
ZCC25	2383
ZCC25A	2383
ZCC25B	2383
ZCC27	0291
ZCC27A	0291
ZCC27B	0291
ZCC30	0305
ZCC30A	0305
ZCC30B	0305
ZCC33	0314
ZCC33A	0314
ZCC33B	0314
ZCC36	0316
ZCC36A	0316
ZCC36B	0316
ZCC39	0322
ZCC39A	0322
ZCC39B	0322
ZCC43	0333
ZCC43A	0333
ZCC43B	0333
ZCC45	0343
ZCC45A	0343
ZCC45B	0343
ZCC47	0343
ZCC47A	0343
ZCC47B	0343
ZCC50	0027
ZCC50A	0027
ZCC50B	0027
ZCC51	0027
ZCC51A	0027
ZCC51B	0027
ZCC52	0027
ZCC52A	0027
ZCC52B	0027
ZCC56	0266
ZCC56A	0266
ZCC56B	0266
ZCC62	0382
ZCC62A	0382
ZCC62B	0382
ZCC68	0401
ZCC68A	0401
ZCC68B	0401
ZCC75	0421
ZCC75A	0421
ZCC75B	0421
ZCC82	0439
ZCC82A	0439
ZCC82B	0439
ZCC91	0238
ZCC91A	0238
ZCC91B	0238
ZCC100	1172
ZCC100A	1172
ZCC100B	1172
ZCC105	1182
ZCC105A	1182
ZCC105B	1182
ZCC110	1182
ZCC110A	1182
ZCC110B	1182
ZCC120	1198
ZCC120A	1198
ZCC120B	1198
ZCC130	1209
ZCC130A	1209
ZCC130B	6696
ZCC140	1870
ZCC140A	1870
ZCC140B	1870
ZCC150	0642
ZCC150A	0642
ZCC150B	0642
ZCC160	1246
ZCC160A	1246
ZCC160B	1246

If replacement code is OEM, contact original manufacturer for replacement.

DEVICE TYPE	REPL CODE
ZCC180	1269
ZCC180A	1269
ZCC180B	1269
ZCC200	0600
ZCC200A	0600
ZCC200B	0600
ZC012	0137
ZCOM3679	0015
ZCOM-5683-0	0015
ZD008	0244
ZD009	1075
ZD010	0064
ZD011	0313
ZD012	0052
ZD013	0361
ZD-015	0002
ZD015	0681
ZD016	0416
ZD018	0371
ZD020	0526
ZD022	0700
ZD024	0398
ZD027	0450
ZD030	0721
ZD033	0166
ZD039	0032
ZD047	0068
ZD056	0125
ZD068	0173
ZD2.7EB1	0755
ZD3.6A	0372
ZD3.6B	0188
ZD3.9	0451
ZD4.3	0528
ZD4.7	0827
ZD-5V	0162
ZD5.1	0162
ZD5.1A	0162
ZD5.1B	0437
ZD5.6	0157
ZD5.6A	0157
ZD5.6B	0157
ZD6.2	0631
ZD6.2A	0631
ZD6.2B	0631
ZD-6.2V	0466
ZD6.8	0205
ZD6.8(STUD)	2713
ZD6.8A	2713
ZD6.8B	2713
ZD6.8R	0920
ZD6.8RA	0920
ZD6.8RB	0920
ZD7.5	0475
ZD7.5(STUD)	2717
ZD7.5A	2717
ZD7.5B	2717
ZD7.5R	0938
ZD7.5RA	0938
ZD7.5RB	0938
ZD8.2	0499
ZD8.2(STUD)	1216
ZD8.2A	1216
ZD8.2B	1216
ZD8.2R	0952
ZD8.2RA	0952
ZD8.2RB	0952
ZD9.1	0679
ZD9.1(STUD)	1228
ZD9.1A	1228
ZD9.1B	1228
ZD9.1R	0988
ZD9.1RA	0988
ZD9.1RB	0988
ZD10	0225
ZD10(STUD)	1243
ZD10A	1243
ZD10B	1243
ZD10R	1003
ZD10RA	1003
ZD10RB	1003
ZD11	0230
ZD11(STUD)	1259
ZD11A	1259
ZD11B	1259
ZD11R	1013
ZD11RA	1013
ZD11RB	1013
ZD12	0234
ZD12(C)	0052
ZD12(STUD)	1267
ZD12A	1267
ZD12B	1267
ZD12C	0052
ZD12R	1761
ZD12RA	0883
ZD12RB	0883
ZD13	0237
ZD13(STUD)	1283
ZD13A	1283
ZD13B	1283
ZD13R	1043
ZD13RA	1043
ZD13RB	1043
ZD14(STUD)	2725
ZD14A	2725
ZD14B	2725
ZD14R	1052
ZD14RA	1052
ZD14RB	1052
ZD-14V	0100
ZD15	0247
ZD15(STUD)	1292
ZD15A	1292
ZD15B	1292
ZD15R	0926
ZD15RA	0926
ZD15RB	0926
ZD16	0251
ZD16(STUD)	1300
ZD16A	1300
ZD16B	1300
ZD16R	1072
ZD16RA	1072
ZD16RB	1072
ZD17(STUD)	2729
ZD17A	2729
ZD17B	2729
ZD17R	1088
ZD17RA	1088
ZD17RB	1088
ZD18	0256
ZD18(STUD)	1314
ZD18A	1314
ZD18B	1314
ZD18R	1098
ZD18RA	1098
ZD18RB	1098
ZD19(STUD)	2731
ZD19A	2731
ZD19B	2731
ZD19R	1115
ZD19RA	1115
ZD19RB	1115
ZD20	0262
ZD20(STUD)	1323
ZD20A	1323
ZD20B	1323
ZD20R	1127
ZD20RA	1127
ZD20RB	1127
ZD22	0269
ZD22(STUD)	1334
ZD22A	1334
ZD22B	1334
ZD22R	1144
ZD22RA	1144
ZD22RB	1144
ZD24	0273
ZD24(STUD)	1346
ZD24-1L	0398
ZD24A	1346
ZD24B	1346
ZD24R	1156
ZD24RA	1156
ZD24RB	1156
ZD25(STUD)	2733
ZD25A	2733
ZD25B	2733
ZD25R	1166
ZD25RA	1166
ZD25RB	1166
ZD27	0291
ZD27(STUD)	1361
ZD27A	1361
ZD27B	1361
ZD27R	1176
ZD27RA	1176
ZD27RB	1191
ZD30	0305
ZD30(STUD)	1377
ZD30A	1377
ZD30B	1377
ZD30R	1201
ZD30RA	1201
ZD30RB	1201
ZD33	0314
ZD33(STUD)	1396
ZD33A	1396
ZD33B	1396
ZD33R	1214
ZD33RA	1214
ZD33RB	1214
ZD36	0316
ZD36(STUD)	1405
ZD36A	1405
ZD36B	1405
ZD36R	1223
ZD36RA	1223
ZD36RB	1223
ZD39	0322
ZD39(STUD)	1419
ZD39A	1419
ZD39B	1419
ZD39R	1237
ZD39RA	1237
ZD39RB	1237
ZD43	0333
ZD43(STUD)	1431
ZD43A	1431
ZD43B	1431
ZD43R	1256
ZD43RA	1256
ZD43RB	1256
ZD45(STUD)	2745
ZD45A	2745
ZD45B	2745
ZD45R	1263
ZD45RA	1263
ZD45RB	1263
ZD47	0343
ZD47(STUD)	1438
ZD47A	1438
ZD47B	1438
ZD47R	1280
ZD47RA	1280
ZD47RB	1280
ZD50(STUD)	2749
ZD50A	2749
ZD50B	2749
ZD50R	1289
ZD50RA	1289
ZD50RB	1289
ZD51	0027
ZD51(STUD)	1452
ZD51A	1452
ZD51B	1452
ZD51R	1297
ZD51RA	1297
ZD51RB	1297
ZD52(STUD)	2752
ZD52A	2752
ZD52B	2752
ZD52R	1312
ZD52RA	1312
ZD52RB	1312
ZD56	0266
ZD56(STUD)	1465
ZD56A	1465
ZD56B	1465
ZD56R	1321
ZD56RA	1321
ZD56RB	1263
ZD62	0382
ZD62(STUD)	0608
ZD62A	0608
ZD62B	0608
ZD62R	1343
ZD62RA	1343
ZD62RB	1343
ZD68	0401
ZD68(STUD)	1502
ZD68A	1502
ZD68B	1502
ZD68R	1355
ZD68RA	1355
ZD68RB	1355
ZD75	0421
ZD75(STUD)	1515
ZD75A	1515
ZD75B	1515
ZD75R	1374
ZD75RA	1374
ZD75RB	1374
ZD82	0439
ZD82(STUD)	1529
ZD82A	1529
ZD82B	1529
ZD82R	1391
ZD82RA	1391
ZD82RB	1391
ZD91	0238
ZD91(STUD)	1541
ZD91A	1541
ZD91B	1541
ZD91R	1402
ZD91RA	1402
ZD91RB	1402
ZD100	1172
ZD100(STUD)	1565
ZD100A	1565
ZD100B	1565
ZD100R	1413
ZD100RA	1413
ZD100RB	1413
ZD105(STUD)	2775
ZD105A	2775
ZD105B	2775
ZD105R	1427
ZD105RA	1427
ZD105RB	1427
ZD110	1182
ZD110(STUD)	2776
ZD110A	2776
ZD110B	2776
ZD110R	1435
ZD110RA	1435
ZD110RB	1435
ZD120	1198
ZD120(STUD)	1499
ZD120A	1499
ZD120B	1499
ZD120R	1448
ZD120RA	1461
ZD120RB	1448
ZD130	1209
ZD130(STUD)	2778
ZD130A	2778
ZD130B	2778
ZD130R	1461
ZD130RA	1461
ZD130RB	1461
ZD140(STUD)	2780
ZD140A	2780
ZD140B	2780
ZD140R	1475
ZD140RA	1475
ZD140RB	1475
ZD150	0642
ZD150(STUD)	2783
ZD150A	2783
ZD150B	2783
ZD150R	1497
ZD150RA	1497
ZD150RB	1497
ZD160	1246
ZD160(STUD)	2788
ZD160A	2788
ZD160B	2788
ZD160R	1513
ZD160RA	1513
ZD160RB	1513
ZD175(STUD)	2791
ZD175A	2791
ZD175B	2791
ZD175R	1523
ZD175RA	1523
ZD175RB	1523
ZD180	1269
ZD180(STUD)	2793
ZD180A	2793
ZD180B	2793
ZD180R	1539
ZD180RA	1539
ZD180RB	1539
ZD200	0600
ZD200(STUD)	2797
ZD200A	2797
ZD200B	2797
ZD200R	1577
ZD200RA	1577
ZD200RB	1577
ZD220(STUD)	OEM
ZD220A	OEM
ZD220B	OEM
ZD220R	OEM
ZD220RA	OEM
ZD220RB	OEM
ZD2008	0499
ZD2009	0679
ZD2010	0225
ZD2011	0230
ZD2012	0234
ZD2013	0237
ZD2015	0247
ZD2016	0251
ZD2018	0256
ZD2020	0262
ZD2022	0269
ZD2024	0273
ZD2027	0291
ZD2028	0269
ZD2030	0305
ZD2033	0314
ZD5008	OEM
ZD5009	OEM
ZD5010	OEM
ZD5011	OEM
ZD5012	OEM
ZD5013	OEM
ZD5015	OEM
ZD5016	OEM
ZD5018	OEM
ZD5020	OEM
ZD5022	OEM
ZD5024	OEM
ZD5027	OEM
ZD5030	OEM
ZD5033	OEM
ZD5036	OEM
ZD5039	OEM
ZD5043	OEM
ZD5047	OEM
ZD5051	OEM
ZD5056	OEM
ZD5062	OEM
ZD5068	OEM
ZD5075	OEM
ZD5082	OEM
ZD5091	OEM
ZD5099	OEM
ZDC7	OEM
ZDDGGZA10Y	0064
ZDRD6.8ENZ	0062
ZDT10	0144
ZDT11	0144
ZDT20	0144
ZDT21	0144
ZDT30	0144
ZDT31	0144
ZDT40	OEM
ZDT41	OEM
ZDX1F	OEM
ZDX1R	OEM
ZDX2F	OEM
ZDX2R	OEM
ZDX3F	OEM
ZDX3R	OEM
ZDX4F	OEM
ZDX4R	OEM
ZDX5	OEM
ZDX6	OEM
ZE1.5	0143
ZE4.7	0140
ZE5.6	0157
ZE6V9	0062
ZE6.8	0025
ZE6.8A	0025
ZE6.8B	0025
ZE7.5	0644
ZE7.5A	0644
ZE7.5B	0644
ZE8.2	0244
ZE8.2A	0244
ZE8.2B	0244
ZE9V4	0057
ZE9.1	0012
ZE9.1A	0012
ZE9.1B	0012
ZE10	0170
ZE10A	0170
ZE10B	0170
ZE11	0313
ZE11A	0313
ZE11B	0313
ZE12	0137
ZE12A	0137
ZE12B	0137
ZE12V7	0053
ZE13	0361
ZE13A	0137
ZE13B	0361
ZE15	0002
ZE15A	0002
ZE15B	0002
ZE16	0416
ZE16A	0416
ZE16B	0416
ZE17V2	0210
ZE18	0490
ZE18A	0490
ZE18B	0490
ZE20	0526
ZE20A	0526
ZE20B	0526
ZE22	0560
ZE22A	0560
ZE22B	0560
ZE23V2	0489
ZE24	0398
ZE24A	0398
ZE24B	0398
ZE27	0436
ZE27A	0436
ZE27B	0436
ZE30	0721
ZE30A	0721
ZE30B	0721
ZE31V	0195
ZE33	0039
ZE33A	0039
ZE33B	0039
ZE36	0814
ZE36A	0814
ZE36B	0814
ZE39	0346
ZE39A	0346
ZE39B	0346
ZE43	0925
ZE43A	0925
ZE43B	0925
ZE47	0993
ZE47A	0993
ZE47B	0993
ZE51	0497
ZE51A	0497
ZE51B	0497
ZE56	0863
ZE56A	0863
ZE56B	0863
ZE62	0778
ZE62A	0778
ZE62B	0778
ZE68	2144
ZE68A	2144
ZE68B	2144
ZE75	1181
ZE75A	1181
ZE75B	1181
ZE82	0327
ZE82A	0327
ZE82B	0327
ZE91	1301
ZE91A	1301
ZE91B	1301
ZE100	0098
ZE100A	0098
ZE100B	0098
ZE110	0149
ZE110A	0149
ZE110B	0149
ZE120	0186
ZE120A	0186
ZE120B	0186
ZE130	0213
ZE130A	0213
ZE130B	0213
ZE150	0028
ZE150A	0028
ZE150B	0028
ZE160	0255
ZE160A	0255
ZE160B	0255
ZE180	0363
ZE180A	0363
ZE180B	0363
ZE200	0417
ZE200A	0417
ZE200B	0417
ZEC3.9	0451
ZEC4.7	0446
ZEC5.6	0157
ZEC6.8	0025
ZEC8.2	0244
ZEC10	0170
ZEC12	0137
ZEC15	0002
ZEC18	0490
ZEC22	0560
ZEC27	0436
ZEC30	0721
ZEN-100	0079
ZEN100	0079
ZEN-101	0126
ZEN101	0126
ZEN-102	0079
ZEN102	0079
ZEN103	0016
ZEN-104	0144
ZEN104	0144
ZEN105	1136
ZEN-106	0527
ZEN106	0527
ZEN107	0037
ZEN108	0224
ZEN-109	0224
ZEN109	0224
ZEN-110	0079
ZEN110	0079
ZEN-111	0016
ZEN111	0016
ZEN-112	0016
ZEN112	0016
ZEN-113	0111
ZEN113	0111
ZEN-114	0016
ZEN114	0016
ZEN-115	0016
ZEN115	0016
ZEN-116	0111
ZEN116	0111
ZEN-117	0127
ZEN117	0127
ZEN-118	0127
ZEN118	0127
ZEN-119	0079
ZEN119	0079
ZEN-120	0079
ZEN120	0079
ZEN121	0079
ZEN-122	0037
ZEN122	0037
ZEN123	0321
ZEN124	0212
ZEN125	0626
ZEN-126	0079
ZEN126	0079
ZEN-127	0079
ZEN127	0079
ZEN-128	0396
ZEN128	0396
ZEN129	1167
ZEN200	0142
ZEN201	0275
ZEN202	0161
ZEN203	0455
ZEN-204	0074
ZEN204	0074
ZEN-205	0488
ZEN205	0488
ZEN206	0637
ZEN207	0626
ZEN208	0334
ZEN-209	0556
ZEN209	0556
ZEN210	0161
ZEN-211	0455
ZEN211	0455
ZEN-300	0086
ZEN300	0279
ZEN-301	0050
ZEN301	0050
ZEN302	0211
ZEN-303	0004
ZEN303	0004
ZEN-304	0164
ZEN304	0164
ZEN-305	0208
ZEN305	0208
ZEN306	0211
ZEN-307	0164
ZEN307	0164
ZEN308	0004
ZEN-309	0211
ZEN309	0211
ZEN310	0004
ZEN-311	0136
ZEN311	0136
ZEN-312	0136
ZEN312	0136
ZEN-313	0136
ZEN313	0136
ZEN-314	0004
ZEN314	0004
ZEN-315	0595
ZEN315	0595
ZEN325	0085
ZEN-326	0160
ZEN326	0160
ZEN327	0435
ZEN328	0969
ZEN-329	1414
ZEN329	1414
ZEN330	0160
ZEN331	0085
ZEN401	0087
ZEN403	0109
ZEN430	0143
ZEN431	0911
ZEN432	0196
ZEN433	0287
ZEN434	0287
ZEN450	0549
ZEN451	0005
ZEN452	0715
ZEN453	0030
ZEN500	0466
ZEN501	0644
ZEN502	0052
ZEN503	0371
ZEN504	0450
ZEN505	0644
ZEN506	0361
ZEN507	0100
ZEN508	0002
ZEN512	0039
ZEN513	0213
ZEN514	0245
ZEN515	0814
ZEN517	0305
ZEN600	OEM
ZEN601	0627
ZEN602	0696
ZEN603	0661
ZEN604	0659
ZEN605	1739
ZEN606	0748
ZEN607	0348
ZEN608	0350
ZEN609	1742
ZEN610	1743
ZENER7-1V	0644
ZENER-132	1596
ZENER-136	0943
ZF2.7	0755
ZF2.7P	0755
ZF3.3	0296
ZF3.6	0188
ZF3.6P	0372
ZF3.9	0188
ZF3.9P	0036
ZF4.3	0528
ZF4.3P	0274
ZF4.7	0140
ZF4.7P	0140
ZF5A	0157
ZF5AR	OEM
ZF5.1	0162
ZF5.6	0157
ZF6A	0298
ZF6.2	0631
ZF6.8	0062
ZF6.8A	0062
ZF6.8B	0062
ZF7.5	0077
ZF7.5A	0077
ZF7.5B	0077
ZF8A	0244
ZF-8.2	0244
ZF8.2	0165
ZF8.2A	0165
ZF8.2B	0165
ZF8.2P	0244
ZF9.1	0057
ZF9.1A	0057
ZF9.1B	0057
ZF10	0064
ZF10A	0064
ZF10B	0064
ZF11	0181
ZF11A	0181
ZF11B	0181
ZF12	0052
ZF12A	0052
ZF12B	0052
ZF13	0053
ZF13A	0053
ZF13B	0053
ZF13.3R	0289
ZF13.6R	0188
ZF15	0681
ZF15A	0681
ZF15B	0681
ZF15.1R	0162
ZF15.6R	0157
ZF-16	0002
ZF16	0440
ZF16A	0440
ZF16B	0440
ZF16.2	0631
ZF17.5	0644
ZF18	0371
ZF18A	0371

If replacement code is OEM, contact original manufacturer for replacement.

DEVICE TYPE	REPL CODE	DEVICE TYPE	REPL CODE	DEVICE TYPE	REPL CODE	DEVICE TYPE	REPL CODE	DEVICE TYPE	REPL CODE	DEVICE TYPE	REPL CODE	DEVICE TYPE	REPL CODE
ZF18B	0371	ZF227	0436	ZG15RA	1264	ZG51RB	0132	ZG220	OEM	ZGL27-82A	OEM	ZGL41-56B	OEM
ZF19.1	0012	ZF230	0721	ZG15RB	1264	ZG52	1863	ZG220A	OEM	ZGL27-82B	OEM	ZGL41-62	OEM
ZF20	0695	ZF233	0039	ZG16	1693	ZG52A	1863	ZG220B	OEM	ZGL27-87	OEM	ZGL41-62A	OEM
ZF20A	0695	ZF236	0814	ZG16A	1693	ZG52B	1863	ZG220R	OEM	ZGL27-87A	OEM	ZGL41-62B	OEM
ZF20B	0695	ZF239	0346	ZG16B	1693	ZG52R	0172	ZG220RA	OEM	ZGL27-87B	OEM	ZGL41-68	OEM
ZF22	0700	ZF262	0778	ZG16R	1392	ZG52RA	0172	ZG220RB	OEM	ZGL27-91	OEM	ZGL41-68A	OEM
ZF22A	0700	ZF282	0327	ZG16RA	1392	ZG52RB	0172	ZG100118	0814	ZGL27-91A	OEM	ZGL41-68B	OEM
ZF22B	0700	ZFT12	OEM	ZG16RB	1392	ZG56	1873	ZG100119	0002	ZGL27-91B	OEM	ZGL41-75	OEM
ZF23.3R	0289	ZFT12A	OEM	ZG17	1630	ZG56A	1873	ZG100120	0560	ZGL27-100	OEM	ZGL41-75A	OEM
ZF23.6R	0372	ZFT14	OEM	ZG17A	1630	ZG56B	1873	ZGL27-6.8	OEM	ZGL27-100A	OEM	ZGL41-75B	OEM
ZF23.9R	0451	ZFT14A	OEM	ZG17B	1630	ZG56R	0207	ZGL27-6.8A	OEM	ZGL27-100B	OEM	ZGL41-82	OEM
ZF24	0489	ZFT16	OEM	ZG17R	1524	ZG56RA	0207	ZGL27-6.8B	OEM	ZGL27-110	OEM	ZGL41-82A	OEM
ZF24A	0489	ZFT18	OEM	ZG17RA	1524	ZG56RB	0207	ZGL27-7.5	OEM	ZGL27-110A	OEM	ZGL41-82B	OEM
ZF24B	0489	ZG2.7	0755	ZG17RB	1524	ZG62	1884	ZGL27-7.5A	OEM	ZGL27-110B	OEM	ZGL41-91	OEM
ZF24.3R	0528	ZG3.3	0296	ZG18	1706	ZG62A	1884	ZGL27-7.5B	OEM	ZGL27-120	OEM	ZGL41-91A	OEM
ZF24.7R	0446	ZG3.9	0542	ZG18A	1706	ZG62B	1884	ZGL27-8.2	OEM	ZGL27-120A	OEM	ZGL41-91B	OEM
ZF25.1R	0162	ZG3.9A	0542	ZG18B	1706	ZG62R	0263	ZGL27-8.2A	OEM	ZGL27-120B	OEM	ZGL41-100	OEM
ZF25.6R	0157	ZG3.9B	0542	ZG18R	1071	ZG62RA	0263	ZGL27-8.2B	OEM	ZGL27-130	OEM	ZGL41-100A	OEM
ZF26.2	0631	ZG3.9R	2024	ZG18RA	1071	ZG62RB	0263	ZGL27-8.7	OEM	ZGL27-130A	OEM	ZGL41-100B	OEM
ZF26.8	0025	ZG3.9RA	2024	ZG18RB	1071	ZG68	1891	ZGL27-8.7A	OEM	ZGL27-130B	OEM	ZGL41-110	OEM
ZF27	0450	ZG3.9RB	2024	ZG19	1709	ZG68A	1891	ZGL27-8.7B	OEM	ZGL27-140	OEM	ZGL41-110A	OEM
ZF27A	0450	ZG4.3	2387	ZG19A	1709	ZG68B	1891	ZGL27-9.1	OEM	ZGL27-140A	OEM	ZGL41-110B	OEM
ZF27B	0450	ZG4.3A	2387	ZG19B	1709	ZG68R	0306	ZGL27-9.1A	OEM	ZGL27-140B	OEM	ZGL41-120	OEM
ZF27.8	0644	ZG4.3B	2387	ZG19R	1701	ZG68RA	0306	ZGL27-9.1B	OEM	ZGL27-150	OEM	ZGL41-120A	OEM
ZF29.1	0012	ZG4.3R	2385	ZG19RA	1701	ZG68RB	0306	ZGL27-10	OEM	ZGL27-150A	OEM	ZGL41-120B	OEM
ZF30	0195	ZG4.3RA	2385	ZG19RB	1701	ZG75	0731	ZGL27-10A	OEM	ZGL27-150B	OEM	ZGL41-130	OEM
ZF30A	0195	ZG4.3RB	2385	ZG20	1720	ZG75A	0731	ZGL27-10B	OEM	ZGL27-160	OEM	ZGL41-130A	OEM
ZF30B	0195	ZG4.7	2101	ZG20A	1720	ZG75B	0731	ZGL27-11	OEM	ZGL27-160A	OEM	ZGL41-130B	OEM
ZF33	0166	ZG4.7A	2101	ZG20B	1720	ZG75R	0325	ZGL27-11A	OEM	ZGL27-160B	OEM	ZGL41-140	OEM
ZF33A	0166	ZG4.7B	2101	ZG20R	1707	ZG75RA	0325	ZGL27-11B	OEM	ZGL27-170	OEM	ZGL41-140A	OEM
ZF33B	0166	ZG4.7R	1429	ZG20RA	1707	ZG75RB	0325	ZGL27-12	OEM	ZGL27-170A	OEM	ZGL41-140B	OEM
ZF36	0010	ZG4.7RA	1429	ZG20RB	1707	ZG82	1898	ZGL27-12A	OEM	ZGL27-170B	OEM	ZGL41-150	OEM
ZF36A	0010	ZG4.7RB	1429	ZG22	0722	ZG82A	1898	ZGL27-12B	OEM	ZGL27-180	OEM	ZGL41-150A	OEM
ZF36B	0010	ZG5.1	2394	ZG22A	0722	ZG82B	1898	ZGL27-13	OEM	ZGL27-180A	OEM	ZGL41-150B	OEM
ZF39	0032	ZG5.1A	2394	ZG22B	0722	ZG82R	0352	ZGL27-13A	OEM	ZGL27-180B	OEM	ZGL41-160	OEM
ZF39A	0032	ZG5.1B	2394	ZG22R	1712	ZG82RA	0352	ZGL27-13B	OEM	ZGL27-190	OEM	ZGL41-160A	OEM
ZF39B	0032	ZG5.1R	2391	ZG22RA	1712	ZG82RB	0352	ZGL27-14	OEM	ZGL27-190A	OEM	ZGL41-160B	OEM
ZF43	0054	ZG5.1RA	2391	ZG22RB	1712	ZG91	1903	ZGL27-14A	OEM	ZGL27-190B	OEM	ZGL41-170	OEM
ZF43A	0054	ZG5.1RB	2391	ZG24	1745	ZG91A	1903	ZGL27-14B	OEM	ZGL27-200	OEM	ZGL41-170A	OEM
ZF43B	0054	ZG5.6	1890	ZG24A	1745	ZG91B	1903	ZGL27-15	OEM	ZGL27-200A	OEM	ZGL41-170B	OEM
ZF47	0068	ZG5.6A	1890	ZG24B	1745	ZG91R	0408	ZGL27-15A	OEM	ZGL27-200B	OEM	ZGL41-180	OEM
ZF47A	0068	ZG5.6B	1890	ZG24R	1725	ZG91RA	0408	ZGL27-15B	OEM	ZGL41-6.8	OEM	ZGL41-180A	OEM
ZF47B	0068	ZG5.6R	1436	ZG24RA	1725	ZG91RB	0408	ZGL27-16	OEM	ZGL41-6.8A	OEM	ZGL41-180B	OEM
ZF51	0092	ZG5.6RA	1436	ZG24RB	1725	ZG100	1155	ZGL27-16A	OEM	ZGL41-6.8B	OEM	ZGL41-190	OEM
ZF51A	0092	ZG5.6RB	1436	ZG25	1757	ZG100A	1155	ZGL27-16B	OEM	ZGL41-7.5	OEM	ZGL41-190A	OEM
ZF51B	0092	ZG6.2	0691	ZG25A	1757	ZG100B	1155	ZGL27-17	OEM	ZGL41-7.5A	OEM	ZGL41-190B	OEM
ZF56	0125	ZG6.2A	0691	ZG25B	1757	ZG100R	0433	ZGL27-17A	OEM	ZGL41-7.5B	OEM	ZGL41-200	OEM
ZF56A	0125	ZG6.2B	0691	ZG25R	1737	ZG100RA	0433	ZGL27-17B	OEM	ZGL41-8.2	OEM	ZGL41-200A	OEM
ZF56B	0125	ZG6.2R	2206	ZG25RA	1737	ZG100RB	0433	ZGL27-18	OEM	ZGL41-8.2A	OEM	ZGL41-200B	OEM
ZF62	0152	ZG6.2RA	2206	ZG25RB	1737	ZG105	1913	ZGL27-18A	OEM	ZGL41-8.2B	OEM	ZGP10-100	1172
ZF62A	0152	ZG6.2RB	2206	ZG27	1771	ZG105A	1913	ZGL27-18B	OEM	ZGL41-9.1	OEM	ZGP10-110	1182
ZF62B	0152	ZG6.8	1591	ZG27A	1771	ZG105B	1913	ZGL27-19	OEM	ZGL41-9.1A	OEM	ZGP10-120	1198
ZF68	0173	ZG6.8A	1591	ZG27B	1771	ZG105R	0459	ZGL27-19A	OEM	ZGL41-9.1B	OEM	ZGP10-130	1209
ZF68A	0173	ZG6.8B	1591	ZG27R	1750	ZG105RA	0459	ZGL27-19B	OEM	ZGL41-10	OEM	ZGP10-140	1870
ZF68B	0173	ZG6.8R	1449	ZG27RA	1750	ZG105RB	0459	ZGL27-20	OEM	ZGL41-10A	OEM	ZGP10-150	0642
ZF75	0094	ZG6.8RA	1449	ZG27RB	1750	ZG110	1922	ZGL27-20A	OEM	ZGL41-10B	OEM	ZGP10-160	1246
ZF75A	0094	ZG6.8RB	1449	ZG30	1783	ZG110A	1922	ZGL27-20B	OEM	ZGL41-11	OEM	ZGP10-160A	OEM
ZF75B	0094	ZG7.5	1606	ZG30A	1783	ZG110B	1922	ZGL27-22	OEM	ZGL41-11A	OEM	ZGP10-160B	OEM
ZF82	0049	ZG7.5A	1606	ZG30B	1783	ZG110R	0483	ZGL27-22A	OEM	ZGL41-11B	OEM	ZGP10-170	2091
ZF82A	0049	ZG7.5B	1606	ZG30R	1761	ZG110RA	0483	ZGL27-22B	OEM	ZGL41-12	OEM	ZGP10-170A	OEM
ZF82B	0049	ZG7.5R	0221	ZG30RA	1761	ZG110RB	0483	ZGL27-24	OEM	ZGL41-12A	OEM	ZGP10-170B	OEM
ZF91	0156	ZG7.5RA	0221	ZG30RB	1761	ZG120	1930	ZGL27-24A	OEM	ZGL41-12B	OEM	ZGP10-180	1269
ZF91A	0156	ZG7.5RB	0221	ZG33	1788	ZG120A	1930	ZGL27-24B	OEM	ZGL41-13	OEM	ZGP10-180A	OEM
ZF91B	0156	ZG8.2	1612	ZG33A	1788	ZG120B	1930	ZGL27-25	OEM	ZGL41-13A	OEM	ZGP10-180B	OEM
ZF100	0189	ZG8.2A	1612	ZG33B	1788	ZG120R	0504	ZGL27-25A	OEM	ZGL41-13B	OEM	ZGP10-190	2210
ZF100A	0189	ZG8.2B	1612	ZG33R	1777	ZG120RA	0504	ZGL27-25B	OEM	ZGL41-15	OEM	ZGP10-190A	OEM
ZF100B	0189	ZG8.2R	1481	ZG33RA	1777	ZG120RB	0504	ZGL27-27	OEM	ZGL41-15A	OEM	ZGP10-190B	OEM
ZF110	0099	ZG8.2RA	1481	ZG33RB	1777	ZG130	1936	ZGL27-27A	OEM	ZGL41-15B	OEM	ZGP10-200	0600
ZF110A	0099	ZG8.2RB	1481	ZG36	1798	ZG130A	1936	ZGL27-27B	OEM	ZGL41-16	OEM	ZGP10-200A	OEM
ZF110B	0099	ZG9.1	0622	ZG36A	1798	ZG130B	1936	ZGL27-28	OEM	ZGL41-16A	OEM	ZGP10-200B	OEM
ZF112	0137	ZG9.1A	0622	ZG36B	1798	ZG130R	0519	ZGL27-28A	OEM	ZGL41-16B	OEM	ZH011TA	OEM
ZF113	0361	ZG9.1B	0622	ZG36R	1785	ZG130RA	0519	ZGL27-28B	OEM	ZGL41-18	OEM	ZH1	OEM
ZF115	0002	ZG9.1R	1608	ZG36RA	1785	ZG130RB	0519	ZGL27-30	OEM	ZGL41-18A	OEM	ZH6.8	0025
ZF116	0416	ZG9.1RA	1608	ZG36RB	1785	ZG140	1942	ZGL27-30A	OEM	ZGL41-18B	OEM	ZH6.8A	0025
ZF120	0089	ZG9.1RB	1608	ZG39	1806	ZG140A	1942	ZGL27-30B	OEM	ZGL41-20	OEM	ZH6.8B	0025
ZF120A	0089	ZG10	0986	ZG39A	1806	ZG140B	1942	ZGL27-33	OEM	ZGL41-20A	OEM	ZH7.5	0644
ZF120B	0089	ZG10A	0986	ZG39B	1806	ZG140R	0537	ZGL27-33A	OEM	ZGL41-20B	OEM	ZH7.5A	0644
ZF122	0560	ZG10B	0986	ZG39R	1793	ZG140RA	0537	ZGL27-33B	OEM	ZGL41-22	OEM	ZH7.5B	0644
ZF124	0398	ZG10R	0505	ZG39RA	1793	ZG140RB	0537	ZGL27-36	OEM	ZGL41-22A	OEM	ZH8.2	0244
ZF127	0436	ZG10RA	0505	ZG39RB	1793	ZG150	1950	ZGL27-36A	OEM	ZGL41-22B	OEM	ZH8.2A	0244
ZF130	0285	ZG10RB	0505	ZG43	1815	ZG150A	1950	ZGL27-36B	OEM	ZGL41-24	OEM	ZH8.2B	0244
ZF130A	0285	ZG11	0989	ZG43A	1815	ZG150B	1950	ZGL27-39	OEM	ZGL41-24A	OEM	ZH9.1	0012
ZF130B	0285	ZG11A	0989	ZG43B	1815	ZG150R	0063	ZGL27-39A	OEM	ZGL41-24B	OEM	ZH9.1A	0012
ZF133	0039	ZG11B	0989	ZG43R	1185	ZG150RA	0063	ZGL27-39B	OEM	ZGL41-27	OEM	ZH9.1B	0012
ZF136	0814	ZG11R	0686	ZG43RA	1185	ZG150RB	0063	ZGL27-43	OEM	ZGL41-27A	OEM	ZH10	0170
ZF139	0346	ZG11RA	0686	ZG43RB	1185	ZG160	0353	ZGL27-43A	OEM	ZGL41-27B	OEM	ZH10A	0170
ZF150	0336	ZG11RB	0686	ZG45	1829	ZG160A	0353	ZGL27-43B	OEM	ZGL41-30	OEM	ZH10B	0170
ZF150A	0336	ZG12	1254	ZG45A	1829	ZG160B	0353	ZGL27-47	OEM	ZGL41-30A	OEM	ZH11	0789
ZF150B	0336	ZG12A	1254	ZG45B	1829	ZG160R	0397	ZGL27-47A	OEM	ZGL41-30B	OEM	ZH11A	0789
ZF156	0863	ZG12B	1254	ZG45R	1810	ZG160RA	0397	ZGL27-47B	OEM	ZGL41-33	OEM	ZH11B	0789
ZF160	0366	ZG12R	0864	ZG45RA	1810	ZG160RB	0397	ZGL27-51	OEM	ZGL41-33A	OEM	ZH12	0137
ZF160A	0366	ZG12RA	0864	ZG45RB	1810	ZG175	0665	ZGL27-51A	OEM	ZGL41-33B	OEM	ZH12A	0137
ZF160B	0366	ZG12RB	0864	ZG47	1842	ZG175A	0665	ZGL27-51B	OEM	ZGL41-36	OEM	ZH12B	0137
ZF162	0778	ZG13	1240	ZG47A	1842	ZG175B	0665	ZGL27-56	OEM	ZGL41-36A	OEM	ZH13	0361
ZF180	0420	ZG13A	1240	ZG47B	1842	ZG175R	0611	ZGL27-56A	OEM	ZGL41-36B	OEM	ZH13A	0361
ZF180A	0420	ZG13B	1240	ZG47R	0022	ZG175RA	0611	ZGL27-56B	OEM	ZGL41-39	OEM	ZH13B	0361
ZF180B	0420	ZG13R	1014	ZG47RA	0022	ZG175RB	0611	ZGL27-60	OEM	ZGL41-39A	OEM	ZH15	0002
ZF182	0327	ZG13RA	1014	ZG47RB	0022	ZG180	0771	ZGL27-60A	OEM	ZGL41-39B	OEM	ZH15A	0002
ZF200	1464	ZG13RB	1014	ZG50	1850	ZG180A	0771	ZGL27-60B	OEM	ZGL41-43	OEM	ZH15B	0002
ZF200A	1464	ZG14	1626	ZG50A	1850	ZG180B	0771	ZGL27-62	OEM	ZGL41-43A	OEM	ZH16	0416
ZF200B	1464	ZG14A	1626	ZG50B	1850	ZG180R	0629	ZGL27-62A	OEM	ZGL41-43B	OEM	ZH16A	0416
ZF210	0170	ZG14B	1626	ZG50R	0070	ZG180RA	0629	ZGL27-62B	OEM	ZGL41-47	OEM	ZH16B	0416
ZF211	0313	ZG14R	1145	ZG50RA	0070	ZG180RB	0629	ZGL27-68	OEM	ZGL41-47A	OEM	ZH18	0490
ZF212	0137	ZG14RA	1145	ZG50RB	0070	ZG200	1065	ZGL27-68A	OEM	ZGL41-47B	OEM	ZH18A	0490
ZF213	0361	ZG14RB	1145	ZG51	1855	ZG200A	1065	ZGL27-68B	OEM	ZGL41-51	OEM	ZH18AR	0363
ZF215	0002	ZG15	1629	ZG51A	1855	ZG200B	1065	ZGL27-75	OEM	ZGL41-51A	OEM	ZH18B	0490
ZF216	0416	ZG15A	1629	ZG51B	1855	ZG200R	0663	ZGL27-75A	OEM	ZGL41-51B	OEM	ZH20	0526
ZF222	0560	ZG15B	1629	ZG51R	0132	ZG200RA	0663	ZGL27-75B	OEM	ZGL41-56	OEM	ZH20A	0526
ZF224	0398	ZG15R	1264	ZG51RA	0132	ZG200RB	0663	ZGL27-82	OEM	ZGL41-56A	OEM	ZH20B	0526

If replacement code is OEM, contact original manufacturer for replacement.

639

DEVICE TYPE	REPL CODE
ZH22	0560
ZH22A	0560
ZH22B	0560
ZH24	0398
ZH24A	0398
ZH24B	0398
ZH27	0436
ZH27A	0436
ZH27B	0436
ZH30	0721
ZH30A	0721
ZH30B	0721
ZH33	0039
ZH33A	0039
ZH33B	0039
ZH36	0814
ZH36A	0814
ZH36B	0814
ZH39	0346
ZH39A	0346
ZH39B	0346
ZH43	0925
ZH43A	0925
ZH43B	0925
ZH47	0993
ZH47A	0993
ZH47B	0993
ZH51	0497
ZH51A	0497
ZH51B	0497
ZH56	1823
ZH56A	1823
ZH56B	1823
ZH62	0778
ZH62A	0778
ZH62B	0778
ZH68	2144
ZH68A	2144
ZH68B	2144
ZH75	1181
ZH75A	1181
ZH75B	1181
ZH82	0327
ZH82A	0327
ZH82B	0327
ZH91	1301
ZH91A	1301
ZH91B	1301
ZH100	0098
ZH100A	0098
ZH100B	0098
ZH102	1302
ZH103	0188
ZH104	0446
ZH105	0157
ZH106	0631
ZH107	0644
ZH109	1075
ZH110	0149
ZH110A	0149
ZH110B	0149
ZH112	0137
ZH115	0416
ZH120	0186
ZH120A	0186
ZH120B	0186
ZH125	1596
ZH130	0213
ZH130A	0213
ZH130B	0213
ZH135	0814
ZH140	0925
ZH150	0028
ZH150A	0028
ZH150B	0028
ZH160	0255
ZH160A	0255
ZH160B	0255
ZH170	2144
ZH180	0363
ZH180A	0363
ZH180B	0363
ZH200	0417
ZH200A	0417
ZH200B	0417
ZH203	2024
ZH204	1429
ZH205	1436
ZH206	1449
ZH209	1481
ZH210	0505
ZH212	0864
ZH225	1737
ZH304	1429
ZH305	1436
ZH306	1449
ZH309	1481
ZH310	0505
ZH312	0864
ZJ4B41	OEM
ZJ6.8	0025
ZJ6.8A	0025
ZJ6.8B	0025
ZJ7.5	0644
ZJ7.5A	0644
ZJ7.5B	0644
ZJ8.2	0244
ZJ8.2A	0244
ZJ8.2B	0244
ZJ9.1	0012
ZJ9.1A	0012
ZJ9.1B	0012
ZJ10	0170
ZJ10A	0170
ZJ10B	0170
ZJ11	0313
ZJ11A	0313
ZJ11B	0313
ZJ12	0137
ZJ12A	0137
ZJ12B	0137
ZJ13	0137
ZJ13A	0137
ZJ13B	0137
ZJ15	0002
ZJ15A	0002
ZJ15B	0002
ZJ16	0416
ZJ16A	0416
ZJ16B	0416
ZJ18	0490
ZJ18A	0490
ZJ18B	0490
ZJ20	0526
ZJ20A	0526
ZJ20B	0526
ZJ22	0560
ZJ22A	0560
ZJ22B	0560
ZJ24	0398
ZJ24A	0398
ZJ24B	0398
ZJ27	0436
ZJ27A	0436
ZJ27B	0436
ZJ30	0721
ZJ30A	0721
ZJ30B	0721
ZJ33	0039
ZJ33A	0039
ZJ33B	0039
ZJ36	0814
ZJ36A	0814
ZJ36B	0814
ZJ39	0346
ZJ39A	0346
ZJ39B	0346
ZJ40	0144
ZJ43	0925
ZJ43A	0925
ZJ43B	0925
ZJ47	0993
ZJ47A	0993
ZJ47B	0993
ZJ51	0497
ZJ51A	0497
ZJ51B	0497
ZJ56	0863
ZJ56A	0863
ZJ56B	0863
ZJ62	0778
ZJ62A	0778
ZJ62B	0778
ZJ68	2144
ZJ68A	2144
ZJ68B	2144
ZJ72	0050
ZJ73	0050
ZJ75	1181
ZJ75A	1181
ZJ75B	1181
ZJ82	0327
ZJ82A	0327
ZJ82B	0327
ZJ91	1301
ZJ91A	1301
ZJ91B	1301
ZJ100	0098
ZJ100A	0098
ZJ100B	0098
ZJ110	0149
ZJ110A	0149
ZJ110B	0149
ZJ120	0186
ZJ120A	0186
ZJ120B	0186
ZJ130	0213
ZJ130A	0213
ZJ130B	0213
ZJ150	0028
ZJ150A	0028
ZJ150B	0028
ZJ160	0255
ZJ160A	0028
ZJ160B	0255
ZJ180	0363
ZJ180A	0363
ZJ180B	0363
ZJ200	0417
ZJ200A	0417
ZJ200B	0417
ZJ224HB	OEM
ZJ224HC	OEM
ZJ224HF	OEM
ZJ224HU	OEM
ZJ224LA	OEM
ZJ224LB	OEM
ZJ224LC	OEM
ZJ224LD	OEM
ZJ224LF	OEM
ZJ224LU	OEM
ZJ227A	OEM
ZJ227B	OEM
ZJ227F	OEM
ZJ227G	OEM
ZJ227U	OEM
ZJ244A	OEM
ZJ244B	OEM
ZJ244C	OEM
ZJ244D	OEM
ZJ244E	OEM
ZJ244F	OEM
ZJ244G	OEM
ZJ244H	OEM
ZJ244U	OEM
ZJ252B	0015
ZJ253A	OEM
ZJ253B	OEM
ZJ253C	OEM
ZJ253D	OEM
ZJ253F	OEM
ZJ255A	OEM
ZJ255B	OEM
ZJ255C	OEM
ZJ255D	OEM
ZJ255F	OEM
ZJ260E	OEM
ZJ260M	OEM
ZJ260N	OEM
ZJ260P	OEM
ZJ260PA	OEM
ZJ260S	OEM
ZJ260T	OEM
ZK3.9	0542
ZK3.9A	0542
ZK3.9B	0542
ZK3.9R	2024
ZK3.9RA	2024
ZK3.9RB	2024
ZK4.3	2387
ZK4.3A	2387
ZK4.3B	2387
ZK4.3R	2385
ZK4.3RA	2385
ZK4.3RB	2385
ZK4.7	2101
ZK4.7A	2101
ZK4.7B	2101
ZK4.7R	1429
ZK4.7RA	1429
ZK4.7RB	1429
ZK5.1	2394
ZK5.1A	2394
ZK5.1B	2394
ZK5.1R	2391
ZK5.1RA	2391
ZK5.1RB	2391
ZK5.6	1890
ZK5.6A	1890
ZK5.6B	1890
ZK5.6R	1436
ZK5.6RA	1436
ZK5.6RB	1436
ZK6.2	0691
ZK6.2A	0691
ZK6.2B	0691
ZK6.2R	2206
ZK6.2RA	2206
ZK6.2RB	2206
ZK6.8	1591
ZK6.8A	1591
ZK6.8B	1591
ZK6.8R	1449
ZK6.8RA	1449
ZK6.8RB	1449
ZK7.5	1606
ZK7.5A	1606
ZK7.5B	1606
ZK7.5R	0221
ZK7.5RA	0221
ZK7.5RB	0221
ZK8.2	1612
ZK8.2A	1612
ZK8.2B	1612
ZK8.2R	1481
ZK8.2RA	1481
ZK8.2RB	1481
ZK9.1	0622
ZK9.1A	0622
ZK9.1B	0622
ZK9.1R	1608
ZK9.1RA	1608
ZK9.1RB	1608
ZK10	0986
ZK10A	0986
ZK10B	0986
ZK10R	0505
ZK10RA	0505
ZK10RB	0505
ZK11	0989
ZK11A	0989
ZK11B	0989
ZK11R	0686
ZK11RA	0686
ZK11RB	0686
ZK12	1254
ZK12A	1254
ZK12B	1254
ZK12R	0864
ZK12RA	0864
ZK12RB	0864
ZK13	1240
ZK13A	1240
ZK13B	1240
ZK13R	1014
ZK13RA	1014
ZK13RB	1014
ZK14	1626
ZK14A	1626
ZK14B	1626
ZK14R	1145
ZK14RA	1145
ZK14RB	1145
ZK15	1629
ZK15A	1629
ZK15B	1629
ZK15R	1264
ZK15RA	1264
ZK15RB	1264
ZK16	1693
ZK16A	1693
ZK16B	1693
ZK16R	1392
ZK16RA	1392
ZK16RB	1392
ZK17	1630
ZK17A	1630
ZK17B	1630
ZK17R	1524
ZK17RA	1524
ZK17RB	1524
ZK18	1706
ZK18A	1706
ZK18B	1706
ZK18R	1071
ZK18RA	1071
ZK18RB	1071
ZK19	1709
ZK19A	1709
ZK19B	1709
ZK19R	1701
ZK19RA	1701
ZK19RB	1701
ZK20	1720
ZK20A	1720
ZK20B	1720
ZK20R	1707
ZK20RA	1707
ZK20RB	1707
ZK22	0722
ZK22A	0722
ZK22B	0722
ZK22R	1712
ZK22RA	1712
ZK22RB	1712
ZK24	1745
ZK24A	1745
ZK24B	1745
ZK24R	1725
ZK24RA	1725
ZK24RB	1725
ZK25	1757
ZK25A	1757
ZK25B	1757
ZK25R	1737
ZK25RA	1737
ZK25RB	1737
ZK27	1771
ZK27A	1771
ZK27B	1771
ZK27R	1750
ZK27RA	1750
ZK27RB	1750
ZK30	1783
ZK30A	1783
ZK30B	1783
ZK30R	1761
ZK30RA	1761
ZK30RB	1761
ZK33	1788
ZK33A	1788
ZK33B	1788
ZK33R	1777
ZK33RA	1777
ZK33RB	1777
ZK36	1798
ZK36A	1798
ZK36B	1798
ZK36R	1785
ZK36RA	1785
ZK36RB	1785
ZK39	1806
ZK39A	1806
ZK39B	1806
ZK39R	1793
ZK39RA	1793
ZK39RB	1793
ZK43	1815
ZK43A	1815
ZK43B	1815
ZK43R	1185
ZK43RA	1185
ZK43RB	1185
ZK45	1829
ZK45A	1806
ZK45B	1829
ZK45R	1810
ZK45RA	1810
ZK45RB	1810
ZK47	1842
ZK47A	1842
ZK47B	1842
ZK47R	0022
ZK47RA	0022
ZK47RB	0022
ZK50	1850
ZK50A	1850
ZK50B	1850
ZK50R	0070
ZK50RA	0070
ZK50RB	0070
ZK51	1855
ZK51A	1855
ZK51B	1855
ZK51R	0132
ZK51RA	0132
ZK51RB	0132
ZK52	1863
ZK52A	1863
ZK52B	1863
ZK52R	0172
ZK52RA	0172
ZK52RB	0172
ZK56	1873
ZK56A	1873
ZK56B	1873
ZK56R	0207
ZK56RA	0207
ZK56RB	0207
ZK62	1884
ZK62A	1884
ZK62B	1884
ZK62R	0263
ZK62RA	0263
ZK62RB	0263
ZK68	1891
ZK68A	1891
ZK68B	1891
ZK68R	0306
ZK68RA	0306
ZK68RB	0306
ZK75	0731
ZK75A	0731
ZK75B	0731
ZK75R	0325
ZK75RA	0325
ZK75RB	0325
ZK82	1898
ZK82A	1898
ZK82B	1898
ZK82R	0352
ZK82RA	0352
ZK82RB	0352
ZK91	1903
ZK91A	1903
ZK91B	1903
ZK91R	0408
ZK91RA	0408
ZK91RB	0408
ZK100	1155
ZK100A	1155
ZK100B	1155
ZK100R	0433
ZK100RA	0433
ZK100RB	0433
ZK105	1913
ZK105A	1913
ZK105B	1913
ZK105R	0459
ZK105RA	0459
ZK105RB	0459
ZK110	1922
ZK110A	1922
ZK110B	1922
ZK110R	0483
ZK110RA	0483
ZK110RB	0483
ZK120	1930
ZK120A	1930
ZK120B	1930
ZK120R	0504
ZK120RA	0504
ZK120RB	0504
ZK130	1936
ZK130A	1936
ZK130B	1936
ZK130R	0519
ZK130RA	0519
ZK130RB	0519
ZK140	1942
ZK140A	1942
ZK140B	1942
ZK140R	0537
ZK140RA	0537
ZK140RB	0537
ZK150	1950
ZK150A	1950
ZK150B	1950
ZK150R	0063
ZK150RA	0063
ZK150RB	0063
ZK160	0353
ZK160A	0353
ZK160B	0353
ZK160R	0397
ZK160RA	0397
ZK160RB	0397
ZK175	0665
ZK175A	0665
ZK175B	0665
ZK175R	0611
ZK175RA	0611
ZK175RB	0611
ZK180	0771
ZK180A	0771
ZK180B	0771
ZK180R	0629
ZK180RA	0629
ZK180RB	0629
ZK200	1065
ZK200A	1065
ZK200B	1065
ZK200R	0663
ZK200RA	0663
ZK200RB	0663
ZK220	OEM
ZK220A	OEM
ZK220B	OEM
ZK220R	OEM
ZK220RA	OEM
ZK220RB	OEM
ZL5	OEM
ZL6	0091
ZL7	OEM
ZL8	OEM
ZLD709	OEM
ZLD709C	OEM
ZLD709CE	OEM
ZLD709CF	OEM
ZLD709CG	OEM
ZLD709F	OEM
ZLD741	OEM
ZLD741C	OEM
ZLD741CE	OEM
ZM3.3	0289
ZM3.3A	0289
ZM3.3B	0289
ZM3.6	0188
ZM3.6A	0188
ZM3.6B	0188
ZM3.9	0451
ZM3.9A	0451
ZM3.9B	0451
ZM4.3	0528
ZM4.3A	0528
ZM4.3B	0528
ZM4.7	0446
ZM4.7A	0446
ZM4.7B	0446
ZM5.1	0162
ZM5.1A	0162
ZM5.1B	0162
ZM5.6	0157
ZM5.6A	0157
ZM5.6B	0157
ZM5.6C	OEM
ZM5.6D	OEM
ZM6	0091
ZM6A	0091
ZM6B	0091
ZM6.2	0631
ZM6.2A	0631
ZM6.2B	0631
ZM6.2C	OEM
ZM6.2D	OEM
ZM6.8	0100
ZM6.8A	0100
ZM6.8B	0025
ZM6.8C	OEM
ZM6.8D	OEM
ZM7.5	0644
ZM7.5A	0644
ZM7.5B	0644
ZM7.5C	OEM
ZM7.5D	OEM
ZM8.2	0244
ZM8.2A	0244
ZM8.2B	0244
ZM8.2C	0244
ZM8.2D	0244
ZM8.7	1075
ZM8.7A	1075
ZM8.7B	1075
ZM9.1	0012
ZM9.1A	0012
ZM9.1B	0012
ZM9.1C	0012
ZM9.1D	OEM
ZM10	0170
ZM10A	0170
ZM10B	0170
ZM10C	OEM
ZM10D	OEM
ZM11	0313
ZM11A	0313
ZM11B	0313
ZM11C	OEM
ZM11D	OEM
ZM12	0137
ZM12A	0137
ZM12B	0137
ZM12C	0137
ZM12D	OEM
ZM13	0361
ZM13A	0361
ZM13B	0361
ZM13C	OEM
ZM13D	OEM
ZM14	0100
ZM14A	0100
ZM14B	0873
ZM14C	OEM
ZM14D	OEM
ZM15	0002
ZM15A	0002
ZM15B	0002
ZM15C	0002
ZM15D	OEM
ZM16	0416
ZM16A	0416
ZM16B	0440
ZM16C	OEM
ZM16D	OEM
ZM17	1639
ZM17A	1639
ZM17B	1639
ZM17C	OEM
ZM17D	OEM
ZM18	0490
ZM18A	0490
ZM18B	0490
ZM18C	OEM
ZM18D	OEM
ZM19	0943
ZM19A	0943
ZM19B	0943
ZM19C	OEM
ZM19D	OEM
ZM20	0526
ZM20A	0526
ZM20B	0526
ZM20C	OEM
ZM20D	OEM
ZM22	0560
ZM22A	0560
ZM22B	0560
ZM22C	OEM
ZM22D	OEM
ZM24	0398
ZM24A	0398
ZM24B	0398
ZM24C	OEM
ZM24D	OEM
ZM25	1596
ZM25A	1596
ZM25B	1596
ZM25C	OEM
ZM25D	OEM
ZM27	0436
ZM27A	0436
ZM27B	0436
ZM27C	OEM
ZM27D	OEM
ZM28	0450
ZM28A	0450
ZM28B	0450
ZM30	0721
ZM30A	0721
ZM30B	0721
ZM30C	OEM
ZM30D	OEM
ZM33	0039
ZM33A	0039
ZM33B	0039
ZM33C	OEM
ZM33D	OEM
ZM36	0814
ZM36A	0814
ZM36B	0814
ZM36C	OEM
ZM36D	OEM
ZM39	0346
ZM39A	0346
ZM39B	0346
ZM39C	OEM
ZM39D	OEM
ZM43	0925
ZM43A	0925
ZM43B	0925
ZM43C	OEM
ZM43D	OEM
ZM45	0993
ZM45A	0993
ZM45B	0993
ZM45C	OEM
ZM45D	OEM
ZM47	0993
ZM47A	0993
ZM47B	0993
ZM47C	OEM
ZM47D	OEM
ZM50	0497
ZM50A	0497
ZM50B	0497
ZM50C	OEM
ZM50D	OEM
ZM51	0497
ZM51A	0497
ZM51B	0497
ZM51C	OEM
ZM51D	OEM
ZM52	0497
ZM52A	0497

If replacement code is OEM, contact original manufacturer for replacement.

DEVICE TYPE	REPL CODE
ZM52B	0497
ZM52C	OEM
ZM52D	OEM
ZM56	0863
ZM56A	0863
ZM56B	0863
ZM56C	OEM
ZM56D	OEM
ZM62	0778
ZM62A	0778
ZM62B	0778
ZM62C	OEM
ZM62D	OEM
ZM68	2144
ZM68A	2144
ZM68B	1258
ZM68C	OEM
ZM68D	OEM
ZM75	1181
ZM75A	1181
ZM75B	1181
ZM75C	OEM
ZM75D	OEM
ZM82	0327
ZM82A	0327
ZM82B	0327
ZM82C	0327
ZM82D	OEM
ZM91	1301
ZM91A	1301
ZM91B	1301
ZM91C	OEM
ZM91D	OEM
ZM100	0098
ZM100A	0098
ZM100B	0098
ZM100C	OEM
ZM100D	OEM
ZM105	0149
ZM105A	0149
ZM105B	0149
ZM105C	OEM
ZM105D	OEM
ZM110	0149
ZM110A	0149
ZM110B	0149
ZM110C	OEM
ZM110D	OEM
ZM120	0186
ZM120A	0186
ZM120B	0186
ZM120C	OEM
ZM120D	OEM
ZM130	0213
ZM130A	0213
ZM130B	0213
ZM130C	OEM
ZM130D	OEM
ZM140	0245
ZM140A	0245
ZM140B	0245
ZM140C	OEM
ZM140D	OEM
ZM150	0028
ZM150A	0028
ZM150B	0028
ZM150C	OEM
ZM150D	OEM
ZM160	0255
ZM160A	0255
ZM160B	0255
ZM160C	OEM
ZM160D	OEM
ZM175	0363
ZM175A	0363
ZM175B	0363
ZM175C	OEM
ZM175D	OEM
ZM180	0363
ZM180A	0363
ZM180B	0363
ZM180C	OEM
ZM180D	OEM
ZM200	0417
ZM200A	0417
ZM200B	0417
ZM200C	OEM
ZM200D	OEM
ZM220	OEM
ZM220A	OEM
ZM220B	OEM
ZM220C	OEM
ZM220D	OEM
ZME60	OEM
ZMIN4935811	OEM
ZMM6.2	0466
ZMM9.1	0057
ZMM12	0052
ZMM15	0681
ZMQ9B	OEM
ZMZ205	0162
ZN6.8	OEM
ZN6.8A	OEM
ZN6.8B	OEM
ZN7.5	OEM
ZN7.5A	OEM
ZN7.5B	OEM
ZN8.2	OEM
ZN8.2A	OEM
ZN8.2B	OEM
ZN9.1	OEM
ZN9.1A	OEM
ZN9.1B	OEM
ZN10	OEM
ZN10A	OEM
ZN10B	OEM
ZN11	OEM
ZN11A	OEM
ZN11B	OEM
ZN12	OEM
ZN12A	OEM
ZN12B	OEM
ZN13	OEM
ZN13A	OEM
ZN13B	OEM
ZN15	OEM
ZN15A	OEM
ZN15B	OEM
ZN16	OEM
ZN16A	OEM
ZN16B	OEM
ZN18	OEM
ZN18A	OEM
ZN18B	OEM
ZN20	OEM
ZN20A	OEM
ZN20B	OEM
ZN22	OEM
ZN22A	OEM
ZN22B	OEM
ZN24	OEM
ZN24A	OEM
ZN24B	OEM
ZN27	OEM
ZN27A	OEM
ZN27B	OEM
ZN30	OEM
ZN30A	OEM
ZN30B	OEM
ZN33	OEM
ZN33A	OEM
ZN33B	OEM
ZN36	OEM
ZN36A	OEM
ZN36B	OEM
ZN39	OEM
ZN39A	OEM
ZN39B	OEM
ZN43	OEM
ZN43A	OEM
ZN43B	OEM
ZN47	OEM
ZN47A	OEM
ZN47B	OEM
ZN51	OEM
ZN51A	OEM
ZN51B	OEM
ZN54L91E	OEM
ZN54L91J	OEM
ZN54L95E	OEM
ZN54L95J	OEM
ZN54L96E	OEM
ZN54L96J	OEM
ZN54L164E	OEM
ZN54L164J	OEM
ZN56	OEM
ZN56A	OEM
ZN56B	OEM
ZN62	OEM
ZN62A	OEM
ZN62B	OEM
ZN68	OEM
ZN68A	OEM
ZN68B	OEM
ZN74L91E	OEM
ZN74L91J	OEM
ZN74L95E	OEM
ZN74L95J	OEM
ZN74L96E	OEM
ZN74L96J	OEM
ZN74L164E	OEM
ZN74L164J	OEM
ZN75	OEM
ZN75A	OEM
ZN75B	OEM
ZN82	OEM
ZN82A	OEM
ZN82B	OEM
ZN91	OEM
ZN91A	OEM
ZN91B	OEM
ZN100	OEM
ZN100A	OEM
ZN100B	OEM
ZN110	OEM
ZN110A	OEM
ZN110B	OEM
ZN120	OEM
ZN120A	OEM
ZN120B	OEM
ZN130	OEM
ZN130A	OEM
ZN130B	OEM
ZN150	OEM
ZN150A	OEM
ZN150B	OEM
ZN160	OEM
ZN160A	OEM
ZN160B	OEM
ZN180	OEM
ZN180A	OEM
ZN180B	OEM
ZN200	OEM
ZN200A	OEM
ZN200B	OEM
ZN219	OEM
ZN219E	OEM
ZN220	OEM
ZN220E	OEM
ZN221	OEM
ZN221E	OEM
ZN222	OEM
ZN222E	OEM
ZN224	OEM
ZN224E	OEM
ZN229	OEM
ZN229E	OEM
ZN230	OEM
ZN230E	OEM
ZN232	OEM
ZN232E	OEM
ZN233	OEM
ZN233E	OEM
ZN244	OEM
ZN244E	OEM
ZN246	OEM
ZN246E	OEM
ZN248	OEM
ZN248E	OEM
ZN262	OEM
ZN262E	OEM
ZN294E	OEM
ZN297E	OEM
ZN319	OEM
ZN319E	OEM
ZN320	OEM
ZN320E	OEM
ZN321	OEM
ZN321E	OEM
ZN322	OEM
ZN322E	OEM
ZN324	OEM
ZN324E	OEM
ZN329	OEM
ZN329E	OEM
ZN330	OEM
ZN330E	OEM
ZN332	OEM
ZN332E	OEM
ZN333	OEM
ZN333E	OEM
ZN342CJ-8	OEM
ZN344	OEM
ZN344E	OEM
ZN346	OEM
ZN346E	OEM
ZN348	OEM
ZN348E	OEM
ZN362	OEM
ZN362E	OEM
ZN394E	OEM
ZN397E	OEM
ZN409CE	OEM
ZN414	OEM
ZN419CE	OEM
ZN423T	OEM
ZN424E	OEM
ZN424P	OEM
ZN424T	OEM
ZN425E-6	OEM
ZN425E-7	OEM
ZN425E-8	OEM
ZN425J-8	OEM
ZN426E-6	OEM
ZN426E-7	OEM
ZN426E-8	OEM
ZN426J-8	OEM
ZN427E-8	OEM
ZN427J-8	OEM
ZN428E-8	OEM
ZN428J-8	OEM
ZN429E-6	OEM
ZN429E-7	OEM
ZN429E-8	OEM
ZN429J-8	OEM
ZN432BJ-8	OEM
ZN432BJ-9	OEM
ZN432CJ-9	OEM
ZN432CJ-10	OEM
ZN432E	OEM
ZN432J-8	OEM
ZN432J-9	OEM
ZN432J-10	OEM
ZN433BJ-8	OEM
ZN433BJ-9	OEM
ZN433BJ-10	OEM
ZN433CJ-8	OEM
ZN433CJ-9	OEM
ZN433J-8	OEM
ZN433J-9	OEM
ZN433J-10	OEM
ZN435E	OEM
ZN435J(A)	OEM
ZN436E(A)	OEM
ZN436J(A)	OEM
ZN458	OEM
ZN458A	OEM
ZN458B	OEM
ZN459	OEM
ZN459C	OEM
ZN459CP	OEM
ZN459CT	OEM
ZN459T	OEM
ZN460	OEM
ZN460C	OEM
ZN460CP	OEM
ZN1004E	OEM
ZN1005E	OEM
ZN1010E	OEM
ZN1010F	OEM
ZN1030E	OEM
ZN1034E	OEM
ZN1034P	OEM
ZN1034T	OEM
ZN1040AE	OEM
ZN1040E	OEM
ZN1060	OEM
ZN2010E	OEM
ZN2010F	OEM
ZN5400E	OEM
ZN5400F	OEM
ZN5401E	OEM
ZN5401F	OEM
ZN5402E	OEM
ZN5402F	OEM
ZN5403J	OEM
ZN5404E	OEM
ZN5404F	OEM
ZN5405E	OEM
ZN5405F	OEM
ZN5408E	OEM
ZN5408J	OEM
ZN5409E	OEM
ZN5409J	OEM
ZN5410E	OEM
ZN5410F	OEM
ZN5412E	OEM
ZN5412J	OEM
ZN5420E	OEM
ZN5420F	OEM
ZN5425E	OEM
ZN5425J	OEM
ZN5427E	OEM
ZN5427J	OEM
ZN5428E	OEM
ZN5428J	OEM
ZN5430E	OEM
ZN5430F	OEM
ZN5432E	OEM
ZN5432J	OEM
ZN5437E	OEM
ZN5437J	OEM
ZN5438E	OEM
ZN5438J	OEM
ZN5440E	OEM
ZN5440F	OEM
ZN5442E	OEM
ZN5442J	OEM
ZN5450E	OEM
ZN5450F	OEM
ZN5451E	OEM
ZN5451F	OEM
ZN5453E	OEM
ZN5453F	OEM
ZN5454E	OEM
ZN5454F	OEM
ZN5460E	OEM
ZN5460F	OEM
ZN5470E	OEM
ZN5470F	OEM
ZN5472E	OEM
ZN5472F	OEM
ZN5473E	OEM
ZN5473F	OEM
ZN5474E	OEM
ZN5474F	OEM
ZN5475E	OEM
ZN5476E	OEM
ZN5486E	OEM
ZN5486J	OEM
ZN5491AE	OEM
ZN5492AE	OEM
ZN5492AJ	OEM
ZN5493AE	OEM
ZN5493AJ	OEM
ZN5494E	OEM
ZN5494J	OEM
ZN5495AE	OEM
ZN5495AJ	OEM
ZN5496E	OEM
ZN5496J	OEM
ZN7400E	0232
ZN7400F	0232
ZN7401E	0268
ZN7401F	0268
ZN7402E	0310
ZN7402F	0310
ZN7403E	0331
ZN7403J	0331
ZN7404E	0357
ZN7404F	OEM
ZN7405E	0381
ZN7405F	OEM
ZN7408E	0462
ZN7408J	0462
ZN7409E	0487
ZN7409J	0487
ZN7410E	0507
ZN7410F	0507
ZN7412E	2227
ZN7412J	2227
ZN7420E	0692
ZN7420F	0692
ZN7425E	3438
ZN7425J	3438
ZN7427E	0812
ZN7427J	0812
ZN7428E	4117
ZN7428J	4117
ZN7430E	0867
ZN7430F	0867
ZN7432E	0893
ZN7432J	0893
ZN7437E	3478
ZN7437J	3478
ZN7438E	0990
ZN7438J	0990
ZN7440E	1018
ZN7440F	1018
ZN7441AE	1032
ZN7442E	1046
ZN7442J	1046
ZN7450E	0738
ZN7450F	0738
ZN7451E	1160
ZN7451F	1160
ZN7453E	1177
ZN7453F	1177
ZN7454E	1193
ZN7454F	1193
ZN7460E	1265
ZN7460F	1265
ZN7470E	1394
ZN7470F	1394
ZN7472E	1417
ZN7472F	1417
ZN7473E	1164
ZN7473F	1164
ZN7474E	1303
ZN7474F	1303
ZN7475E	1423
ZN7476E	1150
ZN7486E	1358
ZN7486J	1358
ZN7490E	1199
ZN7490F	1199
ZN7491AE	OEM
ZN7491AJ	OEM
ZN7492AE	0828
ZN7492AJ	0828
ZN7492E	0828
ZN7492F	0828
ZN7493AE	0564
ZN7493AJ	0564
ZN7493E	0564
ZN7493F	0564
ZN7494E	1692
ZN7494J	OEM
ZN7495AE	1477
ZN7495AJ	OEM
ZN7496E	1705
ZN7496J	OEM
ZN54107E	OEM
ZN54107F	OEM
ZN54121E	OEM
ZN54121J	OEM
ZN54122E	OEM
ZN54122J	OEM
ZN54123E	OEM
ZN54123J	OEM
ZN54154J	OEM
ZN54155E	OEM
ZN54155J	OEM
ZN54161E	OEM
ZN54161J	OEM
ZN54163E	OEM
ZN54163J	OEM
ZN54164E	OEM
ZN54164J	OEM
ZN54165E	OEM
ZN54165J	OEM
ZN54166J	OEM
ZN54174E	OEM
ZN54174J	OEM
ZN54175E	OEM
ZN54175J	OEM
ZN54191E	OEM
ZN54191J	OEM
ZN54192E	OEM
ZN54192J	OEM
ZN54193E	OEM
ZN54193J	OEM
ZN54194E	OEM
ZN54194J	OEM
ZN54197E	OEM
ZN54197J	OEM
ZN74107E	0936
ZN74107F	OEM
ZN74121E	0175
ZN74121J	OEM
ZN74122E	1131
ZN74122J	OEM
ZN74123E	1149
ZN74123J	OEM
ZN74154E	5832
ZN74154J	OEM
ZN74155E	1566
ZN74155J	OEM
ZN74161E	1635
ZN74161J	OEM
ZN74163E	1656
ZN74163J	OEM
ZN74164E	0729
ZN74164J	OEM
ZN74165E	1675
ZN74165J	OEM
ZN74166E	0231
ZN74166J	OEM
ZN74174E	1759
ZN74174J	OEM
ZN74175J	OEM
ZN74191E	1906
ZN74191J	OEM
ZN74192E	1910
ZN74192J	OEM
ZN74193E	1915
ZN74193J	OEM
ZN74194E	OEM
ZN74194J	OEM
ZN74197E	OEM
ZN74197J	OEM
ZN35024712	0919
ZNA234E	OEM
ZNM442E	1046
ZNP100	OEM
ZNP102	OEM
ZNP103	OEM
ZNPCM1CE	OEM
ZNR-3K101	0139
ZNR10K241U	1982
ZNREF025A1	OEM
ZNREF025A2	OEM
ZNREF025A3	OEM
ZNREF025B1	OEM
ZNREF025B2	OEM
ZNREF025B3	OEM
ZNREF025C1	OEM
ZNREF025C2	OEM
ZNREF025C3	OEM
ZNREF040A1	OEM
ZNREF040A2	OEM
ZNREF040A3	OEM
ZNREF040B1	OEM
ZNREF040B2	OEM
ZNREF040B3	OEM
ZNREF040C1	OEM
ZNREF040C2	OEM
ZNREF040C3	OEM
ZNREF050A1	OEM
ZNREF050A2	OEM
ZNREF050A3	OEM
ZNREF050B1	OEM
ZNREF050B2	OEM
ZNREF050B3	OEM
ZNREF050C1	OEM
ZNREF050C2	OEM
ZNREF050C3	OEM
ZNREF062A1	OEM
ZNREF062A2	OEM
ZNREF062A3	OEM
ZNREF062B1	OEM
ZNREF062B2	OEM
ZNREF062B3	OEM
ZNREF062C1	OEM
ZNREF062C2	OEM
ZNREF062C3	OEM
ZNREF100A1	OEM
ZNREF100A2	OEM
ZNREF100A3	OEM
ZNREF100B1	OEM
ZNREF100B2	OEM
ZNREF100B3	OEM
ZNREF100C1	OEM
ZNREF100C2	OEM
ZNREF100C3	OEM
ZNR-K510Z	OEM
ZNV0545L	OEM
ZO6.8	0025
ZO6.8A	0025
ZO6.8B	0025
ZO7.5	0644
ZO7.5A	0644
ZO7.5B	0644
ZO8.2	0244
ZO8.2A	0244
ZO8.2B	0244
ZO9.1	0012
ZO9.1A	0012
ZO9.1B	0012
ZO10	0170
ZO10A	0170
ZO10B	0170
ZO11	0313
ZO11A	0313
ZO11B	0313
ZO-12	0137
ZO12	0137
ZO-12A	0137
ZO12A	0137
ZO-12B	0137
ZO12B	0137
ZO13	0361
ZO13A	0361
ZO13B	0361
ZO-15	0002
ZO15	0002
ZO-15A	0002
ZO15A	0002
ZO-15B	0002
ZO15B	0416
ZO16	0416
ZO16A	0416
ZO16B	0416
ZO18	0490
ZO18A	0490
ZO18B	0490
ZO20	0526
ZO20A	0526
ZO20B	0526
ZO22	0560
ZO22A	0560
ZO22B	0560
ZO24	0398
ZO24A	0398
ZO24B	0398
ZO-27	0436
ZO27	0436
ZO-27A	0436
ZO27A	1664
ZO-27B	0436
ZO27B	1664
ZO30	0721
ZO30A	0721
ZO30B	0721
ZO-33	0039
ZO33	0039
ZO-33A	0039
ZO33A	0039
ZO-33B	0039
ZO33B	0039
ZO36	0814
ZO36A	0814
ZO36B	0814
ZO39	0346
ZO39A	0346
ZO39B	0346
ZO43	0925
ZO43A	0925
ZO43B	0925
ZO47	0993
ZO47A	0993
ZO47B	0993
ZO51	0497
ZO51A	0497
ZO51B	0497
ZO56	0863
ZO56A	0863
ZO56B	0863
ZO-62	0778
ZO62	0778
ZO-62A	0778
ZO62A	2144
ZO-62B	0778
ZO62B	2144
ZO68	2144
ZO68A	2144
ZO68B	2144
ZO75	1181
ZO75A	1181
ZO75B	1181
ZO-82	0327
ZO82	0327
ZO-82A	0327
ZO82A	0327
ZO-82B	0327
ZO82B	0327
ZO91	1301
ZO91A	1301
ZO91B	1301
ZO100	0098
ZO100A	0098
ZO100B	0098
ZO-110	0149
ZO110	0149
ZO-110A	0149
ZO110A	0149
ZO-110B	0149
ZO110B	0149
ZO120	0186
ZO120A	0186
ZO120B	0186
ZO130	0213
ZO130A	0213
ZO130B	0213
ZO150	0028
ZO150A	0028
ZO150B	0028
ZO160	0255
ZO160A	0255
ZO160B	0255
ZO180	0363
ZO180A	0363
ZO180B	0363
ZO200	0417
ZO200A	0417
ZO200B	0417
ZOA2.4	1266
ZOA2.7	0755
ZOB3.6	0188
ZOB5.1	0162
ZOB5.6	0157
ZOB6.2	0631
ZOB12	0137

If replacement code is OEM, contact original manufacturer for replacement.

DEVICE TYPE	REPL CODE
ZOB15	0002
ZOB27	0436
ZOB33	0039
ZOB62	0778
ZOB82	0327
ZOB110	0149
ZOD6.2	0631
ZOD15	0002
ZOD27	0436
ZOD33	0039
ZOD62	0778
ZOD82	0327
ZOD110	0149
ZP2.7	0755
ZP3	OEM
ZP3.3	0296
ZP3.6	0188
ZP3.9	0036
ZP4.3	0528
ZP4.7	0140
ZP5.1	0162
ZP5.6	0157
ZP6.2	0466
ZP6.8	0025
ZP6.8A	0025
ZP6.8B	0025
ZP7.5	0644
ZP7.5A	0644
ZP7.5B	0644
ZP8.2	0244
ZP8.2A	0244
ZP8.2B	0244
ZP9.1	0012
ZP9.1A	0012
ZP9.1B	0012
ZP10	0170
ZP10A	0170
ZP10B	OEM
ZP11	0313
ZP11A	0313
ZP11B	0313
ZP12	0137
ZP12A	0137
ZP12B	0137
ZP13	0361
ZP13A	0361
ZP13B	0361
ZP15	0002
ZP15A	0002
ZP15B	0002
ZP16	0416
ZP16A	0416
ZP16B	0416
ZP18	0490
ZP18A	0490
ZP18B	0170
ZP20	0526
ZP20-0120	0080
ZP20A	0526
ZP20B	0526
ZP22	0560
ZP22A	0560
ZP22B	0560
ZP24	0398
ZP24A	0398
ZP24B	0398
ZP27	0436
ZP27A	0436
ZP27B	0436
ZP30	0721
ZP30A	0721
ZP30B	0721
ZP33	0039
ZP33A	0039
ZP33B	0039
ZP36	0814
ZP36A	0814
ZP36B	0814
ZP39	0346
ZP39A	0346
ZP39B	0346
ZP43	0925
ZP43A	0925
ZP43B	0925
ZP47	0993
ZP47A	0993
ZP47B	0993
ZP51	0497
ZP51A	0497
ZP51B	0497
ZP56	0863
ZP56A	0863
ZP56B	0863
ZP62	0778
ZP62A	0778
ZP62B	0778
ZP68	2144
ZP68A	2144
ZP68B	2144
ZP75	1181
ZP75A	1181
ZP75B	1181
ZP82	0327
ZP82A	0327
ZP82B	0327
ZP91	1301
ZP91A	1301
ZP91B	1301
ZP100	0098
ZP100A	0098
ZP100B	0098
ZP110	0149
ZP110A	0149
ZP110B	0149
ZP120	0186
ZP120A	0186
ZP120B	0186
ZP130	0213
ZP130A	0213
ZP130B	0213
ZP150	0028
ZP150A	0028
ZP150B	0028
ZP160	0255
ZP160A	0255
ZP160B	0255
ZP180	0363
ZP180A	0363
ZP180B	0363
ZP200	0417
ZP200A	0417
ZP200B	0417
ZPB-A	OEM
ZPB-PROM	OEM
ZPD1	OEM
ZPD2.7	0755
ZPD3	1703
ZPD3.3	0296
ZPD3.6	0372
ZPD3.9	0036
ZPD-4.3	OEM
ZPD4.3	0274
ZPD-4.3V	0274
ZPD4.7	0140
ZPD5V1	0162
ZPD5V6	0157
ZPD5.1	0041
ZPD5.6	0253
ZPD6V2	0466
ZPD6V8	0025
ZPD6.2	0466
ZPD6.8	0062
ZPD7V5	0644
ZPD7.1	0644
ZPD7.5	0077
ZPD8V2	0244
ZPD8.2	0244
ZPD9V1	0057
ZPD9.1	0057
ZPD10	0064
ZPD10V	0170
ZPD11	0181
ZPD11V	0313
ZPD12	0052
ZPD12V	0052
ZPD13	0053
ZPD13V	0361
ZPD15	0681
ZPD15V	0681
ZPD16	0440
ZPD16V	0416
ZPD18	0371
ZPD18V	0490
ZPD20	0695
ZPD20V	0526
ZPD22	0700
ZPD22V	0560
ZPD24	0489
ZPD24V	0398
ZPD27	0450
ZPD30	0195
ZPD30V	0721
ZPD33	0166
ZPD33V	0039
ZPD36	0010
ZPD39	0032
ZPD43	0054
ZPD47	0068
ZPD51	0092
ZPE1.5	OEM
ZPFAK-50701	2672
ZPFAK-50801	2672
ZPFAK-50901	2672
ZPFAK-51001	2672
ZPU	OEM
ZPU100	0098
ZPU120	0186
ZPU150	0028
ZPU180	0363
ZPU200	OEM
ZPV0545L	OEM
ZPY1	OEM
ZPY3.9	0012
ZPY4.3	0528
ZPY4.7	0446
ZPY5.1	0162
ZPY5.6	0157
ZPY-6.2	OEM
ZPY6.2	0631
ZPY6.8	0025
ZPY7.5	0644
ZPY8.2	0244
ZPY9.1	0012
ZPY10	0170
ZPY11	0313
ZPY12	0137
ZPY13	0361
ZPY15	0002
ZPY16	0416
ZPY18	0490
ZPY20	0526
ZPY22	0560
ZPY24	0398
ZPY27	0436
ZPY30	0721
ZPY33	0039
ZPY36	0814
ZPY39	0346
ZPY43	0925
ZPY47	0993
ZPY51	0497
ZPY56	0863
ZPY62	0778
ZPY68	1258
ZPY75	1181
ZPY82	0170
ZPY91	1301
ZPY100	0098
ZQ-6	0298
ZQ6.8	0025
ZQ6.8A	0025
ZQ6.8B	0025
ZQ7.5	0644
ZQ7.5A	0644
ZQ7.5B	0644
ZQ8.2	0244
ZQ8.2A	0244
ZQ8.2B	0244
ZQ9.1	0012
ZQ9.1A	0012
ZQ9.1B	0012
ZQ10	0170
ZQ10A	0313
ZQ10B	0170
ZQ11	0313
ZQ11A	0313
ZQ11B	0313
ZQ12	0137
ZQ12A	0137
ZQ12B	0137
ZQ13	0361
ZQ13A	0361
ZQ13B	0361
ZQ15	0002
ZQ15A	0002
ZQ15B	0002
ZQ16	0416
ZQ16A	0416
ZQ16B	0416
ZQ18	0490
ZQ18A	0490
ZQ18B	0490
ZQ20	0526
ZQ20A	0526
ZQ20B	0526
ZQ22	0560
ZQ22A	0560
ZQ22B	0560
ZQ24	0398
ZQ24A	0398
ZQ24B	0398
ZQ27	0436
ZQ27A	0436
ZQ27B	0436
ZQ30	0721
ZQ30A	0721
ZQ30B	0721
ZQ33	0039
ZQ33A	0039
ZQ33B	0039
ZQ36	0814
ZQ36A	0814
ZQ36B	0814
ZQ39	0346
ZQ39A	0346
ZQ39B	0346
ZQ43	0925
ZQ43A	0925
ZQ43B	0925
ZQ47	0993
ZQ47A	0993
ZQ47B	0993
ZQ51	0497
ZQ51A	0497
ZQ51B	0497
ZQ56	0863
ZQ56A	0863
ZQ56B	0863
ZQ62	0778
ZQ62A	0778
ZQ62B	0778
ZQ68	2144
ZQ68A	2144
ZQ68B	2144
ZQ75	1181
ZQ75A	1181
ZQ75B	1181
ZQ82	0327
ZQ82A	0327
ZQ82B	0327
ZQ91	1301
ZQ91A	1301
ZQ91B	1301
ZQ100	0098
ZQ100A	0098
ZQ100B	0098
ZQ110	0149
ZQ110A	0149
ZQ110B	0149
ZQ120	0186
ZQ120A	0186
ZQ120B	0186
ZQ130	0213
ZQ130A	0213
ZQ130B	0213
ZQ150	0028
ZQ150A	0028
ZQ150B	0028
ZQ160	0255
ZQ160A	0255
ZQ160B	0255
ZQ180	0363
ZQ180A	0363
ZQ180B	0363
ZQ200	0417
ZQ200A	0417
ZQ200B	0417
ZR10	0110
ZR10T	OEM
ZR11	0947
ZR11T	OEM
ZR12	0242
ZR12T	OEM
ZR13	0535
ZR13T	OEM
ZR14	0535
ZR14T	OEM
ZR15	1345
ZR15T	OEM
ZR20	1991
ZR21	1241
ZR22	1241
ZR23	OEM
ZR24	OEM
ZR30C	OEM
ZR31C	OEM
ZR32C	OEM
ZR33C	OEM
ZR34C	OEM
ZR35C	OEM
ZR50B793-1	0137
ZR50B793-3	0436
ZR50B849-1	0436
ZR50B921-1	0436
ZR50B921-2	0644
ZR50B921-3	0002
ZR51B155-2	0247
ZR60	0015
ZR61	1345
ZR62	1345
ZR63	1345
ZR64	1345
ZR66	1345
ZR68	0087
ZR200	0084
ZR201	0090
ZR202	0097
ZR203	0188
ZR204	0109
ZR205	0157
ZR206	0122
ZR207	0644
ZR208	0131
ZR209	1075
ZR209T1	1075
ZR209T3	1075
ZR210	1075
ZR212	0137
ZR215	0416
ZR220	0526
ZR225	1596
ZR230	0721
ZR235	0814
ZR240	0925
ZR500	0015
ZR501	OEM
ZR502	OEM
ZR503	OEM
ZR504	OEM
ZR505	OEM
ZR590	0015
ZR590A	0015
ZR601	0947
ZR602	0242
ZR604	0535
ZR606	0959
ZR608	0087
ZR821-5	0466
ZR821-10	0466
ZR821-20	0466
ZR821-50	0466
ZR821-75	0466
ZR821-100	0466
ZR821-120	0466
ZR821-150	0466
ZR823-5	0466
ZR823-10	0466
ZR823-20	0466
ZR823-50	0466
ZR823-75	0466
ZR823-100	0466
ZR823-120	0466
ZR823-150	0466
ZR825-5	0466
ZR825-10	0466
ZR825-20	0466
ZR825-50	0466
ZR825-75	0466
ZR825-100	0466
ZR825-120	0466
ZR825-150	0466
ZR827-5	0466
ZR827-10	0466
ZR827-20	0466
ZR827-50	0466
ZR827-75	0466
ZR827-100	0466
ZR827-120	0466
ZR827-150	0466
ZR829-50	0466
ZR829-75	0466
ZR829-100	0466
ZR829-120	0466
ZR935-20	OEM
ZR935-50	OEM
ZR935-75	OEM
ZR935-100	OEM
ZR935-120	OEM
ZR935-150	OEM
ZR936-20	OEM
ZR936-50	OEM
ZR936-75	OEM
ZR936-100	OEM
ZR936-120	OEM
ZR936-150	OEM
ZR937-20	OEM
ZR937-50	OEM
ZR937-75	OEM
ZR937-100	OEM
ZR937-120	OEM
ZR937-150	OEM
ZR938-50	OEM
ZR938-75	OEM
ZR938-100	OEM
ZR938-120	OEM
ZR939-50	OEM
ZR939-75	OEM
ZR939-100	OEM
ZR939-120	OEM
ZR1025	0015
ZR1031	0015
ZR1035	0015
ZR1076	0015
ZS	OEM
ZS5.6	0157
ZS5.6A	0157
ZS5.6B	0157
ZS6	0466
ZS7	1325
ZS8	0604
ZS8LB	OEM
ZS8.5	OEM
ZS9	OEM
ZS9.1	0012
ZS9.1A	0012
ZS9.1B	0012
ZS10A	0015
ZS-10B	0015
ZS10B	0015
ZS10LB	OEM
ZS11	OEM
ZS11LB	OEM
ZS11.2	OEM
ZS11.4	OEM
ZS12	0137
ZS12A	0137
ZS12B	0137
ZS12.4	OEM
ZS13LB	OEM
ZS14	OEM
ZS14LB	OEM
ZS15	0002
ZS15A	0002
ZS15B	0002
ZS17	OEM
ZS17LB	OEM
ZS18.6	OEM
ZS20A	0015
ZS20B	0015
ZS21	0015
ZS22	0015
ZS23	0015
ZS24	0015
ZS24.8	OEM
ZS25	0015
ZS27	0436
ZS27A	0436
ZS27B	0436
ZS30	0015
ZS30A	0015
ZS30B	0015
ZS31	0015
ZS31A	0015
ZS31B	0015
ZS32	0015
ZS32A	0015
ZS32B	0015
ZS33	0039
ZS33A	0039
ZS33B	0039
ZS34	0015
ZS34A	0015
ZS34B	0015
ZS37	OEM
ZS38	0164
ZS40	0133
ZS40A	1325
ZS40F	OEM
ZS41	OEM
ZS41F	OEM
ZS42	OEM
ZS42F	OEM
ZS43	OEM
ZS50	0133
ZS51	0604
ZS52	0604
ZS53	3855
ZS56	0164
ZS60	1148
ZS61	0466
ZS62	0778
ZS62A	0778
ZS62B	0778
ZS70	1345
ZS71	1345
ZS72	1345
ZS73	1345
ZS74	1345
ZS74B	1345
ZS75	OEM
ZS76	1345
ZS78	0072
ZS78A	0071
ZS78B	0072
ZS82	0327
ZS82A	0327
ZS82B	0327
ZS90	0604
ZS91	0080
ZS92	0604
ZS94	3855
ZS100	0015
ZS101	0080
ZS102	0604
ZS103	0790
ZS104	0790
ZS106	0015
ZS108	0072
ZS110	0149
ZS110A	0149
ZS110B	0149
ZS120	1325
ZS121	0080
ZS122	0604
ZS123	0790
ZS124	0790
ZS142	0133
ZS143	OEM
ZS150	OEM
ZS151	OEM
ZS152	OEM
ZS153	OEM
ZS154	OEM
ZS155	OEM
ZS170	OEM
ZS171	OEM
ZS172	OEM
ZS174	0015
ZS176	OEM
ZS178	OEM
ZS270	0110
ZS271	0947
ZS272	0242
ZS274	0535
ZS605	0466
ZS701	0242
ZS702	0242
ZS704	OEM
ZS706	OEM
ZS708	OEM
ZS901	OEM
ZS902	OEM
ZS905	OEM
ZS6010	0466
ZS6011	0466
ZS6020	0466
ZS6021	0466
ZSA7	OEM
ZSA11	OEM
ZSA49	0050
ZSB364	0004
ZSB439	0004
ZSD51A	OEM
ZSD81A	OEM
ZSF51B	OEM
ZSF51CT	OEM
ZSF81B	OEM
ZSF81CT	OEM
ZSS51A	OEM
ZSS51B	OEM
ZSS53A	OEM
ZSS53B	OEM
ZSS55A	OEM
ZSS55B	OEM
ZSS56B	OEM
ZSS57B	OEM
ZSS59A	OEM
ZSS59B	OEM
ZSS81A	OEM
ZSS81B	OEM
ZSS83A	OEM
ZSS83B	OEM
ZSS85A	OEM
ZSS85B	OEM
ZSS86B	OEM
ZSS87B	OEM
ZSS89A	OEM
ZSS89B	OEM
ZST51A	OEM
ZST52A	OEM
ZST52B	OEM
ZST53A	OEM
ZST53B	OEM
ZST54A	OEM
ZST81A	OEM
ZST82A	OEM
ZST82B	OEM
ZST83A	OEM
ZST83B	OEM
ZST84A	OEM
ZSY0-7	OEM
ZSY0.7	OEM
ZT06	0007
ZT5.6	0157
ZT5.6A	0157
ZT5.6B	0157
ZT6.2	0631
ZT6.2A	0631
ZT6.2B	0631
ZT6.8	0025
ZT6.8A	0025
ZT6.8B	0025
ZT7.5	0644
ZT7.5A	0644
ZT7.5B	0244
ZT8.2	0244
ZT8.2A	0244
ZT8.2B	0244
ZT9.1	0012
ZT9.1A	0012
ZT9.1B	0012
ZT10	0170
ZT10A	0170
ZT10B	0170
ZT11	0313
ZT11A	0313
ZT11B	0313
ZT12	0137
ZT12A	0137
ZT12B	0137
ZT13	0361
ZT13A	0361
ZT13B	0361
ZT15	0002
ZT15A	0002
ZT15B	0002
ZT16	0416
ZT16A	0416
ZT16B	0416
ZT18	0490
ZT18A	0490
ZT18B	0490
ZT20	0016
ZT20(ZENER)	0526
ZT20A	0526
ZT20B	0526
ZT21	0016
ZT22	0016
ZT22(ZENER)	0560
ZT22A	0560
ZT22B	0560
ZT23	0016
ZT24	0016
ZT24(ZENER)	0398
ZT24A	0398
ZT24B	0398
ZT27	0079
ZT27(ZENER)	0436
ZT27A	0436
ZT27B	0436
ZT30	0721
ZT30A	0721
ZT30B	0721
ZT33	0039
ZT33A	0039
ZT33B	0039
ZT36	0814
ZT36A	0814
ZT36B	0814
ZT39	0346
ZT39A	0346
ZT39B	0346
ZT40	0016
ZT41	0016
ZT42	0016
ZT43	0016
ZT43(ZENER)	0925
ZT43A	0925
ZT43B	0925
ZT44	0016
ZT47	0993
ZT47A	0993
ZT47B	0993
ZT50	0016
ZT51	0497
ZT51A	0497
ZT51B	0497
ZT56	0863
ZT56A	0863
ZT56B	0863
ZT60	0016
ZT61	0016
ZT62	0016

If replacement code is OEM, contact original manufacturer for replacement.

DEVICE TYPE	REPL CODE
ZT62(ZENER)	0778
ZT62A	0778
ZT62B	0778
ZT63	0016
ZT64	0016
ZT66	0016
ZT68	0016
ZT68(ZENER)	2144
ZT68A	2144
ZT68B	2144
ZT75	1181
ZT75A	1181
ZT75B	1181
ZT80	0016
ZT81	0016
ZT82	0016
ZT82(ZENER)	0327
ZT82A	0778
ZT82B	0778
ZT83	0016
ZT84	0016
ZT85/38	OEM
ZT86	0086
ZT87	0016
ZT88	0086
ZT89	0016
ZT90	0086
ZT91	1471
ZT91(ZENER)	1301
ZT91A	1301
ZT91B	1301
ZT93	0086
ZT94	0086
ZT100	0098
ZT100A	0098
ZT100B	0098
ZT110	0016
ZT110(ZENER)	0149
ZT110A	0149
ZT110B	0149
ZT111	0016
ZT112	0016
ZT113	0016
ZT114	0016
ZT116	0016
ZT117	0016
ZT118	0016
ZT119	0016
ZT120	0186
ZT120A	0186
ZT120B	0186
ZT130	0213
ZT130A	0213
ZT130B	0213
ZT131	0037
ZT132	OEM
ZT150	0028
ZT150A	0028
ZT150B	0028
ZT152	0037
ZT153	0037
ZT154	0037
ZT160	0255
ZT160A	0255
ZT160B	0255
ZT180	0037
ZT180(ZENER)	0363
ZT180A	0363
ZT180B	0363
ZT181	0037
ZT182	0037
ZT183	0037
ZT184	0037
ZT187	0037
ZT189	0037
ZT190	0086
ZT191	0086
ZT192	0086
ZT193	0086
ZT200	0417
ZT200A	0417
ZT200B	0417
ZT202	0016
ZT202P	0016
ZT203	0016
ZT203P	0016
ZT204	0016
ZT204P	0016
ZT210	0126
ZT211	0126
ZT280	0037
ZT281	0037
ZT282	0037
ZT283	0037
ZT284	0037
ZT286	0126
ZT287	0037
ZT402	0016
ZT402P	0016
ZT403	0016
ZT403P	0016
ZT404	0016
ZT404P	0016
ZT406	0016
ZT502-10	OEM
ZT502-40	OEM
ZT502-60	OEM
ZT600	0555
ZT696	0016

DEVICE TYPE	REPL CODE
ZT697	0016
ZT706	0016
ZT706A	0016
ZT708	0016
ZT709	0144
ZT805	OEM
ZT917	0144
ZT918	0144
ZT929	OEM
ZT930	0111
ZT1420	0016
ZT1479	0086
ZT1481	0086
ZT1483	0042
ZT1484	0042
ZT1485	0042
ZT1486	0042
ZT1487	0103
ZT1488	0103
ZT1489	0103
ZT1490	0103
ZT1511	0556
ZT1512	0556
ZT1513	0556
ZT1514	OEM
ZT1613	0086
ZT1700	0086
ZT1701	0042
ZT1702	0103
ZT1703	OEM
ZT1708	0016
ZT1711	0086
ZT2102	0086
ZT2205	0016
ZT2206	0016
ZT2270	0086
ZT2368	0016
ZT2369	0016
ZT2369A	0016
ZT2475	0144
ZT2476	0016
ZT2477	0016
ZT2631	0617
ZT2708	0007
ZT2857	0144
ZT2876	0042
ZT2938	0016
ZT3053	0590
ZT3229	OEM
ZT3262	OEM
ZT3269A	0144
ZT3375	0555
ZT3439	OEM
ZT3440	0168
ZT3512	0086
ZT3600	0144
ZT3866	0086
ZT7399	OEM
ZT7488/08	OEM
ZT7488/18	OEM
ZT7488/28	OEM
ZTB3-12	OEM
ZTB3-28	OEM
ZTB3-28FL	OEM
ZTB3-28ST	OEM
ZTB12-12	OEM
ZTB12-28	OEM
ZTB12-28FL	OEM
ZTB12-28ST	OEM
ZTB25-12	OEM
ZTB25-28	OEM
ZTB25-28FL	OEM
ZTB25-28ST	OEM
ZTB70-28FL	OEM
ZTC3.12FL	OEM
ZTC238CK	OEM
ZTE1,5	OEM
ZTE1.5	OEM
ZTE2	OEM
ZTE2.4	1266
ZTE2.7	0755
ZTE3	0118
ZTE3.3	0296
ZTE3.6	0372
ZTE3.9	0036
ZTE4.3	0274
ZTE4.7	0140
ZTE5.1	0041
ZTK6,8	OEM
ZTK6.8	OEM
ZTK9	OEM
ZTK11	OEM
ZTK-11W	OEM
ZTK18	OEM
ZTK22	OEM
ZTK22Z	0560
ZTK23	OEM
ZTK27	OEM
ZTK-33	1319
ZTK33	1319
ZTK33A	1319
ZTK33BDPD	0039
ZTP12	OEM
ZTR-1N60	0143
ZTR-B54	0004
ZTR-B56	0004
ZTR-F0R2B	0895
ZTR-FOR2B	0895
ZTR-SFOR2G	OEM

DEVICE TYPE	REPL CODE
ZTR-W06B	0023
ZTR-W06C	0023
ZTR-W06B	0015
ZTW6,8-2	OEM
ZTW6,8-3	OEM
ZTW6.8-1	OEM
ZTW6.8-5	OEM
ZTX3IU	0144
ZTX41	OEM
ZTX42	OEM
ZTX60	OEM
ZTX107	0079
ZTX107A	OEM
ZTX107A-(RED)	0590
ZTX107B	OEM
ZTX108	0079
ZTX108A	OEM
ZTX108A-(RED)	0191
ZTX108B	OEM
ZTX108C	OEM
ZTX109	0079
ZTX109B	OEM
ZTX109C	OEM
ZTX114	0079
ZTX114K	OEM
ZTX114L	OEM
ZTX114M	OEM
ZTX212	0037
ZTX212A-(RED)	0037
ZTX212AK	OEM
ZTX212AL	OEM
ZTX212AM	OEM
ZTX212BK	OEM
ZTX212BL	OEM
ZTX212BM	OEM
ZTX212K	OEM
ZTX212L	OEM
ZTX212M	OEM
ZTX213	0037
ZTX213A-(RED)	0037
ZTX213AK	OEM
ZTX213AL	OEM
ZTX213AM	OEM
ZTX213BK	OEM
ZTX213BL	OEM
ZTX213BM	OEM
ZTX213CK	OEM
ZTX213CL	OEM
ZTX213CM	OEM
ZTX213K	OEM
ZTX213L	OEM
ZTX213M	OEM
ZTX214	0037
ZTX214BK	OEM
ZTX214BL	OEM
ZTX214BM	OEM
ZTX214CK	OEM
ZTX214CL	OEM
ZTX214CM	OEM
ZTX214K	OEM
ZTX214L	OEM
ZTX214M	OEM
ZTX223	OEM
ZTX223AK	OEM
ZTX223AL	OEM
ZTX223AM	OEM
ZTX223BK	OEM
ZTX223BL	OEM
ZTX223BM	OEM
ZTX223K	OEM
ZTX223L	OEM
ZTX223M	OEM
ZTX237AK	OEM
ZTX237AL	OEM
ZTX237AM	OEM
ZTX237BK	OEM
ZTX237BL	OEM
ZTX237BM	OEM
ZTX237K	OEM
ZTX237L	OEM
ZTX237M	OEM
ZTX238AK	OEM
ZTX238AL	OEM
ZTX238AM	OEM
ZTX238BK	OEM
ZTX238BL	OEM
ZTX238BM	OEM
ZTX238CL	OEM
ZTX238CM	OEM
ZTX238K	OEM
ZTX238L	OEM
ZTX238M	OEM
ZTX239BL	OEM
ZTX239BM	OEM
ZTX239CK	OEM
ZTX239CL	OEM
ZTX239CM	OEM
ZTX239K	OEM
ZTX239L	OEM
ZTX239M	OEM
ZTX300	0079
ZTX300K	OEM
ZTX300L	OEM
ZTX300M	OEM
ZTX301	0079
ZTX301K	OEM
ZTX301L	OEM
ZTX301M	OEM
ZTX302	0079

DEVICE TYPE	REPL CODE
ZTX302K	OEM
ZTX302L	OEM
ZTX302M	OEM
ZTX303	0079
ZTX303K	OEM
ZTX303L	OEM
ZTX303M	OEM
ZTX304	0079
ZTX304K	OEM
ZTX304L	OEM
ZTX304M	OEM
ZTX310	0079
ZTX310K	OEM
ZTX310L	OEM
ZTX310M	OEM
ZTX311	0079
ZTX311K	OEM
ZTX311L	OEM
ZTX311M	OEM
ZTX312	0079
ZTX312K	OEM
ZTX312L	OEM
ZTX312M	OEM
ZTX313K	OEM
ZTX313L	OEM
ZTX313M	OEM
ZTX314K	OEM
ZTX314L	OEM
ZTX314M	OEM
ZTX320	0144
ZTX320K	OEM
ZTX320L	OEM
ZTX320M	OEM
ZTX321	0144
ZTX321K	OEM
ZTX321L	OEM
ZTX321M	OEM
ZTX322	OEM
ZTX322M	OEM
ZTX323	OEM
ZTX323K	OEM
ZTX323L	OEM
ZTX323M	OEM
ZTX325	0259
ZTX325K	OEM
ZTX325L	OEM
ZTX325M	OEM
ZTX326	0259
ZTX326A	OEM
ZTX326AK	OEM
ZTX326AL	OEM
ZTX326AM	OEM
ZTX326K	OEM
ZTX326L	OEM
ZTX326M	OEM
ZTX327K	OEM
ZTX327L	OEM
ZTX327M	OEM
ZTX330	0079
ZTX330K	OEM
ZTX330L	OEM
ZTX330M	OEM
ZTX331	0079
ZTX331L	OEM
ZTX331M	OEM
ZTX337	OEM
ZTX337A	OEM
ZTX337AK	OEM
ZTX337AL	OEM
ZTX337AM	OEM
ZTX337B	OEM
ZTX337BK	OEM
ZTX337BL	OEM
ZTX337BM	OEM
ZTX337C	OEM
ZTX337CK	OEM
ZTX337CL	OEM
ZTX337CM	OEM
ZTX338	OEM
ZTX338A	OEM
ZTX338AK	OEM
ZTX338AL	OEM
ZTX338AM	OEM
ZTX338B	OEM
ZTX338BK	OEM
ZTX338BL	OEM
ZTX338BM	OEM
ZTX338C	OEM
ZTX338CK	OEM
ZTX338CL	OEM
ZTX338CM	OEM
ZTX341	0283
ZTX342	0283
ZTX350	OEM
ZTX360	0079
ZTX382	OEM
ZTX382B	OEM
ZTX382BK	OEM
ZTX382BL	OEM
ZTX382BM	OEM
ZTX382C	OEM
ZTX382CK	OEM
ZTX382CL	OEM
ZTX382CM	OEM
ZTX383	OEM
ZTX383B	OEM
ZTX383BK	OEM
ZTX383BL	OEM
ZTX383BM	OEM

DEVICE TYPE	REPL CODE
ZTX383C	OEM
ZTX383CK	OEM
ZTX383CL	OEM
ZTX383CM	OEM
ZTX384	OEM
ZTX384B	OEM
ZTX384BK	OEM
ZTX384BL	OEM
ZTX384BM	OEM
ZTX384C	OEM
ZTX384CK	OEM
ZTX384CL	OEM
ZTX384CM	OEM
ZTX449	OEM
ZTX449K	OEM
ZTX449L	OEM
ZTX449M	OEM
ZTX450	OEM
ZTX451	OEM
ZTX452	OEM
ZTX453	OEM
ZTX454	OEM
ZTX455	OEM
ZTX500	0126
ZTX500K	OEM
ZTX500L	OEM
ZTX500M	OEM
ZTX501	0037
ZTX501K	OEM
ZTX501L	OEM
ZTX501M	OEM
ZTX502	0037
ZTX502K	OEM
ZTX502L	OEM
ZTX502M	OEM
ZTX503	0037
ZTX503K	OEM
ZTX503L	OEM
ZTX503M	OEM
ZTX504	0037
ZTX504K	OEM
ZTX504L	OEM
ZTX504M	OEM
ZTX510	0037
ZTX510K	OEM
ZTX510L	OEM
ZTX510M	OEM
ZTX530	0037
ZTX531	0037
ZTX537	OEM
ZTX537A	OEM
ZTX537AK	OEM
ZTX537AL	OEM
ZTX537AM	OEM
ZTX537B	OEM
ZTX537BK	OEM
ZTX537BL	OEM
ZTX537BM	OEM
ZTX537C	OEM
ZTX537CL	OEM
ZTX537CM	OEM
ZTX538	OEM
ZTX538A	OEM
ZTX538AK	OEM
ZTX538AL	OEM
ZTX538AM	OEM
ZTX538B	OEM
ZTX538BK	OEM
ZTX538BL	OEM
ZTX538BM	OEM
ZTX538C	OEM
ZTX538CK	OEM
ZTX538CL	OEM
ZTX538CM	OEM
ZTX541	0338
ZTX541K	OEM
ZTX541L	OEM
ZTX541M	OEM
ZTX542	0338
ZTX542K	OEM
ZTX542L	OEM
ZTX542M	OEM
ZTX549	OEM
ZTX550	OEM
ZTX550K	OEM
ZTX550L	OEM
ZTX550M	OEM
ZTX551	OEM
ZTX551K	OEM
ZTX551L	OEM
ZTX551M	OEM
ZTX552	OEM
ZTX600	OEM
ZTX600K	OEM
ZTX600L	OEM
ZTX600M	OEM
ZTX601	OEM
ZTX601K	OEM
ZTX601L	OEM
ZTX649	OEM
ZTX650	0079
ZTX650K	OEM
ZTX650L	OEM
ZTX650M	OEM
ZTX650S	OEM
ZTX651	0079
ZTX651K	OEM
ZTX651L	OEM
ZTX651M	OEM

DEVICE TYPE	REPL CODE
ZTX651S	OEM
ZTX652	OEM
ZTX652K	OEM
ZTX652L	OEM
ZTX652M	OEM
ZTX652S	OEM
ZTX653	OEM
ZTX653K	OEM
ZTX653L	OEM
ZTX653M	OEM
ZTX653S	OEM
ZTX749	OEM
ZTX750	OEM
ZTX750K	OEM
ZTX750L	OEM
ZTX750M	OEM
ZTX750S	OEM
ZTX751	OEM
ZTX751K	OEM
ZTX751L	OEM
ZTX751M	OEM
ZTX751S	OEM
ZTX752	OEM
ZTX752K	OEM
ZTX752L	OEM
ZTX752M	OEM
ZTX752S	OEM
ZTX753	OEM
ZTX753K	OEM
ZTX753L	OEM
ZTX753M	OEM
ZTX753S	OEM
ZTX3702	0037
ZTX3703	0037
ZTX3866	OEM
ZTX3905	0037
ZTX4402	0037
ZTX4403	OEM
ZU6.8	0062
ZU6.8A	0062
ZU6.8B	0062
ZU7.5	0077
ZU7.5A	0077
ZU7.5B	0077
ZU8.2	0165
ZU8.2A	0165
ZU8.2B	0165
ZU9.1	0057
ZU9.1A	0057
ZU9.1B	0057
ZU10	0064
ZU10A	0064
ZU10B	0064
ZU11	0181
ZU11A	0181
ZU11B	0181
ZU12	0052
ZU12A	0052
ZU12B	0052
ZU13	0053
ZU13A	0053
ZU13B	0053
ZU15	0873
ZU15A	0681
ZU15B	0681
ZU16	0440
ZU16A	0440
ZU16B	0440
ZU18	0371
ZU18A	0371
ZU18B	0371
ZU20	0695
ZU20A	0695
ZU20B	0695
ZU22	0700
ZU22A	0700
ZU22B	0700
ZU24	0489
ZU24A	0489
ZU24B	0489
ZU27	0450
ZU27A	0450
ZU27B	0450
ZU30	0195
ZU30A	0195
ZU30B	0195
ZU33	0166
ZU33A	0166
ZU33B	0166
ZU36	0010
ZU36A	0010
ZU36B	0010
ZU39	0032
ZU39A	0032
ZU39B	0032
ZU43	0054
ZU43A	0054
ZU43B	0054
ZU47	0068
ZU47A	0068
ZU47B	0068
ZU51	0092
ZU51A	0092
ZU51B	0092
ZU56	0125
ZU56A	0125
ZU56B	0125
ZU62	0152
ZU62A	0152

DEVICE TYPE	REPL CODE
ZU62B	0152
ZU68	0173
ZU68A	0173
ZU68B	0173
ZU75	0094
ZU75A	0094
ZU75B	0094
ZU82	0049
ZU82A	0049
ZU82B	0049
ZU91	0156
ZU91A	0156
ZU91B	0156
ZU100	0189
ZU100A	0189
ZU100B	0189
ZU110	0099
ZU110A	0099
ZU110B	0099
ZU120	0089
ZU120A	0089
ZU120B	0089
ZU130	0285
ZU130A	0285
ZU130B	0285
ZU150	0336
ZU150A	0336
ZU150B	0336
ZU160	0366
ZU160A	0366
ZU160B	0366
ZU180	0420
ZU180A	0420
ZU180B	0420
ZU200	1464
ZU200A	1464
ZU200B	1464
ZV6.8	0025
ZV6.8A	0025
ZV6.8B	0025
ZV7.5	0644
ZV7.5A	0244
ZV7.5B	0244
ZV8.2	0244
ZV8.2A	0244
ZV8.2B	0244
ZV9.1	0012
ZV9.1A	0012
ZV9.1B	0012
ZV10	0170
ZV10A	0170
ZV10B	0170
ZV11	0313
ZV11A	0313
ZV11B	0313
ZV12	0137
ZV12A	0137
ZV12B	0137
ZV13	0361
ZV13A	0361
ZV13B	0361
ZV15	0002
ZV15A	0002
ZV15B	0002
ZV16	0416
ZV16A	0416
ZV16B	0416
ZV18	0490
ZV18A	0490
ZV18B	0490
ZV20	0526
ZV20A	0526
ZV20B	0526
ZV22	0560
ZV22A	0560
ZV22B	0560
ZV24	0398
ZV24A	0398
ZV24B	0398
ZV27	0436
ZV27A	0436
ZV27B	0436
ZV30	0721
ZV30A	0721
ZV30B	0721
ZV33	0039
ZV33A	0039
ZV33B	0039
ZV36	0814
ZV36A	0814
ZV36B	0814
ZV39	0346
ZV39A	0346
ZV39B	0346
ZV43	0925
ZV43A	0925
ZV43B	0925
ZV47	0993
ZV47A	0993
ZV47B	0993
ZV51	0497
ZV51A	0497
ZV51B	0497
ZV56	0863
ZV56A	0863
ZV56B	0863
ZV62	0778
ZV62A	0778
ZV62B	0778

If replacement code is OEM, contact original manufacturer for replacement.

643

DEVICE TYPE	REPL CODE	DEVICE TYPE	REPL CODE	DEVICE TYPE	REPL CODE	DEVICE TYPE	REPL CODE	DEVICE TYPE	REPL CODE	DEVICE TYPE	REPL CODE	DEVICE TYPE	REPL CODE
ZV68	2144	ZVN0535B	OEM	ZVN3306B	OEM	ZVP2206L	OEM	ZW33	OEM	ZX100	OEM	ZY39	0346
ZV68A	2144	ZVN0535L	OEM	ZVN3310A	OEM	ZVP2206M	OEM	ZW400	OEM	ZX110	OEM	ZY43	0925
ZV68B	2144	ZVN0540A	OEM	ZVN3310B	OEM	ZVP2208B	OEM	ZW0-9.1	0012	ZX120	OEM	ZY47	0993
ZV75	1181	ZVN0540B	OEM	ZVN3315A	OEM	ZVP2208L	OEM	ZX012	OEM	ZX130	OEM	ZY51	0497
ZV75A	1181	ZVN0540L	OEM	ZVN3315B	OEM	ZVP2208M	OEM	ZX028B	OEM	ZX150	OEM	ZY56	0863
ZV75B	1181	ZVN0545A	OEM	ZVP0102A	OEM	ZVP2210B	OEM	ZX3.9	OEM	ZX160	OEM	ZY62	0778
ZV82	0327	ZVN0545B	OEM	ZVP0102B	OEM	ZVP2210L	OEM	ZX4.3	OEM	ZX180	OEM	ZY62A	0778
ZV82A	0327	ZVN1306A	OEM	ZVP0102L	OEM	ZVP2210M	OEM	ZX4.7	OEM	ZX200	OEM	ZY62B	0778
ZV82B	0327	ZVN1306B	OEM	ZVP0106A	OEM	ZVP2215L	OEM	ZX5.1	OEM	ZX200A	OEM	ZY68	1258
ZV91	1301	ZVN1308A	OEM	ZVP0106B	OEM	ZVP2215M	OEM	ZX5.6	OEM	ZX204	OEM	ZY75	1181
ZV91A	1301	ZVN1308B	OEM	ZVP0106L	OEM	ZVP2220L	OEM	ZX6.2	OEM	ZX208A	OEM	ZY82	0327
ZV91B	1301	ZVN1320A	OEM	ZVP0108A	OEM	ZVP2220M	OEM	ZX6.8	OEM	ZX432BJ-10	OEM	ZY82A	0327
ZV100	0098	ZVN1320B	OEM	ZVP0108B	OEM	ZVP3302A	OEM	ZX7.5	OEM	ZX609B	OEM	ZY82B	0327
ZV100A	0098	ZVN1404A	OEM	ZVP0108L	OEM	ZVP3302B	OEM	ZX8.2	OEM	ZX655A	OEM	ZY91	1301
ZV100B	0098	ZVN1408A	OEM	ZVP0120A	OEM	ZVP3304A	OEM	ZX9.1	6688	ZX660A	OEM	ZY100	0098
ZV110	0149	ZVN2104A	OEM	ZVP0120B	OEM	ZVP3304B	OEM	ZX10	OEM	ZX906A	OEM	ZY110	1182
ZV110A	0149	ZVN2104B	OEM	ZVP0120L	OEM	ZVP3306A	OEM	ZX11	OEM	ZX907	OEM	ZY110A	0149
ZV110B	0149	ZVN2104L	OEM	ZVP0530A	OEM	ZVP3306B	OEM	ZX12	OEM	ZX908A	OEM	ZY110B	0149
ZV120	0186	ZVN2106A	OEM	ZVP0530B	OEM	ZVP3310A	OEM	ZX13	OEM	ZX9700	OEM	ZY120	0186
ZV120A	0186	ZVN2106B	OEM	ZVP0530L	OEM	ZVP3310B	OEM	ZX15	OEM	ZY1	OEM	ZY130	0213
ZV120B	0186	ZVN2106L	OEM	ZVP0535A	OEM	ZVP3315A	OEM	ZX16	OEM	ZY3.9	0451	ZY150	0028
ZV130	0213	ZVN2110A	OEM	ZVP0535B	OEM	ZVP3315B	OEM	ZX18	OEM	ZY4.3	0528	ZY160	0255
ZV130A	0213	ZVN2110B	OEM	ZVP0535L	OEM	ZW0-9.1	0012	ZX20	OEM	ZY4.7	0446	ZY180	0363
ZV130B	0213	ZVN2110L	OEM	ZVP0540A	OEM	ZW09.1	OEM	ZX22	OEM	ZY5.1	0162	ZY200	0417
ZV150	0028	ZVN2115A	OEM	ZVP0540B	OEM	ZW2	0604	ZX24	OEM	ZY5.6	0157	ZZ3.3	0289
ZV150A	0028	ZVN2115B	OEM	ZVP0540L	OEM	ZW2.7	1302	ZX27	OEM	ZY6.2	0631	ZZ3.6	0188
ZV150B	0028	ZVN2115L	OEM	ZVP0545A	OEM	ZW3	OEM	ZX30	OEM	ZY6.8	0025	ZZ3.9	0451
ZV160	0255	ZVN2202B	OEM	ZVP0545B	OEM	ZW3.3	0289	ZX33	OEM	ZY7.5	0644	ZZ4.1	0162
ZV160A	0255	ZVN2202L	OEM	ZVP1306A	OEM	ZW3.6	0188	ZX36	OEM	ZY8.2	0244	ZZ4.7	0446
ZV160B	0255	ZVN2202M	OEM	ZVP1306B	OEM	ZW3.9	0451	ZX39	OEM	ZY9.1	0012	ZZ5.1	0162
ZV180	0363	ZVN2204B	OEM	ZVP1308A	OEM	ZW4.3	0528	ZX43	OEM	ZY10	0170	ZZ5.6	0157
ZV180A	0363	ZVN2204L	OEM	ZVP1308B	OEM	ZW4.7	0446	ZX47	OEM	ZY11	0313	ZZ6.2	0631
ZV180B	0363	ZVN2204M	OEM	ZVP1320A	OEM	ZW5.1	0162	ZX51	OEM	ZY12	0234	ZZ6.8	0025
ZV200	0417	ZVN2206B	OEM	ZVP1320B	OEM	ZW5.6	0157	ZX56	OEM	ZY12A	0137	ZZ8.2	0244
ZV200A	0417	ZVN2206L	OEM	ZVP2104A	OEM	ZW6.2	0631	ZX62	OEM	ZY12B	0137	ZZ9.1	0012
ZV200B	0417	ZVN2206M	OEM	ZVP2104B	OEM	ZW6.8	0025	ZX68	OEM	ZY13	0361	ZZ10	0170
ZVN0102A	OEM	ZVN2208B	OEM	ZVP2104L	OEM	ZW7.5	0644	ZX74HCT240-2N	OEM	ZY15	0247	ZZ12	0137
ZVN0102B	OEM	ZVN2208L	OEM	ZVP2106A	OEM	ZW8.2	0244	ZX74HCT245-2N	OEM	ZY15A	0002	ZZ15	0002
ZVN0102L	OEM	ZVN2208M	OEM	ZVP2106B	OEM	ZW9.1	0012	ZX74HCT273-2N	OEM	ZY15B	0002	ZZ16	OEM
ZVN0106A	OEM	ZVN2210B	OEM	ZVP2106L	OEM	ZW10	0170	ZX74HCT374-2N	OEM	ZY16	0416	ZZ18	0371
ZVN0106B	OEM	ZVN2210L	OEM	ZVP2110A	OEM	ZW11	0313	ZX74HCTLS240N	3988	ZY18	0490	ZZ22	0700
ZVN0106L	OEM	ZVN2210M	OEM	ZVP2110B	OEM	ZW12	0137	ZX74HCTLS245N	4013	ZY20	0526	ZZ27	0436
ZVN0108A	OEM	ZVN2215B	OEM	ZVP2110L	OEM	ZW13	0361	ZX74HCTLS273N	4063	ZY22	0560	ZZ33	0039
ZVN0108B	OEM	ZVN2215L	OEM	ZVP2115A	OEM	ZW15	0002	ZX74HCTLS374N	4247	ZY24	0398	ZZ36	OEM
ZVN0108L	OEM	ZVN2215M	OEM	ZVP2115B	OEM	ZW16	0416	ZX75	OEM	ZY27	0291	ZZ62	4065
ZVN0117TA	OEM	ZVN2220B	OEM	ZVP2115L	OEM	ZW18	0490	ZX80/05	OEM	ZY27A	0436	ZZ82	0327
ZVN0120A	OEM	ZVN2220L	OEM	ZVP2202B	OEM	ZW20	0526	ZX80/15	OEM	ZY27B	0436	ZZ110	0149
ZVN0120B	OEM	ZVN2220M	OEM	ZVP2202L	OEM	ZW22	0560	ZX82	OEM	ZY30	0305	ZZ160	OEM
ZVN0120L	OEM	ZVN3302A	OEM	ZVP2202M	OEM	ZW24	0398	ZX85	OEM	ZY33	0314	ZZY16	OEM
ZVN0530A	OEM	ZVN3302B	OEM	ZVP2204B	OEM	ZW27	0436	ZX86	OEM	ZY33A	0039	ZZY36	OEM
ZVN0530B	OEM	ZVN3304A	OEM	ZVP2204L	OEM	ZW30	OEM	ZX88	OEM	ZY33B	0039	ZZY62	OEM
ZVN0530L	OEM	ZVN3304B	OEM	ZVP2204M	OEM			ZX91	OEM	ZY36	0814	ZZY160	OEM
ZVN0535A	OEM	ZVN3306A	OEM	ZVP2206B	OEM								

SECTION 2

Replacements
from NTE, ECG, Radio Shack, TCE

REPL. CODE	NTE PART NO.	ECG PART NO.	RADIO SHACK PART NO.	RCA PART NO.
0001	NTE4049	ECG4049	276-2449	SK4049UB
0002	NTE145A	ECG145A	276-564	SK15V
0003	NTE164	ECG164	276-2055	SK3133
0004	NTE102A	ECG102A	.....	SK3004
0005	NTE611	ECG611	.....	SK3324
0006	NTE290A	ECG290A	276-2023	SK3114A
0007	NTE161	ECG161	276-2016	SK3716A
0008	NTE319P	ECG319P	276-2009	SK9432
0009	NTE20	ECG20	.....	SK9668
0010	NTE5037A	ECG5037A	.....	SK36A
0011	NTE974	ECG974	.....	SK3965
0012	NTE139A	ECG139A	276-562	SK9V1
0013	NTE2362	ECG2362	.....	SK10094
0014	NTE13	ECG13	.....	SK9661
0015	NTE116	ECG116	276-1104	SK3313
0016	NTE123A	ECG123A	276-1617	SK3444
0017	NTE558	ECG558	.....	SK3998
0018	NTE293	ECG293	.....	SK3849
0019	NTE109	ECG109	276-1123	SK3088
0020	NTE5369	ECG5369	.....	SK6769
0021	NTE1012	ECG1012	.....	.....
0022	NTE5208A	ECG5208A	.....	SK182
0023	NTE552	ECG552	.....	SK9000
0024	NTE4052B	ECG4052B	.....	SK4052B
0025	NTE5071A	ECG5071A	.....	SK6V8
0026	NTE923D	ECG923D	276-1740	SK3165
0027	NTE5147A	ECG5147A	.....	SK51X
0028	NTE5100A	ECG5100A	.....	SK150V
0029	NTE6008	ECG6008	.....	SK7208
0030	NTE614	ECG614	.....	SK3327
0031	NTE580	ECG580	.....	SK5036
0032	NTE5038A	ECG5038A	.....	SK39A
0033	NTE9944	ECG9944	.....	.....
0034	NTE4053B	ECG4053B	.....	SK4053B
0035	NTE74LS20	ECG74LS20	.....	SK74LS20
0036	NTE5007A	ECG5007A	.....	SK3A9
0037	NTE159	ECG159	276-2023	SK3466
0038	NTE103	ECG103	.....	SK3862
0039	NTE147A	ECG147A	.....	SK33V
0040	NTE213	ECG213	.....	SK3012
0041	NTE5010A	ECG5010A	276-565	SK5A1
0042	NTE152	ECG152	276-2020	SK3893
0043	NTE1094	ECG1094	.....	SK7769
0044	NTE33	ECG33	.....	SK9429
0045	NTE6002	ECG6002	.....	SK7202
0046	NTE1N415E	1N415E	.....	.....
0047	NTE161	ECG161	276-2016	SK3117
0048	.....	.....	.....	SK9411
0049	NTE5047A	ECG5047A	.....	SK82A
0050	NTE160	ECG160	.....	SK3006
0051	NTE8255	ECG8255	.....	.....
0052	NTE5021A	ECG5021A	276-563	SK12A
0053	NTE5022A	ECG5022A	.....	SK13A
0054	NTE5039A	ECG5039A	.....	SK43A
0055	NTE89	ECG89	.....	SK9119
0056	NTE4040B	ECG4040B	.....	SK4040B
0057	NTE5018A	ECG5018A	276-562	SK9A1
0058	NTE5404	ECG5404	276-1067	SK3627
0059	NTE5610	ECG5610	.....	SK10413
0060	NTE377	ECG377	276-2020	SK9112
0061	NTE231	ECG231	.....	SK3857
0062	NTE5014A	ECG5014A	.....	SK6A8
0063	NTE5226A	ECG5226A	.....	SK218
0064	NTE5019A	ECG5019A	.....	SK10A
0065	NTE165	ECG165	276-2055	SK3115
0066	NTE399	ECG399	.....	SK3244
0067	NTE1296	ECG1296	.....	SK9311
0068	NTE5040A	ECG5040A	.....	SK47A
0069	NTE1413	ECG1413	.....	SK9380
0070	NTE5209A	ECG5209A	.....	SK184
0071	NTE125	ECG125	276-1114	SK3081
0072	NTE125	ECG125	276-1114	SK3032A
0073	NTE271	ECG271	.....	SK3936
0074	NTE162	ECG162	.....	SK3559
0075	NTE74LS125A	ECG74LS125A	.....	SK74LS125A
0076	NTE85	ECG85	276-2009	SK3124A
0077	NTE5015A	ECG5015A	.....	SK7A5
0078	NTE9672	ECG9672	.....	.....
0079	NTE123AP	ECG123AP	276-2009	SK3854
0080	NTE116	ECG116	276-1104	SK3311
0081	NTE9945	ECG9945	.....	.....
0082	NTE74LS293	ECG74LS293	.....	SK74LS293
0083	NTE981	ECG981	.....	SK3724
0084	NTE5870	ECG5870	.....	SK3604
0085	NTE104	ECG104	.....	SK3719
0086	NTE128	ECG128	276-2030	SK3024
0087	NTE156	ECG156	276-1114	SK3051
0088	NTE74LS32	ECG74LS32	.....	SK74LS32
0089	NTE5052A	ECG5052A	.....	SK120A
0090	NTE5872	ECG5874	.....	SK3603
0091	NTE5012A	ECG5012A	.....	SK6A0
0092	NTE5041A	ECG5041A	.....	SK51A
0093	NTE1171	ECG1171	.....	SK3565
0094	NTE5046A	ECG5046A	.....	SK75A
0095	NTE5457	ECG5457	276-1020	SK3598
0096	NTE5592	ECG5592	.....	SK6762
0097	NTE5874	ECG5874	.....	SK3603
0098	NTE5096A	ECG5096A	.....	SK100V
0099	NTE5051A	ECG5051A	.....	SK110A
0100	NTE144A	ECG144A	.....	SK14V
0101	NTE4066B	ECG4066B	.....	SK4066B
0102	NTE506	ECG506	.....	SK3925
0103	NTE130	ECG130	276-2041	SK3027
0104	NTE5048A	ECG5048A	.....	SK87A
0105	NTE5876	ECG5878	.....	SK3602
0106	NTE5304	ECG5304	276-1173	SK3106
0107	NTE1569	ECG1569	.....	SK10081
0108	NTE5372	ECG5372	.....	SK6772
0109	NTE5878	ECG5878	.....	SK3602
0110	NTE5800	ECG5800	276-1141	SK9003
0111	NTE199	ECG199	276-2016	SK3245
0112	NTE3098	ECG3098	.....	SK10178
0113	NTE107	ECG107	276-2016	SK3122
0114	.....	ECG5552	.....	SK6651
0115	.....	ECG74HC109	.....	SK7C109
0116	NTE5880	ECG5882	.....	SK3500
0117	NTE7483	ECG7483	.....	SK7483
0118	NTE5004A	ECG5004A	.....	SK3A0
0119	NTE4069	ECG4069	.....	SK4069UB
0120	NTE605A	ECG605A	.....	SK3864
0121	NTE4042B	ECG4042B	.....	SK4042B
0122	NTE5882	ECG5882	.....	SK3500
0123	NTE110MP	ECG110MP	276-1123	SK3709
0124	NTE519	ECG519	276-1122	SK3100
0125	NTE5042A	ECG5042A	.....	SK56A
0126	NTE129	ECG129	.....	SK3025
0127	NTE107	ECG107	276-2016	SK3293
0128	.....	ECG501B	.....	SK3069
0129	NTE4071B	ECG4071B	.....	SK4071B
0130	NTE181	ECG181	.....	SK9134
0131	NTE5886	ECG5886	.....	SK7086
0132	NTE5210A	ECG5210A	.....	SK186
0133	NTE177	ECG177	276-1122	SK9091
0134	NTE270	ECG270	.....	SK3935
0135	NTE74LS40	ECG74LS40	.....	SK74LS40
0136	NTE126	ECG126A	.....	SK3003A
0137	NTE142A	ECG142A	276-563	SK12V
0138	NTE1013	ECG1013	.....	.....
0139	NTE601	ECG601	.....	SK3463
0140	NTE5009A	ECG5009A	276-565	SK4A7
0141	NTE9946	ECG9946	.....	.....
0142	NTE124	ECG124	.....	SK3021
0143	NTE109	ECG109	276-1123	SK3090
0144	NTE108	ECG108	276-2016	SK3452
0145	NTE5890	ECG5890	.....	SK7090
0146	NTE4060B	ECG4060B	.....	SK4060B
0147	NTE5675	ECG5675	.....	SK3508
0148	NTE290A	ECG290A	276-2023	SK9132
0149	NTE151A	ECG151A	.....	SK110V
0150	NTE106	ECG106	.....	SK3984
0151	NTE85	ECG85	276-2009	SK3122
0152	NTE5044A	ECG5044A	.....	SK62A
0153	NTE74LS139	ECG74LS139	.....	SK74LS139
0154	NTE5673	ECG5673	.....	SK5173
0155	NTE289A	ECG289A	276-2009	SK3124A
0156	NTE5049A	ECG5049A	.....	SK91A
0157	NTE136A	ECG136A	.....	SK5V6
0158	NTE506	ECG506	.....	SK3125A
0159	NTE5591	ECG5591	.....	SK6761
0160	NTE121	ECG121	.....	SK3717
0161	NTE184	ECG184	.....	SK3190
0162	NTE135A	ECG135A	276-565	SK5V1
0163	NTE553	ECG553	.....	SK9975
0164	NTE158	ECG158	.....	SK3004
0165	NTE5016A	ECG5016A	.....	SK8A2
0166	NTE5036A	ECG5036A	.....	SK33A
0167	NTE712	ECG712	.....	SK3072
0168	NTE198	ECG198	.....	SK3220
0169	NTE195A	ECG195A	.....	SK3195
0170	NTE140A	ECG140A	.....	SK10V
0171	NTE280	ECG280	276-2041	SK3619
0172	NTE5211A	ECG5211A	.....	SK188
0173	NTE5045A	ECG5045A	.....	SK68A
0174	NTE5412	ECG5412	276-1067	SK3953
0175	NTE74121	ECG74121	.....	SK74121
0176	NTE834	ECG834	276-1712	SK3569
0177	NTE280	ECG280	276-2041	SK3297
0178	NTE175	ECG175	.....	SK3261
0179	NTE5408	ECG5408	276-1067	SK3577
0180	NTE74H108	ECG74H108	.....	.....
0181	NTE5020A	ECG5020A	.....	SK11A
0182	NTE551	ECG551	.....	SK3125A
0183	NTE74LS27	ECG74LS27	.....	SK74LS27
0184	NTE229	ECG229	276-2009	SK3132
0185	NTE5119A	ECG5119A	.....	SK6X2
0186	NTE5097A	ECG5097A	.....	SK120V
0187	NTE396	ECG396	.....	SK3103A
0188	NTE134A	ECG134A	.....	SK3V6
0189	NTE5050A	ECG5050A	.....	SK100A
0190	NTE500A	ECG500A	.....	SK3304
0191	NTE289A	ECG289A	276-2009	SK3122
0192	NTE5590	ECG5590	.....	SK6760
0193	NTE6159	ECG6159	.....	SK7359
0194	NTE36	ECG36	.....	SK9413
0195	NTE5035A	ECG5035A	.....	SK30A
0196	NTE113A	ECG113A	.....	SK9001
0197	NTE5858	ECG5858	.....	SK3599
0198	NTE123	ECG123	276-1617	SK3020
0199	NTE125 N2	ECG125 N2	276-1114 N2	SK3081 N2
0200	NTE5860	ECG5862	.....	SK3584
0201	NTE502	ECG502	.....	SK3067
0202	NTE6163	ECG6163	.....	SK10220
0203	NTE290A	ECG290A	276-2023	SK3932
0204	NTE5862	ECG5862	.....	SK3584
0205	NTE5120A	ECG5120A	.....	SK6X8
0206	NTE5866	ECG5866	.....	SK7066
0207	NTE5212A	ECG5212A	.....	SK190
0208	NTE103A	ECG103A	.....	SK3835
0209	NTE74LS155	ECG74LS155	.....	SK74LS155
0210	NTE5026A	ECG5026A	.....	SK17A
0211	NTE102	ECG102	.....	SK3722
0212	NTE222	ECG222	.....	SK3065
0213	NTE5098A	ECG5098A	.....	SK130V
0214	.....	.....	.....	SK7C112
0215	NTE4011B	ECG4011B	276-2411	SK4011B
0216	NTE161	ECG161	276-2016	SK3018
0217	NTE5577	ECG5577	.....	SK6727
0218	NTE192A	ECG192A	.....	SK3137
0219	NTE186A	ECG186A	.....	SK3357
0220	NTE94	ECG94	.....	SK3559
0221	NTE5182A	ECG5182A	.....	SK130
0222	NTE131	ECG131	.....	SK3198
0223	NTE389	ECG389	.....	SK9411
0224	NTE229	ECG229	276-2058	SK3246A
0225	NTE5125A	ECG5125A	.....	SK10X
0226	NTE5534	ECG5534	.....	.....
0227	NTE5213A	ECG5213A	.....	SK192
0228	NTE152	ECG152	276-2020	SK3054
0229	NTE117	ECG117A	.....	SK5010A
0230	NTE5126A	ECG5126A	.....	SK11X
0231	NTE74166	ECG74166	.....	SK74166
0232	NTE7400	ECG7400	276-1801	SK7400
0233	NTE154	ECG154	.....	SK3044
0234	NTE5127A	ECG5127A	.....	SK12X
0235	NTE3091	ECG3091	.....	SK4929
0236	NTE291	ECG291	276-2020	SK3440
0237	NTE5128A	ECG5128A	.....	SK13X
0238	NTE5155A	ECG5155A	.....	SK91X
0239	NTE230	ECG230	.....	.....
0240	NTE5483	ECG5483	.....	SK3942
0241	NTE5332	ECG5332	.....	SK9230
0242	NTE5802	ECG5802	276-1143	SK9005
0243	NTE74LS74A	ECG74LS74A	.....	SK74LS74A
0244	NTE5072A	ECG5072A	.....	SK8V2
0245	NTE5099A	ECG5099A	.....	SK140V
0246	NTE1V150	ECG1V150	.....	SKMV150H
0247	NTE5130A	ECG5130A	.....	SK15X
0248	NTE5019T1	ECG5019T1	.....	SK9970
0249	NTE2361	ECG2361	276-2009	SK3124A
0250	NTE170	ECG170	.....	SK3649
0251	NTE5131A	ECG5131A	.....	SK16X
0252	NTE5054A	ECG5054A	.....	SK140A
0253	NTE5011A	ECG5011A	.....	SK5A6
0254	NTE5983	ECG5983	.....	SK7183
0255	NTE5101A	ECG5101A	.....	SK160V
0256	NTE5133A	ECG5133A	.....	SK18X
0257	NTE5034A	ECG5034A	.....	SK28A
0258	NTE5991	ECG5991	.....	SK7191
0259	NTE316	ECG316	.....	SK3039
0260	NTE74LS174	ECG74LS174	.....	SK74LS174
0261	NTE399	ECG399	.....	SK9352
0262	NTE5135A	ECG5135A	.....	SK20X
0263	NTE5214A	ECG5214A	.....	SK194
0264	NTE190	ECG190	.....	SK9435
0265	NTE121MP	ECG121MP	.....	SK3718
0266	NTE5148A	ECG5148A	.....	SK56X
0267	NTE5995	ECG5995	.....	SK3518
0268	NTE7401	ECG7401	276-1801	SK7401
0269	NTE5136A	ECG5136A	.....	SK22X
0270	NTE94	ECG94	.....	SK9141
0271	.....	ECG552	.....	.....
0272	NTE3042	ECG3042	.....	SK2042
0273	NTE5137A	ECG5137A	.....	SK24X
0274	NTE5008A	ECG5008A	.....	SK4A3
0275	NTE157	ECG157	.....	SK3747
0276	NTE166	ECG166	276-1171	SK9075
0277	NTE2332	ECG2332	.....	SK10302
0278	NTE5677	ECG5677	.....	SK3520A
0279	NTE100	ECG100	.....	SK3721
0280	NTE6003	ECG6003	.....	SK7203
0281	NTE2322	ECG2322	.....	SK10134
0282	NTE580	ECG580	.....	SK3318A
0283	NTE171	ECG171	.....	SK3201
0284	NTE85	ECG85	276-2009	SK9229
0285	NTE5053A	ECG5053A	.....	SK130A
0286	NTE503	ECG503	.....	SK3068
0287	NTE167	ECG167	.....	SK3647
0288	NTE74LS86	ECG74LS86	.....	SK74LS86
0289	NTE5066A	ECG5066A	.....	SK3V3
0290	NTE173BP	.....	.....	.....
0291	NTE5139A	ECG5139A	.....	SK27X
0292	NTE5013T1	ECG5013T1	.....	SK9969
0293	NTE168	ECG168	276-1173	SK3648
0294	.....	ECG3086	.....	SK2086
0295	.....	ECG56015	.....	.....
0296	NTE5005A	ECG5005A	.....	SK3A3
0297	NTE4082B	ECG4082B	.....	SK4082B
0298	NTE5070A	ECG5070A	276-561	SK6V0
0299	NTE169	ECG169	.....	SK3678
0300	NTE4085B	ECG4085B	.....	SK4085B
0301	NTE864	ECG864	.....	SK9851
0302	.....	ECG3100	.....	SK4930
0303	.....	ECG56016	.....	.....
0304	NTE5438	ECG5438	.....	SK5238
0305	NTE5141A	ECG5141A	.....	SK30X
0306	NTE5215A	ECG5215A	.....	SK196
0307	.....	ECG56017	.....	.....
0308	NTE941M	ECG941M	276-007	SK3552
0309	NTE238	ECG238	276-2055	SK3710

REPL. CODE	NTE PART NO.	ECG PART NO.	RADIO SHACK PART NO.	RCA PART NO.
0310	NTE7402	ECG7402	.....	SK7402
0311	NTE3041	ECG3041	.....	SK2041
0312	NTE6402	ECG6402	.....	SK3628
0313	NTE5074A	ECG5074A	.....	SK11V
0314	NTE5142A	ECG5142A	.....	SK33X
0315	NTE5994	ECG5994	.....	SK3501
0316	NTE5143A	ECG5143A	.....	SK36X
0317	.....	.....	.....	SK9965
0318	NTE5017A	ECG5017A	276-562	SK8A7
0319	NTE5312	ECG5312	.....	SK3985
0320	NTE297	ECG297	.....	SK3449
0321	NTE312	ECG312	276-2055	SK9157
0322	NTE5144A	ECG5144A	.....	SK39X
0323	NTE5468	ECG5468	.....	SK9495
0324	.....	ECG729	.....	SK3074
0325	NTE5216A	ECG5216A	.....	SK198
0326	NTE233	ECG233	276-2009	SK9387
0327	NTE150A	ECG150A	.....	SK82V
0328	NTE1538	ECG1538	.....	SK9403
0329	NTE9099	ECG9099	.....	.....
0330	NTE966	ECG966	276-1771	SK3592
0331	NTE7403	ECG7403	.....	SK7403
0332	NTE5487	ECG5487	.....	SK3944
0333	NTE5145A	ECG5145A	.....	SK43X
0334	NTE191	ECG191	.....	SK3232
0335	NTE584	ECG584	.....	.....
0336	NTE5055A	ECG5055A	.....	SK150A
0337	NTE9963	ECG9963	.....	.....
0338	NTE288	ECG288	.....	SK3434
0339	NTE605A	ECG605A	.....	SK7952
0340	NTE5401	ECG5401	276-1067	SK3638
0341	NTE5378	ECG5378	.....	.....
0342	NTE5409	ECG5409	276-1020	SK3578
0343	NTE5146A	ECG5146A	.....	SK47X
0344	NTE525	ECG525	.....	SK3925
0345	NTE790	ECG790	.....	SK3077
0346	NTE5086A	ECG5086A	.....	SK39V
0347	NTE1580	ECG1580	.....	SK7743
0348	NTE714	ECG714	.....	SK3075
0349	NTE221	ECG221	.....	SK3050
0350	NTE715	ECG715	.....	SK3076
0351	NTE1014	ECG1014	.....	.....
0352	NTE5217A	ECG5217A	.....	SK200
0353	NTE5227AK	ECG5227AK	.....	SK221
0354	NTE9093	ECG9093	.....	.....
0355	NTE19	ECG19	.....	SK9667
0356	NTE778A	ECG778A	276-038	SK3465
0357	NTE7404	ECG7404	276-1802	SK7404
0358	NTE1465	ECG1465	.....	SK3914
0359	NTE283	ECG283	.....	SK3467
0360	NTE780	ECG780	.....	.....
0361	NTE143A	ECG143A	.....	SK13V
0362	NTE4051B	ECG4051B	.....	SK4051B
0363	NTE5103A	ECG5103A	.....	SK180V
0364	NTE85	ECG85	276-2009	SK3356
0365	.....	.....	.....	SK4915
0366	NTE5056A	ECG5056A	.....	SK160A
0367	NTE455	ECG455	.....	SK4915
0368	.....	ECG779A	.....	.....
0369	NTE125	ECG125	276-1114	SK3080
0370	NTE7485	ECG7485	.....	SK7485
0371	NTE5027A	ECG5027A	.....	SK18A
0372	NTE5006A	ECG5006A	.....	SK3A6
0373	.....	ECG782	.....	.....
0374	NTE504	ECG504	.....	SK3108
0375	NTE740A	ECG740A	.....	SK3328
0376	NTE85	ECG85	276-2009	SK3899
0377	NTE5218A	ECG5218A	.....	SK202
0378	NTE189	ECG189	.....	SK3200
0379	NTE85	ECG85	.....	SK9229
0380	.....	ECG454	.....	.....
0381	NTE7405	ECG7405	.....	SK7405
0382	NTE5150A	ECG5150A	.....	SK62X
0383	NTE1002	ECG1002	.....	.....
0384	NTE6800	ECG6800	.....	SK1901
0385	NTE1121	ECG1121	.....	SK7773
0386	NTE186A	ECG186A	.....	SK3248
0387	NTE1771	ECG1771	.....	SK9749
0388	NTE375	ECG375	.....	SK9118
0389	NTE6802	ECG6802	.....	SK9797
0390	NTE5057A	ECG5057A	.....	SK170A
0391	NTE749	ECG749	.....	SK3168
0392	.....	.....	.....	SK3100
0393	NTE5552	ECG5552	.....	SK6652
0394	NTE4050B	ECG4050B	.....	SK4050B
0395	NTE5660	ECG5667A	.....	SK10459
0396	NTE172A	ECG172A	.....	SK9455A
0397	NTE5227A	ECG5227A	.....	SK220
0398	NTE5081A	ECG5081A	.....	SK24V
0399	NTE1062	ECG1062	.....	.....
0400	NTE5661	ECG5667A	.....	SK10459
0401	NTE5151A	ECG5151A	.....	SK68X
0402	NTE291	ECG291	.....	SK3440
0403	NTE5405	ECG5405	276-1020	SK3951
0404	NTE5662	ECG5667A	.....	SK10459
0405	NTE532	ECG532	.....	SK3301
0406	NTE941	ECG941	.....	SK3514
0407	.....	ECG5624	.....	SK3632
0408	NTE5219A	ECG5219A	.....	SK204
0409	NTE4013B	ECG4013B	276-2413	SK4013B
0410	NTE222	ECG454	.....	SK3991
0411	NTE5626	ECG5626	.....	SK3633
0412	NTE1217	ECG1217	.....	SK4801

REPL. CODE	NTE PART NO.	ECG PART NO.	RADIO SHACK PART NO.	RCA PART NO.
0413	NTE973	ECG973	.....	SK3233
0414	NTE278	ECG278	.....	SK3218
0415	.....	.....	.....	SK3567A
0416	NTE5075A	ECG5075A	.....	SK16V
0417	NTE5105A	ECG5105A	.....	SK200V
0418	.....	ECG5667A	.....	SK10459
0419	NTE196	ECG196	276-2020	SK3054
0420	NTE5058A	ECG5058A	.....	SK180A
0421	NTE5152A	ECG5152A	.....	SK75X
0422	NTE74LS138	ECG74LS138	.....	SK74LS138
0423	NTE5374	ECG5374	.....	SK6774
0424	NTE384	ECG384	.....	SK3894
0425	NTE951	ECG941	.....	SK3514
0426	NTE74LS85	ECG74LS85	.....	SK74LS85
0427	NTE40098B	ECG40098B	.....	SK40098B
0428	NTE1052	ECG1052	.....	SK3249
0429	NTE25	ECG25	.....	SK3841
0430	NTE5492	ECG5492	.....	SK6792
0431	NTE298	ECG298	.....	SK3450
0432	NTE213	ECG213	.....	.....
0433	NTE5220A	ECG5220A	.....	SK206
0434	NTE397	ECG397	.....	SK3528
0435	NTE105	ECG105	.....	SK3012
0436	NTE146A	ECG146A	.....	SK27V
0437	NTE5116A	ECG5116A	.....	SK5X1
0438	.....	ECG720	.....	SK9014
0439	NTE5153A	ECG5153A	.....	SK82X
0440	NTE5025A	ECG5025A	.....	SK16A
0441	NTE5315	ECG5315	.....	SK3988
0442	NTE5454	ECG5454	276-1067	SK6754
0443	NTE6821	ECG6821	.....	SK1900
0444	NTE5911	ECG5911	.....	SK7111
0445	NTE1589	ECG1589	.....	SK9911
0446	NTE5069A	ECG5069A	276-565	SK4V7
0447	NTE74LS240	ECG74LS240	.....	SK74LS240
0448	NTE5059A	ECG5059A	.....	SK190A
0449	NTE128	ECG123	276-2009	SK3020
0450	NTE5033A	ECG5033A	.....	SK27A
0451	NTE5067A	ECG5067A	.....	SK3V9
0452	NTE74LS55	ECG74LS55	.....	SK74LS55
0453	NTE74LS244	ECG74LS244	.....	SK74LS244
0454	NTE5380	ECG5380	.....	SK6780
0455	NTE185	ECG185	.....	SK3191
0456	NTE152	ECG152	276-2020	SK3440
0457	NTE1838	ECG1838	.....	SK9750
0458	NTE74LS245	ECG74LS245	.....	SK74LS245
0459	NTE5221A	ECG5221A	.....	SK208
0460	NTE1604	ECG1604	.....	SK4835
0461	NTE9158	ECG9158	.....	.....
0462	NTE7408	ECG7408	.....	SK7408
0463	NTE5574	ECG5574	.....	SK6724
0464	NTE5543	ECG5543	.....	SK3581
0465	NTE1075A	ECG1075A	.....	SK3877
0466	NTE5013A	ECG5013A	276-561	SK6A2
0467	NTE74LS28	ECG74LS28	.....	SK74LS28
0468	NTE5314	ECG5314	.....	SK3987
0469	NTE120	ECG120	276-1101	SK3110
0470	NTE313	ECG313	.....	SK4939
0471	NTE5905	ECG5905	.....	SK7111
0472	NTE383	ECG383	.....	SK9138
0473	NTE4001B	ECG4001B	276-2401	SK4001B
0474	NTE6115	ECG6115	.....	SK10216
0475	NTE5121A	ECG5121A	.....	SK7X5
0476	NTE5651	ECG5651	276-1000	SK3506
0477	NTE331	ECG331	276-2020	SK9234
0478	NTE5387	ECG5387	.....	SK6787
0479	NTE114	ECG114	276-1101	.....
0480	NTE5605	ECG5605	276-1000	SK3666
0481	NTE1856	ECG1856	.....	SK10155
0482	NTE2055	ECG2055	.....	SK10282
0483	NTE5222A	ECG5222A	.....	SK210
0484	NTE1705	ECG1705	.....	SK9950
0485	NTE1416	ECG1416	.....	SK9016
0486	NTE219	ECG219	276-2043	SK3173
0487	NTE7409	ECG7409	.....	SK7409
0488	NTE311	ECG311	.....	SK3195
0489	NTE5031A	ECG5031A	.....	SK24A
0490	NTE5077A	ECG5077A	.....	SK18V
0491	NTE1396	ECG1396	.....	SK9225
0492	.....	ECG1793	.....	.....
0493	NTE4012B	ECG4012B	.....	SK4012B
0494	NTE552	ECG552	.....	SK5002
0495	NTE4030B	ECG4030B	.....	SK4030B
0496	NTE6355	ECG6355	.....	SK6555
0497	NTE5089A	ECG5089A	.....	SK51V
0498	.....	ECG1793	.....	SK9716
0499	NTE5122A	ECG5122A	.....	SK8X2
0500	NTE5463	ECG5463	.....	SK9292
0501	.....	ECG2049	.....	SK10278
0502	.....	.....	.....	SK3245
0503	NTE75188	ECG75188	276-2520	SK5188
0504	NTE5223A	ECG5223A	.....	SK212
0505	NTE5186A	ECG5186A	.....	SK138
0506	NTE75189	ECG75189	276-2521	SK5189
0507	NTE7410	ECG7410	.....	SK7410
0508	NTE4017B	ECG4017B	276-2417	SK4017B
0509	NTE6850	ECG6850	.....	SK9702
0510	NTE5863	ECG5863	.....	SK7063
0511	.....	ECG3017	.....	SK10321
0512	.....	ECG752	.....	.....
0513	NTE289A	ECG289A	276-2009	SK9137
0514	NTE801	ECG801	.....	SK3160
0515	NTE4023B	ECG4023B	.....	SK4023B

REPL. CODE	NTE PART NO.	ECG PART NO.	RADIO SHACK PART NO.	RCA PART NO.
0516	NTE797	ECG797	.....	SK3158
0517	NTE7008	ECG7008	.....	SK10477
0518	NTE2117	ECG2117	.....	SK9832
0519	NTE5224A	ECG5224A	.....	SK214
0520	NTE374	ECG374	.....	SK9042
0521	NTE5371	ECG5371	.....	SK6771
0522	NTE7411	ECG7411	.....	SK7411
0523	NTE1046	ECG1046	.....	SK3471
0524	.....	ECG558	.....	.....
0525	NTE90	ECG90	.....	SK3931
0526	NTE5079A	ECG5079A	.....	SK20V
0527	NTE294	ECG294	.....	SK3841
0528	NTE5068A	ECG5068A	.....	SK4V3
0529	NTE5871	ECG5871	.....	SK7171
0530	NTE4086B	ECG4086B	.....	SK4086B
0531	NTE123A	ECG123A	276-2009	SK3444
0532	NTE85	ECG85	276-2009	SK3245
0533	NTE5879	ECG5879	.....	SK7179
0534	NTE1728	ECG1728	.....	SK9748
0535	NTE5804	ECG5804	276-1144	SK9007
0536	NTE3040	ECG3040	.....	SK2040
0537	NTE5225A	ECG5225A	.....	SK216
0538	NTE284	ECG284	.....	SK3836
0539	NTE2321	ECG2321	.....	SK10119
0540	NTE5887	ECG5887	.....	SK7087
0541	NTE588	ECG588	.....	SK9938
0542	NTE5174AK	ECG5174AK	.....	SK115
0543	.....	ECG3031A	.....	SK24A
0544	NTE108	ECG107	276-2016	SK3293
0545	NTE5891	ECG5891	.....	SK7091
0546	NTE188	ECG188	.....	SK3199
0547	NTE199	ECG199	276-2016	SK3124A
0548	.....	ECG1420	.....	SK9180
0549	NTE610	ECG610	.....	SK3323
0550	NTE5645	ECG5645	.....	SK5545
0551	NTE2331	ECG2331	.....	SK9422
0552	NTE1845	ECG1845	.....	SK10082
0553	NTE253	ECG253	.....	SK3996
0554	NTE74H40	ECG74H40	.....	.....
0555	NTE186	ECG186	276-2017	SK3192
0556	NTE182	ECG182	.....	SK3188A
0557	NTE9962	ECG9962	.....	.....
0558	NTE373	ECG373	.....	SK9041
0559	NTE580	ECG580	276-1114	SK5012
0560	NTE5080A	ECG5080A	.....	SK22V
0561	NTE210	ECG210	.....	SK3202
0562	NTE5522	ECG5522	.....	SK6622
0563	NTE4950	ECG4950	.....	SK10203
0564	NTE7493A	ECG7493A	.....	SK7493
0565	.....	ECG1690	.....	.....
0566	NTE5632	ECG5632	.....	SK3937
0567	NTE5608	ECG5608	276-1000	SK6708
0568	.....	ECG5402	.....	SK3638
0569	NTE5634	ECG5635	.....	SK3533
0570	.....	.....	.....	SK3232
0571	NTE5635	ECG5635	.....	SK3533
0572	NTE5636	ECG5637	.....	SK5137
0573	NTE5631	ECG5631	.....	SK5131
0574	NTE1003	ECG1003	.....	SK3288
0575	NTE5834	ECG5834	.....	SK7042
0576	NTE6889	ECG6889	.....	SK9809
0577	NTE16	ECG16	276-2016	SK9664
0578	NTE15016	ECG1793	.....	SK9716
0579	.....	ECG6090	.....	.....
0580	NTE955MC	ECG955MC	276-1718	SK10449
0581	.....	ECG116	.....	.....
0582	NTE5010T1	ECG5010T1	.....	SK9967
0583	NTE5868	ECG5868	.....	SK7068
0584	NTE5381	ECG5381	.....	SK6781
0585	NTE5942	ECG5944	.....	SK3606
0586	NTE3028	ECG3028	.....	SK4937
0587	NTE74LS266	ECG74LS266	.....	SK74LS266
0588	NTE5633	ECG5633	276-1000	SK3938
0589	NTE5637	ECG5637	.....	SK5137
0590	NTE192	ECG192	.....	SK9142
0591	.....	ECG56010	.....	.....
0592	NTE229	ECG229	276-2009	SK3246A
0593	NTE5228A	ECG5228A	.....	SK222
0594	NTE6154	ECG6154	.....	SK7354
0595	NTE101	ECG101	.....	SK3861
0596	NTE6010	ECG6010	.....	SK7210
0597	NTE262	ECG262	.....	SK3897
0598	.....	.....	.....	SK9405
0599	NTE179	ECG179	.....	SK3642
0600	NTE5166A	ECG5166A	.....	SK200X
0601	NTE1N416E	1N416E	.....	.....
0602	NTE1122	ECG1122	.....	.....
0603	NTE5570	ECG5570	.....	SK6720
0604	NTE116	ECG116	276-1102	SK3311
0605	NTE5572	ECG5572	.....	SK6722
0606	NTE5554	ECG5554	.....	SK6654
0607	NTE5848	ECG5848	.....	SK7048
0608	NTE5280AK	ECG5280AK	.....	SK591
0609	.....	ECG56004	.....	.....
0610	NTE6084	ECG6084	.....	SK9709
0611	NTE5229A	ECG5229A	.....	SK224
0612	NTE56008	ECG56008	.....	SK3660
0613	NTE9660	ECG9660	.....	.....
0614	NTE74145	ECG74145	.....	SK74145
0615	NTE328	ECG328	.....	SK3895
0616	NTE1227	ECG1227	.....	SK3762
0617	NTE282	ECG282	.....	.....
0618	.....	ECG767	.....	.....

REPL. CODE	NTE PART NO.	ECG PART NO.	RADIO SHACK PART NO.	RCA PART NO.
0619	NTE960	ECG960	276-1770	SK3591
0620	NTE987	ECG987	276-1711	SK3643
0621	NTE4081B	ECG4081B	.....	SK4081B
0622	NTE5185AK	ECG5185AK	.....	SK137
0623	NTE613	ECG613	.....	SK3326
0624	NTE943M	ECG943M	.....	SK9993
0625	NTE57	ECG57	.....	SK3913
0626	NTE224	ECG224	.....	SK3049
0627	NTE703	ECG703	.....	.....
0628	NTE126A	ECG126A	.....	SK3003A
0629	NTE5230A	ECG5230A	.....	SK226
0630	.....	.....	.....	SK9456A
0631	NTE137A	ECG137A	276-561	SK6V2
0632	.....	ECG788	.....	SK3829
0633	NTE1089	ECG1089	.....	SK7767
0634	.....	.....	.....	SK7795
0635	NTE552	ECG552	.....	SK3318A
0636	NTE5575	ECG5575	.....	SK6725
0637	NTE163A	ECG163A	.....	SK3439A
0638	NTE376	ECG376	.....	SK3219
0639	NTE282	ECG282	.....	SK3024
0640	NTE16006	.....	.....	SK9720
0641	NTE4006B	ECG4006B	.....	SK4006B
0642	NTE5161A	ECG5161A	.....	SK150X
0643	NTE91	ECG91	.....	SK3932
0644	NTE138A	ECG138A	.....	SK7V5
0645	NTE5231A	ECG5231A	.....	SK228
0646	NTE1214	ECG1214	.....	SK3736
0647	NTE5710	ECG5710	.....	SK10416
0648	NTE1049	ECG1049	.....	SK3470
0649	NTE718	ECG718	.....	SK3159
0650	NTE5368	ECG5368	.....	SK6768
0651	NTE74L93	ECG74L93	.....	.....
0652	NTE6158	ECG6158	.....	SK7358
0653	NTE5579	ECG5579	.....	SK6729
0654	NTE195A	ECG195A	.....	SK3039
0655	.....	.....	.....	SK9067
0656	.....	.....	.....	SK3643
0657	NTE1608	ECG1608	.....	SK9707
0658	NTE1547	ECG1547	.....	SK7676
0659	NTE708	ECG708	.....	SK3135
0660	NTE74LS348	ECG74LS348	.....	SK74LS348
0661	NTE713	ECG713	.....	SK3077
0662	NTE2428	ECG2428	.....	SK9963
0663	NTE5232A	ECG5232A	.....	SK230
0664	NTE74LS640	ECG74LS640	.....	SK7CT640
0665	NTE5229AK	ECG5229AK	.....	SK225
0666	NTE5028A	ECG5028A	.....	SK19A
0667	NTE18	ECG18	276-2030	SK3911
0668	NTE1048	ECG1048	.....	.....
0669	NTE107	ECG107	276-2016	SK3444
0670	.....	ECG1426	.....	.....
0671	NTE5485	ECG5485	.....	SK3943
0672	NTE5003A	ECG5003A	.....	SK2A8
0673	NTE709	ECG709	.....	SK3135
0674	NTE5569	ECG5569	.....	SK6719
0675	.....	ECG74HC132	.....	SK7C132
0676	NTE292	ECG292	.....	SK3441
0677	NTE74H00	ECG74H00	.....	.....
0678	NTE1409	ECG1409	.....	SK9198
0679	NTE5124A	ECG5124A	.....	SK9X1
0680	NTE74H10	ECG74H10	.....	.....
0681	NTE5024A	ECG5024A	276-564	SK15A
0682	NTE5496	ECG5496	.....	SK6796
0683	NTE453	ECG453	276-2055	SK9853
0684	NTE486	ECG486	.....	SK9658
0685	NTE74LS641	ECG74LS641	.....	SK74LS641
0686	NTE5187A	ECG5187A	.....	SK140
0687	NTE725	ECG725	.....	.....
0688	NTE234	ECG234	276-2023	SK3247
0689	NTE519 N2	ECG519 N2	276-1122 N2	SK3100 N2
0690	NTE152	ECG152	276-2020	SK9366
0691	NTE5180AK	ECG5180AK	.....	SK127
0692	NTE7420	ECG7420	.....	SK7420
0693	NTE195A	ECG195A	.....	.....
0694	NTE1689	ECG1689	.....	SK9949
0695	NTE5029A	ECG5029A	.....	SK20A
0696	NTE722	ECG722	.....	SK7812
0697	.....	.....	.....	SK120A
0698	NTE2417	ECG2417	.....	SK10109
0699	NTE74S00	ECG74S00	.....	SK74S00
0700	NTE5030A	ECG5030A	.....	SK22A
0701	NTE1226	ECG1226	.....	SK3763
0702	.....	.....	.....	SK5020
0703	NTE5830	ECG5830	.....	SK7042
0704	NTE74LS373	ECG74LS373	.....	SK74LS373
0705	NTE5465	ECG5465	.....	SK9293
0706	NTE5822	ECG5822	.....	SK3587A
0707	NTE5542	ECG5542	.....	SK6642
0708	NTE74LS374	ECG74LS374	.....	SK1918
0709	NTE5032A	ECG5032A	.....	SK25A
0710	NTE287	ECG287	.....	SK3433
0711	NTE154	ECG154	.....	SK3024
0712	NTE5437	ECG5437	.....	SK5237
0713	NTE55	ECG55	.....	SK9367
0714	NTE74LS642	ECG74LS642	.....	SK74LS642
0715	NTE612	ECG612	.....	SK3325
0716	NTE5544	ECG5545	.....	SK3582
0717	NTE5545	ECG5545	.....	SK3582
0718	NTE754	.....	.....	.....
0719	NTE2408	ECG2408	.....	SK10099
0720	NTE5547	ECG5547	.....	SK3505
0721	NTE5084A	ECG5084A	.....	SK30V
0722	NTE5197AK	ECG5197AK	.....	SK161
0723	NTE379	ECG379	.....	SK9085
0724	NTE5309	ECG5309	.....	SK5028
0725	NTE154	ECG154	.....	SK3040
0726	NTE5541	ECG5541	.....	SK6641
0727	NTE1773	ECG1773	.....	SK9752
0728	NTE289A	ECG289A	276-2009	SK3449
0729	NTE74164	ECG74164	.....	SK74164
0730	NTE585	ECG585	.....	SK9934
0731	NTE5216AK	ECG5216AK	.....	SK199
0732	NTE5310	ECG5310	.....	SK5030
0733	NTE5589	ECG5589	.....	SK6778
0734	.....	ECG123AP	.....	.....
0735	NTE5527	ECG5527	.....	SK6627
0736	NTE5502	ECG5502	.....	SK6502
0737	NTE5311	ECG5311	.....	SK5031
0738	NTE7450	ECG7450	.....	SK7450
0739	NTE56006	ECG56006	.....	SK3659
0740	NTE5504	ECG5504	.....	SK3579
0741	NTE3041	ECG3041	.....	.....
0742	NTE5507	ECG5507	.....	SK3580
0743	NTE5873	ECG5875	.....	SK3517
0744	NTE6104	ECG6104	.....	SK10211
0745	NTE5548	ECG5548	.....	SK6648
0746	NTE739	ECG739	.....	SK3235
0747	NTE5509	ECG5509	.....	SK3504
0748	.....	ECG707	.....	SK3134
0749	NTE1285	ECG1285	.....	SK3922
0750	NTE5424	ECG5424	.....	SK3575
0751	NTE1286	ECG1286	.....	SK3923
0752	NTE505	ECG505	.....	SK3108
0753	.....	ECG56019	.....	.....
0754	NTE1630	ECG1630	.....	SK7827
0755	NTE5002A	ECG5002A	.....	SK2A7
0756	NTE74LS352	ECG74LS352	.....	SK74LS352
0757	NTE5524	ECG5524	.....	SK6624
0758	.....	ECG56020	.....	.....
0759	NTE5529	ECG5529	.....	SK6629
0760	NTE5875	ECG5875	.....	SK7175
0761	NTE5531	ECG5531	.....	SK6631
0762	NTE1411	ECG1411	.....	SK9246
0763	.....	.....	.....	SK9366
0764	NTE5386	ECG5386	.....	SK6786
0765	NTE928M	ECG928M	.....	SK3692
0766	NTE74LS95B	ECG74LS95B	.....	.....
0767	NTE56004	ECG56004	.....	SK3658
0768	NTE74LS353	ECG74LS353	.....	SK74LS353
0769	NTE118	ECG118	.....	SK3066
0770	NTE74LS645	ECG74LS645	.....	SK74LS645
0771	NTE5230AK	ECG5230AK	.....	SK227
0772	NTE5877	ECG5879	.....	SK3517
0773	NTE5546	ECG5547	.....	SK3505
0774	.....	ECG779A	.....	SK3134
0775	NTE74S38	.....	.....	.....
0776	NTE524V48	ECG524V48	.....	SKMV480H
0777	NTE5111A	ECG5111A	.....	SK3X3
0778	NTE149A	ECG149A	.....	SK62V
0779	.....	.....	.....	SK7C137
0780	NTE746	ECG746	.....	SK3234
0781	NTE295	ECG295	.....	SK9041
0782	NTE5307	ECG5307	.....	SK3107
0783	NTE289A	ECG289A	276-2009	SK3132
0784	NTE748	ECG748A	.....	SK3236
0785	.....	.....	.....	SK7CT354
0786	NTE193	ECG193	.....	SK9143
0787	NTE38	ECG38	.....	SK3623
0788	NTE5699	ECG5699	.....	SK10468
0789	NTE141A	ECG141A	276-563	SK11V5
0790	NTE116	ECG116	276-1103	SK3312
0791	NTE5112A	ECG5112A	.....	SK3X6
0792	.....	ECG74HC138	.....	SK7C138
0793	NTE85	ECG85	.....	SK3849
0794	.....	.....	.....	SK7666
0795	NTE9673	ECG9673	.....	.....
0796	NTE5881	ECG5883	.....	SK3517
0797	NTE783	ECG783	.....	.....
0798	NTE7426	ECG7426	.....	SK7426
0799	NTE5360	ECG5360	.....	.....
0800	NTE5990	ECG5990	.....	SK3608
0801	NTE5113A	ECG5113A	.....	SK3X9
0802	NTE395	ECG395	.....	SK9434
0803	.....	ECG74HC139	.....	SK7C139
0804	NTE1510	ECG1510	.....	.....
0805	.....	.....	.....	SK9464
0806	NTE2764	ECG2764	.....	.....
0807	.....	.....	.....	SK7CT356
0808	NTE855	ECG855	.....	SK7616
0809	NTE5240A	ECG5240A	.....	SK510
0810	NTE5883	ECG5883	.....	SK3517
0811	NTE5808	ECG5808	.....	SK9009
0812	NTE7427	ECG7427	.....	SK7427
0813	NTE74LS393	ECG74LS393	.....	SK74LS393
0814	NTE5085A	ECG5085A	.....	SK36V
0815	NTE5114A	ECG5114A	.....	SK4X3
0816	NTE131MP	ECG131MP	.....	SK3840
0817	NTE724	ECG724	.....	SK3525
0818	NTE49	ECG49	.....	SK3178B
0819	NTE19	ECG19	276-2023	SK3912
0820	NTE289A	ECG289A	.....	SK3124A
0821	NTE5241A	ECG5241A	.....	SK512
0822	NTE74LS30	ECG74LS30	.....	SK74LS30
0823	.....	ECG710	.....	SK3102
0824	NTE524V13	ECG524V13	276-568	SKMV130K
0825	NTE4958	ECG4958	.....	SK10205
0826	NTE2355	ECG2355	.....	SK9957
0827	NTE5115A	ECG5115A	.....	SK4X7
0828	NTE7492	ECG7492	.....	SK7492
0829	NTE161	ECG161	276-2016	SK3246A
0830	NTE236	ECG236	.....	SK3239
0831	NTE74LS160A	ECG74LS160A	.....	SK7CT160
0832	NTE2V130	ECG2V130	276-570	SKMV130J
0833	NTE235	ECG235	.....	SK3239
0834	NTE1V130	ECG1V130	.....	SKMV130G
0835	NTE3010	ECG3010	.....	SK2010A
0836	NTE85	ECG85	276-2009	SK3132
0837	NTE1009	ECG1009	.....	SK3499
0838	NTE464	ECG464	.....	SK9159
0839	NTE2011	ECG2011	.....	SK3975
0840	NTE5242A	ECG5242A	.....	SK514
0841	NTE176	ECG176	.....	SK3845
0842	NTE815	ECG815	.....	SK3255
0843	NTE220	ECG220	.....	SK3990
0844	NTE9800	ECG9800	.....	.....
0845	.....	ECG5610	.....	.....
0846	NTE1186	ECG1186	.....	SK3168
0847	NTE5920	ECG5920	.....	SK10426
0848	NTE197	ECG197	.....	SK3083
0849	NTE1080	ECG1080	.....	SK3284
0850	NTE738	ECG738	.....	SK3167
0851	NTE1187	ECG1187	.....	SK3742
0852	NTE74LS161A	ECG74LS161A	.....	SK74LS161
0853	NTE391	ECG391	.....	SK3959
0854	NTE4014B	ECG4014B	.....	SK4014B
0855	NTE194	ECG194	.....	SK3275
0856	.....	.....	276-021	.....
0857	NTE5466	ECG5466	.....	SK9294
0858	NTE1010	ECG1010	.....	SK3376
0859	NTE1483	ECG1483	.....	SK9211
0860	NTE289A	ECG289A	276-2009	SK3849
0861	NTE87	ECG87	.....	SK9237
0862	NTE5243A	ECG5243A	.....	SK516
0863	NTE5090A	ECG5090A	.....	SK56V
0864	NTE5188A	ECG5188A	.....	SK142
0865	NTE5916	ECG5916	.....	SK10424
0866	NTE1434	ECG1434	.....	SK7634
0867	NTE7430	ECG7430	.....	SK7430
0868	NTE9801	ECG9801	.....	.....
0869	NTE56010	ECG56010	.....	SK10265
0870	NTE5117A	ECG5117A	.....	SK5X6
0871	NTE5102A	ECG5102A	.....	SK170V
0872	NTE1004	ECG1004	.....	SK3365
0873	NTE5023A	ECG5023A	.....	SK14A
0874	NTE74LS162A	ECG74LS162A	.....	SK7CT162
0875	NTE1158	ECG1158	.....	.....
0876	NTE1011	ECG1011	.....	.....
0877	NTE5011T1	ECG5011T1	.....	SK9968
0878	.....	ECG1159	.....	SK3290
0879	NTE5244A	ECG5244A	.....	SK518
0880	NTE1183	ECG1183	.....	SK3480
0881	NTE2357	ECG2357	.....	SK9742
0882	NTE9802	ECG9802	.....	.....
0883	NTE5254A	ECG5254A	.....	SK538
0884	NTE373	ECG373	.....	SK3253
0885	NTE165	ECG238	276-2055	SK3710
0886	NTE323	ECG323	.....	SK9369
0887	NTE74LS163A	ECG74LS163A	.....	SK74LS163
0888	NTE74LS273	ECG74LS273	.....	SK74LS273
0889	NTE108	ECG69	276-2016	SK3132
0890	NTE938	ECG938	.....	SK9166
0891	NTE5245A	ECG5245A	.....	SK520
0892	NTE2359	ECG2359	.....	SK9959
0893	NTE7432	ECG7432	.....	SK7432
0894	NTE9803	ECG9803	.....	.....
0895	NTE5402	ECG5402	276-1067	SK3638
0896	.....	ECG6244	.....	.....
0897	NTE596	ECG596	.....	.....
0898	NTE1245	ECG1245	.....	SK3878
0899	NTE218	ECG218	.....	SK3625
0900	NTE74LS243	ECG74LS243	.....	SK74LS243
0901	NTE595	ECG595	.....	SK9944
0902	NTE5679	ECG5679	.....	SK5579
0903	.....	ECG6240	.....	.....
0904	NTE5853	ECG5855	.....	SK7069
0905	NTE1100	ECG1100	.....	SK3223
0906	NTE1545	ECG1545	.....	SK9379
0907	NTE178MP	ECG178MP	276-1122	.....
0908	NTE5246A	ECG5246A	.....	SK522
0909	.....	ECG5679	.....	.....
0910	NTE1216	ECG1216	.....	SK3735
0911	NTE112	ECG112	.....	SK3089
0912	NTE1430	ECG1430	.....	SK9247
0913	NTE9804	ECG9804	.....	.....
0914	NTE507	ECG507	276-1101	SK5014
0915	NTE4078B	ECG4078B	.....	SK4078B
0916	NTE5809	ECG5809	.....	SK9010
0917	NTE962	ECG962	.....	SK3669
0918	NTE174	.....	.....	.....
0919	NTE153	ECG153	276-2027	SK3274
0920	NTE5247A	ECG5247A	.....	SK524
0921	.....	.....	.....	SK9010
0922	NTE56	ECG56	.....	SK3896
0923	NTE9805	ECG9805	.....	.....
0924	.....	ECG1077	.....	.....
0925	NTE5087A	ECG5087A	.....	SK43V
0926	NTE5257A	ECG5257A	.....	SK544
0927	NTE5831	ECG5831	.....	SK7049

REPL. CODE	NTE PART NO.	ECG PART NO.	RADIO SHACK PART NO.	RCA PART NO.
0928	NTE175	ECG175	.....	SK3626
0929	NTE5609	ECG5609	.....	SK6709
0930	NTE235	ECG235	.....	SK3197
0931	NTE107	ECG107	276-2009	SK3293
0932	.....	.....	.....	SK7C147
0933	NTE72	ECG72	.....	SK9272
0934	NTE5455	ECG5455	276-1067	SK3597
0935	.....	.....	.....	SK3565
0936	NTE74107	ECG74107	.....	SK74107
0937	NTE74LS365A	ECG74LS365A	.....	SK7CT365
0938	NTE5248A	ECG5248A	.....	SK526
0939	NTE9806	ECG9806	.....	.....
0940	.....	ECG1076	.....	.....
0941	NTE5835	ECG5835	.....	SK7049
0942	NTE5869	ECG5869	.....	SK7069
0943	NTE5078A	ECG5078A	.....	SK19V
0944	.....	ECG1760	.....	SK10042
0945	NTE85	ECG85	276-2009	SK3449
0946	NTE5556	ECG5556	.....	SK6656
0947	NTE5801	ECG5801	276-1143	SK9004
0948	NTE5613	ECG5613	.....	SK3631
0949	NTE198	ECG198	.....	SK3219
0950	NTE74LS366A	ECG74LS366A	.....	SK7CT366
0951	NTE5615	ECG5616	.....	SK3633
0952	NTE5249A	ECG5249A	.....	SK528
0953	NTE74LS153	ECG74LS153	.....	SK74LS153
0954	NTE5616	ECG5616	.....	SK3633
0955	NTE5617	ECG5618	.....	SK6635
0956	NTE9807	ECG9807	.....	.....
0957	NTE5472	ECG5472	.....	SK10260
0958	NTE1091	ECG1091	.....	SK7768
0959	NTE5806	ECG5806	.....	SK3848
0960	NTE5618	ECG5618	.....	SK6635
0961	NTE74LS168A	ECG74LS168A	.....	SK74LS168A
0962	NTE74109	ECG74109	.....	SK74109
0963	NTE2079	ECG2079	.....	SK9357
0964	NTE5850	ECG5850	.....	SK3601
0965	.....	.....	.....	SK7658
0966	.....	ECG6241	.....	.....
0967	NTE955M	ECG955M	276-1723	SK3564
0968	NTE553	ECG553	.....	SK3322
0969	NTE127	ECG127	.....	SK3764
0970	NTE1674	ECG1674	.....	SK9325
0971	NTE74LS367	ECG74LS367	.....	SK74LS367
0972	NTE5250A	ECG5250A	.....	SK530
0973	NTE74LS123	ECG74LS123	.....	SK74LS123
0974	NTE7491	ECG7491	.....	.....
0975	NTE2416	ECG2416	.....	SK10108
0976	NTE9808	ECG9808	.....	.....
0977	NTE465	ECG465	.....	SK9158
0978	.....	ECG116	.....	SK3313
0979	NTE5851	ECG5851	.....	SK7051
0980	NTE74LS169A	ECG74LS169A	.....	SK74LS169A
0981	NTE74110	ECG74110	.....	SK74110
0982	NTE4008B	ECG4008B	.....	SK4008B
0983	NTE5854	ECG5854	.....	SK3600
0984	NTE5855	ECG5855	.....	SK7055
0985	NTE74LS368	ECG74LS368	.....	SK7CT368
0986	NTE5186AK	ECG5186AK	.....	SK139
0987	NTE5857	ECG5859	.....	SK7069
0988	NTE5251A	ECG5251A	.....	SK532
0989	NTE5187AK	ECG5187AK	.....	SK141
0990	NTE7438	ECG7438	.....	SK7438
0991	NTE5859	ECG5859	.....	SK7059
0992	NTE9809	ECG9809	.....	.....
0993	NTE5088A	ECG5088A	.....	SK47V
0994	NTE5838	ECG5838	.....	SK7038
0995	NTE5861	ECG5863	.....	SK7069
0996	NTE74111	ECG74111	.....	SK74111
0997	.....	ECG74HC151	.....	SK7C151
0998	NTE5417	ECG5417	.....	SK10255
0999	NTE5021T1	ECG5021T1	.....	SK9971
1000	NTE5172AK	ECG5172AK	.....	.....
1001	NTE2012	ECG2012	.....	SK9092
1002	NTE5867	ECG5867	.....	SK7067
1003	NTE5252A	ECG5252A	.....	SK534
1004	NTE226	ECG226	.....	SK3082
1005	NTE9810	ECG9810	.....	.....
1006	NTE5839	ECG5839	.....	SK7039
1007	NTE74162	ECG74162	.....	SK74162
1008	NTE4015B	ECG4015B	.....	SK4015B
1009	NTE125 N1	ECG125 N1	276-1114 N1	SK3081 N1
1010	NTE4532B	ECG4532B	.....	SK4532B
1011	NTE74S20	ECG74S20	.....	SK74S20
1012	NTE1087	ECG1087	.....	SK3477
1013	NTE5253A	ECG5253A	.....	SK536
1014	NTE5189A	ECG5189A	.....	SK144
1015	NTE6085	ECG6085	.....	SK9798
1016	NTE1445	ECG1445	.....	SK9187
1017	NTE6354	ECG6354	.....	SK6554
1018	NTE7440	ECG7440	.....	SK7440
1019	NTE9811	ECG9811	.....	.....
1020	.....	ECG1445	.....	.....
1021	.....	ECG286	.....	SK3194
1022	NTE1781	ECG1781	.....	SK9746
1023	NTE616	ECG616	.....	SK3320
1024	NTE358	ECG358	.....	SK9328
1025	NTE222	ECG221	.....	SK3050
1026	NTE2358	ECG2358	.....	SK9741
1027	NTE74LS51	ECG74LS51	.....	SK74LS51
1028	NTE5418	ECG5418	.....	SK10256
1029	.....	ECG4562B	.....	SK4562B
1030	NTE6356	ECG6356	.....	SK6556
1031	NTE4502B	ECG4502B	.....	SK4502B
1032	NTE7441	ECG7441	.....	SK7441
1033	NTE9812	ECG9812	.....	.....
1034	.....	ECG5329	.....	.....
1035	NTE9932	ECG9932	.....	.....
1036	NTE2329	ECG5329	.....	SK10254
1037	NTE4518B	ECG4518B	.....	SK4518B
1038	NTE5426	ECG5426	.....	.....
1039	NTE5330	ECG5330	.....	SK9972
1040	NTE6358	ECG6358	.....	SK6558
1041	.....	ECG5331	.....	SK10400
1042	NTE1232	ECG1232	.....	SK3852
1043	NTE5255A	ECG5255A	.....	SK540
1044	NTE1155	ECG1155	.....	SK3231
1045	NTE187A	ECG187A	.....	SK9076
1046	NTE7442	ECG7442	.....	SK7442
1047	NTE3084	ECG3084	.....	SK2084
1048	NTE539	ECG539	.....	SK3309
1049	.....	ECG1196	.....	.....
1050	.....	ECG5667A	.....	.....
1051	NTE1231A	ECG1231A	.....	SK9384
1052	NTE5256A	ECG5256A	.....	SK542
1053	.....	.....	.....	SK3043B
1054	NTE7443	ECG7443	.....	SK7443
1055	NTE2338	ECG2338	.....	SK9480
1056	NTE158	ECG158	.....	SK3007A
1057	NTE4538B	ECG4538B	.....	SK4538B
1058	NTE5688	ECG5688	.....	SK5588
1059	.....	.....	.....	SK9766
1060	NTE107	ECG107	276-2016	SK3132
1061	NTE523	ECG523/3306	.....	SK3306
1062	NTE171	ECG171	.....	SK3865A
1063	.....	ECG9914	.....	.....
1064	NTE8308	ECG8308	.....	.....
1065	NTE5232AK	ECG5232AK	.....	SK231
1066	NTE7444	ECG7444	.....	SK7444
1067	NTE5843	ECG5843	.....	SK7043
1068	.....	.....	.....	SK7C157
1069	NTE3161	ECG3161	.....	SK2161
1070	.....	ECG816	.....	.....
1071	NTE5194A	ECG5194A	.....	SK154
1072	NTE5258A	ECG5258A	.....	SK546
1073	NTE115	ECG115	276-1101	SK9002
1074	NTE7445	ECG7445	.....	SK7445
1075	NTE5073A	ECG5073A	276-562	SK8V7
1076	NTE5580	ECG5580	.....	SK6730
1077	NTE376	ECG376	.....	SK9362A
1078	NTE5582	ECG5582	.....	SK6732
1079	NTE173BP	.....	.....	SK3710
1080	.....	.....	.....	SK7C158
1081	NTE5622	ECG5622	.....	SK6630
1082	NTE587	ECG587	.....	SK9937
1083	NTE519 N3	ECG519 N3	276-1122 N3	SK3100 N3
1084	NTE107	ECG107	.....	SK3293
1085	NTE5623	ECG5623	.....	SK3631
1086	NTE1755	ECG1755	.....	SK10038
1087	NTE5625	ECG5626	.....	SK3633
1088	NTE5259A	ECG5259A	.....	SK548
1089	NTE116 N1	ECG116 N1	276-1104 N1	SK9002
1090	NTE7446	ECG7446	.....	SK7446
1091	NTE5627	ECG5628	.....	SK6635
1092	NTE5628	ECG5628	.....	SK6635
1093	NTE2V480	ECG2V480	.....	SKMV480G
1094	NTE5584	ECG5584	.....	SK6734
1095	NTE5481	ECG5481	.....	SK3940
1096	NTE875	ECG875	.....	SK7725
1097	.....	.....	.....	SK15A
1098	NTE5260A	ECG5260A	.....	SK550
1099	NTE5987	ECG5987	.....	SK3698
1100	NTE7447	ECG7447	276-1805	SK7447
1101	NTE3083	ECG3083	.....	SK2083
1102	NTE5470	ECG5470	.....	SK10257
1103	NTE5989	ECG5989	.....	SK7191
1104	NTE5904	ECG5904	.....	SK7104
1105	NTE1N416C	1N416C	.....	.....
1106	NTE109	ECG110A	276-1123	SK3090
1107	NTE1N415C	1N415C	.....	.....
1108	NTE74120	.....	.....	.....
1109	.....	.....	.....	SK7C160
1110	NTE927D	ECG927D	.....	SK7617
1111	NTE5999	ECG5999	.....	SK7199
1112	NTE74LS377	ECG74LS377	.....	SK74LS377
1113	NTE927	ECG927	.....	SK9017
1114	.....	ECG1319	.....	SK4815
1115	NTE5261A	ECG5261A	.....	SK552
1116	NTE5986	ECG5986	.....	SK3609
1117	NTE7448	ECG7448	.....	SK7448
1118	NTE5988	ECG5988	.....	SK3608
1119	NTE597	ECG597	.....	SK9858
1120	NTE1261	ECG1261	.....	SK3872
1121	.....	.....	.....	SK7C161
1122	NTE74LS670	ECG74LS670	.....	SK7CT670
1123	NTE3167	ECG3167	.....	SK2167
1124	NTE5998	ECG5998	.....	SK7198
1125	NTE74LS378	ECG74LS378	.....	SK74LS378
1126	NTE2013	ECG2013	.....	SK9093
1127	NTE5262A	ECG5262A	.....	SK554
1128	.....	ECG56028	.....	.....
1129	NTE5400	ECG5400	276-1067	SK3950
1130	NTE5847	ECG5847	.....	SK7047
1131	NTE74122	ECG74122	.....	SK74122
1132	NTE16	ECG16	276-2016	SK3911
1133	NTE460	ECG460	.....	SK9842
1134	.....	.....	.....	SK7C162
1135	NTE4016B	ECG4016B	.....	SK4016B
1136	NTE229	ECG229	276-2058	SK3132
1137	NTE581	ECG581	.....	SK5001
1138	NTE165	ECG165	276-2055	SK3111
1139	NTE175	ECG175	.....	SK3562
1140	NTE5419	ECG5419	.....	SK10258
1141	NTE178MP	ECG178MP	276-1122	SK3100
1142	NTE389	ECG389	276-2055	SK3115
1143	NTE74LS379	ECG74LS379	.....	SK74LS379
1144	NTE5263A	ECG5263A	.....	SK556
1145	NTE5190A	ECG5190A	.....	SK146
1146	NTE161	ECG161	276-2016	SK3039
1147	NTE466	ECG466	.....	SK9163
1148	NTE5091A	ECG5091A	.....	SK60V
1149	NTE74123	ECG74123	.....	SK74123
1150	NTE7476	ECG7476	.....	SK7476
1151	.....	ECG74HC163	.....	SK7C163
1152	NTE1081A	ECG1081A	.....	SK3474
1153	NTE74LS157	ECG74LS157	.....	SK74LS157
1154	NTE377	ECG377	.....	SK9366
1155	NTE5220AK	ECG5220AK	.....	SK207
1156	NTE5264A	ECG5264A	.....	SK558
1157	NTE54	ECG54	.....	SK9366
1158	NTE3098	ECG3098	.....	SK9763
1159	.....	ECG1867	.....	.....
1160	NTE7451	ECG7451	.....	SK7451
1161	NTE4919	ECG4919	.....	SK10196
1162	NTE1231	ECG1231	.....	SK3832
1163	.....	ECG74HC164	.....	SK7C164
1164	NTE7473	ECG7473	.....	SK7473
1165	NTE302	ECG302	.....	SK3252
1166	NTE5265A	ECG5265A	.....	SK560
1167	NTE6409	ECG6409	.....	SK9124
1168	NTE9935	ECG9935	.....	.....
1169	NTE5140A	ECG5140A	.....	SK28X
1170	NTE5132A	ECG5132A	.....	SK17X
1171	NTE598	ECG598	.....	.....
1172	NTE5156A	ECG5156A	.....	SK100X
1173	.....	.....	.....	SK3569
1174	NTE74125	ECG74125	.....	SK74125
1175	.....	ECG74HC165	.....	SK7C165
1176	NTE5266A	ECG5266A	.....	SK562
1177	NTE7453	ECG7453	.....	SK7453
1178	.....	ECG757	.....	.....
1179	NTE1025	ECG1025	.....	SK3155
1180	NTE5849	ECG5849	.....	SK7049
1181	NTE5093A	ECG5093A	.....	SK75V
1182	NTE5157A	ECG5157A	.....	SK110X
1183	NTE923	ECG923	.....	SK3164
1184	NTE74126	ECG74126	.....	SK74126
1185	NTE5206A	ECG5206A	.....	SK178
1186	NTE5992	ECG5992	.....	SK3501
1187	NTE964	ECG964	.....	SK3630
1188	NTE537	ECG537	.....	SK3903
1189	NTE325	ECG325	.....	SK9607
1190	NTE183	ECG183	.....	SK3189A
1191	NTE5267A	ECG5267A	.....	SK564
1192	NTE1471	ECG1471	.....	SK9194
1193	NTE7454	ECG7454	.....	SK7454
1194	.....	ECG5313	.....	.....
1195	NTE6112	ECG6112	.....	SK10214
1196	NTE5925	ECG5925	.....	SK10429
1197	NTE7406	ECG7406	.....	SK7406
1198	NTE5158A	ECG5158A	.....	SK120X
1199	NTE7490	ECG7490	276-1808	SK7490
1200	.....	ECG286	.....	SK3261
1201	NTE5268A	ECG5268A	.....	SK566
1202	NTE312	ECG451	276-2055	SK9164
1203	NTE261	ECG261	276-2068	SK3896
1204	NTE229	ECG229	276-2058	SK3018
1205	.....	ECG2343	.....	.....
1206	NTE1006	ECG1006	.....	SK3358
1207	NTE5021A	ECG5021A	.....	SK12A
1208	NTE515	ECG515	.....	SK9098
1209	NTE5159A	ECG5159A	.....	SK130X
1210	NTE74128	ECG74128	.....	SK74128
1211	NTE85	ECG85	276-2009	SK3931
1212	NTE199	ECG199	276-2016	SK3899
1213	NTE5456	ECG5457	276-1020	SK3598
1214	NTE5269A	ECG5269A	.....	SK568
1215	NTE289AMP	ECG289AMP	.....	SK10311
1216	NTE5249AK	ECG5249AK	.....	SK529
1217	NTE6110	ECG6110	.....	SK10213
1218	NTE199	ECG199	276-2016	SK3866A
1219	.....	.....	.....	SK3017B
1220	.....	.....	.....	SK16A
1221	NTE74LS386	ECG74LS386	.....	SK74LS386
1222	NTE75450B	ECG75450B	.....	SK9828
1223	NTE5270A	ECG5270A	.....	SK570
1224	NTE350	ECG350	.....	SK3176
1225	.....	.....	.....	SK3460
1226	NTE1000	ECG1000	.....	.....
1227	NTE6240	ECG6240	.....	SK5060
1228	NTE5251AK	ECG5251AK	.....	SK533
1229	NTE5893	ECG5893	.....	SK7093
1230	NTE74LS221	ECG74LS221	.....	SK74LS221
1231	NTE5895	ECG5897	.....	SK7111
1232	NTE5897	ECG5897	.....	SK7097
1233	NTE193A	ECG193A	.....	SK3138
1234	NTE5458	ECG5458	.....	SK9861
1235	NTE75451B	ECG75451B	.....	SK9807
1236	NTE5899	ECG5901	.....	SK7111

REPL. CODE	NTE PART NO.	ECG PART NO.	RADIO SHACK PART NO.	RCA PART NO.
1237	NTE5271A	ECG5271A	.....	SK572
1238	.....	.....	.....	SK7655
1239	NTE1115	ECG1115	.....	SK3184
1240	NTE5189AK	ECG5189AK	.....	SK145
1241	NTE5944	ECG5944	.....	SK3606
1242	NTE5921	ECG5921	.....	SK10427
1243	NTE5252AK	ECG5252AK	.....	SK535
1244	NTE5903	ECG5905	.....	SK7111
1245	NTE1804	ECG1804	.....	SK9894
1246	NTE5162A	ECG5162A	.....	SK160X
1247	NTE4022B	ECG4022B	.....	SK4022B
1248	NTE9910	ECG9910	.....	.....
1249	.....	.....	.....	SK9970
1250	NTE5453	ECG5453	276-1067	SK6753
1251	NTE1248	ECG1248	.....	SK3497
1252	NTE2014	ECG2014	.....	SK9094
1253	NTE75452B	ECG75452B	.....	SK9834
1254	NTE5188AK	ECG5188AK	.....	SK143
1255	NTE5909	ECG5909	.....	SK7109
1256	NTE5272A	ECG5272A	.....	SK574
1257	NTE187	ECG187	.....	SK3193
1258	NTE5092A	ECG5092A	.....	SK68V
1259	NTE5253AK	ECG5253AK	.....	SK537
1260	NTE26	ECG26	.....	SK9477
1261	NTE74132	ECG74132	.....	SK74132
1262	NTE75453B	ECG75453B	.....	SK9827
1263	NTE5273A	ECG5273A	.....	SK576
1264	NTE5191A	ECG5191A	.....	SK148
1265	NTE7460	ECG7460	.....	SK7460
1266	NTE5000A	ECG5000A	.....	SK2A4
1267	NTE5254AK	ECG5254AK	.....	SK539
1268	.....	.....	.....	SK2A4
1269	NTE5164A	ECG5164A	.....	SK180X
1270	NTE312	ECG451	276-2055	SK9157
1271	.....	ECG74HC173	.....	SK7C173
1272	NTE5812	ECG5812	.....	SK3639
1273	.....	.....	.....	SK3006
1274	NTE375	ECG375	.....	SK3929
1275	NTE961	ECG961	.....	SK3671
1276	.....	ECG2117	.....	SK9832
1277	NTE5814	ECG5814	.....	SK9096
1278	NTE74LS390	ECG74LS390	.....	SK7CT390
1279	NTE75454B	ECG75454B	.....	SK75454B
1280	NTE5274A	ECG5274A	.....	SK578
1281	NTE3092	ECG3092	.....	SK9770
1282	NTE5815	ECG5815	.....	SK3640
1283	NTE5255AK	ECG5255AK	.....	SK541
1284	NTE9370	ECG9370	.....	.....
1285	NTE5817	ECG5817	.....	SK9097
1286	NTE4583B	ECG4583B	.....	SK4583B
1287	.....	ECG74HC174	.....	SK7C174
1288	NTE977	ECG977	.....	SK3462
1289	NTE5275A	ECG5275A	.....	SK580
1290	NTE975	ECG975	.....	SK3641
1291	NTE909	ECG909	.....	SK9177
1292	NTE5257AK	ECG5257AK	.....	SK545
1293	.....	ECG119	.....	SK3175A
1294	NTE74LS194	ECG74LS194A	.....	SK74LS194
1295	.....	ECG74HC175	.....	SK7C175
1296	NTE508	ECG508/R-3A3	.....	SK3756
1297	NTE5276A	ECG5276A	.....	SK582
1298	NTE378	ECG378	.....	SK9113
1299	.....	.....	.....	SK9332
1300	NTE5258AK	ECG5258AK	.....	SK547
1301	NTE5095A	ECG5095A	.....	SK91V
1302	NTE5063A	ECG5063A	.....	SK2V7
1303	NTE7474	ECG7474	.....	SK7474
1304	NTE1V015	ECG1V015	.....	SKMV15B
1305	NTE74LS195A	ECG74LS195A	.....	SK74LS195
1306	NTE74136	ECG74136	.....	SK9833
1307	NTE5689	ECG5689	.....	SK5589
1308	NTE1560	ECG1560	.....	SK7620
1309	NTE2V015	ECG2V015	.....	SKMV15C
1310	.....	ECG74LS33	.....	.....
1311	NTE968	ECG968	.....	SK3593
1312	NTE5277A	ECG5277A	.....	SK584
1313	NTE513	ECG513	.....	SK3443
1314	NTE5260AK	ECG5260AK	.....	SK551
1315	.....	ECG389	.....	SK9374
1316	NTE1130	ECG1130	.....	SK3478
1317	NTE399	ECG399	.....	SK3866A
1318	.....	ECG830	.....	.....
1319	NTE615P	ECG615A	.....	SK9976
1320	NTE74LS395A	ECG74LS395A	.....	.....
1321	NTE5278A	ECG5278A	.....	SK586
1322	NTE1V250	ECG1V250	.....	SKMV250H
1323	NTE5262AK	ECG5262AK	.....	SK555
1324	NTE2V250	ECG2V250	.....	SKMV250J
1325	NTE116	ECG116	276-1101	SK3311
1326	NTE524V25	ECG524V25	.....	SKMV250K
1327	NTE791	ECG791	.....	SK3149
1328	.....	.....	.....	SK6V2
1329	NTE7407	ECG7407	.....	SK7407
1330	NTE5279A	ECG5279A	.....	SK588
1331	NTE53	ECG53	.....	SK9140
1332	NTE65	ECG65	.....	SK9373
1333	.....	.....	.....	SK3669
1334	NTE5263AK	ECG5263AK	.....	SK557
1335	NTE723	ECG723	.....	SK3144
1336	NTE1910	ECG1910	.....	
1337	NTE6155	ECG6155	.....	SK7355
1338	NTE290A	ECG290A	276-2023	SK3841
1339	NTE7416	ECG7416	.....	SK7416
1340	.....	ECG9109	.....	.....
1341	.....	.....	.....	SK3592
1342	NTE7417	ECG7417	.....	SK7417
1343	NTE5280A	ECG5280A	.....	SK590
1344	.....	ECG479	.....	SK9651
1345	NTE116	ECG116	276-1104	SK3017B
1346	NTE5264AK	ECG5264AK	.....	SK559
1347	NTE7421	ECG7421	.....	SK9837
1348	NTE3020	ECG3020	.....	SK2020
1349	NTE40160B	ECG40160B	.....	SK40160B
1350	NTE277	ECG277	.....	SK3220
1351	NTE331	ECG331	276-2020	SK3620
1352	.....	ECG576	.....	.....
1353	.....	.....	.....	SK7425
1354	.....	ECG9911	.....	.....
1355	NTE5281A	ECG5281A	.....	SK592
1356	NTE576	ECG576	.....	SK10510
1357	NTE211	ECG211	.....	SK3203
1358	NTE7486	ECG7486	.....	SK7486
1359	NTE332	ECG332	.....	SK9236
1360	.....	.....	.....	SK7430
1361	NTE5266AK	ECG5266AK	.....	SK563
1362	.....	ECG577	.....	.....
1363	NTE40161B	ECG40161B	.....	SK40161B
1364	NTE1V130	ECG1V130	.....	SKMV130H
1365	NTE4585B	ECG4585B	.....	SK4585B
1366	.....	.....	.....	SK7432
1367	NTE74141	ECG74141	.....	SK74141
1368	.....	.....	.....	SK9971
1369	NTE1172	ECG1172	.....	.....
1370	NTE5173AK	ECG5173AK	.....	.....
1371	NTE159MCP	ECG159MCP	276-2009&23	SK10273
1372	NTE74LS26	ECG74LS26	.....	SK74LS26
1373	NTE74LS398	ECG74LS398	.....	SK74LS398
1374	NTE5282A	ECG5282A	.....	SK594
1375	NTE5424	ECG5424	.....	SK3857
1376	NTE382	ECG382	.....	SK9137
1377	NTE5268AK	ECG5268AK	.....	SK567
1378	NTE40162B	ECG40162B	.....	SK40162B
1379	NTE1739	ECG1739	.....	SK10031
1380	NTE74142	ECG74142	.....	SK74142
1381	NTE4018B	ECG4018B	.....	SK4018B
1382	NTE451	ECG451	276-2062	SK9164
1383	NTE1108	ECG1108	.....	.....
1384	NTE249	ECG249	.....	SK9440
1385	NTE743	ECG743	.....	SK3172
1386	NTE5452	ECG5452	276-1067	SK6752
1387	NTE5129A	ECG5129A	.....	SK14X
1388	NTE74LS399	ECG74LS399	.....	SK74LS399
1389	.....	.....	.....	SK13A
1390	NTE195A	ECG195A	.....	SK3024
1391	NTE5283A	ECG5283A	.....	SK596
1392	NTE5192A	ECG5192A	.....	SK150
1393	NTE3086	ECG3086	.....	SK2086
1394	NTE7470	ECG7470	.....	SK7470
1395	NTE4988	ECG4988	.....	SK10207
1396	NTE5269AK	ECG5269AK	.....	SK569
1397	NTE40163B	ECG40163B	.....	SK40163B
1398	NTE4989	ECG4989	.....	SK10208
1399	NTE74143	ECG74143	.....	SK74143
1400	.....	.....	.....	SK9852
1401	NTE237	ECG237	.....	SK3299
1402	NTE5284A	ECG5284A	.....	SK598
1403	NTE5642	ECG5642	276-1000	SK3506
1404	NTE5313	ECG5313	.....	SK3986
1405	NTE5270AK	ECG5270AK	.....	SK571
1406	.....	ECG9371	.....	.....
1407	NTE3100	ECG3100	.....	SK4930
1408	NTE74144	ECG74144	.....	SK74144
1409	NTE85	ECG85	.....	SK3124A
1410	NTE364	ECG364	.....	SK9637
1411	NTE744	ECG744	.....	SK3171
1412	NTE5316	ECG5316	.....	SK3989
1413	NTE5285A	ECG5285A	.....	SK600
1414	NTE176	ECG176	.....	SK3123
1415	NTE878	ECG878	.....	SK4814
1416	NTE552	ECG552	.....	SK3203
1417	NTE7472	ECG7472	.....	SK7472
1418	.....	.....	.....	SK7470
1419	NTE5271AK	ECG5271AK	.....	SK573
1420	NTE1550	ECG1550	.....	SK9249
1421	NTE307	ECG307	.....	SK3203
1422	NTE108	ECG108	276-2016	SK3293
1423	NTE7475	ECG7475	.....	SK7475
1424	NTE9157	ECG9157	.....	.....
1425	NTE5700	ECG5700	.....	SK9811
1426	.....	ECG2406	.....	.....
1427	NTE5286A	ECG5286A	.....	SK602
1428	NTE1338	ECG1338	.....	SK9757
1429	NTE5176A	ECG5176A	.....	SK118
1430	NTE1879	ECG1879	.....	SK10169
1431	NTE5272AK	ECG5272AK	.....	SK575
1432	NTE7413	ECG7413	.....	SK7413
1433	NTE1656	ECG1656	.....	SK7734
1434	NTE737	ECG737	.....	SK3375
1435	NTE5287A	ECG5287A	.....	SK604
1436	NTE5178A	ECG5178A	.....	SK122
1437	NTE1479	ECG1479	.....	SK9188
1438	NTE5274AK	ECG5274AK	.....	SK579
1439	.....	ECG74HC00	.....	SK7C00
1440	NTE511	ECG511/R-2AV2	.....	SK3759
1441	.....	.....	.....	SK3065
1442	NTE74147	ECG74147	.....	SK74147
1443	.....	ECG74HC02	.....	SK7C02
1444	.....	.....	.....	SK7C03
1445	.....	.....	.....	SK7495
1446	.....	ECG74HC04	.....	SK7C04
1447	NTE5646	ECG5646	.....	SK9711
1448	NTE5288A	ECG5288A	.....	SK606
1449	NTE5181A	ECG5181A	.....	SK128
1450	NTE74365	ECG74365	.....	SK74365
1451	.....	ECG74HC08	.....	SK7C08
1452	NTE5276AK	ECG5276AK	.....	SK583
1453	.....	ECG74HC10	.....	SK7C10
1454	.....	ECG74HC11	.....	SK7C11
1455	NTE74148	.....	.....	.....
1456	NTE67	ECG67	.....	SK9509
1457	NTE2380	ECG2380	.....	SK10126
1458	.....	ECG74HC14	.....	SK7C14
1459	NTE96L02	ECG96L02	.....	.....
1460	.....	ECG286	.....	SK3131A
1461	NTE5289A	ECG5289A	.....	SK608
1462	NTE74366	ECG74366	.....	SK74366
1463	NTE21256	ECG4256	.....	SK10191
1464	NTE5060A	ECG5060A	.....	SK200A
1465	NTE5278AK	ECG5278AK	.....	SK587
1466	.....	.....	.....	SK7C20
1467	.....	ECG6157	.....	.....
1468	.....	.....	.....	SK7C21
1469	NTE1142	ECG1142	.....	SK3485
1470	NTE1185	ECG1185	.....	SK3468
1471	NTE324	ECG324	.....	SK9368
1472	NTE9097	ECG9097	.....	SK9788
1473	.....	ECG1864	.....	SK9069
1474	NTE1877	ECG1877	.....	SK10168
1475	NTE5290A	ECG5290A	.....	SK610
1476	.....	.....	.....	SK7C27
1477	NTE7495	ECG7495	.....	SK7495
1478	NTE5494	ECG5494	.....	SK6794
1479	NTE74367	ECG74367	.....	SK74367
1480	.....	.....	.....	SK7C30
1481	NTE5183A	ECG5183A	.....	SK132
1482	NTE990	ECG990	.....	SK9012
1483	.....	ECG580	.....	.....
1484	NTE74150	ECG74150	.....	SK74150
1485	NTE165	ECG165	276-2055	SK9374
1486	.....	ECG74HC32	.....	SK7C32
1487	NTE74151	ECG74151	.....	SK74151
1488	NTE152	ECG152	276-2020	SK3929
1489	.....	.....	.....	SK3132
1490	NTE153	ECG153	276-2027	SK3930
1491	.....	ECG2407	.....	.....
1492	NTE11	ECG11	.....	SK9918
1493	NTE522	ECG522	.....	SK3303
1494	NTE5416	ECG5416	.....	SK3956
1495	.....	ECG2411	.....	.....
1496	NTE175	ECG286	.....	SK3194
1497	NTE5291A	ECG5291A	.....	SK612
1498	NTE2311	ECG2311	.....	SK9131
1499	NTE5288AK	ECG5288AK	.....	SK607
1500	NTE74368	ECG74368	.....	SK74368
1501	NTE1242	ECG1242	.....	SK3483
1502	NTE5281AK	ECG5281AK	.....	SK593
1503	NTE2315	ECG2315	.....	SK4909
1504	NTE5558	ECG5558	.....	SK6658
1505	NTE85	ECG85	276-2009	SK3849
1506	NTE130MP	ECG130MP	.....	SK3029
1507	.....	.....	.....	SK7C42
1508	NTE846	ECG846	.....	SK9178
1509	NTE74152	ECG74152	.....	.....
1510	.....	.....	.....	SK3122
1511	.....	.....	.....	SK74LS195
1512	NTE6007	ECG6007	.....	SK7207
1513	NTE5292A	ECG5292A	.....	SK614
1514	NTE32	ECG32	.....	SK3867A
1515	NTE5282AK	ECG5282AK	.....	SK595
1516	NTE1223	ECG1223	.....	SK3493
1517	NTE4019B	ECG4019B	.....	SK4019B
1518	.....	ECG216	.....	SK9470
1519	NTE74LS00	ECG74LS00	.....	SK74LS00
1520	NTE40175B	ECG40175B	.....	SK40175B
1521	NTE1780	ECG1780	.....	SK9731
1522	NTE6006	ECG6006	.....	SK7206
1523	NTE5293A	ECG5293A	.....	SK616
1524	NTE5193A	ECG5193A	.....	SK152
1525	.....	.....	.....	SK9760
1526	.....	ECG5534A	.....	.....
1527	NTE7480	ECG7480	.....	SK7480
1528	NTE4073B	ECG4073B	.....	SK4073B
1529	NTE5283AK	ECG5283AK	.....	SK597
1530	NTE51	ECG51	.....	SK9118
1531	NTE74153	ECG74153	.....	SK74153
1532	NTE1192	ECG1192	.....	SK3445
1533	NTE2302	ECG2302	.....	SK9422
1534	.....	ECG833	.....	SK7751
1535	NTE4511B	ECG4511B	.....	SK4511B
1536	NTE6094	ECG6094	.....	SK9774
1537	NTE74LS01	ECG74LS01	.....	SK74LS01
1538	NTE5819	ECG5819	.....	SK9286
1539	NTE5294A	ECG5294A	.....	SK618
1540	.....	.....	.....	SK20X
1541	NTE5284AK	ECG5284AK	.....	SK599
1542	NTE40174B	ECG40174B	.....	SK40174B
1543	.....	ECG129&427	.....	.....
1544	NTE4043B	ECG4043B	.....	SK4043B
1545	NTE915	ECG915	.....	SK9090

REPL. CODE	NTE PART NO.	ECG PART NO.	RADIO SHACK PART NO.	RCA PART NO.
1546	NTE74154	ECG74154	.....	SK74154
1547	.....	ECG9372	.....	.....
1548	.....	.....	.....	SK7C194
1549	.....	.....	.....	SK7C73
1550	NTE74LS02	ECG74LS02	.....	SK74LS02
1551	NTE6050	ECG6050	.....	SK7250
1552	.....	.....	.....	SK7C74
1553	NTE31	ECG31	.....	SK3866A
1554	NTE74LS145	ECG74LS145	.....	SK74LS145
1555	.....	.....	.....	SK7C75
1556	.....	.....	.....	SK9668
1557	NTE5818	ECG5818	.....	SK3586A
1558	NTE5295A	ECG5295A	.....	SK620
1559	.....	.....	.....	SK3849
1560	.....	ECG506	.....	.....
1561	NTE1218	ECG1218	.....	SK3740
1562	NTE1732	ECG1732	.....	SK7703
1563	NTE270	.....	ECG270	.....
1564	NTE7482	ECG7482	.....	.....
1565	NTE5285AK	ECG5285AK	.....	SK601
1566	NTE74155	ECG74155	.....	SK74155
1567	NTE5945	ECG5945	.....	SK7145
1568	.....	.....	.....	SK7C195
1569	NTE74LS03	ECG74LS03	.....	SK74LS03
1570	NTE1428	ECG1428	.....	SK9048
1571	NTE5948	ECG5948	.....	SK3605
1572	NTE1400	ECG1400	.....	SK7627
1573	.....	.....	.....	SK7C85
1574	NTE5515	ECG5515	.....	SK6615
1575	NTE1422	ECG1422	.....	.....
1576	NTE5952	ECG5952	.....	SK3585
1577	NTE5296A	ECG5296A	.....	SK622
1578	.....	ECG74HC86	.....	SK7C86
1579	NTE5344	ECG5344	.....	SK9105
1580	NTE1539	ECG1539	.....	SK9404
1581	NTE295	ECG295	.....	SK3253
1582	NTE74156	ECG74156	.....	SK74156
1583	NTE195A	ECG195A	.....	SK3512
1584	.....	.....	.....	SK7C93
1585	NTE74LS04	ECG74LS04	.....	SK74LS04
1586	NTE1737	ECG1737	.....	SK10030
1587	NTE129P	ECG129P	.....	SK9469
1588	NTE285	ECG285	.....	SK3846
1589	NTE9403	ECG9403	.....	SK9063
1590	NTE5912	ECG5912	.....	SK10422
1591	NTE5181AK	ECG5181AK	.....	SK129
1592	NTE74LS107	ECG74LS107	.....	SK74LS107
1593	NTE290A	ECG290A	276-2023	SK3450
1594	NTE1795	ECG1795	.....	SK9879
1595	NTE74157	ECG74157	.....	SK74157
1596	NTE5082A	ECG5082A	.....	SK25V
1597	NTE152	ECG152	276-2020	SK3239
1598	NTE74LS05	ECG74LS05	.....	SK74LS05
1599	NTE5924	ECG5924	.....	SK10428
1600	NTE5928	ECG5928	.....	SK10430
1601	NTE799	ECG799	.....	SK3238
1602	NTE1219	ECG1219	.....	SK3741
1603	NTE290A	ECG290A	276-2023	SK3247
1604	NTE5932	ECG5932	.....	SK10432
1605	NTE3018	ECG3018	.....	SK2018
1606	NTE5182AK	ECG5182AK	.....	SK131
1607	NTE74S112	ECG74S112	.....	SK74S112
1608	NTE5185A	ECG5185A	.....	SK136
1609	NTE9135	ECG9135	.....	.....
1610	NTE74LS122	ECG74LS122	.....	SK74LS122
1611	NTE1039	ECG1039	.....	SK3366
1612	NTE5183AK	ECG5183AK	.....	SK133
1613	NTE74S113	ECG74S113	.....	SK9704
1614	NTE24	ECG24	.....	SK3849
1615	NTE74LS132	ECG74LS132	.....	SK7CT132
1616	.....	.....	.....	SK3505
1617	NTE1520	ECG1520	.....	SK9043
1618	NTE74LS136	ECG74LS136	.....	SK74LS136
1619	NTE74S114	ECG74S114	.....	.....
1620	NTE5981	ECG5981	.....	SK7181
1621	NTE74160	ECG74160	.....	SK74160
1622	NTE9094	ECG9094	.....	SK9789
1623	NTE74LS08	ECG74LS08	.....	SK74LS08
1624	NTE1096	ECG1096	.....	SK3703
1625	NTE5917	ECG5917	.....	SK10425
1626	NTE5190AK	ECG5190AK	.....	SK147
1627	.....	.....	.....	SK3500
1628	NTE21128	.....	.....	.....
1629	NTE5191AK	ECG5191AK	.....	SK149
1630	NTE5193AK	ECG5193AK	.....	SK153
1631	NTE1742	ECG1742	.....	SK9995
1632	NTE74LS09	ECG74LS09	.....	SK1924
1633	NTE5340	ECG5340	.....	SK9101
1634	NTE5993	ECG5993	.....	SK3518
1635	NTE74161	ECG74161	.....	SK74161
1636	NTE74LS151	ECG74LS151	.....	SK74LS151
1637	.....	ECG991	.....	.....
1638	NTE398	ECG398	.....	SK9363
1639	NTE5076A	ECG5076A	.....	SK17V
1640	NTE5517	ECG5517	.....	SK3615
1641	NTE5514	ECG5514	.....	SK3613
1642	NTE276	ECG276	.....	SK3296
1643	.....	ECG2385	.....	.....
1644	NTE74LS156	ECG74LS156	.....	SK74LS156
1645	.....	ECG128	.....	.....
1646	NTE74LS158	ECG74LS158	.....	SK1923
1647	NTE184&185	ECG184&185	.....	SK3190&3191
1648	NTE1V275	ECG1V275	.....	SKMV275A
1649	NTE56017	ECG56017	.....	SK9830
1650	NTE2V275	ECG2V275	.....	SKMV275B
1651	NTE4020B	ECG4020B	.....	SK4020B
1652	NTE74LS10	ECG74LS10	.....	SK74LS10
1653	NTE199	ECG199	276-2016	SK3132
1654	NTE598	ECG598	.....	SK9859
1655	NTE5516	ECG5516	.....	SK6616
1656	NTE74163	ECG74163	.....	SK74163
1657	NTE74LS11	ECG74LS11	.....	SK74LS11
1658	NTE2386	ECG2386	.....	SK10130
1659	NTE6400A	ECG6400B	.....	SK9122
1660	.....	.....	.....	SK4511B
1661	.....	ECG759	.....	.....
1662	NTE74LS175	ECG74LS175	.....	SK74LS175
1663	NTE5342	ECG5342	.....	SK9103
1664	NTE5083A	ECG5083A	.....	SK28V
1665	NTE127	ECG127	.....	SK3035
1666	NTE1573	ECG1573	.....	SK7678
1667	NTE928	ECG928	.....	SK3691
1668	NTE74LS181	ECG74LS181	.....	SK7CT181
1669	NTE74LS12	ECG74LS12	.....	SK74LS12
1670	NTE5701	ECG5701	.....	SK10414
1671	NTE180	ECG180	.....	SK9136
1672	NTE4094B	ECG4094B	.....	SK4094B
1673	NTE5406	ECG5406	.....	SK3952
1674	.....	ECG773	.....	.....
1675	NTE74165	ECG74165	.....	SK74165
1676	NTE74LS190	ECG74LS190	.....	SK7CT190
1677	NTE74LS191	ECG74LS191	.....	SK74LS191
1678	NTE74LS13	ECG74LS13	.....	SK74LS13
1679	NTE74LS192	ECG74LS192	.....	SK7CT192
1680	NTE186	ECG186	.....	SK3192
1681	NTE1V010	ECG1V010	.....	SKMV10B
1682	NTE74LS193	ECG74LS193	.....	SK74LS193
1683	NTE2147	ECG2147	.....	SK10296
1684	NTE2V010	ECG2V010	.....	SKMV10C
1685	NTE74S157	ECG74S157	.....	SK1914
1686	NTE912	ECG912	.....	SK3543
1687	.....	ECG2027	.....	.....
1688	NTE74LS14	ECG74LS14	.....	SK74LS14
1689	NTE778S	ECG778S	.....	SK10139
1690	NTE5377	ECG5377	.....	.....
1691	NTE2027	ECG2027	.....	SK10277
1692	NTE7494	ECG7494	.....	SK7494
1693	NTE5192AK	ECG5192AK	.....	SK151
1694	NTE5567	ECG5567	.....	SK6717
1695	NTE909D	ECG909D	.....	SK3590
1696	NTE526A	ECG526A	.....	SK3306
1697	NTE74LS15	ECG74LS15	.....	SK74LS15
1698	NTE228A	ECG228A	.....	SK9462
1699	NTE8224	ECG8224	.....	.....
1700	NTE533	ECG533	.....	SK3302
1701	NTE5195A	ECG5195A	.....	SK156
1702	NTE308	ECG308	.....	SK3855
1703	NTE5065A	ECG5065A	.....	SK3V0
1704	NTE1167	ECG1167	.....	SK3732
1705	NTE7496	ECG7496	.....	SK7496
1706	NTE5194AK	ECG5194AK	.....	SK155
1707	NTE5196A	ECG5196A	.....	SK158
1708	.....	ECG14	.....	.....
1709	NTE5195AK	ECG5195AK	.....	SK157
1710	NTE1909	ECG1909	.....	SK10051
1711	NTE74170	ECG74170	.....	SK74170
1712	NTE5197A	ECG5197A	.....	SK160
1713	.....	ECG29	.....	.....
1714	NTE5599	ECG5599	.....	SK6749
1715	NTE74LS241	ECG74LS241	.....	SK74LS241
1716	NTE6244	ECG6244	.....	SK9777
1717	NTE74LS242	ECG74LS242	.....	SK74LS242
1718	NTE75491B	ECG75491B	.....	SK9786
1719	NTE74LS37	ECG74LS37	.....	SK74LS37
1720	NTE5196AK	ECG5196AK	.....	SK159
1721	NTE74LS247	ECG74LS247	.....	SK74LS247
1722	NTE2406	ECG2406	.....	SK10097
1723	NTE74LS248	ECG74LS248	.....	SK74LS248
1724	NTE74LS249	ECG74LS249	.....	SK74LS249
1725	NTE5198A	ECG5198A	.....	SK162
1726	NTE74LS251	ECG74LS251	.....	SK1919
1727	.....	ECG931	.....	.....
1728	NTE74LS253	ECG74LS253	.....	SK74LS253
1729	NTE75492B	ECG75492B	.....	.....
1730	.....	ECG8853	.....	.....
1731	NTE2409	ECG2409	.....	SK10100
1732	NTE116	ECG116	276-1102	SK5002
1733	NTE74LS257	ECG74LS257	.....	SK74LS257
1734	NTE6075	ECG6075	.....	SK7075
1735	NTE74LS258	ECG74LS258	.....	SK74LS258
1736	NTE5803	ECG5804	276-1144	SK9007
1737	NTE5199A	ECG5199A	.....	SK164
1738	NTE4021B	ECG4021B	.....	SK4021B
1739	NTE1045	ECG1045	.....	SK3072
1740	NTE321	ECG321	.....	SK3844
1741	NTE2407	ECG2407	.....	SK10098
1742	.....	ECG798	.....	SK3216
1743	.....	ECG779A	.....	SK3170
1744	NTE5601	ECG5601	276-1000	SK6601
1745	NTE5198AK	ECG5198AK	.....	SK163
1746	NTE199	ECG199	276-2016	SK3931
1747	NTE458	ECG458	.....	SK9460
1748	NTE736	ECG736	.....	.....
1749	.....	.....	.....	SK5012
1750	NTE5200A	ECG5200A	.....	SK166
1751	.....	ECG74173	.....	.....
1752	NTE74LS21	ECG74LS21	.....	SK1920
1753	NTE40192B	ECG40192B	.....	SK40192B
1754	NTE5595	ECG5595	.....	SK6745
1755	NTE74173	ECG74173	.....	SK74173
1756	NTE4927	ECG4927	.....	SK10198
1757	NTE5199AK	ECG5199AK	.....	SK165
1758	NTE40194B	ECG40194B	.....	SK40194B
1759	NTE74174	ECG74174	.....	SK74174
1760	NTE5805	ECG5806	.....	SK3848
1761	NTE5202A	ECG5202A	.....	SK170
1762	NTE74LS280	ECG74LS280	.....	SK74LS280
1763	.....	ECG5330	.....	.....
1764	NTE74LS22	ECG74LS22	.....	SK74LS22
1765	NTE40193B	ECG40193B	.....	SK40193B
1766	NTE6357	ECG6357	.....	SK6557
1767	NTE3024	ECG3024	.....	SK2024
1768	NTE74LS283	ECG74LS283	.....	.....
1769	.....	ECG1545	.....	.....
1770	.....	.....	.....	SK3690
1771	NTE5200AK	ECG5200AK	.....	SK167
1772	NTE6077	ECG6077	.....	SK7077
1773	NTE40195B	ECG40195B	.....	SK40195B
1774	NTE126	ECG126A	.....	SK3006
1775	NTE1902	ECG1902	.....	SK3962
1776	NTE74175	ECG74175	.....	SK74175
1777	NTE5203A	ECG5203A	.....	SK172
1778	NTE6359	ECG6359	.....	SK6559
1779	NTE184	ECG184	.....	SK9041
1780	NTE518	ECG518	.....	SK9086
1781	NTE74H50	ECG74H50	.....	.....
1782	NTE2028	ECG2028	.....	SK9814
1783	NTE5202AK	ECG5202AK	.....	SK171
1784	NTE74176	ECG74176	.....	SK74176
1785	NTE5204A	ECG5204A	.....	SK174
1786	NTE910	ECG910	.....	SK9175
1787	NTE6220	ECG6220	.....	SK10434
1788	NTE5203AK	ECG5203AK	.....	SK173
1789	NTE910D	ECG910D	.....	SK9176
1790	.....	.....	.....	SK3629
1791	NTE116 N2	ECG116 N2	276-1104 N2	SK9001
1792	NTE74177	ECG74177	.....	SK74177
1793	NTE5205A	ECG5205A	.....	SK176
1794	.....	.....	.....	SK74LS322
1795	NTE23	ECG23	.....	SK9671
1796	NTE15019E	ECG15019	.....	SK10185
1797	NTE747	ECG747	.....	SK3279
1798	NTE5204AK	ECG5204AK	.....	SK175
1799	.....	ECG9974	.....	.....
1800	NTE4508B	ECG4508B	.....	SK4508B
1801	NTE960	ECG960	.....	SK3591
1802	NTE74178	ECG74178	.....	SK74178
1803	NTE5596	ECG5596	.....	SK6746
1804	NTE922	ECG922	.....	SK3567A
1805	NTE1194	ECG1194	.....	SK3484
1806	NTE5205AK	ECG5205AK	.....	SK177
1807	NTE6079	ECG6079	.....	SK7079
1808	NTE74S133	ECG74S133	.....	.....
1809	NTE74179	ECG74179	.....	SK74179
1810	NTE5207A	ECG5207A	.....	SK180
1811	.....	.....	.....	SK40061
1812	NTE9930	ECG9930	.....	.....
1813	NTE1729	ECG1729	.....	SK9912
1814	NTE314	ECG314	.....	SK3898
1815	NTE5206AK	ECG5206AK	.....	SK179
1816	NTE74S134	ECG74S134	.....	.....
1817	NTE950	ECG950	.....	SK9169
1818	NTE74180	ECG74180	.....	SK74180
1819	NTE4514B	ECG4514B	.....	SK4514B
1820	NTE9936	ECG9936	.....	.....
1821	NTE74LS33	ECG74LS33	.....	SK74LS33
1822	.....	.....	.....	SK3027
1823	NTE148A	ECG148A	.....	SK55V
1824	NTE9937	ECG9937	.....	.....
1825	NTE1903	ECG1903	.....	SK9221
1826	NTE1056	ECG1056	.....	SK3458
1827	NTE967	ECG967	.....	SK3673
1828	NTE74LS38	ECG74LS38	.....	SK74LS38
1829	NTE5207AK	ECG5207AK	.....	SK181
1830	NTE74LS42	ECG74LS42	.....	SK74LS42
1831	NTE74181	ECG74181	.....	SK74181
1832	NTE789	ECG789	.....	SK3078
1833	NTE9949	ECG9949	.....	.....
1834	NTE74LS47	ECG74LS47	.....	SK74LS47
1835	NTE2800	ECG2800	.....	.....
1836	NTE6009	ECG6009	.....	SK7209
1837	NTE5562	ECG5562	.....	SK3655
1838	NTE74LS48	ECG74LS48	.....	SK74LS48
1839	NTE74LS49	ECG74LS49	.....	SK74LS49
1840	NTE6011	ECG6011	.....	SK7211
1841	NTE386	ECG386	.....	SK9039
1842	NTE5208AK	ECG5208AK	.....	SK183
1843	NTE904	ECG904	.....	SK3542
1844	NTE5564	ECG5564	.....	SK3656
1845	NTE74182	ECG74182	.....	SK74182
1846	NTE74LS54	ECG74LS54	.....	SK74LS54
1847	.....	ECG5404	.....	.....
1848	NTE9961	ECG9961	.....	.....
1849	NTE8212	ECG8212	.....	.....
1850	NTE5209AK	ECG5209AK	.....	SK185
1851	NTE226MP	ECG226MP	.....	SK3086
1852	NTE8216	ECG8216	.....	SK9790
1853	NTE74LS63	.....	.....	.....
1854	NTE346	ECG346	.....	SK3529

REPL. CODE	NTE PART NO.	ECG PART NO.	RADIO SHACK PART NO.	RCA PART NO.
1855	NTE5210AK	ECG5210AK	.....	SK187
1856	NTE74LS73	ECG74LS73	.....	SK74LS73
1857	NTE74185	.....	.....	.....
1858	NTE8228	ECG8228	.....	.....
1859	NTE74LS75	ECG74LS75	.....	SK74LS75
1860	NTE5375	ECG5375	.....	SK6775
1861	NTE74LS77	ECG74LS77	.....	SK74LS77
1862	NTE74LS78	ECG74LS78	.....	SK74LS78
1863	NTE5211AK	ECG5211AK	.....	SK189
1864	NTE5332	ECG5332	.....	SK9232
1865	.....	ECG761	.....	.....
1866	NTE2030	ECG2030	.....	.....
1867	.....	ECG819	.....	.....
1868	.....	.....	.....	SK7683
1869	.....	.....	.....	SK9718
1870	NTE5160A	ECG5160A	.....	SK140X
1871	NTE74LS90	ECG74LS90	.....	SK74LS90
1872	.....	.....	.....	SK7698
1873	NTE5212AK	ECG5212AK	.....	SK191
1874	NTE74LS91	ECG74LS91	.....	.....
1875	NTE74S140	ECG74S140	.....	.....
1876	NTE74LS92	ECG74LS92	.....	SK74LS92
1877	NTE74LS93	ECG74LS93	.....	SK74LS93
1878	.....	.....	.....	SK6736
1879	NTE911	ECG911	.....	SK9070
1880	NTE5690	ECG5690	.....	SK5590
1881	NTE2415	ECG2415	.....	SK9962
1882	NTE6410	ECG6410	.....	SK9121
1883	NTE966	ECG966	276-1771	SK9592
1884	NTE5214AK	ECG5214AK	.....	SK195
1885	.....	.....	.....	SK7682
1886	NTE911D	ECG911D	.....	SK9071
1887	NTE2128	ECG2128	.....	SK10519
1888	NTE829	ECG829	.....	SK3891
1889	NTE5587	ECG5587	.....	SK6777
1890	NTE5178AK	ECG5178AK	.....	SK123
1891	NTE5215AK	ECG5215AK	.....	SK197
1892	NTE1345	ECG1345	.....	SK9998
1893	NTE3881	ECG3881	.....	SK2881
1894	NTE6157	ECG6157	.....	SK7357
1895	NTE74LS109A	ECG74LS109A	.....	SK74LS109
1896	NTE74H04	ECG74H04	.....	SK74H04
1897	NTE237	ECG282&427	.....	SK3299
1898	NTE5217AK	ECG5217AK	.....	SK201
1899	.....	.....	.....	SK9073
1900	NTE398	ECG398	.....	SK3930
1901	NTE74190	ECG74190	.....	SK74190
1902	.....	ECG817	.....	.....
1903	NTE5219AK	ECG5219AK	.....	SK205
1904	NTE4934	ECG4934	.....	SK10201
1905	NTE931	ECG931	.....	SK9067
1906	NTE74191	ECG74191	.....	SK74191
1907	NTE74S387	ECG74S387	.....	.....
1908	NTE940	ECG940	.....	SK9171
1909	.....	ECG1118	.....	.....
1910	NTE74192	ECG74192	.....	SK74192
1911	NTE309K	ECG309K	.....	SK3629
1912	.....	ECG5423	276-1067	SK3570
1913	NTE5221AK	ECG5221AK	.....	SK209
1914	NTE600	ECG600	.....	SK3863
1915	NTE74193	ECG74193	.....	SK74193
1916	.....	.....	.....	SK9337
1917	.....	.....	.....	SK5040
1918	.....	ECG9112	.....	.....
1919	.....	ECG1918	.....	SK9338
1920	NTE74S194	ECG74S194	.....	.....
1921	NTE4929	ECG4929	.....	SK10200
1922	NTE5222AK	ECG5222AK	.....	SK211
1923	.....	ECG5655	.....	SK5555
1924	.....	ECG5656	.....	SK5556
1925	.....	ECG109	.....	.....
1926	.....	ECG5657	.....	SK5557
1927	.....	ECG1891	.....	.....
1928	.....	ECG5720	.....	.....
1929	.....	ECG719	.....	.....
1930	NTE5223AK	ECG5223AK	.....	SK213
1931	NTE6090	ECG6090	.....	SK4911
1932	NTE74195	ECG74195	.....	SK74195
1933	NTE74H51	ECG74H51	.....	.....
1934	NTE1409N	ECG1409	.....	SK9198
1935	NTE306	ECG306	.....	SK3251
1936	NTE5224AK	ECG5224AK	.....	SK215
1937	.....	ECG5710	.....	.....
1938	NTE4027B	ECG4027B	.....	SK4027B
1939	NTE74196	ECG74196	.....	SK74196
1940	NTE1382	ECG1382	.....	SK7658
1941	NTE4935	ECG4935	.....	SK10202
1942	NTE5225AK	ECG5225AK	.....	SK217
1943	.....	.....	.....	SK3854
1944	NTE74S151	ECG74S151	.....	.....
1945	NTE74197	ECG74197	.....	SK74197
1946	NTE4024B	ECG4024B	.....	SK4024B
1947	.....	.....	.....	SK7C237
1948	.....	ECG2343	.....	SK10091
1949	.....	ECG1382	.....	SK7658
1950	NTE5226AK	ECG5226AK	.....	SK219
1951	NTE3022	ECG3022	276-041	SK2022
1952	NTE4510B	ECG4510B	.....	SK4510B
1953	NTE74198	ECG74198	.....	SK74198
1954	.....	ECG222	.....	.....
1955	NTE385	ECG385	.....	SK3946
1956	NTE56018	ECG56018	.....	SK10268
1957	NTE2344	ECG2344	.....	SK10092

REPL. CODE	NTE PART NO.	ECG PART NO.	RADIO SHACK PART NO.	RCA PART NO.
1958	.....	ECG598	.....	.....
1959	.....	ECG3173	.....	.....
1960	NTE74199	ECG74199	.....	SK74199
1961	NTE4951	ECG4951	.....	SK10204
1962	NTE6532	ECG6532	.....	.....
1963	NTE320	ECG320	.....	SK9605
1964	NTE941D	ECG941D	.....	SK3552
1965	NTE941SM	ECG941SM	.....	SK10074
1966	NTE351	ECG351	.....	SK3177
1967	NTE315	ECG315	.....	SK3250
1968	.....	ECG74HC240	.....	SK7C240
1969	.....	ECG772A	.....	.....
1970	NTE3000	ECG3000	.....	SK2000
1971	NTE941D	ECG941D	.....	.....
1972	NTE3003	ECG3003	.....	SK2003
1973	NTE322	ECG322	.....	SK3252
1974	NTE3002	ECG3002	.....	SK2002
1975	NTE6156	ECG6156	.....	SK7356
1976	NTE4959	ECG4959	.....	SK10206
1977	NTE1673	ECG1673	.....	SK9402
1978	NTE3001	ECG3001	.....	SK2001
1979	.....	.....	.....	SK7C241
1980	NTE97	ECG97	.....	SK9109
1981	NTE5424	ECG5424	.....	.....
1982	NTE2V150	ECG2V150	.....	SKMV150J
1983	NTE1103	ECG1103	.....	SK3281
1984	.....	.....	.....	SK2162
1985	.....	.....	.....	SK7C242
1986	NTE536A	ECG536A	.....	SK3900
1987	.....	ECG1914	.....	SK9331
1988	NTE4049	ECG4049	.....	SK4009UB
1989	NTE1916	ECG1916	.....	SK9332
1990	.....	.....	.....	SK7C243
1991	NTE5940	ECG5940	.....	SK3607
1992	NTE5941	ECG5941	.....	SK7145
1993	NTE1913	ECG1913	.....	SK9334
1994	.....	ECG74HC244	.....	SK7C244
1995	NTE6034	ECG6034	.....	SK7234
1996	NTE178MP	ECG178MP	276-1122	SK9091
1997	NTE1V014	ECG1V014	.....	SKMV14B
1998	NTE2V014	ECG2V014	.....	SKMV14C
1999	NTE5305	ECG5305	.....	SK3676
2000	NTE61MCP	ECG61MCP	.....	SK9925
2001	.....	.....	.....	SK3244
2002	NTE281	ECG281	276-2043	SK3359
2003	.....	.....	.....	SK7C245
2004	NTE5693	ECG5693	.....	SK3652
2005	NTE300	ECG300	.....	SK3178B
2006	NTE5695	ECG5695	.....	SK3509
2007	NTE5697	ECG5697	.....	SK3522
2008	NTE1234	ECG1234	.....	SK3487
2009	NTE74H52	ECG74H52	.....	.....
2010	NTE187	ECG187	.....	SK9076
2011	NTE852	ECG852	.....	SK9248
2012	.....	.....	.....	SK2168
2013	NTE4000	ECG4000	.....	SK4000UB
2014	NTE1715	ECG1715	.....	SK10021
2015	NTE1714S	ECG1714S	.....	SK9715
2016	.....	ECG755	.....	.....
2017	NTE175	ECG175	.....	SK3538
2018	NTE1045	ECG1045	.....	SK3101
2019	NTE382	ECG382	.....	SK3250
2020	NTE1120	ECG1120	.....	.....
2021	.....	.....	.....	SK9200
2022	.....	.....	.....	SK3466
2023	NTE2V300	ECG2V300	.....	SKMV320B
2024	NTE5174A	ECG5174A	.....	SK114
2025	NTE5569 N4	ECG5569 N4	.....	SK6719 N4
2026	.....	ECG5637	.....	.....
2027	NTE383	ECG383	.....	SK3841
2028	NTE361	ECG361	.....	SK9634
2029	.....	.....	.....	SK7715
2030	NTE346	ECG346	.....	SK9038
2031	NTE1676	ECG1676	.....	SK7653
2032	NTE793	ECG793	.....	.....
2033	.....	ECG56008	.....	SK3660
2034	NTE81	ECG81	.....	SK9114
2035	NTE300	ECG300	.....	SK3464
2036	.....	ECG3157	.....	.....
2037	NTE2114	ECG2114	.....	SK2214
2038	NTE1174	ECG1174	.....	SK3186
2039	NTE299	ECG299	.....	SK3298
2040	NTE165	ECG165	276-2055	SK3710
2041	NTE16001	ECG15	.....	SK3132
2042	NTE4503B	ECG40097B	.....	SK4503B
2043	NTE1532	ECG1532	.....	SK9320
2044	NTE4002B	ECG4002B	.....	SK4002B
2045	NTE74LS643	ECG74LS643	.....	SK7CT643
2046	NTE1104	ECG1104	.....	SK3225
2047	NTE56	ECG56	.....	SK3929
2048	NTE280	ECG87	276-2041	SK3619
2049	NTE5836	ECG5838	.....	SK7038
2050	NTE195A	ECG123	276-2009	SK3024
2051	NTE1135	ECG1135	.....	SK3876
2052	NTE1466	ECG1466	.....	SK9212
2053	.....	ECG35	.....	SK3111
2054	.....	.....	.....	SK7C251
2055	NTE1710	ECG1710	.....	SK9951
2056	NTE1712	ECG1712	.....	SK9953
2057	NTE1713	ECG1713	.....	SK9954
2058	NTE56	ECG56	.....	SK9364
2059	NTE76	ECG76	.....	SK9600
2060	.....	ECG617	.....	.....

REPL. CODE	NTE PART NO.	ECG PART NO.	RADIO SHACK PART NO.	RCA PART NO.
2061	NTE4025B	ECG4025B	.....	SK4025B
2062	NTE1628	ECG1628	.....	SK4834
2063	.....	ECG8233	.....	.....
2064	NTE85	ECG85	276-2009	SK3250
2065	NTE5840	ECG5842	.....	SK7042
2066	.....	ECG579	.....	.....
2067	NTE9951	ECG9951	.....	.....
2068	NTE588	ECG588	.....	SK5014
2069	NTE8234	ECG8234	.....	.....
2070	NTE5842	ECG5842	.....	SK7042
2071	.....	.....	.....	SK7712
2072	NTE509	ECG509/R-3AT2	.....	SK3757
2073	NTE510	ECG510/R-3DB3	.....	SK3758
2074	NTE512	ECG512/R-6DW4	.....	SK3760
2075	NTE6810	ECG6810	.....	SK6810
2076	NTE8235	ECG8235	.....	.....
2077	NTE5846	ECG5846	.....	SK7046
2078	NTE5462	ECG5462	.....	SK9291
2079	NTE1759	ECG1759	.....	SK10003
2080	NTE363	ECG363	.....	SK9636
2081	.....	ECG87	.....	.....
2082	NTE365	ECG365	.....	SK9638
2083	NTE3120	ECG3120	.....	SK10518
2084	NTE5461	ECG5461	.....	SK9290
2085	NTE369	ECG369	.....	SK3131A
2086	NTE9933	ECG9933	.....	.....
2087	.....	ECG80C97	.....	SK4503B
2088	.....	.....	.....	SK9957
2089	NTE760	ECG760	.....	.....
2090	NTE74H53	ECG74H53	.....	.....
2091	NTE5163A	ECG5163A	.....	SK170X
2092	NTE1719	ECG1719	.....	SK7719
2093	NTE922M	ECG922M	.....	SK3668
2094	NTE1558	ECG1558	.....	SK9244
2095	NTE873	ECG873	.....	SK7718
2096	NTE3045	ECG3045	.....	SK10327
2097	NTE528	ECG528	.....	SK3906
2098	NTE374	ECG374	.....	.....
2099	NTE1847	ECG1847	.....	SK10084
2100	NTE74C00	ECG74C00	.....	SK9806
2101	NTE5176AK	ECG5176AK	.....	SK119
2102	NTE74C02	ECG74C02	.....	SK7C02
2103	.....	ECG74HC257	.....	SK7C257
2104	NTE1725	ECG1725	.....	SK7705
2105	NTE6809E	ECG6809E	.....	SK10456
2106	NTE74C08	ECG74C08	.....	SK9785
2107	NTE74C10	ECG74C10	.....	SK74C10
2108	NTE4512B	ECG4512B	.....	SK4512B
2109	NTE1650	ECG1650	.....	SK7606
2110	NTE74C20	ECG74C20	.....	SK74C20
2111	NTE1058	ECG1058	.....	SK3459
2112	NTE283	ECG94	.....	SK3438
2113	NTE74S124	ECG74S124	.....	.....
2114	NTE93L08	ECG93L08	.....	.....
2115	NTE74LS112A	ECG74LS112A	.....	.....
2116	NTE2331	ECG2331	.....	SK10088
2117	NTE178MP	ECG178MP	276-1122	SK3311
2118	NTE90	ECG90	.....	SK3244
2119	NTE74S174	ECG74S174	.....	SK74S174
2120	NTE4903	ECG4903	.....	SK10194
2121	NTE74S132	.....	.....	.....
2122	.....	ECG1492	.....	.....
2123	NTE6401	ECG6401	.....	SK9123
2124	NTE5929	ECG5929	.....	SK10431
2125	NTE74S138	ECG74S138	.....	.....
2126	NTE6118	ECG6118	.....	SK10253
2127	NTE280MP	ECG280MP	.....	SK3360
2128	NTE74S175	ECG74S175	.....	.....
2129	NTE74221	ECG74221	.....	SK74221
2130	NTE74C42	ECG74C42	.....	SK9784
2131	.....	ECG840	.....	.....
2132	.....	ECG56008	.....	.....
2133	.....	.....	.....	SK9118
2134	.....	ECG5589	.....	.....
2135	NTE74C48	ECG74C48	.....	SK74C48
2136	.....	.....	.....	SK74LS266
2137	NTE6408	ECG6408	.....	SK3523
2138	NTE74S153	ECG74S153	.....	SK1915
2139	NTE4026B	ECG4026B	.....	SK4026B
2140	NTE5820	ECG5820	.....	SK9284
2141	NTE74S158	ECG74S158	.....	.....
2142	NTE1021	ECG1021	.....	.....
2143	NTE74S163	.....	.....	.....
2144	NTE5092A	ECG5092A	.....	.....
2145	.....	ECG1113	.....	SK9190
2146	NTE6113	ECG6113	.....	SK10215
2147	NTE705A	ECG705A	.....	SK3134
2148	NTE74C73	ECG74C73	.....	SK74C73
2149	NTE74C74	ECG74C74	.....	SK9783
2150	NTE74C76	ECG74C76	.....	SK74C76
2151	NTE74S181	ECG74S181	.....	.....
2152	NTE74S182	.....	.....	.....
2153	.....	ECG792	.....	.....
2154	.....	ECG870	.....	SK9992
2155	NTE1930	ECG1930	.....	SK7643
2156	NTE349	ECG349	.....	SK9624
2157	NTE74C85	ECG74C85	.....	SK9782
2158	NTE74H54	ECG74H54	.....	.....
2159	.....	ECG74176	.....	.....
2160	NTE74C90	ECG74C90	.....	SK9781
2161	NTE74S288	ECG74S288	.....	.....
2162	.....	ECG2388	.....	SK10131
2163	NTE74C93	ECG74C93	.....	SK74C93

REPL. CODE	NTE PART NO.	ECG PART NO.	RADIO SHACK PART NO.	RCA PART NO.
2164	NTE1754	ECG1754		SK10002
2165	NTE6051	ECG6051		SK7251
2166	NTE74LS76A	ECG74LS76A		SK74LS76A
2167	NTE103&411	ECG103&411		
2168	NTE6055	ECG6055		SK7255
2169	NTE289A	ECG289A	276-2009	SK3479
2170	NTE1575	ECG1575		SK9195
2171	NTE2308	ECG2308		SK4908
2172	NTE1893	ECG1893		
2173		ECG8250		
2174	NTE5521	ECG5521		SK6621
2175		ECG5305		
2176	NTE199	ECG199	276-2016	SK3122
2177	NTE6061	ECG6061		SK7261
2178	NTE6230	ECG6230		SK10435
2179	NTE1211	ECG1211		SK3739
2180	NTE1751	ECG1751		
2181	NTE3026	ECG3026	276-025	SK2026
2182	NTE8301	ECG8301		
2183	NTE6065	ECG6065		SK7265
2184	NTE74S251	ECG74S251		
2185	NTE3079	ECG3079		SK2079
2186	NTE296	ECG296		SK3036
2187	NTE181	ECG181		
2188		ECG5671		SK10467
2189	NTE591	ECG591	276-1122 N1	SK9940
2190	NTE74S257			
2191	NTE74S258	ECG74S258		
2192	NTE3078	ECG3078		SK2078
2193	NTE74S260			
2194	NTE77	ECG77		SK9602
2195	NTE107	ECG107	276-2016	SK3356
2196		ECG74HC273		SK7C273
2197				SK3672
2198	NTE329	ECG329		SK3195
2199	NTE74LS490	ECG74LS490		SK74LS490
2200	NTE277	ECG277		
2201		ECG3020		SK2020
2202	NTE6069	ECG6069		SK7269
2203	NTE74S03	ECG74S03		
2204	NTE74LS83A	ECG74LS83A		SK74LS83
2205	NTE74S280			
2206	NTE5180A	ECG5180A		SK126
2207	NTE924	ECG924		SK9128
2208	NTE15	ECG15		SK9663
2209	NTE74S287	ECG74S287		SK190X
2210	NTE5165A	ECG5165A		
2211		ECG6206		SK9780
2212	NTE74LS295A	ECG74LS295A		
2213	NTE4028B	ECG4028B		SK4028B
2214				SK3265
2215		ECG167		
2216	NTE1133	ECG1133		SK3490
2217	NTE109	ECG109	276-1123	SK3087
2218	NTE4029B	ECG4029B		SK4029B
2219	NTE6246	ECG6246		SK9776
2220	NTE263	ECG263		SK3180
2221	NTE3046	ECG3046		SK2046
2222	NTE264	ECG264		SK3181A
2223	NTE74S02	ECG74S02		SK1917
2224	NTE972	ECG972		SK3670
2225		ECG2344		
2226		ECG5721		
2227	NTE7412	ECG7412		SK7412
2228	NTE7414	ECG7414		SK7414
2229				SK25A
2230	NTE277	ECG277		SK3111
2231	NTE938M	ECG938M		SK9167
2232	NTE992	ECG992		SK3688
2233		ECG5711		
2234				SK7C280
2235				SK3444
2236	NTE5933	ECG5933		SK10433
2237	NTE1488	ECG1488		SK9818
2238	NTE1198	ECG1198		
2239	NTE1912	ECG1912		SK9337
2240		ECG6220		
2241	NTE74LS113	ECG74LS113		SK74LS113
2242	NTE787	ECG787		SK3146
2243	NTE265	ECG265		SK3860
2244	NTE958	ECG958		SK3699
2245		ECG159		
2246	NTE1082	ECG1082		SK3461
2247	NTE1029	ECG1029		SK3368
2248	NTE74S04	ECG74S04		SK74S04
2249	NTE74S373			
2250		ECG5024A		
2251	NTE74S374			
2252	NTE9601	ECG9601		
2253	NTE54	ECG54		SK9391
2254	NTE1794	ECG1794		SK9878
2255	NTE5444	ECG5444		SK3634
2256	NTE2383	ECG2383		SK9507
2257				SK3479
2258		ECG6246		SK3079
2259		ECG6246		
2260	NTE8266	ECG8266		
2261	NTE92	ECG92		SK9446
2262	NTE244	ECG244		SK3183A
2263	NTE2716	ECG2716		SK2716
2264	NTE721	ECG721		SK7747
2265	NTE186A&187A	ECG186A&187A		SK3357&9076
2266		ECG763		
2267	NTE976	ECG976		SK3596
2268	NTE1236	ECG1236		SK7784
2269				SK4515B
2270	NTE9602	ECG9602		
2271	NTE192	ECG192		SK3137
2272				SK7437
2273	NTE1895	ECG1895		
2274	NTE74249	ECG74249		
2275	NTE5897	ECG5897		SK7111
2276	NTE152	ECG152	276-2020	SK3197
2277		ECG74249		
2278	NTE5702	ECG5702		SK10436
2279	NTE2060	ECG2060		SK3966
2280	NTE282	ECG282		SK3049
2281		ECG1318		
2282	NTE5703	ECG5703		SK10437
2283	NTE74251	ECG74251		SK74251
2284	NTE5629	ECG5629	276-1000	SK4918
2285	NTE988	ECG988		SK3973
2286	NTE74LS114	ECG74LS114		SK74LS114
2287	NTE1880	ECG1880		SK10170
2288	NTE1687	ECG1687		SK7711
2289	NTE1110	ECG1110		SK3229
2290	NTE1203	ECG1203		
2291		ECG2117		
2292	NTE4044B	ECG4044B		SK4044B
2293	NTE69	ECG69		
2294				SK9011
2295	NTE5720	ECG5720		SK10417
2296	NTE318	ECG318		SK9604
2297	NTE3032	ECG3032		SK2032
2298		ECG282&427		
2299	NTE6103	ECG6103		SK10210
2300	NTE1092	ECG1092		SK3472
2301	NTE5043A	ECG5043A		SK60A
2302	NTE995	ECG995		SK9209
2303				SK9364
2304	NTE74S472	ECG74S472		
2305	NTE74S05	ECG74S05		
2306	NTE74S474	ECG74S474		
2307	NTE2357	ECG2357		SK10124
2308	NTE74S475	ECG74S475		
2309	NTE1V017	ECG1V017		SKMV17B
2310	NTE2V017	ECG2V017		SKMV17C
2311	NTE230	ECG230		SK3857
2312	NTE1528	ECG1528		
2313	NTE310	ECG310		SK3856
2314				SK9258
2315	NTE4047B	ECG4047B		SK4047B
2316		ECG2410		
2317				SK9036
2318	NTE1883	ECG1883		SK10173
2319				SK9352
2320	NTE239	ECG239		SK4914
2321		ECG279A		
2322		ECG2404		
2323	NTE1659	ECG1659		SK3874
2324	NTE6073	ECG6073		SK7273
2325	NTE66	ECG66	276-2072	SK9165
2326	NTE5403	ECG5404	276-1067	SK3627
2327	NTE5987	ECG5987		SK7111
2328				SK7C00
2329				SK9776
2330	NTE1855	ECG1855		SK10085
2331	NTE4516B	ECG4516B		SK4516B
2332	NTE56014	ECG5679		SK3993
2333	NTE2406	ECG2406		
2334	NTE9670	ECG9670		
2335	NTE151A N3	ECG151A N3		SK110V N3
2336	NTE5650	ECG5650	276-1000	SK5550
2337	NTE5651	ECG5651	276-1000	SK5551
2338	NTE329	ECG329		SK3024
2339	NTE975SM	ECG975SM		SK10455
2340	NTE5652	ECG5652	276-1000	SK5552
2341	NTE2164	ECG2164		SK10297
2342	NTE947D	ECG947D		SK3556
2343	NTE198	ECG198		SK3103A
2344				SKMV373A
2345				SK3261
2346				SK3883
2347	NTE5322	ECG5322		SK3680
2348	NTE1777	ECG1777		SK9870
2349	NTE5901	ECG5901		SK7101
2350	NTE2334	ECG2334		SK9475
2351	NTE2304	ECG2304		SK9985
2352	NTE947	ECG947		SK3526
2353	NTE5324	ECG5324		SK3681
2354	NTE5326	ECG5326		SK3682
2355	NTE284MP	ECG284MP		SK10309
2356	NTE5327	ECG5327		SK9087
2357	NTE5328	ECG5328		SK9088
2358	NTE1733	ECG1733		SK7809
2359	NTE289A	ECG289A	276-2009	SK3244
2360	NTE5905	ECG5905		SK7105
2361	NTE128	ECG123	276-2030	SK3024
2362	NTE3080	ECG3080		SK4832
2363	NTE8098	ECG8098		SK849
2364	NTE1202	ECG1202		SK3087
2365	NTE107	ECG107	276-2016	SK3018
2366				SK9444
2367	NTE5640	ECG5640	276-1000	SK6740
2368	NTE4093B	ECG4093B		SK4093B
2369	NTE1735	ECG1735		SK7811
2370	NTE1667	ECG1667		SK4831
2371	NTE5643	ECG5643		SK3519
2372	NTE74S570	ECG74S570		
2373	NTE74S571	ECG74S571		
2374	NTE74S572	ECG74S572		
2375		ECG289		SK3450
2376	NTE74S573	ECG74S573		
2377	NTE1045	ECG1045		
2378	NTE5641	ECG5641	276-1000	SK3583
2379	NTE5134A	ECG5134A		SK19X
2380	NTE4900	ECG4900		SK9812
2381	NTE5173A	ECG5173A		
2382	NTE74H11	ECG74H11		
2383	NTE5138A	ECG5138A		SK25X
2384	NTE5306	ECG5306		SK3677
2385	NTE5175A	ECG5175A		SK116
2386	NTE123A	ECG123A	276-1617	SK3122
2387	NTE5175AK	ECG5175AK		SK117
2388	NTE1015	ECG1015		SK7754
2389	NTE1822	ECG1822		SK9902
2390	NTE1016	ECG1016		SK7755
2391	NTE5177A	ECG5177A		SK120
2392				SK74LS00
2393				SK7C08
2394	NTE5177AK	ECG5177AK		SK121
2395	NTE42	ECG42		SK9425
2396				SK3577
2397	NTE1881	ECG1881		SK10171
2398	NTE388	ECG388		SK3947
2399	NTE5179A	ECG5179A		SK124
2400	NTE5179AK	ECG5179AK		SK125
2401	NTE1884	ECG1884		SK10174
2402	NTE1823	ECG1823		
2403	NTE1872	ECG1872		SK10164
2404	NTE2350	ECG2350		SK10123
2405	NTE5022A	ECG5022A		
2406	NTE5184A	ECG5184A		SK134
2407				SK3441
2408	NTE5184AK	ECG5184AK		SK135
2409	NTE1679	ECG1679		SK10244
2410		ECG1823		
2411	NTE243	ECG243		SK3182
2412	NTE2349	ECG2349		SK10122
2413				SK7C10
2414	NTE5023A	ECG5023A		
2415	NTE248	ECG248		SK3949
2416	NTE387	ECG387		SK9040
2417	NTE9668	ECG9668		
2418				SK7C11
2419				SK30A
2420	NTE283	ECG283		SK3439A
2421	NTE130	ECG87		SK9237
2422	NTE247	ECG247		SK3948
2423	NTE1017	ECG1017		
2424	NTE389	ECG389		SK9261
2425	NTE5317	ECG5317		SK9037
2426	NTE74S10	ECG74S10		
2427	NTE123A	ECG123A	276-1617	SK3132
2428	NTE74S11	ECG74S11		SK74S11
2429	NTE250	ECG250		SK9441
2430	NTE5491	ECG5491		SK6791
2431	NTE5201A	ECG5201A		SK168
2432	NTE74S15	ECG74S15		
2433	NTE975	ECG975		SK3644
2434	NTE5201AK	ECG5201AK		SK169
2435	NTE1171	ECG1171		SK3645
2436		ECG489		SK10465
2437	NTE199	ECG85	276-2016	SK3124A
2438	NTE731	ECG731		SK3170
2439	NTE454	ECG454		SK3991
2440	NTE123AP	ECG85	276-2016	SK3124A
2441	NTE289	ECG108	276-2016	SK3039
2442	NTE74S22	ECG74S22		SK74S22
2443	NTE1918	ECG1918		SK9338
2444	NTE74H73	ECG74H73		
2445		ECG1026		
2446				SK3899
2447				SK7C14
2448				SK24A
2449	NTE82	ECG82		SK9115
2450	NTE74LS197	ECG74LS197		SK1921
2451	NTE1928	ECG1928		SK7642
2452	NTE18	ECG18	276-2009	SK9666
2453		ECG1111		
2454	NTE6072	ECG6072		SK7272
2455	NTE5213AK	ECG5213AK		SK193
2456	NTE74S40	ECG74S40		
2457		ECG1018		
2458		ECG5018A		
2459	NTE5218AK	ECG5218AK		SK203
2460	NTE810A	ECG810A		SK7730
2461	NTE159	ECG159	276-2023	SK3114A
2462	NTE1112	ECG1112		
2463	NTE382	ECG382		SK9352
2464	NTE17	ECG17	276-2023	SK9665
2465	NTE327	ECG327		SK3945
2466		ECG937		SK3690
2467	NTE604			SK3087
2468	NTE8314	ECG8314		
2469		ECG1706		
2470		ECG2354		
2471	NTE5482	ECG5482		SK3941
2472	NTE74H74	ECG74H74		

REPL. CODE	NTE PART NO.	ECG PART NO.	RADIO SHACK PART NO.	RCA PART NO.
2473	NTE836	ECG836	.....	SK3206
2474	.....	.....	.....	SK3829
2475	NTE236	ECG236	.....	SK3197
2476	NTE74S64	ECG74S64	.....	.....
2477	NTE74S65	ECG74S65	.....	.....
2478	.....	.....	.....	SK3697
2479	NTE5228AK	ECG5228AK	.....	SK223
2480	NTE818	ECG818	.....	SK3207
2481	NTE843	ECG843	.....	SK3208
2482	NTE4068B	ECG4068B	.....	SK4068B
2483	NTE74S74	ECG74S74	.....	SK74S74
2484	NTE1152	ECG1152	.....	.....
2485	NTE360	ECG360	.....	SK9633
2486	NTE5231AK	ECG5231AK	.....	SK229
2487	NTE1019	ECG1019	.....	SK7756
2488	NTE178MP	ECG178MP	276-1122	SK3031A
2489	NTE74S86	ECG74S86	.....	SK74S86
2490	NTE1815	ECG1815	.....	SK9891
2491	.....	ECG587	.....	.....
2492	NTE1453	ECG1453	.....	SK3702
2493	NTE6087	ECG6087	.....	SK9775
2494	NTE4070B	ECG4070B	.....	SK4070B
2495	NTE924M	ECG924M	.....	SK9129
2496	NTE555	ECG555	.....	SK9150A
2497	NTE5501	ECG5501	.....	SK3579
2498	.....	.....	.....	SK3893
2499	NTE5550	ECG5550	.....	SK6650
2500	.....	ECG5013A	.....	.....
2501	NTE506	ECG506	.....	SK5014
2502	NTE4072B	ECG4072B	.....	SK4072B
2503	NTE316	ECG316	.....	SK3018
2504	NTE344	ECG344	.....	SK9620
2505	NTE506	ECG506	.....	SK3318A
2506	NTE506	ECG506	.....	SK3175A
2507	NTE727	ECG727	.....	SK3071
2508	NTE1459	ECG1459	.....	SK7797
2509	NTE4032B	ECG4032B	.....	SK4032B
2510	NTE1215	ECG1215	.....	SK3738
2511	NTE1522	ECG1522	.....	SK9197
2512	NTE1170	ECG1170	.....	SK3874
2513	NTE1609	ECG1609	.....	SK10226
2514	.....	.....	.....	SK3124A
2515	NTE903	ECG903	.....	SK3540
2516	.....	ECG1170	.....	SK3874
2517	NTE1934X	ECG1934X	.....	SK10087
2518	NTE4075B	ECG4075B	.....	SK4075B
2519	NTE74LS540	ECG74LS540	.....	SK7CT540
2520	NTE586	ECG586	.....	SK9935
2521	.....	.....	.....	SKMV130P
2522	.....	ECG471	.....	.....
2523	NTE471	ECG471	.....	SK9643
2524	NTE529	ECG529	.....	SK3307
2525	NTE74LS541	ECG74LS541	.....	SK7CT541
2526	NTE86	ECG86	.....	SK9297
2527	.....	ECG728	.....	.....
2528	NTE47	ECG47	276-2016	SK3245
2529	.....	.....	.....	SK9041
2530	NTE949	ECG949	.....	SK3166
2531	NTE1711	ECG1711	.....	SK9952
2532	.....	ECG1732	.....	SK9760
2533	.....	.....	.....	SK9042
2534	NTE130	ECG87	276-2041	SK3297
2535	NTE804	ECG804	.....	SK3455
2536	NTE4077B	ECG4077B	.....	SK4077B
2537	NTE5963	ECG5963	.....	SK7363
2538	NTE791	ECG791	.....	SK3209
2539	NTE315	ECG315	.....	SK9137
2540	NTE918	ECG918	.....	SK9144
2541	NTE956	ECG956	276-1778	SK9215
2542	.....	ECG9662	.....	.....
2543	NTE918SM	ECG918SM	.....	SK10069
2544	NTE5967	ECG5967	.....	SK7367
2545	NTE918M	ECG918M	.....	SK9145
2546	NTE1005	ECG1005	.....	SK3723
2547	NTE74S08	ECG74S08	.....	.....
2548	NTE919D	ECG919D	.....	SK9218
2549	NTE706	ECG706	.....	SK3101
2550	NTE1179	ECG1179	.....	SK3737
2551	NTE1053	ECG1053	.....	SK7761
2552	NTE919	ECG919	.....	SK9217
2553	.....	.....	.....	SK26V
2554	NTE1054	ECG1054	.....	SK3457
2555	NTE1057	ECG1057	.....	SK7762
2556	NTE1055	ECG1055	.....	SK3494
2557	NTE74H87	ECG74H87	.....	.....
2558	.....	.....	.....	SK3083
2559	NTE1060	ECG1060	.....	SK3460
2560	NTE1061	ECG1061	.....	SK3228
2561	NTE1062	ECG1062	.....	SK3235
2562	.....	ECG1063	.....	SK7763
2563	NTE1064	ECG1064	.....	.....
2564	.....	ECG1065	.....	.....
2565	.....	ECG1066	.....	SK7764
2566	.....	ECG1067	.....	SK7765
2567	NTE1068	ECG1068	.....	.....
2568	NTE1072	ECG1072	.....	SK3295
2569	NTE1074	ECG1074	.....	SK3495
2570	NTE1181	ECG1181	.....	SK3706
2571	NTE1137	ECG1137	.....	SK7776
2572	NTE1634	ECG1634	.....	SK10234
2573	NTE1073	ECG1073	.....	SK3496
2574	NTE9661	ECG9661	.....	.....
2575	.....	ECG80	.....	.....

REPL. CODE	NTE PART NO.	ECG PART NO.	RADIO SHACK PART NO.	RCA PART NO.
2576	.....	ECG1069	.....	SK3227
2577	.....	.....	.....	SKMV18A
2578	.....	ECG1070	.....	SK3874
2579	NTE1168	ECG1168	.....	.....
2580	.....	ECG1071	.....	SK3226
2581	NTE1163	ECG1163	.....	.....
2582	NTE1002	ECG1002	.....	SK3481
2583	NTE978SM	ECG978SM	.....	SK10453
2584	.....	ECG808	.....	.....
2585	.....	.....	.....	SK29V
2586	.....	.....	.....	SK7C32
2587	.....	ECG5460	.....	.....
2588	NTE74290	ECG74290	.....	SK74290
2589	NTE394	ECG394	.....	SK3983
2590	NTE1180	ECG1180	.....	SK3888
2591	NTE5966	ECG5966	.....	SK7366
2592	NTE1255	ECG1255	.....	.....
2593	NTE726	ECG726	.....	SK3129
2594	NTE1188	ECG1188	.....	SK3022
2595	NTE9950	ECG9950	.....	.....
2596	NTE94	ECG86	.....	SK9297
2597	.....	ECG5550	.....	.....
2598	.....	ECG9941	.....	.....
2599	NTE1410	ECG1410	.....	SK9016
2600	NTE704	ECG704	.....	SK3023
2601	NTE1417	ECG1417	.....	SK9315
2602	NTE98	ECG98	.....	SK9111
2603	.....	.....	.....	SKMV132A
2604	NTE3033	ECG3033	.....	SK10324
2605	NTE74LS170	ECG74LS170	.....	.....
2606	NTE1106	ECG1106	.....	SK7771
2607	NTE1085	ECG1085	.....	SK3476
2608	NTE1102	ECG1102	.....	SK3224
2609	NTE1210	ECG1210	.....	SK9074
2610	NTE1101	ECG1101	.....	SK3283
2611	NTE4033B	ECG4033B	.....	SK4033B
2612	NTE3101	ECG3101	.....	SK4931
2613	NTE125	ECG125	276-1114	SK3033A
2614	NTE1241	ECG1241	.....	SK3828
2615	NTE1109	ECG1109	.....	SK3711
2616	NTE3102	ECG3102	.....	SK4932
2617	.....	ECG3103	.....	SK4916
2618	.....	ECG3539	.....	.....
2619	NTE6078	ECG6078	.....	SK9810
2620	NTE74293	ECG74293	.....	SK74293
2621	.....	.....	.....	SK3051
2622	NTE173BP	.....	.....	SK7332
2623	NTE5518	ECG5518	.....	SK3653
2624	NTE963	ECG963	.....	SK3672
2625	NTE5519	ECG5519	.....	SK3654
2626	NTE396	ECG396	.....	SK3104A
2627	.....	.....	.....	SK401B
2628	.....	.....	.....	SK403B
2629	NTE6022	ECG6022	.....	SK7222
2630	.....	.....	.....	SK7609
2631	NTE6044	ECG6044	.....	SK7244
2632	NTE1660	ECG1660	.....	SK3364
2633	NTE6026	ECG6026	.....	SK7226
2634	NTE124	ECG124	.....	SK3261
2635	NTE5484	ECG5485	.....	SK3943
2636	NTE389	ECG389	276-2055	SK9411
2637	NTE73	ECG73	.....	SK9273
2638	NTE74H61	ECG74H61	.....	.....
2639	NTE6030	ECG6034	.....	SK7234
2640	NTE6021	ECG6021	.....	SK7221
2641	NTE1658	ECG1658	.....	SK7736
2642	NTE74S09	ECG74S09	.....	.....
2643	NTE389	ECG389	.....	SK3710
2644	NTE1230	ECG1230	.....	.....
2645	.....	ECG1225	.....	.....
2646	.....	.....	.....	SK74LS32
2647	NTE568	ECG568	.....	SK3909
2648	.....	.....	.....	SK7645
2649	.....	.....	.....	SK7400
2650	NTE4520B	ECG4520B	.....	SK4520B
2651	.....	.....	.....	SK7410
2652	NTE6038	ECG6040	.....	SK7240
2653	.....	.....	.....	SK7420
2654	NTE229	ECG229	276-2058	SK3124A
2655	NTE74S08	ECG74S08	.....	SK74LS08
2656	.....	ECG760	.....	.....
2657	NTE6040	ECG6040	.....	SK7240
2658	.....	ECG1693	.....	.....
2659	.....	.....	.....	SK33A
2660	NTE93L16	ECG93L16	.....	.....
2661	NTE1714M	ECG1714M	.....	SK10019
2662	NTE900	ECG900	.....	SK3547
2663	NTE809	ECG809	.....	SK7727
2664	NTE901	ECG901	.....	SK3549
2665	.....	ECG5538	.....	.....
2666	NTE107	ECG107	276-2058	SK3132
2667	NTE6860	ECG6860	.....	SK9795
2668	NTE1541	ECG1541	.....	.....
2669	NTE1525	ECG1525	.....	SK7604
2670	NTE6023	ECG6023	.....	SK7223
2671	.....	ECG5539	.....	.....
2672	NTE2732	ECG2732	.....	SK1912
2673	NTE905	ECG905	.....	SK3546
2674	NTE784	ECG784	.....	SK3524
2675	NTE329	ECG329	.....	.....
2676	NTE906	ECG906	.....	SK3548
2677	NTE488	ECG488	.....	SK9659
2678	NTE30001	ECG3099	.....	SK10177

REPL. CODE	NTE PART NO.	ECG PART NO.	RADIO SHACK PART NO.	RCA PART NO.
2679	.....	.....	.....	SK3594
2680	NTE908	ECG908	.....	SK3539
2681	NTE785	ECG785	.....	.....
2682	.....	ECG3201	.....	.....
2683	.....	ECG6210	.....	.....
2684	NTE295	ECG295	.....	SK3197
2685	NTE907	ECG907	.....	SK3545
2686	NTE1461	ECG1461	.....	SK9989
2687	NTE121	ECG121	.....	SK3009
2688	.....	ECG786	.....	SK3140
2689	NTE711	ECG711	.....	.....
2690	.....	ECG5340A	.....	.....
2691	NTE121	ECG121	.....	SK3015
2692	.....	.....	.....	SK7710
2693	NTE342	ECG342	.....	SK9618
2694	NTE343	ECG343	.....	SK9619
2695	NTE5240AK	ECG5240AK	.....	SK511
2696	NTE917	ECG917	.....	SK3544
2697	NTE1911	ECG1911	.....	SK10052
2698	NTE5241AK	ECG5241AK	.....	SK513
2699	NTE340	ECG340	276-2009	.....
2700	NTE5242AK	ECG5242AK	.....	SK515
2701	NTE914	ECG914	.....	SK3541
2702	NTE2061	ECG2061	.....	SK7612
2703	NTE5243AK	ECG5243AK	.....	SK517
2704	NTE6408	ECG6408	.....	.....
2705	NTE74H62	ECG74H62	.....	.....
2706	NTE5244AK	ECG5244AK	.....	SK519
2707	NTE5245AK	ECG5245AK	.....	SK521
2708	.....	ECG380MP	.....	.....
2709	NTE957	ECG957	.....	SK9216
2710	NTE935	ECG935	.....	SK9344
2711	NTE5246AK	ECG5246AK	.....	SK523
2712	NTE5424	ECG5424	.....	SK3598
2713	NTE5247AK	ECG5247AK	.....	SK525
2714	NTE288	ECG288	.....	SK3715
2715	NTE834SM	ECG834SM	.....	SK10063
2716	NTE730	ECG730	.....	SK3143
2717	NTE5248AK	ECG5248AK	.....	SK527
2718	NTE1732	ECG1732	.....	SK9761
2719	NTE5250AK	ECG5250AK	.....	SK531
2720	.....	ECG781	.....	.....
2721	NTE902	ECG902	.....	SK9200
2722	NTE916	ECG916	.....	SK3550
2723	NTE2023	ECG2023	.....	SK3694
2724	NTE929	ECG929	.....	SK3695
2725	NTE5256AK	ECG5256AK	.....	SK543
2726	.....	ECG3202	.....	.....
2727	.....	ECG112	.....	.....
2728	NTE788	ECG788	.....	SK3829
2729	NTE5259AK	ECG5259AK	.....	SK549
2730	NTE107	ECG107	276-2016	SK3124A
2731	NTE5261AK	ECG5261AK	.....	SK553
2732	NTE3470	ECG3470	.....	SK7732
2733	NTE5265AK	ECG5265AK	.....	SK561
2734	.....	ECG1691	.....	.....
2735	NTE5267AK	ECG5267AK	.....	SK565
2736	NTE155	ECG155	.....	SK3839
2737	.....	ECG1244	.....	.....
2738	NTE1885	ECG1885	.....	SK10175
2739	NTE2303	ECG2303	.....	SK9485
2740	NTE289MP	ECG289AMP	.....	.....
2741	NTE6027	ECG6027	.....	SK7227
2742	NTE282	ECG282	.....	SK3847
2743	NTE278	ECG278	.....	SK3293
2744	NTE955SM	ECG955SM	.....	SK10450
2745	NTE5273AK	ECG5273AK	.....	SK577
2746	NTE1165	ECG1165	.....	SK3827
2747	.....	ECG76	.....	.....
2748	.....	.....	.....	SK9242
2749	NTE5275AK	ECG5275AK	.....	SK581
2750	NTE4035B	ECG4035B	.....	SK4035B
2751	NTE6074	ECG6074	.....	SK7074
2752	NTE5277AK	ECG5277AK	.....	SK585
2753	.....	ECG834	.....	.....
2754	NTE1166	ECG1166	.....	SK3827
2755	NTE930	ECG930	.....	SK3568
2756	NTE5279AK	ECG5279AK	.....	SK589
2757	NTE2309	ECG2309	.....	SK9488
2758	.....	ECG5304	.....	.....
2759	NTE1175	ECG1175	.....	SK3212
2760	NTE1612	ECG1612	.....	SK9817
2761	.....	.....	.....	SK9243
2762	NTE1176	ECG1176	.....	SK3210
2763	NTE1V020	ECG1V020	.....	SKMV20B
2764	NTE965	ECG965	.....	SK9168
2765	NTE6105	ECG6105	.....	SK10212
2766	NTE87	ECG87	276-2041	SK3297
2767	NTE1375	ECG1375	.....	SK7608
2768	NTE2300	ECG2300	.....	SK9131
2769	NTE2V020	ECG2V020	.....	SKMV20C
2770	NTE46	ECG46	.....	SK9461
2771	NTE1177	ECG1177	.....	SK3213
2772	NTE1619	ECG1619	.....	.....
2773	.....	ECG5340	.....	.....
2774	NTE702	ECG702	.....	SK9025
2775	NTE5286AK	ECG5286AK	.....	SK603
2776	NTE5287AK	ECG5287AK	.....	SK605
2777	NTE531	ECG531	.....	SK3300
2778	NTE5289AK	ECG5289AK	.....	SK609
2779	NTE1932	ECG1932	.....	.....
2780	NTE5290AK	ECG5290AK	.....	SK611
2781	NTE1627	ECG1627	.....	SK9816

REPL. CODE	NTE PART NO.	ECG PART NO.	RADIO SHACK PART NO.	RCA PART NO.
2782	NTE5486	ECG5487	.....	SK3944
2783	NTE5291AK	ECG5291AK	.....	SK613
2784	NTE506	ECG506	.....	SK3130
2785	NTE822	ECG822	.....	SK3919
2786	NTE6076	ECG6076	.....	SK7076
2787	NTE85	ECG85	.....	SK3122
2788	NTE5292AK	ECG5292AK	.....	SK615
2789	NTE948SM	ECG948SM	.....	SK10079
2790	NTE820	ECG820	.....	.....
2791	NTE5293AK	ECG5293AK	.....	SK617
2792	.....	.....	.....	SK9085
2793	NTE5294AK	ECG5294AK	.....	SK619
2794	NTE293	ECG293	.....	SK3250
2795	NTE5295AK	ECG5295AK	.....	SK621
2796	NTE948	ECG948	.....	SK9173
2797	NTE5296AK	ECG5296AK	.....	SK623
2798	NTE340	ECG340	276-2009	SK3842
2799	NTE1413	ECG1413	.....	SK7635
2800	NTE2024	ECG2024	.....	SK3667
2801	.....	.....	.....	SK3830
2802	NTE1721	ECG1721	.....	SK10024
2803	NTE982	ECG982	.....	SK3205
2804	NTE821	ECG821	.....	SK3882
2805	NTE6362	ECG6362	.....	.....
2806	NTE6068	ECG6068	.....	SK7268
2807	NTE74LS196	ECG74LS196	.....	SK74LS196
2808	NTE333	ECG333	.....	SK9609
2809	NTE6206	ECG6206	.....	SK9780
2810	NTE4522B	ECG4522B	.....	SK4522B
2811	NTE970	ECG970	.....	SK9339
2812	NTE1723	ECG1723	.....	SK10026
2813	NTE6054	ECG6054	.....	SK7254
2814	NTE1722	ECG1722	.....	SK10025
2815	NTE1655	ECG1655	.....	SK7687
2816	NTE5594	ECG5594	.....	SK6744
2817	NTE63	ECG63	.....	SK9371
2818	NTE6078	ECG6078	.....	SK7078
2819	NTE4007	ECG4007	.....	SK4007UB
2820	NTE62	ECG62	.....	.....
2821	.....	.....	.....	SK3293
2822	.....	ECG2338	.....	SK9480
2823	NTE6060	ECG6060	.....	SK7260
2824	NTE10	ECG10	.....	SK9139
2825	.....	ECG366	.....	.....
2826	.....	ECG988	.....	.....
2827	NTE1083	ECG1083	.....	.....
2828	NTE6031	ECG6035	.....	SK7245
2829	NTE5149A	ECG5149A	.....	SK60X
2830	.....	.....	.....	SK3362
2831	NTE5104A	ECG5104A	.....	SK190V
2832	.....	.....	.....	SK3249
2833	NTE47	ECG47	.....	SK9459
2834	NTE1090	ECG1090	.....	SK3291
2835	.....	ECG74S479	.....	.....
2836	NTE932	ECG932	.....	SK9340
2837	NTE1148	ECG1148	.....	SK3292
2838	.....	.....	.....	SK9241
2839	NTE102A&103A	ECG102A&103A	.....	SK3004&3835
2840	NTE9924	ECG9924	.....	.....
2841	NTE367	ECG367	.....	SK9640
2842	NTE978C	ECG978C	.....	SK10454
2843	NTE15007	ECG1860	.....	SK9945
2844	NTE6064	ECG6064	.....	SK7264
2845	NTE1140	ECG1140	.....	SK3473
2846	NTE74	ECG74	.....	SK9274
2847	NTE5001A	ECG5001A	.....	SK2A5
2848	NTE5530	ECG5531	.....	SK6631
2849	NTE1027	ECG1027	.....	.....
2850	NTE74LS126A	ECG74LS126	.....	SK7CT126
2851	NTE5722	ECG5722	.....	SK10421
2852	NTE1738	ECG1738	.....	SK9359
2853	.....	.....	.....	SK7C365
2854	NTE928SM	ECG928SM	.....	SK10073
2855	NTE1047	ECG1047	.....	SK7760
2856	.....	ECG346	.....	.....
2857	NTE320F	ECG320F	.....	SK9606
2858	.....	.....	.....	SK7C366
2859	.....	ECG1084	.....	.....
2860	NTE1086	ECG1086	.....	.....
2861	NTE452	ECG452	.....	SK9072
2862	NTE1034	ECG1034	.....	.....
2863	NTE925	ECG925	.....	SK9174
2864	NTE1050	ECG1050	.....	.....
2865	.....	ECG928S	.....	.....
2866	NTE869	ECG869	.....	SK10066
2867	.....	.....	.....	SK7C367
2868	NTE1616	ECG1616	.....	SK7735
2869	NTE254	ECG254	.....	SK3997
2870	.....	.....	.....	SK7C368
2871	.....	ECG9110	.....	.....
2872	NTE5896	ECG5896	.....	SK7096
2873	NTE5982	ECG5982	.....	SK7182
2874	NTE319P	ECG319P	276-2009	SK3246A
2875	NTE178MP	ECG178MP	276-1122	SK9001
2876	.....	.....	.....	SK36A
2877	.....	ECG2321	.....	.....
2878	.....	ECG770	.....	.....
2879	NTE6035	ECG6035	.....	SK7235
2880	NTE2312	ECG2312	.....	SK10000
2881	.....	ECG74S478	.....	SK9703
2882	NTE382	ECG382	.....	SK3849
2883	.....	ECG375	.....	SK3929
2884	NTE1529	ECG1529	.....	SK7804
2885	NTE52	ECG52	.....	SK3995
2886	NTE1160	ECG1160	.....	SK7775
2887	.....	ECG74LS95	.....	.....
2888	NTE1552	ECG1552	.....	SK9314
2889	NTE5506	ECG5507	.....	SK3580
2890	.....	.....	.....	SK9948
2891	NTE2402	ECG2402	.....	SK10095
2892	.....	ECG74HC373	.....	SK7C373
2893	NTE1848	ECG1848	.....	SK10148
2894	.....	ECG928M	.....	.....
2895	NTE55	ECG55	.....	SK3441
2896	NTE40	ECG40	.....	SK9423
2897	.....	ECG5342	.....	.....
2898	NTE1563	ECG1563	.....	SK7648
2899	.....	ECG74HC374	.....	SK7C374
2900	NTE386	ECG386	.....	SK3995
2901	NTE123AP	ECG123A	276-2009	SK3444
2902	NTE745	ECG745	.....	.....
2903	NTE1205	ECG1205	.....	SK3482
2904	NTE5471	ECG5471	.....	SK10259
2905	NTE5473	ECG5474	276-1020	SK10261
2906	NTE96LS02	ECG96LS02	.....	.....
2907	NTE1V035	ECG1V035	.....	SKMV35B
2908	NTE5474	ECG5474	.....	SK10261
2909	.....	ECG8063	.....	SK814
2910	NTE4555B	ECG4555B	.....	SK4555B
2911	.....	ECG380	.....	.....
2912	NTE7497	ECG7497	.....	SK7497
2913	NTE2V035	ECG2V035	.....	SKMV35C
2914	NTE1161	ECG1161	.....	.....
2915	NTE8070	ECG8070	.....	SK821
2916	NTE8076	ECG8076	.....	SK827
2917	NTE461	ECG461	.....	SK9148
2918	NTE317	ECG317	.....	SK9603
2919	NTE44	ECG44	.....	SK9427
2920	NTE8081	ECG8081	.....	SK832
2921	NTE1134	ECG1134	.....	SK3489
2922	NTE457	ECG457	276-2062	SK9161
2923	NTE8085	ECG8085	.....	SK836
2924	NTE195A	ECG195A	.....	SK3479
2925	NTE5012A	ECG5021A	276-563	SK12A
2926	NTE2361	ECG2361	.....	SK10093
2927	NTE8090	ECG8090	.....	SK841
2928	NTE74C240	ECG74C240	.....	SK7C240
2929	NTE1797	ECG1797	.....	SK9753
2930	NTE74C04	ECG74C04	.....	SK74C04
2931	.....	ECG9111	.....	.....
2932	NTE1263	ECG1263	.....	SK3920
2933	NTE8096	ECG8096	.....	SK847
2934	NTE114	ECG114	276-1101	SK3296
2935	NTE8103	ECG8103	.....	SK854
2936	NTE75	ECG75	.....	SK9275
2937	NTE116 N5	ECG116 N5	276-1104 N5	SK3017B N5
2938	NTE116 N7	ECG116 N7	276-1104 N7	SK3313 N7
2939	NTE5823	ECG5823	.....	SK9287
2940	NTE8108	ECG8108	.....	SK859
2941	NTE74H103	ECG74H103	.....	.....
2942	NTE253	ECG253	.....	SK9370
2943	NTE4031B	ECG4031B	.....	SK4031B
2944	NTE8115	ECG8115	.....	SK866
2945	NTE8118	ECG8118	.....	SK869
2946	NTE6039	ECG6041	.....	SK7245
2947	.....	ECG800	.....	.....
2948	NTE8125	ECG8125	.....	SK876
2949	HVD-1	ECG-HIDIV-1	.....	SK3868
2950	HVD-2	ECG-HIDIV-2	.....	SK3869
2951	HVD-4	ECG-HIDIV-4	.....	SK3871
2952	HVD-3	ECG-HIDIV-3	.....	SK3870
2953	NTE4038B	ECG4038B	.....	SK4038B
2954	NTE534	ECG534	.....	SK3305
2955	NTE521	ECG521	.....	.....
2956	NTE538	ECG538	.....	SK3310
2957	NTE535	ECG535	.....	SK3902
2958	.....	ECG802	.....	SK3277
2959	NTE326	ECG326	.....	SK3746
2960	NTE282	ECG282	.....	SK3444
2961	NTE2335	ECG2335	.....	SK10305
2962	NTE8139	ECG8139	.....	SK890
2963	.....	ECG64	.....	.....
2964	.....	ECG9663	.....	.....
2965	.....	.....	.....	SK9374
2966	NTE5721	ECG5721	.....	SK10419
2967	.....	ECG803	.....	SK3278
2968	NTE282	ECG282	.....	SK3265
2969	NTE241	ECG241	276-2020	SK9450
2970	NTE8149	ECG8149	.....	SK900
2971	.....	.....	.....	SK7C86
2972	NTE8213	ECG8213	.....	SK901
2973	NTE2307	ECG2307	.....	SK9483
2974	NTE5013T1	ECG5011T1	.....	.....
2975	NTE5061A	.....	.....	SK2V4
2976	NTE2320	ECG2320	.....	SK10118
2977	.....	ECG814A	.....	.....
2978	NTE64	ECG64	.....	SK9372
2979	.....	ECG735	.....	.....
2980	NTE282	ECG282	.....	SK9368
2981	NTE5064A	.....	.....	SK2V8
2982	NTE5910	ECG5910	.....	SK7110
2983	NTE1636	ECG1636	.....	SK9245
2984	NTE8226	ECG8226	.....	SK914
2985	NTE51	ECG51	.....	SK9452
2986	NTE9669	ECG9669	.....	.....
2987	.....	.....	.....	SK3201
2988	NTE1156	ECG1156	.....	.....
2989	.....	ECG804	.....	SK9068
2990	NTE3007	ECG3007	276-026	SK2007
2991	.....	ECG1008	.....	.....
2992	NTE8242	ECG8242	.....	SK930
2993	.....	.....	.....	SK3617
2994	NTE5318	ECG5318	.....	SK10165
2995	NTE997	ECG997	.....	SK9172
2996	NTE46	ECG46	.....	SK9442
2997	NTE5094A	ECG5094A	.....	SK87V
2998	NTE1799	ECG1799	.....	SK9881
2999	NTE5154A	ECG5154A	.....	SK87X
3000	NTE942	ECG942	.....	SK3924
3001	.....	.....	.....	SK10140
3002	NTE74C14	ECG74C14	.....	SK9805
3003	NTE9664	ECG9664	.....	.....
3004	NTE104MP	ECG104MP	.....	SK3720
3005	NTE8167	ECG8167	.....	SK948
3006	NTE5319	ECG5319	.....	SK10271
3007	NTE8181	ECG8181	.....	SK952
3008	NTE52	ECG52	.....	SK9039
3009	NTE53	ECG53	.....	SK9484
3010	NTE9682	ECG9682	.....	.....
3011	.....	ECG56031	.....	.....
3012	NTE345	ECG345	.....	SK9621
3013	.....	.....	.....	SK22100
3014	.....	ECG74HC390	.....	SK7C390
3015	.....	ECG7018	.....	.....
3016	NTE9681	ECG9681	.....	.....
3017	NTE459	ECG459	.....	SK3112
3018	NTE74C221	ECG74C221	.....	SK74C221
3019	.....	.....	.....	SK22101
3020	NTE293MP	ECG293MP	.....	SK10314
3021	NTE5320	ECG5320	.....	SK10243
3022	NTE6041	ECG6041	.....	SK7241
3023	.....	.....	.....	SK22102
3024	NTE5485	ECG5485	.....	SK10263
3025	.....	ECG9665	.....	.....
3026	NTE5487	ECG5487	.....	SK10264
3027	NTE862	ECG862	.....	SK9822
3028	NTE1565	ECG1565	.....	SK9192
3029	.....	.....	.....	SK9133
3030	.....	.....	.....	SK9335
3031	.....	.....	.....	SK9261
3032	.....	ECG9931	.....	.....
3033	NTE876	ECG876	276-1705	SK10067
3034	NTE823	ECG823	276-1731	SK9210
3035	.....	ECG74HC393	.....	SK7C393
3036	NTE6502	ECG6502	.....	.....
3037	.....	ECG9667	.....	.....
3038	.....	.....	.....	SK3673
3039	NTE1508	ECG1508	.....	SK7638
3040	NTE1509	ECG1509	.....	SK7637
3041	NTE6507	ECG6507	.....	.....
3042	NTE1549	ECG1549	.....	.....
3043	NTE453	ECG453	.....	SK9853
3044	NTE2V025	ECG2V025	.....	SKMV25B
3045	NTE1618	ECG1618	.....	.....
3046	NTE2V030	ECG2V030	.....	SKMV30C
3047	NTE194	ECG194	.....	SK3479
3048	NTE552	ECG552	.....	SK5014
3049	NTE2V040	ECG2V040	.....	SKMV40C
3050	NTE824	ECG824	.....	SK9013
3051	.....	ECG1892	.....	SK10502
3052	NTE390	ECG390	.....	SK3958
3053	NTE36	ECG36	.....	SK9389
3054	NTE15023	ECG1859	.....	SK9946
3055	NTE1610	ECG1610	.....	.....
3056	NTE2V050	ECG2V050	.....	SKMV50C
3057	NTE828	ECG828	.....	SK9127
3058	NTE576	ECG576	.....	.....
3059	NTE2382	ECG2382	.....	SK10128
3060	NTE986	ECG986	.....	SK3918
3061	NTE2V060	ECG2V060	.....	SKMV60B
3062	.....	ECG352	.....	.....
3063	.....	.....	.....	SK9501
3064	.....	.....	.....	SK9453
3065	NTE85	ECG85	.....	SK9465
3066	.....	.....	.....	SK3118
3067	NTE3008	ECG3008	.....	SK2008
3068	NTE1798	ECG1798	.....	SK9745
3069	NTE2311	.....	ECG2311	.....
3070	NTE825	ECG825	.....	SK9126
3071	.....	.....	.....	SK8V2
3072	.....	ECG236	.....	.....
3073	NTE5500	ECG5501	.....	SK3579
3074	NTE1439	ECG1439	.....	SK3964
3075	NTE2V075	ECG2V075	.....	SKMV75B
3076	NTE5503	ECG5504	.....	SK3579
3077	.....	.....	.....	SK40116
3078	.....	.....	.....	SK3247
3079	.....	.....	.....	SK3114A
3080	NTE5505	ECG5507	.....	SK3580
3081	.....	.....	.....	SK9317
3082	NTE37	ECG37	.....	SK9415
3083	NTE54	ECG54	.....	SK3929
3084	.....	.....	.....	SK3929
3085	NTE4902	ECG4902	.....	SK10193
3086	.....	.....	.....	SK9391
3087	NTE2V095	ECG2V095	.....	SKMV95B
3088	NTE6043	ECG6043	.....	SK7243
3089	NTE943SM	ECG943SM	.....	SK10075
3090	NTE477	ECG477	.....	SK9649

REPL. CODE	NTE PART NO.	ECG PART NO.	RADIO SHACK PART NO.	RCA PART NO.
3091	.....	ECG199	.....	.....
3092	NTE7481	ECG7481	.....	SK7481
3093	NTE180MCP	ECG180MCP	.....	.....
3094	NTE2V115	ECG2V115	.....	SKMV115C
3095	NTE3011	ECG3011	.....	SK2011
3096	NTE377	ECG377	276-2020	SK9391
3097	.....	ECG588	.....	SK9938
3098	NTE1680	ECG1680	.....	.....
3099	NTE5118A	ECG5118A	.....	SK6X0
3100	NTE74C30	ECG74C30	.....	SK74C30
3101	.....	.....	.....	SK9205
3102	NTE467	ECG467	.....	SK9162
3103	.....	.....	.....	SK3054
3104	NTE459	ECG459	.....	SK9149
3105	NTE74C32	ECG74C32	.....	SK74C32
3106	.....	ECG1136	.....	.....
3107	.....	ECG2326	.....	SK10137
3108	.....	.....	.....	SK3555
3109	.....	ECG6354	.....	.....
3110	NTE5821	ECG5821	.....	SK9285
3111	.....	ECG6356	.....	.....
3112	NTE74LS624	ECG74LS624	.....	SK74LS624
3113	.....	ECG6358	.....	.....
3114	NTE2358	ECG2358	.....	SK10125
3115	.....	.....	.....	SK3714
3116	NTE4527B	ECG4527B	.....	SK4527B
3117	NTE5680	ECG5681	.....	SK6681
3118	NTE5681	ECG5681	.....	SK6681
3119	NTE5682	ECG5682	.....	SK6682
3120	NTE74LS625	ECG74LS625	.....	SK74LS625
3121	NTE5683	ECG5683	.....	SK6683
3122	NTE5684	ECG5685	.....	SK6685
3123	NTE5685	ECG5685	.....	SK6685
3124	NTE5686	ECG5687	.....	SK6686
3125	NTE74LS626	ECG74LS626	.....	SK74LS626
3126	NTE312	ECG459	.....	SK3448
3127	.....	ECG1850	.....	SK10150
3128	NTE3021	ECG3021	.....	SK2021
3129	NTE74H55	ECG74H55	.....	.....
3130	NTE1787	ECG1787	.....	SK9766
3131	.....	ECG348	.....	.....
3132	NTE1803	ECG1803	.....	SK9884
3133	NTE74LS627	ECG74LS627	.....	SK74LS627
3134	.....	ECG3012A	.....	SK10317
3135	.....	ECG345	.....	.....
3136	NTE242	ECG242	.....	SK9451
3137	.....	ECG74S454	.....	.....
3138	NTE6363	ECG6363	.....	.....
3139	NTE74S188	ECG74S188	.....	.....
3140	.....	ECG3013A	.....	SK10318
3141	.....	ECG344	.....	.....
3142	.....	ECG618	.....	.....
3143	NTE4918	ECG4918	.....	SK10195
3144	NTE584	ECG584	.....	SK3100
3145	NTE4041	ECG4041	.....	SK4041UB
3146	NTE74LS629	ECG74LS629	.....	SK74LS629
3147	.....	ECG580	.....	SK5020
3148	NTE80C95	ECG80C95	.....	.....
3149	.....	ECG377	.....	SK9391
3150	NTE80C96	ECG80C96	.....	.....
3151	NTE80C97	ECG80C97	.....	.....
3152	NTE887M	ECG887M	.....	SK9862
3153	NTE3025	ECG3025	.....	SK2025
3154	.....	.....	.....	SK9454
3155	.....	ECG5344	.....	.....
3156	NTE3035A	ECG3035A	.....	SK2035A
3157	.....	ECG5547	.....	.....
3158	NTE387MP	ECG387MP	.....	.....
3159	.....	ECG577	.....	SK5040
3160	NTE5980	ECG5980	.....	SK3610
3161	NTE1228	ECG1228	.....	SK3889
3162	NTE4926	ECG4926	.....	SK10197
3163	NTE590	ECG590	.....	SK9939
3164	NTE6508	ECG6508	.....	.....
3165	NTE352	ECG352	.....	SK9626
3166	NTE795	ECG795	.....	SK3237
3167	NTE1463	ECG1463	.....	SK9208
3168	NTE4528B	ECG4528B	.....	SK4098B
3169	NTE56022	ECG56022	.....	SK3661
3170	.....	.....	.....	SK3945
3171	NTE4928	ECG4928	.....	SK10199
3172	NTE987SM	ECG987SM	.....	SK10452
3173	NTE123AP	ECG123AP	276-2009	SK9433
3174	NTE5092A	ECG5092A	.....	SK68A
3175	NTE74LS259	ECG74LS259	.....	SK74LS259
3176	.....	ECG461	.....	.....
3177	NTE56024	ECG56024	.....	SK3662
3178	NTE6045	ECG6045	.....	SK7245
3179	NTE51	ECG51	.....	SK9085
3180	.....	.....	.....	SK4014B
3181	NTE2308	ECG2308	.....	SK9131
3182	.....	.....	.....	SK3656
3183	.....	ECG2065	.....	.....
3184	.....	.....	.....	SK9336
3185	NTE5566	ECG5566	.....	SK3657
3186	NTE213	ECG213	.....	SK3003A
3187	NTE2327	ECG2327	.....	SK10138
3188	.....	.....	.....	SK7358
3189	NTE750	ECG750	.....	SK3280
3190	.....	.....	.....	SK3674
3191	.....	ECG1477	.....	.....
3192	NTE56026	ECG56026	.....	SK3663
3193	.....	.....	.....	SK1802
3194	.....	ECG1667	.....	.....
3195	.....	.....	.....	SK9417
3196	NTE58	ECG58	.....	SK9448
3197	NTE87	ECG87	.....	SK3559
3198	NTE1470	ECG1470	.....	SK7799
3199	.....	ECG389	.....	SK9261
3200	.....	ECG601	.....	.....
3201	NTE2309	ECG2309	.....	SK9261
3202	NTE928S	ECG928S	.....	SK10072
3203	NTE3029A	ECG3029A	.....	SK10322
3204	.....	.....	.....	SK3652
3205	.....	ECG56006	.....	.....
3206	NTE1790	ECG1790	.....	SK9850
3207	NTE2057	ECG2057	.....	.....
3208	.....	.....	.....	SK3522
3209	.....	ECG1386	.....	SK7654
3210	NTE74390	ECG74390	.....	SK74390
3211	NTE506	ECG506	.....	SK5012
3212	.....	ECG2307	.....	.....
3213	NTE5508	ECG5509	.....	SK3504
3214	.....	.....	.....	SK4001B
3215	.....	ECG5695	.....	.....
3216	NTE1454	ECG1454	.....	SK9184
3217	NTE297MP	ECG297MP	.....	SK10315
3218	.....	ECG2300	.....	SK9131
3219	NTE312	ECG312	.....	SK3116
3220	NTE1844	ECG1844	.....	SK10147
3221	NTE74H05	ECG74H05	.....	.....
3222	.....	.....	.....	SK4010B
3223	NTE1685	ECG1685	.....	SK9948
3224	NTE292MCP	ECG292MCP	.....	SK10313
3225	NTE74393	ECG74393	.....	SK9835
3226	NTE2V420	ECG2V420	.....	SKMV420
3227	NTE5523	ECG5524	.....	SK6624
3228	.....	ECG328	.....	.....
3229	.....	.....	.....	SK4009UB
3230	.....	.....	.....	SK3971
3231	NTE1239	ECG1239	.....	SK3708
3232	NTE1097	ECG1097	.....	SK3446
3233	NTE74H71	ECG74H71	.....	.....
3234	NTE5943	ECG5945	.....	SK7153
3235	.....	ECG6085	.....	.....
3236	NTE53	ECG53	.....	SK9261
3237	NTE5525	ECG5527	.....	SK6627
3238	NTE1164	ECG1164	.....	.....
3239	NTE984	ECG984	.....	SK9276
3240	NTE5526	ECG5527	.....	SK6627
3241	NTE2419	ECG2419	.....	SK10111
3242	NTE1173	ECG1173	.....	.....
3243	NTE123AP	ECG216	276-2009	SK9433
3244	NTE5947	ECG5949	.....	SK7153
3245	NTE3023	ECG3023	.....	SK2023
3246	NTE5540	ECG5541	.....	SK10408
3247	.....	ECG128&427	.....	.....
3248	.....	.....	.....	SK9389
3249	NTE225	ECG225	.....	SK3045
3250	NTE1669	ECG1669	.....	.....
3251	NTE5949	ECG5949	.....	SK7153
3252	.....	ECG5431	276-1067	.....
3253	.....	ECG5422	276-1067	SK3570
3254	NTE978	ECG978	276-1728	SK3689
3255	NTE33	ECG33	.....	SK9466
3256	NTE5951	ECG5953	.....	SK7153
3257	.....	ECG74S473	.....	.....
3258	NTE195A	ECG195A	.....	SK3529
3259	NTE74LS279	ECG74LS279	.....	SK74LS279
3260	NTE5528	ECG5529	.....	SK6629
3261	NTE238	ECG238	276-2055	SK9411
3262	.....	.....	.....	SK3712
3263	NTE5953	ECG5953	.....	SK7153
3264	.....	ECG74HCT00	.....	.....
3265	.....	ECG74HCT04	.....	SK7CT04
3266	.....	ECG856	.....	SK7708
3267	.....	.....	.....	SK3123
3268	.....	ECG74HCT08	.....	SK7CT08
3269	.....	ECG74HCT14	.....	SK7CT14
3270	NTE85	ECG85	276-2009	SK9407
3271	NTE93MCP	ECG93MCP	.....	SK9931
3272	NTE4055B	ECG4055B	.....	SK4055B
3273	.....	ECG1841	.....	SK10145
3274	.....	ECG74HCT32	.....	SK7CT32
3275	NTE5520	ECG5521	.....	SK6621
3276	.....	.....	.....	SK4059A
3277	NTE6162	ECG6162	.....	SK10219
3278	.....	ECG1741	.....	.....
3279	.....	.....	.....	SK4069UB
3280	.....	ECG879	.....	SK10514
3281	NTE74H72	ECG74H72	.....	.....
3282	NTE290A	ECG290A	276-2023	SK9138
3283	.....	.....	.....	SK4077B
3284	.....	.....	.....	SK3087
3285	NTE5123A	ECG5123A	.....	SK8X7
3286	.....	ECG1193	.....	SK3701
3287	.....	.....	.....	SK3613
3288	NTE889M	ECG889M	.....	SK9864
3289	NTE475	ECG475	.....	SK9647
3290	NTE476	ECG476	.....	SK9648
3291	NTE5415	ECG5415	276-1020	SK3955
3292	NTE4531B	ECG4531B	.....	SK4531B
3293	NTE473	ECG473	.....	SK9645
3294	NTE50	ECG50	.....	SK3179B
3295	.....	.....	.....	SK12A
3296	NTE282	ECG282	.....	SK3512
3297	NTE4099B	ECG4099B	.....	SK4099B
3298	NTE6407	ECG6407	.....	SK3523
3299	NTE1377	ECG1377	.....	SK7808
3300	NTE3017	ECG3017	.....	SK10321
3301	NTE1707	ECG1707	.....	SK10018
3302	.....	ECG282&427	.....	SK3045
3303	.....	ECG9921	.....	.....
3304	NTE53	ECG53	.....	SK9133
3305	.....	ECG2337	.....	.....
3306	NTE1824	ECG1824	.....	SK9899
3307	.....	ECG1824	.....	.....
3308	NTE459	ECG459	276-2055	SK3448
3309	NTE1846	ECG1846	.....	SK10083
3310	NTE1894	ECG1894	.....	.....
3311	.....	ECG256	.....	.....
3312	.....	.....	.....	SK9283
3313	.....	ECG1748	.....	.....
3314	NTE1748	ECG1748	.....	SK9762
3315	NTE5410	ECG5410	.....	SK3503
3316	.....	.....	.....	SK9408
3317	NTE1401	ECG1401	.....	SK9354
3318	.....	ECG1078	.....	SK3498
3319	.....	ECG1825	.....	SK9898
3320	NTE451	ECG451	276-2055	SK9164
3321	NTE1825	ECG1825	.....	SK9898
3322	.....	.....	.....	SK1805
3323	NTE2325	ECG2325	.....	SK9855
3324	.....	ECG560	.....	.....
3325	NTE1403	ECG1403	.....	SK9353
3326	NTE2300	ECG2300	.....	SK9476
3327	NTE1736	ECG1736	.....	SK10029
3328	.....	.....	.....	SK3562
3329	NTE1675	ECG1675	.....	SK9815
3330	.....	.....	.....	SK7CT4002
3331	NTE1800	ECG1800	.....	SK9882
3332	NTE1153	ECG1153	.....	SK3282
3333	NTE3081	ECG3081	.....	SK9965
3334	.....	.....	.....	SK4532B
3335	.....	.....	.....	SK6A8
3336	NTE274	ECG274	.....	SK9107
3337	NTE74LS298	ECG74LS298	.....	SK74LS298
3338	.....	ECG2402	.....	.....
3339	NTE245	ECG245	.....	SK9438
3340	NTE246	ECG246	.....	SK9439
3341	.....	.....	.....	SK9032
3342	NTE300MP	ECG300MP	.....	SK10616
3343	NTE257	ECG257	.....	SK4907
3344	.....	ECG7012	.....	SK10481
3345	NTE2412	ECG2412	.....	SK10107
3346	.....	ECG794	.....	.....
3347	NTE989	ECG989	.....	SK3595
3348	.....	.....	.....	SK5014
3349	NTE5512	ECG5512	276-1020	SK3684
3350	NTE312	ECG312	276-2055	SK3112
3351	NTE238	ECG238	276-2055	SK9261
3352	NTE1786	ECG1786	.....	SK9874
3353	.....	ECG2311	.....	.....
3354	NTE2319	ECG2319	.....	SK10015
3355	.....	ECG1873	.....	SK9764
3356	NTE161	ECG161	276-2016	SK3444
3357	NTE859	ECG859	.....	SK4826
3358	NTE287	ECG287	.....	SK9352
3359	NTE933	ECG933	.....	SK9341
3360	NTE871	ECG871	.....	SK3646
3361	NTE951	ECG951	.....	SK9170
3362	.....	ECG107	.....	SK3132
3363	NTE835	ECG835	.....	.....
3364	.....	ECG382	.....	SK9453
3365	NTE9948	ECG9948	.....	.....
3366	NTE74LS133	ECG74LS133	.....	SK74LS133
3367	NTE74C95	ECG74C95	.....	SK74C95
3368	NTE5446	ECG5446	.....	SK3635
3369	.....	.....	.....	SK9211
3370	NTE5448	ECG5448	.....	SK3636
3371	.....	.....	.....	SK7CT4015
3372	NTE20	ECG20	.....	SK9418
3373	NTE6404	ECG6404	.....	SK7900
3374	.....	ECG5360	.....	.....
3375	.....	.....	.....	SK7CT4016
3376	.....	ECG805	.....	.....
3377	.....	.....	.....	SK9116
3378	.....	.....	.....	SK7CT688
3379	.....	.....	.....	SK43A
3380	.....	ECG5315	.....	.....
3381	NTE524V15	ECG524V15	.....	SKMV150K
3382	.....	.....	.....	SKMV150L
3383	.....	.....	.....	SK7CT4017
3384	.....	ECG9900	.....	.....
3385	NTE5480	ECG5481	.....	SK3940
3386	.....	.....	.....	SK43V
3387	NTE472	ECG472	.....	SK9644
3388	NTE806	ECG806	.....	.....
3389	NTE1578	ECG1578	.....	SK9130
3390	.....	.....	.....	SK9168
3391	NTE983	ECG983	.....	SK3887
3392	.....	.....	.....	SK3024
3393	.....	ECG9976	.....	.....
3394	NTE4046B	ECG4046B	.....	SK4046B
3395	NTE9989	ECG9989	.....	.....
3396	.....	.....	.....	SK7CT4020
3397	NTE4556B	ECG4556B	.....	SK4556B
3398	.....	ECG1277	.....	.....
3399	.....	ECG5826	.....	.....

REPL. CODE	NTE PART NO.	ECG PART NO.	RADIO SHACK PART NO.	RCA PART NO.
3400	NTE944M	ECG944M	.....	SK10077
3401	NTE2305	ECG2305	.....	SK4904
3402	NTE2328	ECG2328	.....	SK9991
3403	NTE1744	ECG1744	.....	SK9732
3404	NTE2301	ECG2301	.....	
3405	NTE5476	ECG5476	.....	SK10262
3406	.....	ECG778A	.....	
3407	NTE607	ECG607	.....	SK9848
3408	NTE4045B	ECG4045B	.....	SK4045B
3409	.....	.....	.....	SK3926
3410	NTE1743	ECG1743	.....	SK9996
3411	.....	ECG377	.....	
3412	.....	ECG2361	.....	
3413	.....	.....	.....	SK7CT4024
3414	.....	ECG51	.....	.....
3415	NTE40085B	ECG40085B	.....	
3416	NTE1292	ECG1292	.....	SK9181
3417	NTE615	ECG615A	.....	SK9976
3418	.....	.....	.....	SK4052B
3419	.....	ECG10	.....	.....
3420	NTE3014	ECG3014	.....	.....
3421	NTE3015	ECG3015	.....	.....
3422	NTE4048B	ECG4048B	.....	.....
3423	NTE4048B	ECG4048B	.....	SK4048B
3424	.....	ECG2339	.....	SK10301
3425	.....	ECG5669A	.....	SK10461
3426	NTE2337	ECG2337	.....	SK10300
3427	.....	.....	.....	SK7CT7030
3428	.....	.....	.....	SK6V8
3429	NTE7423	ECG7423	.....	SK7423
3430	.....	ECG5699	.....	.....
3431	NTE2412	ECG2412	.....	SK10106
3432	.....	.....	.....	SK4724B
3433	NTE2430	ECG2430	.....	SK10114
3434	.....	.....	.....	SK3506
3435	.....	.....	.....	SK3938
3436	.....	.....	.....	SK3736
3437	NTE2301	ECG2301	.....	SK9486
3438	NTE7425	ECG7425	.....	SK7425
3439	NTE2418	ECG2418	.....	SK10110
3440	.....	.....	.....	SK4572UB
3441	NTE3880	ECG3880	.....	SK2880
3442	NTE2414	ECG2414	.....	SK9961
3443	NTE133	ECG312	276-2055	SK9157
3444	.....	ECG1757	.....	.....
3445	.....	ECG966	.....	.....
3446	.....	ECG2324	.....	.....
3447	.....	ECG287	.....	.....
3448	NTE1870	ECG1870	.....	SK10161
3449	NTE70	ECG70	.....	SK9270
3450	NTE3164	ECG3164	.....	SK2164
3451	.....	.....	.....	SK3632
3452	.....	ECG2309	.....	.....
3453	NTE1852	ECG1852	.....	SK10151
3454	NTE2324	ECG2324	.....	SK10136
3455	NTE4076B	ECG4076B	.....	SK4076B
3456	.....	ECG2339	.....	.....
3457	.....	.....	.....	SK9409
3458	NTE5603	ECG5603	276-1000	SK3665
3459	NTE88	ECG88	.....	SK9239
3460	NTE590	ECG590	276-1122 N2	SK9939
3461	NTE1548	ECG1548	.....	SK7646
3462	NTE1546	ECG1546	.....	SK7647
3463	NTE4566B	ECG4566B	.....	SK4566B
3464	.....	.....	.....	SK7CT4040
3465	.....	ECG2302	.....	.....
3466	NTE213	ECG213	.....	SK3035
3467	NTE209	.....	.....	.....
3468	.....	ECG2311	.....	.....
3469	.....	ECG2301	.....	.....
3470	NTE71	ECG71	.....	SK9271
3471	.....	ECG2301	.....	SK9486
3472	.....	ECG2300	.....	.....
3473	NTE7010	ECG7010	.....	SK10479
3474	NTE2330	ECG2330	.....	SK9478
3475	NTE5826	ECG5826	.....	SK7376
3476	NTE1553	ECG1553	.....	SK7720
3477	NTE232	ECG232	.....	SK9443
3478	NTE7437	ECG7437	.....	SK7437
3479	NTE15044	.....	.....	SK9854
3480	.....	.....	.....	SK9994
3481	NTE1752	ECG1752	.....	SK10036
3482	.....	ECG2305	.....	.....
3483	NTE251	ECG251	.....	SK3858
3484	NTE252	ECG252	.....	SK3859
3485	.....	.....	.....	SK7CT7046A
3486	NTE258	ECG258	.....	SK9823
3487	NTE259	ECG259	.....	SK3978
3488	NTE260	ECG260	.....	SK3979
3489	NTE6363	ECG6363	.....	SK6561
3490	NTE266	ECG266	.....	SK9253
3491	NTE267	ECG267	.....	SK9254
3492	NTE268	ECG268	.....	SK9255
3493	NTE269	ECG269	.....	SK9256
3494	NTE125	ECG125	276-1114	SK5010A
3495	NTE272	ECG272	.....	SK9436
3496	NTE273	ECG273	.....	SK9437
3497	NTE275	ECG275	.....	SK9108
3498	NTE5828	ECG5828	.....	.....
3499	NTE2348	ECG2348	.....	.....
3500	.....	.....	.....	SK3930
3501	NTE292	ECG292	.....	SK3930
3502	NTE131&155	ECG131&155	.....	SK3198&3839
3503	NTE5334	ECG5334	.....	SK9233
3504	NTE2313	ECG2313	.....	SK10004
3505	NTE153	ECG153	276-2027	SK3441
3506	NTE1024	ECG1024	.....	SK3152
3507	NTE599	ECG599	.....	SK9860
3508	NTE3036	ECG3036	.....	SK4936
3509	.....	.....	.....	SK3538
3510	.....	.....	.....	SK3619
3511	.....	.....	.....	SK3004
3512	.....	.....	.....	SK7CT4051
3513	.....	ECG2060	.....	.....
3514	.....	.....	.....	SK7CT4052
3515	NTE1272	ECG1272	.....	.....
3516	NTE362	ECG362	.....	SK9635
3517	NTE330	ECG330	.....	SK3012
3518	.....	.....	.....	SK3747
3519	NTE334	ECG334	.....	SK9610
3520	.....	.....	.....	SK7CT4053
3521	NTE335	ECG335	.....	SK9611
3522	.....	.....	.....	SK9016
3523	NTE336	ECG336	.....	SK9612
3524	NTE337	ECG337	.....	SK9613
3525	NTE338	ECG338	.....	SK9614
3526	NTE339	ECG339	.....	SK9616
3527	.....	ECG381	.....	SK3934
3528	NTE341	ECG341	.....	SK9617
3529	NTE1925	ECG1925	.....	SK10056
3530	NTE1840	ECG1840	.....	SK10144
3531	NTE971	ECG971	.....	SK3675
3532	NTE347	ECG347	.....	SK9660
3533	NTE378	ECG378	.....	SK9367
3534	NTE348	ECG348	.....	SK9623
3535	.....	.....	.....	SK4081B
3536	NTE353	ECG353	.....	SK9627
3537	NTE93	ECG93	.....	SK9447
3538	NTE354	ECG354	.....	SK9628
3539	NTE355	ECG355	.....	SK9629
3540	NTE356	ECG356	.....	SK9630
3541	NTE55	ECG55	.....	SK3930
3542	NTE357	ECG357	.....	SK9631
3543	NTE359	ECG359	.....	SK9632
3544	NTE2311	ECG2311	.....	SK9374
3545	NTE366	ECG366	.....	SK9639
3546	.....	ECG2202	.....	.....
3547	NTE368	ECG368	.....	SK9641
3548	.....	.....	.....	SK47A
3549	NTE5620	ECG5620	.....	SK10466
3550	NTE991	ECG991	.....	.....
3551	.....	.....	.....	SK47V
3552	.....	.....	.....	SK3841
3553	.....	.....	.....	SK9001
3554	.....	.....	.....	SK3675
3555	NTE4515B	ECG4515B	.....	SK4515B
3556	NTE6059	ECG6061	.....	SK7261
3557	NTE392	ECG392	.....	SK3960
3558	NTE393	ECG393	.....	SK3961
3559	NTE579	ECG579	.....	SK10163
3560	.....	.....	.....	SK7CT4059
3561	NTE68	ECG68	.....	SK9365
3562	NTE395	ECG395	.....	.....
3563	NTE22	ECG22	.....	SK9670
3564	NTE1485	ECG1485	.....	SK9061
3565	NTE4526B	ECG4526B	.....	SK4526B
3566	NTE4098B	ECG4098B	.....	SK4098B
3567	.....	ECG712	.....	.....
3568	.....	.....	.....	SK3039
3569	.....	.....	.....	SK7CT4060
3570	NTE4034B	ECG4034B	.....	SK4034B
3571	.....	ECG1882	.....	.....
3572	NTE159	ECG159	276-2023	SK9434
3573	.....	ECG4568B	.....	SK4568B
3574	NTE89	ECG89	.....	SK9411
3575	NTE5414	ECG5414	276-1067	SK3954
3576	NTE937	ECG937	.....	SK9146
3577	NTE456	ECG456	.....	SK3977
3578	NTE7057	ECG7057	.....	.....
3579	NTE5513	ECG5513	.....	SK3502
3580	NTE2362	ECG2362	276-2023	SK3114A
3581	NTE40106B	ECG40106B	.....	SK40106B
3582	.....	.....	.....	SK9421
3583	NTE462	ECG462	.....	SK9160
3584	.....	.....	.....	SK7CT4066
3585	NTE34	ECG34	.....	SK9430
3586	NTE470	ECG470	.....	SK9642
3587	NTE474	ECG474	.....	.....
3588	.....	.....	.....	SK7CT4067
3589	.....	ECG955M	.....	.....
3590	NTE7015	ECG7015	.....	SK10484
3591	NTE478	ECG478	.....	SK9650
3592	.....	.....	.....	SK3693
3593	NTE480	ECG480	.....	SK9652
3594	.....	ECG3751	.....	.....
3595	NTE481	ECG481	.....	SK9653
3596	NTE482	ECG482	.....	SK9654
3597	NTE483	ECG483	.....	SK9655
3598	NTE484	ECG484	.....	SK9656
3599	NTE485	ECG485	.....	SK9657
3600	NTE2429	ECG2429	.....	SK9964
3601	NTE59	ECG59	.....	SK9449
3602	.....	ECG4066B	.....	.....
3603	NTE6406	ECG6406	.....	.....
3604	NTE514	ECG514/R-3DS3	.....	SK3761
3605	NTE1920	ECG1920	.....	SK10053
3606	NTE1237	ECG1237	.....	SK3707
3607	NTE524V15	ECG524V15	.....	SK3329
3608	NTE2309	ECG2337	.....	SK10300
3609	NTE290A	ECG290A	276-2023	SK3867A
3610	NTE530	ECG530	.....	SK3308
3611	NTE4539B	ECG4539B	.....	.....
3612	.....	ECG5812	.....	.....
3613	NTE541	ECG541	.....	SK9306
3614	NTE542	ECG542	.....	SK9307
3615	NTE544	ECG544	.....	.....
3616	NTE546	ECG546	.....	SK9300
3617	NTE548	ECG548	.....	SK9305
3618	.....	ECG946	.....	.....
3619	NTE74490	ECG74490	.....	.....
3620	.....	.....	.....	SK7CT4075
3621	NTE556	ECG556	.....	SK3905
3622	NTE557	ECG557	.....	SK3904
3623	.....	ECG3830	.....	.....
3624	NTE565	ECG565	.....	.....
3625	NTE1107	ECG1107	.....	SK7772
3626	NTE5475	ECG5476	.....	SK10262
3627	NTE857M	ECG857M	.....	SK9800
3628	NTE2306	ECG2306	.....	SK4903
3629	NTE56	.....	ECG56	.....
3630	.....	ECG390	.....	.....
3631	NTE6200	ECG6200	.....	SK9773
3632	.....	.....	.....	SK7C533
3633	.....	ECG2328	.....	.....
3634	NTE6202	ECG6202	.....	SK9772
3635	NTE6204	ECG6204	.....	SK9771
3636	.....	.....	.....	SK7C534
3637	NTE379	.....	ECG379	.....
3638	NTE604	.....	.....	.....
3639	NTE606	ECG606	.....	SK9847
3640	NTE1671	ECG1671	.....	SK7841
3641	NTE921	ECG921	.....	SK7615
3642	NTE617	ECG617	.....	.....
3643	NTE618	ECG618	.....	.....
3644	NTE290AMCP	ECG290AMCP	.....	SK10312
3645	.....	ECG7009	.....	SK10478
3646	NTE56	ECG56	.....	SK9431
3647	NTE377	ECG377	276-2020	SK9445
3648	NTE54	ECG54	.....	SK9445
3649	NTE241	ECG241	276-2020	SK9445
3650	NTE1160	ECG1160	.....	.....
3651	NTE5511	ECG5511	276-1067	SK3683
3652	.....	ECG1599	.....	.....
3653	.....	.....	.....	SK3025
3654	.....	ECG293	.....	.....
3655	.....	ECG294	.....	.....
3656	NTE60	ECG60	.....	SK9033
3657	.....	.....	.....	SK9991
3658	.....	.....	.....	SK9370
3659	NTE4536B	ECG4536B	.....	SK4536B
3660	.....	ECG1178	.....	SK3480
3661	NTE4056B	ECG4056B	.....	SK4056B
3662	.....	ECG1598	.....	.....
3663	NTE56031	ECG56031	.....	SK10410
3664	NTE376	ECG376	.....	SK9262A
3665	NTE1374	ECG1374	.....	SK3853
3666	NTE1376	ECG1376	.....	SK7707
3667	NTE132	ECG312	276-2055	SK3834
3668	NTE1567	ECG1567	.....	SK7805
3669	.....	ECG9905	.....	.....
3670	NTE74H20	ECG74H20	.....	.....
3671	NTE1486	ECG1486	.....	SK7607
3672	NTE312	ECG312	.....	SK3448
3673	.....	ECG2387	.....	.....
3674	NTE700	ECG700	.....	SK9028
3675	NTE701	ECG701	.....	SK9026
3676	.....	ECG824	.....	.....
3677	NTE716	ECG716	.....	.....
3678	NTE2336	ECG2336	.....	SK9481
3679	NTE717	ECG717	.....	.....
3680	NTE1842	ECG1842	.....	SK7674
3681	NTE74S30	ECG74S30	.....	.....
3682	NTE4063B	ECG4063B	.....	SK4063B
3683	NTE375	ECG375	.....	SK9452
3684	NTE2001	ECG2001	.....	.....
3685	.....	ECG1718	.....	.....
3686	NTE1703	ECG1703	.....	SK10016
3687	NTE153MCP	ECG153MCP	276-2020&27	SK3274&3893
3688	NTE5852	ECG5854	.....	SK3600
3689	NTE862	ECG862	.....	SK3456
3690	NTE742	ECG742	.....	SK3453
3691	.....	.....	.....	SK7CT4094
3692	NTE1440	ECG1440	.....	SK9056
3693	NTE3016	ECG3016	.....	SK10320
3694	.....	ECG5854	.....	SK3600
3695	NTE858M	ECG858M	276-1715	SK7641
3696	NTE4067B	ECG4067B	.....	SK4067B
3697	NTE5856	ECG5858	.....	SK3599
3698	NTE1551	ECG1551	.....	SK9298
3699	.....	ECG5335	.....	SK7313
3700	NTE214	ECG214	.....	SK9916
3701	NTE1727	ECG1727	.....	SK7618
3702	NTE215	ECG215	.....	SK9421
3703	NTE593	ECG593	.....	SK9942
3704	NTE217	ECG217	.....	SK9471
3705	NTE5900	ECG5900	.....	SK7100
3706	.....	.....	.....	SK3274
3707	NTE1625	ECG1625	.....	SK10232
3708	NTE227	ECG227	.....	SK9472

REPL. CODE	NTE PART NO.	ECG PART NO.	RADIO SHACK PART NO.	RCA PART NO.
3709	.....	ECG56033	.....	.....
3710	.....	.....	.....	SK51V
3711	NTE5902	ECG5904	.....	SK7104
3712	NTE240	ECG240	.....	SK9351
3713	NTE1629	ECG1629	.....	.....
3714	.....	.....	.....	SK4536B
3715	NTE802	ECG802	.....	SK3277
3716	NTE6020	ECG6020	.....	SK7220
3717	NTE803	ECG803	.....	SK3278
3718	NTE255	ECG255	.....	SK9412
3719	NTE256	ECG256	.....	.....
3720	NTE807	ECG807	.....	SK3451
3721	NTE4506B	ECG4506B	.....	SK4056UB
3722	NTE5908	ECG5908	.....	SK7108
3723	.....	ECG1276	.....	.....
3724	NTE812	ECG812	.....	.....
3725	NTE6049	ECG6049	.....	SK7249
3726	NTE1576	ECG1576	.....	SK7672
3727	.....	ECG1862	.....	SK10159
3728	NTE1668	ECG1668	.....	SK9978
3729	NTE108-1	ECG108	276-2016	SK3452
3730	.....	.....	.....	SK10153
3731	.....	ECG753	.....	.....
3732	.....	.....	.....	SK3564
3733	NTE832	ECG832	.....	SK9089
3734	.....	ECG5338	.....	SK7315
3735	NTE841	ECG841	.....	SK9202
3736	NTE1051	ECG1051	.....	.....
3737	NTE1V250	ECG1V250	.....	SKMV250G
3738	.....	.....	.....	SK9047
3739	NTE849	ECG849	.....	.....
3740	NTE55MCP	ECG55MCP	.....	SK9923
3741	NTE851	ECG851	.....	SK9206
3742	NTE853	ECG853	.....	SK7645
3743	NTE2053	ECG2053	.....	SK1911
3744	NTE856	ECG856	.....	SK7708
3745	NTE2312	.....	ECG2312	.....
3746	NTE860	ECG860	.....	SK7731
3747	NTE79	ECG79	.....	.....
3748	NTE926	ECG926	.....	SK7721
3749	NTE48	ECG48	.....	SK4906
3750	.....	.....	.....	SK74LS38
3751	NTE973D	ECG973D	.....	SK3892
3752	.....	ECG918M	.....	.....
3753	.....	.....	.....	SK3970
3754	NTE1199	ECG1199	.....	.....
3755	.....	ECG74HC4053	.....	SK7C4053
3756	NTE107	ECG107	276-2016	SK3854
3757	.....	ECG913	.....	.....
3758	NTE4501	ECG4501	.....	SK4501UB
3759	.....	ECG370A	.....	.....
3760	NTE159	ECG159	276-2023	SK3841
3761	NTE934	ECG934	.....	SK9342
3762	.....	ECG936	.....	.....
3763	NTE1254	ECG1254	.....	SK3880
3764	NTE1557	ECG1557	.....	SK7605
3765	NTE1827	ECG1827	.....	SK9885
3766	NTE939	ECG939	.....	.....
3767	NTE943	ECG943	.....	.....
3768	NTE944	ECG944	.....	SK10076
3769	NTE952	ECG952	.....	SK7752
3770	.....	.....	.....	SK3260
3771	NTE953	ECG953	.....	SK7806
3772	NTE954	ECG954	.....	SK7807
3773	.....	ECG994	.....	.....
3774	NTE959	ECG959	.....	SK9283
3775	NTE994M	ECG994M	.....	SK9224
3776	NTE1716	ECG1716	.....	SK10012
3777	NTE969	ECG969	.....	SK3674
3778	NTE4089B	ECG4089B	.....	SK4089B
3779	NTE980	ECG980	.....	SK4046B
3780	NTE985	ECG985	.....	SK3214
3781	.....	ECG9904	.....	.....
3782	NTE74C107	ECG74C107	.....	SK74C107
3783	.....	ECG993	.....	.....
3784	NTE996	ECG996	.....	SK9201
3785	.....	ECG6013	.....	SK10176
3786	.....	.....	.....	SK9919
3787	.....	ECG463	.....	.....
3788	NTE1141	ECG1141	.....	.....
3789	NTE5023A N9	ECG5023A N9	.....	SK14A N9
3790	.....	ECG468	.....	SK10462
3791	.....	ECG469	.....	SK10463
3792	.....	.....	.....	SK3021
3793	.....	ECG9908	.....	.....
3794	.....	ECG487	.....	SK10464
3795	.....	.....	.....	SK74S32
3796	NTE4095B	ECG4095B	.....	SK4095B
3797	.....	ECG9909	.....	.....
3798	NTE4096B	ECG4096B	.....	SK4096B
3799	NTE5023A N8	ECG5023A N8	.....	SK14A N8
3800	NTE1683	ECG1683	.....	SK7626
3801	NTE5413	ECG5413	276-1067	SK3954
3802	NTE4097B	ECG4097B	.....	SK4097B
3803	.....	.....	.....	SK3764
3804	.....	ECG314	.....	SK3527
3805	NTE521	ECG521	.....	SK3304
3806	NTE524V42	ECG524V42	.....	SK10059
3807	.....	ECG527	.....	SK9035
3808	.....	ECG9903	.....	.....
3809	NTE1402	ECG1402	.....	SK9043
3810	.....	ECG540	.....	.....
3811	.....	ECG543	.....	SK9308
3812	.....	ECG545	.....	SK9303
3813	.....	ECG547	.....	SK9304
3814	NTE549	ECG549	.....	SK3901
3815	.....	ECG550	.....	.....
3816	.....	ECG5462	.....	SK9291
3817	.....	.....	.....	SK7C04
3818	NTE559	ECG559	.....	.....
3819	.....	ECG561	.....	.....
3820	NTE284	ECG284	.....	SK9134
3821	.....	.....	.....	SK9480
3822	.....	ECG562	.....	.....
3823	.....	ECG5463	.....	SK9292
3824	.....	ECG563	.....	.....
3825	NTE3034A	ECG3034	.....	.....
3826	.....	ECG564	.....	.....
3827	.....	.....	.....	SK9119
3828	NTE1924	ECG1924	.....	SK10055
3829	.....	ECG570	.....	.....
3830	NTE1801	ECG1801	.....	SK9883
3831	.....	.....	.....	SK40192B
3832	.....	ECG2409	.....	.....
3833	NTE577	ECG577	.....	SK10511
3834	NTE578	ECG578	.....	SK10162
3835	NTE582	ECG582	.....	SK7332
3836	.....	ECG2342	.....	SK10090
3837	NTE583	ECG583	.....	.....
3838	.....	ECG2341	.....	SK10089
3839	NTE2021	ECG2021	.....	SK9020
3840	NTE591	ECG591	.....	SK9940
3841	NTE592	ECG592	.....	SK9941
3842	NTE594	ECG594	.....	SK9943
3843	.....	ECG9912	.....	.....
3844	NTE519 N8	ECG519 N8	276-1122 N8	SK3100 N8
3845	.....	ECG9915	.....	.....
3846	NTE6042	ECG6042	.....	SK7242
3847	.....	ECG9913	.....	.....
3848	NTE1779	ECG1779	.....	SK9726
3849	NTE182&183	ECG182&183	.....	SK3188A&3189A
3850	.....	ECG153	.....	.....
3851	.....	.....	.....	SK7C123
3852	.....	ECG5440	.....	SK10401
3853	NTE285	ECG285	.....	SK9136
3854	.....	ECG5011T1	.....	.....
3855	NTE116	ECG116	276-1103	SK3031A
3856	NTE74LS148	ECG74LS148	.....	SK74LS148
3857	NTE1778	ECG1778	.....	SK9871
3858	NTE15020E	ECG15020	.....	SK10186
3859	NTE1128	ECG1128	.....	SK3488
3860	NTE1373	ECG1373	.....	SK4822
3861	.....	.....	.....	SK3644
3862	.....	.....	.....	SK3606
3863	NTE293&294	ECG293&294	.....	SK3841&3849
3864	NTE2022	ECG2022	.....	SK9019
3865	.....	ECG1574	.....	.....
3866	NTE1115A	ECG1115A	.....	SK3917
3867	.....	ECG4018B	.....	SK4018B
3868	NTE9926	ECG9926	.....	.....
3869	NTE1810	ECG1810	.....	SK9727
3870	NTE376	.....	ECG376	.....
3871	NTE15046	ECG1861	.....	SK10158
3872	NTE6362	ECG6362	.....	SK6560
3873	NTE83	ECG83	.....	SK3444
3874	.....	.....	.....	SK11V5
3875	.....	ECG758	.....	.....
3876	NTE1311	ECG1311	.....	.....
3877	NTE1300	ECG1300	.....	.....
3878	.....	ECG610	.....	.....
3879	.....	ECG765	.....	.....
3880	NTE1139	ECG1139	.....	.....
3881	NTE69	ECG69	276-2058	SK3246A
3882	NTE24	ECG24	.....	SK9840
3883	.....	ECG5562	.....	.....
3884	.....	ECG768	.....	.....
3885	NTE888M	ECG888M	.....	SK9863
3886	.....	ECG775	.....	.....
3887	.....	ECG776	.....	.....
3888	NTE1521	ECG1521	.....	.....
3889	.....	ECG5107T2	.....	.....
3890	.....	.....	.....	SK3V6
3891	NTE1308	ECG1308	.....	SK3833
3892	NTE332MCP	ECG332MCP	.....	SK10005
3893	.....	.....	.....	SK7C139
3894	NTE1896	ECG1896	.....	SK10505
3895	NTE40100B	ECG40100B	.....	SK40100B
3896	NTE1839	ECG1839	.....	SK10143
3897	NTE1776	ECG1776	.....	SK9743
3898	.....	ECG813	.....	.....
3899	NTE955S	ECG955S	.....	SK9397
3900	NTE15041	ECG1897	.....	.....
3901	NTE1098	ECG1098	.....	SK7770
3902	NTE1778	ECG1778	.....	SK9744
3903	NTE230	ECG230	.....	SK3502
3904	.....	ECG1603	.....	.....
3905	NTE826	ECG826	.....	SK7813
3906	NTE1914	ECG1914	.....	SK9331
3907	NTE1596	ECG1596	.....	.....
3908	.....	ECG831	.....	.....
3909	.....	ECG1594	.....	.....
3910	.....	.....	.....	SK7733
3911	.....	ECG1590	.....	.....
3912	.....	ECG253	.....	SK9370
3913	.....	ECG1586	.....	.....
3914	.....	ECG837	.....	.....
3915	.....	ECG838	.....	.....
3916	NTE1582	ECG1582	.....	.....
3917	.....	ECG839	.....	SK7614
3918	.....	ECG1584	.....	.....
3919	NTE842	ECG842	.....	SK7686
3920	NTE844	ECG844	.....	SK9381
3921	NTE845	ECG845	.....	SK9382
3922	.....	ECG847	.....	.....
3923	NTE1468	ECG1468	.....	SK9322
3924	.....	ECG848	.....	.....
3925	NTE2062	ECG2062	.....	SK10295
3926	NTE850	ECG850	.....	SK9383
3927	NTE1312	ECG1312	.....	.....
3928	NTE1313	ECG1313	.....	.....
3929	.....	ECG854	.....	.....
3930	NTE3121	ECG3121	.....	SK4928
3931	NTE1310	ECG1310	.....	.....
3932	NTE861	ECG861	.....	SK4843
3933	NTE863	ECG863	.....	SK9207
3934	.....	ECG865	.....	.....
3935	.....	ECG1302	.....	.....
3936	.....	ECG74LS77	.....	.....
3937	.....	ECG866	.....	.....
3938	NTE867	ECG867	.....	SK9386
3939	NTE1304	ECG1304	.....	.....
3940	NTE868	ECG868	.....	SK7692
3941	.....	ECG1305	.....	SK7791
3942	.....	ECG872	.....	.....
3943	NTE1306	ECG1306	.....	.....
3944	NTE74C151	ECG74C151	.....	SK7C151
3945	NTE874	ECG874	.....	SK7717
3946	NTE1117	ECG1117	.....	SK9226
3947	.....	ECG1307	.....	.....
3948	NTE877	ECG877	.....	SK9257
3949	NTE1294	ECG1294	.....	SK9394
3950	NTE54	.....	ECG54	.....
3951	NTE880	ECG880	.....	.....
3952	.....	ECG1052	.....	SK3249
3953	.....	ECG5558	.....	.....
3954	NTE12	ECG12	.....	SK9919
3955	NTE28	ECG28	.....	.....
3956	NTE99	ECG99	.....	SK9110
3957	NTE74C154	ECG74C154	.....	SK74C154
3958	.....	ECG5400	.....	SK3950
3959	.....	ECG5401	.....	SK3638
3960	.....	.....	.....	SK40101B
3961	.....	ECG1238	.....	SK3373
3962	NTE5020A	ECG5020A	.....	.....
3963	.....	ECG5404	.....	SK3627
3964	NTE225	ECG396&427	.....	SK3045
3965	NTE3030	ECG3030	276-036	SK2169
3966	.....	ECG1059	.....	.....
3967	.....	ECG920	.....	.....
3968	.....	ECG1125	.....	.....
3969	NTE96	ECG96	.....	SK9259
3970	NTE5568	ECG5568	.....	SK6718
3971	NTE395	ECG395	.....	SK3118
3972	NTE74C157	ECG74C157	.....	SK74C157
3973	NTE1123	ECG1123	.....	SK3743
3974	.....	.....	.....	SK3465
3975	.....	.....	.....	SK3168
3976	NTE945	ECG945	.....	.....
3977	NTE1162	ECG1162	.....	SK3072
3978	NTE1068	ECG1068	.....	SK3226
3979	.....	.....	.....	SK3527
3980	NTE1249	ECG1249	.....	SK3963
3981	.....	.....	.....	SK1822
3982	NTE1487	ECG1487	.....	.....
3983	NTE74C160	.....	.....	SK7C160
3984	NTE74C161	ECG74C161	.....	SK74C161
3985	NTE1450	ECG1450	.....	.....
3986	.....	ECG979	.....	.....
3987	.....	ECG2418	.....	SK10110
3988	.....	.....	.....	SK7CT240
3989	NTE1448	ECG1448	.....	.....
3990	NTE3166	ECG3166	.....	SK2166
3991	.....	ECG5554	.....	.....
3992	.....	ECG5556	.....	.....
3993	.....	ECG1182	.....	SK7779
3994	.....	.....	.....	SK3843
3995	.....	.....	.....	SK7C163
3996	NTE998	ECG998	.....	.....
3997	NTE1406	ECG1406	.....	SK9059
3998	.....	.....	.....	SK40102B
3999	NTE74C164	ECG74C164	.....	SK74C164N
4000	NTE1446	ECG1446	.....	.....
4001	NTE1264	ECG1264	.....	.....
4002	NTE1265	ECG1265	.....	SK7787
4003	.....	.....	.....	SK3238
4004	NTE1266	ECG1266	.....	.....
4005	NTE1444	ECG1444	.....	.....
4006	NTE1240	ECG1240	.....	SK7785
4007	NTE1267	ECG1267	.....	.....
4008	NTE1268	ECG1268	.....	SK3921
4009	NTE1792	ECG1792	.....	SK9877
4010	NTE1250	ECG1250	.....	.....
4011	.....	ECG5312	.....	.....
4012	.....	ECG363	.....	.....
4013	.....	.....	.....	SK7CT245
4014	.....	ECG1070	.....	.....
4015	.....	ECG2345	.....	SK10120
4016	.....	ECG2346	.....	SK10121
4017	NTE1269	ECG1269	.....	SK9054

REPL. CODE	NTE PART NO.	ECG PART NO.	RADIO SHACK PART NO.	RCA PART NO.
4018				SK3831
4019	NTE2026	ECG2026		SK10276
4020	NTE297&298	ECG297&298		SK3449&3450
4021				SK1823
4022		ECG6880		
4023		ECG389		
4024	NTE1224	ECG1224		SK7782
4025	NTE1191	ECG1191		
4026	NTE74C173	ECG74C173		SK74C173
4027	NTE1290	ECG1290		SK9183
4028		ECG383		
4029				SK40103B
4030	NTE74C174	ECG74C174		SK74C174
4031	NTE1037	ECG1037		SK3371
4032	NTE1863	ECG1863		
4033	NTE186&187	ECG186&187		SK9076&3357
4034	NTE74C175	ECG74C175		SK74C175
4035	NTE1395	ECG1395		SK9313
4036	NTE175	ECG175		SK3026
4037	NTE27	ECG27		SK4900
4038	NTE5687	ECG5687		SK3521
4039	NTE703	ECG703		SK3087
4040				SK9713
4041				SK1824
4042		ECG588		
4043	NTE21	ECG21		SK9669
4044	NTE858SM	ECG858SM		SK10064
4045	NTE2004	ECG2004		
4046				SK40104B
4047	NTE1572	ECG1572		SK4825
4048	NTE4597B	ECG4597B		SK4597B
4049	NTE5010A	ECG5010A		SK5A1
4050	NTE1581	ECG1581		SK9360
4051	NTE178MP	ECG178MP	276-1122	SK9009
4052	NTE5806	ECG5806	276-1114	SK3848
4053		ECG87		SK9031
4054	NTE1834	ECG1834		SK9740
4055		ECG1869SM		SK10499
4056	NTE74C192	ECG74C192		SK74C192
4057				SK9748
4058	NTE5604	ECG5605	276-1000	SK3666
4059	NTE74C193	ECG74C193		SK74C193
4060				SK40105B
4061	NTE153		ECG153	
4062	NTE153		ECG153	
4063				SK7CT273
4064				SK3917
4065				SK62V
4066	NTE1782	ECG1782		SK9730
4067	NTE2360	ECG2360		SK9960
4068				SK3233
4069		ECG990		
4070	NTE282	ECG282		SK3299
4071	NTE1496	ECG1496		SK9321
4072	NTE1V115	ECG1V115		SKMV115B
4073	NTE859SM	ECG859SM		SK10065
4074	NTE1775	ECG1775		SK9868
4075	NTE2084	ECG2084		SK4910
4076	NTE234	ECG234	276-2023	SK3841
4077	NTE5832	ECG5834		SK7042
4078	NTE15044			SK9738
4079	NTE9666	ECG9666		
4080		ECG1882		SK10172
4081	NTE61	ECG61		SK9034
4082	NTE8318	ECG8318		SK9831
4083	NTE1740	ECG1740		SK7817
4084	NTE1116	ECG1116		SK3969
4085	NTE5598	ECG5598		SK6748
4086	NTE9671	ECG9671		
4087				SK4016B
4088	NTE1358	ECG1358		SK9987
4089	NTE5340	ECG5340		SK3650
4090				SK40107B
4091		ECG9400		SK9051
4092		ECG399		SK9352
4093		ECG331		
4094		ECG332		
4095	NTE9200	ECG9200		SK10447
4096	NTE5342	ECG5342		SK3651
4097	NTE385	ECG385		SK3559
4098		ECG9674		
4099	NTE9402	ECG9402		SK9062
4100	NTE129MCP	ECG129MCP		SK9932
4101	NTE9675	ECG9675		
4102	NTE1418	ECG1418		SK9214
4103		ECG1665		
4104		ECG598		SK9859
4105		ECG9401		SK10448
4106	NTE922SM	ECG922SM		SK10070
4107	NTE9676	ECG9676		
4108		ECG9677		
4109	NTE2356	ECG2356		SK9958
4110	NTE9678	ECG9678		
4111				SK9751
4112	NTE9679	ECG9679		
4113		ECG2114		
4114		ECG254		
4115	NTE9680	ECG9680		
4116				SK9091
4117	NTE7428	ECG7428		SK7428
4118	NTE6875	ECG6875		SK9794
4119				SK40108B
4120	NTE3027	ECG3027		SK2027A
4121	NTE331MP	ECG331MP		SK10006
4122		ECG9683		
4123				SK4028B
4124		ECG9684		
4125	NTE6208	ECG6208		SK9779
4126	NTE7002	ECG7002		SK10471
4127	NTE3057	ECG3057		SK10329
4128		ECG9685		
4129	NTE5332	ECG5332	276-1161	SK9230
4130	NTE7433	ECG7433		SK7433
4131	NTE1783	ECG1783		SK9873
4132		ECG9686		
4133	NTE1183	ECG1183		
4134	NTE6210	ECG6210		SK9778
4135				SK3176
4136		ECG9688		
4137	NTE9689	ECG9689		
4138				SK3512
4139				SK3199
4140		ECG9690		
4141				SK3200
4142				SK74LS155
4143	NTE9691	ECG9691		
4144	NTE237	ECG237		SK3049
4145	NTE1195	ECG1195		SK3469
4146				SK40109B
4147	NTE116	ECG116		SK3312
4148				SK3588A
4149	NTE711	ECG711		SK3017B
4150				SK3112
4151	NTE74H51	ECG74H51		SK74107
4152	NTE74H53	ECG74H53		SK74LS03
4153				SK4512B
4154		ECG9927		
4155		ECG2002		
4156	NTE153MCP	ECG153MCP		SK9933
4157		ECG9696		
4158	NTE1V060	ECG1V060		SKMV60A
4159				SK3507
4160	NTE1233	ECG1233		SK3732
4161	NTE282	ECG282		SK3045
4162				SK3921
4163				SK7C240
4164		ECG5591		
4165				SK40110B
4166	NTE74C244	ECG74C244		SK74C244
4167	NTE5172A	ECG5172A		
4168	NTE5079A	ECG5079A		
4169	NTE6403	ECG6403		SK9120
4170		ECG9906		
4171		ECG139A		
4172		ECG9907		
4173		ECG455		
4174	NTE1200	ECG1200		SK3714
4175				SK9177
4176				SK3311
4177		ECG7003		SK10472
4178		ECG1588		
4179	NTE373			SK373
4180				SK3611
4181				SK9070
4182	NTE224	ECG224		SK3529
4183	NTE54	ECG54	276-2020	SK3440
4184				SK7CT7266
4185				SK6810
4186	NTE175	ECG152	276-2020	SK3026
4187	NTE95	ECG95		SK9295
4188				SK68V
4189		ECG834SM		SK10063
4190		ECG987SM		
4191		ECG987		
4192				SK3835
4193		ECG125		
4194	NTE1718	ECG1718		SK10023
4195		ECG928SM		
4196	NTE1099	ECG1099		
4197		ECG1601		
4198				SK3514
4199	NTE1V040	ECG1V040		SKMV40B
4200	NTE2361	ECG2361		SK3124A
4201	NTE7066	ECG7066		
4202				SK9747
4203				SK74195
4204				SKMV130L
4205				SK3165
4206				SK3080
4207	NTE282	ECG282		SK3529
4208				SK3526
4209	NTE927SM	ECG927SM		SK10071
4210	NTE1633	ECG1633		SK7729
4211				SK9384
4212				SK10041
4213	NTE15038			
4214	NTE1639	ECG1639		
4215				SK4067B
4216	NTE1512	ECG1512		
4217				SK4078B
4218				SK9460
4219				SK7402
4220	NTE4517B	ECG4517B		SK4517B
4221	NTE6107	ECG6107		
4222	NTE6106	ECG6106		
4223	NTE6362	ECG6362		SK6558
4224		ECG451		SK3116
4225		ECG74HC08		
4226				SK7623
4227	NTE1423	ECG1423		SK7600
4228	NTE96S02	ECG96S02		
4229	NTE196&197	ECG196&197		SK3054&3083
4230		ECG1592		
4231				SK4000UB
4232		ECG404		
4233		ECG127		SK3764
4234				SK40114B
4235		ECG586		
4236			276-065	
4237	NTE4598B	ECG4598B		SK4598B
4238				SK4538B
4239		ECG5033A		
4240			276-066A	
4241	NTE74S51	ECG74S51		
4242	NTE6048	ECG6048		SK7248
4243	NTE1542	ECG1542		SK10274
4244	NTE6058	ECG6060		SK7260
4245				SK8A2
4246	NTE1835	ECG1835		SK9728
4247				SK7CT374
4248				SK4099B
4249		ECG6087		SK9775
4250		ECG6094		
4251		ECG6664		
4252		ECG2056		
4253		ECG326		SK3746
4254		ECG1019		
4255		ECG1584		SK3365
4256				SK2A8
4257		ECG5882		
4258		ECG5886		
4259				SK7CT4316
4260		ECG8212		
4261	NTE7054	ECG7054		
4262	NTE3074	ECG3074		SK2074
4263		ECG8228		
4264	NTE1936	ECG1936		SK7740
4265	NTE261	ECG261	276-2068	SK3180
4266	NTE3076	ECG3076		SK2076
4267	NTE3075	ECG3075		SK2075
4268	NTE3077	ECG3077		SK2077
4269	NTE2317	ECG2317		SK10117
4270		ECG56024		
4271		ECG7014		
4272	NTE5351	ECG5351		
4273				SK3591
4274	NTE74LS164	ECG74LS164		SK74LS164
4275		ECG74S573		
4276				SK3593
4277				SK3699
4278		ECG4049		
4279	NTE30	ECG30		SK9915
4280	NTE29	ECG29		SK9914
4281	NTE1747	ECG1747		SK7619
4282	NTE21	ECG21		SK3841
4283				SK10247
4284	NTE1661	ECG1661		SK4816
4285	NTE1540	ECG1540		SK4837
4286	NTE1772	ECG1772		SK9866
4287		ECG6809E		
4288		ECG1647		SK10493
4289	NTE74LS165	ECG74LS165		SK7CT165
4290		ECG2040		
4291	NTE7039	ECG7039		SK75A
4292		ECG5046A		
4293				SK3212
4294				SK75V
4295	NTE5711	ECG5711		SK10418
4296				SK3259
4297	NTE1V025	ECG1V025		SKMV25A
4298			276-088	
4299				SK3645
4300		ECG4019B		
4301	NTE74LS166	ECG74LS166		SK7CT166
4302	NTE1387	ECG1387		SK7665
4303				SK5V1
4304	NTE6400B	ECG6400B		SK9122
4305	NTE123AP	ECG123AP	276-2016	SK3854
4306	NTE1805	ECG1805		SK9838
4307				SK9754
4308				SK3966
4309	NTE1837	ECG1837		SK9755
4310	NTE1836	ECG1836		SK9756
4311	NTE7004	ECG7004		SK10473
4312	NTE1826	ECG1826		SK9765
4313	NTE1708	ECG1708		SK10017
4314	NTE1788	ECG1788		SK9875
4315		ECG386		
4316	NTE130	ECG130	276-2041	SK3619
4317		ECG962		
4318		ECG21		
4319	NTE1297	ECG1297		SK9265
4320	NTE1043	ECG1043		SK3363
4321		ECG612		
4322				SK7CT4351
4323		ECG598		
4324				SK7CT4352
4325		ECG1189		
4326				SK7CT4353

REPL. CODE	NTE PART NO.	ECG PART NO.	RADIO SHACK PART NO.	RCA PART NO.
4327				SK9140
4328				SK7CT137
4329	NTE74H183	ECG74H183		
4330	NTE74LS147	ECG74LS147		SK7CT147
4331	NTE1169	ECG1169		SK3708
4332				SK6621
4333	NTE552	ECG552		SK3311
4334				SK9422
4335	NTE6405	ECG6405		SK9125
4336				SK7669
4337		ECG524V15		SKMV150K
4338	NTE1038	ECG1038		
4339	NTE1657	ECG1657		SK7673
4340		ECG4053B		
4341	NTE5600	ECG5601	276-1000	SK6601
4342	NTE968	ECG968	276-1771	SK3592
4343	NTE5602	ECG5602	276-1000	SK3664
4344	NTE125	ECG125		SK3081
4345	NTE5606	ECG5607		SK6607
4346	NTE5607	ECG5607		SK6607
4347				SK2041
4348	NTE1127	ECG1127		SK7775
4349	NTE1789	ECG1789		SK9876
4350	NTE116 N6	ECG116 N6	276-1104 N6	SK3017B N6
4351	NTE2708	ECG2708		
4352	NTE74LS290	ECG74LS290		SK74LS290
4353	NTE74LS299	ECG74LS299		SK7CT299
4354				SK3598
4355	NTE1436	ECG1436		
4356				SK9399
4357	NTE378	ECG378		SK3274
4358	NTE3043	ECG3043		SK2043
4359	NTE159	ECG159	276-2023	SK3118
4360		ECG1605		
4361				SK1854
4362	NTE101	ECG101		SK3835
4363		ECG1001		
4364				SK74107
4365	NTE74116			
4366	NTE5614	ECG5614		SK3632
4367	NTE40097B	ECG40097B		SK9787
4368				SK74125
4369		ECG3156		
4370				SK74153
4371				SK74157
4372	NTE74158	ECG74158		SK74158
4373				SK74161
4374				SK74162
4375				SK74163
4376	NTE2310	ECG2310		SK4919
4377				SK74166
4378	NTE107	ECG107		
4379		ECG738		SK9184
4380		ECG738		
4381	NTE5655	ECG5655		SK5555
4382	NTE5656	ECG5656		SK5556
4383				SK74197
4384	NTE5411	ECG5411	276-1067	SK3953
4385				SK7414
4386				SK7CT423
4387		ECG8224		
4388	NTE74C373	ECG74C373		SK74C373
4389	NTE195A	ECG195A		SK3854
4390	NTE195A	ECG195A		SK9645
4391	NTE358A	ECG358A		SK9329
4392	NTE74C374	ECG74C374		SK74C374
4393		ECG157		
4394	NTE1V300	ECG1V300		SKMV300
4395	NTE1V050	ECG1V050		SKMV50B
4396				SK9378
4397	NTE277	ECG277		SK3929
4398	NTE37MCP	ECG37MCP		SK9921
4399	NTE1424	ECG1424		SK7601
4400		ECG188		
4401				SK9377
4402	NTE39	ECG39		SK9260
4403				SK3962
4404	NTE5657	ECG5657		SK5557
4405	NTE1204	ECG1204		
4406		ECG1095		
4407		ECG2348		
4408	NTE4569B	ECG4569B		SK4569B
4409		ECG6247		
4410	NTE2401	ECG2401		SK10103
4411	NTE5552	ECG5552		SK3574
4412		ECG5552		SK3574
4413		ECG5554		SK3575
4414		ECG5556		SK3576
4415		ECG5550		SK3574
4416	NTE1415	ECG1415		SK9058
4417	NTE15045	ECG1873		SK9764
4418		ECG74LS164		SK74LS164
4419	NTE2403	ECG2403		SK10096
4420	NTE88MCP	ECG88MCP		SK9929
4421		ECG988		SK3831
4422		ECG981		SK3724
4423	NTE588	ECG588		SK3043B
4424		ECG950		SK9169
4425		ECG951		SK9170
4426		ECG2164		
4427	NTE1906	ECG1906		SK10048
4428				SK7CT648
4429	NTE1917	ECG1917		SK9219

REPL. CODE	NTE PART NO.	ECG PART NO.	RADIO SHACK PART NO.	RCA PART NO.
4430	NTE1908	ECG1908		SK10050
4431				SK82A
4432	NTE222	ECG222		SK3187
4433		ECG2430		
4434				SK82V
4435		ECG2431		
4436				SK7207
4437	NTE6880	ECG6880		SK9701
4438				SK3356
4439	NTE152	ECG152		SK3893
4440	NTE290A	ECG290A	276-2009	SK3114A
4441	NTE1651	ECG1651		SK7679
4442		ECG5319		
4443	NTE5837	ECG5839		SK7039
4444				SK9946
4445		ECG75452B		
4446	NTE5024A	ECG5024A		SK15A
4447		ECG283		
4448	NTE5015A	ECG5015A		
4449		ECG3041		
4450				SK4054B
4451	NTE4529B	ECG4529B		SK4529B
4452	NTE7007	ECG7007		SK10476
4453				SK7451
4454	NTE285	ECG285		SK9032
4455				SK6632
4456	NTE2074	ECG2074		SK10290
4457				SK9961
4458	NTE9813	ECG9813		
4459		ECG331		SK3188A
4460	NTE386	ECG386		SK9262
4461	NTE9814	ECG9814		
4462		ECG2412		
4463	NTE1124	ECG1124		
4464		ECG2413		
4465	NTE5676	ECG5677		SK3520A
4466		ECG2401		
4467	NTE8080A	ECG8080A		
4468	NTE25	ECG25		SK9841
4469	NTE1437	ECG1437		SK3885
4470		ECG7013		SK10482
4471	NTE995M	ECG995M		SK10451
4472				SK7636
4473	NTE1670	ECG1670		SK10241
4474	NTE74100	ECG74100		
4475	NTE74105			
4476	NTE1022	ECG1022		
4477	NTE1023	ECG1023		
4478				SK6560
4479	NTE1028	ECG1028		SK3436
4480	NTE1480	ECG1480		SK7801
4481	NTE1030	ECG1030		SK3372
4482	NTE1031	ECG1031		
4483	NTE1032	ECG1032		SK7758
4484	NTE1033	ECG1033		SK7759
4485	NTE1035	ECG1035		SK3369
4486	NTE1036	ECG1036		SK3370
4487	NTE2319	ECG2319		SK9261
4488				SK3208
4489	NTE1040	ECG1040		SK3362
4490	NTE1041	ECG1041		SK3361
4491	NTE1042	ECG1042		SK3367
4492		ECG2392		
4493	NTE1288	ECG1288		SK9252
4494	NTE5712	ECG5712		SK10420
4495	NTE1079	ECG1079		SK7766
4496		ECG5460		SK10402
4497	NTE5021A	ECG5021A		
4498	NTE1093	ECG1093		
4499	NTE188&189	ECG188&189		SK3199&3200
4500	NTE173BP			SK3190
4501	NTE5332	ECG5332		SK9231
4502		ECG1105		
4503				SK3189A
4504		ECG189		
4505	NTE6406	ECG6406		SK9082A
4506	NTE1114			
4507				SK3513
4508	NTE5442	ECG5442		SK3634
4509	NTE1119	ECG1119		
4510		ECG2333		SK10299
4511	NTE52	ECG52		
4512	NTE6407	ECG6407		SK9083A
4513	NTE1126	ECG1126		SK7774
4514	NTE1131	ECG1131		SK3286
4515	NTE1132	ECG1132		SK3287
4516	NTE74H22	ECG74H22		
4517	NTE1149	ECG1149		
4518	NTE1150	ECG1150		SK3890
4519		ECG2042		
4520	NTE1154	ECG1154		SK3230
4521	NTE1566	ECG1566		SK7726
4522				SK7CU04
4523	NTE7422	ECG7422		SK7422
4524	NTE65101	ECG65101		SK9829
4525	NTE185MCP	ECG185MCP		
4526	NTE310P	ECG310P		
4527	NTE74C901	ECG74C901		SK7C901
4528	NTE74C902	ECG74C902		SK74C902
4529	NTE74C903	ECG74C903		SK74C903
4530	NTE74C904	ECG74C904		SK74C904
4531	NTE74265			
4532	NTE1184	ECG1184		SK3486

REPL. CODE	NTE PART NO.	ECG PART NO.	RADIO SHACK PART NO.	RCA PART NO.
4533		ECG1768		SK4802
4534	NTE308P	ECG308P		
4535	NTE1190			
4536	NTE74278			
4537		ECG1769		SK4804
4538	NTE74279			
4539	NTE1197	ECG1197		SK3733
4540	NTE74C925	ECG74C925		SK74C925
4541	NTE1201	ECG1201		
4542	NTE1206	ECG1206		SK3160
4543	NTE1208	ECG1208		SK3712
4544	NTE1209	ECG1209		
4545	NTE1212	ECG1212		
4546	NTE1213	ECG1213		SK3704
4547	NTE74298			
4548	NTE15008	ECG15008		SK10183
4549	NTE117	ECG117A	276-1114	SK5010A
4550	NTE1221	ECG1221		SK7781
4551	NTE1229	ECG1229		SK7783
4552	NTE1235	ECG1235		SK3637
4553	NTE1243	ECG1243		SK3731
4554	NTE1246	ECG1246		SK3879
4555	NTE1247	ECG1247		
4556	NTE1251	ECG1251		SK7723
4557	NTE1252	ECG1252		
4558		ECG1253		
4559		ECG1256		SK3873
4560	NTE1257	ECG1257		SK7724
4561	NTE1258	ECG1258		SK7722
4562				SK3365
4563	NTE1260	ECG1260		SK3744
4564	NTE1262	ECG1262		
4565		ECG6885		
4566	NTE6885	ECG6885		SK9793
4567	NTE1271	ECG1271		SK7789
4568	NTE1273	ECG1273		SK3916
4569	NTE1741	ECG1741		SK9994
4570	NTE6886	ECG6886		SK9792
4571	NTE1278	ECG1278		SK3726
4572	NTE1281	ECG1281		SK7661
4573	NTE1282	ECG1282		
4574		ECG6887		
4575	NTE1283	ECG1283		SK9267
4576	NTE1284	ECG1284		SK9268
4577	NTE6887	ECG6887		SK9700
4578	NTE1287	ECG1287		SK9228
4579	NTE40182B	ECG40182B		SK40182B
4580	NTE1289	ECG1289		SK9182
4581	NTE74374			
4582	NTE1291	ECG1291		SK3875
4583	NTE74376			
4584	NTE1293	ECG1293		SK7649
4585		ECG1770		SK4803
4586	NTE6888	ECG6888		SK9791
4587				SK1851
4588	NTE1301	ECG1301		
4589	NTE1303	ECG1303		
4590	NTE1309	ECG1309		
4591	NTE1298	ECG1298		SK9398
4592	NTE1320	ECG1320		
4593		ECG1321		
4594	NTE1322	ECG1322		SK10007
4595	NTE1323	ECG1323		SK3154
4596	NTE1324	ECG1324		
4597	NTE1325	ECG1325		
4598			276-022	SK7659
4599	NTE1326	ECG1326		SK7660
4600	NTE1327	ECG1327		
4601	NTE1328	ECG1328		
4602	NTE1329	ECG1329		
4603	NTE1330	ECG1330		SK9406
4604	NTE1331	ECG1331		SK9189
4605		ECG1332		
4606	NTE1333	ECG1333		
4607		ECG1334		
4608	NTE1335	ECG1335		
4609	NTE1336	ECG1336		
4610	NTE1337	ECG1337		
4611				SK7C107
4612	NTE1339	ECG1339		SK9997
4613	NTE1340	ECG1340		
4614	NTE1341	ECG1341		
4615	NTE1342	ECG1342		
4616	NTE74426			
4617	NTE1343	ECG1343		
4618	NTE1344	ECG1344		
4619		ECG1207		
4620	NTE1346	ECG1346		
4621	NTE1347	ECG1347		
4622	NTE1348	ECG1348		
4623		ECG1349		
4624	NTE1350	ECG1350		
4625		ECG1351		
4626		ECG1352		
4627	NTE1354	ECG1354		
4628		ECG74HC123		SK7C123
4629	NTE1355	ECG1355		
4630		ECG74HC125		SK7C125
4631		ECG74HC126		SK7C126
4632	NTE1361	ECG1361		SK9361
4633	NTE1363	ECG1363		SK7630
4634	NTE1364	ECG1364		
4635	NTE1365	ECG1365		SK9395

REPL. CODE	NTE PART NO.	ECG PART NO.	RADIO SHACK PART NO.	RCA PART NO.
4636	NTE1366	ECG1366		
4637	NTE1367	ECG1367		
4638	NTE1368	ECG1368		
4639	NTE1369	ECG1369		
4640	NTE552 N2	ECG552 N2	276-1102 N2	SK9000 N2
4641	NTE1370	ECG1370		SK4821
4642	NTE1371	ECG1371		
4643	NTE1372	ECG1372		
4644	NTE1378	ECG1378		SK7706
4645	NTE1379	ECG1379		SK7663
4646	NTE1380	ECG1380		SK9251
4647	NTE1381	ECG1381		SK7622
4648	NTE1383	ECG1383		
4649	NTE1384	ECG1384		
4650		ECG74HC153		SK7C153
4651	NTE1385	ECG1385		
4652		ECG74HC154		SK7C154
4653	NTE1388	ECG1388		SK9186
4654	NTE1389	ECG1389		
4655	NTE1391	ECG1391		SK7814
4656	NTE1392	ECG1392		
4657		ECG74HC161		SK7C161
4658	NTE1393	ECG1393		
4659	NTE1394	ECG1394		
4660				SK7C166
4661				SK1852
4662	NTE1404	ECG1404		
4663	NTE1405	ECG1405		SK9018
4664	NTE1407	ECG1407		
4665	NTE1408	ECG1408		SK9064
4666	NTE1412	ECG1412		SK9045
4667				SK7C181
4668				SK7C182
4669	NTE1414	ECG1414		SK9326
4670	NTE1419	ECG1419		SK9046
4671	NTE1421	ECG1421		SK9051
4672				SK7C190
4673				SK7C191
4674				SK7C192
4675				SK7C193
4676	NTE1467	ECG1467		SK4839
4677	NTE1425	ECG1425		SK9049
4678	NTE1427	ECG1427		SK9050
4679	NTE1429	ECG1429		
4680	NTE1431	ECG1431		SK7793
4681	NTE1433	ECG1433		
4682	NTE1435	ECG1435		SK7794
4683	NTE1438	ECG1438		
4684	NTE1441	ECG1441		SK7795
4685	NTE1442	ECG1442		
4686	NTE3163	ECG3163		SK2163
4687	NTE1447	ECG1447		
4688				SK9976
4689	NTE1449	ECG1449		
4690	NTE1451	ECG1451		
4691		ECG2043		
4692	NTE1452	ECG1452		SK7796
4693				SK7C221
4694	NTE1455	ECG1455		
4695	NTE1457	ECG1457		
4696	NTE1458	ECG1458		
4697	NTE1460	ECG1460		SK7798
4698	NTE1462	ECG1462		
4699	NTE1464	ECG1464		
4700	NTE1469	ECG1469		SK9356
4701	NTE552 N1	ECG552 N1	276-1104 N1	SK9000 N1
4702				SK7C238
4703	NTE1472	ECG1472		SK7800
4704	NTE284	ECG284		SK3260
4705	NTE1473	ECG1473		SK9355
4706	NTE1758	ECG1758		SK10041
4707	NTE1474	ECG1474		
4708	NTE1475	ECG1475		SK4838
4709				SK7C244
4710	NTE1476	ECG1476		
4711	NTE1477	ECG1477		
4712	NTE1478	ECG1478		
4713	NTE1724	ECG1724		SK7650
4714	NTE1481	ECG1481		
4715	NTE1482	ECG1482		
4716	NTE1484	ECG1484		
4717				SK7C253
4718				SK7C257
4719	NTE1489	ECG1489		
4720				SK7C258
4721	NTE1490	ECG1490		SK9312
4722				SK7C259
4723	NTE1491	ECG1491		
4724	NTE1492	ECG1492		SK9196
4725	NTE1493	ECG1493		
4726	NTE1494	ECG1494		
4727	NTE1495	ECG1495		
4728	NTE1497	ECG1497		
4729	NTE1498	ECG1498		
4730	NTE1499	ECG1499		SK7667
4731	NTE1500	ECG1500		
4732				SK1853
4733	NTE1501	ECG1501		
4734				SK7668
4735	NTE1502	ECG1502		
4736	NTE1503	ECG1503		SK7802
4737	NTE1504	ECG1504		
4738				SK7C273

REPL. CODE	NTE PART NO.	ECG PART NO.	RADIO SHACK PART NO.	RCA PART NO.
4739	NTE1505	ECG1505		
4740		ECG1507		
4741	NTE1511	ECG1511		
4742	NTE1513	ECG1513		SK9250
4743	NTE1514	ECG1514		
4744				SK7C283
4745		ECG5309		
4746	NTE1515	ECG1515		SK7656
4747	NTE1516	ECG1516		
4748				SK74123
4749		ECG5310		
4750	NTE1517	ECG1517		SK7704
4751	NTE1518	ECG1518		
4752	NTE1519	ECG1519		SK7803
4753		ECG5311		
4754	NTE1523	ECG1523		
4755				SK3544
4756	NTE1626	ECG1626		SK7652
4757		ECG1526		SK4539B
4758	NTE1527	ECG1527		
4759				SK7C297
4760	NTE1530	ECG1530		
4761		ECG74HC299		SK7C299
4762	NTE1531	ECG1531		
4763	NTE1533	ECG1533		
4764				SK18A
4765	NTE1534	ECG1534		
4766	NTE1536	ECG1536		SK3884
4767	NTE1537	ECG1537		
4768				SK9741
4769	NTE1543	ECG1543		
4770	NTE1544	ECG1544		SK9193
4771				SK6649
4772	NTE74H21	ECG74H21		
4773	NTE1615	ECG1615		SK9977
4774		ECG123A		
4775		ECG5015A		
4776				SK7C354
4777				SK7C356
4778	NTE68MCP	ECG68MCP		SK9927
4779		ECG74HC377		SK7C377
4780	NTE524V27	ECG524V27		SK10060
4781	NTE2085	ECG2085		SK9913
4782		ECG1886		SK10086
4783	NTE3052	ECG3052		SK2052
4784	NTE3065	ECG3065		SK2065
4785	NTE524V30	ECG524V30		
4786	NTE3056	ECG3056	276-075	SK2056
4787		ECG166		
4788				SK9306
4789				SK7C423
4790				SK3638
4791		ECG3105		
4792		ECG4510B		SK4510B
4793				SK1855
4794		ECG1910		
4795		ECG1868		
4796		ECG90		SK9370
4797		ECG1917		
4798		ECG1905		
4799	NTE1907	ECG1907		SK10049
4800	NTE54	ECG54		SK9112
4801				SK7C540
4802				SK7C541
4803				SK9401
4804				SK7CT4510
4805				SK7C563
4806				SK7C564
4807				SK7CT4511
4808				SK7206
4809		ECG74HC573		SK7C573
4810		ECG74HC574		SK7C574
4811	NTE123AP	ECG123AP	276-2009	SK3433
4812				SK7C583
4813		ECG5328		SK9088
4814				SK7C597
4815	NTE2107	ECG2107		
4816				SK7CT4514
4817	NTE7488A			
4818		ECG961		SK3671
4819		ECG963		SK3672
4820	NTE5021T1	ECG5021T1		SK9771
4821				SK7CT4515
4822				SK7CT4516
4823				SK7CT02
4824				SK4060B
4825				SK7C640
4826				SK7CT4518
4827				SK7C643
4828				SK7C646
4829				SK7C648
4830		ECG596		
4831				SK7CT4520
4832				SK7C670
4833	NTE580	ECG580		SK3925
4834	NTE1V075	ECG1V075		SKMV75A
4835	NTE6116	ECG6116		SK10217
4836				SK7C688
4837				SK10178
4838	NTE1828	ECG1828		SK9736
4839		ECG753		SK7191
4840	NTE1684	ECG1684		SK9729
4841	NTE389	ECG389		SK3111

REPL. CODE	NTE PART NO.	ECG PART NO.	RADIO SHACK PART NO.	RCA PART NO.
4842	NTE15039			
4843	NTE15042	ECG7019		SK10488
4844	NTE15043			
4845	NTE3044	ECG3044		SK4935
4846	NTE2003	ECG2003		
4847				SK4332
4848	NTE2015	ECG2015		SK9095
4849	NTE2016	ECG2016		SK9077
4850	NTE2017	ECG2017		SK9078
4851				SK16V
4852	NTE2018	ECG2018		SK9079
4853	NTE2019	ECG2019		SK9080
4854	NTE2020	ECG2020		SK9081
4855				SK22A
4856	NTE2025	ECG2025		
4857	NTE280	ECG284	276-2041	SK3836
4858		ECG585		
4859		ECG578		
4860		ECG2029		
4861	NTE580	ECG580	276-1114	SK3081
4862	NTE2031	ECG2031		
4863	NTE2032	ECG2032		SK9203
4864	NTE2050	ECG2050		SK10279
4865	NTE2051	ECG2051		SK10280
4866	NTE7005	ECG7005		SK10474
4867	NTE2054	ECG2054		SK9204
4868	NTE2070	ECG2070		SK10286
4869	NTE2071	ECG2071		SK10287
4870	NTE2072	ECG2072		SK10288
4871				SK7CT4538
4872	NTE2073	ECG2073		SK10289
4873				SK3115
4874	NTE2075	ECG2075		SK10291
4875	NTE2076	ECG2076		SK10292
4876	NTE2077	ECG2077		SK10293
4877		ECG5022A		
4878	NTE2078	ECG2078		SK10294
4879	NTE2080	ECG2080		
4880	NTE2081	ECG2081		
4881	NTE2082	ECG2082		SK9903
4882	NTE2083	ECG2083		SK9906
4883	NTE2087	ECG2087		SK9813
4884				SK7331
4885				SK74LS109
4886	NTE2102	ECG2102		
4887	NTE2104	ECG2104		
4888	NTE129	ECG129		SK3179B
4889	NTE4513B	ECG4513B		SK4513B
4890				SK9002
4891		ECG6155		SK7355
4892				SK7CT4543
4893				SK3533
4894				SK5137
4895				SK3937
4896		ECG61		
4897				SK4007UB
4898	NTE213	ECG213		SK3500
4899	NTE1570	ECG1570		SK7681
4900	NTE3050	ECG3050		SK10403
4901	NTE3051	ECG3051		SK10328
4902	NTE3061	ECG3061		SK2061
4903	NTE4521B	ECG4521B		SK4521B
4904		ECG5983		
4905		ECG5987		
4906		ECG5991		
4907		ECG5995		
4908		ECG5999		
4909		ECG6003		
4910		ECG5818		
4911				SK3912
4912	NTE15007	ECG15007		SK10182
4913	NTE75322			
4914		ECG5994		
4915		ECG5998		
4916		ECG6002		
4917	NTE5913	ECG5913		SK10423
4918			276-145	
4919		ECG519		
4920		ECG129&427		SK3025
4921				SK1861
4922	NTE2410	ECG2410		
4923	NTE1677	ECG1677		SK9769
4924	NTE5827	ECG5827		SK7377
4925				SK5555
4926	NTE5534	ECG5534		SK3505
4927		ECG517		
4928	NTE3131	ECG3131	276-030	SK2170
4929	NTE4541B	ECG4541B		SK4541B
4930	NTE83	ECG83		
4931				SK1862
4932	NTE4543B	ECG4543B		SK4543B
4933	NTE75493	ECG75493		SK75493
4934	NTE75494	ECG75494		SK9825
4935				SK7651
4936	NTE75498	ECG75498		
4937	NTE5426	ECG5426		SK3954
4938	NTE5962	ECG5962		SK7362
4939		ECG216		
4940		ECG9383		
4941	NTE5534	ECG5534		SK6622
4942		ECG5552		
4943	NTE4547B	ECG4547B		SK4547B
4944	NTE2393		ECG2393	

REPL. CODE	NTE PART NO.	ECG PART NO.	RADIO SHACK PART NO.	RCA PART NO.
4945	NTE128P	ECG128P		SK9468
4946		ECG351		SK3177
4947	NTE358B	ECG358B		SK9330
4948		ECG3158		
4949	NTE5875	ECG5875		SK3517
4950	NTE4551B	ECG4551B		SK4551B
4951	NTE4553B	ECG4553B		SK4553B
4952	NTE1905	ECG1905		SK9222
4953		ECG519		SK3100
4954				SK3710
4955	NTE1843	ECG1843		SK10146
4956				SK7CT154
4957	NTE6102	ECG6102		SK10209
4958		ECG1726		
4959	NTE1678	ECG1678		SK9947
4960	NTE4558B	ECG4558B		SK4558B
4961	NTE3047	ECG3047	276-134	SK9708
4962				SK7691
4963				SK1864
4964		ECG1767		
4965				SK7690
4966		ECG35		
4967	NTE41	ECG41		SK9424
4968	NTE43	ECG43		SK9426
4969	NTE45	ECG45		SK9428
4970	NTE66	ECG66		SK9165
4971	NTE14	ECG14		SK9662
4972	NTE78	ECG78		
4973	NTE3171	ECG3171		SK10440
4974	NTE84	ECG84		
4975	NTE3048	ECG3048		SK2048
4976	NTE52	ECG52		SK9261
4977				SK7CT40102
4978				SK7CT40103
4979				SK7CT40104
4980				SK7CT40105
4981		ECG1622		SK9044
4982				SK7C40102
4983				SK7C40103
4984				SK7C40104
4985		ECG74HC40105		SK7C40105
4986				SK7611
4987		ECG5536		
4988	NTE5539	ECG5539		SK10407
4989	NTE5536	ECG5536		SK10405
4990	NTE1151			
4991		ECG5668A		
4992	NTE1164	ECG1164		SK3072
4993		ECG116		SK3032A
4994				SK74LS122
4995		ECG81		
4996		ECG74LS571		
4997				SK1866
4998	NTE152MP	ECG152MP		SK9936
4999		ECG5025A		
5000	NTE4584B			
5001		ECG755		SK3170
5002		ECG48		
5003	NTE1295	ECG1295		SK9299
5004	NTE1299	ECG1299		SK9314
5005	NTE2387	ECG2387		SK10304
5006		ECG2047		
5007	NTE2532	ECG2532		
5008	NTE1356	ECG1356		
5009	NTE1357	ECG1357		
5010	NTE1359	ECG1359		
5011				SK40147B
5012	NTE16007			
5013	NTE1362	ECG1362		SK9396
5014	NTE5426	ECG5426		SK3953
5015	NTE1390	ECG1390		SK7815
5016	NTE1397	ECG1397		SK7603
5017		ECG74S474		
5018	NTE1398	ECG1398		SK9191
5019	NTE1399	ECG1399		SK9269
5020	NTE3004	ECG3004		SK2004
5021	NTE3005	ECG3005		SK2005
5022		ECG3006		SK2006A
5023	NTE3009	ECG3009		SK2009A
5024	NTE3012	ECG3012	276-033	
5025	NTE3013	ECG3013		
5026	NTE1432	ECG1432		
5027	NTE3019	ECG3019		SK2019
5028				SK4098B
5029	NTE1443	ECG1443		SK3967
5030	NTE3031	ECG3031		SK2031
5031	NTE3037	ECG3037		SK10325
5032	NTE3038	ECG3038		SK10326
5033	NTE3039	ECG3039		SK9705
5034	NTE3049	ECG3049		SK2049
5035	NTE3053	ECG3053		SK2053
5036	NTE3054	ECG3054		SK2054
5037	NTE3055	ECG3055		SK2055
5038	NTE3058	ECG3058		SK2058
5039	NTE3059	ECG3059		SK2059
5040	NTE3060	ECG3060		SK2060
5041	NTE128P	ECG128P	276-2009	SK3854
5042	NTE3062	ECG3062		SK2062
5043	NTE3063	ECG3063		SK2063
5044				SK74LS151
5045	NTE3064	ECG3064		SK2064
5046	NTE3068	ECG3068		SK2068
5047	NTE3069	ECG3069		SK2069

REPL. CODE	NTE PART NO.	ECG PART NO.	RADIO SHACK PART NO.	RCA PART NO.
5048	NTE3070	ECG3070		SK2070
5049	NTE3071	ECG3071		SK2071
5050	NTE3082	ECG3082		SK4934
5051		ECG5675		
5052	NTE159	ECG159	276-2023	SK10272
5053				SK1869
5054				SK7CT4046A
5055	NTE290A	ECG290A		SK9132
5056				SK3036
5057				SK7C7046A
5058	NTE580	ECG580		
5059		ECG5331		
5060	NTE3114	ECG3114		SK2114
5061				SK7C4046A
5062	NTE3115	ECG3115	276-081	SK2115
5063	NTE3116	ECG3116		SK2116
5064	NTE3117	ECG3117		SK2117
5065	NTE1535	ECG1535		
5066	NTE1V095	ECG1V095		SKMV95A
5067	NTE1554	ECG1554		
5068	NTE1556	ECG1556		SK7657
5069	NTE1559	ECG1559		
5070	NTE1561	ECG1561		SK7610
5071	NTE1562	ECG1562		
5072	NTE174			SK3130
5073	NTE3150	ECG3150		SK2150
5074				SK74LS161
5075	NTE3151	ECG3151		SK2151
5076	NTE3152	ECG3152		SK2152
5077	NTE1568	ECG1568		
5078	NTE3153	ECG3153		SK2153
5079	NTE3155	ECG3155		
5080	NTE1571	ECG1571		SK7677
5081		ECG5002A		
5082	NTE3160	ECG3160		SK2160
5083	NTE1577	ECG1577		
5084	NTE3162	ECG3162		SK2162
5085	NTE1579	ECG1579		
5086	NTE3165	ECG3165		SK2165
5087	NTE3168	ECG3168		SK2168
5088	NTE1585	ECG1585		
5089	NTE1591	ECG1591		SK7602
5090	NTE1593	ECG1593		
5091	NTE1597	ECG1597		
5092				SK74LS163
5093	NTE1600	ECG1600		SK10221
5094				SK11A
5095	NTE1602	ECG1602		SK10223
5096	NTE1606	ECG1606		SK4828
5097	NTE1607	ECG1607		
5098	NTE156A			
5099	NTE1611	ECG1611		SK9990
5100	NTE1613	ECG1613		SK10010
5101	NTE1620	ECG1620		
5102	NTE1621	ECG1621		SK10230
5103	NTE1624	ECG1624		SK7611
5104				SK3125A
5105	NTE1631	ECG1631		SK10233
5106	NTE1632	ECG1632		SK4812
5107	NTE1635	ECG1635		SK9706
5108	NTE1637	ECG1637		
5109	NTE1641	ECG1641		SK10239
5110	NTE338F	ECG338F		SK9615
5111	NTE1648	ECG1648		SK9053
5112	NTE1649	ECG1649		
5113	NTE1654	ECG1654		SK7670
5114	NTE1659	ECG1659		
5115	NTE1662	ECG1662		
5116	NTE1663	ECG1663		SK9324
5117	NTE1664	ECG1664		SK4833
5118	NTE1666	ECG1666		
5119	NTE3154	ECG3154		SK2154
5120	NTE1672	ECG1672		SK10242
5121				SK3008
5122	NTE1681	ECG1681		SK10246
5123	NTE1682	ECG1682		SK7713
5124		ECG1746		
5125	NTE74LS173A	ECG74LS173		SK1922
5126	NTE1688	ECG1688		SK9725
5127	NTE1690	ECG1690		
5128	NTE1691	ECG1691		
5129	NTE1692	ECG1692		
5130	NTE1693	ECG1693		
5131	NTE5092A	ECG5092A		SK62V
5132	NTE1700	ECG1700		SK9980
5133	NTE1701	ECG1701		SK10008
5134	NTE1702	ECG1702		SK10013
5135		ECG82		
5136		ECG1704		SK9981
5137	NTE1709	ECG1709		SK10080
5138				SK1871
5139	NTE1717	ECG1717		SK10022
5140	NTE1720	ECG1720		SK9983
5141	NTE1726	ECG1726		SK10028
5142				SK4A3
5143	NTE1730	ECG1730		SK9955
5144	NTE1731	ECG1731		
5145	NTE1734	ECG1734		SK7810
5146	NTE1745	ECG1745		SK10033
5147		ECG5455		SK3597
5148	NTE1749	ECG1749		SK10001
5149	NTE1750	ECG1750		SK10035
5150	NTE1753	ECG1753		SK10037

REPL. CODE	NTE PART NO.	ECG PART NO.	RADIO SHACK PART NO.	RCA PART NO.
5151	NTE1757	ECG1757		
5152		ECG4070B		SK4070B
5153	NTE1761	ECG1761		
5154				SK10108
5155	NTE1762	ECG1762		SK10044
5156	NTE1764	ECG1764		
5157	NTE1774	ECG1774		SK9867
5158				SK19A
5159	NTE74H106	ECG74H106		
5160	NTE1785	ECG1785		
5161		ECG5633		
5162	NTE1791	ECG1791		SK9717
5163	NTE1796	ECG1796		SK9880
5164		ECG74S478		
5165	NTE1808	ECG1808		SK9722
5166	NTE1809	ECG1809		SK9724
5167	NTE1811	ECG1811		SK9733
5168	NTE1812	ECG1812		SK9734
5169	NTE1813	ECG1813		SK9735
5170	NTE1814	ECG1814		SK9739
5171				SKMV250L
5172	NTE1816	ECG1816		SK9897
5173				SK1872
5174	NTE1817	ECG1817		SK9890
5175	NTE1818	ECG1818		SK9893
5176	NTE1819	ECG1819		SK9882
5177	NTE1820	ECG1820		SK9889
5178	NTE1829	ECG1829		SK9737
5179	NTE1830	ECG1830		SK9896
5180	NTE1831	ECG1831		SK9895
5181		ECG595		
5182	NTE1849	ECG1849		SK10149
5183	NTE1871	ECG1871		SK10140
5184	NTE1874	ECG1874		SK10141
5185	NTE1875	ECG1875		SK10166
5186	NTE1876	ECG1876		
5187	NTE1900	ECG1900		SK7644
5188	NTE1901	ECG1901		SK10047
5189	NTE5914	ECG5916		SK10424
5190	NTE5918	ECG5920		SK10426
5191		ECG2084		SK4910
5192	NTE5922	ECG5924		SK10428
5193	NTE1915	ECG1915		SK9335
5194				SK1873
5195	NTE1919	ECG1919		SK9336
5196	NTE1923	ECG1923		SK10054
5197	NTE1926	ECG1926		
5198	NTE1927	ECG1927		
5199	NTE1934	ECG1934		SK7739
5200	NTE999SM	ECG999SM		SK10516
5201				SK9037
5202	NTE1938	ECG1938		SK7741
5203	NTE1940	ECG1940		SK7742
5204	NTE999M	ECG999M		SK10515
5205		ECG193A		
5206				SK2214
5207				SK10124
5208	NTE74H76	ECG74H76		
5209	NTE350F	ECG350F		SK9625
5210	NTE943M	ECG943M		SK9721
5211	NTE2000	ECG2000		
5212				SK9431
5213				SK1874
5214				SK3130
5215				SK22859
5216	NTE2047	ECG2047		
5217	NTE2056	ECG2056		
5218	NTE2086	ECG2086		SK9907
5219	NTE2088	ECG2088		SK9908
5220		ECG9615		
5221				SK1875
5222		ECG5596		SK6746
5223				SK6747
5224	NTE1183	ECG1183		SK3328
5225				SK3023
5226	NTE5638	ECG5638		SK5538
5227	NTE56015	ECG56015		SK10266
5228	NTE15043	ECG1807		SK9839
5229	NTE6079	ECG6079		SK9710
5230	NTE56016	ECG56016		SK10267
5231				SK9284
5232				SK9723
5233	NTE383	ECG383		SK3715
5234				SK1876
5235	NTE178MP	ECG178MP	276-1122	SK3088
5236	NTE178MP	ECG178MP	276-1122	SK9002
5237				SK9328
5238				SK9719
5239		ECG85		SK3245
5240				SK7664
5241	NTE74H01	ECG74H01		
5242	NTE3882	ECG3882		SK2882
5243		ECG1170		SK3745
5244	NTE2314	ECG2314		SK9482
5245	NTE2316	ECG2316		SK10116
5246				SK1877
5247		ECG1439		
5248	NTE2318	ECG2318		SK9986
5249	NTE340	ECG340	276-2009	SK3452
5250	NTE213	ECG213		SK3006
5251	NTE2323	ECG2323		
5252	NTE2329	ECG2329		SK9489
5253	NTE2340	ECG2340		SK9479

REPL. CODE	NTE PART NO.	ECG PART NO.	RADIO SHACK PART NO.	RCA PART NO.
5254				SK3925
5255	NTE2351	ECG2351		SK9856
5256	NTE2352	ECG2352		SK9857
5257				SK10111
5258	NTE74H08	ECG74H08		
5259	NTE15006	ECG15006		SK10181
5260		ECG1563		SK7621
5261				SK9935
5262				SK3108
5263	NTE2381	ECG2381		SK10127
5264	NTE2390	ECG2390		SK10132
5265	HVD-12	ECG-HIDIV-12		SK9106
5266	NTE2392	ECG2392		SK10133
5267	NTE2404	ECG2404		SK10104
5268	NTE2405	ECG2405		SK10105
5269	NTE2411	ECG2411		SK10102
5270				SK3715
5271	NTE2413	ECG2413		SK10109
5272	NTE2426	ECG2426		SK10112
5273	NTE2427	ECG2427		SK10113
5274	NTE2431	ECG2431		SK10115
5275	NTE85	ECG85	276-2009	SK9137
5276		ECG19		SK3912
5277		ECG5008A		
5278				SK10110
5279	NTE289AMP	ECG289AMP	276-2009	SK3124A
5280	NTE159	ECG159	276-2023	SK9132
5281				SK3583
5282		ECG3024		SK2024
5283		ECG374		SK9370
5284	NTE74H30	ECG74H30		
5285	NTE74HC02	ECG74HC02		SK7C02
5286		ECG2408		
5287	NTE3026	ECG3026		SK2026
5288	NTE398	ECG398		SK9370
5289		ECG6408		
5290	NTE6411	ECG6411		SK4922
5291		ECG6412		
5292	NTE1890	ECG1890		SK10520
5293		ECG2050		
5294	NTE36MP	ECG36MP		SK9920
5295		ECG5635		
5296		ECG5646		SK9711
5297				SK3857
5298				SK10444
5299		ECG1810		
5300				SK10226
5301		ECG5322		
5302				SK74LS279
5303		ECG5324		
5304		ECG5011A		
5305		ECG5326		
5306		ECG290A		SK3932
5307				SK3031A
5308		ECG2429		
5309	NTE238	ECG238	276-2055	2SD822
5310		ECG2359		SK9959
5311		ECG124		
5312	NTE74H60	ECG74H60		
5313	NTE74HC32	ECG74HC32		
5314		ECG5671		
5315		ECG74HC161		
5316		ECG2319		
5317		ECG127		
5318		ECG199		SK3018
5319		ECG261		
5320	NTE74H78	ECG74H78		
5321				SK9264
5322				SK10094
5323	NTE3085	ECG3085		SK10330
5324	NTE52	ECG52		SK3559
5325	NTE3087	ECG3087		SK2087
5326	NTE3088	ECG3088		SK10331
5327	NTE3089	ECG3089		SK10332
5328	NTE3090	ECG3090		SK4933
5329	NTE3093	ECG3093		SK10334
5330	NTE3095	ECG3095		SK10335
5331	NTE3096	ECG3096		SK10337
5332	NTE3097	ECG3097		SK10336
5333	NTE2324		ECG2324	
5334	NTE213	ECG213		SK3717
5335	NTE3103	ECG3103		SK4916
5336	NTE3111	ECG3111		SK2111
5337	NTE3112	ECG3112		SK2112
5338	NTE3113	ECG3113		SK2113
5339		ECG3174		
5340		ECG3054		SK2054
5341	NTE3130	ECG3130		SK2171
5342		ECG3063		SK2063
5343				SK3993
5344		ECG3059		SK2059
5345		ECG977		
5346	NTE3169	ECG3169		SK10445
5347	NTE3170	ECG3170		SK10439
5348				SK9968
5349	NTE3180	ECG3180		SK10446
5350	NTE3181	ECG3181		SK10441
5351	NTE3182	ECG3182		SK10442
5352				SK10093
5353				SK9457
5354	NTE390	ECG390		SK9389
5355		ECG2326		
5356		ECG270		SK9417

REPL. CODE	NTE PART NO.	ECG PART NO.	RADIO SHACK PART NO.	RCA PART NO.
5357	NTE2411	ECG2411		
5358	NTE7489	ECG7489		SK7489
5359		ECG36		SK9389
5360	NTE263	ECG263		SK3896
5361				SK3105
5362		ECG4901		SK10192
5363		ECG56020		SK9808
5364				SK9972
5365	NTE217	ECG217		SK3466
5366	NTE2351	ECG2351		SK9417
5367				SK9458
5368		ECG130		
5369		ECG282&427		SK9841
5370		ECG398		SK3930
5371		ECG219		
5372	NTE378	ECG378		SK3934
5373	NTE5429	ECG5429		SK3503
5374		ECG199		SK3245
5375				SK3111
5376		ECG383		SK9454
5377	NTE181MP	ECG181MP		SK9984
5378		ECG378		
5379				SK4049UB
5380				SK9390
5381	NTE37	ECG37		SK9390
5382				SK9467
5383		ECG2306		
5384	NTE2300	ECG2300		SK9487
5385	NTE2302	ECG2302		
5386	NTE5322	ECG5322	276-1185	SK3679
5387				SK9944
5388	NTE55		ECG55	
5389				SK3861
5390				SK3452
5391				SK7C4002
5392		ECG288		
5393		ECG1087		SK3477
5394	NTE5915	ECG5917		SK10425
5395	NTE55	ECG55		SK9117
5396		ECG593		
5397		ECG2329		
5398	NTE5919	ECG5921		SK10427
5399	NTE5923	ECG5925		SK10429
5400		ECG186A		
5401	NTE219MCP	ECG219MCP		
5402	NTE156 N6	ECG156 N6	276-1114 N6	SK3051 N6
5403	NTE55	ECG55		
5404		ECG1218		
5405				SK9331
5406	NTE358C	ECG358C		
5407		ECG263		
5408	NTE570	ECG570		
5409				SK7C4015
5410				SK7C4016
5411		ECG11		
5412		ECG1714S		
5413		ECG2428		
5414				SK7C4017
5415				SK7C4020
5416		ECG977		SK3462
5417	NTE5892	ECG5892		SK7092
5418				SK7C4024
5419	NTE3034A	ECG3034		SK2032
5420	NTE5833	ECG5835		SK7049
5421				SK9169
5422				SK7C7030
5423		ECG6362		SK6560
5424	NTE74H101	ECG74H101		
5425				SK9170
5426	NTE74H102	ECG74H102		
5427				SK9508
5428				SK3313
5429	NTE5425	ECG5425		
5430	NTE8309	ECG8309		
5431				SK9762
5432		ECG74HC11		
5433	NTE778SM	ECG778SM		SK10061
5434				SK7C4040
5435	NTE282	ECG282		SK3054
5436		ECG5608		
5437	NTE2353	ECG2353		
5438		ECG74HC86		
5439	NTE179MP	ECG179MP		
5440		ECG184		
5441				SK7C4049
5442		ECG4001B		
5443				SK7C4050
5444				SK3327
5445		ECG54		
5446				SK7C4051
5447				SK7629
5448				SK7C4052
5449		ECG1701		
5450	NTE1314	ECG1314		
5451				SK7C4053
5452	NTE5611	ECG5612		SK6630
5453	NTE5612	ECG5612		SK6630
5454	NTE5621	ECG5622		SK3631
5455		ECG2338		
5456	NTE5649	ECG5649		
5457	NTE5653	ECG5653		
5458		ECG373		
5459				SK7C4059

REPL. CODE	NTE PART NO.	ECG PART NO.	RADIO SHACK PART NO.	RCA PART NO.
5460		ECG4002B		
5461	NTE5672	ECG5672		
5462				SK7C4060
5463		ECG1270		SK9055
5464				SK7714
5465		ECG74LS259		
5466		ECG3007		SK2007
5467	NTE5841	ECG5843		SK7043
5468	NTE195A	ECG195A		SK3444
5469	NTE5340	ECG5340		SK9100
5470				SK9007
5471				SK7C4066
5472				SK7C4067
5473	NTE4164	ECG2164		SK10297
5474	NTE178MP	ECG178MP	276-1122	SK3033A
5475		ECG5605		
5476				SK7C4075
5477	NTE5829	ECG5829		
5478				SK3517
5479	NTE376		ECG376	
5480				SK9635
5481		ECG4034B		SK4034B
5482	NTE5894	ECG5896		SK7096
5483	NTE5898	ECG5900		SK7100
5484		ECG316		
5485	NTE2764	ECG2764		SK2716
5486				SK9960
5487	NTE5946	ECG5948		SK3605
5488		ECG188		SK3199
5489	NTE5950	ECG5952		SK3585
5490				SK1912
5491		ECG189		SK3200
5492		ECG80		SK9351
5493	NTE178MP	ECG178MP	276-1122	SK3087
5494	NTE184MP	ECG184MP		
5495				SK7C4094
5496	NTE74C922	ECG74C922		SK74C922
5497		ECG1169		
5498	NTE74C923	ECG74C923		SK74C923
5499		ECG273		SK9437
5500		ECG7073		
5501				SK3453
5502	NTE54MP	ECG54MP		SK9922
5503	NTE5342	ECG5342		SK9102
5504				SK3450
5505		ECG290A		
5506		ECG56018		
5507		ECG6084		SK9709
5508				SK9383
5509		ECG56030		
5510		ECG125		SK3043B
5511	NTE56020	ECG56020		SK9808
5512		ECG74HC4020		
5513		ECG477		
5514		ECG74HC4040		
5515				SK7744
5516		ECG74HC4053		
5517		ECG1259		
5518		ECG74HC4060		
5519		ECG74HC4067		
5520	NTE2324		ECG2324	
5521				SK3589A
5522		ECG128&427		SK3024
5523				SK6402
5524				SK3521
5525				SK3509
5526		ECG47		
5527				SK6681
5528	NTE605	ECG605A		SK3864
5529				SK3319
5530		ECG106		
5531		ECG568A		SK3910
5532		ECG126A		
5533				SK40181B
5534		ECG285		
5535		ECG284		
5536				SK3667
5537	NTE6412	ECG6412		
5538				SK3462
5539	NTE6415	ECG6415		SK9846
5540	NTE6416	ECG6416		SK9844
5541		ECG468		
5542	NTE6417	ECG6417		SK9843
5543	NTE6418	ECG6418		SK4921
5544	NTE6419	ECG6419		SK4920
5545		ECG457		SK9161
5546				SK10V
5547		ECG129P		SK3715
5548	NTE1595	ECG1595		
5549		ECG2386		SK10130
5550		ECG5690		
5551	NTE116	ECG116		SK3313
5552				SK74LS03
5553				SK3V3
5554				SK3V9
5555				SK4V7
5556		ECG3104		SK10179
5557	NTE5037A	ECG5037A		
5558				SK20V
5559				SK22V
5560			276-018	
5561				SK39V
5562				SK120V

REPL. CODE	NTE PART NO.	ECG PART NO.	RADIO SHACK PART NO.	RCA PART NO.
5563				SK150V
5564				SK3146
5565				SK180V
5566				SK200V
5567				SK5579
5568	NTE3094	ECG3094		SK10404
5569	NTE1595	ECG1595		SK3986
5570		ECG612		SK3325
5571	NTE213	ECG213		SK3444
5572	NTE962	ECG962		
5573	NTE760	ECG760		SK3158
5574		ECG55		
5575	NTE15009	ECG15009		SK10184
5576		ECG1088		
5577		ECG379		
5578		ECG1018		SK3284
5579		ECG3166		
5580		ECG85		
5581		ECG2357		SK10124
5582		ECG830		SK74151
5583				SK4555B
5584		ECG2416		SK10108
5585	NTE1183	ECG1183		SK3704
5586		ECG4012B		
5587	NTE60MP	ECG60MP		SK9924
5588	NTE5314	ECG5314	276-1181	SK3987
5589	NTE3035A	ECG3035A		
5590		ECG5096A		
5591	NTE1218	ECG1220		SK3740
5592		ECG1222		SK3730
5593	NTE5069A	ECG5069A		
5594	NTE5011T1	ECG5011T1		
5595				SK3433
5596		ECG3092		
5597		ECG80C96		
5598		ECG1870		SK10161
5599	NTE61MP	ECG61MP		SK9926
5600		ECG1274		
5601		ECG1275		SK7790
5602		ECG1279		
5603		ECG1280		
5604				SK3438
5605		ECG3017		
5606	NTE397	ECG397		SK3053
5607		ECG5587		
5608		ECG116		SK3017B
5609	NTE1315	ECG1315		
5610	NTE1316	ECG1316		
5611	NTE1317	ECG1317		
5612				SK9187
5613	NTE5092A	ECG5092A		SK3998
5614				SK7CT533
5615		ECG1506		
5616		ECG1332		SK10007
5617		ECG1353		
5618		ECG2388		
5619		ECG1360		
5620		ECG5307		
5621		ECG2388		SK9501
5622	NTE228A	ECG228A		SK3103A
5623				SK9165
5624		ECG5196A		SK159
5625	NTE527A	ECG527A		SK7333
5626				SK3571
5627	NTE116	ECG116		SK3113
5628	NTE125	ECG125		
5629	NTE5335	ECG5335		SK7353
5630				SK3188A
5631	NTE5338	ECG5338		SK7313
5632				SK7CT534
5633	NTE5346	ECG5346		SK7352
5634	NTE5348	ECG5348		SK7303
5635				SK10191
5636		ECG1219		
5637	NTE5019T1	ECG5019T1		
5638	NTE1V030	ECG1V030		SKMV30A
5639	NTE7001	ECG7001		SK10470
5640		ECG1456		
5641	NTE261	ECG261	276-2068	SK9431
5642				SK7315
5643	NTE5427	ECG5427		SK3577
5644	NTE5428	ECG5428		SK3578
5645				SK9893
5646				SK74S20
5647		ECG1555		
5648	NTE74S37			
5649				SK9502
5650	NTE85	ECG85	276-2009	SK9261
5651		ECG1564		
5652				SK3679
5653				SK3680
5654				SK3681
5655				SK74LS138
5656				SK3682
5657				SK9509
5658				SK9087
5659		ECG5314		
5660				SK9088
5661	NTE2385	ECG2385		SK10303
5662		ECG1583		
5663		ECG1587		
5664	NTE74S85			
5665		ECG1614		
5666		ECG1617		
5667		ECG1623		
5668	NTE1761	ECG1761		SK10044
5669	NTE281MCP	ECG281MCP		
5670		ECG1638		
5671		ECG1640		SK10238
5672		ECG1644		
5673		ECG1645		
5674		ECG1646		
5675		ECG1652		SK10252
5676		ECG1653		SK7632
5677	NTE142A	ECG142A		
5678		ECG4017B		
5679		ECG1686		SK10247
5680		ECG74H86		
5681		ECG1706		SK9982
5682				SK74LS153
5683	NTE5075A	ECG5075A		
5684	NTE6241	ECG6241		SK10512
5685	NTE147A	ECG147A		
5686	NTE5016A	ECG5016A		
5687	NTE5665			
5688		ECG136A		
5689		ECG1756		
5690				SK74LS157
5691				SK3214
5692	NTE1763	ECG1763		SK10045
5693	NTE1765	ECG1765		
5694		ECG1766		SK10494
5695		ECG5322		SK3679
5696	NTE139A	ECG139A		
5697	NTE580	ECG580		SK3036
5698		ECG1784		SK9227
5699	NTE1785	ECG1785		SK7635
5700	NTE5704	ECG5704		SK10438
5701	NTE5705	ECG5705		SK10415
5702		ECG1802		
5703		ECG1806		SK9888
5704	NTE568A			
5705		ECG1821		
5706	NTE1832	ECG1832		SK10142
5707	NTE1833	ECG1833		SK9712
5708	NTE1851	ECG1851		
5709		ECG1853		SK10152
5710	NTE230	ECG230		SK3296
5711	NTE1857	ECG1857		SK10156
5712	NTE1858	ECG1858		
5713		ECG1865		SK10509
5714	NTE1866	ECG1866		SK10496
5715		ECG1869		SK10500
5716		ECG1878		SK9757
5717		ECG1887		
5718	NTE1888	ECG1888		
5719		ECG1889		SK10501
5720	NTE1898	ECG1898		SK10507
5721	NTE1899	ECG1899		SK10508
5722	NTE7439	ECG7439		SK7439
5723		ECG1941		SK10058
5724	NTE1942	ECG1942		
5725		ECG4020B		
5726		ECG75497		
5727		ECG2200		
5728		ECG2041		
5729		ECG397		
5730		ECG2045		
5731		ECG2046		
5732		ECG2052		SK10281
5733	NTE2057	ECG2057		SK10190
5734		ECG2063		SK10283
5735		ECG2064		SK10284
5736		ECG2065		SK10285
5737	NTE194	ECG194		SK3433
5738		ECG2090		
5739		ECG1616		
5740	NTE5062A			
5741		ECG1413		
5742	NTE1656	ECG1656		SK7633
5743		ECG2203		
5744				SK74LS193
5745	NTE56030	ECG56030		SK10409
5746				SK10234
5747		ECG4022B		
5748	NTE192&193	ECG192&193		SK9142&9143
5749		ECG2201		
5750		ECG2204		
5751		ECG2205		
5752		ECG2206		
5753		ECG2207		SK10298
5754				SK7C7266
5755				SK7816
5756		ECG40011B		SK4011B
5757		ECG40023B		
5758	NTE329	ECG329		SK3847
5759		ECG5371		
5760		ECG5542		
5761		ECG2354		
5762		ECG4024B		
5763		ECG1048		
5764	NTE2384	ECG2384		SK10129
5765		ECG2400		
5766		ECG2532		
5767	NTE374		ECG374	
5768				SK4520B
5769	NTE5013A N5	ECG5013A N5	276-561 N5	SK6A2 N5
5770		ECG135A		SK5V1
5771				SK7330
5772		ECG1672		
5773		ECG4025B		
5774	NTE6400	ECG6400		SK9122
5775	NTE2362	ECG2362		SK3114A
5776	NTE6408	ECG6408		SK7901
5777				SK9020
5778				SK9504
5779		ECG581		
5780		ECG74HCT00		SK7CT00
5781				SK7CT03
5782				SK7CT10
5783				SK7CT11
5784				SK9137
5785				SK7CT20
5786				SK7CT21
5787				SK3918
5788				SK7CT30
5789				SK3650
5790				SK3651
5791				SK7CT42
5792				SK9388
5793				SK74LS240
5794				SK9019
5795				SK7CT73
5796				SK7CT74
5797				SK7CT75
5798				SK7CT85
5799				SK7CT86
5800	NTE8123	ECG8123		
5801				SK7CT93
5802				SK74LS244
5803	NTE5653	ECG5653		SK3519
5804		ECG5875		
5805		ECG5879		
5806	NTE159	ECG159		SK3466
5807		ECG5883		
5808		ECG5887		
5809		ECG5891		
5810				SK9503
5811				SK158
5812				SK160
5813	NTE8223	ECG8223		
5814	NTE6240		ECG6240	
5815				SK9967
5816	NTE290A	ECG290A		SK3114A
5817				SK7C4316
5818	NTE76MP	ECG76MP		SK9601
5819	NTE8316	ECG8316		
5820	NTE8321	ECG8321		
5821	NTE8328	ECG8328		
5822				SK7626
5823		ECG311		
5824	NTE8368	ECG8368		SK4368
5825	NTE8370	ECG8370		
5826	NTE8374	ECG8374		
5827		ECG237		
5828	NTE6809	ECG6809		SK9796
5829		ECG469		
5830		ECG4021B		SK4021B
5831	NTE74S151	ECG74S151		SK74154
5832				SK2A7
5833		ECG4030B		
5834		ECG5638		
5835	NTE5538	ECG5538		SK10406
5836	NTE8520	ECG8520		
5837	NTE8542	ECG8542		
5838	NTE8546	ECG8546		
5839	NTE8556	ECG8556		
5840		ECG46		
5841		ECG2064		
5842				SK7C4351
5843				SK7C4352
5844				SK3052
5845				SK7C4353
5846		ECG6208		
5847	NTE5018A	ECG5018A		SK9A1
5848		ECG703		
5849		ECG580		SK9000
5850	NTE74LS124			
5851		ECG5020A		
5852		ECG3172		
5853		ECG3200		
5854		ECG291		
5855	NTE6247	ECG6247		SK10513
5856		ECG5080A		
5857	NTE7214	ECG7214		
5858	NTE74LS260	ECG74LS260		SK74LS260
5859		ECG5669A		
5860	NTE74LS283	ECG74LS283		SK7CT283
5861	NTE74LS295	ECG74LS295A		
5862				SK4097B
5863	NTE74LS324			
5864				SK3186
5865	NTE74LS327			
5866	NTE330	ECG330W		SK3012
5867				SK7440
5868	NTE74LS363	ECG74LS363		
5869	NTE74LS364	ECG74LS364		SK74LS364
5870				
5871		ECG40097B		

REPL. CODE	NTE PART NO.	ECG PART NO.	RADIO SHACK PART NO.	RCA PART NO.
5872	NTE74LS396	.....	.....	.....
5873	NTE191	ECG191	.....	SK3865A
5874	.....	ECG1058	.....	.....
5875	NTE74LS445	.....	.....	.....
5876	.....	.....	.....	SK7V5
5877	.....	ECG156	.....	.....
5878	NTE5023A	ECG5023A	276-563	SK24A
5879	.....	.....	.....	SK40208B
5880	.....	ECG937	.....	.....
5881	.....	ECG937M	.....	.....
5882	.....	.....	.....	SK3692
5883	.....	ECG135A	.....	.....
5884	.....	.....	.....	SK3135
5885	NTE966	ECG966	.....	SK3592
5886	NTE552	ECG552	276-1104	SK3313
5887	.....	ECG270	.....	.....
5888	.....	ECG271	.....	.....
5889	.....	ECG74LS138	.....	.....
5890	.....	.....	.....	SK9000
5891	.....	ECG7004	.....	SK10473
5892	.....	.....	.....	SK9213
5893	.....	.....	.....	SK9369
5894	.....	.....	.....	SK9368
5895	.....	.....	.....	SK74LS367
5896	NTE87MP	ECG87MP	.....	SK9928
5897	.....	.....	.....	SK3275
5898	.....	ECG5071A	.....	.....
5899	.....	.....	.....	SK3A3
5900	NTE5021T1	ECG5021T1	.....	.....
5901	NTE937M	ECG937M	.....	SK9147
5902	NTE1747	ECG1747	.....	.....
5903	NTE88MP	ECG88MP	.....	SK9930
5904	.....	.....	.....	SK3A6
5905	.....	.....	.....	SK9343
5906	.....	ECG5065A	.....	SK3A0
5907	.....	ECG138A	.....	.....
5908	.....	ECG960	.....	SK3591
5909	.....	ECG147A	.....	.....
5910	NTE56	ECG56	.....	.....
5911	.....	ECG168	.....	.....
5912	.....	ECG5072A	.....	SK8V2
5913	NTE195A	ECG195A	.....	SK3049
5914	.....	.....	.....	SK3044
5915	.....	.....	.....	SK3104A
5916	.....	.....	.....	SK3894
5917	.....	.....	.....	SK10177
5918	.....	ECG74HC40105	.....	.....
5919	.....	ECG5322	.....	SK3680
5920	.....	ECG5324	.....	SK3681
5921	.....	.....	.....	SK3197
5922	.....	.....	.....	SK3847
5923	.....	ECG5326	.....	SK3682
5924	.....	ECG5327	.....	SK9087
5925	.....	ECG169	.....	.....
5926	.....	.....	.....	SK7674
5927	NTE8214	ECG8214	.....	.....
5928	.....	.....	.....	SK3596
5929	.....	.....	.....	SK9432
5930	NTE8219	ECG8219	.....	.....
5931	.....	.....	.....	SK9236
5932	.....	.....	.....	SK7407
5933	.....	ECG6090	.....	SK4911
5934	.....	ECG964	.....	SK3630
5935	.....	ECG2062	.....	.....
5936	.....	.....	.....	SK9769
5937	.....	.....	.....	SK7473
5938	.....	.....	.....	SK9097
5939	.....	ECG6156	.....	.....
5940	.....	ECG170	.....	.....
5941	.....	ECG4506	.....	.....
5942	.....	ECG1316	.....	.....
5943	NTE832SM	ECG832SM	.....	SK10062
5944	.....	ECG75451B	.....	.....
5945	.....	ECG5569	.....	.....
5946	NTE308&310	ECG308&310	.....	SK3855&3856
5947	.....	.....	.....	SK7C40105
5948	.....	ECG5328	.....	.....
5949	.....	.....	.....	SK7C4510
5950	.....	.....	.....	SK7C4511
5951	NTE2302	ECG2303	.....	SK9422
5952	.....	.....	.....	SK7CT138
5953	NTE8613	ECG8613	.....	.....
5954	.....	.....	.....	SK10033
5955	.....	.....	.....	SK7C4514
5956	.....	.....	.....	SK7C4515
5957	.....	ECG74HCT138	.....	SK7CT158
5958	.....	ECG1409C	.....	.....
5959	.....	.....	.....	SK7C4516
5960	NTE1854M	ECG1854M	.....	SK10154
5961	.....	ECG74HCT161	.....	.....
5962	.....	.....	.....	SK7CT195
5963	.....	ECG74HCT163	.....	.....
5964	.....	.....	.....	SK7C4518
5965	.....	ECG5482	.....	SK3941
5966	.....	.....	.....	SK9959
5967	.....	ECG74HCT174	.....	.....
5968	.....	.....	.....	SK7C4520
5969	.....	ECG74HCT244	.....	SK7CT244
5970	NTE4000	ECG4000	.....	SK4000B
5971	.....	.....	.....	SK7675
5972	.....	ECG74HCT240	.....	.....
5973	.....	ECG5483	.....	SK3942
5974	.....	ECG74HCT273	.....	.....

REPL. CODE	NTE PART NO.	ECG PART NO.	RADIO SHACK PART NO.	RCA PART NO.
5975	.....	.....	.....	SK3998
5976	.....	.....	.....	SK3497
5977	.....	ECG2410	.....	SK10101
5978	NTE717	ECG717	.....	SK3827
5979	.....	ECG4901	.....	.....
5980	.....	ECG597	.....	.....
5981	.....	.....	.....	SK7CT182
5982	.....	.....	.....	SK7706
5983	.....	ECG1854D	.....	SK10153
5984	.....	ECG74HCT373	.....	SK7CT373
5985	NTE859	ECG859	.....	SK4856
5986	.....	.....	.....	SK4A7
5987	.....	.....	.....	SK7C4538
5988	.....	ECG5485	.....	SK3943
5989	NTE15005	ECG15005	.....	SK10180
5990	NTE15021	ECG15021	.....	SK10187
5991	NTE15022	ECG15022	.....	SK10188
5992	.....	ECG74HCT374	.....	.....
5993	NTE15023	ECG15023	.....	SK10189
5994	.....	.....	.....	SK10192
5995	.....	ECG128P	.....	.....
5996	.....	.....	.....	SK7693
5997	.....	ECG5203A	.....	SK172
5998	.....	.....	.....	SK7C4543
5999	.....	ECG5609	.....	.....
6000	NTE56019	ECG56019	.....	SK10269
6001	NTE130	ECG130	276-2041	SK3111
6002	NTE285MCP	ECG285MCP	.....	SK10310
6003	.....	.....	.....	SK7697
6004	.....	.....	.....	SK7694
6005	.....	ECG1409	.....	.....
6006	.....	ECG5424	.....	SK9293
6007	.....	ECG2333	.....	.....
6008	.....	ECG5487	.....	SK3944
6009	.....	ECG74HCT573	.....	.....
6010	.....	ECG74HCT574	.....	.....
6011	.....	.....	.....	SK9046
6012	NTE56033	ECG56033	.....	SK10411
6013	NTE56028	ECG56028	.....	SK10412
6014	.....	ECG5031A	.....	.....
6015	.....	.....	.....	SK10443
6016	.....	.....	.....	SK10457
6017	.....	.....	.....	SK10458
6018	.....	ECG5668A	.....	SK10460
6019	.....	.....	.....	SK3602
6020	NTE7000	ECG7000	.....	SK10469
6021	NTE7006	ECG7006	.....	SK10475
6022	.....	ECG7011	.....	SK10480
6023	NTE7014	ECG7014	.....	SK10483
6024	NTE7016	ECG7016	.....	SK10485
6025	.....	ECG7017	.....	SK10486
6026	NTE7020	ECG7020	.....	SK10489
6027	.....	ECG2004	.....	.....
6028	.....	.....	.....	SK9716
6029	.....	.....	.....	SK6749
6030	.....	ECG5421	276-1067	SK3570
6031	.....	.....	.....	SK3440
6032	.....	ECG5432	276-1067	.....
6033	.....	ECG5433	276-1067	.....
6034	.....	ECG4069	.....	SK4069UB
6035	.....	ECG129P	.....	.....
6036	.....	.....	.....	SK7642
6037	.....	.....	.....	SK9181
6038	.....	.....	.....	SK7CT574
6039	.....	.....	.....	SK74LS04
6040	.....	.....	.....	SK74LS05
6041	.....	ECG2128	.....	.....
6042	.....	.....	.....	SK74LS08
6043	.....	ECG4011B	.....	.....
6044	.....	ECG329	.....	.....
6045	NTE941S	ECG941S	.....	.....
6046	NTE55	ECG55	.....	SK3274
6047	.....	ECG1870	.....	.....
6048	.....	.....	.....	SK3447
6049	.....	.....	.....	SK74LS74A
6050	.....	ECG177	.....	SK3319
6051	.....	.....	.....	SK3501
6052	.....	ECG568A	.....	.....
6053	.....	.....	.....	SK9314
6054	.....	.....	.....	SK5101
6055	.....	.....	.....	SK3931
6056	.....	ECG3881	.....	SK2881
6057	NTE287	ECG287	.....	SK3244
6058	.....	.....	.....	SK74S04
6059	.....	ECG1006	.....	.....
6060	.....	.....	.....	SK3443
6061	.....	.....	.....	SK3724
6062	.....	ECG1580	.....	.....
6063	.....	.....	.....	SK74S11
6064	.....	.....	.....	SK1924
6065	.....	.....	.....	SK5A6
6066	.....	ECG4050B	.....	.....
6067	.....	ECG74C02	.....	.....
6068	.....	ECG74C04	.....	.....
6069	.....	ECG74C08	.....	SK7C08
6070	.....	ECG152	.....	SK3893
6071	.....	ECG74C10	.....	.....
6072	.....	.....	.....	SK2019
6073	.....	ECG74C20	.....	.....
6074	.....	ECG74C42	.....	SK7C42
6075	.....	ECG74C74	.....	SK7C74
6076	.....	.....	.....	SK7354
6077	.....	ECG74C85	.....	SK7C85

REPL. CODE	NTE PART NO.	ECG PART NO.	RADIO SHACK PART NO.	RCA PART NO.
6078	.....	ECG4070B	.....	.....
6079	.....	.....	.....	SK9902
6080	.....	.....	.....	SK5X6
6081	.....	.....	.....	SK9426
6082	.....	.....	.....	SK2880
6083	.....	.....	.....	SK7210
6084	.....	ECG5111A	.....	SK3X3
6085	.....	.....	.....	SK3294
6086	.....	.....	.....	SK3552
6087	.....	.....	.....	SK10073
6088	NTE287&288	ECG287&288	.....	SK3433&3434
6089	.....	.....	.....	SK3853
6090	.....	ECG75453B	.....	.....
6091	.....	.....	.....	SK9132
6092	.....	.....	.....	SK3490
6093	NTE382	ECG382	.....	.....
6094	.....	.....	.....	SK10A
6095	.....	.....	.....	SK3503
6096	.....	.....	.....	SK3502
6097	.....	ECG975	.....	.....
6098	NTE1110R	.....	.....	.....
6099	.....	ECG834	.....	SK3569
6100	.....	ECG525	.....	SK3925
6101	.....	.....	.....	SK4560B
6102	.....	.....	.....	SK2881
6103	.....	.....	.....	SK4019B
6104	NTE5351	ECG5351	.....	SK3857
6105	.....	.....	.....	SK3219
6106	NTE1535	ECG1535	.....	SK9725
6107	.....	ECG1787	.....	SK9766
6108	.....	.....	.....	SK6A2
6109	.....	.....	.....	SK6A0
6110	.....	ECG966	.....	SK3592
6111	.....	ECG7002	.....	SK10471
6112	.....	ECG7021	.....	.....
6113	.....	ECG7022	.....	.....
6114	.....	ECG5804	.....	.....
6115	.....	ECG7023	.....	.....
6116	.....	ECG7024	.....	.....
6117	.....	ECG7025	.....	.....
6118	.....	ECG7026	.....	.....
6119	.....	ECG7027	.....	.....
6120	.....	ECG7028	.....	.....
6121	.....	ECG7029	.....	.....
6122	.....	ECG7030	.....	.....
6123	.....	ECG7031	.....	.....
6124	.....	ECG7032	.....	.....
6125	.....	ECG7033	.....	.....
6126	.....	ECG7034	.....	.....
6127	.....	ECG7035	.....	.....
6128	.....	ECG7036	.....	.....
6129	.....	ECG7037	.....	.....
6130	.....	ECG7038	.....	.....
6131	.....	ECG7039	.....	.....
6132	.....	ECG7040	.....	.....
6133	.....	ECG7041	.....	.....
6134	.....	ECG7042	.....	.....
6135	.....	ECG7043	.....	.....
6136	.....	ECG7044	.....	.....
6137	.....	ECG7045	.....	.....
6138	.....	ECG7046	.....	.....
6139	.....	ECG7047	.....	.....
6140	.....	ECG7048	.....	.....
6141	.....	ECG7049	.....	.....
6142	.....	ECG7050	.....	.....
6143	.....	ECG7051	.....	.....
6144	.....	.....	.....	SK9768
6145	.....	ECG7052	.....	.....
6146	.....	ECG7053	.....	.....
6147	.....	ECG7054	.....	.....
6148	.....	ECG7055	.....	.....
6149	.....	ECG7056	.....	.....
6150	.....	ECG7057	.....	.....
6151	.....	ECG7058	.....	.....
6152	.....	ECG7059	.....	.....
6153	.....	ECG7060	.....	.....
6154	.....	ECG7061	.....	.....
6155	.....	ECG7062	.....	.....
6156	.....	ECG7063	.....	.....
6157	.....	ECG7064	.....	.....
6158	.....	ECG7065	.....	.....
6159	.....	ECG7066	.....	.....
6160	.....	ECG7067	.....	.....
6161	.....	ECG7068	.....	.....
6162	.....	ECG7069	.....	.....
6163	.....	ECG7070	.....	.....
6164	.....	ECG7071	.....	.....
6165	.....	ECG7072	.....	.....
6166	.....	ECG7074	.....	.....
6167	.....	.....	.....	SK7696
6168	.....	.....	.....	SK7695
6169	NTE174	.....	.....	SK3110
6170	.....	ECG858M	.....	.....
6171	.....	ECG1873	.....	.....
6172	.....	ECG5540	.....	.....
6173	.....	ECG123A	.....	SK3444
6174	.....	ECG5174AK	.....	SK115
6175	.....	.....	.....	SK9735
6176	.....	.....	.....	SK4015B
6177	.....	.....	.....	SK6748
6178	NTE74H08	ECG74H08	.....	SK7408
6179	.....	.....	.....	SK7C109
6180	.....	.....	.....	SK3691

REPL. CODE	NTE PART NO.	ECG PART NO.	RADIO SHACK PART NO.	RCA PART NO.
6181				SK9724
6182		ECG1807		SK9886
6183		ECG262		
6184		ECG1529		
6185	NTE56014			SK3993
6186				SK9297
6187		ECG21		SK9720
6188				SK9505
6189				SK7C125
6190				SK3160
6191				SK7C126
6192		ECG74HC4020		SK7C4020
6193	NTE128&401	ECG128&401		
6194				SK7C132
6195		ECG1720		
6196	NTE1160	ECG1160		SK3474
6197				SK7C138
6198	NTE552	ECG515		SK9000
6199	NTE519 N7	ECG519 N7	276-1122 N7	SK3100 N7
6200	NTE519 N9	ECG519 N9	276-1122 N9	SK3100 N9
6201		ECG74HC4040		SK7C4040
6202				SK7C151
6203		ECG912		SK3543
6204				SK7C153
6205				SK7C154
6206		ECG5318		
6207				SK4013B
6208				SK9206
6209	NTE857SM	ECG857SM		SK9799
6210	NTE5022A	ECG5022A		SK5022A
6211				SK4050B
6212				SK7C164
6213	NTE955M	ECG955M		SK3564
6214				SK7C165
6215		ECG177		
6216		ECG74HC4060		SK7C4060
6217				SK9156
6218		ECG2313		
6219				SK9155
6220				SK7A5
6221				SK9424
6222		ECG75491B		
6223				SK7C173
6224		ECG917		SK3544
6225		ECG75492P		
6226				SK7C174
6227				SK7C175
6228		ECG66		
6229				SK7700
6230		ECG2322		
6231		ECG1214		SK3736
6232		ECG5332		
6233		ECG1692		
6234	NTE139A	ECG139A		SK9V1
6235				SK3578
6236		ECG8092		
6237				SK9201
6238				SK3312
6239		ECG1782		
6240		ECG4988		
6241	NTE282	ECG282		SK3192
6242	NTE5018A N6	ECG5018A N6	276-562 N6	SK9A1 N6
6243				SK7671
6244				SK1806
6245		ECG159		SK3466
6246		ECG1397		SK7603
6247				SK1826
6248		ECG2716		SK2716
6249		ECG159		SK3114A
6250	NTE282	ECG282		SK3513
6251				SK1878
6252				SK1879
6253				SK1881
6254				SK1882
6255				SK1883
6256		ECG4072B		SK4072B
6257	NTE180MCP	ECG180MCP		SK9134&9136
6258				SK24V
6259				SK4075B
6260				SK40250B
6261				SK9759
6262		ECG74290		
6263				SK9758
6264	NTE1773	ECG1773		SK7952
6265				SK9849
6266		ECG2318		SK9986
6267		ECG8552		SK2131
6268				
6269				SK2132
6270		ECG8553		
6271		ECG8554		
6272		ECG8555		
6273				SK9028
6274	NTE374			SK374
6275	NTE7068	ECG7068		
6276				SK175
6277	NTE7073	ECG7073		
6278	NTE5075A	ECG5075A		
6279	NTE966	ECG966	276-1771	
6280		ECG230		
6281		ECG5620		
6282				SK9320
6283	NTE2732A			
6284				SK3985
6285				SK5189
6286		ECG3047		
6287				SK3103A
6288	NTE177 N5	ECG177 N5	276-1122 N5	SK9091 N5
6289				SK9394
6290		ECG534		
6291		ECG522		SK3303
6292				SK3668
6293				SK3018
6294				SK9031
6295		ECG506		SK3043B
6296	NTE506	ECG506		SK5003
6297				SK3032A
6298		ECG327		
6299	NTE383	ECG327		SK9040
6300	NTE383	ECG383		SK9464
6301	NTE125 N3	ECG125 N3	276-1114 N3	SK3081 N3
6302				SK7CT22106
6303		ECG7016		
6304				SK3090
6305				SK7C22106
6306	NTE945	ECG945		SK3166
6307				SK9379
6308				SK7C299
6309		ECG6230		
6310		ECG489		SK3201
6311		ECG9301		
6312		ECG9302		
6313		ECG9303		
6314		ECG9304		
6315		ECG9306		
6316		ECG9307		
6317				SK2035A
6318		ECG9311		
6319		ECG9312		
6320		ECG9600		
6321				SK74C245
6322		ECG9321		
6323		ECG9322		
6324		ECG9323		
6325		ECG9324		
6326		ECG9325		
6327		ECG9326		
6328		ECG9331		
6329		ECG9332		
6330		ECG9333		
6331		ECG9334		
6332		ECG9335		
6333		ECG9342		
6334		ECG9343		
6335				SK2716
6336		ECG9347		
6337				SK74LS90
6338		ECG9361		
6339		ECG9362		
6340		ECG9363		
6341				SK9947
6342		ECG9367		
6343		ECG9368		
6344		ECG9375		
6345		ECG9380		
6346		ECG9381		
6347		ECG9382		
6348		ECG9390		
6349		ECG9391		
6350		ECG9392		
6351		ECG9393		
6352		ECG9394		
6353		ECG9400		
6354		ECG126A		SK3008
6355	NTE121	ECG121		
6356	NTE121MP	ECG121MP		SK3015
6357				SK40117B
6358				SK3026
6359				SK3028
6360		ECG386		SK9140
6361	NTE181MP	ECG181MP		SK3037
6362	NTE123A	ECG123A	276-2030	SK3024
6363	NTE123	ECG123A	276-2009	SK3024
6364		ECG131		SK3052
6365	NTE941S	ECG941S		SK9323
6366	NTE760	ECG760		SK3077
6367		ECG162		SK3079
6368	NTE197	ECG197		SK3085
6369		ECG9602		
6370	NTE5304	ECG5304		SK3105
6371		ECG165		SK3111
6372		ECG176		SK3123
6373		ECG1125		SK3827
6374		ECG233		SK3132
6375		ECG146A		SK26V
6376		ECG5084A		SK29V
6377	NTE388	ECG388		SK3559
6378		ECG128		SK3265
6379		ECG3097		
6380	NTE129	ECG129		SK3513
6381	NTE283	ECG283		SK3559
6382	NTE284	ECG284		SK3270
6383	NTE152	ECG152	276-2020	SK3626
6384	NTE291	ECG291		SK3440
6385		ECG5029A		
6386	NTE74116	ECG8308		
6387				SK9222
6388	NTE7060	ECG7060		
6389	NTE6041	ECG6041		SK7245
6390				SK3322
6391		ECG53		
6392		ECG6206		
6393		ECG107		SK3356
6394		ECG1934		SK7739
6395		ECG264		
6396	NTE604	ECG109		SK3087
6397				SK3374
6398	NTE552	ECG552	276-1104	SK9000
6399	NTE1028	ECG1028		SK3435
6400		ECG489		
6401				SK40174B
6402				SK3481
6403				SK10173
6404	NTE178MP	ECG178MP	276-1122	SK3709
6405				SK9A1
6406		ECG5607		SK3507
6407	NTE605	ECG605A		SK7951
6408				SK9218
6409		ECG129		SK3513
6410				SK3325
6411		ECG286		SK3538
6412				SK3557
6413		ECG9982		
6414		ECG175		SK3562
6415		ECG284		SK9134
6416		ECG9990		
6417		ECG5643		SK3570
6418	NTE5554	ECG5554		SK3575
6419	NTE5556	ECG5556		SK3576
6420				SK7C374
6421				SK6746
6422				SK7C377
6423				SK3616
6424				SK3361
6425	NTE328	ECG328		SK3621
6426	NTE54	ECG54		SK3562
6427				SK7406
6428				SK9986
6429	NTE549	ECG549		
6430				SK9277
6431		ECG930		SK3696
6432		ECG2345		SK3996
6433		ECG2345		
6434		ECG2346		
6435		ECG217		
6436				SK7C390
6437				SK3745
6438	NTE40106B	ECG40106B		SK4584B
6439		ECG398		
6440				SK7C393
6441		ECG6204		
6442		ECG2356		SK9958
6443		ECG3020		
6444				SK3842
6445	NTE558	ECG558		SK3843
6446		ECG857M		
6447				SK9639
6448	NTE734			
6449	NTE568	ECG568		SK3910
6450		ECG823		
6451	NTE580	ECG580		SK5016
6452		ECG375		
6453		ECG40194B		SK40194B
6454				SK7CT107
6455				SK7CT109
6456				SK7CT112
6457				SK3116
6458	NTE615P	ECG615A		SK9776
6459		ECG6006		
6460				SK7CT123
6461				SK7CT125
6462				SK7CT126
6463				SK9393
6464				SK9053
6465				SK6631
6466				SK7CT132
6467	NTE125	ECG125	276-1114	SK3311
6468		ECG74HC00		
6469		ECG3181		
6470				SK4311
6471				SK7CT139
6472		ECG4918		
6473				SK4320
6474				SK4325
6475				SK4326
6476		ECG74HC02		
6477		ECG6154		
6478		ECG6158		
6479		ECG74HC04		
6480		ECG6008		
6481		ECG56017		SK9830
6482		ECG1938		SK7741
6483		ECG4926		
6484		ECG74HC109		
6485		ECG74LS132		
6486		ECG4928		
6487				SK7CT147
6488				SK6V0
6489				SK9621

REPL. CODE	NTE PART NO.	ECG PART NO.	RADIO SHACK PART NO.	RCA PART NO.
6490				SK4053B
6491		ECG31		
6492				SK7CT151
6493		ECG74HC14		
6494				SK7CT153
6495		ECG4934		
6496				SK9358
6497		ECG4013B		
6498		ECG467		
6499				SK7CT157
6500	NTE7051	ECG7051		
6501	NTE85	ECG85	276-86535-3	SK31327
6502				SK9982
6503		ECG8316		
6504				SK7CT161
6505				SK7CT160
6506				SK9114
6507		ECG6010		
6508				SK7CT163
6509		ECG116		SK3311
6510				SK7CT164
6511				SK7CT165
6512		ECG967		
6513				SK7CT166
6514	NTE8316	ECG8316		SK74161
6515	NTE1022	ECG1022		SK3481
6516		ECG74HC32		
6517				SK7CT173
6518				SK7CT174
6519				SK7CT175
6520		ECG4950		
6521				SK4503B
6522				SK7CT181
6523		ECG5327		
6524		ECG1191		
6525		ECG159		SK3118
6526		ECG2358		SK9741
6527		ECG1290		SK9183
6528				SK7CT190
6529				SK7CT191
6530	NTE1139	ECG1139		SK3155
6531				SK7676
6532				SK7CT192
6533				SK7CT193
6534	NTE3092	ECG3092		
6535				SK7CT194
6536		ECG4958		
6537	NTE198	ECG198		
6538		ECG992		SK3688
6539	NTE331	ECG331		SK9234
6540	NTE2407	ECG2407		
6541		ECG987		SK3594
6542	NTE159	ECG159		
6543				SK3630
6544				SK3152
6545	NTE123AP	ECG123AP		SK3854
6546	NTE156	ECG156		SK5012
6547				SK3246A
6548		ECG580		SK5032
6549				SK5042
6550				SK5044
6551		ECG199		SK3124A
6552				SK5046
6553				SK5048
6554				SK5050
6555				SK5052
6556				SK5053
6557				SK5054
6558				SK7679
6559		ECG9301		SK9301
6560				SK5114
6561				SK3636
6562				SK7CT221
6563	NTE199	ECG199		SK3132
6564	NTE5073A	ECG5073A		SK8V7
6565		ECG327		SK3945
6566		ECG957		
6567				SK5236
6568		ECG943M		SK9278
6569	NTE6362	ECG6362		SK6561
6570		ECG1940		SK7742
6571				SK3529
6572				SK3089
6573				SK7CT237
6574				SK7CT238
6575		ECG4006B		
6576		ECG527		
6577				SK7CT241
6578				SK7CT242
6579				SK9110
6580		ECG2380		
6581				SK7CT243
6582		ECG379		SK9085
6583		ECG5004A		
6584				SK2068
6585		ECG933		SK9341
6586		ECG427		
6587		ECG2312		
6588				SK7CT251
6589				SK2069
6590				SK7CT253
6591		ECG923		SK9036
6592				SK7CT257

REPL. CODE	NTE PART NO.	ECG PART NO.	RADIO SHACK PART NO.	RCA PART NO.
6593				SK7CT258
6594	NTE5022A	ECG5022A		SK14A
6595				SK7CT259
6596				SK9455A
6597				SK9089
6598		ECG3088		
6599	NTE5160A N3	ECG5160A N3		SK140X N3
6600		ECG5306		
6601		ECG74HC4067		SK7C4067
6602				SK9012
6603	NTE253MCP			
6604				SK7C573
6605				SK3884
6606				SK7C574
6607		ECG128		SK3024
6608		ECG5667A		SK3508
6609		ECG4902		
6610				SK3867A
6611		ECG5463		
6612		ECG955M		SK3693
6613				SK3434
6614		ECG465		SK9158
6615				SK5704
6616				SK9410
6617	NTE552	ECG552		SK3130
6618				SK7CT280
6619		ECG5675		SK3508
6620				SK10098
6621				SK7CT283
6622	NTE783	ECG783		SK5A6
6623				SK7628
6624				SK3072
6625				
6626		ECG5681		SK6681
6627	NTE1230	ECG1230		SK3444
6628	NTE1V150	ECG1V150		SKMV150G
6629		ECG832		
6630				SK9163
6631				SK7CT297
6632				SK7CT299
6633	NTE930#	ECG930#		SK3568
6634	NTE1767	ECG1767		
6635		ECG4046B		SK4046B
6636	NTE7214	ECG7214		SK74LS253
6637				SK4020B
6638		ECG1619		
6639		ECG5146A		
6640		ECG611		
6641				SK9025
6642				SK6117
6643				SK6118
6644		ECG544		
6645				SK5556
6646				SK9934
6647		ECG7015		
6648		ECG1874		
6649	NTE5013A	ECG5013A		SK6A2
6650				SK3066
6651				SK68X
6652		ECG5019A		
6653				SKMV275B
6654		ECG960		
6655	NTE85	ECG85	2009	SK3132
6656				SK3195
6657				SK7616
6658				SK7CT365
6659		ECG525		
6660				SK7701
6661				SK7CT366
6662				SK7CT367
6663				SK7CT368
6664		ECG2320		
6665	NTE5552	ECG5552		SK6651
6666	NTE290A	ECG290A	276-2026	SK3114A
6667		ECG282&427		SK9368
6668				SK9121
6669		ECG2419		SK10111
6670				SK7CT377
6671		ECG2418		SK10108
6672	NTE5608	ECG5608		SK6707
6673				SK6788
6674		ECG2360		SK9960
6675				SK7CT390
6676	NTE4001B	ECG4001B	276-2041	SK4001B
6677		ECG5010T1		
6678		ECG859		
6679				SK7CT393
6680		ECG1766		
6681				SK1922
6682				SK9500
6683	NTE289A	ECG289A		SK3214A
6684		ECG753		SK7226
6685		ECG5567		
6686		ECG5568		
6687		ECG503		SK3068
6688				SK9V1
6689				SK3487
6690	NTE153	ECG152	276-2020	SK3893
6691		ECG2323		
6692	NTE382	ECG382	276-2009	SK9137
6693				SK7621
6694		ECG1569		
6695		ECG2316		

REPL. CODE	NTE PART NO.	ECG PART NO.	RADIO SHACK PART NO.	RCA PART NO.
6696				SK130X
6697		ECG2308		
6698		ECG96L02		
6699		ECG5317		
6700		ECG5427		SK3577
6701	NTE5348	ECG5348		SK7301
6702				SK7305
6703				SK7307
6704		ECG1620		
6705		ECG5019T1		
6706	NTE177	ECG177		SK9091
6707		ECG1234		
6708				SK7317
6709		ECG5428		SK3578
6710		ECG5429		
6711			276-143	
6712				SK9138
6713				SK2027A
6714				SK3574
6715		ECG55		SK9367
6716		ECG5013T1		
6717		ECG963		
6718	NTE174			SK3017B
6719	NTE5159A N3	ECG5159A N3		SK130X N3
6720	NTE5162A N3	ECG5162A N3		SK160X N3
6721	NTE5163A N3	ECG5163A N3		SK170X N3
6722	NTE5165A N3	ECG5165A N3		SK190X N3
6723	NTE5166A N3	ECG5166A N3		SK200X N3
6724		ECG6362		
6725		ECG284		SK3079
6726		ECG2418		
6727				SK9867
6728				SK7613
6729	NTE3098	ECG3081		SK9965
6730		ECG6087		
6731		ECG159		SK7664
6732		ECG1521		SK7671
6733				SK7680
6734				SK7699
6735				SK7702
6736				SK7709
6737				SK3689
6738				SK7738
6739		ECG4900		
6740	NTE1421	ECG1421		SK7792
6741				SK74LS164
6742				SK3610
6743				SK7CT00
6744				SK3609
6745	NTE1398	ECG1398		
6746				SK4V3
6747		ECG1281		
6748				SK9884
6749		ECG2341		
6750				SK9918
6751				SK7951
6752		ECG2414		SK9961
6753				SK7794
6754		ECG74HC123		
6755		ECG74HC125		
6756		ECG74HC126		
6757		ECG74HC132		
6758		ECG74HC138		
6759		ECG74HC139		
6760		ECG74HC151		
6761		ECG74HC153		
6762		ECG74HC154		
6763		ECG74HC163		
6764		ECG74HC164		
6765		ECG74HC165		
6766		ECG74HC173		
6767		ECG74HC174		
6768		ECG74HC175		
6769				SK7C02
6770				SK4040B
6771		ECG74HC244		
6772		ECG74HC257		
6773		ECG74HC259		
6774		ECG74HC273		
6775				SK9157
6776	NTE584	ECG584		SK9091
6777		ECG74HC299		
6778				SK3896
6779	NTE1199	ECG1199		SK9339
6780		ECG5474		SK3943
6781		ECG74HC373		
6782		ECG74HC374		
6783		ECG74HC377		
6784		ECG74HC390		
6785		ECG74HC393		
6786				SK9153
6787	NTE5534	ECG5534		SK6502
6788				SK9294
6789		ECG74HC10		
6790				SK17A
6791				SK7CT540
6792				SK7CT541
6793	NTE282	ECG282		SK3104A
6794		ECG74HC573		
6795		ECG74HC574		
6796		ECG968		SK3593
6797		ECG2003		
6798				SK2V8

REPL. CODE	NTE PART NO.	ECG PART NO.	RADIO SHACK PART NO.	RCA PART NO.
6799				SK7CT563
6800				SK7CT564
6801	NTE195A	ECG195A		SK3124A
6802	NTE195A	ECG195A		SK3004
6803				SK7704
6804				SK4046B
6805				SK7CT573
6806				SK9009
6807				SK4068B
6808				SK7789
6809				SK9075
6810		ECG5702		
6811		ECG5703		
6812		ECG5704		
6813				SK7CT583
6814		ECG5705		
6815	NTE46	ECG46		SK9455A
6816	NTE583	ECG583		SK3311
6817				SK3279
6818				SK7CT597
6819		ECG2303		
6820				SK179
6821		ECG74HCT138		SK7CT138
6822				SK10244
6823		ECG6809		
6824				SK3A0
6825		ECG284		SK9031
6826		ECG285		SK9032
6827	NTE615A	ECG615A		SK9976
6828				SK9057
6829				SK9060
6830				SK9065
6831				SK3866A
6832	NTE804	ECG804		SK9068
6833		ECG744		
6834	NTE5344	ECG5344		SK9104
6835		ECG241		SK9116
6836		ECG242		SK9117
6837		ECG5814		
6838		ECG5817		
6839				SK9152
6840				SK9154
6841				SK3717
6842		ECG109		SK3087
6843				SK110V
6844				SK74LS107
6845		ECG51		SK9263
6846		ECG8546		
6847				SK9278
6848				SK9279
6849				SK9280
6850		ECG1289		SK9282
6851				SK9288
6852				SK9289
6853				SK9301
6854				SK9302
6855				SK9316
6856				SK74LS191
6857				SK9318
6858				SK9319
6859				SK7CT640
6860		ECG941S		SK9323
6861				SK9345

REPL. CODE	NTE PART NO.	ECG PART NO.	RADIO SHACK PART NO.	RCA PART NO.
6862				SK9346
6863				SK9347
6864				SK9348
6865				SK9350
6866				SK7CT643
6867				SK9958
6868				SK74LS243
6869				SK7CT646
6870	NTE5344	ECG5344		SK9388
6871	NTE1471	ECG1471		SK9393
6872		ECG85		SK9407
6873		ECG75492B		
6874		ECG943M		SK9993
6875		ECG6002		SK7202
6876				SK9445
6877		ECG24		SK9453
6878		ECG25		SK9454
6879				SK74LS27
6880				SK9463
6881				SK9465
6882				SK9466
6883	NTE227	ECG227		SK9473
6884				SK9474
6885				SK9486
6886				SK74LS30
6887		ECG2382		SK9502
6888		ECG2383		SK9506
6889	NTE703	ECG703		SK3708
6890		ECG853		
6891				SK100A
6892		ECG1903		
6893	NTE195A	ECG195A		SK3122
6894				SK3235
6895				SK8A7
6896	NTE335	ECG335		SK9608
6897				SK74LS123
6898				SK7CT670
6899	NTE346	ECG346		SK9622
6900		ECG74HCT161		SK7CT161
6901				SK7CT162
6902		ECG74HCT163		SK7CT163
6903		ECG74HCT174		SK7CT174
6904				SK2150
6905				SK9672
6906	NTE102&103	ECG102&103		SK3722&3862
6907				SK2163
6908				SK2166
6909		ECG74HCT240		SK7CT240
6910		ECG74HCT273		SK7CT273
6911				SK3951
6912		ECG797		SK3158
6913		ECG5989		
6914		ECG5988		
6915		ECG5590		
6916		ECG74S475		
6917		ECG74HC7374		SK7CT374
6918				SK7208
6919				SK3986
6920				SK3129
6921	NTE53	ECG53		SK9374
6922				SK74LS75
6923				SK7357
6924		ECG5009A		

REPL. CODE	NTE PART NO.	ECG PART NO.	RADIO SHACK PART NO.	RCA PART NO.
6925	NTE5635	ECG5635	276-1000	SK3533
6926				SK9482
6927		ECG74HCT573		SK7CT573
6928		ECG74HCT574		SK7CT574
6929	NTE5465	ECG5465	276-1020	SK9293
6930				SK9090
6931				SK3763
6932	NTE5463	ECG5463	276-1067	SK9292
6933		ECG382		
6934		ECG1401		
6935				SK68A
6936	NTE5312	ECG5312	276-1146	SK3985
6937	NTE5312	ECG5312	276-1171	SK3985
6938	NTE5314	ECG5314	276-1173	SK9387
6939	NTE5312	ECG5312	276-1181	SK3985
6940				SK2882
6941		ECG2385		SK9509
6942		ECG74LS366A		
6943				SK3543
6944		ECG2319		SK9374
6945				SK3081
6946				SK3131A
6947				SK3143
6948		ECG108		SK3452
6949		ECG961		
6950				SK7CT244
6951	NTE604			SK3004
6952	NTE5534	ECG5534		SK3581
6953				SK3463
6954				SK110A
6955				SK3581
6956				SK3582
6957				SK74LS221
6958				SK7731
6959		ECG5176AK		SK119
6960				SK2161
6961				SK2151
6962		ECG2386		
6963				SK2167
6964		ECG613		SK3326
6965		ECG5481		SK3940
6966				SK9381
6967		ECG782		SK3077
6968	NTE1045	ECG1045		
6969		ECG6502		
6970		ECG943M		
6971				SK9227
6972		ECG89		SK9119
6973				SK7481
6974	NTE5009A	ECG5009A		SK4A7
6975				SK9247
6976				SK3329
6977			276-068	
6978			276-069	
6979	NTE74LS112A	ECG74LS112A		SK7CT112
6980			276-113	
6981			276-142	
6982		ECG5550		SK6650
6983				SK3575
6984				SK3576
6985		ECG5043A		SK60A

MORE TITLES FROM PROMPT® PUBLICATIONS:

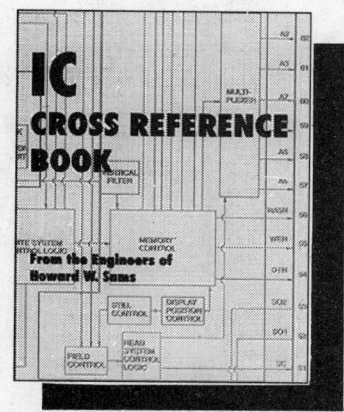

IC Cross Reference Book
Howard W. Sams & Company

The engineering staff of Howard W. Sams & Company has assembled the *IC Cross Reference Guide* to help you find replacements or substitutions for more than 35,000 ICs or modules. It has been compiled from manufacturer's data and from the analysis of consumer electronics devices for PHOTOFACT® service data, which has been relied upon since 1946 by service technicians worldwide. This unique book includes a complete guide to IC and module replacements and substitutions, an easy-to-use cross reference guide, listings of more than 35,000 part and type numbers, part numbers for the United States, Europe, and the Far East.

$19.95
ISBN #: 0-7906-1049-3
Pub. Date 5/94

Tube Substitution Handbook
Complete Guide to Replacements
for Vacuum Tubes and Picture Tubes
William Smith, Barry Buchanan

The most accurate, up-to-date guide available, *Tube Substitution Handbook* will be useful to antique radio buffs, old car enthusiasts, ham operators, and collectors of vintage ham radio equipment. In addition, marine operators, microwave repair technicians, and TV and radio technicians will find this book an invaluable reference tool. Basing diagrams are included as a handy reference to pin numbers for the tubes listed in the *Handbook*.

$16.95
ISBN #: 0-7906-1036-1
Pub. Date 12/92

To Order, Call Our Customer Service Representatives
Toll Free at 800-428-7267.
Be Sure to Ask for Your FREE PROMPT Catalog!